Flower Gardening in the Hot Midwest

Flower Gardening in the Hot Midwest

USDA ZONE 5 AND LOWER ZONE 4

Linda Hillegass

University of Illinois Press

Urbana and Chicago

The photos on pages ii, 14, 138, 170, and 182 are by James L. McKee.
Except where noted, all other photos are by Linda Hillegass.

© 2000 by the Board of Trustees of the University of Illinois
All rights reserved
Manufactured in Canada
♾ This book is printed on acid-free paper.

Library of Congress Cataloging-in-Publication Data
Hillegass, L. L.
Flower gardening in the hot Midwest : USDA zone 5 and lower
zone 4 / Linda Hillegass.
p.   cm.
Includes bibliographical references (p.) and index.
ISBN 0-252-02576-8 (cloth : acid-free paper) —
ISBN 0-252-06885-8 (paper : acid-free paper)
1. Gardening—Middle West. I. Title.
SB453.2.M53.H56   2000
635.9'0977—dc21   99-050670

1 2 3 4 5 C P 5 4 3 2 1

To Jim McKee, the one and only

Contents

Acknowledgments

Thanks to the three gardeners who inspired me to write this book. Clayton Kurkowski called me "gardener extraordinaire" one day and it went to my head. Deb Evnen swelled my head further by asking a thousand gardening questions for which I realized I had answers. Finally, my mother, Catherine MacDonald, told me I should write a gardening book the way I write letters to my loved ones.

Further thanks to two friends who encouraged me to write the book in the first place, gave me invaluable comments when the manuscript was completed, and never flagged in their confidence in the book's worth: Penny Rickard and Kris Gilbertson of Capability's Books. Thanks, too, to Aileen Rodgers and Deb Evnen for reading the manuscript and making suggestions and to Karen Hewitt at the University of Illinois Press for believing in and shaping this book.

And special thanks to my husband, Jim McKee, who gave me a well-timed kick in the pants when writer's block threatened to swamp the whole project.

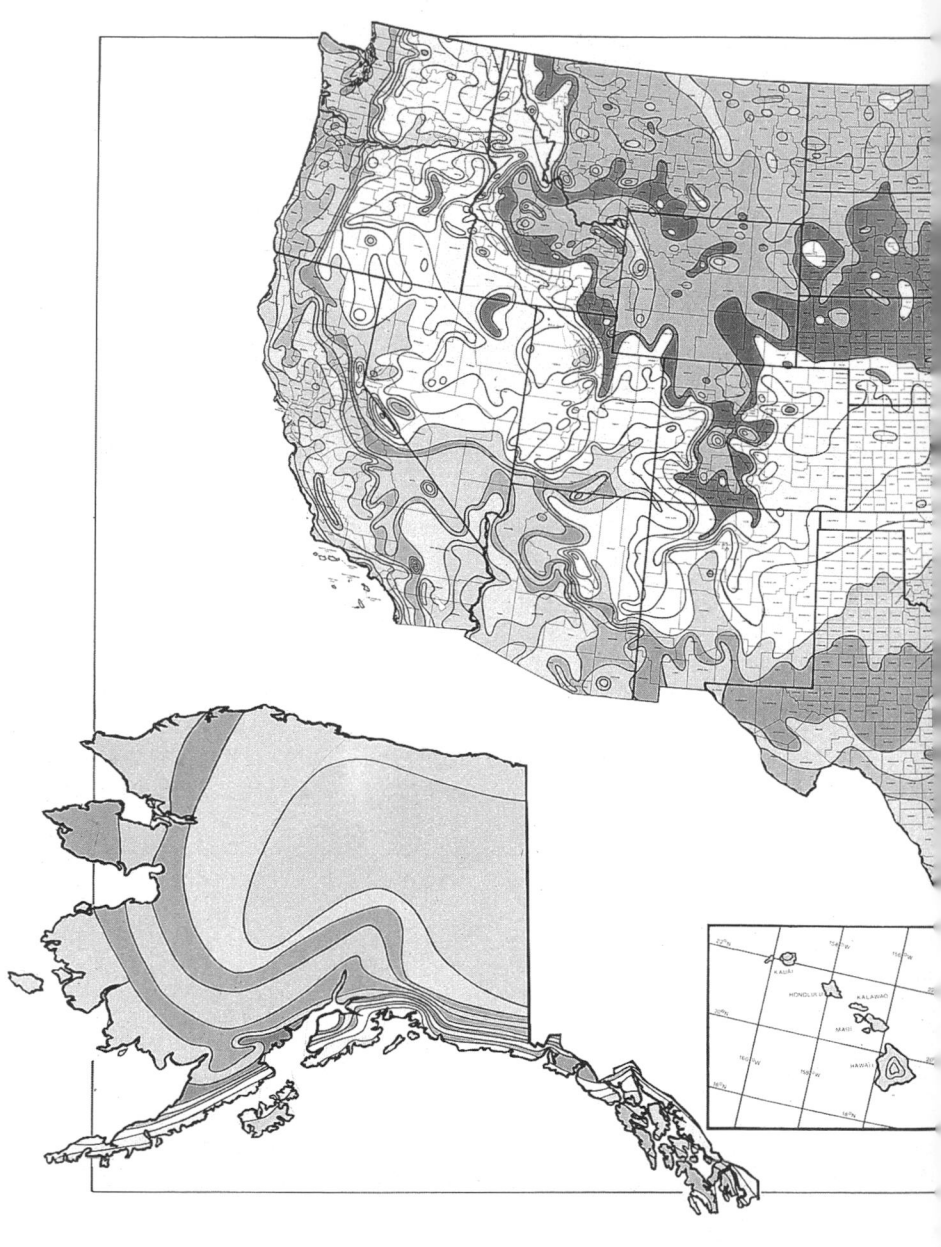

United States Department of Agriculture Plant Hardiness Zone Map (Agricultural Research

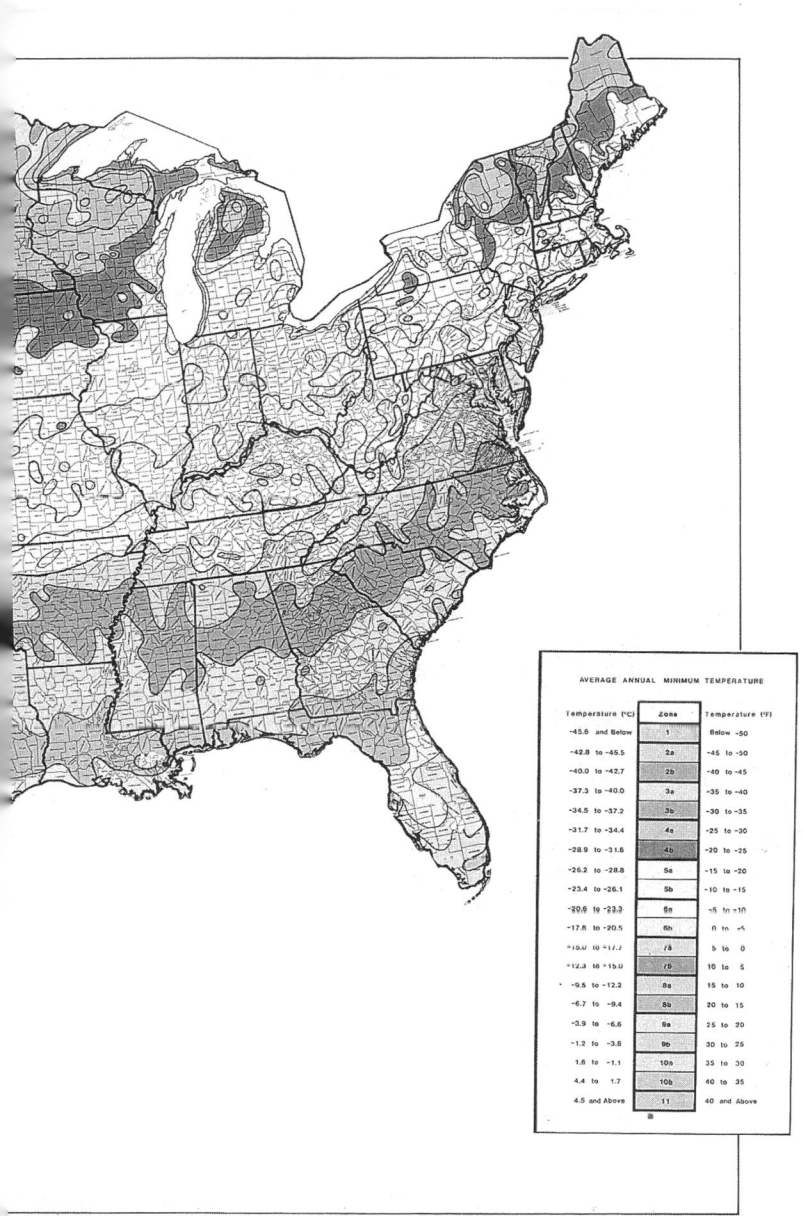

ervice, USDA).

Flower Gardening in the Hot Midwest

1

Coping with the Climate

A garden is often described as a paradise, but if you live in the hot Midwest, the climate can make it seem more like hell. The farm belt that stretches across the heartland of America is great for corn, but raising flowers here can be a challenge. From central Nebraska east to Indiana lies the heart of USDA zones 4 and 5, a strip of blessedly rich soil and a hellish climate of extremes.

Winter temperatures in our area drop as low as -10 to -25 degrees Fahrenheit. Summer temperatures can zoom up over 100 degrees. It's true that many parts of the country experience high heat. Others routinely face icy winters. Only in the hot Midwest are we up against both winter temperatures well below zero and the prolonged scorching heat, drought, and unstoppable winds of summer.

Although parts of the northeastern United States share our USDA hardiness zones and can relate to the challenges of cold weather, our Midwestern summers make New England weather look like sissy stuff. New York sees only *seven to thirty days* a year when the temperature is above 86. By contrast, South Dakota, Nebraska, northern Kansas, southern Iowa, northern Missouri, Illinois, and southern Indiana can expect *thirty to sixty days* in that range.

Putting further demand on flowering plants is our area's propensity to shoot from one extreme of temperature to the other in just a few hours. Our landlocked midcontinental position means we are not subject to the moderating influence that large bodies of water exert on temperature. An unusually warm winter day may be followed by frigidity, the temperature plummeting sixty-five degrees from one day to the next. A summer thunderstorm can drop the temperature from 100 degrees to 60 degrees in a matter of minutes.

Snow is intermittent in a zone 5 winter, providing no reliable insulating cover. Rain on the farm belt is adequate in spring and fall but normally sparse in the blasting heat of summer. Winds are ever present and sometimes violent. The sun's rays are very strong and direct.

You can make your garden a paradise in spite of all this by choosing plants carefully and learning to cope with the climate. Reading about gardening is a great way to learn, but unfortunately most books on the subject are written by gardeners from England or the Pacific Northwest, where less extreme climates and the blessings of reliable rainfall create gardening environments wholly unlike ours. There is also a great outpouring of garden literature from New England. This has much to say about harsh winters, but does not address the heat and drought of summer. Garden books foreign to our region describe, too, a sequence of bloom that doesn't translate to the exceptionally long bloom season of the Midwest.

Heat Wave

Temperatures above 100 degrees do not occur every year, but when they do they can last several days. A flowering plant sited in full sun will experience great stress. Add the wind that can come right along with the heat and only the tough will survive. In a recent Nebraska heat wave, the wags at a local radio station fried eggs on the sidewalk. No wonder your flowers look cooked in this climate. Careful attention to USDA hardiness zones in selecting plants will see your garden reliably through winters, but, oh, those summers.

Extremes of heat create clear visible damage. In 1995 my garden suffered a three-day period of daily highs above 100 degrees. Shade plants fully sheltered were generally unharmed, but those hit by even small amounts of sun for a brief part of the day showed stress. *Hosta* (hosta or plantain lily) in partial shade sported large, gruesome patches of collapsed tissue that browned and finally crisped. Other plants suffered brown and curling edges on their foliage: *Dicentra spectabilis* (bleeding heart), *Astilbe* (false spirea), and *Thalictrum rochebrunianum* (meadow rue). *Alchemilla mollis* (lady's mantle) lay limp and gasping. *Lamium maculatum* 'White Nancy' (spotted deadnettle) had been beautiful in both shade and part sun, but with skyrocketing temperatures dehydrated and died back. Only *Lamium* plants in full shade survived to see the fall. *Digitalis* (foxglove) bloom stalks drooped (*D.* x *mertonensis* and *D. lutea*) or snapped in the middle (*D. purpurea*). Even tough, sun-loving *Hemerocallis* (daylily) plants, especially those on dry sites, showed streaky foliage damage.

Coping

To grow a beautiful flower garden in such a climate you need to be savvy. There are several things you can do to cope. Begin by knowing your USDA hardiness zone. This will tell you which perennial plants will survive the winter in your area. (Perennials are herbaceous—nonwoody—plants that live for several years. Some may die to the ground in winter, but the root survives to send up new growth in spring.) You live in zone 4 or 5. Check the map in the front of this book (or on the back cover) and engrave the number in your mind. Trustworthy catalogs will include a hardiness rating in each plant description. The rating is given as a range, such as 5–8, or as a single figure, such as 6. If your zone number is within the range given, then you can expect the plant to survive winter in your garden. When hardiness is noted as a single digit, it indicates the lowest (coldest) zone number in which a plant is winter hardy. If the single zone listed is 3, then the plant in question can withstand a winter a good deal colder than zone 5 and should breeze through an Iowa January. A 7 means the plant can handle a winter only as cold as the one dished out in zone 7, so zone 5 is definitely too cold.

Once you are an experienced gardener, you can try cheating by one zone. A zone 6 plant, not generally winter hardy in zone 5, might survive planted in a protected spot and given extra winter cover. You could put it against a stone wall, for instance, and apply mulch after the weather turns cold and the ground freezes. Generally, though, you can expect the best vigor, bloom production, and longevity from plants if you stick to your correct zone.

Always check the hardiness of a plant before you make a purchase. To supplement catalog information, you need a couple of good reference books that list perennials and include hardiness ratings. Take a look at the books listed in chapter 9 for suggestions. An English garden book edited for publication in the United States is not a good source of zone information. Unfortunately, some catalogs provide no hardiness rating. This irresponsible habit leads many a novice gardener astray. Not every thrillingly described plant in the listing is suitable for a Midwestern garden. Beware. Planting a perennial with a hardiness rating more than one zone warmer than your own guarantees failure. Don't throw your money away. Take the time to check.

To complicate matters, a second hardiness rating scheme, created by Arnold Arboretum, uses a slightly different numbering system. Though far less common than the USDA system, it does occasionally turn up, so find the map the book or catalog uses and double-check your zone.

Once you have selected a plant appropriate to your zone, the question remains, Will it handle the heat? Until very recently, there has been no heat-zone system comparable to the USDA hardiness zone map. However, in 1997, the American Horticultural Society (AHS) published its Plant Heat-Zone Map assigning zone numbers based on the number of days that temperatures are above 86 degrees. Following the AHS heat-zone scheme, your garden in the hot Midwest is most likely located in heat-zone 5 (thirty to forty-five days above 86 degrees) or heat-zone 6 (forty-five to sixty days above 86 degrees). This breakthrough in recognizing and quantifying the effect of heat on plants should in the long run make it easier to select appropriate specimens for your garden. Presumably nurseries will gradually begin to assign heat ratings to plants just as they now use cold hardiness zones. In some dreamy, utopian future the catalogs will tell you that the plant you're smitten with is cold hardy to USDA zone 5 and heat hardy to AHS heat-zone 6. The AHS suggests that plant listings in catalogs will give a rating such as "3–8, 8–1," showing cold hardiness zone range first, followed by heat-zone range. Check the AHS Plant Heat-Zone Map in the first color photo section of this book for your heat-zone.

Chapter 5 is an encyclopedia of flowering plants that thrive in our climate. The few weaklings included (because they're just too ravishing to omit) are clearly noted. For plants not listed, ask experienced gardeners in your area or consult a nursery professional— one you trust to be honest even when it means losing a sale. A plant's native habitat can also be a clue to the degree of success you can expect in heat. Obviously if it's native to mountain meadows it will sulk in scorching heat. Visit available local public gardens often to observe plant performance.

Plant in full sun are words bandied about loosely by garden writers who dwell in milder climes. In the hot Midwest you must take these words with a large grain of salt. Our full sun is glaring and very strong from mid-June to mid-September. Plants that bloom in the sweet, watery light of spring can be sited in full sun without fear. At that time the sun's rays are low, slanting, and gentle. However, plants that bloom in the more direct and damaging rays of midsummer should be given careful site consideration. Some garden books suggest, for example, planting hostas in sun. Any experienced Midwestern gardener can tell you this is folly.

Fortunately, many plants thrive in hot, direct sun. Even during an extended spell above 100 degrees some plants can be counted on to perform in full sun. *Calamintha nepeta* (lesser calamint), *Nepeta* (catmint), and *Perovskia atriplicifolia* (Russian sage) are completely unaffected by heat and drought, even without watering. *Coreopsis verticillata* 'Moonbeam' (threadleaf tickseed) remains very cool and beautiful in the worst summer heat. *Echinops ritro* (small globe thistle), *Achillea* (yarrow), daylilies, perennial varieties of *Aster, Boltonia asteroides, Rosa* (rose), Siberian irises, *Artemisia stelleriana* (beach wormwood), *Chrysanthemum, Echinacea* (coneflower), *Rudbeckia fulgida* var. *sullivantii* 'Goldsturm' (black-eyed Susan), *Verbascum* (mullein), and *Lilium lancifolium,* syn. *L. tigrinum* (tiger lily) are other examples of plants that can beat the heat and glaring sun. Many annuals, such as *Tagetes* (marigold), *Petunia,* and *Consolida* (larkspur) also flourish in sun.

Still, only the strongest plants can tolerate the full blazing Midwestern sun. Many will need some respite. The most important time to protect plants is afternoon, when the sun is fiercest. You can provide this protection by planting where a physical structure (house, shed, arbor, bench, etc.) or a tree, shrub, or large plant offers shade for some part of the afternoon. A garden on the east side of your house basks in full morning sun, but feels the relief of shade in the afternoon. A garden on the west side receives the same amount of sunlight daily, but the light is stronger (and plants must be tougher) because the garden is shaded in the morning and exposed in the afternoon when sun is most direct. The house gives plants in both gardens protection by reducing the amount of sunlight, but on the west side the protection is less.

A garden close against the north side of your home is somewhat shady all day. This space offers too much sun protection and should be reserved for shade-loving plants. A garden on the south side is hottest of all. In this sun-blasted location, you should put plants that thrive on heat and sun. It is possible, however, to create small areas of sun protection. A shrub or tall perennial within the bed will cast some afternoon shade on its neighbor to the east. A small tree planted on the west end of the bed can create an area of afternoon shade.

July and August

Fortunately your garden won't have to endure a string of days over 100 degrees every summer, even in the blazing Midwest. What you can count on, though, is that somewhere in July and August, possibly much of that period, temperatures will shoot up above 90, the humidity will rise, and the garden will seem faded, wilted, and uninviting. The sweetly fresh darling buds of springtime will be only a faint memory. In May and June your garden bursts with bloom from bulbs and perennials. The list of plants in bloom lengthens each week until the last of June, when flowering is at its peak. In the doldrums of July and August, the loveliest spring bloomers are gone and the fall bloomers have not begun. Nothing much new is happening, and many of the spring perennials that continue to bloom do so only fitfully by midsummer. *Aquilegia* (columbine), roses, yarrow, foxgloves, and *Heuchera* (coral flower or coral bells) are still blooming, but are decidedly over the hill. Heat is bleaching and desiccating much that remains. A few perennials stand up to the heat, but many wilt and refuse to stand upright. You arrive home from work to find the idea of strolling through a dull, limp garden in baking heat insupportable.

How can you make your garden enjoyable at the peak of summer? First, remember to plant lovely and varied foliage. If you do this at the outset, your garden will be attractive in spite of the sun's wilting and fading effect on bloom. Second, plant daylilies. Forget the old orange daylilies your grandmother grew. The modern cultivars are superior in every way. The colors run from an icy pale yellow that suggests white through pinks and melons and salmons to roses, lavenders, deep purples, and reds. A careful mix of these sun lovers can create a gloriously colorful garden in spite of color-fading heat. Third, add to the daylilies a mix of other perennials that thrive and glory in heat and glaring sun so that you build your garden on a framework of these hardy plants. The lavender blue of Russian sage mixes beautifully with the rich red purple of *Hemerocallis* 'Little Grapette.' It's a combination that would make even an English gardener envious, and both plants are tough as nails in our climate. Finally, maximize late summer bloom by planting annuals.

Annuals

If you've begun dipping into garden literature at all, you already know there's a certain cachet to calling yourself a perennial gardener. You get to look down upon those who raise only marigolds, *Zinnia,* and petunias and say sniffishly, "Oh, annuals." The assumption is that if you have the taste and knowledge to grow perennials, you need nevermore sully your hands with mere annuals.

I say baloney. In the blast furnace of a Midwestern summer, annuals are the ideal plants to fill gaps in the perennial border. Annuals live only one season, growing from seed to full size, flowering, and setting seed in just a few months. Many of them achieve their magnificent peak in July and August, just when perennials arc taking a breather. Although most annuals will add no foliage interest, they are robust and reliable bloomers whose showy flowers pep up a sun-faded garden. Hot season annuals include marigolds; petunias; zinnia; *Centaurea cyanus* (bachelor's button); *Nicotiana* (to-bacco plant); *Cleome* (spider flower); *Lobularia maritima,* syn. *Alyssum maritimum* (sweet alyssum); *Heliotropium* (heliotrope); *Borago officinalis* (borage); *Salvia farinacea* (mealycup sage); *Salvia splendens* (scarlet sage); *Salvia viridis,* syn. *S. horminum* (annual clary sage); *Scabiosa atropurpurea* (pincushion flower); and *Celosia* (cockscomb). *Anethum graveolens* (dill), an annual herb, with its lovely sulfur yellow spray of bloom, makes a good cut flower and is utterly unaffected by heat.

By combining these hot weather annuals with daylilies and other perennials that take the heat of July and August you can make a good showing. This mix will carry you through till fall, when temperatures drop (especially at night), and asters, chrysanthemums, *Boltonia asteroides, Buddleia davidii* (butterfly bush), *Solidago* (goldenrod), and other perennials come to the fore again. As a bonus, most of the splendid summer annuals will continue to provide color at least through September.

Don't assume that all annuals are tough, drought-tolerant sun lovers, however. A few are delicate butterflies that look really good only in the cool of autumn and may not thrive long enough to see that season. *Calendula officinalis* (pot marigold), *Clarkia* (also called *Godetia*), *Gerbera,* annual asters, and *Matthiola* (stock) are examples. In an unusually cool, rainy year, they may survive and perform nicely, but most years they will be less than you had hoped. I don't recommend any of these for a hot Midwestern garden, but if you must grow them, try giving them a bit of afternoon sun protection. *Antirrhinum* (snapdragon) is another faint-hearted annual, though planted early it may give some bloom in spring and fall, with poor bloom in between. Look for varieties that indicate they are heat tolerant and provide them with light shade in the afternoon.

Other annuals grow and flower quickly, finishing too early to be useful in filling the hot late summer gap in perennial bloom. Examples are *Viola* (pansy and Johnny-jump-up), *Lobelia*, *Nigella damascena* (love-in-a-mist), and *Papaver* (poppy). If you plant them, expect to enjoy them in spring and early summer only.

The cheater's way to fill late summer gaps requires advance planning. When you plant your garden in spring, you're bound to have a few spare annuals. It's a mystery of the gardening game that if you need four annuals to fill a spot, they will be sold only in six-packs. Pot up the extra annuals and grow them as container plants until holes open up when a plant dies, an early bloomer is cut back, or a mistake in spacing becomes an eyesore. Dig a hole. Tap an annual out of its pot. Pop it into the hole. Problem solved.

Two-Season Garden

Another way to deal with the fiercely hot summer is to focus on the spring and fall garden and let summer be a long vacancy. If you hate heat and spend little time in the garden at summer's peak, then this may be the best approach for you. As a bonus, it gives you a clear time to take your summer vacation without missing anything wonderful in the garden!

Every gardener's goal is a riot of bloom in spring, summer, *and* fall, but this is difficult to achieve over the very long growing season in our area. Because our season is so long, plants that bloom in overlapping profusion elsewhere may be solo performers here. A New York garden starts its bloom with *Galanthus nivalis* (common snowdrop) in March and ends it in September with asters. In eastern Nebraska the snowdrops begin in February and the asters last through October or even longer (consult the sequence of bloom list in chapter 8 for a detailed look at the order of bloom in our area). It's lovely to have a long growing season, but I occasionally yearn for the abundance that a compressed season offers.

Very few plants bloom in all three seasons. In general, you can get one season of bloom in a given space only by sacrificing the other two seasons in that same space. To some extent, of course, you can double up by underplanting with bulbs that go dormant after they bloom in spring. A viable garden design choice is to capitalize on spring bulbs to build a two-season garden. Here's how. First, make a conscious decision to sacrifice summer bloom to gain more space for spring and fall flowering. Then double up bloom over a considerable area by underplanting with spring bulbs. This achieves a garden that is reasonably full of bloom over perhaps three spring months and two fall months, with only a pair of summer months of slight bloom. For example, plant *Narcissus* (daffodil) among daylilies and perennial asters or common snowdrops at the foot of Russian sage.

If a full abandonment of the summer garden seems too rash, you can use just a handful of big showy summer bloomers to create a pleasant summer garden while still concentrating your bloom in the cooler parts of the year. For example, *Rudbeckia fulgida* var. *sullivantii* 'Goldsturm' is a heavy-blooming perennial whose brilliant gold flowers cover the plant in summer. A few of these black-eyed Susans scattered about could single-handedly create the illusion of a garden in bloom at the peak of summer heat. Emphasis on foliage combinations will also help to preserve an attractive garden when bloom is at a low point. By choosing spring and fall bloomers with interesting contrasts of form, foliage texture, and color—the blue of *Baptisia australis* (blue wild indigo, false indigo, or plains false indigo), the fresh green of *Paeonia* (peony), the silvery arched spears of Siberian irises, the fine texture of catmint, the bushy form of asters and chrysanthemums, the silver brocade of *Artemisia stelleriana* (beach wormwood), and the ghostly apparition of Russian sage—you could maintain an attractive summer garden while still reserving plenty of space for show-stopping spring and fall displays.

Using Your Head

Other ways to beat the heat of July and August are just common sense. If the heat is intolerable in late afternoon, why go out into it? Get up an hour early and do your gardening at 6:00 or 7:00 A.M. Even in the hottest part of summer, the heat doesn't become oppressive until somewhere between 9:00 and 10:00 A.M. Spend a pleasurable hour or two watering and deadheading in the cool and quiet morning. The garden is refreshed from the relatively cool night, colors glow in the angled early morning light, and you can enjoy a bit of serenity before going to work. After dinner spend another hour outdoors. The heat has begun to wane and the light is just right to show off color without cooking the gardener. I urge you to heed Noel Coward's warning: "Only mad dogs and Englishmen go out in the mid-day sun."

If you must garden between 10:00 A.M. and 5:00 P.M., wear a hat. You'll be surprised at how much cooler you will feel, and the protection it provides for your skin is vital. Use sunscreen, too, and wear long sleeves. Our Midwestern farmers are often victims of skin cancer. Avoid this and the leathery look of a lifetime of overexposure to the sun by covering up sensibly.

You can continue your commonsense approach to gardening by using the hottest part of summer to perform lighter tasks. Review your garden design and make plans for transplanting. Most of us are all too ready to get a shovel and move a plant the moment the idea strikes. In July and August it's just plain too hot, for gardener and plant alike. It is, however, the perfect time to mull over plans. You don't have to guess how much space plants will take once you move them, because they've reached full size. I commend high summer to you as the time to sit in the shade of a tree with a glass of iced tea and a plate of cookies, contemplating your garden and the changes you will make once the temperature drops to a more reasonable level.

2

Designing a Garden

Making a garden begins and ends with design. Whole books—lots of them—have been written on the subject, and I don't claim to adequately cover it here. After twenty years of shuttling plants from place to place around my garden, I am only just beginning to see it really take shape. I've known the basic precepts of garden design for years (having read lots of those books), but have only now begun to absorb them. Somehow the basics don't make as much sense when you read about them as they do when you stumble over them yourself through years of frustrating trial and error. I offer you here my idea of the most important fundamentals in the hope (probably vain) that you'll absorb and use them without having to make your own twenty years of mistakes.

Design is the most essential part of the garden-making process and the most difficult to learn. You can study design with diligence and learn its elements without ever achieving brilliance in assembling them. Beyond the basics, you need an artistic bent, the courage to express your own personality, and the wit and maturity to

recognize what that means. Though beautiful gardens are made by hand, it is in the eye of the artist that the best of them are created.

I am not among the artistically blessed, but then most of us aren't. When I began gardening in my twenties, I had visions of myself as a sweet young thing, surrounded by a lush and lovely garden, admired by all. It was several years before I realized that gardens are created over time and their craft acquired over many years. As the garden fills with plants and takes shape, the gardener acquires wrinkles. It takes time to shape a garden, but it's worth it, because the process is at least as rewarding as the product.

Know Your Plants

Look at your first ten years in the garden as a period of apprenticeship, a time to learn your craft, and especially a time to learn your plants. When it comes to putting plants together to form a garden, the standard and frequently repeated advice is to make a splash by grouping three or more of the same kind, because perennial borders are said to flow together best if you overlap big drifts of color. Beginners should forget that advice, the sooner the better. In the long run it may be true, but in the short run your primary goal is to become familiar quickly with a large variety of plants since only familiarity will allow you to use plants well in designing a beautiful and vigorous garden. You need to discover what does well for you and what you love. Forget about those groupings of three and just start with one of everything. If you grow thirty different plants you will know far more after three years than you will if you grow three each of ten plants. Over time you can remove the failures and propagate or divide the successes to create mass effects. Most plants by their nature increase in size and number. As they mature they can be divided again and again to make those massed groupings.

As you grow different flowers and gain knowledge about them, make it a point to learn their names. Each of them possesses both a scientific name, also called the Latin or botanical name, and (usually) a common name. To understand garden catalogs and books and other gardeners, you need to learn both. The scientific name is especially important because each plant has only one, while it may have two, three, or even more common names. The first word in the scientific name indicates the genus, the second word names the species (also called the species epithet or the specific epithet). The cultivar, which names a variety produced by cultivation, follows these and is usually enclosed in single quotation marks. Using *Pulmonaria saccharata* 'Mrs. Moon' as an example, *Pulmonaria* is the genus, *saccharata* the species, and 'Mrs. Moon' the cultivar. This plant's common name is lungwort.

Don't let an inability to pronounce Latin stand in your way. *Cleome,* a common annual, is widely pronounced KLEE-ome in my neck of the woods, though plant dictionaries say the correct pronunciation is klay-O-mee. Longer names like *Polygonatum odoratum* 'Variegatum' can be a trifle daunting, but just take them one syllable at a time and give it your best shot. It doesn't really matter whether you can rattle off the correct pronunciation. The person you're addressing is probably at least as unsure as you are yourself. The key is to remember the name with its associated plant and add both to your internal plant encyclopedia.

Remember the Big Picture

In England the term *garden* is applied to the entire landscape around a house. In the Midwest, we call this a *yard* and the flower beds within it our garden. In planning, take your cue from the English. Your property may contain a deck, a fence, gates, a trellis, a shed, and a compost area, in addition to the house and garage. Taken together these create a feel that affects your pleasure in the garden. That flower bed you want to add will not exist in a vacuum. It will be part of a defined space with structures and other plantings and will look best if you try to tie it somehow to its surroundings.

Let's say you plan to extend existing plantings to wrap around one end of a garage. Stop looking down at the space you intend to fill with plants. Instead look up at the overall picture. Perhaps the back of your house is nicely tied to earth by embracing shrubs, but the garage—added later—rises starkly from the surrounding lawn. You can make the garden you plan more attractive and improve the big picture by using shrubs around the garage to echo those around the house. These in turn will make a handsome backdrop for the flowers in your garden.

A board fence may seem a cold, dull background for a flower bed. Cover it with a vigorous *Clematis* or *Parthenocissus tricuspidata* (Boston ivy) and it blends nicely with the big picture—soft, green, and enclosing. A wall may seem unpleasantly hard until draped in green. A plain white garden shed can glare in the harsh Midwestern summer sun, attracting more attention than your loveliest flowers. Paint it sage green, pale gray, or some appropriate soft pastel to quiet it down. A deck needs something to take its edges off and give it a sense of connection to the ground it occupies. A handful of plants in containers, a few shrubs along the edges, accent plants at corners, a shady tree to overhang it can provide this.

As you begin to garden, recognize that the space you devote to flower beds is likely to grow larger. You may start with a little strip of petunias on each side of a walkway, but soon you will be thinking those beds would be very nice doubled in width and planted with a few perennials and bulbs. That's just the beginning. A very few years of flower gardening will leave you firmly convinced that less is more when it comes to lawns.

Consider how you would like your property to develop. Look at pictures in books and magazines to garner ideas. Try to analyze your reaction to other gardens. Why do you love this particular photo or that friend's garden? Is it the color scheme, the arrangement of the beds, the geometric layout, or the flowing curves? Probably the most usual sort of garden in the Midwest is one in which beds are laid out around the perimeter of the property and often against the house, too, leaving a swath of lawn between them. This can be attractive, but there are other approaches to consider. You might create island beds, plantings at sea within your lawn and unattached to architectural features. You could lay out geometrical beds with gravel paths. If you have plenty of space, you might even subdivide your yard into garden rooms, an approach popular on large properties in England. These separate areas, bounded by shrubs or walls, allow you to design several distinct gardens, each with its own color scheme and personality.

Anything added should be seen as a part of the big picture. Consider, of course, how a plant looks with its immediate neighbors, but don't forget the bigger view. How will it look when you sit down to supper in the garden and sweep your eye around? How will it fit into the whole procession when you look down the length of the garden? What view will it affect as you look out a window?

Present a Unified Front

If the front of a flower bed is unified, it does a lot to make the whole bed feel put together. This applies both to the edging material you use and to the plants placed along the front. Use of the same stone, brick, gravel, or wood chip path for edging throughout your yard will help to tie the whole thing together. Choosing the same brick or stone used in the construction of your home enhances that sense of unity.

Repetition of plantings at the front of a flower bed gives an impression of unity and flow. The sublime effect of a repeating edge can hardly be overstated. You don't need to place the same plant monotonously along the entire border or even confine yourself to

three or four. The front of my large sunny border is edged with several different plants, but among them repetitions occur of *Heuchera*
x *brizoides* 'Chatterbox' (coral flower or coral bells), *Coreopsis verticillata* 'Moonbeam' (threadleaf tickseed), and *Nepeta* x *faassenii*,
syn. *N. mussinii* of gardens (catmint). The profusion of bloom on
all three makes them showy, eye-catching plants, good choices for
repetition. The catmint has soft bluish foliage with a flowing quality that speaks of romance, establishing the mood I want. Even when
not in bloom, the distinctive foliage of all three plants gives the
garden rhythm and sweep.

In my smaller shade border, just two dramatic patches of a variegated *Hosta* (hosta or plantain lily) give balance to a whole planting. Many other plants are mixed in along the front, but the repetition is what catches the eye. The white variegation in the dark shade
stands out boldly. Typically, repetition is accomplished with two or
more plants of the same kind, but you can also achieve it with plants
of different kinds that have the same coloring. Since bloom occurs
over only a fraction of a growing season, this works best with foliage color. In shade, for example, yellow-green *Lamium maculatum*
'Aureum,' syn. 'Gold Leaf' (spotted deadnettle) could echo a hosta
of the same color. When you stand back, your eye catches the reit-
eration of color.

An ideal garden is full to bursting with shoulder-to-shoulder
plants, but this doesn't always happen. In the real world, gardens
sometimes have gaps where plants have died or failed to grow robustly. Maintaining close, full planting along the front edge is critical, because fullness here will disguise shortcomings elsewhere.
Likewise, gaps here are much more likely to draw the eye.

Create Vistas

You can add great charm to your garden by providing something
to look at across a distance. Paint a picture with a focal point to-

ward which you will direct your eye. This can be as simple as placing a path so that a particularly beautiful tree lies at one end. You could also make a focal point of a statue or column, a birdbath or birdhouse mounted on a pole, a specimen plant, an arbor, a bench or chair, a gateway, an interesting urn or pot. If you don't have the perfect antique urn or specimen plant on hand, lay out the view anyway and trust time to provide it. Don't forget to look beyond your own garden. A flowering tree in your neighbor's yard, for instance, may feature strongly in your own garden vistas. I was reminded of this after a staggering winter storm damaged many trees in my city. A neighbor inquired anxiously whether the birch tree in my backyard would survive because it is a visually prominent part of her garden.

Provide a Background

The backdrop against which you see a flower bed can be a distraction or an asset. At the planning stage, you must see in your mind's eye not merely the flower bed, but also its setting. A garden is beautiful seen against the background of a stone wall. History and a rocky soil have provided these in abundance for gardeners in England and our own Northeast, but the Midwestern prairie doesn't cough up the raw materials required. Brick makes a nice substitute, but the cost is considerable. Shrubs form a lovely and lasting backdrop, making a garden seem natural and attached to the earth and giving it a strong vertical line.

If you decide to back your flower beds with shrubs, you'll need patience. They are slow growing compared to flowering perennials. The flowers may take three to five years to reach full size, but most shrubs will take more like eight to twelve. Notice shrubs in the gardens you visit. Look for them in catalogs and examine them at your local nursery. Hardiness zones of shrubs refer to the survival of the woody plant, not to the blooms, so it's worth inquiring whether the shrub flowers reliably in your area before you buy. Be especially cautious about plants that bloom on "old wood." This refers to bloom that occurs on the part of the plant that grew in the previous season. If winter creates dieback, you won't see flowers in spring.

As soon as you know what you want and where, get those shrubs in the ground. You'll be rewarded in a few years with a garden blessed with an established and comfortable charm. Early planting of shrubs offers the added advantage of preventing unwise plantings of perennials too close to fences or property lines. It's vital to determine the mature size of shrubs and space them accordingly. A natural tendency is to place them too close together, which achieves an immediate filled-in look, but leads to trouble in a few years when the shrubs begin to crowd one another. Resist the temptation to place large perennials or bulbs in the space between young bushes and encroach upon their growing space. Until the shrubs mature you can dress up overly open areas with annuals or small, easily moved perennials.

Shrubs can be used to create a look of formality when planted in rows to form a hedge and clipped to create straight lines. When planting hedges to create visual pathways, it's essential to know the ultimate size of the shrubs because placing them too closely in their infancy can make an unpleasantly claustrophobic walkway in the future. When in doubt, err on the side of roominess. For informality, try unclipped shrubs. If this is the look you strive for, give them plenty of room, because overcrowding will eventually demand regular pruning.

You can use individual shrubs to create interest in the background of a flower bed or in the bed itself if they are small. *Daphne* x *burkwoodii* 'Carol Mackie' is a small, slow-growing shrub with a variegated leaf and a neat dome shape. It makes a handsome addition to a flower bed and brings light to the shady setting it prefers. Shrubs with yellowish leaves or purple foliage make for nice contrast. Many shrubs can add the dimensions of flower and scent, too.

If your house is part of a garden's background, keep in mind its color. An amazing number of gardeners forget that the house is even in the picture. They fall in love with a shocking magenta rhododendron at the nursery and plant it smack in front of an orange brick house. Or they put a maple at the corner of a house painted mauve, forgetting that in fall the tree will be fiery red and orange. Or they bank the front of their white house with shrubs that bloom in ivory, looking shabby and dirty against their background. The true garden fanatic can always paint a wood house to complement favorite flowers, but if your home is brick or stone, you really do need to stop and think before planting.

Adhere to a Color Scheme

Color scheme is even more important in the garden than it is in your wardrobe, because a great part of your garden wardrobe is on display all at once. To create a sense of unity, pick a color scheme and stick to it. This is surprisingly hard to do. Color is intoxicating and so hugely appealing that I can't imagine choosing just one favorite color. Common color schemes discussed in garden literature are yellow and blue (or purple); white and gray (like Vita Sackville-West's famous White Garden); and pink, white, and blue (said to be English in flavor). There's nothing to stop you, though, from choosing some offbeat scheme to your own liking, say red and gray, or even red and orange. Your garden should be a reflection of the colors you love.

My own first choice color scheme is lots of pink in various shades, along with white and blue, pepped up with lemon yellow in small doses. I use gray foliage to emphasize the soft pastel look. *Crocosmia* 'Lucifer' sings me a siren song with its sharp, hot red, and only by self-discipline and constantly reminding myself that it would be hideous in my color scheme can I resist it. When it comes to color, you must focus. You can't have everything in life, so decide on a color combination and stick with it. If it's red, orange, and gold, you can't go messing about with lavender, pink, and lemon yellow. Satisfy your need for pastels by admiring other people's gardens. Focus on your color scheme whenever you acquire plants, even as gifts. The big difficulty here is that with most of us, taste develops over time. What appeals to you as a neophyte gardener may not as you mature, so your color scheme may shift over the years. This is one reason that mature gardens take so long to form.

It is possible in the Midwest for a single garden to have two color schemes, divided by season. A pastel color scheme of pink, white, blue, and yellow is easy to achieve in spring, but more difficult in the heat of Midwestern summer. A shift to gold, orange, and red might be desirable at that point. In the Midwest this is not as tricky as it sounds because the growing season is very long and a natural pause occurs between spring and summer bloom somewhere around the first of July. When the heat of summer strikes, spring bloomers step hastily aside.

Choosing plants by color descriptions can be confusing, because there is no common understanding of what exact shade any color word describes. A plant described as blue may be anything from royal blue or aquamarine to pale lavender or purple. Capturing flower colors on film is a tricky business, too, so even scrutiny of catalog photos may not help. If you make a habit of looking carefully at plant colors (both leaf and flower) in nurseries, your friends' gardens, and in your own flower beds, you can gradually build up a knowledge of plant color to aid you in garden design. When you choose a color scheme, be clear with yourself about whether you want sky blue or purple or lavender or aquamarine. Then compare book and catalog descriptions and ask experienced gardeners for advice.

As you fine-tune your garden design, you'll probably wind up moving just about every plant at least once. Try to make the decision about a plant's final destination while it is still in bloom. Color memory is surprisingly short, so making a good decision is much easier when you directly compare a plant's blossoms with those of its prospective neighbors.

Unfortunately for your color design, the heat and glaring sunlight of a sunny location in our region dramatically change colors. The sun makes them *appear* faded and the heat fades them *in fact* as well as in appearance. I first became aware of this phenomenon when I visited my sister-in-law's garden in Minneapolis. She cut a handful of annuals for a small bouquet and I was swept away by their jewel-like colors. I particularly recall the luscious tangerine of her *Calendula officinalis* (pot marigold). This was an annual I had never seen before, and based on the brilliant loveliness of hers, I grew some myself the following year, only to be disappointed by their comparatively dull orange. Both in my garden and in bouquets their color lacked the freshness, life, and clarity I remembered. The heat and sun of southeastern Nebraska had sapped the color's vitality. For beautiful color in the hot Midwest, it's best to stick with plants that can handle heat and to bear in mind when selecting colors that the glaring sun will wash them out.

To do a good job of planning, you need to notice colors. It's very easy to err horribly in choosing garden companions because you overlook what is right under your nose. Not all whites, for example, are pure bridal white. Many are really ivory or off-white with a pink or yellow cast. Planting white next to off-white forms an unpleasant combination; the less white plant looks tawdry. *Convallaria* (lily-of-the-valley) planted next to *Tiarella wherryi*, syn. *T. cordifolia* var. *collina* (Wherry's foamflower) is a classic mistake in this department. The lily-of-the-valley is too snowy for the foamflower's cream blushed with dusty pink. Whites (as opposed to creams and ivories) look pure and sweet in the soft sunlight of spring, but seem to glare unpleasantly in the harsh light of summer in the hot Midwest. In early May *Iberis sempervirens* (candytuft) is wonderful in masses, but a month later, in the more direct sun of a later season, white irises and daisies strike the eye keenly and are more attractive used sparingly. You may think of white as a noncolor, but in fact it is a very strong and eye-attracting color in both bright sunlight and shade. In the darkness of shade, this is a desirable quality. Masses of white can lighten a dark place. Just as you wear white when you go for a walk at night so that you are visible to drivers, you can dress your shade garden in white to create visibility.

Plants called "yellow" are often gold instead, and the two do not suit the same color schemes. Gold—an orange shade of yellow—is gorgeous with reds and oranges and purples. However, if you're looking for a dash of yellow to spice up a pastel color scheme, you want yellow green, sulfur, lemon yellow, or perhaps butter yellow, but definitely not gold. Gold stands up very well in brilliant sunlight, while the yellows are somewhat paled by it. *Rudbeckia fulgida* var. *sullivantii* 'Goldsturm' (black-eyed Susan) is a strong perennial whose brilliant gold color never flinches in full sun or heat wave.

Yellow and gold are not happy companions in the garden. One or the other may suit your color plan, but probably not both. Having said that you don't want to put yellows with golds or whites with creams, I should mention the exception. You can make these combinations work if you choose a monochromatic (one-color) scheme. For instance, if you decide on a white garden, you can combine all of the whites—from the purest most blinding white to the creams and even very faint pinks—because the contrasts are dulled by the sheer number of shades. The eye is confused by profusion into seeing a whole instead of individual pairings. It's like looking at a multiple-hued print fabric: you don't notice whether individual colors within the print clash because you see only the colorful whole. If you're mad about the yellow color range, you can create an all-yellow garden using everything from pale butter yellow to the brashest gold.

Flowers described as "blue" are nearly always a shade of purple. Truly sky blue flowers are few in number. Rarest of all is that sumptuous shade of brilliant blue found in *Myosotis alpestris* (alpine forget-me-not) and *Brunnera macrophylla*, syn. *Anchusa myosotid-iflora* (Siberian bugloss). Nature is much more lavish with the violets, purples, and lavenders that are typically called blue in garden catalogs: *Nepeta* (catmint), *Campanula* (bellflower), *Viola* x *wittrockiana* (pansy), irises, asters, *Phlox divaricata* (woodland phlox or wild sweet William), *Baptisia australis* (blue wild indigo, false indigo, or plains false indigo).

"Pink" is used to describe a great range of shades from pale pink or lavender to a vivid, eye-assaulting hot pink. The latter, sometimes described as fuchsia or magenta, is a jolt of color that can perk up a wan pastel color scheme even in very small shots. Magenta is sometimes disparaged as too bright to be easily mixed with other colors. However, this is not a concern in the hot Midwest, where the glare of summer's sun seems to drain away color. Here magenta's brilliance is rather to be sought out than avoided. The paler pinks can become insipid in the blinding light of July and August. Dashes of magenta will enliven them.

Red, gold, orange, and purple can show some oomph in the glare of fierce sunlight. In a climate of milder sunshine they might seem garish, but here they make a warm and cheerful summer color scheme. Certain vividly colored flowers, however, fade under direct sun. I'm speaking here not of a perceived lessening of color caused by excessive light, but of a real sapping of color in heat and full sun. *Hemerocallis* (daylily) is the most obvious example. Some red and purple cultivars fade dramatically unless placed in partial shade.

Gray foliage is actually a pale, soft green, usually with fuzzy leaves that add to the impression of softness. This gray green strikes me as a very relaxing, calming color. It cools and offers pleasant contrast to darker greens. It may have a blue or yellow cast, which you may want to take note of when combining grays.

The Importance of Foliage

Nearly everything you read on garden design will emphasize the importance of foliage. You were probably drawn to gardening in the first place because you love flowers, so you're thinking, phooey on foliage. I once felt the same, but after several years of gardening I've changed my tune. Let me try to convince you of the essential importance of foliage.

Many perennials flower for only one to three weeks, and even those considered long-blooming usually flower for only about six weeks. In zone 5, the garden is in bloom and under scrutiny from February when the *Crocus* bloom until the last asters freeze in October or even November—around thirty-five weeks. Deduct just a couple of weeks for zone 4. This leaves you plenty of time to contemplate the unadorned foliage of even your favorite long bloomers. The phrase *nonstop bloomer* is a fiction of nursery catalogs. No perennial blooms profusely from spring through to fall. That's why leaves are so significant. If foliage is graceful, glossy, fuzzy, silvery, unusually colored, variegated, textured, or exceptionally large or tiny, it introduces dimension and interest to your garden. The satisfying leafy tapestry you weave with it is fresh and beautiful for most of the growing season.

Some wonderful bloomers have uninteresting leaves. The daylily is a prime example. Planting daylilies in masses will make a very dull picture for the many weeks during which they do not bloom. Certainly you don't want to eliminate every plant from your list whose foliage is ho-hum, but you do need to take into consideration all shortcomings. If a plant's foliage is boring, place it in small groupings among plants with handsomer or simply different foliage. The big, straplike green leaves of daylilies are lackluster in masses, but can be contrasted with the rounded leaves of *Heuchera* (coral flower or coral bells), the diminutive leaves of *Calamintha nepeta* (lesser calamint), or the silvery leaves of *Stachys byzantina,* syn. *S. lanata* (lamb's-ears) to create appeal.

Seek plants whose foliage is attractive to your eye. Watch for color, texture, and size that can provide contrast in a scene of unrelenting smooth dark green. Consider planting *Hosta sieboldiana* var. *elegans* for the dramatic effect of its massive leaves, in spite of its unimpressive bloom. Don't worry that shade-loving *Athyrium niponicum* (Japanese painted fern) will never bloom at all; its delicate frosty fronds are reward enough.

On a visit to the garden of a professional horticulturist, I swept my eye over an attractive perennial border and realized what did not at first strike me about the scene: relatively few plants were in bloom. The designer had used varying kinds of foliage—particularly variegated foliage—to produce enduring texture, movement, and interest in the garden. At a different season, masses of bloom would be the frosting on the cake, but this cake was quite satisfying without the frosting.

Make a Plan

It's useful to plan a garden on paper before planting it. Use graph paper with quarter-inch squares and let each square represent a square foot. Measure your existing or planned bed and outline it on graph paper. You can then pencil sketch your plants onto the design, leaving appropriate space for each. A plant that grows thirty-six inches wide will need a space three squares by three squares. You can sketch and erase till you get it right or you can use cutouts. Cut shapes to represent plant sizes out of a different sheet of graph paper. Label them with plant names, then push them around on your garden outline till you're happy with the result. If you like, spray the back of the cutouts with Photo Mount (available at photo shops) before cutting. This makes them tacky enough to stay put in a draft, but they can still be moved around easily.

Putting things on paper lets you stand back and take a look. This is the time to notice that you've put two yellow-blooming plants side by side or plants with very similar foliage too close together. You may also discover that the space where you contemplated putting sixteen plants has room for only eight or that you've planned too many different varieties for your space.

Getting your garden on paper helps you to visualize and think things through. Mistakes can be fixed with an eraser instead of a shovel. A plan on paper is especially useful for beginning and intermediate gardeners who have trouble keeping all the attributes of each plant straight: plant height, width, shape, sun or shade requirements, moisture needs, height of bloom, bloom color, foliage color, foliage shape and texture, bloom shape and form. It's a lot to juggle mentally. A picture helps. As you become more knowledgeable you'll find you can keep all these factors in mind and design more directly in the garden, but it still helps to think the entire design through before you pick up a shovel. It's also a great boon to have a plan on paper when midwinter rolls around. This is when your memory of exact plants and locations is getting dim and you're looking at nursery catalogs, ready to order plants for next year.

Please the Eye

Beyond the flower color and foliage of individual plants, there's plenty that goes into the formation of a pleasing garden picture. A garden is most beautiful when viewed down its length. From this perspective, an illusion of fuller bloom is created by the magic of foreshortening. Empty spots disappear. The garden is especially lovely with the evening light behind it. If you can site your bed so that you see down its length with the setting sun behind it, grab the opportunity. This garden will run east and west lengthwise with your viewing point on the east side, looking west. As the sun angles low in the sky, the flower petals will become stained glass, their jewel colors breathtakingly vivid. If you spend more time in your garden in the morning, reverse the layout to catch the rising sun.

Without constant attention to vertical line in plants, you are likely to find yourself always looking down on a planting about as interesting as wall-to-wall carpet—uniformly low and dull. The occasional *Lilium* (lily), *Verbascum* (mullein), *Thalictrum rochebrunianum* (meadow rue), or *Delphinium* brings the garden up to eye level and adds elegance. Roses, *Buddleia davidii* (butterfly bush), tall perennial asters, *Cleome* (spider flower), and other sizable plants give height, substance, and form. To add interest, vary not only the height of plants but also their general shape. Spikes, clumps, ground huggers, fans, bushy shapes, and so on should mix it up to provide movement. Do the same with bloom size and shape.

For a casual cottage garden look, use annuals and short-lived perennials that self-seed in an unplanned way to fill gaps and soften the overall look: *Consolida* (larkspur), *Viola tricolor* (Johnny-jump-up), *Lychnis coronaria* (rose campion), *Aquilegia* (columbine), *Borago officinalis* (borage). Use weavers—those that spread gradually to close up spaces and work in around their neighbors—to fill in the picture. For this tapestry effect use *Nepeta* (catmint), *Coreopsis verticillata* 'Moonbeam' (threadleaf tickseed), *Lamium maculatum* (spotted deadnettle), *Veronica prostrata* (prostrate speedwell), *Mazus reptans, Artemisia stelleriana* (beach wormwood), *Astilbe chinensis* var. *pumila* (false spirea), or *Galium odoratum,* syn. *Asperula odorata* (sweet woodruff).

Plan ahead to disguise plants not in bloom. Irises make sizable plants that bloom for a brief time, after which the foliage is all too likely to be attacked by disease. Plant irises among daylilies, whose attention-catching blooms come on just as the irises are looking their worst. I grow *Leucanthemum vulgare,* syn. *Chrysanthemum leucanthemum* (ox-eye daisy), a legacy from a previous gardener. In flower the daisies are classic white, but after bloom the foliage becomes rank. I plant my ox-eyes among asters that don't begin to grow large until about the time the daisies fade. I cut back the daisies when the flowering ends and let the asters take over. Obviously all this camouflage is unnecessary when a plant's leaves are beautiful on their own.

If the bad traits of a plant simply can't be disguised, then you must follow an important basic precept of garden design: be ruthless! Your garden will have failures—plants that simply don't perform well. Weak growth or a flopping habit or a color that doesn't quite suit or some other character flaw will cause the plant to seriously disappoint you. Some of these shortcomings may be remedied by maturity, but if you have had a perennial in your garden for three years and still it lets you down, show no mercy. Dig it up and pitch it. This can be unexpectedly difficult to do. You find yourself thinking of the poor old thing as a breathing personality and feel almost as if you are tossing a puppy on the rubbish heap. You must be firm. Take no prisoners. Out it goes. Until you are able to do this your garden will be so full of unsuccessful or second-rate plants that you will have no hope of producing the lovely artistic whole toward which you strive.

In laying out your garden don't forget to give yourself a place to sit down and enjoy it. A bench placed where you can sit in the shade and admire your creation can greatly enhance your delight. Consider at what time of day you are most likely to sit down to contemplate your little paradise and site the bench so that you will not be blinded or baked by sunlight at that hour. A spot for outdoor dining is another very good idea. In the spring and fall when weather is cool and pleasant, nothing is more restful than dinner in the garden. Time seems to stand still as you relax without effort.

3

Dirt

This should have been chapter 1, but frankly, I didn't want to scare you off. Fixing your soil is the first step to a good garden. It's also hard work that many of us would like to avoid. When you paint a house, you start by cleaning and scraping, even though you'd just as soon bypass this arduous and uncreative phase. After a few hours of the tedious stuff, you're finally able to pick up a paintbrush. It's the same in the garden. After a few hours of loosening and amending your soil, you're ready to get creative with the plants. Most beginning gardeners want a yard full of blooms to spring magically from the unaltered earth at their feet. It's not going to happen. Even if you've been gardening for a few years, you may still be trying to scrape by with little or no soil preparation. You need to get serious about giving your perennial plants the rich, loose, moist, fertile soil they deserve.

Sand and Clay

Start with the dirt right under your feet. Unless you have moved onto a property that was formerly owned by a really good gardener, your soil is probably nothing to brag about. If it is sandy, you already have the good drainage that many desirable perennial plants demand. Your soil is easy to work with—loose, light, and gritty. What you lack is the humus (partially decayed vegetable matter) that will supply nutrients and increase moisture retention. Water runs so freely through sandy soil that nutrients wash away quickly and the soil will be dry. The sandy particles hold heat, too, making the soil hotter in warm months and contributing to its dryness.

Many of us in the Midwest are up against clay soil. Clay is solid and heavy. It is difficult to get through with a shovel, hard to lift and turn, sticky when wet, and iron hard when dry. It is a knee-wrecking, backbreaking misery to work with and inhospitable to the many plants that require good drainage. Water soaks into clay soil slowly, making it difficult to water adequately without causing runoff. On the other hand, clay soil is moisture retentive and rich in nutrients. Whining is a favorite pastime of gardeners who must till the clay. No matter how awful your own soil may be, other gardeners will triumphantly insist that theirs is worse. One gardener I know even made a little bowl out of the clay in his garden just to prove its nasty nature.

Whether you're dealing with clay or sand, you can improve it dramatically by adding organic material in generous amounts. This added humus will make clay easier to dig. Plant roots will penetrate more easily and the soil will be more free draining. Sandy soil, improved with humus, will drain more slowly, retain moisture, and have better structure and body. More nutrients will be available and they will leach away more slowly.

Compost

The very best way to add organic material to your soil is to dig in plenty of compost. Compost makes a lovely, healthy garden possible. There are so many ways to use it that you will never truly have enough. Although you may be able to buy this magical ingredient at a local garden shop or even get it free from a municipal composting operation, your best bet for an economical and reliable supply of good quality compost is to make it in your own backyard.

If you start in May, you can have usable compost by September. This may seem like a long time, but the point is that it will be September whether you start composting now or not. If you get moving, it can be September *with compost.*

You may be dragging your feet because you've been taken in by all the detailed baloney about the Science of Composting. Well, you can forget about thermometers, expensive bins, lids, ideal siting, ideal ratios. Composting is really very simple. After all, it's perfectly natural for organic material to rot. All you have to do is speed the process along. Here's how.

Begin by deciding how you'll contain your compost heap. There are various kinds of bins on the market, and garden literature offers plans for building bins. You don't absolutely need a bin at all. You can just pile your materials on the ground. If you choose to use a bin, the type you select probably won't significantly affect the speed with which you turn out compost or the quality of the final product.

I use two kinds of bins. The first is a heavy-duty three-bin beauty my husband built me to the specifications of James Underwood Crockett in *Crockett's Victory Garden* (Boston: Little, Brown, 1977). It is a masterpiece of solid craftsmanship, but it doesn't make compost one whit better than do my other bins, purchased at a local hardware store. They were relatively inexpensive and a snap to assemble. Each bin consists of four sides of coated wire grid held together by four metal skewers that stabilize the bin simply by sticking into the ground. The green wire filled with green and brown materials blends into the garden scene far less obtrusively than the big three-bin job that had to be constructed by someone with building skills. With the wire grid bins it's quick and easy to add another bin, take one down to store, and take the front off to turn the pile.

Siting your pile in a sunny spot will warm it and probably speed the rotting process. Most of us, though, will opt for a hidden location under trees or behind shrubs, where composting will work perfectly well, even if a bit more slowly.

Pay attention now: this paragraph is as technical as I'm going to get. Compost requires just four ingredients: oxygen, water, and two kinds of organic material—carbon-rich and nitrogen-rich. Carbon-rich materials are tough and fibrous, like tree leaves, thick plant stalks, and straw. Nitrogen-rich materials are soft, like grass clippings, fruit and vegetable peelings, garden trimmings, and manure.

Once you've got your containers in place, start filling one of them with carbon-rich materials and nitrogen-rich materials. Simply alternate six-inch layers of the two types. If you use a layer of manure, it will be very high in nitrogen and can be thinner—an inch or two. If the materials you add are dry, sprinkle on a little water, but don't overdo it, because you don't want a sodden mass that squashes oxygen out of the pile.

There is no precise recipe for what you put in the pile. Use grass clippings, trimmings from the garden, fruit and vegetable peelings, horse or cow manure, and tree leaves. Any nonwoody vegetable matter is fine. Steer clear of moldy or diseased plant materials and weed seeds. House pet waste may carry disease and should be avoided. Never put meat, fish, grease or cooking oil, or bones in your compost: you may attract wild animals, including rats.

Oxygen maintains aerobic activity. Without it, rotting slows down and the pile stinks. Keep the oxygen level high by turning the pile every six or eight weeks during the warm season. In cold weather the pile doesn't rot so there's no reason to turn it. The hotter the weather, the faster the pile will rot and the sooner it can be turned.

Work toward making a pile about four feet high and four feet across, but you don't have to build your pile all at once. Just add to the pile as you have materials available. When you put in edibles like kitchen trimmings, cover them with a layer of grass clippings, dirt, or leaves to prevent odors. Sprinkle on a bit of water as you go if the pile seems dry. When the pile reaches four feet high, turn it over. Use a pitchfork to make the work easy. If you have more than one bin, turn the pile into a new bin and start another pile where the first one was. In six or eight weeks you'll have the new pile finished. Then you can move both piles to new bins and start a third heap. About the time the third pile is ready to turn, your first pile will be ready to use.

When the autumn leaves begin to fall they make lovely compost, too. Just use them as a high carbon layer in your regular compost pile. Oak leaves, however, are very tough and slow to break down, so I don't add them to my regular piles unless they are finely chopped. Instead, I make separate oak leaf bins alternating with grass clippings for finished compost in about eighteen months. It may seem like a long time to wait, but the leaves make terrific compost.

Your piles will decompose faster if you chop the materials you add. Cut them up with clippers, run them through a mulcher/shredder (not a chipper, which is designed to chop small branches), or run over them with a mulching mower. You can also hasten breakdown by adding manure, so do that if you have a free supply. Cow manure is ideal. Commercial compost starters or high nitrogen fertilizers can also be used to speed decomposition. The real beauty of compost, though, is that you can make this miraculous product without spending a lot of money. Buy a pitchfork and three bins and you're in business. Everything else you need is free, and if money is really short, you don't absolutely have to have the bins either.

Finished compost is often described as brown and finely crumbled, like chocolate cake crumbs. Don't worry if yours doesn't get that fine. You have usable compost when it has an overall blended, crumbly look, with relatively few distinguishable stems and leaves.

If most of it is crumbly you don't need to worry about a few pieces as big as three or four inches across. The rotting process will continue after you add the compost to your garden. If any of the pieces seem too large, just toss them back onto your newest pile and let them decompose more thoroughly.

Once you've made your first bin of compost, you can start digging it into your soil to improve texture, moisture retention, and drainage. Light, sandy soil will mix easily with the compost, but if you have clay soil, there's one more step to take.

Loosen Clay Soil with Gypsum

You need to mix lots of compost into clay to improve drainage and create a friable soil for plant roots, but mixing anything into the sticky mass of clay is no small chore. You must first break the clay up into smaller particles that will mix more easily with organic materials. You can soften the soil by watering it well the day before you plan to dig it over. If it is still too hard, you can loosen clay soil with gypsum.

Gypsum, available in bags at nurseries, is a powdery or grainy mineral that can work miracles on clay soil. If you've tried it already without success, you probably haven't used it properly. You can't simply sprinkle it over the surface. It must be worked in along with compost. Every time you turn soil and hit heavy clay, sprinkle on gypsum and dig it in. If the clay is so solid that mixing in gypsum is very difficult, do the best you can, then water it in. The next day dig over the area again. It should be much easier to handle. As you work with gypsum, you'll find that the clay begins to break down from solid slabs into smaller, faceted bits.

Notice that I didn't tell you how much gypsum to add. Neither does the bag it comes in, and I've never seen a formula suggested. It all depends. Let's say you're digging a gallon-size hole. Try adding a quarter cup of gypsum and two shovels full of compost. Mix it all up and water it. Come back the next day to dig it over again. Was it enough? You're going for a soil loose enough to allow you to add liberal amounts of compost. Just experiment. It shouldn't take long to get the feel of it. The more solid the clay, the more gypsum you need. Gypsum will work its magic over a period of time. You'll see some initial improvement, followed by great improvement over a few months.

It's a good idea to go slowly when using gypsum because it can raise the pH level of your soil, making it more alkaline. Since most perennials like a slightly acid pH, your garden will not thrive if the soil becomes too alkaline. Add gypsum gradually and have your soil tested periodically to avoid problems. Check with your cooperative extension service office to find out where to get a soil test.

Using Compost

The quickest and most efficient way to improve your soil is to prepare a bed before you plant anything. Obviously, your only chance to do this is when you first plant the bed.

Many garden books suggest double digging. This involves digging a trench twenty to twenty-four inches deep. You then put the turf you removed from the surface upside down in the bottom of the hole to rot. The relatively rich top soil goes on top of it. Over this you shovel the poorer bottom soil. This effectively reverses the soil, putting the richest soil at the bottom to feed the roots. For a modest five-foot-by-ten-foot bed this would require moving one hundred cubic feet of soil twice—once to take it out, once to put it back. You may wish to contemplate this if you have light, sandy soil and the back of an ox, but if you are gardening on clay, the whole idea is laughable.

You don't need to suffer through the amount of brute labor required for double digging. You can provide plants with a reasonable amount of root space in loose soil by what I call single digging.

Loosen and turn the soil to the depth of one shovel plunged well down into the earth. You'll be going down somewhat less than a foot. If you are working with clay soil, add gypsum. Now layer on compost and dig the bed over again, breaking it up and mixing in the gypsum and compost. Ideally your layer of compost would be four to five inches thick, but realistically this amount may not be available. Use what you can lay your hands on. Your city may have a community composting center you can tap. If you're wealthy and have the good sense to spend your money on something really valuable, buy some compost at your local nursery.

If compost isn't available for sale locally and your own compost heap hasn't yet started producing, consider buying sphagnum peat moss. Peat moss is an organic soil amendment available in bales at the nursery. Oddly enough, this material, which is extremely moisture-retentive once moist, is also very difficult to moisten once it becomes thoroughly dried out. Lay your bale on its side, cut open the broad top, and water it. Hot water will be absorbed much more readily than cold. The first water out of a sun-warmed hose on a hot day is good. I sometimes heat water in a teakettle to add along with hose water. One word of caution about peat moss: large amounts of it can make the whole soil difficult to moisten once dried. Compost is definitely preferable when available.

The addition of all this organic matter and the digging and loosening of the soil will raise the level of the bed a few inches, so that between the depth you've dug down and what you've added, you now have rich, loose soil at least a foot deep. This is enough to make just about any perennial very happy. If you've planned ahead, you can dig the bed in the fall and let the freezing and thawing of winter thoroughly mix all of your ingredients for a beautiful soil texture come spring.

Unfortunately, you may be dealing with a flower garden *already established* in unprepared soil. If your bed is already planted and you can't dig and enrich the whole thing at once, it is possible to fix your soil piecemeal. This takes time, but ultimately will result in lovely, loose, rich garden soil. Every time you plant or transplant, loosen the soil thoroughly a full shovel deep, add gypsum if you're working with clay, and enrich the soil with compost. Be especially generous with the compost if you are planting something that likes moisture and rich soil.

In the fall, put a layer of compost over your entire garden—two to four inches. Hoe it lightly into the surface, avoiding roots. Even without any digging, the compost somehow softens and mixes with the soil over the winter.

You can also mulch your beds with compost in the spring to retain moisture and discourage weeds. This works well to give new plants a start, babying them along till their root systems are big enough to weather a bit of drying. About an inch of compost will do it. I don't recommend a thicker layer because it seems to keep moisture out as well as it holds it in. If the compost layer is too thick, thorough watering will moisten its surface without penetrating to the soil beneath it. If you want to add more compost in spring than just an inch, be sure it is well rotted and fine textured. Then hoe it in lightly to blend it with the soil surface while being careful not to damage plant roots. If you find yourself short on compost, *do not* substitute peat moss as a mulch, because it will dry out and prevent moisture from penetrating.

Even enriched loose soil will tend to compact on the surface after a hard rain or following a dry spell. Use a hoe to loosen the surface so that water can penetrate easily. Be careful not to pile compost or any other mulch directly against plant stems. Mulch *around* plants, not *over* them. Allowing mulch materials to crowd against stems or cover foliage will cause the plant to rot and may kill it. Never mulch tall bearded irises, as they like to have their rhizomes (rootstocks) right at surface level.

Routine use of compost (and gypsum on clay) will build and maintain a ravishing garden soil. Apply a heavy layer of compost on new beds, moderate compost in fall, and a thin compost mulch in spring. Add compost in every hole you dig as you plant and transplant. You will notice an immediate improvement in your soil. At the end of three years the difference will be stunning. The quality and texture of your soil will make you the envy of other gardeners, and every time you go out into your garden you will hear a chorus of plants singing, "Thank you, thank you, thank you!"

What about Fertilizer?

If you are considering buying a fertilizer for your flower beds, take a look at the three numbers prominently displayed on the label that indicate the chemical content, such as 5-10-5 or 0-10-10. The first number represents nitrogen, which encourages fast, vigorous leafy growth. Because perennials are slow growing, nitrogen is not needed in quantity. The second number represents phosphorous, which promotes strong roots and stems and encourages flowering. The third number stands for potassium, which makes plants disease resistant. Choose a fertilizer with a low first number and a relatively high second number. If your soil is sandy, it may be potassium deficient, making the third number important.

If you feel you need commercial fertilizer, follow the instructions printed on the container. More is not better. More fertilizer than the package recommends may burn roots and can even kill your plants, especially young ones. Read the instructions and follow them to the letter.

I used to apply fertilizer each spring and was never really happy with the results. Finally one year a nursery employee told me that she used only bonemeal and compost and no commercial fertilizer at all. I tried it, liked it, and have seldom used a bag of fertilizer since. Bonemeal is high in phosphorous, that vital ingredient that encourages bloom and strong root and stem growth. It is slow acting compared to commercial fertilizer. In addition to adding compost and gypsum to my clay soil, I also dig in bonemeal each time I dig a hole. I add about a quarter cup for a small plant, about a half cup for a medium plant, and about one cup for a large plant like a shrub. When I prepare a new bed I sprinkle bonemeal over the entire bed, using the ratio stated on the package, and dig it in.

In the spring, I also like to add composted cow manure, except on plants that prefer a poor soil. Composted manure is sold cheaply in bags at the kind of instant garden shops that spring up at discount stores and drugstores each March. Use the amount recommended on the package. Just spread it on and hoe it in lightly, being careful not to cut into roots. Cow or horse manure straight from farm or stable is even better, but put it in your compost pile instead of applying it directly to the garden, because the high nitrogen in fresh manure can burn plants.

Keeping Your Soil Fixed

It's important to recognize that once you fix soil, your job will not be done. You need to maintain nutrients, texture, and moisture-retentive qualities. The plants in your garden will actually use up the organic matter you put into your soil. You don't put a plate of food in front of your family and expect to be done cooking forever. Once the food is consumed you have to provide more. It's the same with a garden. Once the organic matter, bonemeal, and manure are used up you have to provide more. If you have noticed your garden is not doing as well as it once did, you may be neglecting your soil.

Put down compost each fall. Dig in composted manure, compost, and bonemeal whenever you plant, hoe in composted manure in the spring. It sounds like an enormous amount of work, but you probably need the exercise anyway, and done a little at a time it's not that big a burden. You're going to be digging a hole anyway. You might as well make that small extra effort to enrich the soil you've turned.

Compost, bonemeal, composted manure, and gypsum are the four things I load into my wheelbarrow every time I head into the garden. These ingredients add up to my recipe for rich, moist, loamy soil that is nirvana to perennials.

4

Planting
and Transplanting

When you choose a plant for your garden, start by checking its winter hardiness for your climate zone. Consult the USDA Plant Hardiness Zone Map in the front of this book (or on the back cover) and select only plants that have a hardiness rating no higher than the zone where you live (further detail on climate zones and hardiness is provided in chapter 1).

Next, consider the heat of summer. Read catalog descriptions carefully and supplement them by consulting garden books that give site information for perennial plants. If catalogs and books say the plant requires full sun with some protection from afternoon sun, you may be dealing with a euphemism that really means Midwestern heat will cook this baby. For Midwestern gardeners, "plant in full sun" is the biggest lie in garden literature. Consider the source. Does the author live in one of those sissy places like England or the Pacific Northwest? Full sun in the Midwest, combined with wind, is a blast furnace that only the toughest will survive. Full sun is good siting for *Hemerocallis* (daylily), irises, roses, *Achillea* (yarrow), asters, chrysanthemums, herbs, and *Lilium lancifolium,* syn. *L. tigrinum*

(tiger lily). If you plan to put *Digitalis* (foxglove), *Astilbe* (false spirea), and *Campanula* (bellflower) in the full sun of our region, however, you might just as well stick them in the oven and be done with it. Even with shade protection, some plants that are theoretically appropriate for our region based on their hardiness rating simply will never be vigorous survivors here. Sometimes heeding the advice of a veteran Midwestern gardener is your best bet for success.

Starting Plants from Seed

You can buy the plant you want locally, order it from a nursery catalog, or start it from seed. The general assumption is that starting seed indoors will save you great buckets of money. After many years of tending flats of seedlings, I don't believe this is true. You'll need equipment and supplies that run into serious money: grow lights, seed flats, seed trays, seed starting mix, plastic sheeting to preserve moisture, plant stakes, and expensive seed packets. After all this expense, you'll still have the occasional crop failure that results in a trip to the nursery to buy the plants, too!

Is it worth the fuss and expense? That depends. If all you want is a few annuals easily purchased locally, then you're wasting time and money growing your own. Likewise, if you want two or three perennials, you're probably money ahead to buy the plants. However, there are times when it makes sense to start seed indoors. For design reasons, you may want several annuals of a specific color instead of the ubiquitous mixed colors sold in nurseries. Or you might want to try something new that can't be had except in seed form. Or you might want to plant masses of a particular perennial and don't want to fork over the price for two dozen pots of it. These are all good reasons to start the seeds yourself indoors. There's one more good reason. Tending a few trays of seeds is a great way to counteract the cabin fever of February.

Check each packet to find out when to plant seeds. If the packet suggests starting zinnias six weeks before planting, just count six weeks back from the frost-free date and mark your calendar. It doesn't pay to get in a rush and start seeds early. They will grow large too soon and become leggy from inadequate sunlight. In zone 5, the frost-free date occurs sometime in mid-May; in zone 4, it's later. Ask an experienced gardener or the local nursery staff for the specific date where you live.

If you have a south-facing window, you might just get away with growing a few seedlings without artificial light, but most likely you'll need to invest in light fixtures and special grow light bulbs. Check the nursery or hardware store. Install the lights so they can be adjusted up and down. It's a good idea to get a timer, too, so that lights can be set to go on and off automatically.

Fill your seed flats with a seed starting mix. It will be lightweight, for easy penetration by tiny roots, and moisture retentive. Check the package before you buy to be sure the mix contains some milled sphagnum peat moss to prevent an outbreak of damping off. This fungal disease attacks small seedlings and fells them within hours. The price of a seed starting mix is well worth it to avoid this guilt-producing disaster.

The soil should be moist but not dripping. The easiest way to achieve this is to put water directly into the bag and give the potting mix time to soak it up before you plant. Warm water will soak in faster. If you're in a rush, dump the soil mix into a wheelbarrow, add water, and mix with your gloved hands. Fill the seed flats and allow any excess water to drain off for about thirty minutes.

You can plant seeds in rows or broadcast them over the entire surface of the containers. Cover the seeds with soil or leave them exposed, according to packet instructions. Some seeds require light to germinate and some require darkness, so it's important to check the package. Don't forget to label the seeds. I like to write the planting date and number of days needed for germination right on the plant stake. Later, when the seeds haven't sprouted yet, I can check to see if they're overdue.

Line up your containers under lights and set the lights about three inches above the soil surface. Drape plastic sheeting or kitchen plastic wrap over the trays to retain moisture. You can put a few plastic stakes around the edge of the flat to hold the plastic above the soil. Run the lights about twelve hours a day. When the seeds sprout, remove the plastic. As the seedlings grow, raise the lights to keep them about three to six inches above the plant tops.

Watch the flats closely for drying. When the surface of the seed starter mix looks pale, it needs water. To avoid toppling tiny seedlings, water from the bottom. Put water in the plastic trays and set the seed flats into them. After half an hour dump out any excess water. Once the plants have developed a couple of sets of true leaves, you can water them from above using a gentle spray. I'm speaking here of true leaves, not the rounded cotyledons that first emerge from the seed (cotyledons are the food storage units within the seed that allow a plant to get going before it puts out true leaves to begin photosynthesis).

As the plants grow, thin them to prevent crowding. Remove excess seedlings to leave the remaining ones an inch or two apart. Use your fingers or snip them off with a pair of manicure scissors. Snipping is quicker and prevents damage to the roots of the plants that remain.

Experts usually recommend that you move the seedlings once they have one or two sets of true leaves and pot them individually. This may be ideal, but it is time-consuming. You can skip this step by simply planting directly from the seed flat into the garden. Alternatively, you can plant into small pots in the first place or use the six-packs in which you buy annuals. Plant just two or three seeds in each container and thin them to one plant when it's clear which seedling is strongest. Set the six-packs into a seed flat and put the flat into a tray to make bottom watering easy. Simply lift out the whole flat of six-packs when you're finished watering.

Not every seed you plant will germinate, and some kinds of seed will sprout more completely than others. Seed does best if it's planted fresh. Saving the remains of a partially used packet of seed for a later year can be a disappointing exercise since the old seed may germinate poorly, if at all.

Before setting plants out in the garden, harden them off—in other words, toughen them up a bit. A few days before planting, haul the seed flats outdoors and set them in a protected place where they will get the morning sun, but no direct afternoon sun. A position in dappled shade for the afternoon would do. This accustoms the small plants to stronger light. They will dry out rapidly outdoors, especially if it's windy, so check them a couple of times a day and water as needed. Watch the temperature carefully and run the seedlings back indoors if it looks like temperatures will drop anywhere near freezing. Don't leave seedlings out in the rain because the drops will batter them down and wash the light soil off their roots.

Some plants resent transplanting so strongly that they are best started from seed directly in the garden. *Ocimum basilicum* (basil), *Borago officinalis* (borage), *Lychnis coronaria* (rose campion), *Cleome* (spider flower), and *Consolida* (larkspur) are examples. Others, like early *Tagetes* (marigold) and *Lobularia maritima,* syn. *Alyssum maritimum* (sweet alyssum), shoot up and begin blooming so quickly that starting seed indoors is unnecessary and buying plants is something of an extravagance. If you plant seeds directly into the garden, just follow the instructions printed on the packet. Plant late enough so that the seeds will not germinate before the frost-free date. The larger the seed, the heavier the covering of soil you will put over it. Very fine seeds and those that require light to germinate will not be covered at all. Keep the seed bed moist until germination, then continue to water often until seedlings have at least a couple of pairs of true leaves. Check your seedlings twice a day to be sure they are adequately moist. As they grow more leaves and larger root systems they can withstand more heat and sun. Gradually reduce the amount of water.

Purchasing from a Local Nursery

If you decide to bypass the seed-starting process and purchase plants instead, it's usually best to buy from a local nursery, if possible. When compared to mail-ordered plants, local purchases are likely to be healthier, larger, and less expensive. They haven't been stressed by being wrapped and shut in a box for several days. You have a chance to examine them before buying to assess size and vigor. You don't have to pay the often exorbitant shipping and handling charges. Local nursery staff can advise you and answer questions. Plants found for sale locally are more likely to be suitable to our climate. Add to all these reasons the pleasure of being able to support a local business and your own community and you have ample reason to purchase plants at home.

Be cautious about buying plants locally, however, at places other than established nurseries. The plants available at drugstores, lumberyards, grocery stores, and the other plants stands that pop up in spring are usually shipped from distant nurseries while they're in good condition, but may not receive proper care once they arrive at their destination. Unless you buy the plants on the day they were unloaded from the truck, they're probably going to be stressed.

Serious garden planning gets going in January, right after the frenzy of the holidays. This is when you have the time and peace to consider the coming garden season. Make yourself a pot of tea, sit down, and dream. Once you've made a list of the plants you want to acquire, decide whether to mail order or buy locally. If you have haunted local nurseries in previous years, you already have a good idea whether a specific plant is going to be available. When in doubt, phone the nursery. By midwinter staff there should know what will be in stock come spring.

Ordering by Mail

While there are many reasons to buy locally, there is only one to order by mail: the plant you want isn't offered for sale in your area. When you must order by mail, go slowly. Don't assume that a high price guarantees a fine specimen. For similar prices, you may purchase a daylily from two different mail order nurseries and receive drastically different plants. The roots of one may be the size of half your fist while the other has hardly a tablespoon of root structure. An inflated price may suggest that a plant is exotic or rare, but the very same plant may be available elsewhere for half as much.

One reason prices can be so outrageous is that catalog production is costly. If the catalog before you features page upon page of beautiful color photographs, the price of plants will reflect the cost of its production. If the company does considerable national advertising, that cost, too, will be passed along to you. On the other hand, the big, flashy catalogs represent firms that are long established and likely to stand behind their products. A catalog without illustration is far less enticing, but the prices may be lower, the plants larger, or very possibly both. For my money, careful descriptions of hardiness, mature size, and site and soil needs are worth more than beautiful photographs. Be extremely wary of catalogs that do not include Latin plant names or hardiness zones. To locate a good source for mail-ordered plants, seek advice from gardening friends.

If you plan to order plants like irises and daylilies that are constantly being crossed to create new cultivars, keep in mind that very high prices are often charged for the latest one. While it is different from earlier and cheaper varieties, it isn't necessarily any better—just newer.

Read plant descriptions with care, trolling for nuance. Words like *spreading* and *vigorous* are often used as nursery euphemisms for "relentlessly invasive." *Centaurea montana* (perennial cornflower or mountain bluet), for example, is characterized as "spreading freely" by one catalog in my possession, when the truth is that this hoodlum expands its territory explosively. If you plant it be prepared to jump back.

Talk to other gardeners about their experience with various mail order houses, then test out several sources by ordering just a few plants from each. You can assess plant size and vigor, packaging, speed of delivery, cost, and viability once the plant is in the ground. That way when you're ready to place a big order you can do so with confidence.

Site Selection: Light and Moisture

Siting plants well is key to their success. Start by finding out whether your latest acquisition requires sun, shade, or something in between. If a plant is suggested for "full sun or sun with some afternoon protection," in our climate full sun will probably be too much for it. Assume that the more protective condition applies. Find a spot that receives direct sun only in the morning. Very light shade all day would suit or morning sun and afternoon shade or morning sun and dappled afternoon light. Our sun is extremely hot and direct between about 1:00 and 4:00 P.M. during the summer. At this crucial time of day many perennials require some respite.

For plants requiring shade, remember that not all shade is the same. Under closely planted trees the shade is dense. A single tree casts moderate shade. A shrub or fence may create a temporary area of light shade. The denser the shade the easier it will be to keep the soil moist. Dense shade with numerous tree roots, however, dries out the ground quickly. Some shade plants will not tolerate dense shade. Pay attention to the nuance of description in catalogs and books and plant accordingly, always remembering that sun and part sun are hotter and less hospitable in our area than in other parts of the country that share our hardiness zone. When in doubt, go a degree shadier.

Before you put shovel to dirt, you'll also need to know what a plant wants in the way of moisture. A moisture-retentive soil is great for *Astilbe* (false spirea), Siberian irises, and *Anemone,* but certain death for tall bearded irises. You may notice that certain spots in your garden remain wet longer following a rain. In these poor drainage areas, you must either thoroughly amend the soil to improve drainage or plant only what likes wet feet, such as *Astilbe* or *Iris pseudacorous* (yellow flag).

Locate plants with similar moisture requirements together. It's much easier to water a whole bed with a sprinkler or soaker hose than to water each plant individually according to its own needs.

Allow for Mature Size

At planting time, keep in mind how slowly many perennials grow. Those in small containers (two or three inches across) are probably grown from seed and only a few weeks old. They can't be expected to reach a mature size or to bloom much in their first season or even their second. Plants in containers of quart size or larger, on the other hand, are already a year old and will perform far more quickly. In a hurry to have a show? Buy bigger plants. Want to save money? Buy smaller ones and give them time to mature.

You should, from the beginning, allow the full space your perennial will demand when mature, especially for difficult to move plants like *Hosta* (hosta or plantain lily), *Baptisia australis* (blue wild indigo, false indigo, or plains false indigo), Siberian irises, roses, and shrubs. These quickly become large, heavy, and tough to transplant. During their immature stage, you can put a ground cover at their feet or surround them with annuals to fill the void. Hostas look especially pretty with pansies crowded in amongst them. Alternatively, smaller, easy-to-move perennials can first be planted into a nursery bed. After a year or two when they are more nearly mature size, you can set them into place in a border. This works fine for those that are still a manageable size at maturity, assuming you have the space for a nursery bed. Unless you have a large property, however, this may be a luxury you can't afford.

When to Plant

Perennials can be planted anytime after the ground thaws in spring, usually about four to six weeks before the frost-free date. Because they become established more easily if weather remains cool for about two weeks after they are planted, early is better than late. If you wait until mid-May or later to put perennials in the ground, they are likely to face heat and hot wind during their critical first two weeks, and extra watering will be required.

Most annuals, on the other hand, require warm nights to really begin growing and will not recover if their tops freeze. Wait to plant them until all danger of frost is past. If you are planting seeds rather than plants, you can probably fudge and sow them a week early, as temperatures do not have to be above freezing until the seeds have sprouted. Once you've reached the frost free date, waste no time. Get your annuals into the ground pronto. This gives them a good start before the heat of summer hits. If you plant more than two weeks after the frost-free date, daytime temperatures will have climbed high enough to desiccate tender seedlings and small plants.

Three annuals that fare best if planted very early are *Viola* x *wittrockiana* (pansy), *Antirrhinum* (snapdragon), and sweet alyssum. They thrive in cool weather and need it to do really well, putting on a good show in spring, but sulking in summer. Snapdragons and sweet alyssum will bloom well again in the cool of fall, but often pansies have curled up their toes by then. To take advantage of their lovely spring bloom and give them the best possible start, set out plants very early—about two or three weeks before the frost-free date for snapdragons or sweet alyssum and four to six weeks ahead of the frost-free date for pansies.

Digging the Hole

You've chosen the right plant, checked on its likes and dislikes, decided where to put it; now it's time to get down to business. First, dig a hole. Now, dig it bigger. The adage is, for a dime-size plant, dig a dollar-size hole. To give a plant a good start, dig a hole at least a few inches deeper than the plant is—to accommodate the roots—and several inches wider. If the plant has eight inches of roots, you want a hole that is about twelve inches deep and about sixteen inches wide. The extra-big hole allows you to put loose dirt all the way around and below the root structure, giving roots an easy start. For a shrub or tree, dig the hole extra wide, but only as deep as necessary to accommodate the roots. This allows for plenty of surrounding loose dirt, but prevents the heavy plant from sinking into soft dirt below it.

Now is the time to improve the soil. You've already done the hard work of digging the dirt out of the hole. Take a few extra minutes to improve it. Dig in gypsum if you're working with clay. Add compost, bonemeal, and, if your plant likes a rich soil, add a bit of composted manure. Mix it all up with your shovel and toss some of this beautiful stuff into the bottom of the hole. Next, set the plant in place and fill in all around it with the loose soil you've made. Water the plant in to be sure there are no air pockets left around roots and to give it the moisture it will need to help it survive the shock of transplanting. If you have more soil than you need, use the excess to form a ring around the plant a few inches out from the stem. This will capture water when it rains or when you irrigate. The ring will gradually melt down into the surrounding soil, but meanwhile it helps your plant obtain plenty of moisture while it's getting established.

Transplanting

As you refine your garden design and increase plant stock by dividing, you will do lots of transplanting. Make careful notes while your garden is in bloom about changes you plan to make. Daylilies have a vast range of bloom color, size, and form, but once they stop flowering, their identical foliage makes them indistinguishable. The same is true of irises. You might want to mark plants to be moved with a stake. It's easiest to decide what to move when you can see what is already in flower where you intend to put something new. Pick a leaf and blossom from the plant you want to move and compare them to leaf and blossom of neighbors where you will place it. It's surprising how often a combination imagined in your head is far less attractive when you put the articles in question side by side. Be reasonable in what you plan, because it takes longer to move things with a shovel than it does with your imagination. Unless you have a big, burly, and compliant assistant, you may find you've bitten off more than you can chew.

Time transplanting carefully. Plants are best moved during cool weather after bloom. For spring-blooming plants wait until the cool of fall, probably sometime in September, to transplant. For fall bloomers transplant in the cool of spring. Summer bloomers can be moved in either spring or fall. Foliage plants are best transplanted in spring, when they can be dug and divided before the leaves unfold, minimizing damage. Hostas, for instance, are best moved in spring, when their leaves are newly emerged but still tightly furled in points.

Spring transplanting can be done in the month before the frost-free date—as soon as the ground is warm, workable, and no longer sticky wet from frost and snow. If you transplant in autumn, plants should ideally have six weeks to get over the shock of being moved before freezing temperatures begin. Determine the date of likely first frost and try to do your transplanting six weeks ahead of it.

Having stated the rules, let me add that you probably can manage, if you absolutely must, to transplant most plants even during the heat of summer. Water very frequently until the plant becomes established and provide some shade, especially in the afternoon. Shade can be cast by an overturned box or bushel basket or the woven seat of a lawn chair. It takes a lot of fiddling and personal attention, but it can be done.

Most transplanting is done because you're refining your garden design, but another very good reason to transplant is to increase stock of a desired perennial. With a great many perennials this is surprisingly easy to do. It's just a question of digging up the plant and then literally dividing it into whatever number of plants you need. As violent as it sounds, you can do this by simply plunging your shovel right through, slicing both foliage and roots. With some vigorous growers, like chrysanthemums, asters, and irises, it's best to hack off and replant the outer pieces of new growth, discarding the inner, older parts. Quite small divisions will grow. A *Nepeta* (catmint) plant one foot across could be cut into nine four-inch-square pieces, each of which would make a full-size plant by the end of the second season. The slower growing the plant, the larger the pieces should be if you want a reasonable show quickly.

When you move a plant, do the job in a hurry. Dig a nice big hole and prepare the soil first. Then—and only then—dig the plant to be moved. To decrease root damage, be sure to leave a nice amount of dirt attached to the roots. Put the plant immediately into the hole you've prepared, fill dirt in around the roots, and water well at once. By moving a plant in this way, you can trick it into thinking it's never been moved at all. If for some reason the plant has been dug and a place is not yet prepared, be sure to keep the plant in a shady spot.

Patience

There's an old saying about perennials: The first year they sleep, the second year they creep, the third year they leap. This is an axiom I wish I had heard as a young gardener when I was impatient, booting a plant out if it failed to perform by the end of its first season. Judging a perennial before its third year is like writing a book review without reading beyond the first fifty pages.

I planted a *Filipendula purpurea* (Japanese meadowsweet) that made a mere scrap of a plant its first year, hardly lifting its leaves a foot above ground. The second year it was knee-high and bloomed beautifully, filling its allotted space and displaying lovely pale green maplelike leaves. *Aquilegia canadensis* 'Corbett' (Canada columbine), a dainty pale yellow columbine that looked wildly enticing in a mail order catalog, didn't bloom at all in its first year. The second year it was so loaded with bloom that even my nongardening, color-blind husband commented.

Some plants take more than three years to achieve their full splendor. *Hosta sieboldiana* var. *elegans,* for example, won't reach its colossal shrublike size for six or seven years. I planted two in my shade border and was disappointed with their paltry size after three years. When one of them had to be moved two years later, it required the efforts of two strong men to accomplish the project. *Baptisia australis* (blue wild indigo, false indigo, or plains false indigo), many clematis, and *Polygonatum odoratum* 'Variegatum' (fragrant Solomon's seal) are other examples of slow starters. Conversely, some perennials reach a perfectly respectable size in just two years. There is no hard and fast rule, in spite of the tidy little rhyme quoted above. The point is to have patience. Put your plant in the ground and give it time to reach its full glory.

5

Favorites Flowers for the Hot Midwest . . . & a Few Troublemakers

This is an unabashedly personal catalog of favorite garden plants, not an all-inclusive listing of winter-hardy plants for our region. Most of these have become favorites after years of trial and error for solid reasons—beauty of both flower and foliage, long bloom seasons, the oomph to stand up to heat and humidity, sturdy health, glorious color. I love them and I have my reasons. The plants listed here are suitable for both the cold winters *and* the hot summers in our area. These are four star beauties for your Midwestern paradise.

Difficult Plants for the Hot and Cold Midwest

Not all plants that are theoretically winter hardy in our area will survive severe cold without snow cover or thrive in our scorching heat. Although they are listed as hardy in zones 4 and 5, I specifically warn you against the plants listed below. You may have good luck with them in a mild year or so-so results through year after year of typical weather, but don't expect robust performance over the long haul, particularly if you have heavy clay soil:

Antirrhinum (snapdragon)—except cultivars labeled heat tolerant, like Liberty Series

Calendula officinalis (pot marigold)

Campanula (bellflower)

Centranthus ruber (red valerian)

Clarkia, syn. *Godetia*

Delphinium

Digitalis (foxglove)

Iberis sempervirens (candytuft)

Lavandula (lavender)

Linum (flax)

Lobelia—annual

Matthiola (stock)

Monarda (bee balm or bergamot)—cultivars not labeled disease resistant

Phlox paniculata (garden phlox)—cultivars not labeled disease resistant

Platycodon grandiflorus (balloon flower)

Primula (primrose)

Veronica (speedwell)—except the creepers

In spite of this warning, I have included two of these troublemakers among my favorites: delphiniums and foxgloves. These two are so ravishingly irresistible in spite of their shortcomings that I couldn't leave them out. Although I do not recommend them, some gardeners find them worth the bother and risk when they manage to survive both summer and winter.

Favorites

To make garden planning easy, I've listed the plants chronologically in order of bloom, beginning with the earliest. Since plants have varying and overlapping bloom periods, they are placed in the list according to date they first begin to bloom, but some long bloomers are placed according to their most significant bloom time. These times offer a general guideline only, because weather variations from year to year and your garden's microclimate will cause vagaries in precise dates and length of bloom. Early spring bloomers and the last flowers of fall are especially affected. The specific bloom times mentioned are primarily for zone 5. If you live in zone 4, bloom times are likely to be a couple of weeks later. Bloom time is so important in garden design that you can't start too soon keeping a notebook in which you record weekly what is in bloom in your garden. Chapter 8 presents a sequence of bloom times for these and many more plants to help you in garden planning.

Spring Bulbs

Much of the first wave of spring bloom—some of it actually occurring before winter ends—is made up of bulbs. Because these clever plants form their spring foliage and flower a year ahead, storing them away underground, they are particularly reliable bloomers. They bring the colors we so desperately need after the drab landscape of winter. They can, however, be very tricky to place in a garden design for three reasons. First, their foliage must be left to ripen and brown before it is removed so that next year's flower will form. Second, the dormancy that follows bloom and ripening will, in the case of bulbs planted in groupings, create big empty places in your garden. Third, once dormant, the bulbs' locations become vague in your mind, leading to nasty bulb-jabbing accidents when you start putting your shovel in where it doesn't belong.

The smaller the bulb foliage, the more quickly it will ripen and cease to be unsightly in your garden. Early bulbs like *Galanthus nivalis* (common snowdrop), crocuses, *Puschkinia scilloides* (striped squill), and *Chionodoxa luciliae*, syn. *C. gigantea* (glory of the snow) ripen their small, grassy leaves rapidly. Tulips and particularly daffodils, however, have large leaves that ripen slowly, creating quite a mess in the garden. After years of planting tulip bulbs, I have finally realized that the best way to cope with their postbloom foliage is to plant them in singles or small groupings. A clump of ten or twelve tulips makes quite a patch of ugly brown foliage at a certain stage, unless you can creatively disguise it with growing perennials, groundcover, or annuals. I prefer smaller plantings of one, three, or five tulips, which are far less noticeable when the foliage browns. Fortuitously, this approach also creates a prettier garden. Let's say you have a fifty-foot garden and thirty bulbs to plant. If you plant two clumps of fifteen bulbs, you have two big, widely separated splotches of color. On the other hand, by spacing out three single bulbs, four groupings of three bulbs, and three groupings of five, you can give the impression of bloom throughout the bed. This alone, regardless of what else is in flower, will give your garden a feeling of unity, assuming you stick with some color scheme.

Daffodil foliage is your worst nightmare—lots of leaves that take a long time ripening. Occasionally you will see a garden in which someone has braided the foliage after the bloom ceased. This may interfere with proper ripening of the leaves and thus with flower formation, although I haven't tested the theory myself since I think braided daffodils look idiotic. A better solution is to disguise the foliage with that of surrounding plants.

If you choose to plant tulips and daffodils in clumps, they will leave a considerable empty spot following removal of browned foliage unless you have laid your plans in advance. You can fill the space with annuals. If the bulbs are early bloomers, you'll be able to plant seeds or put annuals right into the vacancy. Later blooming bulbs ripen so late that it will be too hot for seedlings. Try potting up a few annuals and growing them on your patio until they are needed to disguise bulb gaps. Then just tap them out of their pots and plant them without disturbing their roots. Obviously, this method works only with large bulbs, which are planted deep. With shallow bulb plantings, try putting the annuals directly behind the bulbs.

Another way to fill the space is to plant bulbs among bushy perennials that spread out as the season progresses. They need relatively little space while the bulbs are in bloom but will fill in as the bulbs go dormant. This works well with daylilies, asters, and chrysanthemums. You might also try it with *Calamintha* (calamint), *Nepeta* (catmint), *Gypsophila paniculata* (baby's breath), *Buddleia davidii* (butterfly bush), and *Perovskia atriplicifolia* (Russian sage).

Make careful note of exactly where bulbs are planted so that during their dormancy you don't mistakenly plunge a shovel in amongst them. I confess that in spite of garden charts, plant labels, and memories of last spring, I am myself a wanton bulb slicer. I have finally, though, learned to be philosophical about an occasional loss. Once you have whacked a piece off a bulb, discard it and get on with your life.

Galanthus nivalis (common snowdrop), bulb, height four–six inches, spread two–three inches, shade or part shade: A friend who has a breathtaking woodland wildflower garden tells me that snowdrops must always be planted in groups, as they are sociable and do best in company. It's a nice conceit, but in any case they are so small that if you want to make a show, you must follow her advice and plant them in numbers. The delicate, pendant white blooms are the first to appear in my garden, starting near the end of February and lasting about three weeks. Microclimates have a strong influence on these very early bulbs. The aforementioned friend lives less than a mile from my garden and her snowdrops bloom the first of February, nearly a month ahead of mine. It is not at all unusual to experience a snowfall during the snowdrops' bloom, and they appear so charming and gallant blooming with snow at their feet that photographs of them in this situation are almost a cliché of garden literature. Plant them about three inches deep and three inches apart in shade or part shade. They like rich soil with plenty of humus added. Snowdrops will return year after year with no additional care, and if happy will spread themselves from seed.

Crocus, bulb, height four inches, spread one–three inches, sun: In my mother's garden crocuses were the first flowers to bloom each spring, so for me they have a special magic. I've long thought their fat pastel blooms look like the broken shells of Easter eggs. Though all the plants in this large genus of bulbs are no taller than snowdrops, most display disproportionately large blooms, which render them much flashier. *Crocus ancyrensis* (golden bunch crocus), however, is a very early and tiny bright yellow one that always blooms for me at the end of February or early in March. Its bloom is so small that it creates no show at all unless you plant several, but it does weather late spring storms better than the larger crocuses that bloom two weeks later. Crocuses come primarily in white, yellow, and purple shades. I especially admire a wonderful lavender-and-white-striped version: *C. vernus* 'Pickwick' (Dutch crocus). I plant these at the front of my border with perennials behind them that will grow up and spill over the space the crocuses leave behind as they die back. Plant all crocuses three inches deep in a sunny spot or in the shade of deciduous trees (those which drop their leaves each fall). The crocuses will go dormant before the trees cloak themselves in leaves.

Narcissus (daffodil), bulb, size varies, sun: This large genus has about fifty species and hundreds of cultivars split into twelve groups based primarily on flower shape. In a good year, daffodils bloom over a period of several weeks—the very embodiment of springtime in their liquid sunshine yellows and frosty whites. Their fragrance is heavenly sweet and their blossoms, nodding in the spring breeze, seem perpetually filled with sunlight. In a bad year they will be battered to the ground by driving rains, their sod-

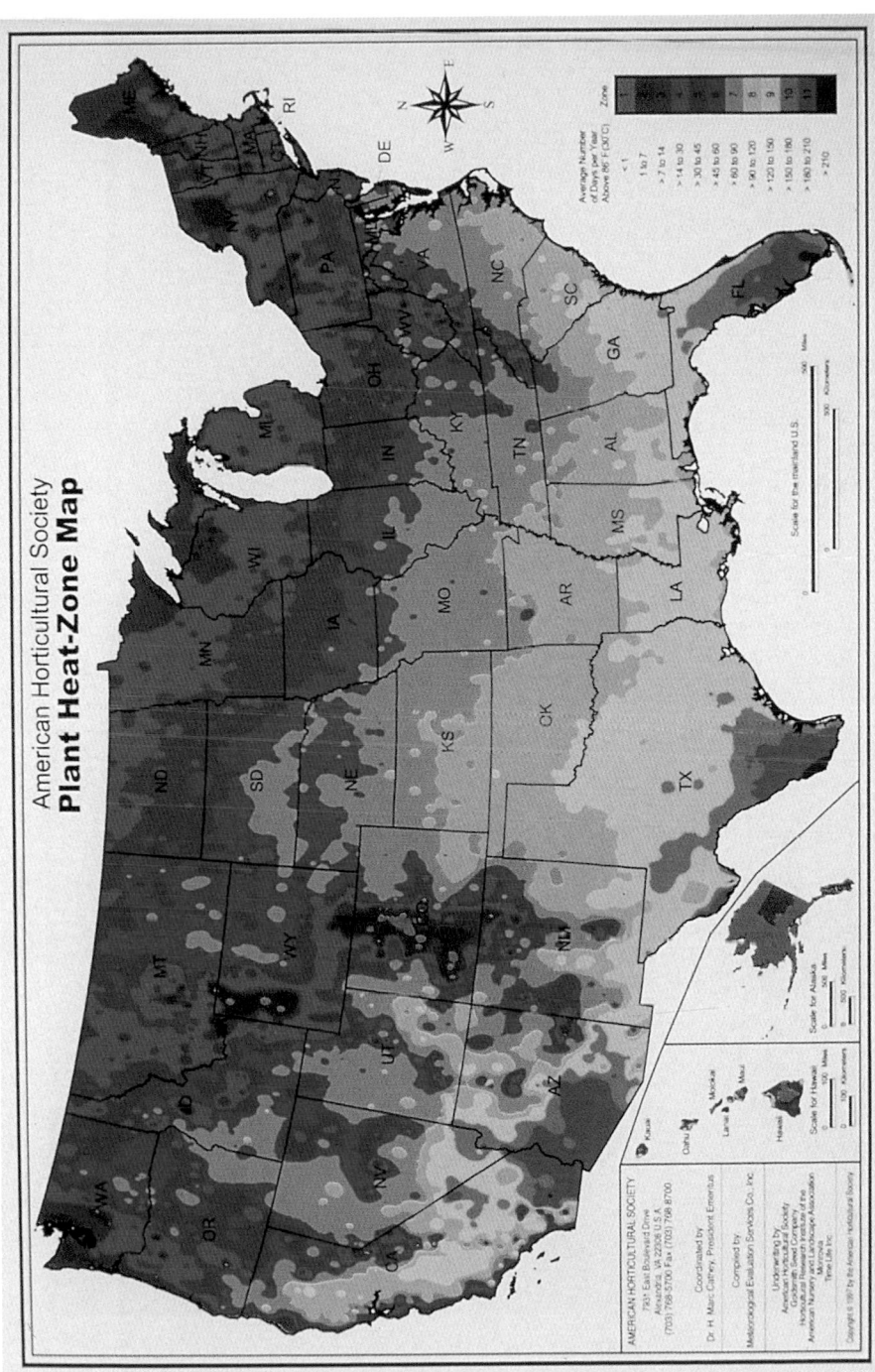

American Horticultural Society Plant Heat-Zone Map (Reprinted by permission of the American Horticultural Society).

Nicotiana sylvestris (garden of Catherine Angle and John Angle).

Sunny border combining various plant shapes and heights to create a pleasing design: *Thymus* (thyme), *Dianthus deltoides* 'Brilliant' (pink), tall bearded *Iris,* and *Lilium* (lily).

Tulipa 'Heart's Delight' with *Narcissus* 'February Gold' (daffodil).

Mixed *Hemerocallis* (daylilies; garden of Aileen Rodgers and Jack Rodgers; photo by Jack Rodgers).

Hosta 'Undulata Albomarginata' (hosta or plantain lily) with *Aquilegia canadensis* (Canada columbine) and *Phlox divaricata* (woodland phlox or wild sweet William).

Right: Hosta 'Krossa Regal'
(hosta or plantain lily), *Athyrium niponicum* (Japanese painted fern), *Cystopteris fragilis*
(fragile fern), *Hosta* 'Frances
Williams.'

Below: Veronica 'Waterperry'
(speedwell) at front. *Geranium*
'Johnson's Blue' at back.

Below: Hosta 'Undulata Albomarginata' (hosta or
plantain lily) with foliage of *Astilbe* 'Brautschleier,'
syn. *A.* 'Bridal Veil' (false spirea) and *Aquilegia
canadensis* (Canada columbine).

den blossoms splattered with mud. The early heat (which comes so often to our part of the country that you have to wonder why we call it unseasonably hot weather) will be accompanied by a blast furnace wind that dries the flowers to a crisp in less than a day. Then there's that endless period while you wait for the foliage to feed the bulb for next year's bloom and *go away.* For several weeks—certainly much longer than the bloom lasted—you must put up with disreputable foliage that flops over, shrivels, and turns yellow. When finally it is brown enough that you can pull it up and compost it, you are left—if you have planted your daffodils in clumps—with great gaping holes in your garden that must be dealt with craftily.

Why would you put up with all this? Simply because daffodils in a good year are stunningly beautiful. They light up the garden and lift the heart. Even in a bad year, you can cut them to enjoy indoors while the rains and winds blast away outside. Furthermore, these bulbs bloom reliably year after year. Plant a tulip and you will most likely enjoy really fine bloom only once. Plant a daffodil and you will watch it bloom and increase for many years to come. (The daffodils planted in the early 1800s by William Wordsworth and his sister, Dorothy, at Rydal Mount, their home in the English Lake District, still bloom each spring.) In addition, unlike many of the bulbs you spend your limited garden budget on, these create large and showy flowers. They are undoubtedly an excellent investment when it comes to beauty and longevity.

We live in a region where heavy snow in April is by no means unheard of, but also where temperatures can reach the nineties in the same season—even in the same year! It seems to me, however, that heat and wind are more the rule when daffodils bloom. For this reason, I think the Midwestern gardener does better to emphasize daffodils that bloom early or midseason and forgo the later-blooming ones. The earlier they put on their show, the less likely they are to be blasted by the hot winds that absolutely ruin them. Fortunately, snow doesn't seem to faze them in the least, as long as temperatures don't plummet. Early bloomers have the added advantage of ripening their foliage and stepping aside earlier.

I have a few favorites among this large group of flowers. *Narcissus* 'Tête-à-Tête' is a miniature daffodil, commonly available in pots at your florist or nursery or even grocery store in winter. Buy a pot to enjoy indoors in February—that dreary month that can scarcely be borne without forced bulbs and cut flowers in the house. After the bloom, keep watering until the foliage has turned brown. By then spring is well begun and you can find a spot in the garden to plant the bulbs five inches deep and four-five inches apart. Unlike many forced bulbs, they will bloom in the garden very nicely the following spring. Just six inches tall, with small golden yellow blooms that begin about mid-March and last about two weeks, they are a treasure indoors and out. *N*. 'February Gold' is an early bloomer that is small (ten–twelve inches tall) but very sturdy. Its flowers, beginning about mid-April, are pure, beautiful yellow. The foliage seems to ripen very rapidly, making far less untidiness than larger daffodils.

N. 'Thalia' never fails to delight garden visitors. Its unusual ivory white blooms, very faintly yellow when first open, four to five to a twelve-inch stem, look like clusters of orchids, very pleasing and elegant. A midseason bloomer, 'Thalia' seems less affected by hot winds than other daffodils. Both 'Thalia' and 'February Gold' are extremely reliable, coming back year after year. Another good return bloomer is 'Carlton,' with a two-toned yellow bloom.

Plant daffodils in full sunlight or light dappled shade, but remember that those with pink or red cups retain their color best if they are given a bit of shade. Depth of planting varies with the size of the bulb, so follow the supplier's instructions. Site daffodils carefully; they are not easy to move and can stay a very long time in one location. If you must transplant them, dig the hole you will put them in first. They don't appreciate being left out of the ground to dry up, so make the move as quickly as possible, being very careful not to leave the exposed bulbs in the sun. Transplanting is best accomplished just as the foliage finishes drying and when the bulbs are dormant, but still easy to find.

Plan ahead to fill the space left behind when daffodils have finished their show. I have a large number of daffodils planted in my herb garden in small patches (about eighteen to twenty-four inches across) between the herbs. As the daffodil foliage emerges from the ground, I cut back the previous year's growth on most of the herbs to a few inches from the ground. After the daffodils have departed, the spreading foliage of *Thymus* (thyme), *Origanum* (oregano), *Salvia officinalis* (common sage), *Allium schoenoprasum* (chives), and *Mentha* (mint) fills the allotted space. In my sunny border, daffodils are planted among daylilies, whose similar straplike foliage helps to disguise the fading leaves of the bulbs. By the time the daffodils finish, the daylilies have increased in size and nicely fill the gaps.

Chionodoxa luciliae, syn. *C. gigantea* (glory of the snow), bulb, height four–five inches, sun: *Chionodoxa luciliae* is a lovely little bulb, less frequently seen in gardens than the similar *Scilla siberica* (Siberian squill). Both have piercingly sapphire blue blooms only about a half inch across. They grow well in sun or in the shade of deciduous trees. Both can be naturalized in grass, where they will ripen their foliage before the first mowing. Both bloom early in April and will spread from seed. A handful will eventually turn into a sheet of blue. From a distance you might easily mistake the one for the other, but the blossom of the Siberian squill is pendant while glory of the snow faces upward and shows a splotch of white at its center. This difference in coloration and orientation makes glory of the snow showier and, I think, a better choice.

Tulipa (tulip), bulb, size varies, sun: This large genus has about a hundred species and hundreds more cultivars separated into fifteen divisions based primarily on flower shape. Thanks to this huge variety, the tulip season runs from about the middle of March until the last of May, starting with the species tulips. If you want tulips throughout that six-week season, plant several different kinds, paying attention to the supplier's comments on bloom time (very early, early, midseason, and so on). Some suppliers offer mixed tulips that give a good span of bloom and may even be available by color scheme.

In general, tulips bloom best in their first year only. Darwin hybrids are said to be the most reliable for return bloom. The small species tulips are second best. Others lose much of their vigor after the first year, with blooms reduced in both size and number. By their third or fourth year, and often by their second, tulips send up leaves, but cease to flower. For this reason, I treat them like annuals and plant new bulbs each fall. This may seem an extravagance, but at an average of fifty cents per bulb, I can make a very nice display for not a large investment. When spring rolls around and I have weeks of overlapping waves of bloom, I never begrudge my fall expenditure.

Tulips are supposed to be planted in full sun. Since deciduous trees may not leaf out until tulips have finished blooming, this leaves some latitude. The flowers finish and the foliage can get some sunshine before the trees leaf out so heavily that they shade the bulbs out. You can plant tulips even in the shade of evergreens if you count on just one season of bloom. The blossom is already in the bulb when you buy it, so the first year of bloom is unaffected by a shady site.

The choice of tulips is very wide, so make your selection based on the colors and shapes you prefer and the bloom time you want. I find the small species tulips especially appealing for their early bloom, their diminutive size, and their indefinable sweetness. *Tulipa* 'Heart's Delight' (Kaufmanniana Group) is a special favorite, with its ruffled leaves faintly striped purplish brown and its dark pink bloom with lighter pink edge and yellow interior base. A wonderful species tulip is *T. clusiana* 'Cynthia' with spindly bluish foliage and narrow blooms that alternate petals of pale yellow and a faded coral red. It clashes—just—with the pink of *Dicentra spectabilis* (bleeding heart) but looks terrific with the purple-bronze leaf of *Heuchera micrantha* var. *diversifolia* 'Palace Purple.' *T. clusiana* blooms in mid-May. Among the late bloomers, I think the lily-flowered tulips are standouts. Their large, flared, and pointed petals and their stately height give them great elegance. As with other tulips, the size of the blossom actually grows after it is fully open (even as a cut flower). At its peak of bloom, the flower can be enormous. The lily-flowered tulips last a long time in the garden and also make lovely and long-lasting cut flowers. I enjoy *T.* 'Ballade' (medium purple, edged with white) and *T.* 'Mariette' (rose). If you like a rich yellow, try *T.* 'West Point.'

Muscari (grape hyacinth), bulb, height eight inches, sun: Grape hyacinths have an unusually long bloom season for spring bulbs. From mid-April until late May they create a wave of color. Most are vivid blue. Each kind (there are about thirty species plus cultivars) blooms about four weeks. They seem unaffected by driving rain, howling wind, or early heat. The dense, cone-shaped clusters of little bells make enchanting bouquets if you can bear to cut short their bloom in your garden.

   Let's be honest, though. There is a drawback—their summer-dormant foliage. Shortly after bloom, their fat leaves and stems die back and the bulb remains dormant until late in the summer when it suddenly puts on fresh new foliage for the last few weeks of the growing season. The difficulty, of course, is that you must somehow fill the space left vacant at the height of the growing season, while still leaving the space open again in late summer for the resurgence of foliage. Tricky.

You can plant your grape hyacinths toward the back of the bed and place something in front of them that will grow up to disguise their absence at midsummer, but not so tall as to shade them out in late summer. In one bed, I have grape hyacinths planted at the feet of *Paeonia* (peony) with *Geum triflorum* (prairie smoke) in front of them. The coloring of the blue *Muscari* is appealing in combination with the emerging dark reddish-purple peony leaves behind it and the soft rose of prairie smoke in the foreground. In front of the prairie smoke is a planting of *Calamintha nepeta* (lesser calamint), which grows up to take center stage with its airy bloom by late July, and with its foliage long before then. In another bed, the grape hyacinths are planted near an *Aster* x *frikartii* 'Mönch,' which grows up and then flops over to cover the gap following the grape hyacinths' bloom, but stays low enough to allow the later rebirth of foliage to poke up through it.

Other Early Spring Bloomers

Vinca minor (dwarf periwinkle, myrtle), perennial, height eight inches, spreading habit, sun or shade: This gradually spreading ground cover bears glossy, dark green leaves. It blooms about four weeks—from mid-April through mid-May—with minor, sporadic bloom likely throughout the summer and fall. The flowers are blue with a hint of lavender. *Vinca minor* makes an excellent ground cover around shrubs, under trees, and in confined areas, but does not mix well with perennials or annuals in a border. It may take some time to get established, but grows densely, puts its roots in firmly, and is difficult to remove. It does seem to coexist with bulbs. Just make sure you choose bulbs whose flowers and foliage will be tall enough to stand above the myrtle. It is remarkably adaptable, growing equally well in full sun and dense shade.

Viola x *wittrockiana* (pansy), annual, height eight inches, sun or
shade: The pansy must be one of the sweetest flowers ever to
grace a garden. The "face" among its petals gives it a special appeal for children, which may explain why so many of us are nos-
talgic about them as adults. Another part of its charm is that
cutting it only encourages further bloom. As my mother (who
adores this flower) always says, "If you want pansies, cut pansies."
They are showy planted in groups of six or more. They make
wonderful filler around junior perennials that have a few years
to go before they expand into their allotted space. My most inspired use of them in my own garden was to surround young
variegated *Hosta* (hosta or plantain lily) with blue pansies. As the
hosta leaves unfurled, the pansies wove their way delicately
among them.

For years, I planted pansies too late, thinking they should go in
the ground with other annuals around mid-May. Pansies revel in
cool weather. Buy them the minute you see them for sale and plant
them promptly. They can take temperatures below freezing without collapsing as other annuals will. This early planting—about
four weeks before the frost-free date—will give you a long cool
season of spring bloom, through the end of June. Admittedly the
strong heat of summer that usually hits in July will cause the pansies to dwindle. Bloom will stop and the plants may gasp their last.
Even so, you've already had six weeks of bloom. In a milder summer, planted in shade, your pansies may survive until fall and give
you a bonus few weeks of late season bloom.

Pansies can be planted in light to moderate shade or in sun with
afternoon protection. The sunnier the site, the earlier in summer
they will cease blooming. Pansies have apparently been bred lately
to be more hardy. In recent years, some cultivars have been developed that live through the winter and bloom well the following year, and even ordinary cultivars sometimes make it. The heat

of our region's summers does sap their strength, though, so it's unwise to rely on this trait. If your ordinary pansies survive through summer to bloom in fall, rejoice. If they make it through winter to bloom a second year, consider it a lucky fluke.

Spring

Pulmonaria (lungwort), perennial, height twelve–eighteen inches, spread twenty-four inches, shade: Its leaves softly speckled with silver, *Pulmonaria* is a very desirable, though short-lived, perennial shade plant. Its beauty and the length of its bloom make it a solid contributor. From early or mid-April till the last of May, lungwort puts on a spring show of bloom. The mottled leaves shimmer on throughout the growing season, bringing light to the darkness of shade. As temperatures skyrocket in the hottest part of summer, the leaves may suffer and die back somewhat, so it is best planted among weaving plants such as *Lamium* (deadnettle) or *Galium odoratum,* syn. *Asperula odorata* (sweet woodruff), which can fill in any weakness.

Different types of *Pulmonaria* have white, pink, blue, red, purple, or violet blooms. The clusters of small bell-shaped flowers of many of them are pink in bud, shifting to blue in bloom. The blue blossoms of *P.* 'Roy Davidson,' *P. saccharata,* and others are truly blue and not some shade of purple. Give lungwort plenty of shade to keep it from collapsing in heat. It appreciates the sort of rich, moist soil that most shade plants find attractive. Powdery mildew is likely to be a problem in the warm and humid part of the season. At best these are short-lived perennials in our climate, not ones that you can divide and increase quickly. Still it takes only two or three to make a nice display.

P. saccharata 'Mrs. Moon' has pale sage speckles on its dark green leaves and flowers about a half inch across. Their blue is a sapphire or cornflower shade. My favorite is *P.* 'Roy Davidson,' which has narrower, firmer leaves with a closely mottled surface and flowers of a subtler sky blue. The splotching on its leaves is very pale silvery green for which the coloring of *Lamium maculatum* 'White Nancy' (spotted deadnettle) is a perfect match.

Mertensia pulmonarioides, syn. *M. virginica* (Virginia bluebells), perennial, height twelve–twenty inches, spread ten–twelve inches, shade: The most noteworthy drawback of Virginia bluebells might also be seen as an asset. Once the plants have finished blooming and the temperature begins to rise, they go dormant, leaving a gap in the garden. You can turn this habit to good use by planning ahead. I plant Virginia bluebells among my larger hostas. The bluebells come up and bloom nicely from mid-April to mid-May. Meanwhile the hosta foliage progresses from tight little points to gradually unfurling leaves. The bluebells cease blooming and begin to go dormant just as the hosta leaves fill in their vacated space. It's a magical transition.

Virginia bluebells have the same trick of turning from pink in bud to blue in full bloom that many *Pulmonaria* (lungwort) display. The clusters of bell-like blooms are also similar in form, making these two a poor choice for companion planting in your shade border because they are too much alike to be interesting when paired. Most lungworts also offer a longer bloom season, handsomer leaves, and foliage interest for the entire growing season. These considerations make *Pulmonaria* the obvious choice between the two, unless you are trying to provide bloom in a spring gap that will be closed by other plants as the season marches on, in which case *Mertensia pulmonarioides* is your clear choice.

Viola tricolor (Johnny-jump-up), annual, height eight inches, spread two–three inches, sun: Now here's a little article that can charm your socks off. In the first place, these annuals bloom from mid-June all the way through August. Admittedly the early bloom is best and by August it is definitely waning. Still, bloom on each plant is profuse, and the plants go to seed wantonly so that left unchecked they will seem an ocean of bloom on which all of your other plants ride. With the look of tiny purple and yellow pansy flowers on plants just a few inches tall, they give the impression of sweet delicacy. In fact they are tough little nuts. They grow in full sun, undisturbed by heat or dry conditions. In one spot in my garden, they have gone to seed in a brick patio where they bake daily in the sun and receive very little water, but still they bloom in profusion until July. Everyone who visits my garden comments on this captivating effect. When the Johnnys die back I pull them out of the brick to let other self-seeded interlopers come to the fore, chiefly *Thymophylla tenuiloba,* syn. *Dyssodia tenuiloba* (Dahlberg daisy or golden fleece). Next spring the Johnnys are back again from seed.

Epimedium (barrenwort), perennial, height twelve inches, spreading habit, light to dense shade: The tissue-thin, elongated, heart-shaped leaves of all *Epimedium* make them top-notch perennials for shade even before you consider their other strong points. They thrive in moist, rich soil if you have it, but are equally at home in dry shade, weathering drought nicely, thank you. Their delicate appearance belies their essential toughness and reliability. The plants are very solid with leaves that look fresh and pretty all season, making this a handsome ground cover. The pale green color of the leaves offers a nice contrast with other foliage, especially when the oncoming cool weather of fall varies the color with purple. Now add to these qualities a pendulous and dainty little inverted cup and saucer of a flower that blooms for only a couple of weeks in the first half of May, but is so fragile and appealing that you would grow the plant just for the privilege of seeing it annually, and you have an all-star perennial. The flowers of the many species range from white and yellow to pink, red, and purple.

Corydalis lutea, syn. *Pseudofumaria lutea,* perennial, height twelve inches, spread eighteen inches, shade: I was first attracted to *Corydalis lutea* (not hardy in zone 4) by catalog descriptions that promoted it as a long bloomer, but once I began to grow it I realized that its pale and lacy bluish foliage is its real charm. The sulfur yellow flowers do last for six weeks in May and June, with sporadic bloom thereafter. They are, however, small and unprepossessing. The foliage, on the other hand, makes a clump that is somehow both solid and dainty at the same time, providing color and texture contrast with other shade plants.

Corydalis lutea* is a very short-lived perennial, but does freely seed itself, so you need only remove seedlings that spring up where you don't want them. Seedlings reach blooming size rapidly and may even bloom the first fall. Two plants side by side will make an imposing clump that looks like one large plant. I enjoy mine in singles, scattered haphazardly through the border to give an overall lacy appearance to the whole bed.

These plants prefer rich, moist soil and a half-shaded position. Mine thrive in morning sun and afternoon shade. They are said to be very adaptable, so may fare well for you in shadier spots. They do require good drainage, however, and do not perform well in clay soil when summers are wet.

Phlox divaricata (woodland phlox or wild sweet William), perennial, height eight inches, spread eighteen inches, shade: Low-growing *Phlox divaricata* makes a dandy perennial for the front of a shady border. It does equally well in dry or moist shade, and its pastel lavender-blue flowers really stand out in the dim light of shade, making the plant unusually showy. This slow creeper has lightly fragrant blooms that last a long time—from early May through mid-June. The foliage may develop powdery mildew after the bloom is over, but the plant seems unharmed by simply cutting it back severely and letting surrounding plants take center stage. It doesn't make a very satisfactory cut flower, as it drops its petals almost at once, so leave it in the garden, where it will last and last.

Veronica 'Waterperry' (speedwell), perennial, height four inches, spreading habit, sun: I've grown several highly touted cultivars of *Veronica,* notably *V. spicata* 'Icicle' and *V.* 'Sunny Border Blue,' without success. These perennials do well at first—blooming beautifully and showing great promise. By midsummer of the first or second season the plants begin to show signs of stress from the heat. The leaves brown and curl. With each season they dwindle, looking scrappier and blooming less. By the third year, they are so disreputable that I dig them up and discard them. I have finally concluded that they are just not reliable plants for a hot climate and I no longer waste time, cash, and gardener's guilt on them.

The creeping forms of *Veronica* seem to be the exception, and I particularly like 'Waterperry.' This very low-growing, slowly creeping plant bears tiny, glossy leaves that look as fresh as springtime throughout the growing season, absolutely regardless of the weather. In the summer of 1995, when my garden was sodden with weeks of almost daily rain and then fried in two heat waves of temperatures above 100 degrees, this plant never faltered. The flowers, which appear from early May through early June, are a profuse and pretty light blue with just a hint of lavender. This nice creeping ground cover spreads at a reasonably fast rate without being invasive.

Lamium maculatum (spotted deadnettle), perennial, height four–six inches, spreading habit, shade: You sometimes see *Aegopodium* (bishop's weed, goutweed) recommended as a ground cover for shade or sun, but this is little more than a noxious weed masquerading as a garden perennial. It is very pretty and also relentlessly invasive. Unless you plant it where it is rigidly controlled by such surroundings as buildings, concrete, and mown lawn, bishop's weed will creep into everything and you will rue the day you made its acquaintance. For a perennial ground cover with the same look of shimmering green and white in shade, plant *Lamium maculatum* instead. This polite plant spreads fairly rapidly, but is easily uprooted when it goes where you don't want it. *L. maculatum* 'Beacon Silver,' with mauve-pink flowers, is commonly available, but I prefer white-blooming 'White Nancy,' which seems to fill in better and has a frostier look. On both of these the bloom is insignificant and not particularly noticeable. 'Pink Pewter,' on the other hand, has slightly larger, far showier blooms in a very appealing clear pink. It flowers from mid-May right on through to frost, making it a charming addition to a shade garden. Also worth trying is *L. maculatum* 'Aureum,' syn. 'Gold Leaf' with acid yellow foliage that makes gorgeous pools of light in shade. It is not as vigorous or as quick to spread as other spotted deadnettles and prefers a shadier location. All of these are good weavers, working their way around nearby plants without threatening their existence. 'White Nancy' is beautiful at the feet of *Pulmonaria* 'Roy Davidson' in one part of my garden. In another, it forms a puddle of light beneath a shaded bench. Spotted deadnettle is well suited to moderate to heavy shade. In light shade or part shade, it will suffer during heat waves.

Dicentra spectabilis (bleeding heart), perennial, height twenty-four to thirty-six inches, spread twenty-four to forty-eight inches, shade to part sun: I confess to harboring tender feelings toward bleeding heart, which I consider one of the loveliest plants available. The pink and white flowers are like a row of ballerinas dangling by their toes from gracefully arched stalks. The leaves are deeply cut and a soft blue-green color. This perennial dies to the ground in fall, but grows rapidly in spring to form a shrublike presence in the garden by early May, when it begins to bloom. *Dicentra spectabilis* can be grown in a variety of shade to part sun conditions. In sunnier spots it often goes dormant with the arrival of hot weather. When the leaves begin to yellow, just cut the plant to the ground and let other plants fill in around it. In shade it shows its lovely foliage at least into August, and in cooler summers until frost. Bleeding heart blooms throughout May into June.

In addition to *D. spectabilis* with its pink flowers, I also grow *D. spectabilis* f. *alba,* a striking plant that never fails to elicit comment from garden visitors. The white blooms have a special elegance and purity that looks somehow classic. The foliage is paler and less blue and the plant has a much longer bloom season if spent blossoms are cut promptly. It begins flowering the first of May and may continue into September. If you leave the blooms on and let the plant go to seed you can easily increase your stock (I have never had the pink form of bleeding heart self-seed in my garden, however).

I've also grown *D. eximia* 'Alba,' which I found very disappointing. Its diminutive size (about eight inches high and eight inches wide) makes it easy to overlook. The blossoms, too, are shaped more like a kernel of corn than a ballerina and their small size and number make them insignificant. There is quite a lot of noise made in the nursery trade about long-blooming cultivars of *D. eximia* like 'Luxuriant.' Their color and bloom form is so inferior to the original that I see nothing to recommend them. Length of bloom isn't everything.

Aquilegia (columbine), perennial, size varies, shade to part sun: It's difficult to think of a group of shade garden plants more enticing than the columbines. These refined perennial beauties have many charms. The foliage is very good-looking—rounded and bluish with scalloped edges. The unique two-part flowers show a face formed of five cups. Graceful spurs shoot backward. The flower may be nodding or face outward. Columbines have a long season of bloom, too, each kind flowering for about six weeks in spring and early summer.

The plant has a very free seeding habit, though it is a matter of opinion whether this is a positive or a negative. On the one hand, it is useful since columbines tend to be short-lived and the oncoming seedlings are ready to fill vacancies as older plants die off. On the other hand, columbines are promiscuous and cultivars and species cross with abandon. If you have a particular color you love and wish to keep true, do not plant any other sort nearby. The two will cross and recross until you have every possible variation on the two parents. Each plant forms a large amount of seed, so your shade garden in spring is likely to be carpeted with seedlings. It's wise to weed these down to just a few, because columbines do not appreciate crowding.

Columbine seed, by the way, must go through a winter before it will germinate. Purchased seed will be ready to plant, but if you are given seed from a friend's garden, either plant it in the fall or store it in the freezer until spring.

Unfortunately, along with their charms, columbines have a pair of serious weak points. They are quite likely to be attacked by fungus and leaf miner. In the maggot form, leaf miner eats its way through leaf surfaces, leaving a clearly identifiable winding white trail. You will never see the insect itself, but the white trail is a dead giveaway. You can remove affected leaves as soon as you see them, and it's a good idea to clear away all foliage in the autumn—this should be destroyed, not added to the compost pile. You can treat leaf miner with a spray, but it is also deadly to bees and other useful insects. The truth is that even if you are so reckless of your garden ecology as to use this insecticide, you will probably not get rid of the leaf miner.

Fungus is likely to attack columbines in mid- to late summer, disfiguring the leaves with gray spots. You can treat the plants with fungicide, but it will not be fully effective. In my opinion, your best bet is to remove and destroy all foliage when it begins to look unsightly. The plant will soon create new leaves. Columbines prefer a rich, moist soil with good drainage. They will be less subject to fungus attack if they are kept adequately moist, but they don't want to sit in water. This means providing them with light to moderate shade and soil rich in organic matter and then watering on a regular basis. They are often recommended for full sun, but will not fare well in such siting in our region. Give them light shade for best results.

The more columbines you plant in close proximity, the more trouble you will have with both fungus and leaf miner, so it's a good idea to limit their number. One type that seems less likely to be attacked by these two problems is *A. canadensis,* the wild columbine seen in the Midwest that is also known as Canada columbine. At about three feet, this is a tall plant, but the loose arrangement of stems and blossoms in its narrow eighteen-inch width gives it an overall airy appearance. The forward, cup-shaped part of the flower is pink to coral pink, the spur portion pale yellow. The nodding blooms last from about the first week in May through mid-June, with slight bloom well into July. A favorite cultivar is *A. canadensis* 'Corbett,' a solid little clump that covers itself in small, pendulous, pale yellow flowers for a long period. Plants stand about twenty to twenty-four inches high and eighteen inches across. 'Corbett' blooms from mid-May until mid-June. In my garden it has not yet fallen victim to either leaf miner or fungus.

If you've admired *A. caerulea,* the Rocky Mountain columbine, on mountain vacations, you can plant it in your own garden. It has white, upward facing cups with sky blue spurs. It is very lovely, though not as heavenly in the hot Midwest as it looks in rarefied mountain air.

Geranium (cranesbill), perennial, size varies, sun to light shade: Those pungently scented plants with large, richly red blooms, commonly grown in containers, treated as annuals, and known as "geraniums," are actually members of the *Pelargonium* genus. The plants in the genus *Geranium* I'm recommending here are perennials—far more subtle plants with smaller leaves and blossoms. Though often suggested for full sun, they fare better in light shade in our climate. They are more interesting than showy, with flowers that are pleasant but not striking or profuse, and a cut leaf shape and rough texture that provide good contrast.

There are lots of species and cultivars to choose from, so if geraniums appeal to you, just start trying them. I like *Geranium* 'Johnson's Blue' for its purple-blue flowers that seem to shimmer with a slight underlying pink. The plants spread at a moderate rate and are a bit loose and gangly, so they look best weaving in among plants with more solidity of form. When in bloom, from mid-May through the end of June, they form sprawling clumps eight to fourteen inches high. *G. x magnificum*, with a purple flower, is a suitable substitute for a more solid, upright form.

G. sanguineum var. *striatum*, syn. *G. sanguineum* var. *lancastriense* is low growing with small leaves. Plants are six or eight inches tall and slowly spreading. Pale pink flowers appear sporadically throughout summer and fall, but make their best show in spring. The flowering season is from the end of May until a week or so before frost.

I enjoy *G. phaeum* (mourning widow) as an oddity. Its small, dark purple flowers are held high above loose and casual foliage. When in flower it stands twenty to twenty-four inches high and twenty inches across. When the blooms fade and stalks are cut back, the basal foliage is eight inches tall. It requires a reasonably moist location and does well in my garden in the shade of a pine tree. Flowering is from mid-May through mid-July.

Convallaria (lily-of-the-valley), perennial, height eight inches, spread five–six inches, shade: Who can resist the blandishments of lily-of-the-valley? This perennial's name alone recommends it. The lavishly fragrant blossoms are perfectly described in that old round song: "White coral bells upon a slender stalk." The broad, basal, ovate leaves look attractive all summer in a shady location, their smooth quality contrasting handsomely with a more textured foliage like *Astilbe chinensis* var. *pumila* (false spirea), *Geranium,* or *Athyrium niponicum* (Japanese painted fern). In autumn the leaves turn a nice gold. Sometimes categorized as a bulb, *Convallaria* actually grows from thick rhizomes.

Once planted in a moist spot, in moderate to heavy shade, lily-of-the-valley requires no further care and nurturing. The plants may begin rather slowly, but in two or three years, they will fill in and start to spread. Eventually you will need to exercise control as they begin to creep beyond their allotted space, sometimes into unlikely spots like the scant quarter inch between a brick patio and a house. This spreading habit gives them a nice, snug, tucked-in look among other plants. A light mulch of compost or manure will increase bloom size.

Though the bloom, which begins in the middle of May, is brief, a handful of the flowers bunched into a small vase on the kitchen windowsill for a few days each spring is reason enough to include them in your shady garden.

Galium odoratum, syn. *Asperula odorata* (sweet woodruff), perennial, height six–eight inches, spreading habit, shade: Sweet woodruff is a delicately pretty ground cover with whorls of dark green leaves. Its spring bloom is lovely but brief, lasting only about three weeks at the end of May. The flowers are tiny and white. Although the whole plant is said to be fragrant, don't count on its scent to be a feature of your garden unless you're willing to crawl on your hands and knees, stick your nose to the ground, and crush the plant to enjoy it. Sweet woodruff's strong point is its foliage. This perennial spreads at a moderate rate, but may take two or three years to take hold. Avoid planting it around low perennials, as they may be swamped by the sweet woodruff. Once established, it weaves cozily in among its neighbors, creating the sort of no-dirt-showing garden that is so particularly appealing. Plant sweet woodruff in moderate to heavy shade. Shear it back after it flowers for a fresh regrowth of foliage.

Tiarella wherryi, syn. *T. cordifolia* var. *collina* (Wherry's foamflower), perennial, shade, height eight–ten inches, spread eight inches: *Tiarella cordifolia* (foamflower) is a pretty little perennial wildflower that rapidly spreads by stolons (horizontal branches from the plant base that spread underground, taking root) to become a pretty little pest. Choose instead *T. wherryi*, which may go to seed on a modest scale—handy for increasing your stock—but is not stoloniferous. It thrives in shade.

This small perennial's bloom is not especially eye-catching or imposing. The little inverted cone of several tiny flowers is creamy white dusted with soft rose. Avoid placing it near a plant of pure white in leaf or flower, where it will look dull and dirty. To create a show, plant *T. wherryi* in groups of at least a half dozen as a companion to hostas or other smooth-leafed plants. The heart-shaped light green leaves with darker serrated edges will contrast beautifully with their neighbors throughout the season. The flowers occur from mid-May until late June.

Baptisia australis (blue wild indigo, false indigo, or plains false indigo), perennial, height forty-eight inches, spread forty-eight inches, sun or light shade: What first attracted me to *Baptisia australis* was the lovely blue of its unusual pea-like flowers. I saw it in bloom in a friend's yard and fell in love. My friend gave me some seeds, and three years later I had a sizable blooming perennial plant. Garden visitors always love it and comment on its pretty flowers, but blue wild indigo has a short bloom season— only about two weeks at the end of May and the beginning of June. What you need to admire if you are going to put this one in your garden are the foliage and form. The oval leaves are a bluish shade that makes for nice contrast with everyday green, and the plant form is quite shrublike.

Blue wild indigo gets larger with each year, so once it reaches and then exceeds the size you want, you need to divide it. The tough mass of roots make this a challenge, and success with transplanted pieces may be mixed. A plant about five years old will be four feet high with an arching vase shape that is roughly four feet across. You can tame the beast by pruning it back hard after bloom, cutting back about half of the growth. The plant will take up less space in the garden when not in bloom and will increase in size more slowly. There is a dwarf variety available for smaller gardens. Blue wild indigo grows very well in full sun, never showing any stress from hot, dry conditions. It is also adaptable for partial shade.

If you are given seeds, be sure to scarify them before planting. I poured boiling water on mine and soaked them overnight. Then with the outer shell of the seed softened, I used a paring knife to carefully nick the coating, making it easier for the seed to sprout.

Heuchera (coral flower or coral bells), perennial, height six–eight inches, spread eight inches, sun or part shade: With a low cluster of scalloped leaves and a myriad of long wiry bloom stalks topped by clusters of tiny bell-shaped pink flowers, coral bells do much to give the early summer garden a look of airy bounty. I planted them in pairs at intervals along the front of a sunny border. When they flower from the last week in May through the middle of July, they tie the whole bed together.

Coral bells are perennial and seem to be unaffected by pests or diseases, but siting is critical. They do not generally fare well in the direct rays of a Midwestern sun. They prefer rich, moist soil in light shade, where they will live longer, bloom better, and have healthier foliage than they will in full sun. Even in the shade, some of them will not last long or look good in our climate. There are exceptions, though. In my sunny border I grow *Heuchera* x *brizoides* 'Chatterbox,' which seems to positively glory in its hot and glaring location. In "Coralbells Get a New Look" published in *Fine Gardening* magazine (November–December 1995, 48–53), Dan Heims recommends three others for sun: *H. americana* 'Garnet,' *H.* 'Strawberry Swirl,' and *H.* 'Winter Red.' Unless a cultivar is specifically suggested for full sun, you'd better stick with light shade.

The pink flowers vary from a muted dusty rose to fiery hot pink. Of those cultivars I have tried, the more muted flowers seemed to grow on the stronger, longer-lived plants. Perhaps this is a coincidence, but much as I love the brilliant pinks, none of these plants has done really well for me. Although the softer pinks may be somewhat less appealing, the mass of bloom created by a couple of plants side by side is most impressive. Even at second best, they are too wonderful to be spared from your garden.

Breeders are now creating cultivars of *Heuchera* with pale green or green-and-white-streaked leaves. These are ideal for lighting up a shady spot and seem well worth investigating. I grow one of the variegated plants called 'Snow Angel,' which seems oblivious to heat. *Heuchera micrantha* var. *diversifolia* 'Palace Purple' has pointed leaves of a dark purplish brown. This leaf color recedes in the shade, so careful placement is important. They are gorgeous combined with chartreuse hostas.

Nepeta (catmint), perennial, size varies, sun: A favorite plant in my garden is *Nepeta* x *faassenii*, syn. *N. mussinii* of gardens. I started it from seeds purchased almost twenty years ago and have divided this perennial and spread it around my garden until its presence scattered along the front edge has become a unifying feature. Garden literature suggests that this plant seeds itself freely, but I haven't found this to be true.

N. x *faassenii* forms a low-growing, soft clump. Its leaves are small, nicely textured, and gray green. The blooms are a hazy lavender blue, not individually showy, but the whole plant has an air of misty delicacy that softens the edges of a garden quite beautifully. It is especially nice grown around the base of roses or clematis or up against any plant that seems too bare at its feet. If you love the way lavender looks in books but have been disappointed in its lack of vigor in our climate, try catmint instead for its similar leaf color, bloom color, romantic look, and general shape and size. Catmint is of the weaver persuasion, making its way in among its neighbors and nicely covering naked earth. The best gardens are those where plants run all together, leaving no visible bare earth around them, and this plant is a good sort for helping to accomplish that look.

Catmint forms a dome-shaped clump that will collapse outward in the first heavy rain or sudden heat. The plant will then grow new foliage at the center to fill in neatly. *N.* x *faassenii* grows about one foot high and two feet across, making it a good choice to spill over the front edge of a border. If you like the look of catmint but want something a bit more stately and substantial, try *N.* 'Six Hills Giant.' Described in most garden books as a three-foot-tall erect plant, this catmint in my garden is more like two feet tall and flopping. This may be due to Farm Belt heat, but a friend who grows her 'Six Hills Giant' in poorer soil has somewhat better results. I have had improved luck getting it to grow upright with thorough and early pea staking.

I'm talking here, by the way, about catmint and not catnip (*N. cataria*). Cats, of course, are known to roll around in catnip until they are positively looped. This destructive behavior does not seem to extend to the ornamental catmints that I have grown. Although my neighborhood rejoices in an extensive population of cats, I have never seen any besotted tomfoolery directed at my catmint.

Cut catmint back in early spring, about six weeks before the frost-free date, to three or four inches from the ground. The plants will come up nicely and bloom from late May into mid-July. Then shear the plant back by about half. It looks a bit hacked for a couple of weeks, but new growth quickly begins to fill in and give it a nice bushy look again. The plant will then bloom sporadically for the rest of the growing season.

Early Summer

Iris, perennial, height varies, spreading, sun: The genus *Iris* has about three hundred species and many, many cultivars divided into a few groupings. When people speak of irises, they're usually talking about tall bearded irises, perennials of great beauty. A healthy and vigorous tall bearded iris at the peak of its bloom is a glorious sight. The blooms are as thrillingly exotic as orchids. The light coming through them in the late afternoon turns the flowers to jewels. With three or five or even more big beautiful blooms on each stalk, they can take your breath away. People who love irises become obsessed, possessed by their rich beauty. My mother is in this category. At the height of her garden life, she had 350 different kinds and was still hungry for more. Her garden at the peak of the iris bloom was a wonderland.

On the flip side, though, many gardeners detest tall bearded irises, and with good reason. First, the flowering period is short. Each plant blooms for about ten days to two weeks, with the entire season spanning only about three weeks from mid-May until the end of the first week in June. While they bloom they are gorgeous, but let's talk about the other thirty-two weeks of the growing season. Their foliage is a light, silvery green that is attractive when healthy, especially when rain makes quicksilver droplets along the leaves. Unfortunately, healthy iris foliage is rarely around for long. The plants require excellent drainage. Without it they are subject to rot, which turns their underpinnings to mush. Even in thoroughly prepared, loose soil, many of mine rotted in the rainy spring of 1995. The foliage is also prey to various leaf spots that disfigure it and can kill the plants. If that isn't discouraging enough, consider the larva of the iris borer, which will enter rhizomes and eat them relentlessly down to a hollow shell.

If you love the tall beardeds, you must deal with these problems. This requires an organized preventive spraying program that would make an organic gardener flinch. When the tulips bloom you will need to start spraying your irises with a fungicide. Spraying should continue (except during bloom time) throughout the growing season. I cannot bring myself to introduce this much spraying into my garden, so I take more natural, less effective measures. As the leaves die or become seriously diseased, I remove and destroy them. I never put any part of the plant into my compost heap. One year when my iris foliage was a mess from leaf spot, I got radical, cutting it all back to the ground and destroying it. The plants put up new leaves and looked better for the rest of the season than they ever had before.

If a plant falls victim to iris borer, dig it up. Break the rhizome apart but leave a fan of leaves attached to each piece. Choose the strongest-looking rhizome and cut off any flower stalk. Cut the foliage back to about five or six inches long. You will wind up with a small fan of trimmed leaves attached to a large rhizome with perhaps a few smaller rhizomes branching off it and a few roots. Discard the remainder of the plant. Wearing rubber gloves, submerge the fan in a bucket of nine parts water and one part bleach plus a fungicide mixed according to package directions. Soak the fan for thirty minutes. Then rinse the plant with a hose and leave it to dry fully in a shady spot before replanting it.

Irises must be planted high. Dig a shallow hole and enrich the soil with superphosphate and bonemeal. Add a small amount of lime, too, since irises do not like an acidic soil. Now mound some of the loose dirt in the center of the hole. Put the iris fan on the mound and fill in with dirt so that the roots are well covered, but the thick rhizome is only barely covered. Some books advise you to leave the top of the rhizome exposed, but I find that this usually results in the plant being pulled out by the first curious squirrel. The base of the leaves must definitely not be covered with dirt.

The iris will gradually grow around, forming a ring of rhizomes and their leaf fans. Once the ring is solid, the rhizomes will begin to be overcrowded and bloom will diminish. At this point, probably after three to five years, you need to dig and divide the plant as described above. It's a good idea to treat it with the bleach and fungicide soak, too.

In spite of all their problems, I do grow several irises because I love their sweet scent. In a good year I enjoy their glories. In a bad year I live with the mess. My favorite is a pastel pink called *I.* 'Vanity' that has an orange beard, large blossoms, and a long bloom period. It is always the first to bloom in my garden and outlasts several that start later. Another good one is *I.* 'Gold Galore,' which is simply the richest, most luscious gold color I've ever seen in a flower.

I once asked my mother which tall bearded iris cultivars she would choose if she could grow only five. She listed 'Vanity,' 'Victoria Falls,' 'Pink Swan,' 'Bubbling Over,' and 'Stepping Out.' After producing this list fairly quickly, she went on to say that she would hate to give up 'Smoke Rings,' 'Sapphire Hills,' 'Persian Berry,' 'Margarita,' 'Gigolo,' 'Mystique,' 'Gay Parasol,' 'Going My Way,' 'Gold Galore,' 'Fort Apache,' 'Conch Call,' 'Copper Classic,' 'Color Splash,' 'Cherry Smoke,' 'Camelot Rose,' and 'Snow Mound.' She went on adding to the list over the next few days until the recitation of her favorites began to sound like a complete iris catalog. Did I mention that some gardeners become obsessed with the tall bearded iris?

For my money the Siberian iris is a better choice for the heat and humidity of the Midwest. This delightful perennial's blooms resemble a flight of butterflies. In fact, one Siberian cultivar bears that name. Though Siberians flower for a relatively short period of time, perhaps only two weeks in late May or early June, their foliage and strong vertical line make them a handsome addition to the perennial garden. The clump of long silvery leaves remains tall, elegant, cool, and attractive throughout the summer and seems impervious to heat, drought, excessive rain, wind, and fungus. In fall the leaves turn a tawny gold, beautiful in sunlight.

Siberians have been so widely hybridized that a seemingly endless selection is available to choose from. You may find a limited choice (or none at all) at local nurseries, but catalogs offer an enormous and bewildering range.

One you may be able to find locally is *Iris* 'Caesar's Brother.' This majestic plant forms a large, vigorous clump, stiffly upright and exceptionally tall. The plant is about three feet high with the profuse, deep blue-violet blooms held another six inches above the foliage. The vivid color adds a piquant note among the more common pastels of this early season. Following bloom the leaves are less strongly vertical, arching gracefully.

I. 'White Swirl' is somewhat smaller with an exquisite flower—delicate and pure white. The lower petals stand out horizontally. The bloom stalks and leaves have a slight tendency to fall over, but the overall effect of the plant is still very pleasing. Use pea staking to prop the plant or position it between sturdy neighbors. Or you can just cut the blooms that flop over for indoor bouquets. Flowering is so profuse that they won't be missed.

Another Siberian that I particularly love is *I.* 'Ego.' The plant is relatively small and its blooms are less profuse than those of either 'Caesar's Brother' or 'White Swirl,' but the color is a thrilling sapphire blue that will stop you in your tracks. I give starts of this one to only my very best friends.

Siberians are generally easy to divide and transplant, though the older, more established clumps are not easy to dig and lift because they are large and heavy. This is a plant you can buy just one of and then divide repeatedly every other year or so to build your stock.

Athyrium niponicum, syn. *A. goeringianum* (Japanese painted fern), perennial, height eighteen inches, spread eighteen inches, shade: Japanese painted fern doesn't flower, so it's difficult to know where to include it in a list of plants arranged chronologically by bloom, but I'll throw it in here, because by early summer the leaves are fully developed and showy. This is quite simply one of the most beautiful plants in my garden. It thrives in the shade of pines or deciduous trees, and is lovely planted with columbines, hostas, lily-of-the-valley, or lungwort. It is especially nice combined with the markedly bluish *Hosta* 'Krossa Regal.' It is relatively low growing and its leaf color is a shimmering mix of green, frosty blue, white, and a suggestion of pink. It has the opalescence of abalone shell and really must be seen to be believed. Grown in the rich, deep soil you can make by mixing plenty of compost into your dirt, it gets about eighteen inches tall. In poorer rocky or sandy soil, it is more of a ground hugger. By late summer heat will take its toll, making the fronds collapse.

Stachys byzantina, syn. *S. lanata* (lamb's-ears), perennial, height twelve inches, spreading habit, sun: This beautiful foliage plant has thick, soft, downy gray leaves that are very attractive placed along the front of a border. They appear fresh and firm in spring, but on the arrival of summer heat and humidity, they droop, rot, and become unsightly. Their unusual bloom spikes of mauve-lavender tubular flowers almost submerged in gray foliage are more interesting than lovely. Heavy or continued rains will knock flower stalks down and plaster the leaves into the mud. The plant is quite nice seen at its best, but in the Midwest where heat, humidity, and summer thunderstorms will take their toll, it is a less than desirable addition to the perennial border. Fortunately, there is a sturdy cultivar called 'Wave Hill' that does not bloom and whose foliage stands up to our weather very well. Give it a try for a nice splash of silver. It spreads moderately rapidly to form a nice ground cover, and it's easy to increase for edging a garden. Tidy it up in spring by removing the dead foliage of the previous season.

Alchemilla mollis (lady's mantle), perennial, height eight inches, spread fifteen inches, light to moderate shade: If you have a shady area in your garden, run (do not walk) to your nearest garden shop to buy *Alchemilla mollis.* Or, better yet, beg the seeds from a gardening friend, as it starts easily from seed, making a full-size blooming perennial plant in the second season. You have no doubt admired it in gardening books for its profuse sprays of tiny, sulfur yellow flowers and its crimped leaves with their pinked edges. The foliage is uniquely formed to catch rain or heavy dew, which rings each leaf with beads of moisture. The stylish leaves, delicate bloom, fresh color, and billowy form make it a must for the romantic look. It is one of those wonderfully touching plants that you find yourself adoring as if it were a kitten or a baby.

Lady's mantle definitely requires a shady spot in our climate. I foolishly planted several in an enclosed garden where they received sun for only about six hours a day, but they soon made it clear that this was too much. Though the plants continued to thrive, the leaves took on a dry and scorched look in summer. They fared better when moved to a shadier site.

The buds appear in late May, giving lady's mantle an illusion of bloom even before the flowering starts about a week later. Bloom continues through mid-July. After bloom, you can cut back the foliage to allow fresh new leaves to take over.

Allium schoenoprasum (chives), perennial, height eighteen inches, spread twelve inches, sun: You know what chives are: you chop them up in salads or stir them into hash-brown potatoes. Relatives of the culinary onion, they are commonly recommended for herb gardens. I think they have a place in the perennial border as well.

Chives are bulbous, each bulb with several leaves, and the bulbs growing together in tight little packs. The leaves are tubular and tapered, like long thick blades of grass. These well-behaved plants spread only very slowly. When you want to reduce or increase your supply, just dig up the clump, divide it with a shovel, and plant or discard the pieces.

The flowers are globe shaped and a soft lavender, lasting a full six weeks from the end of June until the middle of July. They are as ornamental as anything else in flower in the garden at this point, so why not plant them among your late tulips, catmint, irises, coral bells, and roses? After they bloom, the leaves will collapse and become unsightly. When the bloom starts to fade, just shear back the entire plant to near the ground and let new growth shoot up. They soon fill in beautifully. Once the fresh growth comes on, you'll be able to harvest chives for the kitchen—a nice little bonus. Don't disfigure the plant by chopping a small amount off across the whole top. Instead, select just a few leaves and cut off whatever you need near ground level.

Rosa (rose), perennial, size varies, sun: Let me first admit that I know relatively little about roses. Whole books have been written on the hundreds and hundreds of cultivars. Read one or two if you plan to add roses to your garden. Roses are well known for their propensity to become diseased and look dreadful. I didn't even attempt a rose until I had been gardening for a dozen years. Now, after more than twenty, I am just beginning to have the nerve to try several. I regret the wasted years of timidity, too, because nothing adds to the romantic look of a garden like roses. Roses are also fabulous cut flowers and nothing matches their scent.

The kind you most often see are hybrid tea roses. The blooms, which appear repeatedly all summer, are elegantly beautiful. The bushes, however, are not particularly attractive, and they are subject to black spot, powdery mildew, and other diseases. On many, the scent is modest to insignificant. These are the roses with which I was chiefly familiar in my youth and early gardening years. I enjoyed them in other people's gardens, but saw that they required a time-consuming amount of spraying and babying along, and I simply devoted my garden space to less demanding flowers.

On a garden tour of England several years ago, I happened to see Sissinghurst, Hidcote, and other famous gardens at the absolute peak of their late spring bloom when the old roses were in full flower. I was almost literally swept away by the heady fragrance of several of these roses planted in an enclosed garden. It was a powerful lesson in the importance of scent in creating an atmosphere of magical sanctuary. On top of their fragrance, these roses had substantial size in both shrub and flower. They were simply the most billowing, romantic, powerful flowers I had ever encountered. Their only apparent drawback was that they bloomed just once a year.

I returned home yearning to grow them in my own garden, but unable to see where I had space for them. Meanwhile, I began to read about David Austin's English roses. Austin is an English rose breeder who has been crossing old garden roses with hybrid teas and floribundas. By doing so, he has been able to introduce over eighty cultivars that offer the best traits of each. From the old roses they take their large full flowers, heavy fragrance, handsome shrubby form, vigor, and disease resistance. From the moderns, they take their color range and repeat bloom. This seemed like the best of both worlds to me, so when I created an enclosed garden at one side of my house, I framed the gate with a pair of David Austin rose bushes—*Rosa* 'Mary Rose.'

'Mary Rose' is generally described as growing to about four feet tall and four feet across. A friend who owns a local nursery raises this rose at her acreage outside of town, where weather conditions are severe. For her, it reaches only about two and a half to three feet in height. In my enclosed garden in town, planted against a fence with a southern exposure, this rose is a behemoth. Even with drastic pruning throughout the season, it still tops out well over six feet by late autumn. It blooms heavily in spring, beginning about the end of May and continuing until late June. It then takes a brief vacation—three or four weeks—before beginning a period of lighter bloom that lasts from mid-July through late October. This adds up to an impressive sixteen weeks of bloom. The fragrance, which its breeder assesses at only one star (of a possible three), is strong, peppery, and sweet. Though the evident variability in the size of this particular rose gave me pause, I decided to try another David Austin rose.

R. 'Sharifa Asma' is a small rose, just two and a half or three feet tall. The scent is delicious and the shell pink flowers are very beautiful. With lesser calamint and *Geranium sanguineum* var. *striatum* planted at its feet it is truly lovely. In its first year, planted as a mere stick, it bloomed from mid-July until frost.

Much as I love my David Austins, I can't say that I've found them to be completely disease free. When heat and humidity strike they may require spraying for powdery mildew and black spot.

I can also recommend a shrub rose called *R.* 'Bonica.' Though described in books as reaching three feet high and three feet across, after several years in my garden, it grew to about four and a half feet high. 'Bonica' has glossy leaves relatively untroubled by disease. The small, shell-pink flowers appear in sprays so that you can cut one stem and have a miniature bouquet. They are especially lovely in bud. Although this rose blooms continually from mid-June until frost, the heaviest bloom occurs in the first three weeks.

For beautiful foliage you can't beat *Rosa glauca,* syn. *R. rubrifolia* with its bluish leaves, reddish stems, and graceful fountain shape. It grows tall, about six feet, with a spread of four feet or more. Bright pink single flowers appear for just a week in early to mid-June, but the foliage is beautiful all summer and yellow hips gradually turn orange in fall.

Roses like a rich, well-drained soil and plenty of water. Water them gently at the base and avoid wetting the leaves. To promote vigor and bloom, use a liquid rose fertilizer according to package instructions. When the plants become diseased you will have to spray because they don't heal themselves. Seek advice at a good nursery.

Lychnis coronaria (rose campion), biennial or short-lived perennial, height twenty-four inches, spread eighteen inches, sun: The velvety silver foliage of *Lychnis coronaria* contrasts beautifully with darker greens and is reason enough to grow it. This is one plant that can stand up to full sun in our region, but it also manages well in very light shade or in full sun with some afternoon shade. The branching stems bear flowers in snowy white or very dark rose (magenta). The plant blooms from the second week in June through August at least.

Deadheading encourages continued bloom, but be warned: it is a big job because this plant is a profuse bloomer. Rose campion goes to seed with enthusiasm, so if you don't want it to take over, you must remove seed heads or hoe out the small plants as the seeds germinate. This propensity for self-sowing is useful since the plants are short-lived, often lasting just two years. If the plant stops blooming and the foliage begins to look ratty, just pull it up and discard it. Let the seed it has scattered germinate for next year's bloom. Rose campion does not take especially well to transplanting, so plant seed directly in the garden and move any seedlings that require relocation while they are quite small.

Achillea 'Moonshine' (yarrow), perennial, height twelve–eighteen inches, spreading habit, sun: Trying to get a gardener to name a favorite flower is like trying to get a mother to choose her favorite child. Still, if pressed, I might name this standout perennial. Its leaves, like fern fronds painted a silvery sage green, are enough alone to put it on a list of beloved perennials. The bloom heads— flat clusters of tiny flowers—are a shade of yellow so pure and lemony that even the glare of the Midwestern sun can't steal its freshness. In early spring the leaves of *Achillea* 'Moonshine' sparkle with dew or raindrops. In late spring they send up numerous bloom stalks that continue to flower through August.

When the color fades from the flowers, cut them back to encourage a second, less showy and less prolific bloom. After the second bloom fades, cut that back, too, and you still have gorgeous foliage. This remains a pleasurable sight even in winter when frost limns its lacy edges. I can't think of another perennial that is beautiful over so long a stretch.

The only drawback of *Achillea* 'Moonshine' is minor: It weakens as it rapidly increases, making division desirable at least every other year. Frequent division will keep its clump form neater and encourage bloom. Left alone, the plant will grow side clumps and become twiggy and less attractive. On the upside, the roots are not deep and the plant parts are easily distinguished and separated. This perennial is drought tolerant, but will wilt badly if divided in hot weather. Divide in fall when weather cools (late

August or later), or early in spring, four to six weeks ahead of the
frost-free date. Water the divisions carefully until they take hold.

Clematis, perennial vine, size varies, sun: The large genus *Clematis*
is made up of climbers that dress up walls and fences and drape
themselves across gateways, doing much to create a lush ambi-
ance. Some are very vigorous and reliable, while others—at least
in our area—are disappointingly spindly and anemic year after
year. When planting them, remember the old saw that clematis
vines like their feet in the shade and their heads in the sun. Give
them a sunny location, but shade their root runs with something
low and bushy growing at the base, such as catmint. This foundation plant needs to be up and providing cooling shade before
hot weather strikes. Plant clematis in rich, deep soil with plenty
of organic matter and a half cup of lime. All these vines will need
a trellis to ascend, because they climb by winding leaf stems
around something. If it's a bit of a stretch from the ground to the
bottom of the trellis, jam a few twigs into the earth to give the
vine a boost.

Widely in use in the Midwest and very reliable is *C.* x *jackma-
nii,* which has a strong climbing habit and showers of big purple
blossoms in early to midsummer. If you think this is an overused
clematis, remember that it is so common because it is so reliable.
As often as I see it, I still think that a simple mailbox on a post
smothered in this vine is a thoroughly charming sight.

If you want to go for something less widely used, try *C. lanuginosa* 'Candida.' The blooms are very large and flat, about six or
seven inches across, and pure, gleaming white. Flowering lasts a
full month from the second week in June until mid-July. I also
like *C. viticella* (not hardy in zone 4), with its small reddish-purple blooms, each petal twisted slightly. Prune it close to ground
level in April. The flowering is profuse and lasting and the vine
is vigorous. Let it grow over an arbor so you can look up into its

dangling flowers. This one will be in full bloom from mid-June through the end of the first week in July, with some continuation of minor flowering.

A favorite is the fall bloomer called sweet autumn clematis and confusingly named *C. terniflora* or *C. maximowicziana* or *C. paniculata* depending on whose catalog you're perusing. Whatever you call it, it covers itself in small starry white flowers whose fragrance can knock you down from several feet away. The yellow stamens give the flowers a slightly off-white look. Unfortunately, the bloom is brief—only about two weeks in the early half of September. Prune it to one to three feet from the ground four to six weeks before the frost-free date in spring.

The variety of clematis out there waiting to be tried is truly staggering. I suggest watching out for sales late in the spring and then trying several to see what happens. If you get serious about clematis, it's worth buying a book on them, because correct pruning requirements vary.

Digitalis (foxglove), size varies, shade: Foxgloves are those graceful towers of large bells that grow wild in wooded areas of England and always look spectacular pictured in a perennial border. They can't stand winds without staking, will desiccate and topple in heat, and thrive in cool, moist conditions. They do not fare well in our climate. I include the members of this large genus here only because for some gardeners, foxgloves are irresistible. If you are one of the stricken, I offer a few tips for the quixotic task of raising foxgloves in the hot and windy Midwest.

Most foxgloves are biennials—in other words, they live just two years. You grow them from seed one year and they flower, set seed, and die the next year. The plants seldom live beyond the second season. For years I grew foxgloves in my shade border with mixed results. They survived milder winters reasonably well and were statuesque and lovely the following spring. When winters were harsh (i.e., typical), all or nearly all of them would be dead by spring. I grew *D. purpurea* 'Excelsior,' a pretty cultivar of common foxglove that stood four to five feet tall. I also tried a number of others from seed with very little success. As thrillingly beautiful as the foxgloves were when they performed well, their inconsistency was maddeningly disappointing and the gigantic holes left in the garden by the many that died were disastrous.

There is a purportedly annual foxglove, *D. purpurea* 'Foxy,' which is meant to bloom in late summer of its first year from seed. I have grown it twice from seed and bought nursery sets once and never saw any bloom. The foliage did well and by summer's end the plants were large enough to flower, but no bloom appeared. The following spring they were dead.

A relative newcomer in my garden is *D.* x *mertonensis,* a perennial foxglove commonly called strawberry foxglove. Shorter than the sort you see in photos of English country house gardens, it is still pretty and flowers a long time, starting in mid-June. When it finishes, you can cut off the main bloom and side blooms will appear and last into mid-August. The color is a nice mauve pink that looks very soft but is often misleadingly described as crushed strawberry. The leaves are heavily textured, large, and quite beautiful in their own right. *D.* x *mertonensis* lived through one typical Nebraska winter only to die the following winter when temperatures yo-yoed from 50 degrees to -10.

Another modestly successful foxglove for the Midwest is *D. lutea* (straw foxglove). Its pale yellow, tubular flowers are much smaller and stiffer than those of *D.* x *mertonensis* or *D. purpurea* 'Excelsior,' which are soft and dangling. Still, it is a taking little thing that always attracts notice from visitors. The plant is perennial and freely self-sows, so you can expand your colony readily. In my garden, *D. lutea* lived through several winters only to turn up their toes en masse during the aforementioned killer winter. Another perennial foxglove worth trying is *D. grandiflora*, syn. *D. ambigua*, a taller yellow-flowered foxglove.

All foxgloves require rich moist soil. Give them plenty of humus, water them in, and make sure the soil stays moist. If they are inadequately moist, the taller stalks will weaken until the weight of the flowers will break the stalks on a hot day. Plant foxgloves only in shade. They are in no way suited to full or even partial sun in our hot climate. Even with shade protection and diligent watering, high heat may topple bloom stalks. You can try protecting foxgloves over the winter with lots of pine boughs placed over them after the ground has frozen, around Christmas. A mulch of leaves placed *around* them doesn't seem to improve their survival rate. A mulch of leaves placed *over* them will kill them.

Delphinium, perennial, size varies, sun: Here's trouble. Can't live with them. Can't live without them. If you have ever looked at a garden blessed with large, healthy, perennial delphiniums, you surely covet them for your own little plot. They are big, tall, richly colored, bold and yet fragile, stately, regal, breathtaking. Okay, I'm running out of adjectives. Delphiniums simply *make* the garden when they bloom from late June through the middle of July. Cut them back and a secondary flowering occurs, though it is very much a dim shadow of the glorious first bloom.

Here's the downside. Delphiniums will keel over in Midwestern wind, so they must be staked. Don't kid yourself into thinking you can get by without staking or with simple pea staking. These are big mamas and when they fall, they fall hard. Only good strong staking will do. A large cage is best. To make matters worse, their generous size is greatly reduced when the first flush of bloom ends and you trim them back to the side shoots. This leaves a gaping hole in the garden right where you've been focusing attention. Plenty of planning needs to go into how you will disguise this hole that occurs in midsummer. Consider planting your delphiniums behind plants like asters, chrysanthemums, or daylilies that reach their peak in late summer and autumn.

Thrilling as they are, I don't think delphiniums are worth the effort, but if, like sirens, they lure you on, at least do the best you can to keep them happy. All members of this genus like full sun, but in our hot climate you should try to place them where they get the protection of light or dappled shade during part of the afternoon. Too much shade will make the plants grow leggy. Delphiniums demand loose, deep, rich soil with excellent drainage. If you are attempting to garden without properly preparing your soil, don't expect to succeed with delphiniums. They must have moist soil but cannot stand in water, and only proper soil preparation and the addition of plenty of organic matter will give them that condition. When the first growth emerges in spring, thin each clump that is at least a year old to leave only the thickest five to seven stems. Feed them with a granular fertilizer at this point and with a liquid fertilizer when the first bloom is cut off.

Various pests and diseases threaten delphiniums. Slugs find them tasty. Powdery mildew is another hazard. Resign yourself to the reality of spraying regularly with fungicide or putting up with unsightly and damaging fungus. The usual advice is to avoid crowding the plants so that they have good air circulation around them, but in the heat and humidity of our summers, this precaution is unlikely to be effective. When the humidity is 95 percent and there isn't a breath of air stirring you could plant them alone in a square block and they'd probably still get powdery mildew.

If you're tempted by delphiniums take a look at Lynne Rathbone's excellent article "Growing Great English Delphiniums," published in *Fine Gardening* magazine (September–October 1994, 44–49).

Midsummer

Artemisia stelleriana (beach wormwood), perennial, height twelve
inches, spreading habit, full sun: This beautiful perennial foliage
plant bears soft, nappy, silver-white leaves similar to those of
Centaurea cineraria, syn. *C. maritima* (dusty miller) on a low,
spreading perennial plant. The sprays of yellow flowers in summer are more a distraction than a refinement. I cut them off as
soon as they appear. *Artemisia stelleriana* glories in full hot sun
and demands good drainage and dry weather. It won't do well
in a clay soil. It is a master filler plant, closing up the gaps that
can occur in a perennial planting. Get one. I love it. I'm betting
you will, too.

Hosta (hosta or plantain lily), perennial, size varies, shade: Hostas
come in a seemingly endless range of cultivars that offer great
choice of size, form, texture, and leaf color. You could make a very
lovely shade garden with a carefully chosen selection of these
perennials and little else. Their big, broad leaves are their great
feature, varying in color from a green so pale you might as well
go ahead and call it yellow, through darker greens to a rich and
frosty blue. Some are beautifully variegated. Although hostas
send up pretty bloom stalks hung with large bells of white or pale
lavender, the flowering is brief and definitely secondary to the
foliage.

    In choosing hostas, pay attention to form. Most of them pro-
duce a tidy clump with leaves that curve back to earth neatly
covering their feet, but some are vase shaped and will require an
underplanting about their ankles. You also should take note of
the mature size your chosen hosta can be expected to reach. It
may grow slowly, reaching full size in four or five years or even
longer. Once its mature size is realized, though, you don't want

to be moving it to a different location because it will (unless it is a miniature) be extremely heavy. Believe me, transplanting a mature hosta three feet across with roots firmly entrenched in fifteen inches of clay is no small task. The plant may easily weigh fifty pounds, and to dig it, lift it above ground, move it, and make a huge hole to accommodate it is serious work. A better approach is to put the hosta where it will stay and plant annuals or smaller perennials around it while it takes its time putting on girth.

Hostas are well-known plants for shade, but you often see them suggested for partial shade or even sun, too. Variegated hostas in particular may be suggested for sunny locations to maximize their variety of coloration. Beware this advice because our Midwestern sun is just too strong. Site hostas in moist, rich soil in full shade or in constant dappled shade. You can also place them where they receive direct sun only in early morning or very late afternoon. However, if you site them where they are caught out in the full glare of the midday or afternoon sun for even a short time, they will suffer in a heat wave. When temperatures top 100 degrees ugly brown patches will develop and remain for the rest of the season. Meanwhile, hostas in shady locations will show no sign of distress at all.

Among the hostas I've grown, I can especially recommend *H. sieboldiana* var. *elegans, H.* 'Krossa Regal,' and *H. sieboldiana* 'Frances Williams.' *H. sieboldiana* var. *elegans* is a behemoth beauty, a solid three feet high and as much or more across, with gorgeous frosty blue leaves that are rounded, thick, and textured. The first two or three years I had this plant I wondered what all the fuss was about. The darned thing looked green to me, not blue, and it certainly wasn't the flamboyant size I had been lead to expect. Then I read that *H. sieboldiana* var. *elegans* can take as long as seven years to reach maturity, and I settled back to watch patiently. After another couple of years, I saw that it was worth the wait. Both color and size developed over time. I have anchored each end of my shade border with one of these, and they are handsome indeed, creating the effect of a small shrub. The bloom is a solid cluster of white flowers, but it's held too close to the foliage to be showy.

H. 'Krossa Regal' is tall and distinguished by a decided vase shape that demands a low planting close about its feet. The color is a luminous blue gray that must be seen to be believed. The plant is about two feet tall, but the lavender blooms stand up high on four-foot stalks. This hosta is absolutely fearless in a heat wave. In the most scorching days of August it looks fresher than anything else in my garden.

H. 'Frances Williams' possesses leaves that are a slightly blue shade of green edged with a wide band of creamy yellow green that shimmers in dark shade.

If you plan to make a garden in shade, start with hostas and *Astilbe* (false spirea). They make ideal companions. Both are perfectly content in rich, moist shade, and the beautiful contrast of the wide, smooth hosta leaves with the lacy false spirea leaves is quite striking.

Gypsophila paniculata 'Bristol Fairy' (baby's breath), perennial, height thirty-six inches, spread thirty-six inches, sun: To see this perennial in full bloom is to want it—passionately. Baby's breath is that sweet, dainty, airy filler so commonly used in florist's bouquets. A multitude of tiny white blooms creates a three-foot cloud of white like a small blizzard. 'Bristol Fairy' continues this stunning effect for two or three weeks from late June through mid-July, its flowering coinciding with the bloom of *Lilium regale* (regal lily). A large bouquet of regal lilies and baby's breath will absolutely knock your socks off. I have taken this bouquet to a loved one in the hospital and it literally created a sensation. Total strangers stopped to ask about the flowers.

Gypsophila paniculata likes an alkaline soil, so add lime at planting time and be sure to provide good drainage to help prevent crown rot. The difficulty with baby's breath is that it is both so delicate and so large that it will flop horribly, and once flopped will be splattered with mud and ruined by the first hard rain. It's vital to take strong measures early. Instructions for making a girdling cage for baby's breath to grow in are provided in the staking section in chapter 6. It all sounds like a lot of fuss, but once the plant forms that huge cloud of airy white, you will forget all that. This is a truly splendid plant in full flower. I can hardly bear to mar it by picking any of the bloom, but it does make a superb filler in cut flower bouquets. It is also a very desirable dried flower. To dry it, simply cut and arrange it in your hand, then rubber-band or tie the stems together and hang it upside down in a dry, airy location until the stems turn brown. Do not attempt to dry it first and then arrange it, because once it is dry it shatters explosively.

After the first wave of bloom on the plant has faded, cut it back to a point where you see more flower buds forming and you will have a long-lasting secondary bloom. This second flowering, though inferior to the first wave, creates texture in the garden right through August and into September.

A baby's breath is not forever. This short-lived plant is likely to develop crown rot and die rapidly. When it happens, don't worry about it. Just replace your plant as quickly as possible. You don't want to be without this beauty.

Consolida (larkspur), annual, height twenty-four inches, spread twelve inches, sun: I always think of larkspurs as junior delphiniums, lesser in stature, but also free of many of the problems that come with the delphinium package. Larkspur blossoms are similar in form and color, but the plants haven't the dignified elegance of the more regal delphiniums.

Larkspur colors range from white and pink to shades of blue

and purple. The plants self-seed freely, scattering their offspring around your beds at random. Pulling up seedlings that spring up where you don't want them couldn't be easier. Larkspurs thrive in full sun, but will also tolerate light shade for at least part of the day. Their light and airy look is a great part of their charm, but the insubstantial quality of the whole plant means that massing larkspurs is not especially effective. These are casual flowers, not suited to the formal garden. I like them mingled loosely among my perennials. I think they are very good companions for tall bearded irises because they bloom after irises, from late in June through the end of July, filling in the bareness left in the absence of iris bloom.

Lilium (lily), bulb, size varies, sun or part shade: Something about lilies speaks of elegance, purity, and mystery. Their exquisite beauty is so desirable that you somehow feel they are unattainable. They must be terribly tricky and difficult to grow. Their aura daunts you. Or maybe it's the price. Lilies *are* pricey. No doubt about that. A typical tulip bulb costs around fifty cents. A lily can run ten times as much or even more. Never mind. It's worth the price of admission. If your budget is tight, add them gradually.

Lilies are organized into nine divisions and the range available is wide. How will you choose the ones you want? First, consider scent. Many lilies are very strongly and sweetly scented. If a heart beats in your breast you will certainly want some fragrant ones. This eliminates some of the modern hybrids from consideration. For good scent, try Oriental hybrids and trumpet lilies.

To further narrow your choice, consider height. The taller ones—those over about thirty inches—will need staking. The blooms are very large, and their weight might be too much for their stems even in a less windy part of the world. In our climate firm staking is an absolute necessity. If you resent the time spent staking or if accomplishing this sort of task on a timely basis is not your strong suit, avoid the taller lilies. On the other hand, if you want a vertical line, eschew the shorter ones.

The final point to consider is the appearance of the bloom: color and form. The colors include white, cream, pinks from very pale through deep rose, yellow, gold, peach, and orange. Many have edgings or markings of a second color, are freckled, or have yellow or pale green at the throat. On some flowers the stamens are particularly beautiful, but if you don't remove them, they will shed their pollen onto the petals and make an unsightly mess, so try to imagine how the flower will look after a haircut. Pay attention to whether the flowers face upward, downward, or outward. This will make a difference in how you wish to place them in your garden. Obviously the downward-facing blooms are less showy, though they may be quite beautiful cut and placed in a vase at eye level.

Oriental hybrids have rather flat blooms with petals that are curved backward, sometimes tightly, at the tips. Petals may be wide or narrow, smooth or textured. They may ruffle a bit at the edges or twist slightly as they curve backward. The trumpet lilies, though suggested in some reference sources for zones 4–8, may be best grown in areas with warmer winters. If you like the trumpet shape, try *L. regale.* The Asiatic hybrids lack scent, but they do offer plenty of bloom and are the earliest bloomers. The petals are smooth and most have upward-facing flowers. They also thrive in our tough climate and reproduce themselves well.

The commonest garden lily of them all, *L. lancifolium,* syn. *L. tigrinum,* the tiger lily, is very easy to grow and will spread by bulbil. Bulbils are those little black beads that grow up and down the stems at the base of each leaf. Lilies can be propagated by seed, by bulbil, or by separating the bulb into scales and planting them. In the case of tiger lilies, the plants propagate themselves quite freely from the bulbils. When you don't want any more tiger lilies, just start pulling up the seedlings.

Tiger lilies thrive in heat, blooming in August with several flowers on each three-to-five-foot stem. Even the taller ones seldom need staking. Tiger lilies are known to be carriers of lily mosaic virus, and garden books routinely advise against planting them near other kinds of lilies to avoid the spread of this disease. However, if you think you can be satisfied with just one kind of lily and have a taste for flowers in the hot color range, these orange beauties may be just right for you. Their propensity for self-propagation makes them an economical choice. Unfortunately, they have no scent.

L. regale, the regal lily, has a tall stalk that will certainly require staking. Catalogs suggest that it will grow four or five feet tall, but mine routinely reached six feet and occasionally topped out at the eaves of my ranch-style home. The mid-July blooms have the classic white trumpet appearance of florists' Easter lilies. The outsides are pinkish purple to varying extent. This coloration was very faint in my garden and may be reduced by the heat of our climate. Each stem carries several blossoms, making quite a stunning display when at peak bloom. Regal lilies have a potent sweet scent that is especially strong in the evening. When cut, one stem can scent an entire house.

L. 'Casa Blanca' is a stately Oriental hybrid. As with others of this type, plant it in dappled shade or where it is protected from afternoon sun because it suffers when temperatures rise above 90 degrees. In 1995 when two heat waves over 100 degrees were blasting my garden, the 'Casa Blanca' plants that I had sited in full sun developed brown patches on both leaf and petal. If you have been equally foolish in site selection, cut the flower stems as the lower flowers begin to open and take them indoors. They will open and stay fresh in a vase over a remarkably long time. One stem makes a truly majestic bouquet. The flowers are extravagantly large and so shockingly pure white that you need to be careful where you place them because so many other flowers will be dingy in their company. Bloom begins late in July. The wonderful scent reminds me of vanilla.

L. 'Bonnie,' an Asiatic hybrid, is short, about two feet tall, with several pale pink, upward-facing flowers that bloom from the end of June through mid-July. Though unscented, 'Bonnie' does reproduce itself freely and has made a nice show reliably for something like twelve years in my garden. In that time, I have dug and given away excess bulbs twice.

L. 'Pink Virtuoso' is an Oriental hybrid with big white flowers blushed two tones of pink (dark and darker) down the center of each petal and liberally sprinkled with dark rose spots. This lily blooms from late July through mid-August. In our climate it is likely to be damaged in full sun and unlikely to return year after year.

Lilies are perennials. Give them a nice, deep, rich soil with excellent drainage in dappled shade or morning sun with afternoon sun protection. Full sun is fine for tiger lilies, Asiatic lilies, and regal lilies. Fertilize them with a granular fertilizer once a year, in spring when the leaves first emerge from the ground. If you cut them for bouquets, don't take more than a third of the stem because the remaining foliage must nourish the bulb.

Astilbe (false spirea), perennial, size varies, shade: Although these perennials are sometimes suggested for full sun, don't even think about it. These are clearly shade plants in our climate because they need plenty of moisture. Dig in a lot of compost and while you're at it throw in some manure, because *Astilbe* like a very rich soil. They are known as gross feeders, meaning they use up the good stuff in the soil faster than other plants. I scratch in extra manure and compost around them in the spring and give them a second helping after they bloom. They thrive on this treatment. If you don't have the time to enrich your soil with plenty of humus, don't even bother with *Astilbe*. They won't thrive for you.

The fresh and attractive foliage is every bit as good a reason to grow false spirea as the flower. The dark green leaves are deeply cut and reminiscent of ferns. There is a stiff uprightness about the foliage that gives the plants a shrubby presence in the garden in spite of the delicacy of the leaves. A myriad of tiny flowers form the inflorescence, often in the form of an inverted cone that presents a feathery look. This unusual bloom shape adds great interest. Flower colors are white and various shades of pink and purple.

Numerous varieties and cultivars exist, so shop around for those that suit you in size and color. *A. chinensis* var. *pumila* makes a great ground cover because it spreads rapidly to form a dense mass, but not so quickly as to be a nuisance. (You may have to jump back after planting it, but you won't have to run for the ax.) The flowers are lavender pink and less feathery than those of other varieties. The long flowering period begins in mid-July, peaks about the first of August, and ends two weeks later.

A. 'Sprite' is a bit taller (about a foot high and the same across). Its loosely branched pale pink flower heads arch gracefully for a sweetly delicate appearance. Flowering occurs the last two weeks in July.

A. 'Brautschleier,' syn. *A.* 'Bridal Veil' is about two feet high with blooms held another six inches above the plant. The white flowers, in the classic plume form, occur from the last week in June through the middle of July, when seed heads begin to form and the bloom heads turn ecru. You can leave them on for lasting interest and—if you're lucky—even the occasional false spirea from seed.

A. chinensis var. *taquetii* 'Superba' is about four feet high when in bloom and two feet across. The blooms are more tightly placed and do not form the feathery cone of many other *Astilbe*. The pink-purple flowers occur from mid-July into August.

Coreopsis verticillata 'Moonbeam' (threadleaf tickseed), perennial, height ten–twelve inches, spreading habit, sun: The quantity of bloom on this drought-tolerant, carefree gem is quite extraordinary in the world of perennial plants. As a result, it's often used by landscapers to provide a long season of color. You might find it looking stiff and uncomfortable in a mulch of wood chips in the green space around some chain restaurant. To my eye, this plant looks far happier and more graceful at the front of a perennial border where it obligingly weaves in among its neighbors.

Coreopsis verticillata 'Moonbeam' is low-growing, spreading ever wider. It will gradually fill whatever space you allow it, but is readily pulled or dug out if it creeps in where it isn't wanted, so it poses no threat to neighboring perennials. Bits you dig up can be easily moved to fill other spots. The leaves are threadlike. The blooms, produced in showers from late June through September, are small, lemon yellow, and rayed like daisies. Blossoming will lag somewhere in the middle of the bloom season, about mid-August. Some gardeners advise shearing the plant back at this point to promote additional bloom. I find that if I just wait a couple of weeks bloom returns anyway and I haven't sacrificed the plant's shape. Shearing actually removes large numbers of flower buds. Don't take my word on this, though. Shear back half your plants and leave the rest, then stand back and decide what works best in your own garden.

Rudbeckia fulgida var. *sullivantii* 'Goldsturm' (black-eyed Susan), perennial, height twenty inches, spreading habit, sun: This is a workhorse perennial. It blooms from the first of July through late September, most of this period covering itself in blossoms. It makes a nice sturdy bush of a plant that is oblivious to the fierce winds of our region. The stiff stems stand up beautifully and look good even in winter if you forgo cutting the bloom stalks down in fall. The seed heads are a nice presence in the garden in frost and snow.

'Goldsturm' spreads continuously, but doesn't invade and choke its neighbors when you turn your back for a few minutes. It isn't one of those dreaded plants to which the term *vigorous* is so deceptively applied in catalogs. (If crabgrass were offered in nursery catalogs, it would be called "vigorous," as if that were an accolade.) You can divide black-eyed Susans frequently to increase your stock or just dig the plants up every three or four years and replant only a small part if you prefer to keep them contained.

This plant also goes to seed fairly prolifically, and unless you are diligent about removing seedlings, your garden will soon be a sea of gold. Removal of seedlings is quite easy while they are small. Just pay attention to the foliage so you can pick out the 'Goldsturm' seedlings, then pull them by hand as you see them in spring. If you let them grow on a bit, you'll have to get out a hoe to dig them out. To avoid the problem of excess seedlings altogether, you can simply deadhead the flowers as they fade. Of course, this means forgoing the ornamental seed heads in your winter garden.

Zinnia, annual, size varies, sun: Zinnias possess truly uninspiring foliage. Their pallid green leaves of no particular texture or ornamental shape can, however, be excused for the wealth of bloom they support. Zinnias are annuals that begin blooming in late June or early July and keep it up nearly until frost. They come in a range of colors from white, yellow, and orange to varying shades of pink and vivid reds and purples. Most commonly seen in gardens are the mixed colors sold everywhere in the spring. These are bright and cheerful, but if you have a color scheme and aim to do something artistic in your garden, don't expect to find single color six-packs at the nursery. Mix and match or grow your own from seed. You can still buy single colors of some varieties if you order from seed catalogs, though the sad trend seems to be toward nothing but mixes.

You can plant big beds of zinnias for a solid color display from midsummer on. This is certainly a common use of them. I think, though, that they are at their best sprinkled into a perennial border where surrounding plants with more intriguing foliage keep you from noticing the zinnias' weakness in this area. Zinnias are very likely to get a disfiguring powdery mildew in late summer. It strikes me that the more you plant of them in close proximity the more they are likely to be attacked and devastated, so scattering them among your perennials is a good idea from that viewpoint, too. You can spray them to control powdery mildew, but if the disease occurs very late in the summer when flowering is beginning to diminish, you may want to simply pull up the plants, leaving more space for late bloomers. Late season asters, chrysanthemums, *Boltonia asteroides,* and butterfly bushes are taking center stage, so the loss of a few zinnias is no great tragedy.

Zinnias are extremely easy to grow from seed and will germinate in just a few days. You can expect a high percentage of successful germination, so you will probably get more plants than you need from just one seed packet. Give your extras to friends. Plant zinnias in full sun. They are not at all fussy about richness of soil and take only an average amount of water. Because of their susceptibility to powdery mildew, try to water them at the base, not on the leaves.

Petunia, annual, size varies, sun: Petunias thrive in summer heat and fierce sunlight. Their low mounded form makes them ideal for edging borders. They also look great billowing out of pots. Started indoors and set out in mid-May, petunias begin blooming six weeks later and don't quit until frost. Their popularity means they are widely available in a variety of colors from white and yellow to pink, lavender, and purple.

Tagetes (marigold), annual, size varies, sun: Marigolds are very popular annuals, judging by the abundance of six-packs you see in almost every garden shop in spring. They bloom heavily for a very long time, from about the first of July through frost. Most commonly found in the brashest orange, they also come in lemony yellow and clear golds. They've even been bred in a white form. Although marigolds last all right in water, they don't make good cut flowers because they are so closely branched that picking one flower means sacrificing oncoming bloom from the buds that come along with it.

I'm partial to the smaller, single-blossomed marigolds. They are a foot high or less and have flowers only an inch or so across. Look for the ones in the Gem Series or Disco Series. If you choose a shade of yellow or orange that appeals to you, a few small patches of these can add dash to the overall look of your garden. I like the lemon-yellow ones because they suit my favorite color scheme, but if you go in for a hot color scheme, the orange marigolds should fit in nicely.

The dark ferny foliage of marigolds has a pungent odor when bruised. Some people find this smell offensive, others enjoy it. If it's not to your taste, site marigolds where you won't be constantly brushing up against them.

Nicotiana (tobacco plant), size varies, sun to light shade: For heady, powerful scent that permeates a wide area, you can't beat *Nicotiana alata*, syn. *N. affinis* (flowering tobacco). It is in a class with roses on this score. I'm not talking about the modern hybrids that make tidy little clumps good for edging and prolific bloom. For fragrance go straight for the original. *N. alata* is a big, frowzy plant that will sprawl about your garden taking up far more space than you had intended and failing to show the slightest restraint. You will want to stake it somehow, but the stems are so brittle and the leaves so soft that propping efforts won't be successful. By the end of June, just before *N. alata* begins blooming, you will have begun to wonder why you put the darned thing out there in the first place.

Ah, but then the flowers begin. They are like white trumpets flaring into a star at the tip. There whiteness is luminous, making the flowers seem to float above the bed, particularly at night when they emerge startlingly clear from the dusk. This is happy timing, as they also release their staggering perfume in the evening. Walk out after dinner to let it waft over you in sweet waves. The flowering and scent are continuous until frost. This steady display makes *N. alata* a good choice for planting in number to form one strong element of a garden. Its blowzy habit makes it less than desirable for planting in great masses, but it doesn't take masses to create an effect. Half a dozen plants, placed in pairs at intervals along a border, will sweep the area with scent and provide that nice unifying sense of repetition. *N. alata* is a short-lived perennial, best treated as an annual.

Another heavily scented flowering tobacco is *N. sylvestris,* a magnificent thing that makes a shoulder-high plant topped with clusters of pendant white flowers from late summer into fall. Though it blooms for a shorter time, the effect is big and bold. Put a single plant near a gate as a specimen or create the feeling of columns in a border by planting several spaced along both sides of a path with a froth of lower plants at their feet.

If you absolutely insist on something a bit tidier, try *N.* 'Lime Green.' It forms neat little clumps about one foot high and two feet across with pale sulfur yellow flowers all summer. Though it is lovely, it is unscented.

I have admired *N. langsdorfii* in photos, but in my garden the plants were spindly and the flowers seemed to fall off almost before they opened. It is apparently quite variable in height, being described as three to five feet tall. Mine were at the shorter end. The flowers are a pale green, slightly olive, dangling, and less flared at the tips than other types, so they'll look unusual in your garden. Go ahead and try them. Perhaps they will fare better for you. To make a show, you probably need several planted together about one foot apart.

Borago officinalis (borage), annual, height twenty-four to thirty-six inches, spread twelve inches, sun to part shade: Borage is a very nice annual if you like a cottage garden look. It doesn't transplant well, so start it from seed directly in the garden where you want it to grow. You will need to plant it only once, as it seeds itself very freely, and here's where that cottage garden feeling comes into play. Let the plants flourish where the seeds fall for a casual, unplanned look. The plants are a bit lank and lazy and will flop and spill over border edges, giving you a look of happy abundance from late summer on. Borage flowers over a long season from late June through the end of September.

The leaves, stems, and buds are heavily textured, hairy, and a bit prickly, producing an overall misty look. Foliage color is soft green with a blue cast to it. The star-shaped flowers are only one-half to three-quarters inch across, but they are a very intense sapphire blue with a black center. Although the plant is theoretically three feet tall, its floppy habit often means that it is more like two feet off the ground.

Lobularia maritima, syn. *Alyssum maritimum* (sweet alyssum), annual, height four–five inches, spread twelve inches, sun: I read once, I can't recall where, a pooh-poohing of sweet alyssum that suggested it was trite and commonplace and that only the least imaginative gardener would use it. This sweeping condemnation seems to me wildly off-base. Most cultivars of sweet alyssum cover themselves so densely in tiny white flowers that the leaves are all but invisible. The whiteness of the flowers is as pure and snowy as anything you will see anywhere in nature. Sweet alyssum makes this floral offering for an astonishingly long period, from the last week in June through the third week in October. If this were not enough, it is lavishly fragrant. Though the plant is a ground hugger, the scent is very noticeable as you stroll through the garden on a warm day, your nose never closer than five feet away. The fragrance reminds me strongly of honey and I consider it as sweet and fine as that of roses.

Plant sweet alyssum from seed or buy seedlings in the six-packs widely available in nurseries in spring. For about a month after you set them out, they are so insignificant that you may wonder why you bothered with them, but be patient. They soon form lovely floral pools spilling over border edges or down the sides of raised beds. They make very nice pot plants set about the base of some larger, more upright specimen.

Anethum graveolens (dill), annual, size varies, sun: Dill, of course, is an herb. The threadlike leaves can be chopped up to season an egg salad sandwich or a grilled salmon steak. The seeds have their culinary uses, too, so this plant is usually relegated to the herb garden. Its flowers, though, if you take a minute to notice, are quite lovely—airy and graceful and a wonderful acid yellow. The plant is tall but insubstantial with feathery foliage that seems to float weightlessly in the garden. Plants vary considerably in height from about twenty-four to about thirty-six inches. A three-foot-tall plant takes up almost no width, however, so you can toss a few seeds in among perennials.

Dill is a very easy plant that takes no care at all. Site it in full sun. It's an annual that flowers for a few weeks starting in mid-July. The blooms make terrific cut flowers, but leave a few on the plant to form seed. Scatter the seed where you want the plants to grow in next year's garden. If you are lucky, in mid- to late summer you'll notice striped caterpillars on the plants. Allow them to eat their fill and then watch for the swallowtail butterflies to appear. This magical event adds great charm to a garden. Share it with a child. When the caterpillars are through with the dill, just pull it up and toss it on the compost pile.

Echinops ritro (small globe thistle), perennial, height forty-eight inches, spread twenty-four inches, sun: Small globe thistle has a hard edge to it that makes a nifty contrast to all the soft stuff in your border. Its stiffly upright form has a primeval feel. You can imagine *Echinops ritro* in bloom when dinosaurs roamed the Midwest. Though relatively tall, this perennial never needs staking and could in fact be used among floppy plants to help hold them up. Its bloom, from mid-July through the first week in August, is as stiff and prickly as the plant itself. The globe-shaped thistle is about the size of a marshmallow and a color usually described as steely blue, though I think it is too attractive a shade to be so harshly labeled. This is one of those wonderful garden flowers that is truly blue and not the lavender, purple, or violet often called blue in garden literature.

E. *ritro* is a definite conversation starter. Visitors are likely to come to a full, screeching halt in front of it and demand to know what it is. Probably they are startled to see in cultivation something that looks so much like the thistle that is considered a noxious weed by farmers and is actually illegal to have growing on your property in my state. There's nothing weedy about *E. ritro*. Though it will self-sow if you leave the blooms to ripen and form seed, the seedlings are not numerous and are easily pulled. It's a good idea to allow seed to form though, because the ripening seed heads hold the bloom form and some of its color for several weeks, giving the plant at least a semblance of extended bloom. You can dry the flowers for use in wreaths or arrangements, but the trick is to take the flowers just *before* they reach full bloom.

My small globe thistle is planted behind a daylily that has the sunset colors of deep rose layered over apricot (*Hemerocallis* 'Bowl of Roses'). The spiky blooms and angular form of small globe thistle make it the perfect backdrop for the straplike foliage and fat, thick blooms of this daylily. I have only one small globe thistle, but I have seen this plant used at intervals throughout a long border to provide the pleasant unity of spaced repetition, like columns on a grand porch.

E. ritro is very reliable, performing year after year. It increases in size slowly so that it takes quite a while to get too big for its britches. Part of its reliability, unfortunately, is that in my garden I can count on its being attacked by aphids nearly every spring about late May. The good news is that these pests can be easily controlled.

Hemerocallis (daylily), perennial, size varies, sun: If you think you don't like these perennials, you probably don't really know them. Neophyte gardeners often believe that all daylilies are orange, and when it comes to orange daylilies, familiarity breeds contempt. These are the old-fashioned flowers that bloom in ditches and on old farm sites. They bore you silly. I'm talking here about something else again. Modern hybridizers have created a fabulous range of daylilies that includes colors as pale as a frosty yellow that comes very close to white, as vivid as dark reds and purples, as elusive as deep rose layered over apricot. Blooms are made up of wide and heavy petals or of long, thin, and curling ones. They are crimped at their edges or sprinkled with stardust or built around a brilliant green heart. The variety is thrilling. The colors are flashy in the garden. Best of all, these plants bloom well and thrive in the worst heat of summer when much of the rest of the garden is out of flower, wilted, or half dead.

A word of caution about daylilies: the blooms are varied, but the foliage is not. The green straplike leaves are all but identical from one cultivar to the next. Dwarf plants make smaller clumps and perhaps thinner leaves, but the essential character of the foliage does not vary. If you plant a great many of them, the repetition may go unnoticed while the plants bloom, but it will be a great screaming bore when they are not in flower. Furthermore, the leaves rise in an arching fountain that takes up quite a lot of space by midsummer. Unless you plan carefully, this can leave quite a few gaping holes in your spring garden.

I like to plant tall bearded irises among my daylilies. When the daylily plants are small in spring, the irises hold sway with their lovely orchidlike flowers and great swirls of silvery green leaf. By mid- to late summer, the iris foliage is likely to be unattractive. No problem. The daylilies hide it. The irises don't seem to suffer from being slightly shaded for part of the summer. You could also plant bulbs among your daylilies to provide spring bloom because they go dormant by the time the daylilies reach full size.

By the way, though all *Hemerocallis* are called daylilies, they are decidedly not lilies. Lilies are in the genus *Lilium* and are something else entirely. The daylily is a perennial plant with thick roots, numerous leaves emerging from the ground, and several stems of flower buds. Each flower lasts only one day. The lily, on the other hand, is a bulb made up of thick scales. It is planted deeply and produces one stem of flowers with numerous leaves up and down the stem. Each lily flower lasts a few days to two weeks. The only real similarity between lilies and daylilies is in the shape of the bloom.

Each daylily stem produces many flower buds that mature and bloom successively. Though each blossom lasts only one day, there are so many of them that an individual plant blooms over several weeks. The daylily is generally not used as a cut flower because the blossom will last only a few hours and you will have sacrificed the garden bloom of all of the buds picked with that stem.

Most daylilies open in the morning, last through the day, and close in the evening. Because their flowers fade as the day progresses, especially in extreme heat and brilliant sun, particularly if the flowers are in the red-purple range, they are at their best in the morning. If you do most of your gardening in the evening, look for hybrids that open in the afternoon and close the following morning. This will allow you to enjoy your daylilies at their best.

Though not generally thought of as fragrant flowers, many daylilies have a very pleasing, sweet fragrance. This is a characteristic to watch for in selecting daylilies for your garden. Like many other flowers, they are most fragrant in the evening, so selecting for scent is particularly important if you are an after-work gardener.

Often *Hemerocallis* producers' catalogs will picture only a few of their newest offerings. Be warned that these recent introductions are also the most expensive. The longer a daylily is around, the lower the price falls. Some lovely cultivars have been on the market long enough that their prices are quite reasonable. On the other hand, spanking new offerings—so beautiful they make you pant—are often wildly expensive. Get the most for your garden buck by waiting a bit till the price goes down to acquire those lovelies. Meanwhile, purchase the tried and true and economical oldies. I confess that in 1988 I violated my own advice by paying the shocking price of $17.75 for a tempting daylily called *H.* 'Bowl of Roses.' The photo showed a flower of such rich, sunset colors that I could not bear to pass it up. By the second year, it was a large plant with plenty of big beautiful blooms. I thought, and still do, that it lived up completely to that catalog photo and description. Though I have never regretted purchasing it, six years later 'Bowl of Roses' could be had for just $10.50. By comparison, lovely older cultivars like *H.* 'Daydream Believer,' *H.* 'Little Fat Dazzler,' and *H.* 'Prairie Blue Eyes' can be had for $5.00 or $6.00.

Though a few daylilies increase slowly, most become larger at a moderately rapid rate and are relatively easy to dig and divide.

A three- or four-year-old clump can readily be turned into three to five smaller plants that will provide bloom the following year.

You often read in garden books that daylilies are carefree, pest free, and need never be watered. This is a bit of an exaggeration. While daylilies are certainly very tough plants, they are not completely without problems. Although they survive times of drought without water, they definitely bloom best if you water them regularly as you do other perennials. In protracted extreme heat (above 100 degrees), their leaves will scorch somewhat. Following bloom, some of the leaves will die back but will be replaced shortly by fresh new growth. Just pull off and discard the dead leaves.

In some seasons daylilies will form buds nicely but drop many of them before they can bloom. This seems to be the unavoidable result of certain weather conditions. Some years this problem is severe, other times it is negligible.

Your daylilies may also suffer from some pests. Mine are regularly assaulted by tarnished plant bugs (*Lygus lineolaris*). These annoying insects cause buds to shrivel. They dart to the back of a bud or leaf or simply fly away when you try to hand pick them. Although you can control them by spraying with malathion, the spray also is extremely deadly to bees. It's better to simply live with them and the damage they cause. Just turn a blind eye to the little devils. The overall appearance of your plant won't be noticeably affected, and daylilies are such generous bloomers that you can afford to sacrifice a bit for the safety of the bees.

If you plant a new daylily only to have it refuse to bloom, check to see whether it is planted too deeply. Sometimes they sink in soft prepared soil and then refuse to blossom. The top of the root structure should be only about a half inch below the ground's surface.

Thalictrum rochebrunianum 'Lavender Mist' (meadow rue), perennial, height five feet, spread two feet, part shade: This beautiful cultivar of *Thalictrum* is one of those plants whose dimensions in no way indicate its true form. Although it is indeed tall, most of its foliage grows near the ground. The long stems are thick and stout and may need no staking because they support only airy clouds of tiny flowers. As big as this perennial is, it seems light and insubstantial.

You could put one of these smack in front of the border to interrupt the monotony of plants ranked strictly by height. You could throw in four or five scattered along the length of a large border to give vertical line and unity. Or cluster several together for a cool haze of bloom.

'Lavender Mist' likes to grow in a lightly shaded area in moist soil. Flowering starts in mid-July and continues for several weeks before seed forms, which gives the plant interest through most of September.

Aster x *frikartii* 'Mönch,' perennial, height twenty-four to forty inches, spread twenty-four to thirty inches, sun: If you don't already possess this plant (unfortunately not hardy in zone 4), hurry to the nearest nursery to correct this oversight as soon as possible. The color of the blooms alone makes this perennial worth having. Its rayed flowers, roughly two inches across, are a heavenly pale blue that is just faintly lavender. In a world where every dull lavender or purple plant is described as blue, this one truly is. 'Mönch' is also an abundant bloomer. As if this weren't enough, the length of bloom, from mid-July through at least the end of September, is extraordinary. Without pea staking the plant will flop forward, so that the overall clump is lower than described in some garden books. It is not, however, lank, and still looks very solid and full. It's gorgeous draped over the front edge of a raised bed. I have been told by a professional that 'Mönch' can be difficult to establish, but I haven't found it so. If the first plant you try doesn't succeed, try again. And again, if necessary.

When you get a clump going you'll find the show justifies the trouble.

Salvia farinacea 'Victoria' (mealycup sage), annual, height eighteen–thirty inches, spread fourteen inches, sun: This is the first annual blue *Salvia* cultivar that I recall seeing widely offered. Other cultivars have followed it, but I don't think any of them holds a candle to this one. The color is a very pure and piercing blue violet that looks like a rich velvet. The plant is small and compact, unlike some other annual types of sage that are on the rangy side. The flowers are small and spaced along a stalk, creating an overall bloom look that is both nicely textured and vertical. The seed heads are only slightly less blue—like the softly faded upholstery on your favorite chair. You can deadhead mealycup sage early on to keep it blooming. When weather turns cold enough to stop oncoming bloom, allow the seed heads to form, which gives the appearance of extended bloom. The plant will tend to flop over toward the light. I do realize that this should be a fault, but it somehow makes 'Victoria' more compatible for mixing with perennials.

Four plants of *Salvia farinacea* 'Victoria' set out in a diamond shape will make a nice splash of dark blue from mid-July until frost—three solid months, at least. Come August when they are looking absolutely smashing, I guarantee you will wish you had planted more.

Tanacetum parthenium, syn. *Chrysanthemum parthenium* (feverfew), short-lived perennial, height eighteen inches, spread twelve inches, sun or part shade: *Tanacetum parthenium* is a very nice, unassuming little plant that seems able to grow in almost any situation. In my garden it prospers in moist shade, but seems equally happy growing among the bricks of my patio in the full glare of the sun. Feverfew is a low-growing plant with a nice splash of white bloom like a bouquet of small daisies just right to hold in one hand. Flowering doesn't start until late June or mid-July, but continues without a breather until frost. The leaves are dark and lacy and pungently scented.

Although it is a hardy perennial, feverfew is short-lived. Fortunately, though, it will seed itself freely, so that you need plant it only once to enjoy it for many years. Scatter the seed directly in the garden, then pull any that fall where your eye tells you they don't belong. The result is casual and very sweet.

Late Summer

Ocimum basilicum 'Dark Opal' (basil), annual, height fifteen–eighteen inches, spread twelve inches, sun: *Ocimum basilicum* 'Dark Opal' makes attractive foliage for the flower garden. Its dark purple leaves appear spectacular contrasted with the green and gray of other foliage types and look especially beautiful with flowers in the pink range. As an added bonus, you'll be able to harvest some of the leaves for culinary flavoring. Basil strongly dislikes being transplanted, so it's far easier to start it from seed directly in the garden than to buy small sets. Basil is exceptionally tender and susceptible to cold. Don't plant it early, because a late cold snap is very likely to cut its life short. Your plant will show damage from which it may not recover even if temperatures do not drop all the way to freezing.

Perovskia atriplicifolia (Russian sage), perennial, height forty-eight inches, spread forty-eight inches, sun: A friend in the nursery trade says Russian sage can be a tough sell because a young plant looks like a stick in a pot. However unprepossessing it may look at this stage, buy one and plant it in a sunny spot. By the end of the second summer you will be wondering how you lived without it. Russian sage has a big bushy form and airy look that remind me of baby's breath. Though reference books suggest it is not hardy in zone 4, friends who garden north of Minneapolis say they have had good luck getting it through the winter with some shelter.

The stems and narrow toothed leaves are a woolly gray green that is more gray than green. The blooms from late July into September are a grayish blue and are followed for another month by seed pods of very much the same color. The overall effect is soft and hazy in spite of the rigidity of the stems.

P. atriplicifolia tends to lean heavily toward the sun unless you get one of the cultivars that stands more upright, such as 'Longin' or 'Filagran.' 'Longin' is wider and 'Filagran' has more finely cut leaves. I have the plain old species plant *P. atriplicifolia,* an incorrigible flopper. I am very fond of it and think that for some purposes, its arching flop is ideal. I also grow 'Filagran' for its graceful upright habit. It is beautiful with *Hemerocallis* 'Little Grapette,' whose raspberry red blooms are enhanced by association with the soft colors of the Russian sage.

Russian sage likes a sunny position and good drainage. Drought won't faze it, but soggy ground certainly will. If you have difficulty getting it going, improve the drainage of your soil and try again. Don't cut it down in fall, but wait until spring, about six weeks before the frost-free date, when you should prune it hard, cutting it back to just a foot or so off the ground. Its is a pleasant experience, because the stems and foliage have a pungent scent when bruised or cut. The plant soon puts on new foliage to make a nice bushy shape.

Thymophylla tenuiloba, syn. *Dyssodia tenuiloba* (Dahlberg daisy or golden fleece), annual, height six–eight inches, spread six inches, sun: This pleasing annual has half-inch daisylike flowers of clear yellow gold and delicate ferny foliage that delivers a strong, pungent, and delightful fragrance when crushed. As sweet and fragile as it looks, the Dahlberg daisy is a tough little customer that flourishes in strong sunlight or a bit of shade. I enjoy it mixed with other annuals in the containers on my brick patio. Plants from past summers have gone to seed in the brick, where they prosper with no care and very little moisture. You can buy the plants already in flower and set them out in May for continuous bloom through September. Seedlings from these parent plants will start blooming in July the following year.

Buddleia davidii (butterfly bush), shrub, size varies, sun: In milder climates, *Buddleia davidii* live through winter to form sizable shrubs, but in zone 5 they die back severely and must grow from nearly the ground up each season. They are not hardy in zone 4. Leave all of their growth on them until early spring, about four to six weeks before the frost-free date. Then prune them back hard to eight or twelve inches above ground level. They are slow to get started in spring, but will eventually put on growth and reach a height of four to seven feet by late in the season. Because of their slow start, you might want to plant bulbs at their feet to provide some spring show. Small flowers are borne in clusters like tapered bottle brushes from the first of August through frost— about ten weeks. Their sweet scent is unlike anything else in the garden. Butterflies find them irresistible and this, along with their substantial size, is a great part of their appeal. *B. davidii* 'Lo-chinch' has silvery gray leaves and lavender-blue flowers. Other butterfly bushes have dark green leaves and blooms in shades of purple and pink. This plant requires a site in full sun and will languish without it.

Calamintha (calamint), perennial, size varies, sun: Sweetly minty when you brush past it, covered in tiny flowers from late July until frost, absolutely pest-free, *Calamintha nepeta* (lesser calamint) is one terrific perennial. It forms a remarkably tidy clump, like a tiny

Mertensia pulmonarioides, syn. *M. virginica* (Virginia bluebells; garden of Aileen Rodgers and Jack Rodgers).

Right: Baptisia australis (blue wild indigo, false indigo, or plains false indigo).

Below: Artemisia stelleriana 'Silver Brocade' (beach wormwood).

Narcissus 'Thalia' (daffodil) with red tulips.

Below: Spiky *Calamintha nepeta* (lesser calamint) with *Geranium sanguineum* var. *striatum,* syn. *G. sanguineum* var. *lancastriense.*

Lamium maculatum 'Pink Pewter' (spotted deadnettle).

Secret garden with *Iris* 'Caesar's Brother' (Siberian iris) in foreground, *Iris* 'White Swirl' (Siberian iris) in background (photo by James L. McKee).

Right: Coreopsis verticillata 'Moonbeam' (threadleaf tickseed).

Dicentra spectabilis (bleeding heart) at left. At right a yellow *Epimedium* (barrenwort; garden of Aileen Rodgers and Jack Rodgers).

Cleome (spider flower) with *Daphne* x *burkwoodii* 'Carol Mackie' and *Athyrium niponicum* (Japanese painted fern; photo by James L. McKee).

shrub, with stiff and brittle stems. The flowers make pretty filler for the smallest bouquets and can easily be snapped off rather than cut. The overall appearance is sweet, delicate, and graceful. This is an exceptionally fine plant if you strive for a soft romantic look. Bees and wasps find it irresistible. I enjoy the busy hum this adds to the garden.

C. nepeta blooms from the end of July through the third week in October. The flowers are generally described as light blue, but in Midwestern heat they are more likely to be white with only the slightest whiff of blue about them. Then autumn arrives and the cool night air does seem to bring out their color. The plant is about twenty inches high by thirty inches wide.

C. grandiflora 'Variegata' is another very good perennial of the same family. It forms a lower clump (fifteen inches high by eighteen inches wide) and adds sparkle to the front of the border with its small, variegated leaves and purple-pink blooms. Flowering begins in mid-May and runs into early September. Shear the plant back and it may give you some bonus late bloom, too. During a late May tour of my garden, this plant attracted considerable notice.

Site *Calamintha* in full sun or a very little shade. Both kinds are oblivious to heat and dry conditions.

Cleome (spider flower), annual, height sixty inches, spread thirty-six inches, sun to part shade: If you want to make a statement in your garden, plant a few *Cleome.* People will sit up and take notice. These bold annuals start easily from seed the size of a fleck of pepper, growing by late summer into plants as big as you are. The flowers are softball-size exotic clusters of white or shades of rose and purple. These are my husband's favorite flowers, but they aren't to everyone's taste. A friend says they look like they're from outer space and I don't think she means it as a compliment.

Plant the seed directly in the garden, because seedlings do not transplant well. In late summer, the flowers will go to seed, making plenty for future use. Let the seed drop in place to start next year's crop or harvest it and scatter it where you like—no need to scratch the soil or cover the seed. These things are self-starters. Spider flowers positively glory in direct sun and heat, but will also do well in moderate shade. Bloom starts the end of July and continues without hesitation until the first hint of frost.

Fall

Boltonia asteroides 'Snowbank,' perennial, height forty-eight inches, spread twenty-four inches, sun: Like asters, perennial *Boltonia asteroides* blooms only in the late summer and fall, but takes up a sizable space throughout the season. Unlike asters, it has a relatively short bloom period, flowering for most of September but in really blazing full bloom for perhaps just two weeks. Is it worth it? It's a matter of taste, but you might prefer to forgo it if your garden is small.

'Snowbank' increases easily by division, and three plants will make a good showy grouping. The stems are very stiff and strong, so the plant needs no staking even in the windy Midwest. The snowy white rayed flowers are an inch wide or a bit less. They are extremely profuse, blooming all together in a great burst that makes a cloud of white. Bees, butterflies, and other insects are drawn to *Boltonia asteroides,* so no small part of the plant's show is the buzz of activity around it.

Anemone tomentosa 'Robustissima,' syn. *A. vitifolia* 'Robustissima' (grape-leaf anemone), perennial, height thirty inches, spreading habit, shade: This beautiful cultivar is unfortunately not hardy in zone 4, but other plants in this genus are, so if you are a zone 4 gardener, you might want to try the more winter hardy species: *A. canadensis, A. magellanica, A. nemerosa,* and *A. sylvestris.*

Though 'Robustissima' flowers for eight weeks or more from late August through October, its rich green foliage is at least as great an attraction. Grow grape-leaf anemone in shade and its lobed leaves will appear fresh and vigorous from spring until frost. They are remarkably pretty, making for a handsome attention-getting plant even when no bloom is present. The mauve-pink flowers are possessed of a shell-like delicacy and their lack of perfect symmetry somehow makes them particularly appealing. When the petals fall, the small hard centers remain, continuing to make texture in the garden. 'Robustissima' sometimes receives unflattering comments due to its propensity for enlarging its territory. Certainly by the third or fourth year you will need to root out portions that have crept in where they aren't wanted. The plus side is that 'Robustissima' makes a nice healthy clump and can be counted on to fill its allotted space completely, leaving no bare earth at its feet and contributing to a feeling of fullness in the border.

Be sure to give 'Robustissima' a shaded location. If planted where it receives direct sun for even part of the day it will suffer from midsummer on. Leaf edges brown and curl, thus destroying the beautiful foliage that should be one of the plant's chief assets.

A pair of *A.* x *hybrida* hardy to zone 4 are 'Honorine Jobert' and 'Whirlwind.' 'Honorine Jobert' has never been strong in my garden, though I have seen it doing well in a friend's zone 5 garden. For me, the elegant white flowers come on so late that they are routinely nipped by frost before full bloom is achieved. 'Whirlwind,' after three years in my garden, still hasn't formed a healthy clump or bloomed before frost. Both of these may fare better in zone 4, where extremes of heat are somewhat less severe.

Aster novae-angliae 'Andenken an Alma Pötschke,' syn. 'Alma Pötschke' (New England aster), perennial, height thirty-six inches, spread sixty inches or more, sun: For about seven weeks in late summer into fall, from about the beginning of September until frost, 'Alma Pötschke' is the show-stopping queen of the garden. When gardeners get together and talk shop, they refer to this big mama as Alma, as if she were a personal friend, possibly one with an operatic career. Certainly she is a force to be reckoned with. Around three feet tall at maturity in late summer, her matronly girth expands with age. A three-year-old plant is likely to span five feet in autumn. The width is exaggerated by her propensity to flop. A severe girdling of stakes and string might control her sloppy posture, but I have as yet been unable to fully accomplish it. This is a stunningly vigorous perennial.

To control Alma's size, you can dig and divide it every other spring. Although this means Alma is a bit on the high maintenance side, the good news is that the rate at which she grows means getting a free start from a garden friend should be easy. Pinching the plant tips two or three times in the spring and early summer is another way to control the size of a tall aster. Just nip off the last grouping of leaves on each stem when the plant is about six inches high. After every five or six inches of new growth, do it again, but stop pinching by mid-July to allow flower buds to develop. More drastic measures can be applied, if necessary. When massive spring rainfall made my 'Alma Pötschke' knee-high and floppy in June, I took shears to it and whacked it back to about four inches from the ground. By late summer the plant was a bushy but small specimen that bloomed very well.

However much digging, dividing, pinching, and whacking she requires, Alma justifies the effort. The hot pink blooms with which this beauty covers herself are eye-catching, to put it mildly. By mid-October, she is a mass of fiery pink that goes beautifully with the purples and lavenders of other fall asters, the pinks and lavenders of butterfly bushes, the pure white of *Boltonia as-*

teroides 'Snowbank,' the silver of *Artemisia stelleriana* (beach wormwood), and the white-hinting-at-blue of calamint.

Chrysanthemum, perennial, size varies, sun: The genus *Chrysanthemum* includes about twenty different species, but the common name is generally applied to the ubiquitous fall-blooming perennials available at garden centers. These plants can seem a nuisance in the garden all spring and through much of the summer when they are taking up quite a bit of space and not blooming at all. But just wait: In the fall they come into their glory just as many of your favorite perennials are bedding down for winter. Most chrysanthemums get going around the first of September and keep it up until the frost arrives, usually sometime in October.

Potted, blooming chrysanthemums are offered for sale in the fall. It's fun to buy them at this time because you can tell exactly what bloom color you're going to get. Just pop them out of their pots and into the ground for an instant splash of red, yellow, gold, orange, pink, purple, or white. Beware the darker red and purple flowers—they are likely to fade in our hot sun, often to an unpleasant brown. The potted plants won't put on any growth in fall, and you can't absolutely rely on their surviving the winter. Buy as early as possible to give the plants time to develop the root growth they will need to survive. Plant them in soil with good drainage and don't forget to water them often since their pot-size roots won't survive a dry stretch.

Chrysanthemums are said to require division every one to three springs to maintain their vigor. This involves digging the plant just after the leaves emerge, dividing it into pieces about three to six inches across, and replanting as many as you want to keep. Throw out the older inner part of the plant and keep only the newer outside sections. I used to do this with a lavender chrysanthemum that became leggy and flopped if not divided regularly, but I have a brilliant yellow plant that I never divide. It all depends. If your plants become lanky or bloom seems reduced from previous years, divide them. Anytime you want more plants, divide in spring. These plants grow so rapidly and are so easy to increase by division that buying more than one of a color is an extravagance. Buy just one and then increase your stock.

6

Providing Routine Care

Gardens are easiest in spring and early summer—young, tender, sweet, moist, and effortless. Weeds are mere seedlings, rain is adequate, diseases haven't yet gotten a foothold. This, too, is when many of the most beautiful flowers bloom—delicate, profuse and fragrant: *Convallaria* (lily-of-the-valley), *Narcissus* (daffodil), *Tulipa* (tulip), *Paeonia* (peony), irises, *Heuchera* (coral flower or coral bells), *Campanula* (bellflower), *Digitalis* (foxglove), *Viola* x *wittrockiana* (pansy), *Syringa* (lilac), roses. The garden is a delicate fairyland. It seems a paradise and you are in love with it. This is passionate young love when happily-ever-after seems not only attainable, but a lead pipe cinch.

Phase two—reality—hits around the end of June. "I've sort of lost interest in my garden," I heard someone say in July. Well, no wonder. It isn't all roses anymore. The weeds are up, the leaf miner has ravaged the *Aquilegia* (columbine), and mildew has overtaken the *Phlox divaricata* (woodland phlox or wild sweet William). Summer heat has struck the Midwest with its full blast, requiring endless watering. A gap in bloom between the spring flowers and the

late season ones has made the garden seem a wasteland. This is midlife crisis with a vengeance. The strong light of a summer day reveals the garden's every flaw. Autumn will roll around with cooler temperatures, renewed rain, truer colors shown under the sun's angled rays, and mature love will reap its reward. Staying power is the key in the midseason garden. Staying power means keeping on top of routine tasks like watering, weeding, and deadheading to see the garden through the heat of summer.

Weeding

Visitors to my garden often comment on how weed-free it is. In comparison to many flower gardens at midsummer or later it certainly is very clean, but I don't think I spend more time weeding than gardeners who feel they are up to their knees in weeds all the time. I simply do my weeding on a different schedule. If weeds are spotted and removed as seedlings, when they haven't yet put down deep roots, most of them are very easy to pull. The added benefit of moist ground makes springtime especially good for weeding. If weeds are pulled later in the year when they have established root systems, roots often snap off, leaving remnants behind to regenerate the plant. Another advantage of early attention to weeding is that weeds can be removed well before they go to seed, when they reproduce themselves by the hundreds and thousands.

Pulling weeds early doesn't mean you have to make time to go out and weed daily. Just keep an eagle eye out for weeds every time you step into your garden. As you water or cut flowers or put in annuals, watch for weeds and pull them the minute you see them. If you are diligent in scouring the garden for weeds in April, May, and June, you will be amazed at how few there are to deal with in the heat of summer. If you have been very lazy in the spring and find yourself surrounded by weeds in summer, get right on the job of removing them before they go to seed. The day after a rain the softer ground provides ideal weeding conditions. If you're facing a dry spell, plan to weed the day after a good watering.

Even desirable plants can be weeds if they are allowed to go to seed with abandon. If you are pressed for time, steer clear of annuals that go to seed very freely: *Cleome* (spider flower), *Consolida* (larkspur), *Borago officinalis* (borage), *Viola tricolor* (Johnny-jump-up), *Nicotiana alata*, syn. *N. affinis* (flowering tobacco), and others require a controlling hand to keep them from taking over.

To eliminate weeds, you need to be able to recognize them. This is essentially a process of elimination. Whatever is not a known desirable plant must be a weed. To recognize a weed, you first must know your own plants well. Each seedling, whether weed or garden plant, has a distinctive look. Learn that look for each desirable plant in your garden. Start by observing the appearance of the seedlings that emerge when you plant seeds. Notice, too, the sprinkling of seedlings that may appear around a mother plant after midsummer. By studying these you can learn to recognize flowers in their juvenile state. Once the true leaves begin to form, you should be able to see the resemblance to the foliage of mature plants. Don't forget that the nondescript cotyledons appear first. To avoid mistakes, wait until you're sure the first true leaves have appeared, otherwise you may pull a desirable seedling.

What about weeds that just can't be pulled? Some weeds or runaway ground covers, such as dandelions and *Aegopodium* (bishop's weed or goutweed), can be very persistent. No matter how carefully you pull them you always leave behind root fragments to restart the wretches. If these plants or other weeds become a problem in the cracks of pavement or in a gravel or wood chip path, there is an easy and nontoxic way to deal with them. Douse them with boiling water. The more persistent may need a second dousing a week or ten days later, but most will succumb the first time. If persistent weeds are growing among desirable plants, obviously you can't go sloshing about with boiling water. In some cases repeatedly pulling the same weed will progressively weaken and eventually eliminate it. In some situations, such as at the base of a shrub, you may be able to smother the weeds with thick layers of newspaper. A mulch of dirt or grass clippings thrown over the top will prevent the papers from blowing away. This will gradually smother the weeds and the paper will eventually rot into the ground.

A last resort in weed control is to use Roundup carefully. This herbicide will kill everything it touches. The plant absorbs the Roundup into its system through its leaves and slowly, over a period of one to three weeks, dies. Even this harsh treatment may sometimes have to be repeated to fully kill the most determined weeds. Roundup is most effective used in warm weather when plants are growing rapidly. Obviously, since this spray will kill any plant material it touches, you endanger your desirable plants by using it. For this reason you need to exercise great care when spraying it. If you apply it in even the slightest breeze you may kill nearby plants. Wind drift, sloppy spraying, or even wetting a weed that is touching another plant can do considerable damage. This product is also expensive, so use it sparingly and consider other weed removal methods first.

Watering

Appropriate watering is crucial to the survival of a landscape in our hot climate. This is perhaps the most difficult part of the gardener's art to teach through words alone. To a great extent, you just have to get out there and learn it by trial and error.

Flowering plants need at least an inch of water a week. When temperatures are well above 90 degrees, they'll need more. Buy a rain gauge and check it routinely so that you know how much rain your garden is getting. Even though the local weather report tells you how much rain has fallen in your general area, rain can be very spotty, so you should check the rain in your own yard yourself.

When you receive less than an inch a week, you must water. Because they are protected from rain, plants under the eaves of your house or tucked in around tree roots will require watering even during rainy periods. Assessing your garden's need for water is complicated by windy conditions, which dry plants and cause them to need additional moisture.

Soaking a bed thoroughly and letting it dry out is preferable to watering lightly and frequently. This is common advice handed out in garden books. Take it with a grain of salt, because our region's peak summer heat and wind can make actually soaking a bed a near impossibility. Reality comes into play when several consecutive windy days over 95 degrees occur and you just have to get out there and apply all the water you can whenever you can do it.

Plants in sun will normally wilt somewhat during the heat of the afternoon and freshen up in the relative cool of the evening. They look their best and make the nicest cut flowers first thing in the morning when they have had all night to restore moisture to all parts of the plant. Drooping leaves at noon on a hot day do not necessarily mean that water is needed because the plant is simply not pumping water as rapidly as it is losing it. As the sun goes down, the plant will catch up. Overcast skies will slow drying, but under sunny skies more moisture is required. There's a difference between wilting and shriveling, however. Wrinkled leaves, crisp leaf edges, a whole plant lying loose on the ground are all signs of imminent death. The plant requires immediate water and possibly some temporary shade—an upended box or bushel basket or even a leafy twig stuck in the ground next to the plant.

The toughest plants that require little water, such as *Hemerocallis* (daylily), tall bearded irises, *Baptisia australis* (blue wild indigo, false indigo, or plains false indigo), and *Epimedium* (barrenwort) show little if any drooping during periods of drought. Many gray plants (those with a downy surface) are native on dry land and do best if scarcely watered. Even though they tend to wilt in heat, they still probably don't need water. Examples are *Achillea* 'Moonshine' (yarrow), *Lychnis coronaria* (rose campion), *Artemisia stelleriana* (beach wormwood), and *Stachys byzantina,* syn. *S. lanata* (lamb's-ears).

The ideal time to water is morning. Pump the plants full of water so they can get through the heat of the day. Watering in the evening is second best, but may promote fungus. If you have a busy schedule, evening may be your only choice and is better than not watering at all. Midafternoon is not a good time to water because the Midwestern wind will evaporate an enormous amount of what you apply. Even the gentle spray of sprinkler or hose nozzle may cause plants limp from the heat to collapse into the mud.

Shade plants, like *Astilbe* (false spirea) and *Hosta* (hosta or plantain lily), tend to be moisture lovers, but they require less frequent watering than other plants because the lack of sun helps keep them from drying out. The exception to this rule is the dreaded dry shade. Shaded slopes and areas under mature trees, especially evergreens, are likely to be very dry. You can improve the situation by thorough soil preparation and removal of a few tree roots. Adding the humus that shade plants love will create a rich and moisture-retentive soil.

Water each plant at its base as much as possible to help control fungus, to avoid squashing limp plants, and to get more water to the roots. Plants that are especially prone to fungus should never be watered on their leaves: roses, delphiniums, zinnias, *Monarda* (bee balm or bergamot), *Phlox paniculata* (garden phlox), and lilacs. A drip irrigation system is one way to provide water without dampening leaves. Arrange soaker hoses around plants in early spring when they are small. When the garden needs moisture, allow water to drip from the soaker hoses for an extended period of time. This soaks the ground deeply without allowing water to dampen foliage or evaporate.

Plants do soak up water through their leaves and stems, so those not prone to fungus can be refreshed quickly with a light sprinkling if they are excessively stressed by heat and hot wind. Hose attachments that fan water are beneficial because they soften the spray so that you aren't knocking plants down with a stiff blast of water and creating a muddy splatter. The watering attachment that looks like a shower head on a wand is very useful for extending your reach. A shut-off valve for the hose end allows you to turn the water off for limited periods of time without returning to the tap. Avoid using this hose end shutoff for long periods, though, as the water pressure created can cause a hose to spring a leak. A timer can be attached at the tap to set water to run for a specific time and then shut off. This is handy if you want to water in the morning but must leave for work before the watering can be completed.

Soil cracks will open in areas of packed soil during periods of drought. This allows water to penetrate a hard crust. You can't fill the cracks with water and it is useless and a waste of water to try. Water will soak into loose soil best. Create a loose soil to begin with, enriching it with lots of organic material. Mulch it lightly. When the surface of your beds hardens, cultivate lightly with a hoe before watering. This will keep the water from simply rolling off.

Although it is difficult to water too much in our usually hot and dry summers, it can be done by the determined greenhorn. To avoid this, pay attention to the specific wants of your plants. Irises want it hot and dry, as do most herbs. Prepare your soil in the first place so that it is loose and free draining. Don't water in any week when an inch or more of rain has fallen unless temperatures are above 90 degrees. Don't water every time a plant droops. Remember that it takes only an inch of water to penetrate five inches of soil.

The smaller the plant, the more often it will need water. Established trees seldom require irrigation, although a sustained summer drought will require a fall soaking to take trees into winter. Shrubs need weekly watering in their first one or two growing seasons. After that only extended dry spells will necessitate watering.

After a long rainy period, flowering plants wilt and droop almost at once when weather turns dry. It's a temptation to water them even though the ground is saturated. This may be necessary if wilting is severe, but a light sprinkling will usually suffice. Normally, though, plants snap back when the cool of evening arrives. My very unscientific idea is that more than adequate rain makes plants lazy. They haven't put their roots down deep enough to find moisture when incessant rain finally stops. After a few days without rain, plants shift gears, plunge their roots down deeper, and adjust.

The same sort of thing happens if you water excessively, particularly in the spring when you first put plants in the ground. The first week after planting you should probably water annuals and small perennials daily. After a week or two this frequent watering isn't needed and in fact seems to discourage the deep root production plants need to see them through the heat of summer.

Container plants require daily watering in hot weather. Extreme heat—above 95 degrees—may necessitate watering twice a day. Double watering may be needed even at lower temperatures on windy days. This frequent watering leaches nutrients out of the soil, however, so give container plants a liquid fertilizer according to package instructions. Pot plants need bottom drainage to carry off excess water. If for some reason you want the container to sit in a saucer, you'll need to empty the saucer immediately after each watering or rain because a plant left sitting in water will soon expire.

Mulching

You can seriously improve your garden's ability to retain moisture by applying a mulch in the spring after planting. This should be done about midspring after all bulbs and perennials have shown themselves above the soil's surface and annuals have been planted. There are a number of materials you can use for mulch, many of them on sale at garden shops. Bark, cocoa hulls, and straw are examples. You're better off, in my opinion, to use a couple of mulches that are available free on your own property.

Compost can be used as mulch if it is well rotted and fine textured, applied thinly (about one inch), and hoed in lightly. If not thoroughly rotted, though, compost can actually impede water penetration. An alternative is to mulch with grass clippings. Getting rid of them is probably a headache anyway. Why not put them to work? Apply an inch or two of grass clippings around all your plants, being careful not to put them against plant stems, as the heat of decomposing grass can burn the stalks.

A fresh mulch of green grass clippings looks a little strange at first, but within a few days it turns brown and fades into the background. Rain soaks through it easily. It gradually rots down and adds humus to the soil, and as it gets too thin you can just replace it with new clippings.

When a plant is a bit faint of heart, a winter mulch can help pull it through the cold part of the year. If your yard has mature deciduous trees, you'll find that nature provides the mulch for you. The leaves that drop in autumn will blow freely across your smooth lawn to catch on the stalks of plants in your flower beds. Come spring, about eight weeks before the last frost, you can rake the leaves off. Don't strip the beds bare in one afternoon, but peel back a layer at a time in two or three raking sessions over a week or more. You'll avoid shocking the tender shoots making their way out of the ground, and it's easier on your back, too. But be careful: if you wait too long to accomplish this spring cleanup, the weight of the leaves may flatten emerging bulb foliage.

Pinching and Deadheading

Pinching in early spring encourages a plant to branch, creating a fuller form and additional bloom. In some cases it reduces flopping of typically large and untidy plants. Asters and chrysanthemums become bushier and more upright with this treatment, as do zinnias. You can pinch any plant that has a branching habit. To pinch, simply wait until the plant has at least three sets of true leaves. Then pinch or snip off the terminal leaves and the stem end to just above the next set of leaves down. The plant will branch at this point. You can pinch again after the branches have two or three sets of leaves.

For full and tidy growth, some plants respond well to shearing. Use shears or a big pair of scissors to take off no more than about one-third the height of the plant. Plants that form basal clumps (all of their leaves springing individually from one center with no branching) are not suitable for either pinching or shearing. Examples of this type of plant are hostas and *Pulmonaria* (lungwort). *Iberis sempervirens* (candytuft) tends to suffer some winterkill and can be shorn back to green wood. It will then put on a spring growth that soon makes a nice bushy plant. Following bloom, shear it again to encourage fresh foliage. Some plants, like *Nepeta* (catmint), are such prolific bloomers that removing spent flowers individually isn't practical. For these, shearing when bloom wanes is appropriate and may spur a second wave of flowering. *Coreopsis verticillata* 'Moonbeam' (threadleaf tickseed) is often suggested for shearing, but you may find that it does just as well without. In my garden it takes a vacation in late summer, but then blooms again without a haircut.

You must deadhead (remove spent flowers to prevent seed production) routinely. Just a few minutes of deadheading tidies up individual plants and creates a striking improvement in the attractiveness of your flower beds. Deadheading also prevents seed formation, which forces the plant to bloom again in an attempt to produce more seeds. In some plants increased blooming is especially dramatic. Pansies and rose campion are nonstop bloomers if you make the effort to cut off old bloom regularly. In other plants, a first wave of bloom will be followed by a second and smaller, but still handsome bloom, if you remember to cut back the first bloom. Yarrow, foxgloves, and *Gypsophila paniculata* (baby's breath) will all produce that second ripple if deadheaded promptly.

Walk around your garden regularly to remove old bloom, making sure to take the swelling base of the blossom, where seed will form. Collect spent blooms in a grocery bag or basket for the compost bin. If you fall behind on deadheading and seed heads have formed, don't put them on the compost or you may have to contend with thousands of seedlings in the garden next spring. (If compost becomes hot enough in the rotting process, seed will be killed, but don't rely on this happening.) Some plants are easily deadheaded by simply pinching or snapping off the bloom head, but with others you'll need scissors or pruning shears.

Deadheading is best accomplished daily on very prolific bloomers. If you have a large garden, deadheading is a big chore, but doing it daily makes it easier to keep up with it. It can become especially tedious when dealing with really prolific bloomers like petunias, flowering tobacco, or rose campion, but the effort is well worth it, in terms of both additional bloom and the greatly improved appearance of your garden and each plant in it. Deadhead tulips and daffodils promptly so that they put their energy into the bulb that will produce next year's bloom. Leaving the seed heads to develop can rob the bulb of a third of its vigor.

With a few plants, seed formation is desirable to foster reproduction and naturalization. (Naturalization is nothing but the natural formation of a colony through the scattering of a plant's own seed.) *Galanthus nivalis* (common snowdrop), for instance, will gradually spread if left to form seed, as will *Scilla siberica* (Siberian squill), *Chionodoxa luciliae,* syn. *C. gigantea* (glory of the snow), and some *Lilium* (lily). I am very fond of Johnny-jump-ups and allow them to go to seed with abandon. They are such champion bloomers that they don't seem to suffer from the lack of deadheading, and each spring I have a fresh new crop. *Mertensia pulmonarioides,* syn. *M. virginica* (Virginia bluebells) is a lovely thing in the spring garden before it politely steps out of the way by going dormant. I allow it to go to seed because I want to encourage its spread. Likewise,

I never deadhead *Geum triflorum* (prairie smoke), as I want to see the charming little whorls of fuzz its seed heads make. With some short-lived perennials, I may deadhead most of the bloom to keep the plant neat and floriferous, but I allow some seed to form and self-sow to replace the plants that will inevitably die out. Columbines and *Corydalis lutea*, syn. *Pseudofumaria lutea* fall into this category. Some roses form absolutely gorgeous seed heads called hips in late summer. If you want these to develop, stop deadheading midsummer. Try it once to see which roses in your garden make attractive hips. You may find that a lovely pink rose makes a brash orange hip that in no way fits your color scheme. On the other hand, your favorite rose may produce burnished red hips the size of crabapples. You just don't know till you try.

Edging

Maintaining a neat appearance goes a long way toward making a beautiful impression with your flower bed. Edging material will prevent massive invasion by grass, which can be the worst possible weed in a perennial border. No matter what edging material you choose to place as a barrier between flower garden and lawn, some grass will eventually invade. If you edge with stone or brick merely laid in place, once a year you need to lift the edging bit by bit and beat back the intruding lawn. The best time to do this (or to install edging in the first place) is very early in the season when there is little else you can do. I'm talking about that frustrating period about six to ten weeks before the frost-free date when spring signs like crocuses in flower, greening grass, and birds pairing off make a gardener yearn to get going. It's too early to plant perennials or prune, but you can get your annual edging done. It's a good time for it, because later in the season plants at the front of the bed will billow over the edging, making your job more difficult.

Start at one end of the bed and lift a couple of feet of edging. Then take a sharp shovel and jam it into the ground at the outer rim. This will cut off the encroaching grass. Lift to loosen the roots and spreading shoots. Remove them, crumbling excess dirt back into the ground. Then even up the surface and replace the edging material. Repeat along the entire length of edging.

You may have something more permanent in the way of edging, such as stone or brick set in concrete. This forms a more lasting barrier, but as cracks develop, the grass will still manage to creep in. In early spring, push a shovel into the earth at the outer rim of the edging to cut off any roots and shoots trying to get in. Later in the season, when the weather has warmed up, you can use Roundup to kill any bits that have made their way through to the garden side.

Staking

If you don't want your garden to look like a carpet under your feet, you have to throw a few tall plants into the design mix. This creates a problem since very few really stately perennials are going to stand up on their own to the wind that is commonplace in our area, especially when it's combined with heat. You will need to stake. Those pictures you see in gardening books of masses of unstaked foxgloves towering over the mixed border were probably taken in England. They were most certainly not taken in the hot and windy farm belt.

There are a number of ways to accomplish proper staking. The easiest approach is to buy appropriate plant stakes. For plants with a few big bloom stalks, like tall bearded irises, a simple metal rod with an unclosed loop on one end is just the ticket. For tall, bushy plants, grow-through supports that look like a grid mounted on three or four metal rods are handy. You put the support in place over the young plant and simply allow the plant to grow up and through the grid. As foliage develops the grid becomes hidden. This is a very useful kind of support, but also a very expensive one. Less costly is a simple arrangement of two fixed hoops on metal rods. Designed for peonies, these might also be used for asters and other small to midsize bushy plants.

Bamboo stakes can be purchased relatively cheaply in various lengths and used in a number of ways. A tall bamboo stake can be plunged into the ground near each bloom stalk of a regal plant like a delphinium or tall lily. You can then use string to attach the stake to the stalk at three or four points. Arrange the string in a figure 8, with one loop of the 8 around the plant. To close the other loop of the 8 you'll secure the loose ends of the string around the stake with a square knot. Keeping the string loose prevents strangling the plant stalk. This is tricky work. You can make it much easier by using a tip my stepfather, a retired doctor, taught me. As you wrap one end of the string around the other to form the first half of your knot, wrap it around one extra time. Then pull it into place. That extra wrap prevents the first half of the knot from slipping while you form the second half. Apparently surgeons use this method when tying sutures.

I recommend a square knot because it won't slide and come loose in a stiff wind. If you are pathologically incapable of tying a square knot, I offer this advice: right over and under left, then left over and under right. Lead with your right hand as you tie the first half of the knot, going over first, then under. Then lead with your left hand as you tie the second half, again going over, then under. You'll come out with a perfect square knot every time. Confused? Pretend you're tying your shoelaces—the motions are the same.

Bamboo stakes can also be used to form a stout girdling cage for midsize bushy plants. When the foliage is six or eight inches high in the spring, surround the plant closely with half a dozen two-foot bamboo stakes (a sharp pair of pruning shears will make the cutting easy). Jam them well into the ground, leaving about eighteen inches above ground (or enough to equal about half of the plant's mature height). Wrap string around the stakes starting about four inches above the ground and repeating every four or five inches.

Wind the string around two or three times to make it good and stout. As the stems grow taller, make sure they stay inside the cage. The plant will soon fill in and hide the cage. This system works very well for baby's breath and asters and might also be used for peonies if you don't want to invest in a commercially sold peony ring.

Pea staking can support small to medium-size plants prone to flopping. Pea stakes are twiggy branches that you gather in spring from prunings or from dead wood that has fallen from trees or shrubs. They need to be stiff but not so brittle that moderate pressure makes them shatter. Just jam the stem ends into the ground all around the base of a plant and let it grow up through the pea stakes. Climbing plants that will be trained onto a trellis sometimes have a tough time getting started. Pea staking can provide them with an easy boost up onto the trellis.

The key to proper staking is to start early before the plant actually begins to topple. Provide staking sturdy enough to handle the plant at mature size when it is being whipped by wind. Use care not to push stakes and rods into underground roots and bulbs, especially when you're staking lilies.

Pruning

Pruning woody plants is another routine task that helps to keep your garden looking its best, but this one needs to be done only annually at most. You should prune to encourage the plant to have a shape you find attractive or to keep bloom from occurring above your head where you can't enjoy it. Pruning is complicated because different plants have different growth patterns, but a good book on the subject can offer guidance when you decide it's time to prune. Basically, you want to cut just above a leaf bud or the point where a twig meets a main stem of the branch, because this is where a shoot of new growth will develop.

Pruning to make a bush the shape you want is one thing. Pruning to keep a bush smaller than its natural size is quite another. Constant pruning to reduce the size may ultimately reduce the vigor of the shrub and will give it a butchered look. It's better to allow shrubs the vertical and horizontal space they'll need for their full mature growth.

Standard size lilacs, however, respond well to frequent pruning. Without pruning, they will soon be blooming far above your head. To keep them at eye (and nose) level, you'll need to cut them back every three to five years soon after they bloom. If you wait too long or cut them back in spring before bloom, you'll eliminate the flowering for one season. Lilacs put on a good foot or more of growth the first season after pruning, so cut them well back. I like to trim mine down to about four feet high. Simply use pruning shears to cut all branches off at one level. Then use a saw to cut off any stout, tough old stems at the ground. The bush will soon put on fresh growth and look lush again. An old lilac that is very overgrown can be cut back completely to just above the ground. It will regenerate quickly to produce more bloom on a better-looking bush. Lilacs like sun, though, so if an old overgrown lilac is in a shady position due to maturing of nearby trees, it may not do well after a severe pruning.

Forsythia, too, should be pruned back immediately following bloom. Do this when the shrub is getting too large or when bloom diminishes. The wrong way to prune a forsythia is to hack it all back to one uniform height. This is no way to treat an elegant lady. Take the time to prune branches individually to varying lengths to maintain a graceful appearance. The shrub will spring back quickly, so prune a good foot or two below where you want it to be after it begins to grow again.

Roses should be pruned in spring about four to six weeks before the frost-free date. If you do the job earlier, late winter cold is almost sure to kill the plant back further and you'll find yourself repeating the task. Moderate temperatures and blooming crocuses make it very difficult to exercise self-control in this matter. I can assure you from personal experience of succumbing to the temptation to prune on the first warm February or March day that you will do better to wait. When the time is right, prune off all dead wood. If you're not sure what is dead, snip off a little at a time until you can see the green inside the cane, which indicates you have reached live wood. Once the dead wood is off, shape the bush as you want it. In general, cut just above a shoot that is headed in the direction you want the branch to go. Once the plant is in bloom, prune as you deadhead or cut flowers for bouquets by cutting back to just above any leaf that has five leaflets. This is a simplified treatment of a subject that takes up whole chapters in rose books.

When pruning *Hydrangea* and clematis, look to see whether they flower on last year's growth that survived winter or on growth made during the current year. Shrubs that flower on the previous season's growth must be pruned *after* they flower (unless you're willing to sacrifice a year's bloom). If the plant flowers on the current year's growth, you can prune it in spring, along with the roses, about four to six weeks before the frost-free date.

Some shrubs will live through winter to grow larger and larger in milder climates, but in our area they will die back. *Buddleia davidii* (butterfly bush) and *Callicarpa* (beautyberry) are two examples for zone 5. Both grow rapidly enough to make a small shrub each year, so cut them back near ground level in spring.

Many shrubs require only moderate occasional pruning to keep them in the shape you desire. *Viburnum*, for instance, is a handsome family of shrubs whose members grow naturally into nicely shaped bushes, suffering from little or no winter dieback. Given adequate space, these will require very little pruning.

Pest and Disease Control

All of us have in our heads visions of garden perfection toward which we strive. We want our own gardens to match the vision. It's easy to get the idea that any problem in the garden can be dealt with given enough time, energy, spray, dust, fertilizer, fungicide, and money. What's really needed is a liberal dose of realism. Even the most carefully tended garden will have its share of fungus, insect pests, sudden deaths of seemingly healthy plants, disappointing bloom, drought-damaged foliage, rabbits, squirrels, hail and wind damage. A great deal is beyond your control, and many of the controls available to you are dangerous to the natural world you love so much. It's good to remember that perfection is what you aim for, not what you expect to achieve.

Do your best to site plants well and provide them the care that will promote their good health. When garden plans don't pan out, remind yourself that this is nature you're dealing with. It's big, it's unpredictable, it's about death as well as life, and it's beyond your control. In spite of your best efforts, zinnias will mildew late in the season, columbines will be stricken with leaf miners, roses will suffer disease, hostas will be savaged by slugs. Your garden picture— after the first blush of spring—will always include at least one unsightly problem or another. Provide the best care you can, but recognize that sometimes when a problem arises, your best course is to ignore it.

When it comes to pest control, the question is, To spray or not to spray? I am not a proponent of organic gardening, but I do believe that a healthy, luxuriant garden can be achieved with mostly natural methods and scant use of commercial fertilizers, sprays, or fungicides. This view of things began to be shaped one year when I decided I would get ahead of the game, pest-wise. I would spray for insects on a regular basis and would not have to cope with leaf miners or tarnished plant bugs. I was consistent about preventive sprayings but the garden was more plagued by insects than it had ever been. I think I quite simply upset the balance of nature in my little garden ecosystem. Still, if you're not going to spray, how will you handle pest control? Here are a few suggestions.

Slugs and Snails

Slugs and snails are damaging pests that are difficult to dispatch. They are mollusks, not insects, belonging to the same family as the clams you like to stir into chowder. In fact, I once saw a magazine article on trapping snails that included a recipe for cooking them with garlic and butter. Disgusting as it sounds, the best way to get rid of snails is to handpick them and crush them. You can use your thumbnail on small ones and step on the larger specimens. You can't be squeamish and be a gardener.

Larger and far more common are slugs. These slimy, oozing pests amount to snails without the cute little shells. Tiny young slugs are hardly visible. Older slugs, thoroughly fattened on your precious hostas and stretched out as they ooze their way toward another succulent morsel, are as long as four inches.

Snails and slugs feed in the cool of the night, so they are most commonly seen in the garden in the early morning or at twilight. They eat by scraping against plant leaves with their rasplike mouths. During the day, when they are not busy defiling your garden, they hide out in cool, moist, dark cracks and crevices. I often find them huddled up against the cool stone edging of my borders. They prefer shade, cool weather, and moist conditions.

The relatively small number of snails in Midwestern gardens makes them a minor concern, but slugs can become a serious threat. They are dreadful pests on hostas and will also attack a wide range of other plants, including daylilies and pansies.

A frequently recommended slug control method is what I call the slug beer bust. You sink shallow bowls or tuna cans into the garden until their lips are roughly level with the soil surface. The bowls are then filled with beer. The slugs find the scent so bewitching that they slide into the beer for a drink and drown. I do not recommend this means of control. In the first place, it is quite revolting when the beer and slug corpses ferment into a foamy, syrupy, foul-smelling hell-broth that you must dispose of somehow. When I was hosting these beer parties, I buried the old beer and dead slug mix before refilling the containers. The whole process was nasty, nasty, nasty. Still, I kept doing it because there seemed to be an upswing in the slug population and the little sots were becoming a serious problem.

The scent of beer will entice slugs from a very wide area, however, and actually attracts far more slugs to your garden than it kills. This would explain why, in spite of my best efforts with the beer traps, my slug population was thriving. No doubt my neighbors were congratulating themselves on the sudden reduction in the number of slugs in their yards. Every slug in the vicinity had pulled up stakes and headed for my beer garden.

Another commonly suggested method for controlling slugs is a slug bait called Slug-Geta manufactured by Ortho. Available at garden centers, it is moderately successful in limiting the number of slugs in your garden but does not get rid of them completely. It has to be more or less fresh, so every time you get a good rain you have to put out more of it. The chief drawback, though, is that the bait looks enough like dog food to be dangerously attractive to wandering canines. Birds may also be at risk, but cats seem uninterested in the pellets. Slug-Geta is poisonous to humans, too, so using it in a garden visited by small children would be unwise. I use slug bait only very occasionally when slugs get out of hand and begin to cause widespread damage.

My preferred method of controlling slugs is simply to kill them by hand. My husband calls this the two-brick method. When I spot a slug, I pick it up with a stick or a stiff leaf and transfer it to a hard surface, where I either step on it or squash it with a brick. This is a very effective treatment. If I happen to be trimming or deadheading when I spot a slug, I use my pruning shears to cut the slug in half or at least nick its surface. Slugs do not recover from this strategy. Another method of dispatching slugs is to coat the inside of a plastic milk carton with oil. Handpick the slugs from your garden and drop them into the milk bottle. The slippery sides keep them from escaping. When you finish, screw on the cap and throw the bottle in the trash.

Anytime I have reason to turn back a stone in the edging of my garden, I take a look to see if slugs are sheltering there and quickly dispatch any I find. In spring I watch for eggs around hostas and other plants that were attacked by slugs the previous year. The eggs are small, round, and transparent like tiny bubbles and can be easily destroyed by smashing them. These hand methods with occasional use of slug bait (perhaps once a year) seem to keep the slug population within reason.

Aphids

Aphids are common garden pests that you are likely to come up against every year. They cluster on stems and suck the juices from young tender tips. There are many kinds in several colors: green, red, pink, black, gray, and so on. These soft-bodied and usually wingless creatures secrete a sticky substance called honeydew, which attracts ants. You may notice a shiny spattering of this dried honeydew on leaves or find ants around stem ends. You may see wilting on young growth at tips. These are signs that you should examine the plant for aphids.

Aphids are common pests on roses, but they attack a wide range of other plants, too. In my garden they routinely prey on a dwarf crabapple and *Echinops ritro* (small globe thistle). They also occasionally go after the ivy among my container plants.

The simplest way to rid plants of aphids is to first shoot off what you can with a strong squirt of water from the hose (but not on roses, which do not appreciate wet leaves in a humid climate). Then simply squash any remaining aphids by pinching them against the plant stem or between thumb and forefinger. Rinse the plant (and your hands!) with the hose and keep a close eye on it over the next several days, watching for any return. If aphids continue to be a problem, you can use Raid House and Garden spray for further control. Because aphids attack new growth, you need only the small amount of spray it takes to treat the tips. I prefer not to spray if I can help it because spraying risks killing aphid predators like ladybugs.

Other Insect Pests

Many other pests will occasionally visit your garden. They may be a serious threat in one year and hardly noticeable the next. Weather and climate conditions—an especially hard winter or an exceptionally rainy spring—may affect their ability to reproduce and result in a bumper crop one year and a complete absence the next. When you do discover insect pests on your plants, first determine that they are indeed pests and not beneficial or harmless insects. Then start with the easiest, cheapest, and most environmentally sound method of pest control. Simply remove them by hand and squash them. If this is not effective, you need to assess whether the pests are seriously damaging your plants or the appearance of your garden. Is the damage temporary or life threatening? Try to put up with a certain amount of damage, but if havoc is being wrought you may have to take steps.

Before you use any insecticide, determine exactly what kind of insect you are dealing with. If you are unable to identify it by consulting reference books, seek expert advice. The best way to do this is to capture an insect and take it, along with a cutting from the plant that shows the damage it is suffering, to your local nursery. This, of course, assumes that a trained staff is on hand. If this is not the case, consult your cooperative extension service or county extension office. Having identified the specific culprit, use a spray that will kill it. Not all sprays kill all insects, but labels clearly identify which insects a spray is designed to control. Be sure to read the entire label to see what harmless or useful insects will also be killed by the spray. If the insecticide you plan to use will kill off every bee in your yard, you may want to think twice.

Squirrels and Rabbits

Squirrels and rabbits can do enormous amounts of damage. Young trees and shrubs will die if enough of their bark is chewed off, so the immature trunks will need to be wrapped or protected in cages of chicken wire or hardware cloth. A gardening friend of mine tells me that squirrels and rabbits chew young bark to get moisture and will be less destructive if water is set out on the ground for them, but I've had mixed results after following her advice.

Rabbits will chew off the new leaves and buds of crocuses. They also like the tender young shoots of just about anything green, including new growth on shrubs. A simple prevention is to place pine boughs around plants they seem to be targeting. Rabbits apparently don't appreciate having their noses prickled while they snack. If you don't have pines in your yard, recycle a Christmas tree for the purpose. Slivers of soap stuck part way into the ground around a plant victim can help deter rabbits, too, as can a scattering of yew clippings.

Squirrels are especially partial to the buds of clematis. A choice *Clematis* 'Nelly Moser,' planted against a fence, provided a gourmet buffet of some sixty succulent buds one spring, leaving me with a paltry three or four blooms. A mix of hot pepper sauce and water sprayed onto the vine may make the buds distasteful to the squirrels. Both squirrels and rabbits will break off plant stems, sometimes apparently just from curiosity. There is little you can do to prevent this damage, but as plants mature they become sturdier and less vulnerable.

Fungus

Various symptoms caused by fungus may appear on your plants, chiefly leaf spot, powdery mildew, and rust. Leaf spots are relatively easy to identify because, as the name suggests, they make clearly defined spots. If the spotting is widespread it is called leaf blight. Leaf spot is especially common among roses and irises. You encourage fungus when you crowd plantings, water plants from above, plant sun lovers in shady places, or allow diseased foliage to remain in the garden through winter.

Rust is a fungal disease characterized by leaves spotty on their surface and covered on the underside with spore pustules. The spores are likely to be rust colored (hence the name), but may also be brown, black, white, yellow, or orange. Good garden cleanup in the fall to remove affected foliage will help retard the spread of rust. As with leaf spot, overhead watering should be avoided. Rust may exist without seriously damaging its host, so before spraying decide whether the disease is truly harming the plant. A wide variety of perennials may be attacked by this disease, including *Anemone,* columbines, *Campanula* (bellflower), clematis, delphiniums, and *Monarda* (bee balm or bergamot).

Powdery mildew, a common problem, attacks both *Phlox paniculata* (garden phlox) and *Phlox divaricata* (woodland phlox or wild sweet William), as well as zinnias, *Monarda,* asters, and many other flowering plants. Splotches of a grayish, finely textured substance indicate the presence of powdery mildew. The disease first appears in the summer months when soaring heat and humidity encourage its growth. As with other fungal disease, prevention methods include removal of diseased plant materials in fall, watering from below, and avoidance of overcrowded plantings. Ironically, fungus—which you might expect to find in damp places—actually thrives when plants are too dry, so for prevention, be sure to keep plants adequately moist.

Fungal diseases can be so persistent and damaging that they may require spraying. Attempt to identify the specific problem and seek expert advice if you can't. Choose an appropriate spray and read the label carefully before you buy it.

7

Troubleshooting

"I don't have a green thumb" is the biggest cop-out in horticulture.
There is no such thing as a green thumb—some sort of God-given
gardening gift. As with any talent, good gardening begins with a
personal predilection and develops with study and practice. To be
a good gardener, just read, ask questions, and get your hands dirty.

If you are unhappy with the garden you have made, the trouble
probably started with one or more of these problems:

1. You haven't properly prepared your soil. You are turning the soil
   but not amending it or, worse yet, you are just digging a hole in
   your turf, shoving in a plant, and expecting it to flourish. Chapter 3 is your soil preparation Bible. Read it, do it, and marvel at
   the results.

2. You've chosen plants that are not winter hardy for your zone. This
   is a simple question of not doing your homework before buying
   plants, especially those acquired by mail order. Most of what you
   buy locally is suitable for your zone, although nurseries do sell a

few plants that are one zone off for enthusiasts willing to make the extra effort in winter protection and take the risk of loss.

3. You're trying to raise plants that are winter hardy where you live but can't stand the heat of a Midwestern summer. Consult chapter 5 for help.

4. You've failed to meet the light and soil requirements of the plants you are attempting to grow: you've planted shade lovers in sun, plants that require good drainage in unprepared clay soil, sun lovers against a north wall.

5. You are putting plants in the ground too early or too late.

6. You plant too closely, ignoring the plant's mature size. It's a great temptation in spring, when emerging plants are small, to tuck in just one more plant. The result is overcrowding, poor bloom, and disease.

7. You are watering too much or too little—much more likely too little in our hot climate. Lack of water will reduce bloom, dwarf plants, disfigure foliage, encourage fungus, and can, in times of drought, kill plants. Too much water, if you somehow manage to overwater, can drown plants and wash away nutrients.

8. You've ignored routine care, such as deadheading, pruning, and weeding. Neglect in these matters will produce an untidy and unappealing garden.

9. You've set impossibly high standards for your garden. The garden isn't a failure, but your perception of it is.

Like life, a garden is not perfection, but a striving toward it. Even the glorious gardens in books aren't the perfection they appear. One of the big lies of garden literature is that a perennial garden can be created without gap or flaw. The truth is that the right camera angle can hide the problems that occur in even the best plantings. The loveliest garden is transient, and the gardens pictured in books are not as lovely as they appear even at the instant the camera clicks. However, take heart. Your garden will make progress toward perfection as you read, try new plants, discard the inferior, redesign beds, divide and increase favorites, and so on. Every mistake you make teaches you something about the art of gardening.

Flat on My Face

For your inspiration and edification I offer the sad story of one of my own failures. Although this was one of my earliest efforts in the garden, the failure lingered accusingly at the top of my gently sloping backyard for several years until finally a disastrous storm damaged trees so seriously that I was forced to relandscape the whole area.

The problem began as an inherited failure—an ill-conceived flower border that was in place when I moved into my house twenty-one years ago. The bed was about five feet deep and thirty feet long, planted with three lilacs spaced nine feet apart. Between these shrubs were peonies and daylilies. Unfortunately, the entire combination lay squarely in the considerable shade of an oak tree that was more than twenty years old. All of these plants prefer to be sited in full sun and probably were until the oak began to come into its own. In the oak's shade the lilacs bloomed only fitfully and the peonies and daylilies not at all. Poor siting, then, was the first mistake.

To make matters worse, the previous gardener (I had nothing to do with this) had planted three different kinds of lilacs together—one of them fan-shaped, one upright and bushy, and one upright but bare at its feet and knees with most of the foliage beginning about four feet above ground level. As a result of the shade and their incompatible forms, these three never formed the hedge or screen that was probably intended, making instead sadly unattractive companions.

This is where I came on the scene. I noticed that the bed seemed never to have been dug over and the dirt was hard and unyielding.

Even in these early days of my gardening apprenticeship I recognized that the daylilies would never bloom on a densely shaded site. I decided to remove them, enjoy the peonies for their foliage, dig over the rest of the bed, and plant shade-loving *Hosta* (hosta or plantain lily). The result was a miserable flop. My ideas were all right, but they didn't go far enough.

First, I thought preparing a bed meant simply digging it over to loosen the soil. I didn't add compost. I didn't work in bonemeal or gypsum. In short, I did nothing to keep the soil from turning back into a hard moisture-repellent medium after a few hard rains. I then compounded my error by planting hostas—plants that demand a rich, loose, moist soil. Because the bed was on a slight incline, there was even less chance that rain would soak in to root depth. The hostas never reached anything like the full size and vigor that the same variety achieved elsewhere in properly prepared soil.

I also erred in thinking I could remove the daylilies by simply digging out each clump. Daylilies are survivors. It is no accident that they can be found thriving around uninhabited old farmhouses. I should have dug and removed the plants, then carefully dug and sorted the soil to remove the broken bits of their tuberous roots. Then I should have watched the area for emerging leaves and continued to dig up the roots. At some point a couple of applications of Roundup could have been used to finish off the stragglers.

In replanting the bed, I used plants with dark green foliage that simply disappeared into the gloom. Even the *Aquilegia* (columbine) I planted had dark blue blossoms that scarcely showed in the relatively deep shade. I also put in a few shade-loving bulbs, but I chose unwisely, planting *Galanthus nivalis* (common snowdrop) and *Scilla siberica* (Siberian squill). The tiny flowers are invisible from the house when they bloom in the chill of early spring.

My final error was in planting several other shade lovers willy-nilly without establishing big patches and clear areas of leaf contrast. No sense of unity emerged. To make matters worse, the columbine plants spread rapidly from seed, creating a jumble of foliage around the scrappy hostas. The overall impression was dull, formless, and unattractive.

Sometimes It's Not Your Fault

Not all garden failures are the gardener's fault. You may be frantically studying to determine why a plant failed in your garden. Why is it unwell? What did you do to it? What should you have done? The truth is that even when you do all the right things, plants won't always flourish. After a promising start and maybe even years of glorious bloom, a *Gypsophila paniculata* (baby's breath) may begin to dwindle. A few sad weeks later, in spite of all your careful ministrations, it is dead at your feet. *Gypsophila paniculata* is subject to crown rot. Plant two in the same garden and one may live five or six years while the other turns up its toes before its second season ends. Quit feeling guilty and go out and replace the ungrateful wretch.

To say that perennials live for many years is a generalization. Quite a few, generally called short-lived perennials, last only a few years. *Corydalis lutea,* syn. *Pseudofumaria lutea* and some varieties of *Aquilegia* (columbine) may live only two or three years. Fortunately, these are self-seeding and quick to reach mature size and begin blooming, so you may not realize that last year's plants are gone. Some short-lived perennials, though, are not self-sowers and are likely to leave unpleasant gaps when they move on to that great garden in the sky. *Campanula* (bellflower), *Dianthus deltoides* (maiden pinks), and *Aurinia saxatilis,* syn. *Alyssum saxatile* (basket of gold) will disappear from your garden, leaving no progeny behind to carry on their line. Perennials that may last from year to year in other locales seem to lose strength in the blazing heat of a Midwestern summer. Others are simply short-lived by nature. One way to avoid great gaps in the garden is to steer clear of perennials that won't last long and don't seed themselves freely. If you find you can't live without some of them, at least limit their number and plant them carefully to allow surrounding plants to fill the voids they will surely leave.

Some plants are so prone to certain diseases that prevention attempts are spit in the wind. If you grow *Monarda* (bee balm or bergamot) you will have powdery mildew at least some seasons and probably every season. You can try the newer, mildew-resistant cultivars to minimize the problem, but even they are likely to have mildew some of the time. Plant columbines and you can count on seeing leaf miners year after year. This is not your personal failure. This is the nature of the beast.

A number of perennials lavishly praised in garden books and catalogs may be suitable for other climates, but are difficult to grow in the heat of the Midwest: *Leucanthemum* x *superbum,* syn. *Chrysanthemum maximum* of gardens (Shasta daisy), *Gaillardia* 'Burgunder,' syn. 'Burgundy' (blanket flower), *Digitalis* (foxglove), delphiniums, many cultivars of *Heuchera* (coral flower or coral bells), *Veronica* (speedwell; the creeping sort, however, seem to thrive), and most *Primula* (primrose). These enchanting plants are disappointing in a hot climate, where they will sprawl, become diseased, bloom poorly, and live only two or three years at most. Even if they survive longer, they won't have the size, vigor, and healthful beauty they can attain elsewhere. Other plants will be disasters in the clay soil with which many of us are saddled. *Lavandula* (lavender) is highly touted in book after book without much said about the kind of soil it requires. Believe me, it is a disappointment when you plant it on even carefully amended clay soil.

8

Sequence of Bloom and Calendar of Garden Work

One of the most difficult parts of designing a garden is planning attractive groupings of plants that will bloom simultaneously. Plants are generally described vaguely as blooming in "early spring" or "midsummer," but even if you knew exactly when that was or how long it lasted the seasons referred to would probably be in some climate other than your own. To help you plan your Midwestern garden, I'm including this bloom sequence list geared to our part of the country. Obviously specific plants will not flower the same week throughout the Midwest, but they are likely to flower in the same *sequence*. Likewise, plants that bloom as companions in one part of the Midwest are likely to do so, too, in another.

Variations in geographical location, altitude, microclimate, rainfall, and seasonal mildness or severity all affect the timing of bloom, so no list can be definitive. A particular plant will not bloom at exactly the same time throughout our region or even in the same neighborhood. Weather varies year to year, affecting the flowers and how they bloom—both timing and length. This is especially true at the beginning and end of the growing season, when weather is most variable. Crocuses may bloom as early as late February or as late as the third week in March. Early heat combined with wind can stop daffodils in their tracks this year, while next year they may seem to go on forever in cool, cloudy weather. Midseason plants are more likely than others to bloom at about the same time year after year.

So that you can create groupings for effect, use this list to get an idea of which plants are likely to bloom in concert. Plan your garden for constant bloom throughout the growing season or plant for two-season bloom by selecting plants that flower at the appropriate times.

The list here can be a useful guide, but ideally you will begin to keep a sequence of bloom record for your own garden. Much has been written about keeping a garden diary and what to include, but it's a very personal matter. You may include sketches, plans, clippings, poetry, sappy descriptions of your favorite darlings, or arch satirical commentary. It doesn't really matter. The single thing that will make the diary useful to you in coming years is a record of when plants bloom and for how long. Once a week make the rounds of your garden, noting what plants are in bloom. This project will help you to learn not only bloom length and order but also plant names and how plants vary their bloom depending on the amount of sun or shade they get. If you don't want to go to the trouble of keeping a garden journal, just jot your own bloom times on the list here.

Sequence of Bloom

As you use the list for garden planning, remember that certain plants, due to their plant size, bloom size, length of bloom, and showiness, can be used as major design elements. Massed or repeated through a bed or garden, they can create unity at a particular season. Not all long-blooming plants fit this category, however. Some possess uninteresting foliage or flowers that are not particularly showy. Others bloom for a long period, but sporadically. Or a particular plant may be too small to make a splash. The boldface listings below indicate impact plants that might be considered chief features over four weeks or more around which you can build a garden design. In some cases (*Hosta*, for example) this long season of interest is provided by foliage rather than bloom. If several cultivars or species of one plant are named, it may take a mix of them to create several weeks of bloom.

Early Spring

Galanthus nivalis (common snowdrop): Late February to late March (three weeks)

Crocus vernus 'Pickwick' (Dutch crocus): Mid- to late March (two weeks)

Narcissus 'Tête-à-tête' (daffodil): Mid- to late March (one and a half weeks)

Chionodoxa luciliae, syn. *C. gigantea* (glory of the snow): Early to mid-April (two weeks)

Scilla siberica (Siberian squill): Early April to early May (five weeks)

Viola x *wittrockiana* (pansy), planted in bloom: Early April to late July (seventeen weeks)

Spring

Tulipa 'Heart's Delight' (tulip): Early to late April (two weeks)

Pulmonaria 'Roy Davidson' (lungwort): Early April to late May (eight weeks)

Mertensia pulmonarioides, syn. *M. virginica* (Virginia bluebells): Mid- to late April (two weeks)

Narcissus 'February Gold' (daffodil): Mid- to late April (one and a half weeks)

Narcissus **'Thalia' (daffodil):** Mid-April to early May (four weeks)

Muscari (grape hyacinth): Mid-April to late May (five weeks)

Geum triflorum (prairie smoke): Mid-April to early June (seven weeks)

Viola tricolor (Johnny-jump-up): Mid-April to late August (nineteen weeks)

***Pulmonaria saccharata* 'Mrs. Moon' (lungwort):** Late April to late May (four weeks)

Tulipa clusiana 'Cynthia' (tulip): Early May (two weeks)

Epimedium (barrenwort): Early to mid-May (one and a half weeks)

***Tulipa* 'Ballade' (lily-flowered tulip):** Early to mid-May (three weeks)

***Tulipa* 'Mariette' (lily-flowered tulip):** Early to mid-May (three weeks)

***Tulipa* 'West Point' (lily-flowered tulip):** Early to mid-May (three weeks)

Iberis sempervirens (candytuft): Early to late May (three weeks)

***Aquilegia canadensis* 'Corbett' (Canada columbine):** Early May to early June (seven weeks)

Brunnera macrophylla, syn. *Anchusa myosotidiflora* (Siberian bugloss): Early May to early June (four weeks)

***Dicentra spectabilis* (bleeding heart):** Early May to early June (five weeks)

Corydalis lutea, syn. *Pseudofumaria lutea*: Early May to mid-June (six weeks)

Phlox divaricata (woodland phlox or wild sweet William): Early May to early June (five weeks)

Veronica 'Waterperry' (speedwell): Early May to early June (five weeks)

***Dicentra spectabilis* f. *alba* (white bleeding heart):** Early May to early September, if deadheaded (seventeen weeks)

Convallaria (lily-of-the-valley): Mid- to late May (two weeks)

Galium odoratum, syn. *Asperula odorata* (sweet woodruff): Mid- to late May (three weeks)

Aquilegia canadensis (Canada columbine): Mid-May to early June (four weeks)

Geranium 'Johnson's Blue': Mid-May to late June (seven weeks)

Tiarella wherryi, syn. *T. cordifolia* var. *collina* (Wherry's foamflower): Mid-May to late June (seven weeks)

Geranium phaeum (mourning widow): Mid-May to mid-July (nine weeks)

Calamintha grandiflora 'Variegata' (calamint): Mid-May to early September (sixteen weeks)

Baptisia australis (blue wild indigo, false indigo, or plains false indigo): Late May to early June (two weeks)

Iris pseudacorous (yellow flag): Late May to early June (two weeks)

Paeonia (peony): Late May to early June (two weeks)

Iris (tall bearded hybrids): Late May to mid-June (three weeks)

Leucanthemum vulgare, syn. *Chrysanthemum leucanthemum* (ox-eye daisy): Late May to late June (seven weeks)

Heuchera x brizoides 'Chatterbox' (coral flower or coral bells): Late May to mid-July (seven weeks)

Early Summer

Nepeta x faassenii, syn. N. mussinii of gardens (catmint): Late May to late August (fourteen weeks)

Geranium sanguineum var. *striatum,* syn. *G. sanguineum* var. *lancastriense*: Late May to mid-October (twenty-five weeks)

Iris 'Ego' (Siberian iris): Early June (1 week)

Rosa glauca, syn. R. rubrifolia (rose): Flowers, early to mid-June (1 week); hips, July through September (12 weeks)

Digitalis purpurea 'Excelsior' (common foxglove): Early to late June (three weeks)

Iris **'Caesar's Brother' (Siberian iris):** Early to late June (three weeks)

Iris **'White Swirl' (Siberian iris):** Early to late June (three weeks)

Rosa **'Mary Rose' (rose):** Heavy first bloom, early to late June (three weeks); light second bloom, mid-July to late October (thirteen weeks)

Alchemilla mollis **(lady's mantle):** Early June to mid-July (five weeks)

Allium schoenoprasum (chives): Early June to mid-July (six weeks)

Clematis lanuginosa 'Candida': Early June to mid-July (four weeks)

Salvia officinalis (common sage): Early June to mid-July (six weeks)

Lychnis coronaria **(rose campion):** Early June to mid-August (ten weeks)

Achillea **'Moonshine' (yarrow):** Early June to early September (twelve weeks)

Digitalis x *mertonensis:* Early June to early September (twelve weeks)

Rosa **'Bonica' (rose):** Early June to late October (nineteen weeks)

Delphinium: Mid-June to mid-July (five weeks)

Midsummer

Clematis 'Nelly Moser': June (3 weeks)

Clematis viticella: Mid-June to early July (three weeks)

Astilbe **'Brautschleier,' syn. *A.* 'Bridal Veil' (false spirea):** Late June to mid-July (two weeks)

Gypsophila paniculata 'Bristol Fairy' (baby's breath): First bloom, late June to mid-July (two weeks); second bloom, late July to late August (four weeks)

Consolida (larkspur): Late June to late July (four weeks)

Lilium 'Bonnie' (Asiatic hybrid lily): Late June to mid-July (two weeks)

Hosta sieboldiana var. *elegans* (hosta or plantain lily): Late June to late July (three weeks)

Filipendula purpurea (Japanese meadowsweet): Late June to early August (one and a half weeks)

Lilium regale (regal lily): Late June to early August (one and a half weeks)

Nepeta 'Six Hills Giant' (catmint): Late June to mid-August (seven weeks)

Coreopsis verticillata 'Moonbeam' (threadleaf tickseed): Late June to late September (fourteen weeks)

Rudbeckia fulgida var. *sullivantii* 'Goldsturm': Late June to late September (thirteen weeks)

Zinnia: Late June to late September (thirteen weeks)

Antirrhinum Liberty Series (snapdragon): Late June to frost (fifteen to eighteen weeks)

Nicotiana alata, syn. *N. affinis* (flowering tobacco): Late June to frost (fifteen to eighteen weeks)

Petunia: Late June to frost (fifteen to eighteen weeks)

Tagetes (marigold): Late June to frost (fifteen to eighteen weeks)

Borago officinalis (borage): Early July to late September (twelve weeks)

Lobularia maritima, syn. *Alyssum maritimum* (sweet alyssum): Early July to late October (sixteen weeks)

Astilbe 'Sprite' (false spirea): Mid- to late July (two weeks)

Hemerocallis (daylily) 'Little Grapette': Mid- to late July (two weeks)

Anethum graveolens (dill): Mid-July to early August (three weeks)

Astilbe chinensis **var.** *taquetii* **'Superba' (false spirea):** Mid-July to early August (two weeks)

Hemerocallis (daylily) 'Daydream Believer': Mid-July to early August (3 weeks)

Astilbe chinensis **var.** *pumila* **(false spirea):** Mid-July to mid-August (four weeks)

Digitalis lutea (straw foxglove): Mid-July to mid-August (four weeks)

Hemerocallis (daylily) 'Bowl of Roses': Mid-July to mid-August (four weeks)

Hemerocallis (daylily) 'Little Fat Dazzler': Mid-July to mid-August (3 weeks)

Hemerocallis (daylily) 'Prairie Blue Eyes': Mid-July to mid-August (4 weeks)

Echinops ritro **(small globe thistle):** Mid-July to late August (five weeks)

Phlox paniculata (garden phlox): Mid-July to late August (six weeks)

Platycodon grandiflorus (balloon flower): Mid-July to early September (six weeks)

Thalictrum rochebrunianum: 'Lavender Mist' (meadow rue): Mid-July to late September (ten weeks)

Aster x *frikartii* **'Mönch':** Mid-July to frost (thirteen weeks)

Salvia farinacea 'Victoria' (mealycup sage): Mid-July to frost (thirteen to sixteen weeks)

Tanacetum parthenium, syn. *Chrysanthemum parthenium* (feverfew): Mid-July to frost (thirteen to sixteen weeks)

Lilium 'Casa Blanca' (Oriental hybrid lily): Late July to mid-August (two weeks)

Lilium 'Pink Virtuoso' (Oriental hybrid lily): Late July to mid-August (two weeks)

Late Summer

Perovskia atriplicifolia (**Russian sage**): Early August to late September (eight weeks)

Thymophylla tenuiloba, syn. *Dyssodia tenuiloba* (Dahlberg daisy or golden fleece): Early August to late September (eight weeks)

Buddleia davidii '**Lochinch**' (**butterfly bush**): Early August to late October (twelve weeks)

Calamintha nepeta (**lesser calamint**): Early August to late October (twelve weeks)

Cleome (**spider flower**): Early August to late October (twelve weeks)

Fall

Clematis terniflora, syn. *C. maximowicziana* or *C. paniculata* (sweet autumn clematis): Early to mid-September (one and a half weeks)

Boltonia asteroides: September (four weeks)

Anemone tomentosa '**Robustissima,**' syn. *A. vitifolia* '**Robustissima**' (**grape-leaf anemone**): Early September to frost (six to nine weeks)

Aster novae-angliae '**Andenken an Alma Pötschke,**' syn. '**Alma Pötschke**' (**New England aster**): Early September to late October (seven weeks)

Chrysanthemum: Early September to frost (six to nine weeks)

Origanum (oregano): September (four weeks)

Calendar of Garden Work

The following brief outline doesn't cover every last thing you need to do in your garden. This schedule covers only projects that need to be accomplished at specific times, since most garden work can be done as you have time for it. Check to determine the average spring frost-free date and the average fall first frost date in your area.

Spring Projects

Eight weeks before the frost-free date

- Begin raking leaves off flower beds, finishing in about two weeks.

Six weeks before the frost-free date

- Edge flower beds.
- Prune roses.
- Prune shrubs that bloom on new wood. Shrubs that bloom on old wood, such as forsythia and *Syringa* (lilac), should not be pruned until after they bloom.
- Cut back *Buddleia davidii* (butterfly bush) and *Perovskia atriplicifolia* (Russian sage) to about twelve inches from the ground.
- Cut back herbaceous plants that were not cut back in autumn.
- Begin perennial planting, including transplanting perennials that bloom in summer or fall.

Four weeks before the frost-free date

- Plant *Viola* x *wittrockiana* (pansy).
- Prune clematis vines that bloom on new wood.

Two weeks before the frost-free date:

- ❧ Finish planting and transplanting perennials.

- ❧ Plant *Antirrhinum* (snapdragon) and *Lobularia maritima,* syn. *Alyssum maritimum* (sweet alyssum).

Frost-free date:

- ❧ Plant annuals, finishing within two weeks.

Fall Projects

Six weeks before the first frost:

- ❧ Plant perennials and transplant perennials that bloom in spring or summer.

First frost:

- ❧ Cut down and compost healthy foliage of annuals, biennials, and perennials, excluding those that must be pruned back in spring and those that remain green throughout winter.

- ❧ Cut down and dispose of unhealthy foliage.

9

Building a Garden Library

There are three ways to learn about gardening: get some dirt under your fingernails, ask questions of gardeners and experts, and read. Reading is the fastest way to gain a solid base of knowledge. It's also lots of fun. A good garden reference library can go a long way toward filling the gaps and correcting the gaffs of flower catalogs, too. Here are a few suggestions.

Encyclopedias

Brickell, Christopher, ed. *American Horticultural Society Encyclopedia of Garden Plants.* New York: Macmillan, 1989.

This is simply the finest reference around for the passionate gardener. Arranged by scientific name, it also provides an index by common name. The text section at the back provides descriptions of plants and their varieties and refers you to the photographic section for pictures of specific varieties and still more information. The photographic section is arranged by type of plant: Trees, conifers, shrubs, roses, climbers, grasses, ferns, perennials, annuals and biennials, rock plants, bulbs, water plants, and cacti and other succulents. Each type of plant is subdivided. Perennials, for instance, are separated into large, medium, and small, with big subsections on important perennials like chrysanthemums and hostas. These subsections are arranged by color. This way of organizing the pictures makes the book outstanding for design purposes. Inclusion of trees, shrubs, grasses, and so on makes it an invaluable landscaping resource.

Coverage is very thorough: hardiness zone, sun/shade requirements, moisture needs, height and width at maturity, and care information. This is an expensive book, but the cost of color reproduction pushes many garden books to thirty dollars or more. This one, at about twice that figure, is worth half a dozen of the thirty-dollar kind. Buy it. You'll never regret it.

Brickell, Christopher, and Judith D. Zuk, eds. *The American Horticultural Society A-Z Encyclopedia of Garden Plants.* New York: DK Publishing, 1997.

Another great tome from the American Horticultural Society and Christopher Brickell is this more recent volume, very similar in content and coverage, but differently arranged. Brickell and Zuk give a few pages at the beginning to some basics like propagation and pruning, but the vast majority of the book is a straight alphabetical encyclopedia of plants. The arrangement is not useful for design purposes since plants are not grouped by type, size, and color. However, it does cover new plant introductions. Further, all the photos and information on a particular plant appear in one listing. Ideally your garden library would contain both volumes, but if only one fits your budget, this more recent work may be easier to find at a bookstore.

Armitage, Allan M. *Herbaceous Perennial Plants.* Athens, Ga.: Varsity Press, 1989.

Although Armitage includes a handful of color photographs bound together in the center of this work and a scattering of black-and-white illustrations, the real point here is his information-packed text. This is an encyclopedia of important garden perennial plants and their varieties and cultivars. Armitage covers only herbaceous (nonwoody) and bulbous perennial plants. Descriptions include plant height and width, hardiness zone, bloom season, useful care information, and much more. Although this is a sound scholarly work, descriptions are easy to understand and the style is an informal pleasure to read. Armitage frequently offers helpful advice about differing performance of plants in the North and South. This can be a trifle confusing for those of us living in the center of the country, but generally you can assume that plants that suffer from heat and humidity in the South are likely to have some degree of the same problem in the hot Midwest.

Armitage, Allan M. *Armitage's Garden Perennials: A Color Encyclopedia.* Portland, Ore.: Timber Press, 2000.

If a textbook daunts you, try Armitage's popularized work instead. He features what he considers the most interesting, important, or overlooked plants, offers brief and personal comments, and illustrates the book with almost 1,500 color photographs in a handy alphabetical listing.

Cox, Jeffrey. *Perennial All-Stars.* Emmaus, Penn.: Rodale Press, 1998.

This compendium of the author's choice of the 150 best perennial plants gives a generous amount of information in a double-page spread for each plant. This is a first-rate reference for beginners because it offers identifying color photographs, descriptions, care information, propagation techniques, and suggestions for companion planting. The author is an Easterner who gardens in northern California.

Trees and Shrubs

Dirr, Michael A. *Manual of Woody Landscape Plants: Their Identification, Ornamental Characteristics, Culture, Propagation, and Uses.* 4th ed. Champaign, Ill.: Stipes, 1990.

The longer you garden, the more you value shrubs and trees and the more questions you have about them. This book answers all those questions. Known simply as "Dirr" among horticultural professionals, this magnificent tome is a wonderful blend of scientific detail and personal commentary. I especially appreciate the author's comments about how plants fare in different parts of the country. He also gives generous information about mature size. Dirr is invaluable in choosing shrubs and trees. You've decided to plant a *Viburnum* in that shady spot? Check Dirr to decide which one would be best. This is a textbook, so look for it in a university bookstore.

Dirr, Michael A. *Dirr's Hardy Trees and Shrubs: An Illustrated Encyclopedia.* Portland, Ore.: Timber Press, 1997.

This marvelous volume on trees and shrubs from the expert is heavily illustrated with color photographs. Over five hundred species are covered in text and photographs. Though the book lacks the in-depth coverage and detail on propagation and care provided in his other book, the photos in this one make it a valuable tool for selecting trees for the landscape. The text is more accessible for the home gardener, and the book is likely to be easier to find in a bookstore or library, too.

Design

Harper, Pamela J. *Designing with Perennials.* New York: Macmillan, 1991.

This is the best book out there on how to design a garden. Everything you need to know is in this one volume. The sooner in your gardening life you read and absorb it the better because its principles should be applied to your garden as soon as possible. It isn't an easy read for a beginner. Harper refers to many plants you may not have heard of. Keep your *American Horticultural Society Encyclopedia of Garden Plants* handy. Reread the book five years later to soak up its wisdom all over again. By then you'll be familiar with many more plants and the book will be far easier to comprehend.

Harper is English by birth and American by residence. She has had a long career in gardening, half of it in England, half in the United States, where she has gardened in widely different climates. This background gives her a rare perspective. Her range of knowledge is impressive and her artistic flare enviable. The excellent color photos in this book are by the author and clearly illustrate specific points.

Harper, Pamela. *Color Echoes: Harmonizing Color in the Garden.* New York: Macmillan, 1994.

Here Harper expands upon her treatment of color, teaching you to see plant combinations differently and to appreciate the value of color *repetition,* while every other design book seems to speak of color largely in terms of *contrast.*

Cottage and Romantic Gardening

Hensel, Margaret. *English Cottage Gardening for American Gardeners.* New York: W. W. Norton, 1992.

If you yearn for a cottage garden or relish the romantic in garden design, you will love this book. Both text and photographs are full of ideas that help bring into focus exactly what elements combine to create the cozy charm of a cottage garden.

Wilder, Louise Beebe. *Color in My Garden: An American Gardener's Palette.* New York: Atlantic Monthly Press, 1990.

This reprint of a book originally published in 1919 is surprisingly fresh and readable. The author's enjoyable and informal style somehow conveys a solid grasp of what it takes to accomplish the immensely complicated task of creating a lavish, romantic flower garden.

Grooming

DiSabato-Aust, Tracy. *The Well-Tended Perennial Garden: Planting and Pruning Techniques.* Portland, Ore.: Timber Press, 1998.

A practical and unique guide, this book is packed with specific information about how and when to pinch, prune, deadhead, stake, and otherwise groom the garden to achieve maximum bloom and beauty. The author, who lives and gardens in Ohio, amply answers questions about how to care for plants once they're in the ground.

Index

Index

Index

Index

Index

LINDA HILLEGASS was raised in a family of diehard gardeners and has been gardening in the hot Midwest for more than twenty years. A former librarian, she now works full-time in the three bookstores she owns with her husband. Gardening is her passion. Her gardening publications include a chapter in *Perennials: Toward Continuous Bloom,* edited by Ann Lovejoy.

Typeset in 11.5/15 Minion
with Palette display
Designed by Dennis Roberts
Composed by Jim Proefrock
at the University of Illinois Press
Manufactured by Friesens Corporation

University of Illinois Press
1325 South Oak Street
Champaign, IL 61820-6903
www.press.uillinois.edu

E books

Any screen.
Any time.
Anywhere.

Activate the eBook version
of this title at no additional charge.

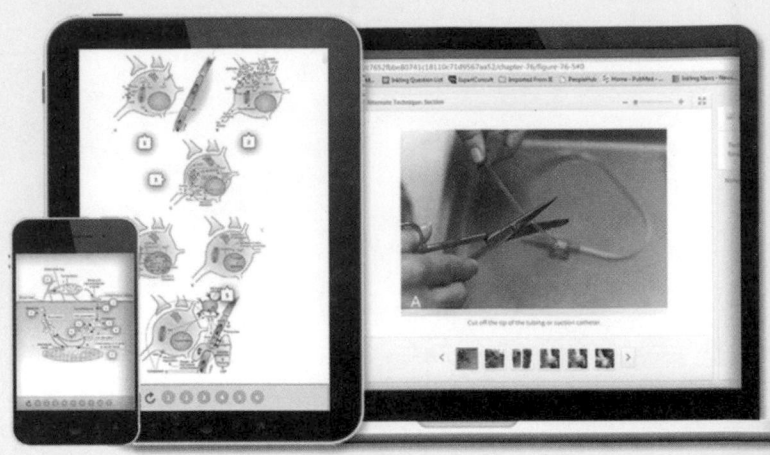

Expert Consult eBooks give you the power to browse and find content,
view enhanced images, share notes and highlights—both online and offline.

Unlock your eBook today.

1. Visit **expertconsult.inkling.com/redeem**

2. Scratch off your code

3. Type code into "Enter Code" box

4. Click "Redeem"

5. Log in or Sign up

6. Go to "My Library"

It's that easy!

Scan this QR code to redeem your
eBook through your mobile device:

FERRI
Scratch Gently
to Reveal Code

3XYQ4NJX2N

For technical assistance:
email expertconsult.help@elsevier.com
call 1-800-401-9962 (inside the US)
call +1-314-447-8200 (outside the US)

ELSEVIER

Bites, snake | I
Botulism | I
Burns | I
Colorado tick fever | I
Contact dermatitis | I
Diarrhea, acute | III
Ehrlichiosis | I
Electrical injury | I
Envenomation, marine | III
Food poisoning, bacterial | I
Frostbite | I
Giardiasis | I
Heat exhaustion and heat stroke | I
High-altitude sickness | I
Hypothermia | I
Leishmaniasis | I
Leptospirosis | I
Lyme disease | I
Malaria | I
Microsporidosis | I
Mushroom poisoning | I
Psittacosis | I
Rabies | I
Radiation exposure | I
Rocky Mountain spotted fever | I
Salmonellosis | I
Shigellosis | I
Tapeworm infestation | I
Tetanus | I
Tularemia | I
Vaccinations for international travel | V
West Nile virus infection | I

GASTROENTEROLOGY

Abdominal compartment syndrome | I
Abdominal pain, chronic lower | II
Abdominal pain, nonsurgical causes | II
Achalasia | I
Acute colonoic pseudo-obstruction | I
Acute liver failure | I
Alcoholic hepatitis | I
Anal abscess and fistula | II
Anorectal fistula | I
Anorexia | II
Appendicitis | I
Ascariasis | I
Ascites | I
Autoimmune hepatitis | I
Bacterial overgrowth, small intestine | II
Barrett's esophagus | I
Bile duct, dilated | II
Bleeding, gastrointestinal, algorithm | III
Bleeding, rectal | II
Bleeding, variceal | III
Budd-Chiari syndrome | I
Calcifications, liver on x-ray | II
Calcifications, pancreas on x-ray | II
Calcifications, spleen on x-ray | II
Celiac disease | I
Cholangitis | I
Cholecystitis | I
Cholelithiasis | I
Cholera | I
Chronic pancreatitis | I
Cirrhosis | I
Cirrhosis, primary biliary | I
Colic, acute abdominal | II
Colorectal cancer | I
Colostridium difficile infection | I
Constipation, adult patient | II
Constipation, algorithm | III
Crohn's disease | I
Cryptosporidium infection | I
Cyclic vomiting syndrome | I
Delayed passage of meconium | II
Diarrhea, acute | III
Diarrhea, acute watery and bloody | II
Diarrhea, chronic | III
Diarrhea, chronic, in patients with HIV infection, algorithm | III
Diarrhea, infectious | II
Diarrhea, non-infectious | II
Diverticular disease (diverticulosis, diverticulitis) | I
Dumping syndrome | I
Dyspepsia | III
Dyspepsia, nonulcerative | I
Dysphagia, oropharyngeal | I
Echinococcosis | I
Epigastric pain | II
Epiploic appendagitis | I
Esophageal tumors | I
Esophageal varices | I
Esophagitis | II
Familial adenomatous polyps and Gardner's syndrome | I
Fetal alcohol syndrome | I
Food poisoning, bacterial | I
Functional gallbladder disorder | I

Gastric cancer | I
Gastric dilatation | II
Gastric emptying, delayed | II
Gastrinoma | I
Gastritis | I
Gastroenteritis | I
Gastroesophageal reflux disease | I
Giardiasis | I
Gilbert's disease | I
Glossitis | I
Glossodynia | II
Helicobacter pylori infection | I
Hematemesis | II
Hemochromatosis | I
Hemoperitoneum | II
Hemoptysis | I
Hemorrhoids | I
Hepatic encephalopathy | I
Hepatitis A | I
Hepatitis, acute | II
Hepatitis B | I
Hepatitis B prophylaxis | V
Hepatitis C | I
Hepatitis, viral | III
Hepatomegaly, algorithm | III
Hepatomegaly, by shape of liver | II
Hepatopulmonary syndrome | I
Hepatorenal syndrome | I
Hiatal hernia | I
Hookworm | I
Hypergastrinemia | II
Hypersplenism, associated conditions | II
Hypoglycemia | II
Incontinence, fecal | II
Irritable bowel syndrome | I
Ischemia, colon | III
Jaundice, classification | II
Jaundice in the adult patient | I
Jaundice, neonatal | I
Jaundice, neonatal, algorithm | III
Lactose intolerance | I
Large bowel stricture | II
Liver abscess | I
Liver disease, pregnancy | II
Liver lesions, benign | II
Lynch syndrome | I
Malabsorption | II
Malabsorption algorithm | III
Mallory-Weiss tear | I
Nonalcoholic fatty liver disease | I
Nutrition assessment and intervention in cancer patient | III
Odynophagia | II
Pancreatic calcifications | II
Pancreatic cancer (exocrine) | I
Pancreatitis, drug-induced | II
Peptic ulcer disease | I
Perianal pain | II
Peritonitis, secondary | I
Peutz-Jeghers syndrome and other polyposis syndromes | I
Pinworms | I
Pneumatosis intestinalis in neonate and older child | II
Portal hypertension | I
Portal vein thrombosis | I
Primary sclerosing cholangitis | I
Pruritus ani | I
Rectal mass, palpable | II
Rectal prolapse | I
Retropharyngeal abscess | I
Shigellosis | I
Short bowel syndrome | I
Small bowel masses | II
Small bowel obstruction | I
Small intestinal bacterial overgrowth | I
Small intestine ulceration | II
Spontaneous bacterial peritonitis | I
Tapeworm infestation | I
Toxic megacolon | I
Traveler's diarrhea | I
Tropical sprue | I
Typhoid fever | I
Ulcerative colitis | I
Vitamin deficiency (hypovitaminosis) | I
Whipple's disease | I
Wilson's disease | I
Zenker's (pharyngoesophageal) diverticulum | I

GYNECOLOGY AND OBSTETRICS

Abruptio placentae | I
Acute fatty liver of pregnancy | I
Amniotic fluid alpha-fetoprotein elevation | II
Bleeding, early pregnancy | III
Bleeding neonate | III
Bleeding, vaginal | III
Bone mineral density, increased | II
Breast cancer | I

Breastfeeding difficulties | III
Breast, nipple discharge evaluation | III
Breast, radiologic evaluation | III
Breast, routine screen or palpable mass evaluation | III
Breech birth | I
Cervical cancer |
Cervical dysplasia |
Cervical insufficiency |
Cervical polyps | I
Cervicitis |
Chancroid | I
Chlamydia genital infections | I
Condyloma acuminatum | I
Contraception | I
Cystitis, acute | III
Delayed passage of meconium | II
Dysfunctional uterine bleeding | I
Dysmenorrhea | I
Dyspareunia | I
Dysuria and/or urethral/vaginal discharge | III
Eclampsia | I
Ectopic pregnancy | I
Emergency contraception | I
Endometrial cancer | I
Endometriosis | I
Endometritis | I
Erosions, genitalia | II
Fibrocystic breast disease | I
Genital lesions or ulcers, algorithm | III
Gonococcal urethritis | I
Gonorrhea | I
Granuloma inguinale | I
Groin masses | II
Heart failure, pregnancy | II
HELLP syndrome | I
Herpes simplex | I
Hot flashes | I
Hyperemesis gravidarum | I
Hypogonadism | III
Immunizations during pregnancy | V
Incontinence (urinary) | I
Infertility | I
Lymphogranuloma venereum | I
Mastitis | I
Mastodynia | I
Meigs' syndrome | I
Menopause | I
Menorrhagia | I
Molar pregnancy | I
Nipple lesions | II
Nongonococcal urethritis | I
Ovarian cancer | I
Ovarian neoplasm, benign | I
Over-the-counter medications in pregnancy | I
Paget's disease of the breast | I
Pelvic abscess | I
Pelvic inflammatory disease | I
Pelvic mass, algorithm | III
Pelvic organ prolapse (uterine prolapse) | I
Pelvic pain, causes in women | II
Pelvic pain, reproductive-age woman | III
Perirectal abscess | I
Placenta previa | I
Polycystic ovary syndrome | I
Postpartum depression | I
Postpartum hemorrhage | I
Preeclampsia | I
Premature labor | I
Premature rupture of membranes | I
Premenstrual dysphoric disorder | I
Premenstrual syndrome | I
Primary ovarian insufficiency | I
Pruritus, pregnant patient | III
Pruritus vulvae | I, II
Rh incompatibility | I
Sexual assault | I
Sexual dysfunction | III
Sexual dysfunction in women | I, II
Sheehan's syndrome | I
Spontaneous miscarriage | I
Syphilis | I
Thrombocytopenia, in pregnancy | II
Toxic shock syndrome | I
Urinary tract infection | I
Uterine fibroids | I
Uterine malignancy | I
Vaginal bleeding during pregnancy | I
Vaginal discharge, algorithm | III
Vaginal fistulas | I
Vaginal malignancy | I
Vaginal prolapse | III
Vaginismus | I
Vaginitis, estrogen-deficient | I
Vaginitis, fungal | I
Vaginitis, prepubertal |
Vaginitis, Trich |
Vaginosis, bac |
Vulvar cancer |

2017

Ferri's CLINICAL ADVISOR

5 BOOKS IN 1

FRED F. FERRI, M.D., F.A.C.P.

Clinical Professor
Alpert Medical School
Brown University
Providence, Rhode Island

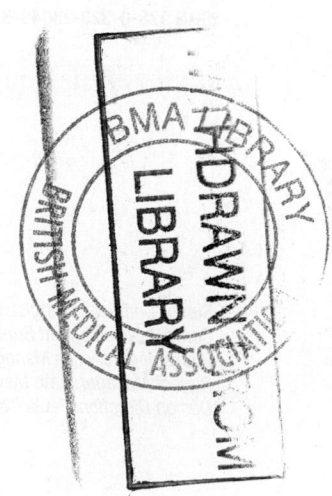

ELSEVIER

ELSEVIER

1600 John F. Kennedy Blvd.
Ste 1800
Philadelphia, PA 19103-2899

FERRI'S CLINICAL ADVISOR, 2017

ISBN: 978-0-323-28048-8

Notices

Knowledge and best practice in this field are constantly changing. As new research and experience broaden our understanding, changes in research methods, professional practices, or medical treatment may become necessary.

Practitioners and researchers must always rely on their own experience and knowledge in evaluating and using any information, methods, compounds, or experiments described herein. In using such information or methods they should be mindful of their own safety and the safety of others, including parties for whom they have a professional responsibility.

With respect to any drug or pharmaceutical products identified, readers are advised to check the most current information provided (i) on procedures featured or (ii) by the manufacturer of each product to be administered, to verify the recommended dose or formula, the method and duration of administration, and contraindications. It is the responsibility of practitioners, relying on their own experience and knowledge of their patients, to make diagnoses, to determine dosages and the best treatment for each individual patient, and to take all appropriate safety precautions.

To the fullest extent of the law, neither the Publisher nor the authors, contributors, or editors, assume any liability for any injury and/or damage to persons or property as a matter of products liability, negligence or otherwise, or from any use or operation of any methods, products, instructions, or ideas contained in the material herein.

ISBN 978-0-323-28048-8

Senior Content Strategist: Suzanne Toppy
Content Development Specialist: Jennifer Horigan
Publishing Services Manager: Catherine Jackson
Project Manager: Kate Mannix
Design Direction: Paula Catalano

Printed in the United States

Last digit is the print number: 9 8 7 6 5 4 3 2 1

Section Editors

RUBEN ALVERO, M.D.
Professor
Obstetrics and Gynecology
Director
Assisted Reproductive Technologies
Section Head
Reproductive Endocrinology and
    Infertility
Vice Chair for Education
University of Colorado Denver
Aurora, Colorado

**RICHARD J. GOLDBERG,
M.D., M.S.**
Psychiatrist-in-Chief
Rhode Island Hospital and
    The Miriam Hospital;
Professor, Department of Psychiatry
    and Human Behavior
Alpert Medical School
Brown University
Providence, Rhode Island

**FRED F. FERRI, M.D.,
F.A.C.P.**
Clinical Professor
Alpert Medical School
Brown University
Providence, Rhode Island

**SIDDHARTH KAPOOR,
M.D., F.A.H.S.**
Assistant Professor of Neurology
Director
Headache Medicine
Program Director
Fellowship in Headache Medicine
Department of Neurology
University of Kentucky College of
    Medicine
Lexington, Kentucky

**GLENN G. FORT, M.D.,
M.P.H., F.A.C.P., F.I.D.S.A.**
Clinical Associate Professor of
    Medicine
Warren Alpert School of Medicine at
    Brown University:
Chief, Infectious Diseases
Our Lady of Fatima Hospital
North Providence, Rhode Island

SAMAAN RAFEQ, M.D.
Director, Interventional Pulmonary
Division of Pulmonary, Critical Care
    and Sleep
Associate Program Director, Internal
    Medicine Residency Program
St. Elizabeth's Medical Center;
Assistant Professor of Medicine
Tufts Medical School
Boston, Massachusetts

Contributors

SONYA S. ABDEL-RAZEQ, M.D.
Assistant Professor of Obstetrics, Gynecology and Reproductive Sciences
Yale School of Medicine
New Haven, Connecticut

TONY ABDO, M.D.
Internal Medicine Resident
Roger Williams Medical Center
Boston University School of Medicine
Providence, Rhode Island

SUBASIT ACHARJI, M.D., F.A.C.P., F.A.C.C.
Fellow in Structural Heart and Endovascular Interventions
Interventional Cardiology
St. Elizabeth's Medical Center
Boston, Massachusetts

CATHLEEN ADAMS, M.D.
Attending Pediatrician and Child and Adolescent Psychiatrist
Department of Psychiatry and Human Behavior, Brown University
Rhode Island Hospital
Providence, Rhode Island

MICHAEL AGUSTIN, M.D.
Fellow: Pulmonary, Critical Care and Sleep Medicine
St. Elizabeth Medical Center/Tufts University
Boston, Massachusetts

MONZR M. AL MALKI, M.D.
Instructor
Department of Hematology and Hematopoietic Cell Transplantation
City of Hope National Medical Center
Duarte, California

ABDULLAH AL-SAWAF, M.D., M.B.B.S.
PGY3 Neurology Resident
Department of Neurology
University of Kentucky
Lexington, Kentucky

TANYA ALI, M.D.
Clinical Assistant Professor of Medicine
Department of Medicine
Alpert Medical School
Brown University
Providence, Rhode Island

SAMAN ALI, M.D.
Community Health Services
Hartford, Connecticut

PHILIP J. ALIOTTA, M.D.
Clinical Instructor
Department of Urology
School of Medicine and Biomedical Sciences
State University of New York at Buffalo
Buffalo, New York;
Medical Director
Center for Urologic Research of Western New York
Williamsville, New York

IHAB ALOMARI, M.D.
Interventional Cardiologist
Cardiovascular Diseases
University of California Irvine
Irvine, California;
Interventional Cardiologist
Cardiovascular Diseases
University of California Medical Center
Orange, California

RASHA B. ALQADI, M.D.
Rheumatology
Roger Williams Medical Center
Providence, Rhode Island

RUBEN ALVERO, M.D.
Professor
Obstetrics and Gynecology
Director
Assisted Reproductive Technologies
Section Head
Reproductive Endocrinology and Infertility
Vice Chair for Education
University of Colorado Denver
Aurora, Colorado

MEL L. ANDERSON, M.D., F.A.C.P.
Assistant Professor of Medicine
University of Colorado School of Medicine
Denver Veterans Affairs Medical Center
Denver, Colorado

THOMAS J.T. ANDERSON, M.D.
Clinical Fellow
Harvard Medical School;
Resident
Diagnostic Radiology
Beth Israel Deaconess Medical Center
Boston, Massachusetts

AUGUSTINE ANDOH-DUKU, M.D.
Steward St Elizabeth Medical Center
Tuft University School of Medicine
Boston, Massachusetts

LAURA M. ANDOLINA, M.S.
Clinical Instructor of Pediatrics
State University of New York at Buffalo
School of Medicine and Biomedical Sciences
Buffalo, New York

GEORGE F. ANDOSCIA, B.S.
Clinical Research Assistant
Rhode Island Hospital
Providence, Rhode Island

KATHRYN TAYLOR ANILOWSKI, M.S., P.T., C.L.T.-L.A.N.A.
Physical Therapist
Kinder Touch Lymphedema Center
Saratoga Springs, New York

ANNGENE G. ANTHONY, M.D., M.P.H., F.A.A.F.P.
Attending Physician
Family Medicine
Morrison Memorial Hospital
Morristown, New Jersey

ETSUKO AOKI, M.D., Ph.D.
Assistant Professor
Department of Leukemia/General Internal Medicine
University of Texas M.D. Anderson Cancer Center
Houston, Texas

NAIM AOUN, M.D.
St Joseph Hospital
Nashua, New Hampshire

GRAYSON W. ARMSTRONG, M.D., M.P.H.
The Warren Alpert Medical School of Brown University
Providence, Rhode Island;
Masters of Public Health Candidate
Health Policy and Management
Harvard School of Public Health
Boston, Massachusetts

RABIA ARSHAD, M.D.
Attending Cardiologist
Cardiology
Mercy Medical Center
Canton, Ohio

DANIEL K. ASIEDU, M.D., Ph.D., F.A.C.P.
Clinical Instructor of Medicine
Alpert Medical School Brown University
Providence, Rhode Island;
Attending Physician
Medicine
Coastal Medical, Inc.
Lincoln, Rhode Island

ARIF ASIF, M.D.
Professor of Medicine
Division of Nephrology and Hypertension
Albany Medical College
Albany, New York

SUDEEP K. AULAKH, M.D.
Assistant Proffesor of Medicine
Tufts University School of Medicine
Boston, Massachusetts;
Director, Ambulatory Education
Baystate Internal Medicine Residency
Co-Director, Baystate Primary Care Program
Baystate Medical Center
Springfield, Massachusetts;
Medical Director, Physician Assistant Program
Bay Path University
Longmeadow, Massachusetts

RUPALI AVASARE, M.D.
Clinical Instructor of Medicine
Department of Medicine
Columbia University Medical Center;
Clinical Instructor of Medicine
Department of Medicine
New York Presbyterian Hospital
New York, New York

TANIA B. BABAR, M.D.
Assistant Professor
Electrophysiology
West Virginia University
Charleston, West Virginia

AMIT BAHIA, M.D.
Clinical Fellow
Division of Cardiology
University of California Medical Center
Orange, California

CRISOSTOMO R. BALIOG Jr., M.D.
Assistant Professor
Department of Internal Medicine
University of South Alabama College of Medicine
Mobile, Alabama

MARYAM BALOUCH, M.D.
Fellow, Cardiovascular Disease
Department of Cardiology
University of California Irvine Medical Center
Irvine, California

PRIYA BANSAL, M.D., M.P.H.
Physician
Internal Medicine
Miriam Hospital/Rhode Island Hospital
Providence, Rhode Island

LUKE BARRÉ, M.D.
Instructor
Department of Medicine
Boston University School of Medicine;
Medical Resident
Department of Medicine
Roger Williams Medical Center
Providence, Rhode Island

ROWLAND P. BARRETT, Ph.D.
Associate Professor of Psychiatry & Human Behavior
Alpert Medical School
Brown University
Providence, Rhode Island

CRAIG L. BASMAN, M.D.
Attending Physician
Department of Medicine
Hospital for Special Surgery
New York, New York

ARNALDO A. BERGES, M.D.
Assistant Clinical Professor
Department of Psychiatry and Human Behavior
Alpert Medical School
Brown University
Rhode Island Hospital
Providence, Rhode Island

VICKY H. BHAGAT, M.D., M.P.H.
Internal Medicine Resident
Boston University
Boston, Massachusetts;
Roger Williams Medical Center
Providence, Rhode Island

HARIKRASHNA B. BHATT, M.D.
Assistant Professor of Medicine
Department of Medicine
Brown University
Providence, Rhode Island

DANISH BHATTI, M.D.
Assistant Professor
Department of Neurological Sciences
University of Nebraska Medical Center
Omaha, Nebraska

RACHAEL M. BIANCUZZO, M.D.
M.S.I.V.
Department of Medicine
University of New England College of Osteopathic Medicine
Biddeford, Maine
Department of Internal Medicine
Roger Williams Medical Center
Providence, Rhode Island

COURTNEY CLARK BILODEAU, M.D., F.A.C.P.
Assistant Professor
Department of Obstetric Medicine
Warren Alpert Medical School of Brown University;
Attending Physician
Internal Medicine–Women's Medicine Collaborative
Miriam Hospital
Providence, Rhode Island

CHRISTOPHER P. BLOMBERG, D.O.
Clinical Instructor
Tufts Medical Center;
Cardiology Fellow
Cardiology
Steward St. Elizabeth's Medical Center
Boston, Massachusetts

NIRALI BORA, M.D.
Assistant Clinical Instructor of Family Medicine
Alpert Medical School
Brown University
Providence, Rhode Island

ALEXANDRA BOSKE, M.D.
Director of Inpatient Neurology
Stroke Program Director
Saint David's Round Rock Medical Center
Round Rock, Texas

LYNN BOWLBY, M.D., F.A.C.P.
Medical Director
Duke Outpatient Clinic
Duke University
Durham, North Carolina

MARK F. BRADY, M.D., M.P.H., M.M.S., D.T.M.&H.
Attending Physician
Emergency Medicine
Baptist Memorial Hospital
Memphis, Tennessee

TINA BRAR, M.D.
Rheumatology Fellow
Brown University
Providence, Rhode Island

MANDEEP K. BRAR, M.D.
Clinical Assistant Professor
Department of Obstetrics and Gynecology
State University of New York at Buffalo
Buffalo, New York

KEITH BRENNAN, M.D.
Geriatric Medicine
Stony Brook University
Stony Brook, New York;
Geriatric Medicine
Winthrop University Hospital
Mineola, New York

ELIZABETH BROWN, M.D.
Assistant Clinical Instructor of Family Medicine
Memorial Hospital of Rhode Island
Pawtucket, Rhode Island;
Alpert Medical School
Brown University
Providence, Rhode Island

GAVIN BROWN, M.D.
General Neurologist
Laureate Medical Group at Northside Hospital
Atlanta, Georgia

JENNIFER BUCKLEY, M.D.
Clinical Instructor of Family Medicine
Family Medicine
Warren Alpert School of Medicine
Brown University
Providence, Rhode Island;
Family Medicine
Memorial Hospital of Rhode Island
Pawtucket, Rhode Island;
Kent Memorial Hospital
Warwick, Rhode Island

JONATHAN BURNS, M.A., M.D.
Clinical Instructor
Population Medicine
Harvard Medical School
Boston, Massachusetts;
Medical Director, Elder Service Plan
Cambridge Health Alliance
Cambridge, Massachusetts

D. BRANDON BURTIS, D.O.
Assistant Professor
Neurology
University of Florida
Gainesville, Florida

DOUGLAS BURTT, M.D.
Clinical Assistant Professor of Medicine
Division of Cardiology
Alpert Medical School
Brown University
Providence, Rhode Island

CLAUDIA S. RODRÍGUEZ CABRERA, M.D.
Department of Medicine
Universidad Tecnológica de Santiago
Hospital Regional Universitario de José María Cabral y Báez
Santiago, Dominican Republic

KATE CAHILL, M.D.
Assistant Professor of Medicine (Clinical)
Division of General Internal Medicine
Warren Alpert Medical School
Brown University
Providence, Rhode Island

ANDREW CARAGANIS, M.D.
Internal Medicine
Boston University School of Medicine
Roger Williams Medical Center
Providence, Rhode Island

AAKRITI CARRUBBA, M.D.
Resident Physician
Obstetrics and Gynecology
University of Colorado Anschutz Medical Campus
Aurora, Colorado

JORGE J. CASTILLO, M.D.
Assistant Professor of Medicine
Harvard Medical School
Boston, Massachusetts

ANDREEA M. CATANA, M.D.
Instructor in Medicine
Gastroenterology and Hepatology
Beth Israel Deaconess Medical Center
Harvard Medical School
Boston, Massachusetts

CAROLINA S. CEREZO, M.D., F.A.A.P.
Department of Pediatrics
Rhode Island Hospital;
Assistant Professor of Pediatrics
The Warren Alpert Medical School
Brown University
Providence, Rhode Island

JOSHUA CHALKELY, M.S., D.O.
Department of Neurology
University of Kentucky Medical Center
Lexington, Kentucky

PHILIP A. CHAN, M.D., M.S.
Assistant Professor
Brown University
Providence, Rhode Island

ARLENE CHAPMAN, M.D.
Professor of Medicine
University of Chicago
Chicago, Illinois

LILY CHEN, M.D.
Resident Physician
Internal Medicine
University of California at Davis Medical Center
Sacramento, California

VICKY CHENG, M.D.
Assistant Professor
Department of Medicine
Division of Endocrinology
Warren Alpert Medical School
Brown University;
Staff Endocrinologist
Department of Medicine
Division of Endocrinology
Rhode Island Hospital
Providence, Rhode Island

SARAH L. CHISHOLM, M.D.
Resident Physician
Department of Obstetrics and Gynecology
University of Colorado Hospital
Denver, Colorado

GEORGE CHOLANKERIL, M.D.
Department of Internal Medicine
Roger Williams Medical Center
Providence, Rhode Island;
Department of Medicine
Boston University School of Medicine
Boston, Massachusetts

NEELESH LALJI CHUDASAMA, M.D.
Postdoctoral Clinical Fellow
Division of Cardiology
Department of Internal Medicine
New York-Presbyterian Hospital
Columbia University Medical Center
New York, New York

LISA COHEN, Pharm.D., C.D.E.
Associate Professor
Department of Pharmacy Practice
University of Rhode Island
Kingston, Rhode Island

KAILA COMPTON, M.D., Ph.D.
Attending Psychiatrist
Alta Bates/Herrick Hospital
Berkeley, California

JESSICA CORIO, Pharm.D. Candidate
University of Rhode Island
Kingston, Rhode Island

JESSICA CORWIN, M.D., M.P.H.
The Permanente Medical Group
Northern California

DAN A. CRISTESCU, M.D.
Arthritis Associates and Osteoporosis Center of Colorado Springs
Colorado Springs, Colorado

PATRICIA CRISTOFARO, M.D.
Assistant Professor of Medicine
Alpert Medical School
Brown University;
Physician
Providence VA Medical Center
Providence, Rhode Island

JOANNE SZCZYGIEL CUNHA, M.D.
Rheumatology Fellow
Rheumatology
The Warren Alpert School of Medicine
Brown University
Providence, Rhode Island

STEPHANIE A. CURRY, M.D.
Tufts University
Boston, Massachusetts;
Endocrinology Fellow
Endocrinology, Diabetes & Metabolism
Lahey Hospital & Medical Center
Burlington, Massachusetts;
Department of Internal Medicine
Roger Williams Medical Center
Providence, Rhode Island

ALICIA J. CURTIN, Ph.D., G.N.P.
Assistant Professor
Division of Geriatrics
Alpert Medical School
Brown University
Providence, Rhode Island

KAUSTUBH C. DABHADKAR, M.D., M.P.H.
Fellow in Cardiovascular Diseases
Division of Cardiology
Department of Medicine
Brown University;
Fellow in Cardiovascular Diseases
Division of Cardiology, Department of Medicine
Rhode Island Hospital;
Fellow in Cardiovascular Diseases
Division of Cardiology
Department of Medicine
VA Providence
Providence, Rhode Island

GANARY DABIRI, M.D., Ph.D.
Dermatology Resident
Dermatology
Boston University School of Medicine
Boston, Massachusetts;
Roger Williams Medical Center
Providence, Rhode Island

KRISTY L. DALRYMPLE, Ph.D.
Assistant Professor (Research)
Alpert Medical School
Brown University;
Staff Psychologist
Rhode Island Hospital
Providence, Rhode Island

CATHERINE D'AVANZATO, Ph.D.
Psychology Fellow
Rhode Island Hospital
Department of Psychiatry and Human Behavior
The Warren Alpert School of Medicine
Brown University
Providence, Rhode Island

ALEXANDRA DEGENHARDT, M.D., M.MSc.
Director
Multiple Sclerosis Center
Pen Bay Medical Center
Rockport, Maine

ANDRE DESOUZA, M.D.
MetroWest Medical Center
Framingham, Massachusetts

JOSEPH A. DIAZ, M.D., M.P.H.
Associate Professor of Medicine
Department of Medicine
Alpert Medical School
Brown University
Providence, Rhode Island;
Department of Medicine
Memorial Hospital of Rhode Island
Pawtucket, Rhode Island

JUAN PABLO DOMECQ, M.D.
Resident Physician
Internal Medicine
Wayne State University;
Resident Physician
Internal Medicine
Henry Ford Hospital
Detroit, Michigan;
Leader Investigator
Epidemiology
Conevid
Lima, Peru

AMANDA C. DORAN, M.D., Ph.D.
Cardiology Fellow
Department of Medicine
Division of Cardiology
Columbia University;
Cardiology Fellow
Department of Medicine
Division of Cardiology
New York Presbyterian Hospital
New York, New York

ANDREW DUKER, M.D.
Associate Professor, Movement Disorders Division Director
Neurology and Rehabilitation Medicine
University of Cincinnati College of Medicine
Cincinnati, Ohio

STUART J. EISENDRATH, M.D.
Professor of Clinical Psychiatry
Director of the UCSF Depression Center
Langley Porter Psychiatric Hospital and Clinics
University of California, San Francisco
San Francisco, California

CHRISTINE EISENHOWER, Pharm.D., B.C.P.S.
Clinical Assistant Professor
Pharmacy Practice
University of Rhode Island College of Pharmacy
Kingston, Rhode Island

PAMELA ELLSWORTH, M.D.
Professor of Urology
Urology
University of Massachusetts Medical Center/University of Massachusetts
   Medical School
Worcester, Massachusetts

ALAN EPSTEIN, M.D.
Assistant Professor of Medicine
Boston University School of Medicine
Providence, Rhode Island

Contributors

JUAN A. ESCARFULLER, M.D., F.A.C.C., F.A.C.P., F.A.S.N.C.
Assistant Clinical Professor
Internal Medicine, Division of Cardiology
Albert Einstein College of Medicine;
Assistant Clinical Professor
Internal Medicine, Division of Cardiology
Montefiore Hospital
New York, New York

PATRICIO SEBASTIAN ESPINOSA, M.D., M.P.H.
Affiliate Associate Professor of Neurology
Department of Clinical Biomedical Science
Charles E. Schmidt College of Medicine
Florida Atlantic University;
Director, General Neurology
Neurology Department
Marcus Neuroscience Institute
Boca Raton Regional Hospital
Boca Raton, Florida

MARK D. FABER, M.D., M.S.
Clinical Associate Professor
Internal Medicine
School of Medicine
Wayne State University;
Senior Staff
Division of Hypertension and Renal Disease
Henry Ford Hospital
Detroit, Michigan

VALERIA FABRE, M.D.
Clinical Instructor
Medicine
Brown University
Providence, Rhode Island;
Medicine
Memorial Hospital of Rhode Island
Pawktucket, Rhode Island

LIORA J. FARBER, M.D.
Physician
Boston University School of Medicine
Boston, Massachusetts;
Internal Medicine Department
Roger Williams Medical Center
Providence, Rhode Island

TIMOTHY W. FARRELL, M.D., A.G.S.F.
Associate Professor of Medicine
Division of Geriatrics
University of Utah School of Medicine
Salt Lake City, Utah

JAMES M. FERGUSON, M.D.
Warren Alpert Medical School
Brown University
Rhode Island Hospital
Providence, Rhode Island

JASON FERREIRA, M.D.
Instructor in Medicine
Gastroenterology
Geisel School of Medicine at Dartmouth
Hanover, Massachusetts;
Gastroenterologist
Dartmouth Hitchcock Medical Center
Lebanon, New Hampshire

FRED F. FERRI, M.D., F.A.C.S.
Clinical Professor
Alpert Medical School
Brown University
Providence, Rhode Island

HEATHER FERRI, D.O.
Medical Resident
Department of Medicine
The Warren Alpert Medical School
Brown University
Rhode Island Hospital
Providence, Rhode Island

AMBER N. FONTENOT FERRISS, M.D.
Anschutz Medical Campus
University of Colorado Denver
Denver, Colorado

ANTONELLA FINE, M.D.
Warren Alpert Medical School of Brown University
Rhode Island Hospital
Providence, Rhode Island

BARRY FINE, M.D., Ph.D.
Fellow in Cardiovascular Medicine
Cardiology
Columbia University;
Clinical Fellow
Medicine
New York Presbyterian Hospital
New York, New York

GLEN FINNEY, M.D.
Neurologist
Geisinger Medical Center
Danville, Pennsylvania

STACI A. FISCHER, M.D.
Associate Professor
Infectious Diseases
Warren Alpert Medical School of Brown University
Providence, Rhode Island

TAMARA G. FONG, M.D., Ph.D.
Assistant Professor of Neurology
Harvard Medical School;
Staff Neurologist
Beth Israel Deaconess Medical Center;
Assistant Scientist
Aging Brain Center
Institute for Aging Research
Hebrew SeniorLife
Boston, Massachusetts

MICHELLE FORCIER, M.D., M.P.H.
Associate Professor of Pediatrics
Division of Adolescent Medicine
Alpert Medical School
Brown University
Providence, Rhode Island

GLENN G. FORT, M.D., M.P.H., F.A.C.P., F.I.D.S.A.
Clinical Associate Professor of Medicine
Warren Alpert School of Medicine
Brown University;
Chief, Infectious Diseases
Our Lady of Fatima Hospital
North Providence, Rhode Island

FRANK G. FORT, M.D., F.A.C.S., R.P.H.S.
Medical Director
Capital Region Vein Centre
Schenectady, New York

JUSTIN F. FRASER, M.D.
Assistant Professor of Cerebrovascular, Endovascular
   and Skull Base Surgery
Department of Neurosurgery
University of Kentucky
Lexington, Kentucky

MICHAEL FRIEDMAN, M.D.
Rhode Island Hosptial
The Miriam Hospital
Brown University School of Medicine
Providence, Rhode Island

DANIEL R. FRISCH, M.D., F.A.C.C.
Associate Professor of Medicine
Electrophysiology Section, Division of Cardiology
Thomas Jefferson University Hospital
Philadelphia, Pennsylvania

SAINATH GADDAM, M.D.
Fellow
Preventive Cardiology
Providence VA Medical Center
Alpert Medical School
Brown University
Providence, Rhode Island

ANTHONY GALLO, M.D.
Assistant Clinical Professor of Psychiatry
Alpert Medical School
Brown University
Providence, Rhode Island

HARSHA V. GANGA, M.D.
Cardiovascular Fellow
Cardiology
Brown University
Providence, Rhode Island

MARINA GARAS, D.O.
Internal Medicine Department
Roger Williams Medical Center
Providence, Rhode Island

LEANNA R. GARBUS, O.M.S. III
University of New England College of Osteopathic Medicine
Biddeford, Maine

EDITH GARNEAU, M.D.
Roger Williams Medical Center
Providence, Rhode Island

PAUL F. GEORGE, M.D., M.H.P.E.
Assistant Professor of Family Medicine
Department of Family Medicine
The Warren Alpert Medical School
Brown University
Providence, Rhode Island

JOYDEEP GHOSH, M.D., F.A.C.C., F.H.R.S.
Assistant Professor of Medicine
Cardiology
Columbia University Medical Center
New York, New York

KATARZYNA GILEK-SEIBERT, M.D., Rh.M.S.U.S.
Associate Program Director, Rheumatology Fellowship
Division of Rheumatology
Roger Williams Medical Center
Providence, Rhode Island

JONATHAN GINNS, M.D.
Assistant Professor of Medicine
Adult Congenital Heart Disease
Columbia University Medical Center
New York, New York

DIMITRI GITELMAKER, M.D.
Internal Medicine Resident
Roger Williams Medical Center
Boston University School of Medicine
Providence, Rhode Island

RICHARD J. GOLDBERG, M.D., M.S.
Psychiatrist-in-Chief
Rhode Island Hospital and The Miriam Hospital'
Professor
Department of Psychiatry and Human Behavior
Alpert Medical School
Brown University
Providence, Rhode Island

ALLA GOLDBURT, M.D.
Clinical Assistant Professor
Family Medicine
Brown University Alpea Medical School
Providence Rhode Island

JESSE GOLDMAN, M.D., F.A.S.H.
Associate Professor of Medicine
Medicine/Nephrology
Drexel University
Hahnemann University Hospital
Philadelphia, Pennsylvania

PAUL GORDON, M.D.
Clinical Assistant Professor of Medicine
Division of Cardiology
Alpert Medical School
Brown University
Providence, Rhode Island

NANCY R. GRAFF, M.D.
Professor of Pediatrics
University of California, San Diego
San Diego, California

JOHN A. GRAY, M.D., Ph.D
Assistant Professor
Department of Neurology
Center for Neuroscience
University of California, Davis
Davis, California

SIMON GRINGUT, M.D.
Fellow
Cardiovascular Medicine
St. Elizabeth's Medical Center
Boston, Massachusetts

Contributors

STEPHEN L. GRUPKE, M.D., M.S.
Chief Resident
Department of Neurosurgery
University of Kentucky
Lexington, Kentucky

PATAN GULTAWATVICHAI, M.D.
Department of Internal Medicine
Roger Williams Medical Center
Providence, Rhode Island

PRIYA SARIN GUPTA, M.D., M.P.H.
Adolescent Medicine Fellow
Division of General Pediatrics and Adolescent Medicine
Department of Pediatrics
Johns Hopkins Hospital
Baltimore, Maryland

NAWAZ HACK, M.D.
Assistant Professor of Neurology
Neurology
F. Edward Hebert School of Medicine
Uniformed Services University of the Health Sciences
Bethesda, Maryland

DENISA HAGAU, M.D.
Clinical Associate
Tufts University School of Medicine;
Cardiology Fellow
Cardiovascular Medicine
St. Elizabeth's Medical Center
Boston, Massachusetts

GREGORY M. HAIDEMENOS, M.D.
Boston University School of Medicine
Boston, Massachusetts;
Internal Medicine Department
Roger Williams Medical Center
Providence, Rhode Island

MOTI HAIM, M.D.
Associate Professor
Cardiology
Faculty of Health Sciences
Ben-Gurion University;
Director of Cardiac Electrophysiology and Pacing
Cardiology
Soroka Medical Center
Beer-Sheva, Israel

LEO HAN, M.D.
Resident
Obstetrics and Gynecology
University of Colorado
Aurora, Colorado

SAJEEV HANDA, M.D., S.F.H.M.
Clinical Assistant Professor
Medicine & Neurology
Alpert Medical School
Brown University;
Director, Division of Hospital Medicine
Department of Medicine
Rhode Island Hospital
Providence, Rhode Island

ERICA HARDY, M.D., M.M.S.
Assistant Professor of Medicine (Clinical)
The Warren Alpert School of Medicine
Brown University;
Attending Physician
Department of Infectious Diseases and Obstetric Medicine
Women & Infant's Hospital
Providence, Rhode Island

TAYLOR HARRISON, M.D.
Assistant Professor of Neurology
Department of Neurology
Emory University
Atlanta, Georgia

DON HAYES JR., M.D., M.S.
Associate Professor
Departments of Pediatrics and Internal Medicine
The Ohio State University;
Section of Pulmonary Medicine
Nationwide Children's Hospital
Division of Pulmonary Allergy, Critical Care, and Sleep Medicine
The Ohio State University Wexner Medical Center
Columbus, Ohio

DWAYNE R. HEITMILLER, M.D.
Department of Psychiatry
Rhode Island Hospital
The Miriam Hospital
Providence, Rhode Island

EMILY Z. HEJAZI, M.D., M.S.
Research Fellow
Dermatology
University of Pennsylvania
Hospital of the University of Pennsylvania
Philadelphia, Pennsylvania

MICHAEL HEUNG, M.D., M.S.
Clinical Associate Professor
Internal Medicine–Nephrology
Universiy of Michigan;
Medical Director, Acute Dialysis Program
Internal Medicine–Nephrology
University of Michigan Health System
Ann Arbor, Michigan

R. SCOTT HOFFMAN, M.D.
Assistant Clinical Professor
Ophthalmology and Visual Sciences
University of Louisville;
Physician
Ophthalmologist
Doctors Eye Institute
Louisville, Kentucky

DAWN HOGAN, M.D.
Clinical Assistant Professor of Family Medicine
Alpert Medical School
Brown University
Providence, Rhode Island

N. WILSON HOLLAND, M.D., F.A.C.P.
Associate Professor of Medicine
Division of Geriatrics and Gerontology
Emory University School of Medicine;
Acting Designated Learning Officer
Atlanta Veterans Administration Medical Center
Atlanta, Georgia

SUSIE L. HU, M.D.
Assistant Professor of Medicine
Division of Renal Diseases
Department of Internal Medicine
Alpert Medical School
Brown University
Rhode Island Hospital
Providence, Rhode Island

ANNE L. HUME, Pharm.D., F.C.C.P., B.C.P.S.
Professor of Pharmacy
Department of Pharmacy Practice
University of Rhode Island
Kingston, Rhode Island;
Adjunct Professor
Department of Family Medicine
Memorial Hospital of Rhode Island
Pawtucket, Rhode Island

DONNY V. HUYNH, M.D.
PGY-5 Hematology-Oncology Fellow
Roger Williams Medical Center
Boston University School of Medicine
Providence, Rhode Island

AHMAD M. ISMAIL, M.D.
Pulmonary and Critical Care Fellows
East Carolina University
Greenville, North Carolina

OLOLADE JAMES, M.D.
3rd-Year Medical Resident
Internal Medicine Department
UCSF-Fresno Campus
San Francisco, California

ROBERT H. JANIGIAN, M.D.
Clinical Assistant Professor of Surgery
Warren Alpert Medical School
Brown University
Providence, Rhode Island

NOEL S.C. JAVIER, M.D.
Assistant Professor of Medicine
Geriatrics and Palliative Medicine
Icahn School of Medicine at Mount Sinai
Mount Sinai Hospital
New York, New York

MICHAEL P. JOHNSON, M.D.
Assistant Professor
Medicine
Warren Alpert Medical School
Rhode Island Hospital
Providence, Rhode Island

KIMBERLY JONES, M.D.
Associate Professor of Child Neurology
Department of Neurology
University of Kentucky
Lexington, Kentucky

SHYAM JOSHI, M.D.
PGY-3
Internal Medicine Residency Program
Brown University
Rhode Island Hospital
Providence, Rhode Island

LUCY KALANITHI, M.D., F.A.C.P.
Stanford Clinical Excellence Research Center
Stanford University School of Medicine
Stanford, California

GARRETT KALMAR, D.P.M.
Department of Podiatric Surgery
Boston University School of Medicine
Roger Williams Medical Center
Providence, Rhode Island

SIDDHARTH KAPOOR, M.D., F.A.H.S.
Assistant Professor of Neurology
Director
Headache Medicine
Program Director
Fellowship in Headache Medicine
Department of Neurology
University of Kentucky College of Medicine
Lexington, Kentucky

EMILY R. KATZ, M.D.
Assistant Professor (Clinical)
Department of Psychiatry & Human Behavior
Alpert Medical School
Brown University;
Director, Child & Adolescent Psychiatry Consultation-Liaison Service
Hasbro Children's Hospital
Rhode Island Hospital
Providence, Rhode Island

ALI KAZIM, M.D.
Clinical Associate Professor
Department of Psychiatry
David Geffen School of Medicine at UCLA
Los Angeles, California;
Associate Chief of Mental Health
Sepulveda Veterans Administration Ambulatory Health Care
Sepulveda, California

SACHIN KEDAR, M.B.B.S., M.D.
Associate Professor
Neurological Sciences; Ophthalmology and Visual Sciences
University of Nebraska Medical School and Truhlsen Eye Institute
Omaha, Nebraska

BROOKE E. KEELEY, D.P.M.
Podiatric Surgeon
Department of Surgery
Newport Hospital
Newport, Rhode Island
South County Hospital
Wakefield, Rhode Island
The Miriam Hospital
PMS-3 Surgical Resident Training
Roger Williams Medical Center
Providence, Rhode Island

ELLIE KELEPOURIS, M.D., F.A.H.A.
Professor of Medicine
Chief of Nephrology and Hypertension
Drexel University College of Medicine
Hahnemann University Hospital
Philadelphia, Pennsylvania

PAUL S. KELLERMAN, M.D.
Professor of Medicine
Department of Internal Medicine
Oakland University
William Beaumont School of Medicine;
Section Head, Nephrology
Department of Internal Medicine
William Beaumont Health System
Royal Oak, Michigan

BEVIN KENNEY, M.D.
Instructor in Medicine
Harvard Medical School;
Department of Medicine
Brigham and Women's Hospital
Boston, Massachusetts

ERIC S. KERNS, M.D.
Assistant Professor of Medicine
Department of Medicine
Alpert Medical School
Brown University;
Attending Physician
Division of Nephrology
Department of Medicine
Rhode Island Hospital
Providence, Rhode Island

BYUNG KIM, M.D.
Internal Medicine Chief Resident
Roger Williams Medical Center
Boston University School of Medicine
Boston, Massachusetts

ROBERT M. KIRCHNER, M.D.
Fellow, Cardiology
Division of Cardiology
Alpert Medical School
Brown University
Providence, Rhode Island

ROBERT KOHN, M.D.
Professor
Department of Psychiatry and Human Behavior
The Warren Alpert School of Medicine
Brown University
Providence, Rhode Island

ARAVIND RAO KOKKIRALA, M.D., F.A.C.C.
Cardiology Staff
Cardiology
Brown University School of Medicine
Rhode Island Hospital
Providence VA Medical Center
Providence, Rhode Island

YUVAL KONSTANTINO, M.D.
Cardiology
Ben Gurion University of the Negev
Soroka University Medical Center
Beer Sheva, Israel

NELSON KOPYT, D.O.
Chief, Division of Nephrology
Lehigh Valley Health Network
Allentown, Pennsylvania

KRISTINA KRAMER, M.D.
Medical Director
Intensive Care Unit
John Muir Medical Center
Walnut Creek, California

PRASHANTH KRISHNAMOHAN, M.B.B.S., M.D.
Neurocritical Care
Stanford University
Palo Alto, California

DEEPA KUMARAIAH, M.D., M.B.A.
Clinical Cardiology Fellow
Cardiology
New York Presbyterian Hospital
New York, New York

DAVID I. KURSS, M.D.
Clinical Assistant Professor
Department of Obstetrics and Gynecology
State University of New York at Buffalo
Buffalo, New York;
Medical Director
Women's Wellness Center of Western New York
Williamsville, New York

PETER LACAMERA, M.D.
Chief, Pulmonary and Critical Care Medicine
St. Elizabeth's Medical Center;
Assistant Professor of Clinical Medicine
Tufts University Medical School
Boston, Massachusetts

ANN S. LACASCE, M.D.
Assistant Professor of Medicine
Medical Oncology
Dana-Farber Cancer Institute
Boston, Massachusetts

CINDY LAI, M.D.
Associate Professor of Clinical Medicine
Intersessions Course Director;
Site Director
Medicine Clerkships
University of California, San Francisco
San Francisco, California

ALISHA LAKHANI, M.D., M.P.H.
Department of Medicine
Brown University & Rhode Island Hospital
Providence, Rhode Island

SYED R. LATIF, M.D.
Clinical Fellow, Cardiovascular Medicine
Internal Medicine
University of California, Davis Medical Center
Sacramento, California

QUANG P. LE, M.D., M.P.H.
Department of Same Day Services
Tufts University School of Medicine
St. Vincent Hospital
Boston, Massachusetts;
Medical Director
Le & Chang Family Urgent Care
Worcester, Massachusetts

KACHIU C. LEE, M.D., M.P.H.
Assistant Professor
Dermatology
Brown University;
Physician
Dermatology
Rhode Island Hospital
Providence, Rhode Island

YOUNG E. LEE, M.D.
Fellow, Cardiovascular Disease
Department of Cardiology
University of California Irvine Medical Center
Irvine, California

ANDRE LEVCHENKO, Ph.D.
Professor of Biomedical Engineering
Johns Hopkins University
Baltimore, Maryland

JIAN LI, M.D., Ph.D.
Clinical Assistant Professor
Internal Medicine
School of Medicine
Wayne State University;
Senior Staff
Division of Hypertension and Renal Diseases
Henry Ford Hospital
Detroit, Michigan

DONITA DILLON LIGHTNER, M.D.
Assistant Professor of Pediatric Neurology
Department of Neurology
University of Kentucky
Lexington, Kentucky

ALBERT LIN, M.D.
Fellow, Cardiovascular Disease
Warren Alpert Medical School
Brown University
Providence, Rhode Island

RICHARD LONG, M.D.
Associate Professor of Family Medicine
Director of Maternal and Child Health
Department of Family Medicine
Boston University School of Medicine
Boston Medical Center
Boston, Massachusetts

ELIZABETH A. LOWENHAUPT, M.D.
Associate Training Director
Child Psychiatry Fellowship & Triple Board Residency
Director, Medical Student Education in Child & Adolescent Psychiatry
Director of Psychiatric Services
Rhode Island Training School;
Clinical Assistant Professor
Department of Psychiatry and Human Behavior
Rhode Isand Hospital
Brown University
Providence, Rhode Island

AMY L. LUNDHOLM, D.O.
Fellow
Department of Rheumatology
Roger Williams Medical Center
Providence, Rhode Island

LAYOLA LUNGHAR, M.D.
Division of Pulmonary, Critical Care and Sleep Medicine
Norwood Hospital
Norwood, Massachusetts

MICHELLE C. MACIAG, M.D.
Department of Pediatrics
Hasbro Children's Hospital;
Department of Internal Medicine
Rhode Island Hospital
Alpert Medical School
Brown University
Providence, Rhode Island

SUSANNA R. MAGEE, M.D., M.P.H.
Assistant Professor
Department of Family Medicine
Alpert Medical School
Brown University
Providence, Rhode Island

DURKHANI MAHBOOB, M.D.
Rheumatology Fellowship
Roger Williams Medical Center
Boston University
Boston, Massachusetts;
Residency
VAMC Bronx
Mount Sinai School of Medicine
New York, New York

MARTA MAJCZAK, M.D.
Clinical Assistant Professor of Psychiatry and Human Behavior
Brown University
Providence, Rhode Island

SHEFALI MAJMUDAR, D.O.
Department of Rheumatology
Assistant Clinical Professor of Medicine
UCSF Fresno
Fresno, California

ABIGAIL K. MANSFIELD, Ph.D.
Department of Psychiatry
Rhode Island Hospital
Providence, Rhode Island

KELLY L. MATSON, B.S.N.U.T.R., Pharm.D.
Clinical Associate Professor
Department of Pharmacy Practice
University of Rhode Island
Providence, Rhode Island
Pediatric Clinical Specialist
UMass Memorial Children's Medical Center
Worcester, Massachusetts

LAUREN MAY, M.D.
Resident in Obstetrics and Gynecology
Department of Obstetrics and Gynecology
University of Colorado
Aurora, Colorado

MAITREYI MAZUMADAR, M.D., M.P.H., M.SC.
Assistant Professor of Neurology
Harvard Medical School;
Staff Physician
Department of Neurology
Boston's Children's Hospital;
Assistant Professor
Department of Environmental Health
Harvard School of Public Health
Boston, Massachusetts

NADINE MBUYI, M.D.
Resident Physician, Internal Medicine
Medicine
Boston University School of Medicine
Roger Williams Medical Center
Providence, Rhode Island

RUSSELL J. MCCULLOH, M.D.
Assistant Professor
Department of Pediatric Infectious Diseases
Children's Mercy Hospitals and Clinics
University of Missouri-Kansas City
Kansas City, Missouri;
University of Kansas School of Medicine
Kansas City, Kansas

ERIN MEDLIN, M.D.
Clinical Instructor
Gynecologic Oncology
Department of Obstetrics and Gynecology
University of Wisconsin School of Medicine and Public Health
Madison, Wisconsin

JOSEPH MEHARG, M.D.
Assistant Professor of Medicine
Department of Medicine
Boston University School of Medicine
Boston, Massachusetts;
Director, Intensive Care Unit
Department of Medicine
Roger Williams Medical Center;
Director, Division of Pulmonary & Critical Care Medicine
Department of Medicine
Roger Williams Medical Center
Providence, Rhode Island

AKANKSHA MEHTA, M.D.
Assistant Professor
Urology
Emory University School of Medicine
Atlanta, Georgia

GAETANE MICHAUD, M.D.
NYU Langone Medical Center
New York, New York

TARO MINAMI, M.D., F.A.C.P., F.C.C.P.
Assistant Professor of Medicine (Clinical)
Warren Alpert Medical School
Brown University
Providence, Rhode Island;
Director, PCCM Simulation and Ultrasound Training
Division of Pulmonary, Critical Care and Sleep Medicine
Memorial Hospital of Rhode Island
Pawtucket, Rhode Island

HASSAN M. MINHAS, M.D.
Child and Adolescent Psychiatry Chief Fellow
The Warren Alpert Medical School
Brown University
Providence, Rhode Island

FARHAN A. MIRZA, M.B.B.S.
PGY III Resident
Department of Neurosurgery
University of Kentucky
Lexington, Kentucky

THERESA A. MORGAN, Ph.D., M.Phil.
Resident in Clinical Psychology
Alpert Medical School
Brown University;
Department of Psychiatry
Rhode Island Hospital
Providence, Rhode Island

ALEEM MUGHAL, M.D.
Cardiovascular Medicine
Tufts University
Steward St. Elizabeth's
Brighton, Massachusetts

SHIVA R. MUKKAMALLA, M.D., M.P.H.
Clinical Fellow
Hematology and Oncology
Roger Williams Medical Center
Providence, Rhode Island

CATHERINE ELIAS NAJEM, M.D.
Internal Medicine Resident
Internal Medicine
Roger Williams Medical Center
Boston University School of Medicine;
Co-Investigator, Clinical Research
Department of Rheumatology
Providence VA Medical Center
Providence, Rhode Island

BILAL H. NAQVI, M.D.
Hematologist/Oncologist
Marshfield Clinic Regional Cancer Center
Eau Claire, Wisconsin

HUSSAIN NASERI, M.D.
Clinical Fellow, Hematology-Oncology
Roger Williams Medical Center
Boston University
Providence, Rhode Island

UZMA NASIR, M.D.
Assistant Professor
Clinical Anesthesia and Pain Management
State University of New York Stony Brook University Hospital
Stony Brook, New York
VA Hospital
Northport, New York

SHAW NATAN, M.D.
Cardiac Electrophysiologist
St Elizabeth Medical Center
Brighton, Massachusetts;
Assistant Professor of Medicine
Tufts University
Medford, Massachusetts

ALI NAYER, M.D.
University of Miami Health System
Miami Transplant Institute
Miami, Florida

LAMA NAZZAL, M.D., M.Sc.
Clinical Instructor
New York University School of Medicine
New York, New York

RABIN NIROULA, M.D.
Roger Williams Medical Center
Boston University School of Medicine
Boston, Massachusetts

MELISSA NOTHNAGLE, M.D., M.Sc.
Associate Professor
Family Medicine
Alpert Medical School
Brown University
Providence, Rhode Island;
Family Medicine Residency Director
Family Medicine
Memorial Hospital of Rhode Island
Pawtucket, Rhode Island

PATRICK NSEREKO, M.D.
Boston University School of Medicine
Boston, Massachusetts;
Internal Medicine Department
Roger Williams Medical Center
Providence, Rhode Island

GAIL M. O'BRIEN, M.D.
Alliance Internal Medicine
Vineyard Haven, Massachusetts

DANIEL W. OESTERLE, B.S.
Research Assistant
Rhode Island Hospital
Department of Psychiatry
Providence, Rhode Island

ALEXANDER B. OLAWAIYE, M.D.
Fellow
Division of Gynecologic Oncology
Vincent Department of Obstetrics
Gynecology and Reproductive Biology
Massachusetts General Hospital
Harvard Medical School
Boston, Massachusetts

ADAM J. OLSZEWSKI, M.D.
Assistant Professor of Medicine
Alpert Medical School of Brown University;
Division of Hematology-Oncology
Rhode Island Hospital
Providence, Rhode Island

LINDSAY M. ORCHOWSKI, Ph.D.
Staff Psychologist
Rhode Island Hospital;
Assistant Professor
Department of Psychiatry
Alpert Medical School of Brown University
Providence, Rhode Island

PAOLO G. PACE, M.A.Sc., M.D.
Resident Physician
Internal Medicine
Roger Williams Medical Center
Providence, Rhode Island

CRISTINA ANTONIO PACHECO, M.D.
Clinical Assistant Professor
Department of Family Medicine
Alpert Medical School
Brown University
Providence, Rhode Island

CHRIS W. PAN, M.D., M.B.A., M.S.
Fellow
Cardiology
University of California, Irvine
University of California, Irvine Medical Center
Orange, California

LISA PAPPAS-TAFFER, M.D.
Assistant Professor of Dermatology
The University of Pennsylvania
Perelman Center for Advanced Medicine
The Hospital of the University of Pennsylvania
Veterans Affairs Hospital
Philadelphia, Pennsylvania

SARIKA PARIKH, D.P.M.
Roger Williams Medical Center
Providence, Rhode Island

BIRJU B. PATEL, M.D., F.A.C.P.
Assistant Professor of Medicine
Department of Medicine
Division of Geriatrics and Gerontology
Emory University School of Medicine
Atlanta Veterans Affairs Medical Center;
Director
Bronze Geriatric Outpatient Clinic
Co-Consultant Network Geriatrics and Extended Care
Atlanta, Georgia

NIKUNJKUMAR PATEL, M.D.
Transplant Nephrology Fellow
Renal Electrolyte and Hypertension Division
University of Pennsylvania
Philadelphia, Pennsylvania

PRANAV M. PATEL, M.D., F.A.C.C., F.S.C.A.I.
Chief
Division of Cardiology
University of California, Irvine;
Director of Cardiac Cath Lab & Cardiac Care Unit
Cardiology/Medicine
University of California Irvine Medical Center
Orange, California

ELENI PATROZOU, M.D.
Research Associate
Medicine
Alpert Medical School
Brown University
Providence, Rhode Island;
Internist-Infectious Diseases Consultant
Medicine
Hygeia Hospital
Maroussi, Athens, Greece

ALISON PATTERSON, M.D.
Resident in Obstetrics and Gynecology
Department of Obstetrics and Gynecology
University of Colorado
Aurora, Colorado

ESHAN PATVARDHAN, M.B.B.S.
Clinical Associate
Interval Medicine
Fellow in Cardiology
Internal Medicine
St. Elizabeth's Medical Center
Boston, Massachusetts

GRACE PAUL, M.D.
Assistant Professor of Pediatrics
Division of Pediatric Pulmonary and Sleep Medicine
Nationwide Children's Hospital
Columbus, Ohio

KATHARINE A. PHILLIPS, M.D.
Director
Body Dysmorphic Disorder Program
Rhode Island Hospital;
Professor of Psychiatry and Human Behavior
Alpert Medical School
Brown University
Providence, Rhode Island

CHRISTOPHER PICKETT, M.D.
Associate Professor of Medicine
Director, Clinical Cardiology
Co-Director, Cardiac Electrophysiology
Pat and Jim Calhoun Cardiology Center
University of Connecticut Health Center
Farmington, Connecticut

WENDY A. PLANTE, Ph.D.
Clinical Assistant Professor of Psychiatry and Human Behavior
Alpert Medical School
Brown University
Rhode Island Hospital
Hasbro Children's Research Center
Providence, Rhode Island

KEVIN V. PLUMLEY, M.D., M.P.H.
Roger Williams Medical Center
Boston University
Providence, Rhode Island

SHARON S. HARTMAN POLENSEK, M.D., Ph.D.
Assistant Professor of Neurology
Center for Dizziness and Balance Disorders
Emory University
Atlanta, Georgia;
Chief
Audiology and Speech Pathology
Atlanta VA Medical Center
Decatur, Georgia

DONN POSNER, Ph.D., C.B.S.M.
Clinical/Research Psychologist
Palo Alto Veterans Institute for Research
Veterans Affairs Palo Alto Health Care System
Palo Alto, California

AMANDA PRESSMAN, M.D.
Assistant Professor of Medicine at Brown University
Rhode Island Hospital and Miriam Hospital
Providence, Rhode Island

KITTICHAI PROMRAT, M.D.
Assistant Professor
Division of Gastroenterology
Department of Medicine
Alpert Medical School
Brown University;
Chief
Gastroenterology Section
Providence VA Medical Center
Providence, Rhode Island

SHAHNAZ PUNJANI, M.D.
Fellow
Preventive Cardiology
Providence VA Medical Center
Alpert Medical School
Brown University
Providence, Rhode Island

IMRANA QAWI, M.D.
Tufts University Medical Center
Boston, Massachusetts

MOHAMMAD U. QAZI, M.D.
Fellow, Cardiovascular Disease
Department of Cardiology
University of California Irvine Medical Center
Irvine, California

JAI RADHAKRISHNAN, M.D.
Professor of Medicine
Department of Medicine
Columbia University Medical Center
New York Presbyterian Hospital
New York, New York

HEIDI RADLINSKI, M.D., M.P.H.
Clinical Instructor
Department of Family Medicine
Alpert Medical School
Brown University
Providence, Rhode Island

WILLIAM M. RAFELSON, M.D., M.B.A.
Department of Internal Medicine
Rhode Island Hospital
Warren Alpert Medical School
Brown University
Providence, Rhode Island

SAMAAN RAFEQ, M.D.
Director, Interventional Pulmonary
Division of Pulmonary, Critical Care and Sleep
Associate Program Director, Internal Medicine Residency Program
St. Elizabeth's Medical Center;
Assistant Professor of Medicine
Tufts Medical School
Boston, Massachusetts

SHALINE D. RAO, M.D.
Fellow in Cardiovascular Disease and Advanced Cardiac Care
Division of Cardiology
Columbia University Medical Center;
Fellow in Cardiovascular Disease and Advanced Cardiac Care
Division of Cardiology
New York Presbyterian
New York, New York

SOMWAIL RASLA, M.D.
Internal Medicine
Memorial Hospital of Rhode Island
Warren Alpert Medical School
Brown University
Providence, Rhode Island

BHARTI RATHORE, M.D.
Program Director, Hematology/Oncology Fellowship
Roger Williams Medical Center;
Assistant Professor of Medicine
Boston University School of Medicine;
Program Director, Hematology/Oncology Fellowship
Department of Medicine
Roger Williams Medical Center
Providence, Rhode Island

RITESH RATHORE, M.D.
Director of Hematology Oncology
Division Director of the Cancer Protocol Office
Roger Williams Cancer Center
Providence, Rhode Island

NEHA P. RAUKAR, M.D., M.S., F.A.C.E.P.
CAQ Primary Care Sports Medicine
Assistant Professor
Director
Division of Sports Medicine
Department of Emergency Medicine
The Warren Alpert School of Medicine
Brown University
Providence, Rhode Island

DHAVAL RAVAL, M.D.
Clinical Associate
St. Elizabeth's Medical Center
Boston, Massachusetts

SUSAN READ, M.D.
School of Medicine
New York Medical College
Valhalla, New York

JOHN L. REAGAN, M.D.
Assistant Professor
Medicine
The Warren Alpert Medical School
Brown University;
Attending Physician
Medicine
Rhode Island Hospital
Providence, Rhode Island

BHARATHI REDDY, M.D.
Assistant Professor of Medicine
University of Chicago
Chicago, IL

CHAKRAVARTHY REDDY, M.D.
University of Utah Health Sciences Center
Salt Lake City, Utah

SNIGHDA T. REDDY, M.D.
Senior Staff Physician
Division of Nephrology and Hypertension
Henry Ford Hospital
Detroit, Michigan

ANTHONY M. REGINATO, Ph.D., M.D.
Rhode Island Hospital
The Miriam Hospital
Providence, Rhode Island

RICHARD REGNANTE, M.D.
Division of Cardiovascular Medicine
Alpert Medical School
Brown University
Providence, Rhode Island

VICTOR I. REUS, M.D.
Professor
Department of Psychiatry
School of Medicine
Langley Porter Psychiatric Institute
University of California, San Francisco
San Francisco, California

HARLAN G. RICH, M.D., F.A.C.P., A.G.A.F.
Associate Professor of Medicine
Department of Medicine
Warren Alpert Medical School
Brown University;
Director of Endoscopy
Department of Medicine
Division of Gastroenterology
Rhode Island Hospital;
Staff Physician
Division of Gastroenterology
University Medicine Foundation, Inc.
Providence, Rhode Island

ROCCO J. RICHARDS, M.D.
Roger Williams Medical Center
Department of Internal Medicine
Boston University School of Medicine
Boston, Massachusetts

PETER RINTELS, M.D.
Kent Hospital
Warwick, Rhode Island,
Hematology & Oncology Associates of Rhode Island
Cranston, Rhode Island

ALVARO M. RIVERA, M.D.
Internal Medicine
Roger Williams Medical Center
Providence, Rhode Island

MICHAEL ROCHON-DUCK, M.D.
Fellow, Cardiovascular Disease
Department of Cardiology
University of California Irvine Medical Center
Irvine, California

DOMINIC RODA, D.P.M
Podiatry Resident
Roger Williams Medical Center
Providence, Rhode Island;
Boston University School of Medicine
Boston, Massachusetts

NICOLETTE RODRIGUEZ, B.A.
Warren Alpert Medical School
Brown University
Providence, Rhode Island

ANDREW ROGERS, M.D.
Department of Medicine
Alpert Medical School
Brown University
Providence, Rhode Island

JAMISON ROGERS, M.D.
Forensic Psychiatry Associate Training Director
Clinical Assistant Professor of Psychiatry and Human Behavior
Warren Alpert Medical School
Brown University
Providence, Rhode Island

ANISHKA S. ROLLE, M.D., F.A.C.R.
Attending Rheumatologist
Internal Medicine
Southside Regional Medical Center
Petersburg, Virginia
John Randolph Medical Center
Hopewell, Virginia;
Rheumatologist
AMDC Physicians Arthritis and Osteoporosis Clinic
Colonial Heights, Virginia

JULIE L. ROTH, M.D.
Assistant Professor
Neurology
Warren Alpert Medical School
Brown University'
Director of Women's Neurology
Neurology
Rhode Island Hospital
Providence, Rhode Island

LAUREN ROTH, M.D.
Assistant Professor
Division of Reproductive Endocrinology and Infertility
Department of Obstetrics and Gynecology
University of Colorado
Aurora, Colorado

STEVEN ROUGAS, M.D., M.S.
Assistant Professor of Emergency Medicine
Alpert Medical School
Brown University
Providence, Rhode Island

AMITY RUBEOR, D.O.
Assistant Professor (Clinical)
Department of Family Medicine
Warren Alpert Medical School
Brown University
Providence, Rhode Island;
Primary Care Sports Medicine Fellow
Department of Family Medicine
Memorial Hospital of Rhode Island
Pawtucket, Rhode Island

PHILLIP RUISI, M.D.
Cardiology Fellow
Cardiology
Brown University School of Medicine
Rhode Island Hospital
Miriam Hospital
Providence VA Medical Center
Providence, Rhode Island

THOMAS M. RÜNGER, M.D., Ph.D.
Professor of Dermatology, Pathology and Laboratory Medicine
Dermatology
Boston University School of Medicine
Boston, Massachusetts;
Chair, Dermatology
Roger Williams Medical Center
Providence, Rhode Island

IMMAD SADIQ, M.D.
Clinical Assistant Professor of Medicine
Division of Cardiology
Alpert Medical School
Brown University
Providence, Rhode Island

TANMAY SAHAI, M.D.
Roger Williams Medical Center
Providence, Rhode Island
Boston University School of Medicine
Boston, Massachusetts

JAVIER RODRIGUEZ SANCHEZ, M.D.
Resident Physician, PGY-3
Internal Medicine
Wayne State University School of Medicine
Henry Ford Hospital
Detroit, Michigan

RUBY K. SATPATHY, M.D.
Fellow
Cardiology
Department of Internal Medicine
Creighton University
Omaha, Nebraska

HEMANT K. SATPATHY, M.D.
Fellow
Division of Maternal Fetal Medicine
Department of Obstetrics and Gynecology
Emory University
Atlanta, Georgia

SYEDA M. SAYEED, M.D.
Clinical Instructor of Medicine,
Alpert Medical School
Brown University
Providence, Rhode Island

DAPHNE SCARAMANGAS-PLUMLEY, M.D.
Resident of Internal Medicine
Roger Williams Medical Center
Boston University School of Medicine
Providence, Rhode Island

HEIKO SCHMITT, M.D., Ph.D.
University Hospital of Connecticut
Farmington, Connecticut

CLAIRE SCHULTZ, M.D.
Resident Physician
Obstetrics and Gynecology
University of Colorado
University of Colorado Anschutz Medical Center
Denver, Colorado

PETER J. SELL, D.O., F.A.A.P.
Assistant Professor
Pediatrics
University of Massachusetts Medical School;
Pediatric Hospitalist
Division of Pediatric Critical Care
UMass Memorial Medical Center
Worcester, Massachusetts;
Pediatric Simulation Educator
Family Medicine
Memorial Hospital of Rhode Island
Pawtucket, Rhode Island;
Adjunct Assistant Professor
Family Medicine
Warren Alpert School of Medicine
Brown University
Providence, Rhode Island

STEVEN SEPE, M.D., Ph.D.
Chair of the Department of Medicine
Roger Williams Medical Center
Providence, Rhode Island;
Clinical Professor of Medicine
Assistant Dean of Clinical Affairs
Boston University School of Medicine
Boston, Massachusetts

CLAUDIA SERRANO, M.D.
Assistant Clinical Professor
Internal Medicine, Division of Cardiology
New York University
New York, New York

REBECCA KURNIK SESHASAI, M.D.
Assistant Professor of Medicine
Department of Medicine
Drexel University College of Medicine
Hahnemann University Hospital
Philadelphia, Pennsylvania

SANJEEV R. SHAH, M.D.
Assistant Professor of Clinical Medicine
Renal Electrolyte and HTN Division
Perelman School of Medicine
Philadelphia, Pennsylvania

APARNA SHARMA, M.D.
Nephrology Fellow
Medicine
University of Chicago
Chicago, Illinois

ASHA SHRESTHA, M.D.
Fellow
Division of Rheumatology
Albert Einstein College of Medicine
Montefiore Medical Center
Bronx, New York

MARK SIGMAN, M.D.
Kristhamurthi Family Professor and Chief of Urology
Surgery (Urology)
Waren Alpert Medical School
Brown University;
Chief of Urology
Surgery (Urology)
Rhode Island Hospital
The Miriam Hospital
Providence, Rhode Island

JOANNE M. SILVIA, M.D.
Clinical Assistant Professor of Family Medicine
Department of Family Medicine
The Warren Alpert Medical School
Brown University
Providence, Rhode Island

DIVYA SINGHAL, M.D.
Clinical Assistant Professor
Neurology
University of Oklahoma
Staff Neurologist/Resident Clinic Director
Neurology and Rehabilitation
VA Oklahoma City
Oklahoma City, Oklahoma

JON SKALECKI, M.D.
Internal Medicine
Roger Williams Medical Center
Providence, Rhode Island

JOHN SLADKY, M.D.
Staff Neurologist
Associate Program Director
Wilford Hall Medical Center
San Antonio, Texas

JEANETTE G. SMITH, M.D.
Assistant Professor of Medicine
Department of Gastroenterology
Alpert Medical School
Brown University
Providence, Rhode Island

JONATHAN H. SMITH, M.D.
Assistant Professor
Neurology
University of Kentucky
Lexington, Kentucky

THOMAS SMITH, M.D.
Assistant Clinical Professor, Cardiovascular Medicine
Internal Medicine
University of California, Davis Medical Center
Sacramento, California

U. SHIVRAJ SOHUR, M.D., Ph.D.
Assistant Professor of Neurology
Harvard Medical School
Boston, Massachusetts

REBECCA SOINSKI, M.D.
Rhode Island Hospital
The Miriam Hospital
Providence, Rhode Island

SANDEEP SOMAN, M.D.
Clinical Associate Professor
Department of Internal Medicine
Wayne State University;
Senior Staff Physician
Division of Nephrology and Hypertension
Henry Ford Hospital
Detroit, Michigan

SCOTT M. SOUTHER, M.D.
Resident
Internal Medicine
Boston University
Boston, Massachusetts
Roger Williams Medical Center
Providence, Rhode Island

MATTHEW J. STANISHEWSKI, D.O.
Rheumatology Fellow
Rheumatology and Internal Medicine
Boston University School of Medicine
Boston, Massachusetts
Roger Williams Medical Center
Providence, Rhode Island

PETER L. STEINBERG, M.D.
Instructor
Surgery (Urology)
Harvard Medical School;
Director of Endourology
Urology
Beth Israel Deaconess Medical Center
Boston, Massachusetts

JOHANNES STEINER, M.D.
Fellow
Cardiovascular Disease
Brown University Medical School
Providence, Rhode Island

PHILIP STOCKWELL, M.D.
Cardiology
Brown University School of Medicine
Rhode Island Hospital
Providence, Rhode Island

LARA STONE, D.P.M.
Chief Resident
PGY-3
Roger Williams Medical Center
Providence, Rhode Island

MELISSA C. STRIGLIO, Pharm.D. Candidate
University of Rhode Island College of Pharmacy
Kingston, Rhode Island

PADMAJA SUDHAKAR, M.B.B.S.
Assistant Professor
Department of Neurology
University of Kentucky
Lecington, Kentucky

MARY BETH SUTTER, M.D.
Maternal, Child, and Reproductive Health Fellow
Department of Family and Community Medicine
University of New Mexico
Albuquerque, New Mexico

ARUN SWAMINATHAN, M.B.B.S.
Resident
Neurology Department
University of Kentucky College of Medicine
University of Kentucky Hospital
Lexington, Kentucky

MAHER TABBA, M.D., F.A.C.P., F.C.C.P.
Associate Professor
Director, Interventional Pulmonology
Director, Pulmonary and Critical Care Fellowship Program
Division of Pulmonary & Critical Care and Sleep Medicine
Tufts Medical Center
Tufts University School of Medicine
Boston, Massachusetts

DOMINICK TAMMARO, M.D.
Warren Alpert Medical School
Brown University
Rhode Island Hospital
Providence, Rhode Island

AFNAN R. TARIQ, M.D., J.D.
Fellow, Cardiovascular Disease
Department of Cardiology
University of California Irvine Medical Center
Irvine, California

TAHIR TELLIOGLU, M.D.
Assistant Professor of Psychiatry and Human Behavior
Alpert Medical School
Brown University;
Director
Substance Abuse Division
Department of Psychiatry
Rhode Island Hospital
Providence, Rhode Island

JIGISHA P. THAKKAR, M.D.
Resident Physician, Neurology
Department of Neurology
University of Kentucky
Lexington, Kentucky

ANTHONY G. THOMAS, M.D.
Clinical Assistant Professor of Medicine
Warren Alpert Medical School
Brown University
Memorial Hospital of Rhode Island
Providence, Rhode Island

ERIN TIBBETTS, Pharm.D. Candidate
University of Rhode Island College of Pharmacy, Class of 2016
Providence, Rhode Island

ALEXANDRA MEYER TIEN, M.D.
Clinical Assistant Professor of Family Medicine
Warren Alpert Medical School
Brown University
Providence, Rhode Island

DAVID ROBBINS TIEN, M.D.
Clinical Associate Professor of Surgery (Ophthalmology)
Warren Alpert Medical School
Brown University
Providence, Rhode Island

IRIS L. TONG, M.D.
Assistant Professor
Department of Medicine
Alpert Medical School
Brown University;
Director
Women's Primary Care
Women's Medicine Collaborative
Providence, Rhode Island

STEVEN P. TREON, M.D., Ph.D.
Associate Professor, Medicine
Harvard Medical School;
Director
Bing Center for Waldenstrom's Macroglobulinemia
Adult Oncology
Dana-Farber Cancer Institute
Boston, Massachusetts

MARGARET TRYFOROS, M.D.
Assistant Professor of Family Medicine (Clinical)
Family Medicine
Warren Alpert Medical School
Brown University
Providence, Rhode Island;
Clinical Team Leader
Family Medicine
Memorial Hospital of Rhode Island
Pawtucket, Rhode Island

HISASHI TSUKADA, M.D., Ph.D.
Instructor of Surgery
Surgery
Harvard Medical School;
Attending Surgeon
Thoracic Surgery
Brigham and Women's Hospital
Boston, Massachusetts

JOSEPH R. TUCCI, M.D.
Professor of Medicine
Medicine
Boston University School of Medicine
Boston, Massachusetts;
Adjunct Professor of Medicine
Medicine
Brown University School of Medicine;
Director, Division of Endocrinology
Director, Bone & Mineral Unit
Medicine
Roger Williams Medical Center
Providence, Rhode Island

MELISSA TUKEY, M.D., M.S.
Warren Alpert Medical School
Brown University
Rhode Island Hospital
The Miriam Hospital
Providence, Rhode Island

SEAN H. UITERWYK, M.D.
Clinical Assistant Professor of Community and Family Medicine
Geisel School of Medicine at Dartmouth
Hanover, New Hampshire;
White River Family Practice
White River Junction, Vermont

NICOLE J. ULLRICH, M.D., Ph.D.
Associate Professor of Neurology
Harvard Medical School;
Director of Neurologic Neuro-oncology
Boston Children's Hospital
Boston, Massachusetts

KAUSIK UMANATH, M.D., M.S.
Assistant Professor
Internal Medicine
Wayne State University;
Section Head, Clinical Trials Research
Nephrology and Hypertension
Henry Ford Hospital
Detroit, Michigan

EMILY VAN KIRK, M.D.
Third Year Internal Medicine Resident
Department of Medicine
Roger Williams Medical Center
Providence, Rhode Island

JENNIFER E. VAUGHAN, M.D.
Fellow
Neurology and Rehabilitation Medicine
University of Cincinnati College of Medicine
University of Cincinnati Medical Center
Cincinnati, Ohio

POOJA VERMA, M.D.
Roger Williams Medical Center
Providence, Rhode Island

JORGE A. VILLAFUERTE, M.D.
Clinical Instructor in Orthopedic Surgery
Harvard Medical School;
Assistant Professor in Orthopedic Surgery
Boston University Medical School;
Associate Chief of Orthopedic Surgery
VA Boston HealthCare System
Boston, Massachusetts

DOUGLAS VON HERZEN, M.D.
Roger Williams Medical Center
Providence, Rhode Island
Boston University
Boston, Massachusetts

MARC PAUL WAASE, M.D., Ph.D.
Cardiology Fellow
Cardiology
Columbia University
New York Presbyterian
New York, New York

CHARLES WANG, M.D.
Gastroenterology Fellow
Gastroenterology
Brown University
Providence, Rhode Island;
Attending Physician
Gastroenterology
Kaiser Permanente - Roseville
Roseville, California

ADAM J. WEINBERG, M.D.
Resident
Internal Medicine
Boston University Medical Center
Boston, Massachusetts

MARY-BETH WELESKO, M.S., A.P.R.N.-B.C., W.C.C.
Teaching Associate
Geriatrics and Palliative Medicine
Warren Alpert Medical School
Brown University
Rhode Island Hospital
Providence, Rhode Island

DENNIS M. WEPPNER, M.D.
Associate Professor of Clinical Gynecology/Obstetrics
State University of New York at Buffalo;
Clinical Chief
Department of Gynecology/Obstetrics
Millard Fillmore Hospital
Buffalo, New York

HILARY B. WHITLATCH, M.D.
Assistant Professor of Medicine
Albert Medical School
Brown University;
Chief of Endocrinology Section
Providence VA Medical Center;
Staff Endocriniologist
Rhode Island Hospital
Providence, Rhode Island

MATTHEW P. WICKLUND, M.D.
Professor
Department of Neurology
Penn State College of Medicine;
Vice-Chair for Education
Department of Neurology
Milton S. Hershey Medical Center
Hershey, Pennsylvania

JEFFREY P. WINCZE, Ph.D.
Department of Pyschiatry
Rhode Island Hospital;
Clinical Assistant Professor
Department of Psychiatry and Human Behavior
Warren Alpert Medical School
Brown University
Providence, Rhode Island

JOHN P. WINCZE, Ph.D.
Clinical Professor
Department of Psychiatry and Human Behavior
The Warren Alpert Medical School
Brown University;
Associate Director
The Men's Health Center
The Miriam Hospital
Providence, Rhode Island

JORDAN WOLFE, M.D.
Resident Physician
Department of Emergency Medicine
Brown University
Lifespan Hospital
Providence, Rhode Isand

MARLENE FISHMAN WOLPERT, M.P.H., C.I.C.
Director
Infection Prevention and Control
St. Joseph Health Services of Rhode Island
North Providence, Rhode Island

TZU-CHING (TEDDY) WU, M.D., M.P.H.
Assistant Professor of Neurology
University of Texas Medical School at Houston
Director of Telemedicine
Mischer Neuroscience Institute
Houston, Texas

JOHN V. WYLIE, M.D., F.A.C.C.
Director, Cardiac Electrophysiology
Steward Health Care System;
Assistant Professor of Medicine
Tufts University School of Medicine
Boston, Massachusetts

NICOLE B. YANG, M.D.
Memorial Hospital of Rhode Island
Warren Alpert Medical School
Brown University
Providence, Rhode Island

JERRY YEE, M.D.
Division Head
Nephrology and Hypertension
Henry Ford Hospital;
Chief Medical Director
Greenfield Health Systems
Detroit, Michigan

LENAR YESSAYAN, M.D., M.S.
Senior Staff Physician
Associate Program Director of Critical Care Medicine
Nephrology and Hypertension, Pulmonary and Critical
   Care Medicine
Henry Ford Hospital
Detroit, Michigan

AGUSTIN G. YIP, M.D., Ph.D.
Clinical Assistant Professor
Butler Hospital
Department of Psychiatry and Human Behavior
Brown University
Providence, Rhode Island

JOHN Q. YOUNG, M.D., M.P.P.
Associate Professor and Vice Chair
Department of Psychiatry
Hofstra North Shore-LIJ School of Medicine
Hempstead, New York

KATHERINE M. YU, M.D.
Cardiology Fellow
Department of Cardiology
University of California, Irvine
University of California, Irvine Medical Center
Orange, California

CANDICE YUVIENCO, M.D.
Director
Division of Rheumatology
University of California San Francisco – Fresno;
Community Regional Medical Center;
Rheumatology, Internal Medicine
UCSF Fresno
Fresno, California

FARIHA ZAHEER, M.D.
Assistant Professor of Neurology
Baylor College of Medicine
Michael. E. DeBakey VA Medical Center
Houston, Texas

TALIA ZENLEA, M.D.
Assistant Professor
Department of Medicine
University of Toronto;
Division of Gastroenterology
Women's College Hospital
Toronto, Ontario, Canada

BERNARD ZIMMERMANN, M.D.
Associate Professor of Medicine
Boston University School of Medicine
Boston, Massachusetts;
Director, Division of Rheumatology
Roger Williams Medical Center
Providence, Rhode Island

MARK ZIMMERMAN, M.D.
Director
Outpatient Psychiatry
Partial Hospital Program
Rhode Island Hospital
The Miriam Hospital;
Professor of Psychiatry and Human Behavior
Alpert Medical School
Brown University
Providence, Rhode Island

RYAN W. ZUZEK, M.D.
Fellow
Clinical Cardiology
Division of Cardiology
Alpert Medical School
Brown University
Providence, Rhode Island

To my sons, Dr. Vito F. Ferri and Dr. Christopher A. Ferri, and my daughter-in-law, Dr. Heather A. Ferri, for their help and constant support, and to my wife, Christina, for her patience during manuscript preparation. A special thanks to all the readers who have personally commented on the merits of this book and through their suggestions have helped make this product a best-seller in the medical field.

Fred F. Ferri, M.D.
Clinical Professor
Alpert Medical School
Brown University
Providence, Rhode Island

Preface

This book is intended to be a clear and concise reference for physicians and allied health professionals. Its user-friendly format was designed to provide a fast and efficient way to identify important clinical information and to offer practical guidance in patient management. The book is divided into five sections and an appendix, each with emphasis on clinical information.

The tremendous success of the previous editions and the enthusiastic comments from numerous colleagues have brought about several positive changes. Each section has been significantly expanded from prior editions, bringing the total number of medical topics covered in this book to more than 1000. Nearly 400 new illustrations and tables have been added to the edition to enhance recollection of clinically important facts. The expedited claims submission and reimbursement ICD-10CM codes have been added to all the topics.

Section I describes in detail more than 800 medical disorders. Nineteen new topics have been added to the 2017 edition. Each medical topic in this section is arranged alphabetically, and the material in each topic is presented in outline format for ease of retrieval. Topics with an accompanying algorithm in Section III are identified with an algorithm symbol (ALG). Similarly, if topics also have a Patient Teaching Guide (PTG) available online, this has been noted. Throughout the text, key quick-access information is consistently highlighted, clinical photographs are used to further illustrate selected medical conditions, and relevant ICD-10CM codes are listed. Most references focus on current peer-reviewed journal articles rather than outdated textbooks and old review articles. Evidence-based medicine data have been added to relevant topics.

Topics in Section I use the following structured approach:

1. Basic Information (Definition, Synonyms, ICD-10CM Codes, Epidemiology & Demographics, Physical Findings & Clinical Presentation, Etiology)
2. Diagnosis (Differential Diagnosis, Workup, Laboratory Tests, Imaging Studies)
3. Treatment (Nonpharmacologic Therapy, Acute General Rx, Chronic Rx, Disposition, Referral)
4. Pearls & Considerations (Comments, Suggested Readings)
5. Evidence-Based Data and References

Section II includes the differential diagnosis, etiology, and classification of signs and symptoms. This section has been significantly expanded for the 2017 edition with the addition of 50 new topics. It is a practical section that allows the user investigating a physical complaint or abnormal laboratory value to follow a "workup" leading to a diagnosis. The physician can then easily look up the presumptive diagnosis in Section I for the information specific to that illness.

Section III includes clinical algorithms to guide and expedite the patient's workup and therapy. Nineteen new algorithms have been added for the 2017 edition. Many physicians describe this section as particularly valuable in today's managed-care environment.

Section IV includes normal laboratory values and interpretation of results of commonly ordered laboratory tests. Several new illustrations and tables have been added to this section. By providing interpretation of abnormal results, this section facilitates the diagnosis of medical disorders and further adds to the comprehensive, "one-stop" nature of our text.

Section V focuses on preventive medicine. Information in this section includes recommendations for the periodic health examination, screening for major diseases and disorders, patient counseling, and immunization and chemoprophylaxis recommendations.

The **Appendix** has been divided into six major sections. Section I contains extensive information on complementary and alternative medicine (CAM). With the material in this appendix, we hope to lessen the current scarcity of exposure of allopathic and osteopathic physicians to the diversity of CAM therapies. Appendix II focuses on nutrition, with an emphasis on dietary supplements, vitamins, and minerals. Appendix III deals with diagnosis and treatment of acute poisoning. Appendix IV is a guide on impairment and disability evaluation. Appendix V, available online, contains an extensive section on primary care procedures. Appendix VI contains several patient teaching guides not linked to Section I topics.

As clinicians, we all realize the importance of patient education and the need for clear communication with our patients. Toward that end, practical patient instruction sheets, organized alphabetically and covering the majority of the topics in this book, are available online and can be easily customized and printed from any computer. They represent a valuable addition to patient care and are useful for improving physician-patient communication, patient satisfaction, and quality of care.

I believe that we have produced a state-of-the-art information system with significant differences from existing texts. It contains five sections and patient education guides that could be sold separately based on their content, yet are available under a single cover, offering the reader a tremendous value. I hope that the *Clinical Advisor*'s user-friendly approach, numerous unique features, and yearly updates will make this book a valuable medical reference, not only to primary care physicians but also to physicians in other specialties, medical students, and allied health professionals.

Fred F. Ferri, M.D., F.A.C.P.

Note: Comments from readers are always appreciated and can be forwarded directly to Dr. Ferri at fred_ferri@brown.edu.

EVALUATION OF EVIDENCE

Ferri's Clinical Advisor evaluates all evidence based on a rating system published by the American Academy of Family Physicians. In order to indicate the strength of the supporting evidence, each summary statement is accorded one of three levels:

LEVEL A

- Systematic reviews of randomized controlled trials, including meta-analyses
- Good-quality randomized controlled trials

LEVEL B

- Good-quality nonrandomized clinical trials
- Systematic reviews not in Level A
- Lower-quality randomized controlled trials not in Level A
- Other types of study: case-control studies, clinical cohort studies, cross-sectional studies, retrospective studies, and uncontrolled studies

LEVEL C

- Evidence-based consensus statements and expert guidelines

SOURCES OF EVIDENCE

Evidence is summarized principally from three critically evaluated, very highly regarded sources:

- **Cochrane Systematic Reviews** are respected throughout the world as one of the most rigorous searches of medical journals for randomized controlled trials. They provide highly structured systematic reviews, with evidence included or excluded on the basis of explicit quality-related criteria, and they often use meta-analyses to increase the power of the findings of numerous studies.
- *Clinical Evidence* is produced by the BMJ Publishing Group. It provides synopses of the best currently available evidence on the treatment and prevention of many clinical conditions, based on searches and appraisals of the available literature.
- **The National Guideline Clearinghouse™** is a comprehensive database of evidence-based clinical practice guidelines and related documents produced by the Agency for Healthcare Research and Quality in partnership with the American Medical Association and the American Association of Health Plans.

In addition, where evidence exists that has not yet been critically reviewed in one of the three sites above, the evidence is summarized briefly, categorized, and fully referenced. Guidelines are also sourced from government and professional bodies.

Mouse icon – Indicates content with additional references, figures, or tables available at www.expertconsult.com

 PTG icon – indicates an accompanying Patient Teaching Guide available at www.expertconsult.com There are also many additional PTGs online not linked to a topic in Section I.

(ALG) ALG icon – indicates a topic with an accompanying Algorithm in Section III or additional Algorithms available at www.expertconsult.com

(EBM) EBM icon – indicates evidence-based medicine data added to relevant topics available at www.expertconsult.com

Contents

Detailed Contents

SECTION I Diseases and Disorders

Additional Topics Available at www.expertconsult.com

SECTION II Differential Diagnosis

SECTION III Clinical Algorithms

Additional Algorithms Available at www.expertconsult.com

SECTION IV Laboratory Tests and Interpretation of Results

SECTION V Clinical Practice Guidelines

APPENDIX I Complementary and Alternative Medicine

Diseases and Disorders

BASIC INFORMATION

DEFINITION

An abdominal aortic aneurysm (AAA) is a focal full-thickness dilation of the abdominal aortic artery to at least 1.5 times the diameter measured at the level of the renal arteries, or exceeding the normal diameter of the abdominal aorta by 50%. The normal diameter at the renal arteries is 2 cm (range 1.4-3.0 cm), and a diameter 3 cm or larger is generally considered aneurysmal.

ICD-10CM CODES
I71.4 Abdominal aortic aneurysm, without rupture
I71.3 Abdominal aortic aneurysm, ruptured

EPIDEMIOLOGY & DEMOGRAPHICS

- Approximately 15,000 deaths/year in the United States are attributed to AAA.
- AAA is predominantly a disease of older adults, affecting men more than women (4:1).
- The prevalence rate ranges from 4% to 9% in men older than age 60.
- Clinically important AAAs ≥4 cm are present in 1% of men between age 55 and 64; and the prevalence rate increases by 2% to 4% per decade thereafter.
- The peak incidence is among men approximately 70 years old.
- The frequency is much higher in smokers than in nonsmokers (8:1); and the risk decreases with smoking cessation.
- Risk factors for AAA are similar to other atherosclerotic cardiovascular diseases. They include age, smoking, male gender, family history, hypertension, hyperlipidemia, peripheral vascular disease, and aneurysm of other large vessels.
- AAA is two to four times more common in first-degree male relatives of known AAA patients.
- Rupture of the AAA occurs in 1% to 3% of men age 65 or older.
  1. Rupture is the 10th leading cause of death in men older than age 55.
  2. Mortality from rupture is 70% to 95%.
  3. Risk factors for rupture include cardiac or renal transplants, severe obstructive lung disease, uncontrolled blood pressure, female sex, and ongoing tobacco use.
- A recent decline in incidence and prevalence of AAA and related mortality has been attributed to reductions in tobacco use.

ETIOLOGY

- Exact etiology is unknown and is likely multifactorial.
  1) Degenerative:
     a. The most common association is atherosclerosis. It is uncertain if atherosclerosis causes or results from AAAs.
     b. Tobacco use: >90% of people who develop an AAA have smoked at some point in their lives.
  2) Inherited: Familial clusters are common. High familial prevalence rate is notable in male individuals. The nature of the genetic disorder is unclear but may be linked to alpha-1-antitrypsin deficiency or X-linked mutation. Connective tissue disorders, such as Marfan's syndrome and Ehlers-Danlos syndrome, have also been strongly associated with AAA.
  3) Inflammatory: AAA is a progressive inflammatory disease of the artery walls. Activated B lymphocytes promote AAA by producing immunoglobulins, cytokines, and matrix metalloproteinases (MMPs), resulting in the activation of macrophages, mast cells (MCs), and complement pathways that lead to the degradation of collagen and matrix proteins and to aortic wall remodeling.
  4) Infection, mycotic: syphilis, *Salmonella*.

NATURAL HISTORY

- The risk of aneurysmal rupture is largely influenced by aneurysm size, rate of expansion, and sex. Other factors associated with increased risk for rupture include continued smoking, uncontrolled hypertension, and increased wall stress.
- AAAs tend to develop in the infrarenal aorta.
- Higher tension in the abdominal aorta (together with histopathologic changes such as accumulation of foam cells, cholesterol crystals, and matrix metalloproteinases) renders the abdominal aortic wall more susceptible to dilation and subsequent rupture.
- The 5-year rupture rate of asymptomatic AAAs is 25% to 40% for aneurysms >5.0 cm in diameter, 1% to 7% for AAAs 4.0 to 5.0 cm, and nearly 0% for AAAs <4.0 cm. The rate of rupture of aneurysms that were 4.0 to 5.5 cm in diameter is four times greater in women compared with men.
- Mortality rate after rupture can be as high as 90% because most patients do not reach the hospital in time for surgical repair. Of those who reach the hospital, the mortality rate is still 50%, compared with the 1% to 4% mortality rate for elective repair of a nonruptured AAA. The U.S. Preventive Services Task Force (USPSTF) also concludes that the current evidence is insufficient to assess the balance of benefits and harms of screening for AAA in women aged 65 to 75 who ever smoked and recommends against routine screening in women who never smoked (most recent update in June 2014).

SCREENING AND MONITORING

- The USPSTF recommends one-time screening for AAA by ultrasonography in men ages 65 to 75 who have a history of smoking, and in those 60 years of age or older with a history of AAA in a parent or sibling. These populations have been shown to have a higher prevalence of AAA, and selectively screening this group has been shown to decrease AAA-specific mortality.
- Monitoring by ultrasound or CT scan should be performed every 6 to 12 months for patients with AAAs measuring 4.0 to 5.4 cm in diameter and by ultrasound every 2 years for those with AAAs measuring <4 cm.

PHYSICAL FINDINGS & CLINICAL PRESENTATION

- Most aneurysms are asymptomatic and incidentally discovered on imaging studies; however, symptomatic aneurysms are at an increased risk for rupture.
- Physical examination has a sensitivity of 76% for detecting AAAs >5 cm and only 29% for AAAs 3.0-3.9 cm.
- Symptomatic patients may present with abdominal, back, flank, or groin pain.
- A pulsatile epigastric mass that may or may not be tender may be present.
- Abdominal pain radiating to the back, flank, and groin.
- Abdominal bruits can be present in case of renal or visceral arterial stenosis.
- Common iliac arteries can be aneurysmal and palpable in the lower abdominal quadrants. In addition, prominent femoral and popliteal pulses warrant an abdominal ultrasound and lower extremity ultrasound.
- Early satiety, nausea, and vomiting may be caused by compression of adjacent bowel.
- Venous thrombosis or insufficiency may occur from iliocaval venous compression.
- Thromboembolization can cause lower extremity pain and discoloration.
- Ureteral obstruction and hydronephrosis can cause flank and groin pain and lead to obstructive renal failure.
- Rupture classically presents as a triad of abdominal or back pain, hypotension, and a pulsatile abdominal mass in 50% of patients.
- Acute blood loss may lead to myocardial infarction; arteriovenous fistulas may present as heart failure; aortoenteric fistulas may present as hematemesis or melena associated with abdominal and back pain.

Dx DIAGNOSIS

DIFFERENTIAL DIAGNOSIS

Almost 75% of patients with AAA are asymptomatic, and the condition is discovered on routine examination or serendipitously when ordering studies for other symptoms. Diagnosis of AAA should be considered in the differential of the following symptoms: abdominal pain, back pain, and/or pulsatile abdominal mass.

LABORATORY TESTS

Not routinely indicated. For suspected infected or inflammatory aneurysms, WBC, ESR/CRP, and blood cultures can be considered. An elevated D-dimer may indicate a thrombus within the aneurysm. Fig 1A-1 describes an algorithm for the diagnosis and treatment of abdominal aortic aneurysms.

IMAGING STUDIES

- Abdominal ultrasound (Fig. 1A-2) has nearly 100% sensitivity and specificity in identifying an aneurysm and estimating the size to

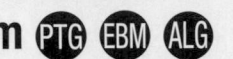
Symptoms of AAA: pulsatile mass; abdominal pain radiating to back, flank, groin; peripheral emboli; flank and/or groin pain; melena thought to be due to aortoenteric fistula; syncope; flank mass or discoloration; lower-extremity paralysis

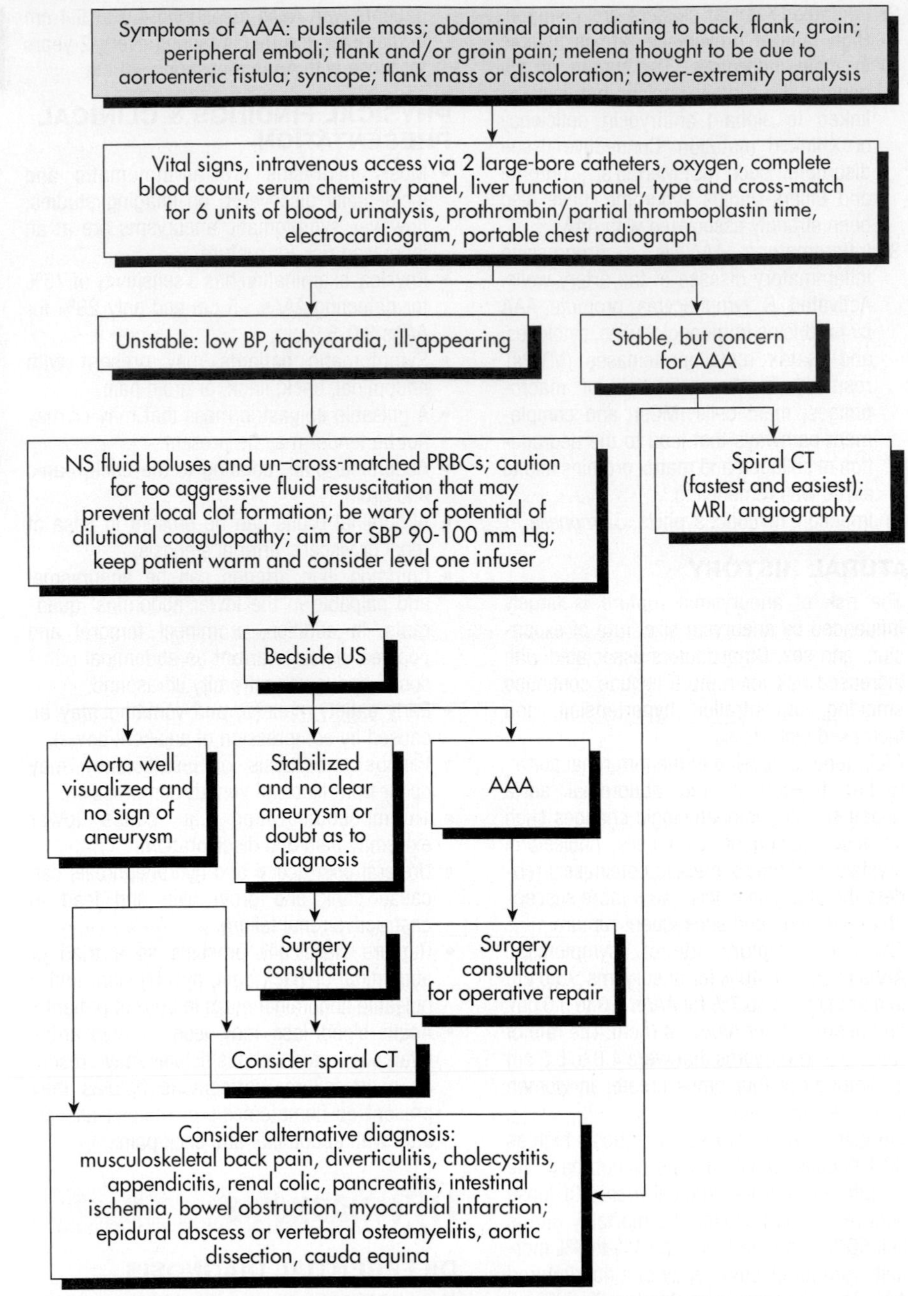

↓

Vital signs, intravenous access via 2 large-bore catheters, oxygen, complete blood count, serum chemistry panel, liver function panel, type and cross-match for 6 units of blood, urinalysis, prothrombin/partial thromboplastin time, electrocardiogram, portable chest radiograph

Unstable: low BP, tachycardia, ill-appearing

Stable, but concern for AAA

NS fluid boluses and un–cross-matched PRBCs; caution for too aggressive fluid resuscitation that may prevent local clot formation; be wary of potential of dilutional coagulopathy; aim for SBP 90-100 mm Hg; keep patient warm and consider level one infuser

Spiral CT (fastest and easiest); MRI, angiography

Bedside US

Aorta well visualized and no sign of aneurysm

Stabilized and no clear aneurysm or doubt as to diagnosis

AAA

Surgery consultation

Surgery consultation for operative repair

Consider spiral CT

Consider alternative diagnosis: musculoskeletal back pain, diverticulitis, cholecystitis, appendicitis, renal colic, pancreatitis, intestinal ischemia, bowel obstruction, myocardial infarction; epidural abscess or vertebral osteomyelitis, aortic dissection, cauda equina

FIGURE 1A-1 Algorithm for the diagnosis and treatment of abdominal aortic aneurysms (AAAs). *BP*, Blood pressure; *CT*, computed tomography; *MRI*, magnetic resonance imaging; *NS*, normal saline; *PRBCs*, packed red blood cells; *SBP*, systolic blood pressure; *US*, ultrasonography. (From Adams JG et al: *Emergency medicine, clinical essentials*, ed 2, Philadelphia, 2013, Elsevier.)

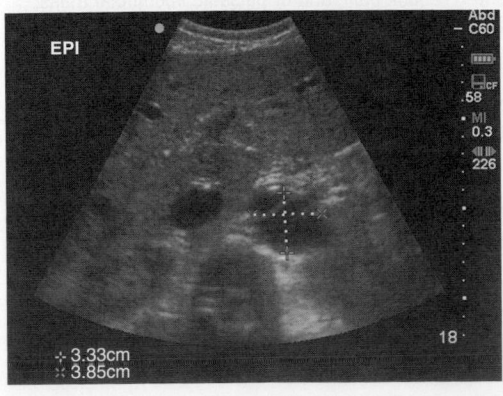

FIGURE 1A-2 Transverse image of an abdominal aortic aneurysm. Note the measurements of 3.35 × 3.85 cm. The inferior vena cava is seen to the patient's right of the aorta, and the vertebral body is seen below the two vessels. Note also that there appears to be an echogenic flap within the aorta, possibly representing an aortic dissection. (From Adams JG et al: *Emergency medicine, clinical essentials*, ed 2, Philadelphia, 2013, Elsevier.)

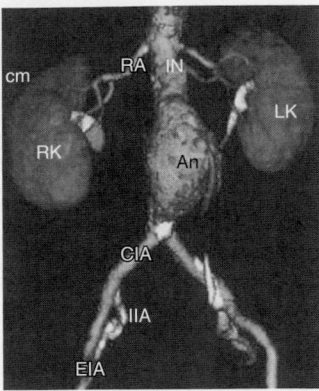

FIGURE 1A-3 Three-dimensional CT image illustrates the presence of an infrarenal abdominal aortic aneurysm. *An*, Aneurysm; *CIA*, common iliac artery; *EIA*, external iliac artery; *IIA*, internal iliac artery; *IN*, infrarenal neck; *LK*, left kidney; *RA*, renal artery; *RK*, right kidney. (From Townsend CM et al [eds]: *Sabiston textbook of surgery*, ed 17, Philadelphia, 2004, Saunders.)

within 0.3 to 0.4 cm. It is not accurate in estimating the extension to the renal arteries or the iliac arteries.

- Computed tomography (CT) (Fig. 1A-3) scan is recommended for preoperative aneurysm imaging and estimates the size of the AAA to within 0.3 mm. There are no false-negative results, and the scan can localize the extent to renal vessels with more precision than ultrasound. CT can also detect the integrity of the wall (Fig. 1A-4) and exclude rupture.
- Magnetic resonance angiography (MRA) may also be used and is at least as accurate as CT.
- Plain radiographs may show the outline of an aneurysm in calcified aortas. This is an insensitive test for diagnosing AAA.
- Diagnostic aortography has essentially been replaced by other noninvasive imaging modalities such as CT or MR angiography. Intraoperative angiography is still used for determining treatment options and post-procedure efficacy.
- Endovascular aneurysm repair (EVAR) needs a close and lifelong imaging surveillance for a timely detection of possible complications, including endoleaks, graft migration, fractures, and enlargement of aneurysm sac size with eventual rupture. Contrast-enhanced computed tomography (CTA) is actually considered the gold standard in EVAR follow-up, but it is accompanied with radiation burden and renal injury because of the use of contrast media. In the past 2 decades, several studies have shown the role of contrast-enhanced ultrasonography (CEUS) in post-EVAR surveillance, with very good diagnostic performance, absence of renal impairment, and no radiation, accompanied by low costs, in comparison with CTA. In numerous prospective studies and meta-analyses, the detection and characterization of endoleaks with CEUS is comparable to that of CTA imaging.

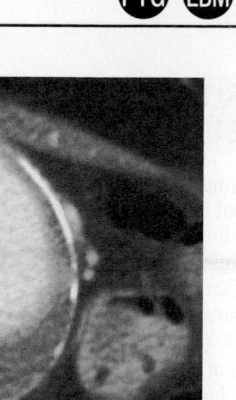

FIGURE 1A-4 Aneurysm of the abdominal aorta. A large aortic aneurysm is evident. The aorta exceeds 5 cm in diameter. A large amount of thrombus (T) partially surrounds the contrast-enhanced patent lumen (L). Note the atherosclerotic calcification (*arrowhead*) in the wall of the aneurysm.

Rx TREATMENT

NONPHARMACOLOGIC THERAPY

- Despite lack of data substantiating reduction in expansion rate through treatment of cardiac risk factors, nonpharmacologic treatment continues to focus on risk factor modification (most importantly smoking cessation, diet, and exercise).
- Serial studies have shown that expansion rates are faster in current smokers than in former smokers. Patients with known AAA or a family history of aneurysms should be advised to stop smoking and be offered smoking cessation interventions.
- Definitive treatment depends on the size of the aneurysm (see "Chronic Rx").

ACUTE GENERAL Rx

- Acute symptomatic or ruptured AAA can be treated with open surgical or endovascular aneurysm repair (EVAR). The choice is determined by anatomic considerations, operative risks, and availability of regular patient follow-up for EVAR.
- Emergent open repair has been the traditional method of treatment. However, multiple trials including Impact of Managed Pharmaceutical care on Resource utilization and Outcomes in Veterans affairs medical centers (IMPROVE) study have shown lower mortality and shorter hospital stay with EVAR. More centers are increasingly using endovascular repair for patients who fit certain anatomic and physiologic criteria.
- The major limitations for EVAR include anatomical issues such as tortuosity or small caliber iliac arteries and inability to follow up of patients to exclude late failure of stents grafts and development of endoleaks.

CHRONIC Rx

- Blood pressure and fasting lipids should be monitored and controlled as recommended for patients with atherosclerotic disease. Statins are associated with decreased mortality after successful AAA repair, and are recommended for those with known AAA to reduce the progression of atherosclerosis.
- The most commonly used predictor of rupture is the maximum diameter of the AAA.
- Monitoring by ultrasound or CT scan should be performed every 6 to 12 months for patients with AAAs measuring 4.0 to 5.4 cm in diameter and by ultrasound every 2 years for those with AAAs measuring <4 cm.
- Long-term beta-blocker therapy has slowed the rate of aortic dilation and decreased the incidence of aortic complications in patients with Marfan's syndrome. Several studies have also suggested that beta-blocker therapy may reduce the rate of expansion and risk of rupture; however, conclusive evidence is lacking. In a Cochrane Database Systematic Review, propranolol was poorly tolerated in all beta-blocker trials and had only minimal, nonsignificant protective benefit.
- Antibiotics such as doxycycline and roxithromycin have shown to limit the expansion of small AAAs.
- Surgical repair to eliminate the risk for rupture should be performed for patients with infrarenal or juxtarenal AAA of approximately 5.5 cm or larger in diameter. All patients who are symptomatic should undergo repair, regardless of size.
- There is no clear advantage to early repair (open or endovascular) for small AAAs (less than 5.5 cm).
- Percutaneous, endovascular, stent-anchored grafts placed with the patient under local anesthesia have provided an alternative approach (Fig. 1A-5) for patients with favorable anatomy. In patients who have undergone endovascular repair, long-term surveillance is required to assess for an endoleak, stent migration, change in aneurysm size, and need for re-intervention.

- Fenestrated endovascular repair is an alternative to open repair in the management of juxtarenal aortic aneurysms (JRAs) and short-neck abdominal aortic aneurysms. Contemporary literature shows that it is a safe and efficacious treatment, particularly for those deemed surgically high risk. Growing experience and innovation of stent grafts are essential for the advancement of fenestrated grafting.[0]
- Randomized trials have shown that endovascular repair of AAA is associated with a significantly lower operative mortality than open surgical repair but it has increased rates of graft-related complications and reintervention, and is more costly. There are no differences between endovascular repair and open surgical repair in total mortality or aneurysm-related mortality in the long term.
- Compared with open aneurysm repair, EVAR is associated with better health-related quality of life up to 12 months postoperatively.
- Most recent meta-analysis concludes that EVAR has lower rates of 30-day mortality, 30-day MI, and length of hospital stay in both elective and ruptured AAA repair.
- Based on current data, less than 1% of endovascular repairs require open conversion and approximately half of all early endoleaks resolve spontaneously within a period of 30 days.
- Open repair still represents a valuable solution for many patients with failed EVAR with relatively low mortality rates when performed electively.
- In high-risk patients undergoing AAA repair, specifically those with coronary artery disease or those with more than one clinical risk factor based on the American Heart Association (AHA) guidelines, preoperative administration of beta-blockers titrated to a goal heart rate of 60 have been shown to decrease incidence of death from cardiac causes or nonfatal myocardial infarctions.
- Patients with chronic obstructive pulmonary disease (COPD) are at higher risk for major clinical complications, particularly if the COPD is suboptimally managed or if it is present in conjunction with cardiac or renal disease. Smoking cessation for 2 months before surgery has also been shown to decrease pulmonary morbidity.
- Renal dysfunction is a strong predictor of mortality, showing up to as high as 41% mortality in those with impaired renal function compared with 6% in those without renal dysfunction.

REFERRAL

- Vascular surgical referral should be made in asymptomatic patients with AAAs that are approximately 4.5 cm.
- In patients with an expansion rate of 0.6-0.8 cm/year, it is reasonable to offer repair, although small studies have shown that using expansion as a criterion for surgical referral is of unclear benefit.
- It is important to optimize any comorbid conditions before surgical referral.

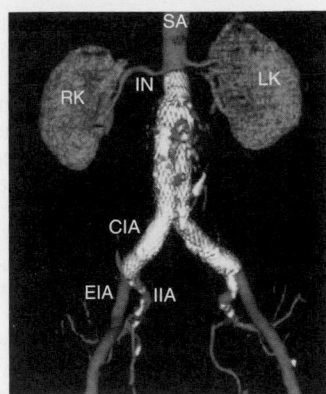

FIGURE 1A-5 Endovascular abdominal aortic aneurysm repair involves aneurysm exclusion with an endoluminal aortic stent-graft introduced remotely, usually through the femoral artery. An endovascular graft extends from the infrarenal aorta to both common iliac arteries, preserving the flow to the internal iliac arteries. *CIA,* Common iliac artery; *IIA,* internal iliac artery; *IN,* infrarenal aortic neck; *LK,* left kidney; *RK,* right kidney; *SA,* suprarenal aorta. (From Townsend CM et al [eds]: *Sabiston textbook of surgery,* ed 17, Philadelphia, 2004, Saunders.)

PEARLS & CONSIDERATIONS

- Repairing asymptomatic AAAs smaller than 5.5 cm has not been shown to improve survival because the risk of rupture is lower than the risk of surgery.
- The results from multiple trials to date demonstrate no advantage to immediate repair for small AAA (4.0-5.5 cm), regardless of whether open or endovascular repair is used and, at least for open repair, regardless of patient age and AAA diameter. Thus, neither immediate open nor immediate endovascular repair of small AAAs is supported by the currently available evidence.
- Five-year survival remains poor after elective AAA repair despite advances in short-term outcomes and is associated with AAA diameter and patient age at the time of surgery. Research in this field should attempt to improve the life expectancy of patients with repaired AAA and to optimize patient selection[0]

COMMENTS

- Most AAAs are infrarenal.
- Surgical risk is increased in patients with coexisting coronary artery disease, pulmonary disease, or chronic renal failure. Evaluation for ischemia and aggressive perioperative hemodynamic monitoring help identify high-risk patients and decrease postoperative complications.
- It is estimated that AAA at <5 cm expand at a rate of 0.4 cm/year.

 ## EVIDENCE

Available at www.expertconsult.com

SUGGESTED READINGS

Available at www.expertconsult.com

RELATED CONTENT

Abdominal Aortic Aneurysm (AAA) (Patient Information)

AUTHORS: **MARYAM BALOUCH, M.D.,** and **PRANAV M. PATEL, M.D.**

Diseases
and Disorders

BASIC INFORMATION

DEFINITION

Abdominal compartment syndrome (ACS) is defined by the presence of organ dysfunction as a result of increased abdominal pressure or intraabdominal hypertension. The increased abdominal pressure reduces blood flow to internal organs, which can lead to multiple system failure and death if not promptly recognized and treated.

ICD-10CM CODES
M79.A3 Nontraumatic compartment
    syndrome of abdomen

EPIDEMIOLOGY & DEMOGRAPHICS

INCIDENCE: Very few studies have examined the incidence of ACS outside of trauma patients, among whom it ranges from 1% to 14%, depending on the population and type of trauma studied. The incidence is the highest among critically ill patients.

RISK FACTORS: The biggest risk factor for developing ACS is critical illness stemming from a wide array of medical and surgical conditions (Table 1A-1). In particular, any illness that requires a patient to undergo large volume intravenous fluid resuscitation can be associated with ACS; the third-spacing of fluid can lead to increased intraabdominal pressures secondary to tissue edema. Due to large volume fluid resuscitation, ACS is commonly seen in severe burns, trauma, post-surgical patients, and sepsis. Other conditions associated with ACS include intraabdominal and retroperitoneal pathologies such as significant bowel distention, liver transplantation, massive ascites, ruptured abdominal aortic aneurysm with resulting hemoperitoneum, pancreatitis, and abdominal surgery (Table 1A-2).

PHYSICAL FINDINGS & CLINICAL PRESENTATION

- The most striking physical exam finding is often massive abdominal distention.
- Difficulty maintaining respiratory support and decreased urine output are also typical hallmarks.
- Other common findings include those associated with poor perfusion states and hypotension such as skin mottling, cool extremities, and obtundation. Patients will often have abdominal tenderness, signs of volume overload such as edema and elevated jugular venous pressures and may present with acute respiratory decompensation.

ETIOLOGY

- ACS can impact nearly every organ system. High intraabdominal pressures are associated with increased intracranial pressures, which can precipitate cerebral ischemia. Elevated abdominal pressures can cause cardiac compression by decreasing ventricular compliance and contractility as well as impairing inferior vena cava venous return, leading to increased central venous and pulmonary pressures. Due to elevation of the diaphragms, patients will often have reduced tidal volumes and lower chest wall compliance, which can lead to atelectasis, pneumonia, hypoxemia, and hypercarbia. Mechanically ventilated patients will also require increased airway pressures that can lead to barotrauma. In addition, renal vein compression and renal artery vasoconstriction lead to decreased urine output. Reduced mesenteric blood flow can lead to intestinal ischemia and lactic acidosis.

 DIAGNOSIS

DIFFERENTIAL DIAGNOSIS

- Mesenteric Ischemia
- Sepsis

- Shock
- Acute kidney injury
- Adult respiratory distress syndrome

WORKUP

- Measurement of intraabdominal pressure is required to make a definitive diagnosis. Bladder pressure is the most common surrogate used to estimate intraabdominal pressures and is measured using a bladder catheter. The most accurate measurements can be obtained with the patient in supine position at end expiration in the absence of abdominal contractions. The threshold abdominal pressure often set for research purposes to define ACS is >20 mm Hg, but patients may have ACS with pressures of >10 mm Hg and above. Oliguria tends to develop at a pressure of 15 mm Hg, and anuria occurs around 30 mm Hg. Intraabdominal pressures can also be estimated using intragastric, intracolonic, and inferior vena cava approaches (Table 1A-3).

LABORATORY TEST(S)

- Laboratory testing is generally not helpful for the diagnosis of ACS. The presence of lactic acidosis would suggest bowel ischemia that would portend a poorer prognosis.

IMAGING STUDIES

- Imaging alone has no diagnostic value in ACS, but chest imaging can be helpful to evaluate for diaphragmatic elevation and evidence of pulmonary complications (atelectasis, volume overload, pneumonia, etc.). Abdominal CT imaging will sometimes show renal displacement, inferior vena cava compression, abdominal wall thickening, or bowel injury related to ischemia but should not be relied upon to make the diagnosis of ACS.

 TREATMENT

Supportive care and, when appropriate, surgical abdominal decompression are the mainstays of ACS treatment.

NONPHARMACOLOGIC THERAPY

- Supportive care, often with hemodynamic and ventilatory support, as well as techniques to improve abdominal wall compliance, are the foundations of ACS management.
- Severe burns to the abdomen leading to ACS will require surgical escharotomy to improve abdominal wall compliance.
- Patients with tense ascites leading to ACS will require large volume paracentesis to decrease intraabdominal pressures.
- Patients should be positioned supine if possible as any elevation of the head will increase abdominal pressures.
- Rectal and nasogastric decompression is required if ACS is due to massive bowel distention.
- Proper sedation and pain control can decrease intraabdominal pressures, and some patients

TABLE 1A-1 Causes of Intraabdominal Hypertension and Abdominal Compartment Syndrome

Increased Abdominal Contents	Decreased Abdominal Volume
Ascites	Reduction of large long-standing hernia
Hemoperitoneum	Direct closure of large, long-standing abdominal wall defect
Abdominal packs	
Peritonitis	
Retroperitoneal edema (pancreatitis)	Retroperitoneal edema (pancreatitis)
Large pelvic, retroperitoneal hematoma	Large pelvic, retroperitoneal hematoma
Intestinal obstruction	
Ileus	
Gastric distention (esophageal ventilation)	
Abdominal aortic aneurysm	
Severe constipation	
Large abdominal tumor (chronic)	
Morbid obesity (chronic)	
Pregnancy (chronic)	

From Vincent JL, et al. *Textbook of critical care,* ed 6, Philadelphia, 2011, Saunders.

TABLE 1A-2 Independent Predictors of Postinjury Primary and Secondary Abdominal Compartment Syndrome

	ED Model Independent Predictors	ICU Model Independent Predictors
Primary ACS	To OR <75 min	Temp ≤34°C
	Crystalloids ≥3 L	GAPco₂ ≥16
		Hb ≤8/dL
		BD ≥12 mEq/L
Secondary ACS	Crystalloids ≥3 L	GAPco₂ ≥16
	No urgent surgery	Crystalloids ≥7.5 L
	PRBC ≥3 units	UO ≤150 mL

From Vincent JL, et al. *Textbook of critical care,* ed 6, Philadelphia, 2011, Saunders.
ACS, Abdominal compartment syndrome; *BD,* arterial base deficit; *CI,* confidence interval; *ED,* emergency department; *GAPco₂,* carbon dioxide gap; *Hb,* hemoglobin concentration; *ICU,* intensive care unit; *OR,* operating room; *PRBC,* packed red blood cells; *Temp,* temperature; *UO,* urine output.

TABLE 1A-3 Classification of Abdominal Compartment Syndrome

Basis of Classification	Subcategories
Time frame	Acute
	Chronic
Relation to peritoneal cavity	Primary
	Secondary
Etiology	Trauma
	Burn
	Postoperative
	Pancreatitis
	Bowel obstruction
	Ileus
	Abdominal aortic aneurysm
	Oncologic
	Gynecologic

From Vincent JL, et al. *Textbook of critical care,* ed 6, Philadelphia, 2011, Saunders.

may require ventilatory support and chemical paralysis to maximize abdominal wall relaxation.
- Mechanical ventilation is often difficult due to the high pressures that need to be generated to overcome the increased intraabdominal pressures. Often a combination of low tidal volumes, permissive hypercapnia, chemical paralysis, and high PEEP are required to ensure adequate ventilatory support.

- Although there is little data to support its use, the administration of colloid may be superior to crystalloid if the patient requires further volume resuscitation. The administration of intravenous fluids will transiently increase renal blood flow, leading to increased urine output and improved organ perfusion and cardiac output. Pressors may also have a role to maintain perfusion pressures, but all of these measures are temporizing and supportive until definitive action through surgical decompression is performed.
- The threshold to perform surgical decompression for ACS has yet to be established; however, data suggest that early decompression prior to the development of ACS may lead to better outcomes. If appropriate, consensus dictates that surgical decompression should be performed on all patients with intraabdominal pressure >25 mm Hg; however, some surgeons are more aggressive and will consider decompression with pressures of 15-25 mm Hg in the right clinical setting. Surgical decompression by incising vertically through the linea alba can be performed at the bedside in emergent situations and most surgeons will then keep the abdomen open through the use of a temporary abdominal closure device that retains heat/fluid and prevents evisceration until the time is appropriate to attempt to close the abdomen again.

ACUTE GENERAL Rx
- There are no direct pharmacologic agents that treat ACS other than pressors, sedatives, pain medications, and paralytics required for supportive care as described above. Despite underlying volume overload, diuretics have no role in therapy. Definitive management is surgical decompression.

DISPOSITION
- Close inpatient monitoring, preferably in an intensive care setting, is indicated as mortality can be extremely high (>40%) with this condition.

REFERRAL
- Patients with ACS often require admission to an intensive care setting with surgical consultation in case decompression is required.

 **PEARLS & CONSIDERATIONS**

COMMENTS
- ACS is seen in critically ill medical and surgical patients, and its diagnosis requires both the presence of intraabdominal hypertension and end organ dysfunction.
- ACS is truly a systemic illness that can lead to multisystem organ failure and is therefore associated with a high mortality.
- Definitive diagnosis of ACS requires measurement of intraabdominal pressure, which is most frequently estimated using bladder pressure as a surrogate.
- Supportive care, including hemodynamic support with colloids and pressors and ventilatory support, is often required, but surgical decompression is the only definitive treatment.
- Surgical decompression is indicated for intraabdominal pressures >25 mm Hg; however, precise thresholds have not been established and earlier decompression may lead to better outcomes.

AUTHORS: **JASON FERREIRA, M.D.,** and **AMANDA PRESSMAN, M.D.**

SUGGESTED READINGS
Available at www.expertconsult.com

ℹ BASIC INFORMATION

DEFINITION

Abruptio placentae is the separation of placenta from the uterine wall before delivery of the fetus. The condition occurs in approximately 1% of pregnancies. There are three classes of abruption based on maternal and fetal status, including an assessment of uterine contractions, quantity of bleeding, fetal heart rate monitoring, and abnormal coagulation studies (fibrinogen, prothrombin time, partial thromboplastin time).

- Grade I: mild vaginal bleeding, uterine irritability, stable vital signs, reassuring fetal heart rate, normal coagulation profile (fibrinogen 450 mg/dl). Approximately half of abruptions are grade I.
- Grade II: moderate vaginal bleeding, hypertonic uterine contractions, orthostatic blood pressure measurements, unfavorable fetal status, fibrinogen 150 to 250 mg. Approximately a quarter of abruptions are grade II.
- Grade III: severe bleeding (may be concealed), hypertonic uterine contractions, overt signs of hypovolemic shock, fetal death, thrombocytopenia, fibrinogen <150 mg/dl. Approximately a quarter of abruptions are grade III.

SYNONYM

Premature separation of placenta

ICD-10CM CODES

O45.8X9 Other premature separation of placenta, unspecified trimester
O45.8X1 Other premature separation of placenta, first trimester
O45.8X2 Other premature separation of placenta, second trimester
O45.8X3 Other premature separation of placenta, third trimester
O45.91 Premature separation of placenta, unspecified, first trimester
O45.92 Premature separation of placenta, unspecified, second trimester
O45.93 Premature separation of placenta, unspecified, third trimester

EPIDEMIOLOGY & DEMOGRAPHICS

INCIDENCE (IN U.S.): One in 86 to 206 births; 80% occur before the onset of labor
RISK FACTORS: Hypertension (greatest association), trauma, polyhydramnios, multifetal gestation, smoking, use of cocaine, chorioamnionitis, preterm premature rupture of membranes. Table 1A-4 summarizes placental abruption risk factors.
RECURRENCE RATE: 5% to 17%, some studies showing a 5- to 10-fold increase in risk; with two prior episodes, 25%

PHYSICAL FINDINGS & CLINICAL PRESENTATION

- Triad of uterine bleeding (concealed or per vagina), hypertonic uterine contractions or signs of preterm labor, and evidence of fetal compromise exists.
- More than 80% of cases have external bleeding; 20% of cases have no bleeding but have indirect evidence of abruption, such as failed tocolysis for preterm labor.
- Tetanic uterine contractions are found in only 17%.

ETIOLOGY

- Primary etiology: unknown
- Hypertension: found in 40% to 50% of grade III abruptions
- Rapid decompression of uterine cavity, as can occur in polyhydramnios or multifetal gestation
- Blunt external trauma (motor vehicle accident, spousal abuse)

Dx DIAGNOSIS

DIFFERENTIAL DIAGNOSIS

- Placenta previa
- Cervical or vaginal trauma
- Labor
- Cervical cancer
- Rupture of membranes
- The differential diagnosis of vaginal bleeding in pregnancy is described in Section III

TABLE 1A-4 Placental Abruption Risk Factors

Increasing parity or maternal age
Cigarette smoking
Cocaine abuse
Trauma
Maternal hypertension
Preterm premature rupture of membranes
Rapid uterine decompression associated with multiple gestation and polyhydramnios
Inherited or acquired thrombophilia
Uterine malformations or fibroids
Placental abnormalities or ischemia
Prior abruption

From Gabbe, SG: *Obstetrics*, ed 6, Philadelphia, 2012, Saunders.

WORKUP

- Placental abruption is primarily a clinical diagnosis that is supported by laboratory, radiographic, and pathologic studies.
- Initial assessment should evaluate for the source of bleeding, ruling out placenta previa that may contraindicate any type of vaginal examination (e.g., pelvic speculum examination).
- Continuous fetal heart monitoring is indicated for all viable gestations (60% incidence of fetal distress in labor); may show early signs of maternal hypovolemia (late decelerations or fetal tachycardia) before overt maternal vital sign changes.
- Actual amount of blood loss is often greater than initially perceived because of the possibility of concealed retroplacental bleeding and apparent "normal" vital signs. The relative hypervolemia of pregnancy initially protects the patient until late in the course of bleeding, when abrupt and sudden cardiovascular collapse can occur.

LABORATORY TESTS

- Baseline hemoglobin helps quantify blood loss and establish baseline values for serial comparisons during expectant management.
- Coagulation profile: platelets, fibrinogen, prothrombin, and partial thromboplastin time. Diffuse intravascular coagulation can develop with severe abruption. If fibrinogen is <150 mg/dl, estimated blood loss is approximately 2000 ml; if fibrinogen is <100 mg/dl, consider fresh frozen plasma to prevent further bleeding.
- Type and antibody screen is important to identify Rh-negative patients who need Rh immune globulin.

IMAGING STUDIES

Ultrasound should include fetal presentation and status, amniotic fluid volume, placental location, as well as any evidence of hematoma (retroplacental, subchorionic, or preplacental) (Fig. 1A-6).

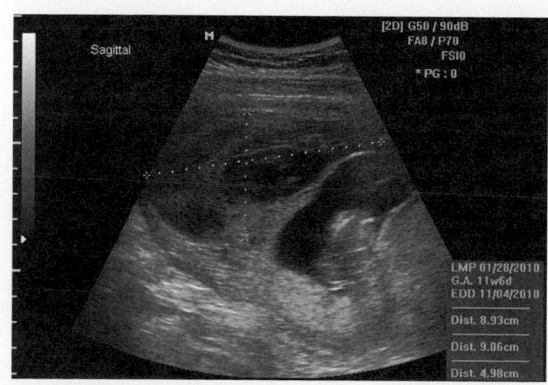

FIGURE 1A-6 Ultrasonic image of a subchorionic abruption. (Courtesy K. Francois; from Gabbe SG: *Obstetrics*, ed 6, Philadelphia, 2012, Saunders.)

Rx TREATMENT

ACUTE GENERAL Rx

- Stabilization of the mother is the first priority.
- Treatment depends on gestational age of the fetus, severity of the abruption, and maternal status.
- Initial assessment for signs of maternal hemodynamic compromise or hemorrhagic shock; large-bore intravenous access, with crystalloid fluid resuscitation using a replacement of 3 ml lactated Ringer's solution for every 1 ml estimated blood loss.
- Indwelling Foley catheter to monitor urine output and maternal volume status, with a goal of 30 ml/hr urine output.
- Assess fetal status and gestational age by sonogram and continuous fetal heart rate monitoring.
- Because of the unpredictable nature of abruptions, cross-matched blood should be made available during the initial resuscitation period.

CHRONIC Rx

- In the term fetus or when lung maturity has been documented, delivery is indicated.
- In the preterm fetus or a fetus with an immature lung profile, consider betamethasone 12.5 mg IM q24h for two doses and then delivery, depending on the severity of the abruption and the likelihood of fetal complications from preterm birth.
- Cesarean section should be reserved for cases of fetal distress or for standard obstetric indications. While cesarean delivery may be needed to stabilize the fetal and/or maternal status, the mother's coagulation status may complicate the procedure and availability of blood products may be critical.
- In select cases, such as severe prematurity with a stable mother and mild contractions, magnesium sulfate can be used for tocolysis, 6 g IV loading dose then 3 g/hr maintenance, to allow for a course of steroids.

DISPOSITION

Because of the unpredictable nature of abruptions, expectant management should occur only under controlled circumstances and is rarely practiced.

REFERRAL

Abruptio placentae places mother and fetus in a high-risk situation and should be managed by a qualified obstetrician in a facility with capability for neonatal and maternal resuscitation, for supporting a preterm infant if delivery is indicated at an early gestational age, and for performing emergency cesarean sections.

RELATED CONTENT

Premature Labor (Related Key Topic)
Vaginal Bleeding During Pregnancy (Related Key Topic)
Abruptio Placentae (Patient Information)

AUTHOR: **RUBEN ALVERO, M.D.**

BASIC INFORMATION

DEFINITION

Acetaminophen (APAP) poisoning is a disorder caused by excessive intake of APAP and is manifested by jaundice, nausea, vomiting, and potential death from hepatic necrosis if not treated appropriately.

SYNONYMS

Paracetamol poisoning

ICD-10CM CODES
T39.1 Poisoning by 4-aminophenol derivatives, accidental
X60   Intentional self-poisoning by 4-aminophenol derivatives

EPIDEMIOLOGY & DEMOGRAPHICS

- APAP is one of the most widely prescribed antipyretics and analgesics in the U.S. Potentially toxic ingestions, both intentional and unintentional, exceed 100,000 cases annually in the U.S.
- APAP toxicity has become the number one cause of acute liver failure in the U.S.
- Death rate is approximately one in 1000 persons. Nearly 50% of exposures occur in children ≤6 yr.
- Hepatic necrosis is most likely to occur in people who are (1) chronically malnourished, (2) regularly abusing alcohol, and (3) using other potentially hepatotoxic medications.

PHYSICAL FINDINGS & CLINICAL PRESENTATION

- The physical examination may vary depending on the amount of time since ingestion.
- Phase I (0 to 24 hr): initial symptoms may be mild or absent and may consist of anorexia, diaphoresis, malaise, nausea, vomiting, and a subclinical rise in transaminase levels.
- Phase II (24 to 72 hr): right upper quadrant pain, vomiting, somnolence, tachycardia, hypotension, and continued increase in transaminases.
- Phase III (72 to 96 hr): hepatic necrosis with abdominal pain, jaundice, hepatic encephalopathy, coagulopathy, hypoglycemia, renal failure, fatality from multi-organ failure.
- Phase IV (4 days to 2 wk): complete resolution of symptoms and resolution of organ failure.
- Table E1A-5 summarizes the four phases/stages of acetaminophen poisoning.

ETIOLOGY

- The amount of APAP necessary for hepatic toxicity varies with the patient's body size and hepatic function. It is recommended that APAP intake should not exceed 4 g for adults and 90 mg/kg in children within a 24-hr period.

- A standardized nomogram is used to determine potential hepatic toxicity by knowing the APAP plasma level and the number of hours after ingestion. See the APAP ingestion algorithm (Fig. E1A-7).

DIAGNOSIS

DIFFERENTIAL DIAGNOSIS

- Liver disease from alcohol abuse or viral hepatitis
- Ingestion of other hepatotoxic substances
- Bacterial/viral gastroenteritis

WORKUP

Initial workup is aimed at confirming APAP overdose with plasma APAP level and assessment of hepatic damage. A careful history should elicit the time of APAP ingestion, amount, preparation (e.g., extended release) and possible co-ingestants (see "Laboratory Tests").

LABORATORY TESTS

- Initial laboratory evaluation should include an initial plasma APAP level with a second level drawn approximately 4 hr after the initial ingestion. Subsequent levels can be obtained every 2 to 4 hr until the levels stabilize or decline. These levels should be plotted on the Rumack-Matthew nomogram (see acetaminophen ingestion algorithm [Fig. E1A-7] to calculate potential hepatic toxicity). The nomogram cannot be used with patients who present >24 hr after ingestion, took extended-release preparations, had chronic ingestions, or when the time of ingestion is unknown.
- Transaminases (AST, ALT), serum glucose, bilirubin level, lipase level, prothrombin time (INR), blood urea nitrogen, creatinine, EKG, and urinalysis should be initially obtained on all patients.
- Serum and urine toxicology screen for other potential toxic substances is also recommended on admission. Screening for infectious hepatitis should also be considered.
- Urine for β-hCG should be obtained from all women of childbearing age.

TREATMENT

NONPHARMACOLOGIC THERAPY

Consultation with a Poison Control Center is recommended for patients who have ingested a large amount of APAP and/or other toxic substances. A single toxic dose of APAP usually exceeds 7 g or 150 mg/kg adults.

ACUTE GENERAL Rx

- Hepatotoxicity is defined as any increase in alanine aminotransferase (ALT) or aspartate aminotransferase (AST) >1000 IU/L, and hepatic failure manifests as hepatotoxicity with hepatic encephalopathy. For

those who cannot be risk stratified using the nomogram, the American College of Emergency Physicians recommends that N-acetylcysteine be administered without delay to those >12 yr and >8 hr after ingestion at presentation.
- Administer activated charcoal 1g/kg PO if the patient is seen within 1 hr of ingestion or the clinician suspects polysubstance ingestion that delays gastric emptying.
- Determine blood levels 4 hr after ingestion; if in the toxic range based on the Rumack-Matthew nomogram, start N-acetylcysteine (NAC) either IV (Acetadote) or PO (Mucomyst). Acetylcysteine IV loading dose is 150 mg/kg ×1 diluted in 200 ml D5W over 15 to 60 min. Maintenance dose is 50 mg/kg diluted in 500 ml D5W over 4 hr, followed by 100 mg/kg diluted in 1000 ml D5W over 16 hr. The dose does not require adjustment for renal or hepatic impairment or for dialysis. Total administration time is 21 hours.
- Oral administration is 140 mg/kg PO as a loading dose, followed after 4 hr by 70 mg/kg PO q4h for a total of 17 doses. N-acetylcysteine therapy should be started within 24 hr of APAP overdose. Total administration time is 72 hours.
- Advantages of IV administration include more reliable absorption, fewer doses, and shorter duration of treatment. Disadvantages include cost and lower hepatic concentrations from first-pass flow as compared to oral acetylcysteine.
- Monitor APAP level; use Rumack-Matthew nomogram to trend hepatic toxicity. Repeat AST/ALT and APAP levels after 12 to 14 hr of IV acetylcysteine infusion and continue infusion longer than 16 hr if transaminases are elevated, if APAP concentration is still measurable, or if coagulopathy exists (INR >1.5-2.0).
- Provide adequate IV hydration (e.g., D5½NS at 150 ml/hr).
- Patients on IV N-acetylcysteine with liver failure require frequent monitoring of vital signs, oxygen saturation by pulse oximetry, and frequent blood draws. Frequent re-assessment for hypoglycemia and infection is also essential.
- If APAP level is nontoxic, N-acetylcysteine therapy may be discontinued.

DISPOSITION

All patients with confirmed APAP poisoning will require admission, usually to an intensive care unit. Most patients (90%) will recover fully without persisting hepatic abnormalities. Hepatic failure is particularly unusual in children <6 yr.

REFERRAL

Psychiatric referral is recommended after intentional ingestions.

RELATED CONTENT

Acetaminophen Overdose (Patient Information)

AUTHOR: **STEVEN ROUGAS, M.D., M.S.**

BASIC INFORMATION

DEFINITION

Acne vulgaris is a chronic disorder of the pilosebaceous apparatus caused by abnormal desquamation of follicular epithelium leading to obstruction of the pilosebaceous canal, resulting in inflammation and subsequent formation of papules, pustules, nodules, comedones, and scarring. Based on their appearance, the acne lesions can be divided into inflammatory (presence of papules, pustules, and nodules) or noninflammatory (open and closed comedones) For inflammatory acne, lesions can be classified as papulopostular, nodular, or both. The American Academy of Dermatology classification scheme for acne denotes the following three levels:

1. Mild acne: characterized by the presence of comedones (noninflammatory lesions), few papules and pustules (generally <10), but no nodules.
2. Moderate acne: presence of several to many papules and pustules (10 to 40) along with comedones (10 to 40). The presence of >40 papules and pustules along with larger, deeper nodular inflamed lesions (up to five) denotes moderately severe acne (Fig. 1A-11).
3. Severe acne (Fig. 1A-12): presence of numerous or extensive papules and pustules as well as many nodular lesions.

SYNONYMS

Acne

ICD-10CM CODES

L70.0	Acne vulgaris
L70.1	Acne conglobata
L70.2	Acne varioliformis
L70.3	Acne tropica
L70.4	Infantile acne
L70.5	Acne excoriee des jeunes filles
L70.8	Other acne
L70.9	Acne, unspecified
L73.0	Acne keloid

EPIDEMIOLOGY & DEMOGRAPHICS

- Acne is the most common skin disease in the U.S.
- It is most common in teenagers, with 85% of all teenagers being affected to some degree.
- Highest incidence between ages of 15 and 18 yr in both genders.
- Involution of the disease usually occurs before age 25 yr, but 12% of women and 3% of men will continue to have clinical acne until the mid-40s.

PHYSICAL FINDINGS & CLINICAL PRESENTATION

- Open comedones (blackheads), closed comedones (whiteheads)
- Greasiness (oily skin)
- Presence of scars from prior acne cysts
- Various stages of development and severity may be present concomitantly
- Common distribution of acne: face, back, and upper chest
- Inflammatory papules, pustules, and ectatic pores

ETIOLOGY

- Acne vulgaris is exclusively a follicular disease, with the principal abnormality being comedone formation.
- Overactivity of the sebaceous glands and blockage in the ducts. The obstruction leads to the formation of comedones, which can become inflamed because of overgrowth of *Propionibacterium acnes.*
- Exacerbated by environmental factors (hot, humid, tropical climate), medications (e.g., iodine in cough mixtures, hair greases), industrial exposure to halogenated hydrocarbons.
- Mechanical or frictional forces can aggravate existing acne (e.g., excessive washing by some patients to help rid them of their blackheads or oiliness).

DIAGNOSIS

DIFFERENTIAL DIAGNOSIS

- Gram-negative folliculitis
- Staphylococcal pyoderma
- Acne rosacea
- Drug eruption
- Sebaceous hyperplasia
- Angiofibromas, basal cell carcinomas, osteoma cutis
- Occupational exposures to oils or grease
- Steroid acne
- Hidradenitis suppurativa
- Perioral dermatitis
- Pseudofolliculitis barbae
- Miliaria
- Seborrheic dermatitis

WORKUP

History and physical examination:
- Inquire about previous treatment
- Careful drug history (including all OTC products)
- Family history, history of cyclic menstrual flares
- History of use of cosmetics and cleansers
- Oral contraceptive use
- Use of medications that may worsen acne such as corticosteroids, anabolic steroids, lithium, neuroleptics, cyclosporine
- Consider the possibility of hyperandrogenic state in all women (hirsutism, irregular menses, androgenic alopecia) or children (seborrhea, acanthosis nigricans, onset of acne between ages 1 and 7 years and no obvious external factors)

LABORATORY TESTS

- Laboratory evaluation is generally not helpful. Patients who are candidates for therapy with isotretinoin should have baseline liver enzymes, cholesterol, and triglycerides checked because this medication may result in elevation of lipids and liver enzymes.
- A negative serum pregnancy test or two negative urine pregnancy tests should also be obtained in females 1 wk before initiation of isotretinoin; it is also imperative to maintain effective contraception during and 1 mo after therapy with isotretinoin ends because of its teratogenic effects. Pregnancy status should be rechecked at monthly visits.
- If hyperandrogenism is suspected in female patients, levels of dehydroepiandrosterone sulfate (DHEAS), testosterone (total and free), and androstenedione should be measured. For women with regular menstrual cycles, serum androgen measurements generally are not necessary.

TREATMENT

NONPHARMACOLOGIC THERAPY

- Blue light (ClearLight therapy system) can be used for treatment of moderate inflammatory acne vulgaris. Light in the violet/blue range can cause bacterial death by a photoreaction in which porphyrins react with

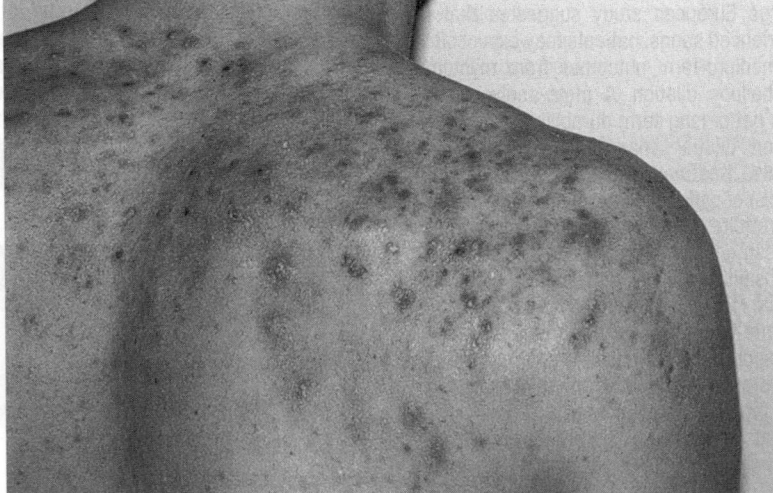

FIGURE 1A-11 Acne on back and shoulders. This acne is typically inflammatory and usually needs oral antibiotics or possibly isotretinoin, but the patient may apply topical medication as well. Heat and sweat may aggravate the condition. (From White GM, Cox NH [eds]: *Diseases of the skin,* ed 2, St Louis, 2006, Mosby.)

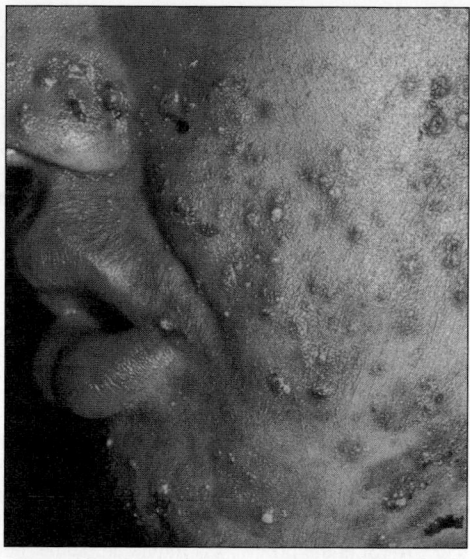

FIGURE 1A-12 Severe acne. Acne this severe on presentation should prompt the consideration of early use of isotretinoin. The dose should be low initially to prevent a severe flare. An oral tetracycline or erythromycin may be helpful to calm the acne before isotretinoin. (From White GM, Cox NH [eds]: *Diseases of the skin,* ed 2, St Louis, 2006, Mosby.)

oxygen to generate reactive oxygen species, which damage the cell membranes of *P. acnes.* Treatment usually consists of 15-min exposures twice weekly for 4 wk. Phototherapy may be effective for short-term treatment of acne, but long-term efficacy and how it compares with conventional acne therapy is unclear.
- Diet: In obese patients, dietary counseling is recommended. A high-glycemic diet may worsen acne, although the strength of its influence is controversial.

ACUTE GENERAL Rx

Treatment generally varies with the type of lesions (comedones, papules, pustules, cystic lesions) and the severity of acne. Use of topical treatments for 6 to 8 weeks is required to judge their efficacy.
- Comedones (noninflammatory acne) can be treated with retinoids or retinoid analogs. Topical retinoids are comedolytic and work by normalizing follicular keratinization. Commonly available agents are Adapalene (Differin, 0.1% gel or cream, applied once or twice daily), tazarotene (Tazorac 0.1% cream or gel applied daily), tretinoin (Retin-A 0.1% cream or 0.025 gel applied once daily), tretinoin microsphere (Retin-A Micro, 0.1% gel, applied at bedtime). Tretinoin is inactivated by ultraviolet light and oxidized by benzoyl peroxide; therefore it should only be applied at night and not used concomitantly with benzoyl peroxide.
- Tretinoin is pregnancy category C and tazarotene is pregnancy category X. Salicylic acid preparations (e.g., Neutrogena 2% wash) have keratolytic and anti-inflammatory properties and are also useful in the treatment of comedones. Large, open comedones (blackheads) should be expressed.
- Patients should be reevaluated after 4 to 6 wk. Benzoyl peroxide gel (2.5% or 5%) may be added if the comedones become inflamed or form pustules. The most common adverse effects are dryness, erythema, and peeling.

Topical antibiotics (erythromycin, clindamycin lotions or pads) can also be used in patients with significant inflammation. They reduce *P. acnes* in the pilosebaceous follicle and have some antiinflammatory effects. The combination of 5% benzoyl peroxide and 3% erythromycin (Benzamycin) or 1% clindamycin with 5% benzoyl peroxide (BenzaClin) is highly effective in patients who have a mixture of comedonal and inflammatory acne lesions.
- Fixed-dose combinations of clindamycin phosphate 1.2% and tretinoin 0.025% are available (Veltin gel, Ziana) and are more effective than either product used alone; however, they are much more expensive than the individual generic components.
- Pustular acne can be treated with tretinoin and benzoyl peroxide gel applied on alternate evenings; drying agents (sulfacetamide-sulfa lotions [Novacet, Sulfacet]) are also effective when used in combination with benzoyl peroxide; oral antibiotics (doxycycline 100 mg qd or erythromycin 1 g qd given in 2 to 3 divided doses) are effective in patients with moderate to severe pustular acne. Patients not responding well to these antibiotics can be switched to minocycline 50 to 100 mg bid; however, this medication is more expensive.
- Patients with nodular cystic acne and those with moderate to severe inflammatory acne unresponsive to topical drugs can be treated with systemic agents: antibiotics (erythromycin, tetracycline, doxycycline, minocycline), isotretinoin (available on a restricted basis), or oral contraceptives. Periodic intralesional triamcinolone (Kenalog) injections by a dermatologist are also effective. The possibility of endocrinopathy should be considered in patients responding poorly to therapy.
- Isotretinoin is the most effective drug available for treatment of severe nodulocystic acne. It is indicated for acne resistant to

antibiotic therapy and severe acne. It inhibits *P. acne's* colonization by reducing sebum production and has antiinflammatory and keratolytic effects. It is available only on a restricted basis. Dosage is 0.5 to 1 mg/kg/day in 2 divided doses (maximum of 2 mg/kg/day); duration of therapy is generally 20 wk for a cumulative dose ≥120 mg/kg for severe cystic acne. Before using this medication patients should undergo baseline laboratory evaluation (see "Laboratory Tests"). This drug is absolutely contraindicated during pregnancy because of its teratogenicity. It should be used with caution in patients with history of depression. Physicians, distributors, pharmacies, and patients must register in the iPLEDGE program (http://www.ipledgeprogram.com) before using isotretinoin.
- Azelaic acid is a bacteriostatic dicarboxylic acid used to normalize keratinization and reduce inflammation. It can be used in pregnant women.
- Oral contraceptives reduce androgen levels and therefore sebum production. They represent a useful adjunctive therapy for all types of acne in women and adolescent girls. Commonly used agents are norgestimate/ethinyl estradiol (Ortho Tri-Cyclen) and drosperinone/ethinyl estradiol (Yasmin).

REFERRAL

Referral for intralesional injection and dermabrasion should be considered in patients with severe acne unresponsive to conventional therapy.

 **PEARLS & CONSIDERATIONS**

- Gram-negative folliculitis should be suspected if inflammatory acne worsens after several months of oral antibiotic therapy.
- Acne may worsen during the first 3 to 4 wk of retinoid therapy before improving.

COMMENTS

Indications for systemic therapy of acne are:
- Painful deep papules or nodules
- Extensive lesions
- Active acne with severe scarring or hyperpigmentation
- Patient's morale

Patients should be educated that in most cases acne can be controlled but not cured and that at least 4 to 6 wk of initial therapy should be required before significant improvement is noted.

 EVIDENCE

Available at www.expertconsult.com

SUGGESTED READINGS
Available at www.expertconsult.com

RELATED CONTENT
Acne (Patient Information)

AUTHOR: **FRED F. FERRI, M.D.**

BASIC INFORMATION

DEFINITION

Acoustic neuroma is a benign proliferation of the Schwann cells that cover the vestibular branch of the eighth cranial nerve (CN VIII). Symptoms are commonly a result of compression of the acoustic branch of CN VIII, the facial nerve (CN VII), and the trigeminal nerve (CN V). The glossopharyngeal nerve (CN IX) and vagus nerve (CN X) are less commonly involved. In extreme cases, compression of the brain stem may lead to obstruction of cerebrospinal fluid (CSF) outflow and elevated intracranial pressure (ICP).

SYNONYMS

Vestibular schwannoma

ICD-10CM CODES
D33.3 Benign neoplasm of cranial nerves

EPIDEMIOLOGY & DEMOGRAPHICS

Overall incidence is approximately 2 in 100,000 person-years, with a higher incidence in patients with neurofibromatosis type 2 (NF2). The prevalence is 2 in 10,000 people. The tumor most commonly presents in the fifth and sixth decades.

PHYSICAL FINDINGS & CLINICAL PRESENTATION

- Most frequently unilateral hearing loss and/or tinnitus. Also balance problems, vertigo, facial pain (trigeminal neuralgia) and weakness, difficulty swallowing, fullness or pain of the involved ear. Headache may occur.
- With elevated ICP, patients may also have vomiting, fever, and visual changes.
- Hearing loss is the most common presenting complaint and is usually high frequency.

ETIOLOGY

The etiology is incompletely understood, but long-term exposure to acoustic trauma has been implicated. Bilateral acoustic neuromas may be inherited in an autosomal-dominant manner as part of NF2. This disease is associated with a defect on chromosome 22q1. Childhood exposure to low-dose radiation for benign head and neck conditions may increase risk for acoustic neuromas. There is inconclusive evidence to link chronic exposure to radiofrequency radiation from cellular telephone use and the risk for developing brain tumors.

DIAGNOSIS

DIFFERENTIAL DIAGNOSIS

- Benign positional vertigo
- Menière's disease
- Trigeminal neuralgia
- Cerebellar disease
- Normal-pressure hydrocephalus
- Presbycusis
- Glomus tumors
- Vertebrobasilar insufficiency

- Ototoxicity from medications
- Other tumors:
  1. Meningioma, glioma
  2. Facial nerve schwannoma
  3. Cavernous hemangioma
  4. Metastatic tumors

WORKUP

- A detailed neurologic examination with special attention to the cranial nerves is crucial.
- Otoscopic evaluation may help rule out other causes of hearing loss.

LABORATORY TESTS

- Audiometry is useful, often showing asymmetric, sensorineural, high-frequency hearing loss.
- CSF protein may be elevated.

IMAGING STUDIES

- MRI with gadolinium (Fig. 1A-13) is the preferred test. It can detect tumors as small as 2 mm in diameter.
- High-resolution CT scan with and without contrast can detect tumors 1 cm in diameter or larger.
- Treatment decisions should be based on the size of the tumor, rate of growth (older patients tend to have slower-growing tumors), degree of neurologic deficit, desire to preserve hearing, life expectancy, age of the patient, and surgical risk. A combination of treatments can also be used.

TREATMENT

NONPHARMACOLOGIC THERAPY

- Surgery is the definitive treatment. Choice of approach (middle cranial fossa, translabyrin-

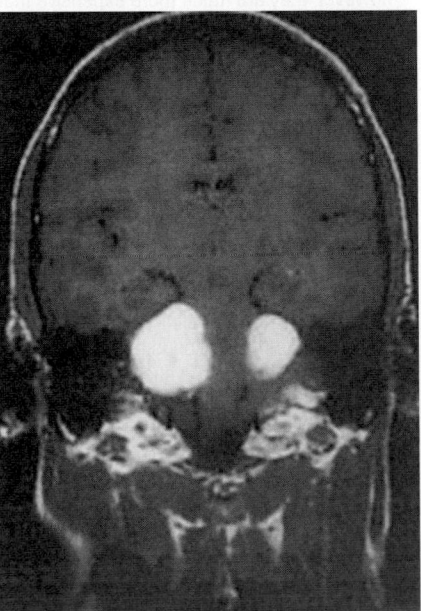

FIGURE 1A-13 MR with enhancement shows bilateral acoustic neuromas. Coronal view. (From Kanski JJ, Bowling B: *Clinical ophthalmology, a systematic approach,* ed 7, Philadephia, 2011, Saunders.)

thine, or retromastoid suboccipital) may vary depending on the size of the tumor, amount of residual hearing desired, and degree of surgical risk that can be tolerated. Partial resection is sometimes undertaken to minimize the risk of injury to nearby structures. Intraoperative facial nerve monitoring is recommended.
- Radiation therapy (stereotactic radiotherapy, stereotactic radiosurgery, or proton beam radiotherapy) is useful for tumors <3 cm in diameter or for those in whom surgery is not an option. Radiotherapy after partial resection has also been used to minimize complications.
- Age alone is not a contraindication to surgery.

GENERAL Rx

- Bevacizumab, an antivascular endothelial growth factor (VEGF) monoclonal antibody, has been shown to improve hearing and reduce the volume of growing acoustic neuromas in some neurofibromatosis type 2 patients.
- Observation with MRI every 6 to 12 mo may be appropriate for frail patients with small tumors, but risk of unrecoverable hearing loss may increase if surgery is delayed. Also, progressive hearing loss may occur despite absence of growth on subsequent imaging.

DISPOSITION

Hearing can be preserved at near-preoperative levels in more than two thirds of patients with small- to medium-sized tumors. Occurrence of secondary radiation-related tumors following radiosurgery is rare. There are no standard posttreatment follow-up recommendations. Therefore, an individualized approach to follow-up imaging and audiometry is recommended.

REFERRAL

Prompt referral to an otolaryngologist or neurosurgeon who is facile with all three surgical approaches is recommended.

PEARLS & CONSIDERATIONS

COMMENTS

- Presents most commonly as unilateral, sensorineural hearing loss.
- Treatment outcomes are generally good, with cure rates approaching 90% at 5 years.
- Of those who are managed with observation only, approximately half have continued enlargement and approximately one fifth eventually have a surgical intervention.

PATIENT/FAMILY EDUCATION

Acoustic Neuroma Association: http://anausa.org.

SUGGESTED READINGS
Available at www.expertconsult.com

RELATED CONTENT

Tinnitus (Related Key Topic)
Acoustic Neuroma (Patient Information)

AUTHOR: **COURTNEY CLARK BILODEAU, M.D.**

Diseases and Disorders

BASIC INFORMATION

DEFINITION

Acquired immunodeficiency syndrome (AIDS) is a disorder caused by infection with the human immunodeficiency virus (HIV) and marked by progressive deterioration of the cellular immune system, leading to secondary (opportunistic) infections and/or malignancies.

SYNONYMS

AIDS

ICD-10CM CODES

B20 Human immunodeficiency virus [HIV] disease

EPIDEMIOLOGY & DEMOGRAPHICS

INCIDENCE (IN U.S.):
- The estimated number of persons diagnosed with AIDS in the U.S. exceeds 30,000/year.
- Almost 50% of new AIDS cases are in black/African Americans, 20% in Hispanics, and 25% in white Americans.
- More than 55% of all new AIDS diagnoses in 2013 were among gay, bisexual, or other men who have sex with men (MSM).

PREVALENCE (IN U.S.):
- The cumulative number of AIDS diagnoses in the U.S. exceeds 1.2 million.

PREDOMINANT SEX: Men constitute 75% of incident AIDS diagnoses in the U.S.; more than 50% of AIDS diagnoses occur in MSM.

PREDOMINANT AGE: The predominant age group diagnosed with AIDS is 30-49 years of age.

PEAK INCIDENCE: Ages 45-49

GENETICS:
- Familial disposition: Although there is no proven genetic predisposition, individuals with deletions in the *CCR5* gene are immune from infection with macrophage tropic virus (the predominant virus in sexual transmission) and may progress to AIDS more slowly.
- Congenital infection:
  1. Transmittable from an infected mother to the fetus in utero in as many as 30% of pregnancies.
  2. No specific congenital malformations associated with infection; low birth weight and spontaneous abortion are possible.
- Neonatal infection: transmission possible to the neonate intrapartum or postpartum through breastfeeding.

PHYSICAL FINDINGS & CLINICAL PRESENTATION

- Nonspecific findings: fever, weight loss, anorexia.
- Specific syndromes:
  1. Seen in association with opportunistic infections and malignancies, so-called indicator diseases; these include:
     a. Opportunistic infections:
        Disseminated strongyloidiasis
        Disseminated toxoplasmosis, cryptococcosis, histoplasmosis, cytomegalovirus (CMV), herpes simplex, or mycobacterial disease
        Candida esophagitis or bronchopulmonary disease
        Chronic *Cryptosporidia* spp. diarrhea
        Pneumocystis jiroveci pneumonia (PJP)
        Extensive pulmonary and extra-pulmonary tuberculosis
        Recurrent bacterial pneumonia
        Progressive multifocal leukoencephalopathy (PML)
     b. AIDS-related neoplasms:
        Kaposi's sarcoma
        Primary brain lymphoma
        Invasive cervical carcinoma
        High-grade B cell non-Hodgkin's lymphoma, Burkitt's lymphoma, undifferentiated non-Hodgkin's lymphoma, or immunoblastic lymphoma
  2. Most common:
     Respiratory infections (*Pneumocystis jiroveci* [formerly known as *Pneumocystis carinii*] pneumonia, TB, bacterial pneumonia, fungal infection)
     CNS infections (toxoplasmosis, cryptococcal meningitis, TB)
     GI (cryptosporidiosis, isosporiasis, CMV); Sections II and III describe organisms associated with diarrhea in patients with AIDS
     Eye infections (CMV, toxoplasmosis)
     Kaposi's sarcoma (cutaneous or visceral) or lymphoma (nodal or extranodal)
- Possibly asymptomatic.
- Diagnosis of AIDS if the CD4 cell count is <200 or <14% of total lymphocyte in the presence of proven HIV infection, even in the absence of other infections.
- The various manifestations of HIV infection are described in Section II.

ETIOLOGY

- Caused by infection with HIV-1 or HIV-2.
- Transmitted by sexual contact, needle-sharing (during IV drug use), transfusion of contaminated blood or blood products, and from infected mother to fetus or neonate as described previously.

DIAGNOSIS

DIFFERENTIAL DIAGNOSIS

- Other wasting illnesses mimicking the nonspecific features of AIDS:
  1. TB
  2. Neoplasms
  3. Disseminated fungal infection
  4. Malabsorption syndromes
  5. Depression
- Other disorders associated with dementia or demyelination producing encephalopathy, myelopathy, or neuropathy.

WORKUP

Prompt evaluation of respiratory, CNS, and GI complaints

LABORATORY TESTS

- HIV antibody testing. See "Human Immunodeficiency Virus" topic for the 2014 revised surveillance case definition for HIV infection.
- T-lymphocyte subset analysis: performed to determine the degree of immunodeficiency (i.e., CD4 cell count).
- Viral load assay: to plan long-term antiviral therapy and to follow progression and success of treatment (i.e., HIV RNA PCR).
- CSF examination: for meningitis (if indicated).
- Serologic tests for syphilis, hepatitis B, hepatitis C, and toxoplasmosis.
- Genotypic resistance testing: used to assess for primary resistance in naïve patients and secondary resistance in patients failing a regimen.
- Eye exam: to evaluate for CMV retinitis in patients with CD4 counts <50 cells/mm^3.
- Cryptococcal antigen: part of the evaluation in AIDS patients with CD4 counts <100 cells/mm^3 who have fever, diffuse pneumonia, or evidence of meningitis.
- Evaluation for infection with mycobacterium (TB or MAI) including PPD, sputum cultures, chest radiograph, and blood cultures for acid-fast bacteria, depending on clinical presentation.

IMAGING STUDIES

- MRI or CT of head for encephalopathy or focal CNS complications (e.g., toxoplasmosis, lymphoma).
  Chest radiography or CT to aid in the diagnosis of *Pneumocystis jiroveci* (*P. carinii*) pneumonia, TB, or bacterial pneumonia

TREATMENT

The most important aspect in management of AIDS due to HIV infection is the timely initiation of antiretroviral therapy (see section on HIV treatment).

NONPHARMACOLOGIC THERAPY

- Maintain adequate caloric intake.
- Encourage good oral hygiene and regular dental care.
- Avoid high-risk behaviors that increase the risk of repeated exposure to HIV and other potential pathogens—safer sexual practices, avoid sharing needles, etc.
- Update vaccines—particularly the pneumococcal and hepatitis B vaccine along with annual influenza vaccines.
- Avoid administration of any live attenuated vaccines that may be a risk to these immunocompromised patients (e.g., MMR, varicella). (See Section V for immunization schedules for HIV-infected children.)
- When feasible, avoid activities that might increase risk of exposure to opportunistic infections (e.g., cleaning out a cat litter box [toxoplasmosis], getting scratched by a cat [*Bartonella* infections], exposure to pet reptiles [salmonellosis], traveling to developing countries [cryptosporidiosis, tuberculosis], eating undercooked foods and drinking from unsafe water supplies, etc.).

ACUTE GENERAL Rx

Acute management of opportunistic infections and malignancies is reviewed elsewhere in this text under specific AIDS-related disorders.

CHRONIC Rx

For all HIV-infected patients, particularly those meeting the case definition of AIDS:

- Preventive therapy for *Pneumocystis jiroveci* pneumonia and TB (see specific chapters elsewhere in this text). With the advent of modern antiretroviral therapy many patients have experienced substantial restoration of cellular immune function. It has become clear that preventive therapy for *Pneumocystis jiroveci* and *Mycobacterium avium* complex as well as suppressive therapy for CMV and cryptococcal infection can often be safely withdrawn if the CD4 cell count rises above 200 for at least six months.
- Based on the Department of Health and Human Services (DHHS) Guidelines of 2015, active antiretroviral therapy (ART) should be started regardless of CD4 cell count. Individuals with CD4 cell counts <350 and especially CD4 cell counts <200 should be strongly encouraged to start ART in a timely fashion.
- ART usually includes three-drug combinations of:
  1. Nucleoside reverse transcriptase inhibitors (NRTI): tenofovir (TDF), zidovudine (AZT), didanosine (DDI), lamivudine (3TC), emtricitabine (FTC), stavudine (D4T), and abacavir (ABC).
  2. Protease inhibitors (PI): saquinavir, amprenavir, indinavir, nelfinavir, agenerase, lopinavir/ritonavir, atazanavir, and darunavir.
  3. Nonnucleoside reverse transcriptase inhibitors (NNRTI): nevirapine, delavirdine, efavirenz (EFV), etravirine, and rilpivirine.
  4. Integrase inhibitors: raltegravir, elvitegravir, and dolutegravir.
  5. Others: maraviroc and enfuvirtide.

The protease inhibitor ritonavir should be used in low dose (100 mg) in combination with other protease inhibitors to obtain more sustained drug levels. Usual initial dosing regimens include two NRTIs and an NNRTI or PI or integrase inhibitor. Currently, integrase inhibitors are recommended as first-line drugs because of tolerability. Examples of initial regimens recommended by the guidelines:

1. Dolutegravir/abacavir/lamivudine (in patients who are HLA-B*5701 NEGATIVE).
2. Dolutegravir plus tenofovir/emtricitabine
3. Elvitegravir/cobicistat/tenofovir/emtricitabine
4. Raltegravir plus tenofovir/emtricitabine
   Darunavir/ritonavir plus tenofovir/emtricitabine

Previous first-line drugs, including efavirenz/tenofovir/emtricitabine and rilpivirine/tenofovir/emtricitabine, are now considered alternative regimens.

All these drugs have unique and class-specific side effects and require careful and expert follow-up to achieve optimal antiviral effects, ensure compliance, and maintain efficacy. Antiviral response should be monitored by baseline HIV viral load and CD4 count and repeat measurement at 2 weeks and 4 weeks into treatment and then periodically (every 3-6 months) to ensure viral suppression.

- An approach to evaluating chronic diarrhea in patients with HIV infection is described in Fig. E1A-14, the approach to the acutely ill HIV-infected patient is outlined in Fig. E1A-15, and the evaluation of HIV-positive patients with respiratory complaints is described in Figs. E1A-16 and E1A-17. The approach to a patient with a suspected CNS lesion is described in Figs. E1A-18 and E1A-19. Fig. E1A-20 presents an approach to cardiac dysfunction.
- Genotypic resistance testing is strongly encouraged for all patients initiating treatment and for any patient failing antiretroviral therapy. Poor adherence to therapy, however, often underlies virologic failure.

DISPOSITION

The outlook for AIDS has changed radically since the advent of ART therapy from an essentially fatal disease to a chronic medical illness compatible with long-term survival and remarkably good quality of life. Patients should be aggressively treated for severe illnesses as outcomes following ICU admissions remain good. This is accomplished through expert and continuous follow-up, use of ART, and careful detail to compliance to medications and lifestyle modification.

REFERRAL

All patients with AIDS: to a physician knowledgeable and experienced in the management of the disease and its complications

SUGGESTED READINGS

Available at www.expertconsult.com

RELATED CONTENT

Acquired Immunodeficiency Syndrome (AIDS) (Patient Information)
Candidiasis, Cutaneous (Related Key Topic)
Candidiasis, Invasive (Related Key Topic)
Cryptosporidium Infection (Related Key Topic)
Cytomegalovirus Infection (Related Key Topic)
Herpes Simplex (Related Key Topic)
Histoplasmosis (Related Key Topic)
HIV Cognitive Dysfunction (Related Key Topic)
Human Immunodeficiency Virus (Related Key Topic)
Kaposi Sarcoma (Related Key Topic)
Pneumocystis jirovecii Pneumonia (Related Key Topic)
Progressive Multifocal Leukoencephalopathy (Related Key Topic)
Toxoplasmosis (Related Key Topic)
Tuberculosis (Related Key Topic)

AUTHOR: **PHILIP A. CHAN, M.D., M.S.**

A

BASIC INFORMATION

DEFINITION

Actinic keratoses (AKs) are common skin lesions usually presenting as multiple erythematous or yellow-brown, dry, scaly lesions in the middle aged or elderly.

SYNONYMS

Solar keratosis
Senile keratosis
AK

ICD-10CM CODES
L57.0 Actinic keratosis

EPIDEMIOLOGY & DEMOGRAPHICS

INCIDENCE: In regions of the northern hemisphere, 11%-25% of adults have a minimum of one AK. In regions closer to the equator, 40%-60% of adults have a minimum of one AK.

PEAK INCIDENCE: The risk of squamous cell carcinoma in patients with AK is 6%-10%. Risk factors associated with increased risk of invasive squamous cell carcinoma arising from actinic keratosis include lesion location (lip, ear, extremities), lesion characteristics (ulceration, induration, hyperkeratotic, proliferative, inflamed, bleeding, large surface area and depth), pigmentation (any rapid changes in presentation, presence of multiple lesions, evidence of greater ultraviolet [UV]-induced skin damage), presence of concomitant illness (lymphoma, leukemia), and use of concomitant medications (immunosuppressive agents, medications that increase sun sensitivity)[1]

PREVALENCE
- In the United States, 58.08 million per year.
- Highest prevalence in those with fair complexions with high sun exposure.
- Approximately 60% of predisposed individuals older than 40 years will have one AK.
- Caucasians' risk increases with age: at age 20-29 prevalence is <10%; at age 80-89, prevalence is approximately 75%.

PREDOMINANT SEX AND AGE: Males > females, age 65-74. Occurs most in those with fair complexions who burn rather than tan following sun exposure.

GENETICS: There is increased frequency of non-melanoma skin cancers connected to squamous cell cancers with the genetic conditions xeroderma pigmentosum, oculocutaneous albinism, epidermodysplasia verruciformis, dystrophic epidermolysis bullosa, Ferguson-Smith syndrome, and Muir-Torre syndrome.

RISK FACTORS:
- Immunosuppression, exposure to UV light, ionizing radiation, arsenic, human papillomavirus, cigarette smoke, chronic ulcers, thermal burns, chronic discoid lupus erythematosus, and nonhealing wounds.
- Lichen planus, lichen sclerosis, linear and classic porokeratosis, and disseminated superficial actinic porokeratosis.
- Age, gender, skin color, and mutations in p53 tumor suppressor gene.

PHYSICAL FINDINGS & CLINICAL PRESENTATION
- Typical lesions occur on sun-damaged skin, usually on the face and neck and the dorsal aspects of hands (Fig. 1A-22) and forearms.
- Advanced lesions are characterized by a hard, spiky scale (Fig. 1A-23) and usually measure 1 cm in diameter or less. Early lesions manifest with redness and minimal scale. With progression, scales become thicker and yellow and may resemble a small squamous cell carcinoma. On examinations, lesions are rough and gritty (Fig. 1A-24).
- The surrounding skin frequently shows additional features of sun damage, including atrophy (Fig. 1A-25), pigment changes, and telangiectasia.
- Classifications
  1. Hypertrophic AK with a cutaneous horn: Biopsy is necessary to distinguish the cutaneous horn from squamous cell carcinoma, seborrheic keratosis, verruca, and trichilemmoma and basal cell carcinoma. Hypertrophic AK has appearance of thick, scaling skin elevations.
  2. Lichenoid AK: Most commonly found on the torso and upper extremities. Must be distinguished from BCC due to pink and pearly characteristics.
  3. Proliferative AK: Often reappear after treatment and are characterized by a diameter >1 cm. Often occurs in same differential as Bowen's disease or SCC.
  4. Spreading pigmented AK: Must be biopsied to distinguish from lentigo maligna–type melanoma in situ as well as solar lentigo.
  5. Actinic cheilitis: Characterized by red and sometimes abrasive lesions around the border of the lips and skin.

ETIOLOGY
- Sun exposure, ionizing radiation.
- Arsenic, polycyclic hydrocarbon exposure.

DIAGNOSIS

DIFFERENTIAL DIAGNOSIS
- Heavily pigmented variants may be clinically mistaken for lentigo maligna.
- Basal cell or squamous cell carcinoma.
- Seborrheic keratosis.
- Eczema.
- Bowen disease (intraepithelial carcinoma).
- Wart.
- Lichenoid keratosis.
- Cutaneous lupus.

WORKUP
- History, physical, and lesion biopsy. Include risk assessment and family or personal history of skin cancers or previous skin lesions.

LABORATORY TESTS
- Skin biopsy in recurrent lesions or when diagnosis is unclear to rule out squamous cell or basal cell carcinoma.
- Microscopy reveals atypical keratinocytes in the lower epidermis basal layers. They are enlarged and often lack normal polarity. The thickness of the epidermis can be compromised with a distribution of atrophic to hyperplastic. Abnormal keratinocytes can cause parakeratosis of the overlying stratum corneum. Visible signs of an alternating orthohyperkeratosis can overlie the spared epithelium, causing the signature "flag sign." Additionally, there is a distinct margin between normal epidermis and the region of AK at lateral edges. Histologic subtypes are hypertrophic, acantholytic, lichenoid, and bowenoid, which are characterized by a thick stratum corneum, lack of intracellular cohesion, presence of lymphocytic infiltrate

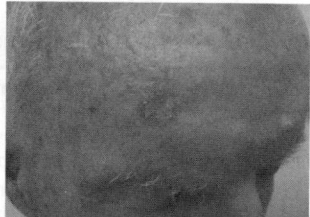

FIGURE 1A-25 Actinic keratosis (shown here on a patient's forehead) is often best appreciated by its rough, tactile quality, similar to that of sandpaper. (From Ferri F et al: *Ferri's fast facts in dermatology,* Philadelphia, 2010, Saunders.)

1. Rigel DS, Stein Goold LF: The importance of early diagnosis and treatment of actinic keratosis. *J Am Acad Dermatol* 68:S20-27, 2013.

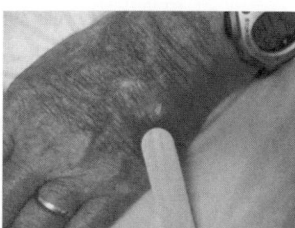

FIGURE 1A-22 Several scaly, adherent, yellow-brown lesions on the sun-exposed dorsum of the hand. (From Ferri F et al: *Ferri's fast facts in dermatology,* Philadelphia, 2010, Saunders.)

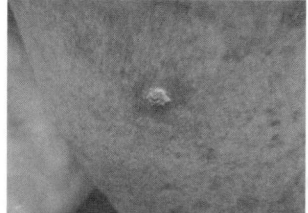

FIGURE 1A-23 Scaly, raised lesion on sun-exposed back. Pain was elicited when scraping this lesion. (From Ferri F et al: *Ferri's fast facts in dermatology,* Philadelphia, 2010, Saunders.)

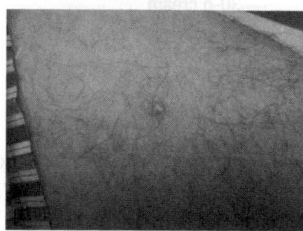

FIGURE 1A-24 Raised, rough, gritty actinic keratosis on the anterior thigh of an outdoorsman. (From Ferri F et al: *Ferri's fast facts in dermatology,* Philadelphia, 2010, Saunders.)

ACUTE GENERAL Rx

- Therapy is generally symptomatic and directed at relief of cough and wheezing.
- Inhaled bronchodilators (e.g., albuterol, metaproterenol) PRN for 1 to 2 wk in patients with wheezing or troublesome cough. Inhaled albuterol has been proven effective in reducing the duration of cough in adults with uncomplicated acute bronchitis.
- Cough suppression with dextromethorphan and guaifenesin is commonly recommended; addition of codeine for cough suppression if cough is severe and is significantly interrupting patient's sleep pattern.
- Use of antibiotics (TMP-SMX, amoxicillin, doxycycline, cefuroxime) for acute bronchitis is generally not indicated; should be considered only in patients with concomitant COPD and purulent sputum or in patients with suspected pertussis. In the few cases of acute bronchitis caused by *B. pertussis* or atypical bacteria such as *C. pneumoniae* or *Mycoplasma pneumoniae,* early use of macrolide antibiotics is reasonable.
- Antibiotics are overused in patients with acute bronchitis (70% to 90% of office visits for acute bronchitis result in treatment with antibiotics); this practice pattern is contributing to increases in resistant organisms.
- Trials have shown that there are no significant differences in patients receiving antibiotics compared with those receiving placebo in overall clinical improvements or limitations in work or other activities. There was a significant increase in adverse effects in the antibiotic group, particularly gastrointestinal symptoms.[1]

CHRONIC Rx

Avoidance of tobacco and other pulmonary irritants

DISPOSITION

- Complete recovery within 7 to 10 days in most patients.
- Patients should be informed to expect to have a cough for 10 to 14 days after the visit.

REFERRAL

For pulmonary function testing only in patients with recurrent bronchitis and suspected underlying pulmonary disease.

[1]Smith SM, Smucny J, Fahey T: Antibiotics for acute bronchitis, *JAMA* 312:2678, 2014.

PEARLS & CONSIDERATIONS

COMMENTS

- Intervention studies reveal that patient and physician education are effective in reducing the use of antibiotic therapy. No offer or delayed offer of antibiotics for acute uncomplicated lower respiratory tract infection is acceptable, is associated with little difference in symptom resolution, and is likely to reduce antibiotic use and beliefs in the effectiveness of antibiotics.
- It is helpful to refer to acute bronchitis as a "chest cold." Patients should be informed that antibiotics are probably not going to be beneficial and may result in significant side effects.

SUGGESTED READINGS

Available at www.expertconsult.com

RELATED CONTENT

Acute Bronchitis (Patient Information)

AUTHOR: **FRED F. FERRI, M.D.**

BASIC INFORMATION

DEFINITION

Ogilvie's syndrome is characterized by acute massive dilation of the cecum and right colon, with occasional extension to the rectum, in the absence of any mechanical obstruction. Oftentimes, acute colonic pseudo-obstruction occurs after surgery, and it can also be seen in patients with significant underlying medical illnesses. Cecal diameter on abdominal radiographs greater than nine centimeters is considered to be the threshold where spontaneous perforation becomes more likely. Medications such as opiates and anti-cholinergics also contribute to the development of this condition.

SYNONYMS

Ogilvie's syndrome
ACPO
Acute megacolon

ICD-10CM CODES
K56.6 Other and unspecified intestinal obstruction

EPIDEMIOLOGY & DEMOGRAPHICS

INCIDENCE: Unknown
PEAK INCIDENCE: Unknown
PREVALENCE: Unknown
PREDOMINANT SEX AND AGE: Although recent data is lacking, data from a retrospective study in 1986 suggested a male predominance with average age of onset in the 6th decade. In general, prevalence is thought to increase with age, although affected females tend to be younger because of the association of acute colonic pseudo-obstruction with obstetric complications
GENETICS: None
RISK FACTORS: Elderly patients seem to be at greatest risk. Other risk factors include significant underlying medical illness, sepsis, electrolyte abnormalities, recent cardiac events, certain medications (opiates, anticholinergics, phenothiazines, benzodiazepines, calcium channel blockers, chemotherapeutic agents, and antiparkinsonian agents), and postoperative patients (Box 1A-1).

PHYSICAL FINDINGS & CLINICAL PRESENTATION

- Acute abdominal distention and crampy abdominal pain are the most common symptoms associated with Ogilvie's syndrome. The distention can be so severe that it may lead to labored breathing. Nausea, vomiting, obstipation, constipation, and, paradoxically, diarrhea, can also be seen but are not consistently present. It has been estimated that 40%-50% of patients continue to pass flatus.
- Physical exam is significant for massive abdominal distention that is tympanic to percussion and varying degrees of abdominal pain or discomfort are also present. Hypoactive or hyperactive bowel sounds are often described. Peritoneal signs are often absent early on but their presence is concerning for imminent perforation.

ETIOLOGY

- Colonic motor and secretory functions are mediated by the autonomic nervous system with the ascending colon receiving parasympathetic innervation from the medulla oblongata via the vagus nerve, which increases gut motility, and sympathetic innervation from the spinal cord, which decreases motility. It is thought that parasympathetic dysfunction is the main driving force that leads to Ogilvie's syndrome but the exact mechanism is unknown.

DIAGNOSIS

DIFFERENTIAL DIAGNOSIS

- Mechanical obstruction
- Volvulus
- Intussusception
- Ileus
- Toxic megacolon

WORK-UP

- History should be focused on the perceived progression of distention and timing of most

BOX 1A-1 Clinical Factors Predisposing to Ogilvie's Syndrome or Acute Colonic Pseudo-Obstruction

Cardiovascular
- Heart failure, stroke
- Gut ischemia
Critical illness
- Severe sepsis
- Acute pancreatitis
- Shock or hypoxemia
Postoperative state or trauma
- Intestinal manipulation
- Peritonitis
- Immobility and dehydration
- Vertebral, pelvic or hip fracture/surgery
- Retroperitoneal hematoma
Metabolic factors
- Hypokalemia and hyperglycemia
- Hypothyroidism, diabetes mellitus
- Liver or renal failure
- Amyloidosis
Drugs
- α-Adrenergic agonists, dopamine
- Clonidine and dexmedetomidine
- Opioids
- Anticholinergics, calcium channel antagonists
- Antipsychotics
- Antidepressants
- High-dose phosphodiesterase inhibitors
Gastrointestinal infections
- Cytomegalovirus, herpes zoster
- Tuberculosis
Neurologic
- Transsection of the spinal cord
- Low spinal cord disease
- Parkinson's disease
Obstetric
- Caesarean section
- Normal delivery

From Vincent JL, Abraham E, Moore FA, Kochanek PM, Fink MP: *Textbook of critical care*, ed 6, Philadelphia, 2011, Saunders.

recent flatus or bowel movement as well as determining any predisposing factors such as recent surgery, severe illness, and recent medication changes. Physical examination should focus on assessing the degree of abdominal distention and percussion to evaluate for tympanic sounds, which is a hallmark of Ogilvie's syndrome. Serial abdominal exams should be performed to ensure no peritoneal signs such a rebound, guarding, or rigidity that would suggest impending or frank perforation.
- Laboratory evaluation should center on metabolic abnormalities as well as lactic acidosis and leukocytosis that can both be used as a barometer of the degree of the patient's underlying illness as well as a marker for impending perforation.
- Imaging of the abdomen with plain radiograph is important for tracking degree of distention.

LABORATORY TESTS

- Metabolic abnormalities such as hypocalcemia, hypomagnesemia, and hypokalemia are commonly present and should be corrected accordingly.
- Leukocytosis as well as lactic acidosis for markers of underlying disease and impending perforation.

IMAGING STUDIES

- Plain and upright abdominal radiographs (Figure 1A-28) are important to establish degree of colonic distention, which often involves the cecum but can also extend to the splenic flexure or rectum. Haustral markings are usually normal.
- CT scan or enema-enhanced radiograph is imperative to confirm the diagnosis and rule out underlying mechanical obstruction.

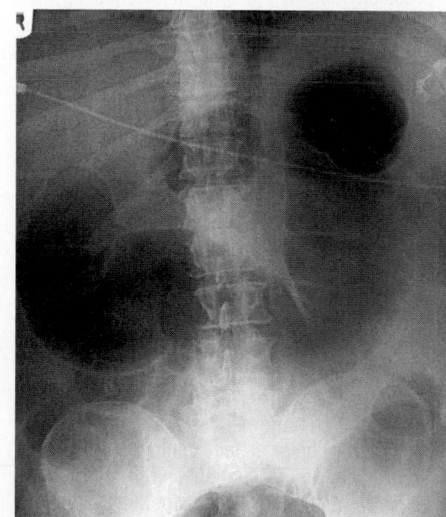

FIGURE 1A-28 Plain abdominal radiograph of patient with Ogilvie's syndrome 11 days after surgery for ruptured aneurysm of abdominal aorta. Dilation (probably due to ischemia) is present in both right and left colon. Syndrome resolved with vasodilators and intravenous neostigmine. (From Vincent JL, Abraham E, Moore FA, Kochanek PM, Fink MP: *Textbook of critical care*, ed 6, Philadelphia, 2011, Saunders.)

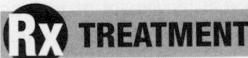 **TREATMENT**

The goals of treatment are to decompress the colon in order to relieve the patient's abdominal discomfort and also mitigate the risk of developing intestinal ischemia or frank perforation.

NONPHARMACOLOGIC THERAPY

- Supportive care with plain radiographs every 12-24 hr, serial abdominal exams, elimination of potential precipitants (medications, treatment of underlying medical illness), correction of electrolyte abnormalities, restricting PO intake, gastric decompression with NG tube to intermittent suction, rectal decompression with rectal tube attached to gravity, IV fluids, encouraging ambulation if possible, and alternating the patient in bed between right and left lateral decubitus as well as prone positioning with hips elevated are all appropriate nonpharmacologic approaches that can be made initially in the absence of colonic distention >12 cm or significant abdominal pain.
- Colonoscopic decompression with or without placement of a decompression tube is often the next step in management although use of this technique remains controversial as some studies indicate that the majority of patients spontaneously resolve within 48 hr. The risk of complication with colonoscopy in this setting is 3%, with a quoted death rate of 1%. Other studies suggest a success rate of 69%-90% with colonoscopic decompression.
- Colonoscopic decompression is indicated when supportive measures fail, there is clinical deterioration, or colonic diameter is between 11-13 cm. Placement of a decompression tube at the time of colonoscopy is thought to reduce the need for repeat colonoscopic decompression, which is required in about 40% of cases, but no trials have been done to compare rates of repeat decompression with and without decompression tube placement.
- Alternative minimally invasive options which are usually reserved for failed colonoscopic decompression include percutaneous tube cecostomy performed under radiologic guidance and percutaneous endoscopic colostomy, which are both techniques that grant percutaneous access to the colon for both decompression and irrigation to promote transit.
- Surgical management is reserved for those who have failed minimally invasive approaches or for patients with peritonitis or perforation. Surgical cecostomy tube or right hemicolectomy can be performed in the absence of perforation whereas ileostomy, colectomy, and Hartmann procedure can be performed in patients who have perforated or who have significant ischemia.

BOX 1A-2   Strategies to Prevent Ogilvie's Syndrome in the Critically Ill

- Early resuscitation of the circulation
- Minimizing prolonged infusion of high doses of α-adrenergic drugs
- Minimizing the use of dopamine
- Minimizing the prolonged use of opioids
- Use of thoracic epidural anesthesia
- Minimally invasive or laparoscopic surgery
- Selective decontamination of the digestive tract
- Avoiding antibiotics that disrupt growth of anaerobic fecal bacteria
- Early oral or enteral feeding
- Avoidance of proton pump inhibitors
- Early mobilization and ambulation
- Promoting timely defecation with
- Oral polyethylene glycol from day 3
- Intravenous neostigmine from day 5

From Vincent JL, Abraham E, Moore FA, Kochanek PM, Fink MP: *Textbook of critical care*, ed 6, Philadelphia, 2011, Saunders.

ACUTE GENERAL Rx

- Neostigmine is an IV anticholinesterase inhibitor that induces rapid colonic decompression in 80%-100% of appropriate candidates with a median response rate of 4 minutes at a starting dose of 2 mg, but requires close cardiovascular monitoring at the time of its administration and has several contraindications. Dose adjustments are required in chronic kidney disease and caution should be used in patients who have bradyarrhythmias, recent myocardial infarction, beta-blocker use, and asthma. Atropine should be made available at bedside and administration of glycopyrrolate, an anticholinergic agent, should be considered to decrease the risk of bradycardia and bronchoconstriction.
- Methylnaltrexone, a peripherally acting opiate receptor antagonist, can also be considered in cases thought to be precipitated by opiates but little data supports its use at this time.

CHRONIC Rx

- None

COMPLEMENTARY AND ALTERNATIVE MEDICINE

- None

DISPOSITION

- Close inpatient monitoring is indicated until there is return of spontaneous bowel function and resolution of abdominal distention.

REFERRAL

- Ogilvie's syndrome is best managed in a team approach involving both surgeons and gastroenterologists. Administration of neostigmine in proper candidates or decompressive colonoscopy should be pursued in patients with absence of peritoneal signs. If there is evidence of perforation, surgical management is indicated.

 **PEARLS & CONSIDERATIONS**

COMMENTS

- Maximal supportive care should be initiated for up to 48 hr barring any significant abdominal pain or massive distention greater than 12 cm on imaging.
- Administration of neostigmine is suggested in appropriate candidates.
- Colonic decompression should be attempted with or without decompression tube placement in patients who fail neostigmine or those who have contraindications to its use.
- Minimally invasive fluoroscopic, endoscopic, or surgical approaches are rarely needed. Surgery is reserved for patients who show signs of perforation.
- Oral laxatives should be discontinued with diagnosis but should be restarted once decompression is achieved.

PREVENTION

Box 1A-2 describes some prevention strategies for Ogilvie's Syndrome in the critically ill.

SUGGESTED READINGS

Available at www.expertconsult.com

AUTHORS: **JASON FERREIRA, M.D.** and **AMANDA PRESSMAN, M.D.**

BASIC INFORMATION

Acute coronary syndrome (ACS) represents a spectrum of clinical disorders that includes unstable angina (UA), non–ST-elevation myocardial infarction (NSTEMI), and ST-elevation myocardial infarction (STEMI). Although the severity of disease will vary between the three subsets of ACS, they share a common clinical presentation and pathophysiology. This syndrome is typically caused by atherosclerotic coronary artery disease (CAD). In this spectrum, UA and NSTEMI are represented electrocardiographically by the absence of ST-segment elevation in the appropriate clinical setting (i.e., chest discomfort). NSTEMI is represented by the addition of positive cardiac biomarkers. STEMI is characterized by ST-segment elevation or presumed new left bundle branch block on electrocardiogram (ECG). ACS should be thought of as a continuous spectrum as UA will often progress to a myocardial infarction if left untreated (Table 1A-10). Because of this continuum, the 2014 American College of Cardiology/American Heart Association (ACC/AHA) guidelines have grouped UA and NSTEMI into a single category called non–ST-elevation ACS (NSTE-ACS).

SYNONYMS

Unstable angina
NSTEMI
STEMI
Acute myocardial infarction

ICD-10CM CODES

I20.0	Unstable angina
I21.0-I21.3	ST elevation (STEMI)
I21.4	non-ST elevation (NSTEMI) myocardial infarction
I24.9	Acute ischemic heart disease, unspecified

EPIDEMIOLOGY & DEMOGRAPHICS

INCIDENCE: In the U.S., there are more than 780,000 cases of ACS yearly. Approximately 70% of myocardial infarctions are listed as NSTEMI, with the remainder being listed as STEMI. Patients with NSTE-ACS have more cardiac and noncardiac comorbidities than patients with STEMI. The underlying etiology, atherosclerotic CAD, is the number one cause of mortality.
PREDOMINANT SEX AND AGE: In evaluating chest pain, male gender and older age are important clinical factors that can identify ACS as a potential cause. In a 2005-2011 study sponsored by National Heart, Lung, and Blood Institute, the average age-adjusted first MI or fatal coronary heart disease rates per 1000 population in patients age 35 to 84 years of age were 3.7 for white men, 5.9 for black men, 2.1 for white women, and 4.0 for black women.
RISK FACTORS: Hypertension, diabetes mellitus, dyslipidemia, tobacco use, family history of premature CAD (CAD in a male first-degree relative younger than 55 years or a female younger than 65 years). Presence of these risk factors causes damage to the vascular endothelium and progression of atherosclerotic coronary artery plaques.

PHYSICAL FINDINGS & CLINICAL PRESENTATION

- Symptoms often, but not always, include chest discomfort described as a pressure that may radiate to the shoulders, neck, jaw, or back. Typical angina is substernal in location, brought on by emotional or physical stress, and relieved with rest and/or nitroglycerin.
- Women, diabetics, and the elderly often have an atypical presentation for ACS.
- Angina is considered unstable if it is new onset (<2 months), increasing in frequency (crescendo pattern), or occurring at rest (typically lasting >20 minutes).
- "Anginal equivalents" may include dyspnea, nausea, vomiting, and fatigue.
- ECG for NSTE-ACS may reveal ST-segment depression and/or T-wave inversion. ECG for definition of STEMI will reveal at least 1-mm ST-segment elevation in two contiguous leads or new left bundle branch block in the appropriate clinical setting.
- Physical exam findings alone are insufficient for the diagnosis of ACS. It is, however, important to assess the patient's hemodynamic stability and volume status. The patient may be diaphoretic and tachycardic. Signs of heart failure may be present, which include elevated jugular venous pressure (JVP), presence of an S3 gallop, and peripheral edema. The degree of heart failure with MI can be represented by the Killip classification: Killip Class 1 is no heart failure; Class 2 includes individuals with rales, elevated JVP, and S3 on exam; Class 3 includes individuals with frank pulmonary edema; Class 3 describes individuals in cardiogenic shock. The greater the Killip class, the worse the prognosis is. Another model that is now infrequently used is an invasive measurement of pulmonary capillary wedge pressure and stratification based on the Forrester classification system.

ETIOLOGY

Atherosclerotic CAD is the underlying etiology. The hallmark of ACS is the vulnerable atherosclerotic plaque, which typically has a thin fibrous cap and a large lipid core. This vulnerable plaque ultimately ruptures, which leads to platelet activation and aggregation, leading to thrombus formation. STEMI typically results from complete thrombotic occlusion of a coronary artery, whereas NSTE-ACS often has partial occlusion. Angiographically, it is often the intermediate coronary artery lesions (30% to 50% diameter vessel stenosis) that lead to subtotal or total vessel occlusion in two thirds of STEMI cases.

DIAGNOSIS

DIFFERENTIAL DIAGNOSIS

Chest pain mimicking ACS may be the result of various underlying disorders, some of which are also accompanied by ECG changes and/or cardiac biomarker release. Examples include acute pulmonary embolism, acute aortic dissection, pericarditis, myocarditis, costochondritis, pneumonia, tension pneumothorax, perforating ulcer, or Boerhaave syndrome.

WORKUP

Focused history and physical exam, 12-lead ECG, cardiac biomarkers, and chest radiograph (CXR). Initial biomarkers may not be positive. Often serial biomarkers are drawn every 6 to 8 hours for a total of three sets for the purposes of ruling out myocardial infarction (MI), or until peak to determine the severity of an established MI. Echocardiogram may reveal new regional wall motion abnormalities. Figure 1A-29 summarizes the evaluation of patients for acute coronary syndrome.

LABORATORY TESTS

- Cardiac biomarkers, which include creatine kinase (CK), its MB isoenzyme, myoglobin, and troponin I or T, will be positive in the setting of NSTEMI or STEMI. See Fig. 1A-30, *A* for timing of release of each biomarker. Troponin I is the most sensitive biomarker for cardiac myocyte damage and also predicts 42-day mortality in ACS and is considered the gold standard biomarker for diagnosis of myocardial infarction. (Fig. 1A-30, *B*). With the advent of high-sensitivity troponins, there is no benefit of CK-MB and myoglobin assays in the diagnosis of MI.
- Testing for B-type natriuretic peptide (BNP) has a class IIb recommendation in the 2014 NSTE-ACS guidelines for use as a prognostic tool in patients presenting with an MI.
- A complete fasting lipid panel should be obtained during the hospital admission.

TABLE 1A-10 Acute Coronary Syndromes

Spectrum of Acute Coronary Syndrome			
	Unstable Angina	**NSTEMI**	**STEMI**
Chest discomfort	1	1	1
Cardiac biomarkers	2	1	1
ECG changes	TWI and/or ST depression	TWI and/or ST depression	ST elevation or presumed new left bundle branch block
Pathophysiology	Partial/transient thrombotic occlusion	Partial/transient thrombotic occlusion	Complete thrombotic occlusion

NSTEMI, Non–ST-segment elevation myocardial infarction; *STEMI,* ST-segment myocardial infarction; *TWI,* T-wave inversion; *ECG,* electrocardiogram.

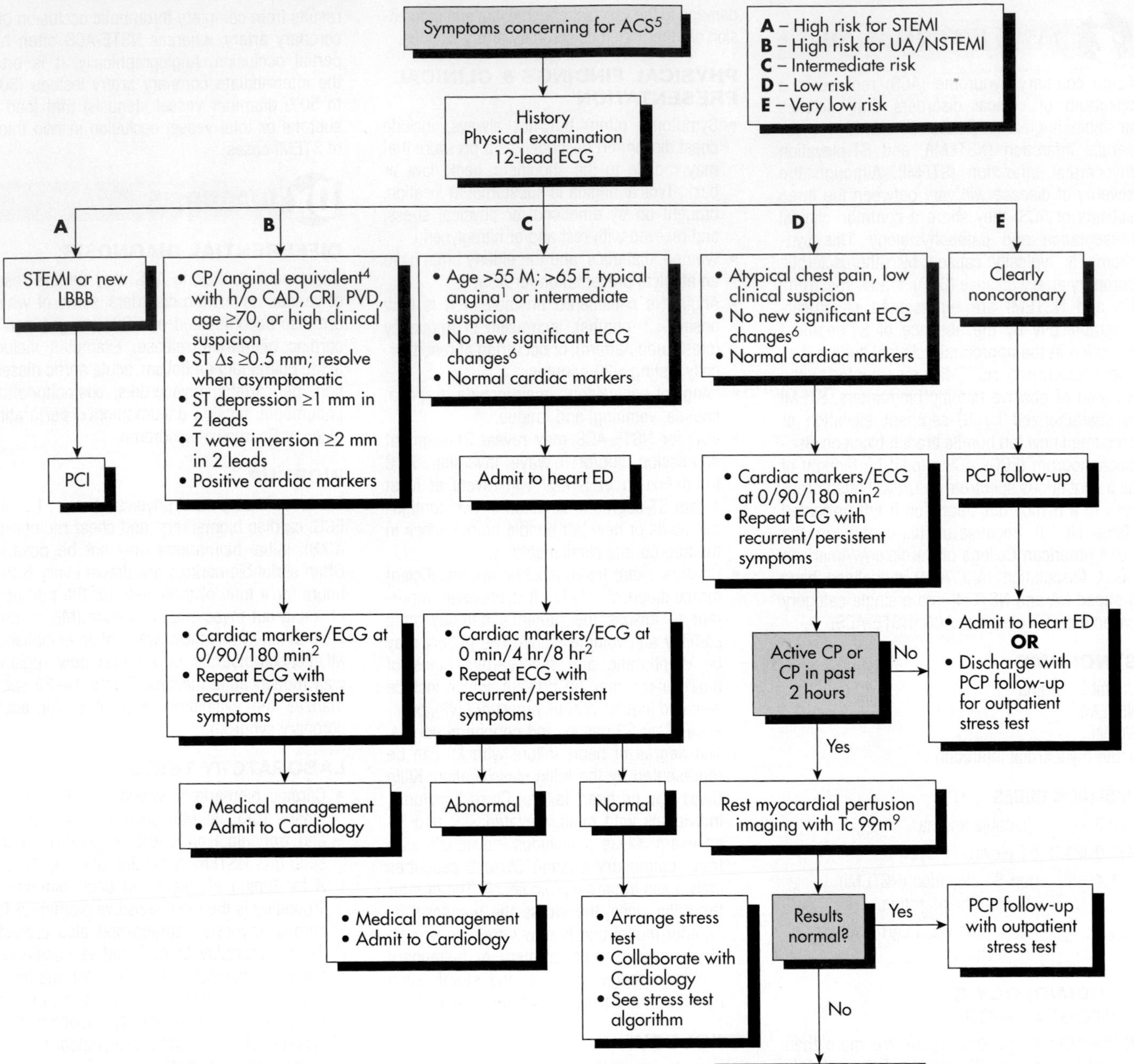

Symptoms concerning for ACS[5]

A	– High risk for STEMI
B	– High risk for UA/NSTEMI
C	– Intermediate risk
D	– Low risk
E	– Very low risk

History
Physical examination
12-lead ECG

A

STEMI or new LBBB

↓

PCI

B

- CP/anginal equivalent[4] with h/o CAD, CRI, PVD, age ≥70, or high clinical suspicion
- ST Δs ≥0.5 mm; resolve when asymptomatic
- ST depression ≥1 mm in 2 leads
- T wave inversion ≥2 mm in 2 leads
- Positive cardiac markers

↓

- Cardiac markers/ECG at 0/90/180 min[2]
- Repeat ECG with recurrent/persistent symptoms

↓

- Medical management
- Admit to Cardiology

C

- Age >55 M; >65 F, typical angina[1] or intermediate suspicion
- No new significant ECG changes[6]
- Normal cardiac markers

↓

Admit to heart ED

↓

- Cardiac markers/ECG at 0 min/4 hr/8 hr[2]
- Repeat ECG with recurrent/persistent symptoms

↓

Abnormal | Normal

Abnormal →
- Medical management
- Admit to Cardiology

Normal →
- Arrange stress test
- Collaborate with Cardiology
- See stress test algorithm

D

- Atypical chest pain, low clinical suspicion
- No new significant ECG changes[6]
- Normal cardiac markers

↓

- Cardiac markers/ECG at 0/90/180 min[2]
- Repeat ECG with recurrent/persistent symptoms

↓

Active CP or CP in past 2 hours — No →
- Admit to heart ED **OR**
- Discharge with PCP follow-up for outpatient stress test

Yes ↓

Rest myocardial perfusion imaging with Tc 99m[9]

↓

Results normal? — Yes → PCP follow-up with outpatient stress test

No ↓

- Medical management
- Admit to Cardiology

E

Clearly noncoronary

↓

PCP follow-up

DEFINITIONS:

[1]Typical angina:
1) Substernal chest pain or discomfort that is 2) provoked by exertion or emotional stress and 3) relieved by rest and/or nitroglycerin

[2]Cardiac marker timing: based on symptom onset; in cases of uncertainty assume symptom onset at ED arrival

[3]ECG normal: no significant ST depression/T wave inversions, BBB, LVH with repolarization, conduction defect, digoxin effect

[4]Anginal equivalent:
- Any symptoms that the physician feels may represent ACS
- Exertional dyspnea—most common anginal equivalent symptom

[5]ACS:
- STE-ACS—1 mm ST elevation in 2 leads
- NSTE-ACS
  – NSTEMI—positive cardiac biomarkers
  – Unstable angina—ischemia with negative biomarkers

[6]New significant ECG changes:
- ST Δs ≥0.5 mm; resolve when asymptomatic
- ST depression ≥1 mm in 2 leads
- T wave inversion ≥2 mm in 2 leads

[7]Regadenoson is preferred agent for chemical nuclear stress test. Technetium Tc-99m tetrofosmin is the preferred tracer.

FIGURE 1A-29 Evaluation of patients for acute coronary syndrome (ACS). *CAD,* Coronary artery disease; *CP,* chest pain; *CRI,* chronic renal insufficiency; *ECG,* electrocardiogram; *ED,* emergency department; *h/o,* history of; *LBBB,* left bundle branch block; *NSTE,* non–ST-segment elevation; *NSTEMI,* non–ST-segment elevation myocardial infarction; *PCP,* primary care physician; *PVD,* peripheral vascular disease; *STE,* ST-segment elevation; *STEMI,* ST-segment elevation myocardial infarction; *UA,* unstable angina. (From Adams JG et al: *Emergency medicine, clinical essentials,* ed 2, Philadelphia, 2013, Elsevier.)

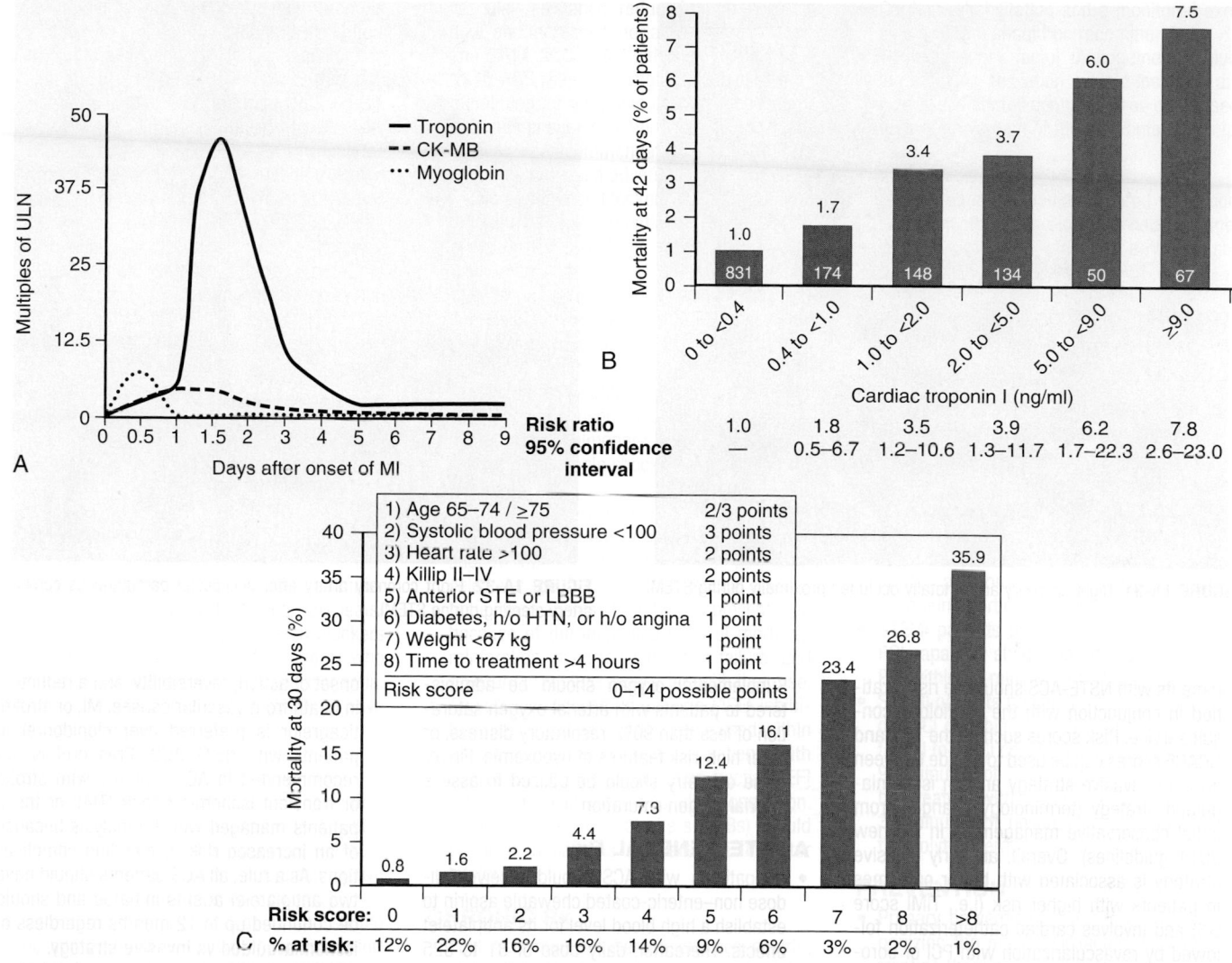

FIGURE 1A-30 Timing of release of cardiac biomarkers in ACS. *ULN,* Upper limit of normal, *MI,* myocardial infarction. (Modified from Shapiro BP, Jaffe AS: Cardiac biomarkers. In: Murphy JG, Lloyd MA [eds]: *Mayo Clinic cardiology: concise textbook,* ed 3, Rochester, MN: Mayo Clinic Scientific Press and New York, 2007, Informa Healthcare USA, pp 773-780; and Anderson JL et al: *J Am Coll Cardiol* 50:e1-e157, 2007, Fig. 5.)

RISK MODELS AND RISK SCORES

Risk models and scores such as TIMI, PURSUIT, and GRACE based on clinical, ECG, and laboratory data at presentation help to discriminate patients at high risk versus low risk for short- and intermediate-term adverse outcomes (Fig. 1A-30, *C*).

IMAGING STUDIES

- CXR to assist in evaluating for volume status and for other possible causes of chest discomfort.
- In patients for whom ECG and cardiac biomarkers are nondiagnostic but the suspicion for ACS is high given the history, an echocardiogram may be helpful to assess left ventricular (LV) function and regional wall motion abnormalities.
- Coronary CT angiography can be performed in patients with possible ACS, a normal 12-lead EKG result, negative troponin results, and no history of coronary artery disease (Class IIa)

- Cardiac stress testing (treadmill ECG, imaging stress studies using echocardiography or nuclear modalities) may further help to diagnose and risk stratify these patients. (See Coronary Artery Disease topic in Section I.)
- Coronary angiogram/cardiac catheterization will reveal coronary artery luminal irregularities/stenotic lesions. In patients with ACS who undergo coronary angiography, approximately 25% will have one vessel disease, 25% will have two vessel disease, 25% will have three vessel disease, 10% will have left main disease, and 15% will have coronary stenosis of <50% or normal coronaries.

🆁🆇 TREATMENT

The overall goal for patients with NSTE-ACS is to relieve myocardial ischemia and to prevent recurrent cardiovascular events. Antithrombotic therapy is needed to reduce thrombus burden, prevent further thrombosis, and improve coronary artery flow. Revascularization is needed

to prevent further events and improve flow within the coronary artery lumen. For patients with STEMI, the goal is immediate reperfusion therapy, whether it is chemical (i.e., thrombolysis) or mechanical (i.e., percutaneous coronary intervention [PCI]), and time from onset of ischemia to revascularization is an important prognostic factor. STEMI patients presenting to a hospital with PCI capability should be treated with primary PCI within 90 minutes of first medical contact (Figs. 1A-31 and 1A-32). At non–PCI-capable hospitals where the first medical contact to balloon time is more than 120 minutes, thrombolytic therapy should be given if no contraindications are present; thrombolytics should not be administered 24 hours after initial diagnosis of STEMI.

NONPHARMACOLOGIC THERAPY

- STEMI is a medical emergency and requires immediate reperfusion therapy; the best outcomes are seen with cardiac catheterization with primary PCI. Guidelines call for a goal door-to-balloon time of ≤90 minutes.

BASIC INFORMATION

DEFINITION

Acute kidney injury (AKI) is a rapid (<48 hr) impairment in kidney function that results in retention of products in the blood that are normally excreted by the kidneys, and is manifested by concurrent extracellular fluid volume and acid-base and mineral metabolism dysregulation. Criteria and staging of AKI are described in Table 1A-11.

SYNONYMS

Acute renal failure (ARF)
Acute renal insufficiency syndrome

ICD-10-CM CODES
N17.9 Acute kidney failure, unspecified
N17.0 Acute kidney failure with tubular necrosis
N17.1 Acute kidney failure with acute cortical necrosis
N17.2 Acute kidney failure with medullary necrosis
N17.8 Other acute kidney failure
N99.0 Postprocedural (acute) (chronic) kidney failure
O90.4 Postpartum acute kidney failure

EPIDEMIOLOGY & DEMOGRAPHICS

- Incidence of AKI is 3 cases/1000 persons in the general population. AKI that requires dialysis develops in 5 in 100,000 persons annually. Among hospitalized patients, approximately 20% develop AKI, and nearly 60% of intensive care unit patients incur AKI.
- Greater than 40% of hospital-associated AKI is iatrogenic.
- Most common cause of AKI in hospitalized patients is intrinsic kidney failure caused by acute tubular necrosis (ATN) and prerenal disease
- Risk factors for AKI include older age, preexisting chronic kidney disease, diabetes mellitus, and proteinuria.
- AKI occurs in 20% of patients with moderate sepsis and >50% of patients with septic shock and positive blood cultures.

PHYSICAL FINDINGS & CLINICAL PRESENTATION

- Frequent presenting symptoms include weakness, anorexia, generalized malaise, and nausea. Early or mild AKI may be asymptomatic.
- Oliguria (i.e., <400 to 500 ml urine/24 hr. However, patients can have nonoliguric renal failure) or anuria.
- Physical examination should focus on volume status. Findings vary with the duration and rapidity of onset of renal failure and the underlying etiology for AKI.
- Peripheral edema resulting from volume overload, heart failure, liver failure, or nephrotic syndrome. Pulmonary rales may also be present.
- Arrhythmias due to electrolyte imbalances and acidosis
- Neurologic findings include altered mental status, delirium, lethargy, myoclonus, seizures, flapping tremors (asterixes)
- Uremic odor, pruritus
- Flank pain, fasciculations, muscle cramps
- Pericardial effusion or pericardial rub (or both) from pericarditis

ETIOLOGY

- **Prerenal:** inadequate renal perfusion caused by hypovolemia, congestive heart failure, cirrhosis, sepsis. Sixty percent of community-acquired cases of AKI are from prerenal conditions.
- **Postrenal:** bladder outlet obstruction from prostatic enlargement, ureteral or urethral fibrosis, ureteral obstruction (stones, bladder masses, retroperitoneal fibrosis), or bilateral renal vein occlusion. In patients with two functioning kidneys, bilateral obstruction is usually required to cause significant AKI. Postrenal causes account for 5% to 15% of community-acquired AKI.
- **Intrinsic renal:** glomerulonephritis, allergic interstitial nephritis (AIN), ATN. Common causes of ATN include ischemia (e.g., hypotension or shock, postcardiac bypass or aorta surgery), rhabdomyolysis, sepsis, drug toxicity (e.g., aminoglycosides), iodinated radiocontrast nephropathy. Contrast-induced nephropathy is the third-most common cause of new AKI in hospitalized patients.

- Causes of AKI are described in Table 1A-12.
- Almost one third of cases of acute kidney injury can be prevented or mitigated by appropriate physician actions.

DIAGNOSIS

DIFFERENTIAL DIAGNOSIS

Refer to "Etiology." Diagnostic tests to distinguish prerenal and renal AKI are described in Table 1A-13. A diagnostic approach to patients with suspected AKI is described in Fig. 1A-33.

LABORATORY TESTS

- Elevated serum creatinine: the rate of rise is approximately 1 mg/dl/day in complete renal failure
- Elevated blood urea nitrogen (BUN): BUN/creatinine ratio is commonly >20:1 in prerenal azotemia, postrenal azotemia, and acute glomerulonephritis. The ratio is <20:1 in acute interstitial nephritis and ATN (Table 1A-14)
- Electrolytes (potassium, phosphate) are elevated; bicarbonate level, sodium, and calcium are decreased; metabolic acidosis is often present
- Complete blood count may reveal anemia from decreased erythropoietin production. Hemoconcentration, hemolysis, or leukocytosis suggesting infection may be present.
- Urinalysis is an important first step in the diagnostic evaluation. Prerenal and postrenal AKI are typically characterized by a normal urinalysis. Conversely, abnormal findings should prompt further work-up for specific intrinsic renal causes of AKI that may require urgent intervention: hematuria and proteinuria suggest a glomerulonephritis, heavy (3+) proteinuria suggests a nephrotic syndrome, and pyuria may suggest AIN. Microscopic examination of urine sediment may facilitate diagnosis: granular casts in ATN, dysmorphic red blood cells or red blood cell casts in acute glomerulonephritis, and white blood cell casts in acute interstitial nephritis.
- In oliguric patients, obtain urinary sodium and urinary creatinine to calculate fractional excretion of sodium [$FE_{Na} = 100\% \times (U_{Na} \times P_{Cr})/(P_{Na} \times U_{Cr})$] $FE_{Na} < 1$ in prerenal AKI and >1 in intrinsic AKI when urine output <400 ml/day. FE_{Na} may be falsely elevated in patients taking diuretics or falsely low in several intrinsic renal conditions, including acute glomerulonephritis, contrast-induced nephropathy, and rhabdomyolysis.
- Urinary osmolarity is 250-300 mOsm/kg in ATN, <400 mOsm/kg in postrenal azotemia, and >500 mOsm/kg in prerenal azotemia and acute glomerulonephritis (Table 1A-15)
- Combined use of cystatin C, a protein that is freely filtered by the glomerulus, and serum creatinine improves glomerular filtration rate (GFR) estimates in AKI
- Fractional excretion of urea (FE_{Urea}) is used to assess renal dysfunction in AKI. FE_{Urea} is calculated as [$100\% \times (U_{Urea} \times PCr) / (P_{Urea} \times UCr)$]. $FE_{Urea} < 35\%$ suggests prerenal acute kidney injury; $FE_{Urea} > 50\%$ indicates intrinsic AKI. FE_{Urea} is more useful than FE_{Na} during diuretic therapy.

TABLE 1A-11 Kidney Disease: Improving Global Outcomes (KDIGO) Criteria for Diagnosis of Acute Kidney Injury

AKI Definition and Staging		
Stage	**Serum Creatinine Criteria**	**Urine Output Criteria**
1	$\Delta S_{Cr} \geq 0.3$ mg/dl (30 μmol/L) or $S_{Cr} \geq 1.5, < 2.0 \times$ baseline*	UO <0.5 ml/kg/h × 6-12 h
2	$S_{Cr} > 2.0, < 3.0 \times$ baseline	UO <0.5 ml/kg/h >= 12 h
3	$S_{Cr} > 3.0 \times$ baseline or $S_{Cr} \geq 4.0$ mg/dl with an acute rise ≥ 0.5 mg/dl (50 μmol/L) or on renal replacement therapy	UO <0.3 ml/kg/h × 24 h or anuria × 12 h

SCr, serum creatinine; *UO*, urinary output.
*To meet criteria, rise of >=0.3mg/dl must be within 48 hours; or increase to ≥1.5 times baseline SCr is known or presumed to have occurred within previous 7 days.
Adapted from KDIGO Clinical Practice Guideline for Acute Kidney Injury, 2012.

TABLE 1A-12 Etiologies of Acute Kidney Injury

Prerenal Causes (Decreased Renal Blood Flow)	Intrinsic Renal Causes	Postrenal Causes
Hypovolemia Renal losses (diuretics, osmotic agents, polyuria) Gastrointestinal losses (vomiting, diarrhea) Cutaneous losses (burns, exfoliative syndromes) Hemorrhage Pancreatitis **Decreased Cardiac Output** Congestive heart failure Pulmonary embolism Acute myocardial infarction Severe valvular heart disease Abdominal compartment syndrome Renal artery obstruction (stenosis, embolism, thrombosis, dissection) **Systemic Vasodilation** Sepsis Anaphylaxis Anesthetics Drug overdose **Afferent Arteriolar Vasoconstriction** Hypercalcemia Drugs (NSAIDs, amphotericin B, calcineurin inhibitors, norepinephrine, radiocontrast agents, aminoglycosides) Hepatorenal syndrome Efferent arteriolar vasodilation (angiotensin converting enzyme inhibitors, aldosterone receptor blockers)	**Vascular: Large and Small Vessels** Trauma Renal vein obstruction (thrombosis, ventilation with high-level PEEP, abdominal compartment syndrome) Microangiopathy (thrombotic thrombocytopenic purpura, hemolytic-uremic syndrome, disseminated intravascular coagulation, preeclampsia) Malignant hypertension Scleroderma renal crisis Transplant rejection Atheroembolic disease **Glomerular** Antiglomerular basement membrane disease (Goodpasture syndrome) Antineutrophil cytoplasmic antibody-associated glomerulonephritis (Wegener granulomatosis) Immune complex glomerulonephritis, systemic lupus erythematosus, postinfectious cryoglobulinemia, primary membranoproliferative glomerulonephritis **Tubular** Ischemic Cytotoxic Heme pigment (rhabdomyolysis, intravascular hemolysis) Crystals (tumor lysis syndrome, seizures, ethylene glycol poisoning, vitamin C megadose, acyclovir, indinavir, methotrexate) Drugs (aminoglycosides, lithium, amphotericin B, pentamidine, cisplatin, ifosfamide, radiocontrast agents), synthetic cannabinoid use **Interstitial** Drugs (penicillins, cephalosporins, NSAIDs, proton pump inhibitors, allopurinol, rifampin, indinavir, mesalamine, sulfonamides) Infection (pyelonephritis, viral infection) **Systemic Disease** Sjögren syndrome, sarcoidosis, systemic lupus erythematosus, lymphoma, leukemia, tubulonephritis, uveitis	**Ureteral Obstruction** Calculus Tumor (intrinsic or extrinsic) Fibrosis Ligation during pelvic surgery **Bladder Neck Obstruction** Benign prostatic hypertrophy Prostate cancer Neurogenic bladder Tricyclic antidepressants Ganglionic blockers Bladder tumor Calculus Hemorrhage/clot **Urethral Obstruction** Strictures Tumor Phimosis Renal calcinosis Obstructed urinary catheter, ureteral stent, or ileal conduit Pelvic trauma, retroperitoneal hematoma

NSAIDs, Nonsteroidal antiinflammatory drugs; *PEEP,* positive end-expiratory pressure.
Modified from Cameron JL, Cameron AM: *Current surgical therapy,* ed 10, Philadelphia, 2011, Saunders.

TABLE 1A-13 Diagnostic Tests to Distinguish Between Prerenal and Renal Acute Kidney Injury

Index	Prerenal Causes	Renal Causes
FENa	<1%	>2%
Urine sodium	<10 mmol/L	>40 mmol/L
Urine/plasma osmolality	>1.5	1 to 1.5
Renal failure index	<1	>2
BUN/creatinine ratio	>20	<10

BUN, Blood urea nitrogen; *FENa,* fractional excretion of sodium. Calculation of FENa: (Urine sodium × Plasma creatinine)/(Plasma sodium × Serum creatinine) × 100. Renal failure index: (Urine sodium × Urine creatinine)/Plasma creatinine.
From Cameron JL, Cameron AM: *Current surgical therapy,* ed 10, Philadelphia, 2011, Saunders.

IMAGING STUDIES

- ECG is done to detect arrhythmias, especially in hyperkalemia: peaked T waves in precordial leads, widening QRS interval, and/or bradycardia with AV nodal blockade
- Chest radiograph to detect signs of congestive heart failure and pulmonary renal syndromes often characterized by pulmonary alveolar hemorrhage (Goodpasture's syndrome, granulomatous polyangiitis)
- Kidney ultrasonography to determine kidney sizes (distinguishes acute from chronic kidney disease), presence of obstruction, and renal vascular status (Doppler study)
- Computed tomography (CT) with radiocontrast administration is typically avoided in AKI. However, unenhanced CT scans may identify obstructing ureteral stones.

℞ TREATMENT

Management of AKI depends on the underlying etiology. Some conditions (e.g., glomerulonephritis) require specific therapy, but the general focus of treatment for established AKI is supportive care and limiting additional injury.

NONPHARMACOLOGIC THERAPY

- Stop nephrotoxic medications
- Appropriate fluid balance
- Dietary modification: (1) energy prescription of 120–150 KJ/kg/day, (2) potassium restriction (60 mEq/day), (3) sodium restriction (90 mEq/day), (4) phosphorus (800 mg/day), and (5) protein supplementation of 0.6 to 1.4 g/kg per day depending on requirement for dialysis
- Daily weight
- Modification of drug dosages or schedules of renally excreted medications

ACUTE GENERAL ℞

- Correct electrolyte abnormalities and metabolic acidosis.
- Administer loop diuretics with volume overload.
- Administer pressors or vasodilators, when applicable, in congestive heart failure.

Specific treatment is variable and dependent on etiology of AKI:

- Prerenal: IV volume expansion with isotonic solutions in hypovolemic patients.
- Intrinsic kidney failure: discontinue all potential nephrotoxins and treat condition(s) causing kidney failure. In severe AIN cases, consider a trial of corticosteroids.
- Postrenal: Eliminate cause of obstruction. Immediate catheter insertion for bladder outlet obstruction and nephrostomy or ureteral stents for upper tract obstruction. Hyperkalemia-related ECG changes: IV calcium to prevent arrhythmias; IV insulin and glucose to shift potassium into cells; and IV bicarbonate therapy for metabolic acidosis to shift potassium into cells. These three treatments are temporary and definitive therapy requires bodily potassium removal via the gastrointestinal (potassium-binding agents) or urinary (diuretics) tracts or dialytic therapy.

ADJUNCTIVE ℞

- Monitoring of renal function parameters and electrolytes
- Renally excreted drugs are adjusted according to creatinine clearance or GFR to prevent further kidney damage or other medication-related toxicities.
- Prevent further renal insult with appropriate volume expansion, particularly before contrast administration, and avoid nephrotoxic agents. Volume expansion with isotonic solutions is more effective than hydration with hypotonic solutions. Isotonic saline or bicarbonate-containing solutions are effective, with or without concomitant N-acetylcysteine prophylaxis, which has shown conflicting results regarding its ability to reduce the risk of iodinated radiocontrast-induced nephropathy. See "Chronic Kidney Disease" entry for indications for initiation of dialysis.

DISPOSITION

- General indications for initiation of dialysis in AKI:
  1. Uremic symptoms (encephalopathy, pericarditis)
  2. Extracellular fluid volume overload refractory to medical management
  3. Severe acid-base imbalance refractory to medical management
  4. Significant electrolyte derangement in (e.g., hyperkalemia, hyponatremia) refractory to medical management
- Intermittent hemodialysis (IHD) and continuous renal replacement therapy (CRRT) have similar outcomes for patients with AKI. However, CRRT is associated with greater hemodynamic stability and fluid removal compared to conventional IHD.
- Renal function recovery (ability to discontinue dialysis) varies from 50% to 75% in AKI survivors.
- Overall mortality rate in AKI is nearly 50%, varying from to 35% in patients with prerenal or postrenal AKI to 60% in patients with ATN.
- The combination of AKI and sepsis is associated with a 70% mortality rate.

❗ PEARLS & CONSIDERATIONS

- Patients with AKI are susceptible to infections and sepsis
- AKI survivors are at risk for development of CKD, and follow-up with monitoring of kidney function is essential even after apparent renal recovery.

EBM EVIDENCE

Available at www.expertconsult.com

SUGGESTED READINGS

Available at www.expertconsult.com

RELATED CONTENT

Acute Renal Failure (Patient Information)
Acute Renal Failure (Patient Information)
Chronic Kidney Disease (Related Key Topic)

AUTHOR: **MICHAEL HEUNG, M.D., M.S.**

BASIC INFORMATION

DEFINITION

Acute liver failure (ALF) is defined as rapid development (<26 wk) of severe hepatic injury, coagulation abnormalities (international normalized ratio [INR] >1.5), and encephalopathy in a patient without preexisting liver disease, in the absence of acute alcoholic hepatitis.

SYNONYMS

Fulminant hepatic failure
Fulminant hepatitis
Fulminant hepatic necrosis
Acute hepatic necrosis
Acute and subacute necrosis of liver

ICD-10CM CODES
72.00 Acute liver failure w/o coma
72.01 Acute liver failure w/ coma

EPIDEMIOLOGY & DEMOGRAPHICS

INCIDENCE (IN U.S.): Affects approximately 2000 people/yr
PREDOMINANT SEX AND AGE: Seen more in women than men (73% vs. 27%)
RISK FACTORS:
- Intentional drug overdose
- Intravenous drug use
- Alcohol use
- Occupational exposure to blood or body fluids
- Hepatotoxic medications

PHYSICAL FINDINGS & CLINICAL PRESENTATION

- Symptoms of ALF include mental status changes, nausea, vomiting, easy bleeding or bruising. Abdominal pain and jaundice are often present.
- Physical findings include some degree of encephalopathy (see Table 1A-16) and may include icteric sclera, jaundice, asterixis, hepatomegaly, decreased hepatic mass on percussion, and ascites. Multisystem organ failure can ensue. In rare cases, cerebral edema and increased intracranial pressure can occur, with abnormal pupillary exam findings, hypertension, bradycardia, seizures, and loss of brainstem reflexes.
- Vesicular skin lesions are suggestive of herpes simplex virus (HSV).

TABLE 1A-16 Grades of Encephalopathy

Grade	Description
I	Changes in behavior with minimal change in level of consciousness
II	Gross disorientation, drowsiness, possibly asterixis, inappropriate behavior
III	Marked confusion, incoherent speech, sleeping most of the time but arousable to vocal stimuli
IV	Comatose, unresponsiveness to pain, decorticate or decerebrate posturing

- Family history of unexplained liver disease/cirrhosis should prompt ocular exam to look for Kayser-Fleischer rings (copper rings around the iris seen in Wilson disease).

ETIOLOGY

- Common causes include:
  1. Acetaminophen toxicity (46%)
  2. Indeterminate (14%)
  3. Idiosyncratic drug reaction (12%)
  4. Viral hepatitis (A, B) (10%)
  Rarer causes include alcoholic hepatitis, autoimmune hepatitis, Wilson disease, ischemic hepatopathy, Budd-Chiari syndrome, acute fatty liver of pregnancy, venoocclusive disease, toxin ingestion (e.g., mushroom poisoning [Amanita phalloides]), sepsis, infiltrative malignancy (breast cancer, lymphoma, myeloma, melanoma, small cell lung cancer), and other viruses (adenovirus, hepatitis E, HSV).

DIAGNOSIS

DIFFERENTIAL DIAGNOSIS

- Severe acute hepatitis (including alcoholic hepatitis): jaundice and coagulopathy without encephalopathy
- Cirrhosis (includes decompensated cirrhosis)
- Hepatocellular carcinoma

WORKUP (BOX 1A-3)

- Fig. 1A-34 describes an algorithm for evaluation of acute liver failure.
- Clinical history is critical and should include medication use (prescriptions, over-the-counter medications, herbal supplements), alcohol use, recreational drug use, prior symptoms of jaundice, onset of symptoms, history of suicide attempts, recent travel to endemic areas of viral hepatitis, and family history of liver failure/disease.
- Laboratory evaluation: complete blood count, liver function tests (LFTs) (AST, ALT, alkaline phosphatase, GGT, total and direct bilirubin, PT/INR, albumin), chemistry panel (sodium, potassium, chloride, bicarbonate, BUN, creatinine, glucose, magnesium, phosphate, calcium), arterial blood gas, arterial lactate, blood type and screen, acetaminophen level, ethanol level, toxicology screen, viral hepatitis serologies (anti–hepatitis A IgM, hepatitis B surface antigen, anti–hepatitis B core IgM, anti–hepatitis C antibody, hepatitis C viral load, anti–hepatitis E Ab, HSV-1 IgM, varicella zoster virus, ceruloplasmin level, pregnancy test, arterial ammonia level, autoimmune markers (ANA, ASMA, total IgG levels), HIV-1, HIV-2, amylase, lipase, ceruloplasmin.
- Abdominal ultrasound with Doppler, CT/MRI of the head.
- Prompt liver biopsy (via transjugular approach to decrease risk of bleeding) should be performed in cases in which:
  1. The etiology remains unknown after initial workup or
  2. It is thought to be secondary to autoimmune hepatitis or malignancy.

LABORATORY TESTS

- Patients with ALF typically have a prolonged prothrombin time (INR >1.5), elevated transaminases, elevated bilirubin, and low platelet count (<150,000).
- Other possible lab findings can include an elevated BUN/creatinine (studies show 30%-50% also have acute kidney injury), hypoglycemia (impairment of gluconeogenesis), hypophosphatemia, hypomagnesemia, hypokalemia, acidosis or alkalosis, elevated LDH, and elevated ammonia.

IMAGING STUDIES

- Abdominal ultrasound with Doppler should be ordered to evaluate for Budd-Chiari syndrome, cirrhosis, portal hypertension, hepatic congestion, and hepatic steatosis.
- CT or MRI scan of the head should be obtained to ensure no other causes for altered mental status.

BOX 1A-3 Investigations in Fulminant Hepatic Failure

Baseline essential investigations
Biochemistry
  ○ Bilirubin, transaminases
  ○ Alkaline phosphatase
  ○ Albumin
  ○ Urea and electrolytes
  ○ Creatinine
  ○ Calcium, phosphate
  ○ Ammonia
  ○ Acid-base, lactate
  ○ Glucose
Hematology
  ○ Full blood count, platelets
  ○ PT, PTT
  ○ Factors V or VII
  ○ Blood group cross-match
Septic screen
Omitting lumbar puncture
  ○ Radiology
  ○ Chest radiograph
  ○ Abdominal ultrasound
  ○ Head CT scan or MRI
Neurophysiology
  ○ Electroencephalogram
Diagnostic investigations
Serum
  ○ Acetaminophen levels
  ○ Cu, ceruloplasmin (>3 yr)
  ○ Autoantibodies
  ○ Immunoglobulins
  ○ Amino acids
  ○ Lactate
  ○ Pyruvate
  ○ Hepatitis A, B, C, E
  ○ EBV, CMV, HSV
  ○ Other viruses
Urine
  ○ Toxic metabolites
  ○ Amino acids, succinylacetone
  ○ Organic acids
  ○ Reducing sugars

CMV, Cytomegalovirus; EBV, Epstein-Barr virus; HSV, herpes simplex virus; PT, prothrombin time; PTT, partial thromboplastin time.
From Fuhrman BP, Zimmerman JJ: Fuhrman and Zimmerman's pediatric critical care, ed 4, Philadelphia, 2011, Mosby.

BASIC INFORMATION

DEFINITION

Acute respiratory distress syndrome (ARDS) is a form of noncardiogenic pulmonary edema that results from acute damage to the alveoli. It is characterized by acute diffuse infiltrative lung lesions with resulting interstitial and alveolar edema, severe hypoxemia, and respiratory failure. The cardinal feature of ARDS, refractory hypoxemia, is caused by formation of protein-rich alveolar edema after damage to the integrity of the lung's alveolar-capillary barrier.

The definition of ARDS based on the American–European Consensus Conference (AECC) from 1994 included the following components:

1. The syndrome must present acutely
2. A ratio of Pao_2 to Fio_2 ≤200 regardless of the level of positive end expiratory pressure (PEEP)
3. The detection of bilateral pulmonary infiltrates on frontal chest radiograph
4. Absence of congestive heart failure (pulmonary artery wedge pressure [PAWP] ≤18 mm Hg or no clinical evidence of elevated left atrial pressure on the basis of chest radiograph or other clinical data)

The Berlin definition of ARDS adopted in 2011 addresses some of the limitations of the AECC definition and establishes the following criteria for ARDS:

- Timing: Within 1 week of a known clinical insult or new or worsening respiratory symptoms
- Chest imaging (chest x-ray or CT scan): Bilateral opacities, not fully explained by effusions, lobar/lung collapse, or nodules
- Origin of edema: Respiratory failure not fully explained by cardiac failure or fluid overload. Need objective assessment (e.g., echocardiography) to exclude hydrostatic edema if no risk factor present
- Oxygenation (if altitude is higher than 1000 m, the correction factor should be calculated as follows: $[Pao_2/Fio_2 \times \{barometric\ pressure/760\}]$
- Mild: 200 mm Hg $<Pao_2/Fio_2$ ≤300 mm Hg with PEEP or CPAP ≥5 cm H_2O (this may be delivered noninvasively in the mild ARDS group)

- Moderate: 100 mm Hg $<Pao_2/Fio_2$ ≤200 mm Hg with PEEP or CPAP ≥5 cm H_2O
- Severe; Pao_2/Fio_2 ≤100 mm Hg with PEEP or CPAP ≥5 cm H_2O

SYNONYMS

ARDS
Adult respiratory distress syndrome

ICD-10CM CODES

J80 Acute respiratory distress syndrome

EPIDEMIOLOGY & DEMOGRAPHICS

- More than 150,000 ARDS cases per year in the U.S. 7.1% of all patients admitted to an ICU and 16.1% of all patients on mechanical ventilation develop ARDS.
- Incidence is 1.5 to 8.3 cases per 100,000 per year.
- Approximately 50% of patients who develop ARDS do so within 24 hours of the inciting event. Mortality rate is 40% to 50%.

PHYSICAL FINDINGS & CLINICAL PRESENTATION

- Signs and symptoms
  1. Dyspnea
  2. Chest discomfort
  3. Cough
  4. Anxiety
- Physical examination
  1. Tachypnea
  2. Tachycardia
  3. Hypertension
  4. Paradoxical breathing and use of accessory muscles
  5. Coarse crepitations or crackles of both lungs
  6. Fever may be present if infection is the underlying etiology

ETIOLOGY

- Sepsis (>40% of cases)
- Aspiration: near-drowning, aspiration of gastric contents (>30% of cases)
- Trauma (>20% of cases)
- Multiple transfusions, blood products
- Drugs (e.g., overdose of morphine, methadone, heroin; reaction to nitrofurantoin)
- Noxious inhalation (e.g., chlorine gas, high O_2 concentration)
- Post-resuscitation

- Cardiopulmonary bypass
- Pneumonia
- Burns
- Pancreatitis
- A history of chronic alcohol abuse significantly increases the risk of developing ARDS in critically ill patients.
- Table 1A-18 describes risk factors associated with development of ARDS.

DIAGNOSIS

DIFFERENTIAL DIAGNOSIS

- Cardiogenic pulmonary edema
- Viral pneumonitis
- Lymphangitic carcinomatosis
- Transfusion-related lung injury
- Acute idiopathic interstitial lung disease (e.g., Hamman-Rich syndrome, acute eosinophilic pneumonitis)

WORKUP

The search for an underlying cause should focus on treatable causes (e.g., infections such as sepsis or pneumonia)

- Arterial blood gases (ABGs)
- Hemodynamic monitoring
- Bronchoalveolar lavage (selected patients)

LABORATORY TESTS

- ABGs:
  1. Initially: varying degrees of hypoxemia, generally resistant to supplemental oxygen
  2. Respiratory alkalosis, decreased Pco_2
  3. Widened alveolar-arterial gradient
  4. Hypercapnia as the disease progresses
- Bronchoalveolar lavage:
  1. The most prominent finding is an increased number of polymorphonucleocytes.
  2. The presence of eosinophilia has therapeutic implications because these patients respond to corticosteroids.
- Blood and urine cultures
- Blood work:
  1. Increased or reduced white blood cell count with left shift if concomitant infectious process
  2. Normal or mildly elevated B-type natriuretic peptide level
  3. Increased lactate level if concomitant sepsis or septic shock

IMAGING STUDIES

Chest radiograph (Fig. 1A-35).

- The initial chest radiograph might be normal in the initial hours after the precipitating event.
- Bilateral interstitial infiltrates are usually seen within 24 hr; they often are more prominent in the bases and periphery.
- "White out" of both lung fields can be seen in advanced stages.
- CT scan of chest: diffuse consolidation with air bronchograms, bullae, pleural effusions. Pneumomediastinum and pneumothoraces

TABLE 1A-18 Risk Factors Associated with Development of Acute Lung Injury and Acute Respiratory Distress Syndrome

Direct Lung Injury	Indirect Lung Injury
Pneumonia	Sepsis
Aspiration of gastric contents	Multiple trauma
Pulmonary contusion	Cardiopulmonary bypass
Fat, amniotic fluid, or air emboli	Drug overdose
Near-drowning	Acute pancreatitis
Inhalational injury	Transfusion of blood products
Reperfusion pulmonary edema	

From Vincent JL et al: *Textbook of critical care*, ed 6, Philadelphia, 2011, Saunders.

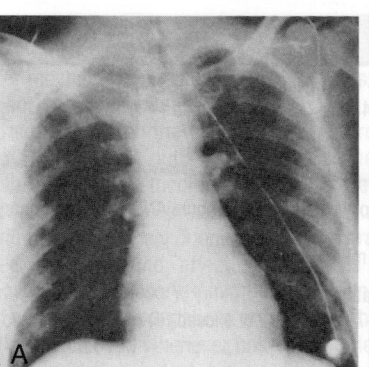 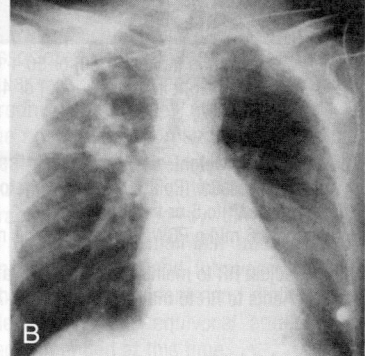 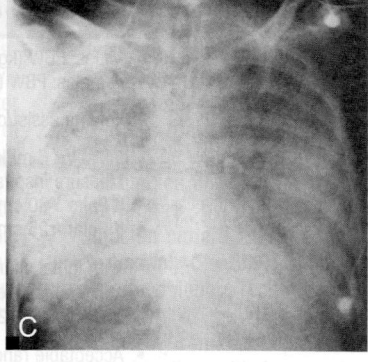

FIGURE 1A-35 Acute respiratory distress syndrome. X-ray of a young man who had sustained severe trauma and blood loss in a road traffic accident; the limbs cover a period of 5 days from a relatively normal x-ray **(A)**, to bilateral infiltrates **(B)**, to bilateral "white out" **(C)**, accompanied by severe hypoxemia. A Swan-Ganz catheter for measurement of pulmonary artery "wedge" pressure (as a reflection of left atrial pressure) can be seen *in situ* on the x-ray in **C**. The patient died shortly after the last film. (From Souhami RL, Moxham J: *Textbook of medicine*, ed 4, London, 2002, Churchill Livingstone.)

may also be present and could result from ventilatory-associated barotrauma.

Rx TREATMENT

NONPHARMACOLOGIC THERAPY

Treatment of ARDS is supportive.

Hemodynamic monitoring:
- Can be used for the initial evaluation of ARDS (in ruling out cardiogenic pulmonary edema) and its subsequent management. However, a pulmonary catheter is not indicated in the routine management of ARDS and trials have shown that clinical management involving the early use of pulmonary artery catheters in patients with ARDS did not significantly affect mortality and morbidity rates and may result in more complications as compared with a central venous catheter.
- Although no dynamic profile is diagnostic of ARDS, the presence of pulmonary edema, a high cardiac output, and a low pulmonary capillary wedge pressure (PCWP) is characteristic of ARDS.
- It is important to remember that partially treated intravascular volume overload and flash pulmonary edema can have the hemodynamic features of ARDS; filling pressures can also be elevated by increased intrathoracic pressures or with fluid administration; cardiac function can be depressed by acidosis, hypoxemia, or other factors associated with sepsis.

Ventilatory support:

Noninvasive positive-pressure ventilation (NIPPV) (i.e., BiPAP) should only be used in selected cases in patients with hypoxic respiratory failure. A recent randomized control study showed that high-flow oxygen by nasal cannula reduced ventilator-free days and mortality compared with NIPPV in patients with hypoxemic respiratory failure without hypercapnia. Either modality should not delay intubation and mechanical ventilation initiation in patients with rapidly progressing clinical deterioration.

Mechanical ventilation is generally necessary to maintain adequate gas exchange (Table 1A-19). General recommendations for ventilator settings in ARDS are described in Table 1A-20. A low tidal volume and low plateau pressure ventilator strategy are recommended to avoid ventilator-induced injury. Assist-control is generally preferred initially with the following ventilator settings:
- Fio_2 1.0 (until a lower value can be used to achieve adequate oxygenation). When possible, minimize oxygen toxicity by maintaining Fio_2 at <60%.
- Tidal volume: Set initial tidal volume at 6 ml/kg of predicted body weight (PBW 5 50.0 1 0.91 [height: 152.4 cm] for men, PBW 5 45.5 1 0.91 [height: 152.4 cm] for women). The concept of using PBW is based on the fact that lung size depends most strongly on height and sex; PBW normalizes the tidal volume to lung size. Aim to maintain plateau pressure (Pplat) at <30 mm Hg.
- PEEP 5 cm H_2O or greater (to increase lung volume and keep alveoli open). PEEP should be applied in small increments of 3 to 5 cm H_2O (see Table 1A-19) to achieve acceptable arterial saturation (>0.9) with nontoxic Fio_2 values (<0.6) and acceptable airway plateau pressures (< 30 to 35 cm H_2O). It is important to remember that an increase in PEEP may lower cardiac output and, despite improvement in Pao_2, may actually have a negative effect on tissue oxygenation (the major determinants of tissue oxygenation are hemoglobin, percent saturation, and cardiac output). The optimal level of PEEP remains unestablished. Although higher levels of PEEP may help prevent life-threatening hypoxemia and be associated with lower hospital mortality in patients meeting criteria for ARDS, such benefit is unlikely in patients with less severe lung injury (paO2/FiO2 >200) and a strategy of treating such patients with high PEEP levels may be harmful.
- Inspiratory flow: 60 L/min.
- Ventilatory rate: high ventilatory rates of up to 35 breaths/min are often necessary in

patients with ARDS to achieve the desired minute ventilation because of their increased physiologic dead space and smaller lung volumes. Patients must be monitored for excessive intrathoracic gas trapping (auto-PEEP or intrinsic PEEP) that can depress cardiac output.
- Permissive hypercapnia: To maintain a low plateau pressure, a low tidal volume is frequently required, leading to a reduced minute ventilation and hypoventilation with consequently a respiratory acidosis (elevated PCO_2 and reduced pH). Most patients (excluding patient with cerebral edema, acute coronary syndrome, seizures, cardiac arrhythmias, and so on) can tolerate a low pH without major consequences. Bicarbonate replacement is suggested when the pH falls to below 7.20.
- Sedation: GABA receptor agonists (including propofol and benzodiazepines such as midazolam) have traditionally been the most commonly administered sedative drugs for ICU patients. Recent trials indicate that the alpha-2 agonist dexmedetomidine (Precedex) may have distinct advantages. At comparable sedation levels, dexmedetomidine-treated patients spent less time on ventilator, experienced less delirium, and developed less tachycardia and hypertension. The most notable adverse effect of dexmedetomidine was bradycardia. Preliminary trials involving early administration of the neuromuscular blocking agent cisatracurium in patients with severe ARDS have shown improvement in the adjusted 90-day survival and increase in the time off the ventilator without increase in muscle weakness. However, patients who receive continuous infusions of sedatives generally need to be on mechanical ventilation longer than those who receive intermittent dosing. Paralysis of patients with neuromuscular blockade (NMB) to facilitate controlled ventilation is associated with protracted mechanical ventilation and postparalysis weakness. It should ideally be conducted for a brief period, and limited to patients with severe ARDS. Daily interruption of sedation

Acute Urinary Retention (AUR)

 BASIC INFORMATION

DEFINITION

The acute cessation of urinary flow; inability to void.

SYNONYMS

Inability to urinate AUR

ICD-10CM CODES
R33.9 Retention of urine, unspecified

EPIDEMIOLOGY & DEMOGRAPHICS

INCIDENCE: Can occur in any age group and both sexes. It is the most common urologic emergency.
PEAK INCIDENCE: Males older than age 60. Over a 5-year period, AUR will occur in 10% of men older than 70 and one third of men older than 80.
PREVALENCE: Increased longevity has caused an increase in prevalence.
PREDOMINANT SEX AND AGE: Men older than 60 years.
GENETICS: None known.
RISK FACTORS: Obstructive risk factors include benign prostatic hypertrophy (BPH) and bladder, pelvic, and urethral masses. Acute trauma, surgery, medications (especially over-the-counter [OTC] antihistamines), neurologic disease, and infection can be contributing or precipitating factors, particularly when superimposed on obstructive risk factors.

PHYSICAL FINDINGS & CLINICAL PRESENTATION

- Patients will present with the acute inability to pass urine.
- Pain in the lower abdomen and suprapubic region is typical (this is not typically present with chronic urinary retention due to the more gradual onset).
- The bladder may be palpable on abdominal or rectal exam. There may be tenderness with deep palpation.
- Patients with cognitive deficits may present with restlessness, discomfort, worsened confusion, or delirium but may not be able to give the history of urinary retention.

ETIOLOGY

- Most commonly the result of obstruction from various causes, including BPH and bladder and pelvic masses.
- Nonobstructive causes include medications, surgery, trauma, neurologic disease, and infection.
- In older patients, cause is frequently multifactorial, with an underlying obstructive risk factor and an acute precipitant.
- In women, AUR may be caused by benign tumors (especially fibroids); malignant tumors of pelvic, urethral, or vaginal origin; postpartum vulvar edema; or labial fusion.
- Infection such as prostatitis, urethritis, and genital herpes and herpes zoster can also cause AUR.

 DIAGNOSIS

DIFFERENTIAL DIAGNOSIS

- AUR is typically self-evident to the cognitively intact patient and physician. Differential diagnosis focuses on the underlying cause of the problem.

WORKUP

- History should focus on urologic symptoms, including dysuria, hematuria, history of retention, and urologic cancer
- History should include a complete list of prescribed and OTC medications
- Review of symptoms (ROS) should include fever, back pain, neurologic symptoms, and rash
- Rectal exam for masses, fecal impaction, perineal sensation, and sphincter tone
- Pelvic exam for female patients
- Neurologic exam to rule out an underlying neurologic cause

LABORATORY TESTS

- Serum creatinine level: In acute retention, creatinine may not be elevated above baseline.
- Urinalysis and culture (obtained via bladder catheterization).
- BUN, electrolytes.
- Prostate-specific antigen testing is not helpful in AUR.

IMAGING STUDIES

- Imaging may not be required when AUR is felt to be reversible.
- Ultrasound is valuable when there is suspicion of a pelvic mass.
- Pelvic computed tomography (CT) scan is done if masses are discovered by exam or imaging.
- Magnetic resonance imaging (MRI) is used when symptoms suggest spinal cord problems.
- Evaluation of bladder function may be considered after initial management, particularly in females with no evidence of anatomic obstruction.

TREATMENT

NONPHARMACOLOGIC THERAPY

- Given that AUR recurs 68% of the time when caused by BPH, consider surgical treatment for this issue. Transurethral resection of the prostate (TURP) should be delayed until at least 30 days after the episode of AUR, to minimize surgical complications.

ACUTE GENERAL Rx

- Prompt bladder decompression and drainage is initial management of AUR.
- Perform immediate urethral catheterization if there is no history of recent genitourinary (GU) surgery.
- Perform suprapubic catheterization if there is a history of recent surgery.
- Partial drainage and clamping of catheter is not indicated and may increase the risk of urinary tract infection (UTI).
- Clean, intermittent catheterization should be considered. In the acute setting, CIC may be limited by patient acceptance and the time requirement for teaching this technique. CIC may improve the rate of spontaneous voiding.

CHRONIC Rx

- Consider catheter removal in 2 to 3 days, particularly in patients younger than 65 years, if catheterized volume is less than 1 L, and if a precipitating event is identified.
- Otherwise, 1 to 2 weeks of catheterization should be considered before voiding trial.
- α-blockers are effective for treatment of BPH symptoms and may increase the success of trials of early catheter removal.
- 5-α reductase inhibitors are not effective for acute management when AUR is caused by BPH, due to slow decrease of prostatic volume.

COMPLEMENTARY & ALTERNATIVE MEDICINE

- None noted.

DISPOSITION

- Patients may be sent home if close follow-up can be assured.
- Hospital admission may be needed, particularly in patients with urosepsis or when urinary retention is due to malignancy or spinal cord compression.

REFERRAL

- Urology for cases where the underlying cause cannot be addressed acutely or is not self-limited.
- Gynecology when gynecologic masses are the underlying cause of AUR.

PEARLS & CONSIDERATIONS

PREVENTION

Patients with BPH should avoid the use of antihistamines, sedatives, and other medications that can precipitate acute retention. Inhaled anticholinergic agents may increase the risk of AUR and should be used cautiously in patients with risk factors, especially BPH.

PATIENT/FAMILY EDUCATION

Education regarding catheter care is helpful in patients who are discharged to home.

SUGGESTED READINGS

Available at www.expertconsult.com

RELATED CONTENT

Benign Prostatic Hypertrophy (Related Key Topic).

AUTHOR: **MARGARET TRYFOROS, M.D.**

BASIC INFORMATION

DEFINITION

Adrenal insufficiency is characterized by inadequate secretion of corticosteroids resulting from partial or complete destruction of the adrenal glands (primary adrenal failure). Inadequate secretion of cortisol from the adrenals due to critical illness and pituitary insufficiency is known as secondary cortisol deficiency.

SYNONYMS

Primary adrenocortical insufficiency
Addison disease

ICD-10CM CODES
E27.1 Primary adrenocortical insufficiency
E27.2 Addisonian crisis
E27.40 Unspecified adrenocortical insufficiency
E27.49 Other adrenocortical insufficiency
E27.3 Drug-induced adrenocortical insufficiency
E23.3 Hypopituitarism

EPIDEMIOLOGY & DEMOGRAPHICS

PREVALENCE: 10 to 15 per 100,000 persons
PREDOMINANT SEX: Female/male ratio of 2:1

PHYSICAL FINDINGS & CLINICAL PRESENTATION

- Adrenal insufficiency may present insidiously with nonspecific symptoms. A high index of suspicion is required for diagnosis. About half of patients may present acutely with adrenal crises. Table 1A-21 summarizes the clinical features of primary adrenal insufficiency.
- Hyperpigmentation of skin (Figs. E1A-36 and E1A-37) and mucous membranes is a cardinal sign of adrenal insufficiency: more prominent in palmar creases, buccal mucosa, pressure points (elbows, knees, knuckles), perianal mucosa, and around areolas of nipples
- Hypotension, postural dizziness
- Generalized weakness, chronic fatigue, malaise, anorexia
- Amenorrhea and loss of axillary hair in females

ETIOLOGY

- Autoimmune destruction of the adrenal glands (80% of cases)
- Tuberculosis (TB) (7%-20% of cases)
- Carcinomatous destruction of the adrenal glands, lymphoma
- Adrenal hemorrhage (anticoagulants, trauma, coagulopathies, pregnancy, sepsis)
- Adrenal infarction (antiphospholipid syndrome, arteritis, thrombosis)

- AIDS (adrenal insufficiency develops in 30% of patients with AIDS, often cytomegalovirus [CMV] adrenalitis)
- Genetic causes: autoimmune polyglandular syndromes (APS) types 1 and 2, X-linked adrenoleukodystrophy, congenital adrenal hyperplasia
- Other: sarcoidosis, amyloidosis, hemochromatosis, Wegener's granulomatosis, postoperative, fungal infections (candidiasis, histoplasmosis)

DIAGNOSIS

DIFFERENTIAL DIAGNOSIS

Sepsis, hypovolemic shock, acute abdomen, apathetic hyperthyroidism in the elderly, myopathies, gastrointestinal malignancy, major depression, anorexia nervosa, hemochromatosis, salt-losing nephritis, chronic infection

WORKUP

- An early morning (8 am) serum cortisol <3 mcg/dl (82.8 mmol/L) is consistent with cortisol deficiency.
- If the clinical picture is highly suggestive of adrenocortical insufficiency, the diagnosis can be confirmed with the rapid adrenocorticotropic hormone (ACTH) test:
  1. Give 250 mcg ACTH (Sinachten, tetracosatrin) by IV push and measure cortisol levels at 0, 30, and 60 min.
  2. An increase in serum cortisol level to peak concentration >500 nmol/L (18 mcg/dl) indicates a normal response. Cortisol level <18 mcg/dl at 30 or 60 min is suggestive of adrenal insufficiency.
  3. Measure plasma ACTH. A high ACTH level (>200 pg/mL [44 pmol/L]) confirms primary adrenal insufficiency.
- Critical illness-related corticosteroid insufficiency (e.g., in sepsis) is best established with the 1-mcg ACTH stimulation test in which cortisol levels are measured at baseline and 30 min after administration of ACTH. A level <25 mcg/dl (690 nmol/L) or an increment over baseline of <9 mcg (250 nmol/L) represents an inadequate adrenal response.
- Secondary adrenocortical insufficiency (caused by pituitary dysfunction) can be distinguished from primary adrenal insufficiency by the following:
  1. Normal or low plasma ACTH level after rapid ACTH
  2. Absence of hyperpigmentation
  3. No significant impairment of aldosterone secretion (because aldosterone secretion is under control of the renin-angiotensin system)
  4. Additional evidence of hypopituitarism (e.g., hypogonadism, hypothyroidism)

LABORATORY TESTS

- Hyponatremia, hyperkalemia
- Decreased glucose
- Increased BUN/creatinine ratio (prerenal azotemia)

TABLE 1A-21 Clinical Features of Primary Adrenal Insufficiency

Feature	Frequency (%)
Symptoms	
Weakness, tiredness, fatigue	100
Anorexia	100
Gastrointestinal symptoms	92
Nausea	86
Vomiting	75
Constipation	33
Abdominal pain	31
Diarrhea	16
Salt craving	16
Postural dizziness	12
Muscle or joint pains	13
Signs	
Weight loss	100
Hyperpigmentation	94
Hypotension (<110 mm Hg systolic)	88-94
Vitiligo	10-20
Auricular calcification	5
Laboratory Findings	
Electrolyte disturbances	92
Hyponatremia	88
Hyperkalemia	64
Hypercalcemia	6
Azotemia	55
Anemia	40
Eosinophilia	17

From Melmed S, Polonsky KS, Larsen PR, Kronenberg HM: *Williams textbook of endocrinology*, ed 12, Philadelphia, 2011, Saunders.

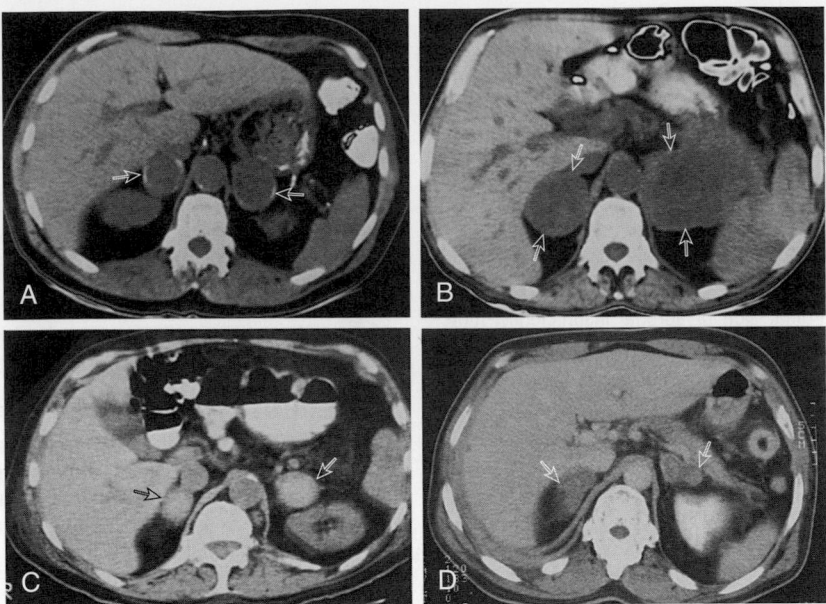

FIGURE 1A-38 Computed tomographic (CT) scans of patients with primary adrenal insufficiency. The affected adrenal glands are indicated by arrows.**A,** CT scan of a 59-year-old man with histoplasmosis. Notice the subcapsular calcium in both glands. **B,** CT scan of a 59-year-old man with metastatic melanoma. **C,** CT scan of an 80-year-old man with bilateral adrenal hemorrhage resulting from anticoagulation for pulmonary emboli. **D,** Bilateral adrenal tuberculomas in a 79-year-old man with tuberculosis affecting the urogenital tract. (**A** and **B** courtesy of Dr. William D. Salmon, Jr.; **C,** courtesy of Dr. Craig R. Sussman.) (From Melmed S, Polonsky KS, Larsen PR, Kronenberg HM: *Williams textbook of endocrinology,* ed 12, Philadelphia, 2011, Saunders.)

- Mild normocytic, normochromic anemia, neutropenia, lymphocytosis, eosinophilia (significant dehydration may mask hyponatremia and anemia), hypercalcemia, metabolic acidosis
- A morning cortisol level >500 mmol/L (18 mcg/dl) generally excludes the diagnosis whereas a level <165 mmol/L (6 mcg/dl) is suggestive of Addison disease and a level <3 mcg/dl requires further evaluation (see "Workup")
- Useful tests in evaluating the cause of adrenal insufficiency are: PPD (rule out TB), adrenal cortex antibodies and 21-hydroxylase antibodies (rule out autoimmune Addison disease), plasma very-long-chain fatty acids (rule out adrenoleukodystrophy)

IMAGING STUDIES

- Imaging is not necessary for diagnosis but may help identify potential causes.
- Abdominal CT scan (Fig. 1A-38): small adrenal glands generally indicate either idiopathic atrophy or longstanding TB, whereas enlarged glands are suggestive of early TB or potentially treatable diseases.
- Chest radiograph may reveal a small heart (Fig. E1A-39).

- Abdominal radiograph: adrenal calcifications may be noted if the adrenocortical insufficiency is secondary to TB or fungal infection.

Rx TREATMENT

NONPHARMACOLOGIC THERAPY

- Perform periodic monitoring of serum electrolytes, vital signs, and body weight; liberal sodium intake is suggested.
- Periodic measurement of bone density may be helpful in identifying patients at risk for the development of osteoporosis.
- Patients should carry a MedicAlert bracelet and an emergency pack containing hydrocortisone 100-mg ampule, syringe, and needle.
- Patients and partners should be educated on how to give IM injection in case of vomiting or coma.

ACUTE GENERAL Rx

- Addisonian crisis is an acute complication of adrenal insufficiency characterized by circulatory collapse, dehydration, nausea, vomiting, hypoglycemia, and hyperkalemia.
  1. Draw plasma cortisol level; do not delay therapy while waiting for confirming laboratory results.

  2. Administer hydrocortisone 100 mg IV immediately, followed by 100 to 200 mg of hydrocortisone every 24 hours divided into 3 or 4 doses; if patient shows good clinical response, gradually taper dosage and change to oral maintenance dose (usually prednisone 7.5 mg/day).
  3. Provide adequate volume replacement with D_5NS solution until hypotension, dehydration, and hypoglycemia are completely corrected. Large volumes (2 to 3 L) under continuous cardiac monitoring may be necessary in the first 2 to 3 hr to correct the volume deficit and hypoglycemia and to avoid further hyponatremia.
- Identify and correct any precipitating factor (e.g., sepsis, hemorrhage).

CHRONIC Rx

- Give hydrocortisone 15 to 20 mg PO every morning and 5 to 10 mg in late afternoon or prednisone 5 mg in morning and 2.5 mg hs.
- Give oral fludrocortisone 0.05 mg/day to 0.20 mg/day: this mineralocorticoid is necessary if the patient has primary adrenocortical insufficiency. The dose is adjusted based on the serum sodium level and the presence of postural hypotension or marked orthostasis.
- Instruct patients to increase glucocorticoid replacement in times of stress and to receive parenteral glucocorticoids if diarrhea or vomiting occurs. Typical supplementation varies from 25 mg PO qd of hydrocortisone for minor medical and surgical stress to 50 to 100 mg IV hydrocortisone q8h for sepsis-induced hypotension or shock.
- The administration of dehydroepiandrosterone (DHEA) is controversial. It is not indicated in men but may be considered in women with primary adrenal failure. A dose of 50 mg PO qd may improve well-being and sexuality in women with adrenal insufficiency.
- Patients with concomitant hypothyroidism should be treated with glucocorticoids first before correcting hypothyroidism because correction of thyroid hormone deficiency will accelerate cortisol clearance and can precipitate adrenal crisis.

SUGGESTED READINGS

Available at www.expertconsult.com

RELATED CONTENT

Addison's Disease (Patient Information)

AUTHOR: **FRED F. FERRI, M.D.**

Diseases and Disorders

BASIC INFORMATION

DEFINITION

Adult-onset Still's disease (AOSD) is a rare systemic autoinflammatory disorder of unknown etiology characterized by high spiking quotidian fever >102 °F, arthralgia or arthritis, evanescent skin rash, and leukocytosis with neutrophilic predominance. Between spikes in fever, temperature will often return to normal.. Articular symptoms can be absent, minimal, or oligoarticular initially, but most patients develop a persistent destructive arthropathy.

SYNONYMS

Adult Still's disease
Wissler's syndrome
Wissler-Fanconi syndrome

ICD-10CM CODES
M06.1 Adult-onset Still disease

EPIDEMIOLOGY & DEMOGRAPHICS

INCIDENCE: 22/10,000,000 in men, 34/10,000,000 in women
PEAK INCIDENCE: Age 16 to 35
PREVALENCE: Unknown
PREDOMINANT SEX AND AGE: Roughly equal sex distribution, bimodal age range 15 to 25 and 36 to 46
GENETICS: Relative risk ranging from 2.1 to 2.9 associated with HLA B17, B18, B35, and DR2. Cytokine production is thought to be implicated in the pathogenesis: IL6, IL2, Interferon gamma, and tumor necrosis factor alpha (TNF-α)
RISK FACTORS: Stress has been proved to be the only known risk factor.

PHYSICAL FINDINGS & CLINICAL PRESENTATION

- Triad: High spiking fevers, characteristic rash, and arthritis/arthralgias
- Fever is >102 °F, transient, quotidian in pattern, usually in the late afternoon or early evening
- Nonspecific symptoms: myalgias, serositis including pleuritis and pericarditis, sore throat
- Rash is typically evanescent, salmon pink, and maculopapular. It is usually located on the trunk and proximal extremities, but it can involve the palms and soles. The rash often accompanies fever and resolves when patient is afebrile.
- Arthritis is symmetric and destructive, involving the wrists, knees, and ankles. Extensive carpal involvement can distinguish this from rheumatoid arthritis (Figs. E1A-40 and E1A-41).

ETIOLOGY
- None identified

DIAGNOSIS

DIFFERENTIAL DIAGNOSIS

- Infection, malignancy, or autoimmune disorders
  1. Infection: Rubella, CMV, EBV, mumps, coxsackie virus, adenovirus
  2. Neoplasms: Leukemia, lymphoma, angioblastic lymphadenopathy
  3. Autoimmune: Reactive arthritis, spondyloarthropathies, dermatomyositis, vasculitis
  4. Periodic fever syndromes: Familial Mediterranean fever (FMF), TNF receptor–associated periodic syndrome (TRAPS)

DIAGNOSTIC CRITERIA

Multiple potential diagnostic criteria have been proposed in the evaluation of patients suspected of having adult-onset Still's disease.
1. Yamaguchi criteria (93.5% sensitivity)
MAJOR CRITERIA:
- Arthralgia >2 weeks
- Fever >102 °F; intermittent >1 week
- Typical rash
- WBC >10,000
MINOR CRITERIA:
- Sore throat
- Lymphadenopathy and/or splenomegaly
- LFT abnormalities
- Negative ANA and RF
Exclusion criteria: infections, malignancies, and rheumatic diseases
   Diagnosis: 4 criteria with at least 2 major criteria
1. Cush criteria (80.6% sensitivity)
MAJOR CRITERIA:
- Quotidian fever >102 °F
- Evanescent rash
- WBC >12 + ESR >40
- Negative ANA and RF
- Carpal ankylosis
MINOR CRITERIA:
- Onset age <35 years
- Arthritis
- Prodromal sore throat
- Reticuloendothelial system involvement
- Abnormal LFTs
- Serositis
- Cervical or tarsal ankylosis
   Probable AOSD: 10 points with 12 weeks of observation
   Definite AOSD: 10 points with 6 months observation
1. Fautrel criteria (80.6% sensitivity, 98.5% specificity)
MAJOR:
- Spiking fever >102 °F
- Arthralgia
- Transient erythema
- Pharyngitis
- PMN >80%
- Glycosylated ferritin <20%
MINOR:
- Maculopapular rash
- Leukocytosis >10
   Diagnosis: 4 major criteria or 3 major + 2 minor criteria

WORKUP
- According to differential diagnosis

LABORATORY TESTS
- CBC generally demonstrates leukocytosis with a predominance of polymorphonuclear leukocytes.
- ANA and RF results are usually negative in AOSD, whereas inflammatory markers are often markedly elevated.
- Liver transaminases are often elevated.
- Ferritin can be markedly elevated beyond the level expected for a typical inflammatory process.
- Glycosylated ferritin (if available)

IMAGING STUDIES
- Radiographs are not helpful at early onset of symptoms; helpful if chronic.
- Radionuclide bone scan and MRI with gadolinium may be used for early diagnosis.

TREATMENT

NSAIDs, corticosteroids, and disease-modifying antirheumatic drugs are generally used to control symptoms.

NONPHARMACOLOGIC THERAPY
- Control of stress factors

ACUTE GENERAL Rx
- NSAIDs at full doses are used initially.
- Systemic glucocorticoids are often required to control systemic inflammation in more severe disease.

CHRONIC Rx
- In patients with persistent symptoms, steroid-sparing immunomodulatory agents are often required.
- Oral or injectable methotrexate is often added to control chronic disease.
- TNF-inhibitors including etanercept and infliximab can be effective at controlling symptoms.
- Anti-IL6 and IL1 blockade may also be effective in controlling disease activity.

DISPOSITION
- Three distinct patterns of its clinical course
  1. Self-limited/monocyclic pattern: systemic symptoms of fever, rash, serositis, organomegaly; remission in 1 year
  2. Intermittent/polycyclic pattern: recurrent fevers with or without articular symptoms; may have complete remission between flares that could be years apart
  3. Chronic articular pattern: severe articular presentation leading to joint destruction; more disability, worst prognosis

REFERRAL
- Rheumatology for diagnosis and treatment
- Dermatology for evaluation and possible biopsy of rash

PEARLS & CONSIDERATIONS

COMMENTS
- Evanescent rash often dissipates when the patient is afebrile; it is therefore important to do a skin exam while the patient is febrile.
- Fever may present before arthritis, complicating accurate diagnosis.

PREVENTION
None

AUTHOR: DOUGLAS VON HERZEN, M.D.

 **BASIC INFORMATION**

DEFINITION

Moderate drinking has been defined as two standard drinks (e.g., 12 oz of beer) per day and one drink per day for women and persons older than 65 yr. Although not generally included under the alcoholism topic, hazardous or at-risk drinking should also be considered. For men, *at-risk drinking* is defined as more than 14 drinks/wk or more than 4 drinks/occasion. For women, at-risk drinking is defined as approximately half that given for men.

The American Psychiatric Association defines diagnostic criteria for *alcohol withdrawal* as follows:

A. Cessation of (or reduction in) alcohol use that has been heavy and prolonged.

B. Two (or more) of the following, developing within several hours to a few days after criterion A:
1. Autonomic hyperactivity (e.g., sweating or pulse rate >100 beats/min)
2. Increased hand tremor
3. Insomnia
4. Nausea and vomiting
5. Transient visual, tactile, or auditory hallucinations or illusions
6. Psychomotor agitation
7. Anxiety
8. Grand mal seizures

C. The symptoms in criterion B cause clinically significant distress or impairment in social, occupational, or other important areas of functioning.

The symptoms are not attributable to a general medical condition and are not better accounted for by another mental disorder.

SYNONYMS

Alcohol abuse
Substance abuse

ICD-10CM CODES
F10   Mental and behavioral disorders due to use of alcohol
F10.1   Mental and behavioral disorders due to use of alcohol: harmful use
F10.2   Mental and behavioral disorders due to use of alcohol: dependence syndrome
F10.3   Mental and behavioral disorders due to use of alcohol: withdrawal state
F10.4   Mental and behavioral disorders due to use of alcohol: withdrawal state with delirium
F10.5   Mental and behavioral disorders due to use of alcohol: psychotic disorder
F10.6   Mental and behavioral disorders due to use of alcohol: amnesic syndrome

EPIDEMIOLOGY & DEMOGRAPHICS

INCIDENCE (IN U.S.):
- The clinical history suggests alcohol problems in 15% to 20% of patients in primary care and hospitalized patients. In the U.S., alcohol abuse generates nearly $223 billion in annual economic costs. An estimated 9% of adults in the U.S. have alcohol dependence.
- 20% achieve abstinence without help; 70% achieve sobriety for 1 yr.

PREVALENCE (IN U.S.): 7% of population ≥18 yr

PREDOMINANT SEX:
- Lifetime risk for males 8% to 10%
- Lifetime risk for females 3% to 5%

PEAK INCIDENCE: 20 to 40 yr. The most common age range for initial treatment of alcohol dependence is 35 to 45 yr. However, the peak period for meeting alcohol dependence criteria is ≥10 years earlier.

GENETICS: More common with a family history of alcoholism and in patients of Irish, Scandinavian, and Native American descent

PHYSICAL FINDINGS & CLINICAL PRESENTATION

- Recurring minor trauma
- Gastrointestinal bleeding from gastritis and/or varices
- Pancreatitis (acute and chronic)
- Liver disease
- Odor of alcohol on breath
- Tremulousness
- Tachycardia
- Peripheral neuropathy
- Recent memory loss

ETIOLOGY

- Social and genetic factors important
- Risk factors:
  1. Broken homes
  2. Unemployment
  3. Divorce
  4. Recurrent depression
  5. Addiction to another substance, including tobacco
  6. Working long hours (≥55 hours/week)

 **DIAGNOSIS**

WORKUP

- The USPSTF recommends that clinicians screen adults 18 years and older for alcohol misuse and provide persons engaged in risky or hazardous drinking with brief behavioral counseling interventions to reduce alcohol misuse. Several screening tests (CAGE, TWEAK, CRAFFT, AUDIT-C) are available. The four-item CAGE (feeling need to Cut down, Annoyed by criticism, Guilty about drinking, and need for an Eye-opener in the morning) is the most popular screening test in primary care (Fig. E1A-42). A positive response should lead to further questioning. The sensitivity of the CAGE ranges from 43% to 94% and its specificity ranges from 70% to 97%. The five-item TWEAK scale (Tolerance, Worry, Eye-openers, Amnesia, [K] cut down) and the TACE questionnaire (Tolerance, Annoyance, Cut down, Eye-opener) are designed to screen pregnant women for alcohol misuse. They detect lower levels of alcohol consumption that may pose risks during pregnancy. The CRAFFT questionnaire (riding in Car with someone who was drinking, using alcohol to Relax, using alcohol while Alone, Forgetfulness, criticism from Friends and Family, Trouble) is useful as a screening tool for adolescents. Its sensitivity is 92% and specificity 64% for alcohol abuse. Single-question screening about alcohol consumption in a day ("When was the last time you had more than X drinks in a day?" [where X is 5 for men and 4 for women]) with the threshold set at "in the past 3 months" is 85% sensitive and 70% specific in men and 82% and 70% in women for unhealthy alcohol use. The 3-question AUDIT-C is a shorter form of the 10-item AUDIT, and the questions center on the quantity and frequency of alcohol use. It asks how often someone has had a drink containing alcohol, how many standard drinks containing alcohol one consumes on a typical day when one is drinking, and how often one has six or more drinks on one occasion. Scoring ranges from 0 to 4 on each question with a total score range of 0 to 12. A total score of 3 or higher for women and 4 or higher for men indicates alcohol use disorder and need for further assessment. Its sensitivity ranges from 85% in Hispanic women to 95% in white men.
- Laboratory evaluation (see below).

LABORATORY TESTS

- Lab tests alone do not accurately detect alcohol problems but can help identify medical complications related to alcohol use, such as pancreatitis or cirrhosis.
- Gamma-glutamyltransferase (GGTP), generally elevated
- Liver transaminases (alanine aminotransferase [ALT], aspartate aminotransferase [AST]), often elevated, may be normal or low in advanced liver disease.
- Low albumin level, hypophosphatemia, hypomagnesemia from malnutrition
- Complete blood count (CBC) reveals elevated mean corpuscular volume from toxic effect of alcohol on erythrocyte development in nutritional deficiencies.
- Stool for occult blood may be positive as a result of gastritis or variceal bleeding
- RBC folate, vitamin B_{12} level, vitamin B_6, vitamin B_1 level

IMAGING STUDIES

Indicated only with a history of trauma. CT or ultrasound of abdomen may reveal fatty liver or cirrhosis in advanced stages.

TREATMENT

NONPHARMACOLOGIC THERAPY

- Twelve-step facilitation, cognitive behavioral therapy, and motivational enhancement therapy improve the chances of recovery in patients with alcohol abuse and dependence.

- Depression, if present, should be treated at same time alcohol is withdrawn.

ACUTE GENERAL Rx

Alcohol withdrawal syndrome (AWS) occurs when a person stops ingesting alcohol after prolonged consumption. It can result in four possible clinical patterns depending on the severity of the patient's alcohol abuse and the time from the patient's previous alcohol ingestion. Fig. 1A-43 illustrates typical symptoms depending on time course of alcohol withdrawal. Blood ethanol level decreases by ~20 mg/dl/hr (Fig. E1A-44) in a normal person. Although discussed separately, these withdrawal states blend together in real life. Table 1A-22 summarizes medications for the treatment of alcohol dependence.

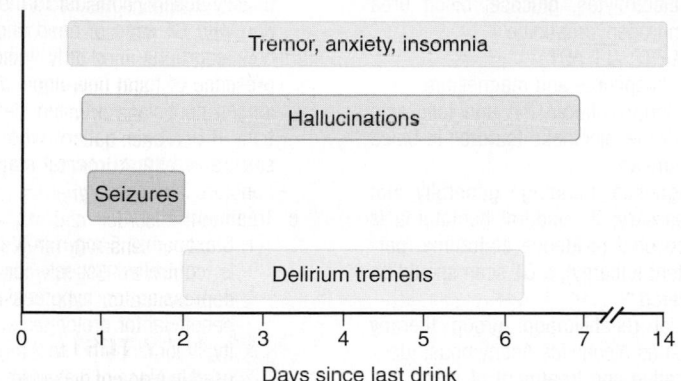

FIGURE 1A-43 Time course of alcohol withdrawal. (From Goldman L, Schafer AI: *Goldman's Cecil medicine,* ed 24, Philadelphia, 2012, Saunders.)

1. **Tremulous state** (early alcohol withdrawal, "impending DTs," "shakes," "jitters").
   a. Time interval: usually occurs 6 to 8 hr after the last drink or 12 to 48 hr after reduction of alcohol intake; becomes most pronounced at 24 to 36 hr.
   b. Manifestation: tremors, mild agitation, insomnia, tachycardia; symptoms are relieved by alcohol.
   c. Detoxification can be in the outpatient (ambulatory) or inpatient setting. Candidates for outpatient detoxification should have a reasonable support system (e.g., reliable contact person) who can monitor progress and lack of any significant comorbid conditions (e.g., suicide risk, seizure disorder, coexisting benzodiazepine dependence, prior unsuccessful outpatient detoxification, pregnancy, cirrhosis) or risk factors for severe withdrawal (age >40 yr, drinking >100 g of ethanol daily [e.g., 1 pint of liquor or eight 12-oz cans of beer, random blood alcohol concentration >200 mg/dl]).
   d. Inpatient treatment:
      (1) Admit to medical floor (private room); monitor vital signs q4h; institute seizure precautions; maintain adequate sedation.
      (2) Administer lorazepam as follows:
         (a) Day 1: 2 mg PO q4h while awake and not lethargic.
         (b) Day 2: 1 mg PO q4h while awake and not lethargic.
         (c) Day 3: 0.5 mg PO q4h while awake and not lethargic.
         (d) NOTE: Hold sedation for lethargy or abnormal vital or neurologic signs. The preceding doses are only guidelines; it is best to titrate the dose case by case.
      (3) In patients with mild to moderate withdrawal and without history of seizures, individualized benzodiazepine administration (rather than a fixed-dose regimen) results in lower benzodiazepine administration and avoids unnecessary sedation. The Clinical Institute Withdrawal Assessment Scale for Alcohol, Revised (CIWA-Ar) scale (Box 1A-6) can be used to measure the severity of alcohol withdrawal. It consists of 10 items: nausea; tremor; autonomic hyperactivity; anxiety; agitation; tactile, visual, and auditory disturbances;

TABLE 1A-22 Medications for the Treatment of Alcohol Dependence*

Medication	Dose and Route	Frequency	Effects	Major Common Adverse Effects
Alcohol Withdrawal				
			Benzodiazepines†	
Chlordiazepoxide*	25-100 mg, PO/IV/IM†	Every 4-6 hr	Decreased severity of withdrawal; stabilization of vital signs; prevention of seizures and delirium tremens	Confusion, oversedation, respiratory depression
Diazepam‡	5-10 mg, PO/IV/IM†	Every 6-8 hr		
Oxazepam‡	15-30 mg, PO†	Every 6-8 hr		
Lorazepam‡	1-4 mg, PO/IV/IM†	Every 4-8 hr		
			β-Blockers	
Atenolol	25-50 mg, PO	Once a day	Improvement in vital signs	Bradycardia, hypotension
Propranolol	10-40 mg, PO	Every 6-8 hr	Reduction in craving	
			α-Agonists	
Clonidine	0.1-0.2 mg, PO	Every 6 hr	Decreased withdrawal symptoms	Hypotension, fatigue
			Antiepileptics	
Carbamazepine	200 mg, PO	Every 6-8 hr	Decreased severity of withdrawal; prevention of seizures	Dizziness, fatigue, red blood cell abnormalities
			Prevention of Relapse	
Disulfiram‡	125-500 mg, PO	Daily	Decreased alcohol use among those who relapse	Disulfiram-alcohol reaction, rash, drowsiness, peripheral neuropathy
Naltrexone‡	50 mg, PO	Daily	Increased abstinence, decreased drinking days	Nausea, abdominal pain, myalgias-arthralgias
	380 mg, IM	Every 4 wk		
Acamprosate‡	666 mg, PO	Three times a day	Increased abstinence	Diarrhea

*Most commonly used medications listed.
†Currently approved by U.S. Food and Drug Administration for the indication noted.
‡Dose and routes given for standard fixed-dose regimens, which include dose tapers over time.
From Goldman L, Schafer AI: *Goldman's Cecil medicine,* ed 24, Philadelphia, 2012, Saunders.

headache; and disorientation. Each item is assigned a score from 0 to 7. For example, in the "agitation" category 0 indicates normal activity, and 7 indicates that the patient constantly thrashes about. For the category of "tremor," 0 indicates that tremor is not present and 7 that tremor is severe, even with arms not extended. The maximum total score is 67. Patients with mild AWS symptoms (CIWA-Ar score <8 can be monitored on an outpatient basis. Benzodiazepines are beneficial for most patients with a CIWA-AR score ≥8 and are strongly recommended in patients with substantial withdrawal symptoms (CIWA-Ar score >12). Patients with CIWA-Ar score of ≥15 should be admitted to detox unit. In-patient treatment is also recommended for patients with history of withdrawal seizures and for those with suicidal ideation and significant comorbidities.

(4) Beta-adrenergic blockers: beta-blockers are useful for controlling blood pressure and tachyarrhythmias. However, they do not prevent progression to more serious symptoms of withdrawal and, if used, should not be administered alone but in conjunction with benzodiazepines. Beta-blockers should be avoided in patients with contraindications to their use (e.g., bronchospasm, bradycardia, or severe congestive heart failure). Centrally acting alpha-adrenergic agonists such as clonidine ameliorate symptoms in patients with mild to moderate withdrawal but do not reduce delirium or seizures.

(5) Vitamin replacement: thiamine 100 mg IV or IM for at least 5 days plus oral multivitamins. The IV administration of glucose can precipitate Wernicke's encephalopathy in alcoholics with thiamine deficiency; therefore thiamine administration should precede IV dextrose.

(6) Hydration PO or IV (high-caloric solution): if IV, glucose with Na^+, K^+, Mg^{2+}, and phosphate replacement prn.

(7) Laboratory studies.
(a) CBC, platelet count, INR.
(b) Electrolytes, glucose, blood urea nitrogen, creatinine.
(c) GGTP, ALT, AST.
(d) Phosphorus and magnesium.
(e) Serum vitamin B_{12} and folic acid (if megaloblastic features in blood smear).

(8) Diagnostic imaging: generally not necessary; if subdural hematoma is suspected (evidence of trauma, persistent lethargy), a CT scan should be ordered.

(9) Social rehabilitation: group therapy such as Alcoholics Anonymous; identification and treatment of social and family problems should be initiated during the patient's hospital stay.

2. **Alcoholic hallucinosis:**
a. Manifestations: hallucinations usually are auditory, but hallucinations occasionally are visual, tactile, or olfactory; usually there is no clouding of sensorium as in delirium (clinical presentation may be mistaken for an acute schizophrenic episode). Disordered perceptions become most pronounced after 24 to 36 hr of abstinence.
b. Treatment: same as for DTs (see "withdrawal seizures").

3. **Withdrawal seizures ("rum fits"):**
a. Time interval: usually occurs 7 to 30 hr after cessation of drinking, with a peak incidence between 13 and 24 hr.
b. Manifestations: generalized convulsions with loss of consciousness; focal signs are usually absent; consider further investigation with CT scan of head and electroencephalography if clearly indicated (e.g., presence of focal neurologic deficits, prolonged postictal confusion state). In addition, in a febrile patient who is having a seizure or altered mental state, a lumbar puncture is necessary.
c. Treatment:
(1) Diazepam 2.5 mg/min IV until seizure is controlled (check for respiratory depression or hypotension) may be beneficial for prolonged seizure activity; IV lorazepam 1 to 2 mg q2h can be used in place of diazepam. Withdrawal

---

BOX 1A-6 Alcohol Withdrawal Assessment Scoring Guidelines (Revised Clinical Institute Withdrawal Assessment for Alcohol Scale)

Nausea and Vomiting (0-7)
0, none; 1, mild nausea with no vomiting; 4, intermittent nausea; 7, constant nausea, frequent dry heaves and vomiting

Tremor (0-7)
0, no tremor; 1, not visible, but can be felt fingertip to fingertip; 4, moderate, with patient's arms extended; 7, severe, even with arms not extended

Paroxysmal Sweats (0-7)
0, no sweats; 1, barely perceptible sweating, palms moist; 4, beads of sweat obvious on forehead; 7, drenching sweats

Anxiety (0-7)
0, no anxiety, patient at ease; 1, mildly anxious; 4, moderately anxious or guarded, so anxiety is inferred; 7, equivalent to acute panic states seen in severe delirium or acute schizophrenic reactions

Agitation (0-7)
0, normal activity; 1, somewhat more than normal activity; 4, moderately fidgety and restless; 7, pacing back and forth during, or constantly thrashing about

Tactile Disturbances (0-7)
Ask, "Have you experienced any itching, pins and needles sensation, burning or numbness, or a feeling of bugs crawling on or under your skin?"
0, none; 1, very mild itching, pins and needles, burning, or numbness; 2, mild itching, pins and needles, burning, or numbness; 3, moderate itching, pins and needles, burning, or numbness; 4, moderately severe tactile hallucinations; 5, severe hallucinations; 6, extremely severe hallucinations; 7, continuous hallucinations

Auditory Disturbances (0-7)
Ask, "Are you more aware of sounds around you? Are they harsh? Do they startle you? Do you hear anything that disturbs you or that you know isn't there?"
0, not present; 1, very mild harshness or ability to startle; 2, mild harshness or ability to startle; 3, moderate harshness or ability to startle; 4, moderate hallucinations; 5, severe hallucinations; 6, extremely severe hallucinations; 7, continuous hallucinations

Visual Disturbances (0-7)
Ask, "Does the light appear to be too bright? Is its color different than normal? Does it hurt your eyes? Are you seeing anything that disturbs you?"
0, not present; 1, very mild sensitivity to light; 2, mild sensitivity; 3, moderate sensitivity; 4, moderate hallucinations; 5, severe hallucinations; 6, extremely severe hallucinations; 7, continuous hallucinations

Headache (0-7)
0, not present; 1, very mild; 2, mild; 3, moderate; 4, moderately severe; 5, severe; 6, very severe; 7, extremely severe

Orientation and Clouding of Sensorium (0-4)
Ask, "What day is this? Where are you? Who am I?"
0, oriented; 1, cannot do serial additions or is uncertain about date; 2, disoriented to date by no more than 2 calendar days; 3, disoriented to date by more than 2 calendar days; 4, disoriented to place and/or person

Total Score
0 to 9: absent or minimal withdrawal
10 to 19: mild to moderate withdrawal
More than 20: severe withdrawal

From Sullivan JT, Sykora K, Schneiderman J, et al: Assessment of alcohol withdrawal: the revised clinical institute withdrawal assessment for alcohol scale (CIWA-Ar). *Br J Addict* 84:1353–1357, 1989.

seizures generally are self-limited and treatment is not required; the use of phenytoin or other anticonvulsants for short-term treatment of alcohol withdrawal seizures is not recommended.

(2) Thiamine 100 mg IV, followed by IV dextrose, should also be administered.

(3) Electrolyte imbalances (increased Mg^{2+}, decreased K^+, increased or decreased Na^+, decreased PO_4^{3-}) that may exacerbate seizures should be corrected.

4. **DTs:**
   a. Time interval: variable; usually occurs within 1 wk after reduction or cessation of heavy alcohol intake and persists for 1 to 3 days. Peak incidence is 72 hr and 96 hr after the cessation of alcohol consumption.
   b. Manifestations: profound confusion, tremors, vivid visual and tactile hallucinations, autonomic hyperactivity; this is the most serious clinical presentation of alcohol withdrawal (mortality rate is approximately 15% in untreated patients).
   c. Treatment
      (1) Admission to a detoxification unit where patient can be observed closely.
      (2) Vital signs q30min (neurologic signs, if necessary).
      (3) Use of lateral decubitus or prone position if restraints are necessary
      (4) NPO: nasogastric tube for abdominal distention may be necessary but should not be routinely used.
      (5) Laboratory studies: same as for early alcohol withdrawal.
      (6) Vigorous hydration (4 to 6 L/day): IV with glucose (Na^+, K^+, PO_4^{3-} and Mg^{2+} replacement [if patient has hypophosphatemia or hypomagnesemia]).
      (7) Vitamins: thiamine 100 mg IV qd. The initial dose of thiamine should precede the administration of IV dextrose; multivitamins (may be added to the hydrating solution).
      (8) Sedation: control of agitation should be achieved with rapid-acting sedative-hypnotic agents in adequate doses to maintain light somnolence for the duration of delirium.
         (a) Initially: lorazepam 2 to 5 mg IM/IV repeated prn.
         (b) Maintenance (individualized dosage): chlordiazepoxide, 50 to 100 mg PO q4-6h, lorazepam 2 mg PO q4h, or diazepam 5 to 10 mg PO tid; withhold doses or decrease subsequent doses if signs of oversedation are apparent.
         (c) Midazolam is also effective for managing DTs. Its rapid onset (sedation within 2 to 4 min of IV injection) and short duration of action (approximately 30 min) make it an ideal agent for titration in continuous infusion.

(9) Treatment of seizures (as previously described).

(10) Diagnosis and treatment of concomitant medical, surgical, or psychiatric conditions.

CHRONIC Rx

- See "Referral."
- Pharmacotherapies for alcoholism include:
  1. Acamprosate is a synthetic compound with a chemical structure similar to the neurotransmitter gamma-aminobutyric acid and the amino acid neuromodulator taurine. Its mechanism of action is not completely understood. It is indicated for the maintenance of abstinence from alcohol in patients with alcohol dependence who are abstinent at treatment initiation. It should be used only as part of a comprehensive psychosocial treatment program. It does not cause a disulfiram-like reaction as a result of ethanol ingestion. Dose is two 333-mg tablets tid. Treatment should be initiated as soon as possible after the period of alcohol withdrawal, when the patient has achieved abstinence, and should be maintained if the patient relapses.
  2. The long-acting opiate antagonist naltrexone inhibits the rewarding effects of alcohol. The starting dose is 25 mg/day, increased to 50 mg PO qd after 1 wk. An extended-release, once-monthly injection of naltrexone is also available and can be used along with psychosocial support to maintain alcohol abstinence. In patients with opioid dependence, naltrexone can precipitate acute withdrawal syndrome and should not be used at least 7 days from last opioid use. There are no established guidelines on the appropriate length of naltrexone treatment for alcohol dependence. One study recommends at least 3 mo of treatment.
  3. In a recent study, gabapentin showed a significant dose-response effect, and estimates of effect sizes were larger than those seen for naltrexone and acamprosate.[1]
  4. Disulfiram (Antabuse). Dosage is 500 mg max qd for 1 to 2 wk, then 125 to 500 mg qd. It interferes with the metabolism of alcohol by inhibiting aldehyde dehydrogenase, causing an accumulation of acetaldehyde. It produces unpleasant symptoms (nausea, flushing, elevated blood pressure, headache, weakness) when alcohol is ingested. It is an older drug that is now rarely used.

DISPOSITION

See "Referral."

[1]Mason BJ et al: Gabapentin treatment for alcohol dependence: a randomized clinical trial, *JAMA Intern Med* 174:70-77, 2014.

REFERRAL

- To Alcoholics Anonymous or Adult Children of Alcoholics
- Family members to Al-Anon or Al-A-Teen
- Many cities have Salvation Army Adult Rehabilitation centers; all patients accepted, regardless of ability to pay

! PEARLS & CONSIDERATIONS

COMMENTS

- Relative indications for inpatient alcohol detoxification are as follows: history of DTs or withdrawal seizures, severe withdrawal symptoms, concomitant psychiatric or medical illness, pregnancy, multiple previous detoxifications, recent high levels of alcohol consumption, and lack of reliable support network.
- Detoxification is not a stand-alone treatment but should serve as a bridge to a formal treatment program for alcohol dependence.
- The cure rate for alcoholism is highly disappointing, regardless of the modality. Only those who want to be helped will be helped. An effective strategy for the primary care physician is a prominently displayed sign in the office that states, "If you think you consume too many alcoholic beverages, please discuss it with me." Those who do open up the discussion can be given the facts in a nonjudgmental way and often can be helped. All too often problem drinkers lie on the questionnaire until they face a life-threatening health issue—and even then denial often reigns supreme.
- In a recent clinical trial, patients receiving medical management with naltrexone (100 mg/day), combined behavioral intervention (CBI), or both fared better on drinking outcomes, whereas acamprosate showed no evidence of efficacy, with or without CBI. No combination produced better efficacy than naltrexone or CBI alone in the presence of medical management.

EBM EVIDENCE

Available at www.expertconsult.com

SUGGESTED READINGS

Available at www.expertconsult.com

RELATED CONTENT

Alcohol Abuse (Patient Information)
Abuse, Drug (Related Key Topic)
Alcoholic Hepatitis (Related Key Topic)
Wernicke Syndrome (Related Key Topic)

AUTHOR: **FRED F. FERRI, M.D.**

A

Diseases and Disorders

BASIC INFORMATION

DEFINITION
Alcoholic hepatitis (AH) is a severe, progressive, inflammatory, and cholestatic liver disease occurring in patients with long-term ethanol abuse.

SYNONYM
AH

ICD-10CM CODES
K70.10 Alcoholic hepatitis without ascites
K70.9 Alcoholic liver disease, unspecified

EPIDEMIOLOGY & DEMOGRAPHICS
- Approximately 2 million people in the U.S. (about 1% of the population) are affected by alcoholic liver disease.
- In 2007, alcoholic hepatitis accounted for 0.71% of all admissions in the U.S.
- Typical presentation age: 40 to 50 yr. Majority occurs before age 60.
- Patients with alcoholic hepatitis typically drink more than 80 g of alcohol daily for at least 5 years.

PREVALENCE: Approximately 25% to 30%
PREDOMINANT SEX AND AGE: The majority of patients are males. Males are two times as likely as women to abuse alcohol. However, women develop alcoholic hepatitis after a shorter time and smaller amount of alcoholic exposure than men.
GENETICS: No genetic predilection for any one race. In the U.S., however, there is increased incidence in minority groups.
RISK FACTORS: Drinking multiple alcohol types, drinking alcohol between meal times, poor nutrition, female gender, obesity, Hispanic ethnicity, long-term ingestion of >10 to 20 g/day of alcohol in women and >20 to 40 g/day in men

PHYSICAL FINDINGS & CLINICAL PRESENTATION
Common presenting symptoms include:
- Rapid onset of jaundice
- Nausea/vomiting
- Malaise
- Low-grade fever
- Anorexia
- Abdominal distention/pain
- Weight loss or malnourishment
- Complications of liver impairment (GI bleed; confusion, lethargy, ascites)
Findings on physical examination include:
- Fever
- Tachycardia
- Hypotension
- Hepatomegaly, with tender liver on palpation
- Jaundice and ascites
- Splenomegaly
- Asterixis (a flapping tremor)
- Peripheral edema
- Abdominal distention with shifting dullness (ascites)
- Hepatic bruit

- With coexistent cirrhosis look for:
  1. Gynecomastia
  2. Proximal muscles wasting
  3. Spider angiomata
  4. Altered hair distribution

DIAGNOSIS

DIFFERENTIAL DIAGNOSIS
- Hepatitis B
- Hepatitis C
- Nonalcoholic steatohepatitis (NASH)
- Chronic pancreatitis
- Drug-induced liver injury
- Hemochromatosis
- Cholangitis

WORK-UP
- A thorough and detailed history is needed.
- Relevant questions may include:
  1. When patients started drinking
  2. Number of times patient drinks per day
  3. How many years of regular/daily drinking
  4. Types of alcohol
  5. Home or bar drinking?
  6. Rehabilitation for drinking?
  7. Social problems (e.g., arrest for public intoxication or driving under the influence, marital discord due to alcoholism)

LABORATORY TESTS
- Elevated transaminase (AST >45 U/L but <300 U/L; AST:ALT ratio >2.0) but some patients may not have elevations in ALT, AST in early phases
- S-bilirubin >2 mg/dl
- Increased prothrombin time (PT)
- Elevated gamma glutamyltransferase (GGT)
- Carbohydrate-deficient transferrin (CDT) is a reliable marker for chronic alcoholism
- Elevated C-reactive protein
- Electrolyte disorder (hypokalemia, hypomagnesemia, low zinc, hypophosphatemia)
- Hypoalbuminemia
- Hyperferritinemia
- CBC (may reveal leukocytosis with bandemia or anemia or thrombocytemia); MCV may be elevated

- Screening tests to rule out other conditions include checking:
  1. Hepatitis B surface antigen (HBsAg)
  2. Anti–hepatic C
  3. Ferritin-transferrin saturation
  4. Alpha-fetoprotein
  5. Alkaline phosphatase
- The severity of AH can be calculated with the Maddrey Discriminant Function (MDF) score, which is calculated as follows:
  MDF = 4.6 × prothrombin time − control prothrombin time + total bilirubin (mg/dl)

IMAGING STUDIES
Ultrasonography is the preferred imaging study. The earliest histologic change in alcoholic liver disease is macrovesicular steatosis.

LIVER BIOPSY
- Liver biopsy is rarely needed.
- Useful to:
  1. Confirm the diagnosis.
  2. Evaluate the effect of coexisting disease.
  3. Rule out cirrhosis.
  4. Exclude other diagnosis (especially other causes of liver diseases).
- Typical finding include:
  1. Macrovascular steatosis
  2. Hepatocyte injury (ballooning degeneration and focal hepatocyte necrosis)
  3. Mallory's bodies (characteristic of alcoholic hepatitis)
  4. Perivenular fibrosis
  5. Portal and lobular inflammation

TREATMENT

Treatment can be divided into three main components:
1. Lifestyle modifications
2. Nutritional support
3. Pharmacologic therapy

LIFESTYLE MODIFICATIONS
- Abstinence from alcohol (this improves both short- and long-term survival). Fig. 1A-45 describes the effect of subsequent alcohol

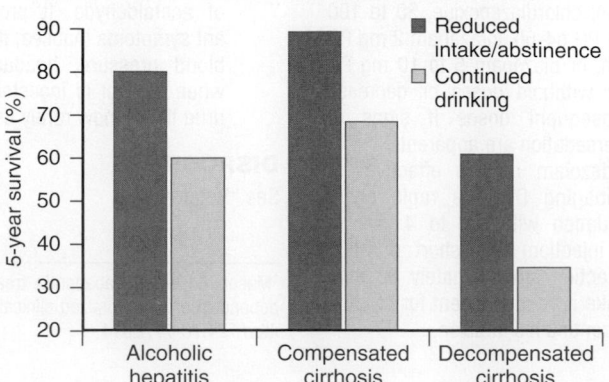

FIGURE 1A-45 Effect of subsequent alcohol intake on 5-year survival in patients with alcoholic hepatitis and cirrhosis. (From Day CP, Liver Disorder Part 1 of 2, *Medicine* 35(1), 2007, p 22–25.)

A

intake on 5-year survival in patients with alcoholic hepatitis
- Smoking cessation (to decrease oxidative stress)
- Treatment of substance abuse

NUTRITIONAL SUPPORT

- Good nutrition is an essential part of treatment because many patients with alcoholic hepatitis are usually in a catabolic state.
- Nutritional support includes:
  1. Liberal vitamin supplementation (especially thiamine, folic acid, vitamin K)
  2. Mineral supplementation (**but not iron**)
  3. Calorie counting is essential. A high calorie intake (1.2 to 1.4 times the normal resting intake) may be required.
  4. Protein intake of 1.2 to 1.5 g/kg of ideal body weight per day will provide adequate support. **Exception: in patients with severe encephalopathy, protein restriction may be required.**

PHARMACOLOGIC THERAPY

Severe alcoholic hepatitis may require treatment. Severity can be assessed by calculating the Model for End-Stage Liver Disease (MELD) score or MDF or the Glasgow score.
- An MDF score >32 indicates significant or severe alcoholic hepatitis (30-day mortality of 50%).
- MELD score can easily be calculated (visit http://www.unos.org/resources/meldpeldcalculator.asp?index=98). This score predicts short-term survival in patients with cirrhosis. A score ≥20 predicts increased short-term mortality.
- Glasgow score: contains four variables (BUN, PT, WBC count, and bilirubin). A score ≥9 indicates increased mortality.

Indications for initiating therapy include:
- MDF >32
- MELD >20
- Glasgow score >8
- Hepatic encephalopathy
  Patients with severe alcoholic hepatitis may be treated with glucocorticosteroids (prednisolone 40 mg/day for 28 days with a 2-wk taper). Glucocorticosteroids reduce hepatic injury, suppress inflammation, and promote liver regeneration. An alternative first-line agent (especially for patients with contraindications to corticosteroids) in patients with severe alcoholic hepatitis is pentoxifylline. There are various other treatments, but these are mainly experimental.

LIVER TRANSPLANTATION

- Usually reserved for patients with end-stage liver disease. Patients whose hepatitis is not responding to medical therapy have a 6-month survival rate of approximately 30%. Since most hepatitis deaths occur within 2 months, early liver transplantation is attractive but controversial.
- Patients with alcoholic hepatitis must be sober for at least 6 mo before they can be eligible for consideration for liver transplantation.

REFERRAL

Severe acute alcoholic hepatitis may require ICU care and referral to different subspecialists:
- GI/hepatology (for patients with evidence of GI hemorrhage)
- Nutritional services
- Nephrology (for acute renal failure, hepatorenal syndrome)
- Neurology (for change in mental status, seizures)
- Infectious disease (for fever/leukocytosis)

PEARLS & CONSIDERATIONS

COMMENTS

- Referral to substance abuse treatment programs may be helpful.
  1. Stress to patients that there are limited long-term drug treatments for alcoholic hepatitis.
  2. Maintaining good general nutrition is important.
  3. Advise patient about the risk of taking certain medications, especially acetaminophen.
- Periodic follow-up to monitor patient's response to check BMP and LFTs.
- Encourage alcohol abstinence. Abstinence improves long-term survival.
- If patient develops liver cirrhosis, check serum alpha-fetoprotein every 6 mo and liver ultrasound annually to rule out hepatocellular carcinoma.
- Vaccinate patient against hepatitis A and B viruses, pneumococci, influenza A virus, and routine adult vaccinations, if appropriate.

SUGGESTED READINGS

Available at www.expertconsult.com

RELATED CONTENT

Alcoholic Hepatitis (Patient Information)

AUTHOR: **DANIEL K. ASIEDU, M.D., PH.D.**

BASIC INFORMATION

DEFINITION

Allergic rhinitis is an IgE-mediated hypersensitivity response to nasally inhaled allergens that involves mucosal inflammation driven by type 2 helper T (Th2) cells that causes sneezing, rhinorrhea, nasal pruritus, and congestion. It may be seasonal or perennial.

SYNONYMS

Hay fever
IgE-mediated rhinitis
Seasonal allergic rhinitis
SAR

ICD-10CM CODES
J30.1 Allergic rhinitis due to pollen
J30.2 Other seasonal allergic rhinitis
J30.3 Other allergic rhinitis
J30.4 Allergic rhinitis, unspecified

EPIDEMIOLOGY & DEMOGRAPHICS

- Allergic rhinitis affects approximately 10% to 20% of the U.S. population and 40% of children.
- Mean age of onset is 8 to 12 yr.
- The prevalence of allergic rhinitis in patients presenting to their primary care provider with nasal symptoms is estimated to be 30% to 60%.

PHYSICAL FINDINGS & CLINICAL PRESENTATION

- Pale or violaceous mucosa of the turbinates caused by venous engorgement (this can distinguish it from erythema present in viral rhinitis)
- Nasal polyps
- Lymphoid hyperplasia in the posterior oropharynx with cobblestone appearance
- Erythema of the throat, conjunctival and scleral injection
- Clear nasal discharge
- Clinical presentation: usually consists of sneezing, nasal congestion, cough, postnasal drip, loss of or alteration of smell, and sensation of plugged ears

ETIOLOGY

- Pollens in the springtime, ragweed in fall, grasses in the summer
- Dust, mites, animal allergens
- Smoke or any irritants
- Perfumes, detergents, soaps
- Emotion, changes in atmospheric pressure or temperature

DIAGNOSIS

DIFFERENTIAL DIAGNOSIS

- Infections (sinusitis; viral, bacterial, or fungal rhinitis)
- Rhinitis medicamentosa (cocaine, sympathomimetic nasal drops)
- Vasomotor rhinitis (e.g., secondary to air pollutants)
- Septal obstruction (e.g., deviated septum), nasal polyps, nasal neoplasms
- Systemic diseases (e.g., Wegener's granulomatosis, hypothyroidism [rare])

WORKUP

- The initial strategy should be to determine whether patients should undergo diagnostic testing or receive empirical treatment.
- Workup is often unnecessary if the diagnosis is apparent. A detailed medical history is useful in identifying the culprit allergen.
- Selected patients with allergic rhinitis that is not controlled with standard therapy may benefit from allergy testing to target allergen avoidance measures or guide immunotherapy. Allergy testing can be performed using skin testing or radioallergosorbent (RAST) testing. Immunoglobulin E (IgE) testing using newest generation assays is also an excellent tool for diagnosing the cause of symptoms related to rhinitis. Allergy testing with skin or blood testing is most useful as confirmatory tests when the patient's history is compatible with an IgE-mediated reaction and should generally be reserved for ambiguous or complicated cases.
- Examination of nasal smears for the presence of neutrophils to rule out infectious causes and the presence of eosinophils (suggestive of allergy) may be useful in selected patients.
- Peripheral blood eosinophil counts are not useful in allergy diagnosis.

TREATMENT

NONPHARMACOLOGIC THERAPY

- Maintain allergen-free environment by covering mattresses and pillows with allergen-proof casings, eliminating carpeting, eliminating animal products, and removing dust-collecting fixtures.
- Use of air purifiers and dust filters is helpful.
- Maintain humidity in the environment below 50% to prevent dust mites and mold.
- Use air conditioners, especially in the bedroom.
- Remove pets from homes of patients with suspected sensitivity to animal allergens.
- Use of acupuncture to treat seasonal allergic rhinitis is controversial. A recent trial showed that acupuncture led to statistically significant improvement in disease-specific quality of life and antihistamine use measures after 8 weeks of treatment compared with sham acupuncture and with rescue medication alone.

ACUTE GENERAL Rx

- Determine if the patient is troubled by swollen turbinates (best treated with decongestants) or blockages secondary to mucus (effectively treated by antihistamines).
- Topical nasal steroids are very effective and are preferred by many as first-line treatment for allergic rhinitis in adults. Patients should be instructed on proper use and informed that improvement might not occur for at least 1 wk after initiation of therapy. Commonly available inhalers follow.
- Beclomethasone dipropionate: one to two sprays in each nostril bid
- Fluticasone: initially two sprays in each nostril qd or one spray in each nostril bid, decreasing to one spray in each nostril qd based on response
- Flunisolide: initially two sprays in each nostril bid
- Budesonide: two sprays in each nostril bid or four sprays in each nostril qam
- Most first-generation antihistamines can cause considerable sedation and anticholinergic symptoms. The second-generation antihistamines (loratadine, fexofenadine, cetirizine, levocetirizine, desloratadine) are preferred because they do not have any significant anticholinergic or sedative effects.
- Montelukast, a leukotriene receptor antagonist commonly used for asthma, is also effective for allergic rhinitis. Usual adult dose is 10 mg qd.
- Azelastine is an antihistamine nasal spray effective for seasonal allergic rhinitis. Olopatadine is an intranasal H_1-antihistamine alternative to azestaline in mild to moderate seasonal allergic rhinitis.

CHRONIC Rx

- Cromolyn sodium: one spray to each nostril three to four times daily can be used for prophylaxis (mast cell stabilizer).
- Immunotherapy is generally reserved for patients responding poorly to the above treatments. Traditionally, immunotherapy consisted of subcutaneous injections of gradually increased doses of allergens. Recently, the FDA has approved 3 allergen extracts for sublingual administration as immunotherapy.

DISPOSITION

Most patients experience significant relief with avoidance of allergens and proper use of medications.

REFERRAL

Allergy testing in patients with severe symptoms who are unresponsive to therapy or when the diagnosis is uncertain

EVIDENCE

Available at www.expertconsult.com

SUGGESTED READINGS
Available at www.expertconsult.com

RELATED CONTENT
Allergic Rhinitis (Patient Information)

AUTHOR: **FRED F. FERRI, M.D.**

ℹ BASIC INFORMATION

DEFINITION

Alopecia is the term used to describe involuntary hair loss, typically on the scalp but can occur anywhere over the body. *Nonscarring alopecia* is hair loss without clinically apparent scarring, inflammation, or skin atrophy. *Scarring alopecia* is characterized by permanent hair loss accompanied by tissue destruction in the form of scarring, inflammation, and/or skin atrophy.

SYNONYMS

Hair loss
Balding

ICD-10CM CODES
L63	Alopecia aerata
L63.0	Alopecia (capitis) totalis
L64	Androgenic alopecia
L64.0	Drug-induced androgenic alopecia
L64.8	Other androgenic alopecia
L64.9	Androgenic alopecia, unspecified
L65	Other nonscarring hair loss
L66	Cicatricial alopecia
L65.9	Nonscarring hair loss, unspecified
L63.8	Other alopecia areata
L65.0	Telogen effluvium

EPIDEMIOLOGY & DEMOGRAPHICS

INCIDENCE: Depends on etiology, for example:
- Alopecia areata affects 1% of the U.S. population by age 50 yr. There is a higher incidence at a younger age and both sexes are affected equally.
- Androgenetic alopecia affects males > females with 50% of Caucasian men affected by age 50 yr. Less common in Asians and African-American men, and often has later onset. By age 70, 40% of females are affected with incidence increasing after menopause.

GENETICS: Depends on etiology, for example:
- Androgenetic alopecia is polygenic with variable penetrance and can be inherited from one or both parents.
- Certain scarring alopecias are more predominant in people with coarser hair.

ETIOLOGY

NONSCARRING:
- Failure of follicle production
- Hair shaft abnormality
- Pattern hair loss, i.e., androgenetic alopecia
- Hair breakage, i.e., trichotillomania, traction alopecia, cosmetic overprocessing
- Problem with cycling (excess shedding), i.e., telogen effluvium, anagen effluvium, loose anagen syndrome, alopecia areata, syphilis

SCARRING:
- Infectious: tinea capitis with inflammation (kerion), bacterial folliculitis as in dissecting folliculitis and folliculitis decalvans
- Neoplasm: alopecia mucinosa in cutaneous T-cell lymphoma or alopecia neoplastica due to metastatic carcinoma (breast cancer)
- Autoimmune: chronic cutaneous lupus erythematosus
- Congenital

CLINICAL FEATURES

HISTORY: A careful history must be taken and should include time course for hair loss, the pattern of hair loss, any recent change in life situation/stresses, any associated medical conditions, new medications, any family history of hair loss, diet, hair care practices, and other skin/nail symptoms.

PHYSICAL EXAMINATION:
- General: patient's emotional response to hair loss
- Hair/skin:
  1. Hair thinning/loss
  2. May have fine downy hairs also referred to as vellus hairs
  3. Skin may show changes consistent with inflammation, infection, and/or atrophy
  4. Women may show virilization (e.g., hirsutism)
  5. Exclamation point hairs can be seen in alopecia areata
  6. Broken hairs of different length may be seen in traumatic alopecia
  7. Hairs that crack or crumble with palpation most often signify shaft damage due to overprocessing

ᴅₓ DIAGNOSIS

WORKUP
- Pull test—no shower for 24 hr, 60 hairs are gently pulled from the scalp, removal of 6 or more hairs is considered positive result and indicates telogen effluvium (active shedding). Look for telogen bulbs on recovered hairs to differentiate from breaking (blunt ends).
- Punch biopsy—Mandatory when suspecting scarring alopecia. Send two punches: one for vertical and one for horizontal sectioning for histopathologic analysis preferably by a dermatopathologist.

- Trichogram—quantifies hair loss. Pull 25-50 hairs and measure proportion of anagen to catagen and telogen hairs under light microscopy. Ten to twenty percent telogen hairs is normal, >35% is highly suspicious for telogen effluvium.
- Fig. E1A-49 describes the evaluation and treatment of alopecia in females.

LABORATORY TESTS

Initiate laboratory studies if not clear based on clinical presentation:
- CBC—rule out Fe deficiency
- Total Fe/ferritin—rule out subclinical Fe deficiency
- TSH—rule out underlying thyroid disease
- ANA—screen for autoimmune disease
- RPR—rule out cutaneous syphilis if history suggestive of increased risk

DIFFERENTIAL DIAGNOSIS

NONSCARRING:
- *Telogen effluvium:* This type of alopecia is usually diffuse thinning that follows significant life stress (death of loved one, high fever, severe infection, crash dieting) or change in hormones (postpartum, change in or cessation of oral contraceptives). Patient often presents with a bag of hair that has fallen out. This is caused by a large number of anagen (growing) hairs entering telogen (dying phase) simultaneously. Telogen effluvium is more common in women.
- *Androgenetic alopecia:* Gradual thinning of hair and a trend toward finer hair, which in men has a typical pattern of receding anterior bitemporal hairline resulting in an M-shaped pattern and hair loss at the vertex and in women has a typical pattern of thinning along vertex with or without frontotemporal thinning. This type of thinning is due to a combination of

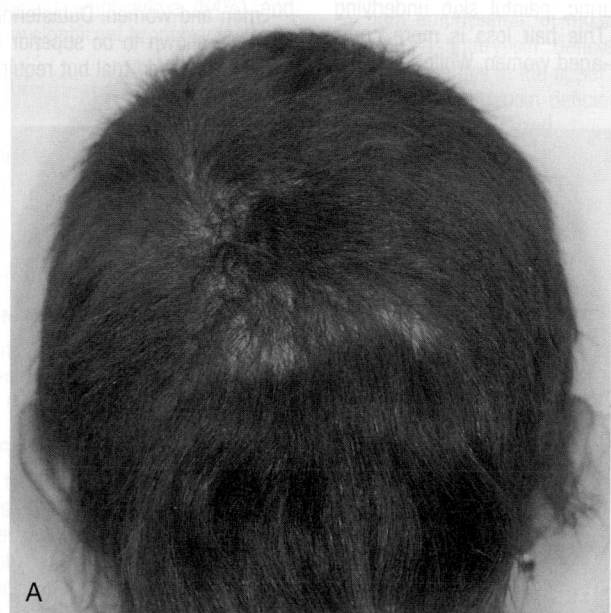

A

FIGURE 1A-50 A Alopecia areata: patchy hair loss. The alopecic area is devoid of hairs, and the scalp does not present inflammatory changes. (From Goldman L, Schafer AI: *Goldman's Cecil medicine*, ed 24, Philadelphia, 2012, Saunders.)

BASIC INFORMATION

DEFINITION
Dementia is a syndrome characterized by progressive loss of previously acquired cognitive skills including memory, language, insight, and judgment. Alzheimer's disease (AD) is believed to account for the majority (50%-75%) of all cases of dementia.

ICD-10CM CODES
G30.0 Alzheimer's disease with early onset
G30.1 Alzheimer's disease with late onset
G30.8 Other Alzheimer's disease
G30.9 Alzheimer's disease, unspecified

EPIDEMIOLOGY & DEMOGRAPHICS
INCIDENCE: Risk doubles every 5 yr after the age of 65; above the age of 85 the incidence is about 8%.
PREVALENCE: Currently an estimated 5.2 million Americans have AD; 6% between the ages of 65 and 74, 44% between 75 and 84, and 46% at 85 years and older.
PREDOMINANT SEX: Female

PHYSICAL FINDINGS & CLINICAL PRESENTATION
- Spouse or other family member, usually not the patient, notes insidious memory impairment.
- Patients have difficulties learning and retaining new information and handling complex tasks (e.g., balancing the checkbook) and have impairments in reasoning, judgment, spatial ability, and orientation (e.g., difficulty driving, getting lost away from home).
- Behavioral changes, such as mood changes and apathy, may accompany memory impairment. In later stages patients may develop agitation and psychosis.
- Atypical presentations include early and severe behavioral changes, focal findings on examination, parkinsonism, hallucinations, falls, or onset of symptoms younger than the age of 65.

DIAGNOSIS

There is no definitive imaging or laboratory test for the diagnosis of AD. Diagnosis is commonly made based on clinical history, a thorough physical and neurologic examination, and use of reliable and valid diagnostic criteria (i.e., DSM or NINDCS-ADRDA) such as the following:
- Loss of memory and one or more additional cognitive abilities (aphasia, apraxia, agnosia, or other disturbance in executive functioning)
- Impairment in social or occupational functioning that represents a decline from a previous level of functioning and results in significant disability
- Deficits that do not occur exclusively during the course of delirium
- Insidious onset and gradual progression of symptoms

- Cognitive loss documented by neuropsychologic tests
- No physical signs, neuroimaging, or laboratory evidence of other diseases that can cause dementia (i.e., metabolic abnormalities, medication or toxin effects, infection, stroke, Parkinson's disease, subdural hematoma, or tumors)

The National Institute on Aging (NIA) and the Alzheimer's Association recommended new diagnostic criteria and guidelines for AD in 2011. These differ from prior DSM or NINDCS-ADRDA criteria in that they recommend that AD be considered a disease well before the onset of symptoms, they incorporate the use of biomarkers in diagnosis, and they define three distinct stages of AD: (1) *preclinical* AD, in which there is measurable biologic evidence of AD pathology but no symptoms; (2) *mild cognitive impairment* (MCI) due to AD, in which there is mild memory loss but no functional impairment at home or work; and (3) *dementia due to AD.*

DIFFERENTIAL DIAGNOSIS
- Cancer (brain tumor, meningeal neoplasia)
- Infection (AIDS, neurosyphilis, PML)
- Toxic/metabolic (EtOH, hypothyroidism, vitamin B_{12} deficiency, mercury exposure, drug effects)
- Organ failure (dialysis dementia, Wilson's disease)
- Vascular disorder (multiple strokes, severe small vessel changes, chronic vasculitides, or chronic subdural hematoma)
- Depression (pseudodementia)

WORKUP
HISTORY & GENERAL PHYSICAL EXAMINATION:
- Medication lists should always be reviewed for drugs or home remedies that may cause mental status changes.
- Patients should be screened for depression, because it can sometimes mimic dementia but also often occurs as a coexisting condition and should be treated.
- On examination, look for signs of metabolic disturbance, presence of psychiatric features, or focal neurologic deficits.

MENTAL STATUS TESTING: Brief mental status testing can be done easily and quickly in the office. Commonly used cognitive tests to detect dementia include the Mini-Mental State Examination (MMSE), the Mini-Cog test, and the Addenbrooke's Cognitive Examination-Revised (ACE-R) test. For detecting mild cognitive impairment and dementia, the Montreal Cognitive Assessment (MoCA, http://www.mocatest.org/) is a highly sensitive 30-point test that takes approximately 10 minutes to administer. Cognitive domains tested include visual-spatial, attention, verbal recall, language, abstraction, and orientation. A score of 25 points or less (26 points if the patient has less than 12 years of education) indicates cognitive impairment. The test is available in over 35 languages and dialects, and multiple forms in English allow for repeated assessments over time.

Mental status testing should include tests that assess the following cognitive functions:

- Orientation: ask the patient to give the day, date, month, year, and place and to name the current president.
- Attention: ask the patient to recite the months of the year forward and in reverse.
- Verbal recall: ask the patient to remember three items; test for recall after a 1- and 5-min delay.
- Language: ask the patient to write and then read a sentence; have the patient name both common and less common objects.
- Visual-spatial: ask the patient to draw a clock and to set the hands of the clock at 11:10.

Patients with AD typically have trouble with verbal recall, plus visual-spatial or language deficits. Attention is usually preserved until the late stages of AD, so consider alternate diagnoses in patients who perform poorly on tests of attention.

LABORATORY TESTS
- CBC
- Serum electrolytes
- Glucose
- BUN/creatinine
- Liver and thyroid function tests
- Serum vitamin B_{12}
- Syphilis serology (RPR), if supported by clinical history
- HIV screening as appropriate
- Lumbar puncture if history or signs of cancer, infectious process, or when the clinical presentation is unusual (i.e., rapid progression of symptoms)
- EEG if there is history of seizures, episodic confusion, rapid clinical decline, or suspicion of Creutzfeldt-Jakob disease
- Measurement of apolipoprotein E genotyping, CSF tau and amyloid, and functional imaging including positron emission tomography (PET) or single proton emission computed tomography (SPECT) are not yet routinely indicated
- Brain biopsy (usually reserved for diagnoses such as prion disease, certain vasculitides). Generally performed post mortem.

IMAGING STUDIES
- CT scan or MRI to rule out hydrocephalus and mass lesions, including subdural hematoma
- Florbetapir-PET imaging of the brain correlates with the presence and density of beta-amyloid

TREATMENT

NONPHARMACOLOGIC THERAPY
- Patient safety, including risks associated with impaired driving, wandering behavior, leaving stoves unattended, and accidents, must be addressed with the patient and family early and appropriate measures implemented.
- Wandering, hoarding or hiding objects, repetitive questioning, withdrawal, and social inappropriateness often respond to behavioral therapies.

ACUTE GENERAL Rx

None

CHRONIC Rx

1. Symptomatic treatment of memory disturbance (Table 1A-23):
   a. Cholinesterase inhibitors (ChEIs):
      FDA approved for the treatment of mild to moderate AD. Common side effects include nausea, diarrhea, and anorexia and may be bothersome enough to require a slower escalation of dosage or switching to another agent.
   b. NMDA receptor antagonist: memantine (Namenda)
      FDA approved for the treatment of moderate to severe AD. Common side effects include constipation, dizziness, or headache. Memantine is contraindicated in patients with renal insufficiency or history of seizures.
2. Symptomatic treatment of neuropsychiatric and behavioral disturbances (Table 1A-24).
3. Depression, agitation, delusions, or hallucinations may respond to medications.

DISPOSITION & REFERRAL

- Patients with complex or atypical presentations or challenging management issues should be referred to a neurologist or another specialist with expertise in dementia.
- Approximately 1 in 8 hospitalized patients with AD who develop delirium will have at least one adverse outcome (e.g., institutionalization, cognitive decline, death) associated with delirium.
- Family education and support may help reduce need for skilled nursing facility and reduce caregiver stress, depression, and burnout.

PEARLS & CONSIDERATIONS

The physician should make a thorough search for the treatable causes of dementia. Current American Academy of Neurology practice parameters recommend:
- Treat cognitive symptoms of AD with ChEIs.
- Treat agitation, psychosis, and depression.
- Encourage caregivers to participate in educational programs and support groups.

COMMENTS

- Ginkgo biloba is marketed widely as effective in delaying cognitive impairment; however, trials have shown that it is not effective in reducing the incidence of Alzheimer dementia or dementia overall.
- Higher midlife fitness levels seem to be associated with lower hazards of developing all-cause dementia later in life independent of cerebrovascular disease.
- Lower plasma beta-amyloid 42/40 is associated with greater cognitive decline among elderly persons without dementia over 9 yr, and this association is stronger among those with low measures of cognitive reserve.
- The *APOE* genotype provides information on the risk for AD, but the genotyping of patients raises ethical and emotional concerns. Because the benefits of genetic testing are often modest, and the tests themselves are often imprecise in identifying risk, the test is generally discouraged. Recent trials, however, reveal that the disclosure of *APOE* genotyping results to adult children of patients with AD did not result in significant short-term psychological risks. Test-related distress was reduced among those who learned that they were *APOE*4 negative. Persons with high levels of emotional distress before undergoing genetic testing are more likely to have emotional difficulties after disclosure.

For additional information for patients, families, and clinicians, contact the following organizations:
- Alzheimer's Association (www.alz.org; 800-272-3900)
- Alzheimer's Disease Education and Referral Center (http://www.nia.nih.gov/Alzheimers; 800-438-4380)

 EVIDENCE

Available at www.expertconsult.com

SUGGESTED READINGS

Available at www.expertconsult.com

RELATED CONTENT

Alzheimer's Disease (Patient Information)
Dementia with Lewy Bodies (Related Key Topic)
Mild Cognitive Impairment (Related Key Topic)

AUTHOR: **TAMARA G. FONG, M.D., PH.D.**

TABLE 1A-23 Symptomatic Treatment of Memory Disturbance

	Initial Dose	Target Dose
Donepezil	5 mg qd for 4-6 weeks	10 mg qd
Rivastigmine	1.5 mg bid with food, increase by 1.5 mg bid weekly	3-6 mg bid
Galantamine	4 mg bid with food, increase by 4 mg bid every 4 weeks	8-12 mg bid
Memantine	5 mg qd, increase by 5 mg weekly	10 mg bid

TABLE 1A-24 Treatment of Behavioral and Neuropsychiatric Symptoms

	Initial Dose	Maximum Dose
Atypical Antipsychotics		
Olanzapine	2.5 mg qd to bid, may increase by 2.5 mg as needed	7.5 mg bid
Quetiapine	25 mg bid, may increase by 25 mg every 2 days	250 mg tid
Antidepressants		
Sertraline	25-50 mg qd, may increase by 25 mg every week	200 mg qd
Citalopram	10 mg qd, may increase after 1 week	20 mg qd

BASIC INFORMATION

DEFINITION

Amebiasis is an infection caused by the protozoal parasite *Entamoeba histolytica*. Although primarily an infection of the colon, amebiasis may cause extraintestinal disease, particularly liver abscess.

SYNONYMS

Amebic dysentery (when severe intestinal infection)

ICD-10CM CODES
A06.9 Amebiasis, unspecified
A06.1 Chronic intestinal amebiasis
A06.7 Cutaneous amebiasis

EPIDEMIOLOGY & DEMOGRAPHICS

INCIDENCE (IN U.S.): 1.2 cases per 100,000 U.S. population. Highest in institutionalized patients, and travelers to/immigrants from developing nations.
PREVALENCE (IN U.S.): 4% (80% of infections asymptomatic)
PREDOMINANT SEX:
• Equal sex distribution in general
• Striking male predominance of liver abscess
PREDOMINANT AGE: 2nd through 6th decades
PEAK INCIDENCE: Peaks at age 2 to 3 yr and >40 yr

PHYSICAL FINDINGS & CLINICAL PRESENTATION

• Often nonspecific
• Approximately 20% of cases symptomatic
  1. Diarrhea, which may be bloody
  2. Abdominal and back pain
• Abdominal tenderness in 83% of severe cases
• Fever in 38% of severe cases
• Hepatomegaly, right upper quadrant tenderness, and fever in almost all patients with liver abscess (may be absent in fulminant cases)

ETIOLOGY

• Caused by the protozoal parasite *E. histolytica*. *E. dispar* and *E. moshkovskii* are 10 times more common but nonpathogenic and difficult to distinguish from *E. histolytica*.
• Transmission by the fecal-oral route
• Infection usually localized to the large bowel, particularly the cecum where a localized mass lesion (ameboma) may form
• Extraintestinal infection in which the organism invades the bowel mucosa and gains access to the portal circulation

DIAGNOSIS

DIFFERENTIAL DIAGNOSIS

• Severe intestinal infection possibly confused with ulcerative colitis or other infectious enterocolitis syndromes, such as those caused by *Shigella*, *Salmonella*, *Campylobacter*, or invasive *Escherichia coli*
• In elderly patients: ischemic bowel possibly producing a similar picture

WORKUP

• Stool antigen testing is more sensitive than ova and parasite examination for the diagnosis of amebiasis
• Three stool specimens over a period of 7 to 10 days to search for cysts or trophozoites has a sensitivity of 85% to 95%, but microscopy cannot differentiate between the species
• Concentration and staining the specimen with Lugol's iodine or methylene blue to increase the diagnostic yield
• Fecal leukocytes not always present

LABORATORY TESTS

• Fecal ELISA antigen detection is specific for *E. histolytica* (87% percent sensitive) and also useful for diagnosis of liver abscess.
• PCR-based assays on stool: 90%-95% sensitive; 95%-100% specific.
• Mucosal biopsy is occasionally necessary to look for cysts or trophozoites.
• Serum antibody assays specific for *E. histolytica* are available and are particularly sensitive and specific for extraintestinal infection or severe intestinal disease but may not distinguish recent from remote infection.
• Aspiration of abscess fluid is used to distinguish amebic from bacterial abscesses.

IMAGING STUDIES

Abdominal imaging studies (sonography or CT scan) to diagnose liver abscess

TREATMENT

ACUTE GENERAL Rx

• *Entamoeba histolytica* causes amoebic dysentery and requires treatment. Other species of *Entamoeba* may colonize the gastrointestinal tract but are not pathogenic and do not mandate treatment.

• Table 1A-25 summarizes drug treatment options for amebiasis in adults and children.
• Liver abscess is generally responsive to medical management but surgical intervention indicated for extension of liver abscess into pericardium or for toxic megacolon.

DISPOSITION

Host immunity incomplete and reinfection rate high for patients remaining at risk

REFERRAL

• For consultation with infectious diseases specialist for extraintestinal infection or persistent or relapsing intestinal infection
• For surgical consultation:
  1. For toxic megacolon
  2. For impending rupture of or extension of liver abscess into adjacent structures

PEARLS & CONSIDERATIONS

COMMENTS

• Infection with other intestinal parasites, particularly *Giardia lamblia*, may coexist with amebiasis.
• There is a high prevalence of *E. dispar* in homosexual males, which is nonpathogenic but may be difficult to distinguish from the pathogen *E. histolytica*.

SUGGESTED READINGS

Available at www.expertconsult.com

RELATED CONTENT

Amebiasis (Patient Information)

AUTHOR: **GLENN G. FORT, M.D., M.P.H.**

TABLE 1A-25 Drug Treatment for Amebiasis

Medication	Adult Dosage (Oral)	Pediatric Dosage (Oral)*
Invasive Disease		
Metronidazole	Colitis or liver abscess: 750 mg tid for 7-10 days	Colitis or liver abscess: 35-50 mg/kg/day in 3 divided doses for 7-10 days
or		
Tinidazole	Colitis: 2 g once daily for 3 days Liver abscess: 2 g once daily for 3-5 days	Colitis: 50 mg/kg/day once daily for 3 days Liver abscess: 50 mg/kg/day once daily for 3-5 days
Followed by:		
Paromomycin (preferred)	500 mg tid for 7 days	25-35 mg/kg/day in 3 divided doses for 7 days
or		
Diloxanide furoate† or	500 mg tid for 10 days	20 mg/kg/day in 3 divided doses for 7 days
Iodoquinol	650 mg tid for 20 days	30-40 mg/kg/day in 3 divided doses for 20 days
Asymptomatic Intestinal Colonization		
Paromomycin (preferred) or Diloxanide furoate† or Iodoquinol	As for invasive disease	As for invasive disease

*All pediatric dosages are up to a maximum of the adult dose.
†Not available in the United States.
From Kliegman RM et al: *Nelson textbook of pediatrics*, ed 19, Philadelphia, 2011, Saunders.

BASIC INFORMATION

DESCRIPTION

Amenorrhea means absence of menstruation. It is classified as either primary or secondary depending on whether the patient has had previous menstrual cycles.

- Primary amenorrhea is defined as the absence of menses by age 16 in the presence of secondary sexual characteristics. However, in the absence of these secondary sexual features by the age of 14 years, one should begin the workup for primary amenorrhea.
- Secondary amenorrhea is the absence of menses for more than six months in a patient who has had previous normal progesterone withdrawal cycles. The duration of amenorrhea required for the diagnosis of secondary amenorrhea varies somewhat depending on the source.

ICD-10CM CODES
N91.0 Primary amenorrhea
N91.1 Secondary amenorrhea
N91.2 Amenorrhea, unspecified

EPIDEMIOLOGY & DEMOGRAPHICS

- Incidence of primary amenorrhea and secondary amenorrhea in the U.S. is <1% and 5% to 7%, respectively.
- There is no racial or ethnic predilection.

ETIOLOGY

- Physiologic amenorrhea
  1. Pregnancy
  2. Lactation
  3. Menopause
- Pathologic amenorrhea
  A. Primary amenorrhea
  1. Hypergonadotropic hypogonadism
     a. Turner's syndrome
     b. Pure gonadal dysgenesis
     c. Autoimmune oophoritis
     d. 17,20-desmolase deficiency or 17-hydroxylase deficiency
     e. Galactosemia
     f. Müllerian agenesis
     g. Eugonadism
  2. Androgen insensitivity (Table 1A-26)
     a. Müllerian agenesis
     b. Transverse vaginal septum
     c. Imperforate hymen
     d. Androgen insensitivity syndrome (AIS) (1%)
     e. 5-alpha reductase deficiency
     f. Polycystic ovarian syndrome (PCOS)
     g. Adult-onset congenital adrenal hyperplasia (CAH)
     h. Cushing's syndrome
     i. Hypothyroidism
  3. Hypogonadotropic hypogonadism
     a. Constitutional delay
     b. Hypothalamic disorders
     c. Pituitary diseases
     d. Other CNS diseases

- Secondary amenorrhea
  1. Ovarian diseases
     a. PCOS
     b. Iatrogenic (oophorectomy, S/P radiation, chemotherapy)
     c. Primary ovarian insufficiency (previously referred to as premature ovarian failure [POF]) and premature menopause; these terms should no longer be used)
     d. Ovarian tumors
  2. Hypothalamic dysfunction
     a. Functional (eating disorders, exercise, stress)
     b. Congenital GnRH deficiency
     c. Infiltrative diseases (sarcoidosis, histiocytosis, lymphoma)
  3. Pituitary diseases
     a. Hyperprolactinemia (drug induced, hypothyroidism, prolactinoma)
     b. Craniopharyngiomas
     c. Empty sella syndrome
     d. Sheehan's syndrome
     e. S/P radiation
     f. Infiltrative diseases
  4. Asherman's syndrome
  5. Others
  Hypothyroidism, Cushing's syndrome, adult-onset congenital adrenal hyperplasia, drug induced (e.g., Lupron Depot, Depo-Provera, levonorgestrel IUD, Danazol), chronic illnesses

PHYSICAL FINDINGS & CLINICAL PRESENTATION

- Turner's syndrome
  1. Usually presents with primary amenorrhea unless mosaic
  2. Short stature
  3. Epicanthic folds
  4. Low-set ears
  5. High-arched palate
  6. Micrognathia
  7. Sensorineural hearing loss
  8. Otitis media
  9. Webbing of the neck
  10. Pigmented nevi
  11. Square/shield chest
  12. Widely spaced nipples
  13. Absent breast development
  14. Bicuspid aortic valve
  15. Coarctation of aorta
  16. Cubit valgus
  17. Short fourth metacarpal
  18. Hyperconvex nails
  19. Leg edema
  20. Renal abnormalities
  21. Autoimmune disorders including thyroiditis
  22. Diabetes mellitus
- Pure gonadal dysgenesis
  1. Unlike Turner's syndrome has no dysmorphic features
- Müllerian agenesis
  1. Sporadic inheritance
  2. Primary amenorrhea
  3. Normal breast development
  4. Normal pubic and axillary hair
  5. Normal female external genitalia
  6. Absent uterus and upper part of vagina
  7. Ovaries present
  8. Renal and vertebral anomalies in some patients; renal agenesis should be evaluated

- Transverse vaginal septum and imperforate hymen
  1. Primary amenorrhea
  2. Progressive cyclic lower abdominal pain
  3. Imperforate hymen or transverse vaginal septum on pelvic examination
  4. Perirectal fullness from hematocolpos
  5. Imaging with MRI identifies level of obstruction
- Androgen insensitivity syndrome
  1. Primary amenorrhea
  2. X-linked recessive inheritance in some patients
  3. Normal breast development
  4. Absent pubic and axillary hair
  5. Testis may be present in the groin or inguinal canal
  6. Uterus and vagina absent
  7. No associated renal or vertebral anomalies
- Adult-onset congenital adrenal hyperplasia
  1. Commonly seen in Ashkenazi Jewish, Inuit Native American, French Canadian, Mexican population
  2. Mimics the presentation of PCOS
  3. Features of hyperandrogenism (virilization, hirsutism, acne)
  4. Hypertension
- 5-alpha reductase deficiency
  1. Primary amenorrhea
  2. Undergo striking virilization at puberty
- PCOS
  1. Usually presents with secondary amenorrhea and oligomenorrhea
  2. Features of hyperandrogenism
  3. Obesity (60% to 80% of PCOS patients)
  4. Infertility
  5. Insulin resistance, predisposition to type II diabetes mellitus
  6. Association with the metabolic syndrome
- Strict diagnosis may also require performance of pelvic ultrasonography
  1. Cushing's syndrome (rare disorder, prevalence 1/1,000,000)
  2. Secondary amenorrhea
  3. Features of hyperandrogenism
  4. Abnormal fat distribution (dorsocervical fat pad [buffalo hump], spider legs, significant central obesity)
  5. Abdominal striae due to weakening of skin integument
  6. Easy bruising
  7. Hypertension
  8. Proximal muscle weakness
- Hypothyroidism
  1. Secondary amenorrhea
  2. Lethargy
  3. Constipation
  4. Decreased appetite
  5. Weight gain
  6. Cold intolerance
  7. Hair loss
  8. Dry skin
  9. Hypotension
  10. Bradycardia
- Primary ovarian insufficiency (previously premature ovarian failure)
  1. Secondary amenorrhea prior to the age of 40 yr and elevated gonadotropins (FSH and LH)
  2. History of oophorectomy or pelvic radiation or chemotherapy

TABLE 1A-37 Treatment Options for Primary and Secondary Warm Autoimmune Hemolytic Anemia and Cold Autoimmune Hemolytic Anemia

Disease or Condition	First Line	Second Line	Beyond Second Line	Last Resort
Primary AIHA	Steroids	Splenectomy Rituximab	Azathioprine, MMF, cyclosporine, cyclophosphamide	High-dose cyclophosphamide, alemtuzumab
B- and T-cell NHL	Steroids	Chemotherapy +/− rituximab (splenectomy in SMZL)		
Hodgkin's lymphoma	Steroids	Chemotherapy		
Solid tumors	Steroids Surgery			
Ovarian dermoid cyst	Ovariectomy			
SLE	Steroids	Azathioprine	MMF	Rituximab Autologous SCT
Ulcerative colitis	Steroids	Azathioprine		Total colectomy
CVID	Steroids + IgG replacement			
ALPD	Steroids	MMF	Sirolimus	
Wiskott Aldrich syndrome	Steroids	Allogeneic SCT		
Allogeneic SCT	Steroids	Rituximab*	Splenectomy T-cells infusion	
Organ transplantation	Reduction of immune suppression, steroids			
Drug induced	Withdrawal	Steroids		
Primary CAD	Protection from cold exposure	Rituximab Chlorambucil	Fludarabine + rituximab	Eculizumab,[†] bortezomib[†]
PCH	Supportive treatment (postinfectious)	Rituximab* (chronic)		

AIHA, Autoimmune hemolytic anemia; *ALPD*, autoimmune lymphoproliferative disorders; *CAD*, cold agglutinin disease; *CVID*, common variable immune deficiency; *IgG*, immunoglobulin G; *MMF*, mycophenolate mofetil; *NHL*, non-Hodgkin lymphoma; *PCH*, paroxysmal cold hemoglobinuria; *SCT*, stem cell transplantation; *SLE*, systemic lupus erythematosus; *SMZL*, splenic marginal zone lymphoma.
*Early second-line treatment because of known poor response to steroids.
[†]Off-label use in single cases.
From Hoffman R: *Hematology, basic principles and practice*, 6th ed, Philadelphia, 2013, Saunders.

TABLE 1A-38 Second-Line Treatment Options After Steroids

Treatment	Dosing and Application	Side Effects	Precautions
Splenectomy (acute)	Preferentially laparoscopic	Infections, thrombosis	Postoperative thromboprophylaxis
Splenectomy (long term)	—	Infections Venous thrombosis	Vaccination, patient information
Rituximab	375 mg/m² on days 1, 8, 15, and 22 IV	Infusional reactions Infections	Premedication with antihistamines (and steroids)
Danazol	200-400/day PO	Hepatotoxicity	None
Cyclophosphamide	PO or IV Dose adjusted to neutrophil count	Neutropenia Mutagenesis	Neutrophil count monitoring, bladder protection after high doses
Azathioprine	2.0-3.mg/kg/day PO Dose adjusted to neutrophil count	Neutropenia	Neutrophil count monitoring; avoid interaction with other drugs (e.g., allopurinol)
Mycophenolate mofetil	1-2 × 1 g/d PO	Gastrointestinal	
Cyclosporine	PO Dose adjusted to blood levels of CyA Target level, 200-400 ng/mL	Nephrotoxicity Gum hyperplasia	Monitoring of CyA levels and creatinine
Alemtuzumab	SC (variable doses)	Neutropenia	Anti-infectious prophylaxis

CyA, Cyclosporine A; *IV*, intravenous; *PO*, oral; *SC*, subcutaneous.
From Hoffman R: *Hematology, basic principles and practice*, 6th ed, Philadelphia, 2013, Saunders.

BASIC INFORMATION

DEFINITION

Inflammatory anemia or anemia of chronic disease is a disorder of iron homeostasis promoted by hepcidin-25 in response to an inflammatory condition.

Iron is carried in the bloodstream shelled by a hollow protein called transferrin (<0.2% of total iron body content) or at the core of hemoglobin in RBCs (60% of total iron body content).

Iron is stored (15%-30% of total iron body content), especially inside the liver, spleen, and skeletal muscle cytoplasm as ferritin (although released to the bloodstream), and in lysosomes as hemosiderin. The rest of the iron body content is trapped in myoglobin in skeletal muscle and cytochromes in mitochondrias. In clinical practice, ferritin is a surrogate for iron stores and TIBC a surrogate for transferrin and carrying capacity of iron.

Cells involved in the defense from the inflammatory insult release cytokines such as IL-6, which stimulates hepatic release of hepcidin-25. Hepcidin is a circulating protein that prevents exit of iron from enterocytes and macrophages by binding to an iron channel called ferroportin. Cytokines also suppress erythrocyte progenitors and induce erythrophagocytosis by activating macrophages. In CKD, not only decreased production of erythropoietin but also decreased renal excretion (and increased level) of hepcidin have a role in ACD.

SYNONYMS

Inflammatory anemia
Anemia of chronic disease
ACD

ICD-10CM CODES
D63.8 Anemia in chronic diseases classified elsewhere
D63.0 Anemia in neoplastic disease
D64.8 Anemia, unspecified

EPIDEMIOLOGY & DEMOGRAPHICS
PREVALENCE
- Second-most prevalent anemia after iron deficiency anemia
  1. Around 11% of men and 10.2% of women ages 65 to 85 yr
  2. >20% of adults older than 85 yr

CLINICAL PRESENTATION
- Besides fatigue, shortness of breath, and generalized weakness from the anemia itself, it is important to consider other complaints if the underlying diagnosis is unknown, such as weight loss (malignancy, chronic infections, connective tissue diseases), anorexia, nausea, paresthesias, pleuritic chest pain, weight gain (CKD), diarrhea, bloody stools, abdominal pain, oral ulcers (IBD), and fevers (HIV, chronic infections).
  - Physical findings may include pallor, lymphadenopathy, stigmatas of connective tissue diseases (malar rash, sclerodactyly), palpable or visible masses, and localized findings for infection or malignancy.

DIAGNOSIS

Isolated ACD:
CBC with diff: normocytic (MCV 80-100 fL), normochromic (<36 g/dL), moderate (Hb rarely <8 g/dL) anemia
Hypoproliferative anemia (low reticulocyte index; reticulocyte count corrected to hematocrit <2%).
Iron studies:
- Low iron concentration as in IDA (iron deficiency anemia)
- Normal/high ferritin (>35 mg/dL) in ACD as it is an acute phase reactant (Fig. 1A-67).
- Low/normal TIBC (as opposed to IDA) and low transferrin saturation (as in IDA)
- Normal soluble transferrin receptor (sTfR, high in IDA)
Combined ACD/IDA
If normal to high ferritin, sTfR/log ferritin <1 defines isolated ACD, and >2 defines combined IDA/ACD

ETIOLOGY

Malignancy
CKD (patients with CKD stage IV [GFR<30 mL/min] should be screened for ACD)
CHF (ACD is the main cause of anemia in CHF patients)
Chronic infections
Anemia of critical illness (develops within days)
Connective tissue diseases

DIFFERENTIAL DIAGNOSIS
- Liver injury (increases ferritin)
  - Iron deficiency anemia
    - Other causes of normocytic anemia
      Red blood cell loss or destruction
      Acute blood loss
      Hypersplenism
      Hemolysis
    - Decreased red blood cell production
      Primary causes
      Bone marrow hypoplasia or aplasia
      Myeloproliferative disease
      Pure red blood cell aplasia
      Secondary causes
      Chronic renal failure
      Liver disease
      Endocrine deficiency states
      Sideroblastic anemia

WORKUP
- CBC, reticulocyte count, peripheral smear, iron level, ferritin, TIBC. Table 1A-39 summarizes characteristic findings in inflammatory anemia.

TREATMENT

Treat the underlying disorder/disease.

ACUTE GENERAL Rx
Blood transfusion is usually reserved for severe anemia (with Hb level <7 g/dl or <8 g/dl in patients with cardiac disease) especially if complicated with ongoing bleeding.

CHRONIC Rx
- Erythropoiesis-stimulating agents (ESA) (epoetin alfa and darbepoetin alfa) are FDA approved for use in patients with anemia resulting from:
  1. CKD
  2. Chemotherapy
  3. Zidovudine therapy.
  Although a 1998 study called Normal Hematocrit Cardiac Trial (NHCT) showed a nonsignificant increase in the combined endpoint death and nonfatal MI in patients with goal hematocrit of 33% versus 27%, subsequent studies (CHOIR, CREATE, and TREAT) suggest that higher doses and higher hematocrit targets are associated with increased cardiovascular events.
  ESA dose should be individualized for each patient, and the lowest sufficient dose to reduce blood transfusions should be used. A hemoglobin target of 10 to 11 g% is widely acceptable. IDA should be ruled out before ESA is started. Transferin saturation <20% and ferritin <100 mg/d indicate supplemental iron. After starting ESA therapy, ASH/ASCO guidelines recommend periodic monitoring of iron status. When no response to oral therapy, parental iron therapy is to be considered before stating that patient is nonresponsive to iron therapy.
  Promising research on the hepcidin–ferroportin axis with novel therapeutics that inhibit the BMP6-HJV-SMAD and the IL-6-STAT3 pathways may lead to better management of ACD.

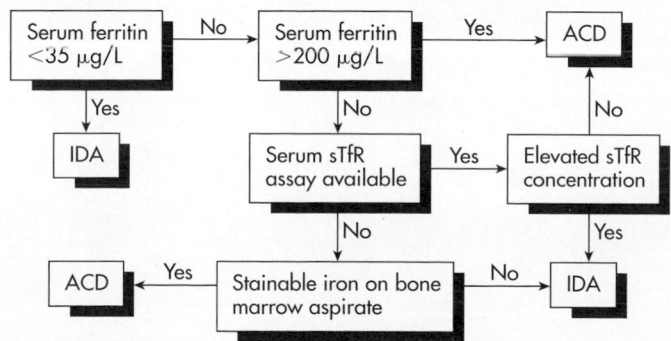

FIGURE 1A-67 Differential diagnosis of anemia with low serum iron. *ACD,* Anemia of chronic disease; *IDA,* iron deficiency anemia; *sTfR,* soluble transferrin receptor. (Modified from Young NS et al [eds]: *Clinical hematology,* St Louis, 2006, Mosby.)

Diseases and Disorders

I

TABLE 1A-39 Laboratory Characteristics of ACD, IDA, and IDA With Inflammation

	Anemia of Chronic Disease (ACD)	Iron Deficiency Anemia (IDA)	IDA with Inflammation
Mean corpuscular volume (MCV)	72-100 fL	<85 fL	<100 fL
Mean corpuscular hemo-globin concentration (MCHC)	<36 g/dl	<32 g/dl	<32 g/dl
Serum iron	Decreased	Decreased	Decreased
Serum total iron-binding capacity (TIBC)	Typical below mid-normal range	Elevated	Less than upper limit of normal range
Transferrin saturation*	2%-20%	<15% (usually <10%)	<15%
Serum ferritin	>35 µg/L	<35 µg/L	>35 µg/L, <200µg/L
Serum soluble transferrin receptor concentration (sTfR)	Normal (may be increased if serum ferritin >200 µg/L)	Increased	Increased
TfR index (sTfR/log ferritin)	<1	>2	>2
Hepcidin	High	Low	Normal
Stainable iron in bone marrow	Present	Absent	Absent

*Serum iron/TIBC * 100.
From Young NS et al (eds): *Clinical hematology*, St Louis, 2006, Mosby.

SUGGESTED READINGS
Available at www.expertconsult.com

AUTHORS: **ANDRE DESOUZA, M.D.,** and **BHARTI RATHORE, M.D.**

BASIC INFORMATION

DEFINITION

Anemia is defined as a hemoglobin level 2 standard deviations below normal for age and sex. Iron deficiency anemia is anemia resulting from inadequate iron supplementation or excessive blood loss.

ICD-10CM CODES
D50.9	Iron deficiency anemia, unspecified
O99.019	Anemia complicating pregnancy, unspecified trimester
D50.0	Iron deficiency anemia secondary to blood loss (chronic)
D50.8	Other iron deficiency anemias

EPIDEMIOLOGY & DEMOGRAPHICS

- Dietary iron deficiency occurs often in infants as a result of unsupplemented milk diets. It is also commonly seen in women during their reproductive years, as a result of heavy menstrual periods, and during pregnancy (increased demand).
- Iron deficiency is the most common nutritional deficiency worldwide.
- The prevalence of iron deficiency is greatest among toddlers ages 1 to 2 yr (7%) from inadequate intake and female individuals ages 12 to 49 yr (9% to 16%) from menstrual losses.
- The prevalence of iron deficiency is 2% in adult men, 9% to 12% in non-Hispanic white women, and 20% in black and Mexican American women.
- GI cancer is diagnosed in 10% of elderly patients with iron deficiency anemia.

PHYSICAL FINDINGS & CLINICAL PRESENTATION

- Most patients have normal examination results.
- Skin pallor and conjunctival pallor may be present.
- Signs and symptoms specific for iron deficiency are koilonychias, pica, pagophagia, blue sclera, glossitis, and angular stomatitis (Fig. 1A-70).

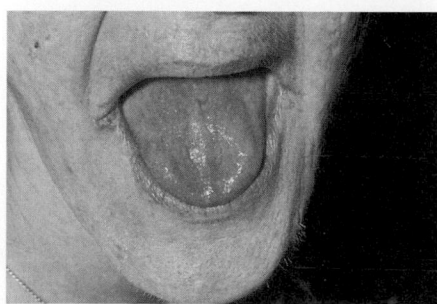

FIGURE 1A-70 Iron deficiency. (From White GM, Cox NH [eds]: *Diseases of the skin, a color atlas and text,* ed 2, St. Louis, 2006, Mosby.)

- Patients with severe anemia can have palpitations, headache, weakness, dizziness, and easy fatigability.

ETIOLOGY

- Blood loss from GI or menstrual bleeding (genitourinary blood loss less often the cause)
- Dietary iron deficiency (rare in adults)
- Poor iron absorption in patients with gastric or small-bowel surgery
- Repeated phlebotomy
- Increased requirements (e.g., during pregnancy)
- Other: traumatic hemolysis (abnormally functioning cardiac valves), idiopathic pulmonary hemosiderosis (iron sequestration in pulmonary macrophages), paroxysmal nocturnal hemoglobinuria (intravascular hemolysis)
- The most common cause worldwide is hookworm infection

 **DIAGNOSIS**

DIFFERENTIAL DIAGNOSIS

- Anemia of chronic disease
- Sideroblastic anemia
- Thalassemia trait
- Lead poisoning

WORKUP

Diagnostic workup consists primarily of laboratory evaluation. Table 1A-40 describes laboratory studies differentiating the most common microcytic anemias. Most patients with iron deficiency anemia are asymptomatic in the early stages. With progressive anemia, the major symptoms are fatigue, dizziness, exertional dyspnea, pagophagia (ice eating), and pica. Patient history may also suggest GI blood loss (melena, hematochezia, hemoptysis).

LABORATORY TESTS

- Laboratory results vary with the stage of deficiency.

- Absent iron marrow stores and decreased serum ferritin are the initial abnormalities.
- Decreased serum iron and increased total iron-binding capacity (TIBC) are the next abnormalities.
- Hypochromic microcytic anemia is present with significant iron deficiency.
- Peripheral smear in patients with iron deficiency generally reveals microcytic hypochromic red blood cells (Fig. 1A-71) with a wide area of central pallor, anisocytosis, and poikilocytosis when severe.
- Laboratory abnormalities consistent with iron deficiency are low serum ferritin level, increased RBC distribution width with values generally >15, low mean corpuscular volume, low mean corpuscular hemoglobin, increased TIBC, and low serum iron.
- In patients diagnosed with iron deficiency anemia, a GI workup including an upper endoscopy and colonoscopy is recommended to look for source of iron loss.

 **TREATMENT**

The goal of therapy is to supply sufficient iron to correct the low hemoglobin and replenish iron stores.

NONPHARMACOLOGIC THERAPY

Patients should be instructed to consume foods that contain large amounts of iron, such as liver, red meat, and legumes.

ACUTE GENERAL Rx

- Treatment consists of ferrous sulfate 325 mg PO daily for at least 6 mo. Doses higher than 325 mg/day are poorly tolerated. Calcium supplements can decrease iron absorption; therefore, these two medications should be staggered.
- Parenteral iron therapy is reserved for patients with poor tolerance, noncompliance with oral preparations, or malabsorption.
- Transfusion of packed RBCs is indicated in patients with severe symptomatic anemia.

TABLE 1A-40 Laboratory Studies Differentiating the Most Common Microcytic Anemias

Study	Iron Deficiency Anemia	α or β Thalassemia	Anemia of Chronic Disease
Hemoglobin	Decreased	Decreased	Decreased
MCV	Decreased	Decreased	Normal-decreased
RDW	Increased	Normal	Normal-increased
RBC	Decreased	Normal-increased	Normal-decreased
Serum ferritin	Decreased	Normal	Increased
Total Fe binding capacity	Increased	Normal	Decreased
Transferrin saturation	Decreased	Normal	Decreased
FEP	Increased	Normal	Increased
Transferrin receptor	Increased	Normal	Increased
Reticulocyte hemoglobin concentration	Decreased	Normal	Normal-decreased

Fe, Ferritin; *FEP,* free erythrocyte protoporphyrin; *MCV,* mean corpuscular volume; *RBC,* red blood cell; *RDW,* red cell distribution width.

From Kliegman RM et al: *Nelson textbook of pediatrics,* ed 19, Philadelphia, 2011, Saunders.

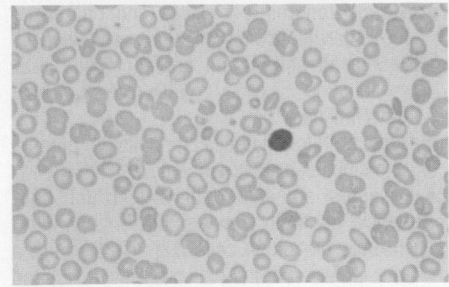

FIGURE 1A-71 Iron deficiency anemia. Many of these red blood cells are microcytic (smaller than the nucleus of the normal lymphocyte near the center of the field) and hypochromic (with central areas of pallor that exceed half the diameter of the cells). (From Goldman L, Schafer AI: *Goldman's Cecil medicine,* ed 24, Philadelphia, 2012, Saunders.)

CHRONIC Rx

Patients should be instructed to continue their iron supplements for at least 6 mo or longer to correct depleted body iron stores.

DISPOSITION

- Most patients respond rapidly to iron supplementation with improvement in CBC and general well-being (Table 1A-41). GI side effects from oral iron therapy are common and may require decreased dosage to once every other day or to change to parenteral iron.
- A differential diagnosis of microcytic anemia that fails to respond to oral iron is described in Table 1A-42.

REFERRAL

GI referral for evaluation of GI malignancy is recommended in all patients with iron deficiency and suspected GI blood loss.

TABLE 1A-41 Responses to Iron Therapy in Iron-Deficiency Anemia

Time after Iron Administration	Response
12-24 hr	Replacement of intracellular iron enzymes; subjective improvement; decreased irritability; increased appetite
36-48 hr	Initial bone marrow response; erythroid hyperplasia
48-72 hr	Reticulocytosis, peaking at 5–7 days
4-30 days	Increase in hemoglobin level
1-3 mo	Repletion of stores

From Kliegman RM et al: *Nelson textbook of pediatrics,* ed 19, Philadelphia, 2011, Saunders.

TABLE 1A-42 Differential Diagnosis of Microcytic Anemia That Fails to Respond to Oral Iron

Poor compliance (true intolerance of iron is uncommon)
Incorrect dose or medication
Malabsorption of administered iron
Ongoing blood loss including gastrointestinal, menstrual, and pulmonary
Concurrent infection or inflammatory disorder inhibiting the response to iron
Concurrent vitamin B_{12} or folate deficiency
Diagnosis other than iron deficiency
- Thalassemias
- Hemoglobin C and E disorders
- Anemia of chronic disease
- Lead poisoning
- Sickle thalassemias, hemoglobin SC disease
- Rare microcytic anemias

From Kliegman RM et al: *Nelson textbook of pediatrics,* ed 19, Philadelphia, 2011, Saunders.

PEARLS & CONSIDERATIONS

COMMENTS

- Iron deficiency may impair aerobic performance and worsen symptoms in patients with heart failure. Treatment with IV iron in patients with chronic heart failure and iron deficiency has been shown to improve symptoms, quality of life, and functional capacity.
- If the diagnosis of iron deficiency anemia is made, locating the suspected site of iron loss is mandatory.

SUGGESTED READINGS

Available at www.expertconsult.com

RELATED CONTENT

Algorithm for diagnosis of anemias (Algorithm in Section III)
Iron Deficiency Anemia (Patient Information)
Anemia (Patient Information)

AUTHORS: **BILAL H. NAQVI, M.D.,** and **FRED F. FERRI, M.D.**

A

Diseases
and Disorders

BASIC INFORMATION

DEFINITION

Pernicious anemia (PA) is an autoimmune disease resulting from antibodies against intrinsic factor and gastric parietal cells.

SYNONYMS

Megaloblastic anemia resulting from vitamin B_{12} deficiency

ICD-10CM CODES

D51.0 Vitamin B12 deficiency anemia due to intrinsic factor deficiency

D51.8 Other vitamin B12 deficiency anemias

D51.9 Vitamin B12 deficiency anemia, unspecified

D51.1 Vitamin B12 deficiency anemia due to selective vitamin B12 malabsorption with proteinuria

EPIDEMIOLOGY & DEMOGRAPHICS

- Increased incidence in females and older adults (diagnosis is unusual before age 35 yr)
- The overall prevalence of undiagnosed PA after age 60 yr is 1.9%
- Prevalence is highest in women (2.7%), particularly in black women (4.3%)

- Increased incidence of autoimmune disease (e.g., type 1 diabetes mellitus, Graves disease, Addison disease), *Helicobacter pylori* infection

PHYSICAL FINDINGS & CLINICAL PRESENTATION

- Mucosal pallor, glossitis
- Peripheral sensory neuropathy with paresthesias initially and absent reflexes in advanced cases
- Loss of joint position sense, pyramidal or long tract signs
- Possible splenomegaly and mild hepatomegaly
- Generalized weakness and delirium/dementia

ETIOLOGY

- Gastric/antiparietal cell antibodies in >70% of patients; antiintrinsic factor antibodies in >50% of patients
- Atrophic gastric mucosa
- Inborn errors of cobalamin-cofactor synthesis are rare. The cobalamin gene *(cblD)* is localized to human chromosome 2q23.2. Mutations in the gene designated MMADHC (methylmalonic aciduria, cblD type, and homocystinuria) are responsible for the cblD defect in vitamin B_{12} metabolism.
- Fig. E1A-72 illustrates the components and mechanism of cobalamin absorption. An etiopathophysiologic classification of cobalamin deficiency is described in Section II.

DIAGNOSIS

DIFFERENTIAL DIAGNOSIS

- Nutritional vitamin B_{12} deficiency
- Malabsorption
- Chronic alcoholism (multifactorial)
- Chronic gastritis related to *H. pylori* infection
- Folic acid deficiency
- Myelodysplasia

WORKUP

- The clinical presentation of PA varies with the stage. Initially, patients may be asymptomatic. In advanced stages patients may have impaired memory, depression, gait disturbances, paresthesias, and reports of generalized weakness.
- Investigation consists primarily of laboratory evaluation. Table 1A-43 describes a stepwise approach to the diagnosis of cobalamin and folate deficiency.
- Endoscopy and biopsy for atrophic gastritis may be performed in selected cases.
- Diagnosis is crucial because failure to treat may result in irreversible neurologic deficits.

LABORATORY TESTS

- Complete blood count generally reveals macrocytic anemia and leukopenia with hypersegmented neutrophils (Fig. E1A-73).
- Mean corpuscular volume (MCV) is generally significantly elevated in the advanced stages.
- Reticulocyte count is low to normal.
- Falsely low serum cobalamin levels can occur in patients with severe folate deficiency, in patients using high doses of ascorbic acid, and when cobalamin levels are measured after nuclear medicine studies (radioactivity interferes with cobalamin radioimmunoassay measurement).
- Falsely high normal levels in patients with cobalamin deficiency can occur in severe liver disease or chronic granulocytic leukemia (Table 1A-44).
- The absence of anemia or macrocytosis does not exclude the diagnosis of cobalamin deficiency. Anemia is absent in 20% of patients with cobalamin deficiency, and macrocytosis is absent in >30% of patients at the time of diagnosis. It can be blocked by concurrent iron deficiency or anemia of chronic disease and may be masked by thalassemia trait.
- Laboratory tests used for detecting cobalamin deficiency in patients with normal vitamin B_{12} levels include serum and urinary methylmalonic acid (MMA) level (elevated), total homocysteine level (elevated), intrinsic factor antibody (positive). Cobalamin is a cofactor for the enzymes L-methylmalonyl-coenzyme A mutase and methionine synthase. Inadequate levels of cobalamin will thus result in increased MMA and homocysteine. MMA level can also be used to differentiate cobalamin from folate deficiency because most patients with folate deficiency have normal or mild elevations of MMA levels.

TABLE 1A-43 Stepwise Approach to the Diagnosis of Cobalamin and Folate Deficiency

Megaloblastic Anemia or Neurologic-Psychiatric Manifestations Consistent With Cobalamin Deficiency *Plus* Test Results on Serum Cobalamin and Serum Folate

Cobalamin* (pg/mL)	Folate† (ng/ml)	Provisional Diagnosis	Proceed With Metabolites?‡
>300	>4	Cobalamin or folate deficiency is unlikely	No
<200	>4	Consistent with cobalamin deficiency	No
200-300	>4	Rule out cobalamin deficiency	Yes
>300	<2	Consistent with folate deficiency	No
<200	<2	Consistent with (1) combined cobalamin plus folate deficiency or (2) isolated folate deficiency	Yes
>300	2-4	Consistent with (1) folate deficiency or (2) an anemia unrelated to vitamin deficiency	Yes

Test Results on Metabolites: Serum Methylmalonic Acid and Total Homocysteine

Methylmalonic Acid (Normal, 70-270 nM)	Total Homocysteine (Normal, 5-14 µM)	Diagnosis
Increased	Increased	Cobalamin deficiency confirmed; folate deficiency still possible (i.e., combined cobalamin plus folate deficiency possible)
Normal	Increased	Folate deficiency is likely
Normal	Normal	Cobalamin and folate deficiency is excluded

*Serum cobalamin levels: abnormally low, less than 200 pg/mL; clinically relevant low-normal range, 200 to 300 pg/mL.
†Serum folate levels: abnormally low, less than 2 ng/mL; clinically relevant low-normal range, 2 to 4 ng/mL.
‡Any frozen-over sample from serum folate/cobalamin determination can be subjected to metabolite tests.
From Hoffman R: *Hematology, basic principles and practice*, 6th ed, Philadelphia, 2013, Saunders.

TABLE 1A-44   Serum Cobalamin: False-Positive and False-Negative Test Results

Falsely Low Serum Cobalamin in the Absence of True Cobalamin Deficiency

Folate deficiency (one-third of patients)
Multiple myeloma
TCI deficiency
Megadose vitamin C therapy

Falsely Raised Cobalamin Levels in the Presence of a True Deficiency*

Cobalamin binders (TCI and II) increased (e.g., myeloproliferative states, hepatomas, and fibrolamellar hepatic tumors)
TCII-producing macrophages are activated (e.g., autoimmune diseases, monoblastic leukemias and lymphomas)
Release of cobalamin from hepatocytes (e.g., active liver disease)
High serum anti-IF antibody titer

IF, Intrinsic factor; *TC,* transcobalamin.
*Although a low serum cobalamin level is not synonymous with cobalamin deficiency, 5% of patients with true cobalamin deficiency have low-normal cobalamin levels, a potentially serious problem because the patient's underlying cobalamin deficiency will progress if uncorrected.
From Hoffman R: *Hematology, basic principles and practice,* 6th ed, Philadelphia, 2013, Saunders, 2013.

- An increased concentration of plasma methylmalonic acid does not predict clinical manifestations of vitamin B_{12} deficiency and should not be used as the only marker for diagnosis of B_{12} deficiency.
- Additional laboratory abnormalities can include elevated lactate dehydrogenase, direct hyperbilirubinemia, and decreased haptoglobin.
- Bone marrow aspirate is not necessary to diagnose cobalamin deficiency. It may show giant C-shaped neutrophil bands and megaloblastic normoblasts (Fig. E1A-74).
- Schilling test: No longer available in most laboratories. It was historically used to identify the locus of cobalamin malabsorption and, in some instances such as pernicious anemia or bacterial overgrowth, the cause of cobalamin deficiency.

(Rx) TREATMENT

NONPHARMACOLOGIC THERAPY
Avoid folic acid supplementation without proper vitamin B_{12} supplementation. Doses of folic acid greater than 0.1 mg/day may result in hematologic remission in patients with vitamin B_{12} deficiency but will not prevent neurologic manifestations.

ACUTE GENERAL Rx
Traditional therapy of a cobalamin deficiency consists of IM injections of vitamin B_{12} 1000 mcg/day for 1 wk, followed by 1000 mcg/mo IM indefinitely. In patients who have no nervous system involvement, intranasal cyanocobalamin may be used in place of IM cyanocobalamin when hematologic parameters have returned to normal range. The initial dose of intranasal cyanocobalamin (Nascobal) is 1 spray (500 mcg) in one nostril once per week. Cost generally exceeds $120/mo. Monitor response and increase dose if serum B_{12} levels decline. Consider return to intramuscular vitamin B_{12} supplementation if decline recurs.

CHRONIC Rx
- Parenteral vitamin B_{12} 1000 mcg/mo or intranasal cyanocobalamin 500 mcg/wk (see "Acute General Rx") for the remainder of life.
- Oral cobalamin (1000-2000 mcg/day) has been reported as also being effective in mild cases of pernicious anemia because approximately 1% of an oral dose is absorbed by passive diffusion, a pathway that does not require intrinsic factor. Cost for 1 mo of therapy is approximately $5.

DISPOSITION
Anemia generally resolves with appropriate treatment. Neurologic deficits, if present at diagnosis, may be permanent.

REFERRAL
Gastrointestinal referral for endoscopy on diagnosis of PA and periodic surveillance endoscopy to rule out gastric carcinoma.

(!) PEARLS & CONSIDERATIONS

COMMENTS
- Early manifestations of negative cobalamin balance are increased serum methylmalonic acid and total homocysteine levels. This occurs when the total cobalamin in serum is still in the low-normal range.
- Patients must understand that therapy is lifelong. Vitamin B_{12} deficiency that is allowed to progress for longer than 3 months may produce permanent degenerative lesions of the spinal cord.
- Vitamin B_{12} deficiency may suppress signs of polycythemia vera; treatment of B_{12} deficiency may unmask this disorder.
- Blunted or impeded therapeutic response to vitamin B_{12} may be due to concurrent iron or folic acid deficiency, uremia, infection, and use of drugs with bone marrow suppressant properties.
- Drugs that interfere with B_{12} absorption include metformin, colchicine, neomycin, and aminosalicylic acid.
- Self-injection of vitamin B_{12} may be taught in selected patients. Cost of monthly injection is less than $5.

SUGGESTED READINGS
Available at www.expertconsult.com

RELATED CONTENT
Pernicious Anemia (Patient Information)

AUTHOR: **FRED F. FERRI, M.D.**

 **BASIC INFORMATION**

DEFINITION

Sideroblastic anemias (SAs) are a heterogeneous group of blood disorders characterized by ring sideroblasts in the bone marrow (abnormal erythroblasts with pathologic iron deposits in the mitochondria distributed in a "ring like" fashion around the nucleus) and impaired heme biosynthesis.

CLASSIFICATION TABLE 1A-45

- Congenital sideroblastic anemia (CSA)
- Acquired clonal sideroblastic anemia (ACSA)
- Acquired reversible sideroblastic anemia (ARSA)
- Sideroblastic anemia

ICD-10CM CODES
D64.0 Hereditary sideroblastic anemia
D64.1 Secondary sideroblastic anemia due to disease
D64.2 Secondary sideroblastic anemia due to drugs and toxins
D64.3 Other sideroblastic anemias

EPIDEMIOLOGY & DEMOGRAPHICS

- X-linked (40% of CSAs); primarily affects males.
- Autosomal recessive (15% of CSAs)
- ACSAs affect middle-aged and older adults.

CLINICAL PRESENTATIONS & PHYSICAL FINDINGS

Symptoms of sideroblastic anemia are similar to those of anemia and iron overload with additional features and variations noted based on the type.

- Mild to moderate anemia with other cytopenias
- Photosensitivity
- Hepatosplenomegaly
- Neurologic deficits
- Cardiomyopathy
- Pancreatic insufficiency
- Hepatic/renal failure

ETIOLOGY

- Congenital forms can be X-linked or autosomal recessive.
- Acquired clonal forms may be associated with chemotherapy or irradiation.
- RARS develops as a subtype of myelodysplasia.
- Reversible sideroblastic anemia can be caused by alcohol, isoniazid, pyrazinamide, cycloserine, chloramphenicol, thiamine deficiency or copper deficiency.

 **DIAGNOSIS**

The principal feature is mild to moderate anemia in middle-aged or elderly patients, although severe anemias have been reported. SAs are usually microcytic, but normocytic and dimorphic smears are not uncommon. Symptoms of iron overload may be the presenting feature in some. History and clinical findings, together with typical laboratory evidence, usually permit accurate diagnosis of different types of SAs. Molecular defects can be identified in several hereditary forms and in some patients with acquired clonal SAs.

DIFFERENTIAL DIAGNOSIS

- Sideroblastic anemia must be differentiated from other causes of microcytic hypochromic anemia: iron deficiency anemia, thalassemia, anemia of chronic disease, and lead poisoning.
- Tissue iron overload from sideroblastic anemia may present similar to hereditary hemochromatosis with liver cirrhosis, diabetes, congestive heart failure, or cardiac arrhythmias.

WORKUP

CBC, peripheral smear, iron studies, free erythrocyte protoporphyrin level, serum copper level, serum lead level, MRI, bone marrow aspiration and biopsy.

- CBC counts reveal anemia, mostly moderate, although severe anemias have been reported,
- Microcytic, normocytic, or macrocytic and classic dimorphic anemias may be seen along with siderocytes with Pappenheimer bodies (mature hypochromic erythrocytes with basophilic iron deposits) (Fig. E1A-75)
- High serum iron levels, low transferrin along with increased transferrin saturation and high serum ferritin.
- Bone marrow shows increased iron stores and the classic ring sideroblasts, not seen in normal bone marrow tissue (Fig. E1A-76). The ring sideroblasts represent pathologic iron deposits in the perinuclear mitochondria of erythroblasts.
- In transfusion-dependent anemias, monitoring of ferritin and transferrin saturation levels is very essential to avoid iron overload.
- Features of ineffective erythropoiesis like increase in indirect bilirubin concentration, decrease in haptoglobin, increase in LDH, and normal or increase in reticulocyte number may be seen.
- MRI of posterior cranial fossa indicated in anemia-ataxia syndromes

TREATMENT

Treatment is directed at controlling symptoms of anemia and preventing organ damage from iron overload.

NONPHARMACOLOGIC THERAPY

Removal of toxic agents including alcohol, lead, zinc, isoniazid, cycloserine, pyrazinamide, chloramphenicol and linezolid is necessary.

ACUTE GENERAL Rx

- A trial of pyridoxine (50-200 mg/day) is indicated for all patients with congenital SAs
- 25% to 50% may show full or partial response to pyridoxine.
- Folic acid given along with pyridoxine ensures adequate substrate availability during increased hemoglobin synthesis
- Patients who do not respond will need to be treated with blood transfusions.
- Chelation therapy is needed for patients with transfusion-dependent anemia to prevent complications of iron overload.
- Erythropoietin and granulocyte colony-stimulating factor may show some success in treating myelodysplasia-associated refractory anemia with ring sideroblasts.
- Secondary sideroblastic anemia caused by medication can be reversed by withdrawing the medication and administering vitamin B_6

CHRONIC Rx

Organ dysfunction resulting from iron overload will require periodic phlebotomy to keep serum

---

TABLE 1A-45 Classification of Sideroblastic Anemias

Congenital (Non-Syndromic)

X-linked (XLSA)
Mitochondrial carrier protein SLC25A38 deficiency
Glutaredoxin 5 deficiency
Erythropoietic protoporphyria

Congenital (Syndromic)

X-linked with ataxia (XLSA/A)
Myopathy, lactic acidosis, and sideroblastic anemia (MLASA)
Sideroblastic anemia, B cell immunodeficiency, fevers, and developmental delay (SIFD)
Pearson marrow-pancreas syndrome
Thiamine-responsive megaloblastic anemia (TRMA)
Unknown cause

Acquired Clonal

Refractory anemia with ring sideroblasts (RARS)
Refractory anemia with ring sideroblasts and thrombocytosis (RARS-T)
Refractory cytopenia with multilineage dysplasia and ring sideroblasts (RCMD-RS)

Acquired Reversible

Alcoholism
Certain drugs (isoniazid, chloramphenicol, linezolid)
Copper deficiency (nutritional, malabsorption, zinc ingestion, copper chelation)
Hypothermia

From Bottomley SS, Fleming MD: Sideroblastic anemia: Diagnosis and management. *Hematol/Oncol Clin N Am,* 28(4), 653-70, 2014.

ferritin level <300 ng/ml, as long as the patient is not anemic.

- Iron chelating therapy for patients with moderate to severe anemia who require regular red cell transfusion: deferoxamine (DESFERAL) subcutaneous infusion or the relatively new oral agent deferasirox (EXJADE).
- Splenectomy should be avoided at all costs.
- Bone marrow transplant in a last resort in young patients who are pyridoxine resistant and transfusion dependent with iron overload.

PROGNOSIS

In patients with anemia alone, life expectancy is normal. In patients dependent on blood transfusions, morbidity from iron overload can be expected.

1. RARS: with dysplasia confined to the erythroid cell lineage; survival similar to age-matched controls; no incidence of leukemic transformation.
2. RCMD-RS; approximately 5% will develop acute leukemia. Erythropoietin and granulocyte colony-stimulating factor therapy do not change survival.

REFERRAL

- Hematologist
- Neurologist (in anemia-ataxia and myopathy-anemia syndromes)
- Families with severe forms of hereditary sideroblastic anemia should receive genetic counseling.

⚠ PEARLS & CONSIDERATIONS

- Sideroblastic anemia can be thought of as an iron-loading anemia secondary to defective heme synthesis.

- A predisposition to leukemia evolution has not been observed in patients with congenital forms.
- Symptoms rather than an absolute hemoglobin level or hematocrit should guide transfusion therapy.

COMMENTS

Vitamin B$_6$, or pyridoxal phosphate, is a required cofactor in heme synthesis, and drugs such as isoniazid, cycloserine, and pyrazinamide can inhibit its function.

SUGGESTED READINGS
Available at www.expertconsult.com

AUTHORS: **SHIVA KUMAR R. MUKKAMALLA, M.D., M.P.H.,** and **BHARTI RATHORE, M.D.**

 BASIC INFORMATION

DEFINITION

Angina pectoris is a term used to describe a clinical syndrome, typically characterized by chest, jaw, shoulder, back or arm discomfort that is caused by myocardial ischemia. This is most commonly related to atheromatous plaque in one or more than one large epicardial coronary artery; however, myocardial ischemia may occur in the absence of obstructive coronary artery disease (CAD), such as uncontrolled hypertension, valvular heart disease, hypertrophic cardiomyopathy, coronary spasm, or endothelial dysfunction. Any situation that causes an imbalance in myocardial oxygen supply and demand can cause an angina syndrome. Angina can be classified as follows:

1. Chronic stable ischemic heart disease (SIHD):
   ○ Predictable. Usually follows a precipitating event (e.g., climbing stairs, sexual intercourse, a heavy meal, emotional stress, cold weather).
   ○ Generally has the same severity as previous attacks; relieved by rest or by the customary dose of sublingual nitroglycerin.
   ○ Caused by a fixed coronary artery obstruction secondary to atherosclerosis. The presence of one or more obstructions in major coronary arteries is likely; the severity of stenosis is usually >70%.
2. Unstable (rest, recent onset, crescendo, acute coronary syndrome; will be reviewed under Acute Coronary Syndrome):
   ○ Rest angina: Angina occurring at rest and usually prolonged >20 min, occurring within 1 week of presentation
   ○ Recent onset. Angina of at least CCS Class III severity occurring less than 2 months after the onset of the symptoms.
   ○ Crescendo angina: Previously diagnosed angina that is distinctly more frequent, longer in duration, or lower in threshold (i.e., increased by >1 CCS class within 2 months of initial presentation to at least CCS Class III severity)
3. Prinzmetal's variant:
   ○ Occurs at rest.
   ○ Cyclical in nature.
   ○ Manifests electrocardiographically as episodic ST-segment elevations.
   ○ Caused by coronary artery spasms with or without superimposed CAD.
   ○ Patients also more likely to develop ventricular arrhythmias.
4. Microvascular angina (syndrome X):
   ○ Refers to patients with angina symptoms, positive exercise test, normal coronary angiograms and no coronary spasm. Defective endothelium-dependent dilation in the coronary microcirculation contributes to the altered regulation of myocardial perfusion and the ischemic manifestations in these patients.
   ○ Patients with chest pain and normal or nonobstructive coronary angiograms are predominantly women, and many have a prognosis that is not as benign as commonly thought (2% risk of death or myocardial infarction [MI] at 30 days of follow-up).
5. Refractory angina:
   ○ Refers to patients whom, despite optimal medical therapy with at least maximal doses, or as tolerated of 2 antianginal medications, in addition to aspirin, aggressive risk factor modification, such as smoking cessation, adequate control of hypertension, diabetes, and hyperlipidemia, still have both angina and objective evidence of ischemia.
6. Other:
   ○ Angina due to aortic stenosis and idiopathic hypertrophic subaortic stenosis, cocaine-induced coronary vasoconstriction.

FUNCTIONAL CLASSIFICATION

Stable angina should be classified using a grading system. The most commonly adopted is that of the Canadian Cardiovascular Society:

- Class I: Ordinary physical activity, such as walking or climbing stairs, does not cause angina. Angina occurs with strenuous, rapid, or prolonged exertion at work or recreation.
- Class II: Slight limitation of ordinary activity. Angina occurs on walking or climbing stairs rapidly; walking uphill; walking or stair climbing after meals, in cold, in wind, or under emotional stress; or only during the few hours after awakening. Angina occurs on walking more than two level blocks and climbing more than one flight of ordinary stairs at a normal pace and in normal conditions.
- Class III: Marked limitations of ordinary physical activity. Angina occurs on walking one to two level blocks and climbing one flight of stairs in normal conditions and at a normal pace
- Class IV: Inability to carry on any physical activity without discomfort; anginal symptoms may be present at rest.

ICD-10CM CODES
I20.8	Other forms of angina pectoris
I20.9	Angina pectoris, unspecified
I20.1	Angina pectoris with documented spasm
I25.110	Atherosclerotic heart disease of native coronary artery with unstable angina pectoris
I25.111	Atherosclerotic heart disease of native coronary artery with angina pectoris with documented spasm
I25.118	Atherosclerotic heart disease of native coronary artery with other forms of angina pectoris
I25.119	Atherosclerotic heart disease of native coronary artery with unspecified angina pectoris
I25.700	Atherosclerosis of coronary artery bypass graft(s), unspecified, with unstable angina pectoris
I25.790	Atherosclerosis of other coronary artery bypass graft(s) with unstable angina pectoris
I25.791	Atherosclerosis of other coronary artery bypass graft(s) with angina pectoris with documented spasm
I25.798	Atherosclerosis of other coronary artery bypass graft(s) with other forms of angina pectoris
I25.799	Atherosclerosis of other coronary artery bypass graft(s) with unspecified angina pectoris

EPIDEMIOLOGY & DEMOGRAPHICS

- It is estimated that 1 in 3 adults in the United States (about 81 million) has some form of cardiovascular disease. Based on the NHANES survey 2007-2010, an estimated 15.4 million have coronary heart disease of which 7.8 million have angina.
- Angina is most common in middle-aged and elderly men. Among persons 60 to 79 years of age, approximately 25% of men and 16% of women have coronary heart disease, and these figures rise to 37% and 23% among men and women >80 years of age, respectively
- The incidence of coronary heart disease and angina in women after menopause is similar to that of men.
- Although the survival rate has steadily improved over time, SIHD remains the number one cause of death in men and women (27% of deaths).
- The initial manifestation of ischemic heart disease is angina pectoris in 50%, and about 50% of patients presenting to the hospital with acute coronary syndrome have preceding angina.
- Two older population-based studies from Olmstead County, MN, and Framingham, MA, showed annual rate of myocardial infarction in patients with symptomatic angina of 3 to 3.5%/year.
- Within 12 months of initial diagnosis, 10% to 20% of patients with diagnosis of stable angina progress to MI or unstable angina.

PHYSICAL FINDINGS & CLINICAL PRESENTATION

- The assessment of chest pain should include quality, location, severity, and duration of pain; radiation; associated symptoms; provocative factors; and alleviating factors. Anginal pain can be described as "squeezing," "griplike," "suffocating," and "heavy," but it is rarely sharp or stabbing and typically does not vary with position or respiration. The classic Levine's sign is placing a clenched fist over the precordium to describe the pain. Many patients do not, however, describe angina as frank pain but as tightness, pressure, or discomfort. Other patients, in particular women and older adults, can present with atypical symptoms such as nausea, vomiting, midepigastric discomfort, sharp (atypical) chest pain, dizziness, or syncope.
- Ischemic pain of more than 20 minutes' duration should raise concern for possible MI.
- Women are more likely than men to report atypical chest pain or discomfort (65% reported on Women's Ischemic Syndrome Evaluation [WISE] study).

- Elderly and diabetics may report symptoms other than chest pain, such as dyspnea, fatigue, or diaphoresis.

ETIOLOGY

RISK FACTORS:

- Advanced age.
- Male sex.
- Genetic predisposition, family history of premature coronary artery disease (CAD) in first-degree relatives (men younger than 55 years of age, and women younger than 65 years of age).
- Smoking (risk of first MI is increased by near threefold)
- Hypertension (risk is double if systolic blood pressure is >180 mm Hg).
- Hyperlipidemia (prevalence remained unchanged from 2002-2008).
- Impaired glucose tolerance or diabetes mellitus (prevalence decreased from 2002-2008).
- History of stroke or peripheral arterial disease.
- Chronic kidney disease (CKD).
- Metabolic syndrome.
- Physical inactivity.
- Obesity (body mass index >30% over ideal). A higher body mass index during childhood is also associated with an increased risk of coronary heart disease (CHD) in adulthood.
- Entities that cause increased oxygen demand include hyperthermia (particularly if accompanied by volume contraction), hyperthyroidism, and cocaine or methamphetamine abuse..
- Cocaine is used by >5 million Americans regularly and is responsible for >64,000 emergency department (ED) evaluations yearly to rule out myocardial ischemia. Cocaine causes sympathomimetic toxicity and not only increases myocardial oxygen demand but also induces coronary vasospasm and can cause infarction in young patients. Long-term cocaine use can cause premature development of SIHD.
- Increased myocardial oxygen demand and decreased subendocardial perfusion are caused by severe uncontrolled hypertension that increases LV wall tension. Hypertrophic cardiomyopathy and aortic stenosis can induce even more severe LV hypertrophy and resultant wall tension.
- Other causes of increased myocardial oxygen demand are ventricular or supraventricular tachycardias, but when paroxysmal, these are difficult to diagnose.
- Entities that limit myocardial oxygen supply such as anemia where the cardiac output rises when the hemoglobin drops to <9 g/dl and ST-T-wave changes (depression or inversion) can occur at levels <7 g/dl.
- Hypoxemia resulting from pulmonary disease (e.g., pneumonia, asthma, chronic obstructive pulmonary disease, pulmonary hypertension, interstitial fibrosis, or obstructive sleep apnea) can also precipitate angina.
- Polycythemia, leukemia, thrombocytosis, and hypergammaglobulinemia.
- Oral contraceptive and HRT use.

- Coronary artery calcium is associated with an increased risk of MI.
- Long-term use of nonsteroidal antiinflammatory drugs (NSAIDs).
- Exposure to air pollution from traffic (dilute diesel exhaust) promotes myocardial ischemia and is associated with adverse cardiovascular events.
- Low serum folate levels required for conversion of homocysteine to methionine are associated with an increased risk of fatal CHD. Hyperhomocysteinemia has a toxic effect on vascular endothelium and interferes with proliferation of arterial wall smooth muscle cells. Elevated plasma homocysteine level is a strong and independent risk factor for CHD events, especially in patients with type 2 diabetes mellitus.
- Elevated levels of highly sensitive C-reactive protein (hs-CRP, cardio CRP), suggesting that diseases associated with systemic inflammation can lead to accelerated atherosclerosis.
- Depression.
- Vasculitis.
- Elevated levels of lipoprotein-associated phospholipase A_2.
- Elevated fibrinogen levels.
- Low level of red blood cell glutathione peroxidase-1 activity.
- Radiation therapy.

Dx DIAGNOSIS

DIFFERENTIAL DIAGNOSIS

Non-ischemic Cardiovascular: Aortic dissection, pericarditis

Pulmonary: Pulmonary embolism, pneumothorax, pneumonia, pleuritis

Gastrointestinal: Esophageal, esophagitis, spasm, reflux, biliary colic, cholecystitis, choledocholithiasis, cholangitis, peptic ulcer, pancreatitis

Chest Wall: Costochondritis, fibrositis, rib fracture, sternoclavicular arthritis, Herpes zoster (before the rash)

Psychiatric: Anxiety disorders, hyperventilation, panic disorder, primary anxiety, affective disorders (i.e., depression), somatiform disorders, thought disorders (i.e., fixed delusions)

WORKUP

- In patients with chest pain, the probability of CAD should be estimated on the basis of patient age, sex, cardiovascular risk factors, and pain characteristics.
- The most important diagnostic factor is the history. Chest pain or left arm pain or discomfort occurring with exertion and relieved by rest in a patient with cardiovascular risk factors is consistent with a high likelihood of CAD.
- In assessing the likelihood of underlying SIHD it is helpful to classify the chest pain as typical angina, atypical angina, and/or noncardiac chest pain.
- Typical angina, (definite) will have the following three features: (1) substernal chest discomfort with a characteristic quality and

duration, (2) provoked by exertion or emotional stress, and (3) relieved by rest and/or sublingual nitroglycerin (NTG).
- Atypical angina, (probable) will have two of the above listed three features.
- Noncardiac chest pain will have one of the above listed features.
- Physical examination may be completely normal in many patients; however, certain findings may be helpful in the assessment of the patient with suspected SIHD. Some findings may identify consequences of ischemia or possible causes of the anginal syndrome other than CAD. The presence of hypertension, arcus senilis, xanthelasma, carotid or peripheral bruits, and a prominent S4 are all physical signs that could raise concern for the presence of CAD. A murmur of mitral regurgitation may be a marker of an ischemic cardiomyopathy or transient ischemia. A murmur suggestive of hypertrophic cardiomyopathy or aortic stenosis may suggest a cause of angina other than CAD.

LABORATORY TESTS

- Initial laboratory tests in patients with chronic SIHD should include a hemoglobin, fasting glucose, and fasting lipid panel.
- Cardiovascular screening: Measurement of total cholesterol, low-density lipoprotein cholesterol (LDL-C), high-density lipoprotein cholesterol (HDL-C), and fasting serum triglycerides. Also, measurement of Non–HDL-C, the ratio of total cholesterol to HDL-C, and apolipoprotein fractions (e.g., apolipoprotein B100, apolipoprotein A1).
- Electrocardiogram should be obtained during pain and when the patient is free of any discomfort. A normal resting electrocardiogram is not unusual in patients with SIHD; in patients who present with chest pain, 1% to 6% who have an acute MI will have a normal or nondiagnostic electrocardiogram.
- Chest x-ray PA and lateral, to rule out heart failure, valvular disease, pericardial disease, aortic aneurysm/dissection.
- Cardio-CRP (hs-CRP): Its elevation is a relatively moderate predictor of CHD, and it adds prognostic information to that conveyed by the Framingham risk score.

EXERCISE TESTING AND IMAGING STUDIES

- The value of further testing is greatest in patients who have an intermediate risk of CAD (10%-90% pretest likelihood).
- Exercise testing is used for the purpose of diagnosis as well as prognosis. If the patient is physically capable to perform at least moderate physical exercise, exercise stress testing (Fig. 1A-77) is useful because of the important prognostic information obtained from exercise performance and the hemodynamic response. Patients who have an intermediate risk of CAD, as patients in a low-risk or high-risk category are more likely to have a false-positive or false-negative result, respectively. Risk assessment is also indicated in patients with SIHD who are being

considered for revascularization of known coronary stenosis of unclear physiological significance.

- Stress echocardiography or stress testing with myocardial perfusion imaging may be employed when baseline electrocardiographic abnormalities are present that render the electrocardiographic response to exercise uninterpretable, such as >1 mm ST segment depression, LBBB, preexcitation, paced ventricular rhythm, digoxin treatment with ST segment changes. Stress echocardiography has the advantage of higher specificity and a lower cost. Stress radionuclide perfusion imaging has a higher sensitivity, particularly for single-vessel coronary disease, and has a higher technical success rate. When the patient is unable to exercise adequately, pharmacologic testing (i.e., dobutamine, adenosine, regadenoson) may be used with these imaging modalities
- A very good predictor of risk for a patient with stable angina is the Duke treadmill score, which incorporates the patient's functional status (METS or time in minutes during the Bruce protocol), ST-segment depression in millimeters, and an angina index (yes or no). Patients with favorable Duke scores (>5) have a 5-year survival rate of >97%; this is independent of other factors such as coronary anatomy and LV function.
- Echocardiography is indicated in patients with murmurs suggestive of aortic stenosis, hypertrophic cardiomyopathy, mitral regurgitation, mitral valve prolapse, previous MI, pathological Q waves, complex ventricular arrhythmias, heart failure, hypertension, diabetes, and abnormal EKG.
- Cardiac computed tomography (CCTA; Fig. E1A-78) is useful for the detection of subclinical CAD in asymptomatic patients with an intermediate Framingham 10-year risk estimate of 10% to 20%. Detects and quantifies coronary calcium and evaluates the lumen and wall of the coronary artery. CCTA can be useful as a first-line test for risk assessment in patients with SIHD who are unable to exercise to an adequate workload regardless of interpretability of ECG. Also can be used when a functional test has an indeterminate result and to assess bypass graft patency or patency of previous stents >3 mm diameter. CCTA CT cost and radiation exposure are limiting factors to recommending widespread routine use of this marker.
- Coronary artery calcium (CAC) score is a strong predictor of incidence of CAD and provides predictive information in patients with low to intermediate pretest probability of CAD beyond that provided by standard risk factors. A score below 100 indicates low risk, and a score above 400 high risk.
- Cardiac magnetic resonance imaging (CMRA), in addition to its use for diagnosis of arrhythmogenic right ventricular dysplasia, can also be used to assess myocardial perfusion and viability as well as function in patients unable to exercise. Additional studies are needed to determine the cost effectiveness of these

studies in patients with ischemic cardiomyopathy.
- Invasive coronary angiography remains the gold standard for the identification of clinically significant CAD. Angiography is performed to define the location and extent of coronary disease; indicated in selected patients who are candidates for coronary revascularization (either coronary artery bypass graft [CABG] surgery or angioplasty).

RX TREATMENT

FIVE FUNDAMENTAL OVERLAPPING STRATEGIES ARE RECOMMENDED

- Patient education: To support active participation of patients in the decision-making process of their treatment.
- Management of comorbid conditions that contribute or worsen SIHD.
- Aggressive modification of preventable risk factors such as smoking cessation, weight reduction in obese patients, regular aerobic exercise program (at least 30 to 60 min/day), correction of folate deficiency, reduced intake of saturated fats (to <7% of total calories), trans fatty acids (to <1% of total calories), cholesterol (to <200 mg/day), low-sodium diet (<2 g/day), and teaching importance of medication adherence. Whole grains as the main form of carbohydrates, an abundance of fruits and vegetables, and adequate omega-3 fatty acids are optimal for prevention of SIHD.
- Evidence-based pharmacologic management to improve quality of life and survival.
- Use appropriate revascularization procedures to improve survival and long-term outcomes in selected patients.

PHARMACOLOGIC THERAPY
Treatment can be classified based on medications that prevent MI and death.

- Aspirin reduces cardiovascular mortality and morbidity rates by 20% to 25% among patients with CAD. Its dose is 75 to 162 mg/day in the absence of contraindications. It inhibits the enzyme cyclooxygenase and synthesis of thromboxane A2 and reduces the risk of adverse cardiovascular events by 33% in patients with unstable angina. Patients intolerant to aspirin can be treated with other antiplatelet agents (see below).
- Clopidogrel irreversibly blocks the P2Y12 adenosine diphosphate receptor on the platelet surface, thereby interrupting platelet activation and aggregation. Clopidogrel can be combined with ASA in high-risk patients with SIHD or can be given alone in patients that are aspirin intolerant. Its dose is 75 mg/day.
- Ticagrelor, the newest CTPT inhibitor (P2Y12 antagonist), in the Pegasus-TIMI-54 reduced the risk of death, cardiovascular MI, or stroke in patients after 1 year of MI. However, it is associated with a slight increased risk of bleeding when compared to placebo.

- Dypiridamole is not recommended as an antiplatelet therapy for the treatment of patients with SIHD.
- Beta-adrenergic blockers, which prevent MI and death, are first-line therapy in the management of angina pectoris. They achieve their major antianginal effect by decreasing myocardial oxygen demand in reducing heart rate and systolic blood pressure product, AV nodal conduction, and myocardial contractility, in this manner contributing to a reduction in angina onset, with improvement in the ischemic threshold during exercise and during the usual daily activities. Absent contraindications, they should be regarded as initial therapy for stable angina for all patients. Their dose should generally be adjusted to reduce the resting heart rate to 55 to 60 beats/min. Despite the difference among the available beta blockers, they all seem to be equally efficacious in SIHD.
- Nitrates cause venodilation and relaxation of vascular smooth muscle; the decreased venous return from venodilation decreases diastolic ventricular wall tension (preload) and thereby reduces mechanical activity (and myocardial oxygen consumption) during systole. Relaxation of vascular smooth muscle increases coronary blood flow and reduces systemic pressure. Dilatation of the arterial wall will not be affected by plaque, but independent of an intact endothelium, leads to reduced resistance across the obstructed lumen. Nitroglycerin contributes to coronary blood flow redistribution by augmenting collateral flow and lowering ventricular diastolic pressure from areas of normal perfusion to ischemic zones. Nitroglycerin also has demonstrated antithrombotic and antiplatelet effects. Sublingual nitroglycerin or nitroglycerin spray should be prescribed to all patients with SIHD for immediate angina relief. Tolerance to nitrates can be minimized by avoiding sustained blood levels with a daily nitrate-free period (e.g., omission of bedtime dose of oral isosorbide dinitrate or 12 hr on/12 hr off transdermal nitroglycerin therapy). Nitrates are relatively contraindicated in patients with hypertrophic obstructive cardiomyopathy, and should also be avoided in patients with severe aortic stenosis. Nitrates should not be used within 24 hr of sildenafil (Viagra) or vardenafil (Levitra) or within 48 hr of tadalafil (Cialis) because of the potential for hypotension.
- Calcium channel blockers are antiischemic medications that have no proven mortality benefit in SIHD. They improve myocardial oxygen supply by decreasing coronary vascular resistance and augmenting epicardial conduit vessel and systemic arterial blood flow. Myocardial demand is decreased by a reduction in myocardial contractility, systemic vascular resistance, and arterial pressure. They are first-line treatment when beta-blockers are contraindicated. They play a major role in preventing and terminating myocardial ischemia induced by coronary

STRESS TEST ALGORITHM

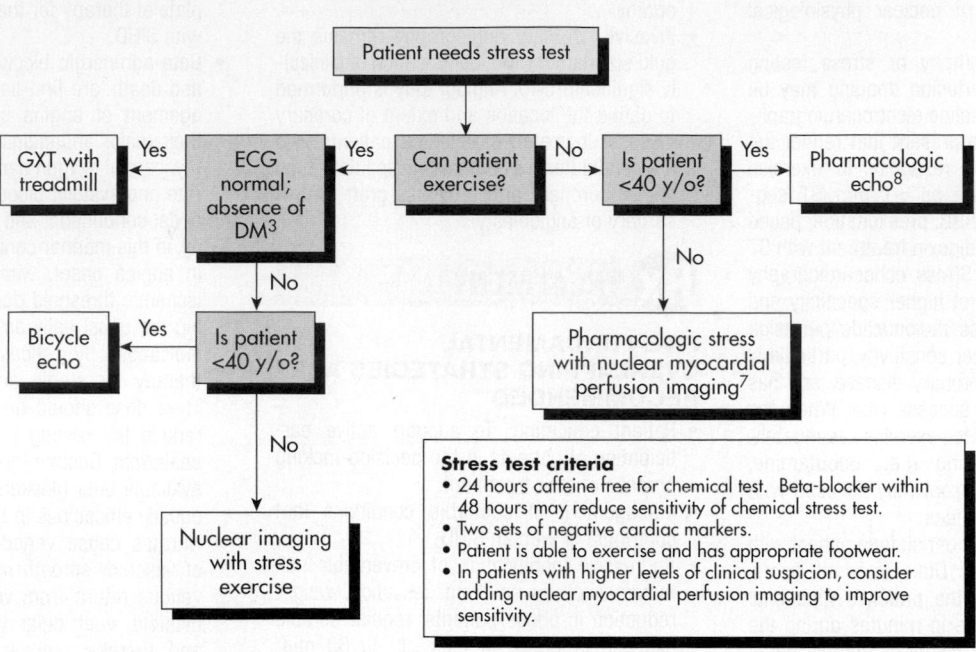

Stress test criteria
- 24 hours caffeine free for chemical test. Beta-blocker within 48 hours may reduce sensitivity of chemical stress test.
- Two sets of negative cardiac markers.
- Patient is able to exercise and has appropriate footwear.
- In patients with higher levels of clinical suspicion, consider adding nuclear myocardial perfusion imaging to improve sensitivity.

DEFINITIONS:

[1]Typical angina:
1) Substernal chest pain or discomfort that is 2) provoked by exertion or emotional stress and 3) relieved by rest and/or nitroglycerin

[2]Cardiac marker timing: based on symptom onset; in cases of uncertainty assume symptom onset at ED arrival

[3]ECG normal: no significant ST depression/T wave inversions, BBB, LVH with repolarization, conduction defect, digoxin effect

[4]Anginal equivalent:
- Any symptoms that the physician feels may represent ACS
- Exertional dyspnea—most common anginal equivalent symptom

[5]ACS:
- STE-ACS—1 mm ST elevation in 2 leads
- NSTE-ACS
  - NSTEMI—positive cardiac biomarkers
  - Unstable angina—ischemia with negative biomarkers

[6]New significant ECG changes:
- ST Δs $\geq$ 0.5 mm; resolve when asymptomatic
- ST depression $\geq$1 mm in 2 leads
- T wave inversion $\geq$2 mm in 2 leads

[7]Regadenoson is preferred agent for chemical nuclear stress test. Technitium Tc 99m tetrofosmin is the preferred tracer.

FIGURE 1A-77 Stress test algorithm. *ACS*, Acute coronary syndrome; *BBB*, bundle branch block; *DM*, diabetes mellitus; *ECG*, electrocardiogram; echo, echocardiography; *ED*, emergency department; *GTX*, graded exercise test; *LVH*, left ventricular hypertrophy; *NSTE*, non–ST-segment elevation; *NSTEMI*, NSTE myocardial infarction; *STE*, ST-segment elevation; *y/o*, years old. (From Adams JG et al: *Emergency medicine: clinical essentials*, ed 2, Philadelphia, 2013, Saunders.)

artery spasm. They are particularly effective in treating microvascular angina. All classes of calcium channel blockers reduce anginal episodes, increase exercise duration, and reduce use of sublingual nitroglycerin in patients with effort-induced angina. Short-acting calcium channel blockers should be avoided. Calcium channel blockers (particularly non-dihydropyridine) should generally also be avoided in patients with CHF secondary to systolic dysfunction due to its negative inotropic effect.

- Ranolazine inhibits the late inward sodium current, indirectly reducing the sodium-dependent calcium current during ischemic conditions and leading to improvement in ventricular diastolic tension and oxygen consumption. It seems to increase the efficiency of energy production in the heart, maintaining cardiac function. Its antianginal and antiischemic effects do not depend on reductions in heart rate or blood pressure. It is indicated for treatment of chronic angina that is inadequately controlled with other

antianginals. It represents a new class of drugs known as metabolic modulators and can be useful when prescribed as substitute for beta-blockers or in combination with them for relief of symptoms when initial treatment with beta-blockers is not successful or is contraindicated. Side effects include prolongation of QT interval. Low doses of diltiazem and verapamil should be used with ranolazine. The extended-release preparation reduces the frequency of angina, improves exercise performance, and delays the development of exercise-induced angina and ST-segment depression.

- Angiotensin-converting enzyme (ACE) inhibition through changes in the physiologic balance between angiotensin II and bradykinin could contribute to the reductions in LV and vascular hypertrophy, atherosclerosis progression, plaque rupture, and thrombosis; the favorable changes in cardiac hemodynamics; and the improved myocardial oxygen supply/demand. It has been shown to be effective in reducing cardiovascular death, MI, and stroke in patients who are at risk for or who had vascular disease. They are indicated in patients with hypertension, diabetes, LVEF <40%, and CKD. Angiotensin receptor blockers (ARBs) can be given to patients with SIHD who are intolerant to ACEI and qualify for them.
- Use of lipid-lowering drugs is recommended in patients with CAD and in patients with hyperlipidemia refractory to diet and exercise. Among patients who have recently had an acute coronary syndrome, an intensive lipid-lowering statin regimen to reduce LDL cholesterol to </0 mg/dl is a reasonable treatment objective. Statins also decrease the level of the inflammatory marker hs-CRP independently of the magnitude of change in lipid parameters.
- Influenza vaccine is recommended for patients with SIHD on annual basis to prevent all-cause mortality, morbidity, and hospitalization caused by the exacerbation of underlying medical conditions produced by influenza.
- Alternative therapies for relief of symptoms in patients with refractory angina that may improve symptoms and quality of life but have not been shown to improve mortality rate:
  - Enhanced external counterpulsation (EECP)
  - Spinal cord stimulation
  - Transmyocardial revascularization (TMR)

The following treatments have NOT been shown to be beneficial in reducing cardiovascular risk or improving clinical outcomes: estrogen therapy, vitamin C, vitamin E, and beta-carotene supplementation; treatment of elevated homocysteine with folate or vitamins B_6 and B_{12}; chelation therapy; garlic; coenzyme Q10; selenium; and chromium.

REFERRAL

Revascularization:

- Revascularization methods should be formulated taking into consideration improved survival or improved symptoms. Revascularization includes either percutaneous coronary intervention (balloon angioplasty and stenting) or CABG. However, note that although the role of percutaneous coronary intervention (PCI) is unquestionable in the presence of an acute myocardial infarction, its role is not so clear in stable CAD. The utilization of PCI for stable CAD was reduced by 51.7% from 2007 to 2011, and hospitals with higher volumes of PCI had the largest reduction of these procedures.

- **To improve survival:**
  1. Perform CABG for patients with significant (>50% diameter stenosis) left main coronary artery stenosis, more than 70% diameter stenosis in proximal left anterior descending artery (LAD), or more than 70% diameter stenosis in three major epicardial vessels, >70% diameter stenosis in two major coronary arteries with severe or extensive myocardial ischemia, and in patients with mild to moderate LV systolic dysfunction (EF 35% to 50%) and significant multivessel CAD. Left internal mammary artery (LIMA) graft improves survival when used to bypass a proximal LAD artery stenosis. CABG is recommended in preference to PCI to improve survival in patients with multivessel CAD and diabetes, particularly if a LIMA graft to LAD is used.
  2. PCI is reasonable as an alternative to CABG in selected stable patients with unprotected left main CAD, low risk of PCI procedural complications, and a high likelihood of good long-term outcome *and* clinical characteristics that predict a significantly increased risk of adverse surgical outcomes (e.g., STS-predicted risk of operative mortality >5).

- **To improve symptoms:**
  1. CABG or PCI to improve symptoms is beneficial in patients with one or more significant (>70% diameter) coronary artery stenosis amenable to revascularization and unacceptable angina despite maximal medical treatment, or in whom increasing medical therapy cannot be implemented because of medication contraindications, adverse effects, or patient preferences.
  2. Hybrid coronary revascularization: LIMA-to LAD artery grafting and of >1 non-LAD coronary artery can be used in patients who have an unfavorable aorta, have poor target vessels for CABG, have unsuitable graft conduits, or have unfavorable LAD for PCI.

- Compared with percutaneous coronary intervention (PCI), CABG is more effective in relieving angina and leads to fewer repeated revascularizations but has a higher risk for procedural stroke. Survival to 10 years is similar for both procedures.

Angioplasty and coronary stents (Fig. E1A-79):

- PCI has an established place in treating angina but is not superior to intensive medical therapy to prevent MI and death in symptomatic or asymptomatic patients. Patients selected for PCI should also be candidates for CABG. Approximately 80% of patients show immediate benefit after PCI. The development of coronary stents has increased the number of patients who can be treated in the cardiac laboratory. Cardiac stents (Fig. E1A-80) are currently used in nearly 95% of all patients with PCI lesions. The rate of restenosis is reduced by placing a stent electively in primary atheromatous lesions. The major limitations of stenting are subacute thrombosis, restenosis within the stent, bleeding

complications when antiplatelets are used after stenting, and higher cost. The combination of aspirin and P2Y12 antagonists is effective in preventing coronary stent thrombosis and the duration of therapy depends on whether bare metal stents (BMS) or drug-eluting stents (DES) are used. Duration of dual antiplatelet therapy can be as short as 4 weeks for BMS, but 12 months of therapy is generally required for DES. This difference in duration is due to the lack of endothelium proliferation in DES initially. New drug-eluting stents with thin struts releasing Limus-family analogs from durable polymers have lowered the risk of stent thrombosis compared with early-generation stents releasing sirolimus or paclitaxel. Current evidence supports the use of drug-eluting stents in most clinical settings without safety concerns (unless there are contraindications to use of dual antiplatelet therapy). Recent data has shown that extending clopidogrel therapy beyond 6 months after stent placement does not reduce death or ischemic events, and it increases the risk of bleeding complications.

PEARLS & CONSIDERATIONS

COMMENTS

- Although nitrate responsiveness is usually an integral part of a diagnostic strategy for SIHD, recent reports question its value and conclude that in a general population admitted for chest pain, relief of pain after nitroglycerin treatment does not predict active CAD and should not be used to guide diagnosis in the acute care setting.
- CABG is associated with higher long-term survival rates and lower rates of repeat revascularization than PCI and stenting; however, patients often prefer stenting because it is less invasive, involves a shorter hospital stay, and has a lower in-hospital mortality rate.

SUGGESTED READINGS

Available at www.expertconsult.com

RELATED CONTENT

Angina (Patient Information)
Unstable Angina (Patient Information)
Acute Coronary Syndrome (Related Key Topic)

AUTHORS: **JUAN A. ESCARFULLER, M.D.,** and **CLAUDIA SERRANO, M.D.**

BASIC INFORMATION

DEFINITION

- The mucocutaneous swelling caused by the release of vasoactive mediators is called urticaria and angioedema.
- Urticaria causes edema of the superficial dermis.
- Angioedema involves the deep layers of the dermis and the subcutaneous tissue.

SYNONYMS

Angioneurotic edema
HAE (hereditary angioedema)

ICD-10CM CODES
T78.3 Angioedema
D84.1 Angioedema, hereditary

EPIDEMIOLOGY & DEMOGRAPHICS

INCIDENCE: 100 to 3000/100,000 persons (for urticaria and angioedema)
LIFETIME PREVALENCE: Approximately 20% of the population experiences urticaria and/or angioedema at some time during life. The prevalence of hereditary angioedema is 1 case per 50,000 persons.
DEMOGRAPHICS:
Race: Slightly more common among African Americans.
Sex: More occurrences in women than men.
Angioedema commonly occurs after adolescence in the third decade of life.
Angioedema can occur together with urticaria (40%) or alone (20%); the remaining 40% have urticaria alone.

PHYSICAL FINDINGS & CLINICAL PRESENTATION

- Angioedema may be acute or chronic.
  1. Acute angioedema is defined as symptoms lasting 6 wk.
  2. Chronic angioedema is defined as symptoms lasting >6 wk.
- Urticaria is commonly known as "hives" and is:
  1. Pruritic
  2. Palpable and well demarcated
  3. Erythematous

4. Millimeters to centimeters in size
5. Multiple in number
6. Fades within 12 to 24 hr
7. Reappears at other sites
- Angioedema is characterized by the following:
  1. Nonpruritic
  2. Burning
  3. Not well demarcated
  4. Involves eyelids (Fig. 1A-81), lips, tongue, and extremities
  5. Can involve the upper airway, causing respiratory distress
  6. Can involve the gastrointestinal tract, leading to cyclic abdominal pain, nausea, vomiting, and diarrhea
  7. Resolves slowly

ETIOLOGY

- Angioedema, with or without urticaria, is classified as acquired (allergic or idiopathic) or hereditary.
- Angioedema is primarily caused by mast cell activation and degranulation with release of vasoactive mediators (e.g., histamine, serotonin, bradykinins), resulting in postcapillary venule inflammation, vascular leakage, and edema in the deep layers of the dermis and subcutaneous tissue.
- Pathologically, angioedema has both immunologic- and nonimmunologic-mediated mechanisms.
  1. Immunoglobulin E–mediated angioedema may result from antigen exposure (e.g., foods [milk, eggs, peanuts, shellfish, tomatoes, chocolate, sulfites] or drugs [penicillin, aspirin, nonsteroidal anti-inflammatory drugs, phenytoin, sulfonamides, recombinant tissue plasminogen activator]).
  2. Complement-mediated angioedema involving immune complex mechanisms can also lead to mast cell activation that manifests as serum sickness.
  3. Hereditary angioedema is an autosomal-dominant disease caused by a deficiency of or mutation in C1 esterase inhibitor (C1-INH). C1-INH is a protease inhibitor normally present in high concentrations in the plasma. C1-INH serves many functions, one of which is

to inhibit plasma kallikrein, a protease that cleaves kininogen and releases bradykinin. Deficient C1-INH activity results in excess concentration of kininogen and the subsequent release of kinin mediators.
  4. Acquired angioedema is usually associated with other diseases, most commonly B-cell lymphoproliferative disorders, but may also result from the formation of autoantibodies directed against C1 inhibitor protein.
  5. Other causes of angioedema include infection (e.g., herpes simplex, hepatitis B, Coxsackie A and B, *Streptococcus, Candida, Ascaris,* and *Strongyloides*), insect bites and stings, stress, physical factors (e.g., cold, exercise, pressure, and vibration), connective tissue diseases (e.g., systemic lupus erythematosus, Henoch-Schönlein purpura), and idiopathic causes. Angiotensin-converting enzyme (ACE) inhibitors can increase kinin activity and lead to angioedema.

DIAGNOSIS

A detailed history and physical examination usually establish the diagnosis of angioedema. Extensive laboratory testing is of limited value.

DIFFERENTIAL DIAGNOSIS

- Cellulitis
- Arthropod bite
- Hypothyroidism
- Contact dermatitis
- Atopic dermatitis
- Mastocytosis
- Granulomatous cheilitis
- Bullous pemphigoid
- Urticaria pigmentosa
- Anaphylaxis
- Erythema multiforme
- Epiglottitis
- Peritonsillar abscess

WORKUP

- An extensive workup searching for the cause of angioedema is often unrevealing (90%).
- Workup, including diagnostic blood tests and allergy testing, is performed according to results of the history and physical examination. Fig. E1A-82 illustrates a diagnostic algorithm for recurrent angioedema.

LABORATORY TESTS

- Complete blood count, erythrocyte sedimentation rate, and urinalysis are sometimes helpful as part of the initial evaluation.
- Stools for ova and parasites.
- Serology testing.
- C4 levels are usually reduced in acquired and hereditary angioedema (occurring without urticaria). If C4 levels are low, C1-INH levels and activity should be obtained. There are isolated reports of hereditary angioedema with normal C4 levels but reduced C1-INH levels.

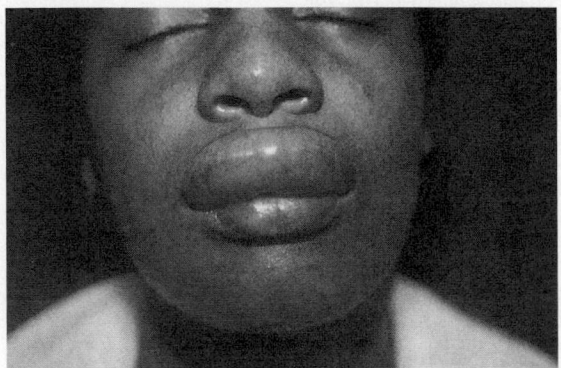

FIGURE 1A-81 Angioedema of the upper lip, with severe swelling of deeper tissues. (From Goldstein BG, Goldstein AO: *Practical dermatology,* ed 2, St Louis, 1997, Mosby.)

- Skin and radioallergosorbent testing may be done if food allergies are suspected.
- Skin biopsy is usually done in patients with chronic angioedema refractory to corticosteroid treatment.

Rx TREATMENT

NONPHARMACOLOGIC THERAPY
- Eliminate the offending agent
- Avoid triggering factors (e.g., cold, stress)
- Cold compresses to affected areas

ACUTE GENERAL Rx
- Acute life-threatening angioedema involving the larynx is treated with:
  1. Epinephrine 0.3 mg in a solution of 1:1000 given SC
  2. Diphenhydramine 25 to 50 mg IV or IM
  3. Cimetidine 300 mg IV or ranitidine 50 mg IV
  4. Methylprednisolone 125 mg IV
- Mainstay therapy in nonhereditary angioedema is H_1 antihistamines
  1. Diphenhydramine 25 to 50 mg q6h
  2. Chlorpheniramine 4 mg q6h
  3. Hydroxyzine 10 to 25 mg q6h
  4. Cetirizine 5 to 10 mg qd
  5. Loratadine 10 mg qd
  6. Fexofenadine 60 mg qd
- H_2 antihistamines can be added to H_1 antihistamines
  1. Ranitidine 150 mg bid
  2. Cimetidine 400 mg bid
  3. Famotidine 20 mg bid
- Tricyclic antidepressants
  1. Doxepin 25 to 50 mg qd
- Corticosteroids are rarely required for symptomatic relief of acute angioedema.

- Antihistamines are probably ineffective in acute hereditary angioedema.
- Purified plasma-derived C1-INH replacement therapy is effective and safe in treating acute attacks of hereditary angioedema caused by C1 inhibitor deficiency. Cost is a limiting factor. Acute attacks can be managed with plasma-derived or recombinant preparations of C1 inhibitor, with ecallantide, a specific plasma kallikrein inhibitor, or with the use of the B2 bradykinin-receptor antagonist icatibant.

CHRONIC Rx
- Chronic angioedema is treated as described under "Acute General Rx." Fig. 1A-83 describes a therapeutic algorithm for chronic angioedema
- Corticosteroids are used more often in chronic nonhereditary angioedema.
- Prednisone 1 mg/kg/day for 5 days and then tapered over a period of weeks.
- Androgens (danazol, stanozolol, oxandrolone, methyltestosterone) and antifibrinolytic agents can be used for the treatment of chronic hereditary angioedema, which does not respond to antihistamines or corticosteroids but are associated with many adverse effects. Long-term prophylaxis with plasma-derived C1 inhibitor is safe and effective and may be used in patients who have frequent or severe attacks. Cost is a limiting factor. C1-INH replacement therapy was approved by the FDA in 2008. Available agents are Cinryze and Berinert. Icatibant is a new bradykinin-receptor antagonist in hereditary angioedema currently undergoing trials. A recent phase 2 study among patients with ACE-inhibitor–induced angioedema revealed that the time to complete resolution of

edema was significantly shorter with icatibant than with combination therapy with a glucocorticoid and an antihistamine.[1]
- Fig. E1A-84 illustrates a hereditary angioedema treatment algorithm.
- Table E1A-46 summarizes approved drugs used to treat hereditary angioedema attacks.

DISPOSITION
- Antihistamines achieve symptomatic relief in more than 80% of patients with nonhereditary acute angioedema.
- In chronic nonhereditary angioedema, corticosteroids are given in addition to antihistamines.
- A small percentage of people will have recurrence of symptoms after steroid treatment.
- Chronic angioedema can last for months and even years.

REFERRAL
Dermatology consultation is recommended in patients with chronic angioedema, hereditary angioedema, and recurring angioedema.

 **PEARLS & CONSIDERATIONS**

ACE inhibitors can cause angioedema up to many months after initiation. There are multiple case reports and case series of angiotensin receptor blocker (ARB)–induced angioedema, although the risk is substantially less than that of ACE inhibitors. (Incidence rates per 1000 person-years are 4.38 cases for ACE inhibitors, 1.66 cases for ARBs.) The incidence rate is also very high for the direct renin inhibitor aliskiren (4.67).

COMMENTS
- Identifying a cause for angioedema in patients is often difficult and met with frustration.
- Chronic angioedema, unlike acute angioedema, is rarely caused by an allergic reaction.

SUGGESTED READINGS
Available at www.expertconsult.com

RELATED CONTENT
Angioedema (Patient Information)

AUTHOR: **MEL L. ANDERSON, M.D.**

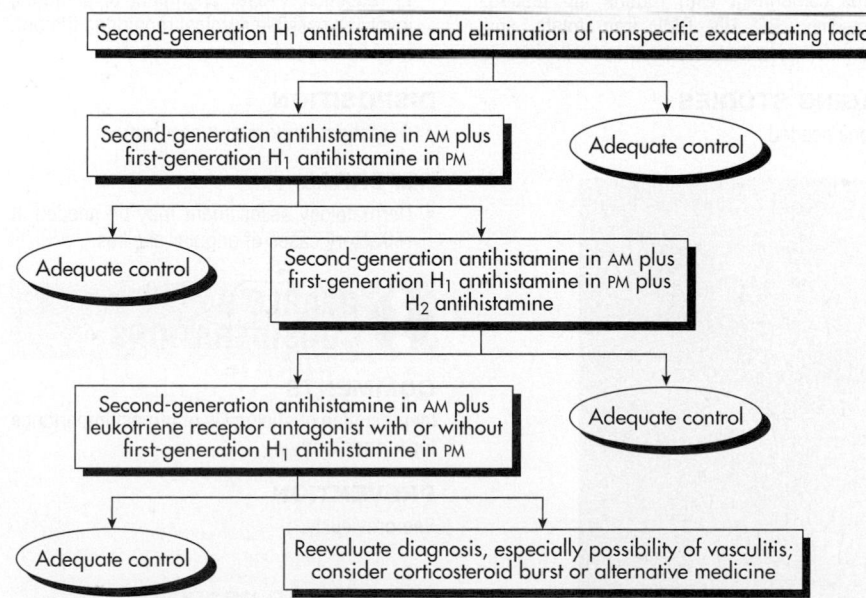

FIGURE 1A-83 Therapeutic algorithm for chronic urticaria/angioedema. (From Leung D, Sampson H, Geha R, Szefler S: *Pediatric allergy: principles and practice*, Chapter 55, 2010, Saunders, p 575-584.)

[1]Bas M et al.: A randomized trial of icatibant in ACE-inhibitor–induced angioedema, *N Engl J Med* 372:418-425, 2015.

 BASIC INFORMATION

DEFINITION

Angular cheilitis refers to inflammation of one, or both, of the corners of the mouth. Most commonly, it represents an infectious etiology, as an opportunistic fungal or bacterial pathogen, and leads to a spectrum of varying severities.

SYNONYM(S)

Angular cheilosis
Rhagades
Commissural cheilitis
Perleche
Angular stomatitis

ICD 10-CM CODE(S)
K13.0 Diseases of lips
B37.83 Candidal cheilitis

EPIDEMIOLOGY & DEMOGRAPHICS

INCIDENCE: Unknown
PEAK INCIDENCE: Advanced age
PREVALENCE: Suspected of causing 0.5-5% of lip infections in adults
PREDOMINANT SEX AND AGE: This form of lip inflammation has a predilection for the elderly, seen with denture use as an example.
GENETICS: No identified correlation
RISK FACTORS: These include dry mouth, nutritional deficiencies (B vitamins, iron), immunosuppression, or chronic irritation as with lip licking, drooling, oral hardware, or dentures.

PHYSICAL FINDINGS & CLINICAL PRESENTATION

- The majority of cases of this lip condition involve both sides of the mouth, which initially involves erythema and swelling (Fig. 1A-85). Over time, the erythema and subsequent linear fissures, or rhagades, may become cracked or ulcerated. Skin thickening is common during the progression of inflammation. It is important to note that this progression may involve strictly the mucosa of the lips or may propagate to the facial dermis, crossing the vermillion border.

ETIOLOGY

- Microorganisms commonly represent underlying infectious causes. These include *Candida* species, *Staphylococcal aureus*, beta-hemolytic *Streptococcus* species, or polymicrobial findings. Another common cause of this condition includes direct irritation of saliva on the corners of the mouth with overclosure of the lower jaw, as evident in edentulous individuals and those who wear dentures. Nearly any condition that leads to chronic irritation or moisture settling in the corners of the mouth, including lip licking, drooling, or habits of oral fixation, may lead to this state. Nutritional deficiencies, specifically of iron, B vitamins, and zinc, are also associated with angular cheilitis. Varying levels of immunosuppression, as seen in diabetes mellitus, HIV, and so on, predispose to subacute infection as well. Patients on medications leading to xerostomia or hypersalivation can develop bilateral involvement.

 DIAGNOSIS

DIFFERENTIAL DIAGNOSIS

- Oral candidiasis or oral-associated angular cheilitis; *S. aureus* infection or impetigo; contact dermatitis; angular herpes simplex

WORK-UP

- Primarily clinical in nature, taking into consideration full details of the patient's medical history and medications

LABORATORY TEST(S)

- If applicable, bacterial and fungal cultures may be beneficial to detect probable infectious component with routine lab testing, including CBC, HIV, BMP, iron, folate, and vitamin B_{12}, to be performed as well.

IMAGING STUDIES

- None needed

℞ TREATMENT

The hallmark of treatment used in this condition revolves around proper identification and understanding of the etiology of the inflammation. With the highest prevalence of this condition seen in those with dentures, proper oral fit and dental hygiene are of the utmost importance.

Certainly, good oral hygiene also includes smoking and tobacco use cessation. Topical antifungal use is at the cornerstone of treatment (details follow). Proper identification may include the presence of *S. aureus*, *Streptococcus* species, and other pathogens, which will need focused treatment. Treatment-refractory cheilitis may require additional workup to identify possible systemic etiology.

NONPHARMACOLOGIC THERAPY

- Dental hygiene, specifically, with a focus on proper cleaning of dentures, plays a pivotal role in prevention. The use of alcohol or bleach-based solutions are commonly available OTC. If significant lag is noted in the corners of the mouth, surgery, and collagen injections have been successful. Petrolatum jelly has been used for preventive measures as well.

ACUTE GENERAL Rx

- With the underlying pathology involving inflammation, topical corticosteroid creams are commonly used. If *S. aureus* has been implicated, topical mupirocin or fusidic acid has a role. Clotrimazole or ketoconazole can be used for combating *Candida albicans*, implicated in >50% of cases.

CHRONIC Rx

- Pending laboratory workup and identification of a nutritional deficiency, iron, B vitamins, or folate supplementation will likely lead to reduction. Proper alignment of dentures, involving possible surgical repair and fitment, may be needed.

DISPOSITION

- Outpatient workup and assessment

REFERRAL

- Dermatology assessment may be needed in refractory cases of angular cheilitis.

⚠ PEARLS & CONSIDERATIONS

COMMENTS

Identification of etiology is of utmost importance for further workup.

PREVENTION

See previously.

SUGGESTED READINGS
Available on www.expertconsult.com

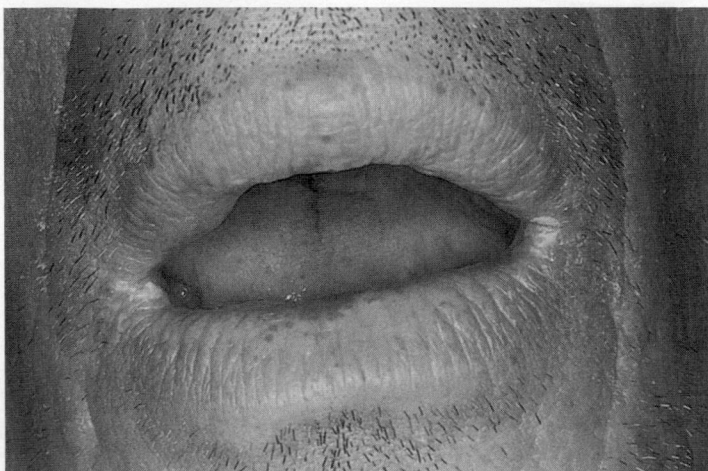

FIGURE 1A-85 Angular cheilitis. (From Swartz MH: *Textbook of physical diagnosis, history and examination,* ed 7, Philadelphia, 2014, Saunders.)

AUTHOR: **GREGORY M. HAIDEMENOS, M.D.**

Diseases
and Disorders

I

BASIC INFORMATION

DEFINITION

An ankle sprain is an injury to the ligamentous structures that support the ankle joint. Most (85%) involve the lateral ligament complex (Fig. 1A-88). The anterior inferior tibiofibular (AITF) ligament, deltoid ligament, and interosseous membrane may also be injured. A severe form of ankle sprain involves disruption of the ankle syndesmosis, known as a high ankle sprain. Lateral ankle sprains classically are graded I, II, or III in respect to specific ligament involvement and their integrity. Table 1A-48 describes a classification of ankle sprains.

ICD-10CM CODES

S93.409A Sprain of unspecified ligament of unspecified ankle, initial encounter
S93.411A Sprain of calcaneofibular ligament of right ankle, initial encounter
S93.411D Sprain of calcaneofibular ligament of right ankle, subsequent encounter
S93.411S Sprain of calcaneofibular ligament of right ankle, sequela
S93.412A Sprain of calcaneofibular ligament of left ankle, initial encounter
S93.412D Sprain of calcaneofibular ligament of left ankle, subsequent encounter
S93.412S Sprain of calcaneofibular ligament of left ankle, sequela

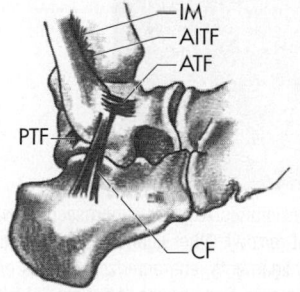

FIGURE 1A-88 The lateral ankle ligaments, anterior and posterior talofibular (ATF, PTF) and calcaneofibular (CF). Also shown are the anterior inferior tibiofibular ligament (AITF) and the beginning of the interosseous membrane (IM). (From Mercier LR [ed]: Practical orthopaedics, ed 4, St Louis, 1995, Mosby.)

S93.419A Sprain of calcaneofibular ligament of unspecified ankle, initial encounter
S93.419D Sprain of calcaneofibular ligament of unspecified ankle, subsequent encounter
S93.419S Sprain of calcaneofibular ligament of unspecified ankle, sequela
S93.421A Sprain of deltoid ligament of right ankle, initial encounter
S93.421D Sprain of deltoid ligament of right ankle, subsequent encounter
S93.421S Sprain of deltoid ligament of right ankle, sequela
S93.422A Sprain of deltoid ligament of left ankle, initial encounter
S93.422D Sprain of deltoid ligament of left ankle, subsequent encounter
S93.422S Sprain of deltoid ligament of left ankle, sequela
S93.429A Sprain of deltoid ligament of unspecified ankle, initial encounter
S93.429D Sprain of deltoid ligament of unspecified ankle, subsequent encounter
S93.429S Sprain of deltoid ligament of unspecified ankle, sequela
S93.431A Sprain of tibiofibular ligament of right ankle, initial encounter
S93.431D Sprain of tibiofibular ligament of right ankle, subsequent encounter
S93.431S Sprain of tibiofibular ligament of right ankle, sequela
S93.432A Sprain of tibiofibular ligament of left ankle, initial encounter
S93.432D Sprain of tibiofibular ligament of left ankle, subsequent encounter
S93.432S Sprain of tibiofibular ligament of left ankle, sequela
S93.439A Sprain of tibiofibular ligament of unspecified ankle, initial encounter
S93.439D Sprain of tibiofibular ligament of unspecified ankle, subsequent encounter
S93.439S Sprain of tibiofibular ligament of unspecified ankle, sequela

EPIDEMIOLOGY & DEMOGRAPHICS

PREVALENCE: One case/10,000 people each day
PREDOMINANT SEX: Varies according to age and level of physical activity

PHYSICAL FINDINGS & CLINICAL PRESENTATION

- Often a history of a "pop"
- Variable amounts of tenderness and hemorrhage (inversion sprains: tender laterally; syndesmotic injury: tender anterior leg about middle third of the leg).
- Anterior talofibular ligament (ATFL) evaluation: anterior drawer test. (With the patient in the sitting position and knee flexed allow the ankle to plantar-flex slightly and apply an anterolateral rotatory force to the heel. Positive if abnormal increase in forward movement of the talus on the tibia.) (Fig. 1A-89)
- Syndesmotic evaluation: manual squeeze test. (Compress the tibia and fibula toward each other at the middle third of the anterior leg. Splaying and pain are indicative of injury.)
- Talar tilt test or inversion stress test (Fig. 1A-90).
- Severe tenderness to direct palpation of ligamentous structure.

ETIOLOGY

- Lateral injuries usually result from inversion and plantar flexion injuries.
- Eversion and rotational forces may injure the deltoid or AITF ligament or the interosseous membrane.

DIAGNOSIS

DIFFERENTIAL DIAGNOSIS

- Fracture of the ankle or foot, particularly involving the distal fibular growth plate in the immature patient
- Avulsion fracture of the fifth metatarsal base

WORKUP

- History and clinical examination are usually sufficient to establish the diagnosis.
- Plain radiographs are not always needed.

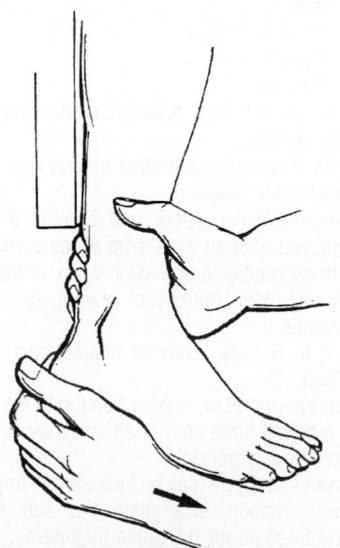

FIGURE 1A-89 Anterior drawer test of the ankle (tests the integrity of the anterior talofibular ligament). (From Brinker MR, Miller MD: Fundamentals of orthopaedics, Philadelphia, 1999, Saunders.)

TABLE 1A-48 Classifications of Ankle Sprains

Grade	Extent of Injury	Physical Findings	Treatments
I	Sprain of ATFL (midstretching of lateral ligament complex	Mild swelling and tenderness; no joint instability	Weight bear as tolerated; free ROM exercises
II	ATFL tear CFL strain	Moderate swelling and tenderness; laxity with positive anterior drawer test	Immobilization (air splint, CAM boot), physical therapy
III	ATFL tear CFL tear	Severe swelling and tenderness; instability with anterior drawer test and talar tilt; inability to bear weight	Immobilization, physical therapy (longer duration than grade II); surgery if symptoms unresolved

ATFL, Anterior talofibular ligament; CAM, controlled ankle movement; CFL, calcaneofibular ligament; ROM, range of motion.

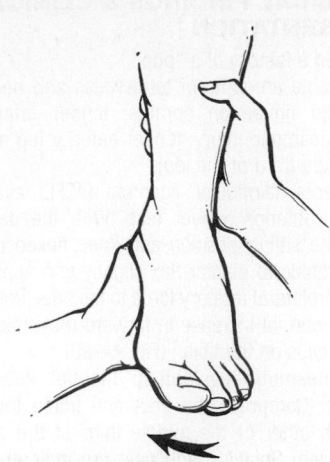

FIGURE 1A-90 Talar tilt test (inversion stress) of the ankle (tests the integrity of the anterior talofibular ligament and the calcaneofibular ligament). (From Brinker MR, Miller MD: *Fundamentals of orthopaedics,* Philadelphia, 1999, Saunders.)

IMAGING STUDIES

Radiographic evaluation (Figs. 1A-91 and 1A-92): According to the Ottawa ankle rules (Table 1A-49), radiography is indicated if there is pain in the malleolar or midfoot zone and either bone tenderness over an area of potential fracture or an inability to bear weight immediately after the injury and in the physician's office. Pearls: palpate entire distal 6 cm of the fibula and tibia; do not use if the patient younger than 18 years of age. Can reduce radiographic evaluation by 30%-40 %. (100% sensitive, 42% specific).[1]

Rx TREATMENT

ACUTE GENERAL Rx

- The first line of treatment is described by the mnemonic *RICE:*
  1. *R*est
  2. *I*ce (3 to 7 days)
  3. *C*ompression
  4. *E*levation
- Pain control with NSAIDs, acetaminophen, mild opioids.
- In 48-2 hr, early controlled motion in a functional ankle brace.
- Compression, support, and bracing is best achieved with an Air-Stirrup brace combined with an elastic compression wrap, or lace-up support alone (functional bracing for active patients).
- In 4 to 5 days, exercise against resistance added.
- Short period of immobilization (up to 10 days) in a below-knee cast or Aircast may shorten the recovery period.
- Physical therapy may be indicated to improve proprioception, strengthen the soft tissue structures about the ankle (ligaments, peroneal tendons), and restore ROM.

[1]Stiell et al: A study to develop clinical decision rules for the use of radiography in acute ankle injuries, *J Ann Emerg Med*, 21:4, 1992.

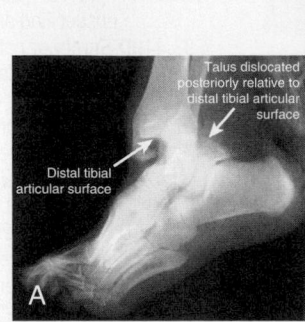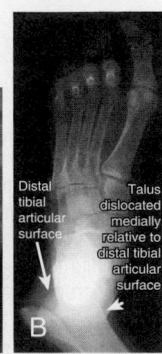

FIGURE 1A-91 Tibiotalar dislocation. This 17-year-old male landed on his left ankle after dunking a basketball, sustaining a deformity. His tibiotalar joint is dislocated, with the talus dislocated posteriorly (visible on the lateral view, **A**) and medially (visible on the anterior-posterior view, **B**). No fractures are present in this case, although fractures are commonly associated with this injury because of the amount of force required to dislocate the ankle. This was an open injury, and the patient underwent exploration, irrigation, and debridement with primary closure. (From Broder JS: *Diagnostic imaging for the emergency physician,* Philadelphia, 2011, Saunders.)

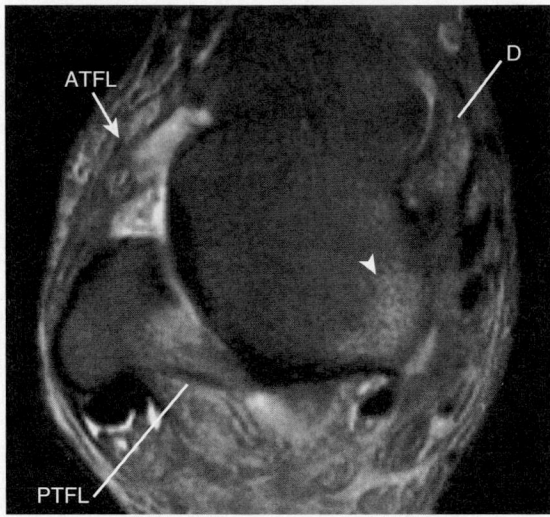

FIGURE 1A-92 Acute lateral ankle sprain with multiple ligamentous injuries. Axial fat-suppressed, T2-weighted MR image shows a tear of the anterior talofibular (ATFL) ligament *(arrow)*. Other ligamentous injuries include sprain to both the posterior talofibular (PTFL) and the deltoid *(D)* ligaments, characterized by loss of normal striation and increased signal on T2-weighted images in these ligaments. Bone bruise of the medial talar dome *(arrowhead)* is present. (From Pope TL, Bloem HL, Beltran J, Morrison WB, Wilson DJ: *Musculoskeletal imaging,* ed 2, Philadelphia, 2014, Saunders.)

TABLE 1A-49 Ottawa Ankle Rules

Accepted Indications: Ankle Radiographs	Accepted Indications: Midfoot Radiographs
Point tenderness about the inferior or posterior aspect of either malleolus (to include the distal 6 cm of the lateral malleolus)	Point tenderness about the navicular or the base of the fifth metatarsal
Inability to bear weight at the time of injury or clinical evaluation (four independent steps)	Inability to bear weight at the time of injury or clinical evaluation (four independent steps)

- Surgery is rarely recommended, even for grade III sprains; reports indicate equally satisfactory outcomes with nonsurgical treatment.

CHRONIC Rx

- Lateral heel and sole wedge to prevent inversion
- Protective taping or bracing during vigorous activities (Fig. 1A-93)

- Strengthening exercises
- Protective bracing or taping indicated for 6 months in patients with symptomatic grade II and III injuries

DISPOSITION

- Lateral sprains of any severity may cause lingering symptoms for weeks and months.

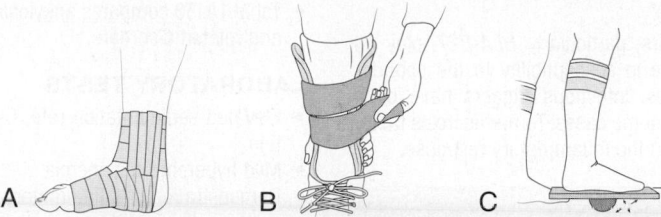

FIGURE 1A-93 **A,** The most effective method of supporting most acute ankle sprains is by using an ACE wrap (BD, Franklin Lakes, NJ) reinforced with 1-inch medial and lateral tape strips. The anterior and posterior aspects of the ankle are left free to allow the patient to flex and extend the ankle. The patient is encouraged to bear weight with crutches. **B,** Diagram of an air splint. Straps are adjusted to heel size, the lower straps are wrapped about the ankle, and the side extensions are centered. The splint is then pressurized and straps adjusted until comfortable support and pressure are attained. **C,** As the ankle pain subsides, about the third to fifth day, balancing exercises can begin to allow the patient to regain ankle proprioception and avoid recurrent instability problems. (From Jardon OM, Mathews MS: Orthopedics. In Rakel RE [ed]: *Textbook of family practice,* ed 5, Philadelphia, 1995, Saunders.)

1. Some syndesmotic sprains take even longer to heal.
2. Heterotopic ossification may even develop in the interosseous membrane, but long-term results do not seem to be affected by such ossification.
- Continuing lateral symptoms may require surgical reconstruction, although late traumatic arthritis or long-term instability is rare regardless of treatment.
- Approximately 15%-20% of patients require surgical intervention after continued lateral ankle instability after 6-8 months of rigorous physical rehabilitation.[2]

REFERRAL
Podiatric and orthopedic consultation for patients who do not respond to conservative treatment. Most ankle sprains resolve in 2 to 6 wk.

[2]Baumhauer JF, O'Brien T: Surgical considerations in the treatment of ankle instability. *J Athl Train.* 37:4, 2002.

PEARLS & CONSIDERATIONS

COMMENTS
If healing seems delayed (more than 6 wk), the following conditions should be considered:
1. Talar dome fracture
2. Reflex sympathetic dystrophy
3. Chronic tendinitis
4. Peroneal tendon subluxation
5. Other occult fracture
6. Peroneal weakness (poor rehabilitation)
7. A "high" (syndesmotic) sprain
   Repeat plain roentgenograms, bone scan, or MRI may be indicated.

EBM EVIDENCE
Available at www.expertconsult.com

SUGGESTED READINGS
Available at www.expertconsult.com

RELATED CONTENT
Ankle Sprain (Patient Information)
Ankle Fracture (Related Key Topic)

AUTHOR: **GARRETT KALMAR, D.P.M.**

Diseases and Disorders

BASIC INFORMATION

DEFINITION

Ankylosing spondylitis is a type of inflammatory arthritis involving the sacroiliac joints and axial skeleton characterized by ankylosis and enthesitis (inflammation at tendon insertions). It is one of a family of overlapping syndromes called seronegative spondyloarthropathies (SpA) that includes reactive arthritis (formerly Reiter syndrome), psoriatic spondylitis, and enteropathic arthritis.

SYNONYMS

Marie-Strümpell disease

ICD-10CM CODES

M45.9   Ankylosing spondylitis of unspecified sites in spine
M08.1   Juvenile ankylosing spondylitis
M45.0   Ankylosing spondylitis of multiple sites in spine
M45.1   Ankylosing spondylitis of occipito-atlanto-axial region
M45.2   Ankylosing spondylitis of cervical region
M45.3   Ankylosing spondylitis of cervicothoracic region
M45.4   Ankylosing spondylitis of thoracic region
M45.5   Ankylosing spondylitis of thoracolumbar region
M45.6   Ankylosing spondylitis lumbar region
M45.7   Ankylosing spondylitis of lumbosacral region
M45.8   Ankylosing spondylitis sacral and sacrococcygeal region

EPIDEMIOLOGY & DEMOGRAPHICS

PREVALENCE: Between 0.1% and 1% of the population. Varies with prevalence of HLA-B27.
PREDOMINANT AGE AT ONSET: 15 to 35 yr
PREDOMINANT SEX: Male/female ratio 2 to 3:1

PHYSICAL FINDINGS & CLINICAL PRESENTATION

- Prolonged morning back stiffness of insidious onset lasting more than 3 mo
- Bilateral sacroiliac tenderness (sacroiliitis)
- Limited lumbar spine motion (Fig. 1A-94)
- Tenderness at tendon insertion sites, especially the Achilles tendons and plantar fascia
- Loss of chest expansion reflecting rib cage involvement
- Occasionally, peripheral joint arthritis, usually involving the large joints of the lower extremities
- In advanced cases the typical posture consists of compensatory hyperextension of neck, fixed flexion of hips, and compensatory flexion of knees (Fig. 1A-95)
- Extraskeletal manifestations may affect the cardiovascular system (aortic insufficiency and cardiovascular disease), lungs (pulmonary fibrosis), and eye (uveitis), but are not usually severe. There is also an increased risk for osteoporosis.

ETIOLOGY

Genetic factors, particularly *HLA-B27*, play an important role in susceptibility to the spondyloarthropathies. Infectious triggers have been implicated in some cases. Tumor necrosis factor is important in the inflammatory response.

DIAGNOSIS

DIFFERENTIAL DIAGNOSIS

- Diffuse idiopathic skeletal hyperostosis (Forestier disease)
- Noninflammatory back pain (A clinical algorithm for the evaluation of back pain is described in Section III.)

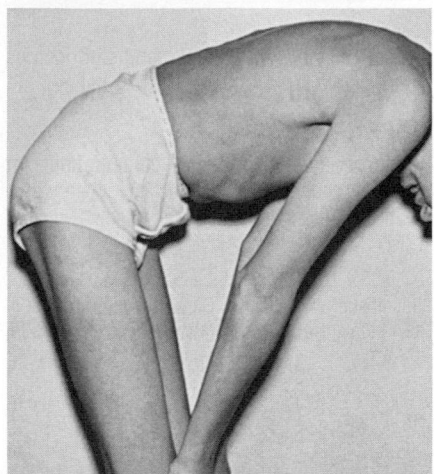

FIGURE 1A-94 Loss of lumbodorsal spine mobility in a boy with ankylosing spondylitis. The lower spine remains straight when the patient bends forward. (From Behrman RE: *Nelson textbook of pediatrics,* ed 17, Philadelphia, 2005, Saunders.)

- Table 1A-50 compares ankylosing spondylitis and related disorders.

LABORATORY TESTS

- Elevated sedimentation rate, C-reactive protein
- Mild hyperchromic anemia
- Demonstration of inflammatory sacroiliitis by radiography or MRI is essential for diagnosis
- HLA/B27 antigen is not useful in the evaluation of noninflammatory back pain because it is present in up to 8% to 10% of the normal population.

IMAGING STUDIES

- Classic features are those of bilateral sacroiliitis on radiographs of the pelvis
- Vertebral bodies lose anterior concave shape and become square
- With progression, calcification of the annulus fibrosus and paravertebral ligaments develop, giving rise to the so-called *bamboo spine* and a "trolley track" appearance (Fig. 1A-96).
- MRI (Fig. 1A-97) may be useful in detecting early inflammatory lesions and is especially helpful when the history is suggestive but radiographs are equivocal.

TREATMENT

NONPHARMACOLOGIC THERAPY

- Exercises primarily to maintain flexibility and aerobic activity are important
- Postural training
  1. Patients must be instructed on spinal extension exercises to avoid fusion in a flexed position
  2. Sleeping should be in the supine position on a firm mattress; pillows should not be placed under the head or knees.

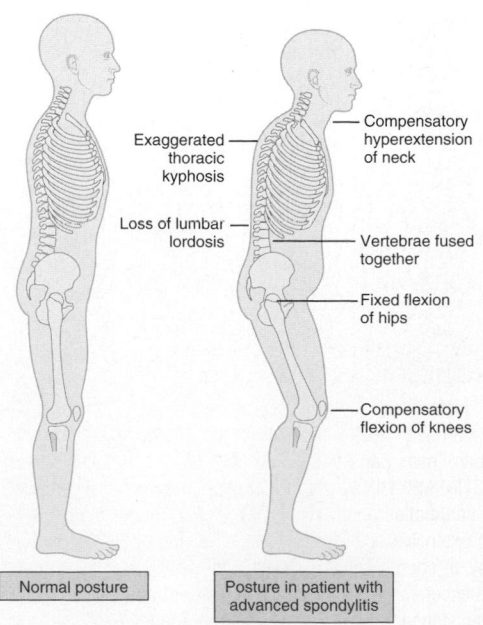

FIGURE 1A-95 Ankylosing spondylitis. Typical posture in advanced cases compared with normal posture. (From Ballinger A: *Kumar & Clark's essentials of clinical medicine,* ed 6, Edinburgh, 2012, Saunders.)

TABLE 1A-50 Comparison of Ankylosing Spondylitis and Related Disorders

Feature	Ankylosing Spondylitis	Psoriatic Arthritis	Reactive Arthritis	Enteropathic Arthropathy
Gender (M:F)	2-3:1	1:1	8:1 (GU) [1:1 (GI)]	1:1
Age at onset	<40	35-55	20-40	Young adult
Sacroiliitis or spondylitis	100%	~20%	~40%	<20%
Symmetry of sacroiliitis	Symmetric	Asymmetric	Asymmetric	Symmetric
Peripheral arthritis	~25%	95%	90%	15%-20%
Distribution	Axial and lower limbs	Any joint	Lower limbs	Variable
HLA-B27	85%-95%	25%	30%-80%	7%
Uveitis	25%-40%	25%	25%	10%-36%

From Hochberg MC et al: *Rheumatology,* ed 5, St Louis, 2011, Mosby.

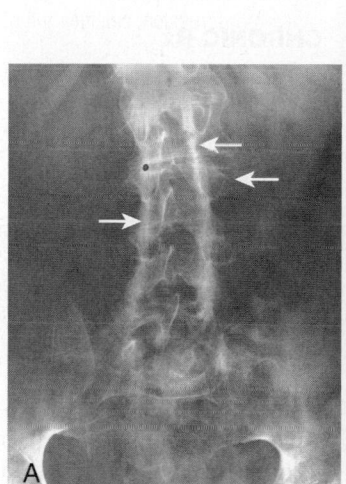
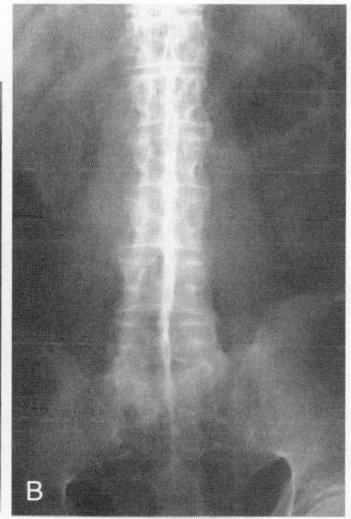

FIGURE 1A-96 Ankylosing spondylitis. A, Fusion of the facet joints and ossification of the adjacent soft tissue have produced a "trolley track" appearance *(arrows).* The sacroiliac joints are fused, and syndesmophytes are present. **B,** In another patient, there is a prominent fusion of the interspinous ligaments producing a "saber sheath" appearance. (From Harris ED: *Kelley's textbook of rheumatology,* ed 7, Philadelphia, 2005, Saunders.)

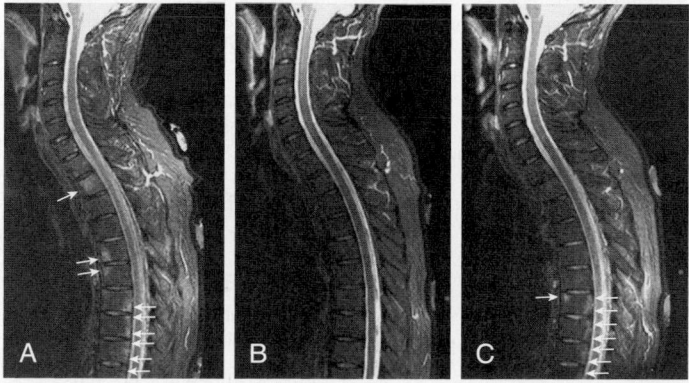

FIGURE 1A-97 Spine inflammation in ankylosing spondylitis (magnetic resonance imaging [MRI]). A 43-year-old man with HLA-B27–positive ankylosing spondylitis with deteriorating symptoms, including inflammatory back pain, had an MRI scan before starting biologic therapy. Baseline sagittal short tau inversion recovery (STIR) MRI **(A)** shows diffuse increased signal (edema) in the T2 vertebral body and multiple foci of corner inflammation anteriorly at T5 and T6, and posteriorly at T7, T8, T9, and T10 *(arrows).* Other images confirmed extensive active inflammation in the spine. The patient responded very well, and after 6 months of therapy, a repeat STIR MRI **(B)** showed complete resolution of bone marrow inflammation. Subsequently, the patient experienced recurrence of symptoms, and a third MRI **(C)** was performed (2 months after anti-TNF therapy was stopped). This MRI shows no edema at T5-T6, a conspicuous new lesion anteriorly at T7, and recurrent inflammation posteriorly in the lower thoracic spine *(arrows).* (From Firestein GS, et al: *Kelley's textbook of rheumatology,* ed 9, Philadelphia, 2013, Saunders.)

PHARMACOLOGIC THERAPY

- NSAIDs: Patients with ankylosing spondylitis should be prescribed full-dose continuous NSAID therapy. There is anecdotal evidence suggesting that indomethacin may be more effective than other NSAIDs, but other NSAIDs are efficacious and may be better tolerated. One study suggested that continuous NSAID therapy may retard the radiographic progression of ankylosing spondylitis.
- Sulfasalazine may be efficacious in some patients, especially for peripheral arthritis
- Tumor necrosis factor (TNF) antagonists such as etanercept, infliximab, and adalimumab have been shown to be very effective for relieving symptoms of spinal inflammatory arthritis in numerous controlled studies. Anti-TNF therapy should be recommended for patients whose symptoms are not completely controlled with NSAIDs, and it sometimes results in dramatic improvement in symptoms, range of motion of the spine, and quality of life for these patients. There is evidence suggesting that anti-TNF therapy slows the radiographic progression of the disease.
- Recent phase 3 trials with secukinumab, an anti-interleukin-17A monoclonal antibody showed significant reductions in the signs and symptoms of ankylosing spondylitis (Baeten et al: *NEJM* 373:2534-2548, 2015).

DISPOSITION

Most patients have a normal life span but many suffer significant disability from loss of spinal mobility.

REFERRAL

All patients with seronegative spondyloarthropathy should be referred to a rheumatologist for consideration of anti-TNF therapy.

 **PEARLS & CONSIDERATIONS**

A family history of seronegative spondyloarthropathy increases the specificity of testing for HLA-B27. Surgical osteotomy may benefit selected patients with severe spinal deformity. Recent data suggest that men with AS have increased risk of vascular mortality.

SUGGESTED READINGS

Available at www.expertconsult.com

RELATED CONTENT

Fig. 3-194 Spondyloarthropathy, diagnosis (Algorithm)
Fig. 3-195 Spondyloarthropathy, treatment (Algorithm)
Ankylosing Spondylitis (Patient Information)

AUTHOR: **BERNARD ZIMMERMANN, M.D.**

BASIC INFORMATION

DEFINITION

A fistula is an inflammatory tract with a secondary (external) opening in the perianal skin and a primary (internal) opening in the anal canal at the dentate line. It originates in an abscess in the intersphincteric space of the anal canal. Fistulas can be classified as follows:

1. Intersphincteric: fistula track passes within the intersphincteric plane to the perianal skin (most common)
2. Transsphincteric: fistula track passes from the internal opening, through the internal and external sphincter, and into the ischiorectal fossa to the perianal skin (frequent)
3. Suprasphincteric: after passing through the internal sphincter, fistula tract passes above the puborectalis and then tracts downward, lateral to the external sphincter, into the ischiorectal space to the perianal skin (uncommon); if abscess cavity extends cephalad, a supralevator abscess possibly palpable on rectal examination
4. Extrasphincteric: fistula tract passes from the rectum, above the levators, through the levator muscles to the ischiorectal space and perianal skin (rare)

With a horseshoe fistula, the tract passes from one ischiorectal fossa to the other behind the rectum.

SYNONYM

Fistula-in-ano

ICD-10CM CODES
K60.3 Anal fistula
K60.5 Anorectal fistula

EPIDEMIOLOGY & DEMOGRAPHICS

- Common in all ages
- Occurs equally in men and women
- Associated with constipation
- Pediatric age group: more common in infants; boys more than girls

PHYSICAL FINDINGS & CLINICAL PRESENTATION

- Acute stage: perianal swelling, pain, and fever
- Chronic stage: history of rectal drainage or bleeding; previous abscess with drainage
- Tender external fistulous opening, within 2 to 3 cm of the anal verge, with purulent or serosanguineous drainage on compression; the greater the distance from the anal margin, the greater the probability of a complicated upward extension
- Goodsall's rule:
  1. Location of the internal opening related to the location of the external opening.
  2. With external opening anterior to an imaginary line drawn horizontally across the midpoint of the anus: fistulous tract runs radially into the anal canal.
  3. With opening posterior to the transanal line: tract is usually curvilinear, entering the anal canal in the posterior midline.
  4. Exception to this rule: an external, anterior opening that is >>3 cm from the anus. In this case the tract may curve posteriorly and end in the posterior midline.
- If perianal abscess recurs, presence of a fistula is suggested.

ETIOLOGY

- Most common: nonspecific cryptoglandular infection (skin or intestinal flora)
- Fistulas more common when intestinal microorganisms are cultured from the anorectal abscess
- Tuberculosis
- Lymphogranuloma venereum
- Actinomycosis
- Inflammatory bowel disease (IBD): Crohn's disease, ulcerative colitis
- Trauma: surgery (episiotomy, prostatectomy), foreign bodies, anal intercourse
- Malignancy: carcinoma, leukemia, lymphoma
- Treatment of malignancy: surgery, radiation

DIAGNOSIS

DIFFERENTIAL DIAGNOSIS

- Hidradenitis suppurativa
- Pilonidal sinus
- Bartholin's gland abscess or sinus
- Infected perianal sebaceous cysts

WORKUP

- Digital rectal examination:
  1. Assess sphincter tone and voluntary squeeze pressure
  2. Determine the presence of an extraluminal mass
  3. Identify an indurated track
  4. Palpate an internal opening or pit
- Gentle probing of external orifice to avoid creating a false tract; 50% do not have clinically detectable opening
- Anoscopy
- Proctosigmoidoscopy to exclude inflammatory or neoplastic disease
- All studies done under adequate anesthesia

LABORATORY TESTS

- Complete blood count
- Rectal biopsy if diagnosis of IBD or malignancy suspected; biopsy of external orifice is useless

IMAGING STUDIES

- Colonoscopy or barium enema if:
  1. Diagnosis of IBD or malignancy is suspected
  2. History of recurrent or multiple fistulas
  3. Patient <<25 yr
- Small bowel series: occasionally obtained for reasons similar to above
- Fistulography: unreliable but may be helpful in complicated fistulas

TREATMENT

NONPHARMACOLOGIC THERAPY

Sitz baths

ACUTE GENERAL Rx

- Treatment of choice: surgery
- Broad-spectrum antibiotic given if:
  1. Cellulitis present
  2. Patient is immunocompromised
  3. Valvular heart disease present
  4. Prosthetic devices present
- Stool softener/laxative

CHRONIC Rx

- Surgery
- Surgical goals are as follows:
  1. Cure the fistula
  2. Prevent recurrence
  3. Preserve sphincter function
  4. Minimize healing time
- Methods for the management of anal fistulas: fistulotomy, setons (maintains fistula patent for drainage while spontaneous healing occurs), rectal advancement flaps, colostomy

DISPOSITION

Outpatient surgery

REFERRAL

Refer to a surgeon with expertise in this area.

PEARLS & CONSIDERATIONS

COMMENTS

- HIV-positive and diabetic patients with perirectal abscesses/fistulas are true surgical emergencies.
- Risk of septicemia, Fournier's gangrene, and other septic complications make immediate drainage imperative.

SUGGESTED READINGS

Available at www.expertconsult.com

RELATED CONTENT

Anal Fissure (Related Key Topic)
Hemorrhoids (Related Key Topic)

AUTHOR: **RUBEN ALVERO, M.D.**

i BASIC INFORMATION

DEFINITION

Anorexia nervosa is a psychiatric disorder characterized by abnormal eating behavior, severe self-induced weight loss, and a specific psychopathology (see "Workup").

ICD-10CM CODES
F50.00 Anorexia nervosa, unspecified
F50.01 Restricting type
F50.02 Binge-eating/purging type

EPIDEMIOLOGY & DEMOGRAPHICS

INCIDENCE/PREVALENCE (IN U.S.):
- Anorexia nervosa occurs in 0.2% to 1.3% of the general population, with an annual incidence of 5 to 10 cases per 100,000 persons.
- Participation in activities that promote thinness (athletics, modeling) is associated with a higher incidence of anorexia nervosa.

PREDOMINANT SEX: Female/male ratio is 9:1. Approximately 0.5% to 1% of women between the ages of 15 and 30 yr have anorexia nervosa.

PREDOMINANT AGE: Adolescence to young adulthood is the predominant age. Mean age of onset is 17 yr. Approximately 0.5% to 1% of college-aged women have anorexia nervosa.

PHYSICAL FINDINGS & CLINICAL PRESENTATION

Eating disorders can affect every organ system. Primary care physicians must be skilled at recognizing this disorder because patients with mild cases usually present with nonspecific symptoms such as asthenia, cold intolerance, lack of energy, or dizziness. Children and adolescents are at particular risk due to their active phase of growth and development. The physical examination may be normal in the early stages or in mild cases. Patients with moderate to severe anorexia have the following physical characteristics:
- Patient is emaciated and bundled in clothing.
- Skin is dry and has excessive growth of lanugo. Skin may also be yellow-tinged from carotenodermia.
- Brittle nails, thinning scalp hair are present.
- Bradycardia, hypotension, hypothermia, and bradypnea are common.
- Female fat distribution pattern is no longer evident.
- Axillary and pubic hair is preserved.
- Peripheral edema may be present.

ETIOLOGY
- Etiology is unknown, but probably multifactorial (sociocultural, psychological, familial, and genetic factors).
- A history of sexual abuse has been reported in as many as 50% of patients with anorexia nervosa.
- Psychological factors: anorexics often have an incompletely developed personal identity. They struggle to maintain a sense of control over their environment, they usually have a low self-esteem, and they lack the sense that they are valued and loved for themselves.

(Dx) DIAGNOSIS

DIFFERENTIAL DIAGNOSIS
- Other eating disorders (bulimia nervosa, binge eating disorder [Table A1-51])
- Substance abuse
- Depression with loss of appetite
- Obsessive compulsive disorder
- Schizophrenia
- Conversion disorder
- Occult carcinoma, lymphoma
- Endocrine disorders: Addison disease, diabetes mellitus, hypothyroidism or hyperthyroidism, panhypopituitarism
- Gastrointestinal disorders: celiac disease, Crohn's disease, intestinal parasitosis
- Infectious disorders: AIDS, tuberculosis
- A clinical algorithm for the evaluation of anorexia is described in Section III

WORKUP
- A diagnosis can be made by using the following DSM-5 diagnostic criteria for anorexia nervosa.
  A. Restriction of energy intake relative to requirements, leading to a significantly low body weight in the context of age, sex, developmental trajectory, and physical health. Significantly low weight is defined as a weight that is less than minimally normal or, for children or adolescents, less than that minimally expected.
  B. Intense fear of gaining weight or becoming fat, or persistent behavior that interferes with weight gain, even though at a significantly low weight.
  C. Disturbance in the way in which one's body or shape is experienced, undue influence of body weight or shape on self-evaluation, or persistent lack of recognition of the seriousness of the current low body weight.

Specify type.
Restricting type: During the last 3 mo, the individual has not engaged in recurrent episodes of binge eating or purging behavior (i.e., self-

TABLE A1-51 Diagnostic Features of Eating Disorders

Anorexia nervosa	Body weight willfully maintained below normal level
	Abnormal perception of body morphology
	Intense fear of weight gain
	Amenorrhea
Bulimia nervosa	Large uncontrolled eating binges at least twice weekly
	Inappropriate compensatory behavior (e.g., vomiting, purging)
Binge eating disorder	Large uncontrolled eating binges at least twice weekly
	No regular inappropriate compensatory disorders
	Marked distress about binges

From Besser CM, Thorner MO: *Comprehensive clinical endocrinology,* ed 3, St Louis, 2002, Mosby.

induced vomiting or the misuse of laxatives, diuretics, or enemas). This subtype describes presentations in which weight loss is accomplished primarily through dieting, fasting, and/or excessive exercise.

Binge-eating/purging type: During the last 3 mo, the individual has engaged in recurrent episodes of binge eating or purging behavior (i.e., self-induced vomiting or the misuse of laxatives, diuretics, or enemas).

Severity level: see "Acute General Rx" section

The SCOFF questionnaire is a screening tool for eating disorders used in England. It consists of the following five questions:
1. Do you make yourself *s*ick because you feel full?
2. Have you lost *c*ontrol over how much you eat?
3. Have you lost more than *o*ne stone (approximately 6 kg) recently?
4. Do you believe yourself to be *f*at when others say you are thin?
5. Does *f*ood dominate your life?

A positive response to two or more questions has a reported sensitivity of 100% for anorexia and bulimia and an overall specificity of 87.5%.

In college-aged women a positive response to any of the following screening questions also warrants further evaluation:
1. How many diets have you been on in the past year?
2. Do you think you should be dieting?
3. Are you dissatisfied with your body size?
4. Does your weight affect the way you think about yourself?

Baseline ECG should be performed on all patients with anorexia nervosa. Routine monitoring of patients with prolonged QT interval is necessary; sudden death in these patients is often caused by ventricular arrhythmias related to QT interval prolongation.

A dual-energy x-ray absorptiometry (DEXA) scan to screen for osteopenia should be considered after 6 mo of amenorrhea in patients suspected of anorexia nervosa.

LABORATORY TESTS
- In mild cases, laboratory findings may be completely normal.
- Endocrine abnormalities:
  1. Decreased follicle-stimulating hormone, luteinizing hormone, T_4, T_3, estrogens, urinary 17-OH steroids, estrone, and estradiol
  2. Normal free T_4, thyroid-stimulating hormone
  3. Increased cortisol, growth hormone, rT_3, T_3RU
  4. Absence of cyclic surge of luteinizing hormone
- Leukopenia, thrombocytopenia, anemia, reduced erythrocyte sedimentation rate, reduced complement levels, and reduced CD4 and CD8 cells may be present.
- Metabolic alkalosis, hypocalcemia, hypokalemia, hypomagnesemia, hypercholesterolemia, and hypophosphatemia may be present.
- Increased plasma b-carotene levels are useful to distinguish these patients from others on starvation diets.

 TREATMENT

NONPHARMACOLOGIC THERAPY

- A multidisciplinary approach with psychological, medical, and nutritional support is necessary.
- A goal weight should be set and the patient should be initially monitored at least once a week in the office setting. The target weight is 100% of ideal BW for teenagers and 90% to 100% for older patients.
- Weight gain should be gradual (1 to 3 lb/wk) to prevent gastric dilation. Begin with 800 to 1200 kcal in frequent small meals (to avoid bloating sensation), then increase calories to 1500 to 3000 depending on height and age.
- Add, as necessary, vitamin and mineral supplements.
- In severe cases, total parenteral nutrition must be used (starting at 800 to 1200 kcal/day).
- Electrolyte levels should be strictly monitored.
- Mealtime should be a time for social interaction, not confrontation.
- Postprandially, sedentary activities are recommended. The patient's access to a bathroom should be monitored to prevent purging.

ACUTE GENERAL Rx

- Criteria to decide on the appropriate initial course of treatment for patients with anorexia nervosa are usually based on the presence of complications, percentage of ideal BW, and severity of body image distortion. According to DSM-5,[1] the minimum level of severity is based, for adults, on current body mass index (BMI; see below) or, for children and adolescents, on BMI percentile. The level of severity may be increased to reflect clinical symptoms, the degree of functional disability, and need for supervision.
  - Mild: BMI ≥17 kg/m²
  - Moderate: BMI 16-16.99 kg/m²
  - Severe: BMI 15-15.99 kg/m²
  - Extreme: BMI <15 kg/m²
- Outpatient treatment is adequate for most patients.

---

[1]American Psychiatric Association: Desk Reference to the Diagnostic Criteria from DSM-5, Arlington, VA, 2013, American Psychiatric Association.

- Indications for hospitalization are described under "Referral" section and summarized in Table A1-52.
- Medically stable patients who are within 85% of ideal BW can be followed up by the primary care physician at 3- or 4-wk intervals, which can be lengthened as the patient improves.
- Pharmacologic treatment generally has no role in anorexia nervosa unless major depression or another psychiatric disorder is present. SSRIs can be used to alleviate the depressed mood and moderate obsessive-compulsive behavior in some individuals.

CHRONIC Rx

- Psychotherapy continued for years and focused specifically on self-image, family and peer interactions, and relapse prevention is an integral part of a successful recovery.
- Family therapy is also recommended, especially in younger patients.

TABLE A1-52   Indications for In-Patient Medical Hospitalization of Patients with Anorexia Nervosa

Physical and Laboratory

Heart rate <45 beats/min

Other cardiac rhythm disturbances

Blood pressure <80/50 mm Hg

Postural hypotension resulting in a >10 mm Hg drop or a >20 beats/min increase

Hypokalemia

Hypophosphatemia

Hypoglycemia

Dehydration

Body temperature <97°F

<80% healthy body weight

Hepatic, cardiac, or renal compromise

Psychiatric

Suicidal intent and plan

Very poor motivation to recover (in family and patient)

Preoccupation with ego-syntonic thoughts

Coexisting psychiatric disorders

Miscellaneous

Requires supervision after meals and while using the restroom

Failed day treatment

From Kliegman RM et al: *Nelson textbook of pediatrics*, ed 19, Philadelphia, 2011, Saunders.

DISPOSITION

- The long-term prognosis is generally poor and marked by recurrent exacerbations. The percentage of patients with anorexia nervosa who fully recover is modest. Most patients continue to have a distorted body image, disordered eating habits, and psychic difficulties.
- Most patients with anorexia nervosa will recover menses within 6 mo of reaching 90% of their ideal BW. It is important to note that patients with anorexia nervosa can become pregnant despite amenorrhea.
- Mortality rates vary from 5% to 20% and are six times that of peers without anorexia. Frequent causes of death are electrolyte abnormalities, starvation, or suicide.
- Factors that predict improved outcome in patients with eating disorders include early age at diagnosis, brief interval before initiation of treatment, good parent-child relationships, and having other healthy relationships with friends or therapists.
- A prolonged QT interval is a marker for risk of sudden death.

REFERRAL

Hospitalization should be considered in the following situations:
1. Severe dehydration or electrolyte imbalance
2. ECG abnormalities (prolonged QT interval, arrhythmias)
3. Significant physiologic instability (hypotension, orthostatic changes)
4. Intractable vomiting, purging, or bingeing
5. Suicidal thoughts
6. Weight loss exceeding 30% of ideal BW and unresponsiveness to outpatient treatment
7. Rapidly progressing weight loss (>2 lb in a week)
8. Failure to progress in nutritional rehabilitation in outpatient treatment

SUGGESTED READINGS

Available at www.expertconsult.com

RELATED CONTENT

Fig. 3-20 Evaluation of anorexia (Algorithm)
Anorexia Nervosa (Patient Information)
Bulimia Nervosa (Related Key Topic)

AUTHOR: **FRED F. FERRI, M.D.**

BASIC INFORMATION

DEFINITION

Anoxic brain injury is cerebral ischemic injury due to decreased blood flow or oxygen to the brain typically caused by interruption of cardiac circulation or respiratory failure, respectively.

SYNONYMS

Hypoxic-ischemic injury
Anoxic encephalopathy
Cerebral hypoxia
Hypoxia of brain

ICD-10CM CODES

G93.1 Anoxic brain damage, not elsewhere classified

EPIDEMIOLOGY & DEMOGRAPHICS

INCIDENCE

- Variable based on diagnostic criteria
- 492,000 out-of-hospital cardiac arrests per year in the U.S.

PREVALENCE

- Vegetative state varies from 40 to 168 per 1 million population, depending on definition used.
- Recovery is rare after 3 months with life expectancy lasting 2 to 5 years.

RISK FACTORS: Same as risk factors for cardiorespiratory arrest: age, race, HTN, hyperlipidemia, tobacco use, drug or alcohol abuse, and physical inactivity.

PHYSICAL FINDINGS & CLINICAL PRESENTATION

- Variable depending on degree of insult
- Minimally conscious state: altered consciousness with normal sleep-wake cycles and intermittent interaction with the environment; intermittently follows simple commands, and maintains visual tracking
- Vegetative state: able to maintain normal sleep-wake cycles; there is loss of cognitive awareness and ability to interact with environment
- Coma: pathologic loss of awareness and ability to interact with the environment; loss of sleep-wake cycles
- Brain death: irreversible loss of cortical and brainstem function manifesting as loss of awareness, cranial reflexes, and motor response, isoelectric EEG

ETIOLOGY

- Ischemia (decreased cerebral perfusion): myocardial infarction, hemorrhage, shock
- Hypoxia (decreased oxygenation): drowning, strangulation, aspiration, carbon monoxide poisoning
- Figure 1A-98 shows categories of mechanisms proposed to be involved in the evolution of secondary damage after severe traumatic brain injury in infants and children.

DIAGNOSIS

DIFFERENTIAL DIAGNOSIS

- Other causes of encephalopathy, including toxic, metabolic, infectious, or neoplastic causes; nonconvulsive status epilepticus; hypothermia

WORKUP

- Neurologic examination (coma examination) to ascertain level of encephalopathy
- Systemic evaluation for causes of cardiorespiratory failure
- Laboratory studies (listed in the following) to evaluate alternate causes of encephalopathy
- Imaging studies: MRI of brain or CT of head (if MRI cannot be obtained)

LABORATORY TESTS

Urine drug screen, serum metabolic profile, ammonia, complete blood count, coagulation panel, finger stick glucose, arterial blood gas, blood alcohol panel, serum neuron-specific enolase (if available)

IMAGING STUDIES

- Imaging is usually not revealing within first 24 hr of an anoxic event.
- Head CT without contrast (Fig. 1A-99): obtain 24 hr after anoxic event to evaluate for stroke, trauma, or hemorrhage
- MRI of brain (Fig. 1A-100): obtain if head CT scan unrevealing; may show cortical necrosis and infarcts of the basal ganglia

OTHER STUDIES

- EEG: to assess for nonconvulsive status epilepticus

- Somatosensory evoked potentials (SSEP; aka, N20 response): obtain 24 to 72 hr after anoxic event

TREATMENT

NONPHARMACOLOGIC THERAPY

- Hypothermia: evidence suggests that inducing hypothermia 32° to 34° C for 24 hr following anoxic brain injury reduces metabolic need and may improve prognosis for recovery.
- Complications from hypothermia include bradycardia, hemodynamic instability, coagulopathy, infection, hyperglycemia, and hypokalemia.
- Contraindications for hypothermia: active hemorrhage, hemodynamic instability, sepsis, or trauma
- Indication for hypothermia: patients who have been resuscitated from a cardiac arrest with VF/VT as the presenting rhythm
- Hyperbaric oxygen is used in carbon monoxide poisoning.

ACUTE GENERAL Rx

- Supportive care: ABCs, secure airway, cardiopulmonary support in the critical care unit
- Control seizures with antiepileptic medications (may need midazolam or propofol drip if severe uncontrolled seizures).
- Treat myoclonus with clonazepam 8 to 12 mg daily in divided doses; levetiracetam and divalproate may be used for myoclonic status epilepticus.

CHRONIC Rx

- Maintain adequate nutrition, infection precautions; provide DVT and gastric ulceration prophylaxis.

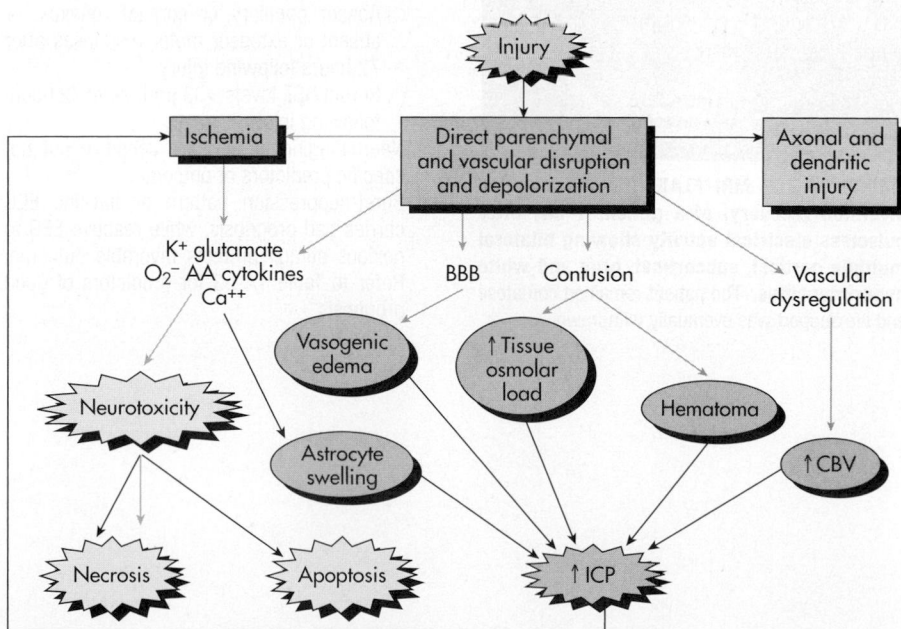

FIGURE 1A-98 Categories of mechanisms proposed to be involved in the evolution of secondary damage after severe traumatic brain injury in infants and children. Three major categories for these secondary mechanisms are (1) ischemia, excitotoxicity, energy failure, and cell death cascades; (2) cerebral swelling; and (3) axonal injury. (From Fuhrman BP: *Pediatric critical care*, ed 4 St. Louis, 2011, Mosby.)

Diseases
and Disorders

I

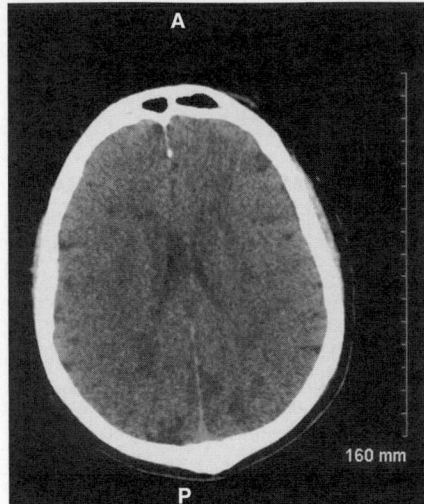

FIGURE 1A-99 CT without contrast of a patient 1 day after pulseless electrical activity showing diffuse sulci effacement and loss of gray-white matter differentiation indicating cerebral edema. Diffuse white and gray matter hypodensities are also present. The patient remained comatose and life support was eventually withdrawn.

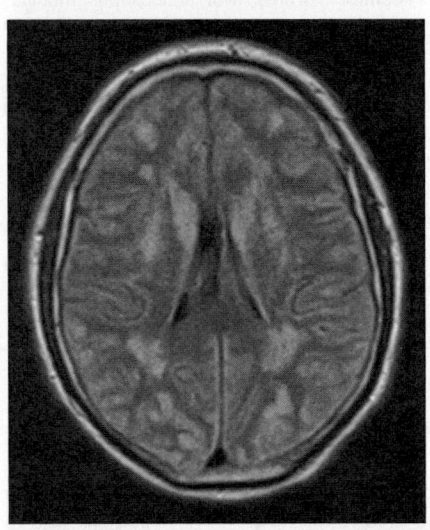

FIGURE 1A-100 MRI FLAIR (fluid attenuated inversion recovery) of a patient 1 day after pulseless electrical activity showing bilateral multiple cortical, subcortical, gray and white hyperintensities. The patient remained comatose and life support was eventually withdrawn.

TABLE 1A-53 Predictors of Good Prognosis

Time from Onset of Anoxic Event	Clinical Exam
Initial exam	Pupils react to light (reflex present), motor response flexor or extensor, and eye movements spontaneous roving conjugate or orienting
24 hr	Motor response withdrawal or better, and eye opening improved at least 2 grades
72 hr	Motor response withdrawal or better and normal spontaneous eye movements present
1 wk	Follows commands
2 wk	Normal oculocephalic response

Composed from data presented in Levy DE et al: Predicting outcome from hypoxic-ischemic coma, *JAMA* 253(10):1420-1426, 1985.

- Physical, occupational, and speech therapy as indicated per prognosis and patient ability
- May consider withdrawal of treatment per prognosis, family consultation, and respect for autonomy and dignity of the patient

PROGNOSIS

- Out-of-hospital cardiopulmonary resuscitation (CPR) for cardiac arrest has a success rate of <10%.
- There is no standardized battery of testing to quantify anoxic injury and reliably predict outcomes.
- Anoxia time, duration of CPR, and cause of cardiac arrest are related to poor outcome after CPR but not sufficient for prognosis.
- Strong predictors of poor outcome (evidence level A or B) are:
  - Presentation with myoclonus status epilepticus within the first 24 hours following injury
  - Absence of bilateral cortical SSEPs (N20 response) anytime
  - Absent papillary or corneal reflexes, or absent or extensor motor responses after 72 hours following injury
  - Serum NSE levels >33 μg/L 24 to 72 hours following injury
- Neuroimaging or EEG are sensitive but not specific predictors of outcome.
- Burst-suppression pattern or flat-line EEG carries bad prognosis, while reactive EEG to noxious stimuli predicts favorable outcome. Refer to Table 1A-53 for predictors of good prognosis.

DISPOSITION: Varies per extent of insult from acute rehabilitation to long-term care facility to return to home

REFERRAL: Referral to a neurologist is appropriate for definitive prognostication.

PEARLS & CONSIDERATIONS

COMMENTS

When assessing prognosis, use caution if patient is being treated with anesthetic agents or depressants including anticonvulsants. Thus serial neurologic exams are substantial.

PREVENTION

CPR, risk factor modification, induced hypothermia

PATIENT/FAMILY EDUCATION

Consult with family members regularly and provide accurate assessment of prognosis.

SUGGESTED READINGS

Available at www.expertconsult.com

AUTHORS: **ABDULLAH AL-SAWAF, M.D., M.B.B.S.,** and **SIDDHARTH KAPOOR, M.D.**

BASIC INFORMATION

DEFINITION

Antiphospholipid antibody syndrome (APS), the most common acquired thrombophilia, is characterized by clinical features of arterial or venous thrombosis and/or pregnancy morbidity *and* the presence of at least one type of antiphospholipid autoantibody (aPL). aPLs are antibodies directed against serum proteins bound to anionic phospholipids. Autoantibodies inhibit the fibrinolytic system and bind to antigenic anticoagulants, which activate endothelial cells, monocytes, and trophoblasts, resulting in complement-mediated thrombosis.

Three types of aPL have been characterized:
- Anticardiolipin antibodies—the most common
- Lupus anticoagulants
- Anti-β2-glycoprotein-1 antibodies

APS can occur with or without associated rheumatic disease, the most common being systemic lupus erythematosus (SLE). APS can affect all organ systems and includes venous and arterial thrombosis, recurrent fetal losses, and thrombocytopenia.

ICD-10CM CODES
D68.61 Antiphospholipid syndrome

EPIDEMIOLOGY & DEMOGRAPHICS

PREVALENCE:
- Up to 5% of healthy individuals have positive aPLs
- Approximately 10% of patients with a deep venous thrombosis have aPLs
- Nearly 20% of women under 50 who have a cerebrovascular accident (CVA) test positive for aPLs
- 10% to 15% of women with recurrent miscarriages have aPLs
- Rule of 40s with systemic lupus erythematosus: 40% of patients with SLE have aPLs but only 40% of patients with antibodies will have thrombosis

TABLE 1A-54 Other Features Suggesting the Presence of Antiphospholipid Antibodies

Clinical

Livedo reticularis

Thrombocytopenia (usually 50,000-100,000 platelets/mm³)

Autoimmune hemolytic anemia

Cardiac valve disease (vegetations or thickening)

Multiple sclerosis–like syndrome, chorea, or other myelopathy

Laboratory

IgA anticardiolipin antibody

IgA anti–β2-glycoprotein I

From Firestein GS, et al: Kelly's *textbook of rheumatology*, ed 9, Philadelphia, 2013, Saunders.

- aPL without APS can be seen in patients with certain medications, infections, malignancies, and autoimmune conditions

PREDOMINANT AGE: Young to middle-aged adults

RISK FACTORS:
- Underlying SLE and collagen-vascular diseases; other autoimmune disorders, including rheumatoid arthritis, Sjögren's syndrome, Behçet's syndrome, primary immune thrombocytopenia (also known as idiopathic thrombocytopenic purpura); AIDS; hypertension (HTN).
- Most individuals are otherwise healthy and have no underlying medical condition.

PROGNOSIS:
- 91% survival at 10 years
- 73% success rate in pregnancy

GENETICS: Some APS-positive families exist, and human leukocyte antigen (HLA) studies have suggested associations with HLA DR7, DR4, and Dqw7+Drw53.

PHYSICAL FINDINGS & CLINICAL PRESENTATION

No pathognomonic findings on examination; Table 1A-54 summarizes other features suggesting the presence of antiphospholipid antibodies, abnormal findings consistent with ischemia or infarction.
- Thrombosis (Fig. 1A-107):
  1. Patients with APS are at risk for both venous and arterial thromboses. Venous thromboses are more common, occurring as the initial manifestation of APS in approximately ~30% of APS patients. Of

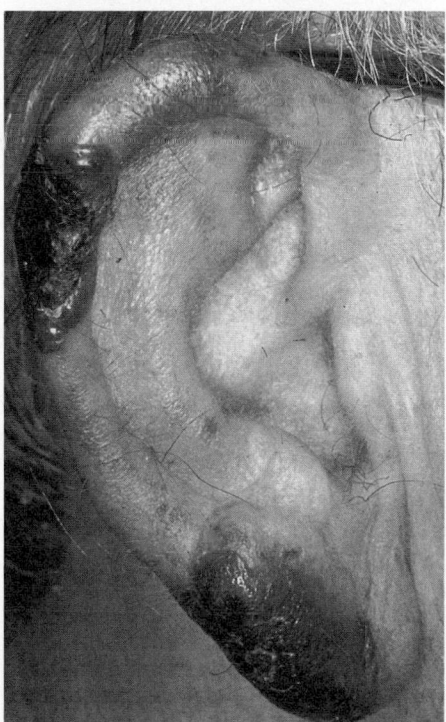

FIGURE 1A-107 Cutaneous thrombosis in antiphospholipid antibody syndrome. (From James WD et al: *Andrews' diseases of the skin*, ed 12, Philadelphia, 2016, Saunders.)

all patients with deep venous thrombosis, approximately 10% have aPL. The most common site for deep vein thrombosis is the calf, but thromboses may also occur in the renal, hepatic, axillary, subclavian, vena cava, and retinal veins. The most common site of arterial thrombosis is the cerebral vessels, followed by the coronary, renal, mesenteric, and bypass arteries. Recurrent thrombosis is common with APS.
- Commonly involved organ systems include:
  1. Central nervous system: stroke, transient ischemic attack, migraine, multi-infarct dementia, epilepsy, movement disorders, transverse myelopathy, depression, Guillain-Barré syndrome, and migraine.
  2. Pulmonary: pulmonary embolism and infarction; pulmonary hypertension; acute respiratory distress syndrome; intraalveolar pulmonary hemorrhage - a postpartum syndrome characterized by fever, pleuritic chest pain, dyspnea, and patchy infiltrates with pleural effusion on chest radiograph.
  3. Cardiology: Libman-Sacks endocarditis, intracardiac thrombosis, coronary artery disease, myocardial infarction, valvulopathy, left ventricular diastolic dysfunction.
  4. Gastrointestinal: abdominal pain, gastrointestinal bleed secondary to ischemia, splenic or pancreatic infarction, hepatic vein thrombosis, Budd-Chiari syndrome (second most common cause of Budd-Chiari syndrome).
  5. Renal: proteinuria, acute renal failure, hypertension, renal infarct, renal artery or vein thrombosis, postpartum hemolytic uremic syndrome.
  6. Hematology: thrombocytopenia, hemolytic anemia, thrombotic microangiopathic hemolytic anemias (HUS, TTP).
  7. Endocrine: Addison's disease secondary to adrenal hemorrhage and, less frequently, thrombosis.
  8. Cutaneous: livedo reticularis, cutaneous necrosis, skin ulcerations, phlegmasia cerulea dolens, gangrene of digits (Fig. 1A-108).
  9. Obstetrics: recurrent spontaneous abortion, premature delivery or fetal growth retardation.
- **Catastrophic APS** (CAPS) (Table 1A-55): CAPS is a rapidly progressive multi-organ thrombotic disease. Approximately 1% of APS is CAPS; approximately 45% of CAPS do not present as APS initially. A 50% mortality rate is seen in patients with CAPS. To make the diagnosis of catastrophic APS, four criteria must be satisfied:
  1. Evidence of involvement of three or more organs, systems, and/or tissues. The most common symptoms are abdominal pain, dyspnea, neurologic symptoms, chest pain, and skin rash.
  2. Development of manifestations simultaneously or in ≤1 week.
  3. Confirmation by histopathology of small-vessel occlusion in at least one organ or tissue.
  4. Laboratory confirmation of the presence of aPL.

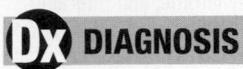

ETIOLOGY

- aPLs react with negatively charged phospholipids.
- Possible mechanisms of thrombosis include effects of aPL on platelet membranes, endothelial cells, and clotting components such as prothrombin, protein C, or protein S. The mammalian target of rapamycin complex (mTORC) has been shown to be involved in the vascular lesions associated with the antiphospholipid syndrome.
- Studies have recently shown that prephospholipids are not immunogenic and that a binding protein (β_2-glycoprotein I) may be the key immunogen in the APS.

Dx DIAGNOSIS

DIFFERENTIAL DIAGNOSIS

Other hypercoagulable states (inherited or acquired):
- Inherited: ATIII, protein C and protein, S deficiencies, factor V Leiden, prothrombin gene mutation.
- Acquired: heparin-induced thrombocytopenia, myeloproliferative syndromes, cancer
- Nephrotic syndrome

WORKUP

Diagnostic criteria of APS include at least one clinical criterion and at least one laboratory criterion. A single clot may not be sufficient, especially with other thrombotic risk factors.
- Clinical:
  1. Venous, arterial, or small vessel thrombosis *or*
  2. Morbidity with pregnancy, defined as:
     1. Fetal death at ≥10 weeks' gestation *or*
     2. ≥1 premature births before 34 weeks' gestation secondary to eclampsia, preeclampsia, or severe placental insufficiency *or*
     3. ≥3 unexplained spontaneous abortions at 10 weeks' gestation.
- Laboratory (see Table 1A-56):
- Screening tests
  1. Partial thromboplastin time (PTT): Elevated, indicating either the presence of a clotting factor deficiency, or the presence of an inhibitor such as a lupus anticoagulant.
  2. Mixing study: Elevated. Normal plasma is incubated with the patient's plasma. In cases of clotting factor deficiencies the PTT will correct. If an inhibitor is present, the PTT will not correct.
  3. Dilute Russell viper venom time: Elevated. Laboratory clotting requires the addition of phospholipids and calcium to plasma samples. Antiphospholipid antibodies bind the phospholipids in the test tube, thereby preventing clot formation. The addition of Russell viper venom to plasma results in immediate activation of Factor X (common pathway). It, therefore, will not be prolonged in intrinsic or extrinsic factor deficiencies but will be prolonged in the presence of an antiphospholipid antibody.

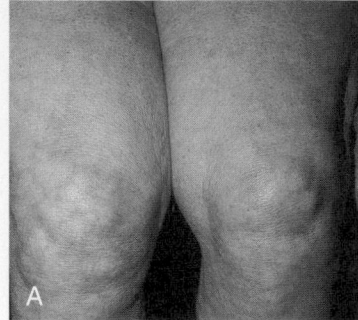
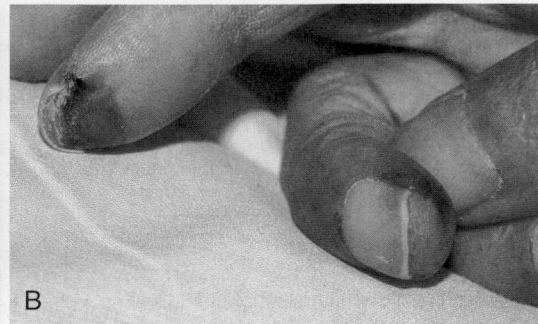

FIGURE 1A-108 Antiphospholipid syndrome. The clinical presentations of this disorder are protean and include those shown here. **A,** Broad bands of livedo around the knees in a patient with anticardiolipin antibodies. Physiologic livedo has a finer patterning and less obvious lesions. **B,** Digital infarcts, a nonspecific feature of several vascular occlusion disorders. (From White GM, Cox NH [eds]: *Diseases of the skin, a color atlas and text,* ed 2, St Louis, 2006, Mosby.)

TABLE 1A-55 Differential Diagnosis of Catastrophic Antiphospholipid Syndrome (CAPS)

Laboratory Abnormalities	CAPS	TTP	DIC
Microangiopathic hemolytic anemia	−	+	+
Thrombocytopenia	+	+	+
Fibrinogen/FDP	Normal/Normal	Normal/Increased	Decreased/Increased
Anticardiolipin antibody	+	−	−
Lupus anticoagulant	+	−	−

TABLE 1A-56 Assays Used to Confirm Diagnosis of Antiphospholipid Syndrome

Assay	Methodology
"Criteria" aPL Assays	
aCL	ELISA
Anti-β_2-GPI	ELISA
LAC	Clotting/functional assays
"Noncriteria" aPL Assays	
Assays to detect antibodies to other phospholipids (i.e., phosphatidylserine, phosphatidylinositol, phosphatidic acid, phosphatidylglycerol, phosphatidylethanolamine, phosphatidylcholine)	ELISA
Annexin A5 resistance assay	Clotting/mechanistic assay
Assays to detect antibodies to prothrombin or prothrombin/phosphatidylserine	ELISA
Assays to detect antibodies to clotting proteins (i.e., protein C, protein S)	ELISA

aCL, Anticardiolipin; *aPL,* antiphospholipid antibody; *ELISA,* enzyme-linked immunosorbent assay; *LAC,* lupus anticoagulant.
From Hochberg MC et al: *Rheumatology,* ed 5, St Louis, 2011, Mosby.

4. The Lupus Anticoagulant screen is the addition of Russell viper venom to plasma. In the Lupus Anticoagulant confirmatory testing, massive doses of phospholipids are added to saturate the antiphospholipid antibody, thereby correcting the prolonged PTT.
- Initial testing for presence of aPL:
  1. Anticardiolipin (aCL) ELISA antibodies in medium or high titers *or*
  2. Lupus anticoagulant activity found *or*
  3. Anti-beta$_2$-glycoprotein (anti-β2GPI) ELISA antibodies no more than 5 years from the clinical event.
- Confirmatory aPL testing: repeat testing after 12 weeks is required to confirm the persistence

of a positive aCL, anti-β2GPI, or LA test because transient elevations of aCL can occur.

LABORATORY TESTS

Diagnostic evaluation of aCL and LA antibodies is indicated in:
- Patient with underlying SLE or collagen-vascular disease with thrombosis.
- Patient with recurrent, familial, or juvenile deep vein thrombosis (DVT) or thrombosis in an unusual location (mesenteric or cerebral).
- One or more unexplained thrombotic events. Do not test those at low risk, e.g., the elderly with clot and other risk factors.
- One or more specific pregnancy events.
- Unexplained thrombocytopenia.

- Patients with an elevated PTT.
  Abnormal tests include:
- False-positive test for syphilis (RPR/VDRL)
- Lupus anticoagulant activity
- Presence of anticardiolipin antibodies (ELISA for anticardiolipin is the most sensitive and specific test [>80%]).
- Presence of anti-b$_2$-glycoprotein I antibody

℞ TREATMENT

ACUTE Rx

Treatment includes use of heparin, low-molecular-weight heparin (LMWH), warfarin, antiplatelet agents, acetylsalicylic acid (aspirin), clopidogrel, hydroxychloroquine. The efficacy of novel oral anticoagulants (NOACs) is currently being evaluated.

- For a patient with positive aPL and venous or arterial thrombosis, treat as any other thrombosis.
  Anticoagulation with heparin or LMWH, then followed by indefinite warfarin treatment, with a target international normalized ratio (INR) of 2.0 to 3.0. There is conflicting evidence on the benefit of a higher INR target (>3.0) or the addition of other agents in patients with arterial clots, especially if they have recurrent events while taking warfarin. Any escalation of therapy should be weighed by the increased hemorrhage risk.
- Length of treatment needed is unknown, but likely indefinite barring no contraindication to anticoagulation, as the lifelong recurrence rate is 11% to 29%.
- Unfractionated heparin (UFH) is preferred if quick reversibility is needed.

PRIMARY PREVENTION

- Aspirin is of no benefit for prevention in patients with a prior clot.
- Aspirin may help patients without a history of clot.
- Patients with a previous history of venous thromboembolism and antiphospholipid antibodies are typically placed on an indefinite course of anticoagulation.
- Adding low-dose warfarin to aspirin for primary prevention seems to confer no benefit.
- Vascular risk factors, such as hypertension and hyperlipidemia, should be controlled.
- Hydroxychloroquine may be useful in those patients with SLE and aPL.
- Avoid oral contraceptive pills; modifiable risk factors for thrombosis such as smoking and immobility should also be addressed.
- For pregnant women with a positive test for aPL antibodies without a history of DVT or pregnancy loss, consider low-dose subcutaneous UFH or LMWH, aspirin 81 mg, or surveillance.

SECONDARY PREVENTION

- For pregnant women with previously diagnosed APS:
  1. Warfarin should be discontinued before pregnancy secondary to its teratogenic effects.
  2. Aspirin 81 mg and subcutaneous UFH or LMWH to therapeutic partial thromboplastin time (PTT) or factor Xa levels, respectively. This is superior to aspirin monotherapy. The evidence for UFH in APS and live birth is more robust than LMWH.
  3. Pregnant patients taking LMWH should be transitioned to unfractionated heparin before delivery due to reversibility.
  4. Intravenous immunoglobulin (IVIG), plasmapheresis, hydroxychloroquine, statins, clopidogrel, dipyridamole, and rituximab have been used when other treatments have failed.
  5. Prednisone, when added to aspirin, seems to confer no benefit to obstetric patients.
  6. Hypertension, if present, should be controlled
- For pregnant women with a positive test for aPL antibodies and a history of fewer than three spontaneous abortions:
  1. Low-dose aspirin at conception, followed by UFH, prophylactically or an intermediate dose at 7 weeks, continuing until 6 weeks' postpartum.
  2. A mid-interval PTT should be checked and should be normal or similar to baseline before therapy.
  3. LMWH can be used in place of unfractionated heparin and should be titrated to factor Xa levels in the recommended prophylactic range. The combination of aspirin (75 mg daily) plus LMWH has been associated with a higher live birth rate when compared with IVIG.

FOR CATASTROPHIC ANTIPHOSPHOLIPID ANTIBODY SYNDROME (CAPS)

- Represents fewer than 1% of all patients with APS; however, the mortality rate approaches 50%.
- Highest survival rates are achieved with the combination of anticoagulation, corticosteroids, and IVIG or plasma exchange.
- Case reports have shown both rituximab and the monoclonal antibody, eculizumab, which inhibits terminal complement activation, to be a successful therapy for patients with life-threatening thrombosis refractory to anticoagulation.

CHRONIC Rx

- Anticoagulation with warfarin therapy.
- Immunosuppressive agents such as corticosteroids and cyclophosphamide have not been shown to be effective.
- Limited data suggest that hydroxychloroquine may be effective in patients with APS and SLE.

DISPOSITION

- APS patients have a 20% to 70% risk for recurrent thrombosis.
- Initial arterial thrombosis tends to be followed by arterial events, and initial venous thrombosis tends to be followed by venous events.
- Catastrophic APS is associated with a high mortality rate, approaching 50%.
- Incidence of developing catastrophic APS is approximately 0.8% among APS patients.

REFERRAL

To hematology, rheumatology, and/or obstetric medicine when diagnosis is made.

! PEARLS & CONSIDERATIONS

COMMENTS

Cerebral features of SLE may be more related to thrombosis than inflammation and may respond better to anticoagulants than immunosuppression.

PREVENTION

Prophylaxis for asymptomatic patients with positive aPL tests without previous thrombosis:
- No routine prophylaxis is recommended.
- Questionable whether low-dose aspirin is effective.
- Antithrombotic prophylaxis for major surgery, prolonged immobilization, and pregnancy
- Avoid oral contraceptive pills in women with positive aPL test.

SUGGESTED READINGS

Available at www.expertconsult.com

RELATED CONTENT

Antiphospholipid Antibody Syndrome (Patient Information)
Deep Vein Thrombosis (Related Key Topic)
Hypercoagulable States (Related Key Topic)
Pulmonary Embolism (Related Key Topic)

AUTHORS: **WILLIAM RAFELSON, M.D., M.B.A.**, and **JOHN L. REAGAN, M.D.**

Diseases and Disorders

BASIC INFORMATION

DEFINITION

Generalized anxiety disorder (GAD) is most likely to present in combination with other psychiatric and medical conditions. Individuals with GAD commonly present with excessive and disproportionately high levels of anxiety, fear, or worry for most days over at least a 6-mo period in a number of areas. The worrying must be greater than would be expected given the situation, and it must cause significant interference in functioning. The subjective anxiety must be accompanied by at least three somatic symptoms in adults, and one in children (e.g., restlessness, irritability, sleep disturbance, muscle tension, difficulty concentrating, or fatigue). GAD cannot be diagnosed if it occurs only in the context of an active mood disorder, such as depression, or if the anxiety is better explained by another active anxiety disorder, such as PTSD or panic disorder.

SYNONYMS

Anxiety neurosis (former name for a subset of anxiety disorders)
Chronic anxiety
GAD

ICD-10CM CODES
F41.1 Generalized anxiety disorder

EPIDEMIOLOGY & DEMOGRAPHICS

INCIDENCE (IN U.S.): 6% to 9% per year in adult primary care clinics; 1-yr incident rate per 100 person-yr of 1.12
PEAK INCIDENCE: Peak incidence tends to occur later relative to other anxiety disorders, such as phobias; cumulative incidence of 4.3% by age 34 in a German community sample
PREVALENCE (IN U.S.):
- In general population: lifetime morbid risk of 9%; 12-month prevalence of 2.9%
- In primary care setting: 3% (the most common anxiety disorder in this setting)
PREDOMINANT SEX: Women are more frequently affected (2:1 ratio) but may present for treatment less often (3:2 female/male).
PREDOMINANT AGE:
- 30% report onset before age 11
- 50% have onset before age 18
- Median age of onset: 30 years
GENETICS: Concordance rates in dizygotic twins and monozygotic twins are not different (0% to 5%)

PHYSICAL FINDINGS & CLINICAL PRESENTATION

- Report of being "anxious" all of their lives.
- Excessive worry, usually regarding family, finances, work, or health.
- Sleep disturbance, particularly early insomnia.
- Muscle tension (typically in the muscles of neck and shoulders) or headache.
- Difficulty concentrating.
- Daytime fatigue.
- GI symptoms compatible with IBS (one third of patients).
- Physical symptoms are the usual reason for seeking medical attention.
- Comorbid psychiatric illness (e.g., dysthymia or major depression) and substance abuse (e.g., alcohol abuse) are frequent.

ETIOLOGY

- Hypotheses include models based on neurotransmitters (catecholamines, indolamines) and developmental psychology (e.g., behavioral inhibition, neuroticism, and harm avoidance).
- Prevalence increased with a family history, increase in stress, history of physical or emotional trauma, and medical illness.

DIAGNOSIS

DIFFERENTIAL DIAGNOSIS

- Wide range of psychiatric and medical conditions:
  1. Cardiovascular and pulmonary disease, such as cardiac arrhythmias or COPD
  2. Hyperthyroidism, hypoglycemia
  3. Substance abuse (e.g., cocaine, amphetamines, and PCP) or withdrawal (e.g., alcohol or benzodiazepines)
  4. Other anxiety disorders (e.g., social anxiety disorder), mood disorder

WORKUP

- Screening tests may enhance detection. A screening tool often used in primary care is the GAD-2. It asks, "During the past month, have you been bothered a lot by: (1) Nerves or feeling anxious or on edge? (2) Worrying about a lot of different things?" The response to each question is given a score of 0 (not at all), 1 (several days), 2 (more than half of the days), 3 (nearly every day). A score of ≥3 has a sensitivity of 86% and a specificity of 83% for detecting GAD. A simple 7-item in-office case finding instrument, the GAD-7, includes additional questions to assess symptom severity and can be used to monitor symptoms.
- Physical examination: additional laboratory and radiologic workup depend on presenting symptoms.
- Iatrogenic cause should be suspected if anxiety follows recent changes in medication.

TREATMENT

NONPHARMACOLOGIC THERAPY

- Cognitive-behavioral therapy
- Acceptance and commitment therapy
- Relaxation training
- Biofeedback
- Psychodynamic psychotherapy

PHARMACOLOGIC THERAPY

- SSRIs/SNRIs
- Azapirones (e.g., buspirone)
- Benzodiazepines (less favored)

ACUTE GENERAL Rx

- Acute treatment is rarely indicated because GAD is a chronic condition.
- If patients are in acute distress, the possibility of another cause, including another anxiety disorder such as panic disorder, should be considered.
- Caution in prescribing benzodiazepines because of the propensity for misuse and dependence. If used, the patient should be educated about the options and the risks.

CHRONIC Rx

- SSRIs and SNRIs (e.g., venlafaxine and duloxetine) are effective typical first-line treatment. Particularly useful if comorbid depression present.
- Buspirone can be effective with minimal potential for tolerance or abuse. May be less effective in patients with previous benzodiazepine exposure and may require a high-dose titration.
- Benzodiazepines can be effective under close supervision; however, they have fallen out of favor as a first-line treatment given their potential for functional impairment, abuse, and dependence.
- Sedating antidepressants, such as mirtazapine, may also be useful for initial insomnia secondary to anxious ruminations.

DISPOSITION

- GAD is chronic with periodic exacerbations.
- Treatment is given to reduce level of symptoms and improve functioning. Suicide risk is higher than in the general population.

REFERRAL

- For refractory symptoms.
- For comorbid psychiatric conditions.

SUGGESTED READINGS
Available at www.expertconsult.com

RELATED CONTENT
Anxiety (Patient Information)
Panic Disorder (Related Key Topic)
Social Anxiety Disorder (Related Key Topic)

AUTHOR: **KRISTY L. DALRYMPLE, PH.D.**

ℹ️ BASIC INFORMATION

DEFINITION

Aortic dissection is part of a spectrum of aortic pathologies (acute aortic syndromes) that includes intramural hematomas and penetrating atherosclerotic ulcers. Aortic dissection occurs when blood passes through an intimal tear, separating the intima from the medial layers and creating a false lumen. Intramural hematoma (IMH) occurs when the vasa vasorum ruptures within the medial wall. IMH does not involve an intimal tearing unless a dissection develops. Seventeen percent of IMH will transform into aortic dissection. Penetrating atherosclerotic ulcers, which occur in the setting of extensive aortic atherosclerosis and hypertension, destroy the aortic intima and dissect into the aortic media. Rupture of atherosclerotic plaques with subsequent blood entry into the median wall forms a pseudoaneurysm. Fig. 1A-109 illustrates acute aortic syndromes.

SYNONYMS

Dissecting aortic aneurysm

ICD-10CM CODES
I71.00	Dissection of unspecified site of aorta
I71.01	Dissection of thoracic aorta
I71.02	Dissection of abdominal aorta
I71.03	Dissection of thoracoabdominal aorta

EPIDEMIOLOGY & DEMOGRAPHICS

INCIDENCE: 2.6-3.5 per 100,000 person-years
PREDOMINANT SEX AND AGE: Males (65%) females (35%), ages 60 to 80 yr; mean, 63 yr

RISK FACTORS:
- Hypertension (found in up to 72% of patients with aortic dissection)
- Atherosclerosis (found in up to 31% of patients with aortic dissection)
- Age (60 to 80 years)
- Family history of aortic aneurysms/dissection
- History of cardiac surgery, aortic valve replacement, intraaortic catheterization
- Disorders of collagen (Marfan's syndrome, Ehlers-Danlos syndrome)
- Vascular inflammation (giant cell arteritis, Takayasu arteritis, rheumatoid arthritis, syphilitic aortitis)
- Aortic coarctation, bicuspid aortic valve
- Turner's syndrome
- Cocaine abuse (usually within 12 hours of last use of cocaine)
- Trauma

CLASSIFICATION

Aortic dissection is generally classified according to anatomic location (Fig. 1A-110):
- Stanford (more commonly used classification system): type A ascending aorta (proximal), type B descending aorta (distal) (Fig. 1A-111)
- DeBakey: type I ascending and descending aorta, type II ascending aorta, type III descending aorta
- Aortic dissection can also be classified by acuity of presentation (acute or chronic), based on the time of onset.

PHYSICAL FINDINGS & CLINICAL PRESENTATION
- Sudden onset of severe sharp, tearing, or ripping chest pain. However, painless dissection occurs in approximately 6.4% of cases.

- Anterior chest pain (83% type A, 71% type B).
- Back pain, abdominal pain (43% type A, 70% type B).
- Syncope (19% type A, 3% type B), generally secondary to cardiac tamponade or stroke.
- Congestive heart failure (CHF).
- May present with hypertension (28% for type A, 66% in type B dissection), although 25% present with hypotension (systolic blood pressure <100 mm Hg), which can indicate bleeding, cardiac tamponade, or severe aortic regurgitation.
- Pulse and blood pressure differentials (>20 mm Hg between arms) in 19% to 31% of cases caused by partial compression of subclavian arteries.
- Aortic regurgitation in 18% to 50% of cases of proximal dissection, often with diastolic decrescendo murmur.
- Myocardial ischemia caused by coronary artery occlusion, most commonly involving the right coronary artery.
- Stroke in 5% to 10% of patients (secondary to dissection into or decreased blood flow to the carotids).
- Mesenteric ischemia occurs in 3% to 5% of cases, with external compression, flap prolapse, or involvement of arterial ostia.
- Horner syndrome (ptosis, miosis, anhidrosis).
- Vocal cord paralysis or hoarse voice (caused by compression of the left recurrent laryngeal nerve).

ETIOLOGY

Genetics, in addition to other risk factors listed above, contribute to the development of aortic dissection.

🅓🅧 DIAGNOSIS

DIFFERENTIAL DIAGNOSIS
- Known as the great imitator: Pulmonary embolism, acute coronary syndrome, aortic stenosis/insufficiency, nondissecting aneurysm, pericarditis, cholecystitis, peptic ulcer disease, pancreatitis, musculoskeletal pain

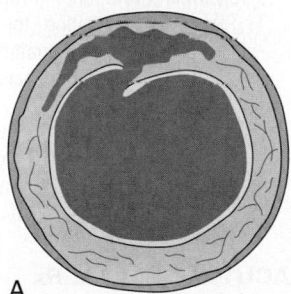

Aortic dissection

A

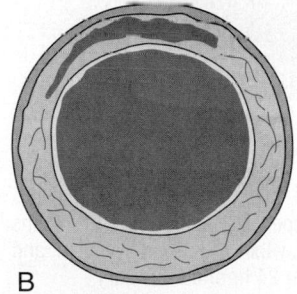

Aortic intramural hematoma

B

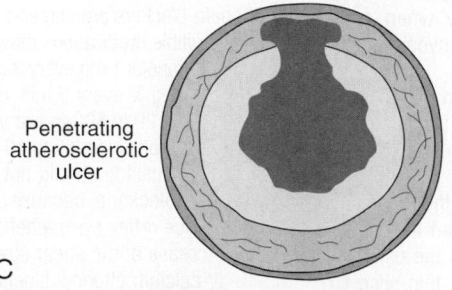

Penetrating atherosclerotic ulcer

C

FIGURE 1A-109 Acute aortic syndromes A, Classic aortic dissection. **B,** Aortic intramural hematoma. **C,** Penetrating atherosclerotic aortic ulcer. (From Bonow RO, et al: *Heart disease*, ed 9, Philadelphia, 2012, Saunders.)

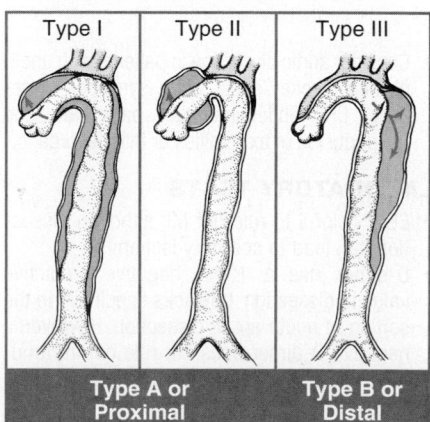

Type I	Type II	Type III

Type A or Proximal		Type B or Distal

FIGURE 1A-110 Classification systems for aortic dissection. (From Isselbacher EM et al: Disease of the aorta. In Braunwald E [ed]: *Heart disease: a textbook of cardiovascular medicine*, ed 5, Philadelphia, 1997, Saunders.)

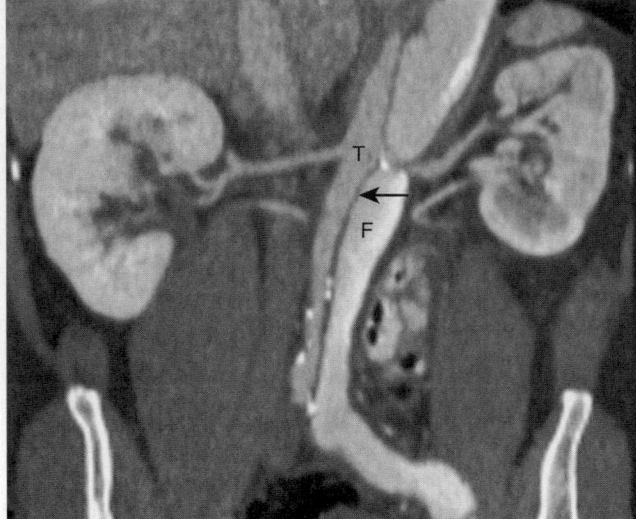

FIGURE 1A-111 Computed tomographic angiogram of the aorta shows type B aortic dissection. The intimal flap *(arrow)* separates the true lumen *(T)* from the false lumen *(F)* and compromises blood flow to the right kidney, causing renal atrophy and cortical thinning. (Image courtesy of Bart Domatch, M.D., Radiology Department, University of Texas Southwestern Medical Center, Dallas, TX; from Andreoli TE et al: *Andreoli and Carpenter's Cecil essentials of medicine,* ed 8, Philadelphia, 2010, Saunders.)

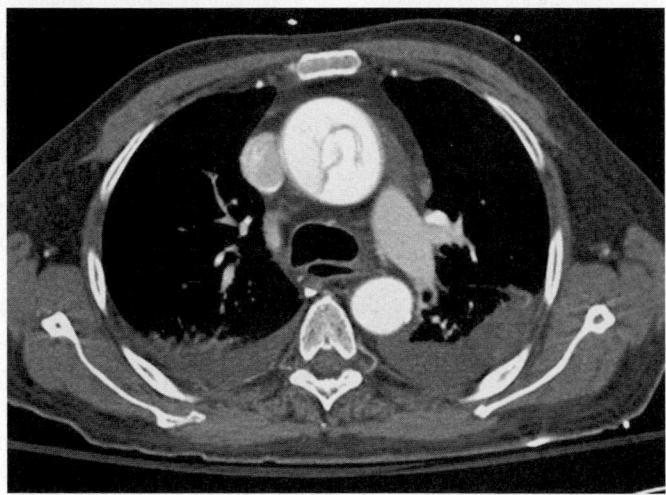

FIGURE 1A-112 Thin-slice CT image of a classic ascending dissection with aneurysmal dilation. (From Cameron JL, Cameron AM: *Current surgical therapy,* ed 10, Philadelphia, 2011, Saunders.)

- Consider aortic dissection in patients with unexplained stroke, chest pain, syncope, acute-onset CHF, abdominal pain, back pain, and malperfusion of extremities or internal organs.

LABORATORY TESTS

- ECG: helpful to rule out MI, although dissection can lead to coronary ischemia
- D-dimer has a 100% negative predictive value in dissection, but lacks specificity in the setting of acute aortic dissection. However, a negative D-dimer does not rule out intramural hematoma or penetrating aortic ulcer.
- Three biomarkers with different diagnostic windows can be used in the diagnosis of aortic dissection:
  ○ Smooth muscle myosin heavy chain protein (released from damaged medial smooth muscle) can be used to detect proximal aortic dissections (91% sensitivity

and 93% specificity). Myosin heavy chains will peak within 3 hr of dissection and clear within 24 hr of aortic injury.
  ○ CK-BB isoenzyme also peaks within 6 hr of dissection.
  ○ Calponin, a smooth muscle troponin counterpart, increases in aortic dissection with a wider diagnostic window when compared to smooth muscle myosin heavy chain and CK-BB.
  ○ C-reactive protein, fibrinogen, and soluble elastin fragments are under investigation.

IMAGING STUDIES

- Multidetector CT is considered the gold standard, but its use may be limited in patients with renal failure as it involves the use of IV contrast. Fig. 1A-112 shows a thin-slice CT image of a classic ascending dissection with aneurysmal dilation.

- TEE, multidetector CT, and MRI are all highly sensitive (98%-100%) and specific (95%-98%). Test of choice depends on clinical circumstances and hospital availability.
- Transesophageal echocardiography (TEE) is study of choice in unstable patients with type A dissection but is operator dependent.
- MRI has high sensitivity and specificity but limited availability; not suitable for unstable patients; contraindicated with pacemakers, metal devices.
- With medium or high pretest probability, a second diagnostic test should be done if the first is negative.
- Coronary computed tomographic angiography (CTA) may be an alternative and useful diagnostic study when evaluating for pulmonary embolism, acute coronary syndrome, and aortic dissection.
- Aortography rarely done, as less sensitive than TEE, CT, or MRI.
- Chest radiograph may show widened mediastinum (62%) and displacement of aortic intimal calcium. It is normal in 29% to 36% of patients with aortic dissection.
- Although the diagnostic sensitivity of transthoracic echocardiography is suboptimal, it is useful in assessing potential high-risk features or complications, such as pericardial effusion, and making other potential diagnoses. A negative transthoracic echocardiography, however, does not exclude aortic dissection.

Rx TREATMENT

- Proximal dissections (acute type A) require emergent surgery to prevent rupture or pericardial effusion.
- Distal dissections (Stanford type B) are usually treated medically unless distal organ involvement or impending rupture occurs.
  1. Surgical intervention for distal dissections is reserved for patients who have a complicated course, including occlusion of a major aortic branch, propagation of the dissection, presence within an aortic aneurysm, and evidence of aortic rupture.
  2. Fig. 1A-113 describes an algorithm for the diagnosis and treatment of aortic dissection.

ACUTE GENERAL Rx

- Admit to ICU for monitoring.
- Target SBP 100 to 120 mm Hg or as low as tolerated; heart rate <60 beats/min to reduce aortic wall stress.
- IV beta-blockers are cornerstones of treatment, but multiple medications may be needed.
  1. Propranolol 1 mg every 3 to 5 min, metoprolol 5 mg IV every 5 min, or labetalol 20 mg IV, then 20 to 80 mg every 10 min, followed by nitroprusside 0.3 to 10 mcg/kg/min.
  2. Nitroprusside should not be used without beta-blockade because vasodilation can induce reflex sympathetic stimulation and increase aortic shear stress.
  3. IV calcium channel blockers with negative inotropy (i.e., verapamil, diltiazem) may be used if beta-blockers are contraindicated.

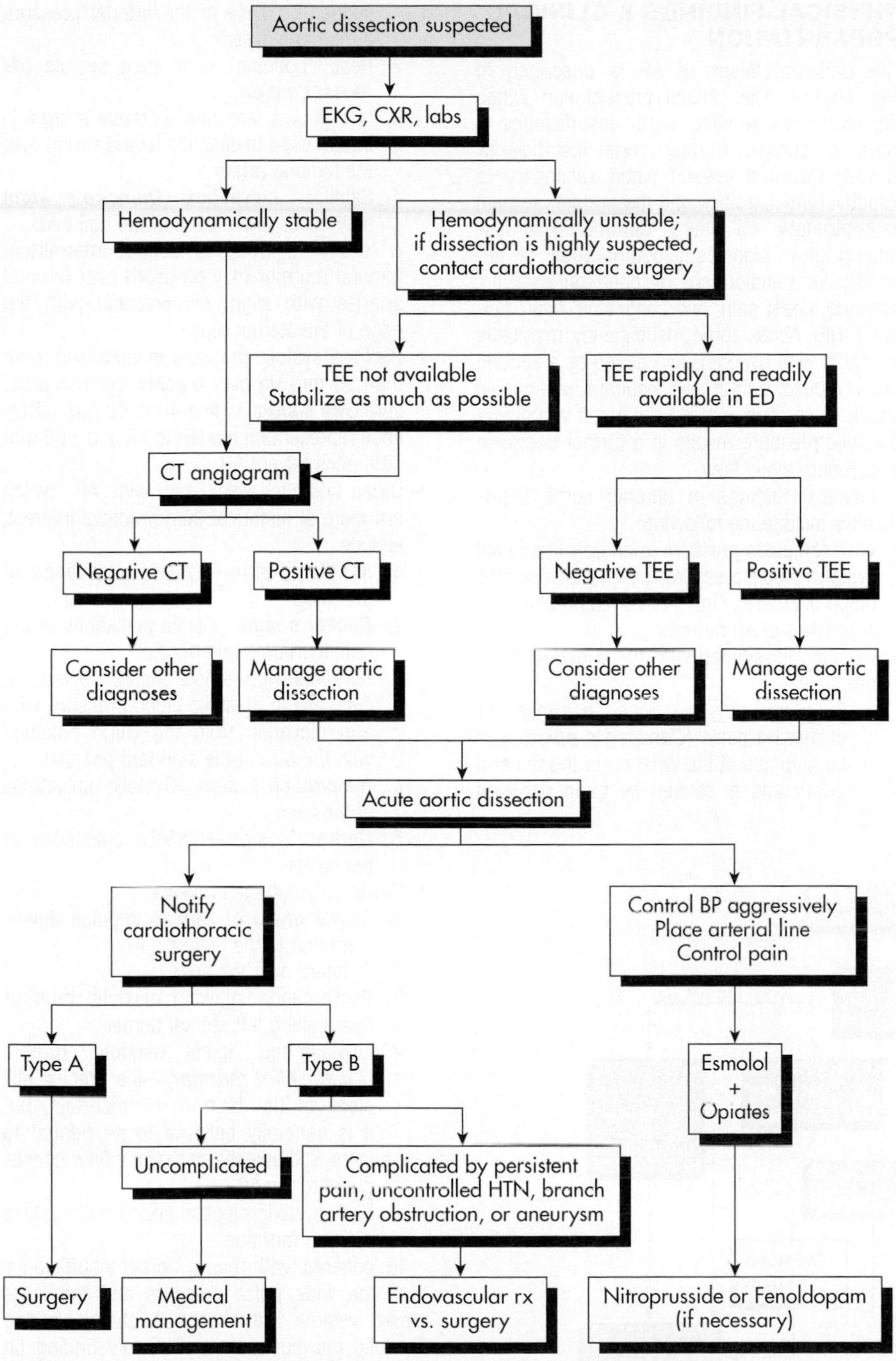

Algorithm

Aortic dissection suspected

↓

EKG, CXR, labs

↓

| Hemodynamically stable | Hemodynamically unstable; if dissection is highly suspected, contact cardiothoracic surgery |

Hemodynamically unstable branch:
- TEE not available — Stabilize as much as possible
- TEE rapidly and readily available in ED

TEE not available → CT angiogram

CT angiogram:
- Negative CT → Consider other diagnoses
- Positive CT → Manage aortic dissection

TEE readily available:
- Negative TEE → Consider other diagnoses
- Positive TEE → Manage aortic dissection

↓

Acute aortic dissection

↓

| Notify cardiothoracic surgery | Control BP aggressively / Place arterial line / Control pain |

Notify cardiothoracic surgery:
- Type A
- Type B

Type A:
- Surgery
- Medical management

Type B:
- Uncomplicated → Medical management
- Complicated by persistent pain, uncontrolled HTN, branch artery obstruction, or aneurysm → Endovascular rx vs. surgery

Control BP aggressively:
- Esmolol + Opiates
- Nitroprusside or Fenoldopam (if necessary)

FIGURE 1A-113 Algorithm for the diagnosis and treatment of aortic dissection. *BP*, Blood pressure; *CT*, computed tomography; *CXR*, chest radiograph; *ECG*, electrocardiography; *ED*, emergency department; *HTN*, hypertension; *labs*, laboratory tests; *TEE*, transesophageal echocardiography. (Adams JG et al: *Emergency medicine, clinical essentials,* ed 2, Philadelphia, 2013, Elsevier.)

- Serial imaging of the aorta, with multidetector CT or MRI should be performed at presentation, at 1 wk, and at 6 wks given the higher risk of instability early on, followed by yearly clinical and imaging follow-up.
- As stated above, endovascular repair should be considered in complicated chronic type B dissections, i.e., when the aortic diameter exceeds 5.5 cm, when there is uncontrolled pain or blood pressure, or when there is rapid growth of the dissecting aneurysm (>4 mm per year).

DISPOSITION
- 90% mortality rate within 2 weeks for an untreated type A dissection.
- Proximal dissection is a surgical emergency. Time is critical; mortality rate is 1% to 3% per hour, approaching 70% after 48 hours.
- Overall, in-hospital mortality rate is 22% with proximal dissections and 14% with distal dissections.

REFERRAL
For ICU management and surgical intervention

⚠ PEARLS & CONSIDERATIONS

- Blood pressure control is essential; beta-blocker is first-line medication.
- Proximal dissection is a surgical emergency.
- Cardiac tamponade is not uncommon in patients with acute type A aortic dissection. Syncope, altered mental status, and a widened mediastinum on chest radiograph on presentation suggest tamponade which warrants urgent operative therapy.
- Surgery for acute type A aortic dissection in patients ≥70 years old can be performed with acceptable outcomes.

SUGGESTED READINGS
Available at www.expertconsult.com

RELATED CONTENT
Aortic Dissection (Patient Information)
Abdominal Aortic Aneurysm (Related Key Topic)

AUTHORS: **ALBERT LIN, M.D.,** and **PHILIP STOCKWELL, M.D.**

- Pain control, often with morphine.
- Thoracic endovascular repair (TEVAR) is a less invasive option for complicated type B aortic dissections, which can occur in up to 31% of cases. Literature has shown significant decrease in short- and mid-term morbidity and mortality with stent grafting when compared to surgery in chronic type B dissections. A meta-analysis found that morbidity and mortality was significantly higher with acute compared to chronic dissections. However, current expert consensus supports TEVAR for first-line treatment in both complicated acute and chronic type B dissection. Long-term outcome data are still under investigation.

CHRONIC Rx
- Chronic aortic dissection (>2 wk) managed with aggressive blood pressure control: target <120/80 mm Hg in most patients.
- Target low-density lipoprotein <70 mg/dl.
- Tobacco cessation.
- Minimize strenuous physical activity such as heavy lifting.

BASIC INFORMATION

DEFINITION

Aortic regurgitation (AR) is retrograde blood flow into the left ventricle from the aorta as a result of an incompetent aortic valve.

SYNONYMS

Aortic insufficiency
AI
AR

ICD-10CM CODES

I35.1 Nonrheumatic aortic (valve) insufficiency
I35.2 Nonrheumatic aortic (valve) stenosis with insufficiency
Q23.1 Congenital insufficiency of aortic valve

EPIDEMIOLOGY & DEMOGRAPHICS

- Prevalence ranges from 4.9% to 10% and increases with age.
- The most common cause of isolated severe AR is aortic root dilation.
- Infectious endocarditis is the most frequent cause of acute AR.

PHYSICAL FINDINGS & CLINICAL PRESENTATION

The pathophysiology of AR is described in Fig. 1A-114. The clinical presentation varies depending on whether aortic insufficiency is acute or chronic. Chronic aortic insufficiency is well tolerated (except when secondary to infective endocarditis), and the patients remain asymptomatic for years. Common manifestations after significant deterioration of left ventricular function are dyspnea on exertion, syncope, chest pain, and congestive heart failure (CHF). Acute aortic insufficiency manifests primarily with hypotension caused by a sudden fall in cardiac output and resultant cardiogenic shock. In addition, a rapid rise in left ventricular diastolic pressure results in a further decrease in coronary blood flow.

Physical findings in chronic aortic insufficiency include the following:

- Widened pulse pressure (markedly increased systolic blood pressure, decreased diastolic blood pressure). Fig. 1A-115 illustrates characteristics of AR murmur.
- Findings associated with the widened pulse pressure:
  1. Bounding pulses, "water hammer" or collapsing pulse (***Corrigan's pulse***), can be palpated at the wrist or on the femoral artery and is caused by rapid rise and sudden collapse of the arterial pressure during late systole.
  2. Head "bobbing" with each systole (***de Musset's sign***).
  3. "Pistol shot femorals" (***Traube's sign***) is a term used to describe a loud sound over the femoral artery
  4. Capillary pulsations (***Quincke's sign***) may occur at the base of the nail beds.
- A to-and-fro Duroziez double intermittent femoral murmur may be heard over femoral arteries with slight compression with the edge of the stethoscope.
- Popliteal systolic pressure is increased more than 20 mm Hg over brachial systolic pressure (***Hill's sign***), with a 40 to 60 mm difference representing moderate AR and >60 mm difference severe AR.
- Other findings associated with AR, which are more of historical than practical interest, include:
  1. ***Mueller's sign***—Systolic pulsations of the uvula.
  2. ***Becker's sign***—Visible pulsations of the retinal arteries and pupils.
  3. ***Mayne's sign***—More than a 15 mm Hg decrease in diastolic blood pressure with arm elevation from the value obtained with the arm in the standard position.
  4. ***Rosenbach's sign***—Systolic pulsations of the liver.
  5. ***Gerhard's sign***—Systolic pulsations of the spleen.
- Cardiac auscultation reveals:
  1. Displacement of cardiac impulse downward and to the patient's left
  2. S_3 heard over the apex
  3. Decrescendo, blowing diastolic murmur heard along left sternal border
  4. Low-pitched apical diastolic rumble (***Austin-Flint murmur***)—the precise etiology of the murmur is uncertain, but it is generally believed to be related to increased velocity of mitral inflow consequent to the AR.
  5. Early systolic ejection sound and systolic ejection murmur.

In patients with acute aortic insufficiency both the wide pulse pressure and the large stroke volume are absent. A short, blowing diastolic murmur may be the only finding on physical examination.

ETIOLOGY

- Leaflet abnormalities:
  1. Infective endocarditis
  2. Rheumatic fibrosis (most common cause in developing countries)
  3. Trauma with valvular rupture
  4. Congenital bicuspid aortic valve (most common cause in the United States)
  5. Myxomatous degeneration
  6. Fenfluramine, dexfenfluramine, pergolide, cabergoline
  7. Ankylosing spondylitis
- Aortic root or ascending aorta abnormalities:
  1. Annuloaortic ectasia
  2. Ehlers-Danlos syndrome
  3. Marfan's syndrome

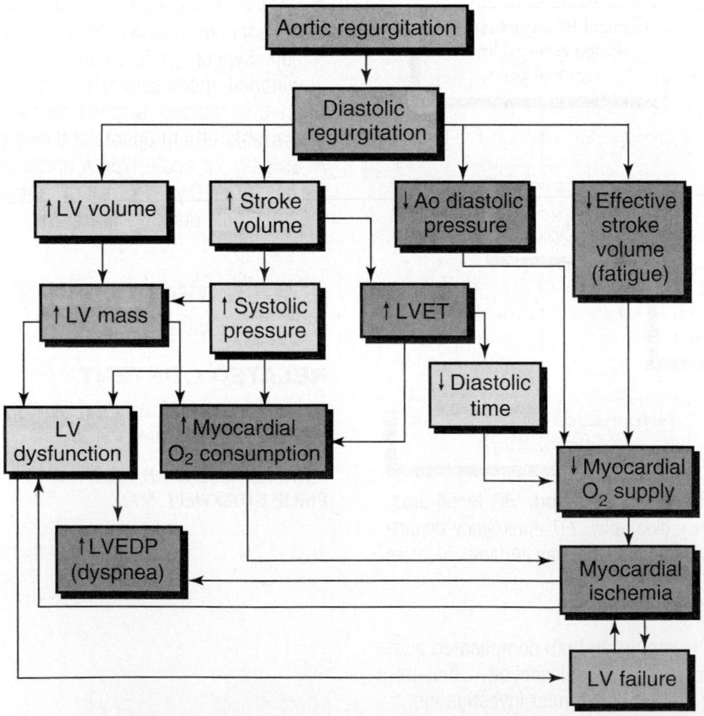

FIGURE 1A-114 Pathophysiology of aortic regurgitation. Aortic regurgitation results in an increased left ventricular *(LV)* volume, increased stroke volume, increased aortic *(Ao)* systolic pressure, and decreased effective stroke volume. Increased LV volume results in an increased LV mass, which may lead to LV dysfunction and failure. Increased LV stroke volume increases systolic pressure and prolongation of LV ejection time *(LVET)*. Increased LV systolic pressure results in a decrease in diastolic time. Decreased diastolic time (myocardial perfusion time), diastolic aortic pressure, and effective stroke volume reduce myocardial O_1 supply. Increased myocardial O_2 consumption and decreased myocardial O_2 supply produce myocardial ischemia, which further deteriorates LV function. *LVEDP,* LV end-diastolic pressure. (From Boudoulas H, Gravanis MB: Valvular heart disease. In Gravanis MB, ed: *Cardiovascular disorders: pathogenesis and pathophysiology,* St Louis, 1993, Mosby.)

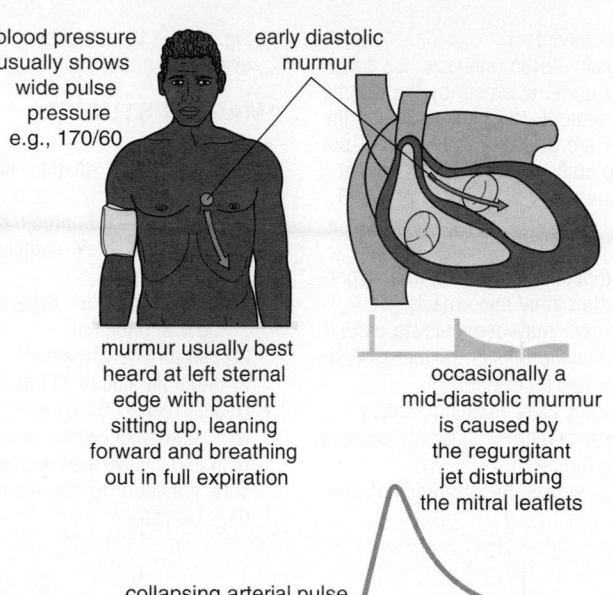

blood pressure usually shows wide pulse pressure e.g., 170/60

early diastolic murmur

murmur usually best heard at left sternal edge with patient sitting up, leaning forward and breathing out in full expiration

occasionally a mid-diastolic murmur is caused by the regurgitant jet disturbing the mitral leaflets

collapsing arterial pulse

FIGURE 1A-115 Aortic regurgitation as an example of an early diastolic murmur. (From Epstein O: *Pocket Guide to Clinical Examination*, ed 4, 2009.)

4. Trauma: ankylosing spondylitis
5. Syphilitic aortitis
6. Systemic hypertension
7. Aortic dissection

DX DIAGNOSIS

DIFFERENTIAL DIAGNOSIS

- Patent ductus arteriosus, pulmonary regurgitation, and other valvular abnormalities.
- The differential diagnosis of cardiac murmurs is described in Section II.

WORKUP

- Echocardiogram, chest radiograph, electrocardiogram (ECG), and cardiac catheterization (selected patients).
- Medical history and physical examination focused on the following clinical manifestations:
  1. Dyspnea on exertion.
  2. Syncope.
  3. Chest pain.
  4. CHF.

IMAGING STUDIES

- Chest radiography:
  1. Left ventricular hypertrophy (LVH) (chronic AR).
  2. Aortic dilation.
  3. Normal cardiac silhouette with pulmonary edema: possible in patients with acute AR.
- ECG: LVH.
- Echocardiography (Fig. E1A-116) is the main imaging modality to diagnose AR and assess left ventricular size and function. Quantification of the severity of regurgitation can be made either qualitatively by Doppler vena contracta width (severe if >0.6 cm) or quantitatively by effective regurgitant orifice

area (severe if >0.30 cm^2) and/or regurgitant volume (severe if >60 mL per/beat).
- Cardiac magnetic resonance is indicated (class 1) in patients with moderate or severe AR and suboptimal echocardiographic images for the assessment of AR severity as well as LV systolic function and volumes.
- Cardiac catheterization is indicated in selected patients to assess the degree of left ventricular dysfunction, to assess the degree of AR when echocardiographic parameters are inconclusive, and to determine if there is coexistent coronary artery disease.

RX TREATMENT

NONPHARMACOLOGIC THERAPY

- Avoidance of competitive sports and heavy weight lifting if the AR is severe and associated with aortic root dilatation.
- Salt restriction.
- In 2007, the American Heart Association (AHA) guidelines for prevention of infectious endocarditis were revised; and routine antibiotic prophylaxis to undergo dental or other invasive procedures is no longer recommended, unless the patient has a prior history of endocarditis.

MEDICAL
ACUTE GENERAL Rx:

- Afterload reduction: angiotensin-converting enzyme (ACE) inhibitors and vasodilators (i.e., nitroprusside) in acute AR; diuretics for pulmonary edema.
- Avoid beta-blockers that can prolong diastole.
- Emergent surgical referral for cardiogenic shock.

CHRONIC Rx:

- Long-term vasodilator therapy with ACE inhibitors or nifedipine in patients who have concomitant hypertension. In one 1994 study [Scognamiglio et al, NEJM 1994] nifedipine delayed the need for aortic valve surgery compared to digoxin, but in a second randomized trial [Evangelista et al, NEJM 2005] comparing placebo to nifedipine and enalapril, there was no reduction in need for aortic valve surgery when followed up to 7 years. Therefore there is no current definitive indication of medical therapy with afterload reduction for aortic regurgitation other than hypertension control.
- Beta-blockers in combination with ACE inhibitors are reasonable in patients with symptomatic severe AR or LV dysfunction when surgery cannot be performed because of concomitant comorbidities. In a retrospective cohort study of 756 patients with chronic AR, beta-blocker therapy was associated with decreased mortality. Patients treated with beta-blockers were more likely to be taking ACE inhibitors and dihydropyridine calcium channel blockers as well (53% vs. 40%). In the same study, patients treated with beta-blockers and undergoing AVR were also noted to have a mortality benefit.
- Diuretics and sodium restriction for CHF.
- Comparable efficacy of losartan and atenolol was shown in curbing aortic root dilatation growth in children and young adults (6 mo-25 yr) with Marfan's syndrome, with similar outcomes of aortic regurgitation severity, surgery, aortic dissection, and death at 3 years.

SURGICAL RESERVED FOR: REFERRAL

Reserved for:
- Patients with acute severe AR (i.e., infective endocarditis) and cardiogenic shock.
- Symptomatic patients with severe AR regardless of LV systolic function (class I).
- Patients with hemodynamically stable severe AR undergoing CABG or surgery on the aorta or other heart valves.
- Evidence of systolic dysfunction with left ventricular ejection fraction of less than 50%.
- Asymptomatic patients with severe AR and left ventricular ejection fraction >50%, but with left ventricular dilation:
  1. Echocardiographic end-systolic dimension >50 mm (Class IIa level of evidence) *or*
  2. Echocardiographic end-diastolic dimension >65 mm with low surgical risk (Class IIb).

SUGGESTED READINGS
Available at www.expertconsult.com

RELATED CONTENT
Aortic Insufficiency (Patient Information)

AUTHOR: NEELESH LALJI CHUDASAMA, M.D.

BASIC INFORMATION

DEFINITION

Aortic stenosis (AS) is obstruction to left ventricular systolic outflow across the aortic valve. Symptoms typically appear when the valve orifice decreases to <1 cm^2 (normal orifice is 3 to 4 cm^2). Criteria for severe AS include a valve area <1.0 cm^2, a mean gradient > 40 mm Hg, or a peak gradient > 4 m/s.

SYNONYMS

Aortic valvular stenosis
AS

ICD-10CM CODES
I35.0   Nonrheumatic aortic (valve) stenosis
I35.2   Nonrheumatic aortic (valve) stenosis
         with insufficiency
Q23.0   Congenital stenosis of aortic valve

EPIDEMIOLOGY & DEMOGRAPHICS

- Aortic stenosis is the most common valve lesion in adults in Western countries.
- Calcific stenosis (most common cause in patients >70 yr) occurs in 75% of patients.

PHYSICAL FINDINGS & CLINICAL PRESENTATION

- Harsh midsystolic, crescendo-decrescendo murmur (Fig. 1A-117) best heard at base of heart and radiating into neck vessels; often associated with a thrill or ejection click; may also be heard well at the apex.
- Signs of severe AS include absent or diminished intensity of the second heart sound and/or late rising carotid upstroke with delayed amplitude (pulsus parvus et tardus), presence of S4, and a reverse splitting of the second heart sound.
- Classic symptoms include angina, syncope, and heart failure.
- Acquired von Willebrand disease is seen in approximately 20% of severe AS, which can lead to GI bleeding from angiodysplasia (Heyde's syndrome) that resolves after aortic valve replacement.

ETIOLOGY

- Idiopathic calcification of the aortic valve (most common cause, presents at ages 60 to 80)
- Progressive stenosis of congenital bicuspid valve (found in 1% to 2% of the population, presents at ages 40 to 60)
- Rheumatic heart disease
- Less common causes include congenital (major cause of AS in patients < 30 yr), radiation, and obstructive vegetations (endocarditis)
- Genetic variation in the LPA locus, mediated by Lp(2) levels, is associated with aortic valve calcification across multiple ethnic groups and with incidental clinical aortic stenosis.

DIAGNOSIS

DIFFERENTIAL DIAGNOSIS

- Hypertrophic cardiomyopathy
- Mitral regurgitation

- Ventricular septal defect
- Aortic sclerosis. Aortic stenosis is distinguished from aortic sclerosis by the degree of valve impairment. In aortic sclerosis, the valve leaflets are abnormally thickened but obstruction to outflow is absent or minimal.
- Subvalvular membrane or supravalvular AS

WORKUP

- ECG: may demonstrate left ventricular hypertrophy and/or left atrial abnormality.
- Chest radiograph: may demonstrate cardiomegaly. Poststenotic dilation of the ascending aorta may also be evident.
- Echocardiography (see "Imaging Studies")
- Cardiac catheterization in selected patients (see "Imaging Studies")
- Dobutamine challenge (for low-gradient, low-flow AS)

- Fig. E1A-118 describes an algorithm for evaluation of AS.

IMAGING STUDIES

- Chest x-ray:
  1. Poststenotic dilation of the ascending aorta
  2. Calcification of aortic cusps
  3. Rounding of left ventricle (LV) apex
- ECG:
  1. Left ventricular hypertrophy (found in 80% of patients)
  2. Left atrial enlargement
  3. Atrial fibrillation (in late disease)
- Doppler echocardiography: thickening of the left ventricular wall; allows calculation of both aortic valve area and estimation of pressure gradients to determine severity of AS. (Fig. 1A-119).

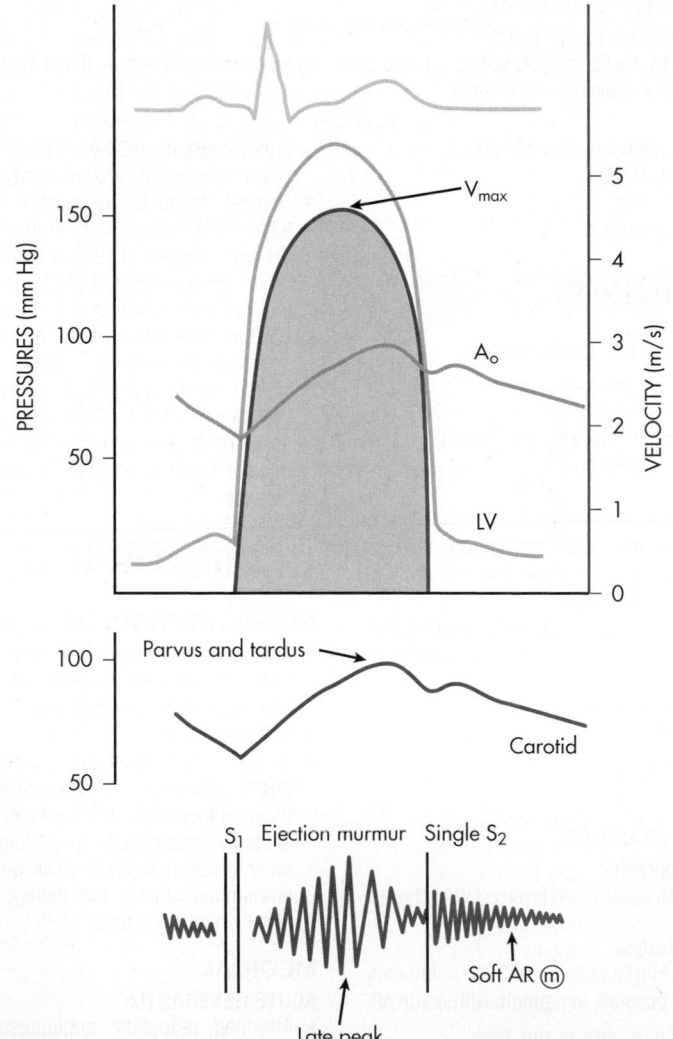

FIGURE 1A-117 Relationship between left ventricle (LV) and aortic (Ao) pressures and the Doppler aortic stenosis velocity curve (in red). The pressure difference between the LV and aorta in systole is four times the velocity squared (the Bernoulli equation). Thus, a maximum velocity (Vmax) of 4.3 m/sec corresponds to a maximum LV to Ao pressure difference of 74 mm Hg and a mean systolic gradient of 44 mm Hg. On physical examination, the slow rate of rise and delayed peak in the carotid pulse (or parvus and tardus) matches the contour of the aortic pressure waveform. The murmur corresponds to the Doppler velocity curve with a harsh crescendo-decrescendo late-peaking systolic murmur, best heard at the aortic region (upper right sternal border). Often, a soft, high-pitched diastolic decrescendo murmur of aortic regurgitation also is appreciated. (From Bonow et al [eds]: *Braunwald's heart disease,* ed 9, Philadelphia, 2012, Saunders.)

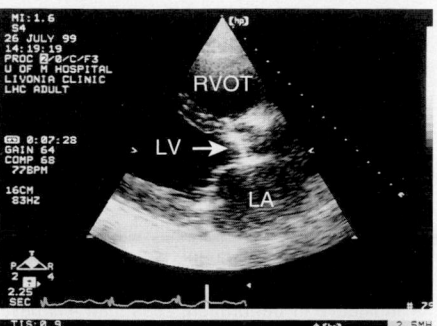

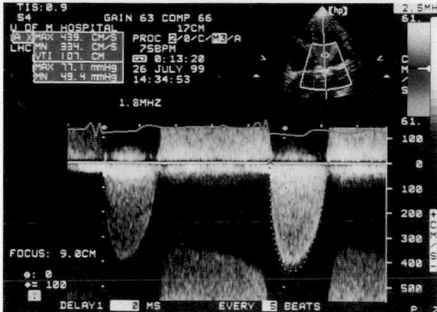

FIGURE 1A-119 Echocardiogram recorded in a patient with severe aortic stenosis. The *top panel* is a parasternal long-axis view recorded in systole. Left ventricular function is diminished. The aortic valve is markedly thickened and partially calcified. Its motion is markedly reduced, and in systole it appears that the valve occludes the orifice *(arrow)*. The *lower panel* is a continuous-wave Doppler recorded from the apex of the left ventricle along a line aimed through the stenotic aortic valve. Note the aortic stenosis signal below the zero crossing line. The peak velocity is 430 cm/sec, which corresponds to a maximum gradient of 77 mm Hg and a mean gradient of 49.4 mm Hg. *LA,* Left atrium; *LV,* left ventricle; *RVOT,* right ventricular outflow tract. (From Zipes DP et al, eds: *Braunwauld's heart disease,* ed 7, Philadelphia, 2005, Saunders.)

- Cardiac catheterization: indicated in symptomatic patients awaiting aortic valve replacement (AVR) in order to detect coexisting coronary artery stenosis that may need bypass at the same time as aortic valve replacement; also indicated in symptomatic patients when noninvasive tests are inconclusive or when there is a discrepancy between noninvasive tests and clinical findings regarding severity of AS because it confirms the diagnosis and the estimates of the severity of the valvular stenosis by directly measuring the gradient across the valve, allowing calculation of the valve area.
- A CT with contrast for imaging the aorta may be needed for annular sizing, aortic measurements, etc., if a transcatheter aortic-valve replacement (TAVR) is planned.

Rx TREATMENT

NONPHARMACOLOGIC THERAPY

- Strenuous activity should be avoided in patients with moderate to severe AS
- Sodium restriction if CHF is present

GENERAL Rx
MEDICAL:
- Once symptomatic, AS is a surgical disease.
- Gentle diuresis for volume overload as preload dependent; control hypertension (HTN) but avoid vasodilators (nitrates), maintain sinus rhythm
- In 2007, the AHA guidelines for prevention of infectious endocarditis were revised and routine antibiotic prophylaxis to undergo dental or other invasive procedures is no longer recommended, unless the patient has prior endocarditis.

SURGICAL:
- Surgical valve replacement is the treatment of choice in symptomatic patients because there is a 50% mortality rate at 2 years with medical therapy alone. Valve replacement is a Class I indication for patients with (a) symptomatic severe AS, (b) asymptomatic severe AS with LV ejection fraction (EF) <50%, and (c) severe AS undergoing CABG or surgery on the aorta or other heart valves. Valve replacement is a class 2a indication for patients with (a) asymptomatic severe AS and abnormal blood pressure response (decrease in systolic blood pressure) or decreased exercise tolerance during exercise; (b) asymptomatic patients with very severe AS (peak velocity > 5 m/s or mean pressure gradient > 60 mm Hg) with low surgical risk; (c) low flow-low gradient (with low ejection fraction <50%) with a positive low dose dobutamine stress echo; (d) symptomatic patients with low-flow/low gradient severe AS with a **normal LVEF** $\geq$ 50%, a valve area $\leq$1.0 cm^2, and a stroke volume index <35 mL/m^2; and (e) patients with moderate AS who are undergoing cardiac surgery for other indications. Patients with asymptomatic severe AS with rapid disease progression and low surgical risk are a class 2b indication for valve replacement surgery.
- Percutaneous aortic balloon valvuloplasty serves best as palliative therapy in severely symptomatic patients who are not surgical candidates and as a bridge to surgery in hemodynamically unstable adult patients. It is not an option in patients who are good candidates for surgical valve replacement because restenosis occurs in most adult patients at 6 mo.
- For patients in whom transcatheter aortic valve replacement (TAVR) or high-risk surgical AVR is being considered, a heart valve team approach is a class I recommendation.
- TAVR is recommended (class I) in patients who have a prohibitive surgical risk and are predicted to survive >12 months after TAVR.
- Percutaneous heart valve replacement is a catheter-based technology that allows for implantation of a prosthetic valve without open heart surgery. TAVR has been shown to reduce mortality by 20% in patients with severe AS and coexisting conditions that exclude them as candidates for surgical replacement of the aortic valve. In another randomized trial involving high-risk patients with severe AS who were candidates for surgery, TAVR was found to be noninferior to surgical valve replacement for short-term

efficacy with similar all-cause mortality at 2 years. The surgical group had double the incidence of new-onset atrial fibrillation and major bleeding, but the TAVR group had a higher rate of paravalvular regurgitation, major stroke, and vascular complications. Clinical trials have shown that among patients with high-risk aortic stenosis undergoing TAVR, the use of a balloon-expandable valve results in a greater rate of device success than use of a self-expandable valve. At 1-year follow-up, the balloon-expandable valve continued to have a higher device success rate and lower paravalvular regurgitation, and there were no statistically significant differences in mortality rates; however, the study had limited statistical power.

DISPOSITION
- The presence of even mild symptoms is an indicator of poor survival for patients with AS. With the average duration of symptoms before death is angina, 5 years; syncope, 3 years; CHF, 2 years.
- Approximately 75% of patients with symptomatic AS will die within 3 yr of symptom onset unless the aortic valve is replaced.

REFERRAL
- Surgical referral for valve replacement in all symptomatic AS patients. There are studies that are examining the presence of moderate or severe valvular calcification, together with a rapid increase in aortic jet velocity and elevated BNP, to identify patients with a very poor prognosis who should be considered for early valve replacement rather than have surgery delayed until symptoms develop. Additionally, patients with severe AS who are asymptomatic should be considered for exercise stress test to see if they are truly without symptoms (low exercise tolerance) or if the BP drops with exercise, both which would be indications for surgical referral. Surgical mortality rate for valve replacement is 3% to 5%; however, it varies with patient's age (>8% in patients >75 yr).
- Referral to cardiology should be considered if patient with low-flow, low-gradient (low ejection fraction) symptomatic aortic stenosis for further work-up (dobutamine stress echo).
- Balloon valvuloplasty is useful in infants and children or poor surgical candidates who do not have calcified valve apparatus; it can be done as an intermediate procedure to stabilize high-risk patients before surgery.
- Patients who are considered high risk for cardiac surgery or have contraindications (porcelain aorta) should be referred to a center with a transcatheter program for TAVR evaluation.

SUGGESTED READINGS
Available at www.expertconsult.com

RELATED CONTENT
Aortic Stenosis (Patient Information)

AUTHORS: **DEEPA KUMARAIAH, M.D., M.B.A,** and **DENISA HAGAU, M.D.**

BASIC INFORMATION

DEFINITION

Appendicitis is the acute inflammation of the vermiform appendix.

ICD-10CM CODES	
K35.2	Acute appendicitis with generalized peritonitis
K35.3	Acute appendicitis with localized peritonitis
K35.80	Unspecified acute appendicitis
K35.89	Other acute appendicitis
K36	Other appendicitis
K37	Unspecified appendicitis

EPIDEMIOLOGY & DEMOGRAPHICS

- Appendicitis occurs in 10% of the population, most commonly between the ages of 10 and 30 yr. Median age is 22 yr. Lifetime risk is 7% to 14%.
- Approximately 300,000 appendectomies are performed in the U.S. each year.
- It is the most common abdominal surgical emergency.
- Incidence of appendicitis has declined over the past 30 yr.
- Male/female ratio is 3:2 until mid-20s; it equalizes after age 30 yr.

PHYSICAL FINDINGS & CLINICAL PRESENTATION

- In children with abdominal pain, fever is the single most useful sign associated with appendicitis. Vomiting, rectal tenderness, and rebound tenderness along with fever are more indicative of appendicitis in children than in adults.
- Abdominal pain: initially the pain may be epigastric or periumbilical in nearly 50% of patients; it subsequently localizes to the right lower quadrant within 12 to 18 hr. Pain can be found in back or right flank if appendix is retrocecal or in other abdominal locations if there is malrotation of the appendix.
- Pain with right thigh extension *(psoas sign)*, low-grade fever: temperature may be >38° C if there is appendiceal perforation.
- Pain with internal rotation of the flexed right thigh *(obturator sign)* is present.
- Right lower quadrant (RLQ) pain on palpation of the left lower quadrant (LLQ) *(Rovsing's sign):* physical examination may reveal right-sided tenderness in patients with pelvic appendix.
- Point of maximum tenderness is in the RLQ *(McBurney's point).*
- Nausea, vomiting, tachycardia, cutaneous hyperesthesias at the level of T12 can be present.

ETIOLOGY

Obstruction of the appendiceal lumen with subsequent vascular congestion, inflammation, and edema; common causes of obstruction are:
- Fecaliths: 30% to 35% of cases (most common in adults)
- Foreign body: 4% (fruit seeds, pinworms, tapeworms, roundworms, calculi)
- Inflammation: 50% to 60% of cases (submucosal lymphoid hyperplasia [most common etiology in children, teens])
- Neoplasms: 1% (carcinoids, metastatic disease, carcinoma)

DIAGNOSIS

DIFFERENTIAL DIAGNOSIS

- Intestinal: regional cecal enteritis, incarcerated hernia, cecal diverticulitis, intestinal obstruction, perforated ulcer, perforated cecum, Meckel's diverticulitis
- Reproductive: ectopic pregnancy, ovarian cyst, torsion of ovarian cyst, salpingitis, tubo-ovarian abscess, mittelschmerz, endometriosis, seminal vesiculitis
- Renal: renal and ureteral calculi, neoplasms, pyelonephritis
- Vascular: leaking aortic aneurysm
- Psoas abscess
- Trauma
- Cholecystitis
- Mesenteric adenitis

WORKUP

Patients with RLQ pain, nausea, vomiting, anorexia, and RLQ rebound tenderness should undergo prompt clinical and laboratory evaluation. Imaging studies are generally not necessary in typical appendicitis and generally reserved for patients with an equivocal likelihood of appendicitis. They are useful when the diagnosis is uncertain. Laparoscopy may be useful as both a diagnostic and a therapeutic modality.

LABORATORY TESTS

- Complete blood count with differential reveals leukocytosis with a left shift in 90% of patients with appendicitis. Total white blood cell (WBC) count is generally lower than 20,000/mm³. Higher counts may be indicative of perforation. Less than 4% have a normal WBC and differential. A WBC count <10,000/mm³ decreases the likelihood of appendicitis. Low hemoglobin and hematocrit levels in an older patient should raise suspicion for GI tract carcinoma.
- Microscopic hematuria and pyuria may occur in <20% of patients.
- HCG to rule out pregnancy in females of reproductive age.

IMAGING STUDIES

- Multidetector computed tomography (Fig. 1A-120) is a useful test for routine evaluation of suspected appendicitis in adults. CT of the abdomen/pelvis without contrast has a sensitivity of >90% and an accuracy >94% for acute appendicitis. A distended appendix, periappendiceal inflammation, and a thickened appendiceal wall are indicative of appendicitis. Table 1A-57 describes CT findings of appendicitis. In children and young adults, exposure to CT radiation is of particular concern. Trials with low-dose CT

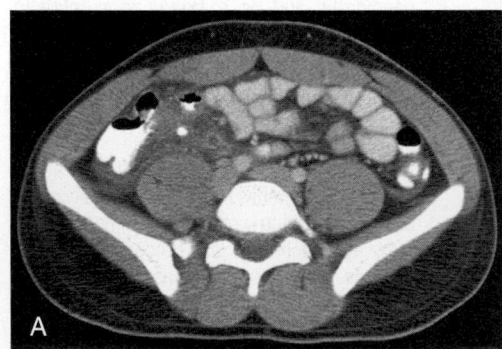

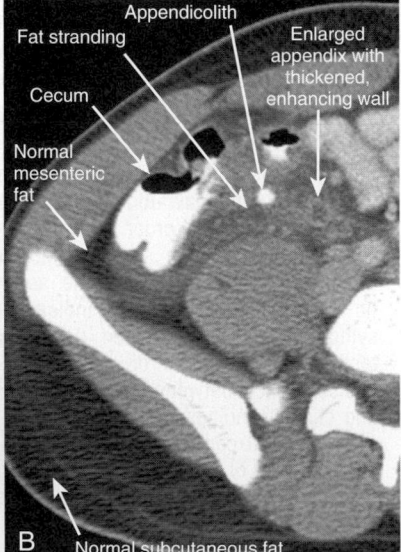

FIGURE 1A-120 Appendicitis, CT with IV and oral contrast. This CT demonstrates classic findings of appendicitis in an 18-year-old male with right lower quadrant pain, as seen with CT with IV and oral contrast. Studies suggest that CT without contrast has similar sensitivity and specificity. An enlarged appendix is seen near the cecum as a right lower quadrant tubular structure in short-axis cross section, giving it a circular appearance. The surrounding fat shows stranding, a smoky appearance indicating inflammation (compare with normal mesenteric and subcutaneous fat, which is nearly black). The appendiceal wall shows enhancement, a brightening after administration of IV contrast. This slice also shows an appendicolith, an occasional finding of appendicitis. It does not appear to be within the appendix in this slice, because the appendix bends in and out of the plane of this slice. An appendicolith usually appears as a calcified (white) rounded structure, visible without any contrast. **A,** Axial CT image. **B,** Close-up. (From Broder JS: *Diagnostic imaging for the emergency physician,* Philadelphia, 2011, Saunders.)

TABLE 1A-57 CT Findings of Appendicitis: SCALPEL Mnemonic

Term	Description
Stranding	Fat stranding suggests regional inflammation, possibly because of appendicitis.
Cecum	The appendix originates from the cecum, which should be identified first to help localize the appendix. The cecum may show wall thickening, suggesting appendicitis.
Air	Air outside of the lumen of the appendix is pathologic and suggests perforation. Air within the appendiceal wall is also abnormal.
Large	The normal appendix is <6 mm; an enlarged appendix >6 mm suggests appendicitis. Wall thickening >1 mm also suggests appendicitis.
Phlegmon	Inflammatory changes surrounding the appendix suggest a perforated appendix. A heterogeneous collection called a phlegmon may be seen. If the appendix has ruptured, a pericecal phlegmon may be the only remaining evidence, because the appendix itself may not be seen.
Enhancement	The wall of an abnormal appendix enhances with IV contrast and appears brighter than the normal bowel or the normal psoas muscle.
Lith	An appendicolith is a calcified stone sometimes found in the lumen of an inflamed appendix.

From Broder JS: *Diagnostic imaging for the emergency physician*, Philadelphia, 2011, Saunders.

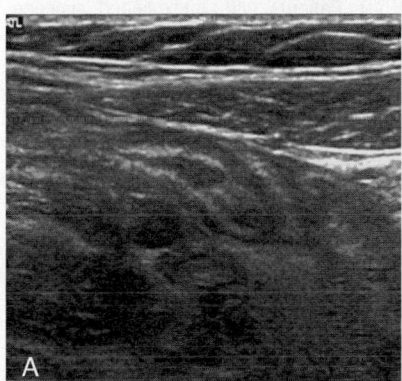
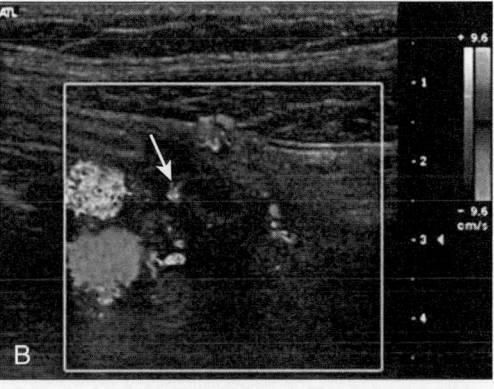

FIGURE 1A-121 Appendicitis. A, Transabdominal ultrasound using a linear transducer demonstrates a thick, tubular, noncompressible structure. **B,** Same imaging method with addition of color Doppler ultrasound shows increased vascularity within the luminal wall consistent with inflammation *(arrow).* (From Fielding JR et al: *Gynecologic imaging,* Philadelphia, 2011, Saunders.)

(116 mGy cm) have shown that low-dose CT is not inferior to standard-dose CT (521 mGy cm) with respect to negative (unnecessary) appendectomy rates in young adults with suspected appendicitis.

- Ultrasonography (Fig. 1A-121) has a sensitivity of 75% to 90% for the diagnosis of acute appendicitis, although it is highly operator dependent and difficult in patients with large body habitus. Ultrasound is useful, especially in pregnancy and in younger women when diagnosis is unclear. Normal ultrasonographic findings should not deter surgery if the history and physical examination are indicative of appendicitis.
- MRI of the abdomen and pelvis can also be used to accurately diagnose acute appendicitis in pregnant patients (100% sensitivity, 93.6% specificity) without exposure to ionizing radiation.

Rx TREATMENT

NONPHARMACOLOGIC THERAPY

- Nothing by mouth
- Do not administer analgesics until the diagnosis is made

ACUTE GENERAL Rx

- Urgent appendectomy (laparoscopic or open), correction of fluid and electrolyte imbalance with vigorous IV hydration and electrolyte replacement
- IV antibiotic prophylaxis to cover gram-negative bacilli and anaerobes (ampicillin/sulbactam 3 g IV q6h or piperacillin/tazobactam 4.5 g IV q8h in adults)

ⓘ PEARLS & CONSIDERATIONS

COMMENTS

- Perforation is common (20% in adult patients). Indicators of perforation are pain lasting >24 hr, leukocytosis >20,000/mm^3, temperature >102° F, palpable abdominal mass, and peritoneal findings.
- In general, prognosis is excellent. Mortality rate is <1% in young adults without complications; however, it exceeds 10% in elderly patients with ruptured appendix.
- In approximately 20% of patients who undergo exploratory laparotomy because of suspected appendicitis, the appendix is normal.

- An increasing amount of evidence supports the use of antibiotics instead of surgery for treating patients with uncomplicated appendicitis. A recent trial assessing the feasibility of nonoperative management for uncomplicated acute appendicitis in children using either IV piperacillin-tazobactam or ciprofloxacin metronidazole therapy for at least 24 hours followed by oral antibiotics for 10 days revealed that 90% of children managed nonoperatively had no progression within 30 days.[1] Another trial among patients with CT-proven, uncomplicated appendicitis revealed that antibiotic treatment did not meet the prescribed criterion for noninferiority compared with appendectomy. Most patients randomized to antibiotic treatment for uncomplicated appendicitis did not require appendectomy during the 1-yr follow-up period, and those who required appendectomy did not experience significant complications.[2] It remains to be determined whether the benefits of potentially avoiding an operation with antibiotics-first approach are outweighed by the burden to the patient related to future appendicitis episodes, more days of antibiotic therapy, lingering symptoms, and uncertainty that may affect quality of life.[3]

ⓔ EVIDENCE

Available at www.expertconsult.com

SUGGESTED READINGS

Available at www.expertconsult.com

RELATED CONTENT

Appendicitis (Patient Information)

AUTHOR: **FRED F. FERRI, M.D.**

[1]Minneci PC et al: Feasibility of a nonoperative management strategy for uncomplicated acute appendicitis in children. J Am Coll Surg 219:272-279, 2014.
[2]Salminen P et al: Antibiotic therapy vs appendectomy for treatment of uncomplicated acute appendicitis, the APPAC Randomized trial. JAMA 313(23):2340-2348, 2015.
[3]Flum DR: Acute appendicitis—appendectomy or the "antibiotics first" strategy. A Engl J Med 372:1937-43, 2015.

BASIC INFORMATION

DEFINITION

Arrhythmogenic right ventricular dysplasia (ARVD) is a cardiomyopathy characterized by replacement of the normal myocardium with fibrofatty tissue, mainly of the right ventricle but also occasionally with involvement of the left ventricle. It is defined clinically by palpitations and syncope and potentially life-threatening ventricular arrhythmias.

SYNONYMS

Arrhythmogenic right ventricular cardiomyopathy (ARVC)

ICD-10CM CODES
I42.8 Arrhythmogenic ventricular dysplasia

EPIDEMIOLOGY & DEMOGRAPHICS

PREVALENCE: 1:2000-5000 persons
PREDOMINANT SEX AND AGE: Mean age, 31 yr (range, 12-50 yr), predominantly male
RISK FACTORS: Family history of ARVD
GENETICS:
- Autosomal dominant (most common) with variable penetrance and polymorphic phenotypic expression.
- Autosomal recessive (rarely, e.g., Naxos disease).
- Several different gene mutations in desmosomal proteins.
- Gene mutations can be identified in 50% of affected individuals.

PHYSICAL FINDINGS & CLINICAL PRESENTATION

- ARVD can present with palpitations, syncope, and chest discomfort and less commonly sudden cardiac arrest and signs of right ventricular failure such as dyspnea, edema, and fatigue. Patients may be clinically asymptomatic for many years.
- Cardiac arrest after physical exertion may be the initial presentation.
- Physical examination will be normal in most patients. Widely split S2 is an important diagnostic clue.

ETIOLOGY

ARVD is characterized by progressive replacement of mainly the right ventricular myocardium with fibrofatty tissue after apoptotic myocardial cell death caused by mutations of desmosomal protein.

 **DIAGNOSIS**

- A major criteria equals 2 points; a minor criteria equals 1 point. The diagnosis of ARVD is considered definite if the patient has 4 points and probable with 3 points. See Table 1A-58 for diagnostic criteria.

DIFFERENTIAL DIAGNOSIS

- Cardiomyopathy with involvement of the right ventricle
- Uhl's anomaly: rare anomaly that presents mainly in childhood with signs and symptoms of right heart failure and characterized by a paper-thin right ventricle resulting from death of the myocytes throughout the right ventricle
- Idiopathic RV tachycardia
- Sarcoidosis
- Right ventricular infarction

WORKUP

- Initial workup includes history with focus on sudden death in the family, resting ECG, 24-Holter ECG, signal-averaged ECG, and imaging studies with echocardiography and MRI.
- ECG will have diagnostic findings in 50% to 90% of patients with ARVD, including T-wave inversions in anterior precordial leads V_1-V_6, epsilon waves, and a QRS duration longer than 110 ms in V1 or >40 ms longer in V1 than v6. (Fig. 1A-122, *A*)
- Ventricular tachycardia (VT) with left bundle branch block pattern and frequent PVCs (>500 in 24 h) might be detected by 24-hr Holter monitoring.
- An abnormal signal-averaged ECG is a minor diagnostic criteria.
- Echocardiography will show right ventricular dilation with regional wall motion abnormalities, aneurysms, and depressed RV function that varies with the severity of the disease.
- MRI is a noninvasive method to detect structural abnormalities (fibrofatty changes) and regional dysfunction. Cardiac MRI (CMR) is the most sensitive method to detect ARVD, but it has high false-positive rates. Cardiac CT angiogram (Fig. E1A-122, *B*) will reveal thinning and aneurysmal dilation of the RV anterior wall and outflow tract.

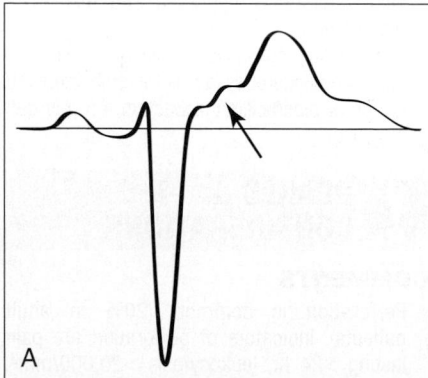

FIGURE 1A-122 A Epsilon waves are small deflections just beyond the QRS complex. Best visualized in leads V_1-V_3. Any potential in leads V_1-V_3 that exceeds the QRS in leads V6 by more than 25 millisecond should be considered epsilon wave. (From Anderson EL: Arrhythmogenic right ventricular dysplasia, *Am Fam Physician* 73(8):1391-1398, 2006.)

If the routine tests are not conclusive, endomyocardial biopsy and electrophysiologic testing can be considered. However, biopsies and radionuclide ventriculography are rarely performed in the U.S.

 **TREATMENT**

No curative treatment is available. The treatment goal is focused on preventing sudden cardiac death, symptomatic treatment of right heart failure, and pharmacologic and invasive treatment of arrhythmias.

NONPHARMACOLOGIC THERAPY

- Avoidance of activity that may trigger ventricular tachycardia and may lead to disease progression.
- ICD implantation needs to be considered in patients who have the definite diagnosis of ARVD. Patients with unexplained syncope, advanced disease, documented ventricular arrhythmias, or a family history of sudden cardiac death or who have been resuscitated from cardiac arrest are at high risk. A subcutaneous ICD might be an alternative option instead of transvenous implantation.
- Radiofrequency catheter ablation is used in cases of refractory VT or frequent tachycardia after defibrillator placement.
- Cardiac transplantation.

PHARMACOLOGIC TREATMENT

- Antiarrhythmic therapy with sotalol (first-line treatment) or amiodarone, often in combination with beta-blockers, is used for tachycardia suppression.

REFERRAL

- Early cardiology and electrophysiology referral
- Consider referring for genetic counseling

! **PEARLS & CONSIDERATIONS**

PREVENTION

All first-degree relatives should be tested if ARVD is confirmed.

SUGGESTED READINGS
Available at www.expertconsult.com

AUTHOR: **HEIKO SCHMITT, M.D., Ph.D.**

TABLE 1A-58 Global or regional dysfunction and structural alterations

Major

2D echo criteria
Regional RV akinesia, dyskinesia, or aneurysm and one of the following measured at end diastole
PLAX RVOT ≥32 mm or
PSAX RVOT ≥36
Fractional area change ≤33%
MRI criteria
Regional RV akinesia or dyskinesia or dyssynchronous RV contraction and one of the following
Ratio of RV end-diastolic volume to BSA >100, <110 mL/m^2 (male) or >100 mL/m2
RV ejection fraction >40% ≤45%
RV angiography criteria
Regional RV akinesia, dyskinesia, or aneurysm

Minor

2D echo criteria
Regional RV akinesia or dyskinesia or dyssynchronous RV contraction and one of the following measured at end diastole
PLAX RVOT ≥29 <32 mm or
PSAX RVOT ≥32 <36
Fractional area change >33% ≤40%
MRI criteria
Regional RV akinesia or dyskinesia or dyssynchronous RV contraction and one of the following
Ratio of RV end-diastolic volume to BSA ≥110 mL/m^2 (male) or _≥100 mL/m^2
RV ejection fraction ≤40%

Tissue characterization of wall

Major

Residual myocytes <60% by morphometric analysis (or <50% if estimated) with fibrous replacement of the RV free wall myocardium in >1 sample, with or without fatty replacement of tissue on endomyocardial biopsy

Minor

Residual myocytes 60%-75% by morphometric analysis (or 50%-65% if estimated), with fibrous replacement of the RV free wall myocardium in >1 sample with or without fatty replacement of tissue on endomyocardial biopsy

Repolarization abnormalities

Major

Inverted T waves in right precordial leads (V1, V2, and V3) or beyond in individuals >14 y of age (in the absence of complete RBBB QRS ≥120 ms)

Minor

Inverted T waves in V1 and V2 in individuals >14 y of age (in the absence of complete RBBB) or in V4, V5, and V6
Inverted T waves in leads V1, V2, V3, and V4 in individuals >14 y of age in the presence of a complete RBBB

Depolarization or conduction abnormalities

Major

Epsilon wave (reproducible low-amplitude signals between end of QRS complex to onset of T wave) in the right precordial leads (V1-V3)

Minor

Late potentials by SAECG in ≥1 of 3 parameters in the absence of a QRSd of ≥110 ms on standard ECG
Filtered QRS ≥114 ms
Duration of terminal QRS <40 mV ≥38 ms
Root-mean-square voltage of terminal 40 ms ≤20µV
Terminal activation duration ≥55 ms measured from the nadir of the end of the QRS, including R', in V1, V2, or V3 in absence of complete RBBB

Arrhythmias

Major

Nonsustained or sustained VT of LBBB morph with superior axis

Minor

Nonsustained or sustained VT of RVOT configuration, LBBB morph with inferior axis or of unknown axis
>500 PVCs per 24 h (Holter)

Family history

Major

ARVD/C in first-degree relative who meets Task Force criteria
ARVD/C confirmed pathologically at autopsy or surgery in first-degree relative
Identification of pathogenic mutation categorized as associated or probably associated with ARVD/C in the patient under evaluation

Minor

History of ARVD/C in first-degree relative in whom it is not possible to determine whether the family member meets Task Force criteria
Premature sudden death (<35 y of age) caused by suspected ARVD/C in a first-degree relative
ARVD/C confirmed pathologically or by current Task Force criteria in second-degree relative.

A major criteria equals 2 points, a minor criteria 1 point. The diagnosis of arrhythmogenic right ventricular dysplasia (ARVD) is considered definite if the patient has 4 points and probable with 3 points.
BSA, body surface area; *MRI*, magnetic resonance imaging; *RBBB*, right bundle branch block; *RV*, right ventricle; *RVOT*, right ventricular outflow tract; *2D*, two dimensional; *VT*, ventricular tachycardia.
From Marcus IM: Diagnosis of arrhythmogenic right ventricular cardiomyopathy/dysplasia proposed modification of the Task Force criteria. *Circulation* 121: 1533-1541, 2010.

A

Diseases
and Disorders

I

BASIC INFORMATION

DEFINITION
Asbestosis is a slowly progressive diffuse interstitial fibrosis resulting from dose-related inhalation exposure to fibers of asbestos in miners, millers, workers of asbestos textiles, and insulators. Clinically, the lung involvement is characterized by bilateral diffuse interstitial fibrosis, more pronounced in the lower lobes, and pleural thickening, leading to shortness of breath and dry cough

ICD-10CM CODES
J61　Pneumoconiosis due to asbestos and other mineral fibers

EPIDEMIOLOGY & DEMOGRAPHICS
- Five to 10 new cases per 100,000 persons per year in the United States.
- Prolonged interval (20 to 30 yr) between exposures to inhaled fibers and clinical manifestations of disease
- Most common in workers involved in the primary extraction of asbestos from rock deposits and in those involved in the fabrication and installation of products containing asbestos (e.g., naval shipyards in World War II; installation of floor tiles, ceiling tiles, acoustic ceiling coverings, wall insulation, and pipe coverings in public buildings)

PHYSICAL FINDINGS & CLINICAL PRESENTATION
- Insidious onset of shortness of breath with exertion is usually the first sign of asbestosis.
- Dyspnea becomes more severe as the disease advances; with time, progressively less exertion is tolerated.
- Cough is frequent and usually paroxysmal, dry, and nonproductive.
- Scant mucoid sputum may accompany the cough in the later stages of the disease.
- Fine end-respiratory crackles (rales, crepitations) are heard more predominantly in the lung bases.
- Digital clubbing, edema, jugular venous distention are present.

ETIOLOGY/PATHOGENESIS
Inhalation of asbestos fibers. Recent work has shown that pathogenesis of pulmonary interstitial inflammation and fibrosis is related to immune mechanisms. Asbestosis is known to be associated with positive serum antinuclear antibody (ANA) and rheumatoid factor (RF). Recently, an important role of interleukin-1beta (IL-1beta) in the pathogenesis of asbestosis and its systemic autoimmune manifestations has been reported.

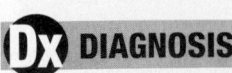

DIAGNOSIS

DIFFERENTIAL DIAGNOSIS
- Silicosis
- Siderosis, other pneumoconioses
- Lung cancer
- Atelectasis

WORKUP
Documentation of exposure history, diagnostic imaging, pulmonary function testing

LABORATORY TESTS
- Generally not helpful
- Possible mild elevation of erythrocyte sedimentation rate (ESR), positive antinuclear antibody (ANA), and rheumatoid factor (RF) (these tests are nonspecific and do not correlate with disease severity or activity)
- Pulmonary function testing: decreased vital capacity, decreased total lung capacity, decreased carbon monoxide gas transfer
- Arterial blood gases: hypoxemia, hypercarbia in advanced stages

IMAGING STUDIES
Chest radiograph (Fig. 1A-123):
　Small, irregular shadows in lower lung zones.
　The imaging findings vary from benign pleural disease (including discrete plaques, pleural calcification, diffuse pleural thickening with blunting of costophrenic angles, and thickening of the interlobar fissure) to asbestosis (diffuse interstitial pulmonary fibrosis.
- Thickened pleura, calcified plaques (present under diaphragm and lateral chest wall).
- CT scan of chest (fig. 1A-124) confirms diagnosis. Typical findings on high-resolution CT of the chest include increased interstitial markings found mainly at the bases. As the disease progresses, honeycombing is noted.

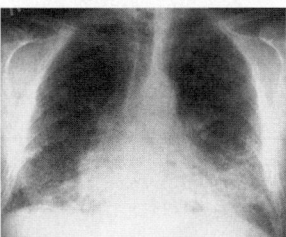

FIGURE　1A-123 Asbestosis. Posteroanterior radiograph shows coarse linear opacities at both lung bases obscuring the cardiac borders. (From McLoud TC: *Thoracic radiology: the requisites*, St Louis, 1998, Mosby.)

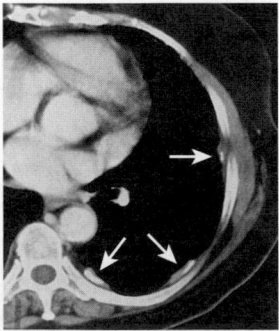

FIGURE　1A-124 Asbestos-related pleural plaques. Typical calcified pleural plaques (*arrows*) are visible. They are often internal to the ribs. (From Webb WR, Brant WE, Major NM: *Fundamentals of body CT*, ed 4, Philadelphia, 2014, Saunders.)

TREATMENT

NONPHARMACOLOGIC THERAPY
- Smoking cessation, proper nutrition, exercise program to maximize available lung function
- Home oxygen therapy PRN
- Removal of patient from further asbestos fiber exposure

GENERAL Rx
- Prompt identification and treatment of respiratory infections
- Supplemental oxygen on a PRN basis
- Annual influenza vaccination, pneumococcal vaccination
　Some new data are coming out targeting IL-1 beta therapy on the progression of lung fibrosis that suggest a new perspective for the treatment of systemic autoimmune features of asbestosis and, possibly, of lung involvement.[1]

DISPOSITION
- There is no specific treatment for asbestosis.
- Death is usually from respiratory failure from cor pulmonale.
- Diffuse pleural thickening and asbestosis are associated with increased risks of malignant peritoneal mesothelioma beyond the risk calculated to be associated with the degree of asbestos exposure.[2]
- None of the benign pleural diseases or asbestosis were associated with an increased risk of malignant pleural mesothelioma.
- Asbestos exposure without asbestosis and smoking increases the risk of lung cancer. The joint effect of asbestos and smoking is additive and depends in part on the presence of asbestosis. Asbestos workers who stop smoking experience a dramatic decline in lung cancer risk, which approaches that of nonsmokers after 30 years.
- Low-dose chest CT scanning offers an excellent opportunity to detect early-stage lung cancers in asbestos-exposed workers.
- Survival in patients after development of mesothelioma is 4 to 6 yr.

SUGGESTED READINGS
Available at www.expertconsult.com

RELATED CONTENT
Asbestosis (Patient Information)

AUTHOR: **IMRANA QAWI, M.D.**

[1]Systemic autoimmune disease in asbestosis rapidly responding to anti-interleukin-1beta antibody canakinumab: a case report. *BMC Musculoskelet Disord* 14(16):146, 2015.

[2]The additional risk of malignant mesothelioma in former workers and residents of Wittenoom with benign pleural disease or asbestosis. *Occup Environ Med* 62:665-669, 2005.

 BASIC INFORMATION

DEFINITION
Ascariasis is a parasitic infection caused by the nematode *Ascaris lumbricoides.* The majority of those infected are asymptomatic; however, clinical disease may arise from pulmonary hypersensitivity, intestinal obstruction, and secondary complications.

SYNONYMS
Round worms
Worms

ICD-10CM CODES
B77.9   Ascariasis, unspecified
B77.81   Ascariasis pneumonia
B77.0   Ascariasis with intestinal
         complications
B77.89   Ascariasis with other complications

EPIDEMIOLOGY & DEMOGRAPHICS
INCIDENCE (IN THE UNITED STATES):
- Unknown. Worldwide, *A. lumbricoides* is the most common helminthic infection of humans, infecting as many as 1 billion or more persons. 71% of persons at risk for infection live in Asia and the Western Pacific.
- Three times the infection rates found in blacks as in whites

PEAK INCIDENCE: Unknown
PREVALENCE (IN THE UNITED STATES): Estimated at 4 million, the majority of which live in the rural southeastern part of the country; ascariasis is associated with poor sanitation
PREDOMINANT SEX: Both sexes probably equally affected, with a possible slight female preponderance
PREDOMINANT AGE: Most common in children from ages 2 to 10 years old and decreases after age 15; infections tend to cluster in families
NEONATAL INFECTION: Probable transmission, though not specifically studied

PHYSICAL FINDINGS & CLINICAL PRESENTATION
- Most people infected with *Ascaris* are asymptomatic.
- Occurs approximately 9 to 12 days after ingestion of eggs (corresponding to the larval migration through the lungs)
- Nonproductive cough
- Substernal chest discomfort
- Fever
- In patients with large worm burdens, especially children, intestinal obstruction associated with perforation, volvulus, and intussusception
- Migration of worms into the biliary tree giving clinical appearance of biliary colic and pancreatitis as well as acute appendicitis with movement into that appendage
- Rarely, infection with *A. lumbricoides* producing interstitial nephritis and acute renal failure
- In endemic areas in Asia and Africa, malabsorption of dietary proteins and vitamins as a consequence of chronic worm intestinal carriage;

1 billion people worldwide are infected with this nematode

ETIOLOGY
- Transmission is usually hand to mouth, but eggs may be ingested via transported vegetables grown in contaminated soil.
- Eggs are hatched in the small intestine, with larvae penetrating intestinal mucosa and migrating via the circulation to the lungs.
- Larval forms proceed through the alveoli, ascend the bronchial tree, and return to the intestines after swallowing, where they mature into adult worms.
- Estimated time until the female adult worm begins producing eggs is 2 to 3 mo.
- Eggs are passed out of the intestines with feces and can survive for years in warm, moist, shaded soil.
- Within human host, adult worm life span is 1 to 2 yr.

Dx DIAGNOSIS

DIFFERENTIAL DIAGNOSIS
- Radiologic manifestations and eosinophilia to be distinguished from drug hypersensitivity and Löffler's syndrome.
- Table E1A-59 compares features of major intestinal nematodes.

LABORATORY TESTS
- Examination of the stool for *Ascaris* ova (Fig. E1A-125)
- Expectoration or fecal passage of adult worm
- Adult male worms: 10 to 30 cm long; adult female worms: larger than male, up to 40 cm
- Eosinophilia: most prominent early in the infection and subsides as the adult worm infestation established in the intestines; usually in 5% to 12% range but can be up to 50%
- Serology: patients develop IgG antibodies, but they cross react with antigens from other helminths and are not protective; thus serology is used more for epidemiologic purposes than for individual diagnosis

IMAGING STUDIES
- Chest x-ray to reveal bilateral oval or round infiltrates of varying size (Löffler's syndrome); NOTE: infiltrates are transient and eventually resolve.
- Plain films of the abdomen and contrast studies to reveal worm masses in loops of bowel.
- Ultrasonography and endoscopic retrograde cholangiopancreatography (ERCP) to identify worms in the pancreaticobiliary tract.
- CT scan with oral contrast can also assist in the detection of GI foreign bodies such as parasites.

Rx TREATMENT

NONPHARMACOLOGIC THERAPY
Aggressive IV hydration, especially in children with fever, severe vomiting, and resultant dehydration

ACUTE GENERAL Rx
- All infected patients, including asymptomatic ones, should be treated

1. Albendazole: 400 mg PO × 3 days is the first-line agent. Single-dose albendazole is used in mass treatment campaigns.
2. Mebendazole 100 mg PO BID y × 3 days: not commercially available in the U.S.
- Cure rate with these agents is 95% to 100%, but they are contraindicated in pregnancy.
- Side effects: GI discomfort, headache, and rarely leukopenia
- Alternative agent or for use in pregnancy: pyrantel pamoate (Antiminth)
  1. Given at a dose of 11 mg/kg PO (maximum dose of 1 g/day)
  2. Considered safe for use in pregnant women
- Other alternative agents:
  1. Ivermectin: 150 to 200 mcg/kg orally once
  2. Nitazoxanide: cure rates in heavy worm burden are only 50% to 80%
  3. Piperazine citrate: no longer first-line agent due to toxicity but still used in cases of intestinal or biliary obstruction, as drug paralyzes the worm, helping its expulsion. Dose: 50 to 75 mg/kg once daily up to maximum of 3.5 g for 2 days.
  4. Levamisole: 2.5 mg/kg once orally is recommended by the WHO as alternative therapy, but not available in the United States.
- Complete obstruction should be managed surgically.

DISPOSITION
Overall prognosis is good. Patients should be reevaluated in 2 to 3 months. Reinfection is common.

REFERRAL
- To gastroenterologist in cases of visualized pancreaticobiliary tract or appendiceal obstruction
- To surgeon in cases of complete obstruction or suspected secondary complication (e.g., perforation or volvulus)

! PEARLS & CONSIDERATIONS

COMMENTS
- Hepatic abscess, containing both viable and dead worms, complicating *Ascaris*-induced biliary duct disease has been documented.
- Given the known transmission of the parasite, routine hand washing with soap and proper disposal of human waste would significantly decrease the prevalence of this disease.
- Other protective measures to avoid ingestion of worm eggs:
  1. Peel or cook food.
  2. Boil drinking water.
  3. Do not place small children directly on soil.

SUGGESTED READINGS
Available at www.expertconsult.com

RELATED CONTENT
Ascariasis (Patient Information)

AUTHOR: **GLENN G. FORT, M.D., M.P.H.**

BASIC INFORMATION

DEFINITION

Ascites is the accumulation of excess fluid (>25 mL) in the peritoneal cavity, most commonly caused by liver cirrhosis.

SYNONYMS

Fluid in peritoneal cavity
Hydroperitoneum
Hydroperitonia
Hydrops abdominis

ICD-10CM CODES
R18   Ascites
C78.6   Malignant ascites
K70.11 Alcoholic hepatitis with ascites
K70.31 Alcoholic cirrhosis of liver with ascites
K71.51 Toxic liver disease with chronic active hepatitis with ascites
R18.8   Other ascites

EPIDEMIOLOGY & DEMOGRAPHICS

Ascites is the most common complication of cirrhosis. Ascites occurs in 60% of individuals with cirrhosis within ten years of diagnosis. Cirrhosis is the cause of 75% of cases of ascites. Other causes include malignancy, heart failure, tuberculosis, pancreatitis, nephrotic syndrome, and Budd-Chiari syndrome.

CLINICAL PRESENTATION

- Important information to elicit within history:
  1. History of viral hepatitis
  2. Alcoholism

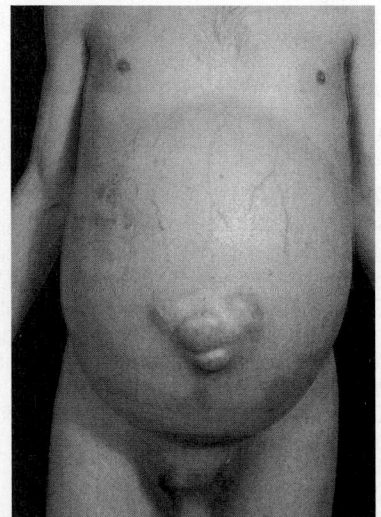

FIGURE 1A-126 Ascites in a patient with alcoholic cirrhosis showing distended abdomen; dilated superficial collateral veins; hemorrhagic scratch marks due to pruritus and coagulopathy; umbilical varices; and plaster in left iliac fossa indicating diagnostic paracentesis. (From Forbes A et al [eds]: *Atlas of clinical gastroenterology*, ed 3, Oxford, 2005, Mosby.)

  3. Increasing abdominal girth
  4. Increasing lower extremity edema
  5. Intravenous drug use
  6. Sexual history (i.e., men who have sex with men)
  7. History of transfusions
- Important physical exam findings:
  1. Bulging flanks
  2. Flank dullness to percussion
  3. Fluid wave on abdominal exam
  4. Lower extremity edema
  5. Shifting dullness on abdominal exam
  6. Physical signs associated with liver cirrhosis: spider angiomas, jaundice, loss of body hair, Dupuytren's contracture, muscle wasting, bruising, palmar erythema, gynecomastia, testicular atrophy, hemorrhoids, and caput medusae (Fig. 1A-126)

ETIOLOGY

Pathophysiology of ascites (Fig. E1A-127): increased hepatic resistance to portal flow leads to portal hypertension. The splanchnic vessels respond by increased secretion of nitric oxide, causing splanchnic artery vasodilation. Early in the disease increased plasma volume and increased cardiac output compensate for this vasodilation. However, as disease progresses the effective arterial blood volume decreases, causing sodium and fluid retention through activation of the renin-angiotensin system. The change in capillary pressure causes increased permeability and retention of fluid in the abdomen.

DIAGNOSIS

DIFFERENTIAL DIAGNOSIS

- Chronic parenchymal liver disease, leading to portal hypertension
- Peritoneal carcinomatosis
- Congestive heart failure
- Peritoneal tuberculosis
- Nephrotic syndrome
- Pancreatitis

LABORATORY TESTS

- Initial evaluation should always include:
  1. Diagnostic paracentesis (Fig. E1A-128). Laboratory tests on this fluid should include a CBC with differential, albumin, total protein, culture, and Gram stain. A serum-ascites albumin gradient (SAAG) should be calculated in all patients.

  a. If the SAAG is greater than 1.1, the cause of ascites can be attributed to portal hypertension.
  b. If SAAG is less than 1.1, a non-portal hypertension etiology of ascites must be sought (see Table 1A-60). Optional tests on paracentesis fluid include amylase, LDH, acid-fast bacilli, and glucose levels.
  2. AST, ALT, total and direct bilirubin, albumin, alkaline phosphatase, GGTP
  3. CBC, coagulation studies
  4. Electrolytes, BUN, creatinine

IMAGING STUDIES

- Abdominal ultrasound (Fig. 1A-129) is the most sensitive measure for detecting ascitic fluid; a CT or MRI scan is a viable alternative.
- Endoscopy of the upper GI tract to evaluate for esophageal varices if ascites is secondary to portal hypertension.

TREATMENT

NONPHARMACOLOGIC THERAPY

- Sodium-restricted diet (<2 g/day).
- Fluid restriction to 1 L/day in patients with hyponatremia (sodium <130 mEq/L).

ACUTE GENERAL Rx

- Patients with moderate-volume ascites causing only moderate discomfort may be treated on an outpatient basis with the following diuretic regimen: spironolactone 50 to 200 mg daily or amiloride 5 to 10 mg daily. Add furosemide 20 to 40 mg/day in the first several days of treatment, monitoring renal function carefully for signs of prerenal azotemia (in patients without edema, goal weight loss is 300 to 500 g/day; in patients with edema it is 800 to 1000 g/day). Furosemide alone is not recommended.
- Patients with large-volume ascites causing marked discomfort or decrease in activities of daily living may also be treated as outpatients if there are no complications. There are two options for treatment in these patients:
  (1) large-volume paracentesis or
  (2) diuretic therapy until loss of fluid is noted (maximum spironolactone 400 mg daily and furosemide 160 mg daily).
  No difference in long-term mortality rate was found; however, paracentesis is faster, more effective, and associated with fewer adverse effects.

TABLE 1A-60 Using the Serum-Ascites Albumin Gradient and the Ascites Total Protein Level to Diagnose the Cause of Ascites

Condition	Serum-Ascites Albumin Gradient*	Ascites Total Protein Level†
Cirrhosis	High	Low
Malignant ascites	Low	High
Cardiac ascites	High	High

*High is greater than 1.1 g/dL; low is less than 1.1 g/dL.
†High is greater than 2.5 g/dL; low is less than 2.5 g/dL.
From Goldman L, Schafer AI: *Goldman's Cecil medicine*, ed 24, Philadelphia, 2012, Saunders.

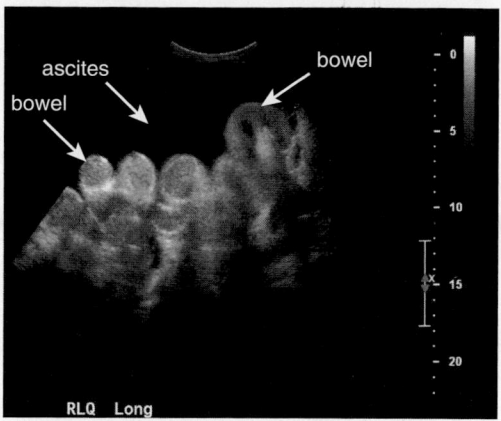

FIGURE 1A-129 Ascites, ultrasound. Ultrasound is useful for detection of ascites. Simple fluids such as ascites are excellent sound transmission media, reflecting almost no sound waves. As a consequence, they appear quite hypoechoic *(black)* on ultrasound. This view of the right lower quadrant shows loops of bowel surrounded by fluid. During the ultrasound, the bowel loops would be seen to undergo peristalsis and drift back and forth in the ascitic fluid with patient movement. Ultrasound cannot distinguish the composition of the fluid; ascites, liquid blood, liquid bile, urine, and infectious fluids have a similar appearance, with a few exceptions. Blood may coagulate and form septations within the fluid collection. Infectious fluids also frequently form loculated fluid collections that may be recognized on ultrasound, although the exact composition cannot be determined. (From Broder JS: *Diagnostic imaging for the emergency physician,* Philadelphia, 2011, Saunders.)

TABLE A1-61 Primary Medical Therapy and Adjunctive Medications Used to Increase the Efficacy of Primary Therapy in the Treatment of Ascites

Class	Medication	Dosing	Relevant Action	Notes
Diuretics	Spironolactone	400 mg + daily*	Aldosterone receptor antagonist	Primary therapy
	Furosemide	160 mg + daily*	Inhibits Na-K-2Cl symporter	Primary therapy
	Mannitol	20%*	Osmotic diuresis	Give dose just prior to furosemide and spironolactone
Vasoconstrictors	Octreotide	300 mcg bid*	Splanchnic vasoconstriction, inhibits RAAS	Also used in combination with midodrine to treat hepatorenal syndrome; given for first 5 days following variceal bleeding to decrease recurrence
	Midodrine	7.5 mg tid*	Inhibits RAAS	Also used in combination with octreotide and albumin to treat hepatorenal syndrome
α2-Agonist	Clonidine	0.075 mg bid*	Inhibits sympathetic outflow, inhibits RAAS	Increases sensitivity to spironolactone
Colloid	Albumin	25 g*	Increased oncotic pressure	Also utilized with large-volume paracentesis and in the treatment of hepatorenal syndrome
Aquaretics	None are FDA approved	N/A	Vasopressin receptor antagonist	May also treat hyponatremia

*The above doses have been derived from various studies and may not be suitable for all patients. Titration is always recommended.
From Cameron JL, Cameron AM: *Current surgical therapy,* ed 10, Philadelphia, 2011, Saunders.

- Table 1A-61 summarizes primary medical therapy and adjunctive medications used to increase the efficacy of primary therapy in the treatment of ascites.

CHRONIC Rx
5% to 10% of patients with large-volume ascites will be refractory to high-dose diuretic treatment. Treatment strategies include repeated large-volume paracentesis with infusion of albumin every 2 to 4 weeks or placement of a transjugular intrahepatic portosystemic shunt (TIPS). A treatment approach to patients with malignant ascites is described in Fig. E1A-130.

DISPOSITION
Monitor closely for worsening liver function and development of spontaneous bacterial peritonitis (SBP).

REFERRAL
Referral to gastroenterology with ascites

 **PEARLS & CONSIDERATIONS**

COMMENTS
- Prevalence of SBP in patients with ascites ranges between 10% and 30%.
  - Presence of at least 250 neutrophils per cubic millimeter of ascitic fluid is diagnostic.
  - Gram negative bacteria such as *E. coli* are the most common isolates.
  - Third-generation cephalosporins are the treatment of choice.
  - By 1 year, 70% of patients have recurrence of SBP and may be prophylaxed with

trimethoprim/sulfamethoxazole DS 1 tab PO bid 5 days/wk or ciprofloxacin 750 mg PO once/wk.

PREVENTION
Prevention of liver cirrhosis through avoidance of long-term use of alcohol, immunization against hepatitis A and B, and treatment of hepatitis C.

SUGGESTED READINGS
Available at www.expertconsult.com

RELATED CONTENT
Ascites (Patient Information)
Cirrhosis (Related Key Topic)

AUTHORS: **JOANNE M. SILVIA, M.D.,** and
PAUL F. GEORGE, M.D, M.H.P.E.

 **BASIC INFORMATION**

DEFINITION

Aspergillosis refers to several forms of a broad range of illnesses caused by infection with *Aspergillus* species.

ICD-10CM CODES
B44.0	Invasive pulmonary aspergillosis
B44.1	Other pulmonary aspergillosis
B44.2	Tonsillar aspergillosis
B44.7	Disseminated aspergillosis
B44.81	Allergic bronchopulmonary aspergillosis
B44.89	Other forms of aspergillosis
B44.9	Aspergillosis, unspecified

EPIDEMIOLOGY & DEMOGRAPHICS

INCIDENCE & PREVALENCE:
- *Aspergillus* species are ubiquitous in the environment internationally and occur as a mold found in soil.
- Cause a variety of illness from hypersensitivity pneumonitis to disseminated overwhelming infection in immunosuppressed patients.
- Frequently cultured from hospital wards from unfiltered outside air circulating through open windows as well as water sources.
- Reach the patient by airborne conidia (spores) that are small enough (2.5 to 3 μm) to reach the alveoli on inhalation.
- Can invade the nose, paranasal sinuses, external ear, or traumatized skin.

RISK FACTORS:
- The clinical syndrome depends on the underlying lung architecture, the host's immune response, and the degree of inoculum.
- Incidence of invasive aspergillosis is increasing with advances in the treatment of life-threatening diseases, such as aggressive chemotherapy or bone marrow and organ transplantation. It also can rarely occur in normal hosts, especially associated with influenza A. Liver and lung transplant recipients are at highest risk for pulmonary disease. Genetic deficiency of the soluble-pattern-recognition receptor known as long pentraxin 3 (PTX3) affects the antifungal capacity of neutrophils and may contribute to the risk of invasive aspergillosis in patients treated with hematopoietic stem-cell transplantation (HSCT).
- Patients with AIDS and a CD4 count <50/mm³ have an increased susceptibility to invasive aspergillosis.
- Pandemic influenza A (H1N1) infection may predispose immunocompromised patients to invasive aspergillosis.

ETIOLOGY
- *A. fumigatus* is the usual cause.
- *A. flavus* is the second most important species, particularly in invasive disease of immunosuppressed patients and in lesions beginning in the nose and paranasal sinuses. *A. niger* can also cause invasive human infection.

ALLERGIC ASPERGILLOSIS:
- Is a hypersensitivity pneumonitis.
- Presents as cough, dyspnea, fever, chills, and malaise typically 4 to 8 hr after exposure.
- Repeated attacks can lead to granulomatous disease and pulmonary fibrosis.

ALLERGIC BRONCHOPULMONARY ASPERGILLOSIS (ABPA):
- Symptoms occur most commonly in atopic individuals during the third and fourth decades of life.
- Hypersensitivity reaction to *Aspergillus* fungal antigens present in the bronchial tree.
- Results from an initial type I (immediate hypersensitivity) and type III reactions (immune complexes).
- Underdiagnosed pulmonary disorder in patients with asthma and cystic fibrosis (reported prevalence in asthmatic patients varies from 6% to 28% and in cystic fibrosis 6% to 25%).

ASPERGILLOMAS ("FUNGUS BALLS"):
- In the absence of invasion or significant immune response, *Aspergillus* can colonize a preexisting cavity, causing pulmonary aspergilloma.
- Forms masses of tangled hyphal elements, fibrin, and mucus.
- Patients typically have a history of chronic lung disease, tuberculosis, sarcoidosis, or emphysema.
- Manifests commonly as hemoptysis.
- Many are asymptomatic.

INVASIVE ASPERGILLOSIS:
- Patients with prolonged and profound granulocytopenia or impaired phagocytic function are predisposed to rapidly progressive *Aspergillus* pneumonia.
- Typically a necrotizing bronchopneumonia, ranging from small areas of infiltrate to intensive bilateral hemorrhagic infarction.
- Most common presentation: unremitting fever and a new pulmonary infiltrate despite broad-spectrum antibiotic therapy in an immunosuppressed patient.
- Dyspnea and nonproductive cough are common; sudden pleuritic pain and tachycardia, sometimes with a pleural rub, may mimic pulmonary embolism; hemoptysis is uncommon.
- Chest radiograph (CXR) may reveal patchy bronchopneumonic, nodular densities, consolidation, or cavitation. High-resolution CT scan is more sensitive and specific than CXR in neutropenic patients.
- Immunocompromised patients: invasive pulmonary *Aspergillus* (IPA) generally is acute and evolves over days to weeks; less commonly, patients with normal or only mild abnormalities of the immune system may develop a more chronic, slowly progressive form of IPA.

EXTRAPULMONARY DISSEMINATION:
- Cerebral infarction from hematogenous dissemination may occur in immunosuppressed individuals.
- Abscess formation from direct extension or invasive disease in the sinuses.
- Esophageal or gastrointestinal ulcerations may occur in the immunosuppressed host.
- Fatal perforation of the viscus or bowel infarction may occur.
- Necrotizing skin ulcers involving the extremities (Fig. 1A-131).
- Osteomyelitis.
- Endocarditis in patients who have recently undergone open heart surgery.
- Infection of an implantable cardioverter-defibrillator has been reported.

 **DIAGNOSIS**

DIFFERENTIAL DIAGNOSIS
- Tuberculosis
- Cystic fibrosis
- Carcinoma of the lung
- Eosinophilic pneumonia
- Bronchiectasis
- Sarcoidosis
- Lung abscess

WORKUP
Physical examination and laboratory data

LABORATORY TESTS

ABPA:
- Peripheral blood eosinophilia and an elevated total serum immunoglobulin E (IgE) level.
- Skin test with *Aspergillus* antigenic extract is usually positive but nonspecific.
- *Aspergillus* serum precipitating antibody is present in 70% to 100% of cases.
- Sputum cultures may be positive for *Aspergillus* spp. but are nonspecific.

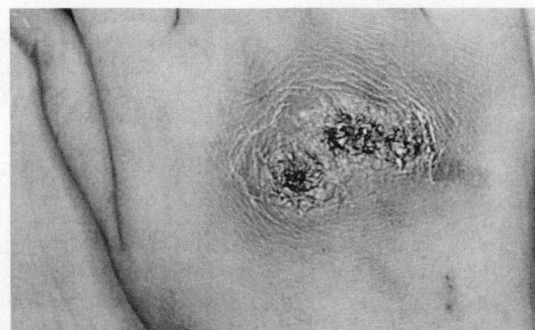

FIGURE 1A1-131 Cutaneous aspergillosis in a patient with acute leukemia and marked neutropenia. The lesion developed at the site where a steel needle had been left for several days of intravenous infusion. (From Mandell GL [ed]: *Mandell, Douglas, and Bennett's principles and practice of infectious diseases,* ed 6, New York, 2005, Churchill Livingstone.)

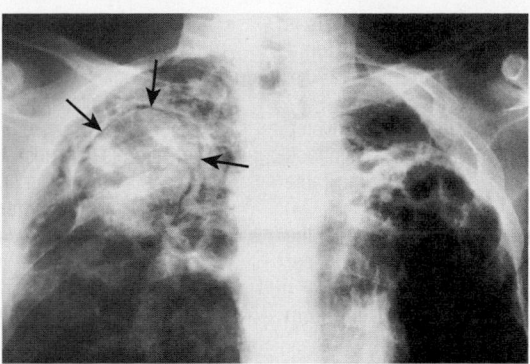

FIGURE 1A-132 Fungus ball or mycetoma caused by *Aspergillus*. Coned-down posteroanterior view of the chest of a patient with biapical fibrocavitary tuberculosis accompanied by volume loss. There is a mass in a large right upper-lobe cavity with air dissecting into the cavity producing "air crescents" *(arrows)*. (From McLoud TC: *Thoracic radiology: the requisites,* St Louis, 1998, Mosby.)

ASPERGILLOMAS:
- Sputum culture
- Serum precipitating antibody
  Invasive aspergillosis: definitive diagnosis requires the demonstration of tissue invasion (i.e., septate, acute angle branching hyphae) or a positive culture from the tissue obtained by an invasive procedure such as transbronchial biopsy.
- Sputum and nasal cultures: in high-risk patients a positive culture is strongly suggestive of invasive aspergillosis.
- Serology: the *Platelia Aspergillus* ELISA assay detects a circulating fungal antigen, galactomannan. Galactomannan is a polysaccharide contained in the cell wall of *Aspergillus*. Its presence in serum or other body fluids is indicative of invasive infection. This immunoassay is often used in some centers in neutropenic patients and for those undergoing stem cell transplantation. The β-D glucan assay can also be used to detect early infection but is not specific for *Aspergillus* species.
- Blood cultures: usually negative.
- Lung biopsy is necessary for definitive diagnosis.
- Biopsy and culture of extrapulmonary lesions.
- Real-time polymerase chain reaction tests are investigational.

IMAGING STUDIES
ABPA:
- CXRs show a variety of abnormalities, from small, patchy, fleeting infiltrates (commonly in the upper lobes) to lobar consolidation or cavitation.
- A majority of patients eventually develop central bronchiectasis.

ASPERGILLOMAS: CXR or CT scans usually show the characteristic intracavity mass partially surrounded by a crescent of air (Fig. 1A-132).
INVASIVE ASPERGILLOSIS: CXR and CT scanning may reveal cavity formation.

 **TREATMENT**

ACUTE GENERAL Rx
ABPA:
- Prednisone (0.5 to 1 mg/kg PO) until the CXR has cleared, followed by alternate-day therapy at 0.5 mg/kg PO (3 to 6 mo).

- If a patient is corticosteroid dependent, prophylaxis for the prevention of *Pneumocystis jiroveci* infection and maintenance of bone mineralization should be considered.
- Bronchodilators and physiotherapy.
- Serial CXR and serum IgE is useful in guiding treatment.
- Itraconazole 200 mg PO bid for 4 to 6 mo, then taper over 4 to 6 mo may be considered as a steroid-sparing agent or if steroids are ineffective.

ASPERGILLOMAS:
- Controversial and problematic; the optimal treatment strategy is unknown.
- Up to 10% of aspergillomas may resolve clinically without overt pharmacologic or surgical intervention.
- Observation for asymptomatic patients.
- Surgical resection/arterial embolization for those patients with severe hemoptysis or life-threatening hemorrhage.
- For those patients at risk for marked hemoptysis with inadequate pulmonary reserve, consider itraconazole 200 to 400 mg/day PO.

INVASIVE ASPERGILLOSIS (IA):
- The guidelines of the Infectious Diseases Society of America recommend the use of voriconazole as the primary therapy for invasive aspergillosis. Voriconazole reduces death compared with amphotericin when used for invasive *Aspergillus* infection. Voriconazole dose is 6 mg/kg IV bid on day 1 followed by 4 mg/kg IV q12h or 200 mg PO q12h for body weight >40 kg but 100 mg PO q12h for body weight <40 kg. Goal trough (day 4): 1.0 to 5.5 mg/l is associated with improved response rates and reduced adverse effects.
  Alternative Treatment:
- Amphotericin B lipid complex (ABLC) 5 mg/kg IV daily in those intolerant of or refractory to amphotericin B
- Liposomal amphotericin B (L-AMB) 3 to 5 mg/kg IV daily; stepwise approach is indicated as empiric therapy for presumed fungal infection in febrile neutropenic patients who are refractory to or intolerant of amphotericin B.
- Posaconazole 200 mg PO 4x/day followed by 400 mg PO bid after stabilization of disease with food or liquid nutritional supplement to enhance absorption is approved in the European Union, but in the United States

is approved only for prophylaxis in leukemic neutropenic patients, those with myelodysplasia, or those who have undergone allogeneic hematopoietic stem cell transplantation; ravuconazole is currently under investigation.
- Caspofungin (Candigas) is an echinocandin approved for the treatment of invasive aspergillosis in patients who do not respond to or are unable to tolerate other antifungal drugs. Starting dose 70 mg IV over 1 hr on day 1, then 50 mg IV daily thereafter (reduce to 35 mg IV daily in cases with moderate hepatic insufficiency). Can switch to oral voriconazole after 2 to 3 wk if the response is favorable. Micafungin 100 mg IV bid daily is another alternative but is investigational.
- Isavuconazole (isavuconazonium sulfate) was recently approved in the U.S. for the treatment of invasive aspergillosis. Initial dose 372 mg IV every 8 hr for six doses followed by a maintenance dose of 372 mg IV daily.
- Because azoles and echinocandins target different cellular sites, combination therapy may have additive activity against *Aspergillus* species. Although still under investigation, some bone marrow transplant units use caspofungin and voriconazole as the preferred initial treatment, especially in patients receiving high-dose corticosteroids. Recent trials (Marr et al., 2015) have shown that compared with voriconazole monotherapy, combination therapy with anidulafungin, and echinocandin antifungal drug that blocks the synthesis of (13)β-D glucan led to higher survival in subgroups of patients with IA.
- Cytokine therapy may offer future treatment options in conjunction with the currently available antifungals.

REFERRAL
To an infectious diseases specialist

 **PEARLS & CONSIDERATIONS**

- Unlike fluconazole, the potential for drug-drug interactions with voriconazole is high. Azoles may interact with drugs used for chemotherapy by increasing toxicity and/or by reducing efficacy.
- Agitation of hospital buildings by renovations or repairs may increase the incidence of *Aspergillus* infections in immunosuppressed individuals.
- Echinocandins should not be used as primary treatment of aspergillosis but only for salvage because there are no data to support its use.

SUGGESTED READINGS
Available at www.expertconsult.com

RELATED CONTENT
Aspergillosis (Patient Information)

AUTHOR: **SAJEEV HANDA, M.D.**

 **BASIC INFORMATION**

DEFINITION

The National Asthma Education and Prevention Program (NAEPP) guidelines define asthma as "a chronic inflammatory disease of the airways in which many cells and cellular elements play a role: in particular mast cells, neutrophils, eosinophils, T lymphocytes, macrophages, and epithelial cells. In susceptible individuals, this inflammation causes recurrent episodes of coughing (particularly at night or early in the morning), wheezing, breathlessness, and chest tightness. The episodes are usually associated with widespread but variable airflow obstruction that is reversible either spontaneously or as a result of treatment." **Status asthmaticus,** or acute severe asthma, is a refractory state that does not respond to standard therapy such as inhaled beta-agonists or subcutaneous epinephrine. It may persist for several hours.

SYNONYMS

Bronchospasm
Reactive airway disease
Asthmatic bronchitis

ICD-10CM CODES

J45.20	Mild intermittent asthma, uncomplicated
J45.21	Mild intermittent asthma with (acute) exacerbation
J45.22	Mild intermittent asthma with status asthmaticus
J45.30	Mild persistent asthma, uncomplicated
J45.31	Mild persistent asthma with (acute) exacerbation
J45.32	Mild persistent asthma with status asthmaticus
J45.40	Moderate persistent asthma, uncomplicated
J45.41	Moderate persistent asthma with (acute) exacerbation
J45.42	Moderate persistent asthma with status asthmaticus
J45.50	Severe persistent asthma, uncomplicated
J45.51	Severe persistent asthma with (acute) exacerbation
J45.52	Severe persistent asthma with status asthmaticus
J45.901	Unspecified asthma with (acute) exacerbation
J45.902	Unspecified asthma with status asthmaticus
J45.909	Unspecified asthma, uncomplicated
J45.991	Cough variant asthma
J45.998	Other asthma

EPIDEMIOLOGY & DEMOGRAPHICS

- Asthma affects more than 12% of the population in the United States, and its prevalence is steadily rising.
- It accounts for around 440,000 hospitalizations and 1.8 million emergency department visits yearly in the United States.

- It is more common in children, but the gap is closing because of a rapid increase in adult-onset asthma (9.5% of children vs 8.2% of adults).
- 50% to 80% of children with asthma develop symptoms before 5 yr of age. Early childhood risk factors for asthma are described in Table 1A-62.
- The overall asthma mortality rate in the United States has slightly improved to 11 per 1 million persons.
- Seniors have a high level of mortality from their asthma.

PHYSICAL FINDINGS & CLINICAL PRESENTATION

Physical examination varies with the stage and severity of asthma and may reveal normal lung examination results in many patients. However, some degree of wheezing and prolonged expiratory phases of respiration are seen with persistent or acute disease. Physical examination during status asthmaticus may reveal:
- Tachycardia and tachypnea
- Use of accessory respiratory muscles
- Pulsus paradoxus (inspiratory decline in systolic blood pressure >10 mm Hg)
- Absence of wheezing (silent chest) or decreased wheezing can indicate worsening obstruction
- Mental status changes: generally secondary to hypoxia and hypercapnia and constitute an indication for urgent intubation
- Paradoxic abdominal and diaphragmatic movement on inspiration (detected by palpation over the upper part of the abdomen in a semirecumbent position) indicates diaphragmatic fatigue, another sign of impending respiratory crisis
- The following abnormalities in vital signs are indicative of severe asthma:
  1. Pulsus paradoxus >18 mm Hg
  2. Respiratory rate >30 breaths/min
  3. Tachycardia with heart rate >120 beats/min

ETIOLOGY

- The pathophysiology of asthma involves a complex interaction among various environmental and genetic factors.

TABLE 1A-62 Early Childhood Risk Factors for Persistent Asthma

Parental asthma
Allergy:
  Atopic dermatitis (eczema)
  Allergic rhinitis
  Food allergy
  Inhalant allergen sensitization
  Food allergen sensitization
Severe lower respiratory tract infection:
  Pneumonia
  Bronchiolitis requiring hospitalization
Wheezing apart from colds
Male gender
Low birthweight
Environmental tobacco smoke exposure
Possible use of acetaminophen (paracetamol)
Exposure to chlorinated swimming pools
Reduced lung function at birth

From Kliegman RM et al: *Nelson textbook of pediatrics,* ed 19, Philadelphia, 2011, Saunders.

- Allergic (extrinsic) asthma is triggered by various aeroallergens or nonspecific (e.g., dust, cigarette smoke, fumes, cold air, exercise) exposures in patients who are prone to develop Ig E antibodies in response to various exposures.
- Non-allergic (intrinsic) asthma commonly manifests as adult-onset asthma in response to respiratory tract infection or psychological stress.
- Occupation exposure to certain organic or non-organic agents can trigger asthma.
- Exercise-induced asthma is seen most frequently in adolescents and manifests with bronchospasm after beginning of exercise and improves with discontinuation of exercise.
- Drug-induced asthma is associated with use of NSAIDs, β-blockers, sulfites, and certain foods and beverages.
- There is a strong association of the *ADAM 33* gene with asthma and bronchial hyper-responsiveness.
- Experimental, genetic, and clinical studies support an important role for Th2 immune pathways in the pathogenesis of severe asthma.

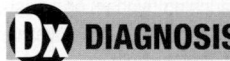 **DIAGNOSIS**

DIFFERENTIAL DIAGNOSIS

- Postinfectious bronchitis
- Rhinitis with postnasal drip
- COPD
- GERD
- Pneumonia and other upper respiratory infections
- Foreign body aspiration (most frequent in younger patients)
- Anxiety disorder
- Diffuse interstitial lung disease
- Hypersensitivity pneumonitis
- CHF
- Pulmonary embolism (in adult and elderly patients)

WORKUP

- Diagnosis of asthma requires documentation of airway obstruction and some degree of reversibility of the obstruction, if and when patient can participate.
- For symptomatic adults and children age >5 yr who can perform spirometry, pre- and postbronchodilator spirometry is the recommended test of choice.
- Airflow reversibility is defined as increase in forced expiratory volume in 1 sec (FEV_1 by at least 12% increase and 200 mL) after inhaling a short bronchodilator.
- The degree of reversibility measured by spirometry correlates with airway inflammation, and patients with a high degree of reversibility have a greater risk of irreversible airflow obstruction in subsequent years.
- For children age<5 yr, spirometry is generally not feasible. Young children with asthma symptoms should be treated as having suspected asthma after alternative diagnoses are ruled out.
- Negative spirometry results do not rule out asthma. Patients with high clinical suspicion should undergo bronchial challenge test using methacholine or other specific agents.

- The clinician should evaluate for environmental causes (e.g., house dust mites, indoor pets) and exposure to other allergens such as tobacco smoke. The degree of reversibility measured by spirometry correlates with airway inflammation, and patients with a high degree of reversibility have a greater risk of irreversible airflow obstruction in subsequent years.
- In the absence of spirometry testing, variability of peak flow measurements by a handheld device can be used to diagnose asthma.
- After the diagnosis of asthma is confirmed, the clinician should evaluate for environmental triggers (e.g., house dust mites, indoor pets) and exposure to other allergens such as tobacco smoke.
- Fig. E1A-133 describes an algorithm for diagnosing asthma.

After diagnosis, the severity of asthma should be classified during the initial assessment before initiating therapy. Patients are divided into four groups based on the severity of their asthma symptoms and number of exacerbations (see Table 1A-63).

- Once therapy is initiated, the emphasis for clinical management should gear toward achievement of asthma control. The level of asthma control should be used to guide decisions either to maintain or adjust therapy.
- Schedule visits at 2- to 6-wk intervals for patients who are just starting therapy or who require a step up in therapy to achieve or regain asthma control. Schedule visits at 6- to 12-mo intervals, after asthma control is achieved, to monitor whether asthma control is maintained. The interval will depend on factors such as the duration of asthma control or the level of treatment required. Consider scheduling visits at 3-mo intervals if step-down therapy is anticipated.

LABORATORY TESTS

Laboratory tests are usually not necessary and the results can be normal if obtained during a stable period.

- Arterial blood gases (ABGs) can be used during acute bronchospasm in staging the severity of an asthmatic attack:
  1. Mild: decreased Pao_2 and $Paco_2$, increased pH
  2. Moderate: decreased Pao_2, normal $Paco_2$, normal pH
  3. Severe: marked decreased Pao_2, increased $Paco_2$, and decreased pH
- Complete blood count: leukocytosis with left shift may indicate the existence of bacterial infection. Elevated eosinophils point toward allergic component of asthma.
- Spirometry is recommended at the initial assessment and at least every 1 to 2 yr after treatment is initiated and when the symptoms and peak expiratory flow have stabilized. Spirometry as a monitoring measure may be performed more frequently, if indicated, based on severity of symptoms and the disease's lack of response to treatment.
- Peak expiratory flow rate (PEFR) can be used to assess severity of an acute exacerbation episode. Value should be compared with individual's personal best number (see asthma action plan).

- Serum IgE levels help guide treatment for patients with severe persistent asthma, and they also help monitor response to treatment in the same group.
- Specific allergy testing may be helpful in a subgroup of patients.

IMAGING STUDIES

- Chest x-ray: usually normal, may show evidence of thoracic hyperinflation (e.g., flattening of the diaphragm, increased volume over the retrosternal air space).
- ECG: tachycardia, nonspecific ST-T wave changes are common during an asthma attack; may also show cor pulmonale, right bundle branch block, right axial deviation, counterclockwise rotation.

 **TREATMENT**

NONPHARMACOLOGIC THERAPY

- Avoidance of triggering factors (e.g., salicylates, sulfites), environmental or occupational triggers
- Encouragement of regular exercise (e.g., swimming)
- Patient education regarding warning signs of an attack and proper use of medications (e.g., correct use of inhalers)

GENERAL Rx

- The 2007 NAEPP guidelines (see Tables 1A-63 to 1A-71) provide treatment options by age groups: 0 to 4 yr, 5 to 11 yr, and >12 yr.

TABLE 1A-63 Classifying Asthma Severity and Initiating Treatment in Youths ≥12 Yr and Adults (Assessing severity and initiating treatment for patients who are not currently taking long-term control medications)

| | | CLASSIFICATION OF ASTHMA SEVERITY (≥12 yr) | | | |
| | | | PERSISTENT | | |
Components of Severity		**Intermittent**	**Mild**	**Moderate**	**Severe**
Impairment Normal FEV_1/ FVC: yr85% yr80% yr75% yr70%	Symptoms	≤2 days/wk	>2 days/wk but not daily	Daily	Throughout the day
	Nighttime awakenings	≤2x/mo	3-4x/mo	>1x/wk but not nightly	Often 7x/wk
	Short-acting beta₂-agonist use for symptom control (not prevention of EIB)	≤2 days/wk	>2 days/wk but not daily, and not more than 1x on any day	Daily	Several times per day
	Interference with normal activity	None	Minor limitation	Some limitation	Extremely limited
	Lung function	Normal FEV_1 between exacerbations			
		FEV_1>80% predicted	FEV_1>80% predicted	FEV_1>60% but <80% predicted	FEV_1<60% predicted
		FEV_1/FVC normal	FEV_1/FVC normal	FEV_1/FVC reduced 5%	FEV_1/FVC reduced>5%
Risk	Exacerbations requiring oral systemic corticosteroids	0-1 per yr	≥2 per yr		
		Consider severity and interval since last exacerbation. Frequency and severity may fluctuate over time for patients in any severity category. Relative annual risk of exacerbations may be related to FEV_1.			
Recommended Step for Initiating Therapy		Step 1	Step 2	Step 3	Step 4 or 5
					and consider short course of oral systemic corticosteroids
		In 2-6 wk, evaluate level of asthma control that is achieved and adjust therapy accordingly.			

The stepwise approach is meant to assist, not replace, the clinical decision-making required to meet individual patient needs.

Level of severity is determined by assessment of both impairment and risk. Assess impairment domain by patient's/caregiver's recall of previous 2-4 wk and spirometry. Assign severity to the most severe category in which any feature occurs.

At present, there are inadequate data to correspond frequencies of exacerbations with different levels of asthma severity. In general, more frequent and intense exacerbations (e.g., requiring urgent, unscheduled care, hospitalization, or ICU admission) indicate greater underlying disease severity. For treatment purposes, patients who had ≥2 exacerbations requiring oral systemic corticosteroids in the past year may be considered the same as patients who have persistent asthma, even in the absence of impairment levels consistent with persistent asthma.

To access the complete *Expert Panel Report 3: Guidelines for the Diagnosis and Management of Asthma*, go to www.nhlbi.nih.gov/guidelines/asthma/asthgdln.pdf.

EIB, Exercise-induced bronchospasm; *FEV₁,* forced expiratory volume in 1 second; *FVC,* forced vital capacity; *ICU,* intensive care unit.

From National Asthma Education and Prevention Program: *Expert panel report 3: Guidelines for diagnosis and management of asthma,* National Institutes of Health, National Heart, Lung, and Blood Institute, August 2007, NIH publication 08-4051.

A step-up approach is described based on the severity of symptoms.

- An approach to home management of acute asthma is described in Fig. E1A-134. Short-acting beta-selective adrenergic agonists (SABAs) administered by inhalation is the most effective therapy for quick relief of asthmatic symptoms. They are recommended for use only as needed for relief of symptoms or before anticipated exposure to known triggers such as exercise. They should not be use as a single agent except for intermittent asthma symptoms. When symptoms become more frequent or more severe, step-up treatment with maintenance inhalers is recommended (see Table 1A-65). Inhaled steroid is the mainstay of treatment for maintenance therapy. Other treatment options include long-acting beta-agonist (LABA), combination of inhaled steroids and LABA, leukotriene receptor antagonist (LTRA), cromalyn, zileuton, and theophylline. Oral corticosteroids are reserved as a last resort for maintenance therapy for recalcitrant cases. Long-acting muscarinic antagonists (LAMAs) are only approved for treatment of COPD, but various studies have showed some degree of benefit when adding LAMA to ICS + LABA. There are several corticosteroid/LABA combination inhalers available (fluticasone/salmeterol [Advair], budesonide/formoterol [Symbicort], mometasone/formoterol [Dulera]) on the market. None of these combinations is indicated for the initial treatment of asthma or for acute therapy of asthma symptoms. There is no evidence that one product is more effective than the others. Omalizumab, an anti-IgE monoclonal antibody, is indicated for the treatment of moderate and severe persistent asthma with elevated Ig E level, which is refractory to other treatment noted earlier. It is administered subcutaneously every 2 or 4 wk. This medicine is expensive ($10,000 to $30,000/yr). Patients should be closely monitored in the first month because omalizumab can result in allergic reactions (anaphylaxis) in 1 to 2 patients/1000. The NIH guidelines recommend considering omalizumab only after consultation with an asthma specialist. Recent trials (Wenzel et al) have also shown that in patients with persistent, moderate to severe asthma and elevated eosinophil levels who used inhaled glucocorticoids and LABAs, therapy with the human monoclonal antibody dupilumab, as compared with placebo, was associated with fewer asthma exacerbations when LABAs and inhaled glucocorticoids were withdrawn, with improved lung function and reduced levels of Th2-associated inflammatory markers. Another recent trial evaluated role of a novel DNA enzyme, which inactivates GATA3 messenger RNA and thus prevents transcription of various cytokines involved in the Th2 pathway. The study showed significant attenuation of both late and early asthmatic responses after allergen

TABLE 1A-64 Assessing Asthma Control and Adjusting Therapy in Youths ≥12 Yr and Adults

	Components of Control	CLASSIFICATION OF ASTHMA CONTROL (≥12 yr)		
		Well Controlled	**Not Well Controlled**	**Very Poorly Controlled**
Impairment	Symptoms	≤2 days/wk	>2 days/wk	Throughout the day
	Nighttime awakenings	≤2×/mo	1-3x/wk	≥4/wk
	Interference with normal activity	None	Some limitation	Extremely limited
	Short-acting beta$_2$-agonist use for symptom control (not prevention of EIB)	≤2 days/wk	>2 days/wk	Several times per day
	FEV$_1$ or peak flow	>80% predicted/personal best	60%-80% predicted/personal best	<60% predicted/personal best
	Validated questionnaires			
	ATAQ	0	1-2	3-4
	ACQ	≤0.75*	≥1.5	N/A
	ACT™	≥20	16-19	≤15
Risk	Exacerbations requiring oral systemic corticosteroids	0-1 per yr	≥2 per yr	
		Consider severity and interval since last exacerbation		
	Progressive loss of lung function	Evaluation requires long-term follow-up care		
	Treatment-related adverse effects	Medication side effects can vary in intensity from none to very troublesome and worrisome. The level of intensity does not correlate to specific levels of control but should be considered in the overall assessment of risk.		
Recommended Action for Treatment		Maintain current step. Regular follow-up every 1-6 mo to maintain control. Consider step down if well controlled for at least 3 mo.	Step up 1 step and reevaluate in 2-6 wk. For side effects, consider alternative treatment options.	Consider short course of oral systemic corticosteroids. Step up 1-2 steps. Reevaluate in 2 wk. For side effects, consider alternative treatment options.

The stepwise approach is meant to assist, not replace, the clinical decision-making required to meet individual patient needs.

The level of control is based on the most severe impairment or risk category. Assess impairment domain by patient's recall of previous 2-4 wk and by spirometry or peak flow measures. Symptom assessment for longer periods should reflect a global assessment, such as inquiring whether the patient's asthma is better or worse since the last visit.

At present, there are inadequate data to correspond frequencies of exacerbations with different levels of asthma control. In general, more frequent and intense exacerbations (e.g., requiring urgent, unscheduled care, hospitalization, or ICU admission) indicate poorer disease control. For treatment purposes, patients who had ≥2 exacerbations requiring oral systemic corticosteroids in the past year may be considered the same as patients who have not-well-controlled asthma, even in the absence of impairment levels consistent with not-well-controlled asthma.

Validated questionnaires for the impairment domain (the questionnaires do not assess lung function or the risk domain)

−ATAQ = Asthma Therapy Assessment Questionnaire

−ACQ = Asthma Control Questionnaire (user package may be obtained at www.qoltech.co.uk or juniper@qoltech.co.uk)

−ACT = Asthma Control Test™

−Minimal Important Difference: 1.0 for the ATAQ; 0.5 for the ACQ; not determined for the ACT

Before step up in therapy:

−Review adherence to medication, inhaler technique, environmental control, and comorbid conditions

−If an alternative treatment option was used in a step, discontinue and use the preferred treatment for that step

EIB, Exercise-induced bronchospasm; FEV$_1$, forced expiratory volume in 1 second; ICU, intensive care unit.

The Asthma Control Test is a trademark of QualityMetric Incorporated.

*ACQ values of 0.76-1.4 are indeterminate regarding well-controlled asthma.

From National Asthma Education and Prevention Program: *Expert panel report 3: Guidelines for diagnosis and management of asthma*, National Institutes of Health, National Heart, Lung, and Blood Institute, August 2007, NIH publication 08-4051.

provocation in patients with allergic asthma who were treated with once daily inhalation of this drug for 28 days.[1] Selected patients with severe persistent asthma who have failed medical treatment may benefit from bronchial thermoplasty. This requires the insertion of a catheter via bronchoscopy and use of radiofrequency heat to reduce bronchial smooth muscle. Long-term follow-up data showed persistent reduction in asthma exacerbation and ED visits over a period of 5 years.

Treatment of status asthmaticus is as follows:
- Oxygen generally started at 2 to 4 L/min by nasal cannula or Venti-Mask at 40% FiO_2; further adjustments are made according oxygen saturations.
- Bronchodilators: Initiate treatment with high-dose SABA plus ipratropium bromide

[1]N Engl J Med 2015;372:1987-1995

administered by means of a nebulizer every 20 min. Use of a metered-dose inhaler with valved holding chamber may be acceptable for patients with mild-to-moderate exacerbations.
- Albuterol nebulizer solution (0.63 mg/3 mL, 1.25 mg/3 mL, 2.5 mg/3 mL, or 5.0 mg/mL): 2.5 to 5 mg every 20 min over the first hr, then 2.5-10 mg every 1-4 hr as needed or 10-15 mg/hr continuously. Other useful medications are levalbuterol nebulizer solution (0.31 mg/3 mL, 0.63 mg/3 mL, 1.25 mg/3 mL) and ipratropium nebulizer solution (0.25/mL [0.025%]).
- Corticosteroids:
  1. Early administration is advised, particularly in patients using steroids at home.
  2. Patients may be started on systemic corticosteroids: methylprednisolone, prednisone, or prednisolone may be used. Dose range is from 40-80 mg/day in one or two divided doses, generally given until peak

expiratory flow reaches 70% of predicted value.
  3. Generally for corticosteroid courses <1 week there is no need to taper the dose.
- IV hydration: judicious use is necessary to avoid congestive heart failure in elderly patients. Aggressive IV hydration is not recommended.
- IV antibiotics are indicated when there is suspicion of bacterial infection (e.g., infiltrate on chest radiograph, fever, or leukocytosis).
- Intubation and mechanical ventilation are indicated when previous measures fail to produce significant improvement (Fig. 1A-135).
- Discharge home from the emergency department is appropriate if the FEV_1 or PEF after treatment is 70% or greater of the personal best or predicted value and if there is sustained improvement in lung function and symptoms for at least 1 hr.

TABLE 1A-65 Stepwise Approach for Managing Asthma in Youths ≥12 Yr and Adults

The stepwise approach is meant to assist, not replace, the clinical decision-making required to meet individual patient needs.
If alternative treatment is used and response is inadequate, discontinue it and use the preferred treatment before stepping up.
Zileuton is a less desirable alternative due to limited studies as adjunctive therapy and the need to monitor liver function. Theophylline requires monitoring of serum concentration levels. In step 6, before oral systemic corticosteroids are introduced, a trial of high-dose ICS + LABA + either LTRA, theophylline, or zileuton may be considered, although this approach has not been studied in clinical trials.
Steps 1, 2, and 3 preferred therapies are based on Evidence A; step 3 alternative therapy is based on Evidence A for LTRA, Evidence B for theophylline, and Evidence D for zileuton. Step 5 preferred therapy is based on Evidence B. Step 6 preferred therapy is based on (EPR-2 1997) and Evidence B for omalizumab.
Immunotherapy for steps 2-4 is based on Evidence B for house-dust mites, animal danders, and pollens; evidence is weak or lacking for molds and cockroaches. Evidence is strongest for immunotherapy with single allergens. The role of allergy in asthma is greater in children than in adults.
Clinicians who administer immunotherapy or omalizumab should be prepared and equipped to identify and treat anaphylaxis that may occur.
This information is directly abstracted from the 2007 NAEPP Expert Panel Report 3: Guidelines for the Diagnosis and Management of Asthma and is not intended to promote or endorse any of the listed products.
To access the complete Expert Panel Report 3: Guidelines for the Diagnosis and Management of Asthma, go to www.nhlbi.nih.gov/guidelines/asthma/asthgdln.pdf.
EIB, Exercise-induced bronchospasm; ICS, inhaled corticosteroid; LABA, inhaled long-acting beta2-agonist; LTRA, leukotriene receptor antagonist; SABA, inhaled short-acting beta2-agonist.
From National Asthma Education and Prevention Program: Expert panel report 3: Guidelines for diagnosis and management of asthma, National Institutes of Health, National Heart, Lung, and Blood Institute, August 2007, NIH publication 08-4051.

TABLE 1A-66 Classifying Asthma Severity and Initiating Treatment in Children 5-11 Yr (Assessing severity and initiating treatment in children who are not currently taking long-term control medications)

Components of Severity		Intermittent	PERSISTENT Mild	PERSISTENT Moderate	PERSISTENT Severe
Impairment	Symptoms	≤2 days/wk	>2 days/wk but not daily	Daily	Throughout the day
	Nighttime awakenings	≤23/mo	3-4×/mo	>1×/wk but not nightly	Often 7×/wk
	Short-acting beta$_2$-agonist use for symptom control (not prevention of EIB)	≤2 days/wk	>2 days/wk but not daily	Daily	Several times per day
	Interference with normal activity	None	Minor limitation	Some limitation	Extremely limited
	Lung function	Normal FEV$_1$ between exacerbations			
		FEV$_1$>80% predicted	FEV$_1$ = >80% predicted	FEV$_1$ 60%-80% predicted	FEV$_1$ <60% predicted
		FEV$_1$/FVC>85%	FEV$_1$/FVC>80%	FEV$_1$/FVC 75%-80%	FEV$_1$/FVC <75%
Risk	Exacerbations requiring oral systemic corticosteroids	0-1 per yr	≥2 per yr		
		Consider severity and interval since last exacerbation. Frequency and severity may fluctuate over time for patients in any severity category.			
		Relative annual risk of exacerbations may be related to FEV$_1$.			
Recommended Step for Initiating Therapy		Step 1	Step 2	Step 3, medium-dose ICS option	Step 3, medium-dose ICS option, or Step 4
				and consider short course of oral systemic corticosteroids	
		In 2-6 wk, evaluate level of asthma control that is achieved and adjust therapy accordingly.			

The stepwise approach is meant to assist, not replace, the clinical decision-making required to meet individual patient needs.

Level of severity is determined by both impairment and risk. Assess impairment domain by patient's/caregiver's recall of previous 2-4 wk and spirometry. Assign severity to the most severe category in which any feature occurs.

At present, there are inadequate data to correspond frequencies of exacerbations with different levels of asthma severity. In general, more frequent and intense exacerbations (e.g., requiring urgent, unscheduled care, hospitalization, or ICU admission) indicate greater underlying disease severity. For treatment purposes, patients who had ≥2 exacerbations requiring oral systemic corticosteroids in the past year may be considered the same as patients who have persistent asthma, even in the absence of impairment levels consistent with persistent asthma.

EIB, Exercise-induced bronchospasm; FEV$_1$, forced expiratory volume in 1 second; FVC, forced vital capacity; ICU, intensive care unit.

From National Asthma Education and Prevention Program: Expert panel report 3: Guidelines for diagnosis and management of asthma, National Institutes of Health, National Heart, Lung, and Blood Institute, August 2007, NIH publication 08-4051.

TABLE 1A-67 Assessing Asthma Control and Adjusting Therapy in Children 5-11 Yr

Components of Control		Well Controlled	Not Well Controlled	Very Poorly Controlled
Impairment	Symptoms	≤2 days/wk but not more than once on each day	>2 days/wk or multiple times on ≤2 days/wk	Throughout the day
	Nighttime awakenings	≤1×/mo	≥2×/mo	≥2×/wk
	Interference with normal activity	None	Some limitation	Extremely limited
	Short-acting beta$_2$-agonist use for symptom control (not prevention of EIB)	≤2 days/wk	>2 days/wk	Several times per day
	Lung function			
	FEV$_1$ or peak flow	>80% predicted/personal best	60%-80% predicted/personal best	<60% predicted/personal best
	FEV$_1$/FVC	>80% predicted	75%-80%	<75% predicted
Risk	Exacerbations requiring oral systemic corticosteroids	0-1 per yr	≥2 per yr	
		Consider severity and interval since last exacerbation		
	Reduction in lung growth	Evaluation requires long-term follow-up care		
	Treatment-related adverse effects	Medication side effects can vary in intensity from none to very troublesome and worrisome. The level of intensity does not correlate to specific levels of control but should be considered in the overall assessment of risk.		
Recommended Action for Treatment		Maintain current step. Regular follow-up every 1-6 mo. Consider step down if well controlled for at least 3 mo.	Step up 1 step and reevaluate in 2-6 wk. For side effects, consider alternative treatment options.	Consider short course of oral systemic corticosteroids. Step up 1-2 steps. Reevaluate in 2 wk. For side effects, consider alternative treatment options.

The stepwise approach is meant to assist, not replace, the clinical decision-making required to meet individual patient needs.

The level of control is based on the most severe impairment or risk category. Assess impairment domain by patient's/caregiver's recall of previous 2-4 wk and by spirometry or peak flow measures. Symptom assessment for longer periods should reflect a global assessment such as inquiring whether the patient's asthma is better or worse since the last visit.

At present, there are inadequate data to correspond frequencies of exacerbations with different levels of asthma control. In general, more frequent and intense exacerbations (e.g., requiring urgent, unscheduled care, hospitalization, or ICU admission) indicate poorer disease control. For treatment purposes, patients who had ≥2 exacerbations requiring oral systemic corticosteroids in the past year may be considered the same as patients who have persistent asthma, even in the absence of impairment levels consistent with persistent asthma.

Before step up in therapy:

−Review adherence to medications, inhaler technique, environmental control, and comorbid conditions.

−If an alternative treatment option was used in a step, discontinue it and use preferred treatment for that step.

EIB, Exercise-induced bronchospasm; FEV$_1$, forced expiratory volume in 1 second; ICU, intensive care unit.

From National Asthma Education and Prevention Program: Expert panel report 3: Guidelines for diagnosis and management of asthma, National Institutes of Health, National Heart, Lung, and Blood Institute, August 2007, NIH publication 08-4051.

TABLE 1A-68 Stepwise Approach for Managing Asthma in Children 5-11 Yr

Intermittent Asthma	Persistent Asthma: Daily Medication
	Consult with asthma specialist if step 4 care or higher is required. Consider consultation at step 3.

Step 6
Preferred:
High-dose ICS + LABA + oral corticosteroid

Alternative:
High-dose ICS + either LTRA or theophylline + oral systemic corticosteroid

Step 5
Preferred:
High-dose ICS + LABA

Alternative:
High-dose ICS + either LTRA or theophylline

Step 4
Preferred:
Medium-dose ICS + LABA

Alternative:
Medium-dose ICS + either LTRA or theophylline

Step 3
Preferred:
Low-dose ICS + either LABA, LTRA, or theophylline

OR

Medium-dose ICS

Step 2
Preferred:
Low-dose ICS

Alternative:
Cromolyn, LTRA, nedocromil, or theophylline

Step 1
Preferred:
SABA prn

Step up if needed
(first, check adherence, inhaler technique, environmental control, and comorbid conditions)

Assess control

Step down if possible

(and asthma is well controlled at least 3 months)

Each step: Patient education, environmental control, and management of comorbidities
Steps 2-4: Consider subcutaneous allergen immunotherapy for patients who have allergic asthma

Quick-Relief Medication for All Patients
- SABA as needed for symptoms. Intensity of treatment depends on severity of symptoms: up to 3 treatments at 20-minute intervals as needed. Short course of oral systemic corticosteroids may be needed.
- Caution: Increasing use of SABA or use >2 days a week for symptom relief (not prevention of EIB) generally indicates inadequate control and the need to step up treatment.

The stepwise approach is meant to assist, not replace, the clinical decision-making required to meet individual patient needs.
If alternative treatment is used and response is inadequate, discontinue it and use the preferred treatment before stepping up.
Theophylline is a less desirable alternative due to the need to monitor serum concentration levels.
Step 1 and step 2 medications are based on Evidence A. Step 3 ICS 1 adjunctive therapy and ICS are based on Evidence B for efficacy of each treatment and extrapolation from comparator trials in older children and adults—comparator trials are not available for this age group; steps 4-6 are based on expert opinion and extrapolation from studies in older children and adults. Immunotherapy for steps 2-4 is based on Evidence B for house-dust mites, animal danders, and pollens; evidence is weak or lacking for molds and cockroaches. Evidence is strongest for immunotherapy with single allergens. The role of allergy in asthma is greater in children than in adults. Clinicians who administer immunotherapy should be prepared and equipped to identify and treat anaphylaxis that may occur.
This information is directly abstracted from the 2007 NAEPP *Expert Panel Report 3: Guidelines for the Diagnosis and Management of Asthma* and is not intended to promote or endorse any of the listed products.
ICS, Inhaled corticosteroid; *LABA*, inhaled long-acting beta₂-agonist; *LTRA*, leukotriene receptor antagonist; *SABA*, inhaled short-acting beta₂-agonist.
From National Asthma Education and Prevention Program: *Expert panel report 3: Guidelines for diagnosis and management of asthma*, National Institutes of Health, National Heart, Lung, and Blood Institute, August 2007, NIH publication 08-4051.

REFERRAL

Box 1A-12 describes indications for referral to an asthma specialist.

ⓘ PEARLS & CONSIDERATIONS

COMMENTS

- The differentiation of asthma from COPD can be challenging. A history of atopy and intermittent, reactive symptoms points toward a diagnosis of asthma, whereas smoking and advanced age are more indicative of COPD. Spirometry is useful in distinguishing asthma from COPD.
- In all asthma patients it is important to treat or prevent comorbid conditions (e.g., rhinosinusitis, vocal cord dysfunction, gastroesophageal reflux disease). However, despite the presumed association between asthma and GERD, trials of PPIs in patients with poorly controlled asthma did not reveal any beneficial effects.

BOX 1A-12 Possible Indications for Referral to an Asthma Specialist

- Severe, acute asthma that has caused loss of consciousness, hypoxia, respiratory failure, convulsions, or near death
- Poorly controlled asthma as indicated by admission to a hospital, frequent need for emergency care, need for oral corticosteroids, absence from school or work, disruption of sleep, interference with quality of life
- Severe, persistent asthma requiring step 4 care (consider for patients who require step 3 care)
- Patient <3 yr who requires step 3 or 4 care (consider for patient <3 yr who requires step 2 care)
- Requirement for continuous oral corticosteroids or high-dose inhaled corticosteroids or more than two

short courses of oral corticosteroids within 1 yr
- Need for additional diagnostic testing such as allergy skin testing, rhinoscopy, provocative challenge, complete pulmonary function testing, bronchoscopy
- Consideration for immunotherapy
- Need for additional education regarding asthma, complications of asthma and treatment of asthma, problems with adherence to management recommendations, or allergen avoidance
- Uncertainty of diagnosis
- Complications of asthma, including sinusitis, nasal polyposis, aspergillosis, severe rhinitis, vocal cord dysfunction, gastroesophageal reflux

Modified from National Asthma Education and Prevention Program, National Heart, Lung, and Blood Institute: *Expert Panel Report 2: guidelines for the diagnosis and management of asthma*, Bethesda, MD, 1997, National Institutes of Health, NIH publication No 97-4051.

TABLE 1A-69 Classifying Asthma Severity and Initiating Treatment in Children 0-4 Yr (Assessing severity and initiating treatment in children who are not currently taking long-term control medications)

Components of Severity		Intermittent	Mild	Moderate	Severe
			PERSISTENT		
Impairment	Symptoms	≤2 days/wk	>2 days/wk but not daily	Daily	Throughout the day
	Nighttime awakenings	0	1-2×/mo	3-4×/mo	>1×/wk
	Short-acting beta₂-agonist use for symptom control (not prevention of EIB)	≤2 days/wk	>2 days/wk but not daily	Daily	Several times per day
	Interference with normal activity	None	Minor limitation	Some limitation	Extremely limited
Risk	Exacerbations requiring oral systemic corticosteroids	0-1 per yr	≥2 exacerbations in 6 mo requiring oral systemic corticosteroids, or ≥4 wheezing episodes/1 yr lasting >1 day AND risk factors for persistent asthma.		
			Consider severity and interval since last exacerbation. Frequency and severity may fluctuate over time. Exacerbations of any severity may occur in patients in any severity category.		
Recommended Step for Initiating Therapy		Step 1	Step 2	Step 3 and consider short course of oral systemic corticosteroids	
			In 2-6 wk, depending on severity, evaluate level of asthma control that is achieved. If no clear benefit is observed in 4-6 wk, consider adjusting therapy or alternative diagnoses.		

The stepwise approach is meant to assist, not replace, the clinical decision-making required to meet individual patient needs.

Level of severity is determined by assessment of both impairment and risk. Assess impairment domain by patient's/caregiver's recall of previous 2-4 wk. Symptom assessment for longer periods should reflect a global assessment such as inquiring whether the patient's asthma is better or worse since the last visit. Assign severity to the most severe category in which any feature occurs.

At present, there are inadequate data to correspond frequencies of exacerbations with different levels of asthma severity. For treatment purposes, patients who had ≥2 exacerbations requiring oral systemic corticosteroids in the past six months, or ≥4 wheezing episodes in the past year, and who have risk factors for persistent asthma may be considered the same as patients who have persistent asthma, even in the absence of impairment levels consistent with persistent asthma.

To access the complete Expert Panel Report 3: Guidelines for the Diagnosis and Management of Asthma, go to www.nhlbi.nih.gov/guidelines/asthma/asthgdln.pdf.

EIB, Exercise-induced bronchospasm.

From National Asthma Education and Prevention Program: *Expert panel report 3: Guidelines for diagnosis and management of asthma,* National Institutes of Health, National Heart, Lung, and Blood Institute, August 2007, NIH publication 08-4051.

TABLE 1A-70 Assessing Asthma Control and Adjusting Therapy in Children 0-4 Yr of Age

Components of Control		Well Controlled	Not Well Controlled	Very Poorly Controlled
		CLASSIFICATION OF ASTHMA CONTROL (0-4 yr of age)		
Impairment	Symptoms	≤2 days/wk	>2 days/wk	Throughout the day
	Nighttime awakenings	≤13/mo	>1×/mo	>1×/wk
	Interference with normal activity	None	Some limitation	Extremely limited
	Short-acting beta₂-agonist use for symptom control (not prevention of EIB)	≤2 days/wk	>2 days/wk	Several times per day
Risk	Exacerbations requiring oral systemic corticosteroids	0-1 per yr	2-3 per yr	>3 per yr
	Treatment-related adverse effects	Medication side effects can vary in intensity from none to very troublesome and worrisome. The level of intensity does not correlate to specific levels of control but should be considered in the overall assessment of risk.		
Recommended Action for Treatment		Maintain current step. Regular follow-up every 1-6 mo. Consider step down if well controlled for at least 3 mo.	Step up 1 step. Reevaluate in 2-6 wk. If no clear benefit in 4-6 wk, consider alternative diagnoses or adjusting therapy. For side effects, consider alternative treatment options.	Consider short course of oral systemic corticosteroids. Step up 1-2 steps. Reevaluate in 2 wk. If no clear benefit in 4-6 wk, consider alternative diagnoses or adjusting therapy. For side effects, consider alternative treatment options.

The stepwise approach is meant to assist, not replace, the clinical decision-making required to meet individual patient needs.

The level of control is based on the most severe impairment or risk category. Assess impairment domain by caregiver's recall of previous 2-4 wk. Symptom assessment for longer periods should reflect a global assessment such as inquiring whether the patient's asthma is better or worse since the last visit.

At present, there are inadequate data to correspond frequencies of exacerbations with different levels of asthma control. In general, more frequent and intense exacerbations (e.g., requiring urgent, unscheduled care, hospitalization, or ICU admission) indicate poorer disease control. For treatment purposes, patients who had ≥2 exacerbations requiring oral systemic corticosteroids in the past year may be considered the same as patients who have not-well-controlled asthma, even in the absence of impairment levels consistent with not-well-controlled asthma.

Before step up in therapy:

–Review adherence to medications, inhaler technique, and environmental control.

–If an alternative treatment option was used in a step, discontinue it and use preferred treatment for that step.

EIB, Exercise-induced bronchospasm; *ICU*, intensive care unit.

From National Asthma Education and Prevention Program: *Expert panel report 3: Guidelines for diagnosis and management of asthma,* National Institutes of Health, National Heart, Lung, and Blood Institute, August 2007, NIH publication 08-4051.

TABLE 1A-71 Stepwise Approach for Managing Asthma in Children 0-4 Yr

Intermittent Asthma	Persistent Asthma: Daily Medication
	Consult with asthma specialist if step 3 care or higher is required. Consider consultation at step 2.

Step 2
Preferred:
Low-dose ICS

Alternative:
Cromolyn or montelukast

Step 1
Preferred:
SABA prn

Step 3
Preferred:
Medium-dose ICS

Step 4
Preferred:
Medium-dose ICS + either LABA or montelukast

Step 5
Preferred:
High-dose ICS + either LABA or montelukast

Step 6
Preferred:
High-dose ICS + either LABA or montelukast

Oral systemic corticosteroid

Step up if needed
(first, check adherence, inhaler technique, and environmental control)

Assess control

Step down if possible

(and asthma is well controlled at least 3 months)

Patient Education and Environmental Control at Each Step

Quick-Relief Medication for All Patients
- SABA as needed for symptoms. Intensity of treatment depends on severity of symptoms.
- With viral respiratory infection: SABA q 4-6 hours up to 24 hours (longer with physician consult). Consider short course of oral systemic corticosteroids if exacerbation is severe or patient has history of previous severe exacerbations.
- Caution: Frequent use of SABA may indicate the need to step up treatment. See text for recommendations on initiating daily long-term-control therapy.

The stepwise approach is meant to assist, not replace, the clinical decision-making required to meet individual patient needs. If alternative treatment is used and response is inadequate, discontinue it and use the preferred treatment before stepping up.

If clear benefit is not observed within 4-6 wk and patient/family medication technique and adherence are satisfactory, consider adjusting therapy or alternative diagnosis.

Studies on children 0-4 yr are limited. Step 2 preferred therapy is based on Evidence A. All other recommendations are based on expert opinion and extrapolation from studies in other children.

This information is directly abstracted from the 2007 NAEPP *Expert Panel Report 3: Guidelines for the Diagnosis and Management of Asthma* and is not intended to promote or endorse any of the listed products.

ICS, Inhaled corticosteroid; *LABA,* inhaled long-acting beta₂-agonist; *SABA,* inhaled short-acting beta₂-agonist.

From National Asthma Education and Prevention Program: *Expert panel report 3: Guidelines for diagnosis and management of asthma,* National Institutes of Health, National Heart, Lung, and Blood Institute, August 2007, NIH publication 08-4051.

- Inhaled low-dose corticosteroids are the single most effective therapy for adult patients with asthma who require more than an occasional use of SABAs to control their asthma.
- Leukotriene modifiers/receptor agonists represent a reasonable alternative in adults unable or unwilling to use corticosteroids; however, these agents are less effective than monotherapy with inhaled corticosteroids.
- Use of LABAs alone without use of a long-term asthma medication, such as an inhaled corticosteroid, is contraindicated. LABAs should also not be used in patients whose asthma is adequately controlled on low- or medium-dose inhaled corticosteroids. Continued use of LABAs may cause down-regulation of the beta-2 receptor with loss of the bronchoprotective effect from rescue therapy with a SABA.
- Patients who remain symptomatic despite inhaled corticosteroids benefit from the addition of LABAs. Trials in patients with poorly controlled asthma despite the use of inhaled glucocorticoids and LABAs have shown that the addition of tiotropium, a long-acting

anticholinergic bronchodilator approved for treatment of COPD, increased the time to the first severe exacerbation and provided modest sustained bronchodilation.
- Therapy with systemic corticosteroids accelerates the resolution of acute asthma and reduces the risk of relapse. There is no evidence that doses >50-100 mg prednisone equivalent are beneficial.
- In patients with allergies and elevated serum immunoglobulin (Ig) E levels, use of anti-IgE therapy is beneficial.
- Bronchial thermoplasty should be considered in selective patients with severe persistent asthma with recurrent exacerbations or ED visits. Biologic modifiers of the Th2 immune pathways (neutralizing monoclonal antibodies, receptor antagonists, soluble receptors) are potential options for the development of new treatments of severe asthma.
- The response to treatment for asthma is characterized by wide individual variability. A functional glucocorticoid-induced transcript 1 gene (GLCCI1) variant is associated with substantial decrements in the response to inhaled glucocorticoids in patients with

asthma. Another potential cause of the variability in response to treatment is heterogeneity in the role of interleukin-13 expression in the clinical asthma phenotype. Patients with asthma who have a certain biochemical signature are more likely to respond to an anti–interleukin-13 monoclonal antibody than those without such a signature. Identification of genetic variants can eventually lead to personalized asthma treatment.

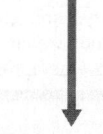 **EVIDENCE**

Available at www.expertconsult.com

SUGGESTED READINGS
Available at www.expertconsult.com

RELATED CONTENT
Asthma (Patient Information)

AUTHOR: **DHAVAL RAVAL, M.D.,** and **SAMAAN RAFEQ, M.D.**

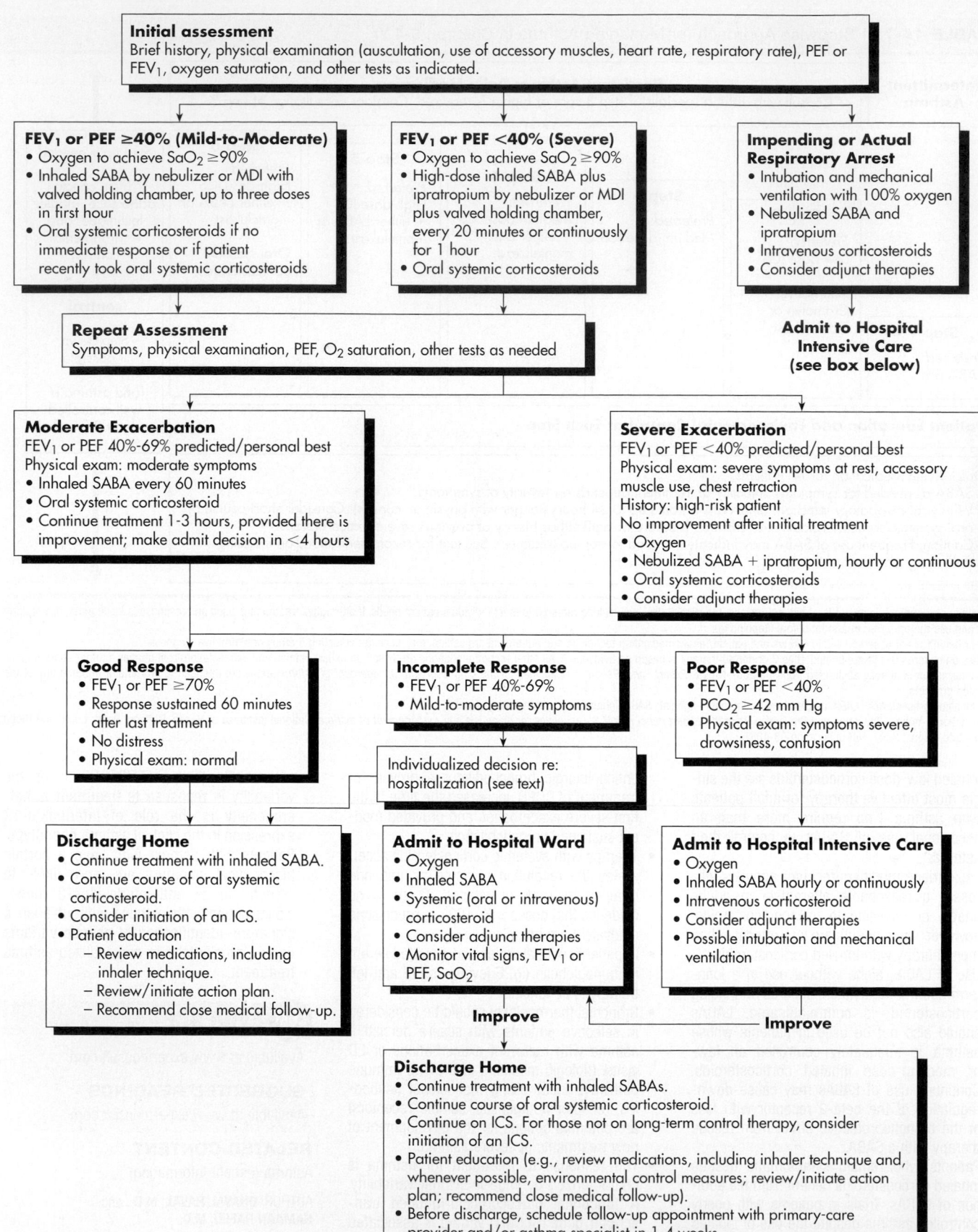

FIGURE 1A-135 Management of asthma exacerbations: emergency department and hospital-based care. *FEV₁*, Forced expiratory volume in 1 second; *ICS*, inhaled corticosteroid; *MDI*, metered-dose inhaler; *PCO₂*, partial pressure carbon dioxide; *PEF*, peak expiratory flow; *SABA*, short-acting beta₂-agonist; *SaO₂*, oxygen saturation. (From National Asthma Education and Prevention Program: *Guidelines for the diagnosis and management of asthma,* 2007, National Institutes of Health, National Heart, Lung, and Blood Institute.)

A

 BASIC INFORMATION

DEFINITION

Astrocytoma is a type of neuroepithelial tumor that arises from astrocytes which is a glial precursor cell According to the current world health organization (WHO) classification astrocytoma is classified as below based on the histopathology
• Grade I: Pilocytic astrocytoma
• Grade II: Diffuse astrocytoma
• Grade III: Anaplastic astrocytoma
• Grade IV: Glioblastoma
• Grades III and IV are considered high-grade astrocytomas (HGAs) or malignant.

The distinction of different grades of astrocytoma provides important clinical prognostic information.

SYNONYMS

Astroglial neoplasms

ICD-10CM CODES
C71.9 Malignant neoplasm of brain, unspecified

EPIDEMIOLOGY & DEMOGRAPHICS

According to SEER registry, the incidence of primary CNS tumor is 6.4 cases per 100,000 persons per year with age adjusted death rate of 4.4 per 100,000 According to the central brain tumor registry of the United States (CBTRUS) astrocytomas constitute about 10% of the central nervous system neoplasms.

ETIOLOGY

• No agent has been definitely implicated in the causation of CNS tumors, and risk factors can be identified only in minority of patients. Farmers and petrochemical workers have been shown to have a higher incidence of primary brain tumors. Exposure to ionizing radiation is a known risk factor for a small percentage of astrocytomas.
• Different hereditary syndromes are associated with increased risk and high frequency of astrocytoma
  A) Neurofibromatosis type 1 is associated with increased frequency of astrocytoma.
  B) Li-Fraumeni syndrome (germ line mutation in one of p53 allele) is associated with increased frequency of malignant gliomas.

GENE AND CHROMOSOMAL ALTERATIONS IN ASTROCYTOMA

• Alteration in p53, a tumor suppressor encoded by the TP53 gene on chromosome 17p plays a key role in the development of at least one third of all grades of astrocytoma. In addition, in high grade astrocytomas, p53 function may be deregulated by alteration of other genes, including amplification of MDM2 or MDM4 and 9p deletions that result in loss of the p14 product of the CDKN2A gene.
• Recently mutations of isocitrate dehydrogenase 1 gene (IDH1) have shown to occur in a large fractions of grade II and grade III

astrocytomas as well as in other gliomas. Antibodies specific to mutant form of IDH1 protein can now be used reliably for glioma diagnosis on routine tissue sections.

PHYSICAL FINDINGS & CLINICAL PRESENTATION

The presenting symptoms of astrocytoma depend, in part, on the location of the lesion and its rate of growth. Astrocytomas classically present with any one or more of the following features:
• Headache (less frequent)
• New-onset partial or generalized seizures (>50%)
• Nausea and vomiting
• Focal neurologic deficit (cranial nerve palsy, hemiplegia, ataxia)
• Change in mental status
• Papilledema (rare)

Dx DIAGNOSIS

A provisional diagnosis of astrocytoma is made on clinical grounds and radiographic imaging studies. Tissue pathology is needed to establish the diagnosis and to grade the astrocytoma.

DIFFERENTIAL DIAGNOSIS

The differential diagnosis is vast and includes any cause of headache, seizures, change in mental status, and focal neurologic deficits.

WORKUP

• The imaging modality of choice for most CNS tumors is contrast enhanced MRI which can demonstrate anatomy and pathological process in detail. CT scan is reserved for patients who are unable or unwilling to get MRI. Biopsy with histological confirmation is required to establish a diagnosis of astrocytoma.
• Stereotactic biopsy under CT or MRI guidance has been reserved for tumors that are deeply seated, multicentric tumors or diffuse nonfocal tumors where surgical resection is not practical. Major objectives of surgical resection are to maximally remove the

tumor bulk, reduce tumor associated mass effect and elevated intracranial pressure and provide tissue for pathological analysis. The surgical resection is carried out in a manner that minimizes the risk to neurological functioning. Surgery can also rapidly reduce the tumor bulk with potential benefits in terms of mass effect, edema and hydrocephalus.

LABORATORY TESTS

There are no diagnostic or supportive blood tests for astrocytoma.

IMAGING STUDIES

• MRI (Fig. 1A-136) is the diagnostic imaging study of choice. MRI with contrast and magnetic resonance angiography are used to locate the margins of the tumor, distinguish vascular masses from tumors, detect LGAs not seen by CT scan, and provide clear views of the posterior fossa.

Rx TREATMENT

ACUTE GENERAL Rx

• Corticosteroids (usually dexamethasone) need to be started immediately preoperatively in all primary CNS tumors unless CNS lymphoma is being suspected. Corticosteroids reduce cerebral edema and thus minimize secondary brain injury from cerebral retraction. Corticosteroids needs to be continued in the immediate postoperative period and tapered as quickly as possible. If there is increased intracranial pressure and impending herniation, patient should be started on IV mannitol, and mechanical ventilation with hyperventilation should be considered if there is depressed consciousness.
• The use of preoperative prophylactic anticonvulsants is less commonly indicated. The practice pattern in US seems to indicate its widespread use.

STAGE SPECIFIC Rx

• Grade I astrocytoma are usually indolent and circumscribed tumors. Complete surgical

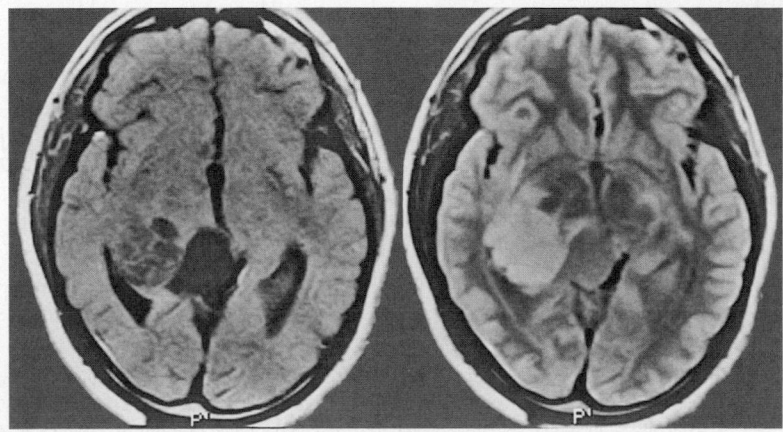

FIGURE 1A-136 MR image of a low-grade astrocytoma, demonstrating a hypointense right temporal lesion without contrast enhancement on T1 and hyperintense signal on T2. (From Goetz CG, Pappert EJ: *Textbook of clinical neurology*, Philadelphia, 1999, Saunders.)

resection, whenever feasible is curative and it is the mainstay therapy for these tumors. If complete surgical resection is not feasible due to location of tumor such as when the tumor is in optic pathway, hypothalamus and in deep midline structures, asymptomatic patients can be observed in these cases until maximally safe resection is feasible upon progression. Unfortunately, despite aggressive near total resection, delayed recurrence and eventual malignant transformation are common.

- In grade II astrocytoma, the extent of postoperative residual disease is an important variable for time to first relapse. The role of postoperative radiotherapy, in particular timing is controversial. Observation with imaging is a reasonable option in patients who are young (<40) and had a gross tumor resection. In patients who have undergone subtotal resection and who are >40 years of age postoperative radiotherapy is recommended. Radiotherapy in this setting has been shown to improve progression-free survival (PFS) without improvement in overall survival.

- In Grade III anaplastic astrocytoma, surgical resection has shown to prolong survival but almost all of these tumors are characterized by postoperative residual disease. So, postoperative radiotherapy is used adjunctively. The role of adjunct chemotherapy is controversial. Most phase 3 clinical trials have demonstrated no benefit compared with radiation alone.

- In Grade IV glioblastoma, surgical resection has been shown to improve median survival. Multiple randomized trials have demonstrated survival benefit with radiotherapy following surgery. Use of chemotherapy as an adjunct to radiation therapy has been shown to improve the median survival in patients with glioblastoma in a randomized phase 3 clinical trial. Hence, radiation therapy concurrent with temozolomide (an alkylating agent) following surgical resection is the standard of care in Grade IV glioblastoma. Unfortunately, even with chemotherapy and radiation therapy, the 2 year survival in these patients is only 16%.

TREATMENT OF RECURRENT DISEASE

- For Grade 1 astrocytoma, re-resection should be considered. For patients who have tumors that are not amenable to resection, chemotherapy or radiotherapy can improve recurrence free survival, although role of chemotherapy in adults remain controversial.

- For Grade 2 astrocytoma, radiation therapy can be considered in the relapsed setting if not given in the adjuvant setting. Data on use of chemotherapy in low grade gliomas in adults is sparse. Although the results are encouraging, number of patients treated in these studies is small and there were a lot of methodological flaws in the studies. For recurrent Grade III anaplastic astrocytoma treated with radiation therapy in the past (Fig. 1A-137), there is a role for chemotherapy. Nitrosoureas based regimen and temozolamide (alkylating agent) have shown efficacy in this setting.

- Various targeted therapies are currently being studied in patients with recurrent Glioblastoma. Irinotecan with bevacizumab or bevacizumab alone have been studied in a phase 2 trial, and a response rate of 38% and 28% respectively was reported in that study. Median survival was 8.7 months and 9.2 months respectively.

PROGNOSIS

- Grade 1 astrocytoma have a good prognosis and they are usually cured with surgical resection
- Grade 2 astrocytoma has a median survival of about 7.5 years with treatment.
- Grade 3 anaplastic astrocytoma has a median survival of approximately 5 years. The patients with 1p and 19q co deletion have superior survival compared to patients without deletion.
- Median survival of Glioblastoma is approximately 14 months.

REFERRAL

A multidisciplinary consultation is indicated in patients diagnosed with astrocytoma. A neurosurgeon, radiation oncologist, and neurooncologist are needed to assist in establishing the diagnosis and to provide immediate and follow-up treatment.

SUGGESTED READINGS

Available at www.expertconsult.com

RELATED CONTENT

Astrocytoma (Patient Information)
Brain Cancer (Patient Information)
Brain Neoplasm, Benign (Related Key Topic)
Brain Neoplasm, Glioblastoma (Related Key Topic)

AUTHORS: **RABIN NIROULA, M.D.,** and **BHARTI RATHORE, M.D.**

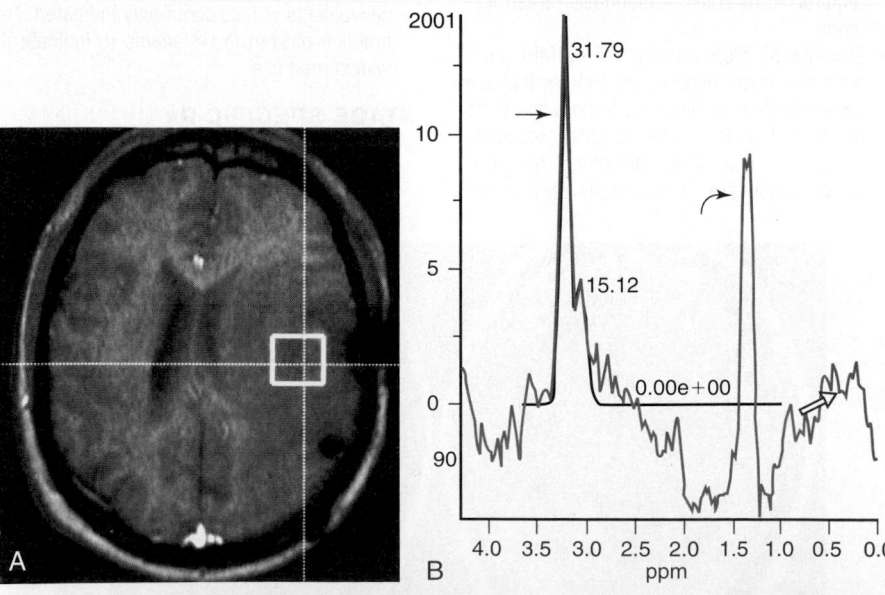

FIGURE 1A-137 Recurrent high-grade astrocytoma. Study performed after radiation therapy (not shown) showed increased edema and mass effect; differential diagnosis included recurrent tumor and radiation necrosis. **A,** Axial MRI scan shows volume of tissue *(box)* selected for spectroscopy. **B,** Proton spectroscopy reveals increase in choline peak *(arrow)*, decrease in *N*-acetyl aspartate peak *(curved arrow)*, and appearance of a lactate peak *(open arrow)*. This appearance is consistent with recurrent tumor, which was verified with repeat surgery and biopsy (From Vincent JL et al: *Textbook of critical care*, ed 6, Philadelphia, 2011, Saunders.)

BASIC INFORMATION

DEFINITION

Ataxia refers to a general incoordination of movement and a disturbance of speech; it is a dysfunction of coordination, force, and tone. It can affect the limbs, structures involved in swallowing, and vision. The most common presentation is a complaint of walking into objects or walls. Gait is the most sensitive test, broad based and inability or difficulty with tandem walking.

SYNONYMS

Gait instability
Loss of balance
Functional impairment

ICD-10CM CODES
R27.0	Ataxia, unspecified
G11.0	Congenital nonprogressive ataxia
G11.1	Early-onset cerebellar ataxia
G11.2	Late-onset cerebellar ataxia
G11.3	Cerebellar ataxia with defective DNA repair
G11.8	Other hereditary ataxias
G11.9	Hereditary ataxia, unspecified
G32.81	Cerebellar ataxia in diseases classified elsewhere
G60.2	Neuropathy in association with hereditary ataxia
I69.093	Ataxia following nontraumatic subarachnoid hemorrhage
I69.193	Ataxia following nontraumatic intracerebral hemorrhage
I69.293	Ataxia following other nontraumatic intracranial hemorrhage
I69.393	Ataxia following cerebral infarction
I69.893	Ataxia following other cerebrovascular disease
I69.993	Ataxia following unspecified cerebrovascular disease

EPIDEMIOLOGY & DEMOGRAPHICS

INCIDENCE: Hereditary ataxia can affect 1 in 50,000 people in the United States.
PEAK INCIDENCE: Can affect all age groups. Hereditary ataxias peak in young adulthood. Ataxia after age 65 is commonly secondary to stroke.
PREVALENCE: 13.9 per 10,000.
PREDOMINANT SEX AND AGE: Ataxia can affect both sexes in equal proportions.
GENETICS: The most common type of inherited ataxia in the United States is Friedreich ataxia (FA), which is autosomal recessive. The second most inherited ataxia is autosomal dominant spinocerebellar ataxia (SCA) type 3.
RISK FACTORS:
- A positive family history of ataxia
- Excessive alcohol use
- Hypothyroidism
- Anticonvulsant use
- A history of celiac disease
- A history of cerebrovascular disease

PHYSICAL FINDINGS & CLINICAL PRESENTATION

- Most individuals will complain of double vision or a sense of the environment moving and then a sense of unsteadiness and eventually frequent falls. Speech may become unintelligible, and they are frequently asked to repeat themselves. A history of difficulty cycling or performing physical activities may be present.
- Physical exam findings include slurred speech, nystagmus, square wave jerks, dysconjugate gaze, and ocular bobbing. Dysmetria and past pointing may be noted in the finger to nose and heel to shin testing. Finger chase may be abnormal. Dysdiadochokinesia may be noted on exam.
- Gait is notable for wide-based and difficulty turning and possible easy falling to one side. Frequent truncal swaying and veering is present. Tandem gait is abnormal.

ETIOLOGY

- Ataxia can be caused by hereditary, structural, and metabolic factors.
- Hereditary factors include mitochondrial diseases such as MELAS (mitochondrial encephalopathy, lactic acidosis, stroke-like episodes) and MIRAS (mitochondrial recessive ataxic syndrome).
- Structural causes may be due to lesions of the cerebellum such as stroke, masses, Arnold-Chiari malformation, and multiple sclerosis.
- Metabolic causes include hypothyroidism and vitamin E, B1, and B12 deficiency, alcohol, and celiac disease.

DIAGNOSIS

DIFFERENTIAL DIAGNOSIS

- Vitamin (B12, B1, B6, or E) deficiency
- Alcoholism
- Anticonvulsant use, such as phenytoin.
- Inherited metabolic disorder, such as Alexander's disease
- Severe neuropathy
- Epilepsy
- Celiac sprue disease
- Wilson's disease
- Cerebral anoxia
- Cerebral tumors
- Stroke
- Cerebellitis
- Conversion disorder

WORK-UP

- The work up for ataxia should be systematic and should always look for easily reversible disorders.
- Always start with a family history and investigate for any family members that were affected. This may guide genetic testing.
- Acute-onset ataxia may warrant consideration of an acute stroke, and a head noncontrast CT scan may be warranted.
- Head imaging, preferably magnetic resonance imaging (MRI), is highly recommended.

- A lumbar puncture may be necessary if infection is suspected. Send the sample for a cell count and bacterial cultures and glucose and protein.
- If a known malignancy is present, then consider a paraneoplastic panel.

LABORATORY TESTS

- Complete metabolic panel, including liver function tests
- Complete blood count and a manual differential
- Thyroid function tests
- HIV and RPR
- Vitamin B12, B1, B6, and E.
- Anti-endomysial antibodies
- Anti-tissue transglutaminase
- Deamidated gliadin peptide
- Serum copper and ceruloplasmin

IMAGING STUDIES

- MRI with contrast is preferable.
- Computed tomography (CT) scan of the head if MRI is not feasible.
- Cardiac echocardiogram is recommended for the inherited ataxias.

TREATMENT

Treatment of ataxia is highly variable. The best way to treat ataxia is to investigate the cause and, if treatable, then treat the underlying condition. For example, if there is a vitamin deficiency, then vitamin replacement is recommended.

However, sometimes the cause is genetic or unknown, and treatment is directed at minimizing complications, such as neuropathy or cardiac disease, and rehabilitative therapy for the ataxia and motor complications.

NONPHARMACOLOGIC THERAPY

- Rehabilitative services such as physical, occupational, and speech therapy are a necessary part of the treatment of all ataxias, and evidence suggests it does improve functional status for individuals affected by ataxia.

ACUTE GENERAL Rx

- Abrupt and sudden ataxia should always be subjected to a stroke workup, which includes a CT of the head within minutes of presenting.

CHRONIC Rx

- Search for the underlying cause and focus on symptomatic management to prevent future disabilities. Rehabilitative services are integral to long-term care. Always evaluate cardiac and renal function and check for signs of developing neuropathy.

COMPLEMENTARY AND ALTERNATIVE MEDICINE

- There are currently no widely accepted or evidence-based forms of complementary medicine for ataxia.

DISPOSITION

- Reversible causes of ataxia may see rapid improvement in symptoms. Genetic ataxias tend to be progressive.

REFERRAL

- Always refer to a neurologist

PEARLS & CONSIDERATIONS

COMMENTS

Look for reversible causes.

PREVENTION

A gluten-free diet would be preferable for people with celiac sprue disease.

PATIENT/FAMILY EDUCATION

Educate families on the need to be supportive and make the home environment safe.

EVIDENCE

Available at www.expertconsult.com

SUGGESTED READINGS

Available at www.expertconsult.com

RELATED CONTENT

Friedreich's Ataxia (Related Key Topic)

AUTHOR: **NAWAZ HACK, M.D.**

Diseases and Disorders

BASIC INFORMATION

DEFINITION

Atelectasis is the collapse of lung with some degree of volume loss.

ICD-10CM CODES
J98.11 Atelectasis

EPIDEMIOLOGY & DEMOGRAPHICS

- Postoperative patients and patients with lung or chest wall injury are at increased risk of atelectasis.
- Asbestos exposure increases risk for a distance entity called "rounded atelectasis."
- Occurs frequently in patients receiving mechanical ventilation.
- Dependent regions of the lung are more prone to atelectasis: they are partially compressed, they are not as well ventilated, and there is no spontaneous drainage of secretions with gravity.

PHYSICAL FINDINGS & CLINICAL PRESENTATION

- Decreased or absent breath sounds
- Abnormal chest percussion
- Cough, dyspnea, decreased vocal fremitus and vocal resonance
- Diminished chest expansion, tachypnea, tachycardia

ETIOLOGY

- Trauma caused by shear force generated by repetitive expansion and collapse during positive-pressure ventilation (e.g., mechanical ventilation)
- Airway obstruction (e.g., endobronchial tumor, foreign bodies, mucus plug)
- Extrinsic bronchial compression (e.g., neoplasms, aneurysms of ascending aorta, enlarged left atrium)
- Pleural disease (e.g., pleural effusion, mesothelioma, rounded atelectasis, pneumothorax)
- Alveolar injury (e.g., toxic fumes, aspiration of gastric contents, infections, ARDS)
- Chest wall abnormalities (e.g. trauma, scoliosis, rib fracture, obesity)
- Impaired respiratory mechanics or decreased cough response (e.g., pain, postanesthetic effect, abdominal distension, neuromuscular disease)

DIAGNOSIS

DIFFERENTIAL DIAGNOSIS

- Neoplasm
- Pneumonia
- Pleural effusion
- Abnormalities of brachiocephalic vein and the left pulmonary ligament

WORKUP

- Chest x-ray (Fig. 1A-139)
- Thoracic ultrasonography
- CT scan and fiberoptic bronchoscopy (selected patients)

IMAGING STUDIES

- Chest radiograph suggests the diagnosis but fails to confirm the diagnosis is many cases.
- Ultrasonography helps differentiate atelectasis from effusion or consolidation.
- CT scan is useful in patients with suspected endobronchial neoplasm or extrinsic bronchial compression.

- Prone images help differentiate true consolidation from dependent atelectasis.
- Fiberoptic bronchoscopy (selected patients) is useful for removal of foreign body or evaluation of endobronchial and peribronchial lesions.

TREATMENT

NONPHARMACOLOGIC THERAPY

- Deep breathing, mobilization of the patient
- Incentive spirometry
- Handheld PEEP devices (e.g., PEEP valve, Acapella®)
- Tracheal suctioning
- Humidification
- Chest physiotherapy with percussion and postural drainage

ACUTE GENERAL Rx

- Positive-pressure breathing (continuous positive airway pressure by face mask, positive end-expiratory pressure for patients on mechanical ventilation)
- Use of mucolytic agents (e.g., acetylcysteine [Mucomyst])
- Recombinant human DNase (dornase alpha) in patients with cystic fibrosis
- Bronchodilator therapy in selected patients
- Pain control in postoperative and trauma cases
- Pleural drainages in cases of large effusions, hemothorax, or empyema

CHRONIC Rx

- Chest physiotherapy
- Humidification of inspired air
- Frequent nasotracheal suctioning

DISPOSITION

Prognosis varies with the underlying etiology

REFERRAL

- Bronchoscopy for removal of foreign body or plugs unresponsive to conservative treatment
- Surgical referral for removal of obstructing neoplasm

PEARLS & CONSIDERATIONS

COMMENTS

Patients should be educated that frequent changes of position are helpful in clearing secretions. Sitting the patient upright in a chair is recommended to increase both volume and vital capacity relative to the supine position. Adequate pain control is paramount after surgical intervention or rib fractures.

RELATED CONTENT

Atelectasis (Patient Information)

AUTHOR: **DHAVAL RAVAL, M.D.,** and **SAMMAN RAFEQ, M.D.**

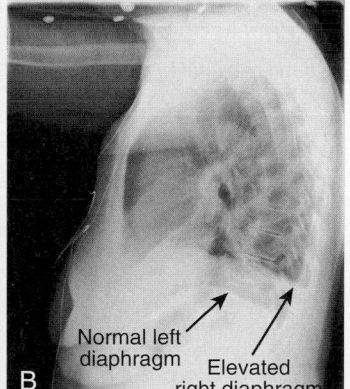

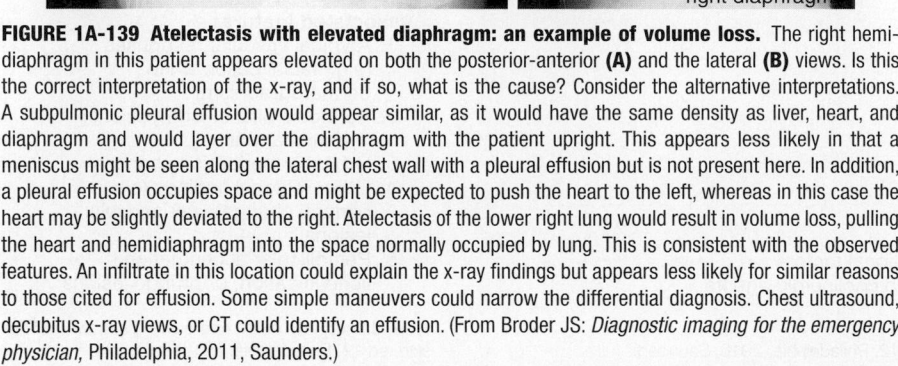

FIGURE 1A-139 Atelectasis with elevated diaphragm: an example of volume loss. The right hemidiaphragm in this patient appears elevated on both the posterior-anterior **(A)** and the lateral **(B)** views. Is this the correct interpretation of the x-ray, and if so, what is the cause? Consider the alternative interpretations. A subpulmonic pleural effusion would appear similar, as it would have the same density as liver, heart, and diaphragm and would layer over the diaphragm with the patient upright. This appears less likely in that a meniscus might be seen along the lateral chest wall with a pleural effusion but is not present here. In addition, a pleural effusion occupies space and might be expected to push the heart to the left, whereas in this case the heart may be slightly deviated to the right. Atelectasis of the lower right lung would result in volume loss, pulling the heart and hemidiaphragm into the space normally occupied by lung. This is consistent with the observed features. An infiltrate in this location could explain the x-ray findings but appears less likely for similar reasons to those cited for effusion. Some simple maneuvers could narrow the differential diagnosis. Chest ultrasound, decubitus x-ray views, or CT could identify an effusion. (From Broder JS: *Diagnostic imaging for the emergency physician,* Philadelphia, 2011, Saunders.)

BASIC INFORMATION

DEFINITION

Atopic dermatitis is a genetically determined eczematous eruption that is pruritic, symmetric, and associated with personal family history of allergic manifestations (atopy). Box 1A-13 summarizes criteria for atopic dermatitis. Modified criteria for children with atopic dermatitis are described in Box 1A-14.

SYNONYMS

Eczema
Atopic neurodermatitis
Atopic eczema

ICD-10CM CODES
L20.9   Atopic dermatitis, unspecified
L20.89   Other atopic dermatitis

EPIDEMIOLOGY & DEMOGRAPHICS

- Incidence is between 5 and 25 cases/1000 persons.
- Highest incidence is among children (10% to 20%). It accounts for 4% of acute care pediatric visits. It affects 1% to 3% of the adult population.
- Onset of disease before age 5 yr in 85% of patients.
- More than 50% of children with generalized atopic dermatitis develop asthma and allergic rhinitis by age 13 yr.
- Concordance in monozygotic twins is 77%.

PHYSICAL FINDINGS & CLINICAL PRESENTATION

- Atopic dermatitis presentation can be subdivided into three phases:
  1. Acute: vesicular, crusting, weeping eruption
  2. Subacute: dry, scaly, erythematous papules and plaques
  3. Chronic: lichenification from repeated scratching
- The lesions are typically on the neck, face, upper trunk, and bends of elbows and knees (symmetric on flexural surfaces of extremities) (Figs. 1A-140 and E1A-141). Atopic dermatitis lesions are usually discrete but vaguely delineated, scaly, and erythematous.
- There is dryness, thickening of the involved areas, discoloration, blistering, and oozing.
- Papular lesions are frequently found in the antecubital and popliteal fossae.
- In children, red scaling plaques are often confined to the cheeks and the perioral and perinasal areas.
- Hertoghe sign: loss of the outer eyebrow from chronic rubbing (Fig. 1A-140, B).
- Constant scratching may result in areas of hypopigmentation or hyperpigmentation (more common in blacks).
- In adults, redness and scaling in the dorsal aspect of the hands or about the fingers are the most common expression of atopic dermatitis; oozing and crusting may be present.
- Secondary skin infections may be present (Staphylococcus aureus, dermatophytosis, herpes simplex).

ETIOLOGY

Unknown; elevated T-lymphocyte activation, defective cell immunity, and B-cell IgE overproduction may play a significant role.

DIAGNOSIS

DIFFERENTIAL DIAGNOSIS

- Scabies
- Psoriasis
- Dermatitis herpetiform
- Contact dermatitis
- Photosensitivity
- Seborrheic dermatitis
- Candidiasis, tinea
- Lichen simplex chronicus
- Other: xerosis, impetigo, Wiskott-Aldrich syndrome, PKU, ichthyosis, HIV dermatitis, nonnummular eczema, histiocytosis X, malignancies (T-cell lymphoma/Mycosis fungoides, Letterer-Siwe disease), graft-versus-host disease, metabolic and nutritional deficiencies (zinc, niacin, pyridoxine deficiencies)

WORKUP

Diagnosis is based on the presence of three of the following major features and three minor features.

BOX 1A-13   Criteria for Atopic Dermatitis

Major criteria
Must have three of the following:
- Pruritus
- Typical morphology and distribution
  - Flexural lichenification in adults
  - Facial and extensor involvement in infancy
- Chronic or chronically relapsing dermatitis
- Personal or family history of atopic disease (e.g., asthma, allergic rhinitis, atopic dermatitis)

Minor criteria
Must also have three of the following:
1. Xerosis
2. Ichthyosis or hyperlinear palms or keratosis pilaris
3. IgE reactivity (immediate skin test reactivity, RAST test positive)
4. Elevated serum IgE
5. Early age of onset
6. Tendency for cutaneous infections (especially Staphylococcus aureus and HSV)
7. Tendency to nonspecific hand/foot dermatitis
8. Nipple eczema
9. Cheilitis
10. Recurrent conjunctivitis
11. Dennie-Morgan infraorbital fold
12. Keratoconus
13. Anterior subcapsular cataracts
14. Orbital darkening
15. Facial pallor or facial erythema
16. Pityriasis alba
17. Itch when sweating
18. Intolerance to wool and lipid solvents
19. Perifollicular accentuation
20. Food hypersensitivity
21. Course influenced by environmental or emotional factors
22. White dermatographism or delayed blanch to cholinergic agents

HSV, Herpes simplex virus; RAST, radioallergosorbent assay.
From James WD et al: Andrews' diseases of the skin, ed 12, Philadelphia, 2016, Saunders.

BOX 1A-14   Modified Criteria for Children with Atopic Dermatitis

Essential features
1. Pruritus
2. Eczema
   - Typical morphology and age-specific pattern
   - Chronic or relapsing history

Important features
1. Early age at onset
2. Atopy
3. Personal or family history
4. IgE reactivity
5. Xerosis

Associated features
1. Atypical vascular responses (e.g., facial pallor, white dermatographism)
2. Keratosis pilaris, ichthyosis, or hyperlinear palms
3. Orbital or periorbital changes
4. Other regional findings (e.g., perioral changes, periauricular lesions)
5. Perifollicular accentuation, lichenification, or prurigo lesions

From James WD et al: Andrews' diseases of the skin, ed 12, Philadelphia, 2016, Saunders.

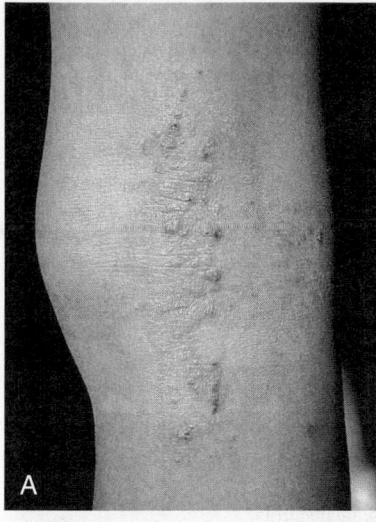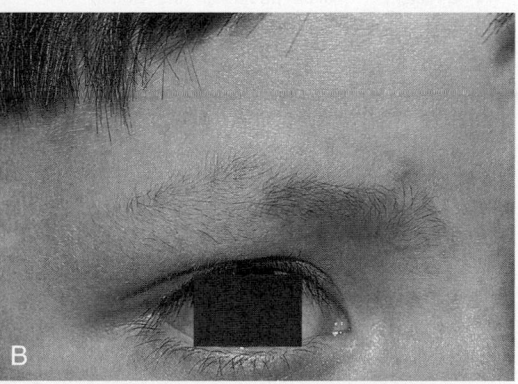

FIGURE 1A-140 A, Flexural atopic dermatitis with lichenification. Many of the skin changes are secondary to scratching. Linear lichenification, as shown here, and excoriations are typical. **B,** Hertoghe sign: loss of the outer eyebrow may occur in the atopic patient as a result of chronic rubbing. (From White GM, Cox NH [eds]: *Diseases of the skin, a color atlas and text,* ed 2, St Louis, 2006, Mosby.)

MAJOR FEATURES:
- Pruritus
- Personal or family history of atopy: asthma, allergic rhinitis, atopic dermatitis
- Facial and extensor involvement in infants and children
- Flexural lichenification in adults

MINOR FEATURES:
- Elevated IgE
- Eczema-perifollicular accentuation
- Recurrent conjunctivitis
- Ichthyosis
- Nipple dermatitis
- Wool intolerance
- Cutaneous *S. aureus* infections or herpes simplex infections
- Food intolerance
- Hand dermatitis (nonallergic irritant)
- Facial pallor, facial erythema
- Cheilitis
- White dermographism
- Early age of onset (after 2 mo of age)

LABORATORY TESTS
- Lab tests are generally not helpful.
- Elevated IgE levels are found in 80% to 90% of atopic dermatitis.
- Consider skin biopsy only in cases unresponsive to treatment.

Rx TREATMENT

NONPHARMACOLOGIC THERAPY
- Clip nails to decrease abrasion of skin
  Avoidance of triggering factors:
- Sudden temperature changes, sweating, low humidity in the winter
- Contact with irritating substance (e.g., wool, cosmetics, some soaps and detergents, tobacco)
- Foods that provoke exacerbations (e.g., eggs, peanuts, fish, soy, wheat, milk)
- Stressful situations
- Allergens and dust
- Excessive hand washing

GENERAL Rx
- Emollients can be used to prevent dryness. Severely affected skin can be optimally hydrated by occlusion in addition to application of emollients.
- Low-potency topical corticosteroids (e.g., 1% to 2.5% hydrocortisone) may be helpful and are generally considered first-line therapy. Use intermediate-potency steroids (e.g., triamcinolone, fluocinolone) for more severe cases and limit potent corticosteroids (e.g., betamethasone, desoximetasone, clobetasol) to severe cases.

- Oral antihistamines (e.g., hydroxyzine, diphenhydramine) are effective in controlling pruritus and inducing sedation, restful sleep, and prevention of scratching during sleep. Doxepin and other tricyclic antidepressants also have antihistamine effect, induce sleep, and reduce pruritus.
- The topical immunomodulators pimecrolimus and tacrolimus are especially useful for treatment of the face and intertriginous sites, where steroid-induced atrophy may occur. However, due to concerns about carcinogenic potential, the FDA recommends limiting their use for short periods in patients who are intolerant or unresponsive to other treatments. Pimecrolimus cream 1% is applied bid and has antiinflammatory effects secondary to blockage of activated T-cell cytokine production. Tacrolimus ointment (0.03% or 0.1%) applied bid is a macrolide that suppresses humoral and cell-mediated immune responses.
- Oral prednisone, IM triamcinolone, Goeckerman regimen, PUVA are generally reserved for severe cases.
- Cyclosporine, azathioprine, mycophenolate, and interferon gamma are sometimes tried for recalcitrant disease in adults by physicians who specialize in severe inflammatory skin conditions.
  Clinical trials have shown that the human monoclonal antibody dupilumab is effective in adults with moderate to severe atopic dermatitis.

DISPOSITION
- Resolution occurs in approximately 70% of patients by adulthood.
- Most patients have a course characterized by remissions and intermittent flares.

SUGGESTED READINGS
Available at www.expertconsult.com

RELATED CONTENT
Dermatitis (Patient Information)
Eczema (Patient Information)

AUTHOR: **FRED F. FERRI, M.D.**

BASIC INFORMATION

DEFINITION

Atrial fibrillation (AF) is a supraventricular tachyarrhythmia characterized by disorganized and rapid atrial activation and uncoordinated atrial contraction. AF occurs when structural and/or electrophysiologic abnormalities alter atrial tissue to promote abnormal impulse formation and/or propagation. The ventricular rate is dependent on the conduction properties of the atrioventricular (AV) node, which can be influenced by vagal/sympathetic tone, medications, or disease of the AV node.

Multiple classification schemes have been used in the past to characterize AF. The current classification scheme (divided into three major types) used by the ACC/AHA guideline committee is as follows:

- Paroxysmal AF—more than one episode of AF that terminate spontaneously or with intervention within 7 days
- Persistent AF—episodes of AF that last longer than 7 days
- Long-standing persistent AF—AF that has persisted for longer than 1 yr, either because cardioversion has failed or because cardioversion has not been attempted
- Permanent AF: When patient and physician decide to stop pursuing restoring sinus rhythm
- In addition to the previous AF categories, which are mainly defined by episode timing and termination, the ACC/AHA/ESC guidelines describe additional AF categories in terms of other characteristics of the patient:
  ○ Lone atrial fibrillation (LAF)—generally refers to AF in younger patients without clinical or echocardiographic evidence of cardiopulmonary disease, diabetes, or hypertension
  ○ Nonvalvular AF—absence of rheumatic mitral valve disease, a mechanical or bioprosthetic heart valve, or mitral valve repair
  ○ Secondary AF—occurs in the setting of a primary condition that may be the cause of the AF, such as acute myocardial infarction, cardiac surgery, pericarditis, myocarditis, hyperthyroidism, pulmonary embolism, pneumonia, or other acute disease. It is considered separately because AF is less likely to recur once the precipitating condition has resolved.

SYNONYMS

AF
PAF
AFib

ICD-10CM CODES
I48.0	Paroxysmal atrial fibrillation
I48.1	Persistent atrial fibrillation
I48.2	Chronic atrial fibrillation
I48.91	Unspecified atrial fibrillation

EPIDEMIOLOGY & DEMOGRAPHICS

- The prevalence of AF increases with age, from 2% in adults <65 yr to 9% of those >65 yr.
- AF affects 2.7 million people in the United States. AF is uncommon in infants and children and, when present, almost always occurs in association with structural heart disease.
- The incidence of AF is significantly higher in men than in women in all age groups (1.1% versus 0.8%). AF appears to be more common in whites than in blacks, who may have lower awareness of the disease.
- Stroke due to thromboembolism is the most common and dreaded complication of AF. The rate of ischemic stroke in patients with non-rheumatic AF averages 5% a year, which is somewhere between two and seven times the rate of stroke in patients without AF. The risk of stroke is not due solely to AF; it increases substantially in the presence of other cardiovascular diseases. The attributable risk of stroke from AF is estimated to be 1.5% for those aged 50 to 59 yr, and it approaches 36% for those aged 80 to 89 yr.

PHYSICAL FINDINGS & CLINICAL PRESENTATION

Clinical presentation is variable:
- Palpitations, dizziness, or lightheadedness
- Fatigue, weakness, or impaired exercise tolerance
- Angina
- Dyspnea
- Some patients are asymptomatic
- Cardiac auscultation revealing irregularly irregular rhythm
- Thromboembolic phenomenon such as stroke

ETIOLOGY

- The most frequent change in AF is the loss of atrial muscle mass and atrial fibrosis.
- Fibrillation is presumed to be caused by multiple wandering wavelets, usually originating from the pulmonary veins. Both reentrant and focal mechanisms have been proposed.
- Vascular causes: hypertensive heart disease
- Valvular heart disease
- Pulmonary causes: pulmonary embolism, chronic obstructive pulmonary disease, obstructive sleep apnea, carbon monoxide poisoning
- Structural cardiac disease: hypertrophic cardiomyopathy, congestive heart failure, coronary artery disease, myocardial infarction, congenital heart disease (especially those that lead to atrial enlargement such as atrial septal defect)
- Pericarditis and myocarditis
- Arrhythmias: atrial tachycardias and atrial flutters have been associated with atrial fibrillation, as has Wolff-Parkinson-White syndrome
- Endocrine: thyrotoxicosis, hyperthyroidism or subclinical hyperthyroidism, pheochromocytoma, obesity
- Surgery: both cardiac and noncardiac
- Electrolytes: hypokalemia, hypomagnesemia
- Systemic stress: fever, anemia, hypoxia, sepsis, infections (e.g., pneumonia)
- Medications/toxins: digitalis, adenosine, theophylline, amphetamines, cocaine, antihistamines, alcohol abuse and/or withdrawal, caffeine, steroidal antiinflammatory drugs (SAIDs), nonsteroidal antiinflammatory drugs (NSAIDs)
- Frequency of vigorous exercise is associated with an increased risk of developing AF in young men and joggers
- Porphyrias have been associated with autonomic dysfunction and increased risk of AF
- Patients with metabolic syndrome, excessive vitamin D intake, or excessive niacin intake have a higher risk of AF

DIAGNOSIS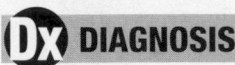

DIFFERENTIAL DIAGNOSIS

- Multifocal atrial tachycardia
- Atrial flutter
- Frequent atrial premature beats
- Atrial tachycardia
- AV nodal reentry tachycardia (AVNRT)
- Wolff-Parkinson-White syndrome

WORKUP

The evaluation of atrial fibrillation involves diagnosis, determination of the etiology, and classification of the arrhythmia. A minimal evaluation includes a history and physical examination, ECG, transthoracic echocardiogram, and case-specific laboratory work to rule out secondary AF.

LABORATORY TESTS

- Thyroid-stimulating hormone, free T_4
- Serum electrolytes
- Toxicity screen
- CBC count (looking for anemia, infection)
- Renal and hepatic function tests
- D-dimer/CT scan of chest PE protocol (if the patient has risk factors to merit a pulmonary embolism workup)

IMAGING STUDIES

- ECG (Fig. 1A-142)
- Absence of P waves
- Fibrillatory or f waves at the isoelectric baseline with varying amplitude, morphology, and intervals
- Irregular ventricular rate
- Echocardiography to rule out structural heart disease (evaluate ventricular size, thickness, and function, atrial size, pericardial disease, and valve function)
- Chest radiography (if pulmonary disease or CHF is suspected)
- Transesophageal echocardiography (TEE): helpful to evaluate for left atrial thrombus (particularly in the LA appendage) to guide cardioversion or ablation (if thrombus is seen, cardioversion should be delayed)
- CT and MRI: in patients with a positive D-dimer result, chest CT angiogram may be necessary to rule out pulmonary embolus. Three-dimensional imaging technologies (CT scan or MRI) are often helpful to evaluate atrial anatomy if AF ablation is planned
- Six-minute walk test or exercise test: six-minute walk or exercise testing can help assess the adequacy of rate control. Exercise testing can also exclude ischemia prior to treatment of

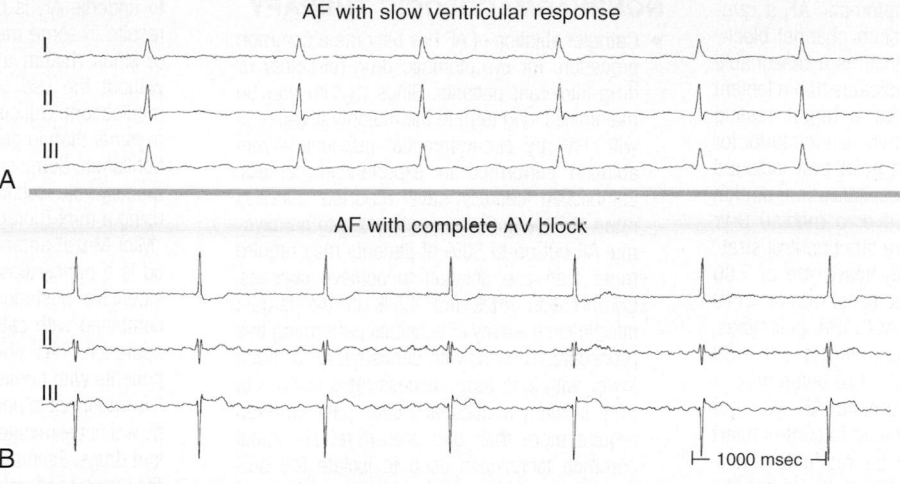

AF with slow ventricular response

I

II

III

A

AF with complete AV block

I

II

III

B

⊢ 1000 msec ⊣

FIGURE 1A-142 Atrial fibrillation (AF) with slow ventricular rate. A, The ventricular rhythm is irregular, indicating that it is the result of conducted atrial beats. **B,** The ventricular rhythm is regular, consistent with the presence of complete atrioventricular *(AV)* block and a regular junctional escape rhythm. (From Issa Z et al: *Clinical arrhythmology and electrophysiology*, ed 2, Philadelphia.)

patients with class Ic antiarrhythmic drugs and can be used to reproduce exercise-induced AF
- Sleep study (if sleep apnea is suspected)
- Holter monitor or event recorder if the diagnosis of AF is in question and to assess AF burden
- Electrophysiologic study: when initiation of AF is secondary to a supraventricular tachycardia, such as AVNRT or Wolff-Parkinson-White syndrome

 **TREATMENT**

ACUTE TREATMENT

ACUTE GENERAL RX: New-onset AF:
- If the patient is hemodynamically unstable (hypotension, congestive heart failure, or angina), perform synchronized cardioversion after immediate conscious sedation with a rapid short-acting sedative (e.g., midazolam). The likelihood of cardioversion-related clinical thromboembolism is low in patients with AF lasting <48 hr. Patients with AF lasting >2 days have a 5% to 7% risk for clinical thromboembolism if cardioversion is not preceded by several weeks of anticoagulation therapy. However, if transesophageal echocardiography reveals no atrial thrombus, cardioversion may be performed safely after therapeutic anticoagulation has been achieved. Alternatively, patients can be safely anticoagulated for approximately 1 month and then undergo cardioversion without transesophageal echocardiogram. Anticoagulant therapy should be continued for at least 1 month after cardioversion to minimize the incidence of adverse thromboembolic events. It can be stopped after 1 month as long as AF has not recurred if the patient is deemed low risk of stroke using the CHA2DS2VASc scoring system (see the following).
- If the patient is hemodynamically stable, a rate-control strategy is typically pursued initially.
- Treatment options for rate control include the following:
  1. Diltiazem 0.25 mg/kg (maximum of 25 mg) given intravenously (IV) over 2 min followed

by a second dose of 0.35 mg/kg (maximum of 25 mg) 15 min later if the rate is not slowed to <100 beats/min. May then follow with IV infusion 10 mg/hr (range, 5-15 mg/h) to achieve a resting heart rate of <100 beats/min. Onset of action after IV administration is usually within 3 min, with peak effect most often occurring within 10 min. After the ventricular rate is slowed, the patient can be changed to oral diltiazem 60 to 90 mg q4 to 6h. High doses of calcium channel blockers can exacerbate heart failure and thus should be used with caution in patients presenting with symptoms of heart failure or depressed ejection fraction.
  2. Verapamil 2.5 to 5 mg IV initially, then 5 to 10 mg IV 10 min later if the rate is still not slowed to <100 beats/min. After the ventricular rate is slowed, the patient can be changed to oral verapamil 80 to 120 mg q6 to 8h. Main concern is hypotension and heart failure with this medication. Because of its poor safety profile, it is infrequently used.
  3. Esmolol, metoprolol, and atenolol are beta-blockers available in IV preparations that can be used in AF. High doses of β-blockers can have negative inotropic effects in heart failure and should be used with caution.
  4. Digoxin is not a potent AV nodal blocking agent and has a potential for toxicity and therefore cannot be relied on for acute control of the ventricular response, but it may be used in conjunction with beta-blockers and calcium channel blockers. However, it can be a useful adjunction to a beta-blocker in the hypotensive or heart failure patient, which is not infrequent. When used, give 0.5 mg IV loading dose (slow) and then 0.25 mg IV 6 hr later. A third dose may be needed after 6 to 8 hr; the daily dose varies from 0.125 to 0.25 mg (decrease dosage in patients with renal insufficiency and elderly patients) depending on the heart rate and signs or symptoms of digoxin toxicity.

Toxicity is manifested by GI and visual complaints, atrial tachyarrhythmias, heart block, and ventricular tachycardia.
  5. Amiodarone has a class IIa recommendation from the ACC/AHA/ESC for use as a rate-controlling agent for patients who are intolerant of or unresponsive to other agents, such as patients with heart failure who may otherwise not tolerate diltiazem or metoprolol. Caution should be exercised in those who are not receiving anticoagulation because amiodarone can promote cardioversion, thereby posing a thromboembolic risk.
- All AV nodal blocking agents should be avoided in patients with Wolff-Parkinson-White syndrome and AF because, by blocking the AV node, AF impulses may be transmitted exclusively down the accessory pathway, which can result in ventricular fibrillation. If this happens, the patient will require immediate defibrillation. Procainamide, flecainide, or amiodarone can be used instead if Wolff-Parkinson-White syndrome is suspected.
- In the acute setting, pharmacologic cardioversion (e.g., ibutilide, dofetilide) is less commonly used than electrical cardioversion. A major disadvantage with pharmacologic cardioversion is the risk of development of ventricular tachycardia and other serious arrhythmias, especially due to acute prolongation of the QT interval.

CHRONIC THERAPY
- Avoidance of alcohol in patients with suspected excessive alcohol use.
- Treatment of underlying source or cause, if any found.
- Per the AFFIRM and RACE trials, either rate control or rhythm control strategies show no difference in composite cardiovascular end points of death, CHF, bleeding, drug side effects, or thromboembolism. Both approaches have similar outcomes as long as appropriate anticoagulation is maintained based on the individual's stroke risk.

- For patients without symptomatic AF, a rate-control strategy with calcium channel blockers, beta-blockers, or digoxin is a reasonable option. The RACE 2 trial indicates that a lenient rate control strategy, with a target resting heart rate of <110 beats/min, is noninferior for a composite primary end point that included CV death, heart failure hospitalization, stroke, and other major events over a median 3-yr follow-up compared with a strict control strategy, with a target resting heart rate of <80 beats/min and an exercise heart rate of <110 beats/min. Most recent ACC/AHA guidelines, however, recommend targeting a HR <80 beats/min over a target of <110 beats/min.

- In patients with symptomatic AF, younger patients, or those with difficult to control heart rate, an attempt should be made to maintain sinus rhythm with antiarrhythmic agents. Options of antiarrhythmic agents include amiodarone, dronedarone, (paroxysmal atrial fibrillation only without heart failure), dofetilide, flecainide, propafenone (contraindicated with structural heart disease), procainamide, or sotalol. The decision of which strategy to follow should be best made in consultation with cardiology. Use of dronedarone should be avoided in patients with persistent or permanent atrial fibrillation because of worsened cardiovascular outcomes, especially in those with concomitant symptomatic heart failure (see Fig. 1A-143 for a proposed algorithm to guide maintenance of sinus rhythm).

NONPHARMACOLOGIC THERAPY

- Catheter ablation of AF has become a common procedure for symptomatic drug-refractory or drug-intolerant patients. Sinus rhythm can be maintained long term in the majority of patients with PAF by circumferential pulmonary vein ablation performed in experienced centers. Established centers have reported success rates of 70% to 85% in patients with paroxysmal AF, but up to 50% of patients may require more than one ablation to achieve success. Complication rates are 4.5% in the largest international survey of hospitals performing this procedure. Success with persistent AF is much lower, with long-term success rates of 40% to 50% in many studies, and such patients often require more than one procedure. The most common techniques used to isolate the pulmonary veins are radiofrequency ablation and cryoballoon ablation, which have shown similar results for patients with PAF.

- Pulmonary vein isolation is being increasingly used to treat AF in patients with heart failure. Trials have shown that pulmonary vein isolation is superior to AV node ablation with biventricular pacing in patients with heart failure who have drug-refractory AF.

- AV nodal ablation with permanent pacemaker implantation may become necessary in some patients in whom rate and rhythm are difficult to control despite drugs and cardioversion, although it is generally used as a therapy of last resort.

- The Cox-Maze III surgical procedure, with its modifications creating electrical barriers to the macroreentrant circuits that are believed to underlie AF, is being performed with good results in some medical centers (preservation of sinus rhythm in 70% to 95% of patients without the use of long-term antiarrhythmic medication). Success rates are higher in paroxysmal than in persistent or permanent atrial fibrillation. Some centers perform surgical pulmonary vein isolation similar to this procedure using a mini-thoracotomy or video thorascopic "Mini-Maze" approach. Another surgical method is a pericardioscopic approach that allows extensive posterior wall ablation and, when combined with catheter ablation in a "hybrid" approach, has shown promising results for patients with persistent AF.

- It is important to understand that ablation therapy will not eliminate the need to take anticoagulant drugs. Even after ablation, patients with AF face increased risk of thromboembolic events and most electrophysiologists suggest lifelong anticoagulation for patients with elevated stroke risk score. Due the increasing success rate of ablation, catheter-based therapy is now considered an acceptable first-line alternative to cardioversion and pharmacologic management to *paroxysmal* atrial fibrillation in the most recent ACC/AHA Guidelines in 2014. It remains second-line therapy for patients in persistent and permanent atrial fibrillation.

STROKE PREVENTION

- The decision whether to pursue long-term anticoagulation must be made in light of the patient's risk for a cardioembolic event versus risk for a bleeding event. In nonvalvular AF, CHA2DS2-VASc has superseded the CHADS2

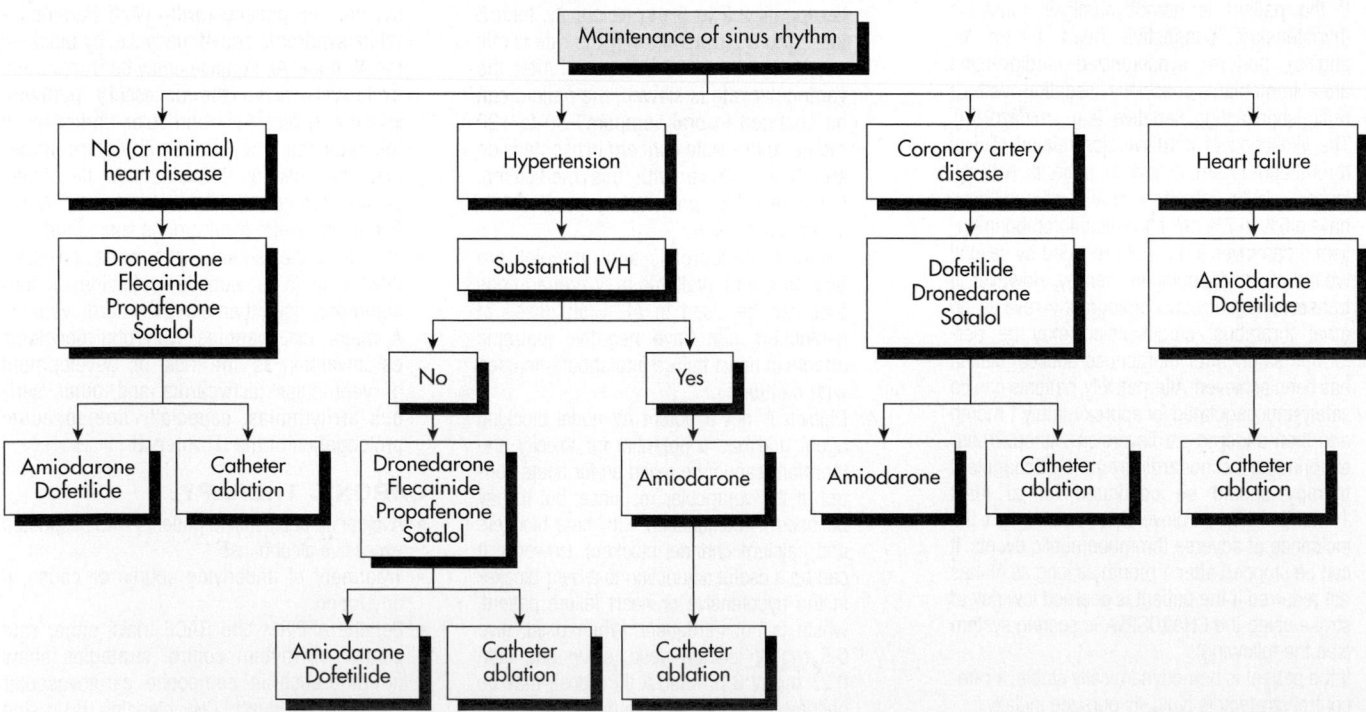

FIGURE 1A-143 Therapy to maintain sinus rhythm in patients with recurrent paroxysmal or persistent atrial fibrillation. Drugs are listed alphabetically and not in order of suggested use. The seriousness of heart disease progresses from left to right, and selection of therapy in patients with multiple conditions depends on the most serious condition present. *LVH,* Left ventricular hypertrophy. (From 2011 ACCF/AHA/HRS Focused Update on the Management of Patients With Atrial Fibrillation [Updating the 2006 Guideline]: A Report of the American College of Cardiology Foundation/American Heart Association Task Force on Practice Guidelines, *J Am Coll Cardiol* 57[2]:223-242, 2011.)

scoring system (C = congestive heart failure; H = hypertension; A = age [>75 years is 2 points]; D = diabetes; S = stroke, transient ischemic attack, or thromboembolic disease [2 points]; V = vascular disease, A = age 65-74 years; and Sc = sex category, with females getting 1 extra point). Patients with a CHA2DS2-VASc score of 0 are considered low risk, 1 to 2 are considered moderate risk, and >2 are considered high risk. Per guidelines, patients with a score of 0 do not merit anticoagulation. Patients with a score of 1 can be treated at the discretion of the physician with either aspirin or an oral anticoagulant (warfarin versus a novel oral anticoagulant). Anticoagulation with either warfarin or a novel oral anticoagulant is recommended for all patients with a CHADS2VASC score of 2 or above.

- Increasing amounts of evidence now show that aspirin likely does not protect a person from stroke in AF and has recently been dropped from most of the ACC/AHA and European Atrial Fibrillation guidelines. Target INR for patients with a CHADS-VASc score of >1 is 2 to 3 and should be diligently monitored to avoid risk of stroke versus bleeding. Patients with hypertrophic cardiomyopathy or thyrotoxicosis with AF also have a high risk of stroke and should be anticoagulated irrespective of their CHADS-VASc score.
- Alternatives to warfarin now include several factor Xa inhibitors and a direct thrombin inhibitor.
  1. Dabigatran is an FDA-approved direct thrombin inhibitor indicated to reduce the risk of stroke and systemic embolism in patients with nonvalvular atrial fibrillation. In the RE-LY trial of 18,113 patients with mean CHADS2 score of 2.1, dabigatran 110 mg BID was noninferior to warfarin, and 150 mg BID was superior to warfarin in prevention of thromboembolic events. Bleeding risk was similar to that of warfarin for both doses.
  2. Factor Xa inhibitors (apixaban, rivaroxaban, edoxaban) are also effective in reducing stroke and systemic embolism in patients with atrial fibrillation. The ARISTOTLE trial in patients at high risk for stroke (mean CHADS2 score 2.1) using apixaban, the ROCKET AF trial using rivaroxaban in patients with CHADS2 score 3.5, and the ENGAGE-AF trial using edoxaban in patients with a CHADS2 score of at least 2, showed that these anticoagulants reduce the risk of stroke, systemic embolism, and serious bleeding compared with warfarin. Rivaroxaban showed noninferior efficacy to warfarin in prevention of thromboembolism. Apixaban showed superior stroke reduction, reduced bleeding events, and an overall mortality benefit when compared with warfarin. Edoxaban showed noninferiority to warfarin with respect to stroke and systemic embolism prevention, with lower rates of bleeding and death from cardiovascular causes, but benefit was limited to patients with moderately impaired renal function. Rivaroxaban and edoxaban are dosed once a day, and apixaban is dosed twice a day.

- The decision to anticoagulate should be made irrespective of whether the atrial fibrillation is paroxysmal, persistent or permanent.
- For patients in whom anticoagulation with warfarin or other anticoagulants is contraindicated due to high bleeding risk, left atrial appendage exclusion is an alternative. Several methods can be used, including the Lariat procedure and the Atriclip, but these are still considered unproven for stroke prevention in AF. The Watchman device is a left atrial appendage occlusion device and is the only device approved by the FDA for stroke prevention specifically for patients with AF that require anticoagulation but have an appropriate reason to seek an alternative.
- Perioperative bridging anticoagulation in patients with AF: current guidelines advise perioperative continuation of warfarin in low-risk patients (CHADS2 score 0 to 2) and bridging anticoagulation in those at highest risk of thromboembolism (CHADS2 score 5 to 6). The recent BRIDGE Study found that for patients who require procedure-related warfarin interruption, forgoing bridging anticoagulation was noninferior to perioperative bridging with LMWH and decrease the risk of major bleeding. Based on this study, a no bridging strategy is responsible for lower-risk AF and minor procedures but in patients having major surgery the answer remains debatable.

PROGNOSIS

- AF is associated with a 1.5- to 1.9-fold higher risk of death, which is in part due to the strong association between AF and thromboembolic events.
- AF is also independently associated with an increased risk of incident MI, especially in women and blacks.
- Development of AF predicts heart failure and is associated with a worse New York Heart Association Heart Failure classification. AF may also worsen heart failure in individuals who are dependent on the atrial component of the cardiac output.
- AF in the setting of acute myocardial infarction was associated with a 40% increase in mortality compared to patients in sinus rhythm.

DISPOSITION

Factors associated with maintenance of sinus rhythm after cardioversion include:
- Left atrium diameter <60 mm
- Absence of mitral valve disease
- Short duration of AF

REFERRAL

Refer to a cardiologist those patients in whom antiarrhythmic therapy or catheter-based/surgical intervention is being considered.

PEARLS & CONSIDERATIONS

COMMENTS

The number of patients anticoagulated in the United States is approximately half the amount

that should be anticoagulated for AF, resulting in a large burden of stroke. The exact burden of AF needed to trigger the need for anticoagulation is not known, though recent pacemaker trials have suggested that as little as 6 min confers significant stroke risk. Reversal agents for the new class of anticoagulation are now available: idarucizumab for reversal of dabigatran; andexanet alfa for reversal of apixaban and rivaroxaban.

The American Academy of Family Physicians and the American College of Physicians provide the following recommendations for the management of newly detected AF:

- Rate control with chronic anticoagulation is the recommended strategy for the majority of asymptomatic patients with chronic AF. Rhythm control has not been shown to be superior to rate control (with chronic anticoagulation) in reducing morbidity and mortality, and may be inferior in some patient subgroups to rate control. Rhythm control is appropriate when based on other special considerations, such as patient symptoms, exercise tolerance, and patient preference.
- Patients with AF should receive chronic anticoagulation, unless they are at low risk for stroke as stated earlier or have specific contraindications.
- For patients with AF, the following drugs are recommended for their demonstrated efficacy in rate control during exercise and while at rest: atenolol, metoprolol, diltiazem, and verapamil (drugs listed alphabetically by class). Digoxin is effective only for rate control at rest and, therefore, should be used only as a second-line agent for rate control in AF.
- For patients who elect to undergo acute cardioversion to achieve sinus rhythm in AF, both direct-current cardioversion and pharmacologic conversion are appropriate options in an otherwise healthy patient.
- Both transesophageal echocardiography with short-term prior anticoagulation followed by early acute cardioversion (in absence of intracardiac thrombus) with postcardioversion anticoagulation vs. delayed cardioversion with preanticoagulation and postanticoagulation are appropriate management strategies for patients who elect to undergo cardioversion.
- Among patients with paroxysmal AF without previous antiarrhythmic drug treatment, ablation compared with antiarrhythmic drugs resulted in a lower rate of recurrent atrial tachyarrhythmias at 2 years. However, recurrence was frequent in both groups.

 **EVIDENCE**

Available at www.expertconsult.com

SUGGESTED READINGS
Available at www.expertconsult.com

RELATED CONTENT
Atrial Fibrillation (Patient Information)

AUTHOR: **TANIA B. BABAR, M.D.**

Diseases and Disorders

I

BASIC INFORMATION

DEFINITION

Typical atrial flutter is the term commonly applied to the atrial macroreentrant circuit that circulates around the tricuspid annulus in the right atrium. The critical isthmus of the circuit is the tissue between the inferior vena cava and the tricuspid annulus, and a more precise name for this arrhythmia is *cavotricuspid isthmus-dependent atrial flutter*, or CTI flutter. Because of its anatomic and physiologic stability, the result is regular atrial depolarizations, typically at a rate of 250 to 350 beats/min. Regular, macroreentrant atrial arrhythmias at this rate that do not use the CTI are referred to as *atypical atrial flutter*. Because of the circuit's stability, conduction through the atrioventicular node (AVN) is often predictable at a common mathematical denominator. For example, when the flutter rate is 300 beats/min, 2:1 conduction results in a ventricular rate of 150 beats/min. By extension, 3:1 conduction results in a ventricular rate of 100 beats/min, 4:1 in a rate of 75 beats/min, and 5:1 in a rate of 60 beats/min. If the regular atrial impulses conduct at a variable rate through the AVN, the result may be an irregular QRS pattern.

ICD-10CM CODES
I48.3   Typical atrial flutter
I48.4   Atypical atrial flutter
I48.92   Unspecified atrial flutter

EPIDEMIOLOGY & DEMOGRAPHICS

- Atrial flutter is the second most common atrial tachyarrhythmia after atrial fibrillation, with an estimated 200,000 new cases annually in the United States.
- Atrial flutter is common in patients with congestive heart failure, COPD, or during the first week after open-heart surgery.
- Atrial flutter occurs more frequently with advancing age (5/10,0000 age <50 vs

587/100,000 age >80 yr) and 2.5 times more frequently in men than in women.
- Patients taking antiarrhythmics for chronic suppression of atrial fibrillation may convert to atrial flutter.
- Atrial flutter is typically seen in patients with underlying structural heart disease and is uncommon in children or young adults.
- More than 50% of patient with atrial flutter will develop atrial fibrillation in 3 years, and more than 80% will develop atrial fibrillation within 5 years.

CLASSIFICATION

Historically, the Wells classification designated atrial flutter as type I and type II. However, it is now recognized that tachycardias satisfying either of the definitions for type I or type II can be caused by reentrant circuits or to rapid focal atrial tachycardia, and this classification is infrequently used. Designating atrial flutter based on whether or not it is CTI dependent is more useful because of the management (i.e., ablation) options. Type I CTI-dependent atrial flutter, also known as common atrial flutter or typical atrial flutter, has an atrial rate of 240 to 350 beats/min. The reentrant loop circles the right atrium, passing through the CTI, a body of fibrous tissue in the lower atrium between the inferior vena cava and the tricuspid valve. CTI flutter can revolve around the tricuspid annulus in either direction (counterclockwise or clockwise) when viewing the tricuspid annulus *en face*.

- Counterclockwise atrial flutter is the more common type (~75%). The flutter waves are "sawtooth" and negative on the surface ECG leads II, III, and aVF; positive in V1; and negative in V6.
- Clockwise atrial flutter is less common (~25%): The reentry loop cycles in the opposite direction; thus, the flutter waves are upright in leads II, III, and aVF; negative in V1; and positive in V6.

Atypical atrial flutter is defined by absence of CTI dependence and may occur in patients with prior cardiac surgery, congenital heart disease,

or prior radiofrequency ablation (especially left atrial ablation for atrial fibrillation) or may be idiopathic. One ECG feature is the lack of discordance between the inferior leads (leads II, III, and aVF) and V1.

PHYSICAL FINDINGS & CLINICAL PRESENTATION

- Palpitations
- Dizziness, lightheadedness, syncope, or near syncope
- Angina
- Congestive heart failure
- Embolic phenomena from intracardiac thrombus

ETIOLOGY

- Age-related degenerative changes
- Rheumatic heart disease
- Congenital heart disease
- Left ventricular dysfunction or congestive heart failure
- Acute myocardial infarction (rarely)
- Thyrotoxicosis
- Pulmonary embolism
- Mitral valve disease
- Cardiac surgery
- Chronic obstructive pulmonary disease
- Obesity
- Pericarditis
- Pulmonary hypertension
- Antiarrhythmic therapy use in patients with atrial fibrillation

DIAGNOSIS

DIFFERENTIAL DIAGNOSIS

- Atrial fibrillation
  Atrial tachycardia:
- Supraventricular tachycardia:
  ○ Atrioventricular node reentry
  ○ Orthodromic reciprocating tachycardia (using a concealed bypass tract)
  ○ Junctional ectopic tachycardia
  ○ Wolff-Parkinson-White syndrome
- Sinus tachycardia

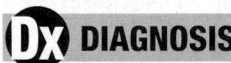
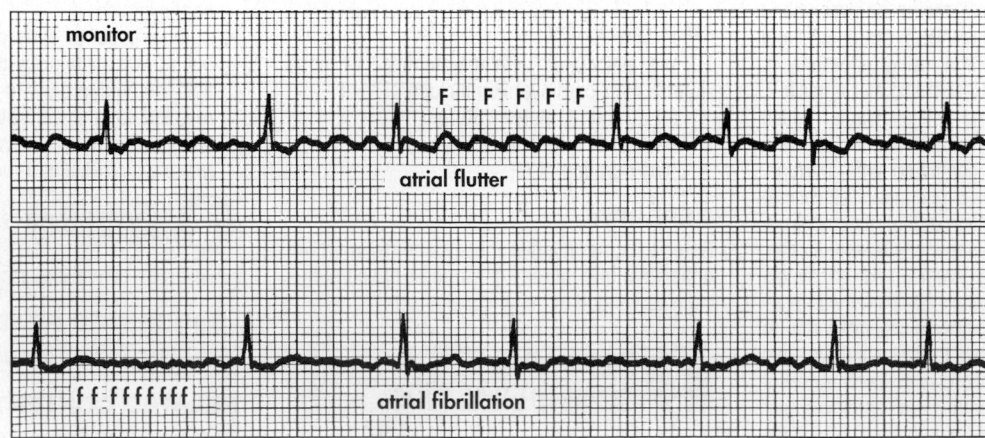

FIGURE 1A-144 Atrial flutter and fibrillation. Notice the sawtooth waves with atrial flutter *(F)* and the irregular fibrillatory waves with atrial fibrillation *(f).* (From Goldberger AL [ed]: *Clinical electrocardiography,* ed 5, St Louis, 1994, Mosby.)

A

WORKUP
- ECG
- Laboratory evaluation
- Assessment of CHA$_2$DS$_2$-VaSc score

LABORATORY TESTS
- Thyroid function studies
- Serum electrolytes, including renal and hepatic tests (anticipating antiarrhythmic therapy use)

IMAGING STUDIES
- ECG (Fig. 1A-144):
  1. Absence of P waves.
  2. Regular, "sawtooth," or "F" (flutter)" wave pattern without an isoelectric baseline in leads II, III, and AVF (seen most commonly with counterclockwise typical CTI-flutter)
  3. There is rarely 1:1 atrioventricular (AV) conduction in atrial flutter (unless pre-excitation is present). Rather, AV conduction is usually in a 2:1, 3:1, or 4:1 fashion, with corresponding usual ventricular rates of 150, 100, or 75 beats/min, respectively (assuming an atrial rate of 300 beats/min).
- Echocardiography (for new diagnoses) to evaluate for structural heart disease (ventricular size, thickness, and function; atrial size, and valve function).
- Transesophageal echocardiography: consider in patients with associated structural or functional heart disease to ascertain the presence of intracardiac thrombi, in the absence of an appropriate duration of anticoagulation.
- Holter monitoring or event recorder to assess for paroxysmal atrial flutter or rate control or to identify the arrhythmia if symptoms are nonspecific or to identify triggering events.
- Electrophysiologic studies: required for a precise diagnosis, for mapping pathway, and for ablation.

Rx TREATMENT

NONPHARMACOLOGIC THERAPY
- Vagal maneuvers (e.g., the Valsalva maneuver or carotid sinus massage) may transiently slow the ventricular rate (by increasing AV block) and may make flutter waves more evident. Adenosine may be similarly helpful for diagnostic purposes, allowing the unmasking of the atrial rhythm in the absence of ventricular activity. Maneuvers that affect AV conduction would be unlikely to terminate atrial flutter.
- Direct current cardioversion is the treatment of choice for acute management of atrial flutter associated with hemodynamic instability or debilitating symptoms such as angina, congestive heart failure, or hypotension. Electrical cardioversion may be successful with energies as low as 25 joules, but because 100 joules is virtually always successful, this may be a reasonable initial shock strength. If the electrical shock results in atrial fibrillation, a second shock at a

higher energy level is used to restore normal sinus rhythm. Sedation of a conscious patient is highly recommended before cardioversion is performed. The use of external defibrillators with biphasic waveforms decreases the amount of energy required for cardioversion and improves cardioversion success rate. Patients should be therapeutically anticoagulated for at least a month or longer depending on their stroke risk (CHA$_2$DS$_2$-VaSc score).
- Overdrive pacing in the atrium may also terminate atrial flutter. This method is especially useful in patients who have recently undergone cardiac surgery and still have temporary atrial pacing wires and in patients who have an implanted pacemaker or defibrillator with an atrial lead.
- Radiofrequency ablation to interrupt the atrial flutter is highly effective for patients with chronic or recurring atrial flutter and is generally considered first-line therapy in those with recurrent episodes of atrial flutter and may be offered for a first-ever episode of atrial flutter. It has been shown to improve health-related quality of life. Despite successful ablation of atrial flutter, however, the risk of future atrial fibrillation remains.

ACUTE Rx
- Treatment choices are based on clinical circumstances. If the patient is unstable, proceed directly to electrical cardioversion.
- In the hemodynamically stable patient, proceed with rate control or rhythm control strategy.
- AV blocking agents such as calcium channel blockers, beta-blockers, and digitalis (second-line treatment) may all be used for rate control. Atrial flutter may spontaneously convert to normal sinus rhythm with this strategy.
- In general, atrial flutter is more difficult to rate control than atrial fibrillation.
- The rate of recurrence of atrial flutter with cardioversion alone is difficult to determine because most published data combine atrial flutter with atrial fibrillation. However, the recurrence rate is substantial, perhaps 50% at 1 yr.
- Intravenous ibutilide is a first-line medication for pharmacologic cardioversion of atrial flutter in patients with normal systolic function and QT intervals. The success rate is approximately 60%, and it is more effective than procainamide, sotalol, or amiodarone.

CHRONIC Rx
- Few data exist to decide on the choice of rate control versus rhythm control in patients with atrial flutter. However, rate control may be difficult in atrial flutter, and ablation success exceeds 90%. Although ablation results in more durable freedom from atrial flutter recurrence, there are several pharmacologic options to help maintain sinus rhythm after cardioversion of atrial flutter, such as dofetilide, amiodarone, flecainide, propafenone, or sotalol. The choice of antiarrhythmic

therapy is, in part, dictated by the presence or absence of underlying structural heart disease.
- Elective outpatient cardioversion or ablation can be performed either immediately preceded by TEE to evaluate the left atrium and the left atrial appendage for thrombus or after a period of at least 3 weeks of documented therapeutic anticoagulation before cardioversion. At least 4 weeks of anticoagulation should be performed after cardioversion, if not longer, depending on the overall thromboembolic risk of the patient as determined by the CHADS$_2$-VASC$_2$ score.

DISPOSITION
More than 85% of patients convert to regular sinus rhythm after cardioversion. Ablation success rates exceed 90%.

REFERRAL
Refer patients who are considered for rhythm control of atrial flutter to cardiologists, especially patients who are candidates for radiofrequency ablation.

! PEARLS & CONSIDERATIONS

COMMENTS
- The surface ECG is the best tool for recognizing atrial flutter and distinguishing atrial flutter from atrial fibrillation.
- Ablation for typical atrial flutter is highly effective, straightforward, and relatively safe. It should be considered for patients with recurrent episodes and even for a first-ever episode.
- Patients with atrial flutter carry a significant risk for subsequent development of atrial fibrillation.
- Anticoagulation should be considered for all patients whose CHA$_2$DS$_2$-VaSc score is ≥2. Anticoagulation is generally not recommended in patients with a CHA$_2$DS$_2$-VaSc score of zero. For patients with a CHA$_2$DS$_2$-VaSc score of 1, low-dose aspirin or oral anticoagulants (warfarin, dabigatran, rivaroxaban, apixaban, or edoxaban) are appropriate options.

SUGGESTED READINGS
Available at www.expertconsult.com

RELATED CONTENT
Palpitations, dizziness, and/or syncope (Algorithm, Section III)
Tachycardia, diagnostic approach (Algorithm, Section III)
Tachycardia, narrow complex (Algorithm, Section III)
Atrial Flutter (Patient Information)
Atrial Fibrillation (Related Key Topic)

AUTHOR: **DANIEL R. FRISCH, M.D.**

BASIC INFORMATION

DEFINITION
Atrial myxoma is a benign neoplasm of mesenchymal origin and is the most common primary tumor of the heart.

SYNONYMS
Cardiac myxoma

ICD-10CM CODES
D15.1 Benign neoplasm of heart

EPIDEMIOLOGY & DEMOGRAPHICS
- Primary cardiac tumors are extremely rare, with an autopsy frequency of 0.001% to 0.03%. The most frequent cardiac tumors are metastases, occurring 30 times more frequently than primary tumors.
- Myxomas are the most common primary cardiac tumors, accounting for 30% to 50% of all benign neoplasms of the heart.
- 65% of cardiac myxomas occur in females. 4.5% to 10% of cardiac myxomas are familial (Carney syndrome).
- Average age of incidence of sporadic cases is 30 to 50 yr but can occur at any age.
- Average age of incidence of familial cases is 25 yr.
- Most arise in the left atrium (75%), but myxomas can also be found in the right atrium (18%), right ventricle (4%), and left ventricle (3%). They are usually pedunculated and attached to the intra-atrial septum.

PHYSICAL FINDINGS & CLINICAL PRESENTATION
Patients with atrial myxomas, when symptomatic, characteristically present in one of three ways:
1. Atrioventricular valve obstruction (e.g., mitral or tricuspid valve): may present with dyspnea, orthopnea, paroxysmal nocturnal dyspnea, wheezing, edema, dizziness, syncope, chest pain, atrial fibrillation, and sudden death (rare). A marked change in the severity of any symptom caused by a change in position of the patient, especially if recumbency relieves dyspnea, is suggestive of myxoma
2. Systemic embolization: leading to cerebrovascular accidents, pulmonary embolism, paradoxical embolism and acute coronary syndrome.
3. Constitutional symptoms: fever, weight loss, arthralgias and Raynaud's phenomenon.
4. Other rare manifestations include peripheral neuropathy, typical angina caused by coronary steal phenomenon (especially large vascularized atrial myxomas), and paraneoplastic syndromes.

On exam there may be widely split loud S1, secondary pulmonary hypertension, murmurs of regurgitation (holosystolic) or stenosis (rumbles), an early diastolic sound 80-120 milliseconds after A2 called "tumor plop" which may resemble an opening snap.

ETIOLOGY:
- Most cases (90%) of atrial myxomas are sporadic with no known cause
- Carney complex, transmitted in an autosomal dominant pattern, accounts for the majority of familial myxomas and as much as 7% of cardiac myxomas. Carney syndrome manifests as cardiac and extracardiac myxomas, pigmented skin discoloration, endocrine hyperactivity, and other tumors, such as schwannomas. There are at least three different genetic loci with two identified genes for this complex.

DIAGNOSIS

DIFFERENTIAL DIAGNOSIS
- Primary valvular diseases: mitral stenosis, mitral regurgitation, tricuspid stenosis, tricuspid regurgitation
- Pulmonary hypertension
- Endocarditis
- Vasculitis
- Atrial thrombus
- Pulmonary embolism
- Cerebrovascular accidents
- Collagen-vascular disease
- Carcinoid heart disease
- Benign tumors of the heart (papillary fibroelastoma, rhabdomyoma, fibroma, teratoma, and lipoma)
- Malignant tumors of the heart (angiosarcoma, rhabdosarcoma, fibrosarcoma, and leiomyosarcoma)
- Metastatic tumors to the heart (melanoma, lung, breast, renal, esophageal, and sarcomas)

WORKUP
A high index of suspicion is needed because the clinical manifestations are nonspecific and similar to many common cardiovascular and pulmonary diseases.

LABORATORY TESTS
Although not very specific, the following laboratory findings may be abnormal in patients with atrial myxomas:
- Complete blood count: anemia, polycythemia, thrombocytopenia may occur
- Erythrocyte sedimentation rate, C-reactive protein, and serum immunoglobulins are commonly elevated
- Electrocardiogram: left or right atrial enlargement, atrial fibrillation, premature ventricular depolarizations, or ventricular tachycardia

IMAGING STUDIES
- Transthoracic echocardiography: With 95% diagnostic sensitivity, it is the initial test of choice in suspected cases of atrial myxoma.
- Chest radiograph: about one third of patients have normal findings. Evidence of altered cardiac contour, pulmonary edema, and chamber enlargement may be present
- Transesophageal echocardiography: is the recommended measure for initial assessment and may better define cardiac masses not clearly visualized by transthoracic echocardiography.

- CT: often used for diagnosis; defines tumor extension and evaluates adjacent cardiac structures.
- MRI (Fig. E1A-145): delineates size, shape, and tissue characteristics, helping distinguish thrombus from tumor.
- Cardiac catheterization: will show neovascularization in 50% of the cases and may be required to rule out concomitant coronary artery disease in anticipation of surgical excision.

TREATMENT

ACUTE GENERAL THERAPY
- Surgical excision is the treatment of choice
- Surgery should be done promptly because systemic embolization and/or sudden death can occur while waiting for the procedure

CHRONIC Rx
Postoperative arrhythmias and conduction abnormalities were present in 26% of patients and can be treated accordingly.

DISPOSITION
- Surgical results have reported a 95% survival rate after a follow-up of 3 yr.
- Careful follow-up is necessary because up to 5% of sporadic cases and 20% of familial cases of atrial myxoma may recur within the first 6 yr after surgery.
- Sudden death in untreated patients may occur in up to 15%, resulting from coronary or systemic embolization or obstruction of the mitral or tricuspid valve.

REFERRAL
- Consultation with a cardiologist is recommended.
- Once the presence of cardiac tumor is confirmed, consultation with a cardiovascular surgeon is needed for prompt surgical excision.

PEARLS & CONSIDERATIONS

- Approximately two thirds of patients present with cardiovascular symptoms, specifically dyspnea, often suggestive of valvular obstruction.
- Nearly one third of patients have evidence of systemic embolization.

COMMENTS
Annual echocardiograms should be performed to monitor for recurrence of atrial myxomas after surgical excision.

SUGGESTED READINGS
Available at www.expertconsult.com

RELATED CONTENT
Atrial Myxoma (Patient Information)

AUTHORS: **ESHAN PATVARDHAN, M.B.B.S.,** and **BARRY FINE, M.D., Ph.D.**

BASIC INFORMATION

DEFINITION

An atrial septal defect (ASD) is a true deficiency in the interatrial septum that allows blood flow between the atria. It should be distinguished from patent foramen ovale (PFO), which is a is a probe-patent defect caused by a failure of the septum primum to fuse to the superior limb of the septum secundum at the edge of the fossa ovalis in postnatal life, leaving a flaplike communication between the two atria. PFO occurs in approximately 20%-25% of the normal adult population. Fig. 1A-146 illustrates the physiology of ASD. There are several forms of ASD (Fig. 1A-147):

- Primum: This type of ASD occurs when there is failure of normal fusion of anterior and posterior endocardial cushions with the septum primum, with resultant deficiency in the inferior portion of the septum primum. The defect frequently coexists with abnormalities of the atrioventricular valves, commonly resulting in a cleft anterior mitral leaflet.
- Secundum: The most common form of ASD; it represents a true deficiency in the septum primum or a septum secundum, or both. This defect most often occurs in the region of the fossa ovalis.
- Sinus venosus defect: This defect is located at the junction of the right atrium and either the superior vena cava or inferior vena cava. In a sinus venosus defect, the wall separating the pulmonary veins and the right atrium is deficient, causing a left-to-right shunt. Most commonly this defect involves the right upper pulmonary vein, which is still anatomically connected to the left atrium but is deficient anteriorly and thus drains anomalously into the right atrium. Less commonly, the right lower pulmonary vein is involved.
- Coronary sinus septal defect (unroofed coronary sinus): This defect results when the wall separating the coronary sinus from the left atrium is deficient, causing a left-to-right shunt. This defect is often associated with a persistent left superior vena cava.

SYNONYMS

ASD
Interatrial septal defect

ICD-10CM CODES
Q21.1 Atrial septal defect
I23.1 Atrial septal defect as current complication following acute myocardial infarction

EPIDEMIOLOGY & DEMOGRAPHICS

- Secundum, 75%; primum, 15%-20%; sinus venosus, 5%-10%; coronary sinus, <1%
- Incidence is greater in females and in patients with Down syndrome
- Accounts for 8% to 10% of congenital heart abnormalities
- Prevalence is 1.6 per 1000 live births
- Holt-Oram syndrome is an autosomal dominant disorder that involves skeletal anomalies, such as absent radial bones in both arms, as well as ASD and cardiac conduction disease, such as AV blocks. Association with other genetic syndromes (e.g., Down syndrome and Noonan syndrome) has been described.
- ASDs may occur as an isolated defect or as part of other congenital cardiac syndromes such as Ebstein's anomaly, Lutembacher syndrome, or fetal alcohol syndrome.

CLINICAL PRESENTATION

- Small ASDs or PFOs may close spontaneously during infancy. The majority of ASDs are small and do not cause any symptoms during infancy. These patients are usually diagnosed by the presence of a cardiac murmur during routine physical examination. Infants with large ASDs may presents with heart failure, recurrent respiratory infections, and failure to thrive.
- Exertional fatigue and dyspnea are usually the main presenting symptoms.
- On rare occasions, young adults may presents with ischemic stroke caused by paradoxical embolism through the ASD or PFO.
- Patients with ASDs caused by congenital syndromes may present with clinical features related to the underlying syndrome. Clinical Features:
- Cyanosis and clubbing (when abnormal right ventricular [RV] compliance has led to right-to-left shunting)
- Increased jugular venous pressure (with RV failure)
- Prominent RV impulse

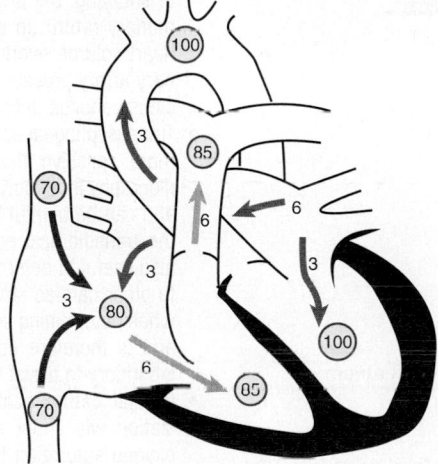

FIGURE 1A-146 Physiology of atrial septal defect (ASD). Circled numbers represent oxygen saturation values. The numbers next to the arrows represent volumes of blood flow (in L/min/m²). This illustration shows a hypothetical patient with a pulmonary-to-systemic blood flow ratio (Qp/Qs) of 2:1. Desaturated blood enters the right atrium from the venae cavae at a volume of 3 L/min/m² and mixes with an additional 3 L of fully saturated blood shunting left to right across the ASD; the result is an increase in oxygen saturation in the right atrium. Six liters of blood flow through the tricuspid valve and cause a mid-diastolic flow rumble. Oxygen saturation may be slightly higher in the RV because of incomplete mixing at the atrial level. The full 6 L flows across the RV outflow tract and causes a systolic ejection flow murmur. Six liters return to the left atrium, with 3 L shunting left to right across the defect and 3 L crossing the mitral valve to be ejected by the left ventricle into the ascending aorta (normal cardiac output). (From Kliegman RM et al: *Nelson textbook of pediatrics*, ed 19, Philadelphia, 2011, Saunders.)

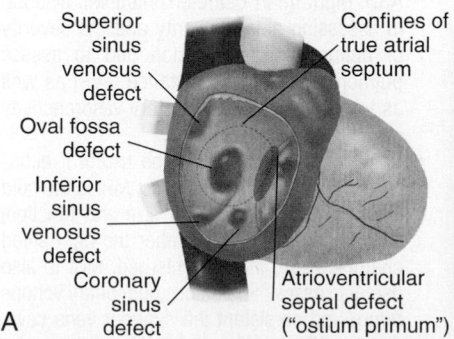
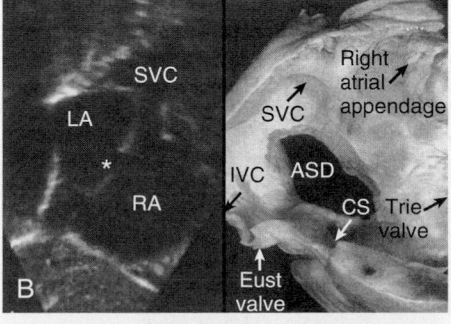

FIGURE 1A-147 A, Schematic diagram outlining the different types of interatrial shunting that can be encountered. Note that only the central defect is suitable for device closure. **B,** Subcostal right anterior oblique view of a secundum atrial septal defect *(ASD) (asterisk)* that is suitable for device closure. The right panel is a specimen as seen in a similar view, outlining the landmarks of defect. *CS,* Coronary sinus; *IVC,* inferior vena cava; *LA,* left atrium; *RA,* right atrium; *SVC,* superior vena cava. (From Zipes DP et al [eds]: *Braunwauld's heart disease*, ed 7, Philadelphia, 2005, Saunders.)

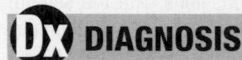
- Visible and palpable pulmonary artery pulsations
- Wide fixed splitting of S_2
- Pansystolic murmur best heard at apex secondary to mitral regurgitation (ostium primum defect)
- Ejection systolic flow murmur (pulmonary valve flow murmur) (Figure 1A-148)
- Diastolic rumble (atrioventricular valve flow murmur)

Dx DIAGNOSIS

DIFFERENTIAL DIAGNOSIS

- Primary pulmonary hypertension
- Pulmonary stenosis
- Rheumatic heart disease
- Mitral valve prolapse
- Cor pulmonale
- Anomalous pulmonary venous connection

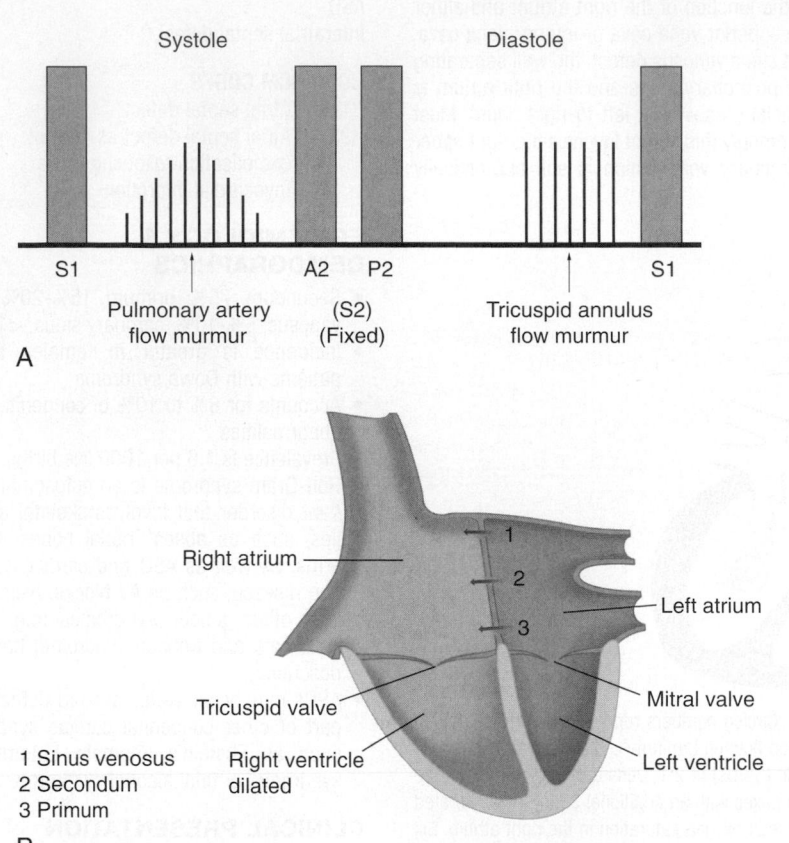

1 Sinus venosus
2 Secondum
3 Primum

Right ventricle dilated

FIGURE 1A-148 Atrial septal defect. **A,** Murmur at the left sternal edge. **B,** Anatomy. (From The patient with a murmur. In Baker T, Nikolic G, O'Connor S [eds]: *Practical cardiology*, Philadelphia, 2008, Elsevier.)

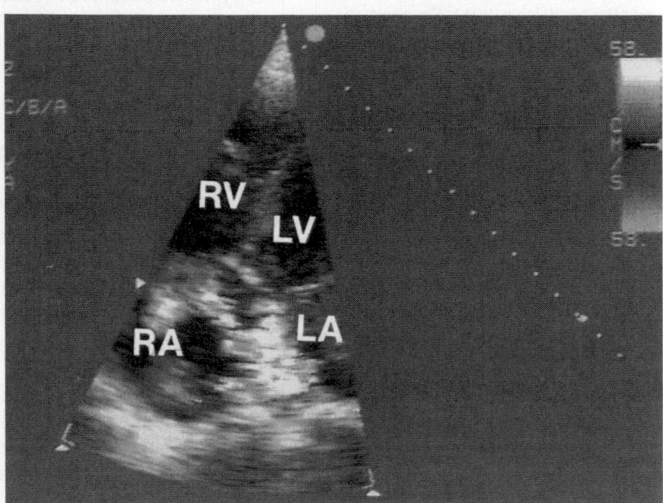

FIGURE 1A-149 Color flow Doppler apical four-chamber view showing blood flow from the left atrium (LA) to the right atrium (RA) through a moderately sized atrial septal defect. *LV,* Left ventricle; *RV,* right ventricle. (From Forbes CD, Jackson WF: *Color atlas and text of clinical medicine,* ed 3, London, 2003, Mosby.)

WORKUP

- ECG:
  1. Ostium primum defect: left axis deviation, incomplete or total right bundle branch block, prolongation of PR interval
  2. Sinus venosus defect: right axis deviation, abnormal P axis
  3. Ostium secundum defect: right axis deviation, incomplete or total right bundle branch block, right atrial enlargement

IMAGING STUDIES

- Chest x-ray: cardiomegaly, right heart enlargement, increased pulmonary vascular pattern
- Echocardiography (Fig. 1A-149): Transthoracic echocardiography has a high degree of sensitivity for diagnosing secundum and primum ASDs. Echocardiography with saline bubble contrast and Doppler flow studies may demonstrate the size of the defect, the direction of shunting, the presence of anomalous pulmonary return (in sinus venosus ASD), right heart volume overload, and elevated pulmonary artery pressures. It should be noted that sinus venosus defects are frequently missed.
- Transesophageal echocardiography: It is much more sensitive than transthoracic echocardiography in identifying sinus venosus defects and can be helpful for all forms of ASD when the transthoracic echo is nondiagnostic. It is also useful to determine defect size, proximity to other cardiac structures, and sizes of rims when determining suitability for device closure and is therefore used in the catheterization laboratory to assist with these issues.
- Cardiac catheterization: Right heart catheterization will show evidence of "step-up" in oxygen saturation from SVC to RA, evidence of elevated PA pressures.
- Cardiac catheterization: Left heart catheterization is not usually a diagnostic necessity; it is only useful when the coronary arteries need to be assessed before surgery. Right heart catheterization will reveal a "step-up" in arterial oxygen saturation in the right atrium compared with the superior vena cava. This may not be the case in patients with partial anomalous pulmonary venous return associated with the sinus venosus type of ASD. Right heart catheterization will also aid in assessing shunt severity and the severity of pulmonary hypertension and to assess pulmonary vascular resistance (PVR) as well as to assess pulmonary artery vasoreactivity in response to vasodilators.
- Cardiac MRI and CT: may be useful if echocardiography is not diagnostic; MRI is the gold standard for assessing RV size and function, and it can determine whether the right-sided chambers are, in fact, enlarged. MRI is also useful to assess anomalous pulmonary venous return and persistent left superior vena cava. Cardiac CT can offer similar information.

Rx TREATMENT

NONPHARMACOLOGIC THERAPY

- Symptomatic patients should avoid strenuous activity.

A

- Asymptomatic patients with small defects with shunts with a pulmonary to systemic flow ratio (Qp/Qs) of <1.5:1 without pulmonary artery hypertension (PAH) and normal RV size require no medical therapy and may be observed. Routine assessment of these patients includes assessment of symptoms, arrhythmias, and embolic events and serial echocardiography.
- A repeat echocardiogram should be obtained every 2 to 3 yr to assess RV size and function and pulmonary pressure; with increasing age, the degree of left-to-right shunting may increase due to progressive noncompliance of the left ventricle with age-related acquired heart disease.

GENERAL Rx

- Children and infants: Closure of ASD before age 10 yr is indicated if Qp/Qs is >1.5:1, ASD size is significantly >5 mm, or if there is evidence of RV dilation.
  1. Small ASDs with a diameter of <5 mm and no evidence of RV volume overload do not impact the natural history of the individual and thus may not require closure unless associated with paradoxic embolism.
  2. Closure of an ASD either percutaneously or surgically is indicated for right atrial and RV enlargement with or without symptoms.
  3. A sinus venosus, coronary sinus, or primum ASD should be repaired surgically rather than by percutaneous closure.
  4. Surgical closure of secundum ASD is appropriate when concomitant surgical repair/replacement of associated defects is needed or when the anatomy of the defect precludes the use of a percutaneous device.
- Adults: Closure of an ASD, either percutaneously or surgically, may be considered in the presence of net left-to-right shunting with Qp/Qs >1.5:1, right-sided chamber enlargement, symptoms, pulmonary hypertension with pulmonary artery pressure less than two-thirds systemic levels, PVR less than two-thirds systemic vascular resistance, or when pulmonary hypertension is responsive to either acute or chronic pulmonary vasodilator therapy. These patients must be treated in conjunction with providers who have expertise in the management of adult congenital heart disease and pulmonary hypertension.
- Patients with severe irreversible PAH and no evidence of a left-to-right shunt should not undergo ASD closure.
- Closure of an ASD, either percutaneously or surgically, is reasonable in the presence of:
  1. Paradoxic embolism (Class 2a indication)
  2. Documented orthodeoxia-platypnea (Class 2a indication)
- Percutaneous catheter device closure is possible in many patients with secundum ASDs (if stretched diameter is <41 mm with adequate rims), with >95% success rate in appropriate candidates. A combination of low-dose aspirin and clopidogrel is usually prescribed for 3-6 months after the procedure to prevent thrombus formation. Early complications include device thrombus formation, atrial arrhythmias,

erosion, and device dislodgement. Potential mid- and long-term complications include late device erosion into the aortic root or pericardium, atrial dysrhythmias, and infective endocarditis. In one study the long-term outcomes of device closure using the Amplatzer septal occluder were excellent as evidenced by no deaths and minimal complication in 151 patients followed for 6.5 years after ASD closure. In October 2013 the Food and Drug Administration (FDA) began alerting health care providers and patients that in very rare instances, tissue surrounding the Amplatzer ASO can erode and result in life-threatening emergencies that require immediate surgery, especially when the rim adjacent to the aortic root is <5 mm. Based on published estimates, these events occur in approximately 1 to 3 of every 1,000 patients implanted with the Amplatzer device. Close clinical follow up and an echocardiogram is recommended predischarge, at 1 wk, at 6 mo, and at 12 mo after implant.
- Percutaneous closure is contraindicated in those with sinus venosus, primum, or unroofed coronary sinus defects. In addition, it is not suitable for secundum defects with unsuitable anatomy (too large; too close to coronary sinus, AV valves, or pulmonary veins; or inadequate rims), presence of sepsis, bleeding disorder, or intracardiac thrombi.
- In adult patients undergoing surgical closure, the surgical mortality should be <1%. Surgical closure of ASD improves function status, exercise capacity, and patient survival; however, it does not prevent atrial fibrillation or stroke, especially if patients are operated on after age 40. Concomitant maze procedure may be considered for intermittent or chronic atrial fibrillation in adults with ASDs who are undergoing surgical repair.

DISPOSITION

- Mortality rate is elevated in patients with large ASDs if left untreated, with complications such as RV failure, arrhythmias, paradoxic embolism, and PAH leading to right-to-left shunting (Eisenmenger syndrome).
- Patients with small shunts (<1.5:1) have a normal life expectancy.
- Basic assessment for adult congenital heart disease patients should include systemic arterial oximetry, an ECG, chest radiograph, transthoracic echocardiography, and blood tests for full blood count and coagulation screen.
- Intracardiac shunts are considered moderate risk for preoperative evaluation for noncardiac procedure. High-risk features include severe systolic dysfunction (ejection fraction <35%), severe pulmonary hypertension whether primary or secondary, cyanotic heart disease, or severe left-side outlet obstruction.
- Annual clinical follow-up is recommended for patients postoperatively if their ASD was repaired as an adult to monitor for PAH, atrial arrhythmias, RV or left ventricular dysfunction, and coexisting valvular lesions.
- Preoperative atrial fibrillation is a risk factor for immediate postoperative and long-term

atrial fibrillation. Patients with a repaired ASD still have an increased risk for development of atrial fibrillation that directly correlates with the age at which the defect is corrected (later correction poses greater risk).
  1. After closure, anticipated benefits include improved functional status and exercise capacity, improved survival after closure as a child, improved quality of life, prevention of right heart failure, and prevention of PAH.
  2. Potential mid- to long-term complications after ASD closure in adulthood include tachyarrhythmias (atrial fibrillation or atrial flutter), bradyarrhythmias (sinus node dysfunction or heart block), stroke (greater risk in older patients), residual ASDs (because of patch dehiscence or incomplete closure by device), right heart failure or PAH (risk is correlated with the size of the original defect and inversely related to age at time of closure), mitral valve regurgitation or subaortic stenosis (in patients with primum ASDs), device migration/erosion, and pulmonary venous congestion (uncommon).
  3. Pregnancy is usually well tolerated in women with ASDs. Follow-up during pregnancy is recommended because of small risk for paradoxic embolus, stroke, arrhythmia, and heart failure. If known, ASDs should be closed before pregnancy is indicated. The sole contraindication to pregnancy in women with an ASD is severe PAH.
  4. Scuba diving is generally contraindicated in patients with unrepaired ASDs because of the risk of paradoxical emboli. In addition, high-altitude climbing should be avoided because it can cause oxygen desaturation from right-to-left shunting in these patients.
- In regard to infective endocarditis prophylaxis for dental procedures:
  1. Prophylaxis is not indicated for an unrepaired ASD.
  2. Prophylaxis is indicated for a repaired ASD or any congenital heart disease with prosthetic material as part of the repair during the first 6 mo after the repair.
  3. Prophylaxis is indicated for a repaired ASD or any congenital heart defect in the presence of residual defects at the site or adjacent to the site of a prosthetic patch or prosthetic device (both of which inhibit endothelialization).

The estrogen-containing oral contraceptive pill is not recommended in acute congenital heart disease patients at risk of thromboembolism, such as those with cyanosis related to an intracardiac shunt, atrial fibrillation, severe PAH, or Fontan repair.

SUGGESTED READINGS
Available at www.expertconsult.com

RELATED CONTENT
Atrial Septal Defect (ASD) (Patient Information)

AUTHORS: **ESHAN PATVARDHAN, M.B.B.S.,** and **JONATHAN GINNS, M.D.**

BASIC INFORMATION

DEFINITION

Atrioventricular (AV) dissociation is defined as a lack of association between the atria and the ventricles or independent function of the atria and ventricles. This simple definition will serve as a reminder that AV dissociation should be considered an umbrella rather than a diagnosis. AV dissociation may occur in the setting of bradycardic rhythms (complete heart block, as well as tachycardic rhythms [ventricular tachycardia, atrial rhythm with associated accelerated junctional rhythm [Figure 1A-150] or AV nodal reentrant tachycardia).

SYNONYMS

Third-degree AV block
CHB
Complete AV block

ICD-10CM CODES

I44.2 Atrioventricular block, complete

EPIDEMIOLOGY & DEMOGRAPHICS

- The prevalence is the sum of the diagnoses that are characterized by AV dissociation

PHYSICAL FINDINGS & CLINICAL PRESENTATION

Physical examination findings may be normal unless the arrhythmia is causing hemodynamic compromise. If the right atrium contracts against a closed tricuspid valve during ventricular systole, Cannon A waves may be seen in the jugular vein. Patients may present with the following clinical manifestations:

- Dizziness, palpitations
- Syncope or presyncope (caused by reduced cardiac output)
- Fatigue, impaired exercise tolerance
- Mental status changes
- Congestive heart failure
- Angina pectoris
- Some patients may be asymptomatic

ETIOLOGY

- Slow rate of firing from sinus node
- Inappropriately fast pacemaker from the ventricle

- Iatrogenic: anesthesia, inotrope infusion, ventricular pacing, radiofrequency ablation of slow pathway, digoxin toxicity
- Sinus node disease, ischemia, hyperkalemia, overactive vagal drive
- Complete heart block: progressive fibrosis of the His-Purkinje system, medications, Lyme disease

DIAGNOSIS

DIFFERENTIAL DIAGNOSIS

- The differential diagnosis should be targeted toward the diagnoses that include AV dissociation.
- Note: The atrium does not need to be faster than the ventricular rate in AV dissociation, as is the case in the definition of complete heart block.
  - Isorhythmic AV dissociation: Atrial and ventricular rates are the same but dissociated.
  - Interference dissociation: Similar atrial and ventricular rates but conduction occurs sometimes.

WORKUP

- Workup such as routine laboratory studies, cardiac biomarkers, and cardiac imaging should be dictated by the clinical circumstances.
  - Laboratory studies: particular attention to electrolyte abnormalities (potassium) and digoxin level
  - Lyme antibody titer in the case of complete heart block

TREATMENT

ACUTE GENERAL Rx

- Initial treatment should focus on the hemodynamic stability and symptoms of the patient.
- Bradycardic rhythms
  - If necessary (i.e., symptoms or hemodynamic compromise), a temporary pacemaker is the most reliable therapy.
  - Hold AV-nodal blocking agents.
  - Chronotropic medications: Atropine, dopamine, dobutamine, or isoproterenol may be used as second-line agents while preparing for a temporary pacemaker.

- Tachycardic rhythms (ventricular tachycardia)
  - In the setting of hemodynamic compromise, cardioversion is the first-line therapy.
  - IV antiarrhythmic drugs: amiodarone or lidocaine to suppress the arrhythmia.
  - Treatment of the underlying cause of ventricular tachycardia: coronary angiogram if ischemia vs electrophysiology (EP) study +/- ablation.

REFERRAL

All patients with AV dissociation should be referred to a cardiologist for diagnostic evaluation of the rhythm.

PEARLS & CONSIDERATIONS

COMMENTS

- Recall that AV dissociation is merely an umbrella that includes multiple diagnoses, including both bradycardic and tachycardic arrhythmias.
- Specific considerations in regards to etiology, treatment, and disposition should be directed toward the rhythm that has caused AV dissociation.

SUGGESTED READINGS

Available at www.expertconsult.com

AUTHORS: **ALEEM MUGHAL, M.D.,** and **JOHN WYLIE, M.D.**

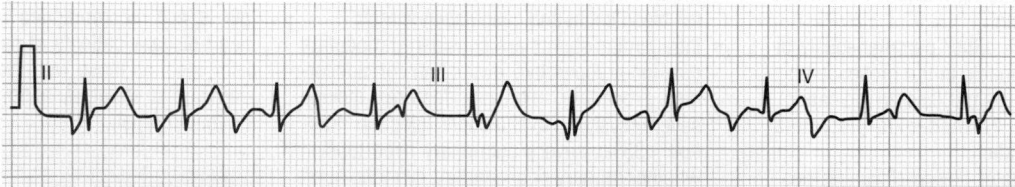

FIGURE 1A-150 Rhythm strip shows a low atrial rhythm at 100 beats/min with a nearly isorhythmic accelerated junctional rhythm at 95 beats/min in a patient with suspected endocarditis.

BASIC INFORMATION

DEFINITION

Attention deficit hyperactivity disorder (ADHD) is a chronic disorder of attention and/or hyperactivity-impulsivity. Symptoms must be present before 12 yr of age, last at least 6 mo, and cause functional impairment in multiple settings. The diagnostic keys for ADHD are described in Table 1A-72.

SYNONYMS

Hyperactivity
Hyperkinetic disorder
Attention deficit disorder (ADD)

ICD-10CM CODES
F90.0 Attention-deficit hyperactivity disorder, predominantly inattentive type
F90.1 Attention-deficit hyperactivity disorder, predominantly hyperactive type
F90.2 Attention-deficit hyperactivity disorder, combined type
F90.8 Attention-deficit hyperactivity disorder, other type
F90.9 Attention-deficit hyperactivity disorder, unspecified type

DSM-V CODES
314.00, 314.01

EPIDEMIOLOGY & DEMOGRAPHICS

PEAK INCIDENCE: Diagnosis is usually first made in school-aged children (6 to 9 yr).
PREVALENCE: Five percent to 10% of school-aged children (most prevalent neurodevelopmental disorder among children) and 2% to 5% of adults. Children from families with low socioeconomic status and children with public insurance are diagnosed with ADHD at higher rates than their peers.
PREDOMINANT SEX: Among children, male predominance with ratio of 2:1 to 4:1. Among adults, ratio is closer to 1:1 (sex difference may reflect referral bias).
PREDOMINANT AGE: Some symptoms must occur before age 12 yr. Symptoms (especially motoric hyperactivity) tend to diminish with age. Up to 70% continue to meet criteria in adolescence, and an estimated 40% to 65% have some symptoms in adulthood.
GENETICS: Strong polygenetic component. First-degree relatives of ADHD patients have 5 times greater risk of ADHD relative to controls. Studies suggest potential involvement of several genes, including those associated with serotonin and glutamate transporters as well as dopamine metabolism.
RISK FACTORS: Possible risk factors include in utero tobacco/drug exposure or hypoxia, low birth weight, prematurity, pregnancy, lead exposure (though most children with elevated lead levels do not develop ADHD), head trauma in young children, family dysfunction, low socioeconomic status. Evidence supports possible association between dietary factors (e.g., refined sugar, food additives) and ADHD in a small percentage of patients. A causal link between environmental toxins and ADHD has not been clearly established.

PHYSICAL FINDINGS & CLINICAL PRESENTATION

- Three types:
  1. Predominantly inattentive: difficulty organizing, planning, remembering, concentrating, starting/completing tasks; symptoms may not be present during preferred activities.
  2. Predominantly hyperactive-impulsive: edgy/restless, talkative, disruptive/intrusive, disinhibited, impatient.
  3. Combined.
- Usually diagnosed in elementary school when achievement is compromised and behavioral problems are not tolerated. Children with academic underproductivity, problems with peer and family relations, or discipline issues are often referred for evaluation. Of the more than 4 million children in the U.S. who have ADHD, most have comorbid conditions (see below) and nearly half use special education and mental health services.
- Up to 50% may have associated disorders such as psychiatric diagnoses (oppositional defiant disorder, conduct disorder, depression, anxiety, eating disorders), learning disabilities, or substance abuse.
- In adults, motoric hyperactivity is less common, but restlessness, edginess, and difficulty relaxing are often seen. Disorganization and difficulty completing tasks are other common complaints.

ETIOLOGY

Strongest evidence exists for genetic inheritance. Other theories include abnormal metabolism of brain catecholamines, structural brain abnormalities, reduced activation in the basal ganglia and anterior frontal lobe, as well as environmental factors (see earlier).

TABLE 1A-72 Diagnostic Keys for Attention Deficit Hyperactivity Disorder

1. Inattention
   a. Careless mistakes in schoolwork, work, or other activities
   b. Seems not to listen when spoken to directly
   c. Poor follow through on schoolwork or chores
   d. Difficulty organizing
   e. Easily distracted by extraneous stimuli and is forgetful
2. Hyperactivity
   a. Trouble sitting still
   b. May act as if "driven by a motor"
   c. May talk excessively
3. Impulsivity
   a. Trouble holding back in class
   b. Trouble taking turns
   c. Interrupts

DIAGNOSIS

DIFFERENTIAL DIAGNOSIS

- Medical: visual/hearing impairment, seizure disorder, head injury, sleep disorder, medication interactions, mental retardation intellectual disability, specific learning disorder, autism spectrum disorder/development delay, thyroid abnormalities, lead toxicity, movement disorders.
- Psychiatric: depression, bipolar disorder, disruptive mood, dysregulation disorder, anxiety, obsessive-compulsive disorder, oppositional defiant disorder, intermittent explosive disorder, conduct disorder, posttraumatic stress disorder, reactive attachment disorder, and substance abuse.
- Psychosocial: mismatch of learning environment with ability, family dysfunction, abuse/neglect.

WORKUP

- Clinical interview should include assessment of symptoms and impact on work/school and relationships; developmental history; personal and family psychiatric history, including substance abuse; social history, including family dysfunction; medical history.
- Physical examination should be performed to investigate medical causes for symptoms, coexisting conditions, and contraindications to treatment. Special focus should be paid to evaluation of dysmorphic features; neurologic examination, including assessment for neurocutaneous findings; and assessment of hearing and vision.
- Information from collateral sources (parents, partners, teachers) is crucial to diagnosis. Many patients will not display symptoms during an office visit and may underreport or overreport symptoms.
- Self-rating scales and standardized symptom-specific questionnaires from collateral sources can help diagnose and assess response to treatment. The use of ADHD-specific rating scales over broadband behavioral scale is associated with improved sensitivity and specificity.
- Laboratory or imaging studies should be undertaken only if indicated by history or physical examination.
- The FDA has approved a quantitative EEG test to aid in the diagnosis of ADHD in children, but sufficient evidence to support its routine use is lacking.
- Ancillary testing (e.g., IQ/achievement testing, language evaluation, and mental health assessment) may be indicated based on clinical findings and may require referral.

TREATMENT

NONPHARMACOLOGIC THERAPY

- The majority of studies comparing the efficacy of pharmacologic vs nonpharmacologic interventions demonstrate the superiority of pharmacologic treatments.

- Studies on combined treatments have not shown significant improvements in core ADHD symptoms when behavioral treatments are added to stimulant medications. However, improvements in related areas of concern such as parent-child relations, aggressiveness, teacher-rated social skills, and reaching achievement have been seen in combined treatment groups.
- Prevailing opinion favors a multimodal approach in which nonpharmacologic behavioral therapies including parent-child behavioral therapy and social skills training can be used to target comorbid conditions or behaviors that have not responded to medication.
- Behavioral therapy alone is often considered when children are under 6 yr, symptoms and impairment are mild, if parents are opposed to or patients cannot tolerate medications, or if there is uncertainty or disagreement about the diagnosis (e.g., between parents and teachers).
- Educational interventions are recommended, particularly in the setting of learning disabilities. Children with ADHD are entitled to reasonable educational accommodations under a 504 Plan or the Individuals with Disabilities Education Act.
- Behavioral interventions (e.g., goal setting and rewards systems) show short-term efficacy and are endorsed by most national organizations (e.g., American Academy of Pediatrics, American Medical Association). Time management and organizational skills appear useful. Social skills training may also be useful.
- Psychotherapy such as cognitive therapy, play therapy, or insight-oriented therapy are unlikely to be useful in addressing the core symptoms of ADHD. However, it may be beneficial in treating comorbid psychiatric conditions.
- Elimination diets are not routinely recommended.
- Many support and advocacy groups provide education and other resources (e.g., Children and Adolescents with ADHD, National ADD Association, American Academy of Child and Adolescent Psychiatry).

ACUTE GENERAL Rx

- Most studies on treatment of ADHD are performed in children; limited data available on adults.
- Mainstay of treatment is stimulant medications. Second-line therapies include antidepressants and alpha-agonists.
- Stimulants:
  1. Release or block uptake of dopamine and norepinephrine.
  2. Include short- and long-acting methylphenidate, dextroamphetamine, and dextroamphetamine/amphetamine combinations (mixed amphetamine salts). A methylphenidate patch (Daytrana) is available, as is a pro-drug form of dextroamphetamine, lisdexamfetamine (Vyvanse), which is designed to limit the abuse potential, and a long-acting oral suspension of methylphenidate (Quillivant XR).

3. All stimulants equally effective; however, not all patients improve with stimulants. Patients who do not respond well to one stimulant may respond to another.
4. Do not cause euphoria or lead to addiction when taken as directed.
5. Improve cognition, inattention, impulsiveness/hyperactivity, and driving skills. Limited impact on academic performance, learning, and emotional problems.
6. Side effects are usually mild, reversible, and dose dependent, including anorexia, weight loss, sleep disturbances, increased heart rate and blood pressure, irritability, moodiness, headache, onset or worsening of motor tics, reduction of growth velocity (but not adult height). Do not worsen seizures in patients on adequate anticonvulsant therapy. Rebound of symptoms can occur with withdrawal of medication.
7. Stimulants have generally been associated with cardiovascular events and death. Patients should be carefully evaluated for cardiovascular disease before beginning therapy and be periodically monitored, including blood pressure checks, while they are treated. However, despite concerns regarding cardiovascular risk, these medications are generally safe. Recent studies have shown that among young and middle-aged adults, current or new use of ADHD medications, compared with nonuse or remote use, is not associated with an increased risk of serious cardiovascular events. Routine, pre-treatment screening with ECGs is not currently recommended by the American Academy of Pediatrics or the American Academy of Child and Adolescent Psychiatry.
- Atomoxetine (Strattera):
  1. Selective norepinephrine reuptake inhibitor.
  2. Generally felt to be less effective than stimulants, but a useful alternative in patients who have not tolerated or responded to stimulants or in the setting of patient or family substance abuse.
  3. Efficacy and safety of use beyond 2 years of treatment have not been studied. There have been reports of behavioral abnormalities and increased suicidality in children and adolescents.
  4. Side effects: gastrointestinal upset, sleep disturbance, decreased appetite, dizziness, sexual side effects in men. Cardiovascular side effects have also been reported.
  5. There have been rare reports of severe liver injury in adults and children.
- Antidepressants (bupropion, imipramine, desipramine, nortriptyline):
  1. May be useful in patients with coexisting psychiatric disorders.
  2. Studies comparing efficacy versus stimulants are inconclusive.
  3. Side effects: arrhythmias, anticholinergic effects, lowering of seizure threshold.
- Alpha-2-adrenergic agonists (clonidine, guanfacine)
  1. Appear to be less effective than stimulants, but may be particularly useful as an

adjunctive treatment to stimulants, particularly in patients with a partial stimulant response or who experience side effects such as sleep disturbance or concurrent symptoms of overarousal, irritability, or aggression.
2. Extended-release formulations of guanfacine (Intuniv) and clonidine (Kapray) have been approved by the FDA for treatment of ADHD in children ages 6 to 17 yr. A transdermal clonidine patch is also available.
3. Potential side effects include sedation, fatigue, headache, bradycardia, hypotension, and depression.
- Use of medications, particularly stimulants (which are monitored under the Controlled Substance Act), requires frequent monitoring.

DISPOSITION

- Although symptoms may change over time, for many patients ADHD represents a chronic condition that requires lifelong management.
- Patients are at higher risk for academic underachievement, lower socioeconomic status, work and relationship difficulties, high-risk behavior, and psychiatric comorbidities.

REFERRAL

- Diagnosis complicated by difficult-to-treat comorbid psychiatric conditions, developmental disorders, or mental retardation
- Lack of adequate response to stimulants/atomoxetine/alpha-adrenergic agents.

PEARLS & CONSIDERATIONS

- The World Health Organization's Adult Self-Report Scale (ASRS) v1.1 has good sensitivity and adaptability to the primary care setting.
- Among adults with persistent ADHD symptoms treated with medication, trials have shown that the use of cognitive behavioral therapy compared with relaxation with educational support resulted in improved ADHD symptoms, which were maintained at 12 mo.
- ADHD has been associated with criminal behavior in some studies. Data analysis has shown that among patients with ADHD, rates of criminality are lower during periods when they receive ADHD medication.
- Recommendations for the diagnosis and management of ADHD have been published by the Centers for Disease Control and Prevention (www.cdc.gov/ncbddd/adhd/treatment/treatment.html).

SUGGESTED READINGS
Available at www.expertconsult.com

RELATED CONTENT
Attention Deficit Hyperactivity Disorder (ADHD) (Patient Information)

AUTHOR: **EMILY R. KATZ, M.D.**

BASIC INFORMATION

DEFINITION

Autism spectrum disorders encompass a continuum of developmental disorders characterized by marked social impairment. Table 1A-73 describes the diagnostic keys. There is usually impairment in several additional domains integral to social functioning, including language and communication. Stereotypic behavior and sensory issues (i.e., hypersensitivity, hyposensitivity) also are prominent. Comorbid intellectual disability and an increased risk of psychiatric disorder are frequently associated with autism spectrum disorder. Onset is typically before age 3 yr and may be diagnosed as early as 12 mo of age if developmental delays are severe. In rare cases, a child may be observed to develop normally to 12 to 24 mo and be diagnosed with autism spectrum disorder at 30 to 36 mo following gradual (or rapid) loss of social and language skills. The diagnosis of autism spectrum disorder without accompanying intellectual and language impairment (aka Asperger's syndrome) is typically made at a later age with 50% of affected children first diagnosed in kindergarten or 1st grade. DSM-5 criteria no longer differentiate autism and Asperger's as separate disorders. Instead, an overarching diagnosis of autism spectrum disorder is applied to both syndromes using severity levels (1, 2, or 3) to identify the magnitude of social and behavioral impairment and the support required to ensure the safety and well-being of the individual.

SYNONYMS

ASD
Autism
Autistic disorder
Early infantile autism
Childhood autism
Kanner's autism
Asperger's disorder
Pervasive developmental disorder PDD NOS

ICD-10CM CODES
F84.0   Autism spectrum disorder
DSM-5 CODE
299.00 Autism spectrum disorder

TABLE 1A-73   Diagnostic Keys for Autism Spectrum Disorder

1. Impairment in social interaction
   a. Uses nonverbal behaviors
   b. Poor peer relationships
   c. Lack of interest in shared activities
   d. Lack of social or emotional reciprocity
2. Impairments in communication
   a. Delay in language
   b. Stereotyped or repetitive language
   c. Lack of age-appropriate social play
3. Repetitive behaviors
   a. Inflexibility
   b. Preoccupation with parts of objects

EPIDEMIOLOGY & DEMOGRAPHICS

INCIDENCE (IN U.S.): Autism spectrum disorder afflicts approximately 1% of children in the United States.
PREVALENCE: 1:88 (1:54 for boys). It is unclear whether the increase in prevalence reflects an expansion of the diagnosis to include subthreshold cases, increased awareness of the disorder, and changes in public policy related to special education eligibility or a true increase in the frequency of autism spectrum disorder.
PREDOMINANT SEX: Male/female ratio of 4:1
PREDOMINANT AGE: Lifelong
PEAK INCIDENCE: Before age 3 yr
GENETICS:
- Autism spectrum disorder is highly inheritable with a heritability index of 82% to 90%.
- De novo mutations account for 15% to 20% of autism spectrum disorder cases. In the remaining cases, the risk appears to be polygenic. Research has identified approximately 1000 gene mutations as being possibly contributory.
- 5% risk rate for siblings of an affected individual, unless fragile X syndrome is determined as the pathway, increasing the risk rate to 50%.
- 90% concordance for autism spectrum disorder in monozygotic twins and 5% for dizygotic pairs.
- Clinical signs correlate with abnormal brain development. Overgrowth and neural dysfunction are evident at young ages and involve an abnormal excess number of neurons in the prefrontal cortex (PFC). This entirely neurobiologic signal of abnormal development (also called the "brain growth dysregulation hypothesis") has been reported to begin at 9 to 18 months of age.

PHYSICAL FINDINGS & CLINICAL PRESENTATION

- Common triad of marked impairment in social interactions (poor social-emotional reciprocity), impaired and atypical verbal and nonverbal communication, and repetitive and unusual behavior or play.
- Marked impairment in the understanding and use of both verbal and nonverbal communication, including unchanging facial expression and lack of gestures during interactions.
- Stereotypic behavior (i.e., hand flapping, body rocking), or language (i.e., echolalia, palilalia).
- Perceptual hypersensitivity (i.e., auditory, tactile, olfactory, gustatory) and avoidance of novel stimuli; or perceptual hyposensitivity (e.g., abnormally high threshold for pain).

ETIOLOGY

- Majority of cases are not associated with a comorbid medical condition. However, two thirds of cases have a comorbid psychiatric feature (ADHD 29%, anxiety 22%, bipolar 20%, depression 20%).
- Significant increase in comorbid seizure disorder (25%) and intellectual disability (75%).
- Sometimes associated with other neurologic conditions (e.g., encephalitis, cytomegalovirus,

toxoplasmosis, tuberous sclerosis, phenylketonuria [PKU], fragile X syndrome), suggesting that it also may result from nonspecific neuronal injury.
- Several studies have shown no association between immunizations (specifically MMR vaccine) or thimerosal-containing vaccines (i.e., DPT) and autism spectrum disorder.
- Maternal use of valproate during pregnancy has been associated with increased risk for autism spectrum disorder and childhood autism in offspring.[1]
- Studies have raised concern about increased risk associated with use of selective serotonin uptake inhibitors (SSRIs) during pregnancy.

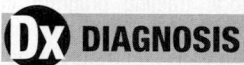

DIAGNOSIS

DIFFERENTIAL DIAGNOSIS

- Rett's syndrome: occurs in females; follows a brief period of normal development (i.e., 12 to 15 mo; characterized by severe neurodevelopmental regression including head growth deceleration, loss of purposeful use of hands, hyperventilation (risk of aerophagia), and motor incoordination
- Childhood disintegration disorder: normal development until age 4 yr, followed by marked neurodevelopmental and behavioral regression beginning with loss of bladder and bowel control
- Childhood-onset schizophrenia: follows period of normal development
- Asperger's syndrome: lacks the language and cognitive deficits characteristic of autism
- Isolated symptoms of autism spectrum disorder: when occurring in isolation, defined as disorders (i.e., Phelan-Mcdermid syndrome, Aciardi syndrome, selective mutism, expressive language disorder, mixed receptive-expressive language disorder, stereotypic movement disorder, severe-to-profound intellectual disability)

WORKUP

- Rule out underlying medical condition including genetic intellectual disability syndromes.
- Administer age-appropriate diagnostic instruments based on questionnaires and observation noting scales. Validated autism spectrum disorder–specific screening tools are available for children age ≥18 mo. All children should be screened specifically for autism spectrum disorder at 18 and 24 mo. General developmental screening tools are currently used in children 9 to 18 mo.

LABORATORY TESTS

- PKU screen (usually done at birth in the United States)
- Lead exposure screening
- Audiology testing for young children with autism spectrum disorder; school-based hearing screening may be sufficient in older children with autism spectrum disorders and without significant language or learning deficits
- Karyotype, microarray analysis, and DNA testing for fragile X syndrome in both boys and girls, as well as for different de novo

copy number variants or de novo mutations in specific genes associated with the disorder.

IMAGING STUDIES

- EEG to diagnose coexisting seizure disorder if seizure is suspected or if language regression is present (i.e., Landau-Kleffner syndrome)
- Brain MRI if tuberous sclerosis or Aicardi syndrome (callosal agenesis) is suspected

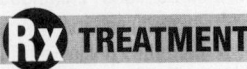 **TREATMENT**

NONPHARMACOLOGIC THERAPY

- Consistent behavioral training program in both the home and school environments
- A number of programs are currently used; many are based on applied behavioral analysis (ABA), others include Pivotal Response Training (PRT), Floortime, and the Early Start Denver Model for Young Children with Autism.
- Special educational program focused on language and communication skills, social and life skills development
- Highly structured home environment
- Education for families and teachers; the Autism Speaks™ website may be helpful in this regard: http://www.autismspeaks.org/about_us.php

ACUTE GENERAL Rx

- Obsessive or ritualistic behaviors: selective serotonin reuptake inhibitors (SSRIs), atypical antipsychotics, valproic acid.
- Aggression, irritability, self-injury: atypical antipsychotic agents (e.g., risperidone), α-agonists, anticonvulsant mood stabilizers, SSRIs, beta-blockers, opiate antagonist (self-injury only).
- Hyperactivity, impulsivity, inattention: stimulants, alpha-agonists, atypical antipsychotics.
- Anxiety: SSRIs, buspirone, mirtazapine.

- Bipolar, mood lability: valproic acid, carbamazepine, lithium, aripiprazole.
- Depression: SSRIs, mirtazapine.

CHRONIC Rx

- Extended use of medications for acute management of comorbid psychiatric disorder.
- Pharmacotherapy is palliative, not curative of autism spectrum disorder.

DISPOSITION

- Most children will require some degree of assistance as adults.
- DSM-5 identifies 3 severity levels based on social communication and restricted, repetitive behaviors: Level 1 (requiring support), Level 2 (requiring substantial support), and Level 3 (requiring very substantial support).
- With early diagnosis and proper treatment/support, the prognosis for children without language and intellectual impairment (aka Asperger's syndrome) is fair to very good despite ongoing symptoms.
- Poorer outcomes include a lack of joint attention by age 4 yr, a lack of functional speech by age 5 yr, intellectual disability, seizures, comorbid medical or psychiatric syndromes, and a pervasive lack of social relatedness.
- Best outcomes are associated with early identification and treatment, the development of oral communication skills, and the cognitive and behavioral capacity for inclusion in regular education settings with typically developing peers.

REFERRAL

Assistance may be needed in diagnosis (child psychiatrist, clinical psychologist, geneticist, pediatric neurologist, developmental pediatrician), management (speech language pathologist, occupational therapist, clinical psychologist), parental teaching (psychiatric social worker), or intervention with the school system (educational advocate, attorney).

PEARLS & CONSIDERATIONS

- There is no scientific evidence of a relation between childhood vaccination and the development of autism spectrum disorder.
- Preliminary evidence suggests that a disproportionate number of children with autism spectrum disorder suffer from sleep difficulties, including obstructive sleep apnea, with sequelae mimicking ADHD.
- The Center for Autism & Developmental Disabilities at Bradley Hospital, an affiliate of the Brown Medical School, is the largest and most comprehensive treatment program in the U.S. for children with autism spectrum disorder and comorbid psychiatric illness (www.bradleyhospital.org). The new U.S. Preventive Services Task Force (USPSTF) recommendation on screening for autism spectrum disorder (ASD) in young children concludes that the current evidence is insufficient to assess the balance of benefits and harms of screening for ASD in young children for whom no concerns of ASD have been raised by their parents or a clinician.[1]

SUGGESTED READINGS
Available at www.expertconsult.com

RELATED CONTENT
Autism (Patient Information)

AUTHOR: **ROWLAND P. BARRETT, PH.D.**

[1]Siu AL, et al.; US Preventive Services Task Force (USPSTF): Screening for Autism Spectrum Disorder in Young Children: US Preventive Services Task Force Recommendation Statement, *JAMA* 315(7):691–696, 2016.

A

BASIC INFORMATION

DEFINITION
Cerebral arteriovenous malformations (AVMs) are congenital vascular lesions that are characterized by blood flow from high-pressure arterial vessels directly into thin-walled veins without passing through an intervening capillary/venule system (Fig. 1A-151, *A*).

SYNONYMS
AVM
Brain AVM

ICD-10CM CODES
Q28.2 Arteriovenous malformations of cerebral vessels

EPIDEMIOLOGY & DEMOGRAPHICS
INCIDENCE
- Detection rates in large prospective studies range from 1.1 to 1.4 per 100,000 person-years.
- Incidence of hemorrhage, the most common and often most clinically dangerous presentation, is estimated to be 2% to 4% per year.

PREVALENCE: Estimated about 1.3 per 100,000.
PREDOMINANT SEX AND AGE
- There is a slight male preponderance; studies of varying populations show 1.04:1 to 1.2:1 M:F ratio.
- Peak age at time of hemorrhage occurrence is about 20 years, but it can occur in younger and older patients.

GENETICS
- Cerebral AVMs are sporadic in most cases.
- AVMs are present in about 20% of cases of Osler-Weber-Rendu syndrome (also known as hereditary hemorrhagic telangiectasia [HHT]), an autosomal dominant disorder that results in abnormal blood vessel formation in the skin, lungs, liver, brain, and other organs.

RISK FACTORS
- Male sex and presence of HHT are risk factors for AVM.
- The risk of hemorrhage is increased with prior hemorrhage, presence of a single draining vein, and diffuse nidus morphology.

PHYSICAL FINDINGS & CLINICAL PRESENTATION
- The most common presentation is hemorrhage; symptoms vary based on location and magnitude of hemorrhage.
- Patients may present with seizures or neurologic deficits related to mass effect of the AVM nidus.
- Headache and pulsatile tinnitus may be present.
- In infants, AVM may present as cyanotic heart failure, macrocephaly, or hydrocephalus.
- A bruit may be auscultated through the scalp or orbit.
- AVMs may also present with associated intracranial aneurysms that occur on distant, unrelated vessels, on a proximal artery that feeds the aneurysm (flow-related aneurysm), or within the AVM nidus itself (intranidal aneurysm). Patients may present with a subarachnoid hemorrhage related to the aneurysm rather than to the AVM.

ETIOLOGY
AVMs are congenital abnormalities caused by failure of formation of a capillary bed between embryonic arterial and venous vascular plexuses during the first trimester of gestation.

DIAGNOSIS

DIFFERENTIAL DIAGNOSIS
The differential diagnosis of cerebral AVMs includes other vascular lesions such as cavernous malformations, dural arteriovenous fistulas, and intracranial aneurysms. Table E1A-74 compares vascular malformations, and Table E1A-75 describes major differences between hemangiomas and vascular malformations.

LABORATORY TESTS
- CBC and BMP with renal function panel prior to contrast dye administration with CT angiography/cerebral angiogram.
- PT/INR/PTT should be drawn and corrected in the case of bleeding diathesis.

IMAGING STUDIES
- In the acute setting, a CT scan of the head to check for hemorrhage and a CT angiogram of the head for characterization of the lesion may be helpful (although calcification may be present and potentially pose as small acute blood).
- MRI of the brain delineates the nidus and its relationship to surrounding soft tissue structures better than a CT scan; however, in the setting of an acute hemorrhage these details will be obscured.
- Four-vessel cerebral angiogram (arteriogram) is the best study to evaluate AVM. Angiography in multiple projections helps identify the number and location of feeding and draining vessels for treatment planning (Fig. 1A-151, *B*). High-resolution images of the nidus may also reveal other irregularities such as aneurysms that often arise given the abnormal histology of the vessel walls and the high-pressure blood flow traversing them.

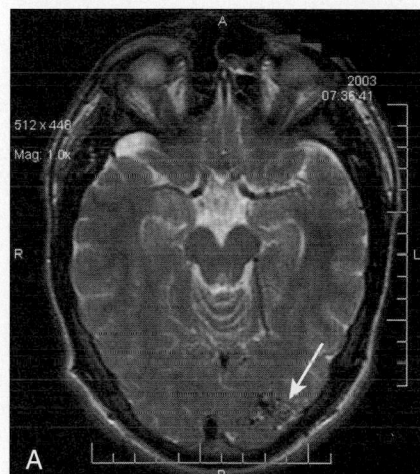
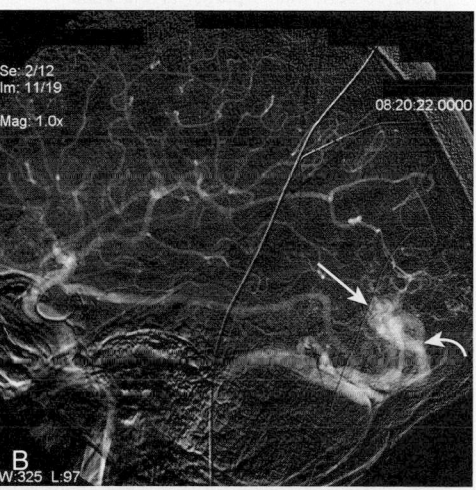
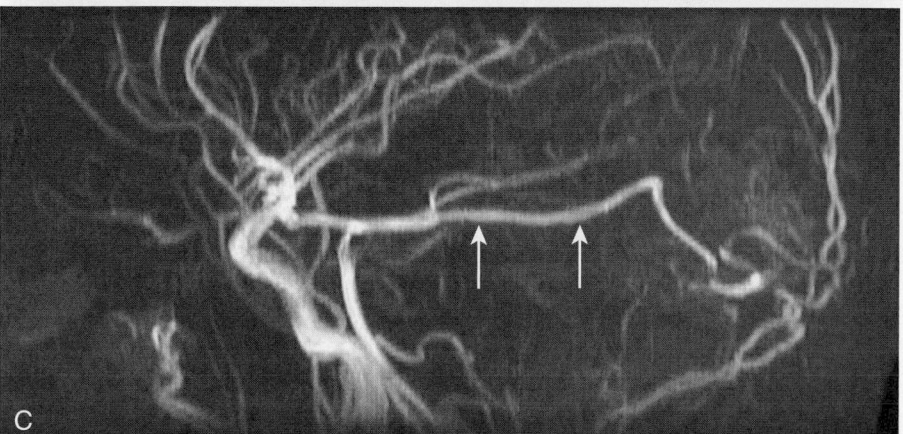

FIGURE 1A-151 A A 14-year-old child with a left occipital arteriovenous malformation (AVM). A, MRI shows multiple flow voids in the left occipital lobe *(arrow).* **B,** Lateral view from catheter angiogram confirms the presence of an AVM *(arrow)* and early draining veins *(curved arrow).* **C,** Lateral maximum intensity projection image from an MR angiogram shows an enlarged posterior cerebral artery branch *(arrows),* which feeds the tangle of abnormal vessels. (From Fuhrman BP et al: *Pediatric critical care,* ed 4, Philadelphia, 2011, Saunders.)

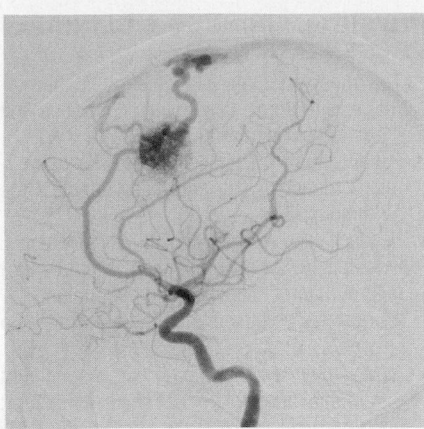

FIGURE 1A-151 B Arteriovenous malformation of the frontal lobe. The anterior cerebral artery provides primary arterial supply with venous drainage superficially into the superior sagittal sinus.

 **TREATMENT**

Pharmacologic management of seizures with antiepilepsy drugs and of headaches with oral analgesics can provide symptomatic relief.

NONPHARMACOLOGIC THERAPY

- Nonemergent outpatient setting: cerebral angiogram provides characterization of the lesion. Based on angiographic characteristics, the Spetzler-Martin AVM grading system may be used to help guide treatment. In general, grade 5 AVMs are considered unresectable; they are not treated because the risks of treatment likely outweigh the risk of hemorrhage. Current tools for the treatment of AVMs include surgical resection, radiosurgery, and endovascular embolization (with liquid glues or embolic agents).
- Surgical resection: in low-grade lesions by an experienced neurosurgeon yields a high cure rate (~95% in published studies). Resection should include removal of all of the nidus of the AVM; failure to remove the complete nidus may increase the risk of recurrence. An increasing Spetzler-Martin grading scale increases risk of neurologic complications. Intraoperative imaging techniques such as indocyanine-green in-field angiography and conventional digital subtraction angiography are used to verify complete resection.

- Radiosurgery: alternative definitive treatment for AVMs. Traditionally employed to treat AVMs in eloquent areas (e.g., brainstem); stereotactic radiosurgery is increasingly used for higher Spetzler-Martin grade AVM. Reported rates of confirmed radiographic obliteration after AVM radiosurgery range from 47% to 90%.
- Endovascular embolization involves transarterial superselective blockage of the AVM. It has become an important adjunctive tool. Currently recommended and approved for use before resection, preoperative embolization can reduce arterial flow and pressure within the AVM, assisting in speed and safety of surgical resection. In addition, embolization may often be used to treat intranidal or flow-related aneurysms in coordination with either resection or radiosurgery. Embolization alone in obliterating an AVM is not routinely recommended.
- Treatment decisions should take into consideration the morbidity associated with the treatment modality versus the risk of future hemorrhage or neurologic deterioration. Disability stemming from intractable seizures or severe headaches may make invasive definitive treatment a more attractive option.
- Acute cerebral hemorrhage: in the case of an acute hemorrhage, airway and breathing must be maintained, with intubation if necessary. Acute neurosurgical intervention for clot evacuation may be warranted. Microsurgical resection of the AVM may or may not be feasible in the acute setting and is controversial.

DISPOSITION

Whether the patient is receiving elective treatment of a known lesion or presenting with an acute hemorrhage, the patient should receive care in a progressive or intensive care unit with experience dealing with cerebrovascular disease. Once the patient is stabilized, appropriate rehabilitation should be arranged.

REFERRAL

- Cerebral AVMs should be managed by a qualified neurosurgeon.
- Referral to radiation medicine for adjuvant radiosurgery should be made when indicated.
- Referral to an interventional radiologist for endovascular treatment may be warranted.

- Treatment in a primary stroke center or other specialized center that offers all treatment modalities is recommended.

 **PEARLS & CONSIDERATIONS**

COMMENTS

No two AVMs are exactly the same; individualization of treatment decisions is the mainstay. Additionally, many AVMs could be effectively treated through one of several modalities or a combination thereof. Factors such as patient age, overall health status, radiographic characteristics, route of surgical access, and potential morbidities of each treatment modality are vital variables in consideration for treatment. The advisability of intervention for unruptured AVMs remains controversial. In a recent randomized trial comparing medical management with specific interventions to obliterate AVMs (neurosurgery, embolization, radiotherapy, or a combination) the rates of neurological disability were much higher in the intervention group than with conservative treatment.[1]

PATIENT/FAMILY EDUCATION

If a patient with a known AVM suffers from acute-onset neurologic deficits or stroke-like symptoms, emergency medical attention is warranted for potential hemorrhage. Presence of AVMs, cerebral or otherwise, in family members should be disclosed to the patient's primary care physician because the presence of a genetic condition predisposing to cerebral AVMs should be considered.

SUGGESTED READINGS

Available at www.expertconsult.com

AUTHORS: **STEPHEN L. GRUPKE, M.D., M.S.,** and **JUSTIN F. FRASER, M.D.**

[1]Mohr JP et al: Medical management with or without interventional therapy for unruptured brain arteriovenous malformations (ARUBA): a multicentre nonblinded, randomized trial, *Lancet* 383:614-621, 2014.

 **BASIC INFORMATION**

DEFINITION

Avascular necrosis (AVN) is ischemic death of bone due to insufficient blood supply. Osteonecrosis is not a specific disease entity but a final common pathway to several disorders that impair blood supply to the femoral head and other locations.

SYNONYMS

AVN
Osteonecrosis
Aseptic necrosis

ICD-10CM CODES

M87 Idiopathic aseptic necrosis of bone
M87.1 Osteonecrosis due to drugs
M87.2 Osteonecrosis due to previous trauma
M87.3 Other secondary osteonecrosis
M87.9 Osteonecrosis, unspecified

EPIDEMIOLOGY & DEMOGRAPHICS

- 15,000 new cases per year in the United States. It is most commonly associated with the hip and accounts for 10% of total hip replacements in the United States.
- Usually occurs in middle age and is more frequent in males than females
- Associated conditions:
  1. Corticosteroid treatment: 35%
  2. Alcohol abuse: 22%
  3. Idiopathic and other: 43%
  4. Hemoglobinopathies, pancreatitis, chronic renal failure, SLE, chemotherapy, decompression sickness
- Common sites involved
  1. Femoral head
  2. Femoral condyle
  3. Humeral head
  4. Navicular and lunate wrist bones
  5. Talus

PHYSICAL FINDINGS & CLINICAL PRESENTATION

- May be asymptomatic in early stages
- Pain in the involved area exacerbated by movement or weight bearing in later stages
- Decreased range of motion as the disease progresses
- Functional limitation

ETIOLOGY

Final common pathway of conditions that lead to impairment of the blood supply to the involved bone. Trauma disrupting the blood supply is the most common cause of AVN. Arterial factors are considered the most common cause of AVN. Table 1A-76 describes proposed mechanism of disease of common conditions associated with osteonecrosis.

TABLE 1A-77 Modified Steinberg Staging System for Osteonecrosis

Stage	Radiographic Appearance	Reversible
I	Normal radiographs, but abnormal bone scan or magnetic resonance image	Yes
II	Lucent and sclerotic changes	Yes
III	Subchondral fracture without flattening	No
IV	Subchondral fracture with flattening or segmental depression of femoral head	No
V	Joint space narrowing or acetabular changes	No
VI	Advanced degenerative changes	No

From Firestein GS, Budd RC, Gabriel SE, et al: *Kelly's textbook of rheumatology*, ed 9, Philadelphia, 2013, Saunders.

STAGING

Table 1A-77 describes the Modified Steinberg Staging System for osteonecrosis.
Stages:
- Stage 0
  1. Asymptomatic
  2. Normal imaging
  3. Histologic findings only (i.e., silent osteonecrosis)
- Stage 1
  1. Asymptomatic or symptomatic
  2. Normal radiographs and CT scan
  3. Abnormal bone scan or MRI
- Stage 2
  1. Abnormal radiographs or CT scan, including linear sclerosis, focal bead mineralization, cysts; however, the overall architecture of the involved bone is normal
- Stage 3
  1. Early evidence of mechanical bone failure (subchondral fracture), but the overall shape of the bone is still intact
- Stage 4
  1. Flattening or collapse of the bone
- Stage 5
  1. Joint space narrowing
- Stage 6
  1. Extensive joint destruction

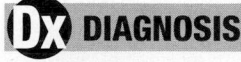 **DIAGNOSIS**

DIFFERENTIAL DIAGNOSIS

- None in late stages
- Early: any condition causing focal musculoskeletal pain, including arthritis, bursitis, tendinitis, myopathy, neoplastic bone and joint diseases, traumatic injuries, pathologic fractures

WORKUP

Fig. 1A-152 describes a diagnostic algorithm for osteonecrosis.

IMAGING STUDIES (FIG. 1A-153)

1. MRI: the most sensitive technology to diagnose early aseptic necrosis. The first sign is a margin of low signal. An inner border of

TABLE 1A-76 Proposed Mechanism of Disease of Common Conditions Associated with Osteonecrosis

Associated Condition	Mechanism of Osteonecrosis							
	Apoptosis	Osteoblast/ Osteoclast Homeostasis	Lipid Abnormalities	Coagulation Abnormalities	Oxidative Stress	Parathyroid/ Calcium Imbalance	Vascular Plugging	Vasoactive Substances
Corticosteroids	X	X	X	X	X			X
Bisphosphonates	X	X	X					
Alcohol abuse	X	X	X	X	X			
Trauma	X	X						X
Renal transplantation	X	X		X		X		
Dialysis						X		
Sickle cell disease							X	

From Firestein GS, Budd RC, Gabriel SE, et al: *Kelly's textbook of rheumatology*, ed 9, Philadelphia, 2013, Saunders.

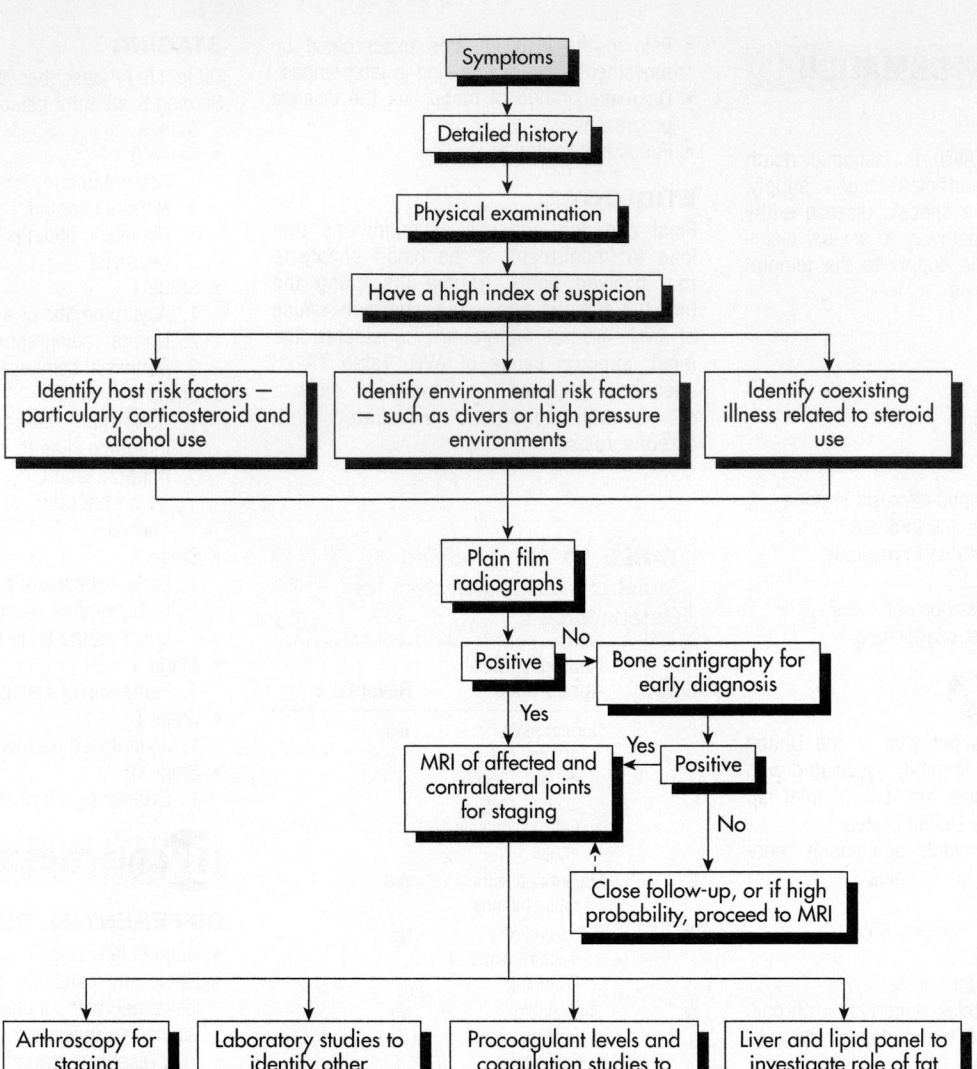

FIGURE 1A-152 Diagnostic algorithm for osteonecrosis. *MRI*, Magnetic resonance image. (From Firestein GS, Budd RC, Gabriel SE, et al: *Kelly's textbook of rheumatology*, ed 9, Philadelphia, 2013, Saunders.)

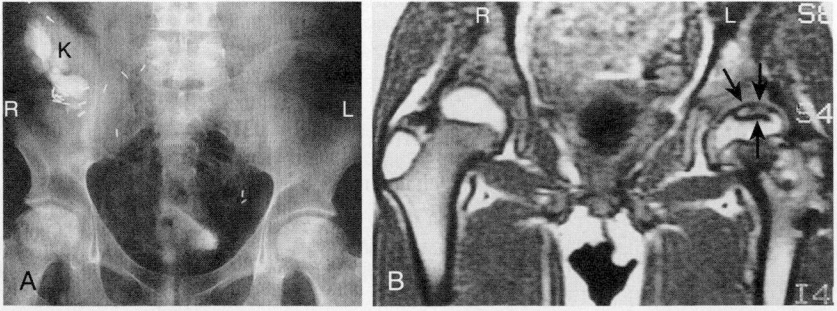

FIGURE 1A-153 Aseptic necrosis of the hips. A, Aseptic necrosis can occur from a number of causes, including trauma and steroid use. In this patient, an anteroposterior view of the pelvis shows a transplanted kidney *(K)* in the right iliac fossa. Use of steroids has caused this patient to have bilateral aseptic necrosis. The femoral heads are somewhat flattened, irregular, and increased in density. **B,** Aseptic necrosis in a different patient is demonstrated on an MRI scan as an area of decreased signal *(arrows)* in the left femoral head. This is the most sensitive method for detection of early aseptic necrosis. (From Mettler FA [ed]: *Primary care radiology*, Philadelphia, 2000, Saunders.)

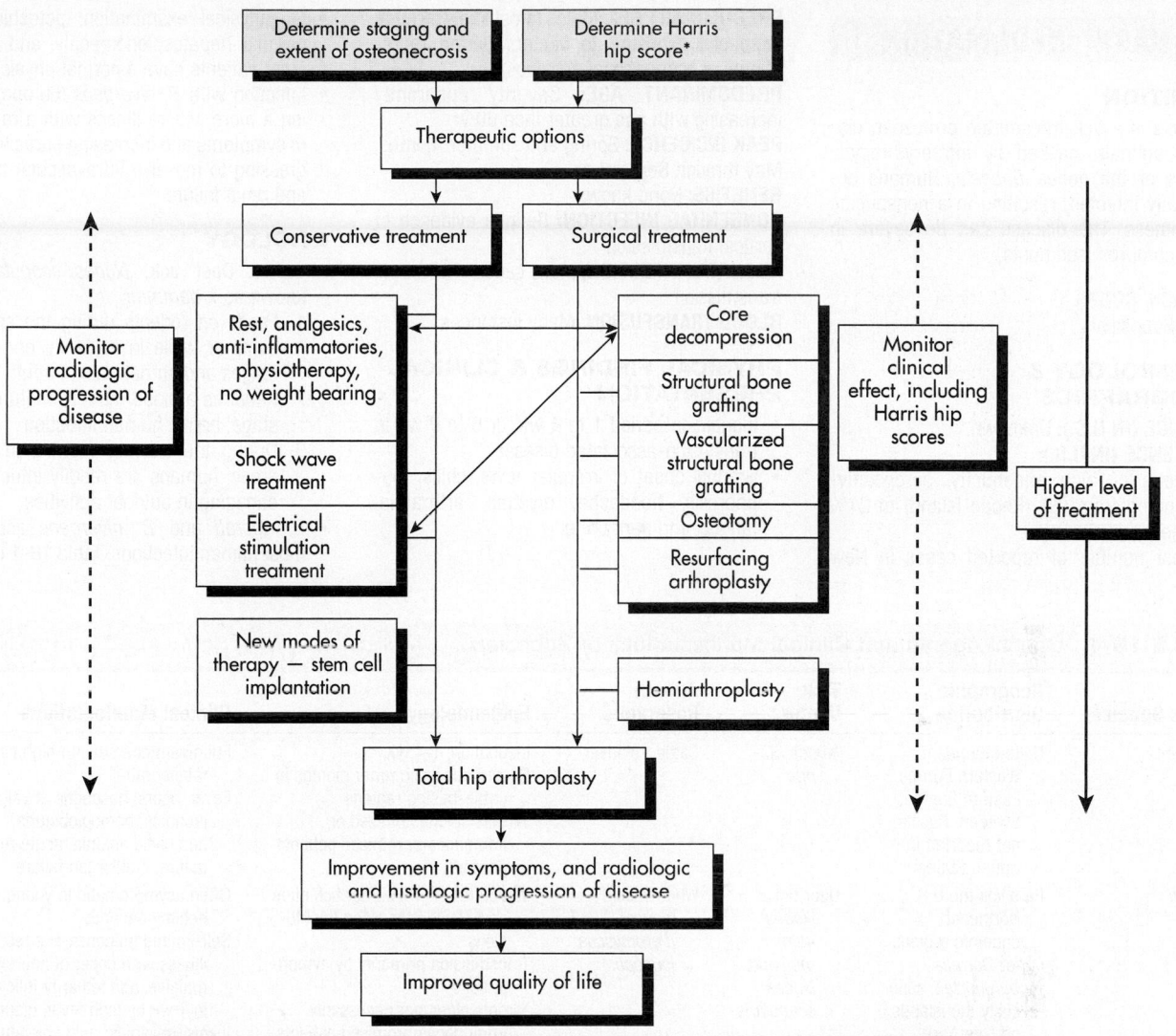

FIGURE 1A-154 Treatment algorithm for osteonecrosis. *www.ncbi.nlm.nih.gov/pubmed/22588745.
(From Firestein GS, Budd RC, Gabriel SE, et al: *Kelly's textbook of rheumatology*, ed 9, Philadelphia, 2013, Saunders.)

high signal associated with a low-signal line is specific for aseptic necrosis ("double line sign"). Sensitivity is 75% to 100%.

2. Radiography: insensitive early in the course. The earliest changes include diffuse osteopenia, areas of radiolucency with sclerotic border, and linear sclerosis. Later, a subchondral lucency (crescent sign) indicates subchondral fracture. More advanced cases reveal flattening, collapsed bone, and abnormal bone contour. In late disease, osteoarthritic changes are seen.

3. Bone scan:
   ○ Early: "cold" area.
   ○ Later: increased radionuclide uptake as a result of remodeling.
   ○ Sensitivity in early disease is only 70% and specificity is poor.

4. CT scan: may reveal central necrosis and area of collapse before those are visible on radiographs.

Rx TREATMENT

PREVENTION
- Manage etiologic conditions
- Minimize corticosteroid use

NONPHARMACOLOGIC THERAPY
- Core decompression: effectiveness 35% to 95% in early phases
- Bone grafting
- Osteotomies
- Joint replacement

ACUTE GENERAL Rx
- Decrease weight bearing of affected area.
- Pulsing electromagnetic fields applied externally (still experimental).
- Peripheral vasodilators (e.g., dihydroergotamine) (unproven).
- Late-stage AVN is most often treated by total joint arthroplasty.

- A treatment algorithm for osteonecrosis is described in Fig. 1A-154.

PROGNOSIS
- When diagnosed at an early stage treatment is appropriate in all cases because 85% to 90% can be expected to progress to a more advanced stage.
- Contralateral joint involvement is common (30% to 70%).

SUGGESTED READINGS
Available at www.expertconsult.com

RELATED CONTENT
Avascular Necrosis (Patient Information)

AUTHOR: **FRED F. FERRI, M.D.**

Babesiosis

BASIC INFORMATION

DEFINITION

Babesiosis is a tick-transmitted protozoan disease of animals, caused by intraerythrocytic parasites of the genus *Babesia*. Humans are incidentally infected, resulting in a nonspecific febrile illness. The disease can be severe in immunocompromised hosts.

ICD-10CM CODES
B60.0 Babesiosis

EPIDEMIOLOGY & DEMOGRAPHICS

INCIDENCE (IN U.S.): Unknown
PREVALENCE (IN U.S.):
- In areas of high endemicity, seropositivity ranging from 9% (Rhode Island) to 21% (Connecticut)
- Highest number of reported cases in New York

PREDOMINANT SEX: Males (most likely through increased exposure to vectors during recreational or occupational activities)
PREDOMINANT AGE: Severity apparently increasing with age greater than 60 yr
PEAK INCIDENCE: Spring and summer months, May through September
GENETICS: None known
CONGENITAL INFECTION: Definite evidence of vertical transmission
NEONATAL INFECTION: Many cases of perinatal transmission
BLOOD TRANSFUSION: Many instances

PHYSICAL FINDINGS & CLINICAL PRESENTATION

- Incubation period 1 to 4 wk, or 6 to 9 wk in transfusion-associated disease
- Gradual onset of irregular fever, chills, diaphoresis, headache, myalgia, arthralgia, fatigue, and dark urine

- On physical examination: petechiae, frank or mild hepatosplenomegaly, and jaundice. Most patients have a normal physical exam.
- Infection with *B. divergens* (Europe) producing a more severe illness with a rapid onset of symptoms and increasing parasitemia progressing to massive intravascular hemolysis and renal failure

ETIOLOGY

- Vector: Deer tick, *Ixodes scapularis* (also known as *I. dammini*)
  1. Feeds on rodents during the spring and summer while in its larval and nymphal stages and on deer as an adult
  2. Requires a blood meal to mature to each stage, hence human infection
  3. During the warmer months in endemic areas, humans are readily infected while engaging in outdoor activities
- *B. microti* and *B. divergens* account for most human infections. Table 1B-1 compares

TABLE 1B-1 Causal Agents and Clinical Manifestations of Babesiosis

Babesia Species	Geographic Distribution	Tick Vectors	Animal Reservoirs	Epidemiology	Clinical Manifestations
B. divergens	United Kingdom, Western Europe, Eastern Europe, Sweden, Russia; not reported in United States	*Ixodes ricinus*	Cattle, reindeer	Incubation, 1-4 wk Occurs during summer months in cattle-raising regions Targets splenectomized or immunocompromised patients primarily	Fulminant course with high case-fatality rate Fever, rigors, headache, myalgia, jaundice, hemoglobinuria, hemolytic anemia, acute renal failure, multiorgan failure
B. microti	Parallels the U.S. Northeast endemic regions for *Borrelia burgdorferi*, especially the islands off New York, Massachusetts, Connecticut, and Rhode Island and focal areas in Connecticut, New Jersey, Wisconsin, and Minnesota	Deer ticks: *Ixodes dammini* and *Ixodes scapularis*	White-footed mouse (*Peromyscus leucopus*)	Incubation, 1-4 wk after tick bites or 4-9 wk after blood transfusions Transmission primarily by nymphal ticks Targets older, not necessarily immunocompromised patients, particularly severe in those immunocompromised by HIV infection, advanced age, coinfections with *B. burgdorferi* Seasonality parallels tick nymph activity; 80% of cases occur from May to August	Often asymptomatic in young, healthy patients Self-limited influenza-like febrile illness with onset of anorexia, malaise, and lethargy followed in 1 wk by high fever, diaphoresis, myalgias; mild splenomegaly, and rarely hepatomegaly Later hemolysis, hemolytic anemia, thrombocytopenia, jaundice, acute renal failure, especially in the splenectomized, older adults, or the immunocompromised Complications include ARDS and DIC Case-fatality rate, 5%
MO-1 (a relative or subspecies of *B. divergens*)	Rural Missouri and Kentucky	*Ixodes dentatus* (rabbit tick)	Rabbits, birds	Incubation, 1-4 wk after tick bites Spring to autumn seasonality Targets the splenectomized, like *B. divergens*	Same as above—often asymptomatic, except in the splenectomized, who will develop high parasitemias and multiorgan failure
WA-1 (a relative or subspecies of *B. gibsoni*)	Rural Washington State	Ixodid ticks, including *Ixodes dentatus*	Unknown—wild canids and ungulates suspected	Incubation, 1-4 wk Targets the splenectomized, older adults, immunocompromised, premature infants May be transmitted by blood transfusion	Same as above—often asymptomatic, except in the splenectomized, who will develop high parasitemias and multiorgan failure
CA-1, CA-2, etc. subspecies (relatives or subspecies of mule deer and bighorn sheep *Babesia* species)	U.S. Pacific coast, primarily rural and semirural areas of California	Ixodid ticks	Unknown—mule deer and big-horn sheep suspected	Incubation, 1-4 wk Targets the splenectomized, elderly, immunocompromised, and premature infants	Same as above—often asymptomatic, except in the splenectomized, who will develop high parasitemias and multiorgan failure

ARDS, Acute respiratory distress syndrome; *DIC*, disseminated intravascular coagulation.
(From Bennett JE, Dolin R, Blaser MJ: *Mandell, Douglas, and Bennett's principles and practice of infectious diseases*, ed 8, Philadelphia, 2015, Saunders.)

causal agents and clinical manifestations of babesiosis.

- In the U.S., cases caused by *B. microti* are acquired on offshore islands of the northeastern coast, including Nantucket Island, Cape Cod, and Martha's Vineyard in Massachusetts; Block Island in Rhode Island; and Long Island, Fire Island, and Shelter Island in New York; as well as the nearby mainland including Connecticut, Rhode Island, and New Jersey.
- Sporadic cases reported from California, Georgia, Maryland, Minnesota, Virginia, Wisconsin, and most recently the WA-1 strain from Washington State and the MO-1 strain from Missouri.
- *B. divergens* is implicated in human disease in Europe, where the disease remains rare and predominantly associated with asplenia.
- Majority of cases are asymptomatic.
- May be transmissible by transfusion, through platelets and erythrocytes.
- Mixed infections (*B. microti* and *Borrelia burgdorferi*, the causative agent of Lyme disease) are estimated to occur in 10% (Rhode Island and Connecticut) to 60% (New York) of cases.

 DIAGNOSIS

DIFFERENTIAL DIAGNOSIS

- Amebiasis
- Ehrlichiosis
- Hepatic abscess
- Leptospirosis
- Malaria
- Salmonellosis, including typhoid fever
- Acute viral hepatitis
- Hemorrhagic fevers
- Subacute bacterial endocarditis

WORKUP

Should be suspected in any febrile patient living or traveling in an endemic area, irrespective of exposure history to ticks or tick bites, especially if asplenic

LABORATORY TESTS

- The preferred method for diagnosing babesiosis is PCR using whole blood specimens.
- Babesial DNA by polymerase chain reaction (PCR) has comparable sensitivity and specificity to microscopic analysis of thin blood smears. PCR is more sensitive than smears at the onset of infection when parasite load may be minimal.
- Diagnosis achieved serologically by indirect immunofluorescence assay (IFA) is specific for *B. microti.*
  1. Assay is hampered by the inability to distinguish between exposed patients and those who are actively infected.
  2. IGG titer of ≥1:64 is indicative of seropositivity, whereas one ≥1:1024 is considered diagnostic of acute infection. IGM titer of 1:64 is considered indicative of acute infection.
  3. Immunoglobulin M indirect immunofluorescent-antibody test may be highly

sensitive and specific for diagnosis. IGM titer of 1:64 is considered indicative of acute infection.
- CBC to reveal mild to moderate thrombocytopenia and anemia. The WBC count may be normal, elevated, or low. Abnormally elevated serum chemistries, including creatinine, liver function profile, lactate dehydrogenase, and indirect and total bilirubin levels; haptoglobin is low.
- Urinalysis to reveal proteinuria and hemoglobinuria
- Examination of Giemsa- or Wright-stained thin blood films for intraerythrocytic parasites
  1. In its classic, though infrequently seen, form a "tetrad" or "Maltese cross" composed of four daughter cells attached by cytoplasmic strands is observed (Fig. 1B-1).
  2. More commonly, smaller forms composed of a single chromatin dot are eccentrically located within bluish cytoplasm.
  3. Parasitized erythrocytes may be multiply infected but not enlarged.
  4. Extra-erythrocytic forms may be seen.

 TREATMENT

NONPHARMACOLOGIC THERAPY
Supportive care with adequate hydration

ACUTE GENERAL Rx
- In patients with intact spleens: predominantly asymptomatic or if symptomatic, generally self-limited
- Therapy reserved for the severely ill patient, especially if asplenic, elderly, or immunosuppressed. Therapy may be offered to any symptomatic patient.
- Combination of atovaquone 750 mg q12h and azithromycin 500 mg on day 1 and 250 mg per day thereafter for 7 to 10 days appears to be as effective as a regimen of clindamycin and quinine with fewer adverse reactions. This is the preferred regimen for mild disease.
- Combination of quinine sulfate 650 mg PO tid plus clindamycin 600 mg PO tid (600 mg parenterally qid) taken for 7 to 10 days: effective but may not eliminate parasites
- Severely ill patients are hospitalized and treated with clindamycin and quinine
- Exchange transfusions in addition to antimicrobial therapy: successful treatment for severe infections in asplenic patients associated with high levels of *B. microti* or *B. divergens* parasitemia. Exchange transfusion is recommended for patients with >10% parasitemia, but may be considered for any severely ill patient.
- Relapsed and immunocompromised patients require a longer duration of therapy.

DISPOSITION
Prognosis is usually good and fatal outcomes are rare.

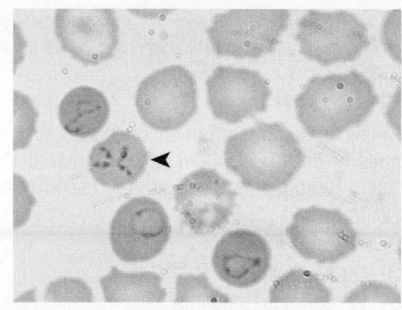

FIGURE 1B-1 Babesia spp. Single and multiple intraerythrocytic parasites can be seen. The *arrow* marks a typical Maltese cross. (From Cohen J, Powderly WG: *Infectious diseases,* ed 2, St Louis, 2004, Mosby.)

REFERRAL
- For prompt consultation with an infectious disease specialist if the diagnosis is acutely suspected, especially in the asplenic, elderly, or immunocompromised patient
- For hospitalization for the severely ill patient who may require exchange transfusions in addition to antibiotic therapy

PEARLS & CONSIDERATIONS

COMMENTS
- Prevention of babesiosis in asplenic or immunocompromised hosts is best achieved by avoidance of areas where the vector is endemic, especially May through September.
- If residence or travel in endemic areas is unavoidable, advise patients to perform daily cutaneous self-examination, wear light-colored clothing (to facilitate removal of ticks), tuck pants into socks, and apply tick repellent (diethyltoluamide and dimethylphthalate) to skin or clothing.
- Advise a daily inspection for ticks in family pets (e.g., cats and dogs).
- Infection with *B. divergens,* especially in the asplenic patient, is often fatal.
- Concurrent cases of babesiosis and Lyme disease have been documented—check for combined infection in severely ill patients.
- A combination of clindamycin and quinine has been successfully used to treat babesiosis during the third trimester of pregnancy without incurring apparent adverse effect on the fetus.
- In 2011 the CDC added babesiosis to the list of nationally notifiable diseases.

SUGGESTED READINGS
Available at www.expertconsult.com

RELATED CONTENT
Babesiosis (Patient Information)

AUTHOR: **PATRICIA CRISTOFARO, M.D.**

BASIC INFORMATION

DEFINITION

Balanitis is an inflammation of the superficial tissues of the penile head (glans penis). If the foreskin (prepuce) is involved, it is called *balanoposthitis*.

ICD-10CM CODES
B37.42 Candidal balanitis
N48.1 Balanitis

EPIDEMIOLOGY & DEMOGRAPHICS

INCIDENCE (IN U.S.): More common in uncircumcised males and in diabetic patients
PREVALENCE (IN U.S.): One study reports that 11% of adult men seen in a urology clinic and 3% of male children (mostly uncircumcised) have balanitis.
PREDOMINANT SEX: Almost exclusive to males but can affect clitoris
PEAK INCIDENCE: All ages, especially in sexually active men. It occurs in ¼ of male sex partners of women infected with *Candida*.

PHYSICAL FINDINGS & CLINICAL PRESENTATION

- Itching and tenderness
- Pain, dysuria, and local edema and erythema (Fig. 1B-4)
- Rarely, ulceration and lymph node enlargement
- Severe ulcerations leading to superimposed bacterial infections
- Inability to void: unusual, but a more distressing and serious complication

ETIOLOGY

- Causes include infectious agents, skin disorders, or miscellaneous.
- Infectious diseases: *Candida species (40%), Neisseria gonorrhoeae,* HPV, herpes simplex, *Gardnerella vaginalis, Treponema pallidum* (syphilis), HIV, *Trichomonas, Staphylococcus aureus,* anaerobic bacteria

- Skin disorders: circinate balanitis of **Reiter's syndrome,** lichen sclerosis
- Miscellaneous: poor hygiene, causing erosion of tissue with erythema and promoting growth of *Candida albicans* (Fig. E1B-5), trauma (zippers, urinary catheters), allergic reactions to condoms or medications

Dx DIAGNOSIS

DIFFERENTIAL DIAGNOSIS

- Leukoplakia
- Nummular eczema
- Balanitis xerotica obliterans
- Psoriasis
- Carcinoma of the penis
- Plasma cell balanitis (noninfectious)
- Erythroplasia of Queyrat
- Nodular scabies
- Circinate balanitis (Reiter's syndrome)

WORKUP

- Sexually active males: assessment for evidence of other sexually transmitted diseases
- Biopsy if lesions do not heal

LABORATORY TESTS

- VDRL, HIV, NAATs for chlamydia and gonorrhea
- FBS, HBA$_{1C}$ to rule out diabetes
- Wet mount for *Trichomonas*
- KOH prep for yeast

Rx TREATMENT

NONPHARMACOLOGIC THERAPY

- Maintenance of meticulous hygiene
- Retraction and bathing of prepuce several times a day
- Warm sitz baths to ease edema and erythema
- Consideration of circumcision, especially when symptoms are severe or recurrent
- With Foley catheters, strict catheter care strongly advised

ACUTE GENERAL Rx

- Metronidazole 2 g PO as a single dose or fluconazole 150 mg PO × 1 or itraconazole 200 mg PO bid × 1 day
- Clotrimazole 1% cream applied topically twice daily to affected areas
- Bacitracin or Neosporin ointment applied topically 4 times daily
- With more severe bacterial superinfection: cephalexin 500 mg PO qid
- Topical corticosteroids added 4 times daily if dermatitis severe
- Patients with suspected urinary tract infections: trimethoprim-sulfa DS twice daily or ciprofloxacin 500 mg PO bid after obtaining appropriate cultures

DISPOSITION

Balanitis is often self-limited and usually responds to conservative therapy; if it does not improve, consider circinate balanitis of Reiter's syndrome, nodular scabies, and primary skin lesions including skin carcinoma.

! PEARLS & CONSIDERATIONS

Don't forget about nodular scabies involving the prepubic area—examine the region carefully for burrows and tracks of *Sarcoptes scabiei.*

REFERRAL

- For surgical evaluation for circumcision if symptoms are recurrent, especially if phimosis or meatitis occurs (note: Severe phimosis with an inability to void may require prompt slit drainage.)
- For biopsy to rule out other diagnoses such as premalignant or malignant lesions if lesions are not healing

SUGGESTED READINGS
Available at www.expertconsult.com

RELATED CONTENT
Balanitis (Patient Information)

AUTHOR: **GLENN G. FORT, M.D., M.P.H.**

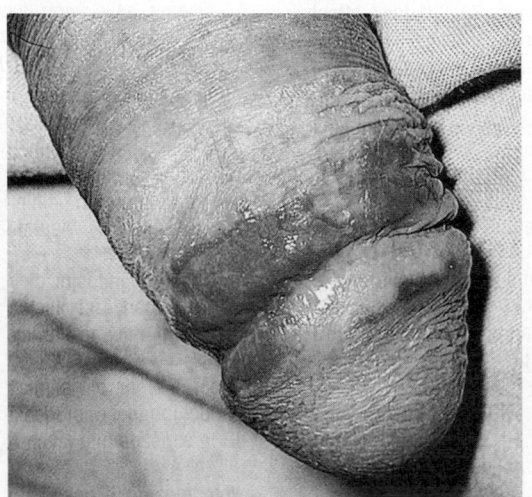

FIGURE 1B-4 Candidal balanitis. (From White GM, Cox NH [eds]: *Diseases of the skin: a color atlas and text,* ed 2, St Louis, 2006, Mosby.)

Diseases and Disorders

DEFINITION

Barrett esophagus occurs when the squamocolumnar junction is displaced proximal to the gastroesophageal junction and the squamous lining of the lower esophagus is replaced by metaplastic columnar epithelium, which predisposes to the development of esophageal adenocarcinoma. While cardia-type epithelium has been shown to predispose to esophageal cancer, the presence of intestinalized epithelium is still considered essential for the diagnosis. Recent data show that the absolute annual risk for esophageal carcinoma in Barrett esophagus is 0.12%, which is much lower than the assumed risk of 0.5% that is the basis for current surveillance guidelines.

SYNONYMS

Barrett's esophagus
Esophagus, Barrett
Esophagus, columnar-lined
Ulcer, Barrett's

ICD-10CM CODES
K22.70   Barrett esophagus without dysplasia
K22.710   Barrett's esophagus with low grade
          dysplasia
K22.711   Barrett's esophagus with high
          grade dysplasia
K22.719   Barrett's esophagus with dysplasia,
          unspecified

EPIDEMIOLOGY & DEMOGRAPHICS

- Male/female ratio of 4:1.
- Mean age of onset is 40 yr, with a mean age range of diagnosis of 55 to 60 yr.
- Occurs more frequently in white and Hispanic individuals than in African American individuals, with a ratio of 10 to 20:1.
- Mean prevalence of 5% to 15% in patients undergoing endoscopy (EGD) for symptoms of gastroesophageal reflux disease (GERD).
- Independent risk factors include chronic reflux (>5 years), hiatal hernia, age >50 years, male gender, white ethnicity, smoking history, and intra-abdominal obesity. A family history with at least one first-degree relative with Barrett esophagus or adenocarcinoma of the esophagus may also be a risk factor.
- It is estimated that 5.6% of adults in the United States have Barrett esophagus. Prevalence rate in asymptomatic cohorts ranges from 5% to 25%.

PHYSICAL FINDINGS & CLINICAL PRESENTATION

SYMPTOMS
- Chronic heartburn
- Dysphagia with solid food
- May be an incidental finding on EGD in patients without reflux symptoms
- Less frequent: chest pain, hematemesis, melena
- Patients may be asymptomatic.

PHYSICAL FINDINGS
- Nonspecific; can be completely normal
- Epigastric tenderness on palpation

ETIOLOGY

- Metaplasia is thought to result from reepithelialization of esophageal tissue injured as a result of chronic GERD.
- Patients with Barrett esophagus tend to have more severe esophageal motility disturbances (decreased lower esophageal sphincter pressure, ineffective peristalsis) and greater esophageal acid exposure on 24-hour pH monitoring.
- Intraesophageal bile reflux may also play a role in the pathogenesis.
- Familial clustering of GERD and Barrett esophagus suggests a genetic predisposition, but no gene has yet been identified. Early data suggest that patients who develop Barrett are genetically predisposed to a severe inflammatory response to GERD. Candidate susceptibility loci include *CRTC1, BARX1,* and *FOXP1.*
- Progression from metaplasia to carcinoma is associated with changes in gene structure and expression, including the caudal-related homeobox family of transcription factors (CDX1 and CDX2) and the tumor suppressors p16 (CDKN2A) and TP53.

 **DIAGNOSIS**

DIFFERENTIAL DIAGNOSIS
- GERD, uncomplicated
- Erosive esophagitis
- Gastritis
- Peptic ulcer disease
- Angina
- Malignancy
- Stricture or Schatzki's ring

WORKUP
- The Practice Parameters Committee of the American College of Gastroenterology (ACG) has suggested that the highest yield for Barrett esophagus screening is in older (age >50 yr) white men with longstanding heartburn. The American Gastroenterological Association Medical Position Panel gave a weak recommendation for screening patients with multiple risk factors, including age over 50, male sex, white race, chronic GERD, hiatal hernia, elevated body mass index, and intraabdominal distribution of body fat. An international consensus group suggested screening men over 60 with GERD symptoms for more than 10 years. General population screening is not currently recommended. The benefit of screening in high-risk populations is not established. Although screening has become standard of practice in some communities, the effectiveness of screening using current techniques is controversial because it may not improve mortality rates from adenocarcinoma or be cost-effective.
- EGD with biopsy is necessary for diagnosis. Ideally, this should be done via high-resolution white-light endoscopy.
- Wireless esophageal capsule endoscopy may detect Barrett esophagus but with a lower sensitivity and specificity than EGD. Imaging studies are not useful. Other modalities under investigation include unsedated transnasal endoscopy and an esophageal cytology device called a *Cytosponge.*
- Diagnosis requires the presence of metaplastic columnar epithelium proximal to the gastroesophageal junction (Fig. 1B-6). Longer-segment (≥3 cm) Barrett esophagus is more readily diagnosed (Fig. 1B-7). Some endoscopists describe the extent of Barrett esophagus using the Prague criteria, describing the circumferential and maximal length via a C and M score. At least two expert gastrointestinal pathologists should concur if any grade of dysplasia is diagnosed.
- Intestinal metaplasia of the gastric cardia is not Barrett esophagus and does not have the same risk for malignancy.
- Biomarkers and advanced imaging techniques such as chromoendoscopy, narrow band imaging, confocal laser endomicroscopy, and optical coherence tomography are being evaluated to assist with diagnosis and to better understand progression of disease, prediction of response to therapy, or prognosis.
- Screening for *Helicobacter pylori* infection in patients with GERD and Barrett esophagus is not recommended.

The goal is to control GERD symptoms and maintain healed mucosa.

NONPHARMACOLOGIC THERAPY
Nonpharmacologic therapy includes lifestyle modifications; elevating head of bed; and avoiding chocolate, tobacco, caffeine, mints, and certain drugs (see "Gastroesophageal Reflux Disease").

ACUTE GENERAL Rx
- Proton pump inhibitors are the most effective treatment for GERD. Therapy should be dosed to control symptoms and/or to promote healing of endoscopic signs of disease.
- If patient is asymptomatic and incidentally found to have Barrett esophagus, proton pump inhibitors may still be considered, as they may reduce the risk of neoplastic progression.

CHRONIC Rx
- Chronic acid suppression is often necessary to control symptoms and maintain healing.
- Antireflux surgery may be considered for management of GERD and associated sequelae, but it has not been proven to be superior to medical therapy. Patients continue to require endoscopic surveillance of their esophagus.
- When GERD is controlled by either medical or surgical therapy, ablation of metaplastic epithelium usually leads to replacement by normal squamous epithelium. Because only a minority of patients with Barrett esophagus progress to high-grade dysplasia or carcinoma, endoscopic eradication therapy is not

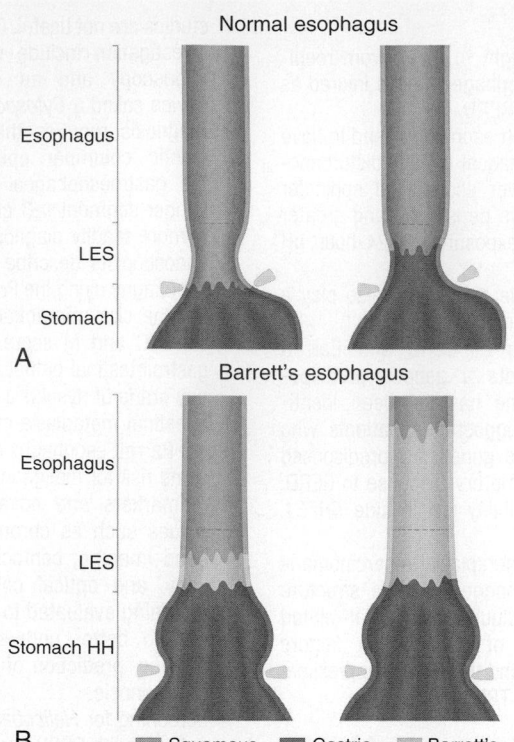

FIGURE 1B-6 Anatomic landmarks of the normal LES region (A) and of Barrett esophagus (B). Note that gastric mucosa is very common and normal in the LES region and that in Barrett esophagus, the squamocolumnar junction is not only proximally displaced within the tubular esophagus, but that the intervening mucosa is composed of intestinalized Barrett's metaplastic epithelium. *HH,* Hiatial hernia. (From Silverburg SG: *Principles of practice of surgical pathology and cytopathology,* ed 4, New York, 2006, Churchill Livingstone.)

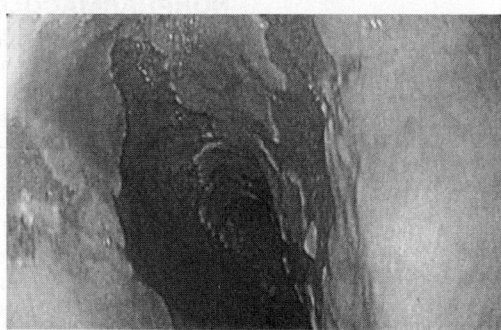

FIGURE 1B-7 Long-segment Barrett esophagus. (From Cameron JL, Cameron AM: *Current surgical therapy,* ed 10, Philadelphia, 2011, Saunders.)

recommended for the general population of patients with nondysplastic Barrett esophagus.

- While endoscopic eradication therapy has been shown to reduce the progression of Barrett esophagus with low-grade dysplasia to high-grade dysplasia and adenocarcinoma in selected patients, a long-term benefit has not been clearly established. As the risk of progression may be increased in patients with several high-risk features (multifocality, persistence over time, or long segment), some authors are recommending ablation therapy in this subgroup.
- Endoscopic eradication therapy is the treatment of choice for high-grade dysplasia. Radiofrequency ablation, thermal ablation techniques, or photodynamic therapy, combined with endoscopic mucosal resection (EMR) or endoscopic submucosal dissection (ESD) of visible mucosal irregularities, are accepted approaches to the treatment of patients with Barrett esophagus and high-grade dysplasia, in conjunction with aggressive surveillance and eradication of all remaining Barrett's epithelium. Endoscopic therapy is preferred over surgical treatment in properly staged individuals. These therapies may even be considered for patients with focal intramucosal carcinoma, if properly staged (T1SM1 or lower). Cryotherapy is being evaluated for the complete eradication of both dysplasia and intestinal metaplasia and reduced risk for disease progression.

All these options run the risk for residual or buried metaplasia.

- Surgical resection is definitive therapy and may be offered for multifocal high-grade dysplasia or carcinoma that has extended into the submucosa. Mortality appears to be lower with experienced surgeons operating in high-volume centers.
- Patients with cardiovascular risk factors may be considered for low-dose aspirin therapy for chemoprevention of esophageal adenocarcinoma.

DISPOSITION

- The relative risk of developing esophageal adenocarcinoma for a patient with Barrett esophagus, as compared with the general population, is 11.3, a substantial drop from the relative risk of 30 or 40 estimated in earlier reports. The risk is greater in men and in patients with longer (≥8 cm) columnar-lined segments.
- The risk of progression from untreated Barrett with high-grade dysplasia to esophageal adenocarcinoma ranges from 6% to 19% per year.
- Frequency of monitoring is controversial. No prospective studies have proven that endoscopic surveillance is cost effective or increases life expectancy. Although some studies have suggested that close adherence to surveillance protocols is associated with higher rates of detection of dysplasia and cancer, a recent case-control study showed no reduction in mortality.
- Patients with Barrett esophagus currently undergo surveillance EGD and systematic four-quadrant biopsy at intervals determined by the presence and grade of dysplasia. Some authors suggest that only high-risk individuals undergo surveillance. All mucosal abnormalities should undergo biopsy. Patients who have had two consecutive EGDs showing no dysplasia should have follow-up every 3 to 5 yr. Patients with low-grade dysplasia should have extensive mucosal sampling within 6 mo and follow-up every 6 to 12 mo. Patients with high-grade dysplasia should have expert confirmation and extensive mucosal sampling. High-grade dysplasia with visible mucosal irregularities should be removed by EMR or ESD. Consider intensive surveillance every 3 mo. Indefinite dysplasia requires aggressive medical therapy and close follow-up and resampling. Endoscopic treatment is preferred over intensive surveillance in patients with high-grade dysplasia.
- Patients should be treated aggressively for GERD before surveillance.

REFERRAL

- Consider EGD with biopsy in patients with multiple risk factors who have not had previous EGD.
- Refer patients with GERD for evaluation if "red flag" symptoms are present (dysphagia, odynophagia, weight loss, vomiting, early satiety, GI bleeding, iron deficiency).

- Refer patients with biopsy-proved Barrett esophagus for surveillance.
- For those with low-grade dysplasia with high-risk features (multifocality, long-segment, or persistence over time), refer for ablative therapy.
- For those with high-grade dysplasia, refer for ablative therapy with EMR or ESD if appropriate, followed by intensive surveillance. Esophageal resection may be considered.

 EVIDENCE

Available at www.expertconsult.com

SUGGESTED READINGS

Available at www.expertconsult.com

RELATED CONTENT

Barrett Esophagus (Patient Information)
Esophageal Tumors (Related Key Topic)

AUTHOR: **HARLAN G. RICH, M.D.**

B

Diseases and Disorders

I

Basal Cell Carcinoma

 **BASIC INFORMATION**

DEFINITION

Basal cell carcinoma (BCC) is a malignant tumor of the skin arising from basal cells of the lower epidermis and adnexal structures. It may be classified as one of six types: nodular, superficial, pigmented, cystic, sclerosing or morpheaform, and nevoid. The most common type is nodular (21%); the least common is morpheaform (1%). A mixed pattern is present in approximately 40% of cases. BCC advances by direct expansion and destroys normal tissue.

SYNONYMS

BCC

ICD-10CM CODES

C44.01	Basal cell carcinoma of skin of lip
C44.111	Basal cell carcinoma of skin of unspecified eyelid, including canthus
C44.112	Basal cell carcinoma of skin of right eyelid, including canthus
C44.119	Basal cell carcinoma of skin of left eyelid, including canthus
C44.211	Basal cell carcinoma of skin of unspecified ear and external auricular canal
C44.212	Basal cell carcinoma of skin of right ear and external auricular canal
C44.219	Basal cell carcinoma of skin of left ear and external auricular canal
C44.310	Basal cell carcinoma of skin of unspecified parts of face
C44.311	Basal cell carcinoma of skin of nose
C44.319	Basal cell carcinoma of skin of other parts of face
C44.41	Basal cell carcinoma of skin of scalp and neck
C44.510	Basal cell carcinoma of anal skin
C44.511	Basal cell carcinoma of skin of breast
C44.519	Basal cell carcinoma of skin of other part of trunk
C44.611	Basal cell carcinoma of skin of unspecified upper limb, including shoulder
C44.612	Basal cell carcinoma of skin of right upper limb, including shoulder
C44.619	Basal cell carcinoma of skin of left upper limb, including shoulder
C44.711	Basal cell carcinoma of skin of unspecified lower limb, including hip
C44.712	Basal cell carcinoma of skin of right lower limb, including hip
C44.719	Basal cell carcinoma of skin of left lower limb, including hip
C44.81	Basal cell carcinoma of overlapping sites of skin
C44.91	Basal cell carcinoma of skin, unspecified

EPIDEMIOLOGY & DEMOGRAPHICS

- Most common cutaneous neoplasm
- 85% of cases appear on the head and neck region
- Most common site: nose (30%)
- Increased incidence with age >40 yr
- Increased incidence in men
- Risk factors: fair skin, increased sun exposure, use of tanning salons with ultraviolet A or B radiation, history of irradiation (e.g., Hodgkin's disease), personal or family history of skin cancer, impaired immune system

PHYSICAL FINDINGS & CLINICAL PRESENTATION

Variable with the histologic type:
- Nodular: dome-shaped, painless lesion that may become multilobular and frequently ulcerates (rodent ulcer); prominent telangiectatic vessels are noted on the surface. Border is translucent, elevated, pearly white (Fig. 1B-8). Some nodular BCCs may contain pigmentation, giving an appearance similar to a melanoma.
- Superficial: circumscribed, scaling, black appearance with a thin, raised, pearly-white border (Fig. 1B-9); a crust and erosions may be present. Occurs most frequently on the trunk and extremities.
- Morpheaform: flat or slightly raised yellowish or white appearance (similar to localized scleroderma); appearance similar to scars; surface has a waxy consistency.

DIAGNOSIS

DIFFERENTIAL DIAGNOSIS

- Keratoacanthoma
- Melanoma (pigmented BCC)

- Xeroderma pigmentosa
- Basal cell nevus syndrome
- Molluscum contagiosum
- Sebaceous hyperplasia
- Psoriasis

WORKUP

Biopsy to confirm diagnosis

TREATMENT

Variable with tumor size, location, and cell type:
- Excision surgery: preferred method for large tumors with well-defined borders on the legs, cheeks, forehead, and trunk.
- Mohs' micrographic surgery: preferred for lesions in high-risk areas (e.g., nose, eyelid), very large primary tumors, recurrent BCCs, and tumors with poorly defined clinical margins.
- Electrodesiccation and curettage: useful for small (>6 mm) nodular BCCs.
- Cryosurgery with liquid nitrogen: useful in BCCs of the superficial and nodular types with clearly definable margins; no clear advantages over the other forms of therapy; generally reserved for uncomplicated tumors.
- Radiation therapy: generally used for BCCs in areas requiring preservation of normal surrounding tissues for cosmetic reasons (e.g., around lips); also useful in patients who cannot tolerate surgical procedures or for large lesions and surgical failures.

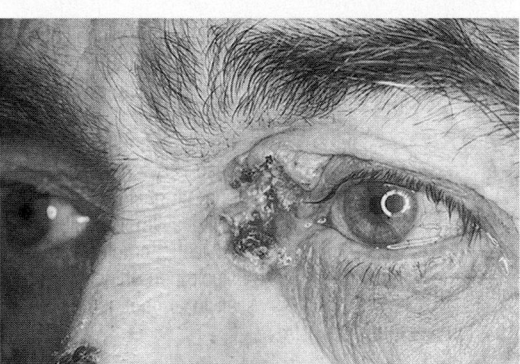

FIGURE 1B-8 Basal cell carcinoma. Note rolled translucent border and central ulceration in typical facial location. (From Noble J et al: *Textbook of primary care medicine,* ed 3, St Louis, 2001, Mosby.)

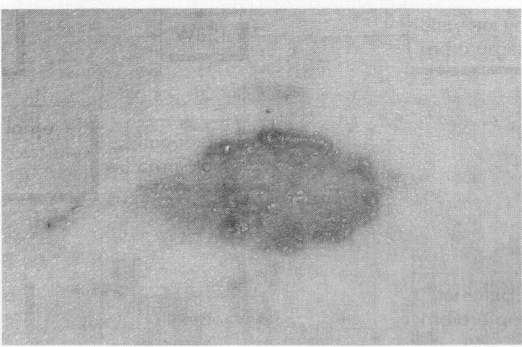

FIGURE 1B-9 Superficial variant of basal cell carcinoma. Multiple lesions are common with this variant, often on the trunk. Closer examination shows the typical raised pearly edge. (From White GM, Cox NH [eds]: *Diseases of the skin: a color atlas and text,*)

- Imiquimod 5% cream can be used for treatment of small, superficial BCCs of the trunk and extremities. Efficacy rate is approximately 80%. Its main advantage is lack of scarring, which must be weighed against higher cure rates with surgical intervention.
- Vismodegib, an orally active hedgehog pathway inhibitor, has been FDA approved for metastatic BCC, recurrent basal cell carcinoma post-surgery, and locally advanced BCC in patients who are not candidates for surgery or radiation. Dose is 150 mg PO qd. Cost of 1-month supply may exceed $7000.

DISPOSITION

- More than 90% of patients are cured; however, periodic evaluation for at least 5 yr is necessary because of increased risk of recurrence of another BCC (<40% risk within 5 yr of treatment).
- A lesion is considered low risk if it is >1.5 cm in diameter, is nodular or cystic, is not in a difficult-to-treat area (H zone of face), and has not been previously treated.
- Nodular and superficial BCCs are the least aggressive.
- Morpheaform lesions have the highest incidence of positive tumor margins (<30%) and the greatest recurrence rate.

PREVENTION

Oral nicotinamide, a form of vitamin B_3 available without prescription (500 mg bid), has been reported to prevent development of new nonmelanoma skin cancer in high risk patients.

SUGGESTED READINGS

Available at www.expertconsult.com

RELATED CONTENT

Basal Cell Skin Cancer (Patient Information)

AUTHOR: **FRED F. FERRI, M.D.**

BASIC INFORMATION

DEFINITION

A bedbug's bite is a wound caused by the penetration of the bedbug mouthpiece into the skin as the insect feeds on blood from vessels or extravasated blood from the damaged surrounding tissue. The saliva of the bedbug contains pharmacologically active substances responsible for a spectrum of undesirable skin reactions depending on the individual. The bugs typically feed during times when an individual is at rest and may feed without being detected. Typically feedings take 5 to 10 minutes.

SYNONYMS

Insect bite
Bedbug *Cimex lectularius* bite

ICD-10CM CODES
T00.9 Multiple superficial (insect bite) injuries, unspecified

EPIDEMIOLOGY & DEMOGRAPHICS

- Traditionally, bedbugs were considered more common in poorer areas, but they are now increasingly found in areas of frequent travel.
- Bedbug infestations may spread among multifamily and institutional facilities with shared walls and are consequently difficult to eradicate.
- Reports of bedbug infestations have increased dramatically in the U.S., as well as worldwide, likely because of the decreased use of pesticides and increased international travel.
- Bedbugs are attracted to carbon dioxide gas and warm bodies.
- Bedbugs do not have a preference for specific age groups, ethnicity, or sex.
- Persons at higher risk include those that have recently stayed overnight in a hotel, dorm room, hospital, or new home.
- Studies have shown increased sensitivity of cutaneous reaction in previous bite victims.

PHYSICAL FINDINGS AND CLINICAL PRESENTATION

- Bites typically occur at night on exposed areas of skin, most often the face, neck, arms, and legs.
- The bites are painless and so do not awaken the individual.
- Onset of signs and symptoms of bites can be immediately on awakening or up to 10 days after the bite.
- Firm, purpuric or erythematous macules, urticaria, papules (Fig. 1B-10), or bullae may be present. Bites are often inflammatory and pruritic, although bedbug-naive individuals may be asymptomatic to their first bites.
- Bite may have a central hemorrhagic punctum.
- Victim may observe a linear series of three bites ("breakfast, lunch, and dinner").
- Bites are typically pruritic.

- The size, degree of itching, and propensity toward vesiculation all increase with repeated bedbug bites.
- Figure 1B-11 illustrates symptoms and behaviors resulting from bed bug bites.

ETIOLOGY

- The *Cimex lectularius* species, also known as the common bedbug (Fig. 1B-12), have flat, oval bodies and retroverted mouth parts used for taking blood meals. It feeds on mammals and birds. *Cimex hemipterus* is a tropical species that bites mostly humans, and hybrid species of the two insects exist. Both generally feed nocturnally on the blood of sleeping humans. The adult bedbug is wingless and about 5 to 7 mm in length. It has a modified mouthpart for piercing and sucking that usually leaves a bite mark of papular urticarial presentation to exposed areas of skin. Bedbugs have weak appendages for latching on to their hosts and are not usually transported from person to person.
- The saliva of the bedbug contains nitrophorin that enables vasodilation, an anticoagulant that interferes with production of coagulation factor Xa, a salivary apyrase that

inhibits platelet aggregation, and an anesthetic. Consequently, the host often does not feel the bite until the effects have worn off.

DIAGNOSIS

DIFFERENTIAL DIAGNOSIS

Scabies, flea and mite bites, vesicular disorders, delusional parasitosis, dermatitis herpetiformis, pemphigus herpetiformis, ecthyma, drug eruptions

WORKUP

- Workup begins with history and physical for clinical symptoms and environmental findings suggestive of insect bites.
- Victims should carefully scrutinize the bedroom for signs of bedbug infestation. One may encounter fecal smears or flecks of

FIGURE 1B-12 Bedbug. (From James WD et al: *Andrews' diseases of the skin*, ed 12, Philadelphia, 2016, Saunders.)

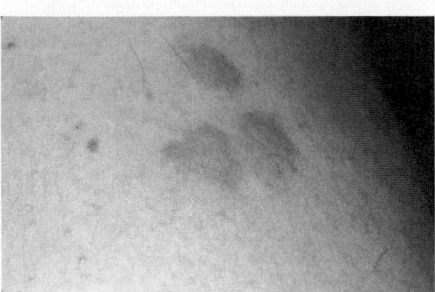

FIGURE 1B-10 Pruritic papules after bedbug bites. (From Kliegman RM et al: Nelson textbook of pediatrics, ed 19, Philadelphia, 2011, Saunders.)

Symptoms and behaviors resulting from bed bug attacks

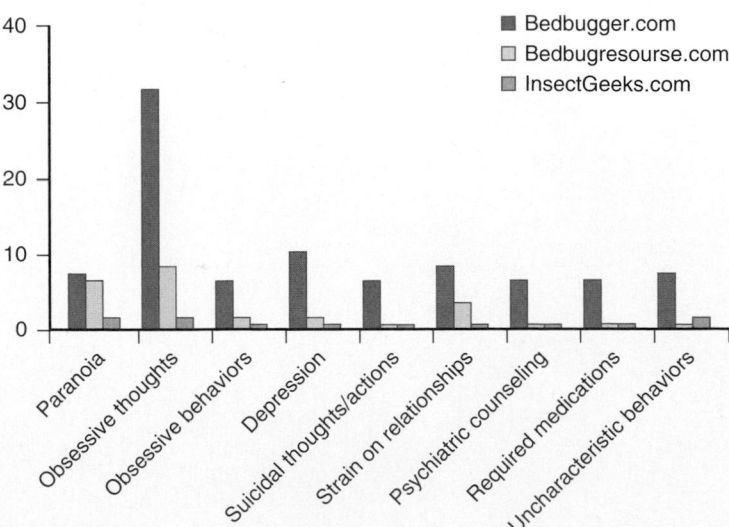

FIGURE 1B-11 Distribution of symptoms in 135 Internet reports describing effects of bed bug bites. (From Goddard J, de Shazo R: Psychological effects of bed bug attacks *(Cimex lectularius L.)*, Am J Med 125:101-103, 2012.)

blood on bed linens, inside furniture cracks and crevices, and behind peeling wallpaper. Bedbugs may travel as far as 20 feet for a meal. Densely infested rooms may also have a distinctive, pungent, soda syrup–like odor.

LABORATORY TESTS

- No specific tests recommended except for identification of the insect.
- The histology of bedbug bites is similar to other insect bites. Perivascular infiltrate of lymphocytes, histiocytes, eosinophils, and mast cells is seen within the upper dermis. One may also observe collagen bundles with interstitial eosinophils, dermal edema, and extravasated erythrocytes.
- Hypersensitivity to bedbug salivary proteins may be tested via intradermal allergy skin testing.
- Skin biopsy results are nonspecific and are not helpful in making the diagnosis.

IMAGING STUDIES
None

 **TREATMENT**

- Specific treatment of bedbug bites is often not necessary. Bites may self-resolve within a week for milder cases and a few weeks for more severe cases. Treatment regimens are based on resolving symptoms of the bites, mainly pruritus.
- To prevent infection, avoid scratching the area.
- Topical glucocorticoids or systemic antihistamines are appropriate in patients with severe pruritus from the bedbug bite.
  1. Triamcinolone cream 0.1%; apply thin film to affected areas bid

  2. Chlorpheniramine 4 mg PO at bedtime (adults), 2 mg PO at bedtime (children)
- Insecticides may be effective in eradicating the bedbug, but growing resistance has been seen and multi-insecticide therapy is recommended.
  1. Use permethrin spray for clothing and bedsheets or bednets
  2. Diethyltoluamide (DEET): Be wary of toxic levels in children when used at high concentrations.
  3. Deltamethrin and chlorfenapyr are two common insecticides used.
  4. Please consult a pest control professional for safe eradication.

NONPHARMACOLOGIC THERAPY

Vacuuming is effective in removing bedbugs but does not remove the eggs. Wash bedsheets and clothing in hot water with detergent with at least 20 minutes in a dryer. Bedbugs have a high thermal death point of 45° C and also may survive at temperatures as low as 7° C. Some companies perform a treatment in which the room is heated above 50° C, which is a lethal temperature for all stages of a bedbug's life cycle. Coating bedposts with antifriction or adhesive substances such as petrolatum or duct tape may hinder bedbugs from gaining access to the bed.

ACUTE GENERAL Rx

Immunologic response is dependent on immunocompetence and individual sensitivity to the salivary components of the bedbug bite. Often, patients with papular urticaria have IgG antibodies to specific bedbug proteins. IgE antibodies may also mediate bullae formation. Anaphylaxis and death from bites is rare but documented in literature.

DISPOSITION

Patient may resume normal activity and lifestyle. Travelers should inspect their clothing and suitcases before returning home.

BEDBUGS AS POTENTIAL VECTORS

The bedbug has been studied extensively as a potential vector for human pathogens such as HIV, hepatitis B, hepatitis C, and Chagas' disease. To date, there is no evidence of transmission from an infected bedbug to a human.

⊘ PEARLS & CONSIDERATIONS

COMMENTS

- Bedbugs are an increasing source of anguish and frustration for humans, and clinicians should evaluate for signs of stress and depression.
- A combination of chemical and physical intervention is often necessary for complete eradication. All hiding areas must be carefully inspected and cleaned. Treatment may include pesticides, laundering, heat, freezing, vacuuming, and hiring a professional service to eradicate bedbugs.

SUGGESTED READINGS
Available at www.expertconsult.com

RELATED CONTENT
Bedbugs (Patient Information)

AUTHOR: **SCOTT M. SOUTHER, M.D.**

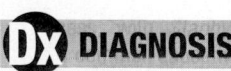 BASIC INFORMATION

DEFINITION
Acute peripheral facial (seventh) nerve palsy

SYNONYMS
Idiopathic facial paralysis
Facial nerve palsy

ICD-10CM CODES
G51.0   Bell palsy

EPIDEMIOLOGY & DEMOGRAPHICS
INCIDENCE: 20-30 cases per 100,000
PEAK INCIDENCE: People <70 yr and pregnant females, especially during the third trimester and/or 1 wk postpartum
PREDOMINANT SEX AND AGE: Sexes are equally affected. Median age is 40 yr.
RISK FACTORS: Diabetes, older age, pregnancy.

PHYSICAL FINDINGS & CLINICAL PRESENTATION
- Dependent on location of facial nerve injury. Onset is usually acute to subacute over hours of unilateral facial paralysis with maximal weakness at 3 wk. One third of patients demonstrate incomplete paralysis, and the remaining two thirds have complete paralysis. Recovery is present within the first 6 mo.
- Based on the following criteria: diffuse facial nerve involvement depicted by paralysis of the facial muscles (Fig. 1B-15), along with variable involvement of taste over the anterior two thirds of the tongue or altered secretion of the lacrimal and salivary glands.
  1. The degree of involvement is dependent on proximity of facial nerve involvement and involvement of associated branches.

ETIOLOGY
Most cases of Bell palsy are thought to be secondary to a viral inflammatory/immune mechanism of injury. Herpes simplex virus is thought to be the most common viral pathogen, followed by herpes zoster. Other infectious causes include EBV, CMV, adenovirus, rubella, and mumps.

(Dx) DIAGNOSIS

DIFFERENTIAL DIAGNOSIS
- Stroke: forehead and periorbital muscles are spared in stroke patients because of bilateral innervation of the upper face. Lyme disease: facial nerve palsy is the most common cranial neuropathy associated with Lyme meningitis; may be unilateral or bilateral.
- HIV
- Ramsay Hunt syndrome: facial nerve paralysis associated with ipsilateral zoster oticus
- Parotid gland tumors
- Trauma/temporal bone fracture
- Meningeal processes
  1. Infectious: Lyme (mentioned earlier), HIV, syphilis, leprosy, tuberculosis

  2. Inflammatory: sarcoid, Sjögren's, Guillain-Barré syndrome
  3. Carcinomatous: breast, lung, lymphoma
- Congenital: Möbius syndrome
- Melkersson-Rosenthal syndrome
- Brainstem stroke: Affecting the nucleus or fascicle of the seventh nerve

WORKUP
- Bell palsy is a clinical diagnosis.
- Additional workup may be necessary in those patients with complete injury or lack of any

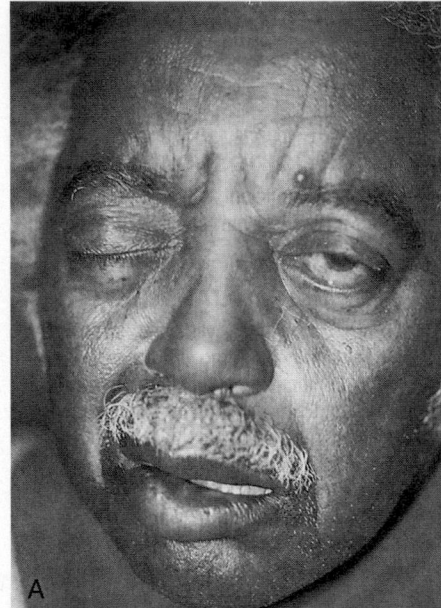

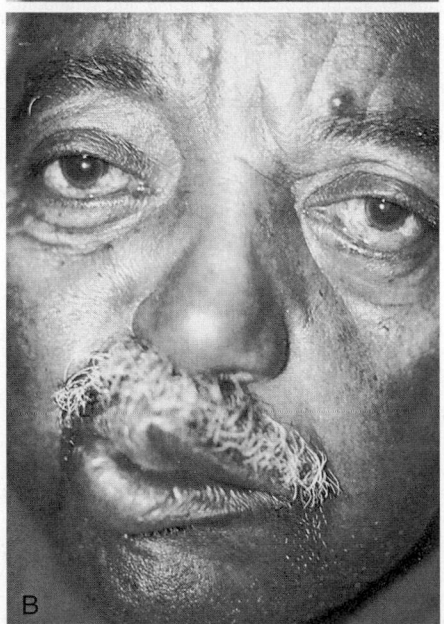

FIGURE 1B-15 A patient with a lesion of the facial nerve. A, The patient has difficulty in closing his left eye, and the left corner of his mouth droops. **B,** The latter defect is especially evident when the patient attempts to purse his lips. (From Haines DE: *Fundamental neuroscience for basic and clinical applications,* ed 3, Philadelphia, 2006, Churchill Livingstone.)

recovery or in whom the diagnosis of Bell palsy is uncertain.

LABORATORY TESTS
Not typically recommended. However, if the diagnosis of Bell palsy versus facial nerve paralysis from secondary causes is in question (especially if the facial paralysis is bilateral), the following are reasonable:
- Lyme antibody followed by Western blot for positive cases
- ACE level
- Glycosylated hemoglobin
- HIV
- VDRL
- ESR

ELECTRODIAGNOSTIC TESTING
May be performed 2 wk after onset to assess prognosis. Facial motor response remains normal for the first 3 days following injury and then rapidly decreases depending on severity of lesion. Facial motor study may be performed at 10 days and compared to contralateral side. A motor response that is 10% the amplitude of the unaffected side has been defined as a critical value in one study in which recovery was poor when associated with 90% degeneration. EMG can be used to visualize any motor units in the affected muscles that would assess the integrity of the facial nerve.

IMAGING STUDIES
Not usually indicated.
- Brain MRI is indicated in certain cases, such as an upper motor neuron pattern (able to wrinkle forehead) where the temporalis branch of the facial nerve is spared.
- Brain MRI with gadolinium is indicated when other cranial nerve palsies are present or when a meningeal process is suspected.
- CT temporal bone: is indicated in cases of trauma or cases with complete facial paralysis in which the surgeon is considering decompression.

(Rx) TREATMENT

NONPHARMACOLOGIC THERAPY
- Reassurance that most patients have a full recovery and that the patient did not sustain a stroke.
- Eye patch: To prevent corneal drying/abrasion and subsequent ulceration.
  1. Lacri-Lube to eye at night and artificial tears during the day.
- A recent study involving acupuncture revealed that in patients with Bell palsy, strong stimulation acupuncture with needle manipulation improved recovery more than acupuncture without needle manipulation.[1]

---

[1]Xu SB et al: Effectiveness of strengthened stimulation during acupuncture for the treatment of Bell palsy: a randomized controlled trial, *CMAJ* 185:473-479, 2013.

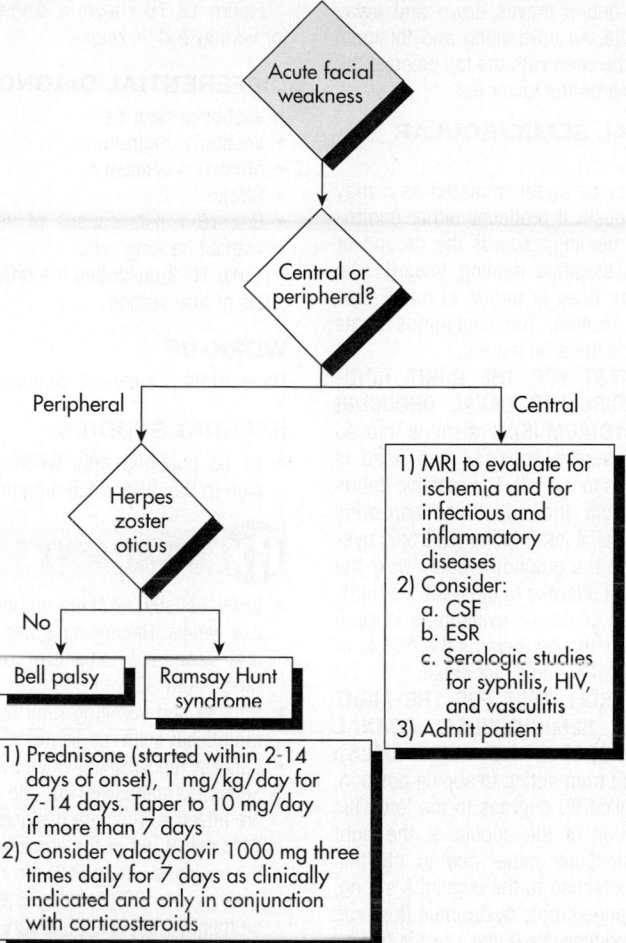

FIGURE 1B-16 Algorithm outlining the treatment of patients with Bell palsy. *CSF,* Cerebrospinal fluid; *ESR,* erythrocyte sedimentation rate; *HIV,* human immunodeficiency virus; *MRI,* magnetic resonance imaging. (Modified from Adams JG et al: *Emergency medicine, clinical essentials,* ed 2, St Louis, 2013, Elsevier.)

The algorithm boxes read:

Acute facial weakness → Central or peripheral?

Peripheral → Herpes zoster oticus → No → Bell palsy / Ramsay Hunt syndrome

1) Prednisone (started within 2-14 days of onset), 1 mg/kg/day for 7-14 days. Taper to 10 mg/day if more than 7 days
2) Consider valacyclovir 1000 mg three times daily for 7 days as clinically indicated and only in conjunction with corticosteroids

Central →
1) MRI to evaluate for ischemia and for infectious and inflammatory diseases
2) Consider:
   a. CSF
   b. ESR
   c. Serologic studies for syphilis, HIV, and vasculitis
3) Admit patient

ACUTE GENERAL Rx

- Corticosteroids started within 72 hr will expedite speed and rate of recovery in most patients. Antiviral therapy alone has no benefit.
  1. Two high-quality randomized trials assessed efficacy of early (<72 hr) treatment with glucocorticoids alone, antiviral treatment alone, and combination therapy of Bell palsy. Glucocorticoid treatment alone was effective, while antiviral therapy showed no benefit when given either alone or with concomitant glucocorticoid therapy.
  2. Largest study compared prednisolone (60 mg daily) versus valacyclovir (1000 mg 3 times daily × 7 days) versus combination therapy versus placebo within 72 hr of presentation.
  3. At 1-year follow-up, time to recovery was shorter in prednisolone-treated group, while valacyclovir therapy efficacy did not differ from placebo. No added benefit was seen with combination therapy.

- Treatment guidelines, in lieu of above, recommend prednisone 60 to 80 mg/day for 1 wk.
  1. Some authors still recommend treatment with valacyclovir (1000 mg 3 times daily for 1 wk) in severe cases (i.e., level IV or greater on the House-Brackmann grading system) despite lack of strong clinical evidence.
- Surgical decompression: Not currently recommended.
  1. AAN Practice Parameter (2001) concluded there was insufficient evidence to make any recommendation regarding surgical decompression for Bell palsy.
  2. AAN Practice Parameter conclusion was further substantiated by Cochrane systematic review in 2011 that looked at two additional studies again citing insufficient evidence regarding surgical decompression for Bell palsy.
- Fig. 1B-16 describes an algorithm for the treatment of patients with Bell palsy.

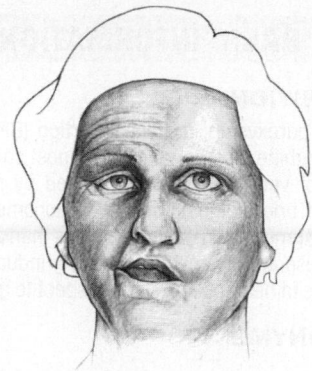

FIGURE 1B-17 Bell palsy. The patient with Bell palsy (facial nerve palsy) will demonstrate an unwrinkled forehead, widely opened eyes (with weakness of eyelid color), flattening of the nasolabial fold, and a droop of the corner of the mouth. (From Remmel KS et al: *Handbook of symptom-oriented neurology,* ed 3, St Louis, 2002, Mosby.)

CHRONIC Rx

Botulinum toxin may be used in cases of hemifacial spasm.

DISPOSITION

- 71% of patients had complete recovery.
- 85% show recovery at 3 wk.
- 13% had slight sequelae.
- 16% had residual weakness, synkinesis, or contracture.
- Prognosis is favorable if recovery is seen within the first 3 wk.
- Recurrence rate is 7%. Average time to recurrence was 10 yr.

REFERRAL

- Neurologist if clinical diagnosis is in question
- Ophthalmologist if concern for corneal abrasion or ulceration

⚠ PEARLS & CONSIDERATIONS

COMMENTS

- Assess wrinkling of forehead (Fig. 1B-17). If present on affected side, need to ensure that the facial weakness is not central.
- Assess for other cranial nerve deficits or long-tract signs because brainstem fascicular lesions of the seventh nerve can show peripheral facial pattern of weakness.

SUGGESTED READINGS

Available at www.expertconsult.com

RELATED CONTENT

Bell Palsy (Facial Palsy) (Patient Information)

AUTHOR: **JOHN SLADKY, M.D.**

BASIC INFORMATION

DEFINITION

Benign paroxysmal positional vertigo (BPPV) is a labyrinthine disorder and is the most common cause of vertigo. It is characterized by paroxysms of brief spinning sensation accompanied by nystagmus that usually lasts less than a minute. These paroxysms are generally induced by changes in head position with respect to gravity.

SYNONYMS

BPPV

CD-10 CM CODES
H81.1 Benign paroxysmal vertigo

EPIDEMIOLOGY & DEMOGRAPHICS

Higher prevalence seen in elderly and women.
INCIDENCE: Incidence increases with advancing age. Unrecognized BPPV can be found in about 10% of certain geriatric populations, and there is a cumulative incidence of nearly 10% by age 80 yr.
PREVALENCE: Lifetime prevalence is 2.4%. Reported prevalence is 10.7 and 64 cases per 100,000 population. BPPV is by far the most common type of vertigo.
PREDOMINANT SEX AND AGE: Female (2:1 to 3:1 ratio); peak onset: 50-60 years.
GENETICS: unknown
RISK FACTORS: Head trauma, inner ear surgery, viral labyrinthitis, Meniere's disease, migraine. The majority are idiopathic.

PHYSICAL FINDINGS & CLINICAL PRESENTATION

- Brief paroxysms of vertigo and nystagmus with certain head positions are seen in 70%.
- Episodes are typically triggered by head position changes such as while getting in or out of bed, rolling over in bed, forward head tilt, or bending forward.
- Episodes are brief usually lasting 30 to 40 seconds but can recur for several days or months.
- Usually no hearing abnormalities are present.
- Direction of nystagmus depends on the canal affected with reversal of direction being seen while sitting up, and fatigability with repeated testing.
- Rarely persistent vertigo and disequilibrium may be seen.

POSTERIOR SEMICIRCULAR CANAL (PCC)

While posterior, horizontal or superior semicircular canal can be affected as isolated or in different combinations, PCC involvement is commonest (60%-90%) and will be discussed in the following sections. Nystagmus is up-beating and torsional and can be elicited by the Dix Hallpike maneuver.
DIX-HALLPIKE MANEUVER: With head turned to one side at an angle of 45 degrees, patient is moved from sitting to supine position with head hanging below the end of the table at an angle of 20 deg. The posterior semicircular canal comes into the sagittal plane and the free

floating otolith debris moves down and away from the ampulla. An up-beating and torsional nystagmus will be seen with the top poles of the eye beating towards the lower ear.

HORIZONTAL SEMICIRCULAR CANAL

Involvement may be underestimated as it may remit spontaneously. It produces either geotropic nystagmus beating towards the ground or apogeotropic nystagmus beating towards the ceiling when the head is turned to either side in the supine position. The nystagmus beats stronger towards the affected ear.
HEAD ROLL TEST FOR THE RIGHT HORIZONTAL SEMICIRCULAR CANAL (INDUCING GEOTROPIC NYSTAGMUS): Patient is moved from sitting to supine position, then head is rolled 90 degrees to the left. The otolithic debris moves away from the cupula of horizontal semicircular canal, a left beating geotropic nystagmus (towards the ground) is seen. Next the head is turned 90 degrees to the right—a right-beating stronger geotropic nystagmus is seen as otolithic debris moves towards the cupula of the right horizontal semicircular canal.
SUPINE HEAD ROLL TEST FOR THE RIGHT HORIZONTAL SEMICIRCULAR CANAL (INDUCING APOGEOTROPIC NYSTAGMUS): Patient is moved from sitting to supine position, then head is rolled 90 degrees to the left. This induces deflection of the cupula of the right horizontal semicircular canal due to otolithic debris near or attached to the cupula. A strong, right-beating apogeotropic nystagmus (towards the ceiling) is induced. Next, the head is turned 90 degrees in the opposite direction. Now the right horizontal semicircular canal cupula is deflected in the opposite direction and a weak, left-beating apogeotropic nystagmus results.

ANTERIOR SEMICIRCULAR CANAL

Involvement is rare as it is located uppermost in the labyrinth and so otolithic debris is unlikely to become trapped. A downbeat and torsional nystagmus where the top poles of the eye beat towards the lower ear is seen. Evaluating for central lesions is a must in these cases.

ETIOLOGY

The fundamental pathologic process is believed to be the movement of otolithic debris in the endolymph of the inner ear. The debris may be present in the cupula (cupulolithiasis) or free floating within the semicircular canal near the cupula (canalithiasis). Static head position changes with respect to gravity, causing the debris to move within the semicircular canal and creating a false sense of rotation.

Dx **DIAGNOSIS**

Elicitation of a typical nystagmus with Dix-Hall pike is the standard for diagnosing posterior canal BPPV. However, 25% of symptomatic patients may not exhibit nystagmus. Appropriate referral to a neurologist or neuro-otologist should be considered in these cases.

Figure 1B-18 shows a diagnostic algorithm for vertigo and dizziness.

DIFFERENTIAL DIAGNOSIS

- Vestibular neuritis
- Vestibular migraine
- Meniere's disease
- Stroke
- Box 1B-1 lists causes of vertigo with and without hearing loss.
- Table 1B-3 describes the differential diagnosis of true vertigo

WORK-UP

None; BPPV is a clinical diagnosis

IMAGING STUDIES

- To be obtained only when stroke remains high in the differential diagnosis.

Rx **TREATMENT**

- BPPV usually resolves without treatment in 2-4 weeks. Recurrences are common in the first year, and long-term recurrence rates range from 30% to 50%.
- Nausea and vomiting may be treated symptomatically with medications.
- Canalith repositioning maneuvers (Epley's and Semont's maneuvers for the posterior canal) are effective. They are designed to "flush" otolithic debris out of the semicircular canals into the vestibule where they are resorbed. Epley's maneuver for BPPV of the posterior canal is recommended as standard of care by the American Academy of Neurology and American Academy of Otolaryngology-Head and Neck Surgery. When patients do not respond, it may be related to the technique, or they may be refractory.

BOX 1B-1 Causes of Vertigo With and Without Hearing Loss

Hearing Loss
Conductive
  Otitis media with effusion
  Chronic suppurative otitis media or cholesteatoma should be considered

Sensorineural
  Perilymphatic fistula
  Tumor
  Ménière's disease
  Migraine headache
  Genetic syndromes
  Temporal bone fracture
  Vestibular concussion

No Hearing Loss
Acute Vertigo
  Perilymphatic fistula
  Benign positional vertigo
  Seizure
  Labyrinthitis

Recurrent or Chronic Vertigo
  Acoustic neuroma
  Multiple sclerosis

From Marx JA et al: *Rosen's emergency medicine: concepts and clinical practice*, ed 7, Philadelphia, 2010, Elsevier.

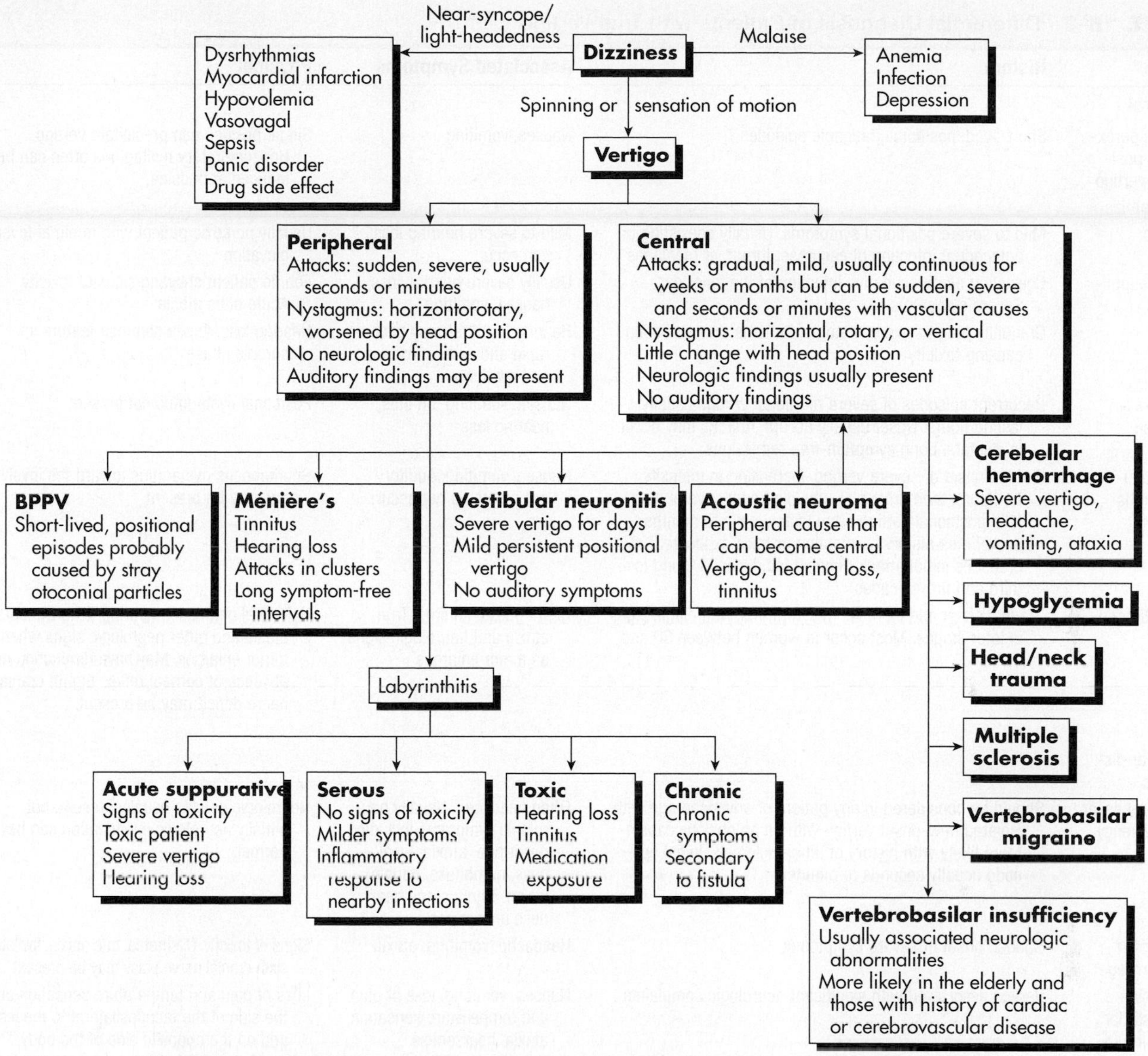

Dizziness

Near-syncope/light-headedness →

Malaise →

Dysrhythmias
Myocardial infarction
Hypovolemia
Vasovagal
Sepsis
Panic disorder
Drug side effect

Anemia
Infection
Depression

Spinning or sensation of motion ↓

Vertigo

Peripheral
Attacks: sudden, severe, usually seconds or minutes
Nystagmus: horizontorotary, worsened by head position
No neurologic findings
Auditory findings may be present

Central
Attacks: gradual, mild, usually continuous for weeks or months but can be sudden, severe and seconds or minutes with vascular causes
Nystagmus: horizontal, rotary, or vertical
Little change with head position
Neurologic findings usually present
No auditory findings

BPPV
Short-lived, positional episodes probably caused by stray otoconial particles

Ménière's
Tinnitus
Hearing loss
Attacks in clusters
Long symptom-free intervals

Vestibular neuronitis
Severe vertigo for days
Mild persistent positional vertigo
No auditory symptoms

Acoustic neuroma
Peripheral cause that can become central
Vertigo, hearing loss, tinnitus

Cerebellar hemorrhage
Severe vertigo, headache, vomiting, ataxia

Hypoglycemia

Head/neck trauma

Multiple sclerosis

Vertebrobasilar migraine

Labyrinthitis

Acute suppurative
Signs of toxicity
Toxic patient
Severe vertigo
Hearing loss

Serous
No signs of toxicity
Milder symptoms
Inflammatory response to nearby infections

Toxic
Hearing loss
Tinnitus
Medication exposure

Chronic
Chronic symptoms
Secondary to fistula

Vertebrobasilar insufficiency
Usually associated neurologic abnormalities
More likely in the elderly and those with history of cardiac or cerebrovascular disease

FIGURE 1B-18 Diagnostic algorithm for dizziness and vertigo. *BPPV*, benign paroxysmal positional vertigo. (From Marx JA et al: *Rosen's emergency medicine: concepts and clinical practice*, ed 7, Philadelphia, 2010, Elsevier.)

There is no clear consensus on how many times the maneuver should be performed at a single visit. Many prefer to do it two or three times if nystagmus is still present with the second maneuver. Other maneuvers such as Barbecue, Vannucchis, and Gufoni's maneuver are used to reposition debris in the horizontal semicircular canal and will not be discussed here.

EPLEY'S MANEUVER:

• Head is turned 90 degrees towards unaffected side. The head and trunk are then turned an additional 90 degrees in the same direction, so that the patient lies on the unaffected side with head pointing towards the floor. The otolithic debris moves in the same direction, producing a brief nystagmus. The patient is then moved to a sitting position, which allows the debris to fall out of the canal into the utricle through the common crus.

• Each position should be maintained for 30 seconds or until the nystagmus or vertigo resolves. Sometimes nystagmus in the opposite direction is seen. It is prudent for patients to sit still in the upright position for about 15 minutes and then to walk cautiously.

NONPHARMACOLOGIC THERAPY

Transection of the ampullary nerve (singular nerve) and plugging of the involved canal are rarely performed for intractable and treatment-resistant cases.

ACUTE GENERAL Rx

Canalith repositioning

CHRONIC Rx

If multiple treatments are needed, patients should be instructed to perform the maneuvers at home.

REFERRAL

To a neuro-otologist, otolaryngologist, neurologist

! PEARLS & CONSIDERATIONS

BPPV is a benign and self-limiting condition but can be disabling.

Diagnosis is clinical and canalith repositioning maneuvers are effective.

PATIENT/FAMILY EDUCATION

• Reassurance
• Fall precautions

RELATED CONTENT

Meniere's Disease (Related Key Topic)
Vestibular Neuritis (Related Key Topic)

SUGGESTED READINGS

Available online at www.expertconsult.com

AUTHORS: **PADMAJA SUDHAKAR, M.B.B.S.,** and **SACHIN KEDAR, M.B.B.S., M.D.**

TABLE 1B-3   Differential Diagnosis of Patients with True Vertigo

Cause	History	Associated Symptoms	Physical
Peripheral			
1. Benign paroxysmal positional vertigo	Short-lived, positional, fatigable episodes	Nausea, vomiting	Single position can precipitate vertigo. Horizontorotary nystagmus often can be induced at bedside.
2. Labyrinthitis			
A. Serous	Mild to severe positional symptoms. Usually coexisting or antecedent infection of ear, nose, throat, or meninges	Mild to severe hearing loss can occur	Usually nontoxic patient with minimal fever elevation
B. Acute suppurative	Coexisting acute exudative infection of the inner ear. Severe symptoms	Usually severe hearing loss, nausea, vomiting	Febrile patient showing signs of toxicity. Acute otitis media
C. Toxic	Gradually progressive symptoms: Patients on medication causing toxicity	Hearing loss that may become rapid and severe, nausea and vomiting	Hearing loss. Ataxia common feature in chronic phase
3. Ménière's disease	Recurrent episodes of severe rotational vertigo usually lasting hours. Onset usually abrupt. Attacks may occur in clusters. Long symptom-free remissions	Nausea, vomiting, tinnitus, hearing loss	Positional nystagmus not present
4. Vestibular neuronitis	Sudden onset of severe vertigo, increasing in intensity for hours, then gradually subsiding over several days. Mild positional vertigo often lasts weeks to months. Sometimes history of infection or toxic exposure that precedes initial attack. Highest incidence is found in third and fifth decades	Nausea, vomiting. Auditory symptoms do not occur	Spontaneous nystagmus toward the involved ear may be present.
5. Acoustic neuroma	Gradual onset and increase in symptoms. Neurologic signs in later stages. Most occur in women between 30 and 60	Hearing loss, tinnitus. True ataxia and neurologic signs as tumor enlarges	Unilateral decreased hearing. True truncal ataxia and other neurologic signs when tumor enlarges. May have diminution or absence of corneal reflex. Eighth cranial nerve deficit may be present.
Central			
1. Vascular disorders			
A. Vertebrobasilar insufficiency	Should be considered in any patient of advanced age with isolated new-onset vertigo without an obvious cause. More likely with history of atherosclerosis. Initial episode usually seconds to minutes	Often headache. Usually neurologic symptoms including dysarthria, ataxia, weakness, numbness, double vision. Tinnitus and deafness uncommon	Neurologic deficits usually present, but initially neurologic examination can be normal.
B. Cerebellar hemorrhage	Sudden onset of severe symptoms	Headache, vomiting, ataxia	Signs of toxicity. Dysmetria, true ataxia. Ipsilateral sixth cranial nerve palsy may be present.
C. Occlusion of posterior inferior cerebellar artery (Wallenberg's syndrome)	Vertigo associated with significant neurologic complaints	Nausea, vomiting, loss of pain and temperature sensation, ataxia, hoarseness	Loss of pain and temperature sensation on the side of the face ipsilateral to the lesion and on the opposite side of the body, paralysis of the palate, pharynx, and larynx. Horner's syndrome (ipsilateral ptosis, miosis, and decreased facial sweating)
D. Subclavian steal syndrome	Classic picture is syncopal attacks during exercise, but most cases present with more subtle symptoms.	Arm fatigue, cramps, mild light-headedness may be only other symptoms than vertigo	Diminished or absent radial pulses in affected side or systolic blood pressure differentials between the two areas occur in most patients.
2. Head trauma	Symptoms begin with or shortly after head trauma. Positional symptoms most common type after trauma. Self-limited symptoms that can persist weeks to months	Usually mild nausea	Occasionally, basilar skull fracture
3. Neck trauma	Usual onset 7–10 days after whiplash injury. Symptoms may last weeks to months. Episodes seconds to minutes when turning head	Neck pain	Neck tenderness, pain on movement, and positional nystagmus and vertigo when head is turned to side of the whiplash
4. Vertebrobasilar migraine	Vertigo almost always followed by headache. Patient has usually had similar episodes in past. Most patients have a family history of migraine. Syndrome usually begins in adolescence	Dysarthria, ataxia, visual disturbances, or paresthesias usually precede headache	No residual neurologic or otologic signs are present after attack.
5. Multiple sclerosis	Vertigo presenting symptoms in 7%–10% and appears in the course of the disease in a third. Onset may be severe and suggest labyrinth disease. Disease onset usually between ages 20 and 40. Often history of other attacks with varying neurologic signs or symptoms	Nausea and vomiting, which may be severe	May have horizontal, rotary, or vertical nystagmus. Nystagmus may persist after the vertiginous symptoms have subsided. Bilateral internuclear ophthalmoplegia and ataxic eye movements suggest multiple sclerosis.
6. Temporal lobe epilepsy	Can be initial or prominent symptom in some patients with the disorder	Memory impairment, hallucinations, trancelike states, seizures	May have aphasia or convulsions
7. Hypoglycemia	Should be considered in diabetics and any other patient with unexplained symptoms	Sweating, anxiety	Tachycardia, mental status change may be present.

From Marx JA et al: *Rosen's emergency medicine: concepts and clinical practice*, ed 7, Philadelphia, 2010, Elsevier.

 BASIC INFORMATION

DEFINITION

Bipolar disorder is an episodic, recurrent, and frequently progressive condition in which the afflicted individual experiences at least one episode of mania, characterized by at least 1 wk of continuous symptoms of elevated, expansive, or irritable mood, in association with three or more of the following symptoms (four if irritability is the presenting mood):
- Decreased need for sleep
- Grandiosity or inflated self-esteem
- Pressured speech
- Flight of ideas or subjective sense of racing thoughts
- Distractibility
- Increased level of goal-directed activity
- Problematic behavior with a high potential for painful consequences

Most individuals with bipolar disorder also experience one or more episodes of major depression over their lifetimes or have symptoms of a depressive episode commingled with those of mania (mixed episode). Hypomanic episodes may also occur.

SYNONYMS

Manic-depression
Cycloid psychosis

ICD-10CM CODES
F42.0 Bipolar affective disorder, current episode hypomanic
F31.1 Bipolar affective disorder, current episode manic without psychotic symptoms
F31.2 Bipolar affective disorder, current episode manic with psychotic symptoms
F31.3 Bipolar affective disorder, current episode mild or moderate depression
F31.4 Bipolar affective disorder, current episode severe depression without psychotic symptoms
F31.5 Bipolar affective disorder, current episode severe depression with psychotic symptoms
F31.6 Bipolar affective disorder, current episode mixed
F31.8 Bipolar II disorder

EPIDEMIOLOGY & DEMOGRAPHICS

INCIDENCE: 0.016% to 0.021%
PREVALENCE (IN U.S.): 0.4% to 1.6% (lifetime); bipolar spectrum disorders: 2.8%; approximately 25% attempt suicide, accounting for 3.4% to 14% of all suicide deaths.
PREDOMINANT SEX: Equal distribution among male and female
PREDOMINANT AGE: Lifelong condition with age of onset 14 to 30 yr
PEAK INCIDENCE: Onset in 20s
GENETICS
- Concordance rates for monozygotic twins: 0.7 to 0.8; for dizygotic twins: 0.2
- Risk of affective disorder in offspring with one affected parent with bipolar disorder:

27% to 29%; with two affected parents: 50% to 74%
- Heritability estimate of 0.85
- No specific causal mutations have been identified. Genome-wide association analyses have suggested a role for *CACNA1C, ODZ4, ZNF 804A,* and *NCAN,* among others, and implicated ion channelopathies, immune and neuronal signaling, and histone methylation in pathogenesis of bipolar disorder. It remains unclear whether the high heritability is the result of the additive effect of many common risk variants or a few higher-risk rare variants.

PHYSICAL FINDINGS & CLINICAL PRESENTATION
- Mania associated with:
  1. Psychomotor activation that is usually goal directed but not necessarily productive
  2. Increase in goal-directed activity and excessive involvement in activities leading to unexpected adverse outcomes
  3. Elevated, euphoric, and frequently labile mood
  4. Decreased need for sleep
  5. Flight of ideas with rapid, loud, pressured speech
- Psychosis may occur, with delusions, hallucinations, and formal thought disorder.
- Depressive episodes resembling major depressive disorder (see "Depression, Major"); however, atypical features (hypersomnia, prominent anxiety, weight gain) may be present.
- Mixed states, characterized by activation, irritability, and dysphoria, also possible.

KEY DIAGNOSTIC CRITERIA DISTINGUISHING BIPOLAR I DISORDER FROM BIPOLAR II DISORDER[1]:
Manic episode (Bipolar I Disorder)
- Distinct period during which there is an abnormally and persistently elevated, expansive, or irritable mood and abnormally and persistently increased goal-directed activity or energy lasting at least 1 wk (or less if hospitalization is required)
- Must be accompanied by at least three of the following symptoms (four if mood is only irritable): inflated self-esteem or grandiosity, decreased need for sleep, pressured speech, racing thoughts, distractibility, increased involvement in goal-directed activity or psychomotor agitation, excessive involvement in pleasurable activities with a high potential for painful consequences
- Symptoms do not meet criteria for a mixed episode
- Disturbance must be sufficiently severe to cause marked impairment in social or occupational functioning or to require hospitalization, or it is characterized by the presence of psychotic features
- Symptoms not due to direct physiologic effect of medication, general medication condition, or substance abuse

[1]Criteria are from the American Psychiatric Association: *Diagnostic and statistical manual of mental disorders,* ed 5, Washington, DC, 2013, American Psychiatric Association.

Hypomanic episode (Bipolar II Disorder)
- Distinct period during which there is an abnormally and persistently elevated, expansive, or irritable mood and abnormally and persistently elevated activity or energy lasting at least 4 consecutive days
- Must be accompanied by at least three of the following symptoms (four if mood is only irritable): inflated self-esteem or grandiosity, decreased need for sleep, pressured speech, racing thoughts, distractibility, increased involvement in goal-directed activity or psychomotor agitation, excessive involvement in pleasurable activities with a high potential for painful consequences
- Hypomanic episodes must be clearly different from the person's usual nondepressed mood, and there must be a clear change in functioning that is not characteristic of the person's usual functioning
- Changes in mood and functioning must be observable by others. In contrast to a manic episode, a hypomanic episode is not severe enough to cause marked impairment in social or occupational functioning or to require hospitalization, and there are no psychotic features
- Symptoms not due to direct physiologic effect of medication, general medication condition, or substance abuse

ETIOLOGY

Hypotheses:
1. Abnormalities of GABAA and G protein–coupled receptor and membrane function, calcium dysregulation
2. Alteration of cAMP, MAP kinase, protein kinase C, arachidonic acid cascade, and glycogen synthase kinase-3 signal transduction pathways; mitochondrial dysfunction
3. Alteration in cell survival pathways, glial and neuronal death and loss of neuroplasticity; proposed biomarkers include BDNF and measures of inflammation, oxidative stress, and endothelial function.

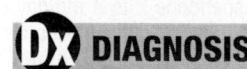 **DIAGNOSIS**

DIFFERENTIAL DIAGNOSIS
- Secondary manias caused by medical disorders (e.g., hyperthyroidism, AIDS, stroke, Cushing syndrome) or pharmacologic treatment (e.g., steroids, stimulants).
- First onset of mania after age 50 yr suggestive of secondary mania.
- Less severe, and possibly distinct, conditions of bipolar type II and cyclothymia.
- Comorbid substance abuse or dependency occurs in 60% to 75% of patients and may confound diagnosis and treatment.
- Presentation can be confused with schizophrenia or paranoid psychosis.

WORKUP
- History
- Physical examination
- Mental status examination
- Mood Disorder Questionnaire (MDQ)

Diseases and Disorders

B

LABORATORY TESTS

Because of high rate of secondary manias, initial evaluation to confirm health of all major organ systems (routine chemistries, complete blood count, urinalysis, sedimentation rate)

IMAGING STUDIES

- Consider brain imaging if late onset or if neurologic examination is abnormal.
- Neuroimaging may show evidence of ventricular enlargement or increased white matter hyperintensities; decrements in prefrontal and temporal lobe cortical thickness also reported. Corresponding changes in neurocognition, including changes in executive function and processing speed, may occur.

 **TREATMENT**

NONPHARMACOLOGIC THERAPY

- Cognitive-behavioral and family-focused psychoeducational psychotherapy to help patients cope with consequences of the disease, improve adherence with medications, and identify possible environmental triggers
- Bright light therapy in the northern latitudes in individuals exhibiting a seasonal pattern of winter depression
- Lifestyle "regularization"; interpersonal and social rhythm therapy; integrated care management for chronic conditions
- Many smartphone mobile apps for bipolar disorder are available to provide information, help monitor symptoms, and deliver interventions.

ACUTE GENERAL Rx

- First-line agents for acute mania and mixed states: lithium 1500 to 1800 mg/day (0.8 to 1.2 mEq/L), valproate 1000 to 1500 mg/day (50 to 125 ng/ml), carbamazepine 600 to 800 mg/day (4 to 12 micrograms/ml), oxcarbazepine 900 to 2400 mg/day, olanzapine 10 to 20 mg/day, risperidone 2 to 4 mg/day, quetiapine 350 to 800 mg/day, ziprasidone 80 to 120 mg/day, asenapine 10 to 20 mg/day, or aripiprazole 10 to 30 mg/day.
- Useful adjuncts to acute treatment of mania: benzodiazepines: lorazepam 1 to 2 mg q4h, clonazepam 1 to 2 mg q4h.
- Traditional antidepressants can induce manic episodes and exacerbate mania in mixed episodes.

- Although best evidence data are limited, first-line options for bipolar depression include lithium, quetiapine, lamotrigine, lurasidone, and olanzapine/fluoxetine combination. Bupropion may have a lower risk for triggering mania, and MAOIs or ECT may be efficacious in treatment-resistant cases.

CHRONIC Rx

- Goal of long-term treatment: prevention of relapse or episode recurrence
- Best agents for prophylaxis of mania: lithium, valproate, and olanzapine (carbamazepine/oxcarbazepine possibly beneficial)
- Best agents for prophylaxis of depression: lamotrigine and lithium
- Risk/benefit of atypical antipsychotics versus traditional mood stabilizers in maintenance unclear
- Long-term use of antidepressants: frequently destabilizes patient and leads to more frequent relapses; depression outweighs mania as the most debilitating dimension over the life span; bipolar disorder accounts for 7% of all disease-related disability-adjusted life years.

DISPOSITION

- Course is variable.
- More than 90% of patients having a single manic episode are likely to experience others.
- Uncontrolled manic or depressive episodes can lead to additional episodes.
- Lithium shown to specifically decrease suicidal risk.
- Socioeconomic consequences of both mania and depression can be severe and disabling.

REFERRAL

- If use of antidepressant contemplated
- If patient is severely manic, rapid cycling, or suicidal or is in a bipolar, mixed episode

⊘ PEARLS & CONSIDERATIONS

COMMENTS

- All patients presenting with depression should be asked about past personal and family history of mania and hypomania; 70% of bipolar patients have previously been misdiagnosed.
- Prompt recognition of the earliest signs of mania in a given individual (e.g., decreased need for sleep, increased rate of speech)

allows earlier intervention and a better likelihood of preventing a full episode.

- Bipolar disorder in children frequently manifests as behavioral disinhibition and temper dysregulation, but current consensus indicates that the condition is overdiagnosed in this age group. Disruptive mood dysregulation disorder (DMDD) describes children who exhibit persistent irritability and severe temper outbursts on a frequent basis (at least three times/week for a year or more).
- Rapid cycling (greater than three episodes/year) is associated with a poorer prognosis, including a longer course, more treatment resistance, more substance use comorbidity, and increased suicidal risk.
- Patients treated with atypical antipsychotic agents should be carefully monitored for development of metabolic syndrome. Independent of medication effect, there is a higher prevalence of metabolic syndrome and abdominal obesity in those with bipolar disorder.
- Despite some variation in prevalence, the severity, impact, and patterns of comorbidity of bipolar disorder are similar in different countries in world health surveys.
- Bipolar disorder often co-occurs with anxiety disorders and attention deficit hyperactivity disorder (ADHD), making attribution of specific symptoms difficult.
- Patients receiving anticonvulsants or antidepressants should be monitored for a possible increase in suicidal thoughts or behavior.
- There is preliminary evidence that nutraceutical agents like omega-3 fatty acids and N-acetyl cysteine (NAC) may have efficacy in the treatment of bipolar disorder.
- Multiple studies show a correlation between bipolar disorder and heightened creativity.

PATIENT/FAMILY EDUCATION

Information available at www.NMHA.org/ and www.dbsalliance.org/.

SUGGESTED READINGS

Available at www.expertconsult.com

RELATED CONTENT

Depression, Major (Related Key Topic)
Bipolar Disorder (Patient Information)

AUTHOR: **VICTOR I. REUS, M.D.**

BASIC INFORMATION

DEFINITION

A bite wound can be animal or human, accidental, or intentional.

ICD-10CM CODES
T14.1	Open wound of unspecified body region
T01.9	Multiple open wounds, unspecified
S31.000A	Unspecified open wound of lower back and pelvis without penetration into retroperitoneum, initial encounter
S41.159A	Open bite of unspecified upper arm, initial encounter

EPIDEMIOLOGY & DEMOGRAPHICS

- Bite wounds account for 1% of emergency department visits, and about 2% of patients need hospitalization.
- More than 1 million bites occur in human beings annually in the U.S.
- Dog bites account for 85% to 90% of all bites and result in 10 to 20 fatalities yearly in the U.S.; most dog bite victims are children. Cat bites account for 10% to 20%. The animal typically is owned by the victim.
- Infection rates are highest for cat bites (30%-50%), followed by human bites (15%-30%) and dog bites (5%).
- The extremities are involved in 75% of bites.

PHYSICAL FINDINGS & CLINICAL PRESENTATION

- The appearance of the bite wound is variable (e.g., puncture wound, tear, avulsion).
- Cellulitis, lymphangitis, and focal adenopathy may be present in infected bite wounds.
- Patient may have fever and chills.

ETIOLOGY

- Increased risk of infection: human and cat bites, closed-fist injuries, wounds involving joints, puncture wounds, face and lip bites, bites with skull penetration, bites in immuno-compromised hosts
- Most frequent infecting organisms:
  1. *Pasteurella* spp.: responsible for majority of infections within 24 hr of dog (*P. canis*) and cat (*P. multocida, P. septica*) bites
  2. *Capnocytophaga canimorsus* (formerly DF-2 bacillus): a gram-negative organism responsible for late infection, usually after dog bites
  3. Gram-negative organisms (*Pseudomonas, Haemophilus*): often found in human bites
  4. *Streptococcus* spp., *Staphylococcus aureus*
  5. *Eikenella corrodens* in human bites

DIAGNOSIS

DIFFERENTIAL DIAGNOSIS

- Bite from a rabid animal (often the attack is unprovoked)
- Factitious injury

WORKUP

- Determination of the time elapsed since the patient was bitten, status of rabies immunization of the animal, and underlying medical conditions that might predispose the patient to infection (e.g., DM, immunodeficiency)
- Documentation of bite site, notification of appropriate authorities (e.g., police department, animal officer)

LABORATORY TESTS

- Generally not necessary
- Hct if there has been significant blood loss
- Wound cultures (aerobic and anaerobic) if there is evidence of sepsis or victim is immunocompromised; cultures should be obtained before irrigation of the wound but after superficial cleaning

IMAGING STUDIES

Radiographs are indicated when bony penetration is suspected or if there is suspicion of fracture or significant trauma; they are also useful for detecting foreign bodies (when suspected).

TREATMENT

NONPHARMACOLOGIC THERAPY

- Local care with debridement, vigorous cleansing, and saline irrigation of the wound; debridement of devitalized tissue
- High-pressure irrigation to clean bite wound and ensure removal of contaminants (e.g., use saline solution with a 30- to 35-mL syringe equipped with a 20-gauge needle or catheter with tip of syringe placed 2 to 3 cm above the wound)
- Avoid blunt probing of wounds (increased risk of infection)
- If the animal is suspected to be rabid: infiltrate wound edges with 1% procaine hydrochloride, swab wound surface vigorously with cotton swabs and 1% benzalcuronium solution or other soap, and rinse wound with normal saline

ACUTE GENERAL Rx

- Avoid suturing of hand wounds and any wounds that appear infected
- Clenched fist injuries that develop after a punch to another's mouth usually require hospitalization, IV antibiotics, and evaluation by a hand specialist.
- Puncture wounds should be left open
- Give antirabies therapy and tetanus immune globulin (250-500 units IM in limb contralateral to toxoid) and toxoid (adult or child older than 5 yr: 0.5 ml DT given IM, child <5 yr 0.5 mL DPT IM) as needed
- Use empiric antibiotic therapy in high-risk wounds (e.g., cat bite, hand bites, face bites, genital area bites, bites with joint or bone penetration, human bites, immunocompromised host): amoxicillin-clavulanate 875 to 1000 mg bid for 7 days or cefuroxime 500 mg bid for 7 days
- In hospitalized patients, IV antibiotics of choice are cefoxitin 1 to 2 g q6h, ampicil-

lin-sulbactam 1.5 to 3 g q6h, ticarcillin-clavulanate 3 g q6h, cefoxitin 2 g IV q8h, or ceftriaxone 1 to 2 g q24h
- Penicillin allergy: animal bite (doxycycline or moxifloxacin or trimethoprim/sulfamethoxazole with either clindamycin or metronidazole); human bite (moxifloxacin plus clindamycin, trimethoprim/sulfamethoxazole plus metronidazole)
- Prophylactic therapy for persons bitten by others with HIV and hepatitis B (see Section V)
- Table 1B-4 summarizes the treatment of mammalian bites

DISPOSITION

- Prognosis is favorable with proper treatment.
- Important prognostic factors are type and depth of wound, which compartments are entered, and pathogenicity of inoculated bacteria.
- Punctures that are difficult to irrigate adequately, carnivore bites over vital structures (arteries, nerves, joints), and tissue crushing that cannot be debrided have a worse prognosis.
- In general, human bites have a higher complication and infection rate than do animal bites.
- Nearly 50% of the anaerobic gram-negative bacilli isolated from human bite wounds may be penicillin resistant and beta-lactamase positive.

PREVENTION

- Box 1B-2 provides advice for avoiding the bites and attacks of common pets.

REFERRAL

- Hospitalization and IV antibiotic therapy for infected human bites; bites with injury to joints, nerves, or tendons; or any animal bites unresponsive to oral therapy.
- Human bites with tendon involvement should go to operating room for washout.
- In the outpatient setting, bite wounds should be reevaluated within 48 hr to assess for signs of infection.

SUGGESTED READINGS
Available at www.expertconsult.com

RELATED CONTENT
Animal and Human Bites (Patient Information)

AUTHOR: **FRED F. FERRI, M.D.**

TABLE 1B-4   Treatment of Mammalian Bites

Type	Wound Care	Antibiotic PR	Tetanus PR	Rabies PR	HIV PR	Hepatitis PR
Human	High-pressure irrigation of the wound with normal saline or dilute (<1%) povidone-iodine solution; débride devitalized tissue or ragged edges	Amoxicillin-clavulanate, second-generation cephalosporin with anaerobic activity, penicillin plus dicloxacillin, clindamycin plus ciprofloxacin or trimethoprim-sulfamethoxazole	Tetanus immunoglobulin (250 units IM) and tetanus toxoid (0.5 mg IM) if never had a tetanus vaccine or have not had 3 doses of tetanus toxoid; tetanus toxoid (0.5 mg IM) if >5 yr since previous tetanus booster	None	ART therapy started within the first 48-72 hr and continued for 28 days or bite source tested HIV negative; refer to the hospital for the specific drugs used in ART therapy	HBIG (0.06 ml/kg IM); HBV given at separate site from HBIG
Cat	High-pressure irrigation of the wound with normal saline or dilute (<1%) povidone-iodine solution; débride devitalized tissue or ragged edges	Amoxicillin-clavulanate, second-generation cephalosporin with anaerobic activity, penicillin plus a first-generation cephalosporin, clindamycin plus a fluoroquinolone or trimethoprim-sulfamethoxazole	Tetanus immune globulin (250 units IM) and tetanus toxoid (0.5 mg IM) if never had a tetanus vaccine or have not had 3 doses of tetanus toxoid; tetanus toxoid (0.5 mg IM) if >5 yr since previous tetanus booster	HRIG (20 IU/kg) injected IM and/or around the bite site; rabies vaccine (1 mL IM) given in the deltoid in adults and in the thigh in children, on days 0, 3, 7, 14, and 28	None	None
Dog	High-pressure irrigation of the wound with normal saline or dilute (<1%) povidone-iodine solution; débride devitalized tissue or ragged edges	Amoxicillin-clavulanate, second-generation cephalosporin with anaerobic activity, penicillin plus a first-generation cephalosporin, clindamycin plus a fluoroquinolone or trimethoprim-sulfamethoxazole	Tetanus immune globulin (250 units IM) and tetanus toxoid (0.5 mg IM) if never had a tetanus vaccine or have not had 3 doses of tetanus toxoid; tetanus toxoid (0.5 mg IM) if >5 yr since previous tetanus booster	HRIG (20 IU/kg) injected IM and/or around the bite site; rabies vaccine (1 mL IM) given in the deltoid in adults and in the thigh in children, on days 0, 3, 7, 14, and 28	None	None

ART, Antiretroviral therapy; *HBIG,* hepatitis B immune globulin; *HBV,* hepatitis B vaccine; *HIV,* human immunodeficiency virus; *HRIG,* human rabies immune globulin; *IM,* intramuscularly; *PR.,* prophylaxis.
From Adams JG et al: *Emergency medicine: clinical essentials,* ed 2, Philadelphia, 2013, Elsevier.

BOX 1B-2   Advice for Avoiding the Bites and Attacks of Common Pets*

Dogs
- Do not leave a young child alone with a dog.
- Never approach or try to pet an unfamiliar dog, especially if it is tied up or confined.
- Always ask the dog's owners if you can pet the dog.
- Do not lean over a dog or pet it directly on the head.
- Do not kiss a dog.
- Avoid quick or sudden movements that may startle a dog.
- Never pet or step over a sleeping dog.
- Never try to take a bone or toy away from a dog (other than your own dog).
- Know the appearance of an angry dog: barking, growling, snarling with teeth showing, ears laid flat, legs stiff, tail up, and hair on the back standing up.
- Never step between two fighting dogs; if you need to separate them, use a bucket of water or a hose.
- Do not approach a female dog that is nursing her pups.
- Teach injury prevention advice to children from an early age.

Cats
- Be aware that some cats do not like prolonged petting.
- Know warning signs of an impending bite: twitching of the tail, restlessness, and "intention" bites (i.e., the cat moves to bite but does not bite).

Ferrets
- Do not sell or adopt a ferret that is known to bite.
- Do not push your fingers through the wires of a ferret cage.
- Reach for a ferret from the side with the palm upward rather than from above.
- Do not handle food and then handle young ferrets without washing your hands first.
- Do not poke a ferret or pull on its tail or ears.
- Never leave a ferret alone with a child or infant.
- If a ferret bites and locks on very tightly, pour cold and fast-running water over its face.

From Auerbach P: *Wilderness medicine, expert consult,* premium edition—Enhanced online features and print, Philadelphia, 2012, Elsevier.

 BASIC INFORMATION

DEFINITION

There are two major classes of arthropods: insects and arachnida. This chapter focuses on the class arachnida. Arachnid bites consist of bites caused by:

- Spiders
- Scorpions
- Ticks

ICD-10CM CODES

T63.301 Toxic effect of unspecified spider venom, accidental (unintentional), initial encounter
T63.2 Toxic effect of venom of scorpion, accidental (unintentional), initial encounter
E906 Bite of nonvenomous arthropod; insect bite NOS

EPIDEMIOLOGY & DEMOGRAPHICS

- Spiders—ubiquitous; only three types potentially significantly harmful:
  1. Sydney funnel web spider—Australia
  2. Black widow (Fig. E1B-24)—worldwide (excluding Alaska)
  3. Brown recluse (Fig. E1B-25)—most common (South Central U.S.)
- Scorpions—various warm climates: Africa, Central South America, Middle East, India; Texas, New Mexico, California, and Nevada in the U.S.
- Ticks—woodlands

PHYSICAL FINDINGS & CLINICAL PRESENTATION

Spiders:

- Sydney funnel web—atracotoxin toxin
  1. Piloerection, muscle spasms leading to tachycardia, hypertension, increased intracranial pressure, coma
- Black widow—females toxic
  1. Initial reaction: local swelling, redness (two fang marks) leading to local piloerection, edema, urticaria, diaphoresis, lymphangitis
  2. Pain in limb leading to rest of body (chest pain, abdominal pain), compartment syndrome
- Brown recluse
  1. Minor sting or burn.
  2. Wound may become pruritic and red with a blanched center with vesicle (Fig. E1B-26). Can necrose, especially in fatty areas (Fig. E1-27). Leaves eschar, which sloughs and leaves ulcer; can take months to heal.
  3. Systemic symptoms: headache, fever, chills, gastrointestinal upset, hemolysis, renal tubular necrosis, disseminated intravascular coagulation possible.

Scorpions:

- Sting leading to sympathetic and parasympathetic stimulation: hypertension, bradycardia, vasoconstriction, pulmonary edema, reduced coronary blood flow, priapism, inhibition of insulin.
- Also possible: tachycardia, arrhythmia, vasodilation, bronchial relaxation, excessive salivation, vomiting, sweating, bronchoconstriction, pancreatitis.
- Clinically significant scorpion envenomation by *Centruroides sculpturatus* produces a severe neuromotor syndrome and respiratory insufficiency that often requires ICU admission.

Ticks: U.S., Europe, Asia

- Very small (<1 mm). Must be attached >36 hr to transmit disease.
- Lyme disease—most common (see "Lyme Disease")
  1. Early: erythema migrans in 60% to 80% of cases
  2. 7 to 10 days: mild to moderate constitutional symptoms; disseminated—secondary skin lesions, fever, adenopathy, constitutional symptoms, facial palsy, peripheral neuropathy, lymphocytic meningitis, meningoencephalitis, cardiac manifestations (heart block)
  3. Late: chronic arthritis, dermatitis, neuropathy, keratitis
- Babesiosis (see "Babesiosis" chapter)
- Ehrlichiosis/anaplasmosis (see "Ehrlichiosis and Anaplasmosis")

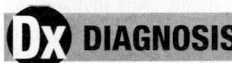 **DIAGNOSIS**

DIFFERENTIAL DIAGNOSIS

- Cellulitis
- Urticaria

Other tick-borne illnesses:

- Babesiosis
- Tick-borne relapsing fever/*Borrelia miyamotoi*
- Tularemia
- Rocky Mountain spotted fever
- Ehrlichiosis/anaplasmosis
- Colorado tick fever
- Tick paralysis
- Community-acquired cutaneous methicillin-resistant *Staphylococcus aureus*

WORKUP

Physical examination: thorough skin examination may reveal fang marks, attached ticks, black eschar.

 **TREATMENT**

ACUTE GENERAL Rx

Spiders:

- Sydney funnel web
  1. Pressure, immediate immobilization, supportive care, antivenin.
- Black widow
  1. Treatment based on severity of symptoms; bite is rarely fatal.
  2. All should receive oxygen, IV, cardiac monitor, tetanus prophylaxis.
  3. Symptomatic/supportive therapy.
  4. 10% calcium gluconate for muscle cramps (controversial).
  5. Antivenin only for more severe reactions; it carries a risk of anaphylaxis.

  1. Dose: one vial in 100 ml 0.9% saline over 20 to 30 min.
  2. Skin test before use.
  3. Give antihistamines with use.
- Brown recluse
  1. Pain management, tetanus, supportive treatment.
  2. No consensus regarding best treatment; some evidence for hyperbaric oxygen.

Scorpions:

- Fluids, supportive care, species-specific antivenin (equine based, risk of serum sickness) is controversial.
- IV administration of scorpion-specific F(ab')2 antivenin has been reported effective in resolving the clinical syndrome within 4 hours and reducing the need for concomitant sedation with midazolam and reducing the levels of circulating unbound venom.

Ticks:

- Prophylactic: tick >36 hr: single dose of doxycycline 200 mg
- Early localized disease
  1. Treatment of choice in children: amoxicillin for 14 days.
  2. Doxycycline preferred in patients with possible concurrent ehrlichiosis.
  3. Early disseminated: treatment depends on manifestation.
  4. Late disease: may require longer-term or IV therapy; controversial for neurologic disease (see "Lyme Disease").

DISPOSITION

- For patients with systemic reactions, send home with emergency epinephrine kit.
- If severe or anaphylactic reaction, admit and observe for 48 hr for cardiac, renal, or neurologic problems.

REFERRAL

For patients with systemic reactions, refer to allergist for immunotherapy; 95% to 98% effective in preventing anaphylaxis.

 **PEARLS & CONSIDERATIONS**

Actual spider bites rare, need witnessed bite, patient should bring spider if possible for confirmation. Bites usually occur in settings of unusually close contact with spider. Bedbugs becoming more prevalent, repeated exposure increases severity of reaction.

SUGGESTED READINGS

Available at www.expertconsult.com

RELATED CONTENT

Bites and Stings, Insect (Related Key Topic)
Bites and Stings (Patient Information)

AUTHOR: **GAIL M. O'BRIEN, M.D.**

BASIC INFORMATION

DEFINITION

Most stinging insects belong to the Hymenoptera order and include honey bees, hornets, bumble-bees, sweat bees, wasps (including yellow jackets), harvester ants, fire ants, and the Africanized honey bee ("killer bee"). Wasps cause 70% of all reactions to stings. Spiders, which are arachnids, not insects, are another cause of bites (Fig. 1B-28) (see "Bites and Stings, Arachnids"). The venom contains vaso-active and proinflammatory mediators that can cause local reactions. A small number of those stung can develop a systemic hypersensitivity reaction. The usual effect of a sting is intense local pain, immediate erythema, and often a small area of edema from the injecting venom. Allergic reactions can be either local or general-ized, which can lead to anaphylactic shock. The majority of reactions occur within the first 6 hr after the sting or bite, but a delayed reaction may occur up to 24 hr after the sting. Delayed reactions are rare and include serum sickness.

SYNONYMS

Venom allergy

ICD-10CM CODES
T63.444 Toxic effect of venom of bees, undetermined, initial encounter
T63.464 Toxic effect of venom of wasps, undetermined, initial encounter
T63.424 Toxic effect of venom of ants, undetermined, initial encounter

EPIDEMIOLOGY & DEMOGRAPHICS

PREVALENCE (OF BEE STINGS AND INSECT BITES):
- Unknown prevalence, very underreported.
- Account for 2.3% of ED visits.5% to 7.5% of the population is hypersensitive, with large local or systemic reactions, to the venom of one or more stinging insects.
- Insect bites are the most common cause of anaphylaxis reactions.
- Most anaphylactic reactions occur during summer months in those most likely to be exposed, including children, males, outdoor

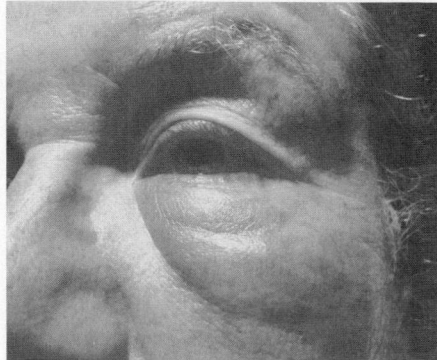

FIGURE 1B-28 Spider bite to lower eyelid.
(From Swartz MH: *Textbook of physical diagnosis,* ed 7, Philadelphia, 2014, Elsevier.)

workers. There are no tests to predict reaction accurately; the reaction to a prior sting is still the best predictor.
- Approximately half of fatal reactions occur without prior allergic response.
- Bites by fire ants are less likely to cause systemic disease.
- Spider bites are rare; only a few of the thousands of spider species cause a reaction in humans. Observation and collection of the spider inflicting the bite is necessary.

INCIDENCE (IN U.S.): Forty to 100 people die each year from insect sting anaphylaxis; ana-phylaxis occurs most often within 10 to 30 min of a sting. Delayed reactions are rare, occurring only in <0.3% of stings.

PHYSICAL FINDINGS & CLINICAL PRESENTATION

Stings:
Local reactions:
- Cutaneous: the skin is the most common site of a local allergic reaction. Manifestations include flushing, urticaria, pruritus, and angioedema. Local reactions may last several days.
Systemic reactions:
- Respiratory: This is the leading cause of anaphylactic death. Anaphylaxis as defined by consensus of the NIH 2006 is a severe life-threatening hypersensitivity reaction. Symptoms of upper and lower airway obstruction including hoarseness, choking, throat tightness or tingling that may progress to stridor, laryngeal edema, laryngospasm, and bronchoconstriction.
- Cardiovascular: Cardiac manifestations are the second leading cause of death from anaphylaxis; the most common reaction is hypotension that can progress to profound hypovolemic shock. Tachycardia and arrhyth-mia may occur. Myocardial infarction is rare.
- General symptoms: abdominal pain, nausea, vomiting, lightheadedness, and diarrhea.
Fire ant bites:
- Initial wheal and flare response.
- Subsequent development of circularly arrayed blisters within 24 hr (Fig. 1B-29).
- Blisters may develop the appearance of pustules, but they are not infected.

ETIOLOGY

Stings:
- Most systemic reactions to insect stings are classic immunoglobulin E (IgE)–mediated reactions. Anaphylaxis can be the presenting sign of indolent mastocytosis.
- Reactions occur in previously sensitized patients who have produced high titers of IgE antibody to insect venom antigens.
- Sensitization to wasp venom can occur after a single sting but is more common after a few stings.
- Sensitization to bee venom occurs mainly in people who have been stung frequently by bees.
- Fig. E1B-30 illustrates representative venom-ous hymenoptera
Bites:
- Fire ant venom contains proteins toxic to the skin.

DIAGNOSIS

DIFFERENTIAL DIAGNOSIS
- Stings: cellulitis, bites, rash
- Bites: stings, cellulitis

WORKUP
The history is essential for accurate diagnosis including timing of sting or bite and type of insect (bee, wasp, spider, or ant) if known.

LABORATORY TESTS (FOR HYPERSENSITIVITY REACTION)
- Skin test: either skin prick test or intradermal method with fire ant or hymenoptera venom.
- Venom skin tests and occasionally radioal-lergosorbent tests (RAST) to provide additional information, only for those with history of a systemic reaction.
- Venom-specific IgE tests
- Basophil activation tests and mast cell medi-ator testing are being developed to identify those with allergy and predict those who will have more severe reactions.

TREATMENT

ACUTE GENERAL Rx

Sting:
- Local Poison Control Center can be contacted
- Removal of the stinger most easily performed with a flat tool such as a credit card within 30 seconds of the sting, followed by cleansing and application of ice.
- Avoid squeezing, which may push venom out of the venom sac and into the tissue.
- Oral antihistamines and nonsteroidal anti-inflammatory medications and topical corti-costeroids for limited reactions.
- Large local reactions (>10 cm) may benefit from oral steroids.
- Patients with previous reactions or multiple stings to the mouth or neck should be evaluated in an emergency department.
- Systemic reactions: Treat with intramuscular epinephrine (no contraindication for use). Increased risk of death if epinephrine delayed. The patient should be supine with 0.30 mg IM in anterior/lateral thigh.
- H1 and H2 antihistamines, oxygen, IV glu-cocorticoids, beta-agonists, pressors, and IV fluids may also be beneficial for anaphylaxis. No data that glucocorticoids improve clinical outcomes.
- Patients should be given 2 units of self-injectable epinephrine pens for home use and referral to allergy indicated after a systemic reaction.
Bite:
- Supportive care—wash with soap and water
- Application of ice or cooling. Calamine lotion may be helpful.
- Surveillance for secondary infection

DISPOSITION
Sting:
- Prognosis for a limited reaction is excellent.

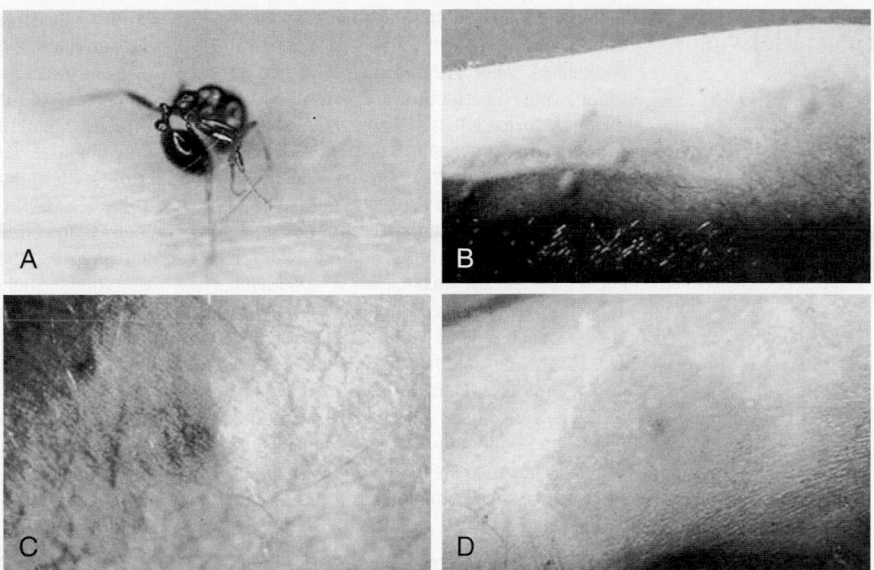

FIGURE 1B-29 A, Stinging fire ant (*Solenopsis invicta*). **B,** Wheal-and-flare reactions 5 minutes after multiple fire ant stings. **C,** Sterile pustule 24 hours after fire ant sting. **D,** Cutaneous late-phase allergic reaction 24 hours after fire ant sting. Excoriated sterile pustule in center of lesion. (From Kemp SF et al: Expanding habitat of the imported fire ant (*Solenopsis invicta*): a public health concern, *J Allergy Clin Immunol* 105(4):683-691, 2000.)

- Subsequent anaphylaxis may occur in up to 65% of patients stung again with history of prior systemic reaction. Large local reaction does not predict a systemic reaction.
- There is no evidence that the next sting will necessarily cause a more severe reaction. Variable outcome is due to the patient's age, comorbidities, time elapsed since prior exposure, dose of venom injected, and site of sting.
- Watch for secondary cellulitis.
- Patients who have a history of a severe systemic reaction:
  1. Should be educated to avoid stinging insects
  2. Carry 2 syringes preloaded with epinephrine for self administration
  3. Undergo testing for serum levels of venom-specific IgE
  4. Refer to allergist for venom immunotherapy (VIT), which reduces chance of serious allergic reaction from 60% to < 5%. VIT is typically needed for 3 to 5 yr.
  5. Carry medical identification for stinging insect hypersensitivity

6. Baseline tryptase level for any patient with an anaphylactic reaction to a sting to evaluate the possibility of an underlying mast cell disorder. Patients with levels >20 ng/mL need further evaluation.

Bite:
- Prognosis for fire ant bite is excellent.
- Large lesions from brown recluse spider bites may take months to heal.
- Watch for secondary cellulitis.

REFERRAL
- Consider a referral to an allergist for venom immunotherapy (VIT).
- Risk of subsequent anaphylaxis with immunotherapy falls to <3%.
- VIT for 3 to 5 yr induces long-term protection in most patients.

 **PEARLS & CONSIDERATIONS**

Hypersensitivity to stings is common. Reactions range from local nonallergic reaction to venom to life-threatening systemic reaction with ana-

phylaxis. This could indicate underlying mast cell disorder; tryptase level is indicated. Venom-specific immunotherapy is highly effective in decreasing subsequent anaphylaxis. Although venom immunotherapy is currently indicated only for systemic reactions, investigation is under way to assess efficacy for prevention of large local reactions, which can result in significant morbidity.

SUGGESTED READINGS
Available at www.expertconsult.com

RELATED CONTENT
Bites and Stings, Arachnids (Related Key Topic)
Bites and Stings (Patient Information)

AUTHOR: **LYNN BOWLBY, M.D.**

ⓘ BASIC INFORMATION

DEFINITION
Injury resulting from a snake biting a human.

ICD-10CM CODES
T63.0   Toxic effect of snake venom
T63.001A Toxic effect of unspecified snake
         venom, accidental (unintentional),
         initial encounter

EPIDEMIOLOGY & DEMOGRAPHICS
- The CDC reports between 7000 and 9000 venomous snakebites annually in the United States, with <1% resulting in death. The southern states have the highest incidence, especially from April to November. Worldwide, farm workers have the highest incidence of snakebites. Men are twice as likely to be bitten, and risk factors for envenomation include intoxication, handling captive snakes, or intentional provocation of snakes. Risk of death is highest in children, the elderly, and in those with delayed presentation to care.
- In the U.S., at least one species of poisonous snake (Fig. 1B-31) has been identified in every state except Alaska, Hawaii, and Maine. Table 1B-5 summarizes medically important snake families.
- The Crotalinae subfamily (Viperidae family), commonly referred to as crotalids or pit vipers, includes rattlesnakes, copperheads, and cottonmouths (water moccasins). Crotalids are responsible for the vast majority of snake envenomations in the U.S. They are characterized by a prominent, diamond-shaped head, a heat-sensing pit between the eye and nostril, long retractable fangs, and, in the case of rattlesnakes, the telltale rattler. Crotalid bites are typically very painful.
- The Elapidae family includes mambas and cobras internationally, but only coral snakes in the U.S. Coral snakes are much less common than crotalids, are less aggressive, and are responsible for only 1% to 2% of venomous snakebites in the U.S. Elapids have smaller heads, shorter fangs, and bright bands of color including red, yellow, and black. The popular saying "red on yellow, kill a fellow; red on black, venom lack" is used to distinguish between venomous and nonvenomous snakes; however, there are venomous coral snakes in South America with red on black coloring which defy this popular axiom. Elapid bites are typically less painful; however, because elapids must "chew" to inject venom, victims may report difficulty dislodging the snake after the bite.
- Exotic, nonnative pets also account for 1% to 2% of snake envenomations.

PHYSICAL FINDINGS & CLINICAL PRESENTATION
The effects of envenomation vary by the type of snake but may include local tissue injury, as well as insults to the cardiovascular, renal, neurologic, and coagulation systems. Crotalids typically cause severe local effects, as well as hematologic symptoms including primary consumptive coagulopathies, with fewer severe neurologic effects. The exception is the Mojave rattlesnake, which causes few local effects and may have severe neurologic effects that can be delayed. Elapids also cause fewer local

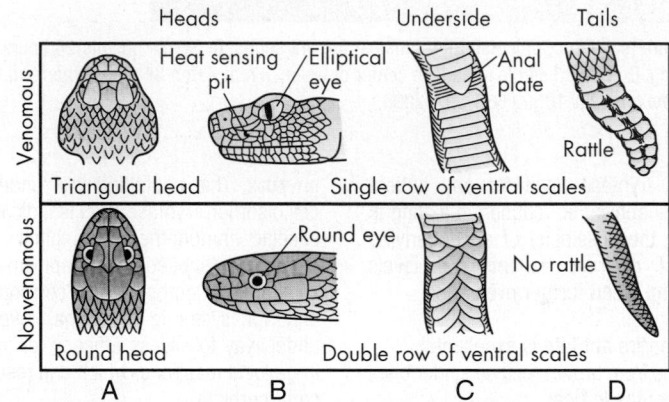

FIGURE 1B-31 Comparison of pit vipers and nonvenomous snakes. Rattle in **D** *(top)* applies to rattlesnakes only. (**A** to **D**, From Sullivan JB et al: North American venomous reptile bites. In Auerbach PS [ed]: *Wilderness medicine: management of wilderness and environmental emergencies,* ed 3, p. 684, St Louis, 1995, Mosby.)

TABLE 1B-5	Medically Important Snake Families			
Family	**Venomous?**	**Location**	**Examples**	**Toxin Effects/Other Comments**
Colubridae	Some species	Most parts of the world	Garter snakes (*Thamnophis* spp.), king snakes and milk snakes (*Lampropeltis* spp.)	Largest family of snakes; most are considered harmless to humans; a few species are dangerously toxic (e.g., African boomslang [*Dispholidus typus*])
Boidae	None	Most parts of the world	*Boa* sp., *Python* sp.	Constrictors; unsupervised children should not be allowed access to large constrictors
Viperidae				
Subfamily Crotalinae (pit vipers)	All	Americas, Asia	Rattlesnakes (*Crotalus* spp.), cottonmouths and copperheads (*Agkistrodon* spp.), Lancehead pit vipers (*Bothrops* spp.)	Heat-sensing "pit" between each eye and nostril
Subfamily Viperinae (true vipers)	All	Europe, Africa, Middle East, Asia	Puff adder (*Bitis arietans*), Gaboon viper (*Bitis gabonica*)	No heat-sensing pits
Elapidae	All	Americas, Africa, Middle East, Asia	Cobras (*Naja* spp.), mambas (*Dendroaspis* spp.), kraits (*Bungarus* spp.), coral snakes (*Micrurus* spp.), and the venomous snakes of Australia	Highly variable venom effects—some largely neurotoxic, others causing severe local tissue damage
Hydrophiidae	All	Warm waters of the Pacific Ocean, Indian Ocean, and Oceania (none in the Atlantic Ocean)	Sea snakes including the pelagic sea snake (*Pelamis platurus*)	Neurotoxins and myotoxins; rarely bite humans unless provoked

From Kliegman RM et al: *Nelson textbook of pediatrics,* ed 19, Philadelphia, 2011, Saunders.

effects but commonly cause severe neurologic symptoms, often with a delayed presentation of up to 12 hours.

CROTALINAE (PIT VIPERS): Local signs and symptoms
- Intense pain within 5 minutes
- Localized edema within 30 minutes
- Erythema, ecchymosis, and serous/hemorrhagic bullae can develop over hours (Fig. 1B-32)
- Compartment syndrome may develop around the site of the bite from significant amounts of soft tissue swelling and subcutaneous tissue fluid accumulation.
- If edema or erythema does not occur within 8 hours of a confirmed crotalid snakebite, it is assumed envenomation did not occur ("dry bite"). Roughly 25% crotalid bites are "dry bites".

Systemic manifestations
- Nonspecific: nausea, vomiting, diarrhea, lightheadedness, weakness, diaphoresis, chills
- Coagulopathy: epistaxis, bleeding from gums, internal hemorrhage
- Neurotoxicity: perioral paresthesias, metallic taste, tingling of fingers or toes (especially with rattlesnake bites), localized/generalized fasciculations, mental status change
- Nephrotoxicity: secondary to rhabdomyolysis
- Increased vascular permeability: severe hypotension, tachycardia, respiratory distress

ELAPIDAE (CORAL SNAKES): Local signs and symptoms
- Absent or minimal local effects, such as mild pain, swelling, or parasthesias at site of bite.

Systemic Manifestations
- May be delayed for up to 12 hours.
- Nonspecific: Nausea, vomiting, abdominal pain, dizziness

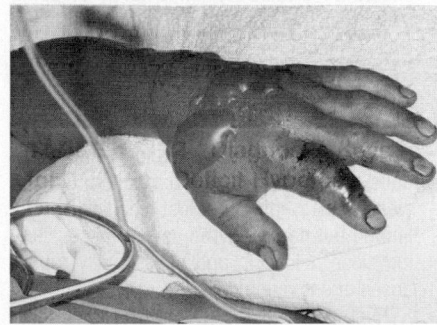

FIGURE 1B-32 Southern Pacific rattlesnake (*Crotalus helleri*) bite wounds. (Courtesy Sean Bush, M.D.)

- Neurotoxic: Cranial neuropathies typically appear first including ptosis, ophthalmoplegia, dysphagia, drooling, and mydriasis with absent or prolonged pupillary light reflex. Descending paralysis and respiratory failure (due to diaphragmatic weakness) can be delayed many hours.

Dx DIAGNOSIS

DIFFERENTIAL DIAGNOSIS
- Bite: nonvenomous snakebite, "dry bite", scorpion bite, insect bite, cellulitis, laceration, puncture wound, necrotizing fasciitis
- Descending paralysis: myasthenia gravis, botulism, shellfish poisoning
- Rhabdomyolysis: crush injury, prolonged immobilization, marked exercise, hyperthermia, metabolic myopathies, drugs or toxins, infections, electrolyte disorders
- Coagulopathy: sepsis, multiple trauma, obstetrical complications, malignancy

WORKUP
1. Stabilize and resuscitate unstable patients.
2. Initial evaluation of the bite (as detailed in the following)
3. Complete physical and neurologic examination
4. Obtain past medical history, including any history of allergic reaction to horse serum in those previously treated for snakebite.
5. Labs and imaging as detailed in the following
6. Determine need for antivenom (see the following and Table 1B-6)
7. Call Poison Control Hotline: 1-800-222-1222
8. Call local zoo when treating patients with envenomations from exotic pets or nonnative snakes
9. Serially reassess, including serial neurologic exams, all cases of suspected envenomation for 8 hours or longer if clinical status deteriorates

LABORATORY TESTS
- CBC with peripheral smear, electrolytes, BUN, creatinine, PT, INR, PTT, fibrinogen, D-dimer, creatine kinase, LFTs, ESR, ABG, type and crossmatch, urinalysis, and ECG.
- Repeat labs every 4 to 6 hours to monitor progression.

IMAGING
- Consider chest x-ray in cases of severe envenomation or in patients over 40 years old with underlying cardiopulmonary disease to rule out pulmonary edema, plain films of bite site

for retained fangs (poor sensitivity), and head CT if concern for intracranial hemorrhage

Rx TREATMENT

ACUTE GENERAL Rx
IN THE FIELD
- Transport immediately to nearest medical facility. No treatments in the field should delay administration of antivenom, when necessary.
- Remove any constricting items including rings, watches, jewelry, or tight clothing.
- Immobilize affected part and keep at the level of the heart.
- Do *not* apply a tourniquet, incise wound, apply mechanical or oral suction, or apply ice.
- In general, do *not* apply a pressure dressing. Since most bites are from crotalids, a pressure dressing can exacerbate local tissue destruction and necrosis. However, if the bite is *known* to be from a coral snake, applying a pressure dressing can prevent the spread of neurotoxin.
- Avoid alcohol, stimulants (caffeine), or agents that can suppress mental status.
- Do *not* pick up a dead snake, as the strike reflexes remain intact and can still envenomate. When possible, a picture can be taken for later classification of the snake.

IN THE HOSPITAL
- Assess ABCs and intervene as needed. Patients with neurotoxic envenomation from elapids or Mojave rattlesnakes can develop respiratory failure (from diaphragmatic paralysis) and may require intubation. Be cautious and repeat the examination as neurotoxic symptoms may be delayed for many hours.
- Place on monitor, obtain vital signs, place 2 large-bore IVs and give crystalloid.
- Unstable patients should be given antivenom immediately. Administration should not be delayed for wound care of bite.
- If patient is stable, obtain a history, including the time of bite and description of snake.
- Inspect bite site for fang marks and local tissue injury. Clean bite site and remove any retained fangs. Bite may appear like two distinct puncture wounds or small scratches.
- Mark leading edge of erythema and edema, and obtain circumferential measurements every 15 minutes to assess for progression.
- Obtain initial labs (as previously mentioned) and repeat every 4 to 6 hours.
- Determine need for antivenom and begin preparation. It can take up to 1 hour to reconstitute antivenom, so this process should be started as early as possible.
- Contact Poison Control at 1-800-222-1222, which will connect you to your local poison control center. They will provide guidance for treatment and use of antivenom, and also track snakebite incidence.
- Immunize against tetanus if no booster within the past 5 years. If never immunized, give immunoglobulin as well as toxoid.
- Aggressive pain control with opioids. Avoid NSAIDs as they increase risk of bleeding and are nephrotoxic.

TABLE 1B-6 Indications for Snake Antivenom Administration	
Evidence of systemic toxicity:	
Hemodynamic or respiratory instability	Hypotension, respiratory distress
Hemotoxicity	Clinically significant bleeding or abnormal coagulation studies
Neurotoxicity	Any evidence of toxicity: usually beginning with cranial nerve abnormalities and progressing to descending paralysis including the diaphragm
Evidence of local toxicity	*Progressive* soft tissue swelling

From Kliegman RM et al: *Nelson textbook of pediatrics*, ed 19, Philadelphia, 2011, Saunders.

ANTIVENOM TREATMENT

CROTALID (RATTLESNAKE, COPPERHEAD, COTTONMOUTH) ENVENOMATIONS

- CroFab (Crotalinae polyvalent ovine immune Fab), made from sheep serum, is the antivenom commercially available in the US for crotalid envenomations.
- Indications for antivenom administration include swelling, pain, and/or ecchymosis extending beyond area immediately adjacent to bite, any progression of local symptoms, any systemic symptoms, any development of coagulation lab abnormalities, or abnormal bleeding.
- Patients with crotalid envenomation who have minimal or nonprogressive symptoms should *not* be given CroFab and instead should be monitored for 8 to 12 hours.
- Dosing:
  - For moderate symptoms, mix 4 to 6 vials of antivenom in 250 mL normal saline and infuse over 60 minutes. Infuse slowly over the first 10 minutes to monitor for allergic reaction.
  - For patients with shock or serious active bleeding, give an initial dose of 8 to 12 vials.
  - If no improvement after first round of antivenom, repeat the initial dose.
- After initial control of symptom progression, give scheduled doses of 2 vials every 6 hours for 3 doses to prevent recurrent toxicity.
- The manufacturer of CroFab maintains a 24/7 hotline: 877-377-3784
- A new Crotalinae antivenom, Anavip, was approved by the FDA in May 2015, with anticipated availability in October 2018. Anavip is approved for use against crotalid envenomations. Anavip is an equine antivenom that has venom specific F(ab')$_2$ fragments of immunoglobulin G (IgG), as opposed to two separate Fab fragments, increasing the half life in the blood and leading to greater binding and therefore greater elimination of the venom. Because of the longer half life, dosing with Anavip also eliminates the need for repeat outpatient antivenom dosing, as is required with CroFab. There is a low risk of adverse reactions and serum sickness because, similar to CroFab, these antivenoms lack the Fc component of the IgG.

ELAPID (CORAL SNAKE) ENVENOMATIONS

- In the U.S., production of coral snake antivenom was discontinued in 2006 and all but one lot of antivenom still exists. After its expiration on April 30, 2016, the only option to obtain antivenom will be to seek compassionate release of expired stock in conjunction with your local Poison Control Center. A potent, safe, sheep-based antivenom for elapid bites exists and is being used internationally but is not yet approved in the U.S. Another option is to contact a zoo that cares for exotic snakes and obtain Mexican coral snake or Australian Tiger snake antivenom, although efficacy for North American coral snake envenomation is unproven.
- In the U.S., only symptomatic patients with confirmed coral snake bites should receive antivenom. The initial dose is 3 to 5 vials given by slow intravenous push, though more may be necessary in children or in envenomations from large coral snakes.

- In the U.S., asymptomatic patients should not receive antivenom. They should be observed, and antivenom should be administered only if symptoms develop.
- There is a high risk of allergic reaction with horse serum-based elapid antivenom so epinephrine, diphenhydramine, IV corticosteroids, and albuterol should be readily available prior to giving antivenom.

NONNATIVE OR EXOTIC SNAKE ENVENOMATIONS

- Contact the Poison Control Center or your local zoo, as zoos with exotic snakes are required to maintain a supply of snake-specific antivenom on their premises.

DISPOSITION

- All patients who are given antivenom must be admitted and monitored in an ICU for further observation and supportive care. Patients should be observed for 18 to 24 hours after initial control of symptom progression and are safe for discharge when symptom progression has resolved and labs have normalized.
- Victims of crotalid envenomations with minimal to no toxicity and normal serial labs should be observed for 8 to 12 hours. Patients are safe for discharge when symptom progression has resolved and labs have normalized. Children, the elderly, those with significant comorbidities, and patients who sustain bites to the legs, face, or neck may require observation for 24 hours.
- Suspected Mojave rattlesnake bites should be observed 12 to 24 hours as their venom predominantly causes neurotoxicity and symptoms may be delayed (similar to elapids).
- Asymptomatic patients with coral snake-bites should be observed for 12 to 24 hours because neurotoxicity may be delayed.

FOLLOW-UP

- All patients who receive antivenom should have repeat labs at 2 to 3 days and 5 to 7 days after discharge to evaluate for delayed hematologic complications or serum sickness.
- Return for worsening, nondependent swelling, abnormal bleeding, or signs of serum sickness, which include fatigue, rash, or arthralgias.
- Have patients adhere to bleeding precautions (no contact sports, elective surgery, etc.) for 2 weeks.

REFERRAL

Refer to a medical facility with an ICU for administration of antivenom. The approach to snake-bites should be multidisciplinary and should include medical toxicology or other physician snakebite specialists, as well as hematology or nephrology consultations if needed. All snake-bites should be reported to Poison Control and the local health department for surveillance.

❗ PEARLS & CONSIDERATIONS

OTHER CONSIDERATIONS

- Dosage of antivenom is based on typical envenomation rather than age or weight,

so the dose is the same for children and adults.
- Antivenom is not contraindicated in pregnancy. Pregnant victims of snakebites have a significantly lower rate of miscarriage when compared to those who did not receive antivenom. Antibiotics are rarely needed and should be reserved for moderate to severe contamination or definite infection. When indicated, broad-spectrum antibiotics should be used to cover gram-negative bacteria (i.e., ampicillin-sulbactam or quinolone derivatives).
- Antivenom is most effective when given within 4 hours of the bite and least effective if delayed beyond 12 hours. Systemic symptoms (coagulopathy, CNS effects, etc.) respond better to treatment than do local symptoms (erythema/edema, bullae, etc.).
- Although local wound effects can be severe, wound management should not take precedence over antivenom administration. Some studies suggest that even in the case of compartment syndrome, antivenom may be more effective than fasciotomy, although both may be necessary.

COMPLICATIONS

- Hypersensitivity reactions and serum sickness can occur following any antivenom administration; however, they are much more common with equine-derived antivenom than with ovine-derived antivenom. Thus, CroFab derived from sheep serum should be used preferentially over equine serum if available given the decreased risk. Risk of allergic reaction and anaphylaxis, however, is still high with elapid antivenom, as it is derived from horse serum.
- Anaphylaxis can occur within 30 minutes and should be treated by immediately stopping the infusion and managing the symptoms. Give epinephrine, diphenhydramine, and hydrocortisone as needed. If the anaphylaxis is well controlled and the envenomation is severe, the infusion can then be resumed.
- Delayed or recurrent hematologic complications are common and can manifest up to 2 weeks post treatment. Most bleeding is self-limited but can rarely be severe, necessitating close follow-up and occasionally repeat doses of antivenom.
- Serum sickness occurs 7 to 14 days after antivenom administration and is characterized by fever, rash, arthralgias, and lymphadenopathy. It can be treated with prednisone 60 mg/d PO, tapered over 7 to 10 days.

SUGGESTED READINGS

Available at www.expertconsult.com

RELATED CONTENT

Snake Bites (Patient Information)

AUTHORS: **JORDAN WOLFE, M.D.,** and **NEHA P. RAUKAR, M.D., M.S.**

B

 **BASIC INFORMATION**

DEFINITION

Bladder cancer is a heterogeneous spectrum of neoplasms ranging from non–life-threatening, low-grade, superficial papillary lesions to high-grade invasive tumors, which often have metastasized at the time of presentation. It is a field change disease in which the entire urothelium from the renal pelvis to the urethra may be susceptible to malignant transformation. The three types of bladder cancer are transitional cell carcinoma (TCCa), squamous cell carcinoma, and adenocarcinoma.

ICD-10CM CODES
C67.9   Malignant neoplasm of bladder, unspecified
C79.11 Secondary malignant neoplasm of bladder
D09.0   Carcinoma in situ of bladder
D30.3   Benign neoplasm of bladder
D41.4   Neoplasm of uncertain behavior of bladder
D49.4   Neoplasm of unspecified behavior of bladder

EPIDEMIOLOGY & DEMOGRAPHICS

Each year over 70,000 new cases are diagnosed and more than 14,000 deaths are attributed to bladder cancer. Overall, bladder cancer is the sixth most prevalent malignancy in the U.S. and the seventh leading cause of solid-cancer–related death.

Until 1990, the incidence of bladder cancer in the U.S. was rising. Since 1990, the incidence of bladder cancer is decreasing at a rate of 0.8% per year (1.2% among men and 0.4% among women).

PREDOMINANT SEX: In males, it is the fourth most common cancer, accounting for 10% of all cancers. In females, it is the tenth most common cancer, accounting for 4% of all cancers.

RISK: The lifetime risk of developing bladder cancer is 2.8% in white males, 0.9% in black males, 1% in white females, and 0.6% in black females.

Smoking:
- Users of "black" tobacco in place of "blond" tobacco have a twofold to threefold increase in developing bladder cancer.
- Smoking risk is based on consumption:
  1. A twofold to threefold increase for subjects smoking at least 10 cigarettes per day
  2. The risk increases again when the daily consumption rises above 40 to 60 cigarettes per day
- Smokers of low-tar and nicotine cigarettes have a lower risk when compared with higher tar and nicotine cigarettes.
- Those who smoke unfiltered cigarettes have a 50% increased risk of bladder cancer compared with those who smoke filtered cigarettes.
- Pipe smokers have a lower risk of bladder cancer compared with cigarette smokers.

- Cigars, snuff, and chewing tobacco, although implicated in nonurologic cancers, are not believed to influence bladder cancer risk.

Diet:
- Diets rich in beef, pork, and animal fat increase risk of bladder cancer.
- There is no indication that consumption of non-beer alcoholic drinks contributes to bladder cancer development.
- Beer consumption has been linked to bladder cancer development as a result of the presence of nitrosamines in the beer. Nitrosamines have also been implicated in the development of rectal cancer.
- Drinking coffee is not believed to contribute to bladder cancer risk. There is additional evidence that coffee consumption is protective for colorectal cancers, possibly by diminishing fecal transit time.

Medications: Long-term (>1 yr) use of pioglitazone and rosiglitazone

PEAK INCIDENCE: Incidence increases with age: higher after age 60 yr, uncommon younger than 40 yr.

GENETICS: It is thought to be multifactorial in etiology, involving both genetic and environmental interactions. Overall, approximately 20% to 25% of the male population in the U.S. with bladder cancer is estimated to have the disease as a result of occupational exposure.

DISTRIBUTION: In North America, transitional cell carcinomas comprise 93%, squamous cell carcinomas comprise 6%, and adenocarcinomas account for 1% of bladder cancers.

PATHOGENESIS: Two pathways exist for bladder cancer (TCCa):
1. Papillary superficial disease occasionally leading to invasive cancer (75%)
2. Carcinoma in situ (CIS) and solid invasive cancer with high risk of disease progression (25%)

Two distinct forms of "superficial cancer" exist:
1. T_a: Papillary low grade tumor with a high rate of recurrence; disease progression occurs in 5%.
2. T_1: Higher-grade papillary tumor that infiltrates the lamina propria; often associated with flat CIS that may involve the urothelium diffusely. Disease progression occurs in 30% to 50%.

Subdivided into:
- T_{1a}: Penetration of tumor up to the muscularis mucosa; disease progression in 5.3%
- T_{1b}: Penetration of tumor through the muscularis mucosa; disease progression 53%

Flat CIS:
- Entirely different and separate pathway of cancer development whose mechanism is manifested by dysplasia, which leads to the occurrence of poorly differentiated malignant cells that replace or undermine the normal urothelium and extend along the plane of the bladder wall. It penetrates the basement membrane and lamina propria in 20% to 30% of cases and is associated with the development of solid tumor growth. A defect in chromosome 17p53 occurs in 50% of the cases.

At presentation, 72% of cancers are localized to the bladder, 20% of the cancers extend to the regional lymph nodes, and 3% present with distant metastases. Eighty percent of superficial TCCa recur, with up to 30% progressing to a higher stage or grade. Younger patients most commonly develop low-grade papillary noninvasive TCCa and are less likely to have recurrences when compared with older patients with similar lesions. Involvement of the upper tracts with tumor occurs in 25% to 50% of the cases.

STAGING (BASED ON THE TNM SYSTEM):
T_0 No tumor in specimen
T_{is} CIS
T_a Papillary TCCa noninvasive
T_1 Papillary TCCa into lamina propria
T_2 TCCa invasive of superficial muscle
T_{3a} Invasive of deep muscle
T_{3b} Invasive of perivesical fat
T_{4a} Invasive of adjacent pelvic organ
T_{4b} Invasive of pelvic wall with fixation
Invasive of nodal status
N_0 No nodal involvement
N_{1-3} Pelvic nodes
N_4 Nodes above bifurcation
N_x Unknown
Invasive of metastatic status
M_0 No distant metastases
M_1 Distant metastases
M_x Unknown

MOLECULAR EPIDEMIOLOGY: TCCa is usually a field change disease with tumors arising at different times and sites in the urothelium, suggesting a polyclonal etiology of bladder cancer. Bladder cancers have been associated with abnormalities on chromosomes 1, 4, 11, 5, 7, 3, 9, 21, 18, 13, 8; with alterations in suppressor genes *P53*, retinoblastoma gene, and *P16*; and with alterations in oncogenes H-ras and epidermal growth factor receptor.

PHYSICAL FINDINGS & CLINICAL PRESENTATION

- Gross, painless hematuria
- Microhematuria
- Frequency, urgency, occasional dysuria
- With locally invasive to distant metastatic disease, the presentation can include:
  1. Abdominal pain
  2. Flank pain
  3. Lymphedema
  4. Renal failure
  5. Anorexia
  6. Bone pain

ETIOLOGY

Bladder cancer is a potentially preventable disease associated with specific etiologic factors:
- Cigarette smoking is associated with 25% to 65% of cases. The risk of developing a TCCa is two to four times higher in smokers than in non-smokers, and that risk persists for many years, being equal to nonsmokers only after 12 to 15 yr of smoking abstinence. Smoking tobacco is associated with tumors that are characterized by higher histologic grade, increased tumor

stage, increase in the numbers of tumor present, and increased tumor size.

- Occupational exposures: dye workers, textile workers, tire and rubber workers, petroleum workers.
- Chemical exposure: O-toluidine, 2-naphthylamine, benzidine, 4-amino-biphenyl, and nitrosamines.
- Exposure to herpes papilloma virus type 16.

Squamous carcinomas are associated with:
- Schistosomiasis
- Urinary calculi
- Indwelling catheters
- Bladder diverticula

Miscellaneous causes:
- Phenacetin abuse
- Cyclophosphamide
- Pelvic irradiation
- Tuberculosis

Adenocarcinomas are associated with:
- Exstrophy
- Endometriosis
- Neurogenic bladder
- Urachal abnormalities
- As a secondary site for distant metastases from other organs (e.g., colon cancer)

Dx DIAGNOSIS

- History and physical examination.
- Urinalysis.
- Cystoscopy with bladder barbotage and biopsy. Fluorescence cystoscopy offers improvement in the detection of flat neoplastic lesions such as carcinoma in situ.
- Transurethral resection of bladder tumor(s).
- There is insufficient evidence to determine whether a decrease in mortality rate from bladder cancer occurs with hematuria testing, urinary cytology, or a variety of other tests on exfoliated urinary cells or other substances.
- In addition to urinary cytology and bladder barbotage, BTA, NMP22, and fibrin degradation products have been approved by the FDA as bladder cancer tumor markers. No marker has general, widespread acceptance because the results are affected by the presence of stents, recent urologic manipulation, stones, infection, bowel interposition, and prostatitis, creating false-positive results.
- Urinary biomarkers: six urinary biomarkers have been approved by the FDA for diagnosis on surveillance of bladder cancer
  - Quantitative nuclear matrix protein 22 (Alere NMP22)
  - Qualitative NMP22 (BladderChek)
  - Qualitative bladder tumor antigen (BTA stat)
  - Quantitative BTA (BTA TRAK)
  - Fluorescence in situ hybridization (FISH)
  - Fluorescent immunohistochemistry (ImmunoCyt)
- Generally urinary biomarkers miss a substantial proportion of patients with bladder cancer and are subject to false-positive results in

others. Accuracy is poor for low-stage and low-grade tumors.[1]

DIFFERENTIAL DIAGNOSIS

- Urinary tract infection
- Frequency-urgency syndrome
- Interstitial cystitis
- Stone disease
- Endometriosis
- Neurogenic bladder

LABORATORY TESTS

- Urine cytology.
- Urine telomerase: telomerase activity in voided urine or bladder washings determined by the telomeric repeat amplification protocol (TRAP) assay. This test has been reported to accurately detect the presence of bladder tumors in men. It represents a potentially useful noninvasive diagnostic innovation for bladder cancer detection in high-risk groups such as habitual smokers or in symptomatic patients.

RADIOLOGIC TESTS

- IVP, renal ultrasound, retrograde pyelography, CT scan, and MRI.
- One or a combination of studies can be used. In the absence of skeletal symptoms, bone scan is not recommended.

Rx TREATMENT

NONPHARMACOLOGIC THERAPY

- Initially, transurethral resection of bladder tumor (TURBT) (Fig. B1-33)
- Loop biopsy of the prostatic urethra if high-grade TCCa is suspected
- If superficial disease, follow-up protocol with repeat TURBT and/or the use of intravesical agents is recommended
- For advanced bladder cancer, radical cystectomy with urethrectomy (unless orthotopic diversion is planned), and either ileal loop conduit or orthotopic diversion

BLADDER PRESERVATION APPROACHES

After cystectomy for muscle-invasive disease, 50% or more of the patients will develop metastases. Most patients develop metastases at distant sites; a third relapse locally. Bladder preservation management is offered in individuals who refuse surgery or who might not be suitable radical cystectomy patients. Bladder-sparing protocols include extensive TURBT or partial cystectomy with external-beam or interstitial radiotherapy and systemic chemotherapy. Radiotherapy as a single treatment modality is not effective. The best predictor of successful bladder preservation is a complete response after the combination of initial TURBT and two cycles of CMV (cisplatin, methotrexate, vinblastine) chemotherapy used with stages T_2 to T_{3a}.

[1]Chou R, et al.: Urinary Biomarkers for Diagnosis of Bladder Cancer: A Systematic Review and Meta-analysis, *Ann Intern Med* 163:922-931, 2015.

INDICATIONS FOR PARTIAL CYSTECTOMY

- Tumor within a bladder diverticulum
- Solitary, primary, and muscle-invasive or high-grade lesion of a region of the bladder that allows complete excision with adequate surgical margins
- Inability to adequately resect tumor by TURBT alone because of size or location
- Tumor overlying a ureteral orifice requiring ureteral reimplantation
- Biopsy of a radiation-induced ulceration
- Palliation of severe local symptoms
- Patient refusal of urinary diversion
- Poor-risk patient who is not a diversion candidate

CONTRAINDICATIONS

- Multiple tumors
- CIS
- Cellular atypia on biopsy
- Prostatic invasion
- Invasion of the trigone
- Inability to achieve adequate surgical margins
- Prior radiotherapy
- Inability to maintain adequate bladder volume after resection
- Evidence of extravesical tumor extension
- Poor surgical risk

ACUTE GENERAL Rx

INDICATIONS FOR INTRAVESICAL CHEMOTHERAPY

- High-grade tumor
- Tumor size >>5 cm
- Multiple tumors
- Presence of CIS
- Positive urinary cytologic findings after a resection
- Incomplete tumor resection

Intravesical agents: thiotepa, Adriamycin, mitomycin C, AD-32, BCG, interferon, bropirimine, Epodyl, interleukin-2, and keyhole-limpet hemocyanin. Photodynamic therapy with hematoporphyrin derivatives has also been used.

INDICATIONS FOR CYSTECTOMY:

- Large tumors not amenable to complete TURBT
- High-grade tumor
- Multiple tumors with frequent recurrences
- Diffuse CIS not responsive to intravesical chemotherapy
- Prostatic urethra involvement
- Irritative bladder symptoms with upper tract deterioration
- Muscle-invasive disease
- Disease outside the bladder

SYSTEMIC CHEMOTHERAPY: Used as neoadjuvant and adjuvant therapy for systemic disease. The most effective agents are cisplatin, methotrexate, vinblastine, Adriamycin (MVAC). Other agents include mitoxantrone, vincristine, etoposide (VP16), 5-fluorouracil, ifosfamide, Taxol, gemcitabine, Piritrexim, mitomycin C, and gallium nitrate. Chemotherapy in combination can provide palliation and modest survival benefit.

RADIOTHERAPY: Conflicting reports suggest that superficial bladder cancer is more sensitive to radiotherapy. Squamous changes within the tumor and secretion of human chorionic

gonadotropin by the lesion are associated with poor response to radiotherapy. Only 20% to 30% of patients with invasive bladder cancer can be cured by external-beam radiation therapy alone.

It is used in combination with surgery or with systemic agents to treat bladder cancer primarily in patients who are not surgical candidates or who refuse surgery. Trials with synchronous

chemotherapy with fluorouracil and mitomycin C combined with radiotherapy have shown significant improved locoregional control of bladder cancer, as compared with radiotherapy alone in patients with muscle-invasive bladder cancer.

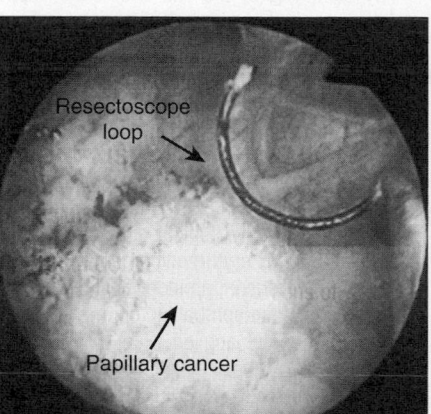

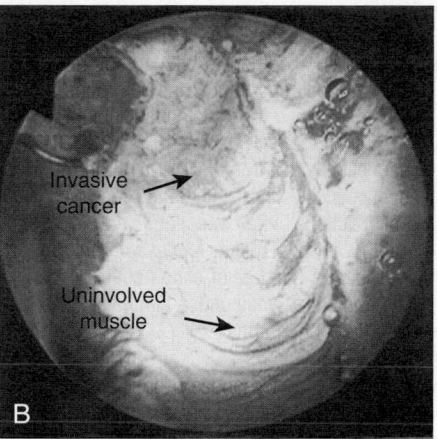

FIGURE B1-33 A, Papillary bladder cancer in right lower aspect of photo with resection loop poised to begin transurethral resection. **B,** Demonstration of grossly uninvolved muscularis propria *(bottom)* and cancer grossly invading the bladder wall *(top)*. (From Abeloff MD: *Clinical oncology*, ed 3, Philadelphia, 2004, Churchill Livingstone.)

BOX 1B-3 American Urological Association Guideline Recommendations

For all index patients
- Standard: Physicians should discuss with the patient the treatment options and the benefits and harms, including side effects, of intravesical treatment.

For a patient who presents with an abnormal growth on the urothelium but who has not yet been diagnosed with bladder cancer
- Standard: If the patient does not have an established histologic diagnosis, a biopsy should be obtained for pathologic analysis.
- Standard: Under most circumstances, complete eradication of all visible tumors should be performed.
- Standard: If bladder cancer is confirmed, periodic surveillance cystoscopy should be performed.
- Option: An initial single dose of intravesical chemotherapy may be administered immediately postoperatively.

For a patient with small volume, low-grade Ta bladder cancer
- Recommendation: An initial single dose of intravesical chemotherapy may be administered immediately postoperatively.

For a patient with multifocal and/or large volume, histologically confirmed, low-grade Ta or a patient with recurrent low-grade Ta bladder cancer
- Recommendation: An induction course of intravesical therapy with bacillus Calmette-Guérin or mitomycin C is recommended for the treatment of these patients with the goal of preventing or delaying recurrence.
- Option: Maintenance bacillus Calmette-Guérin or mitomycin C may be considered.

For a patient with initial histologically confirmed high-grade Ta, T1, and/or carcinoma in situ bladder cancer
- Standard: For patients with lamina propria invasion (T1) but without muscularis propria in the specimen, repeat resection should be performed prior to additional intravesical therapy.
- Recommendation: An induction course of bacillus Calmette-Guérin followed by maintenance therapy is recommended for treatment of these patients.
- Option: Cystectomy should be considered for initial therapy in select patients.

For a patient with high-grade Ta, T1, and/or carcinoma in situ bladder cancer that has recurred after prior intravesical therapy
- Standard: For patients with lamina propria invasion (T1) but without muscularis propria in the specimen, repeat resection should be performed prior to additional intravesical therapy.
- Recommendation: Cystectomy should be considered as a therapeutic alternative for these patients.
- Option: Further intravesical therapy may be considered for these patients.

From the American Urological Association, Guideline Division, http://www.auanet.org.

CHRONIC Rx
FOLLOW-UP RECOMMENDATIONS FOR SUPERFICIAL BLADDER CANCER:
- Cystoscopy, bladder barbotage, and bimanual examination every 3 mo for 2 yr, then every 6 mo for 2 yr, and annually thereafter.
- Upper tract studies are based on the risk of upper tract tumor development, generally every 2 to 5 yr.

FOLLOW-UP RECOMMENDATIONS FOR ADVANCED DISEASE: Bladder preservation:
- Cystoscopy, barbotage, bimanual examination, biopsy (when indicated), every 3 mo for 2 yr, then every 6 mo for 2 yr, yearly thereafter
- CT scan of abdomen and pelvis every 6 mo for 2 yr in addition to chest x-ray examination, liver function testing, and serum creatinine

Cystectomy with ileal loop/orthotopic bladder:
- Neobladder endoscopy and IVP yearly
- CT scan of abdomen and pelvis every 6 mo for 2 yr in addition to chest x-ray examination, liver function tests, and serum creatinine
- Loopogram every 6 mo for 2 yr, then annually

 **PEARLS & CONSIDERATIONS**

COMMENTS
- The most useful prognostic parameters for bladder tumor recurrence and subsequent cancer progression are tumor grade, depth of tumor penetration, multifocal tumors, frequency of recurrence, tumor size, CIS, lymphatic invasion, papillary or solid tumor configuration.
- Box 1B-3 describes the American Urological Association Guideline Recommendations for bladder cancer.

 **EVIDENCE**

Available at www.expertconsult.com

SUGGESTED READINGS
Available at www.expertconsult.com

RELATED CONTENT
Bladder Cancer (Patient Information)

AUTHORS: **PHILIP J. ALIOTTA, M.D., M.S.H.A.** and **RUBEN ALVERO, M.D.**

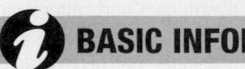
BASIC INFORMATION

DEFINITION
Blepharitis is a chronic inflammation of the eyelid margins that is often refractory to treatment with infectious and noninfectious etiologies.

SYNONYMS
Eyelid infection or inflammation
Eczema of the eyelids
Dermatoblepharitis
Angular blepharitis

ICD-10CM CODES
H01.009 Unspecified blepharitis unspecified eye, unspecified eyelid
H01.019 Ulcerative blepharitis unspecified eye, unspecified eyelid
H01.029 Squamous blepharitis unspecified eye, unspecified eyelid

EPIDEMIOLOGY & DEMOGRAPHICS
- Common in children, particularly those with atopic dermatitis and eczema.
- Adults with seborrhea involving the eyelids.

PHYSICAL FINDINGS & CLINICAL PRESENTATION
- Common symptoms: red eyes, burning sensation, excessive tearing, blurred vision, pruritic eyelids.
- Chronically infected lids are usually diffusely erythematous, with collarettes (fibrin exudate) at the base of the lashes (Fig. 1B-38).
- Lid margins thicken over time, with associated loss of eyelashes (madarosis), misdirected growth of lashes (trichiasis), and overflow or inspissation of the meibomian glands.

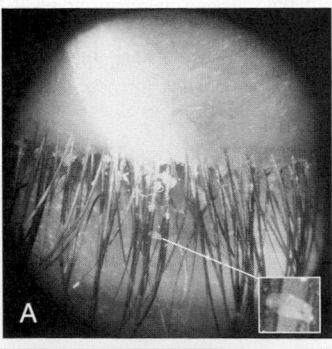
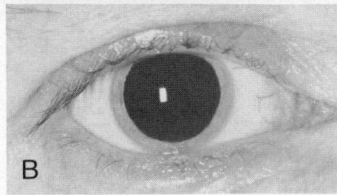

FIGURE 1B-38 A, Seborrheic blepharitis. The typical scales (scurf) are translucent and easily removed. **B,** Staphylococcal blepharitis showing the typical lid margin erythema and discharge. (From Palay D [ed]: *Ophthalmology for the primary care physician,* St Louis, 1997, Mosby.)

- Associated conjunctivitis with erythema, edema but no discharge.
- Chalazion: chronic sterile inflammation of an oil gland of the eyelid.
- Superficial punctate erosions of the inferior corneal epithelium are common.
- More severe findings, such as corneal pannus, ulcerative keratitis, or lid ectropion, are less common.

ETIOLOGY
Multiple: bacterial and nonbacterial causes
- Staphylococcal infection most common but streptococcal, Moraxella, and other bacterial infections; viral infections (e.g., herpes simplex, herpes zoster, *Molluscum contagiosum*); and a number of ecoparasites, including pediculosis, may cause blepharitis
- Seborrheic dermatitis
- Rosacea
- Dry eye (keratoconjunctivitis sicca): decrease in tear volume
- Meibomian gland dysfunction
- Contact lens intolerance
- Two categories of blepharitis:
  1. Anterior blepharitis, most often associated with staphylococcal infection
  2. Posterior blepharitis, associated with meibomian gland dysfunction and seborrheic dermatitis or rosacea

NOTE: Blepharitis patients have normal skin microflora in greater amounts (mostly *S. epidermidis* and *Propionibacterium acnes*). (*S. aureus* and *S. epidermidis* can be cultured in 10% to 35% and 90% to 95% of healthy persons, respectively.)

DIAGNOSIS

DIFFERENTIAL DIAGNOSIS
- Keratoconjunctivitis sicca
- Eyelid malignancies
- Herpes simplex blepharitis
- Molluscum contagiosum
- Phthiriasis palpebrarum
- *Phthirus pubis* (pubic lice)
- *Demodex folliculorum* (transparent mites)
- Allergic blepharitis

WORKUP
Scrapings of the eyelids to show polymorphonuclear leukocytes and gram-positive cocci

LABORATORY TESTS
Eyelid cultures and antibiotic sensitivity testing (usually not done unless patient fails to respond to initial treatment regimen)

TREATMENT

NONPHARMACOLOGIC THERAPY
- Alkaline soaps may be beneficial; alcohol and some detergents remove surface lipids and microflora.

- Hot compresses applied to closed lids for 5 to 10 min: heat loosens debris from lid margins and increases meibomian gland fluidity.
- Firm massage of the lid margins to enhance the flow of secretions from glands, followed by cleansing of the lids with cotton-tipped applicators dipped in a 50:50 mixture of baby shampoo and water.
- Lashes and lid margins scrubbed vigorously while the eyelids are closed, followed by thorough rinsing.
- Following local massage and cleansing, the mainstay of treatment is application of topical antibiotic ointment to the eyelid margins.
  1. Most effective topical antibiotics include bacitracin, erythromycin or 1% azithromycin solution, aminoglycoside and fluoroquinolone ophthalmic ointments.
  2. Ointment is applied 1 to 4 times daily, depending on the severity, for 1 to 2 wk, followed by once daily, at bedtime, for another 4 to 8 wk until all signs of inflammation have disappeared.
- Oral antibiotics: long-term use of doxycycline or tetracycline in a tapering dose may be helpful in severe cases for patients older than 8 years of age.
- Topical glucocorticoids: short-term use in acute exacerbations of blepharitis.
- For patients with rosacea:
- Tetracycline 250 mg orally 4 times daily or doxycycline 100 mg orally bid along with local treatment for several months.
  Recalcitrant cases with antibiotic resistance:
  1. Vancomycin eye drops 1%
  2. Ciprofloxacin or ofloxacin eye drops

CHRONIC Rx
By definition, this is a chronic condition for which there is frequently no cure.

Some newer agents being evaluated are topical cyclosporine 0.05% eye drops, thermal pulsation systems to break up material in meibomian glands, topical metronidazole and topical tacrolimus, and tear lipid substitutes.

DISPOSITION
This condition may be refractory to treatment.

REFERRAL
To an ophthalmologist if patient fails to respond to local therapy.

SUGGESTED READINGS
Available at www.expertconsult.com

AUTHOR: **GLENN G. FORT, M.D., M.P.H.**

BASIC INFORMATION

DEFINITION

Body dysmorphic disorder (BDD) is classified as an obsessive-compulsive and related disorder. It is characterized by preoccupation with one or more perceived defects or flaws in physical appearance that are not observable or appear only slight to others, as well as repetitive behaviors (e.g., excessive grooming, mirror checking) in response to the appearance concerns. The preoccupations cause clinically significant distress or impairment in social, occupational, or other important areas of functioning. The appearance preoccupations are not better explained by concerns with body fat or weight in a person whose symptoms meet diagnostic criteria for an eating disorder.

SYNONYMS

Dysmorphophobia
BDD

ICD-10CM CODES

F45.22 Body dysmorphic disorder

EPIDEMIOLOGY & DEMOGRAPHICS

- Affects 1.7% to 2.4% of the general population (in nationwide epidemiologic studies)
- Prevalence among cosmetic surgery patients (in most studies) is 7% to 16%.
- Prevalence among dermatology patients is 4% to 15% (most studies).
- Slightly higher prevalence among females
- Onset most commonly in adolescence

PHYSICAL FINDINGS & CLINICAL PRESENTATION

- Excessive preoccupation (obsession) with one or more perceived defects in appearance that are not observable or appear slight to others. Patients believe they look abnormal, ugly, or deformed, whereas in reality they look normal. Any part of the body may be a focus of concern; skin, hair, and nose concerns are most common. Most patients are preoccupied with multiple body areas.
- The body areas with which the patient is concerned appear physically normal; if a physical defect is present, it is slight, and the patient's reaction to it is excessive.
- Most patients have poor insight (i.e., mostly convinced) or are delusional (i.e., completely convinced) regarding the accuracy of their belief about the appearance of the perceived defects.
- Over the course of the disorder, all patients engage in repetitive behaviors such as frequent mirror checking, excessive grooming, camouflaging (trying to hide the perceived flaws—e.g., with makeup, a hat, hair), skin picking to try to fix perceived skin flaws, reassurance seeking, and repeatedly measuring or feeling the perceived defect. The intent of these behaviors is to check, try to improve, or be reassured about the appearance of the perceived flaws.

- Nearly all experience impairment in psychosocial functioning and quality of life; impairment is usually substantial.
- Suicidal ideation, suicide attempts, and completed suicide appear common.
- Commonly co-occurring mental disorders are major depressive disorder, substance use disorders, social anxiety disorder, obsessive-compulsive disorder (OCD), and personality disorder.

ETIOLOGY

Likely multifactorial, with both genetic and environmental risk factors (e.g., teasing). Neuropsychological and fMRI studies indicate abnormalities in visual processing consisting of excessive focus on details rather than larger configural elements of visual stimuli.

DIAGNOSIS

Psychiatric interview
Ask:
1. Are you very worried about your appearance in any way? *OR:* Are you unhappy with how you look?
2. Does this concern with your appearance preoccupy you?
3. How much distress does this concern cause you?
4. What effect does this concern have on your life?
5. Is there anything you feel an urge to do over and over again in response to your appearance concerns? (Give examples, such as mirror checking, comparing with others, skin picking to remove perceived skin flaws)
   - Determine that the perceived appearance defects are actually nonexistent or only slight

DIFFERENTIAL DIAGNOSIS

- Often undiagnosed because of patient's reluctance to divulge symptoms due to shame and fear of being misunderstood (e.g., considered vain)
- OCD
- Eating disorder
- Social anxiety disorder
- Major depressive disorder

WORKUP

Clinical evaluation focused on BDD symptoms and associated impairment in functioning.

TREATMENT

NONPHARMACOLOGIC THERAPY

- CBT, with a focus on cognitive restructuring, exposure, and response prevention; CBT must be specifically tailored to BDD's unique symptoms.
- Do not try to talk patients out of their concern; it is ineffective.
- Avoid cosmetic procedures; a majority of patients with BDD receive them, but such treatments do not appear effective for

BDD. Dissatisfied patients may sue or even become violent toward the treating clinician.

ACUTE GENERAL Rx

Precautions/hospitalization if actively suicidal

CHRONIC Rx

- SRIs are medication of choice; relatively high doses often needed.
- Other agents (e.g., neuroleptics, tricyclic antidepressants other than clomipramine) do not appear as beneficial.
- CBT tailored specifically to BDD is recommended, with an SRI if BDD symptoms are more severe, the patient is suicidal because of BDD symptoms, or comorbidity is present that may benefit from an SRI.
- Support groups if available.

DISPOSITION

- Untreated BDD tends to be chronic and can lead to social isolation; school dropout; major depression; unnecessary surgery, dermatologic treatment, or other cosmetic treatment; and even suicide.
- With correct diagnosis and treatment, a majority improve.

REFERRAL

Refer for psychiatric evaluation and treatment if diagnosis is suspected.

PEARLS & CONSIDERATIONS

- In clinical settings, more than 60% have co-occurring major depressive disorder.
- Reassurance that the patient looks normal is rarely helpful.
- Patients often have an unrealistic expectation of improvement with plastic surgery, dermatologic treatment, and other cosmetic procedures; these treatments do not appear to be effective.
- All patients should be screened for suicidality.

PATIENT/FAMILY EDUCATION

- Patients and family members usually benefit from psychoeducation.
- Family support and encouragement of appropriate treatment is important.
- Phillips KA: *Understanding Body Dysmorphic Disorder: An Essential Guide.* Oxford University Press, 2009
  http://www.bodyimageprogram.com
  www.RhodeIslandHospital.org/bdd

SUGGESTED READINGS

Available at www.expertconsult.com

RELATED CONTENT

Obsessive Compulsive Disorder (Related Key Topic)
Body Dysmorphic Disorder (Patient Information)

AUTHOR: **KATHARINE A. PHILLIPS, M.D.**

BASIC INFORMATION

DEFINITION

Borderline personality disorder (BPD) is characterized by a pervasive pattern of instability in interpersonal relationships, self-image, affect regulation, and impulse control that causes significant subjective distress or impairment of functioning. The individual must meet five or more of the following criteria:

1. Frantic efforts to avoid real or imagined abandonment
2. Unstable and intense personal relationships characterized by alternating between extremes of idealization and devaluation
3. Identity disturbance characterized by an unstable self-image
4. Impulsivity in at least two areas that are potentially self-damaging (e.g., overspending, sex, substance abuse, binge eating, reckless driving)
5. Recurrent suicidal behavior, gestures, threats, or self-mutilating behavior
6. Affective instability due to a marked reactivity of mood
7. Chronic feelings of emptiness
8. Inappropriate, intense anger or difficulty controlling anger
9. Transient, stress-related paranoid ideation or severe dissociative symptoms

ICD-10CM CODES
F60.3 Emotionally unstable personality disorder
F60.3 Borderline personality disorder

EPIDEMIOLOGY & DEMOGRAPHICS

PREVALENCE: Affects approximately 1% to 2% of the general population and up to 10% of psychiatric outpatients
PREDOMINANT SEX: Female (3:1)
PREDOMINANT AGE: 20s
GENETICS: BPD is five times as likely if disorder is present in a first-degree relative. Increased prevalence of mood disorders and substance abuse disorders also found in first-degree relatives.
RISK FACTORS: Association with childhood physical, sexual, or emotional abuse and/or neglect

PHYSICAL FINDINGS & CLINICAL PRESENTATION

- No specific associated physical findings.
- Mental status examination may reveal affective lability.
- Clinical presentation may reveal the following:
  1. A pervasive sense of loneliness and emptiness.
  2. Underlying negative affect with dysphoria.
  3. High frequency of comorbid psychiatric disorders, especially posttraumatic stress disorder (PTSD), anxiety disorders generally, mood disorders, attention-deficit/hyperactivity disorder, and substance use disorders.

4. Intense emotions with difficulty returning to emotional baseline.
5. All-or-nothing, either/or cognitive style that is represented by a phenomenon known as "splitting," in which patient sees situations or people as all good or all bad.
6. Difficulty in maintaining commitment to long-term goals; history of numerous stormy relationships and multiple jobs.
7. Reports a high number of sexual partners due to either/both impulsivity and victimization.
8. Reacts with rage, panic, despair to actual or perceived abandonment; may present with suicidality or self-mutilating behavior in response to recent stressor.
9. Attempts to block the experience of pain, which may induce feelings of derealization, depersonalization, changes in consciousness, and/or brief psychotic reactions with delusions and hallucinations.
10. Substance use, gambling, overspending, eating binges, and/or self-mutilation as a way to escape intensely painful affect.

ETIOLOGY

- Interaction of psychosocial adversity plus genetic factors
- Hypotheses:
  1. Genetic: increased risk if first-degree relative with BPD.
  2. Biologic: abnormalities in limbic system and other areas of the brain cause emotional dysregulation. Serotonergic functioning appears to be disturbed.
  3. Environmental: history of childhood abuse (most commonly sexual), invalidation, or neglect.

DIAGNOSIS

DIFFERENTIAL DIAGNOSIS

- Histrionic, antisocial, and narcissistic personality disorders share some common features.

- Dysthymia and other depressive disorders: requires a stability of affective symptoms not seen in BPD.
- Bipolar disorder: mood changes in BPD often triggered by stressors and less sustained than in bipolar disorder. Many patients with BPD are incorrectly diagnosed with bipolar disorder.
- Substance abuse or dependence: often induces impulsive, emotionally labile behavior.
- Posttraumatic stress disorder (PTSD): individuals with BPD often have history of trauma but do not avoid the feared stimulus or reexperience the trauma, as with PTSD.
- Mild cases of schizophrenia may superficially resemble BPD.

WORKUP

- History (helpful to gather collateral information from family and friends)
- Physical examination
- Mental status examination

LABORATORY TESTS

- Toxicology screen; substance use is common and can mimic features of personality disorders.
- Screen for HIV and other sexually transmitted illnesses.

IMAGING STUDIES

Structural and functional MRI demonstrate amygdala hyperactivity (Fig. 1B-40), reduced hippocampus and amygdala volume, greater activation within the insula and posterior cingulate cortex, and less activation in regions extending from the amygdala to the cingulate and prefrontal cortex. PET scans reveal reduced metabolism in prefrontal cortex. Recent PET research reveals dysregulation of endogenous opioid function. Imaging is not recommended as part of routine evaluation.

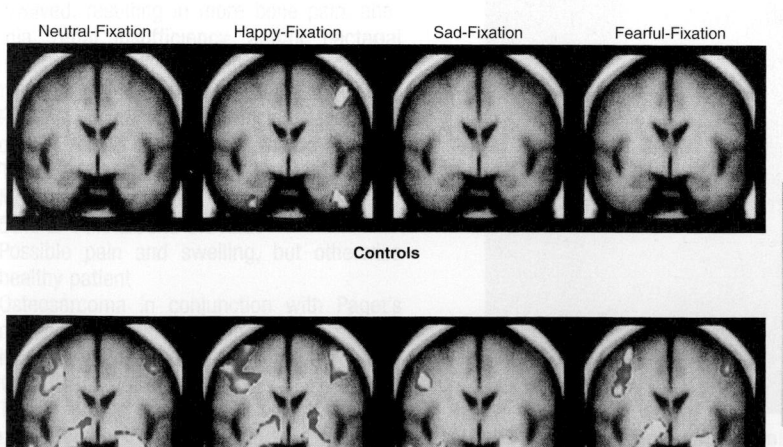

FIGURE 1B-40 Activation map showing regions in an amygdala slice in which activation exceeded the criterion threshold level of $P < .005$ for the normal control and borderline personality disorder groups for each of the four facial expressions. (From Donegan NH et al: Amygdala hyperreactivity in borderline personality disorder: implications for emotional dysregulation, *Biol Psychiatr* 54:1284–1293, 2003.)

 **TREATMENT**

NONPHARMACOLOGIC THERAPY

Psychotherapy is the recommended primary treatment for BPD.

Dialectical behavior therapy (DBT), mentalization-based therapy, variations of cognitive behavior therapy (CBT), and transference-focused psychotherapy, a type of psychodynamic therapy, have the most empirical support from randomized trials. The goal of DBT and most CBT variations is to help patients improve mindful awareness of emotions, control impulsive behaviors and angry outbursts, and develop social skills. In mentalization treatment, the emphasis is on teaching patients to stand outside of their feelings and observe emotions in themselves and others. The focus of transference-focused psychotherapy is on examining the affect-laden themes that emerge in the relationship between patient and therapist. Effective therapeutic treatments typically combine weekly group and individual therapy meetings. Treatment may also include inpatient and partial hospitalization in more severe cases.

ACUTE GENERAL Rx

Low-dose antipsychotics to control impulsivity, brief psychotic episodes.

CHRONIC Rx

- Medications have low to moderate effectiveness and are most effective in improving symptoms of impulsivity, mood instability, and self-destructive behavior. Effectiveness only studied for the first 3 months of treatment.
- SSRIs if concurrent mood disorder. Higher doses may be required than for major depression.
- Low-dose antipsychotics.
- Mood stabilizers (lithium, valproate, carbamazepine, topiramate).
- In preliminary studies, omega-3 fatty acids improve irritability.

DISPOSITION

- Course is variable. The most unstable period is typically in early adulthood; the majority achieve greater stability in social/occupational functioning later in life but often continue with difficulty maintaining intimate relationships.

- Clinically salient features such as alcohol/substance use and self-injury may be less common in older adults.
- No evidence of progression to schizophrenia, but there is a high incidence of concurrent major depression and other psychiatric disorders.
- Patients with high pre-treatment symptom severity who report a strong therapeutic alliance with their providers report highest treatment benefits.
- Drop-out rates are variable in research studies and may be high for individual patients.

REFERRAL

- Referral to mental health specialist:
    1. For diagnosis and management.
    2. Use of pharmacotherapy
    3. Patient is severely impaired or suicidal

! PEARLS & CONSIDERATIONS

COMMENTS

- Consider frequent, brief, scheduled visits for needy, demanding, or somaticizing patients with BPD.
- Validate the patient's feelings while stating the expectation of behavior control.
- Be matter-of-fact; avoid expressing extreme emotions.
- Be alert to the risk of suicide and assess suicide risk often.
- Be alert to the risk of nonsuicidal self-harm, such as cutting.
- Convey a demeanor of competence but openly acknowledge minor errors.
- Have a low threshold for seeking psychiatric consultation.
- Patients commonly present with high functional impairment across multiple settings. Psychosocial impairment as great as, or even greater than, that of bipolar disorder.
- An alternative model of diagnosing borderline personality disorder exists in the DSM-5 section III, consisting of: (1) impairment in personality functioning (identity, self-direction, empathy, or intimacy) and (2) four or more of seven maladaptive personality traits (emotional lability, anxiousness, separation insecurity, depressivity, impulsivity, risk-taking, and hostility).

PREVENTION

- There are no known ways to prevent BPD (or other personality disorders).
- Suicidality should be actively and consistently monitored.
- Benzodiazepines, narcotic analgesics, and other drugs with potential for dependency should be used rarely and with great caution, due to impaired impulse control and risk of addictive behavior.
- Patients should be asked frequently and in detail about parenting practices. Low frustration tolerance, externalization of blame for psychological distress, and impaired impulse control put children at risk for neglect or abuse.

PATIENT & FAMILY EDUCATION

National Alliance for the Mentally Ill (NAMI; http://www.nami.org) provides patient information, online chat groups, and information on support groups throughout the U.S. for people with BPD and their families.

National Education Alliance for Borderline Personality Disorder (NEA, BPD) (http://www.borderlinepersonalitydisorder.com) provides patient, family, and professional information on BPD.

Additional, local and/or online support groups for BPD are common and should be investigated.

SUGGESTED READINGS

Available at www.expertconsult.com

RELATED CONTENT

Borderline Personality Disorder (Patient Information)

AUTHORS: **MARK ZIMMERMAN, M.D.,** and **THERESA A. MORGAN, PH.D, M. PHIL**

- If evidence of edema or mass effect, treatment of elevated intracranial pressure is paramount.
  - Hyperventilation of mechanically ventilated patient.
  - Dexamethasone initially in a dosage of 10 mg IV followed by 4 mg IV q6h until symptoms of cerebral edema subside. Steroids should be discontinued as soon as possible.
  - Mannitol 0.25 to 1 g/kg IV over 20 to 30 min q6 to 8h; maximum of 6 g/kg in 24 hr.
- Medical therapy is never a substitute for surgical intervention to relieve increased intracranial pressure. Neurologic deterioration usually mandates surgery.
- Steroids should be limited to patients with severe cerebral edema or midline shift.

MEDICAL Rx

If abscess <2.5 cm and patient is neurologically stable and conscious, may start antibiotics and observe. Empiric antibiotic therapy guided by:
- Abscess location
- Suspicion of primary source
- Presence of single or multiple abscesses
- Patient's underlying medical conditions (e.g., HIV, immunocompromised)
  Selection of empiric antibiotic therapy:
- Primary infection or contiguous source:
  1. Otitis media/mastoiditis, sinusitis: third-generation cephalosporin (cefotaxime 2 g q4h IV or ceftriaxone 2 g q12h IV) plus metronidazole 15 mg/kg IV as a loading dose, then 7.5 mg/kg q8h IV, not to exceed 4 g per day
  2. Dental infection: penicillin G (20 million to 24 million units per day IV in six divided doses) plus metronidazole (dose as above)

  3. Head trauma: third- or fourth-generation cephalosporin (cefotaxime 2 g IV q4h or ceftriaxone 2 g IV q12h or cefepime 2 g IV q8h) plus vancomycin (30 mg/kg IV in two divided doses adjusted for renal function)
  4. Postoperative neurosurgery: vancomycin (dose as above) plus ceftazidime (2 g IV q8h) or cefepime (2 g IV q8h), or meropenem (1 g IV q8h). Replace vancomycin with nafcillin (2g IV q4h) if susceptibility testing reveals methicillin-sensitive *Staphylococcus aureus.*
- Hematogenous spread (congenital heart disease, endocarditis, urinary tract, lung, intraabdominal): vancomycin (empiric therapy, dose as above) or nafcillin (if susceptibility testing reveals methicillin-sensitive *S. aureus,* dose as above) plus metronidazole plus third-generation cephalosporin (cefotaxime 2 g IV q4h or ceftriaxone 2 g IV q12h)
- HIV infected or immunocompromised patient: metronidazole plus a third-generation cephalosporin, antifungal or antiparasitic agent
  Duration of antibiotic therapy is guided by the clinical course and whether or not the abscess was surgically aspirated or excised. It is usually prolonged. Most recommend parenteral treatment for at least 4 to 8 weeks, with serial neuroimaging to ensure adequate resolution. (Imaging weekly could be considered for first 2 weeks of therapy, then every 2 weeks until resolution.) Surgical therapy may be required for clinical failure (i.e., increasing size of abscess on imaging despite antibiotic therapy).

SURGICAL Rx

- Three indications for surgical intervention:
  1. Collect specimens for culture and sensitivity
  2. Reduce mass effect

  3. Clinical failure with antibiotic therapy alone
- Stereotactic biopsy or aspirate of the abscess if surgically feasible
- Essential to selection of targeted antimicrobial coverage
- Timing and choice of surgery depends on:
  - Primary infection source
  - Number and location of the abscesses
  - Whether the procedure is diagnostic or therapeutic
  - Neurologic status of the patient

DISPOSITION

- Prompt diagnostic consideration, early institution of appropriate antimicrobial therapy, and advanced neuroradiologic imaging have reduced the mortality rate from brain abscesses from 40% to 80% in the preantibiotic era to 10% to 20% at present.
- Morbidity is usually manifest as persistent neurologic sequelae (seizures, intellectual or behavioral impairment, motor deficits).

REFERRAL

Consultation with a neurosurgeon is mandatory.

❗ PEARLS & CONSIDERATIONS

COMMENTS

- It is important to maintain a high index of suspicion because a brain abscess often presents with nonspecific symptoms.
- Rapid imaging and early institution of appropriate antimicrobial therapy improve patient morbidity and mortality.
- Neurosurgical consultation is mandatory.

PREVENTION

Because brain abscesses arise from either contiguous infections or hematogenously from a remote site, early and appropriate treatment of predisposing infections is paramount to prevent brain abscess.

SUGGESTED READINGS

Available at www.expertconsult.com

RELATED CONTENT

Brain Abscess (Patient Information)

AUTHOR: **ERICA HARDY, M.D.**

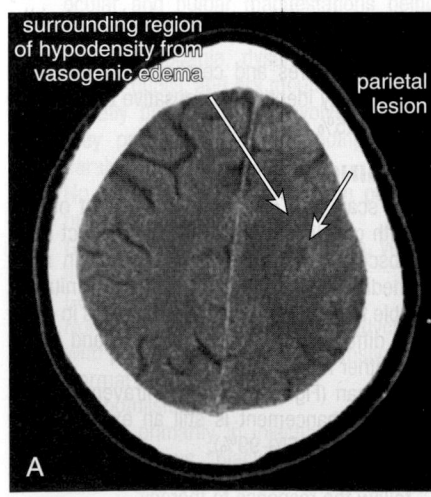
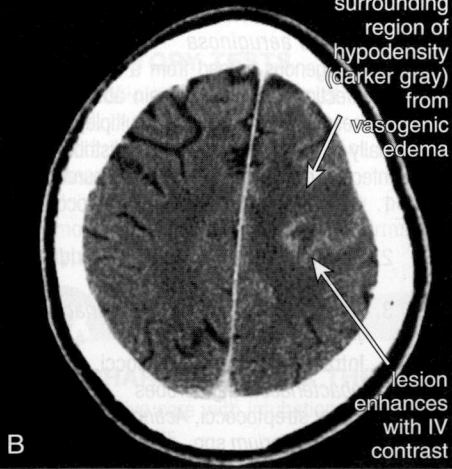

FIGURE 1B-41 Brain abscess. This 48-year-old male presented with status epilepticus. Computed tomography (CT) showed a parietal mass, which at brain biopsy was found to be an abscess. Cultures grew mixed gram-positive and gram-negative organisms and anaerobes. The patient was subsequently found to be human immunodeficiency virus positive. **A,** Noncontrast head CT, brain windows. **B,** CT with intravenous (IV) contrast moments later, brain windows. Abscesses and other infectious, inflammatory, or neoplastic lesions typically have surrounding hypodense regions representing vasogenic edema. When IV contrast is administered **(B),** the lesion may enhance peripherally, often referred to as ring enhancement. (From Broder JS: *Diagnostic imaging for the emergency physician,* Philadelphia, 2011, Saunders.)

 BASIC INFORMATION

DEFINITION

Brain metastases result from a spread of cancers originating in other organs to the brain and are devastating complications of cancer. Brain metastases are the most common intracranial tumors in adults and account for more than one half of brain tumors. They are 10 times more frequent than primary brain tumors.

SYNONYMS

ICD-10CM CODES
C80.0	Malignant neoplasm, primary site unknown
C80.9	Malignant neoplasm, unspecified
C79.89	Secondary malignant neoplasm of other specified sites

EPIDEMIOLOGY & DEMOGRAPHICS

INCIDENCE:
- In the United States, an estimated 98,000 to 170,000 new cases occur each year, which represents 24% to 45% of all cancer patients. The increased incidence is likely due to improved detection and better control of extracerebral disease. The incidence is higher in autopsy series, where 20% of patients with systemic disease have brain metastases.
- The prevalence is thought to be 120,000 to 140,000/yr.

PREDOMINANT SEX AND AGE:
- In patients with systemic malignancies, brain metastases occur in 10% to 30% of adults and 6% to 10% of children. Of these, about 60% of patients are between the ages of 50 to 70.
- There is no gender predilection.

RISK FACTORS
- In adults, the most common malignancies associated with central nervous system spread are lung cancer (16% to 20%), breast cancer (5%), renal cell carcinoma (7% to 10%), colorectal cancers (1% to 2%), and melanoma (7%). These metastatic lesions may or may not be present at the patient's initial presentation, and almost half of patients with metastatic disease present with multiple CNS lesions. The cancers with the highest association of intracranial hemorrhage include renal cell carcinoma, melanoma, and the less common malignancies of thyroid carcinoma and choriocarcinoma.
- In children, metastatic disease is uncommon. The most common primary pediatric solid tumors associated with metastatic spread include sarcomas, neuroblastoma, and germ cell tumors. Leukemias are well known to seed the CNS. Metastatic disease is usually never seen when a child first presents with malignancy, with the occasional exception of leukemia. For solid tumors, metastatic disease is seen at the time of disease recurrence. Neuroblastoma CNS lesions have an association of tumoral hemorrhage.

PHYSICAL FINDINGS & CLINICAL PRESENTATION
- Clinical presentations vary depending on where the lesion is located. Brain metastases should be suspected in any cancer patient who develops acute neurologic signs or symptoms. Neurologic symptoms, however, are common in patients with systemic cancer. In an analysis of more than 800 patients with neurologic symptoms, brain metastases were found in only 16%.
- Symptoms:
  1. Headache occurs in 40% to 50% of patients with brain metastases. Frequency is higher with metastases located in the posterior fossa, which may result in obstructive hydrocephalus. The headache is often accompanied by nausea, vomiting, focal neurologic signs, and postural variation.
  2. Focal neurologic signs/symptoms are the presenting symptom in 20% to 40% of patients. Hemiparesis is the most frequent complaint.
  3. Cognitive dysfunction, including memory problems and/or mood/personality changes, is the presenting problem in 30% to 45% of patients.
  4. The frequency of seizures in patients with metastatic brain tumor is 30% to 40%.
  5. Acute stroke secondary to hemorrhage into a metastasis, hypercoagulability, or local vascular invasion accounts for 5% to 10% of patients.

ETIOLOGY
The most common mechanism of metastasis to the brain is by hematogenous spread. The most common location is at the junction of the gray and white matter and metastases are more frequently seen in the cerebral hemispheres (almost 80%). The blood vessels decrease in diameter in these regions, which is thought to act like a trap for clumps of tumor cells. Different tumor types have a tendency to metastasize to different regions of the brain. For example, metastases of small cell lung carcinoma are equally distributed in all regions, whereas pelvic (prostate and uterine) and gastrointestinal tumors more commonly metastasize to the posterior fossa.

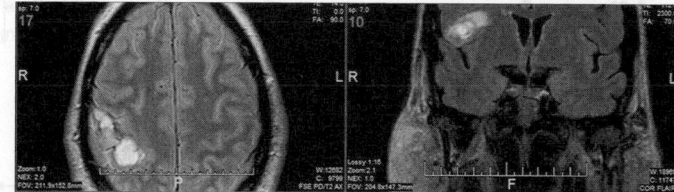 **DIAGNOSIS**

DIFFERENTIAL DIAGNOSIS
- Primary brain tumor
- Infection: abscess/fungal disease
- Progressive multifocal leukoencephalopathy
- Demyelinating disease: multiple sclerosis, postinfectious encephalomyelitis
- Cerebral infarction/bleeding
- Effects of treatment, such as radiation necrosis

LABORATORY TESTS
- Routine laboratory studies are not typically helpful.
- Lumbar puncture is generally contraindicated due to increased intracranial pressure and risk of herniation.
- Brain biopsy is necessary in some cases for a definitive diagnosis, particularly in the case of unknown primary tumor. Illustrating this is a study of cancer patients with solitary lesions in whom, on pathology, what was presumed to be metastatic disease was not. This was seen in about 10% of the individuals.

IMAGING STUDIES
- MRI (Fig. 1B-42) with and without contrast is the imaging study of choice. Important features on MRI that suggest brain metastases include: presence of multiple lesions, localization at the junction of the gray and white matter, circumscribed margins, large amounts of vasogenic edema. CT of head with contrast (Fig. 1B-43) can be used when MRI is contraindicated.
- MR spectroscopy and PET are useful to delineate tumor from other space-occupying lesions or from radiation necrosis.
- Newer experimental imaging studies, such as receptor-targeted and ligand-based molecular imaging, are on the horizon.
- Patients without a known primary tumor. In about 80% of patients, brain metastases develop after the diagnosis of systemic cancer. In the remaining patients, brain metastases are diagnosed simultaneously or before the primary tumor is found. In patients without a known primary tumor, the lung should be the primary focus of evaluation. Other frequent sites include melanoma, colon cancer, and breast cancer. PET scan may be useful in these patients to help identify the primary tumor or to identify other sites of metastatic disease—these latter sites might also be more amenable to biopsy.

TREATMENT

- Management of patients with brain metastases is influenced by the overall prognosis and may include treatments targeted at the metastases, management and prevention of complications (seizures, edema), and treatment of systemic

FIGURE 1B-42 Brain magnetic resonance imaging (axial and coronal fluid-attenuated inversion recovery sequences) showing hemorrhagic metastatic deposition in the inferior right frontoparietal lobe (lobulated high signal focus) in a 40-year-old woman with metastatic choriocarcinoma to the brain. (From Fielding JR et al: *Gynecologic imaging,* Philadelphia, 2011, Saunders.)

IMAGING STUDIES

- MRI with gadolinium enhancement is highly sensitive, though CT scanning is useful if calcification or hemorrhage is suspected. MRI permits visualization of the tumor, as well as the relation to the surrounding tissue. Enhancing tumor can be distinguished from surrounding edema. Low-grade tumors often present as an infiltrating lesion without mass effect. MRI is superior to CT scanning to evaluate the meninges, subarachnoid space, and posterior fossa, and for defining relation to major intracranial vessels. Figure E1B-45 shows the appearance of astrocytoma in imaging studies.
- Magnetic resonance spectroscopy is increasingly being used as a diagnostic tool to define metabolic composition of an area of interest and may be useful to contrast areas of tumor progression from radiation necrosis. N-acetylaspartate is often decreased in brain tumors, whereas choline, a component of cell membranes, is increased because of high cellular turnover.
- PET scan is helpful to distinguish neoplastic lesions (with high rate of metabolism) from other lesions such as demyelination or radiation necrosis (with a much lower metabolic rate). Such lesions take up greater amounts of glucose than surrounding tissues or tumors with slower metabolic rates. May be useful to help map functional areas of the brain before surgery or radiation.
- Functional MRI is now used as an adjunct in perioperative planning for patients whose lesion is in vital regions, such as those responsible for speech, language, and motor control.

Rx TREATMENT

NONPHARMACOLOGIC THERAPY

- Maximal surgical removal or debulking is the initial treatment of choice and provides tissue for diagnosis and molecular characterization. Maximal safe resection is often favored with a trend toward improved survival with this approach.

- Biopsy alone is performed if the tumor is located in eloquent regions of brain or is inaccessible; this is essential for histopathologic diagnosis. Biopsy can be performed under CT or MRI guidance using stereotactic localization.
- If the tumor is benign (e.g., meningioma, acoustic neuroma), often no further therapy is required.

ACUTE GENERAL Rx

Antiseizure medications have been used perioperatively and to control seizures resulting from focal lesions. Prophylactic use of anticonvulsants is not typically recommended without clear history of seizures.

CHRONIC Rx

- Chemotherapy (combination or single agent) may be used before, during, or after surgery and radiation therapy. (In children, chemotherapy is often used to delay radiation therapy.) Radiosensitizers may help increase the therapeutic effect of radiation therapy.
- Radiation is useful for certain types of tumors and is often used if there is residual tumor after surgery; conventional radiation uses external beams over a period of weeks, whereas stereotactic radiosurgery delivers a single, high dose of radiation to a well-defined area (usually <1 cm). Long-term effects of radiation therapy include radiation necrosis (particularly of white matter), blood vessel hyalinization, and secondary tumors (usually meningiomas, sarcomas, and malignant astrocytomas).
- Experimental therapies are continually in development and are typically based on molecular characterization of tumors and small molecule blockers of signal transduction cascades. Some of these therapies involve antisense molecules, biologic agents, immunotherapies, or angiogenesis inhibitors. Intratumoral drug infusions and convection-enhanced delivery of novel agents are currently under study.

DISPOSITION

In general, younger age, high performance status, and lower pathologic grade have more favorable prognosis. For all histologic subtypes of brain tumors, pediatric and young adult patients have a better survival rate.

REFERRAL

- All cases warrant evaluation by an oncologist and neurosurgeon.
- Patients should be evaluated for physical and occupational therapy.
- Children should undergo neuropsychologic evaluations and screening for learning disabilities.

COMMENTS

In general, younger age, high performance status, and lower pathologic grade have more favorable prognosis. For all histologic subtypes of brain tumors, pediatric and young adult patients have a better survival.

PATIENT/FAMILY EDUCATION

American Brain Tumor Association (http://www.abta.org)
National Brain Tumor Society (http://www.braintumor.org)
Pediatric Low Grade Astrocytoma (PLGA) (http://fightplga.org)

SUGGESTED READINGS

Available at www.expertconsult.com

RELATED CONTENT

Brain Cancer (Patient Information)
Astrocytoma (Related Key Topic)
Meningioma (Related Key Topic)

AUTHOR: **NICOLE J. ULLRICH, M.D., PH.D.**

DEFINITION

Glioblastoma (GBM) is the most aggressive diffuse glioma of astrocytic lineage and corresponds to grade IV based on the World Health Organization's (WHO) Classification. GBM is the most common brain and central nervous system (CNS) malignancy, accounting for 45.2% of malignant primary brain and CNS tumors, 54% of all gliomas, and 16% of all primary brain and CNS tumors.

GBM represents a molecularly heterogeneous disease with numerous subclassifications. GBMs comprise primary and secondary subtypes that evolve through different genetic pathways, affect patients at different ages, and have differences in outcomes. Primary (de novo) GBMs account for 80% of GBMs and occur in older patients (mean age 62 years). Secondary GBMs develop from lower-grade astrocytoma or oligodendrogliomas and occur in younger patients (mean age 45 years).

ICD-10CM CODES
C71.9 Malignant neoplasm of brain, unspecified

EPIDEMIOLOGY & DEMOGRAPHICS

INCIDENCE: Based on the 2014 CBTRUS report, the average annual age-adjusted incidence rate (IR) of GBM is 3.19/100,000 population.
PREDOMINANT SEX AND AGE: GBM is primarily diagnosed at older ages, with the median age of diagnosis at 64 years. It is uncommon in children, accounting for ~3% of all brain and CNS tumors reported among infants to 19-year-olds. A higher incidence of GBM has been reported in men compared to women; the incidence rate is 1.6 times higher in males [3.97 versus 2.53]. Whites have the highest incidence rates for GBM compared to any other race in the US.
RISK FACTORS: Many genetic and environmental factors have been studied in GBM, but no risk factor that accounts for a large proportion of GBM has been identified. Like many cancers, the causes are sporadic. Factors associated with GBM risk are prior therapeutic radiation, decreased susceptibility to allergy, immune factors and immune genes, and some single nucleotide polymorphisms (SNPs) detected by genome-wide association studies (GWAS). There is no substantial evidence of GBM association with lifestyle characteristics such as cigarette smoking, alcohol consumption, drugs, or dietary exposure to N-nitroso compounds (cured or smoked meat or fish). Inconsistent and nondefinitive results have been published regarding the risk of glioma with use of mobile phones.

PHYSICAL FINDINGS & CLINICAL PRESENTATION

Patients present with a variety of symptoms, including headache, seizures, symptoms of increased intracranial pressure, and cognitive disturbances.

Dx DIAGNOSIS

IMAGING STUDIES

Initial work up includes imaging studies. MRI with and without contrast is the study of choice, and demonstrates a contrast-enhancing tumor. Functional MRI is now used as an adjunct modality in perioperative planning for patients whose lesion is in vital regions (eloquent regions), such as those responsible for speech, language, and motor control. Pathologically, GBM is a high-grade astrocytoma characterized by hypercellularity, mitotic activity, nuclear atypia, pseudopalisading necrosis, and microvascular proliferation. Various molecular markers have been identified that help distinguish it from other astrocytomas and between primary and secondary subtypes of GBM.

Rx TREATMENT

- GBM is an aggressive neoplasm which has a median survival of 3 months if untreated.
- Combined modality therapy with surgery, RT, and chemotherapy has significantly improved survival of GBM patients. Treatment is complex and initially consists of maximal-safe surgical resection followed by RT with concurrent temozolomide (TMZ) chemotherapy followed by six cycles of maintenance TMZ.
- Surgical intervention has decompressive and cytoreductive effects and there is increasing evidence of a significant survival advantage with complete resection.
- Various emerging treatment modalities under investigation seem promising, including immunotherapy and tumor treating fields.
- Symptomatic treatment includes corticosteroids to reduce cerebral edema, antiepileptic drugs for seizures, and painkillers for headache.

REFERRAL

Treatment involves a multidisciplinary team approach including oncology, neurosurgery, neurology, and radiation oncology.

PROGNOSIS

Survival: GBM has a poor prognosis with a low relative survival estimate; only a few patients reach long-term survival status of 2.5 years, and less than 5% of patients survive 5 years post-diagnosis. The relative survival for the first year after diagnosis is 35%, and it falls in the second year post-diagnosis to 13.7%, and continues to fall thereafter. Median survival of GBM post-diagnosis is 15 months following standard therapy. Several variables affect the prognosis of patients with GBM, including age, preoperative performance status, tumor location, preoperative imaging characteristics of the tumor, and the extent of resection.

Prognostic molecular markers in GBM: All GBMs are WHO grade IV but exhibit significant genetic heterogeneity, and tumor subtypes with genetic alterations exist within this larger homogeneous histologic category that carry prognostic significance. These markers include methylation status of the gene promoter for O^6-methylguanine-DNA

methyltransferase (MGMT), isocitrate dehydrogenase enzyme 1/2 (IDH1/2) mutation, epidermal growth factor receptor (EGFR) overexpression and amplification, tumor protein (TP53) mutation, ATRX mutation and genetic losses of chromosomes.

- Primary GBMs show EGFR overexpression, phosphatase and tensin homolog gene (PTEN) mutations, and loss of heterozygosity (LOH) 10q, p16 deletions; less frequently shown are mouse double-minute 2 (MDM2) amplification, high frequency of telomerase reverse transcriptase (hTERT) promoter mutations, and absence of IDH1 mutation. The hallmark of secondary GBMs is TP53, alpha thalassemia/mental retardation syndrome X-linked (ATRX) and IDH1 mutations; additionally, they show LOH 10q.
- The MGMT promoter is methylated in approximately 50% of newly diagnosed GBMs. MGMT methylation is more common in secondary than primary GBM (75% versus 36%, respectively) and has prognostic and predictive significance of better overall survival in patients with GBM, irrespective of treatment choices.
- IDH1/2 mutations are far more common in grades II and III astrocytomas and oligodendrogliomas compared to GBMs, and more than 90% of the mutations involve IDH1. IDH1/2 mutations are a selective molecular marker of secondary GBMs, help distinguish them from primary GBMs, and are a marker of more favorable prognosis in high-grade gliomas.
- In GBMs, EGFR signaling promotes cell division, tumor invasiveness, and resistance to radiation therapy (RT) and chemotherapy. About 40% of all GBMs have EGFR amplification, and it is more common in primary as compared to secondary GBMs.
- Mutation of the *TP53* gene has been found in 60% to 70% of secondary GBMs and 25% to 30% of primary GBMs, and it occurs more frequently in younger patients. Studies of *TP53* mutations as a prognostic marker have not been definitive.
- *ATRX* is frequently mutated in grade II-III astrocytomas (71%), oligoastrocytomas (68%), and secondary GBMs (57%), but is infrequent in primary (4%) and pediatric GBMs (20%) as well as pure oligodendroglial tumors (14%). In a prospective cohort of patients with astrocytic tumors, those harboring *ATRX* loss had a significantly better prognosis than the ones that expressed *ATRX* and had IDH mutation.
- *TERT* mutation is one of the most frequent genetic alterations in primary adult GBMs and is significantly higher in these tumors as compared to secondary adult or any pediatric GBMs. GBMs with *TERT* mutation have a shorter survival than those without *TERT* mutations. However, when adjusted for GBM subtype (primary and secondary), they do not have a significant impact on survival.

SUGGESTED READINGS
Available at www.expertconsult.com

AUTHOR: **JIGISHA P. THAKKAR, M.D.**

TABLE 1B-10 Pathological Staging of Breast Cancer*

Primary Tumor (pT)

pT0: No evidence of primary tumor

pTis (DCIS): Ductal carcinoma in situ

pT1: Tumor ≤20 mm in greatest dimension

pT1mi: Tumor ≤1 mm in greatest dimension (microinvasion)

pT1a: Tumor >1 mm but ≤5 mm in greatest dimension

pT1b: Tumor >5 mm but ≤10 mm in greatest dimension

pT1c: Tumor >10 mm but ≤20 mm in greatest dimension

pT2: Tumor >20 mm but ≤50 mm in greatest dimension

pT3: Tumor >50 mm in greatest dimension

pT4: Tumor of any size with direct extension to the chest wall and/or to the skin

pT4a: Extension to chest wall, not including only pectoralis muscle adherence/invasion

pT4b: Ulceration and/or ipsilateral satellite nodules and/or edema of the skin

pT4c: Both T4a and T4b

pT4d: Inflammatory carcinoma (a clinical-pathologic entity characterized by diffuse erythema and edema [peau d'orange] involving one-third or more of the skin of the breast; the skin changes are due to lymphedema caused by tumor emboli within dermal lymphatics)

Regional Lymph Nodes (pN)

pNX: Regional lymph nodes cannot be assessed (eg, previously removed, or not removed)

pN0: No regional lymph node metastasis identified histologically

Note: Isolated tumor cell (ITC) clusters are defined as small clusters of cells not greater than 0.2 mm or single tumor cells, or a cluster of fewer than 200 cells in a single histologic section. ITCs may be detected by routine histology or by immunohistochemical (IHC) methods. Nodes containing only ITCs are excluded from the total positive node count for purposes of N classification but should be included in the total number of nodes evaluated.

pN0 (i-): No regional lymph node metastases histologically, negative IHC

pN0 (i+): Malignant cells in regional lymph node(s) no greater than 0.2 mm and no more than 200 cells (detected by H&E or IHC including ITC)

pN1mi: Micrometastases (greater than 0.2 mm and/or more than 200 cells, but none greater than 2.0 mm)

pN1a: Metastases in 1 to 3 axillary lymph nodes

pN2a: Metastases in 4 to 9 axillary lymph nodes

pN3a: Metastases in 10 or more axillary lymph nodes

Distant Metastasis (M)

pMX: Metastatic sites cannot be assessed

pM0: No metastases

pM1: Distant detectable metastasis

Stage Groupings in Breast Cancer

Stage	T	N	M
0	Tis	N0	M0
IA	T1	N0	M0
IB	T0-T1	N1mi	M0
IIA	T0-T1	N1	M0
	T2	N0	M0
IIB	T2	N1	M0
	T3	N0	M0
IIIA	T0-T2	N2	M0
	T3	N1-N2	M0
IIIB	T4	N0-N2	M0
IIIC	Any T	N3	M0
IV	Any T	Any N	M1

*AJCC 7th Edition

- Table 1B-11 compares ductal versus lobular carcinoma in situ. Adjuvant treatment guidelines for patients with early-stage invasive breast cancer are described in Table 1B-12.
- Among patients with limited sentinel lymph nodes (SNL) who are treated with breast conservation and systemic therapy, the use of sentinel lymph node dissection (SNLD) alone compared with axillary lymph node dissection (ALND) did not result in inferior survival.
- DCIS: Local breast-conserving therapy (lumpectomy plus radiation therapy) or mastectomy followed by tamoxifen therapy in estrogen receptor-positive cases
- Invasive breast cancer: Mastectomy and sentinel lymph node evaluation *or* lumpectomy and sentinel lymph node evaluation plus whole breast radiation therapy

- Invasive breast cancer may require adjuvant endocrine therapy and chemotherapy. Endocrine therapy is recommended alone or after chemotherapy in patients with hormone-receptor positive tumors. Adjuvant hormone therapy with anti-estrogen drugs reduces disease recurrence and mortality in women with breast cancer. Aromatase inhibitors decrease the agonist effect of estrogen by inhibiting estrogen synthesis and have become preferred first-line hormonal treatment agents over the selective estrogen receptor modulator tamoxifen.
- Standard adjuvant chemotherapy regimens include first-generation regimens such as CMF (cyclophosphamide, methotrexate, and fluorouracil) and second-generation regimens such as AC (cyclophosphamide plus doxorubicin). Third-generation regimens such as ACT (standard doxorubicin and cyclophosphamide plus taxane) are also in routine use. Fig. 1B-49 illustrates considerations for adjuvant chemotherapy in breast cancer.
- Neoadjuvant combination chemotherapy results in pathologic complete responses in significant number of cases, causes downstaging, provides an assessment of chemosensitivity, and provides no deleterious effect on survival.
- The benefit of adjuvant chemotherapy or hormone therapy can be assessed by commercially available multi-gene assays which have demonstrated utility in determining prognostic and predictive benefit with both hormonal therapy and chemotherapy in breast cancer.
- Metastatic breast cancer is approached based on the extent of bone-only or visceral disease sites as well as the rate of symptomatic progression. Typically, bone-only metastatic disease is approached with upfront, sequential hormonal therapy consisting of tamoxifen and aromatase inhibitors or activators. Patients with advanced bone disease or those with visceral disease are treated with typically single-agent chemotherapy and occasionally with combination chemotherapy regimens. The chemotherapy agents are the same as those used in early stages of disease. Sequential chemotherapy with different classes of chemotherapy agents are usually used to provide palliation with improvement in survival and symptoms.
- Recent trials in patients with HER2-positive metastatic breast cancer have shown that the addition of pertuzumab to trastuzumab and docetaxel, as compared with the addition of placebo, significantly improved the median overall survival to 56.6 months and extended the results of previous analyses showing the efficacy of the drug combination.

CHRONIC Rx

Follow-up after treatment of primary breast cancer includes:

- Regular clinical evaluations as delineated by medical oncologist or surgeon

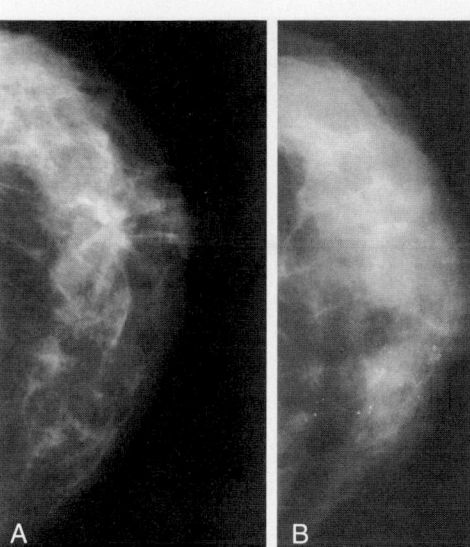
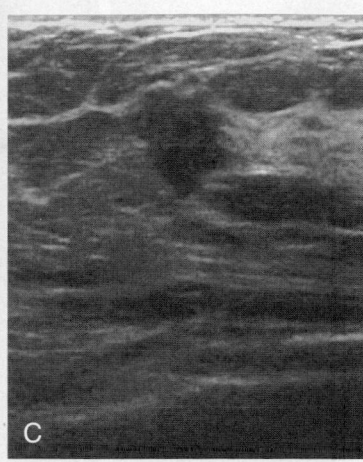

FIGURE 1B-47 Mammogram and ultrasound findings of breast disease. A, A stellate mass in the breast. The combination of a density with spiculated borders and distortion of surrounding breast architecture suggests a malignancy. **B,** Clustered microcalcification. Fine, pleomorphic, and linear calcifications that cluster together suggest the diagnosis of ductal carcinoma in situ (DCIS). **C,** An ultrasound image of breast cancer. The mass is solid, containing internal echoes, and displaying an irregular border. Most malignant lesions are taller than they are wide. (From Townsend CM et al [eds]: *Sabiston textbook of surgery*, ed 17, Philadelphia, 2004, Saunders.)

- Annual mammograms and breast MRI as indicated
- Laboratory tests as indicated
- Tumor markers and CT scans for surveillance are not recommended
- Patient instruction in monthly breast self-examination
- Prognosis after curative therapy: depends on size of tumor, extent of nodal metastasis, and pathologic grade of tumor
- Systemic adjuvant therapy: improves prognosis significantly. Women who take tamoxifen for 10 yr lower their risk of recurrence by 26% and dying of breast cancer by 27% compared with those who took it for just 5 yr. Adjuvant therapy with an aromatase inhibitor improves outcomes, compared with tamoxifen, in postmenopausal women with hormone receptor–positive breast cancer. Recent trials have shown that in premenopausal women with hormone receptor–positive early breast cancer, adjuvant treatment with the aromatase inhibitor exemestane plus ovarian suppression, compared with tamoxifen plus ovarian suppression, significantly reduced recurrence.
- Isolated tumor cells or micrometastases in regional lymph nodes is associated with a reduced 5-yr rate of disease-free survival among women with favorable early-stage breast cancer who do not receive adjuvant therapy. Survival is improved in patients with isolated tumor cells or micrometastases who received adjuvant therapy.
- Retrospective analyses suggest that occult lymph-node metastases are an important prognostic factor for disease recurrence or survival among patients with breast cancer; however, recent trials indicate that the magnitude of the difference in outcome at 5 yr is small (1.2 percentage points). These data do not favor a clinical benefit of additional evaluation (including immunohistochemical analysis) of initially negative sentinel nodes in patients with breast cancer.
- The addition of zoledronic acid to adjuvant endocrine therapy improves disease-free survival in premenopausal patients with estrogen-responsive early breast cancer.

REFERRAL

Referral to a multidisciplinary team consisting of a breast surgeon, reconstructive surgeon, medical oncologist, and radiation oncologist is necessary as soon as breast cancer is suspected.

(!) PEARLS & CONSIDERATIONS

BREAST CANCER IN PREGNANCY AND LACTATION

1. Frequency in women 40 yr or younger reported to be 15%
2. May carry worse prognosis because disease discovery delayed by engorged and nodular breast changes and/or because disease progression more rapid in pregnancy
3. Survival rates similar to those for nonpregnant early-stage breast cancer patients in same age group
4. Mass usually found by patient or obstetrician
5. Expedient workup recommended, including mammography and sonography
6. Choice of mastectomy or lumpectomy with axillary dissection for treatment
7. Adjuvant chemotherapy delayed until third trimester or after delivery
8. Irradiation to breast after lumpectomy delayed until after delivery

DUCTAL CARCINOMA IN SITU (DCIS, INTRADUCTAL CARCINOMA) (SEE TABLE 1B-11)

1. Discovered by mammogram as cluster of microcalcifications and/or density
2. Presents less often as a palpable mass or nipple discharge
3. Before mammogram screening, DCIS accounted for 1% of all breast cancers
4. Now 15% to 20% or even higher proportion have DCIS
5. Treated with lumpectomy with cure rates 98% to 99%
6. Higher-risk cases require breast radiation and adjuvant hormone therapy
7. Mastectomy possibly required with multifocal and/or high-grade DCIS

INFLAMMATORY CARCINOMA

1. Rare, rapidly progressive and often lethal form of breast cancer
2. Presents as erythematous and edematous breast resembling mastitis
3. Biopsy required, including that of the skin
4. Treatment with upfront combination chemotherapy followed by surgery and radiotherapy
5. Prognosis once dismal, now 5-yr disease-free survival approaches 50%

COMMENTS

- The U.S. Preventive Services Task Force (USPSTF) now recommends against automatic "routine" screening of younger women (age range 40 to 49). The task force recommends biennial screening mammography for all middle-aged women (age range 50 to 74). It also states that current evidence is insufficient to assess the benefits and harms of screening mammography in older women (aged 75 and older). The task force also discourages women from performing breast self-examination. Several other U.S. organizations, such as the American Congress of Obstetricians and Gynecologists, however, still recommend annual screening beginning at age 40 yr.
- The 2015 American Cancer Society guidelines for breast cancer screening are summarized in the following:
  1. Women with an average risk of breast cancer should undergo regular screening mammography starting at age 45 years. (Strong recommendation*)
     a. Women aged 45 to 54 years should be screened annually. (Qualified recommendation†).
     b. Women 55 years and older should transition to biennial screening or have the opportunity to continue screening annually. (Qualified recommendation)
     c. Women should have the opportunity to begin annual screening between

*A strong recommendation conveys the consensus that the benefits of adherence to that intervention outweigh the undesirable effects that may result from screening
†Qualified recommendations indicate that there is clear evidence of benefit of screening but less certainty about the balance of benefits and harms, or about patients' values and preferences, which could lead to different decisions about screening.

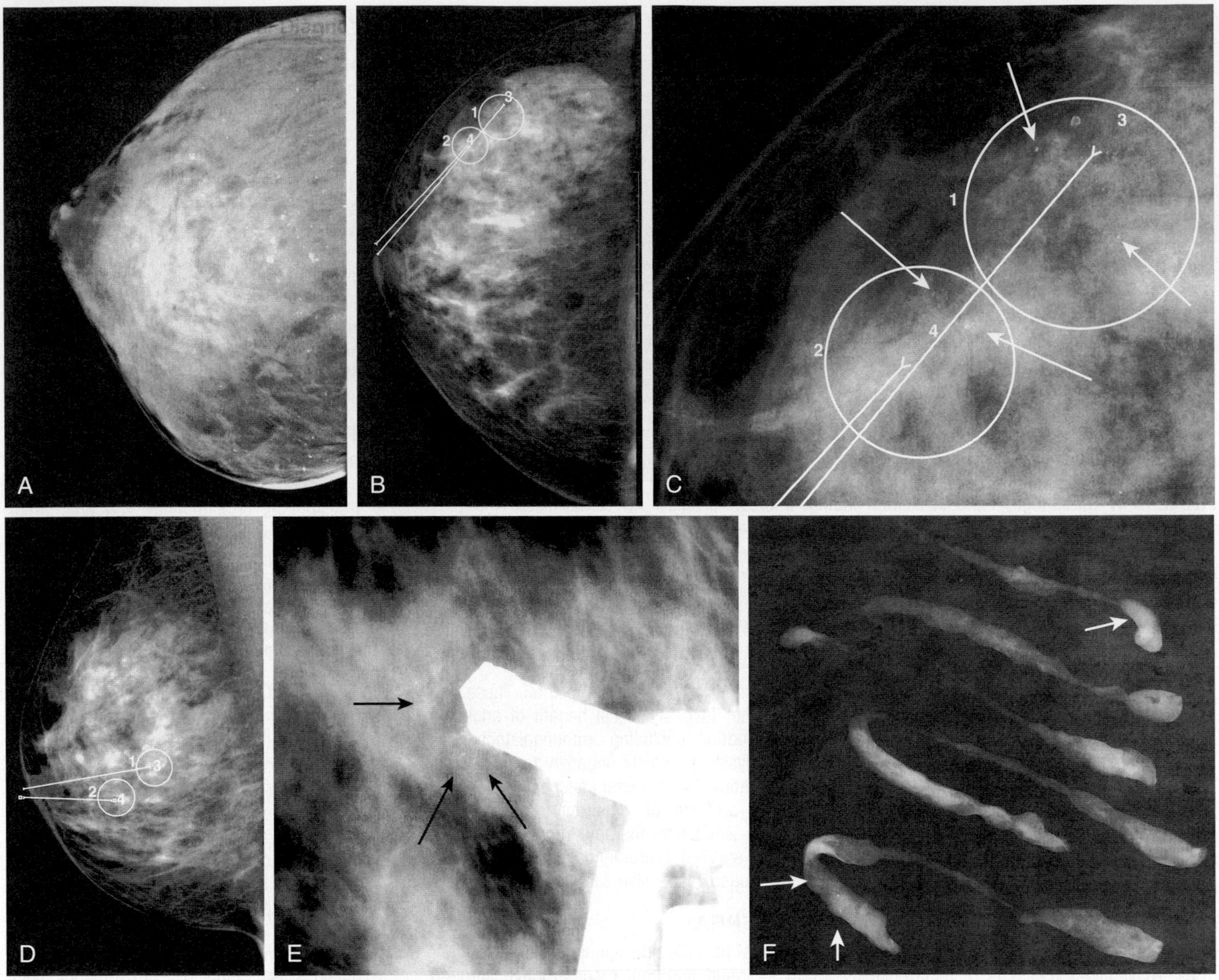

FIGURE 1B-48 Digital mammography and workup of breast calcifications. A, Craniocaudal (CC) view in a routine screening of a 43-year-old woman. Digital mammography penetrates dense breast tissue better than film-screen mammography, clearly showing diffuse benign pattern of large and small calcifications throughout the breast. **B,** CC view in a routine screening of a 46-year-old woman. Digital mammography shows two areas of very faint calcification in the outer breast that require further workup. **C,** Close-up view of **B,** showing the calcifications (*arrows*) to be variable in size and shape, which is worrisome for malignancy, particularly ductal carcinoma in situ. Such tiny calcifications in a background of dense breast stroma are easier to see on digital mammography than on film-screen mammography. Computer-assisted diagnosis programs also help the radiologist to locate even tiny groups of faint calcifications such as these. **D,** Mediolateral view in the same patient as in **B,** showing that the calcifications are in the lower breast. **E,** Image from stereo core biopsy procedure in the same patient as in **B,** showing the core needle immediately proximal to one of the groups of calcifications. Stereo core biopsy allows histologic sampling of tiny groups of calcifications, which can be very helpful in planning surgical approach. This interventional procedure can decrease the total number of surgeries that a patient must undergo to achieve definitive treatment. **F,** Radiograph of specimen from stereo core biopsy procedure on the same patient as in **B,** showing that there are several tiny calcifications (*arrows*) within some of the core samples. Pathologic analysis of the core biopsy revealed ductal carcinoma in situ, high grade, with comedo features. (From Skarin AT: *Atlas of diagnostic oncology*, ed 4, Philadelphia, 2010, Elsevier.)

the ages of 40 and 44 years. (Qualified recommendation)

2. Women should continue screening mammography as long as their overall health is good and they have a life expectancy of 10 years or longer. (Qualified recommendation)

3. The ACS does not recommend clinical breast examination for breast cancer screening among average-risk women at any age. (Qualified recommendation)

- Physicians should be familiar with the risks and benefits of various competing recommendations in order to better counsel patients.

- Breast radiologic evaluation, evaluation of nipple discharge, and evaluation of palpable mass are described in Section III.

- Exposure of the heart to ionizing radiation during breast cancer radiotherapy increases risk of ischemic heart disease. The increased rate of ischemic heart disease begins within a few years of exposure and continues for at least 20 yr. The increase is proportional to the mean radiation dose to the heart.

RISK REDUCTION STRATEGIES

- Prophylactic bilateral mastectomy reduces the risk for invasive breast cancer by > 90%.

- Selective estrogen receptor modulators (SERM) reduce the incidence of hormone receptor-positive invasive breast cancer by 50%.

- Ovarian failure is a common toxic effect of chemotherapy. Administration of the gonadotropin-releasing hormone (GnRH) agonist Goserelin appears to protect against ovarian failure, reducing the risk of early menopause and improving prospects for fertility.

EVIDENCE

Available at www.expertconsult.com

TABLE 1B-11 Carcinoma in Situ: Lobular Versus Ductal

Feature	Lobular Carcinoma in Situ	Ductal Carcinoma in Situ
Age	Younger	Older
Palpable mass	No	Uncommon
Mammographic appearance	Not detected on mammography	Microcalcifications, mass
Immunophenotype	E-cadherin negative	E-cadherin positive
Usual manifestation	Incidental finding on breast biopsy	Microcalcifications on mammography or breast mass
Bilateral involvement	Common	Uncertain
Risk and site of subsequent breast cancer	25% risk for invasive breast cancer in either breast over remaining lifespan	At site of initial lesion; 0.5% risk/yr of invasive breast cancer in opposite breast
Prevention	Consider tamoxifen or raloxifene	Consider tamoxifen or raloxifene if estrogen-receptor positive
Treatment	Yearly mammography and breast examination	Lumpectomy ± radiation; mastectomy for large or multifocal lesions

From Goldman L, Schafer AI: *Goldman's Cecil medicine,* ed 24, Philadelphia, 2012, Saunders.

TABLE 1B-12 Adjuvant Treatment Guidelines for Patients with Early-Stage Invasive Breast Cancer*

Patient Group*	Treatment
Favorable Histology (Tubular or Colloid)	
ER- and/or PR-Positive Breast Cancer	
<1 cm	No adjuvant therapy
1-2.9 cm	Consider adjuvant hormonal therapy†
≥3 cm or node-positive	Adjuvant hormonal therapy + adjuvant chemotherapy†
ER- and PR-Negative Breast Cancer	
<1 cm	No adjuvant therapy
1-2.9 cm	Consider adjuvant chemotherapy
≥3 cm or node-positive	Adjuvant chemotherapy
Hormone Receptor-Positive (ER- and/or PR-Positive) Breast Cancer	
Lymph Nodes Negative	
≤0.5 cm	No adjuvant therapy
0.6-1.0 cm well differentiated and no unfavorable features‡	Consider adjuvant hormonal therapy
0.6-1.0 cm moderate/ poorly differentiated or unfavorable features	Adjuvant hormonal therapy ± adjuvant chemotherapy
>1 cm	Adjuvant hormonal therapy ± adjuvant chemotherapy
Lymph Nodes Positive	
All sizes	Adjuvant hormonal therapy + adjuvant chemotherapy
Hormone Receptor-Negative (ER- and PR-Negative) Breast Cancer	
≤0.5 cm	No adjuvant therapy
0.6-1.0 cm	Consider chemotherapy
>1 cm or lymph-node positive	Adjuvant chemotherapy
HER2 Positive	
	Trastuzumab should be added to the suggested treatment above for all node-positive patients; trastuzumab not recommended for tumors ≤1 cm for most node-negative patients; for tumors >1 cm, trastuzumab should be considered for most patients

ER, Estrogen receptor; *HER2,* human epidermal growth factor receptor 2; *PR,* progesterone receptor.

*Data are insufficient to make chemotherapy recommendations for patients ≥70 yr. Treatment should be individualized for these patients based on life expectancy and comorbidity.

†In ER-positive or PR-positive patients, decisions regarding the added value of chemotherapy in addition to hormonal therapy alone can be aided by accurately assessing the added value of chemotherapy in individual patients using a web-based model: www.adjuvantonline.com or Oncotype Dx assay.

‡Unfavorable characteristics include high-grade tumor, blood vessel or lymphatic invasion by tumor, and high tumor proliferation rate (high S phase by flow cytometry or high Ki-67 value by immunohistochemistry) or HER2-positive status.

Modified from National Comprehensive Cancer Network Guidelines. Available at www.nccn.org.

SUGGESTED READINGS
Available at www.expertconsult.com

RELATED CONTENT

Breast Cancer (Patient Information)
Breast Cancer: For Men (Patient Information)
Breast Abscess (Related Key Topic)
Fibrocystic Breast Disease (Related Key Topic)

AUTHORS: **BHARTI RATHORE, M.D.**

B

Diseases and Disorders

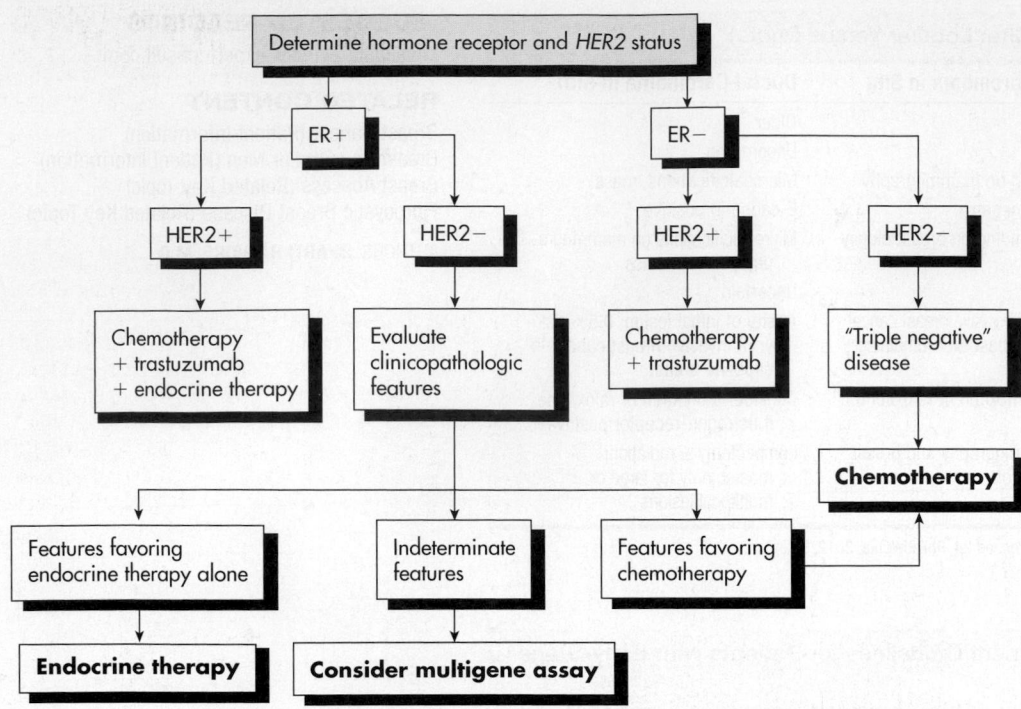

FIGURE 1B-49 Management of recurrent and metastatic breast cancer. Considerations for adjuvant chemotherapy. (From Cameron JL, Cameron AM: *Current surgical therapy*, ed 10, Philadelphia, 2011, Saunders.)

BASIC INFORMATION

DEFINITION

Bronchiectasis is an irreversible pathologic dilatation of the bronchi or bronchioles. Radiographically, it is often divided into cylindrical, varicose, and cystic varieties, although these variants have no significant etiologic or prognostic relevance.

ICD-10CM CODES
J47.0 Bronchiectasis with acute lower respiratory infection
J47.1 Bronchiectasis with (acute) exacerbation
J47.9 Bronchiectasis, uncomplicated
Q33.4 Congenital bronchiectasis

EPIDEMIOLOGY & DEMOGRAPHICS

- The exact prevalence of bronchiectasis is unknown.
- Cystic fibrosis is responsible for nearly 50% of all cases of bronchiectasis.
- Acquired primary bronchiectasis is uncommon because of rapid diagnosis of pulmonary infections and frequent use of antibiotics.
- Effective childhood immunizations have led to a significant decrease in the incidence of bronchiectasis resulting from pertussis.
- Declining incidence of pulmonary tuberculosis has also resulted in a decline in bronchiectasis without apparent causes.
- In developed countries, an increasing proportion of patients with an identifiable cause of bronchiectasis is being seen.

PHYSICAL FINDINGS & CLINICAL PRESENTATION

- Moist crackles at lung bases
- Chronic cough, typically with expectoration of large amount of purulent sputum
- Fever, night sweats, generalized malaise, weight loss
- Hemoptysis
- Halitosis, skin pallor
- Clubbing (infrequent)

ETIOLOGY

- Cystic fibrosis
- Lung infections (pneumonia, lung abscess, TB, nontubercular mycobacterial infections, fungal infections, viral infections)
- Impaired host defense (panhypogammaglobulinemia, primary ciliary dyskinesia/Kartagener's syndrome, AIDS, chemotherapy)
- Localized airway obstruction (congenital structural defects, foreign bodies, neoplasms)
- Inflammation (inflammatory pneumonitis, granulomatous lung disease, allergic aspergillosis)
- Rheumatoid arthritis, ulcerative colitis, and so on
- Congenital disorders such as tracheobronchomegaly (Mounier Kuhn syndrome), cartilage deficiency (Williams-Campbell syndrome)

DIAGNOSIS

DIFFERENTIAL DIAGNOSIS

- TB
- Asthma
- Chronic bronchitis or chronic rhinosinusitis
- Interstitial fibrosis
- Chronic lung abscess
- Foreign body aspiration
- Cystic fibrosis
- Lung carcinoma
- GERD

LABORATORY TESTS

- Sputum for Gram stain, culture and sensitivity, and acid-fast bacteria
- Complete blood count with differential (leukocytosis with left shift, anemia)
- Serum protein electrophoresis to evaluate for hypogammaglobulinemia
- Antibody test for aspergillosis
- Sweat test in patients with suspected cystic fibrosis
- Pulmonary function tests: mild to moderate airflow obstruction

IMAGING STUDIES

- Chest radiograph: hyperinflation, crowded lung markings, small cystic spaces at the base of the lungs.
- High-resolution CT scan of the chest (Fig. 1B-51) has become the best tool to detect cystic lesions and exclude underlying obstruction from neoplasm with a sensitivity and specificity exceeding 90%. The CT study should be a noncontrast study with the use of 1- to 1.5-mm window every 1 cm with acquisition time of 1 sec. Typical findings on CT include enlarged internal bronchial diameter, bronchi appearing larger than accompanying artery, lack of tapering of an airway toward periphery, ballooned cysts at the end of bronchus, and varicose constrictions along airways.
- Bronchoscopy may be helpful to evaluate hemoptysis, rule out obstructive lesions, and remove mucus plugs.
- Table 1B-13 summarizes diagnostic studies for the classification and management of patients with bronchiectasis.

TREATMENT

NONPHARMACOLOGIC THERAPY

- Postural drainage (reclining prone on a bed with the head down on the side) and chest percussion with use of inflatable vests or mechanical vibrators applied to the chest may enhance removal of respiratory secretions.
- Adequate hydration.
- Supplemental oxygen for hypoxemia.
- Inhaled hypertonic saline in conjunction with chest physiotherapy improves airway clearance.

ACUTE GENERAL Rx

- Antibiotic therapy is based on the results of sputum, Gram stain, and culture and sensitivity; in patients with inadequate or inconclusive results, empiric therapy with amoxicillin/clavulanate 500 to 875 mg q12h, TMP-SMX q12h, doxycycline 100 mg bid, or cefuroxime 250 mg bid for 10 to 14 days is recommended.
- Bronchodilators are useful in patients with demonstrable airflow obstruction.

CHRONIC Rx

- Avoidance of tobacco.
- Maintenance of proper nutrition and hydration.
- Prompt identification and treatment of infections.
- Pneumococcal vaccination and annual influenza vaccination.
- In patients with cystic fibrosis, using rhDNase and aerosolized antipseudomonal antibiotics should be considered.

FIGURE 1B-51 High-resolution computed tomographic image of nodular bronchiectasis due to nontuberculous mycobacterium infection. (From Goldman L, Schafer AI: *Goldman's Cecil medicine,* ed 24, Philadelphia, 2012, Saunders.)

DISPOSITION

Prognosis is variable with severity of the disease and underlying etiology of bronchiectasis.

REFERRAL

Surgical referral for partial lung resection in patients with localized, severe disease unresponsive to medical therapy or in patients with massive hemoptysis.

SUGGESTED READINGS

Available at www.expertconsult.com

RELATED CONTENT

Bronchiectasis (Patient Information)

AUTHOR: **LAYOLA LUNGHAR, M.D.**

TABLE 1B-13 Diagnostic Studies for the Classification and Management of Patients with Bronchiectasis

Test	Comments
Routine, Universal Studies	
Computed tomography lung scan (CTLS)	If bronchiectasis (BXSIS) is suspected, CTLS is the definitive test. Thin-section, high-resolution images may help detect subtle airway dilation before bronchial walls are grossly thickened. Contrast is generally not helpful and may, in fact, compromise the overall resolution of the study. CTLS may also identify esophageal abnormalities.
Pulmonary function tests (PFTs)	For patients with significant bronchiectasis, comprehensive PFTs, including spirometry, bronchodilator responsiveness, lung volumes, and diffusion capacity, are important studies that aid in management and prognosis. PFTs may also provide useful hints regarding predisposing conditions.
Complete blood count	Anemia may reflect effects of chronic infection or blood loss (consider inflammatory bowel disorders). Leukocytosis may mark severity of infection. Eosinophilia may suggest ABPA/M.
ESR, C-reactive protein	Nonspecific markers of inflammation; very high levels may suggest underlying connective tissue disease or vasculitis.
Routine sputum culture	Antibiotic therapy in bronchiectasis should generally be directed against specific pathogens and guided by in vitro susceptibility. The presence of mucoid strains of *Pseudomonas aeruginosa* and *Staphylococcus aureus* may raise suspicions for CF. *Stenotrophomonas maltophilia, Alcaligenes xylosoxidans,* and *Burkholderia cepacia* are gram-negative bacilli that may prove problematic pathogens in patients with long-standing bronchiectasis. Isolation of *B. cepacia* and *Helicobacter pylori* requires special laboratory techniques.
Mycobacterial sputum culture	Environmental mycobacteria such as *Mycobacterium avium* complex, *M. chelonae,* and *M. abscessus* appear to be increasingly common in contemporary bronchiectasis. May be commensal but often are pathogenic.
Fungal sputum culture	In patients with an asthmatic component, the presence of *Aspergillus* species (or other molds including Pseudallescheria or penicillium) may be suggestive of etiology.
CT scan of sinuses	Many patients with bronchiectasis also suffer chronic rhinosinusitis. The presence of extensive sinus involvement suggests possible CF, immunoglobulin deficiencies, or ciliary disorders. Also, optimal management often entails aggressive sinus care.
Specific, Directed Studies	
Sweat chloride, CF genotyping, and nasal potential differences	For bronchiectasis patients with bilateral disease, recurrent sinusitis, and no other identified risk factor, mild variants of CF appear to be relatively common. Sweat chloride is regarded as the primary screening test for CF, but a considerable portion of adults with CF have borderline or normal results. Nasal potential difference may be useful for identifying CF in equivocal cases.
Alpha$_1$-antitrypsin (AAT) levels and phenotype	AAT anomalies appear to be a substantial risk factor for bronchiectasis, especially with white females. Abnormal proteinase inhibitor (Pi) phenotypes, even heterozygous patterns such as MS, appear to confer risk even with normal levels of AAT. Repletion of AAT may enhance resistance to lower respiratory tract infections.
Immunoglobulin (Ig) levels	Deficiencies of IgG or IgA may promote bronchiectasis; IgG subclass deficiencies may also be a factor. Elevated levels of IgE may suggest ABPA/M or Job's syndrome. Hyper-IgM may be associated, as well, with chronic infections.
Ciliary morphology or function	For individuals with suggestive stories, a nasal ciliated epithelium biopsy with transmission electron microscopy may identify primary ciliary dyskinesia. Other studies including ex- vivo ciliary activity, the saccharine test, or spermatozoa analysis may aid in this diagnosis.
Nasal nitric oxide (NNO) levels	Patients with documented PCD have significantly lower levels of NNO than normal or patients with CF. Although not universally available, such testing may prove highly useful in identifying PCD. Paradoxically, exhaled NO levels have been elevated in bronchiectasis of diverse etiologies except CF.
Barium swallow (BaS)	The BaS may detect disturbed deglutition, esophageal diverticula, obstructing lesions (tumors or strictures), hypomotility, achalasia, hiatal hernias, or lower esophageal sphincter (LES) incompetence with reflux. The absence of reflux on a BaS, however, does not exclude this problem (see pH probe).
pH probe	For patients suspected of gastroesophageal reflux, an 18- to 24-hour study with a transnasal pH probe may identify, quantitate, and characterize reflux. Medications that inhibit acid production must be stopped before such tests.
Esophageal manometry	For patients being considered for surgical repair of the LES, manometry should be performed to determine that the esophagus generates sufficient pressure to propel food and liquids through the tightened sphincter.
Tailored hypopharyngography (TH)	TH is useful in detecting abnormalities of the initial phase of swallowing, deglutition. Persons particularly prone to problems include those with prior strokes, Parkinson's disease, bulbar disorders including postpolio syndrome, and those with prior laryngeal or pharyngeal surgery. Note that some patients have gross aspiration without clinical manifestations (choking, coughing); this may occur in individuals with none of the above risk factors.
Less Common, Exotic Studies	
Collagen vascular disease (CVD) serologies	Various CVDs may contribute to the risk for bronchiectasis, including RA, ankylosing spondylitis, and systemic lupus erythematosus. Thus, for patients with compatible histories or physical findings, assays for rheumatoid factor, HLA-B27, and ANA may provide insight into predisposing conditions. CVD serologies may also suggest the diagnosis of Sjögren syndrome, particularly SSA/Ro and/or SSB/La.
Schirmer's test	For patients with histories suggestive of "sicca syndrome" (dry eyes, dry mouth, oral ulcers), a positive Schirmer test may indicate the presence of either primary or secondary (associated with a CVD) Sjögren's syndrome.

ABPA/M, Allergic bronchopulmonary aspergillosis/other mycoses; *ANA,* antinuclear antibody; *CF,* cystic fibrosis; *ESR,* erythrocyte sedimentation rate; *HLA,* human leukocyte antigen; *PCD,* primary ciliary dyskinesia; *RA,* rheumatoid arthritis.
From Mason, RJ: *Murray & Nadel's textbook of respiratory medicine,* 5th ed, Philadelphia, 2010, Saunders.

 **BASIC INFORMATION**

DEFINITION

Brugada syndrome (BRS) is a genetically determined channelopathy characterized by typical electrocardiographic abnormalities. Patients with a Brugada pattern on ECG and symptoms such as palpitations, syncope, or sudden death are deemed to have BRS. BRS predisposes one to sudden cardiac death (SCD) secondary to polymorphic ventricular tachycardia (PVT)/ventricular fibrillation (VF) in the absence of structural heart disease.

SYNONYMS

BRS

ICD-10CM CODES
I49.9 Cardiac arrhythmia, unspecified
I47.2 Ventricular tachycardia

EPIDEMIOLOGY & DEMOGRAPHICS

INCIDENCE: The incidence ranges from 1 to 5:10,000 people in Europe and 12:10,000 in Southeast Asia.
PREVALENCE: It comprises 4% of SCD and 20% of SCD in structurally normal hearts. Although found in every population, the prevalence is much higher in Asian and Southeast Asian countries; in fact in some Southeast Asian countries, such as Laos and Thailand, it may be the most common form of natural death in younger males.
PREDOMINANT SEX AND AGE: BRS is more common in males (80% of patients). Mean age at presentation is 40 to 45.
GENETICS: The disease is autosomal dominant with variable expression.
- *SCN5A,* the gene that encodes for the alpha subunit of the cardiac sodium channel, accounts for about 20% to 30% of cases of BRS.
- *SCN10a,* the gene that encodes the Nav1.8 subunit of the sodium channel, has been found in 17% of BRS patients, making it the second most common known mutation.
- Known genetic abnormalities are only found in half of patients; thus the impact of genetic testing is limited. When available, it may be useful in identifying silent carriers.
- In all genotypes, the basic abnormality is either a decrease in the inward sodium or calcium current or an increase in the outward potassium current.

RISK FACTORS:
- First-degree relatives with the disease

PHYSICAL FINDINGS & CLINICAL PRESENTATION
- Physical exam is usually benign.
- Classic ECG finding is a pattern of right bundle branch block (RBBB) with persistent ST elevation of cove-like morphology and T-wave inversion in the anterior leads (V_1-V_2)

- Often an incidental finding diagnosed from a typical ECG pattern
- Palpitations
- Nocturnal agonal respirations
- Syncope
- Sudden cardiac arrest (SCA)/SCD secondary to rapid PVT that frequently degenerates into VF more often at night
- Three ECG patterns were described. Type 1 is the most common and characteristic (Fig. 1B-54, *A*).
- Type 1 ECG pattern can be transient and may be provoked (sodium channel blockers, vagal maneuvers, increased alpha-adrenergic tone, beta-blockers, tricyclic or tetracyclic antidepressants, fever, hypokalemia, hyperkalemia, hypercalcemia, and alcohol and cocaine toxicity). Type 2 (formerly known as types 2 and 3) can change to type 1 pattern with these triggers as well. Table 1B-15 describes drugs used to unmask Brugada ECG pattern.

ETIOLOGY
- Autosomal dominant inheritance with variable penetration.

Dx **DIAGNOSIS**

Diagnosis is made by the presence of a type 1 ECG and symptoms.
- ST segment elevation with type 1 morphology ≥2 mm in one or more right-sided leads (V_1-V_2), occurring either spontaneously or after provocative drug testing
- Type 2 ECG that converts into type 1 following sodium channel blocker (procainamide/flecainide/ajmaline) challenge (Fig. 1B-54, *A*)

DIFFERENTIAL DIAGNOSIS

A number of diseases can lead to a BRS-like abnormality on the surface ECG, including the following:
- Atypical RBBB
- Early repolarization
- Acute pericarditis
- Acute myocardial infarction or ischemia
- Pulmonary embolism
- Various central and autonomic system abnormalities
- Duchenne's muscular dystrophy
- Electrolyte abnormalities such as hyperkalemia and hypercalcemia
- Arrhythmogenic right ventricular cardiomyopathy
- Pectus excavatum

WORKUP
- Clinical history with special emphasis on syncope, palpitations, nocturnal agonal respirations, and family history.
- Echocardiography to rule out structural heart disease. While no structural heart disease is usually apparent, there are some recent reports indicating mild abnormalities in the right ventricle (RV) and left ventricle (LV).
- MRI, especially to rule out ARVC (arrhythmogenic right ventricular cardiomyopathy).
- Electrophysiology study. No consensus exists on the value of arrhythmia induction in predicting future clinical events in individual patients. However, findings such as HV (His ventricular) conduction interval >60 ms and VERP (ventricular effective refractory period) <200 ms during electrophysiology study can help in supporting a diagnosis. Repeated trials have failed to show

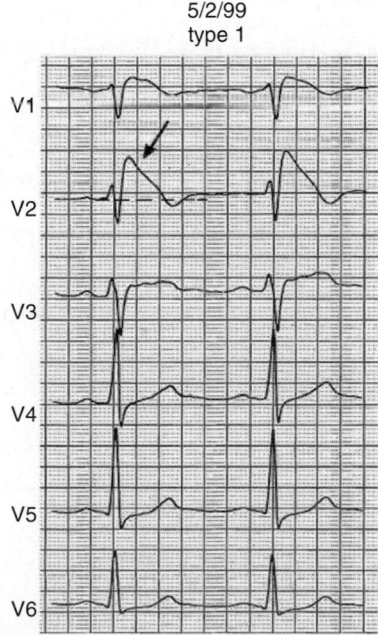

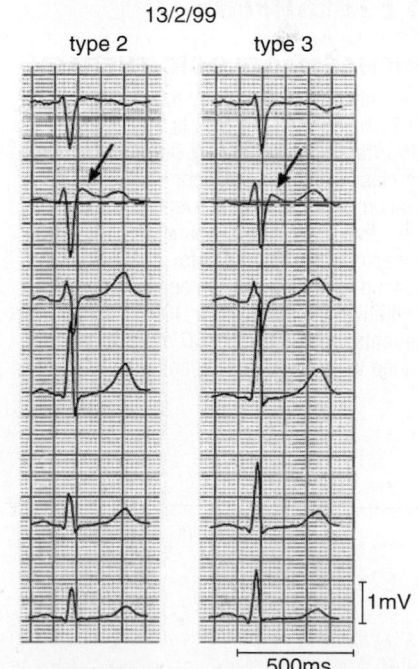

FIGURE 1B-54 A ECG changes in Brugada syndrome. ST elevation occurs in the anterior precordial leads, leads V1 and V2. Type 1 (coved) ECGs with 1 mV of ST elevation have the most prognostic significance. (From Strickberger SA et al: AHA/ACCF scientific statement on the evaluation of syncope, *J Am Coll Cardiol* 47:473-484, 2006.)

TABLE 1B-15 Drugs Used to Unmask Brugada ECG Pattern

Drug	Dose
Ajmaline	1-mg/kg IV infusion over 5 min
Flecainide	2-mg/kg IV infusion over 10 min, maximum 150 mg; or 400 mg PO
Procainamide	10-mg/kg IV infusion over 10 min
Pilsicainide	1-mg/kg IV infusion over 10 min

From Issa Z et al: *Clinical arrhythmology and electrophysiology,* ed 2, Philadelphia, 2012, Saunders.

a predictive power of electrophysiology study, and although it still exists as a IIb recommendation in the most recent consensus statement, the data supporting this practice are extremely limited.

- Laboratory tests are unhelpful. Genetic testing may be helpful but not necessary for diagnostic purposes.
- First-degree relatives should obtain ECG and be evaluated for symptoms.
- Risk stratification in the asymptomatic patient
- The following are considered indicators of high risk
  1. Spontaneous type 1 ECG at baseline
  2. Presence of fragmented QRS on ECG
  3. RVERP (right ventricular effective refractory period) <200 ms on EPS
  4. Male sex
  5. Spontaneous atrial fibrillation
Note that family history of sudden death is not considered a high-risk feature in BRS.

 TREATMENT

NONPHARMACOLOGIC THERAPY

- The only effective strategy that prevents sudden cardiac death in BRS is implantable cardioverter-defibrillator (ICD). Currently there are no class I recommendations for primary prevention because clinical events are extremely rare, even in high-risk patients. Fig. 1B-54, *B* depicts the algorithm for clinical decision making regarding recommendation of an ICD.
- Definitive candidates for ICD (class I) are patients who survived SCD or have had sustained VT (secondary prevention).

- ICD can be useful (class IIa) for patients who have type 1 ECG pattern in the absence of class IC drug test associated with history of syncope.
- ICD may be considered (class IIb) if there is inducible VF on electrophysiologic (EP) study, but the literature on EP study in patients with BRS does not support this practice.
- Patients with spontaneous type 1 ECG without syncope or inducible VF on EP study or asymptomatic patients with drug-induced type 1 ECG pattern are considered a lower risk group for SCD, and ICD is not indicated in these patients.

ACUTE GENERAL RX:
- Isoproterenol (class IIa) may be used for electrical storm.
- Quinidine, which blocks both Ito and IKr currents in the RV epicardium, is used in patients with a history of multiple appropriate ICD shocks, as well as for electrical storms and treatment of supraventricular tachycardia (SVT) in these patients. It is also useful in cases where the patient refuses an ICD implant or when an ICD implant is contraindicated.
- Radiofrequency ablation: There are a few published case reports of radiofrequency ablation of premature ventricular contractions (PVCs) leading to reduced clinical events. These have been performed in patients already implanted with an ICD. In addition, epicardial substrate ablation in the right ventricular outflow tract (RVOT) has been shown to prevent VF inducibility.

REFERRAL

Consultation with cardiology is strongly recommended if BRS is suspected.

⚠ PEARLS & CONSIDERATIONS

COMMENTS

- The clinical manifestations, such as syncope and SCD, are rare in the pediatric group, but fever can acutely predispose to cardiac arrest. Mean age of presentation is 40 to 45 years.
- Cardiac events may occur during sleep, at rest, or after a large meal.

BRS patients should be advised to avoid all drugs that may induce a type 1 ECG pattern and/or be known to trigger ventricular arrhythmias and avoid unnecessary use of drugs (a drug that is not yet identified as potentially dangerous for these patients does not make its use safe). For up-to-date information on this matter, a full list can be found at www.brugadadrugs.org.

- Fever may induce the appearance of a type 1 BRS ECG pattern and may trigger episodes of PVT/VF in BRS patients. In the case of fever, close ECG monitoring is appropriate in combination with lowering of the body temperature.
- The classic ECG changes in BRS can be transient with patients having normal ECGs in between highly abnormal ones.
- The appearance of syncope, seizures, or nocturnal agonal respiration must lead to prompt medical evaluation.
- Family screening of BS in first-degree relatives is strongly recommended.
- Although participation in sports is not strictly prohibited, competitive training can lead to development of strong vagal tone and subsequent higher risk of clinical events. Hence, participation in sports at a competitive or professional level is not advised.
- Once diagnosed initially by an ECG pattern, all patients must be followed up on a regular basis by an electrophysiologist.

PREVENTION

Identification of patients with BRS, risk stratification, and appropriate screening of family members are paramount to the prevention of SCD. Patients with known BRS should have fevers aggressively treated with antipyretics and avoid drugs associated with drugs that induce a type 1 pattern.

PATIENT/FAMILY EDUCATION

Immediate family members should be notified and be screened for BRS.

SUGGESTED READINGS

Available at www.expertconsult.com

AUTHOR: **JOYDEEP GHOSH, M.D.**

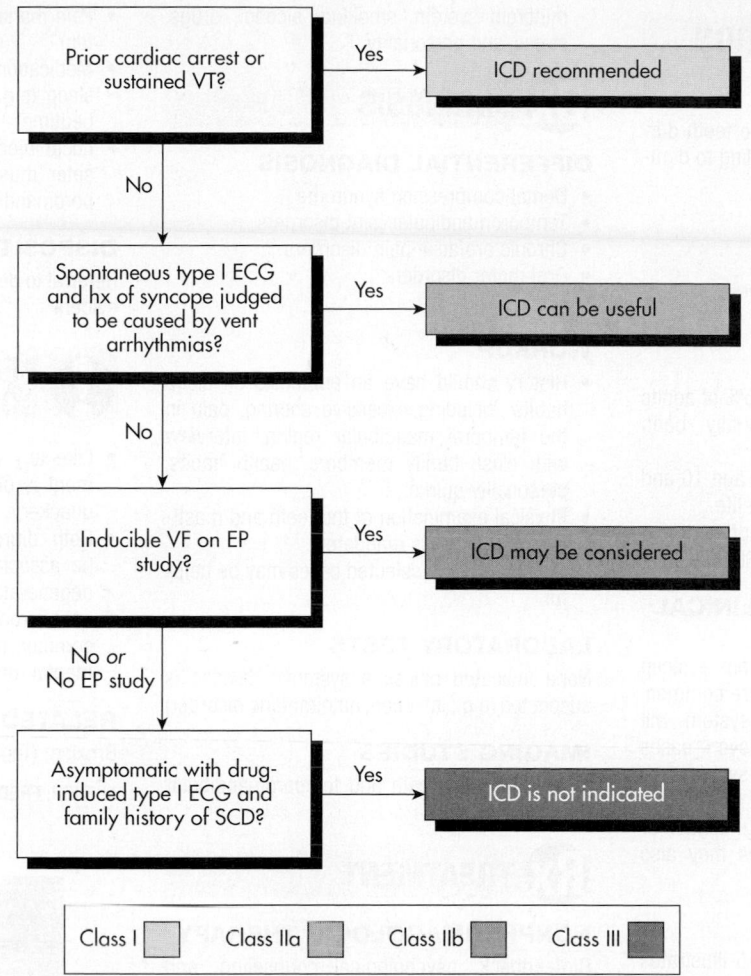

Prior cardiac arrest or sustained VT? — Yes → ICD recommended

No ↓

Spontaneous type I ECG and hx of syncope judged to be caused by vent arrhythmias? — Yes → ICD can be useful

No ↓

Inducible VF on EP study? — Yes → ICD may be considered

No or No EP study ↓

Asymptomatic with drug-induced type I ECG and family history of SCD? — Yes → ICD is not indicated

Class I   Class IIa   Class IIb   Class III

FIGURE 1B-54 B Consensus recommendations for ICDs in patients diagnosed with Brugada syndrome. (Priori SG et al: HRS/EHRA/APHRS expert consensus statement on the diagnosis and management of patients with inherited primary arrhythmia syndromes, *Heart Rhythm* 10:1932-1963, 2013.)

BASIC INFORMATION

DEFINITION

Forcible clenching or grinding of the teeth during sleep or wakefulness, often leading to damage of the teeth.

ICD-10CM CODES
G47.63 Sleep related bruxism
F45.8   Other somatoform disorders

EPIDEMIOLOGY & DEMOGRAPHICS

- Occurs in 15% of children and 75% of adults
- Familial cases have occasionally been described.
- Bruxism often presents between age 10 and 20 yr but may persist throughout life.
- Nocturnal bruxism is noted most often during stages I and II NREM sleep and REM sleep.

PHYSICAL FINDINGS & CLINICAL PRESENTATION

Complaints of grinding of teeth from a sleep partner or members of the family are common. In many cases the masticatory system will adapt to the phenomenon, but in severe cases nearly every part of the masticatory system may be damaged. Excessive wearing of dentition is the most common physical finding. Tender or hypoatrophied masticatory muscles may also be observed.

ETIOLOGY

- Cause is controversial. Fig. 1B-55 illustrates the cascade of physiologic events in the genesis of sleep bruxism and rhythmic masticatory muscle activity and course of action for management.
- Possible causes include occlusal discrepancies, anatomy of the bony structures of the orofacial region, part of the sleep arousal response, disturbances of the central dopaminergic system, smoking, alcohol, drugs, stress, and personality.

DIAGNOSIS

DIFFERENTIAL DIAGNOSIS

- Dental compression syndrome
- Temporomandibular joint disorders
- Chronic orofacial pain disorders
- Oral motor disorders
- Malocclusion

WORKUP

- History should have an emphasis on sleep habits, including excessive snoring, pain in the temporal mandibular region, interview with close family members, health habits, personality quirks.
- Physical examination of the teeth and masticatory muscles is mandatory.
- Sleep studies in selected cases may be helpful.

LABORATORY TESTS

None indicated unless a systemic disease is suspected (e.g., infection, autoimmune disorder)

IMAGING STUDIES

X-ray studies of teeth and temporomandibular joints

TREATMENT

NONPHARMACOLOGIC THERAPY

Biofeedback, psychological counseling, and elimination of harmful health habits have been used with limited success.

GENERAL Rx

- Oral splints (Fig. 1B-56); night guard to protect teeth may be useful
- Correction of malocclusion
- Pain management (e.g., gabapentin, ibuprofen)
- Medication to relieve anxiety and improve sleep (e.g., benzodiazepine or trazodone at bedtime)
- Local injections of botulinum toxin into masseter muscles to prevent dental and temporomandibular joint complications

DISPOSITION

Referral to dentist mandatory if damage to teeth evident

PEARLS & CONSIDERATIONS

- Like any poorly understood disease, treatment is often unsatisfactory and subject to quackery.
- Both diurnal and nocturnal bruxism may be associated with various movement and degenerative disorders (e.g., Huntington disease, oromandibular dystonia) and are quite common in children with cerebral palsy and mental retardation.

RELATED CONTENT

Bruxism (Tooth Grinding) (Patient Information)

AUTHOR: **FRED F. FERRI, M.D.**

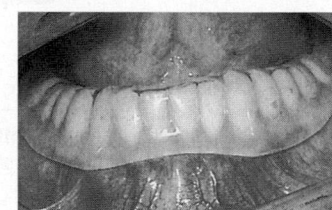

FIGURE 1B-56 Occlusal splint. (From Hochberg MC et al [eds]: *Rheumatology,* ed 3, St Louis, 2003, Mosby.)

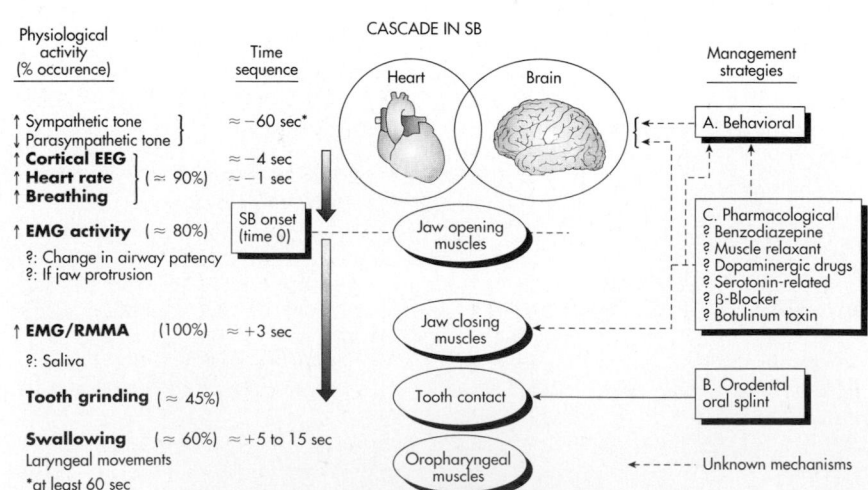

FIGURE 1B-55 Cascade of physiologic events in genesis of sleep bruxism and rhythmic masticatory muscle activity (*left*) and courses of action for management (*right*). (From Lavigne G et al: Sleep bruxism. In Kryger MH, Roth T, Dement WC [eds]: *Principles and practice of sleep medicine,* ed 5, Philadelphia, 2011, Elsevier, pp 1128–1139.)

Diseases
and Disorders

I

BASIC INFORMATION

DEFINITION

Budd-Chiari syndrome (BCS) is a rare disease defined by the obstruction of hepatic venous outflow anywhere from the small hepatic veins to the junction of the inferior vena cava (IVC) and the right atrium. Primary BCS is defined by endoluminal obstruction as seen in thromboses or webs. Secondary BCS occurs when the obstruction is caused by compression or invasion by a lesion originating outside the veins (tumor, abscess, cyst, etc.). It can also be a postoperative complication of orthotopic liver transplantation.

SYNONYMS

Hepatic vein thrombosis
Obliterative endophlebitis of the hepatic veins
IVC thrombosis (obliterative hepatocavopathy)
Chiari-Budd syndrome
Budd's syndrome
Chiari's disease
Rokitansky's disease

ICD-10CM CODE
I82.0 Budd-Chiari syndrome

EPIDEMIOLOGY & DEMOGRAPHICS

INCIDENCE: 1/2.5 million persons per yr
PREDOMINANT SEX: In Western countries, women are more commonly affected (approximately 2/3 of cases).

In Asia, men are slightly more affected.
PREDOMINANT AGE: In Western countries, presentation is usually in the third and fourth decades of life, with the median age being 35 yr.

In Asia, presentation is usually at a median age of 45 yr.

PHYSICAL FINDINGS & CLINICAL PRESENTATION

Clinical presentation and characteristics vary with geography. In Africa and South Asia, intravascular webs are more often associated with IVC thrombosis with a stronger association with subsequent hepatocellular carcinoma. In the United States, BCS is more commonly associated with primary myeloproliferative disorders and underlying hypercoagulable states. Underlying factors that contribute to BCS can be identified in ~85% of cases; multiple causative factors are identified in 50% of cases.

- Clinical manifestations can be caused by complete or partial occlusion of any or all of the three major hepatic veins or the inferior vena cava.
- Presentation is variable according to the degree, location, acuity of obstruction, and presence of collateral circulation:
  1. Fulminant/acute (20%): severe right upper quadrant abdominal pain, fever, nausea, vomiting, mild jaundice, hepatomegaly, transudative and intractable ascites, marked elevation in serum aminotransferases (ALT >5 times the upper limit of

normal), elevation of alkaline phosphatase to 300 to 400 IU/L, increase in the serum-ascitic fluid albumin gradient with total protein greater than 2.5 g/dl, decrease in coagulation factors, variceal bleeding, encephalopathy within 8 wk of onset of jaundice. Biopsy, if performed, would reveal hepatic necrosis. Early recognition and treatment are essential for survival; a slow decrease in ALT is associated with poor survival.
  2. Subacute/chronic (60%): vague abdominal discomfort, gradual progression to caudate lobe hypertrophy with atrophy of the rest of the liver, portal hypertension with or without cirrhosis and its sequelae, transudative ascites, lower-extremity edema, esophageal varices, splenomegaly, coagulopathy, hepatorenal syndrome in up to half of patients, hepatopulmonary syndrome in up to 28% of patients, and rarely, encephalopathy; biopsy, if performed, could reveal minimal hepatic necrosis.
  3. Asymptomatic (5% to 20%): usually discovered incidentally by abnormal liver function tests or imaging attained for other reasons

ETIOLOGY
- Primary myeloproliferative diseases: 20% to 53%
  1. Polycythemia vera, responsible for 10% to 40% of cases
  2. Essential thrombocythemia and idiopathic myelofibrosis are less common causes
  3. *JAK2* mutations are implicated in cases of idiopathic BCS (identified in 26%-59% of cases)
  4. Rare but recently reported: idiopathic hypereosinophilia syndrome
- Hypercoagulable states (inherited and acquired) often coexist with other causes, 30% to 65%
  1. Factor V Leiden (12%-31%)
  2. Anticardiolipin antibodies (25%)
  3. Hyperhomocysteinemia (22%)
  4. Paroxysmal nocturnal hemoglobinuria (19%)
  5. Factor II gene mutation (5%)
- Protein C, protein S, and antithrombin III deficiency are difficult to interpret because the presence of liver disease may confound results. However, recent studies show that they account for 3.8%, 3.0%, and 2.3% of BCS, respectively.
- Heterozygosity for G20210A prothrombin gene mutation or methylene-tetrahydrofolate reductase (MTHFR) mutation may be seen in BCS
- Pregnancy and oral contraceptive pills (cases reported after <2 wk of use)
- Malignancy (up to 10% of cases, causing external compression or invasions of vascular structures)
  1. Most commonly due to hepatocellular carcinoma but also can be due to neoplasms of the kidney, adrenal gland, pancreas, stomach, and sarcomas of the right atrium, inferior vena cava, and hepatic veins

- Rare but reported: sickle cell anemia, infections with liver abscess, hydatid cyst (echinococcosis), schistosomiasis, sarcoidosis, Behçet's disease (<5%), membranous webs of IVC or hepatic veins (more common in Africa and South Asia, can be congenital or acquired secondary to underlying myeloproliferative disorder), abdominal trauma, liver torsion, granulomatous venulitis, ulcerative colitis, celiac disease, systemic lupus erythematous, minimal change nephrotic syndrome, neurofibromatosis, alpha-1 antitrypsin deficiency, idiopathic (10%-20%)

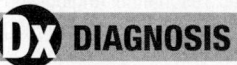 DIAGNOSIS

DIFFERENTIAL DIAGNOSIS
- Hepatitis from ischemia, viral infection, toxin, alcohol
- Cholecystitis
- Hepatic venoocclusive disease (sinusoidal obstruction syndrome)
- Congestive hepatopathy, also known as *cardiac cirrhosis,* from tricuspid regurgitation, right atrial myxoma, constrictive pericarditis
- Cirrhosis from any etiology

LABORATORY TESTS
- Assessment of liver injury and function: serum aminotransferases, alkaline phosphatase, prothrombin time (PT), albumin, bilirubin
- Exclusion of another form of liver disease: viral hepatitis panel, autoantibodies (antinuclear antibody, anti–smooth muscle antibody, anti-mitochondrial antibody), serum iron, transferrin saturation, ferritin, ceruloplasmin, and α-1 antitrypsin
- Ascites protein content >3.0 g/dl and serum ascites albumin gradient ≥1.1 g/dl are suggestive of transudative ascites from BCS, cardiac, or pericardial disease
- Evaluation for underlying myeloproliferative disorder and hypercoagulable state: CBC, bone marrow biopsy, tests for hypercoagulable states (Factor V Leiden, prothrombin gene G20210A mutation, protein C, protein S, and antithrombin deficiencies, antiphospholipid antibodies, hyperhomocysteinemia, paroxysmal nocturnal hemoglobinuria, and MTHFR C677T mutation); protein C, protein S, and antithrombin deficiencies may be difficult to interpret in the setting of liver dysfunction, but levels <20% of normal are suggestive of a true deficiency; thrombophilia screening for the JAK2 V617F mutation may be useful if no other cause for myeloproliferative disorders/ hypercoagulable states identified

IMAGING STUDIES
- Diagnosis of BCS is made by radiographic imaging.
- Ultrasound and color and pulsed Doppler are the first-line tests. Diagnostic sensitivity and specificity are 85% to 90%. Findings include large hepatic vein with an absent flow signal, or with reversed or turbulent flow; large intrahepatic collateral vessels; enlarged, stenotic, thickened, or tortuous

hepatic veins; and caudate lobe hypertrophy (as the caudate lobe has an alternate blood supply through anastomoses).

- MRI with gadolinium contrast is the second-line test. It is superior to contrast-enhanced CT (Fig. E1B-57), with a sensitivity and specificity of approximately 90%. Findings include obstructed hepatic veins or IVC, large intrahepatic or subcapsular collaterals, and caudate lobe hypertrophy. MRI is beneficial to visualize the entire length of the IVC and distinguish between acute, subacute, and chronic BCS. Three-dimensional contrast-enhanced magnetic resonance angiography (MRA, see Fig. E1B-58) rivals hepatic venography in sensitivity.
- Contrast-enhanced CT may reveal similar findings as Doppler ultrasound, as well as delayed or absent filling of the hepatic veins, parenchymal opacification of the liver, and narrowing of the inferior vena cava. However, ultrasonography is more accurate than CT for detecting lesions in the hepatic veins and IVC.
- CT image reconstruction of vasculature is becoming available.
- Venography: not essential for diagnosis; it should be performed when other noninvasive imaging tests are nondiagnostic in the setting of strong clinical suspicion for BCS. Measurement of pressure gradients can help predict success of percutaneous or surgical shunt intervention and plan surgical intervention. Confirms the pathognomonic web pattern caused by collateral venous flow.
- Liver biopsy: not necessary to diagnose BCS but may be helpful in patients with cirrhosis in whom the diagnosis remains uncertain and is critical for differentiating from hepatic venoocclusive disease. Findings include hepatic congestion, hepatocyte necrosis and fibrosis in centrilobular areas, and compensatory nodular regenerative hyperplasia with progression to fibrosis and cirrhosis. In advanced BCS, may also see infarction caused by concomitant thrombosis of the intrahepatic, extrahepatic, and portal veins. There are conflicting studies regarding the association of histologic findings and prognosis.

℞ TREATMENT

NONPHARMACOLOGIC THERAPY
- Goal of therapy is decompression of hepatic congestion.
- In general, therapeutic procedures should be introduced by order of increasing invasiveness based on response/failure to therapy rather than disease severity.
- Hypercoagulable states should be investigated in all patients.

ACUTE GENERAL RX:
- Anticoagulation, first with low-molecular-weight heparin (LMWH), followed by warfarin, even in the absence of an underlying hypercoagulable disorder

- In situ thrombolysis: can be successful when performed in patients with recently thrombosed veins (clot less than 3 to 4 wk old) that are well defined on venography and do not involve the inferior vena cava or in patients with a large clot in the hepatic veins or intrahepatic vena cava. Mature clots are nonresponsive to thrombolysis, and bleeding risk is high if portal hypertension has developed.
- Balloon angioplasty: complicated by 50% restenosis rate; effective when membranous webs are the etiology.
- Stenting: may improve long-term patency rates to 90%, but if placed above the intrahepatic IVC, may complicate future liver transplantation.
- Transjugular intrahepatic portosystemic shunt (TIPS) has been increasingly used in recent years; usually performed in patients with no improvement on anticoagulation therapy or when a dilatable lesion cannot be found. TIPS has replaced surgical shunting as the most common invasive therapeutic procedure; recently, polytetrafluoroethylene (ePTFE)-coated stents have improved TIPS-patency rates, especially in patients with underlying hypercoagulable defects.
- Surgical portal systemic shunts: feasibility depends on technical factors, long-term patency of the stent, the extent of liver damage before surgery, as well as on locating a center with well-trained surgeons.
- Liver transplant may be indicated in patients with fulminant hepatic failure and in patients who fail to respond to TIPS; 10-year survival reported to range between 69% and 84%.
- Supportive measures

CHRONIC Rx
- Lifelong anticoagulation: Warfarin therapy with a target international normalized ratio (INR) of 2 to 3 lessens, but does not completely prevent, recurrence. This should be continued permanently unless the patient has an adverse event to anticoagulation, the obstruction is because of an anatomic cause that has been corrected, or anticoagulation is contraindicated.
- In patients with an underlying myeloproliferative disorder, treatment with hydroxyurea and aspirin, or anagrelide, may be given instead of traditional anticoagulation.
- Treat liver dysfunction and complications related to portal hypertension, such as ascites (diuretics and low-sodium diet).
- Invasive interventions should be reserved for symptomatic patients who do not improve with medical therapy.
- Manage shunt thrombosis, which is a common complication.
- Liver transplantation is another treatment option; up to 27% recurrence of BCS after transplant has been recognized.
- Monitor for development of hepatocellular carcinoma and transformation of myeloproliferative disease in patients with longstanding, well-controlled BCS.

DISPOSITION

Prognosis is variable and depends on multiple factors, including time to recognition and treatment, etiology, acuity, the type of intervention, and the condition of the patient at the time of treatment. Overall mortality rates are decreasing with the use of anticoagulation and early diagnosis of asymptomatic cases. Survival rates have been reported as 77%, 65%, and 57% at 1, 5, and 10 yr from diagnosis. A prognostic index called the *Rotterdam BCS Index* has been described: $1.27 \times$ Encephalopathy $+ 1.04 \times$ Ascites $+ 0.72 \times$ PT $+ 0.004 \times$ Bilirubin. Encephalopathy and ascites are scored as 1 for present or 0 as absent, and PT is scored as greater (1) or less than (0) an INR of 2.3. An index of >1.1 correlates to low risk (5-yr survival rate, 89%), 1.1 to 1.5 with intermediate risk (5-yr survival rate, 74%), and <1.5 with high risk (5-yr survival rate, 42%).

REFERRAL

Fulminant presentations should immediately be referred to a center capable of liver transplantation. All cases benefit from referral to a hepatologist, a hematologist, an interventional radiologist, and a surgeon specializing in hepatobiliary disease.

❗ PEARLS & CONSIDERATIONS

COMMENTS
- Look for one or more underlying causes, especially hypercoagulable or hematologic disorders, and malignancies or space-occupying lesions that may compress or invade the hepatic outflow tract.
- Myeloproliferative disorders are most common.
- Diagnosis relies on imaging, beginning with Doppler ultrasound.
- Treatment with anticoagulation comes first, followed by invasive interventions as needed. Prophylaxis of portal hypertension can reduce the risk of major bleeding associated with anticoagulation therapy.
- Referral for liver transplantation may be necessary.
- Prognosis depends on presence of ascites, encephalopathy, PT, and serum bilirubin levels.

PREVENTION

In the setting of known risk factors, such as a hypercoagulable state or myeloproliferative disorder, any additional risks, such as smoking or oral contraceptive therapy, should be avoided.

SUGGESTED READINGS
Available at www.expertconsult.com

RELATED CONTENT
Hypercoagulable States (Related Key Topic)
Budd-Chiari Syndrome (Patient Information)

AUTHORS: **JEANETTE G. SMITH, M.D.,** and **NICOLETTE RODRIGUEZ, B.A.**

ⓘ BASIC INFORMATION

DEFINITION

Bulimia nervosa is a prolonged illness characterized by a specific psychopathology. According to the *Diagnostic and Statistical Manual of Mental Disorders,* 5th edition, bulimia nervosa can be diagnosed by: (A) recurrent episodes of binge eating. An episode of binge eating is characterized by both of the following:
1. Eating, in a discrete period of time, an amount of food that is definitely larger than what most individuals would eat in a similar period of time under similar circumstances.
2. A sense of lack of control over eating during the episode.

(B) Recurrent inappropriate compensators/behaviors in order to prevent weight gain, such as self-induced vomiting; misuse of laxatives, diuretics, or other medications; fasting; or excessive exercise. (C) The binge eating and inappropriate compensatory behaviors both occur, on average, at least once a week for 3 mo. (D) Self-evaluation is unduly influenced by body shape and weight. (E) The disturbance does not occur exclusively during episodes of anorexia nervosa.

ICD-10CM CODES
F50.2 Bulimia nervosa

EPIDEMIOLOGY & DEMOGRAPHICS

INCIDENCE/PREVALENCE: Affects 1% to 3% of female adolescents and young adults
PREDOMINANT SEX: Female/male ratio of 10:1
PREDOMINANT AGE: Adolescence to young adulthood; mean age of onset: 17 yr

PHYSICAL FINDINGS & CLINICAL PRESENTATION

- Parotid and salivary gland swelling
- Scars on the back of the hand and knuckles (Russell sign) from rubbing against the upper incisors when inducing vomiting
- Eroded enamel, particularly on the lingual surface of the upper teeth; pyorrhea and other gum disorders possible
- Petechial hemorrhages of the cornea, soft palate, or face possibly noted after vomiting
- Loss of gag reflex, well-developed abdominal musculature
- Often no emaciation; normal physical examination possible

ETIOLOGY

- Etiology is unknown but likely multifactorial (sociocultural, psychological, familial factors).
- Bulimia is much more common in Western societies, where there is a strong cultural pressure to be slender.
- According to the American Psychiatric Association, patients with eating disorders display a broad range of symptoms that occur along a continuum between those of anorexia nervosa and bulimia.

Ⓓ DIAGNOSIS

DIFFERENTIAL DIAGNOSIS

- Schizophrenia
- Gastrointestinal disorders
- Neurologic disorders (seizures, Kleine-Levin syndrome, Klüver-Bucy syndrome)
- Brain neoplasms
- Psychogenic vomiting

WORKUP

- The following questions are useful to screen patients for bulimia:
  1. "Are you satisfied with your eating habits?"
  2. "Do you ever eat in secret?"
- Answering "no" to the first question and/or "yes" to the second question has 100% sensitivity and 90% specificity for bulimia. The SCOFF questionnaire can also be used as a screening tool for eating disorders (see "Anorexia Nervosa").
- According to DSM-5, the level of severity is based on the frequency of inappropriate compensatory behaviors and may be increased to reflect other symptoms and degree of functional disability, as noted below:
  ○ Mild: An average of 1 to 3 episodes of inappropriate compensatory behaviors per week.
  ○ Moderate: An average of 4 to 7 episodes of inappropriate compensatory behaviors per week
  ○ Severe: An average of 8 to 13 episodes of inappropriate compensatory behaviors per week
  ○ Extreme: An average of ≥14 inappropriate compensatory behaviors per week
- Table 1B-16 describes eating and weight control habits commonly found in children and adolescents with an eating disorder.

LABORATORY TESTS

- Electrolyte abnormalities from vomiting (hypokalemia and metabolic alkalosis) or diarrhea from laxative abuse (hypokalemia and hyperchloremic metabolic acidosis)
- Hyponatremia, hypocalcemia, hypomagnesemia (caused by laxative abuse)
- Elevated cortisol, decreased luteinizing hormone, decreased follicle-stimulating hormone

℞ TREATMENT

NONPHARMACOLOGIC THERAPY

- Cognitive behavioral therapy, particularly interpersonal therapy to control abnormal behaviors
- Use of food diaries, nutritional counseling, and planning meals at least 1 day in advance are useful measures to counter abnormal eating behaviors
- Correction of electrolyte abnormalities

ACUTE GENERAL Rx

- Selective serotonin reuptake inhibitors are generally considered to be the safest medication option in these patients. They are useful in severely depressed patients and in those who do not benefit from cognitive behavioral therapy.
- Prompt recognition and treatment of complications:
  1. Ipecac cardiotoxicity from laxative abuse
  2. Electrolyte abnormalities (see "Laboratory Tests")
  3. Esophagitis and Mallory-Weiss tears; esophageal rupture from repeated vomiting
  4. Aspiration pneumonia and pneumomediastinum
  5. Menstrual irregularities (including amenorrhea)
  6. Gastrointestinal abnormalities: acute gastric dilation, pancreatitis, abdominal pain, constipation

CHRONIC Rx

- Psychotherapy continued for years and focused specifically on self-image and family and peer interactions is an integral part of successful recovery.
- Family therapy is also recommended, especially in younger patients.

DISPOSITION

Course is variable and marked by frequent recurrence of exacerbations.

REFERRAL

- In addition to the primary care physician, the multidisciplinary team should include a dietician, a psychiatrist, and a family therapist.
- Hospitalization should be considered for patients with severe electrolyte abnormalities or those with suicidal thoughts.

❗ PEARLS & CONSIDERATIONS

COMMENTS

- Bulimia has a close association with depression, bipolar disorder, obsessive-compulsive disorder, alcoholism, and substance abuse.
- Bulimia should be considered in all patients (especially adolescents) with unexplained hypokalemia and metabolic alkalosis.

SUGGESTED READINGS
Available at www.expertconsult.com

RELATED CONTENT
Bulimia (Patient Information)
Anorexia Nervosa (Related Key Topic)

AUTHOR: **FRED F. FERRI, M.D.**

TABLE 1B-17 Immunobullous Skin Diseases

Immunobullous Disease	Clinical Presentation	Serum Autoantibodies	Targeted Protein or Structure	Tissue Immunofluorescence*
Pemphigus				
Pemphigus vulgaris	Flaccid bullae on noninflamed skin, crusting, positive Nikolsky sign[†]; commonly affects scalp, chest, intertriginous areas, and oral mucosa	IgG epithelial cell surface; correlates with disease activity	Desmoglein 3 and desmoglein 1 of the desmosome	Epidermal IgG and C3 cell surface staining
Pemphigus foliaceous	Superficial bullae, erosions, and scale with crusting, positive Nikolsky sign[†]	IgG epithelial cell surface; correlates with disease activity	Desmoglein 1 of the desmosome	Epidermal IgG and C3 cell surface staining
Paraneoplastic pemphigus	Flaccid bullae, lichenoid or erythema multiforme-like, usually involves mucosa, often extensively includes esophageal and respiratory areas	IgG epithelial cell surface and basement membrane zone (staining on rodent bladder epithelium is characteristic); correlates with disease activity	Desmoglein 3, desmoplakin 1, desmoplakin 2, BPAG1, envoplakin, periplakin, other proteins of the desmosome and hemidesmosome	Epidermal IgG and C3 cell surface and basement membrane zone staining
IgA pemphigus	Flaccid bullae, similar to pemphigus vulgaris	IgA epithelial cell surface; correlates with disease activity	Desmocollin 1 of the desmosome	Epidermal IgA cell surface staining
Pemphigoid				
Bullous pemphigoid	Tense bullae, often on urticarial base, prominent pruritus	IgG basement membrane zone, epidermal	BPAG2, BPAG1, hemidesmosome, lamina lucida	Linear basement membrane zone IgG and C3
Cicatricial pemphigoid	Tense bullae and erosions, scarring sequelae	IgG basement membrane zone, epidermal	BPAG2, laminin 5, hemidesmosome, lamina lucida	Linear basement membrane zone IgG and C3
Herpes gestationis	Tense bullae, similar to bullous pemphigoid; onset during or immediately after pregnancy	Complement fixing, basement membrane zone, epidermal	BPAG2, BPAG1, hemidesmosome, lamina lucida	Linear basement membrane zone C3
Epidermolysis bullosa acquisita	Tense bullae; commonly occurs in areas of trauma and in oral mucosa	IgG basement membrane zone, dermal[‡]	Type VII collagen, anchoring fibrils	Linear basement membrane zone IgG and C3; may show linear IgA and IgM
Linear IgA bullous dermatosis and chronic bullous disease of childhood	Tense bullae, similar to bullous pemphigoid; oral involvement common in adult disease	IgA basement membrane zone, epidermal (rarely dermal)	97-kD portion of BPAG2, hemidesmosome, lamina lucida	Linear basement membrane zone IgA
Dermatitis herpetiformis	Small bullae on extensor surfaces (elbows and knees); markedly pruritic; associated with intestinal gluten sensitivity	IgA endomysial and transglutaminase antibodies; correlates with disease activity and compliance with gluten-free diet	Epidermal transglutaminase	Granular basement membrane zone IgA with stippling in dermal papillae
Bullous lupus erythematosus[§]	Tense bullae, photodistributed	IgG basement membrane zone, dermal	Type VII collagen, anchoring fibrils	Linear basement membrane zone IgG; may show granular IgM and C3 basement membrane zone as in lupus band

BPAG1, 230-kD bullous pemphigoid antigen 1; *BPAG2*, 180-kD bullous pemphigoid antigen 2; *C3*, complement component 3; *cell surface*, intercellular substance; *Ig*, immunoglobulin.
*In all suspected immunobullous disease, the biopsy for diagnosis should be obtained from perilesional tissue because immunoreactants may not be present in lesional tissue; perilesional skin is the area immediately adjacent to but not involving a lesion. Serum studies are also essential to differentiate diseases.
[†]The Nikolsky sign is the formation of a new blister or extension of a blister from shearing pressure applied on normal-appearing skin or at the edge of an existing blister.
[‡]*Dermal* and *epidermal* refer to localization of antibodies on human split skin by indirect immunofluorescence of serum.
(From Adkinson NF et al: *Middleton's allergy principles and practice*, ed 8, Philadelphia, 2014, Saunders.)

B

 BASIC INFORMATION

DEFINITION

- Cutaneous burns can be classified by type of injury (e.g., thermal vs. chemical), burn depth (e.g., 1st, 2nd, 3rd degree), extent of burn (total burn surface area [TBSA]), and burn severity (e.g., minor vs. major). Types of burn injury include thermal (flames, scalds, hot contactants), chemical, electrical, and radiation burns. This chapter will focus on thermal and electrical burns.
- Burns can affect skin and respiratory, ocular, oral, and genital mucosa.

SYNONYMS

Thermal injury
Chemical injury
Electrical injury
Radiation injury

ICD-10CM CODES

T29.0	Burns of multiple regions, unspecified degree
T30.0	Burn of unspecified body region, unspecified degree
T30.1	Burn of first degree, body region unspecified
T30.2	Burn of second degree, body region unspecified
T30.3	Burn of third degree, body region unspecified
T31.0	Burns involving less than 10% of body surface
T31.1	Burns involving 10-19% of body surface
T31.2	Burns involving 20-29% of body surface
T31.3	Burns involving 30-39% of body surface
T31.4	Burns involving 40-49% of body surface
I31.5	Burns involving 50-59% of body surface

EPIDEMIOLOGY & DEMOGRAPHICS

PREVALENCE (IN U.S.):

- More than 1.2 million individuals experience burns in the U.S., and burn injuries account for approximately 500,000 emergency department visits, with 9% (45,000) requiring hospitalization and 0.8% (4000) resulting in death annually.
- Of thermal injury, scald burn from liquid is most common—followed by flame, flash burn, and then contact burn.

PREDOMINANT AGE & SEX:

- Children ages 2-4 years have the greatest frequency of burns (most commonly scald burns), with male adolescent and young adults ages 17 to 25 with second greatest frequency (most commonly from flammable liquids).

PHYSICAL FINDINGS & CLINICAL PRESENTATION

- It is important to note that burns occur unevenly—often with various depths (Table 1B-18).
- 1st-degree (superficial) burns—penetrate epidermis only (minimal barrier loss)
  1. Very painful, intact, erythematous skin with minimal to no edema and no blistering.
- 2nd-degree (partial-thickness) burns—epidermis and part of dermis is affected.
  1. Moist, very painful skin with edema and blistering/blebs
  2. Superficial partial-thickness burns—cherry red with two-point discrimination intact, incredibly painful
  3. Deep partial-thickness burns—mottled white and cherry red; only the sensation of pressure is intact in these areas
- 3rd-degree (full-thickness) burns—entire epidermis and dermis are affected, with destruction of hair follicles and sweat glands.
  1. The skin is dry, charred, pale, painless, and leathery. Charred vessels may be visible beneath, little or no pain, and hair pulls out easily.

DIAGNOSIS

CLASSIFICATION

- Burns are classified by (1) depth of injury, (2) extent of injury, and (3) severity, according to the American Burn Association.
- Depth of injury (see Table 1B-18)
  1. Indicates how the wound will heal and whether grafting will be needed
- Extent of TBSA
  1. The TBSA is best classified by using age-specific burn charts and the "rule of nines" (Fig. 1B-60).
  2. For scattered burns, utilizing patient's palm including fingers to equate 1% body surface area can be helpful.
  3. TBSA indicates how aggressively the patient will need to be resuscitated.
- Severity—determined by burn depth, TBSA, age, location, type of injury, and presence/absence of coexisting conditions. Severity classification helps triage patients to outpatient, inpatient, or burn unit care (see Table 1B-19).
  1. Minor burns—outpatient management.
  2. Moderate burns—admission to hospital with experience managing burns or burn center referral.
  3. Major burns—referral to burn center.

LABORATORY STUDIES (MODERATE OR MAJOR BURNS)

- CBC, electrolytes, BUN, creatinine, glucose, liver function tests, venous blood gas, blood coagulation, and type and screen in anticipation of blood transfusion
- *If smoke inhalation expected:* serial ABG carboxyhemoglobin and continuous ECG
- *If electrical burn or if concern for rhabdomyolysis:* urinalysis, urine myoglobin, and CPK levels
- *If severe lactic acidosis:* consider checking cyanide level

IMAGING STUDIES

- If smoke inhalation suspected: chest radiograph and bronchoscopy
- If high-voltage electrical burn: cardiac monitoring first 24 hours

TABLE 1B-18 Categorization of Burn by Depth

Burn Type	Histologic Depth	Clinical Presentation	Treatment	Healing Time/Prognosis
1st degree	Epidermis	Erythematous but intact skin, no blisters, pain may range in severity	Topical salves, cold compresses, NSAIDs for pain control	2-5 days with no scarring
Superficial 2nd degree (partial thickness)	Papillary dermis	Erythematous with superficial blisters, intense pain	Topical antimicrobials with gauze dressing or biosynthetic dressing (if widespread), pain control	5-21 days with no grafting
Deep 2nd degree (partial thickness)	Reticular dermis	Erythematous with superficial/deep blisters, range of pain depending on nerve involvement	Same	21-35 days with no infection; if infected, converts to full-thickness burn
3rd degree (full thickness)	Through dermis to subcutaneous tissue. Can involve fascia, muscle and bone.	White or black, possible eschar, may or may not be painful depending on nerve damage	Usually requires grafting, may require resuscitation depending on TBSA affected, pain control	Large areas require grafting, but small areas may heal from the edges after weeks

From Kliegman RM et al: *Nelson textbook of pediatrics*, ed 19, Philadelphia, 2011, Saunders; and Kessides MC, Skelsey MK: Management of acute partial-thickness burns, *Cutis* 86:249-257, 2010.

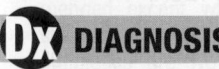 **BASIC INFORMATION**

DEFINITION

Bursitis is an inflammation of bursa, which is a thin-walled sac lined with synovial tissue. Bursae facilitate movement of tendons and muscles over bony prominences.

SYNONYMS

Student's elbow (olecranon bursitis)
Housemaid's knee (prepatellar bursitis)
Weaver's bottom (ischial gluteal bursitis)
Baker's cyst (gastrocnemius-semimembranosus bursa)

ICD-10CM CODES
M75.80	Other shoulder lesions, unspecified shoulder
M70.20	Olecranon bursitis, unspecified elbow
M70.60	Trochanteric bursitis, unspecified hip
M70.70	Other bursitis of hip, unspecified hip
M76.899	Other specified enthesopathies of unspecified lower limb, excluding foot
M70.40	Prepatellar bursitis, unspecified knee
M71.20	Synovial cyst of popliteal space [Baker], unspecified knee
M77.50	Other enthesopathy of unspecified foot

PHYSICAL FINDINGS & CLINICAL PRESENTATION

- Local swelling, tenderness, erythema, warmth over the site of bursa
- Pain with active joint movement or at rest
- Range of motion less painful and less restricted in septic bursitis than in septic arthritis
- Referred pain

ETIOLOGY

- Direct trauma or repetitive injury
- Infection (septic bursitis)—from hematogenous seeding or spread from contiguous infection (*Staphylococcus aureus* >80%)
- Crystal diseases (e.g., gout, pseudogout)

- Systemic inflammatory arthritis, such as rheumatoid arthritis (RA)
- Bleeding

 **DIAGNOSIS**

DIFFERENTIAL DIAGNOSIS

- Acute monoarthritis due to septic arthritis or crystal arthritis (gout, pseudogout)
- Tendinitis, tenosynovitis
- Cellulitis

WORKUP

- Bursal fluid aspiration: send for Gram stain; culture and sensitivity; cell count; and crystal analysis

IMAGING STUDIES

- Plain radiography can rule out foreign body penetration and other bone or joint problems such as fracture (Fig. 1B-62)
- MRI to define soft tissue involvement
- Musculoskeletal ultrasound for visualizing superficial and deep bursae can guide aspiration/injection

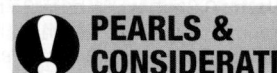 **TREATMENT**

NONPHARMACOLOGIC THERAPY

- Avoid direct pressure or repetitive irritation
- Joint protection (e.g., kneeling pads)
- Rest, ice, elevation for acute phase
- Physical therapy

ACUTE GENERAL Rx

- Septic:
  1. Appropriate antibiotic coverage and drainage. If MSSA, use nafcillin or oxacillin 2 g IV q4h or dicloxacillin 500 mg PO qid. If MRSA, use vancomycin 15 to 20 mg/kg IV q8-12h or linezolid 600 mg PO bid.
  2. Serial aspirations of purulent fluid or surgical drainage may be indicated.
- Nonseptic:
  1. Aspiration of bursal fluid or blood from acute trauma

2. Nonpharmacologic therapy
3. Traumatic bursitis may respond well to aspiration and corticosteroid injection.
4. Crystal-related bursitis: systemic anti-inflammatories or injection of corticosteroid

CHRONIC Rx

- Aspiration of fluid, followed by compression dressing to prevent fluid reaccumulation (repeat aspiration may be required)
- Steroid injection into bursa (40 mg triamcinolone mixed with 1 to 3 ml lidocaine, depending on size of bursa)
- Oral NSAIDs, although steroid injection may be more effective in certain types of bursitis

DISPOSITION

- Nonsurgical treatment is effective in most cases. Surgical drainage may be indicated for loculated bursitis. Recurrent bursitis may require open bursectomy.

REFERRAL

Orthopedic consultation may be needed to assist in treatment of septic bursitis or for excision of chronic enlarged bursa when indicated.

⚠ **PEARLS & CONSIDERATIONS**

- Bursae in patients with RA are not usually the sole site of active flare. Therefore, in patients with RA, acute bursitis should be considered septic bursitis until proven otherwise.

COMMENTS

- Scapulothoracic bursitis is under-recognized and undertreated. It results from friction between superomedial angle of scapula and adjacent second and third ribs. Crepitus, snapping, and tenderness are suggestive findings; it can also cause chest wall pain.
- Do not incise and drain sterile bursae because chronic draining sinus tract may develop.
- In bursitis caused by infectious or systemic inflammatory disorders, the leukocytosis in bursal fluid may be substantially less intense than the elevations in the joint fluid.
- Investigate crystal-induced bursitis for underlying metabolic or hematologic diseases (hemochromatosis, hyperparathyroidism [calcium pyrophosphate deposition disease]), and for hyperuricemia (gout).

SUGGESTED READINGS
Available at www.expertconsult.com

RELATED CONTENT
Bursitis (Patient Information)

AUTHOR: **CANDICE YUVIENCO, M.D.**

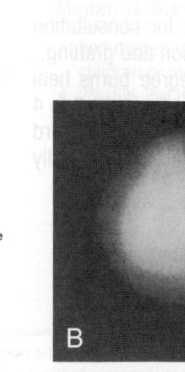

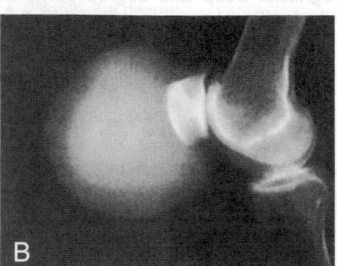

FIGURE 1B-62 A, Bursae around the knee. **B,** Markedly swollen prepatellar bursa. (From Scudieri G [ed]: *Sports medicine principles of primary care,* St Louis, 1997, Mosby.)

Suprapatellar bursa
Superficial prepatellar bursa
Deep infrapatellar bursa
Superficial infrapatellar bursa
Pes anserine bursa

A

B

BASIC INFORMATION

DEFINITION

Infection caused by the species of the genus *Candida,* mainly *Candida albicans. Candida* species are ubiquitous. They are the most common fungal pathogens affecting mankind. Cutaneous candidiasis comprises superficial *Candida* infections of the skin and mucosal membranes.

Cutaneous candidiasis can be classified into two subgroups: cutaneous candidiasis syndromes and chronic mucocutaneous syndromes. Cutaneous candidiasis syndromes include:
- Generalized cutaneous candidiasis
- Intertrigo
- *Candida* folliculitis
- Paronychia/onychomycosis
- Perianal candidiasis
- Erosio interdigitalis blastomycetica
- Balanitis

Chronic mucocutaneous syndromes include:
- Oropharyngeal candidiasis
- Esophageal candidiasis
- Vulvovaginal candidiasis
- GI candidiasis (gastric/intestines/perianal)
- *Candida* cystitis

SYNONYMS

Yeast infection
Candidosis
Moniliasis
Oidiomycosis

ICD-10CM CODES
B37.2   Candidiasis of skin and nail
B37.8   Candidiasis, unspecified
B37.89   Other sites of candidiasis

EPIDEMIOLOGY & DEMOGRAPHICS

- *Candida* species: it is the most common fungal infection in immunocompromised people.
- Most females (75%) experience an episode of vulvovaginal candidiasis in their lifetime.

INCIDENCE: Estimated to be 50 cases per 100,000 persons

PREVALENCE: Colonizes more than 50% of U.S. population

PREDOMINANT SEX AND AGE:
- Female > male
- No predominant age, but neonates and the elderly (adults >65 yr) are susceptible to *Candida* colonization and to getting mucocutaneous candidiasis.

RISK FACTORS: Risk factors that allow *Candida* infection include:
- Age >65 yr
- Females in the third trimester
- Defects in the mucocutaneous barrier (e.g., wounds, burns, ulcerations)
- Decreased/defective granulocytes/monocytes
- Diseases of white blood cells (e.g., chronic granulomatous disease)

- Complement deficiency
- Certain diseases associated with cell-mediated immunity (e.g., HIV, DM)
- Use of certain medications (e.g., broad-spectrum antibiotics, high doses of corticosteroids)
- Increased skin pH due to panty liners and occlusive attire
- **Chronic mucocutaneous candidiasis** (CMC) is characterized by susceptibility to *Candida* infection of skin, nails (Fig. 1C-1), and mucous membranes. Patients with recessive CMC and autoimmunity have mutations in the autoimmune regulator *AIRE.* Mutations in the CC domain of *STAT1* underlie autosomal-dominant CMC and lead to defective Th1 and Th17 responses, which may explain the increased susceptibility to fungal infections (van de Veerdonk et al).

Anatomical sites predisposed to *Candida* infection include:
- Axilla
- Beneath the breast, abdominal fold, intertriginous areas
- Periungual creases
- Inguinal creases
- Back and buttocks of bedridden persons

PHYSICAL FINDINGS & CLINICAL PRESENTATION

There are several clinical presentations of cutaneous candidiasis. A few are presented here.

A. Cutaneous candidiasis
- Presents as erythematous, sometimes shiny with flakes and fluid lesions at the edge of the redness (satellite pustules). It is itchy and the skin becomes inflamed. Pustules may be present in candidiasis of the scrotal and perineal skin.

B. Gastrointestinal tract candidiasis
1. Oropharyngeal candidiasis
   - Usually seen in diabetics, after exposure to inhaled steroids or broad-spectrum antibiotics and in immunosuppressed individuals (e.g., patients with a history of HIV infection).
   Symptoms include:

○ White thick patches on the oral mucosa (Fig. 1C-2)
○ Dysphagia, mouth soreness, and pain
○ Tongue burning
1. Physical examination shows:
   ○ Erythema of the buccal mucosa
   ○ White patches on buccal cavity surfaces
   ○ Transverse fissuring
2. Esophageal candidiasis:
   - History of oropharyngeal candidiasis
   Symptoms include:
   ○ Dysphagia
   ○ Odynophagia
   ○ Epigastric pain
   ○ Retrosternal pain
   Physical examination shows:
   ○ Affects mainly the distal one third of the esophagus
   Endoscopy shows areas of the erythema and edema; scattered white patches or ulcers
3. Perianal candidiasis
   ○ Skin maceration
   ○ Itching
   ○ Frequently extends to the perineum

C. Paronychia/onychomycosis
- Fungal infection of the nail and surrounding tissues
- Associated with diabetes mellitus and immersion of hands or feet in water
- History: pain and redness around and beneath the nail and nail bed
- Physical exam: inflammation around the toe nail. There may also be nail thickening and discoloration (dystrophic nails). Nail loss may also occur.

D. Respiratory tract candidiasis
1. Usually seen in hospitalized patients
2. About 25% of outpatients have their respiratory tract colonized by *Candida* species

E. Genitourinary tract candidiasis
1. Vulvovaginal candidiasis
   - It causes itching, curdy white discharge, and occasionally dysuria and dyspareunia.

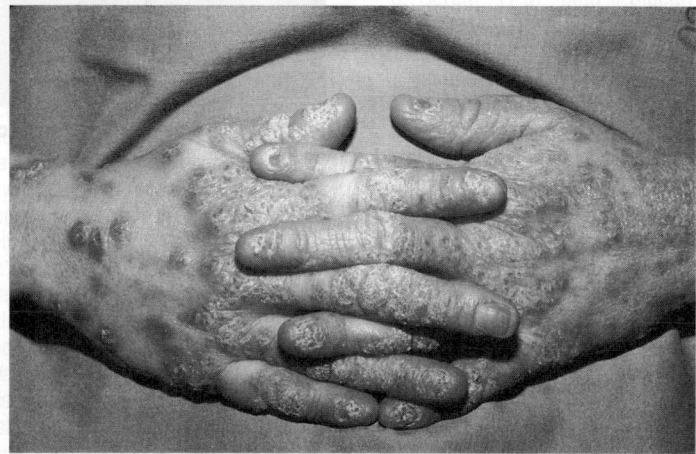

FIGURE 1C-1 Hand and nail involvement in chronic mucocutaneous candidiasis. (From James WD, et al: *Andrews' diseases of skin,* ed 12, Philadelphia, 2016, Saunders.)

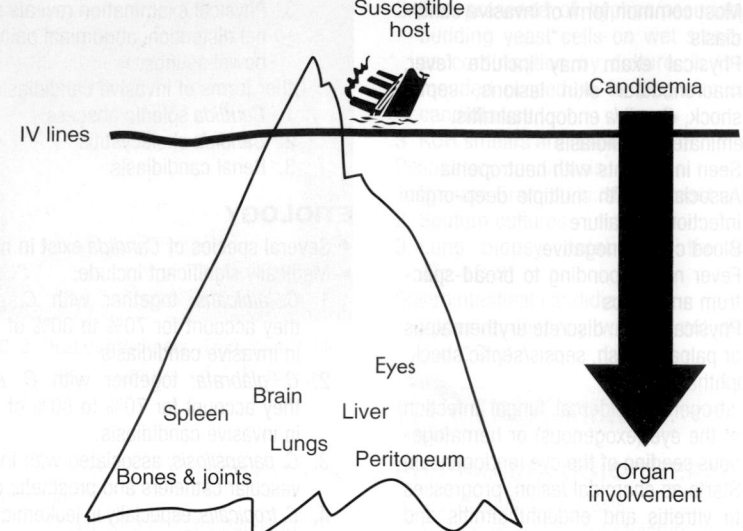

FIGURE 1C-5 Spectrum of disease of invasive candidiasis. Candidemia represents the tip of the iceberg with respect to the more invasive forms of candidiasis. Central lines often contribute to the propagation of candidemia. From the blood, infection can spread to almost any organ. (From Ostrosky-Zeichner L et al: Deeply invasive candidiasis, *Infect Dis Clin North Am* 16:821-835, 2002.)

Rx TREATMENT

- To successfully treat invasive *Candida* infection, it is important to start antifungal medication as early as possible. A small delay (approximately 12-24 hr) in starting treatment may result in a significantly excessive mortality rate.
  1. Do not dismiss Candida spp as a contaminant when it is isolated in blood cultures or other sterile sites.
  2. Before treatment, also consider removal of an intravenous catheter.
- Antifungals available include:
  1. Azoles (e.g., fluconazole, posaconazole, itraconazole, voriconazole). They inhibit the synthesis of ergosterol, a fungal cell component.
  2. Echinocandins (e.g., caspofungin, micafungin, anidulafungin). These are glucan synthesis inhibitors. Glucan is an important component of fungal cell walls. Most studies have provided reasonable support for echinocandins as treatment of choice for the majority of patients with invasive candidiasis.
  3. Polyenes (e.g., amphotericin B, lipid formulation of amphotericin B, nystatin). Broad spectrum. Their mechanism of action is to increase cytoplasmic permeability.
  4. Antimetabolites (e.g., flucytosine). Flucytosine is deaminated to 5-fluorouracil in fungal cell. 5-Fluorouracil inhibits RNA and protein synthesis.

TREATMENT PLANS
CANDIDEMIA:
- Treatment depends on whether the patient is neutropenic or not.
  1. Nonneutropenic adult patients: drug of choice is fluconazole; 800 mg as loading dose then 400 mg/day for at least 2 wk after clinical improvement or negative blood culture. Amphotericin B is equally efficacious.

  2. Neutropenic adult patients: an echinocandin is the drug of choice (e.g., caspofungin 70 mg IV loading dose then 50 mg/day IV or micafungin 100 mg/day IV or anidulafungin 200 mg IV loading dose then 100 mg IV all for at least 2 wk after clear blood culture and after clinical improvement.

DISSEMINATED CANDIDIASIS: Fluconazole is the drug of choice.
DISSEMINATED CANDIDIASIS WITH END-ORGAN INFECTION:
- Treatment is the same as for candidemia of nonneutropenic patients. In most cases, therapy is prolonged for at least 4 to 6 wk.
- The echinocandins are the first-line therapy.

OSTEOMYELITIS OR SEPTIC ARTHRITIS:
- Fluconazole 400 mg IV or PO *or*
- Lipid-based amphotericin B 3-5 mg/kg qd

ENDOCARDITIS:
- Caspofungin 50-150 mg/day or
- Micafungin 100-150 mg/day or
- Anidulafungin 100-200 mg/day

MYOCARDITIS:
- Lipid-based amphotericin B 3-5 mg/kg daily *or*
- Fluconazole 400-800 mg daily IV or PO

ESOPHAGITIS:
- Fluconazole 200-400 mg/day or
- Caspofungin 50 mg IV daily

PERICARDITIS:
- Lipid-based amphotericin B 3-5 mg/kg daily *or*
- Fluconazole 400-800 mg PO qd IV or PO

SURGICAL CARE: Include:
- Drainage
- Removal of any foreign bodies
- Surgical debridement
- Organ-specific care (e.g., valve replacement for endocarditis, splenectomy for splenic abscess, or vitrectomy for fungal endophthalmitis)

DISPOSITION
- Several factors affect prognosis: infection site, degree of immune suppression, and how quickly diagnosis and therapy is initiated

- Overall mortality rate: 30% to 40%

REFERRAL
- Always involve an infectious disease specialist.
- Referral to specialist will depend on the organ involved. For example:
  1. Endocarditis will require a cardiothoracic surgeon.
  2. Endophthalmitis will require an ophthalmologist.

FOLLOW-UP CARE
- Prolonged periods, mainly in the hospital, of antifungal treatment may be necessary.
- Closely monitor patients on amphotericin B because of the high incidence of side effects. Check basic metabolic panel, magnesium, and CBC at least twice a week.

! PEARLS & CONSIDERATIONS

PREVENTION
Basic preventive measures are similar to those used for nosocomial infections. This includes:
- Maximizing hand hygiene recommendations:
  1. Hand washing
  2. Using alcohol/chlorhexidine solution
- Adhering strictly to recommendations for placement and care of central lines and catheters.
- Judicious use of antimicrobials

PROPHYLAXIS
Antifungal prophylaxis should be limited to patients in whom it has proved beneficial: patients with gastrointestinal anastomotic leakage, patients undergoing transplantation of the pancreas or small bowel, selected patients undergoing liver transplantation who are at high risk for candidiasis and extremely low-birth-weight neonates in settings with a high incidence of neonatal candidiasis (Kullberg BJ, Arendrup MC: *NJEM* 373:1445-1456, 2015.)

PATIENT/FAMILY EDUCATION
- Inform them about the risk factors for invasive candidiasis.
- Inform them of the seriousness of the disease and the associated high morbidity/mortality rates, thus requiring aggressive treatment.
- Side effects and toxicities associated with treatment

EBM EVIDENCE

Available at www.expertconsult.com

SUGGESTED READINGS
Available at www.expertconsult.com

RELATED CONTENT
Candidiasis (Patient Information)
Candidiasis, Cutaneous (Related Key Topic)

AUTHOR: **DANIEL K. ASIEDU, M.D., PH.D.**

C

 BASIC INFORMATION

DEFINITION

Carbon monoxide (CO) is a colorless, odorless, tasteless, nonirritating gas. When inhaled it produces toxicity by causing cellular hypoxia and damage.

ICD-10CM CODES
T68   Toxic effect of carbon monoxide
T58.01 Toxic effect of carbon monoxide from motor vehicle exhaust, accidental (unintentional), initial encounter

EPIDEMIOLOGY & DEMOGRAPHICS

- A leading cause of accidental and intentional poisoning in the U.S.
- Can occur because of acute toxicity or chronic exposure.
- CO poisoning is seen more frequently during the fall and winter months in cold climates. Frequently seen after storm-related power outages, mostly due to the use of portable gasoline-powered electrical generators.
- In adults, 20% of CO poisonings occur in occupational settings.

PHYSICAL FINDINGS & CLINICAL PRESENTATION

- Depends on the severity and duration of exposure. The brain and heart are most sensitive to CO poisoning.
- Presentation is often nonspecific and may be mistaken for a flulike illness.
- Severity of poisoning does not correlate with carboxyhemoglobin (COHb) levels.
- Mild to moderate poisoning may present with headache, malaise, dizziness, nausea, dyspnea, difficulty concentrating, confusion, and blurred vision. Patients may have tachypnea and tachycardia.
- Severe poisoning may present with hypotension, arrhythmias, myocardial ischemia, pulmonary edema, lethargy, ataxia, loss of consciousness, seizure, coma, or rarely, cherry-red skin.
- Delayed neurologic sequelae may develop days to weeks after apparent recovery from acute poisoning. Patients may present with neurologic or psychiatric symptoms (cognitive deficits, memory loss, personality changes, movement disorders, Parkinson's, psychosis, neurologic deficits).

ETIOLOGY

- CO results from the incomplete combustion of carbon-containing compounds. CO poisoning occurs from inhaling smoke from fires, motor vehicle/motor boat exhaust, or the burning of fuel (oil, wood, coal, gasoline, natural gas) in poorly functioning or improperly ventilated devices (heating systems, stoves/grills, portable generators, etc.). Methylene chloride (paint stripper) fumes are converted to CO by the liver.

- CO toxicity results from tissue hypoxia and direct CO-mediated damage at the cellular level. This may explain why COHb levels alone are not predictive of clinical toxicity. The mechanisms of CO toxicity are not completely understood.
- CO impairs oxygen delivery. CO reversibly binds hemoglobin with an affinity 250 times greater than oxygen, displacing oxygen from hemoglobin and decreasing the oxygen-carrying capacity of blood. By binding to hemoglobin, CO changes the structure of the hemoglobin molecule and decreases oxygen release to tissue.
- CO also interferes with peripheral oxygen utilization. It binds to other heme-containing proteins including cytochromes and myoglobin. Cellular respiration is depressed by inhibition of mitochondrial function. By binding to myoglobin, CO decreases its ability to use and store oxygen.
- Neurologic toxicity is not explained by hypoxia alone and is related to the complex intracellular actions of CO. CO precipitates an inflammatory cascade that results in oxidative damage and brain lipid peroxidation.

 DIAGNOSIS

DIFFERENTIAL DIAGNOSIS

- Viral syndromes
- Cyanide, hydrogen sulfide
- Methemoglobinemia
- Amphetamines and derivatives
- Cocaine, phencyclidine (PCP)
- Cyclic antidepressants
- Phenothiazines
- Theophylline

WORKUP

History (duration and source of CO exposure, loss of consciousness), physical examination (detailed neurologic examination), laboratory and imaging tests

LABORATORY TESTS

- COHb level (measured by CO-oximetry on arterial blood; venous blood may be used to screen large populations exposed to CO or monitor change in COHb with treatment). COHb level >3% in nonsmokers confirms exposure. Heavy smokers may have baseline levels of up to 10%. Levels may be low if the patient has already received supplemental oxygen or if delays occur between exposure and testing.
- Direct measurement of arterial carboxyhemoglobin (by CO-oximetry): Pulse oximetry and arterial blood gas (ABG) may be falsely normal because neither measures oxygen saturation of hemoglobin directly. Pulse oximetry is inaccurate because of the similar absorption characteristics of oxyhemoglobin and COHb. An ABG is inaccurate because it measures oxygen dissolved in plasma (which is not affected by CO) and then calculates oxygen saturation of hemoglobin.

- Electrolytes, glucose, BUN, creatinine, cardiac biomarkers, ABG (lactic acidosis and rhabdomyolysis may develop), CBC (polycythemia from hypoxia in chronic CO poisoning).
- ECG (ischemia, arrhythmia).
- Pregnancy test (fetus at high risk).
- Consider toxicology screen.

IMAGING STUDIES

- Chest x-ray (noncardiogenic edema)
- Brain CT, MRI if neurologic abnormalities are present

Rx TREATMENT

ACUTE GENERAL Rx

- Remove from site of CO exposure.
- Ensure adequate airway.
- Continuous ECG monitor.
- Fetal monitoring if pregnant.
- 100% oxygen by nonrebreather mask or endotracheal tube (decreases half-life of COHb from 4 to 6 hr to 60 to 90 min) until COHb level is <10% and patient is asymptomatic. Table 1C-1 describes the half-life of COHb.
- Hyperbaric oxygen (2.5 to 3 atm).
  1. Questionable beneficial effect over normobaric oxygen. Disparate findings in various studies: some suggest hyperbaric oxygen treatment reduces the incidence of neurologic sequelae, and others have found it worsens neurologic outcomes compared to normobaric oxygen treatment.
  2. Decreases half-life of COHb to 20 to 30 min; increases amount of oxygen dissolved in plasma. It also reduces CO binding to other heme-containing proteins.
  3. Consider for:
     1. Severe intoxication (COHb >25%, history of loss of consciousness, neurologic symptoms or signs, cardiovascular compromise, severe metabolic acidosis)
     2. Pregnant women with COHb >20% or signs of fetal distress. CO elimination is slower in fetus than mother, fetal Hgb has greater affinity for CO than adult Hgb
     3. Should be instituted quickly if deemed necessary
- Consider concomitant poisoning with other toxic/irritant gases that may be present in smoke (e.g., cyanide) or thermal injury to airway. Toxic effects of CO and cyanide are synergistic.

TABLE 1C-1   Half-Life of COHb

Oxygen Concentration	Half-Life
21% (room air)	4-5 hr
100% (mask or endotracheal)	60-90 min
100% (hyperbaric molecular oxygen)	20-30 min

From Fuhrman BP et al: *Pediatric critical care*, ed 4, Philadelphia, 2011, Saunders.

Carbon Monoxide Poisoning

- Identify source of exposure and determine if poisoning was accidental. Fig. 1C-6 illustrates a suggested management algorithm for carbon monoxide poisoning.

DISPOSITION

- Patients with mild accidental poisoning can be treated in an ambulatory setting. Those with moderate/severe poisoning or coexisting illness require hospitalization.

- Survivors of severe poisoning are at 14% to 40% risk for neurologic sequelae.
  1. Deficits are usually apparent within 3 wk of poisoning but may present months later.
  2. Risk of developing sequelae is greater if patient lost consciousness during acute poisoning and with older age.
  3. Brain MRI and functional CT may reveal changes; damage is seen most often in the globus pallidus and deep white matter.

4. Recovery may occur over months to years.
- CO-mediated cardiac damage is associated with increased long-term mortality.
- High risk of fetal demise

REFERRAL

- American Association of Poison Control Centers: 1-800-222-1222
- Hyperbaric unit; accredited facilities are listed on the Undersea & Hyperbaric Medical Society website (www.uhms.org)
- Psychiatric evaluation if intentional poisoning

! PEARLS & CONSIDERATIONS

- Severity of poisoning and prognosis do not correlate with COHb levels.
- Neuropsychometric testing is an objective measure of cognitive function but is not universally used.
- Imaging techniques and biomarkers to define severity of CO poisoning, early prediction of CNS damage and prognosis are being studied, but are not ready for application.
- Pulse CO-oximetry measurement of CO saturation has limited clinical use.
- Treatment with hydroxocobalamin (for cyanide toxicity) may make subsequent COHb testing unreliable.
- Contact local fire department to assess environment and identify source of CO.

SUGGESTED READINGS

Available at www.expertconsult.com

RELATED CONTENT

Carbon Monoxide Poisoning (Patient Information)

AUTHOR: **SUDEEP K. AULAKH, M.D.**

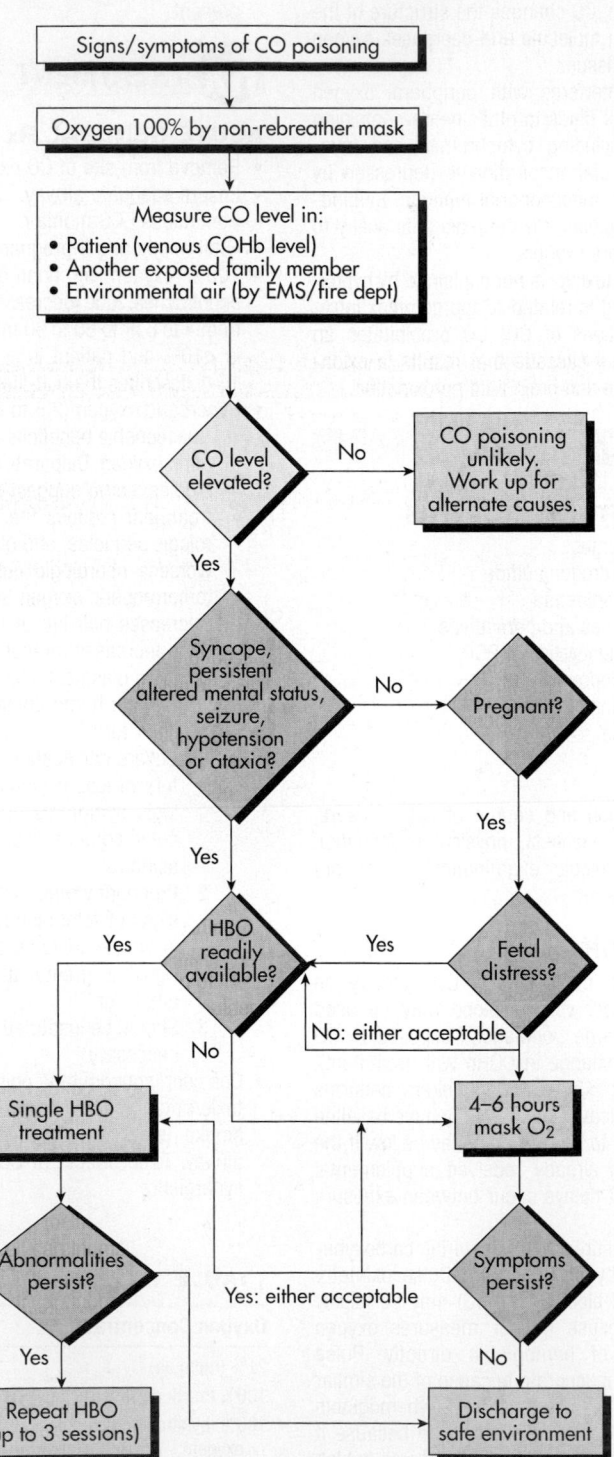

FIGURE 1C-6 Suggested management algorithm for carbon monoxide poisoning. (From Lavonas EJ: Carbon monoxide poisoning. In Shannon M.W., Borron S.W., Burns M. (eds): *Haddad and Winchester's clinical management of poisoning and drug overdose*, Philadelphia, 2007, Elsevier.)

 BASIC INFORMATION

DEFINITION

Carcinoid syndrome is a symptom complex characterized by paroxysmal vasomotor disturbances, diarrhea, and bronchospasm. It is caused by the action of amines and peptides (serotonin, bradykinin, histamine) produced by tumors arising from neuroendocrine cells.

SYNONYMS

Flush syndrome
Argentaffinoma syndrome

ICD-10CM CODES
E34.0 Carcinoid syndrome

EPIDEMIOLOGY & DEMOGRAPHICS
INCIDENCE:

- Carcinoid tumors are found incidentally in 0.5% to 0.75% of autopsies.
- Carcinoid tumors are principally found in the following organs: appendix (40%); small bowel (20%; 15% in the ileum); rectum (15%); bronchi (12%); esophagus, stomach, and colon (10%); and ovary, biliary tract, and pancreas (3%).
- The incidence of carcinoids is 2.47 to 4.48/100,000, depending on race and sex, and is highest in black men. The overall incidence has increased over the last 30 years due in part to improved diagnostic modalities.
- Carcinoid tumors can be classified using the WHO classification as follows:
  1. WHO I: Well-differentiated, <2 cm diameter, low proliferation index (<2%), confined to mucosa and submucosa
  2. WHO II: Differentiated, >2 cm diameter, invasive growth, high proliferation index (2% to 15%)
  3. WHO III: Poorly differentiated carcinomas with metastases and proliferation index >15%

PHYSICAL FINDINGS & CLINICAL PRESENTATION

- Cutaneous flushing (75% to 90%)
  1. The patient usually has red-purple flushes starting in the face, then spreading to the neck and upper trunk (Fig. E1C-7).
  2. The flushing episodes last from a few minutes to hours (longer-lasting flushes may be associated with bronchial carcinoids).
  3. Flushing may be triggered by emotion, alcohol, or foods or may occur spontaneously.
  4. Dizziness, tachycardia, and hypotension may be associated with the cutaneous flushing.
- Diarrhea (>70%): often associated with abdominal bloating and audible peristaltic rushes
- Intermittent bronchospasm (25%): characterized by severe dyspnea and wheezing
- Facial telangiectasia
- Tricuspid insufficiency, pulmonic stenosis from carcinoid heart lesions

ETIOLOGY

- Carcinoid syndrome is caused by neoplasms originating from neuroendocrine cells.
- Carcinoid tumors do not usually produce the syndrome unless liver metastases are present or the primary tumor does not involve the gastrointestinal tract.

 **DIAGNOSIS (FIG. 1C-8)**

DIFFERENTIAL DIAGNOSIS

- Flushing: Carcinoid syndrome must be distinguished from idiopathic flushing (IF); patients with IF more often are female, are younger, and have a longer duration of symptoms; palpitations, syncope, and hypotension occur primarily in patients with IF. Additional causes of flushing that need to be ruled out are menopause, medications (niacin, nitrates), alcohol, renal cell carcinoma, medullary cancer of thyroid, VIPoma, mastocytosis, and chronic use of food additives (nitrites, sulfites)
- Diarrhea: IBD, IBS, laxative abuse, infectious colitis
- Bronchospasm: asthma, foreign body, GERD, lung neoplasm

LABORATORY TESTS

- The biochemical marker for carcinoid syndrome is increased 24-hr urinary 5-hydroxy-indoleacetic acid, a metabolite of serotonin (5-hydroxytryptamine).
- False elevations can be seen with ingestion of certain foods (bananas, pineapples, eggplant, avocados, walnuts) and certain medications (acetaminophen, caffeine, guaifenesin, reserpine); therefore patients should be on a restricted diet and avoid these medications when the test is ordered.
- Falsely low results can occur with use of alcohol, aspirin, MAO inhibitors, and St. John's wort.
- Liver function studies are an unreliable indicator of liver involvement.

IMAGING STUDIES

- CT scan of chest is useful to detect bronchial carcinoids.
- CT scan or MRI of abdomen or a liver and spleen radionuclide scan is useful to detect liver metastases (palpable in >50% of cases).
- Iodine-123–labeled somatostatin can detect carcinoid endocrine tumors with somatostatin receptors.
- Scanning with radiolabeled octreotide (Fig. 1C-9) can visualize previously undetected or metastatic lesions.
- PET scan.

 **TREATMENT**

NONPHARMACOLOGIC THERAPY

Avoidance of ethanol ingestion (may precipitate flushing)

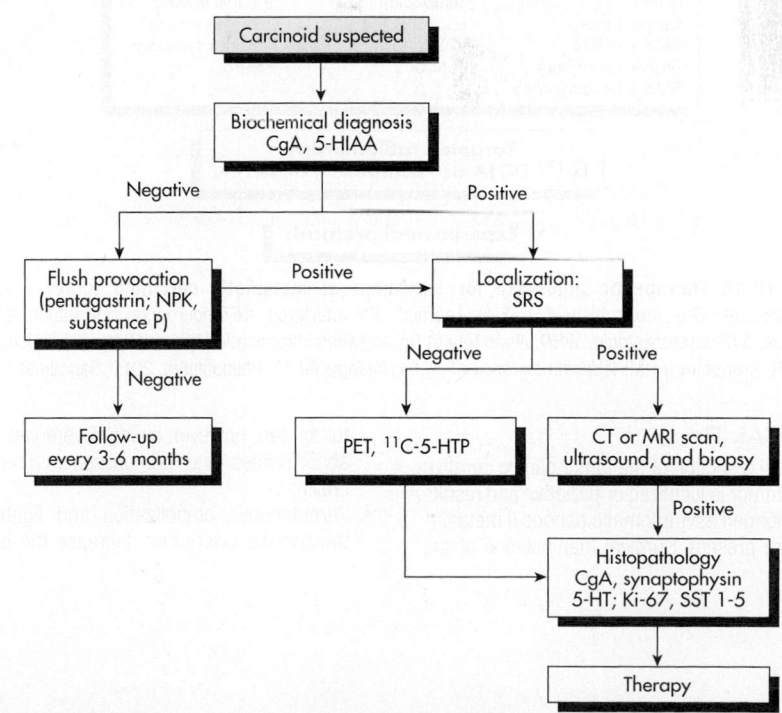

FIGURE 1C-8 Diagnostic algorithm for patients with carcinoid tumors. *CgA,* Chromogranin A; *C-5-HTP,* C-5-hydroxytryptophan; *CT,* computed tomography; *5-HIAA,* 5-hydroxyindoleacetic acid; *5-HT,* 5-hydroxytryptamine; *MRI,* magnetic resonance imaging; *NPK,* neuropeptide K; *PET,* positron emission tomography; *SRS,* somatostatin receptor scintigraphy; *SST 1-5,* somatostatin receptor subtypes 1 through 5. (From Melmed S, Polonsky KS, Larsen PR, Kronenberg HM: *Williams textbook of endocrinology,* ed 12, Philadelphia, 2011, Saunders.)

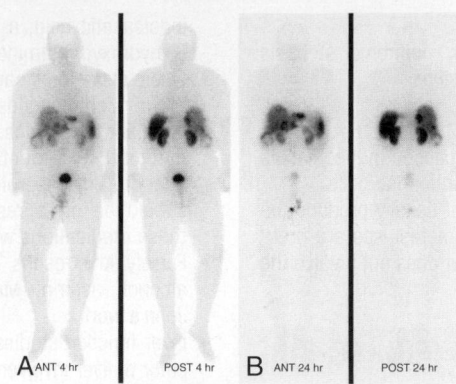

FIGURE 1C-9 A and B, Octreoscan illustrating uptake pattern in liver metastases from a small bowel carcinoid. (From Cameron JL, Cameron AM: *Current surgical therapy*, ed 10, Philadelphia, 2011, Saunders.)

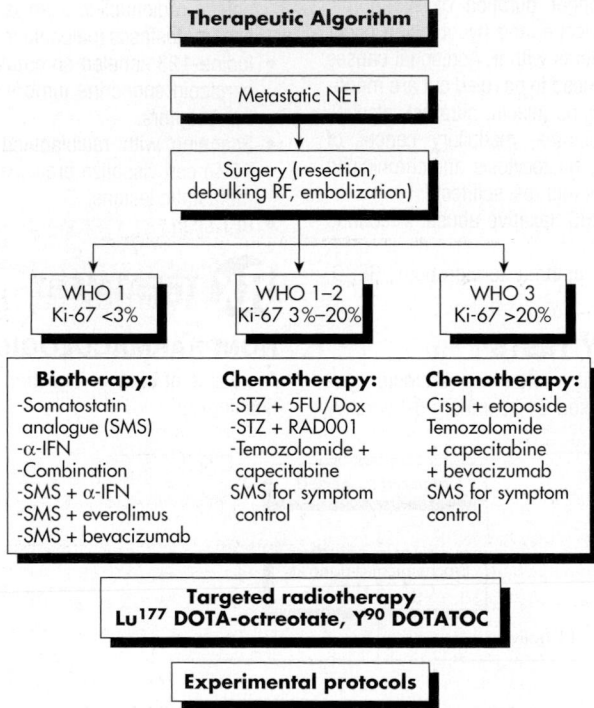

FIGURE 1C-10 Therapeutic algorithm for treatment of metastatic carcinoid tumor. *DOTATOC,* DOTA-octreotide; *Dox,* doxorubicin; *5FU,* 5-fluorouracil; *IFN,* interferon; *NET,* neuroendocrine tumor; *RAD001,* everolimus; *STZ,* streptozotocin; *WHO,* World Health Organization classification. (From Melmed S, Polonsky KS, Larsen PR, Kronenberg HM: *Williams textbook of endocrinology*, ed 12, Philadelphia, 2011, Saunders)

GENERAL Rx

- Surgical resection of the tumor can be curative if the tumor is localized or palliative and results in prolonged asymptomatic periods if metastases are present. Surgical manipulation of the tumor can, however, cause severe vasomotor abnormalities and bronchospasm (carcinoid crisis).
- Percutaneous embolization and ligation of the hepatic artery can decrease the bulk of the tumor in the liver and provide palliative treatment of tumors with hepatic metastases.
- Cytotoxic chemotherapy: combination chemotherapy with 5-fluorouracil and streptozocin can be used in patients with unresectable or recurrent carcinoid tumors; however, it has only limited success. Fig. 1C-10 describes a therapeutic algorithm for treatment of metastatic carcinoid tumor.
- Control of clinical manifestations:
  1. Somatostatin analogues (octreotide and lanreotide) are effective for both flushing and diarrhea in most patients. Interferon alfa may be useful as an additive therapy for persistent symptoms despite use of somatostatin analogues; however, data remain inconclusive.
  2. Flushing may be controlled by the combination of H_1- and H_2-receptor antagonists (e.g., diphenhydramine 25 to 50 mg PO q6h and ranitidine 150 mg bid).
  3. Diarrhea may respond to diphenoxylate with atropine (Lomotil).
  4. Bronchospasm can be treated with aminophylline and/or albuterol.
- Nutritional support: supplemental niacin therapy may be useful to prevent pellagra because the tumor uses dietary tryptophan for serotonin synthesis, resulting in a nutritional deficiency in some patients.
- Interferon alfa may be useful as an additive to control symptoms unresponsive to somatostatin analogues.
- Echocardiography and monitoring for right-sided congestive heart failure are recommended for patients with unresectable disease because endocardial fibrosis, involving predominantly the endocardium, chordae, and valves of the right side of the heart, can occur.

DISPOSITION

Carcinoids of the appendix and rectum have a low malignancy potential and rarely produce the clinical syndrome; metastases are also uncommon if the size of the primary lesion is <2 cm in diameter.

RELATED CONTENT

Carcinoid Syndrome (Patient Information)

AUTHOR: **FRED F. FERRI, M.D.**

 **BASIC INFORMATION**

DEFINITION

Cardiac tamponade is a life-threatening condition where an accumulation of fluid within the pericardial sac causes equal elevation of atrial, end diastolic pressures in the ventricles, and pericardial pressures, as well as an exaggerated inspiratory decrease in arterial systolic pressure (pulsus paradoxus) along with arterial hypotension.

ICD-10CM CODES
I31.4 Cardiac tamponade

PHYSICAL FINDINGS & CLINICAL PRESENTATION

- Chest pain
- Tachypnea/dyspnea
- Beck's triad
  1. Absolute or relative hypotension
  2. Elevated jugular venous pressure (with prominent *x* descent and blunted *y* descent)
  3. Muffled heart sounds
- Tachycardia (except in uremia or hypothyroid patients)
- Pulsus paradoxus (decrease in systolic arterial pressure of 10 mm Hg or more during normal inspiration while in normal sinus rhythm)
- Pericardial friction rub may or may not be present
- Reduced or absent apical cardiac impulse

ETIOLOGY

I. Acute (rapidly accumulating pericardial effusion leading to cardiac tamponade): does not need a large amount of effusion to cause tamponade, rather it is the rapidity of fluid accumulation that leads to tamponade. Usually resembles clinical presentation of cardiogenic shock requiring urgent reduction of pericardial pressure. Causes for acute cardiac tamponade include:
  1. Penetrating trauma
  2. Aortic dissection
  3. Postinfarction myocardial rupture and/or hemorrhagic pericarditis
  4. Iatrogenic (central line and pacemaker insertions, cardiac ablation, post–coronary bypass surgery or post–percutaneous coronary intervention)
II. Subacute or chronic: occurs over days to weeks, and the effusion is usually large; causes include the following:
  1. Malignancy (e.g., lung, breast, lymphoma)
  2. Viral pericarditis (e.g., Coxsackie, human immunodeficiency virus, enterovirus, HSV 6, parvovirus, etc.)
  3. Bacterial, fungal, or tuberculous pericarditis
  4. Uremia
  5. Hypothyroidism/myxedema (rare)
  6. Collagen vascular disease (e.g., lupus, rheumatoid arthritis, scleroderma)
  7. Radiation

8. Post–myocardial infarction or post–cardiac ablation inflammation
9. Idiopathic
III. Regional cardiac tamponade occurs when the localized or loculated hematoma compresses only selected cardiac chambers

DIAGNOSIS

Cardiac tamponade is a clinical diagnosis made at the bedside from history and physical examination. The echocardiogram will help confirm or reject the clinical diagnosis. Tamponade can be confirmed invasively by the measurement of elevated intrapericardial pressures with an intrapericardial catheter and right-sided heart catheterization. Typical findings are diastolic equalization of pressures, usually ranging from 10 to 30 mm Hg (diastolic pulmonary artery pressure = right ventricular diastolic pressure = right atrial pressure = intrapericardial pressure), and lowering of the intrapericardial pressure with fluid drainage. Thereafter, the underlying etiology must be determined with specific laboratory work (see "Laboratory Tests").

DIFFERENTIAL DIAGNOSIS

Other conditions that can also lead to elevated jugular venous pressure, decreased systemic pressure, and pulsus paradoxus include:
- Chronic obstructive pulmonary disease and asthma exacerbations
- Constrictive pericarditis (Table 1C-2)
- Restrictive cardiomyopathy
- Right ventricular infarction
- Pulmonary embolism
- Chronic biventricular heart failure

LABORATORY TESTS

- Electrolytes, blood urea nitrogen, creatinine, erythrocyte sedimentation rate, thyroid function tests, antinuclear antibody, rheumatoid factor, PPD, blood cultures, viral titers, and pericardial fluid analysis including cytology and cultures
- Possible 12-lead ECG findings:
  1. Sinus tachycardia
  2. PR depression and/or diffuse ST elevations if acute pericarditis is present
  3. Electrical alternans (beat to beat alternations in the QRS complex heights) (Fig. E1C-11)

4. Low voltage if massive effusion is present. (QRS complex <0.5 mV in the limb leads and <1.0 mV in precordial leads)

IMAGING STUDIES

- Chest radiograph (enlarged cardiac silhouette with clear lung fields) (Fig. 1C-12)
- Chest CT (may overestimate size of the effusion) (Fig. 1C-13)
- Echocardiogram findings (Fig. 1C-14):
  1. Pericardial effusion
  2. Diastolic collapse of the right atrium (late diastole) is virtually 100% sensitive but has low specificity.
  3. Diastolic collapse of the right ventricle (early diastole) is pathognomonic and very specific.
  4. >25% mitral and >50% tricuspid valve inflow variation with respiration
  5. Plethoric inferior vena cava (IVC dilation and <50% decrease in the diameter of the IVC during inspiration)
  6. Left atrial collapse (high specificity)
- Cardiac catheterization as discussed earlier will see equalization of intracardiac diastolic

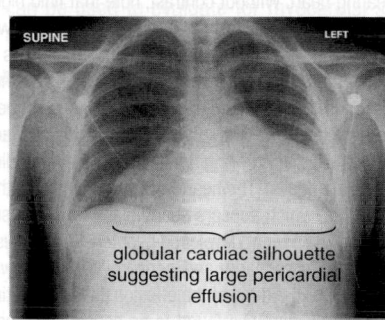

globular cardiac silhouette suggesting large pericardial effusion

FIGURE 1C-12 Massive pericardial effusion and tamponade. This 23-year-old male has a history of aortic valve replacement for infective endocarditis. He presented with increased chest pain and dyspnea. His chest x-ray shows a globular cardiac silhouette, suggesting a large pericardial effusion. The lung fields and right costophrenic angle appear clear, although the left costophrenic angle is hidden behind the heart and cannot be assessed. The patient underwent chest computed tomography to evaluate his aorta, as he complained of severe interscapular pain as well (see Fig. 1C-13). (From Broder JS: *Diagnostic imaging for the emergency physician,* Philadelphia, 2011, Saunders.)

TABLE 1C-2 Hemodynamics in Cardiac Tamponade and Constrictive Pericarditis

	Tamponade	Constriction
Paradoxical pulse	Usually present	Present in ~1/3
Equal left- and right-sided filling pressures	Present	Present
Systemic venous wave morphology	Absent *y* descent	Prominent *y* descent (M or W shape)
Inspiratory change in systemic venous pressure	Decrease (normal)	Increase or no change (Kussmaul sign)
"Square root" sign in ventricular pressure	Absent	Present

From Bonow RO: *Heart disease,* ed 9, Philadelphia, 2012, Saunders.

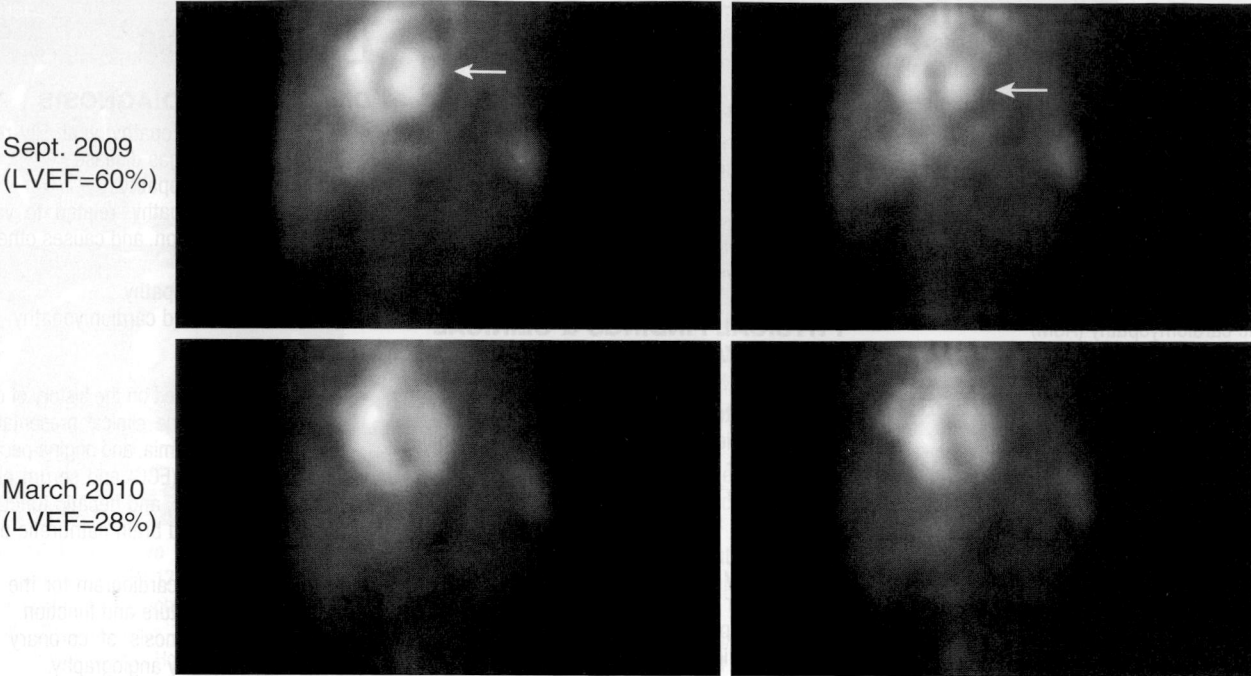

Sept. 2009
(LVEF=60%)

March 2010
(LVEF=28%)

End-Diastole   End-Systole

FIGURE 1C-15 Technetium-99m-pertechnetate multigated acquisition scans in a 47-year-old woman with breast cancer treated with doxorubicin. The top scan was taken before initiation of doxorubicin and cyclophosphamide therapy in September 2009. The left ventricular ejection fraction (left ventricular end-diastolic counts minus left ventricular end-systolic counts/left ventricular end-diastolic counts 100) was calculated at 60%. The bottom scan was taken in March 2010 after treatment with a total doxorubicin dose of 451 mg/m^2. Left ventricular ejection fraction was calculated at 28%. Left ventricle (*white arrows*) during end-diastole and end-systole. (From Figuerado VM: Chemical cardiomyopathies: the negative effects of medications and nonprescribed drugs on the heart, *Am J Med* 124:480-488, 2011.)

2. Global longitudinal strain imaging (GSLI) is an emerging echocardiographic measurement that may predict early cardiotoxicity before an actual drop in LVEF occurs.
- Radionuclide imaging (Figure 1C-15).
  1. If baseline LVEF ≤55%, the cardiac risks vs. oncological benefits should be discussed with the patient, cardiologist, and oncologist before initiating therapy. Cardioprotective agents such as ACE inhibitors and beta-blockers should be initiated and serial LVEF measurements done after each dose.
  2. Even after chemotherapy is completed, annual LVEF measurements with echocardiograms or MUGA scans should be done for 5 years to detect late anthracycline cardiotoxicity.

Rx TREATMENT

NONPHARMACOLOGIC THERAPY
- The noninvasive assessment of LV function before, during, and after anthracycline-containing chemotherapy by means of echocardiograms and MUGA scan.
- To reduce the risk of anthracycline-induced cardiotoxicity, the lifetime cumulative dosage should be limited to <350 mg/m^2 in adults.
- Other approaches include the use of infusion other than bolus, liposomal encapsulated doxorubicin, less cardiotoxic analogs of doxorubicin such as epirubicin, and co-administration of protective agents such as dexrazoxane.

- Termination of 5-FU treatment if cardiac symptoms manifest and re-administration is not recommended

ACUTE GENERAL Rx
- Treat decompensated CHF with diuresis and inotropes if low cardiac output.
- For angina in acute cocaine intoxication, benzodiazepines, nitrites, and calcium channel blockers are the first line of therapy. Once myocardial infarction is indicated by ECG and serum troponin, patients should be evaluated by cardiac catheterization.

CHRONIC Rx
- Nitrates, beta-blockers, and calcium channel blockers for angina caused by 5-FU.
- Dexrazoxane is an ethylenediaminetetraacetic acid–like chelator that acts by binding to iron, which prevents anthracycline cardiotoxicity. Cardio-oncology experts suggest a 10:1 ratio of dexrazoxane to anthracycline, administered 15 to 30 minutes before doxorubicin administration. However, the routine use of the drug is currently not approved in adults except in cases of cumulative dose of doxorubicin of 300 mg/m^2 or greater.
- Those developing anthracycline cardiomyopathy should never be re-challenged with the drug as the cardiac damage is usually irreversible due to cell death (Type I cardiotoxicity). The cardiotoxicity from trastuzumab, however, is reversible (Type II cardiotoxicity).
- Beta-blocker: In one study, carvedilol preserved LV diastolic function and chamber size after doxorubicin treatment, compared to placebo.

- ACE inhibitor: Enalapril and ramipril can improve myocardial contractility after doxorubicin or epirubicin treatment.
- Thiamine, folic acid, and multivitamins are adjunctive treatment for alcoholic cardiomyopathy. Abstinence can usually reverse the cardiomyopathy.

DISPOSITION
Prognosis depends on the dosage of chemicals and the severity of LV dysfunction.

REFERRAL
Close follow-up with cardiologist.

! PEARLS & CONSIDERATIONS

The presentation of chemotherapy-induced cardiac toxicity ranges from asymptomatic decline in LVEF to heart failure. The incidence is dose-dependent in the case of anthracyclines and may manifest itself up to 10 years after initial exposure. Therefore, a regular clinical follow-up of such patients is advised and echocardiographic surveillance is possibly indicated to detect late cardiotoxicity.

SUGGESTED READINGS
Available at www.expertconsult.com

AUTHORS: **KAUSTUBH C. DABHADKAR, M.D., M.P.H.,** and **ARAVIND RAO KOKKIRALA, M.D.**

 BASIC INFORMATION

DEFINITION

Dilated cardiomyopathy describes a group of diseases involving the myocardium and characterized by myocardial dysfunction that is not wholly the result of hypertension, coronary atherosclerosis, valvular dysfunction, congenital, or other structural heart disease. As a result, the heart is enlarged and the ventricles are dilated with impaired systolic function.

SYNONYMS

Congestive cardiomyopathy
Idiopathic cardiomyopathy

ICD-10CM CODES	
B33.24	Viral cardiomyopathy
I11.0	Hypertensive heart disease with heart failure
I42.0	Dilated cardiomyopathy (includes congestive cardiomyopathy)
I42.9	Cardiomyopathy, unspecified (includes cardiomyopathy [primary] [secondary] NOS)
I43	Cardiomyopathy in diseases classified elsewhere
I50.20 to I50.9	(Unspecified, Acute, Chronic, or Acute on Chronic) + (systolic, diastolic, or combined) (congestive) heart failure
O90.3	Peripartum cardiomyopathy

EPIDEMIOLOGY & DEMOGRAPHICS

- The estimated prevalence of dilated cardiomyopathy in the general adult population is approximately 1:2500. The incidence is approximately 4 to 8 per 100,000 persons per yr.
- The incidence of dilated cardiomyopathy is greatest in middle age and among men.
- African Americans have a three-fold increased risk for developing DCM, irrespective of comorbidities or socioeconomic factors, compared with whites.
- It is the most common cardiomyopathy and accounts for 25% of cases of congestive heart failure.

PHYSICAL FINDINGS & CLINICAL PRESENTATION

The patient will present with common symptoms of congestive heart failure, which may be of insidious or sudden onset. The patient may also be asymptomatic and the diagnosis made by the unexpected finding of cardiomegaly on a chest x-ray. The history should focus also on information that could help determine the etiology. Classical signs of heart failure may be absent. When present, findings are indistinguishable from other heart failure syndromes, including:
- Increased jugular venous pressure
- Narrow pulse pressure
- Pulmonary rales, hepatomegaly, peripheral edema
- S3, S4

- Mitral regurgitation, tricuspid regurgitation (less common)

ETIOLOGY

In approximate order of occurrence:
- Idiopathic (often a viral infection that cannot be confirmed)
- Infections (viral [Coxsackie B, adenovirus, parvovirus, HIV], rickettsial, mycobacterial, toxoplasmosis, trichinosis, Chagas' disease)
- Alcoholism (15% to 40% of all cases in Western countries)
- Uncontrolled tachyarrhythmia ("tachycardia-mediated")
- Peripartum (greatest risk from last trimester of pregnancy to 6 mo postpartum)
- Chemotherapeutic (anthracycline, doxorubicin, daunorubicin) or pharmacologic agents (antiretrovirals, phenothiazines) (see "Cardiomyopathy, Chemical-Induced")
- Substance abuse (cocaine, heroin, organic solvents "glue-sniffer's heart")
- Postmyocarditis
- Toxins (cobalt, lead, phosphorus, carbon monoxide, mercury)
- Collagen-vascular disease (systemic lupus, rheumatoid arthritis, polyarteritis, dermatomyositis, sarcoidosis)
- Heredofamilial neuromuscular disease (e.g., muscular dystrophy)
- Excess hormones (acromegaly, osteogenesis imperfecta, myxedema, thyrotoxicosis, diabetes)
- Hematologic (e.g., sickle cell anemia, hemochromatosis, hypereosinophilia)
- Stress-induced (i.e., takotsubo or broken heart syndrome)
- LV noncompaction
- TTN truncating mutations (mutations in TTN, the gene encoding the sarcomere protein titin) are a common cause of dilated cardiomyopathy, occurring in approximately 25% of familial cases of idiopathic dilated cardiomyopathy and in 18% of sporadic cases.

Dx **DIAGNOSIS**

Dilated cardiomyopathy is a diagnosis of exclusion, made after ruling out other potential causes of myocardial dysfunction.

DIFFERENTIAL DIAGNOSIS

- Coronary atherosclerosis, that is, left ventricular dysfunction secondary to ischemia and/or myocardial infarction
- Valvular dysfunction (especially aortic and mitral regurgitation)
- Other cardiomyopathies (restrictive, hypertrophic)
- Pulmonary disease (embolism, obstructive, restrictive)
- Pericardial abnormalities (constrictive pericarditis, tamponade)
- Hypothyroidism/myxedema
- Athlete heart

WORKUP

- Medical history: emphasis on symptoms of dyspnea, orthopnea, paroxysmal nocturnal

dyspnea, weight gain, palpitations, or signs of systemic and pulmonary embolism, substance abuse history, possible toxin exposures (especially occupational)
- Physical exam (see "Physical Findings & Clinical Presentation")
- Testing (see "Laboratory Tests" and "Imaging Studies" for more detail): laboratory, chest x-ray, ECG, echocardiogram, cardiac catheterization; myocardial biopsy is not routinely recommended, unless acute myocarditis requiring immunosuppressive therapy is considered (e.g., giant cell myocarditis)

LABORATORY TESTS

- Chemistries/metabolites (deficiencies), renal function tests (renal dysfunction)
- Cardiac biomarkers (elevation of cardiac troponin or BNP)
  1. Persistently increased cardiac troponin T levels are a marker of poor outcome in cardiomyopathy patients
- Endocrine (particularly thyroid)
- Iron studies (hemochromatosis, deficiency)
- Rheumatologic and inflammatory (ANA, ESR, CRP)
- Others as indicated (HIV, Lyme, neurohormonal)

IMAGING STUDIES

Chest x-ray:
- Cardiac silhouette enlargement (particularly left ventricle)
- Pulmonary vascular redistribution and congestion (Kerley B lines, cephalization of vasculature), pleural effusion (may appear as unilateral, most often on the right side)

ECG:
- ECG findings are typically nonspecific, and sinus tachycardia is usually a reflection of underlying heart failure. Large voltage in precordial leads and low voltage in limb leads may be seen in advanced disease.
- Intraventricular conduction defects and left bundle branch block
- Arrhythmias (atrial fibrillation, premature ventricular or atrial contractions, ventricular tachycardia)

Echocardiogram (Fig. E1C-16, *B*):
- Low ejection fraction with global hypokinesis
- Four-chamber enlargement (LV enlargement usually predominates)
- Mitral or tricuspid regurgitation (tethering due to incomplete leaflet closure caused by ventricular dilation)

Cardiac catheterization:
- On initial presentation to exclude obstructive epicardial coronary artery disease

Cardiac magnetic resonance imaging (CMRI):
- Particularly if infiltrative or inflammatory etiology suspected

Rx **TREATMENT**

NONPHARMACOLOGIC THERAPY

- Treatment of underlying disease (systemic lupus, alcoholism)
- Dietary sodium restriction (<2 g/day).

C

I

- Exercise training has been shown to be associated with reduced risk for hospitalization and death in patients with history of heart failure in limited trials; enrollment in a formal cardiac rehabilitation program may be beneficial in improving patient's functional status

ACUTE GENERAL Rx

- Treat the etiology of the acute exacerbation, when able. A helpful mnemonic is FAILURE: **f**ailure to take medications, **a**nemia/**a**rrhythmia, **i**schemia/**i**nfection/**i**nfarction, **l**ifestyle (dietary indiscretion), **u**pregulation of cardiac output (hyperthyroidism or pregnancy), **r**enal failure, **e**mbolus (pulmonary).
- Diuretics are indicated for all patients with current symptoms or history of heart failure and reduced left ventricular ejection fraction (LVEF) with evidence of volume overload (see "Physical Findings and Clinical Presentation") to improve symptoms. It is important to note that diuretics have not been shown to improve mortality rates.
- Patients with associated coronary atherosclerosis (angina, ECG changes, reversible defects on myocardial perfusion imaging) may benefit from percutaneous or surgical revascularization.

CHRONIC Rx

- Diuretics and digoxin as noted in "Acute General Rx."
- ACE inhibitors (and angiotensin receptor blockers) have been shown to have favorable effects on ventricular remodeling in patients with cardiomyopathy and a demonstrable mortality benefit in these patients. They also reduce afterload and improve cardiac output. Therefore, they are recommended in all patients with reduced LV systolic function (EF ≤40%), regardless of symptoms unless specific contraindications exist.
- Beta-blockers work by inhibiting the adverse effects of the sympathetic nervous system in patients with ventricular systolic dysfunction (EF ≤40%). *Only* carvedilol, long-acting metoprolol succinate, and bisoprolol have shown a mortality benefit in patients with LV systolic dysfunction. Unless specifically contraindicated, they should be started after the acute exacerbation has resolved and titrated to the maximum tolerated dose.
- Aldosterone antagonists (spironolactone and eplerenone) have shown mortality benefit along with a decreased rate of hospitalization for heart failure in patients with symptomatic heart failure and reduced LV systolic function (EF ≤35%). They should be used following label guidelines and with close monitoring of renal function and potassium.
- Additional medical therapies (hydralazine/nitrates, digitalis) can be considered in certain patient subpopulations with persistent symptoms on otherwise optimal medical management.
- Digoxin has no mortality benefit but has been shown to improve patients' quality of life in appropriately selected patients.

- The angiotensin receptor-neprilysin inhibitor LCZ696 on top of optimal medical therapy in patients with class II-IV heart failure and an EF of 40% or less was found to significantly reduce multiple heart failure endpoints, including death, hospitalizations, and CV death in comparison to enalapril. This medication was approved in the U.S. in 2015.
- Ivabradine was FDA approved in 2015 for patients with stable, symptomatic chronic heart failure with left ventricular ejection fraction ≤35% who are in sinus rhythm with resting heart rates ≥70 beats/min and either on are on maximally tolerated doses of beta-blockers or have a contraindication to beta-blocker use. It acts by blocking the hyperpolarization-activated cyclic nucleotide-gated (HCN) channel responsible for the cardiac pacemaker I_f current, which regulates heart rate.

DISPOSITION

- Annual mortality rate is 20% in patients with moderate heart failure, and it exceeds 50% in patients with severe heart failure. Once symptomatic, hospitalizations are frequent and readmission rates are high (>50% at 3 mo). A multispecialty treatment approach (e.g., primary care, cardiology, nutrition, cardiac rehabilitation) is recommended.
- Factors associated with an adverse outcome in dilated cardiomyopathy are described in Table 1C-3.

REFERRAL

- Implantation of a cardiac defibrillator for primary prevention of sudden cardiac death can be considered for patients with LVEF <35% on optimal medical therapy regardless of symptom status.
- Patients with LVEF <35%, left bundle branch block on ECG (QRS ≥0.13 sec), and persistent heart failure symptoms may benefit from cardiac resynchronization therapy via a biventricular pacemaker.

- Consider heart transplantation for relatively young patients (there is no precise age threshold) free of other significant comorbid conditions who are unresponsive to medical therapy. Dilated cardiomyopathy is the reason for 45% of all heart transplantations in the U.S.

PEARLS & CONSIDERATIONS

COMMENTS

- Patients should be encouraged to restrict or eliminate alcohol and reduce sodium intake (<2 g daily).
- Patients may benefit from daily weight checks as a means of early detection of volume overload and decompensated heart failure.
- Vulnerability to cardiomyopathy among chronic alcohol abusers is partially genetic and related to the presence of the ACE DD genotype.
- Idiopathic dilated cardiomyopathy is often familial, and apparently healthy relatives may have latent, early, or undiagnosed disease. Echocardiographic evaluation of family members is recommended.
- Incorporation of sequencing approaches that detect TTN truncations into genetic testing for dilated cardiomyopathy may substantially increase test sensitivity and allow earlier diagnosis of dilated cardiomyopathy.

SUGGESTED READINGS

Available at www.expertconsult.com

RELATED CONTENT

Dilated Cardiomyopathy (Patient Information)

AUTHOR: **CHRISTOPHER P. BLOMBERG, D.O.**

TABLE 1C-3 Factors Associated with an Adverse Outcome in Dilated Cardiomyopathy

Clinical	Noninvasive	Invasive
NYHA Class III/IV	Low LV ejection fraction	High LV filling pressures
Increasing age	Marked LV dilation	
Low exercise peak oxygen consumption	Low LV mass	
Marked intraventricular conduction delay	≥Moderate mitral regurgitation	
Complex ventricular arrhythmias	Abnormal diastolic function	
Abnormal signal-averaged ECG	Abnormal contractile reserve	
Evidence of excessive sympathetic stimulation	Right ventricular dilation or dysfunction	
Protodiastolic gallop (S₃)		
Elevated serum BNP		
Elevated uric acid		
Decreased serum sodium		

BNP, Brain natriuretic peptide; *ECG,* electrocardiogram; *LV,* left ventricular; *NYHA,* New York Heart Association.
From Hare JM: The dilated, restrictive, and infiltrative cardiomyopathies. In Bonow RO et al (eds): *Braunwald's heart disease—a textbook of cardiovascular medicine,* ed 9, St Louis, 2011, Saunders.

BASIC INFORMATION

DEFINITION

Hypertrophic cardiomyopathy (HCM) is an autosomal dominant myocardial disorder characterized by disorganized myocyte architecture and marked thickening (hypertrophy) of the left ventricular wall (>15 mm), without dilation, not explained by another cardiac or systemic disorder. The interventricular septum is the most common site of enlargement, though hypertrophy may involve other focal regions or may be concentric. HCM may result in hemodynamically significant obstruction within the left ventricular outflow tract (LVOT) and/or impairment of the diastolic function of the left ventricle. However, about one third of patients have no obstruction at rest or with provocation.

SYNONYMS

HCM
Hypertrophic cardiomyopathy
Idiopathic hypertrophic subaortic stenosis (IHSS)
Hypertrophic obstructive cardiomyopathy (HOCM)
Hypertrophic nonobstructive cardiomyopathy
Asymmetric septal hypertrophy (ASH)
Familial hypertrophic cardiomyopathy

ICD-10CM CODES
I42.1 Obstructive hypertrophic cardiomyopathy (Includes hypertrophic subaortic stenosis)
I42.2 Other hypertrophic cardiomyopathy (Includes nonobstructive hypertrophic cardiomyopathy)
I42.8 Other cardiomyopathies
I42.9 Cardiomyopathy, unspecified (includes cardiomyopathy [primary] [secondary] NOS)

EPIDEMIOLOGY & DEMOGRAPHICS

- Prevalence in the general population in the U.S., China, and Japan is estimated to be between 1/500 to 1/200 (the most common genetically transmitted cardiovascular disease).
- HCM is the most common cause of sudden cardiac death in young athletes (more commonly among blacks).
- There is equal prevalence in men and women (probably underdiagnosed in women).
- It occurs across ethnicities, perhaps underdiagnosed among blacks.
- Mortality rate is approximately 1%/yr, as high as to 2%/yr in children.
- The most common form of the disease is familial (60% to 70% of cases), and it follows an autosomal dominant inheritance pattern with variable expression.
- Spontaneous mutations can also occur, accounting for approximately 20% of cases. It is otherwise indistinguishable from the familial form.
- A variant form seen in the elderly (5%-10% of cases) has a better prognosis, and it is not typically associated with sudden cardiac death.
- The familial form is usually diagnosed in young patients. It is most often caused by a mutation in one of the contractile protein genes of the cardiac sarcomere. See "Etiology" under the "Genetic" section for more details.
- Nonsarcomeric genetic mutations that cause storage disease (e.g., Fabry disease) have a very similar clinical presentation.
- Apical HCM is a variant more common among Asians: as many as 41% of Chinese HCM and 15% of Japanese HCM patients. Clinically there is no LVOT obstruction.

PHYSICAL FINDINGS & CLINICAL PRESENTATION

Patients may have subtle symptoms of progressive congestive heart failure (CHF). At time of diagnosis, most patients are asymptomatic, referred and diagnosed based on family history. HCM may be suspected on the basis of abnormalities found on physical examination. Classic findings include:

- Harsh, systolic, crescendo-decrescendo murmur at the left sternal border or apex. The murmur increases with maneuvers that decrease venous return or LV size (Valsalva, standing), and decreases with those that increase venous return or afterload (squatting, hand grip, post-Valsalva release).
- Paradoxical splitting of S2 (if left ventricular obstruction is present).
- S4 may be present.
- Double or triple LV apical impulse ("triple ripple": atrial contraction, early rapid ejection, and late slow ejection).
- Pulsus bisferiens (double pulsation on palpation of the carotid pulse).

Increased obstruction can occur with:
- Drugs: digitalis, β-adrenergic stimulators (isoproterenol, dopamine, epinephrine), nitroglycerin, vasodilators, diuretics, alcohol, inhalation of amyl nitrate
- Hypovolemia
- Tachycardia
- Valsalva maneuver
- Standing position

Decreased obstruction is seen with:
- Drugs: β-adrenergic blockers, calcium channel blockers, disopyramide, α-adrenergic stimulators
- Volume expansion
- Bradycardia
- Hand-grip exercise
- Squatting position
- Release phase of the Valsalva maneuver

Clinical manifestations are as follows:
- Syncope or presyncope (usually seen with exercise)
- Angina
- Palpitations
- Sudden cardiac death
- Heart failure (typically with advanced stages): dyspnea on exertion, orthopnea, edema, increased jugular venous pressure, paroxysmal nocturnal dyspnea

ETIOLOGY

- Genetic: Autosomal dominant trait with variable penetrance caused by mutations in multiple genes encoding proteins of the cardiac sarcomere and calcium regulation. To date, >1400 mutations have been identified among at least 13 genes, with variable phenotypes, expressivity, and penetrance. The most vigorous evidence indicates that 8 genes are known to definitively cause HCM: beta myosin heavy chain, myosin binding protein C, troponin T, troponin I, alpha tropomyosin, actin, regulatory light chain, and essential light chain. HCM may be caused by a single mutation in one of two alleles; however, 5% of patients have at least two mutations.
- Sporadic occurrence.

DIAGNOSIS

DIFFERENTIAL DIAGNOSIS

- Hypertensive heart disease
- Valvular disease, especially aortic stenosis
- Cardiac amyloidosis
- Fabry disease
- Non–sarcomeric protein mutations: γ-2-regulatory subunit of AMP-activated protein kinase (PRKAG2) mutation
- X-linked lysosome-associated membrane protein 2 (LAMP2) mutation: Danon disease
- Athlete's heart

WORKUP

- Medical history: Unexplained "Clinical Manifestations" and/or family history of sudden death.
- Physical exam: See "Physical Findings & Clinical Presentation."
- Genetic counseling with or without testing.
- ECG is abnormal in 75% to 95% of patients, although there are no pathognomonic findings. Typical findings include:
  1. LV hypertrophy (abnormally tall R waves in the precordial leads) in up to 80% of patients
  2. Abnormal Q waves in lateral and inferior leads (Fig. 1C-17)
  3. T wave inversions (associated with the apical hypertrophy predominant variant)
- Echocardiography (Fig. 1C-18) is usually diagnostic as the majority of patients have significant LV hypertrophy (See "Imaging Studies" for details) and should be repeated every 12 to 24 months or as clinically needed.
- 24-hour Holter monitor to screen for potentially lethal ventricular arrhythmias (principal cause of syncope or sudden death in obstructive cardiomyopathy) should be performed at the initial diagnosis and in patients that subsequently develop palpitations, lightheadedness, or syncope. The presence of these arrhythmias identifies patients who are candidates for ICD therapy.
- In the absence of significant LVOT obstruction, exercise testing is indicated at diagnosis and annually thereafter to evaluate for symptoms and response to exercise.

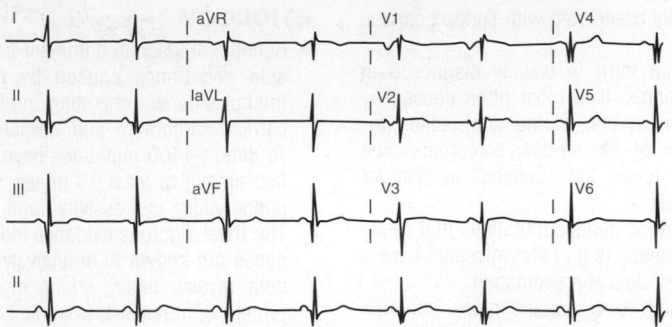

FIGURE 1C-17 Surface ECG in a patient with hypertrophic cardiomyopathy. Note the deep narrow Q waves in the inferolateral leads. (From Issa Z et al: *Clinical arrhythmology and electrophysiology*, ed 2, Philadelphia, 2012, Saunders.)

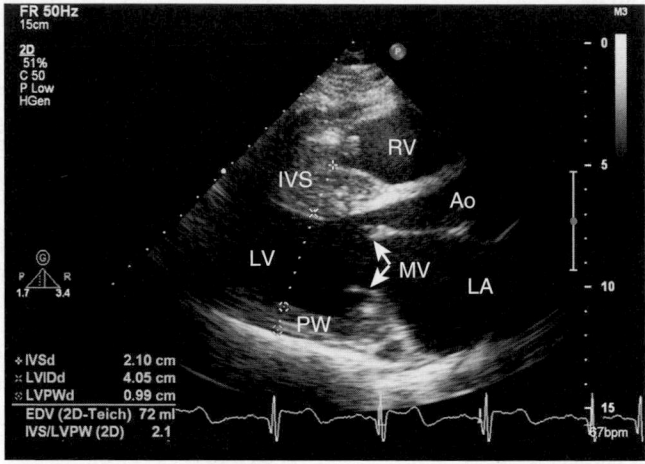

FIGURE 1C-18 Echocardiographic appearance of hypertrophic cardiomyopathy. Parasternal long-axis view from a patient with hypertrophic cardiomyopathy demonstrating asymmetrical septal hypertrophy. The interventricular septum (marked by *arrow*) measures 2.1 cm; the posterior wall measures 0.99 cm. *Ao*, Aorta; *IVS*, interventricular septum; *LA*, left atrium; *LV*, left ventricle; *MV*, mitral valve; *PW*, posterior wall; *RV*, right ventricle. (From Issa Z et al: *Clinical arrhythmology and electrophysiology*, ed 2, Philadelphia, 2012, Saunders.)

A drop in systolic blood pressure by at least 20 mm Hg or failure to augment by at least 20 mm Hg with exercise are markers of poor prognosis and are indicators for referral for myotomy/myomectomy. Cardiopulmonary exercise testing can provide objective evidence for worsening diseases, but need only be performed every 2 to 3 years.

- Biomarkers of myocardial fibrosis in HCM include BNP and high-sensitivity cardiac troponin T and I. Other labs include CBC, BMP, LFTs, TSH, SPEP, UPEP, Kappa/Lambda.
- Screening for sarcomere protein gene mutations in family members of patients with HCM can identify a broad subgroup of patients with increased propensity toward long-term impairment of left ventricular function and adverse outcome, irrespective of the myofilament (thick, intermediate, or thin) involvement.
- In individuals with pathogenic mutations who do not express the HCM phenotype, it is recommended to perform serial electrocardiogram (ECG), transthoracic echocardiogram (TTE), and clinical assessment at periodic intervals (12 to 18 months in children and adolescents and about every 5 years in adults), based on the patient's age and change in clinical status.
- Endomyocardial biopsy may be helpful to rule out diseases other than HCM if a diagnosis remains inconclusive after extensive testing.

IMAGING STUDIES

- Chest x-ray may be normal or show cardiomegaly.
- Two-dimensional echocardiography is used to establish the diagnosis and assess the severity of obstruction when present. LV wall thickness will usually be >15 mm (although some may be genetically positive but phenotype negative), and most patients (up to 95%) will have asymmetric (ratio of septum thickness to left ventricular wall thickness >1.3:1) LV wall hypertrophy. Symmetric LV hypertrophy is less common. The septum is most often affected, followed by the left ventricular mid-cavity and apex. In addition, 25% to 30% of patients will manifest systolic anterior motion (SAM) of the anterior leaflet of the mitral valve, causing obstruction of the LVOT and mitral regurgitation. Two-dimensional strain imaging echocardiography is useful for differentiation of HCM and cardiac amyloidosis from other causes of ventricular wall thickening. Up to 80% of HCM patients will also have diastolic dysfunction as evidenced by pulsed mitral valve inflow pattern and tissue Doppler.

- Cardiac MRI or cardiac CT may be of diagnostic value when echocardiographic studies are technically inadequate. MRI is also useful in identifying unusual segmental hypertrophy undetectable by standard echocardiography and can detect myocardial replacement fibrosis (an independent predictor of adverse cardiac outcomes and ventricular arrhythmias) using late gadolinium enhancement. CMR evaluation may be considered every 5 years or every 2 to 3 years in patients with progressive disease.

Rx TREATMENT

NONPHARMACOLOGIC THERAPY

- Avoid volume depletion: HCM patients experience decrease in stroke volume and consequent increase in left ventricular outflow gradient with exercise. This may lead to hypotension, dizziness, and syncope.
- Exercise restriction: The risk of sudden cardiac death is increased by exercise in HCM patients. Participation in competitive sports and intense physical activity should be avoided. As a part of a healthy lifestyle, low-intensity aerobic exercise is reasonable.
- Avoidance of alcohol: Alcohol use (even in small amounts) may result in increased obstruction of the left ventricular outflow tract. Other stimulants such as cocaine and other sympathomimetic recreational drugs should also be avoided.

GENERAL Rx

- Therapy for HCM is directed at blocking the effect of catecholamines and avoiding vasodilator or diuretic agents that can exacerbate the dynamic left ventricular outflow tract obstruction.
- Beta-blockers' beneficial effects on symptoms (principally dyspnea and chest pain) and exercise tolerance appear to be largely a result of a decrease in the heart rate with consequent prolongation of diastole and increased passive ventricular filling. By reducing the inotropic response, beta-blockers may also reduce myocardial oxygen demand and decrease the outflow gradient during exercise, when sympathetic tone is increased.
- Nondihydropyridine calcium channel blockers (e.g., verapamil, diltiazem) can also decrease left ventricular outflow obstruction through a mechanism similar to beta-blockers. However, they are mainly second-line agents used in patients who cannot tolerate beta-blockers as they also theoretically have vasodilatory properties that may worsen severe outflow tract gradients.
- Disopyramide is an antiarrhythmic that is also a negative inotrope, resulting in further

decrease in outflow gradient. It is sometimes used in combination with beta-blockers.
- Prophylactic antibiotics before dental, GI, and genitourinary procedures are no longer recommended according to the 2007 American Heart Association (AHA) guidelines.
- Avoid use of digitalis, intravenous inotropes, dihydropyridine calcium channel blockers (e.g., nifedipine, amlodipine), nitrates, and vasodilators.
- Diuretics, angiotensin-converting enzyme inhibitors, and angiotensin receptor blockers should be used with caution.
- Intravenous phenylephrine (or another pure vasoconstricting agent) is recommended for the treatment of acute hypotension in patients with obstructive HCM who do not respond to fluid administration.
- Implantable cardiac defibrillators (ICDs) are a safe and effective therapy in HCM patients prone to ventricular arrhythmias. In their practice guidelines, the major cardiology societies (AHA/ACC/HRS) give a strong recommendation (Class I) for ICD implantation in all patients with HCM who have had an episode of sustained ventricular tachycardia or fibrillation. In addition, they endorse the prophylactic placement of an ICD (Class IIa recommendation) for patients with one or more of the major risk factors for sudden cardiac death (outlined in "Disposition").
- Dual-chamber pacing may provide symptomatic relief of symptoms attributable to LVOT obstruction and refractory to medical therapy.
- HCM patients are at an increased risk of atrial fibrillation (AF) as well as systemic thromboembolization. AF occurs in over 20% of the HCM population. AF is an important source of symptoms, morbidity, and mortality and correlates to a worse prognosis. AF therapy should aim for thromboembolic risk mitigation with a vitamin K antagonist (unless contraindicated) and symptom alleviation via rate or rhythm control. Direct thrombin and factor Xa inhibitor use has not yet reached societal guidelines for this population given the lack of data.
- Fig. 1C-19 describes management strategies for subgroups of patients within the broad HCM clinical spectrum.

DISPOSITION
HCM is not a static disease. Some adults may experience subtle regression in wall thickness, whereas others (~5% to 10%) paradoxically evolve into an end-stage cardiomyopathy resembling dilated cardiomyopathy, characterized by cavity enlargement, left ventricular wall thinning, and systolic dysfunction. Patients with HCM are at increased risk for sudden death, especially if the onset of symptoms began during childhood. Severe left ventricular outflow obstruction at rest is also a strong, independent predictor of severe symptoms of heart failure and death. ICD implantation for primary prevention should be considered if patients (particularly the young) have any of the following high risk features:
- Personal history of sudden cardiac death or out of hospital cardiac arrest (major risk factor)
- Spontaneous sustained ventricular tachycardia or ventricular fibrillation (major risk factor)
- Family history of premature death in a first-degree relative possibly caused by HCM
- Unexplained syncope

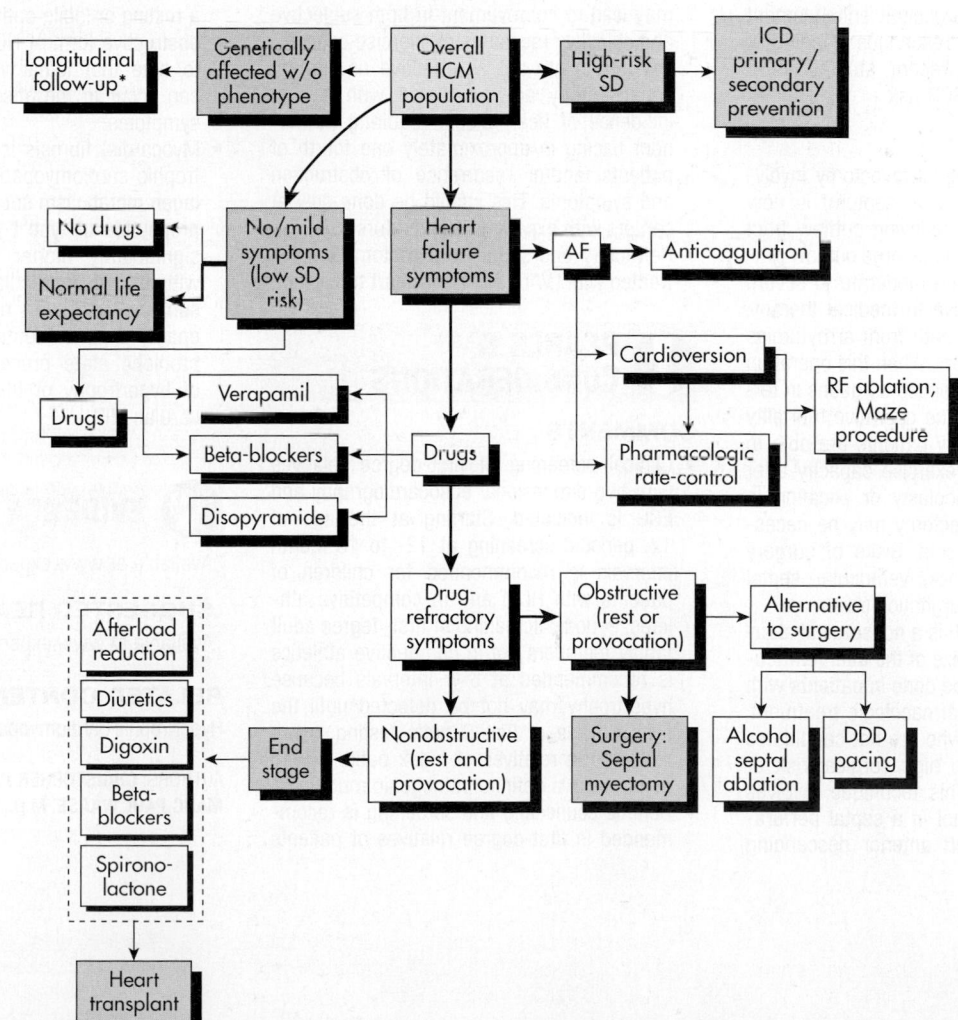

FIGURE 1C-19 Management strategies for subgroups of patients within the broad HCM clinical spectrum. *Generally no specific treatment or intervention indicated. *AF*, Atrial fibrillation; *DDD*, dual-chamber defibrillator; *ICD*, implanted cardioverter-defibrillator; *RF*, radiofrequency; *SD*, sudden death. (From Bonow RO et al: *Braunwald's heart disease—a textbook of cardiovascular medicine*, ed 9, St Louis, 2011, Saunders.)

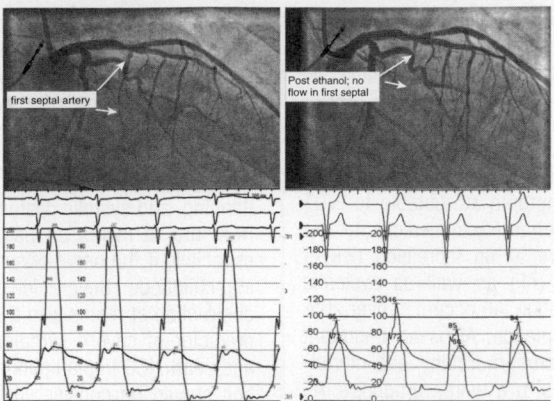

FIGURE 1C-20 Septal ablation for obstructive hypertrophic cardiomyopathy. *Left*, Large pressure gradient between the left ventricle and aorta. A large proximal septal perforating artery is identified. *Right*, Following selective injection of ethanol, there is no flow within the septal artery and the gradient is dramatically reduced. (From Bonow RO et al: *Braunwald's heart disease—a textbook of cardiovascular medicine,* ed 9, St Louis, 2011, Saunders.)

- Nonsustained ventricular tachycardia during Holter monitoring
- Substantial septal hypertrophy (>30 mm)
- Abnormal blood pressure response during exercise
- Increased delayed gadolinium enhancement on cardiac magnetic resonance imaging is suggested in some recent studies as a marker of increased SCD risk

REFERRAL

- Surgical treatment (septal myectomy involving resection of the basal septum) is now the gold standard for relieving outflow tract obstruction in patients with large outflow gradient (≥50 mm Hg) and moderate to severe symptoms unresponsive to medical therapy. The risk for sudden death from arrhythmias is not altered by surgery. When this operation is performed by experienced surgeons in tertiary referral centers, the operative mortality rate is <1%, and many patients are able to achieve near-normal exercise capacity after surgery. Mitral valvuloplasty or plication in combination with myectomy may be necessary in <5% of patients. Risks of surgery include AV nodal block, ventricular septal defect, and aortic regurgitation (AR).
- Alcohol septal ablation is a nonsurgical alternative to reduce the size of the interventricular septum. This can be done in patients with HCM refractory to pharmacologic treatment, particularly in those who are not candidates for myectomy due to high surgical risk or patient preference. This technique involves the injection of ethanol in a septal perforator branch of the left anterior descending coronary artery (Fig. 1C-20), producing a controlled myocardial infarction of the interventricular septum, and thereby reducing septal mass and consequently the left ventricular outflow tract gradient. This method may lead to improvement in both subjective and objective measures of exercise capacity, but results are not as effective as surgery because they are associated with a high incidence of heart block, requiring permanent pacing in approximately one fourth of patients, and/or recurrence of obstruction and symptoms. This should be done only at centers with experienced operators.
- Refractory end-stage HF symptoms can be treated with LVAD, BiVAD, or heart transplant.

 **PEARLS & CONSIDERATIONS**

COMMENTS

- Clinical screening of first-degree relatives with two-dimensional echocardiography and ECG is indicated. Starting at the age of 12, periodic screening at 12- to 18-month intervals is recommended for children of patients with HCM and in competitive athletes. Periodic screening of first-degree adult family members not in competitive athletics is recommended at 5-yr intervals because hypertrophy may not be detected until the sixth decade of life. Genetic testing is not indicated in relatives of index patients who do not have a definite pathogenic mutation.
- Genetic counseling and screening is recommended in first-degree relatives of patients with HCM. Genetic screening of first-degree relatives can refine or eliminate the need for periodic clinical screening. At least 13 genes are known to cause HCM, among them: cardiac myosin binding protein-C, beta-myosin heavy chain, troponin T, troponin I, alpha tropomyosin, actin regulatory light chain, and essential light chain. Clinical predictors of positive genotype, such as the presence of ventricular arrhythmias, age at diagnosis, degree of left ventricular wall hypertrophy, and family history of HCM, may aid in patient selection for genetic testing and increase the yield of cardiac sarcomere gene screening. Currently a mutation can be identified in 40% to 60% of all cases, sporadic or familial.
- All HCM patients who wish to become pregnant should be given prenatal counseling about the risk of transmission (about 50%) to their offspring and should be followed at a tertiary care center that specializes in high-risk pregnancies. Most patients with HCM tolerate pregnancy well due to the higher circulating blood volume.
- The mortality rate in HCM is approximately 1% to 2% per yr.
- About one third of HCM patients will not have a resting or labile outflow gradient (i.e., nonobstructive form of HCM), but it is important to note that lethal ventricular arrhythmias can occur in the absence of obstruction or symptoms.
- Myocardial fibrosis is a hallmark of hypertrophic cardiomyopathy. Biomarkers of collagen metabolism such as serum C-terminal propeptide of type I procollagen (PICP) are significantly higher in mutation carriers without left ventricular hypertrophy and in subjects with overt hypertrophic cardiomyopathy than in controls, indicating that a probiotic state precedes the development of hypertrophy of fibrosis identifiable with cardiac MRI.

(EBM) **EVIDENCE**

Available at www.expertconsult.com

SUGGESTED READINGS

Available at www.expertconsult.com

RELATED CONTENT

Hypertrophic Cardiomyopathy (Patient Information)

AUTHORS: **CHRISTOPHER P. BLOMBERG, D.O.,** and **MARC PAUL WAASE, M.D., Ph.D**

Diseases
and Disorders

 BASIC INFORMATION

DEFINITION

Restrictive cardiomyopathy refers to either an idiopathic or a systemic myocardial disorder (in the absence of ischemic, hypertensive, valvular, or congenital heart disease) characterized by restrictive filling (Fig. 1C-21), normal or reduced left ventricular (LV) and right ventricular (RV) volumes, and normal or near normal systolic LV and RV function. Pathophysiologically, the heart muscle is abnormally stiff, resulting in decreased compliance, abnormal relaxation in diastole, and increased filling pressures. Except for primary nonhypertrophic cardiomyopathy and a few infiltrative diseases, restrictive cardiomyopathies are secondary.

SYNONYMS

Idiopathic restrictive cardiomyopathy
Infiltrative cardiomyopathy

ICD-10CM CODES
D86.XX	Sarcoidosis-related codes
E83.11X	Hemochromatosis-related codes
E85.X	Amyloidosis-related codes
I42.5	Other restrictive cardiomyopathy
I42.8	Other cardiomyopathies
I43.1	Cardiomyopathy in metabolic diseases
I42.9	Cardiomyopathy, unspecified

EPIDEMIOLOGY & DEMOGRAPHICS

- A relatively uncommon cardiomyopathy, accounting for 5% of all primary myocardial diseases.
- Most frequently caused by amyloidosis or myocardial fibrosis (following open heart surgery, transplantation or radiation).
- Patients classified as having "idiopathic" restrictive cardiomyopathy may have mutations in the gene for cardiac troponin I, and restrictive cardiomyopathy may represent an overlap with hypertrophic cardiomyopathy in many familial cases.

PHYSICAL FINDINGS & CLINICAL PRESENTATION

Restrictive cardiomyopathy presents with symptoms of progressive left-sided and right-sided heart failure:

- Fatigue, weakness (caused by low output as patients are unable to augment cardiac output by increasing heart rate without compromising ventricular filling).
- Progressively worsening exercise intolerance and dyspnea.
- Anginal chest pain can be seen (particularly in patients with amyloidosis) from myocardial compression of small coronaries.
- Palpitations (atrial fibrillation is common), dizziness or syncope (from orthostasis, heart block, or malignant arrhythmia).
- Edema, ascites, hepatomegaly, distended neck veins (from elevated heart pressures).
- Kussmaul sign may be present (rise, or failure to fall, of the jugular veins on inspiration).
- On auscultation: murmurs of mitral or tricuspid regurgitation may be heard; an S3 may be present.
- Apical impulse may be palpable (can help distinguish it from constrictive pericarditis) and nondisplaced.

ETIOLOGY

Disease may be classified according to pathophysiologic processes:
Infiltrative:
1. Amyloidosis (most common overall): The main types include AA, AL, Aß (ß amyloid), and ATTR (transthyretin-mutated or wild type [commonly known as senile systemic]).
2. Sarcoidosis (usually results in a dilated cardiomyopathy with regional wall motion abnormalities)
Noninfiltrative:
1. Idiopathic (familial subtypes may have genetic overlap with hypertrophic cardiomyopathy)
2. Scleroderma
3. Diabetic cardiomyopathy
4. Pseudoxanthoma elasticum
Storage diseases:
1. Hemochromatosis (unusual as it is commonly associated with a dilated cardiomyopathy)
2. Glycogen or other storage diseases (Gaucher, Hurler, Fabry—all rare)
Endomyocardial:
1. Endomyocardial fibrosis
2. Hypereosinophilic syndrome (Loeffler's)
Carcinoid heart disease
Radiation
Metastatic cancers
Drug related (anthracyclines, serotonin, ergotamine, busulfan, methysergide)

DX DIAGNOSIS

DIFFERENTIAL DIAGNOSIS

- Constrictive pericarditis (see Table E1C-4)
- Valvular dysfunction (especially aortic stenosis)
- Hypertrophic cardiomyopathy
- Hypertensive heart disease

WORKUP

- Blood count (to identify eosinophilia), iron studies, serum renal function studies, chest x-ray, ECG, echocardiogram.
- Cardiac catheterization, magnetic resonance imaging, and computed tomography (selected cases).
- Aspiration biopsy of subcutaneous fat to detect amyloidosis.
- Endomyocardial biopsy if diagnostic confirmation needed.
- Brain natriuretic peptide (BNP) serum levels: there is data suggesting that BNP levels are markedly elevated in restrictive cardiomyopathy but near normal in patients with constrictive pericarditis, despite nearly identical clinical and hemodynamic features,

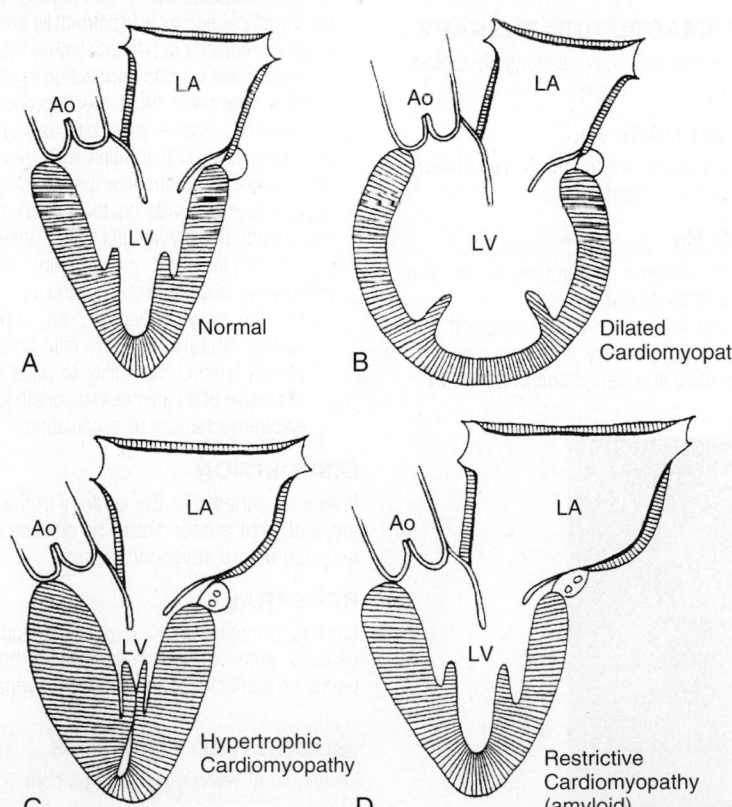

FIGURE 1C-21 Cardiomyopathies. A, Normal. **B,** Dilated. **C,** Hypertrophic. **D,** Restrictive. *Ao,* Aorta; *LA,* left atrium; *LV,* left ventricle. (Modified from Roberts WC, Ferrans VJ: Pathologic anatomy of the cardiomyopathies. *Hum Pathol* 6:289–342, 1975.)

most likely resulting from the lack of myocardial stretching in constriction that is required for BNP release.
- Genetic testing.

IMAGING STUDIES
- Chest x-ray:
  1. Ranges from normal cardiomediastinal silhouette to moderate cardiomegaly (primarily because of biatrial enlargement).
  2. Evidence of heart failure may be present.
  3. Presence of pericardial calcification favors alternative diagnosis of constrictive pericarditis.
- ECG:
  1. Nonspecific ST-T wave abnormalities are the most common finding. Voltage may be low in infiltrative etiologies such as amyloidosis.
  2. Frequent atrial and ventricular ectopy are often present. Atrial fibrillation may be present.
  3. High-degree atrioventricular block, intraventricular conduction delay may be seen in advanced cases.
- Echocardiogram (Fig. 1C-22):
  1. Biatrial enlargement almost always present.
  2. Wall thickness depends on etiology; often thickened in infiltrative disease such as amyloidosis.
  3. Myocardial appearance may be altered (speckled pattern suggestive of infiltration).
  4. Ventricular chamber sizes and systolic function are often normal or reduced.
  5. Echo Doppler shows evidence of diastolic dysfunction. Tissue Doppler demonstrates low mitral annular velocities.
- Cardiac catheterization:
  1. Characteristic hemodynamic findings are a dip and plateau, or square-root sign, in the left ventricular tracing where a deep and rapid decline in ventricular pressure at the onset of diastole is immediately followed by rapid rise and plateau in early diastolic phase.
  2. To distinguish restrictive cardiomyopathy from constrictive processes (Fig. 1C-23):
     - Constrictive: Usually involves both ventricles and leads to equalization of diastolic pressures between all four cardiac chambers to within 5 mm Hg. There is discordance in RV and LV pressures generated during inspiration, which is due to increased ventricular interdependence and decreased left atrial filling (caused by a decreased gradient in inspiration between the pulmonary veins, which are outside the constrictive process and the left atrium).
     - Restrictive cardiomyopathy: Impairs the left ventricle more than the right, often with left-sided end-diastolic pressures of 5 mm Hg greater than the right. The presence of increased pulmonary arterial systolic pressures is also suggestive of restrictive disease. Simultaneous RV and LV pressure tracings demonstrate concordant patterns during the respiratory cycle.
- Cardiac computed tomographic scan may be helpful to identify a thickened and calcified pericardium, consistent with constrictive pericarditis.
- Cardiac magnetic resonance imaging (CMRI) may also be useful to distinguish restrictive cardiomyopathy from constrictive pericarditis (thickness of the pericardium greater than 4 mm in the latter). CMRI is particularly helpful in the diagnosis of the amyloid or sarcoid variants and may have value in other variants as well. Late gadolinium enhancement can be seen with infiltrative diseases.

(Rx) TREATMENT

NONPHARMACOLOGIC THERAPY
Congestive symptoms may respond to dietary sodium restriction (<2 g/day).

ACUTE GENERAL Rx
Treatment of volume overload and heart failure symptoms with diuretic therapy.

CHRONIC Rx
- Treatment involves management of the underlying disease if it exists:
  1. Hemochromatosis may respond to repeated phlebotomy and iron chelators to decrease iron deposition in the heart.
  2. Sarcoidosis may respond to corticosteroid therapy.
  3. Primary amyloidosis may respond to chemotherapy (high-dose melphalan with autologous stem cell therapy or bortezomib-based regimens). ATTR may be treated with liver transplant or other promising novel therapeutic agents that are currently being tested in clinical trials.
  4. Eosinophilic cardiomyopathy may respond to corticosteroid and cytotoxic drugs.
  5. There is no effective therapy for other causes of restrictive cardiomyopathy.
- Overall, the goal of treatment is to reduce symptoms by decreasing filling pressures while preserving cardiac output. Since there is currently no drug available to specifically act on myocardial relaxation, therapy centers on low-dose diuretics to lower the preload.
- Beta-blockers or calcium channel blockers have not been demonstrated to improve symptoms or alter the course of disease.
- ACE inhibitors (or angiotensin receptor blockers [ARBs]) and vasodilators should be avoided in patients with amyloidosis as they are poorly tolerated. Even small doses can trigger profound hypotension (probably due to associated autonomic neuropathy).
- Atrial fibrillation is common and patients with it or with a history of embolization should be anticoagulated. Tachycardia (of any cause) is poorly tolerated and a common cause of decompensation. Rate control is of paramount importance. Cardioversion in case of rapid atrial fibrillation should be considered. Of note, digoxin should be used with caution as it is potentially arrhythmogenic (particularly in patients with amyloidosis).
- Fibrosis of the cardiac conduction system may result in complete heart block presenting as dizziness or syncope (especially in amyloidosis) and pacemaker implantation may be required. The course of restrictive cardiomyopathy is variable and depends on the underlying etiology. Death usually results from heart failure or arrhythmias, and interventions aimed at addressing these are recommended.
  1. For the amyloid variant, an implantable cardiac defibrillator offers little prophylactic benefit beyond the ability to pace because the cause of sudden cardiac death is usually electromechanical disassociation.

DISPOSITION
Prognosis varies with the etiology of the cardiomyopathy but is poor overall as disease is rarely detected before advanced stages.

REFERRAL
Cardiac transplantation can be considered in patients with refractory symptoms and idiopathic or familial restrictive cardiomyopathies.

SUGGESTED READINGS
Available at www.expertconsult.com

RELATED CONTENT
Restrictive Cardiomyopathy (Patient Information)

AUTHORS: **CHRISTOPHER P. BLOMBERG, D.O,** and **BARRY FINE, M.D., Ph.D**

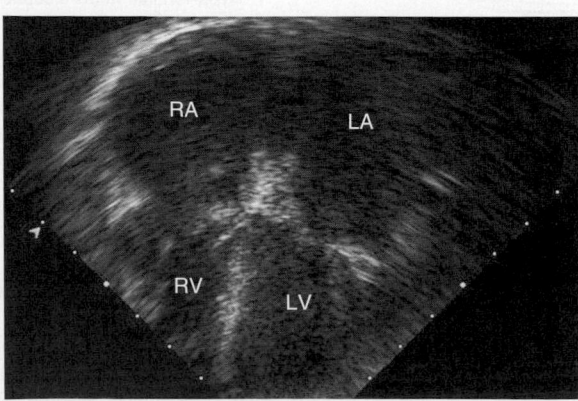

FIGURE 1C-22 Echocardiogram of a patient with restrictive cardiomyopathy. The optical four-chamber view shows the markedly enlarged right and left atria, compared to the normal-sized left and right ventricular chambers. *LA,* Left atrium; *LV,* left ventricle; *RA,* right atrium; *RV,* right ventricle. (From Kliegman RM et al: *Nelson textbook of pediatrics,* ed 19, Philadelphia, 2011, Saunders.)

DIFFERENTIATION OF RESTRICTIVE CARDIOMYOPATHY FROM CONSTRICTIVE PERICARDITIS

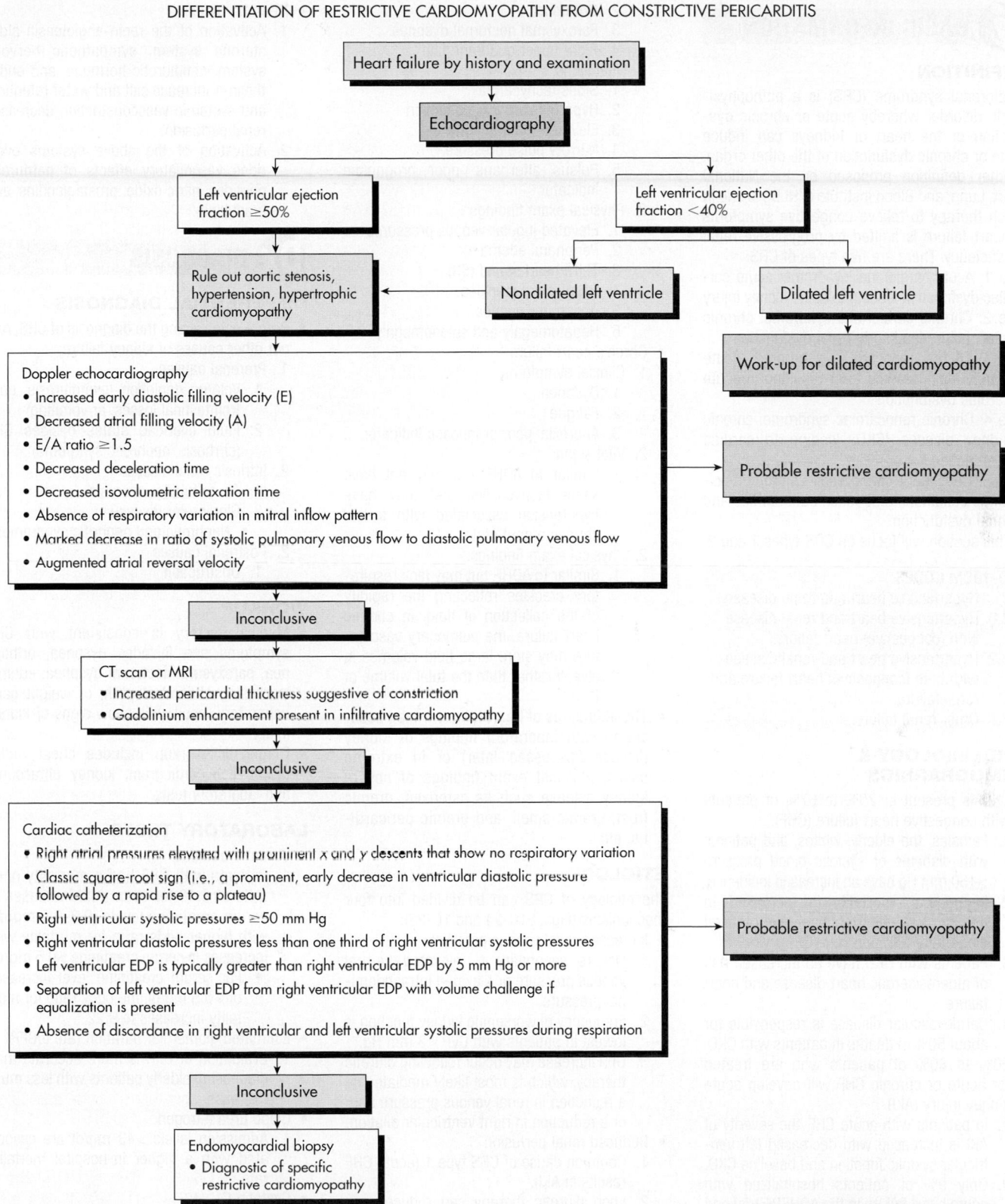

FIGURE 1C-23 Differentiation of restrictive cardiomyopathy from constrictive pericarditis. *CT,* Computed tomography; *MRI,* magnetic resonance imaging; *EDP,* end-diastolic pressure. (From Pereira NL, Dec GW: Restrictive and infiltrative cardiomyopathies. In Crawford MH et al: *Cardiology,* Philadelphia, 2010, Elsevier.)

BASIC INFORMATION

DEFINITION

Cardiorenal syndrome (CRS) is a pathophysiologic disorder whereby acute or chronic dysfunction of the heart or kidneys can induce acute or chronic dysfunction of the other organ. Another definition proposed by the National Heart, Lung, and Blood Institute (NHLBI) is one in which therapy to relieve congestive symptoms of heart failure is limited by progressive renal insufficiency. There are five types of CRS:

Type 1: Acute cardiorenal syndrome: acute cardiac dysfunction leading to acute kidney injury

Type 2: Chronic cardiorenal syndrome: chronic heart failure leading to renal dysfunction

Type 3: Acute renocardiac syndrome: acute kidney injury leading to or resulting in acute cardiac dysfunction

Type 4: Chronic renocardiac syndrome: chronic kidney disease (CKD) leading to cardiac dysfunction

Type 5: Secondary cardiorenal syndrome: systemic conditions that cause both cardiac and renal dysfunction

This section will focus on CRS types 1 and 2.

ICD-10CM CODES

I13	Hypertensive heart and renal disease
I13.0	Hypertensive heart and renal disease with (congestive) heart failure
I13.2	Hypertensive heart and renal disease with both (congestive) heart failure and renal failure
I17.8	Other renal failure

EPIDEMIOLOGY & DEMOGRAPHICS

- CKD is present in 20% to 67% of patients with congestive heart failure (CHF).
  1. Females, the elderly, whites, and patients with diabetes or systolic blood pressure >160 mm Hg have an increased incidence.
  2. In general, mortality is increased in patients with heart failure and reduced glomerular filtration rate (GFR).
  3. Patients with CKD have an increased risk of atherosclerotic heart disease and heart failure.
  4. Cardiovascular disease is responsible for about 50% of deaths in patients with CKD.
- 20% to 30% of patients who are treated for acute or chronic CHF will develop acute kidney injury (AKI).
  1. In patients with acute CHF, the severity of AKI is increased with decreased left ventricular systolic function and baseline CKD.
  2. Only 9% of patients hospitalized with acute heart failure in the ADHERE trial had normal renal function with GFR >90 ml/min/1.73 m² on admission

PHYSICAL FINDINGS & CLINICAL PRESENTATION

- Acute/subacute decompensated heart failure (ADHF)
  1. Clinical symptoms:
     1. Dyspnea with exertion or at rest

2. Orthopnea
3. Paroxysmal nocturnal dyspnea
4. Right upper quadrant pain
  2. Vital signs:
     1. Sinus tachycardia
     2. Hypertension or hypotension
     3. Elevated respiratory rate
     4. Narrow pulse pressure
     5. Pulsus alternans: poor prognostic indicator
  2. Physical exam findings:
     1. Elevated jugular venous pressures
     2. Peripheral edema
     3. Third heart sound (S3)
     4. Respiratory crackles
     5. Abdominal ascites
     6. Hepatomegaly and splenomegaly
- Chronic heart failure
  1. Clinical symptoms:
     1. Dyspnea
     2. Fatigue
     3. Anorexia: poor prognostic indicator
  2. Vital signs:
     1. Similar to ADHF, but may not have sinus tachycardia, and may have hypotension associated with a low cardiac output state.
  2. Physical exam findings:
     1. Similar to ADHF, but may lack respiratory crackles reflecting the rapidity of the collection of fluid. In chronic heart failure, the pulmonary vasculature may store large fluid volumes in alveoli rather than the total volume of fluid.
- These findings of heart failure will be associated with laboratory findings of kidney disease (discussed later) or in extreme cases, physical exam findings of severe kidney disease such as asterixes, uremic frost, uremic smell, and uremic pericarditis, etc.

ETIOLOGY

The etiology of CRS can be divided into four mechanisms (Figs. E1C-24 and 1C-25):

- Increased renal venous pressure
  1. Occurs secondary to elevated central venous pressure or elevated intraabdominal pressure.
  2. Frequency of worsening kidney function is lowest in patients with CVP <8 mm Hg.
  3. GFR increase may occur following diuretic therapy, which is most likely mediated by a reduction in renal venous pressure and/or a reduction in right ventricular dilation.
- Reduced renal perfusion
  1. Common cause of CRS type 1 (acute CHF results in AKI).
  2. Loop diuretic therapy can reduce ventricular preload and reduce cardiac output by as much as 20%.
- Right ventricular dilation and dysfunction
  1. Increases central venous pressure that increases renal venous pressure and reduces GFR
  2. Right ventricular dilation and dysfunction reduce left ventricular filling and renal blood

- Neurohormonal
  1. Activation of the renin-angiotensin-aldosterone system, sympathetic nervous system, antidiuretic hormone, and endothelin-1 increase salt and water retention, and systemic vasoconstriction decreases renal perfusion.
  2. Activation of the above systems overrides vasodilatory effects of natriuretic peptides, nitric oxide, prostaglandins, and bradykinin.

DIAGNOSIS

DIFFERENTIAL DIAGNOSIS

- Before establishing the diagnosis of CRS, rule out other causes of kidney failure:
  1. Prerenal causes
     1. Volume depletion (overdiuresis, gastrointestinal losses, or vomiting)
     2. Fluid overload states besides CHF (cirrhosis, nephrotic syndrome)
  2. Intrinsic renal disease
     1. Acute tubular necrosis
     2. Glomerular disease
        - Nephrotic and nephritic syndromes
  2. Postrenal causes
     1. Obstruction

WORKUP

- Medical history is consistent with CHF symptoms and includes dyspnea, orthopnea, paroxysmal nocturnal dyspnea, edema, increasing abdominal girth, or weight gain. Laboratory results will show signs of kidney injury.
- Diagnostic workup includes chest radiograph, echocardiogram, kidney ultrasound, and laboratory tests.

LABORATORY TESTS

- Serum creatinine
  1. Patients with CRS had a mortality odds ratio of 1.48 for even mild increases in serum creatinine levels (0.3-0.5 mg/dl), with higher odds ratio for mortality with increases in serum creatinine >0.5 mg/dl.
     - For serum creatinine level increases of >0.5 mg/dl, the odds ratio for mortality increases to 3.22.
- Estimated glomerular filtration rate (eGFR)
  1. Evaluation of GFR is more accurate than diagnosing elderly patients with less muscle mass.
- Blood urea nitrogen
  1. Admission levels >43 mg/dl are associated with a higher in-hospital mortality rate.
- Cystatin C
  1. GFR calculations are moderately less accurate than cystatic C assays.
- Beta natriuretic peptide (BNP)
  1. Initial admission values >480 pg/ml are associated with a 51% chance of death, hospital readmission, or an emergency department visit within 6 months compared with patients whose levels were <230 pg/ml.

INTERACTIONS BETWEEN THE HEART AND THE KIDNEY IN CARDIORENAL SYNDROME

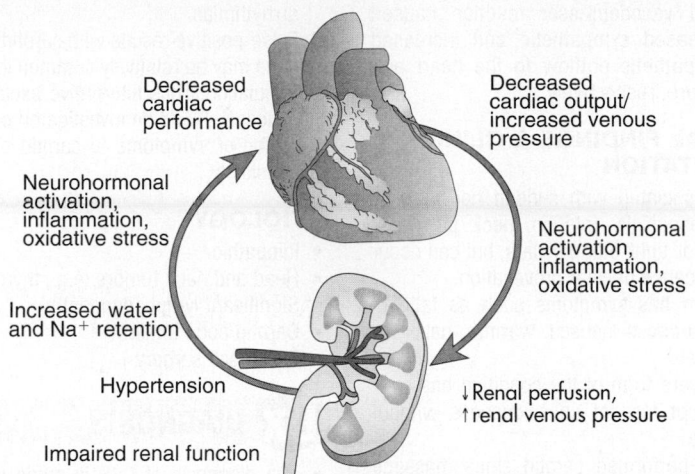

FIGURE 1C-25 Interactions between the heart and the kidney in cardiorenal syndrome. (From Pereira NL, Dec GW: Special problems in chronic heart failure. In Crawford MH et al [eds]: *Cardiology,* Philadelphia, 2010, Elsevier.)

- It can be difficult to distinguish between CKD and impaired kidney function due to cardiorenal syndrome, especially if prior renal function is unknown. Some patients have both underlying CKD and CRS. Findings that support underlying CKD include significant proteinuria (>1000 mg/day), urine sediment with hematuria and/or pyuria, cellular casts, and/or small echogenic kidneys on ultrasound

IMAGING STUDIES

- Chest radiograph
  1. May demonstrate signs of fluid overload, including pulmonary edema, effusions, or fluid in the fissures
- Echocardiogram
  1. Determines if there is underlying systolic or diastolic dysfunction and/or significant valvular disease present
- Kidney ultrasound
  1. Distinguishes between acute and chronic kidney disease and determine if obstruction may be causing worsening kidney function

Rx TREATMENT

NONPHARMACOLOGIC THERAPY

- Sodium and fluid restriction
- Hemodialysis/ultrafiltration
  - Used when there is insufficient response to pharmacologic treatment or if pharmacologic agents are limited by hemodynamics or worsening laboratory values
- Left ventricular assist device/cardiac resynchronization therapy (CRT)
  - Improve cardiac output and reverses cardiac dyssynchrony. CRT improves ejection fraction by 7% and CHF symptoms in patients with NYHA class II-IV heart failure with ejection fractions ≤35% and left bundle branch block morphology and QRS duration >150 milliseconds.

ACUTE GENERAL Rx

There is no medical treatment that directly improves GFR in the setting of CRS, but improving cardiac function improves kidney function by alleviating any of the mechanisms of CRS listed previously.

- Diuretics
  1. Extracellular fluid volume reduction returns hemodynamics to a more optimal position on the Frank-Starling curve.
  2. Reducing volume overload improves renal perfusion pressure by decreasing central venous pressure, renal venous pressure, and right ventricular dilation, which improves right ventricular function that increases left ventricular performance.
  3. Twice-daily intravenous furosemide that is 2.5 times the daily oral furosemide equivalent dose is a reasonable starting point.
  4. High-dose intravenous bolus loop diuretic therapy improves cardiopulmonary congestion more effectively than low-dose loop diuretics, but continuous infusion loop diuretics are not more effective than frequently bolused loop diuretic regimens.
  5. Diuretic resistance is common, and a combination of diuretics with different sites of action may optimize treatment.
- Inhibitors of the renin-angiotensin-aldosterone system
  1. Angiotensin-converting enzyme (ACE) inhibitors, angiotensin II receptor blockers, aldosterone receptor antagonists, and newer direct renin inhibitors
     1. Use limited by worsening kidney function, especially when serum creatinine is greater than 2.5 mg/dl.
     2. Permit decreased diuretic therapy.
     3. Efficacy of anti-renin-angiotensin-aldosterone system therapy in management of decompensated HF is established, but its role in CRS is unproven.

- Vasodilators
  1. Include nitroglycerin and nitroprusside
     1. Increase renal perfusion pressure by improving Frank-Starling curve relationships with improving cardiac output
- Inotropic agents
  1. Include dobutamine, dopamine, and milrinone.
  2. Improve cardiac output and renal perfusion by vasodilation. Used to treat cardiogenic shock and low cardiac output states with normal blood pressure.
  3. Caution: Dobutamine and milrinone may lower systemic blood pressures.
- Mechanical fluid removal such as extracorporeal ultrafiltration (UF) may be required to achieve control of fluid retention, particularly in patients resistant to diuretic therapy. UF removes plasma salt and water isotonically by convection through a highly permeable filter in an extracorporeal circuit through central venous catheterization. Newer technologies permit vascular access via peripheral veins. With slow continuous UF, the patient's intravascular fluid volume remains stable as fluid shifts from the extravascular to intravascular space without affecting cardiac hemodynamics. UF may be indicated in highly refractory HF with diuretic resistance.

DISPOSITION

Based on improvements in heart failure and kidney function.

REFERRAL

Consultations by a cardiologist and nephrologist are recommended

SUGGESTED READINGS

Available at www.expertconsult.com

RELATED CONTENT

Acute Kidney Injury (Related Key Topic)
Heart Failure (Related Key Topic)

AUTHORS: **SANDEEP SOMAN, M.D.**

 **BASIC INFORMATION**

DEFINITION

Light-headedness, dizziness, presyncope, or syncope in a patient with carotid sinus hypersensitivity is defined as carotid sinus syndrome (CSS). Carotid sinus hypersensitivity is the exaggerated response to carotid stimulation resulting in bradycardia, hypotension, or both. CSS is often considered a variant of neurocardiogenic syncope. The 2013 European Guidelines (ESC) defines CSS as syncope with reproduction of symptoms during carotid sinus massage of 10-second duration. There are two components of CSS: cardioinhibitory and vasodepressor.

SYNONYMS

Carotid sinus syncope
CSS
Carotid sinus hypersensitivity

ICD-10CM CODES
G90.01 Carotid sinus syncope
R55   Syncope and collapse

EPIDEMIOLOGY & DEMOGRAPHICS

- Carotid sinus hypersensitivity accounts for 1% of syncopal episodes.
- Carotid sinus hypersensitivity is frequently associated with atherosclerosis and diabetes mellitus.
- Incidence increases with age, with an average age of onset at 61 to 74 yr. Fig. 1C-26 illustrates age distribution of the patients with carotid sinus syndrome.
- Men are affected more often than women (2:1).
- CSS is rarely found in patients younger than 50 yr.

MECHANISM

- The carotid sinus is located in the internal carotid artery.
- There is a reflex loop between the mechanoreceptors of the carotid sinus and the vagal nucleus in the midbrain.

- There is an exaggerated cardioinhibitory and vasodepressor reaction caused by decreased sympathetic and increased parasympathetic outflow to the heart and vasculature, respectively.

PHYSICAL FINDINGS & CLINICAL PRESENTATION

- Often associated with sudden neck movements, especially rotation, neck palpation, shaving, or tight-fitting collars, but can occur in the absence of clear provocation.
- Mild form has symptoms such as fatigue, lightheadedness, nausea, warmth, pallor, or diaphoresis.
- More severe form of the condition has sudden abrupt loss of consciousness without prodrome.

Properly performed carotid sinus massage (CSM) at the bedside is diagnostic. European Society of Cardiology recommends carotid sinus massage as part of the exam in patients with syncope of unknown etiology and age over 40. This maneuver can elicit three types of responses in patients with carotid sinus hypersensitivity (see "Diagnosis").
1. CSM should be performed with the patient in the supine and upright positions while monitoring the patient's blood pressure by cuff and heart rate by ECG.
2. CSM should be performed on both the right and left sides but on only one carotid artery at a time.
3. Vigorous pressure is applied over the carotid artery, directed posterior to compress the artery against the spinous process of the vertebrae, at the level of the cricoid cartilage for 10 seconds. Repeat on the opposite side if no effect is produced.
4. Contraindications to CSM include the presence of carotid artery bruits, documented carotid artery stenosis >70%, history of stroke or transient ischemic attack <3 mo, history of myocardial infarction <6 mo, history of serious ventricular arrhythmia, or prior carotid endarterectomy.
5. Complications of CSM are rare (0.1%-1%) and may include transient visual disturbance,

transient paresis, tachyarrythmias, or bradyarrhythmias.
6. False-positive results with carotid sinus massage may be relatively common in the elderly population. Thus alternative explanations for syncope should be investigated prior to attribution of symptoms to carotid sinus hypersensitivity.

ETIOLOGY

- Idiopathic
- Head and neck tumors (e.g., thyroid)
- Significant lymphadenopathy
- Carotid body tumors
- Prior neck surgery

Dx DIAGNOSIS

- The diagnosis of CSS is made in a patient with a history of syncope when carotid sinus hypersensitivity is demonstrated by CSM and no other cause of syncope is identified.
- CSM can elicit three types of responses diagnostic of carotid sinus hypersensitivity:
  1. Cardioinhibitory type: CSM producing (1) asystole for at least 3 sec in the absence of symptoms or (2) reproduction of symptoms occurring with a decline in heart rate of 30% to 40% or asystole of up to 2 sec in duration. Symptoms should not recur when CSM is repeated after atropine infusion.
  2. Vasodepressor type: CSM producing (1) a decrease in systolic blood pressure of 50 mm Hg in the absence of symptoms or 30 mm Hg in the presence of neurologic symptoms; (2) no evidence of asystole; or (3) neurologic symptoms that persist after infusion of atropine.
  3. Mixed type: CSM producing both types of responses.

DIFFERENTIAL DIAGNOSIS

All causes of syncope

WORKUP

- CSS is a diagnosis of exclusion.
- Exclude other causes of syncope or presyncope: detailed history, physical examination including orthostatic vital signs, ECG. Other tests should be considered depending on the clinical setting.

Rx TREATMENT

NONPHARMACOLOGIC THERAPY

Reassurance and education are important. Avoid applying neck pressure from tight collars, shaving, or rapid head turning.

ACUTE GENERAL Rx

Treatment will vary according to the type of carotid hypersensitivity response and symptoms present (see "Chronic Rx").

CHRONIC Rx

Therapy is divided into three classes: medical, surgical (carotid denervation), and cardiac pacing.

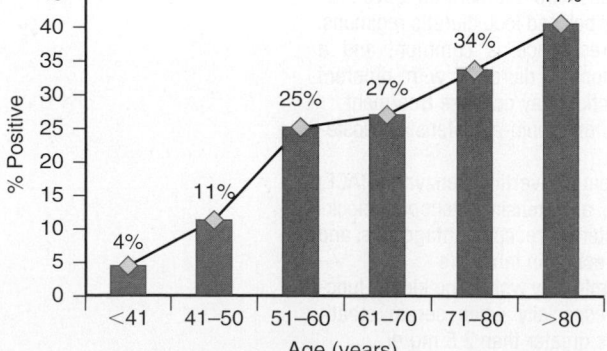

FIGURE 1C-26 Age distribution of patients with carotid sinus syndrome. (From Puggioni E et al: Results and complications of the carotid sinus massage performed according to the "method of symptoms," *Am J Cardiol* 89:599–601, 2002.)

- Surgical therapy has been largely abandoned except in cases of compressing tumors or masses responsible for CSS.
- For infrequent and mildly symptomatic carotid sinus hypersensitivity of either the cardio-inhibitory or vasodepressor type, treatment is generally not necessary.
- Cardiac pacing is indicated in patients with recurrent syncope in whom CSM induces ventricular asystole of more than 3 seconds, especially if accompanied by reproduction of symptoms.

Permanent pacing is not indicated for carotid sinus hypersensitivity with no, or only vague, symptoms.

For symptomatic patients with a vasodepressor response to CSM:

- No medical treatment is proven to be effective
- Drugs, such as vasodilators, that would worsen the response should be discontinued or reduced if feasible
- Permissive hypertension
- Increased fluids (≥2 L) and salt intake (>6 g/day)
- Sympathomimetics: midodrine, titrate from 2.5 to 10 mg tid based on BP and therapeutic response (major side effect in urinary retention in elderly males)
- Serotonin-specific reuptake inhibitors
- Fludrocortisone

- Elastic knee-high or thigh-high stockings
- Carotid sinus denervation

For symptomatic patients with CSS with a mixed response to CSM:

- Combination of dual-chamber permanent pacemaker and agents used to treat vasodepressor response

DISPOSITION

- Up to 50% of the patients have recurrent symptoms.
- No increased mortality rate in patients with idiopathic CSS compared with the general population.

REFERRAL

Cardiology referral is indicated if cardiac testing, such as tilt-table test, or pacemaker placement is being considered.

PEARLS & CONSIDERATIONS

The most common type of CSS is cardio-inhibitory, followed by mixed and vasodepressor responses.

Driving restrictions in the 2009 ESC syncope update and 2006 AHA/ACCF consensus document on syncope are stratified according to whether patients have mild or severe syncope.

Mild carotid sinus syndrome is defined as infrequent mild symptoms (without syncope), with clear precipitating causes (usually standing), warning signs, and infrequent occurrence. For patients with mild sinus hypersensitivity, no driving restrictions are recommended for private or commercial driving.

Severe carotid sinus syndrome is marked by syncope without warning occurring in any position, without precipitating causes and frequent occurrences. For patients with severe hypersensitivity, all driving is prohibited. If symptoms are controlled, driving is permitted 1 to 6 months after, based on the modality of treatment.

COMMENTS

Prognosis depends on the underlying cause.

SUGGESTED READINGS
Available at www.expertconsult.com

RELATED CONTENT

Syncope (Patient Information)
Orthostatic Hypotension (Related Key Topic)
Syncope (Related Key Topic)

AUTHORS: **CHRISTOPHER PICKETT, M.D.,** and **BARRY FINE, M.D., PH.D.**

C

Diseases and Disorders

Carotid Stenosis

BASIC INFORMATION

DEFINITION
Carotid stenosis is narrowing of the arterial lumen within the carotid artery that is typically a result of atherosclerosis.

SYNONYMS
Atherosclerotic disease of the carotid artery

ICD-10CM CODES
I65.29 Occlusion and stenosis of unspecified carotid artery
I65.21 Occlusion and stenosis of right carotid artery
I65.22 Occlusion and stenosis of left carotid artery
I65.23 Occlusion and stenosis of bilateral carotid arteries

EPIDEMIOLOGY & DEMOGRAPHICS
INCIDENCE: 2.2 to 8/1000 persons per yr
PREVALENCE: 1. 1 to 77/100,000 persons; it is estimated that 5/1000 persons aged 50 to 60 yr and 100/1000 persons >80 yr have carotid stenosis >50%. (*Note:* The incidence of carotid stenosis is unknown as screening is not routine. However, the incidence of transient ischemic attack [TIA], a common presenting symptom of carotid stenosis, is well known.)
PREDOMINANT SEX AND AGE: Male/female ratio of 2:1; more common in whites than African Americans and Asians
PEAK INCIDENCE: Peak incidence is between 50 and 60 yr.
GENETICS: Multifactorial; twin studies (monozygous versus dizygous) suggest a familial influence
RISK FACTORS: Hypertension, dyslipidemia, diabetes mellitus, and smoking are the four major risk factors.

PHYSICAL FINDINGS & CLINICAL PRESENTATION
Patients with carotid stenosis are often asymptomatic, but many have the presence of a carotid bruit or TIA.
- Carotid bruit: In general, the presence of a carotid bruit is a better indicator of generalized atherosclerosis and as such, is a better predictor of ischemic heart disease than future stroke.
- TIA: Carotid stenosis is classically heralded by ipsilateral transient monocular blindness (amaurosis fugax), contralateral numbness or weakness, contralateral homonymous hemianopsia, aphasia, or syncope (if bilateral disease is present).

ETIOLOGY
- Atherosclerosis (most common by far).
- Aneurysm.
- Arteritis.
- Carotid dissection.
- Fibromuscular dysplasia.
- Postradiation necrosis.
- Vasospasm.

DIAGNOSIS

DIFFERENTIAL DIAGNOSIS
Aneurysm, arteritis, and carotid dissection.

WORKUP
Systematic history, examination, and diagnostic studies to assess for carotid stenosis and other risk factors of TIA.

LABORATORY TESTS
CBC, basic metabolic panel, fasting lipid profile, PT/international normalized ratio, APTT, CRP.

IMAGING STUDIES
- Four imaging modalities are available for the evaluation of carotid stenosis (Table 1C-5).
- Patients who have neurologic sequelae suggestive of carotid stenosis should be screened via carotid duplex. If carotid stenosis is suspected on carotid duplex, but inconclusive, magnetic resonance angiography, computed tomography angiography, or conventional angiography should be obtained to confirm the degree of stenosis (Fig. 1C-27).
- Screening of asymptomatic patients without any risk factors for atherosclerosis is not routinely recommended.
- When required, carotid duplex is considered the imaging modality of choice for screening.
- Screening with carotid duplex may be considered in asymptomatic patients with carotid bruit and in those with multiple risk factors for atherosclerosis or those with known atherosclerotic disease at other sites such as coronary artery disease, peripheral arterial disease, or abdominal aortic aneurysms.
- Patients identified to have >50% stenosis on carotid duplex may be re-imaged annually to assess progression.

TREATMENT

ACUTE GENERAL Rx
- General medical therapy should be aimed at risk factor reduction. As stated earlier, the major risk factors for carotid stenosis are hypertension, diabetes mellitus, dyslipidemia, and smoking (see "Stroke, Secondary Prevention").
- Antiplatelet therapy: Three antiplatelet options are available for patients with carotid stenosis: ASA, ASA plus dipyridamole, and clopidogrel.

NONPHARMACOLOGIC THERAPY
Carotid endarterectomy (CEA) and carotid angioplasty and stenting (CAS) are the options available. The decision favoring revascularization procedures is dependent upon the presence or absence of symptoms, degree of stenosis, and medical co-morbidities.

TABLE 1C-5 Imaging Modalities for Carotid Stenosis

Imaging Modality	Benefit	Drawback
Cerebral angiography	• Gold standard • Assesses plaque morphology • Assesses presence of collaterals	• Invasive • High cost • 4% incidence rate of complications • 1% incidence rate of serious complications or death
Carotid duplex	• Sensitive in detecting high-grade stenosis (>70%) • Less invasive • Lower cost	• Can be limited by body habitus • Technician dependent • Overestimates degree of stenosis
Magnetic resonance angiography (MRA)	• Sensitive in detecting high-grade stenosis (>70%) • Less operator dependent	• Overestimates degree of stenosis • Cannot be performed in patients who are critically ill, unable to tolerate supine positioning, have pacemaker or other ferromagnetic hardware, or are claustrophobic* • Expensive • Takes much longer to obtain compared with other modalities
Computed tomography angiography (CTA)	• Sensitive for high-grade stenosis	• Contraindicated in patients with serum creatinine concentration >1.5 mg/dl

*One study revealed that ~17% of patients are unable to tolerate MRA secondary to claustrophobia or are unable to lie still for procedure.

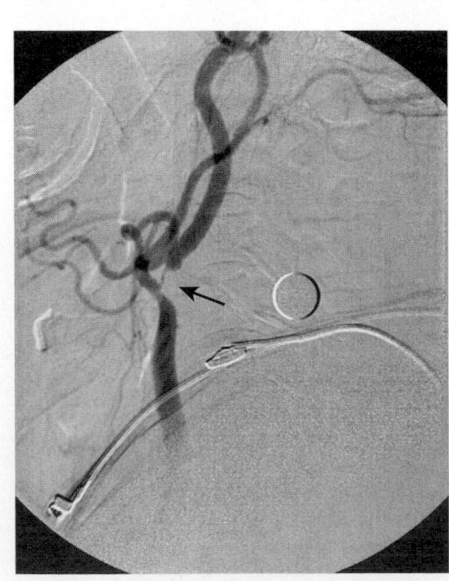

FIGURE 1C-27 Conventional angiography demonstrating severe stenosis of the internal carotid artery at the bifurcation.

C

ASYMPTOMATIC CAROTID STENOSIS

With significant improvements in medical therapy, the benefit of surgical revascularization of the carotids in asymptomatic patients with either CEA or CAS is not well established.

According to the most recent guidelines, revascularization procedures may be considered in asymptomatic patients with >70% stenosis if the anticipated perioperative risk is low, but this should be done only after considering their medical comorbidities, life expectancy, and after discussing the risks and benefits in detail with the patients.

SYMPTOMATIC CAROTID STENOSIS

In patients who have suffered a nondisabling ischemic stroke or TIA in the preceding 6 months, surgical revascularization by CEA is recommended if the degree of stenosis is >70% by noninvasive imaging or >50% by catheter angiogram and if the anticipated rate of perioperative stroke or mortality is <6%.

All patients undergoing CEA should be started on aspirin (ASA; 81 or 325 mg daily) before surgery and this should be continued indefinitely.

CAS can be an alternative to CEA in select patients considered to be at high surgical risk or with unfavorable neck anatomy for surgery.

CEA is preferred over CAS in older patients.

For patients undergoing CAS, dual antiplatelet therapy is recommended for a minimum of 30 days.

When feasible, early revascularization within 14 days might be undertaken unless there are definite contraindications.

Surgical revascularization is not recommended in <50% stenosis, total occlusion or in patients with major disabling strokes.

In patients who are considered high surgical risk for either CEA or CAS, the role of medical therapy alone compared with surgical revascularization is not well established.

DISPOSITION

Disposition and prognosis depend on several variables (Table 1C-6): the degree of stenosis, the presence of symptoms, medication compliance, and the type of intervention (if any).

PEARLS & CONSIDERATIONS

There are ongoing studies concerning the best treatment of patients with carotid artery stenosis. Based on the results of these studies, guidelines may change rapidly.

SPECIAL CONSIDERATION

Some studies have shown that in patients with bilateral hemodynamically significant stenosis (>70%), reduction of blood pressure resulted in worse outcome in terms of stroke. These patients would likely be candidates for CEA.

Carotid artery occlusion (100% blockage), for which there is no routine treatment, is being reexamined in the national Carotid Occlusion Surgery Study (http://www.cosstrial.org). Consider referring symptomatic carotid occlusion patients for consideration of this study.

PREVENTION

Prevention of carotid stenosis should be guided at pursuing a healthy lifestyle and management of risk factors for development of atherosclerosis.

PATIENT/FAMILY EDUCATION

Patients should be counseled on pursuing a healthy lifestyle to include exercise and smoking cessation. In addition, patients should take an active role in controlling blood pressure and blood glucose. Further educational materials can be found online at: http://www.strokecenter.org/education.

 **EVIDENCE**

Available at www.expertconsult.com

SUGGESTED READINGS

Available at www.expertconsult.com

RELATED CONTENT

Carotid Stenosis (Patient Information)
Transient Ischemic Attack (Related Key Topic)

AUTHOR: **PRASHANTH KRISHNAMOHAN, M.B.B.S., M.D.**

Diseases and Disorders

I

TABLE 1C-6 Carotid Stenosis Management

Degree of Carotid Stenosis	<50%	50%-69%	70%-99%
Asymptomatic	• Medical management	• Medical management • Inconclusive evidence base to favor surgical treatment. May be considered in select patients with >60% stenosis.*	• Medical management • CEA in highly selected patients*
Symptomatic	• Medical management	• CEA • CAS can be an alternative	• CEA • CAS can be an alternative

CAS, Carotid artery stenting; *CEA,* carotid endarterectomy.
*CEA can be considered in asymptomatic patients with >70% stenosis if the anticipated rate of perioperative complications (Stroke, MI, and death) is low, after considering their life expectancy (minimum 5 years), medical co-morbidities and after a thorough discussion of the risks and benefits involved with the patients and their families.

 BASIC INFORMATION

DEFINITION

Carpal tunnel syndrome (CTS) is a compressive neuropathy of the median nerve as it passes under the transverse carpal ligament at the wrist (Figs. E1C-28 and E1C-29). It is the most common entrapment neuropathy.

SYNONYMS

CTS

ICD-10CM CODES
G56.0 Carpal tunnel syndrome, unspecified upper limb
G56.01 Carpal tunnel syndrome, right upper limb
G56.02 Carpal tunnel syndrome, left upper limb

EPIDEMIOLOGY & DEMOGRAPHICS

INCIDENCE: 3.8% of the general population (most common entrapment neuropathy)
PREVALENT AGE: 30 to 60 yr
PREVALENT SEX: Females are affected two to five times as often as males.

PHYSICAL FINDINGS & CLINICAL PRESENTATION

- Pain, paresthesia in 1st, 2nd, 3rd, and lateral ½ of 4th fingers, worse at night.
- Tinel's sign at wrist (Fig. 1C-30): tapping lightly over the median nerve on the volar surface of the wrist produces a tingling sensation radiating from the wrist to the hand.
- Phalen's sign (Fig. 1C-31): reproduction of symptoms after 1 min of gentle, unforced wrist flexion.

FIGURE 1C-30 Tinel's sign. The wrist is held in extension while gentle percussion is performed over and just proximal to the transverse carpal ligament. (From Hochberg MC et al: *Rheumatology,* ed 5, St Louis, 2011, Mosby.)

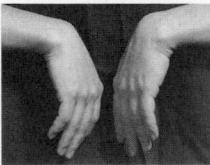

FIGURE 1C-31 Phalen's (wrist flexion) test. With the wrists held in unforced flexion for 30 to 60 seconds, a positive test reproduces or worsens the patient's symptoms. (From Hochberg MC et al: *Rheumatology,* ed 5, St Louis, 2011, Mosby.)

- Carpal compression test: direct pressure over the patient's carpal tunnel for 30 sec elicits symptoms.
- Thenar atrophy in longstanding cases with weakness of thumb abduction and opposition.
- Findings may be bilateral in up to 65% of patients.

ETIOLOGY

- Idiopathic in most cases
  1. Increased intracarpal tunnel pressure
  2. Ischemia, friction, or angulation of median nerve
- Space-occupying lesions in carpal tunnel (tenosynovitis, ganglia, aberrant muscles)
- Can be associated with diabetes, hypothyroidism, pregnancy, connective tissue diseases, acromegaly, amyloidosis
- Repetitive strain or job-related mechanical overuse may be a risk factor

 DIAGNOSIS

DIFFERENTIAL DIAGNOSIS

- Cervical radiculopathy
- Chronic tendinitis
- Other arthritides
- Complex regional pain syndrome
- Brachial plexopathy, thoracic outlet syndrome
- Polyneuropathy
- Other entrapment neuropathies
- Traumatic wrist injuries
- Vascular disorders (Raynaud syndrome)
- Cervical myelopathy
- Pronator teres syndrome
- Anterior interosseous syndrome

IMAGING STUDIES

Carpal tunnel syndrome is a clinical diagnosis but imaging may assist workup in uncertain situations. Musculoskeletal ultrasound has been very effective in supporting the diagnosis and may help identify the structural cause of nerve compression. Roentgenograms or MRI may be helpful in ruling out other conditions.

ELECTRODIAGNOSTIC STUDIES

Nerve conduction velocity tests (NCS) demonstrate impaired sensory conduction across the carpal tunnel. Electromyography may show active denervation muscle potentials. Specificity of NCS and electromyography for CTS is >95%, and sensitivity is >85%

 TREATMENT

ACUTE GENERAL Rx

- Activity modification
- Nocturnal wrist splint
- No evidence for effectiveness of NSAIDs
- Corticosteroid injection of carpal canal on ulnar side of palmaris longus tendon proximal to wrist crease (Figs. E1C-32 and E1C-33): can be done with palpation guidance or under ultrasound guidance. A recent

trial[1] has shown that methylprednisolone injections for CTS have significant benefits in relieving symptoms at 10 wk and reducing the rate of surgery 1 yr after treatment, but 3 out of 4 patients had surgery within 1 yr.
- Low-dose oral corticosteroids can be considered.
- Short-term benefit from ultrasound therapy (physical therapy modality)
- Ergonomic keyboards

DISPOSITION

Clinical course may have remissions and exacerbations. Some may progress from intermittent to persistent sensory complaints (numbness, tingling, paresthesia) and then to motor symptoms. In pregnancy, symptoms usually resolve spontaneously weeks after delivery.

REFERRAL

Surgical referral is needed if conservative treatment fails. It is usually reserved for severe symptoms or presence of weakness/thenar atrophy. Surgery (sectioning of transverse carpal ligament) to release pressure on the median nerve is done by open or endoscopic approach, with good long-term results. Carpal tunnel release is one of the most common surgeries performed, with approximately 400,000 conducted per year.

⚠ PEARLS & CONSIDERATIONS

- The sensory changes of carpal tunnel syndrome spare the thenar eminence. This distinctive pattern occurs because the palmar sensory cutaneous branch of the median nerve arises proximal to the wrist, passing over, rather than through, the tunnel.
- Role of repetitive hand or wrist use and workplace factors in the development of carpal tunnel syndrome remains controversial.

EBM EVIDENCE

Available at www.expertconsult.com

SUGGESTED READINGS

Available at www.expertconsult.com

RELATED CONTENT

Carpal Tunnel Syndrome (Patient Information)

AUTHOR: **CANDICE YUVIENCO, M.D.**

[1]Methylprednisolone injections for the carpal tunnel syndrome: a randomized, placebo-controlled trial, *Ann Int Med* 159:309-317, 2013.

ℹ️ BASIC INFORMATION

DEFINITION

Cataracts are the clouding and opacification of the normally clear crystalline lens of the eye. The opacity may occur in the cortex, the nucleus of the lens, or the posterior subcapsular region, but it is usually in a combination of areas.

SYNONYMS

Congenital cataracts (e.g., from rubella)
Metabolic cataracts (e.g., caused by diabetes)
Hereditary cataracts
Age-related senile cataracts (nuclear sclerotic and cortical cataracts)
Traumatic cataracts
Toxic or drug-induced cataracts (e.g., caused by steroids)
Lenticular opacities

ICD-10CM CODES

H26.9	Cataract, unspecified
H25.0	Senile incipient cataract
H25.1	Senile nuclear cataract
H26.0	Infantile, juvenile and presenile cataract
E11.36	Type 2 diabetes mellitus with diabetic cataract
E13.36	Other specified diabetes mellitus with diabetic cataract
H25.011	Cortical age-related cataract, right eye
H25.012	Cortical age-related cataract, left eye
H25.013	Cortical age-related cataract, bilateral
H25.019	Cortical age-related cataract, unspecified eye
H25.039	Anterior subcapsular polar age-related cataract, unspecified eye
H25.049	Posterior subcapsular polar age-related cataract, unspecified eye
H25.099	Other age-related incipient cataract, unspecified eye
H25.10	Age-related nuclear cataract, unspecified eye
H25.9	Unspecified age-related cataract
H26.019	Infantile and juvenile cortical, lamellar, or zonular cataract, unspecified eye
H26.039	Infantile and juvenile nuclear cataract, unspecified eye
H26.041	Anterior subcapsular polar infantile and juvenile cataract, right eye
H26.042	Anterior subcapsular polar infantile and juvenile cataract, left eye
H26.043	Anterior subcapsular polar infantile and juvenile cataract, bilateral
H26.069	Combined forms of infantile and juvenile cataract, unspecified eye
H26.09	Other infantile and juvenile cataract
H26.101	Unspecified traumatic cataract, right eye
H26.102	Unspecified traumatic cataract, left eye
H26.103	Unspecified traumatic cataract, bilateral
H26.109	Unspecified traumatic cataract, unspecified eye
H26.8	Other specified cataract
H26.9	Unspecified cataract

EPIDEMIOLOGY & DEMOGRAPHICS

INCIDENCE (IN U.S.): Most common cause of treatable blindness; cataract removal is the most frequent surgical procedure in patients >65 yr (1.3 million operations per year, with an annual cost of approximately $3 billion). By year 2020 more than 30 million Americans will have cataracts. Of Americans >40 yr, 20.5 million (17.2%) have cataracts. Of these, 5% have had surgery.

PEAK INCIDENCE:

- In early life: congenital and hereditary causes predominant; consider drug related, diabetes, and trauma
- In older age group: senile cataracts (after 40 yr)

PREDOMINANT AGE: Elderly; some stage of cataract development is present in >50% of persons 65 to 74 yr and in 65% of those >75 yr. Lens opacification and sclerosis begins around age 40 yr and then usually progresses either slowly or rapidly depending on individual and health.

GENETICS: Hereditary with syndromes such as galactosemia, homocystinuria, diabetes

PHYSICAL FINDINGS & CLINICAL PRESENTATION

- Cloudiness and opacification of the crystalline lens of the eye (Figs. 1C-34 and 1C-35)
- Decrease or absence of the red reflex (important in pediatric ages, since visual acuity is more difficult to assess)
- Painless decreased visual acuity (difficulty reading, seeing road signs; usually gradual, over months to years)
- Glare and decreased night vision (early symptom: difficulty with night driving)

ETIOLOGY

- Heredity
- Trauma

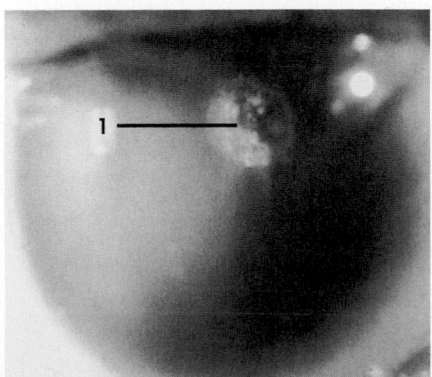

FIGURE 1C-34 The central location of a posterior subcapsular cataract (1). (From Palay D [ed]: *Ophthalmology for the primary care physician*, St Louis, 1997, Mosby.)

- Age related
- Drug related (e.g., corticosteroids, smoking)
- Radiation (UV B and ionizing)
- Congenital (genetic, metabolic, or infections)
- Inflammatory (e.g., history of uveitis or previous ocular surgery)
- Diabetes
- Collagen vascular disease

🅳🆇 DIAGNOSIS

DIFFERENTIAL DIAGNOSIS

- Corneal lesions
- Retinal lesions, detached retina, tumors
- Vitreous disease, chronic inflammation

WORKUP

- Complete eye examination, including visual acuity and measurement of refractive error, slit lamp examination, dilated funduscopic examination, and brightness acuity testing
- Complete physical examination for other underlying causes

LABORATORY TESTS

- Rarely, urinary amino acid screening and central nervous system imaging studies with congenital cataracts
- Fasting glucose in young adults with cataracts
- Diabetes, collagen vascular disease, other metabolic diseases in younger patients
- Genetic and hereditary evaluation

🆁🆇 TREATMENT

There is no evidence that antioxidants or drugs will slow or treat cataracts.

NONPHARMACOLOGIC THERAPY

- Wait until vision is compromised before doing surgery
- Plan cataract removal with intraocular lens implantation when vision is compromised and limiting activities of daily living, such as driving at night or reading. Removal of the cataract should be expected to improve the ability of the patient to perform these activities. Another indication to remove cataracts might be to improve the examination view for treatment and assessment of retinal diseases.
- Decision for timing of surgery depends upon patient complaints, best corrected visual acuity (e.g., 20/50), and glare measurements (brightness acuity test decreases vision significantly).

ACUTE GENERAL Rx

None necessary except when acute glaucoma or inflammation occurs

CHRONIC Rx

- Change glasses as cataracts develop.
- Myopia is common, and glasses can be adjusted until surgery is contemplated.

DISPOSITION

Refer if sight is compromised or the eye is red or inflamed.

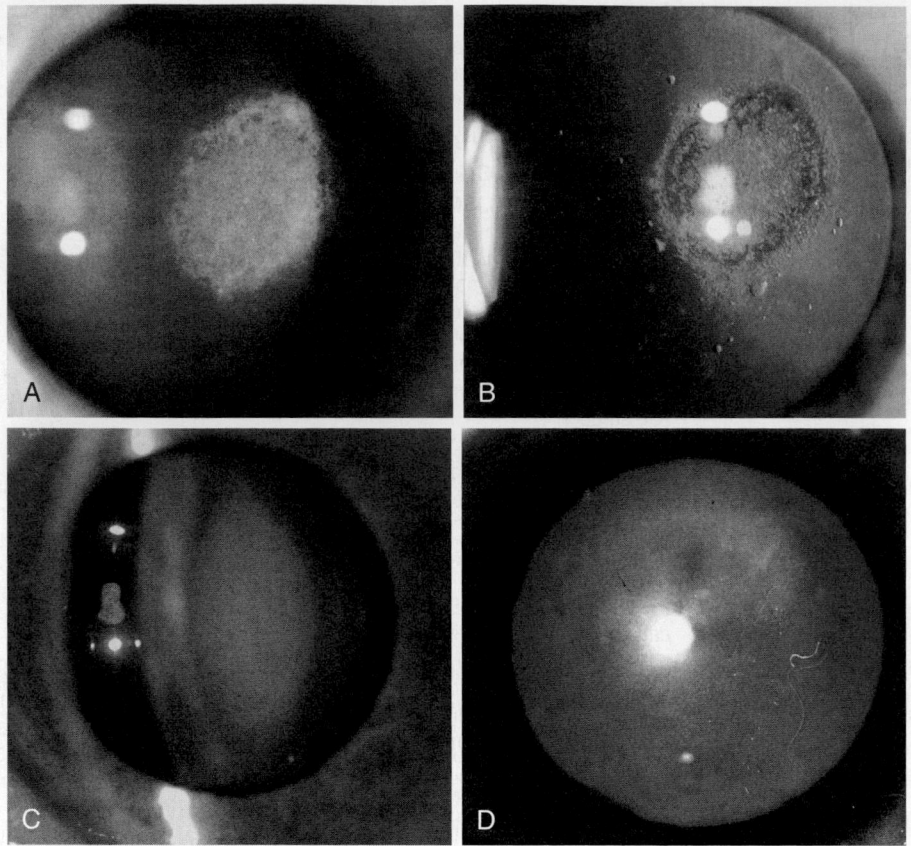

FIGURE 1C-35 Age-related cataract. A, Posterior subcapsular. **B,** On retroillumination. **C,** Nuclear. **D,** On retroillumination. (Courtesy Schuman V et al: from Lens and glaucoma. In *Rapid diagnosis in ophthalmology,* St Louis, 2008, Mosby.)

REFERRAL

Refer to ophthalmologist for evaluation for extraction when vision is compromised (see "Nonpharmacologic Therapy").

! PEARLS & CONSIDERATIONS

- Patients want to know five things about cataracts:
  1. Chance for vision improvement
  2. When vision will improve
  3. Risk from surgery (such as infection, hemorrhage, retinal detachment, corneal problems)
  4. Effect of surgery, including reduction of refractive errors
  5. Types of complications
- Men planning cataract surgery should, if feasible, delay the use of alpha blockers until after surgery has been completed. The risk of intraoperative floppy iris syndrome is substantial among men taking tamsulosin. This is often unavoidable, and discontinuation of alpha blockers does not help, although intraoperative techniques have improved to make floppy iris syndrome less complicated.

 **EVIDENCE**

Available at www.expertconsult.com

SUGGESTED READINGS

Available at www.expertconsult.com

RELATED CONTENT

Cataracts (Patient Information)

AUTHOR: **R. SCOTT HOFFMAN, M.D.**

Diseases
and Disorders

BASIC INFORMATION

DEFINITION

Cat-scratch disease (CSD) is an infectious disease consisting of gradually enlarging regional lymphadenopathy occurring after contact with a feline. Atypical presentations are characterized by a variety of neurologic manifestations as well as granulomatous involvement of the eye, liver, spleen, and bone. The disease is usually self-limiting, and recovery is complete; however, patients with atypical presentations, especially if immunocompromised, may suffer significant morbidity and mortality.

SYNONYMS

Cat-scratch fever
Benign inoculation lymphoreticulosis
Nonbacterial regional lymphadenitis

ICD-10CM CODES
A28.1 Cat-scratch disease

EPIDEMIOLOGY & DEMOGRAPHICS

PREVALENCE: Unknown
INCIDENCE (IN U.S.):
- 9 to 10 cases per 100,000 persons per year (22,000 cases per year)
- Majority of reported cases occur in persons <21 yrs

PEAK INCIDENCE: August through January

PHYSICAL FINDINGS & CLINICAL PRESENTATION

- Classic, most common finding: regional lymphadenopathy occurring within 2 wk of a scratch or contact with felines; usually a new kitten in the household
- Tender, swollen lymph nodes most commonly found in the head and neck (Fig. E1C-36), followed by the axilla and the epitrochlear, inguinal, and femoral areas
- Erythematous overlying skin, showing signs of suppuration from involved lymph nodes
- On careful examination, evidence of cutaneous inoculation in the form of a nonpruritic, slightly tender pustule or papule
- Fever in most patients
- Malaise and headache in fewer than a third of patients
- Atypical presentations in fewer than 15% of cases
  1. Usually in association with lymphadenopathy and a low-grade or frank fever (>101 °F, >38.3 °C)
  2. Include granulomatous involvement of the conjunctiva (Parinaud's oculoglandular syndrome) and focal masses in the liver, spleen, and mesenteric nodes
- CNS involvement: neuroretinitis, encephalopathy, encephalitis, transverse myelitis, seizure activity, and coma
- Osteomyelitis in adults and children
- Can be a cause of culture-negative endocarditis
- In HIV-infected and other immunocompromised patients, Bartonella henselae is the cause of bacillary angiomatous and peliosis hepatis

ETIOLOGY

- Major cause: Bartonella henselae, possibly Afipia felis and Bartonella clarridgeiae
- Mode of transmission: predominantly by direct inoculation through the scratch, bite, or lick of a cat, especially a kitten
- Also can be transmitted by flea bite (with the flea obtaining the bacteria from a bacteremic cat); rarely after exposure to a dog, probably secondary to flea bites
- Approximately 2 wk after introduction of the bacteria into the host, regional lymphatic tissues displaying granulomatous infiltration associated with gradual hypertrophy
- Possible dissemination to distant sites (e.g., liver, spleen, and bone), usually characterized by focal masses or discrete parenchymal lesions

DIAGNOSIS

DIFFERENTIAL DIAGNOSIS

Granulomas of this syndrome must be differentiated from those associated with:
- Tularemia
- Tuberculosis or other mycobacterial infections
- Brucellosis
- Sarcoidosis
- Sporotrichosis or other fungal diseases
- Toxoplasmosis
- Lymphogranuloma venereum
- Benign and malignant tumors such as lymphoma

WORKUP

Diagnosis should be considered in patients who present with a predominant complaint of gradually enlarging regional (focal) lymphadenopathy, often with fever and a recent history of having contact with a cat. A primary ulcer at the site of the cat scratch may or may not be present at the time lymphadenopathy becomes manifest.

LABORATORY TESTS

- Serologies: An IFA or EIA Bartonella serology (titer ≥1:64) is diagnostic. A PCR assay on tissue or blood is also available.
- Lymph node biopsy: granulomatous inflammation consistent with CSD.
- Warthin-Starry silver stain on biopsy can identify the bacteria.
- Histopathologically, Warthin-Starry silver stain has been used to identify the bacillus.
- Culture: B. henselae is a fastidious, slow-growing, gram-negative rod that requires specific culture techniques for tissue or blood.
- Routine laboratory findings:
  1. Mild leukocytosis or leukopenia
  2. Infrequent eosinophilia
  3. Elevated ESR or CRP
- Abnormalities of bilirubin excretion and elevated hepatic transaminases are usually secondary to hepatic obstruction by granuloma, mass, or lymph node.
- In patients with neurologic manifestations, lumbar puncture usually reveals normal CSF, although there may be a mild pleocytosis and modest elevation in protein.
- CSD skin test is no longer used for clinical purposes.

TREATMENT

NONPHARMACOLOGIC THERAPY

- Warm compresses to the affected nodes
- In cases of encephalitis or coma: supportive care

ACUTE GENERAL Rx

- This disease is typically self-limited and generally resolves within 2 to 6 months. Most studies show no additional benefit from antibiotic therapy.
- It would be prudent to treat severely ill patients, especially if immunocompromised, with antibiotic therapy, because these patients tend to suffer dissemination of infection and increased morbidity.
- Bartonella is usually sensitive to a 5-day course of azithromycin (500 mg on day 1 followed by 250 mg for 4 days for weight >45.5 kg; 10 mg/kg on day 1 followed by 5 mg/kg for 4 days for weight <45.5 kg) or alternatively tetracycline, sulfa, and the quinolones can be used for 7 to 10 days.
- Hepatosplenic disease, neuroretinitis, and endocarditis require longer courses of therapy..
- Antipyretics and NSAIDs may also be used for lymphadenitis.

DISPOSITION

Overall prognosis is good.

REFERRAL

- For diagnostic aspiration or excision in presence of regional lymphadenopathy, bone lesions, and mesenteric lymph nodes and organs
- Infectious diseases specialist for organ involvement including endocarditis
- To ophthalmologist for ocular granulomas

PEARLS & CONSIDERATIONS

COMMENTS

- A presentation of this syndrome, especially in patients with HIV infection or impaired cellular immunity, may be fever of unknown origin.
- Hepatic and splenic granulomas, coronary valve infections may offer few physical clues to diagnosis, emphasizing the need for a complete history.
- CSD should be considered in the differential diagnosis of school-aged children presenting with status epilepticus.
- Chronically immunocompromised patients considering the acquisition of a young feline should be made aware of the possible risk of infection.
- No signs of illness may be apparent in bacteremic kittens.

SUGGESTED READINGS

Available at www.expertconsult.com

RELATED CONTENT

Cat-Scratch Disease (Patient Information)

AUTHOR: **GLENN G. FORT, M.D., M.P.H.**

 **BASIC INFORMATION**

DEFINITION

Cavernous sinus thrombosis (CST) is a late complication of facial or paranasal sinus infection, resulting in thrombosis of the cavernous sinus and inflammation of its surrounding anatomic structures, including cranial nerves III, IV, V (ophthalmic and maxillary branch), and VI, and the internal carotid artery.

SYNONYMS

Cavernous sinus thrombosis (CST)
Intracranial venous sinus thrombosis or thrombophlebitis
Dural sinus thrombosis

ICD-10CM CODES
G08 Intracranial and intraspinal phlebitis and thrombophlebitis

EPIDEMIOLOGY & DEMOGRAPHICS

- CST is rare in the postantibiotic era.
- Before antibiotics the mortality rate was 80% to 100%.
- With antibiotics and early diagnosis, mortality rates have fallen to ~20%.
- Reported morbidity rates have also declined from between 50% and 70% to about 20% to 30% with advances in imaging modalities and aggressive medical care.

PHYSICAL FINDINGS & CLINICAL PRESENTATION

- Can be either an acute and fulminant disease or an indolent and subacute presentation.
- Septic cases of CST commonly present with high-grade fever (picket fence pattern) and signs of sepsis.
- Headache, although not specific, is the most common presenting symptom and may precede fever and periorbital edema by several days. Elderly patients, however, may only demonstrate alteration in mental status without antecedent headache. The triad of unilateral or bilateral progressive chemosis, periorbital edema, and proptosis with headache is a classical presentation in patients with CST. These signs and symptoms are related to the anatomic structures affected within the cavernous sinus, notably cranial nerves III to VI, as well as impaired venous drainage from the orbit and eye.

Other common signs and symptoms include:
- Ptosis.
- Cranial nerve palsies (III, IV, V, VI).
  1. Ophthalmoplegia caused by involvement of cranial nerves III, IV, and VI is present in most cases. Sixth nerve palsy can occur early in some cases of septic CST, especially when originating from the sphenoid sinus owing to its anatomic proximity.
  2. Hypoesthesia or hyperesthesia of the ophthalmic and maxillary branch of the fifth nerve is common. Periorbital sensory loss and impaired corneal reflex may be noted.

- Papilledema, retinal hemorrhages, and decreased visual acuity progressing to blindness may occur from venous congestion within the retina.
- Pupil may be dilated and sluggishly reactive.
- Headache with nuchal rigidity and changes in mental status may occur if the infection spreads intracranially to the meninges and brain parenchyma.
- Infection can spread to the contralateral cavernous sinus through the intercavernous sinuses within 24 to 48 hr of initial presentation.
- Patients may also develop signs and symptoms of pituitary insufficiency.

ETIOLOGY

- CST most commonly results from contiguous spread of an infection from the sinuses (sphenoid, ethmoid, or frontal) or the medial third of the face (areas around the eyes and nose that drain to the ophthalmic vein). Nasal furuncles are the most common facial infection to produce this complication. Less-common primary sites of infection include dental abscess, tonsils, soft palate, middle ear, or orbit (orbital cellulitis).
- CST also can result from hematogenous spread of infection to the cavernous sinus by the superior and inferior ophthalmic veins or through the lateral and sigmoid sinuses. It can spread in a retrograde direction depending on the pressure gradients, because the dural sinuses are valveless.
- *Staphylococcus aureus* is the most commonly identified pathogen, found in 60% to 70% of the cases.
- *Streptococcus* is the second leading cause.
- Gram-negative rods and anaerobes may also lead to CST.
- Rarely, *Aspergillus fumigatus* and mucormycosis cause CST.
- Risk factors for dural sinus thrombosis include venous hypercoagulable disorders, infections (see above), trauma, malignancies, systemic inflammatory disorders, pregnancy, and dehydration.

Dx **DIAGNOSIS**

- The diagnosis of CST is made by clinical suspicion and confirmed by appropriate imaging studies.
- Proptosis, ptosis, chemosis, and cranial nerve palsy beginning in one eye and progressing to the other eye establish the diagnosis.

DIFFERENTIAL DIAGNOSIS

- Orbital or periorbital cellulitis.
- Internal carotid artery aneurysm or fistula.
- Cerebrovascular disease.
- Migraine headache.
- Allergic blepharitis.
- Thyroid ophthalmopathy.
- Orbital neoplasm.
- Meningitis.
- Epidural and subdural infections.
- Epidural and subdural hematoma.
- Subarachnoid hemorrhage.

- Acute angle-closure glaucoma.
- Trauma.

WORKUP

CST is a clinical diagnosis, with laboratory tests and imaging studies confirming the clinical impression.

LABORATORY TESTS

- Complete blood count, erythrocyte sedimentation rate, blood cultures, and sinus cultures help establish and identify an infectious primary source. Metabolic panel to look for electrolyte imbalances in cases of suspected pituitary involvement (DI/SIADH).
- Lumbar puncture (LP) helps to distinguish CST from more localized processes (e.g., sinusitis, orbital cellulitis). LP reveals inflammatory cells in 75% of cases. In half of these cases, the cerebrospinal fluid profile is typical for a parameningeal focus (high white blood cells with polymorphonuclear and/or mononuclear cells, normal glucose, normal protein, culture negative), and in one third may be similar to that of a bacterial meningitis.

IMAGING STUDIES

- MRI with gadolinium, including magnetic resonance angiography and magnetic resonance venogram (Fig. 1C-37), is more sensitive than CT scan and is the imaging study of choice to diagnose CST. Findings may include deformity of the internal carotid artery within the cavernous sinus and an obvious signal hyperintensity within thrombosed vascular sinuses.
- Noncontrast CT scan of the head and orbits may demonstrate increased density in the region of the cavernous sinus but has relatively low sensitivity. Contrast-enhanced CT scan may reveal underlying sinusitis, thickening of the superior ophthalmic vein, and irregular filling defects within the cavernous sinus; however, findings may be normal early in the disease course.

Rx **TREATMENT**

NONPHARMACOLOGIC THERAPY

Recognizing the primary source of infection (i.e., facial cellulitis, middle ear, and sinus infections) and treating the primary source expeditiously is the best way to prevent CST.

ACUTE GENERAL Rx

- Appropriate therapy should take into account the primary source of infection as well as possible associated complications such as brain abscess, meningitis, or subdural empyema.
- Broad-spectrum intravenous antibiotics are used as empiric therapy until a definite pathogen is found. Treatment should include vancomycin to cover hospital or community-acquired methicillin-resistant *Staphylococcus aureus* or resistant *Streptococcus pneumoniae* plus a third- or fourth-generation cephalosporin:

1. Vancomycin (1 g q12h with normal renal function) plus either ceftriaxone (2 g q12h) or cefepime (2 g q8 to 12h).
2. Metronidazole 500 mg IV q6h should be added if anaerobic bacterial infection is suspected (dental or sinus infection).

- Most experts recommend anticoagulation with heparin after the diagnosis is confirmed, unless surgical intervention is planned or there is evidence of an expanding hematoma. Spontaneous intracranial hemorrhage should first be ruled out before initiating heparin therapy. Early heparinization has been suggested in patients with unilateral CST to prevent clot propagation. Coumadin therapy should be avoided in the acute phase of the illness, but should ultimately be instituted to achieve an INR of 2 to 3 and continued until the infection, symptoms, and signs of CST have resolved or significantly improved. Retrospective case reports and case series have demonstrated a favorable outcome in terms of decreased mortality and morbidity in the anticoagulated patients.
- Steroid therapy is also controversial but may prove helpful in reducing cranial nerve dysfunction or when progression to pituitary insufficiency occurs. Corticosteroids should only be instituted after appropriate antibiotic

coverage. Dexamethasone 10 mg q6h is the treatment of choice.
- Emergent surgical drainage with sphenoidotomy is indicated if the primary site of infection is believed to be the sphenoid sinus.

CHRONIC Rx

- Patients with CST are usually treated with prolonged courses (3 to 4 wk) of IV antibiotics. If there is evidence of complications such as intracranial suppuration, 6 to 8 wk of total therapy may be warranted.
- All patients should be monitored for signs of complicated infection, continued sepsis, or septic emboli while antibiotic therapy is being administered. Relapse of septic CST can occur after an initial improvement weeks after stopping antibiotic treatment.

DISPOSITION

- CST can be a life-threatening, rapidly progressive infectious disease with high morbidity and mortality rates (30%) despite antibiotic use. Morbidity and mortality rates are increased in cases of sphenoid sinus infection.
- Complications of untreated CST include extension of thrombus to other dural sinuses, carotid thrombosis with concomitant strokes,

subdural empyema, brain abscess, or meningitis. Septic embolization may also occur to the lungs, resulting in acute respiratory distress syndrome, pulmonary abscess, empyema, and pneumothorax.
- Thirty percent of treated patients develop long-term sequelae, including cranial nerve palsies, blindness, pituitary insufficiency, and hemiparesis.

REFERRAL

If suspected, CST should be considered a medical emergency. Depending on source of infection, appropriate consultation should be made (i.e., ear-nose-throat, ophthalmology, and infectious disease).

PEARLS & CONSIDERATIONS

COMMENTS

CST is a medical emergency and should be suspected with progressing chemosis, proptosis, and cranial neuropathy in a patient with headaches with or without fever.

The anatomy of the cavernous sinus explains the clinical findings: CS lies just above and lateral to the sphenoid sinus and drains the middle portion of the face by the superior and inferior ophthalmic veins; cranial nerves III, IV, V, and VI pass alongside or through the cavernous sinus.

SUGGESTED READINGS
Available at www.expertconsult.com

RELATED CONTENT
Cavernous Sinus Thrombosis (Patient Information)

AUTHOR: **PRASHANTH KRISHNAMOHAN, M.B.B.S., M.D.**

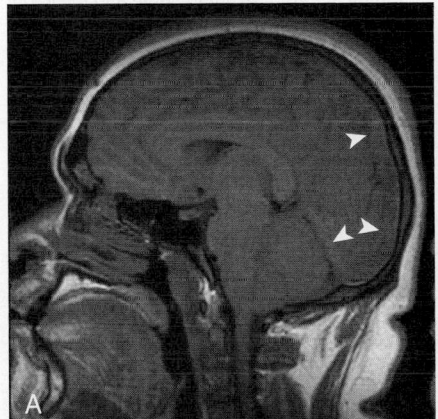
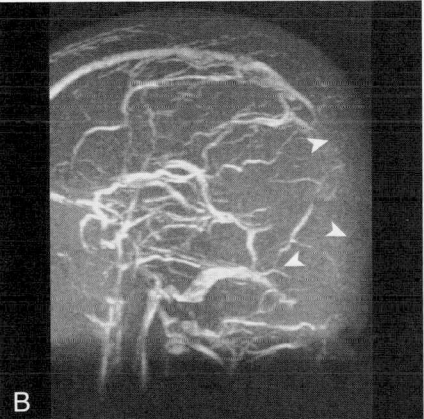
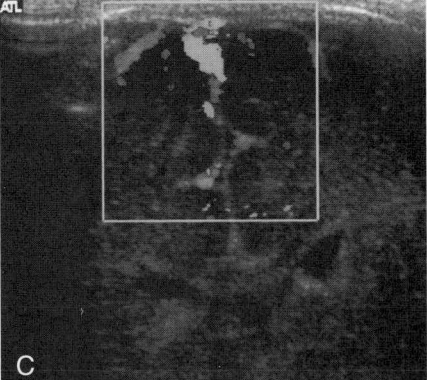

FIGURE 1C-37 Superior sagittal sinus (SSS) thrombosis on magnetic resonance venogram (MRV). Sagittal T1 magnetic resonance imaging **(A)** shows intermediate signal intensity in sagittal and straight sinuses *(arrowheads)*. No flow is seen on MRV **(B)** in these vessels *(arrowheads)*, which is consistent with thrombosis. Color Doppler evacuation **(C)** of the SSS in another 6-mo-old patient with suspected thrombosis demonstrated a patent SSS with normal draining cortical veins. (From Fuhrman BP et al: *Pediatric critical care,* ed 4, Philadelphia, 2011, Saunders.)

BASIC INFORMATION

DEFINITION

Celiac disease is a chronic autoimmune disease characterized by malabsorption and diarrhea precipitated by ingestion of food products containing gluten. Gluten is a protein complex found in wheat, rye, and barley.

SYNONYMS

Gluten-sensitive enteropathy
Celiac sprue
Nontropical sprue

ICD-10CM CODES
K90.0 Celiac disease

EPIDEMIOLOGY & DEMOGRAPHICS

- The prevalence of celiac disease is 0.5% to 1% in the general population in North America and Western Europe and 5% in high-risk groups such as first-degree relatives of persons with the disease. The prevalence of celiac disease in the U.S. has increased fourfold over the past three decades. Worldwide celiac disease affects 0.6% to 1% of the population. Celiac disease is significantly more common in persons with type 1 DM and is associated with greater risk of retinopathy and nephropathy in this population.
- Incidence is highest during infancy and the first 36 mo of life (after introduction of foods containing gluten), in the third decade (frequently associated with pregnancy and severe anemia during pregnancy), and in the seventh decade.
- There is a slight female predominance.
- The average age of diagnosis is in the fifth decade of life.
- The risk for celiac disease is 5% to 10% in newborn children of parents with the disease and nearly 20% in siblings.
- It is estimated that only 10% to 15% of persons with celiac disease in the U.S. have been diagnosed.

PHYSICAL FINDINGS & CLINICAL PRESENTATION

- Physical examination may be entirely within normal limits.
- Weight loss, dyspepsia, short stature, and failure to thrive may be noted in children and infants (Fig. 1C-38).
- Weight loss, fatigue, and diarrhea are common in adults.
- Abdominal pain, nausea, and vomiting are unusual.
- Pallor as a result of iron-deficiency anemia is common.

- Atypical forms of the disease are being increasingly recognized and include osteoporosis, short stature, anemia, infertility, and neurologic problems. Manifestations of calcium deficiency, such as tetany and seizures, are rare and can be exacerbated by coexistent magnesium deficiency.
- Angular cheilitis, aphthous ulcers, atopic dermatitis, and dermatitis herpetiformis are frequently associated with celiac disease.
- Table 1C-7 summarizes the clinical spectrum of celiac disease.

ETIOLOGY

- Celiac sprue is considered an autoimmune-type disease, with tissue transglutaminase (tTG) suggested as a major autoantigen. It results from an inappropriate T-cell–mediated immune response against ingested gluten in genetically predisposed individuals who carry either HLA-DQ2 or HLA-DQ8 genes. There is sensitivity to gliadin, a protein fraction of gluten found in wheat, rye, and barley. In patients with celiac disease, immune responses to gliadin fractions promote an inflammatory reaction, mainly in the upper small intestine, manifested by infiltration of the lamina propria and the epithelium with chronic inflammatory cells and villous atrophy.
- Seroconversion to celiac autoimmunity may occur at any time.
- Timing of introduction of gluten into the infant diet is associated with the appearance of celiac disease in children at risk. Children initially exposed to gluten in the first 3 mo of life have a fivefold increased risk. Current recommendations are to delay introduction of gluten into the diet of a genetically susceptible infant until 4 to 6 mo of age while the mother continues to breastfeed.

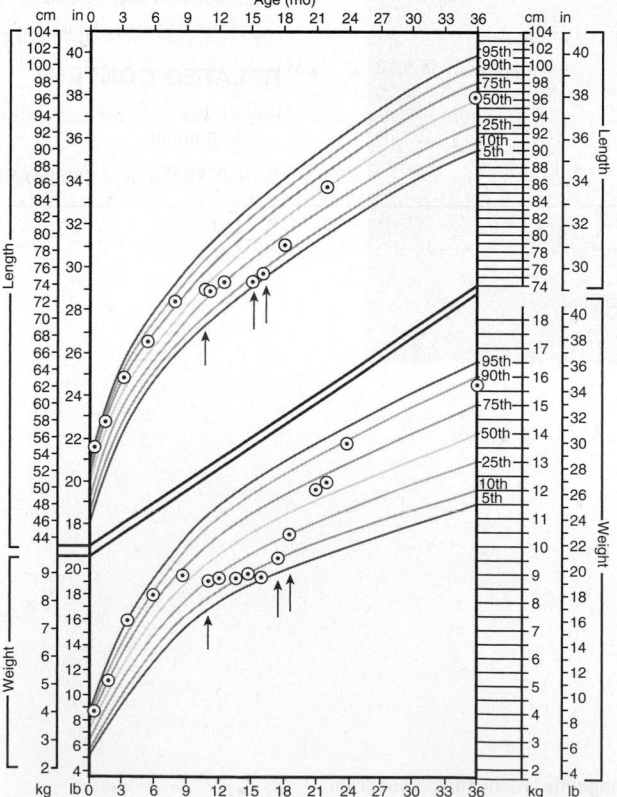

FIGURE 1C-38 Gluten-sensitive enteropathy. Growth curve demonstrates initial normal growth from 0 to 9 mo, followed by onset of poor appetite with intermittent vomiting and diarrhea after initiation of gluten-containing diet *(single arrow)*. After biopsy-confirmed diagnosis and treatment with gluten-free diet *(double arrow)*, growth improves. (From Kliegman RM et al: *Nelson textbook of pediatrics*, ed 19, Philadelphia, 2011, Saunders.)

TABLE 1C-7   Clinical Spectrum of Celiac Disease

Symptomatic

Frank malabsorption symptoms: chronic diarrhea, failure to thrive, weight loss

Extraintestinal manifestations: anemia, fatigue, hypertransaminasemia, neurologic disorders, short stature, dental enamel defects, arthralgia, aphthous stomatitis

Silent

No apparent symptoms in spite of histologic evidence of villous atrophy

In most cases identified by serologic screening in at-risk groups (see laboratory tests)

Latent

Subjects who have a normal histology, but at some other time, before or after, have shown a gluten-dependent enteropathy

Potential

Subjects with positive celiac disease serology but without evidence of altered jejunal histology

It might or might not be symptomatic

From Kliegman RM et al: *Nelson textbook of pediatrics*, ed 19, Philadelphia, 2011, Saunders.

Diseases
and Disorders

I

 **DIAGNOSIS**

Diagnostic criteria for celiac disease require at least four out of five or three out of four if the *HLA* genotype is not performed:
1. Typical symptoms of celiac disease
2. Positivity of serum celiac disease Ig A class autoantibodies at high titer
3. *HLA-DQ2* or *HLA-DQ8* genotypes
4. Celiac enteropathy at the small intestinal biopsy
5. Response to gluten-free diet

DIFFERENTIAL DIAGNOSIS

- Inflammatory bowel disease
- Laxative abuse
- Intestinal parasitic infestations
- Lactose intolerance
- Other: irritable bowel syndrome, tropical sprue, chronic pancreatitis, Zollinger-Ellison syndrome, cystic fibrosis (children), lymphoma, eosinophilic gastroenteritis, short bowel syndrome, Whipple's disease
- Intestinal lymphoma, tuberculosis, radiation enteritis, HIV enteropathy

LABORATORY TESTS

- IgA anti-tTG antibody by enzyme-linked immunosorbent assay (tissue transglutaminase [tTG] test) is the best screening serologic test for celiac disease. IgA antiendomysial antibodies (EMA) test is also a good screening test for celiac disease but is best used as a confirmatory test in cases of borderline positive results. In patients with IgA deficiency, the IgG DPG test (deamidated gliadin peptides) can be used for diagnosis. Screening of close relatives is initially done with PCR testing for *HLA DQ2* or *HLA DQ8*. Those that are positive should then have serum tTG IgA screening. All diagnostic serologic testing for celiac disease should be performed before a gluten-free diet is initiated.
- CBC, ferritin level: Iron-deficiency anemia (microcytic anemia, low ferritin level) may be present.
- Celiac disease can lead to malabsorption: Screen for vitamin B_{12} level, folate level, vitamin D level, serum calcium, albumin, magnesium; vitamin B_{12} deficiency, vitamin D deficiency, hypomagnesemia, and hypocalcemia are not uncommon in celiac disease.
- Biopsy of the small bowel, considered the gold standard, has been questioned as a reliable and conclusive test in all cases. It may be reasonable in children with significant elevations of tTG levels (>100 U) to first try a gluten-free diet and consider biopsy in those who do not improve with diet. Repeat small-bowel biopsies are no longer required to show healing when there is a clear response to a gluten-free diet.
- The HLA-DQ2 allele is identified in >90% of patients with celiac disease, and HLA-DQ8 is identified in most of the remaining patients. These genes occur in only 30% to 40% of the general population. Their greatest diagnostic value is in their negative predictive value, making them useful when negative in ruling out the disease.

IMAGING STUDIES

- Consider bone density in newly diagnosed adult patients.
- Capsule endoscopy can be used to evaluate mucosa of the small intestine, especially if future innovations will allow mucosal biopsy.

 **TREATMENT**

NONPHARMACOLOGIC THERAPY

Patients should be instructed on a gluten-free diet (avoidance of wheat, rye, and barley). Safe grains (gluten-free) include rice, corn, oats, buckwheat, millet, amaranth, quinoa, sorghum, and teff (an Ethiopian cereal grain). The lowest amount of daily gluten that causes damage to the celiac intestinal mucosa is 10-15 mg/day. One slice of bread contains 1.6 g of gluten.

GENERAL Rx

- Correct nutritional deficiencies with iron, folic acid, calcium, vitamin D, and vitamin B_{12} as needed.
- Prednisone 20 to 60 mg qd gradually tapered is useful in refractory cases.
- Lifelong gluten-free diet is necessary. A referral to a nutritionist experienced in celiac disease and gluten-free diet is recommended at initial diagnosis.

DISPOSITION

- Prognosis is good with adherence to a gluten-free diet. Rapid improvement is usually seen within a few days of treatment. Healing of the intestinal damage typically occurs within 6 to 24 mo after initiation of the diet. Lack of response to gluten-free diet occurs in 5% of patients and is due to unintentional ingestion of gluten or presence of coexisting GI disorders such as IBD, lactose or other carbohydrate intolerance, and pancreatic insufficiency.
- Serial antigliadin or antiendomysial antibody tests can be used to monitor the patient's adherence to a gluten-free diet.
- Repeat small-bowel biopsy after treatment generally reveals significant improvement. It is also useful to evaluate for increased risk of small-bowel T-cell lymphoma in these patients, especially untreated patients. Some experts recommend a repeat biopsy only in selected patients who have an unsatisfactory response to a strict gluten-free diet; however, recent data (Lebwohl et al) show that the risk for lymphoproliferative malignancy (LPM) is affected by the results of follow-up intestinal biopsy performed to document mucosal healing. Increased risk for LPM in CD is associated with the follow-up biopsy results, with a higher risk among patients with persistent villous atrophy. Follow-up biopsy may effectively stratify patients with CD by risk for subsequent LPM.

PEARLS & CONSIDERATIONS

COMMENTS

- The presence of dermatitis herpetiformis is pathognomonic for celiac disease.

- In close relatives, repeated serum tTG IgA testing may be useful in those with positive *HLA-DQ2* or *HLA-DQ8* tests because celiac disease may not manifest until later in life, and initial negative results do not preclude the possibility of future onset of celiac disease.
- Celiac disease should be considered in patients with unexplained metabolic bone disease, osteoporosis, transaminasemia, or hypocalcemia, because gastrointestinal symptoms are absent or mild. Clinicians should also consider testing children and young adults for celiac disease if unexplained weight loss, abdominal pain or distention, or chronic diarrhea is present.
- Screening for celiac disease is recommended in first-degree relatives. It should also be considered in patients with type 1 diabetes mellitus and in those with certain autoimmune disorders such as primary biliary cirrhosis, primary sclerosing cholangitis, autoimmune hepatitis, IBD, thyroid disease (hypothyroidism occurs in up to 15% of patients with celiac disease), SLE, RA, and Sjögren's syndrome due to increased risk of celiac disease in these populations. Screening persons with Down syndrome or Turner syndrome has also been recommended.
- The prevalence of celiac disease in patients with dyspepsia is twice that of the general population. Screening for celiac disease should be considered in all patients with persistent dyspepsia.
- Patients with celiac disease have an overall risk of cancer that is almost twice that of the general population. The risk of adenocarcinoma of the small intestine is increased manifold compared with the risk in the general population. Celiac disease is also associated with an increased risk for non-Hodgkin's lymphoma, especially of T-cell type and primarily localized in the gut. Lymphoma is 4 to 40 times more common, and death from lymphoma is 11 to 70 times more common in patients with celiac disease.
- Patients with celiac disease who have followed a gluten-free diet for prolonged periods may not experience relapse of symptoms for several months after gluten is reintroduced.

Trials involving randomized feeding intervention in infants at high risk for celiac disease have shown that as compared to placebo, the introduction of small quantities of gluten at 16 to 24 weeks of age did not reduce the risk of celiac disease by 3 years of age.

EBM **EVIDENCE**

Available at www.expertconsult.com

SUGGESTED READINGS
Available at www.expertconsult.com

RELATED CONTENT
Celiac Disease (Patient Information)
Dermatitis Herpetiformis (Related Key Topic)

AUTHOR: **FRED F. FERRI, M.D.**

BASIC INFORMATION

DEFINITION

Cellulitis is a superficial inflammatory condition of the skin and underlying tissues characterized by erythema, warmth, and tenderness of the involved area.

SYNONYMS

Erysipelas (cellulitis generally caused by group A β-hemolytic streptococci [GABHS])
SSSIs (skin and skin structure infections)
ABSSSIs (acute bacterial skin and skin structure infections)

ICD-10CM CODES

H05.011 Cellulitis of right orbit
H05.012 Cellulitis of left orbit
H05.013 Cellulitis of bilateral orbits
H05.019 Cellulitis of unspecified orbit
H60.10 Cellulitis of external ear, unspecified ear
H60.11 Cellulitis of right external ear
H60.12 Cellulitis of left external ear
H60.13 Cellulitis of external ear, bilateral
K12.2 Cellulitis and abscess of mouth
L03.011 Cellulitis of right finger
L03.012 Cellulitis of left finger
L03.019 Cellulitis of unspecified finger
L03.031 Cellulitis of right toe
L03.032 Cellulitis of left toe
L03.039 Cellulitis of unspecified toe
L03.111 Cellulitis of right axilla
L03.112 Cellulitis of left axilla
L03.113 Cellulitis of right upper limb
L03.114 Cellulitis of left upper limb
L03.115 Cellulitis of right lower limb
L03.116 Cellulitis of left lower limb
L03.119 Cellulitis of unspecified part of limb
L03.211 Cellulitis of face
L03.221 Cellulitis of neck
L03.311 Cellulitis of abdominal wall
L03.312 Cellulitis of back [any part except buttock]
L03.313 Cellulitis of chest wall
L03.314 Cellulitis of groin
L03.315 Cellulitis of perineum
L03.316 Cellulitis of umbilicus
L03.317 Cellulitis of buttock
L03.319 Cellulitis of trunk, unspecified
L03.811 Cellulitis of head [any part, except face]
L03.818 Cellulitis of other sites
L03.90 Cellulitis, unspecified

EPIDEMIOLOGY & DEMOGRAPHICS

- Occurs most frequently in diabetics, immunocompromised hosts, and patients with venous and lymphatic compromise.
- Frequently found near skin breaks (trauma, surgical wounds [surgical site infections develop in 2% to 5% of all surgical procedures], ulcerations, tinea infections). Edema, animal or human bites, subadjacent osteomyelitis, and bacteremia are potential sources of cellulitis.

- Skin and soft-tissue infections account for >14 million outpatient visits in the U.S./yr.

PHYSICAL FINDINGS & CLINICAL PRESENTATION

Variable with the causative organism:
- Erysipelas (Fig. 1C-39): superficial-spreading, warm, erythematous lesion distinguished by indurated, elevated margin; lymphatic involvement, vesicle formation common.
- Staphylococcal cellulitis: area involved is erythematous, hot, and swollen; differentiated from erysipelas by nonelevated, poorly demarcated margin; local tenderness and regional adenopathy are common; up to 85% of cases occur on the legs and feet.
- *Haemophilus influenzae* cellulitis: area involved is a blue-red/purple-red color; occurs mainly in children; generally involves the face in children and the neck or upper chest in adults.
- *Vibrio vulnificus:* larger hemorrhagic bullae, cellulitis, lymphadenitis, myositis; often found in critically ill patients in septic shock.
- Table 1C-8 describes anatomic variants of or predispositions to cellulitis. Typically, nonpurulent cellulitis is caused by β-hemolytic streptococci, whereas cellulitis with purulent drainage is caused by MRSA.

ETIOLOGY

- Group A β-hemolytic streptococci (may follow a streptococcal infection of the upper respiratory tract). β-hemolytic streptococci are implicated in most cases of non-traumatic cellulitis.
- Staphylococcal cellulitis: Diabetics, athletes, men who have sex with men, people living in public housing, and incarcerated men are at greater risk for methicillin-resistant *Staphylococcus aureus* (MRSA) infection. A community-acquired MRSA strain, USA 300, is replacing nosocomial strains of MRSA in hospitals.
- IV drug use: MRSA, *Pseudomonas aeruginosa.*
- *V. vulnificus:* higher incidence in patients with liver disease (75%) and in immunocompromised hosts. *V. vulnificus* infection is the leading cause of death related to seafood consumption in the U.S.
- *Erysipelothrix rhusiopathiae:* common in people handling poultry, fish, or meat.
- *Aeromonas hydrophila:* generally occurs in contaminated open wounds in fresh water.
- Fungi *(Cryptococcus neoformans):* in immunocompromised granulopenic patients.
- Gram-negative rods *(Serratia, Enterobacter, Proteus, Pseudomonas):* may be present in immunocompromised or granulopenic patients.
- Hot tub exposure: *P. aeruginosa*; fish tank exposure: *Mycobacterium marinum.*
- Bites: human *(Eikenella corrodens),* dog *(Pasteurella multocida, C. canimorsus),* cat *(P. multocida),* rat *(Streptobacillus moniliformis).*

DIAGNOSIS

DIFFERENTIAL DIAGNOSIS

- Necrotizing fasciitis (reddish-purple discoloration of skin, rapid increase in size, woody induration and pale appearance rather than erythema, violaceous bullae, pain out of proportion to appearance, sepsis)
- Deep vein thrombosis
- Peripheral vascular insufficiency
- Paget disease of the breast
- Thrombophlebitis
- Acute gout
- Psoriasis
- *Candida* intertrigo
- Pseudogout
- Osteomyelitis
- Insect bite
- Fixed drug eruption
- Lymphedema
- Contact dermatitis
- Olecranon bursa infection
- Herpetic whitlow, early herpes zoster (before blisters)
- Erythema migrans (Lyme disease)
- Rare: *Vaccinia* vaccination, Kawasaki disease, pyoderma gangrenosum, Sweet syndrome, carcinoma erysipeloides, anaerobic myonecrosis, erythromelalgia, eosinophilic cellulitis (Well's syndrome), familial Mediterranean fever

LABORATORY TESTS

- Gram stain, culture (aerobic and anaerobic):
  1. Aspirated material from:
     a. Advancing edge of cellulitis
     b. Any vesicles
  2. Swab of any drainage material
  3. Punch biopsy (in selected patients)
- Blood cultures in hospitalized patients, patients with cellulitis superimposed on lymphedema, patients with buccal or periorbital cellulitis, and patients suspected of having a salt- or fresh-water source of infection. Bacteremia uncommon in cellulitis (positive blood cultures in 4% of patients).
- Anti-streptolysin O (ASLO) titer (in suspected streptococcal disease)

The cause of cellulitis remains unidentified in most patients. Patients with recurrent lower-extremity cellulitis should be inspected for tinea pedis. If found it should be treated.

IMAGING STUDIES

CT or MRI in patients with suspected necrotizing fasciitis (deep-seated infection of the subcutaneous tissue that results in the progressive destruction of fascia and fat).

TREATMENT

NONPHARMACOLOGIC THERAPY

Immobilization and elevation of the involved limb. Cool sterile saline dressings to remove purulence from any open lesion. Support stockings in patients with peripheral edema.

ACUTE GENERAL Rx

Erysipelas:
- PO: dicloxacillin 500 mg PO q6h
- IV: cefazolin 1 g q6 to 8h or nafcillin 1.0 or 1.5 g IV q4 to 6h
  NOTE: Use vancomycin 1 g IV q12h in patients allergic to penicillin.

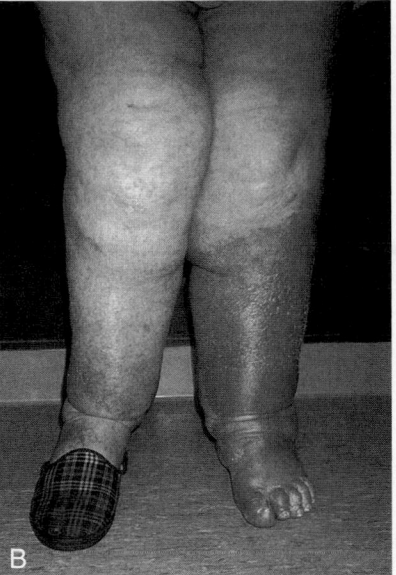

FIGURE 1C-39 Erysipelas of the leg. A, Note the open wound on the proximal thigh, which gave rise to this infection. The patient should be monitored closely for more severe skin changes (e.g., purpura, bulla, postbullous ulceration, necrosis, hypoesthesia, fluctuance), which may suggest necrotizing fasciitis or pyomyositis. **B,** Chronic lymphedema has predisposed to cellulitis in this elderly patient. (From White GM, Cox NH, eds: *Diseases of the skin,* ed 2, St Louis, 2006, Mosby.)

TABLE 1C-8 Anatomic Variants of or Predispositions to Cellulitis

Anatomic Variant or Predisposition	Location	Likely Bacterial Cause
Periorbital cellulitis	Periorbital	*Staphylococcus aureus, Streptococcus pneumoniae,* group A streptococci
Buccal cellulitis	Cheek	*Haemophilus influenzae* type b
Cellulitis complicating body piercing	Ear, nose, umbilicus	*S. aureus,* group A streptococci
After mastectomy (with axillary node dissection)[63]	Ipsilateral upper extremity	Non–group A β-hemolytic streptococci
After lumpectomy (with limited axillary node dissection, breast irradiation)[64]	Ipsilateral breast	Non–group A β-hemolytic streptococci
After saphenous vein harvest for coronary artery bypass	Ipsilateral leg	Group A or non–group A β-hemolytic streptococci
After radical pelvic surgery, radiation therapy	Vulva, inguinal areas, legs	Group B and group G streptococci
After liposuction	Thigh, abdominal wall	Group A streptococci, peptostreptococci
Postoperative (very early) wound infection	Abdomen, chest, hip	Group A streptococci
Injection drug use ("skin popping")	Extremities, neck	*S. aureus,* streptococci (groups A, C, F, G)*
Perianal cellulitis	Perineum	Group A streptococcus

*Other bacteria to consider based on isolation from skin or abscesses in this setting include *Enterococcus faecalis,* viridans group streptococci, coagulase-negative staphylococci, anaerobes (including *Bacteroides* and *Clostridium* spp.), and Enterobacteriaceae. (From Bennett JE, Dolin R, Blaser MJ: *Mandell, Douglas, and Bennett's Principles and Practice of Infectious Diseases,* ed 8, Philadelphia, 2015, Saunders.)

Staphylococcal cellulitis:
- PO: dicloxacillin 250 to 500 mg qid
- IV: nafcillin 1 to 2 g q4 to 6h
- Cephalosporins (cephalothin, cephalexin, cephradine) also provide adequate antistaphylococcal coverage, except for MRSA.
- Trimethoprim-sulfamethoxazole (160 mg/800 mg 1 PO bid) may be appropriate in mild MRSA infections. Use vancomycin 1.0 to 2.0 g IV qd or linezolid 0.6 g IV q12h in patients allergic to penicillin or cephalosporins and in patients with moderate/severe MRSA. Daptomycin (Cubicin), a cyclic lipopeptide, can be used as an alternative to vancomycin for complicated skin and skin structure infections. Usual dose is 4 mg/kg IV given over 30 min every 24 hr. Telavancin is a new glycopeptide derivative of vancomycin effective for gram-positive skin and skin structure infections, including those caused by MRSA. Tedizolid is an oxazolidinone effective in ABSSSI as an alternative to linezolid. Ceftaroline fosamil (Teflaro) is a new IV cephalosporin also effective against MRSA. Dalbavancin and tedizolid are two new drugs recently FDA-approved for skin and skin structure infections, including those caused by MRSA. Trials involving once-weekly IV dalbavancin have shown non-inferiority to daily IV vancomycin in adults with acute bacterial skin and skin-structure infection (SSSI).[1]

H. influenzae cellulitis:
- PO: cefixime or cefuroxime
- IV: cefuroxime or ceftriaxone

Vibrio vulnificus:
- Doxycycline 100 mg IV bid + ceftazidime 2 g IV q8h or IV ciprofloxacin 400 mg bid. Mild cases treated with oral antibiotics (doxycycline 100 mg bid + ciprofloxacin 750 mg bid).
- IV support and admission into intensive care unit (mortality rate >50% in septic shock).

E. rhusiopathiae:
- Penicillin

A. hydrophila:
- Aminoglycosides
- Chloramphenicol
- Complicated skin and skin structure infections in hospitalized patients can be treated with daptomycin (Cubicin) 4 mg/kg IV q24h

 **EVIDENCE**

Available at www.expertconsult.com

SUGGESTED READINGS

Available at www.expertconsult.com

RELATED CONTENT

Cellulitis (Patient Information)
Erysipelas (Related Key Topic)

AUTHOR: **FRED F. FERRI, M.D.**

[1] Boucher HW, Wilcox M, Talbot GH et al: Once-weekly dalbavancin versus daily conventional therapy for skin infections. N Engl J Med 370: 2169-79, 2014

Cervical Cancer

 BASIC INFORMATION

DEFINITION

Cervical cancer is the penetration of the basement membrane and infiltration of the stroma of the uterine cervix by malignant cells.

ICD-10CM CODES
C53.8 Malignant neoplasm of overlapping sites of cervix uteri
C53.9 Malignant neoplasm of cervix uteri, unspecified
D06.7 Carcinoma in situ of other parts of cervix
D06.9 Carcinoma in situ of cervix, unspecified

EPIDEMIOLOGY & DEMOGRAPHICS

INCIDENCE: Approximately 12,000 new cases annually, with 4000 to 5000 associated deaths. Mean age at diagnosis is 48 years. U.S. has age-adjusted mortality rate of 2.6 per 100,000 persons.
PREDOMINANCE: Higher incidence rates occur in developing countries. Among the U.S. population, Hispanics have a higher incidence than African Americans, who likewise have a higher incidence than whites. Worldwide, cervical cancer is the third most common cancer in women.
RISK FACTORS: Smoking, early age at first intercourse, multiple sexual partners, immunocompromised state, nonbarrier methods of birth control, infection with high-risk human papillomavirus (HPV; types 16 and 18), and multiparity.

PHYSICAL FINDINGS & CLINICAL PRESENTATION

- Unusual vaginal bleeding, particularly post-coital
- Vaginal discharge and/or odor
- Advanced cases may present with lower-extremity edema or renal failure
- In early stages, there may be little or no obvious cervical lesion; more advanced cases may have large, bulky, friable lesions encompassing majority of vagina

ETIOLOGY

- Infection with high-risk HPV types is a necessary, although not sufficient, cause of almost all cases of cervical cancer. Persistent HPV infection leads to precancerous changes of cervix (cervical intraepithelial neoplasia [CIN]). CIN can progress to invasive cervical cancer.
- Both squamous cell and adenocarcinoma of cervix are associated with HPV infection.
- More than 40 HPV types can infect the cervix. Most cases are believed to be linked to presence of HPV 16, 18, 45, and 56 by interaction of E6 oncoprotein on p53 gene product.
- There may be an association with past infection with *Chlamydia trachomatis.*

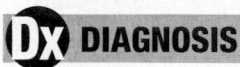 DIAGNOSIS

DIFFERENTIAL DIAGNOSIS

- Cervical polyp or prolapsed uterine fibroid
- Preinvasive cervical lesions
- Neoplasia metastatic from a separate primary neoplasia

WORKUP

- Thorough history and physical examination.
- Pelvic examination with careful rectovaginal examination.
- Compared with Pap testing, HPV testing has greater sensitivity for detection of CIN. Addition of HPV test for high-risk types to Pap test to screen women in mid-30s for cervical cancer reduces incidence of grade 2 or 3 CIN or cancer detected by subsequent screening examinations.
- Colposcopy with directed biopsy and endocervical curettage.
- FIGO staging described in Table 1C-10.

LABORATORY TESTS

- Complete blood count, chemistry profile
- SCC antigen in research setting
- Carcinoembryonic antigen

IMAGING STUDIES

- Chest x-ray
- Depending on stage, may need CT scan, MRI (Fig. 1C-43), PET/CT
- Intravenous pyelogram

 TREATMENT

NONPHARMACOLOGIC THERAPY

- FIGO stage IA: cone biopsy or simple hysterectomy
- FIGO stage IB or IIA: type III radical hysterectomy and pelvic lymphadenectomy or pelvic radiation therapy
- Advanced or bulky disease: multimodality therapy (radiation, chemotherapy, and/or surgery); platinum use before radiation therapy

ACUTE GENERAL Rx

Table 1C-10 summarizes treatment according to tumor stage. Chemotherapy is cisplatin-based. In advanced cases, cervical cancer may present with massive and acute vaginal bleeding requiring volume and blood replacement, vaginal packing or other hemostatic modalities, and/or high-dose local radiotherapy.

CHRONIC Rx

- Physical examination with Pap smear every 3 mo for 2 yr, every 6 mo for 3 to 5 yr, annually thereafter
- Chest x-ray annually (optional)
- Other imaging done only as clinically indicated
- Localized pelvic recurrence may be treated and cured with pelvic exenteration

DISPOSITION

Five-year survival varies by stage:
- Stage I: 90% to 95%
- Stage II: 40% to 80%
- Stage III: <60%
- Stage IV: <15%

Early detection by Pap smear is imperative for long-term improvements in survival.

TABLE 1C-10   FIGO Staging of Cervical Cancer

Stage	Invasion	Prognosis: 5-yr Survival	Treatment
1A1	Depth of invasion ≤3 mm and width ≤7 mm (includes early stromal invasion of ≤1 mm)	84% to 90% if tumor <3 cm; 85% will have negative pelvic nodes, and 95% of these patients will be "cured"	Local excision; if margins of cone clear (i.e., no residual tumor or CIN), then conization is adequate, with no need for pelvic lymphadenectomy
1A2	Depth of invasion between 3 and 5 mm (i.e., 3.1-5 mm) and width up to 7 mm		Simple hysterectomy and pelvic lymphadenectomy
1B1	Tumor confined to cervix and diameter <4 cm	66% if tumor >3 cm	Radical hysterectomy or radiotherapy
1B2	Tumor confined to cervix and diameter >4 cm		Radical hysterectomy or radiotherapy
IIA	Upper third of the vagina		Radical hysterectomy or radiotherapy
IIB	Upper two thirds of the vagina plus parametrial disease	62%	Radiotherapy ± chemotherapy
IIIA	Lower third of the vagina		Radiotherapy ± chemotherapy
IIIB	Pelvic sidewall and/or hydronephrosis	40%	Radiotherapy ± chemotherapy
IVA	Bladder, rectum		Radiotherapy ± chemotherapy
IVB	Beyond pelvis	15%	Radiotherapy ± chemotherapy

From Drife J, Magowan B: *Clinical obstetrics and gynecology,* Philadelphia, 2004, Saunders.

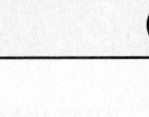

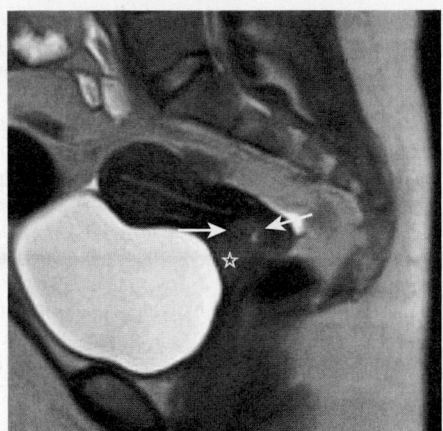

FIGURE 1C-43 Cervical carcinoma. T2-weighted sagittal image through the cervix shows an intermediate signal mass *(arrows)* disrupting the normally intense low signal ring of the cervical stroma with areas of high signal. The mass infiltrates the upper vagina *(star)*. (From Fielding JR et al: *Gynecologic imaging,* Philadelphia, 2011, Saunders.)

REFERRAL

Gynecologic oncologist for all invasive disease

PEARLS & CONSIDERATIONS

- HPV vaccination is indicated in males and females age 9 to 26 yr for the prevention of cervical cancer caused by HPV types 6, 11, 16, and 18. HPV vaccination is over 90% effective in preventing infection and cervical cancer.

- Available evidence supports discontinuation of cervical cancer screening among women aged 65 yrs or older who have had adequate screening and are not otherwise at high risk.
- Updated recommendations from the American College of Physicians on screening for cervical cancer in average-risk women are as follows[1]

[1] Sawaya GF, et al.: Cervical cancer screening in average-risk women: Best practice advice from the Cervical Guidelines Committee of the American College of Physicians, Ann Intern Med 162(12):851-859, 2015.

1. Women should be screened with cervical cytology every 3 years beginning at age 21.
2. After age 30, women can be screened with cytology and HPV testing every 5 years.
3. Before age 21, women should not be scanned at all.
4. Before age 30, women should not be screened with HPV testing.
5. At age 65, screening can stop in women with three consecutive negative cytology results or two consecutive negative cytology results combined with a negative HPV test within the last 10 years (with the most recent test within 5 years).
6. Women without a cervix should not be screened.

 EVIDENCE

Available at www.expertconsult.com

SUGGESTED READINGS

Available at www.expertconsult.com

RELATED CONTENT

Cervical Dysplasia (Related Key Topic)
Cervical Cancer (Patient Information)

AUTHORS: **RUBEN ALVERO, M.D.** and **FRED F. FERRI, M.D.**

Diseases and Disorders

C

I

Cervical Dysplasia

 **BASIC INFORMATION**

DEFINITION

Cervical dysplasia refers to atypical development of immature squamous epithelium that does not penetrate the basement epithelial membrane. Characteristics include increased cellularity, nuclear abnormalities, and increased nuclear/cytoplasmic ratio. A progressive loss of squamous differentiation exists beginning adjacent to the basement membrane and progressing to the most advanced stage (severe dysplasia), which encompasses the complete squamous epithelial layer thickness. The revised 2001 Bethesda System terminology was used in a National Institutes of Health consensus conference, sponsored by the American Society for Colposcopy and Cervical Pathology (ASCCP) and its partner professional organizations in 2006. The conference updated therapeutic options for women based on studies such as the **A**SC-US (atypical squamous cells of undetermined significance)/**L**SIL (low-grade squamous intraepithelial lesions) **T**riage **S**tudy (ALTS) that appeared after revision of the Bethesda classification. Fig. 1C-46 provides a comparison of grading systems for cervical squamous dysplasia.

In 2012, the American Cancer Society (ACS), ASCCP, and American Society for Clinical Pathology (ASCP) published a new set of recommendations for lifetime assessment and early diagnosis of cervical dysplasia and cancer. The recommendations attempted to reduce the number of lifetime assessments, thereby reducing the possible morbidity associated with excess testing and also optimizing the co-evaluation with Pap smear and HPV testing. In brief, women younger than 21 yr of age should not have any screening. Women 21-29 yr of age should have testing every 3 yr with only cytology. With negative cytology or HPV-negative ASC-US, patients can repeat every 3 yr. For HPV-positive ASC-US or cytology with

LG-SIL, follow-up is as per the 2006 guidelines (essentially a colposcopic examination as the initial step with follow-up steps depending on the findings). Women between the ages of 30 and 65 yr should have co-testing every 5 yr with both Pap cytology and HPV testing. Alternatively, it is also acceptable to perform cytology alone, but then the testing interval should be every 3 yr. With negative cytology or HPV-negative ASC-US, patients can repeat with co-testing every 5 yr. For HPV-positive ASC-US or cytology with LG-SIL, follow-up is as per the 2006 guidelines, as previously documented. For patients with positive HPV but negative cytology, the patient can repeat testing 12 months later with co-testing; patients can also specifically test for HPV 16 or HPV 16/18 genotypes and, if positive, should be referred for colposcopy. Patients with positive HPV but negative 16 and/or 18 should be retested in 12 months with co-testing.

Women older than the age of 65 yr and those with a history of hysterectomy (including removal of cervix) should no longer be tested unless they had previous diagnosis of cervical intraepithelial neoplasia (CIN) 2 or more severe; these women should be tested for at least 20 yr. Women who have been vaccinated for HPV should still use age-specific recommendations for screening.

BETHESDA 2001 UPDATED CLASSIFICATION: The Bethesda 2001 System was the result of a year-long iterative process held to update the original 1991 system and to broaden participation in the consensus process, clarify reporting of abnormalities, and incorporate data that had been collected since the initial system was created.

The reporting system includes the following areas:

Specimen adequacy: The system defines the specimen as either satisfactory for evaluation or unsatisfactory and then specifies the reason for inadequacy if necessary.

General categorization (optional): This serves to triage the specimen into normal finding (negative for intraepithelial lesion or

malignancy) or identifies it as an "epithelial abnormality." The descriptions are meant to be mutually exclusive.

Interpretation/result: Makes a distinction between "interpretation" and "diagnosis" of the specimen so that the interpretation may be incorporated into the overall clinical context for the particular patient being evaluated.

Negative for intraepithelial lesion or malignancy: In this screening test, no intraepithelial lesion or malignancy is identified. Non-neoplastic findings such as organisms or reactive cellular findings may be specified but are still considered to be a negative result.

Epithelial cell abnormalities:

Squamous cell:

Atypical squamous cell (ASC) of undetermined significance (ASC-US) emphasizing the unusual but still possible association with underlying CIN II/III and extremely rare possibility of squamous cell carcinoma

ASC cannot exclude high-grade squamous intraepithelial lesion (HSIL) (ASC-H), suggesting a risk for CIN II/III that is intermediate between ASC-US and HSIL

Low-grade squamous intraepithelial lesion (LSIL) suggests a transient viral infection with a greater likelihood for regression, more likely to encompass human papillomavirus (HPV) infection and CIN I histologically

HSIL suggestive of a more persistent viral infection and with a greater risk for progressive disease, more likely to encompass CIN II/III and carcinoma in situ (CIS) histologically

Squamous cell carcinoma

Glandular cell

Atypical glandular cells (should specify endocervical, endometrial, or not otherwise specified)

Histological features	Traditional system	WHO system	British Society for Cervical Cytology	Bethesda system
Atypical squamous cells not meeting the criteria for dysplasia	Mild atypia	Mild atypia	Borderline nuclear abnormality	Atypical squamous cells (ASC)
Koilocytes plus mild atypia	HPV infection	HPV infection	HPV plus borderline change	Low-grade squamous intraepithelial lesion (SIL)
Dysplasia limited to lower third of epithelium	Mild dysplasia	CIN 1	Mild dyskaryosis (low-grade dyskaryosis)	Low-grade SIL
Dysplasia limited to lower two-thirds of epithelium	Moderate dysplasia	CIN 2	Moderate dyskaryosis (high-grade dyskaryosis)	High-grade SIL
Dysplasia extending into upper third of epithelium	Severe dysplasia	CIN 3	Severe dyskaryosis (high-grade dyskaryosis)	High-grade SIL
Dysplasia of full thickness of epithelium	Carcinoma in situ	CIN 3	Severe dyskaryosis (high-grade dyskaryosis)	High-grade SIL

FIGURE 1C-46 Comparison of grading systems (From Young B et al: Female reproductive system. In *Wheater's basic pathology,* Philadelphia, 2011, Elsevier, pp 216-315.)

C

Atypical glandular cell, favor neoplasia (should specify endocervical or not otherwise specified)

Endocervical adenocarcinoma in situ (AIS)

Adenocarcinoma

Other: Endometrial cells in a woman ≥>40 yr of age. Because menopausal status is sometimes uncertain, age was chosen to discriminate women who might, with the findings of endometrial cells on cytology, warrant further evaluation with endometrial sampling

KEY POINTS:

1. The cytologic distinctions of low grade (LSIL) and high grade (HSIL) do not necessarily equate to the histologic classifications CIN I and CIN II/III.
2. The 2006 conference notes that one cytologic abnormality can have different histologic risk in different women and highlights "special populations" such as adolescent and young women, and those women who are pregnant. In young women, spontaneous HPV clearance rates are exceptionally high. The new testing recommendations essentially remove the possibility of testing women younger than 21 yr of age.
3. DNA testing for high-risk HPV types is incorporated into the evaluation and treatment algorithms for women with cytologic cervical abnormalities.

Histologically, a two-tiered system is developed in this guideline that distinguishes between the lower-risk CIN I and higher-risk CIN II/III diagnoses.

ICD-10CM CODES

N87.9	Dysplasia of cervix uteri, unspecified
R87.610	Atypical squamous cells of undetermined significance on cytologic smear of cervix (ASC-US)
R87.611	Atypical squamous cells cannot exclude high grade squamous intraepithelial lesion on cytologic smear of cervix (ASC-H)
R87.612	Low grade squamous intraepithelial lesion on cytologic smear of cervix (LGSIL)
R87.613	High grade squamous intraepithelial lesion on cytologic smear of cervix (HGSIL)
R87.614	Cytologic evidence of malignancy on smear of cervix
R87.615	Unsatisfactory cytologic smear of cervix
R87.618	Other abnormal cytological findings on specimens from cervix uteri
R87.619	Unspecified abnormal cytological findings in specimens from cervix uteri
Z12.4	Encounter for screening for malignant neoplasm of cervix

EPIDEMIOLOGY & DEMOGRAPHICS

PREDOMINANT AGE:

- Dysplasia: peak age, 26 yr (3600 cases/100,000 persons)
- CIS: peak age, 32 yr (1100 cases/100,000 persons)

- Invasive cancer: peak age <>60 yr (800 cases/100,000 persons)

PEAK INCIDENCE:

- Age 35 yr
- Abnormal Pap smear rate revealing dysplasia approximates 2% to 5% depending on population risk factors and false-negative rate variance
- False-negative rate approaching 40%
- Average age-adjusted incidence of severe dysplasia is 35 cases/100,000 persons
- Approximately half of the cases of new cervical cancer had never been screened, and another 10% had not been screened in more than 5 yr. Many of these women come from underserved or underresourced communities. The single biggest impact in reducing the morbidity and mortality from cervical cancer would come from appropriately addressing these health disparities.

PHYSICAL FINDINGS & CLINICAL PRESENTATION

- Cervical lesions associated with dysplasia often are not visible to the naked eye; therefore, physical findings are best viewed by colposcopy of a 3% acetic acid–prepared cervix.
- Patients evaluated by colposcopy are identified by abnormal cervical cytology screening from Pap smear screening.
- Colposcopic findings:
  1. Leukoplakia (white lesion seen by the unaided eye that may represent condyloma, dysplasia, or cancer)
  2. Acetowhite epithelium with or without associated punctation, mosaicism, abnormal vessels
  3. Abnormal transformation zone (abnormal iodine uptake, "cuffed" gland openings)

ETIOLOGY

- Strongly associated and initiated by oncogenic HPV infection (high-risk HPV types are 16, 18, 31, 33, 35, 45, 51, 52, 56, and 58; low-risk HPV types are 6, 11, 42, 43, and 44)
- Risk factors:
  1. HPV
  2. Any heterosexual coitus
  3. Coitus during puberty (transformation-zone metaplasia peak)
  4. Diethylstilbestrol exposure
  5. Multiple sexual partners
  6. Lack of prior Pap smear screening
  7. History of STD
  8. Other genital tract neoplasia
  9. HIV
  10. Tuberculosis
  11. Substance abuse
  12. "High-risk" male partner (HPV)
  13. Low socioeconomic status
  14. Early first pregnancy
  15. Tobacco use

Dx DIAGNOSIS

DIFFERENTIAL DIAGNOSIS

- Metaplasia
- Hyperkeratosis

- Condyloma
- Microinvasive carcinoma
- Glandular epithelial abnormalities
- Vulvar intraepithelial neoplasm
- Vaginal intraepithelial neoplasm
- Metastatic tumor involvement of the cervix

WORKUP

- Periodic history and physical examination (including cytologic screening) depending on age, risk factors, and history of preinvasive cervical lesions
- Consider screening for sexually transmitted disease (gonorrhea, *Chlamydia,* herpes, HIV, HPV)
- Abnormal cytology (HSIL/LSIL, initial ASC/ASC-US/ASC-H in high-risk patients, recurrent in low-risk/postmenopausal patients) and grossly evident suspicious lesions; refer for colposcopy and possible directed biopsy/endocervical curettage (ECC; examination should include cervix, vagina, vulva, and anus)
- For glandular cell abnormalities (AGCs): refer for colposcopy and possible directed biopsy/ECC, and consider endometrial sampling
- In pregnancy, abnormal cytology followed by colposcopy in the first trimester and at 28 to 32 wk; only high-grade lesions suspicious for carcinoma biopsied; ECC is contraindicated

LABORATORY TESTS

- Gonorrhea, chlamydia to rule out STD
- Pap cytology screening (requires appropriate sampling, preparation, cytologist interpretation, and reporting)
- Colposcopy and directed biopsy, ECC for indications (see "Workup")
- HPV DNA typing if identified abnormal cytology
- As compared with Pap testing, HPV testing has greater sensitivity for the detection of intraepithelial neoplasia

IMAGING STUDIES

- Cervicography
- Computer-enhanced Pap cytology screening (e.g., PAPNET)

MANAGEMENT

Refer to the literature for a more comprehensive approach. The following treatment paradigms in Table 1C-11 give a general outline for care.

DISPOSITION

- Because of the large number of women in high-risk groups, the prevalence of HPV, and the high false-negative Pap smear rate, routine Pap smear screening should be strongly encouraged for all women, especially those with a history of cervical dysplasia. The addition of an HPV test to the Pap test reduces the incidence of CIN II or III, or cancer detected by subsequent screening.
- Success rates for treatment approach 80% to 90%.
- Detection of persistence of recurrence requires careful follow-up.
- Cervical treatment possibly results in infertility (cervical stenosis or incompetence), which

BASIC INFORMATION

DEFINITION

Cervicitis is an infection of the cervix. It may result from direct infection of the cervix, or it may be secondary to uterine or vaginal infection.

SYNONYMS

Endocervicitis
Ectocervicitis
Mucopurulent cervicitis

ICD-10CM CODES

N72	Inflammatory disease of cervix uteri
A54.03	Gonococcal cervicitis, unspecified
A74.89	Other chlamydial diseases
A60.03	Herpesviral cervicitis
O86.11	Cervicitis following delivery

EPIDEMIOLOGY & DEMOGRAPHICS

Cervicitis accounts for 20% to 25% of patients with abnormal vaginal discharge. It is most common in adolescents, but it can be found in any sexually active woman. Practicing unsafe sex with multiple partners increases the risk of developing cervicitis as well as other sexually transmitted diseases.

PHYSICAL FINDINGS & CLINICAL PRESENTATION

Cervicitis is usually asymptomatic or associated with mild symptoms. Copious purulent or mucopurulent vaginal discharge (Fig. 1C-52), pelvic pain, and dyspareunia may be present if cervicitis is severe. The cervix can be erythematous and tender on palpation during bimanual examination. The cervix may also bleed easily when obtaining cultures or a Pap smear. Patients may have postcoital bleeding. The CDC emphasizes that the two diagnostic signs are either mucopurulent discharge or sustained cervical bleeding with gentle trauma.

ETIOLOGY

- *Chlamydia trachomatis*
- *Neisseria gonorrhoeae*
- *Trichomonas*

- Herpes simplex
- *T. vaginalis*
- Human papillomavirus

DIAGNOSIS

DIFFERENTIAL DIAGNOSIS

- Carcinoma of the cervix
- Cervical erosion
- Cervical metaplasia
- Cervical ectropion

WORKUP

The patient usually presents with a vaginal discharge or history of postcoital bleeding. Otherwise the patient is asymptomatic and diagnosed during routine examination. On examination there is gross visualization of yellow, mucopurulent material on the cotton swab.

LABORATORY TESTS

A finding of leucorrhea (>10 WBC per high-power field on microscopic examination of vaginal fluid) has been associated with chlamydial and gonococcal infection of the cervix. Positive Gram stain is found. Nucleic acid amplification tests (NAAT) should be used for diagnosing *C. trachomatis* and *N. gonorrhoeae* in women with cervicitis; this testing can be performed in vaginal, cervical, or uterine samples. Use a wet mount to look for trichomonads, but because the sensitivity of microscopy to detect *T. vaginalis* is relatively low (~50%), symptomatic women with cervicitis and negative microscopy for trichomonads should receive further testing with culture. Obtain a Pap smear. HIV testing is recommended in all patients with supposed cervicitis. Although HSV-2 infection has been associated with cervicitis, the utility of specific testing (i.e., culture or serologic testing) for HSV-2 in this setting is unknown.

TREATMENT

NONPHARMACOLOGIC THERAPY

- Cervicitis is treated in an outpatient setting. Safe sex should be practiced with the use of condoms.

- Partners should be treated in all cases of infection proven by culture.

ACUTE GENERAL Rx

Because *Chlamydia* and *N. gonorrhoeae* cause 50% of cases of infectious cervicitis, if it is suspected treat without waiting for test results. Administer ceftriaxone 125 mg IM single dose followed by azithromycin 1 g single dose or doxycycline 100 mg PO bid for 7 days. If the patient is pregnant, treat with azithromycin 1 g single dose instead of using doxycycline, which is contraindicated in pregnant or nursing mothers. If *Trichomonas* is the etiologic agent, treat with metronidazole 2 g single dose. For herpes, treat with acyclovir 200 mg PO five times daily for 7 days.

DISPOSITION

Bacterial cervicitis responds well to antibiotics. Possible complications to watch for are a subsequent pelvic inflammatory disease (PID) and infertility (found in 5%-10% of patients with increasing rates with repeat episodes of PID). Repeat cultures should be performed after treatment. Sexual relations can be resumed after negative cultures.

REFERRAL

If subsequent PID develops, consider hospital admission for IV antibiotics.

PEARLS & CONSIDERATIONS

COMMENTS

- Management of sex partners of women tested for cervicitis should be appropriate for the identified or suspected STD.
- Repeat testing 3 to 6 mo after treatment is recommended for all women diagnosed with chlamydia or gonorrhea, and all sex partners in the preceding 60 days should be evaluated and treated for the STDs for which the index patient received treatment.
- Limited data indicate that infection with *M. genitalium* or bacterial vaginosis and frequent douching might cause cervicitis.
- *M. genitalium* might be considered for cases of clinically significant cervicitis that persist after azithromycin or doxycycline therapy in which reexposure to an infected partner or medical nonadherence is unlikely. If *M. genitalium* infection is confirmed, treatment is with moxifloxacin.

SUGGESTED READINGS

Available at www.expertconsult.com

RELATED CONTENT

Cervicitis (Patient Information)
Chlamydia Genital Infections (Related Key Topic)
Gonorrhea (Related Key Topic)
Nongonococcal Urethritis (Related Key Topic)

AUTHOR: **RUBEN ALVERO, M.D.**

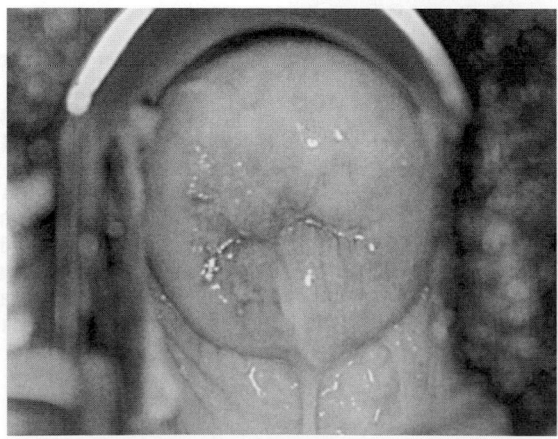

FIGURE 1C-52 Colposcopy of a woman with mucopurulent cervicitis and purulent discharge from endocervical os. (Courtesy Dr. David Soper, Richmond, VA. From Mandell GL [ed]: *Mandell, Douglas, and Bennett's principles and practice of infectious diseases*, ed 6, New York, 2005, Churchill Livingstone.)

C

BASIC INFORMATION

DEFINITION

Charcot-Marie-Tooth disease (CMT) is a heterogeneous group of noninflammatory inherited peripheral neuropathies characterized by chronic motor and sensory polyneuropathy. It is the most common inherited neuromuscular disorder (see also "Neuropathy, Hereditary").

SYNONYMS

Peroneal muscular atrophy
Hereditary motor and sensory neuropathy (HMSN)
CMT

ICD-10CM CODES
G60.0 Hereditary motor and sensory
neuropathy

EPIDEMIOLOGY & DEMOGRAPHICS

PREVALENCE: 1:2500; CMT type 1 and type 2 are the major divisions with an estimated prevalence of 40 per 100,000
PREDOMINANT AGE: Onset usually 10 to 20 yr; may present in infants
GENETICS: Transmission may be autosomal dominant, autosomal recessive, or X-linked, with some sporadic cases reported. Duplication of *peripheral myelin protein 22* (PMP22) is the most common cause of CMT. CMT is classified into types 1 through 7 and is genetically heterogeneous with at least 43 CMT genes known.

PHYSICAL FINDINGS & CLINICAL PRESENTATION

- Wide variation in clinical presentation, but affected individuals in a family tend to have similar symptoms.
- Symmetric, slowly progressive distal motor neuropathy resulting in weakness and atrophy in legs, often progresses to involve hands.
- High-arched feet (pes cavus), claw toe deformities (Fig. 1C-57), and hammer toes.
- Atrophy of the lower legs producing a stork-like appearance (muscle wasting does not involve the upper legs) (Fig. 1C-58).
- Nerve enlargement.
- Mild to moderate distal sensory loss; uncommonly can have painful paresthesias.
- Decreased proprioception and weakness of ankle dorsiflexors often interfere with balance and gait (steppage gait).

- Depressed or absent deep tendon reflexes in many cases.
- Hearing loss and hip dysplasia are under-recognized manifestations.
- Ambulation usually maintained throughout life.
- CMT has been reported to be associated with renal diseases, mostly focal segmental glomerulosclerosis (FSGS).

ETIOLOGY

Genetic abnormalities cause defects in either peripheral nerve myelination, or result in axonal degeneration. Mutations in one of several myelin genes result in defects in myelin structure, maintenance, and formation. Duplication of the PMP22 gene causes CMT1A, the most common type of hereditary motor sensory neuropathy (~40% overall). INF_2 mutations appear to cause many cases of FSGS-associated CMT.

DIAGNOSIS

DIFFERENTIAL DIAGNOSIS

- Other inherited neuropathies.
- Acquired peripheral neuropathies such as toxic, metabolic, infectious, endocrine, inflammatory, immune-mediated, and nutritional polyneuropathies.

WORKUP

- Clinical diagnosis is based on family history, characteristic presentation, and findings on detailed physical and neurologic examination.
- Electrophysiologic studies are often diagnostic and may help define various subtypes of CMT.
- Occasionally, sural nerve biopsy is helpful in establishing diagnosis.

TREATMENT

ACUTE GENERAL Rx

- Symptomatic and supportive, managed by multidisciplinary team including physical and occupational therapy.
- Special shoes with good ankle support, ankle/foot orthoses.
- Some require crutches/cane for gait stability; <5% need wheelchair.
- Daily heel cord stretching exercises and hand grip exercises.
- Musculoskeletal pain may respond to acetaminophen or NSAIDs; neuropathic pain may respond to tricyclic antidepressants or drugs such as carbamazepine or gabapentin.

CHRONIC Rx

Occasionally, orthopedic surgery is required to correct severe pes cavus deformity or hip dysplasia. Avoiding obesity is essential as this makes walking difficult; avoiding potentially neurotoxic medications is also important, particularly *Vinca* alkaloids.

DISPOSITION

- Disability is usually compatible with a long life.
- 10% to 20% of patients are asymptomatic.

REFERRAL

- Orthopedic consultation for bracing and surgical treatment of deformity.
- Genetic counseling and family planning.

PEARLS & CONSIDERATIONS

COMMENTS

Patient information on CMT disease is available from the Muscular Dystrophy Association, 3300 East Sunrise Drive, Tucson, AZ 85718; (520) 529-2000.

EVIDENCE

Available at www.expertconsult.com

SUGGESTED READINGS
Available at www.expertconsult.com

RELATED CONTENT
Charcot-Marie-Tooth Disease (Patient Information)

AUTHOR: **CANDICE YUVIENCO, M.D.**

I

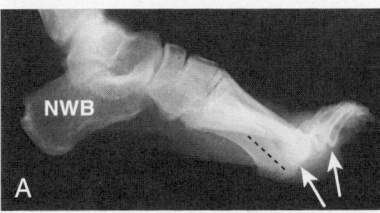
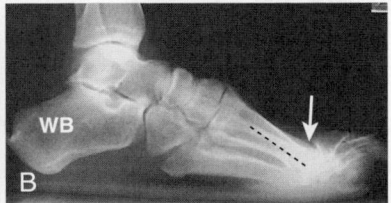

FIGURE 1C-57 A, Non–weight-bearing view of cavus and claw toe deformities in a patient with Charcot-Marie-Tooth disease. **B,** On weight-bearing view, plantar flexion of first ray is less noticeable, but clawed hallux remains, indicating fixed extension contracture at first metatarsophalangeal joint. (From Canale ST, Beaty JH: *Campbell's operative orthopedics,* ed 11, Philadelphia, 2007, Mosby.)

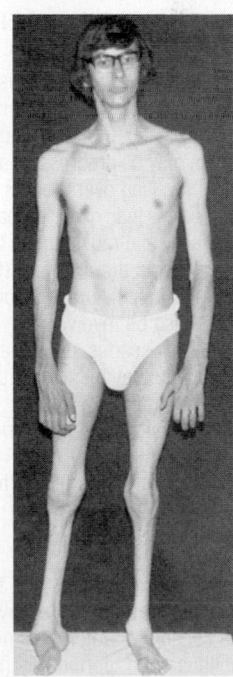

FIGURE 1C-58 Patient with Charcot-Marie-Tooth disease showing marked wasting of calf muscles and intrinsic foot muscles. (From Dubowitz V: *Muscle disorders in childhood,* London, 1995, Saunders.)

BASIC INFORMATION

DEFINITION

Charcot's joint was first described by Jean Martin Charcot in reports of patients with tabes dorsalis. The term now describes a chronic progressive arthropathy that is associated with peripheral neuropathy and commonly results in destruction of the bone and soft tissues at peripheral weight-bearing joints. It is characterized early on by acute inflammation that often leads to joint degeneration, instability from joint dislocation and pathologic fractures, and gross deformities.

SYNONYMS

Neuropathic arthropathy
Charcot osteoarthropathy
Charcot neuroosteoarthropathy

ICD-10CM CODES
A52.16 Charcot's arthropathy

EPIDEMIOLOGY & DEMOGRAPHICS
PREVALENCE:
- Estimated as 0.08% to 13% in patients with diabetes mellitus.
- 5 cases per 100 of those with peripheral neuropathy, primarily affecting the foot.
- 20% to 40% of patients with syringomyelia (shoulder, elbow, and wrist are most commonly involved).
- 5% to 10% of patients with tabes dorsalis (spine, hip, knee, and ankle are most commonly involved).
- Average age of onset is 50 to 60 years.
- No definite sex predilection and ethnic variance is unknown.

PHYSICAL FINDINGS & CLINICAL PRESENTATION
- Initial presentation is with a diffusely warm, erythematous, and swollen joint with or without associated pain. Continual attacks may occur, or there may be progressive arthropathy and insidious swelling over months to years.
- Pain is typically less than expected based on the severity of clinical and radiographic findings.
- It commonly affects the mid-foot (tarsus and tarsometatarsal joints), but the forefoot and hind foot can also be involved.
- Joint instability, osseous debris around the joint, and crepitus may be seen with progressive disease.
- Frank dislocation, fracture, and subsequent bony deformity may occur over time. Additionally, plantar ulcers may affect neuropathic foot joints.

ETIOLOGY

The most common identifiable risk factors for Charcot osteoarthropathy include any condition that causes a sensory or autonomic neuropathy. Diabetes mellitus with peripheral neuropathy is the most common cause (Fig. 1C-59). Other, more common lower extremity causes include tertiary syphilis, chronic alcoholism, and congenital insensitivity to pain. Upper extremity causes include syringomyelia, neoplasms, and

trauma. Less common associations include renal dialysis, Charcot-Marie-Tooth disease, poliomyelitis, leprosy, familial amyloid neuropathy, spinal or peripheral nerve surgery, and spinal dysraphism. Two theories contribute to the underlying processes involved in the disease:
1. Neurotraumatic theory:
   1. Impairment or loss of protective joint sensation with continued weight bearing and repetitive stress.
   2. Rapid and extensive bone destruction leads to joint subluxation, dislocation, and possible deformity.
   3. Chronic inflammation eventually contributes to joint instability and incongruity.
2. Neurovascular theory:
   1. Autonomic neuropathy leads to increased blood flow to the affected joints.
   2. Enhanced osteoclastic bone resorption contributes to osteopenia and further susceptibility to bone destruction.

DIAGNOSIS

DIFFERENTIAL DIAGNOSIS
- Osteomyelitis
- Cellulitis
- Inflammatory arthritides, particularly gout or pseudogout
- Deep vein thrombosis
- Infectious arthritis/septic joint
- Osteoarthritis
- Complex regional pain syndrome

WORKUP

History and physical examination findings are important to establishing the diagnosis.

Early diagnosis, before radiographic changes are evident, requires a high index of suspicion because the acute phase is characterized by the classical signs of edema, increased warmth, and erythema as seen in an acute inflammatory process.
- Patients should be tested for an underlying peripheral neuropathy.
- It may be helpful to diagnose or rule out a previously unrecognized contributing condition or risk factor for the above.

LABORATORY TESTS

There are no specific lab criteria for diagnosis. Labs can help to exclude infection and identify underlying risk factors.

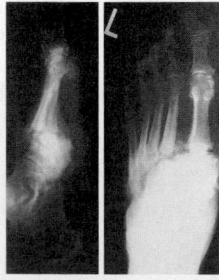

FIGURE 1C-59 Diabetes mellitus and neuropathic arthritis. Note lateral displacement of metatarsals *(left)* and fragmentation and osseous debris *(right).* (From Goldman L, Ausiello D [eds]: *Cecil textbook of medicine,* ed 22, Philadelphia, 2004, Saunders.)

- Complete blood count and metabolic panel, and additional testing may include vitamin B_{12}, folate, RPR, ALP, and PTH
- In questionable cases, aspiration, sometimes including biopsy, to rule out soft tissue or bone infection and a septic joint

IMAGING STUDIES

Plain x-rays
- May reveal variable degrees of destruction and joint disruption. This is usually sufficient to establish the diagnosis in most cases.
- Three radiographic stages correspond to clinical progression of the disease: fragmentation, coalescence, and reconstruction.
- MRI can detect changes early on and has the highest diagnostic accuracy. Features include the center of signal enhancement within the joints and subchondral bone, disrupted ligaments, and joint deformity.
- PET-CT hybrid useful to rule out osteomyelitis in extremely difficult cases and is reported to have a sensitivity of nearly 100%.

TREATMENT

ACUTE GENERAL Rx

The cornerstone of therapy involves offloading, which is best achieved with cessation of weight-bearing activities and use of total contact casts, typically for a period of 8 to 12 weeks. After an acute phase, prescriptive shoes, boots, and weight-bearing braces are used in cases of lower extremity involvement.
SURGERY: In some cases, operative treatment might be necessary. This involves superconstructs in the treatment of Charcot foot. Preoperative diabetic and infection control and vascular assessment are extremely important to a successful outcome.

PHARMACOLOGIC THERAPY

Antiresorptives such as bisphosphonates and calcitonin have shown improved symptom control and decreased bone turnover markers in controlled trials.

DISPOSITION

Early diagnosis of Charcot's joint is imperative to avoid compromise of bone and joint integrity. In general, it typically takes 1 to 2 yr for complete healing of a Charcot's joint. Once bony changes set in they are very difficult if not impossible to reverse. Timely, appropriate treatment can greatly reduce the risk of irreversible damage and enhance future ability to walk.

REFERRAL

Patient should be referred to a high-risk foot clinic with foot and ankle specialists.

SUGGESTED READINGS
Available at www.expertconsult.com

RELATED CONTENT

Charcot Joint (Patient Information)

AUTHOR: **ANISHKA S. ROLLE, M.D.**

C

Diseases and Disorders

 **BASIC INFORMATION**

DEFINITION

Chemotherapy-induced nausea and vomiting (CINV) refers to adverse emetic effects associated with the use of drugs used to treat cancer. There are three recognized subtypes:

- Acute-phase CINV: nausea and vomiting start within minutes to hours after receiving chemotherapy.
- Delayed-phase CINV: nausea and vomiting begin or return 24 hours or more after receiving chemotherapy.
- Anticipatory CINV: symptoms begin before receiving therapy as a conditioned response in patients who have developed significant nausea and vomiting during previous chemotherapy.

SYNONYMS

Drug-induced nausea and vomiting
Chemotherapy-induced emesis
CINV

ICD-10CM CODES
R11.2	Nausea with vomiting, unspecified
R11.0	Nausea
R11.10	Vomiting, unspecified
Z51.11	Encounter for antineoplastic chemotherapy

EPIDEMIOLOGY & DEMOGRAPHICS

- The patient's risk for development of nausea and vomiting is most strongly dependent on the chemotherapy agent used.
- Chemotherapy drug emetogenicity is classified into four major categories: highly emetic, moderately emetic, low emetic, and minimally emetic.
- With certain chemotherapy regimens, nausea and vomiting will occur in almost 100% of patients. However, patients' tolerance may vary, and symptoms can be as low as 10%.
- Symptoms may be dose dependent (the higher the dose, the greater the risk for symptoms).
- CINV is more likely to affect female and younger patients.
- Patients expecting CINV before receiving therapy are at greater risk of experiencing symptoms (anticipatory emesis).
- Patients with a history of alcohol consumption are at lower risk.
- Patients with a history of motion sickness are at greater risk.

INCIDENCE: The highest incidence is before or during the first cycle of chemotherapy.

GENETICS: Some rapid metabolizers of certain 5-HT3 receptor antagonists and polymorphisms in the 5-HT3 receptor confer greater risk for CINV.

RISK FACTORS:
- Previous history of CINV.
- History of motion sickness or vestibular dysfunction.
- Higher levels of anxiety.
- History of alcohol use decreases risk.

PHYSICAL FINDINGS & CLINICAL PRESENTATION

- Symptoms may include anxiety and light-headedness.
- The most common physical findings are elevated pulse and abnormal blood pressure (elevated if the person is highly anxious, reduced if the patient is dehydrated).
- Symptoms such as diarrhea, fever, headache, and abdominal pain may suggest an alternative diagnosis; physical examination findings such as increased blood pressure, abdominal tenderness, or focal neurologic deficits may suggest symptoms caused by cancer progression or other acute illness such as infection.

PATHOPHYSIOLOGY

CINV is probably the result of chemotherapy drugs acting in two places: directly in the gastrointestinal tract and in the vomiting center of the brain. In both areas, nausea and vomiting are mediated by the actions of certain neurotransmitters, with serotonin, dopamine, and neurokinin-1 being the most important.

 **DIAGNOSIS**

DIFFERENTIAL DIAGNOSIS

- The two main considerations are progression of cancer and infection
- Intestinal/gastric: obstruction or partial obstruction of the digestive tract from tumor
- Neurologic: metastases to the brain causing vomiting; metastatic infiltration of nerves affecting the digestive tract
- Infectious: acute bacterial, viral, or parasitic infections of the digestive tract causing symptoms (usually diarrhea will be present)
- Renal: dehydration leading to acute kidney injury and failure, causing a worsening of nausea and vomiting

WORKUP

No workup is indicated if patient's symptoms and onset of nausea and vomiting fit the usual presentation for CINV. If other symptoms or unexpected physical examination findings are present, then other causes need to be ruled out. A combination of blood work and imaging may be helpful.

LABORATORY TESTS

- If the onset of symptoms is not typical for CINV, then blood tests such as a CBC, liver function tests, and kidney function tests may be indicated.
- Stool studies looking for infections from bacteria or parasites may be ordered if diarrhea is also present.

IMAGING STUDIES

- Abdominal radiographs may be ordered to look for obstruction of the digestive tract but will not provide any information about tumor progression.
- Abdominal CT scan will provide more detailed information about local cancer progression/invasion in the proximity of the digestive tract and whether obstruction of the digestive tract is present.

- Brain CT scan or magnetic resonance imaging (MRI) will provide information about possible metastases to the brain.

Rx **TREATMENT**

- Treatment depends on the likelihood of a given drug or drug regimen to cause CINV and is preventive in nature.
- For chemotherapy agents with a high probability of causing CINV, adding anti-nausea medications has proven to be highly effective in symptom prevention.
- Drug of choice and its duration of use is highly dependent on the chemotherapy regimen used.
- The most common treatment combination includes a serotonin-receptor antagonist (ondansetron, granisetron, dolasetron, or palonosetron), a corticosteroid (methylprednisolone or dexamethasone), and a neurokinin-1 receptor antagonist (aprepitant, roaprepitant, or fosaprepitant).
- Many other drugs are available, such as olanzapine, prochlorperazine, metoclopramide, haloperidol, and marinol, but they are less effective and have greater potential for adverse effects.
- Benzodiazepines (usually lorazepam) may help in patients with significant anxiety levels that lead to anticipatory CINV.
- Patients with uncontrolled symptoms may require hospitalization for supportive care including intravenous medications and fluids.

NONPHARMACOLOGIC THERAPY

For those patients with a significant anxiety component to their CINV, cognitive behavioral therapy may help.

DISPOSITION

Although CINV is one of the most feared complications of cancer therapy, its treatment has been revolutionized in the last 20 years, with most patients achieving adequate symptom control.

! **PEARLS & CONSIDERATIONS**

COMMENTS

- Aggressive symptom control in the acute phase of CINV is the key initial therapeutic approach. Prevention of the acute phase has led to much improved control of the delayed phase, which, in turn, has greatly decreased the incidence of anticipatory CINV.
- Prevention of symptoms is much easier to achieve than controlling or treating symptoms once they have begun.

SUGGESTED READINGS
Available at www.expertconsult.com

AUTHORS: **BYUNG KIM, M.D.,** and **BHARTI RATHORE, M.D.**

ⓘ BASIC INFORMATION

DEFINITION

Definition from the Federal Child Abuse Prevention and Treatment Act (CAPTA): any recent act or failure to act on the part of a parent or caretaker that results in death, serious physical or emotional harm, sexual abuse or exploitation of a child; or an act or failure to act that presents an imminent risk of serious harm to a child. More specific definitions may be found in individual states.

- Neglect: failure to provide for the basic needs of a child
  1. Physical neglect: failure to provide necessary food, shelter, and supervision
  2. Medical neglect: failure to provide necessary medical or mental health care
  3. Educational neglect: failure to meet educational needs
  4. Emotional neglect: failure to attend to emotional needs, exposure to domestic violence
- Physical abuse: physical injury inflicted by a parent or caregiver intentionally or in the course of excessive discipline
- Sexual abuse: sexual act inflicted by parent or caretaker; includes exploitation and pornography
- Emotional/psychological abuse: pattern of behavior of caretaker toward a child that impairs emotional development. This includes verbal abuse, cruelty, and threats. Difficult to prove. Almost always present when other forms of abuse occur.
- Abandonment: child left and parents' whereabouts unknown.
- Substance abuse: includes: prenatal exposure to mother's use of illicit drugs; manufacture of drugs, e.g., methamphetamine in the presence of a child; selling or giving drugs to a child; use of mood-altering substance by caregivers that impairs their ability to provide care for their child.

SYNONYMS

Child maltreatment syndrome
Physical abuse
Sexual abuse
Battered child syndrome
Shaken baby syndrome
Shaken impact syndrome
Abusive head trauma

ICD-10 CM CODES
T74	Adult and child abuse, neglect or other maltreatment, confirmed
T74.02	Child neglect or abandonment, confirmed
T74.12	Child physical abuse, confirmed
T74.32	Child psychological abuse, confirmed
T74.22	Child sexual abuse, confirmed
Z62.811	Personal history of psychological abuse in childhood
Z62.819	Personal history of unspecified abuse in childhood

T76.32XA	Child psychological abuse, suspected, initial encounter
T76.22XA	Child sexual abuse, suspected, initial encounter
T76.12XA	Child physical abuse, suspected, initial encounter

EPIDEMIOLOGY & DEMOGRAPHICS

INCIDENCE (IN U.S.): Any reports of incidence are underestimates because many cases are not recognized or reported. The following data are based on Child Protective Services (CPS) state aggregate as reported in *Child Maltreatment 2013*. In 2013 roughly 679,000 unique children were determined to be victims of abuse or neglect. This is a rate of 9.1 unduplicated victims per 1000 children.

- Types of abuse by percentage (note the total is greater than 100% since children are often victims of more than one type of abuse).
  1. Neglect: 79.5%
  2. Physical abuse: 18%
  3. Sexual abuse: 9%
  4. Psychological abuse: 8.7%
  5. Medical neglect: 2.3%
  6. Other: 10% (e.g., abandonment, threats of harm, congenital drug addiction)
- For 2013, an estimated 1520 child deaths were caused by abuse or neglect.
  1. Overall annual death rate resulting from abuse or neglect is estimated to be 2 deaths/100,000 children.
  2. 71% of these deaths were due to neglect alone or in combination with other forms of abuse; 46.8% were due to physical abuse; alone or in combination.
  3. 73.9% of these children were younger than 3 yr of age with 46% less than 1 yr old.
  4. Most fatalities were directly caused by one or both parents (78.9%).
  5. Many child abuse fatalities are underreported because of misdiagnosis or variations in state definitions and coding.
- 91% of abused children were victimized by one or both of their parents.
- One fifth of adult women report history of molestation or sexual assault as a child or adolescent.

PREDOMINANT SEX: There is a slight predominance of girls as victims. However, boys have a higher child fatality rate than girls (2.36/100,000 for boys and 1.77/100,000 for girls).

PREDOMINANT AGE: Youngest children (0 to 3 yr old) have the highest rates of victimization with 27% being younger than the age of 3.

GENETICS: No known genetic factors.

ETIOLOGY

Multiple factors contribute to the incidence. No factor or combination of factors can definitively predict which children will be victimized. Factors contributing to risk of abuse or neglect include the following:

- Parent
  1. Substance abuse
  2. Mental illness
  3. Intellectual impairment
  4. Parental history of being abused as a child
  5. Young age of parent
  6. Poor knowledge of child development leading to unrealistic expectations
- Child
  1. Low birth weight or prematurity
  2. Chronic physical disability or illness
  3. Prior CPS report
  4. Unplanned, unwanted child
- Family
  1. Social isolation
  2. Poor parent-child bonding
  3. Stress: unemployment, chronic illness, eviction, arrest, poverty, military deployment
  4. Domestic violence
  5. Nonbiologically related adult male living in household
- Community/society
  1. Limited transportation
  2. Limited day care
  3. Unsafe neighborhoods
  4. Poverty

Ⓓⓧ DIAGNOSIS

Careful history and physical examination are the most important aspects of the evaluation. Careful documentation of any statements regarding origin of injuries or history of abuse is crucial. Careful history of behavior before and after the event and activities leading up to the event are also critical, especially in infants and toddlers. Chart and photographic documentation of injuries is also essential. The following are keys to the final diagnosis:

- Patterned bruising (e.g., loop-shaped, square, oval) is indicative of being struck with an object (Fig. E1C-60).
- Bruising to nonbony areas: torso, ears, face, neck and upper arms, especially in children younger than the age of 4 yr.
- Injury observed is incompatible with the history provided.
- History of injury provided is incompatible with the developmental capabilities of the child.
- Delay in seeking care for a significant injury (e.g., callus formation on a fracture, eschar formation on a burn).
- Any injury (bruise, mouth injury, fracture, internal hemorrhage) is rare in healthy preambulatory infants and warrants further investigation.
- Multiple significant injuries of different ages.
- Infant with clinically significant head trauma attributed to a trivial cause (e.g., a short fall). Often associated with retinal hemorrhages and skeletal fractures, which are indicative of shaken baby syndrome or abusive head trauma.
- No history or explanation in a child with significant injury.
- Changing histories as investigation continues.
- Certain fractures in infants without a history of significant trauma (e.g., motor vehicle accident) are characteristic of abuse: metaphyseal, rib, sternum, scapula, vertebral body.
- Inflicted contact burns are indicated by an impression of the burning object: lighter, iron, cigarette (Fig. E1C-61).

- Inflicted immersion burns are indicated by "stocking" burns of the feet or "glove" burns of the hands. Stocking burns are often associated with buttocks/perineal burns from immersion of a minor in a flexed position.
- Most sexual abuse victims will have a normal or nonspecific genital examination. A normal genital examination does not mean the child was not abused. History is the most important part of the diagnosis. Forensic interview by a trained professional is recommended, as is an examination by a health care provider experienced in child sexual abuse evaluations for child and adolescent victims of sexual abuse.
- The identification of a sexually transmitted disease in a prepubertal child who is beyond the neonatal period is highly suspicious and, in some instances, diagnostic of sexual abuse. Reporting and further careful investigation are mandatory. Consult current CDC guidelines and a child sexual abuse expert for further guidance.

DIFFERENTIAL DIAGNOSIS

In all categories, accidental injury is the most common entity to be distinguished from abuse. Accidental injuries are most common over bony prominences: forehead, elbows, knees, shins; soft, fleshy areas are more common for inflicted injury: buttocks, thighs, upper arms. Neck and ears are also more common locations for inflicted injury. Table 1C-12 describes patterns of injury.

BRUISING:
- Bleeding disorder (idiopathic thrombocytopenic purpura, hemophilia, leukemia, hemorrhagic disease of the newborn, von Willebrand's disease)
- Connective tissue disorder (Ehlers-Danlos syndrome, vasculitis)
- Pigments (Mongolian spots)
- Dermatitis (phytophotodermatitis, nickel allergy)
- Folk treatment (coining, cupping)

BURNS:
- Chemical burn
- Impetigo
- Folk treatment (moxibustion)
- Dermatitis (phytophotodermatitis)

INTRACRANIAL HEMORRHAGE:
- Bleeding disorder
- Perinatal trauma (should resolve by 4 wk)
- Arteriovenous malformation rupture
- Glutaric aciduria

TABLE 1C-12   Patterns of Injury

Accidental	Nonaccidental
Unilateral	Bilateral/symmetrical
Isolated injury	Multiple injuries
Amorphous shape	Well-defined shape
Prominent bone areas	Soft tissue areas
Posterior aspect of body	Anterior aspect of body
One age of injury	Multiple ages of injury

From Fuhrman BP et al: *Pediatric critical care*, ed 4, Philadelphia, 2011, Saunders.

FRACTURES:
- Osteogenesis imperfecta
- Rickets
- Congenital syphilis
- Very low birth weight (osteopenia of prematurity)

SEXUAL ABUSE:
- Normal variants
- Lichen sclerosis et atrophicus
- Congenital abnormalities
- Urethral prolapse
- Hemangioma
- Nonsexually acquired infection (group A *Streptococcus, Shigella*)

WORKUP (FIG. E1C-62)

History and physical examination:
- Careful history from all caretakers and child.
- Scene investigation may be necessary.
- Complete physical examination.
- Sexual abuse: forensic interview and magnified examinations by trained professionals are the standard for evaluation and evidence collection. This is especially important to avoid further psychological or physical trauma to the child.

Laboratory tests to assess for bleeding disorder in the case of children with suspicious bruising. These tests may not be necessary if the abuse was witnessed or if the child has clear patterned bruising or other indicators of physical abuse:
- CBC with differential and platelets.
- Prothrombin time, activated partial thromboplastin time.
- Von Willebrand factor antigen and activity
- Factor VIII and IX levels
- Alanine aminotransferase, amylase, urinalysis should be considered in infants or other children with abdominal bruising to look for evidence of internal injury to the liver, pancreas, or kidneys.

Laboratory tests to assess for bleeding disorder in the case of children with suspicious ICH. These tests may not be necessary if the abuse was witnessed or if the child has clear patterned bruising or other indicators of physical abuse:
- CBC with differential and platelets.
- Prothrombin time, activated partial thromboplastin time.
- Factor VIII and IX levels
- DIC Panel
- Consultation with a child abuse expert physician should be strongly considered in children with suspicion of abusive head trauma.

Laboratory tests for sexual abuse:
- If within 72 hr of acute sexual assault/abuse, swabs are obtained from the oropharynx, areas of skin exposure (use an alternate light source to ID), genitalia, and rectum to send to the crime lab for DNA and other testing. Also collect samples of foreign hair, blood, saliva, or other tissue if present. A wet mount from cervical/vaginal specimen should be done to look for motile sperm.
- Per current CDC recommendations, adolescent victims of acute assault should have appropriate specimens collected from sites of penetration or attempted penetration for *Neisseria gonorrhoeae* and *Chlamydia*. Nucleic acid amplification tests (NAATs) may be used and are preferred. In females, wet mount and culture or POC testing of vaginal swab for *T. vaginalis* should also be done. If there is itching, vaginal discharge or malodor present, wet mount for bacterial vaginosis and *Candida* should also be done. Serum should be obtained for HIV, hepatitis B, and syphilis testing acutely. If negative, HIV and syphilis testing should be repeated 6, 12, and 24 wk after the assault.
- Child victims (i.e., prepubertal) should have specimens collected if considered high risk for a sexually transmitted infection (STI) per current CDC recommendations. Cervical specimens are not collected and vaginal specimens must be collected with care by an experienced provider to avoid further trauma to the child. Gonorrhea and *Chlamydia* culture is the gold standard for diagnosis and legal purposes. However, many providers now analyze specimens using urine or vaginal NAAT followed by culture confirmation or 2nd NAAT if any positive results are obtained. However, extragenital sites should have cultures obtained when assessing for gonorrhea and *Chlamydia*. Any culture testing positive for *N. gonorrhoeae* should be confirmed by at least two laboratory tests that are based on different principles. Specimens should be collected for gonorrhea and *Chlamydia*, wet mount, and blood for serologic testing (HIV, hepatitis B, syphilis) in the following cases:
  1. Child has a past or current symptom of an STI, such as vaginal discharge, genital ulcer, or vaginal pain or currently diagnosed STI
  2. Alleged assailant is known to have an STI or be at high risk for an STI
  3. A sibling or adult in the same household has a known STI
  4. Evidence of ejaculation or of oral, genital, and/or anal penetration is present on the examination
  5. Child was assaulted by a stranger
  6. Child lives in an area with a high rate of STI
  7. Child or parent requests testing

IMAGING STUDIES

Physical abuse:
- Radiographic skeletal survey for all children with suspicious injuries up to 2 yr. Additionally, any twin of an abused infant or toddler younger than 2 yr or a child younger than 2 yr of an abused sibling. For children 2 to 5 yr, done only for severe abuse. Consider repeat skeletal survey in 2 wk if severe physical injury is present. Adjunct imaging (MRI, ultrasound, bone scan) may be useful to further define suspicious lesions seen on plain films. Skeletal survey should conform to American College of Radiology Standards.

- Noncontrast head CT scan or MRI for all children <1 yr; for children over 1 yr, clinical judgment should be used.
- Head MRI for children with significant abusive head trauma. This is used as an adjunct a few days after initial head CT.
- Abdominal CT scan if indicated by clinical examination or laboratory evaluation.
- Box 1C-1 describes the specificity of radiologic findings for child abuse.

 **TREATMENT**

ACUTE GENERAL Rx

- Stabilize and treat acute medical injuries.
- Report to Child Protective Services. HIPAA allows reports for suspected child abuse without parental authorization.
- Early report to law enforcement for suspected physical abuse or sexual abuse to allow scene investigation.
- Disposition, once medically stable, is dependent on CPS. The child cannot be returned home if the environment is not safe.
- Physician should remain available to discuss with investigators. This is often critical to

---

BOX 1C-1 Specificity of Radiologic Findings for Child Abuse

High Specificity
Classic metaphyseal lesions
Rib fractures, especially posterior
Scapular fractures
Spinous process fractures
Sternal fractures

Moderate Specificity
Multiple fractures, especially bilateral
Fractures of different ages
Epiphyseal separations
Vertebral body fractures and subluxations
Digital fractures
Complex skull fractures

Common but Low Specificity
Subperiosteal new bone formation
Clavicular fractures
Long bone shaft fractures
Linear skull fractures

From Manaster BJ: *Musculoskeletal imaging—the requisites,* ed 3, Philadelphia, Mosby, 2006.

---

determining the outcome of the case and placement of the child.

- Because follow-up of adolescent sexual assault victims can be difficult, many experts recommend offering empiric treatment for STIs: gonorrhea, *Chlamydia, Trichomonas,* and bacterial vaginosis. Pregnancy prophylaxis should also be offered. Hepatitis B immunization should be offered if not previously given. HIV prophylaxis is offered in certain situations depending on local epidemiology and type of assault. Consult local infectious disease experts for current recommendations. Repeat examination should be done in 2 wk for all victims of sexual assault, especially if they declined empiric treatment. If empiric treatment was not done, STI testing should be repeated at the 2-week follow-up visit.
- Empiric treatment of child victims of sexual abuse is generally not recommended. This is especially important if NAATs are used for screening for STIs because confirmation is necessary for any positive results. Careful follow-up within 2 wk and treatment based on culture results are indicated. HIV prophylaxis is offered in certain circumstances according to local epidemiology and risk. Consult with a local infectious disease expert for further recommendations.

CHRONIC Rx

- Often depends on CPS and court-ordered interventions
- Treatment of parental mental illness
- Treatment of parental substance abuse, including requirements for random drug testing
- Instruction for parents in behavior management skills, including appropriate limit setting and discipline
- Anger management classes for parents
- Trauma-focused cognitive-behavioral therapy is an evidence-based practice for victims of sexual abuse and exposure to domestic violence; useful to include nonoffending parent/caregiver
- Ongoing individual and family therapy
  1. Parent-child interactive therapy is an evidence-based practice that is used with young children with behavioral problems and parent-child relationship problems

  2. Child-parent psychotherapy is an evidence-based practice that is for young children (<5 yr) who have experienced a trauma and their caregivers
- May need long-term placement in foster care before it is safe to return home. In extreme cases of abuse, parental rights may be terminated without offering services.

OUTCOMES

- Victims of chronic abuse and neglect:
  1. Have higher rates of mental illness (depression, suicide, posttraumatic stress disorder, eating disorders)
  2. Have more cognitive difficulties, often impaired academic performance
  3. Are more likely to become aggressive
  4. Are more likely as adults to have adverse physical health outcomes (cardiovascular disease, cancer, STDs)
- Victims of abusive head trauma:
  1. One third die, one third have severe disability, one third appear normal in the short term.

 **PEARLS & CONSIDERATIONS**

PREVENTION

- Home visitation by a specially trained nurse to high-risk families during pregnancy and infancy has shown positive outcomes (Nurse-Family Partnership).
- Anticipatory guidance at health visits to teach normal developmental expectations and appropriate discipline.
- Screening to identify at-risk or abused children.
- Targeted education in the newborn nursery for shaken baby prevention has been shown to be effective.
- Substance abuse prevention and treatment.
- Identification and intervention for domestic violence before children are born.

SUGGESTED READINGS
Available at www.expertconsult.com

RELATED CONTENT
Protecting Children from Abuse (Patient Information)

AUTHOR: **NANCY R. GRAFF, M.D.**

C

 **BASIC INFORMATION**

DEFINITION

Genital infection with *Chlamydia trachomatis* may result in urethritis, epididymitis, cervicitis, and acute salpingitis, but often it is asymptomatic in women (see "Pelvic Inflammatory Disease"). In men, urethritis, mucopurulent discharge, dysuria, and urethral pruritus are noted.

ICD-10CM CODES
A56.01 Chlamydial cystitis and urethritis
N34.1 Nonspecific urethritis
N45.4 Abscess of epididymis or testis
A74.89 Other chlamydial diseases

EPIDEMIOLOGY & DEMOGRAPHICS

- *C. trachomatis* is the most common sexually transmitted disease in the U.S. More than 4 million infections occur annually, although the exact number is unknown because reporting is not required in all states. Occurrence is common worldwide and has been increasing steadily over the last 2 decades in the U.S., Canada, Australia, and Europe.
- Most women with endocervical or urethral infections are asymptomatic.
- Up to 45% of cases of gonococcal infection may have concomitant chlamydial infection.
- Infertility or ectopic pregnancy can result as a complication from symptomatic or asymptomatic chronic infections of the endometrium and fallopian tubes.
- Conjunctival and pneumonic infection of the newborn may result from infection in pregnancy.
- In men 15% to 55% of cases are caused by *C. trachomatis*. Complications of nongonococcal urethritis in men infected with *C. trachomatis* include epididymitis and Reiter's syndrome.
- Table 1C-13 summarizes clinical characteristics of common *C. trachomatis* infections.

PHYSICAL FINDINGS & CLINICAL PRESENTATION

Clinical manifestations may be similar to those of gonorrhea: mucopurulent endocervical discharge, with edema, erythema, and easily induced endocervical bleeding caused by inflammation of endocervical columnar epithelium. Less-frequent manifestations may include bartholinitis, urethral syndrome with dysuria and pyuria, and perihepatitis (Fitz-Hugh–Curtis syndrome).

ETIOLOGY

- *C. trachomatis,* serotypes D through K
- Obligate, intracellular bacteria

Dx DIAGNOSIS

DIFFERENTIAL DIAGNOSIS

Gonorrhea, nongonococcal urethritis (nonchlamydial etiologies)

WORKUP

Diagnosis based on laboratory demonstration of evidence of infection in intraurethral or endocervical swab by various tests. The intracellular organism is less readily recovered from the discharge. Diagnosis can be made in both men and women using first catch urine void specimens.

LABORATORY TESTS

- Cell culture is the reference method for diagnosis (single culture sensitivity 80% to 90%), but it is labor intensive and takes 48 to 96 hr; it is not suited for large screening programs.
- Nonculture methods:
  1. NAATs are very sensitive tests for cervical and male urethral specimens and are FDA-approved for use with urine.
  2. Direct fluorescent antibody tests
  3. Enzyme immunoassay
  4. DNA probes
  5. Polymerase chain reaction (PCR)
- With the exception of PCR, the other tests are probably less specific than cell culture and may yield false-positive results.
- Because this is an intracellular organism, purulent discharge is not an appropriate specimen. An adequate sample of infected cells must be obtained.
- >Ten white blood cells per high-power field (mucopurulent discharge, presumptive diagnosis).

Rx TREATMENT

ACUTE GENERAL Rx

Nongonococcal urethritis, urethritis, cervicitis, conjunctivitis (except for lymphogranuloma venereum):
- Azithromycin 1 g PO ×single dose therapy *or*
- Doxycycline 100 mg PO bid for 7 days
- Alternatives
  1. Erythromycin base 500 mg PO qid for 7 days *or*
  2. Erythromycin ethylsuccinate 800 mg PO qid for 7 days *or*
  3. Levofloxacin 500 mg PO qd for 7 days *or*
  4. Ofloxacin 300 mg PO bid for 7 days

Infection in pregnancy:
- Azithromycin 1 gm PO single dose therapy
Alternatives:
- Amoxicillin 500 mg PO tid for 7 days *or*
- Erythromycin base 250 mg PO qid for 7 days *or*
- Erythromycin ethylsuccinate 800 mg PO qid for 7 days
- Erythromycin ethylsuccinate 400 mg PO qid for 14 days

NOTE: Doxycycline and ofloxacin are contraindicated in pregnancy. Safety and efficacy of azithromycin are not established in pregnancy and lactation, although preliminary data indicate that it may be safe and effective. Erythromycin estolate is contraindicated in pregnancy because of drug-related hepatotoxicity.

FOLLOW-UP: Observed single-dose therapy should be offered to individuals for whom compliance is a concern. Reculture after therapy completion and refer partners for evaluation and treatment.

RECURRENT AND PERSISTENT URETHRITIS: Retreat noncompliant patients with the above regimens. If patient was initially compliant, recommended regimens: metronidazole 2 g PO in single dose plus erythromycin base 500 mg PO qid for 7 days or erythromycin ethylsuccinate 800 mg PO qid for 7 days.

CLINICAL PEARL

When treating *Chlamydia,* it is best to assume concomitant gonorrhea because co-infection is common. Combination of ceftriaxone 125 mg IM single dose plus azithromycin 1 g PO single dose will treat both.

REFERRAL

Refer to infectious disease specialist if persistent infection or gynecologist if salpingitis is suspected.

SUGGESTED READINGS
Available at www.expertconsult.com

RELATED CONTENT
Cervicitis (Related Key Topic)
Gonococcal Urethritis (Related Key Topic)
Gonorrhea (Related Key Topic)
Nongonococcal Urethritis (Related Key Topic)
Pelvic Inflammatory Disease (Related Key Topic)

AUTHOR: **RUBEN ALVERO, M.D.**

Diseases and Disorders

I

TABLE 1C-13 Clinical Characteristics of Common *Chlamydia trachomatis* Infections

	Infection	Symptoms and Signs	Presumptive Diagnosis	Definitive Diagnosis	Treatment
Men	Nongonococcal urethritis	Urethral discharge, dysuria	Urethral leukocytosis; no gonococci seen	Urine or urethral NAAT	Azithromycin, 1 g PO (single dose) *or* Doxycycline, 100 mg PO bid, for 7 days
	Epididymitis	Unilateral epididymal tenderness, swelling; pain; fever, presence of NGU	Urine or urethral NAAT	Urethral leukocytosis; pyuria on urinalysis	STI likely: Ceftriaxone 250 mg IM plus doxycycline, 100 mg PO bid, for 10 days *History of insertive anal intercourse:* Ceftriaxone, 250 mg IM, plus levofloxacin, 500 mg bid for 10 days
	Proctitis (non-LGV)	Rectal pain, discharge and bleeding; history of receptive anal intercourse	≥1 PMN/OIF on rectal Gram stain; no gonococci seen	Urine or urethral NAAT; rectal culture or NAAT	Doxycycline, 100 mg PO bid, for 7 days
	LGV	Painful, tender inguinal lymphadenopathy, fever	"Groove sign"	Urine, urethral, lymph node or rectal NAAT; rectal or lymph node culture; LGV-specific testing if available	Doxycycline, 100 mg PO bid, for 21 days
	LGV proctitis	Rectal pain, discharge, and bleeding in MSM; absence of inguinal lymphadenopathy	≥1 PMN/OIF on rectal Gram stain; no gonococci seen	Urine, urethral, or rectal NAAT; rectal culture; LGV-specific testing if available	Doxycycline, 100 mg PO bid, for 21 days
	Conjunctivitis	Ocular pain, redness, discharge; simultaneous genital infection	Gram stain of conjunctival swab negative for bacterial pathogens; PMNs on smear	Rectal culture or NAAT; NAAT of conjunctivae	Azithromycin, 1 g PO (single dose) *or* Doxycycline, 100 mg PO bid, for 7 days
Women	Cervicitis	Mucopurulent cervical discharge; ectopy, easily induced bleeding	≥20 PMN/OIF on cervical Gram stain	Urine or cervical NAAT	Azithromycin, 1 g PO (single dose) *or* Doxycycline, 100 mg PO bid, for 7 days
	Urethritis	Dysuria, frequency; no hematuria	Pyuria on UA; negative urine Gram stain and culture	Urine, cervical, or urethral NAAT	Azithromycin, 1 g PO (single dose) *or* Doxycycline, 100 mg PO bid for 7 days
	PID	Lower abdominal pain, adnexal pain, cervical motion tenderness	Evidence of mucopurulent cervicitis	Urine or cervical NAAT	Outpatient: Ceftriaxone 250 mg IM as a single dose, plus doxycycline 100 mg PO bid for 14 days, with or without metronidazole, 500 mg PO bid for 14 days
Adults	Conjunctivitis	Ocular pain, redness, discharge; simultaneous genital infection	Gram stain of conjunctival swab negative for bacterial pathogens; PMNs on smear	DFA or NAAT on conjunctival swab	Azithromycin, 1 g PO (single dose) *or* Doxycycline, 100 mg PO bid for 7 days
Newborns	Conjunctivitis	Ocular pain, redness, discharge; simultaneous genital infection	Gram stain of conjunctival swab negative for bacterial pathogens; PMNs on smear	DFA or NAAT on conjunctival swab; vagina, rectum, pharynx also often positive	Erythromycin base 50 mg/kg/day, orally divided into four doses daily for 14 days; evaluate and treat parents as well
	Pneumonia	Staccato cough, tachypnea, hyperinflation	Diffuse interstitial infiltrate, eosinophilia	Nasopharyngeal NAATs or culture; MIF serology (IgM)	Erythromycin base 50 mg/kg/day, orally divided into four doses daily for 14 days; evaluate and treat parents as well

DFA, Direct fluorescent antibody; *IgM,* immunoglobulin M; *LGV,* lymphogranuloma venereum; *MIF,* microimmunofluorescence; *MSM,* men who have sex with men; *NAAT,* nucleic acid amplification test; *NGU,* nongonococcal urethritis; *OIF,* oil immersion field; *PMN,* polymorphonuclear neutrophil; *STI,* sexually transmitted infection; *UA,* urinalysis.

From Bennett JE, Dolin R, Blaser MJ. *Mandell, Douglas, and Bennett's principles and practice of infectious diseases,* ed 8, Philadelphia, 2015, Saunders.

 **BASIC INFORMATION**

DEFINITION

Cholangitis refers to an inflammation and/or infection of the hepatic and common bile ducts associated with obstruction of the common bile duct.

SYNONYMS

Biliary sepsis
Ascending cholangitis
Suppurative cholangitis

ICD-10CM CODES
K83.0 Cholangitis
K80.30 Calculus of bile duct with cholangitis, unspecified, without obstruction
K80.31 Calculus of bile duct with cholangitis, unspecified, with obstruction
K80.32 Calculus of bile duct with acute cholangitis without obstruction
K80.33 Calculus of bile duct with acute cholangitis with obstruction
K80.34 Calculus of bile duct with chronic cholangitis without obstruction
K80.35 Calculus of bile duct with chronic cholangitis with obstruction
K80.36 Calculus of bile duct with acute and chronic cholangitis without obstruction
K80.37 Calculus of bile duct with acute and chronic cholangitis with obstruction
K80.50 Calculus of bile duct without cholangitis or cholecystitis without obstruction
K80.51 Calculus of bile duct without cholangitis or cholecystitis with obstruction

EPIDEMIOLOGY & DEMOGRAPHICS

INCIDENCE (IN U.S.): Complicates approximately 1% of cases of cholelithiasis
PEAK INCIDENCE: Seventh decade
PREVALENCE (IN U.S.): 2 cases/1000 hospital admissions
PREDOMINANT SEX:
- Females, for cholangitis secondary to gallstones
- Males, for cholangitis secondary to malignant obstruction and HIV infection
PREDOMINANT AGE: Seventh decade and older; unusual <50 yr of age

PHYSICAL FINDINGS & CLINICAL PRESENTATION

- Usually acute onset of fever, abdominal pain (RUQ), and jaundice (Charcot's triad) or Reynolds pentad (Charcot triad plus hypotension and mental status changes)
- All signs and symptoms in only 50% to 85% of patients
- Often, dark coloration of the urine resulting from bilirubinuria
- Complications:
  1. Bacteremia (50%) and septic shock
  2. Hepatic abscess and pancreatitis

ETIOLOGY

Obstruction of the common bile duct causing rapid proliferation of bacteria in the biliary tree
- Most common cause of common bile duct obstruction: stones, usually migrated from the gallbladder
- Other causes: prior biliary tract surgery with secondary stenosis, tumor (usually arising from the pancreas or biliary tree), and parasitic infections from *Ascaris lumbricoides* or *Fasciola hepatica*
- Iatrogenic after contamination of an obstructed biliary tree by endoscopic retrograde cholangiopancreatoscopy (ERCP) or percutaneous transhepatic cholangiography (PTC)
- Primary sclerosing cholangitis (PSC)
- HIV-associated sclerosing cholangitis: associated with infection by CMV, *Cryptosporidium*, Microsporida, and *Mycobacterium avium* complex

 **DIAGNOSIS**

DIFFERENTIAL DIAGNOSIS

- Biliary colic
- Acute cholecystitis
- Liver abscess
- Peptic ulcer disease (PUD)
- Pancreatitis
- Intestinal obstruction
- Right kidney stone
- Hepatitis
- Pyelonephritis

WORKUP

- Blood cultures
- CBC
- Liver function tests

LABORATORY TESTS

- Usually, elevated WBC count with a predominance of polymorphonuclear forms
- Elevated alkaline phosphatase and bilirubin in chronic obstruction
- Elevated transaminases in acute obstruction
- Positive blood cultures in 50% of cases, typically with enteric gram-negative aerobes (e.g., *Escherichia coli*, *Klebsiella pneumoniae*), enterococci, or anaerobes

IMAGING STUDIES

- Magnetic retrograde cholangiopancreatography (MRCP) or endoscopic ultrasound are most reliable diagnostic modalities for common bile duct stones
- Abdominal ultrasound:
  1. Allows visualization of the gallbladder and bile ducts to differentiate extrahepatic obstruction from intrahepatic cholestasis
  2. Insensitive but can visualize common duct stones
- CT scan:
  1. Less accurate for gallstones
  2. More sensitive than ultrasound for visualization of the distal part of the common bile duct
  3. Also allows better definition of neoplasm
- ERCP:
  1. Confirms obstruction and its level

  2. Allows collection of specimens for culture and cytology
  3. May be indicated in therapy (see "Treatment")

 **TREATMENT**

NONPHARMACOLOGIC THERAPY

Biliary decompression
- May be urgent in severely ill patients or those unresponsive to medical therapy within 12 to 24 hr
- May also be performed semielectively in patients who respond
- Options:
  1. ERCP with or without sphincterotomy or placement of a draining stent
  2. Percutaneous transhepatic biliary drainage for the acutely ill patient who is a poor surgical candidate
  3. Recently, EUS-guided biliary drainage has been proven as an alternative to percutaneous transhepatic biliary drainage in specialized centers when ERCP fails or is not available.
  4. Surgical exploration of the common bile duct

ACUTE GENERAL Rx

- Nothing by mouth
- Intravenous hydration
- Broad-spectrum antibiotics directed at gram-negative enteric organisms, anaerobes, and enterococcus such as carbapenems (meropenem: 1 g q8h or imipenem: 500 mg IV q6h if life threatening), piperacillin/tazobactam: 3.375 or 4.5 g IV q6h, or ampicillin-sulbactam, or ticarcillin-clavulanate; if infection is nosocomial, post-ERCP, or the patient is in shock, broaden antibiotic coverage.

REFERRAL

- To biliary endoscopist if obstruction is from stones or a stent needs to be placed
- To interventional radiologist if external drainage is necessary
- To a general surgeon in all other cases
- To an infectious disease specialist if blood cultures are positive or the patient is in shock or otherwise severely ill

⚠ PEARLS & CONSIDERATIONS

- Cholangitis is a life-threatening form of intraabdominal sepsis, though it may appear to be rather innocuous at its onset.
- Antibiotics alone will not resolve cholangitis in the presence of biliary obstruction because high intrabiliary pressures prevent antibiotic delivery. Decompression and drainage of the biliary tract to alleviate the obstruction with antimicrobial therapy is the therapy of choice.

SUGGESTED READINGS

Available at www.expertconsult.com

AUTHOR: **GLENN G. FORT, M.D., M.P.H.**

BASIC INFORMATION

DEFINITION
Cholecystitis is acute or chronic inflammation of the gallbladder generally caused by gallstones (>95% of cases).

SYNONYMS
Gallbladder attack

ICD-10CM CODES
K81.9   Acute cholecystitis
K80.00   Calculus of gallbladder with acute cholecystitis without obstruction
K81.9   Cholecystitis, unspecified

EPIDEMIOLOGY & DEMOGRAPHICS
- Acute cholecystitis occurs most commonly in women during the fifth and sixth decades. Approximately 120,000 cholecystectomies are performed for acute cholecystitis annually in the U.S.
- The incidence of gallstones is 0.6% in the general population and much higher in certain ethnic groups (>75% of Native Americans by age 60 yr). Most patients with gallstones are asymptomatic. Of such patients, biliary colic develops in 1% to 4% annually.

PHYSICAL FINDINGS & CLINICAL PRESENTATION
- Pain and tenderness in the right hypochondrium or epigastrium; pain possibly radiating to the infrascapular region
- Palpation of the right upper quadrant (RUQ) eliciting marked tenderness and stoppage of inspired breath (*Murphy's sign*)
- Guarding
- Fever (33%)
- Jaundice (25% to 50% of patients)
- Palpable gallbladder (20% of cases)
- Nausea and vomiting (>70% of patients)
- Fever and chills (>25% of patients)
- Medical history often revealing ingestion of large, fatty meals before onset of pain in the epigastrium and RUQ

ETIOLOGY
- Gallstones (>95% of cases)
- Ischemic damage to the gallbladder, critically ill patient (acalculous cholecystitis)
- Infectious agents, especially in patients with AIDS (cytomegalovirus, *Cryptosporidium*)
- Strictures of the bile duct
- Neoplasms, primary or metastatic
- Risk factors for cholelithiasis include age, obesity, female sex, rapid weight loss, ethnicity/race (Native American), use of contraceptives, pregnancy, diabetes mellitus, hemolysis, total parenteral nutrition, biliary parasites

Dx DIAGNOSIS

DIFFERENTIAL DIAGNOSIS
- Hepatic: hepatitis, abscess, hepatic congestion, neoplasm, trauma

- Biliary: neoplasm, stricture, sphincter of Oddi dysfunction
- Gastric: pelvic ulcer disease, neoplasm, alcoholic gastritis, hiatal hernia, non-ulcer dyspepsia
- Pancreatic: pancreatitis, neoplasm, stone in the pancreatic duct or ampulla
- Renal: calculi, infection, inflammation, neoplasm, ruptured kidney
- Pulmonary: pneumonia, pulmonary infarction, right-sided pleurisy
- Intestinal: retrocecal appendicitis, intestinal obstruction, high fecal impaction, irritable bowel syndrome (IBS), inflammatory bowel disease (IBD)
- Cardiac: myocardial ischemia (particularly involving the inferior wall), pericarditis
- Cutaneous: herpes zoster
- Trauma
- Fitz-Hugh-Curtis syndrome (perihepatitis), ruptured ectopic pregnancy
- Subphrenic abscess
- Dissecting aneurysm
- Nerve root irritation caused by osteoarthritis of the spine

WORKUP
Workup consists of detailed history and physical examination coupled with laboratory evaluation and imaging studies. No single clinical finding or laboratory test is sufficient to establish or exclude cholecystitis without further testing.

LABORATORY TESTS
- Leukocytosis (12,000 to 20,000) is present in >70% of patients.
- Elevated alkaline phosphatase, ALT, AST, bilirubin; bilirubin elevation >4 mg/dl is unusual and suggests presence of choledocholithiasis.
- Elevated amylase may be present (consider pancreatitis if serum amylase elevation exceeds 500 U).

IMAGING STUDIES
- Ultrasound of the gallbladder (Fig. E1C-63) is the preferred initial test; it will demonstrate the presence of stones and also dilated gallbladder with thickened wall and surrounding edema in patients with acute cholecystitis.
- Nuclear imaging (HIDA scan) (Fig. E1C-64) is useful for diagnosis of cholecystitis when sonogram is inconclusive: sensitivity and specificity exceed 90% for acute cholecystitis. This test is only reliable when bilirubin is <5 mg/dl. A positive test result (absence of gallbladder filling within 60 min after the administration of tracer) will demonstrate obstruction of the cystic or common hepatic duct; the test will not demonstrate the presence of stones.
- CT scan of abdomen is useful in cases of suspected abscess, neoplasm, or pancreatitis.
- Plain radiograph of the abdomen generally is not useful because <25% of stones are radiopaque.

Rx TREATMENT

NONPHARMACOLOGIC THERAPY
Provide IV hydration; withhold oral feedings.

ACUTE GENERAL Rx
- Laparoscopic (percutaneous) cholecystectomy (PC) is considered the treatment of choice for most patients. The rate of conversion to open cholecystectomy is higher when laparoscopic cholecystectomy (CCY) is performed for acute cholecystitis rather than for uncomplicated cholelithiasis; conservative management with IV fluids and antibiotics (ampicillin-sulbactam 3 g IV q6h or piperacillin-tazobactam 4.5 g IV q8h) may be justified in some high-risk patients to convert an emergency procedure into an elective one with a lower mortality rate.
- Endoscopic retrograde cholangiopancreatography with sphincterectomy and stone extraction can be performed in conjunction with laparoscopic cholecystectomy for patients with choledochal lithiasis; approximately 7% to 15% of patients with cholelithiasis also have stones in the common bile duct.

DISPOSITION
- Prognosis is good; elective laparoscopic cholecystectomy can be performed as outpatient procedure.
- Hospital stay (when necessary) varies from overnight with laparoscopic cholecystectomy to 4 to 7 days with open cholecystectomy.
- Complication rate is approximately 1% (hemorrhage and bile leak) for laparoscopic cholecystectomy and <0.5% (infection) with open cholecystectomy.

REFERRAL
Surgical referral in all patients with acute cholecystitis

 PEARLS & CONSIDERATIONS

COMMENTS
- Patients should be instructed that stones may recur in bile ducts.
- Gallbladder aspiration, in which all fluid visualized by ultrasound is aspirated, represents a nonsurgical treatment when patients who are at high operative risk develop acute cholecystitis. Salvage cholecystectomy is reserved for nonresponders.

SUGGESTED READINGS
Available at www.expertconsult.com

RELATED CONTENT
Gallbladder Attack (Cholecystitis) (Patient Information)
Cholelithiasis (Related Key Topic)
Cholangitis (Related Key Topic)

AUTHOR: **FRED F. FERRI, M.D.**

C

Diseases and Disorders

I

 BASIC INFORMATION

DEFINITION

Cholelithiasis is the presence of stones in the gallbladder

SYNONYMS

Gallstones

ICD-10CM CODES
K80.80 Other cholelithiasis without obstruction
K80.81 Other cholelithiasis with obstruction
K91.86 Retained cholelithiasis following cholecystectomy

EPIDEMIOLOGY & DEMOGRAPHICS

- Gallstone disease can be found in 12% of the U.S. population. Of these, 2% to 3% (500,000 to 600,000) are treated with cholecystectomies each year.
- Annual medical expenditures for gallbladder surgeries in the U.S. exceed $5 billion.
- Incidence of gallbladder disease increases with age. Highest incidence is in the fifth and sixth decades. Predisposing factors for gallstones are female sex, pregnancy, age >40 yr, family history of gallstones, obesity, ileal disease, oral contraceptives, diabetes mellitus, rapid weight loss, estrogen replacement therapy. Risk factors for the development of cholelithiasis are described in Table E1C-14.
- Patients with gallstones have a 20% chance of developing biliary colic or its complications at the end of a 20-yr period.

PHYSICAL FINDINGS & CLINICAL PRESENTATION

- Physical examination is entirely normal unless patient is having biliary colic; 80% of gallstones are asymptomatic.
- Typical symptoms of obstruction of the cystic duct include intermittent, severe, cramping pain affecting the right upper quadrant.
- Pain occurs mostly at night and may radiate to the back or right shoulder. It can last from a few minutes to several hours.

ETIOLOGY

- 75% of gallstones contain cholesterol and are usually associated with obesity, female sex, and diabetes mellitus; mixed stones are most common (80%); pure cholesterol stones account for only 10% of stones.
- 25% of gallstones are pigment stones (bilirubin, calcium, and variable organic material) associated with hemolysis and cirrhosis. These tend to be black-pigmented stones that are refractory to medical therapy.
- 50% of mixed-type stones are radiopaque.

Dx DIAGNOSIS

DIFFERENTIAL DIAGNOSIS

- Peptic ulcer disease
- Gastroesophageal reflux disease
- Irritable bowel disease
- Pancreatitis
- Neoplasms
- Nonnuclear dyspepsia
- Inferior wall myocardial infarction
- Hepatic abscess

LABORATORY TESTS

Generally normal unless patient has biliary obstruction (elevated alkaline phosphatase, bilirubin).

IMAGING STUDIES

- Ultrasound of the gallbladder (Fig. E1C-65) will detect small stones and biliary sludge (sensitivity, 95%; specificity, 90%); the presence of dilated gallbladder with thickened wall is suggestive of acute cholecystitis.
- Nuclear imaging (HIDA scan) can confirm acute cholecystitis (>90% accuracy) if gallbladder does not visualize within 4 hr of injection and the radioisotope is excreted in the common bile duct.
- Common bile duct stones can be detected noninvasively by magnetic resonance cholangiopancreatography or invasively by endoscopic retrograde cholangiopancreatography (ERCP) and intraoperative cholangiography.

Rx TREATMENT

NONPHARMACOLOGIC THERAPY

Lifestyle changes (avoidance of diets high in polyunsaturated fats, weight loss in obese patients; however, avoid rapid weight loss)

ACUTE GENERAL Rx

- The management of gallstones is affected by the clinical presentation.
- Asymptomatic patients do not require therapeutic intervention. Proposed criteria for prophylactic cholecystectomy are described in Table 1C-15.

TABLE 1C-15 Proposed Criteria for Prophylactic Cholecystectomy

Life expectancy >20 years

Calculi >2 cm in diameter

Calculi >3 mm and patent cystic duct

Radiopaque calculi

Gallbladder polyps >15 mm

Nonfunctioning or calcified gallbladder ("porcelain" gallbladder)

Women <60 years

Patients in areas with high prevalence of gallbladder cancer

From Cameron JL, Cameron AM: *Current surgical therapy,* ed 10, Philadelphia, 2011, Saunders.

- Surgical intervention is generally the ideal approach for symptomatic patients. Laparoscopic cholecystectomy is preferred over open cholecystectomy because of the shorter recovery period and lower mortality rate. Between 5% and 26% of patients undergoing elective laparoscopic cholecystectomy will require conversion to an open procedure. Most common reason is the inability to clearly identify the biliary anatomy.
- Laparoscopic cholecystectomy after endoscopic sphincterectomy is recommended for patients with common bile duct stones and residual gallbladder stones. Where possible, single-stage laparoscopic treatments with removal of duct stones and cholecystectomy during the same procedure are preferable. Percutaneous cholecystectomy is an alternative for patients who are critically ill with gallbladder empyema and sepsis.
- Patients who are not appropriate candidates for surgery because of coexisting illness or patients who refuse surgery can be treated with oral bile salts: ursodiol or chenodiol. Candidates for oral bile salts are patients with cholesterol stones (radiolucent, noncalcified stones), with a diameter of ≤15 mm and having three or fewer stones. Candidates for medical therapy must have a functioning gallbladder and must have absence of calcifications on CT scans.
- Extracorporeal shock wave lithotripsy (ESWL) is another form of medical therapy. It can be used in patients with stone diameter of ≤3 cm and having three or fewer stones.

DISPOSITION

- Complicated gallstone events develop in 8% of patients with incidentally discovered gallstones after 17 years (Shabanzadeh DM, et al: *Gastroenterology* 150:156, 2016).
- After ESWL, stones recur in approximately 20% of patients after 4 yr.
- Patients with at least one gallstone <5 mm in diameter have a greater than fourfold increased risk of presenting with acute biliary pancreatitis. A policy of watchful waiting in such cases is generally warranted.
- A potential serious complication of gallstones is acute cholangitis. ERCP and endoscopic sphincterectomy followed by interval laparoscopic cholecystectomy are effective in acute cholangitis.

SUGGESTED READINGS

Available at www.expertconsult.com

RELATED CONTENT

Gallstones (Patient Information)
Cholecystitis (Related Key Topic)

AUTHOR: **FRED F. FERRI, M.D.**

 **BASIC INFORMATION**

DEFINITION

Chronic fatigue syndrome (CFS), also known as myalgic encephalomyelitis/chronic fatigue syndrome (ME/CFS) is characterized by at least three of the following symptoms, present concurrently for at least 6 mo:

- Impaired memory or concentration (cognitive impairment)
- Sore throat
- Tender cervical or axillary lymph nodes
- Muscle pain
- Multijoint pain
- New headaches
- Unrefreshing sleep
- Postexertion malaise for longer than 24 hr
- Orthostatic intolerance

There are currently several sets of clinical criteria to define ME/CFS, yet there is no consensus regarding which set of criteria best identifies patients with this condition.

SYNONYMS

Yuppie flu
CFS
Chronic Epstein-Barr syndrome
Myalgic encephalomyelitis/chronic fatigue syndrome (ME/CFS)
Systemic exertion intolerance disease (SEID)

ICD-10CM CODES
R53.82 Chronic fatigue, unspecified
F45.8   Other somatoform disorders

EPIDEMIOLOGY & DEMOGRAPHICS

PREVALENCE IN U.S: Prevalence rates of CFS in the U.S. range from 0.3% to 2.5%. It is estimated that 800,000 to 2.5 million Americans have CFS.
PREDOMINANT AGE: Young adulthood and middle age
PREDOMINANT SEX: Females affected more often than males
ECONOMICS: The estimated annual cost of lost productivity is estimated to be between $17 billion and $24 billion annually.

PHYSICAL FINDINGS & CLINICAL PRESENTATION

- There are no physical findings specific for CFS.
- The physical examination may be useful to identify fibromyalgia and other rheumatologic conditions that may coexist with CFS.

ETIOLOGY

- The etiology of CFS is unknown.
- Some theorize that a viral illness may trigger certain immune responses that lead to the various symptoms. Most patients often report the onset of their symptoms with a flulike illness.

- The presence of numerous psychiatric comorbidities in CFS have led some experts to question the existence of any organic etiology.

 **DIAGNOSIS**

DIFFERENTIAL DIAGNOSIS

- Psychosocial depression, dysthymia, anxiety-related disorders, and other psychiatric diseases
- Sleep apnea
- Infectious diseases (subacute bacterial endocarditis, Lyme disease, fungal diseases, mononucleosis, HIV, chronic hepatitis B or C, tuberculosis (TB), chronic parasitic infections)
- Autoimmune diseases: systemic lupus erythematosus, myasthenia gravis, multiple sclerosis, thyroiditis, rheumatoid arthritis
- Endocrine abnormalities: hypothyroidism, hypopituitarism, adrenal insufficiency, Cushing's syndrome, diabetes mellitus, hyperparathyroidism, pregnancy, reactive hypoglycemia
- Occult malignant disease
- Substance abuse
- Systemic disorders: chronic renal failure, chronic obstructive pulmonary disease, cardiovascular disease, anemia, electrolyte abnormalities, liver disease
- Other: inadequate rest, sleep apnea, narcolepsy, fibromyalgia, sarcoidosis, medications, toxic agent exposure, Wegener's granulomatosis, vitamin deficiency

LABORATORY TESTS

- No specific laboratory tests exist for diagnosing CFS. Initial laboratory tests are useful to exclude other conditions that may mimic or may be associated with CFS.
  1. Screening laboratory tests: CBC, ESR, ALT, total protein, albumin, globulin, alkaline phosphatase, calcium, phosphorus, glucose, BUN, creatinine, electrolytes, TSH, and urinalysis are useful.
  2. Serologic tests for Epstein-Barr virus, *Candida albicans,* human herpesvirus 6, and other studies for immune cellular abnormalities are not useful; these tests are expensive and generally not recommended.
- Other tests may be indicated depending on the history and physical examination (e.g., ANA, RF in patients presenting with joint complaints or abnormalities on physical examination, Lyme titer in areas where Lyme disease is endemic).

IMAGING STUDIES

Generally not recommended unless history and physical examination indicate specific abnormalities (e.g., chest radiography in any patient suspected of TB or sarcoidosis)

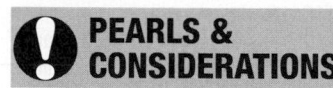 **TREATMENT**

NONPHARMACOLOGIC THERAPY

- Patients should be reassured that the illness is not fatal and that most patients improve over time.
- An initially supervised exercise program to preserve and increase strength is beneficial for most patients and can improve symptoms.
- Cognitive behavioral therapy trials have shown positive effects on fatigue levels, work, depression/anxiety, and social adjustment.

GENERAL Rx

Therapy is generally palliative. The following medications may be helpful; however, evidence is conflicting:

- Antidepressants: The choice of antidepressant varies with the desired side effects. Patients with difficulty sleeping or fibromyalgia-like symptoms may benefit from low-dose tricyclics (doxepin 10 mg hs or amitriptyline 25 mg qhs). When sedation is not desirable, low-dose SSRIs (paroxetine 20 mg qd) often help alleviate fatigue and associated symptoms.
- NSAIDs can be used to relieve muscle and joint pain and headaches.
  "Alternative" medications (herbs, multivitamins, nutritional supplements) are very popular with many CFS patients but are generally not very helpful.

 **PEARLS & CONSIDERATIONS**

COMMENTS

- In CFS the symptoms are serious enough to reduce daily activities by >50% in the absence of any other medically identifiable disorders.
- Moderate to complete recovery at 1 yr occurs in 22% to 60% of patients with CFS.

EVIDENCE

Available at www.expertconsult.com

SUGGESTED READINGS

Available at www.expertconsult.com

RELATED CONTENT

Evaluation of Fatigue (Algorithm, Section III)
Chronic Fatigue Syndrome (Patient Information)

AUTHOR: **FRED F. FERRI, M.D.**

BASIC INFORMATION

DEFINITION

Chronic inflammatory demyelinating polyneuropathy (CIDP) is an autoimmune neuropathy manifesting with symmetric proximal and distal weakness with associated sensory loss along with reduced or absent reflexes for >2 mo

SYNONYMS

Chronic inflammatory demyelinating polyradiculoneuropathy CIDP

ICD-10CM CODES
G61.81 Chronic inflammatory demyelinating polyneuritis

EPIDEMIOLOGY & DEMOGRAPHICS

PREVALENCE: 0.5/100,000 children; 1 to 2/100,000 adults
PREDOMINANT SEX AND AGE: Slightly higher in males
RISK FACTORS: Association with certain systemic medical conditions (see under "Differential Diagnosis"), but association is unclear

PHYSICAL FINDINGS & CLINICAL PRESENTATION

- Occurrence of symmetrical weakness in both proximal and distal muscles that progressively increases over 2 mo
- Associated with impaired sensation, postural instability, reduced or absent deep tendon reflexes, and variable craniofacial-bulbar involvement

ETIOLOGY

Immune-mediated disorder emerging from interplay of both cell-mediated and humoral immune responses directed against incompletely characterized peripheral nerve antigens. May also be associated with various concurrent illnesses (Table 1C-17), although the pathogenetic significance is unclear.

DIAGNOSIS

There is no universal consensus regarding diagnostic criteria for CIDP. The three most widely used are the American Academy of Neurology (AAN), Saperstein, and Inflammatory Neuropathy Cause and Treatment (INCAT) criteria.

- The AAN and INCAT criteria are the least stringent regarding clinical criteria and require motor and sensory function in one limb, whereas the Saperstein criteria are more stringent, requiring both symmetrical proximal and distal weakness.
  1. Therefore, a patient with DADS (distal acquired demyelinating symmetric neuropathy) could fulfill AAN and INCAT criteria for CIDP.
- All require cerebral spinal fluid analysis to assess for albuminocytologic dissociation.
- Nerve conduction study (NCS): All require some features of demyelination including prolonged distal latencies and F-waves, slowed velocities, and at least one nerve demonstrating partial conduction block (feature of acquired demyelination).
- INCAT criteria do not require a nerve biopsy.
- See Table 1C-17 for complete review of differences.

DIFFERENTIAL DIAGNOSIS

- Other demyelinating neuropathies such as:
  1. Distal acquired demyelinating symmetric neuropathy (DADS)
  2. Multifocal motor neuropathy (MMN)
  3. Multifocal acquired demyelinating sensory and motor neuropathy (MADSAM; Lewis-Sumner syndrome)
- Inherited neuropathies: family history, genetic testing, and lack of acquired demyelinating features on NCS will help differentiate it from CIDP

- Metabolic neuropathies: diabetes, uremia
- Paraneoplastic neuropathy: associated with lymphoma or carcinoma
- Neuropathy associated with monoclonal gammopathy: associated with osteosclerotic myeloma, MGUS, and Waldenström's macroglobulinemia
- Neuropathy associated with infectious diseases: HIV and leprosy
- Neuropathy associated with systemic inflammatory or immune-mediated diseases:
  1. Sarcoidosis
  2. Amyloidosis
  3. Vasculitis: PAN, Behçet's, Sjögren's, cryoglobulinemia, lupus, Castleman's disease, granulomatosis with polyangiitis, Churg-Strauss
- Toxic neuropathies: ETOH, acrylamide, drugs (platinum-based agents, amiodarone, tacrolimus, perhexiline)

WORKUP

Nerve conduction studies and EMG to assess for demyelinating polyneuropathy with features of acquired demyelination (temporal dispersion) and conduction block (Fig. 1C-67)

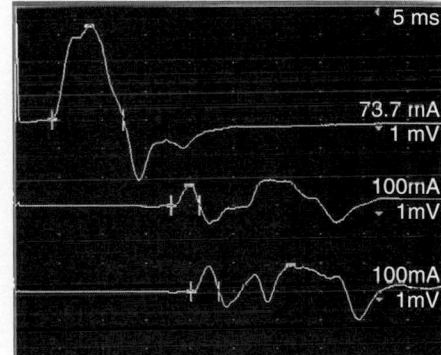

5 ms

73.7 mA
1 mV

100mA
1mV

100mA
1mV

FIGURE 1C-67 Conduction block.

Feature	American Academy of Neurology (AAN) Criteria	Saperstein Criteria	Inflammatory Neuropathy Cause and Treatment Criteria
Clinical involvement	Motor dysfunction, sensory dysfunction of >1 limb or both	Major: Symmetric proximal and distal weakness; minor: exclusively symmetrical distal weakness or sensory loss	Progressive or relapsing motor and sensory dysfunction of >1 limb
Time course	≥2 mo	≥2 mo	≥2 mo
Reflexes	Reduced or absent	Reduced or absent	Reduced or absent
Electrodiagnostics	Any 3 of the following 4 criteria: partial conduction block of ≥1 motor nerve, reduced velocity of ≥2 motor nerves, prolonged distal latency of ≥2 motor nerves, or prolonged F-waves of ≥2 motor nerves	2 of the 4 AAN electrodiagnostic criteria	Partial conduction block of ≥2 motor nerves and abnormal conduction velocity or distal latency or F-wave latency in 1 other nerve; or, in the absence of partial conduction block, abnormal conduction velocity, distal latency, or F-wave latency in 3 motor nerves; or electrodiagnostic abnormalities indicating demyelination in 2 nerves and histologic evidence of demyelination
CSF analysis	WBC count <10, negative CSF VDRL, and elevated protein (supportive)	Protein >45, WBC <10 (supportive)	CSF recommended but not mandatory
Biopsy findings	Evidence of demyelination and remyelination	Predominant features of demyelination; inflammation (not required)	Not mandatory (except in cases with electrodiagnostic abnormalities in only 2 motor nerves)

TABLE 1C-17 Diagnostic Criteria

LABORATORY TESTS

- CSF analysis to assess for albumin-cytologic dissociation (i.e., elevated protein with normal cell count), along with appropriate laboratory studies to exclude associated conditions.
- Nerve biopsy specimens (rarely done now) also reveal signs of demyelination with variable degrees of inflammation and secondary axonal loss.

IMAGING STUDIES

MRI with/without gadolinium may show enlargement and enhancement of the proximal nerve root segments, respectively (Figs. 1C-68 and 1C-69)

Rx TREATMENT

Therapies are directed at blocking the underlying immune processes to arrest demyelination and inflammation and to prevent secondary axonal degeneration. The most widely used forms of immunomodulatory therapy are IV immunoglobulin (IVIg), plasmapheresis/plasma exchange (PE), and corticosteroids. There is no difference in efficacy between these three modalities of treatment. Azathioprine, mycophenolate mofetil, cyclophosphamide, rituximab, and cyclosporine may be used as secondary agents.

NONPHARMACOLOGIC THERAPY

Orthotics/braces for significant distal weakness

ACUTE GENERAL Rx

IVIg 2 g/kg divided over 2 to 5 days; plasmapheresis (5 to 6 exchanges)

CHRONIC Rx

- Oral prednisone (1 mg/kg daily starting dose). Typically changed to every other day after 1 mo or when strength plateaus. Reduce by 10 mg every month until 20 mg every other day. Then reduce by 5 mg/mo. Get tuberculin skin test prior to administration. Treat with calcium and vitamin D; low-sodium/high-protein diet, routine ophthalmologic evaluation for cataract and glaucoma screening, and surveillance for diabetes and GERD symptoms/signs.

- PREDICT study: compared dexamethasone (Decadron) 40 mg daily × 4 days per month with prednisone 60 mg daily × 2 months and then tapered over 27 wk. No difference in efficacy was found between the two groups. Less weight gain and cushingoid features occurred with pulsed steroids but possibly more sleep and psychological disturbances.
- Pulsed Solu-Medrol: no standard regimen. However, 1000 mg × 3 days can be used, followed by 1000 mg wk with the goal of reduced frequency to every 2 to 12 wk.
- IVIg: 0.4 to 1 g/kg administered monthly. Check baseline IgA level. Check renal function panel and survey for hypercoagulable states and development of headache.
- Mycophenolate mofetil: Start 500 mg bid and increase in 2 to 4 wk to 1 g bid (check CBC, LFTs, and CBC monthly for first 3 mo, then every 3 mo thereafter). May cause GI upset.
- Imuran: Start 25 to 50 mg bid and increase in 4 wk to 100 mg bid (check baseline LFTs and CBC for first 3 mo, then every 3 mo thereafter). Watch for idiosyncratic reaction of fever, GI upset. If occurs, cannot re-challenge patient.
- Cytoxan: used for severe cases. 1000 mg/m^2 monthly for 6 months (moderate dose) or 50 mg/kg daily × 4 days (high dose).
- Other treatments used (case reports/anecdotal evidence): etanercept, rituximab, tacrolimus, interferon beta-1a.

DISPOSITION

- In one series, 90% of patients with CIDP improved. However, relapse rate was approximately 50%. In Mayo Clinic series, 64% of the patients were either improved or in remission and able to work, 8% were ambulatory but unable to work, 11% were bedridden or wheelchair bound, and 11% died from the disease.
- Patients with CIDP associated with IgM monoclonal gammopathy often respond poorly to treatment.

- Younger age, female gender, and relapsing-remitting course may portend a more favorable prognosis.

REFERRAL

- Neurologist, physical therapy/occupational therapy, orthotics

! PEARLS & CONSIDERATIONS

- Patients are compliant with Imuran treatment if MCV >100.
- Always place PPD prior to initiation of steroid treatment.
- Consider Bactrim 3 times weekly in patients concomitant with steroids and other immunosuppressant agent for *Pneumocystis* pneumonia prophylaxis (especially in patients with coexisting lung disease).
- NCS: Look for acquired features of demyelination
  1. Conduction block
  2. Temporal dispersion
- CSF: albuminocytologic dissociation; high CSF protein with normal cell count.
- CIDP can present like Guillain-Barré syndrome but sensory symptoms and proximal weakness are more common in CIDP and symptoms do not stabilize after 4 wk and continue to evolve over more than 8 wk.

PATIENT/FAMILY EDUCATION

CIDP is a chronic illness usually characterized by a relapsing-remitting course that typically responds well to treatment. Early referral to a neurologist is important, and education on steroid side effects and mitigating factors is paramount.

SUGGESTED READINGS

Available at www.expertconsult.com

AUTHOR: **JOHN SLADKY, M.D.**

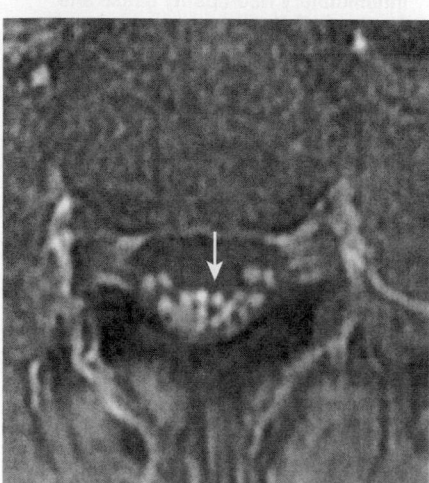

FIGURE 1C-68 Contrast-enhanced MRI shows enhancement of nerve roots.

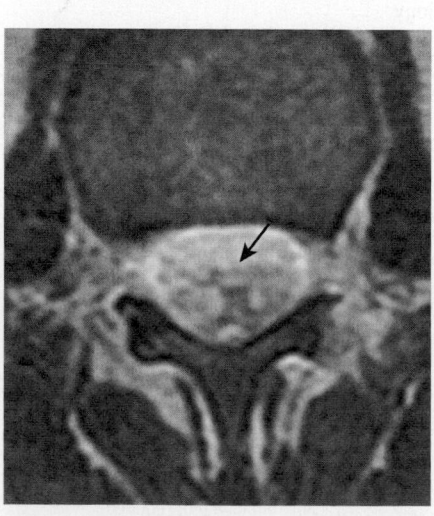

FIGURE 1C-69 T2-weighted axial MRI shows enlarged nerve roots.

 **BASIC INFORMATION**

DEFINITION

Chronic kidney disease (CKD) is generally diagnosed when there is evidence for more than 3 months of **kidney damage** (urine albumin >30 mg/g creatinine, or hematuria, congenital malformations, and so on) and/or **decreased kidney function** (glomerular filtration rate, GFR <60 ml/min/1.73 m^2). CKD is characterized by accumulation of metabolic waste products in blood, electrolyte abnormalities, mineral and bone disorders, and anemia. The manifestations of CKD are summarized in Table 1C-18.

SYNONYMS

CKD
CRF
Chronic kidney disease
Chronic renal failure

ICD10CM CODES
N18.1 Chronic kidney disease, stage 1
N18.2 Chronic kidney disease, stage 2
N18.3 Chronic kidney disease, stage 3
N18.4 Chronic kidney disease, stage 4
N18.5 Chronic kidney disease, stage 5
N18.6 End-stage renal disease
N18.9 Chronic kidney disease, unspecified

EPIDEMIOLOGY & DEMOGRAPHICS

- Prevalence of CKD in the U.S. is 10% to 14%. Today, more than 26 million Americans have CKD stages 1 through 5.
- Incidence of end-stage renal disease (ESRD) is 7% to 9% per year in the U.S., primarily because of diabetes mellitus and hypertension, the leading risk factors for CKD. Annually, 2 in 10,000 persons develop ESRD, and more than 100,000 patients begin dialysis each year.
- In the U.S., >250,000 people per year receive dialysis treatment for ESRD.
- Kidney transplantation is the best option for kidney replacement therapy, but many patients are not eligible for transplantation.

PHYSICAL FINDINGS & CLINICAL PRESENTATION

- Skin pallor, ecchymosis.
- Sleep disorder
- Hypertension
- Edema, leg cramps, restless legs, peripheral neuropathy
- Emotional lability, depression, decreased cognitive function
- Clinical presentation varies with the degree of kidney disease and its underlying etiology. Common symptoms are generalized fatigue, nausea, anorexia, pruritus (Fig. E1C-70), sleep disturbances, smell and taste disturbances, hiccups, and seizures
- Manifestations of uremic encephalopathy are described in Table 1C-18

ETIOLOGY

- Diabetes (37%), hypertension (30%), chronic glomerulonephritis (12%)
- Failed kidney transplant
- Polycystic kidney disease
- Interstitial nephritis (e.g., drug hypersensitivity, analgesic nephropathy), obstructive nephropathies (e.g., nephrolithiasis, prostatic disease)
- Vascular diseases (renal artery stenosis, hypertensive nephrosclerosis)
- Autoimmune diseases

DIAGNOSIS

- CKD is primarily distinguished from acute kidney injury by time (progression over 3 or more months). When using eGFR equations to diagnose CKD, the serum creatinine must be trended to establish a diagnosis of CKD during steady-state creatinine production. Trend analysis prevents misdiagnosis of acute kidney injury.

TABLE 1C-18 Pathophysiology of Chronic Kidney Disease

Manifestation	Mechanisms
Accumulation of nitrogenous waste products	Decrease in glomerular filtration rate
Acidosis	Decreased ammonia synthesis Impaired bicarbonate reabsorption Decreased net acid excretion
Sodium retention	Excessive renin production Oliguria
Sodium wasting	Solute diuresis Tubular damage
Urinary concentrating defect	Solute diuresis Tubular damage
Hyperkalemia	Decrease in glomerular filtration rate Metabolic acidosis Excessive potassium intake Hyporeninemic hypoaldosteronism
Renal osteodystrophy	Impaired renal production of 1,25-dihydroxycholecalciferol Hyperphosphatemia Hypocalcemia Secondary hyperparathyroidism
Growth retardation	Inadequate caloric intake Renal osteodystrophy Metabolic acidosis Anemia Growth hormone resistance
Anemia	Decreased erythropoietin production Iron deficiency Folate deficiency Vitamin B$_{12}$ deficiency Decreased erythrocyte survival
Bleeding tendency	Defective platelet function
Infection	Defective granulocyte function Impaired cellular immune functions Indwelling dialysis catheters
Neurologic symptoms (fatigue, poor concentration, headache, drowsiness, memory loss, seizures, peripheral neuropathy)	Uremic factor(s) Aluminum toxicity Hypertension
Gastrointestinal symptoms (feeding intolerance, abdominal pain)	Gastroesophageal reflux Decreased gastrointestinal motility
Hypertension	Volume overload Excessive renin production
Hyperlipidemia	Decreased plasma lipoprotein lipase activity
Pericarditis, cardiomyopathy	Uremic factor(s) Hypertension Fluid overload
Glucose intolerance	Tissue insulin resistance

From Kliegman RM et al: *Nelson textbook of pediatrics*, ed 19, Philadelphia, 2011, Saunders.

TABLE 1C-19 Criteria for Definition of Chronic Kidney Disease

Kidney damage for ≥3 months, as defined by structural or functional abnormalities of the kidney, with or without decreased GFR, that can lead to decreased GFR, manifest by either:
- Pathologic abnormalities
- Markers of kidney damage, including abnormalities in the composition of blood or urine, or abnormalities in imaging tests
- GFR <60 ml/min/1.73 m^2 for ≥3 months, with or without kidney damage

GFR, Glomerular filtration rate.
From Floege J et al: *Comprehensive clinical nephrology*, ed 5, Philadelphia, 2015, Saunders.

Diseases and Disorders

WORKUP

- Laboratory evaluation and imaging studies can identify reversible causes of acute GFR declines (e.g., volume depletion, urinary tract obstruction, heart failure)
- Ultrasound evaluation of the kidneys often reveals small kidneys (<9 cm sagittal length) with increased echogenicity
- Kidney biopsy is generally not conducted if kidneys are small or CKD is advanced.

LABORATORY TESTS

- Elevated blood urea nitrogen (BUN), creatinine, and low GFR, are the best overall indicators of kidney function. GFR is estimated by multivariable (creatinine, age, sex, race) prediction equations that are normalized to body surface area. GFR calculators are available online (http://www.kidney.org/kls/professionals/gfr_calculator.cfm).
- Urinalysis may reveal proteinuria, hematuria, or formed elements such as casts.
- Serum chemistries: elevated BUN and creatinine, hyperkalemia, hyperuricemia, hypocalcemia, hyperphosphatemia, hyperglycemia, decreased bicarbonate.
- Urinary protein excretion. A urine total protein-to-creatinine ratio >1000 mg/g indicates glomerular disease.
- Special studies: serum and urine immunoelectrophoresis (multiple myeloma), antinuclear antibody (systemic lupus erythematosus).
- Cystatin C measurement or direct glomerular filtration clearance methods may confirm CKD in situations when serum creatinine–based GFR equations are less accurate (e.g., HIV, malnutrition) or more precise measurement is desired (e.g., kidney transplant organ donation).

IMAGING STUDIES

- Ultrasound of kidneys for size measurements and to rule out obstruction.
- Plain radiographs of the aorta and extremities ordered for other reasons may reveal vascular and extraskeletal calcification (Fig. E1C-71).

CLASSIFICATION

The 2012 Kidney Disease: International Global Outcomes classifies CKD with a CGA format: **c**ause (etiology), **G**FR (G1 to G5), and **a**lbuminuria (A1 to A3) by urine albumin-to-creatinine ratio. The term *microalbuminuria* is no longer used; the term *moderate* is used (30-300 mg/g or 2.5-30 mg/mmol).

 **TREATMENT**

Management varies according to stage (Table 1C-22).

NONPHARMACOLOGIC THERAPY

- Provide adequate nutrition and calories (147–168 kJ/kg/day energy intake, chiefly from carbohydrate and polyunsaturated fats). Table 1C-22 describes nutritional recommendations in CKD. Referral to a dietitian for nutritional therapy for patients with GFR <50 ml/1.73 m^2 is recommended and is a Medicare-covered service.
- Sodium restriction (~100 mmol/day), potassium (≤60 mmol/day), and phosphorus (<800 mg/day).
- Blood pressure: Target blood pressure of ≤140/90 mm Hg if CKD (diabetic and nondiabetic) and urine albumin excretion ≤30 mg/24 hr. If CKD (diabetic and nondiabetic) and albumin excretion >30 mg/24 hr, irrespective of age, consider a target blood pressure ≤130/80 mm Hg.
- Adjust medication doses for reduced GFR.
- Restrict fluid if significant edema or hyponatremia (serum Na <130 mEq/L) is present.
- Resistance exercise training can preserve lean body mass, nutritional status, and muscle function in patients with moderate CKD.
- Avoid radiocontrast agents. Volume expansion with sodium chloride or sodium bicarbonate before dye exposure is equally effective.
- Smoking cessation.
- Prompt referral to a nephrologist is helpful. Late evaluation of patients with CKD is associated with greater burden and severity of comorbid disease and complications and lesser survival. Suggested criteria for nephrology referral are described in Table 1C-23.
- Kidney transplantation in selected patients.

GENERAL Rx

- Angiotensin-converting enzyme inhibitors (ACEIs) and angiotensin II receptor blockers (ARBs) reduce proteinuria and slow progression of CKD, especially in hypertensive diabetic patients. The combination of ACEI and ARB is not recommended due to increased risks of hyperkalemia, hypotension, and acute kidney injury.
- Addition of chlorthalidone to CKD patients with difficult-to-treat hypertension may reduce blood pressure and proteinuria. Consistent with loop diuretic therapy, successful blood pressure–lowering is associated with weight loss and the complication of hypokalemia.
- Initiation of dialysis:
  1. Urgent indications: uremic pericarditis, neuropathy, neuromuscular abnormalities, CHF, hyperkalemia, seizures
  2. Other indications: GFR 10 to 15 mL/min; progressive anorexia, weight loss, disordered sleep, pruritus, uncontrolled fluid gain with hypertension and signs of heart failure.
  3. General indications for initiation of dialysis are summarized in Table 1C-24. Suggested steps for resolving conflict in the shared decision-making regarding dialysis initiation are described (Fig. E1C-72). Early initiation of dialysis when the GFR is 10 to 14 mL/min per 1.73 m^2 does not enhance survival compared with a symptom-driven strategy for initiation of dialysis at eGFR <8-10 ml/min per 1.73 m^2.
- Erythropoiesis-stimulating agents (ESAs), epoetin alfa and darbepoetin alfa, are used to reduce transfusions in anemic CKD patients. Anemia of CKD should not be fully corrected to avoid adverse cardiovascular events. A target hemoglobin of 10 to 11 g/dl is reasonable to avoid premature and excessive ESA use. Iron repletion therapy must be present, defined as transferrin saturation ≤20% and ferritin ≤100 ng/ml, before ESA therapy is contemplated.
- Diuretics for edema or cardiopulmonary congestion (loop diuretics preferred).
- ACEIs or ARBs retard progression of CKD and lower blood pressure but may reduce GFR and renal potassium excretion.
- Treat metabolic acidosis with sodium bicarbonate to attain a goal serum HCO$_3$ level of 22 to 26 mEq/L.
- Statin or statin and ezetimibe combination is recommended in adults age ≥50 years with eGFRs <60 mL/min/1.73 m^2. Lipid management focuses on absolute risk for coronary events, and there are no target cholesterol levels.
- Control of renal osteodystrophy with calcium supplementation and vitamin D. Starting dose of calcium carbonate is 0.5 g with each

---

TABLE 1C-20 Classification of Chronic Kidney Disease Based on GFR

CKD Stage	Definition
1	Normal or increased GFR; some evidence of kidney damage reflected by microalbuminuria, proteinuria, and hematuria as well as radiologic or histologic changes
2	Mild decrease in GFR (89 to 60 ml/min per 1.73 m^2) with some evidence of kidney damage reflected by albuminuria, proteinuria, and hematuria as well as radiologic or histologic changes
3	GFR 59 to 30 ml/min per 1.73 m^2
3A	GFR 59 to 45 ml/min per 1.73 m^2
3B	GFR 44 to 30 ml/min per 1.73 m^2
4	GFR 29 to 15 ml/min per 1.73 m^2
5	GFR <15 ml/min per 1.73 m^2; when renal replacement therapy in the form of dialysis or transplantation has to be considered to sustain life

Classification and prognosis of chronic kidney disease from 2012 KDIGO guidelines.
CKD, Chronic kidney disease; *GFR,* glomerular filtration rate; *KDIGO,* Kidney Disease: Improving Global Outcomes
From Floege J et al: *Comprehensive clinical nephrology,* ed 5, Philadelphia, 2010, Saunders.

meal, increased until the serum phosphorus concentration is normalized (most patients require 5-10 g/day). Calcitriol 0.125 to 0.25 mcg PO daily increases serum calcium and phosphorus while suppressing parathyroid concentration. Paricalcitol, a vitamin D analogue, also reduces parathyroid hormone levels but induces less hypercalcemia and hyperphosphatemia than calcitriol.

- Dietary phosphate restriction is recommended for nearly all CKD patients. For additional management of hyperphosphatemia, calcium-based agents are inexpensive, well tolerated, and first-line phosphate binders for patients undergoing dialysis. Sevelamer carbonate and lanthanum carbonate are effective as phosphate binders but are more expensive. Two iron-based phosphate-binding agents have recently been approved by the FDA.
- General considerations in the continuing assessment of the CKD patient are described in Table 1C-25.
- A sequential approach to the uremic patient with pruritus is described in Fig. E1C-73.

DISPOSITION

- Prognosis is influenced by CKD stage and burden of comorbid illness. Late referral of patients to a nephrologist is associated with greater morbidity and mortality. Despite recommendations for early referral, up to 64% of CKD patients are referred late.
- Genetic susceptibility for CKD is prominent in African Americans. Apolipoprotein E allele status predicts CKD progression, independent of diabetes, race, lipid, and nonlipid factors. Whereas an e2 allele moderately

TABLE 1C-21 Management Plan for Patients with Chronic Kidney Disease, According to Stage

KDOQI Classification	GFR (ml/min)	Typical Serum Creatinine in 65-kg Subject	Consequences	Actions to Consider
3	30-59	2 mg/dl (170 μmol/L)	Hypertension, secondary hyperparathyroidism	6 monthly eGFR initially 12 monthly eGFR if stable Annual Hb, K+, Ca, P Treat hypertension Immunize against hepatitis B
4	15-29	4 mg/dl (350 μmol/L)	*Plus* anemia, hyperphosphatemia	3 monthly eGFR initially 6 monthly eGFR if stable 6 monthly Hb, K+, Ca, P, and PTH Start phosphate-restricted diet and phosphate binders Correct vitamin D deficiency Start vitamin D analogue Plan renal replacement therapy, including vascular access
5	<15	8 mg/dl (700 μmol/L)	*Plus* sodium and water retention, anorexia, vomiting, reduced higher mental function	Plan elective start of dialysis or preemptive renal transplant
5	<5	17 mg/dl (1500 μmol/L)	*Plus* pulmonary edema, coma, fits, metabolic acidosis, hyperkalemia, death	Start dialysis or provide palliative care

The table gives a rough guide to the level of serum creatinine corresponding to each stage of CKD in a typical 65-kg subject and shows the approximate timing of the anticipated clinical problems and interventions required as CKD progresses. At each stage, the action plan for the previous CKD stage should be followed if it has not already been initiated. *eGFR*, Estimated glomerular filtration rate; *PTH*, parathyroid hormone.
From Floege J et al: *Comprehensive clinical nephrology*, ed 4, Philadelphia, 2010, Saunders.

TABLE 1C-22 Nutritional Recommendations in Renal Disease

Daily Intake	Predialysis CKD	Hemodialysis	Peritoneal Dialysis
Protein (g/kg ideal BW) (see KDOQI for estimation of adjusted edema-free body weight)	0.6-1.0 Level depends on the view of the nephrologist 1.0 for nephrotic syndrome	1.1-1.2	1.0-1.3
		This is a broad recommendation as protein intake would be individualized for the patient's nutritional status, serum phosphate levels, and dialysis adequacy	
Energy (kcal/kg BW)	35 (<60 yr) 30-35 (>60 yr)	35 (<60 yr) 30-35 (>60 yr)	35 including dialysate calories (<60 yr) 30-35 including dialysate calories (<60 yr)
Sodium (mmol)	<100 (more if salt wasting)	<100	<100
Potassium	Reduce if hyperkalemic	Reduce if hyperkalemic	Reduce if hyperkalemic; potassium restriction is generally not required
	If hyperkalemic, advice will take the form of decreasing certain foods (e.g., some fruits and vegetables) and giving information about cooking methods		
Phosphorus	Reduce; level dependent on protein intake Advice will take the form of reducing certain foods (e.g., dairy, offal, some shellfish) and giving information about the timing of binders with high-phosphorus meals and snacks		
Calcium	In CKD stages 3-5, total intake of elemental calcium (including dietary calcium) should not exceed 2000 mg/day	Total intake of elemental calcium (including dietary calcium) should not exceed 2000 mg/day	Total intake of elemental calcium (including dietary calcium) should not exceed 2000 mg/day

Recommendations are for typical patients but should always be individualized on the basis of clinical, biochemical, and anthropometric indices.
BW, Body weight; *CKD*, chronic kidney disease; *CRF*, chronic renal failure; *KDOQI*, Kidney Disease Outcomes Quality Initiative.
From Floege J et al: *Comprehensive clinical nephrology*, ed 5, Philadelphia, 2015, Saunders.

C

Diseases and Disorders

I

TABLE 1C-23 Suggested Criteria for Referral of Patients with Chronic Kidney Disease to a Nephrologist

New Diagnosis	Stage 3	Stage 4
eGFR <30 ml/min/per 173 m²	eGFR falling by >4 ml/min per year	eGFR <20 ml/min per 173 m²
Hemoglobin <11 g/dl	eGFR <50 ml/min in patient younger than 50 years	eGFR falling by >4 ml/min per year
K⁺ >6 mmol/L	Hemoglobin <11 g/dl	Hemoglobin <11 g/dl
Ca <2.1 mmol/L	K⁺ >6 mmol/L	K⁺ >6 mmol/L
Pi >1.5 mmol/L	Ca <2.1 mmol/L	Ca <2.1 mmol/L
PTH >3× upper limit normal	Pi >1.5 mmol/L	Pi >1.5 mmol/L
Hematuria		PTH >3× upper limit normal
Urine ACR >30 mg/mmol		
Suspected renovascular disease		

ACR, Albumin to creatinine ratio; *eGFR,* estimated glomerular filtration rate; *PTH,* parathyroid hormone.
From Floege J et al: *Comprehensive clinical nephrology,* ed 5, Philadelphia, 2015, Saunders.

TABLE 1C-24 When to Initiate Dialysis

Indications for early start on dialysis

- Intractable fluid overload
- Intractable hyperkalemia
- Malnutrition due to uremia
- Uremic neurologic dysfunction
- Uremic serositis
- Functional deterioration otherwise unexplained

Uremic cognitive dysfunction can affect learning

Therefore, home-based self-dialysis may need to start earlier than center-assisted dialysis.

Start of dialysis may be delayed if patient is

asymptomatic, awaiting imminent kidney transplant, awaiting imminent placement of permanent HD or PD access, or, after appropriate education, has chosen conservative therapy.

If start of dialysis is delayed,

patient should be re-evaluated regularly to see if dialysis has become necessary.

Patients who choose PD

should not be required to have HD access placed, but venous sites for possible future HD access in arms should be preserved since HD may be required in the future.
Incremental start on PD may be considered if there is significant residual renal function.

Nephrologists should consider conservative (non dialysis) treatment of kidney failure an integral part of their clinical practice.

HD, Hemodialysis; *PD,* peritoneal dialysis.
Modified from NKF KDOQI Clinical Practice Guideline for initiation of dialysis. http://www.kidney.org/professional/Kdoqi/guideline_upHD_PD_VA/pd_rec1.htm. From Floege J et al: *Comprehensive clinical nephrology,* ed 5, Philadelphia, 2015, Saunders.

TABLE 1C-25 Continuing Assessment of the Chronic Kidney Disease Patient

Kidney Function

Has kidney function declined?

Has kidney function declined at the predicted rate?

If not, are there exacerbating factors?

Should dialysis be started?

Are there life-threatening complications?
Pericarditis
Fluid overload
Resistant hypertension
Hyperkalemia
Uncompensated metabolic acidosis

Should access be created or transplantation planned?

Supportive Treatment

Can salt, potassium, and fluid balance be improved by diet or diuretics?

Is the phosphate controlled?

Is the dose of vitamin D compound appropriate?

Should erythropoietin (EPO) be prescribed?

Are nutritional supplements needed?

Does the patient need counseling?

Questions to be posed in evaluation of the patient.
From Floege J et al: *Comprehensive clinical nephrology,* ed 5, Philadelphia, 2010, Saunders.

TABLE 1C-26 Principles Underlying Withdrawal of Dialysis

The ultimate responsibility for the decision rests with the physician, not the relative.

The patient's interests and dignity should be protected at all times.

The process should not be rushed. If there is any doubt about the correctness of the decision, treatment should continue.

There should be an open discussion among the multidisciplinary team to avoid any damaging disagreements.

The psychological needs of the health care team should not be overlooked.

Palliative care must be given in the most appropriate environment, e.g., a hospice or, ideally, the patient's own home.

From Floege J et al: *Comprehensive clinical nephrology,* ed 5, Philadelphia, 2010, Saunders.

increases the risk of kidney disease progression, an e4 allele decreases risk.
- Kidney transplantation in selected patients improves survival. Whereas the 2-year kidney graft survival rate for living related donor transplantations is >80%, the 2-year graft survival rate for cadaveric donor transplantation is nearly 70%.
- Principles underlying withdrawal from dialysis treatment are described in Table 1C-26.

 **EVIDENCE**

Available at www.expertconsult.com

SUGGESTED READINGS

Available at www.expertconsult.com

AUTHOR: **SNIGDHA T. REDDY, M.D.** and **JERRY YEE, M.D.**

BASIC INFORMATION

DEFINITION

Chronic obstructive pulmonary disease (COPD) is an inflammatory respiratory disease usually caused by exposure to tobacco smoke. It is characterized by the presence of airflow limitation that is not fully reversible. The pathophysiology of COPD is related to enhanced inflammatory response to noxious particles and gases, chronic airway irritation, mucus production, and pulmonary scarring and changes in pulmonary vasculature.

Acute exacerbations and comorbidities contribute to the overall severity and prognosis of the disease in individual patients.

Traditionally, COPD was described as encompassing *emphysema*, characterized by loss of lung elasticity and destruction of lung parenchyma with enlargement of air spaces, and *chronic bronchitis*, characterized by obstruction of small airways and productive cough >3 months for more than 2 successive years. These terms are no longer included in the formal definition of COPD, although they are still used clinically. Although emphysema and chronic bronchitis are commonly associated with COPD, neither is required to make the diagnosis.

SYNONYMS

COPD
Emphysema
Chronic bronchitis

ICD-10CM CODES
J44.9 Chronic obstructive pulmonary
        disease, unspecified
J43.9 Emphysema, unspecified

EPIDEMIOLOGY & DEMOGRAPHICS

- COPD affects more than 5% of adults in the U.S.
- Between 10% and 20% of COPD in the U.S. is due to occupational or other exposure to chemical vapors, irritants, and fumes; 80% to 90% is due to cigarette smoking.
- COPD is the third leading cause of death in the U.S.
- Highest incidence is in males >40 yr.
- 16 million office visits, 500,000 hospitalizations, 120,000 deaths annually, and >$18 billion in direct health care costs annually can be attributed to COPD.
- Patients with COPD living in isolated rural areas of the U.S. are at greater risk for COPD exacerbation-related mortality than those living in urban areas, independent of hospital rurality and volume.

PHYSICAL FINDINGS & CLINICAL PRESENTATION

- Patients with COPD have historically been classically subdivided in two major groups based on their phenotype
  1. *Blue bloaters* are patients with chronic bronchitis; the name is derived from the bluish tinge of the skin (as a result of chronic hypoxemia and hypercapnia) and from the frequent presence of peripheral edema (from cor pulmonale); chronic cough with production of large amounts of sputum is characteristic.
  2. *Pink puffers* are patients with emphysema; they have a cachectic appearance but pink skin color (adequate oxygen saturation); shortness of breath is manifested by pursed-lip breathing and use of accessory muscles of respiration.
- COPD may present with combinations of the following signs and symptoms:
  1. Cyanosis, chronic cough (usually productive but may be intermittent and may be unproductive), tachypnea, tachycardia.
  2. Dyspnea (persistent, progressive), pursed-lip breathing with use of accessory muscles for respiration, decreased breath sounds, wheezing.
  3. Chronic sputum production.
  4. Chest wall abnormalities (hyperinflation, "barrel chest," protruding abdomen).
  5. Flattening of diaphragm.
- Systemic manifestations and comorbidities of COPD are described in Table 1C-27.
- Acute exacerbation of COPD is mainly a clinical diagnosis and generally manifests with worsening dyspnea, increase in sputum purulence, and increase in sputum volume. Respiratory symptom status, however, is not a reliable indicator of the presence of airflow obstruction. Individuals with normal spirometric values may report respiratory symptoms, whereas individuals who have severe to very severe airflow obstruction by spirometry may report no symptoms. Individuals with sedentary lifestyles may underestimate their symptoms and careful history taking is important to elicit symptoms suggestive of COPD.

ETIOLOGY

- Tobacco exposure
- Occupational exposure to pulmonary toxins (e.g., dust, noxious gases, vapors, fumes, cadmium, coal, silica). The industries with the highest exposure risk are plastics, leather, rubber, and textiles.
- Atmospheric pollution.
- Alpha-1-antitrypsin deficiency (rare; <1% of COPD patients).

TABLE 1C-27 Systemic Manifestations and Comorbidities of COPD

Cardiovascular	Infarction
	Arrhythmia
	Congestive heart failure
	Aortic aneurysm
Hypercoagulability	Stroke
	Pulmonary embolism
	Deep vein thrombosis
	Atrophy
Systemic	Weight loss
	Osteoporosis
	Skin wrinkling
	Anemia
	Fluid retention
Lung cancer	Depression

From Mason RJ: *Murray & Nadel's textbook of respiratory medicine*, 5th ed, Philadelphia, 2010, Saunders.

DIAGNOSIS

DIFFERENTIAL DIAGNOSIS

- Heart failure (HF)
- Asthma
- Tuberculosis, other respiratory infections
- Bronchiectasis
- Cystic fibrosis
- Neoplasm
- Pulmonary embolism
- Obliterative bronchiolitis
- Diffuse panbronchiolitis
- Sleep apnea, obstructive
- Hypothyroidism <50% predicted
- Neuromuscular disease

DIAGNOSTIC WORKUP

Chest x-ray is seldom diagnostic but useful to visualize significant hyperinflation and to exclude alternative diagnosis (e.g., CHF, TB).

Pulmonary function testing (spirometry).

Oxygen saturation and arterial blood gases (useful in selected patients with FEV_1 <50% predicted or with acute exacerbation).

Alpha-1-antitrypsin deficiency screening may be useful in whites with suspected COPD and no clear risk factors.

LABORATORY TESTS

- CBC: generally not helpful, may reveal leukocytosis with left shift during acute exacerbation and secondary polycythemia in COPD with significant, chronic hypoxia. Recent trials have shown that eosinophilia in COPD patients predicts response to corticosteroids.
- Sputum may be purulent with bacterial respiratory tract infections. Sputum staining and cultures are usually reserved for cases refractory to antibiotic therapy.
- Arterial blood gases: normocapnia, mild to moderate hypoxemia may be present. ABGs and pulse oximetry are usually used to determine if a patient is a candidate for long-term oxygen therapy or if hypercapnia is present (ABGs).
- Spirometry pulmonary function testing (PFT) with measurement of forced vital capacity (FVC) and forced expiratory volume in 1 s (FEV_1). Spirometry should be obtained to diagnose airflow obstruction in clinically stable patients with respiratory symptoms. It should not be used to screen for airflow obstruction in individuals without respiratory symptoms. Spirometry reveals that the primary physiologic abnormality in COPD is an accelerated decline in FEV_1 from the normal rate in adults >30 yr of approximately 30 mL/yr to nearly 60 mL/yr. PFT results in COPD reveal abnormal diffusing capacity, increased total lung capacity and/or residual volume, and fixed reduction in FEV_1 in patients with emphysema; normal diffusing capacity and

reduced FEV$_1$ are found in patients with chronic bronchitis. Stage and severity of COPD according to post-bronchodilator spirometry are described in Table 1C-28. It is important to note that FEV$_1$ does not correlate well with individual patients' severity of dyspnea, exercise limitations, or health status. Evaluation of patients should also focus on symptom control and risk for adverse events in addition to FEV$_1$.

- Patients with COPD can generally be distinguished from asthmatics by their incomplete response to short-acting beta agonist (change in FEV$_1$ <200 ml and 12%) and absence of an abnormal bronchoconstrictor response to methacholine or other stimuli. Nearly 40% of patients with COPD will, however, respond to bronchodilators.

ASSESSMENT

- The global initiative for chronic obstructive lung disease (GOLD) assigns patients with COPD into four groups (A, B, C, D) based on (1) the degree of airflow restriction (Table 1C-28), (2) a patient symptom score using one of two symptom questionnaires (CAT or mMRC), or (3) the number of COPD exacerbations in one year.[1]

IMAGING STUDIES

Chest x-ray:
- Hyperinflation with flattened diaphragm, tenting of the diaphragm at the rib, and increased retrosternal chest space (Fig. 1C-74)
- Decreased vascular markings and bullae in patients with emphysema
- Thickened bronchial markings and enlarged right side of the heart in patients with chronic bronchitis
- Computed tomography: Emphysematous lung, tracheobronchomalacia

Rx TREATMENT

NONPHARMACOLOGIC THERAPY

- Avoidance of tobacco and elimination of air pollutants.
- Supplemental oxygen, usually through a face mask/nasal cannula, to ensure oxygen saturation >90% as measured by pulse oximetry. Continuous oxygen therapy should be prescribed for patients with COPD who have arterial partial pressure of oxygen 55 mm Hg or less, or oxygen saturation 88% or less as measured by pulse oximetry.
- Pulmonary secretion clearance: careful nasotracheal suction is indicated only in patients with excessive secretions and an inability to expectorate. Mechanical percussion of the chest as applied by a physical or respiratory therapist is ineffective with acute exacerbations of COPD.
- Pulmonary rehabilitation should be considered in COPD patients who remain symptomatic

[1]Lee H, Kim J, Tagmazyan K: Treatment of stable chronic obstructive pulmonary disease: the GOLD guidelines, *Am Fam Physician* 88(10):655-663, 2013.

despite optimal medical management. Medicare will cover up to 36 sessions of pulmonary rehabilitation in COPD patients.
- Weight loss in obese patients.
- Preliminary trials involving lung volume reduction using bronchoscopic treatment with nitinol coils have shown improved exercise capacity in patients with severe emphysema (Deslee G, et al: *JAMA* 315(2):175-184, 2016).
- Endobronchial valve (EBV) placement via bronchoscopy to reduce lung volume with one way valves that are allowed to leave but not enter a lung segment has been used in Europe but is not yet approved in the U.S. (Klooster K, et al: *NEJM* 373:2325, 2015).

TABLE 1C-28 Stage and Severity of COPD According to Postbronchodilator Spirometry

GOLD Stage and Severity	Definition
I: Mild	FEV$_1$/FVC <0.70, FEV$_1$ ≥80% of predicted
II: Moderate	FEV$_1$/FVC <0.70, 50%≤FEV$_1$ <80% of predicted
III: Severe	FEV$_1$/FVC <0.70, 30%≤FEV$_1$ <50% of predicted
IV: Very severe	FEV$_1$/FVC <0.70, FEV$_1$ <30% of predicted or FEV$_1$ <50% of predicted plus chronic respiratory failure

Data from the Global Initiative for Chronic Obstructive Lung Disease. Goldman L, Schafer AI: *Goldman's Cecil medicine,* ed 24, Philadelphia, 2012, Saunders.

GENERAL Rx

- Pharmacologic treatment should be administered in a stepwise approach according to the severity of disease and patient's tolerance for specific drugs. Fig. 1C-75 describes general management approaches for COPD. When using the COLD assessment criteria, pulmonary rehabilitation is recommended for patients in groups B, C, and D. Those in group A should receive a short-acting anticholinergic or short-acting β$_2$-agonist for mild intermittent symptoms. For patients in group B, long-acting anticholinergics or long-acting β$_2$-agonists should be added. Patients in group C or D are at high risk of exacerbations and should receive a long-acting anticholinergic or a combination of an inhaled corticosteroid and a long-acting β$_2$-agonist.

1. Bronchodilators improve symptoms, quality of life, and exercise tolerance and decrease incidence of exacerbations. Inhaled bronchodilators *may be used* for stable COPD patients with respiratory symptoms and FEV$_1$ between 60% and 80% of predicted. They are *recommended* for stable COPD patients with respiratory symptoms and FEV$_1$ <60% of predicted. Recent guidelines from ACP, ACCP, ATS, and ERS recommend that clinicians prescribe monotherapy using either long-acting inhaled anticholinergics or long-acting inhaled β-agonists for symptomatic patients with COPD and FEV$_1$ <60% of predicted. Clinicians should base the choice of specific monotherapy on patient preference, cost, and adverse effect profile.

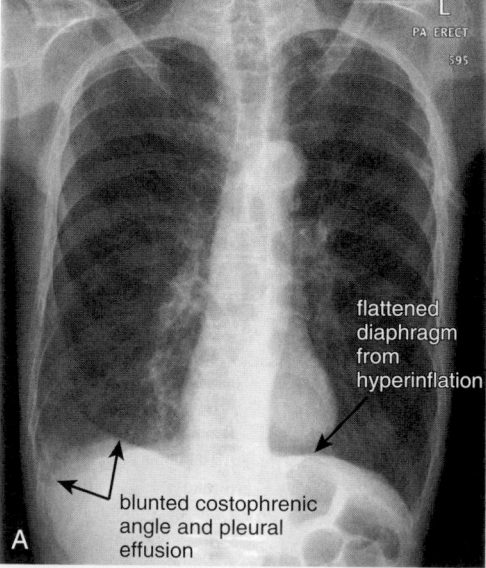
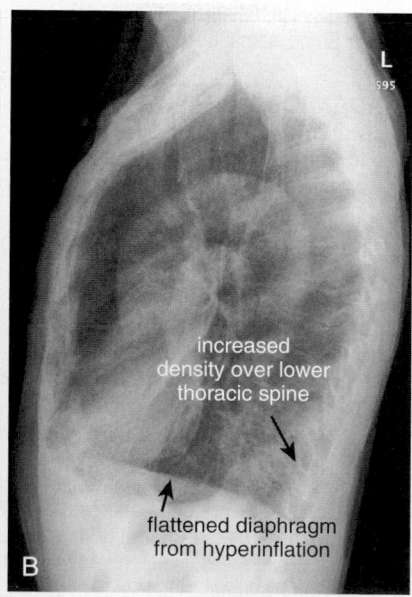

FIGURE 1C-74 Chronic obstructive pulmonary disease (COPD). A, Posterior-anterior (PA) upright chest x-ray. **B,** Lateral upright chest x-ray. This 63-year-old man with a history of COPD presented with 2 weeks of worsening cough with yellow sputum and dyspnea. His oxygen saturation was 87% in the emergency room. He has evidence of hyperinflation with flat diaphragms (particularly evident on the lateral x-ray, **(B)**. The patient also has a blunted right costophrenic angle with an apparent effusion and increased densities in both the right and the left lung base **(A)**. The lateral x-ray also shows increased density overlying the inferior thoracic spine, an abnormal spine sign. (From Broder JS: *Diagnostic imaging for the emergency physician,* Philadelphia, 2011, Saunders.)

2. Short-acting β₂-agonists (e.g., albuterol metered-dose inhaler 1 to 2 puffs q4 to 6h prn) or short-acting anticholinergic agents (e.g., ipratropium inhaler 2 puffs qid) are acceptable in patients with mild, variable symptoms. Anticholinergics are also effective and are available in combination with albuterol (e.g., Combivent). Long-acting inhaled agents are preferred in patients with mild to moderate or continuous symptoms. Tiotropium is an excellent long-acting bronchodilator. It is very effective for long-term, once-a-day use. It has been shown to be superior to salmeterol, an inhaled long-acting β-agonist (LABA) in patients with moderate to severe COPD and may possibly slow the rate of decline in FEV1. Some recent trials, however, have shown higher hospitalization rates and mortality with tiotropium compared to LABAs. Indacaterol, olodaterol, and vilanterol are other available LABAs for long-term maintenance treatment of bronchospasm associated with COPD. Indacaterol provides the convenience of once-daily dosing. Aclidinium, unlike tiotropium, is another long-acting anticholinergic that is predominantly renally excreted, can be used safely in renal impairment. Olodaterol is also for once-a-day use. As with other LABAs, these medications should not be used with other sympathomimetic drugs, medications that can prolong the QT interval, or beta-blockers. LABA and long-acting anticholinergic in different combinations are now available in the market. A combination of Umeclidinium and vilanterol in once-a-day dosing was found to achieve greater increases in trough FEV₁ and mean peak FEV₁ over the 6 hours after dosing compared with monotherapy or placebo.

3. Addition of inhaled steroids (fluticasone, budesonide, triamcinolone) is used to reduce exacerbations in patients with moderate to severe COPD. Inhaled steroids are reserved for patients with either ≥2 exacerbations annually or FEV₁ <50% of predicted. The role of inhaled corticosteroids (ICS) in COPD is controversial. Although some trials have demonstrated mild improvement in patients' symptoms and decreased frequency of exacerbations, most pulmonologists believe that these drugs are ineffective in most patients with COPD but should be considered for patients with moderate to severe

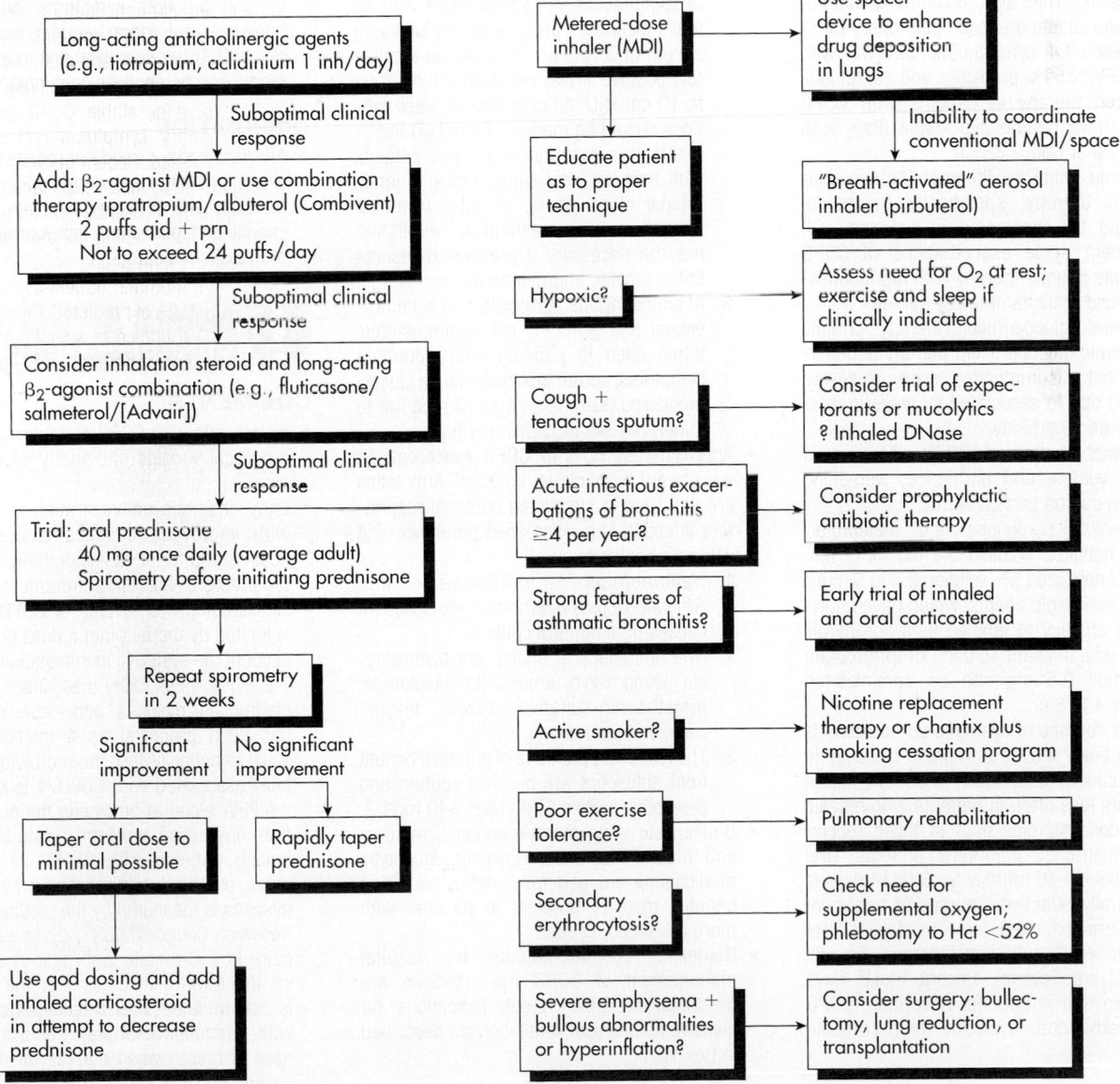

FIGURE 1C-75 Managed care guide: pharmacotherapy and general management approaches for chronic obstructive pulmonary disease (COPD). *DNase,* Deoxyribonuclease; *Hct,* hematocrit; *prn,* as needed; *qid,* four times a day; *qod,* every other day. (Modified from Noble J: *Primary care medicine,* ed 3, St Louis, 2001, Mosby.)

airflow limitation who have persistent symptoms despite optimal bronchodilator therapy. ICS therapy does not affect 1-yr all-cause mortality among patients with COPD and is associated with a higher risk of pneumonia.

4. Roflumilast is a selective oral PDE4 inhibitor useful to reduce the risk of COPD exacerbations in patients with severe COPD associated with chronic bronchitis and a history of exacerbations. It is not a bronchodilator and is not indicated for the relief of acute bronchospasm.

5. Recent guidelines from ACP (American College of Physicians), ACCP (American College of Chest Physicians), ATS (American Thoracic Society), and ERS (European Respiratory Society) suggest that clinicians may administer combination inhaled therapies for symptomatic patients with stable COPD and FEV_1 <60% predicted. They also recommend that clinicians should prescribe pulmonary rehabilitation for symptomatic patients with an FEV_1 <50% predicted and continuous oxygen therapy in patients with COPD who have resting hypoxemia (PaO_2 <55 mm Hg or SpO_2 <88%).

6. Chronic antibiotic therapy: Chronic antibiotic therapy, specifically macrolide, should be considered in patients with frequent acute exacerbations of COPD despite optimal therapy with bronchodilators and antiinflammatory agents.

7. Systemic glucocorticoid therapy: Chronic systemic glucocorticoid therapy is generally not recommended even in severe COPD due to associated increase in mortality and morbidity.

- Acute exacerbation of COPD (increase in sputum volume and purulence, worsening dyspnea) can be treated with:
  1. Aerosolized β_2-agonists (e.g., metaproterenol nebulizer solution 5% 0.3 ml or albuterol nebulized 5% solution 2.5 to 5 mg).
  2. Anticholinergic agents, which have equivalent efficacy to inhaled beta-adrenergic agonists. Inhalant solution of ipratropium bromide 0.5 mg can be administered every 4 to 8 hr.
  3. Short courses of systemic corticosteroids have been shown to improve spirometric and clinical outcomes. Treatment failure occurs less often in patients who receive low-dose steroids than in those receiving high-dose parenteral steroids. Oral prednisone 40 mg/day for 5 to 14 days is generally effective. Courses of treatment that are extended for >14 days confer no added benefit and increase the risk of adverse events. Recent trials[2] have shown that in patients with acute COPD exacerbations, systemic glucocorticoid

treatment for 5 days is not inferior to treatment for 14 days.

4. Use of noninvasive positive pressure ventilation (NIPPV) decreases the risk of endotracheal intubation and decreases intensive care unit admission rates. Contraindications to its use are uncooperative patient, decreased level of consciousness, hemodynamic instability, inadequate mask fit, and severe respiratory acidosis. Increased airway pressure can be delivered by using inspiratory positive airway pressure, continuous positive airway pressure, or bilevel positive airway pressure, which combines the other modalities. When using NIPPV, the nasal mask is usually tolerated the best; however, patients must be instructed to keep their mouths closed while breathing with the nasal apparatus. Oxygen can be delivered at 10 to 15 L/min and started in spontaneous ventilation mode with an initial expiratory positive airway pressure setting of 3 to 5 cm H_2O and an inspiratory positive airway pressure setting of up to 10 cm H_2O. Adjustments in these settings should be made in 2-cm H_2O increments. It is important to monitor patients with frequent vital signs measurements, arterial blood gases, or pulse oximetry. Intubation and mechanical ventilation may be necessary if previous measures fail to provide improvement.

5. IV aminophylline administration is controversial and generally not recommended. When used in patients with refractory symptoms, serum levels should be closely monitored (keep level 8 to 12 mcg/ml) to minimize risks of tachyarrhythmias.

- Approximately 50% of COPD exacerbations are caused by bacterial infection. Antibiotics are indicated in suspected bacterial respiratory infection (e.g., increased purulence and volume of phlegm).
  1. *Haemophilus influenzae* and *Streptococcus pneumoniae* are frequent causes of acute bronchitis.
  2. Oral antibiotics of choice are azithromycin, levofloxacin, amoxicillin-clavulanate, trimethoprim-sulfamethoxazole, doxycycline, and cefuroxime.
  3. The two best predictors of potential benefit from antibiotics are purulent sputum and C-reactive protein (CRP) level >40 mg/L.[3]
- Guaifenesin may improve cough symptoms and mucus clearance; however, mucolytic medications are generally ineffective. Their benefits may be greatest in patients with more advanced disease.
- Guideline recommendations for hospital management of COPD exacerbations are described in Table 1C-29. Indications for invasive mechanical ventilation are described in Box 1C-2.

- Lung volume reduction surgery has been proposed as a palliative treatment for severe emphysema. Overall it increases the chance of improved exercise capacity but does not confer a survival advantage over medical therapy. It is most beneficial in patients with both predominantly upper-lobe emphysema and low baseline exercise capacity.
- Single-lung transplantation should be considered a surgical option in patients with end-stage emphysema who have an FEV_1 <25% of predicted normal value after administration of bronchodilator and additional complications such as severe hypoxemia, hypercapnia, and pulmonary hypertension.
- Trials involving endobronchial valves that allow air to escape from a pulmonary lobe but not to enter it have been done to improve lung function by reducing lobar volume in patients with advanced heterogeneous emphysema. Results have shown modest improvements in lung function, symptoms, and exercise tolerance, but more frequent exacerbations of COPD, Other complications included pneumonia and hemoptysis postimplantation.

DISPOSITION

- After the initial episode of respiratory failure, 5-yr survival is approximately 25%.
- Development of cor pulmonale or hypercapnia and persistent tachycardia are poor prognostic indicators.

COMMENTS

- All patients with COPD should receive pneumococcal vaccine and yearly influenza vaccine.
- Early antibiotic administration is associated with improved outcomes among patients hospitalized for acute exacerbations of COPD regardless of the risk of treatment failure.
- In assessing the severity of COPD, the FEV_1 is limited by the fact that it does not take into account the systemic manifestations of COPD. The BODE index (body mass index, degree of obstruction, dyspnea, and exercise capacity) has been proposed as a multidimensional scale to better assess the morbidity and mortality associated with COPD. It is better than the FEV_1 alone at predicting the risk of death from any cause and from respiratory causes among patients with COPD. In the BODE index, obstruction is measured by FEV_1 and dyspnea is measured by the modified Medical Research Council (MMRC) dyspnea questionnaire in a 6-minute walk test. A score of 0 on the MMRC indicates that the individual is not troubled with breathlessness except with strenuous exercise, 1 indicates shortness of breath when hurrying or walking up a slight hill, and 2 means the individual walks slower than people of the same age due to breathlessness or has to stop for breath when walking at own pace on level ground. A score of 3 means severe dyspnea because

[2]Leuppi JD et al: Short-term vs conventional glucocorticoid therapy in acute exacerbations of chronic obstructive pumonary disease: the REDUCE randomized clinical trial, *JAMA* 309:2223-2231, 2013.

[3]Miravilles M et al: Is it possible to identify exacerbations of mild to moderate COPD that do not require antibiotic treatment? *Chest* 144:1571, 2013.

Diseases
and Disorders

I

TABLE 1C-29 Guideline Recommendations for Hospital Management of COPD Exacerbations

	Global Initiative for Chronic Obstructive Lung Disease*	American Thoracic Society/ European Respiratory Society†	National Institute for Clinical Excellence‡
Date of statement	2010	2004	2010
Diagnostic testing	Chest radiograph, oximetry, ABGs, and ECG. Other testing as warranted by clinical indication.	Chest radiograph, oxygen saturation, ABGs, ECG, sputum Gram stain and culture.	Chest radiograph, ABG, ECG, complete blood count, sputum smear and culture, blood cultures if febrile.
Bronchodilator therapy	Inhaled short-acting β_2-agonist is recommended. Consider ipratropium if inadequate clinical response. Consider theophylline or aminophylline as second-line intravenous therapy.	Inhaled short-acting β_2-agonist and/ or ipratropium with spacer or nebulizer, as needed.	Administer inhaled drugs by nebulizer or handheld inhaler. Specific agents and dosing regimens not specified. Consider theophylline if inadequate response to inhaled bronchodilators.
Antibiotics	Recommended if (1) increases in dyspnea, sputum volume, and sputum purulence all are present; (2) increase in sputum purulence along with increase in either dyspnea or sputum volume; or (3) need for assisted ventilation. See original document for complex treatment algorithm.	Base choice on local bacterial resistance patterns. Consider amoxicillin/clavulanate or respiratory fluoroquinolones. If *Pseudomonas* species and/or other Enterobacteriaceae are suspected, consider combination therapy.	Administer only if history of purulent sputum. Initiate with an aminopenicillin, a macrolide, or a tetracycline, taking into account local bacterial resistance patterns. Adjust therapy according to sputum and blood cultures.
Systemic corticosteroids	Daily prednisolone 30-40 mg (or its equivalent) orally for 7-10 days.	Daily prednisone 30-40 mg orally for 10-14 days. Equivalent dose intravenously if unable to tolerate oral intake. Consider inhaled corticosteroids.	Daily prednisolone 30 mg (or its equivalent) orally for 7-14 days.
Supplemental oxygen	Maintain oxygen saturation >90%. Monitor ABGs for hypercapnia and acidosis.	Maintain oxygen saturation >90%. Monitor ABGs for hypercapnia and acidosis.	Maintain oxygen saturation within the individualized target range. Monitor ABGs.
Assisted ventilation	Indications for NPPV include severe dyspnea, acidosis (pH ≤7.35) and/or hypercapnia (PCO₂ >45 mm Hg), and respiratory rate >25 breaths/ min. Contraindications to NPPV include respiratory arrest, hemodynamic instability, impaired mental status, copious bronchial secretions, and extreme obesity. Intubate if contraindication to NPPV or failure of NPPV (worsening ABGs or clinical status). Consider likelihood of recovery and patient's wishes and expectations before intubation.	Consider with pH <7.35 and PCO₂ >45-60 mm Hg and respiratory rate >24 breaths/min. Institute NPPV in a controlled environment, unless there are contraindications (e.g., respiratory arrest, hemodynamic instability, impaired mental status, copious bronchial secretions, and extreme obesity). Intubate if contraindication to NPPV or failure of NPPV (worsening ABGs or clinical status).	NPPV treatment of choice for persistent hypercapnic respiratory failure. Consider functional status, body mass index, home oxygen, comorbidities, prior ICU admissions, age, and FEV₁ when assessing suitability for intubation and ventilation.

ABGs, Arterial blood gases; *ECG*, electrocardiogram; *ICU*, intensive care unit; *NPPV*, noninvasive positive pressure ventilation.
*Data from http://www.goldcopd.com.
†Data from MacNee W. Standards for the diagnosis and treatment of patients with COPD: a summary of the ATS/ERS position paper. *Eur Respir J* 23:932-946, 2004.
‡Data from http://www.nice.org.uk.
From Goldman L, Schafer AI: *Goldman's Cecil medicine*, ed 24, Philadelphia, 2012, Saunders.

BOX 1C-2 Indications for Invasive Mechanical Ventilation

Severe dyspnea, with use of accessory muscles and paradoxical abdominal motion
Respiratory frequency >35 breaths/min
Life-threatening hypoxemia (Pao₂ <40 mm Hg or Pao₂/Fio₂ <200 mm Hg)
Severe acidosis (pH <7.25) and hypercapnia (Paco₂ >60 mm Hg)
Respiratory arrest
Somnolence, impaired mental status
Cardiovascular complications (hypotension, shock, heart failure)
Other complications: metabolic abnormalities, sepsis, pneumonia, pulmonary embolism, barotrauma, massive pleural effusion
Noninvasive positive-pressure ventilation failure (or exclusion criteria)

Fio₂, Inspired oxygen fraction; *Pao₂*, partial pressure of carbon dioxide in arterial blood; *Pao₂*, partial pressure of oxygen in arterial blood.
From Vincent JL et al: *Textbook of critical care*, ed 6, Philadelphia, 2011, Saunders.

the person has to stop for breath after walking approximately 100 meters or after a few minutes on level ground, and a score of 4 indicates very severe dyspnea and is given when the individual is too breathless to leave the house or is breathless when dressing or undressing.

• Pulmonary artery enlargement as determined by a ratio of the diameter of the pulmonary artery to the diameter of the aorta [PA:A ratio] of >1 detected by CT is associated with severe exacerbations of COPD.
• The average person with COPD has one or two acute exacerbations each year.

Prophylactic use of macrolide antibiotics (azithromycin 250 mg/day) has been shown to decrease the frequency of exacerbations and improve quality of life among selected patients with COPD; however, it leads to hearing decrements in a small percentage of patients and increased prevalence of macrolide-resistant bacteria colonizing the airway and is therefore not recommended.

 **EVIDENCE**

Available at www.expertconsult.com

SUGGESTED READINGS

Available at www.expertconsult.com

RELATED CONTENT

Chronic Obstructive Pulmonary Disease (Patient Information)
Emphysema (Patient Information)

AUTHOR: **LAYOLA LUNGHAR, M.D.**

 **BASIC INFORMATION**

DEFINITION

- Chronic urticaria (CU) is the occurrence of hives (edematous, pruritic pink wheals of variable size and shape) that have been present continuously or intermittently for at least 6 wk. Some patients may also experience angioedema (deep swelling, often painful). CU can be associated with autoimmune conditions but is often idiopathic. When no underlying cause is found, CU has been referred to as chronic idiopathic urticaria (CIU).

SYNONYMS

Chronic hives
CU
CIU
Chronic idiopathic urticaria

ICD 10-CM CODES
ICD 10 L50.8 Other Urticaria: Chronic
Urticaria

EPIDEMIOLOGY & DEMOGRAPHICS

INCIDENCE: 1.4 % per year.
PREVALENCE: Lifetime prevalence is 1.8%. The period prevalence in the last 12 months is 0.6% to 0.8%. CU occurs in 0.1% to 0.3% of children.
PREDOMINANT SEX AND AGE: There is a 2:1 female to male predominance. The mean age is 40 yr.
GENETICS: Patients with demonstrable histamine-releasing autoantibodies have a very strong association with HLA-DR4 and the associated allele HLA-DQ8.
RISK FACTORS: None

PHYSICAL FINDINGS & CLINICAL PRESENTATION

- CU lesions are edematous, pink or red wheals of variable size and shape with surrounding erythema and are usually pruritic. Individual urticarial lesions usually resolve within 24 hr, but new lesions may be developing simultaneously.
- Angioedema typically appears as brawny nonpitting edema, often without well-defined margins and erythema commonly affecting the lips, tongue, eyelids, and genitalia. This is often described as painful rather than pruritic.

ETIOLOGY

- CU results from cutaneous mast cells releasing histamine. It is often triggered by immunoglobulin E (IgE), components of the complement cascade, endogenous peptides, endorphins, and enkephalins.
- More than 30% of patients have autoimmune manifestations, including specific IgG antibodies against the FcεRIα subunit of the high-affinity IgE receptor or IgG antibodies against IgE itself, thyroid autoimmunity, or positive autologous serum skin test (ASST) result.

- Activation of the coagulation cascade, including increased levels of prothrombin fragment F112 and D-dimer, has been noted in patients with CU and may be a marker for CU severity.
- Chronic infections such as hepatitis B and C, Epstein-Barr virus (EBV), herpes simplex virus, and helminthic parasitic infections have been implicated.

 **DIAGNOSIS**

DIFFERENTIAL DIAGNOSIS

- Urticarial vasculitis
- Erythema multiforme
- Drug eruptions
- Still's disease
- Insect bites

WORKUP

- Complete history and physical exam: Questioning about new drugs, travel, infection, health status, and a complete review of systems (including fever, arthralgias, abdominal pain, bone pain, weight loss, and cold/heat sensitivity) is important. Determining if an individual lesion resolves within 24 hr, whether lesions are tender or itchy, and whether lesions leave a purpuric mark is important (to screen for urticarial vasculitis).
- Fig. 1C-76 describes an algorithm for the diagnosis and management of chronic urticaria.

LABORATORY TEST(S)

- In a recent systemic review analyzing 29 studies (6462 patients), a causative internal disease was detected in 1.6% of patients with CU, with no association between the number of tests ordered and the detection rate.
- Aside from a complete history and physical examination, a trial of antihistamine therapy without further diagnostic testing is recommended.
- In those who fail antihistamine therapy, there is consensus for a limited laboratory workup:
  - CBC with differential, complete metabolic panel (creatinine, liver function tests), ESR, TSH.
  - The authors typically also check G6PD, hepatitis B and C, HIV, and age-appropriate malignancy screening.
- A skin biopsy may be performed in cases of suspected urticarial vasculitis or urticaria with atypical historical or physical findings.
- NOTE:
Testing for autoantibodies to the high-affinity IgE receptor, autoantibodies to IgE, ASST, and the autologous plasma skin test (APST) is not routinely recommended because it has not been clearly demonstrated that these tests identify a distinct subgroup of patients with CU nor that there is a different response to therapy based on these results.
- C4 testing is recommended in patients with isolated angioedema (without urticaria) to rule out C1 inhibitor deficiency.

IMAGING STUDIES
None

Rx TREATMENT

NONPHARMACOLOGIC THERAPY
Elimination of any suspected medications, herbal products, etc.

ACUTE GENERAL Rx

- Oral corticosteroids are not recommended as long-term treatment because of their detrimental effects over prolonged periods. However, they may be necessary for 3-7 days to abort severe, acute flares.

CHRONIC Rx
FIRST-LINE TREATMENT:
- Second-generation nonsedating H1-antagonist antihistamines
  - Loratidine 10 mg, fexofenadine 180 mg, cetirizine 10 mg, levocetirizine 2.5 mg, desloratadine (5 mg).
  - These are the mainstay of treatment (50%-95% of patients achieve satisfactory disease control with one or a combination of antihistamines only). The typical starting dose is twice daily. If no improvement after 2 weeks, there is current data supporting dose-escalation to fourfold on-label dosing. Studies have shown routine (rather than episodic) use is important for efficacy.
- Sedating H1-antagonist antihistamines (diphenhydramine, hydroxyzine) are no longer recommended as first-line treatment given their potential for sedation and anticholinergic effects, as well as the availability of second-generation agents. However, these can be used as adjuncts at bedtime.

SECOND-LINE TREATMENT:
- For those who do not respond to monotherapy H1-antagonist, a combination of antihistamines, both second-generation H1 and H2 antagonists, may be necessary:
  - A second nonsedating H1 antihistamine.
  - Addition of H2 blockade (ranitidine, famotidine, cimetidine).
  - Addition of doxepin 25-50 mg at night or twice daily (which is a potent H1/H2 blocker) may be necessary. Of note, doxepin can prolong PR interval and worsen conduction defects; an EKG before therapy may be warranted.

THIRD-LINE TREATMENT: Choice of agent depending on histologic infiltrate (e.g. neutrophilic), patient's comorbidities, and preferences. If failed the above treatments, patients are typically considered refractory CIU.

IMMUNOMODULATING AGENTS

- Addition of leukotriene-receptor antagonist (e.g., monoleukast 10 mg/day).
- Dapsone 25-500 mg/day (typically 100 mg/day starting dose). Must check for G6PD and monitor labs. Limited use in patients with anemia. Side effects include peripheral

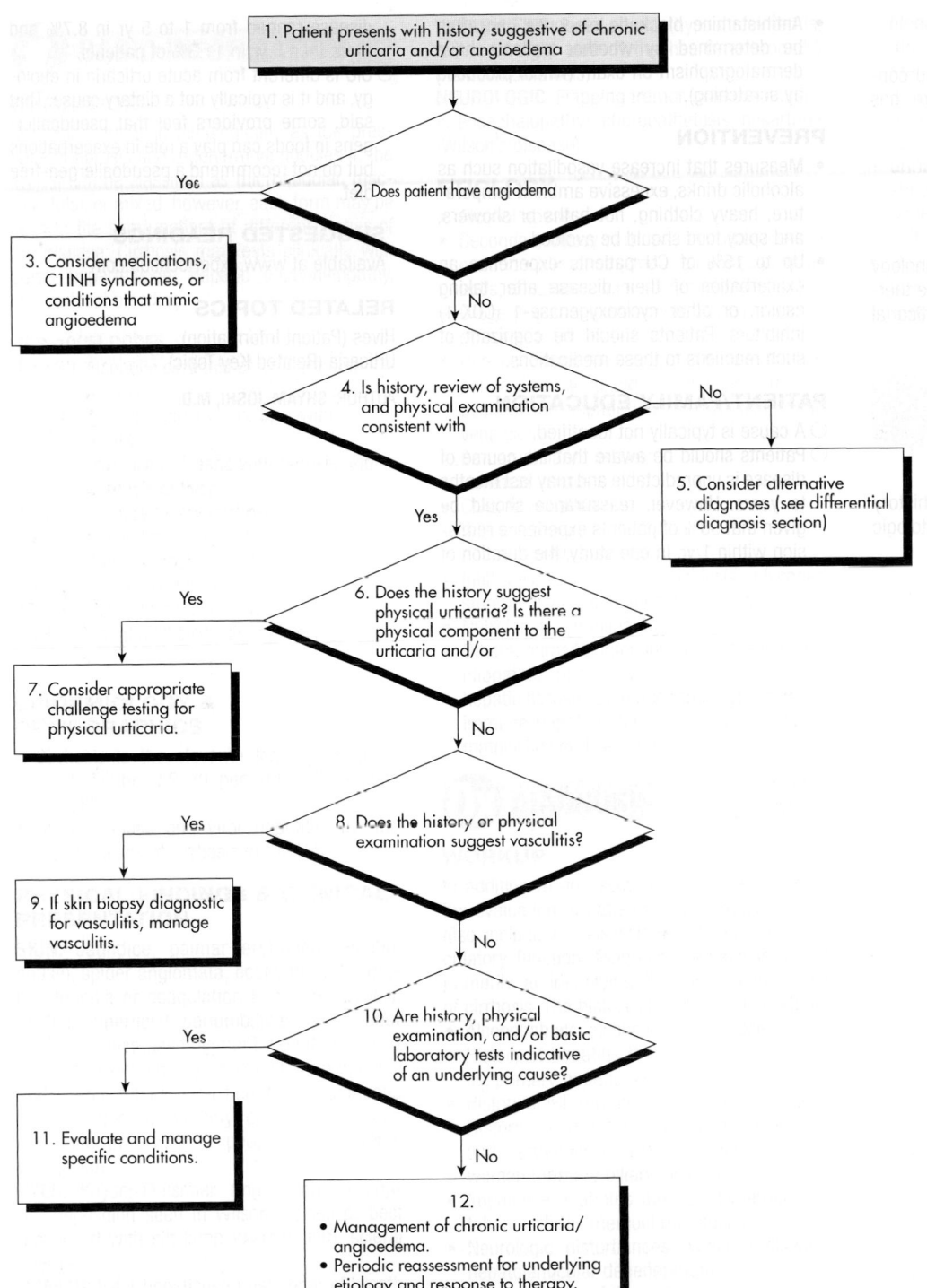

FIGURE 1C-76 Algorithm for the diagnosis and management of chronic urticaria. (From Bernstein JA, Lang DM, Khan DA, et al. The diagnosis and management of acute and chronic urticaria: 2014 update, *J Allergy Clin Immunol* 133[5]:1270-1277, 2014.)

Diseases
and Disorders

neuropathy, methemaglobinemia, agranulocytosis, and systemic drug hypersensitivity. Improvement is generally noted within days to weeks.
- Hydroxychlorquine 200 mg twice daily (can start with dapsone or sulfasalazine because of slow onset on the order of 3 months). Must monitor for retinal toxicity.

- Sulfasalazine 500 mg twice daily (then uptitrate to 1 g twice daily). Good option if patient is anemic and cannot tolerate dapsone.

BIOLOGIC AGENTS
- Omalizumab 300 mg subcutaneous injection every 4 weeks
  - A monoclonal IgG antibody that binds free IgE. Approved in both the U.S. and EU for

the treatment of antihistamine-resistant CIU in March 2014.

IMMUNOSUPPRESSIVE AGENTS
- Mycophenolate mofetil 500-1500 mg twice daily
- Cyclosporine (3-5 mg/kg per day for 3-6 months). Limited by nephrotoxic potential. Should not be used longer than a year.

500 mg qid can be used. It can also be supplemented with vancomycin 500 mg by nasogastric tube with intermittent clamping or retention enema.

- Fidaxomicin, has shown non-inferiority to vancomycin and a lower rate of CDI recurrence (25% with vancomycin vs. 15% with fidaxomicin); however, its higher cost and the fact that a lower risk of recurrence was not seen among patients infected with the BI/NAP1/027 strain (found in 38% of isolates) has limited its use.
- IV tigecycline (a broad-spectrum antibiotic used for skin or soft-tissue infection) can be used as adjunctive or alternative therapy for severe refractory *C. difficile* toxin infection.
- The addition of monoclonal antibodies against *C. difficile* toxins to antibiotic agents has been shown to reduce the recurrence of *C. difficile* infection.
- Fecal transplantation: When standard treatment has failed, intestinal microbiota transplantation (IMT) is an effective alternative therapy (eradication rate is 94%). It involves infusing intestinal microorganisms (in a suspension of healthy donor stool) into the intestine of a sick patient via enema, gastroscope/colonoscope, or nasojejunal tube to restore the microbiota. Trials comparing fresh versus frozen fecal microbiota transplantation have shown equal efficacy.

SURGICAL MANAGEMENT OF CDI

- Indications: CDI unresponsive to medical therapy, fulminant colitis
- Clinical features: colonic distention, severe abdominal pain/tenderness, systemic inflammatory response syndrome. Diarrhea may be absent because of ileus.
- Surgical approaches:
  1. Traditional (subtotal or total colectomy), high mortality (50%)
  2. Colon-sparing (loop ileostomy with intraoperative colonic lavage using warmed polyethylene glycol solution via the ileostomy and instillations of postoperative vancomycin flushes via the ileostomy); lower mortality compared to traditional approach

CHRONIC Rx

- Judicious future use of antibiotics to prevent recurrences (e.g., avoid prolonged antibiotic therapy)
- Probiotics have been shown mildly effective in reducing the risk for CDI among patients prescribed antibiotics.
- Alcohol-based hand gels are inadequate for eradication of spores. They are inferior to soap and water for eradication of spores.

DISPOSITION

- Most patients recover completely with appropriate therapy. Fever resolves within 48 hr

and diarrhea within 4 to 5 days. Overall mortality rate is 1% to 2.5% but exceeds 10% in untreated patients. CDI recurrence after an initial episode is 20% to 25% regardless of initial treatment with metronidazole or vancomycin. Each recurrence increases risk of repeat episodes (65% chance of recurrence after 3 CDI episodes). Recurrent CDI usually represents relapse rather than reinfection, no matter how long between episodes. Recurrent episodes are best treated with a prolonged course of oral vancomycin tapered off over several weeks to months.

- Hospital-acquired CDI is independently associated with an increased risk of in-hospital death. All hospitalized patients with CDI should be placed in contact isolation at least until resolution of diarrhea.

 EVIDENCE

Available at www.expertconsult.com

SUGGESTED READINGS

Available at www.expertconsult.com

RELATED CONTENT

Clostridium difficile Infection (Patient Information)
Pseudomembranous Colitis (Patient Information)

AUTHOR: **FRED F. FERRI, M.D.**

BASIC INFORMATION

DEFINITION

Cocaine is an alkaloid derived from the coca plant *Erythroxylum coca,* native to South America, which contains approximately 0.5% to 1% cocaine. The drug produces physiologic and behavioral effects when administered orally, intranasally, intravenously, or by inhalation after smoking. Cocaine has potent pharmacologic effects on dopamine, norepinephrine, and serotonin neurons in the central nervous system (CNS) involving alteration and blockade of cellular membrane transport and prevention of reuptake. Cocaine's second action involves the blockage of voltage-gated sodium ion membrane channels, which is responsible for its anesthetic effect. The mechanisms by which cocaine may induce myocardial ischemia or infarction are described in Fig. E1C-80. Table 1C-33 describes the pharmacokinetics of cocaine according to route of administration.

SYNONYMS

Cocaine hydrochloride: topical solution (FDA approved as a topical anesthetic)

Crack: this is produced when the hydrochloride molecule is removed by ether extraction, which frees the basic cocaine molecule or "free base." Heating does not destroy the free base; rather, it melts at 98° F and vaporizes at higher temperatures allowing it to be smoked.

Freebase: aqueous solution of cocaine hydrochloride converted to a more volatile base state by the addition of alkali, thereby extracting the cocaine base in a residue or precipitate.

Street names include Bernice, Blow, C, Carrie, Cecil, Charlie, Coke, Dust, Dynamite, Flake, Gin, Girl, Gold dust, Green gold, Jet, Powder, Star dust, Paradise, Pimp's drug, Snow, Stardust, White girl, Yay, Yayo

Liquid lady: alcohol + cocaine

Speedball: heroin + cocaine

Street measures: hit (2 to 200 mg), snort, line, dose, spoon (approximately 1 g)

ICD-10CM CODES
T40.5 Poisoning, cocaine
F14.20 Cocaine dependence, uncomplicated

EPIDEMIOLOGY & DEMOGRAPHICS

- The 2010 National Survey on Drug Use and Health (NSDUH) indicates that there were 1 million individuals age 12 yr or older who had dependence or abuse of cocaine in the preceding year. This compares with 1.1 million in 2009, 1.4 million in 2008, and 1.6 million in 2007.
- The most recent NSDUH (2012) reports that there were 1.6 million individuals aged 12 yr or older who had dependence or had abuse of cocaine in the preceding year compared with 1.4 million in 2011.

PHYSICAL FINDINGS & CLINICAL PRESENTATION

PHASE I:
- CNS: euphoria, agitation, headache, vertigo, twitching, bruxism, unintentional tremor
- Nausea, vomiting, fever, hypertension, tachycardia

PHASE II:
- CNS: lethargy, hyperreactive deep tendon reflexes, seizures (status epilepticus)
- Sympathetic overdrive: tachycardia, hypertension, hyperthermia
- Incontinence

PHASE III:
- CNS: flaccid paralysis, coma, fixed dilated pupils, loss of reflexes
- Pulmonary edema
- Cardiopulmonary arrest

Psychological dependence manifests with habituation, paranoia, and hallucinations (cocaine "bugs").

CNS: Cerebral ischemia and infarction, cerebral arterial spasm, cerebral vasculitis, cerebral vascular thrombosis, subarachnoid hemorrhage, Intraparenchymal hemorrhage, seizures, cerebral atrophy, movement disorders, and hyperthermia

Cardiac: Acute myocardial ischemia and infarction (Table 1C-34), arrhythmias (Table 1C-35), and sudden death, dilated cardiomyopathy and myocarditis, infective endocarditis, aortic rupture, acceleration of coronary atherosclerosis

Pulmonary: Inhalation injuries (secondary to smoking crack cocaine): cartilage and nasal septal perforation, oropharyngeal ulcers; immunologically mediated diseases: hypersensitivity pneumonitis, bronchiolitis obliterans; pulmonary vascular lesions and hemorrhage, pulmonary infarction, pulmonary edema secondary to left ventricular failure, pneumomediastinum, and pneumothorax

Gastrointestinal: Gastroduodenal ulceration and perforation; intestinal infarction or perforation, colitis

Renal: Acute renal failure secondary to rhabdomyolysis and myoglobinuria; renal infarction; focal segmental glomerulosclerosis

Obstetric: Placental abruption, low infant weight, prematurity, microcephaly

Psychiatric: Anxiety, depression, paranoia, delirium, psychosis, suicide

Adulterants such as levamisole (an immunomodulator) and clenbuterol (a beta-adrenergic agonist) have been found mixed with cocaine. Levamisole can cause agranulocytosis, leukoencephalopathy, and cutaneous vasculitis leading to necrosis of the skin. Clenbuterol may cause tachycardia, hyperglycemia, and hypokalemia.

ETIOLOGY

Cocaine may be absorbed through different routes with varying degrees of speed:
- Nasal insufflation/snorting: 2.5 min
- Smoking: <30 sec
- Oral: 2 to 5 min
- Mucosal: <20 min
- Intravenous injection: <30 sec

TABLE 1C-34 Characteristics of Patients with Cocaine-Induced Myocardial Infarction

Dose of Cocaine

Five or six lines (150 mg), up to 2 g

Serum concentration, 0.01-1.02 mg/liter

Frequency of Use

Reported in chronic, recreational, and first-time users

Route of Administration

Occurs with all routes of administration

75% of reported MIs occurred after intranasal use

Age

Mean, 34 yr (range, 17-71 yr)

20% younger than 25 yr

Sex

80%-90% male

Timing

Often within minutes of cocaine use

Reported as late as 5-15 hr after use

From Bonow RO et al: *Heart disease,* ed 9, Philadelphia, 2012, Saunders.

TABLE 1C-35 Cardiac Dysrhythmias and Conduction Disturbances Reported with Cocaine Use

Sinus tachycardia

Sinus bradycardia

Supraventricular tachycardia

Bundle branch block

Complete heart block

Accelerated idioventricular rhythm

Ventricular tachycardia

Ventricular fibrillation

Asystole

Torsades de pointes

Brugada pattern (right bundle branch block with ST-segment elevation in leads V_1, V_2, and V_3)

From Bonow RO et al: *Heart disease,* ed 9, Philadelphia, 2012, Saunders.

TABLE 1C-33 Pharmacokinetics of Cocaine According to Route of Administration

Route of Administration	Onset of Action	Peak Effect	Duration of Action
Inhalation (smoking)	3-5 sec	1-3 min	5-15 min
Intravenous	10-60 sec	3-5 min	20-60 min
Intranasal or other mucosal	1-5 min	15-20 min	60-90 min

From Bonow RO et al: *Heart disease,* ed 9, Philadelphia, 2012, Saunders.

 **DIAGNOSIS**

DIFFERENTIAL DIAGNOSIS

- Methamphetamine ("speed") abuse
- Methylenedioxyamphetamine ("ecstasy") abuse
- Cathinone ("khat") abuse
- Lysergic acid diethylamide (LSD) abuse

WORKUP

Physical examination and laboratory evaluation

LABORATORY TESTS

- Toxicology screen (urine): cocaine is metabolized within 2 hr by the liver to major metabolites, benzoylecgonine and ecgonine methyl ester, which are excreted in the urine. Metabolites can be identified in urine within 5 min of IV use and up to 48 hr after oral ingestion.
- Blood: CBC, electrolytes, glucose, BUN, creatinine, calcium
- Arterial blood gas analysis
- ECG
- Serum creatine kinase and troponin concentration

 **TREATMENT**

There is no specific antidote, and at present, no drug therapy is uniquely effective in treating cocaine abuse and dependence. Modifying cocaine's pharmacokinetic properties by sequestering or hydrolyzing it in serum and limiting its access to its sites of action may prove helpful by using a bacterial cocaine esterase, currently investigational. Adulterants (such as levamisole and clenbuterol, discussed earlier), contaminants, and other drugs may be admixed with street cocaine and should be kept in mind with patients presenting with unusual manifestations. Amantadine may provide effective treatment for cocaine-dependent patients with severe cocaine withdrawal symptoms, as well as the other dopamine agonist bromocriptine (1.5 mg PO tid), which may alleviate some of the symptoms of craving associated with acute cocaine withdrawal.

ACUTE GENERAL Rx

Acute cocaine toxicity requires following advanced poisoning treatment and life support. A suspected "body packer" should have an abdominal radiograph to detect the continued presence of cocaine-containing condoms in the intestinal tract. If present, gentle catharsis with charcoal and mineral oil should be performed with ICU admission and monitoring.

SPECIFIC TREATMENT

INHALATION: Wash nasal passages
AGITATION:
- Check STAT glucose
- Diazepam 15 to 20 mg PO or 2 to 10 mg IM or IV for severe agitation

HYPERTHERMIA:
- Check rectal temperature, creatine kinase, electrolytes
- Monitor with continuous rectal probe; bring temperature down to 101° F within 30 to 45 min

RHABDOMYOLYSIS:
- Vigorous hydration with urine output at least 2 ml/kg
- Mannitol or bicarbonate for rhabdomyolysis resistant to hydration

SEIZURE MANAGEMENT (STATUS EPILEPTICUS):
- Diazepam 5 to 10 mg IV over 2 to 3 min; may be repeated every 10 to 15 min.
- Lorazepam 2 to 3 mg IV over 2 to 3 min; may be repeated.
- Phenytoin loading dose 15 to 18 mg/kg IV at a rate not to exceed 25 to 50 mg/min under cardiac monitoring.
- Phenobarbital loading dose 10 to 15 mg/kg IV at a rate of 25 mg/min; an additional 5 mg/kg may be given in 30 to 45 min if seizures are not controlled.
- For refractory seizures, consider:
  1. Pancuronium 0.1 mg/kg IV
  2. Halothane general anesthesia
  3. Both require EEG monitoring to determine brain seizure activity.

HYPERTENSION: Cocaine-induced hypertension usually responds to benzodiazepines. If this fails:
- Consider arterial line for continuous blood pressure monitoring
- Avoid the use of calcium channel blockers because they may potentiate the incidence of seizures and death, especially in body packers.
- The use of beta-blockers may exacerbate cocaine-induced vasoconstriction.
- Phentolamine (unopposed adrenergic effects) or nitroglycerin may be required.
- If diastolic pressure >120 mm Hg: hydralazine hydrochloride 25 mg IM or IV; may repeat q1h.
- If hypertension is uncontrolled or hypertensive encephalopathy is present: sodium nitroprusside initially at 0.5 mg/kg/min not to exceed 10 mg/kg/min.

CHEST PAIN:
- Chest radiograph, ECG, cardiac enzymes
- Benzodiazepines for agitation
- Acetylsalicylic acid and nitroglycerin for ischemic pain (Aspirin is contraindicated if dissection is suspected.)
- Percutaneous transluminal coronary angioplasty possibly better than thrombolysis for cocaine-associated myocardial infarction
- Phentolamine will reverse cocaine-induced vasoconstriction and may be administered 5 to 10 mg every 5 to 10 minutes.
- The use of beta-adrenergic blockers remains controversial because of the unopposed alpha-adrenergic effects of cocaine.
- If beta-blockers are to be used, this should be preceded by administration of phentolamine to prevent unopposed alpha-adrenergic stimulation. Many authors recommend not using beta-blockers until the cocaine has been systemically eliminated.

VENTRICULAR ARRHYTHMIAS (CONSIDERATIONS):
- Antiarrhythmic agents should be used with caution during the early period after cocaine exposure as a result of their proarrhythmic and proconvulsant effects.
- Lidocaine 1.5 mg/kg IV bolus followed by IV infusion (controversial: may be proarrhythmic and proconvulsant)
- Termination of ventricular arrhythmias may be resistant to lidocaine and even cardioversion.
- $NaHCO_3-$ is under investigation in cocaine-mediated conduction abnormalities and rhythm disturbances.
- In a cardiac arrest situation secondary to cocaine toxicity, vasopressin offers a theoretical advantage over epinephrine as it increases coronary blood flow and myocardial oxygen availability.

DISPOSITION

Although many patients who use cocaine may not require treatment because of the short half-life of the drug, others may require specific treatment for possible cocaine-related complications.

REFERRAL

Consider psychotherapy or behavioral therapy once stable. There is some evidence that topiramate 300 mg orally daily added to cognitive behavioral therapy may be beneficial in patients with severe withdrawal symptoms.

 **PEARLS & CONSIDERATIONS**

- Cocaine-induced vasoconstriction may be exacerbated by the use of selective and non-selective beta-adrenergic blocking agents.
- The use of lidocaine in treating ventricular arrhythmias may precipitate seizures and further arrhythmias.

SUGGESTED READINGS

Available at www.expertconsult.com

RELATED CONTENT

Cocaine Abuse and Dependence (Patient Information)
Drug Abuse (Patient Information)
Drug Abuse (Related Key Topic)

AUTHOR: **SAJEEV HANDA, M.D.**

BASIC INFORMATION

DEFINITION

Colorectal cancer (CRC) is a neoplasm arising from the luminal surface of the large bowel; locations include descending colon (40% to 42%), rectosigmoid and rectum (30% to 33%), cecum and ascending colon (25% to 30%), and transverse colon (10% to 13%).

ICD-10CM CODES
C18	Malignant neoplasm of colon
C18.2	Malignant neoplasm of colon, ascending colon
C18.4	Malignant neoplasm of colon, transverse colon
C18.6	Malignant neoplasm of colon, descending colon
C18.7	Malignant neoplasm of colon, sigmoid colon
C19	Malignant neoplasm of rectosigmoid junction

EPIDEMIOLOGY & DEMOGRAPHICS

- Worldwide, CRC accounts for about 1.4 million new cases and almost 700,000 deaths annually. The highest incidence is in North America, Australasia, Europe, and South Korea.
- CRC is the third most common cancer and the third leading cause of cancer deaths in the U.S. (132,000 new cases and almost 50,000 deaths annually).
- Peak incidence is in the seventh decade of life. The lifetime risk for development of CRC is 1 in 17, with 90% of cases occurring after age 50 yr.
- CRC accounts for 14% of all cases of cancer (excluding skin malignancies) and 8% of all yearly cancer deaths.
- Risk factors:
  1. Hereditary polyposis syndromes
  2. Familial polyposis (high risk)
  3. Gardner's syndrome (high risk)
  4. Turcot's syndrome (high risk)
  5. Peutz-Jeghers syndrome (low to moderate risk)
  6. Inflammatory bowel disease (IBD), both ulcerative colitis and Crohn's disease
  7. Family history of "cancer family syndrome"
  8. Heredofamilial breast cancer and colon carcinoma
  9. Pelvic irradiation history
  10. First-degree relatives with colorectal carcinoma
  11. Age >50 years
  12. Dietary factors (diet high in fat or red meat, alcohol use, low vegetable intake)
  13. Hereditary nonpolyposis colon cancer (HNPCC): autosomal dominant disorder characterized by early age of onset (mean age, 44 yr) and right-sided or proximal colon cancers, synchronous and metachronous colon cancers, mucinous and poorly differentiated colon cancers; accounts for 1% to 5% of all cases of CRC
  14. Previous endometrial or ovarian cancer, particularly when diagnosed at an early age

PHYSICAL FINDINGS & CLINICAL PRESENTATION

- Physical examination may be completely unremarkable.
- Digital rectal examination can detect approximately 50% of rectal cancers.
- Palpable abdominal masses may indicate metastasis or complications of colorectal carcinoma (abscess, intussusception, volvulus).
- Abdominal distention and tenderness are suggestive of colonic obstruction.
- Hepatomegaly may be indicative of hepatic metastasis.

ETIOLOGY

CRC can arise through two mutational pathways: microsatellite instability or chromosomal instability. Germline genetic mutations are the basis of inherited colon cancer syndromes; an accumulation of somatic mutations in a cell is the basis of sporadic colon cancer.

DIAGNOSIS

DIFFERENTIAL DIAGNOSIS

- Diverticular disease
- Strictures or adhesions
- IBD
- Infectious or inflammatory lesions
- Arteriovenous malformations
- Metastatic carcinoma
- Extrinsic masses (cysts, abscesses)

WORKUP

The clinical presentation of colorectal malignancies may be nonspecific symptoms (weight loss, anorexia, malaise) or with specific symptoms related to mass effect or bleeding. It is useful to divide colon cancer symptoms into those usually associated with the right- or left-sided cancers because the clinical presentation can vary with the location.

- Right side of colon:
  1. Anemia (from chronic blood loss).
  2. Abdominal pain may be present, or the patient may be completely asymptomatic.
  3. Rectal bleeding is often missed because blood is mixed with feces.
  4. Obstruction and constipation are unusual because of large lumen and more liquid stools.
- Left side of colon:
  1. Change in bowel habits (constipation, diarrhea, tenesmus, pencil-thin stools).
  2. Rectal bleeding (bright red blood coating the surface of the stool).
  3. Intestinal obstruction is frequent because of small lumen.

CLASSIFICATION AND STAGING

AJCC classification for CRC:
A. Confined to the mucosa-submucosa (stage I)
B. Invasion of muscularis propria (stage II)
C. Local node involvement (stage III)
D. Distant metastasis (stage IV)

TNM Classification:

Stage	TNM Classification
I	T1-2, N0, M0
IIA	T3, N0, M0
IIB	T4a, N0, M0
IIC	T4b, N0, M0
IIIA	T1-2, N1, M0
	T1, N2a, M0
IIIB	T3-4, N1, M0
	T2-3, N2a, M0
	T1-2, N2b, M0
IIIC	T4a, N2a, M0
	T3-4a, N2b, M0
	T4b, N1-2, M0
IVA	T(any), N(any), M1a
IVB	T(any), N(any), M1b

LABORATORY TESTS

- Positive fecal occult blood test (FOBT): Many primary care physicians use single digital FOBT as their primary screening test for CRC. Single FOBT has low specificity for detecting human hemoglobin, is a poor screening method for CRC (sensitivity, 4.9%), and is inappropriate as the only test because negative results do not decrease the odds of advanced neoplasia. The American College of Gastroenterology recommends fecal immunochemical test (FIT) as a replacement for guaiac-based FOBT for CRC detection. FIT measures intact human globin protein (as opposed to heme) in the stool. It detects more advanced adenomas than FOBT. Fecal DNA testing is emerging as a newer screening method for CRC. It detects colonic cells shed into the fecal stream that possess specific genetic or epigenetic changes and has a reported sensitivity of 97% and a specificity of 90% for CRC stages I to III. In trials involving asymptomatic persons at average risk for colorectal cancer, multitarget stool DNA testing detects significantly more cancers than FIT but has more false-positive results. Cost ($500) and rate of false positives are the main obstacles inhibiting broader adoption of fecal DNA testing. A recent clinical study in asymptomatic persons ≥50 years old at average risk for colorectal cancer revealed that one-time screening with stool DNA test (Cologuard) detected 92% of cases of colorectal cancer, but it detected less than half of advanced precancerous lesions and produced a substantial number of false-positive results.[1]
- Microcytic anemia on CBC may be indicative of chronic blood loss.
- Increased plasma carcinoembryonic antigen (CEA) level: CEA is not useful for screening because it can be increased in nonmalignant conditions (smoking, IBD, alcoholic liver disease). A normal CEA result does not exclude the diagnosis of CRC.

[1]The Medical Letter on Drugs and Therapeutics, October 13, 2014; 56(1453):100-101.

- CDX2 is a useful prognostic biomarker in stage II colon cancer. Lack of CDX2 expression identifies a subgroup of patients with high-risk stage II colon cancer who appear to benefit from adjuvant chemotherapy.[2]

IMAGING STUDIES

- Colonoscopy with biopsy (primary assessment tool): The American College of Physicians (ACP) recommends that patients should be offered a colonoscopy beginning at age 50, and it should be repeated every 10 yr in average-risk patients. Screening is recommended in African Americans beginning at age 45 yr. Persons with only one first-degree relative with CRC or advanced adenomas diagnosed at 60 yr or older may be screened as at average risk. A family history of small tubular adenomas in first-degree relatives is not considered to increase the risk for CRC. The U.S. Preventive Services Task Force guidelines state that screening should not be routinely recommended in persons older than 75 yr, and it should not be recommended at all in persons older than 85 yr. If persons between the ages of 75 and 85 yr have never undergone screening, the decision about screening should be individualized according to health status. The ACP recommends that clinicians stop screening for colorectal cancer in adults over age 75 yr or in adults with a life expectancy of <10 yr. Table 1C-38 describes CRC screening and surveillance recommendations.

[2]Dalerba P, et al: CDX2 as a prognostic marker in stage II and stage III colon cancer. *N Engl J Med* 374:211-222, 2016.

- Computed tomography colonoscopy (CTC) virtual colonoscopy (VC) uses helical (spiral) CT scanning to generate a two- or three-dimensional virtual colorectal image (Fig. 1C-82). CTC does not require sedation, but, like optical colonoscopy, it requires some bowel preparation (either bowel cathartics or ingestion of iodinated contrast medium with meals during the 48 hr before CT) and air insufflation. It also involves substantial exposure to radiation. In addition, patients with lesions detected by VC will require traditional colonoscopy. Compared with colonoscopy, CTC sensitivity for detection of polyps >10 mm ranges from 70% to 96%, and specificity ranges from 72% to 96%. CTC has replaced double-contrast barium enema as the radiographic screening alternative when patients decline colonoscopy.
- Capsule endoscopy allows visualization of the colonic mucosa but is not recommended as a screening procedure because its sensitivity for detecting colonic lesions is low compared with colonoscopy.
- CT scanning of the abdomen (Fig. 1C-83), pelvis, and chest assists in preoperative staging.
- PET scanning can display functional information and is accurate in the detection of CRC and its distant metastases. Combined PET/CT scanners are increasingly available and are useful to detect and characterize malignant lesions. Colonography composed of a combined modality of PET and CT is a newer diagnostic modality that can provide whole-body tumor staging in a single session.

Rx TREATMENT

GENERAL Rx

- Surgical resection is the definitive and curative upfront treatment for stages I-III colon cancers. Selected patients (high-risk stage II, all stage III) are often recommended for adjuvant chemotherapy.
- The standard chemotherapy regimen for adjuvant therapy of resected CRC is the combination of oxaliplatin with a fluoropyrimidine (5-fluorouracil or capecitabine) Older patients and patients who are not considered candidates for aggressive therapy are often treated with single-agent fluoropyrimidine therapy.
- The combination of neoadjuvant chemotherapy and radiation therapy is used to downsize and downstage rectal cancers before definitive resection and has been proven to improve overall survival and local disease control in stage II-III cancers.
- The use of adjuvant chemotherapy in stage II disease (no nodal involvement) is estimated to provide an improvement in overall survival by 3% to 4% with current 5-yr survival rates in the 80% range. Given the limited benefit, current guidelines recommend consideration of adjuvant chemotherapy in this setting only in high-risk patients. The magnitude of survival benefit is higher in stage III patients and combination chemotherapy regimen as above is associated with 5-year overall survival in the 70% range with wide variation in the subgroups.
- The outlook for patients with metastatic and relapsed CRC has improved dramatically in the past few years. Median overall survival is now expected in the 30+ month range with modern chemotherapeutic regimen usage. Patients with limited and resectable metastases in sites such as the liver have even better survivals with 5-year survival ranges in the 50% range.
- Current chemotherapy agents which are used in the metastatic setting include 5-fluorouracil (5-FU), capecitabine, irinotecan, oxaliplatin, and mitomycin. Two-drug chemotherapy regimens using a combination of antimetabolite (5-FU or capecitabine) in combination with either oxaliplatin or irinotecan form the backbone of systemic therapy approaches.
- Molecularly targeted therapy against the epidermal growth factor receptor (EGFR) and the angiogenesis pathway are used in combination with the chemotherapy backbone in metastatic CRC. Antiangiogenesis agents include monoclonal antibodies bevacizumab, aflibercept, and ramucirumab. Cetuximab and panitumumab are EGFR receptor blockers which are active in metastatic CRC patients whose tumors do not harbor mutated RAS oncogenes.
- The liver is generally the initial and most common site of CRC metastases. Resection of metastases limited to the liver followed by systemic chemotherapy is curative in more

TABLE 1C-38 Colorectal Cancer (CRC) Screening and Surveillance Recommendations*

Indication	Recommendations
Average risk	Beginning at age 50 yr: Colonoscopy every 10 yr Computed tomographic colonography every 5 yr Flexible sigmoidoscopy every 5 yr Double-contrast barium enema every 5 yr Stool blood testing annually or stool DNA testing acceptable but not preferred
One or two first-degree relatives with CRC at any age or adenoma at age <60 yr	Colonoscopy every 5 yr beginning at age 40 yr, or 10 yr younger than earliest diagnosis, whichever comes first
Hereditary nonpolyposis CRC	Genetic counseling and screening[†] Colonoscopy every 1 to 2 yr beginning at age 25 yr and then yearly after age 40 yr[‡]
Familial adenomatous polyposis and variants	Genetic counseling and testing[†] Flexible sigmoidoscopy yearly beginning at puberty[‡]
Personal history of CRC	Colonoscopy within 1 yr of curative resection; repeat at 3 yr and then every 5 yr if normal
Personal history of colorectal adenoma	Colonoscopy every 3 to 5 yr after removal of all index polyps
Inflammatory bowel disease	Colonoscopy every 1 to 2 yr beginning after 8 yr of pancolitis or after 15 yr if only left-sided disease

*Recommendations proposed by the American Cancer Society and U.S. Multi-Society Task Force on Colorectal Cancer; recommendations for average-risk patients also endorsed by the American College of Radiology.
[†]Whenever possible, affected relatives should be tested first because of potential false-negative results.
[‡]Screening recommendation for individuals with positive or indeterminate tests as well as for those who refuse genetic testing.
From Andreoli TE et al: *Andreoli and Carpenter's Cecil essentials of medicine*, ed 8, Philadelphia, 2010, Saunders.

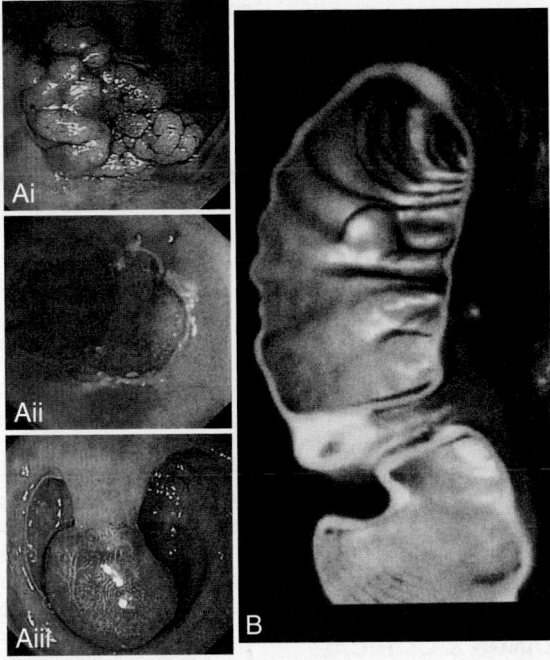

FIGURE 1C-82 Colon polyps seen at (Ai–iii) colonoscopy and (B) computed tomography (CT) colonography. Aii is after endoscopic resection of the polyps in Ai. (From Ballinger A: *Kumar & Clark's essentials of medicine*, ed 5, Edinburgh, 2012, Saunders.)

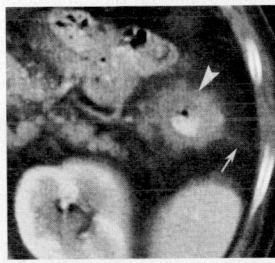

FIGURE 1C-83 Colon carcinoma: wall thickening. A carcinoma of the descending colon near the splenic flexure causes thickening of the colon wall (*arrowhead*) and narrowing of the lumen. Stranding densities (*arrow*) extending into the pericolonic fat suggest tumor extension through the bowel wall. (From Webb WR, Brant WE, Major NM: *Fundamentals of body CT*, ed 4, Philadelphia, 2015, Saunders.)

than 30% of selected patients. Metasectomy of limited pulmonary metastases can also be considered in selected cases.
- Unresectable multiple liver metastases are often approached by locoregional therapeutic approaches such as transarterial chemoembolization (TACE), selective internal radiation therapy (SIRT) using yttrium-90 brachytherapy, or hepatic arterial infusional chemotherapy.

CHRONIC Rx
Follow-up is indicated with:
- Physician visits with a focus on clinical and disease-related history, directed physical examination, coordination of follow-up, and counseling every 3 to 4 mo for the first 3 yr and then every 6 months for 2 yr.
- Colonoscopy at end of first year, then after 3 yr and subsequently every 5 yr.

- Baseline CEA level can be obtained; if elevated, it can be used after surgery as a measure of completeness of tumor resection. It is used to monitor tumor recurrence and is obtained every 3 to 6 mo for up to 5 yr.

DISPOSITION
The 5-yr survival rate varies with the stage of the carcinoma:
- TNM stage:

Stage	5-yr Survival Rate (%)
I	>90
IIA-C	60-85
IIIA-C	25-65
IV	5-10%

- Overall 5-yr disease-free survival rate has increased from 50% to 63% during the past two decades.
- High-frequency microsatellite instability in CRC is independently predictive of a relatively favorable outcome and reduces the likelihood of metastases.
- In patients with high-risk stage II and with stage III CRC, there is improved 5-yr survival among patients treated with adjuvant chemotherapy.
- Expression patterns of microRNA are systemically altered in colon adenocarcinomas. High miR-21 expression is associated with poor survival and poor therapeutic outcome.
- The optimal timing from surgery to initiation of adjuvant chemotherapy is 4 to 8 wk. A longer time to initiation of adjuvant chemotherapy is associated with worse survival rates.
- Regular aspirin use after the diagnosis of CRC has been reported to be associated

with lower risk for CRC-specific and overall mortality, especially among individuals with tumors that overexpress cyclooxygenase-2. Regular aspirin use is associated with lower BRAF-wild type colorectal cancer but not with BRAF-mutated cancer risk. All aspirin doses starting with 75 mg daily had similar effects on CRC incidence and mortality.

REFERRAL
- Multidisciplinary referral to colorectal surgery or surgical oncology, medical oncology, radiation oncology

PEARLS & CONSIDERATIONS

COMMENTS
- Metastases of tumor cells to regional lymph nodes is the single most important prognostic factor in patients with colon cancer.
- Decreased fat intake to 30% of total energy intake, increased fiber through fruit and vegetable consumption may reduce CRC risk.
- Chemoprophylaxis with aspirin (81 mg/day) reduces the incidence of colorectal adenomas in persons at risk.
- The National Cancer Institute has published consensus guidelines for universal screening for HNPCC in patients with newly diagnosed CRC. Tumors in mutation carriers of HNPCC typically exhibit microsatellite instability, a characteristic phenotype caused by expansion or contraction of short nucleotide repeat sequences. These guidelines (Bethesda Guidelines) are useful for selective patients for microsatellite instability testing. Screening patients with newly diagnosed CRC for HNPCC is cost effective, especially if the benefits to their immediate relatives are considered.
- The use of either annual or biennial FOBT significantly reduces the incidence of CRC.
- The detection of mutations in the *APC* gene from stool samples is a promising new modality for early detection of colorectal neoplasms.

SUGGESTED READINGS
Available at www.expertconsult.com

RELATED CONTENT
Colon Cancer (Patient Information)

AUTHOR: **RITESH RATHORE, M.D.**

BASIC INFORMATION

DEFINITION

Compartment syndrome is a condition that occurs when elevated pressure within a limited space compromises the circulation, with increased risk of irreversible damage to its contents and their function. Acute compartment syndrome is a surgical emergency.

ICD-10CM CODES

958.90	Compartment syndrome unspecified
958.90	Compartment syndrome, not otherwise specified
T79.A0	Compartment syndrome, unspecified, initial encounter
M79.A11	Nontraumatic compartment syndrome of right upper extremity
M79.A12	Nontraumatic compartment syndrome of left upper extremity
M79.A19	Nontraumatic compartment syndrome of unspecified upper extremity
M79.A21	Nontraumatic compartment syndrome of right lower extremity
M79.A22	Nontraumatic compartment syndrome of left lower extremity
M79.A29	Nontraumatic compartment syndrome of unspecified lower extremity
M79.A9	Nontraumatic compartment syndrome of other sites
T79.A19A	Traumatic compartment syndrome of unspecified upper extremity, initial encounter
T79.A21A	Traumatic compartment syndrome of right lower extremity, initial encounter
T79.A22A	Traumatic compartment syndrome of left lower extremity, initial encounter
T79.A29A	Traumatic compartment syndrome of unspecified lower extremity, initial encounter

EPIDEMIOLOGY & DEMOGRAPHICS

- Occurs most commonly after acute trauma, especially with long bone fractures, comprising 75% of cases.
- It usually occurs in persons <35 yr.
- Incidence is higher in males.
- It can occur in other parts, such as the foot, thigh, gluteal region, and abdomen.
- Supracondylar fractures in children can commonly lead to compartment syndrome.
- 6% to 9% of open tibial fractures are complicated by compartment syndrome.
- It is seen in all races and ethnicities.

PATHOPHYSIOLOGY

Compartment syndrome occurs when the blood flow is less than the tissue metabolic demands, causing tissue injury. It occurs when the intracompartmental pressure increases limiting venous outflow with rising venous pressure, resulting in compromise of the local circulation and tissue hypoxia with decreased arteriovenous pressure gradient. Venous congestion additionally leads to tissue edema and interstitial pressure, and the compartment pressure continues to increase. Compartment pressure ranges between 10 and 30 mm Hg of diastolic pressure are able to cause the condition.

Different conditions are known to cause compartment syndrome:

- Conditions that limit compartment volume, such as when patients have fracture casts, when sedated or comatose patients lie on a limb for a prolonged period, or when patients have tight dressings that are applied externally.
- Conditions that cause increased compartment content, such as bleeding in the compartment from vascular injury or diathesis, fractures or finger injuries, reperfusion after ischemic injury such as embolectomy and arterial bypass grafting, severe bruising of muscle, and thermal or electrical burn injuries.
- Other injuries, such as extravasation of intravenous fluids, injection of recreational drugs, and snake bites.

PHYSICAL FINDINGS & CLINICAL PRESENTATION

Signs and symptoms are usually apparent but can be unreliable and can lead to delayed diagnosis. Acute compartment syndrome can worsen within hours; therefore serial examination is important in a patient with suspected compartment syndrome. Patients with tense painful limbs are considered to have acute compartment syndrome; however, diagnosis is confirmed with the assessment of elevated compartment pressure. Clinical signs and symptoms include the following:

- Pain disproportional to injury (the earliest sign)
- Constant deep pain and pain that is referred to the compartment on passive stretching of the muscles of the affected compartment (Fig. E1C-84, *A*)
- Reduced sense of touch or sensation (hypesthesia) within the territory of the nerve passing the compartment (in acute anterior compartment syndrome, the patient may have hypesthesia in the territory of the first webspace)
- Tense and swollen compartment (Figs. E1C-84, *B* and 1C-84, *C*)
- Muscle weakness
- Paresis (late finding) that suggests permanent muscle damage
- Capillary refill can be slow but normal.
- Peripheral pulses that are normally palpable even in severe conditions
- Tingling and numbness in the affected limb. Hypesthesia or paresthesia should be evaluated with pinprick, light touch, and two-point discrimination tests.
- Difficulty moving the extremities.

DIAGNOSIS

Diagnosis is based on clinical signs and symptoms along with compartment pressure. Compartment pressure testing may be unnecessary if the diagnosis is clinically obvious.

DIFFERENTIAL DIAGNOSIS

- Muscle strains
- Cellulitis
- Gangrene
- Peripheral vascular injury
- Necrotizing fasciitis
- Stress fractures
- Deep vein thrombosis and thrombophlebitis
- Tendinitis
- Muscle contusion
- Tarsal tunnel syndrome
- Posterior ankle syndrome
- Popliteal artery impingement
- Claudication
- Tumor
- Venous insufficiency

LABORATORY TESTS

Diagnosis is based on clinical findings and the measurement of compartment pressures. Laboratory values are not useful in the diagnosis of compartment syndrome but are important for other diagnoses or associated conditions.

- CBC with differential for evaluation of infection
- Creatine phosphokinase (CK) levels, which can rise as muscle injury develops
- Metabolic panel for the assessment of electrolytes and renal function
- Coagulation profile for bleeding diathesis
- Urinalysis for rhabdomyolysis
- Urine and serum myoglobin levels

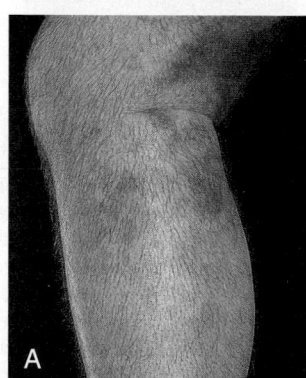
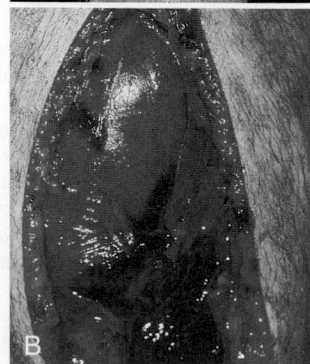

FIGURE 1C-84 C: A, Severe calf swelling due to anterior and posterior compartment syndromes after ischemia-reperfusion. **B,** Appearance after emergency fasciotomy. Note edematous muscle and hematoma. (Courtesy Michael J. Allen, FRCS, Leicester, UK. From Floege J et al: *Comprehensive clinical nephrology,* ed 4, Philadelphia, 2010, Saunders.)

IMAGING STUDIES

- Direct intracompartmental pressure measurement can be done by handheld manometer, wick or slit catheter technique, and simple needle manometer system. Compartment syndrome is diagnosed when the difference between diastolic blood pressure and compartment pressure (Δ pressure) is ≤30 mm Hg.
- Ultrasonography can be used to rule out deep vein thrombosis, or Doppler ultrasonography can be used to evaluate blood flow to the extremity. Arteriography should be used to evaluate the adequate blood flow through a compartment.
- Near-infrared spectroscopy and technetium-99m methoxyisobutylisonitrile scintigraphy can also be used.
- Radiography can be used on the affected limb for fracture or foreign body evaluation.

 **TREATMENT**

Treatment goal is to keep intracompartmental pressure low and prevent tissue injury (Fig. 1C-84, *D*).

NONPHARMACOLOGIC THERAPY

- Immediate relieving of all external pressure on the affected compartment
- Removal of casts, splints, and dressings
- Placing limb at heart level to avoid decreased or increased blood flow

ACUTE GENERAL Rx

- Analgesics for pain
- Hyperbaric oxygen
- Hypotension can worsen tissue ischemia and thus should be treated with IV isotonic saline.
- Fasciotomy of the affected compartment is indicated if there has been >6 hr of limb ischemia, or immediate decompression should be performed when the compartment pressure > 30 to 35 mm Hg.
- Measurement of compartment pressure is not necessary to perform fasciotomy if clinical suspicion is high depending on history and clinical examination.
- When compartment pressures are trending downward, it is often safe to delay emergent fasciotomy, provided the Δ pressure is also improving.

CHRONIC Rx

- Aftercare of fasciotomy wound: Wound is inspected after 48 hours and dead tissue is removed.
- Wounds are left open, requiring later skin grafting or delayed wound closure.
- Opsite sheet and boot lace techniques are also used for closing fasciotomy wounds.
- Concomitant fractured bones should also be stabilized with plating, external fixation, or intramedullary nailing.

DISPOSITION

With early diagnosis and treatment, the prognosis is excellent for recovery of the muscles and nerves inside the compartment. The following conditions can be prevented:

- Permanent nerve damage/paralysis
- Muscle contracture
- Gangrene
- Amputation
- Muscle necrosis
- Fracture nonunion
- Rhabdomyolysis that leads to renal failure
- Compartment syndrome that can occur in open fractures
- Permanent nerve injury, which can occur after 12 to 24 hr of compression; mortality rates in patients who need fasciotomy is ≈15%.

REFERRAL

Patients with suspected compartment syndrome should be referred promptly to orthopedic and general surgery.

 **PEARLS & CONSIDERATIONS**

- Universal precautions and aseptic measures are necessary for patients undergoing fasciotomy because the risk of local and systemic infection is high with the procedure.
- Invasive monitoring techniques should be undertaken with adequate analgesia so that patient immobility is ensured while the pressure is measured.
- Injection of local anesthetics into the compartment can increase the pressure and pain and therefore should be avoided.
- Patients with fracture casts should be informed about the risks of swelling, and patients should also be encouraged to wear appropriate equipment while playing sports.
- A history of coagulation disorders and the use of anticoagulants should be mentioned in a patient's medical history.

EBM EVIDENCE

Available at www.expertconsult.com

SUGGESTED READINGS

Available at www.expertconsult.com

RELATED CONTENT

Compartment Syndrome (Patient Information)

AUTHOR: **SYEDA M. SAYEED, M.D.**

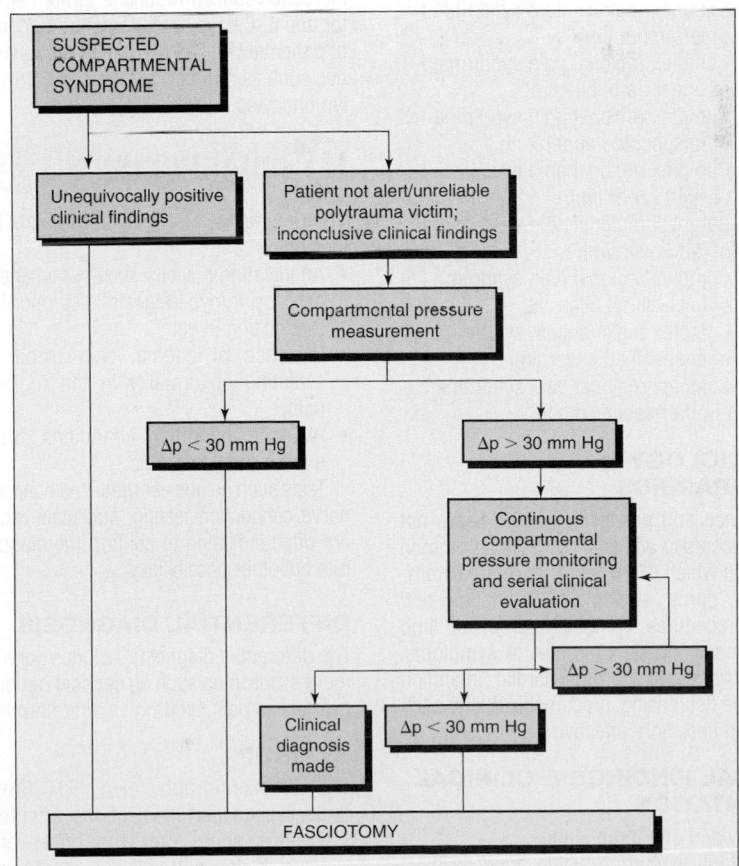

FIGURE 1C-84 D, Algorithm for management for a patient with suspected compartment syndrome. Δp is defined as the difference between the diastolic pressure and the measured compartment pressure in mm Hg as documented by McQueen and Court-Brown. (From Browner BD et al [eds]: *Skeletal trauma*, ed 4, Philadelphia, 2009, Saunders.)

 **BASIC INFORMATION**

DEFINITION

Complex regional pain syndrome (CRPS) is a pain disorder characterized by constant and intense limb pain associated with vasomotor and neurosensory abnormalities, skin changes, and demineralization of bone. CRPS has been divided into type I, in which there is usually an initiating noxious event but no distinct nerve lesion, and type II, in which a definable (usually traumatic) nerve lesion exists. CRPS type I generally correlates with the syndrome formerly known as reflex sympathetic dystrophy (RSD), and CRPS type II equates with what was previously termed causalgia. The term *shoulder-hand syndrome* has been used to describe CRPS in the setting of myocardial infarction or ischemia.

SYNONYMS

Reflex sympathetic dystrophy
Shoulder hand syndrome
CRPS

ICD-10CM CODES
M89.0	Algoneurodystrophy
G90.59	Complex regional pain syndrome I of other specified site
G90.511	Complex regional pain syndrome I of right upper limb
G90.512	Complex regional pain syndrome I of left upper limb
G90.513	Complex regional pain syndrome I of upper limb, bilateral
G90.519	Complex regional pain syndrome I of unspecified upper limb
G90.521	Complex regional pain syndrome I of right lower limb
G90.522	Complex regional pain syndrome I of left lower limb
G90.523	Complex regional pain syndrome I of lower limb, bilateral
G90.529	Complex regional pain syndrome I of unspecified lower limb
G90.59	Complex regional pain syndrome I of other specified site

EPIDEMIOLOGY & DEMOGRAPHICS

The incidence and prevalence of CRPS are not known. It occurs in adults and children. Common situations in which CRPS is seen include extremity trauma, burns, stroke, and orthopedic and podiatric procedures. Immobilization of the limb often precedes the development of symptoms. CRPS in the setting of myocardial infarction seems to be decreasing, presumably due to early mobilization and more effective pain control.

PHYSICAL FINDINGS & CLINICAL PRESENTATION

CRPS is divided into three stages:
1. Acute stage (occurring within hours to days after the injury).
   - Burning or aching pain occurring over the injured extremity.
   - Hyperalgesia (exaggerated response to nociceptive stimuli).
   - Edema.
   - Dysthermia.
   - Increased hair and nail growth.
2. Dystrophic stage (3 to 6 months after injury).
   - Burning pain radiating both distally and proximally from the site of injury.
   - Brawny edema (Fig. E1C-85).
   - Hyperhidrosis.
   - Hypothermia and cyanosis.
   - Muscle tremors and spasms.
   - Increased muscle tone and reflexes.
3. Atrophic stage (6 months after injury).
   - Spread of pain proximally.
   - Allodynia (pain response to stimuli that are not normally painful).
   - Cold, pale, cyanotic skin.
   - Tropic skin changes with subcutaneous atrophy.
   - Contractures.

ETIOLOGY

The exact pathogenetic mechanisms underlying CRPS have not been fully elucidated, but most theories include the formation of an abnormal reflex arc in the sympathetic nervous system that is modulated by cortical centers to produce peripheral vascular disturbances. Persistent pain in the peripheral nervous system is modulated by inflammatory neuropeptides including substance P, which has been shown to be elevated in the serum of patients with CRPS-I. Increased concentrations of tumor necrosis factor and IL-6 have been demonstrated in the skin of patients with CRPS-I, and immune abnormalities such as reduced numbers of CD8-positive T lymphocytes have also been seen.

 **DIAGNOSIS**

Criteria proposed for the diagnosis of CRPS type I include:
- An initiating noxious event, spontaneous pain or alloying/hyperalgesia disproportionate to the inciting event.
- Evidence of edema, skin blood flow, or sweating abnormality in the region of the pain.
- Absence of other conditions that could explain the symptoms.

Tests such as nuclear medicine bone scanning, nerve conduction testing, and plain radiographs are often indicated to confirm the diagnosis and rule out other possibilities.

DIFFERENTIAL DIAGNOSIS

The differential diagnosis includes nerve entrapment syndromes such as cervical radiculopathy, myofascial pain syndromes, and fibromyalgia.

WORKUP

- Bone scintigraphy (Fig. E1C-86) shows decreased perfusion of the affected areas if done soon after the onset of symptoms. If done after 6 weeks of symptoms, bone scan may show increased uptake in the region of the peripheral joints of the involved extremity.
- Electrophysiologic testing is useful to identify nerve injury in patients with type II CRPS.
- Plain radiographs show diffuse patchy osteopenia (Fig. E1C-87).
- Skin temperature measurements can be used as a diagnostic test.
- Autonomic testing, although not commonly done, has been proposed.
  1. Measuring resting sweat output.
  2. Measuring resting skin temperature.
  3. Quantitative sudomotor axon reflex test.

Rx TREATMENT

Treatment of CRPS is largely empiric, based mostly on anecdotal reports, extrapolation from drug trials for other painful conditions, and clinical experience. Therapy should be tailored to stage of disease progression and severity of symptoms.

NONPHARMACOLOGIC THERAPY
- Physical therapy.
- Patient education.

PHARMACOLOGIC THERAPY

Suggested regimens:
Stage 1
   Tricyclic antidepressants (amitriptyline 25 to 150 mg or doxepin 5 to 20 mg).
   Prednisone 1 mg/kg for 2 weeks, then taper by 10 mg every 2 weeks.
   Alendronate 70 mg PO weekly.
Stage II
   Topical capsaicin.
   Gabapentin 300 mg tid.
   Regional nerve blocks.
Stage III
   Sympathetic ganglion blocks.
   Refer to multidisciplinary pain center.
   NOTE: High-dose vitamin C may decrease the incidence of CRPS following wrist fracture and foot and ankle surgery or trauma.

DISPOSITION

Spontaneous remission can occur after several weeks to months.

REFERRAL

Cases in which the diagnosis is not clear or there is suboptimal response to therapy should promptly be referred to a multidisciplinary pain clinic.

! PEARLS & CONSIDERATIONS

COMMENTS
- CRPS is a common clinical entity without clear definition, pathophysiologic features, or treatment.
- Early mobilization in high-risk situations is important for prevention of CRPS.
- Prompt diagnosis and aggressive physical and pharmacologic therapy may prevent progression to chronic, intractable pain.

SUGGESTED READINGS
Available at www.expertconsult.com

AUTHOR: **BERNARD ZIMMERMANN, M.D.**

BASIC INFORMATION

DEFINITION

Bereavement is a universal human experience, and grieving after the loss of a loved one is recognized as a normal and healthy response to loss. Normal grieving typically resolves on its own over time. In a small proportion of bereaved individuals, the process of grieving does not resolve on its own. In complicated or prolonged grief, intense grieving symptoms significantly impair functioning. Complicated grief was proposed as a diagnosis for DSM 5, and prolonged grief disorder has been recommended for inclusion in the ICD-11. Persistent complex bereavement disorder is included in the DSM 5 appendix in the section for conditions needing further study.

SYNONYM(S)

Prolonged grief disorder
Persistent complex bereavement disorder

ICD-10CM CODES
Complicated grief and prolonged grief are not included as diagnoses in the DSM 5 or the ICD-10.

EPIDEMIOLOGY & DEMOGRAPHICS

INCIDENCE: Studies indicate that of bereaved individuals, around 10% experience bereavement symptoms that grow or persist with the passage of time and significantly impair functioning.
PREDOMINANT SEX AND AGE: Prolonged grief is more common among women than men, and more common in the elderly, who are exposed to more losses as they age.

PHYSICAL FINDINGS & CLINICAL PRESENTATION

The key feature of prolonged or complicated grief is impaired functioning in occupational, social, or other contexts beyond 6 to 12 mo after the loss, with symptoms that center around feelings of loss. Individuals struggling with prolonged or complicated grief may present with intense longing for the deceased, feelings of emptiness, prolonged reactivity to reminders of the loss, unwillingness to adopt new roles, difficulty engaging in social relationships, isolation and social disengagement, and fixation on the past and on reminders of the past. They may have difficulty envisioning life without the diseased person and may experience suicidal ideation or intent as a result.

ETIOLOGY

The etiology is not known, but complications such as isolation or attentional biases impede normal resolution of grief and lead to prolonged or intensified grief symptoms. Risk factors include a history of trauma or loss, a history of mood or anxiety disorders, insecure attachment style, low perceived social support, increased stress, having been a caregiver for the deceased, pessimistic temperament, and violent cause of death of the deceased.

DIAGNOSIS

Proposed criteria for prolonged difficulties with bereavement differ, but commonalities include having been bereaved (lost a loved one) and experiencing a constellation of the symptoms below for at least 6 mo (different sets of criteria propose different minimum lengths of time ranging from 6-12 mo);
- Experiencing intense yearning, sorrow, or pain, or preoccupation with the deceased
- Feeling stunned or having difficulty accepting the death of the loved one
- Feelings of emptiness or lack of self
- Emotional numbness
- Bitterness about the loss
- Avoidance of reminders of the loss
- Difficulty moving on with life and forging new friendships or pursuing hobbies or interests
- Difficulty engaging in relationships
- Difficulty imagining life without the deceased
- Impairment in social, occupational, or other areas of functioning

DIFFERENTIAL DIAGNOSIS

- Major depression: Whereas in major depression, a globally pessimistic outlook prevails, with prolonged or complicated grief, negative feelings tend to be specifically centered on the loss of the loved one.
- PTSD. Whereas PTSD is characterized predominantly by fear, horror, anger, guilt, shame, and hyperarousal, prolonged or complicated grief is characterized by yearning, loss, and emptiness.

WORKUP

A comprehensive clinical interview should assess when symptoms began, whether symptoms and negative feelings center on the loss of the loved one, impairment in functioning, and hopelessness or suicidal ideation or intent. The assessment should also explore attachment history and the history or presence of other psychiatric disorders.

IMAGING STUDIES

Imaging studies have shown activation of the nucleus accumbens on exposure to cues of the deceased in cases of complicated grief but not in cases of normal grief.

TREATMENT

Studies have demonstrated the efficacy of various grief-specific therapies. Commonalities across treatments that have demonstrated efficacy include:
- Psychoeducation about grief
- A focus on processing the loss of the loved one, including feelings of loss and positive reminiscing about the loved one
- A focus on restoring functioning and purposeful engagement in life
- A focus on challenging thoughts that worsen negative feelings

Some studies have found that antidepressant medications are not effective for prolonged grief symptoms, but more research is needed on psychopharmacology and prolonged grief.

Psychotherapies for depression, including interpersonal psychotherapy, have not been effective for prolonged or complicated grief.

DISPOSITION

Compared with normal grief, prolonged or complicated grief is associated with debilitating distress and disability, suicidal ideation, and negative health outcomes.

PEARLS & CONSIDERATIONS

- It is important to assess patients 6 to 12 mo after a loss of a loved one and to determine whether they might be experiencing prolonged or complicated grief.
- For patients with prolonged or complicated grief, grief-specific therapy has demonstrated efficacy and should be encouraged.
- Treatments for depression that do not specifically address the loss have not been shown to be effective for complicated grief.
- Suicidality must be assessed.

SUGGESTED READINGS
Available online at www.expertconsult.com

AUTHOR: **ABIGAIL K. MANSFIELD, Ph.D.**

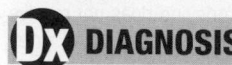
BASIC INFORMATION

DEFINITION

- Concussion is a mild traumatic brain injury that manifests with self-limited symptoms at the less severe end of the brain injury spectrum.
- It is a complex pathophysiologic process affecting the brain, induced by traumatic biomechanical forces. It may be caused by a direct blow to the head, face, neck, or elsewhere on the body with an "impulsive" force transmitted to the head.
- Concussion typically results in the rapid onset of short-lived impairment of neurologic function that resolves spontaneously. It may result in neuropathologic changes, but the acute clinical symptoms largely reflect a functional disturbance rather than a structural injury.
- The fourth International Conference on Concussion (2012) defines concussion as "a complex pathophysiological process affecting the brain, induced by traumatic biomechanical forces," characterized by the following features: (1) caused by a direct blow to the head or blow to the body that transmits an "impulsive" force to the head; (2) results in rapid onset of short-lived neurotic impairment that resolves spontaneously; (3) variable clinical symptoms that may not include loss of consciousness; (4) symptoms that largely reflect a functional disturbance rather than structural injury (thus, no abnormalities are seen on standard structural neuroimaging studies); and (5) symptom resolution that typically follows a sequential course but may be prolonged in a small percentage of cases.[1]

SYNONYMS

Sports-related mild traumatic brain injury (mTBI)

ICD-10CM CODES

S06.0	Concussion
S06.0X0A	Concussion without loss of consciousness, initial encounter
S06.0X0D	Concussion without loss of consciousness, subsequent encounter
S06.0X0S	Concussion without loss of consciousness, sequela
S06.0X1A	Concussion with loss of consciousness of 30 minutes or less, initial encounter
S06.0X9A	Concussion with loss of consciousness of unspecified duration, initial encounter

EPIDEMIOLOGY & DEMOGRAPHICS

INCIDENCE: 3.8 million sports- and recreation-related concussions occur each year in the U.S.

It is estimated that as many as 50% of concussions go unreported.

PREVALENCE: Each year, U.S. emergency departments treat an estimated 135,000 sports- and recreation-related TBIs, including concussions, among children ages 5 to 18.

PREDOMINANT SEX AND AGE: Children and teens are more likely to get a concussion and take longer to recover than adults. Limited studies have shown that in sports that are played by both men and women, women are at more risk of sustaining a concussion.

RISK FACTORS: High-impact sports and recreation; six times more likely in organized sports than leisure physical activity. Individuals who have sustained a concussion previously are at a higher risk of sustaining another concussion. Athletes with a body mass index (BMI) >27 kg/m^2 and those who train <3 hr/wk are also at greater risk.

PHYSICAL FINDINGS & CLINICAL PRESENTATION

See Table 1C-39.

TABLE 1C-39 Symptoms and Signs of Concussion

Mental Status Changes

Amnesia

Confusion

Disorientation

Easily distracted

Excessive drowsiness

Feeling dinged, stunned, or foggy

Impaired level of consciousness

Inappropriate play behaviors

Poor concentration and attention

Seeing stars or flashing lights

Slow to answer questions or to follow directions

Physical or Somatic

Ataxia or loss of balance

Blurry vision

Decreased performance or playing ability

Dizziness

Double vision

Fatigue

Headache

Lightheadedness

Nausea, vomiting

Poor coordination

Ringing in the ears

Seizures

Slurred, incoherent speech

Vacant stare/glassy-eyed

Vertigo

Behavior or Psychosomatic

Emotional lability

Irritability

Low frustration tolerance

Personality changes

Nervousness, anxiety

Sadness, depressed mood

From Patel DR et al: Sports related concussions in adolescents, *Pediatr Clin N Am* 57:652, 2010.

ETIOLOGY

- Concussion occurs when rotational or angular acceleration forces are applied to the brain, resulting in shear strain of the underlying neural elements, including altered autonomic function and impaired control of cerebral blood flow.
- This may be associated with a blow to the skull; however, direct impact to the head is not required.

DIAGNOSIS

DIFFERENTIAL DIAGNOSIS

- Migraine
- Cervical strain
- Posttraumatic vestibular injury

WORKUP

- Sideline assessment:
  1. No athlete with a suspected concussion should return to play that day.
  2. Neurologic assessment using a standardized tool, such as s SCAT3 (Sports Concussion Assessment Tool), which includes the BESS (Balance Error Scoring System) and Maddocks Questions or SAC (Standardized Assessment of Concussion) (Fig. 1C-88)
  3. Monitor for deterioration; no athlete should be left alone
- Neurocognitive testing:
  1. Computer-based programs, such as ImPACT, ANAM, CogSport
  2. Neuropsychiatric testing administered by a neuropsychologist
- Gait/balance testing with a tool such as the Balance Error Scoring System (BESS)
- When used in combination, symptom assessment, balance assessment, and neurocognitive testing provide a sensitivity of >90% for the identification of concussion.
- Consider the Buffalo Concussion Treadmill Test, which identifies physiologic dysfunction in concussion, rules out other diagnoses, and can quantify a safe level of activity in concussion recovery.

IMAGING STUDIES

- CT imaging is indicated in any athlete with a Glasgow Coma Scale score of ≤15 or a rapidly changing neurologic exam.
- Imaging should be reserved for athletes in whom intracerebral bleeding is suspected; PECARN guidelines.

TREATMENT

ACUTE GENERAL Rx

- Removal from game
- Physical rest
  1. No return to play until asymptomatic for 24 hr
  2. Follow return-to-play guidelines (Table 1C-40)
- Cognitive rest to limit symptoms
  1. Modifications at school
  2. Modifications at home/recreation
  3. Encourage sleep

[1]McCrory P et al.: Consensus statement on concussion in sport: the 4th International Conference on Concussion in Sport held in Zurich, November 2012. *Clin J Sport Med* 23:89-117, 2013.

FIGURE 1C-88 Standardized assessment of concussion (SAC). (Redrawn from McCrea M et al: Standard assessment of concussion in football players. *Neurology* 48:586–588, 1997.)

The SAC form contains the following sections:

NAME: _____

AGE: ____ SEX: ____ EXAMINER: _____

Nature of Injury: _____

Date of Exam: _____ Time: _____ No. ____

1) ORIENTATION:

Month: _____	0	1
Date: _____	0	1
Day of Week: _____	0	1
Year: _____	0	1
Time (within 1 hour): _____	0	1

Orientation Total Score _____ /5

2) IMMEDIATE MEMORY: (all 3 trials are completed regardless of score on trials 1 & 2; score equals sum across all 3 trials)

LIST	TRIAL 1	TRIAL 2	TRIAL 3
Elbow	0 1	0 1	0 1
Apple	0 1	0 1	0 1
Carpet	0 1	0 1	0 1
Saddle	0 1	0 1	0 1
Bubble	0 1	0 1	0 1
Total			

Immediate Memory Score _____ /15

3) CONCENTRATION:

Digits Backward: (if correct, go to next string length. If incorrect, read trial 2. Stop after incorrect on both trials.)

4–9–3	6–2–9	0	1
3–8–1–4	3–2–7–9	0	1
6–2–9–7–1	1–5–2–8–6	0	1
7–1–8–4–6–2	5–3–9–1–4–8	0	1

Months in Reverse Order: (entire reverse sequence correct for 1 point)
DEC–NOV–OCT–SEP–AUG–JUL
JUN–MAY–APR–MAR–FEB–JAN   0   1

Concentration Total Score _____ /5

EXERTIONAL MANEUVERS
(when appropriate):

5 jumping jacks	5 push-ups
5 sit-ups	5 knee-bends

4) DELAYED RECALL

Elbow	0	1
Apple	0	1
Carpet	0	1
Saddle	0	1
Bubble	0	1

Delayed Recall Score _____ /5

SUMMARY OF TOTAL SCORES:

Orientation	_____ /5
Immediate Memory	_____ /15
Concentration	_____ /5
Delayed Recall	_____ /5
OVERALL TOTAL SCORE	_____ **/30**

CHRONIC Rx

See "Postconcussive Syndrome"

DISPOSITION

- Table 1C-40 summarizes the American Academy of Neurology, American Medical Society for Sports Medicine, and International Conference on Concussion recommendations on returning to play after a concussion.
- If concussion symptoms occur with activity at one level, the athlete should stop the activity, rest until symptoms resolve, and then restart his or her progression at the level that did not elicit symptoms.
- There are no evidence-based guidelines for disqualifying or retiring an athlete from sport after a concussion. Each case should be individually considered.

REFERRAL

Sports-medicine physician, neuropsychology or concussion center

PEARLS & CONSIDERATIONS

PREVENTION

- Preparticipation evaluations for all athletes

- Preparticipation neurocognitive and balance testing to establish a baseline
- There is currently no evidence to support the use of concussion prevention headbands or mouth guards.

PATIENT/FAMILY EDUCATION

Centers for Disease Control and Prevention: http://www.cdc.gov/concussion/support.html

SUGGESTED READINGS

Available at www.expertconsult.com

RELATED CONTENT

Concussion (Patient Information)
Traumatic Brain Injury (Related Key Topic)
Post-Concussion Syndrome (Related Key Topic)

AUTHORS: **PETER J. SELL, D.O.,** and **AMITY RUBEOR, D.O.**

TABLE 1C-40 Graduated Return to Play Protocol

Rehabilitation Stage	Functional Exercise at Each Stage of Rehabilitation	Objective of Each Stage
1. No activity	Complete physical and cognitive rest	Recovery
2. Light aerobic exercise	Walking, swimming, or stationary cycling, keeping intensity <70% maximum predicted heart rate. No resistance training	Increase heart rate
3. Sport-specific exercise	Skating drills in ice hockey, running drills in soccer. No head impact activities	Add movement
4. Noncontact training drills	Progression to more complex training drills, e.g., passing drills in football and ice hockey. May start progressive resistance training	Exercise, coordination, and cognitive load
5. Full contact practice	After medical clearance, participate in normal training activities	Restore confidence and assess functional skills by coaching staff
6. Return to play	Normal game play	

From Putukian M: The acute symptoms of sports-related concussion: diagnosis and on-field management, *Clin Sports Med* 30(58), 2011.

🛈 BASIC INFORMATION

DEFINITION

Contraception refers to the various modalities that a sexually active couple use to prevent pregnancy. These options can be either medical or nonmedical and used by men or women or both. An algorithm for helping couples select a contraceptive method is described in Fig. E1C-96. Online Appendices A-F summarize U.S. medical eligibility criteria for contraceptive use. The options are as follows:

- No contraception (unprotected intercourse) failure rate 85% both typical use and perfect use
- Abstinence
  1. 12.4% of unmarried men
  2. 13.2% of unmarried women
  3. More frequently practiced before age 17 yr
  4. No intercourse experienced by 13% of women ages 30 to 34 yr
  5. Failure rate 0%
- Withdrawal
  1. Used in only 2% of sexually active women
  2. Failure rate with perfect use, 4%; with typical use, 19%
- Rhythm method (natural family planning)
  1. Failure rate with perfect use, 1% to 9%; with typical use, 20%
  2. Symptothermal type: mucus method and ovulation pain combined with basal body temperature
  3. Ovulation (Billings' method): takes into account mucus quality
  4. Basal body temperature method: uses biphasic temperature chart
  5. Lactation amenorrhea method: effective in fully breastfeeding women, especially 70 to 100 days after delivery; depends on number of feedings per day
- Barriers
  1. Diaphragm and cervical cap: failure rate 5% to 9% in nulliparous women, 20% in multiparous women
  2. Female condom: failure rate with perfect use, 5.1%; with typical use, 12.4%; FDA labeling states 25% failure rate
  3. Male condom: failure rate with perfect use, 3%; with typical use, 12%
  4. Spermicides (aerosols, foam, jellies, creams, tabs): failure rate with perfect use, 3%; with typical use, 21%
- Oral contraceptives
  1. Failure rate with perfect use, <<1%; with typical use, 3%
  2. Come in combinations of estrogen/progestin or as progestin only
- Hormonal implants and injectables
  1. Implanon (etonogestrel) implant 2-yr cumulative pregnancy rate 0.05%. Nexplanon is essentially the same as Implanon but with a barium sulfate core for easier radiologic detection and a preloaded applicator to facilitate insertion.
  2. Depo-Provera: failure rate 0.3% in first year of use
  3. Lunelle failure rate 0.2% in first year

  4. Nestorone-releasing single implant: not yet available
  5. Jadelle implant: Successor to the Norplant implant, which has been discontinued in the U.S. The Jadelle implant is not available in the U.S.
- Mini pill (progesterone only pill)
  1. Failure rate with typical use, 1.1% to 13.2%
  2. With perfect use, 5 pregnancies per 1000 women
     - Requires precise timing of daily use for effectiveness
- Emergency postcoital contraception
  1. Decreases pregnancy rate by 75% with women treated immediately postcoitally
  2. Involves dedicated hormonal (Plan B, which contains levonorgestrel) use or intrauterine device (IUD) insertion
- IUD (available over the counter in some states)
  1. Progestasert: failure rate with perfect use, 2%; with typical use, 3%
  2. Copper T (30-A): failure rate with perfect use, 0.8%; with typical use, 3%
  3. Levonorgestrel Intrauterine System (Mirena)
     1. 1-yr failure rate, 1%
     2. 5-yr cumulative failure rate, 0.71 per 100 women
- Skyla, a smaller version of the Mirena, and that also releases Levonorgestrel, targeted for younger users, was released in 2014. In 2015, the FDA approved Liletta, which also releases levonorgestrel. Liletta is marketed by Medicine 360, a nonprofit pharmaceutical firm, and is intended for use by women with fewer economic resources. Cost, which limits access to long-acting reversible contraceptives for many women, has been cited as a public health problem. Although Liletta has been approved for a 3-yr lifespan, the lower initial cost may allow many more women access to affordable contraception.
- Female sterilization (tubal ligation): failure rate with perfect use, 0.2%; with typical use, 3%
- Male sterilization (vasectomy): failure rate of 0.1% in first year
- Vaginal ring (Nuva ring): failure rate pearl index 0.77
- Contraceptive patch (Ortho Evra): failure rate 0.4% to 0.7%

SYNONYMS

Birth control
Family planning

ICD-10CM CODES	
Z30.011	Encounter for initial prescription of contraceptive pills
Z30.018	Encounter for initial prescription of other contraceptives
Z30.09	Encounter for other general counseling and advice on contraception
Z30.430	Encounter for insertion of intrauterine contraceptive device
Z30.2	Encounter for sterilization

 DIAGNOSIS

WORKUP

- Thorough medical history
- Thorough surgical history
- Obstetric history (was fertility desired with conception?)
- Gynecologic history, including:
  1. History of previous sexually transmitted diseases
  2. Number of partners
  3. Previous difficulties with contraception
  4. Frequency of intercourse
- Family history

LABORATORY TESTS

- Pap smear
- Cultures, aerobic and *Chlamydia*
- Pregnancy test if suspected pregnancy
- Lipid profile if family history of premature vascular event

Ⓡ TREATMENT

NONPHARMACOLOGIC THERAPY

- Male condoms
  - 95% latex (rubber), 5% skin or natural membrane
  - Proper use: place on an erect penis and leave ½-inch empty space at the tip of the condom; use with non–oil-based lubricants
  - Effectiveness increased when used with spermicides
- Female condoms
  - Composed of polyurethane, with one end open and one end closed
  - Proper use: place closed end over cervix, open end hanging out of vagina to cover penis and scrotum
  - Highly effective against HIV
- Spermicides
  - Types: nonoxynol, octoxynol
  - Forms: jellies, creams, foams, suppositories, tablets, soluble films
  - Proper use: put in immediately before intercourse; may be used with other barrier methods
- Diaphragm and cervical cap
  - Must be fitted by practitioner, used with contraceptive gels, and refitted with weight gain or loss of 4.5 kg. Must also be refit after pregnancy.
  - Diaphragm sizes: 50 to 105 mm; cervical cap sizes 26, 28, and 30 mm
  - The correct fit allows the woman to remain ambulatory without feeling the device
  - Proper use of diaphragm: put in immediately before intercourse and keep in for 6 hr after intercourse; must not remain in the vagina for longer than 24 hr
  - Proper use of cervical cap: fit over the cervix exactly; must not remain in place for longer than 48 hr

- Lactation amenorrhea method
  - Depends on number of feedings per day; effective as birth control for 6 mo if 15 or more feedings, lasting 10 min each, are accomplished daily. If woman meets criteria (e.g., breastfeeding only source of infant feeding) 0.5%-2.0% failure rate in the first 6 months after delivery.
  - Not a common practice in the U.S.
- Withdrawal
  - Withdrawal of the penis from the vagina before ejaculation.
  - Depends on self-control, but even with withdrawal, there is a high typical use failure rate.
- Rhythm method
  - Depends on awareness of physiology of male and female reproductive tracts
  - Sperm viable in vagina for 2 to 7 days
  - Ovum life span 24 hr
- Sterilization
  1. Male:
     - Vasectomy to interrupt vas deferens and block passage of sperm to seminal ejaculate
     - Scalpel and nonscalpel techniques available
     - More easily performed procedure than female sterilization and does not require general anesthesia
  2. Female:
     - Leading method of birth control in U.S. in women older than 30 yr
     - Interrupts fallopian tubes, blocking passage of ovum proximally and sperm distally through tube
     - Several types; modified Pomeroy done during cesarean section or interval laparoscopic using clips (Filshie, Hulka) or banding
     - Essure-tubal occlusion through hysteroscopic placement of micro-inserts into the fallopian tubes.

ACUTE GENERAL Rx

- Combination oral contraceptives
  - Taken daily for 21 days, pill-free interval of 7 days
  - Less than 50 mcg ethinyl estradiol in most common combination oral contraceptives; progestins most commonly used in combination pills are norethindrone, levonorgestrel, norgestrel, norethindrone acetate, ethynodiol diacetate, norgestimate, or desogestrel; triphasic combination oral contraceptives (give varying doses of progestin and estrogens throughout cycle); monophasic oral contraceptives: offer same dose of progestin and estrogen throughout cycle, taken daily at same time; estrophasic pill (constant progesterone with variation of estrogen throughout the cycle).
  - If pill taken with antibiotics, efficacy affected by inadequate gastrointestinal absorption in most cases; only rifampin truly reduces pill's effectiveness.
  - Increased body weight decreases effectiveness.

- Table E1C-45 describes oral contraceptive formulations available in the U.S. Guidelines for use of combination estrogen-progestin contraceptives in women 35 yr of age and older are described in Table E1C-46
- Mini pill
  - Progestin only; taken without a break.
  - Causes much irregular bleeding because of the lack of estrogen effect on the lining of the uterus.
  - Table E1C-47 provides a summary and recommendations for progestin-only oral contraceptive use.
- Hormonal implants and injectables
  1. Implanon/Nexplanon
  Single etonogestrel-secreting device that is inserted underneath the skin
  Among the most effective contraceptive available
  Approved by FDA in 2006 and effective over 3-yr period
  2. Depo-Provera
     - Medroxyprogesterone acetate given every 3 mo in IM injection form
     - Major side effect: irregular bleeding
     - Fertility return possibly delayed up to 1 year or longer after last injection
     - Table E1C-48 provides a summary and recommendations for depot medroxyprogesterone acetate (DMPA) use.
  3. Lunelle: monthly injectable administered intramuscularly. Contains 0.5 ml aqueous, 5 mg estradiol cypionate, and 25 mg medroxyprogesterone acetate
- Postcoital contraception
  - Done on emergency basis, usually as a result of noncompliance with birth control or failure of birth control (e.g., condom breakage) at the time of ovulation
  - Methods:
    - Hormonal methods:
      - Levonorgestrel is available either as two 0.75 mg tablets taken 12 hr apart (next choice) or as a 1.5 mg tablet taken once (Plan B, one step). It is indicated for emergency contraception to be used within 72 hr after unexpected intercourse. It can be obtained OTC by women >15 yr of age and by prescription by younger patients
      - Ulipristal (ELLA) is a progesterone-receptor agonist/antagonist available by prescription only. It is a 30-mg, single-dose tablet and can be taken up to 5 days after unexpected intercourse
      - Copper IUD insertion within 5 days of coitus
- IUD
  - Device inserted into uterus to prevent sperm and ovum from uniting in fallopian tube
  - Types available in the U.S.:
    - ParaGard (Copper T/30-A): a polyethylene T wrapped with a fine copper wire effective for 10 yr
    - Mirena Levonorgestrel Intrauterine System: a T-shaped system with a chamber that contains levonorgestrel. Releases 20 mcg/day; is effective for 5 yr

- Vaginal ring (NuvaRing)
  - Provides daily dose of 120 mcg of etonogestrel and 15 mcg ethinyl estradiol
  - Stays in vagina 3 wk and is removed the fourth for a contraceptive-free interval analogous to the placebo pills in oral contraceptive pills
  - Increased body weight decreases effectiveness
- Contraceptive patch (Ortho-Evra)
  - Provides low daily dose of steroids
  - Releases a progestin and estrogen (ethinyl estradiol)
  - Patch size 20 cm^2
  - Each patch contains 6 mg norelgestromin and delivers an estimated continuous systemic dose of 150 mcg norelgestromin and 20 mcg of ethinyl estradiol; common dose 250 mcg/day progestin and 25 mcg/day estrogen
  - Worn 3 out of 4 wk
  - Increased body weight decreases effectiveness
  - Concern for increased risk of thromboembolic events

CHRONIC Rx

- With all the previously mentioned types of birth control, patient is followed up at least yearly, or as necessary, if problems arise.
- Full history, physical examination, and Pap smear, including cultures when needed, are performed yearly.
- Patients with medical problems are followed up approximately every 6 mo when taking hormonal therapy.

DISPOSITION

- Follow yearly or more frequently according to patient's side effects.
- Tailor birth control to patient according to different needs or side effects present at different times in life. Effective counseling also requires an understanding of a woman's preference and medical risks, benefits, side effects, and contraindications of each contraceptive method.

COMMENTS

- With hormonal contraception, if neurologic or cardiac symptoms arise, stop method immediately, evaluate, and refer to internist when appropriate.
- The effectiveness of long-acting reversible contraception (IUDs and implants) is superior to that of contraceptive pills, patch, or ring and is not altered in adolescents and young women.

 **EVIDENCE**

Available at www.expertconsult.com

SUGGESTED READINGS
Available at www.expertconsult.com

RELATED CONTENT
Contraception (Patient Information)
Emergency Contraception (Related Key Topic)

AUTHOR: **RUBEN ALVERO, M.D.**

TABLE 1C-49 Therapeutic Strategies for Cor Pulmonale

Diet and Lifestyle

Smoking cessation
Weight loss
Sodium restriction
Judicious exercise training
Structured rehabilitation and breathing training programs
Avoidance of overexertion
Avoidance of pregnancy
Avoidance of high altitudes

Interventions

Treatment of underlying condition
  COPD (bronchodilators, corticosteroids, antibiotics, oxygen)
  Interstitial lung disease (immunosuppression, oxygen, interferon gamma [investigational])
  Sleep-disordered breathing and alveolar hypoventilation disorders (CPAP, BiPAP, surgery)
  Chronic exposure to high altitudes (return to sea level)
  Chronic thromboembolic disease (anticoagulation, inferior vena cava filters, thromboendarterectomy)
Supplemental oxygen
Pulmonary vasodilators
Anticoagulation
Diuretics
Digitalis glycosides (chronic therapy)
Nonglycoside inotropes (low-dose dobutamine or dopamine in acute severe right heart decompensation with
  hypoperfusion)
Lung volume-reduction surgery
Lung transplantation
Heart-lung transplantation (PAH secondary to complex congenital heart disease)
Percutaneous blade-balloon atrial septostomy (investigational)
  Severe right-sided heart failure
  Recurrent syncope

BiPAP, Bilevel positive airway pressure; *CPAP*, continuous positive airway pressure; *PAH*, pulmonary arterial hypertension.
(From Mason RJ: *Murray & Nadel's textbook of respiratory medicine*, ed 5, Philadelphia, 2010, Saunders.)

- Right ventricular volume overload should be treated with loop diuretics (e.g., furosemide) and potassium-sparing diuretics such as spironolactone.
- Anticoagulation with warfarin has been shown to have a proven survival benefit in patients with idiopathic pulmonary arterial hypertension and is recommended in other causes of cor pulmonale as well, with a target international normalized ratio (INR) of 1.5-2.5, unlike the target for thromboembolic disease, provided there are no obvious contraindications to long-term anticoagulation but can cause toxicity and arrhythmias.
- Digoxin, though controversial, may be employed as an oral inotropic agent to improve right heart contractility and control atrial arrhythmias.
- Selective oral or parenteral pulmonary vasodilators such as oral calcium channel blockers (CCBs), prostanoids, and endothelin receptor blockers may be used after a right heart catheterization that establishes pulmonary hypertension. If vasoreactivity to calcium channel blockers is established, CCBs may be used to combat pulmonary hypertension. However, if there is no vasoreactivity, prostanoids such as epoprostenol or treprostinil or endothelin receptor blockers such as bosentan may be tried. However, such agents have been shown to be beneficial in the treatment of idiopathic PAH, PAH related to connective tissue disease, and PAH due to congenital heart disease. Pulmonary vasodilators are sometimes considered in other forms of PAH when primary disease management strategies have failed to improve right heart failure.
- Phosphodiesterase inhibitors such as sildenafil and tadalafil are newer vasodilators that improve symptoms, functional class, and mean pulmonary artery pressures as alternatives or in addition to prostanoids.
- Pulmonary thromboendarterectomy may be curative in the special case of cor pulmonale due to chronic thromboembolic pulmonary hypertension.
- Atrial septostomy is a salvage option for patients with ongoing decompensated right heart failure from PAH despite pulmonary vasodilators. Such patients should undergo rapid assessment for possible transplantation.
- Lung transplantation or heart-lung transplantation should be considered in the setting of cor pulmonale from lung diseases or from pulmonary vascular disease.

DISPOSITION

Patients with cor pulmonale should have regular assessment of their functional class (e.g., NYHA or WHO functional class); worse functional class indicates a poorer prognosis. Other poor prognostic features include high right atrial pressure, impaired cardiac output, presence of hyponatremia, elevated BNP levels, low systemic blood pressure, and poor exercise tolerance as demonstrated by a 6-minute walk test.

REFERRAL

Patients with pulmonary disease who have progressed to cor pulmonale should be followed up by a pulmonologist and a tertiary care center that specializes in treatment of advanced pulmonary hypertension.

 **PEARLS & CONSIDERATIONS**

- Identification and treatment of the underlying cause of cor pulmonale is key
- Prognosis and treatment are related to the underlying cause, whereas the presence of cor pulmonale is merely a marker of the underlying disease severity.
- Right heart catheterization is the gold standard to establish diagnosis and to determine treatment, including response to calcium channel blockers, prostanoids, and endothelin receptor blockers.

COMMENTS

There is increasing interest in selective pulmonary vasodilators to improve right ventricular heart function in patients with cor pulmonale outside of the setting of idiopathic PAH, PAH related to connective tissue disease, and PAH related to congenital heart disease. However, more data on the safety and efficacy of these agents, especially in the setting of hypoxemic lung disease, is needed.

The importance of maintaining or improving right heart function, rather than solely lowering pulmonary pressures, is becoming increasingly apparent in the therapeutic management of patients with pulmonary hypertension and right heart failure.

Long-term survival is related to improved pulmonary artery hemodynamics (lower PAP). Improved pulmonary hemodynamics are apparent within the first 6 months of oxygen therapy. Twenty-four-hour oxygen therapy improves pulmonary hemodynamics more than 12 hr/day therapy.

SUGGESTED READINGS

Available at www.expertconsult.com

RELATED CONTENT

Pulmonary Hypertension (Related Key Topic)

AUTHOR: **RABIA ARSHAD, M.D.**

C

Diseases
and Disorders

I

BASIC INFORMATION

DEFINITION

A corneal abrasion is a loss of surface epithelial tissue of the cornea caused by trauma.

SYNONYMS

Corneal erosion
Corneal contusion
Corneal epithelial defect

ICD-10CM CODES
S05.00XA Injury of conjunctiva and corneal abrasion without foreign body, unspecified eye, initial encounter
S05.01XA Injury of conjunctiva and corneal abrasion without foreign body, right eye, initial encounter
S05.02XA Injury of conjunctiva and corneal abrasion without foreign body, left eye, initial encounter

EPIDEMIOLOGY & DEMOGRAPHICS

INCIDENCE (IN U.S.): A universal problem. Corneal abrasions comprise 8% of all eye presentations in primary care.
PEAK INCIDENCE: Childhood through active adulthood and older and debilitated patients
PREDOMINANT AGE: Any age

PHYSICAL FINDINGS & CLINICAL PRESENTATION

- Haziness of the cornea
- Disruption of the corneal surface (Fig. 1C-99)
- Redness and injection of the conjunctiva
- Pain
- Light sensitivity
- Tearing
- Gritty feeling
- Pain on opening or closing eyes
- Sensation of a foreign body

ETIOLOGY

- Trauma (direct mechanical event)
- Foreign body
- Contact lenses
- Chemical or flash ultraviolet burns

DIAGNOSIS

DIFFERENTIAL DIAGNOSIS

- Acute-angle glaucoma
- Herpes ulcers and other corneal ulcers
- Foreign body in the cornea (be certain it is not a keratitis)
- Infective keratitis

WORKUP

- Fluorescein staining, slit lamp evaluation. After fluorescein staining of the cornea, an abrasion will appear yellow under normal light and green in cobalt blue light.
- Assessment of visual acuity. Vision loss requires referral.
- Intraocular pressure.
- Rule out corneal laceration (flattened anterior chamber with perforation; refer urgently).
- Rule out other eye pathology. Inspect anterior chamber for blood (hyphema) or pus (hypopyon). If present, refer immediately to ophthalmologist.
- Examine for foreign bodies and remove them if present. (Evert upper eyelid to locate foreign body on the palpebral conjunctiva.)
- Confirm red reflex to rule out significant globe injury.

TREATMENT

NONPHARMACOLOGIC THERAPY

- Bandage contact lens can help to speed healing for large epithelial abrasions.
- Warm compresses.
- Pressure dressing (patching) is controversial. Although eye patching traditionally has been recommended in the treatment of corneal abrasions, several studies show that patching does not help and may hinder healing.
- Removal of any foreign particles if present.

ACUTE GENERAL Rx

- Topical antibiotics such as 10% sulfacetamide or ofloxacin 0.3% solution 2 drops qid are commonly prescribed to prevent bacterial superinfection, but evidence for their use is lacking. Ointment forms are often used (e.g., erythromycin, bacitracin ophthalmic

QID) to also improve corneal surface lubrication. Antipseudomonal topical antibiotics are, however, recommended for contact lens–related abrasions.
- Pressure patching of eye with eyelid closed is no longer recommended because it can result in decreased oxygen delivery, increased moisture, and a higher chance of infection.
- Cycloplegics such as 5% homatropine are often prescribed to relieve ciliary muscle spasm; however, their benefit has been questioned and they are no longer routinely recommended.
- Topical nonsteroidal anti-inflammatory drugs (NSAIDs) (e.g., diclofenac 0.1% or ketorolac 0.5%) 1 drop qid may be used for pain relief.
- Topical anesthetic drops immediately improve comfort for purposes of examination, but repeated use can lead to severe problems, delayed or arrested healing, infections, perforations, and loss of the eye.
- Oral NSAIDs may be used for severe pain.

DISPOSITION

Follow-up in 24 hr and then every 3 days until abrasion has cleared and vision has returned to normal. Less frequent follow-up is appropriate for abrasions ≤4 mm or for uncomplicated abrasions.

REFERRAL

To ophthalmologist if patient has no relief within 24 hr or for patients with deep eye injuries, foreign bodies that cannot be removed, or suspected recurrent corneal erosion or infections.

PEARLS & CONSIDERATIONS

COMMENTS

- Never give the patient topical anesthetic to use at home because these can cause decompensation of the cornea, severe delay of epithelial healing, and permanent damage.
- Corticosteroid drops (e.g., dexamethasone, prednisolone) should be avoided, since they can delay healing and exacerbate some corneal infections (herpes viral keratitis, pseudomonas, and fungal ulcers)
- Most corneal abrasions heal in 24 to 48 hr and rarely progress to corneal erosion or infection.
- Improvement in pain is a good indication of corneal epithelial healing. Severe worsening of pain could indicate corneal bacterial infection (keratitis) and should be evaluated urgently.

SUGGESTED READINGS

Available at www.expertconsult.com

RELATED CONTENT

Corneal Foreign Body or Abrasion (Patient Information)

AUTHOR: **R. SCOTT HOFFMAN, M.D.**

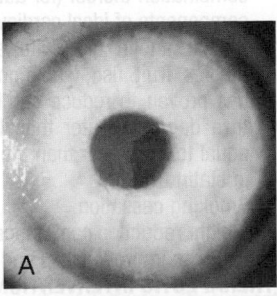
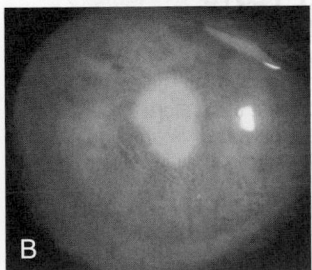

FIGURE 1C-99 Corneal epithelial abrasion. A, Epithelial defect without fluorescein highlighting the defect. An irregularity in the otherwise smooth corneal surface is the key to identifying the defect if no fluorescein is available. **B,** Classic fluorescein staining of an epithelial defect. (From Palay D [ed]: *Ophthalmology for the primary care physician,* St Louis, 1997, Mosby.)

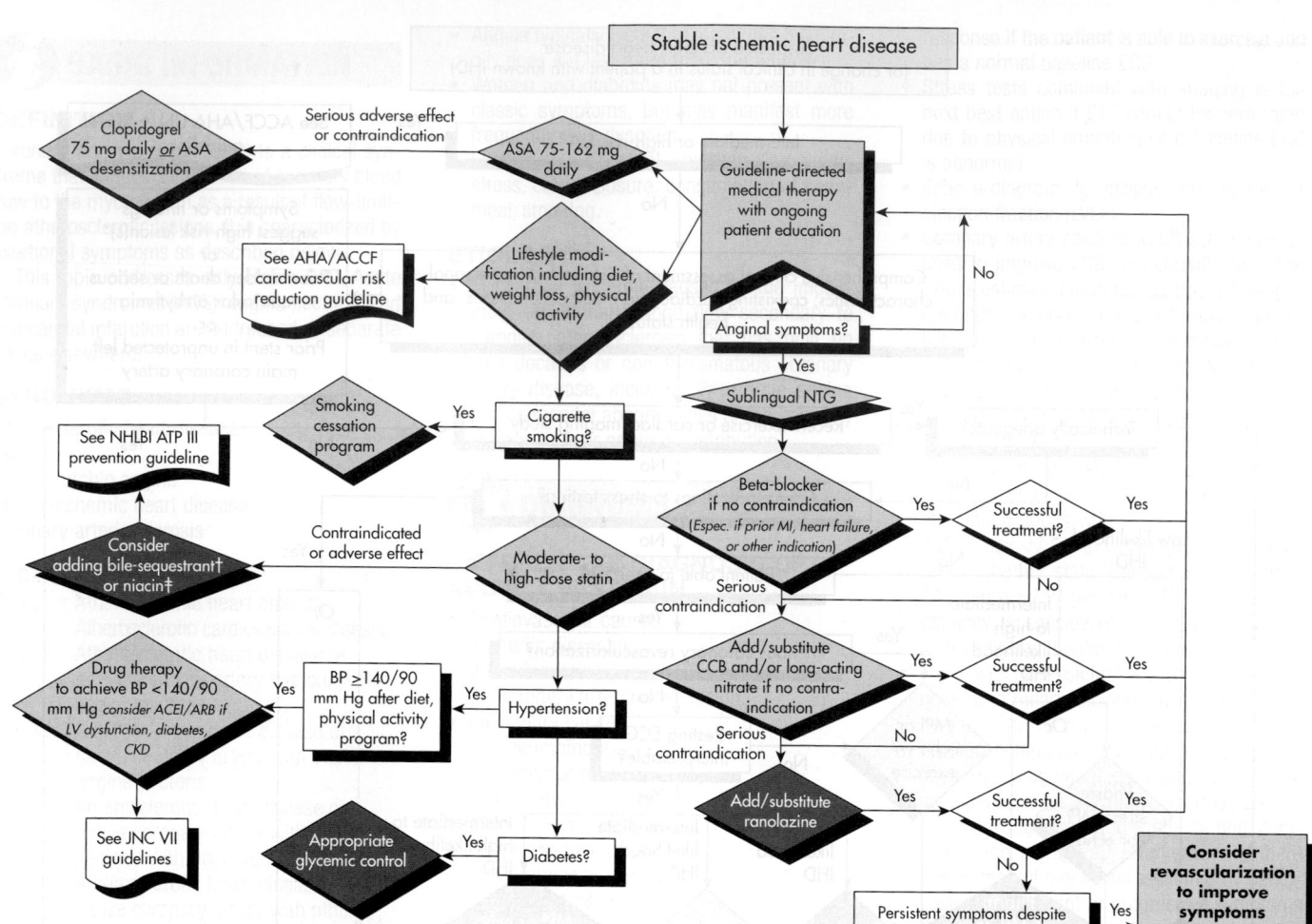

FIGURE 1C-102 Algorithm for guideline-directed medical therapy for patients with SIHD.*

*The algorithms do not represent a comprehensive list of recommendations (see text for all recommendations).

†The use of bile acid sequestrant is relatively contraindicated when triglycerides are ≥200 mg/dl and is contraindicated when triglycerides are ≥500 mg/dl.

‡Dietary supplement niacin must not be used as a substitute for prescription niacin. *ACCF,* American College of Cardiology Foundation; *ACEI,* angiotensin-converting enzyme inhibitor; *AHA,* American Heart Association; *ARB,* angiotensin-receptor blocker; *ASA,* aspirin; *ATP III,* Adult Treatment Panel 3; *BP,* blood pressure; *CCB,* calcium channel blocker; *CKD,* chronic kidney disease; *HDL-C,* high-density lipoprotein cholesterol; *JNC VII,* Seventh Report of the Joint National Committee on Prevention, Detection, Evaluation, and Treatment of High Blood Pressure; *LDL-C,* low-density lipoprotein cholesterol; *LV,* left ventricular; *MI,* myocardial infarction; *NHLBI,* National Heart, Lung, and Blood Institute; *NTG,* nitroglycerin. (From 2012 ACCF/AHA/ACP/AATS/PCNA/SCAI/STS Guideline for the Diagnosis and Management of Patients With Stable Ischemic Heart Disease: A report of the American College of Cardiology Foundation/American Heart Association Task Force on Practice Guidelines, and the American College of Physicians, American Association for Thoracic Surgery, Preventive Cardiovascular Nurses Association, Society for Cardiovascular Angiography and Interventions, and Society of Thoracic Surgeons, *J Am Coll Cardiol* 60:e44-e164, 2012.)

• Coronary angiography with PCI or CABG for patients on optimal medical therapy with persistent symptoms.

ACUTE GENERAL Rx FOR STABLE ANGINA

• Rest.
• Sublingual nitroglycerin if rest does not provide adequate relief.

CHRONIC Rx

• Antianginal therapy
  1. Nitrates (isosorbide mononitrate and isosorbide dinitrate). These medications treat ischemia by venodilation to decrease preload, dilate epicardial coronary arteries, and recruit coronary collaterals. Furthermore, they attenuate platelet aggregation. Although they do not influence survival or decrease cardiovascular death in patients with chronic CAD, they do lower the rate of angina frequency and increase time to ischemic ECG findings on treadmill testing.
  2. Beta-adrenergic antagonists (metoprolol, atenolol, carvedilol, or any other beta-blockers with the exception of those with intrinsic sympathomimetic activity). These medications work to relieve angina by decreasing myocardial oxygen demand by reducing heart rate, blood pressure, and contractility. Drugs should be titrated to a heart rate of 50 to 60 beats/min at rest and ≤100 beats/min with exercise
  3. Calcium channel blockers (CCBs; amlodipine or verapamil). The antianginal efficacy of CCBs is comparable to beta-blockers; however, the efficacy of monotherapy for reducing MI or cardiac death has not been demonstrated.
  4. Ranolazine. This is a selective inhibitor of late sodium influx into myocytes, which leads to decreased myocardial contractility. It can be used in combination with beta-blockers and significantly reduces frequency of angina and increases exercise duration and time to onset of angina (CARISA trial). Although it rarely may cause QT prolongation, it has not been linked to any clinically important arrhythmias.
  5. May benefit from combination therapy of the above.

BOX 1C-3   Noninvasive Risk Stratification

High risk (>3% annual mortality rate)
1. Severe resting left ventricular dysfunction (LVEF <35%).
2. High-risk treadmill score (≤–11).
3. Severe exercise left ventricular dysfunction (exercise LVEF <35%).
4. Stress-induced large perfusion defect (particularly if anterior).
5. Stress-induced multiple perfusion defects of moderate size.
6. Large, fixed perfusion defect with LV dilation or increased lung uptake (thallium-201).
7. Stress-induced moderate perfusion defect with LV dilation or increased lung uptake (thallium-201).
8. Echocardiographic wall motion abnormality (involving >2 segments) developing at low dose of dobutamine (≤10 mg/kg/min) or at a low heart rate (<120 beats/min).
9. Stress echocardiographic evidence of extensive ischemia.

Intermediate risk (1% to 3% annual mortality rate)
1. Mild/moderate resting left ventricular dysfunction (LVEF 35% to 49%).
2. Intermediate-risk treadmill score (score between –11 and <5).
3. Stress-induced moderate perfusion defect without LV dilation or increased lung intake (thallium-201).
4. Limited stress echocardiographic ischemia with a wall motion abnormality only at doses of dobutamine involving ≤2 segments.

Low risk (<1% annual mortality rate)
1. Low-risk treadmill score (≥5).
2. Normal or small myocardial perfusion defect at rest or with stress.
3. Normal stress echocardiographic wall motion or no change of limited resting wall motion abnormalities during stress.

- Antiplatelet therapy
  1. Aspirin therapy (71-162 mg/day).
  2. Clopidogrel for those intolerant to aspirin therapy.
  3. Combination of aspirin and clopidogrel does not reduce cardiovascular events (CHARISMA trial).
  4. Newer antiplatelet drugs such as prasugrel and ticagrelor have been studied in ACS but not in stable CAD.
- Statins
  1. HMG-CoA reductase inhibitors (statins) (atorvastatin, rosuvastatin) with high-intensity therapy for a target LDL reduction of >50% if safely achieved in high-risk patients; if not a candidate for high-intensity therapy, patient should receive at least moderate-intensity statin therapy that lowers LDL by 30% to 50% as advised by the new ATP IV cholesterol guidelines from the 2013 ACC/AHA expert panel.
- PCSK9 Inhibitors
  1. This is a novel class of monoclonal antibodies that inhibit proprotein convertase subtilisin/kexin type 9. In the recent OSLER trial, PCSK9 inhibition in addition to standard therapy reduced LDL cholesterol by 61%. The rate of cardiovascular events at 1 yr reduced to 0.98% with therapy versus 2.18% in the standard therapy group.
- ACE-inhibitors (captopril, enalapril, lisinopril) are a class I recommendation for patients with chronic CAD with LV dysfunction LVEF <40% or diabetes and a class II recommendation for CAD patients without these features.

CORONARY ARTERY REVASCULARIZATION

- Patients with symptoms refractory to optimal medical therapy (OMT) as above or those with high clinical, stress testing, or an angiographic risk profile and suitable coronary anatomy may benefit from revascularization with either PCI (percutaneous coronary intervention) or CABG (coronary artery bypass graft) surgery.
- ACC/AHA class I indications for CABG surgery in chronic CAD patients include the following:
  1. High grade (>50%) left main CAD.
  2. Left main CAD-equivalent anatomy including >70% luminal stenosis in the left anterior descending artery and left circumflex arteries.
  3. Three-vessel disease with LVEF <50%.
  4. Single- or two-vessel CAD with a large area of viable myocardium at risk.
  5. Severe angina despite medical therapy if CABG can be performed with acceptable risk.
- PCI has not been shown to reduce long-term rates of MI and death in patients with stable chronic CAD and therefore has no class I indications in this group. PCI is suitable in patients with suitable anatomy with refractory or lifestyle-limiting angina who have failed optimal medical therapy (OMT). Recent trials such as the COURAGE Trial have demonstrated no significant difference between OMT and PCI in overall survival, MI, and ACS over 5 years in patients with chronic stable CAD. A recent meta-analysis demonstrated no objective reduction in death, nonfatal MI, unplanned revascularization, or angina versus medical therapy alone.
- The SYNTAX trial, which used a numerical score based on qualitative plaque features on angiography, showed that surgical revascularization was associated with a lesser risk of stroke and major cardiac events if the SYNTAX score was high (>33).
- The FREEDOM trial showed that in diabetic patients with multivessel disease, CABG is superior to PCI with drug-eluting stents in chronic CAD and should remain the revascularization strategy of choice in this patient population. CABG resulted in lower rates of death and MI but a higher risk of stroke. This is true for patients with either insulin-dependent or non–insulin-dependent DM.

DISPOSITION

- Coronary artery disease is a common chronic condition with which many patients can live for years with good symptom control on optimal medical therapy.

REFERRAL

- Cardiovascular disease specialist.

⊘ PEARLS & CONSIDERATIONS

COMMENTS

- The transition from stable coronary artery disease to unstable angina must be carefully monitored. Symptoms of concern include more frequent episodes of chest pain, exertional dyspnea, chest pain that is less responsive to nitroglycerin, or first episode of chest pain. Regarding unstable angina, please refer to section on acute coronary syndromes.

SUGGESTED READINGS
Available at www.expertconsult.com

RELATED CONTENT
Coronary Artery Disease (Patient Information)
Acute Coronary Syndrome (Related Key Topic)
Angina Pectoris (Related Key Topic)
Hyperlipidemia (Related Key Topic)
Myocardial Infarction (Related Key Topic)

AUTHORS: **SYED R. LATIF, M.D., LILY CHEN, M.D.,** and **THOMAS SMITH, M.D.**

BASIC INFORMATION

DEFINITION
Clinical condition characterized by pain and tenderness at costochondral or chondrosternal joints of the anterior chest wall without obvious swelling or induration.

SYNONYMS
Anterior chest wall syndrome
Chest wall pain syndrome
Costosternal syndrome
Parasternal chondrodynia

ICD-10CM CODES
M94.0 Chondrocostal junction syndrome

EPIDEMIOLOGY & DEMOGRAPHICS
PREVALENCE: Fairly common, comprises approximately 28% of undifferentiated noncardiac chest pain patients.
PREDOMINANT SEX: Women more than men.
PREDOMINANT AGE: >40 years of age.

PHYSICAL FINDINGS & CLINICAL PRESENTATION
SYMPTOMS:
- Anterior chest wall pain, usually described as sharp, aching, or pressure-like. Pain is usually aggravated by coughing, sneezing, deep inspiration, or any chest wall movement.
- Pain is usually self-limited.
- May radiate to arms and shoulders mimicking cardiac pain.

SIGNS:
- Reproducible tenderness of costochondral (mostly second through fifth) or costosternal junction without localized swelling or induration.

- Pain on crossed-chest adduction of arm and backward extension of arm from 90 degrees of abduction signifies pain of musculoskeletal origin. Reproduction of symptoms during dry needling also suggests pain from musculoskeletal origin.

DIAGNOSIS

DIFFERENTIAL DIAGNOSIS
Usually self-limited and benign; however, it needs to be distinguished from other potentially serious conditions.
- Cardiac pain: primary concern; ischemic chest pain, acute pericarditis, aortic dissection.
- Gastrointestinal: gastroesophageal reflux disease.
- Pulmonary embolism, pneumonia, pneumothorax.
- Musculoskeletal (Table 1C-50): Tietze's syndrome, cervical or thoracic spine disease, fibromyalgia, arthritis.
- Involvement of ribs by trauma, infections *(Candida albicans)* or neoplasms (breast cancer, prostate cancer, sarcoma, plasma cell cytoma, non-Hodgkin's lymphoma).
- Miscellaneous: fibromyalgia syndrome, panic attack.

WORKUP
- A diagnosis of exclusion for chest pain after ruling out more serious conditions including cardiac chest pain. Keys to diagnosis are a detailed history, a meticulous physical examination, and a few rationally selected diagnostic studies, including electrocardiogram and chest x-ray to rule out cardiopulmonary causes. Usefulness of nuclear scanning with technetium-99m scintigraphy, gallium, or bone scanning to assist diagnosis of costochondritis is not clear.

TREATMENT

ACUTE GENERAL Rx
- Often self-limiting, so reassurance is important.
- Symptomatic treatment includes local application of heat, minimizing of activities that aggravate symptoms, stretching exercises for chest wall muscles, and nonsteroidal anti-inflammatory drugs or acetaminophen.
- Refractory cases can be treated with local injections of combined lidocaine and corticosteroid (may be a useful diagnostic and therapeutic tool). Dry needling by a trained physical therapist may be helpful.
- Recurrent costochondritis may respond to sulfasalazine; however, there are no clinical trials of pharmacologic therapy for costochondritis.

PEARLS & CONSIDERATIONS

Presence of costochondritis in a patient with chest pain does not exclude more serious problems including cardiac pain. Further testing is required as clinically indicated.

SUGGESTED READINGS
Available at www.expertconsult.com

RELATED CONTENT
Costochondritis (Patient Information)

AUTHOR: **ASHA SHRESTHA, M.D.**

TABLE 1C-50 Musculoskeletal Chest Pain

Disorder	Clinical Features	Comments
Tietze's syndrome	Painful swelling of usually 2nd or 3rd costochondral junctions.	Less common than costochondritis; commonly affects young people of either sex. Exact cause is unknown, but a traumatic pathogenesis has been associated. The disease course is mostly self-limited. Non-Hodgkin's lymphoma of medial clavicular head has been reported to mimic Tietze's syndrome.
Costochondritis	Pain and tenderness at the costochondral or chondrosternal junctions without a notable swelling. The 2nd-5th costal cartilages are most commonly involved.	Certain maneuvers like "crowing rooster" maneuver (extension of the cervical spine and traction on the posteriorly extended arm) and traction on the adducted arm with head rotated to ipsilateral side may reproduce the pain.
Slipping rib syndrome	Pain at the lower costal cartilages, associated with increased mobility of the anterior end of a costal cartilage. Most commonly affects 10th rib and occasionally 8th and 9th ribs.	Maneuver such as hooking the fingers under the anterior costal margin and pulling the rib cage anteriorly may produce a palpable click of the cartilages slipping over one another.
Cervical, thoracic disc disease	Referred regional pain from affected areas. Often aggravated by spine motion and may be accompanied by radicular pain into arm if cervical origin or along intercostal nerve if thoracic origin. Symptoms reproduced by Spurling's maneuver (steady pressure to head causing increased axial loading on the nerve root).	May mimic chest disease if spinal complaints are minimal and referred or radicular symptoms predominate.
Fibromyalgia	Widespread pain with multiple other peripheral tender points.	Female/male ratio of 9:1. Prevalent age 30-50 yr. Frequently associated with tension headache, irritable bowel syndrome, and psychiatric symptoms.
Sternoclavicular or manubriosternal joint involvement in osteoarthritis, inflammatory conditions (rheumatoid arthritis, ankylosing spondylitis, psoriatic arthritis), and infection	Dull, aching local pain with tenderness. Occasional bony joint enlargement with soft tissue swelling.	Crepitus may rarely be present.

C

BASIC INFORMATION

DEFINITION

Craniopharyngiomas are tumors arising from squamous cell remnants of Rathke's pouch, located in the infundibulum or upper anterior hypophysis.

SYNONYMS

Subset of nonadenomatous pituitary tumors

ICD-10CM CODES
D44.3 Neoplasm of uncertain behavior of pituitary gland

EPIDEMIOLOGY & DEMOGRAPHICS

PEAK INCIDENCE: Occurs at all ages; peak during the first 2 decades of life, with a second small peak occurring in the sixth decade.
PREDOMINANT SEX:
- Both sexes are usually equally affected.
- Craniopharyngiomas are the most common nonglial tumors in children and account for 3% to 5% of all pediatric brain tumors.

PHYSICAL FINDINGS & CLINICAL PRESENTATION

- The typical onset is insidious and a 1- to 2-year history of slowly progressive symptoms is common.
- Presenting symptoms are usually related to the effects of a sella turcica mass. Approximately 75% of patients report headache and have visual disturbances.
- The usual visual defect is bitemporal hemianopsia. Optic nerve involvement with decreased visual acuity and scotomas and homonymous hemianopsia from optic tract involvement may also occur.
- Other symptoms include mental changes, nausea, vomiting, somnolence, or symptoms of pituitary failure. In adults, sexual dysfunction is the most common endocrine complaint, with impotence in men and primary or secondary amenorrhea in women. Diabetes insipidus is found in 25% of cases. In children, craniopharyngiomas may present with dwarfism.
- More than 70% of children at the time of diagnosis present with growth hormone deficiency, obstructive hydrocephalus, short-term memory deficits, and psychomotor slowing.

ETIOLOGY

Craniopharyngiomas are believed to arise from nests of squamous epithelial cells that are commonly found in the suprasellar area surrounding the pars tuberalis of the adult pituitary.

DIAGNOSIS

DIFFERENTIAL DIAGNOSIS

- Pituitary adenoma.
- Empty sella syndrome.
- Pituitary failure of any cause.
- Primary brain tumors (e.g., meningiomas, astrocytomas).

- Metastatic brain tumors.
- Other brain tumors.
- Cerebral aneurysm.

LABORATORY TESTS

- Hypothyroidism (low FT_4, FT_3 with high thyroid-stimulating hormone).
- Hypercortisolism (low cortisol) with low adrenocorticotropic hormone.
- Low sex hormones (testosterone, estriol) with low follicle-stimulating hormone and luteinizing hormone.
- Diabetes insipidus (hypernatremia, low urine osmolarity, high plasma osmolarity).
- Prolactin may be normal or slightly elevated.
- Pituitary stimulation tests may be required in some cases.

IMAGING STUDIES

- MRI (Fig. 1C-103) or head CT if MRI is contraindicated. MRI features include a multicystic and solid enhancing suprasellar mass. Hydrocephalus may also be present if the mass is large. CT usually reveals intratumoral calcifications.
- Visual field testing for bitemporal hemianopsia.
- Skull film may show:
  1. Enlarged or eroded sella turcica (50%)
  2. Suprasellar calcification (50%)

TREATMENT

GENERAL Rx

- Traditionally, surgery has been the main treatment for craniopharyngioma. However, radiation treatment instead of surgery may be an option in selected cases.
- Surgical resection (curative or palliative).
  1. Transsphenoidal surgery for small intrasellar tumors.
  2. Subfrontal craniotomy for most patients.

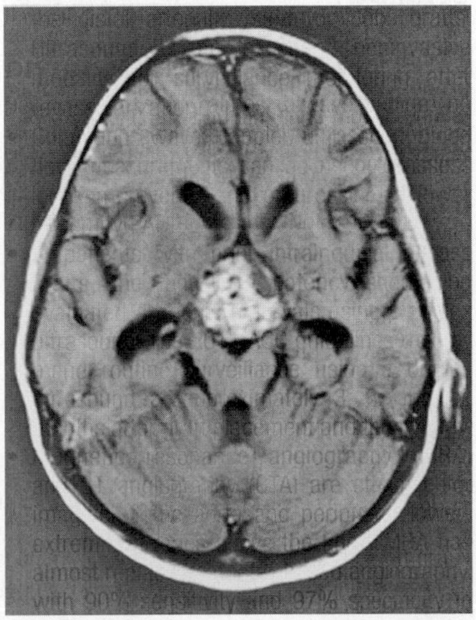

FIGURE 1C-103 MRI scan of a craniopharyngioma, demonstrating a cystic contrast-enhancing mass in the suprasellar area extending upward and compressing the hypothalamus. (From Goetz CG: *Textbook of clinical neurology*, Philadelphia, 1999, Saunders.)

- Overall prognosis is good with 80% to 90% chance of permanent cure.
- Postoperative radiation.
- Intralesional ^{32}P irradiation or bleomycin for unresectable tumors. Long-term complications of radiation include secondary malignancies, optic neuropathy, and vascular injury.

PROGNOSIS

- Overall prognosis is good with 80% to 90% chance of permanent cure.
- Operative mortality rate: 3% to 16% (higher with large tumors).
- Postoperative recurrence rate: <20% of cases after total resection and 60% of cases after subtotal resection. Most recurrences occur within the first 2 yr after surgery.
- 5-yr and 10-yr survival: 88% and 76%, respectively, with surgery and radiation.
- The most important factors that correlate with prognosis are the extent of resection and postoperative radiation.
- Long-term post-treatment hormonal, visual, and neurological problems occur in a significant percentage of patients.

RELATED CONTENT

Craniopharyngioma (Patient Information)

AUTHOR: **FRED F. FERRI, M.D.**

BASIC INFORMATION

DEFINITION

Crohn's disease is an inflammatory disease of the bowel of unknown etiology, most commonly involving the terminal ileum and manifesting primarily with diarrhea, abdominal pain, fatigue, and weight loss.

SYNONYMS

Regional enteritis
Inflammatory bowel disease (IBD)

ICD-10CM CODES

K50.00	Crohn's disease of small intestine without complications
K50.011	Crohn's disease of small intestine with rectal bleeding
K50.012	Crohn's disease of small intestine with intestinal obstruction
K50.013	Crohn's disease of small intestine with fistula
K50.014	Crohn's disease of small intestine with abscess
K50.018	Crohn's disease of small intestine with other complication
K50.019	Crohn's disease of small intestine with unspecified complications
K50.10	Crohn's disease of large intestine without complications
K50.111	Crohn's disease of large intestine with rectal bleeding
K50.112	Crohn's disease of large intestine with intestinal obstruction
K50.113	Crohn's disease of large intestine with fistula
K50.114	Crohn's disease of large intestine with abscess
K50.118	Crohn's disease of large intestine with other complication
K50.119	Crohn's disease of large intestine with unspecified complications
K50.80	Crohn's disease of both small and large intestine without complications
K50.811	Crohn's disease of both small and large intestine with rectal bleeding
K50.812	Crohn's disease of both small and large intestine with intestinal obstruction
K50.813	Crohn's disease of both small and large intestine with fistula
K50.814	Crohn's disease of both small and large intestine with abscess
K50.818	Crohn's disease of both small and large intestine with other complication
K50.819	Crohn's disease of both small and large intestine with unspecified complications
K50.90	Crohn's disease, unspecified, without complications
K50.911	Crohn's disease, unspecified, with rectal bleeding
K50.912	Crohn's disease, unspecified, with intestinal obstruction
K50.913	Crohn's disease, unspecified, ewith flstula
K50.914	Crohn's disease, unspecified, with abscess
K50.918	Crohn's disease, unspecified, with other complication
K50.919	Crohn's disease, unspecified, with unspecified complications

EPIDEMIOLOGY & DEMOGRAPHICS

PREVALENCE:

- One case per 1000 persons; most common in whites and Jews.
- Crohn's disease affects approximately 380,000 to 480,000 persons in the United States.
- Incidence: bimodal with a peak in the third decade of life and another in the fifth decade.

PHYSICAL FINDINGS & CLINICAL PRESENTATION

- Physical exam findings vary depending on disease location and severity.
- Abdominal tenderness, mass, or distention.
- Chronic or nocturnal diarrhea.
- Weight loss, fever, night sweats.
- Hyperactive bowel sounds in patients with partial obstruction, bloody diarrhea.
- Delayed growth and failure of normal development in children.
- Perianal and rectal abscesses, multiple sinuses and scarring (Fig.E1C-104), mouth ulcers, cobblestone appearance of oral mucosa (Fig. E1C-105), and atrophic glossitis.
- Extraintestinal manifestations (Table E1C-52): joint swelling and tenderness, hepatosplenomegaly, erythema nodosum, clubbing, tenderness to palpation of the sacroiliac joints.
- Symptoms may be intermittent with varying periods of remission.
- Overall 40% of patients have ileocolonic inflammation, 30% have isolated small bowel disease, 25% have isolated colonic disease, and 5% have isolated upper GI or perianal manifestations.

ETIOLOGY

Unknown. Pathophysiologically, Crohn's disease involves an immune system dysfunction.

DIAGNOSIS

DIFFERENTIAL DIAGNOSIS

- Ulcerative colitis (see Table 1C-51).
- Infectious diseases (tuberculosis, *Yersinia, Salmonella, Shigella, Campylobacter*).
- Parasitic infections (amebic infection).
- Pseudomembranous colitis.
- Ischemic colitis in elderly patients.
- Lymphoma.
- Colon carcinoma.
- Diverticulitis.
- Radiation enteritis.
- Collagenous colitis.
- Fungal infections (*Histoplasma, Actinomyces*).
- Gay bowel syndrome (in homosexual patient).
- Carcinoid tumors.
- Celiac sprue.
- Mesenteric adenitis.

LABORATORY TESTS

- Decreased hemoglobin and hematocrit from chronic blood loss, effect of inflammation on bone marrow, and malabsorption of vitamin B_{12}.
- Hypokalemia, hypomagnesemia, hypocalcemia, and low albumin in patients with chronic diarrhea.
- Vitamin B_{12} and folate deficiency.
- Elevated erythrocyte sedimentation rate and CRP.
- Positive anti–*Saccharomyces cerevisiae* antibodies.
- Elevated INR (due to vitamin K malabsorption).
- Fecal calprotectin has been reported as useful in screening of patients with suspected IBD. Based on a pretest probability of 32% in adults, an abnormal calprotectin test result increases the posttest probability to 91%, and a normal result reduces the probability of IBD to 3%. False elevations may occur with other gastrointestinal diseases such as bacterial, viral, and protozoal causes of infective diarrhea.

TABLE 1C-51 Differentiating Features

	Ulcerative Colitis	Crohn's Disease
Site of involvement	Only involves colon Rectum almost always involved	Any area of the gastrointestinal tract Rectum usually spared
Pattern of involvement	Continuous	Skip lesions
Diarrhea	Bloody	Usually nonbloody
Severe abdominal pain	Rare	Frequent
Perianal disease	No	In 30% of patients
Fistula	No	Yes
Endoscopic findings	Erythematous and friable Superficial ulceration	Aphthoid and deep ulcers Cobblestoning
Radiologic findings	Tubular appearance resulting from loss of haustral folds	String sign of terminal ileum RLQ mass, fistulas, abscesses
Histologic features	Mucosa only Crypt abscesses	Transmural Crypt abscesses, granulomas (about 30%)
Smoking	Protective	Worsens course
Serology	p-ANCA more common	ASCA more common

ASCA, Anti–*Saccharomyces cerevisiae* antibodies; *p-ANCA*, perinuclear antineutrophil cytoplasmic antibody; *RLQ*, right lower quadrant.
From Andreoli TE et al: *Andreoli and Carpenter's Cecil essentials of medicine*, ed 8, Philadelphia, 2010, Saunders.

C

I

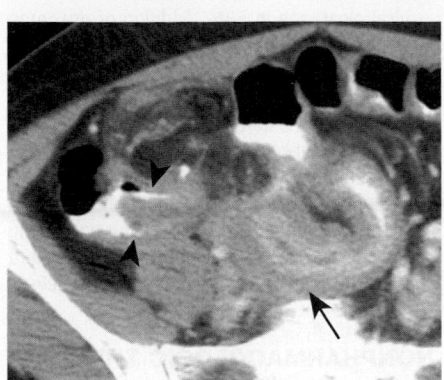

FIGURE 1C-106 Crohn's disease: fistulas. The ileum (*arrow*) in the right lower quadrant exhibits marked wall thickening and matting of bowel loops caused by inflammation of the mesentery. A double-tract bowel lumen (*arrowheads*) is seen, indicating the formation of an ileo–ileal fistula. (From Webb WR, Brant WE, Major NM: *Fundamentals of body CT*, ed 4, Philadelphia, 2015, Saunders.)

ENDOSCOPIC EVALUATION

Endoscopic features of Crohn's disease include asymmetric and discontinued disease, deep longitudinal fissures, cobblestone appearance, and presence of strictures. Crypt distortion and inflammation are also present. Granulomas may be present.

IMAGING STUDIES

- CT of abdomen may show thickening of the terminal ileum and is helpful in identifying abscesses, fistulas (Fig. 1C-106), and other complications.
- Magnetic resonance enterography (MRe) is superior to other imaging modalities in its ability to distinguish active from chronic fibrotic disease. It is, however, more expensive.
- In 10% to 15% of patients with IBD, a clear distinction between ulcerative colitis and Crohn's disease cannot be made. In general, Crohn's disease can be distinguished from ulcerative colitis by the presence of transmural involvement and the frequent presence of noncaseating granulomas and lymphoid aggregates on biopsy.

Rx TREATMENT

The medical management of Crohn's disease is based on disease activity. According to Hanauer and Sanborn, disease activity can be defined as follows:
- Mild to moderate disease: The patient is ambulatory and able to take oral alimentation. There is no dehydration, high fever, abdominal tenderness, painful mass, obstruction, or weight loss of >10%.
- Moderate to severe disease: Either the patient has not responded to treatment for mild to moderate disease or has more pronounced symptoms, including fever, significant weight loss, abdominal pain or tenderness, intermittent nausea and vomiting, or significant anemia.
- Severe fulminant disease: Either the patient has persistent symptoms despite outpatient steroid

therapy or has high fever, persistent vomiting, evidence of intestinal obstruction, rebound tenderness, cachexia, or evidence of an abscess.
- Remission: The patient is asymptomatic or without inflammatory sequelae, including patients responding to acute medical intervention.

NONPHARMACOLOGIC THERAPY

- Nutritional supplementation is needed in patients with advanced disease. Total parenteral nutrition may be necessary in selected patients.
- Low-residue diet is necessary when obstructive symptoms are present.
- If diarrhea is prominent, increased dietary fiber and decreased fat in the diet are sometimes helpful.
- Psychotherapy is useful for situational adjustment crises. A trusting and mutually understanding relationship and referral to self-help groups are very important because of the chronicity of the disease and the relatively young age of the patients.
- Avoid oral feedings during acute exacerbation to decrease colonic activity: a low-roughage diet may be helpful in early relapse.

ACUTE GENERAL Rx

- Corticosteroids are used to induce remission. They have been the mainstay for treating moderate to severe active Crohn's disease. Prednisone 40 to 60 mg/day is useful for acute exacerbation. Steroids are usually tapered over approximately 2 to 3 mo. Some patients require a low dose for a prolonged period of maintenance.
- Steroid analogues are locally active corticosteroids that target specific areas of inflammation in the gastrointestinal tract. Budesonide is available as a controlled-release formulation and is approved for mild to moderate active Crohn's disease involving the ileum and/or ascending colon. The adult dose is 9 mg qd for a maximum of 8 wk.
- Patients responding to glucocorticoids are transitioned to immunomodulators as their glucocorticoid is tapered.
- Immunosuppressants such as azathioprine or mercaptopurine are used for maintenance of remission. Methotrexate is an alternative agent.
- Metronidazole 500 mg qid may be useful for colonic fistulas and treatment of mild to moderate active Crohn's disease. Ciprofloxacin 1 g qd has also been found to be effective in decreasing disease activity.
- TNF inhibitors are agents useful to induce remission and maintain remission in patients with moderate to severe Crohn's disease. Infliximab, a chimeric monoclonal antibody targeting tumor necrosis factor-α, is effective in the treatment of enterocutaneous fistulas. This medication can induce clinical improvement in 80% of patients with Crohn's disease refractory to other agents. It can be used in combination with other medications such as azathioprine in patients with severe Crohn's disease. A PPD test should be done before using this medication. Adalimumab

and certolizumab are other TNF inhibitors also effective in inducing remissions and may be useful in adult patients with Crohn's disease who cannot tolerate infliximab or have symptoms despite receiving infliximab therapy. Efficacy is better when an anti-TNF is used together with an immunomodulator.
- Natalizumab, a selective adhesion-molecule inhibitor, has been reported to be effective in increasing the rate of remission and response in patients with active Crohn's disease. It is effective for patients in whom anti-TNF therapy has been unsuccessful. Prior to using natalizumab, serologic testing should be done for JC virus, which causes multifocal leukoencephalopathy (PML), and if the patient is seronegative, the risk of PML from natalizumab is low. Vedolizumab is another IV integrin receptor antagonist recently FDA approved for moderate to severe Crohn's disease patients who have not responded to or cannot tolerate standard treatment. Vedolizumab use is not associated with high risk of PML.
- Hydrocortisone enema bid or tid is useful for proctitis.
- Most patients who have anemia associated with Crohn's disease respond to iron supplementation. Erythropoietin is useful in patients with anemia refractory to treatment with iron and vitamins.

CHRONIC Rx

- Monitor disease activity with symptom review and laboratory evaluation (complete blood count and sedimentation rate).
- Liver tests and vitamin B_{12} levels monitored on a yearly basis.

DISPOSITION

One tenth of patients have prolonged remission, three quarters have a chronic intermittent disease course, and one eighth have an unremitting course. Patients with IBD are at increased risk of colon cancer.

REFERRAL

- Surgical referral is needed for complications such as abscess formation, obstruction, fistulas, toxic megacolon, refractory disease, or severe hemorrhage. Approximately 40% to 50% of patients will require some type of bowel surgery within the first 5 years of Crohn's disease. A conservative surgical approach is necessary because surgery is not curative. Multiple surgeries may also result in short bowel syndrome.

 **EVIDENCE**

Available at www.expertconsult.com

SUGGESTED READINGS
Available at www.expertconsult.com

RELATED CONTENT
Crohn's Disease (Patient Information)

AUTHOR: **FRED F. FERRI, M.D.**

BASIC INFORMATION

DEFINITION

Cryoglobulins are serum immunoglobulins that precipitate when cooled and redissolve when heated. A classification of cryoglobulins is described in Table E1C-55. Cryoglobulinemia is a clinical syndrome that results from systemic inflammation caused by cryoglobulin-containing immune complexes. Mixed cryoglobulinemia is a vasculitis of small and medium-sized arteries and veins due to the deposition of complexes of antigen, cryoglobulin, and complement in the vessel walls.

SYNONYMS

Cryoglobulinemic vasculitis
Cryoproteinemia
Mixed cryoglobulinemia
Essential cryoglobulinemia

ICD-10CM CODES
D89.1 Cryoglobulinemia

EPIDEMIOLOGY & DEMOGRAPHICS

PREVALENCE:
- Prevalence of mixed cryoglobulinemia is approximately 1:100,000.
- Approximately 50% of patients with HCV are found to have mixed cryoglobulinemia; only 5% to 10% develop vasculitis.
- Three types: I (monoclonal), II (IgM monoclonal and IgG polyclonal), and III (polyclonal).

PREDOMINANT SEX AND AGE: Female:male ratio of 3:1.

PREDOMINANT AGE: Mean age reported is 42 to 52 yr.

RISK FACTORS:
- Hepatitis C virus (HCV) infection
- Connective tissue disorders
- Lymphoproliferative disorders

PHYSICAL FINDINGS & CLINICAL PRESENTATION

- **Meltzer triad** of purpura, arthralgias/myalgia, and weakness.
- Other symptoms include dyspnea, cough, numbness, abdominal pain, acrocyanosis.

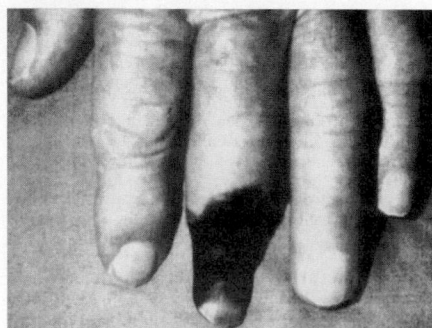

FIGURE 1C-108 Cryoglobulinemia. (From Hoffman R et al: *Hematology, basic principles and practice*, ed 6, New York, 2013, Elsevier.)

- Hypertension, hepatosplenomegaly, Raynaud's phenomenon, and in severe cases, distal necrosis and ulcerations of lower limbs (Fig. 1C-108).

ETIOLOGY

- Cryoglobulins cause hyperviscosity, resulting in noninflammatory thrombosis and immune complex deposition, leading to complement fixation and vascular inflammation.
- Infections: HCV, mycosis fungoides, HBV, HIV, Epstein-Barr virus, cytomegalovirus, *Treponema pallidum, Mycobacterium leprae,* and in post-streptococcal glomerulonephritis
- Lymphoproliferative disorders: chronic lymphocytic leukemia, Waldenström's macroglobulinemia, multiple myeloma
- Connective tissue disorders: rheumatoid arthritis, systemic lupus erythematosus (SLE), scleroderma, Sjögren's syndrome, vasculitis
- Renal diseases including proliferative glomerulonephritis

DIAGNOSIS

DIFFERENTIAL DIAGNOSIS

- Antiphospholipid syndrome
- SLE
- Churg-Strauss syndrome
- Cirrhosis
- Glomerulonephritis
- Goodpasture syndrome
- Hemolytic uremic syndrome
- Hepatitis
- Lymphoma
- Sarcoidosis
- Waldenström's hypergammaglobulinemia

WORKUP

History and physical examination; laboratory tests; imaging tests depending on patients' presentation.

LABORATORY TESTS

- Serum cryoglobulins, rheumatoid factor, serum complement, hepatitis C titer, urinalysis, CBC, ALT, AST, BUN, creatinine.
- Electromyogram/nerve conduction studies may demonstrate axonal changes and distal muscle denervation.
- Sural nerve and skin biopsy.

IMAGING STUDIES

Chest x-ray for pulmonary involvement, CT scan to evaluate for malignancy, and angiography for vasculitis.

TREATMENT

- Control of the underlying disease and immunosuppressive therapies such as corticosteroids are the mainstay treatment for mixed cryoglobulinemia. In patients with HCV, antiviral treatment with interferon alfa and ribavirin results in remission in 62% of cases and

viral clearance in 58%. Addition of rituximab results in decreased production of immune complexes and remission in 83% of patients with hepatitis C.
- Use of corticosteroids is initiated in severe cases, but tapering occurs quickly because infection is a leading cause of death.
- In cases of mixed cryoglobulinemia caused by other conditions, control of the underlying disease is paramount followed by treatment with rituximab and corticosteroids in severe cases.

NONPHARMACOLOGIC THERAPY

Avoidance of cold exposure

ACUTE GENERAL Rx

NSAIDs in those with general fatigue and arthralgia; see "Treatment" for further management.

DISPOSITION

Overall prognosis is worse with concomitant renal disease. Mean survival rate is ~50% at 10 yr.

REFERRAL

Consider referring to a
1. Nephrologist if there is renal involvement
2. Hematologist in patients with lymphoproliferative disorders
3. Gastroenterologist/hepatologist in patients with hepatitis
4. Rheumatologist in patients with connective tissue disease cases
5. Clinical immunologist in severe cases

PEARLS & CONSIDERATIONS

COMMENTS

Always look for underlying causes of cryoglobulinemia.

PREVENTION

Avoidance of cold exposure, avoidance of late complications.

PATIENT/FAMILY EDUCATION

Inform patients about early signs/symptoms of cryoglobulinemia so that treatment can be rendered before the development of complications.

SUGGESTED READINGS
Available at www.expertconsult.com

AUTHORS: **REBECCA SOINSKI, M.D.;**
QUANG P. LE, M.D., M.P.H.

BASIC INFORMATION

DEFINITION

Cryptococcosis is an infection caused by the fungal organism *Cryptococcus neoformans*.

SYNONYMS

C. neoformans var. *neoformans* infection
C. neoformans var. *gatti* infection
C. neoformans var. *grubii* infection

ICD-10CM CODES

B45.9 Pulmonary cryptococcosis
B45.1 Cerebral cryptococcosis
B45.2 Cutaneous cryptococcosis
B45.3 Osseous cryptococcosis
B45.7 Disseminated cryptococcosis
B45.9 Cryptococcosis, unspecified

EPIDEMIOLOGY & DEMOGRAPHICS

INCIDENCE (IN U.S.):
- 0.8 cases/million persons/year; *C. neoformans* is an important opportunistic infection in patients with deficits in cell-mediated immunity.
- 6% to 7% in HIV-infected persons with AIDS.

PEAK INCIDENCE: 20 to 40 yr (parallel to AIDS epidemic).

PREDOMINANT SEX: Equal sex distribution when corrected for HIV status.

PREDOMINANT AGE: Less than 2 yr of age; 20 to 40 yr of age.

NEONATAL INFECTION: Very uncommon.

PHYSICAL FINDINGS & CLINICAL PRESENTATION

- More than 90% present with meningitis; almost all have fever and headache.
- Meningismus, photophobia, mental status changes are seen in approximately 25%.
- Increased intracranial pressure.
- Most common infections outside the CNS:
  1. In the lungs (fever, cough, dyspnea).
  2. In the skin (cellulitis, papular eruption).
  3. In the lymph nodes (lymphadenitis).
  4. Potential involvement of virtually any organ.

ETIOLOGY

- Caused by the fungal organism *C. neoformans*. There are 3 varieties of *Cryptococcus* spp. and 4 capsular serotypes: Serotype A is *Cryptococcus neoformans* var. *grubii* and Serotype D is known as *Cryptococcus neoformans* var. *neoformans*. Both cause disease primarily in immunocompromised patients. Serotype B and C are known as *C. neoformans* var. *gatti*. This organism causes disease primarily in normal hosts. *C. gatti* infections are much less common and the majority of cases in the U.S. have been diagnosed in California.
- Infection originates by inhalation into the respiratory tract followed by dissemination to the CNS in most cases, usually without recognizable lung involvement.

- Almost always in the setting of AIDS or other disorders of cellular immune function.
- Neutropenia alone poses a much lower risk of significant cryptococcal infection.

DIAGNOSIS

DIFFERENTIAL DIAGNOSIS

- Subacute meningitis (caused by *Listeria monocytogenes, Mycobacterium tuberculosis, Histoplasma capsulatum,* viruses).
- Intracranial mass lesion (neoplasms, toxoplasmosis, TB).
- Pulmonary involvement confused with *Pneumocystis jiroveci* pneumonia when diffuse or confused with TB or bacterial pneumonia when focal or involving the pleura.
- Skin lesions confused with bacterial cellulitis or molluscum contagiosum.

WORKUP

- Lumbar puncture to exclude cryptococcal meningitis. In cryptococcal meningitis, CSF reveals lymphocytic pleocytosis.
- CT scan of the head when focal lesion or increased intracranial pressure is suspected.
- Biopsy of enlarged lymph nodes and skin lesions if feasible.

LABORATORY TESTS

- Culture and India ink stain (60% to 80% sensitive in culture-proven cases [Fig. 1C-109]); examination of the CSF in all cases when CNS involvement is suspected.
- Blood and serum cryptococcal antigen assay (>90% sensitivity and specificity in immunocompromised patients; lower sensitivity in immunocompetent patients).
- Culture and histologic examination of biopsy material.
- HIV.

IMAGING STUDIES

- CT scan or MRI of the head if focal neurologic involvement is suspected.
- Chest x-ray examination to exclude pulmonary involvement.

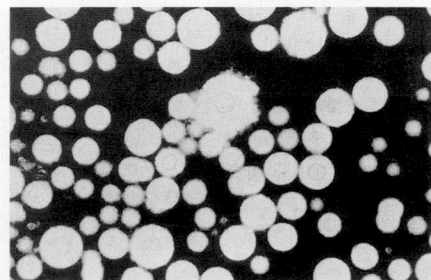

FIGURE 1C-109 India ink preparation of cerebrospinal fluid revealing encapsulated cryptococci. Note the large capsules surrounding the smaller organisms. (From Andreoli TE [ed]: *Cecil essentials of medicine,* ed 4, Philadelphia, 1997, Saunders.)

TREATMENT

ACUTE GENERAL Rx

- Induction therapy for CNS disease (meningitis) is initiated with IV amphotericin B (0.5 to 0.8 mg/kg/day) with flucytosine 37.5 mg/kg PO q6h until afebrile and cultures negative (≈6 wk), then stop amphotericin B/flucytosine and start fluconazole 200 mg PO q24h or fluconazole 400 mg PO q24h for 8-10 wk or longer (up to 2 yr) to reduce relapse rate. Maintenance therapy is indicated in patients with AIDS until these patients have been receiving antifungal therapy for at least 1 year and they have responded to antiretroviral therapy (CD4 cell count ≥100/microliter for ≥3 mo). In patients without HIV, the duration of maintenance therapy is 6 to 12 months. Lifelong antifungal therapy is needed in organ transplant patients.
- Alternative: IV fluconazole for initial therapy in patients unable to tolerate amphotericin B.
- If symptomatic increased intracranial pressure, consider multiple therapeutic lumbar taps or intraventricular shunt.

CHRONIC Rx

- Fluconazole (200-400 mg PO qd) is highly effective in preventing a relapse in HIV-infected patients; development of resistance may occur. Itraconazole is an alternative agent.
- Immune reconstitution syndrome following the institution of ART can cause transient worsening of meningitis and necessitate the use of a short course of corticosteroids.

DISPOSITION

Without maintenance therapy, relapse rate is >50% among AIDS patients.

REFERRAL

- For consultation with infectious diseases specialist in all cases.
- For neurologic consultation if level of consciousness is depressed or focal lesion is present.

SUGGESTED READINGS

Available at www.expertconsult.com

RELATED CONTENT

Cryptococcosis (Patient Information)

AUTHOR: **PHILIP A. CHAN, M.D., M.S.**

Diseases and Disorders

BASIC INFORMATION

DEFINITION

The intracellular protozoan parasite *Cryptosporidium parvum* is associated with gastrointestinal disease and diarrhea, especially in AIDS patients or immunocompromised hosts. It is also associated with sporadic infections and waterborne outbreaks in immunocompetent hosts. Cryptosporidiosis is a nationally notifiable disease.

Other species, including *C. hominis, C. felis, C. muris,* and *C. meleagridis,* are now described to be pathogens as well.

SYNONYMS

Cryptosporidiosis

ICD-10CM CODES
A07.2 Cryptosporidiosis

EPIDEMIOLOGY & DEMOGRAPHICS

INCIDENCE:
• Approximately 2% in industrial countries, 5% to 10% in developing countries
• Immunocompromised patients, especially those with HIV/AIDS, are particularly susceptible to infection. 10% to 20% of HIV patients in the United States may excrete cyst
• Cryptosporidiosis was the leading cause of all waterborne outbreaks in the U.S. during 2001-2010. An estimated 748,000 cryptosporidiosis cases occur annually, although fewer than 2% are reported. In 2011, more than 9000 cases of cryptosporidiosis were reported in the U.S. The highest overall reporting rates were observed in the Midwest.[1]

PREVALENCE: Worldwide, especially third world countries; associated with poor hygiene as a waterborne pathogen

PREDOMINANT SEX: Male = female.

TRANSMISSION:
• Person to person (daycare, family members).
• Animal to person (pets, farm animals). Fig. E1C-111 describes the life cycle of *Cryptosporidium.*
• Environmental (water-associated outbreaks, including travel associated with swimming in or drinking contaminated water or eating contaminated food).
• May be significant pathogen causing diarrhea in AIDS.

PHYSICAL FINDINGS & CLINICAL PRESENTATION

• Spectrum of illness ranging from asymptomatic to severe enteritis. Typical cases in immunocompetent hosts reveal self-limited diarrhea, whereas immunocompromised hosts are characterized by profuse, watery, nonbloody diarrhea that may lead to dehydration and weight loss.
• Usually limited to gastrointestinal tract.
• Diarrhea, severe abdominal pain (2-28 days).
• Impaired digestion, dehydration.

• Fever, malaise, fatigue, nausea, vomiting.
• Pneumonia if aspirated.

ETIOLOGY

C. hominis, C. parvum, C. felis, C. muris, C. meleagridis.

DIAGNOSIS

Clinical presentation of acute gastrointestinal illness, especially associated with HIV or with travel and waterborne outbreaks.

DIFFERENTIAL DIAGNOSIS

• *Campylobacter*
• *Clostridium difficile*
• *Entamoeba histolytica*
• *Giardia lamblia*
• *Salmonella*
• *Shigella*
• Microsporidia
• Cytomegalovirus
• *Mycobacterium avium*

Disease may cause cholecystitis, reactive arthritis, hepatitis, pancreatitis, pneumonia in immunocompromised or HIV-infected patients.

WORKUP

• Stool evaluation looking for characteristic oocyst by modified acid-fast stain (Fig. 1C-112).
• Direct immunofluorescence using monoclonal antibodies is the gold standard for stool exams.
• HIV.

TREATMENT

• May be self-limited in normal host over several weeks. Antidiarrheal agents Pepto-Bismol, Kaopectate, or loperamide may give symptomatic relief.
• Pharmacologic treatment with antibiotics has been largely unsatisfactory in AIDS patients. Antiviral therapy is the treatment of choice to restore the immune system. Oocyst excretion reduction has been shown with nitazoxanide 500 mg PO bid for 3 days in immunocompetent patients. If treatment fails, consider a trial of paromomycin, metronidazole, or trim-

ethoprim/sulfamethoxazole. However, these medications have not been approved for treatment of *Cryptosporidium.*
• Nitazoxanide elixir has been approved for the treatment of cryptosporidiosis in children ages 1 to 11 yr.
• Biliary cryptosporidiosis can be treated with antiretroviral therapy in the HIV setting.

DISPOSITION

• A self-limited disease in immunocompetent patients with complete recovery over 2 to 3 weeks.
• In patients with AIDS, chronic infection often clears with initiation of antiretroviral therapy.
• Chronic arthralgia, headache, malaise, and weakness may persist after cryptosporidial infection even in immunologically normal people.
• If severe and prolonged disease (>30 days), testing for HIV and other immunocompromised states is appropriate along with a referral to an infectious disease specialist or gastroenterologist.

REFERRAL

• To an infectious disease specialist if symptoms persist and if HIV infection is found.
• To a gastroenterologist if chronic malabsorption or biliary or pancreatic complications occur.

PEARLS & CONSIDERATIONS

• Chronic cryptosporidiosis (>30 days of diarrhea from *Cryptosporidium* spp. infection) in a patient with HIV is an AIDS-qualifying opportunistic infection.
• *Cryptosporidium hominis* has a limited host range (humans), whereas *Cryptosporidium parvum* has a wide host range including humans, horses, cattle, other domesticated animals, and wild animals; both species present a similar illness in humans.

SUGGESTED READINGS
Available at www.expertconsult.com

AUTHOR: **PHILIP A. CHAN, M.D., M.S**

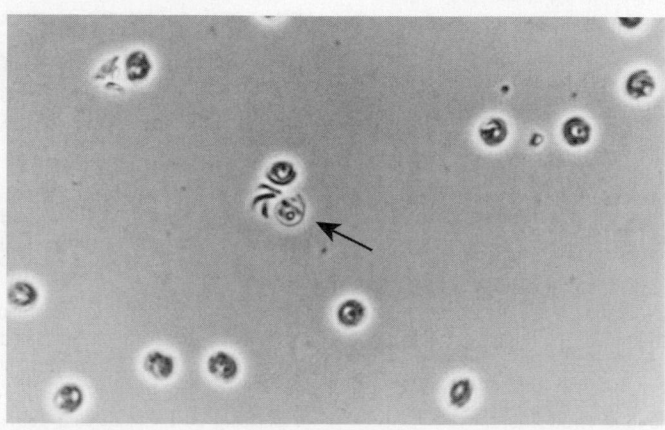

FIGURE 1C1-112 Human stool-derived Cryptosporidium oocysts. Excysting oocyst (arrow) is releasing three of its four sporozoites. (Phase-control microscopy ×630.) (From Gorbach SL: *Infectious diseases,* ed 2, Philadelphia, 1998, Saunders.)

---

[1]Cryptosporidiosis surveillance, United States, 20111-2012. MMWR 64 3 (2015).

C

BASIC INFORMATION

DEFINITION

- Cushing's syndrome is the occurrence of clinical abnormalities associated with glucocorticoid excess as a result of exaggerated adrenal cortisol production or long-term glucocorticoid therapy.
- Cushing's disease is Cushing's syndrome caused by pituitary adrenocorticotropic hormone (ACTH) excess.

ICD-10CM CODES
E24	Cushing syndrome
E24.2	Drug-induced Cushing syndrome
E24.3	Ectopic ACTH syndrome
E24.8	Other Cushing syndrome
E24.9	Cushing syndrome, unspecified
E24.9	Pituitary-dependent Cushing's disease

PHYSICAL FINDINGS & CLINICAL PRESENTATION

- Hypertension.
- Central obesity with rounding of the facies (moon facies); thin extremities.
- Hirsutism, menstrual irregularities, hypogonadism.
- Skin fragility, ecchymoses, red-purple abdominal striae (Fig. E1C-116), acne, poor wound healing, hair loss, facial plethora, hyperpigmentation (with ACTH excess).
- Psychosis, emotional lability, paranoia.
- Muscle wasting with proximal myopathy.

NOTE: The previous characteristics are not commonly present in Cushing's syndrome caused by ectopic ACTH production. Many of these tumors secrete a biologically inactive ACTH that does not activate adrenal steroid synthesis. These patients may have only weight loss and weakness.

ETIOLOGY

- Iatrogenic from long-term glucocorticoid therapy (common).
- Pituitary ACTH excess (Cushing's disease; 60%).
- Adrenal neoplasms (30%).
- Ectopic ACTH production (neoplasms of lung, pancreas, kidney, thyroid, thymus; 10%).
- Table E1C-56 summarizes the incidence of tumors associated with the ectopic adrenocorticotropic hormone syndrome.
- A classification of causes of Cushing's syndrome is described in Table 1C-57.

DIAGNOSIS

DIFFERENTIAL DIAGNOSIS

- Alcoholic pseudo-Cushing's syndrome (endogenous cortisol overproduction).
- Obesity associated with diabetes mellitus.
- Adrenogenital syndrome.

WORKUP (TABLE E1C-58)

- Initial tests include the overnight low-dose dexamethasone suppression test (LDST), 24-hour urine free cortisol (UFC), and late-night (LN) salivary cortisol. The LN and UFC tend to be more convenient.
- In patients with a clinical diagnosis of Cushing's syndrome the initial screening test is the overnight dexamethasone suppression test:
  1. Dexamethasone 1 mg PO given at 11 PM.
  2. Plasma cortisol level measured 9 hr later (8 AM).
  3. Plasma cortisol level <5 mcg/100 ml excludes Cushing's syndrome.
- Late-night (LN) salivary cortisol: a single midnight serum cortisol level (normal diurnal variation leads to a nadir around midnight) >7.5 mcg/dl has been reported as 96% sensitive and 100% specific for the diagnosis of Cushing's syndrome.
- Serial measurements (two or three consecutive measurements) of 24-hr urinary free cortisol and creatinine (to ensure adequacy of collection) are undertaken if overnight dexamethasone test is suggestive of Cushing's syndrome. Persistent elevated cortisol excretion (>300 mcg/24 hr) indicates Cushing's syndrome.
- The low-dose (2 mg) dexamethasone suppression test is useful to exclude pseudo-Cushing's syndrome if the previous results are equivocal. Corticotropic-releasing hormone (CRH) stimulation after low-dose dexamethasone administration (dexamethasone-CRH test) is also used to distinguish patients with suspected Cushing's syndrome from those who have mildly elevated urinary free cortisol level and equivocal findings.
- The high-dose (8 mg) dexamethasone test and measurement of ACTH by radioimmunoassay are useful to determine the etiology of Cushing's syndrome.
  1. ACTH undetectable or decreased and lack of suppression indicate adrenal cause of Cushing's syndrome.
  2. ACTH normal or increased and lack of suppression indicate ectopic ACTH production.
  3. ACTH normal or increased and partial suppression suggest pituitary excess (Cushing's disease).

Bilateral inferior petrosal sinus sampling (BIPSS) can be used to distinguish pituitary Cushing's disease from the ectopic ACTH syndrome (Fig. 1C-117).

LABORATORY TESTS

- Hypokalemia, hypochloremia, metabolic alkalosis, hyperglycemia, hypercholesterolemia.
- Increased 24-hr urinary free cortisol (>100 mcg/24 hr).

IMAGING STUDIES

- CT scan or MRI of adrenal glands in suspected adrenal Cushing's syndrome (Fig. E1C-118).
- MRI of pituitary gland with gadolinium is the preferred procedure for localizing a pituitary edema in suspected pituitary Cushing's syndrome.
- Additional imaging studies to localize neoplasms of the lung, pancreas, kidney, thyroid, or thymus in patients with ectopic ACTH production.

TREATMENT

GENERAL Rx

The definitive treatment of Cushing's syndrome is surgical removal of the tumor causing excessive production of cortisol:

- Pituitary adenoma: transsphenoidal microadenomectomy is the therapy of choice in adults. Pituitary irradiation is reserved for patients not cured by transsphenoidal surgery. In children, pituitary irradiation may be considered as initial therapy because 85% of children are cured by radiation. Stereotactic radiotherapy (photon knife or gamma knife) is effective and exposes the surrounding neuronal tissues to less irradiation than conventional radiotherapy. Total bilateral adrenalectomy is reserved for patients not cured by transsphenoidal surgery or pituitary irradiation.
- Adrenal neoplasm:
  1. Surgical resection of the affected adrenal.
  2. Glucocorticoid replacement for approximately 9 to 12 mo after the surgery to allow time for the contralateral adrenal gland to recover from its prolonged suppression.
  3. In nonsurgical candidates, suppression of adrenal steroid production can be accomplished with ketoconazole. Mifepristone, an antiprogestin, can also be used for control of hyperglycemia secondary to hypercortisolism in adults with endogenous Cushing's syndrome. It should be avoided in women who are or who could become pregnant.
- Bilateral micronodular or macronodular adrenal hyperplasia: bilateral total adrenalectomy.
- Ectopic ACTH:
  1. Surgical resection of the ACTH-secreting neoplasm.
  2. Control of cortisol excess with metyrapone, aminoglutethimide, mifepristone, or ketoconazole.
  3. Control of the mineralocorticoid effects of cortisol and 11-deoxycorticosteroid with spironolactone.
  4. Bilateral adrenalectomy: a rational approach to patients with indolent, unresectable tumors.

DISPOSITION

Prognosis is favorable in patients with surgically amenable disease.

PEARLS & CONSIDERATIONS

COMMENTS

- Screening for multiple endocrine neoplasia type I should be considered in patients with Cushing's disease.

SUGGESTED READINGS

Available at www.expertconsult.com

RELATED CONTENT

Cushing's Syndrome (Patient Information)

AUTHOR: **FRED F. FERRI, M.D.**

Diseases and Disorders

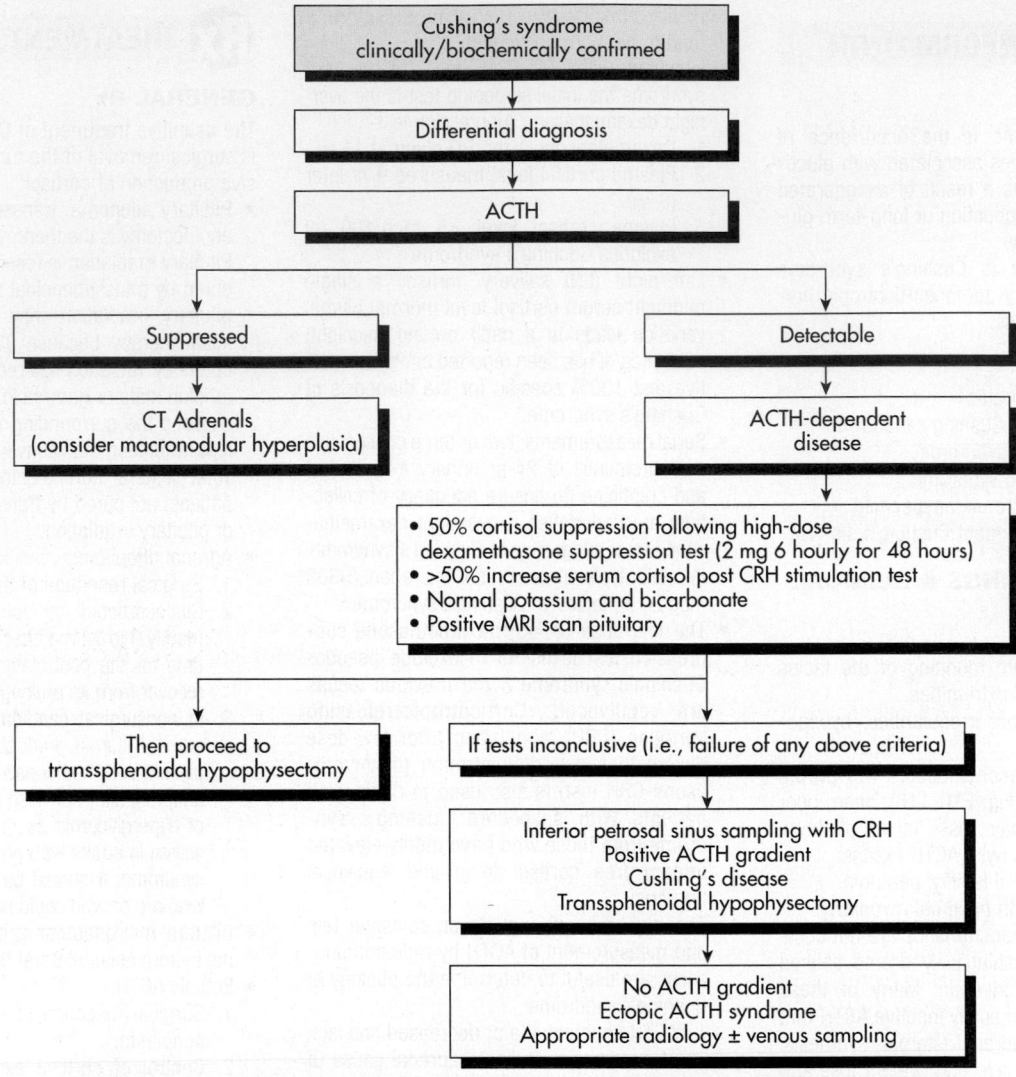

FIGURE 1C-117 The tests to uncover the cause of Cushing's syndrome are debatable and differ in any given center depending on many factors, including familiarity and turnaround time of hormone assays and local expertise in techniques such as inferior petrosal sinus sampling. Depicted here is an algorithm in use within many endocrine units based on the reported sensitivity and specificity of each endocrine test. *ACTH,* Adrenocorticotropin; *CT,* computed tomography; *MRI,* magnetic resonance imaging. (From Melmed S, Polonsky KS, Larsen PR, Kronenberg HM: *Williams textbook of endocrinology,* ed 12, Philadelphia, 2011, Saunders.)

C

 BASIC INFORMATION

DEFINITION

Cyclic vomiting syndrome (CVS), an idiopathic disorder primarily seen in children, is characterized by recurrent, stereotypical episodes of vomiting with varying asymptomatic periods.

SYNONYM(S)

CVS

ICD-10CM CODES
G43.A0 Cyclical vomiting, not intractable
G43.A1 Cyclical vomiting, intractable

EPIDEMIOLOGY & DEMOGRAPHICS

INCIDENCE & PREVALENCE:
- Incidence and prevalence are unknown because no national population studies have been done.
- Cross-sectional study of school-age children in Aberdeen, Scotland, estimated that 1.6% fulfilled diagnostic criteria.
- Average age of time of diagnosis: 9.6 years.
- Average age of onset of symptoms: 5.3 years.
- This study showed gender ratio was equivalent, although isolated reports say it may be more common in girls.
- In adults, no population studies exist to extrapolate prevalence. In one study with 17 patients followed over a 10-yr interval, it was found that average age of onset was 35 years, but diagnosis was 41 years. Gender distribution was again found to be equal.

GENETICS: Mutations in mitochondrial DNA (mtDNA) have been associated with cyclical vomiting syndrome and neuromuscular disease in pediatric patients. These mutations were also more commonly associated with migraines, irritable bowel syndrome, and hypothyroidism. Evidence shows that the mtDNA mutations seen in pediatric patients have a maternal inheritance pattern.

PHYSICAL FINDINGS & CLINICAL PRESENTATION

- There is a stereotypical pattern to the vomiting episodes. They normally begin in the early morning hours and may involve a prodrome that includes pallor, nausea, abdominal pain, or lethargy.

- High rates of emeses per hour with the peak in the first hour with a decline in the next 4 to 8 hr. These episodes normally last up to 24 hr.
- Many patients may have neurologic symptoms, including headache, photophobia, or vertigo, which supports the genetic relation between CVS and migraines.

ETIOLOGY

- mtDNA mutations that were also associated with migraines in pediatric patients with 2 mtDNA polymorphisms in particular, 16519T and 3010A, that are expressed in high frequency in subjects with CVS. In adults, CVS is not associated with these polymorphisms.
- Sympathetic hyperresponsiveness and autonomic dysregulation may contribute to the pathogenesis of CVS. Elevated corticotropin, cortisol, vasopressin, and catecholamines have been described in patients with vomiting, lethargy, and hypertension. Studies in animals suggest that corticotropin-releasing factor induces gastric stasis, leading to emesis. Stress responses, which are mediated by the hypothalamic-pituitary-adrenal axis, can therefore potentially induce episodes of vomiting. Triggers of stress responses can be infectious, psychological, or physical.

 DIAGNOSIS

DIFFERENTIAL DIAGNOSIS

- Acute porphyria
- Abdominal migraines
- Diabetic ketoacidosis
- *Helicobacter pylori* infection
- Cannabis hyperemesis syndrome
- Jamaican vomiting sickness
- Munchausen syndrome by proxy
- Mechanical obstruction
- Gastrointestinal malignancies
- Intestinal malrotation

WORKUP

CVS is a clinical diagnosis because there are no biochemical markers or imaging that exists to make the diagnosis. The North American Society of Pediatric Gastroenterology, Hepatology, and Nutrition (NASPGHAN) has set forth criteria (all criteria must be met). Box 1C-4 summarizes criteria. In adults, Rome III criteria should be met to make diagnosis. Box 1C-5 summarizes

Rome III criteria. Supportive criteria in addition to either set of guidelines include a personal or family history of migraine headaches.

LABORATORY TESTS

In the evaluation for possible GI disease as an etiology of vomiting, screening blood work should be performed. CBC, BMP, liver function tests, pancreatic amylase and lipase, and ESR should be done. Screening for endocrine and metabolic disorders is also warranted and can include lactic acid, ammonia, amino acids, ACTH, and ADH as well as urinary ketones, organic acids, porphobilinogen, and aminolevulinic acid.

IMAGING STUDIES

An upper GI series with small bowel follow-through, CT/MRI of the head, and endoscopy should be performed in between episodes. In adults, a CT of the abdomen and pelvis should be done in addition to the mentioned testing to exclude malignancy.

℞ TREATMENT

Treatment of CVS includes avoidance of certain triggers that precipitate attacks as well as pharmacologic therapy divided into prophylactic, abortive, and supportive treatment.

NONPHARMACOLOGIC THERAPY

- Avoidance of dietary triggers such as chocolate, cheese, or monosodium glutamate (MSG) may prevent episodes.
- Stress management techniques for psychosocial stressors may decrease the frequency of episodes exacerbated by stress.

ACUTE GENERAL Rx

Treatment can be considered as prophylactic, abortive, or supportive.
- Prophylactic therapy is reserved for patients who have more than one attack per month or with attacks that are severe enough to cause hospitalization. A trial of prophylactic antimigraine medications is recommended even in the absence of personal or family history of migraine headaches. Prophylactic therapy includes cyproheptadine, amitriptyline, propranolol, erythromycin, and topiramate. Some specialists recommend starting amitriptyline at 0.5 mg/kg per day in children older than 5 yr. It often is increased to 1 mg/kg per day with effects typically taking a few months to become evident.
- There is emerging evidence that carnitine and coenzyme Q10 along with strict dietary protocol can reduce episodes.
- Abortive therapy is used during episodes. Agents that are used in migraine attacks such as triptans have also been found to effective in aborting episodes in CVS. If abortive therapy fails, antiemetic therapy with ondansetron can be used as supportive therapy. If attack is severe, ondansetron may be used in conjunction with a benzodiazepine or diphenhydramine.

BOX 1C-4 North American Society for Pediatric Gastroenterology, Hepatology, and Nutrition (NASPGHAN) Criteria for Cyclic Vomiting Syndrome

- At least five episodes over any interval or a minimum of three attacks over a 6-mo period
- Episodic attacks of intense nausea and vomiting lasting from 1 hour to 10 days and occurring at least 1 week apart
- Stereotypical in the individual patient
- Vomiting during attacks occurs at least 4 times/hr for at least 1 hour
- A return to baseline health between episodes

BOX 1C-5 ROME III Diagnostic Criteria for Cyclic Vomiting Syndrome

Must include all of the following:
- Stereotypical episodes of vomiting regarding onset (acute) and duration (<1 week)
- Three or more discrete episodes in 1 year
- Absence of nausea and vomiting between episodes

Supportive Criterion
- History or family history of migraine headaches

DISPOSITION

If episode is severe, the patient may need hospital admission. Treatment includes IV fluids, antiemetics, and analgesics. Otherwise, this can be managed on an outpatient basis.

REFERRAL

Referral should be made to gastroenterologist for thorough investigation of vomiting until definitive diagnosis of CVS can be established. If certain neurologic findings or laboratory study results suggest a metabolic disorder, early referral to a metabolic specialist or neurologist should be considered.

 **PEARLS & CONSIDERATIONS**

COMMENTS

CVS is a clinical diagnosis that is seen in pediatric and adult populations. Laboratory testing and appropriate imaging should be done to rule out other differential diagnoses. A thorough history including family history, onset and duration of episodes, alarming symptoms, and so on as well as a complete physical examination will allow clinician to narrow differential diagnoses.

PREVENTION

There is emerging evidence of carnitine and coenzyme Q10 in a certain subtype of patients to prevent frequent attacks. Prophylactic therapy includes pharmacologic agents stated earlier. Avoidance of stress and dietary triggers are also warranted if this can be identified as causative etiology.

PATIENT/FAMILY EDUCATION

Families are encouraged to view www.cvsaonline.org for more information and education about the disease.

SUGGESTED READINGS

Available online at www.expertconsult.com

AUTHOR: **TANMAY SAHAI, M.D.**

BASIC INFORMATION

DEFINITION

Cystic fibrosis (CF) is an autosomal recessive disorder characterized by dysfunction of exocrine glands.

ICD-10CM CODES
E84.0   Cystic fibrosis with pulmonary manifestations
E84.11 Meconium ileus in cystic fibrosis
E84.19 Cystic fibrosis with other intestinal manifestations
E84.8   Cystic fibrosis with other manifestations
E84.9   Cystic fibrosis, unspecified

EPIDEMIOLOGY & DEMOGRAPHICS

- CF is the most common fatal hereditary disorder of whites in the United States (one case per 2500 whites) and second most common life-shortening childhood-onset inherited disorder in the United States, behind sickle cell disease.
- Median age at diagnosis is 5.3 mo. Median survival is 37 yr.
- Carrier screening is associated with a decrease in incidence of CF.

PHYSICAL FINDINGS & CLINICAL PRESENTATION

- Failure to thrive in children
- Increased anterior/posterior chest diameter
- Basilar crackles and hyperresonance to percussion
- Digital clubbing
- Chronic cough
- Abdominal distention
- Greasy, smelly feces

ETIOLOGY

Chromosome 7 gene mutations (*CFTR* gene). There are more than 1000 mutations in the gene. About half of patients in the U.S. with CF are homozygous for the Phe508del mutation in *CFTR*, and more than 90% have at least one Phe508del

TABLE 1C-60   Diagnostic Criteria for Cystic Fibrosis (CF)

Presence of typical clinical features (respiratory, gastrointestinal, or genitourinary)
OR
A history of CF in a sibling
OR
A positive newborn screening test
PLUS
Laboratory evidence for CFTR (CF transmembrane regulator) dysfunction:
Two elevated sweat chloride concentrations obtained on separate days
OR
Identification of two CF mutations
OR
An abnormal nasal potential difference measurement

From Kliegman RM et al: *Nelson textbook of pediatrics*, ed 19, Philadelphia, 2011, Saunders.

allele. These mutations result in abnormalities in chloride transport and water flux across the surface of epithelial cells; the abnormal secretions cause obstruction of glands and ducts in various organs and subsequent damage to exocrine tissue (recurrent pneumonia, atelectasis, bronchiectasis, diabetes mellitus, biliary cirrhosis, cholelithiasis, intestinal obstruction, increased risk of gastrointestinal malignancies).

DIAGNOSIS

DIFFERENTIAL DIAGNOSIS

- Immunodeficiency states
- Celiac disease
- Asthma
- Recurrent pneumonia
- Primary ciliary dyskinesia

WORKUP

A diagnosis of CF requires a positive quantitative pilocarpine iontophoresis test with one or more phenotypic features consistent with CF (e.g., chronic suppurative obstructive lung disease, pancreatic insufficiency) or documented CF in a sibling or first cousin. Table 1C-60 describes diagnostic criteria for CF. Conditions suggesting the diagnosis of CF in adults and recommended diagnostic studies are described in Table 1C-61.

LABORATORY TESTS

- Pilocarpine iontophoresis (sweat chloride test): diagnostic of CF in children if sweat chloride is >60 mmol/L (>80 mmol/L in adults) on two separate tests on consecutive days. Repeat testing may be necessary because not all infants have sufficient quantities of sweat for reliable testing. Table 1C-63 describes conditions associated with false-positive and false-negative sweat test results.
- DNA testing may be useful for confirming the diagnosis and providing genetic information for family members.

TABLE 1C-61   Approach to Diagnosis of Cystic Fibrosis in Adult Patients

Conditions Suggesting the Diagnosis of Cystic Fibrosis in Adults
Recurrent pancreatitis
Male infertility
Chronic sinusitis
Nasal polyposis
Nontuberculous mycobacterial infection
Allergic bronchopulmonary mycosis
Bronchiectasis

Recommended Diagnostic Studies
Sweat electrolyte determination
Extended CFTR mutation analysis
Nasal potential difference
High-resolution CT scan to identify bronchiectasis
CT scan of sinuses for polyposis
Sputum induction or bronchoalveolar lavage to identify bacterial and fungal pathogens

CFTR, Cystic fibrosis transmembrane conductance regulator; *CT,* computed tomography.
From Goldman L, Schafer AI: *Goldman's Cecil medicine*, ed 24, Philadelphia, 2012, Saunders.

- Sputum culture and sensitivity and Gram stain (frequent bacterial infections with *Staphylococcus aureus, Pseudomonas aeruginosa* [most common virulent respiratory pathogen], *Haemophilus influenzae* and *Burkholderia cenocepacia*). Bronchoalveolar lavage (BAL) is used at times to aid in the early diagnosis of pulmonary infection in non-expectorating patients. However, evidence for its clinical benefit is lacking. Trials have shown that among infants diagnosed with CF, BAL-directed therapy did not result in a lower prevalence of *P. aeruginosa* infection or lower total CF-CT score when compared with standard therapy at age 5 years.
- Low albumin level, increased 72-hr fecal fat excretion.
- Pulse oximetry or arterial blood gases: hypoxemia.
- Pulmonary function studies: decreased total lung capacity, forced vital capacity, pulmonary diffusing capacity.

IMAGING STUDIES

- Chest x-ray (Fig. 1C-120): may reveal focal atelectasis, peribronchial cuffing, bronchiectasis, increased interstitial markings, hyperinflation
- High-resolution chest CT scan: bronchial wall thickening, cystic lesions, ring shadows (bronchiectasis)

TABLE 1C-62   Conditions Associated with False-Positive and False-Negative Sweat Test Results

With False-Positive Results
Eczema (atopic dermatitis)
Ectodermal dysplasia
Malnutrition/failure to thrive/deprivation
Anorexia nervosa
Congenital adrenal hyperplasia
Adrenal insufficiency
Glucose-6-phosphatase deficiency
Mauriac syndrome
Fucosidosis
Familial hypoparathyroidism
Hypothyroidism
Nephrogenic diabetes insipidus
Pseudohypoaldosteronism
Klinefelter's syndrome
Familial cholestasis syndrome
Autonomic dysfunction
Prostaglandin E infusions
Munchausen syndrome by proxy

With False-Negative Results
Dilution
Malnutrition
Edema
Insufficient sweat quantity
Hyponatremia
Cystic fibrosis transmembrane conductance regulator (CFTR) mutations with preserved sweat duct function

From Kliegman RM et al: *Nelson textbook of pediatrics*, ed 19, Philadelphia, 2011, Saunders.

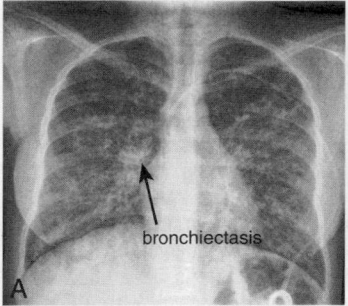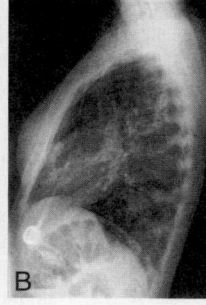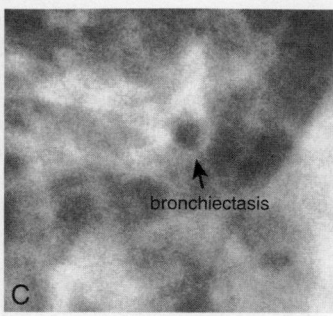

FIGURE 1C-120 Cystic fibrosis. Cystic fibrosis is aptly named. Chest x-ray findings include increased interstitial density of fibrosis and cystic changes of lung parenchyma similar to chronic obstructive pulmonary disease. Bronchiectasis (dilation of bronchi, potentially eroding into bronchial arteries and presenting with hemoptysis) may be visible on chest x-ray as large and thickened bronchioles particularly when viewed in short axis (when bronchioles are oriented perpendicular to the frontal plane). This I5-year-old with cystic fibrosis presented with cough and dyspnea. Does she have pneumonia? Comparison with prior x-rays showed no changes. **A,** Posterior-anterior chest x-ray. **B,** Lateral chest x-ray. **C,** Close-up from A showing bronchiectasis. (From Broder JS: *Diagnostic imaging for the emergency physician,* Philadelphia, 2011, Saunders.)

℞ TREATMENT

NONPHARMACOLOGIC THERAPY

- Mucus clearance (using postural drainage techniques, chest percussion, Therapy Vest, Acapella, and so on).
- Encouragement of regular exercise and proper nutrition (daily caloric intake of 120%-200% of healthy population).
- Psychosocial evaluation and counseling of patient and family members.

ACUTE GENERAL Rx

- Antibiotic therapy based on results of Gram stain and culture and sensitivity of sputum (PO quinolones for *Pseudomonas,* cephalosporins for *S. aureus,* IV aminoglycosides [tobramycin] plus ceftazidime or ticarcillin for life-threatening *Pseudomonas* infections). Inhaled antibiotics (aztreonam or tobramycin) can also be used and can achieve high airway concentration with lower systemic side effects. Macrolides are also active against *Pseudomonas aeruginosa.* For *S. aureus* infection, use oxacillin or nafcillin 2 g IV p4h if MSSA; if dealing with MRSA, use IV vancomycin 1 g q12h. A recent study using azithromycin maintenance in children with CF for 6 mo found less use of additional antibiotics and improvement in some aspects of pulmonary function. Additional studies may be necessary to determine if azithromycin should be used as a primary therapy or rescue treatment.
- Bronchodilators for patients with airflow obstruction.
- Long-term pancreatic enzyme replacement.
- Alternate-day prednisone (2 mg/kg) possibly beneficial in children with CF (decreased hospitalization rate, improved pulmonary function); routine use of corticosteroids not recommended in adults; among children with CF who have received alternate-day treatment with prednisone, boys, but not girls, have persistent growth impairment after treatment is discontinued.
- Proper nutrition and vitamin supplementation (ADEK).

- Recombinant human deoxyribonuclease (DNase [dornase alfa]) 2.5 mg qd or bid given by aerosol for patients with viscid sputum. It lowers the viscosity of sputum. It is useful to improve mucociliary clearance by liquefying difficult-to-clear pulmonary secretions. It is, however, very expensive; it is most beneficial in patients with forced vital capacity values >40% of predicted. Its cost can be decreased by using alternate-day rhDNase therapy.
- Intermittent administration of inhaled tobramycin has been reported beneficial in CF.
  Newer treatment modalities involve increasing the activity of CF transmembrane conductance regulator (CFTR) protein. Ivacaftor (a CFTR potentiator) is FDA approved for oral treatment of CF in patients 6 years and older with the G551D mutation (5% of patients with CF). It can decrease the frequency of pulmonary exacerbations and improve lung function. Dose is 150 mg PO BID. Cost is a significant limiting factor. A new oral combination treatment of Lumacaftor 400 mg (CFTR-corrector)-Ivacaftor 250 mg every 12 hr has been FDA approved in patients ages 12 yr and older who are homozygous for the F508del mutation in the *CFTR* gene. If the patient's genotype is unknown, an FDA-cleared CF mutation test should be used to detect the presence of the F508del mutation on both alleles of the *CFTR* gene.
  Limitations of use: Efficacy and safety have not been established in patients with CF other than those homozygous for the F508del mutation.
- Treatment of impaired glucose tolerance and diabetes mellitus.

CHRONIC Rx

Pneumococcal and influenza vaccination

DISPOSITION

- Bronchiectasis develops early in the course of cystic fibrosis, being detectable in infants as young as 10 wk of age, and is persistent and progressive. Recent data[1]

[1]Sly PD et al: Risk factors for bronchiectasis in children with cystic fibrosis, *N Engl J Med* 368:1963-1970, 2013.

reveal that neutrophil elastase activity in BAL fluid in early life is associated with early bronchiectasis in children with cystic fibrosis.
- More than 50% of children with CF live beyond age 20 yr. During the past 2 decades, survival among patients with late-stage CF has lengthened substantially. Survival has improved at the rate of 1.8% annually during the past decade. This is believed due to increased use of NBH DNase.
- Lung transplantation is the only definitive treatment; 3-yr survival after transplantation exceeds 50%.
- Obstructive azoospermia is present in >98% of postpubertal males.
- The SERPINA Z allele is a risk factor for liver disease in CF. Patients that carry the Z allele are at a greater risk of developing severe liver disease with portal hypertension.

REFERRAL

- For lung transplantation in selected patients. Indications for lung transplantation are FEV_1 <30% of predicted, rapidly progressive respiratory deterioration, increasing number of hospital admissions, massive hemoptysis, recurrent pneumothorax, arterial partial pressure of oxygen <55 mm Hg, arterial partial pressure of carbon dioxide >50 mm Hg, multiresistant organisms, wasting. Young female patients should be referred earlier because of overall poor prognosis.
- For screening of family members with DNA analysis.

ⓘ PEARLS & CONSIDERATIONS

COMMENTS

- Clinicians should think of CF in any patient with bronchiectasis plus any of the following: male infertility, recurrent idiopathic pancreatitis, recurrent nasal polyposis.
- Genetic testing for CF should be offered to adults with a positive family history of CF, couples currently planning a pregnancy, and couples seeking prenatal care.
- Inhalation of hypertonic saline (5 mL of 7% sodium chloride qid) has been reported to produce a sustained acceleration of mucus clearance and improved lung function.
- The prevalence of MRSA in the respiratory tract of individuals with CF has increased dramatically over the past decade and is associated with worse survival.

EBM EVIDENCE

Available at www.expertconsult.com

SUGGESTED READINGS

Available at www.expertconsult.com

RELATED CONTENT

Cystic Fibrosis (Patient Information)
Bronchiectasis (Related Key Topic)

AUTHORS: **AUGUSTINE ANDOH-DUKU, M.D.,** and **SAMAAN RAFEQ, M.D.**

 BASIC INFORMATION

DEFINITION

Cysticercosis is an infection caused by the tissue deposition of larval forms of the pork tapeworm *Taenia solium*. *T. solium* cysts, or cysticerci, may accumulate in any human tissue, including the eyes, spinal cord, skin, muscle, heart, and brain. Central nervous system (CNS) involvement is common and is known as neurocysticercosis. Humans most commonly acquire cysticercosis via fecal-oral transmission from human tapeworm carriers or via ingestion of larval cysts in infected pork or tapeworm eggs in contaminated water or soil. Larvae in the gastrointestinal tract migrate hematogenously to tissues, where they encyst, forming cysticerci.

SYNONYMS

Cysticerciasis
Taeniasis
Pork tapeworm

ICD-10CM CODES
B69	Cysticercosis
B69.0	Cysticercosis of central nervous system
B69.1	Cysticercosis of eye
B69.81	Myositis in cysticercosis
B69.89	Cysticercosis of other sites
B69.9	Cysticercosis, unspecified

EPIDEMIOLOGY & DEMOGRAPHICS

- *T. solium* infection is worldwide in distribution. Tapeworm infection and cysticercosis are endemic in developing countries where pigs are raised as a food source, including developing countries of Central America, South America, and parts of Africa and Asia.
- Serologic studies from endemic areas of Latin America have demonstrated seroprevalence rates of 4% to 24% in native populations.
- Neurocysticercosis is most common in the United States in states with large immigrant populations from countries where the disease is endemic.

PHYSICAL FINDINGS & CLINICAL PRESENTATION

- After ingestion of *T. solium* eggs or cysts, humans may remain asymptomatic for years.
- Cysticerci in muscles and skin may form asymptomatic "cold" nodules without erythema or tenderness that may calcify and be seen on radiographs.
- Neurocysticercosis, the presence of cysts within the brain parenchyma, is usually asymptomatic. Symptoms develop due to the inflammatory response to degeneration of cysts, which can result in focal encephalitis, vasculitis, chronic meningitis, and cranial nerve palsies.
- Seizures are the most common manifestation of neurocysticercosis, occurring in 70% to 90% of symptomatic cases. Headache and focal neurologic deficits can also occur.

- In 10% to 20% of cases of neurocysticercosis, cysts lodge within the ventricular system and result in obstructive hydrocephalus, causing acute intracranial hypertension. Symptoms are caused by the presence of the parasite itself, ependymal inflammation, and/or fibrosis, each of which blocks the circulation of cerebrospinal fluid (CSF). Death may occur from progressive hydrocephalus, cerebral edema, or intractable seizures.
- Ocular cysticercosis occurs in less than 5% of infections and is generally asymptomatic. Inflammation in response to degenerating cysticerci may result in chorioretinitis, vasculitis, or retinal detachment, threatening vision.

ETIOLOGY

- *T. solium* has a complex two-host life cycle.
- Humans are the only definitive host and harbor the adult worm in the intestine (taeniasis). However, both humans and pigs can serve as intermediate hosts and harbor the larvae or cysticerci.

Dx **DIAGNOSIS**

DIFFERENTIAL DIAGNOSIS

- Epilepsy of unknown etiology
- Migraine
- CNS vasculitis
- Primary neoplasia of CNS
- Chronic CNS infections, including toxoplasmosis, coccidioidomycosis, tuberculosis, and cryptococcosis
- Brain abscess
- CNS involvement with sarcoidosis or systemic lupus erythematosus

WORKUP

Comprehensive clinical history: obtain information on current and previous travel and residence, including geographic area, sanitary conditions, and consumption of undercooked pork.

LABORATORY TESTS

- Serum antibody detection by enzyme-linked immunoelectrotransfer blot (EITB) assay has a sensitivity of 98% and a specificity of 100% in patients with more than one cyst but has less predictive value in patients with a single cyst, in which up to 38% can be falsely negative. The same assay can be performed in CSF, with lower sensitivity. Antibodies detected by EITB can persist for years after successful therapy, limiting the usefulness of this assay in following patients after treatment. In endemic regions, a negative test result is useful in ruling out disease but a positive result is a marker of exposure, not necessarily symptomatic infection.
- Circulating cysticercus antigens can be detected in blood and CSF, providing a marker of viable organisms, even when CNS lesions are calcified and presumed to be inactive. This method may be particularly useful in monitoring patients after therapy.

Antigen levels usually fall within 3 months of successful treatment.
- Polymerase chain reaction (PCR) detection of *T. solium* DNA has been developed, with a reported sensitivity of 96.7%, but it is not widely available.
- Definitive diagnosis is based on the histopathologic demonstration of cysticerci in the tissue involved.
- Peripheral eosinophilia is usually absent.
- Stool examination for ova and proglottids of *T. solium* is insensitive and not specific for the diagnosis of cysticercosis.
- CSF examination in neurocysticercosis is usually unremarkable, but may demonstrate pleocytosis, with lymphocytic or eosinophilic predominance, low glucose, and elevated protein.

IMAGING STUDIES

- Plain radiographs of the extremities may reveal calcified cysts in patients with soft tissue or muscle involvement.
- For diagnosis of neurocysticercosis, CT and MRI are most commonly used.
- Brain CT (Fig. 1C-121) has a sensitivity and specificity of 95% and can identify living cysticerci, which appear as hypodense lesions, as well as degenerating cysts, which appear as isodense or hyperdense lesions with surrounding edema. CT is the best method for detecting calcification associated with prior infection, which suggests inactivity.
- Brain MRI is the most accurate technique to assess the extent of infection, location, and evolutionary stage of the parasites. MRI provides detailed images of living and degenerating cysts, perilesional edema, as well as small cysts or those located in the ventricles, brainstem, and cerebellum. However, MRI has a low sensitivity for detecting calcified lesions, which are the most common neuroimaging finding in endemic populations.

Rx **TREATMENT**

ACUTE GENERAL Rx
Asymptomatic cysticercosis:
- There is no evidence that administering antiparasitic therapy is beneficial.

Symptomatic neurocysticercosis:
The goals of treatment are to control seizures and mass effect from cysticercal lesions, control intracranial hypertension, and reduce the size of active cysts.
- Treatment decisions in neurocysticercosis should be individualized. Initial measures should focus on the symptomatic management considering antiparasitic therapy when appropriate.
- Patients with active lesions, with evidence of surrounding edema and/or inflammation, generally warrant treatment with antiparasitics, corticosteroids, and anticonvulsants.
  1. Patients who have seizures or are considered at risk for recurrent seizures based on imaging should be treated with anticonvulsants.

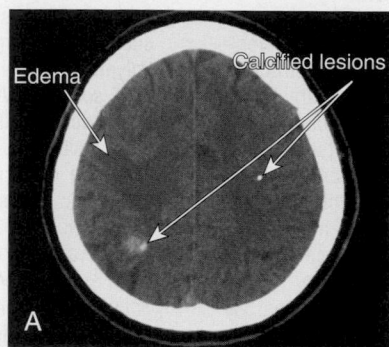

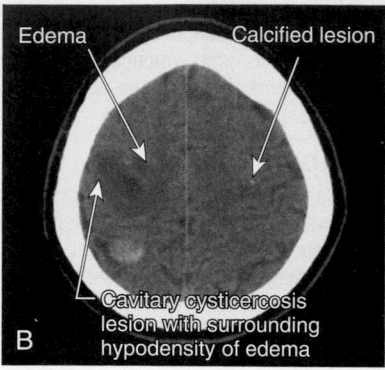

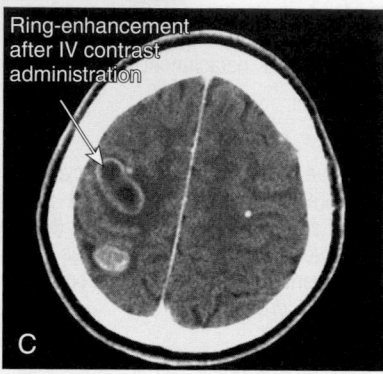

FIGURE 1C-121 Neurocysticercosis. This 40-year-old Bolivian man presented with left-hand weakness. **A, B,** Noncontrast head computed tomography (CT) scan, brain windows. **C,** CT scan with contrast moments later; compare this with (**B**). A slice through the same level of the brain before contrast administration. Hypodense lesions are present, with surrounding hypodensity (*dark gray*) representing edema. Scattered calcifications are also seen, which are a common feature of old neurocysticercosis lesions. Administration of intravenous contrast leads to ring enhancement, a feature of many infectious and inflammatory conditions, including neurocysticercosis, brain abscess, and toxoplasmosis. (From Broder JS: *Diagnostic imaging for the emergency physician,* Philadelphia, 2011, Saunders.)

2. Corticosteroids may decrease inflammation and edema, and should be given whenever antiparasitic therapy is given.
3. Antiparasitic therapy is indicated in the treatment of symptomatic patients with multiple viable brain parenchymal cysticerci. Despite treatment, only 30% to 50% of lesions resolve within 6 months.
4. Calcified cysticerci are generally inactive and do not warrant antiparasitic treatment.
5. Antiparasitic therapy is often unnecessary in patients with single cysts, which are usually self-limited and resolve spontaneously within 6 months.

Antiparasitic therapy:
1. Patients with viable parenchymal or subarachnoid cysts should be treated with albendazole 15 mg/kg/day PO divided twice daily for 7 days or praziquantel 50 mg/kg/day divided three times daily for 28 days. Albendazole is preferred since praziquantel management is more complicated due to an interaction with anticonvulsants such as phenytoin. Patients should receive prednisolone (2 mg/kg/day) or dexamethasone (0.15 mg/kg/day) orally before initiation of antiparasitic therapy. Antiparasitics should be used cautiously in patients with massive cysticercal infection of the brain parenchyma (≥50 cysts) or cysticercal encephalitis. These patients should be managed initially with corticosteroids, and perhaps mannitol, to control intracranial hypertension. Once the inflammation and edema have resolved by MRI, antiparasitics can be administered.
2. Albendazole is considered to be the drug of choice due to slightly better efficacy, greater availability, fewer drug interactions, and lower cost.
3. Combination therapy with praziquantel (50 mg/kg/day) and albendazole (15 mg/kg/day) with dexamethasone (0.1 mg/kg/day) has recently been demonstrated to be more efficacious than albendazole and steroids alone for cyst resolution; seizures persisted despite treatment in many cases.

Surgical therapy:
1. Surgery may be indicated in patients with obstructive hydrocephalus or giant cysts with associated intracranial hypertension.
2. Minimally invasive neurosurgery (neuroendoscopy) for cyst removal and ventricular shunt formation has greatly improved the management of intraventricular neurocysticercosis.

3. Extraparenchymal neurocysticercosis, including ocular, subarachnoid, and intraventricular disease, carries a poor prognosis and requires a more aggressive approach. When feasible, complete surgical excision of lesions remains the definitive therapy.

CHRONIC Rx
- Prolonged antiparasitic therapy does not improve outcomes in neurocysticercosis and may delay calcification of lesions. Antiepileptic medications should be continued for 2 years or 6 to 12 months after CT/MRI resolution of viable cysts, before tapering. In some cases, antiepileptic therapy needs to be continued indefinitely.
- Rare patients with neurocysticercosis develop chronic or recurrent perilesional inflammation, requiring long-term, high-dose steroid therapy. Methotrexate has been reported to be of use as a steroid-sparing agent in this setting.

DISPOSITION
- In seizure-free, stable neurocysticercosis, outpatient management is appropriate.
- Patients with seizures should be restricted from driving.

REFERRAL
- Infectious diseases consultation.
- Neurology consultation in patients with seizures.
- Neurosurgical consultation if extraparenchymal neurocysticercosis or obstructive hydrocephalus is present.

PREVENTION
- Eradication of taeniasis/cysticercosis is possible with implementation of meat inspection, improvement of pig husbandry, and improvement of socioeconomic conditions in endemic areas.
- A porcine vaccine against *T. solium* has been developed and successfully implemented in Peru, Mexico, and Australia.
- There is currently no human vaccine to prevent tapeworm infection or cysticercosis.

PATIENT & FAMILY EDUCATION
- Pork should be inspected for the presence of cysticerci, which are visible in raw meat.
- Pork must be well cooked.
- Proper disposal of human excreta and handwashing are of utmost importance to break the transmission cycle in households.

RELATED CONTENT
Cysticercosis (Patient Information)

AUTHORS: **ELENI PATROZOU, M.D.,** and **STACI A. FISCHER, M.D.**

BASIC INFORMATION

DEFINITION

Infection with cytomegalovirus (CMV), a herpes virus, is common in the general population, with multiple mechanisms for transmission, often during childhood and adolescence. CMV is associated with pregnancy and can be a congenital disease. CMV is also associated with immunocompromised states and may be life threatening.

SYNONYMS

CMV
Heterophil-negative mononucleosis
Cytomegalic inclusion disease virus

ICD-10CM CODES

B25.9	Cytomegaloviral disease, unspecified
P35.1	Congenital cytomegalovirus infection
Z20.820	Contact with and (suspected) exposure to varicella

EPIDEMIOLOGY & DEMOGRAPHICS

- Seroprevalence is widespread: 40% to 100% antibody positivity in adults.
- Increased infection develops perinatally, in day care exposure, and then during reproductive age, related to sexual activity.

ROUTES OF TRANSMISSION

- Blood transfusions.
- Sexually (STDs) via uterus, cervix, and semen.
- Perinatally via breast milk.
- Transplant of organs—bone marrow, kidneys, liver, heart, or lung.
- Saliva.

PHYSICAL FINDINGS & CLINICAL PRESENTATION

CHILDREN: Congenital—25% of infected children with symptoms if congenital:
- Petechial rash.
- Jaundice and/or hepatosplenomegaly.
- Lethargy.
- Respiratory distress.
- CNS involvement, seizures.
Postnatal acquisition:
- CMV mononucleosis.
- Pharyngitis, croup, bronchitis, pneumonia.
HEALTHY ADULTS: Common
- May be asymptomatic.
- CMV mononucleosis similar to EBV mononucleosis.
- Fever—lasting 9 to 30 days—mean of 19 days.
Less common
- Exudative pharyngitis.
- Lymphadenopathy, hepatitis, splenomegaly.
- Interstitial pneumonia (rare).
- Nonspecific rash.
- Thrombocytopenia/hemolytic anemia.
Rare
- Guillain-Barré syndrome.
- Meningoencephalitis.
- Myocarditis.
IMMUNOSUPPRESSED PATIENTS:
- Febrile mononucleosis.

- GI ulcerations, hepatitis, pneumonitis, retinitis, encephalopathy, meningoencephalopathy.
- HIV associated—dementia, demyelination, retinitis, acalculous cholecystitis, adrenalitis, diarrhea, enterocolitis, esophagitis.
- Diabetes associated with pancreatitis.
- Adrenalitis associated with HIV.

ETIOLOGY

CMV infection can remain latent, reactive with immunosuppression.

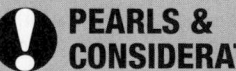 DIAGNOSIS

DIFFERENTIAL DIAGNOSIS

Congenital:
- Acute viral, bacterial, parasitic infections including other congenitally transmitted agents (toxoplasmosis, rubella, syphilis, pertussis, croup, bronchitis).
Acquired:
- EBV mononucleosis.
- Viral hepatitis—A, B, C.
- Cryptosporidiosis.
- Toxoplasmosis.
- *Mycobacterium avium* infections.
- Human herpesvirus 6.
- Acute HIV infection.

WORKUP

- Laboratory confirmation combined with clinical findings often with leukopenia, thrombocytopenia, lymphocytosis. Diagnostic modalities include serologic assays, PCR, detection of CMV PP25 antigen in leukocytes, isolation of virus from body fluids and urine, and cytopathic demonstration of "owl eye" intracellular inclusions.
- Serology:
  1. Detection of CMV-IgM antibodies suggests recent infection. CMV-IgG antibodies usually appear 2 to 3 weeks after infection.
  2. Molecular assays (PCR viral loads): on plasma.
  3. CMV antigenemia assays: detects antibodies to the pp65 protein of the virus in peripheral blood leukocytes. These tests and the PCR tests are used in immunocompromised, AIDS, and transplant patients.
- Cultures: using human fibroblast cultures of blood, CSF, urine, BAL, and biopsy specimens but can take 1 to 6 weeks.
- Funduscopic—necrotic patches with white granular component of retina.
- Biopsy—"owl's eye" inclusion bodies on tissue sample.
- HIV.

IMAGING STUDIES

- Chest radiograph—if pneumonitis suspected, consider bronchoscopy.
- Endoscopy—if GI involvement.
- CT scan/MRI—if CNS involvement.

TREATMENT

NONPHARMACOLOGIC THERAPY

- Strict hand washing and standard precautions limit CMV transmission in health care facilities.

- Antiretroviral therapy (ART) in patients with CD4 count <50/mm^3 for the goal of CD4 >100/mm^3 for a 3- to 6-mo period.

ACUTE GENERAL Rx

For compromised hosts with CMV retinitis or pneumonitis:
- Ganciclovir 5 mg/kg q12h IV x 14 to 21 days, then valganciclovir: 900 mg PO q24h or alternative regimen.
- Ganciclovir intraocular implant plus valganciclovir 900 mg PO q24h or alternative regimen.
- Foscarnet 90 mg/kg q12h x 14 to 21 days, then 90 mg to 120 mg/kg IV q24h or alternative regimen.
- Cidofovir 5 mg/kg IV q day x 14 days, then 5 mg/kg IV q 2 weeks.
- Fomivirsen-salvage therapy for CMV retinitis 300 µg injected into vitreous.

DISPOSITION

- CMV infection in patients who are immunocompromised (especially those with AIDS, bone marrow and solid organ transplant recipients, and disorders of cell-mediated immune function) will need expert, long-term follow-up by an infectious disease specialist or immunologist familiar with the care of such patients.
- CMV mononucleosis, hepatitis, pharyngitis, etc. in immunologically normal hosts are usually self-limiting infections requiring no special follow-up plans.

REFERRAL

- To an ophthalmologist if CMV retinitis is present.
- To an infectious disease specialist or AIDS specialist for patients who are HIV-positive with CMV disease.
- To a cellular immunologist or transplant specialist in the case of CMV infection in a transplant recipient.
- To a pediatric infectious disease specialist for congenital CMV infection.

⚠ PEARLS & CONSIDERATIONS

CMV is ubiquitous in the environment and is asymptomatically shed by latently infected persons with CMV infection, making it difficult to protect patients who are immunocompromised from acquiring this infection.

EBM EVIDENCE

Available at www.expertconsult.com

SUGGESTED READINGS

Available at www.expertconsult.com

AUTHOR: **GLENN G. FORT, M.D., M.P.H.**

ℹ️ BASIC INFORMATION

DEFINITION

Venous thromboembolism is any thromboembolic event occurring within the venous system. Deep vein thrombosis (DVT) is the development of thrombi in the deep veins of the extremities or pelvis.

SYNONYMS

DVT
Venous thromboembolism (VTE) (VTE includes DVT and pulmonary embolism [PE])
Deep venous thrombosis
VTE

ICD-10CM CODES

I82.401	Acute embolism and thrombosis of unspecified deep veins of right lower extremity
I82.402	Acute embolism and thrombosis of unspecified deep veins of left lower extremity
I82.403	Acute embolism and thrombosis of unspecified deep veins of lower extremity, bilateral
I82.621	Acute embolism and thrombosis of deep veins of right upper extremity
I82.622	Acute embolism and thrombosis of deep veins of left upper extremity
I82.623	Acute embolism and thrombosis of deep veins of upper extremity, bilateral

EPIDEMIOLOGY & DEMOGRAPHICS

- Annual incidence of VTE is 0.1% to 0.27%, affecting up to 5% of the population during their lifetimes.
- The risk of recurrent thromboembolism is higher among men than women.
- In the U.S., there are approximately 900,000 DVT events annually. About 5% to 15% of persons with untreated DVT die from pulmonary embolism.
- Venous thromboembolism occurs in nearly 2 cases per 1000 pregnancies and is a leading cause of maternal mortality and morbidity

PHYSICAL FINDINGS & CLINICAL PRESENTATION

- Pain and swelling of the affected extremity
- In lower extremity DVT: leg pain on dorsiflexion of the foot (***Homans' sign***)
- Physical examination may be unremarkable in early DVT

ETIOLOGY

The etiology is often multifactorial (prolonged stasis, coagulation abnormalities, vessel wall trauma). The following are risk factors for DVT:

- Prolonged immobilization (>3 days)
- Postoperative state
- Trauma to pelvis and lower extremities for lower extremity DVT; central line placement for upper extremity DVT
- Birth control pills, high-dose estrogen therapy; conjugated equine estrogen but not esterified estrogen is associated with increased risk of DVT; estrogen plus progestin is associated with doubling the risk of venous thrombosis. The use of bevacizumab is also significantly associated with an increased risk of developing DVT in cancer patients receiving this drug.
- Visceral cancer (lung, pancreas, alimentary tract, genitourinary tract)
- Age >60 yr
- History of thromboembolic disease
- Hematologic disorders (e.g., factor V Leiden mutation [FVL], antithrombin III deficiency, protein C deficiency, protein S deficiency, heparin cofactor II deficiency, sticky platelet syndrome, G20210A prothrombin mutation, lupus anticoagulant, dysfibrinogenemias, anticardiolipin antibody, hyperhomocysteinemia, concurrent homocystinuria, high levels of factors VIII, XI, and single nucleotide polymorphisms [SNPs] such as CYP4V2)
- Pregnancy and early puerperium
- Obesity (BMI >30)
- Congestive heart failure
- Surgery, fracture, or injury involving lower leg or pelvis
- Plaster cast immobilization
- Surgery requiring >30 min of anesthesia
- Gynecologic surgery (particularly gynecologic cancer surgery)
- Recent travel (within 2 wk, lasting ≥2 hr). Every 2 hr spent traveling increases VTE risk by 18%.
- Smoking and abdominal obesity
- Central venous catheter or pacemaker insertion
- Superficial vein thrombosis (10% risk of DVT within 3 mo), varicose veins
- Collagen vascular disease
- Nephrotic syndrome
- Myeloproliferative disorders
- Long-term exposure to particulate air pollution is also associated with altered coagulation function and DVT risk.

🆚 DIAGNOSIS

DIFFERENTIAL DIAGNOSIS

- Postphlebitic syndrome
- Superficial thrombophlebitis
- Ruptured Baker's cyst
- Cellulitis, lymphangitis, Achilles tendinitis
- Hematoma
- Muscle or soft tissue injury, stress fracture
- Varicose veins, lymphedema
- Arterial insufficiency
- Abscess
- Claudication
- Venous stasis

WORKUP

- The clinical diagnosis of DVT is inaccurate. Pain, tenderness, swelling, or color changes are not specific for DVT.
- Clinical prediction rules can be used to establish pretest probability of DVT. The Wells prediction rules for DVT and for pulmonary embolism are described in Box 1D-1. These rules perform better in younger patients without a history of DVT and in those without comorbidities. In younger patients without associated comorbidities and a low pretest probability using Wells criteria and a negative high-sensitivity D-dimer test, the diagnosis of DVT can be reasonably excluded.
- Compression ultrasonography (CUS; Fig. E1D-1) is preferred as the initial study to diagnose DVT in patients with intermediate to high pretest probability. An initial negative test limited to the proximal leg should be repeated after 5 days (if the clinical suspicion of DVT persists) to exclude DVT that is propagating proximally from the calf. Comprehensive ultrasonography (whole-leg CUS) is a more extensive test that examines the deep veins from the inguinal ligament to the level of the malleolus. Literature reports indicate that it may be safe to withhold anticoagulation after negative results on comprehensive duplex ultrasonography in nonpregnant patients with a suspected first episode of symptomatic DVT of the leg.

LABORATORY TESTS

- Laboratory tests are not specific for DVT. Baseline prothrombin time (INR), partial thromboplastin time, and platelet count should be obtained on all patients before starting anticoagulation. D-dimer testing is

---

BOX 1D-1 Wells Prediction Rule for Diagnosing Deep Venous Thrombosis: Clinical Evaluation Table for Predicting Pretest Probability of Deep Venous Thrombosis*

Clinical Characteristic	Score
Active cancer (treatment ongoing, within previous 6 mo, or palliative)	1
Paralysis, paresis, or recent plaster immobilization of the lower extremities	1
Recently bedridden >3 days or major surgery within 12 wk requiring general or regional anesthesia	1
Localized tenderness along the distribution of the deep venous system	1
Entire leg swollen	1
Calf swelling 3 cm larger than asymptomatic side (measured 10 cm below tibial tuberosity)	1
Pitting edema confined to the symptomatic leg	1
Collateral superficial veins (nonvaricose)	1
Alternative diagnosis at least as likely as deep venous thrombosis	22

*Clinical probability: low, ≤0; intermediate, 1-2; high, ≥3. In patients with symptoms in both legs, the more symptomatic leg is used.
Reprinted from Wells PS et al: Value assessment of pretest probability of deep-vein thrombosis in clinical management, *Lancet* 351:1795-1798, 1997.

sensitive but not specific for DVT. A negative result (D-dimer <0.5 mcg/ml) can exclude the diagnosis in a patient with low probability of DVT, but a positive result (≥0.5 mcg/ml) mandates additional testing with venous ultrasonography.

- Use of D-dimer assay by ELISA is useful in the management of suspected DVT. The combination of a normal D-dimer study on presentation together with a normal compression venous ultrasound is useful to exclude DVT. DVT can be ruled out in patients who are clinically unlikely to have DVT and who have a negative D-dimer test. Compressive ultrasonography can be safely omitted in such patients. Fig. E1D-2 is an algorithm for the diagnosis of DVT.
- Laboratory evaluation of young patients with DVT, patients with recurrent thrombosis without obvious causes, and those with a family history of thrombosis should include protein S (both total and free PS), protein C, fibrinogen, antithrombin III level, lupus anticoagulant, anticardiolipin antibodies, anti-b2 glycoprotein1, factor V Leiden, factor VIII, factor IX, and fasting plasma homocysteine levels. HIT antibody may also be useful in the correct context (heparin exposure and abrupt onset of unexplained decrease in platelet count, whether thrombocytopenic or not). It is important to remember that the lupus anticoagulant assay and antithrombin, protein C, protein S, and dysfibrinogenemia testing cannot be properly interpreted if the patient is already on warfarin, whereas anticardiolipin antibody test, prothrombin G20210A factor VII:C, factor V Leiden, and PT polymorphism can be performed when the patient is on warfarin.

IMAGING STUDIES

- Compression ultrasonography (CUS) is generally preferred as the initial study because it is noninvasive and can be repeated serially (useful to monitor suspected acute DVT); it offers good sensitivity for detecting proximal vein thrombosis (in the popliteal or femoral vein) (see Fig. E1D-1). Its disadvantages are poor visualization of deep iliac and pelvic veins and poor sensitivity in isolated or nonocclusive calf vein thrombi. Whole-leg compression ultrasound can generally exclude proximal and distal DVT in a single evaluation. Withholding anticoagulation following a single negative whole-leg CUS is associated with a relatively low risk of venous thromboembolism (3.5% of inpatients will develop DVT) during a 3-mo follow-up.
- Contrast venography is the gold standard for evaluation of DVT of the lower extremity. It is, however, invasive and painful. Additional disadvantages are the increased risk of phlebitis, new thrombosis, renal failure, and hypersensitivity reaction to contrast media; it also gives poor visualization of the deep femoral vein in the thigh and the internal iliac vein and its tributaries.
- Magnetic resonance direct thrombus imaging (MRDTI) is an accurate noninvasive test for diagnosis of DVT. It is particularly useful in

suspected DVT patients with leg casts, which prevent CUS, and in pregnant patients with positive D-dimer and negative CUS (Fig. E1D-3). Current limitations are its cost and lack of widespread availability.

Rx TREATMENT

NONPHARMACOLOGIC THERAPY

- Gradual resumption of normal activity. Immobility promotes stasis and propagation of DVT. Patients should get up and walk as tolerated. The theoretical risk that ambulation may dislodge thrombi in the legs, precipitating PE, is unfounded.
- Patient education on anticoagulant therapy and associated risks.

ACUTE GENERAL Rx

- Initial treatment of DVT requires therapeutic doses of heparin (low-molecular-weight heparin [LMWH] or unfractionated). LMWH is preferred due to ease of administration, less hemorrhage, and significantly fewer deaths. Unfractionated heparin is recommended in patients with renal insufficiency because LMWH is predominantly excreted in the urine.
- LMWH is generally administered for 5 to 7 days. Recommended dose of enoxaparin is 1 mg/kg q12h SC. Once-daily fondaparinux, a synthetic analogue of heparin, is also as effective and safe as twice-daily enoxaparin in the initial treatment of patients with symptomatic DVT. Once systemic anticoagulation is initiated, vitamin K antagonist warfarin or oral factor V inhibitors are initiated. When using warfarin, it is normally started on the same day as heparin and is titrated to maintain an INR between 2 and 3. Warfarin therapy at 10 mg daily for 2 days may be initiated in healthy patients with acute DVT. This higher dose helps to achieve therapeutic INR sooner and decreases LMWH doses needed as compared to the 5 mg/day dose. After ≥5 days, heparin is stopped and warfarin is continued as monotherapy. Long-term LMWH may be preferable to warfarin in patients with cancer or those whose INR is difficult to control. Alternatives to warfarin may include the oral factor Xa inhibitors rivaroxaban, apixaban, or edoxaban, or dabigatran, a direct oral thrombin inhibitor. These new anticoagulants are noninferior to warfarin, do not require periodic lab monitoring, and have a relatively low bleeding risk. They may eventually become preferred agents for extended treatment of venous thromboembolism.
- Outpatient treatment of DVT is appropriate for patients without prior DVT, thrombophilic conditions, or substantial comorbidity, but not for those who are pregnant or likely not to adhere to therapy.
- Exclusions from outpatient treatment of DVT include patients with potential high complication risk (e.g., hemoglobin <7, platelet count <75,000, guaiac-positive stool, recent cerebrovascular accident or noncutaneous surgery, noncompliance).

- Compression stockings are effective in reducing the incidence of postthrombotic syndrome and should be used starting within 1 mo of proximal DVT and continued for at least 1 yr after diagnosis.
- Insertion of an inferior vena cava filter to prevent pulmonary embolism is recommended in patients with contraindications to anticoagulation (e.g., hemorrhagic stroke, active internal bleeding, pregnancy), HIT in a patient with an active VTE/PE, recurrent PE despite adequate anticoagulant therapy, emergent surgery in patient with DVT, presence of free-floating iliofemoral thrombus, lower IVC thrombosis (incipient embolization), and chronic pulmonary (thromboembolic) hypertension with limited pulmonary reserve.
- Thrombolytic therapy (streptokinase) can be used in rare cases (unless contraindicated) in patients with extensive iliofemoral venous thrombosis and a low risk of bleeding. There are concerns about hemorrhagic complications related to the large doses of thrombolytics required in systemic thrombolysis for DVT (2% to 10% risk of major hemorrhagic complications).
- Other treatment modalities for DVT include surgical thrombectomy and catheter-directed thrombolysis (CDT). Thromboreduction by surgical thrombectomy is effective but invasive and expensive. CDT is also invasive, carries a bleeding risk, and will generally require ICU admission.

CHRONIC Rx

- The optimal duration of anticoagulant therapy varies with the cause of DVT and the patient's risk factors. The risk of recurrence is low if VTE is provoked by surgery, intermediate if provoked by a nonsurgical risk factor, and high if unprovoked. These risks should determine whether patients with VTE should undergo short-term vs. indefinite treatment.
- Therapy for 3 mo is generally satisfactory in patients with reversible risk factors (low-risk group). A high D-dimer level measured after 3 mo of anticoagulation in patients with unprovoked DVT should favor a longer duration of therapy. The American College of Chest Physicians Guidelines suggests that patients with first unprovoked VTE receive indefinite anticoagulation unless their bleeding risk is high.
- The risk of recurrence in patients with a first unprovoked VTE who have negative D-dimer results is not low enough to justify stopping anticoagulant therapy in men but may be low enough in some cases to justify stopping therapy in women who were taking estrogen at the time of initial VTE.[1]
- Anticoagulation for 6 mo is recommended for patients with idiopathic venous thrombosis or medical risk factors for DVT (intermediate-risk group). About 20% of patients with

[1]Kearon C, et al: D-Dimer testing to select patients with a first unprovoked venous thromboembolism who can stop anticoagulant therapy: A cohort study. *Ann Intern Med* 162:27–34, 2015.

unprovoked venous thromboembolism have a recurrence within 2 yr after the withdrawal of oral anticoagulant therapy. Use of daily low-dose aspirin after discontinuation of anticoagulant treatment may provide a modest reduction in DVT risk.

- Indefinite anticoagulation is necessary in patients with DVT associated with active cancer; long-term anticoagulation is also indicated in patients with inherited thrombophilia (e.g., deficiency of antithrombin III, protein C or S antibody), high factor VIII levels, antiphospholipid antibody, and those with recurrent episodes of idiopathic DVT (high-risk group). Long-term anticoagulation should also be considered in the presence of comorbidities such as paroxysmal nocturnal hemoglobinuria (PNH), SLE (especially with nephrotic syndrome), some myeloproliferative disorders, IBD, and Cushing's syndrome.

- Measurement of D-dimer after withdrawal of oral anticoagulation may be useful to estimate the risk of recurrence in selected patients. In patients with a first unprovoked DVT, positive D-dimer test results after cessation of anticoagulation predict recurrence, regardless of test timing or patient's age. Patients with a first spontaneous DVT and a D-dimer level <250 mg/ml after withdrawal of oral anticoagulation have a low risk of DVT recurrence. Risk is lower in women than in men. Recent trials show that in patients who have completed at least 3 mo of anticoagulation for a first episode of unprovoked DVT and after approximately 2 yr of follow-up, a negative D-dimer result is associated with a 3.5% annual risk of recurrent disease, whereas a positive D-dimer result is associated with an 8.9% annual risk for recurrence. Hence, elevated D-dimer levels would be an indication for prolonged therapy (for 1 or 2 more yr at a minimum).

- The presence of residual thrombosis on ultrasonography when warfarin therapy is discontinued is also associated with an increased risk for subsequent recurrent DVT; a recent trial showed that tailoring the duration of anticoagulation on the basis of the persistence of residual thrombi on ultrasonography may reduce the rate of recurrent DVT. Additional trials are needed before this approach can be adapted for all patients.

- Patients with DVT and pulmonary embolism are at high risk of recurrence whenever anticoagulation is discontinued; therefore, many experts recommend prolonged anticoagulation in this population group, especially if other risk factors for recurrence are present.

ⓘ PEARLS & CONSIDERATIONS

COMMENTS

- The prevalence of occult cancer is low among patients with a first unprovoked venous embolism. Routine screening with CT

of the abdomen and pelvis does not provide a clinically significant benefit.[2]

- When using heparin, there is a risk of heparin-induced thrombocytopenia (HIT) (with unfractionated more so than with LMWH). Platelet count should be obtained initially and repeated every 3 days while on heparin.

- ***PROPHYLAXIS OF DVT:*** Recommended in all patients at risk (e.g., low-molecular-weight heparin [enoxaparin 30 mg SC bid or fondaparinux 2.5 mg SC daily] after major trauma, postsurgery of hip and knee; enoxaparin 40 mg SC qd post-abdominal surgery in patients with moderate to high DVT risk; gradient elastic stockings alone or in combination with intermittent pneumatic compression [IPC] boots following neurosurgery). Graduated compression stockings (GCSs) are effective for preventing air-travel-related DVT and in reducing the risk of DVT in patients hospitalized for conditions other than stroke. The type of GCSs is also important because proximal DVT occurs more often in patients with stroke who wear below-knee stockings than in those who wear high-length stockings. The new oral anticoagulants (rivaroxaban, apixaban, etc.) are effective for thromboprophylaxis after THR and TKR. However, their clinical benefits over LMWH are marginal, they are more expensive, and they lack antidotes for timely reversal in case of bleeding.

- ***RECURRENT THROMBOEMBOLISM:*** The risk of recurrent venous thromboembolism in heterozygous carriers of factor V Leiden and a first spontaneous venous thromboembolism is similar to that of non-carriers of factor V Leiden; therefore, heterozygous patients should receive secondary thromboprophylaxis for a similar length of time as patients without factor V Leiden.

- ***POSTTHROMBOTIC SYNDROME:*** Approximately 20% to 50% of patients with DVT develop postthrombotic syndrome characterized by leg edema, pain, venous ectasia, skin induration, and ulceration. Patients with extensive DVT and those with more severe postthrombotic manifestations 1 month after DVT have poorer long-term outcomes. Recent trials have shown that compression stockings after DVT do not prevent postthrombotic syndrome.

- Exercise following DVT is reasonable because it improves flexibility of the affected leg and does not increase symptoms in patients with postthrombotic syndrome.

- Previously undiagnosed cancer is frequent in patients with newly diagnosed DVT. A cancer screening strategy should be considered in all patients with unprovoked venous thromboembolism.

- ***UPPER EXTREMITY DVT:*** It is less common than lower extremity DVT and is seen more frequently in patients requiring central venous catheters or wires. It confers risk for

---

[2]Carrier M, Lazo-Langner A, Shivakumar S et al: Screening for occult cancer in unprovoked venous thromboembolism, N Engl J Med 373:697-704, 2015

mortality, recurrent thromboembolic events, and post-thrombotic syndrome similar to that of lower extremity DVT. It is classified as primary upper extremity DVT ***(Paget-Schroetter syndrome)***, defined as a thrombus in the axillary and subclavian veins in absence of identifiable thrombosis risk factors. It accounts for 20% of upper extremity DVT cases and may be due to an underlying anatomic abnormality at the thoracic outlet in combination with local hypercoagulability due to venous stretching or perivascular fibrosis from recurrent venous compression. Secondary upper extremity DVT is defined as any DVT related to a predisposing factor (e.g., insertion of central venous catheter, wires, or other devices, malignancy). In patients with secondary upper extremity DVT removal of the catheter is not routinely recommended but is warranted if there is a catheter malfunction or infection, if anticoagulation therapy is contraindicated or has failed, or if the catheter is no longer needed. Anticoagulation therapy in upper extremity DVT consists of use of vitamin K antagonists except in patients with cancer, for whom low-molecular-weight heparin is preferred. Optimal duration of anticoagulation treatment in upper extremity DVT is 3 to 6 mo (including in those in whom a central catheter has been removed).

- ***DVT THERAPY IN PREGNANCY***
Vitamin K antagonists such as warfarin are contraindicated in pregnancy. Low-molecular-weight heparins are safe and effective. Typical agents used in pregnancy include dalteparin (200 IU per kilogram of body weight daily or 100 IU per kilogram twice daily) or enoxaparin (1.5 mg per kilogram daily or 1 mg per kilogram twice daily).

- ***REVERSAL OF ANTICOAGULATION:***
-Vitamin K (1 mg PO or 2 mg IV) can be used to reverse elevated INR (3 to 6) from warfarin when elective or urgent procedures are needed. The administration of vitamin K can take more than 24 hr to fully restore vitamin K dependent coagulation factors II, VII, IX, and X. The American College of Chest Physicians recommends the following guidelines for managing elevated INRs or bleeding in patients receiving vitamin A antagonist therapy:

1. INR between 4.5 and 10 and no significant bleeding: omit dose and monitor the next day, routine use of vitamin K is not recommended

2. INR >10 and no significant bleeding: hold vitamin K antagonist, give 5 to 10 mg orally of vitamin K. Monitor the next day and use additional vitamin K if necessary. Resume therapy at lower dose when INR therapeutic.

3. Serious bleeding at any elevation of INR: hold vitamin K antagonist and supplement with prothrombin complex concentrates (PCC). Give vitamin K (10 mg by slow IV infusion over 30 min to reduce the risk of anaphylaxis). Vitamin K can be repeated

every 12 hr. PCC composition in the United States (3-factor PCC) includes clotting factors II, IX, and X but minimal amounts of factor VII (unlike PCC products available outside of the United States [4-factor PCC], which have a significant amount of factor VII). In order to replace the low factor VII some clinicians in the United States will also give fresh frozen plasma (FFP) in addition to vitamin K and PCC in patients with life-threatening warfarin-related bleeding.

- **SPECIFIC REVERSAL AGENTS FOR NON–VITAMIN K ANTAGONIST ANTICOAGULANTS**
  - Idarucizumab, an antibody fragment given at a dose of 5 g IV, has been shown to completely reverse the anticoagulant effect of dabigatran within minutes.[3]

[3]Pollack CV, Reilly PA, Eikleboom J et al: Idarucizumab for dabigatran reversal, N Engl J Med 373:511-20, 2015

- The anticoagulant activity of factor Xa inhibitors apixaban, rivaroxaban, and edoxaban can be rapidly reversed with IV administration of andexanet alfa.[4]

 **EVIDENCE**

Available at www.expertconsult.com

SUGGESTED READINGS

Available at www.expertconsult.com

[4]Siegal DM, et al.: Andexanet Alfa for the Reversal of Factor Xa Inhibitor Activity, N Engl J Med 373:2413-2424, 2015.

RELATED CONTENT

Deep Vein Thrombosis (DVT) (Patient Information)
Antiphospholipid Antibody Syndrome (Related Key Topic)
Hypercoagulable State (Related Key Topic)
Pulmonary Embolism (Related Key Topic)

AUTHOR: **FRED F. FERRI, M.D.**

BASIC INFORMATION

DEFINITION

Delayed puberty is clinically defined as the absence of or incomplete development of secondary sexual characteristics by an age at which 95% of the population begins to mature sexually. For girls, a delay is defined as an absence of breast development by age 13 or primary amenorrhea by age 16. For boys, a delay is classified as an absence of testicular enlargement by age 14.

SYNONYMS

Pubertal delay

ICD-10CM CODES
E30.0 Delayed puberty

EPIDEMIOLOGY & DEMOGRAPHICS

PREVALENCE: The actual prevalence and incidence for children presenting with delayed puberty is unknown. Delayed puberty is more common in boys.

GENETICS: Constitutional pubertal delay (CPD) often runs in families. Although specific gene mutations have yet to be identified, studies have shown that 50% to 75% of patients with CPD have at least one parent who experienced a delay in puberty. The inheritance pattern for CPD is thought to be autosomal dominant.

PHYSICAL FINDINGS & CLINICAL PRESENTATION

- Girls with pubertal delay have an absence of breast development by age 13, absence of menarche by age 16, or absence of menarche within 3 years of thelarche. Boys with pubertal delay show no evidence of testicular enlargement, further defined as testes <2.5 cm, by age 14. Absence of pubic and/or axillary hair is common, as is lack of growth spurt.
- Patients with a constitutional delay in puberty are short in stature with a normal growth rate and otherwise good health.
- Boys often fall below the 10th percentile on a height chart with normal rate of growth between 4 and 6 cm per yr.

ETIOLOGY

Causes for pubertal delay (Fig. 1D-4) can be separated into four categories (from most to least common):
1. Constitutional delay, which is a temporary delay in puberty that is seen mostly in boys and is genetic. Patients are typically short in stature with normal growth rate and appropriate skeletal age.
2. Functional hypogonadotropic hypogonadism secondary to malnutrition or chronic disease. Celiac sprue, inflammatory bowel disease (IBD), hypothyroidism, diabetes mellitus, cystic fibrosis, and eating disorders such as anorexia nervosa are examples of illnesses that may cause a temporary, reversible delay in puberty.

Clinical suspicion is warranted when underweight children present with pubertal delay.
3. Hypergonadotropic hypogonadism caused by primary gonadal failure. Congenital disorders such as cryptorchidism; chromosomal disorders such as gonadal dysgenesis, Klinefelter's syndrome, and Turner's syndrome; and acquired causes secondary to chemotherapy, pelvic radiation, and gonadal surgery are organic dysfunctions that result in gonadal failure despite adequate hypothalamic-pituitary function. In this group of disorders, luteinizing hormone (LH) and follicle-stimulating hormone (FSH) levels are elevated yet cannot stimulate ovaries and testicles to produce estrogen and testosterone, respectively, leading to hypogonadism and absence of secondary sex characteristics.
4. Permanent hypogonadotropic hypogonadism secondary to genetic or acquired defects along the hypothalamic-pituitary-gonadal (HPG) axis. Kallmann's syndrome is a genetic mutation in *KAL1* on the X chromosome and is responsible for the migration of gonadotropin-releasing hormone and olfactory neurons into the hypothalamus. Children with Kallmann's syndrome typically present with pubertal delay and anosmia. Other mutations such as *FGFR1* and *DAX1* have been linked to congenital gonadotropin deficiencies and pubertal delay. Acquired defects such as hemochromatosis, sickle cell anemia, and pituitary tumors can cause delayed puberty and other hypothalamic syndromes, including Prader-Willi. Table E1D-1 provides a classification of puberty and sexual infantilism.

DIAGNOSIS

DIFFERENTIAL DIAGNOSIS

Normal or low serum LH and FSH
- Constitutional pubertal delay
- Functional hypogonadotropic hypogonadism
  1. Malnutrition or eating disorder
  2. Strenuous exercise
  3. Chronic illness (e.g., hypothyroidism, celiac disease, IBD, cystic fibrosis)
- Hypopituitarism
  1. Panhypopituitarism
  2. Isolated gonadotropin deficiency
  3. Kallmann's syndrome (associated with anosmia)
  4. Prader-Willi syndrome
- Hyperprolactinemia
  1. Pituitary adenoma
  2. Drug-associated (e.g., cannabis, cocaine)

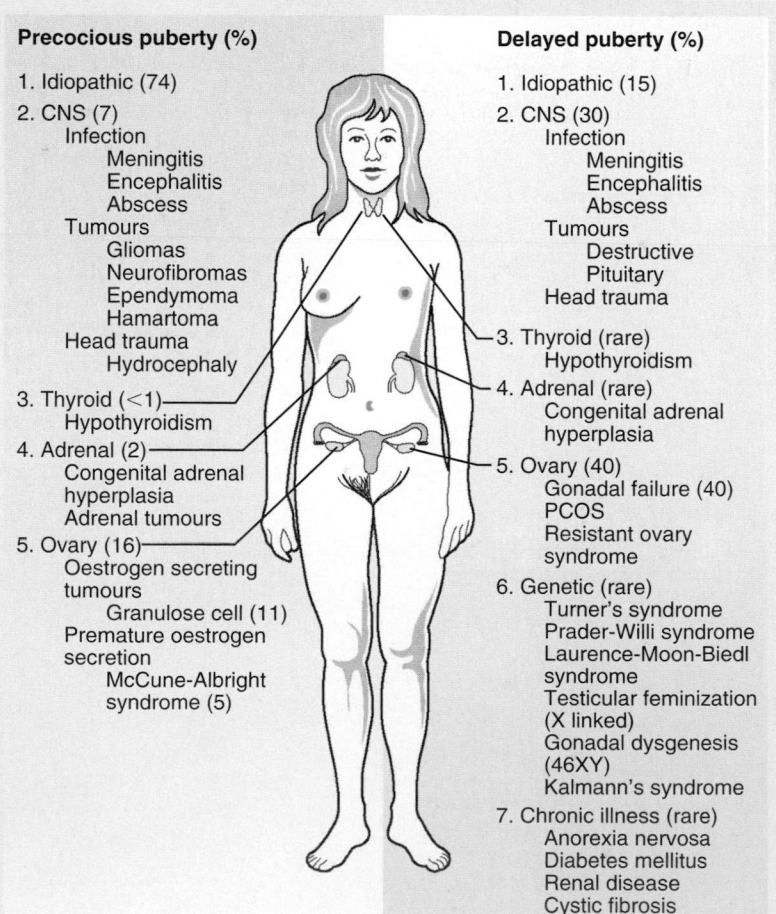

Precocious puberty (%)

1. Idiopathic (74)
2. CNS (7)
   Infection
       Meningitis
       Encephalitis
       Abscess
   Tumours
       Gliomas
       Neurofibromas
       Ependymoma
       Hamartoma
   Head trauma
       Hydrocephaly
3. Thyroid (<1)
   Hypothyroidism
4. Adrenal (2)
   Congenital adrenal hyperplasia
   Adrenal tumours
5. Ovary (16)
   Oestrogen secreting tumours
       Granulose cell (11)
   Premature oestrogen secretion
       McCune-Albright syndrome (5)

Delayed puberty (%)

1. Idiopathic (15)
2. CNS (30)
   Infection
       Meningitis
       Encephalitis
       Abscess
   Tumours
       Destructive
       Pituitary
   Head trauma
3. Thyroid (rare)
   Hypothyroidism
4. Adrenal (rare)
   Congenital adrenal hyperplasia
5. Ovary (40)
   Gonadal failure (40)
   PCOS
   Resistant ovary syndrome
6. Genetic (rare)
   Turner's syndrome
   Prader-Willi syndrome
   Laurence-Moon-Biedl syndrome
   Testicular feminization (X linked)
   Gonadal dysgenesis (46XY)
   Kalmann's syndrome
7. Chronic illness (rare)
   Anorexia nervosa
   Diabetes mellitus
   Renal disease
   Cystic fibrosis

FIGURE 1D-4 Causes of precocious puberty and delayed puberty. (From Pariseai M: Gynaecological endocrinology. In *Obstetrics and gynaecology*, St. Louis, 2008, Mosby.)

Increased serum gonadotropins
- Hypergonadotropic hypogonadism
  1. Turner's syndrome (gonadal dysgenesis)
  2. Klinefelter's syndrome
  3. Gonadal dysgenesis
  4. Noonan syndrome
  5. Bilateral gonadal failure
     1. Primary testicular failure
     2. Anorchia
     3. Premature ovarian failure
     4. Resistant ovary syndrome
     5. Radiation, chemotherapy
     6. Trauma
     7. Infections (e.g., mumps, orchitis)
  Other conditions
- Androgen sensitivity syndrome
- Steroidogenic enzyme defects

WORKUP

- Given the extensive differential diagnosis for pubertal delay, a systematic and focused approach is necessary. Table E1D-2 describes differential diagnostic features of delayed puberty and sexual infantilism. A careful history, including family and social history, can identify eating, exercise habits, chronic illnesses, weight loss, poor weight gain, changes in bowel habits, and parental history of pubertal delay. Figs. 1D-5 and 1D-6 describe an algorithm for the evaluation of delayed puberty in males and females.

- Growth measurement should include height and weight, a growth chart to assess rate of growth, and calculation of the sex-adjusted midparental height that represents the statistically probable adult height for the child.
  1. For boys, add 2.5 inches (6.5 cm) from the mean of the parents' heights. For girls, subtract 2.5 inches (6.5 cm) from the mean of the parents' heights.
  2. Physical exam can reveal signs of sexual maturation, stigmata of congenital syndromes, and nutritional deficiencies. It is important to include a neurologic (visual fields, ophthalmologic), thyroid, respiratory, cardiovascular, and abdominal examination, in addition to evaluation of the Tanner stages of sexual characteristics.

LABORATORY TESTS

- Serum LH, FSH, testosterone, and estradiol can help distinguish disorders of congenital or acquired gonadal failure from other causes. By the age of 10 to 12 yr gonadal failure produces elevated levels of serum LH and FSH. If levels are low or normal, constitutional delay is the most common diagnosis.
- Chromosomal analysis is indicated if there is a suspicion of gonadal dysgenesis or Klinefelter's syndrome.

- Screening studies include complete blood count, erythrocyte sedimentation rate, prolactin, thyroid-stimulating hormone, and free thyroxine level.
- Endocrinologist may incorporate further studies such as IGF-1 to screen for growth hormone disorders and GnRH stimulation testing.

IMAGING STUDIES

Bone age skeletal radiograph of the left hand and wrist determines skeletal age, which is delayed in constitutional delay and GnRH deficiency. MRI of the head should be considered if there is high clinical suspicion for tumors of pituitary or hypothalamic origin. Pelvic ultrasound can be helpful in detecting intraabdominal testes and evaluating müllerian anatomy.

Rx TREATMENT

- Treat underlying cause.
- Constitutional delay can be managed with reassurance that the delay will have no effect on the final adult height or overall development. Short-term hormonal therapy can be used to hasten puberty if the delay is causing severe psychosocial difficulties. Oxandrolone orally can be given daily or IM depot testosterone q6wk for 3-6 mo for boys to improve velocity of growth. Girls can receive oral estradiol once daily for 3-6 mo.

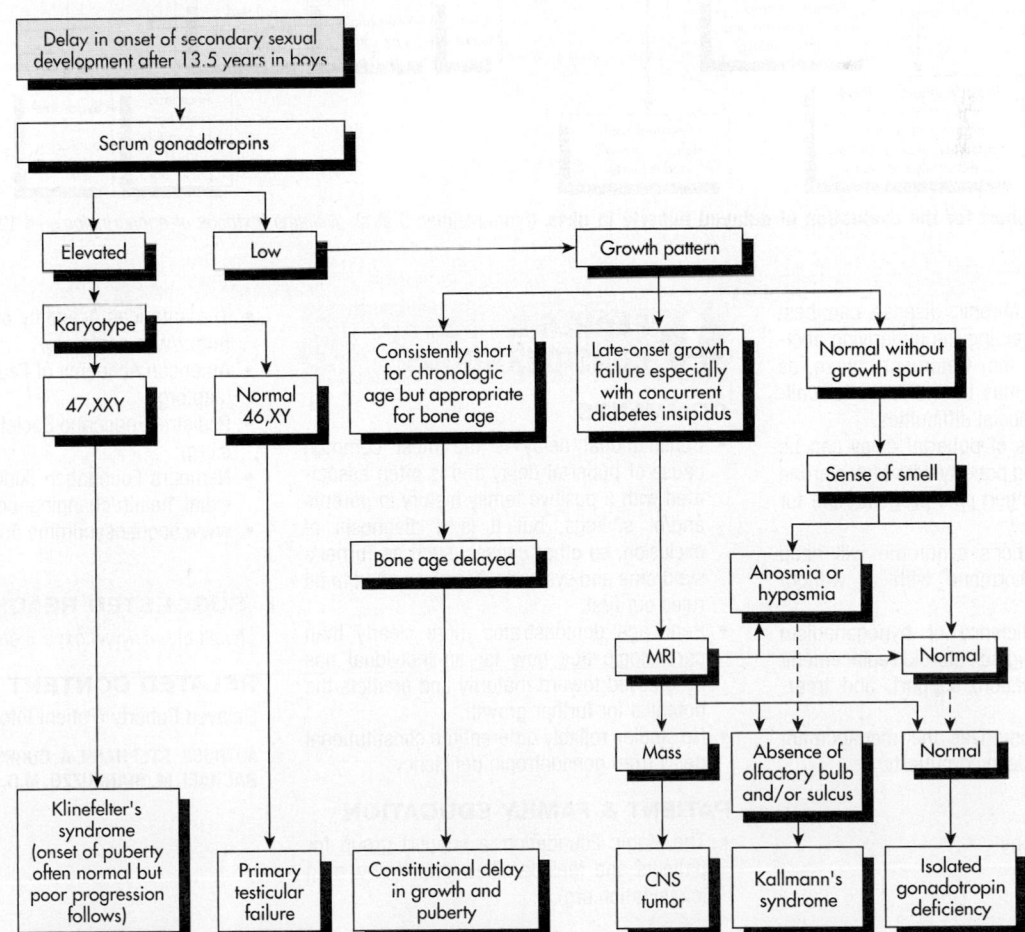

FIGURE 1D-5 Flow chart for the evaluation of delayed puberty in boys. (From Melmed S et al: *Williams textbook of endocrinology*, ed 12, Philadelphia, 2011, Saunders.)

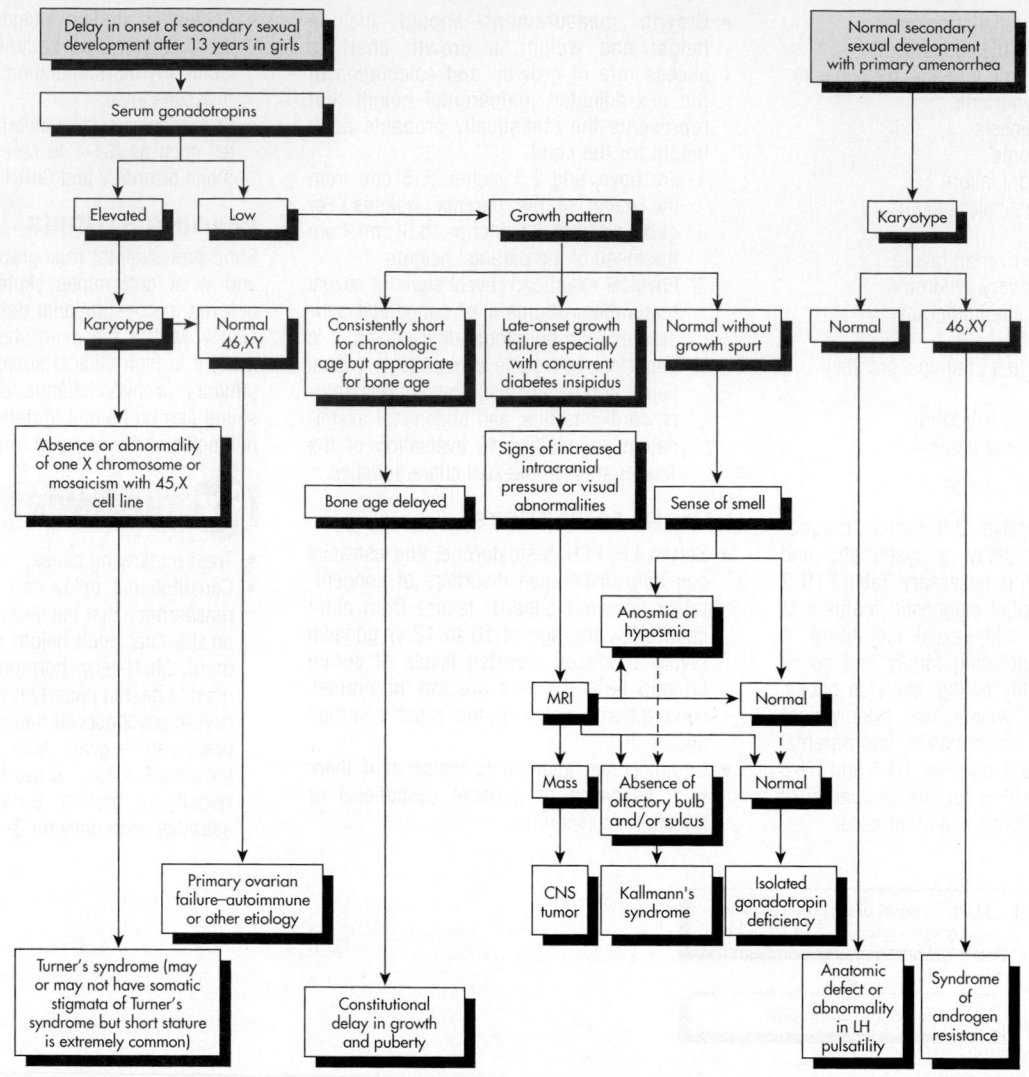

FIGURE 1D-6 Flow chart for the evaluation of delayed puberty in girls. (From Melmed S et al: *Williams textbook of endocrinology*, ed 12, Philadelphia, 2011, Saunders.)

- Malnutrition and chronic disease can best be treated by correcting the underlying etiology. A short (3-6 mo) treatment course, as described above, may be indicated for children with psychosocial difficulties.
- Permanent causes of pubertal delay can be treated by inducing puberty with testosterone for boys and estrogen plus progesterone for girls.
- Patients with Turner's syndrome will need adjunct growth hormone with or without oxandrolone.
- Gonadotropin deficiency or hypogonadism may require lifelong sex steroid replacement.
- Psychosocial evaluation, support, and treatment as needed.
- Table E1D-3 summarizes the management and treatment of delayed puberty.

REFERRAL

Pediatric endocrinology

 **PEARLS & CONSIDERATIONS**

COMMENTS

- Constitutional delay is the most common cause of pubertal delay and is often associated with a positive family history in parents and/or siblings, but it is a diagnosis of exclusion, so other causes, such as Turner's syndrome and systemic disorders, need to be ruled out first.
- Bone age demonstrates more clearly than chronologic age how far an individual has progressed toward maturity and predicts the potential for further growth.
- No studies reliably differentiate constitutional delay from gonadotropin deficiency.

PATIENT & FAMILY EDUCATION

- The Magic Foundation, a support group for patients and their families (http://www.magicfoundation.org)

- The American Academy of Family Physicians (http://www.aafp.org)
- American Academy of Pediatrics (http://www.aap.org)
- Pediatric Endocrine Society (http://www.lwpes.org)
- Nemours Foundation (kiddshealth.rog/teen/sexual_health/changing_body/puberty)
- www.noonansyndrome.org

SUGGESTED READINGS

Available at www.expertconsult.com

RELATED CONTENT

Delayed Puberty (Patient Information)

AUTHORS: **STEPHANIE A. CURRY, M.D.,** and **RACHAEL M. BIANCUZZO, M.D.**

Diseases and Disorders

I

 **BASIC INFORMATION**

DEFINITION

The American Psychiatric Association's *Diagnostic and Statistical Manual*, 5th edition (DSM 5) defines delirium as:
- Disturbance of consciousness with reduced ability to focus, sustain, or shift attention.
- The disturbance develops over a short period of time (usually hours to days) and tends to fluctuate during the course of a day.
- An additional disturbance in cognition (e.g., memory deficit, disorganization, language, visuospatial ability, or perception).
- A change in cognition or development of a perceptual disturbance that is not better accounted for by a preexisting, established, or evolving dementia.
- There is evidence from history, physical exam, or lab findings that the disturbance is caused by medical condition, substance intoxication or withdrawal (i.e., due to a drug of abuse or to a medication), or exposure to a toxin, or is due to multiple etiologies.

SYNONYMS

Acute confusional state
Toxic or metabolic encephalopathy

THEORIES REGARDING PATHOPHYSIOLOGY

- Neuroinflammation, with increased permeability of the blood-brain barrier.
- Acetylcholine deficiency.
- Other neurotransmitter imbalances, including excesses of norepinephrine, serotonin, and, most important, dopamine.

CLASSIFICATION

Hyperactive, hypoactive, and mixed subtype.

ICD-10CM CODES
F05	Delirium, not induced by alcohol and other psychoactive substances
F05.9	Delirium, unspecified
F06.0	Organic hallucinosis
F05.8	Other delirium
F05.0	Delirium not superimposed on dementia
F05.1	Delirium superimposed on dementia

EPIDEMIOLOGY & DEMOGRAPHICS

Nearly 30% of older patients experience delirium at some time during the hospital course. In old surgical patients, the risk varies from 10% to 50%. Hypoactive is more common. Delirium is the most common mental disorder in patients with medical illness. Any age, race, or gender can be affected. Pediatric delirium is often missed but remains important because delirium is associated with longer hospital stays, decreased cognitive performance, and increased mortality. Risk factors include extremes of age, severe pain, illicit substance use, surgery, dementia, and kidney or liver failure (Tables E1D-1 and 1D-2).

PHYSICAL FINDINGS & CLINICAL PRESENTATION

- One of the earliest symptoms is change in level of awareness and ability to focus, sustain, or shift attention. Symptoms may differ both among patients and within one patient. Family members or caregivers report that the patient "isn't acting quite right." Symptoms may include poor attention, sleepiness, agitation, or psychosis.
- Acuteness of presentation helps in differentiating delirium with dementia. Change in cognition, perceptual problems (such as visual, auditory, or somatosensory hallucination usually with lack of insight), memory loss, disorientation, difficulty with speech and language. It is important to ascertain from family member or caregivers the patient's level of functioning before onset of delirium.
- Elderly patients with delirium often do not look sick, but patients with delirium are sick by definition.
- There is often a prodrome phase that later blends into hypoactive delirium or erupts into an agitated confusional state.
- Physical examination should be performed, focusing on signs of infection, dehydration, or chronic disease that may be exacerbated. Vital signs are key. Consider using the Mini-Mental Status Exam or the Montreal Cognitive Assessment.
- Fig. 1D-1 describes an algorithm for evaluation of mental status changes in an older patient.

ETIOLOGY

Can be multifactorial; often falls into one of the following categories:
- Drugs: benzodiazepines are the worst offenders, but other drugs such as narcotics, anticholinergics, beta-blockers, steroids, nonsteroidal anti-inflammatory drugs, digoxin, cimetidine can cause delirium; also, withdrawal states such as alcohol withdrawal or benzodiazepine withdrawal can cause delirium.
- Infection or inflammation.
- Metabolic: kidney or liver failure, thyroid, adrenal, or glucose dysregulation, anemia, vitamin deficiency such as Wernicke's encephalopathy or vitamin B_{12} deficiency, inborn metabolic errors such as porphyrias or Wilson's disease.
- Stress: surgery, sleep problems, pain, fever, hypoxia, anesthesia, environmental changes, fecal or urinary retention, burns.
- Fluids, electrolytes, nutrition (FEN): dysregulation of calcium, magnesium, potassium, or sodium; dehydration; volume overload; altered pH.
- Brain disorder: CNS infection, head injury, hypertensive encephalopathy.

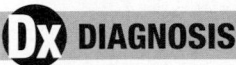 **DIAGNOSIS**

DIFFERENTIAL DIAGNOSIS

- Primary psychiatric illness.
- Focal syndromes.
- Dementia.
- Sundowning.
- Nonconvulsive status epilepticus.
  Remember, delirium may coexist with any of the above. Table 1D-3 describes clinical factors that help differentiate delirium and dementia from psychiatric disease.

LABORATORY TESTS

- Complete blood count, electrolytes, liver function tests, ammonia, drug levels (digoxin, lithium).
- Toxicology screen, urinalysis, urine culture.
- Thyroid function tests, vitamin B_{12}, and folate levels.
- Rapid plasma reagin for syphilis, blood, urine, and spinal fluid culture.
- Arterial blood gas.
- Lumbar puncture is mandatory when cause of delirium is not obvious.

IMAGING STUDIES

- Consider head CT (to look for bleed, trauma, tumor, atrophy, dementia, stroke)
- Chest radiograph (to look for tumor, infection).

TABLE 1D-2 Mnemonic for Risk Factors for Delirium and Agitation

Iwatchdeath	Delirium
Infection	**D**rugs
Withdrawal	**E**lectrolyte and physiologic abnormalities
Acute metabolic	**L**ack of drugs (withdrawal)
Trauma/pain	**I**nfection
Central nervous system pathology	**R**educed sensory input (blindness, deafness)
Hypoxia	**I**ntracranial problems (CVA, meningitis, seizure)
Deficiencies (vitamin B_{12}, thiamine)	**U**rinary retention and fecal impaction
Endocrinopathies (thyroid, adrenal)	**M**yocardial problems (MI, arrhythmia, CHF)
Acute vascular (hypertension, shock)	
Toxins/drugs	
Heavy metals	

CHF, Congestive heart failure; *CVA*, cerebrovascular accident; *MI*, myocardial infarction.
From Vincent JL et al: *Textbook of critical care*, ed 6, Philadelphia, 2011, Saunders.

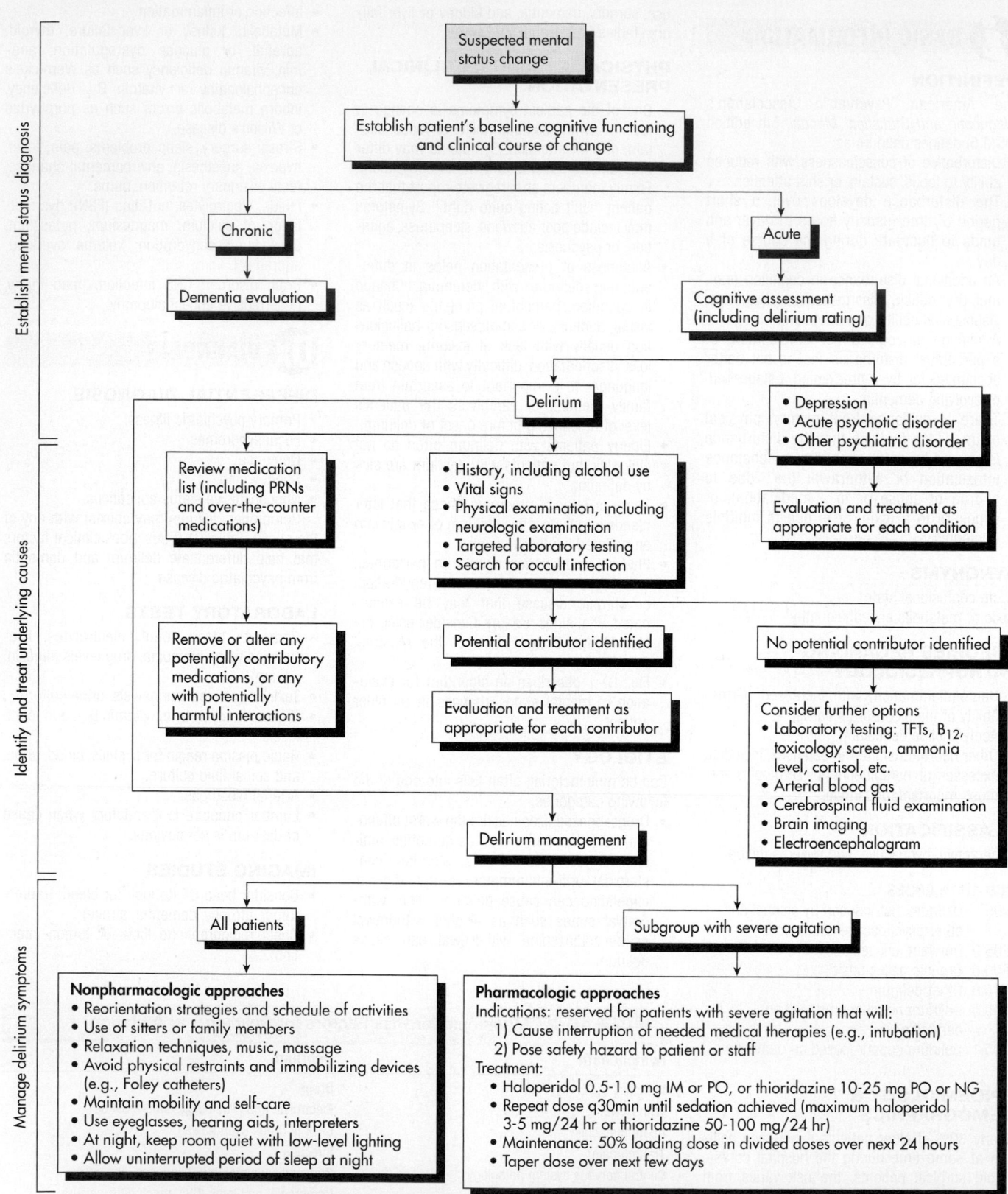

FIGURE 1D-1 Algorithm for evaluation of suspected mental status change in an older patient. *IM,* Intramuscular; *NG,* nasogastric; *PO,* by mouth; *PRN,* as needed; *TFTs,* thyroid function tests. (From Goldman L, Ausiello D [eds]: *Cecil textbook of medicine,* ed 24, Philadelphia, 2012, Saunders.)

TABLE 1D-3 Clinical Factors That Help Differentiate Delirium and Dementia from Psychiatric Disease

Characteristic	Delirium	Dementia	Psychiatric Illness
Symptoms			
Age at onset	<12 or >40 yr	Usually elderly, >50 yr	13-40 yr
Onset	Acute	Gradual or insidious	Gradual
Symptom course	Rapid, fluctuating	Stable and progressive	Stable
Duration	Days to weeks	Months to years	Months to years
Reversibility	Usually	Rarely	Rarely
History			
Past medical history	Substance abuse, medical illness	Comorbid conditions of aging	Previous psychiatric history
Family history	Unusual	History of dementia	History of psychiatric illness
Physical Examination			
Vital signs	Usually abnormal	Usually normal	Usually normal
Involuntary activity	May have tremors, asterixis, etc.	None unless coexistent disease	None
Mental Status			
Affect	Emotional lability	Flat affect with advanced disease	Flat affect
Orientation	Usually impaired	Impaired with advanced disease	Rarely impaired
Attention	Impaired	Slow to focus	Disorganized
Hallucinations	Primarily visual	Rare	Primarily auditory
Speech	Slow, incoherent, dysarthric	Usually coherent	Usually coherent
Consciousness	Decreased to impaired	Normal (clear)	Alert
Intellectual function	Usually impaired	Impaired	Intact

From Adams JG et al: *Emergency medicine, clinical essentials*, ed 2, Philadelphia, 2013, Elsevier.

ELECTROENCEPHALOGRAM

- To exclude seizure, confirm diagnosis of metabolic encephalopathy.

 **TREATMENT**

NONPHARMACOLOGIC THERAPY

- The most important consideration is to keep the patient safe by using a variety of methods, including frequent reorientation.
- A quiet, restful, simplified environment with cues to time and location such as clock or calendar is helpful, as well as consistent staff providing both personal and medical care. If possible, encourage familiar family members and friends to keep the patient company.
- Early mobilization and minimized use of physical restraints (use of physical restraints if necessary to ensure safety).
- Visual and hearing aids for patients with these impairments.

ACUTE GENERAL Rx

- Reverse any treatable cause, such as volume repletion for patients with dehydration, antibiotics for urinary tract infection.
- Haloperidol can be used with caution to control agitation, with doses ranging from 0.25 to 2 mg IM/IV twice daily, repeating the dose

every 20 to 30 min until patient has calmed and using lower doses for the elderly.
- Risperidone 0.5 mg twice daily (off-label use, non-FDA approved) can also be used with caution with a slow increase to desired dose, not to exceed 1.0 to 2.0 mg.
- Avoid benzodiazepines and meperidine. Drug toxicity accounts for approximately 30% cases of delirium.

CHRONIC Rx

Delirium is not a chronic condition; if assessing a more long-term mental status change, consider other diagnoses.

DISPOSITION

Requires frequent monitoring often necessitating hospital level of care to ensure safety and assess etiology.

REFERRAL

Consider neurologic or psychiatric consultation if not improved in several days or in complicated cases.

 **PEARLS & CONSIDERATIONS**

COMMENTS

Although benzodiazepines are frequently used in hospitalized patients for sedation and are the

mainstay of therapy for alcohol withdrawal, they must be used with caution in the elderly because they can have a paradoxical effect on agitation.

PREVENTION

- Avoid polypharmacy as much as possible.
- Optimize chronic medical conditions.
- Provide frequent reorientation and a soothing environment for high-risk patients (e.g., lights on during the day, off at night; open curtains during the day so patient can see the weather).
- In patients over 70 without dementia, regular exercise has been associated with lower risk for developing delirium, and early return to physical activity can improve outcomes in ill patients.

PATIENT & FAMILY EDUCATION

Inform about the above preventive techniques, especially polypharmacy risks.

SUGGESTED READINGS

Available at www.expertconsult.com

RELATED CONTENT

Delirium Tremens (Related Key Topic)

AUTHORS: **CRISTINA ANTONIO PACHECO, M.D.,** and **POOJA VERMA, M.D.**

BASIC INFORMATION

DEFINITION

Delirium tremens, also known as withdrawal delirium, is overactivity of the central nervous system after cessation of alcohol intake. The time interval is variable; it usually occurs within 1 wk after reduction or cessation of heavy alcohol intake and persists for 1 to 3 days.

SYNONYMS

Withdrawal delirium
Alcohol withdrawal syndrome
DTs
Alcoholic delirium

ICD-10CM CODES
F10.231 Alcohol dependence with withdrawal delirium

EPIDEMIOLOGY & DEMOGRAPHICS

INCIDENCE (IN U.S.): Up to 500,000 cases annually, 3% to 5% of patients who are hospitalized for alcohol withdrawal meet the criteria for withdrawal delirium
PEAK INCIDENCE: 30 yr and older
PREDOMINANT SEX: Male
PEAK AGE: Teenage years and older
GENETICS: More common with patients who have relatives who are alcoholics

PHYSICAL FINDINGS & CLINICAL PRESENTATION

- Ethanol withdrawal symptoms usually begin within 8 hours after blood alcohol levels decrease, peak at about 72 hours, and are markedly reduced by days 5 to 7 of abstinence.
- Initially: anxiety, insomnia, tremulousness
- Early: tachycardia, sweating, anorexia, agitation, headache, gastrointestinal distress
- Late: seizures, visual hallucinations, delirium

ETIOLOGY

Alcoholism

DIAGNOSIS

DIFFERENTIAL DIAGNOSIS

- Coexisting illness.
- Trauma.
- Drug use.

WORKUP

- Frequent rating of symptoms (hallucinations, tremor, sweating, agitation, orientation).
- The Clinical Institute Withdrawal Assessment-Alcohol (CIWA-A) scale can be used to measure the severity of alcohol withdrawal. It consists of the 10 following items:
  1. Nausea.
  2. Tremor.
  3. Autonomic hyperactivity.
  4. Anxiety.

  5. Agitation.
  6. Tactile disturbances.
  7. Visual disturbances.
  8. Auditory disturbances.
  9. Headache.
  10. Disorientation.

The maximum score is 67. Scores <8 indicate mild symptoms; scores 8-15 indicate moderate withdrawal symptoms; and scores >15 indicate severe withdrawal symptoms.

LABORATORY TESTS

- Electrolytes (including magnesium, phosphate).
- Close monitoring of glucose levels.
- Drug screen (blood and urine).

IMAGING STUDIES

CT scan of head if there is a history of head trauma.

TREATMENT

NONPHARMACOLOGIC THERAPY

Refer to drug rehabilitation program after patient recovers.

ACUTE GENERAL Rx

- Admission to a detoxification unit where patient can be observed closely.
- Vital signs q30min initially (neurologic signs, if necessary).
- Use of lateral decubitus or prone position if restraints are necessary.
- Nothing by mouth: nasogastric tube for abdominal distention may be necessary but should not be routinely used.
- Vigorous hydration (4 to 6 L/day): IV with glucose (Na^+, K^+, PO_4^{-3}, and Mg^{2+} replacement). May be necessary in some patients but commonly there is little support for routine administration of magnesium. Use vigorous hydration with caution in patients with CHF.
- Vitamins: thiamine 500 mg infused IV over the course of 30 minutes daily for 3 days. The initial dose of thiamine should precede the administration of IV dextrose; multivitamins (may be added to the hydrating solution).
- Sedation (sedation can be achieved using fixed-dose regimen or individualized benzodiazepine administration [see CIWA-Ar score] in Alcohol-Related Disorders):
  1. Initially: lorazepam 8 mg IM/IV every 15 minutes as needed, after the patient has received 16 mg. If delirium is still severe, administer an 8 mg bolus IV, then administer 10-30 mg/hr.[1]
  2. Maintenance (individualized dosage): chlordiazepoxide, 50 to 100 mg PO q4 to 6h, lorazepam 2 mg PO q4h, or diazepam 5 to 10 mg PO tid; withhold doses or decrease subsequent doses if signs of oversedation are apparent.

3. Midazolam is also effective for managing DTs. Its rapid onset (sedation within 2 to 4 min of IV injection) and short duration of action (approximately 30 min) make it an ideal agent for titration in continuous infusion.
- In addition to benzodiazepines, administer medications such as the antipsychotic agent haloperidol for uncontrolled agitation or hallucinations (0.5-5 mg IV/IM every 30-60 minutes as needed for severe agitation or hallucinations, not to exceed 20 mg.
- Treatment of seizures: diazepam 2.5 mg/min IV until seizure is controlled (check for respiratory depression or hypotension) may be beneficial for prolonged seizure activity; IV lorazepam 1 to 2 mg q2h can be used in place of diazepam. In general, withdrawal seizures are self-limited and treatment is not required; the use of phenytoin or other anticonvulsants for short-term treatment of alcohol withdrawal seizures is not recommended.
- Diagnosis and treatment of concomitant medical, surgical, or psychiatric conditions.

CHRONIC Rx

Alcoholics Anonymous has the best record in breaking addiction, but the results are still disappointing.

DISPOSITION

Refer to drug rehabilitation program.

REFERRAL

If cardiac arrhythmias are prominent or respiratory distress develops.

PEARLS & CONSIDERATIONS

COMMENTS

- This is a potentially lethal disease if not carefully treated. Mortality rate is 15% in untreated patients, and approximately 1% to 6% of hospitalized patients who have withdrawal delirium die.

SUGGESTED READINGS

Available at www.expertconsult.com

RELATED CONTENT

Delirium Tremens (Patient Information)
Alcohol Abuse (Related Key Topic)
Delirium (Related Key Topic)
Wernicke's Syndrome (Related Key Topic)

AUTHOR: **FRED F. FERRI, M.D.**

---

[1]Schuckit MA: Recognition and management of withdrawal delirium (delirium tremens). *N Engl J Med* 371:2109-2113, 2014.

 **BASIC INFORMATION**

DEFINITION

A fixed belief characterized by a person's preoccupation that his or her skin is infested by insects, worms, or other living organisms.

SYNONYMS

Morgellon's disease, Ekbom syndrome

ICD-10CM CODE
F22   Delusional disorders

EPIDEMIOLOGY & DEMOGRAPHICS

INCIDENCE: Unknown
PEAK INCIDENCE: Occurs more often later in life
PREVALENCE: Unknown
PREDOMINANT SEX AND AGE: For patients less than age 50, the male/female ratio is 1:1; for patients older than 50, females predominate by a ratio of 3:1
GENETICS: Unknown
RISK FACTORS: None known

PHYSICAL FINDINGS & CLINICAL PRESENTATION

- Patients complain of living organisms infesting their skin, sometimes including mucosal tissues.
- Patients have often been to specialists, including dermatologists, allergists, and infectious disease specialists.
- Patients may bring in samples of skin or hair, stating that they have looked at tissue under a microscope and have seen organisms. These samples are often brought in a matchbox ("matchbox sign") or wrapped in plastic wrap ("Saran sign"). This is generally called the "specimen sign."
- Skin may show areas of excoriation.

ETIOLOGY

Unknown: Thought to be mediated through dopaminergic pathways in the brain given the known etiology of other psychotic disorders and the ability of cocaine use to create symptoms of formication (see the following).

 **DIAGNOSIS**

DIFFERENTIAL DIAGNOSIS

- Primary psychiatric disorders include formication, in which patients experience crawling and biting sensations on their skin, although they are not delusional about the cause.
- Substance abuse should be considered. Case reports exist of cocaine and amphetamine use leading to these delusions.

- Neuropsychiatrically, B12 deficiency, dementia, diabetic neuropathy, cardiovascular disease, multiple sclerosis, hyperthyroidism, and brain lesions can all cause similar delusions.
- Other medical causes that deserve workup include primary skin lesions, systemic diseases that may present with skin lesions, and disorders of infestation.
- Dopaminergic agents, such as those that treat Parkinson's disease, have also been shown to cause these symptoms.

WORKUP

- Skin biopsy may exclude dermatitis herpetiformis (although many patients have already been to their primary care doctor and dermatologist and have had a skin biopsy done, likely many times).
- Mineral oil preparation may exclude scabies, and a microscopic examination may exclude louse infestation.
- Thorough history is likely to yield the very fixed nature of the belief and an unwillingness to come to terms with the lack of findings on the exam.

LABORATORY TESTS

- Pruritus workup: iron studies, LFTs, CBC, UA, TSH, Chem 7, Folate, B12
- Lumbar puncture (especially when multiple sclerosis is highly suspected)
- CRP (especially when an infectious etiology is suspected)
- Urine toxicology screen to evaluate substance use

IMAGING STUDIES

- Head CT, without contrast
- MRI

Rx TREATMENT

- Antipsychotics have been shown to lead to full to partial remission in 60% to 100% of cases.
- Classically, Orap was the treatment of choice, although it has been associated with QTc prolongation.
- Multiple studies describe the use of second-generation antipsychotics, but these have been shown to cause weight gain and metabolic syndrome.
- Numerous antipsychotics have a black box warning about the risk of sudden death in the elderly and must be administered carefully for patients who have issues with QTc.
- Given all of these issues, a careful risk/benefit analysis is needed, including the assistance of family members of elderly patients.

TABLE 1D-4   Antipsychotics

Antipsychotic Drug	Dosage
Haloperidol	0.5-10 mg PO bid
Pimozide	2-12 mg PO qam
Perphenazine	4-16 mg PO tid
Olanzapine	2.5-10 mg PO bid
Aripiprazole	2.5-20 mg PO qam
Quetiapine	12.5-200 mg PO bid
Ziprasidone	20-80 mg PO bid
Risperidone	0.5-3 mg PO bid

NONPHARMACOLOGIC THERAPY

- Given the fixed nature of the belief, patients often refuse referral to a mental health specialist.
- A treatment (e.g., Permethrin) should not be recommended "just in case" because it may reinforce the patient's belief.
- Repeat visits with medical providers may be helpful to provide assurance and prevent harm from further workup.

ACUTE GENERAL Rx

Antipsychotics (Table 1D-4)

COMPLEMENTARY & ALTERNATIVE MEDICINE

There is no evidence on the use of complementary or alternative medicine for this disorder.

REFERRAL

Referral to an outpatient psychiatrist may be helpful, but patients are often resistant.

PREVENTION

No preventive measures have been identified.

PATIENT/FAMILY EDUCATION

Psychoeducation may be helpful for the patient and family, although resistance from the patient can be expected.

SUGGESTED READINGS

Available at www.expertconsult.com

RELATED CONTENT

Alcoholism (Related Key Topic)
Cocaine Overdose (Related Key Topic)
Delirium (Related Key Topic)
Schizophrenia (Related Key Topic)

AUTHOR: **ANTHONY GALLO, M.D.**

D

Diseases and Disorders

I

BASIC INFORMATION

DEFINITION

A neurodegenerative disease characterized by dementia concurrent with or preceding parkinsonian symptoms typically by 1 yr with other core features including fluctuations in attention and alertness and recurrent visual hallucinations. Diagnostic criteria for dementia syndrome associated with Lewy body pathology are described in Box 1D-1. The disease characteristically responds to cholinesterase inhibitors, is relatively unresponsive to L-dopa, and is very sensitive to neuroleptics.

SYNONYMS

Lewy body dementia
Diffuse Lewy body disease
Lewy body type senile dementia
Cortical Lewy body disease

ICD-10CM CODES
G31.83 Dementia with Lewy bodies

EPIDEMIOLOGY & DEMOGRAPHICS

INCIDENCE: Accounts for 10% to 22% of all dementias.
PEAK INCIDENCE: Affects individuals in their sixth decade or older.
PREVALENCE: Estimated 0.7% of individuals older than age 65.
PREDOMINANT SEX AND AGE
- Sex: Male predominance
- Mean age of onset: 75 yr. On average, 10 yr greater for dementia with Lewy bodies (DLB) than Parkinson's disease (PD).

GENETICS
- Most cases are sporadic with a discordance among monozygotic twins, which suggests that environment or other epigenetics play a major role in the incidence of DLB.
- Multiplication of alpha-synuclein gene (SNCA) has been reported in families with DLB.
- Other factors include glucocerebrosidase genetic mutations, high prevalence of Lewy bodies with presenilin-1 mutations, and polymorphisms of the coding region for the synuclein genes.

RISK FACTORS
- Male sex
- Advanced age

PHYSICAL FINDINGS & CLINICAL PRESENTATION

- Importance of recognizing DLB relates to its pharmacologic management, including responsiveness to cholinesterase inhibitors, sensitivity to side effects of neuroleptics, and relative unresponsiveness to L-dopa.
- Insidious onset of dementia with core features of fluctuations in cognition, recurrent visual hallucinations, and extrapyramidal motor symptoms, along with other features either suggestive or supportive of the clinical diagnosis. Refer to "Revised Criteria for the Clinical Diagnosis of Dementia with Lewy Bodies" (McKeith I et al, *Neurology*, 2005).

- Detailed neuropsychological assessment demonstrates a characteristic profile of impairments in visuoperceptual, attentional, and executive functions, which reflects a combination of cortical and subcortical damage.

ETIOLOGY

- SNCA is a protein normally found at the synapse with a role in vesicle production. In its insoluble form, SNCA aggregates into Lewy bodies found at the cortical and subcortical levels.
- Lewy bodies (Fig. 1D-2) are round, eosinophilic, intracytoplasmic inclusions in the nuclei of neurons.
- Cortical Lewy bodies are found in deep cortical layers of the anterior frontal and temporal lobes, the cingulate gyrus, and insula.
- As in PD, Lewy bodies aggregate in the following structures: substantia nigra, locus coeruleus, raphe nuclei, nucleus basalis of Meynert, and brainstem nuclei.
- Figure 1D-3 shows the relationships among the subtypes of dementia.

DIAGNOSIS

DIFFERENTIAL DIAGNOSIS

- Similar to Parkinson's disease with dementia, including fluctuation in neuropsychological function, neuropsychiatric features, and extrapyramidal motor features

- Diagnosis of DLB when dementia occurs before or concurrently with extrapyramidal features—arbitrarily set as the "1-yr rule" vs. Parkinson's disease with dementia, which occurs after 1 yr
- Dementia: Alzheimer's disease (AD), vascular dementia
- Parkinsonian features: progressive supranuclear palsy, multisystem atrophy, corticobasal degeneration
- Rapidly progressive form: Creutzfeldt-Jakob disease. Lack of cerebellar signs may help distinguish DLB from classic CJD (but not variant form of CJD)
- Psychiatric features: late-onset psychosis or depression with psychotic features
- Hallucinations with fluctuations in consciousness: temporal lobe epilepsy (TLE)

WORKUP

- Lumbar puncture to rule out underlying chronic infections. Protein 14-3-3 may be present in both DLB and CJD.
- EEG to rule out potential TLE. However, either DLB or TLE may show nonspecific slowing or periodic complexes.

LABORATORY TESTS

- Rule out other potential reversible causes for dementia including:
  1. Hormonal dysregulation: thyroid stimulating hormone, free thyroxine
  2. Vitamin deficiency: thiamine, cyanocobalamin, folate

BOX 1D-1   Diagnostic Criteria for the Dementia Syndrome Associated With Lewy Body Pathology

The cognitive disturbance is of insidious onset and is progressive, based on evidence from the history or serial cognitive examination
The presence of at least two of the following:
  Parkinsonism (rigidity, resting tremor, bradykinesia, postural instability, parkinsonian gait disorder)
  Prominent, fully formed visual hallucinations
  Substantial fluctuations in alertness or cognition
  Rapid eye movement sleep behavior disorder
  Severe worsening of parkinsonism by antipsychotic drugs
  The disturbance is not better accounted for by a systemic disease or another brain disease

From Goldman L, Schafer AI: *Goldman's Cecil medicine,* ed 24, Philadelphia, 2012, Saunders.

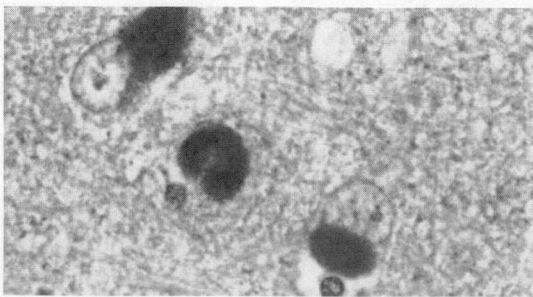

FIGURE 1D-2 Cortical Lewy bodies present in cerebral cortex, as opposed to Parkinson's disease without dementia, in which Lewy bodies are found in the substantia nigra. Immunostain for Alpha synuclein is characteristic for Lewy body immunohistological profile. (From MacDonald AB: Spirochetal cyst forms in neurodegenerative disorders, hiding in plain sight, *Medical Hypotheses* 67(4) 819–832, 2006.)

FIGURE 1D-3 Relationships among Alzheimer's disease (AD), the three subtypes of dementia with Lewy bodies (DLB), and Parkinson's disease (PD). Parkinsonism refers to the clinical symptoms of PD (hypokinesia, tremor, and muscular rigidity). *LBV*, Lewy body variant of Alzheimer's disease; *DLBD*, diffuse Lewy body disease; *PD*, Parkinson's disease; *PDD*, Parkinson's disease dementia; *LBs*, Lewy bodies. (From Lewis KA et al: Abnormal neurites containing C-terminally truncated α-synuclein are present in Alzheimer's disease without conventional Lewy body pathology. *Am J Pathol* 177(6) 3037–3050, 2010.)

3. Vascular risk factors: lipid profile, Hgb A_{1c}, homocysteine, syphilis (FTA-ABS), or ApoE genotype

IMAGING STUDIES

- MRI typically shows a relative preservation of the hippocampi and medial temporal lobe volumes (as found in AD) but generalized atrophy and white matter changes.
- Functional imaging including single photon emission computed tomography (SPECT) demonstrates hypoperfusion of the occipital region.

Rx TREATMENT

Patient and caregiver education on benefits, side effects, and limitations of treatment is very important. Based on the preference of the patient and caregiver, a fine balance between psychosis and Parkinsonism features confounds the treatment choices.

NONPHARMACOLOGIC THERAPY

- Social interaction and environmental novelty may improve cognitive dysfunction and psychiatric features often exacerbated by low levels of arousal and attention.
- Behavioral methods, such as avoiding previously exposed environmental triggers known to cause anxiety, agitation, or aggression.
- Physical therapy, mobility aids, and daily exercise.

ACUTE GENERAL Rx

Neuroleptic for disabling, persistent psychotic features despite initiation of a cholinesterase inhibitor. A very low dose of an atypical antipsychotic (quetiapine 12.5 mg daily) may be started after patient/caregiver education regarding the sensitivity to neuroleptics.

CHRONIC Rx

- Cholinesterase inhibitors for cognitive and behavioral symptoms. Rivastigmine (6 to 12 mg per day orally or 9.5 mg per day by transdermal patch) has shown in RCT a significant reduction in anxiety, delusions, and hallucinations, as well as significantly improved performance on neuropsychological testing.
- Antiparkinson medications for disabling parkinsonian features. L-Dopa is reported to be more effective with fewer side effects than dopamine agonists. Begin at a low dose of L-dopa (25/100 mg tid), and slowly titrate over several weeks as tolerated and according to response.
- Selective serotonin reuptake inhibitors are commonly used for depression.
- If REM sleep disorder remains disabling (or patient has not responded to an atypical antipsychotic initiated for psychosis), a trial of low-dose clonazepam (0.25 to 0.5 mg) or melatonin (3 mg) at bedtime remains an option.
- Orthostatic hypotension may be aided by nonpharmacologic therapy, such as supportive stockings, or pharmacologically by midodrine and/or fludrocortisone.
- Memantine demonstrated an improvement in clinical global measure and remains well tolerated but may worsen hallucinations or delusions.

- Avoid anticholinergics (including tricyclic antidepressants) and benzodiazepines.

DISPOSITION

- Survival resembles the progression of AD, but a minority of cases may have a rapid disease course.
- Progression in cognitive decline, similar to AD, by an approximate 10% per year on cognitive testing.

REFERRAL

DLB requires a multidisciplinary approach including the general practitioner, neurologist, neuropsychologist, and/or neuropsychiatrist.

(!) PEARLS & CONSIDERATIONS

COMMENTS

- Clinical presentation helps differentiate DLB from AD. AD presents with early signs of anterograde episodic memory loss without the benefit of recognition on neuropsychological testing due to cortical atrophy at the medial temporal lobe region.
- Vascular dementia may also present with evidence of frontal-subcortical features but typically without the core features listed in the criteria above.
- Bed partners may report that individuals with DLB "act out their dreams," sometimes violently, leading to sleeping in separate beds. A history of REM sleep behavior may precede the diagnosis by many years.

PATIENT/FAMILY EDUCATION

- Visual hallucinations (VH) typically consist of innocuous, well-formed, detailed images of animate figures. Unless VH lead to a potential threat to self or others, avoid antipsychotics due to the sensitivity of neuroleptics. Family/ friends are often more alarmed by the VH than the patient with DLB.
- Apathy is a common clinical feature of DLB and mimics changes in mood, including depression, or excessive daytime somnolence. These features are often noticed by family/friends.

SUGGESTED READINGS

Available at www.expertconsult.com

AUTHORS: **D. BRANDON BURTIS, D.O.,** and **GLEN FINNEY, M.D.**

Depression, Major  PTG ALG EBM

BASIC INFORMATION

DEFINITION

Major depression is an episodic, frequently recurring syndrome. The diagnosis requires that five of nine criteria be present for 2 wk. One of these nine criteria must be either a persistent depressed mood or pervasive anhedonia (loss of interest or pleasure in all, or almost all, usual interests or activities). Other symptoms include sleep disturbance (insomnia or hypersomnia), appetite loss/gain or weight loss/gain, fatigue, psychomotor retardation or agitation, difficulty concentrating or indecisiveness, feelings of guilt or worthlessness, and recurrent thoughts of death or suicidal ideation.

SYNONYMS

Unipolar affective disorder
Clinical depression
Melancholia
Manic-depressive illness, depressed type
Depressive episode

Codes depend on whether the episode is single or recurrent, and also on clinical severity.

ICD-10CM CODES
F32.9 Depressive episode, unspecified
F33.0 Recurrent depressive episode, current episode mild
F33.1 Recurrent depressive disorder, current episode moderate
F33.2 Recurrent depressive disorder, current episode severe without psychotic symptoms
F33.3 Recurrent depressive disorder, current episode severe with psychotic symptoms
F33.4 Recurrent depressive disorder, currently in remission
F33.9 Recurrent depressive disorder, unspecified

EPIDEMIOLOGY & DEMOGRAPHICS

LIFETIME RISK (IN U.S.): 10% of men, 20% of women
PREVALENCE (IN U.S.): Point prevalence in a community sample is 3% of men, 4.5% to 9.3% of women, and 1% of children. Prevalence of 20% to 40% in patients with comorbid medical conditions.
PREDOMINANT SEX: Female/male ratio 2:1
PREDOMINANT AGE: 25 to 44 yr; 5% of adolescents
PEAK INCIDENCE: 30 to 40 yr; 13% of postpartum women
GENETICS:
- Clear evidence of familial predominance
- Prevalence is 2 to 3 times greater among first-degree relatives.
- Concordance among monozygotic twins approximately 50%
- No established pattern of inheritance; MDD with anxious features may be uniquely associated with family history of bipolar disorder, but further studies are needed.

PHYSICAL FINDINGS & CLINICAL PRESENTATION

- Clinical evaluation facilitated by organizing the major symptoms into four hallmarks: (1) depressed mood, (2) anhedonia, (3) physical symptoms (sleep disturbance, appetite problem, fatigue, psychomotor changes), and (4) psychological symptoms (difficulty concentrating or indecisiveness, guilt or worthlessness, and suicidal ideation).
- A stressful life event, typically a serious loss, may trigger a depressive episode. DSM-5 recommends that clinical judgment be used to determine if depression in the context of a loss should be used to determine if a diagnosis of a disorder is warranted.
- Patients often present with somatic complaints such as pain, fatigue, insomnia, dizziness, headache, or gastrointestinal problems. Somatic complaints may be reported more frequently among certain ethnic groups than depressed mood, increasing risk for underdetection in these groups.
- May be associated with mood-congruent delusional thinking (paranoid and melancholic themes).
- May be associated with active or passive suicidal ideation.
- Serious misconduct may appear in adolescents.
- May be underdiagnosed in elderly patients, with signs and symptoms attributed to normal aging.
- May be underdiagnosed in medically ill patients, with signs and symptoms attributed to medical illness or considered appropriate reaction to medical condition.

ETIOLOGY

- A heterogeneous group of disorders probably arising from various etiologies.
- Genetic and environmental experiences, and their interaction, each contribute.
- Significant psychosocial stressors, especially loss, often trigger depression, particularly for first episodes.
- Numerous biologic correlates have been identified, though none is considered causative or diagnostic. Genes that influence the production and reuptake of serotonin, norepinephrine, and dopamine, as well as nerve cell growth in brain regions underlying memory and emotional processing, are of greatest interest. Abnormalities in brain regions underlying executive functioning, emotion regulation, and reward processing, as well as irregularities in cortisol responding and inflammation, appear to play a role.
- Cognitive risk factors include a pessimistic style of explaining negative events, a tendency to ruminate, and biases in processing emotional information and events.

DIAGNOSIS

DIFFERENTIAL DIAGNOSIS

- Anxiety disorders (e.g., social phobia, PTSD, obsessive compulsive disorder), substance abuse, and personality disorders often present with depressive symptoms.
- Important to determine if a depressive episode is part of major depression or part of bipolar disorder.
- Important to distinguish from adjustment disorder. Depression in the context of a stressful life event is diagnosed as major depressive disorder if the symptom criteria are met and adjustment disorder if the symptom criteria are not met. There is no evidence that medication is effective for adjustment disorder.
- Approximately 10% to 15% of depression caused by general medical illnesses, such as Alzheimer's disease, Parkinson's disease, stroke, end-stage renal failure, cardiac disease, HIV infection, and cancer.
- Some medical conditions present as depression (e.g., hypothyroidism, hyperthyroidism or neurosyphilis).
- Premenstrual dysphoric disorder.
- In elderly, depression often coexists with dementia.

WORKUP

- Careful medical history is required
- Physical examination reveals no specific diagnostic signs of depression
- Mental status examination
- Self-report scales can assist in screening.
- Commonly used validated screening tools include the 15-item Geriatric Depression Scale in the elderly and the Patient Health Questionnaire (PHQ)-2 and PHQ-9. The PHQ-2 has a 97% sensitivity and 67% specificity in adults. If it is positive for depression, the PHQ-9 should be administered. The PHQ-9 has a 61% sensitivity and 94% specificity for depression in adults.

LABORATORY TESTS

- No laboratory studies are diagnostic.
- The following can assist in ruling out other confounding issues:
  1. Routine blood chemistry evaluation
  2. CBC with differential
  3. Thyroid function studies
  4. Vitamin B_{12} levels

IMAGING STUDIES

With unusual presentations (e.g., associated with new-onset severe headache, focal neurologic signs, a cognitive or sensory disturbance), the following may be performed:
- EEG (diffuse slowing indicates metabolic encephalopathy)
- Anatomic brain imaging (CT scan or MRI)

TREATMENT

NONPHARMACOLOGIC THERAPY

- Good evidence that cognitive-behavioral therapy is as effective as antidepressant medication in achieving significant reduction or remission (Table 1D-8).
- Problem solving and interpersonal psychotherapies have efficacy rates of 50% to 60%.
- "New wave" cognitive-behavioral therapies (e.g., acceptance and commitment therapy,

mindfulness-based CBT) have demonstrated efficacy in numerous studies. It is unclear as of yet whether new-wave versus traditional behavioral therapies differ in mechanisms of action, as well as in suitability for particular patient populations.

- Growing evidence indicates that Internet-based CBT and brief therapy interventions integrated into primary care to expand access to therapy are efficacious, but further research is needed.
- By 12 wk or earlier, psychotherapy and medication approaches are equally effective.
- Augmentation of standard depression treatment with CBT to address insomnia (CBT-I) was found to significantly improve response rates.
- Patients with severe symptoms should generally not be treated by psychotherapy alone.
- Evidence, although mixed, that combined psychotherapy and medication may be more effective than either treatment alone. Psychotherapy or augmentation with psychotherapy appears to reduce the risk for future recurrences compared to medication alone, particularly when medication is discontinued after symptomatic remission.
- Factors, including history of childhood maltreatment, presence of precipitant stressful life events, family psychiatric history, the presence of anhedonia, and depression severity, may affect treatment response and risk of recurrence. Numerous genetic and neurobiologic variables that predict treatment response have been identified, particularly in combination with one another or with clinical characteristics. However, as of yet there are no universally accepted markers that can aid clinicians in matching individuals to particular medications or interventions.

ACUTE GENERAL Rx

- Concurrent medical or psychiatric illnesses, history of prior response, cost, patient preference, and side effects should be considered when selecting initial treatment.
- Antidepressants are helpful in approximately 60% to 70% of cases, though sustained remission rates are lower.
- Selective serotonin reuptake inhibitors (SSRIs) generally are first-line.
- According to the STAR-D trial, approximately 30% achieve remission with the first prescribed medication after 3 months of treatment.

Another 25% to 30% respond to treatment, but do not achieve remission. Treatment-refractory patients should be switched to another SSRI or to another class of medication, offered adjunctive medication such as bupropion, or referred for evidence-based counseling. Approximately 25% more patients will achieve remission with this secondary intervention.

- Response to antidepressants for many patients is seen as early as 2 wk, and among patients showing little to no response, the odds of later response decrease the longer patients remain unimproved.
- To date no benefit of combining antidepressants as first-line treatment. Also no clear advantage has been identified for switching medications within vs. across different classes, or to switching vs. augmentation.
- Therapy should be continued for 4 to 9 mo after the full remission of symptoms.
- Electroconvulsive therapy is the most effective means available for the treatment of severe, refractory depression. Transcranial magnetic stimulation has also shown evidence of efficacy though the magnitude of effects is more variable. To date electroconvulsive therapy has shown superior efficacy; research is underway to investigate whether higher-intensity TMS may enhance its efficacy.
- Antipsychotic medication should be added for psychotic depression. Antipsychotic medication has also been shown to be helpful in augmenting antidepressants for nonpsychotic depression.
- Ketamine found to be rapidly effective in treatment-resistant depression. However, treatment remains experimental and effects do not persist.

CHRONIC Rx

Long-term treatment, in some cases, lifelong recommended for multiple depressive episodes, an episode duration longer than 2 yr, a severe episode or significant suicidality, or a strong family history of severe depression or bipolar disorder.

DISPOSITION

- Major depression is often a relapsing and remitting illness.
- Physical symptoms predict a favorable response to biologic intervention.

- Additional episodes experienced by >50% after one episode, with each additional episode linked to increased risk for subsequent episodes.
- Without treatment, episodes last an average of 6 to 12 mo; risk of recurrence higher without treatment.
- For many depressed individuals, subthreshold residual symptoms are present between episodes and define the majority of an individual's course of depression. Such symptoms may lead to impairment and warrant prolonged treatment.

REFERRAL

- If treatment refractory
- If patient suicidal or psychotic
- For suspected bipolar depression

PEARLS & CONSIDERATIONS

COMMENTS

- All threats of suicide should be taken very seriously. Clinicians can use the mnemonic SAL: Is the method specific? Is it available? Is it lethal?
- Rule out bipolar affective disorder before initiating antidepressant medication. Screening scales for bipolar disorder can be helpful in primary care settings to identify patients at increased risk for bipolar disorder, although unclear benefit in mental health settings.
- Many patients and families reluctant to acknowledge depression because of stigma.
- A two-question screener is as effective as longer instruments. A positive answer to either question warrants a full assessment.
  1. Over the past 2 weeks, have you ever felt down, depressed, or hopeless?
  2. Over the past 2 weeks, have you felt little interest or pleasure in doing things?
- Depression screening programs without treatment programs are unlikely to improve depression outcomes.
- Strict monitoring of patients who initiate antidepressant therapy is necessary both for safety and to ensure optimal treatment. Use of self-report scales to measure symptom severity are helpful in monitoring outcome and may result in improved outcomes.

SUGGESTED READINGS
Available at www.expertconsult.com

RELATED CONTENT
Bipolar Disorder (Related Key Topic)
Depression (Patient Information)

AUTHORS: **MARK ZIMMERMAN, M.D.,** and **CATHERINE D'AVANZATO, Ph.D.**

TABLE 1D-8 Treatments of Depression

Name of Psychotherapy	Approach
Cognitive psychotherapy	Identify and correct negativistic patterns of thinking.
Interpersonal psychotherapy	Identify and work through role transitions or interpersonal losses, conflicts, or deficits.
Problem-solving therapy	Identify and prioritize situational problems; plan and implement strategies to deal with top-priority problems.
Psychodynamic psychotherapy	Use therapeutic relationship to maximize use of the healthiest defense mechanisms and coping strategies.

From Goldman L et al: *Goldman's Cecil medicine*, ed 24, Philadelphia, 2012, Saunders.

BASIC INFORMATION

DEFINITION

De Quervain's tenosynovitis is a stenosing tenosynovitis of the first dorsal retinacular compartment containing the abductor pollicis longus and extensor pollicis brevis tendons.

SYNONYMS

Stenosing tenosynovitis of the radial styloid process
Stenosing tenovaginitis of the first dorsal compartment
De Quervain's disease
De Quervain's stenosing tenosynovitis
Tendinosis
Styloid tenovaginitis

ICD-10CM CODES
M65.4 Radial styloid tenosynovitis [de Quervain]
M65.9 Synovitis and tenosynovitis, unspecified
M65.849 Other synovitis and tenosynovitis, unspecified hand

EPIDEMIOLOGY & DEMOGRAPHICS

- More common in women than in men (10:1)
- Usually occurs between the ages of 30 and 50
- May be associated with systemic inflammatory diseases
- Can be seen in new mothers or daycare providers due to holding the babies with an outstretched thumb
- Seen more frequently in certain occupations involving repetitive wrist motion (e.g., clerical, assembly, and manual labor)

PHYSICAL FINDINGS & CLINICAL PRESENTATION

- Pain over the styloid process of the radius with grasping and isometric thumb abduction
- Pain may radiate up to the volar aspect of the wrist or to the thumb
- Swelling on the radial styloid
- Tenderness and swelling of the first extensor (dorsal) compartment.
- Positive Finkelstein's test (Fig. 1D-8)
- Crepitance
- Rarely, numbness of dorsum of thumb
- Absence of local heat on examination

ETIOLOGY

- Repetitive use or overuse of the hand and thumb involving pinching with the thumb while moving wrist in radial and ulnar directions (e.g., typing, writing, nailing, golfing, fly-fishing).
- Acute trauma to the first extensor dorsal compartment.
- Anatomic abnormality or variation
- Increased volume states, such as occurring during pregnancy

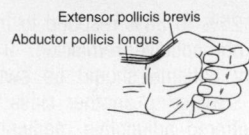

FIGURE 1D-8 Finkelstein's test is positive in de Quervain's stenosing synovitis. Ulnar flexion of the wrist produces pain over the dorsal compartment containing the extensor pollicis brevis and abductor pollicis longus. (From Noble J [ed]: *Textbook of primary care medicine,* ed 2, St Louis, 1996, Mosby.)

DIAGNOSIS

- The diagnosis of de Quervain's tenosynovitis is based on the clinical triad of:
  1. Tenderness over the radial styloid
  2. Pain over the first extensor compartment on resisted thumb abduction or extension
  3. Pain on ulnar movement of the wrist with the thumb adducted and flexed (Finkelstein's test; see Fig. 1D-8)
- Consideration can be given to injecting 1.5 mL of 1% Xylocaine into the tenosynovial sac, and if all three physical signs resolve, the diagnosis is confirmed, allowing for differentiation from carpometacarpal (CMC) osteoarthritis (OA).
- Finkelstein maneuver can also be present in first CMC joint OA.

DIFFERENTIAL DIAGNOSIS

- Carpal tunnel syndrome
- Arthritis (OA or RA)
- Gout
- Infiltrative tenosynovitis
- Instability of the thumb
- Compression neuropathy (e.g., superficial branch of the radial nerve "bracelet syndrome")
- Ganglia
- Infection (e.g., tuberculosis, bacterial)
- Saphead or radial styloid fracture

LABORATORY TESTS

- ESR is usually normal in patients with de Quervain's tenosynovitis.
- Arthrocentesis may be indicated to rule out crystal-induced arthritis and infection.

IMAGING STUDIES

- Imaging of wrist and thumb not necessary unless fracture or arthritis suspected.

TREATMENT

NONPHARMACOLOGIC THERAPY

- Avoid repetitive movements of hand or thumb
- Splinting (thumb spica)
- Icing (4 to 6 times a day for 15 min)
- Physiotherapy

ACUTE GENERAL Rx

- Corticosteroid injection using 20 to 40 mg triamcinolone acetonide and 1% xylocaine is often effective in relieving pain.
- Oral NSAIDs (ibuprofen 800 mg tid or naproxen 500 mg bid)
- Topical NSAIDs or hydrocortisone

CHRONIC Rx

- Once signs of active inflammation have resolved after 3 to 4 wk, gentle stretching exercises involving abductor and extensor tendons usually help recovery.
- Surgical release is generally reserved for patients not responding to NSAIDs and corticosteroid injection therapy.
- Surgery includes first extensor (dorsal) compartment release with or without tenosynovectomy.

DISPOSITION

- ~90% of patients have relief of symptoms with steroid injection.
- Rarely, steroid injection use can cause infection, skin hypopigmentation, and tendon rupture.
- Accidental injection of the glucocorticoid in the subcutaneous tissue instead of sheath of first extensor (dorsal) compartment should be avoided to prevent fat and dermal atrophy.
- If left untreated, can lead to fibrosis and decrease in mobility (stenosing tenosynovitis).
- Surgical control of symptoms achieved in 90% of referred cases
- Complications of surgery include:
  1. Radial nerve damage
  2. Paresthesia (10%)
  3. Neuroma
  4. Scarring
- Recovery rates are higher with early treatment to ~80% after 6 wk but <40% after 4 yr.

PEARLS & CONSIDERATIONS

- Steroid injection is generally recommended after failure of conservative treatment for 2 to 6 weeks.
- Pain relief usually noted within 48 hr, with patient becoming asymptomatic 1 to 2 wk after corticosteroid injection
- If no improvement by 6 weeks after second corticosteroid injection, refer to orthopedic hand surgeon.
- Condition can recur if triggering activity continues.

SUGGESTED READINGS

Available at www.expertconsult.com

RELATED CONTENT

De Quervain's Tenosynovitis (Patient Information)

AUTHOR: **RASHA B. ALQADI, M.D.**

BASIC INFORMATION

DEFINITION

Dermatitis herpetiformis (DH) is an autoimmune blistering disease that is considered to be a cutaneous manifestation of celiac disease (CD). It is associated with gluten-sensitive enteropathy in nearly all cases, although only 20% of patients have gastrointestinal symptoms. Approximately 25% of patients with CD will have DH.

SYNONYMS

Duhring disease

ICD-10CM CODES

L13.0 Dermatitis herpetiformis

EPIDEMIOLOGY & DEMOGRAPHICS

PREVALENCE (IN U.S.): 11.2 cases per 100,000 persons; prevalence for CD is one in 133 adults
PREDOMINANT SEX: Male predominance (2:1); however, female predominance in children
PREDOMINANT AGE: Fourth decade of life, but can occur at any age
PREDOMINANT RACE: Most common in Caucasians of Northern European ancestry
GENETICS: Both CD and DH have a strong genetic component. 11% of patients with DH have a first-degree relative with either DH or CD. Specific HLA genes (involved in processing gliadin antigen in genetically susceptible individuals) have also been shown to predispose to developing DH (HLA-DQ2 in 90%, DQ8 in the remaining 10%). However, less than 50% of genetic predisposition is attributed to HLA genes.

PHYSICAL FINDINGS & CLINICAL PRESENTATION

- Classically, the lesions of DH are small, grouped, "herpetiform" vesicles that are distributed symmetrically on extensor surfaces (elbows, knees, scalp, back, and buttocks) (Fig. 1D-9). However, due to intense pruritus and scratching, pinpoint erosions and excoriations are often the most prominent findings on examination, with intact vesicles rarely seen.
- Spontaneous improvement with cyclic exacerbations is common.
- Celiac-type enamel defects to permanent teeth, oral vesicles, or palmoplantar purpura have been reported as potential associated findings.

PATHOGENESIS

CD and DH are both autoimmune-mediated by IgA class autoantibodies. Dietary gluten is central to the pathogenesis in both. It is hypothesized that gluten byproduct, gliadin, complexes with tissue transglutaminase (tTG) in the gut, binding as an antigen to HLA-DQ2 on T-cells, creating an immune response resulting in anti-tTG IgA antibodies (i.e., anti-endomysial antibodies) in the blood. However, unlike CD, patients with DH also have high-affinity antibodies against epidermal transglutaminase (eTG). Antigenetic cross-reactivity has been hypothesized.

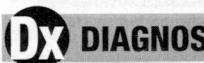

DIAGNOSIS

Physical examination and routine histopathology are often suggestive of DH; however, direct immunofluorescence (DIF) of a perilesional skin biopsy has pathognomonic findings and is the gold standard for diagnosis. Fig. 1D-10 describes an approach to the patient with suspected dermatitis herpetiformis.

DIFFERENTIAL DIAGNOSIS

- Clinically and histologically, the differential diagnosis includes linear IgA dermatosis, bullous pemphigoid, and bullous lupus. These diagnoses can be differentiated by DIF on perilesional skin biopsy,

- Other clinical diagnoses to consider:
  1. Scabies (check for interdigital burrows, involvement of genitalia)
  2. Arthropod bite (papular urticaria over exposed areas)
  3. Eczematous dermatitis (ill-defined, weeping erythematous plaques)
  4. Herpes simplex or zoster infection (painful, not symmetric)
  5. Generalized pruritus (no blister history)

WORKUP, LABORATORY TESTS

- Evaluation for gastrointestinal symptoms, family history of DH or CD, and pruritus should be sought in patients with suspected DH.
- **Lesional skin biopsy:** will demonstrate a neutrophil-rich subepidermal bulla and rule out many conditions.
- **DIF of normal-appearing perilesional skin biopsy:** will demonstrate pathognomonic IgA deposits localized to the dermal papillae and dermal-epidermal junction in a granular pattern.
- Checking for circulating antibodies in the blood (anti-gliadin, anti-endomysial, or anti-reticulin IgA antibodies) is not recommended as part of the diagnostic workup for DH. However, they can be helpful in confirming the diagnosis of DH in cases where linear IgA cannot be excluded on DIF.

TREATMENT

A gluten-free diet (GFD) and dapsone are considered first-line therapy and are often started in conjunction.
1. GFD improves symptoms of both GI and skin disease, with GI responding quicker (skin responds after 2 months).
2. Dapsone results in improvement of skin manifestations within days but does not treat GI manifestations. Dapsone is often tapered over time, while lifelong gluten avoidance is often necessary.
   A recent small study demonstrated that a GFD alone was comparable to a GFD plus dapsone in the treatment of DH; hence GFD is an essential component in the treatment of DH.

NONPHARMACOLOGIC THERAPY

- First line: GFD
  1. Avoid barley, rye, wheat (can consume rice, corn, and oats)
  2. Consultation with a dietitian recommended
  3. Most patients need to follow diet indefinitely; however, cases of spontaneous remission have been reported.
- Second line: elemental diet (controversial)
  1. Can consider elemental diet (avoidance of whole proteins) in those patients who do not adequately respond to a strict GFD; however, data are limited.

ACUTE GENERAL Rx

- First line: dapsone
  1. Initial dose 25-50 mg PO daily with gradual increase to an average maintenance dose of 0.5-1 mg/kg daily (often maintenance dose of 100 mg daily).

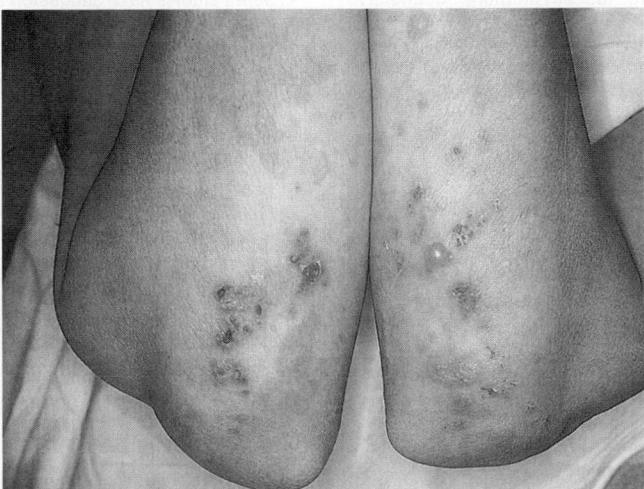

FIGURE 1D-9 Dermatitis herpetiformis is an immunologically mediated blistering disease. There is a strong association of dermatitis herpetiformis with HLA-B8, DR3. Gluten-sensitive enteropathy is a common associated finding. The lesions are grouped (herpetiform) and extremely pruritic. (From Callen JP [ed]: *Color atlas of dermatology*, ed 2, Philadelphia, 2000, Saunders.)

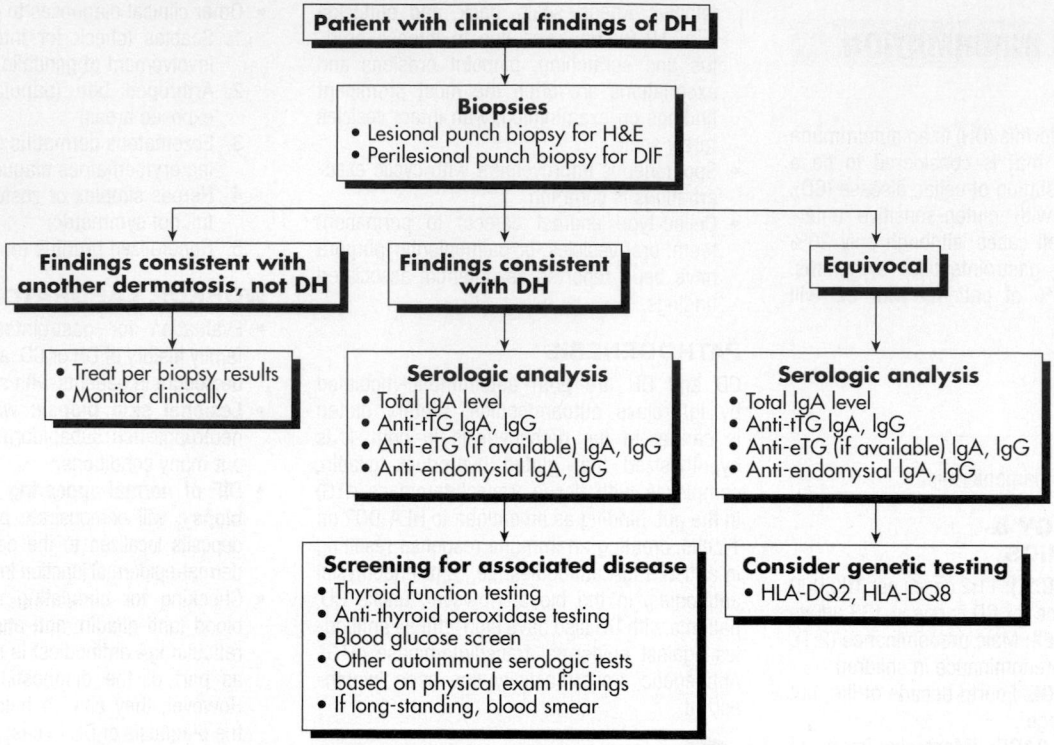

FIGURE 1D-10 Approach to the patient with suspected dermatitis herpetiformis. (From Bolotin D, Petronic-Rosic V: Dermatitis herpetiformis: Part II. Diagnosis, management, and prognosis. *J Am Acad Dermatol* 64(6), 1027–1033, 2011.)

2. Clinical monitoring weekly is recommended to optimize dose (optimal dose is when 1-2 new lesions/wk)
3. Caution: dapsone may produce hemolysis (especially if G6PD deficiency), agranulocytosis, methemoglobinemia, systemic drug hypersensitivity reaction (DRESS), and a peripheral neuropathy.
4. Baseline labs: CBC, LFTs, G6PD levels. After the initiation of therapy, monitor CBC every week ×1 month, then every other week ×2 months, monthly ×3 months, then every 3-4 months. Monitor LFTs every 3-4 months.
- Second-line alternatives
  1. Sulfapyridine (500-1500 mg/day) or sulfasalazine (500-1000 mg bid) may be substituted in cases of dapsone intolerance.
  2. Reported efficacy in uncontrolled studies and case reports have suggested efficacy with tetracyclines, nicotinamide, cyclosporine, colchicine, and heparin
- Symptomatic relief for pruritus
  1. Potent and superpotent topical corticosteroids (atrophy with prolonged use, limit to 14 days per month), non-sedating antihistamines twice daily, sedating antihistamines at bedtime, sarna lotion

CHRONIC Rx

- As DH is considered to represent the cutaneous manifestations of CD, lifelong avoidance of gluten is typically recommended. Information about educational resources, such as national and local support groups, should be provided (www.celiac.org).

- Patients with DH and CD have an increased risk of developing Hashimoto's thyroiditis, non-Hodgkin lymphoma, and GI lymphomas. An increased incidence of other autoimmune disorders (type 1 diabetes mellitus, pernicious anemia, Addison's disease, vitiligo, systemic lupus erythematosus, rheumatoid arthritis, and Sjögren's syndrome) and osteoporosis have also been reported.
  1. Screening for thyroid disease (TSH, antithyroid peroxidase antibody titers) is typically recommended
  2. Screening for autoimmune connective tissue diseases should be considered if suspicious signs or symptoms
  3. Routine screening for GI lymphomas is controversial

REFERRAL

- Dermatologist for skin biopsy and management of cutaneous disease
- Gastroenterologist for evaluation of CD
- Nutritionist to educate patients about gluten-free diet
- National support groups (www.celiac.org) and local support groups

! PEARLS & CONSIDERATIONS

- Classic areas involved are those that are exposed if in a "fetal position."
- Lesions may be worsened by iodides and certain NSAIDs; systemic steroids ineffective.

- Location of biopsies is important! False-negative DIF can result if biopsies are taken from lesional skin (should be taken from normal-appearing skin adjacent to lesion) as diagnostic IgA deposits are usually destroyed by the blistering process.
- GFD results in reduced IgA in skin on DIF (with eventual disappearance) and reduced anti-endomysial antibodies in the blood. Hence, serologies (e.g., anti-endomysial antibodies) can be used to monitor degree of compliance to dietary gluten restriction.
- Some studies have suggested a possible protective effect of GFD against intestinal lymphoma. First-degree relatives do not appear to be at increased risk for GI or systemic lymphomas in the absence of DH or CD.

SUGGESTED READINGS

Available at www.expertconsult.com

RELATED CONTENT

Celiac Disease (Related Key Topic)

AUTHOR: **LISA PAPPAS-TAFFER, M.D.**

 **BASIC INFORMATION**

DEFINITION

Diabetes insipidus is a polyuric disorder resulting from insufficient production of vasopressin (pituitary [neurogenic] diabetes insipidus) or unresponsiveness of the renal tubules to vasopressin (nephrogenic diabetes insipidus).

ICD-10CM CODES
E23.2 Diabetes insipidus

EPIDEMIOLOGY & DEMOGRAPHICS

GENETICS:
- Nephrogenic diabetes insipidus can be inherited as a sex-linked recessive trait.
- There is also a rare autosomal-dominant form of neurogenic diabetes insipidus.

PHYSICAL FINDINGS & CLINICAL PRESENTATION

- Central diabetes insipidus is usually abrupt in onset whereas in compulsive water drinking there is a more vague history of onset
- Nocturia is unusual in compulsive water drinkers and more common in central diabetes insipidus
- Polyuria: urinary volumes ranging from 2.5 to 6 L/day
- Polydipsia (predilection for cold or iced drinks)
- Neurologic manifestations (seizures, headaches, visual field defects)
- Evidence of volume contractions

NOTE: The physical findings and clinical manifestations are generally not evident until vasopressin secretory capacity is reduced to <20% of normal.

ETIOLOGY

Neurogenic diabetes insipidus:
- Idiopathic (Autoimmune hypophysitis)
- Malignancy: Neoplasms of brain or pituitary fossa (craniopharyngiomas, metastatic neoplasms from breast or lung)
- Posttherapeutic neurosurgical procedures (e.g., hypophysectomy)
- Head trauma (e.g., basal skull fracture)
- Granulomatous disorders (sarcoidosis, granulomatosis with polyangiitis, or tuberculosis)
- Histiocytosis (Hand-Schüller-Christian disease, eosinophilic granuloma)
- Familial (autosomal dominant); some cases autosomal recessive
- Other: interventricular hemorrhage, aneurysms, meningitis, postencephalitis, multiple sclerosis, Guillain-Barré syndrome, IgG4-related disease, lymphocytic hypophysitis
Nephrogenic diabetes insipidus:
- Drugs: lithium, aminoglycosides, antivirals (foscarnet, didanosine), amphotericin B, demeclocycline, ifosfamide, methoxyflurane anesthesia
- Familial: X-linked
- Metabolic: hypercalcemia or hypokalemia
- Other: sarcoidosis, urinary tract infection, amyloidosis, Sjögren syndrome, pyelonephritis, nephronophthisis, polycystic disease, sickle cell nephropathy, postobstructive, low-protein diets (protein malnourishment)

Dx DIAGNOSIS

DIFFERENTIAL DIAGNOSIS

- Diabetes mellitus, nephropathies
- Primary polydipsia, medications (e.g., chlorpromazine)
- Osmotic diuresis (glucose, mannitol, anticholinergics)
- Psychogenic polydipsia, electrolyte disturbances

WORKUP

- The diagnostic workup is aimed at showing that polyuria is caused by the inability to concentrate urine and determining whether the problem is the result of decreased vasopressin or insensitivity to vasopressin. This is done with the water deprivation test (Table E1D-6):
1. After baseline measurement of weight, vasopressin, plasma sodium, and urine and plasma osmolarity, the patient is deprived of fluids under strict medical supervision.
2. Frequent (q2h) monitoring of plasma and urine osmolarity follows.
3. The test is generally terminated when plasma osmolarity is >295 mOsm/kg or the patient loses ≥3.5% of initial body weight.
4. Diabetes insipidus is confirmed if the plasma osmolarity is >295 mOsm/kg and the urine osmolarity is <500 mOsm/kg.
5. To distinguish nephrogenic from neurogenic diabetes insipidus, the patient is given 5 U of vasopressin and the change in urine osmolarity is measured. A significant increase (>50%) in urine osmolarity after administration of vasopressin is indicative of neurogenic diabetes insipidus.
- A diagnostic algorithm for diabetes insipidus is described in Fig. E1D-11.

LABORATORY TESTS

- Decreased urinary specific gravity (≤1.005)
- Baseline plasma osmolality >295 mOsm/kg is suggestive of central diabetes mellitus whereas values below 270 mOsm/kg favor compulsive water drinking. Decreased urinary osmolarity (usually <200 mOsm/kg) even in the presence of high plasma osmolality
- Hypernatremia, increased plasma osmolarity, hypercalcemia, hypokalemia

IMAGING STUDIES

MRI of the pituitary if neurogenic diabetes insipidus is confirmed

Rx TREATMENT

NONPHARMACOLOGIC THERAPY

- Patient education regarding control of fluid balance and prevention of dehydration with adequate fluid intake or IV D_5W
- Daily weight

ACUTE GENERAL Rx

Therapy varies with the degree and type of diabetes insipidus (Table E1D-7).
- Neurogenic diabetes insipidus:
1. Desmopressin acetate (DDAVP) 20-40 mcg qd intranasally in 1 to 3 divided doses or in tablet form 0.1 to 1.2 mg. Usual oral dose is 0.1 to 1.2 mg/day in 2 to 3 divided doses. Desmopressin is also available in injectable form given as 2 to 4 mcg/day SC or IV in 2 divided doses.
2. Vasopressin tannate in oil: 2.5 to 5 U IM q24 to 72h; useful for long-term management because of its long half-life.
3. In mild cases of neurogenic diabetes insipidus, polyuria may be controlled with HCTZ 50 mg qd (decreases urine volume by increasing proximal tubular reabsorption of glomerular infiltrate).
- Nephrogenic diabetes insipidus:
1. Removal of the underlying cause. However, prolonged lithium therapy can lead to irreversible nephrogenic diabetes insipidus even after lithium therapy is withdrawn.
2. Amiloride 5 mg/day for lithium-related disease
3. Low-sodium diet and chlorothiazide to induce mild sodium depletion

CHRONIC Rx

Patients should be aware of the danger of dehydration and the need for liberal water intake.

REFERRAL

Endocrinology consultation for diagnostic testing

 **PEARLS & CONSIDERATIONS**

COMMENTS

- Patients should be instructed to wear a medical identification tag or bracelet identifying their medical illness.
- In central diabetes insipidus, the use of DDAVP has become the standard of care. Extensive clinical experience has shown it to be both safe and effective in the treatment of this disorder.
- The treatment of nephrogenic diabetes insipidus is more complicated than the central form, and opinion varies among experts in the field. Consultation with a specialist is always recommended in this setting.

SUGGESTED READINGS
Available at www.expertconsult.com

RELATED CONTENT
Diabetes Insipidus (Patient Information)

AUTHOR: **FRED F. FERRI, M.D.**

BASIC INFORMATION

DEFINITION

- Diabetes mellitus (DM) refers to a syndrome of hyperglycemia resulting from many different causes (see "Etiology"). It is broadly classified into type 1 and type 2 DM. The terms "insulin-dependent" and "non–insulin-dependent" diabetes are obsolete because when a person with type 2 diabetes needs insulin, he or she remains labeled as type 2 and is not reclassified as type 1. Table 1D-8 provides a general comparison of the two types of DM.
- The American Diabetes Association (ADA) defines DM as follows:
  1. A fasting plasma glucose (FPG) ≥126 mg/dl, which should be confirmed with repeat testing on a different day. Fasting is defined as no caloric intake for at least 8 hr.
  2. Symptoms of hyperglycemia and a casual (random) plasma glucose ≥200 mg/dl. Classic symptoms of hyperglycemia include polyuria, polydipsia, and unexplained weight loss.
  3. An oral glucose tolerance test (OGTT) with a plasma glucose ≥200 mg/dl 2 hr after a 75 g (100 g for pregnant women) glucose load.
  4. A hemoglobin A_{1c} (HbA1c) value ≥6.5%.
- Individuals with glucose levels higher than normal but not high enough to meet the criteria for diagnosis of DM are considered to have "prediabetes," the diagnosis of which is made as follows:
  1. A fasting plasma glucose 100 to 125 mg/dl; this is referred to as impaired fasting glucose.
  2. After OGTT, a 2-hr plasma glucose 140 to 199; this is referred to as impaired glucose tolerance.
  3. A hemoglobin A_{1c} value 5.7% to 6.4%.

- Table 1D-9 describes diagnostic categories for DM and at-risk states.

SYNONYMS

IDDM (insulin-dependent diabetes mellitus)
NIDDM (non–insulin-dependent diabetes mellitus)
Type 1 diabetes mellitus (insulin-dependent diabetes mellitus)
Type 2 diabetes mellitus (non–insulin-dependent diabetes mellitus)

ICD-10CM CODES

E11.5	Type 2 diabetes mellitus with peripheral circulatory complications
E11.7	Type 2 diabetes mellitus with multiple complications
E11.8	Type 2 diabetes mellitus with unspecified complications
E11.9	Type 2 diabetes mellitus without complications
E10.69	Type 1 diabetes mellitus with other specified complication
E10.8	Type 1 diabetes mellitus with unspecified complications
E10.9	Type 1 diabetes mellitus without complications
E11.69	Type 2 diabetes mellitus with other specified complication
E11.8	Type 2 diabetes mellitus with unspecified complications
E11.9	Type 2 diabetes mellitus without complications

EPIDEMIOLOGY & DEMOGRAPHICS

- DM affects 9% to 10% of the U.S. population. Prevalence rates vary considerably by race/ethnicity.
- Incidence rate increases with age, varying from 2% in persons age 20 to 44 yr to 18% in persons 65 to 74 yr. Type 2 DM can have a long presymptomatic phase, leading to a 4- to 7-yr delay in diagnosis.

- Diabetes accounts for 8% of all legal blindness in the United States and is the leading cause of end-stage renal disease (ESRD).
- Patients with diabetes are 2-4 times more likely than nondiabetic patients to experience development of cardiovascular disease.

PHYSICAL FINDINGS & CLINICAL PRESENTATION

1. Physical examination varies with the presence of complications and may be normal in early stages
2. Diabetic retinopathy:
   a. Nonproliferative (background diabetic retinopathy):
      (1) Initially: microaneurysms, capillary dilation, waxy or hard exudates, dot and flame hemorrhages, atrioventricular shunts
      (2) Advanced stage: microinfarcts with cotton wool exudates, macular edema
   b. Proliferative retinopathy: characterized by formation of new vessels, vitreous hemorrhages, fibrous scarring, and retinal detachment
3. Cataracts and glaucoma occur with increased frequency in patients with diabetes
4. Diabetic neuropathy
   a. Distal sensorimotor polyneuropathy
      (1) Symptoms include paresthesia, hyperesthesia, or burning pain involving bilateral distal extremities, in a "stocking-glove" distribution. This can progress to motor weakness and ataxia.
      (2) Physical examination may reveal decreased pinprick sensation, sensation to light touch, vibration sense, and loss of proprioception. Motor disturbances such as decreased deep tendon reflexes and atrophy of interossei muscles can also be seen.

TABLE 1D-8 General Comparison of the Two Types of Diabetes Mellitus

	Type 1	Type 2
Previous terminology	Insulin-dependent diabetes mellitus (IDDM), type I, juvenile-onset diabetes	Non–insulin-dependent diabetes mellitus, type II, adult-onset diabetes
Age of onset	Usually <30 yr, particularly childhood and adolescence, but any age	Usually >40 yr, but any age
Genetic predisposition	Moderate; environmental factors required for expression; 35%-50% concordance in monozygotic twins; several candidate genes proposed	Strong; 60-90% concordance in monozygotic twins; many candidate genes proposed; some genes identified in maturity-onset diabetes of the young
Human leukocyte antigen associations	Linkage to DQA and DQB, influenced by DRB (3 and 4) (DR2 protective)	None known
Other associations	Autoimmune; Graves' disease, Hashimoto's thyroiditis, vitiligo, Addison's disease, pernicious anemia	Heterogenous group, ongoing subclassification based on identification of specific pathogenic processes and genetic defects
Precipitating and risk factors	Largely unknown; microbial, chemical, dietary, other	Age, obesity (central), sedentary lifestyle, previous gestational diabetes
Findings at diagnosis	85%-90% of patients have one and usually more autoantibodies to ICA512/IA-2/IA-2b, GAD_{65}, insulin (IAA)	Possibly complications (microvascular and macrovascular) caused by significant preceding asymptomatic period
Endogenous insulin levels	Low or absent	Usually present (relative deficiency), early hyperinsulinemia
Insulin resistance	Only with hyperglycemia	Mostly present
Prolonged fast	Hyperglycemia, ketoacidosis	Euglycemia
Stress, withdrawal of insulin	Ketoacidosis	Nonketotic hyperglycemia, occasionally ketoacidosis

GAD, Glutamic acid decarboxylase; *IA-2/IA-2b,* tyrosine phosphatases; *IAA,* insulin autoantibodies; *ICA,* islet cell antibody; *ICA512,* islet cell autoantigen 512 (fragment of IA-2).
From Andreoli TE (ed): *Cecil essentials of medicine,* ed 6, Philadelphia, 2005, Saunders.

TABLE 1D-9 Diagnostic Categories*: Diabetes Mellitus and At-Risk States

Fasting Plasma Glucose Level	2-Hour (75-g) OGTT Result		
	<140 mg/dl	140-199 mg/dl	≥200 mg/dl
<100 mg/dl	Normal	IGT[†]	DM
100-125 mg/dl	IFG[†]	IGT[†] and IFG[†]	DM
≥126 mg/dl	DM	DM	DM
HbA$_{1C}$ Level	<5.7%	5.7-6.4%	≥6.5%
	Normal	High-risk[†]	DM

DM, Diabetes mellitus; *IFG,* impaired fasting glucose; *IGT.* impaired glucose tolerance.
*These diagnostic categories are based on the combined fasting plasma glucose level and a 2-hour, 75-g oral glucose tolerance test (OGTT) result. Note that a confirmed random plasma glucose level of 200 mg/dl or higher in the appropriate clinical setting is diagnostic of diabetes and precludes the need for further testing.
[†]May be referred to as prediabetes.
From Goldman L, Schafer AI: *Goldman's Cecil medicine,* ed 24, Philadelphia, 2012, Saunders.

b. Autonomic neuropathy:
   (1) GI disturbances: esophageal motility abnormalities, gastroparesis, diarrhea (usually nocturnal)
   (2) Genitourinary (GU) disturbances: neurogenic bladder (hesitancy, weak stream, and dribbling), impotence
   (3) Cardiovascular (CV) disturbances: orthostatic hypotension, tachycardia, decreased heart rate variability (HRV). Decreased heart rate variability is associated with increased cardiac mortality, independent of ejection fraction.
c. Polyradiculopathy: painful weakness and atrophy in the distribution of ≥1 contiguous nerve roots.
d. Mononeuropathy involving cranial nerves III, IV, or VI or peripheral nerves can also occur.
5. Diabetic nephropathy: pedal edema, pallor, weakness, uremic appearance
6. Foot ulcers: occur in 15% of individuals with diabetes (annual incidence rate 2%) and are the leading causes of hospitalization; they are usually secondary to a combination of factors, including peripheral vascular insufficiency, repeated trauma (unrecognized because of sensory loss), and superimposed infection.
   a. Patient symptoms are usually less than would be expected from clinical findings, due to loss of sensation related to peripheral neuropathy.
   b. Comprehensive foot exams include visual inspection, assessment of pedal pulses, and assessment of protective sensation using a 10-g monofilament to test sensation.
   c. Prevention of foot ulcers in an individual with diabetes includes strict glucose control, patient education, prescription footwear, intensive podiatric care, and evaluation for surgical interventions
7. Neuropathic arthropathy (Charcot's joints): bone or joint deformities from repeated trauma (secondary to peripheral neuropathy; Fig. E1D-12).
8. Necrobiosis lipoidica diabeticorum: plaquelike reddened areas with a central area that fades to white-yellow found on the anterior surfaces of the legs (Fig. E1D-13); in these areas, the skin becomes very thin and can ulcerate easily.

ETIOLOGY

IDIOPATHIC DIABETES: Type 1 DM: results from autoimmune beta-cell destruction, usually leading to absolute insulin deficiency

- Hereditary factors:
  1. Islet cell antibodies (found in 90% of patients within the first yr of diagnosis)
  2. Higher incidence of human leukocyte antigen (HLA) types DR3, DR4
  3. 50% concordance rate in identical twins
- Environmental factors: viral infection (possibly Coxsackie virus, mumps virus)
  Type 2 DM: results from insulin resistance and a progressive defect in insulin secretion.
- Hereditary factors: 90% concordance rate in identical twins
- Environmental factors: obesity, sedentary lifestyle, high carbohydrate content in food

DIABETES SECONDARY TO OTHER FACTORS:

- Hormonal excess: Cushing's syndrome, acromegaly, glucagonoma, pheochromocytoma
- Drugs: glucocorticoids, diuretics, oral contraceptives
- Insulin receptor unavailability (with or without circulating antibodies)
- Pancreatic disease: pancreatitis, pancreatectomy, hemochromatosis, cystic fibrosis
- Genetic syndromes: maturity onset diabetes of the young (MODY, monogenetic diabetes accounting for 2% to 5% of diabetes), familial hyperlipidemias, myotonic dystrophy, lipoatrophy
- Gestational diabetes (GDM): diabetes diagnosed during pregnancy that is due to pregnancy-related insulin resistance

Dx DIAGNOSIS

DIFFERENTIAL DIAGNOSIS

- Diabetes insipidus
- Stress hyperglycemia
- Diabetes secondary to hormonal excess, drugs, pancreatic disease

LABORATORY TESTS

- Diagnosis of DM is made on the basis of the following tests:
  1. Fasting glucose ≥126 mg/dl on two occasions
  2. Non-FPG ≥200 mg/dl and symptoms of DM
  3. OGTT (75 g glucose load for nonpregnant individuals) with 2-hr value >200 mg/dl
  4. Glycosylated hemoglobin (HbA$_{1c}$) ≥6.5%

- Screening for prediabetes and diabetes in asymptomatic patients (see Table 1D-10):
  1. Should be considered in adults of any age who are overweight (body mass index [BMI] >25 kg/m^2) or obese (BMI >30) and who have one or more additional risk factors for diabetes.
  2. In those who are without these risk factors, testing should begin at age 45 yr.
  3. If screen is normal, repeat testing should be carried out at least at 3-yr intervals.
- Detection and diagnosis of gestational diabetes mellitus (GDM)
  1. Screen for GDM using risk factor analysis and use of an OGTT. Pregnant women who are not known to have diabetes should be screened for gestational diabetes at 24 to 48 weeks' gestation with a 75 g oral glucose tolerance test. A diagnosis of GDM is made if any of the following levels of plasma glucose are exceeded: ≥92 mg/dl (5.1 mmol/L) when fasting, ≥80 mg/dl (10 mmol/L) at 1 hour, or ≥153 mg/dl (8.5 mmol/L) at 2 hours.
  2. Women with GDM should be screened for diabetes 6 to 12 wk postpartum and should be followed with subsequent screening for the development of diabetes or prediabetes at least every 3 yr
- Screening for diabetic nephropathy (Fig. E1D-14)
  1. Screening should be done at diagnosis and then yearly for type 2 diabetes and 5 yr after diagnosis then yearly in type 2 diabetics.
  2. Screening can be performed using a albumin:creatinine ratio (microalbumin) in a random spot urine collection or by measurement of a 24 hr urine collection for albumin, and creatinine clearance. The urine albumin to creatinine ratio (ACR) is independently associated with mortality at all levels of estimated glomerular filtration rate (eGFR) in older adults with diabetes.
  3. The diagnosis of microalbuminuria (ACR 30-299 mg/24 hr) should be based on 2 to 3 elevated levels within a 3- to 6-mo period because there is a marked variability in day-to-day albumin excretion. Patients with overt macroalbuminuria (>300 mg albumin/24 hr or albumin:creatinine ratio >300) should be followed by urine protein:creatinine ratio.
- A fasting serum lipid panel, serum creatinine, and electrolytes should be obtained yearly on all adult patients with diabetes.
- Self-monitoring of blood glucose (SMBG) is crucial for assessing the effectiveness of the management plan. The frequency and timing of SMBG varies with the needs and goals of each patient. In most patients with type 1 DM and pregnant women taking insulin, SMBG is recommended at least 3 times/day. In patients with type 2 DM not on insulin, recommendations are unclear for SMBG, but testing once or twice/day is acceptable in most patients.

TABLE 1D-10 Criteria for Diabetes Screening in Asymptomatic Individuals

1. Testing should be considered in all adults who are overweight (BMI >25 kg/m2*) and have additional risk factors:
   o Physical inactivity
   o A first-degree relative with diabetes
   o High-risk ethnic population (e.g., African American, Hispanic American, Native American, Asian American, Pacific Islander)
   o Delivered a baby weighing more than 9 lb or diagnosed with gestational diabetes mellitus
   o Systemic hypertension (blood pressure >140/90 mm Hg or on antihypertensive therapy)
   o High-density lipoprotein cholesterol level <35 mg/dl or triglyceride level >250 mg/dl
   o Polycystic ovary syndrome
   o Hemoglobin A_{1c} ≥5.7%, impaired glucose tolerance or impaired fasting glucose on prior testing
   o Other clinical conditions associated with insulin resistance (e.g., severe obesity, acanthosis nigricans)
   o History of cardiovascular disease
2. If none of the above criteria are present, screening for diabetes should begin at age 45 yr.
3. If the results are normal, screening should be repeated at least every 3 yr. Depending on initial results and risk status, more frequent testing may need to be considered.

*In some ethnic groups, such as Asians, at-risk body mass index (BMI) may be lower.
Modified from American Diabetes Association, Diagnosis and classification of diabetes mellitus *Diabetes Care* 33(Suppl. 1):S14, 2010. Borrowed from Goldman L, Schafer AI: *Goldman's Cecil medicine*, ed 24, Philadelphia, 2012, Saunders.

- Screening for thyroid dysfunction (TSH level), Vitamin B_{12} deficiency, and celiac disease should be considered in type 1 diabetes due to the increased frequency of other autoimmune diseases in these individuals.

Rx TREATMENT

- Type 1 diabetes requires immediate initiation of insulin therapy.
- The ADA and European Association for the Study of Diabetes recommend lifestyle intervention (diet and exercise) and metformin initiation (unless contraindication exist such as serum creatinine levels ≥1.5 mg/dL in males or ≥1.4 mg/dL in females or patients ≥30 years of age with reduced renal function as measured by creatinine clearance.) at the time of diagnosis of type 2 diabetes. Therapy should then be augmented with additional agents (including early initiation of insulin therapy) to achieve adequate glycemic control.
- In Type 1 diabetes, intensive glycemic control (HbA1c <7) has been shown in randomized controlled trials (RCT) to reduce the risk of microvascular (neuropathy, retinopathy, nephropathy) and macrovascular (cardiovascular events) complications.
- In Type 2 diabetes, intensive glycemic control (HbA1c <7) has been shown in RCT to reduce the risk of microvascular complications. While intensive glucose control reduced the risk of some cardiovascular disease outcomes (such as nonfatal MI), it did not reduce the risk of cardiovascular death or all cause mortality and increased the risk of severe hypoglycemia.
- It is important to remember that tight glycemic control may burden patients with complex treatment programs, hypoglycemia, weight gain, and costs. Clinicians should individualize HbA1c targets so that they are reasonable and reflect patients' personal and clinical contexts and their informed values and preferences. A target HbA1c <7 is reasonable for motivated new diabetic patients with long life expectancies, whereas less stringent controls (HbA1c 7.5 or higher) may be reasonable in elderly patients with limited life expectancy and elevated risk of hypoglycemia. The American Geriatrics Society recommends a general goal for glycated hemoglobin in older adults of 7.5% to 8.0%. Higher HbA1c targets (8%-9%) are appropriate for older adults with multiple comorbidities, poor health, and limited life expectancy.[1]

NONPHARMACOLOGIC THERAPY

1. Diet
   a. Calories
      (1) The patient with diabetes can be started on 15 calories/lb of ideal body weight; this number can be increased to 20 calories/lb for an active person and 25 calories/lb if the patient does heavy physical labor.
      (2) The calories should be distributed as 45% to 65% carbohydrates, <30% fat, with saturated fat limited to <7% of total calories, and 10% to 30% protein. Daily cholesterol intake should not exceed 300 mg.
      (3) The emphasis should be on complex carbohydrates rather than simple and refined starches, and on polyunsaturated instead of saturated fats in a ratio of 2:1.
   b. Seven food groups
      (1) The exchange diet of the ADA includes bread or starches, meat or proteins, vegetables, fruits, fats, milk, and free foods (e.g., black tea, sugar-free gelatin).
      (2) The name of each exchange is meant to be all-inclusive (e.g., cereal, muffins, spaghetti, potatoes, rice are in the bread group; meats, fish, eggs, cheese, peanut butter are in the protein group).
      (3) The glycemic index compares the increase in blood sugar after the ingestion of simple sugars and complex carbohydrates with the increase that occurs after the absorption of glucose; equal amounts of starches do not give the same increase in plasma glucose (pasta equal in calories to a baked potato causes less of an increase than the potato); thus, it is helpful to know the glycemic index of a particular food product.
      (4) Fiber: Insoluble fiber (bran, celery) and soluble globular fiber (pectin in fruit) delay glucose absorption and attenuate the postprandial serum glucose peak; they also appear to reduce the increased triglyceride level often present in patients with uncontrolled diabetes. A diet high in fiber should be emphasized (20 to 35 g/day of soluble and insoluble fiber).
   c. Other principles
      (1) Modest sodium restriction to 2400 to 3000 mg/day. If hypertension is present, restrict to <2400 mg/day; if nephropathy and hypertension are present, restrict to <2000 mg/day.
      (2) Moderation of alcohol intake recommended (≤2 drinks/day in men, ≤1 drink/day in women).
      (3) Non-nutritive artificial sweeteners are acceptable in moderate amounts.
2. Exercise: increases the cellular glucose uptake by increasing the number of insulin receptors. The following points must be considered:
   a. Exercise program must be individualized and built up slowly. Consider beginning with 15 min of low-impact aerobic exercise 3 times per wk and increasing the frequency and duration to 30 to 45 min of moderate aerobic activity (50% to 70% of maximum age predicted heart rate) to 3 to 5 days/wk.
      (1) In the absence of contraindications, resistance training three times per wk should be encouraged.
   b. Insulin is more rapidly absorbed when injected into a limb that is then exercised, and this can result in hypoglycemia.
   c. Physical activity can result in hypoglycemia if medication dose or carbohydrate consumption is not modified. Ingestion of additional carbohydrates is recommended if pre-exercise glucose levels are <100 mg/dl.
3. Weight loss: to ideal body weight if the patient is overweight. Recent trials have shown that although weight loss has many positive health benefits for people with type 2 DM, such as slower decline in mobility, it does not reduce the number of cardiovascular events.
4. Screening for nephropathy, neuropathy, and retinopathy: annual serum creatinine and urine albumin excretion; initial comprehensive eye examination and at least annually thereafter
5. Diabetes self-management education: could also address psychosocial issues
6. Self-monitoring of blood glucose should occur three to four times per day for patients using multiple insulin injections or on insulin pump therapy
7. Perform HbA1c at least two times a year in patients who are meeting treatment goals and who have stable glycemic control

[1]Huang ES, Davis AM: Glycemic Control in Older Adults With Diabetes Mellitus, *JAMA* 314:1509-1510, 2015.

1. HbA1c quarterly in patients whose therapy has changed or who are not meeting glycemic goals
2. The HbA1c goal for nonpregnant adults in general is <7%
3. In the elderly, those with comorbidities, or those at risk for complications from hypoglycemia, a more moderate glycemic target (HbA1c 7-8) may be appropriate

GENERAL Rx

- When the previous measures fail to normalize the serum glucose, oral hypoglycemic agents should be added to the regimen in type 2 DM. Tables 1D-11 and 1D-12 compare therapies for type 2 DM and classes of antihyperglycemic agents.
- The primary mechanism of metformin is to decrease hepatic glucose production and improve insulin sensitivity. Because metformin does not produce hypoglycemia when used as a monotherapy, it is preferred initially for most patients. Metformin reduces mean HbA1c level by 1.1%. It is contraindicated in patients with severe renal insufficiency with an estimated glomerular filtrate rate <30 ml/min, serum creatinine level of 1.5 per dl or greater in men or 1.4 per dl or greater in women, heart failure, or other clinical states of hypoperfusion, and in patients with significant liver disease.
- Sitagliptin, saxagliptin, vildagliptin, alogliptin, and linagliptin inhibit the enzyme DPP-4, responsible for inactivation and degradation of glucagon-like peptide-1 (GLP-1) and glucose-dependent insulinotropic polypeptide (GIP). These drugs, known as "gliptins," raise blood incretin levels, thereby inhibiting glucagon release and lowering blood glucose levels. When used with metformin they do not cause hypoglycemia and are preferred over sulfonylureas as second line agents. Linagliptin does not require a dosage adjustment in renal insufficiency. Cost is a major barrier to their use.
- Exenatide, dulaglutide, albiglutide, and liraglutide are glucagon-like peptide-1 (GLP-1) agonists. They are incretin mimetics that stimulate release of insulin from pancreatic beta cells and can be used as adjunctive therapy for patients with type 2 DM. GLP-1 agonists are not indicated in type 1 DM and are contraindicated in patients with severe renal impairment. Cost is a barrier to their use.
- Sulfonylureas increase insulin secretion and work best when given before meals. All sulfonylureas are contraindicated in patients who are allergic to sulfa.
- Sodium-glucose co-transporter 2 (SGLT$_2$) inhibitors (e.g., canagliflozin, dapagliflozin, empagliflozin) are useful for oral treatment of type 2 DM. By inhibiting SGLT$_2$,, these medications decrease glucose reabsorption, increase urinary glucose excretion, and lower blood glucose levels (decrease HbA$_{1c}$ by 0.7%). Side effects include increased risk of genital mycotic infections, UTIs, and volume depletion. Higher cost and limited drug formulary availability are limiting factors.
- Acarbose and miglitol inhibit pancreatic amylase and small intestinal glucosidases, thereby delaying carbohydrate absorption in the gut and reducing associated postprandial hyperglycemia. The major side effects are flatulence, diarrhea, and abdominal cramps.
- The meglitinides nateglinide and repaglinide and the bile acid sequestrant colesevelam can also be used to lower glucose levels but are expensive and generally poorly tolerated.

TABLE 1D-11 Comparison of Therapies for Type 2 Diabetes

Property	Lifestyle	Insulins	Sulfonylureas	Metformin	α-Glucosidase Inhibitors	Glitazones	Glinides	Exenatide	Pramlintide
Target tissue	Muscle or fat	Beta cell supplement	Beta cell	Liver	Gut	Muscle	Beta cell	Various	Brain
ΔHbA$_{1c}$ (%) as (monotherapy)	Variable	1->2	1-2	1-2	0.5-1	0.5-2	Re: 1-2 N: 0.5-1	~1	~0.5
Fasting effect	Good	Excellent	Good	Good	Poor	Good	Re: Moderate N: Poor	Poor	Poor
Postprandial effect	Good	Excellent	Good	Good	Excellent	Good	Re: Good N: Excellent	Excellent	Excellent
Severe hypoglycemia	No	Yes	Yes	No	No	No	Re: Yes N: No	No	No
Dosing interval	Continuous	qd to continuous	qd to tid	bid or tid	bid to qid	P: qd Ro: qd or bid	tid to qid with meals	bid	tid
ΔWeight (lb/yr)	+1	+3	+1 to 3	0 to −6	0 to −10	+1 to 13	+1 to 3	−6 to −12	−3 to −6
ΔInsulin	Variable	Increase	Increase	Modest decrease	Modest decrease	Decrease	Increase	Increase	None
ΔLDL	Minimal decrease	Minimal decrease	None	Decrease	Minimal decrease	Increase	None	None	None
ΔHDL	Minimal increase	None	None	Increase	None	Increase	None	Decrease	None
ΔTG	Minimal decrease	Decrease	None	Decrease	Minimal decrease	P: Decrease Ro: None	None	Decrease	None
Common problem	Recidivism, injury	Hypoglycemia, weight gain	Hypoglycemia, weight gain	Transient GI	Flatulence	Weight gain, edema, anemia	Hypoglycemia	GI	GI
Rare problem	—	—	—	Lactic acidosis	—	Hepatotoxicity?	—	—	—
Contraindications	None	None	Allergy	Renal failure, Liver failure, CHF (>80 yr old)	Intestinal disease	Hepatocellular disease	—	None	None
Cost ($/mo)	0-200	30-450	10-15	30-60	40-80	75-180	70-110	170-200	200-400
Maximum effective dose	—	1-2 U/kg per day	maximum or double starting	1000 mg bid	50 mg tid	P: 45 mg qd Ro: 4 mg bid	Re: 2 mg tid N: 120 mg tid	10 μg bid	120 μg ac

Δ, Change; ac, before food; CHF, congestive heart failure; GI, gastrointestinal disturbance; HbA$_{1c}$, glycosylated hemoglobin; HDL, high-density lipoprotein; LDL, low-density lipoprotein; N, nateglinide; P, pioglitazone; Re, repaglinide; Ro, rosiglitazone; TG, triglycerides.
From Melmed S, Polonsky KS, Larsen PR, Kronenberg HM: Williams textbook of endocrinology, ed 12, Philadelphia, 2011, Saunders.

TABLE 1D-12 Classes of Antihyperglycemic Therapy

Class	Representative Agents	Major Action	HbA1c Lowering (%)	Fasting or Prandial Effect	Usual Dosing Frequency (Doses/Day)	Route	Hypoglycemia	Weight Effect	CVD Risk Factor Benefits	Important Contraindications	Daily Cost ($)
Lifestyle	—	Broad	>1	Both	—	—	No	Loss	Yes	—	—
Biguanide	Metformin	Liver sensitizer	>1	Fasting	1-2	Oral	No	Neutral	Modest	Renal or hepatic failure	<$1
Sulfonylurea	Glimepiride, glipizide	Insulin secretagogue	>1	Fasting	1-2	Oral	Yes	Gain	Negligible	—	<<$1
Meglitinide	Repaglinide	Insulin secretagogue	>1	Both	With meals	Oral	Yes	Gain	Negligible	—	~$5
Benzoic acid–derived	Nateglinide	Insulin secretagogue	<1	Prandial	With meals	Oral	Minimal	Minimal	Negligible	—	~$5
Basal insulin	NPH, glargine, detemir	Insulin supplement/substitute	>1	Fasting	1	SQ	Yes++	Gain++	Lowers TG	—	~$5
Bolus insulin	R, lispro, aspart, glulisine	Insulin supplement/substitute	>1	Prandial	With meals	SQ	Yes++	Gain++	Lowers TG	—	~$5
Thiazolidinediones	Pioglitazone, rosiglitazone	Peripheral sensitizer	>1	Fasting	1	Oral	No	Gain++	Variable (see text)	Heart or liver failure	~$5
α-Glucosidase inhibitors	Acarbose, miglitol	Slow carbohydrate absorption	<1	Prandial	With meals	Oral	No	Neutral	Negligible	—	~$3
Amylinomimetics	Pramlintide	Broad	<1	Prandial	With meals	SQ	No	Loss	Negligible	—	~$10
GLP1 receptor agonists	Exenatide	Broad	~1	Prandial	2	SQ	No	Loss	Modest with weight loss	Pancreatitis, renal failure	~$9
Long-acting GLP1 receptor agonists	Liraglutide, albiglutide, dulaglutide	Broad	>1	Both	1	SQ	No	Loss	Lowers BP	Pancreatitis, medullary thyroid cancer	~$13
DPP4 inhibitors	Sitagliptin, saxagliptin	Improved insulin/glucagon secretion	<1	Both	1	Oral	No	Neutral	Negligible	Pancreatitis	~$7
Bile acid sequestrants	Colesevelam	Uncertain	<1	Prandial	1-2	Oral	No	Neutral	Lowers LDL	Hypertriglyceridemia	~$9
SGLT2 inhibitor	Canagliflozin, dapagliflozin, empagliflozin	Decrease renal glucose reabsorption, increase urinary glucose excretion	<1	Both	1	Oral	No	Loss	Negligible	Volume dilution	~$10

BP, Blood pressure; CVD, cardiovascular disease; LDL, low-density lipoprotein; SGLT2, sodium–glucose co-transporter 2; SQ, subcutaneous; TG, triglyceride.
Modified from Melmed S, Polonsky KS, Larsen PR, Kronenberg HM: Williams textbook of endocrinology, ed 12, Philadelphia, 2011, Saunders.

- Pramlintide is a synthetic analog of human amylin, which is synthesized by pancreatic beta cells and cosecreted with insulin in response to food intake. It suppresses glucagon secretion and slows stomach emptying and can be used as an adjunctive treatment for patients with type 1 or type 2 DM who inject insulin at mealtime. Nausea is its major side effect.
- Thiazolidinediones (pioglitazone and rosiglitazone) increase insulin sensitivity and have been used in the therapy of type 2 diabetes. Serum transaminase levels should be obtained before starting therapy and monitored periodically. Thiazolidinediones, in general, result in moderate weight gain and increase the risk for heart failure and osteoporosis/fractures. Rosiglitazone has an FDA black box warning for heart failure exacerbations and myocardial ischemia. Pioglitazone and rosiglitazone cause increased incidence of bladder cancer.
- Combination therapy of various hypoglycemic agents is commonly used when monotherapy results in inadequate glycemic control.
- Insulin is indicated for the treatment of all type 1 DM and for type 2 DM patients whose condition cannot be adequately controlled with diet and oral agents. The American College of Endocrinology and the American Association of Clinical Endocrinologists recommend initiation of insulin therapy in patients with type 2 diabetes and an initial HbA1c level >9%, or if the diabetes is uncontrolled despite optimal oral glycemic therapy. Insulin therapy may be initiated as augmentation, starting at 0.3 unit/kg, or as replacement, starting at 0.6 to 1.0 unit/kg. Table 1D-13 describes commonly used types of insulin.
  1. The risks of insulin therapy include weight gain, hypoglycemia, and in rare cases, allergic or cutaneous reactions.
  2. Replacement insulin therapy should mimic normal release patterns.
     a. Approximately 50% to 60% of daily insulin can be given as a long-acting insulin (NPH, ultralente, glargine, detemir) injected once or twice daily
     b. The remaining 40% to 50% can be short-acting (regular) or rapid-acting (lispro, aspart, glulisine) to cover mealtime carbohydrates and correct increased current glucose levels.
- Continuous subcutaneous insulin infusion (CSII, or insulin pump) provides comparable or slightly better control than multiple daily injections. It should be considered for diabetes presenting in childhood or adolescence and during pregnancy. The guidelines for insulin pump therapy from the American Association of Diabetes Educators include "frequent and unpredictable fluctuations in blood glucose" and "patient perceptions that diabetes management impedes the pursuit of personal or professional goals."
- Low-dose aspirin (ASA; 81 mg/day) has been proven to lower the risk of subsequent myocardial infarction, stroke, or vascular death in secondary prevention studies. The ADA recommends low-dose aspirin for primary prevention in diabetic patients with one additional cardiovascular risk factor, including age older than 40 yr, cigarette smoking, hypertension, obesity, albuminuria, hyperlipidemia, and family history of coronary artery disease.
- Measure fasting lipid profile at least annually in adults.
  1. All patients with diabetes with one or more additional risk factors for cardiovascular disease should be on statin therapy together with lifestyle modification regardless of baseline lipid levels.
  2. Diabetic patients aged 40 to 75 with LDL cholesterol of 70 to 189 mg/dl and without clinical atherosclerotic cardiovascular disease (ASCVD) should receive at least moderate-intensity statin therapy and consider high-intensity statin therapy if 10-year ASCVD risk is >=7.5%.
- Aggressive antihypertensive therapy is recommended to keep systolic blood pressure (BP) <130 and diastolic BP <80 mm Hg. Use of angiotensin-converting enzyme (ACE) inhibitors or angiotensin receptor blockers (ARBs) to decrease albuminuria and for prevention of progression of kidney disease should be considered regardless of presence of hypertension. Combination therapy with an ACE inhibitor and an ARB should be avoided due to increased risk of adverse effects among patients with diabetic nephropathy.
- Bariatric surgery should be considered in adults with BMI >35 kg/m^2 and type 2 diabetes, especially if the diabetes is difficult to control with lifestyle and pharmacologic therapy.
- Treat hypoglycemia in a conscious person with glucose tab or gel 15 to 20 g, and intramuscular injection of glucagon if unconscious. Patient and family members should be instructed on the administration of glucagon for individuals at significant risk for severe hypoglycemia.

DISPOSITION

- Diabetic retinopathy occurs in nearly 15% of patients with diabetes after 15 yr of diagnosis and increases 1%/yr after diagnosis. Retinal laser photocoagulation and vitrectomy are effective treatment modalities. Prevention is best accomplished by strict glucose and BP control. Early blockade of the renin-angiotensin system has been shown to slow progression of retinopathy in patients with type 1 diabetes.
- The frequency of neuropathy in patients with type 2 diabetes approaches 70% to 80%. It can be subdivided into sensorimotor neuropathy and autonomic neuropathy. Duloxetine, a selective serotonin and norepinephrine reuptake inhibitor, is effective and

TABLE 1D-13 Types of Insulin[a]

Preparation	Brand	Onset (hr)[b]	Peak (hr)	Duration (hr)[c]	Route
Insulin Aspart	NovoLog[d]	<0.25	1-3	3-5	SC, IV, CSII
Insulin Aspart Protamine/Insulin Aspart	Novol og Mix 70/30[d]	<0.25	1-4	24	SC
Insulin Detemir	Levemir	1-4	None	24	SC
Insulin Glargine	Lantus[d]	1-4	None	≥24	SC
Insulin Degludec	Tresiba	1-9	None	>42	SC
Insulin Glulisine	Apidra[d]	≤0.25	1	2-4	SC, IV
Insulin Lispro	Humalog[d]	<0.25	1	3.5-4.5	SC
Insulin Lispro Protamine/Insulin Lispro	Humalog Mix 75/25[d]	≤0.25	0.5-1.5	24	SC
	Humalog Mix 50/50[d]	≤0.25	1	16	SC
Insulin Injection Regular (R)	Humulin R[f]	0.5	2-4	6-8	SC, IM, IV
	Novolin N[e]	0.5	2.5-5	8	SC, IM, IV
Insulin Isophane Suspension (NPH)/ Regular Insulin (R)	Humulin 70/30[f]	0.5	2-12	24	SC
	Humulin 50/50[f]	0.5	3-5	24	SC
	Novolin 70/30[e]	0.5	2-12	24	SC
Insulin Isophane Suspension (NPH)	Humulin N[f]	1-2	6-12	18-24	SC
	Novolin N[e]	1.5	4-12	24	SC

CSII, Continuous subcutaneous infusion; *IM*, intramuscularly; *IV*, intravenously.

[a]Injectable insulins listed are available in a concentration of 100 U/ml; Humulin R, in a concentration of 500 U/ml for SC injection. SC injection only is available by prescription from Lilly for insulin-resistant patients who are hospitalized or in need of medical supervision.

[b]Onset for injectable formulations is always for the subcutaneous (SC) route. All times are approximate.

[c]Maximum effect occurs between these times; actual effect may last longer.

[d]Recombinant human insulin analogue (using *E. coli*).

[e]Recombinant (using *S. cerevisiae*).

[f]Recombinant (using *E. coli*).

BOX 1D-6 Equivalent Daily Doses of Oral Progestins for the Treatment of Dysfunctional Uterine Bleeding

Medroxyprogesterone acetate (Provera, Cycrin)	10 mg
Micronized progesterone (Prometrium)	400 mg
Norgestrel (Ovrette)	150 µg
Norethindrone acetate (Micronor, Nor-QD)	0.7 to 1.0 mg

From Carlson KJ et al: *Primary care of women*, ed 2, St Louis, 2002, Mosby.

2. For prolonged bleeding that is not life threatening: Premarin 1.25 mg (Estrace 2 mg) q4h for 24 hr, followed by Provera to bring on withdrawal bleeding; then sequential regimen of estrogen and progestin (Premarin 1.25 mg qd for 24 days, Provera 10 mg for last 10 days) or oral contraceptives

- Surgical treatment
1. Hysteroscopy with or without dilation and curettage (D&C)
2. Endometrial ablation
3. Hysterectomy

CHRONIC Rx

- Progestational agents
1. Medroxyprogesterone acetate 10 mg qd for 12 days, then cyclically to induce monthly withdrawal bleeding
2. Norethindrone 2.5 to 10 mg qd for 12 days
3. Depo-Provera 150 mg IM and then 150 mg every 3 mo
4. Oral contraceptives, 1 tablet qd either cyclically or continuously using only active pills
5. Levonorgestrel-releasing intrauterine device (Mirena, currently has an FDA indication for heavy menstrual bleeding in women who use an IUD for contraception)

- Letrozole or clomiphene citrate: patients with anovulatory bleeding who want to become pregnant. Recent studies suggest that progesterone withdrawal may be counterproductive in patients wishing to start an ovulation induction regimen. Pregnancy rates are lower when patients undergo withdrawal compared to when random ovulation induction start is used. A recent large, multicenter trial demonstrated that letrozole is superior to clomiphene citrate in ovulation induction in women with PCOS. Human menopausal gonadotropin (HMG) can be used for women who do not ovulate with oral agents or who have hypothalamic dysfunction.
- Others.
1. Antiprostaglandins
2. Danazol (rarely used due to side-effect profile).
3. Gonadotropin-releasing hormone analogues (GnRH); often used to reduce bleeding and ameliorate anemia and in preparation for a surgical procedure.
4. Tranexamic acid (Lysteda) is an antifibrinolytic agent FDA approved for cyclic heavy menstrual bleeding. Dosage in normal renal function is 3900 mg daily (650 mg tablets, 2 tablets tid) for up to 5 days during menses.
- Surgical treatment
1. D&C and hysteroscopy
2. Endometrial ablation
3. Hysterectomy

DISPOSITION

Cyclical treatment on birth control pills or Provera for several cycles, then discontinue pill and watch patient for onset of regular menses. If the patient does not want to conceive, continued cycle management with oral contraceptives is commonly used.

REFERRAL

To gynecologist in case of failure of treatment

ⓘ PEARLS & CONSIDERATIONS

COMMENTS
- Table 1D-23 describes management options for DUB.
- Patient education material may be obtained from the American College of Obstetricians and Gynecologists, 409 12th Street SW, Washington, DC 20024-2188; phone 202-638-5577.

SUGGESTED READINGS
Available at www.expertconsult.com

RELATED CONTENT
Evaluation of ovulatory bleeding (Algorithm, Section III)
Evaluation of anovulatory bleeding (Algorithm, Section III)
Dysfunctional Uterine Bleeding (Patient Information)
Endometrial Cancer (Related Key Topic)
Uterine Fibroids (Related Key Topic)

AUTHORS: **MANDEEP K. BRAR, M.D.**, and **RUBEN ALVERO, M.D.**

TABLE 1D-23 Management of Dysfunctional Uterine Bleeding (DUB)

Bleeding Pattern	Cause	Treatment
Ovulatory DUB		
Heavy menstrual bleeding	Imbalance in endometrial prostacyclins and prostaglandins	Nonsteroidal antiinflammatory drugs Combination oral contraceptive pill Progestin intrauterine device Endometrial ablation
Midcycle spotting	Periovulatory estrogen decline	None
Delayed menses	Persistent corpus luteum	None (rule out pregnancy)
Anovulatory DUB		
Irregular menses	Unopposed estrogen stimulation of endometrium	Combination oral contraceptive pill Cyclic progestins Endometrial ablation
Postmenopausal bleeding	Endometrial atrophy	Hormone replacement therapy Endometrial ablation

From Carlson KJ, Eisenstat SA, et al: *Primary care of women*, ed 2, St Louis, 2002, Mosby.

BASIC INFORMATION

DEFINITION

Dysmenorrhea is pain with menstruation, usually cramping and usually centered in the lower abdomen. It is defined as *primary dysmenorrhea* when there is no associated organic pathology and *secondary dysmenorrhea* when there is demonstrable organic pathology.

SYNONYMS

Menstrual cramps
Painful periods

ICD-10CM CODES
N94.3 Primary dysmenorrhea
N94.5 Secondary dysmenorrhea
N94.6 Dysmenorrhea, unspecified

EPIDEMIOLOGY & DEMOGRAPHICS

- Approximately 50% of menstruating women are affected by dysmenorrhea, with approximately 10% of them having severe dysmenorrhea with incapacitation for 1 to 3 days/mo.
- Dysmenorrhea is most common in the age group from 20 to 24 yr, and primary dysmenorrhea usually appears within 6 to 12 mo after menarche.
- Dysmenorrhea is more common in women who have menarche at an earlier age and in those with a longer duration of menstruation.

PHYSICAL FINDINGS & CLINICAL PRESENTATION

- Sharp, crampy, midline, lower abdominal pain without a lower quadrant or adnexal component but possible radiation to the lower back and upper thighs
- Unremarkable pelvic examination in non-menstruating patient
- Accompanying symptoms: nausea, vomiting, headaches, anxiety, fatigue, diarrhea, fainting, and abdominal bloating
- Cramps usually lasting $<<$24 hr and seldom lasting $>>$2 to 3 days
- Secondary dysmenorrhea: dyspareunia is a common complaint, and bimanual pelvic-abdominal examination may demonstrate uterine or adnexal tenderness, fixed uterine retroflexion, uterosacral nodularity, a pelvic mass, or an enlarged, irregular uterus

ETIOLOGY

Prostaglandin $F_2\alpha$ is the agent responsible for dysmenorrhea. It stimulates uterine contractions and cervical stenosis (narrowing) and increases vasopressin release. Behavior and psychological factors have also been implicated in the etiology of primary dysmenorrhea. Primary dysmenorrhea only occurs in ovulatory cycles. Secondary dysmenorrhea is usually caused by endometriosis, adenomyosis, leiomyomas and, less commonly, chronic salpingitis, intrauterine device (IUD) use, or congenital or acquired outflow tract obstruction, including cervical stenosis.

DIAGNOSIS

DIFFERENTIAL DIAGNOSIS

- Adenomyosis
- Adhesions
- Allen-Masters syndrome
- Cervical structures or stenosis
- Congenital malformation of müllerian system
- Ectopic pregnancy
- Endometriosis
- Endometritis
- Imperforate hymen
- IUD use
- Leiomyomas
- Ovarian cysts
- Pelvic congestion syndrome, pelvic inflammatory disease
- Polyps
- Transverse vaginal septum
- Interstitial cystitis

WORKUP

- Primary dysmenorrhea: characteristic history, physical examination normal with the absence of an identifiable cause of pelvic pain
- Secondary dysmenorrhea: history of onset generally $>>$2 yr after menarche; physical examination may reveal uterine irregularity, cul-de-sac tenderness, or nodularity or pelvic masses

LABORATORY TESTS

- No specific tests diagnostic for dysmenorrhea
- Elevated white blood cell count in the presence of infection
- Human chorionic gonadotropin to rule out ectopic pregnancy

IMAGING STUDIES

- Ultrasound scan of the pelvis to evaluate the presence of leiomyomas, ovarian cysts, or ectopic pregnancy
- Hysterosalpingogram or saline ultrasonography to assess the uterine cavity to rule out endometrial polyps or submucosal or intraluminal leiomyomas
- Cystoscopy for evaluation of interstitial cystitis

TREATMENT

NONPHARMACOLOGIC THERAPY

- Applying heat to the lower abdomen with hot compresses, heating pads, or hot water bottles seems to offer some relief.
- Offer reassurance that this is a treatable condition.

ACUTE GENERAL Rx

- Nonsteroidal anti-inflammatory drugs such as ibuprofen 400 to 600 mg q4 to 6h or naproxen sodium 500 mg q12h, mefenamic acid 500 mg initial dose followed by 250 mg q6h prn.
- Oral contraceptives cyclically or continuously (taking only active pills), primarily in women with primary dysmenorrhea.
- The levonorgestrel-containing IUD is increasingly being used to ameliorate symptoms of dysmenorrhea. Pain improvement has been shown in many cases to be even better than oral contraceptive pills.
- Nifedipine 30 mg qd in difficult cases of dysmenorrhea.
- Vitamin E supplements may reduce pain compared to placebo.
- Magnesium supplements have been found likely to be beneficial.
- Thiamine supplements may reduce pain.
- The Chinese herbal remedy toki-shakuyaku-san may be effective in reducing pain. However, few studies have been of good quality.
- Secondary dysmenorrhea: treatment directed to the specific underlying condition; surgery may be indicated if pathology is found on physical examination or by imaging.

CHRONIC Rx

Acupuncture and transcutaneous electrical nerve stimulation may be tried. However, there is not enough evidence to support the use of yoga, acupuncture, or massage. In cases in which medical therapy has not worked, laparoscopy or other surgical treatments should be considered depending on the secondary cause of the dysmenorrhea. A directed physical examination, looking for gynecologic masses or nodularity should be performed. Nontraditional approaches such as acupuncture have been tried with relief in some patients. The levonorgestrel IUD has been shown to effectively reduce pain in women with primary dysmenorrhea.

DISPOSITION

The majority of patients are satisfactorily treated with good outcomes. Possible chronic complications with primary dysmenorrhea that has not been adequately treated can lead to anxiety and depression. With certain causes of secondary dysmenorrhea, infertility can become a problem.

REFERRAL

If a secondary cause of dysmenorrhea is revealed, refer to the appropriate specialist for further medical or surgical treatment (e.g., gynecologist, urogynecologist, pain management center).

SUGGESTED READINGS
Available online at www.expertconsult.com

RELATED CONTENT
Dysmenorrhea (Patient Information)
Dyspareunia (Related Key Topic)
Endometriosis (Related Key Topic)
Premenstrual Syndrome (Related Key Topic)

AUTHOR: **RUBEN ALVERO, M.D.**

BASIC INFORMATION

DEFINITION

Persistent and/or recurrent pain associated with sexual activity that causes marked distress or interpersonal conflict.

SYNONYMS

Painful intercourse

ICD-10CM CODES
N94.1 Dyspareunia
F52.6 Dyspareunia not due to a substance or known physiological condition

EPIDEMIOLOGY & DEMOGRAPHICS

PREVALENCE (IN U.S.): Affects 10% to 20% of women
PREDOMINANT SEX: Female
AT-RISK POPULATION: No consistent findings regarding:
- Age
- Parity
- Educational status
- Race
- Income
- Marital status

RISK FACTORS: Lower:
- Frequency of intercourse
- Levels of desire and arousal
- Orgasmic response
- Physical and emotional satisfaction
- General happiness

HISTORICAL FACTORS:
- Pain parameters
  1. Character
  2. Location (introital, middle, deep)
  3. Onset
  4. Duration
  5. Timing
  6. Chronicity
  7. Cyclicity
  8. Recurrence
- Gynecologic history
  1. History of sexually transmitted disease
  2. History of herpes simplex virus (HSV) or human papillomavirus (HPV)
  3. Other sexual dysfunctions
  4. Prior abdominal or gynecologic surgery
  5. Prior pelvic or abdominal radiation
  6. History of endometriosis, fibroids
  7. History of genital or uterine prolapse
  8. History of gynecologic infection
  9. History of pelvic pain
  10. History of menopausal symptoms
  11. Sexual misinformation
- Obstetric history
  1. Lacerations
  2. Episiotomy
- General medical causes
  1. History of chronic diseases
  2. Gastrointestinal or genitourinary symptoms
  3. Medications
  4. History of psychological disorders
  5. History of dermatologic condition

  6. Religious beliefs
  7. Generalized anxiety

PHYSICAL FINDINGS & CLINICAL PRESENTATION

- Primary versus secondary dyspareunia
  1. Latter with history of pain-free coitus
- Visual inspection of lower genital tract
  1. Discoloration
  2. Ulcerations
  3. Discharge
  4. Prolapse
  5. Dysplastic changes
  6. Infestations
- Physical examination
  1. Sensitivity to light touch
  2. Tenderness to palpation
  3. Genital prolapse
     a. Uterus
     b. Bladder
     c. Cervix
     d. Vagina
     e. Adnexa
     f. Rectum
     g. Bowel
  4. Longitudinal or transverse vaginal septum
  5. Levator muscle tone
  6. Evidence of previous surgery
  7. Vaginal length, depth, caliber constrictions: assess for shortened or absent vagina

ETIOLOGY

- Pathology or alteration or reduction of genital-associated tissue
- Psychosocial factors
- Marital or relationship discord
- History of sexual abuse

DIAGNOSIS

DIFFERENTIAL DIAGNOSIS

- Congenital deformities (septa/agenesis)
- Imperforate hymen
- Menopausal changes
- Atrophic tissue
- Impaired lubrication
- Psychogenic
- Vaginismus
- Inadequate foreplay
- Endometriosis
- Levator ani myalgia
- Chronic pelvic pain
- Previous surgery (posterior colporrhaphy, perineorrhaphy)
  1. Alteration in vaginal length, depth, caliber
  2. Adhesions
- Infectious
  1. HPV
  2. HSV
  3. Candidiasis
  4. *Tinea cruris*
  5. Acute or chronic salpingitis or endometritis
- Pelvic carcinoma
- Previous radiation
- Adnexal attachment or tubal prolapse
- Pelvic tumor

- Uterine prolapse, malposition, enlargement, or retroversion
- Genital prolapse
- Cystocele, rectocele, enterocele
- Urethral or bladder pathology
- Pelvic congestion (controversial)
- Vulvar vestibulitis
- Postcoital cystitis
- Broad ligament pathology
- Neuroma at the site of previous episiotomy
- Previous sexual abuse
- Vulvodynia
- Contact or allergic dermatitis
- Vitamin A, B, or C deficiency
- Equestrian dyspareunia
- Interstitial cystitis
- Pudendal neuralgia
- Myofascial pain syndrome
- Rectal pathology
- Structural abnormalities or alterations
  1. Muscle
  2. Bone
  3. Ligament

WORKUP

- History and physical examination are key
- If needed:
  1. Colposcopy
  2. Cystoscopy
  3. Consider laparoscopy for unexplained deep dyspareunia

LABORATORY TESTS

- Erythrocyte sedimentation rate
- White blood cell count
- Wet mount
- Cultures
  1. Cervical
     a. Gonorrhea
     b. *Chlamydia*
  2. Vaginal
  3. Lesions
  4. Urine
- Vulva, vaginal, or cervical biopsy
- Pap smear
- HSV antibodies
- Gonadotropin levels

IMAGING STUDIES

Pelvic or abdominal ultrasonography. Transvaginal ultrasonography provides for greater resolution of uterus and ovaries due to proximity to pelvic organs. MRI when diagnosis is unclear with other diagnostic modalities (Fig. 1D-44).

TREATMENT

NONPHARMACOLOGIC THERAPY

- Patient education
- Discontinue exacerbating activity and irritants
- Lubrication with coitus
- Coital position changes to reduce deep thrust discomfort
- Warm or cool soaks
- Reassurance to patient of nonmalignant condition

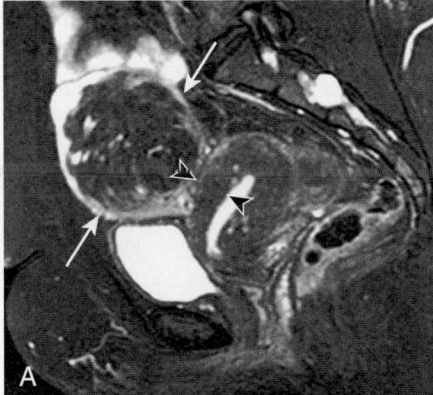

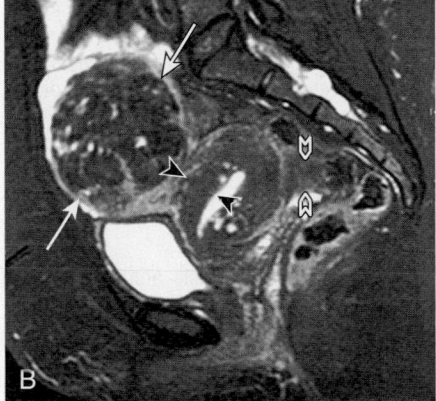

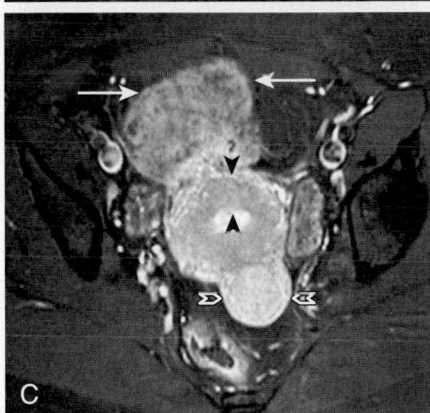

FIGURE 1D-44 Adenomyosis and leiomyomata in a 41-year-old woman with pelvic pain, irregular menses, menorrhagia, and dyspareunia. A and **B,** Sagittal T2-weighted fat-suppressed images show a large anterior subserosal fibroid with mixed but predominantly low signal *(arrows)* and a smaller posterior subserosal fibroid with low to intermediate signal *(chevrons).* There is also widening of the junctional zone *(black arrowheads)* with areas of increased T2 signal, indicative of adenomyosis. **C,** Axial three-dimensional gradient echo postcontrast image with fat suppression shows enhancement of the leiomyomata *(white arrowheads and chevrons)* and the thickened junctional zone *(black arrowheads).* (From Fielding JR et al: *Gynecologic imaging,* Philadelphia, 2011, Saunders.)

- Psychosocial interventions
  1. Systemic desensitization techniques
  2. Behavior modification
- Vaginal dilators
- Vaginal muscle exercises and relaxation techniques
- Excision of pathologic tissue
- Surgical correction of altered, reduced, or deformed tissues

ACUTE GENERAL Rx

- Topical lidocaine, nonhormonal moisturizers and lubricants.
- Corticosteroids.
- Antiinfective agents if vaginitis found.
- Trigger point injections.
- Massage or physical therapy.
- Acupuncture.
- Transcutaneous electrical nerve stimulation.
- Stress reduction techniques.
- Safe sexual practices.
- Hormonal replacement therapy. The FDA has approved ospemifene (Osphena), an oral estrogen agonist/antagonist for treatment of moderate to severe dyspareunia in postmenopausal women with suspected vaginal atrophy. Dosage is 60 mg tablet daily.
- Antiviral agents.
- Intralesional interferon.
- Mild analgesics.
- Antidepressants.

CHRONIC Rx

All the previous plus:
- Set supportive visits as needed
- Oral contraceptives
- Regular sexual activity
- Balanced diet
- Vitamin supplementation
- Proper hygiene

DISPOSITION

Most patients will have a reduction and/or resolution of their symptoms by using the appropriate therapeutic approaches.

REFERRAL

As with other chronic pain conditions, a multidisciplinary approach using the expertise of psychologists, dermatologists, gynecologic surgeons, infectious disease specialists, or urologists is helpful.

! PEARLS & CONSIDERATIONS

- Dyspareunia is a symptom complex resulting from a multitude of etiologies, some of which act simultaneously.
- Uncovering the etiology of dyspareunia is predominantly based on a comprehensive history and physical examination.
- The differential diagnoses can be sorted into superficial, intermediate, and deep dyspareunia categories.
- As with the physical evaluation of any painful condition, attempt—by precise touching (moistened cotton swab), palpation, or applied pressure—to reproduce the patient's chief complaint.
- Performing a one-finger pelvic examination without concurrent abdominal palpation allows a more precise assessment of the source of genital pain.
- Individualize therapy.
- Initiate and maintain an honest diagnosis and compassionate demeanor with the patient and her partner.
- Be open minded, approachable, nonjudgmental, and diligent in your search for a solution to help these often silently suffering patients.

SUGGESTED READINGS

Available at www.expertconsult.com

RELATED CONTENT

Painful Intercourse (Patient Information)
Dysmenorrhea (Related Key Topic)
Endometriosis (Related Key Topic)
Sexual Dysfunction in Women (Related Key Topic)

AUTHORS: **DAVID I. KURSS, M.D.,** and
RUBEN ALVERO, M.D.

D

Diseases and Disorders

BASIC INFORMATION

DEFINITION
Nonulcerative dyspepsia is a term used to describe signs and symptoms of persistent or recurrent dyspepsia centered in the upper abdomen that have no identifiable organic cause

SYNONYMS
Nonulcer dyspepsia
Functional dyspepsia
Idiopathic dyspepsia

ICD-10CM CODES
K30 Functional dyspepsia

EPIDEMIOLOGY & DEMOGRAPHICS
- Up to 25% of the general population will experience dyspepsia each year. Of these, 75% will have no evident causative agent.

PHYSICAL FINDINGS & CLINICAL PRESENTATION
Typical clinical presentation is dyspepsia without findings on physical examination to explain the symptoms

ETIOLOGY
The etiology and pathophysiology are still unclear. Research is focused on abnormalities of gastric motor function and visceral hypersensitivity, as well as
- *Helicobacter pylori* infection
- Psychosocial factors—associated with anxiety and depression

RISK FACTORS
Risk factors include:
- Genetic predisposition: homozygous GNB3 gene.
- Dietary habits such as caffeine, alcohol, or smoking.
- Medications such as NSAIDs, calcium channel blockers, methylxanthines, alendronate, orlistat, acarbose, and potassium supplements.
- Psychological disorders such as anxiety, depression, somatization, or personal history of childhood sexual or physical abuse.

DIAGNOSIS

DIFFERENTIAL DIAGNOSIS
Nonulcerative dyspepsia is diagnosed when all other organic causes have been excluded, including:
- PUD
- Gastroesophageal reflux
- Gastric/esophageal/other abdominal cancers
- Biliary tract disease
- Gastroparesis, including diabetic gastroparesis
- Pancreatitis
- Medications (i.e., NSAIDs, erythromycin)
- Metabolic disturbances (i.e., hypercalcemia, heavy metals, or hyperkalemia)
- Ischemic bowel disease

- Systemic disorders (i.e., eosinophilic gastritis, Crohn's disease, sarcoidosis, celiac disease, thyroid disorders)

DIAGNOSIS
Developed in 2006 in conjunction with the American Gastroenterological Association, the Rome III criteria lists the following factors, which must be present at least 3 months and first noticed within 6 months of diagnosis:
- At least one of the following:
  1. Postprandial fullness, *or*
  2. Early satiety, *or*
  3. Epigastric pain, *or*
  4. Epigastric burning
- *and* no evidence of structural disease likely to explain the symptoms

WORKUP
The American Gastroenterological Association, as well as the Maastricht III and the IV European consensus, suggest the following:
- The pattern of symptoms overlaps considerably for all types of dyspepsia; therefore, the history and physical should focus on finding specific symptoms that help exclude other causes of dyspepsia.
- Endoscopy should be performed only in patients >55 years old and in younger patients with alarming symptoms (e.g., weight loss, progressive dysphagia, recurrent vomiting, evidence of gastrointestinal bleeding, or family history of cancer) presenting with new-onset dyspepsia. Findings consistent with diagnosis of nonulcerative dyspepsia are not conclusive, no presence of *H. pylori*, no signs of gastroesophageal reflux disease, no mucosal inflammation. NOTE: Patients <55 years old and without any alarming symptoms can be treated without endoscopy.

LABORATORY TESTS
H. pylori: Laboratory methods include serologic tests[1], monoclonal stool antigen, or urea breath test.

TREATMENT

ACUTE GENERAL Rx
PHARMACOLOGIC THERAPY: Primary treatment is usually initiated with proton pump inhibitors (PPIs), which can be started without performing endoscopy, especially if the patient comes from a population with low prevalence of *H. pylori* infection. If symptoms persist, a trial of antidepressants can be started.

Treatment of accompanying symptoms includes:

Predominant Symptom	Possible Etiology	Medication Recommended
Nausea	Motility dysfunction	Prokinetic agent
Bloating	Motility dysfunction	Simethicone and/or prokinetic agent

[1]Serologic testing for *H. pylori* has a low predictive value because colonization is lifelong; it can therefore determine prevalence better than incidence.

Predominant Symptom	Possible Etiology	Medication Recommended
Pain	Mucosal disease or *H. pylori* infection	Antibiotic trial
Somatic complaints	Psychosocial	Psychotropic medication trial

Medication categories:
- Antacids (i.e., aluminum hydroxide, calcium carbonate)
- Gas-reducing agents, such as those containing simethicone
- H_2-receptor antagonists (i.e., cimetidine)
- PPIs (i.e., omeprazole)
- Prokinetic agents (i.e., metoclopramide)
- Antidepressants (i.e., selective serotonin receptor inhibitors)
- *H. pylori* therapy/antibiotic therapy (various antibiotic regimens, usually 1 PPI) if *H. pylori* present

CHRONIC Rx
Controversy currently exists around the long-term use of PPIs. Due to the high association with psychological factors, patients with functional dyspepsia should undergo psychological intervention, even if there is good response to pharmacotherapeutic approaches.

COMPLEMENTARY & ALTERNATIVE THERAPIES
Peppermint and caraway oil may be helpful, as well as acupuncture; however, no definitive trials have been performed.

REFERRAL
- Referral to gastroenterology if patient has alarming symptoms (such as GI bleeding, dysphagia, odynophagia, unexplained anemia, change in appetite, and weight loss) or when endoscopy is indicated—although controversy exists about the workup of younger patients.
- Referral to cardiology if cardiac etiology suspected.

PEARLS & CONSIDERATIONS

PREVENTION
Avoid excessive amounts of caffeine, alcohol, smoking, or long-term use of steroids and NSAIDs.

PATIENT AND FAMILY EDUCATION
http://www.mayoclinic.com/health/stomach-pain/DS00524

SUGGESTED READINGS
Available at www.expertconsult.com

RELATED CONTENT
Approach to the patient with dyspepsia (Algorithm, Section III)

AUTHORS: **ALVARO M. RIVERA, M.D.,** and **NADINE MBUYI, M.D.**

 BASIC INFORMATION

DEFINITION

The term "dysphagia" is derived from the Greek words *dys* (with difficulty) and *phagia* (to eat). It is characterized by abnormal transfer of food from mouth to the stomach, which may involve the oral, pharyngeal, or esophageal stages of swallowing.

ICD-10CM CODES
R13.10	Dysphagia, unspecified
D50.1	Sideropenic dysphagia
I69.091	Dysphagia following nontraumatic subarachnoid hemorrhage
I69.191	Dysphagia following nontraumatic intracerebral hemorrhage
I69.291	Dysphagia following other nontraumatic intracranial hemorrhage
I69.391	Dysphagia following cerebral infarction
I69.891	Dysphagia following other cerebrovascular disease
I69.991	Dysphagia following unspecified cerebrovascular disease
R13.11	Dysphagia, oral phase
R13.12	Dysphagia, oropharyngeal phase
R13.13	Dysphagia, pharyngeal phase
R13.14	Dysphagia, pharyngoesophageal phase
R13.19	Other dysphagia

EPIDEMIOLOGY & DEMOGRAPHICS

- This is seen in 10% of individuals above the age of 50 yr. Its prevalence increases with advancing age.
- Nearly 12% of hospitalized patients have symptoms of dysphagia.
- Up to 30% to 60% of nursing home patients have some form of dysphagia.
- Special populations, including patients with head injury, stroke, or Parkinson's disease, have 30% to 50% prevalence of oropharyngeal dysphagia.

ETIOLOGY

- Oropharyngeal
  1. Neuromuscular causes
     1. Stroke.
     2. Parkinson's disease.
     3. Multiple sclerosis.
     4. Myasthenia gravis.
     5. Amyotrophic lateral sclerosis.
     6. CNS tumors.
     7. Muscular dystrophy.
     8. Thyroid dysfunction.
     9. Polymyositis and dermatomyositis.
     10. Sarcoidosis.
     11. Cerebral palsy.
     12. Head trauma.
     13. Metabolic encephalopathy.
     14. Dementia.
     15. Bell's palsy.
  2. Structural causes
     1. Oropharyngeal tumors.
     2. Zenker's diverticulum.
     3. Infection of pharynx or neck (mucositis from *Candida,* herpes, and CMV).
     4. Thyromegaly.

5. Prior surgery or radiotherapy.
6. Osteophytes and other spinal disorders.
7. Proximal esophageal disorders.
8. Congenital anomalies (e.g., cleft palate).
9. Poor dentition.

- Esophageal
  1. Neuromuscular disorders
     1. Achalasia.
     2. Diffuse esophageal spasm.
     3. Nutcracker esophagus.
     4. Hypertensive lower esophageal sphincter.
     5. Ineffective esophageal motility.
     6. Scleroderma.
     7. Reflex-associated dysmotility.
  2. Structural disorder
     1. Peptic stricture.
     2. Esophageal rings and webs.
     3. Diverticuli.
     4. Carcinoma and benign tumors.
     5. Foreign bodies.
     6. Vascular compression.
     7. Mediastinal masses.
     8. Spinal osteophytes.
     9. Mucosal injury (from pills, infection, gastroesophageal reflux disease [GERD], etc.).

PATHOGENESIS

The inability to swallow is caused either by a problem in strength or coordination of the muscles required to move material from the mouth to stomach or by a fixed obstruction somewhere between the mouth and the stomach.

CLINICAL FEATURES

Oropharyngeal dysphagia
- Problem arises within 2 seconds of initiating the voluntary phase of swallowing.
- Typical symptoms include drooling, spillage of food, postnasal regurgitation, difficulty in initiation of swallowing, sialorrhea, sensation of food stuck in the neck, coughing or choking during swallowing, the need to swallow repeatedly to clear food or fluid from the pharynx, dysphonia, nasal speech, hoarseness of voice, and dysarthria.
- A thorough physical examination including that of the nervous system, oral cavity, and the head/neck is very important in patients with oropharyngeal dysphagia.

Esophageal dysphagia
- Problem usually arises several seconds after swallowing.
- Patients often complain of food being stuck in lower substernal area.
- Dysphagia to solids suggests mechanical obstruction.
- Neuromuscular causes result in dysphagia to both solids and liquids. Particularly, patients with achalasia tend to drink a lot of fluids while eating or apply maneuvers such as straightening the back, raising their arms over their heads, or standing to increase intraesophageal pressure to facilitate the emptying of food into the stomach.
- Oftentimes, ingestion of very cold or very hot foods precipitates the dysphagia associated with neuromuscular disorder.

- Delayed regurgitation of food, heartburn, and chest pain are usually present.
- Weight loss is usually associated with malignancy or achalasia.
- Symptoms are intermittent in patients with esophageal dysphagia from benign causes of structural obstruction or diffuse esophageal spasm. However, it is progressive in patients with peptic stricture, esophageal carcinoma, scleroderma, and achalasia.
- In patients with structural obstruction, when the luminal diameter is more than 18 to 20 mm, they are rarely symptomatic, whereas those with a diameter of less than 13 mm are nearly always symptomatic.
- These patients with esophageal dysphagia usually do not have any characteristic physical findings.

 **DIAGNOSIS**

Laboratory evaluation
- CBC.
- Thyroid studies.
- Nutritional assessment by checking serum protein and albumin levels.
- Other studies based on specific clinical conditions.

Special studies
- Oropharyngeal dysphagia
  1. Videofluoroscopy is the first test often ordered in evaluation of patients with oropharyngeal dysphagia.
  2. Double contrast modified barium swallow study (Fig. E1D-45).
  3. Fiberoptic flexible nasopharyngeal laryngoscopy is mandatory in all cases when a structural lesion, particularly malignancy, is suspected.
  4. Pharyngeal and upper esophageal manometry (Fig. E1D-46) is occasionally of value to predict which patients will have a favorable outcome from cricopharyngeal myotomy or dilation.
  5. Radiography of head and neck when indicated.
- Esophageal dysphagia
  1. Barium esophagography should precede upper endoscopies to identify patients at risk from potential perforation with an endoscopy and to help plan fluoroscopically guided dilation. It is often the first step in evaluating patients with dysphagia, especially if an obstructive lesion is suspected.
  2. EGD.
  3. Esophageal manometry is indicated if no abnormality is identified by barium study or EGD.
  4. Esophageal pH monitoring in patients with suspected reflux disease.
  5. Endoscopic ultrasonography.
  6. Radiograph, CT, and MRI of chest.

DIFFERENTIAL DIAGNOSIS (FIG. 1D-47)

- Globus pharyngeus.
- Odynophagia.
- Phagophobia.
- GERD.

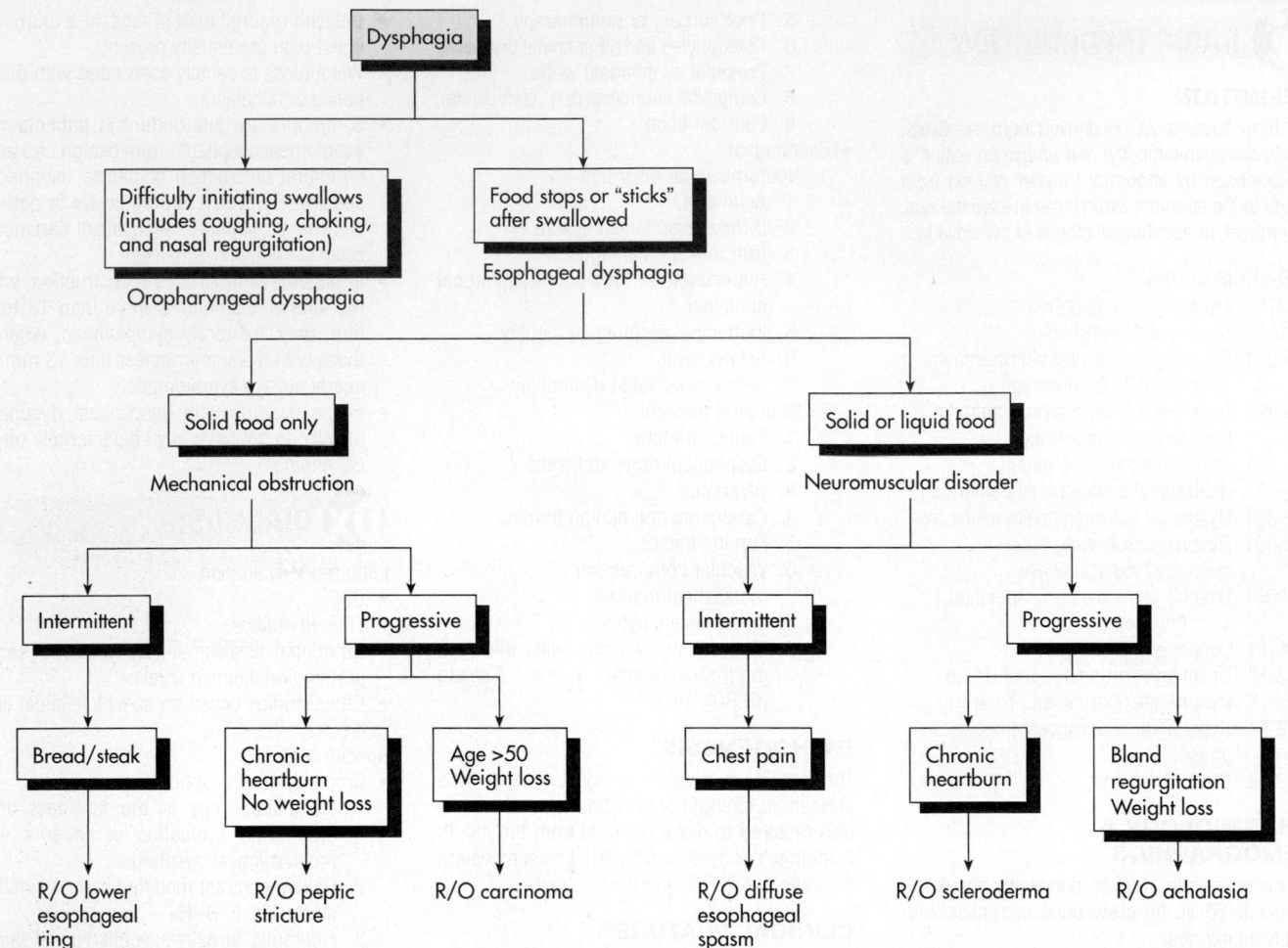

FIGURE 1D-47 Differential diagnosis of dysphagia. *RO,* Rule out. (Modified from Andreoli TE [ed]: *Cecil essentials of medicine,* ed 7, Philadelphia, 2008, Saunders.)

℞ TREATMENT

- Treatment should be approached with the help of specialists of multiple disciplines (ENT, head and neck surgeon, radiologist, speech pathologist, physical therapist, dietitian, gastroenterologist, physical medicine and rehabilitation specialist, dentist, neurologist, etc.).
- Goal of therapy is airway protection and maintenance of nutrition.
- Alteration of food consistency, volume, and delivery rate plays a major role.
- The goal of direct therapy is to change swallowing physiology with medical treatment of primary disease, maxillofacial prosthesis, and cricopharyngeal myotomy.
- Indirect therapies include exercise programs for tongue coordination and chewing under the guidance of a speech therapist.
- Maintenance of oral feeding often requires compensatory techniques such as chin-tuck position, rotation of head to the affected side, tilting of head to the strong side, and lying on one's back or on one's side during swallowing.
- Some of the voluntary maneuvers applied include supraglottic swallow, effortful swallow, Mendelson maneuver, Shaker exercise, and the Heimlich maneuver.
- Placement of nasogastric tube, jejunostomy tube, or percutaneous endoscopic gastrotomy

(PEG) tube is considered for enteral feeding when other measures fail and the patient remains at significant risk for aspiration or nutrition becomes compromised.
- Treatment of associated GERD should not be forgotten.
- Surgery for chronic aspiration may involve tracheostomy, medialization, laryngeal suspension, laryngeal closure, and/or laryngotracheal separation-diversion.
- Other measures include esophageal dilation removal of foreign body, esophageal resection, chemotherapy, radiotherapy, endoscopic ablation of tumor, photodynamic therapy, esophageal prosthesis/stents, diverticulectomy, intrasphincteric injection of botulinum toxin, surgical myotomy, and others. Smooth muscle relaxants such as nitrates and calcium channel blockers have been used to effectively treat patients with diffuse esophageal spasm and nutcracker esophagus.
- Several scales have been suggested to determine patients' functional outcome. One of them is the "Swallowing Rating Scale."

COMPLICATIONS

- Dehydration.
- Malnutrition.
- Aspiration pneumonia.
- Airway obstruction.
- Death resulting from pulmonary complications.

PROGNOSIS

- Depends on the etiology.
- Nursing home patients with oropharyngeal dysphagia and a history of aspiration have an approximately 45% mortality rate over 1 yr.
- All patients, especially the elderly, should take their medications with a full glass of water while in upright position well before bedtime.
- Dysphagia should be considered an alarm symptom, indicating the need for immediate evaluation.

PATIENT EDUCATION

Elderly patients with dysphagia should not attribute their symptoms to aging.

SUGGESTED READINGS

Available at www.expertconsult.com

RELATED CONTENT

Dyspepsia, Nonulcerative (Related Key Topic)
Esophageal Tumors (Related Key Topic)
Gastroesophageal Reflux Disease (Related Key Topic)

AUTHOR: **HEMANT K. SATPATHY, M.D.**

BASIC INFORMATION

DEFINITION

Dystonia refers to a group of disorders characterized by involuntary muscle contractions (sustained or spasmodic) that lead to abnormal body movements or postures. Dystonia can be generalized or focal, of early (<20 yr) or late onset, and primary or secondary.

SYNONYMS

Blepharospasm
Oromandibular (orofacial) dystonia
Spasmodic (limb or axial) dystonia
Torticollis
Writer's cramp

ICD-10CM CODES
G24 Dystonia
G24.1 Idiopathic familial dystonia
G24.0 Drug induced dystonia
G24.3 Spasmodic torticollis

EPIDEMIOLOGY & DEMOGRAPHICS

PREVALENCE: Estimated at one in 3000 persons.
PREDOMINANT SEX: Cervical dystonia has a 3:2 female preponderance.
PREDOMINANT AGE:
- Onset of focal cervical dystonia is usually in the fifth decade.
- Hereditary forms may have an onset in childhood or adulthood and tend to be more severe.
GENETICS: Autosomal-dominant, autosomal-recessive, and X-linked forms of dystonia have been identified. Ashkenazi Jews are particularly susceptible to primary early-onset dystonia. Metabolic conditions in which dystonia is a feature can be inherited or, more frequently, caused sporadic mutations.

CLINICAL PRESENTATION

Focal dystonias produce abnormal sustained muscle contractions in a single region of the body:
- Neck (*torticollis*): most commonly affected site with a tendency for the head to turn to one side.
- Eyelids (*blepharospasm*): involuntary closure of the eyelids that leads to excessive eye blinking, sometimes with persistent eye closure and functional blindness.
- Mouth (*oromandibular dystonia*): involuntary contraction of muscles of the mouth, tongue, or face.
- Hand (*writer's cramp*) (Fig. 1D-48).
Generalized dystonia affects multiple areas of the body and can lead to marked joint deformities. Isolated foot dystonia is very rare and may suggest an underlying parkinsonian disorder or brain structural abnormality.

ETIOLOGY

Exact pathophysiology of primary dystonia is unknown but believed to involve abnormalities of basal ganglia. Specifically, reduced abnormal patterns of neuronal activity the basal ganglia result in disinhibition of motor thalamus and cortex, leading to abnormal movement.

- Fifteen hereditary forms have been described, including the severe progressive form, dystonia musculorum deformans.
- Secondary dystonia results from central nervous system (CNS) disease of the basal ganglia (stroke, demyelination, hypoxia, trauma), Huntington's disease, Wilson's disease, Parkinson syndromes, and lysosomal storage diseases.
- Acute dystonia can occur with drugs that block dopamine receptors, such as phenothiazines or butyrophenones.
- Tardive dyskinesia can result from long-term treatment with antiemetics (e.g., phenothiazines), antipsychotics (e.g., haloperidol), levodopa, anticonvulsants, or ergots.

DIAGNOSIS

DIFFERENTIAL DIAGNOSIS
- Drug effects.
- Parkinson's disease.
- Progressive supranuclear palsy.
- Wilson's disease.
- Huntington's disease.
- Table 1D-24 describes selected causes of primary and secondary dystonia in childhood.

WORKUP

History (family history, birth history, trauma, medication use, age of onset, and temporal pattern), physical examination to determine associated features (weakness, myoclonus, tremor) and to determine pattern of dystonia—focal (single body region), segmental (two or more body contiguous body regions), multifocal (two or more noncontiguous body regions), generalized (involving the trunk and at least two other sites), or hemidystonia (involving more regions but restricted to one body side).

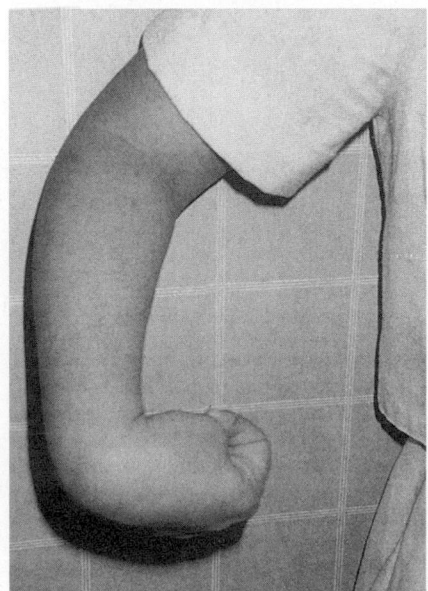

FIGURE 1D-48 Focal dystonia of the distal right arm. (From Goldman L, Ausiello D [eds]: *Cecil textbook of medicine,* ed 22, Philadelphia, 2004, Saunders.)

LABORATORY TESTS
- Usually not helpful for diagnosis
- Serum ceruloplasmin if Wilson's disease is suspected
- Genetic testing (DYT gene mutations, inborn errors of metabolism, or mitochondrial disease) if indicated
- Comprehensive toxicology screen indicated if causative drugs suspected (dopamine-blocking agents) and history unavailable

IMAGING STUDIES
- Primary dystonias are generally not associated with structural CNS abnormalities. CT scan or MRI of brain if a CNS lesion is suspected as a cause of secondary dystonia.
- Electrophysiologic testing can provide diagnostic support for the diagnosis, but dystonia is a clinical diagnosis.

TREATMENT

NONPHARMACOLOGIC THERAPY
- Heat, massage, physical therapy to relieve pain
- Splints to prevent contractures.
- "Sensory trick" (geste antagoniste) can relieve discomfort: Application of light touch to the affected body part can abolish the dystonia; this also aids in diagnosis.

ACUTE GENERAL Rx

For acute dystonic reactions to phenothiazines/butyrophenones, use diphenhydramine 50 mg IV or benztropine 2 mg IV. For patients presenting with subacute or chronic dystonia, a trial of L-dopa can be useful in distinguishing dopa-responsive dystonia from other causes.

CHRONIC Rx
- For treatment of drug-induced dystonia, slowly withdraw offending agents (antiemetics, antipsychotics most commonly).
- For generalized dystonia, a trial of carbidopa/levodopa may be beneficial and diagnostic of dopa-responsive dystonia.
- Trihexyphenidyl or benztropine may be helpful in up to 50% of tardive dystonias; these are the mainstay of treatment for generalized dystonias not responsive to dopa.
- Diazepam, clonazepam, or baclofen may be helpful.
- Injections of botulinum toxin into the affected muscles are the standard treatment for focal dystonias. Both type A and type B toxins produced by *Clostridium botulinum* block cholinergic transmission at the neuromuscular junction by inhibiting release of acetylcholine.
- Surgical procedures, including denervation, myectomy, rhizotomy, thalamotomy (pallidotomy), or deep brain stimulation, may be helpful for severe, refractory cases, depending on the etiology.
- Intrathecal baclofen can be useful for spastic or truncal dystonia.

DISPOSITION

Spontaneous remission of focal cervical dystonia can occur, but dystonia is generally progressive and pharmacologic therapy is often ineffective.

REFERRAL

Neurology (movement disorders) and/or neurosurgery for severe or refractory cases.
Physical therapy for maintaining flexibility.

PEARLS & CONSIDERATIONS

COMMENTS

- Avoid triggers/exacerbating factors.
- Early physical therapy and splinting to prevent contractures.
- Consider botulism injections.

TABLE 1D-24 Selected Causes of Primary and Secondary Dystonia in Childhood

Diagnosis	Additional Clinical Features	Diagnosis
Aicardi-Goutieres syndrome	Encephalopathy, developmental regression Acquired microcephaly Sterile pyrexias Lesions on the digits, ears (chilblain) Epilepsy CT: calcification of the basal ganglia	Leigh syndrome
Alternating hemiplegia of childhood	Episodic hemiplegia/quadriplegia Abnormal ocular movements Autonomic symptoms Epilepsy Global developmental impairment Environmental triggers for spells	Lesch-Nyhan syndrome (X-linked)
Aromatic amino acid decarboxylase deficiency (AADC)	Developmental delay Oculogyric crises Autonomic dysfunction Hypotonia	Myoclonus dystonia
ARX gene mutation (X-linked)	Male Cognitive impairment Infantile spasms, epilepsy Brain malformation	Niemann-Pick type C
Benign paroxysmal torticollis of infancy	Episodic Cervical dystonia only Family history of migraine	Neuroacanthocytosis
Complex regional pain syndrome	Lower limb involvement Prominent pain	Neurodegeneration with brain iron accumulation
Dopa-responsive dystonia (DRD)	Diurnal variation	Rapid onset dystonia parkinsonism (DYT12)
Drug-induced dystonia		Rett syndrome
Dystonia-deafness optic neuropathy syndrome	Sensorineural hearing loss in early childhood Psychosis Optic atrophy in adolescence	
DYT1 dystonia	Lower limb onset followed by generalization	
Glutaric aciduria type 1	Macrocephaly Encephalopathic crises MRI: striatal necrosis	Spinocerebellar ataxia 17 (SCA17)
GM1 gangliosidosis type 3	Short stature, skeletal dysplasia Orofacial dystonia Speech/swallowing disturbance Parkinsonism MRI: putaminal hyperintensity	Tics
Huntington disease (HD)	Parkinsonism Epilepsy Family history of HD	Tyrosine hydroxylase deficiency
Kernicterus	Jaundice in infancy Hearing loss Impaired upgaze Enamel dysplasia MRI: hyperintense lesions in the globus pallidus	

From Kliegman RM et al: *Nelson textbook of pediatrics*, ed 19, Philadelphia, 2011, Saunders.

D

I

(i) BASIC INFORMATION

DEFINITION

The term "dysphagia" is derived from the Greek words *dys* (with difficulty) and *phagia* (to eat). It is characterized by abnormal transfer of food from mouth to the stomach, which may involve the oral, pharyngeal, or esophageal stages of swallowing.

ICD-10CM CODES

R13.10	Dysphagia, unspecified
D50.1	Sideropenic dysphagia
I69.091	Dysphagia following nontraumatic subarachnoid hemorrhage
I69.191	Dysphagia following nontraumatic intracerebral hemorrhage
I69.291	Dysphagia following other nontraumatic intracranial hemorrhage
I69.391	Dysphagia following cerebral infarction
I69.891	Dysphagia following other cerebrovascular disease
I69.991	Dysphagia following unspecified cerebrovascular disease
R13.11	Dysphagia, oral phase
R13.12	Dysphagia, oropharyngeal phase
R13.13	Dysphagia, pharyngeal phase
R13.14	Dysphagia, pharyngoesophageal phase
R13.19	Other dysphagia

EPIDEMIOLOGY & DEMOGRAPHICS

- This is seen in 10% of individuals above the age of 50 yr. Its prevalence increases with advancing age.
- Nearly 12% of hospitalized patients have symptoms of dysphagia.
- Up to 30% to 60% of nursing home patients have some form of dysphagia.
- Special populations, including patients with head injury, stroke, or Parkinson's disease, have 30% to 50% prevalence of oropharyngeal dysphagia.

ETIOLOGY

- Oropharyngeal
  1. Neuromuscular causes
     1. Stroke.
     2. Parkinson's disease.
     3. Multiple sclerosis.
     4. Myasthenia gravis.
     5. Amyotrophic lateral sclerosis.
     6. CNS tumors.
     7. Muscular dystrophy.
     8. Thyroid dysfunction.
     9. Polymyositis and dermatomyositis.
     10. Sarcoidosis.
     11. Cerebral palsy.
     12. Head trauma.
     13. Metabolic encephalopathy.
     14. Dementia.
     15. Bell's palsy.
  2. Structural causes
     1. Oropharyngeal tumors.
     2. Zenker's diverticulum.
     3. Infection of pharynx or neck (mucositis from *Candida,* herpes, and CMV).
     4. Thyromegaly.

  5. Prior surgery or radiotherapy.
  6. Osteophytes and other spinal disorders.
  7. Proximal esophageal webs.
  8. Congenital anomalies (e.g., cleft palate).
  9. Poor dentition.
- Esophageal
  1. Neuromuscular disorders
     1. Achalasia.
     2. Diffuse esophageal spasm.
     3. Nutcracker esophagus.
     4. Hypertensive lower esophageal sphincter.
     5. Ineffective esophageal motility.
     6. Scleroderma.
     7. Reflex-associated dysmotility.
  2. Structural disorder
     1. Peptic stricture.
     2. Esophageal rings and webs.
     3. Diverticuli.
     4. Carcinoma and benign tumors.
     5. Foreign bodies.
     6. Vascular compression.
     7. Mediastinal masses.
     8. Spinal osteophytes.
     9. Mucosal injury (from pills, infection, gastroesophageal reflux disease [GERD], etc.).

PATHOGENESIS

The inability to swallow is caused either by a problem in strength or coordination of the muscles required to move material from the mouth to stomach or by a fixed obstruction somewhere between the mouth and the stomach.

CLINICAL FEATURES

Oropharyngeal dysphagia
- Problem arises within 2 seconds of initiating the voluntary phase of swallowing.
- Typical symptoms include drooling, spillage of food, postnasal regurgitation, difficulty in initiation of swallowing, sialorrhea, sensation of food stuck in the neck, coughing or choking during swallowing, the need to swallow repeatedly to clear food or fluid from the pharynx, dysphonia, nasal speech, hoarseness of voice, and dysarthria.
- A thorough physical examination including that of the nervous system, oral cavity, and the head/neck is very important in patients with oropharyngeal dysphagia.

Esophageal dysphagia
- Problem usually arises several seconds after swallowing.
- Patients often complain of food being stuck in lower substernal area.
- Dysphagia to solids suggests mechanical obstruction.
- Neuromuscular causes result in dysphagia to both solids and liquids. Particularly, patients with achalasia tend to drink a lot of fluids while eating or apply maneuvers such as straightening the back, raising their arms over their heads, or standing to increase intraesophageal pressure to facilitate the emptying of food into the stomach.
- Oftentimes, ingestion of very cold or very hot foods precipitates the dysphagia associated with neuromuscular disorder.

- Delayed regurgitation of food, heartburn, and chest pain are usually present.
- Weight loss is usually associated with malignancy or achalasia.
- Symptoms are intermittent in patients with esophageal dysphagia from benign causes of structural obstruction or diffuse esophageal spasm. However, it is progressive in patients with peptic stricture, esophageal carcinoma, scleroderma, and achalasia.
- In patients with structural obstruction, when the luminal diameter is more than 18 to 20 mm, they are rarely symptomatic, whereas those with a diameter of less than 13 mm are nearly always symptomatic.
- These patients with esophageal dysphagia usually do not have any characteristic physical findings.

(Dx) DIAGNOSIS

Laboratory evaluation
- CBC.
- Thyroid studies.
- Nutritional assessment by checking serum protein and albumin levels.
- Other studies based on specific clinical conditions.

Special studies
- Oropharyngeal dysphagia
  1. Videofluoroscopy is the first test often ordered in evaluation of patients with oropharyngeal dysphagia.
  2. Double contrast modified barium swallow study (Fig. E1D-45).
  3. Fiberoptic flexible nasopharyngeal laryngoscopy is mandatory in all cases when a structural lesion, particularly malignancy, is suspected.
  4. Pharyngeal and upper esophageal manometry (Fig. E1D-46) is occasionally of value to predict which patients will have a favorable outcome from cricopharyngeal myotomy or dilation.
  5. Radiography of head and neck when indicated.
- Esophageal dysphagia
  1. Barium esophagography should precede upper endoscopies to identify patients at risk from potential perforation with an endoscopy and to help plan fluoroscopically guided dilation. It is often the first step in evaluating patients with dysphagia, especially if an obstructive lesion is suspected.
  2. EGD.
  3. Esophageal manometry is indicated if no abnormality is identified by barium study or EGD.
  4. Esophageal pH monitoring in patients with suspected reflux disease.
  5. Endoscopic ultrasonography.
  6. Radiograph, CT, and MRI of chest.

DIFFERENTIAL DIAGNOSIS (FIG. 1D-47)

- Globus pharyngeus.
- Odynophagia.
- Phagophobia.
- GERD.

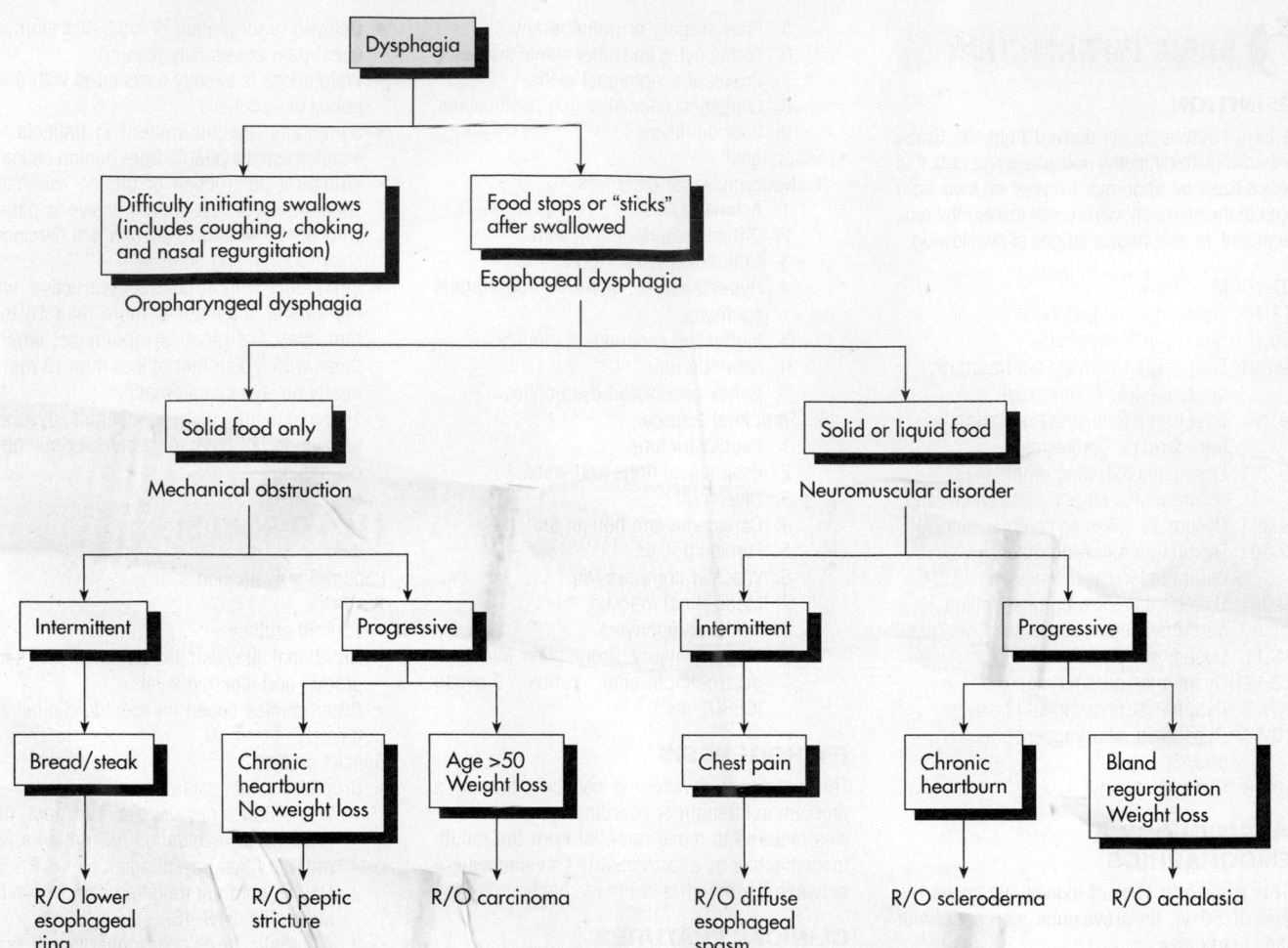

FIGURE 1D-47 Differential diagnosis of dysphagia. *RO,* Rule out. (Modified from Andreoli TE [ed]: *Cecil essentials of medicine,* ed 7, Philadelphia, 2008, Saunders.)

(Rx) TREATMENT

- Treatment should be approached with the help of specialists of multiple disciplines (ENT, head and neck surgeon, radiologist, speech pathologist, physical therapist, dietitian, gastroenterologist, physical medicine and rehabilitation specialist, dentist, neurologist, etc.).
- Goal of therapy is airway protection and maintenance of nutrition.
- Alteration of food consistency, volume, and delivery rate plays a major role.
- The goal of direct therapy is to change swallowing physiology with medical treatment of primary disease, maxillofacial prosthesis, and cricopharyngeal myotomy.
- Indirect therapies include exercise programs for tongue coordination and chewing under the guidance of a speech therapist.
- Maintenance of oral feeding often requires compensatory techniques such as chin-tuck position, rotation of head to the affected side, tilting of head to the strong side, and lying on one's back or on one's side during swallowing.
- Some of the voluntary maneuvers applied include supraglottic swallow, effortful swallow, Mendelson maneuver, Shaker exercise, and the Heimlich maneuver.
- Placement of nasogastric tube, jejunostomy tube, or percutaneous endoscopic gastrostomy

(PEG) tube is considered for enteral feeding when other measures fail and the patient remains at significant risk for aspiration or nutrition becomes compromised.
- Treatment of associated GERD should not be forgotten.
- Surgery for chronic aspiration may involve tracheostomy, medialization, laryngeal suspension, laryngeal closure, and/or laryngotracheal separation-diversion.
- Other measures include esophageal dilation removal of foreign body, esophageal resection, chemotherapy, radiotherapy, endoscopic ablation of tumor, photodynamic therapy, esophageal prosthesis/stents, diverticulectomy, intrasphincteric injection of botulinum toxin, surgical myotomy, and others. Smooth muscle relaxants such as nitrates and calcium channel blockers have been used to effectively treat patients with diffuse esophageal spasm and nutcracker esophagus.
- Several scales have been suggested to determine patients' functional outcome. One of them is the "Swallowing Rating Scale."

COMPLICATIONS

- Dehydration.
- Malnutrition.
- Aspiration pneumonia.
- Airway obstruction.
- Death resulting from pulmonary complications.

PROGNOSIS

- Depends on the etiology.
- Nursing home patients with oropharyngeal dysphagia and a history of aspiration have an approximately 45% mortality rate over 1 yr.
- All patients, especially the elderly, should take their medications with a full glass of water while in upright position well before bedtime.
- Dysphagia should be considered an alarm symptom, indicating the need for immediate evaluation.

PATIENT EDUCATION

Elderly patients with dysphagia should not attribute their symptoms to aging.

SUGGESTED READINGS

Available at www.expertconsult.com

RELATED CONTENT

Dyspepsia, Nonulcerative (Related Key Topic)
Esophageal Tumors (Related Key Topic)
Gastroesophageal Reflux Disease (Related Key Topic)

AUTHOR: **HEMANT K. SATPATHY, M.D.**

 **BASIC INFORMATION**

DEFINITION

Dystonia refers to a group of disorders characterized by involuntary muscle contractions (sustained or spasmodic) that lead to abnormal body movements or postures. Dystonia can be generalized or focal, of early (<20 yr) or late onset, and primary or secondary.

SYNONYMS

Blepharospasm
Oromandibular (orofacial) dystonia
Spasmodic (limb or axial) dystonia
Torticollis
Writer's cramp

ICD-10CM CODES
G24   Dystonia
G24.1 Idiopathic familial dystonia
G24.0 Drug induced dystonia
G24.3 Spasmodic torticollis

EPIDEMIOLOGY & DEMOGRAPHICS

PREVALENCE: Estimated at one in 3000 persons.
PREDOMINANT SEX: Cervical dystonia has a 3:2 female preponderance.
PREDOMINANT AGE:
- Onset of focal cervical dystonia is usually in the fifth decade.
- Hereditary forms may have an onset in childhood or adulthood and tend to be more severe.
GENETICS: Autosomal-dominant, autosomal-recessive, and X-linked forms of dystonia have been identified. Ashkenazi Jews are particularly susceptible to primary early-onset dystonia. Metabolic conditions in which dystonia is a feature can be inherited or, more frequently, caused by sporadic mutations.

CLINICAL PRESENTATION

Focal dystonias produce abnormal sustained muscle contractions in a single region of the body:
- Neck (***torticollis***): most commonly affected site with a tendency for the head to turn to one side.
- Eyelids (***blepharospasm***): involuntary closure of the eyelids that leads to excessive eye blinking, sometimes with persistent eye closure and functional blindness.
- Mouth (***oromandibular dystonia***): involuntary contraction of muscles of the mouth, tongue, or face.
- Hand (***writer's cramp***) (Fig. 1D-48).
Generalized dystonia affects multiple areas of the body and can lead to marked joint deformities.
- Isolated foot dystonia is very rare and may suggest an underlying parkinsonian disorder or brain structural abnormality.

ETIOLOGY

- Exact pathophysiology of primary dystonia is unknown but believed to involve abnormalities of basal ganglia. Specifically, reduced and abnormal patterns of neuronal activity in the basal ganglia result in disinhibition of the motor thalamus and cortex, leading to abnormal movement.

- Fifteen hereditary forms have been described, including the severe progressive form, dystonia musculorum deformans.
- Secondary dystonia results from central nervous system (CNS) disease of the basal ganglia (stroke, demyelination, hypoxia, trauma), Huntington's disease, Wilson's disease, Parkinson syndromes, and lysosomal storage diseases.
- Acute dystonia can occur with drugs that block dopamine receptors, such as phenothiazines or butyrophenones.
- Tardive dyskinesia can result from long-term treatment with antiemetics (e.g., phenothiazines), antipsychotics (e.g., haloperidol), levodopa, anticonvulsants, or ergots.

Dx DIAGNOSIS

DIFFERENTIAL DIAGNOSIS

- Drug effects.
- Parkinson's disease.
- Progressive supranuclear palsy.
- Wilson's disease.
- Huntington's disease.
- Table 1D-24 describes selected causes of primary and secondary dystonia in childhood.

WORKUP

History (family history, birth history, trauma, medication use, age of onset, and temporal pattern), physical examination to determine associated features (weakness, myoclonus, tremor) and to determine pattern of dystonia—focal (single body region), segmental (two or more body contiguous body regions), multifocal (two or more noncontiguous body regions), generalized (involving the trunk and at least two other sites), or hemidystonia (involving more regions but restricted to one body side).

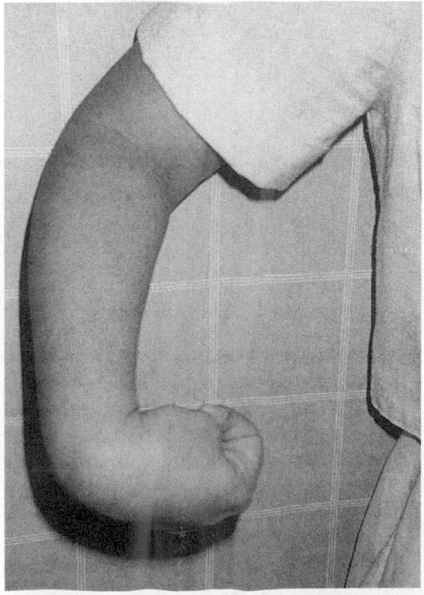

FIGURE 1D-48 Focal dystonia of the distal right arm. (From Goldman L, Ausiello D [eds]: *Cecil textbook of medicine,* ed 22, Philadelphia, 2004, Saunders.)

LABORATORY TESTS

- Usually not helpful for diagnosis
- Serum ceruloplasmin if Wilson's disease is suspected
- Genetic testing (DYT gene mutations, inborn errors of metabolism, or mitochondrial disease) if indicated
- Comprehensive toxicology screen indicated if causative drugs suspected (dopamine-blocking agents) and history unavailable

IMAGING STUDIES

- Primary dystonias are generally not associated with structural CNS abnormalities. CT scan or MRI of brain if a CNS lesion is suspected as a cause of secondary dystonia.
- Electrophysiologic testing can provide diagnostic support for the diagnosis, but dystonia is a clinical diagnosis.

Rx TREATMENT

NONPHARMACOLOGIC THERAPY

- Heat, massage, physical therapy to relieve pain
- Splints to prevent contractures.
- "Sensory trick" (geste antagoniste) can relieve discomfort: Application of light touch to the affected body part can abolish the dystonia; this also aids in diagnosis.

ACUTE GENERAL Rx

For acute dystonic reactions to phenothiazines/butyrophenones, use diphenhydramine 50 mg IV or benztropine 2 mg IV. For patients presenting with subacute or chronic dystonia, a trial of L-dopa can be useful in distinguishing dopa-responsive dystonia from other causes.

CHRONIC Rx

- For treatment of drug-induced dystonia, slowly withdraw offending agents (antiemetics, antipsychotics most commonly).
- For generalized dystonia, a trial of carbidopa/levodopa may be beneficial and diagnostic of dopa-responsive dystonia.
- Trihexyphenidyl or benztropine may be helpful in up to 50% of tardive dystonias; these are the mainstay of treatment for generalized dystonias not responsive to dopa.
- Diazepam, clonazepam, or baclofen may be helpful.
- Injections of botulinum toxin into the affected muscles are the standard treatment for focal dystonias. Both type A and type B toxins produced by *Clostridium botulinum* block cholinergic transmission at the neuromuscular junction by inhibiting release of acetylcholine.
- Surgical procedures, including denervation, myectomy, rhizotomy, thalamotomy (pallidotomy), or deep brain stimulation, may be helpful for severe, refractory cases, depending on the etiology.
- Intrathecal baclofen can be useful for spastic or truncal dystonia.

DISPOSITION

Spontaneous remission of focal cervical dystonia can occur, but dystonia is generally progressive and pharmacologic therapy is often ineffective.

REFERRAL

Neurology (movement disorders) and/or neurosurgery for severe or refractory cases.
Physical therapy for maintaining flexibility.

PEARLS & CONSIDERATIONS

COMMENTS

- Avoid triggers/exacerbating factors.
- Early physical therapy and splinting to prevent contractures.
- Consider botulism injections.
- Consider deep brain stimulation surgery for severe or refractory dystonia and for focal dystonias.

SUGGESTED READINGS

Available at www.expertconsult.com

AUTHOR: **JULIE L. ROTH, M.D.**

TABLE 1D-24   Selected Causes of Primary and Secondary Dystonia in Childhood

Diagnosis	Additional Clinical Features	Diagnosis	Additional Clinical Features
Aicardi-Goutieres syndrome	Encephalopathy, developmental regression Acquired microcephaly Sterile pyrexias Lesions on the digits, ears (chilblain) Epilepsy CT: calcification of the basal ganglia	Leigh syndrome	Motor delays, weakness, hypotonia Ataxia, tremor Elevated lactate MRI: bilateral symmetric hyperintense lesions in the basal ganglia or thalamus
Alternating hemiplegia of childhood	Episodic hemiplegia/quadriplegia Abnormal ocular movements Autonomic symptoms Epilepsy Global developmental impairment Environmental triggers for spells	Lesch-Nyhan syndrome (X-linked)	Male Self-injurious behavior Hypotonia Oromandibular dystonia, inspiratory stridor Oculomotor apraxia Cognitive impairment Elevated uric acid
Aromatic amino acid decarboxylase deficiency (AADC)	Developmental delay Oculogyric crises Autonomic dysfunction Hypotonia	Myoclonus dystonia	Myoclonus Head, upper limb involvement
ARX gene mutation (X-linked)	Male Cognitive impairment Infantile spasms, epilepsy Brain malformation	Niemann-Pick type C	Hepatosplenomegaly Hypotonia Supranuclear gaze palsy Ataxia, dysarthria Epilepsy Psychiatric symptoms
Benign paroxysmal torticollis of infancy	Episodic Cervical dystonia only Family history of migraine	Neuroacanthocytosis	Oromandibular and lingual dystonia
Complex regional pain syndrome	Lower limb involvement Prominent pain	Neurodegeneration with brain iron accumulation	Cognitive impairment Retinal pigmentary degeneration, optic atrophy
Dopa-responsive dystonia (DRD)	Diurnal variation	Rapid onset dystonia parkinsonism (DYT12)	Acute onset Distribution face>arm>leg Prominent bulbar signs
Drug-induced dystonia		Rett syndrome	Female Developmental regression following a period of normal development Stereotypic hand movements Acquired microcephaly Epilepsy
Dystonia-deafness optic neuropathy syndrome	Sensorineural hearing loss in early childhood Psychosis Optic atrophy in adolescence		
DYT1 dystonia	Lower limb onset followed by generalization	Spinocerebellar ataxia 17 (SCA17)	Ataxia Dementia, psychiatric symptoms Parkinsonism
Glutaric aciduria type 1	Macrocephaly Encephalopathic crises MRI: striatal necrosis	Tics	Stereotyped movements Premonitory urge, suppressible
GM1 gangliosidosis type 3	Short stature, skeletal dysplasia Orofacial dystonia Speech/swallowing disturbance Parkinsonism MRI: putaminal hyperintensity	Tyrosine hydroxylase deficiency	Infantile encephalopathy, hypotonia Oculogyric crises, ptosis Autonomic symptoms Less diurnal fluctuation than DRD
Huntington disease (HD)	Parkinsonism Epilepsy Family history of HD		
Kernicterus	Jaundice in infancy Hearing loss Impaired upgaze Enamel dysplasia MRI: hyperintense lesions in the globus pallidus		

From Kliegman RM et al: *Nelson textbook of pediatrics*, ed 19, Philadelphia, 2011, Saunders.

BASIC INFORMATION

DEFINITION

Echinococcosis is a chronic infection caused by the larval stage of several animal cestodes (tapeworms) of the genus *Echinococcus.*

SYNONYMS

Hydatid disease

ICD-10CM CODES
B67.8 Echinococcosis, unspecified, of liver
B67.90 Echinococcosis, unspecified
B67.99 Other echinococcosis

EPIDEMIOLOGY & DEMOGRAPHICS

INCIDENCE (IN U.S.): Seen primarily in immigrants, but local transmission can occur in southwestern U.S., California, and Alaska.
PEAK INCIDENCE: Presumed to be acquired in childhood or early adulthood in most cases.
PREVALENCE (IN U.S.): See Incidence
PREDOMINANT SEX: Male = female
PREDOMINANT AGE: 0 to 50 yr of age

PHYSICAL FINDINGS & CLINICAL PRESENTATION

- Signs of an enlarging mass lesion in a visceral site such as the liver, lungs, kidneys, bone, or CNS
- Occasional cyst rupture causing allergic manifestations such as urticaria, angioedema, or anaphylaxis that bring the patient to medical attention
- Incidental discovery of cysts by abdominal or thoracic imaging studies performed for other reasons

ETIOLOGY

- Four species of *Echinococcus: E. granulosus, E. multilocularis, E. oligarthrus,* and *E. vogeli.*
  1. *E. granulosus* is the cause of cystic hydatid disease.
  2. *E. multilocularis* and *E. vogeli* are the causes of alveolar and polycystic disease.
- The disease is transmitted to humans by infected canines (domestic or wild dogs, wolves, foxes), which are the definitive hosts, and seen most commonly in livestock-producing areas of the Middle East, Africa, Australia, New Zealand, Europe, and the Americas, including the southwestern U.S., whereby sheep, goats, camels, or cattle serve as intermediate hosts to humans. Humans are incidental hosts and do not play a role in the transmission cycle.
- The adult tapeworm resides in the small intestine of the canine definitive hosts. Eggs are then shed in the feces of infected canines; human infection occurs by ingestion of viable eggs in contaminated food from intermediate hosts or direct fecal-oral transmission.
- After ingestion of the eggs by intermediate hosts or humans, eggs hatch and release onchospheres, which migrate through intestinal mucosa to definitive organs and develop into enlarging fluid-filled cysts known as hydatid cysts (metacestode) (Fig. 1E-1). The cyst is acellular and is surrounded by fibroblasts and lymphocytic infiltrate (Fig. E1E-2).
- It is common in many areas of the world, especially the Middle East.

DIAGNOSIS

DIFFERENTIAL DIAGNOSIS

- Cystic neoplasms (see Table 1E-1)
- Abscess (amebic or bacterial)
- Congenital polycystic disease

WORKUP

- Antibody assay
- Imaging study (CT scan [Fig. 1E-3], ultrasonography)
- Classification (Fig. 1E-4): Table 1E-2 describes the World Health Organization Informal Working Group on Echinococcosis classification of hepatic echinococcal cysts.
- Histologic examination of cyst or contents obtained by aspiration or resection (if possible) to confirm diagnosis

LABORATORY TESTS

Antibody assays (ELISA or Western blot) available through CDC: 80% to 100% sensitive and 88% to 96% specific for liver cysts, but less accurate for cysts in other sites, such as lung. A PCR assay is now available for problematic cases. Eosinophilia is not consistently seen and thus not a reliable test.

IMAGING STUDIES

Ultrasonography, CT, and MRI:
- All are extremely sensitive for the detection of cysts, especially in the liver.
- All lack specificity and are inadequate to establish the diagnosis of echinococcosis with certainty.

TREATMENT

ACUTE GENERAL Rx

- Albendazole 400 mg PO bid followed by percutaneous aspiration-injection-reaspiration (PAIR) for uncomplicated larval cysts. It consists of puncture (P) and needle aspirate (A) of cyst content followed by inspiration (I) of hypertonic saline (15%-30%) or absolute alcohol, waiting 20 to 30 minutes, then reaspirating (R) with final irrigation. Albendazole is continued for 28 days. Cure rate is 96%.
- Surgical resection: cure rate 90%
- Alternatives to albendazole include mebendazole and praziquantel alone or in combination with mebendazole.

DISPOSITION

- Long-term follow-up is necessary following surgical or medical therapy because of the potential for late relapse.
- Antibody assays and imaging studies are repeated every 6 to 12 mo for several years following successful surgical or medical therapy.

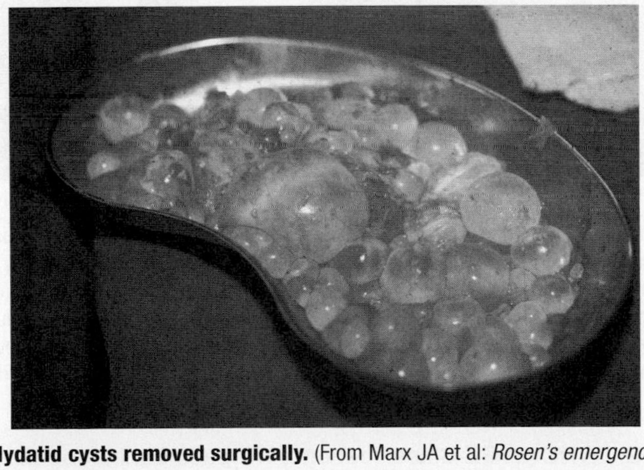

FIGURE 1E-1 Hydatid cysts removed surgically. (From Marx JA et al: *Rosen's emergency medicine,* ed 8, Philadelphia, 2014, Saunders.)

TABLE 1E-1 Hepatic Cyst Disease: Differential Features on Imaging Studies

Characteristics	Hydatid Cyst	Congenital Cyst	Cystadenoma
Configuration	Cyst within cyst	Single or multiple ± septations	Single ± septations
Wall character	Thick, uniform ± calcification	Thin, uniform	Mural nodules
Cyst contents	Daughter cystsHydatid sand	Low density	Low density

From Cameron JL, Cameron AM: *Current surgical therapy,* ed 10, Philadelphia, 2011, Saunders.

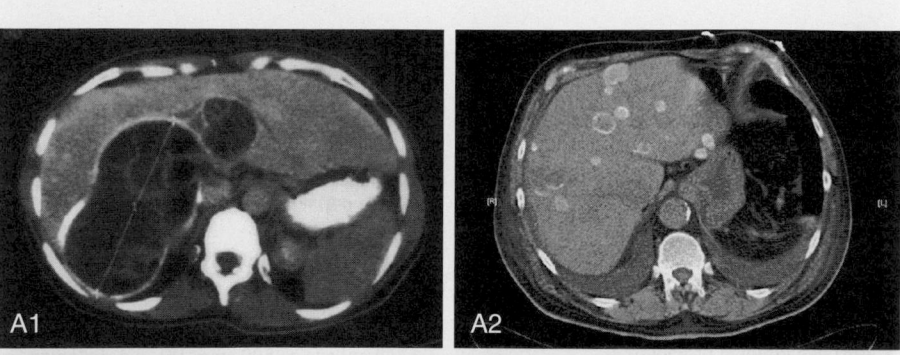

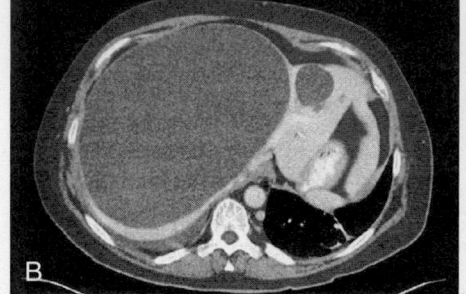

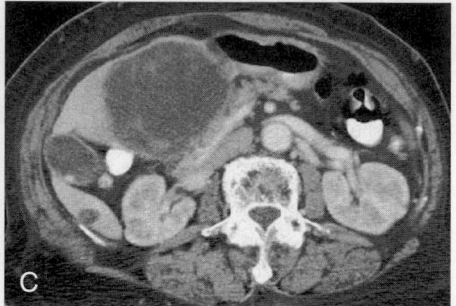

FIGURE 1E-3 A comparison of computed tomography scans. A, Hepatic echinococcal cysts. **B,** Congenital cyst. **C,** Cystadenoma. For echinococcal cyst. **A1** demonstrates a single cyst with calcification and daughter cyst caused by *E. granulosa*. **A2** shows multiple small cysts characteristic of *E. multilocularis* infection. (Courtesy Barbara M. Kadell, MD, Professor of Radiology, David Geffen School of Medicine at University of California, Los Angeles. From Cameron JL, Cameron AM: *Current surgical therapy*, ed 10, Philadelphia, 2011, Saunders.)

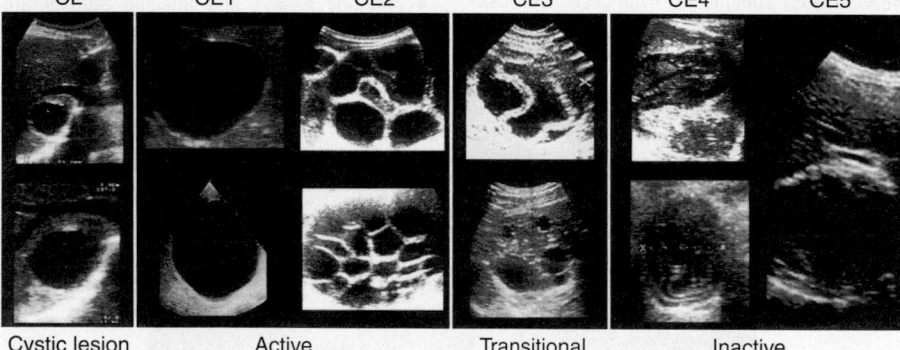

FIGURE 1E-4 WHO Informal Working Group on Echinococcosis standardized ultrasound classification of cystic echinococcosis. CL lesions are cystic lesions lacking a distinct wall and may have other diagnoses. CE1 lesions are cystic lesions with a visible wall that may demonstrate protoscolices ("hydatid sand"). CE2 lesions include internal septation. CE3 lesions may be detached from the wall or have daughter cysts with internal thickening. CE4 lesions are heterogeneous lesions with degeneration. CE5 lesions show thick calcification. (From Goldman L, Schafer AI: *Goldman's Cecil medicine*, ed 24, Philadelphia, 2012, Saunders.)

REFERRAL

All patients for evaluation for possible surgical resection of cysts versus PAIR

! PEARLS & CONSIDERATIONS

COMMENTS

Cyst resection, if indicated, should be performed by surgeons experienced with this procedure.

SUGGESTED READINGS

Available at www.expertconsult.com

RELATED CONTENT

Echinococcosis (Patient Information)

AUTHOR: **GLENN G. FORT, M.D., M.P.H.**

TABLE 1E-2 WHO-IWGE Classification of Hepatic Echinococcal Cysts

Type of Cyst	Status	Ultrasound Features	Remarks
CL	Active	Signs not pathognomonic, unilocular, no cyst wall	Usually early stage, not fertile; differential diagnosis necessary
CE 1	Active	Cyst wall, hydatid sand	Usually fertile
CE 2	Active	Multivesicular, cyst wall, rosette-like	Usually fertile
CE 3	Transitional	Detached laminated membrane, "water lily" sign, less round, decreased intracystic pressure	Starting to degenerate, may produce daughter cyst
CE 4	Inactive	Heterogeneous hypoechogenic or hyperechogenic degenerative contents; no daughter cyst	Usually no living protoscolices; differential diagnosis necessary
CE 5	Inactive	Thick, calcified wall, calcification partial to complete; not pathognomonic but highly suggestive of diagnosis	Usually no living protoscolices

WHO-IWGE, World Health Organization Informal Working Group on Echinococcosis.
From Cameron JL, Cameron AM: *Current surgical therapy*, ed 10, Philadelphia, 2011, Saunders.

BASIC INFORMATION

DEFINITION

Eclampsia is the occurrence of seizures or coma in a woman with preeclampsia, occurring at >>20 wk of gestation or <<48 hr postpartum. Atypical eclampsia occurs at <<20 wk of gestation or as much as 14 days postpartum.

SYNONYMS

Toxemia
Seizures of pregnancy

ICD-10CM CODES
015.00 Eclampsia in pregnancy, unspecified trimester
015.02 Eclampsia in pregnancy, second trimester
015.03 Eclampsia in pregnancy, third trimester
015.1 Eclampsia in labor
015.2 Eclampsia in the puerperium
015.9 Eclampsia, unspecified as to time period

EPIDEMIOLOGY & DEMOGRAPHICS

INCIDENCE: One case per 1500 to 3000 pregnancies; 2% to 4% of those with preeclampsia.; one large Australian series found 8.6 cases per 10,000 live births.
GENETICS: Increased incidence with a first-degree relative (sister or mother) having had eclampsia.
RISK FACTORS: Multifetal gestation (3.6% in twin gestation), molar pregnancy, nonimmune hydrops fetalis, uncontrolled hypertension, pre-existing hypertension, renal disease.

PHYSICAL FINDINGS & CLINICAL PRESENTATION

- Seizure begins as facial twitching, then spreads to generalized tonic-clonic state, with cessation of respiration followed by a postictal period of amnesia, agitation, and confusion.
- 40% have severe hypertension, 40% have mild to moderate hypertension, and 20% are normotensive.
- Generalized edema with rapid weight gain (>2 lb/wk) may be one of the earliest signs of eclampsia.
- Persistent occipital headache and hyper-reflexia with clonus occur in 80% of patients with eclampsia; epigastric pain occurs in 20% of these patients.

ETIOLOGY

- Exact etiology unknown.
- Common pathway relates to abnormalities in autoregulation of cerebral blood flow. This may involve transient vasospasm, ischemia, cerebral hemorrhage, and edema occurring by a mechanism involving hypertensive encephalopathy, decreased colloid osmotic pressure, and prostaglandin imbalance.

DIAGNOSIS

DIFFERENTIAL DIAGNOSIS

- Preexisting seizure disorder

- Metabolic abnormalities (hypoglycemia, hyponatremia, hypocalcemia)
- Substance abuse
- Head trauma, infection (meningitis, encephalitis)
- Intracerebral bleeding or thrombosis
- Amniotic fluid embolism
- Space-occupying brain lesions or neoplasms
- Pseudoseizure
- Hypertensive encephalopathy
- Venous or arterial thrombosis, arterial embolism
- Posterior reversible vasoconstriction syndrome
- Vasculitis, angiopathy

WORKUP

- Rule out other causes of seizures during pregnancy.
- Atypical presentations such as prolonged postictal state; status epilepticus; gestational age <20 wk or >48 hr postpartum; or signs of meningitis, substance abuse, or severe uncontrolled hypertension should prompt a search for other seizure etiologies.

LABORATORY TESTS

- Proteinuria: severe (49%), mild to moderate (29%), absent (22%).
- HCT: elevated as a result of hemoconcentration.
- Platelet count: decreased; LFTs elevated in HELLP syndrome (hemolysis, elevated liver enzymes, and low platelet count).
- BUN and creatinine: elevated with renal involvement.
- Serum electrolytes, glucose, calcium, toxicology profile: Rule out other causes of seizures.
- Hyperuricemia: >6.9 mg/dl found in 70% of eclamptics.
- ABG: maternal acidemia and hypoxia.

IMAGING STUDIES

- CT scan or MRI indicated in atypical presentation, suspected intracerebral bleeding, or focal neurologic deficit.
- There are abnormal findings, including cerebral edema, hemorrhage, and infarction, in 50% of patients.

 TREATMENT

NONPHARMACOLOGIC THERAPY

- Airway protection (risk of aspiration)
- Supportive care during acute event

ACUTE GENERAL Rx

- Maintain airway, adequate oxygenation, and IV access.
- Fetal resuscitation, involving maternal oxygenation, left lateral positioning, and continuous fetal heart rate monitoring, is needed.
- Magnesium sulfate is the drug of choice. Give magnesium sulfate 6 g IV load over 20 min, then 3 g/hr maintenance, for recurrent seizure prophylaxis. If repeated convulsions, may give an additional 2 g IV over 3 to 5 min. Approximately 10% to 15% of patients will have a second seizure after initial loading dose. Check magnesium level 1 hr after loading dose, then q6h (therapeutic range 4 to 7 mEq/L). Clinical signs of progressive Mg^{2+}

toxicity, such as loss of reflexes, should also be followed. Respiratory and cardiac arrest occur at extremely high levels. Antidote for toxicity is calcium gluconate 10 ml of 10% solution. Phenytoin has been used as an alternative in patients in whom magnesium sulfate is contraindicated (renal insufficiency, heart block, myasthenia gravis, hypoparathyroidism).
- Give sodium amobarbital 250 mg IV over 3 min for persistent seizures.
- Treat blood pressure if >160 mm Hg/110 mm Hg with labetalol 20- to 40-mg IV bolus, hydralazine 10 mg IV, or nifedipine 10 to 20 mg sublingual q20 min.
- Evaluate patient for delivery.

CHRONIC Rx

- The first priority is stabilization of the mother in terms of adequate oxygenation, hemodynamics, and laboratory abnormalities, such as associated coagulopathies.
- Cervical status and gestational age should be assessed. If unfavorable cervix and <30 wk of gestation, consider C-section; otherwise consider induction.
- Controlled epidural is the anesthesia of choice for labor or C-section.
- Avoid general anesthesia in uncontrolled hypertension to minimize risk of catastrophic cerebral events.

DISPOSITION

The maternal mortality rate for eclampsia averages 5% to 6%. Morbidity rate is 25%, including placental abruption (10%), maternal apnea with fetal asphyxia, aspiration pneumonia, pulmonary edema (4%), renal failure, cardiopulmonary arrest, and coma.

REFERRAL

Because of the potential for serious permanent maternal and fetal sequelae, all cases should be managed by a team approach of obstetrician, neonatologist, and intensivist.

PEARLS & CONSIDERATIONS

COMMENTS

- Eclampsia antepartum, 50%; intrapartum, 20%; and postpartum, 30%.
- Postseizure there is an associated period of fetal bradycardia from 1 to 9 min; if there is evidence of fetal compromise beyond that time, consider alternative etiologies such as placental abruption (23% incidence).

SUGGESTED READINGS

Available at www.expertconsult.com

RELATED CONTENT

Eclampsia (Patient Information)
HELLP Syndrome (Related Key Topic)
Preeclampsia (Related Key Topic)

AUTHOR: **RUBEN ALVERO, M.D.**

BASIC INFORMATION

DEFINITION

An ectopic pregnancy (EP) occurs when a fertilized ovum implants outside the endometrial lining of the uterus.

SYNONYMS

Abdominal pregnancy (0.03% to 1%)
Cervical pregnancy (0.5%)
Interstitial pregnancy (1% to 2%)
Ovarian pregnancy (1%)
Tubal pregnancy (97%)

ICD-10CM CODES
O00.9 Ectopic pregnancy, unspecified
O00.8 Other ectopic pregnancy

EPIDEMIOLOGY & DEMOGRAPHICS

- 1% to 2% of pregnancies
- 13% of maternal deaths

PREVALENCE (IN U.S.): Increasing number of EPs; 17,800 reported cases in 1970 and currently over 100,000 reported cases/year.

RISK FACTORS: Previous salpingitis, previous EP, previous tubal ligation, previous tuboplasty, intrauterine device use, progestin-only pill, assisted reproductive techniques

PHYSICAL FINDINGS & CLINICAL PRESENTATION

- Abdominal tenderness: 95%
- Adnexal tenderness: 87% to 99%
- Peritoneal signs: 71% to 76%
- Adnexal mass: 33% to 53%
- Enlarged uterus: 6% to 30%
- Shock: 2% to 17%
- Amenorrhea or abnormal vaginal bleeding: 75%
- Shoulder pain: 10%
- Tissue passage: 6% to 7%

ETIOLOGY

- Anatomic obstruction to zygote passage
- Abnormalities in tubal motility
- Transperitoneal migration of the zygote

Dx DIAGNOSIS

DIFFERENTIAL DIAGNOSIS

- Corpus luteum cyst
- Rupture or torsion of ovarian cyst
- Threatened or incomplete abortion
- Pelvic inflammatory disease
- Appendicitis
- Gastroenteritis
- Dysfunctional uterine bleeding
- Degenerating uterine fibroids
- Endometriosis

WORKUP

1. The classic presentation of EP includes the triad of abnormal vaginal bleeding, pelvic pain, and an adnexal mass. Fig. 1E-5 describes a diagnostic approach to suspected EP. Fig. 1E-6 *(top)* describes potential sites of ectopic implantations. Consider in all women with abdominopelvic pain and a positive pregnancy test.
2. Transvaginal ultrasound.
3. Quantitative serum human chorionic gonadotropin level.
4. Laparoscopy in equivocal situations and possibly for treatment.

LABORATORY TESTS

- Quantitative human chorionic gonadotropin (qhCG): If normal intrauterine pregnancy (IUP), 85% have doubling time of 2 days. If abnormal gestation, will show <>66% increase of qhCG within 2 days. However, 13% of ectopic pregnancies have a normal doubling time.
- Progesterone: decreased production in EP; <<5 ng/ml strongly predictive of abnormal pregnancy. If >>25 ng/ml, strongly predictive of normal IUP.
- Dropping hematocrit associated with tubal rupture, resolving EP, or abnormal intrauterine pregnancy.
- Leukocytosis.

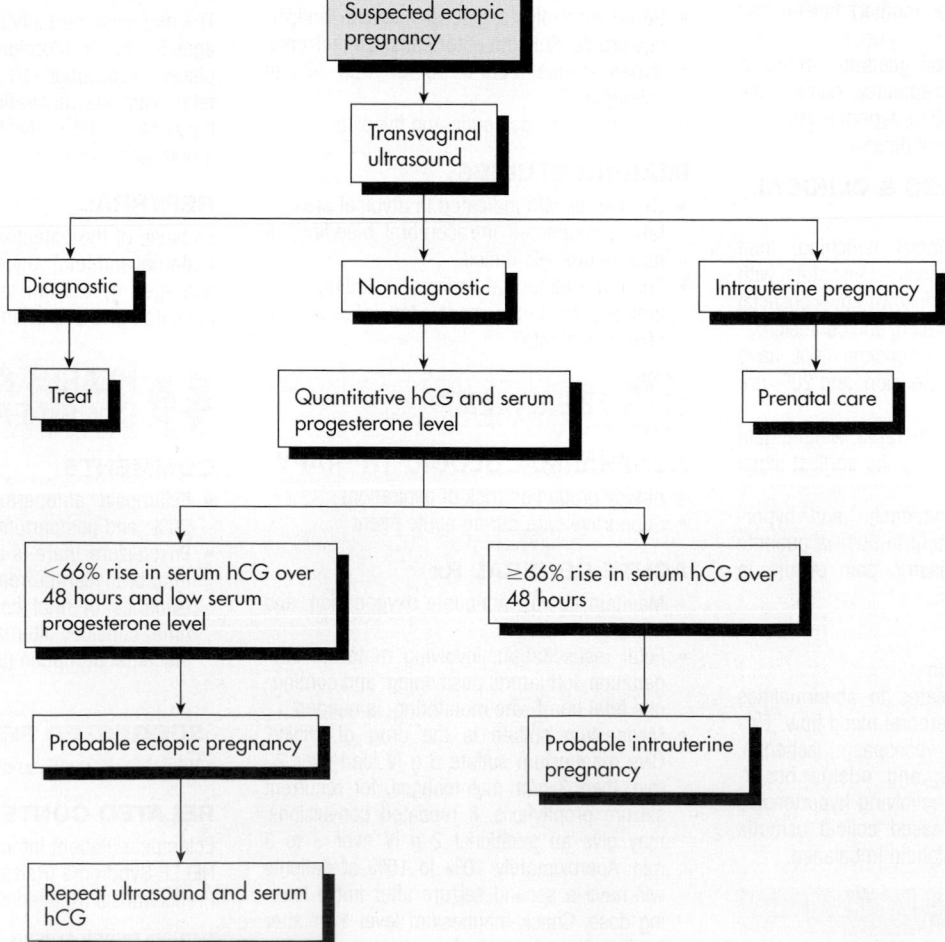

FIGURE 1E-5 Ectopic pregnancy. *hCG*, Human chorionic gonadotropin.

IMAGING STUDIES

- Ultrasound: presence of an IUP makes EP extremely unlikely. However, if the patient used assisted reproductive technologies, a heterotopic pregnancy (a pregnancy in the uterus as well as in the fallopian tube) is much more likely to occur (Fig. 1E-6, *A* and *B*). A repeat ultrasonographic examination 2 to 7 days after presentation may identify the location of a pregnancy that was not identified on initial ultrasonographic examination.
- If >qhCG >6000 mIU/ml, should see IUP on abdominal scan; >qhCG >1500 mIU/ml for transvaginal scan. Since transvaginal ultrasonography is overwhelmingly the preferred modality for imaging, the latter value is clearly the discriminatory threshold that is used in diagnosis.
- Findings on ultrasound in EP include:
  1. Empty uterus.
  2. Adnexal mass.
  3. Cul-de-sac fluid.
  4. Fetal sac in tube.
  5. Fetal cardiac activity in adnexa.

Rx TREATMENT

NONPHARMACOLOGIC THERAPY

Surgery can be performed by laparoscopy if patient is stable or rarely, by laparotomy if patient is very unstable. Salpingiosis is the direct injection of chemotherapy into the EP by laparoscopy, transvaginal ultrasound, or hysteroscopy. Direct injection of methotrexate, and possibly KCl if there is active cardiac activity, may be performed when the pregnancy is in a location where there is high morbidity, such as the cervix or cornu.

- Conservative surgery, salpingostomy or segmental resection, depends on tubal location and size of EP.
- Salpingectomy should be considered in the following circumstances:
  1. Ruptured tube
  2. Future fertility not desired
  3. Recurrent EP in the same tube
  4. Uncontrolled hemorrhage

ACUTE GENERAL Rx

- If the patient is stable and compliant, consider medical management with methotrexate. Patient should not have contraindications to methotrexate such as hepatic or renal disease, thrombocytopenia, leukopenia, or significant anemia. There should be no evidence of hemoperitoneum on transvaginal ultrasound. EP should be <<3.5 cm mass with <qhCG <6,000 to 15,000 mIU/mL, but these are relative contraindications. Presence of cardiac activity in the fetus is also a relative contraindication to methotrexate.
- Most common regimen is methotrexate 50 mg/m^2 of body surface area. May require second dose or surgical intervention if qhCG increases or plateaus (<(<15% drop) when comparing values from the fourth through seventh day after treatment (day 1 is the day that methotrexate is given). Absolute contraindications to methotrexate include breast feeding, preexisting blood dyscrasias, known sensitivity to methotrexate, active pulmonary disease, chronic liver disease, alcoholism, laboratory evidence of immunodeficiency, renal disease, and peptic ulcer disease.

CHRONIC Rx

Persistent EP results from residual trophoblastic tissue or secondary implantation after conservative surgery. There is a 5% incidence of persistent EP with conservative treatment.

DISPOSITION

If diagnosed and treated early (before rupture), prognosis is excellent for good recovery. Monitor qhCG weekly until negative. Use reliable contraception until hCG is negative. With subsequent pregnancies, follow qhCG and perform early ultrasound to confirm IUP. There is a 12% recurrence rate for EP.

REFERRAL

Should obtain gynecologic consultation if EP is suspected.

SUGGESTED READINGS

Available at www.expertconsult.com

RELATED CONTENT

Ectopic Pregnancy (Patient Information)
Spontaneous Miscarriage (Related Key Topic)
Vaginal Bleeding During Pregnancy (Related Key Topic)

AUTHOR: **RUBEN ALVERO, M.D.**

E

Diseases
and Disorders

I

Sites of Ectopic Implantations

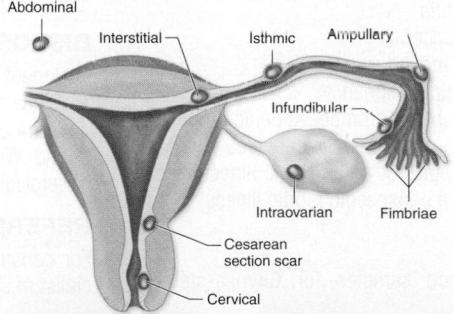

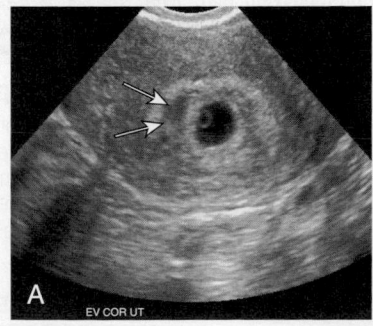 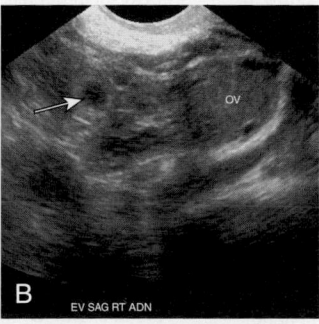

FIGURE 1E-6 *Top,* Schematic drawing depicting implantation sites of ectopic pregnancies. **A** and **B,** Heterotopic pregnancy. This pregnant patient presented with vaginal bleeding at 5 to 6 wk of gestational age. **A,** Transverse transvaginal ultrasound (TVUS) image of the uterus reveals an intrauterine gestational sac containing a yolk sac. Note small subchorionic hemorrhage (*arrows*), most likely accounting for the vaginal bleeding. **B,** Sagittal TVUS image of the right adnexa reveals an echogenic tubal ring (*arrow*) clearly separate from the right ovary (*OV*), which was surgically confirmed to be an ectopic pregnancy. (From Fielding JR et al: *Gynecologic imaging,* Philadelphia, 2011, Saunders.)

BASIC INFORMATION

DEFINITION

Human monocytic ehrlichiosis (HME) and human granulocytic anaplasmosis (HGA) are tick-borne rickettsial diseases. HGA was formerly known as human granulocytic ehrlichiosis (HGE). Table 1E-4 describes the agent, vector, and geographic prevalence of these diseases.

SYNONYMS

Human granulocytic ehrlichiosis (HGE)
Ehrlichiosis
Human monocytic ehrlichiosis (HME)
Human granulocytic anaplasmosis (HGA)
Anaplasmosis
Ehrlichia phagocytophila
Anaplasma phagocytophilum

ICD-10CM CODES
A77.40 Ehrlichiosis, unspecified
A77.41 Ehrlichiosis chaffeensis [E. chaffeensis]
A77.49 Other ehrlichiosis

EPIDEMIOLOGY & DEMOGRAPHICS

INCIDENCE (IN U.S.): Highest overall incidence in Rhode Island (36.5 per 1 million), New York, New Jersey, Connecticut, Wisconsin, Minnesota, and northern California; >3000 cases identified in the United States since 2006.
PREDOMINANT SEX: Males outnumber females by 2 to 1.
PREDOMINANT AGE: Most severe disease 50 to 70 yr
PEAK INCIDENCE: Occurs throughout the year, with peak incidence between May and July and again in November.

PHYSICAL FINDINGS & CLINICAL PRESENTATION

- Most common initial symptoms
  1. Fever
  2. Chills, rigor
  3. Headache
  4. Myalgia
- Subsequent symptoms
  1. Anorexia, nausea
  2. Arthralgia
  3. Cough
  4. Confusion (meningoencephalitis in 20% of patients with HME)
  5. Abdominal pain
  6. Rash (erythematous to pustular) <30% in HME, uncommon in HGA
- Complications
  1. Hepatitis
  2. Interstitial pneumonitis; acute respiratory distress syndrome
  3. Renal and respiratory failure
  4. Demyelinating polyneuropathy
  5. Toxic shock–like syndrome
  6. Life-threatening opportunistic infections

ETIOLOGY

- The causative agents are *Ehrlichia chaffeensis* and *Anaplasma phagocytophilum*
- Vector

1. Almost certainly tick-borne, recently confirmed to be rarely transmitted by infected blood (including nosocomial infection).
2. Transmitted by *Ixodes scapularis* in the northeastern states and *Amblyomma americanum* in the south central, southeastern, and mid-Atlantic states. Fig. 1E-8 illustrates the life cycles of human monocytic ehrlichiosis (HME, with *Ehrlichia chaffeensis*) and human granulocytic ehrlichiosis (anaplasmosis).
3. Tick exposure reported in >90% of patients, with ~60% reporting tick bite.
- Mammalian host: deer, horses, dogs, white-footed mice, cattle, sheep, goats, bison
- Host inflammatory and immune responses define final spectrum of disease beyond granulocytes, including hepatitis, interstitial pneumonitis, and nephritis with mild azotemia
- Between 6% and 21% of patients with HGE also have serologic evidence of other *Ixodes* spp. tick-borne diseases: Lyme disease or babesiosis
- Recovery is usual outcome; fatality rate of HGE is about 1%
- ICU care required: 7%

DIAGNOSIS

DIFFERENTIAL DIAGNOSIS

- Rocky Mountain spotted fever, Colorado tick fever, Q fever, relapsing fever
- Babesiosis
- Leptospirosis
- Lyme disease
- Tularemia
- Typhoid fever, paratyphoid fever
- Brucellosis
- Viral hepatitis
- Meningococcemia
- Infectious mononucleosis
- Hematologic malignancy
- TTP (thrombotic thrombocytopenic purpura)
- Table 1E-5 describes clinical clues suggesting a diagnosis of a tick-borne illness manifesting as a nonspecific febrile illness

WORKUP

- Acute blood samples for Giemsa-stained smears
- CBC (leukopenia, thrombocytopenia), liver function (elevated), BUN/creatinine
- Acute serum samples for serology. Antibodies are seldom detected at time of acute infection (they usually appear 2-4 weeks following clinical illness).
- Chest radiograph examination
- Bone marrow rarely needed

LABORATORY TESTS

- Polymerase chain reaction (PCR) to facilitate early diagnosis: detection of *Ehrlichia* DNA in blood or CSF by PCR (Table 1E-6)
- Giemsa-stained smear demonstrating morulae of the organism within granulocytes (sensitivity 20% to 75%) (Fig. 1E-9)
- CBC: progressive leukopenia and thrombocytopenia with nadir near day 7

- C-reactive protein concentration is generally elevated
- Liver function tests (LFTs): increase in hepatic transaminases, lactate dehydrogenase, and alkaline phosphatase
- Elevated plasma creatinine concentration may be seen
- Serologic titer (IFA) >80 or fourfold increase in titer to *E. equi* antigen
- Culture on the first 7 days of illness; not readily available in most clinical laboratories

IMAGING STUDIES

- Chest radiograph examination to show interstitial pneumonitis (unusual)
- MRI of the brain

TREATMENT

ACUTE GENERAL Rx

- Immediate therapy to limit extent of acute illness and complication
- Doxycycline: 100 mg twice a day for 7 to 14 days is therapy of choice for adults and children >8 yr (4 mg/kg/day in 2 divided doses).
- Rifampin: 300 mg twice a day for 7 to 10 days can be used in pregnancy and for children <8 yr at 10 mg/kg twice per day
- Most patients defervesce within 24 to 48 hr given appropriate treatment.

PROGNOSIS

Poor prognostic indicators include:
- Advanced age
- Concomitant chronic illness (such as diabetes mellitus, collagen-vascular disease)
- Lack of diagnosis recognition
- Delayed onset of specific antibiotic therapy
- Concomitant HIV or organ transplant status

DISPOSITION

- Repeat CBC every 2 to 4 wk until normal.
- A new pathogenic *Ehrlichia* species, close relative of *E. muris* has been identified in Minnesota and Wisconsin. Organism-specific PCR and serologic testing can be used for identification.

REFERRAL

For consultation with infectious diseases specialist in suspected cases

PEARLS & CONSIDERATIONS

COMMENTS

- Duration of time tick must be attached to produce illness as few as 4 hr
- Delay in antibiotic treatment results in poorer outcome. Antibiotic treatment should be initiated as soon as infection is suspected.

SUGGESTED READINGS

Available at www.expertconsult.com

RELATED CONTENT

Anaplasmosis (Patient Information)

AUTHOR: **PATRICIA CRISTOFARO, M.D.**

TABLE 1E-4 Human Ehrlichioses and Anaplasmosis

	Human Monocytotropic Ehrlichiosis	Human Granulocytotropic Ehrlichiosis	Human Granulocytotropic Anaplasmosis
Former disease nomenclature	Human monocytic ehrlichiosis	Human granulocytic ehrlichiosis	Human granulocytic ehrlichiosis
Causative agent(s)	*Ehrlichia chaffeensis*	*Ehrlichia ewingii, Ehrlichia cani*—one asymptomatic human case reported in Venezuela	*Anaplasma phagocytophilum*
Leukocyte targets	Monocytic cell phagosomes	Neutrophil phagosomes	Granulocyte-neutrophil phagosomes
Tick vectors	*Amblyomma americanum* (lone star ticks)	*Amblyomma americanum* (lone star ticks), *Dermacentor variabilis* (American dog ticks)	*Ixodes persulcatus* complex (American deer ticks)—*I. scapularis, I. ricinus, I. pacificus*
Animal reservoirs	White-tailed deer, coyotes, dogs	White-tailed deer, dogs	Rodents, deer, ruminants, horses
U.S. regional distribution	Southeastern and south central United States	South central United States	Northeastern United States, upper Midwest, northern California
U.S. regional prevalence	2-5 cases/100,000	≤10% of presumed HME cases have *E. ewingii* infections in south central United States	50-60 cases/100,000; high seroprevalence rates in children (>20%) who have had subclinical infections
Seasonal occurrences	April-September, peaking in July	Spring-fall	May-July
Incubation periods (wk)	1-4	1-4	1-4
Modes of transmission	Tick bite, blood product transfusion	Tick bite, blood product transfusion	Tick bite, blood product transfusion, nosocomial
Frequently presenting clinical manifestations	Fever, malaise, headache, myalgias, rash in <40%	Same initial manifestations, but much milder, except in immunocompromised individuals	Fever, malaise, headache, myalgias; rarely rash
Laboratory abnormalities	Leukopenia, thrombocytopenia, transaminitis	Leukopenia, thrombocytopenia, transaminitis	More pronounced and prolonged leukopenia, thrombocytopenia, transaminitis
Potential complications, especially in immunocompromised individuals	Meningoencephalitis, acute renal and respiratory failure, hepatitis, myocarditis	Milder and less likely, except in patients immunocompromised by HIV/AIDS, organ transplantation, prolonged corticosteroid therapy	May be significant in immunocompromised patients with high fevers, seizures, confusion, hemorrhagic diathesis, rhabdomyolysis, shock, acute tubular necrosis, adult respiratory distress syndrome; some specific CNS complications may include eighth nerve palsy, brachial plexopathy, demyelinating polyneuropathy
Case-fatality rate (CFR)	3%, higher in immunocompromised individuals	No deaths reported	0.5%, higher CFR in immunocompromised individuals
Recommended confirmatory diagnostic tests	Wright-stained peripheral blood smears with characteristic intracytoplasmic morulae in monocytes, DNA detection by PCR assay, culture	Wright-stained peripheral blood smears with characteristic intracytoplasmic morulae in neutrophils, DNA detection by PCR	Wright-stained peripheral blood smears with characteristic intracytoplasmic aggregates in neutrophils, DNA detection by PCR assay, increased immunofluorescent antibodies in initial and paired serum samples
Current antibiotic resistance	Fluoroquinolones	Fluoroquinolones	Fluoroquinolones
Currently recommended antibiotic therapy, adults	Doxycycline, 100 mg PO bid, or tetracycline, 250-500 mg PO qid, for minimum of 3 days after defervescence to maximum of 14-21 days	Doxycycline, 100 mg PO bid, or tetracycline, 250-500 mg PO qid, for minimum of 3 days after defervescence to maximum of 14-21 days	Doxycycline, 100 mg PO bid, or tetracycline, 250-500 mg PO qid for minimum of 3 days after defervescence to maximum of 14-21 days
Currently recommended antibiotic therapy, children	Doxycycline, 4.4 mg/kg PO bid, or tetracycline, 25-50 mg/kg PO qid, for minimum of 3 days after defervescence to maximum of 14-21 days	Doxycycline, 4.4 mg/kg PO bid, or tetracycline, 25-50 mg/kg PO qid, for minimum of 3 days after defervescence to maximum of 14-21 days	Doxycycline, 4.4 mg/kg PO bid, or tetracycline, 25-50 mg/kg PO qid, for minimum of 3 days after defervescence to maximum of 14-21 days

CNS, Central nervous system; *HIV/AIDS,* human immunodeficiency virus infection/acquired immunodeficiency syndrome; *PCR,* polymerase chain reaction.
From Bennett JE, Dolin R, Blaser MJ: *Mandell, Douglas, and Bennett's principles and practice of infectious diseases,* ed 8, Philadelphia, 2015, Saunders.

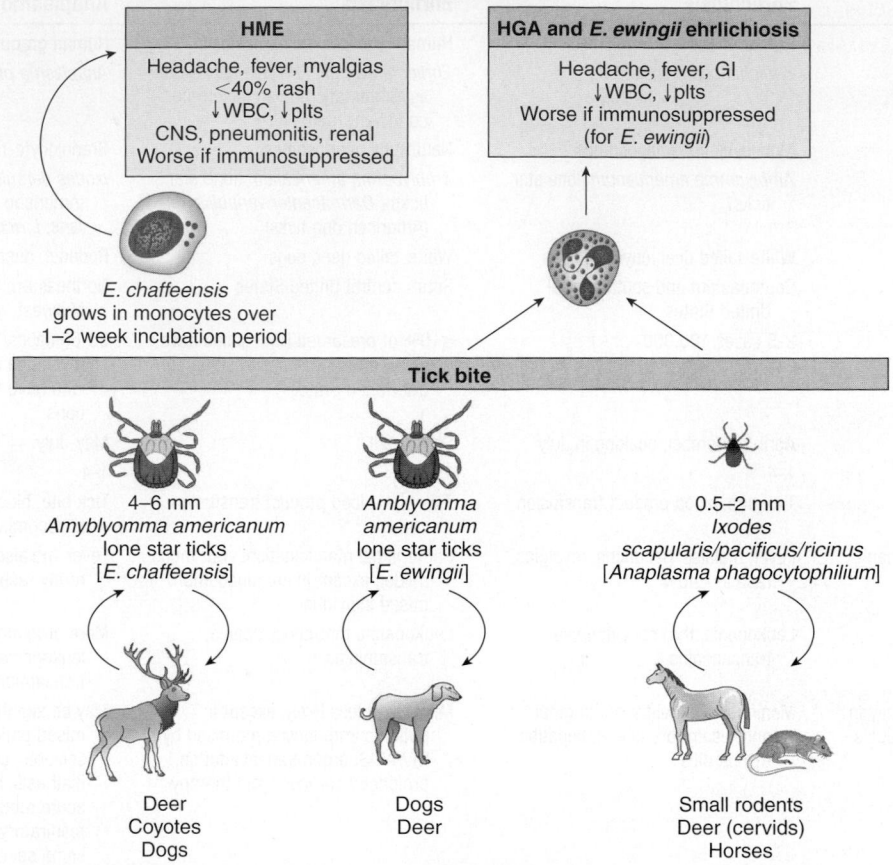

FIGURE 1E-8 Life cycles of human monocytic ehrlichiosis (HME, with *Ehrlichia chaffeensis*) and human granulocytic ehrlichiosis (anaplasmosis, HGA with *Anaplasma phagocytophilum*) or infection with *E. ewingii*. *CNS*, Central nervous system; *GI*, gastrointestinal; *WBC*, white blood cell count. (From Dumler JS: Ehrlichioses and anaplasmosis. In Guerrant RL, Walker DH, Weller PF (eds) *Tropical infectious diseases: principles, pathogens and practice*, 3rd ed, Philadelphia, 2011, Elsevier, pp. 339-343.)

TABLE 1E-5 Clinical Clues (History, Physical Examination, or Laboratory) Suggesting the Diagnosis of a Tick-Borne Illness Manifesting as a Nonspecific Febrile Illness*

Disease	Clues
Anaplasmosis	Faint rash possible Low white blood cell or platelet count Elevated hepatic transaminases
Babesiosis	Findings of hemolysis History of splenectomy Presence of faint rash, hepatomegaly, or splenomegaly
Lyme disease	Careful skin examination for any rash consistent with erythema migrans Bradycardia from heart block Associated seventh nerve palsy or lymphocytic meningitis
Colorado tick fever	Saddle-back fever curve
Rocky Mountain spotted fever	Maculopapular or petechial rash Normal white blood cell count or low platelet count Hyponatremia Peripheral edema
Relapsing fever	Recurring episodes of fever with afebrile intervals
Tularemia	Acrally located ulcer Regional lymphadenopathy Possible associated pneumonia

*Apart from an epidemiologic context suggesting a tick-borne disease.

TABLE 1E-6 Diagnostic Tests for Human Monocytic Ehrlichiosis with the Corresponding Sensitivities and Specificities in Relation to Disease Course

Diagnostic Test	Time Course	Sensitivity (%)	Specificity (%)
Peripheral smear showing morulae	Early (first week)	3-2	>90%
Polymerase chain reaction (PCR)	Early (first week)	55-87	99
Serology with immunofluo-rescence assay (IFA)	Late (after 7-14 days) and requires documented 4-fold rise in 2-3 wk	94-100	99

From Hilal T, Snapp WK: The perils of country life: human monocytic ehrlichiosis. *Am J Med* 128(8), 2015.

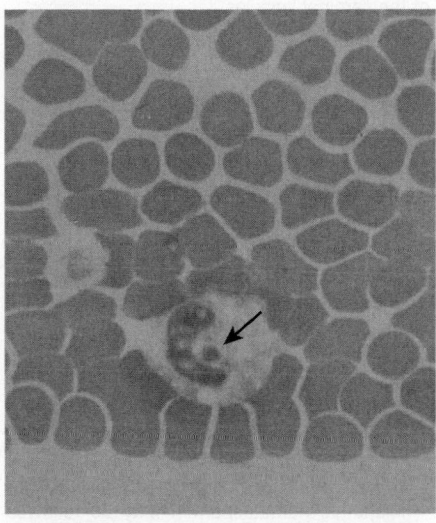

FIGURE 1E-9 White blood cells infected with the agent of human granulocytic ehrlichiosis (*Anaplasma phagocytophilum*). (Courtesy Dr. Daniel Caplivski, Division of Infectious Diseases, Mount Sinai School of Medicine.)

BASIC INFORMATION

DEFINITION

Clinically significant disorders of ejaculation include failure of emission, retrograde ejaculation, premature ejaculation, delayed ejaculation, painful ejaculation, hematospermia, and anorgasmia. Failure of emission occurs when semen is not propulsed into the urethra during orgasm, resulting in a dry ejaculate. Retrograde ejaculation is a backward flow of semen into the bladder. Premature ejaculation refers to ejaculation that occurs sooner than desired, either before or shortly after penetration, causing distress to either one or both partners. Hematospermia is the appearance of blood in the ejaculate. Anorgasmia is the inability to achieve orgasm in a timely manner.

SYNONYMS

Ejaculatory dysfunction
Retarded or delayed ejaculation
Early or rapid ejaculation
Inhibited ejaculation
Anejaculation

ICD-10CM CODES
N53.14 Retrograde ejaculation
R36.1   Hematospermia
F45.8   Other somatoform disorders
F52.4   Premature ejaculation
F52.32 Male orgasmic disorder

EPIDEMIOLOGY & DEMOGRAPHICS

INCIDENCE: Not well understood, due to variability in definitions and reporting.
PEAK INCIDENCE: Not well understood.
PREVALENCE: Premature ejaculation is the most prevalent male sexual complaint, affecting 20%-30% of men, and may be primary (lifelong) or acquired. Retarded or delayed ejaculation is the least common, least studied, and least understood of the male sexual dysfunctions.
PREDOMINANT SEX AND AGE: These disorders have been reported among men aged 18-70 years.
GENETICS: No known genetic predisposition.
RISK FACTORS: Men with ejaculatory dysfunction of any type usually indicate higher levels of relationship stress, sexual dissatisfaction, anxiety about sexual performance, and general health issues, compared to sexually functional men.

PHYSICAL FINDINGS & CLINICAL PRESENTATION

- Failure of emission: no ejaculate is produced during orgasm. Physical findings may reveal nervous system dysfunction (e.g., spinal cord injury); present with infertility.
- Retrograde ejaculation: little or no ejaculate is expelled out of the urethra at orgasm. Patients may report cloudy postcoital urine. Physical examination is usually normal; may present with infertility.
- Premature ejaculation: ejaculation occurs sooner than desired, either before or shortly after penetration. Physical examination is

normal. Up to 30% of patients may report concomitant erectile dysfunction.
- Delayed ejaculation: ejaculation requires prolonged sexual stimulation, often 30 minutes or longer. Physical examination is normal.
- Painful ejaculation: perineal, scrotal, or testicular pain during or shortly after ejaculation. Physical examination may demonstrate pain on examination of external genitalia, or with digital rectal examination; may present with infertility.
- Hematospermia: reddish-brown ejaculate, usually painless. Physical findings are usually unremarkable; not associated with malignancy.
- Anorgasmia: patient is not able to achieve orgasm despite appropriate stimulation.

ETIOLOGY

- Failure of emission may result from pelvic surgery, trauma, or radiation; from neurologic diseases such as Parkinson's disease, multiple sclerosis, spinal cord injury, or diabetes mellitus; from bilateral ejaculatory duct obstruction; or from psychological stress and anxiety.
- Retrograde ejaculation is most commonly caused by the use of medications (e.g., alpha-blockers) or surgical procedures (e.g., transurethral resection of prostate) that relax the bladder neck, but it can also be the result of retroperitoneal surgery and the previously mentioned neurologic diseases.
- Premature and delayed ejaculation represent opposite ends of the spectrum of ejaculatory disorders. The underlying etiology is complex and multifactorial and includes organic and psychogenic contributions.
- Causes of painful ejaculation may be infectious (e.g., epididymo-orchitis, urethritis, prostatitis), obstructive (e.g., vasectomy, prostatectomy, hernia repair), or psychological.
- Hematospermia may be idiopathic, secondary to prolonged abstinence, or due to infection or inflammation of the genitourinary tract.
- Anorgasmia may be caused by spinal cord injury, psychological factors, dysfunctional sexual techniques, or medications, particularly serotonin reuptake inhibitors.

 **DIAGNOSIS**

DIFFERENTIAL DIAGNOSIS

- Erectile dysfunction
- Hypogonadism
- Ejaculatory duct obstruction
- Urethral stricture disease
- Urethritis or sexually transmitted infection

LABORATORY TESTS

- Fig. 1E-10 describes an algorithm for the evaluation of the patient with low-volume or absent (aspermia) ejaculate.
- For a low-volume ejaculate, post-ejaculate urine should be evaluated for the presence of spermatozoa to differentiate failure of emission from retrograde ejaculation.

- Hematuria, in the setting of hematospermia or painful ejaculation, may signal an underlying inflammatory disorder or a malignancy and should prompt a complete evaluation.
- A fasting blood glucose test may be considered if diabetes is suspected as a cause of lack of emission or retrograde ejaculation.
- Urinalysis, urine culture, and screening for sexually transmitted diseases, when indicated, can rule out an infectious etiology of painful ejaculation.

IMAGING STUDIES

Transrectal ultrasonography or pelvic MRI can rule out ejaculatory duct obstruction or absence of the seminal vesicles.

TREATMENT

NONPHARMACOLOGIC THERAPY

- Retrograde ejaculation and failure of emission do not require treatment unless fertility is desired.
- In the setting of retrograde ejaculation, viable sperm can be recovered from the postejaculate urine and used for intrauterine insemination or in vitro fertilization.
- Premature ejaculation can improve with psychotherapy and behavioral interventions (e.g., "coronal squeeze" or "start-and-stop" technique) and effective partner communication. These approaches may be more effective when combined with pharmacologic therapy.
- Idiopathic hematospermia may be followed expectantly and is usually self-limited to 10 to 15 ejaculations.
- Anorgasmia caused by serotonin reuptake inhibitors usually improves with withdrawal of the medication. Sexual therapy and counseling can improve anorgasmia caused by dysfunctional sexual techniques or psychological issues. Vibratory or electrical stimulation of emission is helpful in selected cases.

ACUTE GENERAL Rx

- Retrograde ejaculation: pharmacologic therapy is only effective in patients without an anatomic disturbance of the bladder neck. Sympathomimetic medications (phenylpropanolamine, ephedrine, pseudoephedrine) and imipramine may be useful in converting retrograde ejaculation to antegrade ejaculation.
- Failure of emission: may be converted to retrograde ejaculation by oral sympathomimetic therapy, as listed above.
- Premature ejaculation: selective serotonin reuptake inhibitors (SSRI) (e.g., sertraline, fluoxetine) and the tricyclic antidepressant clomipramine can successfully delay ejaculation when taken daily. Dapoxetine, a short-acting SSRI, may be used as an "on-demand" treatment for premature ejaculation. Topical anesthetics such as lidocaine cream and topical sprays have been used with variable success. The use of phosphodiesterase inhibitors (PDE5i) (e.g., sildenafil, vardenafil, tadalafil) with SSRIs may be beneficial in men with concomitant erectile dysfunction and premature ejaculation.

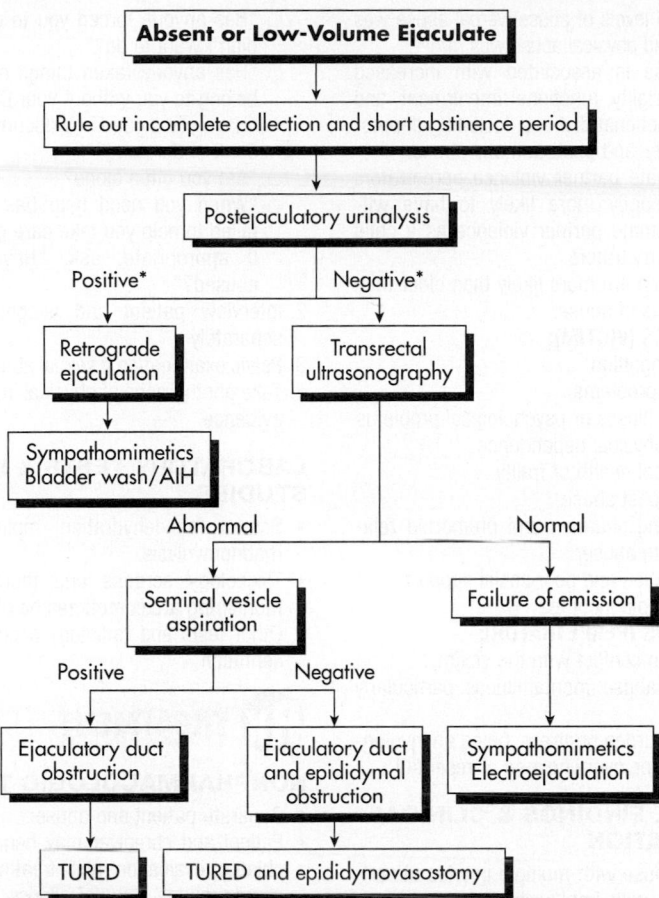

FIGURE 1E-10 Algorithm for the evaluation of the patient with low-volume or absent (aspermia) ejaculate. *AIH*, Artificial insemination using husband's sperm; *TURED*, transurethral resection of the ejaculatory ducts. *See text. (From Wein AJ; Male infertility. In Wein AJ et al (eds): *Campbell-Walsh urology*, Philadelphia, 2007, Elsevier.)

- Antimicrobial treatment (if indicated), NSAIDs, and muscle relaxants may help decrease discomfort associated with painful ejaculation.
- The use of the pharmacologic therapies listed above for the treatment of various disorders of ejaculation is strictly off label and does not carry FDA approval.

CHRONIC Rx

Rarely, painful ejaculation due to long-standing obstructive causes may show improvement with surgical intervention (e.g., vasectomy reversal). The pharmacologic therapies listed previously can also be used for the chronic treatment of disorders of ejaculation and orgasm.

COMPLEMENTARY AND ALTERNATIVE MEDICINE

- A variety of nutritional supplements and herbs have been used for the treatment of erectile dysfunction, but their benefit for the specific treatment of ejaculation and orgasm disorders is unknown.
- Acupuncture and traditional Chinese medicine may be helpful in treating underlying hormonal imbalances.
- Yoga and meditation can reduce the effects of stress and relieve anxiety about sexual dysfunction.
- Therapeutic massage can decrease stress.

DISPOSITION

Prognosis varies with etiology. Ejaculatory dysfunction attributable to sexual techniques or psychological issues can improve with psychotherapy. Pharmacologic treatment is helpful in treating premature, retrograde, or painful ejaculation.

REFERRAL

All fertility issues and suspected anatomic problems should be referred to a urologist. Professional psychotherapy should be considered for appropriate patients.

COMMENTS

Ejaculatory and orgasmic disorders are common male sexual dysfunctions and include failure of emission, retrograde ejaculation, premature ejaculation, delayed ejaculation, painful ejaculation, hematospermia, and anorgasmia

PREVENTION

Preventing sexually transmitted infections and treating other inflammatory disorders of the genitourinary tract may be of some benefit in reducing the incidence of these sexual disorders.

PATIENT/FAMILY EDUCATION

These sexual disorders can exert a significant psychological burden on affected men and their partners. A combination of pharmacologic and nonpharmacologic therapies, including a urologic and psychologic evaluation, when indicated, may be helpful in the treatment of these complaints.

SUGGESTED READINGS
Available at www.expertconsult.com

RELATED CONTENT

Erectile Dysfunction (Patient Information)
Premature Ejaculation (Patient Information)
Erectile Dysfunction (Related Key Topic)

AUTHORS: **AKANKSHA MEHTA, M.D.,** and **MARK SIGMAN, M.D.**

BASIC INFORMATION

DEFINITION

Elder abuse includes abuse committed by someone in a trust relationship whether in the community or institutional setting.

- Physical abuse: inflicting physical pain or injury
- Sexual abuse: inflicting nonconsensual sexual activity
- Psychological abuse: inflicting mental anguish, including intimidation, humiliation, or threats
- Financial abuse: improper use of resources, property, or assets without the person's consent
- Neglect: abandonment, failure to fulfill a care-taking obligation, including provision of food, safe shelter, physical health and mental health care, or basic custodial care

SYNONYMS

Battered elder syndrome
Elder mistreatment
Domestic violence in the elderly
Diogenes syndrome

Adult maltreatment and neglect problems cover a range of diagnostic codes depending on whether the issue is confirmed or suspected and whether the problem is physical, psychological, or sexual
Core Codes:
ICD-10-CM CODES
T74   Maltreatment syndrome
T74.0 Neglect or abandonment
T74.1 Physical abuse
T74.2 Sexual abuse
T74.3 Psychological abuse
T74.8 Other maltreatment syndromes
T74.9 Maltreatment syndromes, unspecified

EPIDEMIOLOGY & DEMOGRAPHICS

INCIDENCE: 2013 CDC report estimates 500,000 adults 60 and older are subject to elder maltreatment yearly in the U.S.
PEAK INCIDENCE: >75 yr; more recent studies now suggest <75 yr
PREVALENCE:
- About 7.6% to 11% of those 60 yr or older
- Emotional followed by financial abuse are the most common forms.
- 12-month U.S. prevalence rates: emotional abuse 9.0% and 4.6%; physical abuse 0.2% and 1.6%; sexual abuse 0.6%; neglect 0.5%; and financial abuse 3.5% and 5.2%.
- Family members reported 21% of nursing home residents were neglected on one or more occasion in the past 12 months, and over 24% had been subjected to physical abuse during their entire stay.
- Among caregivers of patients with dementia in the U.K., one half reported behaving abusively at least some of the time, and one third reported

"important" levels of abuse. Verbal abuse was common and physical abuse was rare.
- Elder abuse is associated with increased risk of mortality, functional impairment, and greater emotional distress, including depression, anxiety, and posttraumatic stress.
- Adult intimate partner violence perpetrators are significantly more likely to have witnessed intimate partner violence as a child than nonperpetrators.
- Older women are more likely than older men to be victims of abuse.

RISK FACTORS (VICTIM):
- Impaired cognition
- Behavioral problems
- Psychiatric illness or psychological problems
- Mental or physical dependence
- Poor physical health or frailty
- Trauma or past abuse
- Shared living situation and premorbid relationship with abuser
- Social isolation and poor social support
- Low household income

RISK FACTORS (PERPETRATOR):
- Relationship conflict with the victim
- Substance abuse, mental illness, particularly depression
- Caregiver burden or stress, being an involuntary caregiver, overwhelmed or resentful

PHYSICAL FINDINGS & CLINICAL PRESENTATION

- Physical abuse with multiple injuries at various stages with implausible descriptions of their origins.
- Fear, hypervigilance, or withdrawal.
- Evidence of poor nutrition, dehydration, poor hygiene, multiple or neglected pressure ulcers, genital or anal pain, neglected medical conditions, or evidence of restraint use (bruises around wrists or ankles).
- Toxicologic evidence of unprescribed medications.
- Poor adherence, frequent no-shows, or little contact with health care system.
- Caregiver not allowing interviewing the patient alone.

DIAGNOSIS

DIFFERENTIAL DIAGNOSIS

- Dementia
- Depression, substance misuse, or other psychiatric disorder
- Malnutrition from intrinsic causes
- Nonadherence to medical treatment
- Relationship distress
- Falling

WORKUP

1. Ask direct specific questions such as:
   ○ "Has anyone close to you called you names or put you down recently?"
   ○ "Are you afraid of anyone who lives with you or cares for you?"
   ○ "Has anyone at home ever hurt you?"
   ○ "Has anyone touched you without your consent?"

   ○ "Has anyone forced you to do things you didn't want to do?"
   ○ "Has anyone taken things or money that belong to you without your OK?"
   ○ "Have you signed any documents that you don't understand?"
   ○ "Are you often alone?"
   ○ "When you need help has anyone ever failed to help you take care of yourself?"
   ○ If appropriate, ask, "Have you been abused?"
2. Interview patient and alleged perpetrator separately.
3. Pelvic examination if sexual abuse suspected.
4. Take photographs of physical injuries as legal evidence.

LABORATORY TESTS & IMAGING STUDIES

- Screen for dehydration, malnutrition, and rhabdomyolysis.
- Toxicology screens and therapeutic drug monitoring are sometimes helpful.
- Other tests and radiology according to presentation.

TREATMENT

NONPHARMACOLOGIC THERAPY

- Separate patient and abuser.
- Patient and caregiver may benefit from psychiatric evaluation and treatment for substance abuse, mental illness, or cognitive impairment.
- If appropriate, assess the patient's capacity.
- Fig. 1E-11 describes a management algorithm for elder abuse.

ACUTE GENERAL Rx

- As indicated for injury or pain relief
- As indicated for mental disorders, dementia, or delirium

DISPOSITION

If the patient's level of disability does not allow independent living, institutionalization may be required. Guidelines vary at the state and county levels regarding guardianship and conservatorship requirements.

REFERRAL

- For outpatients, report to local adult protective services agency. Reporting is mandatory in most states.
- For nursing home patients, report to regional long-term care ombudsman. Reporting is mandatory under federal law.
- Mental health services may be needed.

PEARLS & CONSIDERATIONS

COMMENTS

Care should be taken in interacting with the alleged abuser so that access to the victim is not lost.

PREVENTION

- Offer social services (e.g., respite care or homecare) for stressed caregivers.
- Make financial arrangements and arrange durable power of attorney for health care and finances while patient is still cognitively intact.

PATIENT & FAMILY EDUCATION

In the U.S., the elder care help line is 1-800-677-1116.

National Center on Elder Abuse: http://www.ncea.aoa.gov

JAMA Patient Page: Hildreth CJ et al: JAMA patient page. Elder abuse, *JAMA* 302(5):588, 2009

SUGGESTED READINGS

Available at www.expertconsult.com

RELATED CONTENT

Elder Abuse (Patient Information)

AUTHOR: **ROBERT KOHN, M.D.**

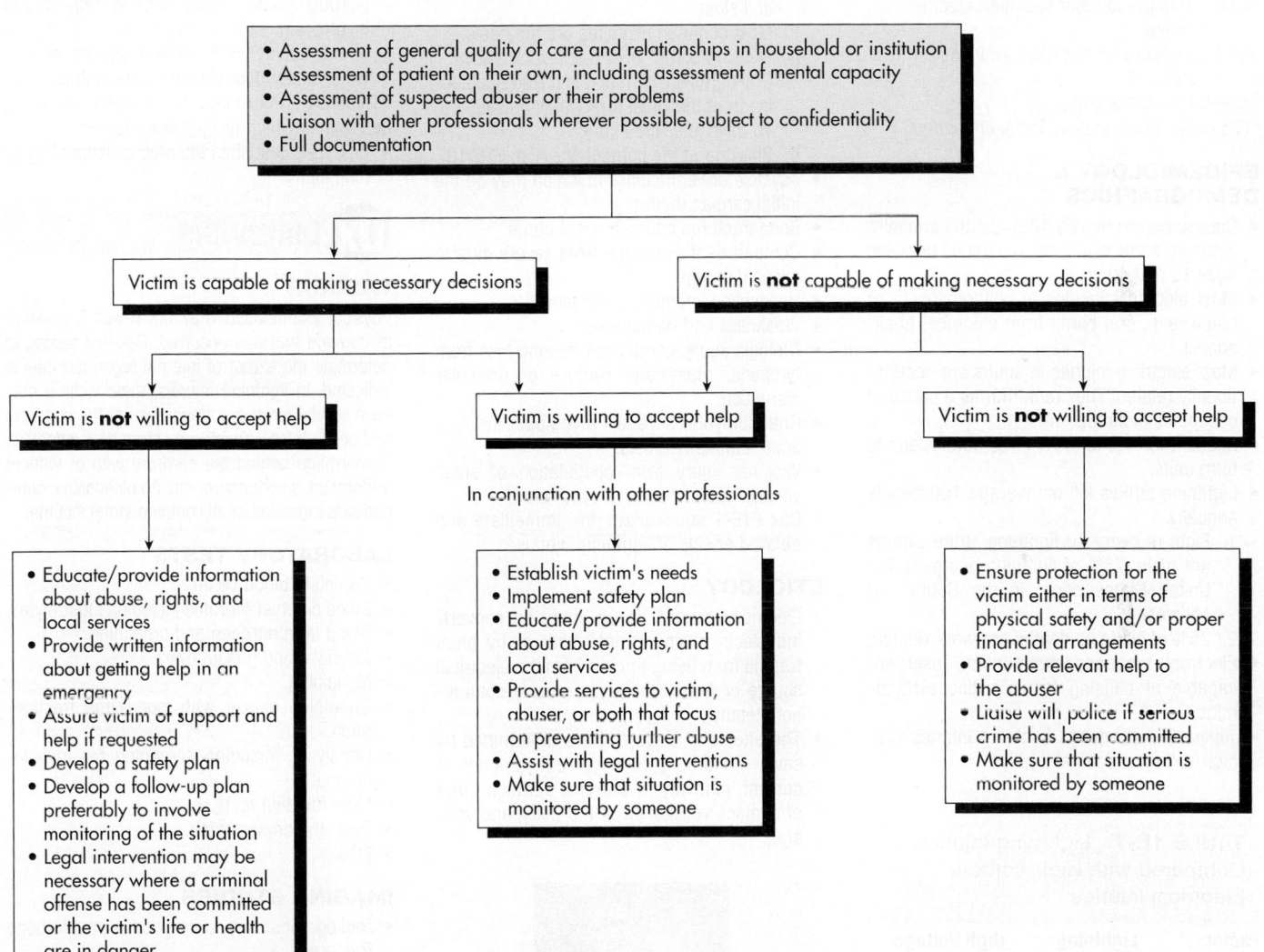

FIGURE 1E-11 Management of elder abuse. (From Tallis RC, Fillit HM [eds]: *Brocklehurst's textbook of geriatric medicine and gerontology*, ed 6, London, 2003, Churchill Livingstone.)

 BASIC INFORMATION

DEFINITION

Injuries or wounds that occur as a result of contact with an electrical current or lightning.

ICD-10CM CODES

W87 Exposure to unspecified electric current
W86 Exposure to other specified electric current
W85 Exposure to electric transmission lines
X33 Victim of lightning
T75.4XXA Electrocution, initial encounter

EPIDEMIOLOGY & DEMOGRAPHICS

- Causes approximately 1000 deaths annually, with two thirds occurring in persons between ages 15 and 40 yr.
- Most electrical injuries in children occur at home (e.g., oral burns from electrical appliances).
- Most electrical injuries in adults are occupationally related. They rank fifth as a cause of occupational death.
- Account for 4% to 6.5% of all admissions to burn units.
- Lightning strikes kill on average 100 people annually.
  1. Eight of every 10 lightning strike victims are male; 75% of lightning deaths in the United States occur in the South and Midwest.
  2. 25% of lightning deaths are work related.
- Electronic weapons (stun gun and Taser) are capable of causing fatal cardiac arrhythmias.
- Table 1E-7 compares lightning injuries with high-voltage electrical injuries.

TABLE 1E-7 Lightning Injuries Compared with High-Voltage Electrical Injuries

Factor	Lightning	High Voltage
Energy level	30 million volts, 50,000 Å	Usually much lower*
Time of exposure	Brief, instantaneous	Seconds
Pathway	Flashover, orifice	Deep, internal
Burns	Superficial, minor	Deep, major injury
Renal	Rare myoglobinuria or hemoglobinuria	Myoglobinuric renal failure common
Fasciotomy	Rarely if ever necessary	Common, early, and extensive
Blunt injury	Explosive thunder effect	Falls, being thrown

*Range is 500 V up to millions of volts in transmission lines.
From Auerbach P: *Wilderness medicine, expert consult* Premium Edition—Enhanced Online

PHYSICAL FINDINGS & CLINICAL PRESENTATION

- Cognitive changes: depending on the extent of injury, the patient may be unconscious, seizing, or confused and unable to present a history.
- Extensive skin burns (>10% of the body surface).
  1. Located over the entry and exit sites (Fig. 1E-12).
  2. Most common entry sites are the hands and skull.
  3. Most common exit sites are the heels.
  4. "Kissing burns" over the flexor creases.
  5. Oral burns are common in children; bleeding from the labial artery may present 7 to 10 days after the injury.
  6. Charring at the contact site (Fig. E1E-13).
- Asystole or ventricular fibrillation may be the initial cardiac rhythm.
- Bone fractures and periosteal burns.
- Compartment syndrome from severe muscle tissue damage.
- Headaches, memory disturbances.
- Weakness and paresthesias.
- Otologic injury, conductive hearing loss from tympanic membrane rupture or ossicular disruption.
- Rhabdomyolysis and myoglobin-induced acute tubular necrosis.
- Vascular injury from coagulation of small vessels or compartment syndrome.
- Box E1E-1 summarizes the immediate and delayed effects of lightning injuries.

ETIOLOGY

- Electricity causes tissue injury by converting electrical energy into heat or by blunt trauma from being thrown from the electrical source or from continuous muscle contraction (tetany).
- The effects of electricity are determined by seven factors: type of current, amount of current, pathway of current, duration, area of contact, resistance of the body, and voltage.

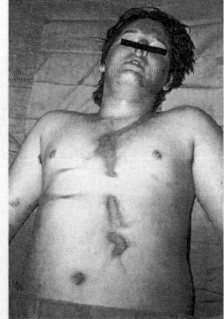

FIGURE 1E-12 The arborescent current markings on the face, neck, and anterior trunk of this young patient, which are characteristic of lightning injury, healed without the need for grafting. Note the focal lesions on the right arm, indicating the spread of the current that produced the marks on the right anterolateral aspect of the chest wall. (From Goldman L, Schafer AI: *Goldman's Cecil medicine*, ed 24, Philadelphia, 2012, Saunders.)

- Tissue damage is greater with higher voltage and longer duration of contact.
- Direct current (DC) contact causes a single muscle contraction, throwing the patient away from the source. Alternating current (AC) contact precipitates a tetanic contraction, not allowing the patient to withdraw from the source and prolonging the duration of contact. AC contact is more ominous than DC contact.
- Electrical injuries are arbitrarily divided into high-voltage (>1000 volts) and low-voltage (<1000 volts) burns. Low-voltage burns involve almost exclusively either the hands or oral cavity. High-voltage injuries have a wide variety of systemic manifestations.
- The entry and exit path of the electrical current determines which tissues are affected.
- Box 1E-2 describes the mechanisms of lightning injury.

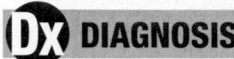 **DIAGNOSIS**

WORKUP

Physical examination may not reveal the extent of damage that has occurred. Detailed testing to determine the extent of internal organ damage is indicated. In lightning injuries, male victims may have scrotal (on the undersurface of the scrotum) and penile burns, which may often be overlooked. Hemorrhage behind the eardrum with or without perforation is not uncommon. An otoscopic examination is indicated in all lightning strike victims.

LABORATORY TESTS

- Complete blood count.
- Blood chemistry profile including electrolytes.
- Blood urea nitrogen and creatinine.
- Arterial blood gas analysis.
- Myoglobin.
- Creatinine kinase with isoenzyme fractionation.
- Urinalysis, including screening for myoglobinuria.
- Liver function tests.
- Type and cross-match.
- ECG.

IMAGING STUDIES

- Radiographs: any suspicious area for bone fractures.
- CT scan of the head and cervical spine in patients with suspected head injury, coma, or neurologic deficit.

 **TREATMENT**

NONPHARMACOLOGIC THERAPY

- At the scene: ensure the electrical power source of injury is turned off before approaching patients.
- Basic and advanced cardiac life support with cervical spine precautions. Prolonged cardiopulmonary resuscitation should be undertaken regardless of the initial cardiac rhythm.
- Cardiac monitoring.
- Oxygen.
- Tetanus prophylaxis.

BOX 1E-2   Mechanisms of Lightning Injury

Electrothermal Effects
1. Direct strike.
2. Contact potential.
3. Side flash, sometimes called "splash" (1 to 3 may include surface arcs over the body surface).
4. Step voltage (also termed "Earth potential rise" or "ground current").
   a. Transmitted through the ground.
   b. Surface arcing.
5. Upward streamer current (also called "fifth mechanism").

Blunt Force Trauma Effects
1. Barotrauma.
2. Concussive injury.
3. Musculoskeletal injury from muscle contraction, falls.

From Auerbach P: *Wilderness medicine, expert consult* Premium Edition—Enhanced Online Features and Print, Philadelphia, 2012, Saunders, Elsevier.

ACUTE GENERAL Rx

- IV fluids to maintain urine output of 50 to 100 ml/hr (IV hydration should be reassessed with central nervous system expert in patients at risk of developing cerebral edema).
- Alkalinization of the urine (sodium bicarbonate 50 mEq in 1 L of normal saline) in patients with or at risk of myoglobinuria.
- Furosemide 20 to 40 mg PO or IV and/or mannitol 12.5 g/kg/hr may be used to force diuresis.
- Seizures are treated in the standard fashion.
- Treat burns with sulfadiazine silver dressings.

CHRONIC Rx

- Hospitalization is indicated in patients with high-voltage injuries, extensive burns, central nervous system symptoms, myonecrosis (creatine kinase level more than twice normal, high serum myoglobin levels, or myoglobinuria), new cardiac arrhythmia or ECG changes, or any internal organ damage.
- Ophthalmology consultation at the follow-up to screen for cataract formation (occurs within 1 to 24 mo of a high-voltage electrical injury in 5% to 20% of patients).

DISPOSITION

- Patients with severe burns should be transferred to the regional burn center.
- Complications of electrical injuries include:
  1. Infection.
  2. Renal failure from rhabdomyolysis.
  3. Seizure disorder.
  4. Fasciotomies.
  5. Amputation.
- Delayed neurologic damage may present as ascending paralysis, amyotrophic lateral sclerosis, or transverse myelitis weeks to years after the injury.
- Vascular damage may also present in a delayed fashion.

REFERRAL

- Referrals to general surgery, burn surgery, trauma surgery, orthopedic surgery, and/or

BOX 1E-3   Myths Commonly Cited as Facts in Litigation

These apply to electrical injury as well as lightning injury.

Behavior of Current in the Body
- Current seeks earth.
- Current seeks the path of lowest resistance.
- Nerve tissue is a good conductor, or alternatively, current is preferentially conducted by nerve tissue.
- When a person touches a source of potential, current flows through the skin to other parts of the skin in contact with the same conductor (i.e., current passage is local only).

The Severity of Electric Shock
Myth: If the following are absent, the shock cannot be severe and no deleterious effect can result:
- Being thrown (i.e., if a person is not thrown, the shock is not severe).
- Burns (i.e., if burns are not present, the shock is not severe).
- If the only surface change is a blister, the shock was not severe.
- Entry and exit wounds:
  ○ Must be present.
  ○ Demonstrate the current path.
  ○ If not present, indicate no shock occurred.
- Fuses being blown (i.e., if a fuse does not blow, the shock is not severe enough to harm a victim).
- Low voltage cannot harm.
- Electroconvulsive therapy does not give long-term post–electric-shock symptoms (also false), so any other electric shock cannot be harmful.

Investigations
- If computed tomography (CT) and magnetic resonance imaging (MRI) scans are normal, there are no injuries.
- Negative investigations (e.g., nerve conduction study, electroencephalogram, CT, MRI) mean a victim has not sustained an electric shock.
- Neuropsychological testing is objective and easily interpreted.
- Burns of electrical origin can be distinguished on histologic examination.

Remote Symptoms
- Remote symptoms do not exist.
- Remote symptoms are proportional to the size of the shock.
- Symptoms of the shock that are not present immediately after the shock are not related to it.
- A person getting remote symptoms was psychologically vulnerable all the time.

Miscellaneous
- Litigation increases the potency of the claimed symptoms. Corollary: resolving litigation terminates symptoms.
- Medical specialists understand electricity or lightning.
- Electrical experts can predict lightning or electrical injury.
- A diagnosis of depression, post-traumatic stress disorder, adjustment disorder, and so on negate an electrical injury causation.
- Residual current devices (RCDs) eliminate the possibility of all shocks. Corollary: a shock occurring when an RCD breaks the circuit cannot be severe.

From Auerbach P: *Wilderness medicine, expert consult* Premium Edition—Enhanced Online Features and Print, Philadelphia, 2012, Saunders, Elsevier.

critical care specialists as appropriate in any patient that meets hospitalization criteria. Ophthalmology and ear-nose-throat specialist referral may be indicated.
- Plastic surgery is recommended in children with oral burns.

! PEARLS & CONSIDERATIONS

COMMENTS

- The size of external skin burns can often underestimate the degree of internal injury.
- Lightning Strike and Electric Shock Survivors International is a support group that serves people from around the world who have sustained an electric injury (http://www.lightning-strike.org).

- Home safety education provided one to one in a clinical setting or at home, especially with the provision of safety equipment, is effective in increasing the range of safety practices.
- Box 1E-3 describes myths regarding electrical and lightning injury commonly cited as facts in litigation.

SUGGESTED READINGS

Available at www.expertconsult.com

RELATED CONTENT

Electrical Injury (Patient Information)

AUTHORS: **ROBERT M. KIRCHNER, M.D.**, and **PAUL GORDON, M.D.**

BASIC INFORMATION

DEFINITION

An accumulation of pus in the pleural space, most often caused by bacterial infection.

SYNONYMS

Infected pleuritis
Infected pleural effusion
Purulent pleural effusion

ICD-10CM CODES
J86 Pyothorax
A16.5 Empyema due to tuberculosis

EPIDEMIOLOGY & DEMOGRAPHICS

- Empyema is most commonly a complication of bacterial pneumonia, especially in association with pneumococcal or anaerobic infection (40% to 60% of cases of empyema).
- Occurs as a complication of thoracic surgery (<20% of cases).
- Penetrating chest trauma (4% to 10% of cases).
- Bronchopleural fistulae resulting from malignancy or lung biopsy.

PHYSICAL FINDINGS & CLINICAL PRESENTATION

- May be abrupt or chronic and insidious depending on the etiologic agent and host factors.
- Typically presents as progressive pleuritic chest pain, persistent fever, and other sustained signs and symptoms of infection.
- In anaerobic empyema, particularly that caused by the actinomycetes, the clinical picture is dominated by systemic symptoms and signs: weight loss, malaise, and low grade fever.
- A slowly enlarging chest wall mass.
- As a complication of thoracic trauma or surgery, empyema typically results from contamination of blood within the pleural space several days following the event.
- The physical findings of empyema are those of pleural effusion. Decreased breath sounds and dullness to percussion over the involved part of the thorax is typical. Systemic signs include fever, tachycardia, leukocytosis, and warmth and erythema over the involved area.

ETIOLOGY

Infection of the lung parenchyma spreading to pleural space caused by
- *Streptococcus pneumoniae.*
- *Haemophilus influenzae.*
- *Staphylococcus aureus.*
- *Legionella* species.
- *Mycobacterium tuberculosis.*
- *Actinomyces* spp.
- A variety of oral anaerobic bacteria have been cultured in 36% to 37% of empyemas: *Bacteroides fragilis, Prevotella* species, *Fusobacterium nucleatum,* and *Peptostreptococcus* are the most common.

DIAGNOSIS

DIFFERENTIAL DIAGNOSIS

- Uninfected parapneumonic effusion.
- Lung abscess (see Fig. 1E-14)
- Congestive heart failure.
- Malignancy involving the pleura.
- Tuberculous pleurisy.
- Collagen vascular disease (particularly rheumatoid lung and systemic lupus erythematosus).

LABORATORY TESTS

- Complete blood count; arterial blood gas.
- Blood cultures.
- Pleural fluid analysis in empyema has the characteristics of an exudate with a ratio of pleural fluid to serum protein >0.5 or pleural fluid to serum LDH >0.6. Characteristically, empyema fluid is grossly purulent with visible organisms on Gram stain with glucose <50 mg/dl and pH <7. These findings justify immediate drainage by chest tube or surgery because of the high risk of loculation and progressive systemic infection.

IMAGING STUDIES

- Chest x-ray (Fig. E1E-15, *A*).
- Lateral decubitus view to establish the presence of free fluid in the pleural space.
- Computed tomography (Fig. E1E-15, *B*) to establish the presence of fluid loculation, underlying mass lesions, and other intrathoracic pathology.

TREATMENT

NONPHARMACOLOGIC THERAPY

Prompt drainage by thoracostomy (chest tube) or open thoracotomy. Video-assisted thorascopic surgery (VATS) has greatly improved surgical management of empyemas.

ACUTE GENERAL Rx

- Maintenance of drainage until infection controlled.
- Antibiotics directed at suspected or proven bacterial or fungal pathogens. Initial regimens include cefotaxime or ceftriaxone for suspected *S. pneumoniae* or group A *Streptococcus,* nafcillin or oxacillin for suspected methicillin-sensitive *S. aureus,* vancomycin or linezolid for suspected MRSA, ceftriaxone for suspected *H. influenzae,* and clindamycin plus ceftriaxone when suspecting anaerobes.
- Thoracoscopy or instillation of thrombolytic agents (streptokinase or urokinase) may be considered in refractory, loculated empyema.

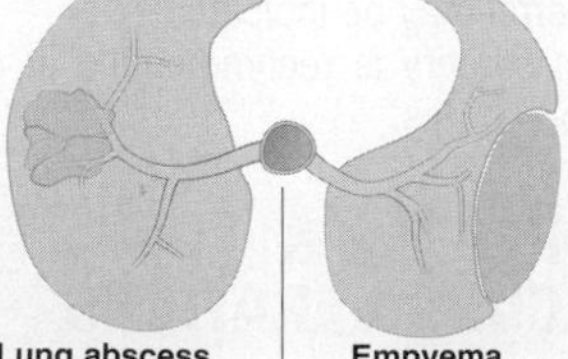

CHRONIC Rx

- If thorough drainage cannot be accomplished, open thoracotomy with pleural decortication may be required.
- Lung function should be monitored following completion of therapy.

DISPOSITION

Hospitalization with supplemental oxygen with ventilatory support if necessary

REFERRAL

Consultation by infectious diseases, pulmonary, or thoracic surgery specialists as needed.

PEARLS & CONSIDERATIONS

COMMENTS

- Empyema caused by actinomycetes may present with erosion through the chest wall and formation of a fistulous tract.
- Nosocomial infection caused by relatively resistant bacterial or fungal pathogens may result in empyema in patients with indwelling thoracostomy tubes.

SUGGESTED READINGS
Available at www.expertconsult.com

AUTHOR: **GLENN G. FORT, M.D., M.P.H.**

Lung abscess	Empyema
Poorly defined	Well defined
Irregular wall	Smooth, uniform wall
Spherical	Elliptical
Multiple cavities	"Split pleura"
Acute angles	Acute or obtuse angles
Vessels not displaced	Vessels displaced

FIGURE 1E-14 Empyema versus lung abscess. (From Webb WR, Brant WE, Major NM: *Fundamentals of body CT,* ed 4, Philadelphia, 2015, Saunders.)

 **BASIC INFORMATION**

DEFINITION

Acute viral encephalitis is an acute febrile syndrome with evidence of meningeal involvement and of derangement of the function of the cerebrum, cerebellum, or brain stem.

SYNONYMS

Arboviral encephalitis
Brain stem encephalitis
Acute necrotizing encephalitis
Rasmussen encephalitis
Encephalitis lethargica

ICD-10CM CODES

A86	Unspecified viral encephalitis
A83.0	Japanese encephalitis
A83.1	Western equine encephalitis
A83.2	Eastern equine encephalitis
A83.3	St Louis encephalitis
A83.4	Australian encephalitis
A83.5	California encephalitis
A83.8	Other mosquito-borne viral encephalitis
A83.9	Mosquito-borne viral encephalitis, unspecified
A84.8	Other tick-borne viral encephalitis
A84.9	Tick-borne viral encephalitis, unspecified
A85.0	Enteroviral encephalitis
A85.1	Adenoviral encephalitis
A85.2	Arthropod-borne viral encephalitis, unspecified
A85.8	Other specified viral encephalitis
A92.31	West Nile virus infection with encephalitis
B00.4	Herpesviral encephalitis
B01.11	Varicella encephalitis and encephalomyelitis
B02.0	Zoster encephalitis
B05.0	Measles complicated by encephalitis
B06.01	Rubella encephalitis
B10.01	Human herpesvirus 6 encephalitis
B10.09	Other human herpesvirus encephalitis
B26.2	Mumps encephalitis
B94.1	Sequelae of viral encephalitis
G04.00	Acute disseminated encephalitis and encephalomyelitis, unspecified
G04.81	Other encephalitis and encephalomyelitis
G04.90	Encephalitis and encephalomyelitis, unspecified
G05.3	Encephalitis and encephalomyelitis in diseases classified elsewhere

EPIDEMIOLOGY & DEMOGRAPHICS

INCIDENCE (IN U.S.):
- About 20,000 cases/yr are reported to the CDC. In 2014, there were 2205 cases of West Nile Virus with 97 deaths..

PEAK INCIDENCE: Any age, but children and older adults are more likely to have significant morbidity

PREVALENCE (IN U.S.):
- Arbovirus infections are transmitted by mosquitoes and thus cause infection when mosquitoes

are active, especially summer and fall. Herpes simplex infections can occur at any time.
- Geography also plays a role: Whereas eastern equine encephalitis is more likely on the East Coast of U.S., West Nile Virus has spread to 48 states. Powassan virus is more common in northern New England and Canada. La Crosse virus is more common in the upper Midwestern and mid-Atlantic and southeastern states. There was a recent outbreak of enterovirus type 71 in Colorado.

PREDOMINANT SEX: Male = female
PREDOMINANT AGE: Any age
GENETICS: No specific genetic or congenital predisposition

ETIOLOGY
- Can be caused by a host of viruses, with herpes simplex the most common virus identified.
- Arboviruses transmitted by mosquitoes include Eastern equine encephalitis, Western equine encephalitis, St. Louis encephalitis, Venezuelan equine encephalitis, California virus encephalitis, Japanese B encephalitis, La Crosse encephalitis, Murray Valley and West Nile encephalitis. Tick-borne diseases include Russian spring-summer encephalitis, Powassan encephalitis, and other lesser known agents.
- Also implicated: rabies-causing agents, CMV, Epstein-Barr, varicella-zoster, echo virus, mumps, adenovirus, coxsackie, rubeola, and herpes viruses.
- Meningoencephalitis: acute retroviral infection from HIV.
- In the U.S., the most commonly identified etiologies are herpes simplex virus, West Nile virus, and the enteroviruses.

PHYSICAL FINDINGS & CLINICAL PRESENTATION
- Initially, fever and evidence of meningeal irritation
- Headache and stiff neck
- Later, development of signs of cortical dysfunction: lethargy, coma, stupor, weakness, seizures, facial weakness, as well as brainstem findings
- Cerebellar findings: ataxia, nystagmus, hypotonia, myoclonus, cranial nerve palsies, and abnormal tendon reflexes
- Patients with rabies: hydrophobia, anxiety, facial numbness, psychosis, coma, or dysarthria
- Rarely, movement disorders, such as chorea, hemiballismus, or dystonia
- Recall of a prodromal viral-like illness (this finding is not at all uniform)

 **DIAGNOSIS**

DIFFERENTIAL DIAGNOSIS
- Bacterial infections: brain abscess, toxic encephalopathies, TB
- Protozoal infections
- Behçet's disease
- Lupus encephalitis
- Sjögren's syndrome
- Multiple sclerosis
- Syphilis

- Cryptococcus
- Toxoplasmosis
- Brucellosis
- Leukemic or lymphomatous meningitis
- Other metastatic tumors
- Lyme disease
- Cat-scratch disease
- Vogt-Koyanagi-Harada syndrome
- Mollaret's meningitis

WORKUP
- Lumbar puncture to reveal pleocytosis, usually lymphocytic, although neutrophils may be seen early on
- Usually, elevated CSF protein
- Normal or low CSF glucose
- In herpes simplex encephalitis: RBCs and xanthochromia
- Selected tests on CSF fluid in viral encephalitis are described in Table 1E-9
- EEG changes showing periodic high-voltage sharp waves in the temporal regions and slow wave complexes suggestive of herpes encephalitis (Fig. 1E-16).
- CT scan and MRI to reveal edema and hemorrhage in the frontal and temporal lobes
- Temporal lobe involvement suggests herpes simplex encephalitis
- Basal ganglia and thalami are areas involved as generally seen in Eastern equine encephalitis
- With West Nile infection, MRI changes have shown changes in basal ganglia, thalami, mesial temporal structures, brain stem, and cerebellum
- Arboviral infections suspected during outbreaks in specific areas
- Rising titers of neutralizing antibodies from the acute to the convalescent stage demonstrated but often not helpful in the acutely ill patient
- Polymerase chain reaction (PCR) that amplifies DNA from the CSF for herpes simplex encephalitis
- Rarely, brain biopsy to assist in the diagnosis; viral culture of cerebral tissue obtained if biopsy done
- Classic herpetic skin lesions suggestive of herpes encephalitis
- In diagnosing arboviral encephalitis:
  1. Presence of antiviral IgM within the first few days of symptomatic disease; detected and quantified by ELISA
  2. Unusual to recover an arbovirus from the blood or CSF

LABORATORY TESTS
- Aside from the lumbar puncture, most other laboratory studies are nonspecific.
- Skin lesions and urine may be cultured for herpes simplex and CMV.

TREATMENT

ACUTE GENERAL Rx
- Supportive care, frequent evaluation, and neurologic examination
- Ventilatory assistance for patients who are moribund or at risk for aspiration
- Avoidance of infusion of hypotonic fluids to minimize the risk of hyponatremia

TABLE 1E-9 Selected Tests for Viral Encephalitis

Organism/Syndrome	Test	Comment
West Nile Virus		
West Nile encephalitis	IgM in CSF	Diagnostic of CNS invasive disease or acute flaccid paralysis
Herpes Simplex Virus Type 1		
Herpes simplex encephalitis	PCR in CSF	Sensitive and specific in the acute phase
	CSF–serum antibody ratio	Useful 2 weeks to 3 months after onset
Herpes Simplex Virus Type 2		
Neonatal encephalitis	PCR in CSF	Confirmatory, high sensitivity
Relapsing meningitis	PCR in CSF	Sensitive and specific in first 3 days of illness
Varicella-Zoster Virus		
Meningoencephalitis	PCR in CSF	Confirmatory when used with clinical and spinal fluid findings; sensitivity unclear
Epstein-Barr Virus		
EBV encephalitis	PCR in CSF	Suggests CNS invasion by virus
JC Virus		
Progressive multifocal leukoencephalopathy	PCR in CSF	Diagnostic but incompletely (70%) sensitive
Cytomegalovirus		
CMV ventriculitis	PCR in CSF	Sensitive and specific

CMV, Cytomegalovirus; *CNS,* central nervous system; *CSF,* cerebrospinal fluid; *EBV,* Epstein-Barr virus; *PCR,* polymerase chain reaction.
From Goldman L, Schafer AI: *Goldman's Cecil medicine,* ed 24, Philadelphia, 2011, Saunders.

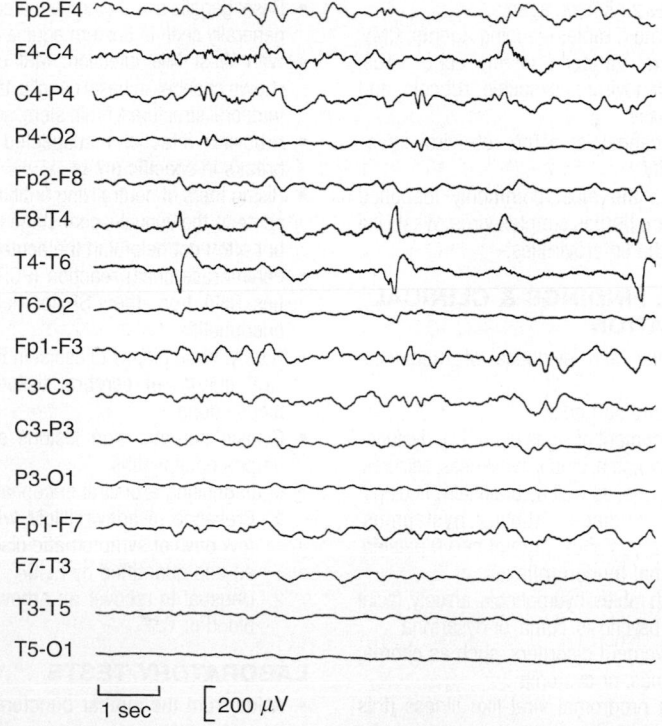

FIGURE 1E-16 Repetitive complexes occurring in the right temporal region of a child with herpes simplex encephalitis. (From Goetz CG, Pappert EJ: *Textbook of clinical neurology,* Philadelphia, 1999, Saunders.)

- For patients who develop seizures: anticonvulsant therapy and follow-up in a critical care setting
- For comatose patients:
  1. Aggressive care to avoid decubitus ulcers, contractures, and DVT
  2. Close attention to weights, input/output, and serum electrolytes
- Acyclovir 30 mg/kg/day IV total dose divided in q8 hour intervals for 14 days for herpes simplex encephalitis
- Short courses of corticosteroids to control brain edema and prevent herniation
- In patients with suspected rabies:
  1. Human rabies immune globulin (HRIG) should be given at a dose of 20 U/kg.
  2. Active immunization may be stimulated by rabies vaccine, which is grown on a human diploid cell line (HDCV) and has reduced the number of doses needed to five.
  3. If suspect animal is a dog or cat and can be found, observe closely for 10 days to detect rabid behavior; any significant illness in the animal should promptly initiate humane sacrifice of the animal with the brain submitted to local or state health departments for pathology and immunologic testing for rabies. Any wild animal suspected of rabies should be humanely sacrificed, if possible, and submitted for rabies testing immediately.
  4. If signs are seen, animal should be euthanized and its brain examined for signs of rabies.
- No specific pharmacologic therapy for most other viral pathogens

CHRONIC Rx

Some patients may develop permanent neurologic sequelae; these patients will benefit from intensive rehabilitation programs, including physical, occupational, and speech therapy.

DISPOSITION

- Patients with suspected encephalitis of any cause should generally be admitted for initial diagnostic workup and specific treatment (if available).
- Long-term management of patients with significant neurologic sequelae from encephalitis (e.g., memory defects, depression, difficulty with organization of thoughts, movement disorders) may benefit from rehabilitation services, home care, or nursing home placement.

REFERRAL

- To a neurologist for initial workup and management
- To an infectious disease specialist for diagnostic and therapeutic plan
- To a rehabilitation service for long-term evaluation and convalescent services

! PEARLS & CONSIDERATIONS

- West Nile virus encephalitis occurs primarily in elderly patients >65 years of age.
- Rabies may occur months after contact with the rabid animal, and the exposure (especially bat rabies) may have been seemingly insignificant and even inapparent.
- Experimental therapies are worthy of consideration for some forms of viral encephalitis (e.g., immune plasma, ribavirin, interferons), and expert consultation should be obtained early on for possible treatment interventions with promising experimental therapies (e.g., Milwaukee protocol for rabies).

SUGGESTED READINGS

Available at www.expertconsult.com

RELATED CONTENT

Herpes Encephalitis (Patient Information)
Rabies (Related Key Topic)
West Nile Virus Infection (Related Key Topic)

AUTHOR: **GLENN G. FORT, M.D., M.P.H.**

BASIC INFORMATION

DEFINITION

Encephalopathy is a clinical syndrome of global cognitive impairment characterized by impaired arousal, inattention, and disorientation.

SYNONYMS

Delirium, acute confusional state

ICD-10CM CODES

G93.40	Encephalopathy, unspecified
G93.41	Metabolic encephalopathy
G93.49	Other encephalopathy
G92	Toxic encephalopathy
E51.2	Wernicke's encephalopathy
G04.30	Acute necrotizing hemorrhagic encephalopathy, unspecified
G04.31	Postinfectious acute necrotizing hemorrhagic encephalopathy
G04.32	Postimmunization acute necrotizing hemorrhagic encephalopathy
G04.39	Other acute necrotizing hemorrhagic encephalopathy
G93.49	Other encephalopathy
I67.4	Hypertensive encephalopathy
I67.83	Posterior reversible encephalopathy syndrome
J10.81	Influenza due to other identified influenza virus with encephalopathy
J11.81	Influenza due to unidentified influenza virus with encephalopathy
P91.60	Hypoxic ischemic encephalopathy [HIE], unspecified
P91.61	Mild hypoxic ischemic encephalopathy [HIE]
P91.62	Moderate hypoxic ischemic encephalopathy [HIE]
P91.63	Severe hypoxic ischemic encephalopathy [HIE]

EPIDEMIOLOGY & DEMOGRAPHICS

POINT PREVALENCE: 1.1% of adults in the general population >55 yr, 10% to 40% of hospitalized elderly, and 60% of nursing home patients >75 yr; 100,000 to 200,000 cases annually with anoxic encephalopathy

RISK FACTORS: Age, cancer, AIDS, terminal illness, bone marrow transplant, surgery

PHYSICAL FINDINGS & CLINICAL PRESENTATION

- The essential feature of encephalopathy is the patient's inability to maintain a coherent stream of thought or action.
- The history may often suggest a waxing and waning of the level of arousal and general cognitive ability.
- Because toxins and metabolic disturbances are common causes of encephalopathy, the history should focus on exposure to toxins (especially medications) and symptoms suggesting a concurrent illness such as a urinary tract infection or pneumonia.
- Common to all encephalopathies is a fluctuating level of arousal, poor attention, and disorientation.
- Some patients may appear agitated and others lethargic.
- Delusions (fixed false beliefs) and hallucinations are common.
- Asterixis (negative myoclonus) is common.
- Other physical findings may vary depending on the underlying cause of encephalopathy, such as fever, ascites, jaundice, or tachycardia.

ETIOLOGY

The final common pathway of all causes of encephalopathy is widespread, neuronal dysfunction from structural or functional causes. Many conditions are reversible and carry a good prognosis if treated in a timely manner.

- Organ failure (e.g., hepatic encephalopathy, hypoxia, hypercapnia, uremia)
- Infection: systemic (e.g., urinary tract, pneumonia, sepsis) or involving the central nervous system (e.g., meningitis, encephalitis)
- Toxin ingestion or withdrawal (e.g., alcohol, medications [especially psychotropics and neuroleptics], recreational drugs)
- Metabolic disturbances: hyperosmolar states, hypernatremia, hyponatremia, hyperglycemia, hypoglycemia, hypercalcemia, hypophosphatemia, acidosis, alkalosis, inborn errors of metabolism
- Endocrinopathy: hyperthyroidism, hypothyroidism, Cushing's syndrome, adrenal insufficiency, pituitary failure
- Neoplasm: tumors of the central nervous system, primary or metastatic; also effect of distant tumors (e.g., paraneoplastic limbic encephalitis)
- Nutritional deficiency, mostly in alcoholics and chronically ill patients, such as vitamin B_1 deficiency (Wernicke's encephalopathy)
- Seizures: postictal state, nonconvulsive status epilepticus, complex partial seizures, absence seizures
- Trauma: concussion, contusion, subdural hematoma, epidural hematoma, diffuse axonal injury
- Vascular: ischemic and hemorrhagic strokes, vasculitis, venous thrombosis
- Postanoxic encephalopathy
- Psychiatric disease: acute psychosis, depression with psychiatric features
- Acute disease: acute disseminating myelitis, tumefactive multiple sclerosis
- Other: hypertensive encephalopathy, postoperative status, sleep deprivation

DIAGNOSIS

DIFFERENTIAL DIAGNOSIS

Differential diagnosis for encephalopathy is broad. It is typically helpful to distinguish toxic metabolic causes from primary neurologic causes.

- Dementia: distinguished from encephalopathy by a history of slowly progressive cognitive decline over time (fluctuating cognitive function is rare except in diffuse Lewy body disease).
- Hypersomnia
- Aphasia: distinguished from encephalopathy by virtue of it representing a specific disorder of language rather than a global disturbance of cognitive function.
- Depression
- Psychosis: some overlap with encephalopathy because delusions and hallucinations may be common to both.
- Mania
- Vegetative state from cerebral injury; these patients appear awake (eyes are open) but there is no content to their consciousness.
- Akinetic mutism: these patients do not talk and do not move; there is little fluctuation in their state and there is no asterixis or other focal deficit.
- Locked-in syndrome: may be distinguished from encephalopathy by the presence of fixed neurologic deficits (e.g., paralysis of all four limbs); however, the patient is aware of his or her environment.

WORKUP

The best tool in the evaluation of encephalopathy is a good history and physical exam, which will help tailor the remainder of the diagnostic workup. Interview family members and other providers to identify preceding events, medication changes, and medical history. Evaluate focal deficits.

LABORATORY TESTS

- General chemistry: electrolytes, glucose, creatinine, ammonia, blood urea nitrogen, transaminases, amylase, lipase
- Complete blood count
- Drug screen and alcohol level (must order ethylene glycol separately if suspected)
- Lumbar puncture if meningitis, encephalitis, or subarachnoid hemorrhage with negative imaging is suspected
- HIV testing
- Endocrine testing: cortisol level, thyroid function test
- Urinalysis and microscopy, urine culture, blood cultures
- Arterial blood gases

IMAGING STUDIES

The following imaging studies may be indicated depending on history and physical examination:

- Chest radiograph to rule out pneumonia
- Head CT to rule out bleeding, hydrocephalus, tumors
- Brain MRI with diffusion-weighted images for suspected encephalitis, tumors, and acute strokes
- Magnetic resonance angiography/venography for strokes, arterial dissection, venous thrombosis
- Conventional angiography for central nervous system (CNS) vasculitis and aneurysms
- EEG: evaluate for subclinical status epilepticus

TREATMENT

The encephalopathy itself is a symptom of these underlying problems. In general, it is best to avoid treating the symptom of encephalopathy with antipsychotics or sedatives.

- The best approach is to treat the underlying toxic or metabolic disturbance.
- Thiamine supplementation
- Glucose for hypoglycemia
- Antibiotics in cases of infections (choose an agent with good CNS penetration in cases of primary CNS infections)
- Insulin in hyperglycemic conditions (e.g., diabetic ketoacidosis, hyperosmolar nonketosis, and sepsis)
- Ensure hemodynamic stability (blood pressure and heart rate)

SUGGESTED READINGS

Available at www.expertconsult.com

RELATED CONTENT

Delirium (Related Key Topic)
Encephalitis, Acute Viral (Related Key Topic)
Hepatic Encephalopathy (Related Key Topic)

AUTHOR: **JOSHUA CHALKELY, M.S., D.O.**

BASIC INFORMATION

DEFINITION/DIAGNOSTIC CRITERIA (DSM 5; ROME III)

A. Reverted passage of feces into inappropriate places (e.g., clothing, floor), whether involuntary or intentional
B. At least one such event occurs each month for at least three months
C. The behavior is not attributable to the physiologic effects of a substance (e.g., laxatives) or another medical condition except through a mechanism involving constipation

Encopresis may be classified into two types based on published guidelines of the Multinational Working Teams to Develop Criteria for Functional Disorders (Rome III). Definition of functional retentive encopresis requires two of six criteria: 2 or fewer defecations per week, at least 1 episode of incontinence after acquisition of toileting skills, history of excessive fecal retention and or painful or hard bowel movements, presence of large fecal mass in the rectum, history of large diameter stools that may obstruct the toilet. Non-retentive encopresis is fecal incontinence without evidence of constipation or fecal retention in the absence of underlying disease process that explains the symptoms .

SYNONYMS

Stool/fecal incontinence; soiling

ICD-10 CODES
R15.9 Full incontinence of feces
F98.1 Encopresis not due to a substance or known physiological condition
DSM 5 CODES
307.7 Encopresis with or without constipation and overflow incontinence

EPIDEMIOLOGY & DEMOGRAPHICS

PEAK INCIDENCE: Preschool age (though also occurs during school age and adolescence)
PREVALANCE (IN U.S.): 1.5% to 7.5% of children 4 to 12 yr old
PREDOMINANT SEX: More often in males (estimates range from 1.9:1 to 9:1)

PHYSICAL FINDINGS & CLINICAL PRESENTATION

- Most children are toilet-trained for stool by age 4. Traditionally, in primary encopresis, fecal continence is never fully established; in secondary encopresis, soiling is preceded by a period of fecal continence. However, definitions of "primary" vs. "secondary" do not reliably correlate with etiology or outcome.
- Constipation and withholding of stool are significant factors in 80% to 90% of cases ("retentive encopresis"). In 10% to 20%, constipation is not a factor ("nonretentive" encopresis).
- When constipation is longstanding, soft or liquid stool may flow around the retained feces, resulting in overflow incontinence.

This may occur several times per day and mistakenly be interpreted as diarrhea.
- Children may report a lack of awareness of stool passage when longstanding constipation/impaction has resulted in loss of rectal tone and sensation. Furthermore, some children habituate to the odor.

ETIOLOGY

- Approximately 96% of children have bowel movements between three times daily to once every other day. When bowel movements are less frequent, stool becomes drier and harder and much more uncomfortable or painful to pass. Children may avoid the discomfort or pain by avoiding elimination, resulting in worsening constipation and overflow incontinence.
- Constipation may begin gradually as a result of a decrease in elimination frequency, or more acutely after an illness or changes in diet.
- Toilet training practices that increase anxiety may also play a role in stool retention, the development of constipation, and eventual encopresis.

DIAGNOSIS

DIFFERENTIAL DIAGNOSIS

- Hirschsprung's disease
- Endocrine disease (hypothyroidism)
- Cerebral palsy
- Myelomeningocele
- Pseudoobstruction
- Anorectal lesions (rectal stenosis)
- Malformations
- Trauma
- Rectal prolapse
- Celiac disease
- Hypothyroidism
- Medications

WORKUP

- History: frequency of elimination, character of the stool, associated pain, and presence of enuresis (with which it is frequently associated).
- Evaluate for other developmental or psychiatric problems.
- Common physical findings in retentive encopresis: abdominal fecal mass, stool impacted rectum, loose anal sphincter, fecal material in the perianal area, anal tags or fissures.
- Perform a complete neurologic examination to exclude sensory-neural or spinal cord abnormalities

LABORATORY TESTS

- Consider thyroid function tests, celiac screening tests, electrolytes, calcium, urinalysis, and urine culture.
- If concerned about the possibility of Hirschsprung's disease, obtain rectal biopsy.

IMAGING STUDIES

- Abdominal imaging to determine extent of obstruction or megacolon

- Anorectal manometric studies or barium enema can support suspicion of Hirschsprung's disease

TREATMENT

ACUTE GENERAL Rx

- Disimpaction is a necessary first step, by oral or rectal route (or combination).
- For oral disimpaction, polyethylene glycol, magnesium citrate or high doses of mineral oil are effective (avoid use of mineral oil in patients at risk for aspiration
- Adding stimulant laxatives such as senna or bisacodyl can sometimes make oral disimpaction more effective.
- For rectal disimpaction, phosphate soda, saline, or mineral oil enemas are effective.
- When medical workup determines that constipation is not present ("nonretentive encopresis"), consider implementing toilet-training routines or referral to behavioral health provider.

CHRONIC Rx

- Prevent recurrence of constipation with oral stool softeners (e.g., polyethylene glycol or lactulose) or stool lubricants (mineral oil).
- In immediate post disimpaction period (1 mo after acute treatment), stimulant laxatives may be needed because bowel tone remains low; taper use as quickly as possible to avoid dependence.
- Family documentation of stool passage, including location and amount, on a chart or calendar helps inform medication changes and best times for toilet sitting.
- Praise and other small incentives for positive toileting routines and taking medication can help to maintain good bowel habits. Balanced diet and Increased fiber intake/supplementation may also help.
- Formal behavioral treatment (education, reinforcement of treatment adherence and exercises to improve anal sphincter control) increases treatment success. Biofeedback to improve sphincter function is advocated by some, with 1-yr results comparable to behavioral treatment. Adjunctive Internet-based interventions that incorporate behavioral therapy and medical management are also beginning to show promise.

DISPOSITION

Encopresis may be self-limited or relatively brief in duration; may require prolonged maintenance therapy. Relapses are common.

REFERRAL

Behavioral family therapy should be considered for patients who do not respond to medical treatment within a few months or who have significant contributing psychiatric or family factors.

Diseases and Disorders

TABLE 1E-10 Clinical Manifestations of Infective Endocarditis Myalgia/Arthralgia

Symptoms	Patients Affected (%)	Signs	Patients (%)
Fever	80	Fever	90
Chills	40	Heart murmur	85
Weakness	40	Changing murmur	5-10
Dyspnea	40	New murmur	3-5
Sweats	25	Embolic phenomenon	>50
Anorexia	25	Skin manifestations	18-50
Weight loss	25	Osler nodes	10-23
Malaise	25	Splinter hemorrhages	15
Cough	25	Petechiae	20-40
Skin lesions	20	Janeway lesion	<10
Stroke	20	Splenomegaly	20-57
Nausea/vomiting	20	Septic complications	20
Headache	20	(e.g., pneumonia, meningitis)	
Myalgia/arthralgia	15	Mycotic aneurysms	20
Edema	15	Clubbing	12-52
Chest pain	15	Retinal lesion	2-10
Abdominal pain and delirium/coma	15	Signs of renal failure	10-25
Delirium/coma	10-15		
Hemoptysis	10		
Back pain	10		

From Mandell GL et al: *Principles and practice of infectious diseases*, ed 6, Philadelphia, 2005, Churchill Livingstone.

- Gram-negative bacilli.
- Group D streptococci.

PROSTHETIC VALVE ENDOCARDITIS (LATE):
- *S. epidermidis.*
- Viridans streptococci.
- *S. aureus.*
- Enterococci and group D streptococci.

NOSOCOMIAL ENDOCARDITIS:
- Coagulase-negative staphylococci
- *S. aureus*
- Streptococci: viridans, group B, enterococcus

HACEK ORGANISMS:
- Fastidious gram-negative bacilli.
- *H. parainfluenzae.*
- *H. aphrophilus.*
- *A. actinomycetemcomitans.*
- *Cardiobacterium hominis.*
- *Eikenella corrodens.*
- *Kingella kingae.*

RISK FACTORS
- Poor dental hygiene.
- Long-term hemodialysis.
- Diabetes mellitus.
- HIV infection.
- Mitral valve prolapse.

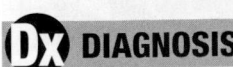 **DIAGNOSIS**

DIFFERENTIAL DIAGNOSIS
- Brain abscess.
- FUO.
- Pericarditis.
- Meningitis.
- Rheumatic fever.
- Osteomyelitis.
- *Salmonella.*

- TB.
- Bacteremia.
- Pericarditis.
- Glomerulonephritis.

WORKUP

Physical examination to evaluate for the previous physical findings followed by laboratory testing (see "Laboratory Tests"). Fig. 1E-20 describes a diagnostic evaluation of suspected endocarditis. The modified Duke criteria for diagnosis of endocarditis defines "major criteria" as persistently positive blood cultures of organisms typical of endocarditis or endocardial involvement (new valvular regurgitation or positive echocardiogram). "Minor criteria" are defined as presence of predisposing condition or injection drug use, fever, embolic vascular pneumonia (e.g., glomerulonephritis, rheumatoid factor), or positive blood cultures not meeting major criteria. Definite endocarditis is 2 major criteria or 1 major criteria and 3 minor criteria or 5 minor criteria or presence of organisms by culture or histologic examination of a vegetation.

LABORATORY TESTS
- Blood cultures: three sets in first 24 hr. Table 1E-11 describes causes of culture-negative endocarditis.
- More culturing if patient has received prior antibiotic.
- CBC (anemia possibly present, subacute).
- WBC (leukocytosis is higher in acute endocarditis).
- ESR and C-reactive protein (elevated).
- Positive rheumatoid factor (subacute endocarditis).
- Proteinuria, hematuria, RBC casts.

IMAGING STUDIES
- Echocardiogram: two-dimensional. Transthoracic echocardiography (TTE) (Fig. E1E-21) is noninvasive and more easily available but has less-than-optimal sensitivity (50%-80%) for endocarditis.
- Transesophageal echocardiography (TEE): more sensitive in detecting vegetations and preferred diagnostic modality. It is especially helpful with prosthetic valves or in detecting perivalvular disease.
- Electrocardiogram: look for cardiac conduction abnormalities, injury pattern, or evidence of pericarditis—any such new findings are suggestive of myocardial abscess.

 **TREATMENT**

Initial IV antibiotic therapy (before culture results) is aimed at the most likely organism. The American Heart Association has developed guidelines based on the most frequently encountered bacteria.

- **Native valve** endocarditis caused by penicillin-susceptible *S. viridians, S. bovis,* and other streptotcocci (MIC of penicillin ≤0.12 mcg/ml): Pen G 12-18 million U IV q24h continuous or divided q4h for 4 weeks **or** ceftriaxone 2 g IV or IM q day for 4 weeks for penicillin allergic patients. Vancomycin at 30 mg/kg per 24 hr in 2 equally divided doses assuming normal kidney function, for 4 weeks.
- **Native valve** endocarditis caused by strains of viridians streptococci and *S. bovis* relatively resistant to penicillin (MIC >0.12 mcg/ml): Pen G: 24 million units per 24 hr IV either continuously or in 4 or 6 equally divided doses for 4 weeks **or** ceftriaxone 2 g per 24 hr IV or IM for 4 weeks **plus** gentamicin 3 mg/kg per 24 hr IV or IM in one dose or in 2 to 3 equally divided doses for two weeks or monotherapy with vancomycin 30 mg/kg per 24 hr IV in 2 equally divided doses for 4 weeks not to exceed 2 g per 24 hr unless concentrations in serum too low.
- **Native valve** endocarditis due to *Staphylococcus:*
  1. **MSSA:** nafcillin (or oxacillin) 12 per 24 hr IV in 4 or 6 equally divided doses for 6 weeks **plus** optional addition of gentamicin 3 mg/kg per 24 hr IV or IM in 2 or 3 equally divided doses for 3 to 5 days **or** cefazolin 6 g per 24 hr IV in 3 equally divided doses for 6 weeks, **plus** optional addition of gentamicin 3 mg/kg per 24 hr IV or IM in 2 or 3 equally divided doses for 3 to 5 days. A newer antibiotic daptomycin has an indication for right-sided endocarditis with MSSA at 6 mg/kg IV q24h.
  2. **MRSA:** vancomycin 30 mg/kg per 24 hr in 2 equally divided doses for 6 weeks; not to exceed 2 g per 24 hr unless concentrations in serum are low.
- For culture negative native valve endocarditis one of the following regimens is suggested: ampicillin-sulbactam: 12 g per 24 hr IV in 4 equally divided doses for 4 to 6 weeks

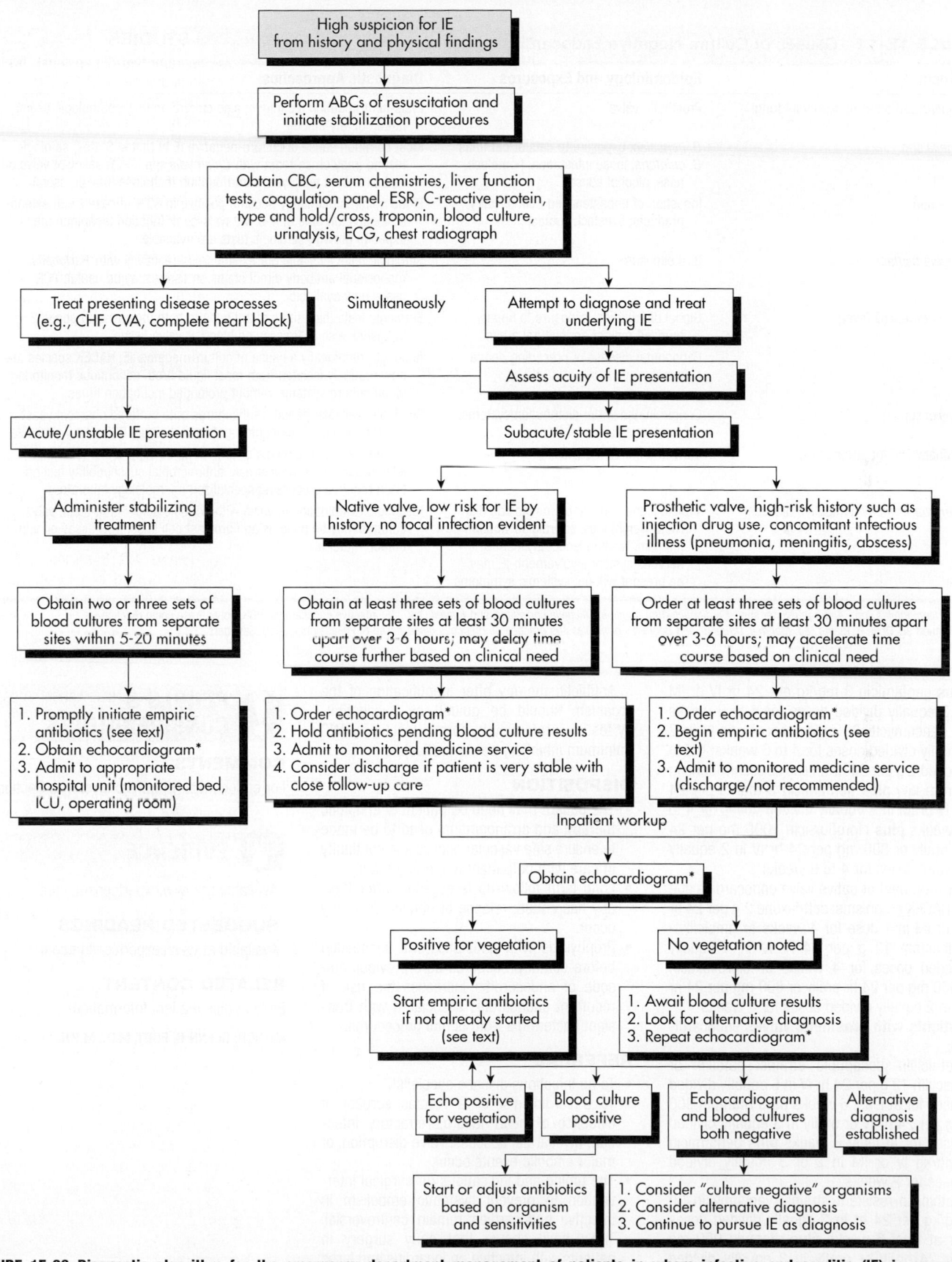

FIGURE 1E-20 Diagnostic algorithm for the emergency department management of patients in whom infective endocarditis (IE) is suspected.
*Echocardiography can be performed via either the transthoracic (TTE) or transesophageal (TEE) technique. TEE is more invasive but is more sensitive for detecting vegetations and complications of IE, such as perivalvular abscesses; it is recommended for prosthetic valves; for situations in which optimal visualization by TTE will be difficult, such as emphysema and morbid obesity; for high suspicion of IE but normal TTE findings; and for high suspicion of a complication of IE, such as perivalvular abscess. Normal findings with either technique do not exclude IE if clinical suspicion is high. Echocardiograms can be repeated in an attempt to identify problems such as vegetations and abscesses that may not be noted initially. *ABCs*, Airway, breathing, and circulation; *CBC*, complete blood count; *CHF*, congestive heart failure; *CVA*, cerebrovascular accident; *ECG*, electrocardiogram; *ESR*, erythrocyte sedimentation rate; *ICU*, intensive care unit. (From Adams JG et al: *Emergency medicine, clinical essentials*, ed 2, Philadelphia, 2013, Elsevier.)

TABLE 1E-11 Causes of Culture-Negative Endocarditis

Organism	Epidemiology and Exposures	Diagnostic Approaches
Aspergillus and other noncandidal fungi	Prosthetic valve	Lysis-centrifugation technique; also culture and histopathologic examination of any emboli
Bartonella spp.	*B. henselae:* exposure to cats or cat fleas *B. quintana:* louse infestation; homelessness, alcohol abuse	Most common cause of culture-negative IE in United States; serologic testing (may cross-react with *Chlamydia* spp.); PCR assay of valve or emboli is best test; lysis-centrifugation technique may be useful
Brucella spp.	Ingestion of unpasteurized milk or dairy products; livestock contact	Blood cultures ultimately become positive in 80% of cases with extended incubation time of 4-6 wk; lysis-centrifugation technique may expedite growth; serologic tests are available
Chlamydia psittaci	Bird exposure	Serologic tests available but exhibit cross-reactivity with *Bartonella;* monoclonal antibody direct stains on tissue may be useful; PCR assay now available
Coxiella burnetii (Q fever)	Global distribution; exposure to unpasteurized milk or agricultural areas	Serologic tests (high titers of antibody to both phase 1 and phase 2 antigens); also PCR assay on blood or valve tissue
HACEK spp.	Periodontal disease or preceding dental work	Although traditionally a cause of culture-negative IE, HACEK species are now routinely isolated from most liquid broth continuous monitoring blood culture systems without prolonged incubation times
Legionella spp.	Contaminated water distribution systems; prosthetic valves	Serology available; periodic subcultures onto buffered charcoal yeast extract medium; lysis-centrifugation technique; PCR assay available
Nutritionally variant streptococci	Slow and indolent course	Supplemented culture media or growth as satellite colonies around *Staphylococcus aureus* streak; antimicrobial susceptibility testing often requires processing specialized microbiology laboratory
Tropheryma whipplei (Whipple's disease)	Typical signs and symptoms include diarrhea, weight loss, arthralgias, abdominal pain, lymphadenopathy, central nervous system involvement; IE may be present without systemic symptoms	Histologic examination of valve with periodic acid–Schiff stain; valve cultures may be done using fibroblast cell lines; PCR assay on vegetation material

HACEK, *Haemophilus* spp., *Aggregatibacter* spp., *Cardiobacterium hominis, Eikenella corrodens,* and *Kingella* spp.; IE, infective endocarditis; PCR, polymerase chain reaction.
From Bennett JE, Dolin R, Blaser MJ: *Mandell, Douglas, and Bennett's principles and practice of infectious diseases,* ed 8, Philadelphia, 2015, Saunders.

plus gentamicin 3 mg/kg per 24 hr IV or IM in 3 equally divided doses for 4 to 6 weeks **or** vancomycin 30 mg/kg per 24 hr IV in 2 equally divided doses for 4 to 6 weeks; not to exceed 2 g per 24 hr unless concentrations in serum low **plus** gentamicin 3 mg/kg per 24 hr IV or IM in 3 equally divided doses for 4 to 6 weeks **plus** ciprofloxacin 1000 mg per 24 hr orally or 800 mg per 24 hr IV in 2 equally divided doses for 4 to 6 weeks.

- For treatment of native valve endocarditis due to HACEK organisms: ceftriaxone 2 g per 24 hr IV or IM in 1 dose for 4 weeks **or** ampicillin-sulbactam 12 g per 24 hr IV in 4 equally divided doses for 4 weeks **or** ciprofloxacin 1000 mg per 24 hr orally or 800 mg per 24 hr IV in 2 equally divided doses for 4 weeks
- **Patients with prosthetic valves** endocarditis:
- methicillin-susceptible strains: nafcillin or oxacillin 12 g per 24 hr IV in 6 equally divided doses for at least 6 weeks **plus** rifampin 900 mg per 24 hr IV or orally in 3 equally divided doses for at least 6 weeks **plus** gentamicin 3mg/kg IV or IM in 2 or 3 equally divided doses for 2 weeks.
- Methicillin-resistant strains: vancomycin 30 mg/kg per 24 hr in 2 equally divided doses for at least 6 weeks **plus** rifampin 900 mg per 24 hr IV or orally in 3 equally divided doses for at least 6 weeks **plus** gentamicin 3 mg/kg per 24 hr IV or IM in 2 or 3 equally divided doses for 2 weeks.

Antibiotic therapy after identification of the organism should be guided by susceptibility testing, preferably by formal testing by MIC (minimum inhibitory concentration).

DISPOSITION

- The patient may need outpatient IV antibiotic therapy, and arrangements need to be made to ensure safe vascular access and continuity of care with outpatient IV therapy team.
- Long-term follow-up is essential after therapy has ended; relapse of endocarditis may occur.
- Prophylaxis with antibiotics will be needed before dental procedures as a previous episode of endocarditis increases the risk of recurrent endocarditis associated with transient bacteremia from dental procedures.

REFERRAL

- To an infectious disease specialist.
- To a cardiologist or a cardiac surgeon if evidence of heart failure, refractory infection, myocardial abscess, valve disruption, or major embolic events occur.
- The timing and indications for surgical intervention to prevent systemic embolism in infective endocarditis remain controversial. Trials have shown that early surgery in patients with infective endocarditis and large vegetations significantly reduced death and embolic events by decreasing the risk of systemic embolism.

PEARLS & CONSIDERATIONS

COMMENTS
For endocarditis prophylaxis refer to Section V.

EVIDENCE

Available at www.expertconsult.com

SUGGESTED READINGS
Available at www.expertconsult.com

RELATED CONTENT
Endocarditis (Patient Information)

AUTHOR: **GLENN G. FORT, M.D., M.P.H.**

BASIC INFORMATION

DEFINITION

Endometrial cancer (EC) is a malignant transformation of endometrial stroma and/or glands typified by irregular nuclear membranes, nuclear atypia, mitotic activity, loss of glandular pattern, and irregular cell size. The two main histologic subcategories of EC, endometrioid and nonendometrioid EC, show unique molecular aberrations and differing clinical behaviors.

SYNONYMS

Uterine cancer (some forms)

ICD-10CM CODES
C54.1 Malignant neoplasm of endometrium
C55 Malignant neoplasm of uterus, part unspecified
C54.9 Malignant neoplasm of corpus uteri, unspecified

EPIDEMIOLOGY & DEMOGRAPHICS

INCIDENCE: 21.2 cases per 100,000 persons; approximately 30,000 new cases annually. It is the most common gynecologic malignancy in the U.S.
PREDOMINANCE: Median age at onset: 60 yr; only 5% occur in women <40 yr
RISK FACTORS: Obesity, diabetes, nulliparity, early menarche and late menopause, unopposed estrogen therapy, tamoxifen use, oligoovulation with chronic unopposed estrogen exposure such as with polycystic ovary syndrome (PCOS), endometrial atypical hyperplasia, endometrial polyps (malignancy is found in 3.6% of endometrial polyps)

PHYSICAL FINDINGS & CLINICAL PRESENTATION

- Abnormal uterine bleeding or postmenopausal bleeding in 90%
- Pyometra or hematometra
- Abnormal Pap smear

ETIOLOGY

Endogenous or exogenous chronic unopposed estrogen stimulation of the endometrium

DIAGNOSIS

DIFFERENTIAL DIAGNOSIS

- Atypical hyperplasia
- Other genital tract malignancy
- Uterine polyps
- Atrophic vaginitis
- Granuloma cell tumor
- Fibroid uterus

WORKUP

- Complete history and physical examination
- Endometrial biopsy or dilation and curettage
- Assessment of operative risk
- Staging (Table 1E-12)

LABORATORY TESTS

- Complete blood count
- Chemistry profile including liver function tests
- Consider CA-125 level

IMAGING STUDIES

- Chest x-ray
- CT scan, and/or pelvic ultrasound (Fig. 1E-22)
- Endovaginal ultrasound (Fig. 1E-23) in postmenopausal women with vaginal bleeding

TREATMENT

NONPHARMACOLOGIC THERAPY

- Surgery is the mainstay of treatment, with or without radiation, depending on tumor stage and grade. Laparoscopic surgery for early-stage EC is as safe and effective as laparotomy. Robotic laparoscopy procedures have increased significantly in recent years for this indication.
- Surgery generally consists of pelvic washings, total abdominal hysterectomy and bilateral salpingo-oophorectomy, omental biopsy, and selective pelvic and periaortic lymphadenectomy, depending on stage and grade.
- Brachytherapy and/or teletherapy are added in an advanced stage.
- Chemotherapy (cisplatin, Adriamycin) or tamoxifen may also be used, especially for advanced or recurrent endometrial cancers.
- Aromatase inhibitors, currently primarily used for breast carcinoma, are being investigated as adjuvant therapy for endometrial cancer.
- Hormonal therapy is an option for some young women with early-stage EC who wish to preserve fertility. This choice should be discussed with a gynecologic oncologist.

ACUTE GENERAL Rx

- A thorough workup should be completed before any therapy for EC.
- Surgery is the treatment of choice.

CHRONIC Rx

- Physical and pelvic examination every 3 mo for 2 yr, then every 6 mo for 2 yr, annually thereafter
- Yearly Pap smear
- Hormone replacement (combination) a consideration in low-risk patients (stage I or early stage II)

DISPOSITION

The majority of cases present early, and the 5-yr survival is generally good:

Stage I (Fig. 1E-24) 75%-100%
Stage II 65%
Stage III 40%
Stage IV 10%

Some histologic types (clear cell, serous papillary) have worse survival rates.

Patients with prolonged unopposed estrogen, such as with polycystic ovary syndrome (PCOS), should have an endometrial biopsy performed, especially if the patient has few ovulatory cycles per year. Although no clear thresholds have been established, patients with three or four or fewer cycles per year should be considered for sampling, even in younger women.

TABLE 1E-12 FIGO Staging of Endometrial Carcinoma

Stage	Definition	Stage at Presentation	Pelvic Nodes	5-Year Survival
I$_A$	Tumor limited to the endometrium	73%	>20%	85%
I$_B$	Growth that has invaded <50% of myometrial thickness			
I$_C$	Growth that has invaded >50% of myometrial thickness			
II$_A$	Endocervical glandular involvement only	11%	20%	65%
II$_B$	Cervical stroma involved			
III$_A$	Invades seroserosal surface of uterus, 6 adnexa, 6 positive washings	13%	35%	40%
III$_B$	Vaginal metastases			
III$_C$	Metastases to pelvic or para-aortic nodes			
IV$_A$	Tumor invasion of bladder and/or bowel	3%	50%	10%
IV$_B$	Distant metastases, including intra-abdominal and/or inguinal lymph nodes			

Histopathology: Degree of Differentiation

Uterine adenocarcinoma should be grouped according to the degree of differentiation as follows:

G1: 5% or less of a solid growth pattern
G2: 6%-50% of a solid growth pattern
G3: More than 50% of a solid growth pattern

From Drife J, Magowan B: *Clinical obstetrics and gynecology*, Philadelphia, 2004, Saunders.

Diseases and Disorders

E

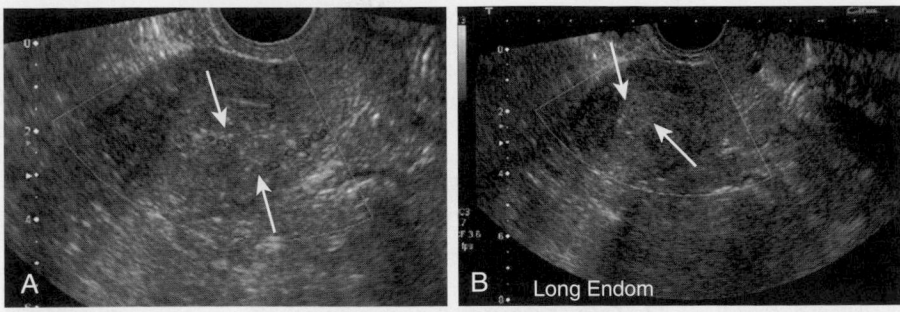

FIGURE 1E-22 A 48-year-old woman with endometrial carcinoma. A, Endovaginal ultrasound (US) showing thickened, heterogeneous, cystic, and vascular hyperechoic tissue filling the endometrial cavity *(arrows)*. **B,** Second, sagittal US image showing the same. (From Fielding JR et al: *Gynecologic imaging*, Philadelphia, 2011, Saunders.)

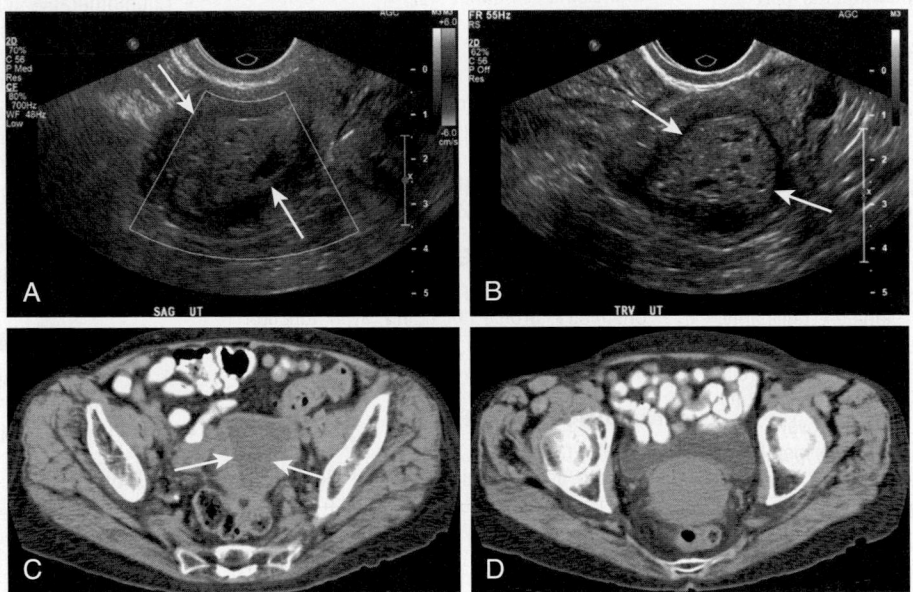

FIGURE 1E-23 A 56-year-old woman with endometrial carcinoma. A, Sagittal ultrasound (US) image showing thickened cystic echogenic soft tissue filling the endometrial cavity *(arrows)*. **B,** Axial US image showing thickened cystic echogenic soft tissue filling the endometrial cavity *(arrows)*. **C,** Non–contrast-enhanced axial computed tomographic (CT) image showing low-attenuation tissue filling the endometrial canal *(arrows)* in a postmenopausal patient. Note fundal thinning. **D,** Non–contrast-enhanced axial CT image showing cervical soft tissue fullness. (From Fielding JR et al: *Gynecologic imaging*, Philadelphia, 2011, Saunders.)

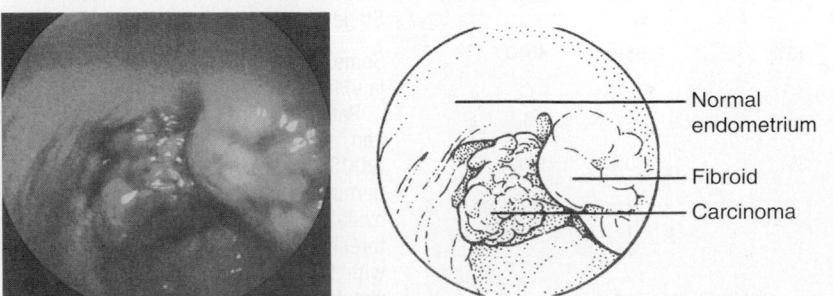

FIGURE 1E-24 Stage I endometrial carcinoma. A small carcinoma can be seen adjacent to a uterine fibroid in this hysteroscopy photograph. Occasionally, a tumor this small may be missed on curettage. (From Skarin AT: *Atlas of diagnostic oncology*, 4th ed, St Louis, 2010, Mosby.)

EVIDENCE

Available at www.expertconsult.com

SUGGESTED READINGS

Available at www.expertconsult.com

RELATED CONTENT

Endometrial Cancer (Patient Information)
Dysfunctional Uterine Bleeding (Related Key Topic)
Uterine Malignancy (Related Key Topic)

AUTHOR: **RUBEN ALVERO, M.D.**

BASIC INFORMATION

DEFINITION

Endometriosis is defined as the presence of functioning endometrial glands and stroma outside the uterine cavity (Fig. 1E-25).

ICD-10-CM CODES
N80.0 Endometriosis of uterus
N80.1 Endometriosis of ovary
N80.2 Endometriosis of fallopian tube
N80.3 Endometriosis of pelvic peritoneum
N80.4 Endometriosis of rectovaginal septum and vagina
N80.5 Endometriosis of intestine
N80.6 Endometriosis in cutaneous scar
N80.8 Other endometriosis
N80.9 Endometriosis, unspecified

EPIDEMIOLOGY & DEMOGRAPHICS

PREVALENCE:
- Endometriosis affects 10% of reproductive-aged women.
- Women with dysmenorrhea: 40% to 60%.
- Subfertile women: 20% to 30%.
- Incidence peaks at approximately 40 yr.

MOST COMMON AGE AT DIAGNOSIS: 25 to 29 yr.

GENETICS:
- Multifactorial inheritance pattern.
- 6.9% occurrence rate in first-degree female relatives.

PHYSICAL FINDINGS & CLINICAL PRESENTATION
- Classic triad is dysmenorrhea, dyspareunia, and infertility.
- Presence of pelvic pain not correlated with the total area of endometriosis, type of lesion, or volume of disease, but is correlated with the depth of infiltration.

- Other symptoms include abnormal bleeding (premenstrual spotting, menorrhagia), cyclic abdominal pain, intermittent constipation/diarrhea, dyschezia, dysuria, hematuria, and urinary frequency.
- Rare manifestations: catamenial hemothorax, bloody pleural effusion, massive ascites occurring during menses.
- Most severe discomfort is associated with lesions >>1 cm in depth.
- Bimanual examination may reveal tender uterosacral ligaments, cul-de-sac nodularity, induration of the rectovaginal septum, fixed retroversion of the uterus, adnexal mass, and generalized or localized tenderness.

ETIOLOGY
- Reflux and direct implantation theory: retrograde menstruation with implantation of viable endometrial cells to surrounding pelvic structures (Sampson's theory).
- Coelomic metaplasia theory: transformation of multipotential cells of the coelomic epithelium into endometrium-like cells.
- Vascular dissemination theory: transport of endometrial cells to distant sites by the uterine vascular and lymphatic systems.
- Autoimmune disease theory: disorder of immune surveillance allows growth of endometrial implants.

DIAGNOSIS

DIFFERENTIAL DIAGNOSIS
- Ectopic pregnancy
- Acute appendicitis
- Chronic appendicitis
- Pelvic inflammatory disease (PID)
- Pelvic adhesions
- Hemorrhagic cyst
- Hernia

- Psychologic disorder
- Irritable bowel syndrome
- Uterine leiomyomata
- Adenomyosis
- Nerve entrapment syndrome
- Scoliosis
- Muscular/skeletal strain
- Interstitial cystitis

WORKUP
- Thorough history and physical examination, including inquiry about physical and emotional abuse. Defining diagnosis of endometriosis can be made only by histology of lesions that have been removed surgically.
- Laparoscopy for definitive diagnosis. (the gold standard).
- Revised American Fertility Society (renamed American Society for Reproductive Medicine) scale to classify endometriosis (since 1985):

Stage I	Minimal
Stage II	Mild
Stage III	Moderate
Stage IV	Severe

LABORATORY TESTS
Cancer antigen 125 (CA125): limited overall value in the diagnosis of endometriosis
- Also elevated in ovarian epithelial neoplasm, myomas, adenomyosis, acute PID, ovarian cysts, pancreatitis, chronic liver disease, menstruation, and pregnancy.
- CA125 value >35 U/ml: positive predictive value of 0.58 and a negative predictive value of 0.96 for the presence of endometriosis.

IMAGING STUDIES
- Ultrasound: for evaluating adnexal mass; ultrasound characteristics may suggest endometriomas versus other benign or malignant ovarian conditions but persistent solid or cystic-solid ovarian masses require definitive tissue diagnosis with laparoscopy.
- MRI:
  1. Highly accurate in detecting endometriomas.
  2. Limited sensitivity in detecting diffuse pelvic endometriosis, especially if sessile lesions.
- CT scan may show adnexal masses of varying density (Fig. 1E-26).

TREATMENT

NONPHARMACOLOGIC THERAPY
Expectant management (observation for 5 to 12 mo) for stage I or stage II endometriosis-associated infertility. Evaluation should take place if the couple meet the diagnostic criteria for infertility.

ACUTE GENERAL Rx
Nonsteroidal anti-inflammatory drugs for symptomatic relief of dysmenorrhea.

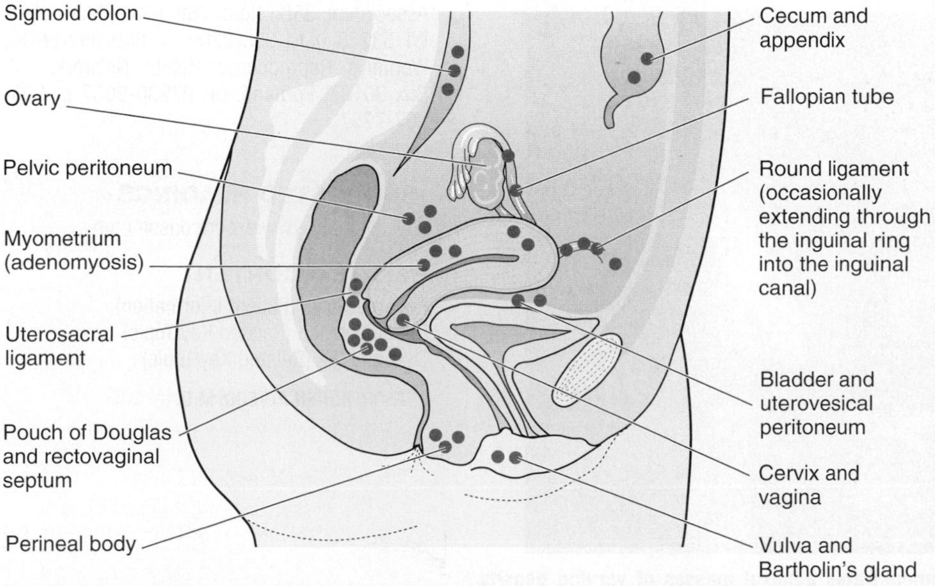

FIGURE 1E-25 Common sites for endometriotic deposits in the pelvis. (From Drife J, Magowan B: *Clinical obstetrics and gynecology,* Philadelphia, 2004, Saunders.)

Sigmoid colon
Ovary
Pelvic peritoneum
Myometrium (adenomyosis)
Uterosacral ligament
Pouch of Douglas and rectovaginal septum
Perineal body

Cecum and appendix
Fallopian tube
Round ligament (occasionally extending through the inguinal ring into the inguinal canal)
Bladder and uterovesical peritoneum
Cervix and vagina
Vulva and Bartholin's gland

CHRONIC Rx

PHARMACOLOGIC MANAGEMENT: Estrogen-progesterone:

- State of "pseudopregnancy" created by continuous (discarding pill pack when placebo pills remaining and starting active pills from new pill pack) use of combination oral contraceptives for minimum of 6 mo and continuing indefinitely.
- Breakthrough bleeding treated by administering conjugated estrogens 1.25 mg/day for 2 wk.

Progestins:

- Medroxyprogesterone acetate 10 to 30 mg orally qd and occasionally up to 100 mg orally qd.
- Alternatively, 100 mg IM q2wk for four doses, followed by 200 mg IM monthly for 4 mo.
- Breakthrough bleeding treated with ethinyl estradiol (20 mcg/day) or conjugated estrogens (1.25 mg/day) for 1 to 2 wk.
- Comparison with danazol: progestins cost less, have a more tolerable side-effect profile, and have comparable efficacy with regard to pain relief and so are often the first-line drug. Very little justification for the use of danazol.

Gonadotropin-releasing hormone (GnRH) agonists:

- Use usually limited to 6-12 mo due to hypoestrogenic effects such as osteopenia or osteoporosis but can be given longer in certain circumstances, particularly when paired with estrogen add-back therapy. Referral to specialist strongly advised.
- Leuprolide acetate depot 3.75 mg IM monthly or 11.25 mg IM q3mo or nafarelin 200 mcg nasal puffs bid or goserelin 3.6 mg SC monthly.
- As effective as danazol for relief of pelvic pain.
- Add-back therapy for protection against vasomotor symptoms and bone loss: norethindrone acetate 5 mg PO qd alone or in combination with conjugated estrogen 0.625 mg orally qd.
- Add-back therapy allows gonadotropin-releasing hormone (GnRH) agonist use to be extended to 1 yr based on limited studies available.

Alternative therapies for inhibition of estrogen action currently under investigation are:

- Aromatase inhibitors: anastrozole, letrozole
- SERM: raloxifene
- Agents enhancing cell-mediated immunity are cytokines (interleukin-12 and interferon-α2b)
- Immunomodulators (loxoribine, levamisole)
- Anti-inflammatory: pentoxifylline

SURGICAL MANAGEMENT: Conservative:

- Directed at enhancing fertility or treating pain unresponsive to first-line medical treatment.
- Usually accomplished through laparoscopy.
- Removal or destruction of endometriotic implants by excision, electrocautery, or laser.
- Cystectomy for endometrioma; must remove cyst wall to be effective long-term.
- Laparoscopic uterosacral nerve ablation for midline pain such as dysmenorrhea or dyspareunia (evidence does not support its use).
- Unless pregnancy is desired, patient is usually started on GnRH agonist therapy or continuous OCP immediately after surgery.
- For those desiring pregnancy, surgery alone results in significant increase in fertility.

Definitive:

- Directed at relieving endometriosis-associated pain.
- Total abdominal hysterectomy with bilateral salpingo-oophorectomy and complete excision or ablation of endometriosis.
- Thorough abdominal exploration to ensure removal of all disease.
- Must be prepared to manage possible gastrointestinal and urinary tract endometriosis.
- 90% effective in pain relief; patient must be counseled that pain relief is not guaranteed.

- Estrogen replacement therapy (ERT) to be considered in all women undergoing definitive surgical management; after ERT, recurrence rate is 0% to 5% in women with endometriosis confined to the pelvis but 18% in women with bowel involvement.
- Concern for malignant degeneration exists in implants if unopposed estrogen is used after definitive surgical therapy.

MANAGEMENT OF ENDOMETRIOSIS-ASSOCIATED INFERTILITY:

Conservative surgery:

- Yields significantly higher pregnancy rate than does expectant management, in part because of correction of mechanical factors such as adhesions.

Assisted reproductive technologies:

- Can be used to circumvent unknown mechanism of endometriosis-associated infertility.
- Superovulation with clomiphene citrate or human menopausal gonadotropins; clomiphene citrate results in threefold pregnancy rate over either danazol or expectant management.
- Further improvement with intrauterine insemination combined with superovulation.
- In vitro fertilization if above procedures are unsuccessful.

DISPOSITION

Tends to recur unless definitive surgery is performed, and should be considered a chronic condition.

REFERRAL

To a reproductive endocrinologist for advanced surgical management or infertility management.

PEARLS & CONSIDERATIONS

COMMENTS

Patient information can be obtained through the following organizations: Endometriosis Association, 8585 North 76th Place, Milwaukee, WI 53223, 414-355-2200 or 800-992-ENDO; Women's Reproductive Health Network, P.O. Box 30167, Portland, OR 97230-9067 or 503-667-7757.

SUGGESTED READINGS

Available at www.expertconsult.com

RELATED CONTENT

Endometriosis (Patient Information)
Dysmenorrhea (Related Key Topic)
Dyspareunia (Related Key Topic)

AUTHOR: **RUBEN ALVERO, M.D.**

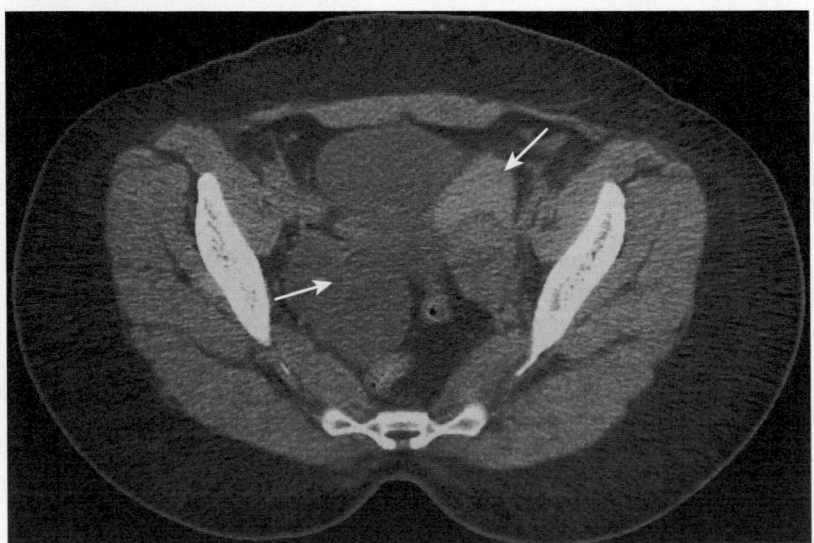

FIGURE 1E-26 Computed tomographic scan demonstrates adnexal masses of varying density, subsequently proven to be endometriomas. (From Fielding JR et al: *Gynecologic imaging,* Philadelphia, 2011, Saunders.)

Diseases and Disorders

 **BASIC INFORMATION**

DEFINITION

Endometritis is defined as a uterine infection after delivery or abortion.

SYNONYMS

Endomyometritis
Metritis

ICD-10CM CODES
085   Puerperal sepsis
086   Other puerperal infections
086.1 Other infection of genital tract following delivery
086.8 Other specified puerperal infections

EPIDEMIOLOGY & DEMOGRAPHICS

- Overall rate of postpartum infection: estimated between 1% and 8%
- Most common genital tract infection after delivery
- Usually presents early in postpartum period; more commonly seen after cesarean section than vaginal delivery; also seen with an incomplete abortion (spontaneous abortion, legal abortion, or illegal abortion)
- More common in preterm deliveries
- Possible after any uterine manipulation in the presence of undiagnosed cervicitis or vaginitis

PHYSICAL FINDINGS & CLINICAL PRESENTATION

- Postpartum oral temperature >37.8° C
- Localized uterine tenderness, purulent or foul lochia; physical examination revealing uterine or parametrial tenderness
- Nonspecific signs and symptoms such as malaise, abdominal pain, chills, and tachycardia

ETIOLOGY

Endometritis is usually associated with multiple organisms: group A or B streptococci, *Staphylococcus aureus* and *Bacteroides* species, *Neisseria gonorrhoeae, Chlamydia trachomatis,* enterococci, *Gardnerella vaginalis, Escherichia coli,* and *Mycoplasma.*

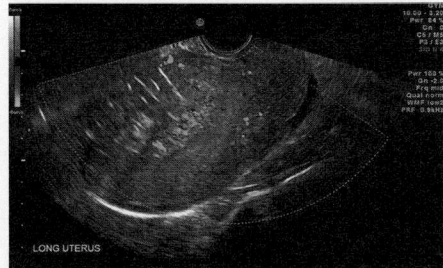

FIGURE 1E-27 Endometritis. Patient with uterine tenderness and fever 7 days after classic cesarean section for premature rupture of membranes, chorioamnionitis, and fundic presentation at 27 weeks' gestational age. Sagittal transvaginal ultrasound shows increased vascularity within the endometrium, which can be seen with endometritis. Linear echogenic foci within the anterior myometrium likely represent air and suture material in the vertical uterine incision. Patient's symptoms resolved with antibiotics. (From Fielding JR et al: *Gynecologic imaging,* Philadelphia, 2011, Saunders.)

DIAGNOSIS

DIFFERENTIAL DIAGNOSIS

Causes of postoperative or postprocedural infections

WORKUP

Diagnosis based on symptoms of fever, malaise, abdominal pain, uterine tenderness, and purulent, foul vaginal discharge.

LABORATORY TESTS

Complete blood count, blood cultures, and uterine culture

IMAGING STUDIES

Ultrasound (Fig. 1E-27) may be useful if retained products are considered a possible source of infection.

TREATMENT

ACUTE GENERAL Rx

Treatment options include doxycycline plus one of the following:
1. Cefoxitin.
2. Ticarcillin-clavulanate.
3. Ertapenem.
4. Imipenem-cilastatin.
5. Meropenem.
6. Ampicillin-sulbactam.
7. Piperacillin-tazobactam.
    An alternative regimen is clindamycin plus aminoglycoside or ceftriaxone.
    Regimen should be continued for at least 48 hr after substantial clinical improvement. If response is not adequate (Table 1E-13), check cultures and treat with appropriate antibiotics.

CHRONIC Rx

Watch for recurrent infection.

DISPOSITION

With appropriate antibiotic therapy, 95% to 98% cure rate.

REFERRAL

For patients who do not respond within 48 to 72 hr of appropriate antibiotic therapy, obtain an infectious disease consultation or gynecologic consultation.

SUGGESTED READINGS
Available online at www.expertconsult.com

AUTHOR: **RUBEN ALVERO, M.D.**

TABLE 1E-13 Identified Causes of Poor Response to Antibiotic Therapy in Patients with Endometritis

Cause	Approximate Prevalence (%)
Infected mass, including abscess, hematoma, septic pelvic thrombophlebitis, pelvic cellulitis, retained placenta	40-50
Resistant organisms, commonly enterococci, in a patient receiving clindamycin-aminoglycoside or a cephalosporin	20
Additional cause, including catheter phlebitis, inadequate dose of antibiotics	10
No cause evident but response to empirical change in antibiotic therapy	20-30

From Gorbach SL: *Infectious diseases,* ed 2, Philadelphia, 1998, Saunders.

BASIC INFORMATION

DEFINITION

Enteropathic arthritis (EA) is a spondyloarthritis that occurs in patients with inflammatory bowel diseases (Crohn's disease [CD] and ulcerative colitis [UC]). It also includes inflammatory arthritis seen in other gastrointestinal diseases such as Whipple's disease, celiac disease, and after intestinal bypass surgery. Arthritis is the most common extraintestinal manifestation of inflammatory bowel diseases (IBDs).

SYNONYM(S)

IBD-related spondyloarthropathy (SpA), enteroarthritis, arthritis associated with gastrointestinal disease

ICD 10-CM CODE(S)

M.07.60	Enteropathic arthropathies, unspecified sites
M.07.69	Enteropathic arthropathies, multiple sites
M.07.68	Enteropathic arthropathies, vertebra
M07.611	Enteropathic arthropathies, right shoulder
M07.612	Enteropathic arthropathies, left shoulder
M07.619	Enteropathic arthropathies, unspecified shoulder
M07.621	Enteropathic arthropathies, right elbow
M07.622	Enteropathic arthropathies, left elbow
M07.629	Enteropathic arthropathies, unspecified elbow
M07.631	Enteropathic arthropathies, right wrist
M07.632	Enteropathic arthropathies, left wrist
M07.639	Enteropathic arthropathies, unspecified wrist
M07.641	Enteropathic arthropathies, right hand
M07.642	Enteropathic arthropathies, left hand
M07.649	Enteropathic arthropathies, unspecified hand
M07.651	Enteropathic arthropathies, right hip
M07.652	Enteropathic arthropathies, left hip
M07.659	Enteropathic arthropathies, unspecified hip
M07.661	Enteropathic arthropathies, right knee
M07.662	Enteropathic arthropathies, left knee
M07.669	Enteropathic arthropathies, unspecified knee
M07.671	Enteropathic arthropathies, right ankle and foot
M07.672	Enteropathic arthropathies, left ankle and foot
M07.679	Enteropathic arthropathies, unspecified ankle and foot
M07.68	Enteropathic arthropathies, vertebrae
M07.69	Enteropathic arthropathies, multiple sites

EPIDEMIOLOGY AND DEMOGRAPHICS

Arthritis occurs in 6% to 46% of patients with IBD. Inflammatory back pain usually presents before the age of 45 yr. Onset of peripheral arthritis is usually between 25 and 45 yr of age.

PREDOMINANT SEX AND AGE: Males and females equally affected. Whereas women more frequently have a peripheral joint involvement, men tend to have an axial involvement (sacroiliac and/or spine joint arthritis).

GENETICS: The presence of HLA-B27 is the strongest association with spondyloarthropathies.

RISK FACTORS:
- Active large bowel disease
- Family history of IBD
- Appendectomy
- Cigarette smoking
- Other extraintestinal manifestations such as erythema nodosum, pyoderma gangrenosum, uveitis, and complicating intestinal manifestations such as abscesses and perianal disease

PHYSICAL FINDINGS & CLINICAL PRESENTATION

- Axial: affects the spine in the form of sacroiliitis with or without spondylitis; can be similar to ankylosing spondylitis or other idiopathic spondyloarthropathies (e.g. psoriatic arthritis, reactive arthritis, undifferentiated SpA).
- Peripheral: affects peripheral joints, predominantly lower limb joints.
- Axial involvement is found more commonly in CD than in UC) The axial disease is independent of IBD activity.
- Peripheral arthritis is the most frequent finding in both CD and UC, equally affecting both sexes.
- Periarticular and other extraintestinal manifestations include enthesitis (inflammation of tendon insertion sites into bone such as Achilles or plantar fascia), dactylitis (flexor tenosynovitis of a finger or toe causing sausage-like swelling of digit), uveitis, psoriasis.
- Main complaints are inflammatory back pain, buttock pain, joint pain (with prolonged morning stiffness and fatigue); symptoms worse with rest or inactivity and improve with exercise.
- Examination reveals evidence of synovitis, progressive limitation of spinal mobility.
- Type 1 arthropathy or pauciarticular (less than five joints): usually acute and self-limited asymmetric inflammatory arthritis; commonly affects large joints of legs such as the knee; occurs early in the course of IBD and commonly parallels the disease activity or flares of IBD.
- Type 2 arthropathy or polyarticular (five or more joints): affects mainly the metacarpophalangeal (MCP) joints; bilateral and symmetric; may be migratory. Symptoms may take a more chronic course, independent of IBD activity.
- Type 3 includes patients with both axial and peripheral forms.

ETIOLOGY

- Theorized that in genetically predisposed individuals with bacterial gut infections, the occurrence of joint inflammation provides an important evidence for a possible relationship between inflammation of the gut mucosa and arthritis.

DIAGNOSIS

DIFFERENTIAL DIAGNOSIS

- Hypertrophic osteoarthropathy
- Osteonecrosis (avascular necrosis)
- Septic arthritis
- Erythema nodosum
- Other idiopathic seronegative spondyloarthropathies
- Behçet's disease
- Rheumatoid arthritis

WORK-UP

- Diagnosis mainly relies on clinical evidence and imaging data. There is no gold standard for diagnosis

LABORATORY TEST(S)

- Laboratory testing: Markers of inflammation such as sedimentation rate and CRP may reflect underlying disease activity of bowel disease and thus may not be useful to track for EA activity. CBC can reveal leukocytosis, anemia, thrombocytosis; suggestive of inflammatory response.
- Synovial fluid is nonspecific; shows mild to marked inflammation: WBC 1500-50,000/mm^3.
- Serologic tests are negative for rheumatoid factor, and antinuclear antibodies (ANA) are absent.

IMAGING STUDIES

- Plain x-ray of the spine and pelvis may appear normal in early disease but with progression may show evidence of sacroiliitis, spondylitis, or ankyloses.
- X-ray of peripheral joints may show soft tissue swelling, periostitis, or joint effusion.
- MRI may be used to assess early changes of spondyloarthritis when plain x-rays are negative. MRI is the most sensitive method of detecting sacroiliitis in IBD patients.
- Musculoskeletal ultrasonography is a noninvasive, safe, and easily reproducible means of detecting early pathological changes in SpA patients. It can identify characteristic features of enthesitis, bone erosions, synovitis, bursitis, and tenosynovitis.

TREATMENT

- Treatment is generally directed toward treating underlying GI illness, which may also improve the associated extraintestinal manifestations.
- The goal of treatment of EA is reducing inflammation to relieve suffering and prevent joint deformity and disability.

NONPHARMACOLOGIC THERAPY

- Rest, physical therapy, and exercise such as swimming

ACUTE GENERAL Rx

- Axial and peripheral arthritis symptoms respond to NSAIDs and physical therapy.
- There has been concern that NSAIDs exacerbate IBD and that NSAID-related adverse events such as ulcers and GI bleeding may mimic IBD flares. COX-2 inhibitors may be preferred to traditional NSAIDs, but similar concerns and cautions apply.
- Intra-articular steroid injections may help treat joint synovitis.
- Systemic steroids can help reduce polyarticular joint and IBD activity but should be used at the lowest effective dose and ideally for only short courses.

CHRONIC Rx

- Immunomodulatory agents such as sulfasalazine, azathioprine, 6-mercaptopurine, methotrexate, and cyclosporine can be used to treat active IBD and peripheral arthritis. Peripheral joint disease responds better to these agents than axial disease.

- TNF inhibitors, particularly infliximab or adalimumab, are useful to treat both arthritis (axial or peripheral) and severe, refractory IBD. Golimumab and certolizumab are also in use for refractory IBD and used for arthritis, but there is no clear data on its use in EA. Etanercept is effective only to control the arthritis but not IBD.
- For highly active IBD, particularly UC, colectomy has been found to ameliorate peripheral joint inflammatory disease but does not influence axial involvement.

REFERRAL

Rheumatology and gastroenterology

⚠ PEARLS & CONSIDERATIONS

- When a single joint is affected, consider joint aspiration to rule out septic arthritis. Signs of infection may be atypical in those receiving anti-inflammatory or immunosuppressive medications.
- Other extraintestinal manifestations of enteropathic arthritis include skin and mucous membrane involvement, anterior uveitis, Hashimoto's thyroiditis, genitourinary involvement (nephrolithiasis), aortic insufficiency, and cardiac conduction abnormalities. These are often seen in patients with prolonged disease activity and with positive HLA-B 27.
- Pyoderma gangrenosum is the most severe skin manifestation in IBD.

RELATED TOPICS

Ankylosing Spondylitis (Related Key Topic)
Psoriatic Arthritis (Related Key Topic)
Ulcerative Colitis (Related Key Topic)
Crohn's Disease (Related Key Topic)

AUTHORS: **CANDICE YUVIENCO, M.D.,** and **OLOLADE JAMES, M.D.**

Diseases and Disorders

I

BASIC INFORMATION

DEFINITION

Enuresis refers to the voiding of urine into clothes or in bed that is either voluntary or involuntary in individuals who are expected to be continent (>5 yr of age). The diagnosis is made if voiding occurs at least twice a week for 3 months. Primary enuresis refers to enuresis without a period of continence, whereas secondary enuresis occurs after a 6-month period of normal bladder control.

SYNONYMS

Urinary incontinence
Bedwetting
Nocturia

ICD-10CM CODES
N39.44 Nocturnal enuresis
F98.0   Enuresis not due to a substance or known physiological condition

EPIDEMIOLOGY & DEMOGRAPHICS

PEAK INCIDENCE: Ages 5 to 10 yr. 5 to 7 million children in the U.S. have enuresis.
PREVALENCE (IN U.S.):
- Age 5 yr: 7% of males and 3% of females.
- Age 10 yr: 3% of males and 2% of females.
- Ages 15 and older: 1% of males and females.
PREDOMINANT SEX: Twice as many males as females at all ages
PREDOMINANT AGE: Highest prevalence at age 5 with a steady decrease thereafter at a rate of approximately 12% to 15% per year
GENETICS:
- Approximately 75% of children with enuresis have a first-degree relative with enuresis.
- Almost twice as common in monozygotic than dizygotic twins.

PHYSICAL FINDINGS & CLINICAL PRESENTATION

Three enuresis subtypes are defined in DSM-5:
- Nocturnal only (also known as monosymptomatic enuresis): occurs in each sleep stage in proportion to the time spent in the particular stage. May occur during transition from deep sleep to REM and is without other lower urinary tract symptoms.

- Diurnal only (also referred to as nonmonosymptomatic or urinary incontinence): more frequent in girls and rarely after age 9 yr; voiding occurs in early afternoon on school days. Within this subtype, individuals have "urge incontinence" with sudden symptoms of urgency and detrusor instability or "voiding postponement" where individuals ignore urges until the point of incontinence.
- Combined nocturnal and diurnal.

ETIOLOGY

- Enuresis often correlates with other maturational delays, particularly language, motor skills, and social development.
- May be related to toilet training issues, stress (secondary enuresis), inability to concentrate urine, altered smooth muscle physiology, small bladder capacity, or dysfunction of the arousal system.
- Diurnal enuresis associated with a higher rate of urinary tract infections.

DIAGNOSIS

DIFFERENTIAL DIAGNOSIS

- The pathophysiology of primary enuresis involves the inability to awaken from sleep in response to full bladder, or a decreased functional capacity of the bladder with possible excessive nighttime urine production.
- May be associated with encopresis and sleep disorders such as sleep terrors; much less likely to be a primary psychological disorder.
- Organic causes of enuresis include diabetes mellitus, diabetes insipidus, bladder outlet obstruction, small bladder capacity, detrusor instability, urethral valves, meatal stenosis, cerebral palsy, spina bifida, pelvic mass, impacted stool, sedating medications, nocturnal seizures, urinary tract infections, kidney disease, hyperthyroidism, pinworms, and obstructive sleep apnea.

WORKUP

- History and physical examination to rule out anatomic abnormalities, look for signs of obstructive sleep apnea. Fluid intake, voiding diaries, and stooling histories may be useful.

Family history of enuresis, particularly for nocturnal enuresis.
- Children frequently experience shame, so gentleness and care must be exercised when questioning or examining the child.
- Observation of voiding stream is useful.

LABORATORY TESTS

- Urinalysis with specific gravity and urine culture if white cells or nitrites to rule out infection.
- Serum studies to rule out diabetes, electrolyte abnormalities, or renal dysfunction.

IMAGING STUDIES

- In complicated cases, or if there is evidence of obstructive sleep apnea, sleep studies may be useful.
- If an anatomic abnormality is suspected, urologic imaging, including voiding cystourethrogram and renal sonogram is possibly indicated: an abdominal x-ray may demonstrate stool retention; MRI of the spine if evidence of abnormalities of lower spine or perineum is found on examination.

TREATMENT

NONPHARMACOLOGIC THERAPY

Behavioral treatment:
- Scheduled voiding to reduce the frequency of enuretic episodes.
- Motivational therapy including sticker or star charts to reward child for dry nights.
- Alarm and pad technique: 66% response rate (compared with 4% of control participants), although about half relapse.
- Punishment for enuresis is not effective.

ACUTE GENERAL Rx

- Desmopressin (DDAVP) administered orally at bedtime significantly reduces the incidence of bedwetting with complete response in 30% of patients and another 40% with dramatic reduction in symptoms. Relapse rate is as high as 70% after discontinuation. Of note, the intranasal preparation is associated with a greater risk for water intoxication and is not recommended.

TABLE 1E-14   Medications for Treatment of Monosymptomatic Nocturnal Enuresis

Generic Name (Trade Name)	Dosage Formulation	Dosage Regimen	Mechanisms of Action	Comments
Desmopressin acetate (DDAVP)	Tablets: 0.1 mg, 0.2 mg	0.2 mg PO qhs, increasing up to 0.4 mg	Decreased urine volume Possible effect on sleep arousal through its action as a central nervous system neurotransmitter	Risk of water intoxication (headache, seizures); hence, limit fluids 1 hr before and 3 hours after the dose Stop treatment during illness or conditions necessitating increased fluid intake
Imipramine hydrochloride (Tofranil)	Tablets: 10 mg, 25 mg, 50 mg; Tofranil PM capsule 75, 100, 125, 150 mg	1.5-2 mg/kg 2 hr before bedtime, not to exceed 50 mg in children less than 12 yr and 75 mg in older children	Anticholinergic effect on bladder Increased resistance of bladder outlet Possible central inhibition of micturition reflex Possible effect on sleep arousal by central noradrenergic facilitation	Can cause sleep disturbance, mood alteration, decreased appetite Risk of cardiac arrhythmia with overdose

Modified from Chandra MM: Enuresis and voiding dysfunction. In Burg FD et al (eds): *Current pediatric therapy*, ed 18, Philadelphia, 2006, Saunders.

Diseases
and Disorders

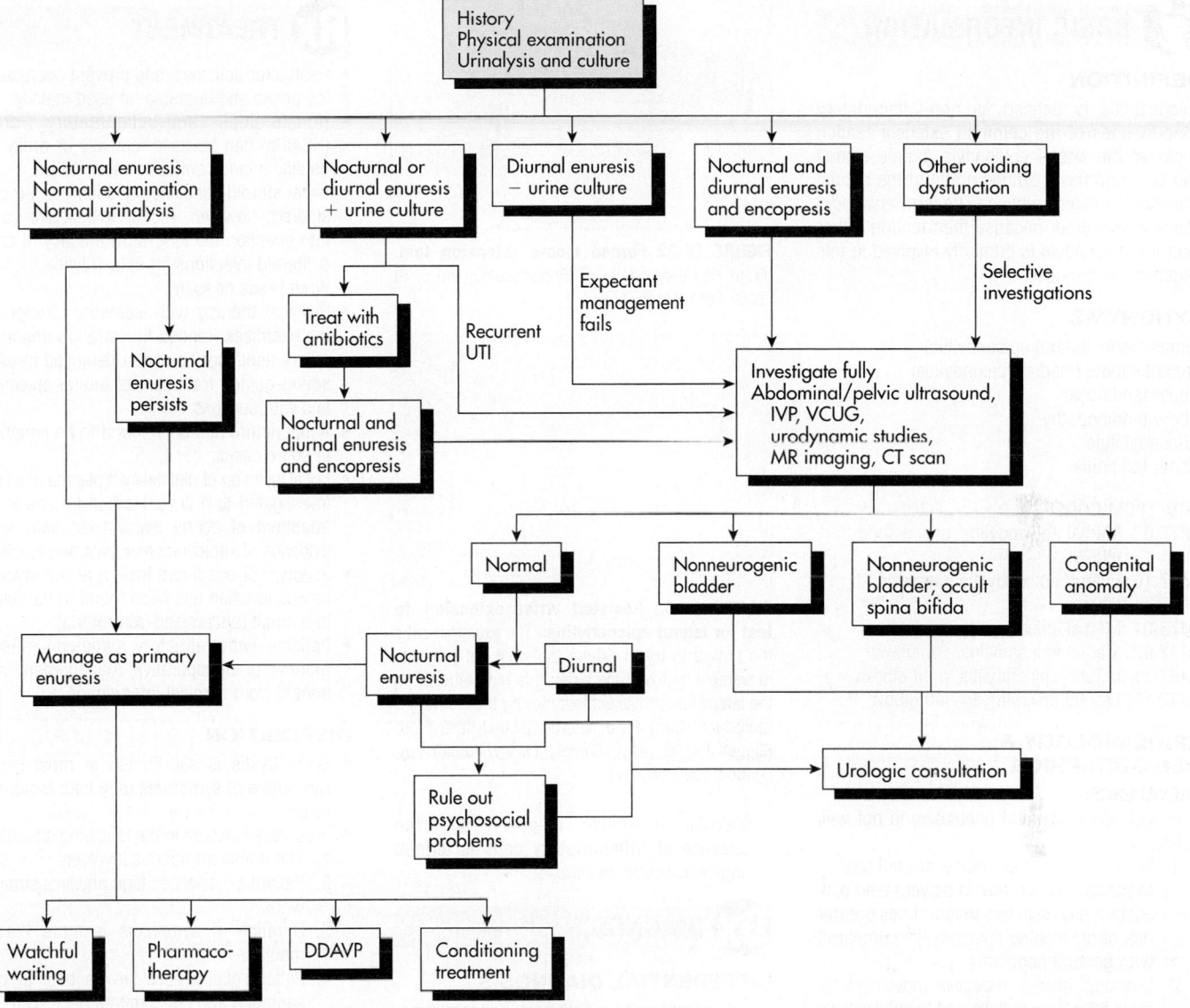

FIGURE 1E-28 Algorithm of management of pediatric enuresis and voiding dysfunction. *CT,* Computed tomography; *DDAVP,* desmopressin acetate; *IVP,* intravenous pyelogram; *MR,* magnetic resonance; *UTI,* urinary tract infection; *VCUG,* voiding cystourethrogram. (From Nseyo UO [ed]: *Urology for primary care physicians,* Philadelphia, 1999, Saunders.)

- Tricyclic antidepressants (imipramine): efficacy supported by randomized control trials. Use with care in children, given the side effect profile.
- Serotonin reuptake inhibitors: lack of adequate trials is notable.
- Indomethacin suppositories may reduce normal prostaglandin inhibitory effects on antidiuretic hormone.
- Table 1E-14 summarizes medications commonly used for treatment of monosymptomatic nocturnal enuresis. Fig. 1E-28 describes an algorithm for management of pediatric enuresis and voiding dysfunction.

DISPOSITION

- After age 5 yr, the rate of spontaneous remissions is approximately 12% to 15% per year.
- The disorder usually resolves by adolescence. However, effective treatment spares considerable misery.
- Fewer than 1% will have enuresis as adults.

REFERRAL

- If coexisting, a psychiatric condition complicates the course of treatment.
- Referral to a pediatric urologist is indicated for primary enuresis refractory to therapy and for selected secondary causes (e.g., urinary tract malformations, neurologic disorders).

! PEARLS & CONSIDERATIONS

Illness, hospitalization, and family stressors may precipitate recurrent enuresis after a period of dryness.

PATIENT & FAMILY EDUCATION

American Academy of Pediatrics www.healthy children.org/English/ages-stages/toddler/toilet-training/Pages/default.aspx

Kidshealth http://kidshealth.org/parent/general/sleep/enuresis.html

SUGGESTED READINGS

Available at www.expertconsult.com

RELATED CONTENT

Bedwetting (Patient Information)

AUTHORS: **MARTA MAJCZAK, M.D.,** and **CATHLEEN ADAMS, M.D.**

BASIC INFORMATION

DEFINITION

Epicondylitis is defined as non-inflammatory abnormalities of the common extensor tendon origin at the lateral epicondyle (tennis elbow) and common flexor tendon origin at the medial epicondyle (golfer's elbow)) The term *epicondylitis* is a misnomer because then tendon rather than the epicondyle is primarily involved in this degenerative process.

SYNONYMS

Tennis elbow (lateral epicondylitis)
Golfer's elbow (medial epicondylitis)
Elbow tendinosis
Elbow tendinopathy
Epicondylalgia
Elbow tendinitis

ICD-10CM CODES

M77.00 Medial epicondylitis, unspecified elbow
M77.10 Lateral epicondylitis, unspecified elbow
M77.01 Medial epicondylitis, right elbow
M77.02 Medial epicondylitis, left elbow
M77.11 Lateral epicondylitis, right elbow
M77.12 Lateral epicondylitis, left elbow

EPIDEMIOLOGY & DEMOGRAPHICS

PREVALENCE:
- Prevalence in general population in not well known.
  1. 90% cases of tennis elbow are not related to playing tennis. Tennis players who play >2 hr a day have two to four times greater risk of developing epicondylitis compared with general population.
  2. Smoking, obesity, repetitive movement for more than 2 hours daily, and forceful activity are risk factors in the general population.
- The lateral side is involved more often than the medial.

PREVALENT AGE AND SEX:
- Affects middle-aged women more often than men.
- More common in individuals 40 to 60 years old.

PHYSICAL FINDINGS & CLINICAL PRESENTATION

- Main symptom is pain in lateral or medial elbow.
  1. Pain is typically related to activity.
  2. Physical examination maneuver to provoke pain: wrist extension against resistance tests for lateral epicondylitis and wrist flexion against resistance for medial epicondylitis. Local tenderness is experienced over the affected epicondyle (Figs. 1E-32 and 1E-33)

ETIOLOGY

- Epicondylitis is thought to be secondary to degeneration, tendinosis, and possibly tendon tear. This process is most often from trauma or overuse.
- Disorganization of normal collagen by invading fibroblasts in association with an immature

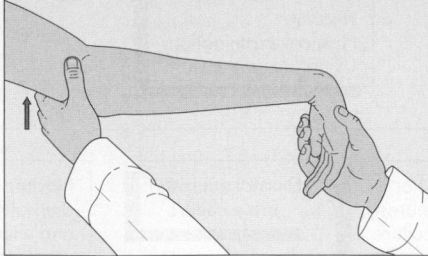

FIGURE 1E-32 Forced elbow extension test. (From Hochberg MC et al: *Rheumatology,* ed 5, St Louis, 2011, Mosby.)

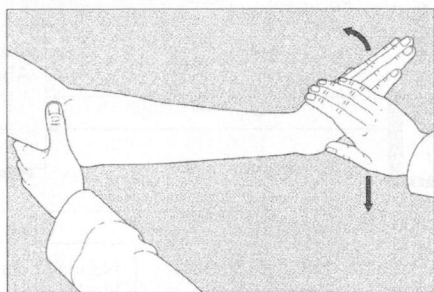

FIGURE 1E-33 Resisted wrist extension to test for lateral epicondylitis. The examiner asks the patient to try to extend the wrist but prevents movement by fixing the wrist; this puts tension on the lateral epicondyle without moving the elbow and reproduces the pain of lateral epicondylitis. (From Klippel J et al [eds]: *Primary care rheumatology,* London, 1999, Mosby.)

vascular reparative response and the **absence of inflammatory cells** is termed *angiofibroblastic tendinosis.*

DIAGNOSIS

DIFFERENTIAL DIAGNOSIS

- Intraarticular elbow pathology (osteoarthritis, osteochondritis dissecans, loose body).
- Radial tunnel syndrome (compression of the posterior interosseous nerve).
- Cubital tunnel syndrome (compression of the median nerve)
- Medial collateral ligament instability
- Valgus extension overload
- Ulnar neuritis
- Tumors
- Avascular necrosis
- Thoracic outlet syndrome
- Cervical radiculopathy

IMAGING STUDIES

- Plain radiography is useful for chronic cases to evaluate for osteoarthritis, exostosis, or other bony abnormalities.
- Musculoskeletal ultrasound (MSK US) may show tendinosis as hypoechoic swelling of involved tendon, possible hyperechoic calcification and bony abnormality. Power or color Doppler signal is variable.
- MRI is the gold standard in detecting epicondylitis. MRI is the most sensitive test, showing tendon thickening and high T2 signal intensity.

TREATMENT

- Rest, alter activities, and prevent overuse.
- Ice packs and heat can be used initially.
- Nonsteroidal anti-inflammatory drugs (NSAIDs) can be used topically or orally but usually provide only short-term relief.
- Local steroid/lidocaine injection can be considered; however, recent trials have called into question the long-term efficacy of corticosteroid injections for epicondylitis.
- Wrist brace or splint.
- Physical therapy with isometric strengthening exercises. Tendon fenestration (tenotomy or dry needling) has been deployed in ultrasound-guided treatment of lateral epicondylitis with success.
- Acupuncture has been found to be beneficial in some cases.
- Local injection of platelet-rich plasma has been investigated to a limited extent for use in the treatment of lateral epicondylitis with some evidence of improvement in pain and function.
- Injection of botulinum toxin A at the myotendinous junction has been found to be helpful in a small randomized-control trial.
- Patients with refractory symptoms after 6 months of nonoperative management may benefit from surgical intervention.

DISPOSITION

- Epicondylitis is self-limited in most cases. Resolution of symptoms may take months to years.
- Prognosis is worse in the following situations:
  1. The dominant hand is involved.
  2. Patient experiences high physical strain at work.
  3. Duration of symptoms is more than 3 months.
  4. Patient experiences severe pain at presentation and concomitant neck pain.

REFERRAL

If symptoms do not respond to injections or a 6-month trial of conservative therapy, surgical referral is appropriate.

PEARLS AND CONSIDERATIONS

The lateral epicondyle may be harder to localize than bony medial epicondyle

EVIDENCE

Available at www.expertconsult.com

SUGGESTED READINGS
Available at www.expertconsult.com

RELATED CONTENT
Golfer's Elbow (Patient Information)
Tennis Elbow (Patient Information)

AUTHOR: **KATARZYNA GILEK-SEIBERT, M.D., Rh.M.S.U.S.**

 **BASIC INFORMATION**

DEFINITION

- Epididymitis is an inflammatory reaction of the epididymis caused by either an infectious agent or local trauma. In most cases of acute epididymitis, the testis is also involved (orchitis).
- Epididymitis is considered chronic if lasting ≥6 wk. Chronic epididymitis has been subcategorized into inflammatory chronic epididymitis, obstructive chronic epididymitis, and chronic epididymalgia.

SYNONYMS

Nonspecific bacterial epididymitis
Sexually transmitted epididymitis

ICD-10CM CODES
N45.1   Epididymitis
A54.00 Gonococcal infection of lower genitourinary tract, unspecified

EPIDEMIOLOGY & DEMOGRAPHICS

INCIDENCE (IN U.S.): Cause of >600,000 visits to physicians per year
PEAK INCIDENCE: Sexually active years
PREDOMINANT SEX: Exclusive to males
PREDOMINANT AGE: All ages affected but usually in sexually active men or older males
CONGENITAL: Congenital urologic structural disorders possibly predisposing to infections

PHYSICAL FINDINGS & CLINICAL PRESENTATION

- Tender swelling of the scrotum with erythema, usually unilateral testicular pain and tenderness
- Dysuria and/or urethral discharge
- Fever and signs of systemic illness (less common)
- Pain and redness on scrotal examination
- Hydrocele or even epididymoorchitis, especially late
- Chronic draining scrotal sinuses with a "beadlike" enlargement of the vas deferens in tuberculous disease

ETIOLOGY

- In young, sexually active men (<35 years of age), the most common infectious agents isolated are *Neisseria gonorrhoeae* and *Chlamydia trachomatis*.
- In older men (>35 years of age) or with underlying urologic disease:
  1. Gram-negative aerobic rods are predominant (i.e., *Escherichia coli*).
  2. Similar organisms are found in men following invasive urologic procedures.
  3. Gram-positive cocci are rarely seen in these groups.
  4. Mycobacteria may also be a cause of epididymitis.
- Acute epididymitis caused by sexually transmitted enteric organisms (e.g., *Escherichia coli*) also occurs among men who are the insertive partner during anal intercourse.
- Young, prepubertal boys may present with epididymitis caused by coliform bacteria; almost always a complication of underlying urologic disease such as reflux.
- In AIDS patients, CMV and *Salmonella* epididymitis have been described. CMV may have a negative urine culture. Toxoplasmosis and *Cryptococcus* should also be considered as a cause of epididymitis in AIDS patients.
- Chronic infectious epididymitis is mostly frequently seen in conditions associated with granulomatous reaction; mycobacterium tuberculosis is the most common granulomatous disease affecting the epididymis.

 **DIAGNOSIS**

DIFFERENTIAL DIAGNOSIS

- Orchitis
- Testicular torsion, trauma, or tumor
- Epididymal cyst
- Hydrocele
- Varicocele
- Spermatocele
- Testicular torsion should be considered in all cases (Table E1E-16).

WORKUP

- Consideration of a full assessment of the urologic tract in patients with bacterial infection, especially if recurrent
- If discharge is present, cultures and Gram stain smear of urethral exudate. Gram stain will demonstrate >5 WBC per oil immersion field.
- In sexually active men: gonococcal cultures of the throat and rectum possibly of value
- If testicular torsion a consideration: radionuclear imaging
- Examination of first void uncentrifuged urine for leukocytes if the urethral Gram stain is negative. Positive leukocyte esterase test on first-void urine or microscopic examination of first-void urine sediment will demonstrate ≥10 WBC per high power field. A culture and Gram-stained smear of this urine specimen should be obtained along with nucleic acid amplification studies (ligase chain reaction [LCR]) from urine samples for gonorrhea and *Chlamydia* spp.
- Imaging with sonogram

LABORATORY TESTS

- All suspected cases of acute epididymitis should be tested for *C. trachomatis* and for *N. gonorrhoeae* by NAAT. Urine is the preferred specimen for NAAT testing.
- Urinalysis and urine culture if dysuria is present or if urinary tract infection is suspected
- HIV testing and counseling
- PPD placed and chest x-ray viewed if TB suspected (rare cases)
- Rarely, biopsy to ensure the diagnosis of tuberculous epididymitis

TREATMENT

ACUTE GENERAL Rx

- Ice packs and scrotal elevation for relief of pain
- Analgesia with acetaminophen with or without codeine or NSAIDs
- Antibiotics to cover suspected pathogens. Empiric therapy is indicated before laboratory test results are available.
- Recommended regimens are ceftriaxone 250 mg IM in a single dose plus doxycycline 100 mg bid for 10 days. For acute epididymitis most likely caused by enteric organisms, treatment options are levofloxacin 500 mg qd × 10 days or ofloxacin 300 mg bid × 10 days. Add ceftriaxone 250 mg IM single dose to levofloxacin or ofloxacin in men who practice insertive anal sex and are suspected to have chlamydia and gonorrhea and enteric organisms.
- Best treatment for older men with gram-negative bacteriuria: ofloxacin 300 mg PO bid for 10 days or levofloxacin 500 mg PO qd for 10 days
- *Pseudomonas* covered by ciprofloxacin PO or IV or cefepime (2 g IV q12h)
- Consider ampicillin-sulbactam, 3rd-generation cephalosporin, ticarcillin-clavulanate, or piperacillin-tazobactam in toxic-appearing patients.
- Surgical aspiration of local abscesses or even open surgical drainage
- Diabetics: especially prone to develop more extensive scrotal infections, including Fournier's gangrene
- Reinforcement of compliance with antibiotics to avoid partial treatment

CHRONIC Rx

- Repair of underlying structural defects is considered especially if infections are severe or recur.
- Surgical repair of reflux in young boys should be undertaken promptly and at a young age when possible.
- Sex partners of patient should be referred for evaluation and treatment.

REFERRAL

- If abscess or chronic structural problems suspected
- If another diagnosis, such as testicular torsion, is suspected

PEARLS & CONSIDERATIONS

- Recurrent epididymitis in sexually active men is usually related to failure to simultaneously treat sexual partners for STDs.
- Recurrent epididymitis in non-sexually active men is generally related to structural-anatomic defects in the genitourinary system or relapsing disease from inadequate initial treatment or antimicrobial resistance.
- Tuberculous epididymitis fails to respond to seemingly adequate antimicrobial therapy even without characteristic radiographic changes on chest films.

SUGGESTED READINGS
Available at www.expertconsult.com

RELATED CONTENT
Epididymitis (Patient Information)

AUTHOR: **PHILIP A. CHAN, M.D., M.S.**

E

Diseases and Disorders

I

BASIC INFORMATION

DEFINITION

Epidural abscess is a suppurative infection of the central nervous system localized between the dura mater and the overlying skull or vertebral column. There are two types of epidural abscess: spinal epidural abscess (SEA) and intracranial epidural abscess (IEA), depending on the location within the central nervous system.

SYNONYMS

Spinal epidural abscess
Intraspinal abscess
Epidural abscess

ICD-10CM CODES
G06.2 Extradural and subdural abscess, unspecified

EPIDEMIOLOGY & DEMOGRAPHICS

INCIDENCE: Spinal epidural abscess: 2 to 25 patients per 100,000 admissions; spinal epidural abscess is 9 times more common than intracranial abscess
PEAK INCIDENCE: Median age at onset of spinal epidural abscess: 50 years old
PREVALENCE: Greatest between 50 and 70 years of age
PREDOMINANT SEX: More common in men
RISK FACTORS: Bacteremia, secondary to distant infection; epidural catheter placement (0.5% to 3% risk), paraspinal injections of glucocorticoids or for pain management, contiguous bone or soft tissue infection, intravenous drug abuse, diabetes, immunosuppressive therapy, HIV

PHYSICAL FINDINGS & CLINICAL PRESENTATION

- Initially nonspecific, such as fever and malaise
- Classic triad: fever, spinal pain, and neurologic deficits are not common
- More commonly:
  1. Localized and significant back pain is present.
  2. Nerve root pain is present ("shooting" or "electrical" from involved nerve root).
  3. Motor weakness, sensory changes, and even paralysis can occur.
  4. Fever may not be a prominent sign.

ETIOLOGY

- Bacteria enter the epidural space most often secondary to hematogenous spread from foci elsewhere in the body (25% to 50% of cases)

or by direct extension from nearby infected tissues such as vertebral body or psoas muscle. A local intervention such as injection can also cause infection.
- Hematogenous foci include furuncles, cellulitis, urinary tract infection, pharyngitis, and pneumonia.
- Microbiology:
  1. *Staphylococcus aureus*, including methicillin-resistant S. *aureus* (MRSA), accounts for 50% to 90% of cases.
  2. Aerobic and anaerobic streptococci account for 8% to 17% of cases.
  3. Aerobic gram-negative rods (*Escherichia coli* and *Pseudomonas*) account for 10% to 17% of cases.
  4. Coagulase-negative staphylococci can be seen with spinal procedures.

DIAGNOSIS

DIFFERENTIAL DIAGNOSIS

- Disc and degenerative bone disease
- Metastatic tumors
- Vertebral discitis and osteomyelitis

WORKUP

Includes a combination of physical exam with neurologic evaluation, blood work, and radiographic studies

LABORATORY TESTS

- Blood cultures
- Culture of fluid or pus by CT-guided aspiration if possible
- Erythrocyte sedimentation rate and/or C-reactive protein
- CBC with differential

IMAGING STUDIES

- MRI with gadolinium is the diagnostic test of choice and imperative if diagnosis is considered.
- CT is an alternative but not as good as MRI for visualizing spinal cord and epidural space.
- CT myelography can be performed if MRI is not available.

TREATMENT

NONPHARMACOLOGIC THERAPY

- Immediate surgery is required if neurologic deficits occur or the patient worsens with medical therapy.
- CT-guided aspiration of abscess with antimicrobial therapy is an alternative treatment to surgery for patients without neurologic deficits.

ACUTE GENERAL Rx

- Empiric antibiotic regimen should include antibiotics effective against staphylococci (including MRSA), streptococci, and gram-negative rods.
- Examples are vancomycin (30 to 60 mg/kg daily divided in q12h doses adjusted for creatinine clearance *plus* metronidazole (500 mg IV q8h) *plus* ceftriaxone (2 g IV q12h) or ceftazidime (2 g IV q8h) if *Pseudomonas* is suspected.
- If cultures reveal methicillin-sensitive S. *aureus*, use nafcillin 2 g IV q4h.

CHRONIC Rx

Antimicrobial therapy tailored to culture results may have to be continued for 4 to 6 weeks depending on whether or not there was surgical or CT-guided drainage. If osteomyelitis is suspected, treat for 6 to 8 weeks.

DISPOSITION

- Mortality rates vary from 5% to 32%. Irreversible paralysis can affect 4% to 22% of patients.
- Complete recovery is more likely if neurologic signs are present less than 24 hours before the start of treatment.
- Final functional capacity may continue to improve for up to 1 year after the end of treatment.

REFERRAL

- Neurosurgery should be involved early when this diagnosis is considered.
- Refer to an interventional radiologist for possible aspiration.
- An infectious diseases evaluation is needed for antimicrobial therapy.

PEARLS & CONSIDERATIONS

COMMENTS

It is important to think of spinal epidural abscess early to permit early treatment and prevent permanent neurologic deficits.

SUGGESTED READINGS
Available at www.expertconsult.com

RELATED CONTENT
Abscess, Brain (Related Key Topic)

AUTHOR: **GLENN G. FORT, M.D., M.P.H.**

BASIC INFORMATION

DEFINITION

Epidural hematoma (EDH) is the accumulation of blood in the potential space surrounding the brain, between the dura mater and the inner surface of the skull.

SYNONYMS

Extradural hematoma/hemorrhage
EDH

ICD-10CM CODES

S06.4	Epidural hemorrhage
I62.1	Non-traumatic extradural hemorrhage
S06.4X0A	Epidural hemorrhage without loss of consciousness, initial encounter
S06.4X1A	Epidural hemorrhage with loss of consciousness of 30 minutes or less, initial encounter
S06.4X9A	Epidural hemorrhage with loss of consciousness of unspecified duration, initial encounter

EPIDEMIOLOGY & DEMOGRAPHICS

INCIDENCE: Exact incidence is unknown; however, it is found in 1% to 4% of traumatic head injury cases and 5% to 15% of autopsy series.
PREDOMINANT SEX AND AGE: Male > female
PEAK INCIDENCE: Peak incidence is among adolescents and young adults. It is rarely found in patients older than 50-60 years old.
GENETICS: There is a role for genetics in spontaneous (nontraumatic) EDH caused by coagulopathies and vascular malformations.
RISK FACTORS: Head trauma, especially in cases involving skull fracture.

PHYSICAL FINDINGS & CLINICAL PRESENTATION

- History of head trauma is present.
- Signs and symptoms vary depending on severity.
- Symptoms: altered mental status, nuchal rigidity, headache, drowsiness, confusion, aphasia, photophobia, and paralysis
- Signs: transient loss of consciousness, followed by a "lucid interval" in 47% of cases, in which the patient is free of any neurologic signs or symptoms. This is followed by clinical deterioration including, vomiting, lethargy, confusion, or seizures. Other signs include focal neurologic deficits such as paralysis of limbs, unequal pupils, and coma. Signs of increased intracranial pressure could be found including the Cushing reflex of hypertension, bradycardia, and respiratory distress. External signs of skull fracture—lacerations, ecchymoses, cerebrospinal fluid (CSF) rhinorrhea or otorrhea—may be observed. Skull fractures can be found in 75% to 95% of EDH patients.

ETIOLOGY

- Traumatic: commonly caused by arterial injury (the middle meningeal artery) (Fig. 1E-34) but may also be injury of the anterior meningeal artery, a dural arteriovenous (AV) fistula at the vertex, or from venous bleeding
- Nontraumatic: caused by an infection/eroding abscess, coagulopathy, hemorrhagic tumors, vascular malformations, postsurgical procedures, and in special populations (e.g., pregnant women, patients receiving hemodialysis)

DIAGNOSIS

DIFFERENTIAL DIAGNOSIS

In the setting of head trauma: subdural hematoma, subarachnoid hemorrhage, cerebral contusion, brain laceration, diffuse brain swelling

WORKUP

- Imaging is the mainstay of diagnosis.
- Serial head CT is the test most commonly used due to its simplicity, widespread use, and availability. Typical appearance is a "lens shaped," or "lentiform" hyperdensity (Fig. 1E-35). Box 1E-5 describes CT findings of EDH.
- Note: Head CT is not conclusive in 8% of cases possibly due to severe anemia, early scanning (before blood has time to accumulate), and severe hypotension.
- Brain MRI: more sensitive. Indicated in situations in which there is a strong clinical suspicion but no evidence of EDH on head CT (Fig. 1E-36).
- Angiography: rarely necessary but may be used to evaluate an underlying vascular lesion.
- NOTE: lumbar puncture (LP) is contraindicated in EDH due to risk of brain stem herniation.

LABORATORY TESTS

- Laboratory tests are helpful as adjunct to diagnosis but are not the mainstay of diagnosis or treatment.
- CBC may be helpful to evaluate for anemia, although in an acute onset of bleeding, hemoglobin levels can be normal.

- Other tests: renal functions, electrolytes, liver functions, INR may be helpful depending on the case scenario.

TREATMENT

Acute symptomatic EDH is a neurologic emergency that requires surgical treatment to prevent permanent brain injury.

NONPHARMACOLOGIC THERAPY

- Immediate surgical decompression, ideally within 1-2 hr after traumatic event
- Craniotomy and hematoma evacuation is the treatment of choice. When indicated, identify and ligate the bleeding vessel.

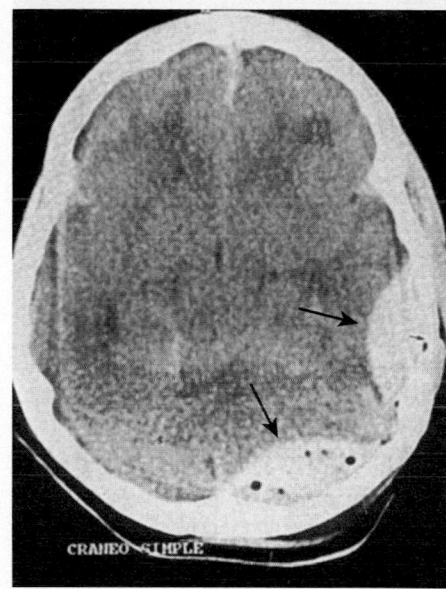

FIGURE 1E-35 Head CT showing two epidural hematomas in 23-year-old involved in a motor vehicle accident. Note air bubbles that are a result of linear fracture in the left temporal bone *(short arrow)*.

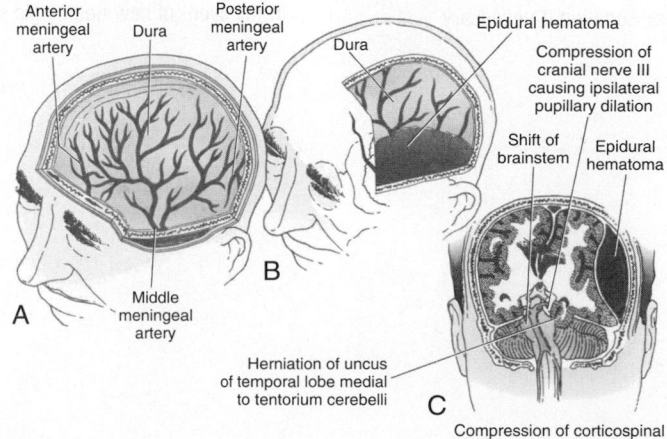

FIGURE 1E-34 Epidural hematoma is typically caused by trauma resulting in laceration of the middle meningeal artery. **A,** The middle meningeal artery. The typical traumatic epidural hematoma is caused by a laceration of this vessel. **B** and **C,** A linear fracture of the squamous portion of the temporal bone has torn the middle meningeal artery, which has resulted in an epidural hematoma. (From Rothrock, JC: Neurosurgery. In Rothrock, JC (ed): *Alexander's care of the patient in surgery*, 13th edition, Philadelphia, 2007, Elsevier.)

Diseases and Disorders

BOX 1E-5 CT Findings of Epidural Hematoma

- CT appearance: variable white to gray on brain windows
- Location: peripheral to brain, variable but usually temporal region
- Shape: biconvex disc or lens
- Pearl: does not cross suture lines
- White swirl sign means active bleeding

- Significance: may cause mass effect and herniation
- Look for midline shift
- Look for effacement of ventricles and sulci
- Surgical indications: 15-mm thickness or 5-mm midline shift

From Broder JS: *Diagnostic imaging for the emergency physician*, Philadelphia, 2011, Saunders.

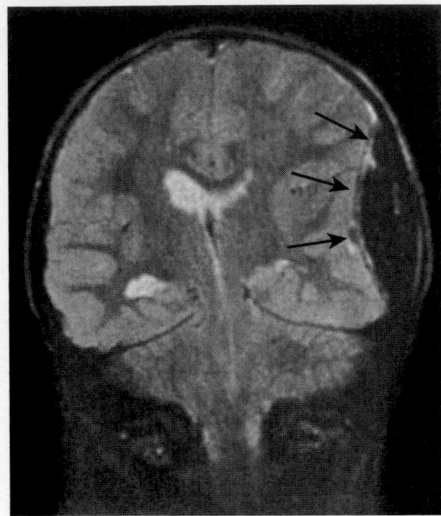

FIGURE 1E-36 Epidural hematoma on MRI. Coronal T2-weighted images show hypointense biconvex extraaxial collection in the left temporal region.

- Burr hole evacuation: this involves drilling a hole in the skull to evacuate the hematoma. It is a lifesaving procedure that is indicated if surgical expertise is limited.

ACUTE GENERAL Rx

- Cardiopulmonary resuscitation and assessment for disability.
- Medical resuscitation maneuvers: head elevation, hyperventilation, monitoring of vital signs and avoidance of hypotension and hyperthermia, sedation if necessary.

- Medications: osmotic diuresis with IV mannitol, cerebrosedating medications, antiepileptics may be used to treat or, in some situations, prevent seizures. The patient should also be started on a proton pump inhibitor to decrease risks of developing an upper gastrointestinal bleed.
- Reversing anticoagulation should be weighed in terms of advantages versus disadvantages.
- NOTE: glucocorticoid therapy is *not* indicated following head injury and may be related to increased mortality.
- Evaluation for surgery: the best available evidence points toward advantages of decompression procedures. Nonoperative treatment may only be indicated if the patient has no symptoms, no focal neurologic deficit, no coma (Glasgow coma score >8), and EDH volume is less than 30 ml by CT scan, with clot thickness <15 mm and midline shift of less than 5 mm.
- Nonoperative treatment involves close monitoring, hourly neurologic checks, and serial head CT scans.

CHRONIC Rx

- There is a risk of permanent brain damage whether the disorder is treated or not. Most recovery occurs in the first 6 months with some improvement over 2 years.
- Children have a tendency to recover more quickly.
- Patients should be educated on rehabilitative exercises and to alert medical professionals in the event of new neurologic symptoms.

- Support and encouragement to patient and family should always be provided.

REFERRAL

Neurosurgery should be the first service consulted. If not available, then general surgery needs to be called. Clinical nurse practitioners, pastoral care staff, and social workers to help patients and families are also appropriate.

- Acute symptomatic EDH is a neurologic emergency.
- EDH should be suspected in any patient with a history of blow to the head leading to a period of loss of consciousness.
- Initial resuscitation is extremely important, but surgery is the mainstay of treatment for acute symptomatic EDH.

PREVENTION

Should be directed toward preventing head trauma: use of appropriate safety equipment (e.g., helmets, hard hats, safe driving, avoiding diving into unknown depths)

PATIENT/FAMILY EDUCATION

Online head injury support groups are helpful: www.headinjury.com/linktbisup.htm, www.headinjury.com/,www.dailystrength.org/c/Brain-Injury/support-group.

SUGGESTED READINGS

Available at www.expertconsult.com

AUTHOR: **SCOTT M. SOUTHER, M.D.**

E

DEFINITION

Epiglottitis is a rapidly progressive cellulitis of the epiglottis and adjacent soft tissue structures with the potential to cause abrupt airway obstruction, which can be life-threatening.

SYNONYMS

Supraglottitis
Cherry-red epiglottitis

ICD-10CM CODES
J05.1 Acute epiglottitis

EPIDEMIOLOGY

INCIDENCE (IN U.S.): Due to vaccination against *Haemophilus influenzae* type B, this is a rare infection in children estimated at between 0.6 to 0.8 per 100,000 in one study and for adults at 1.6 per 100,000.
PEAK INCIDENCE: Now highest in children ages 6 to 12
PREDOMINANT SEX: Males

PHYSICAL FINDINGS & CLINICAL PRESENTATION

- Irritability, fever, dysphonia, and dysphagia.
- Respiratory distress, with child tending to lean up and forward.
- Often, drooling or oral secretions.
- Often, presence of tachycardia and tachypnea.
- On visualization, edematous and cherry-red epiglottis.
- Often, no classic barking cough as seen in croup.
- Possibly fulminant course (especially in children), leading to complete airway obstruction.

ETIOLOGY

- In children, *Haemophilus influenzae* type b, still most common cause but now rare due to vaccination *Streptococcus pyogenes,* (group A Streptococcus) *Streptococcus pneumoniae, Staphylococcus aureus* (includes MRSA).

- In adults, *Streptococcus pyogenes* (group A Streptococcus), *H. influenzae* (can be isolated from blood and/or epiglottis [about 26% of cases]).
- Pneumococci, streptococci, and staphylococci are also implicated.
- Role of viruses in epiglottitis unclear.

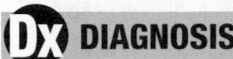 **DIAGNOSIS**

DIFFERENTIAL DIAGNOSIS

- Croup (Table E1E-17)
- Angioedema
- Retropharyngeal or peritonsillar abscess
- Diphtheria
- Foreign body aspiration
- Lingual tonsillitis
- Bacterial tracheitis

WORKUP

- Cultures of blood and urine.
- Lateral neck radiograph to show an enlarged epiglottis, ballooning of the hypopharynx, and normal subglottic structures (Fig. 1E-37).
  1. Radiographs are of only moderate sensitivity and specificity and take time to perform.
  2. Visualization of the epiglottis may be safer in adults than in children.
- Cultures of the epiglottis.

LABORATORY TESTS

- CBC: may reveal a leukocytosis with a shift to the left.
- Chest radiograph examination: may reveal evidence of pneumonia in close to 25% of cases.
- Cultures of blood, urine, and the epiglottis, as noted previously.

 **TREATMENT**

ACUTE GENERAL Rx

- Maintenance of adequate airway is critical. Fig. E1E-38 describes the optimal assessment and management of upper airway

obstruction caused by epiglottitis or severe croup. It is crucial to have a tracheostomy set "at bedside."
- Early placement of an endotracheal or nasotracheal tube in a child is advised.
- Closely follow the adult patient, if no signs of airway obstruction, and defer intubation.
- In children, visualization and intubation are best done in the most controlled environment.
- *H. influenzae* in children is much less common in large part due to the HIB vaccine.

Empiric antibiotics:
1. **In children:** use cefotaxime 50 mg/kg IV q8h or ceftriaxone 50 mg/kg IV q24h *plus* vancomycin for its coverage of MRSA. If penicillin allergy, use levofloxacin 10 mg/kg IV q24h *plus* clindamycin 7.5 mg/kg IV q6h.
2. **In adults:** ceftriaxone 2 g IV q24h or cefotaxime *plus* vancomycin.
3. If possible, obtain cultures before initiating antibiotics.
4. If there is an unvaccinated child for *H. influenzae* at home (or in a day care center) who is >4 yr and living with an index case, give close family contacts of the patient (including adults) rifampin 20 mg/kg/day for 4 days (up to 600 mg/day) for prophylaxis.
5. Role of epinephrine or corticosteroids in the management of epiglottitis is not firmly established.

DISPOSITION

Invasive *H. influenzae* infections and epiglottitis are reportable illnesses; this may be particularly important in recognizing an outbreak in a day care center with unvaccinated children.

REFERRAL

- Close cooperation between the pediatrician or internist, anesthesiologist, and otorhinolaryngologist, especially when epiglottis is visualized and when the patient requires endotracheal intubation.
- Best managed in a critical care setting or ICU.

 **PEARLS & CONSIDERATIONS**

The incidence of epiglottitis has diminished markedly since the introduction of the conjugate vaccine against *H. influenzae* serotype B into routine childhood immunization.

SUGGESTED READINGS
Available at www.expertconsult.com

RELATED CONTENT
Epiglottitis (Patient Information)

AUTHOR: **GLENN G. FORT, M.D., M.P.H.**

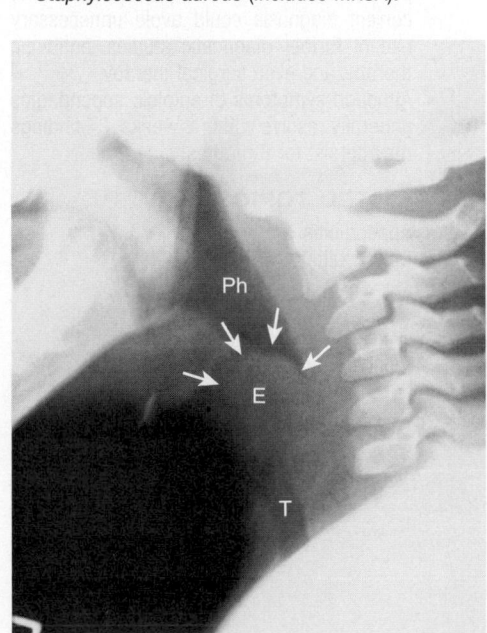

FIGURE 1E-37 Epiglottitis. A lateral soft tissue view of the neck shows a ballooned pharynx *(Ph)* with swollen epiglottis *(E)* in the shape of a large thumbprint *(arrows). T,* Trachea. (From Mettler FA [ed]: *Primary care radiology,* Philadelphia, 2000, Saunders.)

Diseases and Disorders

I

BASIC INFORMATION

DEFINITION

Epiploic appendagitis is an ischemic infarction of an epiploic appendage caused by the torsion or spontaneous thrombosis of the epiploic appendage central draining vein. Epiploic appendages are fat-containing, peritoneum-bounded sites containing blood vessels that extend from the serosa of the colon. They vary in size from 5 mm to 5 cm and occur throughout the colon but are most numerous in the sigmoid colon. Epiploic appendagitis is usually a benign self-limited condition but can mimic other causes of acute abdomen such as diverticulitis or acute appendicitis.

SYNONYM(S)

Appendicitis epiploica
Epiplopericolitis
Hemorrhagic epiploitis
Appendagitis

ICD-10CM CODES

K55.0 Acute vascular disorders of the intestine

EPIDEMIOLOGY & DEMOGRAPHICS

INCIDENCE: Reported in 2% to 7% of patients suspected of diverticulitis and 0.3% to 1% of patients suspected of appendicitis.
PEAK INCIDENCE: Reported age range of 12 to 82 yr with a peak incidence in the fifth decade of life
PREDOMINANT SEX AND AGE: Four times higher in men than women
RISK FACTORS: Obesity and strenuous exercise

PHYSICAL FINDINGS & CLINICAL PRESENTATION

- Patients present with acute or subacute onset of lower abdominal pain.
- Pain is left sided in 60% to 80% of cases and is nonmigratory, but worsens with cough and abdominal stretching.
- Less frequent are nausea and vomiting, low grade fever, diarrhea, and bloating.
- Patients do not appear acutely ill, rebound tenderness is not common, and a mass is only palpable in 10% to 30% of patients.

ETIOLOGY

- Epiploic appendage: small, fat-filled, serosa-covered sacs, attached on the external surface of the colon by vascular stalks, from cecum to rectosigmoid junction. There are about 50 to 100 of these, they measure 1 to 2 cm thick and 2 to 5 cm long, and they may serve as a protective and defensive mechanism
- Primary epiploic appendagitis: ischemic infarction of an epiploic appendage either by torsion or spontaneous thrombosis of the epiploic appendage central draining vein, causing vascular occlusion and focal inflammation
- Secondary epiploic appendagitis: inflammation of the epiploic appendage is caused by an external process such as diverticulitis, appendicitis, pancreatitis, or cholecystitis

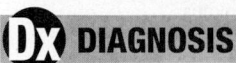

DIAGNOSIS

DIFFERENTIAL DIAGNOSIS

- Appendicitis
- Diverticulitis
- Ovarian torsion, ovarian cyst rupture, ectopic pregnancy
- Secondary epiploic appendagitis: pancreatitis, and cholecystitis are predisposing conditions

WORKUP

- Physical exam, bloodwork and radiology

LABORATORY TEST(S)

- CBC, ESR, C-reactive may be normal or mildly elevated

IMAGING STUDIES

- Abdominal CT: characteristic finding of round or ovoid lesions of fatty density measuring 1.5 to 3 cm in diameter with a hyperattenuating rim (Fig. 1E-39) and ill-defined fat stranding are seen in mesenteric fat adjacent to the colon. At times the thrombosed vein can be seen as a high attenuated dot within the appendage.
- Abdominal ultrasound: At the site of maximum tenderness, a noncompressible hyperechoic small ovoid or round solid mass of adipose tissue is identified between the colon and abdominal wall.

TREATMENT

PHARMACOLOGIC THERAPY

- Ibuprofen: 600 mg po q 8 hr for 4 to 6 days
- Opiates for pain for 4 to 6 days if needed

ACUTE GENERAL Rx

- Epiploic appendagitis is usually a self limited, benign condition lasting 3 to 14 days.

DISPOSITION

- Patients usually do not require hospitalization or antibiotics.
- Recurrence rates are low.

REFERRAL

- Surgery is only required for patients who do not improve or who have a complication such as abscess or bowel obstruction.

PEARLS & CONSIDERATIONS

- It is important to consider this entity in patients with abdominal pain because the correct diagnosis could avoid unnecessary use of further diagnostic studies, antibiotic therapy, and even surgical therapy.
- Although symptoms of epiploic appendagitis generally resolve within 2 weeks, CT findings may persist for 6 months.

RELATED TOPICS

- Appendicitis
- Diverticulitis

SUGGESTED READINGS

Available at www.expertconsult.com

AUTHOR: **GLENN G. FORT, M.D., M.P.H.**

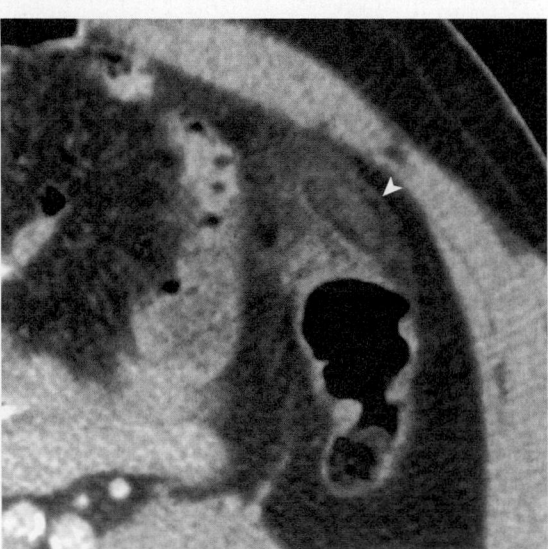

FIGURE 1E-39 Epiploic appendagitis. Axial computed tomography shows a pericolonic focus of inflammation enveloping a focus of fat (*arrowhead*). This finding is characteristic of epiploic appendagitis. (From Webb WR, Brant WE, Major NM: *Fundamentals of body CT*, ed 4, Philadelphia, 2015, Saunders.)

BASIC INFORMATION

DEFINITION

Episcleritis is an inflammation of the episclera (Fig. 1E-40), the thin layer of vascular elastic tissue between the sclera and conjunctiva.

ICD-10CM CODES
H15.1 Episcleritis

EPIDEMIOLOGY & DEMOGRAPHICS

INCIDENCE (IN U.S.): Relatively rare in an ophthalmologic practice.
PEAK INCIDENCE: Most common in middle and old age.
PREDOMINANT SEX: None.
PREDOMINANT AGE: 40s.

PHYSICAL FINDINGS & CLINICAL PRESENTATION

- Red, vascular injection of conjunctiva with engorged and enlarged blood vessels beneath the conjunctiva (Fig. 1E-41).
- Pain in area of inflammation that is usually localized (severe pain suggests deeper inflammation, see Scleritis).
- Can be diffuse or nodular inflammation.

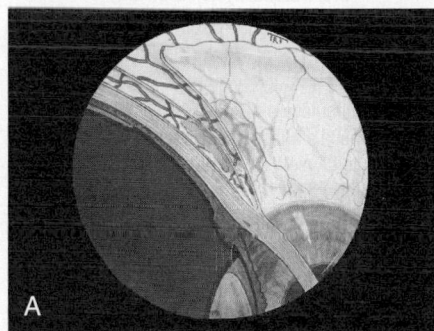

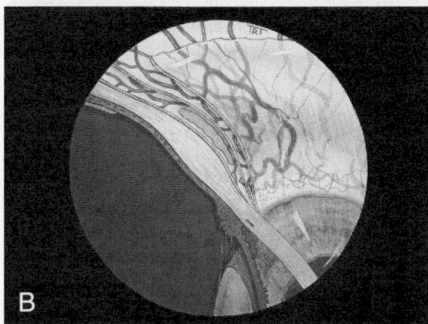

FIGURE 1E-40 A, Episcleritis with maximal vascular congestion of the superficial episcleral plexus; **B,** scleritis with scleral thickening and maximal vascular congestion of the deep vascular plexus. (From Kanski JJ, Bowling B: *Clinical ophthalmology, a systematic approach,* ed 7, Philadelphia, 2010, Saunders.)

ETIOLOGY

Associated with collagen-vascular diseases, vasculitis, trauma; usually idiopathic

 **DIAGNOSIS**

DIFFERENTIAL DIAGNOSIS

- Acute glaucoma.
- Conjunctivitis and blepharoconjunctivitis.
- Scleritis.
- Subconjunctival hemorrhage.
- Congenital or lymphoid masses.
- The differential diagnosis of "red eye" is described in Section II.
- Table 1E-18 compares immunologic diseases of the eye.

WORKUP

Eye examination, general check-up for collagen-vascular disease or other autoimmune diseases.

LABORATORY TESTS

Studies for collagen-vascular disease (e.g., ANA, ESR, RF).

 **TREATMENT**

NONPHARMACOLOGIC THERAPY
Warm compresses.

ACUTE GENERAL Rx

- Topical steroids, 1% prednisolone if no glaucoma; nonsteroidal eye drops if there is a tendency for glaucoma.
- Nonsteroidal anti-inflammatory drugs (NSAIDs): treat underlying systemic disease.

CHRONIC Rx

NSAID eye drops (diclofenac eye drops, ketorolac ophthalmic solution).

DISPOSITION

Close follow up needed.

REFERRAL

To ophthalmologist if patient unresponsive to treatment after a few days.

 **PEARLS & CONSIDERATIONS**

COMMENTS

- Can rarely be associated with collagen-vascular disease.
- Episcleritis has tendency to recur.
- May occur with systemic autoimmune disease. Workup for autoimmune disease is often negative, more likely with scleritis (50%). Ask about other symptoms to find autoimmune disorders, helps to guide workups.
- Episcleritis is a benign and self-limiting condition; loss of vision only occurs with steroid-induced cataracts. Prolonged topical steroid treatment is worse than the condition itself.

SUGGESTED READINGS
Available at www.expertconsult.com

RELATED CONTENT
Episcleritis (Patient Information)

AUTHOR: **R. SCOTT HOFFMAN, M.D.**

Diseases and Disorders

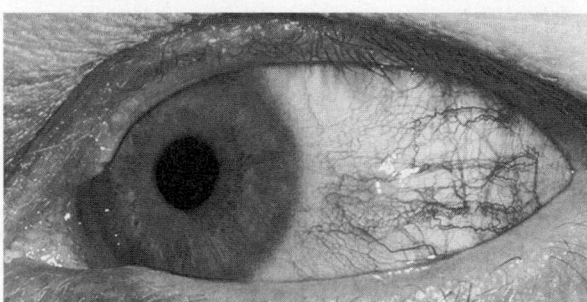

FIGURE 1E-41 Nodular episcleritis in a patient with gout. (From Palay D [ed]: *Ophthalmology for the primary care physician,* St Louis, 1997, Mosby.)

TABLE 1E-18 Immunologic Diseases of the Eye

Disease	Clinical Parameters	Signs/Symptoms	Treatment
Ocular cicatricial pemphigoid	Systemic pemphigoid Females predominate Peak incidence: 60-70 yr of age	Severe conjunctival redness Chronic conjunctivitis Mucous discharge Conjunctival scarring Inturning eyelids and eyelashes Breakdown of corneal and conjunctival epithelium Sight threatening	*Mild*: Dapsone *Severe*: Systemic steroids Immunosuppressive drugs
Peripheral ulcerative keratitis	*Mild*: Both females and males affected Any age Example: associated with staphylococcal blepharitis *Necrotizing*: Mooren ulcer Both females and males affected Adults Unilateral involvement (worldwide) Bilateral involvement (males of African descent) History of infectious ocular disease History of rheumatic disease	*Mild*: Pain Photophobia Tearing Redness Peripheral infiltrate on ocular exam Not sight-threatening *Necrotizing*: Pain Photophobia Tearing Redness Perilimbal ulceration Sight-threatening	*Mild*: Topical steroids and antibiotics *Necrotizing*: Topical steroids Systemic steroids and other immunosuppressive drugs Surgical intervention
Episcleritis	Females predominate Peak incidence: 40 yr of age	Conjunctival redness Diffuse or nodular Minimal pain Not sight threatening	Cool compress Treat associated blepharitis Artificial tears Topical NSAIDs Topical steroids
Scleritis	Females predominate Peak incidence: 40 yr of age; rare in children *Anterior scleritis*: diffuse, nodular, necrotizing *Posterior scleritis*: Scleritis associated with systemic disease, rarely with ocular infection (40%)	*Anterior scleritis*: Deep, boring pain Diffuse ocular redness Raised nodules Scleral ulceration *Necrotizing scleritis*: Sight threatening *Posterior scleritis*: Pain with eye movement Sight threatening	Topical steroids ineffective Periocular steroid injection acceptable Oral NSAIDs, systemic steroids, immunosuppressive drugs
Uveitis	Associated with systemic and infectious disease (40%) All ages Occurrence rates: *Anterior uveitis*: 70% *Intermediate uveitis*: 20% *Posterior uveitis*: 10%	*Anterior*: Redness Pain Photophobia Anterior chamber cells and fibrin Pupil miotic *Intermediate*: Bilateral involvement Mildly hazy/blurry vision *Posterior*: Photophobia Pain Sight threatening	*Anterior*: Topical steroids *Intermediate*: Periocular steroids Systemic steroids *Posterior*: Systemic steroids Immunosuppressive drugs

NSAIDs, Nonsteroidal antiinflammatory drugs.
From Adkinson NF et al: *Middleton's allergy principles and practice*, ed 8, Philadelphia, 2014, Saunders.

BASIC INFORMATION

DEFINITION
Epistaxis is defined as bleeding from the nose or nasal hemorrhage and is classified as either anterior or posterior.

SYNONYMS
Nosebleed

ICD-10CM CODES
R04.0 Epistaxis

EPIDEMIOLOGY & DEMOGRAPHICS
- Epistaxis accounts for one of every 200 emergency department visits in the U.S. annually.
- It increases in frequency after age 20 yr and reaches the highest levels among the elderly population.
- More than 80% of cases of epistaxis are anterior in origin (Little's area) and occur from Kiesselbach's plexus.
- Only 5% of patients with epistaxis have posterior bleeds.

PHYSICAL FINDINGS & CLINICAL PRESENTATION
- Nosebleed
- Hypotension and hemodynamic instability with acute, severe epistaxis

ETIOLOGY
- Approximately 90% of epistaxis events are idiopathic.
- Common identifiable causes are:
  1. Cold, dry environment
  2. Trauma (nose picking, accidents, and physical altercations)
  3. Structural deformities (septal deviations or spurs, chronic perforations)
  4. Inflammatory (rhinosinusitis, nasal polyposis)
  5. Allergies
  6. Foreign bodies in the nasal cavity
  7. Tumors (juvenile angiofibroma)
  8. Irritants
  9. Hypertension
  10. Coagulopathy (hemophilia, von Willebrand's disease, thrombocytopenia)
  11. Osler-Weber-Rendu disease
  12. Renal failure
  13. Drugs: aspirin, nonsteroidal antiinflammatory drugs, warfarin, alcohol, sildenafil, and tadalafil
  14. Blood vessel disorders (connective tissue disease, hereditary hemorrhagic telangiectasia)
  15. Pseudoaneurysm and aneurysm of the internal carotid artery might present as epistaxis

DIAGNOSIS

A good attempt should be made to directly visualize the source of bleeding to confirm the diagnosis and determine the best treatment. Fig. 1E-42 illustrates anatomical sites for epistaxis.

DIFFERENTIAL DIAGNOSIS
Pseudoepistaxis must be ruled out. Common extranasal sites of bleeding that can simulate epistaxis include:
1. Pulmonary hemoptysis
2. Bleeding esophageal varices
3. Tumor bleeding from the pharynx, larynx, or trachea

WORKUP
The workup should include laboratory blood testing to exclude obvious causes. Type and cross in anticipation of transfusion if the bleeding is severe.

LABORATORY TESTS
- Hemoglobin and hematocrit
- Platelet count
- Blood urea nitrogen and creatinine
- Coagulation studies (prothrombin time and partial thromboplastin time)
- Type and crossmatching of blood products

IMAGING STUDIES
Radiographic studies are usually not helpful.

TREATMENT

NONPHARMACOLOGIC THERAPY
- Digital compression or pinching of the lower soft cartilaginous part of the nose for 10 min is the method of choice.
- Use cotton or tissue plug.
- The patient should be sitting and leaning forward, breathing through the mouth, allowing blood to flow out of the nostrils as opposed to bending backward, which would allow the blood to flow down the throat.
- Application of cold compresses to the bridge of the nose to cause a vasoconstrictive effect; the patient may also suck on ice to achieve this effect.

ACUTE GENERAL Rx
Anterior epistaxis:
- Local vasoconstriction is performed by moistening a cotton pledget with either:
  1. 4% lidocaine with 1:1000 epinephrine
  2. 4% lidocaine with 1% phenylephrine (Neo-Synephrine)
  3. 4% lidocaine with 0.05% oxymetazoline (Afrin)
  4. 4% cocaine or cocaine 25% in paraffin base ointment and inserting the pledget into the nasal cavity with bayonet forceps.
- Cauterization with silver nitrate or trichloroacetic acid is performed once hemostasis is achieved.

E

Diseases and Disorders

I

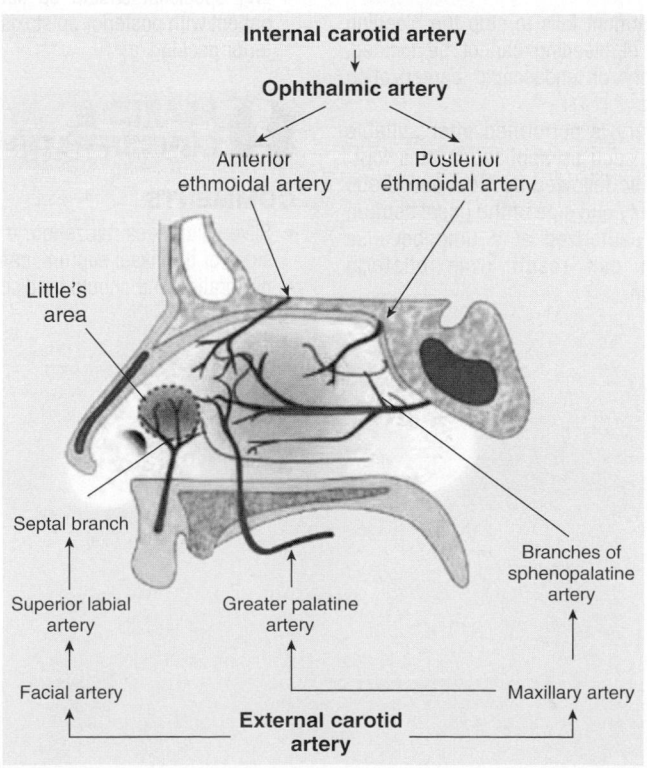

FIGURE 1E-42 Anatomical sites for epistaxis. (From McLarnon CM, Carrie S: Epistaxis. *Surgery (Oxford)* 30(11): 584–589, 2012.)

- Anterior nasal packing is needed when local measures are unsuccessful. Nasal packing is performed under local anesthesia and is done by inserting Vaseline gauze strips in layers from the floor of the nasal cavity to the front entrance of the nasal orifice. Enough pressure is placed to tamponade the epistaxis.
- Other commercially available nasal packing uses sponge packs that expand when exposed to blood or moisture and can be used for anterior epistaxis.

Posterior epistaxis:

- Posterior nasal packing
  1. Commercially available nasal sponge packing can be applied
  2. Rolled gauze technique
- Foley catheter balloon insertion into the nasopharynx can be tried in patients with posterior epistaxis.

Newer agents in the treatment of epistaxis:

- Quick clot hemostatic agent, available OTC. When it comes in contact with blood in and around a wound, it absorbs the smaller water molecules from the blood to promote rapid clotting
- FloSeal hemostatic matrix, a combination of human thrombin, gelatin matrix, and calcium chloride, which are mixed together and placed at bleeding site
- Recombinant factor VIIa, generally reserved for uncontrolled epistaxis

CHRONIC Rx

- If acute treatment fails to stop the bleeding or the site of bleeding cannot be located, electrocautery or endoscopic cauterization can be used.
- Electrocautery is performed after suitable anesthesia, such as application of a topical anesthetic followed by local anesthetic injection. Only one side of the nasal septum should be cauterized at a time because perforation can result from bilateral cauterization.

- Arterial ligation or embolization has been used in refractory posterior epistaxis.
- For cases involving irritated or inflamed mucosa, a conservative regimen of triamcinolone 0.025%, Nemdyn, Nasalate, or equivalent cream should be applied once a week, combined with nightly application of a small quantity of petroleum jelly to the septum before bedtime.

DISPOSITION

- Most cases of anterior epistaxis from Kiesselbach's plexus can be stopped by nasal compression and local vasoconstriction or cauterization.
- Nasal packing with gauze or sponge can control 90% of anterior epistaxis.
- Anterior and posterior packs are removed in 2 to 3 days. Hospital admission should be considered in patients who cannot be expected to return for prompt follow-up because prolonged packing increases the risk of pressure necrosis, toxic shock syndrome, sinus infections, and other complications.
- Although rare, epistaxis can lead to death by aspiration of blood, hemodynamic compromise from rapid excessive blood loss, or toxic shock syndrome.

REFERRAL

- If epistaxis cannot be controlled, an ear-nose-throat (ENT) specialist should be called for assistance.
- ENT specialist should be consulted in any patient with posterior epistaxis requiring posterior packing.

❗ PEARLS & CONSIDERATIONS

COMMENTS

- Silver nitrate cauterization, if done on both sides of the nasal septum, can lead to septal perforation and should be discouraged.

- If anterior nasal packing is done, broad-spectrum antibiotics (e.g., amoxicillin-clavulanate 250 mg PO tid or trimethoprim-sulfamethoxazole 1 tablet PO bid) are used until the anterior packs are removed. Although it is customary to place patients on antibiotics to prevent sinusitis from obstruction, there is no proof that this is effective.
- Complications of nasal packing include:
  1. Aspiration
  2. Dislodged packing
  3. Infection
  4. Nasal trauma
- Traditional risk factors for epistaxis, including nasal perforation, nasal septum deviation, rhinitis, sinusitis, and upper respiratory tract infection, do not increase the risk of recurrent epistaxis. Significant risk factors for recurrent epistaxis include congestive heart failure, diabetes mellitus, hypertension, and a history of angina. Warfarin use also increases risk of recurrence, independent of INR. Aspirin and clopidogrel do not increase the risk of recurrent epistaxis.[1]

SUGGESTED READINGS
Available at www.expertconsult.com

RELATED CONTENT
Nosebleeds (Patient Information)

AUTHOR: **TANYA ALI, M.D.**

[1]Abrich V, Brozek A, Boyle TR, et al.: Risk factors for recurrent spontaneous epistaxis, *Mayo Clin Proc* 89(12):1636-1643, 2014.

BASIC INFORMATION

DEFINITION

Epstein-Barr virus infection refers to a disease caused by Epstein-Barr virus (EBV), a human herpesvirus.

SYNONYMS

Infectious mononucleosis (IM)
Kissing disease

ICD-10CM CODES

B27.80 Other infectious mononucleosis without complication
B27.81 Other infectious mononucleosis with polyneuropathy
B27.82 Other infectious mononucleosis with meningitis
B27.89 Other infectious mononucleosis with other complication
B27.90 Infectious mononucleosis, unspecified without complication
B27.91 Infectious mononucleosis, unspecified with polyneuropathy
B27.92 Infectious mononucleosis, unspecified with meningitis
B27.99 Infectious mononucleosis, unspecified with other complication

EPIDEMIOLOGY & DEMOGRAPHICS

INCIDENCE (IN U.S.): 5 cases/100,000 persons per yr of IM.
PREDOMINANT SEX: Neither, although peak incidence occurs about 2 yr earlier in women.
PREDOMINANT AGE:
- Clinical evidence of IM: occurs most commonly at ages 15 to 24 yr.
- EBV infection: occurs earlier in life in lower socioeconomic groups.

PHYSICAL FINDINGS & CLINICAL PRESENTATION

- Most EBV infections either are asymptomatic or cause a nonspecific viral illness.
- Incubation period is 1 to 2 mo, possibly followed by a prodrome of anorexia, low-grade fever, malaise, headache, and chills; after several days, clinical triad of pharyngitis, moderate to high fever, and adenopathy may appear, accompanied by fatigue and malaise.
- Pharyngitis is usually the most severe symptom; white or necrotic exudates are common.
- Symmetrical lymphadenopathy is most prominent in the posterior more than anterior cervical region but may be diffuse.
- Splenomegaly (50% of cases) is possible, most commonly during the second week of illness.
- Maculopapular or morbilliform rash is uncommon but will occur in patients who receive ampicillin. Patients may have palatal petechiae, periorbital, or palpebral edema. Mucocutaneous oral hairy leukoplakia (OHL), which is associated with intense EBV replication and the action of

EBV-encoded proteins such as latent membrane protein-1, may occur.
- Possible IM presentation: fever and adenopathy without pharyngitis.
- Nausea, vomiting, and anorexia are frequent in patients with IM, probably reflecting mild hepatitis encountered in 90% of infected individuals.
- Although complications such as spleen rupture, airway obstruction, and malignancy may be severe and fatal, they are uncommon and tend to resolve completely.
- Hematologic involvement includes hemolytic or aplastic anemia, thrombocytopenia, thrombotic thrombocytopenic purpura/hemolytic-uremic syndrome, and disseminated intravascular coagulation (DIC). Pneumonia, myocarditis, pancreatitis, mesenteric adenitis, myositis, and glomerulonephritis may occur as well. Nervous system involvement includes Guillain-Barré syndrome, facial nerve palsy, meningoencephalitis, aseptic meningitis, transfer myelitis, peripheral neuritis, and optic neuritis.
- IM is usually a self-limited illness. Acute symptoms resolve in 1 to 2 wk, but symptoms of malaise and fatigue often persist for months.
- EBV is related to lymphoproliferative syndromes in transplant recipients and in AIDS patients.
- Increasing evidence showing an association between EBV infection and African Burkitt's, B-cell, T-cell lymphoma, and nasopharyngeal carcinoma. Table 1E-19 describes EBV-associated malignancies.

ETIOLOGY

- EBV is a ubiquitous virus.
- Infection during childhood is much less likely to cause significant illness.
- Frequency of IM in late adolescence is attributed to the onset of social contact between the sexes.
- Close personal contact is usually necessary for transmission, although EBV is occasionally transmitted by blood transfusion; transfer via saliva while kissing may be responsible for many cases.

DIAGNOSIS

DIFFERENTIAL DIAGNOSIS

- Heterophile-negative IM caused by cytomegalovirus (CMV).
- Although clinical presentation similar, CMV more frequently follows transfusion.
- Bacterial and viral causes of pharyngitis.
- Toxoplasmosis.
- Acute retroviral syndrome of HIV.
- Lymphoma.
- Lyme disease.

WORKUP

Heterophile antibody and CBC with blood smear. Table 1E-20 describes frequently determined EBV-specific antibodies.

LABORATORY TESTS

- Increased WBC common, with a relative lymphocytosis of more than 50% and neutropenia identified.
- Hallmark of IM: atypical lymphocytes of more than 10% (not pathognomonic) are found.
- Mild thrombocytopenia is present.
- Falling hematocrit signals the possibility of splenic rupture or immune hemolytic anemia.
- Elevated hepatocellular enzymes and cryoglobulins are found in most cases.
- Heterophile antibody:
  1. As measured by the monospot test, may be positive at presentation or may appear later in the course of illness.
  2. Negative test is repeated in 1 wk if clinical suspicion is high.
  3. A positive test has been reported with primary HIV infection.
- Viral capsid antigen (VCA) IgG and IgM are rarely used for diagnosis, but better value in children because heterophile antibody is negative in most children younger than 8 years.
- PCR DNA for CMV is the test of choice in transplant recipients who develop lymphoproliferative syndromes.

TABLE 1E-19 Epstein-Barr Virus (EBV)-Associated Malignancies

Malignancy	EBV Frequency (%)
Hodgkin disease	~40
Non-Hodgkin lymphomas	
Burkitt's lymphoma	20-95
Diffuse large B-cell lymphoma and CD30+ Ki-1+ anaplastic large cell lymphoma	10-35
Lymphomatoid granulomatosis	80-95
T-cell–rich B-cell lymphoma	20
Angioimmunoblastic lymphoma	>80
T-cell, NK-cell, and T/NK-cell lymphomas	30-90
Nasopharyngeal carcinoma	>95
Gastric adenocarcinoma	5-10
Pyothorax-associated lymphoma	>95
Leiomyosarcoma in immunocompromised patients	>95

From Hoffman R et al: *Hematology: basic principles and practice*, ed 5, Philadelphia, 2009, Churchill Livingstone.

TABLE 1E-20 Frequently Determined EBV-Specific Antibodies

Antibody Specificity	Positive in IM (%)	Time of Appearance in IM	Persistence	Comments
Viral Capsid Antigen				
VCA-IgM	100	At clinical presentation	4-8 weeks	Highly sensitive and specific; of major diagnostic utility
VCA-IgG	100	At clinical presentation	Lifelong	Useful for documentation of past EBV infection
Early Antigen				
Anti-D	70	Peaks 3-4 weeks after onset	3-6 months	Correlates with disease severity; seen in NPC patients
Anti-R	Low	2 weeks to several months after onset	2 months to >3 years	Occasionally seen with unusually severe cases; seen in African Burkitt's lymphoma patients
EBNA	100	3-4 weeks after onset	Lifelong	Presence excludes primary EBV infection

EBNA, EBV nuclear antigen; *EBV*, Epstein-Barr virus; *IM*, infectious mononucleosis; *NPC*, nasopharyngeal carcinoma; *VCA*, viral capsid antigen.
Adapted from Schooley RT: Epstein-Barr virus (infectious mononucleosis). In Mandell GL et al (eds): *Principles and practice of infectious diseases*, Philadelphia, 2010, Churchill Livingstone.

IMAGING STUDIES

Chest radiograph examination:
- May rarely show infiltrates.
- Possible elevated left hemidiaphragm with splenic rupture.

 **TREATMENT**

NONPHARMACOLOGIC THERAPY
- Supportive including rest.
- Splenectomy if rupture occurs.
- Transfusions for severe anemia or thrombo-cytopenia.

ACUTE GENERAL Rx
- Pharmacologic therapy is not indicated in uncomplicated illness.
- Avoid aspirin due to the risk of Reye's syndrome.
- Avoid ampicillin and amoxicillin as their use can frequently precipitate a nonallergic rash.

- Use of steroids is suggested in patients who have severe thrombocytopenia, hemolytic anemia, impending airway obstruction resulting from enlarged tonsils, or fulminant liver failure. Prednisone 60 to 80 mg PO qd for 3 days, then tapered over 1 to 2 wk.
- Although it may reduce initial viral shedding, there is little evidence to support the use of antiviral agents such as acyclovir in the management of IM.

CHRONIC Rx

An extremely rare, chronic form of IM with persistent fevers and fatigue has been described and should be differentiated from chronic fatigue syndrome, which is not related to EBV.

DISPOSITION

Eventual resolution of all symptoms.

REFERRAL

If more than mild illness.

PEARLS & CONSIDERATIONS

COMMENTS

Avoidance of contact sports during the first month of illness because splenic rupture can occur even in the absence of clinically detectable splenomegaly.

SUGGESTED READINGS

Available at www.expertconsult.com

RELATED CONTENT

Epstein-Barr Virus Infection (Patient Information)
Mononucleosis (Related Key Topic)

AUTHOR: **MONZR M. AL MALKI, M.D.**

BASIC INFORMATION

DEFINITION

Erectile dysfunction (ED) is the persistent inability to achieve or sustain a penile erection of adequate rigidity to make sexual penetration possible or satisfactory.

SYNONYMS

ED
Impotence
Male erectile disorder
Sexual dysfunction (a nonspecific term)

ICD-10CM CODES
N48.4 Impotence of organic origin
F52.2 Failure of genital response
F52.9 Unspecified sexual dysfunction, not caused by organic disorder or disease
N52.01 Erectile dysfunction due to arterial insufficiency
N52.02 Corporo-venous occlusive erectile dysfunction
N52.03 Combined arterial insufficiency and corporo-venous occlusive erectile dysfunction
N52.1 Erectile dysfunction due to diseases classified elsewhere
N52.2 Drug-induced erectile dysfunction
N52.31 Erectile dysfunction following radical prostatectomy
N52.32 Erectile dysfunction following radical cystectomy
N52.33 Erectile dysfunction following urethral surgery
N52.34 Erectile dysfunction following simple prostatectomy
N52.39 Other post-surgical erectile dysfunction
N52.8 Other male erectile dysfunction
N52.9 Male erectile dysfunction, unspecified

EPIDEMIOLOGY & DEMOGRAPHICS

PREVALENCE (IN U.S.):
- Increases with age and presence of specific medical comorbidities.
- Approximately 8% in the 20s to 30s, 18% in the 50s, 25% in the 60s, 37% in the 70s, 80% in the 80s.

PREDOMINANT SEX: By definition, only in males

PREDOMINANT AGE: Increases with age

RISK FACTORS: Age, coronary artery disease, peripheral vascular disease, hypertension, hypogonadism, diabetes mellitus, hypercholesterolemia, prostate surgery, neurologic injury, numerous medications, alcohol, smoking or drug abuse, obesity, obstructive sleep apnea, systemic sclerosis

ETIOLOGY

- Most cases involving men older than 50 yr are caused by organic problems related to neurologic, hormonal, or vascular abnormalities or prescription or recreational drugs. In organic ED, nocturnal penile tumescence is generally abnormal, and ED is also experienced during private masturbation and across partners.
- Psychogenic ED results from mental stress, depression, a stressful partner relationship, a partner's sexual and mental health problems, and performance anxiety. Performance anxiety is extremely common and is characterized by a focus on the performance outcome of sex (i.e., obtaining and maintaining an erection) rather than a focus on the process and enjoyment of sex. Psychogenic ED is characterized by normal nocturnal penile tumescence and otherwise negative test results.
- Vascular disease: history of hypertension (HTN), peripheral vascular disease, ischemic heart disease, diabetes, smoking. In approximately 40% of men >50 yr, the primary cause of ED is related to atherosclerotic disease, diabetes mellitus (DM), neuropathy, or vascular disease.
- Medication side effects: antihypertensives such as thiazides and clonidine, guanethidine or methyldopa (consider change to ACE inhibitors and calcium channel blockers with lower reported incidence of ED); antiandrogens such as spironolactone, finasteride, ketoconazole; cimetidine (but not ranitidine or famotidine); antidepressants such as selective serotonin reuptake inhibitors [SSRIs]; and antipsychotics.
- Excessive alcohol and nicotine use.
- Recreational drugs, including cocaine, heroin, amphetamines, and marijuana. These may increase libido but impair performance.
- Hormonal dysfunction such as testosterone deficiency (decreases libido and erection), hypothyroidism or hyperthyroidism, hyperprolactinemia, and adrenal insufficiency.
- Neurogenic causes including spinal cord lesions, cortical lesions, and peripheral neuropathics.
- Trauma or pelvic surgeries such as radical prostatectomy or cystectomy.

DIAGNOSIS

DIFFERENTIAL DIAGNOSIS

- A useful tool to diagnose/evaluate ED severity is the Sexual Health Inventory for Men.
- Distinguish psychogenic from organic ED.
- Evaluate for underlying etiology of organic ED and comorbid psychiatric condition.

WORKUP

- Clinical history should include time course (abrupt onset may correlate with reversible cause such as medications, psychosocial stress, psychiatric complaint, trauma. Nonsustained erection may be secondary to anxiety or vascular steal syndrome), cause (psychogenic vs. organic), and change in libido.
- Report of spontaneous nocturnal or morning erections indicate intact neurologic reflexes and penile blood flow.
- Decreased libido may indicate endocrinologic or psychogenic cause.
- If possible, interview partner regarding sexual function, relationship satisfaction, and mental health history.

- Medical and social history should address cardiac disease symptoms and risk factors (HTN, DM, hyperlipidemia, smoking, and substance abuse), pelvic surgery, medications, and mental health.
- Physical examination to check blood pressure, visual field defects to evaluate for pituitary tumors; femoral and peripheral pulses, femoral bruits; gynecomastia; neuronal damage (genital sensation, cremasteric reflex); direct penile damage (e.g., plaque formation such as Peyronie's disease); prostate examination; or testicular atrophy and other secondary sexual characteristics.

LABORATORY TESTS

Screen for diabetes mellitus with fasting glucose. Consider lipid panel, thyroid-stimulating hormone, morning serum testosterone (free and total). If decreased testosterone, check prolactin, follicle-stimulating hormone, and luteinizing hormone.

IMAGING STUDIES

Imaging studies are rarely performed except in situations of pelvic trauma or surgery.

OTHER STUDIES

- Nocturnal penile tumescence testing very specific for distinguishing psychogenic versus organic causes.
- Neurogenic etiologies examined by the cremasteric reflex (inner-thigh touch elicits scrotal contraction), the bulbocavernosus reflex, or the pudendal-evoked response.
- Intracorporeal injection of prostaglandin E_1 to distinguish vascular and nonvascular etiologies (erection is achieved in patients with normal vascular systems). If no erection with direct injection of vasoactive substance, consider duplex ultrasound of penile vasculature.
- In patients without an obvious cause of ED, consider screening for cardiovascular disease prior to starting treatment.

TREATMENT (FIG. 1E-43)

NONPHARMACOLOGIC THERAPY

- Various psychotherapeutic approaches: cognitive-behavioral therapy preferred; success rates decrease with advancing age and duration of symptoms.
- Psychosexual therapy is first line for psychogenic ED. Psychosexual therapy may be used as for adjunctive therapy in ED from any cause to address contributing, performance anxiety, social, and relationship issues.
- Performance anxiety is best addressed by sensate focus in which a couple is asked to refrain from sexual penetration but enjoy erotic touching.
- Mechanical vacuum devices (function by drawing blood into corpus cavernosum) are 70% to 90% effective but are difficult to use.
- Incorporate vascular risk factor reduction including counsel on diet, exercise, smoking cessation, ETOH Intake and screening/treatment for HTN, insulin resistance, and

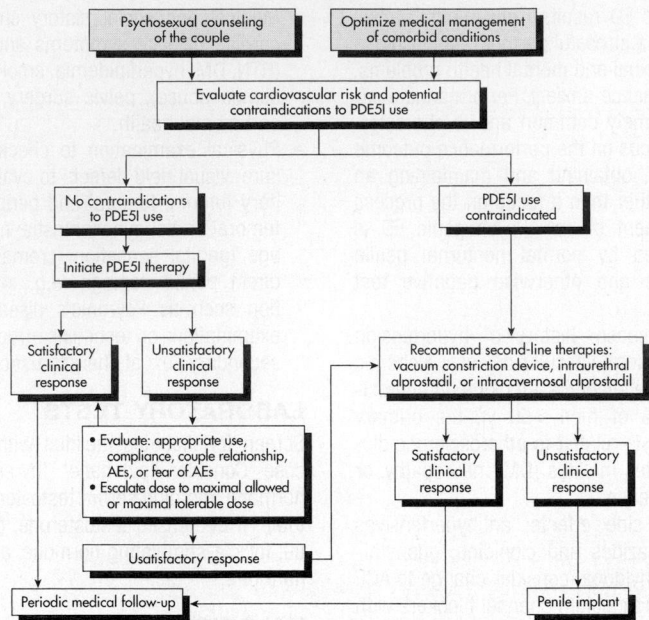

FIGURE 1E-43 An algorithmic approach to the treatment of erectile dysfunction in men. *AE,* Adverse effects; *PDE5I,* phosphodiesterase 5 inhibitor. (From Melmed S, Polonsky KS, Larsen PR, Kronenberg HM: *Williams textbook of endocrinology,* ed 12, Philadelphia, 2011, Saunders.)

hypercholesterolemia as appropriate. Trials have shown that lifestyle modification and pharmacotherapy for cardiovascular risk factors are effective in improving sexual function in men with ED.

ACUTE GENERAL Rx

- First-line treatment: In setting of sexual stimulation, four selective phosphodiesterase type 5 (PDE5) inhibitors prolong nitric oxide–induced vasodilation by increase of intracavernosal cyclic guanosine monophosphate levels. Sildenafil (Viagra) and vardenafil (Levitra, Staxyn) can be taken 30 to 60 min before sexual activity, and both are effective for about 4 hr. Avanafil (Stendra) can be taken 15 to 30 min before sexual activity and is effective for about 6 hr. Tadalafil (Cialis) can be taken several hours before sexual activity (although 50% respond within 30 min) and lasts up to 36 hr. All four PDE5 inhibitors have similar efficacy and tolerability, but tadalafil has a longer duration of action and is less affected by high-fat meals and alcohol. Counsel patients to avoid high-fat meals and excessive alcohol when taking PDE5 inhibitors, as they may impede effectiveness.
- With PDE5 inhibitors, avoid concomitant use of nitrates (absolute contraindication), drugs that inhibit or induce cytochrome P450 CYP3A4, and drugs that prolong the QT interval. Caution in men on alpha-adrenergic blocker therapy because of concern for hypotension; start the lowest dose of PDE5 inhibitor. Caution in men who have had myocardial infarction in the past 6 mo, resting hypotension or uncon-

trolled hypertension, unstable angina, positive exercise stress test or poor exercise tolerance. Counsel on side effects of headache, flushing, dyspepsia, nasal congestion, changes in color perception (including blue vision for sildenafil and vardenafil but not tadalafil), sudden hearing loss, and priapism (rare). Nonarteritic anterior ischemic optic neuropathy is also a rare association with sildenafil and tadalafil. Consider counseling on safe sexual practices when prescribing PDE5 inhibitors.
- Second-line treatment if PDE5 inhibitors fail: self-injection with intraurethral alprostadil (prostaglandin E_1 [medicated urethral suppository]) applied into meatus of penis before intercourse; or intracavernosal injections of vasodilators (e.g., papaverine or prostaglandin E_1). Consider combining intraurethral alprostadil with PDE5 inhibitor. Relatively high success with self-injection, but attrition is high (Table E1E-21).
- Second-line treatment alternative: vacuum constriction pump; has variable satisfaction rate.

CHRONIC Rx

- Psychosexual therapy is helpful as an adjunctive treatment.
- Psychogenic impotence: PDE5 inhibitors are effective in patients with depression because tissues, nerves, hormones, and vasculature are normal. PDE5 inhibitors are also effective as a way of providing positive experiences and building sexual confidence. Full psychologic evaluation is recommended before starting treatment.

- For men not responding to other approaches: surgical implantation of penile prosthesis may be considered. Full psychological evaluation is recommended to evaluate the possibility of unrealistic expectations or partner problems contributing to ED.
- Testosterone therapy in men with low testosterone (i.e., hypogonadal); evaluate for prostate cancer before prescribing testosterone.
- Aerobic exercise may improve ED along with pharmacologic treatment.

DISPOSITION

- Psychogenic-acquired ED will remit spontaneously in 15% to 30% of cases.
- Lifelong ED is usually a chronic and unremitting condition.
- Situational ED may remit with changes in social environment and reducing performance anxiety.

REFERRAL

- Refer if psychotherapy, sex therapy, or invasive organic treatment required
- Refer to urology if PDE5 inhibitors fail or sudden onset occurs after penile trauma

ⓘ PEARLS & CONSIDERATIONS

- ED is commonly evaluated and treated by primary care physician; refer to urologist if oral therapy fails or surgery is required.
- PDE5 inhibitors are treatment of choice for most causes of ED. Main contraindications are nitrate use and decompensated cardiac disease. Caution in patients on alpha-adrenergic blockers and with blood pressures at extreme ends (significant hypotension or hypertension).
- For optimal response, patients should be appropriately informed of proper use, precautions, and adverse effects of PDE5 inhibitors. Try six to eight times at optimal doses before declaring PDE5 inhibitors a failure. Consider switching among the four PDE5 inhibitors if one fails.
- Men with ED are at increased risk of coronary, cerebrovascular, and peripheral vascular diseases. Screen for cardiovascular risk factors in these patients.

SUGGESTED READINGS

Available at www.expertconsult.com

RELATED CONTENT

Erectile Dysfunction (Patient Information)
Ejaculation Disorders (Related Key Topic)

AUTHORS: **JOHN P. WINCZE, Ph.D.,** and **CINDY LAI, M.D.**

BASIC INFORMATION

DEFINITION

Erysipelas is a type of cellulitis caused by infection of the superficial layers of the skin and cutaneous lymphatics. Erysipelas is characterized by redness, induration, and a sharply demarcated, raised border.

SYNONYMS

St. Anthony's fire

ICD-10CM CODES
A46 Erysipelas

EPIDEMIOLOGY & DEMOGRAPHICS

PREDOMINANT AGE: Occurs most often in the young or old
RISK FACTORS: Patients with impaired lymphatic or venous drainage (mastectomy, saphenous vein harvesting) and immunocompromised patients. Athlete's foot is a common portal of entry.
RECURRENCE RATE: Relatively common

PHYSICAL FINDINGS & CLINICAL PRESENTATION

- Distinctive red, warm, tender skin lesion with induration and a sharply defined, advancing, raised border (Fig. 1E-44)
- Most common sites are lower extremities and face.
- Systemic signs of infection (fever) are often present.
- Vesicles or bullae may develop.
- After several days lesions may appear ecchymotic.
- After 7 to 10 days, desquamation of affected area may occur.

ETIOLOGY

- Usually group A β-hemolytic streptococci (GABHS)
- Less often group B, C, or G streptococci
- Rarely *Staphylococcus aureus*

COMPLICATIONS

- Abscess
- Necrotizing fasciitis
- Thrombophlebitis
- Gangrene
- Metastatic infection

DIAGNOSIS

DIFFERENTIAL DIAGNOSIS

- Other types of cellulitis
- Necrotizing fasciitis
- Deep vein thrombosis
- Contact dermatitis
- Erythema migrans (Lyme disease)
- Insect bite
- Herpes zoster
- Erysipeloid
- Acute gout
- Pseudogout

WORKUP

History, physical examination, and laboratory evaluation

LABORATORY TESTS

Diagnosis is usually made by characteristic clinical setting and appearance.
- Complete blood count and white blood cell count often elevated
- Blood cultures positive in 5% of patients
- Gram stain and culture of any drainage from skin lesions
- Culture of aspirated fluid from leading edge of skin lesion has low yield

IMAGING STUDIES

- Not routinely indicated
- Duplex ultrasound for patients suspected of having deep vein thrombosis
- CT scan or MRI for patients with suspected necrotizing fasciitis

TREATMENT

NONPHARMACOLOGIC THERAPY

- Elevation of the affected limb
- Warm compresses

ACUTE GENERAL Rx

Typical erysipelas of extremity in nondiabetic patient:
- PO: penicillin V 500 mg qid. Use azithromycin in patients who are allergic to penicillin.
- IV: penicillin G (aqueous) 1 to 2 million units q6h. Use vancomycin 15 mg/kg IV q12h in penicillin-allergic patients.

Facial erysipelas (include coverage for *Staphylococcus aureus*):
- PO dicloxacillin 500 mg q6h
- IV nafcillin or oxacillin 2 g q4h
- IV vancomycin 1 g q12h
- Daptomycin 4 mg/kg IV q24h
- Linezolid 600 mg IV q12h

DISPOSITION

Prognosis is good with antibiotic treatment but recurrence is common.

REFERRAL

For surgical debridement for patients with necrotizing fasciitis or for drainage of abscess

PEARLS & CONSIDERATIONS

- Consider early surgical referral when necrotizing fasciitis suspected. Consider skin biopsy when not responding to appropriate antibiotics.
- Look for tinea pedis as portal of entry in erysipelas of lower extremities. Treat if present.

SUGGESTED READINGS

Available at www.expertconsult.com

RELATED CONTENT

Erysipelas (Patient Information)
Cellulitis (Related Key Topic)

AUTHOR: **GAIL M. O'BRIEN, M.D.**

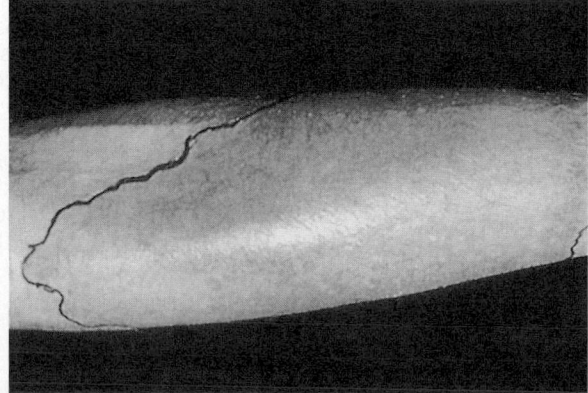

FIGURE 1E-44 Erysipelas. Note well-demarcated erythematous plaque on arm. (From Goldstein B [ed]: *Practical dermatology,* ed 2, St Louis, 1997, Mosby. Courtesy Department of Dermatology, University of North Carolina at Chapel Hill.)

BASIC INFORMATION

DEFINITION

Erythema multiforme is an inflammatory disease characterized by eruption of annular, maculopapular lesions with dark raised, erythematous, or vesiculobullous center surrounded by a pale zone. It is believed to be caused by immune complex formation and subsequent deposition in the skin and mucous membranes. It is considered a hypersensitivity reaction to infection or drugs.

SYNONYMS

EM

ICD-10CM CODES
L51.9 Erythema multiforme, unspecified
L51.0 Nonbullous erythema multiforme
L51.8 Other erythema multiforme

EPIDEMIOLOGY & DEMOGRAPHICS

PREDOMINANT AGE: 20 to 40 yr.
RISK FACTORS: Often associated with herpes simplex and other infectious agents, drugs, or connective tissue diseases.

PHYSICAL FINDINGS & CLINICAL PRESENTATION

- Prodromal symptoms are mild or absent. Itching or burning at the site of eruption may occur.
- Symmetric skin lesions with a classic "target" appearance (caused by the centrifugal spread of red maculopapules to circumference of 1 to 3 cm with a purpuric, cyanotic, or vesicular center) are present (Fig. 1E-45). The papules may enlarge into plaques measuring a few centimeters in diameter with a dark or red central portion. Target lesions may not be apparent for several days.

- Lesions are most common on the back of the hands and feet and extensor aspect of the forearms and legs. Trunk involvement can occur in severe cases.
- Urticarial papules, vesicles, and bullae may also be present and generally indicate a more severe form of the disease.
- Individual lesions heal in 1 to 2 wk without scarring.
- Bullae and erosions may also be present in the oral cavity. The most common sites are the lips and buccal mucosa.

ETIOLOGY

- Immune complex formation and subsequent deposition in the cutaneous microvasculature may play a role in the pathogenesis of erythema multiforme.
- The majority of cases follow outbreaks of herpes simplex virus 1 and 2.
- *Mycoplasma pneumoniae,* fungal infections, medications (bupropion, sulfonamides, penicillins, nonsteroidal antiinflammatory drugs, barbiturates, phenothiazines, hydantoins).
- In >50% of patients no specific cause is identified.

DIAGNOSIS

DIFFERENTIAL DIAGNOSIS

- Chronic urticaria.
- Pityriasis rosea.
- Contact dermatitis.
- Pemphigus vulgaris.
- Lichen planus.
- Serum sickness.
- Drug eruption.
- Granuloma annulare.
- Polymorphic light eruption.
- Viral exanthema.
- Stevens-Johnson syndrome (SJS).
- Toxic epidermal necrolysis (TEN).
- Bullous pemphigoid.

- Viral exanthems.
- Leukocytoclastic vasculitis.
- Lupus erythematosus.
- Secondary syphilis.

WORKUP

- Medical history with emphasis on drug ingestion.
- Laboratory evaluation in patients with suspected collagen-vascular diseases.
- Skin biopsy when diagnosis is unclear.

LABORATORY TESTS

- Complete blood count with differential elevated ESR.
- Antinuclear antibody.
- Serology for *Mycoplasma pneumoniae,* HSV-1, HSV-2.
- Biopsy for atypical cases.
- Direct immunofluorescence if suspecting bullous diseases.

TREATMENT

NONPHARMACOLOGIC THERAPY

- Mild cases generally do not require treatment; lesions resolve spontaneously within 1 mo.
- Potential drug precipitants should be removed.

ACUTE GENERAL Rx

- Treatment of associated diseases (e.g., valacyclovir or famciclovir for herpes simplex, erythromycin for *Mycoplasma* infection).
- Dapsone, antimalarials or azathioprine for severe or resistant cases.
- Prednisone 40 to 80 mg/day for 1 to 3 wk may be tried in patients with many target lesions; however, the role of systemic steroids remains controversial.
- Levamisole, an immunomodulator, may be effective in the treatment of patients with chronic or recurrent oral lesions (dose is 150 mg/day for 3 consecutive days used alone or in combination with prednisone).
- IV immunoglobulins in severe cases.

DISPOSITION

The rash generally evolves over a 2-wk period and resolves within 3 to 4 wk without scarring. A severe bullous form can occur (see entry for "Stevens-Johnson Syndrome").

REFERRAL

Hospital admission in patients with suspected Stevens-Johnson syndrome

PEARLS & CONSIDERATIONS

COMMENTS

The risk of recurrence of erythema multiforme exceeds 30%. Recurrence may be treated with valacyclovir 500 to 1000 mg/day, famciclovir 125 to 250 mg/day, or acyclovir 400 mg bid. Dapsone, antimalarials, azathioprine, or cyclosporine use is reserved for cases resistant to antivirals.

FIGURE 1E-45 Iris and arcuate lesions of erythema multiforme. Note erythematous lesions with multiform configurations: target, arcuate, and vesicles. (From Noble J et al: *Textbook of primary care medicine,* ed 2, St Louis, 1995, Mosby.)

SUGGESTED READINGS
Available at www.expertconsult.com

RELATED CONTENT

Erythema Multiforme (Patient Information)
Stevens-Johnson Syndrome (Related Key Topic)

AUTHOR: **FRED F. FERRI, M.D.**

BASIC INFORMATION

DEFINITION

Erythema nodosum (EN) is an acute, tender, erythematous, nodular skin eruption resulting from inflammation of subcutaneous fat, often associated with bruising. It is the most common form of panniculitis.

ICD-10CM CODES
L52 Erythema nodosum

EPIDEMIOLOGY & DEMOGRAPHICS

INCIDENCE: Two to three cases/100,000 persons per yr.
PREDOMINANT SEX: Female/male ratio of 3 to 4:1.
PREDOMINANT AGE: 25 to 40 yr.

PHYSICAL FINDINGS & CLINICAL PRESENTATION

- Prodromal symptoms of fatigue, malaise, upper respiratory infection symptoms may precede eruption by 1 to 2 weeks.
- Acute onset of tender nodules typically located on the shins (Fig. 1E-46) and occasionally seen on the thighs and forearms.
- The nodules are usually 1/8 to 1 inch in diameter but can be as large as 4 inches; they begin as light red lesions, then become darker and often ecchymotic. The nodules heal within 8 wk without ulceration.
- Associated findings:
  1. Fever (60%).
  2. Lymphadenopathy (<50%).
  3. Arthralgia (64%).
  4. Signs of the underlying illness.

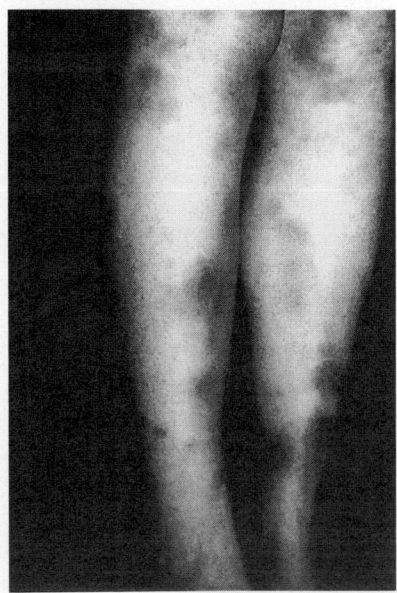

FIGURE 1E-46 Erythema nodosum. (From Arndt KA et al: *Cutaneous medicine and surgery, vol 1,* Philadelphia, 1997, Saunders.)

ETIOLOGY

Cell-mediated hypersensitivity reaction is seen more frequently in persons with human leukocyte antigen (HLA) B8. The lesion results from an exaggerated interaction between an antigen and cell-mediated immune mechanisms leading to granuloma formation. Up to 55% of cases of EN are idiopathic.
Infections:
- Bacteria
  Campylobacter.
  Streptococcal pharyngitis (28% to 48%).
  Salmonella enteritis.
  Yersinia enteritis.
  Psittacosis.
  Chlamydia pneumoniae infection.
  Mycoplasma pneumonia.
  Meningococcal infection.
  Gonorrhea.
  Syphilis.
  Lymphogranuloma venereum.
  Tularemia.
  Cat-scratch disease.
  Leprosy.
  Tuberculosis.
- Fungi
  Histoplasmosis.
  Coccidioidomycosis.
  Blastomycosis.
  Trichophyton verrucosum.
- Viruses
  Cytomegalovirus.
  Hepatitis B.
  Epstein-Barr virus.
- Drugs (3% to 10%)
  Sulfonylureas.
  Sulfonamides.
  Penicillins.
  Oral contraceptives.
  Gold salts.
  Prazosin.
  Aspirin.
  Bromides.
- Sarcoidosis (11% to 25%).
- Inflammatory bowel disease.
- Hodgkin's disease, non-Hodgkin's lymphoma.
- Ankylosing spondylosis and reactive arthropathies (e.g., associated with inflammatory bowel disease)
- Behcet's disease.
- Lofgren's syndrome.
- Acute myelogenous leukemia.

DIAGNOSIS

DIFFERENTIAL DIAGNOSIS

- Insect bites.
- Posttraumatic ecchymoses.
- Vasculitis.
- Weber-Christian disease.
- Fat necrosis associated with pancreatitis.
- Necrobiosis lipoidica.
- Scleroderma.
- Lupus panniculitis.
- Subcutaneous granuloma.

WORKUP

- Physical examination.
- Diagnosis of underlying illness by history, physical examination, and laboratory tests as indicated.

LABORATORY TESTS

- Erythrocyte sedimentation rate.
- Throat culture and antistreptolysin O titer.
- PPD.
- Others depending on index of suspicion (e.g., stool culture and evaluation for ova and parasites in patients with diarrhea and gastrointestinal symptoms).
- Skin biopsy in doubtful cases:
  1. Early lesion: inflammation and hemorrhage in subcutaneous tissue.
  2. Late lesion: giant cells and granulomata.

IMAGING STUDIES

Chest radiograph to rule out sarcoidosis and tuberculosis.

 TREATMENT

- The disease is self-limited and treatment is symptomatic. EN nodules develop in pretibial locations and resolve spontaneously over several weeks without scarring or ulceration.
- Treatment of underlying disorders.
- Avoidance of contact irritation of affected areas.
- Nonsteroidal anti-inflammatory drugs for pain.
- Systemic steroids (prednisone 1 mg/kg of body weight/day, tapered over several days) may be useful in severe cases if underlying risk of sepsis and malignancy have been excluded.
- Potassium iodide given as tablet 300 mg tid or as a supersaturated solution (5 drops 3 times/day in orange juice) has been reported as effective for symptom control.
- Intralesional corticosteroid injections for persistent lesions.

PROGNOSIS

Typical case:
- Pain for 2 wk.
- Resolution within 8 wk.

SUGGESTED READINGS
Available at www.expertconsult.com

RELATED CONTENT
Erythema Nodosum (Patient Information)
Sarcoidosis (Related Key Topic)

AUTHOR: **FRED F. FERRI, M.D.**

E

I

BASIC INFORMATION

DEFINITION

Esophageal varices are dilated submucosal veins that occur in patients with underlying portal hypertension, function as a shunt between the portal venous and systemic venous circulation, and can result in severe upper GI hemorrhage.

ICD-10CM CODES
I85.00 Esophageal varices without bleeding
I85.01 Esophageal varices with bleeding

EPIDEMIOLOGY & DEMOGRAPHICS

INCIDENCE:
- Esophageal varices: 5% to 15% per year in patients with cirrhosis
- Hemorrhage:
  1. One third of all patients with varices will develop hemorrhage.
  2. Variceal hemorrhage occurs in 25% to 40% of patients with cirrhosis
  3. The risk of bleeding from varices is approximately 15% at 1 year.
  4. Survivors of an episode of active bleeding have a 70% risk of recurrent hemorrhage within 1 year.

PREVALENCE: Approximately 50% of patients with cirrhosis have varices at the time of diagnosis.

RISK FACTORS: Cirrhosis, low platelet count and advanced Child-Pugh class, hepatitis C with advanced fibrosis

PHYSICAL FINDINGS & CLINICAL PRESENTATION

- Often asymptomatic until acute upper GI hemorrhage: hematemesis, hypovolemia
- No physical findings specific for esophageal varices
- Stigmata of cirrhosis and portal hypertension may be evident: palmar erythema, telangiectasias, gynecomastia, testicular atrophy, jaundice, caput medusae, lower extremity edema, ascites, splenomegaly, hemorrhoids, asterixis

ETIOLOGY

- Portal hypertension results from obstruction to portal venous outflow, and varices subsequently develop in order to decompress the hypertensive portal vein and return blood to the systemic circulation.
- Varices may appear when portal vein pressures rise above 10 to 12 mm Hg.
- Cirrhosis is the most common cause of portal hypertension.

DIAGNOSIS

DIFFERENTIAL DIAGNOSIS

- Budd-Chiari syndrome, cirrhosis, portal vein thrombosis, schistosomiasis, Wilson's disease
- Other causes of upper GI bleeding: duodenal or gastric ulcers, gastric cancer, Mallory-Weiss tear

WORKUP
Upper endoscopy, laboratory tests, and imaging

LABORATORY TESTS
- CBC
  1. Anemia (blood loss, nutritional deficiencies, alcohol myelosuppression)
  2. Thrombocytopenia (hypersplenism, alcohol myelosuppression)
- Renal function panel
  1. BUN: often increased in setting of upper GI bleeding
  2. Creatinine: often elevated by hypovolemia, monitor for hepatorenal syndrome
  3. Sodium: dilutional hyponatremia
- Heme-positive stools
- Type and Crossmatch: in preparation for blood transfusion
- INR/PT and PTT: coagulation factors produced in liver and may be prolonged in liver disease or impairment
- Liver function tests: ALT/AST may be normal in cirrhotic patients due to longstanding fibrosis; elevated alkaline phosphatase and a direct hyperbilirubinemia may be present if cholestatic liver disease is present
- Serum albumin: severe liver disease results in hypoalbuminemia

IMAGING STUDIES (FIG. 1E-47)
Invasive:
- Esophagogastroduodenoscopy (EGD) (upper endoscopy):
  1. In all patients with cirrhosis, screen for the presence or absence of varices and determine subsequent risk for variceal hemorrhage.
  2. In patients with compensated cirrhosis who do not have varices, screening is repeated every 2 to 3 years.
  3. In patients with decompensated cirrhosis (ascites, hepatic encephalopathy, variceal hemorrhage, or jaundice), it is repeated every year or at the time of first decompensation.
  4. Emergently performed if there is evidence of acute upper GI bleeding to diagnose and treat variceal hemorrhage.
Noninvasive:
- Esophagography with barium can diagnose esophageal varices (Fig. 1E-47).
- Capsule endoscopy can also diagnose esophageal varices, although sensitivity is not yet established.
- CT scan (Figs. 1E-47, E1E-48).

 TREATMENT

NONPHARMACOLOGIC THERAPY
- Endoscopic variceal ligation (Fig. 1E-49) is an alternative to nonselective beta-blockers for primary prophylaxis against variceal hemorrhage.
  1. Typically for patients with medium or large varices at highest risk for hemorrhage (Child-Pugh B/C or red wale markings viewed on endoscopy)
  2. Usually 2 to 4 sessions

3. May not be a permanent solution because varices can recur after initial eradication
4. Associated with significant complications, including hemorrhage from banding-induced ulcerations
   1. Therefore should be performed by endoscopists with expertise in prophylactic banding
   2. First surveillance endoscopy 1-3 months after obliteration, then every 6 to 12 months indefinitely

ACUTE GENERAL Rx
- Variceal hemorrhage: acute hemodynamic resuscitation with packed red blood cell transfusion, correct coagulopathy and thrombocytopenia, airway protection and intubation as necessary, antibiotics (ceftriaxone or norfloxacin) for SBP prophylaxis, octreotide maintained for 2 to 5 days in conjunction with endoscopic therapy
- EGD to treat bleeding esophageal varices by esophageal band ligation or sclerotherapy

CHRONIC Rx
Primary prophylaxis:
- Nonselective beta-blockers such as propranolol (20 mg twice daily) and nadolol (40 mg once daily)
  1. Increase as tolerated for goal heart rate of approximately 55 beats/min
  2. Blocks the adrenergic dilatory tone in mesenteric arterioles, resulting in unopposed alpha-adrenergic mediated vasoconstriction and therefore a decrease in portal inflow
Secondary prophylaxis:
- All patients with compensated cirrhosis who have bled from esophageal varices should receive esophageal band ligation and beta-blockers, unless beta-blockers are contraindicated.
  1. Transjugular intrahepatic portosystemic shunt or surgical shunt may be performed if bleeding from esophageal varices continues or recurs despite this dual therapy.
- For patients with decompensated cirrhosis there is evidence, although limited, against the use of prophylactic beta-blockers due to the risk for increased mortality.

REFERRAL: Consultation with a gastroenterologist is recommended in all patients with cirrhosis or portal hypertension in order to screen for esophageal varices.

PEARLS & CONSIDERATIONS

Besides variceal size, risk factors for variceal hemorrhage include Child-Pugh class B/C or variceal red wale markings on endoscopy.

PREVENTION
Treatment of the underling liver disease may help to prevent variceal development. However, treatment with nonselective beta-blockers is not recommended because they do not prevent the development of varices.

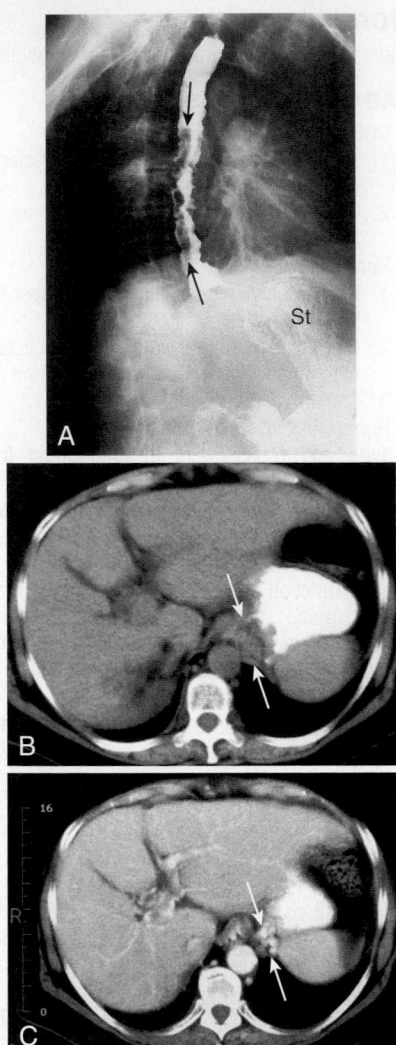

FIGURE 1E-47 Esophageal varices. In an oblique view from an upper gastrointestinal examination (**A**) performed on an alcoholic patient, a large, dark, wormlike filling density *(arrows)* is seen in the distal esophagus. It is caused by varices protruding into the lumen of the esophagus. The stomach *(St)* also is seen. Varices also can be seen on computed tomography (CT) scan. On a CT scan without intravenous contrast (**B**), they are seen as small rounded structures *(arrows)*, and they may indent the fundus of the stomach. When intravenous contrast is given (**C**), they enhance and become whiter *(arrows)*. (From Mettler FA: *Essentials of radiology*, 3rd ed, Philadelphia, 2014, Saunders.)

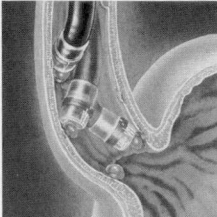

FIGURE 1E-49 Esophageal varices. Endoscopic band ligation performed with a multiple-band ligating device. The endoscopist makes circumferential contact between the end of the ligating device and the varix to be ligated. Endoscopic suction draws the varix into the device, after which the elastic band is ejected to ensnare the varix. The ligated tissue sloughs after 3 to 5 days, leaving a shallow ulceration that generally heals within 1 week. (Courtesy Bard Endoscopic Technologies, Billerica, Mass.)

EVIDENCE

Available at www.expertconsult.com

SUGGESTED READINGS

Available at www.expertconsult.com

RELATED CONTENT

Cirrhosis (Related Key Topic)
Portal Hypertension (Related Key Topic)

AUTHOR: **ADAM J. WEINBERG, M.D.**

🛈 BASIC INFORMATION

DEFINITION

Esophageal tumors include benign and malignant neoplasms of the esophageal mucosa and wall. Carcinomas of the esophageal epithelium, both squamous cell and adenocarcinoma, are by far the most common tumors of the esophagus (see Table 1E-22). Rare esophageal tumors include both malignant (spindle cell, small cell, sarcoma, lymphoma) and benign neoplasms (leiomyoma, papilloma, and fibrovascular polyps). Approximately 15% of esophageal tumors arise in the proximal esophagus, 50% in the middle third of the esophagus, and 35% in the lower third.

SYNONYMS

Neoplasm of the esophagus.
Malignancy of the esophagus.

ICD-10CM CODES
C15.X Malignant neoplasm of the esophagus (X defines location)
C15.3 Malignant neoplasm of upper third of esophagus
C15.4 Malignant neoplasm of middle third of esophagus
C15.5 Malignant neoplasm of lower third of esophagus
D00.2 Carcinoma of esophagus, in situ

EPIDEMIOLOGY & DEMOGRAPHICS

INCIDENCE: It is the eighth most common cancer and the seventh leading cause of cancer death worldwide. Rates are increasing every decade and are highest in the Asian esophageal cancer belt, extending from the Caspian Sea to northern China, with certain high-incidence pockets in Finland, Ireland, southeast Africa, and northwest France. Incidence has increased six-fold since 1975. Rates of squamous cell carcinoma are decreasing while those of adenocarcinomas are dramatically increasing.

TABLE 1E-22 Classification of Esophageal Cancer

Epithelial

Squamous cell
  Ordinary squamous cell
  Verrucous squamous cell
  Spindle cell (carcinosarcoma)
Adenocarcinoma
  Ordinary
  Adenoacanthoma
  Mucoepidermoid
  Adenoid cystic
Small cell
Melanoma
Choriocarcinoma

Metastatic Disease

Lymphoma
Sarcoma

From Abeloff MD: *Clinical oncology,* ed 3, Philadelphia, 2004, Churchill Livingstone.

PREVALENCE: In the United States, there will be an estimated 17,000 new cases and 15,600 deaths in 2015, making it the seventh leading cause of death by cancer among men. The majority of cases are diagnosed at an advanced stage (unresectable or metastatic disease).

RACE, AGE, & SEX PREDOMINANCE: In the United States, squamous cell esophageal cancer is more common among blacks than whites, whereas adenocarcinoma is more common in whites than blacks. The overall male/female ratio is 3 to 4:1; the highest male/female ratio is in the Hispanic population. It usually develops in the seventh and eighth decades and is associated with lower socioeconomic status.

GENETICS: Increasing evidence shows that genetics may play a role by increasing susceptibility to esophageal cancer. One well-identified disease associated with esophageal cancer is tylosis (focal non-epidermolytic palmoplantar keratoderma), linked to loss of heterozygosity on chromosome 17q. Familiar clustering of Barrett's esophagus and the recent identification of germline mutations in affected sibling pairs support a genetic link to esophageal adenocarcinoma.

CLINICAL PRESENTATION

Symptoms and signs:
- Dysphagia (74%): initially with solid foods, gradually progresses to semisolids and liquids; the latter signs usually indicate incurable disease with tumor involving more than 60% of the esophageal circumference. It may be felt as chest pain.
- Unintentional weight loss: usually of short duration. Losing >10% of body mass predicts poor outcome.
- Hoarseness: suggests recurrent laryngeal nerve involvement.
- Odynophagia and halitosis: unusual symptoms.
- Cervical adenopathy: usually involving supraclavicular lymph nodes.
- Dry cough: suggests tracheal involvement.
- Aspiration pneumonia: caused by fistula between the esophagus and trachea.
- Iron deficiency anemia: related to chronic GI blood loss.
- Massive hemoptysis or hematemesis from the invasion of vascular structures.
- Advanced disease spreads to lymph nodes, liver, lungs, peritoneum, and pleura.
- Hypercalcemia: associated with squamous cell carcinoma from secretion of a parathyroid-like tumor peptide.
Clinical findings:
- 50% to 60%of patients present with locally advanced, regional, or metastatic disease.

ETIOLOGY

Pathogenesis of esophageal cancers is attributable to chronic recurrent oxidative damage from any of the following etiologic agents, which cause inflammation, and esophagitis, increased cell turnover, and, ultimately, initiation of the carcinogenic process.

ETIOLOGIC AGENTS: Squamous cell carcinoma
- Excess alcohol consumption is strongly associated with squamous cell esophageal cancer in the United States; hard liquor is associated with a higher incidence than wine or beer.
- Tobacco and alcohol synergistically increase risk for squamous cell cancer.
- Other ingested carcinogens:
  1. Nitrates (converted to nitrites): South Asia, China.
  2. Smoked opiates: Northern Iran.
  3. Fungal toxins in pickled vegetables.
  4. Betel nut chewing.
- Mucosal damage:
  1. Long-term exposure to extremely hot tea (>70° C).
  2. Lye ingestion.
- Radiation-induced strictures.
- Achalasia: incidence of esophageal cancer is seven times greater in this population.
- Host susceptibility as a result of precancerous lesions:
  1. Plummer-Vinson syndrome (Paterson-Kelly): glossitis with iron deficiency.
  2. Congenital hyperkeratosis and pitting of palms and soles (tylosis).
- Human papillomavirus infection (particularly types 16 and 18) has been variably detected in squamous cell carcinoma of the esophagus, sometimes associated with p53 tumor suppressor gene mutations.
- Questionable relationship with prolonged bisphosphonate use (≥10 prescriptions, or use >3 yr).
- Possible association with celiac sprue or dietary deficiencies of molybdenum, selenium, zinc, vitamin A.

ADENOCARCINOMA:
- Smoking may increase the risk of developing adenocarcinoma, particularly in patients with Barrett's.
- Obesity, hiatal hernia, and diets lacking in fresh fruit and vegetables and high in fat (particularly from red meat and processed foods).
- Chronic GERD leading to Barrett's metaplasia and adenocarcinoma via immune cell infiltration and production of inflammatory mediators and reactive oxygen species. The annual rate of transformation from Barrett's to adenocarcinoma is <0.5%.
- *H. pylori* infection may reduce the risk of adenocarcinoma.

Dx DIAGNOSIS

DIFFERENTIAL DIAGNOSIS
- Achalasia.
- Scleroderma of the esophagus.
- Diffuse esophageal spasm.
- Esophageal rings and webs.

LABORATORY TESTS

Complete blood cell count, blood chemistry, liver enzymes. No biomarkers are available currently to diagnose, monitor, or predict outcomes.

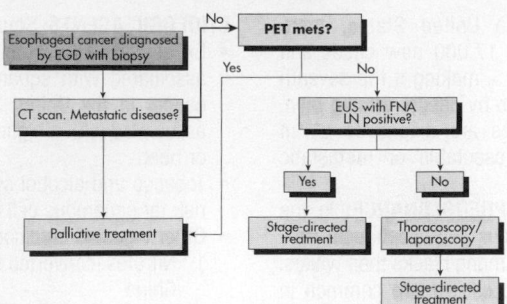

FIGURE 1E-50 Algorithm for staging esophageal cancer. *CT,* Computed tomography; *EGD,* esophago-gastroduodenoscopy; *mets,* metastases; *PET,* positron emission tomography. (From Cameron JL, Cameron AM: *Current surgical therapy,* ed 10, Philadelphia, 2011, Saunders.)

IMAGING STUDIES

Imaging studies are important not only for diagnosis but for accurate staging (Fig. 1E-50):

- Esophagogastroduodenoscopy (EGD) (Fig. E1E-51) should be performed initially to visualize smaller tumors, which may be missed by esophagogram, and to allow histopathologic confirmation.
- Endoscopic inspection of the larynx, trachea, and bronchi may identify concomitant cancers of head, neck, and lung ("triple endoscopy").
- Endoscopic ultrasound (EUS) (Fig. E1E-51) is the most accurate method for locoregional staging: to determine the depth of tumor invasion and to assess for and possibly obtain fine needle aspiration biopsies of suspicious lymph nodes.
- Double-contrast esophagogram effectively identifies large esophageal lesions (Fig. E1E-52).
  1. In contrast to benign esophageal leiomyomata, which cause narrowing with preservation of normal mucosal pattern, esophageal carcinomas cause ragged ulcerating mucosal changes in association with deeper infiltration.
- Chest and abdominal CT and/or integrated CT-PET scans can determine tumor spread for preoperative staging and may help restage patients after initial induction therapy.
- Staging laparoscopy may alter treatment plans in 20% to 30% of cases by more accurately staging regional lymph nodes and detecting occult peritoneal metastases.

STAGING

Table 1E-23 describes the TNM staging system for cancer of the esophagus from the American Joint Committee on Cancer Criteria.

 **TREATMENT**

TREATMENT OF ALL STAGES OF ESOPHAGEAL CANCER

SURGICAL RESECTION:

- Surgical resection of squamous cell carcinoma and adenocarcinoma of the middle esophagus and lower third of the esophagus is an acceptable initial modality for local

and resectable disease in the absence of widespread metastases detected by CT-PET and transesophageal ultrasound (T1 and T2 tumors). Gastric pull-through or colonic interposition typically is used to provide luminal continuity.

- Endoscopic mucosal resection may replace radical surgical resection in very early tumors with no lymph node involvement (Tis or T1a), but a recent Cochrane review found no studies comparing endoscopic treatment vs. surgery. This may be performed in conjunction with ablative therapies, including radiofrequency ablation, thermal ablation techniques, or photodynamic therapy.
- Complications of surgery:
  1. Anatomic fistula (usually with colon interposition, subphrenic abscesses).
  2. Respiratory complications.
  3. Cardiovascular complications are most common, including MI, CVA, and PE.
  4. Mortality is lower and clinical outcomes are better at high-volume hospitals and with minimally invasive surgery.

PRE-TREATMENT PATIENT PREPARATION

The patient needs to stop smoking and drinking alcohol if at all possible. Before neoadjuvant or definitive chemoradiotherapy, the patient should have placement of an intravenous access device (port-a-cath or PICC line) and a feeding tube (J-tube is preferable before surgical resection).

RADIATION THERAPY:

- Squamous cell carcinomas are more radiosensitive. Radiotherapy achieves good local control but is generally only used as monotherapy in a palliative mode for obstructive symptoms in patients with unresectable or advanced cancer or those with multiple comorbidities that limit treatment. It is best used for cervical esophageal tumors, but response rates are best when combined with chemotherapy.
- Radiotherapy in the preoperative/neoadjuvant setting is taken to a total dose of 40-50 Gy. For definitive therapy, the dose range is 50-65 Gy.
- Palliative radiotherapy for bone metastasis is also effective.

- Complications of radiotherapy: can best be avoided by 3D conformal therapy.
  1. Esophageal stricture, fistula formation, radiation-induced pulmonary fibrosis, and transverse myelitis are the most common.
  2. Radiotherapy-induced cardiomyopathy and skin changes are rare.

COMBINATION CHEMOTHERAPY, RADIOTHERAPY RX, & SURGICAL RX:

- Chemotherapy is most often given with concurrent radiotherapy (chemoradiotherapy). Chemotherapy acts as a radiosensitizer and makes tumor cells more vulnerable to the effects of ionizing radiation thus improving tumoricidal effects on cancer. Neoadjuvant chemoradiotherapy followed by surgery is the most common approach for patients with resectable disease, but employed primarily for patients with stage IIA or higher disease. Five-year survival is improved with neoadjuvant chemoradiotherapy (39%) versus surgery alone (16%). Several trials have now shown that preoperative chemoradiotherapy improves survival among patients with potentially curable esophageal or esophagogastric junction cancer. Neoadjuvant chemotherapy alone is another

---

TABLE 1E-23 TNM Staging System for Cancer of the Esophagus (American Joint Committee on Cancer Criteria)

Primary Tumor (T)*

TX	Primary tumor cannot be assessed
T0	No evidence of primary tumor
Tis	High-grade dysplasia[†]
T1	Tumor invades lamina propria, muscularis mucosae, or submucosa
T1a	Tumor invades lamina propria or muscularis mucosae
T1b	Tumor invades submucosa
T2	Tumor invades muscularis propria
T3	Tumor invades adventitia
T4	Tumor invades adjacent structures
T4a	Resectable tumor invading pleura, pericardium, or diaphragm
T4b	Unresectable tumor invading other adjacent structures, such as aorta, vertebral body, trachea, etc.

Lymph Node (N)[‡]

NX	Regional lymph nodes cannot be assessed
N0	No regional lymph node metastasis
N1	Metastasis in 1-2 regional lymph nodes
N2	Metastasis in 3-6 regional lymph nodes
N3	Metastasis in 7 or more regional lymph nodes

Distant Metastasis (M)

MX	Metastasis cannot be assessed
M0	No distant metastasis
M1	Distant metastasis

*(1) At least maximal dimension of the tumor must be recorded and (2) multiple tumors require the T(m) suffix.
[†]High-grade dysplasia includes all noninvasive neoplastic epithelia that was formerly called carcinoma in situ.
[‡]Number must be recorded for total number of regional nodes sampled and total number of reported nodes with metastasis.
From Edge S et al (eds): *AJCC cancer staging manual,* ed 7, New York, 2010, Springer.

option for locally advanced disease, but results are not as good as neoadjuvant chemoradiotherapy.

- Chemoradiotherapy followed by surgery should be offered to late stage I (T1bN0 or higher), stage II, and stage III esophageal cancer patients as the current standard of care. In several studies, this approach significantly improved local control, reduced recurrence, and reduced mortality compared with surgery alone in patients with resectable esophageal cancer. Trimodality therapy is the preferred treatment for most esophageal cancers.
- Chemoradiotherapy alone may be offered as the definitive treatment for patients who are not surgical candidates.
- Combination chemotherapy utilizing a platinum doublet (platinum agent plus second agent) can achieve significant tumor reduction in 30% to 60% of patients. Cisplatin, oxaliplatin or carboplatin is usually given with 5-FU (5-fluorouracil) or paclitaxel to obtain the desired tumoricidal effects.
- Capecitabine in combination with either cisplatin or oxaliplatin is as effective as 5FU in the neoadjuvant or definitive treatment setting.
- Complications of chemotherapy primarily include mucositis, nausea, vomiting, diarrhea, myelosuppression, nephrotoxicity, ototoxicity, and neurotoxicity. These can occur to varying degrees and are certainly more significant in the elderly and otherwise infirmed.
- Postoperative adjuvant chemotherapy with or without radiation therapy may be offered to node-positive patients who underwent initial surgery alone.

TREATMENT OF UNRESECTABLE, LOCALLY ADVANCED, OR METASTATIC DISEASE

- Combination chemotherapy regimens as a rule have a higher response rate than single agent therapy. Response rates can be as high as 50% but that does not always translate into prolonged survival.
- Neoadjuvant chemotherapy regimens can also be utilized in locally advanced or metastatic settings. Cisplatin is probably the most active agent, and this combined with 5FU can yield response rates shown in several studies of 20% to 50%. If a taxane is added to this regimen in the metastatic setting, the triple drug regimen can lead to a prolongation in disease progression by about 2 months, which may translate into prolonged survival. However, the patients have to be carefully chosen for this triple drug regimen because of increased toxicity. Other active double regimens can combine cisplatin with irinotecan, etoposide, or gemcitabine. Again, capecitabine can be substituted for 5FU in these regimens.

TARGETED MOLECULAR THERAPY

- Ramucirumab is a recombinant monoclonal IgG1 antibody that is a vascular endothelial growth factor receptor 2 (VEGFR-2) antagonist. It inhibits ligand proliferation and migration of endothelial cells and ultimately inhibits angiogenesis. It is indicated for second line therapy in conjunction with paclitaxel or as third line as monotherapy.
- Trastuzumab, in combination with cisplatin and 5FU, can be used as first line therapy for metastatic esophageal cancer in patients with HER-2 overexpressing adenocarcinoma. Approximately 22% of adenocarcinomas will overexpress the type II epidermal growth factor receptor HER2. The overall response rate is 47%.

FOLLOW-UP CARE

The majority of recurrences develop within 12 months. Clinical monitoring, lab tests, imaging, and endoscopic evaluation where appropriate (particularly Barrett's), are performed for postoperative surveillance, without clear benefit in earlier detection or decreased mortality. For patients who have undergone definitive therapy, it is recommended that endoscopic surveillance be performed every 3 months for the first year, and then annually. Palliative procedures such as repeated endoscopic dilation, endoscopic ablation, endoscopic mucosal resection, photodynamic therapy, brachytherapy, feeding tube insertion, or placement of expandable metal stents or polyvinyl prostheses to bypass tumors have been used for unresectable patients. The morbidity and mortality associated with resection in patients with advanced disease and/or for palliation argues against offering this modality to most of these patients.

SURVIVORSHIP

- Overall 5-yr survival for all stages at presentation is 15% (39% for localized disease, 21% for regional disease, and 4% for distant disease).
- Endoscopic therapy for highly selected stage 0 or stage I patients with disease limited to the submucosa may have 5-year survival rates of 70% to 90%.
- Surgical resection without neoadjuvant treatment: 5-yr survival rate is 5% to 30%, with higher survival (up to 45%-50%) in early stage cancers.
- Radiation therapy without chemotherapy or surgery: 5-yr survival rate of 6% to 20%.
- Chemoradiation without surgery: 5-year survival up to 30%.
- Combined trimodality treatment: up to 45% to 50% 5-year survival rates (all stages of disease treated).
- Patients with metastatic disease have median survivals of less than 1 year with palliative chemotherapy.

REFERRAL

- To gastroenterologist for endoscopy for patients with dysphagia, odynophagia, or unexplained weight loss, or for palliative care.
- To medical oncologist for evaluation of preoperative chemotherapy and care of the metastatic patient.
- To radiation oncologist for palliative therapy if tumor is unresectable or obstruction is present.
- To hospice if appropriate.

PEARLS & CONSIDERATIONS

COMMENTS

More than 50% of patients with esophageal cancer are diagnosed when the disease is metastatic or unresectable.

PREVENTION

- A diet high in fruits, vegetables, and antioxidants may be associated with lower risk of esophageal cancer.
- Avoid tobacco and excessive alcohol use.
- Avoid ingested toxins known to cause esophageal cancers.
- Aspirin may have a chemopreventive role in Barrett's but is only currently recommended for patients with other (e.g., cardiac) indications.
- There is no evidence that vitamins, Chinese herbal regimens, or green tea prevent esophageal cancer.
- Screening the general population is not recommended. If Barrett esophagus is detected, regularly scheduled surveillance endoscopies are necessary, with consideration for radiofrequency or other ablation therapy if dysplasia is detected.

PATIENT/FAMILY EDUCATION

Provide education and support about the likely prognosis because most esophageal cancers are diagnosed at an advanced stage.

SUGGESTED READINGS

Available at www.expertconsult.com

RELATED CONTENT

Barrett Esophagus (Related Key Topic)
Esophageal Cancer (Patient Information)

AUTHORS: **HARLAN G. RICH, M.D.,** and **ANTHONY G. THOMAS, D.O.**

BASIC INFORMATION

DEFINITION

A predominantly postural and action tremor that is bilateral and tends to progress slowly over the years in the absence of other neurologic abnormalities.

SYNONYMS

Benign essential tremor
Familial tremor

ICD-10CM CODES
G25.0 Essential tremor

EPIDEMIOLOGY & DEMOGRAPHICS

PREDOMINANT AGE: Can begin at any age, but incidence increases after age 40 yr. Prevalence is 6% to 9% for those >60 yr.
GENETICS: No gender or racial predominance.

PHYSICAL FINDINGS & CLINICAL PRESENTATION

- Patients complain of tremor that is most bothersome when writing or holding something such as a newspaper or trying to drink from a cup. Worsens under emotional distress.
- Tremor, 4 to 12 Hz, bilateral postural and action tremor of the upper extremities. May also affect the head, voice, trunk, and legs. Typically it is the same amplitude throughout the action, such as bringing a cup to the mouth. No other neurologic abnormalities on examination except difficulty with tandem gait. Patients often note improvement with intake of small amounts of alcohol.

ETIOLOGY

Often an inherited disease, autosomal dominant; sporadic cases without a family history are frequently encountered

DIAGNOSIS

DIFFERENTIAL DIAGNOSIS (SEE TABLE 1E-24)

- Parkinson's disease—tremor is usually asymmetric, especially early on in the disease, and is predominantly a resting tremor. Patients

with Parkinson's disease will often also have increased tone, decreased facial expression, slowness of movement, and shuffling gait.
- Cerebellar tremor—an intention tremor that increases at the end of a goal-directed movement (such as finger to nose testing). Other associated neurologic abnormalities include ataxia, dysarthria, and difficulty with tandem gait.
- Drug-induced—there are many drugs that enhance normal, physiologic tremor. These include caffeine, nicotine, lithium, levothyroxine, β-adrenergic bronchodilators, amiodarone, valproate, and SSRIs.
- Wilson's disease—wing-beating tremor that is most pronounced with shoulders abducted, elbows flexed, and fingers pointing toward each other. Usually there are other neurologic abnormalities including dysarthria, dystonia, and Kayser-Fleischer rings on ophthalmologic examination.
- Physiologic tremor

WORKUP

- Essential tremor is a clinical diagnosis
- All imaging studies (MRI, CT) are unnecessary unless there are other associated neurologic abnormalities
- Obtain TSH (rule out hyperthyroidism)
- In patients younger than 40 yr with other neurologic abnormalities, send ceruloplasmin, serum Cu, 24-hr urine Cu to rule out Wilson's disease

TREATMENT

Treat essential tremor when it is functionally impairing. Treatments are up to 75% effective.

NONPHARMACOLOGIC THERAPY

- Stress management
- Minimize use of caffeine if consumption is correlated with worsened symptoms.
- Small quantities of alcohol at social functions may be beneficial.

ACUTE GENERAL Rx

Propranolol (20-40 mg) may be used in preparation for specific event.

CHRONIC Rx

First-line agents:
- Propranolol/Inderal LA: usual starting dose is 30 mg. The usual therapeutic dose is 160 to

320 mg. Although not contraindicated, they must be used with caution in those with asthma, depression, cardiac disease, and diabetes.
- Primidone: usual starting dose is 12.5 to 25 mg qhs. Usual therapeutic dose is between 62.5 and 750 mg daily (assuming side effects are tolerated). Sedation and nausea are common at treatment initiation.
- Topiramate: 25 mg qhs, may titrate up to about 400 mg

Other agents:
- Gabapentin: 400 mg qhs, usual therapeutic dose is 1200 to 3600 mg
- Alprazolam: 0.75 to 2.75 mg
- Botulinum toxin injected focally may decrease tremor
- Atenolol, sotalol

SURGICAL Rx

Thalamic deep brain stimulation (or possibly thalamotomy) contralateral to side of tremor is reserved for resistant tremor or for patients who do not tolerate drug therapy.

DISPOSITION

Patients should be reassured that the condition is not associated with other neurologic disabilities; however, it can become quite functionally disabling over time.

REFERRAL

This is a condition that usually can be treated by the primary care physician; however, if patient fails first-line therapies then patient should be referred to specialists for other drug trials and other possible surgical options.

PEARLS & CONSIDERATIONS

- Essential tremor is the most common of all movement disorders.
- In addition to motor dysfunction, essential tremor can cause significant psychological impact on patients in social situations.

SUGGESTED READINGS
Available at www.expertconsult.com

RELATED CONTENT
Essential Tremor (Patient Information)

AUTHOR: **U. SHIVRAJ SOHUR, M.D., PH.D.**

TABLE 1E-24 Overlapping Features of Various Types of Tremor

Feature	Parkinson's Syndrome	Cerebellar Tremor	Essential Tremor
Present at rest	Yes	No	Yes
Increased tone	Yes	No	No
Decreased tone	No	Yes	No
Postural abnormality	Yes	Yes	No
Head involvement	Yes	Yes	Yes
Intentional component	No	Yes	Yes
Incoordination	No	Yes	No

From Remmel KS et al: *Handbook of symptom-oriented neurology*, ed 3, St Louis, 2002, Mosby.

BASIC INFORMATION

DEFINITION

Failure to thrive (FTT) describes a delay in growth and development among children. FTT is a cluster of symptoms rather than a specific disease.

SYNONYMS

Pediatric undernutrition
Faltering growth
Weight faltering
Growth failure
FTT

ICD-10CM CODES
R62.51 Failure to thrive (child)

EPIDEMIOLOGY & DEMOGRAPHICS

INCIDENCE: FTT is a common problem, though its incidence in the community is unclear. A total of 1% to 5% of inpatient pediatric admissions are for evaluation of FTT.

PREDOMINANT SEX AND AGE: FTT most commonly occurs among children ages 6 to 12 months, with 80% presenting before 18 months of age. Most FTT patients present before 3 years of age. Males and females are equally affected.

RISK FACTORS: Poverty is the single greatest risk factor. Nonmedical: poverty, food insecurity, social isolation, neglect, and physical or emotional abuse. Medical: Intrauterine growth restriction (IUGR), prematurity, medical conditions leading to inadequate food intake, food malabsorption, or increased metabolic demand.

PHYSICAL FINDINGS & CLINICAL PRESENTATION

Children have blunted growth in height, weight, head circumference, or any combination of these. Children may have pallid, dry, or cracked skin, sparse hair growth, poorly developed musculature, lack of subcutaneous fat, swollen abdomen, or evidence of vitamin deficiencies.

ETIOLOGY

FTT is the result of inadequate nutrition, which may be due to a wide range of medical or psychosocial causes. FTT can be thought of as stemming from inadequate nutritional intake, malabsorption of nutrients, or increased caloric expenditure, though the actual cause is commonly multifactorial.

DIAGNOSIS

DIFFERENTIAL DIAGNOSIS

- Inadequate nutritional intake: food insecurity, poor parent knowledge of child's needs, formula dilution, excessive juice, breastfeeding difficulties, neglect, behavioral feeding problem, oromotor dysfunction, developmental delay, emesis, gastroesophageal reflux, volvulus, increased intracranial pressure, genetic disease (trisomy 13, 18, 21), and psychiatric conditions

- Malabsorption: cystic fibrosis, celiac disease, eosinophilic esophagitis, food protein insensitivity or intolerance, and inflammatory bowel disease
- Increased metabolic demand: insulin resistance, congenital infection, other infection, genetic syndrome, hyperthyroidism, chronic disease, and malignancy

WORKUP

- Evaluation should include the child's eating habits, caloric intake, parent-child interactions, psychosocial history, past medical history, medications, family history to include parent stature and weight, review of systems, and physical exam. Fig. 1F-1 illustrates an algorithm for management of a child with failure to thrive (FTT).
- Height, weight, and weight-to-length measurements are most sensitive, whereas head circumference and body mass index (BMI) may be useful. Common FTT criteria for children younger than 2 years are below, but clinical judgment should be used because normal causes and biologic variants may exist.
  1. Length, weight, or BMI below the 3rd or 5th percentile on more than one consecutive visit
  2. Weight that drops below two major percentile lines
  3. Weight less than 80% of the ideal weight for age
  4. Weight-to-length below the 5th percentile or weight-for-length less than 70% to 79% of the median
  5. Weight velocity below the 3rd or 5th percentile
  6. Weight less than 70% of the 50th percentile; may require hospitalization
- Obtain caliper measurements of skinfold thickness and midarm muscle circumference.
- Observation of a meal being taken to assess potential feeding difficulties.
- A 3-day food diary is helpful, as well as consultation by a nutritionist, to calculate the child's intake of energy, protein, vitamins, and minerals.
- Assess stool frequency, consistency, quantity, as well as fat, blood, or mucus content.
- Routine hospitalization for FTT evaluation is not recommended. Rarely, hospitalization for observed feedings and further workup is warranted.

LABORATORY TESTS

- Laboratory tests should be based on medical history and physical exam findings and should consider the risk for refeeding syndrome and other medical complications.
- Consider CBC with red blood cell indices, complete chemistry panel including phosphorus, thyroid function, urinalysis, HIV testing, C-reactive protein or erythrocyte sedimentation rate, celiac screening, stool

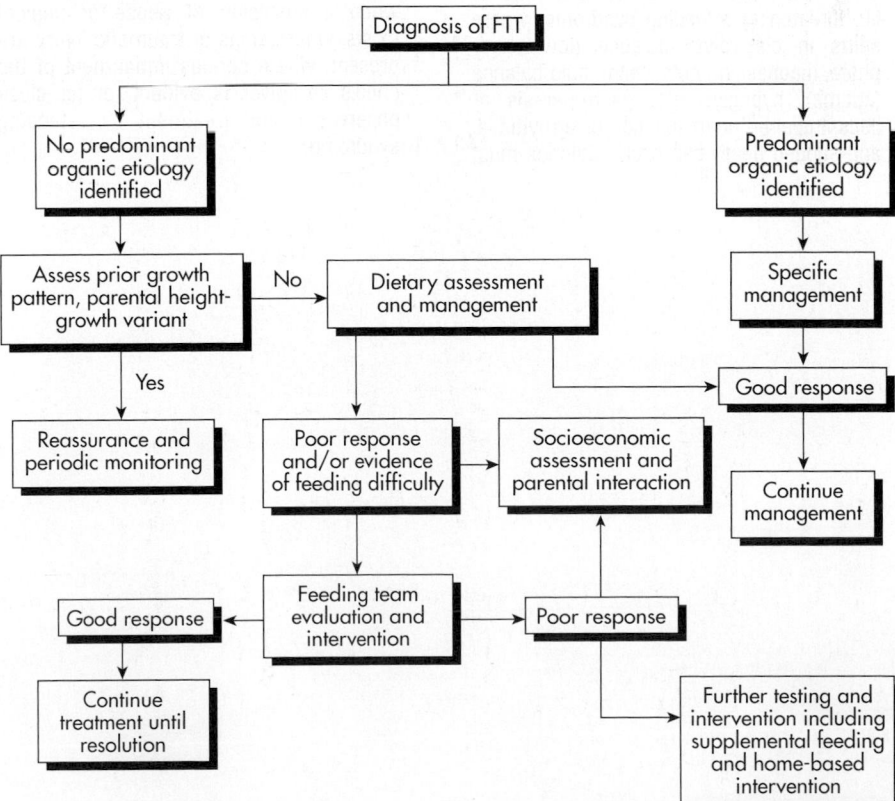

FIGURE 1F-1 Algorithm for management of a child with failure to thrive (FTT). (Shashidhar H, Tolia V: Failure to Thrive. *In* Wyllie R, Hyams, JS (eds): *Pediatric gastrointestinal and liver disease*, 4th ed, Philadelphia, 2011, Elsevier, pp. 136–145.e3.)

examination for fats or reducing substances, or sweat chloride testing. If clinically indicated, growth hormone level and genetic sequencing can be checked.

IMAGING STUDIES

Imaging tests are not routinely performed but may be warranted depending on underlying medical cause.

 **TREATMENT**

Identification and management of underlying causes should be implemented. In cases in which there is no underlying medical condition, providing nutrition repletion will, by definition, correct FTT. A multidisciplinary team (including, but not limited to, social workers, occupational/speech therapists, nutritionists/dietitians, nurses, advanced practice nurses, and pediatricians) should be used.

NONPHARMACOLOGIC THERAPY

- Add calorie-dense foods or increase the number of feedings.
- Enteral feeding, percutaneous endoscopic gastrostomy (PEG), and nasogastric feeding tubes can be used to accelerate weight gain, and results should be seen within 2 to 7 days. Caloric intake should be titrated up to goal over 5 to 7 days. Caloric goals by age group: 0 to 6 months: 108 kcal/kg/day, 6 to 12 months: 98 kcal/kg/day, and 1 to 3 years: 102 kcal/kg/day.
- Swift restoration of nutrition can lead to life-threatening refeeding syndrome, where shifts in electrolyte balance (low phosphate, magnesium, potassium), fluid balance (edema), hypoglycemia, gastroparesis or ileus, impaired heart function or arrhythmia, and sudden death can occur. Calories must

therefore be titrated slowly to goal with close monitoring.
- Treat underlying medical conditions, including mental health disorders.
- Assist with family psychosocial stressors.
- Follow up closely, including home nursing visits.
- In cases where economic, psychosocial, or parental issues are suspected and the child's growth is not maintained, state and federal legislation regarding reporting to child protection services must be followed.

ACUTE GENERAL Rx

Multivitamins including iron and zinc

CHRONIC Rx

Nutrient repletion with the goal of accelerated growth should be continued for 4 to 9 months

DISPOSITION

Children with FTT commonly remain small in height and weight. Studies consistently find that children with FTT are more prone to long-term cognitive, learning, and behavioral abnormalities.

REFERRAL

- Indicated based on the cause of FTT
- Hospitalization should be considered in cases of FTT in which a child is less than 70% of predicted weight for length, where outpatient management has failed, when a suspicion of abuse or neglect exists, where signs of traumatic injury are present, where serious impairment of the child's caregiver is evident, or for close observation and treatment for refeeding syndrome.

 **PEARLS & CONSIDERATIONS**

COMMENTS

- FTT is a common childhood symptom encountered in the outpatient and inpatient pediatric populations, is caused by undernutrition, and is associated with inadequate nutritional intake, malabsorption, or increased metabolic demand.
- A thorough multidisciplinary approach to assessment, diagnosis, and management should be used to manage nutrient status and any underlying cause(s).
- Child height/length, weight, and weight-for-length measurements with comparison to standard growth curves are useful in the identification of potential cases of FTT.
- FTT treatment should include restoration of nutrition along with treatment of the underlying cause(s), including psychosocial factors.
- Although FTT can usually be managed effectively in the outpatient setting, specific indications for inpatient treatment should be considered.

PREVENTION

Nutritional counseling and anticipatory guidance should be provided at each well-child visit. Growth parameters should be measured during serial clinical assessments and compared with growth standards. Enlist dietitians and visiting nurses to provide support to families with children at high risk of FTT.

SUGGESTED READINGS
Available at www.expertconsult.com

AUTHOR: **GRAYSON W. ARMSTRONG, M.D., M.P.H.**

 **BASIC INFORMATION**

DEFINITION

A fall is an "event which results in a person coming to rest inadvertently on the ground and other than a consequence of the following: loss of consciousness, sudden onset of paralysis, or epileptic seizure" (Kellogg International Work Group, *Danish Medical Bulletin,* 34, 1-24).

SYNONYMS

Syncope
Collapse

ICD-10CM CODES
E880-E888.9 Accidental fall
R29.6 Repeated falls

EPIDEMIOLOGY & DEMOGRAPHICS

INCIDENCE:
- Trauma is the fifth leading cause of death in persons >65 years of age, and falls are responsible for 70% of accidental deaths in persons ≥75 yr.
- The incidence of falls among community-dwelling older adults is 30% to 40%. Two thirds of falls in the community are preventable; 6% to 7% of these falls result in fracture.
- The incidence of falls for nursing home and hospitalized older adults is three times the rate of community-dwelling older adults. Over 50% of nursing home residents fall during their stay.
- 20% to 30% of older adults who fall suffer significant injury leading to immobility, dependence, and an increased risk of early death.

HEALTHCARE COST:
- In 2006, patients ≥65 had over 2.1 million visits to the ED for injurious falls, which was 10.5% of all ED visits among the elderly and 29.6% of these visits required hospital admission. In those that were admitted, the mean length of stay was 5.5 days with a mean cost of $10,800. The aggregate hospital cost for those requiring admission in 2006 was $6.8 billion. (Source: Healthcare Cost and Utilization Project).

PREDOMINANT SEX & AGE:
- Fall-related mortality is highest among older white men followed by white women, black men, and black women.
- The incidence rates of falls increase with advancing age.
- Older adults ≥85 years are 10 to 15 times more likely to have a fracture compared with those aged 60 to 65 years.

RISK FACTORS: Four groups of risk factors for falls have been identified (Table 1F-1):
1. Intrinsic factors inherent in the older adult who falls.
2. Extrinsic factors circumstantial to the older adult who falls.
3. Falls in nursing homes.
4. Situational or the activity in which the older adult is engaged in when a fall occurs.

CLINICAL PRESENTATION
- Older adults who fall may present with minor soft tissue injuries, such as lacerations or bruising, hip fracture, or head trauma; however, most falls are not reported unless an injury has occurred.
- If an older adult presents for medical attention for a fall or reports recurrent falls in the past year or difficulties in walking or balance, a multifactorial fall risk assessment should be completed.
- The multifactorial fall risk assessment should include:
  1. Focused history: A detailed history of events and circumstances surrounding fall, relevant risk factors including review of medications, acute and chronic medical problems (e.g., osteoporosis, urinary incontinence, and cardiovascular disease), and whether the fall was witnessed.
  2. Physical examination
     1. Vital signs including orthostatics.
     2. Cardiovascular examination assessing for arrhythmias, carotid bruits, or new murmurs.
     3. Neurologic examination including vision assessment, evaluation of lower extremity strength, peripheral nerves, proprioception, and testing of cortical, extrapyramidal, and cerebellar function.
     4. Gait and balance assessment: "Get up and go test" is a rapid assessment that will quickly tell you if the patient needs rehabilitation and what to work on. (Ask patient to stand from a seated position without use of hands, walk 10 feet forward, turn around, and return to chair and sit).
     5. Musculoskeletal exam with attention to joints of lower extremity, feet, and footwear.
  2. Functional assessment including the older adult's activities of daily living skills, use of adaptive equipment, and fear of falling
  3. Environmental assessment of home safety

ETIOLOGY
- Falls are a multifactorial syndrome resulting from the cumulative effects of impaired gait and balance, aging, polypharmacy, depression, cognitive impairment, acute medical illness, or environmental factors (Fig. E1F-2).

TABLE 1F-1 Risk Factors for Falls in the Elderly

Intrinsic

Aging

Age-related decline in vestibular function might lead to loss of balance, dizziness, and falls. Aging of the vision system (e.g., glaucoma, cataracts, retinopathy) may result in decreased visual acuity, inability to discriminate dark/light, and decreased spatial perception.

Cardiac

Cardiac arrhythmias, carotid sinus hypersensitivity, neurocardiogenic syncope

Neurologic

Parkinson's disease, normal pressure hydrocephalus (NPH), sensory neuropathy, dementia/impaired cognition, cervical myelopathy, senile gait disorder, prior stroke (One third of the elderly have abnormal position sense)

Musculoskeletal

Lower extremity weakness, impaired knee extension and ankle plantar flexion strength contribute to abnormalities in gait velocity and step length, deconditioning, arthritis, foot abnormalities (such as bunions, calluses, or nail abnormalities)

Vascular

Vertebrobasilar insufficiency, postural hypotension, postprandial hypotension

Metabolic

Hypoglycemia, hypothyroidism, hyponatremia

Psychiatric

Depression

Medications

Use of more than four medications may be associated with an increased risk of falls. Medications that may increase fall risk include benzodiazepines, sleeping medications, neuroleptics, antidepressants, anticonvulsants, class I antiarrhythmics, and antihypertensives (Rao, 2005).

Extrinsic

Environmental

Environmental hazards cause >50% of falls in the elderly (cords, furniture, small objects, ill-fitting shoes, slippery surfaces, loose rugs, uneven steps, optical patterns on escalators). Majority occurs with mild-moderate activity (walking, stepping up/down, changing position); 70% occur at home and 10% on stairs (descending > ascending).

Nursing Home Falls

20% have a cardiovascular cause (hypotension: drug induced, postprandial, postural, or bradycardia)
5% are the result of an acute illness such as PNA, febrile illness, UTI, CHF.
3% are from an overwhelming intrinsic event such as syncope, seizure, stroke, psychoactive drugs.

Situational

Tripping over obstacles, carrying heavy items, descending/ascending stairs, rapid turning, reaching overhead, climbing ladders, ill-fitting shoes, lack of assistive devices

- Most falls among community-dwelling older adults are due to environmental factors, whereas falls among nursing home residents are a result of confusion, gait impairment, or postural hypotension.

Dx DIAGNOSIS

DIFFERENTIAL DIAGNOSIS

Falls are often a nonspecific symptom of an acute illness (such as delirium, urinary tract infection, acute anemia, or pneumonia) or an exacerbation of a chronic disease (chronic heart failure [CHF] or chronic obstructive pulmonary disease [COPD]). The mnemonic "DELIRIUMS" can be used to assess the differential diagnosis in acute delirium. (**D**rugs, **E**motional [depression], **L**ow PaO_2 [CHF, COPD], **I**nfection, **R**etention [urinary, fecal], **I**ctal status, **U**nder nutrition/hydration, **M**etabolic, **S**ubdural/Sensory [all neurologic causes] workup).

WORKUP

- Older adults presenting with a noninjurious fall need a detailed history and physical exam to identify acute medical illnesses and potential modifiable risk factors. Laboratory and neuroimaging studies may be necessary if the history and physical exam indicate a specific problem. ECG and Holter monitoring may be considered if cardiac arrhythmia is suspected.
- See Fig. E1F-2.

LABORATORY TESTS

CBC, stool guaiac, blood chemistries, thyroid function, liver function, vitamin B_{12} level, folate level, erythrocyte sedimentation rate, vitamin D level, drug levels, and urinalysis depending on physical/historical findings.

IMAGING STUDIES

- CT or MRI of the brain or cervical spine films in the presence of neurologic or gait impairment.
- Chest x-ray if pulmonary pathology (pneumonia, pulmonary edema) is suspected.
- Consider ECG, echocardiography, or Holter monitor if suspicious for structural cardiac abnormality or syncope.

Rx TREATMENT

NONPHARMACOLOGIC THERAPY

- Physical therapy evaluation for gait and balance training, evaluation of appropriate assisted devices (e.g., cane, walker), the use of fall prevention equipment (e.g., low beds, bed alarms).
- Home safety assessment: studies show that 50% of recurrent fallers fell doing the same activity that caused them to fall the first time.

This can be prevented by creating a home safety evaluation checklist (preferably done by family member to improve compliance) or arranging for a home safety inspection by a visiting nurse or occupational therapist.
- Minimization or discontinuation of certain medications associated with falls (psychotropics).
- Customized exercise program to improve strength, gait, and balance
- Evaluation of proper footwear, hard sole, and low heel height.

ACUTE GENERAL Rx

Hospitalization may be necessary for treatment of hip fracture, subdural hematoma, lacerations, or trauma as well as the treatment of underlying cause of the fall such as infection, metabolic disturbances, cardiovascular (e.g., carotid sinus hypersensitivity, vasovagal syndrome, bradyarrhythmias, and tachyarrhythmias) or neurologic abnormality.

CHRONIC Rx

- Screen and treat for osteoporosis as low bone density increases the risk of hip or other fractures.
- Optimize treatment of chronic illnesses such as CHF, COPD, osteoarthritis, Parkinson's disease, dementia, postural hypotension, and visual problems.
- Vitamin D supplementation of at least 800 IU per day. Epidemiological studies reveal that compared with usual care, short-term intervention with oral nutritional supplementation and dietetic counseling significantly decrease falls in malnourished older adults.

COMPLEMENTARY & ALTERNATIVE MEDICINE

T'ai chi has been shown to reduce the risk of falls in community-dwelling study participants.

DISPOSITION

Falls increase the older adult's risk of hospitalization, institutionalization, and mortality.

REFERRAL

- Referral may be appropriate to cardiologist, ophthalmologist, neurologist, or podiatrist depending on the presence of a specific condition.
- Consider referral to physical therapist for gait and balance training, evaluation for assisted device, or strengthening program.

 PEARLS & CONSIDERATIONS

COMMENTS

- Fear of falling may lead to restriction of activities, social isolation, and dependence.

- Older adults with four or more risk factors have a 78% chance of falling.
- Mortality from falls has increased by 42% over the past decade.

PREVENTION

The U.S. Preventive Services Task Force recommends exercise or physical therapy and vitamin D supplementation to prevent falls in community-dwelling adults aged ≥65 who are at increased risk for falls. It does not recommend automatically performing an in-depth multifactorial risk assessment in conjunction with comprehensive management of identified risks to prevent falls in community-dwelling adults aged 65 or older because the likelihood of benefit is small. In determining whether this service is appropriate in individual cases, patients and clinicians should consider the balance of benefits and harms on the basis of the circumstances of prior falls, comorbid medical conditions, and patient values.

SCREENING

The "get up and go test" is a quick assessment of balance and gait. A more in-depth screening tool for falls is the Tinetti gait and balance assessment, which evaluates normal and adaptive ability to maintain balance when rising from a chair, standing with eyes closed, turning, and receiving a sternal nudge. It also evaluates several components of gait (step height, postural sway, path deviation). The test is scored on the patient's ability to perform specific tasks. Scoring is done on a 3-point scale with a range of 0 to 2. Individual scores are combined to form three measures: an overall gait assessment score (maximum score = 12), an overall balance assessment score (maximum score = 16), and a gait and balance score (maximum score = 28). In general, patients who score below 19 are at high risk for falls, and those who score 19-24 are at risk for falls.

PATIENT/FAMILY EDUCATION

Providing education and information for the patient and caregiver regarding fall prevention strategies in addition to multifactorial risk reduction strategies

EVIDENCE

Available at www.expertconsult.com

SUGGESTED READINGS

Available at www.expertconsult.com

AUTHORS: **SEAN H. UITERWYK, M.D., ALICIA J. CURTIN, PH.D.** and **KEITH BRENNAN, M.D.**

BASIC INFORMATION

DEFINITION

Familial adenomatous polyposis (FAP) is a highly penetrant autosomal-dominant condition characterized by hundreds of colorectal adenomatous polyps that inevitably progress to cancer (Fig. 1F-3). Gardner's syndrome is a subset of FAP, with prominent extraintestinal manifestations including dental abnormalities, soft tissue lesions, desmoid tumors, and osteomas.

SYNONYMS

Familial adenomatous polyposis
Gardner's syndrome

ICD-10CM CODES

D12.5 Benign neoplasm of sigmoid colon
D12.4 Benign neoplasm of descending colon
D12.3 Benign neoplasm of transverse colon
D12.2 Benign neoplasm of ascending colon
D12.6 Benign neoplasm of colon, unspecified

EPIDEMIOLOGY & DEMOGRAPHICS

- FAP occurs in approximately 1 in 10,000 births.
- FAP accounts for <1% of all colorectal cancers.
- Individuals develop hundreds to thousands of adenomatous colorectal polyps.
- Polyps usually present in adolescence.
- 100% lifetime risk for colorectal cancer; most diagnosed by 40 yr of age.
- Gastric, duodenal, periampullary, and small bowel polyps occur but have lower malignant potential.
- Increased risk for other tumors: desmoid (15%), duodenal/periampullary (7%), thyroid (2%), brain (1%), childhood hepatoblastoma (1%), nasopharyngeal angiofibroma (benign), pancreatic (2%), adrenal adenoma (10%), and gastric (1%).

PHYSICAL FINDINGS & CLINICAL PRESENTATION

Phenotypic variability is seen in individuals and families with the same mutation. Soft tissue and bone abnormalities may precede intestinal disease. These findings are reported in at least 20% of individuals with FAP.

- Congenital hypertrophy of the retinal pigment epithelium (CHRPE): benign fundus lesions, usually present at birth
- Dental abnormalities: supernumerary or unerupted teeth
- Soft tissue lesions: epidermal or sebaceous cysts, fibromas, lipomas, desmoid tumors (benign, locally invasive, aggressive connective tissue tumor)
- Osteomas (benign bone growths): skull, mandible, long bone
- Anemia, occult blood in stool, bowel obstruction, weight loss

ETIOLOGY

- FAP is caused by mutations of the tumor suppressor gene adenomatous polyposis coli (APC) on chromosome 5q21-q22; more than 1000 disease-causing mutations identified. The site of the mutation may explain the prominent extraintestinal lesions found in Gardner's syndrome.
- De novo mutations are responsible for approximately 20% of FAP cases. These may be due to germline mutations or somatic cell mosaicism, which is seen when a new mutation occurs in the APC gene post-fertilization and is present in only a subset of cell types or tissues.

DIAGNOSIS

In individuals with a family history, more than 100 adenomatous colorectal polyps, CHRPE lesions, or genetic testing confirms diagnosis. In those without a family history, more than 100 adenomatous colorectal polyps suggest the diagnosis, and genetic testing confirms it.

DIFFERENTIAL DIAGNOSIS

- Turcot's syndrome
- Attenuated FAP
- MUTYH-associated polyposis
- Peutz-Jeghers syndrome
- Juvenile polyposis syndrome
- Cowden Disease
- Hereditary mixed polyposis syndrome
- POLE or POLD1 polyposis
- Hyperplastic polyposis

WORKUP

History, physical examination, laboratory tests, imaging studies

DIAGNOSTIC SCREENING OPTIONS

GENETIC TESTING: NOTE: Genetic counseling should be performed, and written informed consent obtained before testing. Refer to a specialized center for counseling and evaluation.

- Should be offered to first-degree relatives of affected individuals (with an identified mutation) at age 10 to 12 yr and clinically suspected individuals.
- Able to identify a mutation in approximately 80% of families. To ensure that the family has a detectable mutation, test an affected family member first.
- If positive in the affected individual, the test can differentiate with 100% accuracy affected and unaffected family members. If negative in the affected individual, screening family members will not be useful in determining disease status.
- If no known family history exists, screening the clinically suspected individual is reasonable. A positive test rules in FAP but a negative test does not rule it out.
- Numerous testing techniques available; may require multiple tests to identify the mutation.

SIGMOIDOSCOPY:

- Individuals with a positive genetic test, untested at-risk family members, or patients from families with an unidentified APC mutation: annual flexible sigmoidoscopy or colonoscopy beginning at 10 to 12 yr of age.
- Once adenomatous polyps are detected, patients should undergo colonoscopy and evaluation for colectomy.
- Negative genetic test in patients from families with an identified mutation: average risk screening.

CHRPE: Lesions occur in up to 80% of families and are a reliable indicator of affected status in these families.

TREATMENT

- Prophylactic colectomy or proctocolectomy: timing determined by polyp number, size, and degree of dysplasia. Postsurgical endoscopic surveillance annually.
- Consider celecoxib therapy to reduce polyposis.

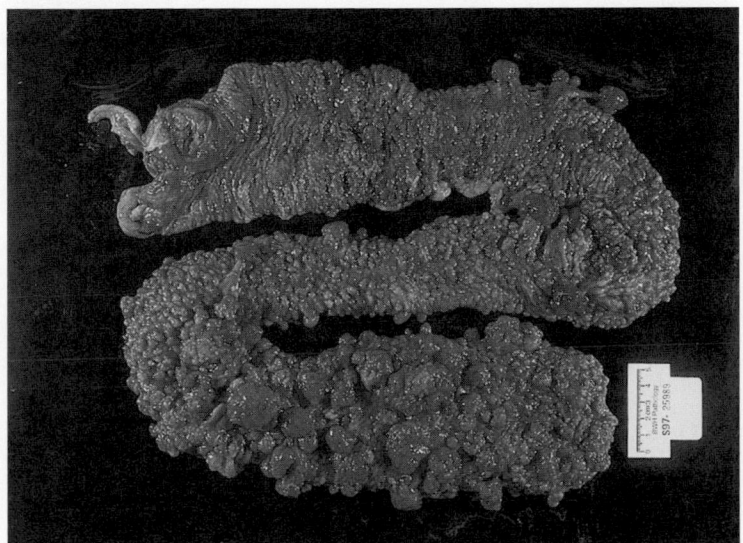

FIGURE 1F-3 Familial adenomatous polyposis with innumerable adenomatous polyps, increasing in size and density from proximal *(upper left)* to distal *(lower right)*. (From Skarin AT: Atlas of diagnostic oncology, 4th ed, St. Louis, 2010, Mosby.)

- Screening of remaining GI tract and screening for extraintestinal manifestations continues after colectomy
  1. Annual physical examination: history, examination (including thyroid), and blood tests
  2. Upper endoscopy to screen for gastric/duodenal polyps: baseline at age 25 yr (earlier if colon polyps detected) and repeated every 0.5 to 4 yr based on findings
  3. Some recommend annual thyroid ultrasound
  4. Other possible cancer sites imaged if symptoms occur or if these cancers have occurred in relatives
- Treat soft tissue lesions and osteomas for symptoms or cosmetic concerns. Treat desmoid tumors if they pose a risk to adjacent structures.

DISPOSITION

- 100% chance of colorectal cancer in untreated individuals. Many other neoplasms occur at higher rates.

- Metastatic colorectal cancer is the leading cause of death (58%), followed by desmoid tumors (11%), and duodenal/periampullary adenocarcinoma (8%).

REFERRAL

- Patients should be managed at centers with expertise in FAP, including a gastroenterologist, medical geneticist, and surgeon.
- Genetic counselors can be found at www.nsgc.org.
- Genetic testing sites can be found at www.genetests.org.

! PEARLS & CONSIDERATIONS

- Management should be individualized based on genotype, phenotype, and individual preferences.
- Sulindac (NSAID) and celecoxib (COX-2 inhibitor) cause polyp regression in individuals with FAP. Celecoxib is FDA approved for this indication. Cancer risk remains; neither replaces colon resection for cancer

prevention. Small studies suggest combination therapies and dietary supplements may also be effective in reducing polyposis.
- Desmoid tumors usually present in the 30s, frequently occur in the abdomen, and are difficult to treat with high rates of recurrence. Growth and recurrence are stimulated by surgery.
- Screen children of affected parents (from infancy to age 7 yr) biannually with alpha-fetoprotein level and liver ultrasound to rule out hepatoblastoma.
- Preimplantation and prenatal genetic testing is available.

SUGGESTED READINGS
Available at www.expertconsult.com

RELATED CONTENT
Familial Adenomatous Polyposis and Polyposis Syndromes (Patient Information)
Colorectal Cancer (Related Key Topic)
Peutz-Jeghers Syndrome (Related Key Topic)

AUTHOR: **SUDEEP K. AULAKH, M.D.**

BASIC INFORMATION

DEFINITION

Acute fatty liver of pregnancy (AFLP) is characterized histologically by microvesicular fatty cytoplasmic infiltration of hepatocytes with minimal hepatocellular necrosis.

SYNONYMS

Acute fatty metamorphosis
Acute yellow atrophy
Fatty liver of pregnancy

ICD-10CM CODES

O26.611 Liver and biliary tract disorders in pregnancy, first trimester
O26.612 Liver and biliary tract disorders in pregnancy, second trimester
O26.613 Liver and biliary tract disorders in pregnancy, third trimester
O26.619 Liver and biliary tract disorders in pregnancy, unspecified trimester

EPIDEMIOLOGY & DEMOGRAPHICS

INCIDENCE:
- Approximately one in 10,000 pregnancies
- Equal frequencies in all races and at all maternal ages

AVERAGE GESTATIONAL AGE: 37 wk (range 28 to 42 wk)

RISK FACTORS:
- Primiparity
- Multiple gestation
- Male fetus

GENETICS: Some with a familial deficiency of long-chain 3-hydroxyacyl-coenzyme A dehydrogenase (LCHAD)

PHYSICAL FINDINGS & CLINICAL PRESENTATION

- Initial manifestations:
  1. Nausea and vomiting (70%)
  2. Pain in right upper quadrant or epigastrium (50% to 80%)
  3. Malaise and anorexia
- Jaundice often in 1 to 2 wk
- Late manifestations:
  1. Fulminant hepatic failure
  2. Encephalopathy
  3. Renal failure
  4. Pancreatitis
  5. Gastrointestinal and uterine bleeding
  6. Disseminated intravascular coagulation
  7. Seizures
  8. Coma
- Liver:
  1. Usually small
  2. Normal or enlarged in preeclampsia, eclampsia, HELLP syndrome (hemolysis, elevated liver enzymes, and low platelets), and acute hepatitis
  3. Coexistent preeclampsia in up to 46% of patients

ETIOLOGY

- Postulated that inhibition of mitochondrial oxidation of fatty acids may lead to microvesicular fatty infiltration of liver
- Fatty metamorphosis of preeclamptic liver disease believed to be of different etiology

DIAGNOSIS

DIFFERENTIAL DIAGNOSIS

- Acute gastroenteritis
- Preeclampsia or eclampsia with liver involvement
- HELLP syndrome
- Acute viral hepatitis
- Fulminant hepatitis
- Drug-induced hepatitis caused by halothane, phenytoin, methyldopa, isoniazid, hydrochlorothiazide, or tetracycline
- Intrahepatic cholestasis of pregnancy
- Gallbladder disease
- Reye's syndrome
- Hemolytic-uremic syndrome
- Budd-Chiari syndrome
- Systemic lupus erythematosus

WORKUP

- A clinical diagnosis is based predominantly on physical and laboratory findings.
- Most definitive diagnosis is through liver biopsy with oil red O staining and electron microscopy.
- Liver biopsy is reserved for atypical cases only and only after any existing coagulopathy is corrected with fresh frozen plasma because of concerns for excessive bleeding.

LABORATORY TESTS

Tests to determine the following:
- Hypoglycemia (often profound <60 mg/dl).
- Hyperammonemia.
- Elevated aminotransferases (usually <500 U/mL).
- Thrombocytopenia.
- Leukocytosis (white blood cell count >15,000).
- Hyperbilirubinemia (usually <10 mg/dl).
- Low albumin.
- Hypofibrinogenemia (<300 mg/dl).
- Disseminated intravascular coagulation (DIC) (in 75%).

IMAGING STUDIES

- Ultrasound: best used to rule out other diseases in the differential diagnosis such as gallbladder disease
- CT scan: plays minimal role because of a high false-negative rate

TREATMENT

NONPHARMACOLOGIC THERAPY

- Patient is admitted to intensive care unit for stabilization.
- Fetus is delivered; spontaneous resolution usually follows delivery.
- Mode of delivery is based on obstetric indications and clinical assessment of disease severity.

ACUTE GENERAL Rx

- Decrease in endogenous ammonia through dietary protein restriction; neomycin 6 to 12 g/day PO to decrease presence of ammonia-producing bacteria; magnesium citrate 30 to 50 mL PO or enema to evacuate nitrogenous wastes from colon.
- Administration of IV fluids with glucose to keep glucose levels >60 mg/dl.
- Coagulopathy corrected with fresh frozen plasma.
- Avoidance of drugs metabolized by liver.
- Aggressive avoidance and treatment for nosocomial infections; consideration of prophylactic antibiotics.
- Monitor closely for development of complications such as hepatic encephalopathy, pulmonary edema, DIC, and respiratory arrest.

CHRONIC Rx

Orthotopic liver transplantation is the only treatment for irreversible liver failure.

DISPOSITION

- Before 1980, both maternal and fetal mortality rates were approximately 85%.
- Since 1980, both maternal and fetal mortality rates are less than 20%.
- Usually rapid return of liver function to normal after delivery.
- Minimal risk of recurrence with future pregnancies.

REFERRAL

- To tertiary health care facility as soon as diagnosis is suspected.
- Infants of mothers with AFLP should be evaluated for LCHAD deficiency.

SUGGESTED READINGS

Available at www.expertconsult.com

RELATED CONTENT

Eclampsia (Related Key Topic).
Preeclampsia (Related Key Topic).

AUTHOR: **RUBEN ALVERO, M.D.**

F

Diseases and Disorders

BASIC INFORMATION

DEFINITION

- Adverse effects of alcohol on developing humans represent spectrum of structural anomalies and behavioral and neurocognitive disabilities, most accurately termed fetal alcohol spectrum disorder (FASD) (Table 1F-2).
- Children at severe end of spectrum defined as having fetal alcohol syndrome (FAS).

ICD-10CM CODES
Q86.0 Fetal alcohol syndrome (dysmorphic)
P04.3 Newborn (suspected to be) affected by maternal use of alcohol

EPIDEMIOLOGY & DEMOGRAPHICS

- Alcohol considered to be most common teratogen to which the fetus is liable to be exposed.
- 10% report drinking alcohol during pregnancy and 2% to 4% admit to binge drinking.
- Most common form of mental retardation in the United States.
- Prevalence is 1 to 2/1000 live births across the United States.
- Each year 40,000 babies are born with FASD.

RISK FACTORS

- Advanced maternal age (>30 yr).
- High parity.
- African-American, Alaskan Natives, and Native Indian race.
- Binge drinking (>4 drinks per occasion).
- History of prior affected child.
- Genetic susceptibility.
- Undernutrition.
- Low socioeconomic group.

PHYSICAL FINDINGS & CLINICAL PRESENTATION

Typical features:
- Growth retardation.
  1. Prenatal or postnatal.
  2. Height and/or weight <10%.
- Facial dysmorphia
  1. Smooth philtrum.
  2. Thin vermilion border.
  3. Small palpebral fissure (<10%).
  4. Others: epicanthic folds, ptosis of eyelids, flat nasal bridge and midface, upturned nose, railroad track ears, and so forth.
- CNS abnormalities
  1. Structural
     1. Head circumference, 10%.
     2. Clinically significant brain abnormalities observable through imaging.
  2. Neurologic
     1. Neurologic problems not due to a postnatal insult or fever.
  3. Functional
     1. Intellectual deficit.
     2. Cognitive or developmental deficits.
     3. Executive function deficits.
     4. Motor function delays.
     5. Problem with attention and hyperactivity.
     6. Social skills.
     7. Other problems such as sensory, pragmatic language, and memory.
Rare birth defects:
- Cardiac
  1. Ventricular septal defect (VSD).
  2. Atrial septal defect (ASD).
  3. Tetralogy of Fallot.
  4. Aberrant great vessels.
- Skeletal
  1. Radioulnar synostosis.
  2. Hypoplastic nails.
  3. Clinodactyly.
  4. Shortened fifth digit.
  5. Pectus excavatum and carinatum.

6. Klippel-Feil syndrome.
7. Hemivertebrae.
8. Camptodactyly.
9. Scoliosis.
- Renal
  1. Aplastic kidneys.
  2. Dysplastic kidneys.
  3. Ureteral duplication.
  4. Hypoplastic kidneys.
  5. Hydronephrosis.
  6. Horseshoe kidneys.
- Ocular
  1. Strabismus.
  2. Refractive problems.
  3. Retinal vascular abnormalities.
- Auditory
  1. Conductive hearing loss.
  2. Neurosensory hearing loss.
- Others
  1. Hockey stick–like palmar crease.

ETIOLOGY

- Prenatal damage comes about primarily by direct action of ethanol or its metabolites (e.g., acetaldehyde) on the fetus.
- Exact damaging mechanism is unclear.
- Although the damaging effect of alcohol is different in the various phases of pregnancy, it is by no means limited to first trimester.
- No exact dose-response relationship between alcohol consumed during prenatal period and extent of damage inflicted on infant.
- An occasional drink during pregnancy carries no risk to the fetus, but no level of drinking is known to be safe during pregnancy.
- The least significant effect recognized at 2 drinks/day is smaller birth weight (160 g less than average).
- Until 4 to 6 drinks/day are consumed, no additional subtle clinical features are evident.
- Most children who have FAS have been born to frankly alcoholic mothers whose intake is ≥8 to 10 drinks/day, and those who engage in binge drinking.
- The risk of serious problem in the offspring of a chronically alcoholic woman is ~30% to 50%; the greatest risk is mental retardation.

SECONDARY DISABILITIES

- Mental health problems.
- Dependent living.
- Employment problems.
- Disruptive school problems.
- Trouble with law.
- Confinement.
- Inappropriate sexual behavior.
- Alcohol or drug problems.

DIAGNOSIS

- It is a diagnosis of exclusion.
- Diagnosis is difficult prenatally and at birth. Most cases are not diagnosed until school age.
- As the characteristic facial features tend to become decreasingly recognizable as the child reaches adolescence, the diagnosis becomes increasingly difficult with advancing age.

TABLE 1F-2 Institute of Medicine's Diagnostic Criteria for Fetal Alcohol–Related Abnormalities

Category 1

FAS with confirmed maternal alcohol exposure	Presence of classic triad of growth retardation, characteristic facial dysmorphology, and neurodevelopmental abnormalities. This is often defined as full-blown FAS.

Category 2

FAS without confirmed maternal alcohol exposure	Triad in category 1 is present without confirmed maternal drinking

Category 3

Partial FAS with confirmed maternal alcohol exposure	Presence of some of the characteristic facial anomalies plus growth retardation or CNS neurodevelopmental abnormalities or behavioral/cognitive abnormalities

Category 4

FAS with confirmed maternal alcohol exposure and alcohol-related birth defects	Some congenital anomalies as a result of alcohol toxicity

Category 5

FAS with confirmed maternal alcohol exposure and alcohol-related neurodevelopmental disorder	Evidence of CNS neurodevelopmental abnormalities, a complex pattern of behavioral/cognitive abnormalities, or both, but not necessarily any obvious physical changes

CNS, Central nervous system; *FAS*, fetal alcohol syndrome.

- Prenatal exposure to alcohol is not sufficient to warrant a diagnosis. According to the CDC, diagnosis of FAS requires 3 specific findings and history of prenatal alcohol exposure:
  1. Growth restriction (intrauterine or postnatal)
  2. CNS involvement
  3. Documentation of all three facial abnormalities (smooth philtrum, thin vermilion border, and short palpebral fissure)
- Imaging recommendation during pregnancy with alcohol exposure:
  1. High-risk anatomy scan.
  2. Serial growth scan.
  3. Fetal echocardiogram at 22 to 24 weeks' intrauterine pregnancy.
- Measurement of the ethyl esters of fatty acids in the meconium and hair of the newborn can substantiate maternal alcohol exposure.
- In school-aged children, the diagnostic process should include a thorough psychological evaluation that assesses multiple domains. Also, supplement the observation by obtaining standardized testing through early intervention programs, public schools, and psychologists in private practice.

DIFFERENTIAL DIAGNOSIS

- Other causes of symmetric growth retardation including intrauterine infection and aneuploidy.
- Aneuploidy (T21, T18, T13).
- Syndromes with overlapping features of FAS:
  1. Fetal anticonvulsant syndrome.
  2. Maternal phenylketonuria.
  3. Toluene embryopathy.
  4. Velocardiofacial syndrome (deletion 22q11).
  5. Williams syndrome.
  6. Dubowitz syndrome.
  7. Cornelia de Lange syndrome.

℞ TREATMENT

- As there is no cure for FAS, we need to emphasize prevention.
- For women who are planning pregnancy or who could become pregnant, the United States Surgeon General recommends the safest course: to avoid alcohol entirely during pregnancy.
- Women of childbearing age who are not pregnant should drink ≤7 alcoholic drinks/wk and ≤3 drinks on any one occasion.
- Preconception counseling should be offered to women of childbearing age who are at risk for an alcohol-exposed pregnancy.
- Screen all pregnant women for alcohol use.
- The National Institute on Alcohol Abuse and Alcoholism recommends that any woman who reports drinking >7 drinks/wk or >3 drinks on a given day be further assessed for alcohol-related problems.
- The T-ACE (Table 1F-3) and TWEAK (Table 1F-4) questionnaires are used to identify women drinking enough to potentially damage the fetus. The CAGE questionnaire is less sensitive for screening pregnant women.

- Effective treatment alternatives for women who screen positive for hazardous alcohol use include brief interventions to promote reductions in alcohol use and that facilitate referral to specialized treatment programs.
- Discontinuation or reduction of alcohol consumption at any point in pregnancy may be beneficial.
- The use of alcohol-containing tonics and medications should be avoided. This applies to medications with an alcohol base when the concentration exceeds 10%.
- Alcoholism is one of the few situations in which pregnancy interruption may be discussed with the patient as it may result in FAS.
- Early diagnosis and appropriate treatment may decrease secondary disabilities and recurrence in future pregnancies.
- A child should be referred for full FAS evaluation when substantial prenatal alcohol use by the mother has been confirmed (>7 drinks/wk, >3 drinks on multiple occasions, or both).
- If substantial prenatal exposure is known, with no other positive criteria, the physician should document exposure and closely monitor the child's growth and development.

TABLE 1F-3   T-ACE Questions*

T (tolerance)	How many drinks does it take to make you feel high? (3 or more drinks = 2 points)
A (annoyed)	Have people annoyed you by criticizing your drinking? (Yes = 1 point)
C (cut down)	Have you felt you ought to cut down on your drinking? (Yes = 1 point)
E (eye opener)	Have you ever had to drink first thing in the morning to steady your nerves or to get rid of a hangover? (Yes = 1 point)

*A score of 2 or more indicates heavy or problem drinker. Its sensitivity is 70% and specificity is 85%.

TABLE 1F-4   TWEAK*

T (tolerance)	How many drinks does it take before you begin to feel the first effects of alcohol? (3 or more drinks = 2 points)
W (worried)	Have close friends or relatives worried about your drinking in the past year? (Yes = 2 points)
E (eye opener)	Do you sometimes take a drink in the morning when you first get up? (Yes = 1 point)
A (amnesia)	Has a friend or family member ever told you about things you said or did while you were drinking that you could not remember? (Yes = 1 point)
K (kut down)	Do you sometimes feel the need to cut down on your drinking? (Yes = 1 point)

*A total of 3 or more points indicates the woman is likely to be a heavy or problem drinker. Its sensitivity is 79% and specificity is 83%.

- When information about prenatal exposure is unknown, a child should be referred for full FAS if any of the following conditions are present: (1) all three dysmorphic facial features (smooth philtrum, thin vermilion border, and small palpebral fissure), (2) one or more of these facial features with growth deficit, (3) one or more facial features with one or more CNS abnormalities, (4) one or more dysmorphic facial features with growth deficit and one or more CNS abnormalities, or (5) any report of concern by a caregiver or parent that a child has or may have FAS.
- Infants and children who are diagnosed with FAS should be evaluated by a physician who is knowledgeable and competent in the evaluation of neurodevelopment and psychosocial problems associated with the diagnosis.
- A multidisciplinary team including a clinical geneticist, developmental pediatrician, mental health professional, social worker, and education specialist is often necessary for management.
- Treatment options include:
  1. Medications to help with symptoms
  2. Behavior and education therapy
     Friendship training
     Specialized math training
     Executive function training
     Parent-child interaction training
     Parenting and behavior management training
  3. Parenting training
     Concentrate on child's strengths and talents.
     Accept child's limitations.
     Be consistent with everything.
     Use concrete language and examples.
     Use stable routine that does not change daily.
     Keep everything simple.
     Be specific (i.e., say exactly what you mean).
     Structure your child's world to provide a foundation for daily living.
     Use visualized aids, music, and hands-on activities to help your child learn.
     Use positive reinforcement often.
     Supervise.
     Repeat, repeat, and repeat.
  4. Emphasis on the following protective factors helps reduce the effects and also assists people with this condition to reach their full potential:
     Diagnosing before 6 yr
     Living in stable nurturing home environment in school years
     Absence of violence
     Involvement in special education and social services
  5. Alternative approaches such as biofeedback, auditory training, relaxation therapy, visual imagery, yoga/exercise, acupuncture/acupressure, massage, Reiki, energy healing, animal-assisted therapy, and so forth may play a role.

SUGGESTED READINGS

Available at www.expertconsult.com

AUTHOR: **HEMANT K. SATPATHY, M.D.**

BASIC INFORMATION

DEFINITION

Fever of undetermined origin (FUO) was defined by Petersdorf and Beeson in 1961 as an illness characterized by temperatures >38.3° C (101° F) on several occasions for >3 wk with no known cause despite extensive workup.

- Persistence for >2 wk separates an FUO from an insignificant viral illness.
- Traditionally, diagnosis was made only after a 1-wk inpatient workup. In contemporary practice, much of the workup is performed as an outpatient.

FUO can be classified into classic, nosocomial (health-care associated), neutropenic (immune deficient), and HIV-associated. Table 1F-5 provides a summary of definitions and major features of subtypes of FUO.

SYNONYMS

Fever of unknown origin

ICD-10CM CODES
R50.9 Fever, unspecified

EPIDEMIOLOGY & DEMOGRAPHICS

- The incidence of undiagnosed FUO dropped to <10% in the 1950s but has steadily increased since then.

- True FUOs are uncommon.

CLINICAL PRESENTATION

Fever 38.3° C (101° F or higher) on several occasions >3 wk.

ETIOLOGY

- Infection (16%-23%).
  1. Abscess: abdominal, pelvic
  2. Tuberculosis
  3. HIV infection
  4. Nosocomial: urinary tract infection, pneumonia, line-related bacteremia, *Clostridium difficile* colitis, sinusitis
  5. Bacterial endocarditis (especially caused by difficult-to-isolate organisms)
  6. Biliary tract infection
  7. Osteomyelitis, vertebral and mandibular
  8. Less common infections: Q fever, leptospirosis, psittacosis, tularemia, secondary syphilis, gonococcemia, chronic meningococcemia, Whipple's disease, yersiniosis, fungal infections
- Malignancy (7%-10%): lymphoma (especially non-Hodgkin lymphoma), leukemia, renal cell carcinoma, hepatocellular carcinomas, other tumors metastatic to liver
- Noninfectious inflammatory disease (22%-31%)
  1. Adult Still's disease (young to middle-aged patients)
  2. Temporal arteritis (elderly patients)

  3. Other vasculitis: polyarteritis nodosa, Takayasu's arteritis, Wegener's granulomatosis, mixed cryoglobulinemia
- Other
  1. Drug-induced fever
  2. Inflammatory bowel disease
  3. Sarcoidosis
  4. Pulmonary embolism
  5. Alcoholic hepatitis
- No diagnosis

DIAGNOSIS

DIFFERENTIAL DIAGNOSIS

Factitious fever

WORKUP

- Accurate history and careful physical examination are essential. Fig. E1F-4 describes an approach to the patient with FUO.
- Laboratory tests and imaging dependent on medical history clues and physical findings.
- When in doubt, perform another complete history and physical examination. Examples of subtle physical findings in patients with FUO are described in Table 1F-6.

MEDICAL HISTORY CLUES

- Fever duration, tempo; inciting factors
- Rash, myalgia, weight loss, pain

TABLE 1F-5 Summary of Definitions and Major Features of the Four Subtypes of Fever of Undetermined Origin

Feature	Classic FUO	Health Care–Associated FUO	Immune-Deficient FUO	HIV-Related FUO
Definition	>38.0° C, >3 wk, >2 visits or 1 wk in hospital	≥38.0° C, >1 wk, not present or incubating on admission	≥38.0° C, >1 wk, negative cultures after 48 hr	≥38.0° C, >3 wk for outpatients, >1 wk for inpatients, HIV infection confirmed
Patient location	Community, clinic, or hospital	Acute care hospital	Hospital or clinic	Community, clinic, or hospital
Leading causes	Cancer, infections, inflammatory conditions, undiagnosed, habitual hyperthermia	Health care–associated infections, postoperative complications, drug fever	Majority due to infections, but cause documented in only 40%-60%	HIV (primary infection), typical and atypical mycobacteria, CMV, lymphomas, toxoplasmosis, cryptococcosis, immune reconstitution inflammatory syndrome (IRIS)
History emphasis	Travel, contacts, animal and insect exposure, medications, immunizations, family history, cardiac valve disorder	Operations and procedures, devices, anatomic considerations, drug treatment	Stage of chemotherapy, drugs administered, underlying immunosuppressive disorder	Drugs, exposures, risk factors, travel, contacts, stage of HIV infection
Examination emphasis	Fundi, oropharynx, temporal artery, abdomen, lymph nodes, spleen, joints, skin, nails, genitalia, rectum or prostate, lower limb deep veins	Wounds, drains, devices, sinuses, urine	Skinfolds, IV sites, lungs, perianal area	Mouth, sinuses, skin, lymph nodes, eyes, lungs, perianal area
Investigation emphasis	Imaging, biopsies, sedimentation rate, skin tests	Imaging, bacterial cultures	CXR, bacterial cultures	Blood and lymphocyte count; serologic tests; CXR; stool examination; biopsies of lung, bone marrow, and liver for cultures and cytologic tests; brain imaging
Management	Observation, outpatient temperature chart, investigations, avoidance of empirical drug treatments	Depends on situation	Antimicrobial treatment protocols	Antiviral and antimicrobial protocols, vaccines, revision of treatment regimens, good nutrition
Time course of disease	Months	Weeks	Days	Weeks to months
Tempo of investigation	Weeks	Days	Hours	Days to weeks

CMV, Cytomegalovirus; *CXR*, chest radiograph; *FUO*, fever of undetermined origin.
Adapted from Mandell GL, Bennett JE, Dolin R (eds): *Mandell, Douglas, and Bennett's principles and practice of infectious diseases*, ed 7, Philadelphia, 2010, Churchill Livingstone. Borrowed from Kliegman RM et al: *Nelson textbook of pediatrics*, ed 19, Philadelphia, 2011, Saunders.

- Sick contacts
- Past medical history: tuberculosis, HIV, malignancies, surgeries
- Medications
- Family history: tuberculosis, malignancies, familial Mediterranean fever
- Social history: daily routine, rural versus urban, pets and animal contacts, arthropod bites, recent and remote travel, socioeconomic status, occupation, military service, sexual history

PHYSICAL FINDINGS

- HEENT (head, ears, eyes, nose, throat): sinus tenderness, dental abscesses, funduscopic lesions.
- Neck: adenopathy, palpable thyroid
- Lungs: auscultate for rales
- Heart: murmur
- Abdomen: organomegaly
- Rectal: prostate tenderness
- Pelvic: cervical motion tenderness, fundal or adnexal masses or pain, inguinal adenopathy
- Extremities: clubbing, splinter hemorrhages, tenderness or fluctuance at IV access site.
- Musculoskeletal: joint effusions
- Skin: rashes, wounds

LABORATORY TESTS

- Most FUO workups include:
  1. Blood cultures (three sets from different sites)
  2. Complete blood count with differential
  3. Erythrocyte sedimentation rate or C-reactive protein
  4. Urinalysis with microscopic exam and culture
  5. Transaminases
  6. Serum lactate dehydrogenase
  7. PPD testing
- Consider
  1. HIV antibody testing
  2. Creatinine phosphokinase
  3. Rheumatoid factor
  4. Serum protein electrophoresis
  5. Lumbar puncture
  6. Thyroid function testing
  7. Stool culture and *C. difficile* assay
  8. Biopsy (bone marrow, skin, liver lymph nodes, pleural, etc., based on clinical and laboratory findings)
  9. Antinuclear antibody testing
  May need to repeat tests at regular intervals until diagnosis is established.

IMAGING STUDIES

- Most workups eventually include chest radiograph and abdominal CT scan.
- Further imaging is based on medical history clues and physical findings.
- FDG-PET is very sensitive to detect anatomic sites of inflammation or malignancy. It may help to identify sites requiring further investigation. Further data are needed to evaluate efficacy.

Rx TREATMENT

ACUTE GENERAL Rx

Antibiotics and other treatment indicated only after definitive or highly probable diagnosis is established unless patient is neutropenic, severely ill, or septic.

DISPOSITION

In some cases a diagnosis is not made for years. At 5-yr follow-up, mortality rate among patients with undiagnosed FUO was only 3.2% in one study.

REFERRAL

To an infectious disease specialist, hematologist, or rheumatologist if no diagnosis after thoughtful workup.

! PEARLS & CONSIDERATIONS

COMMENTS

Because of improvements in imaging and laboratory tests, fewer cases of FUO are attributed to infectious causes and more are diagnosed as attributable to tumors and collagen-vascular diseases.

SUGGESTED READINGS

Available at www.expertconsult.com

RELATED CONTENT

Fever of Unknown Origin (Patient Information).

AUTHOR: **ETSUKO AOKI, M.D., PH.D.**

F

Diseases and Disorders

TABLE 1F-6 Examples of Subtle Physical Findings Having Special Significance in Patients with Fever of Undetermined Origin

Body Site	Physical Finding	Diagnosis
Head	Sinus tenderness	Sinusitis
Temporal artery	Nodules, reduced pulsations	Temporal arteritis
Oropharynx	Ulceration	Disseminated histoplasmosis
	Tender tooth	Periapical abscess
Fundi or conjunctivae	Choroid tubercle	Disseminated granulomatosis*
	Petechiae, Roth's spot	Endocarditis
Thyroid	Enlargement, tenderness	Thyroiditis
Heart	Murmur	Infective or marantic endocarditis
Abdomen	Enlarged iliac crest lymph nodes, splenomegaly	Lymphoma, endocarditis, disseminated granulomatosis*
Rectum	Perirectal fluctuance, tenderness	Abscess
	Prostatic tenderness, fluctuance	Abscess
Genitalia	Testicular nodule	Periarteritis nodosa
	Epididymal nodule	Disseminated granulomatosis
Lower extremities	Deep venous tenderness	Thrombosis or thrombophlebitis
Skin and nails	Petechiae, splinter hemorrhages, subcutaneous nodules, clubbing	Vasculitis, endocarditis

*Includes tuberculosis, histoplasmosis, coccidioidomycosis, sarcoidosis, and syphilis.
From Mandell GL et al (eds): *Mandell, Douglas, and Bennett's principles and practice of infectious diseases*, ed 7, Philadelphia, 2010, Churchill Livingstone.

 BASIC INFORMATION

DEFINITION

Fibrocystic breast disease (FCD) is a "nondisease" that includes nonmalignant breast lesions such as microcystic and macrocystic changes, fibrosis, ductal or lobular hyperplasia, adenosis, apocrine metaplasia, fibroadenoma, papilloma, papillomatosis, and other changes. Atypical ductal or lobular hyperplasia is associated with a moderate increase in breast cancer risk.

SYNONYMS

Cystic changes
Chronic cystic mastitis
Mammary dysplasia

ICD-10CM CODES
N60.01 Solitary cyst of right breast
N60.02 Solitary cyst of left breast
N60.09 Solitary cyst of unspecified breast
N60.11 Diffuse cystic mastopathy of right breast
N60.12 Diffuse cystic mastopathy of left breast
N60.19 Diffuse cystic mastopathy of unspecified breast

EPIDEMIOLOGY & DEMOGRAPHICS

- Ubiquitous in premenopausal women after 20 yr of age
- Palpable nodular changes in the breast termed FCD clinically; such changes observable in more than half of adult women aged 20 to 50 yr

PHYSICAL FINDINGS & CLINICAL PRESENTATION

- Tender breasts
- Nodular areas
- Dominant mass
- Thickening
- Nipple discharge
- Can vary with menstrual cycle

ETIOLOGY

- Although it is frequently seen and diagnosed, mechanism of development is not understood.
- Because it is found in the majority of healthy breasts, it is regarded as a nonpathologic process.
- With hormone replacement therapy, the condition may be carried into menopause.

 DIAGNOSIS

DIFFERENTIAL DIAGNOSIS

Table 1F-7 differentiates breast masses. Characteristics of breast masses suspect for cancer (90% sensitivity, 40%-60% specificity) are fixed mass, poorly defined mass, and hard mass.

WORKUP

- Exclude breast carcinoma if breast mass, thickening, discharge, and/or pain are present.
- Perform biopsy of suspected area for histologic confirmation.

IMAGING STUDIES

Mammography and ultrasound studies required:
- For mammographic changes (suspicious densities, microcalcifications, architectural distortion): careful evaluation, including possibly biopsy to exclude breast cancer.
- Ultrasound study: to establish cystic nature of clinical or mammographic mass lesion.

TREATMENT

NONPHARMACOLOGIC THERAPY

- Not considered a "disease" and does not require treatment.
- Surgical intervention diagnostic to eliminate possibility of breast cancer.
- Periodic physician examination to monitor patients with FCD who have pronounced nodular features.

- Aspiration for palpable cysts (NOTE: Cysts often recur; repeat aspiration is not always required unless pain is a problem).

ACUTE GENERAL Rx

The majority of women require no treatment.

CHRONIC Rx

For breast pain:
- Danocrine (Danazol): limited success reported but significant side effect profile of medication
- Bromocriptine or tamoxifen: used less frequently
- Limited caffeine intake: not as successful in controlling pain or nodularity as originally suggested

DISPOSITION

- Careful evaluation to exclude suspicious changes for breast cancer, then reassurance and periodic reevaluation as required
- Regular self-examination, annual physician examination, and annual mammograms for women with atypical ductal or lobular hyperplasia

REFERRAL

- For further evaluation and/or biopsy if there are suspicious changes that may be associated with FCD (including changing of dominant mass or thickening, persistent or spontaneous discharge, suspicious mammographic changes or lesions)
- To alleviate anxiety associated with breast symptoms or changes

RELATED CONTENT

Fibrocystic Breast Changes (Patient Information)
Breast Cancer (Related Key Topic)
Mastodynia (Related Key Topic)

AUTHOR: **RUBEN ALVERO, M.D.**

TABLE 1F-7   Differentiation of Breast Masses

Characteristic	Cystic Disease	Benign Adenoma	Malignant Tumor
Patient age	25-60 yr	10-55 yr	25-85 yr
Number	One or more	One	One
Shape	Round	Round	Irregular
Consistency	Elastic, soft to hard	Firm	Stony hard
Delimitation	Well delimited	Well delimited	Poorly delimited
Mobility	Mobile	Mobile	Fixed
Tenderness	Present	Absent	Absent
Skin retraction	Absent	Absent	Present

From Swartz, MH: *Textbook of physical diagnosis*, ed 7, Philadelphia, 2014, Saunders.

 **BASIC INFORMATION**

DEFINITION

Fibromyalgia (FM) is a syndrome characterized by chronic, widespread musculoskeletal pain without evidence of soft tissue inflammation. Key features also include fatigue, sleep disruption, and psychiatric and somatic symptoms, as well as cognitive disturbance. Research suggests that FM is a disorder of pain regulation, which is often classified as a form of central sensitization.

SYNONYMS

"Fibrositis" is a term that is no longer used because there is no evidence of connective tissue inflammation in FM.

ICD-10CM CODES
M79.7 Fibromyalgia

EPIDEMIOLOGY & DEMOGRAPHICS

Worldwide, the prevalence of FM is believed to be 2% to 8%, and it increases with age. In the U.S., FM is the most common cause of musculoskeletal pain in women ages 20 to 55 yr. Using the 2010 American College of Rheumatology (ACR) diagnostic criteria for FM, the female-to-male ratio is approximately 2:1.

PHYSICAL FINDINGS & CLINICAL PRESENTATION

Patients with FM often report the following symptoms:
- Chronic (>3 months) widespread (affecting both sides of the body, above and below the waist, and involving the axial spine) musculoskeletal pain
- Cognitive disturbances
- Fatigue and sleep disturbances (e.g., unrefreshed sleep, easy fatigability)
- Psychiatric symptoms (e.g., anxiety, depression)
- Headache (present in more than half of patients with FM; this includes migraine and tension-type headaches)

- Paresthesias
- Associated disorders: irritable bowel syndrome, interstitial cystitis/painful bladder syndrome

On physical examination, patients with FM may have tenderness in particular soft tissue locations called tender points (Fig. 1F-5). Examination of tender points requires that the examiner be familiar with the areas to palpate and that they apply enough pressure (4 kg/cm^2 or enough pressure to whiten the nail bed of the finger tips of the examiner).

ETIOLOGY

Although the exact cause of FM is unknown, many factors are believed to contribute to the development of this disorder:
- Genetic and environmental factors predispose individuals to FM. Evidence suggests that both the ascending and descending pain pathways operate abnormally, resulting in central amplification of pain signals. Familial associations of FM provide strongest evidence that reflect both these factors.
- In those predisposed, FM may be precipitated by stressful events such as abuse, injury from accidents, illnesses (including autoimmune disorders), infections, surgical procedures, and psychological stressors.
- Psychosocial, neuroendocrine, hormonal, and sociocultural factors also influence symptom expression.

PATHOGENESIS

Much remains to be discovered about the pathogenesis of FM, even though significant advances have been made in our understanding of this syndrome over the past few decades. Researchers have shown that biochemical, metabolic, and immunoregulatory abnormalities exist in patients with FM. Hence, this condition is now believed to be neurosensory in nature.
- Augmented pain and sensory processing is a hallmark, resulting in diffuse pain, allodynia (pain brought on by nonpainful stimuli), and hyperalgesia (more intense and prolonged pain perception).

- Afflicted persons show altered physiologic responses to painful stimulation at spinal and supraspinal levels.
- Brain neuroimaging studies found differences in brain structure, neurochemical concentrations, and functional brain networks in FM compared with control subjects.
- Pain augmentation may also result from a loss of tonic inhibition by descending inhibitory pathways from the brain to the spinal cord.

 **DIAGNOSIS**

DIFFERENTIAL DIAGNOSIS

The presence of any of the disorders mentioned below does not necessarily exclude a diagnosis of FM because it may coexist with many conditions:
- Other functional somatic or "central sensitivity" syndromes: myofascial pain, chronic fatigue syndrome, irritable bowel syndrome, headache/migraines, chronic pelvic and bladder pain disorders, and temporomandibular disorder.
- Disorders that can mimic FM and must be ruled out include metabolic (e.g., hypothyroidism), infectious, and neurologic disorders. Arthritis and rheumatic diseases (e.g., rheumatoid arthritis, systemic lupus erythematosus, osteoarthritis, Sjögren's syndrome)
- Myalgias and other muscle disease (e.g., inflammatory and metabolic myopathies).
- Mood and anxiety disorders.
- Sleep disorders (e.g., sleep apnea, restless leg syndrome).
- Neurologic disorders.
- Medications: statin-induced muscle pain, opioid-induced hyperalgesia.

WORKUP

A thorough history, physical examination, and appropriately selected laboratory or imaging studies can usually differentiate FM from connective tissue or other systemic diseases.
- Chronic (>3 mo), widespread pain is the hallmark symptom of FM, but fatigue, tenderness, depression/anxiety, nonrestorative sleep, cognitive difficulties (the so-called "fibrofog"), and functional impairment are other key symptoms.
- The 1990 American College of Rheumatology (ACR) FM Classification Criteria was used for clinical studies:
  1. Chronic, widespread pain in all four quadrants of the body and the axial skeleton.
  2. Pain on digital palpation of at least 11 of 18 tender points (see Fig. 1F-5).
- The 2010 ACR preliminary diagnostic criteria for FM do not require a tender point examination; it requires the exclusion of other disorders that would otherwise explain the pain (Table 1F-8)
- A diagnostic screening tool (Fibromyalgia Diagnostic Screen) developed by Arnold and colleagues was found to accurately screen for FM. This tool includes a patient self-reported questionnaire and an abbreviated physical examination with targeted lab tests.

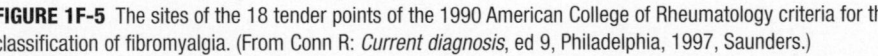

right | left | left | right
1. Occiput
2. Low cervical
3. Trapezius
4. Supraspinatus
5. Second rib
6. Lateral epicondyle
7. Gluteal
8. Greater trochanter
9. Knees

right | left

FIGURE 1F-5 The sites of the 18 tender points of the 1990 American College of Rheumatology criteria for the classification of fibromyalgia. (From Conn R: *Current diagnosis*, ed 9, Philadelphia, 1997, Saunders.)

Table 1F-8: 2010 Fibromyalgia Diagnostic Criteria

Criteria

A patient satisfies diagnostic criteria for fibromyalgia if the following three conditions are met:

1. Widespread pain index (WPI) 7 and symptom severity (SS) scale score of 5 or WPI 3-6 and SS scale score of 9.
2. Symptoms have been present at a similar level for at least 3 months.
3. The patient does not have a disorder that would otherwise explain the pain.

Ascertainment

1. WPI: Note the number of areas in which the patient has had pain over the past week. In how many areas has the patient had pain?

Score will be between 0 and 19

Shoulder girdle, left	Hip (buttock, trochanter), left	Jaw, left	Upper back
Shoulder girdle, right	Hip (buttock, trochanter), right	Jaw, right	Lower back
Upper arm, left	Upper leg, left	Chest	Neck
Upper arm, right	Upper leg, right	Abdomen	
Lower arm, left	Lower leg, left		
Lower arm, right	Lower leg, right		

2. SS scale score:
   -Fatigue
   -Waking unrefreshed
   -Cognitive symptoms
   For the each of the three symptoms above, indicate the level of severity over the past week using the following scale:
0 No problem
1 Slight or mild problems, generally mild or intermittent
2 Moderate, considerable problems, often present at a moderate level
3 Severe: pervasive, continuous, life-disturbing problems
Considering somatic symptoms in general, indicate whether the patient has:*
0 no symptoms
1 Few symptoms
2 A moderate number of symptoms
3 A great deal of symptoms
The SS scale score is the sum of the severity of the three symptoms (fatigue, waking unrefreshed, cognitive symptoms) plus the extent (severity) of somatic symptoms in general. The final score is between 0 and 12.

*Somatic symptoms that might be considered include muscle pain, irritable bowel syndrome, fatigue or tiredness, thinking or remembering problem, muscle weakness, headache, pain or cramps in the abdomen, numbness or tingling, dizziness, insomnia, depression, constipation, pain in the upper abdomen, nausea, nervousness, chest pain, blurred vision, fever, diarrhea, dry mouth, itching, wheezing, Raynaud's phenomenon, hives or welts, ringing in ears, vomiting, heartburn, oral ulcers, loss of or change in taste, seizures, dry eyes, shortness of breath, loss of appetite, rash, sun sensitivity, hearing difficulties, easy bruising, hair loss, frequent urination, painful urination, and bladder spasms.
Table adapted from Wolfe et al, 2010.

LABORATORY TESTS

- Selective use of ancillary tests complements the history and physical examination in the diagnosis of FM. Testing should be highly focused on the exclusion of FM mimickers or suspected concurrent diseases.
- Complete blood cell count, routine chemistries, thyroid-stimulating hormone (TSH), 25-hydroxy vitamin D level (low levels can cause muscle pain), vitamin B_{12} level (low levels can cause fatigue and pain), iron studies (low levels can cause fatigue and depressive symptoms), and magnesium levels (low levels can cause muscle spasms).
- Erythrocyte sedimentation rate (ESR), and C-reactive protein (CRP) are normal in FM.
- Routine testing for antinuclear antibody (ANA) and/or rheumatoid factor should be avoided unless history and physical examination suggest an autoimmune disease.

 TREATMENT

GENERAL Rx (FIG. 1F-6)

The goal in treating patients with fibromyalgia is to reduce the main symptoms of the syndrome (musculoskeletal pain, fatigue, depression, anxiety, poor sleep).

- Best approach may be combination of drug and nondrug therapies.
- FM can be due to abnormalities in many different neurotransmitter systems, thus, approaches and treatment responses may vary.
- Best evidence for tricyclics (low-dose amitriptyline and cyclobenzaprine), serotonin-norepinephrine reuptake inhibitors (milnacipran and duloxetine), and gabapentinoids (gabapentin and pregabalin).
- Second-tier drug classes include SSRIs.
- "Start low, go slow" approach is best to avoid side effects from medications.

- The only analgesic that has demonstrated efficacy in FM has been tramadol, either alone or in combination with acetaminophen.
- There is no evidence that NSAIDs or corticosteroids are effective in FM.
- Avoid narcotic use. There is concern that opioid use and abuse may aggravate chronic widespread pain.
- Nonpharmacologic: strong evidence to support exercise (aerobic, strengthening, and stretching exercises), cognitive behavioral therapy, physical therapy, and patient education (e.g., regarding the disease, importance of good sleep hygiene)

DISPOSITION

- The pain and symptoms of FM can wax and wane, vary in physical location and in intensity day to day; many patients continue to have chronic pain and fatigue regardless of therapy.
- Disability rates vary from 10% to 30%.

REFERRAL

Referral to rheumatology, neurology, mental health professionals, physical medicine and rehabilitation, including physical therapy, may be helpful for a multidisciplinary team approach.

 PEARLS & CONSIDERATIONS

- Fibromyalgia is a neurosensory disorder whereby affected individuals have abnormal central nociceptive processing.
- Diagnosis is based on the presence of chronic musculoskeletal pain in the absence of physical or laboratory evidence of inflammation and in the absence of any other condition that would explain the symptoms.
- Treatment options are varied, but a combination of drug and nondrug options is likely to provide optimal results.
- Myofascial pain syndrome may represent a localized form of FM. It is associated with trigger points (rather than tender points as seen in FM). Some patients with myofascial pain syndrome may progress to FM.

COMMENTS

FM occurs frequently in patients with some rheumatic diseases such as rheumatoid arthritis, ankylosing spondylitis, and systemic lupus erythematosus, in which prevalence of FM may reach 20%.

SUGGESTED READINGS
Available at www.expertconsult.com

RELATED CONTENT
Fibromyalgia (Patient Information)

AUTHOR: **NADINE MBUYI, M.D.**

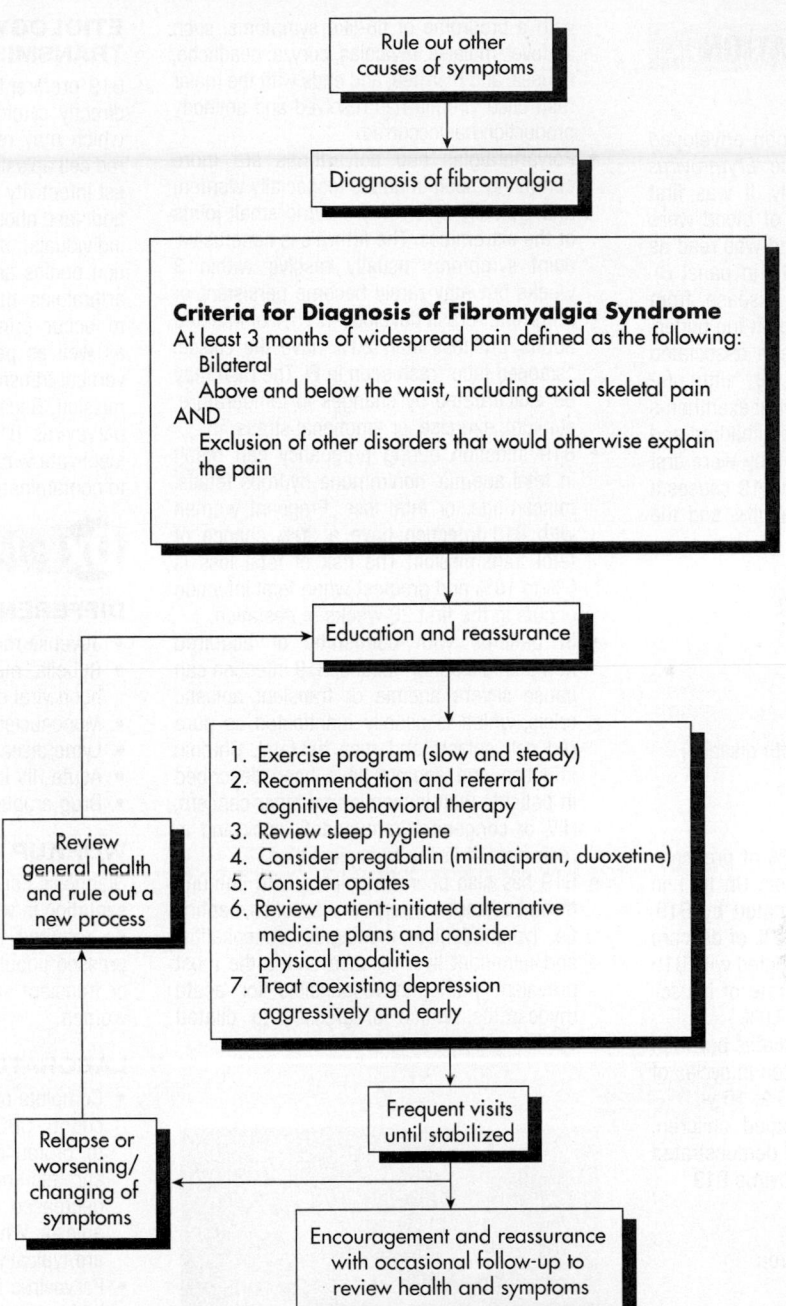

FIGURE 1F-6 Treatment algorithm for fibromyalgia. (Modified from Harris ED et al: *Kelley's textbook of rheumatology*, ed 7, Philadelphia, 2005, Saunders.)

BASIC INFORMATION

DEFINITION

Parvovirus B19 is a small, non-enveloped ssDNA virus that belongs to the *Erythrovirus* genus of the *Parvoviridae* family. It was first discovered in 1975 when units of blood were being screened for hepatitis B and was read as a false-positive result (sample 19 in panel B). It causes a spectrum of human disease, from asymptomatic to fatal, depending on the underlying host. Classically, it has been associated with erythema infectiosum (EI), or "fifth disease," the fifth in a series of six viral exanthems that commonly affect school-aged children and are named in order of the dates they were first described. In addition, parvovirus B19 causes a variety of diseases in fetuses, adults, and the immunocompromised.

SYNONYMS

Parvovirus B19
Erythema infectiosum
Fifth disease

ICD-10CM CODES
B08.3 Erythema infectiosum [fifth disease]

EPIDEMIOLOGY & DEMOGRAPHICS

INCIDENCE: Between 1% and 9% of pregnancies are affected by B19 infection. Up to 1 in 200 units of blood are contaminated by B19, and 16% of schoolteachers and 9% of daycare workers and homemakers are infected with B19 during epidemics. The infection rate of household contacts may be as high as 50%.
PEAK INCIDENCE: Temperate climates between late winter and early summer, often in cycles of local epidemics that peak every 3 to 10 yr.
PREVALENCE: 15% of school-aged children, and 30% to 85% of adults have demonstrated protective IgG antibodies to parvovirus B19.
PREDOMINANT AGE: 5 to 18 yr
RISK FACTORS:
- Exposure to school-aged children
- Immunosuppression
- Congenital or acquired hematologic abnormalities,
- Blood transfusion
- Tissue transplantation

PHYSICAL FINDINGS & CLINICAL PRESENTATION

- Approximately 25% of those infected are asymptomatic, 50% have nonspecific flu-like symptoms, and 25% have the classic symptoms of B19 infection, including rash and/or arthralgias.
- Parvovirus B19 is the most common viral agent associated with rashes in school-aged children. EI is characterized by a bright red, nontender rash most prominent on the cheeks with a circumoral pallor producing the classic "slapped face" appearance (Fig. 1F-7), which is often followed by a reticular, lacelike rash on the trunk and extremities. This is typically a transient, self-limited illness that begins

with a prodrome of flu-like symptoms, such as fever, malaise, myalgias, coryza, headache, nausea, and diarrhea, and ends with the malar rash once viremia has resolved and antibody production has occurred.
- Polyarthralgias and polyarthritis are more commonly seen in adults (especially women) and typically involve symmetric small joints of the extremities. The arthritis is nonerosive. Joint symptoms usually resolve within 3 weeks but may rarely become persistent or recurrent. A rash develops in 75% of infected adults, but less than 20% have the classic "slapped face" rash seen in EI. The rash may be exacerbated by changes in temperature, sunlight, exercise, or emotional stress.
- B19 infection during pregnancy can result in fetal anemia, nonimmune hydrops fetalis, miscarriage, or fetal loss. Pregnant women with B19 infection have a 30% chance of fetal transmission. The risk of fetal loss is 5% to 10% and greatest when fetal infection occurs in the first 20 weeks of gestation.
- In patients with congenital or acquired hematologic abnormalities, B19 infection can cause severe anemia or transient aplastic crisis, which is usually manifested as pure red cell aplasia and may be fatal. Chronic infection and anemia have been described in patients with leukemia and other cancers, HIV, or congenital immunodeficiency and in recipients of tissue transplantation.
- B19 has also been associated with immune thrombocytopenic purpura, vasculitis, nephritis, lymphadenitis, meningitis, encephalitis, and fulminant liver disease and is the most prevalent pathogen responsible for acute myocarditis, which progresses to dilated cardiomyopathy in 21% of cases.

FIGURE 1F-7 Fifth disease (erythema infectiosum). Facial erythema "slapped face." The red plaque covers the cheek and spares the nasolabial and the circumoral region. (From Habif TP: *Clinical dermatology: a color guide to diagnosis and therapy,* ed 3, St Louis, 1996, Mosby.)

ETIOLOGY, INFECTIVITY, & TRANSMISSION

B19 preferentially infects, replicates in, and is directly cytotoxic to erythroid progenitor cells, which may result in profound anemia or pure red cell aplasia. Viremia and the period of greatest infectivity occur 7 to 10 days after exposure and last about 1 week in immunocompetent individuals, after which time antibody production begins and typical symptoms of rash and arthralgias manifest. Transmission is thought to occur primarily through droplet exposure, as well as person-to-person contact, fomites, vertical transmission, and hematogenous transmission. Because of its non-enveloped capsid, parvovirus B19 is heat stable and difficult to inactivate with solvent detergents, often leading to contamination of blood products.

DIAGNOSIS

DIFFERENTIAL DIAGNOSIS
- Juvenile rheumatoid arthritis (Still's disease)
- Rubella, measles (rubeola), and other childhood viral exanthems
- Mononucleosis
- Lyme disease
- Acute HIV infection
- Drug eruption

WORKUP

Diagnosis can be made by typical clinical presentation in well children. Laboratory tests may be required for confirmation in immunosuppressed populations, those with severe anemia or transient aplastic crisis (TAC), and pregnant women.

LABORATORY TESTS
- Complete blood count (CBC) and reticulocyte count: CBC evaluation ranges from mild to profound classically normocytic normochromic anemia. Reticulocytes are markedly decreased or absent in pure red blood cell aplasia. White blood cell and platelet counts are typically unchanged.
- Parvovirus B19 IgM and IgG: Parvovirus B19 IgM enzyme immunoassay is widely available and the preferred method of diagnosis in immunocompetent individuals. IgM can be found within 7 to 10 days of exposure and may persist for several months. IgG antibodies are detectable about 15 days after exposure and persist long term.
- Parvovirus B19 viral DNA polymerase chain reaction (PCR): Nucleic acid antigen testing (NAAT) of B19 DNA by PCR is the most sensitive method of infection detection and the preferred method for diagnosis in immunocompromised individuals, fetuses, immunocompetent patients with suspected persistent infection, and blood products.
- Bone marrow biopsy: Bone marrow examination in patients with pure red cell aplasia demonstrates complete or near-complete absence of red cell precursors. Characteristic giant proerythroblasts containing large eosinophilic nuclear inclusions can be seen.

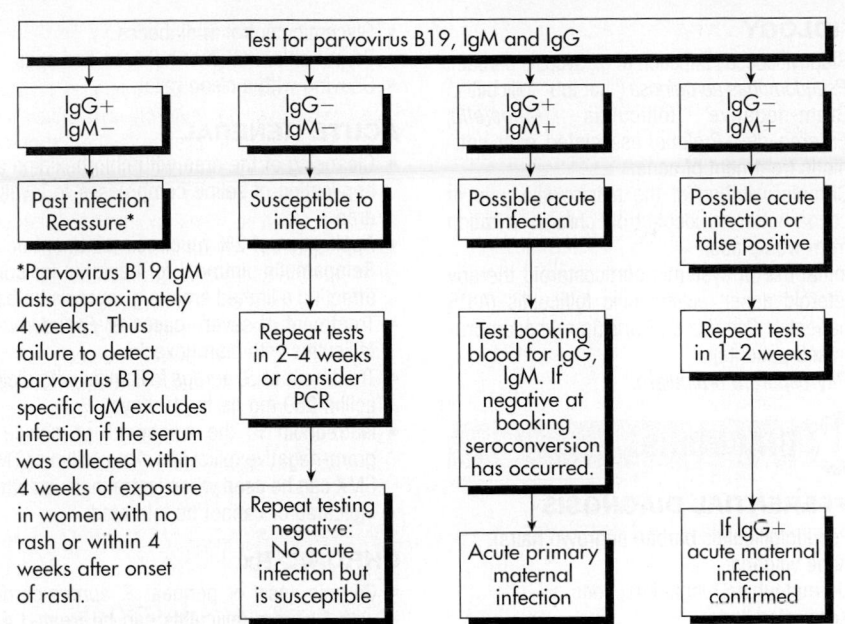

Test for parvovirus B19, IgM and IgG

| IgG+ IgM− | IgG− IgM− | IgG+ IgM+ | IgG− IgM+ |

IgG+ IgM−: Past infection Reassure*

*Parvovirus B19 IgM lasts approximately 4 weeks. Thus failure to detect parvovirus B19 specific IgM excludes infection if the serum was collected within 4 weeks of exposure in women with no rash or within 4 weeks after onset of rash.

IgG− IgM−: Susceptible to infection → Repeat tests in 2–4 weeks or consider PCR → Repeat testing negative: No acute infection but is susceptible

IgG+ IgM+: Possible acute infection → Test booking blood for IgG, IgM. If negative at booking seroconversion has occurred. → Acute primary maternal infection

IgG− IgM+: Possible acute infection or false positive → Repeat tests in 1–2 weeks → If IgG+ acute maternal infection confirmed

FIGURE 1F-8 Investigations for parvovirus B19 infection. (From Stephen G, Gillham J: Fetal infection: a pragmatic approach to recognition and management. *Obstetr Gynecol Reprod Med* 22(10): 299–303, 2012.)

- Fig. 1F-8 illustrates investigations for parvovirus B19 infection in pregnancy.
- Prenatal testing: Fetal nuchal translucency measurement and ductus venosus Doppler velocimetry may indicate the presence of severe fetal anemia. Ultrasound may show fetal edema, ascites, pleural effusions, and cardiomegaly in hydrops fetalis.

 **TREATMENT**

NON-PHARMACOLOGIC THERAPY

- Treatment for Fifth disease is generally supportive because the majority of B19 infections are asymptomatic or mild and self-limited. Nonsteroidal antiinflammatory drugs may be used for relief of joint symptoms, antipyretics for fever, and adequate hydration.

ACUTE GENERAL TREATMENT

- No antiviral drug is available.
- Blood transfusion is often required in cases of severe anemia and pure red cell aplasia until red blood cell (RBC) production returns; intrauterine transfusion may be required in fetal infection.
- Initiation of antiretroviral therapy (ART) has been associated with resolution of B19-induced anemia in HIV-infected patients.

- Bone marrow transplantation has been used in individuals with nonresolving aplastic crisis.
- The mainstay of fetal therapy is delivery, which may be followed by resuscitation and ventilation in cases of severe hydrops.

CHRONIC GENERAL TREATMENT

- IV immunoglobulin (IVIG) treatment may be considered for immunocompromised patients with chronic B19 infection and chronic anemia.

DISPOSITION

- B19 infection is typically self-limited, with symptoms usually resolving within a few weeks and most often only requiring supportive care.
- Children in whom EI develops are no longer contagious and may attend school and day-care.
- Patients in whom persistent arthritis with or without joint erosion develops should be evaluated by a rheumatologist.
- In immunocompetent patients, anemia is typically transient with spontaneous resolution and return of RBC production in days to weeks. In patients with hematologic abnormalities, however, anemia may be severe and may be the result of transient aplastic crisis or pure red cell aplasia, which warrants immediate hematologic evaluation and transfusion.

- Patients with TAC or chronic parvovirus B19 infection pose a risk for nosocomial spread and, when hospitalized, should be isolated with droplet precautions.
- Patients with chronic infection and anemia may require evaluation for possible IVIG treatment.
- Pregnant women with B19 infection have a 30% risk of fetal transmission; they should undergo close monitoring of fetal health and development and may require fetal transfusion or referral to a tertiary care center for delivery in the case of hydrops fetalis.
- Vaccines have not progressed beyond phase I/II clinical trials.

REFERRAL

- To hematologist if signs of marrow suppression
- To rheumatologist if signs of severe or erosive arthritis
- To cardiologist if suspicion of myocarditis

 **PEARLS & CONSIDERATIONS**

- Generally self-limited disease lasting up to 3 weeks in immunocompetent individuals.
- Symmetric arthritis involving small joints is common in adults, whereas facial rash is common in children.
- Can cause severe anemia with or without transient aplastic crisis that may become chronic in patients with hematologic abnormalities, immunocompromise, malignancy, or a history of organ transplantation.
- Infection during pregnancy can cause fetal anemia, hydrops fetalis, or fetal loss.

PREVENTION

- Hand-washing and not sharing food or drinks during epidemics.
- Testing of plasma pools and blood products for B19 contamination.

SUGGESTED READINGS

Available at www.expertconsult.com

RELATED CONTENT

Fifth Disease (Patient Information)

AUTHORS: **ANTONELLA FINE, M.D.,** and **DOMINICK TAMMARO, M.D.**

BASIC INFORMATION

DEFINITION

Folliculitis is inflammation of the hair follicle as a result of infection, physical injury, or chemical irritation.

SYNONYMS

Sycosis barbae

ICD-10CM CODES
L72.9   Follicular cyst of skin and subcutaneous tissue, unspecified
L73.1   Pseudofolliculitis barbae
L73.8   Other specified follicular disorders
L66.2   Folliculitis decalvans
L66.4   Folliculitis ulerythematosa reticulata
L66.3   Perifolliculitis capitis abscedens

EPIDEMIOLOGY & DEMOGRAPHICS

PREVALENCE: Staphylococcal folliculitis is the most common form of infectious folliculitis; it occurs most commonly in persons with diabetes. Gram-negative folliculitis occurs in patients who have had moderately inflammatory acne for long periods and have been treated with long term antibiotics such as tetracycline.
PREDOMINANT SEX: Sycosis barbae occurs most frequently in men who have commenced shaving.

PHYSICAL FINDINGS & CLINICAL PRESENTATION

- The lesions generally consist of painful yellow pustules surrounded by erythema; a central hair is present in the pustules. Furuncles with pus may be present (Fig. 1F-11).
- Patients with sycosis barbae may initially present with small follicular papules or pustules that increase in size with continued shaving; deep follicular pustules may occur surrounded by erythema and swelling; the upper lip is frequently involved.
- "Hot tub" folliculitis occurs within 1 to 4 days after the use of a hot tub with poor chlorination. It is characterized by papules and pustules (Fig. 1F-12) with surrounding erythema generally affecting the torso, buttocks, and limbs.

ETIOLOGY

- Staphylococcus infection (e.g., sycosis barbae), *Pseudomonas aeruginosa* ("hot tub" folliculitis.)
- Gram-negative folliculitis *(Klebsiella, Enterobacter, Proteus)* associated with antibiotic treatment of acne.
- Chronic irritation of the hair follicle (use of cocoa butter or coconut oil, chronic irritation from workplace).
- Initial use of systemic corticosteroid therapy (steroid acne), eosinophilic folliculitis (AIDS patients), *Candida albicans* (immunocompromised patients).
- *Pityrosporum orbiculare.*

DIAGNOSIS

DIFFERENTIAL DIAGNOSIS

- Pseudofolliculitis barbae (ingrown hairs).
- Acne vulgaris.
- Dermatophyte fungal infections.
- Keratosis pilaris.
- Cutaneous candidiasis.
- Superficial fungal infections.
- Miliaris.

WORKUP

- Physical examination and medical history (e.g., use of hot tub: "hot tub" folliculitis; adolescent patients who have started shaving: sycosis barbae; use of occlusive topical steroid therapy: *Staphylococcus* folliculitis).
- Gram-negative folliculitis in acne patients on prolonged antibiotic treatment manifests with superficial pustules 3 to 6 mm in diameter flaring out from anterior nares or fluctuant, deep seated nodules.

LABORATORY TESTS

- Generally not necessary.
- Gram stain is useful to identify the infective organisms in infectious folliculitis and to differentiate infectious folliculitis from noninfectious.

TREATMENT

NONPHARMACOLOGIC THERAPY

- Prevention of chemical or mechanical skin irritation.

- Glycemic control in diabetics.
- Proper chlorination of hot tubs and spas.
- Shaving with a clean razor.

ACUTE GENERAL

- Cleansing of the area with chlorhexidine and application of saline compresses to involved area.
- Application of 2% mupirocin ointment or 1% Retapamulin ointment for bacterial folliculitis affecting a limited area (e.g., sycosis barbae).
- Treatment of severe cases of *Pseudomonas* folliculitis with ciprofloxacin.
- Treatment of *S. aureus* folliculitis with dicloxacillin 250 mg qd for 10 days.
- Isotretinoin is the treatment of choice in gram-negative folliculitis. Amoxicillin or TMS-SMX can be used when isotretinoin is contraindicated or cannot be tolerated.

CHRONIC Rx

- Chronic nasal or perineal *S. aureus* carriers with frequent folliculitis can be treated with rifampin 300 mg bid for 5 days.
- Mupirocin or Retapamulin ointment applied to nares bid is also effective for nasal carriers.

DISPOSITION:
- Most cases of bacterial folliculitis resolve completely with proper treatment.
- Steroid folliculitis responds to discontinuation of steroids.

PEARLS & CONSIDERATIONS

COMMENTS

Patients should be instructed in good personal hygiene and avoidance of sharing razors, towels, and washcloths.

SUGGESTED READINGS

Available at www.expertconsult.com

RELATED CONTENT

Folliculitis (Patient Information)

AUTHOR: **FRED F. FERRI, M.D.**

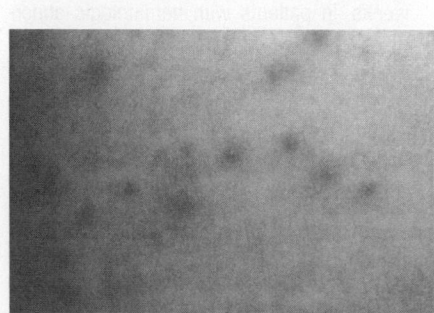

FIGURE 1F-11 Rupture and discharge of pus in a furuncle. (From Kliegman RM et al: *Nelson textbook of pediatrics*, ed 19, Philadelphia, 2011, Saunders.)

FIGURE 1F-12 Papules and pustules in hot tub folliculitis. (From Kliegman RM et al: *Nelson textbook of pediatrics*, ed 19, Philadelphia, 2011, Saunders.)

🛈 BASIC INFORMATION

DEFINITION

Food allergies are divided into IgE-mediated and immunologically mediated non-IgE reactions. They include a spectrum of disorders that involve adverse immunologic responses to dietary antigens.

ICD-10CM CODES

T78.0	Adverse food reaction (including anaphylactic shock)
T78.1	Other adverse food reactions, not elsewhere classified
L27.2	Dermatitis due to ingested food
Z91.010	Allergy to peanuts
Z91.011	Allergy to milk products
Z91.012	Allergy to eggs
Z91.013	Allergy to seafood
Z91.018	Allergy to other foods
Z91.02	Food additives allergy status

EPIDEMIOLOGY & DEMOGRAPHICS

INCIDENCE: Food allergies have a cumulative incidence of 6% to 8% for the first 3 yr of life.
PREVALENCE:
- Overall prevalence is 1% to 2% in general population, ~3.9% to 8% in children.
- Patient self-reported food allergies have a prevalence of 12% to 13%, demonstrating the importance of objective measures in assessing food allergies.
- Nearly 40% of children with food allergy have a history of severe reactions that, if not treated immediately with proper medication, can lead to hospitalization or even death.[1]
- There is insufficient evidence to conclude a racial predilection (Greenhawt, 2013).

PREDOMINANT SEX: Males are more affected than females among children, and among adults, females are more frequently affected.
GENETICS: Children with parents or close relatives with allergies may have a tendency to become allergic to foods.

PHYSICAL FINDINGS & CLINICAL PRESENTATION

- IgE-mediated reactions: (within minutes to a few hours) pruritus, urticaria or angioedema, atopic dermatitis, GI symptoms, conjunctival injection, sneezing, nasal congestion, rhinorrhea, bronchospasm, and anaphylaxis.
- Non–IgE-mediated reactions: food-induced enterocolitis, celiac disease, Crohn's disease, dermatitis herpetiformis, and pulmonary reactions such as Heiner syndrome. These illnesses are discussed separately.
- Signs, symptoms, and presentation reflect specific allergic manifestation, but in food allergies there is a reproducible temporal relationship to ingested food allergens.

ETIOLOGY

Failure to establish tolerance to food antigens. IL-33 mediated epithelial permeability and Th2

[1]Gupta RS et al: The prevalence, severity, and distribution of childhood food allergy in the United States, *Pediatrics* 128(l):e9-e17, 2011.

skewing result in sensitization to food proteins which are presented to primed T cells. Food processing conditions that may affect allergenic activity are described in Table E1F-9.

🅳🅧 DIAGNOSIS

- Thorough history and physical exam should be performed.
- The temporal relationship and reproducibility of the symptoms are most important to establishing the diagnosis.
- A review of ingredient labels may be helpful.
- Confirmatory testing can include skin testing or in vitro testing.
- Skin prick testing (SPT): positive predictive value <50%, but negative predictive value >95%. Thus a negative skin test effectively rules out an IgE-mediated process.
- In vitro testing: RAST testing: Historically it is less sensitive than skin testing, but sensitivity has improved with cut off points indicating a positive predictive value of 95% for allergies to eggs, milk, peanuts, wheat, and fish.
- Atopy patch test: used in conjunction with RAST and skin testing in multiallergic children to plan widening the elimination diet. However, it is not recommended in the routine evaluation of food allergies.
- Double-blind, placebo-controlled food challenges are the gold standard test for determining food allergies. These need to be done in a supervised and controlled setting.
- In summary, if the history and lab tests are suggestive of a specific food allergy, that food should be confirmed by SPT, RAST, or food challenge and, once confirmed, eliminated from the diet.

DIFFERENTIAL DIAGNOSIS

- Gastrointestinal disorders
- Irritable bowel syndrome
- Carcinoid syndrome
- Giardiasis
- Structural abnormalities like hiatal hernia, pyloric stenosis, Hirschsprung's disease, tracheoesophageal fistula
- Disaccharidase deficiencies: lactase, sucrase-isomaltase complex, glucose-galactose complex
- Pancreatic insufficiency: cystic fibrosis
- Gallbladder disease
- Peptic ulcer disease
- Malignancy
- Metabolic disorders
- Galactosemia
- Phenylketonuria
- Pharmacologic-related conditions
- Gustatory rhinitis
- Auriculotemporal syndrome (facial flush from tart food)

🆁🆇 TREATMENT

NONPHARMACOLOGIC THERAPY

- Elimination diet should be used in conjunction with nutritional counseling. Fig. 1F-13 illustrates an algorithm for the management of food allergy

- Formula-fed infants: brief trial of hydrolyzed milk formula as most children with milk allergy–induced skin symptoms will respond to the change of formula. Nonresponders may require amino acid–based formula.
- In older children: elimination of one to two suspected foods is appropriate for 2 wk or longer and then reintroducing the foods to determine if symptoms recur.

ACUTE GENERAL Rx

- Antihistamines (both H_1 and H_2 antihistamines), albuterol if wheezing, epinephrine and glucocorticoids in patients with anaphylaxis.
- Patients with documented IgE-mediated reactions should receive and be counseled on the use of epinephrine autoinjector.

NEW TREATMENTS FOR FOOD ALLERGIES

- Oral and sublingual immunotherapy may play a role in management of food allergies, but this is currently under investigation.
- Recombinant vaccines and other immunomodulatory strategies are under development, although monoclonal anti-IgE antibody has shown benefit in adults with peanut allergy.

❗ PEARLS & CONSIDERATIONS

- Eczema that develops in first 6 to 12 mo of life is usually the first manifestation of atopy.
- Egg allergy or sensitization is the strongest recognized predictor of respiratory allergies in children and asthma in adults.
- Neither the size of the wheal in skin prick testing nor the IgE antibody level correlates with severity. However, there may be increased positive predictive value with larger wheals and higher titers.
- Consultation with trained dietitian is critical to avoid potentially adverse nutritional consequences in children with multiple food allergies.
- Skin testing is the preferred method for identifying food-specific IgE. RAST is useful if there is chance of severe food reaction causing risk to the patient.
- American Academy of Pediatrics recommends avoiding influenza vaccine in patients with severe systemic allergic reactions to egg. Skin prick testing using influenza vaccine containing egg is recommended before vaccination in children with egg allergy and asthma. Skin prick testing not required before MMR vaccine in children with egg allergy.

COMMENTS

- Milk allergy usually resolves by age 5. Risk factors for persistence are early cutaneous manifestations following milk ingestion, development of other atopic conditions, and persistence of milk-specific high IgE titers. Soy milk is recommended for these children, keeping in mind that about 15% of these children can develop soy allergy.
- Egg allergy has been thought to resolve in 66% of children by 5 yr of age and in 75% of children by 7 yr of age. Trials have shown

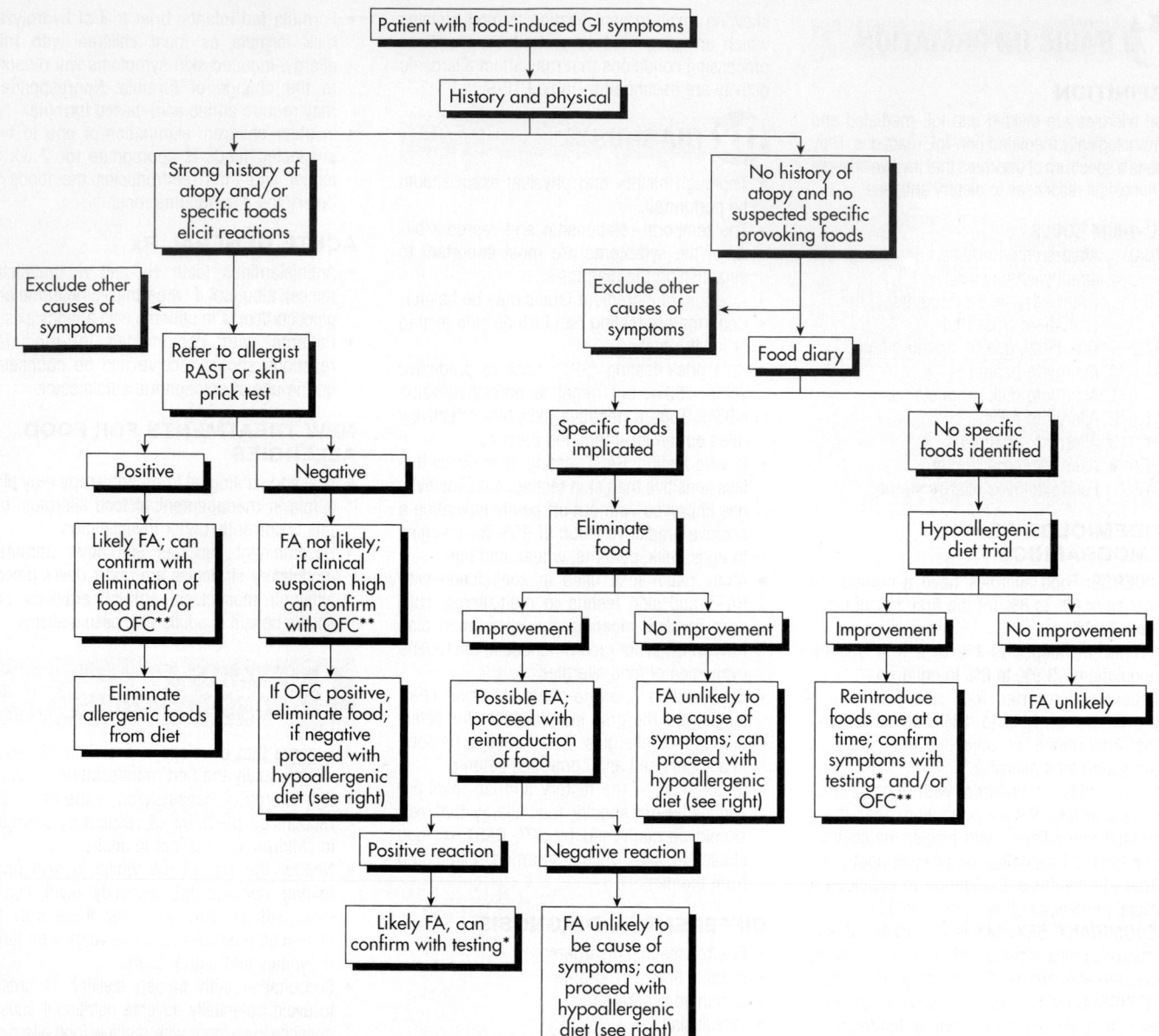

FIGURE 1F-13 Algorithm for the management of food allergy. *Testing indicates skin-prick testing, radioallergosorbent tests (RAST), IgG₄ assay, and/or patch testing. Note that clinical symptoms must be associated with the food(s) that test positive before the food(s) should be eliminated from the diet. **Oral food challenge (OFC) involves reintroducing the food and observing for signs/symptoms of food allergy (FA). Treatment of food allergy involves elimination of the causative food(s) from the diet. (From Stephen G, Gillham J: Fetal infection: a pragmatic approach to recognition and management. *Obstetr Gynaecolo Rep Med* 22(10) 299–303, 2012.)

that oral immunotherapy can desensitize a high proportion of children with egg allergy and induce sustained unresponsiveness in a clinically significant subset.

- Wheat allergy found to resolve by 5 yr of age and soybean allergy by 2 yr of age.

PREVENTION

- There is conflicting evidence regarding the protective effect of breastfeeding on food allergies.
- There is no evidence to suggest that exclusive breastfeeding for 6 mo or more is superior to exclusive breastfeeding for 4 to 6 mo in terms of developing food allergies.
- In high-risk infants who are not exclusively breast fed, there is limited evidence to suggest that feeding with hydrolyzed formula compared to cow's milk formula reduces allergies.

- Currently, there is no evidence to support the use of prebiotics, probiotics, or synbiotics for the prevention of allergic diseases.
- No current evidence exists to support delaying the introduction of solid foods beyond 4 to 6 mo.
- The early introduction of peanuts significantly decreases the frequency of the development of peanut allergy among children at high risk for this allergy and modulated immune responses to peanuts.[2]

PATIENT/FAMILY EDUCATION

Information can be found on American Academy of Allergy, Asthma and Immunology

[2]DuToit G et al.: Randomized trial of peanut consumption in infants at risk for peanut allergy, *N Engl J Med* 372:803-13, 2015

(www.aaaai.org), the Food Allergy and Anaphylaxis Network (www.foodallergy.org), and the Anaphylaxis Campaign (www.anaphylaxis.org.uk).

REFERRAL

Patients may be referred to an allergy/immunology specialist when the diagnosis is uncertain or if avoidance measures are not successful.

SUGGESTED READINGS
Available at www.expertconsult.com

RELATED CONTENT
Food Allergies (Patient Information)

AUTHOR: **LUKE BARRÉ, M.D.**

BASIC INFORMATION

DEFINITION

Food poisoning is an illness caused by ingestion of food contaminated by bacteria and/or bacterial toxins. Table 1F-10 describes pathogenic mechanisms in bacterial foodborne disease.

SYNONYMS

Enterotoxin-poisoning
Epidemic vomiting disease

ICD-10CM CODES
A05.9 Bacterial foodborne intoxication, unspecified

EPIDEMIOLOGY & DEMOGRAPHICS
INCIDENCE (IN U.S.):
- CDC estimates that each year one in six Americans will experience a foodborne illness.
- CDC reported 13,405 foodborne disease outbreaks from 1998 to 2008 in the United States.
- Majority of identifiable causes are bacterial, although more than 250 known diseases can be transmitted through food.

PEAK INCIDENCE: Varies with specific organism.
- Summer: *Staphylococcus aureus, Salmonella, Shigella* spp.
- Summer and fall: *Clostridium botulinum, Vibrio parahaemolyticus.*
- Spring and fall: *Campylobacter jejuni.*
- Winter: *Clostridium perfringens, Yersinia enterocolitica.*

PREDOMINANT AGE: Varies with specific agent.
NEONATAL INFECTION: Rare but severe with *Shigella* and *Salmonella* spp.

PHYSICAL FINDINGS & CLINICAL PRESENTATION
- Any combination of GI symptoms and fever. Orthostatic pulse and blood pressure changes should be noted.
- Specific organisms suspected on the basis of the incubation period and predominant symptoms (Table E1F-11), although a great deal of overlap exists.
  1. Short incubation period (1 to 6 hr): involve the ingestion of preformed toxin; noninvasive.
     a. *S. aureus:* nausea, profuse vomiting, and abdominal cramps common; diarrhea possible, but fever uncommon; usually resolves within 24 hr; foods

implicated in outbreaks include meats, mayonnaise, and cream pastries.
     b. *B. cereus:* two forms, a short incubation (emetic) form (characterized by vomiting and abdominal cramps in virtually all patients, diarrhea in one third of patients, fever uncommon) and a long incubation (diarrheal) form; illness usually mild, resolves within 12 hr; unrefrigerated rice most often implicated as vehicle. Other sources include gravy, meats, stews, vanilla, and sauces.
  2. Moderate incubation period (8 to 16 hr): involves the in vivo production of toxin; noninvasive.
     a. *C. perfringens:* severe crampy abdominal pain and watery diarrhea common; fever and vomiting unlikely; symptoms usually resolving within 24 hr; outbreaks invariably related to cooked meat or poultry that is allowed to cool without refrigeration; most cases in the fall and winter months. *C. perfringens* is the third most common cause of foodborne illness in the United States.
     b. *B. cereus:* diarrheal (or long incubation) form most commonly beginning with diarrhea, abdominal cramps, and occasionally vomiting; fever uncommon; usually resolves within 24 hr; the responsible food is usually fried rice.
  3. Long incubation period (>16 hr): some toxin-mediated, some invasive.
- Toxin-producing organisms include:
  (1) *C. botulinum:* should be considered when a diarrheal illness coincides with or precedes paralysis; severity of illness related to the quantity of toxin ingested; characteristic cranial nerve palsies progressing to a descending paralysis; fever usually absent; usually associated with home-canned foods.
  (2) Enterotoxigenic *E. coli* (ETEC): most common cause of travelers' diarrhea; after 1- to 2-day incubation period, abdominal cramps and copious diarrhea occur; vomiting and fever uncommon; usually resolves after 3 to 4 days; vehicle usually unbottled water or contaminated salad or ice.
  (3) Enterohemorrhagic *E. coli* (EHEC): can cause severe abdominal cramps and watery diarrhea, which may eventually

become bloody; bacteria (strain 0157:H7) are noninvasive; no fever; illness may be complicated by hemolytic-uremic syndrome; associated with contaminated beef (especially hamburger), unpasteurized milk or juice.
  (4) *V. cholerae:* varies from a mild, self-limited illness to life-threatening cholera; diarrhea, nausea, and vomiting, abdominal cramps, and muscle cramps; no fever; severe cases may progress to shock and death within hours of onset; survivors usually have resolution of symptoms in 1 wk; U.S. cases are either imported or result from ingestion of imported food.
- Invasive organisms include:
  (1) *Salmonella:* associated most often with nontyphoidal strains; incubation period generally 12 to 48 hr; nausea, vomiting, diarrhea, and abdominal cramps typical; fever possible; outbreaks of gastroenteritis related to contaminated poultry, meat, and dairy products.
  (2) *Shigella:* asymptomatic infection possible, but some with fever and watery diarrhea that may progress to bloody diarrhea and dysentery; with mild illness, usually self-limited, resolves in a few days; with severe illness, may develop complications; transmission usually from person to person but can occur via contaminated food or water.
  (3) *C. jejuni:* the most common food-borne bacterial pathogen; incubation period is about 1 day, then a prodrome of fever, headache, and myalgias; intestinal phase marked by diarrhea associated with fever, malaise, and abdominal pain; diarrhea mild to profuse and bloody; usually resolves in about 7 days, but relapse is possible; associated with undercooked meats and poultry, unpasteurized dairy products, and drinking from freshwater streams.
  (4) *Y. enterocolitica* and *Y. pseudotuberculosis:* infrequent causes of enteritis in the United States; children affected more often than adults; fever, diarrhea, and abdominal pain lasting 1 to 3 wk; some with mesenteric adenitis that mimics acute appendicitis; contaminated food or water is usually responsible.
  (5) *V. parahaemolyticus:* In the United States, most outbreaks in coastal states or on cruise ships during the summer months;

TABLE 1F-10 Pathogenic Mechanisms in Bacterial Foodborne Disease

Preformed Toxin	Toxin Production in Vivo	Tissue Invasion	Toxin Production and/or Tissue Invasion
Staphylococcus aureus	*Clostridium perfringens*	*Campylobacter jejuni*	*Vibrio parahaemolyticus*
Bacillus cereus (short incubation)	*B. cereus* (long incubation)	*Salmonella*	*Yersinia enterocolitica*
Clostridium botulinum	*C. botulinum* (infant botulism)	*Shigella*	
	Enterotoxigenic *Escherichia coli*	Invasive *E. coli*	
	Vibrio cholerae 01 or 0139		
	V. cholerae non-01		
	Shiga toxin–producing *E. coli*		

From Mandell GL et al: *Principles and practice of infectious diseases*, ed 6, Philadelphia, 2005, Churchill Livingstone.

incubation period usually >1 day, followed by explosive watery diarrhea in the majority of cases; nausea, vomiting, abdominal cramps, and headache also common; fever less common; usually resolves by 1 wk; related to ingestion of seafood.

(6) Enteroinvasive *E. coli* (EIEC): a rare cause of disease in the United States; high incidence of fever and bloody diarrhea; may resemble bacillary dysentery.

(7) *V. vulnificus:* may cause serious, often fatal illness in persons with chronic liver disease; GI symptoms usually absent, but fever, chills, hypotension, and hemorrhagic skin lesions possible; patients with liver disease or at increased risk of developing liver disease should avoid eating raw oysters.

ETIOLOGY

Classically categorized as either inflammatory (invasive) or noninflammatory:

- Noninflammatory: *B. cereus, S. aureus, C. botulinum, C. perfringens, V. cholerae,* enterotoxigenic *E. coli* (ETEC), and enterohemorrhagic *E. coli* (EHEC); toxin-producing organisms that are noninvasive; fecal leukocytes are not seen.
- Inflammatory: *Campylobacter,* enteroinvasive *E. coli* (EIEC), *Salmonella, Shigella, V. parahaemolyticus,* and *Yersinia;* cause disease by invasion of intestinal tissue; fecal leukocytes are seen.

 **DIAGNOSIS**

DIFFERENTIAL DIAGNOSIS

Gastroenteritis caused by viruses (Norwalk, Noro, or rotavirus), parasites *(Amoeba histolytica, Giardia lamblia),* or toxins (ciguatoxins, mushrooms, heavy metals).

LABORATORY TESTS

- Watchful waiting is often the most appropriate option and ancillary testing is usually not necessary.
- In severe or persistent cases stool test for fecal leukocytes may help narrow the differential diagnosis:
  1. Send stool for culture and for ova and parasites.
  2. Send stool for *C. difficile* toxin in patients with current or recent antibiotic use.
  3. Note: Some pathogens are not identified on routine stool culture; laboratory should be advised if *Yersinia, C. botulinum, Vibrio,*

or enterohemorrhagic *E. coli* (0157:H7) are suspected.
4. Finding *B. cereus, C. perfringens,* or *E. coli* in stool is of little value, because these may be part of the normal bowel flora.
5. Stool cultures are positive in less than 40% of cases.
6. Newer techniques such as polymerase chain reaction (PCR) testing provide a more rapid and reliable determination of specific pathogens.

- If botulism suspected, send food, serum, and stool for toxin assay.
- Blood cultures should be considered for all febrile patients.
- Consider toxic megacolon (identified on plain abdominal sonography).
- Consider sigmoidoscopy to obtain tissue and histology in hospitalized patients with bloody diarrhea.
- Consider lactoferrin measurement if an inflammatory etiology is suspected.

 **TREATMENT**

NONPHARMACOLOGIC THERAPY

Adequate rehydration is the mainstay of therapy.

ACUTE GENERAL Rx

- Most cases of acute infectious diarrhea are viral and antibiotics are not indicated.
- Gastroenteritis caused by the following bacterial organisms requires no antimicrobial treatment: *B. cereus, S. aureus, C. perfringens, V. parahaemolyticus, Yersinia,* and enterohemorrhagic and enteroinvasive *E. coli.*
- The usual cause of traveler's diarrhea is enterotoxigenic *E. coli.* Although usually a self-limited illness, antibiotics can shorten the course in patients with fever or dysentery.
  1. Azithromycin 1000 mg in a single oral dose or
  2. SMX/TMP one DS tab bid for 3 days or
  3. Ciprofloxacin 500 mg PO bid for 3 days.
- The mainstay of therapy for cholera is fluid replacement. Antibiotics should be given to decrease shedding and duration of illness.
  1. Doxycycline 300 mg in a single dose or 100 mg PO bid for 3 days.
  2. SMX/TMP one DS tab bid for 3 days.
- Treatment is not indicated for *Salmonella* gastroenteritis. Patients who are at high risk of developing bacteremia may be treated for 48 to 72 hr (see "Salmonellosis").
- Although shigellosis tends to be a self-limited illness, antibiotics shorten the course of illness

and may limit transmission of the illness (see "Shigellosis").
- Those with moderate or severe *Campylobacter* diarrhea may benefit from treatment.
  1. Azithromycin 500 mg qd for 3 days or
  2. Erythromycin 500 mg PO qid for 5 days or
  3. Ciprofloxacin 500 mg PO bid for 5 days.
- *V. vulnificus* sepsis should be treated with:
  1. Doxycycline 100 mg IV bid for 2 wk.
  2. Ceftazidime 2 g IV q8h for 2 wk.
- For suspected botulism, antitoxin should be administered early (see "Botulism").

CHRONIC Rx

Patients with *Salmonella* infections may become carriers and may require treatment (see "Salmonellosis").

DISPOSITION

- Most infections are self-limited and do not require therapy.
- In immunocompromised host or patient with underlying disease, serious complications are possible.
- Postinfectious syndromes are important with some infections:
  1. Reiter's syndrome: *Salmonella, Shigella, Campylobacter, Yersinia* spp.; more common in genetically susceptible host (HLA-B27+).
  2. Guillain-Barré syndrome: *Campylobacter* spp.

REFERRAL

If more than a mild illness.

 **PEARLS & CONSIDERATIONS**

COMMENTS

- Grossly underreported and undiagnosed.
- All cases to be reported to the local health department.
- Table E1F-12 summarizes control and prevention measures of foodborne diseases.

SUGGESTED READINGS

Available at www.expertconsult.com

RELATED CONTENT

Bacterial Food Poisoning (Patient Information)
Salmonellosis (Related Key Topic)

AUTHOR: **GLENN G. FORT, M.D., M.P.H.**

Diseases and Disorders

 BASIC INFORMATION

DEFINITION
Friedreich's ataxia is the most common hereditary neurodegenerative ataxic disorder, caused by degeneration of dorsal root ganglions, posterior columns, spinocerebellar and corticospinal tracts, and large sensory peripheral neurons.

ICD-10CM CODES
G11.1 Early-onset cerebellar ataxia

EPIDEMIOLOGY & DEMOGRAPHICS
INCIDENCE (IN U.S.): Estimated at one in 30,000 whites
PEAK INCIDENCE: 8 to 15 yr
PREVALENCE (IN U.S.): Two to four per 100,000. Carrier rate 1:120 to 1:160; lower prevalence in Asians and people of African descent.
PREDOMINANT SEX: Males and females affected equally
GENETICS: Autosomal recessive; 96% of affected patients are homozygous and 4% are compound heterozygous (two different mutations). Trinucleotide repeat expansion accounts for 94% to 98% of cases, whereas point mutations account for 2% to 6% of cases.

PHYSICAL FINDINGS & CLINICAL PRESENTATION
- Onset of progressive appendicular and gait ataxia, with absent muscle stretch reflexes in the lower extremities.
- With disease progression (within 5 yr): dysarthria, distal loss of position and vibration sense, pyramidal leg weakness, areflexia in all four limbs, and extensor plantar responses.
- Common findings: progressive scoliosis, distal atrophy, pes cavus, and cardiomyopathy (symmetric concentric hypertrophic form in most cases).
- Insulin-requiring diabetes mellitus may occur in 10% of patients, with glucose intolerance occurring in an additional 10% to 20%.

ETIOLOGY
- Genetic: frataxin gene is localized to the centromeric region of chromosome 9q13.
- Normal sequence has six to 27 repeats; abnormal sequence has 120 to 1700 GAA repeats.
- Frataxin deficiency leads to impaired mitochondrial iron homeostasis.

DIAGNOSIS

DIFFERENTIAL DIAGNOSIS
- Charcot-Marie-Tooth disease type 2
- Abetalipoproteinemia
- Severe vitamin E deficiency with malabsorption
- Early-onset cerebellar ataxia with retained reflexes
- Autosomal-dominant cerebellar ataxia (spinocerebellar ataxia)

WORKUP
- Diagnostic criteria include electrophysiologic evidence for a generalized axonal sensory or sensorimotor neuropathy.
- ECG may show widespread T-wave inversion and evidence of left ventricular hypertrophy. ECG abnormalities are present in 65% of patients.
- Sural nerve biopsy shows loss of large myelinated fibers.
- Specific gene testing for the expanded GAA trinucleotide repeat.

LABORATORY TESTS
- Electromyography or nerve conduction study
- ECG and echocardiogram
- Peripheral blood smear for acanthocytes
- Lipid profile
- Two-hour glucose tolerance test
- Vitamin E levels (if necessary)

IMAGING STUDIES
MRI of the spinal cord may demonstrate spinal cord atrophy with essentially normal cerebrum, brainstem, and cerebellum (Fig. 1F-14).

TREATMENT

NONPHARMACOLOGIC THERAPY
- Surgical correction of scoliosis and foot deformities in selected patients

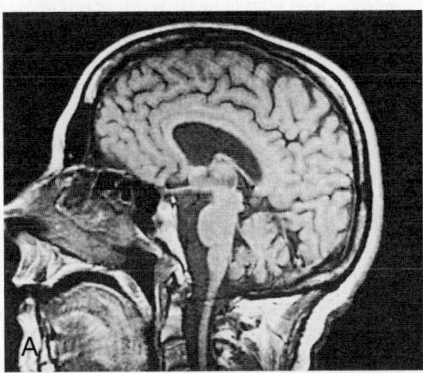
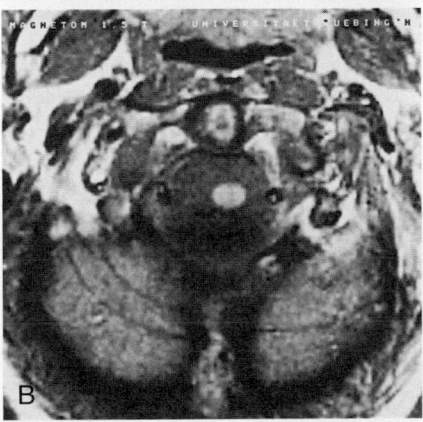

FIGURE 1F-14 T1 MRI of the brain (midsagittal section) and spinal cord (axial slice at level of the dens) showing severe shrinkage of the cervical cord, but the cerebellum and brainstem are of normal size. (From Goetz CG: *Textbook of clinical neurology*, Philadelphia, 1999, Saunders.)

- Prosthetic devices as required (e.g., ankle-foot orthosis for footdrop)
- Physical therapy
- Communication devices for patients with severe dysarthria

ACUTE GENERAL Rx
None established.
- An antioxidant, idebenone (short-chain analogue of coenzyme Q10), administered orally at 5 to 20 mg/kg/day with or without vitamin E has demonstrated inconsistent effects on neurologic, cardiac, and psychosocial outcome measures in clinical trials.
- Further research with various antioxidants and iron chelators is ongoing. An open-label pilot study of antioxidants (coenzyme Q10, 400 mg/day, and vitamin E, 2100 U/day) in a small cohort demonstrated slowing in progression of generalized ataxia and kinetic dysfunction and significant improvement in cardiac function with unaltered deterioration in posture, gait, and hand dexterity.

CHRONIC Rx
Chronic management of congestive heart failure is required. Cardiac arrhythmias will warrant pacemaker implantation.

DISPOSITION
- Loss of ambulation typically occurs within 15 yr of symptom onset, and 95% are wheelchair bound by age 45 yr.
- Life expectancy is reduced, particularly if heart disease with or without diabetes mellitus is present.
REFERRAL:
- If uncertain about diagnosis
- For genetic counseling (recommended if available)

 PEARLS & CONSIDERATIONS

Friedreich's ataxia should be considered in all preadolescent and adolescent children presenting with progressive ataxia. Early recognition of cardiac failure and arrhythmias and institution of appropriate therapy helps prolong survival.

SUGGESTED READINGS
Available at www.expertconsult.com

RELATED CONTENT
Friedreich's Ataxia (Patient Information)

AUTHOR: **FARIHA ZAHEER, M.D.**

BASIC INFORMATION

DEFINITION
Frostbite represents tissue injury (or death) from freezing and vasoconstriction induced by severe environmental cold exposure.

SYNONYMS
Cold-induced tissue injury.

ICD-10CM CODES
T35.0 Superficial frostbite involving multiple body regions
T34 Frostbite with tissue necrosis
T345 Frostbite with tissue necrosis of wrist and hand
T34.8 Frostbite with tissue necrosis of ankle and foot
T34.9 Frostbite with tissue necrosis of other and unspecified sites
T35.4 Superficial frostbite involving multiple body regions
T33.9 Superficial frostbite of unspecified sites, initial encounter

EPIDEMIOLOGY & DEMOGRAPHICS
- Environmental factors include windchill factor, temperature, duration of exposure, altitude, and degree of wetness. Hands and feet account for 90% of injuries; nose, cheeks, ears, and male genitalia are also more susceptible.
- Host factors include psychiatric illness, neuroleptic and sedative drugs (especially alcohol), immobility, previous frostbite, malnutrition, tobacco use, peripheral neuropathy, peripheral vascular disease, diabetes, exhaustion, and constricting clothing and footwear.
  Patients at the extremes of age are at greatest risk, but frostbite is more common in adults ages 30 to 49 yr, and African Americans may be more susceptible than whites.

PHYSICAL FINDINGS & CLINICAL PRESENTATION
- Frostbite may be classified into four degrees of injury severity or, more practically, into *superficial* (corresponding to first and second degree) and *deep* (corresponding to third and fourth degree) groups. In both cases, the degree of frostbite can only be accurately determined after rewarming as initially most frostbite injuries appear similar.
- *Superficial* frostbite involves the skin and subcutaneous tissue. The frozen part is waxy, white (or mottled), and firm but soft and resilient below the surface when gently depressed. After rewarming, there is an initial hyperemia that may be followed by swelling and formation of superficial blisters with clear or milky fluid within 6 to 24 hr (Fig. 1F-15). There is no ultimate tissue loss.
- *Deep* frostbite extends into the dermis and may involve muscles, nerves, tendons, or bones. The skin may be hard or wooden, without tissue resilience. Nonblanching cyanosis, hemorrhagic blisters, tissue necrosis (Fig. 1F-16), and gangrene may develop. Affected tissue has

a poor prognosis and debridement or amputation is generally required.
- Patients initially feel numbness, prickling, and itching. More severe injury can produce paresthesias and stiffness, with burning or throbbing pain upon thawing.

PATHOPHYSIOLOGY
Two phases of tissue injury:
1. During cold exposure when cellular damage is caused by the formation of extracellular ice crystals, which cause osmotic shifts, cellular dehydration, cell membrane lysis, and cell death.
2. During thawing in which damaged endothelial cells release a cascade of inflammatory mediators (e.g., prostaglandin F, thromboxane A2, bradykinins, histamine) that contribute to reperfusion injury and thrombus formation and ultimately lead to destruction of the microcirculation and cell death.

DIAGNOSIS

DIFFERENTIAL DIAGNOSIS
- Frostnip: a superficial nonfreezing cold injury associated with intense vasoconstriction and characterized by frost forming on the surface of the skin. Transient numbness, tingling, and pallor resolve quickly with warming
- Pernio (chilblains): self-limited, cold-induced vasculitis associated with purple plaques or nodules, often affecting dorsum of hands and feet; seen with prolonged cold exposure to above-freezing temperatures
- Cold immersion (trench foot): caused by ischemic injury resulting from sustained, severe vasoconstriction in appendages exposed to wet cold at temperatures above freezing

WORKUP
- Laboratory workup is not indicated unless the patient has systemic hypothermia.
- Early presentation (<24 hr from thawing): If there is deep frostbite with potential significant morbidity, angiography should be done emergently in anticipation of potential thrombolysis treatment.
- Late presentation (>24 hr from thawing): Noninvasive imaging with MRA or triple-phase bone scan (with technetium) can be

used to predict the likely levels of tissue viability for amputation.

TREATMENT (3 PHASES)

1. FIELD MANAGEMENT
- Prioritize treatment of hypothermia (core body temperature <35° C) with systemic and adjunctive rewarming measures if available (e.g., warmed, humidified oxygen, heated IV saline [45° C], and warming blankets) before thawing frostbitten extremities.
  - Shelter patient out of wind and give warm fluids.
- Remove constricting or wet clothing and jewelry from affected digits.
  - Place cold extremity in a companion's axilla or groin for 10 minutes, then replace dry gloves/boots.
- Insulate, splint, and elevate affected areas if practical to do so.
  - Never rub or massage the affected area. Avoid dry heat (e.g., fires and heaters).
- Avoid thawing if there is any risk of refreezing and if possible avoid ambulation on thawed lower extremities (unless only distal toes affected).
- Administer pain medication and topical aloe if available.
- Box 1F-1 describes the Alaska State Guidelines for prehospital treatment of frostbite.

2. REWARMING
- Rapid rewarming (with warm water) is the key objective with better outcomes than slow rewarming (e.g., moving to a warmer location).
- Rapid rewarming is achieved by immersing the affected area in circulating warm water bath with or without a mild antibacterial agent (e.g., chlorhexidine or povidone-iodine) maintained at 37° to 39° C for at least 15 to 30 min up to 1 hour, until all tissues are thoroughly rewarmed and pliable with a red-purple color. Active motion during rewarming is advisable; massage is not.
- Analgesics recommended during rewarming (ibuprofen and possibly narcotics).

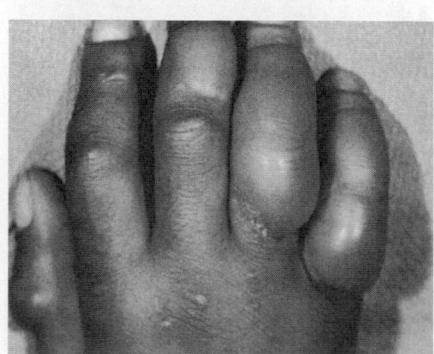

FIGURE 1F-15 Large, clear frostbite blisters on the right hand. (From Rosen P [ed]: *Emergency medicine*, ed 4, St Louis, 1998, Mosby.)

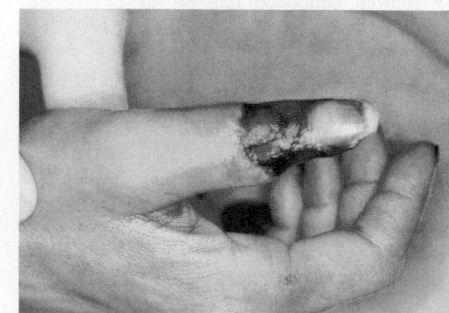

FIGURE 1F-16 Third- and fourth-degree frostbite with tissue death. Note demarcation beyond the interphalangeal joint. (From Cameron, JL, Cameron AM: *Current surgical therapy*, ed 10, Philadelphia, 2011, Saunders.)

BOX 1F-1   Alaska State Guidelines for Prehospital Treatment of Frostbite

First Responder/Emergency Medical Technician—I, II, III/Paramedic/Small Bush Clinic
Evaluation and Treatment

A   Anticipate, assess, and treat the patient for hypothermia, if present.
B   Assess the frostbitten area carefully because the loss of sensation may cause the patient to be unaware of soft tissue injuries in that area.
C   Obtain a complete set of vital signs and the patient's temperature.
D   Remove jewelry and clothing, if present, from the affected area.
E   Obtain a patient history, including the date of the patient's last tetanus immunization.
F   If there is frostbite distal to a fracture, attempt to align the limb unless there is resistance. Splint the fracture in a manner that does not compromise distal circulation.
G   Determine whether rewarming the frostbitten tissue can be accomplished in a medical facility. If it can, transport the patient while protecting the tissue from further injury from cold or impacts.
H   If the decision is made to rewarm frostbitten tissue in the field, you should prepare a warm water bath in a container large enough to accommodate the frostbitten tissues without them touching the sides or bottom of the container. The temperature of the water bath should be 99° to 102° F (37° to 39° C).
 ○ Generally, patients with frostbite do not require opiates for pain relief; they occasionally need non-opiate pain medication or anxiolytics. If possible, consult a physician regarding the administration of oral analgesics, such as acetaminophen, ibuprofen or aspirin. Aspirin or ibuprofen may help improve outcomes by blocking the arachidonic acid pathway.
 ○ Immersion injury or frostbite with other associated injuries may produce significant edema and high pain levels. These patients may need opiate pain medications for initial treatment. In this case, advanced life support personnel should administer morphine or other analgesics in accordance with physician-signed standing orders or online medical control.
I   A source of additional warm water must be available.
J   Water should be maintained at approximately at 99° to 102° F (37° to 39° C) and gently circulated around the frostbitten tissue until the distal tip of the frostbitten part becomes flushed.
K   Pain after rewarming usually indicates that viable tissue has been successfully rewarmed.
L   After rewarming, let the frostbitten tissues dry in the warm air. Do **not** towel dry.
M   After thawing, tissues that were deeply frostbitten may develop blisters or appear cyanotic. Blisters should not be broken and must be protected from injury.
N   Pad between affected digits and bandage affected tissues loosely with a soft, sterile dressing. Avoid putting undue pressure on the affected parts.
O   Rewarmed extremities should be kept at a level above the heart, if possible.
P   Protect the rewarmed area from refreezing and other trauma during transport. A frame around the frostbitten area should be constructed to prevent blankets from pressing directly on the injured area.
Q   Do not allow an individual who has frostbitten feet to walk except when the life of the patient or rescuer is in danger. Once frostbitten feet are rewarmed, the patient becomes nonambulatory.

3.   POST-THAW Rx

- Tetanus prophylaxis and topical antibiotics if potentially contaminated skin wound.
- Consider systemic antibiotics for patients with significant trauma or signs of infection.
- Debride broken clear vesicles and avoid disrupting intact blisters (especially hemorrhagic ones) unless they interfere with mobility.
- Topical aloe vera (a potent anti-prostaglandin agent) q6h and ibuprofen (a thromboxane inhibitor) 400 to 600 mg bid to tid (or daily aspirin) can be given until wounds are healed or surgery occurs.

- Thrombolytic therapy: If <24 hr from thawing in a patient with severe frostbite involving an extremity (e.g., extending proximally to PIP joints), imaging with angiography (or possibly MRA) to assess for arterial compromise followed by intraarterial or intravenous tPA if perfusion defects are demonstrated and there is no contraindication to thrombolysis. This use of early thrombolytic therapy appears to improve reperfusion considerably and reduce subsequent digit amputation significantly.
- Heparin is recommended in addition to tPA to prevent recurrent local thrombosis.

- Vasodilator therapy: Various vasodilators (prostacyclin or analog iloprost), NTG, pentoxifylline, phenoxybenzamine, nifedipine, reserpine, and buflomedil) have been tried, with the best evidence favoring prostacyclin (or ilprost, which is available in Europe) If iloprost is available, at least one study shows superior efficacy to tPA, and it is easier to administer, has a better safety profile, has fewer contraindications, and can be managed on a general ward.
- Daily dressing changes with dry, sterile, noncompressive, and nonadherent dressings. Splint and elevate hands and feet to reduce edema and separate digits with cotton gauze. Avoid any abrasion to limit risk of infection.
- Whirlpool hydrotherapy: 1 to 2 times per day for 30 minutes with warm water (37°-39° C), +/- an antiseptic solution if severe edema is present, until there is a clear demarcation of necrotic tissues or evidence of tissue healing.
- Gentle, progressive physical therapy after edema resolves.
- Keep site warm, and avoid all vasoconstrictors, including nicotine.
- Dextran, warfarin, sympathectomy, and hyperbaric oxygen are of potential but unproven benefit.

DISPOSITION

A majority of patients have long-term residual symptoms, including cold hypersensitivity, neuropathic pain, sensory deficits, hyperhidrosis, secondary Raynaud's disease, localized osteoporosis, edema, hair or nail deformities, and (rarely) arthritis. Treatment with tricyclics, gabapentin, calcium channel blockers, and careful protection from further cold exposure may be helpful.

REFERRAL

- Hospitalize for hypothermia or deep frostbite; a burn unit is best.
- Surgical decisions regarding amputation should be deferred until demarcation of viable tissue is clear (6 to 12 weeks), unless refractory pain, sepsis, or gangrene occurs.

SUGGESTED READINGS
Available at www.expertconsult.com

RELATED CONTENT
Frostbite (Patient Information)

AUTHOR: **MICHAEL P. JOHNSON, M.D.**

BASIC INFORMATION

DEFINITION

Gastric cancer is an adenocarcinoma arising from the stomach. It is subdivided into intestinal and diffuse histology. The diffuse form of gastric cancer is more common in women and young patients, whereas the intestinal type is predominantly related to environmental factors.

SYNONYMS

Gastric adenocarcinoma
Stomach cancer
Linitis plastica

ICD-10CM CODES

C16   Malignant neoplasm of stomach
C16.0 Malignant neoplasm of cardia of
       stomach
C16.1 Malignant neoplasm of stomach
C16.2 Malignant neoplasm of body of stomach
C16.3 Malignant neoplasm of pyloric antrum
C16.5 Malignant neoplasm of lesser
       curvature of stomach, unspecified
C16.6 Malignant neoplasm of greater
       curvature of stomach, unspecified
C16.8 Malignant neoplasm of overlapping
       sites of stomach

EPIDEMIOLOGY & DEMOGRAPHICS

- Gastric cancer is the fourth commonest cancer in the world, with an annual incidence of approximately 950,000 cases annually; of these, 70% occur in developing countries. The highest incidence is in Asia (80 cases per 100,000 persons in Japan) and the lowest in North America.

- Annual estimated deaths due to gastric cancer are 723,000 worldwide.
- The incidence of distal stomach tumors has greatly declined, whereas that of proximal tumors of the cardia and fundus is on the rise.
- Gastric cancer occurs most commonly in male patients >65 yr (70% of patients are >50 yr).
- Incidence of gastric cancer has been declining over the past 30 yr.
- Male/female ratio is 3:2.
- Familial diffuse gastric cancer is a disease with autosomal-dominant inheritance in which gastric cancer develops at a young age. Germ-line truncating mutations in the E-cadherin gene *(CDH1)* are found in these families. It is associated with an 80% lifetime risk of gastric cancer. Increased risk of gastric cancer is also seen with Lynch syndrome, FAP, Peutz-Jeghers, juvenile polyposis syndrome, and hyperplastic gastric polyps.

PHYSICAL FINDINGS & CLINICAL PRESENTATION

- Medical history may reveal complaints of postprandial fullness with significant weight loss (70% to 80%), nausea/emesis (20% to 40%), dysphagia (20%), and dyspepsia, usually unrelieved by antacids; epigastric discomfort, usually lessened by fasting and exacerbated by food intake, is also common.
- Epigastric or abdominal mass (30% to 50%), epigastric pain.
- Anemia from tumor bleeding and hemoccult-positive stools.
- Hard, nodular liver: generally indicates metastatic disease to the liver.
- Ascites, lymphadenopathy, or pleural effusions: may indicate metastasis.

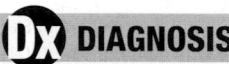

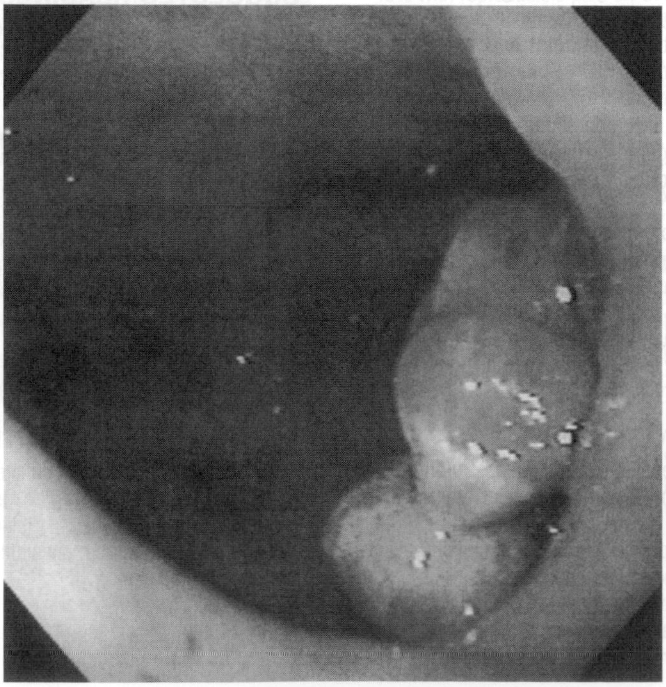

ETIOLOGY

Risk factors:
- Chronic *Helicobacter pylori* gastritis. Gastric cancer develops in persons infected with *H. pylori* but not in uninfected persons. Those with histologic findings of severe gastric atrophy, corpus-predominant gastritis, or intestinal metaplasia are at increased risk. Persons with *H. pylori* infection and duodenal ulcer are not at risk, whereas those with gastric ulcers, nonulcer dyspepsia, and gastric hyperplastic polyps are. Eradication of *H. pylori* reduces gastric cancer risk.
- Tobacco abuse, alcohol consumption.
- Food additives (nitrosamines), smoked foods, occupational exposure to heavy metals, rubber, asbestos.
- Chronic atrophic gastritis with intestinal metaplasia, hypertrophic gastritis, and pernicious anemia.

DIAGNOSIS

DIFFERENTIAL DIAGNOSIS

- Gastric lymphoma (5% of gastric malignancies).
- Hypertrophic gastritis.
- Peptic ulcer.
- Reflux esophagitis.

WORKUP

Upper endoscopy (Fig. 1G-3) with biopsy will confirm diagnosis. Endoscopic ultrasonography in combination with CT scanning and operative lymph node dissection can be used in staging of the tumor. Table 1G-1 describes staging systems for gastric carcinoma.

LABORATORY TESTS

- Microcytic anemia.
- Hemoccult-positive stools.
- Hypoalbuminemia.
- Abnormal liver enzymes in patients with metastasis to the liver.
- Up to 20% of gastric cancers overexpress the HER2 growth factor receptor.
- Mutation-specific predictive genetic testing by polymerase chain reaction amplification followed by restriction: enzyme digestion and DNA sequencing for truncating mutations in *CDH1* is recommended in families of patients with familial diffuse cancer because gastric cancer develops in three of every four carriers of a mutant *CDH1* gene.

IMAGING STUDIES

Chest and abdomen CT scan (Fig. 1G-4) to evaluate for metastases .

TREATMENT

ACUTE GENERAL Rx

- Gastrectomy with regional lymphadenectomy is performed in patients who have early cancers with curative potential (<30% of patients at time of diagnosis).

FIGURE 1G-3 Polypoid gastric cancer. A trilobed polyp is apparent at the angularis. (From Feldman M, Friedman LS, Brandt LJ [eds]: *Sleisenger & Fordtran's gastrointestinal and liver disease: pathophysiology/diagnosis/management,* ed 8, Philadelphia, 2006, Saunders.)

TABLE 1G-1 Staging Systems for Gastric Carcinoma*

Modified Astler-Coller	TNM	Characteristics
A	TisN0	Nodes negative; lesion limited to mucosa
B1	T1–2N0	Nodes negative; extension of lesion beyond mucosa but still within gastric wall
B2	T3N0	Nodes negative; extension beyond the entire wall (including serosa if present) without adherence to or invasion of surrounding organs or structures
B3	T4N0	Nodes negative; beyond wall with adherence to or invasion of surrounding organs or structures
C1	Tis–2N1–3	Nodes positive; lesion limited to wall
C2	T3N1–3	Nodes positive; extension of lesion through the entire wall (including serosa)
C3	T4N1–3	Nodes positive; beyond wall with adherence to or invasion of surrounding organs or structures

*Comparison of TNM system with a modification of the Astler-Coller rectal system by Gunderson and Sosin.
From Abeloff MD: *Clinical oncology,* ed 3, Philadelphia, 2004, Elsevier.

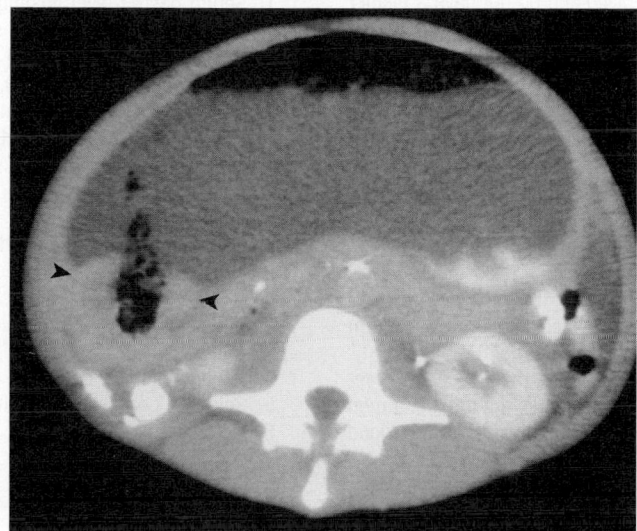

FIGURE 1G-4 Gastric outlet obstruction—cancer of the antrum. A markedly distended stomach with an air-fluid level is seen on computed tomography. In this case a mass in the distal end of the antrum is apparent *(arrowheads)*. (From Grainger RG, Allison DJ, Dixon AK [eds]. *Grainger & Allison's diagnostic radiology: a textbook of medical imaging,* ed 4, St. Louis, 2001, Churchill Livingstone.)

- In patients with operable gastric cancer, a perioperative regimen of epirubicin, cisplatin, and infused fluorouracil decreases tumor size and stage and significantly improves progression-free and overall survival.

- Postoperative adjuvant chemoradiation therapy using 5-fluorouracil (5-FU) and leucovorin is now the standard of care for resected patients able to tolerate such treatment. Postoperative chemotherapy and radiotherapy, compared with surgical resection alone, can extend the survival rate of patients with gastric cancer in those who are able to complete adjuvant therapy.
- When surgical cure is not possible, palliative resection may prolong duration and quality of life.
- Chemotherapy (5-FU, Adriamycin, and mitomycin C) may provide some palliation; however, it generally does not prolong survival. Chemotherapy with docetaxel, cisplatin, and 5-FU can be used for chemotherapy-naive patients with metastatic or locally recurrent gastric cancer.
- The addition of trastuzumab to cisplatin plus 5-FU or capecitabine may prolong survival in gastric cancer patients expressing HER2.

DISPOSITION
- 5-yr survival rate of gastric carcinoma is 28% overall.
- 5-yr survival for early gastric cancers (usually detected incidentally with endoscopy in populations where screening is recommended) is >35%.

ⓘ PEARLS & CONSIDERATIONS

COMMENTS
- Gastrectomy patients will need vitamin B$_{12}$ replacement. They are also at risk for dumping syndrome and should be advised to ingest frequent, small meals.
- Prophylactic gastrectomy should be considered in young, asymptomatic carriers of germ-line truncating *CDH1* mutations who belong to families with highly penetrant heredity diffuse gastric cancer.
- Gastric cancer screening for average-risk patients is not recommended in the United States.

SUGGESTED READINGS
Available at www.expertconsult.com

RELATED CONTENT
Stomach Cancer (Patient Information)

AUTHOR: **FRED F. FERRI, M.D.**

Gastrinoma

 BASIC INFORMATION

DEFINITION

Gastrinoma is a pancreatic or extrapancreatic non-beta islet cell tumor that secretes gastrin. The hypergastrinemic state caused by a gastrinoma results in peptic ulcer disease and is known as Zollinger-Ellison (ZE) syndrome

SYNONYMS

Zollinger-Ellison (ZE) syndrome

ICD-10CM CODES
C25.4 Malignant neoplasm of endocrine pancreas
E16.4 Abnormal secretion of gastrin

EPIDEMIOLOGY & DEMOGRAPHICS

- Incidence is unknown, but 0.1% of all duodenal ulcers are believed to be caused by ZE.
- Occurs in both genders and at any age (most common in ages 30 to 50 yr).
- Two thirds of gastrinomas are sporadic, and one third are associated with multiple endocrine neoplasia type 1 (MEN-1), an autosomal-dominant genetic disorder that also includes hyperparathyroidism and pituitary tumors.
- Approximately 60% of gastrinomas are malignant.
- The incidence and prevalence of pancreatic neuroendocrine tumors are increasing. They represent 1.3% of all cases of pancreatic cancer.

PHYSICAL FINDINGS & CLINICAL PRESENTATION

- The majority of patients (95%) present with symptoms of peptic ulcer (see Section I, "Peptic Ulcer Disease").

- 60% of patients have symptoms related to gastroesophageal reflux disease (see Section I, "Gastroesophageal Reflux Disease").
- One third of patients with ZE have diarrhea and, less commonly, steatorrhea.

The following circumstances warrant suspicion of ZE syndrome:
- Ulcers distal to the first portion of the duodenum.
- Multiple peptic ulcers.
- Ineffective treatment for peptic ulcer disease with the usual drug doses and schedules.
- Peptic ulcer and diarrhea.
- Familial history of peptic ulcer.
- Patients with a personal or family history suggesting parathyroid or pituitary tumors or dysfunction.
- Peptic ulcer and urinary tract calculi.
- Patients with peptic ulcer who are negative for *Helicobacter pylori* and do not have a history of nonsteroidal anti-inflammatory drug use.

ETIOLOGY

- The pathophysiologic manifestations of ZE syndrome are related to the effects of hypergastrinemia. Gastrin stimulates gastric acid secretion, which in turn is responsible for the development of duodenal ulcers and diarrhea. Gastrin also promotes gastric mucosal epithelial cell growth and resulting parietal cell hyperplasia.
- Gastrinomas are usually small (0.1 to 2 cm) but sometimes large (>20 cm) tumors.
- 60% of gastrinomas are malignant, with liver and regional lymph nodes the most common site of metastases. Histology is not a good predictor of the biology of gastrinomas.
- 60% of patients with MEN-1 have gastrinomas.
- 10% of patients with ZE syndrome have islet cell hyperplasia rather than gastrinomas; in 10% to 20% of patients with gastrinoma the tumors cannot be located because of small size.

 DIAGNOSIS

DIFFERENTIAL DIAGNOSIS

- Peptic ulcer disease (see Section I, "Peptic Ulcer Disease").
- Gastroesophageal reflux disease (see Section I, "Gastroesophageal Reflux Disease").
- Diarrhea (see Section III, "Diarrhea, Acute" and "Diarrhea, Chronic").
- Other endocrine tumors of the pancreas (see Table 1G-2).

WORKUP

- Diagnosis of peptic ulcer:
  1. Upper gastrointestinal series (may also show prominent gastric rugal folds).
  2. Endoscopy
- Gastric acid secretion:
  1. Serum gastrin level (fasting) >150 pg/ml (criterion for diagnosis is serum gastrin >1000 pg/ml) (causes of false-positive results: pernicious anemia, renal failure, retained gastric antrum syndrome, diabetes mellitus, rheumatoid arthritis).
- Provocative gastrin level tests:
  1. Secretin stimulation.
  2. Calcium stimulation.
  3. Standard test meal stimulation.
- Gastrinoma localization:
  1. Arteriography.
  2. Abdominal sonography.
  3. Abdominal CT scan.
  4. Abdominal MRI/PET scan.
  5. Selective portal vein branch gastrin level.
  6. Octreotide scan.

RX TREATMENT

- Surgical resection of the gastrinoma (NOTE: 90% of gastrinomas can be located, resulting in a 40% overall cure rate).
- Total gastrectomy or vagotomy (palliative in some patients).

TABLE 1G-2 Characteristics of Endocrine Tumors of the Pancreas

Tumor Type	Major Clinical Symptoms	Predominant Hormone	Islet cell Type	Malignant (%)	Localization	Other Clinical Features
Insulinoma	Hypoglycemia (fasting or nocturnal)	Insulin	β	10	Usually pancreatic; rarely extrapancreatic	Catecholamine excess
Glucagonoma	1. Diabetes mellitus 2. Migratory necrolytic erythema	Glucagon	α	90	Usually pancreatic; rarely extrapancreatic	Panhypoaminoaciduria Thromboembolism Weight loss
Gastrinoma	Recurrent peptic ulcer disease	Gastrin	γ	90	Usually pancreatic but frequently extrapancreatic	Diarrhea/steatorrhea
Somatostatinoma	1. Diabetes mellitus 2. Diarrhea, steatorrhea	Somatostatin	δ	80	Pancreatic and duodenal	Hypochlorhydria Weight loss Gallbladder disease
VIPoma	Watery diarrhea, hypokalemia, achlorhydria (WDHA syndrome)	Vasoactive intestinal polypeptide (VIP)	δ	50	Usually pancreatic but frequently extrapancreatic	Metabolic acidosis Hyperglycemia Hypercalcemia Flushing
PPoma	1. Hepatomegaly 2. Abdominal pain	Pancreatic polypeptide (PP)	PP cells	80	Usually pancreatic; rarely extrapancreatic	Occasional watery diarrhea

From Besser GM, Cudworth AG: *Clinical endocrinology,* Philadelphia/London, 1987, Lippincott/Gower Medical Publishing, p. 20.

- Medical treatment.
  1. Proton pump inhibitors (e.g., omeprazole, lansoprazole).
  2. Somatostatin or octreotide.
  3. Chemotherapy for metastatic gastrinoma with streptozotocin, 5-fluorouracil, and doxorubicin.
  4. Early trials with everolimus, an oral inhibitor of mammalian target of rapamycin (mTOR) have shown antitumor activity in patients with advanced pancreatic neuroendocrine tumors with significant prolongation of progression-free survival and low rates of severe adverse events.

5. Preliminary trials with the tyrosine kinase inhibitor sunitinib have shown encouraging results on prolongation of survival.
- Fig. 1G-5 describes a treatment algorithm for gastrinoma.

PROGNOSIS

Five-year survival:
- Two thirds of all patients.
- 20% with liver metastases.
- 90% without liver metastases.

REFERRAL

To gastroenterologist and surgeon.

EBM **EVIDENCE**

Available at www.expertconsult.com

SUGGESTED READINGS

Available at www.expertconsult.com

RELATED CONTENT

Gastrinoma (Zollinger-Ellison Syndrome) (Patient Information)

AUTHOR: **FRED F. FERRI, M.D.**

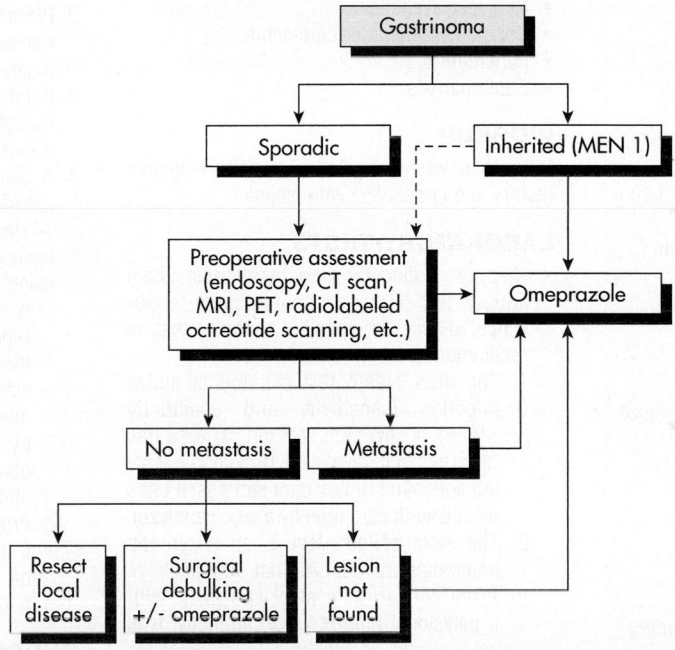

FIGURE 1G-5 Treatment algorithm for the management of a patient with gastrinoma. In some circumstances, patients with familial gastrinoma may also be candidates for surgical resection if disease is highly limited *(dotted line)*. *CT,* computed tomography; *MEN 1,* multiple endocrine neoplasia type 1; *MRI,* magnetic resonance imaging; *PET,* positron emission tomography. (From Melmed S et al: *Williams textbook of endocrinology,* ed 12, Philadelphia, 2011, Saunders.)

Diseases and Disorders

G

Gastritis

 BASIC INFORMATION

DEFINITION

Histologically, *gastritis* refers to inflammation in the stomach. Endoscopically, gastritis refers to a number of abnormal features such as erythema, erosions, and subepithelial hemorrhages. Gastritis can also be subdivided into erosive, nonerosive, and specific types of gastritis with distinctive features both endoscopically and histologically.

SYNONYMS

Erosive gastritis
Hemorrhagic gastritis
Helicobacter pylori gastritis

ICD-10CM CODES

K29.00 Acute gastritis without bleeding
K29.01 Acute gastritis with bleeding
K29.20 Alcoholic gastritis without bleeding
K29.21 Alcoholic gastritis with bleeding
K29.30 Chronic superficial gastritis without bleeding
K29.31 Chronic superficial gastritis with bleeding
K29.40 Chronic atrophic gastritis without bleeding
K29.41 Chronic atrophic gastritis with bleeding
K29.50 Unspecified chronic gastritis without bleeding
K29.51 Unspecified chronic gastritis with bleeding
K29.60 Other gastritis without bleeding
K29.61 Other gastritis with bleeding
K29.70 Gastritis, unspecified, without bleeding
K29.71 Gastritis, unspecified, with bleeding
K52.81 Eosinophilic gastritis or gastroenteritis

EPIDEMIOLOGY & DEMOGRAPHICS

- Erosive and hemorrhagic gastritis is most commonly seen in patients taking nonsteroidal anti-inflammatory drugs (NSAIDs), alcoholics, and critically ill patients (usually on ventilator support).
- *H. pylori* infection with gastritis is believed to be present in 30% to 50% of the population; however, the majority are asymptomatic.
- The prevalence of *H. pylori* infection increases with age from <10% in whites <40 yr to >50% in patients >50 yr.

PHYSICAL FINDINGS & CLINICAL PRESENTATION

- Patients with gastritis generally present with nonspecific clinical signs and symptoms (e.g., epigastric pain, abdominal tenderness, bloating, anorexia, nausea [with or without vomiting]). Symptoms may be aggravated by eating.
- Epigastric tenderness in acute alcoholic gastritis (may be absent in chronic gastritis).
- Foul-smelling breath.
- Hematemesis ("coffee grounds" emesis).

ETIOLOGY

- Alcohol, NSAIDs, stress (critically ill patients usually on mechanical respiration), hepatic or renal failure, multiorgan failure.
- Infection (bacterial, viral).
- Bile reflux, pancreatic enzyme reflux.
- Gastric mucosal atrophy, portal hypertension gastropathy.
- Irradiation.

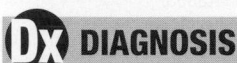 DIAGNOSIS

DIFFERENTIAL DIAGNOSIS

- Peptic ulcer disease.
- Gastroesophageal reflux disease.
- Nonulcer dyspepsia.
- Gastric lymphoma or carcinoma.
- Pancreatitis.
- Gastroparesis.

WORKUP

Diagnostic workup includes a comprehensive history and endoscopy with biopsy.

LABORATORY TESTS

- *H. pylori* testing by urea breath test, stool antigen test (*H. pylori* stool antigen), endoscopic biopsy, or specific antibody test is recommended.
  1. The urea breath test documents active infection (sensitivity and specificity >90%). A new card test for ^{14}C urea has recently been developed, providing a testing option in primary care settings. It uses a flat breath card read by a small analyzer.
  2. The stool antigen test is an enzymatic immunoassay (ELISA) that identifies *H. pylori* antigen in a stool specimen with a polyclonal anti–*H. pylori* antibody. It is as accurate as the urea breath test for diagnosis of active infection and follow-up evaluation of patients treated for *H. pylori*. A negative result on the stool antigen test 8 wk after completion of therapy identifies patients in whom eradication of *H. pylori* was unsuccessful.
  3. Histologic evaluation of endoscopic biopsy samples is considered by many the gold standard for accurate diagnosis of *H. pylori* infection. However, detection of *H. pylori* depends on the site and number of biopsy samples, the method of staining, and experience of the pathologist.
  4. Serologic testing for antibodies to *H. pylori* is easy and inexpensive; however, the presence of antibodies demonstrates previous but not necessarily current infection. Antibodies to *H. pylori* can remain elevated for months to years after infection has cleared; therefore antibody levels must be interpreted in light of patient's symptoms and other test results (e.g., peptic ulcer disease [PUD] seen on upper gastrointestinal series).
- Vitamin B_{12} level in patients with atrophic gastritis.
- Hematocrit (low if significant bleeding has occurred).

 TREATMENT

NONPHARMACOLOGIC THERAPY

- Avoidance of mucosal irritants such as alcohol and NSAIDs
- Lifestyle modifications with avoidance of tobacco and foods that trigger symptoms

ACUTE GENERAL Rx

Eradication of *H. pylori*, when present, can be accomplished with various regimens:
1. Proton pump inhibitor (PPI) (omeprazole 20 mg, lansoprazole 30 mg, pantoprazole 40 mg, rabeprazole 20 mg) bid *plus* amoxicillin 1000 mg bid *plus* metronidazole 500 mg for 10 to 14 days.
2. PPI bid *plus* clarithromycin 500 mg bid *and* metronidazole 500 mg bid for 10 to 14 days. This regimen is useful in those with penicillin allergy.
3. Ranitidine 150 mg bid plus bismuth subsalicylate 525 mg qid plus metronidazole 250 mg qid plus doxycycline 100 mg bid.
4. A combination of levofloxacin 250 mg bid, amoxicillin 1000 mg bid, and a PPI bid for 10 to 14 days can be used as salvage therapy after unsuccessful attempts to eradicate *H. pylori* using other regimens.
   - A 10-day sequential therapy has been reported to be superior to standard triple therapy for eradication of *H. pylori*. It consists of 5 days of treatment with a PPI and one antibiotic (usually amoxicillin) followed by 5-day treatment with the PPI and two other antibiotics (usually clarithromycin and metronidazole).
   - Prophylaxis and treatment of stress gastritis with sucralfate suspension 1 g orally q4-6h, H_2-receptor antagonists, or PPIs in patients on ventilator support.

CHRONIC Rx

- Omeprazole 20 mg/qd in patients receiving long-term NSAIDs.
- Avoidance of alcohol, tobacco, and prolonged NSAID or corticosteroid use.

DISPOSITION

- Undetectable stool antigen tested at least 4 wk after therapy accurately confirms cure of *H. pylori* infection in initially seropositive healthy subjects with reasonable sensitivity. PPI therapy should be stopped at least 2 weeks prior to testing.
- Surveillance gastroscopy in patients with atrophic gastritis (increased risk of gastric cancer).

RELATED CONTENT

Gastritis (Patient Information)
Helicobacter pylori Infection (Related Key Topic)

AUTHOR: **FRED F. FERRI, M.D.**

G

I

BASIC INFORMATION

DEFINITION

- Gastroenteritis is a broad term used for various gastrointestinal pathologic states. The main manifestation is diarrhea, defined as daily stool of at least 200 g, often accompanied by nausea, vomiting, malaise, anorexia, fever, abdominal pain, and dehydration. Gastroenteritis is usually self-limited, but if it is not managed properly, it can lead to a prolonged course.
- Gastroenteritis is a common cause of morbidity/mortality around the world. In the developing world, it is a leading cause of death.

ICD-10CM CODES
K52.9 Non-infective gastroenteritis and colitis
558.3 Allergic gastroenteritis and colitis
K52.1 Infectious gastroenteritis and colitis
K52.0 Gastroenteritis and colitis due to radiation

EPIDEMIOLOGY & DEMOGRAPHICS

- Frequency is difficult to determine. Gastroenteritis is underreported in adults.
- Statistics on sporadic cases of adult viral gastroenteritis are not known
- It is estimated that there are 1.5 billion cases a year worldwide.
- It is the leading cause of death in many developing countries. Children under the age of 5 yr are most vulnerable.
- Traveler's diarrhea affects 20% to 50% of residents of industrialized countries who travel to developing countries.

SEX: Higher mortality seen in women.

Females have a higher incidence of *Campylobacter* infections.

AGE:

- May occur at any age
- High morbidity and mortality in the very young (younger than 5 yr), the elderly (people aged 65 or older), and the immunosuppressed.

PHYSICAL FINDINGS & CLINICAL PRESENTATION

- A well-taken history is important. The onset, duration, and frequency of diarrhea should be noted. The aim of the physical examination is to assess the patient's degree of hydration. This helps to identify the cause of diarrhea and identify patients at risk of complications. Viral gastroenteritis has a short prodome with vomiting, mild fever, nonbloody and watery diarrhea, usually for 1 to 4 days.
- Bacterial gastroenteritis presents with high fever, bloody diarrhea, severe abdominal pain, and at least 6 stools in a 24-hour period.
- Patients usually present with:
  1. Diarrhea: usually more than 6 stools a day indicates bacterial cause of gastroenteritis
  2. Vomiting
  3. Abdominal pain

4. Mucus and/or blood in stool: indicating bacterial or parasitic infection
5. Fever
6. Dehydration: this is the main cause of morbidity and mortality. Check for lethargy, dry mucous membrane, poor skin turgor, sunken eyes as signs of dehydration.
7. Malnutrition: this occurs when diarrhea is chronic. There is reduced muscle and fat mass.
8. Abdominal pain: this is a very common symptom in gastroenteritis.
9. Borborygmi: there is significantly increased peristaltic activity, which may cause audible or palpable bowel activity.
10. Perianal erythema: secondary to constantly wet area. Wet buttock and perianal area may result in redness and skin breakdown.

ETIOLOGY

- Bacterial gastroenteritis: The top three leading cause of bacterial diarrhea worldwide are *Salmonella, Shigella,* and *Campylobacter* spp.
  1. *Salmonella*
  2. *Shigella*
  3. *Campylobacter*
  4. *Aeromonas* species
  5. *Yersinia*
  6. Enterohemorrhagic *Escherichia coli*
  7. *E. coli*
  8. *Clostridium perfringens*
- Viral gastroenteritis (in adults)
  1. The caliciviruses such as *Norovirus* genogroup I (e.g., Norwalk), *Norovirus* genogroup II (e.g., South Hampton), *Sapovirus* (e.g., Sapporo).
  2. Non-group A *Rotavirus*
  3. *Astrovirus*
  4. Adenovirus

 DIAGNOSIS

DIFFERENTIAL DIAGNOSIS

- Amebiasis
- Appendicitis
- Celiac disease
- Inflammatory bowel disease
- Colon cancer
- Bowel obstruction
- Botulism
- Hemolytic uremic syndrome
- Food poisoning
- Intraabdominal abscess
- Crohn's disease

WORKUP

- In most cases laboratory tests are not indicated.
- Further workup is indicated in patients who:
  1. Have persistent diarrhea
  2. Are extremely dehydrated
  3. Appear seriously ill
  4. Have high fever
  5. Present with severe abdominal pain
  6. Have bloody diarrhea
  7. Have persistent nausea

LABORATORY TESTS

- Routine laboratory tests
  1. Tests such as CBC and BMP may not be indicated in making a diagnosis. However, electrolytes and BUN are indicated in patients with severe diarrhea or dehydration.
  2. CBC is indicated with severe diarrhea or toxicity. WBC is increased in *Salmonella* infection; eosinophilia is present in parasitic infections.
- Stool studies
  1. Presence of blood/leukocytes in stool may indicate inflammatory diarrhea.
  2. In *Salmonella* or *Shigella* infections there is an increased fecal leukocyte.
  3. Stool leukocytes are absent in viral diarrhea.
- Stool culture
  1. Are only useful when positive
  2. Usually not necessary in most cases of diarrhea
  3. Indications for stool cultures include: bloody stools; prolonged, untreated diarrhea; fever; leukocytes in stool; immunosuppressed patients; immunocompromised patients; and patients who have traveled to remote, exotic, or developing nations. It should also be considered in patients with concurrent or very recent use of antibiotics to rule out *Clostridium difficile* infection as a cause of the diarrhea.
- Examination for ova and parasites (O&P) is indicated in immunosuppressed patients, immunocompromised patients, and patients who have traveled to remote, exotic, or developing nations

IMAGING STUDIES

- In patients with suspected bowel obstruction, perforation, or toxic megacolon, abdominal series is warranted.
- Consider CT scan of the abdomen in older patients with severe abdominal pain.

TREATMENT

GENERAL CONSIDERATIONS

- Most infectious diarrhea is self-limited. Medical care is mainly supportive. Fig. 1G-6 describes an approach to the management of gastroenteritis.
- It is important to assess the degree of dehydration by checking BP, pulse, HR, skin turgor, mucous membrane, thirst, urine output, and mental status change.
- Oral rehydration therapy is very important in diarrhea treatment.
- Consider intravenous rehydration when oral rehydration fails. Watch out for potassium depletion.
- Early re-feeding decreases recovery time.

Principles of treatment include:

- Rehydration: orally or intravenously, PRN
- Treatment of symptoms such as fever, abdominal pain, nausea, vomiting as needed
- Identify and treat complications

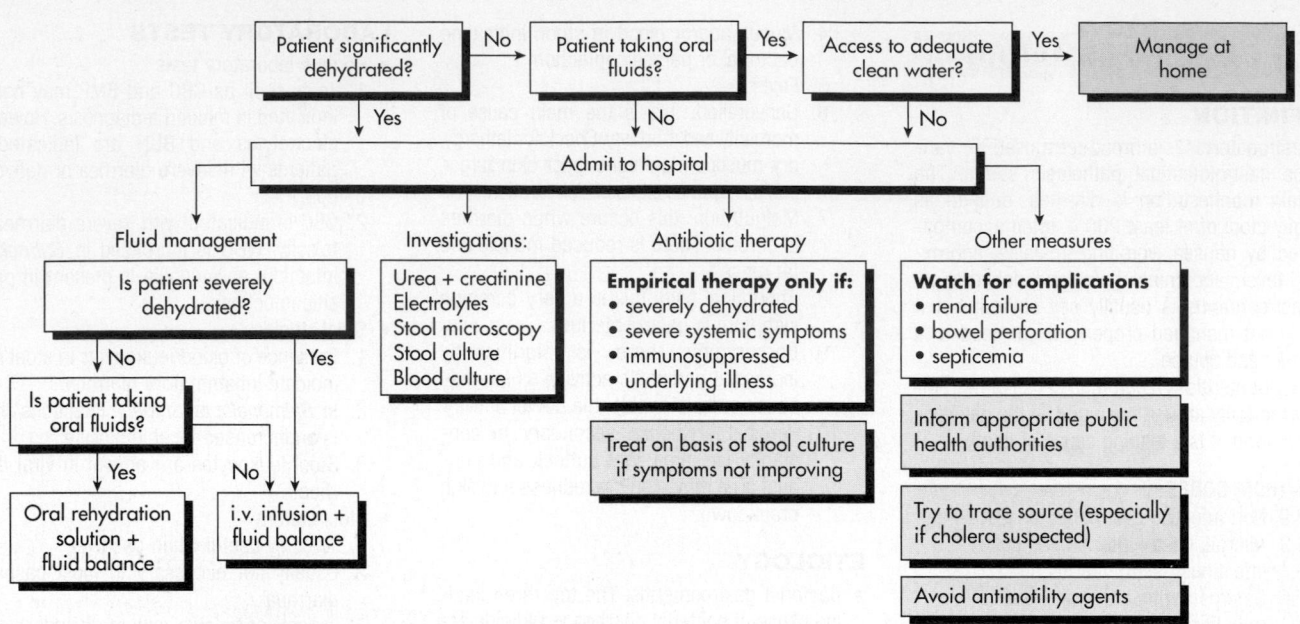

FIGURE 1G-6 Management of gastroenteritis. (From Currie G, Douglas G: *Flesh and bones of medicine*, St. Louis, 2011, Mosby, pp 8-9.)

REHYDRATION:
- Oral hydration products include Naturalyte, Rehydralyte.
- Intravenous solutions used include dextrose 5% in 0.5 isotonic NaCl with 50 mEq NaHCO$_3$ and 10-20 mEq KCl.
  1. Indications for IV hydration include intractable vomiting, severe dehydration, change in mental status or consciousness, and ileus.
  2. Oral hydration is not appropriate due to environmental conditions

TREATMENT OF SYMPTOMS:
- Infectious diarrhea sometimes requires empiric treatment with antibiotics. Foodborne toxigenic diarrhea usually does not.
- Traveler's diarrhea: patients without fever or dysentery may be treated with rifaximin 200 mg thrice daily for 3 days, or ciprofloxacin 500 mg twice daily or 750 mg daily for 1 to 3 days; patients with fever or dysentery can be treated with azithromycin 1000 mg in a single dose.
- *C. difficile* diarrhea and parasitic infestations with *Giardia* or *Entamoeba* are treated with metronidazole or vancomycin. For *C. difficile*, it is important to discontinue the causative antibiotic.
- Treat severe nausea and vomiting with antiemetics.
- Antidiarrheal agents may be useful for systemic relief in mild to moderate diarrhea.
- Loperamide (Imodium) or bismuth subsalicylate (Pepto-Bismol) may provide limited relief in traveler's or non-bloody diarrhea.

Dietary measures may include:
- Start with banana, rice, applesauce, toast diet (BRAT diet)
- As early as possible introduce lean meats and clear liquid

  In recent years the use of probiotics (non-pathogenic live microorganism) has increased. They are known to provide beneficial effects on the host's health. Beneficial effects have been noted with *Lactobacillus casei GG* and *S. boulardii*.

REFERRAL

Referral to infectious disease or gastroenterologist specialist may be indicated in patients:
- With chronic diarrhea
- In whom a parasitic etiology is suspected
- With *C. difficile* resistant to treatment with metronidazole and vancomycin
- With HIV/AIDS
- Who relapse

ⓘ PEARLS AND CONSIDERATIONS

PREVENTION
- Perform proper hand washing before and after eating and after each bowel movement to prevent spread to family members.
- Avoid (raw) shellfish served in certain unregulated places.
- Avoid raw or undercooked eggs and/or poultry.
- Wash all produce before consumption.

- For travelers to high-risk areas:
  1. Eat only cooked foods.
  2. Drink hot or carbonated beverages.
  3. Avoid water, raw peeled fruits/vegetables, green leafy vegetables, and street food sold by street vendors.
  4. Vaccines are available for *Salmonella typhi* and *Vibrio cholerae* (the latter provides about 50% protection for 3-6 months).

PATIENT EDUCATION
- Stress the importance of oral rehydration.
- Stress the need for early appropriate feeding.
- Relapse occurs due to dietary noncompliance.
- Travelers to developing areas should be educated on proper avoidance measures and treatment.
- Also stress the importance of good hygiene, hand washing, safe food preparation, and access to clean water as key in preventing gastroenteritis.

SUGGESTED READINGS

Available at www.expertconsult.com

RELATED CONTENT

Gastroenteritis (Patient Information)

AUTHOR: **DANIEL K. ASIEDU, M.D., Ph.D.**

BASIC INFORMATION

DEFINITION

Gastroesophageal reflux disease (GERD) is a motility disorder characterized primarily by heartburn and caused by the reflux of gastric contents into the esophagus. A current definition is a condition that develops when the reflux of stomach contents causes at least two heartburn episodes per week and/or complications.

SYNONYMS

Peptic esophagitis
Reflux esophagitis
GERD

ICD-10CM CODES
K21.9 Gastroesophageal reflux disease without esophagitis
R12 Heartburn

EPIDEMIOLOGY & DEMOGRAPHICS

- GERD is one of the most prevalent gastrointestinal disorders. It is the most common GI diagnosis recorded during visits to outpatient clinics. From 14% to 20% of adults are affected.
- Nearly 7% of persons in the United States have heartburn daily, 20% have it monthly, and 60% have it intermittently. Incidence in pregnant women exceeds 80%.
- Nearly 20% of adults use antacids or over-the-counter H_2 blockers at least once a week for relief of heartburn.

PHYSICAL FINDINGS & CLINICAL PRESENTATION

- Physical examination: generally unremarkable.

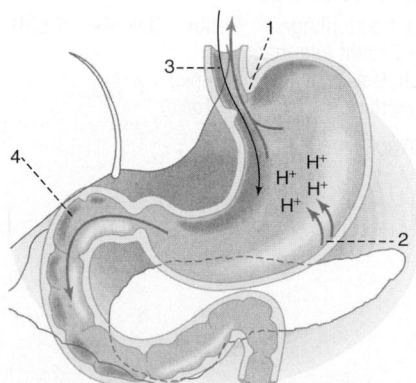

FIGURE 1G-7 Pathogenesis of gastroesophageal reflux disease: *(1)* impaired lower esophageal sphincter—low pressures or frequent transient lower esophageal sphincter relaxation; *(2)* hypersecretion of acid; *(3)* decreased acid clearance resulting from impaired peristalsis or abnormal saliva production; *(4)* delayed gastric emptying or duodenogastric reflux of bile salts and pancreatic enzymes. (From Andreoli TE et al: *Andreoli and Carpenter's Cecil essentials of medicine*, ed 8, Philadelphia, 2010, Saunders.)

- Clinical signs and symptoms: heartburn, dysphagia, sour taste, regurgitation of gastric contents into the mouth.
- Chronic cough and bronchospasm.
- Chest pain, laryngitis, early satiety, abdominal fullness, and bloating with belching.
- Dental erosions in children.

ETIOLOGY

- Incompetent lower esophageal sphincter (LES) (see Fig. 1G-7).
- Medications that lower LES pressure (calcium channel blockers, alpha-adrenergic antagonists, nitrates, theophylline, anticholinergics, sedatives, prostaglandins).
- Foods that lower LES pressure (chocolate, yellow onions, peppermint).
- Tobacco abuse, alcohol, coffee.
- Pregnancy.
- Gastric acid hypersecretion.
- Hiatal hernia (controversial) present in >70% of patients with GERD; however, most patients with hiatal hernia are asymptomatic.
- Obesity is associated with a statistically significant increase in the risk for GERD symptoms, erosive esophagitis, and esophageal carcinoma.

DIAGNOSIS

DIFFERENTIAL DIAGNOSIS

- Peptic ulcer disease.
- Unstable angina.
- Esophagitis (from infections such as herpes, *Candida*), medication induced (doxycycline, potassium chloride).
- Esophageal spasm (nutcracker esophagus).
- Cancer of esophagus.

WORKUP

- Aimed at eliminating the conditions noted in the differential diagnosis and documenting the type and extent of tissue damage. Generally, when symptoms of GERD are typical and the patient responds to therapy, there is no need for further diagnostic tests to verify the diagnosis.
- Upper GI endoscopy is useful to document the type and extent of tissue damage in persistent GERD and to exclude potentially malignant conditions such as Barrett esophagus. The American College of Physicians recommends endoscopy in the setting of GERD in people with heartburn and alarm symptoms (dysphagia, bleeding, anemia, weight loss, and recurrent vomiting). It is also indicated in people with GERD symptoms that persist despite a therapeutic trial of 4 to 8 weeks of bid PPI therapy in patients with severe erosive esophagus after a 2-month course of PPI therapy to assess healing and rule out Barrett esophagus.
- Fig. E1G-8 describes an approach to patients with heartburn.

LABORATORY TESTS

- 24-hr esophageal pH monitoring and Bernstein test are sensitive diagnostic tests;

however, they are not practical and generally not done. They are useful in patients with atypical manifestations of GERD, such as chest pain or chronic cough.
- Esophageal manometry is indicated in patients with refractory reflux in whom surgical therapy is planned.
- *Helicobacter pylori* testing is not indicated in GERD.

IMAGING STUDIES

An upper GI series is useful in patients unwilling to have endoscopy or with medical contraindications to the procedure. It can identify ulcerations and strictures; however, it may miss mucosal abnormalities. Only one third of patients with GERD have radiographic signs of esophagitis on an upper GI series.

TREATMENT

NONPHARMACOLOGIC THERAPY

- Lifestyle modifications with avoidance of foods (e.g., citrus- and tomato-based products, onions, spicy foods, carbonated beverages, mint, chocolate, fried foods) and drugs that exacerbate reflux (e.g., caffeine, β-blockers, calcium channel blockers, α-adrenergic agonists, theophylline).
- Avoidance of tobacco and alcohol use.
- Elevation of head of bed (4 to 8 in) with blocks.
- Avoidance of lying down directly after late or large evening meals, consumption of smaller and more frequent meals.
- Weight reduction to BMI <25, decreased fat intake.
- Avoidance of clothing that is tight around the waist.

GENERAL Rx

- Proton pump inhibitors (PPIs) (esomeprazole 40 mg qd, omeprazole 20 mg qd, lansoprazole 30 mg qd, rabeprazole 20 mg qd, or pantoprazole 40 mg qd, or dexlansoprazole 30 mg) are generally safe, tolerated, and highly effective in most patients (Table 1G-3). Omeprazole and esomeprazole are inhibitors of CYP2C19 and can increase serum concentrations of phenytoin and diazepam. Concomitant use of clopidogrel should also be avoided with omeprazole and esomeprazole.
- H_2 blockers (nizatidine 300 mg qhs, famotidine 40 mg qhs, ranitidine 300 mg qhs, or cimetidine 800 mg qhs) can be used but are generally much less effective than PPIs.
- Antacids (may be useful for relief of mild symptoms; however, they are generally ineffective in severe cases of reflux).
- Prokinetic agents (metoclopramide) are indicated only when PPIs are not fully effective. They can be used in combination therapy; however, side effects limit their use.
- For refractory cases: surgery with Nissen fundoplication. Potential surgical candidates should have reflux esophagitis documented by esophagogastroduodenoscopy and normal esophageal motility as evaluated by

TABLE 1G-3 Drug Therapy for Esophageal Disorders

Agent	Dose
Antacids: Liquid (to Buffer Acid and Increase LESP)	
For example, Mylanta II/Maalox TC (acid-neutralizing capacity, 25 mEq/5 mL)*	15 mL qid 1 hr after meals and at bedtime or as needed
Gaviscon (to Decrease Reflux via a Viscous Mechanical Barrier and Buffer Acid)	
$Al(OH)_3$, $NaHCO_3$, Mg trisilicate, alginic acid	2-4 tablets qid at bedtime or as needed
H_2-Receptor Antagonists (to Decrease Acid Secretion)	
Cimetidine	800 mg bid, 400 mg qid, ≈13 mL bid
Ranitidine	150 mg qid or 10 mL qid; maintenance dose, 150 mg bid, 10 mL bid
Famotidine	20-40 mg bid or 2.5-5 mL bid
Nizatidine	150 mg bid
Proton Pump Inhibitors (to Decrease Acid Secretion and Gastric Volume)†	
Omeprazole	20 mg/day; maintenance dose, 20 mg/day
Lansoprazole	30 mg/day; maintenance dose, 15 mg/day
Pantoprazole	40 mg/day; maintenance dose, 40 mg/day
Rabeprazole	20 mg/day; maintenance dose, 20 mg/day
Esomeprazole	20-40 mg/day; maintenance dose, 20 mg/day
Dexlansoprazole	30-60 mg/day; maintenance dose, 30 mg/day

LESP, Lower esophageal sphincter pressure.

*Patients with reflux are not generally hypersecretors of gastric acid, so the therapeutic doses of antacids are based on their capacity to buffer (normal) basal acid secretion rates of approximately 1 to 7 mEq/hr (mean, 2 mEq/hr) and peak meal-stimulated acid secretion rates of about 10 to 60 mEq/hr (mean, 30 mEq/hr).

†High-dose therapy is a twice-daily administration of the usual daily dose.

From Goldman L, Schafer AI: *Goldman's Cecil medicine*, ed 24, Philadelphia, 2012, Saunders.

manometry. Surgery generally consists of reduction of hiatal hernia when present and placement of a gastric wrap around the gastroesophageal (GE) junction (fundoplication). Although laparoscopic fundoplication is now widely used, long-term medical therapy is a better choice for most patients who are willing to remain on daily acid-reduction medication. In patients preferring surgical intervention, surgery should not be advised with the expectation that patients with GERD will no longer need to take antisecretory medications or that the procedure will prevent esophageal cancer among those with GERD and Barrett esophagus.

- Endoscopic radiofrequency heating of the GE junction (Stretta procedure) is a newer treatment modality for GERD patients unresponsive to traditional therapy. Its mechanism of action remains unclear. Endoscopy gastroplasty (EndoCinch procedure) is also aimed at treating GERD. Initial results appear encouraging; however, long-term studies are needed before recommending these procedures.

- Lifestyle modification must be followed for life because this is generally an irreversible condition.

DISPOSITION

- Recurrence of reflux is common if treatment is discontinued.
- The majority of patients respond well to therapy. In patients with chronic GERD, long-term outcomes are similar between medical therapy with PPIs and anti-reflux surgery. Prolonged use of PPIs is associated with increased risk of fractures of hip, wrist, and spine; increased risk of diarrhea from *Clostridium difficile;* pneumonia; and possible iron deficiency from impaired iron absorption. PPIs also block the effects of clopidogrel by inhibiting cytochrome P450 2C19 isozyme. Therefore all PPIs (other than pantoprazole) should be avoided in patients using clopidogrel. H_2 blockers (e.g., ranitidine) can be used for patients with GERD taking clopidogrel.

- Postsurgical complications occur in nearly 20% of patients (dysphagia, gas, bloating, diarrhea, nausea). Long-term follow-up studies also reveal that within 3 to 5 yr, 52% of patients who had undergone antireflux surgery are taking antireflux medications again.

REFERRAL

- There is a strong and probably causal relation between symptomatic prolonged and untreated GERD, Barrett esophagus, and esophageal adenocarcinoma. GI referral for upper endoscopy is needed when there are concerns about associated peptic ulcer disease, Barrett esophagus, or esophageal cancer.
- Patients with Barrett esophagus should undergo surveillance endoscopy with mucosal biopsy every 2 yr or less because the risk of developing adenocarcinoma of esophagus is at least 30 times greater than that of the general population.
- Testing and treating for *Helicobacter pylori* in patients with GERD has not been shown to improve symptoms.
- All children with dental erosions should be evaluated for GERD.

 EVIDENCE

Available at www.expertconsult.com

SUGGESTED READINGS

Available at www.expertconsult.com

RELATED CONTENT

Gastroesophageal Reflux Disease (GERD) (Patient Information)
Achalasia (Related Key Topic)
Dysphagia (Related Key Topic)

AUTHOR: **FRED F. FERRI, M.D.**

BASIC INFORMATION

DEFINITION

Gender nonconformity or transgender identity results when a person's perceived and innate sense of being male or female (i.e., gender identity) is at odd with the natal assigned gender based on chromosomes, hormones, organs, and eventually secondary sexual characteristics. Gender dysphoria may result when an individual's gender identity is incongruent with the person's assigned gender, with discomfort and dislike of one's external gender characteristics and a desire to be physically different from the gender born into or assigned at birth.

Historically, gender and sexuality are related but separate concepts: gender is who a person is and how they identify as male, female, or somewhere on the continuum; sexuality is about who a person is attracted to or the behaviors involved during intercourse. Although discomfort and dislike of one's biologic and anatomic gender and secondary gender characteristics are a major component of gender dysphoria disorder, some individuals who identify as transgender do not express clinically disabling dysphoria or psychopathology. Careful evaluation of each patient's unique perspective and gender experience guides options for care. Transition is a process of moving the external gender characteristics and presentation to the individual's asserted gender identity. Transition is typically divided into three types (reversible, partially reversible, and irreversible), but should be tailored to the individual throughout the lifespan.

SYNONYMS

Gender nonconformity
Transgender
Gender dysphoria in children, adolescents, adults
Transsexual

ICD-10CM CODES

For the purposes of medical care for transgender individuals, ICD-10 codes are already inaccurate and do not represent and reflect current standards and understanding of gender development. The diagnostic entity of gender identity disorder has been rejected as pathologizing and inappropriate per DSM 5 psychiatric coding. Transsexualism is older terminology that perpetuates confusion between gender and sexuality. This author regrets that ICD-10 neglects developmental aspects of health, and its classifying detail within codes focuses on pathology and classification for billing and reimbursement priorities.
F64.0 Transsexualism
F64.2 Gender identity disorder of childhood
F64.9 Gender identity disorder, unspecified
F64.8 Other gender identity disorder
E34.9 Endocrine, Hormones
Disease of, Disorder(s), Dysfunction(s), Disturbance, Complication(s) from

EPIDEMIOLOGY & DEMOGRAPHICS

DEVELOPMENT & BACKGROUND: Gender development begins as early as 18 months. By age 2 to 4 yr, children understand gender differences and use pronouns such as "him" and "her." Toddlers identify their own gender, and most consider gender a stable personal trait at age 5 to 6 yr. All children partake in gender play and explore gender activities, behaviors, and roles. Gender play does not mean a child is dysphoric, dislikes his or her gender, or identifies as the other gender.

PREDOMINANT AGE:
- Gender nonconformity in prepubertal years is more than gender play; nonconforming prepubertal children exhibit *consistent, persistent, and insistent* play, dress, attributes, and activities of the other gender. Some of these children, but not all, experience dysphoria regarding their genitalia or express mild to intense discomfort and dislike of their biologic gender. Some, but not all, gender nonconforming prepubertal children may verbally assert that they are or need to be the other gender. In the prepubertal years, males who present to medical providers with this experience outnumber females by 3:1.
- With puberty, attaining a mature and adult gender (who you are, your male or female persona, and role in society) and exploring one's sexuality (attraction, orientation, behaviors, sexual partner preference) become core developmental tasks of adolescence. At this age, gender nonconforming youth who present for care changes to a ratio of 1:1 male to female.
- Incidence may be heavily associated with cultural expectations. It is generally less acceptable to be a feminized boy than a prepubertal girl who is a "tomboy." A peripubertal spike in gender dysphoria also occurs as pubertal females lose their androgenous appearance, develop breasts, and begin menses.

PREVALENCE: Overall estimates are between 1 in 10,000 to 1 in 100,000. Most believe these numbers vastly underestimate prevalence because they originate from adult surgical or gender specialty clinics.

GENETICS: There is no known single or specific genetic basis for gender dysphoria or a gender nonconforming identity. There appear to be no specific relationships between transgender identity with socioeconomic status, race, or ethnicity. There may be a link between autism spectrum disorders and gender nonconformity.

RISK FACTORS: Most children and adults benefit from medical care models that do not pathologize their innate sense and experience of self. However, children and teens who are gender nonconforming have historically experienced higher rates of child abuse, bullying, mental health concerns (e.g., anxiety, depression, suicidality), and substance use. Transgender adult populations have poorer health outcomes, such as depression, anxiety, self-harm and suicide, substance use, underemployment, homelessness, incarceration, and positive HIV status.

Poorer health outcomes are explained by using minority stress theory (chronic stress related to stigma and dysphoria) rather than gender variance as a pathology itself.

PHYSICAL FINDINGS & CLINICAL PRESENTATION

Gender nonconforming prepubertal children present with *consistent, persistent, and insistent* interest and expression of other or opposite-gendered activities and behaviors. Boys may be considered more feminine than their same-age peers; they may prefer to wear long hair, nail polish, makeup, girls' jewelry, and clothing. Girls may be considered "tomboys" and reject wearing dresses and skirts, prefer short hair, wear boys' clothing, and participate in traditionally masculine play and activities. During the school-age years, children become sensitive to social expectations and norms as well as both explicit and implicit criticism, and some may suppress their feelings of being in the wrong body and assume cisgender expression. Many gender dysphoric children who do conform in their gender play and expression, however, still experience underlying problems with their external gender expression at odds with their internal gender identity.

Adolescents and adults may present at any point along the lifespan, though a majority express having cross-gender feelings and identities earlier in life. Many gender dysphoric persons will not present directly with gender dysphoria but present with mood, behavior, or social problems. For many persons, gender dysphoria or the disclosure of gender nonconformity is first elicited as a result of mental health counseling.

DIAGNOSIS

- Gender nonconformity and transgender identity is not considered pathologic or requiring psychiatric evaluation and care. Developmental models instead view gender along a biologic spectrum with diverse presentations and expression. Persons may assert a nonconformity identity without severe self-hatred or significant dysphoric presentation. Psychiatric evaluations are no longer considered necessary or essential to "diagnose" gender nonconforming persons. Transgender individuals may have a range of expression, from an inherent, longstanding belief and feeling that one's psyche is more congruent with the opposite gender, to feeling androgenous and non-gendered, to strongly desiring not to have or to be rid of one's primary and secondary gender's physical characteristics.
- Changes in DSM 5 focus on "gender dysphoria" and inherent distress in one's natal gender and biologic gender characteristics rather than creating a "disorder" of identity. For an individual to be diagnosed with gender dysphoria, marked differences between the individual's natal or assigned gender and expressed/experienced gender must exist for at least six months; cause clinically

Diseases and Disorders

G

I

significant distress or impairment in social, occupational, or other important areas of functioning; with strong and consistent desire to be the other gender. Persons with severe dysphoria and sequelae from the mismatch in biology with identity usually benefit from participating in therapy, building skills to create successful transition plans, and/or obtaining treatment for commonly associated comorbid psychiatric concerns, such as anxiety and depression.

- Gender dysphoria has a chapter in DSM 5 separate from Sexual Dysfunctions and Paraphilic Disorders. Many gender specialists focus on paradigms using physical or endocrine conditions to avoid stigma and allow for improved access to hormonal and surgical therapies.
- DSM 5 changes add a posttransition specifier for people who are living full time as the desired gender identity so as to ensure treatment access for hormone therapy, related surgeries, or counseling.

WORKUP

- Ideally, this interview is in the context of interviewing the individual as a person and part of a holistic health assessment. Persons with various degrees and experience in behavioral health can perform these interviews. While some patients may benefit from additional therapy or psychiatric evaluation, many transgender individuals should not be "required" to seek psychiatric care. Patients may benefit from additional psychiatric services for comorbid mental health concerns, social and emotional skill building, and creating a safe and successful transition plan. Parents of a gender nonconforming child may benefit from receiving support and their own counseling services so that they may successfully focus on the child's issues and needs.
- Clinical interview includes assessment of gender experience from childhood until present; desired name, pronoun, and past and current place on the gender spectrum; past and current attempts to feminize or masculinize with clothing, hair, makeup, hormones, and surgeries; future goals of transitioning, gender identity, and expression. For many children, many parents may provide insight as to early childhood gender identity and expression. For some children, parental distress and denial of a consistent cross-gender identity is the most problematic aspect of providing care.
- Review for known comorbidities by asking mental health specific questions about: depression, anxiety, self-harm (cutting and suicidal ideation), psychiatric hospitalization, substance use. Patient history should also include: sexual attraction and behaviors and risk for sexually transmitted infections and pregnancy; social history, experience of bullying, hate crimes, physical or emotional/verbal abuse, homelessness, joblessness, and survival sex. Resiliency theory also promotes focusing on patient strengths and identifying social support systems

- An initial visit may include a physical examination, depending on the provider and patient goals. Many gender dysphoric persons are exquisitely uncomfortable with their genitalia and genital examination. If the evaluation is a consultation for information and counseling, an exam may be deferred until the patient is more comfortable and familiar with the provider.
- A general physical examination may be performed as with any new patient, but detailed examination of secondary sexual characteristics (breasts, vulva, penis, testicles) often is deferred at an initial visit. Tanner staging genitalia to determine which peripubertal youth are most appropriate for gonadotropin releasing hormone (GnRH) analogues ("puberty blockers") or cross-gender hormones is important. Those young children who are not peripubertal or those teens who are well into Tanner stage 5 (by chronologic age, years post menarche, or adult secondary sexual characteristics) may be allowed to defer the genital exam during these initial visits.
- Luteinizing hormone is a preferred lab for evaluating prepubertal children and GnRH analogue use, but additional laboratory studies may include follicle stimulating hormone, testosterone, or estradiol. For older youth or adults starting cross-gender hormones, baseline laboratory values include CBC, lipid panel, and liver function tests. Cross-gender hormones may affect hematopoiesis, cholesterol levels, and irritate the liver. Testosterone may be useful to measure androgen suppression in asserted women receiving estrogen therapy. Prolactin is an additional baseline lab for continued estradiol therapy and has been rarely associated with prolactinoma. Potassium and blood pressure monitoring is useful in transwomen using spironolactone to block male pattern hair growth. Asserted transmales taking testosterone may get routine total testosterone levels with a goal within average adult male range.
- Screening for sexually transmitted infections (urine, rectal, and oral *Chlamydia* and gonorrhea; syphilis; herpes simplex virus; HIV; hepatitis B and C), and pregnancy is indicated according to sexual practices.
- Ancillary testing may include various psychiatric screening and diagnostic tools for comorbid depression, anxiety, suicidality, substance use, and interpersonal violence.
- Additional preventive care screening and testing may be deferred. Over time, patients should receive typical preventive and screening tests for both natal and asserted gender.

Rx TREATMENT

Treatment is determined by patient age and development (including Tanner stage) and desired place on the gender spectrum. Moving from biologic gender to asserted gender identity or transition is typically described as: reversible, partially reversible, and irreversible.

REVERSIBLE TRANSITION

- Social transition includes taking a name and pronoun in the identified gender, as well as clothing, shoes, hair, make-up, and other gender identifying social cues. For prepubertal, androgenous children, social transition does not require hormones, but does require extensive planning for disclosure, social support, and peer- and school-based activities.
- Gonadotropin releasing hormone (GnRH) agonists act to block the hypothalamic pituitary gonadal axis and put a "pause" on endogenous gender hormone secretion. Puberty blockers in puberty are completely reversible and best when used at very early Tanner stage II breast and testicular development. When used in early puberty, blockers stop puberty with regression to prepubertal hormones and secondary gender characteristics. This often "buys time" for additional support and assessment or allowing the family to determine a safe and supportive social transition plan.
- GnRH analogues may be used for patients later in puberty according to genital exam but are still androgenous in regard to other secondary gender characteristics, such as voice, facial and body hair, bone, muscle, and fat deposition. Blockers can also be used to stop penile function or menses, which can be highly distressing to some gender dysphoric persons.
- GnRH analogues are *completely reversible*. If stopped, a person can continue into biologic puberty with no impact on future gender characteristics or fertility. Most teens who opt to start GnRH agonists to block puberty continue to create a transition plan and eventually move to cross-gender hormones and puberty in their asserted gender. The current literature from the past 30 or more years demonstrates that it is unlikely that an adolescent who is consistently, persistently, and insistently gender nonconforming or transgender will return to his or her natal gender or regret either blockers or cross-gender hormones. This can be both of concern and relief to parents as they determine how to best to support their child.

PARTIALLY REVERSIBLE TRANSITION:

- Cross-gender or gender affirming hormone therapies include testosterone for masculinization and estradiol for feminization. Both hormones may have reversible effects on skin, fat deposition, and muscle mass. Irreversible testosterone effects may include masculine voice changes, changes in facial and body hair, and clitoromegaly. Irreversible estradiol effects include areolar enlargement and breast tissue growth. These changes are usually desired by transgender individuals and desired for continued transition into their asserted gender.
- Estradiol creates softer skin, female body fat deposition (hips/thighs), and breast development. It may impair erectile function, which may or may not be desired because some male-to-female persons still want or depend on penile function (masturbation, sexual

relationships, and/or sex work. Estradiol is typically administered sublingually but can be taken intramuscularly, orally, or topically. Topical medicines are expensive and time consuming, run the risk of undesired feminization (or masculinization) of sex partners or others in close physical contact, but are likely have the lowest thromboembolic risks.

- Testosterone masculinizes by inducing male hair patterns, deepening the voice, and inducing male-pattern fat and muscle deposition (bulk and abdominal girth) and clitoromegaly. It can lead to vaginal atrophy, resulting in dyspareunia for transgender female-to-male persons who use the vagina for sex. Testosterone comes in a variety of vehicles, including subcutaneous, intramuscular, and topical. Testosterone is teratogenic in pregnancy. Both gender hormones should not be used in lieu of contraception as current evidence suggests that estrogen or testosterone are not sufficiently effective as a contraceptive. Persons taking testosterone who are having unprotected egg–sperm sex should be counseled and offered birth control in addition to testosterone.

- Individuals who feel strongly about having future genetic children or child bearing may wish to consult reproductive endocrinology and infertility specialists to discuss sperm and oocyte preservation strategies. For male-to-female persons, sperm banking offers future options for biologic children, although at some expense. For female-to-male persons, oocyte banking is extremely expensive and has not yet demonstrated reliable successful outcomes. For many transgender persons, transition to their asserted identity is more important than creating or carrying genetic children. Many transgender persons would prefer to parent or adopt in their identified or asserted gender.

- Consent to what we know and do not know is an important part of beginning the cross-gender hormone process. We currently do not have strong guidelines or outcome studies for ongoing preventive care and anticipatory guidance.

IRREVERSIBLE TRANSITION: Includes mostly surgical options for masculinization (mastectomy and male chest reconstruction, hystero-oophrectomy, and orchi-peniplasty) or feminization (orchiectomy-penectomy with vulvovaginal reconstruction, breast implants, and other cosmetic surgeries). Many patients opt for partial surgical transition due to expense. At present, many surgeries are not covered under many insurance plans. The U.S. Department of Health and Human Services Departmental Appeals Board ruled Medicare's categorical exclusion of gender confirmation medical and surgical treatments was unreasonable and contrary to medical standards of care. Several states have adopted legislation that also prevents insurers from excluding transgender care services. While Medicare can no longer categorically exclude gender surgeries as it has done since the 1980s,

there is, as yet, no consensus or plan for how to include and cover these services by Medicare. Lack of insurance, under-insurance and lack of available providers are additional reasons that many transgender individuals may not opt for irreversible surgical care. Male-to-female genitoplasty surgeons in the United States are rare, and many patients travel overseas for surgical care. Top surgery is more with asserted males seeking specific male chest reconstructive surgeries and asserted females opting for breast implants. It is important to ask specific goals for surgery because they vary by individual patient.

ADDITIONAL THERAPIES: Anti-androgens such as spironolactone prevent male-pattern hair growth. Vocal coaching, tracheal shaving, and other facial feminizing surgeries are some options for male-to-female. Progesterone is used by some asserted females to promote increased breast development, although there is no evidence pointing to side effects or its effectiveness. Topical androgen therapies do not seem to improve clitoral growth. Individual, family, and marital counseling and therapies can be important for dysphoric individuals or for parents and/or partners struggling to unconditionally accept a loved one's transition. Support is important to family members who are involved in a patient's transition. Medications for anxiety, depression, and other mental health concerns may facilitate self-esteem, mood, cognitive function, and social skills building as persons and families negotiate the process of transition. Social support and activity groups may help gender nonconforming persons find a sense of community, feel and become less isolated, and improve transition experiences. Reparative therapy is *universally* rejected as *unethical and harmful* by all the national medical and psychological boards and associations.

DISPOSITION

Support is important to both patients and family members who are involved in transition. Medications for anxiety, depression, and other mental health concerns may facilitate self-esteem, mood, cognitive function, and social skills building as persons and families negotiate the process of transition. Social support and activity groups may help gender nonconforming persons find a sense of community, feel and become less isolated, and improve transition experiences. Reparative therapy is *universally* rejected as *unethical and harmful* by all the national medical and psychological boards and associations.

- Gender is a physical, emotional, social, and cultural construct across the lifespan that every person experiences. Newer paradigms of gender focus on the brain as the most important "source" of gender. When brain and body gender are not congruent a person may experience gender nonconforming or transgender identity. Some transgender individuals experience a severe degree of gender dysphoria, but dysphoria is not a prerequisite for gender nonconforming persons to receive care. Gender dysphoria and social stigma

may create lifelong implications for physical, emotional, and social well-being.

- Younger prepubertal gender nonconforming patients may grow up and be cisgender or transgender, hetero or homosexual. Patients who have early consistent, persistent, insistent dysphoria or cross-gender identification are more likely to continue this into puberty and eventually transition.

- Peripubertal youth who begin hormone blockers are likely to continue to cross-gender hormones and may desire more permanent surgical interventions.

- Youth who are transitioned early both socially and hormonally, and experience puberty in their identified gender, and have family support may have improved ability to be accepted in their asserted gender, decreased suicidality, and less risk of nonmedical use of street hormones and drugs, as well as fewer future surgeries. "Passing" in one's asserted gender can have significant and demonstrated protective effects for victimization from hate crimes and interpersonal violence, low socioeconomic status, underemployment, and isolation. Early identification and early transition in a person's identified gender, along with a better likelihood of acceptance, may offer significant psychosocial benefits to many gender dysphoric persons.

- Regardless of the timing of transition, safety and ongoing support is a priority in transition planning and important to consider along the lifespan.

REFERRALS

- Providers who are not comfortable with gender or behavioral assessments may want to refer to medical or mental health providers with experience and expertise in gender issues and care. This group may include pediatric, family medicine, medicine-pediatrics, endocrinology and psychiatry providers. Similarly, there are therapists and social workers with expertise in gender dysphoria assessment and management.

- There are few contraindications to transitioning for most transgender or gender dysphoric persons. Active psychosis and inability to consent to care would require further psychiatric evaluation but are extremely rare. For older persons, some medical issues involving cardiac, liver, and thromboembolic risks complicate hormone use and need to be taken into consideration.

ⓘ PEARLS & CONSIDERATIONS

- Periodic assessment of a person's place on the gender spectrum can begin in toddler age children and can continue into adulthood as a potentially effective way of helping identify and support gender nonconforming or gender dysphoric persons earlier, and earlier identification and parental support for gender dysphoric and nonconforming persons may lead to improved mental and physical health outcomes.

- Hormone blockers and cross-gender hormones typically offer far more benefit than risk in the treatment of gender dysphoria when a person desires to transition to the opposite gender.
- Federal and state changes in mandated insurer coverage of gender care, including gender affirming surgeries, may offer substantial benefit for a growing population of transgender identified persons.

PATIENT & FAMILY EDUCATION

- The World Professional Association for Transgender Health promotes the highest standards of health care for individuals through the articulation of Standards of Care (SOC) for the Health of Transsexual, Transgender, and Gender Nonconforming People. The SOC are based on the best available science and expert professional consensus: http://www.wpath.org/site_page.cfm?pk_association_webpage_menu=1351
- Center of Excellence for Transgender Health, the mission of which is to increase access to comprehensive, effective, and affirming health care services for trans communities: http://transhealth.ucsf.edu/

- The Trans Health Program at Fenway helps to ensure access to high-quality, informed care for trans women, trans men, genderqueer, gender nonconforming, nonbinary individuals, affirmed men and women, people with trans histories, and anyone with health needs unique to their diverse gender expressions and identities: http://fenwayhealth.org/care/medical/transgender-health/

AUTHOR: **MICHELLE FORCIER, M.D., M.P.H**

BASIC INFORMATION

DEFINITION

- Glucose intolerance that begins, or is first recognized, during pregnancy.
- In the United States, the "two-step" approach is commonly used and is currently endorsed by the American College of Obstetricians and Gynecologists (ACOG) and the National Institutes of Health (NIH). Women are first screened with a 1-hr, nonfasting 50 g oral glucose tolerance test. If the result is ≥ 130 mg/dl, a 3-hr, 100 g oral glucose tolerance test is ordered. The diagnosis is made if two or more of the glucose values are met or exceeded:
  Fasting: 95 mg/dl
  1-hr: 180 mg/dl
  2-hr: 155 mg/dl
  3-hr: 140 mg/dl
- The International Association of Diabetes in Pregnancy Study Group has recommended a simplified "one-step" approach to screening and diagnosing gestational DM (GDM). It involves a fasting 75 g, 2-hr oral glucose tolerance test. A diagnosis of GDM is made if any of the following levels of plasma glucose are exceeded: ≥92 mg/dl when fasting, ≥180 mg/dl at 1 hr, or ≥153 mg/dl at 2 hr. Although this approach is endorsed by the American Diabetes Association, the NIH Consensus on GDM did not endorse these guidelines in 2013 because of increases in the prevalence of GDM, along with corresponding costs and interventions without clear evidence of improvement in outcomes.
- Pregnant women with diabetes mellitus (DM) (gestational or preexisting) are classified according to White's classification (Table 1G-4).

SYNONYMS

Gestational diabetes
Diet-controlled gestational diabetes (A1)
Medication-treated gestational diabetes (A2)

ICD-10CM CODES
024.410 Gestational diabetes mellitus in pregnancy, diet controlled
024.414 Gestational diabetes mellitus in pregnancy, insulin controlled
024.419 Gestational diabetes mellitus in pregnancy, unspecified control
099.810 Abnormal glucose complicating pregnancy

EPIDEMIOLOGY & DEMOGRAPHICS

INCIDENCE: Approximately 5% to 6% of pregnancies using the two-step approach and 15% to 20% using the one-step approach.
PREDOMINANT SEX AND AGE: Women of childbearing age.
GENETICS: Higher rate in women with family history of GDM or type 2 diabetes; specific HLA alleles (DR3 or DR4) predispose to the development of DM type 1 after delivery.

RISK FACTORS

- Obesity.
- Family history of GDM or type 2 diabetes.
- Polycystic ovarian syndrome.
- Multiple gestation.
- Hypertension.
- Chronic systemic steroid use.
- Previous infant weighing >9 lb or with shoulder dystocia.
- Unexplained perinatal loss or malformation.
- Personal history of abnormal glucose tolerance or GDM.
- Hispanic, Native American, African American, Asian, or Pacific Islander ethnicity.

POTENTIAL RISK FACTORS

- Limited physical activity the year before pregnancy.
- Prepregnancy diet low in fiber and high in glycemic load.

PHYSICAL FINDINGS & CLINICAL PRESENTATION

Suspect GDM if:
- Fetal size greater than dates.
- Macrosomia or polyhydramnios on ultrasound.
- Marked maternal obesity or weight gain.

ETIOLOGY

- During normal pregnancy there is increased insulin resistance because of placental secretion of diabetogenic hormones in the late second and third trimesters. Pancreatic beta-cell secretion increases to compensate for the increased insulin resistance. GDM occurs when this need cannot be met.
- Insulin resistance is also exacerbated by an increase in maternal adipose deposition, decreased exercise, and increased caloric intake.

DIAGNOSIS

DIFFERENTIAL DIAGNOSIS

Preexisting type 1 or 2 DM not previously diagnosed.

WORKUP

- History with focus on personal medical history, prior pregnancy history, and family history.
- Routine prenatal examination.
- Laboratory evaluation (see the following).

LABORATORY TESTS

- "Two-step" approach.

1. For screening without risk factors, order a 1-hr glucose tolerance test (Nonfasting; 50 g oral glucose load) at 24 to 28 wk.
2. For screening with risk factors, order at first prenatal visit, then repeat at 24 to 28 wk if initial screen was normal. If abnormal at intake, consider possibility of undiagnosed preexisting DM and check hemoglobin A1c.
- If 1-hr test result is abnormal (≥130 mg/dl), order 3-hr glucose tolerance test (Fasting: 100 g oral glucose load).
  1. Performed after 3 days of unrestricted diet (carbohydrate load is probably not necessary).
  2. Carpenter and Coustan Criteria National Diabetes Data Group Criteria.
  3. GDM is diagnosed if two or more of the glucose values are met or exceeded:
- If one of four values on 3-hr glucose tolerance test is abnormal, repeat testing in 1 month and consider beginning a diabetic diet.
- "One-step" approach
  1. Rule out overt diabetes at the initial prenatal visit. A diagnosis of diabetes is made if a woman meets any of the following criteria: fasting plasma glucose >126 mg/dl, A1c >6.5%, random plasma glucose >200 mg/dl.
  2. Perform a one-step screening at 24 to 28 wk on all pregnant patients who have not already been diagnosed with diabetes or GDM. This is a 2-hr, 75 g oral glucose tolerance test performed after an overnight fast. A diagnosis of GDM is made if one or more of the following values are met or exceeded:
     Fasting: ≥92 mg/dl
     1-hr plasma glucose ≥180 mg/dl
     2-hr plasma glucose ≥153 mg/dl
- The U.S. Preventive Services Task Force (USPSTF) recommends screening for gestational diabetes in all pregnant women after 24 weeks' gestation. The current evidence is insufficient to assess the balance between the benefits and harms of screening women for GDM in asymptomatic women before 24 weeks' gestation. Clinicians should discuss early screening for GDM with their patients and make case-by-case decisions. The discussion should include information about the uncertain benefits and harms as well as the frequency and uncertain meaning of a positive screening test result.

TABLE 1G-4 White's Classification for Pregnant Women with Diabetes (Gestational or Preexisting)

Class	Description
A1	DM diagnosed during pregnancy and controlled by diet
A2	DM diagnosed during pregnancy and requiring medication
B	Insulin-requiring DM diagnosed before pregnancy, age >20 yr, lasting <10 yr
C	Insulin-requiring DM, onset at age 10 to 19 yr, with a duration 10 to 19 yr
D	Onset >10 yr or duration >20 yr, or associated with hypertension or background retinopathy
F	DM with renal disease
H	DM with coronary artery disease
R	DM with proliferative retinopathy
T	DM with renal transplant

DM, Diabetes mellitus.

- Women with GDM have an increased risk of developing diabetes during their lifetime. Women with GDM should be screened at 6 to 12 weeks postpartum with a 75 g 2-hour GTT to diagnose impaired glucose tolerance or diabetes.

IMAGING STUDIES

Ultrasound for fetal size at least once at 36 to 37 wk; more frequently (every 3 to 4 weeks) if macrosomia suspected.

 **TREATMENT**

NONPHARMACOLOGIC THERAPY

- Glucose monitoring:
  1. Four times daily: fasting and 2-hr postprandial.
  2. Goals: fasting ≤95 mg/dl; 2-hr postprandial <120 mg/dl.
  3. Can also use 1-hr postprandial goal of <140 mg/dl.
- Dietary modifications aimed at glycemic control:
  1. Follow a low-fat, high-fiber diet; avoid sugar and concentrated sweets; and eat small, frequent meals.
  2. Nutrition counseling for diet that adequately meets the needs of pregnancy but restricts carbohydrates to 35% to 40% of daily calories.
  3. Normal BMI: 30 kcal/kg/day; BMI above 30 to 25 kcal/kg/day and morbid obesity 12 to 14 kcal/kg/day.
- Regular moderate exercise.

PHARMACOLOGIC Rx

Begin if >20% of fasting or postprandial glucose values are elevated after trial of diet control:

- Oral hypoglycemics:
  1. Oral hypoglycemics are equivalent in efficacy to insulin and can be appropriate first-line agents. There is no consistent evidence from randomized trials showing any increase in short-term adverse maternal or neonatal outcomes with oral medications vs insulin. There are no long-term trials available, and both metformin and glyburide may cross the placenta.
  2. Glyburide: begin at 2.5 mg qd and titrate up to a maximum of 20 mg qd (10 mg bid). Increase dose as needed by 2.5 to 5 mg/wk.
  3. Metformin is typically used pre-pregnancy for polycystic ovarian syndrome or preexisting diabetes and may be continued into pregnancy. Studies show that up to 50% of women may require insulin to achieve glycemic control; however, no adverse outcomes have been described. Comparisons of glyburide versus metformin similarly show more women on metformin will require addition of insulin to achieve glycemic control.
- Insulin:
  ○ There are no randomized controlled trials on insulin regimens, and therapy is largely guided by expert opinion.
  ○ Insulin may be started first line or added when oral medications have failed to achieve glycemic control.

1. One commonly used regimen:
   1. Insulin 0.7–1.0 U/kg/day SQ (based on current pregnant weight), with two thirds of the total daily dose given in the morning and one third of the total daily dose given in the evening
   2. One third of each dose is given as short-acting (regular, lispro, or aspart) insulin and the remaining two thirds as NPH insulin
2. Another option:
   1. If fasting values are elevated, use NPH at bedtime with initial dose of 0.2 U/kg
   2. If postprandial values are elevated, use rapid-acting insulin before meals with initial dose 1.5 U/10 g carbohydrate at breakfast and 1 U/10 g carbohydrate at lunch and dinner
   3. Long-acting insulin such as glargine (Lantus) does not have sufficient data to determine whether it crosses the placenta; it may be continued in persons with preexisting diabetes who are well controlled but is not recommended in patients with newly diagnosed GDM

ANTENATAL TESTING

Antepartum testing is recommended for women with pre-gestational diabetes. There is no consensus regarding antepartum testing in gestational diabetes, and this should be guided by local standards.

ONE COMMONLY USED REGIMEN

- Class A1: NST/AFI at 40 wk.
- Class A2: weekly NST/AFI beginning at 32 wk or when medications are initiated.
- Poorly controlled diabetes, vascular complications, or hypertension: biweekly NST/AFI beginning at 28 wk and consider admission for initial glycemic control.

TIMING AND ROUTE OF DELIVERY

- Women with preexisting diabetes should be induced at 39 weeks.
  ACOG states that there is no evidence-based recommendation that can be made regarding timing of delivery in women with GDM. Decisions should be guided by local standards of care, and well-controlled A1 or A2 women should not be induced before 39 weeks.
- Counseling regarding elective cesarean section at or after 39 weeks if estimated fetal weight is over 4500 g.
- Consider delivery earlier than 39 weeks if poor control or other medical indications such as growth restriction or preeclampsia.

INTRAPARTUM MANAGEMENT

- Goal is normoglycemia (80 to 120 mg/dl) using insulin and D5 lactated Ringer's IV fluid if needed.
- Monitor glucose every 1 to 2 hours.
- Preparation for shoulder dystocia
- If on glyburide, discontinue in labor or 12 hr before a scheduled induction
- If on insulin consider decreased long-acting insulin by one third to one half before scheduled induction

NEONATAL MANAGEMENT

- Check 30- and 60-min glucose.
- Watch for signs of hypoglycemia, hypocalcemia, hyperbilirubinemia, and polycythemia.

POSTPARTUM MANAGEMENT

- Class A2: check fasting level before discharge; if abnormal, continue checking at home and early follow-up with primary care physician to confirm diagnosis of DM.
- 6-wk postpartum visit: screen for impaired glucose tolerance and diabetes in A1 and A2 women with a 75 g, 2-hr glucose tolerance test
- If no evidence of DM, screen annually for DM and counsel on risk factor modification

REFERRAL

- Nutritionist.
- High-risk obstetrician.
- Maternal-fetal medicine.
- Diabetes educator.

COMPLICATIONS

- Maternal: preeclampsia, future type 2 DM or GDM, operative delivery.
- Fetal: polyhydramnios, macrosomia, shoulder dystocia, birth trauma, congenital malformations.
- Neonatal: hypoglycemia, hypocalcemia, hyperbilirubinemia, polycythemia, perinatal death, future obesity and DM, impaired fine and gross motor functions; increased rates of inattention and hyperactivity.

⊘ PEARLS & CONSIDERATIONS

- Trials have shown that although treatment of mild gestational DM did not significantly reduce the frequency of a composite outcome that included stillbirth or perinatal death and several neonatal complications, it did reduce the risks of fetal overgrowth, shoulder dystocia, cesarean delivery, and hypertensive disorders.
- Lactation improves glucose metabolism and may prevent DM after GDM delivery. Higher lactation intensity and longer duration are independently associated with lower 2-year incidences of DM after GDM pregnancy.[1]

PREVENTION

Regular exercise, maintenance of ideal body weight, and high-fiber low-glycemic diet

SUGGESTED READINGS
Available at www.expertconsult.com

RELATED CONTENT

Gestational Diabetes (Patient Information)
Diabetes Mellitus (Related Key Topic)

AUTHORS: **MARY BETH SUTTER M.D., NIRALI BORA, M.D., SUSANNA R. MAGEE, M.D., M.P.H.,** and **HEIDI RADLINSKI, M.D., M.P.H.**

[1]Gunderson EP, et al.: Lactation and Progression to Type 2 Diabetes Mellitus After Gestational Diabetes Mellitus: A Prospective Cohort Study, Ann Intern Med 163:889-898, 2015.

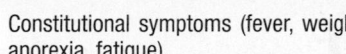 **BASIC INFORMATION**

DEFINITION

Giant cell arteritis (GCA) is a segmental systemic granulomatous arteritis affecting medium and large arteries in individuals >50 yr. Inflammation primarily targets extracranial blood vessels (external carotids, temporal arteries, ciliary and ophthalmic arteries). Subclavian and brachial arteries can also be affected. Intracranial arteritis is rare.

SYNONYMS

Temporal arteritis
Cranial arteritis
GCA
Horton's disease

ICD-10CM CODES
M31.5 Giant cell arteritis with polymyalgia rheumatica
M31.6 Other giant cell arteritis

EPIDEMIOLOGY & DEMOGRAPHICS

INCIDENCE: 17 to 23.3 new cases per 100,000 persons >50 yr; peak incidence is in patients ages 60 to 80 yr.
PREVALENCE: 10 cases per 100,000 persons; it is the most common primary vasculitis; female/male predominance of twofold to fourfold; more common in Caucasians.

PHYSICAL FINDINGS & CLINICAL PRESENTATION

GCA can present with the following clinical manifestations:
• Headache, often associated with marked scalp tenderness—noticed while brushing hair (hair comb allodynia).

TABLE 1G-5 Atypical Manifestations of Giant Cell Arteritis

Fever of unknown origin
Respiratory symptoms (especially cough)
Otolaryngeal manifestations
  Glossitis
  Lingual infarction
  Throat pain
  Hearing loss
Large-artery disease
  Aortic aneurysm
  Aortic dissection
  Limb claudication
  Raynaud's phenomenon
Neurologic manifestations
  Peripheral neuropathy
  Transient ischemic attack (TIA) or stroke
  Dementia
  Delirium
Myocardial infarction
Tumorlike lesions
  Breast mass
  Ovarian and uterine mass
Syndrome of inappropriate antidiuretic hormone secretion (SIADH)
Microangiopathic hemolytic anemia

From Harris ED et al: *Kelly's textbook of rheumatology*, ed 7, Philadelphia, 2005, Saunders.

• Constitutional symptoms (fever, weight loss, anorexia, fatigue).
• Polymyalgia rheumatica (aching and stiffness of the trunk and proximal muscle groups).
• Visual disturbances (transient or permanent monocular or binocular visual loss).
• Intermittent claudication of jaw and tongue on mastication that is especially prominent when solid food such as steak is chewed.
• Table 1G-5 describes atypical manifestations of GCA.
  Important physical findings in GCA:
• Vascular examination: The temporal artery demonstrates tenderness, decreased pulsation, and nodulation (ropy) (Fig. 1G-9); diminished or absent pulses in upper extremities may be seen.

ETIOLOGY

Vasculitis of unknown etiology.

Dx **DIAGNOSIS**

Clinical history and vascular examination remain cornerstones of diagnosis. An algorithm for diagnosing GCA is described in Fig. 1G-10. The American College of Rheumatology has proposed the following criteria for the diagnosis of GCA. Presence of three or more of these criteria in a patient with suspected vasculitis is considered to be diagnostic for GCA.

• Age of onset of symptoms >50 yr.
• New-onset of or new type of localized headache.
• Temporal artery abnormalities including tenderness or decreased pulsation.
• Westergren erythrocyte sedimentation rate (ESR) elevated (typically >50 mm/hr).
• Temporal artery biopsy with vasculitis and mononuclear cell infiltrate or granulomatous changes.

DIFFERENTIAL DIAGNOSIS

• Other vasculitic syndromes.
• Nonarteritic anterior ischemic optic neuropathy (NAION).
• Pituitary apoplexy.
• Primary amyloidosis.
• Transient ischemic attack, stroke.
• Infections.
• Occult neoplasm, multiple myeloma.

LABORATORY TESTS

• ESR elevated although up to 22.5% of patients with GCA have normal ESR before treatment.
• C-reactive protein (CRP) is typically included in laboratory investigation; it may have greater sensitivity than ESR. CRP typically rises before the ESR.
• Mild to moderate normochromic normocytic anemia, elevated platelet count.

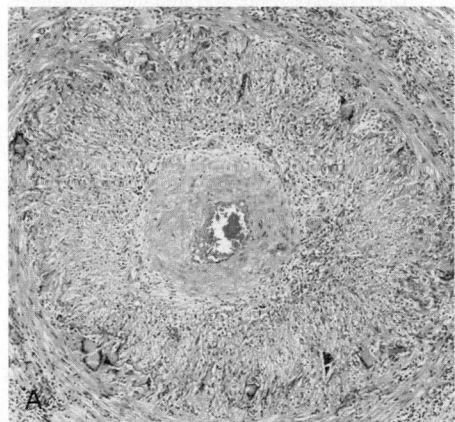
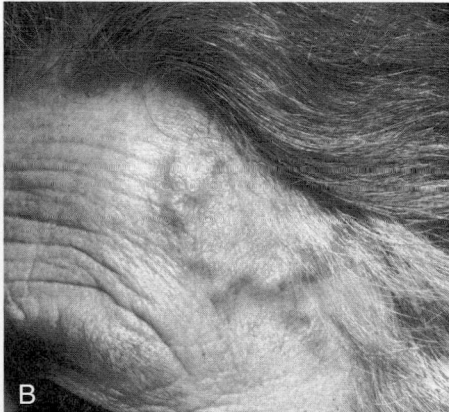
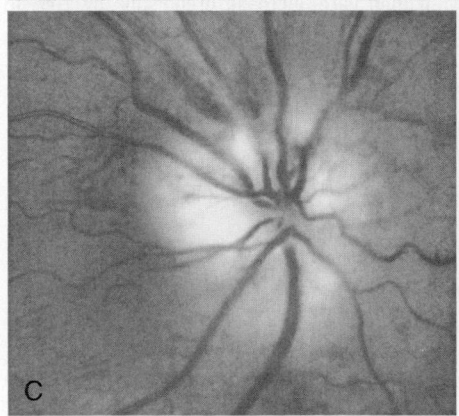
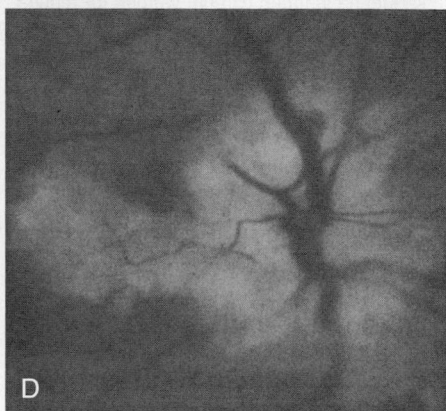

FIGURE G1-9 Giant cell arteritis. A, Histology shows transmural granulomatous inflammation, disruption of the internal elastic lamina, proliferation of the intima, and gross narrowing of the lumen. **B,** The superficial temporal artery is pulseless, nodular, and thickened. **C,** Ischemic optic neuropathy. **D,** Ischemic optic neuropathy and cilioretinal artery occlusion. (From Kanski JJ, Bowling B: *Clinical ophthalmology, a systematic approach,* ed 7, Philadelphia, 2010, Saunders.)

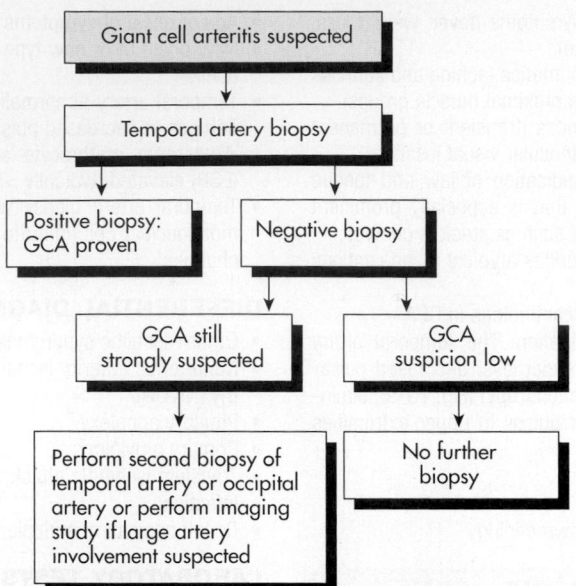

FIGURE G1-10 Algorithm for diagnosing giant cell arteritis (GCA). (From Firestein GS et al: *Kelly's textbook of rheumatology*, ed 9, Philadelphia, 2013, Saunders.)

IMAGING STUDIES

- Color duplex ultrasonography of temporal artery produces three characteristic features—periluminal "halo" over the temporal artery involved, segmental arterial stenosis, and arterial luminal occlusion in severe cases. Clinical utility is not superior to clinical examination with biopsy.
- Contrasted MRI of temporal artery may be performed in patients with contraindications to surgical biopsy of the superficial temporal artery, if treatment with steroids has not been initiated.
- Angiography of the arms is indicated in patients with peripheral vascular insufficiency.

Rx TREATMENT

ACUTE GENERAL Rx

- If there is clinical suspicion of GCA, treatment should be initiated without waiting for results of laboratory or imaging studies.
- IV methylprednisolone (250-1000 mg for 1-3 days) is considered standard of care in patients with severe clinical manifestations such as visual loss from ischemic optic neuropathy.
- Oral prednisone (1 mg/kg/day): high-dose oral regimen should be continued at least

until symptoms resolve and ESR returns to normal. Steroid taper is very slow (10%-20% per month) with monitoring of clinical features as well as ESR and CRP. When dose <10 mg/day, taper by 1 mg/month. Treatment may last up to 2 yr or more.

Corticosteroids are the treatment of choice. There is no evidence for the role of steroid-sparing agents. Methotrexate, tocilizumab, and cyclophosphamide may be considered in cases of contraindications to or failure of corticosteroid therapy. Evidence for their efficacy is limited.

DISPOSITION

With steroid therapy there is a dramatic improvement of systemic symptoms, but not vision in patients with ischemic optic neuropathy. In one study only 4% of eyes improved in both visual acuity and central visual field.

Management of flares: Repeat prednisone induction if patient experiences severe flare. If mild flare, increase prednisone by 10% to 20%.

REFERRAL

- Surgical or ophthalmologic referral for biopsy of temporal artery.
- Rheumatology referral for long-term immunosuppressive treatment management.

ⓘ PEARLS & CONSIDERATIONS

- Treatment of GCA should be started if there is clinical suspicion of the disease. This usually includes patients above the age of 55 presenting with a severe headache and systemic features that suggest GCA as well. Physicians should not wait for laboratory or pathologic confirmation before starting treatment as the risk of visual loss increases.
- Temporal artery biopsy should be performed as soon as possible, but within 2 weeks of initiating treatment with steroids.
- Treatment should not be withheld pending temporal artery biopsy.

COMMENTS

- The relation between polymyalgia rheumatica and GCA is unclear, but the two frequently coexist. They are considered to be different points along the gradient or spectrum of the same disease.
- Clinical picture rather than ESR should be the prime yardstick for continuing prednisone therapy. A rising ESR in a clinically asymptomatic patient with normal hematocrit should raise suspicion for alternate explanations (e.g., infections, neoplasms).
- GCA is associated with a markedly increased risk for the development of aortic aneurysm, which is often a late complication and may cause death. Annual chest radiograph in chronic CGA patients has been suggested, as well as emergent chest CT or MRI for clinical suspicion.
- GCA is also associated with increased risk of myocardial infarction, stroke, and peripheral vascular disease.
- Coadministration of low dose aspirin (81 mg/day) has been reported by some as effective for further reduction of risk of blindness. Additional trials may be needed before it can be recommended as standard therapy.

SUGGESTED READINGS

Available at www.expertconsult.com.

RELATED CONTENT

Giant Cell Arteritis (Patient Information)
Temporal Arteritis (Patient Information)

AUTHORS: **ARUN SWAMINATHAN, M.B.B.S.**, and **SACHIN KEDAR, M.B.B.S., M.D.**

 BASIC INFORMATION

DEFINITION

Giardiasis is an intestinal and/or biliary tract infection caused by the protozoal parasite *Giardia intestinalis* (also known as *G. lamblia* or *G. duodenalis*). The organism is a widespread zoonotic parasite and frequently contaminates fresh water sources worldwide.

SYNONYMS

Giardiasis
Giardia duodenalis
Giardia intestinalis

ICD-10CM CODES
A07.1 Giardiasis [lambliasis]

EPIDEMIOLOGY & DEMOGRAPHICS

INCIDENCE (IN U.S.):
- Exact incidence unknown. CDC estimates 20,000 cases a year in the U.S.
- Frequently occurs as water-borne outbreaks in international adoptees, travelers, and immunocompromised patients
- *G. lamblia* has been demonstrated in 4% to 7% of submitted stool specimens, making it the most commonly identified intestinal parasite.

PREVALENCE (IN U.S.): 4%
PREDOMINANT SEX: Male = female
PREDOMINANT AGE:
- Preschool children, especially if in day care
- 20 to 40 yr of age, especially among sexually active homosexual men

PEAK INCIDENCE:
- Varies with risk factors, outbreaks, but peak onset from early summer through early fall
- All age groups affected

GENETICS: Familial disposition: Patients with common variable immunodeficiency or X-linked agammaglobulinemia are at increased risk of infection.

PHYSICAL FINDINGS & CLINICAL PRESENTATION
- More than 70% with one or more intestinal symptoms (diarrhea, flatulence, cramps,

TABLE 1G-6 Clinical Signs and Symptoms of Giardiasis

Symptom	Frequency (%)
Diarrhea	64-100
Malaise, weakness	72-97
Abdominal distention	42-97
Flatulence	35-97
Abdominal cramps	44-81
Nausea	14-79
Foul-smelling, greasy stools	15-79
Anorexia	41-73
Weight loss	53-73
Vomiting	14-35
Fever	0-28
Constipation	0-27

From Kliegman RM et al: *Nelson textbook of pediatrics*, ed 19, Philadelphia, 2011, Saunders.

bloating, nausea). Table 1G-6 summarizes clinical signs and symptoms of giardiasis
- Incubation period averages 7 to 14 days but can be longer
- Fever in <30%
- Chronic diarrhea, malabsorption, and weight loss, which can be up to 10% of body weight, are common
- GI bleeding is unusual
- Continuous or intermittent symptoms, lasting for 2 to 4 weeks
- Of infected patients, 20% to 25% are asymptomatic and can shed cysts for months

ETIOLOGY

Infection is acquired by ingestion of viable cysts of the organism (Fig. 1G-11), typically in contaminated water or food or by fecal-oral contact. *Giardia* cysts are resistant to chlorination and survive well in cold mountain streams.

 DIAGNOSIS

DIFFERENTIAL DIAGNOSIS
- Other agents of infective diarrhea (amebae, *Salmonella* sp., *Shigella* sp., *Staphylococcus aureus, Cryptosporidium,* etc.)
- Noninfectious causes of malabsorption

WORKUP
- Stool specimen (three specimens yield 90% sensitivity) as a saline suspension or duodenal aspirate for microscopic examination to establish diagnosis and exclude other pathogens
- Immunoassays for *Giardia* sp. Antigens in stool samples such as the DFA or ELISA are now routinely used in most clinical laboratories. These assays are 85% to 98% sensitive and 90% to 100% specific. They also have a faster turnaround time.

LABORATORY TESTS

Serum albumin, vitamin B_{12} levels, and stool fat test to exclude malabsorption

IMAGING STUDIES
- Not necessary unless biliary obstruction is suspected

- In detection of organism, possible interference by barium in stool from radiographic studies

Rx TREATMENT

NONPHARMACOLOGIC THERAPY

Avoidance of milk products to reduce symptoms of transient lactase deficiency that occur in many patients and can last for weeks to months

GENERAL Rx

Adult and pediatric:
- Tinidazole: 2 g single dose (50 mg/kg in children over 3 years of age).
- Metronidazole 250 mg PO three times daily for 5 to 7 days. Pediatric dose: 5 mg/kg tid × 7 days (metronidazole should be avoided in pregnancy).
- Nitazoxanide: aged 12 to 47 mo: 100 mg bid × 3 days. Aged 4 to 11 yr: 200 mg bid × 3 days
- Albendazole 400 mg PO qd x 5 days
- Paromomycin 25 to 35 mg/kg/day in three doses for 5 to 10 days
- Can be used in pregnancy

DISPOSITION

Reinfection is possible.

! PEARLS & CONSIDERATIONS

COMMENTS

Travelers to endemic areas (developing world, wilderness areas) should be cautioned to boil drinking water or use water purification tablets. Chronic giardiasis as seen in developing nations can cause delays in growth and development in children due to malabsorption and diarrhea.

SUGGESTED READINGS
Available at www.expertconsult.com

RELATED CONTENT
Giardiasis (Patient Information)

AUTHOR: **GLENN G. FORT, M.D., M.P.H.**

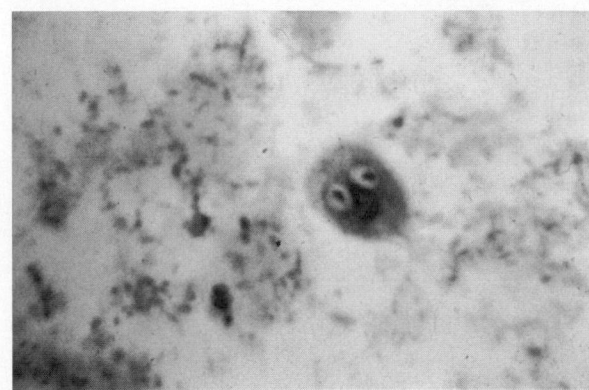

FIGURE 1G-11 *Giardia lamblia* trophozoite is demonstrated in a trichrome stain of fecal material. Note the prominent nuclei in the trophozoite. (Bennett JE, Dolin R, Blaser MJ: *Mandell, Douglas, and Bennett's principles and practice of infectious diseases*, ed 8, Philadelphia, 2015, Saunders.)

 **BASIC INFORMATION**

DEFINITION

Gilbert's syndrome is an autosomal-dominant disorder characterized by indirect hyperbilirubinemia caused by impaired glucuronyl transferase activity.

SYNONYMS

Gilbert's disease

ICD-10CM CODES

E80.4 Gilbert's syndrome

EPIDEMIOLOGY & DEMOGRAPHICS

INCIDENCE (IN U.S.): Probable autosomal-dominant disease affecting >5% of the U.S. population
PREDOMINANT SEX: Male/female ratio of 3:1
GENETICS: Most common hereditary hyperbilirubinemia (genotypic prevalence 12%)

PHYSICAL FINDINGS & CLINICAL PRESENTATION

- No abnormalities on physical examination other than mild jaundice when bilirubin exceeds 3 mg/dl.

- A family history of unconjugated hyperbilirubinemia may be present.

ETIOLOGY

- Decreased elimination of bilirubin in bile is caused by inadequate conjugation of bilirubin.
- Alcohol consumption and starvation diet can increase bilirubin level.
- The pathogenesis of Gilbert's syndrome has been linked to a reduction in the bilirubin UGT-1 gene *(HUG-Brl)* transcription, resulting from a mutation in the promoter region.

 **DIAGNOSIS**

DIFFERENTIAL DIAGNOSIS

- Hemolytic anemia.
- Liver disease (chronic hepatitis, cirrhosis).
- Crigler-Najjar syndrome.

WORKUP

- Most patients are diagnosed during or after adolescence, when isolated hyperbilirubinemia is detected as an incidental finding on routine biochemical testing.
- Laboratory evaluation to exclude hemolysis and liver diseases as a cause of the elevated bilirubin level (Table 1G-7).

LABORATORY TESTS

Elevated indirect (unconjugated) bilirubin (rarely exceeds 5 mg/dl).

 **TREATMENT**

ACUTE GENERAL Rx

Treatment is generally unnecessary. Phenobarbital (if clinical jaundice is present) can rapidly decrease serum indirect bilirubin level.

DISPOSITION

Prognosis is excellent. Treatment is generally unnecessary.

REFERRAL

Referral is generally not necessary.

❗ PEARLS & CONSIDERATIONS

COMMENTS

- Patients should be reassured about the benign nature of their condition.
- Fasting for 2 days or significant dehydration may raise the bilirubin level and result in the clinical recognition of jaundice.

AUTHOR: **FRED F. FERRI, M.D.**

TABLE 1G-7 Characteristic Patterns of Liver Function Tests

Disorder	Bilirubin	Alkaline Phosphatase	AST	ALT	Prothrombin Time	Albumin
Gilbert's syndrome (abnormal bilirubin metabolism)	↑	NL	NL	NL	NL	NL
Bile duct obstruction (pancreatic cancer)	↑↑↑	↑↑↑	↑	↑	↑-↑↑	NL
Acute hepatocellular damage (toxic, viral hepatitis)	↑-↑↑↑	↑-↑↑	↑↑↑	↑↑↑	NL-↑↑↑	NL-↓↓
Cirrhosis	NL-↑	NL-↑	NL-↑	NL-↑	NL-↑↑	NL-↓↓

ALT, Alanine aminotransferase; *AST,* aspartate aminotransferase; *NL,* normal; ↑ increase; ↓, decrease (arrows indicate extent of change: ↑-↑↑↑, slight to large).
From Andreoli TE (ed): *Cecil essentials of medicine,* ed 6, Philadelphia, 2005, Saunders.

BASIC INFORMATION

DEFINITION

Inflammation of the gums covering the maxilla and mandible.

SYNONYMS

None

ICD-10CM CODES
K05.0 Acute gingivitis
K05.1 Chronic gingivitis
K05.6 Other disorders of gingiva and
edentulous alveolar ridge

EPIDEMIOLOGY & DEMOGRAPHICS

Gingivitis generally occurs in adults.

PHYSICAL FINDINGS & CLINICAL PRESENTATION

- Inflammation is usually painless. Red velvety gingiva may be present (Fig. 1G-12).
- Bleeding may occur with minor trauma such as brushing teeth.
- A bluish discoloration of the gums and halitosis are sometimes present.
- Subgingival plaque may be seen on close examination, and in time, there is detachment of soft tissue from the tooth surface.
- Long-standing infection may lead to destructive periodontal disease, which may involve teeth and bones.
- A dramatic form of gingivitis called acute ulcerative necrotizing gingivitis (ANUG or "trench mouth") can occur. This is manifested by acute, painful inflammation of the gingivae, with bleeding, ulceration, and halitosis. At times this is accompanied by fever and lymphadenopathy.
- Linear gingival erythema ("HIV gingivitis") presents as a brightly inflamed band of marginal gingiva. It may be painful, with easy bleeding and rapid destruction.
- Severe periodontitis can occur in patients with diabetes mellitus or HIV infection and in primary HIV infection (acute retroviral syndrome).

- Pregnancy may be associated with an acute form of gingivitis. Gingivae become inflamed and hypertrophic; this is likely the result of hormonal shifts.

ETIOLOGY

- A variety of organisms may be found in the environment of plaque. Anaerobes play a predominant role in periodontal disease.
- Improper hygiene and poorly fitting dentures may contribute to the development of gingivitis.
- Excessive use of tobacco and alcohol may predispose individuals to gingival disease.
- In patients with HIV infection, gram-negative anaerobes, enteric organisms, and yeast predominate.
- Appropriate oral hygiene, such as flossing and tooth brushing, can prevent the accumulation of bacterial plaque; once dense plaque is present, adequate hygiene becomes more difficult.

DIAGNOSIS

DIFFERENTIAL DIAGNOSIS

Gingival hyperplasia, which may be caused by long-term use of phenytoin or nifedipine.

WORKUP

Oral examination.

LABORATORY TESTS

Elevated serum glucose in diabetics.

IMAGING STUDIES

Radiographs of the teeth and facial bones may reveal extension of infection to these structures.

TREATMENT

NONPHARMACOLOGIC THERAPY

Removal of plaque, and at times, debridement of soft tissue.

ACUTE GENERAL Rx

- Penicillin VK, 500 mg PO qid for 1 to 2 wk or
- Clindamycin, 300 mg PO qid for 1 to 2 wk.
- For linear gingival erythema, chlorhexidine gluconate rinses and nystatin rinses or troches may be used.

CHRONIC Rx

Extensive or recurrent infection may require periodic evaluation and debridement.

DISPOSITION

Continued inflammation can eventually lead to destruction of teeth and bone.

REFERRAL

Patients should be referred to a dentist or periodontist.

PEARLS & CONSIDERATIONS

COMMENTS

- Presence of periodontal disease is associated with an increased incidence of anaerobic pleuropulmonary infections.
- Existing data support the recommendation to change a toothbrush every 3 mo. Worn brushes seem to be less effective in plaque reduction.

SUGGESTED READINGS

Available at www.expertconsult.com

RELATED CONTENT

Gingivitis (Patient Information)
Gingivitis, Necrotizing Ulcerative (Related Key Topic)

AUTHOR: **GLENN G. FORT, M.D., M.P.H.**

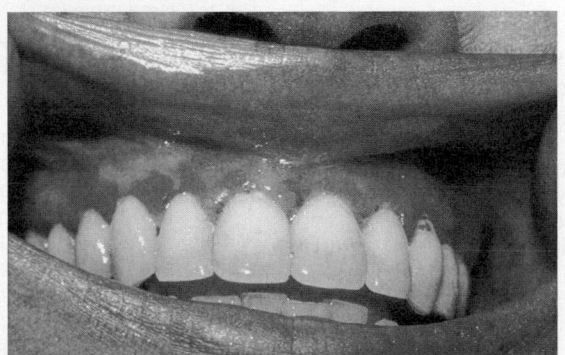

FIGURE 1G-12 Gingivitis in a patient with cicatricial pemphigoid. This pattern of periodontal, chronic, red, velvety gingivitis is very suggestive of this disorder but may occur in other blistering diseases. (From White GM, Cox NH [eds]: *Diseases of the skin, a color atlas and text*, ed 2, St Louis, 2006, Mosby.)

BASIC INFORMATION

DEFINITION

Glaucoma is a chronic degenerative optic neuropathy (or the high potential for such degeneration due to risk factors) in which the neuro-retinal rim of the optic nerve becomes progressively thinner, thereby enlarging the optic-nerve cup. The classification of glaucoma is based on the appearance of the iridocorneal angle (open angle vs. closed angle) and is further subdivided into primary and secondary types. Primary open-angle glaucoma can occur with or without elevated intraocular pressure (IOP). Normal tension glaucoma refers to primary open-angle glaucoma without elevated intraocular pressure.

SYNONYMS

Primary open-angle glaucoma (POAG)
Open-angle glaucoma (OAG)
Secondary open-angle glaucoma (e.g., pseudoexfoliation, pigment dispersion, trauma, inflammatory)
Chronic open-angle glaucoma

ICD-10CM CODES
H40.10X0	Unspecified open-angle glaucoma, stage unspecified
H40.10X1	Unspecified open-angle glaucoma, mild stage
H40.10X2	Unspecified open-angle glaucoma, moderate stage
H40.10X3	Unspecified open-angle glaucoma, severe stage
H40.10X4	Unspecified open-angle glaucoma, indeterminate stage
H40.11X0	Primary open-angle glaucoma, stage unspecified
H40.11X1	Primary open-angle glaucoma, mild stage
H40.11X2	Primary open-angle glaucoma, moderate stage
H40.11X3	Primary open-angle glaucoma, severe stage
H40.11X4	Primary open-angle glaucoma, indeterminate stage

EPIDEMIOLOGY & DEMOGRAPHICS

INCIDENCE (IN U.S.): Third most common cause of vision loss (75% to 95% of all forms of glaucoma are open angle)
PEAK INCIDENCE:
- Increases after age 40 yr
- Three million cases expected by 2020 because of the rapid increase in aging population

PREVALENCE (IN U.S.):
- Overall prevalence in U.S. population aged >40 yr is estimated to be 1.86%, with 1.57 million white and 398,000 black patients affected. By 2020, we may expect more than 3 million cases in the U.S.
- 150,000 patients have bilateral blindness.
- Prevalence is higher in diabetics, those with high myopia, and older persons.
- More common in African-American population (three times the age-adjusted prevalence than whites). There is a genetic tendency to

OAG; multiple genes have been isolated that are associated with development of high IOP and optic nerve damage.

PREDOMINANT AGE:
- Persons >50 yr
- Can occur in 30s and 40s, and juvenile forms are rare

PHYSICAL FINDINGS & CLINICAL PRESENTATION

- High intraocular pressures and/or large optic nerve cup (Ocular Hypertension Treatment Study results very important).
- Abnormal visual fields (with advanced glaucoma damage to the optic nerve).
- Open anterior chamber angle—evaluated with gonioscopy.
- Since early treatable stages of OAG normally have no symptoms, it's important to have routine eye exams, especially patients with family history and patients over 60 yr.
- Secondary forms of OAG may exhibit ocular findings such as pseudo-exfoliation, pigment dispersion, blood in anterior chamber, inflammation.

ETIOLOGY

- Uncertain hereditary tendency (multifactorial genetics).
- Topical steroids can induce high IOP and cause glaucoma.
- Trauma.
- Inflammatory (e.g., history of uveitis).
- High-dose oral corticosteroids taken for prolonged periods.

DIAGNOSIS

DIFFERENTIAL DIAGNOSIS

- Other optic neuropathies (previous retinal vascular disorders, optic nerve pits, or coloboma).
- Ocular hypertension: IOP is chronically elevated, but not causing optic nerve damage, must monitor closely.
- Secondary glaucoma from inflammation and steroid therapy.
- Trauma.

WORKUP

- Comprehensive eye examination
- Intraocular pressure
- Slit lamp examination
- Visual fields
- Gonioscopy: to determine the type of glaucoma
- Nerve fiber analysis (e.g., GDx, OCT, and HRT)
- Corneal thickness (thick central cornea will result in possible overestimation of the true physiologic IOP, and vice versa, so this is important information in diagnosis and treatment of OAG)

LABORATORY TESTS

Blood sugar

IMAGING STUDIES

- Optic nerve photography—stereo photographs.
- Visual field testing.

- Laser scan of nerve fiber layer, OCT, HRT. Rarely, MRI of orbits if the glaucoma findings are atypical or suspicious of other causes of optic nerve atrophy.

TREATMENT

ACUTE GENERAL Rx

- β-blockers (e.g., timolol) qd to bid depending on individual response to drug.
- Carbonic anhydrase inhibitors (e.g., Diamox 250 mg qid or 500 mg bid).
- Prostaglandin analogues (latanoprost, bimatoprost, travoprost, tafluprost) are commonly used as first-line treatment. They lower intraocular pressure by 25% to 30% by increasing uveoscleral outflow and reducing aqueous production.
- Alpha-2 agonists and cholinergic agonists.
- Hyperosmotic agents (mannitol) in acute treatment (IV).
- Selective laser trabeculoplasty (SLT) may delay or forestall need for second eyedrop. The effect may be temporary but the laser can be repeated.

CHRONIC Rx

- At least biannual checks of intraocular pressure and adjustment of medication.
- Surgical trabeculectomy and filter valve surgeries can be considered for glaucoma that progresses (optic nerve changes or visual field progression) despite maximal tolerated medical therapies. Recently, minimally invasive glaucoma surgeries (MIGS) have been advocated for IOP control. Some are performed at the time of cataract procedures and some are independent procedures. The effort is to reduce the risks associated with traditional trabeculectomy.

DISPOSITION

Must be followed by ophthalmologist.

REFERRAL

Immediately to ophthalmologist.

PEARLS & CONSIDERATIONS

COMMENTS

- Glaucoma is a serious blinding disease that must be monitored professionally by an ophthalmologist. It is mostly asymptomatic until late in the disease when visual problems arise. Even in developed countries half of glaucoma cases are undiagnosed.
- Risk factors that should prompt referral to an ophthalmologist for evaluation of glaucoma are high intraocular pressure, family history of glaucoma, use of systemic or topical corticosteroids, older age, and black race.
- Vision loss from glaucoma cannot be recovered. Early diagnosis and treatment may minimize visual loss.
- Glaucoma is not solely caused by increased intraocular pressure because approximately

20% of patients with glaucoma have normal intraocular pressure. However, high pressure is definitely a risk factor to be considered. Potential sites of increased resistance to aqueous flow are described in Fig. 1G-13.

EBM EVIDENCE

Available at www.expertconsult.com

SUGGESTED READINGS

Available at www.expertconsult.com

RELATED CONTENT

Glaucoma (Patient Information)

AUTHOR: **R. SCOTT HOFFMAN, M.D.**

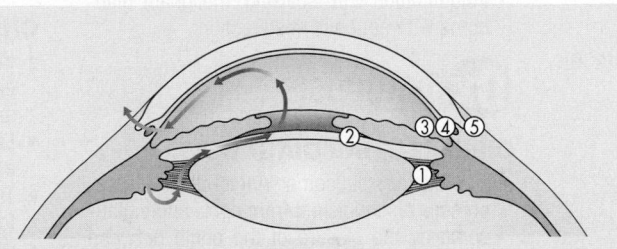

1 Ciliary body processes (when ciliary body swollen by congestion), fibrin debris, vitreous face against the lens equator
2 Pupillary block by anterior position of lens or swollen lens
3 Pretrabecular by neovascular or cellular membranes
4 Trabecular by abnormal accumulation of extracellular matrix
5 Post-trabecular by increased episcleral venous pressure

FIGURE 1G-13 Potential sites of increased resistance to aqueous flow. (From Yanoff M, Duker JS: *Ophthalmology*, ed 2, St Louis, 2004, Mosby.)

BASIC INFORMATION

DEFINITION
Primary angle-closure glaucoma occurs when elevated intraocular pressure is associated with closure of the filtration angle or obstruction in the circulating pathway of the aqueous humor.

SYNONYMS
Acute glaucoma, angle-closure glaucoma (ACG)
Pupillary block glaucoma
Narrow-angle glaucoma
Angle-closure glaucoma

ICD-10CM CODES
H40.061 Primary angle closure without glaucoma damage, right eye
H40.062 Primary angle closure without glaucoma damage, left eye
H40.063 Primary angle closure without glaucoma damage, bilateral
H40.069 Primary angle closure without glaucoma damage, unspecified eye

EPIDEMIOLOGY & DEMOGRAPHICS
INCIDENCE (IN U.S.):
- 2% to 8% of all patients with glaucoma.
- Higher incidence among those with hyperopia, small eyes, dense cataracts, shallow anterior chambers.

PEAK INCIDENCE: Greater >50 yr; high association with hyperopia, cataracts, and eye trauma
PREDOMINANT SEX: Females are affected more often than males.
PREDOMINANT AGE: 50 to 60 yr.
GENETICS: Family history is not particularly helpful; far-sighted (hyperopes) individuals with thickening lenses (i.e., cataracts) are often those with angle-closure attacks

PHYSICAL FINDINGS & CLINICAL PRESENTATION
- Although angle-closure glaucoma can present with an acute painful crisis associated with blurred vision, more than 75% of patients present with an asymptomatic course with progressive loss of the visual field (similar to that in patients with primary open-angle glaucoma; referred to as intermittent, subacute, or chronic angle closure).
- Hazy cornea.
- Narrow angle (Fig. E1G-14).
- Red eyes.
- Pain may be present (supraorbital headache is typical.)
- Injection of conjunctiva.
- Shallow anterior chamber.
- Thick cataract.
- Pupil may be mid-dilated and nonreactive to light.

ETIOLOGY
- Narrow angles with acute closure: blockage of circulatory path of the aqueous humor causing increase in intraocular pressure (IOP). ACG occurs more commonly in eyes with shorter axial length (farsightedness), shallower anterior chamber, and a relatively larger lens (enlarging cataract).
- Secondary angle-closure glaucoma resulting from neovascularization of iris, iris tumors, lens induced, iris scarring, trauma, chronic inflammation with scarring, malignant glaucoma with aqueous misdirection

 **DIAGNOSIS**

DIFFERENTIAL DIAGNOSIS
- Open-angle glaucoma: Angle-closure glaucoma is distinguished from open-angle glaucoma by the closure of the angle between the iris and cornea, obstructing outflow of aqueous humor.
- High pressure.
- Optic nerve cupping.
- Shallow chamber.
- Open-angle glaucoma.
- Conjunctivitis.
- Corneal disease, keratitis.
- Uveitis.
- Scleritis.
- Allergies.
- Contact lens wearing with irritation.

WORKUP
Comprehensive eye examination: if one suspects narrow angle or angle closure, avoid pupil dilation since this may exacerbate the attack
- Intraocular pressure.
- Gonioscopy.
- Slit lamp examination.
- Visual field examination.
- GDx examination (laser scan of nerve fiber layer), OCT.
- Optic nerve evaluation.
- Anterior chamber depth.

LABORATORY TESTS
- Blood sugar and complete blood count (if diabetes or inflammatory disease is suspected).
- Visual field.
- GDx nerve fiber analysis, OCT, Heidelberg retinal tomography.

IMAGING STUDIES
- Fundus photography (optic nerve photos).
- Fluorescein angiography for neovascular disease such as diabetic retinopathy, retinal vein occlusions.
- Ultrasound biomicroscopy and anterior OCT can show relationships of anterior eye structures.

 **TREATMENT**

The goal of treatment is to acutely lower pressure on the eye and keep it down.

NONPHARMACOLOGIC THERAPY
Laser iridotomy early in disease process.

ACUTE GENERAL Rx
- IV mannitol.
- Pilocarpine.
- β-blockers.
- Diamox.
- Laser iridotomy.
- Anterior chamber paracentesis (as emergency treatment).

CHRONIC Rx
- Iridotomy: When there is an adequate peripheral hole in the iris, the chance for future angle closure is usually eliminated.
- Lens removal (cataract extraction) can also eliminate the possibility of ACG.
- Trabeculectomy and filter valve procedures for non-responsive cases.
- Other laser procedures.

DISPOSITION
Refer to ophthalmologist immediately.

REFERRAL
If acute angle-closure episode is suspected, should refer emergently to ophthalmologist.

 **PEARLS & CONSIDERATIONS**

COMMENTS
- Do not use antihistamines or vasodilators with narrow-angle glaucoma.
- After iridotomy, the majority of patients will be totally cured and will need no further medication and have no visual loss.
- Lower socioeconomic status and higher levels of social deprivation are risk factors for delayed detection and probable worse outcomes in glaucoma.
- Risk factors that should prompt referral to an ophthalmologist for evaluation of glaucoma are high intraocular pressure, family history of glaucoma, use of systemic or topical corticosteroids, older age, and black race.
- Glaucoma is undiagnosed in 9 out of 10 affected people worldwide and is undiagnosed in 50% of those in developed countries.

EBM **EVIDENCE**

Available at www.expertconsult.com

SUGGESTED READINGS
Available at www.expertconsult.com

RELATED CONTENT
Glaucoma (Patient Information).

AUTHOR: **R. SCOTT HOFFMAN, M.D.**

BASIC INFORMATION

DEFINITION

Glenohumeral dislocation (Fig. 1G-15) is complete separation or displacement of the humeral head from the glenoid surface (partial separation is termed *subluxation*). Most often the cause is traumatic, and the humeral head dislocates anteriorly and inferiorly. This may cause a tear of the glenoid labrum (the Bankart lesion). Less commonly the head dislocates posteriorly.

Rarely, multidirectional instability may be present in which dislocation or subluxation, often bilateral, may occur in multiple directions, usually the result of excessive joint laxity and generally without trauma.

ICD-10CM CODES

S43.016A	Anterior dislocation of unspecified humerus, initial encounter
S43.026A	Posterior dislocation of unspecified humerus, initial encounter
S43.036A	Inferior dislocation of unspecified humerus, initial encounter
M24.419	Recurrent dislocation, unspecified shoulder
M24.819	Other specific joint derangements of unspecified shoulder, not elsewhere classified

PHYSICAL FINDINGS & CLINICAL PRESENTATION

Traumatic:
- The arm is held in external rotation with anterior dislocation and internal rotation with posterior dislocation.
- Little movement is possible without pain.
- The acromion may appear more prominent, and there is absence of the normal "fullness" beneath the acromion.

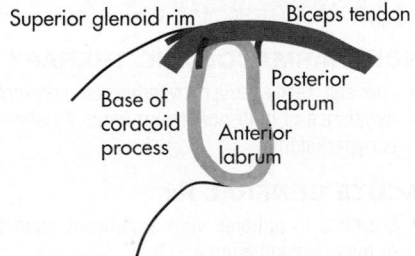

FIGURE 1G-15 Glenohumeral dislocation. (From Weisslederer R et al: *Primer of diagnostic imaging*, St Louis, 2007, Mosby.)

- The status of the axillary nerve must always be checked (sensation to the mid-deltoid should be assessed).
- The apprehension test may become positive if anterior instability persists (pain and apprehension that the shoulder will dislocate when the relaxed arm is manually placed in the "throwing position" of external rotation and abduction).
- Recurrent episodes of anterior dislocation may occur with minor movement, such as putting on a coat or turning off a light.

Multidirectional:
- Often difficult to diagnose, especially if only subluxation occurs.
- Recurrent episodes of giving out and weakness, often bilateral and without trauma.
- Sulcus sign is often positive (the arms are pulled downward with the patient standing; a sulcus [indentation] will form between the acromion and humeral head, indicating excessive inferior movement of the head).
- Other signs of generalized joint laxity may be present, such as joint hyperextensibility and the ability of the patient to touch the thumb against the flexor aspect of the forearm.

ETIOLOGY
- Trauma.
- Generalized joint laxity (multidirectional).
- Seizures (posterior dislocations).

DIAGNOSIS

DIFFERENTIAL DIAGNOSIS
- Rotator cuff rupture.
- Frozen shoulder (posterior dislocation).
- Suprascapular nerve paralysis.
- Anterior Instability.

IMAGING STUDIES
- Acute shoulder injury: true anteroposterior roentgenogram plus lateral view of the glenohumeral joint, either transaxillary or transscapular.
- MRI: to determine soft tissue status, especially the presence of Bankart lesion or rotator cuff tear; may be indicated after a second episode of dislocation.

TREATMENT

- Reduction of the acute dislocation by gentle straight traction in the relaxed patient followed by light immobilization.
- Gentle limited range-of-motion exercises as pain subsides followed by strengthening exercises at 2 wk.

DISPOSITION
- Recurrence of anterior dislocation is common in the young; these patients may have to avoid the arm position associated with dislocation (external rotation with abduction).
- Primary dislocations in patients >40 yr are not generally complicated by recurrence but may result in shoulder stiffness and associated rotator cuff injuries.
- There is an almost 100% recurrence after the third dislocation.

REFERRAL

Surgical reconstruction may be required in the recurrent dislocator.

PEARLS & CONSIDERATIONS

COMMENTS
- It is important to know if there was an injury involved in the first episode and if a radiograph was taken to determine direction of the dislocation.
- Up to 50% of posterior dislocations are missed by the first examiner, usually the result of an inadequate lateral radiograph of the glenohumeral joint.
- "Voluntary" posterior dislocators should always be treated nonsurgically.
- Sports activities may be resumed when there is pain-free full flexibility and normal strength.
- Multidirectional instabilities are usually treated nonsurgically with strengthening exercises.
- Dislocations in either direction are occasionally overlooked. If the injury is over 2 to 4 weeks old, enough tissue healing will have occurred to make closed reduction fail. Open reduction or arthroplasty will then be needed in the young. Older patients may improve with therapeutic exercises, and the resultant disability is often acceptable.

EVIDENCE

Available at www.expertconsult.com

SUGGESTED READINGS
Available at www.expertconsult.com

AUTHOR: **FRED F. FERRI, M.D.**

 **BASIC INFORMATION**

DEFINITION

Acute glomerulonephritis is an immunologically mediated inflammation of the filtering unit of the kidney called the glomerulus. The inflammation may result in damage to the basement membrane, mesangium, and/or capillary endothelium.

SYNONYMS

Acute nephritic syndrome

ICD-10CM CODES

N00.0 Acute nephritic syndrome with minor glomerular abnormality
N00.1 Acute nephritic syndrome with focal and segmental glomerular lesions
N00.2 Acute nephritic syndrome with diffuse membranous glomerulonephritis
N00.3 Acute nephritic syndrome with diffuse mesangial proliferative glomerulonephritis
N00.4 Acute nephritic syndrome with diffuse endocapillary proliferative glomerulonephritis
N00.5 Acute nephritic syndrome with diffuse mesangiocapillary glomerulonephritis
N00.6 Acute nephritic syndrome with dense deposit disease
N00.7 Acute nephritic syndrome with diffuse crescentic glomerulonephritis
N00.8 Acute nephritic syndrome with other morphologic changes
N00.9 Acute nephritic syndrome with unspecified morphologic changes

EPIDEMIOLOGY & DEMOGRAPHICS

- Incidence rates of primary glomerulonephritis vary between 0.2/100,000/yr and 2.5/100,000/yr.
- Immunoglobulin A (IgA) nephropathy (Berger's disease) is the most common glomerulonephritis worldwide.
- Glomerulonephritis accounts for 25% of end-stage renal disease cases.
- Glomerulonephritis affects adults and children.

PHYSICAL FINDINGS & CLINICAL PRESENTATION

- Acute onset of hypertension.
- Dark, "tea-colored" urine.
- Edema (peripheral, periorbital, or pulmonary).
- Fatigue.
- Joint pains, oral ulcers, and malar rash are frequently seen with systemic lupus erythematosus.
- Palpable purpura may be found in patients with systemic vasculitis such as Henoch-Schönlein purpura, ANCA-associated vasculitis, or cryoglobulinemia.
- Heart murmurs may indicate endocarditis.
- History of impetigo or preceding pharyngitis may indicate infection-related glomerulonephritis.
- Concurrent upper respiratory tract infection "synpharyngitic" is commonly associated with flares of IgA nephropathy.

- Nonspecific flu-like symptoms, fatigue, and achiness may indicate ANCA-associated vasculitis.

ETIOLOGY

Acute glomerulonephritis may occur as a kidney-limited disease or a systemic disease. The three mechanisms of primary glomerulonephritis are immune-complex deposition, anti–glomerular basement membrane disease antibodies, and vasculitis with minimal immune staining ("pauci immune" glomerulonephritis)

Immune Complex	Pauci-Immune	Anti–Glomerular Basement Membrane
IgA nephropathy/Henoch Schonlein purpura (IgA Vasculitis)	MPO (ANCA) associated vasculitis	Goodpasture's disease
Lupus nephritis	PR3 (ANCA)-associated vasculitis	
Infection-related glomerulonephritis, including poststreptococcal GN and endocarditis-associated GN	Eosinophilic vasculitis	
Membranoproliferative GN		
Cryoglobulinemic vasculitis		

Table 1G-8 summarizes primary renal diseases that present as acute glomerulonephritis (GN). Diseases associated with rapidly progressive glomerulonephritis and pertinent laboratory findings are described in Table 1G-9.

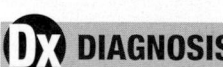 **DIAGNOSIS**

DIFFERENTIAL DIAGNOSIS

- Cirrhosis with edema and ascites.
- Congestive heart failure.
- Acute interstitial nephritis.
- Acute tubular necrosis.
- Severe hypertension.
- Thrombotic microangiopathy.
- Nephrotic syndrome, diabetic nephropathy, amyloidosis, preeclampsia, scleroderma renal crisis.
- Nephrolithiasis.

WORKUP

Initial evaluation of suspected glomerulonephritis consists of laboratory testing.

LABORATORY TESTS

- Urinalysis (hematuria [dysmorphic erythrocytes and red cell casts], proteinuria).
- Serum creatinine (to estimate glomerular filtration rate [GFR]), blood urea nitrogen.
- 24-hr urine for protein excretion and creatinine clearance (to document degree of renal dysfunction and amount of proteinuria). Random urine (spot specimen) protein-to-creatinine ratio is also acceptable in place of a 24-hour collection. Proteinuria in acute glomerulonephritis typically ranges from 500 mg/day to 3 g/day, but nephrotic-range proteinuria (>3.5 g/day) may be present.
- Streptococcal tests (Streptozyme), anti-streptolysin O (ASO) quantitative titer (highest in 3 to 5 wk); ASO titer, however, is not related to severity of renal disease, duration, or prognosis.

- Additional serologic testing: anti-DNA antibodies (rule out SLE), C3 complement, C4 complement, cryoglobulins, rheumatoid factor, hepatitis B and C serologies, antineutrophil cytoplasmic antibodies (MPO and PR3), and antiglomerular basement membrane (type alpha[3] IV collagen) antibodies, serum and urine protein electrophoresis, and serum kappa and lambda free light chains.
- Hematocrit and platelet count (decreased in thrombotic microangiopathy).
- Blood cultures are indicated in all febrile patients.

- Antigens identified in glomerulonephritis are described in Table 1G-10.

IMAGING STUDIES

- Chest x-ray: Pulmonary involvement may be seen in ANCA-associated vasculitis and Goodpasture's syndrome.
- Renal ultrasound to evaluate renal size. A kidney size of <9 cm is suggestive of extensive scarring and low likelihood of reversibility.
- Echocardiogram in patients with new cardiac murmurs or positive blood cultures to rule out endocarditis and pericardial effusion.
- Renal biopsy with light (Fig. 1G-16), electron, and immunofluorescence microscopy to confirm diagnosis.
- Biopsy of other affected organs if systemic vasculitis is suspected.

 **TREATMENT**

NONPHARMACOLOGIC THERAPY

- Low-salt diet if edema or hypertension is present
- Avoidance of high-potassium foods if patient is hyperkalemic

ACUTE GENERAL Rx

- Diuretics in patients with significant edema or hypertension edema
- Correction of electrolyte abnormalities (hypocalcemia, hyperkalemia) and acidosis
- High-dose steroids for rapidly progressive glomerulonephritis
- Additional immunosuppressive treatment with alkylating agents, calcineurin inhibitors, or biologic agents (e.g., rituximab) may be necessary depending on the underlying disease
- Treatment of streptococcal infection with penicillin (or erythromycin in penicillin-allergic patients). Hemodialysis in patients with diuretic-resistant volume overload, hyperkalemia, uremic symptoms, and encephalopathy. Plasma exchange therapy

Diseases
and Disorders

TABLE 1G-8 Summary of Primary Renal Diseases That Manifest as Acute Glomerulonephritis

Diseases	Poststreptococcal Glomerulonephritis	IgA Nephropathy	Goodpasture Syndrome	Idiopathic Rapidly Progressive Glomerulonephritis
Clinical Manifestations				
Age and sex	All ages, mean 7 yr, 2:1 male	10-35 yr, 2:1 male	15-30 yr, 6:1 male	Adults, 2:1 male
Acute nephritic syndrome	90%	50%	90%	90%
Asymptomatic hematuria	Occasionally	50%	Rare	Rare
Nephrotic syndrome	10%-20%	Rare	Rare	10%-20%
Hypertension	70%	30%-50%	Rare	25%
Acute renal failure	50% (transient)	Very rare	50%	60%
Other	Latent period of 1-3 wk	Follows viral syndromes	Pulmonary hemorrhage; iron deficiency anemia	None
Laboratory findings	↑ ASO titers (70%) Positive Streptozyme (95%)↓ C3-C9; normal C1, C4	↑ Serum IgA (50%) IgA in dermal capillaries	Positive anti-GBM antibody	Positive ANCA in some
Immunogenetics	HLA-B12, D "EN" (9)*	HLA-Bw 35, DR4 (4)*	HLA-DR2 (16)*	None established
Renal Pathology				
Light microscopy	Diffuse proliferation	Focal proliferation	Focal → diffuse proliferation with crescents	Crescentic GN
Immunofluorescence	Granular IgG, C3	Diffuse mesangial IgA	Linear IgG, C3	No immune deposits
Electron microscopy	Subepithelial humps	Mesangial deposits	No deposits	No deposits
Prognosis	95% resolve spontaneously 5% RPGN or slowly progressive	Slow progression in 25%-50%	75% stabilize or improve if treated early	75% stabilize or improve if treated early
Treatment	Supportive	Uncertain (options include steroids, fish oil, and ACE inhibitors)	Plasma exchange, steroids, cyclophosphamide	Steroid pulse therapy

ACE, Angiotensin-converting enzyme; *ANCA*, antineutrophil cytoplasmic antibody; *ASO*, anti–streptolysin O; *GBM*, glomerular basement membrane; *GN*, glomerulonephritis; *HLA*, human leukocyte antigen; *Ig*, immunoglobulin; *RPGN*, idiopathic rapidly progressive glomerulonephritis.
*Relative risk.
From Kliegman RM et al: *Practical strategies in pediatric diagnosis and therapy*, ed 2, Philadelphia, 2004, Saunders.

TABLE 1G-9 Diseases Associated with Rapidly Progressive Glomerulonephritis and Pertinent Laboratory Studies

Disease	Studies
Renal Limited	
IgA nephropathy	
Infection-related glomerulonephritis	Low complement, streptococcal serologies, bacterial cultures Echocardiography
ANCA-associated glomerulonephritis (pauci-immune glomerulonephritis)	ANCA titers
Anti-GBM disease (Goodpasture's syndrome)	Anti-GBM antibodies
Systemic Disorders	
Lupus nephritis	Low complement, ANA, dsDNA antibodies
ANCA-associated small-vessel vasculitis	ANCA titers
Goodpasture disease	Anti-GBM antibodies
Henoch-Schönlein purpura	None
Cryoglobulinemic vasculitis	Low complement, cryoglobulins, rheumatoid factor, hepatitis C serologies

ANCA, Antineutrophil cytoplasmic antibody; *ANA*, antinuclear antibodies; *dsDNA*, double-stranded DNA; *GBM*, glomerular basement membrane; *IgA*, immunoglobulin A.
From Vincent JL et al: *Textbook of critical care*, ed 6, Philadelphia, 2011, Saunders.

for concurrent diffuse alveolar hemorrhage or rapidly progressive glomerulonephritis with a low GFR
- Table 1G-11 summarizes suggested management

CHRONIC Rx
- Frequent monitoring of blood pressure, urinalysis, serum creatinine, serum albumin, and random urine for protein-to-creatinine ratio
- Angiotensin-converting enzyme (ACE) inhibitors or angiotensin receptor II blockers (ARBs) are used in patients with persistent proteinuria
- Lipid management with statins and fibrates as indicated
- Monitoring for side effects related to immunosuppression, such as infections, leukopenia and anemia, osteoporosis or osteopenia, gastrointestinal ulcers, high blood pressure, and tumors

- Routine health maintenance with vaccinations for influenza and pneumococcal pneumonia, age-appropriate vaccinations, as well as age-appropriate malignancy screening. Live-vaccines are contraindicated in patients on immunosuppression

DISPOSITION
- Prognosis is generally related to histology, with excellent prognosis in patients with minimal change in glomerulonephritis and focal segmental proliferative glomerulonephritis.
- In general, prognosis is worse in patients with heavy proteinuria, low GFR at presentation, severe hypertension, and crescentic glomerulonephritis.
- Recovery of renal function occurs within 8 to 12 wk in 95% of patients with poststreptococcal glomerulonephritis.

REFERRAL
- Nephrology consultation for all patients with suspected glomerulonephritis. Urgent consultation is recommended if GFR is significantly abnormal or rapidly deteriorating or if the patient has systemic symptoms.

PEARLS & CONSIDERATIONS

COMMENTS
- Kidney biopsy is necessary when the diagnosis will alter the treatment plan; this is usually the case in patients with systemic

TABLE 1G-10 Antigens Identified in Glomerulonephritis

Poststreptococcal GN	Streptococcal pyrogenic exotoxin B, plasmin receptor
Anti-GBM disease	α3 type IV collagen (likely induced by molecular mimicry)
IgA nephropathy	Possibly no antigen but rather polymerized polyclonal IgA (?superantigen driven)
Membranous nephropathy	Phospholipase A_2 receptor (idiopathic), neutral endopeptidase in podocyte (congenital), HBeAg (hepatitis associated)
Staphylococcus aureus–associated GN	*Staphylococcus* superantigens induce polyclonal response; not necessarily antigen in glomeruli
Membranoproliferative GN	HCV and HBsAg in hepatitis-associated MPGN
ANCA-associated vasculitis	Proteinase 3 (c-ANCA) and myeloperoxidase (p-ANCA) in neutrophils; antibodies to lysosome-associated membrane protein 2 on endothelial cells (likely induced by molecular mimicry to fimbriated bacterial antigens)

ANCA, Antineutrophil cytoplasmic antibody; *GBM*, glomerular basement membrane; *GN*, glomerulonephritis; *HBeAg*, hepatitis B virus early antigen; *HBsAg*, hepatitis B surface antigen; *HCV*, hepatitis C virus; *IgA*, immunoglobulin A; *MPGN*, membranoproliferative glomerulonephritis.
From Floege J et al: *Comprehensive clinical nephrology*, ed 4, Philadelphia, 2010, Saunders.

illnesses or significant proteinuria (>500 mg to 1 g) or rising creatinine. Diagnosis of glomerulonephritis is made on kidney biopsy. However, not all patients with suspected glomerulonephritis need a kidney biopsy because of success with supportive therapies (e.g., infection-related GN). A search for systemic illness, including infections, autoimmune disease, and malignancy is needed with careful history, physical examination, and serologic tests.

- Nephrology consultation is necessary before initiation with immunosuppressive therapy. In the absence of contraindications to their use, ACE inhibitor or ARB therapy is essential for proteinuria reduction. Aldosterone receptor antagonists may be used for additional reduction in proteinuria.
- Monitoring of lipids and aggressive treatment of hyperlipidemia is recommended when persistent disease is present.
- Close monitoring of side effects of immunosuppressive drugs and complications of corticosteroids is necessary.

SUGGESTED READINGS

Available at www.expertconsult.com

RELATED CONTENT

Glomerulonephritis (Patient Information)
Acute Kidney Injury (Related Key Topic)

AUTHORS: **RUPALI AVASARE, M.D.,** and **JAI RADHAKRISHNAN, M.D.**

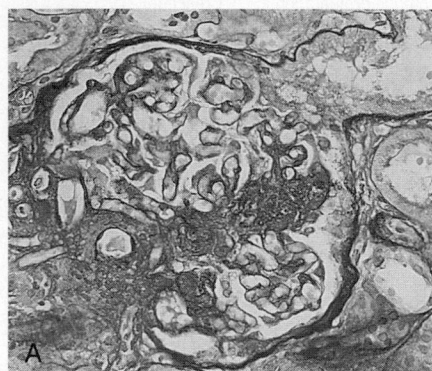 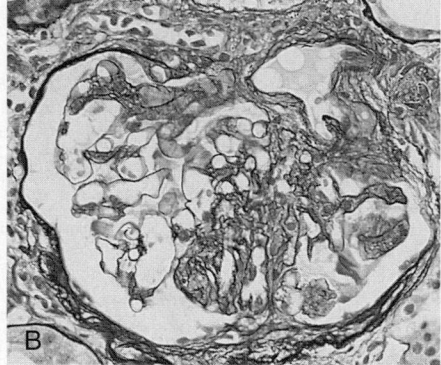

FIGURE 1G-16 Light microscopic appearances in focal segmental glomerulosclerosis. Segmental scars with capsular adhesions in otherwise normal glomeruli. A, Periodic acid-Schiff, ×3300. **B,** Methenamine silver stain, ×3300. (Courtesy Dr. D. Davies. From Johnson RJ, Feehally J: *Comprehensive clinical nephrology,* ed 2, St Louis, 2000, Mosby.)

TABLE 1G-11 Suggested Management of Membranoproliferative Glomerulonephritis

Type	Treatment
All types	Supportive therapy following the recommendations discussed in text
Idiopathic MPGN in children	Non-nephrotic proteinuria, normal renal function: follow with 3-month visits Normal renal function and moderate proteinuria (>3 g/day): prednisone 40 mg/m² on alternate days for 3 months Nephrotic or impaired renal function: prednisone 40 mg/m² on alternate days (80 mg maximum) for 2 years, tapering to 20 mg on alternate days for 3-10 years
Idiopathic MPGN in adults	Non-nephrotic, normal renal function: follow with 3-month visits Nephrotic or impaired renal function: 6-month course of corticosteroid with/without cytotoxic agents (cyclophosphamide) or other drugs used: cyclosporine, tacrolimus, mycophenolate mofetil Rapidly progressive renal failure with diffuse crescents: treat as for idiopathic rapidly progressive glomerulonephritis In the presence of chronic renal failure or nephrotic proteinuria: angiotensin-converting enzyme inhibitors
Hepatitis C–associated glomerulonephritis	Non-nephrotic, normal renal function: treat with interferon alpha based on severity of liver disease (diagnosed by biopsy) Nephrotic syndrome, reduced renal function, or signs of cryoglobulinemia: pegylated interferon alfa-2b (1 mg/kg weekly) and ribavirin (15 mg/kg/day) for 12 months, followed by a short-term course of low-dose corticosteroids; if relapse occurs, consider high-dose interferon alfa (10 million U daily for 2 weeks, then every other day for 6 more weeks). Direct-acting antiviral combination therapy may be considered (e.g., ledipasvir 90 mg/sofosbuvir 400 mg, 1 tablet daily for 12 weeks) Rapidly progressive renal failure or severe symptoms of vasculitis (heart failure, pulmonary disease): methylprednisolone 1 g daily for 3 days, followed by oral prednisone 60 mg/daily with slow taper during 2-3 months Rituximab 375 mg/m² weekly x4 weeks or cyclophosphamide (2 mg/kg/day with adjustment for renal function) and plasmapheresis may be added as adjunctive therapy; when the prednisone is reduced to 20 mg/day and the cyclophosphamide is discontinued, antiviral therapy (as above) should be considered.

MPGN, Membranoproliferative glomerulonephritis.
From Floege J et al: *Comprehensive clinical nephrology,* ed 4, Philadelphia, 2010, Saunders.

G

 **BASIC INFORMATION**

DEFINITION

Glossitis is an inflammation of the tongue that can lead to loss of filiform papillae.

ICD-10CM CODES
K14.0 Glossitis
K14.2 Median rhomboid glossitis

EPIDEMIOLOGY & DEMOGRAPHICS

Glossitis is seen more frequently in patients of lower socioeconomic status, malnourished patients, alcoholics, smokers, elderly patients, immunocompromised patients, and patients with dentures.

PHYSICAL FINDINGS & CLINICAL PRESENTATION

- The appearance of the tongue varies depending on the etiology of the glossitis (Fig. 1G-17, A). Loss of filiform papillae results in a red, smooth-surfaced tongue.
- The tongue may appear pale in patients with significant anemia.
- Pain and swelling of the tongue may be present when glossitis is associated with infections, trauma, or lichen planus.
- Ulcerations may be present in patients with herpetic glossitis, pemphigus, or streptococcal infection.
- Excessive use of mouthwash may result in a "hairy" appearance of the tongue (Fig. 1G-17, B)

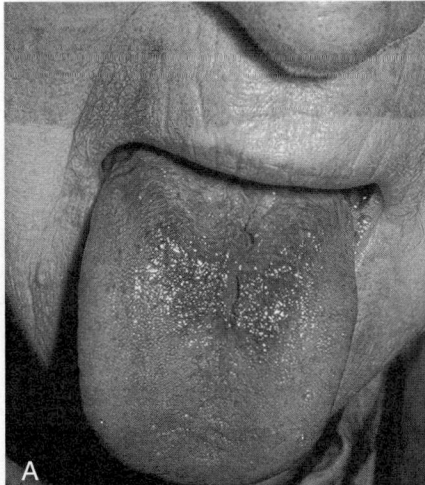

FIGURE 1G-17A Median rhomboid glossitis. (From White GM, Cox NH [eds]: *Diseases of the skin, a color atlas and text,* ed 2, St Louis, 2006, Mosby.)

ETIOLOGY

- Nutritional deficiencies (vitamin E, riboflavin, niacin, vitamin B$_{12}$, iron).
- Infections (viral, candidiasis, tuberculosis, syphilis).
- Trauma (generally caused by poorly fitting dentures).
- Irritation of the tongue from toothpaste, medications, alcohol, tobacco, citrus.
- Lichen planus, pemphigus vulgaris, erythema multiforme.
- Neoplasms.

 **DIAGNOSIS**

DIFFERENTIAL DIAGNOSIS

- Infections.
- Use of chemical irritants.
- Neoplasms.
- Skin disorders (e.g., Behçet's syndrome, erythema multiforme).

WORKUP

- Laboratory evaluation to exclude infectious processes, vitamin deficiencies, and systemic disorders,
- Biopsy of lesion only when there is no response to treatment,

LABORATORY TESTS

- Complete blood count: decreased hemoglobin and hematocrit, low mean corpuscular volume (MCV) (iron-deficiency anemia), elevated MCV (vitamin B$_{12}$ deficiency).

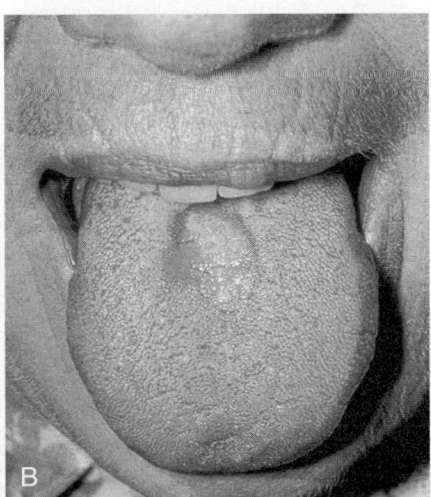

FIGURE 1G-17B Black hairy tongue. (From White GM, Cox NH [eds]: *Diseases of the skin, a color atlas and text,* ed 2, St Louis, 2006, Mosby.)

- Vitamin B$_{12}$ level.
- 10% KOH scrapings in patients with white patches suspect for candidiasis.

 **TREATMENT**

NONPHARMACOLOGIC THERAPY

Avoidance of primary irritants such as hot foods, spices, tobacco, and alcohol.

ACUTE GENERAL Rx

Treatment varies with the etiology of the glossitis.
- Malnutrition with avitaminosis: multivitamins.
- Candidiasis: fluconazole 200 mg on day 1, then 100 mg/day for at least 2 wk or nystatin 400,000 U suspension qid for 10 days or 200,000 pastilles dissolved slowly in the mouth four to five times qd for 10 to 14 days.
- Painful oral lesions: rinsing of the mouth with 2% lidocaine viscous, 1 to 2 tablespoons q4h prn; triamcinolone 0.1% applied to painful ulcers prn for symptomatic relief.

CHRONIC Rx

- Lifestyle changes with elimination of tobacco, alcohol, and other primary irritants.
- Dental evaluation for correction of ill-fitting dentures.
- Correction of associated metabolic abnormalities such as hyperglycemia from diabetes mellitus.

DISPOSITION

Most patients experience prompt improvement with identification and treatment of the cause of the glossitis.

REFERRAL

Surgical referral for biopsy of solitary lesions unresponsive to treatment to rule out neoplasm.

 **PEARLS & CONSIDERATIONS**

COMMENTS

If the primary cause of glossitis is not identified or cannot be corrected, enteric nutritional replacement therapy should be considered in malnourished patients.

RELATED CONTENT

Glossitis (Patient Information)

AUTHOR: **FRED F. FERRI, M.D.**

Diseases and Disorders

I

BASIC INFORMATION

DEFINITION

Gonorrhea is a sexually transmitted bacterial infection with a predilection for columnar and transitional epithelial cells. It commonly manifests as urethritis, cervicitis, or salpingitis. Infection may be asymptomatic. It differs between males and females in course, severity, and ease of recognition.

SYNONYMS

Gonococcal urethritis
Gonococcal vulvovaginitis
Gonococcal cervicitis
Gonococcal bartholinitis
GC

ICD-10CM CODES

A54.9	Gonococcal infection, unspecified
O98.211	Gonorrhea complicating pregnancy, first trimester
O98.212	Gonorrhea complicating pregnancy, second trimester
O98.213	Gonorrhea complicating pregnancy, third trimester
O98.219	Gonorrhea complicating pregnancy, unspecified trimester
O98.22	Gonorrhea complicating childbirth
O98.23	Gonorrhea complicating the puerperium
A54.03	Gonococcal cervicitis, unspecified
A54.00	Gonococcal infection of lower genitourinary tract, unspecified

EPIDEMIOLOGY & DEMOGRAPHICS

- The disease is common worldwide, affects both sexes and all ages, especially younger adults; highest incidence is in inner-city areas, with an estimated 820,000 new cases annually. Gonorrhea is the second most commonly reported communicable disease.
- Asymptomatic anterior urethral carriage may occur in 12% to 50% of cases in men.
- Asymptomatic in 50% to 80% of cases in women. Most common dissemination by mucosal passage to fallopian tubes, resulting in pelvic inflammatory disease (PID) in 10% to 15% of infected women. Hematogenous spread may result in septic arthritis and skin lesions. Conjunctivitis rarely occurs but may result in blindness if not rapidly treated. Infection can occur in both men and women in oropharynx and anorectally.
- 700,000 new infections per year (second most commonly reported bacterial STD).

PHYSICAL FINDINGS & CLINICAL PRESENTATION

- Males: purulent discharge from anterior urethra (Fig. 1G-18), with dysuria appearing 2 to 7 days after infecting exposure. May have rectal infection causing pruritus, tenesmus, and discharge or may be asymptomatic.
- Females: initial urethritis or cervicitis may occur a few days after exposure, frequently mild. Infections may be asymptomatic or may not produce recognizable symptoms until complications have occurred. In approximately 20% of cases uterine invasion occurs after menstrual period with signs and symptoms of endometritis, salpingitis, or pelvic peritonitis. The patient may have purulent discharge or inflamed Skene's or Bartholin's glands.
- Classic presentation of acute gonococcal PID is fever, abdominal and adnexal tenderness, and often absence of purulent discharge. Physical examination may be normal if asymptomatic. Disseminated gonococcal infection (DGI) may manifest with petechial or pustular acral skin lesions (Fig. 1G-19), asymmetric polyarthralgias, tenosynovitis, or oligoarticular septic arthritis. The infection is complicated occasionally by perihepatitis and rarely endocarditis or meningitis.

ETIOLOGY

- *Neisseria gonorrhoeae* is the gonococcus. Plasmids coding for β-lactamase render some strains resistant to penicillin or tetracycline. There is an increasing frequency of chromosomally mediated resistance to penicillin, tetracycline, fluoroquinolones, and cefoxitin. In the Far East, high-level resistance to spectinomycin is endemic.
- There are a rising number of cases of quinolone-resistant *N. gonorrhoeae* worldwide, with the expected number to rise in the U.S. from importation.
- Men who have sex with men are vulnerable to the emerging threat of antimicrobial-resistant *N. gonorrhoeae.*

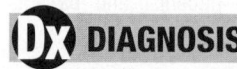

DIAGNOSIS

DIFFERENTIAL DIAGNOSIS

- Nongonococcal urethritis (NGU).
- Nongonococcal mucopurulent cervicitis.
- *Chlamydia trachomatis.*

WORKUP

Diagnosis depends on bacteriologic investigation. Culture and nucleic acid amplification tests (NAAT) are available for the detection of genitourinary infection with *N. gonorrhoeae.*

- NAATs are preferred testing modalities for the detection of genitourinary infection with *N. gonorrhoeae.* The performance of NAATs with respect to overall sensitivity, specificity, and ease of specimen transport is better than that of any of the other tests available for the diagnosis of gonococcal infections. NAATs should be used to detect gonorrhea except in cases of child sexual assault involving

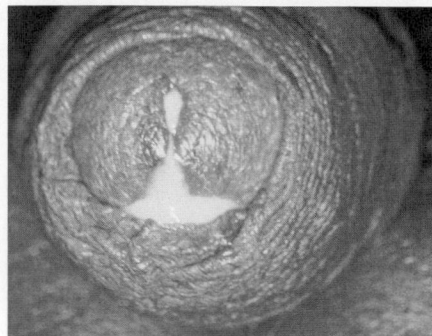

FIGURE 1G-18 Purulent urethral discharge from a man with gonococcal urethritis. (From Mandell GL et al: *Principles and practice of infectious diseases,* ed 6, Philadelphia, 2005, Churchill Livingstone.)

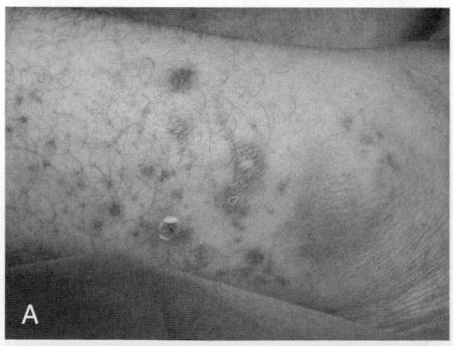
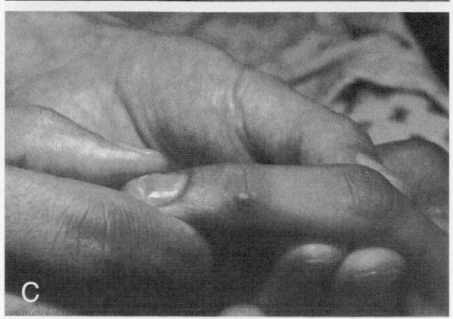
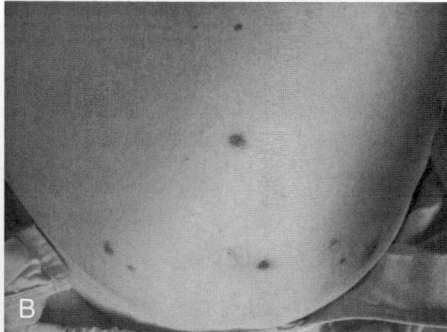

FIGURE 1G-19 Disseminated gonococcal infection: skin lesions. A, Macules, papules, and pustules over an ankle. **B,** Hemorrhagic papules localized in trunk. **C,** Hemorrhagic vessel over a distal interphalangeal joint. (**C** Courtesy of Dr. Peter Schlessinger. From Hochberg MC et al: *Rheumatology,* ed 5, St Louis, 2011, Mosby.)

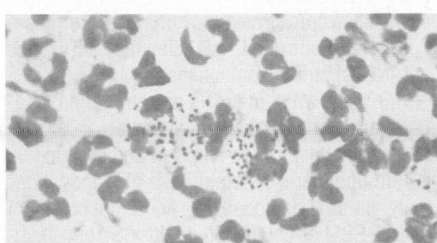

FIGURE 1G-20 _Neisseria gonorrhoeae._ Gram stain of urethral exudate in gonorrhea, showing intracellular gram-negative reniform diplococci. (Courtesy of Dr S.E. Thompson. From Hochberg MC et al: _Rheumatology,_ ed 5, St Louis, 2011, Mosby.)

boys and rectal and oropharyngeal infections in prepubescent girls and when evaluating a potential gonorrhea treatment failure, in which case culture and susceptibility testing might be required. NAATs allow testing of the widest variety of specimen types including endocervical swabs, vaginal swabs, urethral swabs (men), and urine (from both men and women).

- Culture: Gonorrhea culture on Thayer-Martin medium (organism is fastidious; requires aerobic conditions with increased carbon dioxide atmosphere; incubate ASAP). Culture has a sensitivity of 95% or more for urethral specimens from men with symptomatic urethritis and 80% to 90% for endocervical infection in women. Gram-negative intracellular diplococci are diagnostic in male urethral smears (Fig. 1G-20). There is a false-negative rate of 60% to 70% in female cervical or urethral smears.
  - ○ Concomitant serologic testing for syphilis for all patients
  - ○ Concomitant _Chlamydia_ testing for all patients
  - ○ Offer of HIV testing and counseling to all patients

LABORATORY TESTS

- Gonorrhea culture on Thayer-Martin medium (organism is fastidious; requires aerobic conditions with increased carbon dioxide atmosphere; incubate ASAP). Culture has a sensitivity of 95% or more for urethral specimens from men with symptomatic urethritis and 80% to 90% for endocervical infection in women.
- NAATs: These tests have largely replaced culture in many settings where persons are screened for asymptomatic genital infection. They are not more sensitive than culture for detecting _N. gonorrhoeae_ in cervical or urethral specimen; however, they have specificities >>99% and retain sensitivity when used to test voided urine or self-collected vaginal swabs.
- Nonamplified DNA probe tests are less sensitive than culture or NAATs and are not useful in the diagnosis of rectal or pharyngeal infection or for testing urine; however, they are

inexpensive, readily available and offered in many laboratories in combination assays for _C. trachomatis._
- Concomitant serologic testing for syphilis on all patients.
- Concomitant _Chlamydia_ testing on all patients.
- Offer of HIV testing and counseling to all patients.

Rx TREATMENT

ACUTE GENERAL Rx

Uncomplicated infections of the cervix, urethra, and rectum. Critical for the practitioner to know local resistance characteristics to best treat the patient:
- Ceftriaxone 250 mg IM × 1 dose _plus_ azithromycin 1 g PO single dose. Doxycycline 100 mg PO bid for 7 days can be substituted for azithromycin in patients with azithromycin allergy.

Alternative regimens if ceftriaxone is not available:
- Ceftizoxime (500 mg IM), cefoxitin (2 gm IM with probenecid 1 gm orally), and cefotaxime (500 mg IM). None of these injectable cephalosporins offer any advantage over ceftriaxone.
- Cefixime 400 mg PO × 1 dose _plus_ azithromycin 1 g orally single dose. Doxycycline 100 mg PO bid for 7 days can be substituted for azithromycin in patients with azithromycin allergy.
- If the patient has severe cephalosporin allergy, then azithromycin 2 g PO single dose _plus_ single-dose gemifloxacin 320 mg PO or gentamicin 240 mg IM.
- A test-of-cure is not needed for persons who receive a diagnosis of uncomplicated urogenital or rectal gonorrhea who are treated with any of the recommended or alternative regimens.

Uncomplicated gonococcal infections of the pharynx:
- Ceftriaxone 250 mg IM × 1 dose _plus_ azithromycin 1 g PO single dose. Doxycycline 100 mg PO bid for 7 days can be substituted for azithromycin in patients with azithromycin allergy.
- Treatment of the cephalosporin-allergic patient: oral azithromycin 2 gm _plus_ single dose gemifloxacin 320 mg PO _or_ 240 mg IM of gentamicin is effective.
- Any person with pharyngeal gonorrhea who is treated with an alternative regimen should return 14 days after treatment for a test-of-cure using either culture or NAAT.

Treatment of arthritis and arthritis-dermatitis syndrome:
- Recommended regimen: Ceftriaxone 1 gm IM or IV every 24 hours plus azithromycin 1 gm orally as a single dose.
- Alternative regimens: Cefotaxime 1 gm IV every 8 hours or ceftizoxime 1 gm IV every 8 hours _plus_ azithromycin 1 gm orally in a single dose.

DISPOSITION

- Pregnant women infected with _N. gonorrhoeae_ should be treated with dual therapy consisting of ceftriaxone 250 mg in a single IM dose or azithromycin 1 g PO as a single dose. When cephalosporin allergy or other considerations preclude treatment and spectinomycin is not available, consultation with an ID specialist is recommended.
- To reduce development of drug resistance reculture should be done for patients who show continued symptoms despite treatment. These patients should be tested with a culture-based gonorrhea test that can detect antibiotic resistance.
- All sexual partners should be identified, examined, tested, and receive presumptive treatment.

REFERRAL

PID requiring hospitalization, disseminated gonococcal infection.

❗ PEARLS & CONSIDERATIONS

COMMENTS

- This is a reportable disease.
- The proportion of gonorrhea cases in heterosexual men who are fluoroquinolone resistant (QRNG) has reached 6.7%, an 11-fold increase from 0.6% in 2001. Fluoroquinolone antibiotics are no longer recommended to treat gonorrhea in the U.S.
- The use of azithromycin as the second antimicrobial is preferred over doxycycline due to the high prevalence of tetracycline resistance.
- The U.S. Preventive Services Task Force (USPSTF) recommends screening for gonorrhea in sexually active females 24 years or younger and in older women who are at increased risk for infection. The USPSTF also concludes that the current evidence is insufficient to assess the balance of benefits and harms of screening for gonorrhea in men.
- High-intensity counseling on sexual risk reduction has been shown to reduce sexually transmitted infections (STIs) in primary care and related settings.

SUGGESTED READINGS
Available at www.expertconsult.com

RELATED CONTENT
Gonorrhea (Patient Information)
Cervicitis (Related Key Topic)
Chlamydia Genital Infections (Related Key Topic)
Pelvic Inflammatory Disease (Related Key Topic)

AUTHOR: **RUBEN ALVERO, M.D.**

BASIC INFORMATION

DEFINITION

Goodpasture's syndrome is defined as the coexistence of pulmonary alveolar hemorrhage and rapidly progressive glomerulonephritis (RPGN). Goodpasture's *disease* refers specifically to alveolar hemorrhage and RPGN caused by an anti–glomerular basement membrane (anti-GBM) antibody.

SYNONYMS

Anti-GBM disease

ICD-10CM CODES
N01.7 Rapidly progressive nephritic syndrome with diffuse crescentic glomerulonephritis
N00.7 Acute nephritic syndrome with diffuse crescentic glomerulonephritis

EPIDEMIOLOGY & DEMOGRAPHICS

- Goodpasture's disease affects predominantly young, white, male smokers
- Male-to-female ratio is 6:1
- Goodpasture's disease accounts for 5% of all cases of RPGN
- HLA-BR2 positive is positive in 80% of patients
- Goodpasture disease may occur in up to 5% of syndrome patients with Alport disease who undergo kidney transplantation.

PHYSICAL FINDINGS & CLINICAL PRESENTATION

- Dyspnea, cough, hemoptysis
- Skin pallor, fever, arthralgias (may be mild or absent at the time of initial presentation)

ETIOLOGY

Goodpasture's disease is caused by autoantibodies directed against type IV collagen or the GBM. Antibody deposition leads to immune cell- and complement-mediated tissue damage that results in pulmonary hemorrhage and glomerulonephritis.

DIAGNOSIS

DIFFERENTIAL DIAGNOSIS

- Granulomatosis with polyangiitis
- Systemic lupus erythematosus
- Churg-Strauss syndrome
- Essential mixed cryoglobulinemia
- Idiopathic rapidly progressive glomerulonephritis
- Drug-induced renal pulmonary disease (e.g., penicillamine)

WORKUP

Laboratory evaluation, diagnostic imaging, and kidney biopsy

LABORATORY TESTS

- Serum anti-GBM antibodies

- Absence of circulating immune complexes, antineutrophil, cytoplasmic antibodies (ANCAs), and cryoglobulins
- Urinalysis with microscopic hematuria, proteinuria, and red blood cell casts
- Elevated blood urea nitrogen and creatinine
- Immunofluorescence studies of kidney biopsy material demonstrates linear deposition of anti-GBM antibody, often with C3 deposition
- Anemia and iron deficiency from blood loss and iron sequestration in the lungs

IMAGING STUDIES

Chest radiograph with airspace disease composed of alveolar infiltrates or evidence of pulmonary hemorrhage (Fig. 1G-21)

TREATMENT

ACUTE GENERAL Rx

- Apheresis with albumin replacement for 1 to 2 weeks with ongoing immunosuppressive and medical therapy consisting of prednisone (1 mg/kg/day) and oral cyclophosphamide (2 mg/kg/day).
- Dialysis support in patients with renal failure.
- Factors influencing the decision to treat or not to treat aggressively in Goodpasture's disease are described in Table 1G-12.

DISPOSITION

Life-threatening pulmonary hemorrhage and irreversible glomerular damage are the major causes of death.

REFERRAL

- Referral for kidney biopsy to guide the management.
- Consider kidney transplantation in patients with end-stage renal disease.

SUGGESTED READINGS
Available at www.expertconsult.com

RELATED CONTENT
Goodpasture's Syndrome (Patient Information)

AUTHOR: **KAUSIK UMANATH, M.D., M.S.**

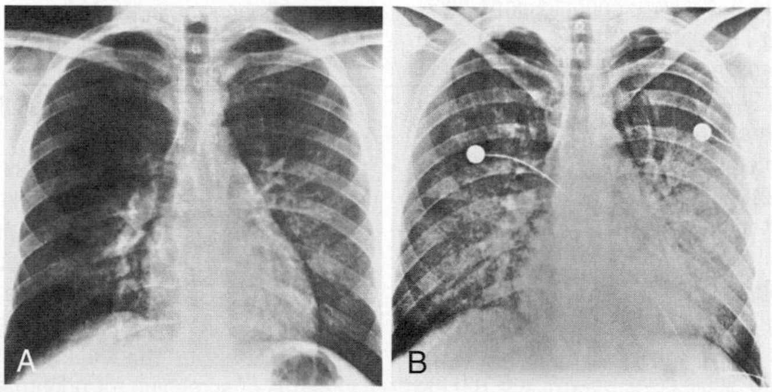

FIGURE 1G-21 Lung hemorrhage. A, Patient with early pulmonary hemorrhage. The chest radiograph still appears normal. **B,** Radiograph taken 4 days later shows the evolution of alveolar shadowing caused by lung hemorrhage. (From Floege J et al: *Comprehensive clinical nephrology*, ed 4, Philadelphia, 2010, Saunders, p. 285.)

TABLE 1G-12 Factors Influencing Decision to Treat Aggressively in Goodpasture's Disease

	Factors Favoring Aggressive Treatment	Factors Against Aggressive Treatment
Pulmonary hemorrhage	Present	Absent
Oliguria	Absent	Present
Creatinine	<5.5 mg/dl (~500 µmol/L)	>5.5–6.5 mg/dl (~500–600 µmol/L) and ANCA negative Severe damage on kidney biopsy No desire for early kidney transplantation
Other factors	Creatinine >5.5–6.5 mg/dl (~500–600 µmol/L) Rapid and recent progression ANCA positive status Glomerular damage less severe than expected Crescents recent, nonfibrous Early renal transplantation desired	
Associated disease	Absent	Unusually high risk from immunosuppression

ANCA, Antineutrophil cytoplasmic antibody.
From Floege J et al: *Comprehensive clinical nephrology*, ed 4, Philadelphia, 2010, Saunders.

BASIC INFORMATION

DEFINITION

Gout is a term used to refer to a group of disease states caused by tissue deposition of monosodium urate due to prolonged hyperuricemia. Clinical manifestations of gout include acute and chronic arthritis, soft tissue inflammation, tophus formation, gouty nephropathy, and nephrolithiasis. Untreated hyperuricemia in patients with gout may lead to chronic destructive deforming arthritis.

ICD-10CM CODES
M10   Gout
M10.0 Idiopathic gout
M10.2 Drug induced gout
M10.3 Gout due to impairment of renal
       function
M10.4 Other secondary gout
M10.9 Gout, unspecified
M10.1 Lead-induced gout

EPIDEMIOLOGY & DEMOGRAPHICS

PREVALENCE: 5 cases per 1000 persons in the United States. Globally 8 cases per 10,000. Incidence is rising.
PREDOMINANT SEX: Male/female ratio ~4:1.
PREDOMINANT AGE: 30 to 50 years in men. Older than 60 years in women.

ETIOLOGY

- Gout is induced by inflammation from monosodium urate (MSU) crystal deposition. The primary risk factor for MSU deposition is hyperuricemia, though local factors such as temperature, pH, and mechanical stress may play a role.
- Hyperuricemia and gout develop from excessive uric acid production, a decrease in the renal excretion of uric acid, or both.
- Primary hyperuricemia results from an inborn error of metabolism and may be attributed to several biochemical defects.
- Secondary hyperuricemia may develop as a complication of acquired disorders (e.g., leukemia) or as a result of the use of certain drugs (e.g., diuretics). Consumption of alcohol, especially beer, increases the risk of gout, and fructose-rich beverage intake is associated with hyperuricemia.

PHYSICAL FINDINGS & CLINICAL PRESENTATION

ACUTE GOUT:
- Rapid onset of pain and swelling and erythema of a distal joint and/or periarticular

TABLE 1G-13   Key Components of Gout Flares

- Marked tenderness and swelling of affected joint
- Acute onset with maximum pain in 4-12 hr
- Recurrent pattern of similar attacks
- Marked impairment of physical function
- Resolution of symptoms within 3-14 days

From Hochberg MC et al: *Rheumatology*, ed 5, St Louis, 2011, Mosby.

soft tissue. Table 1G-13 summarizes key components of gout flares.
- May present as monoarthritis of any joint. Acute gout of the first metatarsophalangeal (MTP) joint (Fig. 1G-22) is known as *podagra*.
- 10% to 15% of attacks are polyarticular.
- Spontaneous resolution occurs over days to weeks.

CHRONIC TOPHACEOUS GOUT (FIG. 1G-23):
- Insidious onset of painless arthritis and soft tissue swelling.
- Distal small joints characteristic.
- May be confused with nodal osteoarthritis.

DIAGNOSIS

DIFFERENTIAL DIAGNOSIS OF ACUTE GOUT

- Infectious arthritis.
- Cellulitis.
- Pseudogout.
- Trauma.

DIFFERENTIAL DIAGNOSIS OF CHRONIC GOUT

- Osteoarthritis (especially nodal OA in women).
- Rheumatoid arthritis.
- Psoriatic arthritis.

Section II describes the differential diagnosis of acute monoarticular and oligoarticular arthritis.

WORKUP

Arthrocentesis and examination of synovial fluid

LABORATORY TESTS

- Uric acid: All patients with gout are hyperuricemic at some time, but during an acute attack the serum uric acid may be normal or low.
- Synovial aspirate: usually cloudy and markedly inflammatory in nature. Urate crystals in fluid are needle-shaped and strongly negatively birefringent under polarized microscopy (Fig. E1G-24).
- CBC: mild leukocytosis often present.
- Inflammatory markers: ESR and CRP often elevated.

IMAGING STUDIES

- Plain radiography for diagnosis and evaluation. Not generally indicated in typical gout presentation.

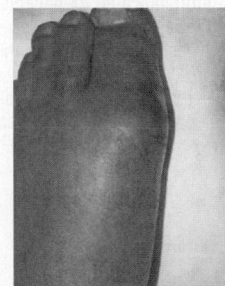

FIGURE 1G-22 Podagra or acute gout of the first metatarsophalangeal (MTP) joint is shown. The hyperintense erythema with a dusky hue is characteristic. The area of inflammation usually extends beyond the area of the involved joint. (From Hochberg MC et al: *Rheumatology,* ed 5, St Louis, 2011, Mosby.)

- No typical findings in early gouty arthritis but late disease is associated with characteristic punched-out marginal erosions and overhanging edges.
- Musculoskeletal ultrasound has been shown to be an effective means of detecting monosodium urate crystal deposition. Ultrasound can differentiate urate crystals which are found on the surface of articular cartilage from CPPD crystals that are seen within the substance of the cartilage (Fig. 1G-25).

TREATMENT OPTIONS FOR ACUTE GOUT

- Nonsteroidal anti-inflammatory medication (see Table 1G-14).
  1. Indomethacin 75 mg bid.
  2. Ibuprofen 800 mg tid.
  3. Naproxen 500 mg bid.
  4. Celecoxib 800 mg, then 400 mg/day.
- Low-dose colchicine (less toxic and as effective as traditional high-dose colchicine): 1.2 mg colchicine PO, followed by 0.6 mg PO 1 hr later.
- Intraarticular corticosteroid injection (treatment of choice for monoarticular large joint attack): triamcinolone acetonide 40 mg or equivalent for knee.
- Systemic corticosteroid therapy: prednisone 40 mg PO for 3 days, then taper over 10 days (effective and safe, but evidence is lacking).

NONPHARMACOLOGIC THERAPY

Lifestyle and dietary modification may be effective in highly motivated patients. Recommendations include reducing ingestion of red meat, kidney, liver, yeast extract, shellfish, and overall protein along with restricting alcohol intake. These recommendations should be attempted only in patients with modestly elevated uric acid, as dietary modification can only lower uric acid 1 mg%. Discontinuation of diuretic therapy may help.

PHARMACOLOGIC TREATMENT OF SYMPTOMATIC HYPERURICEMIA

ALLOPURINOL: Allopurinol is very effective and safe when used properly. Correct dosing and

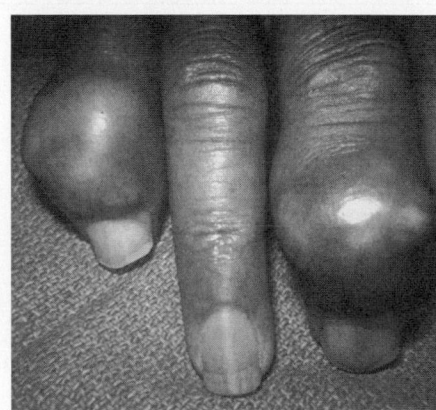

FIGURE 1G-23 Large tophi involving the distal interphalangeal joints are commonly seen in gouty patients with preexisting Heberden's nodes. This is particularly characteristic of late-onset gout. (From Hochberg MC et al: *Rheumatology,* ed 5, St Louis, 2011, Mosby.)

patient compliance are essential elements in the prevention of erosive and tophaceous gout. Patients with renal insufficiency are at increased risk for allopurinol hypersensitivity, which manifests as fever, rash, and hepatitis occurring most commonly in the first 3 months of therapy. The rash may progress to life-threatening toxic epidermal necrolysis if not recognized early.

Traditionally, therapy with allopurinol is initiated several weeks after the acute attack has resolved. However, initiation of allopurinol at presentation may improve long-term compliance without reducing the efficacy of acute treatment. The initial dose should be low (≤100 mg/day depending on creatinine clearance) in patients with renal insufficiency and those with

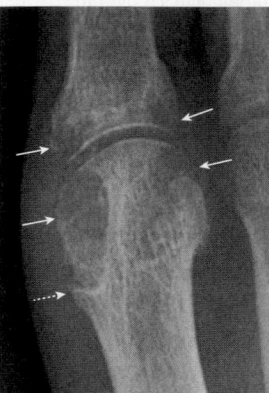

FIGURE 1G-25 Classic radiographic findings of gout in a 69-year-old man. Note the asymmetric, well-marginated erosions in the head of the first metatarsal and lesser erosions in the opposing phalanx *(solid arrows)*. The medial erosions are characteristically larger than the lateral erosions. There is a "hook" sign on the inferior margin of the large medial erosion of the head of the metatarsal *(dashed arrow)*. The joint space is preserved, and there is no osteopenia. (Pope TL , Bloem HL, Beltran J, Morrison WB, Wilson DJ: *Musculoskeletal imaging*, ed 2, Philadelphia, 2014, Saunders.)

very high uric acid levels. High initial doses are associated with increased incidence of allopurinol hypersensitivity. The serum uric acid should be reevaluated after 4 to 6 wk of therapy, and the allopurinol dose adjusted to reduce the serum uric acid to less than 6 mg%. The most common therapeutic dosage of allopurinol is 300 mg/day, but dose may be increased by 50 to 100 mg every two to three weeks until the target serum uric acid level is achieved. There is evidence that increasing allopurinol doses in patients with renal insufficiency does not result in significant toxicity, but concurrent use with statins and colchicine is associated with a higher incidence of adverse effects. Some authors have reported using doses as high as 800 mg daily without excess toxicity.

FEBUXOSTAT: Febuxostat is a xanthine oxidase inhibitor that has been shown to be more potent than allopurinol 300 mg daily for reducing serum uric acid. The chemical structure of febuxostat is different from allopurinol, making cross-reactive allergy unlikely. The metabolism of febuxostat is primarily hepatic, which obviates the need for dose adjustments due to renal insufficiency. Some cases of hepatic toxicity have been reported, and it is recommended that liver function tests be monitored periodically. Febuxostat may help preserve renal function in patients with chronic kidney disease (CKD) but has not been tested in patients with severe renal failure.

The primary indication for febuxostat is demonstrated allergy to allopurinol. The cost of febuxostat may be as much as 40 times that of allopurinol.

BENEMID AND SULFINPYRAZONE: These uricosuric agents may only be used in patients with good renal function and urinary uric acid less than 600 mg in a 24-hr collection. Compliance is poor due to necessity of taking drugs more often than once daily.

PEGLOTICASE: Intravenous pegylated uricase was approved by the FDA in 2010 for treatment of severe refractory tophaceous gout.

It is a pegylated recombinant mammalian uricase that rapidly degrades urate when given intravenously. Use is limited by very high cost and significant toxicities including frequent gout flares and anaphylaxis.

PATIENT/FAMILY EDUCATION

It is essential that patients, families, physicians, and other members of the health care team appreciate the importance of compliance with a daily allopurinol regimen if recurrent flares and progression to chronic arthritis and tophi are to be avoided. Allopurinol should be discontinued only for symptoms suggesting the hypersensitivity syndrome. It should be continued during flares, medical illnesses, and surgical procedures.

REFERRAL

- Rheumatologist if diagnosis is not clear or therapy is complicated.
- Podiatrist for management of pedal complications.

PEARLS & CONSIDERATIONS

Do not stop allopurinol during hospitalizations, surgery, or acute attacks unless there is evidence of drug allergy.

EVIDENCE

Available at www.expertconsult.com

SUGGESTED READINGS

Available at www.expertconsult.com

RELATED CONTENT

Gout (Patient Information)
Hyperuricemia (Related Key Topic)

AUTHOR: **BERNARD ZIMMERMANN, M.D**

TABLE 1G-14 Treatment of Gout

Acute Gout	Interval Gout	Treatment of Hyperuricemia
NSAIDs (preferred): Indomethacin 50 mg qid or ibuprofen 800 mg tid (or other NSAID in full doses). Contraindicated in patients with renal insufficiency and gastrointestinal disorders. *Or* **Colchicine, oral:** 1.2 mg followed by a second dose of 0.6 mg 1 hr later. Contraindicated in patients with renal insufficiency and gastrointestinal disorders *Or* **Intraarticular steroids** (Treatment of choice for large joint monoarthritis): Triamcinolone 40 mg or equivalent for knee *Or* Systemic steroid therapy (for patients in whom NSAIDs and colchicine are contraindicated) Prednisone 30-50 mg PO daily or in divided doses. May use lower dose in diabetic or postsurgical patients.	**Colchicine, oral:** 0.6-1.2 mg/day as prophylaxis against recurrent attacks. **NSAIDs may also be used for prophylaxis.** **Hypouricemic agent:** Indicated for patients with recurrent attacks despite prophylaxis, severe hyperuricemia, presence of tophi, urolithiasis, or gouty arthritis **Other:** Weight loss, reduce alcohol (especially beer), diet low in seafood, red meat, organ meat, and fructose	**Colchicine, oral:** 0.6-1.2 mg/day for 4-6 wk before initiating hypouricemic therapy and for several months afterward to prevent recurrent attacks during initiation of hypouricemic therapy. *And* **Allopurinol:** Initial dose 100 mg/day in patients with renal insufficiency or very high uric acid levels. Increase dose as needed to attain uric acid less than 6 mg/dl. *Or* **Uricosuric agent** (Use only in patients with good renal function and <600 mg uric acid in a 24-hr collection): probenecid, 0.5-1 g bid, or sulfinpyrazone 100 mg tid or qid **Other:** Consider febuxostat for patients allergic to allopurinol. Pegloticase may be useful for selected patients with severe tophaceous gout.

NSAIDs, Nonsteroidal anti-inflammatory drugs.

G

BASIC INFORMATION

DEFINITION
Granuloma annulare (GA) is a chronic, usually self-limited, inflammatory disorder of the dermis that classically presents as arciform to annular plaques located on the extremities.

SYNONYMS
Pseudorheumatoid nodule—subcutaneous granuloma annulare
GA

ICD-10CM CODES
L92.0 Granuloma annulare

EPIDEMIOLOGY & DEMOGRAPHICS
- Most common in children and young adults; most cases of localized GA are diagnosed in patients <30 yr.
- Female predominance (2:1).
- Disseminated form associated with diabetes mellitus.
- Recurrent in 40% of affected individuals.
- A generalized form of GA can occur in up to 15% of patients.

PHYSICAL FINDINGS & CLINICAL PRESENTATION
- The main clinical variants of GA are localized (75%), disseminated (>10 lesions), subcutaneous (occurring primarily in children aged 2 to 5 yr), patch-type or macular GA, and perforating (rare form manifesting with 1- to 4-mm papules with a central crust usually appearing on the dorsal hands).
- Localized GA starts as a small ring of colored skin or pale erythematous papules. More common in children and young to middle-age adults. Usually, only one or a few lesions occur at any one time.
- Lesions coalesce and evolve into annular plaques over several weeks.
- Plaques undergo central involution and increase in diameter over several months (0.5 to 5 cm) (Fig. 1G-26).
- Most frequently found on the lateral and dorsal surfaces of the hands and feet.
- Most lesions resolve spontaneously after several months.
- The generalized form of GA is characterized by hundreds of small (lesions rarely exceed 5 cm in diameter), flesh-colored papules in a symmetric distribution on the trunk and extremities. It most commonly affects women in the fifth or sixth decades but can also be seen in adolescents and children. Some patients are completely asymptomatic, whereas others complain of severe pruritus.
- Macular GA is more common in women between ages 30 to 70 and manifests with flat or slightly palpable erythematous or red-brown lesions on upper medial thighs and in bathing-trunk distribution.
- Deep dermal GA (subcutaneous GA) presents as large, painless, skin-colored nodules

that are frequently mistaken for rheumatoid nodules.

ETIOLOGY
Unknown, but may be related to vasculitis, trauma, monocyte activation, or delayed hypersensitivity.

DIAGNOSIS

DIFFERENTIAL DIAGNOSIS
- Tinea corporis.
- Lichen planus.
- Necrobiosis lipoidica diabeticorum.
- Sarcoidosis.
- Rheumatoid nodules.
- Late secondary or tertiary syphilis.
- Arcuate and annular plaques of mycosis fungoides.
- Papular GA can simulate insect bites, secondary syphilis, xanthoma.
- Annular elastolytic giant cell granuloma.

WORKUP
- Diagnosis based on clinical appearance and presentation.
- Biopsy when diagnosis is unclear.

LABORATORY TESTS
- No laboratory tests will help confirm the diagnosis.
- Biopsy shows focal degeneration of collagen and elastic fibers, mucin deposition, and perivascular and interstitial lymphohistiocytic infiltrate in the upper and middle dermis.

TREATMENT

NONPHARMACOLOGIC THERAPY
Reassurance, given the self-limited and benign nature of GA

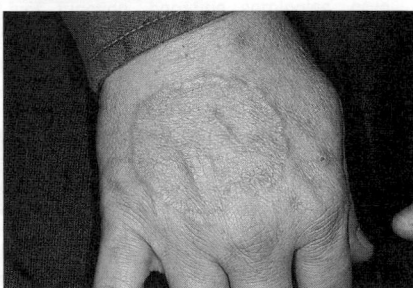
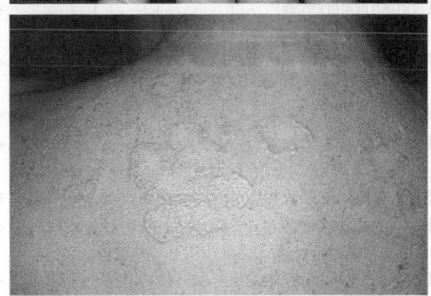

FIGURE 1G-26 Granuloma annulare. (From Callen JP [ed]: *Color atlas of dermatology,* ed 2, Philadelphia, 2000, Saunders.)

CHRONIC Rx
High-potency topical corticosteroids with or without occlusion and intralesional steroid injection into elevated border with triamcinolone 2.5 to 10 mg/ml are useful first-line local therapies.
- Cryosurgery, psoralen ultraviolet-A (UVA) range or UVA-1 therapy, and carbon dioxide laser treatment can also be used.
- Systemic agents (e.g., niacinamide, hydroxychloroquine, chloroquine, cyclosporine, dapsone) are generally reserved for severe cases. Recent case reports indicate positive outcomes with tacrolimus and pimecrolimus and the tumor necrosis factor infliximab.

DISPOSITION
Most lesions resolve spontaneously within 2 yr.

REFERRAL
Dermatology referral recommended for symptomatic, disseminated disease

PEARLS & CONSIDERATIONS

COMMENTS
GA has been described as a paraneoplastic granulomatous reaction to Hodgkin's disease, non-Hodgkin's lymphoma, solid organ tumors, and mycosis fungoides.

SUGGESTED READINGS
Available at www.expertconsult.com

RELATED CONTENT
Granuloma Annulare (Patient Information)

AUTHOR: **FRED F. FERRI, M.D.**

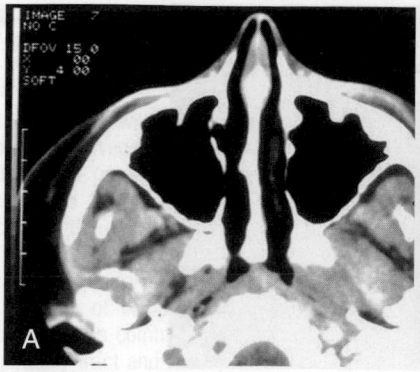
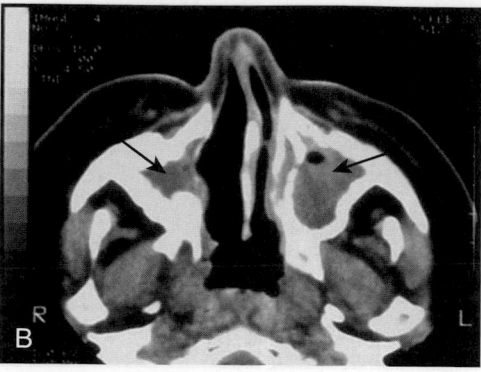

FIGURE 1G-31 Computed tomography (CT) scans of the sinuses. A, Normal maxillary sinuses in a recently diagnosed Wegener's granulomatosis (WG) patient. **B,** Sinus CT scan of a patient with long-standing WG: nasal septal deviation to the left, destruction of the medial walls of the right maxillary sinus, opacification of both sinuses with soft tissue densities *(arrows)*, and neo-ossification of all maxillary bony structures due to chronic inflammation. (From Hochberg MC et al: *Rheumatology,* ed 5, St Louis, 2011, Mosby.)

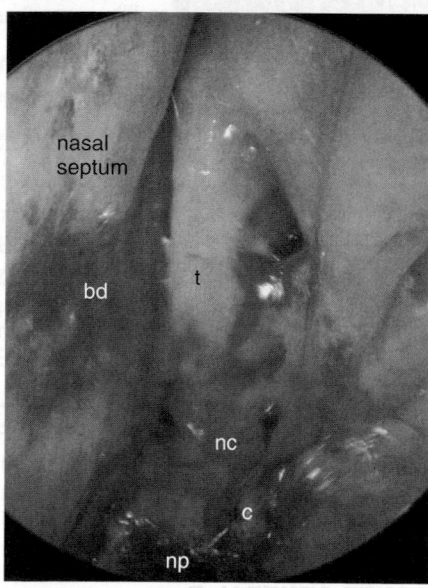

FIGURE 1G-33 Endoscopic view of nasal cavity of GPA patient showing crusting and bloody discharge. (From Holle et al; *Rheum Dis Clin North Am* 36(3):507-526, 2010).

studies used concurrent methylprednisone followed by prednisone.

- Methotrexate and glucocorticoids alone may be used with mild extrarenal disease or little to no renal involvement.

- Potentially useful agents for maintenance therapy include rituximab, methotrexate, azathioprine, and mycophenolate mofetil. The MAINRITSAN trial showed that rituximab may be preferable for maintenance therapy, and the CYCAZAREM (for azathioprine) and LEM (for leflunomide) trials showed that these agents can also be used. The WEGENT study showed oral methotrexate and azathioprine were also noninferior for maintenance than intravenous cyclophosphamide.
- Maintenance therapy should generally be continued for 18 to 24 months, and, if ANCA positivity remains, even as long as 5 years.
- TMP-SMX therapy has a limited role in patients with lesions confined to the upper or lower respiratory tracts in absence of vasculitis or nephritis. Treatment with TMP-SMX (160 mg/800 mg bid) may reduce the incidence of relapses in patients with granulomatosis with polyangiitis in remission. It is also useful in preventing *Pneumocystis jirovecii* pneumonia (PJP), which occurs in 10% of patients receiving induction therapy. When used for prophylaxis, dose of TMP-SMX (160 mg/800 mg) is 1 tablet three times/week.
- In patients unable to tolerate TMP-SMX, often because of rash or allergy, PJP prophylaxis can also be achieved with dapsone, atovaquone, or inhaled pentamidine.

DISPOSITION

- Five-year survival with aggressive treatment is approximately 80%; without treatment 2-yr survival is 20%.
- Age >50 yr, impaired renal function, pulmonary involvement at diagnosis, and lack of ENT changes at diagnosis are all associated with worse outcomes and increased mortality rate.
- With standard therapy, remission is achieved by 90% to 94% of patients, but relapse is frequent (from 18% to 40% at 24 months.).

REFERRAL

- Rheumatology referral for continued treatment.
- ENT, surgical referral for biopsy

PEARLS & CONSIDERATIONS

COMMENTS

- Granulomatosis with polyangiitis is characterized by granulomatous lesions and vasculitis involving the respiratory tract, lung, and kidneys.
- C-ANCA levels should not dictate changes in therapy, because they correlate erratically with disease activity.
- The incidence of venous thrombotic events in patients with granulomatosis with polyangiitis is significantly higher than in the general population. Clinicians should maintain a heightened awareness of the risks of venous thrombosis and a lower threshold for evaluating patients for possible DVT or pulmonary embolism.
- Disease relapse remains a major problem in the course of the disease.

SUGGESTED READINGS

Available at www.expertconsult.com

RELATED CONTENT

Wegener's Granulomatosis (Patient Information).

AUTHOR: **ANTHONY M. REGINATO, PH.D., M.D.**

BASIC INFORMATION

DEFINITION

Graves' disease is a hypermetabolic state caused by circulating IgG antibodies that bind to and activate the G-protein–coupled thyrotropin receptor. This activation stimulates follicular hypertrophy and hyperplasia, causing thyroid enlargement as well as increases in thyroid hormone production. It is characterized by thyrotoxicosis, diffuse goiter, and infiltrative ophthalmopathy (edema and inflammation of the extraocular muscles and an increase in orbital connective tissue and fat); infiltrative dermopathy characterized by lymphocytic infiltration of the dermis; accumulation of glycosaminoglycans; and occasionally edema.

SYNONYMS

Thyrotoxicosis

ICD-10CM CODES
E05.00 Thyrotoxicosis with diffuse goiter without thyrotoxic crisis or storm
E05.01 Thyrotoxicosis with diffuse goiter with thyrotoxic crisis or storm

EPIDEMIOLOGY & DEMOGRAPHICS

INCIDENCE/PREVALENCE: Graves' disease is the most common cause of hyperthyroidism. It affects 3% of women and 0.5% of men during their lifetime. There is a slight increased incidence among young African Americans.
PREDOMINANT AGE: Peak incidence is between 30 and 60 yr.
GENETICS: Patients often report a family history of Hashimoto thyroiditis, Graves' disease, or other autoimmune conditions. Increased prevalence of HLA-B8 and HLA-DR3 in whites with Graves' disease. Concordance rate is 20% among monozygotic twins.

PHYSICAL FINDINGS & CLINICAL PRESENTATION

- Elevated systolic blood pressure with a widened pulse pressure.
- Diffusely enlarged thyroid. Thyroid bruit may be present.
- Tachycardia, palpitations, tremor, hyperreflexia.
- Exophthalmos (50% of patients), lid retraction (lid lag), in which contraction of the levator palpebrae muscles of the eyelids shows immobility of the upper eyelid with downward rotation of the eye.
- Nervousness, weight loss, heat intolerance, atrial fibrillation.
- Increased sweating, brittle nails, clubbing of fingers.
- Localized infiltrative dermopathy (1% to 2% of patients) is most frequent over the anterolateral aspects of the legs, commonly over the pretibial area (pretibial myxedema) (Fig.1G-34) but can be found at other sites

(especially after trauma). It is typically patchy with a peau d'orange appearance to the skin.
- Men may have gynecomastia, reduced libido, and erectile dysfunction. Women often have irregular menses.

ETIOLOGY

Autoimmune etiology: the activity of the thyroid gland is stimulated by the action of T cells, which induce specific B cells to synthesize antibodies against thyroid-stimulating hormone (TSH) receptors in the follicular cell membrane.

DIAGNOSIS

DIFFERENTIAL DIAGNOSIS

- Anxiety disorder.
- Premenopausal state.
- Thyroiditis.
- Other causes of hyperthyroidism (e.g., toxic multinodular goiter, toxic adenoma).
- Other: metastatic neoplasm, diabetes mellitus, pheochromocytoma.

WORKUP

- The diagnosis is made clinically on most instances.
- The diagnostic workup includes a detailed medical history followed by laboratory and imaging studies and ECG. Patients often present with anxiety, heat intolerance, menstrual dysfunction, increased appetite, and weight loss. Elderly patients can have an atypical presentation (apathetic hyperparathyroidism). For additional information, refer to the topic "Hyperthyroidism."
- Table 1G-16 describes the clinical assessment of the patient with Graves' ophthalmopathy.

LABORATORY TESTS

- Increased free thyroxine (T_4) and free triiodothyronine (T_3).
- Decreased TSH.
- Measurement of thyroid-stimulating antibodies (TSI) is generally reserved for patients without classic presentation of thyrotoxicity (see "Clinical Findings") to differentiate Graves' disease from toxic nodular goiter.

IMAGING STUDIES

- 24-hr radioactive iodine uptake (RAIU): increased homogeneous uptake.
- CT or MRI of the orbits (Fig. 1G-35) is useful if there is uncertainty about the cause of ophthalmopathy.

TREATMENT

NONPHARMACOLOGIC THERAPY

- Patient education and discussion of therapeutic options.
- Smoking cessation: smoking is associated with an increased risk of progression of Graves' ophthalmopathy.

ACUTE GENERAL Rx

- Antithyroid drugs (ATDs) to inhibit thyroid hormone synthesis or peripheral conversion of T_4 to T_3:
  1. Methimazole or propylthiouracil (PTU) are available. Methimazole is generally preferred because it has a longer half-life, allowing for once-daily dosing. PTU is preferred during pregnancy.
  2. Side effects: skin rash (3% to 5%), arthralgias, myalgias, granulocytopenia (0.5%); rare side effects: aplastic anemia, hepatic necrosis (PTU), cholestatic jaundice.
  3. Thionamide antithyroid drug therapy results in a remission in 40% to 50% of patients treated for 12 to 18 months.
- Radioactive iodine (RAI):
  1. Treatment of choice for patients >21 yr and younger patients who have not achieved remission after 1 yr of ATD therapy
  2. Contraindicated during pregnancy and lactation
  3. Following radioactive therapy there may be an acute elevation of thyroid antibody titers and exacerbation of ocular symptoms in 15% to 20% of patients.
- Surgery: near-total thyroidectomy. Indications: obstructing goiters despite RAI and ATD therapy, patients who refuse RAI and cannot be adequately managed with ATDs, and pregnant women inadequately managed with ATDs. Complications of surgery include hypoparathyroidism (4%) and vocal cord paralysis (1%).
- Adjunctive therapy: Beta-adrenergic receptor blockers (e.g., atenolol 50 to 100 mg/day) to alleviate the beta-adrenergic symptoms of hyperthyroidism (tachycardia, tremor); contraindicated in patients with bronchospasm.
- Graves' ophthalmopathy. methylcellulose eye drops to protect against excessive dryness, sunglasses to decrease photophobia, intraocular and systemic high-dose corticosteroids for severe exophthalmos. Worsening of ophthalmopathy after RAI therapy is often transient and can be prevented by the administration of prednisone. Other treatment options include antiinflammatory and immunosuppressive agents, radiation, and corrective surgical procedures. The admin-

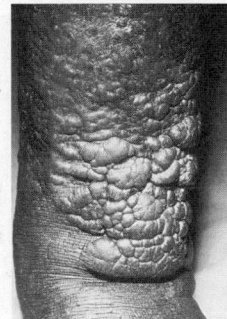

FIGURE 1G-34 Chronic pretibial myxedema in a patient with Graves' disease and orbitopathy. The lesions are firm and nonpitting, with a clear edge to feel. (Courtesy of Dr. Andrew Werner, New York, NY.)

istration of the antioxidant selenium (100 µg PO bid) has been recently reported as effective in improving quality of life, reducing ocular involvement, and slowing progression of the disease in patients with mild Graves' orbitopathy. Its mechanism of action is believed to be an effect on the oxygen free radicals and cytokines that play a pathogenic role in Graves' orbitopathy.

CHRONIC Rx

Patients undergoing treatment with ATDs should be seen every 1 to 3 mo until euthyroidism is achieved and every 3 to 4 mo while they are receiving ATDs.

DISPOSITION

- ATDs induce sustained remission in <60% of cases.
- The incidence of hypothyroidism after RAI is >50% within the first year and 2% per year thereafter.
- Complications of surgery include hypothyroidism (28% to 43% after 10 yr), hypoparathyroidism (4%), and vocal cord paralysis (1%).
- Successful treatment of hyperthyroidism requires lifelong monitoring for the onset of hypothyroidism or the recurrence of thyrotoxicosis.

- RAI therapy is followed by the appearance or worsening of ophthalmopathy more often than is therapy with methimazole, particularly in patients who are cigarette smokers. It can be prevented with the administration of prednisone 0.5 mg/kg body weight per day starting 2 to 3 days after RAI, continued for 1 mo, then tapered off over 2 mo.
- Mild to moderate ophthalmopathy often improves spontaneously. Severe cases can be treated with high-dose glucocorticoids, orbital irradiation, or both. Orbital decompression may be used in patients with optic neuropathy and exophthalmos (see "Hyperthyroidism").

 **EVIDENCE**

Available at www.expertconsult.com

SUGGESTED READINGS
Available at www.expertconsult.com

RELATED CONTENT
Graves' Disease (Patient Information)
Hyperthyroidism (Related Key Topic)

AUTHOR: **FRED F. FERRI, M.D.**

TABLE 1G-16 Clinical Assessment of the Patient with Graves' Ophthalmopathy

Activity Measures*

Spontaneous retrobulbar pain

Pain on attempted up or down gaze

Redness of the eyelids

Redness of the conjunctiva

Swelling of the eyelids

Inflammation of the caruncle and/or plica

Conjunctival edema

Severity Measures

Lid aperture: distance between lid margins in millimeters with the patient looking in the primary position, sitting relaxed, and with distant fixation

Swelling of the eyelids (absent/equivocal, moderate, severe)

Redness of the eyelids (absent/present)

Redness of the conjunctivae (absent/present)

Conjunctival edema (absent, present)

Inflammation of the caruncle or plica (absent, present)

Exophthalmos: measured in millimeters using the same Hertel exophthalmometer and the same intercanthal distance for an individual patient

Subjective diplopia score[†]

Eye muscle involvement (ductions in degrees)

Corneal involvement (absent/punctate keratopathy/ulcer)

Optic nerve involvement: best-corrected visual acuity, color vision, optic disk, relative afferent pupillary defect (absent/present), plus visual fields if optic nerve compression is suspected

---

*Based on the seven classic features of inflammation in Graves' ophthalmopathy. The clinical activity score (CAS) is the total number of items present; a CAS ≥3 indicates active ophthalmopathy.
†Subjective diplopia score: 0 = no diplopia; 1 = intermittent (i.e., diplopia in primary position of gaze, when tired, or when first awakening); 2 = inconstant (i.e., diplopia at extremes of gaze); 3 = constant (i.e., continuous diplopia in primary or reading position).
From Melmed S, Polonsky KS, Larsen PR, Kronenberg HM: *Williams textbook of endocrinology,* ed 12, Philadelphia, 2011, Saunders.

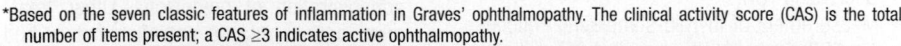

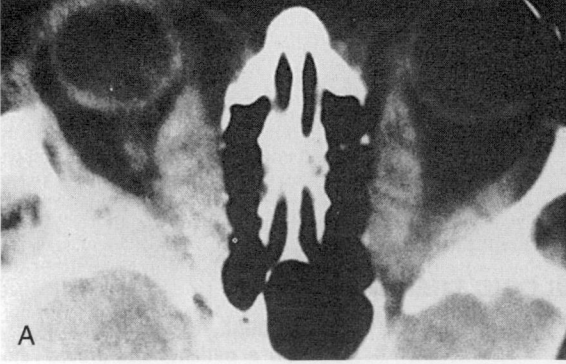
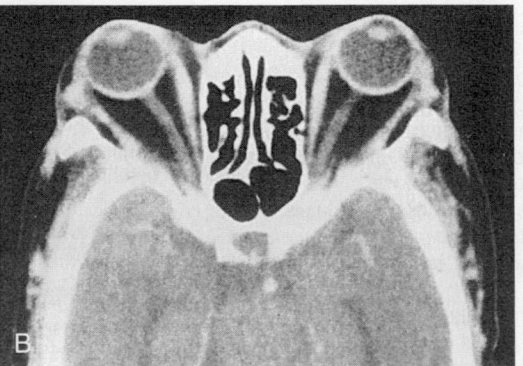

FIGURE 1G-35 Computed tomographic scans of orbits in two patients with Graves' orbitopathy. A, Notice the obviously grossly swollen medial rectus extraocular muscles in both orbits and the resulting proptosis. **B,** The patient shows considerable proptosis with only minimal muscle enlargement, suggesting the presence of a large amount of retroorbital fat. (Courtesy of Dr. Peter Som, New York, NY.)

ℹ BASIC INFORMATION

DEFINITION

Guillain-Barré syndrome (GBS) is an acute immune-mediated polyradiculoneuropathy (affects nerve roots and peripheral nerves), with predominant motor involvement. It is the most common cause of acute flaccid paralysis in the Western hemisphere and probably worldwide. By definition, maximal clinical weakness occurs within 4 wk of disease onset.

SYNONYMS

AIDP (acute inflammatory demyelinating polyradiculoneuropathy)
Acute polyneuropathy
Ascending paralysis
GBS
Postinfectious polyneuritis

ICD-10CM CODES
G61.0 Guillain-Barré syndrome

EPIDEMIOLOGY & DEMOGRAPHICS

INCIDENCE: 0.6 to 1.9 cases/100,000 persons annually without geographic variation. Incidence increases with age. A slight peak in incidence occurs between late adolescence and early adulthood. A slight male preponderance (1.25:1) also exists.
PREDISPOSING FACTORS: Viral (HIV, CMV, EBV, influenza) and bacterial *(Campylobacter jejuni, Mycoplasma pneumoniae)* infections; systemic illness (Hodgkin's lymphoma, immunizations). Major antecedents of GBS are described in Box 1G-1.

ETIOLOGY

- Unknown, but believed to be caused by infection-induced aberrant immune response.
- Preceding infectious illness 1 to 4 wk before disease onset has been noted. The most frequent antecedent infection is *C. jejuni* infection (associated with 30% of cases of GBS and 20% of cases of Miller-Fisher syndrome).
- Humoral and cell-mediated immune attack of peripheral nerve myelin, Schwann cells; sometimes with primary axonal involvement

PHYSICAL FINDINGS & CLINICAL PRESENTATION

- Symmetric weakness, most commonly involving proximal muscles initially, subsequently involving both proximal and distal muscles; difficulty in ambulating, getting up from a chair, or climbing stairs.
- Depressed or absent reflexes bilaterally.
- Minimal to moderate glove and stocking paresthesias/dysesthesia/anesthesia or back pain.
- Pain (caused by involvement of posterior nerve roots) may be prominent.
- Autonomic abnormalities (bradyarrhythmias or tachyarrhythmias, hypotension or hypertension).
- Respiratory insufficiency (caused by weakness of bulbar/intercostal muscles).
- Facial paresis, ophthalmoparesis, dysphagia (secondary to cranial nerve involvement).

BOX 1G-1 Major Antecedents of Guillain-Barré Syndrome

Frequent
Upper respiratory tract infections
Campylobacter jejuni enteritis
Cytomegalovirus infection
Epstein-Barr virus infection
Hepatitis A infection
Hepatitis B infection
Hepatitis C infection
HIV infection

Infrequent
Mycoplasma pneumoniae infection
Haemophilus influenzae infection
Leptospira icterohaemorrhagiae infection
Salmonellosis
Rabies vaccine
Tetanus toxoid
Bacille Calmette-Guérin immunization
Sarcoidosis
Systemic lupus erythematosus
Lymphoma
Trauma
Surgery

Questionable
Hepatitis B vaccine
Influenza vaccine
Hyperthermia
Epidural anesthesia

From Vincent JL et al: *Textbook of critical care*, ed 6, Philadelphia, 2011, Saunders.

- GBS consists of several clinical variants based on the pattern of clinical involvement and electrophysiologic findings. These include:
  1. AIDP (most common form in Europe and North America)
  2. Acute motor axonal neuropathy (AMAN; most prevalent form in China and Japan)
  3. Acute motor and sensory axonal neuropathy (AMSAN; has more severe sensory involvement and is associated with more severe clinical course and poorer prognosis)
  4. **Miller Fisher syndrome** (MFS; triad of ophthalmoplegia, ataxia, and areflexia)
  5. Acute pandysautonomia (rapid onset of parasympathetic and sympathetic failure without motor or sensory involvement)
  6. Regional variants (e.g., pharyngeal-cervical-brachial GBS, pure ataxic GBS)

Ⓓ DIAGNOSIS

DIFFERENTIAL DIAGNOSIS

- Toxic peripheral neuropathies: heavy metal poisoning (lead [microcytic anemia], thallium [alopecia], arsenic [typically accompanied by acute GI illness]), medications (vincristine, disulfiram), organophosphate poisoning, hexacarbon (glue sniffer's neuropathy)
- Nontoxic peripheral neuropathies: acute intermittent porphyria, fulminant vasculitic polyneuropathy, infectious (poliomyelitis, diphtheria, Lyme disease, West Nile virus); tick paralysis

- Neuromuscular junction disorders: myasthenia gravis, botulism, snake envenomations
- Myopathies such as polymyositis, acute necrotizing myopathies caused by drugs
- Metabolic derangements such as hypermagnesemia, hypokalemia, hypophosphatemia
- Acute CNS disorders such as basilar artery thrombosis with brainstem infarction, brainstem encephalomyelitis, transverse myelitis, or spinal cord compression
- Hysterical paralysis or malingering

WORKUP

1. Exclude other causes based on clinical history, examination, and laboratory tests.
2. Lumbar puncture (may be normal in the first 1 to 2 wk of the illness). Typical findings include elevated CSF protein with few mononuclear leukocytes (albuminocytologic dissociation) in 80% to 90% of patients. Elevated CSF cell counts is an expected feature in cases associated with HIV seroconversion.
3. EMG/nerve conduction study (NCS): may be normal in the first 10 to 14 days of the disease. The earliest electrodiagnostic abnormality is prolongation or absence of H-reflexes. NCS evidence of demyelination (prolonged distal latency, conduction velocity slowing, conduction block, temporal dispersion, and prolonged F-waves) in two or more motor nerves confirms diagnosis of AIDP in the appropriate clinical context.

LABORATORY TESTS

- CBC may reveal early leukocytosis with left shift. Electrolytes are tested to exclude metabolic causes.
- Heavy metal testing, urine porphyria screen, creatine kinase, HIV titers, neuroimaging of the brain and spinal cord if diagnosis is uncertain. Nerve root enhancement may be seen on MRI of the lumbosacral spine.
- Antibodies against ganglioside GQ1b may be present in up to 90% of patients with MFS. IgG antibodies against ganglioside GM1 may be associated with AMAN. There are no anti-ganglioside antibodies commonly associated with AIDP.
- In equivocal cases (especially if peripheral nerve vasculitis is a concern), nerve biopsy may aid in confirming a diagnosis of GBS. Sensory nerve biopsy demonstrates segmental demyelination with infiltration of monocytes and T cells into the endoneurium. Axonal loss is commonly seen in sensory nerve biopsy specimens in GBS.

Ⓡ TREATMENT

NONPHARMACOLOGIC THERAPY

- Close monitoring of respiratory function (frequent measurements of vital capacity, negative inspiratory force, and tidal volume) and pulmonary toilet should be done because respiratory failure is the major complication in GBS.
- Frequent repositioning of patient to minimize formation of pressure sores.

- Prevention of thromboembolism with anti-thrombotic stockings and SC heparin (5000 U q12h) in nonambulatory patients.
- Emotional support and social counseling for patient and family.

ACUTE GENERAL Rx

- Infusion of IV immunoglobulins (IVIG; 0.4 g/kg/day for 5 days). Always check serum IgA levels before infusion to prevent anaphylaxis in IgA deficient patients.
- Early therapeutic plasma exchange (TPE or plasmapheresis: 200 to 250 ml/kg over five sessions every other day), started within 7 days of onset of symptoms, is beneficial in reducing the need for mechanical ventilation in patients with rapidly progressive disease and results in improved rate of recovery. It is contraindicated in patients with cardiovascular disease (recent MI, unstable angina), active sepsis, and autonomic dysfunction.
- Both therapies are equally effective and may shorten recovery time by 50%. There is no proven benefit from combining IVIG and plasma exchange.
- Mechanical ventilation may be needed if FVC is <12 to 15 mL/kg, vital capacity is rapidly decreasing or is <1000 ml, negative inspiratory force <20 cm H_2O, PaO_2 is <70, the patient is having significant difficulty clearing secretions or is aspirating.

CHRONIC Rx

- Ventilatory support may be necessary in 10% to 20% of patients. Adequate fluid/electrolyte support and nutrition are necessary, especially in patients with dysautonomia or bulbar dysfunction.
- Aggressive nursing care to prevent decubitus, infections, fecal impactions, and pressure nerve palsies.

- Monitoring and treatment of autonomic dysfunction (bradyarrhythmias or tachyarrhythmias, orthostatic hypotension, systemic hypertension).
- Treatment of back pain and dysesthesia with low-dose tricyclics, gabapentin, and so on. Opiate narcotics can be used cautiously in the short term but may compound dysautonomia.
- Stress ulcer prevention in patients receiving ventilator support.
- Physical and occupational therapy rehabilitation, including supportive devices.

DISPOSITION

- Mortality rate is approximately 5% to 10% worldwide. Causes of death include cardiac arrest, pulmonary embolism, and fulminant infections. A recent study showed 62% complete motor recovery, 14% mild weakness, 9% moderate weakness, 4% bed-bound or ventilated, and 8% dead at 1 yr. Another study suggested that about 33% of patients were free from sensory symptoms at 1 yr, with residual sensory loss present in the lower extremities in 67% and 36% in the upper extremities. About 32% had to change their work, 30% were unable to function at home as well as they could before the disease, and 52% had to alter their leisure activities 1 yr after GBS onset. Excessive fatigue is a common complaint in patients during the recovery phase of GBS. This may be treated with exercise therapy (e.g., bicycle exercise training).
- Predictors for poor recovery (inability to walk independently at 1 yr): age >60 yr, preceding diarrheal illness, recent CMV infection, fulminant or rapidly progressing course, ventilatory dependence, reduced motor amplitudes (<20% normal), or inexcitable

nerves on NCS. Outcomes may also be influenced by complications of medical therapy.
- GBS is typically a monophasic illness. Recurrence may occur in <5% of patients following full recovery.

REFERRAL

Tracheostomy may be necessary in patients with prolonged ventilatory support. Percutaneous endoscopic gastrostomy may be temporarily required.

- GBS is the most common cause of acute flaccid paralysis.
- Close monitoring of ventilatory function with respiratory mechanics (FVC and NIF) is of paramount importance in all patients with suspected GBS.
- Glucocorticoids are not indicated in GBS and may even slow recovery.

PATIENT/FAMILY EDUCATION

Patient education information may be obtained from the Guillain-Barré Foundation International, The Holly Building, 104 1/2 Forrest Avenue, Narberth, PA 19072; phone: (610) 667-0131; fax: (610) 667-7036; toll-free: (866) 224-3301; E-mail: info@gbs-cidp.org

SUGGESTED READINGS

Available at www.expertconsult.com

RELATED CONTENT

Guillain-Barre Syndrome (Patient Information)

AUTHOR: **DIVYA SINGHAL, M.D.**

BASIC INFORMATION

DEFINITION

Gynecomastia is a benign enlargement of male breast, resulting from proliferation of glandular breast tissue.

ICD-10CM CODES
N62 Hypertrophy of breast

EPIDEMIOLOGY

- Most common reason for male breast evaluation.
- Seen in patients of all age groups.
- 60% to 90% of infants have transient gynecomastia due to high estrogenic state of pregnancy.
- Prevalence during adolescence ranges from 4% to 69%. It results from transient increase of estradiol concentration at the onset of puberty.
- Higher incidence in body builders due to use of anabolic steroids.
- 24% to 65% of older men have gynecomastia. It is secondary to decreased testosterone production with advanced age, increased peripheral conversion of testosterone to estrogen, and at times from side effects of medications.

PATHOPHYSIOLOGY

Altered estrogen-androgen balance, in favor of estrogen.

ETIOLOGY

- Physiologic
  Infancy
  Puberty
  Persistent pubertal gynecomastia seen in 25% of cases
  Elderly
- Pathologic
  Idiopathic (25%)
  Increased estrogen production or action
  Testicular tumors (3%)
  Chronic liver disease
  Malnutrition
  Hyperthyroidism
  Adrenal tumors
  Familial gynecomastia
  Decreased testosterone production or action (10%)
  Testicular trauma
  Testicular torsion
  Viral orchitis
  Congenital anorchia
  Renal failure (1%)
  Hyperthyroidism (1.5%)
  Malnutrition
  Androgen insensitivity syndrome
  Five-alpha reductase deficiency
  Pituitary tumors
  Kallmann syndrome
  Klinefelter's syndrome
  Medications (10% to 25%)

Estrogen, gonadotropins, clomiphene, phenytoin, ketoconazole, metronidazole, metoclopramide, alkylating agents, busulfan, methotrexate, cisplatin, cimetidine, ranitidine, omeprazole, flutamide, finasteride, etomidate, HAART therapy, INH, tricyclic antidepressants, phenothiazines, diazepam, haloperidol, calcium channel blocker, ACE inhibitors, spironolactone, digoxin, amiodarone, methyldopa, alcohol, marijuana, heroin, methadone, amphetamine, anabolic steroids Table E1G-17 summarizes the various causes of gynecomastia.

CLINICAL FEATURES

- Although gynecomastia is usually bilateral, it could be unilateral.
- Characterized by concentric rubbery to firm disk of tissue, which is often mobile and located directly beneath the areola (Fig. 1G-36).
- Pain is usually not severe. Varying degree of tenderness and nipple sensitivity are more common than pain, usually in the first 6 mo.

DIAGNOSIS

- Good history and physical examination including review of all medications the patient is taking is helpful.
- Mammogram is recommended for suspected breast cancer.
- Serum concentration of hCG, LH, testosterone, and estradiol should be measured, preferably in the morning, unless the cause is clearly apparent. There is no uniformity of opinion regarding what biochemical evaluation, if any,

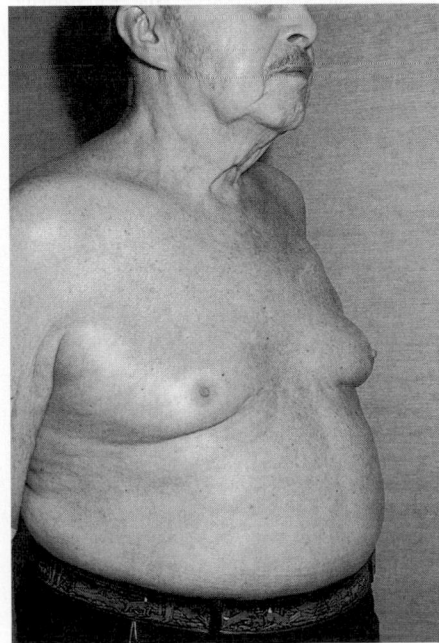

FIGURE 1G-36 Gynecomastia. (From Swartz, MH: *Textbook of physical diagnosis*, ed 7, Philadelphia, 2014, Saunders.)

should be performed in patients with asymptomatic gynecomastia. Fig. E1G-37 describes an algorithm for evaluation of gynecomastia.

DIFFERENTIAL DIAGNOSIS

- Breast cancer
  1. Mass is usually firm to hard
  2. Unilateral
  3. Eccentric in location
  4. Could be associated with nipple discharge and retraction, lymphadenopathy, and skin dimpling
- Pseudogynecomastia or lipomastia
  1. Characterized by fat deposition without glandular proliferation
  2. Seen in obese men
  3. Bilateral
  4. Remain unchanged over time

TREATMENT

- Observation is recommended for most patients with physiologic gynecomastia. They often regress spontaneously. Reassurance and follow-up examination in 3 to 6 mo usually suffice.
- Treat the underlying cause, and stop the offending medications.
- Treatment is most effective in the early stages (first 6 mo). Medical therapy often fails when given for longstanding (>12 mo) cases because of the presence of fibrosis.
- Potential indications of early therapy include severe breast enlargement, pain, tenderness, and psychological embarrassment. Consider giving tamoxifen 10 mg orally twice a day to these patients for up to 3 mo. It is not FDA-approved for this purpose. It results in regression of gynecomastia in approximately 80% of patients and, of which, only 60% had complete regression. As far as breast symptoms, such as pain and tenderness, some improvement is usually seen within a month of therapy.
- Surgery is offered for symptomatic gynecomastia that does not respond to medical therapy. However, for adolescents, surgery is deferred until puberty is completed. The different surgical options include subcutaneous mastectomy, ultrasound-guided liposuction, and suction-assisted lipectomy.
- For prevention of gynecomastia in patients with prostate cancer using antiandrogen therapy, one could offer tamoxifen or radiotherapy.

SUGGESTED READINGS

Available at www.expertconsult.com

RELATED CONTENT

Gynecomastia (Patient Information)

AUTHOR: **HEMANT K. SATPATHY, M.D.**

 **BASIC INFORMATION**

DEFINITION

Hand-foot-mouth disease (HFMD) is a viral illness characterized by superficial lesions of the oral mucosa and skin of the extremities. HFMD is primarily caused by coxsackie or enterovirus infection and can be transmitted by either respiratory droplet contact or fecal-oral contact. Although young children are predominantly affected, adults are also at risk. This disease is usually self-limited and benign, although outbreaks in the Asia Pacific region have been increasingly complicated by neurologic and cardiopulmonary sequelae.

SYNONYMS

Vesicular stomatitis with exanthema
Coxsackie virus infection
Enterovirus infection

ICD-10CM CODES
B08.4 Enteroviral vesicular stomatitis with exanthem

EPIDEMIOLOGY & DEMOGRAPHICS

- HFMD most often affects children <10 yr.
  - Children <5 yr are at the highest risk of infection and have the most severe cases.
- HFMD is contagious. Close contacts of affected children, including family members and health care workers, are the most commonly infected adults.
- Infection is spread from person to person by direct contact with saliva, respiratory secretions, fluid in vesicles, or stool.
- A person is most contagious during the first week of illness.
- Outbreaks tend to occur during the summer.
- Infection leads to immunity, but a second episode may occur after infection with a different etiologic virus or type.

PHYSICAL FINDINGS & CLINICAL PRESENTATION

Symptoms:
- After a 4- to 6-day incubation period, patients may report odynophagia, sore throat, malaise, and fever (38.3° to 40° C).
- 1 to 2 days later, the characteristic oral lesions appear (small red spots that blister and may ulcerate). The fluid from these lesions is infectious, and disease can be transmitted through contact with the fluid.
- In 75% of cases, skin lesions on the extremities accompany these oral manifestations (small flat or raised red bumps, sometimes with blisters).
- 11% of adults have cutaneous findings.
- Lesions appear over the course of 1 or 2 days.
Physical findings:
- Oral lesions are common and are usually found on the tongue, buccal mucosa, gingivae, and hard palate.

- Oral lesions initially start as 1- to 3-mm erythematous macules and evolve into gray vesicles on an erythematous base.
- Vesicles are frequently broken by the time of presentation and appear as superficial, gray ulcers with surrounding erythema.
- Skin lesions of the palms of the hands and soles of the feet are common and start as linear erythematous papules (3 to 10 mm in diameter) that evolve into gray vesicles that may be mildly painful (Fig. E1H-1). These vesicles are usually intact at presentation and remain so until they desquamate within 2 wk.
- Involvement of the buttocks and genital area is also common (present in 31% of cases).
- Although rare, atypical findings such as fingernail or toenail loss (nail separation from the nail matrix, otherwise known as onychomadesis) after HFMD (notably with the A6 strain of coxsackie virus) has been reported in children. The nail loss is temporary, and nails grow back without intervention.
- Another atypical skin manifestation is that of "eczema coxsackium," which is described as the typical skin lesions of coxsackie virus but with a more extensive distribution involving the trunk and extremities, localized to areas of active or past atopic dermatitis.
- In rare cases, encephalitis, meningitis, myocarditis, poliomyelitis-like paralysis, and pulmonary edema may develop. Sporadic acute paralysis and long-term neurologic sequelae have been reported with enterovirus 71.
- Although information is limited, there is no clear evidence that pregnancy outcomes are affected.

ETIOLOGY

- Coxsackie virus group A, type 16, was the first and is the most common cause of HFMD.
- Enterovirus 71 is the second leading cause of HFMD. Enterovirus 71 is neurotropic and has a predilection for the brainstem, leading to more severe cases of the disease. Infection rates have been rising in the Asia Pacific region.
- Coxsackie viruses A5, A6, A7, A9, A10, B1, B2, B3, and B5 have also been implicated.
- Coxsackie A6 has been known to cause a severe skin rash and self-limited nail abnormalities (onychomadesis). Patients with this strain may lack oral lesions.
- Epidemic outbreaks have been reported with coxsackie A16 and enterovirus 71.

 **DIAGNOSIS**

DIFFERENTIAL DIAGNOSIS
- Aphthous stomatitis
- Herpes simplex infection
- Herpangina
- Behçet's disease
- Erythema multiforme
- Pemphigus
- Gonorrhea

- Acute leukemia
- Lymphoma
- Allergic contact dermatitis

WORKUP

The diagnosis is made on the basis of typical history and characteristic physical examination.

LABORATORY TESTS

- Not indicated unless the diagnosis is in doubt such as for a suspected case with an atypical presentation.
  - Oropharyngeal specimen, stool specimen, or vesicular fluid may be obtained to identify the presence of enterovirus or coxsackie virus by polymerase chain reaction (PCR), but may take from 2 to 4 weeks for results.
    - Identification of a certain strain is only available in public health laboratories.

 **TREATMENT**

ACUTE GENERAL Rx

- Symptomatic therapy is given for this usually self-limited disease.
- There are currently no available approved therapies for more severe cases. Antivirals and IV immunoglobulin have been evaluated for enterovirus 71 infections, but these treatments have not been evaluated in randomized, placebo-controlled studies.
- Systemic steroids should be avoided because they have been associated with more severe disease and higher viral loads.

DISPOSITION

Prognosis is excellent except in rare cases of central nervous system or cardiac involvement. Most are managed as outpatients.

REFERRAL

Not usually needed

PEARLS & CONSIDERATIONS

- Frequent handwashing, disinfection of contaminated surfaces, and washing of soiled articles of clothing can help reduce transmission.
- HFMD has no relation to hoof and mouth disease in cattle.

SUGGESTED READINGS
Available at www.expertconsult.com

RELATED CONTENT
Hand, Foot, and Mouth Disease (Patient Information)

AUTHOR: **ERICA HARDY, M.D., M.M.S.**

BASIC INFORMATION

DEFINITION

The term *cluster headache* refers to attacks of severe, unilateral pain that is orbital, supraorbital, temporal, or any combination of these sites, lasting 15 to 180 minutes, and occurring from once every other day to eight times a day. The attacks are associated with one or more of the following, all of which are ipsilateral: conjunctival injection, lacrimation, nasal congestion, rhinorrhea, forehead and facial sweating, miosis, ptosis, and eyelid edema. Most patients are restless or agitated during an attack.

SYNONYMS

Cluster headache
Ciliary neuralgia
Erythromelalgia of the head
Erythroprosopalgia of Bing
Horton's headache

ICD-10CM CODES
G44.001 Cluster headache syndrome, unspecified, intractable
G44.009 Cluster headache syndrome, unspecified, not intractable
G44.011 Episodic cluster headache, intractable
G44.019 Episodic cluster headache, not intractable
G44.021 Chronic cluster headache, intractable
G44.029 Chronic cluster headache, not intractable

EPIDEMIOLOGY & DEMOGRAPHICS

INCIDENCE: Estimated to occur in 0.05% to 1% of the population
PREDOMINANT SEX: Occurs in males at least five times more commonly than in females
PREDOMINANT AGE: Peak age of onset between 20 and 40 yr
GENETICS: May be inherited (autosomal dominant) in approximately 5% of cases

PHYSICAL FINDINGS & CLINICAL PRESENTATION

- During attack: ipsilateral conjunctival injection, lacrimation, nasal congestion, rhinorrhea, facial sweating, Horner's syndrome.
- In contrast to migraine sufferers, patients are agitated and active during an attack.
- Permanent partial Horner's syndrome in 5% of patients; otherwise examination is normal.

ETIOLOGY

Activation of the posterior hypothalamic gray matter resulting in trigeminal activation coupled with parasympathetic activation. The pathophysiology remains controversial.

DIAGNOSIS

- Severe or very severe unilateral orbital, supraorbital, and/or temporal pain lasting 15 to 180 minutes.

- Frequency of every other day to eight per day; they may cluster seasonally or at a certain time in a patient's life.
- Headache is accompanied by at least one of the following (ipsilateral):
  1. Conjunctival injection and/or lacrimation
  2. Nasal congestion and/or rhinorrhea
  3. Eyelid edema
  4. Forehead and facial sweating
  5. Miosis and/or ptosis
  6. Restlessness or agitation

DIFFERENTIAL DIAGNOSIS

- Migraine
- Trigeminal neuralgia
- Temporal arteritis
- Post-herpetic neuralgia
- Venous sinus thrombosis
- Carotid-cavernous fistula or other cavernous sinus lesions
- Other trigeminal autonomic cephalalgias
- Section II describes the differential diagnosis of headaches

WORKUP

Diagnosis is usually established by characteristic history.

IMAGING STUDIES

- None, unless history or examination suggests focal neurologic deficit or headaches change in character or are of new onset.
- MRI of the brain along with vascular imaging may be necessary to exclude secondary headaches at the time of initial diagnosis.

 # TREATMENT

NONPHARMACOLOGIC THERAPY

Avoidance of alcohol, histamine, nitroglycerin, and tobacco during clusters

ABORTIVE Rx

- Inhalation of 100% oxygen by face mask for 15 min often aborts an attack.
- About 75% of users of triptans (sumatriptan, zolmitriptan) will be pain free within 20 minutes. Only injectable and nasal formulations achieve a rapid response to be efficacious.
- Cafergot, octreotide, intranasal lidocaine, or dihydroergotamine may abort an attack or prevent one if given just before a predictable episode. Acute episode is typically resolved before oral analgesics become effective, although indomethacin and other NSAIDs may also be effective in prolonged attacks.
- Capsaicin nasal spray, available as a homeopathic OTC preparation, may be effective in aborting some cluster episodes, although double-blind, randomized, controlled trials are lacking due to lack of inert placebo.

PROPHYLAXIS Rx

Various medications have been tried without great success, although good responses may be obtained in up to 50% of cases. Examples include:

- Valproic acid: start at 500 mg/day
- Topiramate: up to 50 mg bid
- Verapamil: up to 480 mg/day as tolerated. Verapamil can be used as first-line prophylactic therapy and can also be used to treat chronic cluster headaches.
- Lithium: 200 mg tid with frequent monitoring and adjustment to maintain therapeutic serum level of 0.4 to 1 mEq/L. Equally effective as verapamil, but with more side effects
- Methysergide: 1 to 2 mg tid; requires familiarity with the potential adverse effects and use of "drug holidays" to decrease risk of fibrosis
- Ergotamine tartrate: 3 to 4 mg/day during clusters
- Prednisone: 60 mg PO daily for 1 wk followed by taper; headaches can return during taper
- Greater and lesser occipital nerve blocks, with the use of local anesthetics including lidocaine and bupivacaine along with steroids like Depo-Medrol, dexamethasone, or triamcinolone, may be used to shorten the duration of the cluster period. Consensus guidelines from the American Headache Society have been published recently.
- There is emerging evidence for benefit of a sphenopalatine ganglion block that may be available at some centers, for treatment and prophylaxis of cluster attacks.

DISPOSITION

Headache-free periods tend to increase with increasing age.

REFERRAL

Refractory cluster headaches may require referral to a headache specialist.

PEARLS & CONSIDERATIONS

COMMENTS

- Cluster headaches are divided into episodic (attacks lasting up to 1 yr with more than 1 mo pain-free periods) and chronic (>1 yr without remission). Episodic cluster headache is six times more common than the chronic form.
- Home oxygen therapy is reasonable for cluster headache sufferers.

SUGGESTED READINGS

Available at www.expertconsult.com

RELATED CONTENT

Cluster Headaches (Patient Information)

AUTHOR: **SIDDHARTH KAPOOR, M.D.**

BASIC INFORMATION

DEFINITION

Migraine headaches are recurrent headaches that are either preceded by a focal neurologic symptom (migraine with aura), occur independently without preceding focal neurologic symptoms (migraine without aura), or have atypical presentations (migraine variants). The migraine aura typically is characterized by visual or sensory symptoms that develop over 5 to 60 min. If aura includes motor weakness, the migraine is referred to as hemiplegic. In migraine with and without aura, the headache is typically unilateral, pulsatile, and associated with nausea and vomiting, photophobia, and phonophobia. Migraines that occur ≥15 days every month for ≥3 months are known as chronic; otherwise, they are referred to as episodic.

ICD-10CM CODES
G43.909	Migraine, unspecified, not intractable, without status migrainosus
G43.1	Migraine with aura (classical migraine)
G43.0	Migraine without aura (common migraine)
G43.2	Status migrainosus
G43.3	Complicated migraine

EPIDEMIOLOGY & DEMOGRAPHICS

INCIDENCE: Increases from infancy, peaks during the third decade of life, then decreases
PREVALENCE (IN U.S.): Females: 18%; males: 6%. More than 50% of persons affected by migraine headaches report reduced work or school productivity.
AGE: Peak prevalence between ages of 18 and 49
PREDOMINANT SEX: Female/male ratio of 3:1
GENETICS
- Familial predisposition: more than 50% of migraine sufferers have an affected family member
- Autosomal-dominant transmission for some rare migraine variants (familial hemiplegic migraine, cerebral autosomal-dominant arteriopathy with subcortical infarcts and leukoencephalopathy [CADASIL]); familial hemiplegic migraines have been associated with calcium channelopathy, sodium channelopathy, and Na$^+$/K$^+$- ATPase dysfunction.

PHYSICAL FINDINGS & CLINICAL PRESENTATION

- Normal between episodes
- Normal for migraine without aura.
- Focal motor or sensory abnormalities possible for migraine with aura or migraine variants.
- Common aura types include scintillating scotoma, bright zigzags, homonymous visual disturbance such as paresthesia, speech disturbances, or hemiparesis (familial or sporadic hemiplegic migraine). Other visual phenomena include image distortion or "Alice in Wonderland" effect

ETIOLOGY

The pathophysiology of migraines is not clearly understood. It is believed that a primary neuronal event results in a trigeminovascular reflex causing neurogenic inflammation. Serotonin, substance P, nitric oxide, and calcitonin gene-related peptide also play a role, but the exact mechanism is unknown. Cortical spreading depression is probably responsible for the aura.

DIAGNOSIS

Migraine without aura:
- Five attacks fulfilling criteria
- Headache attacks lasting 4 to 72 hr
- Headache has at least two of the following characteristics:
  1. Unilateral location
  2. Pulsating quality
  3. Moderate or severe pain intensity
  4. Aggravation or causing avoidance of routine physical activity
- At least one of the following during headache:
  1. Nausea and/or vomiting
  2. Photophobia and phonophobia

Migraine with aura:
- At least two attacks
- Aura consisting of at least one of the following, but no motor weakness:
  1. Fully reversible visual symptoms, including positive and/or negative features
  2. Fully reversible sensory symptoms, including positive and/or negative features
- At least two of the following:
  1. Homonymous visual symptoms and/or unilateral sensory symptoms
  2. At least one aura symptom develops gradually over >5 min and/or different aura symptoms occur in succession over >5 min
- A migraine occurring during or within 60 min of the aura

DIFFERENTIAL DIAGNOSIS

- A diagnosis of migraine is possible only after five recurrent episodes.
- The first or the worst headache should always be investigated and the differential includes headaches from all secondary causes.
- Headache red flags can be remembered by the mnemonic SNOOP:
  1. S: systemic symptoms of fever, weight loss
  2. S: secondary risk factors of immunosuppression from any cause, cancer
  3. N: neurologic deficits, altered consciousness
  4. O: onset is sudden, abrupt, or split second
  5. O: older, age >50 for new-onset headache should be worked up for giant cell arteritis
  6. P: previous headache history is different or there is a change to headache
- Section II describes the differential diagnosis of headaches

WORKUP

- In general, no additional investigation is needed with recurrent, typical attacks with usual age of onset, family history, and a normal physical examination.

- If there is an unusual presentation and/or unexpected findings on examination, investigation for other causes is required.

LABORATORY TESTS

Lumbar puncture for history of abrupt-onset headaches and uncertain diagnosis of migraine

IMAGING STUDIES

- Imaging should be done in patients with headaches and an unexplained abnormal finding on the neurologic examination.
- Imaging should be considered in patients with rapidly increasing headache frequency, history of dizziness or incoordination, headache causing wakening from sleep, or headaches worsening with Valsalva maneuver.

TREATMENT

Consider the use of a headache log/diary to identify triggers of headaches, record efficacy of treatments, and track history of headaches.

NONPHARMACOLOGIC THERAPY

- Avoid any identifiable provoking factors: caffeine, tobacco, and alcohol may trigger attacks, as may dietary or other environmental precipitants (less common)
- Avoid stressors in life and minimize variations in daily routine with regular sleep, meals, and exercise
- Relaxation training, behavioral therapy, and biofeedback. Trials have shown that among young persons with chronic migraine, the use of cognitive behavior therapy (CBT) plus amitriptyline results in greater reductions in days with headaches and migraine-related disability compared with use of headache education plus amitriptyline.[1]

ACUTE ANALGESIC Rx

- Many oral agents are ineffective because of poor absorption from migraine-induced gastric stasis. Non-oral route of administration should be selected in patients with severe nausea or vomiting.
- NSAIDs such as ketorolac, combination analgesics, or barbiturates may be used.

ACUTE ABORTIVE Rx

- IV antiemetic (prochlorperazine, metoclopramide, domperidone): Acute dystonic reactions and akathisia are rare side effects. These are generally not used as monotherapy.
- Ergotamine and ergotamine combinations (PO/PR) and dihydroergotamine (DHE 45) (SC, IV, IM, intranasal) have well-documented efficacy against migraines. DHE is usually administered in combination with an antiemetic drug (Table 1H-2).
- Triptans (SC, PO, and intranasal) are now considered the drug class of choice for abortive therapy. Meta-analysis suggests that

---

[1]Powers SW et al: Cognitive behavioral therapy plus amitriptyline for chronic migraine in children and adolescents, *JAMA* 310(24):2622-2630, 2013.

TABLE 1H-2 Abortive and Analgesic Therapy for Migraine*

Drug	Route	Dose
Triptans (Serotonin Agonists)		
Sumatriptan	Subcutaneous	6 mg, repeat in 2 hr (max 2 doses/day)
Sumatriptan	Oral	25 mg, 50 mg, 100 mg, repeat in 2 hr (max 200 mg/day)
Sumatriptan	Nasal spray	5 mg, 20 mg, repeat in 2 hr (max 40 mg/day)
Zolmitriptan	Oral	1.25, 2.5 mg, 5 mg, repeat in 2 hr (max 10 mg/day)
Zolmitriptan	Nasal spray	5 mg, repeat in 2 hr (max 10 mg/day)
Zolmitriptan	Orally disintegrating tab	2.5, 5 mg, repeat in 2 hr (max 10 mg/day)
Naratriptan	Oral	1 mg, 2.5 mg, repeat in 4 hr (max 5 mg/day)
Rizatriptan	Oral	5 mg, 10 mg, repeat in 2 hr (max 30 mg/day)
Almotriptan	Oral	6.25 mg, 12.5 mg, may repeat in 2 hr (max 25 mg/day)
Eletriptan	Oral	20 mg, 40 mg, may repeat in 2 hr (max 80 mg/day)
Frovatriptan	Oral	2.5 mg, may repeat in 2 hr (max 7.5 mg/day); may also be used for mini prophylaxis
Ergotamine Preparations		
Ergotamine and caffeine	Oral	2 tablets, may repeat 1 tab q30 min (max 6/day)
Ergotamine and caffeine	Rectal	1 suppository, repeat in 1 hr (max 2/day)
Ergotamine	Sublingual	1 tablet, repeat in 1 hr (max 2/day)
Dihydroergotamine	Intramuscular	0.5-1.0 mg, repeat twice at 1-hr intervals (max 3 mg/attack)
	Subcutaneous	
	Intravenous	
	Nasal spray	
Sympathomimetics (with or without Barbiturates or Codeine)		
Isometheptene+ dichloralphenazone+ acetaminophen	Oral	1 to 2 capsules, repeat in 4 hr (max 8/day)
Nonsteroidal Antiinflammatory Drugs		
Acetaminophen+ (should not be used alone)	Oral	2 tablets, repeat in 6 hr (max 8/day aspirin+caffeine)
Naproxen	Oral	550-750 mg, repeat in 1 hr (max 3 times/wk)
Meclofenamate	Oral	100-200 mg, repeat in 1 hr (max 3 times/wk)
Flurbiprofen	Oral	50-100 mg, repeat in 1 hr (max 3 times/wk)
Ibuprofen	Oral	200-300 mg, repeat in 1 hr (max 3 times/wk)
Antiemetics		
Promethazine	Oral	50-125 mg
	Intramuscular	No clear benefit in migraine, may be used
Prochlorperazine	Oral	1-25 mg
	Rectal	2.5-25 mg (suppository)
	Intramuscular/IV	5-10 mg, good evidence for strong benefit
Chlorpromazine	Oral	10-25 mg
	Rectal	50-100 mg (suppository)
	Intravenous	Up to 35 mg, use with monitoring, some evidence for good benefit
Trimethobenzamide	Oral	250 mg
	Rectal	200 mg
Metoclopramide	Oral	5-10 mg
	Intramuscular	10 mg
	Intravenous	5-10 mg
Dimenhydrinate	Oral	50 mg

*For side effects and contraindications consult the manufacturer's drug insert before prescribing any of these drugs.
Modified from Wiederholt WC: *Neurology for non-neurologists*, ed 4, Philadelphia, 2000, Saunders.

10 mg rizatriptan, 40 mg eletriptan, and 12.5 mg almotriptan are most effective.
- Early administration improves effectiveness.
- There is an emerging role for the use of IV magnesium (1 g), IV valproate infusions to abort migraine headaches. IV dexamethasone up to 12 mg may be used for headaches lasting more than 72 hours.
- Greater and lesser occipital nerve blocks may also be performed to alleviate pain in the acute setting. This may be combined with auriculotemporal, supraorbital, and supratrochlear nerve block to achieve anesthesia in the area of perceived pain. Steroids should generally be avoided with these nerve blocks because of lack of benefit.
- Recently an OTC preparation classified as a homeopathic drug has become available. It is derived from capsaicin, is used as a nasal spray, and is reported to be beneficial in both migraine and cluster headaches.
- Single pulse transcranial magnetic stimulation has also been approved by the FDA but is only available in Europe at the current time.

PROPHYLAXIS Rx
- Prophylactic treatment is generally indicated when headaches occur more than once a week or when symptomatic treatments

are contraindicated or not effective. They are most effective when initiated during a headache-free period. All prophylaxis should be maintained for at least 3 months before deeming the medication a failure.

- Well-established options for prophylactic treatment include β-blockers (propranolol, timolol, atenolol, metoprolol), tricyclic antidepressants (amitriptyline), and the antiepileptic drugs topiramate and valproic acid.
- Less-established options include calcium channel blockers, selective serotonin reuptake inhibitors, and the antiepileptic drug gabapentin.
- Supraorbital transcutaneous electrical stimulation has been approved by the FDA for prophylaxis of episodic migraine and is widely available with a prescription in Europe and North America.
- The FDA has approved injection of onabotulinum toxin A (Botox) for prevention of headaches in adult patients with chronic migraines only (≥15 headache days/mo for ≥3 mo). The recommended total dose is 155 total units administered intramuscularly every 12 wk divided among 31 sites in head and neck area (frontalis, corrugator, procerus, occipitalis, temporalis, trapezius, cervical paraspinal muscle group). A maximum of 195 units is allowed.
- Surgical treatment for migraine using nerve decompression has been advocated recently but remains highly controversial, with poorly established results. This should be pursued only in collaboration with a headache specialist.

DISPOSITION

With advancing age, many patients will have sustained reduction of migraine headaches.

REFERRAL

To neurologist if uncertain about diagnosis or treatment not effective

PEARLS & CONSIDERATIONS

- Avoid overuse of narcotics, barbiturates, caffeine, and benzodiazepines because they are habit-forming.
- Long-term use of analgesic medications can result in drug-induced or rebound headaches.
- Useful mnemonic for migraine is POUND: *P*ulsatile, *O*ne-day in duration, *U*nilateral, *N*ausea/vomiting, *D*isabling.
- Migraine with aura is a significant contributor to stroke risk in women.

SUGGESTED READINGS

Available at www.expertconsult.com

RELATED CONTENT

Migraine Headache (Patient Information)

AUTHOR: **SIDDHARTH KAPOOR, M.D.**

BASIC INFORMATION

Tension-type headache (TTH) is a highly prevalent primary headache disorder that is not associated with nausea or vomiting. Although previously thought to be caused by psychological factors and muscle contraction, current thinking implicates neurobiological mechanisms.

ICD-10CM CODES
G44.209 Tension-type headache,
        unspecified, not intractable
G44.201 Tension-type headache,
        unspecified, intractable

EPIDEMIOLOGY & DEMOGRAPHICS

Most common type of headache, representing 70% of all headaches presenting to primary care physicians. Women are affected more often than men.

PHYSICAL FINDINGS & CLINICAL PRESENTATION

Headaches have an insidious progression, ranging from infrequent (<1 day per month) to chronic. Although considered a "featureless" headache disorder, either one symptom of photo- or phonophobia may still be present. Concurrent problems, such as anxiety, depression, and analgesic overuse, may aggravate the headaches. Patients may have pericranial tenderness to palpation on exam, which should otherwise be normal.

PATHOPHYSIOLOGY

- TTH is no longer thought to be due to a psychological problem or abnormal muscle contraction. Similar to migraine, TTH is likely a heterogeneous disorder with several possible pathophysiologic mechanisms.
- In episodic TTH, peripheral mechanisms are predominant, whereas central mechanisms are involved in chronic TTH.

(Dx) DIAGNOSIS

Tension-type headache:
- At least 10 headaches
- Lasting from 30 minutes to 7 days
- Having at least two of the following features:
  1. Bilateral
  2. Pressure or tightening (nonpulsating) quality
  3. Mild or moderate intensity
  4. Not aggravated by routine physical activity such as walking or climbing stairs

- Both of the following:
  1. No nausea or vomiting
  2. No more than one of photophobia or phonophobia
- Not better accounted for by another diagnosis

DIFFERENTIAL DIAGNOSIS

- Migraine (would expect associated symptoms; see topic "Headache, Migraine").
- Cervical spine disease.
- Intracranial mass (may present with focal neurologic signs, seizures, or headache awakening patient from sleep).
- Idiopathic intracranial hypertension (found more often in obese women of childbearing age).
- Medication overuse headache.
- Secondary headache (e.g., obstructive sleep apnea, temporomandibular joint syndrome, thyrotoxicosis, drug side effects).
- Section II describes the differential diagnosis of headaches.

WORKUP

- Routine testing is not needed; the diagnosis may be established clinically.
- Thorough history to identify any red flag features (see topic "Headache, Migraine", SNOOP mnemonic in differential diagnosis) and physical examination (looking for papilledema) for all patients being evaluated for headache
- Neuroimaging, preferably with contrast-enhanced MRI, should be performed when red flag features are identified by history or unexplained neurologic findings are present on examination.
- Erythrocyte sedimentation rate in patients 50 yr or older (to screen for giant cell arteritis).

(Rx) TREATMENT

Current evidence supports synergistic benefits of combined nonpharmacologic and pharmacologic interventions. Nonpharmacologic therapy may include behavioral sleep modification, acupuncture, cognitive-behavioral therapy, relaxation training, and biofeedback.

ACUTE Rx

- Simple analgesics (i.e., NSAID, acetaminophen).
- Combination analgesics containing caffeine may be used a second-line treatment, although use on more than 10 days per month may lead to medication overuse headache.
- Narcotic and barbiturate-containing analgesics should be avoided.

PREVENTIVE Rx

- Tricyclic antidepressants (e.g., amitriptyline 10-50 mg qhs) (first choice)
  Other options: mirtazapine, venlafaxine, and tizanidine

DISPOSITION

The headache prognosis is generally favorable. Some patients will not respond to treatment.

REFERRAL

If red flags are present on history or exam or if the patient is not improving with treatment

(!) PEARLS & CONSIDERATIONS

It is imperative to avoid overuse of caffeine-, narcotic-, and barbiturate-containing medications because of the risk of rebound headaches.

SUGGESTED READINGS
Available at www.expertconsult.com

RELATED CONTENT
Tension Headache (Patient Information)

AUTHOR: **JONATHAN H. SMITH, M.D.**

BASIC INFORMATION

DEFINITION

Complete heart block (CHB) is the absence of electrical impulse transmission from the atria to the ventricles when atrioventricular (AV) junction is not physiologically refractory, due to a functional or anatomical impairment of the conduction system, resulting in a bradycardia characterized by AV dissociation. It may be acquired or congenital. CHB can be permanent or reversible.

SYNONYMS

Third-degree AV block
CHB
Complete AV block

ICD-10CM CODES

I44.2 Atrioventricular block, complete

EPIDEMIOLOGY & DEMOGRAPHICS

- The prevalence of CHB is 0.04%.
- The prevalence of CHB increases with age.

PHYSICAL FINDINGS & CLINICAL PRESENTATION

Physical examination may be normal. Cannon A waves may appear in the jugular vein periodically due to the right atrium contracting during ventricular systole. Patients may present with the following clinical manifestations:

- Dizziness, palpitations
- Syncope or presyncope (due to reduced cardiac output)
- Fatigue, impaired exercise tolerance
- Mental status changes
- Congestive heart failure
- Angina pectoris
- Some patients may be asymptomatic (e.g., congenital CHB)

ETIOLOGY

- Fibrosis or sclerosis of the conduction system, Lenegre and Lev disease
- Acute myocardial infarction—inferior (14%) or anterior (2%) wall of patients, usually within 24 hours
- Drug effect (digitalis, calcium channel blockers, beta-blockers, amiodarone)
- Cardiomyopathy and myocarditis
- Infiltrative processes of the myocardium (amyloidosis, sarcoidosis, scleroderma, tumor)
- Metabolic abnormalities (hyperkalemia, hypoxia, hypothyroidism)

- Lyme carditis, rheumatoid nodules, polymyositis, Chagas' disease
- Neuromuscular disorders (Becker muscular dystrophy, myotonic muscular dystrophy)
- Congenital (birth from mothers with systemic lupus)
- Hyperkalemia
- Familial: SCN5 sodium channel mutations have been associated with CHB
- Iatrogenic (cardiac surgery, catheter ablation of arrhythmias, percutaneous coronary intervention). Transcatheter aortic valve implantation (TAVI) is shown to be frequently associated with new conduction abnormalities; patients with preexisting right bundle-branch block are at increased risk of CHB (resolves over time in most patients).
- Paroxysmal due to phase 4 block of the His-Purkinje system

DIAGNOSIS

DIFFERENTIAL DIAGNOSIS

- The differential diagnosis includes lesser degree of AV block, automatic accelerated junctional rhythms, and nonconducted premature atrial contractions.
- The atrial rate must be faster than the ventricular rate (more As than Vs) and the junctional or ventricular rate is regular. Episodes of AV dissociation with an accelerated ventricular or junctional pacemaker overtaking

the sinus node can often look like heart block on a single electrocardiogram.

WORKUP

- Workup such as routine labs, cardiac biomarkers, and cardiac imaging should be dictated by the clinical circumstances.
- ECG: diagnostic of the disease (Figs. 1H-2 and 1H-3):
  1. P waves are present with a regular atrial rate that is faster than the ventricular rate.
  2. P waves are not related to the QRS complexes. The PR intervals are variable.
  3. RR intervals are regular.
  4. QRS complexes may be narrow with rate of 40 to 60 beats/min (block proximal to His bundle) or wide with a rate of <40 beats/min (block distal to His bundle)—depending on the location of the block in the conduction system.
  5. Complete AV block can result from block at the level of AV node, within the His bundle, or distal to it, in the Purkinje system.

TREATMENT

ACUTE GENERAL Rx

- Initial treatment should focus on the hemodynamic stability and symptoms of the patient.
- Consider temporary pacemaker insertion if ventricular escape rate is slow (<40 beats/min) and associated with symptoms or hemo-

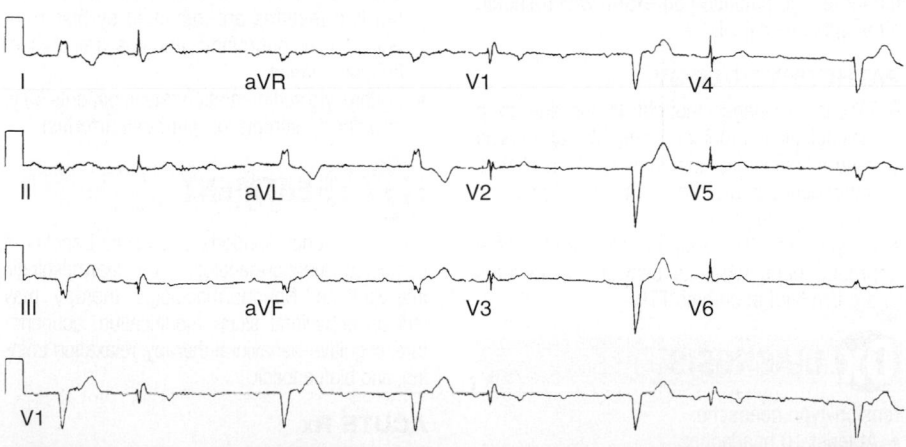

FIGURE 1H-3 High-grade atrioventricular block. Note that only three P waves conducted to the ventricle in the whole tracing. Conducted P waves were associated with normal PR intervals and right bundle branch block, a finding suggesting infranodal block. All other P waves were blocked, and ventricular escape rhythm with a left bundle branch block pattern is observed. Note that the block is not caused by retrograde concealment in the atrioventricular node or His-Purkinje system from the ventricular escape complexes because the conducted P waves occurred at a short cycle following the escape complexes. (From Issa Z et al: *Clinical arrhythmology and electrophysiology,* ed 2, Philadelphia, 2012, Saunders.)

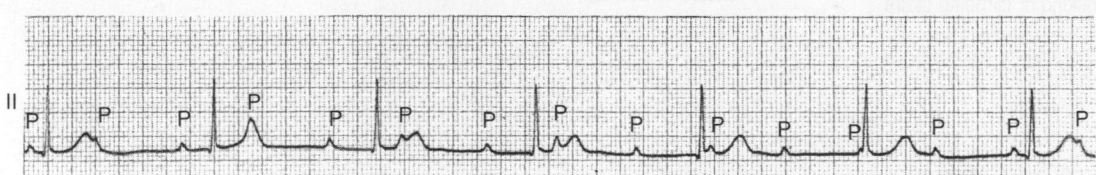

FIGURE 1H-2 Third-degree (complete) atrioventricular heart block is characterized by independent atrial (P) and ventricular (QRS) activity. The atrial rate is always faster than the ventricular rate. The PR intervals are completely variable. Some P waves fall on the T wave, distorting its shape. Others may fall in the QRS complex and be "lost." Notice that the QRS complexes are of normal width, indicating that the ventricles are being paced from the atrioventricular junction. (From Goldberger AL [ed]: *Clinical electrocardiography,* ed 5, St Louis, 1994, Mosby.)

dynamic compromise as well as wide QRS escape rhythms, which can be unstable, and QT prolongation above 500 ms, increasing the risk of torsade de pointes ventricular tachycardias.

- CHB as a complication of inferior MI usually only requires temporary pacing; however, a CHB as a result of anterior MI often requires permanent pacing (Table 1H-3).
- Acquired CHB usually requires pacing, but patients with congenital CHB often have sufficiently rapid escape rhythm to prevent symptoms and avoid permanent pacemaker implantation.
- Withdraw AV-nodal blocking agents if any.
- Short-term therapy (until adequate pacing therapy is established)
  1. Vagolytic agents such as atropine may be used to increase the rate of the escape rhythm (for AV nodal level blocks)
  2. Catecholamines such as isoproterenol transiently used for a CHB at any site

(use with extreme caution or not at all in patients with coronary artery disease or in patients with digitalis toxicity).
  3. Percutaneous external cardiac pacing (uncomfortable for patients and not always reliably capturing the ventricle).
- Drugs cannot be relied on to increase HR for more than several hours or days without side effects; therefore, temporary or permanent pacemaker insertion is indicated.
- Symptomatic CHB in the absence of a condition that is likely to resolve is an ACC/AHA/HRS Class I indication for permanent pacemaker (PPM) placement.
- Class 1 indications for PPM placement in asymptomatic patients according to the ACC/AHA guidelines include:
  1. Patients in sinus rhythm, with documented asystolic pauses greater than or equal to 3.0 sec or an escape rate <40 beats/min, or with an escape rhythm that is below the AV node

  2. Patients with atrial fibrillation and bradycardia with one or more pauses of at least 5 sec or longer
  3. After catheter ablation of the AV junction
  4. If cardiomegaly or LV dysfunction is present with ventricular rates of 40 beats/min or faster
  5. Postoperative CHB that is not expected to resolve
  6. When it is associated with neuromuscular diseases, such as Erb dystrophy (limb-girdle muscular dystrophy), Kearns-Sayre syndrome, myotonic muscular dystrophy, and peroneal muscular atrophy
  7. CHB present during exercise in the absence of myocardial ischemia
- Therapy is directed toward the underlying etiology if there is a reversible source (i.e., IV antibiotics for Lyme disease).

CHRONIC Rx

Dual-chamber pacemaker implantation. Patients with PPM need regular follow-up and pacemaker monitoring to ensure proper device functioning.

DISPOSITION

- Mortality is highest in the neonatal period in congenital CHB.
- Prognosis is favorable after insertion of pacemaker and related to the underlying etiology of complete AV block (e.g., myocardial infarction, cardiomyopathy).
- Nonrandomized studies have shown that PPM insertion improves survival in patients with CHB.

REFERRAL

All patients with CHB should be referred to a cardiologist for consideration of temporary and/or PPM implantation.

TABLE 1H-3 Indications for Pacing in AV Block

Class I

1. Third-degree or advanced second-degree AV block at any anatomic level associated with any one of the following conditions:
   a Symptoms (including heart failure) attributable to AV block (*Level of Evidence: C*)
   b Arrhythmias and other medical conditions that require drugs that result in symptomatic bradycardia (*Level of Evidence: C*)
   c Documented periods of asystole >3.0 seconds, any escape rate <40 beats/min, or any escape rhythm below the AV junction (e.g., a wide QRS morphology) in awake, asymptomatic patients in sinus rhythm (*Level of Evidence: C*)
   d A documented period of asystole >5 seconds in awake, asymptomatic patients in atrial fibrillation (*Level of Evidence: C*)
   e After catheter ablation of the AV junction (*Level of Evidence: C*)
   f Postoperative AV block that is not expected to resolve after cardiac surgery (*Level of Evidence: C*)
   g Neuromuscular diseases, such as myotonic muscular dystrophy, Kearns–Sayre syndrome, Erb (limb-girdle) dystrophy, and peroneal muscular atrophy, with or without symptoms of bradycardia (*Level of Evidence: B*)
2. Asymptomatic third-degree AV block at any anatomic site with an average awake ventricular rate >40 beats/min in patients with cardiomegaly or left ventricular dysfunction
3. Second-degree or third-degree AV block during exercise in the absence of myocardial ischemia (*Level of Evidence: C*)
4. Symptomatic second-degree AV block regardless of type or site of block (*Level of Evidence: B*)

Class IIa

1. Advanced second-degree or third-degree AV block at any anatomic site with an average ventricular rate >40 beats/min in the absence of cardiomegaly (*Level of Evidence: C*)
2. Asymptomatic second-degree AV block at intra- or infra-His levels found at electrophysiologic study (*Level of Evidence: B*)
3. First-degree or second-degree AV block with symptoms similar to those of pacemaker syndrome (*Level of Evidence: B*)
4. Asymptomatic type II second-degree AV block with a narrow QRS. When type II second-degree AV block occurs with a wide QRS, including isolated right bundle branch block, pacing becomes a Class I recommendation. (*Level of Evidence: B*)

Class IIb

1. AV block due to drug use or toxicity when the block is expected to recur even after withdrawal of the drug (*Level of Evidence: B*)
2. Neuromuscular diseases, such as myotonic muscular dystrophy, Kearns–Sayre syndrome, Erb (limb-girdle) dystrophy, and peroneal muscular atrophy with any degree of AV block (including first-degree AV block), with or without symptoms of bradycardia (*Level of Evidence: B*)

Class III

1. Asymptomatic first-degree AV block (*Level of Evidence: B*)
2. Asymptomatic type I second-degree AV block at a site above the His (i.e., the AV node) level or not known to be intra- or infra-Hisian by electrophysiologic study (*Level of Evidence: B*)
3. AV block expected to resolve and unlikely to recur (e.g., drug toxicity, Lyme disease, nocturnally in sleep apnea, early postoperative status, transient increases in vagal tone) (*Level of Evidence: B*)

Bonow RO, et al. *Heart disease*, ed 9, Philadelphia, 2012, Saunders.

 **PEARLS & CONSIDERATIONS**

COMMENTS

- Patients should be instructed to avoid activities that may damage the pacemaker (e.g., contact sports).
- Pacemaker manufacturers do not recommend any special restrictions regarding proximity to typical household items.
- The presence of a permanent pacemaker is a strong relative contraindication to MRI, although now many MRI-compatible pacemakers are available.
- Some medical procedures, such as lithotripsy, hyperbaric chamber, and electrocautery used during surgery, may require pacemaker programming and testing perioperatively.
- Table E1H-4 describes the five-letter pacemaker code, and Table E1H-5 summarizes common permanent pacemakers.

SUGGESTED READINGS

Available at www.expertconsult.com

RELATED CONTENT

Complete Heart Block (Patient Information)

AUTHORS: **BARRY FINE, M.D., Ph.D.,** and **HEIKO SCHMITT, M.D., Ph.D.**

 **BASIC INFORMATION**

DEFINITION

Second-degree heart block or second-degree atrioventricular (AV) heart block is characterized by a failure of one or more, but not all, atrial impulses to conduct to the ventricles. The block may be at any level of AV conduction system. In both types of second-degree heart block, the sinus rate will continue at regular intervals resulting in a constant sinus rate. When more than one atrial impulse is present for each ventricular complex, the rhythm may be described as a ratio of the number of atrial impulses to the number of ventricular complexes. Electrocardiographically there are three types of second-degree block:

- Mobitz type I (Wenckebach):
  1. Characterized by a progressive prolongation of the PR interval prior to a blocked nonconducted beat and a shorter PR interval after that blocked beat; the conducted impulse will generally be narrow. The cycle may repeat periodically, leading to "grouped beating."
  2. Site of block is usually AV node (proximal to the His bundle).
- Mobitz type II:
  1. Characterized by fixed PR intervals before and after blocked beats and may be associated with a wide QRS morphology (right bundle branch block [RBBB] or left bundle branch block [LBBB] patterns).
  2. Site of block is usually infranodal, especially when QRS is wide.
  3. It has a greater propensity for progressing to third-degree AV block.
- Pure 2:1 conduction patterns cannot be reliably classified as Mobitz type I or type II because there are not enough P waves to characterize prolongation of the PR interval.

SYNONYMS

Wenckebach block (Mobitz type I block)
Mobitz type II block
AV block

ICD-10CM CODES
I44.1   Atrioventricular block, second degree
I45.5   Other specified heart block
Q24.6   Congenital heart block

EPIDEMIOLOGY & DEMOGRAPHICS

Mobitz type I block is more common and may occur in individuals with heightened vagal tone or as a side effect of medications, such as β-blockers or calcium channel blockers.

PHYSICAL FINDINGS & CLINICAL PRESENTATION

- Patients with Mobitz type I are usually asymptomatic. Patients with either type may feel palpitations or the feeling of "missing a beat." Sudden loss of consciousness without warning (Adams-Stokes attack) can occur in patients with Mobitz type II; however, it is much more common in patients with complete heart block.
- Type I block: there is gradual decrease in the intensity of the first heart sound with widening of the a-c interval in the central venous waveform, ending in a pause, and an a wave not followed by a v wave in the neck along with an irregular pulse.
- Type II block: the first heart sound retains a constant intensity, with intermittent ventricular pauses and a waves not followed by v waves in the neck. There is an irregular pulse for most times with intermittent pauses.

ETIOLOGY

- High vagal tone (young patients, athletes at rest)
- Degenerative changes in the AV conduction system
- Ischemia at the AV nodes (type I with inferior wall myocardial infarction [MI] and type II with anterior wall MI)
- Drugs (digitalis, quinidine, procainamide, adenosine, calcium channel blockers [nondihydropyridines], β-blockers)
- Cardiomyopathies, collagen vascular diseases, infiltrative diseases (amyloidosis, sarcoidosis, hematochromatosis)
- Myocarditis/endocarditis (infectious, e.g., Lyme disease, Chagas disease; and noninfectious, e.g., systemic lupus erythematosus)
- Hyperkalemia, hypermagnesemia
- Hypothyroidism
- Prior cardiac valve surgery
- Catheter trauma, catheter ablation for arrhythmias

Dx DIAGNOSIS

DIFFERENTIAL DIAGNOSIS

The ECG easily and reliably distinguishes Mobitz type I from Mobitz type II block and from other conduction abnormalities. It should be distinguished from the less common phenomenon of second-degree sinoatrial node exit block.

Mobitz type I block with a normal QRS complex tends to be benign and usually does not progress to more advanced forms of AV conduction within a short period of time because the disease is mostly confined to within the AV node. Mobitz type II block often precedes the development of Adams-Stokes syncope, symptoms are frequent, prognosis is compromised, and progression to third-degree AV block is common and sudden. Thus, type II second-degree AV block with a wide QRS typically indicates diffuse conduction system disease involving even the infranodal His-Purkinje system.

WORKUP

ECG, ambulatory monitoring (Holter or external loop recorders) in selected patients
- Mobitz type I (Fig. 1H-4) ECG shows:
  1. Sequential and gradual prolongation of PR interval leading to a nonconducted P wave
  2. Shortened PR interval following the pause as compared to the pre-pause PR interval
  3. Progressive shortening of the R-R interval prior to nonconducted atrial impulse
  4. Usually see "grouped beating" pattern.
- Mobitz type II ECG shows (Fig. 1H-5):
  1. Fixed duration of PR interval with constant P-P and R-R intervals
  2. Sudden nonconducted P wave
  3. Abnormal QRS duration or fascicular blocks are common.
- In 2:1 AV block (Fig. 1H-6), it cannot be determined based on the 12-lead ECG whether there is Mobitz type I or type II AV block, although a wide QRS complex is suggestive of Mobitz type II.
  1. Administering atropine can improve AV conduction if the AV block is type I or within the AV node; however, if it is infranodal (i.e., type II), the increased sinus rate caused by atropine may worsen the ratio of AV conduction, resulting in worsening bradycardia.
  2. Exercise stress testing may function in the same way as atropine above. If the disease is confined to the AV node, it may improve with exercise, but in cases of Mobitz type II AV block, the degree of AV block will worsen.

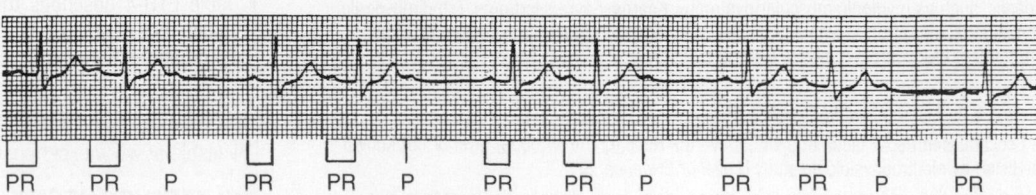

FIGURE 1H-4 Wenckebach (Mobitz type I) second-degree atrioventricular block. Notice the progressive increase in PR intervals, with the third P wave in each sequence not followed by a QRS. Wenckebach block produces a characteristically syncopated rhythm with grouping of the QRS complexes (group beating). (From Goldberger AL [ed]: *Clinical electrocardiography*, ed 5, St Louis, 1994, Mosby.)

Lead v₁

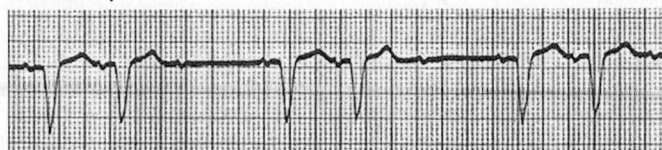

2nd degree AV block (type II) with LBBB

FIGURE 1H-5 Mobitz type II AV block with left bundle branch block (LBBB). Note the fixed P-P intervals with no change in PR intervals followed by a sudden nonconducted P wave. The LBBB indicates infranodal disease in the His-Purkinje system that is suggestive of Mobitz type II block.

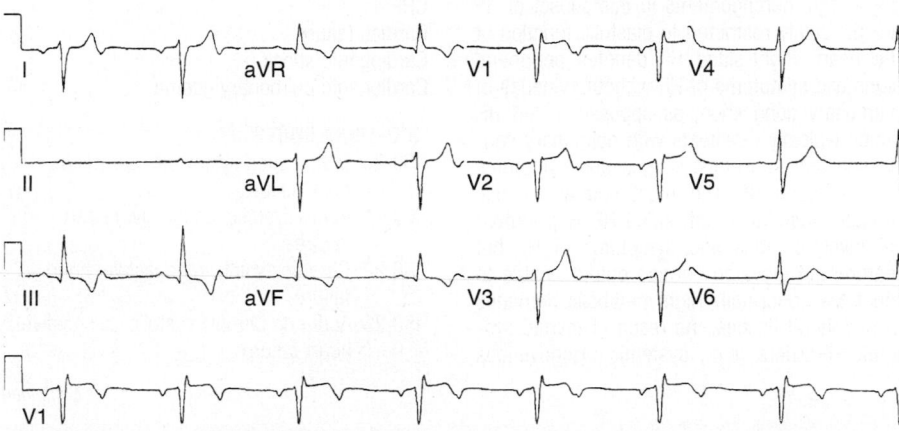

FIGURE 1H-6 Second-degree 2:1 atrioventricular block. Notice the short PR interval during conducted complexes and the wide QRS complexes, suggesting block in the His-Purkinje system. (From Issa Z et al: *Clinical arrhythmology and electrophysiology,* ed 2, Philadelphia, 2012, Saunders.)

3. Carotid sinus stimulation and other vagal maneuvers may worsen the AV block if it is at the level of the AV node (i.e., Mobitz type I) but will paradoxically improve the ratio of AV conduction by slowing down the sinus rate if it is a Mobitz type II or infranodal AV block.

 **TREATMENT**

NONPHARMACOLOGIC THERAPY
Elimination of drugs that may induce AV block such as digoxin, beta-blockers, and calcium channel blockers

ACUTE GENERAL Rx
- Treatment is usually not necessary unless the resting heart rate is <40 beats per min (bpm) while awake.
- If symptomatic (e.g., dizziness), atropine 1 mg (may repeat once after 5 min) may be tried to increase AV conduction; if no response, trial of dobutamine or isoproterenol may be helpful prior to insertion of a pacemaker.

- Atropine
  1. Reduces heart block due to hypervagotonia but not due to AV node ischemia
  2. Does not increase infranodal conduction (third-degree and second-degree AV block that is below the AV node)
  3. Should be used with caution in Mobitz type II AV block due to possible paradoxical decrease in heart rate (as atrial rate increases, AV conduction decreases)
  4. Is ineffective in heart transplantation patients
- If associated with anterior wall MI and wide QRS complex, consider insertion of a temporary pacemaker.
- Indications for permanent pacemaker (PPM) implantation by ACC/AHA/HRS 2008 guidelines:
  1. Second-degree AV block with associated symptomatic bradycardia regardless of the type or site of the block (class I; level of evidence: B).
  2. Second-degree AV block provoked by exercise in the absence of myocardial ischemia (class I; level of evidence: C).
  3. Asymptomatic second-degree AV block at intra- or infra-His levels found at electrophysiologic study (class IIa; level of evidence: B).
  4. First- or second-degree AV block with symptoms similar to those of pacemaker syndrome or hemodynamic compromise (class IIa; level of evidence: B).
  5. Asymptomatic type II second-degree AV block with a wide QRS, including isolated right bundle-branch block (class I; level of evidence: B).
  6. PPM is not indicated for asymptomatic type I second-degree AV block at supra-His (AV node) level or that which is not known to be intra- or infra-Hisian (class III; level of evidence: C)

DISPOSITION
Prognosis is good with insertion of a pacemaker.

REFERRAL
Referral for pacemaker insertion (see "Acute General Rx")

ⓘ PEARLS & CONSIDERATIONS

COMMENTS
Patients with symptomatic Mobitz type II should be referred for a pacemaker. Asymptomatic patients should be referred if the AV block worsens with exercise and should be followed up routinely for potential development of high-grade AV block.

SUGGESTED READINGS
Available at www.expertconsult.com

RELATED CONTENT
Second-Degree Heart Block (Patient Information)

AUTHOR: **AMANDA C. DORAN, M.D., Ph.D.**

Diseases and Disorders

H

BASIC INFORMATION

DEFINITION

Heart failure (HF) is a complex clinical syndrome that can result from any structural or functional cardiac disorder that impairs the ability of the ventricle to fill with or eject blood. The cardinal manifestations of heart failure are dyspnea and fatigue that can limit exercise tolerance. The pathophysiology of HF is related to progressive activation of the neuroendocrine system to compensate for decreased effective circulating volume, leading to total body volume overload and circulatory insufficiency. These events culminate in the development of pulmonary congestion as well as peripheral edema. Specifically, the renin-angiotensin-aldosterone system (RAAS) is implicated as being activated in HF, leading to volume expansion (sodium retention) and cardiac fibrosis (mediated through angiotensin II). Disordered adrenergic stimulation has also been recognized as a key component of progression of disease. The term "congestive heart failure" (CHF) usually denotes a volume-overloaded status as a result of HF. Given that not all patients have volume overload at the time of the evaluation, "congestive heart failure" should be distinguished from the broader term "heart failure."

CLASSIFICATION: The American College of Cardiology/American Heart Association (ACC/AHA) describes the following four stages of HF. This staging model was designed to emphasize the evolution and progression of HF over a continuum and the preventability of HF in at-risk patients.

Stage A: Patients at high risk (e.g., with hypertension, atherosclerotic disease, diabetes mellitus, metabolic syndrome, cytotoxin, family history) for HF but without structural heart disease or symptoms of HF

Stage B: Patients with structural heart disease (e.g., left ventricular [LV] dysfunction) but without symptoms of HF

Stage C: Patients with structural heart disease with prior or current symptoms of HF

Stage D: Patients with refractory HF requiring specialized interventions

In addition to the ACC/AHA stages described above, the New York Heart Association (NYHA) defines four functional classes of HF designed to describe the symptoms of stage C and D HF. The functional classes are intended to assess the symptoms of HF and may fluctuate with therapy. It should be noted that current guidelines employ the functional classes to aid in determination of appropriate treatment.

I. Asymptomatic or symptomatic only at activity levels that would limit normal individuals

II. Symptomatic with ordinary exertion (e.g., 2 city blocks or 1 flight of stairs in a faster than usual pace)

III. Symptomatic with less than ordinary exertion (e.g., less than 2 city blocks or 1 flight of stairs)

IV. Symptomatic at rest

TERMINOLOGY: HF has been traditionally dichotomized as systolic versus diastolic (see Table 1H-6), which has now been replaced with the terms HF with preserved ejection fraction (HFpEF) and HF with reduced ejection fraction (HFREF). Other common classifications include right-sided versus left-sided and high-output versus low-output. Systolic HF or HFREF is defined by the presence of impaired contractility of the LV, as measured by ejection fraction (EF) with clinical signs or symptoms of HF. In contrast, HFpEF or has been described as evidence (clinical) of HF with an EF above 50% with or without evidence of diastolic dysfunction. The term "HF with preserved EF" is preferred over the term "diastolic HF," given that many of the physiologic derangements in this subset of HF are not solely restricted to diastolic function of the heart. Right-sided HF denotes peripheral signs and symptoms of HF without evidence of pulmonary congestion, as opposed to left HF, which typically manifests with pulmonary congestion and subsequent signs and symptoms of right-sided HF. The most common cause of right-sided HF is left-sided HF. High-output HF involves signs and symptoms of HF but features an elevated cardiac output unable to meet the abnormally high metabolic demands of peripheral tissues, the result of myriad systemic disorders (e.g., systemic arteriovenous fistulas, hyperthyroidism, anemia). The term "acute decompensated HF" (ADHF) refers to worsening of signs or symptoms of HF due to a wide range of causes. Of note, HF is not equivalent to cardiomyopathy or LV dysfunction. These latter terms describe the possible structural or functional reasons for the development of HF, whereas HF is a clinical syndrome characterized by specific symptoms and signs.

SYNONYMS

HF
Congestive heart failure
CHF
Cardiac failure
Cardiogenic shock
Cardiogenic pulmonary edema

ICD-10CM CODES

I50.20 Unspecified systolic (congestive) heart failure
I50.21 Acute systolic (congestive) heart failure
I50.22 Chronic systolic (congestive) heart failure
I50.23 Acute on chronic systolic (congestive) heart failure

Continued

TABLE 1H-6   Systolic versus Diastolic Heart Failure*

Parameters	Systolic (HFrEF)	Diastolic (HFpEF)
History		
Coronary artery disease	+++[†]	++
Hypertension	++	++++
Diabetes	++	++
Valvular heart disease	++++	+
Paroxysmal dyspnea	++	+++
Physical Examination		
Cardiomegaly	+++	+
Soft heart sounds	++++	+
S_3 gallop	+++	+
S_4 gallop	+	+++
Hypertension	++	++++
Mitral regurgitation	+++	+
Rales	++	+
Edema	+++	+
Jugular venous distention	+++	+
Chest Radiograph		
Cardiomegaly	+++	+
Pulmonary congestion	+++	+++
Electrocardiogram		
Left ventricular hypertrophy	++	++++
Q waves	++	+
Low voltage	+++	-
Echocardiogram		
Left ventricular hypertrophy	++	++++
Left ventricular dilation	++	-
Left atrial enlargement	++	++
Reduced ejection fraction	++++	-

*Certain aspects of the history and physical examination, along with clinical measurements, may help to distinguish diastolic from systolic heart failure. For example, patients with hypertensive heart disease and severe left ventricular hypertrophy often experience heart failure because of diastolic dysfunction.

†*Plus signs* indicate "suggestive" (the number reflects relative weight). *Minus signs* indicate "not very suggestive." *HFpEF,* Heart failure with preserved ejection fraction; *HFrEF,* heart failure with reduced ejection fraction.

From Zipes DP et al (eds): *Braunwald's heart disease,* ed 7, Philadelphia, 2005, Saunders.

I50.30 Unspecified diastolic (congestive) heart failure

I50.31 Acute diastolic (congestive) heart failure

I50.32 Chronic diastolic (congestive) heart failure

I50.33 Acute on chronic diastolic (congestive) heart failure

I50.40 Unspecified combined systolic (congestive) and diastolic (congestive) heart failure

I50.41 Acute combined systolic (congestive) and diastolic (congestive) heart failure

I50.42 Chronic combined systolic (congestive) and diastolic (congestive) heart failure

I50.43 Acute on chronic combined systolic (congestive) and diastolic (congestive) heart failure

I50.9 Heart failure, unspecified

EPIDEMIOLOGY & DEMOGRAPHICS

- There is variability in the reported demographics of HF due to heterogeneous definitions and classifications of HF. African Americans have the highest risk for HF of the demographic groups. Incidence rate is lowest among white women and highest among black men, with blacks having a greater 5-yr mortality rate than whites.
- The lifetime risk of developing HF is 20% for Americans ≥40 years of age.
  1. In the United States, HF incidence has largely remained stable over the past several decades, with >650,000 new HF cases diagnosed annually.
- HF is primarily a condition of the elderly. Approximately 80% of patients hospitalized with HF are older than 65 yr. HF is the most common inpatient diagnosis in the U.S. for patients aged >65 yr.
- HF incidence increases with age, rising from approximately 20 per 1,000 individuals 65 to 69 yr to >80 per 1,000 individuals among those >85 yr. Before age 75, the incidence of HF is higher in males, but both sexes are equally affected after this age cutoff.
- In the U.S., 1.1 million hospital discharges and 3.2 million hospitalizations/ambulatory care visits were associated with HF in 2007.
- Prevalence: 5.1 million persons in the U.S. and an estimated 23 million persons worldwide. The prevalence of HF is rising, especially in the elderly, particularly due to aging of the population and improved survival from other conditions.
- The estimated (direct and indirect) cost of HF in the U.S. was >$40 billion in 2012, with over half of these costs spent on hospitalizations. The mean cost of HF-related hospitalizations is $23,077 per patient and is higher when HF was a secondary rather than the primary diagnosis.
- HFrEF and HFpEF each make up about half of the overall HF burden.
- Among patients with HF in one large population study, hospitalizations were common after HF diagnosis, with 83% of patients hospitalized at least once and 43% hospitalized at least 4 times. More than half of the hospitalizations were related to non-cardiovascular causes.

PHYSICAL FINDINGS & CLINICAL PRESENTATION

The clinical and physical exam findings should be given the highest priority when determining the diagnosis of HF. These signs and symptoms are dependent on the severity of disease, precipitant factors, comorbid conditions, and whether the HF symptoms are predominantly right-sided or left-sided.

- Common clinical manifestations are:
  1. Dyspnea on exertion, that can progress to dyspnea at rest, caused by increasing pulmonary vascular congestion
  2. Orthopnea, caused by increased venous return in the recumbent position and further elevated pulmonary venous pressure
  3. Paroxysmal nocturnal dyspnea (PND) resulting from multiple factors including increased venous return in the recumbent position, decreased Pao_2 and decreased adrenergic stimulation of myocardial function during sleep
  4. Nocturnal angina resulting from increased myocardial oxygen demand (secondary to increased venous return in the recumbent position causing increased preload) in patients with concomitant coronary artery disease (CAD)
  5. ***Cheyne-Stokes respiration*** (alternating phases of apnea and hyperventilation) caused by prolonged circulation time from lungs to brain as a result of impaired cardiac output
  6. Fatigue, lethargy, and decreased functional capacity resulting from low cardiac output and hypoperfusion of peripheral tissues
- Physical examination:
  1. Fine pulmonary crackles, wheezes, tachypnea, hypoxia (due to elevated pulmonary pressures). Crackles may be absent in chronic and longstanding high pulmonary venous pressure because it allows for lymphatic drainage in the lungs to increase.
  2. Tachycardia and narrowed pulse pressure (due to increased sympathetic tone)
  3. S_3 gallop, paradoxical splitting of S_2, jugular venous distention, peripheral edema in dependent tissues, congestive hepatomegaly, ascites, and hepatojugular reflux (due to volume overload)
  4. Perioral and peripheral cyanosis, decreased capillary refill, pulsus alternans, and cool extremities (due to decreased cardiac output)
- Six common clinical presentations identified by European Society of Cardiology of Acute Heart Failure Syndromes:
  1. ADHF presenting with hypertension (SBP >160): the hypertension leads to increased afterload causing pulmonary vascular congestion.
  2. Worsening or decompensation of chronic HF
  3. Flash pulmonary edema
  4. Cardiogenic shock
  5. Acute coronary syndrome (ACS) and ADHF
  6. Isolated RV failure
- Each of these scenarios may require different therapies to effectively stabilize and treat the patient.

Acute precipitants of HF decompensation include noncompliance with salt restriction or medications (most common cause), infection, arrhythmias (e.g., atrial fibrillation), ischemia or infarction, uncontrolled hypertension, new medications (e.g., negative inotropic agents such as calcium channel blockers/antiarrhythmic agents), nonsteroidal anti-inflammatory drugs (NSAIDs), renal dysfunction, toxins (e.g., ethanol and anthracyclines), cardiac surgery, or valvular catastrophe.

ETIOLOGY

LEFT VENTRICULAR FAILURE: The dichotomy of whether HF occurs in the setting of preserved or reduced LV systolic function plays an important role in treatment strategies. Patients with heart failure with preserved ejection fraction (HFpEF) may have significant abnormalities in active relaxation and passive stiffness of the LV as well as valvular disease. HF with reduced systolic function denotes poor pump function.

- Abnormal LV systolic function
  1. CAD (acute or chronic ischemia, myocardial infarction [MI], LV aneurysm), the most common cause of cardiomyopathy in the U.S., comprising 50% to 75% HF patients.
  2. Increased afterload or pressure overload (severe hypertension, aortic stenosis)
  3. Increased preload or volume overload (mitral regurgitation, aortic regurgitation)
  4. Cardiomyopathy: Idiopathic, infiltrative (non-ischemic)
  5. Infectious (Chagas, myocarditis)
  6. Infiltrative (amyloidosis, sarcoidosis, hemochromatosis)
  7. Toxins (ethanol, cocaine, anthracyclines)
  8. Tachycardia induced (e.g., with atrial fibrillation)
- Preserved LV systolic function
  1. Impaired relaxation (myocardial ischemia, diabetes mellitus, metabolic syndrome)
  2. Tachyarrhythmia (featuring reduced diastolic filling time)
  3. Restrictive cardiomyopathy (myocardial stiffness, such as hypereosinophilic syndrome, amyloidosis, hemochromatosis)
  4. High cardiac output (thiamine deficiency, anemia, thyrotoxicosis, arteriovenous malformations)
  5. Increased afterload (uncontrolled hypertension, aortic stenosis, hypertrophic obstructive cardiomyopathy)
  6. Hypervolemia (oliguric renal failure, iatrogenic)

RIGHT VENTRICULAR FAILURE:

- Left-sided HF
- Chronic hypoxemic pulmonary disease

H

Diseases and Disorders

I

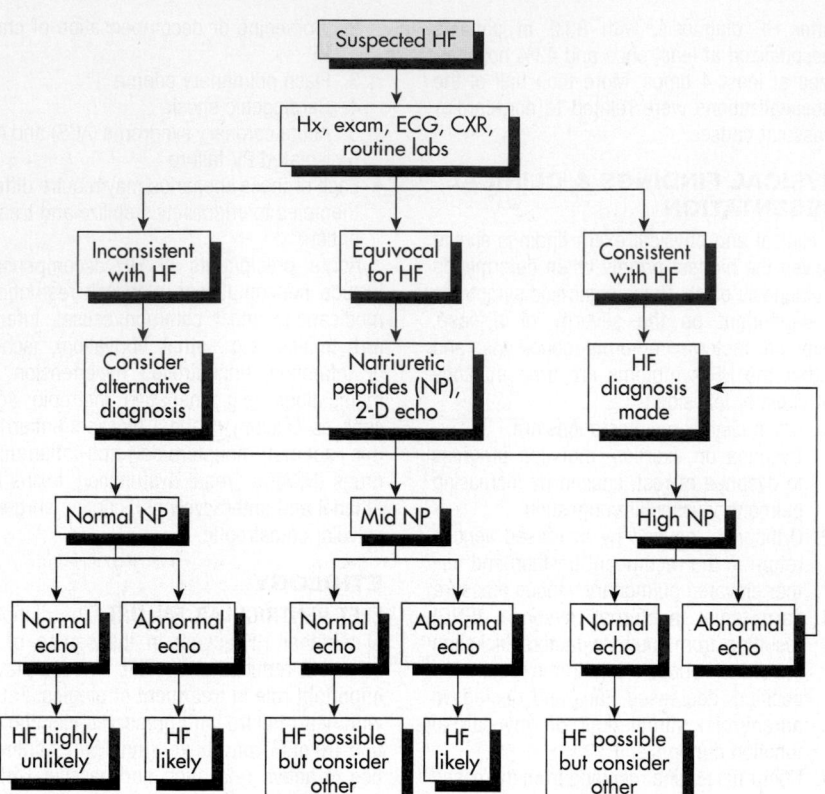

FIGURE 1H-7 Flow chart for the evaluation of patients with heart failure. *CXR*, Chest radiograph; *ECG*, electrocardiograph; *echo*, echocardiograph; *HF*, heart failure; *Hx*, history; *NP*, natriuretic peptides. (From Bonow RO et al: Braunwald*'s heart disease:a textbook of cardiovascular medicine*, ed 9, St Louis, 2011, Saunders.)

- Valvular heart disease (mitral stenosis or regurgitation)
- Pulmonary embolism
- Primary pulmonary hypertension
- Right-to-left shunts that cause systemic hypoxemia (e.g., large patent foramen ovale and tetralogy of Fallot)
- Left-to-right shunts that cause volume overload (e.g., atrial and ventricular septal defects)
- Bacterial endocarditis (right-sided)
- Right ventricular infarction

 **DIAGNOSIS**

DIFFERENTIAL DIAGNOSIS
- COPD, asthma
- Cirrhosis
- Nephrotic syndrome
- Venous insufficiency
- Pulmonary embolism
- ARDS (adult respiratory distress syndrome)
- Pneumonia
- Heroin overdose

WORKUP
- A flow chart for the evaluation of patients with heart failure is outlined in Fig. 1H-7. Fig. 1H-8 describes the stages and treatment options for HF.
- Blood work (to diagnose potentially reversible causes, identify comorbidities, and assess disease severity)

1. CBC (to evaluate for anemia, infections), urinalysis, blood urea nitrogen (BUN), creatinine, electrolytes (worsening hyponatremia is a marker of disease severity and is associated with higher mortality rates), liver enzymes (hepatic congestion), thyroid function (especially in the elderly or patients with comorbid atrial fibrillation or known thyroid disease)
2. B-type natriuretic peptide (BNP) is a cardiac neurohormone secreted from the ventricles in response to elevated LV end-diastolic pressure. The sensitivity is low in asymptomatic patients (but elevated BNP levels have been shown to have a negative predictive value up to 90% in symptomatic patients), and BNP elevation generally correlates with severity of disease and parallels closely morbidity and mortality outcome measures. The cleavage remnant N-terminal-pro-BNP (NT-pro-BNP) has a longer half-life and is cleared through the kidneys, making it susceptible to alterations in renal function. A level of <300 pg/mL has an age-independent 98% negative predictive value.
3. Cardiac biomarkers may be elevated if ischemia is the precipitant factor. However, slight elevations are very common and may not always be due to obstructive coronary disease. These elevations could be due to subendocardial ischemia (due to increased end diastolic

pressure resulting in decreased perfusion) and necrosis, or cardiomyocyte damage from the inflammatory cytokines or oxidative stress. Impaired renal function is very common, and decreased clearance of the biomarkers can contribute to their elevation. Therefore these elevations should be interpreted in the context of the clinical setting. Despite that, in patients with acute decompensated heart failure (ADHF), a positive cardiac troponin test (from whatever mechanism) is associated with worse prognosis.
4. Screening for dyslipidemia and glucose intolerance, which are risk factors for CAD.
5. If hemochromatosis is suspected (specifically in Northern European patients), consider checking a transferrin saturation and ferritin level.
6. Consider HIV testing in high-risk patients.
- Electrocardiogram (ECG)
1. Look for signs of prior MI, chamber enlargement, hypertrophy, heart block, arrhythmia, and evidence of pericardial effusion.
2. More than 25% of patients with HF have some form of intraventricular conduction abnormality that is manifest as an increased QRS duration. The most common pattern seen is left bundle-branch block.
- Chest x-ray (Fig. 1H-9)
1. Evaluate for pulmonary venous congestion, pulmonary edema, pleural effusion, cardiomegaly, chamber dilation, and Kerley B lines.
- Echocardiography
1. Plays a critical diagnostic role in patients with HF and is useful in assessment of systolic, diastolic function in addition to assessment of valvular structure and function
- Exercise stress testing
1. May be useful in evaluating concomitant ischemic etiologies and assessment of degree of disability in stable compensated patients.
- Cardiac catheterization
1. Left heart catheterization can help to identify coronary artery disease as a cause of HF. Right heart catheterization can help to evaluate intracardiac filling pressures, estimates of valvular areas, presence of intracardiac shunts, and calculation of hemodynamic properties such as cardiac output, systemic vascular resistance, and pulmonary artery wedge pressure to further guide management.
- Cardiac MRI
1. Useful modality in accurately estimating EF (with less variability than conventional 2D echocardiography). MRI is also useful in excluding pericardial disease, identifying infiltrative disease, and assessing viability in cases of HF caused by underlying ischemic heart disease

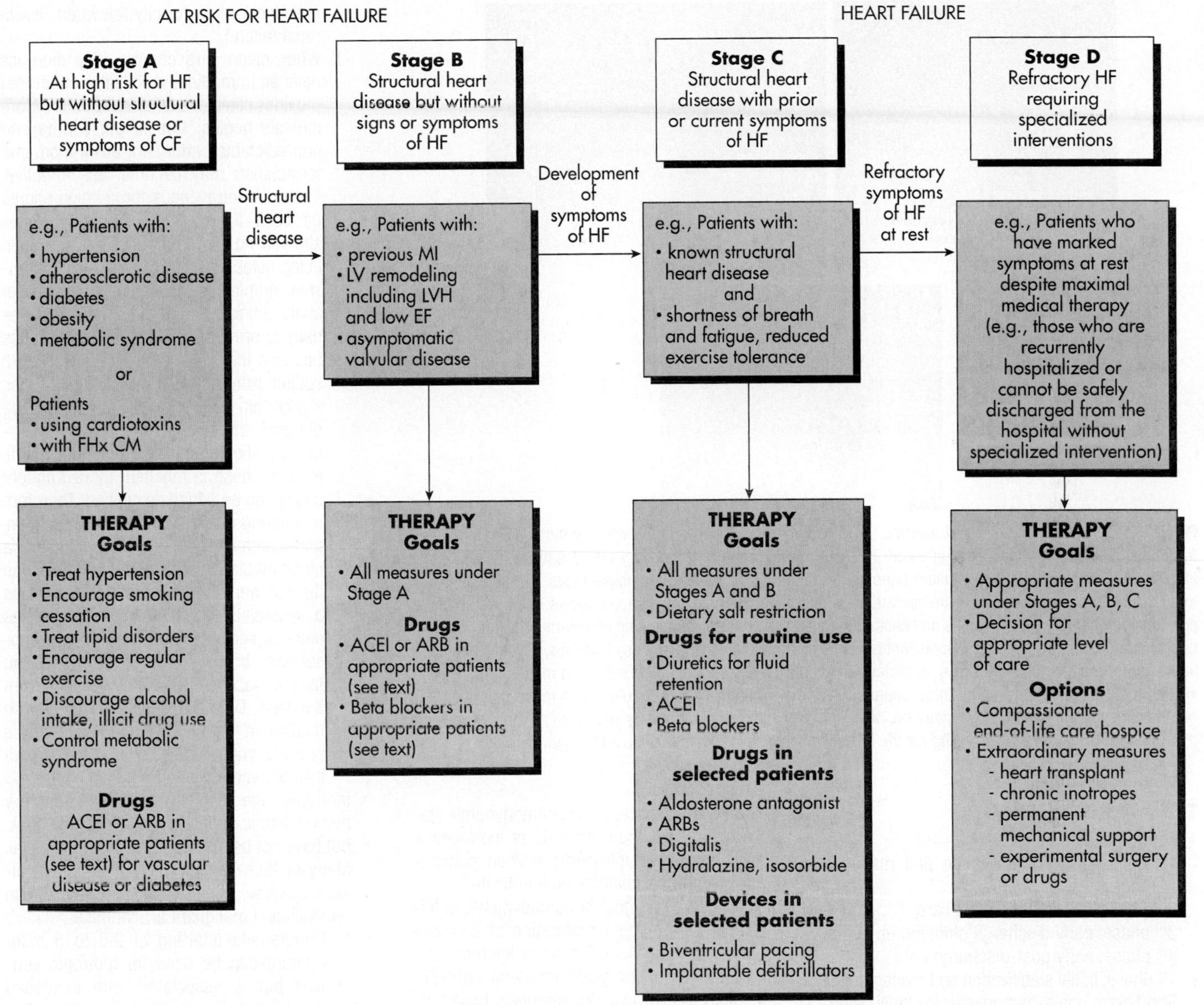

Diseases
and Disorders

AT RISK FOR HEART FAILURE   HEART FAILURE

Stage A
At high risk for HF
but without structural
heart disease or
symptoms of CF

Stage B
Structural heart
disease but without
signs or symptoms
of HF

Stage C
Structural heart
disease with prior
or current symptoms
of HF

Stage D
Refractory HF
requiring
specialized
interventions

Structural
heart
disease

Development
of
symptoms
of HF

Refractory
symptoms
of HF
at rest

e.g., Patients with:
- hypertension
- atherosclerotic disease
- diabetes
- obesity
- metabolic syndrome

or

Patients
- using cardiotoxins
- with FHx CM

e.g., Patients with:
- previous MI
- LV remodeling
  including LVH
  and low EF
- asymptomatic
  valvular disease

e.g., Patients with:
- known structural
  heart disease
  and
- shortness of breath
  and fatigue, reduced
  exercise tolerance

e.g., Patients who
have marked
symptoms at rest
despite maximal
medical therapy
(e.g., those who are
recurrently
hospitalized or
cannot be safely
discharged from the
hospital without
specialized intervention)

THERAPY
Goals
- Treat hypertension
- Encourage smoking
  cessation
- Treat lipid disorders
- Encourage regular
  exercise
- Discourage alcohol
  intake, illicit drug use
- Control metabolic
  syndrome

Drugs
ACEI or ARB in
appropriate patients
(see text) for vascular
disease or diabetes

THERAPY
Goals
- All measures under
  Stage A

Drugs
- ACEI or ARB in
  appropriate patients
  (see text)
- Beta blockers in
  appropriate patients
  (see text)

THERAPY
Goals
- All measures under
  Stages A and B
- Dietary salt restriction
Drugs for routine use
- Diuretics for fluid
  retention
- ACEI
- Beta blockers

Drugs in
selected patients
- Aldosterone antagonist
- ARBs
- Digitalis
- Hydralazine, isosorbide

Devices in
selected patients
- Biventricular pacing
- Implantable defibrillators

THERAPY
Goals
- Appropriate measures
  under Stages A, B, C
- Decision for
  appropriate level
  of care

Options
- Compassionate
  end-of-life care hospice
- Extraordinary measures
  - heart transplant
  - chronic inotropes
  - permanent
    mechanical support
  - experimental surgery
    or drugs

FIGURE 1H-8 Stages in the evolution of heart failure (HF) and recommended therapy by stage. *ACEI,* Angiotensin-converting enzyme inhibitor; *ARB,* angiotensin receptor blocker; *EF,* ejection fraction; *FHx CM,* family history of cardiomyopathy; *IV,* intravenous; *LV,* left ventricular; *LVH,* left ventricular hypertrophy; *MI,* myocardial infarction. (From Hunt SA, Baker DW, Chin MH, et al: ACC/AHA guidelines for the evaluation and management of chronic heart failure in the adult: Executive summary. A report of the American College of Cardiology/American Heart Association Task Force on Practice Guidelines [Committee to Revise the 1995 Guidelines for the Evaluation and Management of Heart Failure]. *J Am Coll Cardiol* 104:2996, 2001.)

Rx TREATMENT

NONPHARMACOLOGIC GENERAL MEASURES

- Assess the etiology and severity of disease. Educate the patient and family about the nature of the disorder. Assess the home setting and if patient has social support to ensure compliance, especially for patients with dementia.
- Identify and correct precipitating factors (e.g., increased sodium load, medication noncompliance, ischemia, infections, anemia, thyrotoxicosis) and address lifestyle modification (e.g., smoking and alcohol cessation, weight reduction, avoiding use of nonsteroidal antiinflammatory drugs [NSAIDs]). Anemia is common in patients with HF. However, treatments with erythropoiesis-stimulating agents (ESAs) have not shown improved clinical outcomes

in patients with systolic HF and mild-to-moderate anemia and are thus not recommended.
- Review list of medications and discontinue the ones that can contribute to HF (e.g., NSAIDs, antiarrhythmic drugs, calcium channel blockers, thiazolidinediones)
- Dietary sodium restriction of <2 g/day is commonly recommended to patients with HF and is endorsed by many guidelines.
- Restrict fluid intake to <2 L/day in patients with hyponatremia.
- Caloric supplementation should be provided to patients with advanced HF with weight loss and muscle wasting due to cardiac cachexia. Weight loss may reflect cachexia caused by the higher total energy expenditure associated with HF compared with that of healthy sedentary subjects. The diagnosis of cardiac cachexia independently predicts a worse prognosis.

- For patients with coexisting obstructive sleep apnea, continuous positive airway pressure (CPAP) is often recommended after polysomnography, thereby reducing systolic blood pressure and improving LV function (Class IIa recommendation).
- Exercise training (or regular physical activity) is recommended as safe and effective for patients with class I to III HF who are able to participate to improve functional status (Class I recommendation). Cardiac rehabilitation is unfortunately an underused preventive measure, although it has been shown to reduce morbidity and mortality. Cardiac rehabilitation can be useful in clinically stable patients with HF to improve functional capacity, exercise duration, health-related quality of life, and mortality (Class IIa recommendation).
- Pneumococcal vaccination and annual influenza vaccination.

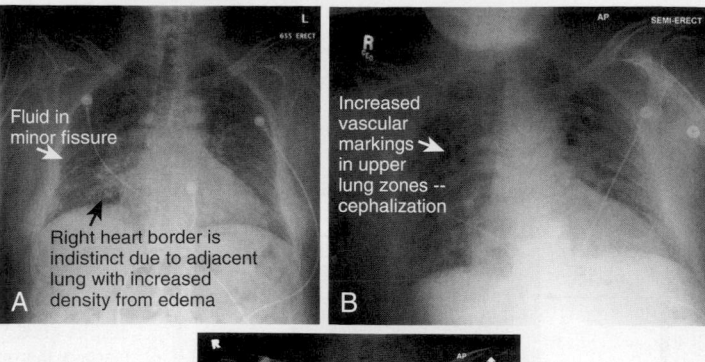

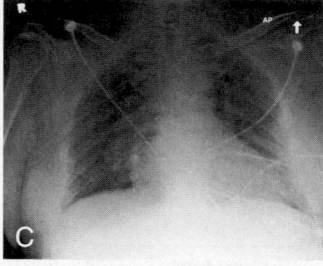

FIGURE 1H-9 Congestive heart failure. Mild left ventricular hypertrophy with restricted filling, ejection fraction >55%, and no pericardial effusion. This 63-year-old man with coronary artery disease, chronic renal insufficiency, and diastolic heart failure (ejection fraction >55%) presented multiple times for dyspnea (**A, B,** and **C,** first through third clinical presentations). Each of these three radiographs shows signs of moderate pulmonary edema. The diaphragms and costophrenic angles are clear, suggesting no pleural effusion. The right heart border in all three images is indistinct because of interstitial edema in these locations. Portions of the left heart border are also indistinct. The upper lung fields have a hazy appearance indicating mild edema. Fluid is visible in the minor fissure on all three images. Does the similarity of these radiographs mean that edema is not the cause of the patient's dyspnea? No, he simply presented with pulmonary edema on all three occasions. (From Broder JS: *Diagnostic imaging for the emergency physician,* Philadelphia, 2011, Saunders.)

TREATMENT OF ADHF

- Four phases in treatment of ADHF (Fig 1H-8):
  1st phase: initial stabilization and management
  2nd phase: inpatient hospital care
  3rd phase: early discharge planning and care
  4th phase: early post-discharge care
- 1st phase: Initial stabilization and management
  Short-term goals: hemodynamic stabilization, stabilization of respiratory status, symptom relief, optimization of tissue perfusion, and recognition of more immediately life-threatening conditions (e.g., arrhythmias, valvular catastrophe, MI, cardiac tamponade). Initial therapy of ADHF is contingent on appropriate determination of clinical scenario.
  Management as per clinical scenario:
  1. ADHF-associated hypertension: goal is afterload reduction and decrease of systemic hypervolemia. Mode of treatment: diuresis (IV loop diuretics) and vasodilators (acutely nitrates and morphine followed by treatment with ACE inhibitors or angiotensin receptor blockers [ARBs])
  2. Worsening or decompensation of chronic HF (HFREF or HFpEF): goal is control of volume status. Treatment is accomplished with vasodilators and diuretics.
  3. Flash pulmonary edema: goal is afterload reduction (vasodilators such as nitrates acutely), respiratory status stabilization, and diuresis (IV loop diuretics). Rate control can be initiated in patients with atrial fibrillation or tachyarrhythmias as it may improve cardiac filling and function.

  4. Cardiogenic shock: goal is hemodynamic stabilization. Treatment consists of inotropes + vasopressors ± intraaortic balloon pump ± emergent revascularization if indicated.
  5. ACS and ADHF: goal is hemodynamic stabilization + emergent restoration of coronary perfusion. See "Acute Coronary Syndromes."
  6. Isolated RV failure: goals are identification of etiology: (1) valvular, (2) pulmonary hypertension, and (3) primary RV failure secondary to ischemia. Treatment: depends on etiology, either corrective surgery vs. treatment of pulmonary hypertension (endothelin antagonists, calcium channel blockers, phosphodiesterase inhibitors) vs. coronary reperfusion therapies.

ACUTE PHARMACOLOGIC TREATMENTS:

- Vasodilators are appropriate in most patients with ADHF (contraindicated in cardiogenic shock and severe aortic stenosis)
  1. Nitroglycerin (0.4 to 0.8 mg sublingually every 3 to 5 min, or by intravenous infusion starting at 0.2 to 0.4 mcg/kg/min with subsequent up titration) may be administered in the emergency setting until relative hypotension ensues. Nitrates are contraindicated after use of phosphodiesterase inhibitors such as sildenafil due to risk of hypotension.
  2. Sodium nitroprusside (0.1 to 0.2 mcg/kg/min as an intravenous infusion) is a potent vasodilator with balanced venous and arteriolar effects that usually requires hemodynamic monitoring with an arterial line and may precipitate coronary steal

and thiocyanate toxicity (elevated risk in renal failure).
3. When given intravenously, loop diuretics have an immediate vasodilator effect that provides clinical relief of symptoms before diuresis begins. Due to gut edema and unpredictable patterns of absorption, oral formulation may become less effective. Therefore intravenous formulation should be used in the acute setting. Studies showed no difference in outcome when using bolus dosing vs. continuous IV infusion. Administration of smaller doses of short-acting loop diuretics multiple times daily is preferable to a single large dose because the kidneys can avidly reabsorb sodium after the initial diuresis. However, if a certain dose is not adequate to force diuresis, the dose, rather than the frequency, should be increased until a single effective dose is reached; more frequent doses can be added as needed. Therefore monitoring of urine output, renal function, and electrolytes is key. The addition of a distal tubule inhibitor such as metolazone 30 min prior to loop diuretic dosing has a synergistic effect and often enhances diuresis because it inhibits sodium reabsorption in the distal segment in the face of increased sodium delivery from the loop. Diuretics should be used with caution in patients with aortic stenosis and are contraindicated in patients with severe hypotension or cardiogenic shock.
- Inotropic agents are used for temporary hemodynamic support in cardiogenic shock, but have not been shown to improve survival. Many of these agents have serious associated adverse events including myocardial necrosis and malignant arrhythmias.
  1. Dobutamine (starting at 2.5 to 5 mcg/kg/min) can be used for inotropic support but is associated with increased myocardial oxygen demand and cardiac arrhythmias and may result in hypotension from decreased systemic vascular resistance.
  2. Milrinone (37.5 to 75 mcg/kg loading dose, followed by 0.375 to 0.75 mcg/kg/min) can be used as a vasodilator and inotropic agent, but is associated with increased oxygen demand and cardiac arrhythmias, and may result in hypotension from decreased systemic vascular resistance.
  3. Levosimendan is a calcium-sensitizing drug, which also inhibits potassium channels leading to inotropy. However, this agent is not FDA approved for use in the U.S. Currently, this inotrope has been associated with an elevated risk of malignant arrhythmia and higher mortality.
- Renal replacement therapy (can be used as an alternative to pharmacologic diuresis in ADHF when renal function is significantly compromised).
- ACE inhibitors or ARBs, if part of a patient's chronic medication regimen, should be continued in the absence of hypotension, acute renal failure, or hyperkalemia.

- Beta-blockers, if part of a patient's chronic medication regimen, may be continued or reduced in dosage in mild exacerbations of HF but should be discontinued in patients with hypotension or those requiring inotropic support. Beta-blockers should not be initiated in patients who are not on chronic beta-blocker therapy until euvolemia is achieved unless used for rate control.
- Morphine sulfate can cause venodilation and thus reduce cardiac preload. It may be used to reduce patient work of breathing and anxiety, but recent retrospective studies have suggested increased incidence of mechanical ventilation and in-hospital mortality in patients who received morphine.
- If ADHF with preserved EF is suspected, therapy is usually aimed at relief of symptoms and correction of any potential precipitating etiologies (e.g., tachycardia, hypertension, ischemia). Treatment generally involves diuretics to reduce pulmonary congestion with caution to not overdiurese given the need for elevated filling pressures in these patients to ensure adequate stroke volume and cardiac output. Nitrates may be useful in providing symptomatic relief but may precipitate hypotension. Ventricular rate should be controlled in the presence of atrial fibrillation, which, at rapid rates, is poorly tolerated in patients with impaired diastolic filling. Negative inotropic agents such as beta-blockers and calcium channel blockers can be used with caution.
- Nesiritide (recombinant brain natriuretic protein) does not reduce morbidity or mortality (ASCEND-HF trial)
- 2nd phase: Inpatient hospital care

This phase of treatment includes further diuresis and stabilization of volume status. The patient should be carefully brought to euvolemia with daily volume status and electrolyte monitoring. The patient should also be transitioned to oral diuretics when stabilized. Whilst inpatient, the patient should have his/her medical and device management optimized with the therapies discussed later.

3rd phase: Early discharge planning and care

The patient should be transitioned to oral diuretics and be placed on optimum outpatient maintenance therapy. If the patient was on IV inotropic therapy, oral regimens should be adjusted while these infusions are tapered off. Prolonged physiologic effects of these IV inotropic agents after their discontinuation before discharge may mask the inadequate diuretic regimen and intolerance to the vasodilator doses. This can result in readmission, especially with milrinone due to its long half-life that can be further prolonged by the common coexisting impaired renal function. Therefore it may be recommended that patients who received inotropic infusions remain hospitalized for at least 48 hours after inotropic agents are discontinued, and optimize the oral regimen.

4th phase: Early post-discharge care

The patient will require reevaluation and constant monitoring in order to avoid another episode of ADHF. Emphasis should be placed on importance of compliance with instructions regarding dietary restrictions and daily body weight monitoring. Early follow-up should be scheduled as well as outpatient electrolyte monitoring if required after medication adjustments.

CHRONIC TREATMENT OF HF SECONDARY TO SYSTOLIC DYSFUNCTION: The goals of HF therapy are clinical improvement followed by stabilizing, slowing, or even reversing deterioration in myocardial function, and ultimately a reduction in risk of morbidity (including hospitalization rates) and mortality.

- ACE inhibitors
  1. Reduce morbidity and mortality.
  2. Produce both venous and arterial vasodilation acutely, thereby reducing both preload and afterload.
  3. Potential mechanism of long-term benefit is attenuation of RAAS activation and decreased myocardial remodeling and fibrosis.
  4. Used as first-line therapy for asymptomatic LV dysfunction (LVEF <40%) and symptomatic systolic HF (ACC/AHA grades A-D).
  5. Therapy should be initiated at low doses to prevent hypotension and rapidly titrated to higher doses as tolerated.
  6. Contraindications to the use of ACE inhibitors are renal insufficiency (creatinine clearance <30 ml/min), bilateral renal artery stenosis, hyperkalemia, hypotension, or adverse reactions (e.g., angioedema).
- ARBs
  1. Receptor antagonists to the angiotensin II receptor.
  2. Clinical trials have not shown any superiority compared to ACE inhibitors in patients with systolic HF (LVEF <40%).
  3. Reserved for patients who are ACE inhibitor intolerant.
  4. There are conflicting data on the utility of combination therapy with ARBs and ACE inhibitors in addition to beta-blockers for patients who remain symptomatic in the absence of renal dysfunction, hyperkalemia, and outside the post-MI period.
  5. Have a similar contraindication profile to ACE inhibitors. Routine combined use of an ACE inhibitor, ARB, and aldosterone antagonist is potentially harmful for patients with HFrEF.
- Beta-adrenergic blockers (beta-blockers)
  1. Reduce morbidity and mortality. Such benefits observed with bisoprolol (CIBIS II trial), metoprolol succinate (MERIT-HF trial), and carvedilol (COPERNICUS trial).
  2. Benefit is believed to be conferred by blockade of sympathetic effects of neurohormonal stimulation due to HF.
  3. Are considered first-line therapy for symptomatic patients with systolic HF (NYHA class ≥II and LVEF <35%).
  4. Only carvedilol, bisoprolol, and metoprolol succinate (long acting) have been approved for the medical treatment of chronic HF; these agents are generally started in patients judged to be euvolemic and dosage is to be slowly uptitrated as tolerated.
  5. Adverse effects include worsening HF (due to negative inotropic effects), fatigue, dizziness, bradycardia, hypotension, and bronchospasm.
- Aldosterone receptor antagonists
  1. Reduce morbidity and mortality
  2. Indicated in patients with NYHA class II-IV HF, with LVEF ≤35%, already treated with ACE inhibitors and beta-blockers without significant renal insufficiency or hyperkalemia. Patients with NYHA class II should have a history of prior cardiovascular hospitalization or elevated plasma natriuretic peptide levels to be considered for aldosterone receptor antagonists. Creatinine should be ≤2.5 mg/dL in men or ≤2.0 mg/dL in women (or estimated glomerular filtration rate >30 mL/min/1.73 m2), and potassium should be <5.0 mEq/L. They are also indicated for post-MI patients with EF ≤40% who have either symptomatic HF or diabetes mellitus.
  3. Spironolactone may cause gynecomastia, galactorrhea, and hyperkalemia (especially in patients with baseline renal insufficiency or type 4 renal tubular acidosis).It has been best studied in chronic HF with NYHA class III to IV symptoms (RALES study).
  4. Eplerenone is associated with fewer endocrine side effects and has especially been studied in postmyocardial infarction left ventricular dysfunction (EPHESUS trial) and in chronic systolic HF with only class II symptoms (EMPHASIS-HF trial).
  5. Inappropriate use of aldosterone receptor antagonists is potentially harmful because of life-threatening hyperkalemia or renal insufficiency when serum creatinine is >2.5 mg/dL in men or >2.0 mg/dL in women (or estimated glomerular filtration rate <30 mL/min/1.73 m^2), and/or potassium >5.0 mEq/L.
- Diuretics
  1. Are used to maintain euvolemia and to improve symptoms as discussed previously.
  2. Although data on diuretic efficacy are limited, a meta-analysis of a few small trials found that they were associated with reduction in mortality as well as reduced hospitalization for HF.
  3. Of note, loop diuretics with better bioavailability, such as torsemide and bumetanide, may be used in diuretic-resistant patients but are generally more expensive.
- Combination of isosorbide dinitrate and hydralazine
  1. Cause venous (nitrates) and arteriolar (hydralazine) vasodilation resulting in decreased preload and afterload.
  2. The combination of hydralazine and isosorbide dinitrate is recommended to reduce morbidity and mortality for patients self-described as African Americans with NYHA class III–IV HFrEF receiving optimal therapy with ACE inhibitors and beta blockers, unless contraindicated.

3. A combination of hydralazine and iso-sorbide dinitrate can be useful to reduce morbidity or mortality in patients with current or prior symptomatic HFrEF who cannot be given an ACE inhibitor or ARB because of drug intolerance, hypotension, or renal insufficiency, unless contraindicated.

4. Adverse effects of nitrates include hypotension, headaches, and tolerance as well as reflex tachycardia and lupus-like syndrome with hydralazine.

- Digoxin
  1. Positive inotropic and negative chronotropic drug that works by inhibition of the sodium-potassium transmembrane exchange pump and through its vagomimetic action
  2. Commonly used in patients with concomitant atrial fibrillation
  3. Has been shown to reduce HF-related hospitalizations but does NOT confer any mortality benefit (DIG trial). However, there is evidence suggesting that digoxin may actually have an effect on survival that varies with the serum digoxin level; survival was improved when the level was between 0.5 and 0.8 ng/ml (most often in men) and significantly worsened when it was $\geq$1.2 ng/ml and >0.9 mg/ml in women.
  4. Caution must be used in patients with abnormal renal function to avoid digoxin toxicity and life-threatening arrhythmia. Avoid hypokalemia because potassium competes with digoxin on the same site of the Na^+-K^+-ATPase pump.

- Sacubitril/valsartan
  1. Combination of ARB and neprilysin inhibitor was superior to ACE-I alone in the PARADIGM-HF trial, with 20% reduction in death and CHF hospitalization and 16% reduction in death.
  2. Approved by the FDA in 2015.
  3. Consider use for patients with heart failure symptoms despite optimal medical therapy with an ACE-I or ARB and beta blocker.

- Cardiac resynchronization therapy (CRT)
  1. Improves morbidity and mortality rates in selected patients.
  2. The presence of a bundle-branch block or other intraventricular conduction delay (IVCD) can cause ventricular dyssynchrony, which induces regional loading disparities and reduces the efficiency of ventricular contraction, thereby further impairing the systolic function of a failing ventricle.
  3. CRT is indicated for patients who have LVEF $\leq$35%, sinus rhythm, left bundle-branch block with a QRS duration of 150 ms or greater, and NYHA class II, III, or ambulatory IV symptoms on guideline-directed medical therapy. CRT is NOT indicated in patients whose functional status and life expectancy are limited predominantly by chronic noncardiac conditions. Life expectancy should be >1 yr.

4. In the appropriate subset of patients, CRT in addition to optimal medical therapy has been shown in numerous clinical trials to improve symptoms by at least one NYHA class, improve 6-min walk distance and quality of life, reduce rate of HF-related hospitalization, and reduce rate of all-cause and cardiovascular mortality.

5. Detailed guidelines for CRT are beyond the scope of this chapter. Consultation with cardiology service may be indicated.

- Implantable cardioverter-defibrillators (ICDs)
  1. Sudden cardiac death (SCD) is a common cause of death in patients with HF in both ischemic and nonischemic cardiomyopathies. Ventricular tachycardia (VT) degenerating into ventricular fibrillation (VF) is the culprit in the majority of patients with SCD, although bradyarrhythmias do also occur with less frequency.
  2. ICD therapy is recommended for primary prevention of SCD to reduce total mortality in selected patients with nonischemic dilated cardiomyopathy or ischemic heart disease at least 40 days post-MI with LVEF $\leq$35% and NYHA class II or III symptoms on chronic guideline-directed medical therapy, who have reasonable expectation of meaningful survival for >1 year.
  3. Patients with HF who survive an episode of sudden cardiac arrest or experience sustained VT in the presence of LVEF <35% are at high risk for future arrhythmic events and SCD and obtain a mortality benefit from ICD placement for secondary prevention, with or without adjunctive therapies such as antiarrhythmic drugs, radiofrequency ablation, surgery, or transplant.

- In the absence of an indication (e.g., atrial fibrillation), routine use of anticoagulation is currently not recommended in patients with HF. Even with the increased risk for LV thrombus formation in dilated cardiomyopathy and subsequent thromboembolization, data are conflicting about benefits of antithrombotic (antiplatelet or anticoagulant) therapy for primary prevention to reduce thromboembolic events or mortality in patients with systolic HF who are in sinus rhythm (SOLVD, V-HeFT, SAVE, HELAS, and WASH trials). It may be reasonable to consider anticoagulation for secondary prevention in patients with HF who had a prior thromboembolic event; however, risks and benefits should be carefully assessed.

- Antiplatelet agents are recommended for patients with concomitant CAD.

- Statins are not beneficial as adjunctive therapy when prescribed solely for the diagnosis of HF in the absence of other indications for their use.

- Calcium channel blocking drugs are not recommended as routine treatment for patients with HFrEF.

- Omega-3 polyunsaturated fatty acid supplementation is reasonable to use as adjunctive therapy in patients with NYHA class II-IV symptoms and HFrEF or HFpEF, unless con-

traindicated, to reduce mortality and cardiovascular hospitalizations.

- Percutaneous coronary intervention (PCI) or surgical revascularization should be considered in patients with HF and significant CAD who are revascularization candidates.

- In general, the following sequence of drugs is recommended:
  1. Loop diuretics to provide symptom relief and achieve a euvolemic state.
  2. ACE or ARB started at low doses, then increased to a moderate dose in 1-2 weeks.
  3. Beta-blockers after the patient is stable on ACE/ARB treatment. Start a low dose, then uptitrate to goal based on trial data or maximal dose tolerated. Once achieved, uptitration of ACE or ARB to goal doses can be completed.

- The following drugs can be added in selected patients in the absence of contraindications:
  1. Aldosterone antagonists improve survival in NYHA class II with LVEF <30% or NYHA class III-IV with EF <35%. Kidney function should be stable with eGFR $\geq$30 ml/min and potassium <5 mEq/L.
  2. Combination of hydralazine with a nitrate in patients (particularly African Americans) with a reduced EF.
  3. Digoxin reduces hospitalizations for HF and controls HR rate in atrial fibrillation. It can also help control symptoms.

CHRONIC TREATMENT OF HF WITH PRESERVED SYSTOLIC FUNCTION:

- To date, there is a relative dearth of clinical trials examining effective chronic treatment strategies in this subset of patients with HF. Current therapies are mainly for symptomatic relief.

- Therapy centers on relief of volume overload with judicious diuretic use, treatment of ischemia via coronary revascularization, management of atrial fibrillation, controlling heart rate and blood pressure to prevent acute decompensation, and restriction of sodium and fluid to prevent volume overload.

- Diuretics should be used for relief of symptoms due to volume overload in patients with HFpEF.

- The use of beta-blocking agents, ACE inhibitors, and ARBs in patients with hypertension is reasonable to control blood pressure in patients with HFpEF.

- The use of ARBs might be considered to decrease hospitalizations for patients with HFpEF.

- HF hospitalization was less frequent in the spironolactone group compared with the placebo group (TOPCAT trial); therefore, spironolactone may be considered in HPpEF patients who can be reliably and carefully monitored for changes in potassium and creatinine, and they should have potassium levels <5 meq/L and glomerular filtration rate <30 mL/min per 1.73m² at baseline.

- Omega-3 polyunsaturated fatty acid supplementation is reasonable, unless contraindicated, to reduce mortality and cardiovascular hospitalizations.

- There is no evidence to support routine use of nutritional supplements and they are not recommended for patients with HFpEF.
- Surgical options for contributing critical aortic stenosis, constrictive pericarditis, and hypertrophic cardiomyopathy (HCM) should be entertained in appropriate patients.

DISPOSITION

- Annual mortality of systolic HF ranges from 10% in stable patients with mild symptoms to 50% in patients with NYHA class IV disease (a mortality rate rivaling some malignancies). The Seattle Heart Failure Model provides an accurate estimate of 1-, 2-, and 3-year survival before and after different therapies. This model can be useful to assess the need for LV assist device implantation or urgent

transplantation. The calculator is available online at http://depts.washington.edu/shfm/.
- Cardiac transplantation has a 5-yr survival rate of ~70% and represents a viable option in selected patients.
- The use of an LV assist device (LVAD) in patients with advanced HF can result in a clinically meaningful survival benefit and improve quality of life in patients who are not candidates for cardiac transplantation. There are two approved uses of LVADs specifically as a bridge to transplant and as destination therapy. There are two major categories of LVAD pulsatile flow devices vs. continuous flow devices. Continuous flow devices are associated with increased survival as destination therapy as compared to medically managed controls (REMATCH trial).

 EVIDENCE

Available at www.expertconsult.com

SUGGESTED READINGS

Available at www.expertconsult.com

RELATED CONTENT

Heart Failure (Patient Information)

AUTHORS: **HARSHA V. GANGA, M.D.,** and **ARAVIND RAO KOKKIRALA, M.D.**

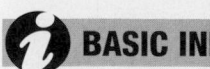 **BASIC INFORMATION**

DEFINITION

Heat exhaustion and heat stroke are part of a continuum of heat-related illness, and unless factors leading to heat exhaustion are corrected swiftly, affected patients can progress to heat stroke.

- *Heat exhaustion:* an illness resulting from prolonged, heavy activity in a hot environment with subsequent dehydration, electrolyte depletion, and rectal temperature >37.8° C but ≤40° C.
- *Heat stroke:* a life-threatening heat illness characterized by extreme hyperthermia (core temperature >40° C [104.0° F]), dehydration, and neurologic manifestations. Heat stroke can be further subdivided into "exertional heat stroke" occurring in generally healthy individuals undergoing strenuous physical activity in warm conditions and "non-exertional heat stroke" often seen in elderly and/or debilitated patients with impaired thermal regulations due to illness or medications (see Etiology).

SYNONYMS

Heat illness
Hyperthermia

ICD-10CM CODES
T67.5 Heat exhaustion, unspecified
T67.0 Heatstroke and sunstroke
T67.1 Heat syncope
T67.2 Heat cramp
T67.3 Heat exhaustion, anhydrotic
T67.6 Heat fatigue, transient

EPIDEMIOLOGY & DEMOGRAPHICS

INCIDENCE (IN U.S.): Incidence of heat stroke is approximately 20 cases/100,000 population.
PREDOMINANT AGE: Heat exhaustion and stroke occur more frequently in elderly patients, especially those taking diuretics or medications that impair heat dissipation (e.g., phenothiazines, anticholinergics, antihistamines, beta-blockers). Table 1H-7 describes factors predisposing to serious heat illness.

PHYSICAL FINDINGS & CLINICAL PRESENTATION

Heat exhaustion:
- Generalized malaise, weakness, headache, muscle and abdominal cramps, nausea, vomiting, hypotension, tachycardia.
- Rectal temperature is usually normal.
- Sweating is usually present.
Heat stroke:
- Neurologic manifestations (seizures, tremor, hemiplegia, coma, psychosis, other bizarre behavior).
- Evidence of dehydration (poor skin turgor, sunken eyeballs).
- Tachycardia, hyperventilation.
- Skin is hot, red, and flushed.

- Sweating is often (not always) absent, particularly in elderly patients.
- Classic heat stroke generally develops slowly over days and occurs predominantly in older persons and in those with chronic illness. Exertional heat stroke is more common in young, healthy persons, has a more rapid onset, and is associated with higher core temperatures. Table 1H-8 compares classic and exertional heat stroke. Box 1H-2 summarizes organ dysfunction seen in patients with heat stroke.

ETIOLOGY

- Exogenous heat gain (increased ambient temperature).
- Increased heat production (exercise, infection, hyperthyroidism, drugs).

TABLE 1H-7 Factors Predisposing to Serious Heat Illness

Individual Factors

Lack of acclimatization
Low physical fitness
Excessive body weight
Dehydration
Advanced age
Young age

Health Conditions

Inflammation and fever
Viral infection
Cardiovascular disease
Diabetes mellitus
Gastroenteritis
Rash, sunburn, and previous burns to large areas of skin
Seizures
Thyroid storm
Neuroleptic malignant syndrome
Malignant hyperthermia
Sickle cell trait
Cystic fibrosis
Spinal cord injury

Drugs

Anticholinergic properties (atropine)
Antiepileptic (topiramate)
Antihistamines
Glutethimide (Doriden)
Phenothiazines
Tricyclic antidepressants
Amphetamines, cocaine, "Ecstasy"
Ergogenic stimulants (e.g., ephedrine, ephedra)
Lithium
Diuretics
β-Blockers
Ethanol

Environmental Factors

High temperature
High humidity
Little air motion
Lack of shade
Heat wave
Physical exercise
Heavy clothing
Air pollution (nitrogen dioxide)

From Goldman L, Schafer AI: *Goldman's Cecil medicine*, ed 24, Philadelphia, 2012, Saunders.

- Impaired heat dissipation (high humidity, heavy clothing, neonatal or elderly patients, drugs [phenothiazines, anticholinergics, antihistamines, butyrophenones, amphetamines, cocaine, alcohol, β-blockers]).
- Diuretics, laxatives.
- Fig. E1H-10 describes an algorithm of the pathophysiology of heat stroke.

 **DIAGNOSIS**

DIFFERENTIAL DIAGNOSIS

- Infections (meningitis, encephalitis, sepsis).
- Head trauma.
- Epilepsy.
- Thyroid storm.
- Acute cocaine intoxication.
- Malignant hyperthermia.
- Heat exhaustion can be differentiated from heat stroke by the following:
  1. Essentially intact mental function and lack of significant fever in heat exhaustion.
  2. Mild or absent increases in creatine phosphokinase (CPK), aspartate aminotransferase (AST), lactate dehydrogenase (LDH), and alanine aminotransferase (ALT) in heat exhaustion.

WORKUP

- Heat stroke: comprehensive history, physical examination, and laboratory evaluation.
- Heat exhaustion: in most cases, laboratory tests are not necessary for diagnosis.

LABORATORY TESTS

Laboratory abnormalities may include the following:
- Elevated BUN, creatinine, hematocrit.
- Hyponatremia or hypernatremia, hyperkalemia or hypokalemia.
- Elevated LDH, AST, ALT, CPK, bilirubin.
- Lactic acidosis, respiratory alkalosis (from hyperventilation).
- Myoglobinuria, hypofibrinogenemia, fibrinolysis, hypocalcemia.

Rx **TREATMENT**

- Treatment of heat exhaustion consists primarily of placing the patient in a cool, shaded area and providing rapid hydration and salt replacement.
  1. Fluid intake should be at least 2 L q4h in patients without history of CHF.
  2. Salt replacement can be accomplished by using one-quarter teaspoon of salt or two 10-grain salt tablets dissolved in 1 L of water.
  3. If IV fluid replacement is necessary, young athletes can be given normal saline IV (3 to 4 L over 6 to 8 hr); in elderly patients, consider using D5½NS IV with the rate titrated to cardiovascular status.
- Patients with heat stroke should undergo rapid cooling.

TABLE 1H-8 Comparison of Classic and Exertional Heat Stroke

Patient Characteristics	Classic	Exertional
Age	Young children or elderly	15-55 yr
Health	Chronic illness	Usually healthy
Fever	Unusual	Common
Prevailing weather	Frequent in heat waves	Variable
Activity	Sedentary	Strenuous exercise
Drug use	Diuretics, antidepressants, anticholinergics, phenothiazines	Ergogenic stimulants or cocaine
Sweating	Often absent	Common
Acid-base disturbances	Respiratory alkalosis	Lactic acidosis
Acute renal failure	Uncommon	Common ($\approx$15%)
Rhabdomyolysis	Uncommon	Common ($\approx$25%)
CK	Mildly elevated	Markedly elevated (500-1000 U/L)
ALT, AST	Mildly elevated	Markedly elevated
Hyperkalemia	Uncommon	Common
Hypocalcemia	Uncommon	Common
DIC	Mild	Marked
Hypoglycemia	Uncommon	Common

ALT, Alanine aminotransferase; *AST,* aspartate aminotransferase; *CK,* creatine kinase; *DIC,* disseminated intravascular coagulation.
From Goldman L, Schafer AI: *Goldman's Cecil medicine,* ed 24, Philadelphia, 2012, Saunders.

BOX 1H-2 Organ Dysfunction Seen in Patients with Heat Stroke

Encephalopathy
Rhabdomyolysis
Acute renal failure
Acute respiratory distress syndrome
Myocardial injury
Hepatocellular injury
Intestinal ischemia and infarction
Pancreatic injury
Hemorrhagic complication (e.g., disseminated intravascular coagulation)

From Adams JG et al: *Emergency medicine, clinical essentials,* ed 2, Philadelphia, 2013, Elsevier.

1. Remove the patient's clothes and place the patient in a cool and well-ventilated room.
2. If patient is unconscious, position on his or her side and clear the airway. Protect airway and augment oxygenation (e.g., nasal O_2 at 4 L/min to keep oxygen saturation >90%).
3. Monitor body temperature every 5 min. Measurement of the patient's core temperature with a rectal probe is recommended. The goal is to reduce the body temperature to 39° C (102.2° F) in 30 to 60 min. Advantages, disadvantages, and efficacy of various cooling methods are described in Table E 1H-9.
4. Spray the patient with a cool mist and use fans to enhance airflow over the body (rapid evaporation method).
5. Immersion of the patient in ice water, stomach lavage with iced saline solution, intravenous administration of cooled fluids, and inhalation of cold air are advisable only when the means for rapid evaporation are not available. Immersion in tepid water (15° C, 59° F) is preferred over ice water immersion to minimize risk of shivering.
6. Use of ice packs on axillae, neck, and groin is controversial because they increase peripheral vasoconstriction and may induce shivering.
7. Antipyretics are ineffective because the hypothalamic set point during heat stroke is normal despite the increased body temperature.
8. Intubate a comatose patient, insert a Foley catheter, and start nasal O_2. Continuous ECG monitoring is recommended.
9. Insert at least two large-bore IV lines and begin IV hydration with NS or Ringer's lactate.
10. Draw initial laboratory studies: electrolytes, complete blood count, blood urea nitrogen, creatinine, AST, ALT, CPK, LDH, glucose, PT (INR), PTT, platelet count, Ca^{2+}, lactic acid, and arterial blood gases.
11. Treat complications as follows:
    a. Hypotension: vigorous hydration with normal saline or Ringer's lactate.
    b. Convulsions: diazepam 5 to 10 mg IV (slowly).
    c. Shivering: chlorpromazine 10 to 50 mg IV.
    d. Acidosis: use bicarbonate judiciously (only in severe acidosis).
- Observe for evidence of rhabdomyolysis and hepatic, renal, or cardiac failure and treat accordingly.

DISPOSITION

Most patients recover completely within 48 hr. Central nervous system injury is permanent in 20% of cases. Mortality rate can exceed 30% in patients with prolonged and severe hyperthermia. Delayed access to cooling is the leading cause of morbidity and mortality in persons with heat stroke.

SUGGESTED READINGS

Available at www.expertconsult.com

RELATED CONTENT

Heat Exhaustion and Heat Stroke (Patient Information)

AUTHOR: **FRED F. FERRI, M.D.**

Diseases and Disorders

I

BASIC INFORMATION

DEFINITION

Infection of the human gastric mucosa with the organism *Helicobacter pylori,* a spiral-shaped gram-negative organism with unique features that allow it to survive in the hostile gastric environment.

SYNONYMS

Previously known as *Campylobacter pylori*

ICD-10CM CODES
B96.81 *Helicobacter pylori (H. pylori)* as the cause of diseases classified elsewhere

EPIDEMIOLOGY & DEMOGRAPHICS

H. pylori is the most common chronic bacterial infection in human beings, probably affecting 50% of the earth's population in all age groups and probably 30% to 40% of the U.S. population. In developing nations, infection is acquired at an earlier age and occurs more frequently.

CLINICAL PRESENTATION

- *H. pylori* causes histologic gastritis in all affected individuals. The majority of cases are asymptomatic and unlikely to proceed to serious consequences.
- *H. pylori* is a causative agent in peptic ulcer disease (PUD), gastric adenocarcinoma, and gastric mucosa-associated lymphoid tissue lymphoma, and may be a risk factor for iron-deficiency anemia and chronic idiopathic thrombocytopenic purpura. It may present with the signs and symptoms of these

disorders, including abdominal pain, bloating, anorexia, and early satiety. Figure 1H-11 describes association of *H. pylori* infection and disease states.
- "Alarm symptoms" that should prompt more immediate and aggressive workup include weight loss, dysphagia, protracted nausea or vomiting, anemia, melena, and palpable abdominal mass.

ETIOLOGY

- Route of acquisition is unknown but is presumed to be person to person by oral-oral or fecal-oral exposure.
- The majority of cases are acquired in childhood. Socioeconomic status and living conditions in childhood affect risk of acquisition of infection. These factors include housing density, number of siblings, overcrowding, sharing a bed, and lack of running water.
- *H. pylori* does not invade gastroduodenal tissue, but disrupts the mucous layer, causing the underlying mucosa to be more vulnerable to acid peptic damage.
- What differentiates the subset of patients with *H. pylori* who go on to develop ulcers or cancer remains unclear.

DIAGNOSIS

DIFFERENTIAL DIAGNOSIS

- Infection with *H. pylori* should be considered in the face of PUD, gastric cancer, gastritis, and gastric MALT lymphoma.
- *H. pylori* should be considered in the differential diagnosis of upper gastrointestinal (GI) tract disease, along with non-ulcer dyspepsia, reflux esophagitis, biliary tract disease,

gastroparesis, pancreatitis, and ischemic bowel.

WORKUP

- Workup is indicated in patients with active PUD, a past history of documented peptic ulcer, or gastric MALT lymphoma. The role of routine screening in high-risk populations is not clear. However, numerous studies suggest that *H. pylori* eradication is protective against progression of premalignant lesions. Consider testing for *H. pylori* in patients with idiopathic thrombocytopenic purpura, with otherwise unexplained iron deficiency anemia or unexplained B12 deficiency, as well as patients facing long-term NSAID or PPI therapy. Consider a test-and-treat approach in asymptomatic first-degree relatives of gastric cancer patients.
- Routine identification and treatment of *H. pylori* in cases of non-ulcer dyspepsia, gastroesophageal reflux disease (GERD), nonsteroidal antiinflammatory drug (NSAID) use, and in asymptomatic individuals in populations at high risk for gastric cancer is considered controversial, although it may be indicated in specific cases. A test-and-treat strategy may be used in patients younger than 55 with uncomplicated dyspepsia who have no alarm symptoms.
- Results of testing must be interpreted in relation to the individual patient's likelihood of *H. pylori* infection based on demographic risk factors. In the U.S. population, increased probability of infection exists in African Americans, Hispanics/Latinos, immigrants from developing nations, patients with poor socioeconomic status, Native Americans from Alaska, and persons >50 yr.
- Routine screening for *H. pylori* is not indicated in asymptomatic patients who are at low risk of infection.
- Infected patients with functional dyspepsia often benefit from treatment and should be evaluated for *H. pylori.*

LABORATORY TESTS

- Testing may be invasive or noninvasive depending on the need for endoscopy for other indications. There is no indication for endoscopy solely to diagnose *H. pylori.*
- Tests for *H. pylori* are differentiated as active or passive. Active tests provide direct evidence that *H. pylori* infection is currently present and include urea breath testing and stool antigen testing. Passive testing, which includes all serologic testing for *H. pylori,* gives indirect evidence of its presence by detecting the presence of antibodies to the organism. Serologic testing is limited by its inability to distinguish between active current infection and prior infection that has resolved.
- Tests that use urease as a marker (urea breath and stool antigen tests and biopsy for urease activity) may result in false-negative results in patients taking antibiotics, bismuth, or antisecretory therapy, as well as those with active ulcer bleeding. Patients should be

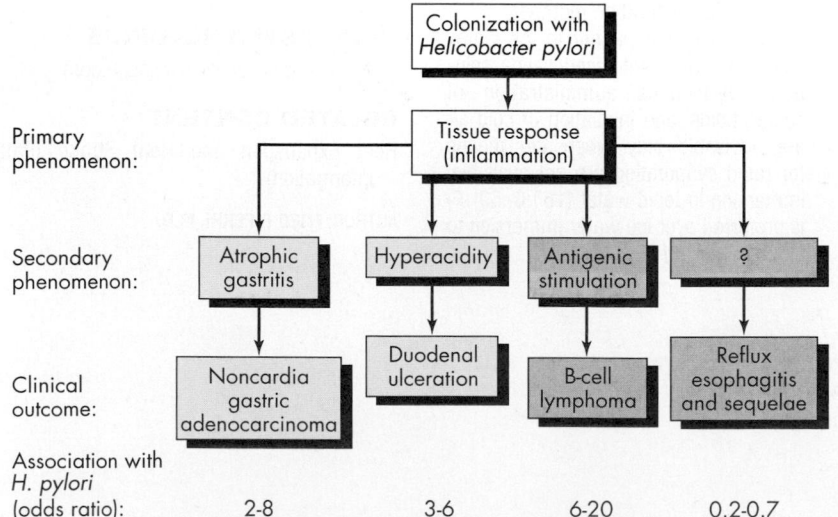

FIGURE 1H-11 Association of *Helicobacter pylori* colonization and disease states. After *H. pylori* acquisition, virtually all persons develop persistent colonization that lasts for life. Colonization induces tissue responses termed *chronic gastritis.* This process affects gastric physiology, including glandular structure, acid secretion, and antigen processing, which in turn affect disease risk. Colonization with *H. pylori* increases the risk for certain diseases (duodenal ulcer, gastric ulcer, noncardia gastric adenocarcinoma, and B-cell lymphomas) but appears to decrease the risk for gastroesophageal reflux disease and its complications, including Barrett's esophagus, and adenocarcinoma of the esophagus or gastric cardia. (From Mandell GL et al: *Principles and practice of infectious diseases,* ed 7, Philadelphia, 2010, Churchill Livingstone.)

off antibiotics for 4 wk and off protein pump inhibitors for 2 wk before urea breath or stool antigen testing.

- When diagnostic endoscopy is indicated (for suspicion or follow-up of PUD or gastric MALT), antral biopsy should be tested for urease activity. If urease testing is likely to show a false-negative result because of recent proton pump inhibitor (PPI), bismuth, or antibiotic use or active ulcer bleeding, the sample should undergo histologic examination.

- In cases in which biopsy is not indicated, urea breath testing or stool antigen testing is indicated to evaluate for active infection. The sensitivities and specificities of these two tests are similar (>90%). Urea breath testing is slightly more expensive than stool antigen testing, but both costs are in the modest range. Choice can be made based on patient preference and availability.

- In cases in which biopsy is not indicated, consider using serologic testing as the initial approach. However, in individuals with a low pretest probability of infection, positive results should be confirmed with another testing method.

Rx TREATMENT

ACUTE GENERAL Rx

- Test only patients whom you intend to treat if positive (see "Workup"). At this time, the value of eradicating *H. pylori* infection is proven in patients with PUD or gastric MALT lymphoma.

- The optimal antibiotic regimen has not been defined. In addition to efficacy, side effects, cost, and ease of administration must be considered.

- Due to increasing resistance to clarithromycin, decisions regarding appropriate regimens should take into account local rates of clarithromycin resistance.

- The following regimens may be considered for first-line therapy:
  1. PPI twice daily, with twice-daily clarithromycin (500 mg) and amoxicillin (1 g) may be used in areas of low clarithromycin resistance.
  2. In cases of penicillin allergy, metronidazole (500 mg bid) may be substituted for amoxicillin.
  3. PPI twice daily, combined with bismuth four times daily, as well as tetracycline (500 mg) and metronidazole (250 mg), both four times daily, is now recommended as first-line therapy in areas of high clarithromycin resistance. Sequential

therapy, consisting of 5 days of treatment with a PPI and one antibiotic (usually amoxicillin) followed by 5-day treatment with the PPI and two other antibiotics (usually clarithromycin and metronidazole), may be used in areas of high clarithromycin resistance when bismuth-based therapy is not available.

- Duration of treatment remains controversial. Extending therapy to 10 to 14 days may improve eradication rates. Use of combination capsules may improve compliance but is likely to be more expensive.

- Prior exposure to a macrolide or metronidazole, for any reason, is associated with increased resistance. A preferable regimen would include medications to which the patient has not been previously exposed.

- Diarrhea and abdominal cramping are commonly observed with many of the regimens. (Probiotics may diminish this effect.) Other side effects may include a metallic taste with metronidazole or clarithromycin, neuropathy, seizures, and disulfiram-like reaction with metronidazole, diarrhea with amoxicillin, photosensitivity with tetracycline, and *Clostridium difficile* infection with any antibiotic exposure. Bismuth may cause black stool and constipation. Tetracycline is contraindicated in pregnant patients.

- 20% of patients may not respond to initial therapy. Optimal retreatment regimens are under investigation. It is important to reinforce compliance. Second-line therapy should be either bismuth-containing quadruple therapy or levofloxacin-containing triple therapy (regardless of local clarithromycin resistance patterns). When possible, management of those who do not respond to two courses of therapy should be guided by antimicrobial sensitivity testing (although this is not indicated before initial treatment).

CHRONIC Rx

- Accepted indications for confirming eradication include *H. pylori*–associated ulcers, MALT lymphoma, and early gastric cancer. It may be considered in those with persistent dyspepsia despite a test-and-treat management strategy (as well as consideration of other causes for the dyspeptic symptoms). Given the increasing prevalence of antibiotic resistance and the decreasing cost of testing, consider confirming eradication of *H. pylori* in all treated patients.

- Serology does not reliably revert to undetectable levels after treatment and should not be used to determine eradication.

- Active tests (urea breath test and stool antigen testing) are preferable. They are equally accurate in confirming eradication, and either may be used depending on availability and patient preference. To reduce the likelihood of false-negative results, testing should be performed at least 4 wk after eradication therapy with PPI and antibiotics or at least 2 wk after the cessation of PPI therapy alone.

DISPOSITION

Consider further evaluation in patients with recurrent symptoms after appropriate treatment.

REFERRAL

- Patients with gastric MALT lymphoma should be followed by a gastroenterologist and oncologist with expertise in the care of lymphoid neoplasms.

- Patients with dyspepsia who have tested positive for *H. pylori* and been treated without resolution should be referred for endoscopy.

- Consider referral for biopsy for culture and sensitivity in patients who have not responded to two attempts at treatment.

PEARLS & CONSIDERATIONS

- Whether *H. pylori* eradication reduces the risk of gastric cancer is unclear.

- Outcomes in PUD and gastric MALT lymphoma are improved with treatment of associated *H. pylori* infection.

- Tests that provide direct evidence of active *H. pylori* infection (urea breath and stool antigen testing) are preferred but may result in false-negative results in patients taking antibiotics, bismuth, or antisecretory agents.

- Serologic testing does not differentiate active from prior infection. It may be useful when active tests are not indicated, particularly in high-risk patients.

- Be aware of high-risk populations in low-prevalence settings, including immigrants from Mexico, South America, Southeast Asia, and Eastern Europe.

SUGGESTED READINGS

Available at www.expertconsult.com

RELATED CONTENT

Helicobacter pylori Infection (Patient Information)
Gastritis (Related Key Topic)
Peptic Ulcer (Related Key Topic)

AUTHOR: **MARGARET TRYFOROS, M.D.**

BASIC INFORMATION

DEFINITION

The HELLP syndrome is a serious variant of preeclampsia. HELLP is an acronym for **h**emolysis, **e**levated **l**iver function, and **l**ow **p**latelet count. It is the most frequently encountered microangiopathy of pregnancy. There are three classes of the syndrome based on the degree of maternal thrombocytopenia as a primary indicator of disease severity:

Class 1: Platelets ≤50,000/mm³
Class 2: Platelets >50,000/mm³ to 100,000/mm³
Class 3: Platelets >100,000/mm³

SYNONYMS

Hemolysis
Elevated liver function
Low platelet syndrome

ICD-10CM CODES

O26.892	Other specified pregnancy related conditions, second trimester
O14.2	HELLP syndrome
O26.893	Other specified pregnancy related conditions, third trimester
O26.899	Other specified pregnancy related conditions, unspecified trimester
O26.90	Pregnancy related conditions, unspecified, unspecified trimester
O26.91	Pregnancy related conditions, unspecified, first trimester
O26.92	Pregnancy related conditions, unspecified, second trimester
O26.93	Pregnancy related conditions, unspecified, third trimester

BOX 1H-3 Medical and Surgical Disorders Often Confused with HELLP Syndrome

- Acute fatty liver of pregnancy
- Appendicitis
- Gallbladder disease
- Glomerulonephritis
- Hemolytic uremic syndrome
- Hepatic encephalopathy
- Hyperemesis gravidarum
- Idiopathic thrombocytopenia
- Pyelonephritis
- Systemic lupus erythematosus
- Antiphospholipid antibody syndrome
- Thrombotic thrombocytopenic purpura
- Viral hepatitis
- HELLP (hemolysis, elevated liver enzymes, and low platelets) syndrome

From Gabbe SG: *Obstetrics*, ed 6, Philadelphia, 2012, Saunders.

EPIDEMIOLOGY & DEMOGRAPHICS

- Among women with severe preeclampsia, 6% will manifest with one abnormality suggestive of HELLP syndrome, 12% will develop two abnormalities, and approximately 10% will develop all three.
- The HELLP syndrome, like preeclampsia, is rare before 20 wk of gestation.
- One third of all cases occur postpartum; of these, only 80% are typically diagnosed with preeclampsia before delivery.

RISK FACTORS: Women >35 yr, white, multiparity
RECURRENCE RATE: 3% to 25%

PHYSICAL FINDINGS & CLINICAL PRESENTATION

- Definitive laboratory criteria remain to be validated prospectively.
- Most commonly used criteria include hemolysis defined by the presence of an abnormal peripheral smear with schistocytes, lactate dehydrogenase (LDH) >600 U/L, and total bilirubin >1.2 mg/dl; elevated liver enzymes as serum aspartate aminotransferase (AST) >70 U/L and LDH >600 U/L; low platelet count as less than 100,000/mm³.
- Although many women with HELLP syndrome are asymptomatic, 80% report right upper quadrant pain and 50% to 60% present with excessive weight gain and worsening edema.

ETIOLOGY

As with other microangiopathies, endothelial dysfunction, with resultant activation of the intravascular coagulation cascade, has been proposed as the central pathogenesis of HELLP syndrome.

DIAGNOSIS

DIFFERENTIAL DIAGNOSIS

- Appendicitis.
- Gallbladder disease.
- Peptic ulcer disease.
- Enteritis.
- Hepatitis.
- Pyelonephritis.
- Systemic lupus erythematosus.
- Thrombotic thrombocytopenic purpura/hemolytic-uremic syndrome.
- Acute fatty liver of pregnancy.
- Box 1H-3 summarizes medical and surgical disorders often confused with HELLP syndrome.

WORKUP

Because HELLP syndrome is a disease entity based on laboratory values, initial assessment is detailed below.

LABORATORY TESTS

- Initial assessment of suspected HELLP syndrome should include a complete blood count to evaluate platelets, urinalysis, serum creatinine, LDH, uric acid, indirect and total bilirubin levels, and AST/alanine aminotransferase (ALT).
- Tests of prothrombin time, partial thromboplastin time, fibrinogen, and fibrin split products are reserved for women with a platelet count well below 100,000/mm³.

IMAGING STUDIES

No imaging modalities aid in diagnosis.

TREATMENT

Treatment depends on gestational age of the fetus, severity of condition, and maternal status. Stabilization of the mother is the first priority. Fig. 1H-12 describes an algorithm for the management of HELLP syndrome.

ACUTE GENERAL Rx

- Assess gestational age thoroughly. Fetal status should be monitored with nonstress tests, contraction stress tests, and/or biophysical profile.

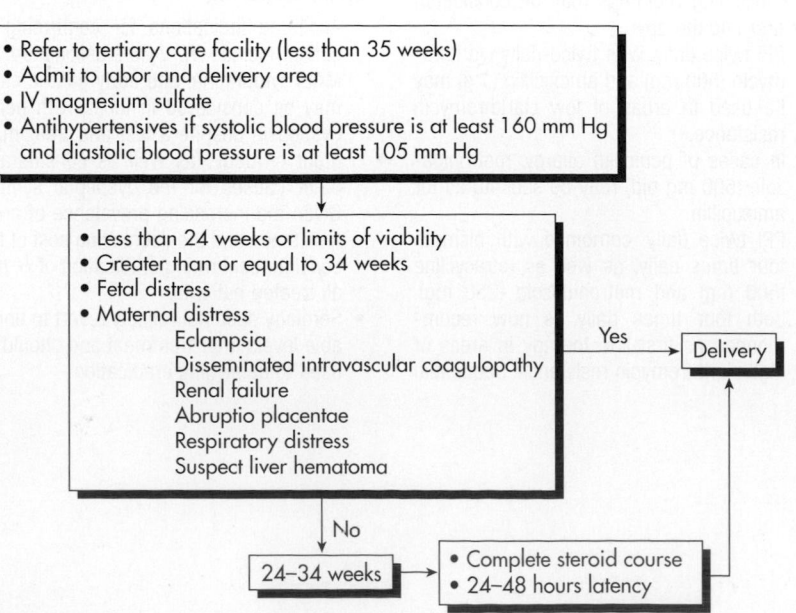

FIGURE 1H-12 An algorithm for the management of HELLP syndrome. (From Gabbe SG: *Obstetrics*, ed 6, Philadelphia, 2012, Saunders.)

- Maternal status should be evaluated by history, physical examination, and laboratory testing.
- Magnesium sulfate is administered for seizure prophylaxis regardless of blood pressure.
- Blood pressure control is achieved with agents such as hydralazine or labetalol.
- Indwelling Foley catheter to monitor maternal volume status and urine output.

CHRONIC Rx

- In pregnancies of 34 wk or with class 1 HELLP syndrome, delivery, either vaginal or abdominal, within 24 hr is the goal.
- In the preterm fetus corticosteroid therapy to enhance fetal lung maturation is indicated.
- Some reports have shown temporary amelioration of HELLP severity with the administration of high-dose steroids measured by increased urine output, improvement in platelet count, and liver function test. However, a 2010 Cochrane review found no benefit of steroids in improving the clinical outcome.
- Judicious use of blood products, especially in those requiring surgery.
- The patient requires intensive observation for 48 hr postpartum; laboratory levels should begin to improve during this time.

DISPOSITION

The natural history of this disorder is a rapidly deteriorating condition requiring close monitoring of maternal and fetal well-being.

REFERRAL

Preterm patients with HELLP syndrome should be stabilized hemodynamically and transferred to a tertiary care center. Term patients can be treated at a local hospital depending on the availability of obstetric, neonatal, and blood banking services.

 PEARLS & CONSIDERATIONS

- Not all women with HELLP have hypertension or proteinuria.
- Life-threatening hemorrhage is a rare event in HELLP syndrome. Identifiable risk factors predictive of a major hemorrhage are thrombocytopenia ($<100,000/mm^3$), AST>70 IU/L, and previous gestations.
- The most effective therapy for HELLP is emergent delivery of the fetus.

SUGGESTED READINGS
Available at www.expertconsult.com

RELATED CONTENT
Eclampsia (Related Key Topic)
Preeclampsia (Related Key Topic)

AUTHORS: **SONYA S. ABDEL-RAZEQ, M.D.,** and **RUBEN ALVERO, M.D.**

Diseases and Disorders

H

BASIC INFORMATION

DEFINITION

Hemochromatosis is an autosomal-recessive disorder that disrupts the body's regulation of iron and is characterized by increased accumulation of iron in various organs (adrenals, liver, pancreas, heart, testes, kidneys, pituitary) and eventual dysfunction of these organs if not treated appropriately.

SYNONYMS

Bronze diabetes

ICD-10CM CODES
E83.110 Hereditary hemochromatosis
E83.111 Hemochromatosis due to repeated red blood cell transfusions
E83.118 Other hemochromatosis
E83.119 Hemochromatosis, unspecified

EPIDEMIOLOGY & DEMOGRAPHICS

INCIDENCE: In whites, approximately 1 in 385 persons.

PREDOMINANT SEX AND AGE:

Generally diagnosed in males in their fifth decade. Diagnosis in females is generally not made until 10 to 20 yr after menopause.

GENETICS:

Most common genetic disorder in North European ancestry. Homozygosity for the *C282Y* mutation is now found in approximately 5 of every 1000 persons of European descent.

PHYSICAL FINDINGS & CLINICAL PRESENTATION

- In earlier stages patients completely asymptomatic and diagnosed due to abnormal laboratory tests.
- Hepatic dysfunction leading to hepatomegaly, fibrosis, and eventually cirrhosis.
- Arthritis.
- Gonadal insufficiency leading to loss of libido and testicular atrophy.
- Diabetes mellitus: risk greater in patients with family history.
- Iron-induced cardiac disease resulting in cardiomyopathy, heart failure, and arrhythmias.
- Skin pigmentation.

ETIOLOGY

- The majority of the patients diagnosed with hemochromatosis have mutation in the *HFE* gene and are either homozygous for the *C282Y* mutation *(C282Y/C282Y)* or compound heterozygote for the *C282Y* mutation and either the mutation *H63D (C282Y/H63D)* or less commonly the *S65C (C282Y/S65C).*
- The remainder of the patients are classified as non–*HFE*-associated hemochromatosis.

DIAGNOSIS

DIFFERENTIAL DIAGNOSIS
- Hereditary anemias with defect of erythropoiesis.

- Cirrhosis, chronic liver disease, porphyria cutanea tarda.
- Repeated blood transfusions.
- African dietary iron overload.

WORKUP

Medical history, physical examination, and laboratory evaluation should be focused on affected organ systems (see "Physical Findings & Clinical Presentation"). Figure 1H-13 outlines evaluation for possible hereditary hemochromatosis in an individual with negative family history. Liver biopsy is the gold standard for diagnosis; it reveals iron deposition in hepatocytes, bile ducts, and supporting tissues.

LABORATORY TESTS

- Transferrin saturation is the best screening test. Values >45% are an indication for further testing.
- Elevated serum ferritin is good evidence of iron overload, but other causes like chronic inflammatory conditions, malignancy, and so forth need to be ruled out as ferritin is also an acute phase reactant.
- Genotypical screening for *C282Y* and *H63D* mutation in *HFE* gene should be done in patients with high transferrin saturation, elevated ferritin, or both.

- Liver biopsy (Fig. 1H-14) is the gold standard but is not needed in somebody who has a persistently elevated transferrin saturation, elevated ferritin, or both.
- Hepatic iron index can help differentiate between various causes of iron overload.
- Elevated aspartate aminotransferase, alanine aminotransferase, and alkaline phosphatase are seen.
- Hyperglycemia is found.
- Endocrine abnormalities (decreased testosterone, luteinizing hormone, follicle-stimulating hormone) are noted.
- Table 1H-10 describes laboratory findings in patients with hereditary hemochromatosis.

IMAGING STUDIES

Routine radiologic imaging is not needed.

TREATMENT

The goal of therapy is the removal of excess iron and maintaining it at a normal or near-normal level.

NONPHARMACOLOGIC THERAPY

Phlebotomy is the treatment of choice.

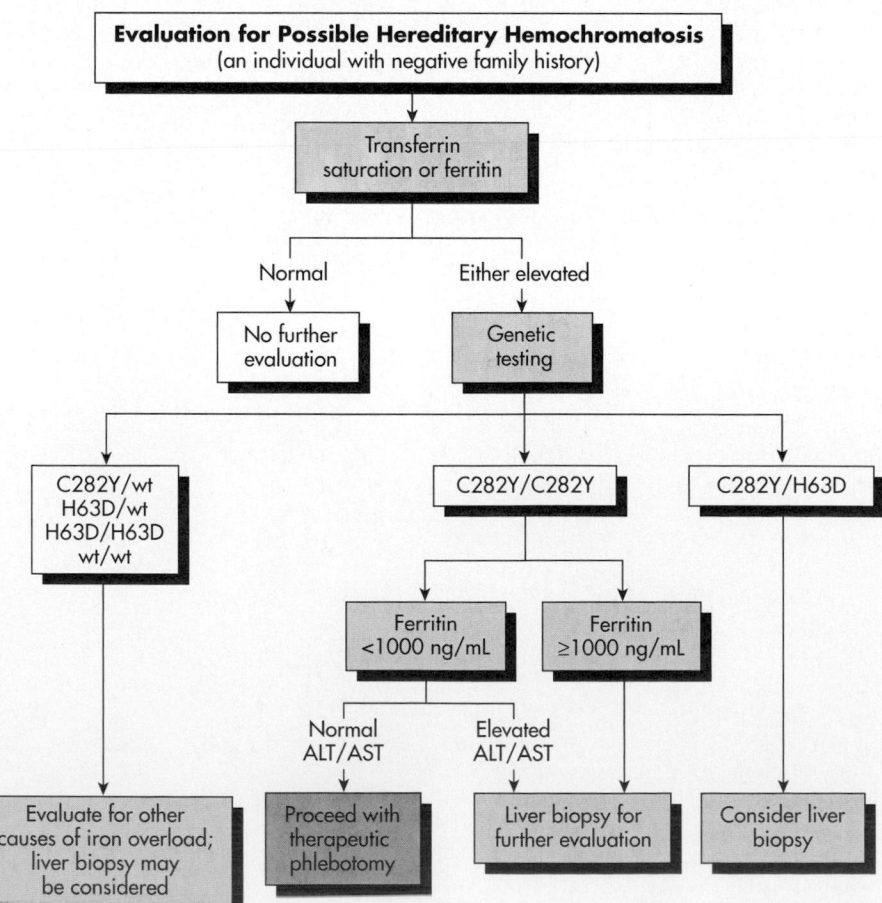

FIGURE 1H-13 Algorithm for evaluation of possible hereditary hemochromatosis in a person with a negative family history. *ALT,* Alanine transminase; *AST,* aspartate transminase. (From Goldman L, Schafer AI: *Goldman's Cecil medicine,* ed 24, Philadelphia, 2012, Saunders.)

ACUTE GENERAL Rx

- The timing and frequency of phlebotomy needs to be individualized for each patient.
- For patients with heavy iron overload twice-weekly phlebotomies should be started. In most patients, weekly phlebotomy is adequate.
- The effectiveness of treatment is monitored by periodic ferritin measurement. The goal is to bring ferritin level below 50 ng/mL.
- Patients with iron overload due to transfusion-dependent anemias may not tolerate phlebotomy. For these patients iron chelation may be needed.
- The chelating agent deferoxamine has to be given daily as a 9- to 12-hr IV or SC infusion and compliance is difficult.
- The oral chelating agent deferasirox (Exjade) is effective, but should not be used in patients with high-risk myelodysplastic syndrome because it can cause renal impairment, hepatic impairment, or gastrointestinal hemorrhage, which can be fatal.

CHRONIC Rx

After the ferritin has been brought to less than 50 ng/mL, phlebotomy is needed on an as-needed basis to keep the ferritin at that level.

DISPOSITION

- Serum ferritin measurement is the most useful prognostic indicator of disease severity.
- Prognosis is good if phlebotomy is started early (before onset of cirrhosis or diabetes mellitus); women can have the full phenotypic expression of the disease, including cirrhosis, and should also be aggressively treated.

REFERRAL

For liver biopsy if diagnosis is uncertain.

 **PEARLS & CONSIDERATIONS**

COMMENTS

- Persons who are homozygous for the HFE gene mutation *C282Y* comprise 85% to 90% of phenotypically affected individuals.
- Patients with hemochromatosis and serum ferritin levels <1000 ng/mL are unlikely to have cirrhosis. Liver biopsy to screen for cirrhosis may be unnecessary in such patients.
- Cirrhotic patients must be periodically monitored (ultrasound or CT scan) because of their increased risk of hepatocellular carcinoma.
- *HFE* gene testing for *C282Y* mutation is a cost-effective method of screening relatives of patients with hereditary hemochromatosis. The American College of Gastroenterology recommends genotyping persons who have abnormal iron screening tests and first-degree relatives of those identified with *C282Y* homozygosity.
- Established cirrhosis, hypogonadism, destructive arthritis, and insulin-dependent diabetes mellitus secondary to hemochromatosis cannot be reversed with repeated phlebotomy, but their progress can be slowed.
- In patients who are heterozygotes for *C282Y* or *H63D* mutation, clinically meaningful iron overload does not develop.
- Screening for hepatocellular carcinoma is reserved for those with hereditary hemochromatosis and cirrhosis.

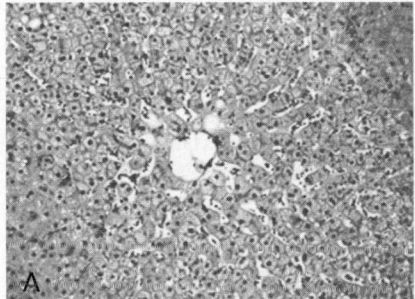 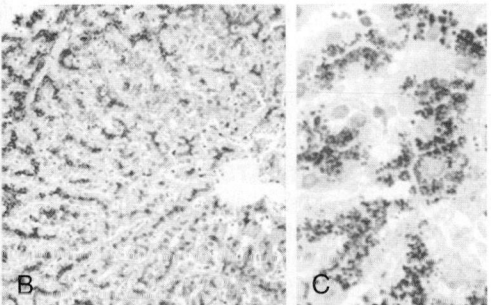

FIGURE 1H-14 Hemochromatosis. Liver biopsy sample from a 46-year-old man with homozygous hemochromatosis. Hematoxylin and eosin stain of the liver **(A)** shows intact hepatic architecture. Iron stain **(B, C)** shows marked diffuse iron deposits in the hepatocytes throughout the lobules. A normal liver would show essentially no iron in the hepatocytes. (From Hoffman R et al: *Hematology, basic principles and practice,* ed 5, Philadelphia, 2009, Churchill Livingstone.)

SUGGESTED READINGS

Available at www.expertconsult.com

RELATED CONTENT

Hemochromatosis (Patient Information)

AUTHOR: **FRED F. FERRI, M.D.**

TABLE 1H-10 Laboratory Findings in Patients with Hereditary Hemochromatosis

Measurements	Normal Subjects	Patients With Hereditary Hemochromatosis	
		Asymptomatic	Symptomatic
Blood (Fasting)			
Serum iron level (μg/dl)	60-180	150-280	180-300
Serum transferrin level (mg/dl)	220-410	200-280	200-300
Transferrin saturation (%)	20-45	45-100	80-100
Serum ferritin level (ng/ml)			
Men	20-200	150-1000	500-6000
Women	15-150	120-1000	500-6000
Genetic (*HFE* Mutation Analysis)			
C282Y/C282Y	wt/wt‡	*C282Y/C282Y*	*C282Y/C282Y*
*C282Y/H63D**	wt/wt	*C282Y/H63D*	*C282Y/H63D*
Liver			
Hepatic iron concentration			
μg/g dry weight	300-1500	2000-10,000	8000-30,000
μmol/g dry weight	5-27	36-179	140-550
Hepatic iron index†	<1	1 to >1.9	>1.9
Liver histology			
Perls' Prussian blue stain	0, 1+	2+ to 4+	3+, 4+

*Compound heterozygote.
†Calculated by dividing the hepatic iron concentration (in μmol/g dry weight) by the age of the patient (in yr). With the increased use of genetic testing in patients with iron overload, the specificity of the hepatic iron index has diminished.
‡wt/wt: wild type (normal).
From Goldman L, Schafer AI: *Goldman's Cecil medicine,* ed 24, Philadelphia, 2012, Saunders.

BASIC INFORMATION

DEFINITION

Hemolytic-uremic syndrome (HUS) is a life-threatening form of thrombotic microangiopathy (TMA). HUS generally occurs in two different settings. A bacterial infection antedates the onset of HUS in the majority of cases. A preceding bacterial infection is not identified in approximately 5% to 10% of patients with atypical HUS (aHUS).

SYNONYMS

HUS

ICD-10CM CODES
D59.3 Hemolytic-uremic syndrome

EPIDEMIOLOGY & DEMOGRAPHICS

HUS affects mainly young children less than 5 years of age and has an incidence of 1 to 2 cases per 100,000 in the United States. At times, HUS cases cluster in rural populations during the summer months. Atypical HUS can occur at any age. The prevalence of aHUS is estimated to be 1 to 9 cases per million.

PHYSICAL FINDINGS AND CLINICAL PRESENTATION

TMAs are characterized by microangiopathic hemolytic anemia, thrombocytopenia, and ischemic organ injury. HUS is preceded by an infection such as bacterial gastroenteritis in nearly 90% of cases. HUS occurs 2 to 10 days following the onset of diarrhea that is often bloody (~75%) and accompanied by abdominal pain, vomiting, and fever. Oligoanuric acute kidney injury and hypertension are common. Neurologic manifestations, including altered mental status and seizure, occur in ~20% of cases. Stroke and coma are associated with increased mortality. Hepatomegaly and abnormal liver function tests may be present.

aHUS occurs in sporadic and familial forms. While aHUS is usually abrupt in onset, it can be insidious in ~20% of cases. aHUS often leads to severe renal dysfunction necessitating renal replacement therapy. Hypertension, proteinuria, and hematuria are frequently noted. C3 hypocomplementemia is present in ~20% of cases. Extrarenal manifestations are increasingly recognized in cases of aHUS, with neurologic, gastrointestinal, and cardiovascular manifestations.

ETIOLOGY

Endothelial injury and microvascular thrombosis are the common findings of HUS and aHUS. Endothelial injury in HUS is secondary to toxins produced by pathogenic bacteria such as Shiga toxin-producing *E. coli* (STEC), usually *E. coli* serotype O157:H7. Endothelial injury in aHUS is secondary to enhanced complement activity. Complement activation via the alternative pathway is the result of defective complement regulation in aHUS. Complement activity is normally regulated by several soluble and membrane-bound proteins. Loss-of-function genetic mutations involving complement regulators are found in 40% to 60% of patients with aHUS.

DIAGNOSIS

The first step in making a diagnosis of HUS/aHUS is establishing the presence of a TMA. While most cases of HUS occur following a bacterial infection such as acute gastroenteritis due to STEC, aHUS remains a diagnosis of exclusion.

DIFFERENTIAL DIAGNOSIS

A TMA also occurs in a variety of other settings such as thrombotic thrombocytopenic purpura (TTP), malignant hypertension, scleroderma renal crisis, and antiphospholipid antibody syndrome. TMAs are also associated with drugs (cyclosporine, tacrolimus, clopidogrel, quinine, mitomycin, gemcitabine), pregnancy, malignancy, bone marrow transplantation, HIV infection, and systemic lupus erythematosus.

WORKUP

The workup for suspected HUS/aHUS includes blood and stool tests.

LABORATORY TESTS

Anemia in HUS/aHUS primarily due to microangiopathic hemolysis. Therefore, haptoglobin is low to undetectable, LDH is increased, and the peripheral blood smear reveals fragmented erythrocytes (schistocytes) and reticulocytosis. Indirect (unconjugated) bilirubin may be elevated. Intravascular thrombosis with platelet consumptions leads to relative (>25% reduction) or absolute (<150.000/mm^3) thrombocytopenia. In the absence of blood transfusion or autoimmunity, the direct Coombs test is typically negative. Increased blood urea nitrogen and creatinine indicate reduced kidney function. Urinalysis may show proteinuria and hematuria. Stool culture using special agar plates may detect STEC, especially during the first week of diarrhea. Specific immunoassays and genetic studies for detection of Shiga toxin from stool specimens are available. If plasma activity of the von Willebrand factor-cleaving protease ADAMTS-13 (*a disintegrin and metalloproteinase with a thrombospondin type 1 motif, member 13*) is <5% to 10%, thrombotic thrombocytopenic purpura is suspected.

IMAGING STUDIES

Imaging studies are not very helpful in the diagnosis of HUS/aHUS.

TREATMENT

While the treatment of HUS is primarily supportive, pharmacological complement inhibition is the mainstay of therapy for aHUS.

NONPHARMACOLOGIC THERAPY

Careful attention should be paid to volume status and electrolyte derangements. Severe anemia may require blood transfusions. Platelet transfusion is reserved for patients with clinically significant bleeding and those who require invasive procedures. Antibiotics and antimotility agents are avoided. Corticosteroids and plasma exchange therapy have no proven benefit in STEC-HUS. Plasma exchange therapy is accepted as first- or second-line therapy for aHUS, either as standalone treatment or in conjunction with other treatment modalities.

ACUTE GENERAL Rx

The treatment of HUS is supportive. Plasma exchange is the standard of care for HUS in adults. Eculizumab has been successfully used for the treatment of aHUS. Eculizumab is a humanized monoclonal antibody that acts a terminal complement inhibitor by blocking complement component 5 or C5 activation.

CHRONIC Rx

Kidney replacement therapy as dialysis or kidney transplantation may be required for kidney failure in HUS/aHUS. Long-term plasma therapy or eculizumab may be required for aHUS.

DISPOSITION

STEC-HUS has a mortality rate of <5%. The prognosis in adults is less favorable than in children. aHUS has a grave prognosis. While aHUS mortality approaches 25% during the acute phase, end-stage renal disease develops in nearly half of patients within a year. aHUS has a high recurrence rate after renal transplantation, and recurrent disease often leads to graft loss.

REFERRAL

Local health department if STEC is isolated. Large food-borne outbreaks have occurred as a result of contaminated commercial beef products and asparagus. Hematology. Nephrology consultation is recommended when renal manifestations are present.

PEARLS & CONSIDERATIONS

- Children testing positive for STEC should not return to school or day care facilities until two consecutive stool specimens test are negative. STEC is transmissible person-to-person, and universal precautions and handwashing are recommended.
- The clinical presentation of HUS overlaps with thrombotic thrombocytopenic purpura (TTP). However, HUS is more common in children, has more kidney manifestations, and fewer neurologic manifestations.

SUGGESTED READINGS
Available at www.expertconsult.com

RELATED CONTENT
Hemolytic-Uremic Syndrome (Patient Information)
Thrombotic Thrombocytopenic Purpura (Related Key Topic)

AUTHORS: **ALI NAYER, M.D.,** and **ARIF ASIF, M.D.**

BASIC INFORMATION

DEFINITION

Hemophilia is a hereditary bleeding disorder caused by low factor VIII coagulant activity (hemophilia A) or low levels of factor IX coagulant activity (hemophilia B).

SYNONYMS

Hemophilia A: Classic hemophilia, factor VIII deficiency hemophilia
Hemophilia B: Christmas disease, factor IX hemophilia

ICD-10CM CODES
D66   Hereditary factor VIII deficiency
D67   Hereditary factor IX deficiency
D68.311 Acquired hemophilia
Z14.01 Asymptomatic hemophilia A carrier
Z14.02 Symptomatic hemophilia A carrier

EPIDEMIOLOGY & DEMOGRAPHICS

INCIDENCE/PREVALENCE (IN U.S.): Hemophilia A: 100 cases per 1 million males; hemophilia B: 20 cases per 1 million males. Approximately 400,000 patients have severe hemophilia worldwide.

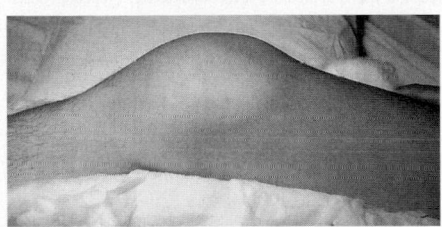

FIGURE 1H-15 Acute hemarthrosis of the knee is a common complication of hemophilia. It may be confused with acute infection unless the patient's coagulation disorder is known because the knee is hot, red, swollen, and painful. (From Forbes CD, Jackson WF. *Color atlas and text of clinical medicine,* ed 3, London, 2003, Mosby.)

GENETIC: Both hemophilias have an X-linked recessive pattern of inheritance with only males affected.

PHYSICAL FINDINGS & CLINICAL PRESENTATION

- The clinical features of hemophilia A and B are generally indistinguishable from each other. The clinical symptoms are determined by the baseline factor activity in each patient. Spontaneous bleeding can occur with those with severe hemophilia (<1% factor VIII or IX activity). Trauma-induced bleeding can occur in those with moderate hemophilia (factor levels 1%-5%) and mild disease (factor levels >5%).
- Bleeding is most commonly seen in joints (knees, ankles, elbows), resulting in hot, swollen, painful joints (Fig. 1H-15) and subsequent crippling joint deformity (Fig. 1H-16).
- Bleeding can also occur into the muscles and the gastrointestinal tract.
- Compartment syndrome can occur from large hematomas.
- Hematuria may be present.

ETIOLOGY

- Both disorders are congenital. X-linked recessive disorders of hemostasis.
- Hemophilia A: low factor VIII coagulant (VIII:C) activity; can be classified as mild if factor VIII:C levels are >5%, moderate if levels are 1% to 5%, and severe if levels are <1%.
- Hemophilia B: low levels of factor IX coagulant activity.
- Spontaneous acquisition of factor VIII inhibitors (acquired hemophilia) is rare.

DIAGNOSIS

DIFFERENTIAL DIAGNOSIS

- Other clotting factor deficiencies.
- Platelet function disorders.
- Vitamin K deficiency.

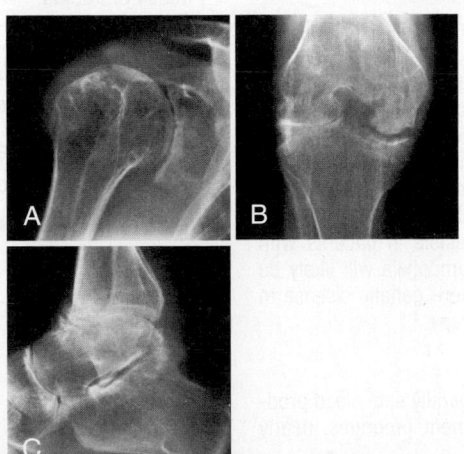

FIGURE 1H-16 Radiographic changes associated with hemophilic arthropathy. A, Radiograph of the shoulder showing multiple subchondral cysts in the head of the humerus, an early finding in hemophilic arthropathy. The glenohumeral joint space is fairly well preserved, and range of motion is normal. **B,** Widening of the intercondylar notch and near fusion of the femur and medial tibial condyle in the knee joint affected by hemophilic arthropathy. **C,** Narrowing and fusion of the tibiotalar joint in the ankle. (From Hoffman R et al: *Hematology, basic principles and practice,* ed 5, Philadelphia, 2009, Churchill Livingstone.)

WORKUP

Patients with mild hemophilia bleed only in response to major trauma or surgery and may not be diagnosed until young adulthood. Diagnostic workup includes laboratory evaluation (see "Laboratory Tests").

LABORATORY TESTS

- Partial thromboplastin time (aPTT) is prolonged. Prothrombin time (PT) is normal, and the aPTT mixing study will fully correct.
- Reduced factor VIII: C level distinguishes hemophilia A from other causes of prolonged PTT.
- Factor VIII antigen, fibrinogen level, and bleeding time are normal.
- Factor IX coagulant activity levels are reduced in patients with hemophilia B.
- Coagulation factor activity measurement is useful to correlate with disease severity. Normal range is 50 to 150 U/dl; 5 to 20 U/dl indicates mild disease, 2 to 5 U/dl indicates moderate disease, and <2 U/dl indicates severe disease with spontaneous bleeding episodes.

TREATMENT

NONPHARMACOLOGIC THERAPY

- Avoidance of contact sports.
- Patient education regarding the disease; promotion of exercises such as swimming.
- Avoidance of aspirin or other NSAIDs.
- Orthopedic evaluation and physical therapy evaluation in patients with joint involvement.
- Hepatitis vaccination.

ACUTE GENERAL Rx

(See Table 1H-11).
HEMOPHILIA A:
- Reversal and prevention of acute bleeding in hemophilia A and B are based on adequate replacement of deficient or missing factor protein.
- The choice of the product for replacement therapy is guided by availability, capacity, concerns, and cost. Recombinant factors cost two to three times as much as plasma-derived factors, and the limited capacity to produce recombinant factors often results in periods of shortage. In the United States 60% of patients with severe hemophilia use recombinant products.
- Factor VIII concentrates are effective in controlling spontaneous and traumatic hemorrhage in severe hemophilia. The new recombinant factor VIII is stable without added human serum albumin (decreased risk of transmission of infectious agents).
- Alloantibodies (inhibitors) that neutralize factor VIII clotting function occur in nearly 30% of patients with severe hemophilia A after exposure to factor VIII. In these patients, bypassing agents (anti-inhibitor coagulant complex [AICC] and recombinant activated factor VII [rFVIIa]) can be used to treat bleeding. AICC can also be used prophylactically to decrease the frequency of joint and other bleeding events in patients with severe hemophilia A and factor VIII inhibitors.
- Recombinant activated factor VII is useful to stop spontaneous hemorrhages and prevent excessive bleeding during surgery in 75%

TABLE 1H-11 Treatment of Hemophilia

Type of Hemorrhage	Hemophilia A	Hemophilia B
Hemarthrosis*	50 IU/kg factor VIII concentrate[†] on day 1; then 20 IU/kg on days 2, 3, 5 until joint function is normal or back to baseline. Consider additional treatment every other day for 7-10 days. Consider prophylaxis.	80-100 IU/kg on day 1; then 40 IU/kg on days 2, 4. Consider additional treatment every other day for 7-10 days. Consider prophylaxis.
Muscle or significant subcutaneous hematoma	50 IU/kg factor VIII concentrate; 20 IU/kg every-other-day treatment may be needed until resolved.	80 IU/kg factor IX concentrate[‡]; treatment every 2-3 days may be needed until resolved.
Mouth, deciduous tooth, or tooth extraction	20 IU/kg factor VIII concentrate; antifibrinolytic therapy; remove loose deciduous tooth.	40 IU/kg factor IX concentrate[‡]; antifibrinolytic therapy[§]; remove loose deciduous tooth.
Epistaxis	Apply pressure for 15-20 min; pack with petrolatum gauze; give antifibrinolytic therapy; 20 IU/kg factor VIII concentrate if this treatment fails.[l]	Apply pressure for 15-20 min; pack with petrolatum gauze; antifibrinolytic therapy; 30 IU/kg factor IX concentrate[‡] if this treatment fails.
Major surgery, life-threatening hemorrhage	50-75 IU/kg factor VIII concentrate, then initiate continuous infusion of 2-4 IU/kg/hr to maintain factor VIII >100 IU/dl for 24 hr[l] then give 2-3 IU/kg/hr continuously for 5-7 days to maintain the level at >50 IU/dl and an additional 5-7 days to maintain the level at >30 IU/dl.[¶]	120 IU/kg factor IX concentrate[‡], then 50-60 IU/kg every 12-24 hr to maintain factor IX at >40 IU/dl for 5-7 days, and then at >30 IU/dl for 7 days.
Iliopsoas hemorrhage	50 IU/kg factor VIII concentrate, then 25 IU/kg every 12 hr until asymptomatic, then 20 IU/kg every other day for a total of 10-14 days.**	120 IU/kg factor IX concentrate[‡]; then 50-60 IU/kg every 12-24 hr to maintain factor IX at >40 IU/dl until patient is asymptomatic; then 40-50 IU every other day for a total of 10-14 days.[#] **
Hematuria	Bed rest; 1½ × maintenance fluids; if not controlled in 1-2 days, 20 IU/kg factor VIII concentrate; if not controlled, give prednisone (unless patient is HIV-infected).	Bed rest; 1½ × maintenance fluids; if not controlled in 1-2 days, 40 IU/kg factor IX concentrate[‡]; if not controlled, give prednisone (unless patient is HIV-infected).
Prophylaxis	20-40 IU/kg factor VIII concentrate every other day to achieve a trough level ≥1%.	30-50 IU/kg factor IX concentrate[‡] every 2-3 days to achieve a trough level ≥1%.

*For hip hemarthrosis, orthopedic evaluation for possible aspiration is advisable to prevent avascular necrosis of the femoral head.

[†]For mild or moderate hemophilia, desmopressin, 0.3 µg/kg, should be used instead of factor VIII concentrate, if the patient is known to respond with a hemostatic level of factor VIII; if repeated doses are given, monitor factor VIII levels for tachyphylaxis.

[‡]Stated doses apply for recombinant factor IX concentrate; for plasma-derived factor IX concentrate, use 70% of the stated dose.

[§]Do not give antifibrinolytic therapy until 4 to 6 hr after a dose of prothrombin complex concentrate.

[l]Over-the-counter coagulation-promoting products may be helpful.

[¶]Alternatively, give 25 IU/kg every 12 hr to maintain a trough level >50% for 5 to 7 days followed by 25-30 IU/kg for an additional 5 to 7 days to maintain trough >25%.

[#]Repeat radiologic assessment should be performed before discontinuation of therapy.

**If repeated doses of factor IX concentrate are required, use highly purified, specific factor IX concentrate.

Adapted from Montgomery RR et al: Hemophilia and von Willebrand disease. In Nathan DG, Orkin SH (eds): *Nathan and Oski's hematology at infancy and childhood,* ed 5, Philadelphia, 1998, Saunders.

of patients with inhibitors. Recommended dose is 90 µg/mg of body weight every 2 to 3 hr for treatment of life-threatening hemorrhage. It is, however, very expensive ($1 per µg).

- Desmopressin acetate 0.3 µg/kg q24h (causes release of factor VIII:C) may be used in preparation for minor surgical procedures in mild hemophiliacs.
- Aminocaproic acid (EACA, Amicar) 4 g PO q4h can be given for persistent bleeding that is unresponsive to factor VIII concentrate or desmopressin.

HEMOPHILIA B:

- Infuse factor IX concentrates. It is important to remember that factor IX concentrates contain other proteins that may increase the risk of thrombosis with recurrent use. Therefore factor IX concentrates must be used only when clearly indicated.
- Daily administration of oral cyclophosphamide and prednisone without empirical factor VIII therapy is an effective and well-tolerated treatment for acquired hemophilia.

CHRONIC Rx

- The aim of chronic treatment is to prevent spontaneous bleeding and excessive bleeding during any surgical intervention. Monitoring and treatment of patients with hemophilia at comprehensive hemophilia treatment centers is cost-effective and decreases morbidity and mortality.
- Prophylaxis with recombinant factor VIII can prevent joint damage and decrease the frequency of joint and other hemorrhages in young boys with severe hemophilia A. The estimated annual cost for treatment of one patient with recombinant factor VIII is $300,000.
- Implantation of genetically altered fibroblasts that produce factor VIII is safe and well tolerated. This form is feasible in patients with severe hemophilia. Hemophilia will likely be the first common, severe genetic disease to be cured by gene therapy.

DISPOSITION

- Despite the advent of virally safe blood products and blood treatment programs, nearly

70% of hemophiliacs are HIV seropositive. Survival is of normal expectancy in HIV-negative patients with mild disease.
- Intracranial bleeds are the second most common cause of death in hemophiliacs after AIDS. They are fatal in 30% of patients, occur in 10% of patients, and are generally the result of trauma.

SUGGESTED READINGS
Available at www.expertconsult.com

RELATED CONTENT
Hemophilia (Patient Information)

AUTHOR: **FRED F. FERRI, M.D.**

BASIC INFORMATION

DEFINITION

Hemoptysis is coughing up of blood originating from the lower respiratory tract, ranging from blood-streaked sputum to gross blood. If greater than 100 to 600 mL in 24 hours or if the bleeding rate is >100 mL/hr, it is considered massive hemoptysis.

ICD-10CM CODES
R04.2 Hemoptysis

EPIDEMIOLOGY & DEMOGRAPHICS

INCIDENCE: Unknown, varies based on underlying pathology
RISK FACTORS: Tobacco smoking predisposes to lung cancer, a common cause of hemoptysis. Systemic processes (rheumatologic, renal hematologic) may contribute to alveolar hemorrhage or vasculitis. Anticoagulation can worsen bleeding.

PHYSICAL FINDINGS & CLINICAL PRESENTATION

- Presentation of hemoptysis is variable and can range from minimal blood-tinged sputum to more than 500 mL of gross blood in 24 hr. Other symptoms depend on the underlying etiology and can include cough, sputum production, fever, shortness of breath, weight loss, night sweats, wheezing, and chest pain.
- There are no specific exam findings, but clues to the etiology may be present, for example, focal wheezing, rhonchi or rales on pulmonary exam, murmur of mitral stenosis on cardiac exam.

ETIOLOGY

- There are many potential causes of hemoptysis including airway disease (bronchitis, bronchiectasis, lung neoplasm), infection (necrotizing pneumonia, lung abscess, tuberculosis, fungal infection), inflammatory diseases (granulomatosis with polyangiitis, Goodpasture's syndrome, lupus), cardiac disease (mitral stenosis after rheumatic heart disease, congenital heart diseases), and others (pulmonary embolism, cocaine use, foreign body, airway trauma, iatrogenic and cryptogenic).
- Acute respiratory tract infections, asthma, COPD, malignancy, and bronchiectasis are the most common diagnoses in outpatient primary care.
- Worldwide tuberculosis accounts for 7% to 85% of cases of massive hemoptysis. Highest incidence is in South Africa; lowest incidence in the U.S.

DIAGNOSIS

DIFFERENTIAL DIAGNOSIS

- Various potential causes of lower respiratory tract bleeding.
  1. Airway disease (bronchitis, bronchiectasis, lung neoplasm).
  2. Infection (necrotizing pneumonia, lung abscess, tuberculosis, fungal infection).
  3. Inflammatory diseases (granulomatosis with polyangiitis, Goodpasture's syndrome, lupus).
  4. Cardiac disease (mitral stenosis after rheumatic heart disease, congenital heart diseases).
  5. Pulmonary embolism.
  6. Cocaine use.
  7. Foreign body.
- Bleeding from upper respiratory tract.
- Hematemesis or epistaxis
- Coagulopathy.

WORKUP

- The initial history should focus on determining the anatomic origin of bleeding.
- Complete history and physical exam may suggest a particular etiology; important to ask about duration and quantity of hemoptysis and smoking history.

LABORATORY TESTS

- Complete blood count.
- Coagulation profile.
- Serum chemistries including creatinine, urinalysis.
- If indicated, consider vasculitis serologies (i.e., ANA, ANCA, anti-GBM).
- Arterial blood gas to assess oxygenation.
- Sputum for cultures and cytologic studies.
- PPD

IMAGING STUDIES

- Chest x-ray: all patients with hemoptysis should have a chest x-ray but will likely need additional studies to localize site of bleeding.
- Chest CT: chest CT scan combined with flexible bronchoscopy has the highest yield for localizing the site of bleeding.

TREATMENT

Varies based on underlying etiology and non-massive versus massive hemoptysis

NONPHARMACOLOGIC THERAPY

Massive hemoptysis:
- Arteriographic embolization of bronchial arteries and/or collateral systemic vessels.
- Surgical resection of affected lung.

ACUTE GENERAL Rx

Massive hemoptysis:
- Stabilize hemodynamic status and oxygenation.
- Reverse any coagulopathy.
- Bronchoscopy can be used to identify cause of hemoptysis (e.g., neoplasm), as well as to help isolate a site/segment of bleeding.
- If site of bleeding is known, place patient with bleeding lung in dependent position to prevent blood from spilling into non-affected lung and consider selective intubation with large-bore single-lumen endotracheal tube or double-lumen endotracheal tube.
- Bronchoscopic lavage with iced saline or topical application of epinephrine can be tried as a temporizing measure.
- Bronchoscopic balloon tamponade of bleeding site can be used as temporizing measure.
- Early consultation with interventional radiology, interventional pulmonology, and/or thoracic surgery for definitive intervention is recommended.

Submassive hemoptysis:
For submassive hemoptysis, identify and treat underlying condition. Referral to pulmonologist or hematologist if indicated.

CHRONIC Rx

For patients requiring anticoagulation or antiplatelet therapy for another disorder, consider risks/benefits of continued anticoagulation or antiplatelet therapy.

DISPOSITION

Generally, patients have a good prognosis after an episode of hemoptysis, but those with massive bleeding and/or malignancy tend to have a poorer prognosis.

SUGGESTED READINGS
Available at www.expertconsult.com

RELATED CONTENT
Evaluation of hemoptysis (Algorithm, Section III)

AUTHOR: **GAETANE MICHAUD, M.D.**

BASIC INFORMATION

DEFINITION

Henoch-Schönlein purpura (HSP) is a systemic, small-vessel, IgA immune complex–mediated leukocytoclastic vasculitis characterized by a tetrad of palpable purpura (without thrombocytopenia), abdominal pain, renal disease, and arthritis/arthralgias. It may also present with gastrointestinal (GI) bleeding.

SYNONYMS

Anaphylactoid purpura
Allergic purpura
HSP

ICD-10CM CODES

D69.0 Allergic purpura

EPIDEMIOLOGY & DEMOGRAPHICS

INCIDENCE: Annual incidence of 20 cases/100,000 population in children. Approximately 1/100,000 in adults
PEAK INCIDENCE: Late autumn to early spring, rarely in summer. Seasonal variation is not seen in adults.
PREVALENCE: Most common vasculitis seen in children and younger age groups; seen in white and Asian populations 3 to 4 times more commonly than black patients.
PREDOMINANT SEX AND AGE: 2:1 male/female ratio. Seen mostly from ages 3 to 12, although can be seen in older adolescents and young adults; 90% of all patients <10 years old.
GENETICS: Recent studies have identified genetic susceptibility factors, but familial recurrence is very rare. An association has been seen with the "Mediterranean fever" (MEFV) gene; HSP seen in up to 7% of gene carriers.

RISK FACTORS

No formally identified risk factors.

PHYSICAL FINDINGS & CLINICAL PRESENTATION

- Palpable purpura (Fig. 1H-22) of dependent areas, especially lower extremities (palms and soles) and areas subjected to pressure, such as the beltline in adults or buttocks in toddlers.
- GI symptoms are seen in up to two thirds of patients. Common findings are abdominal pain, nausea, vomiting, diarrhea, cramping, hematochezia, and melena. Complications include GI bleeding (20% to 30%), bowel ischemia, intussusception (1%-5%), and bowel perforation (<1%).
- Subcutaneous edema
- Arthralgias and arthritis in 60% to 85%. Typically oligoarticular, affecting lower extremity and large joints. Periarticular swelling and tenderness also noted.
- Renal involvement is seen in as many as 80% of older children, usually within the first month of illness. Fewer than 5% progress to end-stage renal failure, a major cause of morbidity. Renal manifestations may range from isolated hematuria or proteinuria to acute nephropathy with renal insufficiency.
- 10% to 20% of male children can present with orchitis that can mimic testicular torsion.

ETIOLOGY

- Presumptive etiology is exposure to a trigger antigen that causes antibody formation.
- Antigen-antibody (immune) complex deposition then occurs in arteriole and capillary walls of skin, renal mesangium, and GI tract. Immunoglobulin (Ig) A deposition is most common.
- Antigen triggers postulated include drugs, foods, immunization, and upper respiratory and other viral illnesses. Group A streptococcal infection is the most common precipitant in children, seen in up to one third of cases. A recent adult case triggered by pantoprazole has also been reported.
- 30% to 65% of cases reviewed in children were preceded by an unspecified upper respiratory infection.
- Serologic and pathologic evidence suggests an association between parvovirus B19 and HSP, which may explain observed cases of HSP that do not respond to corticosteroids or other immunosuppressive therapy.
- Case reports have been published describing development of HSP after treatment with a variety of medications including immunosuppressive agents (e.g., etanercept) and more widely used medications such as pantoprazole.

DIAGNOSIS

- Diagnosis is based on the finding of IgA in the affected vessels. Nonthrombocytopenic purpura (see Figure 1H-23) is essential to the diagnosis.
- Skin manifestations are most common. See Table 1H-13 for common clinical manifestations of HSP.

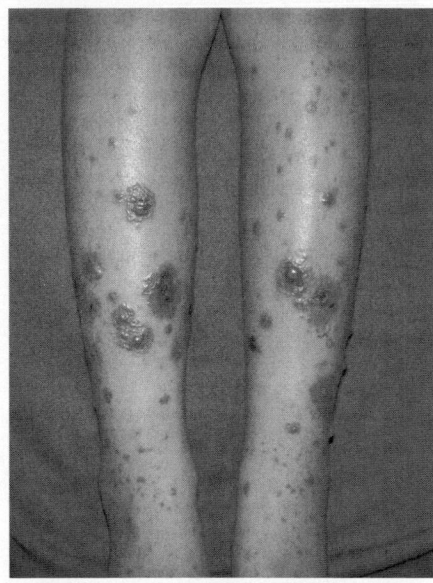

FIGURE 1H-23 Extensive palpable purpura over the lower extremities in a 7-yr-old girl with Henoch-Schönlein purpura. (From Hochberg MC et al: *Rheumatology,* ed 5, St Louis, 2011, Mosby.)

TABLE 1H-13 Clinical Manifestations of Henoch-Schönlein Purpura

	% at Onset	% during Course
Purpura (nl platelet count)	50	100
Subcutaneous edema	10-20	20-50
Arthritis (large joints)	25	60-85
Gastrointestinal	30	85
Renal	?	10-50
Genitourinary (ddx torsion)	?	2-35
Pulmonary (T_LCO)	?	95
Pulmonary hemorrhage	?	Rare, may be fatal
Central nervous system (headache, organic brain syndrome, seizures)	?	Rare, may be fatal

From Hochberg MC et al: *Rheumatology,* ed 5, St Louis, 2011, Mosby.

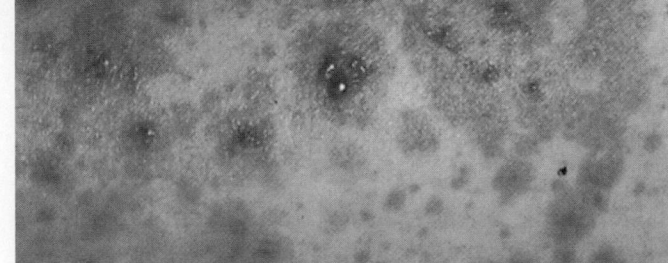

FIGURE 1H-22 Palpable purpura in a patient with Henoch-Schönlein purpura. (From Hoffman R et al [eds]: *Hematology: basic principles and practice,* ed 4, Philadelphia, 2005, Saunders.)

- Skin biopsy shows leukocytoclastic vasculitis. Renal biopsy shows mesangial IgA deposition.
- The presence of two of the following four American College of Rheumatology criteria yields a diagnostic sensitivity of 87.1% and specificity of 87.7%:
  1. Palpable purpura unrelated to thrombocytopenia
  2. Age <20 yr at onset of first symptoms
  3. Bowel angina or ischemia
  4. Granulocytic infiltration of arteriole or venule walls on biopsy
- In 2010, a European consortium published a set of validated diagnostic criteria that showed 100% sensitivity and 87% specificity. Their criteria described purpura with lower limb predominance and one or more of the following:
  ○ Abdominal pain
  ○ Predominant IgA deposits of histopathology
  ○ Arthritis or arthralgia
  ○ Renal involvement

DIFFERENTIAL DIAGNOSIS

- Polyarteritis nodosa
- Acute abdomen
- Meningococcemia
- Thrombocytopenic purpura
- Hypersensitivity vasculitis
- Microscopic polyangiitis
- Granulomatosis with polyangiitis (Wegener granulomatosis)

WORKUP

History, physical examination, laboratory testing, skin or renal biopsy.

LABORATORY TESTS

- Electrolytes, blood urea nitrogen, and creatinine
- Urinalysis
- Complete blood count
- Prothrombin time, fibrinogen, and fibrin degradation products
- Blood cultures
  Laboratory abnormalities are not specific for HSP but may help identify complications and rule out other diseases. Leukocytosis and eosinophilia may be seen. IgA levels are elevated in approximately 50% of patients. Glomerulonephritis may be present (microscopic hematuria, proteinuria, and red blood cell casts).

IMAGING STUDIES

Imaging studies are generally not useful in the diagnosis of HSP. Arteriography or magnetic resonance angiography may be helpful in distinguishing from polyarteritis nodosa. Abdominal ultrasound is recommended for patients with severe abdominal pain to detect increased bowel wall thickness, peritoneal fluid, or intussusception.

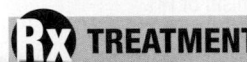 **TREATMENT**

NONPHARMACOLOGIC THERAPY

- Supportive care with pain management, adequate hydration, and nutrition is the primary intervention as up to 94% of cases in children and 87% cases in adults will resolve spontaneously.

ACUTE GENERAL Rx

Prednisone 1 to 2 mg/kg PO daily for two weeks is typically given for severe arthritis and/or abdominal pain. An equivalent dose of methylprednisolone can be used with same efficacy.
  ○ A double-blind, randomized, controlled trial found that early treatment with prednisone reduced abdominal pain and joint symptoms but did not prevent development of renal disease. It was effective in the treatment of renal disease once it was established.
  ○ Another recent trial showed no evidence that early treatment with prednisolone reduces the prevalence of proteinuria 12 months after disease onset in children with HSP.
- Corticosteroids and azathioprine may be beneficial if rapidly progressive glomerulo nephritis is present. Pulse methylprednisolone therapy has also been proposed in patients with glomerulonephritis, mesenteric vasculitis, or pulmonary involvement. Recent reports describe improvement in rapidly progressive glomerulonephritis and nephrotic-range proteinuria after treatment with mycophenolate mofetil. The combination of cyclosporin A with corticosteroids appears to be effective in inducing remission of nephrotic syndrome in adult patients with HSP nephritis. Recent studies show no benefit to the use of cyclophosamide alone or in combination with steroids in patients with renal manifestations of HSP.

CHRONIC Rx

- Even if renal involvement is not present after initial episode, urinalysis and blood pressure should be checked every 2 to 4 weeks for first 6 months to detect development and progression of kidney disease.

COMPLEMENTARY AND ALTERNATIVE MEDICINE:

- No complementary or alternative treatment modalities proven to be effective for HSP.

DISPOSITION

- Prognosis excellent, with spontaneous recovery within 4 weeks in most patients.
- Hospitalization is recommended for significant GI or renal involvement.
- Increased age of onset generally correlates with morbidity. While end-stage renal disease (ESRD) occurs in 10% to 30% of adult patients with HSP at 15 years, chronic renal insufficiency is the most common long-term morbidity and affects adults more than children.
- Recurrences in up to one third of patients, especially within first 4 to 6 mo after initial episode and most commonly in patients with renal involvement. Recurrences are characteristically less severe than initial episode.

REFERRAL

Rheumatologist, Nephrology, or General Surgery consultation based on clinical manifestations

 **PEARLS & CONSIDERATIONS**

- HSP is an IgA-related vasculitis.
- Organ systems involved are skin, joints, GI tract, and kidneys.
- Palpable purpura without thrombocytopenia more common in adults; GI symptoms more common in children.
- GI symptoms and arthritis may precede rash. Skin and renal manifestations occur at same time.
- Most with spontaneous recovery within 4 weeks of onset of symptoms.
- End-stage renal disease occurs in only 5% of patients.
- Corticosteroids have been proven to shorten the duration and intensity of arthritis and GI symptoms but do not prevent nephritis or recurrences.

SUGGESTED READINGS

Available at www.expertconsult.com

RELATED CONTENT

Henoch-Schönlein Purpura (Patient Information)

AUTHORS: **JAMES M. FERGUSON, M.D.,** and **DOMINICK TAMMARO, M.D.**

BASIC INFORMATION

DEFINITION

There are two forms of heparin-induced thrombocytopenia (HIT). Type 1 HIT is a mild, transient decrease in platelet count that occurs during the first few days of heparin exposure due to platelet agglutination. This form is a benign, non–immune-mediated reaction, and the platelet count will return to normal while heparin is continued. This section will refer to Type 2 HIT, an antibody-mediated thrombocytopenia that is associated with a high risk of developing thrombosis.

SYNONYMS

Type II heparin-induced thrombocytopenia
Heparin-induced thrombocytopenia and thrombosis (HITT)
White clot syndrome
Heparin-associated immune thrombocytopenia

ICD-10CM CODES

D75.82 Heparin-induced thrombocytopenia (HIT)

EPIDEMIOLOGY & DEMOGRAPHICS

INCIDENCE: Occurs in 0.2% to 5% of patients exposed to heparin. Unfractionated heparin is associated with a 5 to 10 times higher risk of HIT compared with low-molecular-weight heparin. Initially, there was an overwhelming underdiagnosis of HIT; however, since the introduction of HIT antibody ELISA test, there is a propensity to overdiagnose HIT irrespective of the clinical scenario.
PREDOMINANT SEX AND AGE: Females are at slightly higher risk than males. More common in adults but may also occur in children.
RISK FACTORS: Longer duration of exposure to heparin, type of heparin (unfractionated heparin has a greater risk), type of patient (surgical patients, especially cardiac and orthopedic surgery, are at higher risk than medical patients).

PHYSICAL FINDINGS & CLINICAL PRESENTATION

Suspect in a patient with:
- Exposure to heparin for 4 to 14 days OR who was exposed to heparin in the prior 3 mo.
- Unexplained platelet count decrease to 50% below pretreatment baseline.
- Onset of thrombocytopenia 5 to 10 days after heparin initiation.
- Evidence of acute venous or arterial thrombosis.
- Skin lesions or necrosis at heparin injection sites.
- Acute anaphylactoid reaction during administration of heparin bolus.
- Adrenal hemorrhage.

ETIOLOGY

Occurs due to the formation of IgG antibodies, directed against heparin in complex with platelet factor 4, which bind to and activate platelets. Activated platelets release platelet factor 4 (leading to more antibody production) and undergo aggregation and premature removal from the circulation (resulting in thrombocytopenia). This platelet activation and antibody formation also can lead to thrombosis. Fig. E1H-24 illustrates the mechanism of HIT.

DIAGNOSIS

DIFFERENTIAL DIAGNOSIS

Thrombocytopenia due to other causes including:
- Sepsis
- Disseminated intravascular coagulation
- Thrombocytopenic thrombotic purpura
- Hemolytic uremic syndrome
- Drug-induced thrombocytopenia (other than heparin)
- Antiphospholipid antibody syndrome
- Liver failure
- Splenic sequestration

WORKUP

HIT is first and foremost a clinical diagnosis that is confirmed with laboratory testing. See Table 1H-14 for workup based on pretest probability. If the patient has a low pretest probability score, heparin can be safely continued, and there is no need to send for further testing for HIT. If the patient has a moderate to high pretest probability, HIT testing (Table 1H-15), imaging studies for lower-extremity deep venous thrombosis (also consider imaging of upper extremities if swelling

---

TABLE 1H-14 A Diagnostic and Treatment Approach to Heparin-Induced Thrombocytopenia

Suspicion of HIT Based upon the "4 T's"	Score	Pre-Test Probability Score Criteria 2	1	0
Thrombocytopenia	☐	nadir 20-100, or >50% platelet fall	nadir 10-19, or 30%-50% platelet fall	nadir <10, or <30% platelet fall
Timing of onset of platelet fall	☐	day 5-10, or ≤day 1 with recent heparin*	>day 10 or timing unclear (but fits with HIT)	≤day 1 (no recent heparin)
Thrombosis or other sequelae	☐	proven thrombosis, skin necrosis, or ASR†	progressive, recurrent, or silent thrombosis; erythematous skin lesions	none
Other cause of platelet fall	☐	none evident	possible	definite
Total Pre-Test Probability Score	☐	periodic reassessment as new information can change pre-test probability (e.g., positive blood cultures)		

Total Pre-Test Probability Score		
High	**Moderate**	**Low**
8 | 7 | 6	5 | 4	3 | 2 | 1 | 0
Stop heparin‡, give alternative non-heparin anticoagulant argatroban¶ or lepirudin# or danaparoid** (or bivalirudin†† or fondaparinux‡‡)	Physician judgment	Continue (LMW) heparin

Positive test for HIT antibodies
Continue non-heparin anticoagulant until platelet count recovery
← **HIT Test** →
Negative test for HIT antibodies
Consider continuing or switching back to (LMW) heparin ##

Thrombosis* **
If **HIT**, continue non-heparin anticoagulant until platelet count recovery, then **cautious coumarin overlap¶¶**
← **Imaging studies for lower-limb DVT†††** →
No Thrombosis
If **HIT**, consider anticoagulating until platelet count recovery, even if no thrombosis apparent (± coumarin¶¶)

- -

*recent heparin indicates exposure within the past 30 days (2 points) or past 30-100 days (1 point)
†ASR, acute systemic reaction following *i.v.* heparin bolus
‡stop all heparin, including catheter "flushes" and, possibly, heparin-coated catheters
¶argatroban: approved (U.S., Canada) for isolated HIT and HIT complicated by thrombosis (2 μg/kg/min *i.v.*, adjusted to 1.5-3.0X patient's baseline aPTT or the mean of the laboratory normal range); reduce dose for hepatobiliary compromise: may increase INR more than the other direct thrombin inhibitors, thus requiring care in managing coumarin overlap (see ¶¶ below)
#lepirudin: approved (U.S., Canada, E.U., elsewhere) for treatment of thrombosis complicating HIT (±0.4 mg/kg *i.v.* bolus, then 0.15 mg/kg/h adjusted to 1.5-2.5X patient's baseline aPTT or mean of the laboratory normal range); used (off-label) also to treat isolated HIT (0.1 mg/kg/h, adjusted by aPTT); to avoid overdosing and anaphylaxis, it may be preferable to omit the bolus, and begin as *i.v.* infusion (except when facing life- or limb-threatening thrombosis); reduce dose for renal insufficiency
**danaparoid: usual *i.v.* bolus, 2250 U (body weight 60-75 kg) followed by infusion (400 U/hr for 4 h, then 300 U/h for 4 h, then 200 U/h, adjusted by anti-factor Xa levels); this therapeutic-dose regimen is appropriate both for isolated HIT and for HIT complicated by thrombosis (though higher than approved dose in some jurisdictions); withdrawn from U.S. market (2002)
††bivalirudin: no bolus, *i.v.* infusion 0.15 mg/kg/h adjusted by aPTT; limited experience (off-label)
‡‡fondaparinux: dosing for HIT not established; limited experience (off-label)
¶¶delay coumadin pending substantial platelet count recovery (at least >100, preferably >150); begin coumadin in low doses, with at least 4-5 day overlap, stopping alternative anticoagulant when INR therapeutic for 2 days and platelets recovered
##depending on physician confidence in the laboratory's ability to rule out HIT antibodies (usually, negative PF4-dependent enzyme-immunoassay and/or washed platelet activation assay performed by an experienced laboratory)
***some thrombi may require special treatment, e.g., thrombectomy for large limb artery thrombosis
†††routine ultrasound of lower-limb veins recommended, since many HIT patients have subclinical deep-vein thrombosis (DVT)

From Warkentin TE.; et al. Platelet-endothelial interactions: sepsis, HIT, and antiphospholipid syndrome. *Hematology (Am Soc Hematol Educ Prog)* 497-519, 2003.

TABLE 1H-15 Laboratory Assays for Heparin-Induced Thrombocytopenia

Assay	Sensitivity (%)	Specificity (%)	Positive Predictive Value (%)	Negative Predictive Value (%)
Functional assay (e.g., serotonin release assay)	88	~100	~100	81
PF4/heparin enzyme immunoassay (ELISA)	95-98	86	93	95

ELISA, Enzyme-linked immunosorbent assay; *PF4*, platelet factor 4.
From Goldman L, Schafer AI: *Goldman's Cecil medicine*, ed 24, Philadelphia, 2012, Saunders.

is present or venous catheters are in place), cessation of heparin products, and alternative anticoagulation should all be performed. Patients with intermediate and high pretest probability but no HIT antibodies or intermediate pretest probability and only weakly positive HIT antibodies (based on optical density, see below) can resume heparin use as HIT is unlikely in these scenarios. Patients with high pretest probability and weakly positive antibodies or intermediate/high pretest probability and moderate to strongly positive antibodies likely have HIT and should be treated as such.

LABORATORY TESTS

These can be broadly divided into immunoassays (high sensitivity) and functional assays (high specificity). In the appropriate clinical setting, testing for HIT antibodies with an enzyme-linked immunosorbent assay, or ELISA, can be useful. This test is very sensitive, but not specific. The majority of patients with positive testing for HIT antibodies will not develop clinical HIT. Thus, HIT antibody testing is more effective for ruling out rather than confirming the diagnosis of HIT. More recently, use of the HIT antibody optical density as well as the immunoglobulin subtypes of the HIT antibody have entered the diagnostic realm. Higher optical density levels are associated with increased likelihood of a positive functional assay, higher pretest probability score, and increased risk of thrombosis. Weakly positive optical densities (0.4 to 1.0) are only rarely associated with functional assay positivity. In contrast, optical densities >2.0 almost always show heparin-dependent platelet activation. Optical densities are thus defined as weakly positive (0.4-1.0), moderately positive (1.0-2.0), or strongly positive (>2.0). The HIT antibody IgG subtype is the pathologic antibody for HIT. Hence, use of IgG-specific ELISA kits increases the test specificity over the polyspecific (IgA/M/G) antibody. Patients with low pretest probability via the 4T clinical prediction score should not have HIT antibody testing performed because it has a more than 99% negative predictive value, while all patients with intermediate and high pretest probability of HIT benefit from HIT antibody testing.

The gold standard test for HIT is to measure heparin-dependent platelet activation via the functional serotonin release assay (14C-SRA).

This is both a highly sensitive and specific test. Donor platelets are incubated with radiolabeled serotonin. The platelets internalize the serotonin and are then exposed to the patient's serum and heparin at a therapeutic concentration. If antibodies to the platelet factor 4-heparin complex are present in the patient's serum, the platelets react and released radioactive serotonin is then measured. Availability and turn-around time of this test is dependent on the institution, which can influence the test's clinical utility. Cases where there is intermediate pretest probability, but only a weakly positive HIT antibody optical density, benefit the most from confirmatory SRA testing. Here, a positive SRA test result will argue for HIT; a negative SRA test result suggests the absence of HIT.

IMAGING STUDIES

Doppler sonography of the extremities in the correct clinical setting.

 **TREATMENT**

- For patients with a moderate or high pretest probability, discontinue all heparin exposure. Even if the patient does not have a clinically evident thrombosis, he or she is at a 50% risk of developing an incident clot within the subsequent 30 days. Thus, the patient must be started on an alternate anticoagulant.
- Three agents, all direct thrombin inhibitors, are approved for this indication:
  1. Argatroban (avoid in liver dysfunction).
  2. Bivalirudin (approved only for patients with HIT or at risk of HIT who are undergoing PCI).
     Note: Lepirudin is no longer available; manufacturing has been discontinued.
- These drugs should be continued as a single agent until the platelet count returns to baseline (generally a platelet count of 150 × 10⁹/L but it is important to consider the individual patient's baseline), then warfarin can be added at a maximum dose of 5 mg/day. This overlap therapy should continue until the platelet count has reached a stable plateau, the INR has reached the intended target (remember that argatroban artificially elevates the INR), and after a minimum overlap of 5 days of both the direct thrombin inhibitor

and warfarin. The length of treatment is controversial, but most clinicians agree that 1 month of alternate anticoagulation is sufficient in the absence of thrombosis, while 3 to 6 months of treatment are required in the presence of thrombosis.

- Argatroban has been shown to be safely used in hemodialysis patients with HIT.
- Care should be taken when initiating warfarin in HIT because the risk of warfarin-induced skin and limb necrosis is increased in this setting.
- There are emerging data showing similar efficacy and lower bleeding risk in HIT for fondaparinux when compared with the direct thrombin inhibitors. Fondaparinux is a synthetic pentasaccharide that binds antithrombin, causing long-acting inhibition of activated factor X, but not thrombin. It is not FDA approved for HIT, but its use in HIT has been reported. It can initiate the formation of anti-PF4 antibodies, but it does not support platelet activation by the newly formed immune complexes.
- The use of novel oral anticoagulants (e.g., rivaroxaban, dabigatran, apixaban) is being studied.
- Outside of the U.S., the Xa inhibitor danaparoid may be used.

NONPHARMACOLOGIC THERAPY

All nonpharmacologic therapies including surgical procedures.

REFERRAL

Request a hematology consultation.

! **PEARLS & CONSIDERATIONS**

COMMENTS

HIT paradoxically causes thrombocytopenia and *clotting*, not bleeding.

It is unclear whether patients who have had HIT should be considered heparin allergic lifelong. If a patient with history of HIT requires a life-saving procedure that uses heparin (e.g., on-pump cardiac bypass), he or she may be pretreated with a direct thrombin inhibitor or factor X inhibitor.

PREVENTION

Consider the use of low-molecular-weight heparin (as opposed to unfractionated heparin) as DVT prophylaxis. It can be safely administered to patients not on dialysis and with a creatinine clearance (CrCl) greater than 30 mL/min.

SUGGESTED READINGS

Available at www.expertconsult.com

AUTHORS: **WILLIAM M. RAFELSON, M.D., M.B.A.,** and **JOHN L. REAGAN, M.D.**

H

Diseases and Disorders

I

BASIC INFORMATION

DEFINITION

Hepatic encephalopathy is a neuropsychiatric syndrome occurring in patients with severe impairment of liver function and consequent accumulation of toxic products not metabolized by the liver. It is characterized by gradual impairment of the ability to perform mental tasks and to react to external stimuli. *Minimal hepatic encephalopathy* refers to patients with hepatic cirrhosis and mild cognitive impairment, but no history of overt encephalopathy.

SYNONYMS

Hepatic coma

ICD-10CM CODES
K72.0	Acute and subacute hepatic failure
K72.1	Chronic hepatic failure
K72.9	Hepatic failure, unspecified
G92	Toxic encephalopathy
G93.40	Encephalopathy, unspecified
G93.41	Metabolic encephalopathy
K70.40	Alcoholic hepatic failure without coma
K70.41	Alcoholic hepatic failure with coma
K72.00	Acute and subacute hepatic failure without coma
K72.01	Acute and subacute hepatic failure with coma
K72.10	Chronic hepatic failure without coma
K72.11	Chronic hepatic failure with coma
K72.90	Hepatic failure, unspecified without coma
K72.91	Hepatic failure, unspecified with coma
K91.82	Postprocedural hepatic failure

EPIDEMIOLOGY & DEMOGRAPHICS

INCIDENCE/PREVALENCE: Hepatic encephalopathy occurs in >40% of all cases of cirrhosis.

PHYSICAL FINDINGS & CLINICAL PRESENTATION

Hepatic encephalopathy can be classified by clinical stages described in Table 1H-16.

The physical examination in hepatic encephalopathy varies with the stage and may reveal the following abnormalities:
- Skin: jaundice, palmar erythema, spider angiomata, ecchymosis, dilated superficial periumbilical veins (caput medusae) in patients with cirrhosis.
- Eyes: scleral icterus, Kayser-Fleischer rings (Wilson's disease).
- Breath: fetor hepaticus.
- Chest: gynecomastia in men with chronic liver disease.
- Abdomen: ascites, small nodular liver (cirrhosis), tender hepatomegaly (congestive hepatomegaly).
- Rectal examination: hemorrhoids (portal hypertension), guaiac-positive stool (alcoholic gastritis, bleeding esophageal varices, peptic ulcer disease, bleeding hemorrhoids).
- Genitalia: testicular atrophy in males with chronic liver disease.
- Extremities: pedal edema from hypoalbuminemia.
- Neurologic: flapping tremor (asterixis), obtundation, coma with or without decerebrate posturing.

ETIOLOGY

- Hepatic encephalopathy is thought to be caused mainly by accumulation of unmetabolized ammonia.
- Precipitating factors in patients with underlying cirrhosis (upper gastrointestinal bleeding, hypokalemia, hypomagnesemia, analgesic and sedative drugs, sepsis, alkalosis, increased dietary protein).
- Acute fulminant viral hepatitis.
- Drugs and toxins (e.g., isoniazid, acetaminophen, diclofenac and other NSAIDs, statins, methyldopa, loratadine, propylthiouracil, lisinopril, labetalol, halothane, carbon tetrachloride, erythromycin, nitrofurantoin, troglitazone, herbal products, flavocoxid).
- Reye's syndrome.
- Shock and/or sepsis.
- Fatty liver of pregnancy.
- Metastatic carcinoma, hepatocellular carcinoma.
- Other: autoimmune hepatitis, ischemic venoocclusive disease, sclerosing cholangitis, heat stroke, amebic abscesses.

DIAGNOSIS

DIFFERENTIAL DIAGNOSIS

- Delirium caused by medications or illicit drugs.
- Cerebrovascular accident, subdural hematoma.
- Meningitis, encephalitis.
- Hypoglycemia.
- Uremia.
- Cerebral anoxia.
- Hypercalcemia.
- Metastatic neoplasm to brain.
- Alcohol withdrawal syndrome.

WORKUP

Hepatic encephalopathy should be considered in any patient with cirrhosis who presents with neuropsychiatric manifestations. Exclude other etiologies with comprehensive history (obtained from patient, relatives, and others), physical examination, and laboratory and imaging studies. A pertinent history should include exposure to hepatitis, ethanol intake, drug history, exposure to toxins, IV drug abuse, measles or influenza with aspirin use (Reye's syndrome), and history of carcinoma (primary or metastatic). Minimal hepatic encephalopathy may not be obvious on clinical examination, but can be detected with neurophysiologic and neuropsychiatric testing.

LABORATORY TESTS

- Alanine aminotransferase, aspartate aminotransferase, bilirubin, alkaline phosphatase, glucose, calcium, electrolytes, blood urea nitrogen, creatinine, albumin.
- Complete blood count, platelet count, prothrombin time, partial thromboplastin time.
- Serum and urine toxicology screen in suspected medication or illegal drug use.
- Blood and urine cultures, urinalysis.
- Venous ammonia level. Measurement of serum ammonia level is useful in the evaluation of acute liver failure because levels correlate with the severity of encephalopathy and elevated levels are predictive of severe encephalopathy and cerebral edema. It is not useful for the evaluation or screening of hepatic encephalopathy in patients with chronic liver disease because it can neither rule in nor rule out hepatic encephalopathy, and levels do not correlate with the degree of encephalopathy.
- Arterial blood gases.

IMAGING STUDIES

CT scan or MRI of the brain may be useful in selected patients to exclude other etiologies when diagnosis is unclear.

TREATMENT

NONPHARMACOLOGIC THERAPY

- Identification and treatment of precipitating factors.
- Restriction of protein intake (30 to 40 g/day) to reduce toxic protein metabolites.

TABLE 1H-16 Clinical Stages of Hepatic Encephalopathy

Stage	Asterixis	EEG Changes	Clinical Manifestations
I (prodrome)	Slight	Minimal	Mild intellectual impairment, disturbed sleep-wake cycle
II (impending)	Easily elicited	Usually generalized	Drowsiness, confusion, coma/inappropriate behavior, disorientation, mood swings
III (stupor)	Present if patient cooperative	Grossly abnormal slowing of rhythm	Drowsy, unresponsive to verbal commands, markedly confused, delirious, hyperreflexia, positive Babinski sign
IV (coma)	Usually absent	Appearance of delta waves, decreased amplitudes	Unconscious, decerebrate or decorticate response to pain present (stage IVA) or absent (stage IVB)

EEG, Electroencephalogram.
From Fuhrman BP et al: *Pediatric critical care*, ed 4, Philadelphia, 2011, Saunders.

H

Diseases and Disorders

I

TABLE 1H-17 Management of Fulminant Hepatic Failure

No sedation except for procedures
Minimal handling
Enteric precautions until infection ruled out
Monitor:
- ○ Heart and respiratory rate
- ○ Arterial BP, CVP
- ○ Core/toe temperature
- ○ Neurologic observations
- ○ Gastric pH (>5.0)
- ○ Blood glucose (>4 mmol/L)
- ○ Acid-base
- ○ Electrolytes
- ○ PT, PTT
Fluid balance
- ○ 75% maintenance
- ○ Dextrose 10%-50% (provide 6-10 mg/kg/min)
- ○ Sodium (0.5-1 mmol/L)
- ○ Potassium (2-4 mmol/L)
Maintain circulating volume with colloid/FFP
Coagulation support only if required
Drugs
- ○ Vitamin K
- ○ H_2 antagonist
- ○ Antacids
- ○ Lactulose
- ○ N-acetylcysteine for acetaminophen toxicity
- ○ Broad-spectrum antibiotics
- ○ Antifungals
Nutrition
- ○ Enteral feeding (1-2 g protein/kg/day)
- ○ PN if ventilated

BP, Blood pressure; *CVP,* central venous pressure; *FFP,* fresh frozen plasma; *PN,* parenteral nutrition; *PT,* prothrombin time; *PTT,* partial thromboplastin time.
From Fuhrman BP et al: *Pediatric critical care,* ed 4, Philadelphia, 2011, Saunders.

ACUTE GENERAL Rx

Table 1H-17 summarizes the management of fulminant hepatic failure.

Reduction of colonic ammonia production:

- Lactulose 30 ml of 50% solution qid initially; dose is subsequently adjusted depending on clinical response. Ornithine aspartate 9 g tid is also effective. Lactulose may improve hepatic encephalopathy but may be less effective than antibiotics.
- Neomycin 1 g PO q4 to 6h or given as a 1% retention enema solution (1 g in 100 ml of isotonic saline solution); neomycin should be used with caution in patients with renal insufficiency. Metronidazole 250 mg qid may be as effective as neomycin and is not nephrotoxic; however, long-term use can be associated with neurotoxicity.
- A combination of lactulose and neomycin can be used when either agent is ineffective alone.
- The oral antibiotic rifaximin (550 mg PO bid) is effective in reducing the risk of recurrent hepatic encephalopathy in patients with cirrhosis. It can be taken with lactulose, and the combination of lactulose and rifaximin is superior to lactulose alone in reversing hepatic encephalopathy. Rifamaxin has also been shown to be effective in improving psychometric performance and health-related quality of life in patients with minimal hepatic encephalopathy. It is well tolerated but expensive.
- Probiotics (e.g., 1 capsule containing 112.5 billion viable lyophilized bacteria tid) might also be beneficial in altering gut flora to reduce ammonia production.

Treatment of cerebral edema:

- Cerebral edema is often present in patients with acute liver failure, and it accounts for nearly 50% of deaths. Monitoring intracranial pressure by epidural, intraparenchymal, or subdural transducers and treatment of cerebral edema with mannitol (100 to 200 ml of 20% solution [0.3 to 0.4 g/kg of body weight]) given by rapid IV infusion are helpful in selected patients (e.g., potential transplantation patients).
- Dexamethasone and hyperventilation (useful in head injury) are of little value in treating cerebral edema from liver failure.

CHRONIC Rx

- Avoidance of any precipitating factors (e.g., high-protein diet, medications).
- Consideration of liver transplantation in selected patients with progressive or recurrent encephalopathy (Box 1H-4). Liver transplantation remains the only curative therapeutic option.

DISPOSITION

Prognosis varies with the underlying etiology of the liver failure and the grade of encephalopathy (generally good for grades 1 or 2; poor for grades 3 or 4). Without proper therapy, the survival rate at 1 yr is 42% and decreases to 23% at 3 yr.

REFERRAL

The early stages of hepatic encephalopathy can be managed in the outpatient setting, whereas stages 3 or 4 require hospital admission.

 **PEARLS & CONSIDERATIONS**

COMMENTS

- Long-acting benzodiazepines should not be used to treat anxiety and sleep disorders in patients with cirrhosis, as they may precipitate encephalopathy.
- Patients not responding to supportive therapy should be evaluated for liver transplantation.
- Not all patients with cirrhosis develop hepatic encephalopathy. It has been shown that 40% of persons with cirrhosis and minimal hepatic encephalopathy do not develop overt hepatic encephalopathy in long-term follow-up. There are genetic factors associated with development of hepatic encephalopathy in patients with cirrhosis. Genetic analyses have shown that glutaminase TACC and CACC haplotypes are linked to the risk for overt hepatic encephalopathy.

 EVIDENCE

Available at www.expertconsult.com

SUGGESTED READINGS

Available at www.expertconsult.com

RELATED CONTENT

Hepatic Encephalopathy (Patient Information)
Cirrhosis (Related Key Topic)
Encephalopathy (Related Key Topic)

AUTHOR: **FRED F. FERRI, M.D.**

BOX 1H-4 Various Prognostic Criteria Used for Liver Transplantation in Patients with Fulminant Hepatic Failure

King's College Criteria
Acetaminophen overdose:
- Arterial pH <7.3 (irrespective of grade of encephalopathy) or
- PT >100 sec (INR >6.5)
- Serum creatinine >3.4 mg/dl (>300 μmol/L)
- Patients with grade III and IV hepatic encephalopathy
Nonacetaminophen liver injury:
- PT >100 sec (INR >6.5) (irrespective of grade of encephalopathy) or any three of the following variables:
  1. Age <10 or >40 years
  2. Non-A, non-B hepatitis, halothane hepatitis, idiosyncratic drug reactions
  3. Jaundice >7 days before onset of encephalopathy
  4. Serum bilirubin 17.4 mg/dl (300 μmol/L)
  5. PT >50 sec

Cliché Criteria
Factor V <20% in persons <30 years or both of the following:
- Factor V <30% in patients >30 years
- Grade III or IV encephalopathy

Serum Gc Globulin Levels
- Decreasing Gc levels due to dying hepatocytes

Serum α-Fetoprotein Level
- Serial increase from day 1 to day 3 has shown correlation with survival

Liver Biopsy[32]
70% necrosis is discriminant of 90% mortality

Gc, Plasma group-specific component protein; *INR,* international normalized ratio; *PT,* prothrombin time.
From Vincent JL et al: *Textbook of critical care,* ed 6, Philadelphia, 2011, Saunders.

BASIC INFORMATION

DEFINITION

Hepatitis A is generally an acute self-limiting infection of the liver by an enterically transmitted picornavirus, hepatitis A virus (HAV). Infection may range from asymptomatic to fulminant hepatitis.

SYNONYMS

Infectious hepatitis
Short incubation hepatitis
Type A hepatitis
HAV (hepatitis A virus)

ICD-10CM CODES
B15.9 Hepatitis A without hepatic coma
B15.0 Hepatitis A with hepatic coma

EPIDEMIOLOGY & DEMOGRAPHICS

INCIDENCE:
- Hepatitis A occurs worldwide, affecting 1.4 million people annually and accounting for 20% to 40% of cases of viral hepatitis in the United States.
- The seroprevalence increases with age, ranging from 10% in individuals aged <5 yr to 74% in those aged >50 yr.
- In the United States, average disease rate was ~15 cases/100,000 persons/yr before routine vaccination of all children in certain states. The incidence after 2005 is about 1 case/100,000.
- The incidence is relatively higher in some regions in the United States, including Arizona, Alaska, California, Idaho, Nevada, New Mexico, Oklahoma, Oregon, South Dakota, and Washington.
- At-risk groups include:
  1. Residents and staff of group homes.
  2. Children and employees of day care centers.
  3. People who engage in oral-anal contact, regardless of sexual orientation.
  4. IV drug abusers.
  5. Travel to endemic areas.
  6. Areas of overcrowding, poor sanitation, inadequate sewage treatment.

PREVALENCE:
- Approximately three fourths of the U.S. population has serologic evidence of prior infection.
- Anti-HAV prevalence has an inverse relation to income and household size.

PREDOMINANT SEX: None, except higher infection rates seen in homosexual males who engage in oral-anal contact.

PREDOMINANT AGE/PEAK INCIDENCE:
- In areas of high rates of hepatitis A, virtually all children are infected while younger than 10 yr, but disease is rare.
- In areas of moderate rates of hepatitis A, disease occurs in late childhood and young adults.
- In areas of low rates of hepatitis A, most cases occur in young adults.

INCUBATION PERIOD: Averages 30 days (15 to 50)

PHYSICAL FINDINGS & CLINICAL PRESENTATION

- Infection with HAV may have acute or subacute presentation, icteric or anicteric. Severity of illness seems to increase with age (90% of infection in children aged <5 yr may be subclinical).
- The incubation period of HAV is 2 to 6 weeks.
- A preicteric, prodromal phase of approximately 1 to 14 days; 15% no apparent prodrome. Symptoms are usually abrupt in onset and may include anorexia, fatigue, malaise, nausea, vomiting, fever, headache, and mild abdominal pain.
- Less common symptoms are chills, myalgias, arthralgias, upper respiratory symptoms, constipation, diarrhea, pruritus, urticaria.
- Jaundice occurs in >70% of patients. Patients older than 30 years are more likely than younger individuals to have jaundice.
- The icteric phase is preceded by dark urine.
- Bilirubinuria is typically followed a few days later by clay-colored stools and icterus.

PHYSICAL EXAMINATION

- Jaundice: Peaks in severity 2 wk after onset.
- Hepatomegaly.
- Splenomegaly.
- Cervical lymphadenopathy.
- Evanescent rash.
- Petechiae.
- Cardiac arrhythmias.

COMPLICATIONS

- Cholestasis.
- Fulminant hepatitis.
- Arthritis.
- Myocarditis.
- Optic neuritis.
- Transverse myelitis.
- Thrombocytopenic purpura.
- Aplastic anemia.
- Red cell aplasia.
- Henoch-Schönlein purpura.
- IgA dominant glomerulonephritis.

ETIOLOGY

- Caused by HAV, a 27-nm, nonenveloped, icosahedral, positive-stranded RNA virus.
- Transmission is fecal-oral route, from person to person. Transmission occurs with close contact or with food- or water-borne outbreaks with inadequately purified water or cooked foods. Recent outbreaks have involved green onions and tomatoes.
- Parenteral transmission is considered rare.
- Vertical transmission has also been reported.

DIAGNOSIS

DIFFERENTIAL DIAGNOSIS

- Other hepatitis virus (B, C, D, E).
- Infectious mononucleosis.
- Cytomegalovirus infection.
- Herpes simplex virus infection.
- Leptospirosis.
- Brucellosis.
- Drug-induced liver disease.

- Ischemic hepatitis.
- Autoimmune hepatitis.

WORKUP

- IgM antibody specific for HAV.
- Liver function tests; ALT and AST elevations are sensitive for liver damage but not specific for HAV.
- Elevated ESR.
- CBC; may find mild lymphocytosis.

LABORATORY TESTS

- Diagnosis confirmed by IgM anti-HAV; it is detectable in almost all infected patients at presentation and remains positive for 3 to 6 mo.
- A fourfold rise in titer of total antibody (IgM and IgG) to HAV confirms acute infection.
- HAV detection in stool and body fluids by electron microscopy.
- HAV RNA detection in stool, body fluids, serum, and liver tissue.
- ALT and AST usually more than 8 times normal in acute infection.
- Bilirubin usually 5 to 15 times normal.
- Alkaline phosphatase minimally elevated but higher level in cholestasis.
- Albumin and prothrombin time are generally normal; if elevated, they may herald hepatic necrosis.
- Fig. 1H-25 illustrates the typical course of hepatis A.

IMAGING STUDIES

- Rarely useful.
- Sonogram (fulminant hepatitis).

TREATMENT

- Usually self-limited.
- Supportive care.
- Those with fulminant hepatitis may require hospitalization and treatment of associated complications.
- Activity as tolerated.
- Advise to avoid alcohol and hepatotoxic drugs.
- Patients with fulminant hepatitis should be assessed for liver transplantation.

CHRONIC Rx

No chronic HAV and no chronic carrier state. The majority of patients have resolution of symptoms and liver abnormalities within 3 months.

DISPOSITION

- Follow-up as outpatient.
- Most patients recover within 3 months of infection, although 5% to 10% of patients will experience a relapse in the first 6 months.
- HAV is a self-limited infection and does not cause chronic hepatitis.

REFERRAL

- To a hepatologist if severe, fulminant hepatitis develops
- To a transplant surgeon if liver transplant becomes a consideration for fulminant hepatitis and liver failure

PEARLS & CONSIDERATIONS

- All cases of hepatitis A should be reported to the public health authorities because food-borne or water-borne outbreaks may occur, and public health efforts (mass vaccination or immunoglobulin therapy) may prevent secondary cases.
- Hepatitis A is a common illness in internationally traveled and developing countries. Pretravel vaccination is strongly recommended for travelers who are HAV susceptible.

PREVENTION

- Improvement in hygiene and sanitation.
- Heating food.
- Avoidance of water and foods from endemic area.

PASSIVE IMMUNIZATION

- Immunoglobulin provides protection against HAV through passive transfer of antibody.
- Preexposure prophylaxis indicated for people traveling to endemic areas (Ig 0.02 or 0.06 ml/kg given IM) who have not received or cannot receive the hepatitis A vaccine before departure. The lower dose is effective for up to 3 mo, and the higher dose is effective for up to 5 mo.
- Postexposure prophylaxis (Ig 0.02 ml/kg given IM) is indicated for people with recent exposure (within 2 wk) to HAV and who have not been previously vaccinated. In high-risk patients, vaccine may be administered with immunoglobulin.

ACTIVE IMMUNIZATION

- There are several inactivated and attenuated hepatitis vaccines; only the inactivated vaccines are currently available for use and they have been found to be safe and highly immunogenic: HAVRIX or VAQTA. These can be used in adults and children older than 12 mo. They are given as a two-dose regimen 6 mo to 1 yr apart. A combined hepatitis A and hepatitis B vaccine called TWINRX is also available.
- Protective antibody levels were reached in 94% to 100% of adults 1 mo after the first dose; similar results have been found for children and adolescents.
- Theoretic analyses of antibody levels estimate duration of immunity to be 10 to 20 yr.
- Vaccine should be considered for persons who are at risk: those traveling to or working in endemic areas, homosexual men, illegal drug users, persons with chronic liver disease, children in areas with high rates of hepatitis A infection.
- The Advisory Committee on Immunization Practices recommends routine hepatitis A vaccination for all children beginning at 12 to 23 mo of age.
- Clinical trials have shown equivalency between use of Ig and hepatitis A vaccine for postexposure prophylaxis in preventing symptomatic hepatitis A in healthy persons 2 to 40 yr of age. The Advisory Committee guidelines now provide for the use of Ig or the vaccine for this population. Those patients who are immunocompromised, have chronic liver disease, or are <1 yr of age should receive Ig.

SUGGESTED READINGS
Available at www.expertconsult.com

RELATED CONTENT
Hepatitis A (Patient Information)

AUTHOR: **GLENN G. FORT, M.D., M.P.H.**

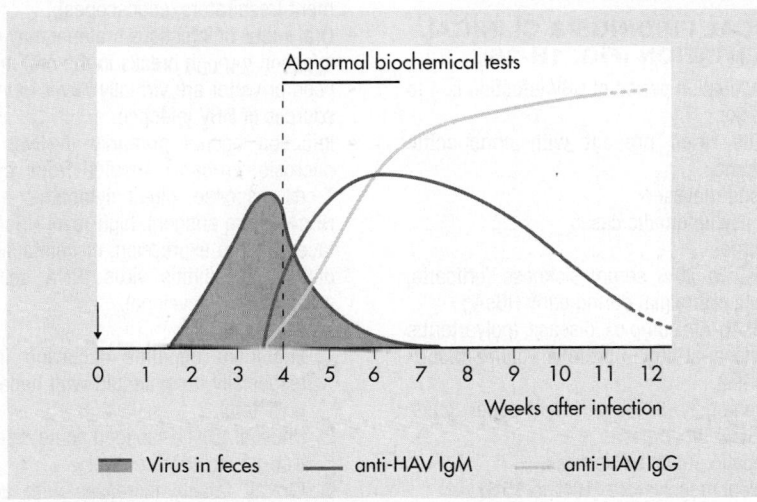

FIGURE 1H-25 Course of acute hepatitis A. (From Cohen J, Powderly WG: *Infectious diseases,* ed 2, St Louis, 2004, Mosby.)

BASIC INFORMATION

DEFINITION
Hepatitis B is an acute infection of the liver parenchymal cells caused by the hepatitis B virus (HBV).

SYNONYMS
Serum hepatitis
Long incubation (30 to 180 days) hepatitis HBV

ICD-10CM CODES
B16	Acute hepatitis
B16.9	Acute hepatitis B without delta agent and without hepatic coma
B16.1	Acute hepatitis B with delta agent (coinfection) without hepatic coma
B18.0	Chronic hepatitis B with delta agent
B18.1	Chronic hepatitis B without delta agent
B19.10	Unspecified viral hepatitis B without hepatic coma

EPIDEMIOLOGY & DEMOGRAPHICS
INCIDENCE (IN U.S.):
- ~200,000 to 300,000 infections annually in the United States.
- Much higher incidence in Europe (~1 million new cases annually) and in areas of high endemicity.
- In the United States, transmission is mainly horizontal (percutaneous and mucous membrane exposure to infectious blood and other body fluids [e.g., sexual transmission, either homosexual or heterosexual]); also from needle sharing among drug abusers; occupational exposure to contaminated blood and blood products; persons receiving transfusions of blood and blood products; and hemodialysis patients.

NOTE: Improved screening of blood and blood products has greatly reduced, although not eliminated, the risk of posttransfusion HBV infection.
- In areas of high endemicity, transmission is largely vertical (perinatal): HBV exists in the blood and body fluids. Perinatal transmission from HBsAg-positive mothers is as high as 90% unless immunoprophylaxis is given.

PREVALENCE (IN U.S.):
- The WHO estimates that 400 million people worldwide (6% of the population) are chronic HBV carriers. North America, Western Europe, and Australia are areas of low prevalence, <2%. In the United States an estimated 800,000 to 1.4 million people have chronic HBV infection.
- Africa, Asia, and the Western Pacific region are areas of high prevalence, ≥8%.
- Southern and Eastern Europe have intermediate rates, 2% to 7%.
- Chronically infected persons, those with positive HBsAg for >6 mo, represent the major source of infection.

- As many as 95% of infants and children aged <5, who typically have subclinical acute infection, will become chronic HBV carriers.
- Adults are more likely to have clinically evident acute infection, but only 1% to 5% will develop chronic infection.
- ~0.1% of patients with acute infection will develop fulminant acute hepatitis resulting in death.

PREDOMINANT SEX:
- Predominant in males because of increased IV drug abuse, homosexuality.
- Females more commonly terminate in chronic carrier state.

PREDOMINANT AGE: 20 to 45 yr.
PEAK INCIDENCE: 30 to 45 yr of age, at rates of 5% to 20%.
GENETICS: Neonatal infection:
- Rare in the United States.
- High (up to 90%) in areas of high endemicity (only 5% to 10% of perinatal infections occur in utero).

PHYSICAL FINDINGS & CLINICAL PRESENTATION (FIG. 1H-26)
- The incubation period of HBV infection is 4 to 24 weeks.
- Patients often present with nonspecific symptoms.
- Profound malaise.
- Many asymptomatic cases.
- Prodrome:
  1. 15% to 20% serum sickness (urticaria, rash, arthralgia) during early HBsAg.
  2. HBsAg-Ab complex disease (polyarteritis nodosa–arthritis, arteritis, glomerulonephritis).
- Hepatomegaly (87%) with right upper quadrant (RUQ) tenderness.
  1. Hepatic punch tenderness.
  2. Splenomegaly: rare (10% to 15%).
- Jaundice, dark urine, with occasional pruritus.
- Variable fever (when present, generally precedes jaundice and rapidly declines following onset of icteric phase).

- Spider angiomata: rare; resolves during recovery.
- Rare polyarteritis nodosa, cryoglobulinemia.

ETIOLOGY
- Caused by HBV (42-nm hepadnavirus with an outer surface coat [HBsAg], inner nucleocapsid core [HBcAg; HBeAg]; DNA polymerase; and partially double-stranded DNA genome). There are eight genotypes (A to H) based on nucleotide sequence. The prevalence of each genotype varies widely.
- Transmission by parenteral route (needle use, tattooing, ear piercing, acupuncture, transfusion of blood and blood products, hemodialysis, sexual contact), perinatal transmission.
- Infection may result from contact of infectious material with mucous membranes and open skin breaks (e.g., HBV is stable and can be transmitted from toothbrushes, utensils, razors, baby toys, assorted medical equipment [respirators, endoscopes]).
- Oral intake of infectious material may result in infection through breaks in the oral mucosa.
- Food or water are virtually never found to be sources of HBV infection.
- Infection occurs primarily in liver, where necrosis probably results from cytotoxic T-cell response, direct cytopathic effect of HBcAg (core antigen), high-level HBsAg (surface antigen) expression, or coinfection with delta (D) hepatitis virus (RNA delta core within HBsAg envelope).
- Recovery (>90%):
  1. Fulminant hepatitis occurring in <1% (especially if coinfected with hepatitis D); 80% fatal.
  2. Unusual (5%) prolonged acute disease for 4 to 12 mo, with recovery.
  3. Overall fatality increases with age and viral inoculation (e.g., transfusions).
- Chronic infection (1% to 2%):
  1. Persistent carrier state without hepatitis (HBsAg positive).

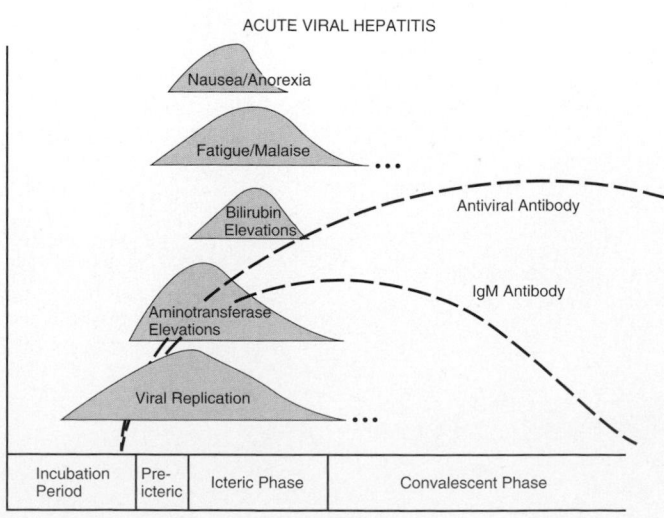

ACUTE VIRAL HEPATITIS

FIGURE 1H-26 The typical course of acute viral hepatitis. (From Goldman L, Ausiello D [eds]: *Cecil textbook of medicine,* ed 22, Philadelphia, 2004, Saunders.)

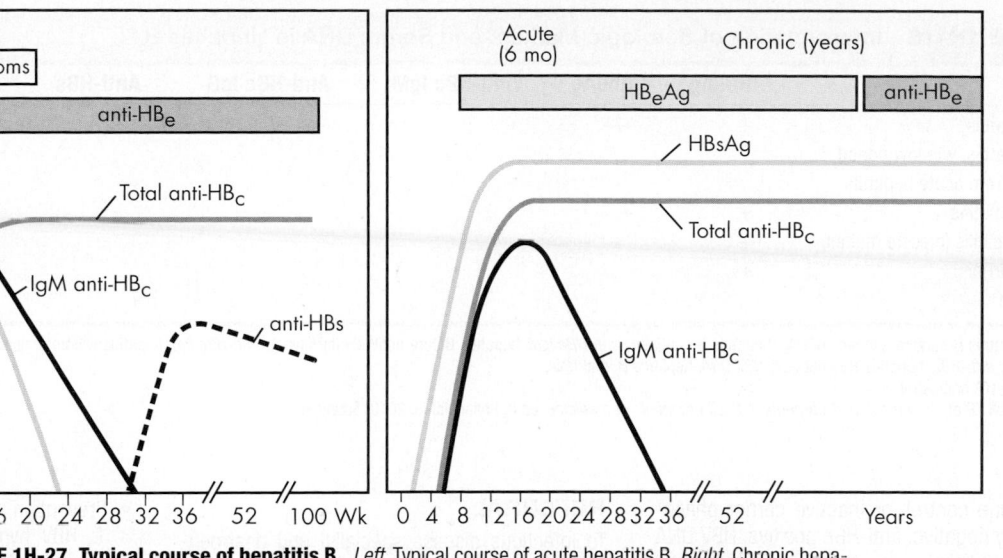

FIGURE 1H-27 Typical course of hepatitis B. *Left,* Typical course of acute hepatitis B. *Right,* Chronic hepatitis B. *HBc,* Hepatitis B core; *HBe,* hepatitis B early; *HBsAg,* hepatitis B surface antigen; *IgM,* immunoglobulin M. (From Mandell GL et al: *Principles and practice of infectious diseases,* ed 7, Philadelphia, 2010, Saunders.)

2. Chronic persistent hepatitis (CPH) (clinically well), or chronic active hepatitis (CAH) (HBsAg positive and HBeAg positive).
3. Cirrhosis.
4. Hepatocellular carcinoma (especially after neonatal infection).
5. Chronic infection: more common following low-dose exposure and mild acute hepatitis, with earlier age of infection, in males, and in immunosuppressed patients.
6. One third to one quarter of chronically infected will develop progressive liver disease (cirrhosis, hepatocellular carcinoma).

Dx DIAGNOSIS

DIFFERENTIAL DIAGNOSIS
- Acute disease confused with other viral hepatitis infections (A, C, D, E).
- Any viral illness producing systemic disease and hepatitis (e.g., yellow fever, EBV, CMV, HIV, rubella, rubeola, coxsackie B, adenovirus, herpes simplex or zoster).
- Nonviral causes of hepatitis (e.g., leptospirosis, toxoplasmosis, alcoholic hepatitis, drug-induced [e.g., acetaminophen, INH], toxic hepatitis [carbon tetrachloride, benzene]).

WORKUP
- Acute serum specimen for hepatitis B serology (HBsAg, HBsAb, HBcAb, HBeAg, HBeAb), HBDNA by PCR.
- LFTs.
- CBC.
- Liver biopsy: rarely indicated for diagnosis of fulminant viral hepatitis, chronic hepatitis, cirrhosis, carcinoma.

LABORATORY TESTS
- Diagnosis of acute HBV infection is best confirmed by IgM HBcAb in acute or early convalescent serum or by HBDNA by PCR.

1. Generally, IgM present during onset of jaundice.
2. Coexisting HBsAg.
- HBsAg and IgG-HBcAb during acute jaundice are strongly suggestive of remote HBV infection and another cause for current illness (Fig. 1H-27).
- HBsAb alone is suggestive of immunization response.
- With recovery, HBeAg is rapidly replaced by HBeAb in 2 to 3 mo, and HBsAg is replaced by HBsAb in 5 to 6 mo.
- In chronic HBV hepatitis, HBsAg and HBeAg are persistent without corresponding Ab.
- In chronic carrier state, HBsAg is persistent, but HBeAg is replaced by HBeAb.
- HBcAb develops in all outcomes.
- HBeAg correlation with highest infectivity; appearance of HBeAb heralds recovery.
- LFTs:
  1. ALT and AST: usually more than eight times normal (often 1000 U/L) at onset of jaundice (minimal acute ALT/AST rises often followed by chronic hepatitis or hepatocellular carcinoma).
  2. Bilirubin: variably elevated in icteric viral hepatitis.
  3. Alkaline phosphatase: minimally elevated (one to three times normal) acutely.
- Albumin and prothrombin time:
  1. Generally normal.
  2. If abnormal, possible harbinger of impending hepatic necrosis (fulminant hepatitis).
- WBC and ESR: generally normal.

IMAGING STUDIES
- Sonogram to document rapid reduction in liver size during fulminant hepatitis or mass in hepatocellular carcinoma.
- Fibroscan (transient elastography): A noninvasive test to quantify liver fibrosis without liver biopsy.

Rx TREATMENT

NONPHARMACOLOGIC THERAPY
- Symptomatic treatment as necessary.
- Activity as tolerated.
- High-calorie diet preferred; often best tolerated in morning.

ACUTE GENERAL Rx
- In most cases of acute HBV infection no treatment necessary; >90% of adults will spontaneously clear infection.
- Hospitalization advisable for any patient in danger from dehydration caused by poor oral intake, whose PT is prolonged, who has rising bilirubin level >15 to 20 µg/dl, or who has any clinical evidence of hepatic failure.
- IV therapy needed (rarely) for hydration during severe vomiting.
- Avoid hepatically metabolized drugs.
- No therapeutic measures are beneficial.
- Steroids not shown helpful.

CHRONIC Rx
- Chronic HBV infection can be subdivided into "immune tolerant" or "immune active."
- Immune tolerant is often seen in those who acquire HBV infection at birth (vertical transmission) and is characterized by positive HBeAg, very high HBV DNA (>1 million), and normal ALT. Liver biopsy or hepatic Fibroscan generally shows no inflammation or fibrosis. Vertical transmission patients in immune tolerant phase can reactivate into an immune active phase after several years.
- Immune active patients demonstrate elevated ALT, HBeAg positivity, anti-HBe negative, HBV DNA >10,000 IU/mL, and inflammation and fibrosis on liver biopsy or hepatic Fibroscan.
- HBV treatment is not recommended in immune tolerant patients and in those in

TABLE 1H-18 Interpretation of Serologic Markers and Serum DNA in Hepatitis B

	HBsAg	HbeAg	Anti-HBc IgM	Anti-HBc IgG	Anti-HBs	Anti-HBe	HBV DNA*
Acute hepatitis	+	+/–	+				+
Acute hepatitis, window period			+				
Recovery from acute hepatitis			+	+	+	+/–	
Chronic hepatitis	+	+					+
Chronic hepatitis (precore mutant)	+					+	+
Inactive carrier	+					+/–	
Vaccinated					+		

HBsAg, Hepatitis B surface antigen; *HBeAg*, hepatitis Be antigen; *anti-HBc IgM*, hepatitis B core antibody (IgM type); *anti-HBc IgG*, hepatitis B core antibody (IgG type); *anti-HBs*, hepatitis B surface antibody; *anti-HBe*, hepatitis Be antibody; *HBV DNA*, hepatitis B viral DNA.
*HBV DNA >10^5 copies/mL.
From Andreoli TE et al: *Andreoli and Carpenter's Cecil essentials of medicine*, ed 8, Philadelphia, 2010, Saunders.

"immune control, or inactive carrier phase" (HBeAg negative, anti-HBe positive, HBV DNA <10,000 IU/mL, normal ALT, variable fibrosis but no inflammation on liver biopsy or hepatic Fibroscan).

- Treatment for hepatitis B is recommended for patients with acute liver failure (ALF), those with elevated ALT and HBV DNA >10,000 IU/mL, and in patients receiving immunosuppressive therapy.
- Treatment consists of entecavir or tenofovir.
- The goal of treatment is a decline in HBV DNA level to <50 IU/mL and normalization of ALT level.
- If some patients without cirrhosis who can tolerate the side effects of pegylated interferon, it may be used if they have elevated ALT levels and low HBV DNA levels.
- Liver transplantation (should be considered for fulminant hepatitis).

DISPOSITION

- Follow-up as outpatient.
- Acute disease: infection will resolve (defined as clearance of hepatitis B surface antigen within 6 months) in 90% of adult patients.
- Rare fatalities (fulminant hepatitis).
- Possible chronic carrier state, cirrhosis, hepatocellular carcinoma.
- Cure of HBV is an unrealistic goal for most patients with chronic infection since only a few patients will become HBsAg with current treatment modalities.

REFERRAL

To infectious disease specialist and gastroenterologist for consultation regarding fulminant hepatitis or prolonged cholestasis, for cases of uncertain etiology, or for treatment of CAH.

PEARLS & CONSIDERATIONS

COMMENTS

- Virus and HBsAg in high titers in blood for 1 to 7 wk before jaundice and for a variable time thereafter.
- Transmission is possible during entire period of HBsAg (and especially during HBeAg) in serum.
- Universal precautions should be followed for all contacts with blood or secretions/excretions contaminated with blood.
- Preventing before exposure:
  1. Lifestyle changes
  2. Meticulous testing of blood supply (although some chronically infected, infectious donors are HBsAg negative).
  3. Sterilization via steam or hypochlorite.
  4. Hepatitis B vaccine for high-risk groups given IM in deltoid to induce HBsAb (response should be confirmed) is protective (>90% effective).
  5. Recommendation for universal childhood immunization with doses at birth, 1 mo, and 6 mo.

- Prevention after exposure:
  1. HBV hyperimmune globulin (HBIG) (0.06 ml/kg IM) given immediately after needlestick, within 14 days of sexual exposure, or at birth, followed by HBV vaccination. A second dose of HBIG is given in 28 days for those refusing vaccine or vaccine nonresponders.
  2. Standard immune globulin: nearly as effective as HBIG
- Preventive therapy with lamivudine or entecavir or tenofovir for patients who test positive for HBsAg and are undergoing chemotherapy may reduce the risk for HBV reactivation and HBV-associated morbidity and mortality,
- Hepatitis B prophylaxis is described in Section V.
- Table 1H-18 summarizes interpretation of serologic markers and serum DNA in hepatitis B.

SUGGESTED READINGS
Available at www.expertconsult.com

RELATED CONTENT
A flow diagram showing the use of specific serologic tests for the diagnosis of acute viral hepatitis in relation to the clinical and epidemiologic setting (Algorithm in Section III)
Hepatitis B (Patient Information)

AUTHOR: **GLENN G. FORT, M.D., M.P.H.**

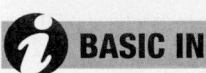 **BASIC INFORMATION**

DEFINITION

Hepatitis C is an acute liver parenchymal infection caused by hepatitis C virus (HCV).

SYNONYMS

Transfusion-related non-A, non-B hepatitis (incubation period averages 6 wk, intermediate between hepatitis A and B)

ICD-10CM CODES
B17.1	Acute hepatitis C
B18.2	Chronic viral hepatitis C
B17.10	Acute hepatitis C without hepatic coma
B17.11	Acute hepatitis C with hepatic coma
B19.20	Unspecified viral hepatitis C without hepatic coma
B19.21	Unspecified viral hepatitis C with hepatic coma

EPIDEMIOLOGY & DEMOGRAPHICS

Hepatitis C infection is the most common chronic blood-borne infection in the United States. About 3% of baby boomers test positive for the virus. The CDC now recommends testing for hepatitis C for anyone born from 1945 to 1965.
INCIDENCE (IN U.S.): HCV infects more than 185 million individuals worldwide. Approximately 20% of patients chronically infected with HCV progress to cirrhosis.

- 150,000 new cases/yr (37,500 symptomatic; 93,000 later chronic liver disease; 30,700 cirrhosis). The incidence of acute HCV has declined substantially over the past 30 yr (from 7.4/100,000 to 0.7/100,000).
- ~9000 of these ultimately die of HCV infection; most common (40%) cause of nonalcoholic liver disease in the United States

PREVALENCE (IN U.S.):

- Overall prevalence of anti-HCV antibody is 1% to 1.2% (an estimated 2.7 million persons nationwide).
- Highest prevalence in hemophiliacs transfused before 1987 and users of injection drugs, 72% to 90%. Over past 30 yr, blood transfusion as a risk factor declined from 15% of cases to 1.9%.
- Among low-risk groups, prevalence 0.6%.

PREDOMINANT SEX: Slight male predominance.
PREDOMINANT AGE: Highest prevalence in 30- to 49-yr age group (65%).
PEAK INCIDENCE:

- 20 to 39 yr of age.
- African Americans and whites have similar incidence of acute disease; Hispanics have higher rates.
- Prevalence is substantially higher among non-Hispanic blacks than among non-Hispanic whites.

GENETICS: Neonatal infection is rare; increased risk with maternal HIV-1 coinfection.

PHYSICAL FINDINGS & CLINICAL PRESENTATION

- Symptoms usually develop 7 to 8 wk after infection (range of 2 to 26 wk), but 70% to 80% of cases are subclinical.
- 10% to 20% report acute illness with jaundice and nonspecific symptoms (abdominal pain, anorexia, malaise).
- Fulminant hepatitis may rarely occur during this period.
- After acute infection, 15% to 25% have complete resolution (absence of HCV RNA in serum, normal ALT).
- Progression to chronic infection is common, 50% to 84%. 74% to 86% have persistent viremia; spontaneous clearance of viremia in chronic infection is rare. 60% to 70% of patients will have persistent or fluctuating ALT levels; 30% to 40% with chronic infection have normal ALT levels.
- 15% to 20% of those with chronic HCV will develop cirrhosis over a period of 20 to 30 yr; in most others, chronic infection leads to hepatitis and varying degrees of fibrosis. Table 1H-19 describes factors associated with cirrhosis in persons with hepatitis C infection.

- 0.4% to 2.5% of patients with chronic infection develop hepatocellular carcinoma (HCC).
- 25% of patients with chronic infection continue to have an asymptomatic course with normal LFTs and benign histology.
- In chronic HCV infection, extrahepatic sequelae include a variety of immunologic and lymphoproliferative disorders (e.g., cryoglobulinemia, membranoproliferative glomerulonephritis, and possibly Sjögren's syndrome, autoimmune thyroiditis, polyarteritis nodosa, aplastic anemia, lichen planus, porphyria cutanea tarda, B-cell lymphoma, others).

ETIOLOGY

- Caused by HCV (single-stranded RNA flavivirus).
- Most HCV transmission is parenteral.
- In the United States, advances in screening of blood and blood products have made transfusion-related HCV infection rare (the risk is estimated to be 0.001% per unit transfused).
- Injecting-drug use accounts for most HCV transmission in the United States (60% of newly acquired cases, 20% to 50% of chronically infected persons).
- Occupational needlestick exposure from an HCV-positive source has a seroconversion rate of 1.8% (range 0% to 7%).
- Nosocomial transmission rates (from surgery and procedures such as colonoscopy and hemodialysis) are extremely low.
- Sexual transmission and maternal-fetal transmission are infrequent (estimated at 5%).
- No identifiable risk in 40% to 50% of community-acquired hepatitis C, but snorting of cocaine by shared use of straw or rolled-up paper has been identified as a risk factor because it causes microscopic bleeding of nasal mucosa.
- HCV infection may stimulate production of cytotoxic T lymphocytes and cytokines (INF-γ), which probably mediate hepatic necrosis.

TABLE 1H-19 Factors Associated With Cirrhosis in Persons With Hepatitis C Infection

Factor	Impact	Comment
Environmental		
Alcohol use	+4	The importance of minimal alcohol ingestion (<20 g/day) has not been established
Host		
HIV infection	+4	Increasingly important as HIV-related survival improves; may be masked by competing mortality
HBV infection	+3	Strong effect when HBsAg positive; relatively uncommon
Age	+4	Strong effect; increases as low as 40 yr. Hard to distinguish from infection duration
Body mass index	+2	Associated with metabolic syndrome
Duration of HCV infection	+3	Cirrhosis is rare before 10 yr
HLA type	+1?	HLA B54 is correlated with increased risk of cirrhosis; DRB1*0301 with lack of cirrhosis
Viral		
Quasispecies complexity	+1	Cross-sectional studies cannot assess causality and complexity may be confounded by duration of infection
HCV genotype 1	+1?	Genotype 1b in some, but not other studies, could be confounded by longer duration of 1b infections
Quantitative measures of viremia (serum or plasma HCV RNA level)	+2	Not always detected or lost in multivariate analysis of age or HIV

HCV, Hepatitis C virus; *HIV,* human immunodeficiency virus; *HLA,* human leukocyte antigen; *RNA,* ribonucleic acid.
From Bennett JE, Dolin R, Blaser MJ: *Mandell, Douglas, and Bennett's principles and practice of infectious diseases,* ed 8, Philadelphia, 2015, Saunders.

Dx DIAGNOSIS

DIFFERENTIAL DIAGNOSIS

- Other hepatitis viruses (A, B, D, E).
- Other viral illnesses producing systemic disease (e.g., yellow fever, EBV, CMV, HIV, rubella, rubeola, coxsackie B, adenovirus, HSV, HZV).
- Nonviral hepatitis (e.g., leptospirosis, toxoplasmosis, alcoholic hepatitis, drug-induced hepatitis [acetaminophen, INH], toxic hepatitis).

WORKUP

- Acute hepatitis C antibody, viral genotyping, viral titers.
- LFTs; CBC.

NOTE: ALT is an easy and inexpensive test to monitor infection and efficacy of therapy. However, ALT levels may fluctuate or even be normal in active or chronic infection and even with cirrhosis, and ALT may remain elevated even after clearance of viremia.

- Liver biopsy with histologic staging is the gold standard for assessing the degree of disease activity and the likelihood of disease progression, and also to help rule out other causes of liver disease.
- Transient elastography (Fibroscan) is a non-invasive test to quantify liver fibrosis and is being increasingly used in place of liver biopsy in many institutions.

LABORATORY TESTS

- Diagnosis is often by exclusion, because it takes 6 wk to 12 mo to develop anti-HCV antibody (70% positive by 6 wk, 90% positive by 6 mo).
- Diagnostic tests include serologic assays for antibodies and molecular tests for viral particles.
  1. Enzyme immunoassay is the test for anti-HCV antibody:
     The current version can detect antibody within 4 to 10 wk after infection.
     False-negative rate in low-risk populations is 0.5% to 1%.
     False negatives also occur in immune-compromised persons, HIV-1, renal failure, HCV-associated essential mixed cryoglobulinemia.
     False positives in autoimmune hepatitis, paraproteinemia, and persons with no risk factors.
- The recombinant immunoblot assay that was previously recommended as a follow-up to positive antibody test is no longer available. The CDC now recommends that anyone who tests positive for HCV antibodies receive a follow-up HCV RNA test.
- Qualitative and quantitative HCV RNA tests using PCR: Lower limit of detection is <43 IU/mL.
- Used to confirm viremia and to assess response to treatment.
- Qualitative polymerase chain reaction (PCR) useful in patients with negative enzyme immunoassay in whom infection is suspected.
- Quantitative tests use either branched-chain DNA or reverse transcription PCR; the latter is more sensitive.
- Viral genotyping can distinguish among genotypes 1, 2, 3, 4, 5, and 6, which is helpful in choosing therapy; most of these tests use PCR (genotypes 1, 2, 3, and 4 predominate in the United States and Europe [genotype 1 is especially common in North America (60% to 75% of Hep C infections in the United States).
- LFTs: ALT and AST may be elevated to more than eight times normal in acute infection; in chronic infection ALT may be normal or fluctuate.
- Bilirubin may be five to 10 times normal.
- Albumin and prothrombin time generally normal; if abnormal, may be harbinger of impending hepatic necrosis.
- WBC and erythrocyte sedimentation rate (ESR) are generally normal.
- HIV testing. Infection with HCV is seen in 15% to 30% of individuals with HIV infection due to shared risk factors.

IMAGING STUDIES

- Transient elastography (Fibroscan) to quantify liver fibrosis.
- Sonogram: rapid liver size reduction during fulminant hepatitis or mass in HCC.

Rx TREATMENT

NONPHARMACOLOGIC THERAPY

Activity and diet as tolerated; avoid saw palmetto and green tea leaf herbs.

ACUTE GENERAL Rx

- Supportive care.
- Avoid hepatically metabolized drugs.

CHRONIC Rx

Response to therapy is influenced by HCV genotype. Recommendations for the treatment of hepatitis C in adults are changing constantly as new therapies come to the market. The advent of direct-acting antiviral agents (DAAs) has drastically changed treatment options and improved cure rates to greater than 95%. The most up-to-date guidance is available at the website www.hcvguidelines.org. The following is a brief summary of the guidelines based on genotype as of August 2015. Newer agents are expected to be FDA approved in the next few years. Currently, these treatment regimens are extremely expensive.

Genotype 1a: Options for treatment-naïve patients with similar efficacy in alphabetical order:
A. Daily daclatasvir (60 mg) and sofosbuvir (400 mg) [Sovaldi] for 12 wk (no cirrhosis) or 4 wk with or without weight-based ribavirin (1000 mg [<75 kg]) to 1200 mg [75 kg]) (cirrhosis)
B. Elbasvir (50 mg)/grazoprevir (100 mg) combination (Zepatier): one tablet once/day for 12 weeks
C. Daily fixed-dose combination of ledipasvir (90 mg)/sofosbuvir (400 mg) [Harvoni] for 12 wk
D. Daily fixed-dose combination of paritaprevir (150 mg)/ritonavir (100 mg)/ombitasvir (25 mg) plus twice-daily dasabuvir (250 mg) [Viekira] and weight-based ribivirin for 12 wk (no cirrhosis) or 24 wk (cirrhosis)
E. Daily simeprevir (150 mg) and sofosbuvir (400 mg) for 12 wk (no cirrhosis) or 24 wk (cirrhosis without the Q80K polymorphism) with or without weight-based ribivirin

Genotype 1b:Options with similar efficacy for treatment-naïve patients in alphabetical order:
A. Daily daclatasvir (60 mg) and sofosbuvir (400 mg) for 12 wk (no cirrhosis) or 24 wk with or without weight-based ribivirin (cirrhosis) (1000 mg [<75 kg] to 1200 mg [>75 kg])
B. Daily fixed-dose combination of ledipasvir (90 mg)/sofosbuvir (400 mg) for 12 wk
C. Daily fixed-dose combination of paritaprevir (150 mg)/ritonavir (100 mg)/ombitasvir (25 mg) plus twice-daily dosed dasabuvir (250 mg) for 12 wk
D. Daily simeprevir (150 mg) plus sofosbuvir (400 mg) for 12 wk (no cirrhosis) or 24 wk with or without weight-based ribivirin (cirrhosis)

Genotype 2: Treatment-naïve regimens:
A. Daily daclatasvir (60 mg) and sofosbuvir (400 mg) for 12 wk for patients who cannot tolerate ribivirin
B. Daily sofosbuvir (400 mg) and weight-based ribivirin (100 mg [<75 kg] to 1200 mg [>75 kg])
C. Extending treatment to 16 wk is recommended in patients with cirrhosis

Genotype 3: Treatment-naïve regimens:
A. Daily daclatasvir (60 mg) and sofosbuvir (400 mg) for 12 wk (no cirrhosis) or 24 wk with or without weight-based ribavirin (1000 mg [<75kg] to 1200 mg [>75 kg])
B. Daily sofosbuvir (400 mg) and weight-based ribivirin plus weekly PEG-IFN (pegylated interferon 2a:180 mcg SQ) for 12 wk for interferon-eligible patients (interferon has numerous limiting side effects)
C. Daily sofosbuvir (400 mg) and weight-based ribivirin for 24 wk is an alternative regimen for patients who are interferon ineligible.

Genotype 4: Treatment-naïve options in alphabetical order with similar efficacy:
A. Elbasvir (50 mg)/grazoprevir (100 mg) combination (Zepatier): one tablet once/day for 12 weeks
B. Daily fixed-dose combination of ledipasvir (90 mg)/sofosbuvir (400 mg) for 12 wk.
C. Daily fixed-dose combination of paritaprevir (150 mg)/ritonavir (100 mg)/ombitasvir (25 mg) and weight-based ribivirin (1000 mg [<75 kg] to 1200 mg [>75kg])
D. Daily sofosbuvir (400 mg) and weight-based ribavirin (1000 mg [<75 kg] to 1200 mg [>75 kg])

Genotypes 5 and 6: There are few data to guide therapy, but the following is recommended.
A. Daily fixed-dose combination of ledipasvir (90 mg)/sofosbuvir (400 mg for 12 wk
B. Alternative regimen: daily sofosbuvir (400 mg) and weight-based ribivirin (1000 mg [<75 kg] to 1200 mg [>75 kg] plus weekly PEG-IFN [pegylated interferon 2a]: 180 mcg SQ)

Drug interactions can be significant with these regimens (http://www.hep-druginteractions.org). With DAA regimens, viral loads are measured at 4 wk into the therapy to monitor success and at the end of therapy. A final viral load is measured 12 wk after completing the treatment, and if undetectable, the patient is considered to have a sustained virologic response (SVR), which equates to a cure.

- Liver transplantation:
  1. Hepatitis C is the main indication for liver transplantation in the United States.
  2. It is the only option for patients with deteriorating HCV-related cirrhosis and for some patients with HCC.
  3. Recurrent infection occurs in almost all patients with progressive fibrosis and cirrhosis; as many as 20% progress to cirrhosis within 5 yrs posttransplant.

DISPOSITION

- SVR after treatment among HCV-infected persons at any stage of fibrosis is associated with reduced HCC.
- Periodic abdominal ultrasonography for HCC screening.
- Recent guidelines recommend against measurement of alpha-fetoprotein (AFP) to screen for HCC in patients with chronic hepatitis C due to lack of sensitivity, specificity, and predictive values.

REFERRAL

- To a hepatologist or infectious disease specialist for treatment for hepatitis C.
- To a transplant surgeon for consideration of liver transplant if indicated.

⚠ PEARLS & CONSIDERATIONS

- More rapid progression of disease in persons who drink alcohol regularly, persons of advanced age at time of infection, and those coinfected with other viruses (HIV, hepatitis B). All persons with identified HCV infection should receive a brief alcohol screening and intervention as clinically indicated.
- Major depression is a common (20%-40%) side effect of treatment with interferons. Use of the SSRI escitalopram has been found safe and effective for prevention of interferon-associated depression in these patients.
- Regression of cirrhosis has been demonstrated after antiviral therapy in some patients with chronic hepatitis C. Regression is associated with decreased disease-related morbidity and improved survival.
- The presence of interleukin (IL)-28B and HLA class II is independently associated with spontaneous resolution of HCV infection, and single nucleotide polymorphism IL-28B and DQB1*03:01 may explain approximately 15% of spontaneous resolution of HCV infection.

SUGGESTED READINGS

Available at www.expertconsult.com

RELATED CONTENT

Hepatitis C (Patient Information)

AUTHOR: **GLENN G. FORT, M.D., M.P.H.**

ⓘ BASIC INFORMATION

DEFINITION

Autoimmune hepatitis is a chronic inflammatory condition of the liver characterized by elevated serum globulin levels (IgG), presence of circulating autoantibodies, interface hepatitis on histology, and plasma cell rich infiltrate. Two types have been described:

- Type 1, or "classic," autoimmune hepatitis is the most predominant form in the United States and worldwide (80%) and has a bimodal age distribution with peaks between 10 to 20 and 45 to 70 years of age. Patients are positive for antinuclear antibodies (ANA) and/or antismooth muscle antibodies (SMA) and have specific associated HLA haplotypes: B8, DR3, DR4.
- Type 2 is rare in the United States and primarily affects young children between 2 and 14 years of age and is characterized by the presence of antibodies to liver/kidney microsomes (anti-LKM-1) or liver cytosol 1. Patients have associated HLA haplotypes: B14, DR. This form is generally more advanced at presentation and is more difficult to treat.

SYNONYMS

Autoimmune chronic active hepatitis
Chronic active hepatitis
Lupoid hepatitis
Plasma cell hepatitis

ICD-10CM CODES
K75.4 Autoimmune hepatitis
K73.2 Chronic active hepatitis, not elsewhere classified

EPIDEMIOLOGY & DEMOGRAPHICS

- Annual incidence (estimated): 0.2 to 2.0 cases per 100,000, similar to PBC, more common than PSC.
- Point prevalence (estimated): 16.9 per 100,000
- Type 1: age of onset has a bimodal distribution with peaks between 10 to 20 and 45 to 70 years
- Type 2: more common in young children 2 to 14 years of age.
- Female/male ratio is 3.6:1; type 1 has an 80% female predominance whereas type 2 has a 90% female predominance.
- Approximately 100,000 to 200,000 persons affected in the United States.
- Accounts for 4% to 6% of liver transplants in United States.
- Associated with HLA-DRB1*0301 and HLA-DRB1*0401 alleles.

CLINICAL PRESENTATION

- Varies from intermittent asymptomatic elevations of liver enzymes to advanced cirrhosis. Cirrhosis is often the presenting stage. AIH can also present initially as a fulminant hepatitis.
- Symptoms may include fatigue, anorexia, nausea, abdominal pain, pruritus, and arthralgia.

- Autoimmune findings may include arthritis, xerostomia, keratoconjunctivitis, cutaneous vasculitis, and erythema nodosum.
- Patients with advanced disease can show hepatosplenomegaly, ascites, peripheral edema, abnormal bleeding, and jaundice.

ETIOLOGY

- Exact etiology is unknown; liver histology demonstrates cell-mediated immune attack against hepatocytes.
- Presence of a variety of autoantibodies suggests an autoimmune mechanism.
- There are likely two components involved: genetic predisposition and an inciting environmental trigger.
- Potential triggering agents such as viruses (hepatitis A, B, C) or drugs (minocycline, nitrofurantoin) likely possess some homology similar to liver-specific antigens.

ⓓⓧ DIAGNOSIS

- A simplified diagnostic criteria for routine clinical practice has been developed by the International Autoimmune Hepatitis Group (see Table 1H-20).
- Histology: lymphoplasmacytic infiltrate invading the hepatocyte boundary surrounding the portal triad (limiting plate). Also, a periportal infiltrate may be seen (interface hepatitis).

DIFFERENTIAL DIAGNOSIS

- Acute viral hepatitis (A, B, C, D, E, cytomegalovirus, Epstein-Barr, herpes)
- Chronic viral hepatitis (B, C)
- Toxic hepatitis (alcohol, drugs)
- Primary biliary cirrhosis
- Primary sclerosing cholangitis
- Hemochromatosis
- Nonalcoholic steatohepatitis
- SLE
- Wilson's disease
- Alpha-1 antitrypsin deficiency

WORKUP

- History and physical examination with attention to the presence of autoimmune abnormalities such as autoimmune thyroiditis, Graves' disease, inflammatory bowel disease, celiac sprue, and rheumatoid arthritis.
- Liver function tests and serum gamma-globulins.

- Tests for autoantibodies: ANA, SMA, anti-LKM.
- Liver biopsy for establishing diagnosis and disease severity.

LABORATORY TESTS

- Aminotransferases generally elevated and may fluctuate
- Bilirubin and alkaline phosphatase moderately elevated or normal
- Elevation of gamma globulin (>2.0 g/dl [20 g/L]) and immunoglobulin G
- Circulating autoantibodies often present:
  1. Rheumatoid factor
  2. ANAs
     a. Present in two thirds of patients
     b. Typical pattern is homogeneous or speckled
     c. Titer does not correlate with the stage, activity, or prognosis
  3. Anti-SMAs
     a. Present in 87% of patients
     b. Titer does not correlate with course or prognosis
  4. Anti-LKM antibodies
     a. Typically found in patients who are ANA negative and SMA negative
     b. Characterizes type 2 AIH
     c. Present in pediatric population and up to 20% of adults in Europe; also present in patients with drug-induced hepatitis
  5. Autoantibodies against soluble liver antigen and liver-pancreas antigen (anti-SLA/LP)
     a. Present in 10% to 30% of patients
     b. Associated with higher rate of relapse after corticosteroid therapy
     c. Several studies suggest that patients with anti-SLA/LP have a more severe course
     Serum p-ANCA levels are useful for diagnosis of the 10% to 15% of patients with negative SMA, ANA, and low gamma globulin levels.
- Hypoalbuminemia and prolonged prothrombin time with advanced disease.
- There is a well-described overlap syndrome with primary biliary cirrhosis (7%), primary sclerosing cholangitis (6%), and autoimmune cholangitis (11%). In patients who do not respond to therapy after 3 months, consider cholangiographic studies to evaluate for primary sclerosing cholangitis.

TABLE 1H-20 Simplified Diagnostic Criteria for Autoimmune Hepatitis

Variable	Cutoff	Points	Cutoff	Points
ANA or SMA	≥1:40	1	≥1:80	2
LKM			≥1:40	2
SLA			Positive	2
IgG	≥ULN	1	≥1.1 × ULN	2
Histology	Compatible with AIH	1	Typical of AIH	2
Absence of viral hepatitis			Yes	2

Maximum number of points for all antibodies = 2, total = 8.
Probable AIH ≥6 points, definite AIH ≥7 points. 88% sensitivity and 97% specificity.
AIH, Autoimmune hepatitis; *ANA,* antinuclear antibody; *IgG,* immunoglobulin G; *LKM,* liver/kidney microsomes; *SLA,* soluble liver antigen; *SMA,* smooth muscle antibody; *ULN,* upper limit of normal.

IMAGING STUDIES

- Ultrasound of liver and biliary tree to rule out obstruction or hepatic mass.
- Cirrhosis secondary to AIH is a risk factor for development of hepatocellular carcinoma (although less so than viral hepatitis). Patients with cirrhosis should get ultrasonography and AFP every 6 months.

Rx TREATMENT

NONPHARMACOLOGIC THERAPY

- Avoid alcohol and hepatotoxic medications.
- Liver transplantation is an option for end-stage disease or fulminant hepatic failure.

PHARMACOLOGIC THERAPY

- Initial treatment:
  1. Prednisone or prednisolone 40 to 60 mg/day PO or combination treatment with prednisone 30 mg PO daily plus azathioprine 50 mg PO daily, with a gradual taper to prednisone 10 mg PO daily over 2 to 3 months as liver function test (LFT) results normalize. A combination of oral budesonide (6 to 9 mg/day) and azathioprine (1-2 mg/kg/day) can be used to induce and maintain remission in patients with non-cirrhotic AIH, with a lower rate of steroid-specific side effects. Steroids are contraindicated in brittle diabetes mellitus, uncontrolled hypertension, prior steroid intolerance, severe osteopenia, and psychosis. Azathioprine is contraindicated by thiopurine S-methyltransferase (TPMT) deficiency, leukopenia, or thrombocytopenia. Budesonide is contraindicated in cirrhosis because portal systemic shunting and abnormal hepatic metabolism prevent complete hepatic first-pass extraction, reducing therapeutic efficacy and causing systemic steroid side effects.
  2. Combination therapy allows lower prednisone doses, fewer steroid side effects, and faster normalization of LFTs.

  The primary goal of therapy in AIH is to achieve remission. The 2010 AASLD Practice Guideline (2010 PG) redefined remission to require: normal levels of AST, ALT (optimally <19 U/L in women and <30 U/L in men), total bilirubin, gamma-globulin or IgG and absence of inflammatory activity on liver biopsy. Secondary goals of therapy are the prevention of progression of fibrosis to cirrhosis and reversion of cirrhosis to a lower stage of fibrosis which has been documented.

- Indications for treatment:
  1. Serum aminotransferases more than 10 times greater than the upper limit of normal
  2. Serum aminotransferases more than five times the upper limit of normal, with serum gamma-globulin level twice the upper limit of normal

  3. Histologic features of bridging necrosis
  4. Symptomatic disease: incapacitating symptoms such as fatigue and arthralgia
- Relative indications:
  - Asymptomatic patients with elevated liver enzymes or limited histological activity
- Treatment not indicated:
  - Inactive cirrhosis
- Evaluation of treatment response:
  1. Goals are the absence of symptoms, normalization of liver function tests, and absence of inflammatory activity on liver biopsy. Generally, this is a steroid-responsive condition, but up to 20% do not respond.
  2. Patients whose transaminase levels normalize may continue to have ongoing active hepatitis involving inflammation and fibrosis.
  3. Histologic improvement may lag behind clinical and laboratory improvement by as much as 6 months. Because of this, repeat liver biopsy should be considered after normalization of transaminase levels. A review of AIH studies between 1972 and 2013 shows that hepatic fibrosis improves in 53% to 57% of cases and progressive fibrosis slows or is prevented in 79% of patients.
  4. After initial remission is achieved, one may consider tapering medications. Steroid withdrawal should be done only if liver function tests normalize and histologic quiescence is achieved. About 50% to 86% of patients will relapse after this and require long-term maintenance medications.
  5. Complete normalization on biopsy is associated with a 15% to 20% risk of relapse, whereas persistent interface hepatitis is associated with a 90% risk of relapse. Do not attempt multiple treatment withdrawals. The risk of developing cirrhosis with single relapse is 9.5%, whereas multiple relapses are associated with 37.5% risk of developing cirrhosis. The patient with sustained remission has a risk of cirrhosis of 4.5%.

DISPOSITION

- Follow up as outpatient.
- Long-term treatment may be necessary for sustained remission in individuals who continuously relapse and in partial responders. Sixty-five percent of patients achieve remission by 18 months; 80% achieve remission by 3 years.
- Approximately 10% to 15% of patients do not respond to conventional therapy. The risk factors for nonresponse include presence of underlying cirrhosis, younger age, or longer duration of disease, HLA-B8 or DR3. High-dose therapy can achieve remission in 70%: prednisone 60 mg or dual therapy with prednisone 30 mg and AZA 150 mg. Other alternatives such as mycophenolate,

the calcineurin inhibitors (CNIs), tacrolimus (TAC) and cyclosporine (CSA), sirolimus (SIR), everolimus (EVR), rituximab, and infliximab, have been used successfully. However, none of the alternative therapies has been studied in multicenter, randomized, controlled trials.

- Orthotopic liver transplantation (OLT) is a life-saving option for AIH patients with ALF, decompensated cirrhosis, or HCC. Allograft and patient survival are excellent; however, AIH recurs in the allograft in a minority (25% probability in first 5 years, 50% in 10 years).

REFERRAL

Patients with advanced cirrhosis or who progress to end-stage liver disease are candidates for liver transplantation and should be referred to appropriate medical centers that provide liver transplantation services.

! PEARLS & CONSIDERATIONS

COMMENTS

- ANA and SMA are observed together in 60% of cases. Serum titers >1:40 suggest autoimmune hepatitis.
- A variety of autoimmune conditions can be seen in association with autoimmune hepatitis, including thyroiditis, Graves' disease, ulcerative colitis, rheumatoid arthritis, uveitis, pernicious anemia, Sjögren's syndrome, mixed connective tissue disease, CREST syndrome, and vitiligo.
- Variant forms of autoimmune hepatitis (overlap syndrome) have clinical and serologic findings of autoimmune hepatitis plus features of other forms of chronic liver disease such as primary biliary cirrhosis (PBC) or primary sclerosing cholangitis (PSC).

PREVENTION

None

PATIENT & FAMILY EDUCATION

- American Liver Foundation (ALF): Phone: 800-GO-LIVER (465-4837); Internet: www.liverfoundation.org
- National Digestive Diseases Information clearinghouse: http://digestive.niddk.nih.gov/ddiseases/pubs/autoimmunehep

EBM EVIDENCE

Available at www.expertconsult.com.

SUGGESTED READINGS

Available at www.expertconsult.com.

RELATED CONTENT

Autoimmune Hepatitis (Patient Information).

AUTHORS: **ANDREEA M. CATANA, M.D.,** and **KITTICHAI PROMRAT, M.D.**

BASIC INFORMATION

DEFINITION
Hepatocellular carcinoma (HCC) is a malignant neoplasm of the hepatocytes.

SYNONYMS
Hepatoma
HCC

ICD-10CM CODES
C22.0 Liver cell carcinoma

EPIDEMIOLOGY & DEMOGRAPHICS
HCC is the fifth most common cancer worldwide (~600,000 new cases/year) and third most common cause of cancer deaths. Incidence varies worldwide:
- Areas with high rates of hepatitis B and C (East Asia, sub-Saharan Africa) have highest incidence.
- Males more affected than females, with ratios between 2:1 and 4:1.
- Peak incidence: fifth and sixth decades in Western countries, earlier in areas with perinatal transmission of hepatitis B.
- Incidence rapidly growing in the U.S. due to chronic hepatitis C, increasing obesity, and diabetes mellitus.
  1. During the past two decades, the incidence of HCC in the U.S. doubled. The greatest proportional increase in cases has been among Hispanics and whites between 45-60 years of age
  2. Mean age of diagnosis approximately 65 years
  3. HCC is the fastest-rising cause of cancer-related deaths in the U.S.
- Risk factors:
  1. Chronic hepatitis B infection accounts for 50% of all cases and virtually all childhood cases.
  2. Chronic hepatitis C infection markers are found in 80% to 90% of patients with HCC in Japan and 30% to 50% in the U.S.
  3. Cirrhosis from other causes: alcoholic liver disease, nonalcoholic steatohepatitis, primary biliary cirrhosis, hemochromatosis, α1-antitrypsin deficiency, and autoimmune hepatitis.
  4. Hepatotoxins: aflatoxin B1.
  5. Systemic diseases affecting the liver: tyrosinemia.
  6. Obesity and diabetes mellitus.

PHYSICAL FINDINGS & CLINICAL PRESENTATION
- One third of patients are asymptomatic.
- Abdominal pain may be the initial presentation.
- Signs of underlying cirrhosis and portal hypertension are often present.
- Previously compensated cirrhosis with new ascites, encephalopathy, jaundice, or bleeding.
- Paraneoplastic syndromes (hypoglycemia, erythrocytosis, hypercalcemia, severe diarrhea, dermatomyositis) may be present.

DIAGNOSIS

DIFFERENTIAL DIAGNOSIS
- Metastatic cancers to liver
- Intrahepatic cholangiocarcinoma
- Benign liver neoplasms (adenomas, focal nodular hyperplasia, and hemangiomas)
- Focal fatty infiltration

WORKUP
- History regarding risk factors
- Physical examination with attention to signs of chronic liver disease
- Laboratory evaluation and imaging studies
- Imaging studies: ultrasound for initial testing; -phase CT scan or dynamic contrast-enhanced MRI

LABORATORY TESTS
- Liver function tests
- α-Fetoprotein (AFP) levels can be elevated in 70% of patients. An AFP level of 400 ng/mL or greater is highly suggestive of HCC; however, elevations may not be seen in up to 40% of patients with small lesions (1-2 cm).
- Paraneoplastic syndromes associated with HCC may cause hypercalcemia, hypoglycemia, and polycythemia
- Elevated serum HBV DNA level (≥10,000 copies/mL) is a strong risk predictor of HCC independent of HBeAg, serum aminotransferase level, and liver cirrhosis

IMAGING STUDIES
Ultrasound (US), CT scan (Fig. 1H-28), or MRI. Ultrasound is most commonly used as a screening test for HCC in high-risk patients every 6 months. Fig. E1H-29 shows a laparoscopic view of a cirrhotic liver with a nodular hepatoma.

The following imaging modalities are recommended based on US findings:
- Hepatic lesion <1 cm needs to be followed with a repeat US every 3 months to ensure

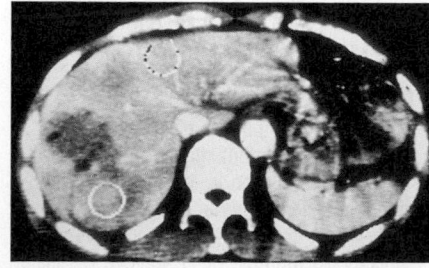

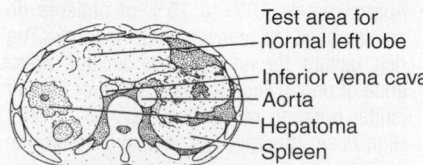

FIGURE 1H-28 Hepatoma. CT scan shows a diffuse lesion in the right lobe of an otherwise normal liver. (From Skarin AT: *Atlas of diagnostic oncology,* ed 3, St Louis, 2003, Mosby.)

the lesion does not change in size. If stable for 24 months, the interval for US can be increased back to every 6 months.
- Hepatic lesion >1 cm needs further confirmatory imaging with either a CT scan or a MRI scan. If the chosen imaging modality shows characteristics typical of HCC (hypervascular in the arterial phase with washout in the portal venous or delayed phase) the diagnosis of HCC is confirmed with no need for additional diagnostic testing or biopsy. If the imaging modality is inconclusive or atypical for HCC then the alternate imaging test must be performed. If the second imaging modality is also inconclusive, an image-guided biopsy is recommended.

BIOPSY: Percutaneous biopsy under ultrasound or CT scan is obtained in the event that imaging studies are nondiagnostic or atypical for HCC, or if no cirrhosis is present. Negative biopsy results should be followed and the hepatic nodule reassessed every 3 to 6 months until it is no longer seen, enlarges, or shows diagnostic characteristics.

SCREENING: Screening high-risk patients with US every 6 months is currently recommended to identify early-stage HCC. The use of AFP in addition to US is debatable; though it does increase detection rate it also increases false-positive results. The use of AFP alone should be discouraged due to limited sensitivity and specificity. Patients on transplant waiting lists should be regularly screened for HCC because in the U.S. the development of HCC gives increased priority for liver transplantation. Screening for HCC is recommended in the following groups:
- Hepatitis B carriers (HBsAg positive): Asian males >40 years, Asian females >50 years, all cirrhotic hepatitis B carriers, family history of HCC and North American blacks/Africans older than age 20 years
- Cirrhosis (nonhepatitis B): hepatitis C, alcoholic cirrhosis, hemochromatosis, primary biliary cirrhosis, and possibly α1-antitrypsin deficiency, autoimmune hepatitis, and nonalcoholic steatohepatitis

STAGING: The commonly used Barcelona Clinic Liver Cancer (BCLC) staging system includes patient performance status, cancer symptoms, number and size of nodules, and liver function. Treatment is determined according to stage:
- Early stage (A): asymptomatic single tumor 5 cm or 3 nodules, each ≤3 cm (
- Intermediate stage (B): patients with tumors that exceed early criteria but do not yet show cancer-related symptoms, vascular invasion, or metastases
- Advanced stage (C): patients with mild cancer-related symptoms and/or vascular invasion or extrahepatic spread
- End-stage (D): patients with advanced, symptomatic disease

TREATMENT

- Fig. 1H-30 describes a treatment algorithm for HCC.
- Early stage: curative treatment (surgical resection or liver transplantation). Patients who have

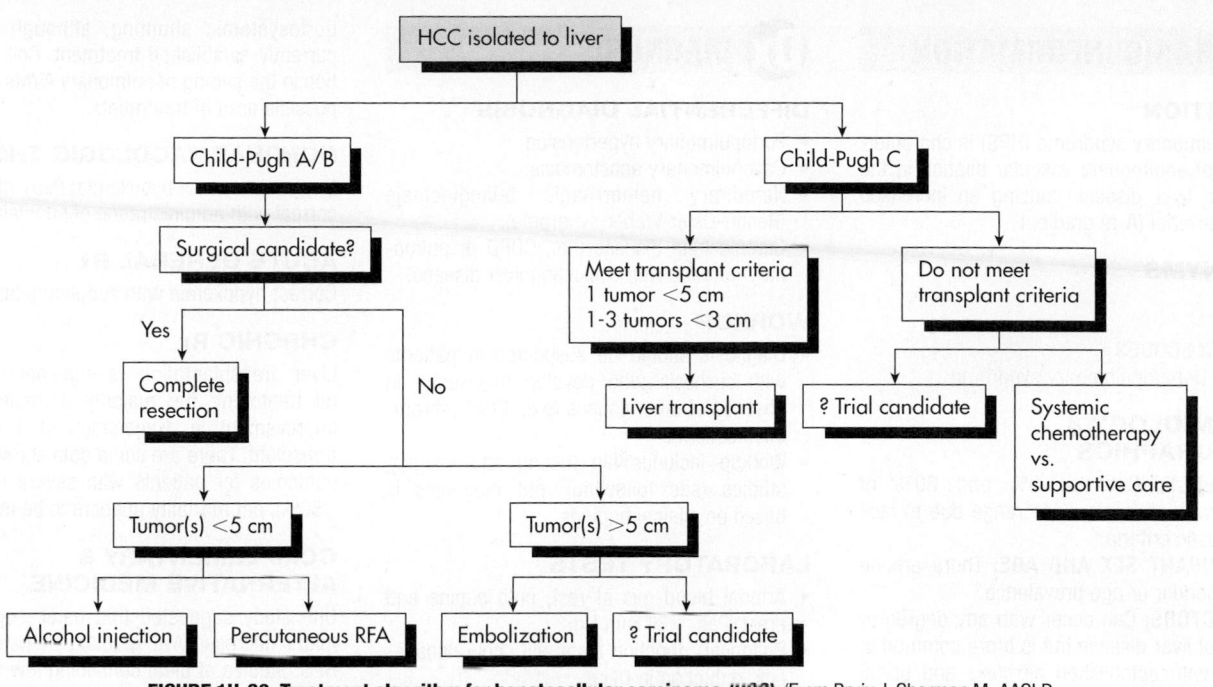

FIGURE 1H-30 Treatment algorithm for hepatocellular carcinoma (HCC). (From Druix J, Sherman M. AASLD practice guideline. Management of hepatocellular carcinoma: An update. *Hepatology* 53(3):1020-1022, 2011.)

TABLE 1H-21 Milan Criteria of Eligibility for Liver Transplantation

Presence of a tumor ≤5 cm in diameter in patients with single hepatocellular carcinomas
Or
≤3 tumor nodules, each 3 cm or less in diameter, in patients with multiple tumors

From Cameron JL, Cameron AM: *Current surgical therapy*, ed 10, Philadelphia, 2011, Saunders.

---

a single lesion can be offered surgical resection if they are non-cirrhotic or have cirrhosis with well-preserved liver function, normal bilirubin, and no significant portal hypertension. Liver transplantation is an effective option for patients with HCC corresponding to the Milan criteria (Table 1H-21). Living donor transplantation can be offered for HCC if the waiting time is expected to be long. Local ablation is safe and effective therapy for patients who cannot undergo resection or as a bridge to transplantation. With these options, survival at 5 year ranges from 50% to 70%. Radiofrequency ablation (RFA) is used in patients with early HCC who are not surgical candidates, and very high local control rates at 2 years are obtained (>90%), but eventual recurrence rates can approach 70% at 5 years.
- Intermediate stage: Transarterial chemoembolization (TACE) is recommended as first-line, noncurative therapy for nonsurgical patients with large/multifocal HCC who do not have vascular invasion or extrahepatic spread. More recently, transarterial use of selective internal radiation therapy (SIRT) with yttrium-90 radiolabeled glass microspheres is an alternative to traditional TACE approaches in this setting. Median survivals exceed 2 years.
- Advanced stage: Palliative therapy or clinical trials are used in this stage. Sorafenib, an oral multikinase inhibitor, is the standard

of care and has been shown to improve overall survival. The effectiveness has been demonstrated in patients with Child-Pugh A cirrhosis and the greatest benefit is seen in patients with hepatitis C related HCC. Doxorubicin chemotherapy may be considered, although survival benefits are unclear.
- End stage: palliative care.

DISPOSITION
- For resectable HCC, the 5-year survival after liver transplantation is 50% to 70% and 30% to 50% with surgical resection. For unresectable HCC, the overall prognosis is poor.
- Tumor size is an independent prognostic factor for resected small HCC (≤50 mm in diameter). Patients with tumors of 0-35 mm diameter have a better 60-month HCC specific survival rate than do those with larger tumors (36-50 mm).[1]
- In the U.S. the 5-year overall survival rate for HCC is 10% to 12%.

REFERRAL
Multidisciplinary gastrointestinal cancer team for treatment planning

---

[1]Zhang W, et al.: Effect of Tumor Size on Cancer-Specific Survival in Small Hepatocellular Carcinoma, *Mayo Clin Proc* 90(9):1187–1195, 2015.

! PEARLS & CONSIDERATIONS

PREVENTION
- Universal hepatitis B vaccination in children in endemic areas has been shown to decrease the incidence of HCC.
- Treatment of patients with chronic hepatitis B–associated cirrhosis with lamivudine reduces the incidence of HCC. Treatment with entecavir in chronic hepatitis B-HCC can improve hepatic function and MELD score.
- Treatment with interferon-based therapy in patients with noncirrhotic hepatitis C reduces risk of HCC in patients demonstrating a sustained viral response
- HCC screening is recommended in high-risk patients because curative therapies are available only for small and early HCC.
- Patients diagnosed with HCC with an AFP >1000 are at increased risk for recurrence after transplantation regardless of tumor size.
- There are numerous ongoing trials with new tyrosine kinase inhibitors and monoclonal antibodies for advanced HCC in patients who are intolerant or resistant to sorafenib. The future of therapy for advanced HCC will likely lead to the personalized combination of multiple agents targeting different oncogenic pathways to optimize treatment success.

SUGGESTED READINGS
Available at www.expertconsult.com

RELATED CONTENT
Liver Cancer (Patient Information)

AUTHOR: **BHARTI RATHORE, M.D.**

BASIC INFORMATION

DEFINITION

Hepatopulmonary syndrome (HPS) is characterized by intrapulmonary vascular dilation in the setting of liver disease causing an increased alveolar-arterial (A-a) gradient.

SYNONYMS

HPS

ICD-10CM CODES
K76.81 Hepatopulmonary syndrome

EPIDEMIOLOGY & DEMOGRAPHICS

PREVALENCE: Between 5% and 30% of patients with cirrhosis; wide range due to lack of diagnostic criteria.
PREDOMINANT SEX AND AGE: There are no data on gender or age prevalence.
RISK FACTORS: Can occur with any degree or etiology of liver disease but is more common in patients with established cirrhosis and portal hypertension. There is no clear relationship between severity of hepatic dysfunction and level of hypoxemia. One recent study suggests that HPS is more common in patients with history of viral hepatitis than in patients with alcoholic cirrhosis.
GENETICS: There are new data suggesting that genes involved in the regulation of angiogenesis are associated with the risk of HPS.

PHYSICAL FINDINGS & CLINICAL PRESENTATION

- Dyspnea.
- Platypnea: worsened dyspnea when sitting upright compared with supine position due to further ventilation-perfusion mismatch.
- Orthodeoxia: decreased Pao_2 when the patient is sitting upright compared with supine position due to ventilation-perfusion mismatch.
- Spider angiomata seen in high number.
- Signs of severe hypoxemia (e.g., cyanosis and clubbing of the digits).

ETIOLOGY

Dilation of intrapulmonary arterioles and dilated vascular channels between pulmonary arteries and veins leading to a ventilation-perfusion mismatch and right-to-left shunting (Fig. E1H-31). Research shows that nitric oxide plays a role in vasodilation. The relationship of vasodilation to liver disease is unclear. New areas of research include endothelin-1, which is produced by proliferating cholangiocytes, pulmonary angiogenesis, and opiate receptors' influence on NO production.

 **DIAGNOSIS**

DIFFERENTIAL DIAGNOSIS

- Portopulmonary hypertension.
- Cavopulmonary anastomosis.
- Hereditary hemorrhagic telangiectasia (Rendu-Osler-Weber syndrome).
- Chronic lung disease (i.e., COPD or pulmonary fibrosis) with coexisting liver disease.

WORKUP

- Diagnosis should be suspected in patients with cirrhosis who develop hypoxemia in absence of other causes (e.g., COPD, thromboembolism).
- Workup includes lab testing and imaging studies (see following), but diagnosis is based on clinical findings.

LABORATORY TESTS

- Arterial blood gas at rest, both supine and erect; Pao_2 <80 mm Hg.
- Pulmonary function tests will show nonspecific reduction in DLco.

There is new evidence showing that blood testing for elevated von Willenbrand factor antigen is a good screening test for HPS because it is a surrogate marker for endothelial dysfunction.

IMAGING STUDIES

- The most effective screening tool is transthoracic echocardiogram with bubble study to rule out right-to-left cardiac shunt; microbubble opacification in left atrium shows vasodilation of pulmonary vascular bed.
- Chest x-ray may show nonspecific bibasilar interstitial pattern.
- Scintigraphic perfusion scanning: technetium-99m–labeled albumin found in brain or spleen indicates dilated pulmonary vasculature or cardiac right-to-left shunt.
- Pulmonary angiography rarely used unless there is potential to embolize arteriovenous malformation (AVM).

TREATMENT

Ideal treatment would be targeted against pulmonary vasodilation. Most medications have targeted NO production, the activity of NO synthase or endothelin-1, pulmonary angiogenesis, or even bacterial translocation, but no controlled trials exist. Liver transplantation is the only successful treatment, which leads to improvement in gas exchange or complete resolution in gas exchange in the majority of patients. However, severe hypoxemia with Pao_2 <50 has been associated with a high posttransplant mortality. Some studies have shown benefit of transjugular

portosystemic shunting, although it is not currently established treatment. Coil embolization in the setting of pulmonary AVMs is another possible area of treatment.

NONPHARMACOLOGIC THERAPY

Oxygen to correct hypoxemia; Pao_2 will partially correct with administration of supplemental O_2.

ACUTE GENERAL Rx

Correct hypoxemia with supplemental O_2.

CHRONIC Rx

Liver transplantation is the only successful treatment; the majority of patients show improvement in oxygenation at 1 year post transplant. There are some data showing worse outcomes for patients with severe HPS (PaO_2 <50%), but mortality appears to be improving.

COMPLEMENTARY & ALTERNATIVE MEDICINE

One study suggested that garlic supplements might decrease A-a gradient in patients with HPS. Studies of diets containing low amount of L-arginine have not shown benefit.

DISPOSITION

The diagnosis of HPS confers a poor prognosis. Patients with HPS have high mortality and shorter median survival than other patients with liver disease, even after adjusting for severity of liver disease. According to one natural history study, compared with patients with similar severity of liver disease and comorbidities whose 5-yr survival was estimated at 63%, those patients with the diagnosis of HPS had a 5 yr survival rate of 23%.

REFERRAL

- Referral to pulmonologist to help in establishing diagnosis.
- Referral to a liver transplant center.

PEARLS & CONSIDERATIONS

COMMENTS

Consider the diagnosis of HPS in patients with cirrhosis who present with dyspnea without signs of pulmonary edema from fluid overload.

SUGGESTED READINGS
Available at www.expertconsult.com.

RELATED CONTENT

Cirrhosis (Related Key Topic)

AUTHOR: **BEVIN KENNEY, M.D.**

BASIC INFORMATION

DEFINITION

Hepatorenal syndrome (HRS) is a condition in which severe liver dysfunction leads to increased production or activity of vasodilators. Vasodilation is more pronounced in the splanchnic circulation, and this leads to intense renal vasoconstriction, hypoperfusion, and a decline in kidney function (see Fig. 1H-32).

There are two types of HRS (see Table 1H-22):
1. Type 1: progressive impairment in renal function as defined by a doubling of initial serum creatinine >2.5 mg/dl in <2 weeks
2. Type 2: stable or slowly progressive impairment of renal function not meeting the previous criterion.

SYNONYMS

Hepatic nephropathy
Oliguric renal failure of cirrhosis
HRS

ICD-10CM CODES
K76.7 Hepatorenal syndrome

EPIDEMIOLOGY & DEMOGRAPHICS

The probability of HRS in cirrhotic patients is 18% at 1 year and 39% at 5 years. HRS is associated with poor prognosis. HRS type 1 is associated with more than 90% mortality rate in 3 months, and HRS type 2 is associated with a 30% mortality rate within 3 months and 60% in 1 year.

PHYSICAL FINDINGS & CLINICAL PRESENTATION

There are no specific physical findings associated with HRS, although it is usually associated with symptoms of acute or chronic decompensated liver failure such as jaundice, spider angiomas, splenomegaly, ascites, fetor hepaticus, pedal edema, asterixes, encephalopathy, or coma. Usually HRS is associated with oliguria and bland urine sediment. However, a nonoliguric state or an active (blood and/or protein) urine sediment does not exclude the diagnosis of HRS.

PRECIPITANTS

Precipitating events are identified in 70% to 100% of cases of HRS. Contributory factors include bacterial infection, alcoholic hepatitis, and GI bleeding. By definition, overdiuresis or large and rapid fluid removal does not cause HRS because HRS is a condition in which volume depletion is not present or has been treated appropriately (see "Treatment"). Unlike HRS, prerenal azotemia, irrespective of its etiology (diuretics or fluid removal), improves with the cessation of the therapy and/or fluid repletion. Nevertheless, HRS may present in the absence of a clear precipitating factor.

DIAGNOSIS

HRS is a diagnosis of exclusion. Tables 1H-23 and 1H-24 summarize the classic and the revised diagnostic criteria for HRS.

DIFFERENTIAL DIAGNOSIS

- Prerenal azotemia: must be excluded or treated appropriately before establishing HRS. HRS typically responds positively to volume expansion and cessation of diuretic therapy, if present. Prerenal conditions and HRS are often associated with low fractional excretions of sodium (FENa) <1%.

- Acute tubular necrosis: urine sodium >30 mEq/L, FENa >1.5%, urine-to-plasma creatinine ratio <30, urine-to-plasma osmolality ratio = 1, urine sediment reveals brown casts and cellular debris and no significant response to sustained plasma expansion.
- Other: Renal artery or vein thrombosis, cardiorenal syndrome, urinary tract obstruction, and drug toxicity from drugs, organic solvents, heavy metals, heme pigments, and intravenous contrast medium.

WORKUP

Acute azotemia and oliguria in the setting of liver disease requires laboratory evaluation to differentiate HRS from acute tubular necrosis.

TABLE 1H-22 Definition of Hepatorenal Syndrome Type 1 and Type 2

Type 1 Hepatorenal Syndrome

Doubling of serum creatinine >2.5 mg/dl (220 μmol/L) or a 50% reduction in 24-hour creatinine clearance to <20 ml/min in <2 weeks
Frequently follows a precipitating event (e.g., infection)
Median survival without treatment is 2 weeks

Type 2 Hepatorenal Syndrome

Less rapid renal functional deterioration than type 1
Mainly presents with refractory ascites
Median survival without treatment is 4–6 months

From Floege J et al: *Comprehensive clinical nephrology,* ed 4, Philadelphia, 2010, Saunders.

TABLE 1H-23 Diagnostic Criteria for Hepatorenal Syndrome

Major Criteria

Chronic or acute liver disease with advanced hepatic failure and portal hypertension
Low glomerular filtration rate, as indicated by serum creatinine >1.5 mg/dl (135 μmol/L) or 24-hour creatinine clearance <40 ml/min
Absence of shock, ongoing bacterial infection, and current or recent treatment with nephrotoxic drugs
Absence of gastrointestinal fluid losses (repeated vomiting or intense diarrhea)
Absence of renal fluid losses (weight loss >500 g/day for several days in patients with ascites without peripheral edema or 1000 g/day in patients with peripheral edema)
No sustained improvement in renal function (decrease in serum creatinine to 1.5 mg/dl [135 μmol/L] or less or increase in creatinine clearance to 40 ml/min or more) following diuretic withdrawal and expansion of plasma volume with 1.5 liters of isotonic saline
Proteinuria <500 mg/day and no ultrasonographic evidence of obstructive uropathy or parenchymal renal disease

Additional Criteria

Urine volume <500 ml/day
Urine sodium <10 mmol/L
Urine osmolality greater than plasma osmolality
Urine red blood cells <50 per high-power field
Serum sodium concentration <130 mmol/L

From Floege J et al: *Comprehensive clinical nephrology,* ed 4, Philadelphia, 2010, Saunders.

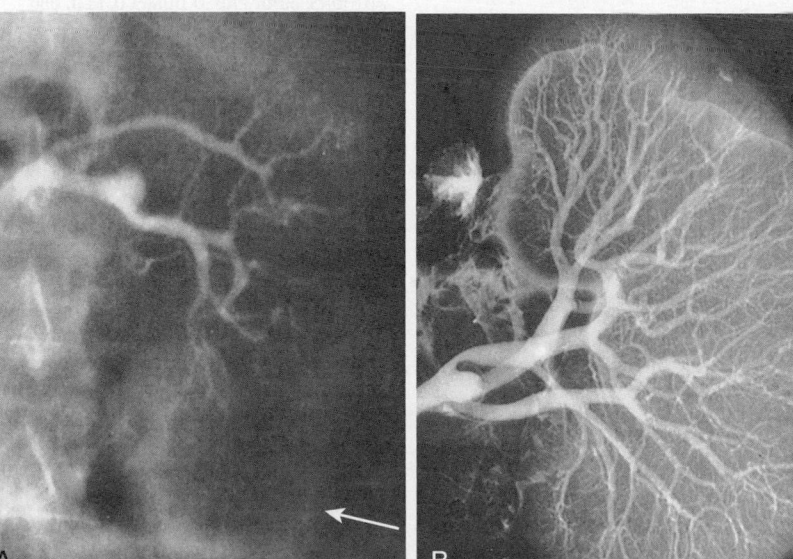

FIGURE 1H-32 Hepatorenal syndrome (HRS). A, Renal angiogram (the *arrow* marks edge of the kidney). **B,** Angiogram carried out in the same kidney at autopsy. Note complete filling of the renal arterial system throughout the vascular bed to the periphery of the cortex. The vascular attenuation and tortuosity of **A** are no longer present. The vessels are also histologically normal. This indicates the functional nature of the vascular abnormality in HRS. (From Floege J et al: *Comprehensive clinical nephrology,* ed 4, Philadelphia, 2010, Saunders.)

TABLE 1H-24 Revised Diagnostic Criteria for Hepatorenal Syndrome

Cirrhosis with ascites

Serum creatinine >1.5 mg/dl (133 μmol/L)

No improvement in serum creatinine (decrease to a level of 1.5 mg/dl) after at least 2 days with diuretic withdrawal and volume expansion with albumin. The recommended dose of albumin is 1 g/kg of body weight per day up to a maximum of 100 g/day.

Absence of shock

No current or recent treatment with nephrotoxic drugs

Absence of parenchymal kidney disease as indicated by proteinuria >500 mg/day, microhematuria (>50 red blood cells per high-power field) and/or abnormal renal ultrasound

From Floege J et al: *Comprehensive clinical nephrology*, ed 4, Philadelphia, 2010, Saunders.

Extracellular fluid volume challenge may be required to differentiate HRS from prerenal azotemia. Rule out concurrent bacterial infection.

LABORATORY TESTS

- Serum electrolytes, blood urea nitrogen, creatinine, osmolality.
- Urinalysis, urinary sodium, urinary creatinine, urine osmolality.
- FENa will not adequately differentiate between HRS from other common etiologies associated with kidney failure in liver dysfunction. Only a minority of patients with HRS have high urine sodium values
- Urine sodium <10 mEq/L, FENa <1%, urine-to-plasma creatinine ratio >30, urine plasma-to-urine osmolality ratio >1.5, bland urine sediment.

IMAGING STUDIES

Kidney, bladder, and ureter ultrasound may be indicated if obstructive uropathy is suspected. CT scans may be required to diagnose occult infection(s), and prophylaxis directed at preventing contrast-induced nephropathy is recommended.

 **TREATMENT**

ACUTE GENERAL Rx

- Avoidance of precipitating factors and their appropriate therapy are cornerstones of HRS management.
- Improvement in liver function from partial resolution of the primary disorder or successful liver transplantation is the optimal treatment. Liver transplantation leads to resolution of HRS type 1 in 76% of cases.
- Splanchnic vasoconstrictor agents (e.g., terlipressin, norepinephrine, midodrine).
- Ornipressin prevents further deterioration of renal function in patients awaiting liver transplantation.
- Dopamine and prostaglandins are generally ineffective in treating patients with HRS.

PHARMACOLOGIC THERAPY

CRITICALLY ILL PATIENTS: Patients admitted to a critical intensive care unit should be adequately volume resuscitated and treated with systemic vasoconstriction agents in the following manner:

a. Norepinephrine (0.5-3.0 mg/hr IV) or

b. Terlipressin* (0.2-2.0 mg IV every 4-12 hours, with a maximum dosage of 12 mg daily) plus

c. Albumin 1 g/kg IV on day 1 followed by 20 to 40 g daily until discontinuation of norepinephrine or terlipressin or clinical evidence of volume overload

---

*A systematic review of four randomized, controlled trials showed no significant difference in effectiveness between norepinephrine and terlipressin. The latter is more expensive and showed higher incidence of non–life-threatening side effects.

NON–CRITICALLY ILL PATIENTS:

a. Terlipressin* (0.2-2.0 mg IV q4–12h) or

b. Midodrine (7.5 mg PO three times daily, increased to 12.5 mg three times daily if needed) in combination with octreotide 100 μg SC three times a day (increase to 200 μg three times a day if needed) plus

c. Albumin 1 g/kg IV on day 1 followed by 20–40 g daily until discontinuation of terlipressin or midodrine plus octreotide or clinical evidence of volume overload

NONPHARMACOLOGIC THERAPY

- Transjugular, intrahepatic, portosystemic shunts

REFERRAL

Referral for hepatology, nephrology, and liver transplantation as indicated (see "Comments")

❗ PEARLS & CONSIDERATIONS

COMMENTS

Liver transplantation may be indicated in an otherwise healthy patient (age, preferably <65 years) with sclerosing cholangitis, chronic hepatitis with cirrhosis, or primary biliary cirrhosis. Contraindications to liver transplantation are AIDS, most metastatic malignancies, active substance abuse, uncontrolled sepsis, and uncontrolled cardiac or pulmonary disease.

SUGGESTED READINGS

Available at www.expertconsult.com

RELATED CONTENT

Hepatorenal Syndrome (Patient Information)

AUTHORS: **JUAN PABLO DOMECQ, M.D.** and **JERRY YEE, M.D.**

 **BASIC INFORMATION**

DEFINITION

Herpangina is a self-limited upper respiratory tract infection associated with a characteristic vesicular rash on the soft palate.

SYNONYMS

Vesicular stomatitis
Acute lymphonodular pharyngitis

ICD-10CM CODES
B08.5 Enteroviral vesicular pharyngitis

EPIDEMIOLOGY & DEMOGRAPHICS

PREDOMINANT SEX: Male = female.
PREDOMINANT AGE: 3 to 10 yr.

PHYSICAL FINDINGS & CLINICAL PRESENTATION

- Characterized by ulcerating lesions typically located on the soft palate (Fig. 1H-33).
- Usually fewer than six lesions that evolve rapidly from a diffuse pharyngitis to erythematous macules and subsequently to vesicles that are moderately painful.
- Fever, vomiting, and headache in the first few days of illness but subsiding spontaneously.
- Pharyngeal lesions typical for several more days.

ETIOLOGY

- Most cases caused by coxsackie A viruses (most frequently A8, A10, and A16).
- Occasional cases caused by other enteroviruses (echovirus and enterovirus 71).

 **DIAGNOSIS**

DIFFERENTIAL DIAGNOSIS

- Herpes simplex.
- Bacterial pharyngitis.
- Tonsillitis.
- Aphthous stomatitis.
- Hand-foot-mouth disease.

WORKUP

Diagnosis is typically based on characteristic lesions on the soft palate.

LABORATORY TESTS

- Viral and bacterial cultures of the pharynx to exclude herpes simplex infection and streptococcal pharyngitis if the diagnosis is in doubt.
- The type-specific antibodies appear in the blood about 1 week after infection has occurred and attain their maximum titer in 3 weeks.

 **TREATMENT**

- Give symptomatic treatment for sore throat: saline gargles and analgesics, and encourage oral fluids.
- No antiviral therapy indicated; avoid antibacterial agents because they are ineffective, increase cost, might result in side effects, and promote antibiotic resistance.

NONPHARMACOLOGIC THERAPY

Analgesic throat lozenges are helpful in some cases.

ACUTE GENERAL Rx

Antipyretics when indicated.

CHRONIC Rx

Self-limited infection.

DISPOSITION

- Generally, resolution of symptoms within 1 wk.
- Persistence of fever or mouth lesions beyond 1 wk suggestive of an alternative diagnosis (see "Differential Diagnosis").

REFERRAL

For consultation with otolaryngologist or infectious disease specialist if the diagnosis is in doubt.

PEARLS & CONSIDERATIONS

COMMENTS

Household outbreaks may occur, especially during the summer months.

SUGGESTED READINGS

Available at www.expertconsult.com

RELATED CONTENT

Herpangina (Patient Information)

AUTHOR: **GLENN G. FORT, M.D., M.P.H.**

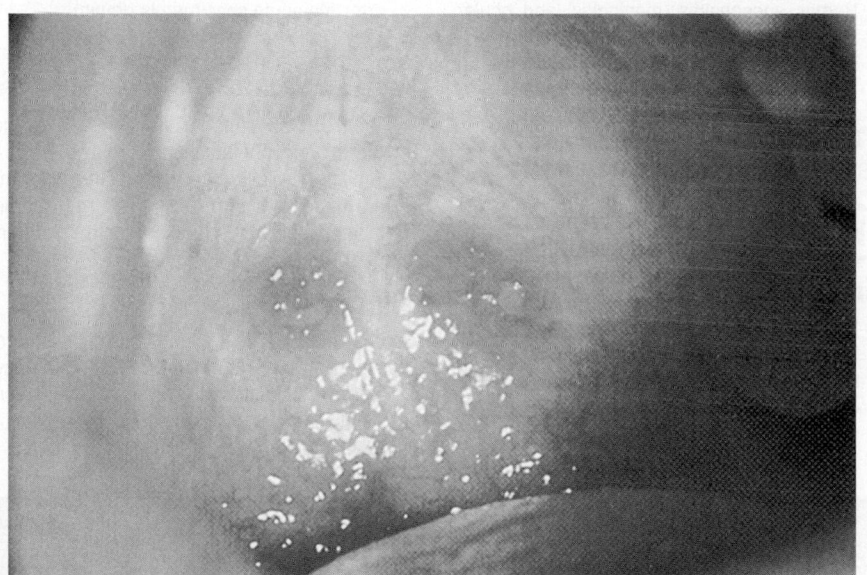

FIGURE 1H-33 Herpangina with shallow ulcers in the roof of the mouth. (Courtesy Marshall Guill, M.D. From Goldstein B [ed]: *Practical dermatology,* ed 2, St Louis, 1997, Mosby.)

BASIC INFORMATION

DEFINITION

Herpes simplex is a viral infection caused by the herpes simplex virus (HSV). HSV-1 is associated primarily with oral infections, and HSV-2 causes mainly genital infections. However, either type can infect any site. After the primary infection, the virus enters the nerve endings in the skin directly below the lesions and ascends to the dorsal root ganglia, where it remains in a latent stage until it is reactivated.

SYNONYMS

Genital herpes
Herpes labialis
Herpes gladiatorum
Herpes digitalis

ICD-10CM CODES

B00.1	Herpesvirus vesicular dermatitis
B00.0	Eczema herpeticum
A60.9	Anogenital herpesviral infection, unspecified
B00.9	Herpesviral infection, unspecified
B00.82	Herpes simplex myelitis
P35.2	Congenital herpesviral [herpes simplex] infection

EPIDEMIOLOGY & DEMOGRAPHICS

- More than 85% of adults have serologic evidence of HSV-1 infection. The seroprevalence of adults with HSV-2 in the United States is 25%; however, only approximately 20% of these persons recall having symptoms of HSV infection.
- Most cases of eye or digital herpetic infections are caused by HSV-1.
- Frequency of recurrence of HSV-2 genital herpes is higher than HSV-1 oral labial infection.
- The frequency of recurrence is lowest for oral labial HSV-2 infections.
- The incidence of complications from herpes simplex (e.g., herpes encephalitis) is highest in immunocompromised hosts.
- Male circumcision significantly reduces the incidence of HSV-2.

PHYSICAL FINDINGS & CLINICAL PRESENTATION

Primary infection
- Symptoms occur from 3 to 7 days after contact (respiratory droplets, direct contact).
- Constitutional symptoms include low-grade fever, headache and myalgias, regional lymphadenopathy, and localized pain.
- Pain, burning, itching, and tingling last several hours.
- Grouped vesicles (Fig. 1H-34), usually with surrounding erythema, appear and generally ulcerate or crust within 48 hr.
- The vesicles are uniform in size (differentiating it from herpes zoster vesicles, which vary in size). Scattered erosions covered with exudate may be noted on genitals (Fig. E1H-35).
- During the acute eruption the patient is uncomfortable; involvement of lips and inside

of mouth may make it unpleasant for the patient to eat; urinary retention may complicate involvement of the genital area.
- Lesions generally last from 2 to 6 wk and heal without scarring.
Recurrent infection:
- Generally caused by alteration in the immune system; fatigue, stress, menses, local skin trauma, and exposure to sunlight are contributing factors.
- The prodromal symptoms (fatigue, burning and tingling of the affected area) last 12 to 24 hr.
- A cluster of lesions generally evolves within 24 hr from a macule to a papule and then vesicles surrounded by erythema; the vesicles coalesce and subsequently rupture within 4 days, revealing erosions covered by crusts.
- The crusts are generally shed within 7 to 10 days, revealing a pink surface.
- The most frequent location of the lesions is on the vermilion border of the lips (HSV-1), the penile shaft or glans penis and the labia (HSV-2), buttocks (seen more frequently in women), fingertips (herpetic whitlow), and trunk (may be confused with herpes zoster).
- Rapid onset of diffuse cutaneous herpes simplex (eczema herpeticum) may occur in certain atopic infants and adults. It is a medical emergency, especially in young infants, and should be promptly treated with acyclovir.
- Herpes encephalitis, meningitis, and ocular herpes can occur in patients with immunocompromised status and occasionally in normal hosts.

ETIOLOGY

HSV-1 and HSV-2 are both DNA viruses.

 DIAGNOSIS

DIFFERENTIAL DIAGNOSIS

- Impetigo.
- Behçet's syndrome.
- Coxsackie virus infection.
- Syphilis.
- Stevens-Johnson syndrome.

- Herpangina.
- Aphthous stomatitis.
- Varicella.
- Herpes zoster.

WORKUP

Diagnosis is based on clinical presentation. Laboratory evaluation confirms diagnosis.

LABORATORY TESTS

- Direct immunofluorescent antibody slide tests provide a rapid diagnosis.
- Viral culture is the most definitive method for diagnosis; results are generally available in 1 or 2 days. The lesions should be sampled during the vesicular or early ulcerative stage; cervical samples should be taken from the endocervix with a swab.
- Tzanck smear is a readily available test that will demonstrate multinucleated giant cells. However, it is not a highly sensitive test.
- Pap smear will detect HSV-infected cells in cervical tissue from women without symptoms.
- Serologic tests for HSV: immunoglobulin (Ig) G and IgM serum antibodies. Antibodies to HSV occur in 50% to 90% of adults. The presence of IgM or a fourfold or greater rise in IgG titers indicates a recent infection (convalescent sample should be drawn 2 to 3 wk after the acute specimen is drawn).

 TREATMENT

- Table 1H-25 summarizes antiviral chemotherapy for HSV infection.
- Topical acyclovir, penciclovir, and docosanol are optional treatments for recurrent herpes labialis, but they are less effective than oral treatments.

DISPOSITION

Most patients recover from the initial episode or recurrences without complications; immunocompromised hosts are at risk for complications (e.g., disseminated herpes simplex infection, herpes encephalitis).

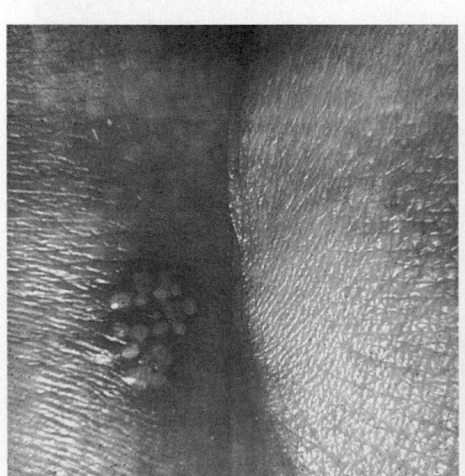
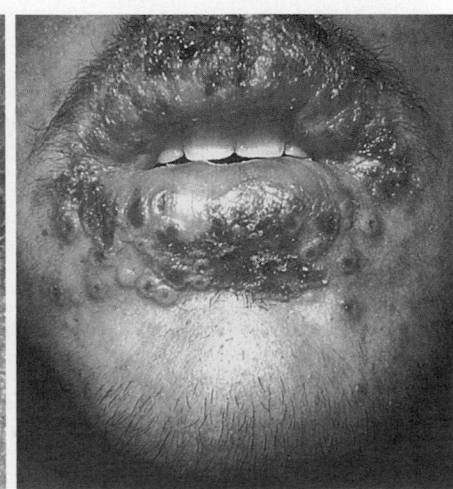

FIGURE 1H-34 Herpes simplex. (From Scuderi G [ed]: *Sports medicine: principles of primary care,* St Louis, 1997, Mosby.)

REFERRAL

- Hospital admission in patients with herpes encephalitis or herpes meningitis and in immunocompromised hosts with diffuse herpes simplex infection.
- Ophthalmology referral in patients with suspected ocular herpes.

PEARLS & CONSIDERATIONS

COMMENTS

- Provide patient education regarding transmission of HSV.
- Condom use offers significant protection against HSV-1 infection in susceptible women.
- Patients should be instructed on the use of condoms for sexual intercourse and on avoiding kissing or sexual intercourse until lesions are crusted. Pericoital application of tenofovir gel, an antiretroviral vaginal gel, has also been shown to reduce the risk of HSV-2 in women. This may be useful in regions of the world where use of condoms is shunned upon.
- Patients should also avoid contact with immunocompromised hosts or neonates while lesions are present.
- Proper handwashing techniques should be explained.
- Patients with herpes gladiatorum (cutaneous herpes in athletes involved in contact sports) should be excluded from participation in active sports until lesions have resolved.
- Many new HSV-2 infections are asymptomatic. Since HSV-2 antibody tests have become commercially available, an increasing number of persons have learned that they have genital herpes through serologic testing. Persons with asymptomatic HSV-2 infection shed virus in the genital tract less frequently than persons with symptomatic infection, but much of the difference is attributable to less frequent genital lesions because generally lesions are accompanied by frequent viral shedding.
- Suppressive treatment of HSV-2 infection lowers the incidence of genital lesions by 70% to 80%, but cuts the rate of HSV-2 transmission to uninfected partners by only 50%.
- Trials involving investigational herpes simplex vaccine have found it to be effective in preventing HSV-1 genital disease and infection, but not in preventing HSV-2 disease or infection.

SUGGESTED READINGS

Available at www.expertconsult.com

RELATED CONTENT

Genital Herpes (Patient Information)
Oral Herpes (Patient Information)

AUTHOR: **FRED F. FERRI, M.D.**

TABLE 1H-25 Antiviral Chemotherapy for Herpes Simplex Virus Infection

Mucocutaneous HSV Infections

Infections in Immunosuppressed Patients

Acute symptomatic first or recurrent episodes: IV acyclovir (5 mg/kg q8h) and oral acyclovir (400 mg qid), famciclovir (500 mg PO tid), or valacyclovir (500 mg PO bid) for 7-10 days are effective. Treatment duration may vary from 7-14 days.

Suppression of reactivation disease: IV acyclovir (5 mg/kg q8h), valacyclovir (500 mg PO bid), or oral acyclovir (400-800 mg 3-5 times per day) prevents recurrences during the immediate 30-day post-transplantation period. Longer-term suppression is often used for persons with continued immunosuppression. In bone marrow and renal transplant recipients, valacyclovir 2 g 4 times daily is also effective in preventing CMV infection. Valacyclovir 4 g 4 times daily has been associated with TTP after extended use in HIV-positive persons. In HIV-infected persons, oral famciclovir (500 mg bid) is effective in reducing clinical and subclinical reactivations of HSV-1 and -2.

Genital Herpes

First episodes: Oral acyclovir (200 mg five times per day or 400 mg tid), oral valacyclovir (1000 mg bid), or famciclovir (250 mg bid) for 10-14 days is effective. IV acyclovir (5 mg/kg q8h for 5 days) is given for severe disease or neurologic complications such as aseptic meningitis.

Symptomatic recurrent genital herpes: Oral acyclovir (200 mg 5 times per day for 5 days, 800 mg PO tid for 2 days), valacyclovir (500 mg bid for 3 or 5 days), or famciclovir (125 mg bid for 5 days). All these therapies are effective in shortening lesion duration.

Suppression of recurrent genital herpes: Oral acyclovir (200-mg capsules bid or tid, 400 mg bid, or 800 mg qd), famciclovir (250 mg bid), or valacyclovir (500 mg or 1000 mg qd or 500 mg bid) prevents symptomatic reactivation. Persons with frequent reactivation (<9 episodes/year) can take 500 mg daily; those with >9 episodes/year should take 1000 mg/daily or 500 mg bid.

Oral-Labial HSV Infections

First episode: Oral acyclovir (200 mg) is given 4 or 5 times per day. Famciclovir (250 mg bid) or valacyclovir (1000 mg bid) has been used clinically.

Recurrent episodes: Valacyclovir 1000 mg bid for 1 day or 500 mg bid for 3 days is effective in reducing pain and speeding healing. Self-initiated therapy with six times daily topical 1% penciclovir cream is effective in speeding the healing of oral-labial HSV; topical acyclovir cream has also been shown to speed healing.

Suppression of reactivation of oral-labial HSV: Oral acyclovir (400 mg bid), if started before exposure and continued for the duration of exposure (usually 5-10 days), prevents reactivation of recurrent oral-labial HSV infection associated with severe sun exposure.

Herpetic Whitlow

Oral acyclovir (200 mg) 5 times daily for 7-10 days.

HSV Proctitis

Oral acyclovir (400 mg five times per day) is useful in shortening the course of infection. In immunosuppressed patients or in patients with severe infection, IV acyclovir (5 mg/kg q8h) may be useful.

Herpetic Eye Infections

In acute keratitis, topical trifluorothymidine, vidarabine, idoxuridine, acyclovir, penciclovir, and interferon are all beneficial. Debridement may be required; topical steroids may worsen disease.

CNS HSV Infections

HSV encephalitis: Intravenous acyclovir (10 mg/kg q8h; 30 mg/kg per day) for 14-21 days is preferred.

HSV aseptic meningitis: No studies of systemic antiviral chemotherapy exist. If therapy is to be given, IV acyclovir (15-30 mg/kg/day) should be used.

Autonomic radiculopathy: No studies are available.

Neonatal HSV infections: Acyclovir (60 mg/kg/day, divided into three doses) is given. The recommended duration of treatment is 21 days. Monitoring for relapse should be undertaken, and some authorities recommend continued suppression with oral acyclovir suspension for 3 to 4 mo.

Visceral HSV Infections

HSV esophagitis: IV acyclovir (15 mg/kg per day). In some patients with milder forms of immunosuppression, oral therapy with valacyclovir or famciclovir is effective.

HSV pneumonitis: No controlled studies exist. IV acyclovir (15 mg/kg per day) should be considered.

Disseminated HSV infections: No controlled studies exist. Intravenous acyclovir (10 mg/kg q8h) nevertheless should be tried. No definite evidence indicates that therapy decreases the risk of death.

Erythema multiforme-associated HSV: Anecdotal observations suggest that oral acyclovir (400 mg bid or tid) or valacyclovir (500 mg bid) suppresses erythema multiforme.

Surgical prophylaxis: Several surgical procedures such as laser skin resurfacing, trigeminal nerve root decompression, and lumbar disk surgery have been associated with HSV reactivation. Intravenous acyclovir (3 mg/kg) and oral acyclovir 800 mg bid, valacyclovir 500 mg bid, or famciclovir 250 mg bid is effective in reducing reactivation. Therapy should be initiated 48 hours before surgery and continued for 3-7 days.

Infections with acyclovir-resistant HSV: Foscarnet (40 mg/kg IV q8h) should be given until lesions heal. The optimal duration of therapy and the usefulness of its continuation to suppress lesions are unclear. Some patients may benefit from cutaneous application of trifluorothymidine or 5% cidofovir gel.

CMV, Cytomegalovirus; *CNS*, central nervous system; *HIV*, human immunodeficiency virus; *HSV*, herpes simplex virus; *TTP*, thrombotic thrombocytopenic purpura.
From Mandell GL et al: *Principles and practice of infectious diseases*, ed 6, Philadelphia, 2005, Churchill Livingstone.

ℹ️ BASIC INFORMATION

DEFINITION
Herpes zoster is a disease caused by reactivation of the varicella-zoster virus, with spread of the virus alone from the sensory nerve to the dermatome. After the primary infection (chickenpox), the virus becomes latent in the dorsal root ganglia and reemerges when there is a weakening of the immune system (as a result of disease or advanced age).

SYNONYMS
Shingles
HZ

ICD-10CM CODES
B02 Herpes zoster
B02.7 Disseminated zoster
B02.8 Zoster with other complications
B02.9 Zoster without complications
B02.39 Other herpes zoster eye disease
B02.0 Zoster encephalitis
B02.1 Zoster meningitis
B02.30 Zoster ocular disease, unspecified
B02.31 Zoster conjunctivitis
B02.32 Zoster iridocyclitis
B02.33 Zoster keratitis
B02.34 Zoster scleritis
B02.39 Other herpes zoster eye disease

EPIDEMIOLOGY & DEMOGRAPHICS
- Herpes zoster occurs during the lifetime of 10% to 20% of the population.
- There is an increased incidence in immunocompromised patients (AIDS, malignancy), the elderly, and children who acquired chickenpox when younger than 2 mo.

PHYSICAL FINDINGS & CLINICAL PRESENTATION
- Pain generally precedes skin manifestation by 3 to 5 days and is generally localized to the dermatome that will be affected by the skin lesions.
- Constitutional symptoms are often present (malaise, fever, headache).
- The initial rash consists of erythematous maculopapules generally affecting one dermatome (thoracic region in majority of cases [Fig. 1H-36]). Typically the rash does not cross the midline. Some patients (<30%) may have scattered vesicles outside the affected dermatome. In rare cases the rash can be generalized (Fig. 1H-37).
- The initial maculopapules evolve into vesicles and pustules by the third or the fourth day.
- The vesicles have an erythematous base (Fig. 1H-38), are cloudy, and have various sizes (a distinguishing characteristic from herpes simplex, in which the vesicles are of uniform size) and may have a classic appearance of grouped vesicles (Fig. H1-39).
- The vesicles subsequently become umbilicated and then form crusts that generally fall off within 3 wk; scarring may occur.

- Pain during and after the rash is generally significant. Post-herpetic neuralgia occurs after herpes zoster in approximately one third of patients aged 60 years and older and can persist for months or years.
- Secondary bacterial infection with *Staphylococcus aureus* or *Streptococcus pyogenes* may occur.
- Regional lymphadenopathy may occur.
- Herpes zoster may involve the trigeminal nerve (most frequent cranial nerve involved); involvement of the geniculate ganglion can cause facial palsy and a painful ear, with the presence of vesicles on the pinna and external auditory canal (Ramsay Hunt syndrome).

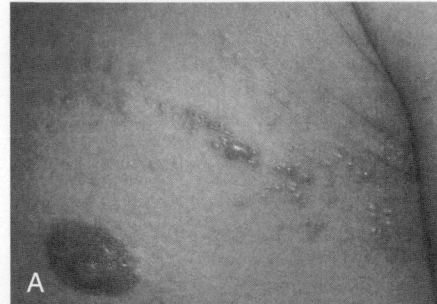
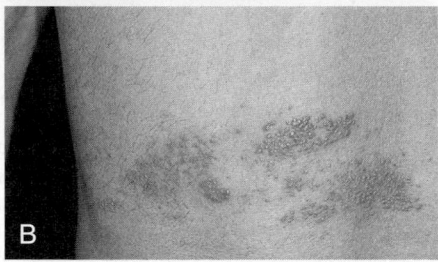

FIGURE 1H-36 A and **B,** Herpes zoster lesions in T3 distribution. (From Swartz, MH: *Textbook of physical diagnosis*, ed 7, Philadelphia, 2014, Saunders.)

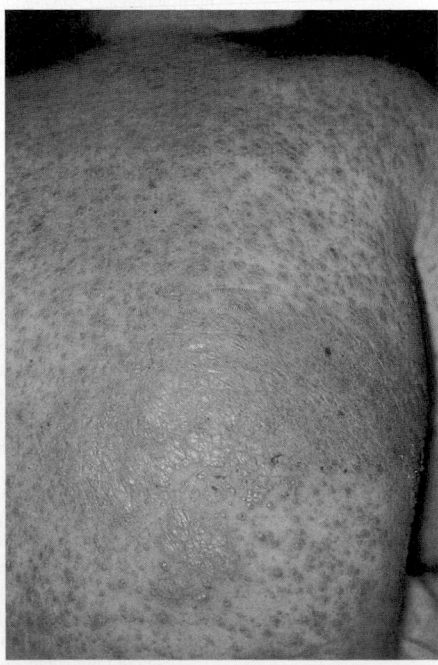

FIGURE 1H-37 Herpes zoster, generalized. (From Swartz, MH: *Textbook of physical diagnosis*, ed 7, Philadelphia, 2014, Saunders.)

ETIOLOGY
Reactivation of varicella virus (human herpes virus III)

🆁 DIAGNOSIS

DIFFERENTIAL DIAGNOSIS
- Rash: herpes simplex and other viral infections
- Pain from herpes zoster: may be confused with acute myocardial infarction, pulmonary embolism, pleuritis, pericarditis, renal colic

LABORATORY TESTS
Laboratory tests are generally not necessary (viral cultures and Tzanck smear will confirm diagnosis in patients with atypical presentation).

🆁 TREATMENT

NONPHARMACOLOGIC THERAPY
- Wet compresses (using Burow's solution or cool tap water) applied for 15 to 30 min five to 10 times a day are useful to break vesicles and remove serum and crust.
- Care must be taken to prevent any secondary bacterial infection.

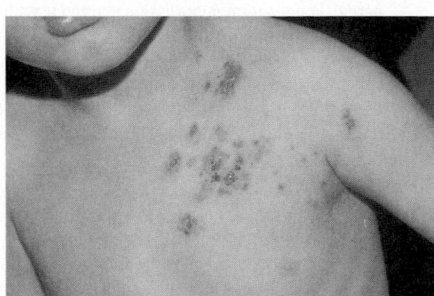

FIGURE 1H-38 Herpes zoster occurred in this 3-year-old. She had chickenpox at age 18 months. The varicella-zoster virus causes both conditions. Spontaneous resolution can be expected. (From White GM, Cox NH [eds]: *Diseases of the skin, a color atlas and text,* ed 2, St Louis, 2006, Mosby.)

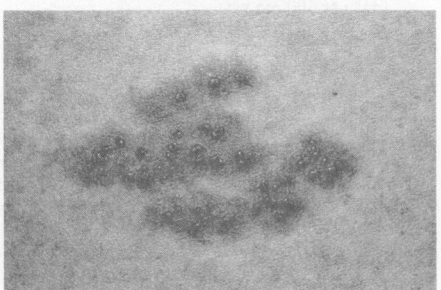

FIGURE 1H-39 Herpes zoster. Classic appearance of grouped vesicles. (From White GM, Cox NH [eds]: *Diseases of the skin, a color atlas and text,* ed 2, St Louis, 2006, Mosby.)

ACUTE GENERAL Rx

- Oral antiviral agents can decrease acute pain, inflammation, and vesicle formation when treatment is begun within 48 hr of onset of rash. Treatment options are:
  1. Valacyclovir 1000 mg tid for 7 days
  2. Famciclovir 500 mg tid for 7 days
  3. Acyclovir 800 mg 5 times daily for 7 to 10 days
- Corticosteroids should be considered in older patients within 72 hr of clinical presentation or if new lesions are still appearing if there are no contraindications. Initial dose is prednisone 40 mg/day decreased by 5 mg/day until finished. When used there is a decrease in the use of analgesics and time to resumption of usual activities, but there is no effect on the incidence and duration of postherpetic neuralgia.
- Immunocompromised patients should be treated with IV acyclovir 500 mg/m^2 or 10 mg/kg q8h in 1-hr infusions for 7 days, with close monitoring of renal function and adequate hydration; vidarabine (continuous 12-hr infusion of 10 mg/kg/day for 7 days) is also effective for treatment of disseminated herpes zoster in immunocompromised hosts.
- Patients with AIDS and transplant recipients may develop acyclovir-resistant varicella-zoster; these patients can be treated with foscarnet (40 mg/kg IV q8h) continued for at least 10 days or until lesions are completely healed.
- Postherpetic neuralgia
  1. Gabapentin 100 to 600 mg tid is effective in the treatment of pain and sleep interference associated with postherpetic neuralgia. Other effective agents are pregabalin, duloxetine, and tricyclic antidepressants.

2. Lidocaine patch 5% is also effective in relieving postherpetic neuralgia. Patches are applied to intact skin after resolution of blisters and crusts to cover the most painful area for up to 12 hr within a 24-hr period.
3. Capsaicin cream can be useful for treatment of postherpetic neuralgia. It is generally applied 3 to 5 times daily for several weeks after the crusts have fallen off. A topical 8% patch formulation of capsaicin is now available by prescription for postherpetic neuralgia.
4. Sympathetic blocks (stellate ganglion or epidural) with 0.25% bupivacaine and rhizotomy are reserved for severe cases unresponsive to conservative treatment.

DISPOSITION

- The incidence of postherpetic neuralgia (defined as pain that persists more than 90 days after onset of rash) increases with age (<30% by age 40 yr, >70% by age 70 yr); antivirals reduce the risk of postherpetic neuralgia.
- Incidence of disseminated herpes zoster is increased in immunocompromised hosts (e.g., 15% to 50% of patients with active Hodgkin's disease).
- Immunocompromised hosts are also more prone to neurologic complications (encephalitis, myelitis, cranial and peripheral nerve palsies, acute retinal necrosis). The mortality rate is 10% to 20% in immunocompromised hosts with disseminated zoster.
- Motor neuropathies occur in 5% of all cases of zoster; complete recovery occurs in >70% of patients.
- Rates of HZ recurrence are more frequent than previously reported and are comparable

to rates of first HZ occurrence in immunocompetent individuals.

REFERRAL

- Hospitalization for IV acyclovir in patients with disseminated herpes zoster.
- Patients with herpes zoster ophthalmicus should be referred to an ophthalmologist.
- Vaccination: In the absence of the herpes zoster vaccine, persons who live to 85 yr of age have a 50% risk of herpes zoster. Immunocompetent adults ≥60 yr are appropriate candidates for a single dose of varicella-zoster vaccine (VZV) whether or not they have had a previous episode of herpes zoster. Immunization with VZV (Zostavax) boosts waning immunity in older adults and reduces the severity and duration of pain caused by herpes zoster by 61%. Adults who are VZV seronegative (never had varicella) should be immunized against varicella with two doses of varicella vaccine (Varivax). Despite its efficacy and safety, use of this vaccine remains low (<8% of potential recipients).

 **EVIDENCE**

Available at www.expertconsult.com

SUGGESTED READINGS

Available at www.expertconsult.com

RELATED CONTENT

Shingles (Patient Information)
Post-Herpetic Neuralgia (Related Key Topic)

AUTHOR: **FRED F. FERRI, M.D.**

Diseases and Disorders

I

BASIC INFORMATION

DEFINITION

Hidradenitis suppurativa (HS) is a chronic, relapsing suppurative cutaneous disease affecting skin that bears apocrine glands and manifested by abscesses, fistulating sinus tracts, and chronic infection leading to scarring.

SYNONYMS

Acne inversa
Apocrinitis
Verneuil's disease
HS

ICD-10CM CODES

L73.2 Hidradenitis suppurativa

EPIDEMIOLOGY & DEMOGRAPHICS

Onset is postpubertal, with an average age of onset of 23 yr; rates decline after age 55 yr.
PREVALENCE: Overall prevalence in the United States is ~1% to 2%.
PREDOMINANT SEX: Female to male ratio is 3:1.
PREDOMINANT AGE: HS most often manifests after puberty, usually in the second or third decade of life. It is rare in the elderly.
RISK FACTORS:
- Obesity and metabolic syndrome.
- Family history (approximately 30%).
- Hyperandrogenism in women.
- Cigarette smoking.

PHYSICAL FINDINGS & CLINICAL PRESENTATION

The diagnosis is primarily clinical based on the development of typical lesions in a characteristic distribution, with a relapsing nature. The course of HS is prolonged and marked by intermittent periods of activity and remission.
- Early symptoms include pain, itching, burning, erythema, and hyperhidrosis.
- Typical lesions include:
  1. Painful erythematous papules and nodules leading to painful abscesses with foul-smelling discharge.
  2. Dermal contractures and ropelike elevation of the skin.
  3. Comedones in the apocrine, gland-bearing skin.
- Classified into Hurley Stages
  1. Stage I: abscesses without sinus tracts or scarring.
  2. Stage II: multiple abscesses plus sinus tracts and scarring.
  3. Stage III: diffuse involvement of entire area with abscesses, sinus tracts, and scarring.
- The axilla is the most common site (Fig. 1H-43).
- Less common sites include the inguinal region, the breasts more often in women, and the perineal or perianal skin more often in men.
- There is a strong tendency toward relapse and recurrence.

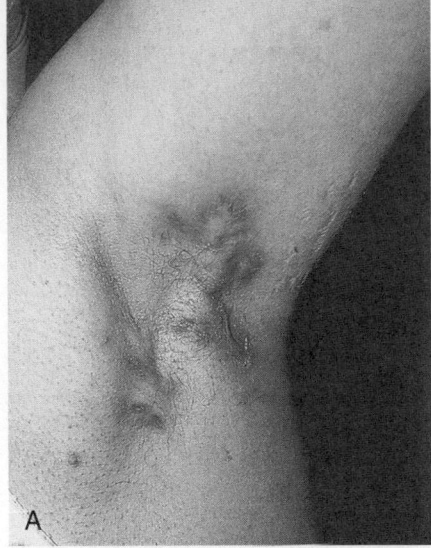

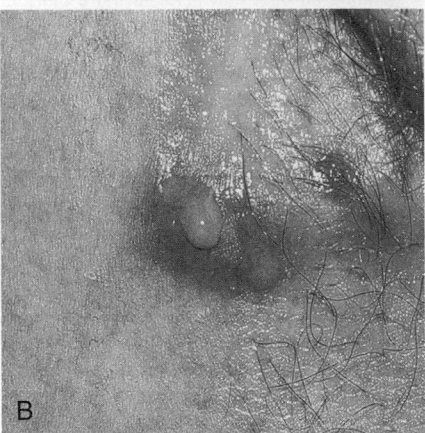

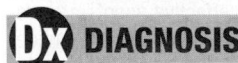

FIGURE 1H-43 Hidradenitis suppurativa (HS). A, HS of the axilla. This is the classic appearance with inflammatory nodules and scarred areas. This condition is commonly misdiagnosed as a bacterial infection. **B,** HS of the axilla; a close-up view of the draining pus. When intact, the lesions represent sterile abscesses. Once open, they may become secondarily infected. (From White GM, Cox NH [eds]: *Diseases of the skin: a color atlas and text,* ed 2, St Louis, 2006, Mosby.)

- There is often a poor response to conventional antibiotics and no pathogens isolated from cultures of lesions.
- The disease is often mistaken for a simple infection and a long delay in diagnosis is common.
- Three clinical subtypes of HS have been recently proposed[1]:
  1. A classic axillary-mammary HS subtype, representing 48% of cases and characterized by breast and axillary involvement and hypertrophic scarring.
  2. A follicular HS subtype, representing 26% of cases manifesting primarily in male smokers with a family history of HS and characterized by follicular lesions,

[1]Woodruff CM, Charlie AM, Leslie KS: Hidradenitis suppurative: a guide for the practicing physician, *Mayo Clin Proc* 90(12):1679–1693, 2015.

including epidermal cysts, pilonidal sinus, comedones, and severe acne.
  3. A gluteal HS subtype, representing 26% of cases, most often seen in smokers with lower body mass index (BMI) and with a morphology characterized by follicular papules, folliculitis, and gluteal involvement.

ETIOLOGY

- Keratinous materials plug apocrine glands in hair follicles leading to stasis, dilation, rupture, and re-epithelialization.
- Bacteria are trapped and multiply leading to gland rupture with surrounding inflammation and local bacterial infection.
- Over time, repeated nodules and infections cause scarring, which can lead to deep tissue damage and sinus tracts.
- Infectious agents such as *Streptococcus, Staphylococcus,* and *Escherichia coli,* and enteric flora have been identified in cultures, but are likely a secondary component of the disease.
- There is likely a significant genetic component to the disease. 35% to 40% of patients report a family history of HS. An HS spectrum of different phenotypes has been characterized involving genetic factors that are not yet well described but may be important for future therapy.
- HS has been associated with other endocrine and autoimmune disorders such as diabetes, Cushing's disease, acromegaly, Crohn's disease, and inflammatory arthritis.
- Metabolic syndrome affects as many as 50% of patients with HS and may exacerbate the associated inflammation.

DIAGNOSIS

DIFFERENTIAL DIAGNOSIS

- Follicular pyodermias such as folliculitis, furuncles, carbuncles, and pilonidal cysts.
- Noduloulcerative syphilis.
- Cat scratch disease.
- Granuloma inguinale.
- Perianal and vulvar manifestations of Crohn's disease.
- Actinomycosis.
- Lymphogranuloma venereum.
- Dermoid, epidermoid, or Bartholin's cysts.
- Tuberculous inflammation of the skin.
- Lymphadenitis.
- Erysipelas.

WORKUP

Primarily a clinical diagnosis based on typical lesion (see "Physical Findings & Clinical Presentation").

LABORATORY TESTS

- Patients with acute lesions may have an elevated erythrocyte sedimentation rate or WBC.
- Febrile and toxic-appearing patients should have complete blood count, chemistries, and blood cultures.
- Any pus should be sampled for bacterial culture and sensitivity.

TREATMENT

There is no definitive cure for hidradenitis.

NONPHARMACOLOGIC THERAPY

- Weight loss and control of metabolic syndrome.
- Smoking cessation.
- Avoidance of shaving, depilatory creams, deodorants.
- Avoidance of tight-fitting clothing.
- Warm compresses.
- Incision and drainage of nonpurulent lesions is *not* recommended due to recurrence and scarring.
- Laser therapy, radiotherapy, and cryotherapy currently under study.
- Wide local excision for stage III disease with or without vacuum-assisted closure device.

ACUTE AND CHRONIC Rx

- NSAIDs for inflammation and pain, consider gabapentin, pregabalin, SSRIs for chronic pain management.
- Antibiotics never proven to be effective; however, are mainstay of treatment. Can base treatment on the basis of aspirate culture and sensitivities or empirically.
  1. Clindamycin is the only topical antibiotic proven to be effective in randomized controlled trial and is appropriate for stage I disease.
  2. For oral therapy in stage II: consider clindamycin and rifampin in combination.

Cephalosporins, dicloxacillin, erythromycin, minocycline, and tetracycline have also been used.
  3. Severe, recurrent disease can require up to 3 to 6 mo of antibiotics.
- Oral contraceptives with low androgenic progesterone (norgestimate, desogestrel, or gestodene) for women show mixed effectiveness. They are especially advantageous for female patients of childbearing age who also require some form of birth control.
- Isotretinoin has been used with mixed effectiveness. They should be avoided in women of childbearing age.
- Metformin has mixed effectiveness, possibly due to related metabolic syndrome and hyperandrogenism.
- Trials using zinc gluconate 75 to 118 mg/day in patients with mild (grade 1) disease have shown mixed effectiveness
- Corticosteroids and other immune suppressants such as cyclosporin, infliximab, and etanercept have been used for stage II disease, with mixed results.
- Adalimumab, an anti–tumor necrosis factor-α antibody given once per week (dose 40 mg/wk) has been used with mixed results, and further studies are needed. Infliximab has also been used in trials with variable success rates, with most patients exhibiting clinical improvement within 8 weeks.

COMPLICATIONS

- Squamous cell carcinoma.
- Scarring leading to restricted limb mobility or lymphedema.

- Rectal or urethral fistulas.
- Psychological effects related to disfiguring nature of disease.

REFERRAL

- Referral to dermatology during stage I to II disease.
- Referral to a surgeon is indicated for stage III disease.
- Surgical approaches include laser surgery and excisional surgery.

PEARLS & CONSIDERATIONS

COMMENTS

- Patients with hidradenitis are at risk for severe depression, social isolation, and negatively impacted sexuality as a result of their disease.
- There is an average delay in diagnosis of 12 years and most patients are diagnosed in stage II of the disease.
- It is important to maximize nonmedical treatment, start medical treatment, and refer to a surgeon early in the disease course to ensure the best quality of life for patients.
- The only definitive treatment for hidradenitis is wide excision of the involved skin.

SUGGESTED READINGS

Available at www.expertconsult.com

AUTHOR: **MARY BETH SUTTER, M.D.**

H

Diseases and Disorders

I

High-Altitude Sickness (PTG)

BASIC INFORMATION

DEFINITION

High-altitude illness refers to a spectrum of cerebral and pulmonary syndromes related to hypoxemia occurring during rapid ascension to high altitudes. Common acute syndromes include high-altitude pulmonary edema (HAPE), acute mountain sickness (AMS), and high-altitude cerebral edema (HACE). The latter two are thought to represent different points of severity along the same pathophysiologic process in the brain.

SYNONYMS

Altitude sickness
High-altitude headache
Acute mountain sickness
High-altitude pulmonary edema
High-altitude cerebral edema

ICD-10CM CODES

W94   Exposure to high and low air pressure and changes in air pressure
T70.2 Other and unspecified effects of high altitude

EPIDEMIOLOGY & DEMOGRAPHICS

- More than 30 million people are at risk of developing altitude sickness.
- 80% of people who ascend to high altitudes have HAH_2.
- AMS is the most common of the altitude diseases. It affects approximately 40% to 50% of people ascending to 14,000 ft (4200 m) from lowland.
- The incidence of HACE is reported to be 0.1% to 2% at elevations in excess of 12,000 ft (3000 m). HACE is often complicated by concomitant HAPE.
- Men are five times more likely to develop HAPE than are women.
- AMS and HACE affect men and women equally.

PHYSICAL FINDINGS & CLINICAL PRESENTATION (TABLE E1H-26)

HAH_1
- Headache that develops within 24 hr of ascent.
- Bilateral, frontal or frontotemporal, dull or pressing quality.
- Mild to moderate intensity and aggravated by exertion, movement, straining, coughing, or bending.
- Headache resolves within 8 hr of descent.
- HAH should resolve with analgesics and/or 10 to 15 min of supplementary oxygen.
- Difficult to distinguish from headaches secondary to dehydration.

AMS
- AMS is thought to be a progression of HAH_2.
- Occurs within 6 to 12 hours after rapid ascent to 8000 ft (2500 m) in 10% to 25% of unacclimatized persons.
- Headache is the most common symptom.

- Dizziness and lightheadedness.
- Nausea, vomiting, and loss of appetite.
- Fatigue.
- Sleep disturbance from an exaggerated hyperventilatory phase of Cheyne-Stokes respiration in response to hypoxemia and alkalosis.
- AMS can evolve into HAPE and HACE.
- Retinal hemorrhages can be present from increased blood flow or breakdown in the blood-retina barrier.
- Supplemental oxygen may be used to support the clinical diagnosis.

HAPE (Fig. E1H-44, *A*)
- Typically occurs 2 to 4 days after ascent over 8000 ft (2500 m).
- Dyspnea, loss of stamina.
- Dry cough or cough with frothy rust- or pink-tinged sputum.
- Chest tightness.
- Tachycardia, tachypnea, rales, cyanosis.

HACE
- Usually presents several days after AMS.
- Confusion, irritability, drowsiness, stupor, hallucinations, mild fever.
- Headache, nausea, vomiting.
- Truncal ataxia, paralysis, and seizures.
- The sixth cranial nerve is the most commonly affected from the compression of the trunk adjacent to brain swelling.
- Coma and death from brain herniation may develop within hours of the first symptoms.

ETIOLOGY

- During ascent to altitudes above sea level, the atmospheric pressure decreases. Although the percentage of oxygen in the air remains the same, the partial pressure of oxygen decreases with increased altitude, and can cause hypoxemia. Fig. E1H-44, *B* illustrates the effect of altitude on alveolar Pao_2 and oxygen saturation.
- Increased cerebral blood flow and the loss of autoregulation of intracranial pressure may contribute to increased cerebral vascular permeability and subsequent brain edema.
- Hypobaric hypoxia can trigger elevated pulmonary pressures, resulting in protein-rich, hemorrhagic exudates into the lung alveoli due to a breakdown in the pulmonary blood-gas barrier (HAPE).
- The body responds to low oxygen partial pressures through a process of acclimatization (see "Comments").

DIAGNOSIS

Made by clinical presentation and physical findings.

DIFFERENTIAL DIAGNOSIS

- Dehydration.
- Carbon monoxide poisoning.
- Hypothermia.
- Infection.
- Substance abuse.
- Congestive heart failure.
- Pulmonary embolism.
- Cerebrovascular accident.
- Box 1H-5 summarizes the differential diagnosis of high-altitude illnesses.

WORKUP

Typically the diagnosis is self-evident after history and physical examination. Laboratory tests and imaging studies help monitor cardiopulmonary and central nervous system status in patients admitted to the intensive care unit for pulmonary and/or cerebral edema. In patients with HAPE occurring at lower altitudes (<8000 ft), an evaluation of preexisting pulmonary hypertension or a left-to-right shunt should be considered.

LABORATORY TESTS

Not useful, unless to rule out an alternative diagnosis.

IMAGING STUDIES

- Chest x-ray showing Kerley B-lines and patchy edema (see Fig. E1H-44, *A*).
- CT scan of the head showing diffuse or patchy edema.
- MRI of the head showing characteristic intense T2 signal in the white matter.

TREATMENT

NONPHARMACOLOGIC THERAPY

- Stop the ascent to allow acclimatization or start to descend until symptoms have resolved. Descent is the definitive treatment and should begin immediately at the first suspicion of HACE.
- Oxygen 4 to 6 L/min is used for severe AMS, HAPE, and HACE.
- Portable hyperbaric bags are useful if available at the site.

BOX 1H-5   Differential Diagnosis of High-Altitude Illnesses

Acute mountain sickness and high-altitude cerebral edema	Dehydration, exhaustion, viral or bacterial infection, alcohol hangover, hypothermia, carbon monoxide poisoning, migraine, hyponatremia, hypoglycemia, diabetic ketoacidosis, CNS infection, transient ischemic attack, arteriovenous malformation, stroke, seizures, brain tumors, ingestion of toxins or drugs, acute psychosis
High-altitude pulmonary edema	Asthma, bronchitis, pneumonia, mucus plugging (secondary to previous), hyperventilation syndrome, pulmonary embolus, heart failure, myocardial infarction

CNS, Central nervous system.
From Auerbach P: *Wilderness medicine, expert consult* Premium Edition—Enhanced Online Features and Print, Philadelphia, 2012, Saunders.

- Altitude can cause diuresis that may be mediated by enhanced release of atrial natriuretic peptide. When coupled with the increased fluid loss through increased ventilation, there is a higher risk for dehydration, and adequate hydration should be maintained.

ACUTE PHARMACOLOGIC Rx

- Nonsteroidal anti-inflammatory drugs (e.g., ibuprofen 600 mg every 6 hours, beginning 6 hours before ascending) are effective prophylaxis of traditional altitude sickness and in treating headaches in AMS.
- Acetazolamide 125 to 250 mg PO bid has been effective for both prevention and acute therapy in patients with AMS and HACE.
- Nifedipine 10 mg sublingual followed by long-acting nifedipine 30 mg bid is used for patients with HAPE who cannot descend immediately.
- Dexamethasone 4 mg PO every 6 hr is used in patients with severe AMS, HAPE, or HACE.

CHRONIC Rx

Prevention is the most prudent therapy.
1. Slow, staged ascent to avoid altitude sickness.
2. Start the ascent below 8000 feet.
3. Ascend 1000 feet/day (300 m/day).
4. Spend two nights at the same altitude every 3 days.
5. Sleep at lower heights than the altitude climbed ("climb high, sleep low").
6. Prophylactic therapy with NSAIDs (ibuprofen 600 mg every 6 hours, beginning 6 hours before ascending) or acetazolamide up to 750 mg daily and/or dexamethasone 8 to 16 mg daily

decreases the risk of developing AMS (combination may have additive benefit). The drugs should be used until acclimatization occurs.
7. Prophylactic inhalation of a β-adrenergic agonist, salmeterol 125 mcg q12h, or the use of slow-release nifedipine 20 mg bid have both been shown to reduce the risk of HAPE in susceptible individuals.
8. Tadalafil, a long-acting phosphodiesterase inhibitor, has recently been shown to decrease the incidence of HAPE in susceptible individuals.
9. Box 1H-6 summarizes field treatment of high-altitude illness.

DISPOSITION

- AMS improves over a period of 2 to 3 days.
- HAPE is the most common cause of death among patients with altitude illnesses.
- More than 60% of patients with HAPE will have recurrence of symptoms on subsequent climbs.
- In HACE, neurologic deficits may persist for weeks but eventually resolve. If coma occurs, prognosis is poor.

REFERRAL

Cardiology and neurology referrals are made in patients with pulmonary edema and central nervous system findings, respectively.

PEARLS & CONSIDERATIONS

COMMENTS

- Acclimatization is the process in which an individual who normally resides at low alti-

tude adapts to hypobaric hypoxia to improve tolerance and performance at higher altitude. These mechanisms include:
1. An increase in respiratory rates and tidal volume. This hyperventilation allows lowering of arterial carbon dioxide to preserve oxygen delivery, even at extreme altitudes.
2. An early increase in heart rate and stroke volume to improve oxygen delivery. After 1 wk, both parameters decrease because of diuresis and lower catecholamine levels.
3. Pulmonary hypertension develops in response to hypoxemia, resulting in improvement of the ventilation-perfusion mismatch but may be maladaptive and lead to the development of HAPE.
4. Cerebral vasodilation to increase blood flow to the brain.
5. Rise in hemoglobin and hematocrit. This is a long-term process that takes up to 1 wk to occur in response to the need for improved oxygen delivery.
- Adaptation to altitude is different from acclimatization and refers to physiologic differences in permanent residents at high altitude (e.g., an increased oxygen diffusion capacity).
- High altitude illness can generally be prevented by ascending to 300 to 500 meters per day at altitudes above 3000 meters and including a rest day every 3 to 4 days.
- Risk factors for the development of altitude sicknesses are:
1. Rapid ascent.
2. Previous history of altitude sickness.
3. Strenuous exertion on arrival.
4. Obesity.
5. Male gender.
- Physical fitness is not protective against high-altitude illness.
- Both dexamethasone and tadalafil decrease systolic pulmonary artery pressure and may reduce the incidence of HAPE in adults with a history of HAPE. Dexamethasone prophylaxis may also reduce the incidence of AMS in these adults.
- Descent is mandatory for all persons with HACE or HAPE.
- The American College of Chest Physicians has released a primer on caring for passengers with a variety of health conditions who are traveling to high-altitude places or areas (http://www.accpstorage.org/newOrganization/patients/TravelingwithOxygen.pdf). Specific indications for supplemental oxygen are provided in the document.

SUGGESTED READINGS

Available at www.expertconsult.com

RELATED CONTENT

Altitude Sickness (Patient Information)

AUTHORS: **AUGUSTINE ANDOH-DUKU, M.D.,** and **SAMAAN RAFEQ, M.D.**

BOX 1H-6 Field Treatment of High-Altitude Illness

High-Altitude Headache and Mild Acute Mountain Sickness
- Stop ascent, rest, acclimatize at same altitude.
- Symptomatic treatment as necessary with analgesics and antiemetics.
- Consider acetazolamide, 125 to 250 mg bid, to speed acclimatization.
- OR descend 500 m (1640 feet) or more.

Moderate to Severe Acute Mountain Sickness
- Low-flow oxygen, if available.
- Acetazolamide, 125 to 250 mg bid, with or without dexamethasone, 4 mg PO, IM, or IV q6h.
- Hyperbaric therapy.
- OR immediate descent.

High-Altitude Cerebral Edema
- Immediate descent or evacuation.
- Oxygen, 2 to 4 L/min.
- Dexamethasone, 8 mg PO, IM, or IV, then 4 mg q6h.
- Hyperbaric therapy.

High-Altitude Pulmonary Edema
- Minimize exertion and keep warm.
- Immediate descent or hyperbaric therapy.
- Oxygen, 4 to 6 L/min until improving, then 2 to 4 L/min. If above unavailable, one of the following:
- Nifedipine, 30 mg extended release q12h.
- Sildenafil 50 mg q8h.
- Tadalafil 10 mg q12h.
- Consider inhaled β-agonist.

Periodic Breathing
- Acetazolamide, 62.5 to 125 mg at bedtime as needed.

IM, Intramuscularly; *IV,* intravenously; *PO,* orally.
From Auerbach P: *Wilderness medicine, expert consult* Premium Edition—Enhanced Online Features and Print, Philadelphia, 2012, Saunders.

Diseases and Disorders

ⓘ BASIC INFORMATION

DEFINITION

Hip fractures are classified as intracapsular or extracapsular. Intracapsular fractures include femoral head and femoral neck fractures (Fig. 1H-45, Table 1H-27). These fractures are further categorized as either displaced or nondisplaced. Extracapsular fractures include intertrochanteric and subtrochanteric fractures, as well as the less common greater and lesser trochanteric fractures. These fractures can be further categorized by the degree of comminution.

SYNONYMS

Hip fracture
Intracapsular fracture
Subcapital fracture
Extracapsular fracture
Intertrochanteric fracture

ICD-10CM CODES
S72.0	Fracture of neck of femur
S72.1	Pertrochanteric fracture
S72.2	Subtrochanteric fracture
S72.3	Fracture of shaft of femur
S72.4	Fracture of lower end of femur
S72.7	Multiple fractures of femur
S72.8	Fractures of other parts of femur
S72.009	A fracture of unspecified part of neck of unspecified femur, initial encounter for closed fracture

EPIDEMIOLOGY & DEMOGRAPHICS

PREVALENCE: Lifetime risk in women ~16%.
PREDOMINANT SEX: Female/male ratio of 3:1.
PREDOMINANT AGE: 90% >60 yr.

PHYSICAL FINDINGS & CLINICAL PRESENTATION

- Hip or groin pain.
- Affected limb usually shortened and externally rotated in displaced fractures.
- Impacted fractures: possibly no deformity and only mild pain with hip motion.
- Mild external bruising.

RISK FACTORS

- Osteoporosis.
- Age >75.
- Gait instability, foot deformities, muscular weakness.
- Sensory impairment.
- Polypharmacy.
- Impaired cognition, depression.
- Use of alcohol or benzodiazepines.
- Orthostatic hypotension.
- Environmental hazards at home (e.g., loose rugs, loose cords).
- Subclinical hyperthyroidism.

ETIOLOGY

- Trauma.
- Age-related bone weakness, usually caused by osteoporosis.
- Increased risk of fractures in elderly (decline in muscle function, use of psychotropic medication, etc.).

ⓧ DIAGNOSIS

DIFFERENTIAL DIAGNOSIS

- OA of hip, RA of hip.
- Hip dislocation.
- Pathologic fracture.
- Lumbar disk syndrome with radicular pain.
- Insufficiency fracture of pelvis.
- Trochanteric bursitis.
- Septic hip joint.
- Pelvic fracture.
- Lateral femoral cutaneous nerve entrapment (meralgia paresthetica).
- Osteitis deformans (Paget's disease).

WORKUP

Diagnosis is usually obvious based on clinical and radiographic findings (Figs. 1H-46 and 1H-47). Fig. E1H-48 illustrates the Garden classification of femoral neck fractures.

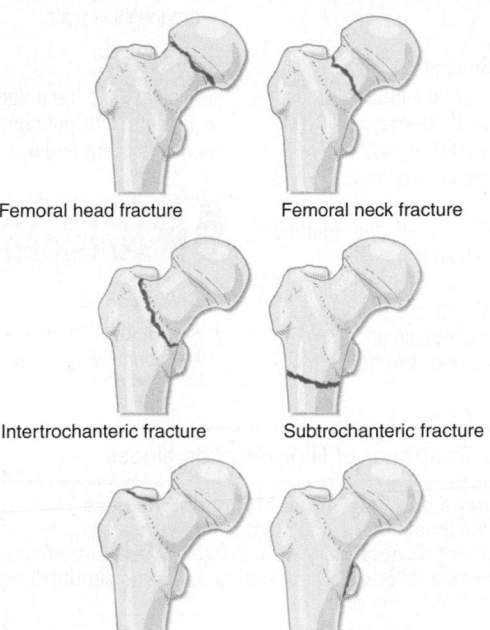

Femoral head fracture　　Femoral neck fracture

Intertrochanteric fracture　　Subtrochanteric fracture

Greater trochanter fracture　　Lesser trochanter fracture

FIGURE 1H-45 Types of hip fractures. (From Adams JG.; et al. *Emergency medicine, clinical essentials,* ed 2, Philadelphia, 2013, Elsevier.)

IMAGING STUDIES

- Standard roentgenograms consisting of an anteroposterior view of the pelvis and a cross-table lateral view of the hip to confirm the diagnosis.
- If initial roentgenograms are negative and diagnosis of an occult femoral neck fracture is suspected, hospital admission and further radiographic assessment with either bone scanning or MRI are recommended.
- Bone scanning is sensitive after 48 to 72 hr.

℞ TREATMENT

- Orthopedic consultation.
- Surgery indicated in most cases, usually within 24 hr. Treatment depends on type of fracture:
  1. Femoral neck, non-displaced, impacted valgus: cannulated screws.

TABLE 1H-27	Garden's Classification of Femoral Neck Fractures
Type I	Nondisplaced, slightly impacted, incomplete fracture line The medial trabeculae of the femoral head and neck form an angle of 180 degrees The femoral head is tilted into valgus The distal fragment lies in external rotation
Type II	Nondisplaced, complete fracture line The medial trabeculae of the femoral head and neck form an angle of 160 degrees Nondisplaced femoral head Normal distal alignment
Type III	Complete fracture line, with displacement <50% The femoral head trabeculae are not in alignment with those of the pelvis The femoral head is tilted into varus and medially rotated The distal fragment lies in external rotation
Type IV	Complete fracture line, with displacement >50% and dissociation The femoral head trabeculae lie in alignment with those of the pelvis The femoral head is detached and frequently realigns with the acetabulum The distal fragment is proximally displaced and lies in external rotation

From Pope TL, Bloem HL, Beltran J, Morrison WB, Wilson DJ: *Musculoskeletal imaging,* ed 2, Philadelphia, 2014, Saunders.

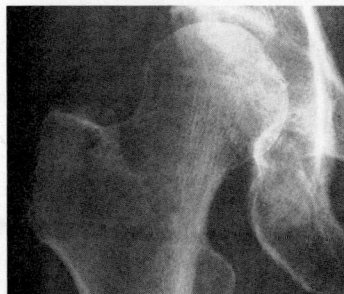

FIGURE 1H-46 Intertrochanteric femur fracture: three parts (proximal, distal, and one trochanter).

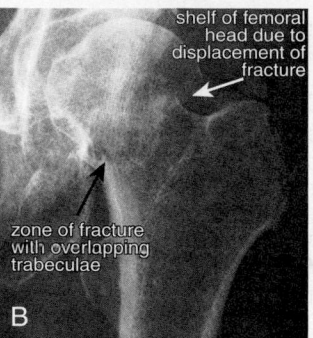

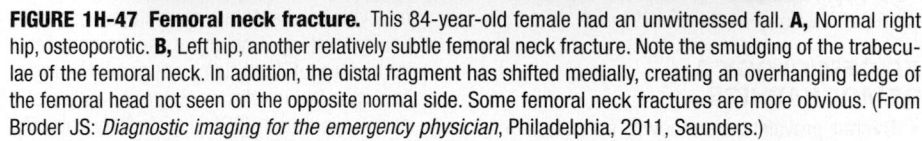

FIGURE 1H-47 Femoral neck fracture. This 84-year-old female had an unwitnessed fall. **A,** Normal right hip, osteoporotic. **B,** Left hip, another relatively subtle femoral neck fracture. Note the smudging of the trabeculae of the femoral neck. In addition, the distal fragment has shifted medially, creating an overhanging ledge of the femoral head not seen on the opposite normal side. Some femoral neck fractures are more obvious. (From Broder JS: *Diagnostic imaging for the emergency physician*, Philadelphia, 2011, Saunders.)

FIGURE 1H-46 Intertrochanteric femur fracture: three parts (proximal, distal, and one trochanter). Intertrochanteric femur fractures are common, with the mechanism often being a fall from standing in an elderly patient. The major fracture line usually runs obliquely between the greater and the lesser trochanters. These fractures may have two, three, or four parts classically, although badly comminuted combinations are also possible. Two-part fractures consist of the proximal and distal fragments. Three-part fractures also include a fragment of one trochanter. Four-part fractures include fragments of both trochanters. This 86-year-old female had an unwitnessed fall. She has a typical 3-part fracture, with a fragment of the lesser trochanter visible. Note her generalized severe osteopenia. (From Broder JS: *Diagnostic imaging for the emergency physician*, Philadelphia, 2011, Saunders.)

2. Displaced: <50 yr, emergent reduction, cannulated screws; >50 yr: hemiarthroplasty, unipolar versus bipolar or total hip arthroplasty if preexisting degenerative changes.
3. Intertrochanteric: stable, 2 and 3 parts, dynamic hip screw (DHS) versus trochanteric femoral nail (TFN); unstable, 4 parts, subtrochanteric extension, TFN.
4. Reverse obliquity: TFN, blade plate, dynamic condylar screw, not DHS.
- Deep vein thrombosis prophylaxis (fondaparinux, LMWH, vitamin K antagonist). Mechanical prophylaxis is contraindicated. Prophylaxis is usually continued for 28 to 35 days postop.
- Pain management: effective pain management is a primary goal in hip fracture. Opioid analgesics have a high incidence of delirium and constipation. Nerve blockade is effective in reducing acute pain after hip fracture.
- Prophylactic antibiotics should be initiated before surgery and continued for 24 hours after surgical repair.
- Rehabilitation is a major component of hip fracture treatment and should be initiated on the first postoperative day.

- Conservative therapy in patients who are not surgical candidates (too ill for surgery, bed or wheelchair-bound patients before injury).

DISPOSITION
- Surgical mortality after hip fracture repair is 2% to 3%. Older adults have a 5- to 8-fold increased risk for all-cause mortality during the first 3 mo after hip fracture. Mortality rate within 1 yr in elderly patients is 25% to 30%. Excess annual mortality persists over time for both women and men, but at any given age, excess annual mortality after hip fracture is higher in men than in women.
- Dementia is a particularly poor prognostic sign.

REFERRAL
For surgical consideration when the diagnosis is made.

PEARLS & CONSIDERATIONS

COMMENTS
- Complications: nonunion, avascular necrosis, DVT, infection, delirium, decubitus ulcers, incontinence, persistent pain, loosening of prosthesis.
- Intracapsular fractures: occasionally occur in nonambulatory patients.
  1. Usually treated nonsurgically, especially in the patient with dementia and limited pain perception.
  2. Early bed-to-chair mobilization and vigilant nursing care to avoid skin breakdown.
  3. Fracture usually pain free in a short time even if solid bony healing does not occur.
- As a result of the increasing life span of the female population, femoral neck fractures are becoming more common. The initial physical examination and roentgenographic

studies may be completely negative. Groin pain, sometimes quite severe, may be the only early clue to the diagnosis.
- The rate of hip fracture could be reduced by:
  1. Elimination of environmental hazards (poor lighting, loose rugs).
  2. Regular exercise for balance and strength.
  3. Patient education about fall prevention.
  4. Medication review to minimize side effects.
  5. Prevention and treatment of osteoporosis.
- In the United States, hip fracture rates and subsequent mortality among persons aged 65 yr and older are declining, and comorbidities among patients with hip fractures are very expensive ($40,000 in the first year following hip fracture for direct medical costs and $5000 in subsequent years).
- Fragility (or low-trauma) hip fractures, common in elderly patients with reduced bone density, carry a 1-yr mortality of 26%, while another 58% require long-term care in a nursing facility. Previous fragility hip fracture is associated with a second osteoporotic fracture within the subsequent 5 yr.
- Concurrent prolonged use of proton-pump inhibitors (≥1 yr) is associated with reduced effectiveness of alendronate for preventing hip fractures in older adults.

EBM EVIDENCE
Available at www.expertconsult.com

SUGGESTED READINGS
Available at www.expertconsult.com

RELATED CONTENT
Hip Fracture (Patient Information)

AUTHOR: **FRED F. FERRI, M.D.**

BASIC INFORMATION

DEFINITION

Hirsutism is the development of stiff, pigmented (terminal) facial and body hair (male distribution) in women as a result of excess androgen production.

SYNONYMS

Excessive hair growth

ICD-10CM CODES
L68.0 Hirsutism

EPIDEMIOLOGY & DEMOGRAPHICS

- Overall prevalence unknown, estimated 5% to 10% in reproductive age women.
- Race and genetics should be considered. Some distinct ethnic populations have minimal body hair and others (Mediterranean, Middle Eastern, South Asian) have moderate to large amounts of body hair while serum androgen levels are similar.
- Social norms and culture also determine how much body hair is cosmetically acceptable.
- Half of all cases of mild hirsutism do not have hyperandrogenemia. "Patient-important hirsutism" refers to hirsutism causing woman sufficient distress to seek care.
- Incidence and presentation of hirsutism is dependent on underlying cause of androgen excess (see "Differential Diagnosis").
- Most women with hirsutism have polycystic ovary syndrome.

PHYSICAL FINDINGS & CLINICAL PRESENTATION

- Timing of symptoms: abrupt onset, short duration, rapid progression, progressive worsening, more severe signs of virilization (Fig. 1H-49), or later age of onset suggest androgen-producing tumor, late-onset congenital adrenal hyperplasia, or Cushing's syndrome. Weight increases may produce increased androgen production.
- Menstrual history: menarche, cycle regularity and symptoms of ovulation, fertility, and contraception use. Anovulatory cycles are the most common underlying cause of androgen excess.
- Medication use history: some drugs cause hirsutism or produce androgenic effects (danazol, phenytoin, valproic acid, androgenic progestins (e.g., norgestrel), cyclosporin, minoxidil, metoclopramide, phenothiazines, methyldopa, diazoxide, penicillamine).
- Family history: known or suspected family history of hirsutism, congenital adrenal hyperplasia, insulin resistance, polycystic ovary syndrome (PCOS), infertility, obesity, menstrual irregularity may be found.
- Physical exam reveals deepening voice, body habitus, increased muscle mass, galactorrhea; abdominal and pelvic exam.
- Associated cutaneous manifestations (Fig. 1H-50) are acne, acanthosis nigricans, striae, hair distribution, location and quantity, frontotemporal balding, muscle mass, clitoromegaly.
- Ferriman-Gallwey scale, a simple, pictorial system of scoring nine body areas, is the most common tool used to quantify hirsutism. It may be unreliable in non-Caucasian women of other ethnicities.

ETIOLOGY

- Presence of hirsutism indicates androgen excess. Total testosterone may be normal, but free testosterone is elevated.
- Androgens induce vellus hair follicles (soft, unpigmented hair) in sex-specific areas (upper lip, chin, midsternum, upper abdomen, back, buttocks) to develop into thicker, more heavily pigmented terminal hairs.
- Anovulatory ovaries are usual source of excess androgens through thecal cell steroidogenesis and conversion of androstenedione to testosterone. The most common cause of hirsutism is polycystic ovary syndrome, which accounts for three out of every four cases.
- Conditions that decrease hepatic production of sex hormone binding globulin (SHBG) decrease protein-bound testosterone and increase free testosterone fraction (e.g., low estrogen, high androgen, and hyperinsulinemic states).
- Late-onset, congenital adrenal hyperplasia enzyme deficiency (most commonly 21-hydroxylase deficiency) produces excess 17 hydroxyprogesterone (17-OHP) and overproduction of androstenedione.
- Rare ovarian tumors primarily derived from Sertoli-Leydig cells, granulosa theca cells, or hilus cells produce excess androgens.
- Rare adrenal tumors produce excess androgens.
- Rare pituitary or hypothalamic tumors produce excess prolactin and can lead to anovulation.
- Box 1H-7 summarizes causes of androgen excess in women of reproductive age.

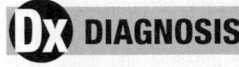

DIAGNOSIS

DIFFERENTIAL DIAGNOSIS

- Androgen-independent vellus hair: soft, unpigmented hair that covers entire body
- Hypertrichosis: diffusely increased total body hair (vellus or lanugo-type) not restricted to androgen-dependent areas often an adverse response to a medication or systemic illness (e.g., anorexia nervosa, porphyria, malnutrition, hypothyroidism)
- PCOS 75%
- Idiopathic 5% to 15%
- Congenital adrenal hyperplasia 1% to 8%
- Insulin resistance syndrome 3% to 4%
- Cushing's syndrome <1%
- Drug induced <1%
- Ovarian tumor <1%
- Adrenal tumor <1%
- Hyperthecosis <1%
- Hyperprolactinemia <1%

WORKUP

- Hirsutism is a clinical diagnosis.
- Management of hirsutism is largely independent of the etiology.
- Workup in selected hirsute women is directed to determine underlying cause of androgen excess.
- See specific conditions for more detailed workup of individual diagnoses.

LABORATORY TESTS

Establishing laboratory evidence of excess androgens in women with moderate or severe hirsutism, sudden onset, rapid progression, or associated menstrual dysfunction, central obesity, clitoromegaly, or acanthosis nigricans is an approach consistent with guidelines from the Endocrine Society, the American College of Obstetricians and Gynecologists, the Androgen Excess and Polycystic Ovary Syndrome Society and the American Association of Clinical Endocrinologists.

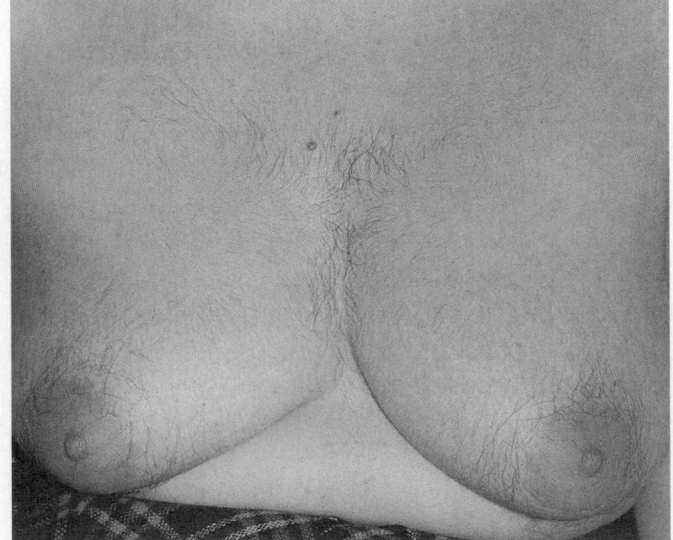

FIGURE 1H-49 Hirsutism. (From James WD et al: *Andrews' diseases of the skin*, ed 12, Philadelphia, 2016, Saunders.)

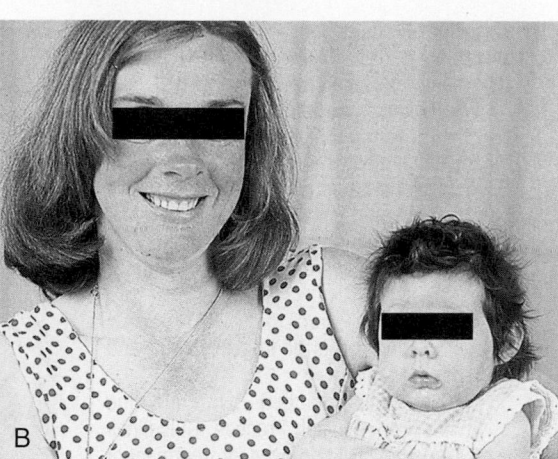

FIGURE 1H-50 A patient with an arrhenoblastoma with associated polycystic ovaries before and after treatment. **A,** Before treatment, the patient had marked facial hirsutism. **B,** The patient is shown successfully treated. The tumor was resected and ovulation ensued with clomiphene and human chorionic gonadotropin therapy. (From Besser CM, Thorner MO: *Comprehensive clinical endocrinology*, ed 3, St Louis, 2002, Mosby.)

BOX 1H-7   Causes of Androgen Excess in Women of Reproductive Age

Ovarian
Polycystic ovary syndrome (PCOS)
Hyperthecosis (a severe PCOS variant)
Ovarian tumor (e.g., Sertoli-Leydig cell tumor)

Adrenal
Nonclassic adrenal hyperplasia
Cushing's syndrome
Glucocorticoid resistance
Adrenal tumor (e.g., adenoma, carcinoma)

Specific Conditions of Pregnancy
Luteoma of pregnancy
Hyperreaction luteinalis
Aromatase deficiency in fetus

Other
Hyperprolactinemia, hypothyroidism
Medications (danazol, testosterone, anabolizing agents)
Idiopathic hirsutism (normal serum testosterone in an ovulatory woman)
Idiopathic hyperandrogenism (patients who do not fall into any of the other categories listed)

From Melmed S et al: *Williams textbook of endocrinology,* ed 12, Philadelphia, 2011, Saunders.

- Total plasma testosterone (normal range 20-60 ng/dl [0.69-2.1 nmol/L]) or free testosterone: early morning on day 4 to 10 of menstrual cycle to screen for testosterone-secreting tumors. If moderately or markedly elevated (total testosterone >150 ng/dl [5.2 nmol/L], free testosterone >2 ng/dl [0.07 nmol/L]) may image adrenals and ovaries for androgen-secreting tumors.
  Other laboratory test considerations if appropriate:
- Prolactin: moderately elevated values should prompt imaging of pituitary-hypothalamic region
- 17-OHP (17 α-hydroxyprogesterone): screen for adrenal enzyme deficiencies. Morning value >200 ng/dl in early follicular phase suggests nonclassic (late onset) congenital adrenal hyperplasia due to 21-hydroxylase deficiency and may be confirmed with high-dose (250 mcg) ACTH stimulation test.
- Thyroid-stimulating hormone (TSH): rule out hypothyroidism

- Dehydroepiandrosterone sulfate (DHEA-S): screen for adrenal androgen production as almost entirely produced by adrenals. Levels >700 mcg/dl (13.6 nmol/L) raise suspicion for adrenal androgen-secreting tumor.
  Additional laboratory test considerations if appropriate:
- Follicle-stimulating hormone: (FSH): rule out hypoestrogenic state (perimenopausal).
- Luteinizing hormone: (LH): typically elevated in PCOS with low or normal FSH.
- 24-hour urinary free cortisol: rule out Cushing's syndrome and overproduction of cortisol.
- Overnight single-dose dexamethasone suppression test: rule out Cushing's syndrome and adrenal hyperfunction.
- Fasting blood sugar (FBS), 2-hr 75-g oral glucose tolerance test, fasting insulin levels: rule out insulin resistance syndrome.

IMAGING STUDIES

Imaging study considerations if appropriate:

- Pelvic ultrasound (high resolution, transvaginal): rule out ovarian tumor if total testosterone is elevated.
- Abdominal CT/MRI: rule out adrenal tumor if elevated DHEA-S.
- Pituitary-hypothalamic region CT/MRI: rule out pituitary tumor if prolactin elevated.
- Laparoscopy/laparotomy: rule out small ovarian tumor in cases of elevated testosterone levels without radiologic evidence of adrenal or ovarian pathology.

Rx TREATMENT

NONPHARMACOLOGIC THERAPY

- Weight reduction: can reduce androgen production indirectly by reducing insulin-stimulated theca cell androgen production and improve menstrual function, and slow hair growth in obese women.
- Cosmetic: temporary.
  1. Shaving: does not stimulate hair growth; lasts days, leaves stubble.
  2. Epilation: electronic plucking.
  3. Bleaching: removes hair pigment. May cause skin irritation.
  4. Mechanical waxing/plucking.
  5. Depilatories: gels, lotions, or creams that chemically disrupt sulfide bonds of hair causing dissolution of hair shaft. No stubble.
  6. Photoepilation (laser and intense pulsed light [IPL]): hair follicles destroyed by wavelengths of light absorbed by melanin. Good for pigmented hair; laser treatment is more effective than shaving, waxing, and electrolysis. It lasts 3 to 6 months as vellus follicles remain and can be converted to terminal pigmented hair under excess androgens.
- Cosmetic: permanent. Electrolysis: destroys individual hair follicles. May be expensive and time consuming.

ACUTE GENERAL Rx

See "Pharmacologic Therapy."

CHRONIC Rx

See "Pharmacologic Therapy."

PHARMACOLOGIC THERAPY

- Usually second-line treatment following nonpharmacologic, physical methods of hair control, and in consideration of patient's comorbidities and risk factors, patient preferences, area of excess hair amenable to treatment, and access and affordability of treatments.
- Pharmacologic treatments categorized as topical, oral contraceptive pills (OCPs), antiandrogens (potential adverse effects on a developing male fetus, so use with reliable contraception), other treatments directed at specific underlying etiology.
- Topical: Eflornithine topical cream 13.9%: unclear mechanism of action; may inhibit ornithine decarboxylase, retarding hair growth. Temporary cosmetic treatment for

facial hair. Applied directly to unwanted facial hair bid with at least 8 hr spaced applications. Does not remove hair, rather slows growth. Slow response over 4 to 8 wk. Hair growth returns upon discontinuation of treatment.

- OCPs: Suppress ovarian steroidogenesis and LH through low-dose estrogen and low androgenic progestational agents. Slow response to treatment. Suppresses new hair growth. Established hair unaffected. Low-dose OCPs with low androgenic progestational agents, for example, desogestrel, drospirenone, norgestimate. Avoid norgestrel and levonorgestrel (higher androgenic progestational agents).

- Antiandrogens: Spironolactone: when OCPs unacceptable or may be added for disappointing results after 6 mo of OCP treatment.
  1. Aldosterone-antagonist diuretic inhibits adrenal and ovarian biosynthesis of androgens. May result in ovulation, so consider contraception needs.
  2. Slow response usually 6 mo or more.
  3. 200 mg PO qd, then decrease to 25 to 50 mg qd maintenance.
  4. May cause hyperkalemia.
  5. Anovulatory, unopposed estrogen states require progestin management.

REFERRAL

- To endocrinologist if difficulty in determining diagnosis, achieving therapeutic goals, or resistant to first-line therapies. Prepubertal and postmenopausal hirsutism is suspicious for neoplastic or secondary endocrine causes and should be referred for further evaluation.

- Consider referral or consultation for following therapies:
  1. Finasteride: antiandrogen, in hair follicle blocks 5α-reductase conversion of testosterone to intranuclearly active 5α-dihydrotestosterone (DHT).
     1. Use only with reliable contraception because DHT necessary for normal male fetus urogenital development.
     2. Not FDA approved for treatment of hirsutism.
     3. 1 to 5 mg PO qd.
  2. Flutamide: inhibits androgen uptake and receptor binding
     1. Not recommended by Endocrine Society Clinical Practice Guidelines and not FDA approved for treatment of hirsutism, but used by some European endocrinologists.
     2. Use only with reliable contraception.
     3. Reserved for women with severe, resistant hirsutism because of risk of hepatic dysfunction.
     4. 250 mg PO bid.
  3. Cyproterone acetate (not available in the United States): antiandrogen that competes with DHT for binding androgen receptors. Used as progestin component of OCPs outside the United States.
- Other treatments directed at specific underlying etiology:
  1. Metformin/thiazolidinediones: therapy reserved for documented insulin-resistant states.
  2. GnRH agonists: recommended only in women with severe hyperandrogenemia (e.g., ovarian hyperthecosis) with subop-

timal response to combination low-dose estrogen/progestin pills and antiandrogen treatment. Inhibits gonadotropin and consequently ovarian androgen and estrogen secretion.
3. Dexamethasone: adrenal glucocorticoid suppression is reserved for diagnosis of adrenal enzyme deficiency.
4. Total abdominal hysterectomy/bilateral salpingo-oophorectomy reserved for recalcitrant hirsutism in older female with hyperthecosis and undesired fertility.

PEARLS & CONSIDERATIONS

COMMENTS

- Hirsutism is both an endocrine and cosmetic problem for patients.
- Ovulation induction therapy is indicated in women desiring pregnancy.
- Delay checking serum androgens until oral contraceptives have been discontinued for 2 to 3 mo.
- Evaluation of incidental adrenal mass is always warranted.

SUGGESTED READINGS

Available at www.expertconsult.com

RELATED CONTENT

Hirsutism (Patient Information)

AUTHOR: **RICHARD LONG, M.D.**

BASIC INFORMATION

DEFINITION

Histoplasmosis is caused by the fungus *Histoplasma capsulatum* and characterized by a primary pulmonary focus with occasional progression to chronic pulmonary histoplasmosis (CPH) or various forms of dissemination. Progressive disseminated histoplasmosis (PDH) may present with a diverse clinical spectrum, including adrenal necrosis, pulmonary and mediastinal fibrosis, and ulcerations of the oropharynx and GI tract. In those patients coinfected with HIV, it is a defining disease for AIDS.

SYNONYMS

North American histoplasmosis
Ohio Valley fever
Vanderbilt disease

ICD-10CM CODES

B39.0 Acute pulmonary histoplasmosis capsulati
B39.1 Chronic pulmonary histoplasmosis capsulati
B39.2 Pulmonary histoplasmosis capsulati, unspecified
B39.3 Disseminated histoplasmosis capsulati
B39.4 Histoplasmosis capsulati, unspecified
B39.5 Histoplasmosis duboisii
B39.9 Histoplasmosis, unspecified

EPIDEMIOLOGY & DEMOGRAPHICS

INCIDENCE (IN U.S.):
- Unknown for acute pulmonary disease
- For CPH, estimated at 1/100,000 cases in endemic areas
- For PDH in immunocompetent adults, estimated at 1/2000 cases of histoplasmosis

PREVALENCE: Unknown

PREDOMINANT SEX: Clinically evident disease is most common in males; male/female ratio of 4:1

PREDOMINANT AGE:
- CPH is most often seen in males >50 yr old with an associated history of COPD.
- Presumed ocular histoplasmosis syndrome (POHS) is seen between ages of 20 and 40 yr.

PEAK INCIDENCE: Unknown

PHYSICAL FINDINGS & CLINICAL PRESENTATION

- Conidia are deposited in alveoli then converted to yeast forms where they spread to regional lymph nodes and other organs, especially liver and spleen.
- 1 to 2 wk later, a granulomatous inflammatory response begins to contain the yeast in the form of discrete granulomas.
- Delayed-type hypersensitivity to *Histoplasma* antigens occurs 3 to 6 wk after exposure.
- Clinical disease manifests in various forms, depending on host cellular immunity and inoculum size:
  1. Acute primary pulmonary histoplasmosis
     a. An overwhelming number of patients are asymptomatic.
     b. Most clinically apparent infections manifest by complaints of fever, headache, malaise, pleuritic chest pain, nonproductive cough, and weight loss.
     c. Less than 10%, mainly women, complain of arthralgias, myalgias, and skin manifestations such as erythema multiforme or erythema nodosum.
     d. Acute pericarditis presents in a smaller percentage of patients.
     e. Hepatosplenomegaly is most commonly observed in children.
     f. With particularly heavy exposure, there is severe dyspnea, marked hypoxemia, impending respiratory failure.
     g. Most patients are asymptomatic within 6 wk.
  2. CPH
     a. Presents insidiously with low-grade fever, malaise, weight loss, cough, sometimes with blood-streaked sputum or frank hemoptysis.
     b. Most patients with cavitary lesions present with associated COPD or chronic bronchitis, masking underlying fungal disease.
     c. Tends to worsen preexisting pulmonary disease and further contribute to eventual respiratory insufficiency.
  3. PDH
     a. In both acute and subacute forms, constitutional symptoms of fever, fatigue, malaise, and weight loss are common.
     b. Acute form (seen in infants and children) presents with respiratory symptoms, fever >101° F (38.3° C), generalized lymphadenopathy, marked hepatosplenomegaly, and fulminant course resembling septic shock associated with a high fatality rate.
     c. Subacute form is more common in adults and associated with lower temperatures, hepatosplenomegaly, oropharyngeal ulceration, focal organ involvement (including adrenal destruction, endocarditis, chronic meningitis, and intracerebral mass lesions).
     d. Course of subacute form is relentless, with untreated patients dying within 2 yr.
     e. Chronic PDH is found in adults and marked by gradual symptoms of weight loss, weakness, easy fatigability; low-grade fever when present; oropharyngeal ulcerations and hepatomegaly and/or splenomegaly in one third of patients.
     f. Less clinical evidence of focal organ involvement in chronic form than in subacute form.
     g. Natural history of chronic form is protracted and intermittent, spanning months to years.
- Histoplasmoma
  1. A healed area of caseation necrosis surrounded by a fibrous capsule
  2. Usually asymptomatic
- Mediastinal fibrosis
  1. A rare consequence of a fibroblastic process that encases caseating mediastinal lymph nodes producing severe retraction, compression, and distortion of mediastinal structures
  2. Constriction of the bronchi resulting in bronchiectasis, also esophageal stenosis associated with dysphagia, and superior vena cava syndrome
- POHS
  1. Diagnosis characterized by distinct clinical features, including atrophic choroidal scars and maculopathy in patients with histories suggestive of exposure to the fungus (e.g., residence in an endemic area)
  2. Patient complains of distortion or loss of central vision without pain, redness, or photophobia
  3. Usually no evidence of infection except for a positive skin reaction to histoplasmin
- In patients with AIDS
  1. Possible presentation as overwhelming infection similar to acute PDH seen in children
  2. Constitutional symptoms: fever, weight loss, malaise, cough, dyspnea
  3. About 10% with cutaneous maculopapular, erythematous eruptions or purpuric lesions on face, trunk, and extremities
  4. Up to 20% with CNS involvement, manifesting as intracerebral mass lesions, chronic meningitis, or encephalopathy

ETIOLOGY

- *H. capsulatum* is a dimorphic fungus present in temperate zones and river valleys worldwide.
- In the U.S., it is highly endemic in southeastern, mid-Atlantic, and central states.
- Exists as mold at ambient temperature and favors soils enriched with bird or bat droppings.

 DIAGNOSIS

DIFFERENTIAL DIAGNOSIS

- Acute pulmonary histoplasmosis
  1. *Mycobacterium tuberculosis*
  2. Community-acquired pneumonias caused by *Mycoplasma* and *Chlamydia*
  3. Other fungal diseases, such as *Blastomyces dermatitidis* and *Coccidioides immitis*
- Chronic cavitary pulmonary histoplasmosis: *M. tuberculosis*
- Histoplasmomas: true neoplasms

WORKUP

- Suspect diagnosis in patients who present with a history of residence or travel in an endemic area, especially if engaged in occupations (e.g., outside construction or street cleaning) or hobbies (e.g., cave exploring) that increase the likelihood of exposure to fungal spores.
- Suspect diagnosis in immunosuppressed patients with remote history of exposure, especially if associated with characteristic calcifications on chest x-ray.

LABORATORY TESTS

- Demonstration of organism on culture from body fluid or tissues biopsy (Fig. E1H-52) to make definitive diagnosis
  1. Especially high yield in patients with AIDS
  2. Characteristic oval yeast cells in neutrophils with Giemsa stain from peripheral smear
  3. Preparations of infected tissue with Gomori's silver methenamine for revealing yeast forms, especially in areas of caseation necrosis
- Serologic tests, including complement-fixing (CF) antibodies and immunodiffusion assays
- Detection of *Histoplasma* antigen in urine: may be influenced by infections with *Blastomyces* and *Coccidioides*
- In PDH
  1. Pancytopenia
  2. Marked elevations in alkaline phosphatase and alanine aminotransferase (ALT) common
- In chronic meningitis (majority of cases)
  1. CSF pleocytosis with either lymphocytes or neutrophils predominating
  2. Elevated CSF protein levels
  3. Hypoglycorrhachia

IMAGING STUDIES

- Chest radiograph examination in acute pulmonary histoplasmosis
  1. Singular or multiple patchy infiltrates, especially in the lower lung fields
  2. Hilar or mediastinal lymphadenopathy with or without pneumonitis
  3. Diffuse nodular or confluent bilateral miliary infiltrates characteristic of heavier exposure
  4. Infrequent pleural effusions, except when associated with pericarditis
- Chest radiograph examination in histoplasmoma: coin lesion displaying central calcification, ranging from 1 to 4 cm in diameter, predominantly located in the subpleural regions
- Chest radiograph examination in CPH (Fig. E1H-53):
  1. Upper lobe disease frequently associated with cavities
  2. Preexisting calcifications in the hilum associated with peribronchial streaking extending to the parenchyma
- Chest radiograph examination in acute PDH: hilar adenopathy and/or diffuse nodular infiltrates
- CT scan of adrenals to reveal bilateral enlargement and low-attenuation centers

TREATMENT

NONPHARMACOLOGIC THERAPY

For life-threatening disease seen in acute disseminated disease or infection in patients with AIDS: supportive therapy with IV fluids

ACUTE GENERAL Rx

- No drug therapy is required for asymptomatic pulmonary disease.
- A course of therapy with itraconazole 200 mg PO tid for 3 days, then 200 mg/day PO for 6-12 wk may be beneficial in some patients with acute pulmonary distress. Avoid fluconazole because it is not as active.
- Same therapy appropriate for immunocompetent, mild to moderately symptomatic patients with CPH and subacute and chronic forms of PDH, but duration for 6 to 12 mo.
- Use amphotericin B 0.7 to 1 mg/kg IV q day for initial therapy in moderate to severe disease and then transition to oral itraconazole within 1 to 2 wk. Lipid formulations of amphotericin can be used to avoid nephrotoxicity of amphotericin B.
- (Liposomal amphotericin: 3mg/kg/day IV or amphotericin B lipid complex: 5 mg/kg/day)
- Posaconazole and voriconazole are highly effective as well, but echinocandins such as micafungin are not effective.
- Chronic cavitary pulmonary histoplasmosis: itraconazole 200 mg PO tid for 3 days, then once or twice daily for at least 12 mo.
- CNS histoplasmosis: liposomal amphotericin B, 5 mg/kg/day for a total of 175 mg/kg over 4 to 6 wk, then itraconazole 200 mg 2 to 3×/day for at least 12 mo.
- Endocarditis: surgical treatment with excision of infected valve or graft combined with amphotericin for a total dose of 35 mg/kg or 2.5 g.
- For pericardial disease:
  1. Antifungal therapy: no apparent benefit
  2. Best managed with NSAIDs
- For POHS:
  1. Antifungal therapy: no apparent benefit
  2. May respond to laser therapy

CHRONIC Rx

- In patients with AIDS: lifelong suppressive therapy with either itraconazole, given 200 mg PO q day, or IV amphotericin B at a dose of 50 mg once weekly; a triazole compound posaconazole (400 mg PO bid) may be useful in refractory cases, but clinical experience is limited at this point.
- Prophylaxis in HIV-infected patients with <150 CD4 cells/mm^3: itraconazole 200 mg PO qd

DISPOSITION

For those with chronic or progressive disease, especially if immunocompromised, prognosis is dependent on prompt recognition and timely administration of appropriate antifungal drugs.

REFERRAL

- To an infectious disease specialist in suspected cases of disseminated disease, especially if immunocompromised
- To a pulmonologist for patients with CPH form because of progressive respiratory compromise
- To a thoracic surgeon for decompression procedures for progressive mediastinal fibrosis

PEARLS & CONSIDERATIONS

- *H. capsulatum*, variety *duboisii*, also known as African histoplasmosis, is restricted to Senegal, Nigeria, Zaire, and Uganda.
- Unlike *H. capsulatum*, pulmonary forms of *duboisii* are not seen, and the disease is limited to the skin, soft tissues, and bone.

COMMENTS

- Patients living in endemic areas, especially if immunocompromised, should take appropriate respiratory precautions when disposing of bird waste from rooftop or home aviaries.
- Appropriate respiratory precautions should also be taken when leisure traveling to areas that act as a natural haven for the fungus, such as bat caves.

SUGGESTED READINGS

Available at www.expertconsult.com

RELATED CONTENT

Histoplasmosis (Patient Information)

AUTHOR: **GLENN G. FORT, M.D., M.P.H.**

BASIC INFORMATION

DEFINITION

Patients with histrionic personality disorder present with a pervasive pattern of excessive emotionality and attention-seeking behavior that generally begins in early adulthood. The individual must meet five or more of the following criteria:

1. Is uncomfortable in situations where he or she is not the center of attention.
2. Interaction with others is often characterized by inappropriate sexually seductive or provocative behavior.
3. Displays rapidly shifting and shallow expression of emotions.
4. Consistently uses physical appearance to draw attention to self.
5. Has a style of speech that is excessively impressionistic and lacking in detail.
6. Shows self-dramatization, theatricality, and exaggerated expression of emotion.
7. Is suggestible (i.e., easily influenced by others or circumstances).
8. Considers relationships to be more intimate than they actually are.

SYNONYMS

Hysterical personality disorder
Psycho-infantile personality disorder
Personality disorder (nonspecific)
Personality disorder (trait specified)

ICD-10CM CODES
F60.4 Histrionic personality disorder

EPIDEMIOLOGY & DEMOGRAPHICS

PREVALENCE (IN U.S.):
- Diagnosed more often in women (85%); rarely found in men.
- Prevalence: 1% to 3%.

PREDOMINANT SEX: Female. Cultural factors (e.g., attention-seeking behavior not as acceptable in men) may lead to more common diagnosis in women.

PREDOMINANT AGE: Generally begins in early adulthood.

GENETICS: Limited research using interview and self-report methods suggests histrionic personality disorder has a moderate genetic component.

PHYSICAL FINDINGS & CLINICAL PRESENTATION

- No specific physical findings

- Exaggerated emotionality
- Clinical presentation:
  1. Exaggerated, shallow, and/or rapidly shifting emotions
  2. A pattern of repeated attention-seeking behavior, often suggestive or provocative
  3. Theatrical
  Eccentric

ETIOLOGY

- Unknown
- Hypothesized that childhood events, psychosocial adversity, and genetics are contributory

DIAGNOSIS

DIFFERENTIAL DIAGNOSIS

- Narcissistic and borderline personality disorders share common features.
- Other personality disorders (e.g., antisocial personality disorder, dependent personality disorder)
- Personality change attributable to general medical condition.
- Symptoms in association with chronic substance abuse.

WORKUP

There is no formal test to establish diagnosis.

TREATMENT

NONPHARMACOLOGIC THERAPY

- Long-term individual psychotherapy is treatment of choice.
- One controlled study exists, suggesting patients in schema therapy experience greater functional improvement and symptom reduction compared with treatment-as-usual and clarification-oriented psychotherapy.
- Unlike other people who have personality disorders, these individuals often seek treatment and exaggerate their symptoms and difficulties in functioning.
- Patients tend to be more emotionally needy and are often reluctant to terminate therapy.

ACUTE GENERAL Rx

- No placebo-controlled trials.
- Care should be given when prescribing medications because of the potential for self-destructive or otherwise harmful behaviors.

DISPOSITION

- Therapeutic approaches should not focus on the long-term personality change, but rather short-term alleviation of specific difficulties and deficits within the person's life.
- Therapeutic approaches that emphasize vague somatic, anxious, or depressive symptoms often fail.
- Patients are likely to be intolerant or drop out of treatment approaches that use delayed gratification.
- Symptoms are moderately stable over adulthood and may remit or decrease in intensity with age.

REFERRAL

Primarily treated by mental health professionals.

PEARLS & CONSIDERATIONS

- This disorder is difficult to treat.
- Like most personality disorders, patients present for treatment only when stress or other situational factors within their lives have made their ability to function and cope effectively impossible.
- Suicidality and risk of self-injury should be assessed on a regular basis, and suicidal threats and self-mutilation should not be ignored or dismissed. Patients may present with a higher risk for (or history of) suicidal gestures.
- An alternative model in DSM 5, section III, reconceptualizes histrionic personality disorder as "Personality Disorder, Trait Specified," which rates: (1) impairment in personality functioning (identity, self-direction, empathy, and/or intimacy) and (2) pathologic trait domains such as attention seeking, grandiosity, and manipulativeness.

PATIENT & FAMILY EDUCATION

Group and family therapy approaches are generally not recommended because individuals with this disorder often try to draw attention to themselves and exaggerate every action and reaction.

SUGGESTED READINGS
Available at www.expertconsult.com

AUTHORS: **MARK ZIMMERMAN, M.D.,** and **THERESA A. MORGAN, PH.D., M.PHIL.**

H

Diseases and Disorders

I

 BASIC INFORMATION

- HIV cognitive dysfunction covers a spectrum of disorders ranging from asymptomatic to clinically severe (including AIDS dementia complex or HIV encephalopathy).
- Cognitive, motor, and behavioral abnormalities

SYNONYMS

HIV-associated neurocognitive disorder (HANDS)
AIDS dementia complex
HIV-1 encephalopathy

ICD-10CM CODES

B20	Human immunodeficiency virus [HIV] disease
R41.8	Other and unspecified symptoms and signs involving cognitive functions and awareness
B97.35	Human immunodeficiency virus, type 2 [HIV 2] as the cause of diseases classified elsewhere

EPIDEMIOLOGY

- Presenting complaint in 3% to 10% of cases
- Incidence: occurs in 15% of patients with AIDS; however, as more HIV-infected patients live longer, prevalence may be increasing.
- Minor cognitive disorders known as HIV-1-associated minor cognitive/motor disorder (MND) are more common and seen in 20% to 25% of patients; not necessarily progressive
- Rarely precedes clinical evidence of HIV infection

CLINICAL FEATURES

- Cognitive changes: forgetfulness, poor attention and concentration, increased difficulty performing complex tasks, slowed psychomotor speed.
- Behavioral changes: apathy, lack of initiative, social withdrawal, irritability, occasionally agitation, psychosis or obsessive compulsive disorder.
- Motor problems: clumsiness, unsteady gait, poor balance, tremor, leg weakness.
- Progressive/later stages: bedbound, severe dementia, bowel/bladder incontinence.
- Subcortical dementia (aphasia, apraxia, and agnosia) is uncommon.
- Results from inflammation triggered by HIV itself (not related to opportunistic infection) and immune activation of microglia and brain macrophages.
- Clinically may resemble Parkinson's disease.
- In children: developmental delay, microcephaly, and spasticity are common.
- Table 1H-29 summarizes features of HIV-associated neurocognitive disorder.

RISK FACTORS

- Low CD4 count (less than 200 cells/mm³)
- High viral load
- Anemia
- Injection drug use
- Hepatitis C
- Female gender
- Older age

Dx DIAGNOSIS

DIAGNOSTIC EVALUATION

- Diagnosis is based on clinical examination and neuropsychometric tests
- CT of brain may show greater subcortical atrophy than cortical atrophy, which is not proportional to the degree of infection
- MRI head (Fig. 1H-54): diffuse, confluent, periventricular white matter lesions on T2 weighted images with normal T1 images
- Lumbar puncture: CSF analysis helps to rule out opportunistic infections. In HIV-related cognitive dysfunction the CSF may show a nonspecific increase in cell count and protein.
- Subtle electrophysiologic abnormalities can be found in early HIV-1 infection (on electroencephalography, evoked potentials, nerve conduction studies), but they do not seem to have a predictive value for the later onset of AIDS dementia, which generally occurs when the CD4+ T-lymphocyte counts are less than 200 cells/microliter.[1]
- Potential causes for cognitive impairment that must be ruled out include:
  1. Opportunistic infections (toxoplasmosis, CNS lymphoma)
  2. Vitamin B_{12} deficiency
  3. Substance use
  4. Organic affective disorder (such as depression and mania)
  5. Side effects of prescribed medications

Rx TREATMENT

Early treatment with antiretroviral therapy (ART) may lead to clinical improvement in some patients, but in most cases, cognitive dysfunction persists despite ART.

! PEARLS & CONSIDERATIONS

- Initiation of ART can lead to rapid improvement in cognitive function in early stages (untreated, life span is typically 4-6 mo)
- Most common presenting complaint in children infected with HIV
- Mini-mental status examination (MMSE): baseline scores in HIV patients are very helpful
- Usually cognitive symptoms precede motor abnormalities
- Four HIV-related opportunistic infections that commonly cause cognitive impairment are: toxoplasmosis, cryptococcal meningitis, progressive multifocal leukoencephalopathy, and CNS lymphoma

REFERRALS

- Upon diagnosis/clinical suspicion for HIV-associated cognitive dysfunction, referral to neurology is recommended
- Referral to neuropsychology may be considered

SUGGESTED READINGS

Available at www.expertconsult.com

AUTHOR: **DIVYA SINGHAL, M.D.**

TABLE 1H-29 Clinical Triad in Human Immunodeficiency Virus Type 1–Associated Neurocognitive Disorder

Cognition	Behavioral	Motor
Forgetfulness	Apathy	Gait instability
Mental slowing	Social withdrawal	Poor coordination
Decreased concentration	Lack of spontaneity	Leg weakness

From Bennett JE, Dolin R, Blaser MJ: *Mandell, Douglas, and Bennett's principles and practice of infectious diseases*, ed 8, Philadelphia, 2015, Saunders.

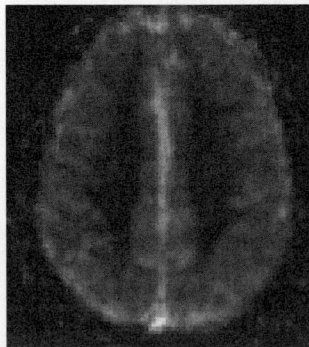 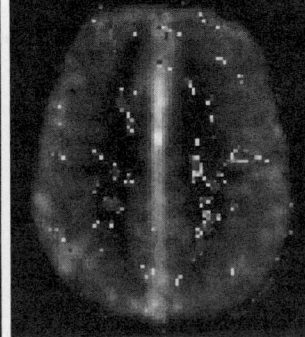 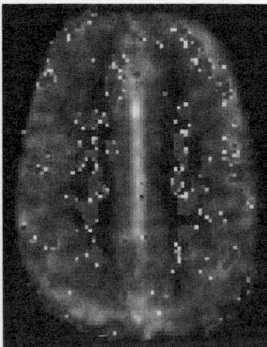

Asymptomatic   MCMD   HAD

FIGURE 1H-54 Perfusion MRI (pMRI) maps showing regions of increasing cerebral blood volume (CBV) with advancing HIV groups: asymptomatic, minor cognitive–motor disorder (MCMD), and HIV-associated dementia (HAD). Areas of red indicate >2 standard deviations elevation in CBV. (Tucker KA et al: Neuroimaging in human immunodeficiency virus infection. *J Neuroimmunol* 157(1–2): 153–162, 2004.)

 **BASIC INFORMATION**

DEFINITION

Compulsive hoarding is defined as the acquisition of and failure to discard a large number of possessions that appear to be useless or of limited value, with living spaces sufficiently cluttered so as to preclude activities for which those spaces were designed and significant distress or impairment in functioning caused by the hoarding. Hoarding has historically been a criterion of obsessive-compulsive personality disorder. With the publication of the DSM 5 (2013), compulsive hoarding is now recognized as a distinct form of psychopathology.

DSM 5 CRITERIA FOR HOARDING DISORDER:

A. Persistent difficulty discarding or parting with possessions, regardless of the value others may attribute to these possessions. (The Work Group is considering alternative wording: "Persistent difficulty discarding or parting with possessions, regardless of their actual value.")

B. This difficulty is due to strong urges to save items and/or distress associated with discarding.

C. The symptoms result in the accumulation of a large number of possessions that fill up and clutter active living areas of the home or workplace to the extent that their intended use is no longer possible. If all living areas become decluttered, it is only because of the interventions of third parties (e.g., family members, cleaners, authorities).

D. The symptoms cause clinically significant distress or impairment in social, occupational, or other important areas of functioning (including maintaining a safe environment for self and others).

E. The hoarding symptoms are not due to a general medical condition (e.g., brain injury, cerebrovascular disease).

F. The hoarding symptoms are not restricted to the symptoms of another mental disorder (e.g., hoarding due to obsessions in obsessive-compulsive disorder, decreased energy in major depressive disorder, delusions in schizophrenia or another psychotic disorder, cognitive deficits in dementia, restricted interests in autism spectrum disorder, food storing in Prader–Willi syndrome).

Specify if:
- With excessive acquisition: If discarding possessions is accompanied by excessive acquisition of items that are not needed or for which there is no available space.

Specify if:
- With good or fair insight
- With poor insight
- With absent insight/delusional beliefs

SYNONYM(S)

Hoarding
Obsessive-compulsive disorder
Obsessive-compulsive personality disorder
Anankastic personality disorder
Saving
Collecting
Clutter

ICD-10CM CODES:
ICD-10: Hoarding Disorder is not found in the ICD-9 or ICD-10; however, it is being considered as a new diagnostic category for the ICD-11.

EPIDEMIOLOGY, PREVALENCE, & DEMOGRAPHICS

- Community surveys suggest that the prevalence of clinically significant compulsive hoarding is estimated to be somewhere between 2% and 6%. National studies on prevalence are not yet available.
- Clinical samples suggest a higher prevalence among females, but some epidemiologic studies suggest a higher prevalence among males.
- Hoarding onset typically starts in early adolescence.
- Late-onset hoarding is rare.
- Available data outside of the United States suggest that hoarding is a universal phenomenon.
- Hoarding tendencies tend to begin in childhood or adolescence and become clinically significant by middle age.
- Hoarding may have a sudden onset in adulthood after experiencing a traumatic event.
- A large percentage of individuals who hoard report having at least one first-degree relative who experiences hoarding problems.
- It is estimated that one in four people with OCD are hoarders.
- Hoarding tends to be a chronic condition with spontaneous remission a rarity.
  Associated with Axis I (Major Depressive Disorder, Social Phobia, Obsessive-Compulsive Disorder, Generalized Anxiety Disorder, and Attention-Deficit Hyperactivity Disorder) and Axis II (Borderline Personality Disorder and Avoidant Personality Disorder).

RISK FACTORS

- Genetic vulnerabilities and early attachment experiences are thought to contribute to hoarding behavior.
- Social isolation can lead to hoarding behavior as a way to provide comfort.
- A sudden traumatic event can lead to hoarding behavior as a coping mechanism.
- Family history.
- Age.

ETIOLOGY

Although the etiology is unknown, hoarders share a number of characteristics, including problems with emotional attachments to possessions (i.e., viewing their possessions as extensions of themselves), behavioral avoidance (i.e., a fear of making a decision about what to do with a possession), beliefs about the nature of possessions (i.e., an exaggerated desire for control over possessions and a sense of responsibility to take care of the possessions and to be prepared for the future), perfectionism (i.e., possessions must be used perfectly such as a belief that a newspaper must be thoroughly read), and information processing deficits (i.e., deficits in decision making, difficulty in memory functions, and deficits in categorization and organization).

 **DIAGNOSIS**

DIFFERENTIAL DIAGNOSIS
WORKUP:

- Hoarding disorder is not diagnosed if the hoarding behavior is determined to be the direct consequence of another medical condition, including traumatic brain injuries, surgery for seizure control, cerebrovascular disease, infections of the central nervous system, neurogenetic conditions, autism, schizophrenia, major depressive episode, obsessive-compulsive disorder, or neurocognitive disorders.

TREATMENT

NONPHARMACOLOGIC THERAPY

- Frost and Hartl developed a cognitive-behavioral model of hoarding, which conceptualizes hoarding as a consequence of: (1) information-processing deficits, (2) problems in forming emotional attachments, (3) behavioral avoidance, and (4) erroneous beliefs about the nature of possessions.
- Steketee and Frost published a specialized cognitive-behavioral therapy (CBT) compulsive hoarding treatment manual that uses cognitive-behavioral strategies to address these areas. The authors recommend 26 therapy sessions over a period of 1 year. Treatment can be individual or group therapy with a combination of office and in-home sessions. Family consultation is recommended, with an emphasis on education and the treatment of hoarding behavior.

ACUTE GENERAL Rx

Antidepressants may be helpful for underlying mood or anxiety disorders.

CHRONIC Rx

CBT is the preferred treatment for hoarding disorder, but selective serotonin reuptake inhibitors (SSRIs) are the preferred pharmacologic intervention for severe cases.

DISPOSITION

Long-term follow-up is essential for recurring hoarding behavior and to address underlying mood disorders.

REFERRAL

- CBT is the preferred treatment.
- If underlying mood symptoms such as depression and anxiety interfere with treatment, a referral for medication is encouraged.

PEARLS & CONSIDERATIONS

Patients with hoarding disorder can be challenging to treat because many with the disorder do not recognize that they have a problem nor do they understand the negative impact hoarding has on their lives and the lives of their loved ones. They often do not believe that they need treatment, and they take great comfort in their possessions. Patient and family education is an important first step in the treatment of hoarding disorder. Family members are often frustrated and angry at the individual who hoards because of a perception that the hoarder is simply "messy," "lazy," and so on. Psychoeducation helps family members understand the complicated nature of the illness. They can be instructed on how to become "surrogate therapists" rather than distress the family member who hoards by taking it upon themselves to throw items away. It is essential that they work with a therapist who has expertise with hoarding behavior.

PATIENT/FAMILY EDUCATION

International OCD Foundation: http://208.88.128.33/hoarding/

SUGGESTED READINGS
Available at www.expertconsult.com

AUTHOR: **JEFFREY P. WINCZE, PH.D.**

BASIC INFORMATION

DEFINITION

Hodgkin lymphoma is a malignant disorder arising from germinal center B cells and characterized histologically by the presence of multinucleated giant cells (Reed-Sternberg cells) in a mixed inflammatory background.

ICD-10CM CODES

C81.90 Hodgkin lymphoma, unspecified, unspecified site
C81.00 Nodular lymphocyte predominant Hodgkin lymphoma, unspecified site
C81.10 Nodular sclerosis classical Hodgkin lymphoma, unspecified site
C81.20 Mixed cellularity classical Hodgkin lymphoma, unspecified site
C81.30 Lymphocyte depleted classical Hodgkin lymphoma, unspecified site
C81.79 Other classical Hodgkin lymphoma, extranodal and solid organ sites
C81.90 Hodgkin lymphoma, unspecified, unspecified site
C81.91 Hodgkin lymphoma, unspecified, lymph nodes of head, face, and neck
C81.92 Hodgkin lymphoma, unspecified, intrathoracic lymph nodes
C81.93 Hodgkin lymphoma, unspecified, intra-abdominal lymph nodes
C81.94 Hodgkin lymphoma, unspecified, lymph nodes of axilla and upper limb
C81.95 Hodgkin lymphoma, unspecified, lymph nodes of inguinal region and lower limb
C81.96 Hodgkin lymphoma, unspecified, intrapelvic lymph nodes
C81.97 Hodgkin lymphoma, unspecified, spleen
C81.98 Hodgkin lymphoma, unspecified, lymph nodes of multiple sites
C81.99 Hodgkin lymphoma, unspecified, extranodal and solid organ sites

EPIDEMIOLOGY & DEMOGRAPHICS

- There is a bimodal age distribution (15-34 yr and >50 yr).
- Incidence is 4 in 100,000 cases; >8000 new cases of Hodgkin lymphoma diagnosed annually in the U.S.
- Concordance for Hodgkin lymphoma in identical twins suggests that a genetic susceptibility underlies Hodgkin lymphoma in young adulthood.
- There is association between certain HLA haplotypes, especially HLA-A1.
- The disease is more common in males (in childhood Hodgkin lymphoma, >80% occur in males), whites, and higher socioeconomic groups.
- There is an increased risk in smokers and HIV-infected individuals.

PHYSICAL FINDINGS & CLINICAL PRESENTATION

- Painless palpable lymphadenopathy is the most common presenting symptom.

- The most common site of involvement is the neck region.
- Fever and night sweats: fever in a cyclical pattern (days or weeks of fever alternating with afebrile periods) is known as Pel-Ebstein fever.
- Unexplained weight loss, generalized malaise.
- Persistent, nonproductive cough.
- Lymph node pain associated with alcohol ingestion often because of heavy eosinophil infiltration of the tumor sites is relatively uncommon.
- Generalized pruritus.
- Hepatosplenomegaly.
- Other: superior vena cava syndrome, spinal cord compression (rare), erythema nodosum, ichthyosis.

ETIOLOGY

Evidence implicating Epstein-Barr virus remains controversial.

DIAGNOSIS

DIFFERENTIAL DIAGNOSIS

- Non-Hodgkin lymphoma.
- Sarcoidosis.
- Infections (e.g., cytomegalovirus, Epstein-Barr virus, toxoplasmosis, HIV, tuberculosis).
- Drug reaction.

WORKUP

Diagnosis is confirmed by lymph node biopsy. The World Health Organization classifies Hodgkin lymphoma into two groups: classical Hodgkin lymphoma (92%-97%) and nodular lymphocyte-predominant Hodgkin lymphoma (3%-8%). Classical Hodgkin lymphoma has four main histologic subtypes based on the number of lymphocytes, Reed-Sternberg cells, and the presence of fibrous tissue:
1. Nodular sclerosis (60%-80%) (Fig. E1H-55).
2. Mixed cellularity (15%-30%) (Fig. E1H-56).

3. Lymphocyte rich (2%-7%).
4. Lymphocyte depleted (1%-6%).
   Nodular sclerosis occurs mainly in young adulthood, whereas the mixed cellularity type is more prevalent after age 50 yr.
   Staging: Table 1H-30 describes the Cotswolds staging classification.
   Proper staging requires the following:
- Detailed history (with documentation of "B symptoms" and physical examination).
- Excisional biopsy with histologic, immunophenotypic and immunohistochemical analysis.
- Laboratory evaluation (complete blood count, erythrocyte sedimentation rate, blood urea nitrogen, creatinine, liver function tests, albumin, lactate dehydrogenase, HIV test), immunophenotypic markers (see Table 1H-31). Gene-expression profiling for tumor-associated macrophages is a new biomarker for risk stratification.
- CT scan of chest, abdomen, pelvis, neck.
- Positron emission tomography scan (18F-FDG PET scan).
- Unilateral bone marrow biopsy in selected patients.
  Box 1H-8 summarizes recommended staging procedures for Hodgkin lymphoma.

TREATMENT

ACUTE GENERAL Rx

The main therapeutic modality includes chemotherapy with or without radiotherapy depending on stage and other risk factors. In general, chemotherapy plus involved-field radiotherapy can be used as standard treatment for Hodgkin lymphoma in the early stages. Chemotherapy is used for advanced stage disease with radiotherapy in selected patients, such as those with bulky disease.

Most oncologists prefer the combination of adriamycin (doxorubicin), bleomycin, vinblastine, and dacarbazine (ABVD). ABVD does not cause infertility or stem cell damage and has

TABLE 1H-30 Cotswolds Staging Classification for Hodgkin Lymphoma

Classification	Description
Stage I	Involvement of a single lymph node region or lymphoid structure (e.g., spleen, thymus, Waldeyer ring) or involvement of a single extralymphatic site (IE)
Stage II	Involvement of two or more lymph node regions on the same side of the diaphragm (hilar nodes, when involved on both sides, constitute stage II disease); localized contiguous involvement of only one extranodal organ or site and lymph node regions on the same side of the diaphragm (IIE). The number of anatomic regions involved should be indicated by a subscript (e.g., II$_3$)
III$_1$	With or without involvement of splenic, hilar, celiac, or portal nodes
III$_2$	With involvement of paraaortic, iliac, and mesenteric nodes
Stage IV	Diffuse or disseminated involvement of one or more extranodal organs or tissues, with or without associated lymph node involvement
	Designations applicable to any disease stage
A	No symptoms
B	Fever (temperature, >38° C [100.4° F]), drenching night sweats, unexplained loss of >10% of body weight within the preceding 6 mo
X	Bulky disease (a widening of the mediastinum by more than one third of the presence of a nodal mass with a maximal dimension <10 cm)
E	Involvement of a single extranodal site that is contiguous or proximal to the known nodal site

From Hoffman R et al: *Hematology: basic principles and practice*, ed 5, Philadelphia, 2009, Churchill Livingstone.

TABLE 1H-31 Selected Immunophenotypic Markers and Histologic Characteristics of Use in the Differential Diagnosis of Hodgkin Lymphoma and Other Lymphoid Neoplasms

Marker	Classical HL	Nodular Lymphocyte Predominant HL	TCRBCL	ALCL
CD30	+	–	–	+
CD15	+	–	–	–
CD20	–/+*	+	+	–
CD45	–	+	+	+/–
CD79a	–	+	+	–
ALK	–	–	–	+/–
EMA	–	+	+	+
Nodular growth protein	+/–†	+	–	–

+, >90% of cases positive; +/–, majority of cases positive; –/+, minority of cases positive; –, <10% of cases positive; *ALCL*, anaplastic large cell lymphoma; *HL*, Hodgkin lymphoma; *TCRBCL*, T-cell rich B-cell lymphoma.
*CD20 positivity in classical Hodgkin lymphoma is quite heterogeneous, with a wide range in brightness of staining.
†In classical Hodgkin lymphoma, a nodular growth pattern is confined to the nodular sclerosing subtype.
From Abeloff MD: *Clinical oncology*, ed 3, Philadelphia, 2004, Saunders.

BOX 1H-8 Recommended Staging Procedures for Hodgkin Lymphoma

The following staging procedures are recommended for the initial workup of Hodgkin lymphoma:
1. Adequate surgical biopsy reviewed by an experienced hematopathologist
2. Cytologic examination of any effusion in selected cases
3. Detailed history, with attention to the presence or absence of systemic symptoms, and a careful physical examination, emphasizing node chains, size of the liver and spleen, and inspection of Waldeyer ring
4. Routine laboratory tests: complete blood cell count, erythrocyte sedimentation rate, and liver function tests
5. Neck, chest, and abdominal CT imaging fused with 18-FDG PET scan (Fig. 1H-57)

From Hoffman R. et al. *Hematology: basic principles and practice,* ed 5, Philadelphia, 2009, Churchill Livingstone.

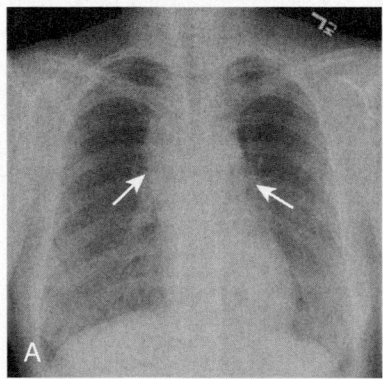
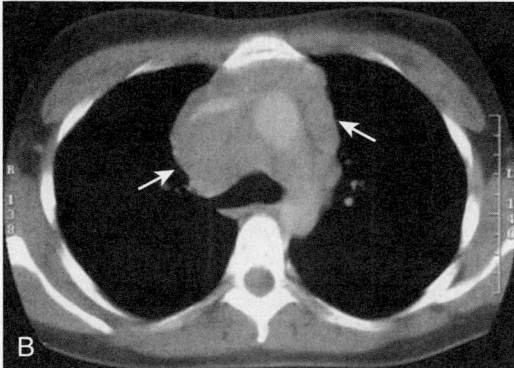
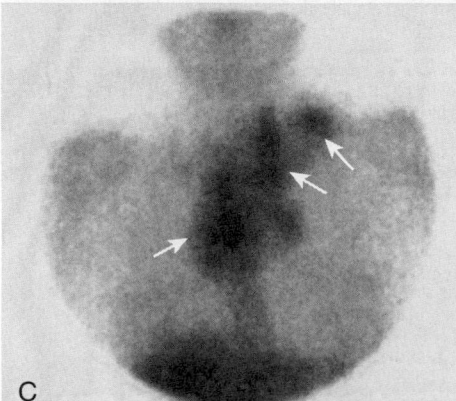
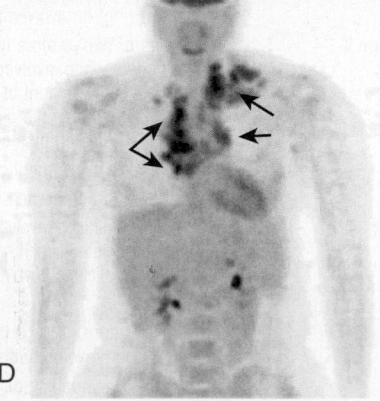

FIGURE 1H-57 Imaging of Hodgkin lymphoma. Bulky Hodgkin disease as seen on chest radiograph (**A**), computed tomography (CT) of the chest (**B**), gallium scan (**C**), and positron emission tomography (PET) (**D**). The *arrows* indicate sites of disease. Note that the PET and CT scans provide more detailed information than the chest radiograph and gallium scan. (From Goldman L , Schafer AI. *Goldman's Cecil medicine*, ed 24, Philadelphia, 2012, Saunders.)

TABLE 1H-32 Characteristics of the ABVD Regimen

Agents: doxorubicin, bleomycin, vinblastine, dacarbazine
All intravenous, total compliance
80% complete response rate
10% primary refractory disease
60%-65% overall disease-free survival
Most relapses occur within the first 4 yr; however, about 10% of all relapses occur beyond 5 yr
Major side effects are nausea, phlebitis, myelosuppression, less cumulative myelotoxicity than MOPP
No infertility
No leukemia

ABVD, Adriamycin (doxorubicin), bleomycin, vinblastine, dacarbazine; *MOPP*, mechlorethamine, Oncovin (vincristine), procarbazine, prednisone.
From Abeloff MD: *Clinical oncology*, ed 3, Philadelphia, 2004, Saunders.

also shown to be effective in patients with HIV infection and Hodgkin lymphoma. Table 1H-32 describes characteristics of the ABVD regimen.

Recent trials have shown that in patients with early-stage Hodgkin lymphoma and favorable prognosis, defined by fewer than three nodal sites without bulky or extranodal disease in the absence of ESR >50 without symptoms or 30 with symptoms, treatment with two cycles of ABVD followed by 20 Gy of involved-field radiation therapy may be as effective as, and less toxic than, four cycles of ABVD followed by 30 Gy of involved-field radiation therapy. For patients with early stage disease who do not meet these criteria, options include three or four cycles of ABVD plus involved site radiotherapy to 30 Gy. In addition, chemotherapy alone, in the absence of bulky disease, is an alternative approach, especially in young women younger than the age of 30 yr, given the increased risk of including breast cancer, as well as cardiac and thyroid disease. Although the risk of disease recurrence is slightly higher in patients who receive chemotherapy alone, there is no difference in overall survival.

BEACOPP, an intensified regimen consisting of bleomycin, etoposide, doxorubicin, cyclophosphamide, vincristine, procarbazine, and prednisone, has been advocated by some as the new standard for treatment of advanced Hodgkin lymphoma in place of ABVD. Recent trials have shown that treatment with BEACOPP, as compared with ABVD, results in better initial tumor control, but the long-term clinical outcome does not differ significantly between the two regimens. In addition, with the use of the escalated BEACOPP regimen, the rate of complications is higher (3% treatment-related death, 20% rate of hospitalization, and 3% rate of secondary leukemia, and near-universal infertility). Thus, if the goal is cure with the least overall toxic effects, it is best to favor ABVD therapy, reserving rescue therapy with high-dose chemotherapy and autologous hematopoietic stem-cell transplantation for the small

TABLE 1H-33   Definition of Treatment Groups According to the EORTC/GELA and GHSG

Treatment Group	EORTC/GELA	GHSG	NCIC/ECOG
Early-stage favorable	CS I-II without risk factors (supradiaphragmatic)	CS I-II without risk factors	Standard risk group: favorable CSD I-II (without risk factors)
Early-stage unfavorable (intermediate)	CS I-II with ≥1 risk factors (supradiaphragmatic)	CS I, CSIIA ≥1 risk factors; CS IIB with C/D but without A/B	Standard risk group: unfavorable CS I-II (at least one risk factor)
Advanced stage	CS III-IV	CS IIB with A/B;CS III-IV	High-risk group: CS I or II with bulky disease; intraabdominal disease; CS III, IV
Risk factors (RF)	A large mediastinal mass	A large mediastinal mass	A ≥40 years
	B age ≥50 yr	B extranodal disease	B not NLPHL or NS histology
	C elevated ESR*	C elevated ESR*	C ESR ≥50 mm/h
	D ≥4 involved regions	D ≥3 involved areas	D ≥4 involved nodal regions

CS, Clinical stage; *ECOG*, Eastern Cooperative Oncology Group; *EORTC*, European Organization for Research and Treatment of Cancer; *GELA*, Groupe d'Etude des Lymphomes de l'Adulte; *GHSG*, German Hodgkin Study Group; *NCIC*, National Cancer Institute of Canada.
*Erythrocyte sedimentation rate (≥50 mm/h without or ≥30 mm/h with B-symptoms).
From Hoffman R et al: *Hematology, basic principles and practice*, ed 5, New York, 2009, Churchill Livingstone.

TABLE 1H-34   Recommendations for the Primary Treatment of Hodgkin Lymphoma Outside of Clinical Trials

Group	Stage	Recommendation
Early stages (favorable)	CS I-II A/B, no RFs	2 cycles ABVD ± IF RT (20-30 Gy)
	Early stages (unfavorable, intermediate)	4-6 cycles ABVD plus-30Gy or 6 cycles of ABVD in selected cases
	CS I-II A/B + RFs	
Advanced stages	CS IIB + RFs, CS III A/B, CS IV A/B	6 cycles ABVD; BEACOPP-escalated *or* BEACOPP-14 ± RT, 20-30 Gy for residual tumor (PET positive) and/or bulky disease

ABVD regimen, Adriamycin (doxorubicin), vinblastine, bleomycin, and dacarbazine; *BEACOPP-baseline* regimen, bleomycin, etoposide, Adriamycin (doxorubicin), cyclophosphamide, Oncovin (vincristine), procarbazine, and prednisone; *BEACOPP-escalated* regimen, bleomycin, etoposide, Adriamycin (doxorubicin), cyclophosphamide, Oncovin (vincristine), procarbazine, prednisone, and G-CSF; *BEACOPP-14* regimen, bleomycin, etoposide, Adriamycin (doxorubicin), cyclophosphamide, Oncovin (vincristine), procarbazine, prednisone, and G-CSF; *CS*, clinical stage; *IF*, involved field; *MOPP* regimen, mechlorethamine, Oncovin (vincristine), procarbazine, and prednisone; *PFT*, positron emission tomography; *RF*, risk factors; *RT*, radiation therapy; *Stanford V* regimen, nitrogen mustard, doxorubicin, vinblastine, bleomycin, vincristine, etoposide, and prednisone.
From Hoffman R et al: *Hematology, basic principles and practice*, ed 5, New York, 2009, Churchill Livingstone.

TABLE 1H-35   Prognostic Factors of Importance in Advanced Hodgkin Lymphoma*

Gender	Male
Age	>45 yr
Stage	IV
Hemoglobin	<105 g/L
White blood cell count	>15 × 10⁹/L
Lymphocyte count	<0.6 × 10⁹/L or <8% of the white cell differential
Serum albumin	<40 g/L

*Identified by the International Prognostic Factors Project on Advanced Hodgkin Disease.
From Abeloff MD: *Clinical oncology*, ed 3, Philadelphia, 2004, Saunders.

number of patients in whom the primary treatment fails.
- Definitions of treatment groups are described in Table 1H-33.
- Recommendations for the primary treatment of Hodgkin lymphoma outside of clinical trials are described in Table 1H-34.
- The FDA has approved the use of brentuximab vedotin for the treatment of patients with relapsed Hodgkin lymphoma. Brentuximab vedotin is an antibody–drug conjugate that links the chemotherapeutic agent auristatin to an anti-CD30 monoclonal antibody. Brentuximab is associated with overall response rates of 75% in patients with HL who have relapsed after autologous stem cell transplantation.

DISPOSITION
- Cure rates as high as 85% to 90% in early stage patients and 75% in stage III/V disease are now possible with appropriate initial therapy.
- Poor prognostic features (Table 1H-35) include presence of B symptoms, advanced age, advanced stage at initial presentation, mixed cellularity and lymphocyte depletion histology, and increased number of tumor-associated macrophages.
- Unlikely escalated BEACOPP, ABVD is not associated with a risk of leukemia. Chemotherapy significantly increases the risk of leukemia.

- Mediastinal irradiation increases the risk of subsequent cardiac disease, including valvular and pericardial disease, accelerated coronary artery disease, and conduction abnormalities.
- Radiation therapy increases the risk of developing secondary solid tumors, especially breast cancer in women younger than age 30 yr (Table 1H-36).
- Table 1H-37 describes potential late complications of Hodgkin lymphoma treatment and appropriate clinical responses and preventive strategies.

REFERRAL
- To surgery for lymph node biopsy
- Fertility clinic for sperm banking
- Hematology/Oncology
- Radiation oncology, in selected cases

⊘ PEARLS & CONSIDERATIONS

COMMENTS
- Young male patients should consider sperm banking before the initiation of therapy even though the risk of infertility with ABVD is low. Symptomatic males, particularly with advanced stage Hodgkin lymphoma, may have disease-related oligospermia at diagnosis.

- Chemotherapy with or without involved-field radiotherapy should be the standard treatment for Hodgkin lymphoma with early stage disease. Chemotherapy with radiation in selected cases should be the standard of care for advanced stage.
- After failure of ABVD therapy, more than 60% of patients who have had a relapse and about 30% of patients with initially refractory lymphoma can be reliably cured with high-dose chemotherapy and autologous hematopoietic stem-cell transplantation.
- Preclinical studies suggest that Reed-Sternberg cells exploit the programmed death 1 (PD-1) pathway to evade immune detection. Phase 1 trials with nivolumab, a PD-1 blocking antibody, have shown substantial therapeutic activity and an acceptable safety profile in patients with previously treated relapsed or refractory Hodgkin lymphoma.

SUGGESTED READINGS
Available at www.expertconsult.com

RELATED CONTENT
Hodgkin Lymphoma (Patient Information)

AUTHORS: **JORGE J. CASTILLO, M.D.,** and **ANN S. LACASCE, M.D.**

TABLE 1H-36 Second Neoplasms Seen with Increased Frequency After Successful Hodgkin Lymphoma Treatment

Acute myelogenous leukemia/myelodysplasia (BEACOPP)
Non-Hodgkin lymphoma
Melanoma
Soft tissue sarcoma
Adenocarcinoma
  Breast
  Thyroid
  Lung
Stomach and esophagus
  Squamous cell carcinoma
  Skin
  Uterine cervix
  Head and neck

From Abeloff MD: *Clinical oncology*, ed 3, Philadelphia, 2004, Saunders.

TABLE 1H-37 Potential Late Complications of Hodgkin Lymphoma Treatment and Appropriate Clinical Responses and Preventive Strategies

Risk/Problem	Incidence/Response
Dental caries	Neck or oropharyngeal irradiation can cause decreased salivation. Patients should have careful dental care follow-up and should make their dentist aware of the previous irradiation.
Hypothyroidism	After external beam irradiation that encompasses the thyroid with doses sufficient to cure Hodgkin lymphoma, at least 50% of patients will eventually become hypothyroid. All patients whose TSH level becomes elevated should be treated with lifelong thyroxine replacement in doses sufficient to suppress TSH levels to low normal. This is also necessary to ensure that the radiation-damaged thyroid is not subjected to long-term stimulation by thyroid-stimulating hormone, which can increase the risk of thyroid neoplasm.
Infertility	ABVD is not known to cause any permanent gonadal toxicity, although oligospermia for 1-2 yr after treatment is common. Direct or scatter radiation to gonadal tissue can cause infertility, amenorrhea, or premature menopause, but this seldom occurs with the current fields used for the treatment of Hodgkin lymphoma. Thus, with the current chemotherapy regimens and radiation fields used, most patients will not develop these problems. In general, after treatment, women who continue menstruating are fertile, but men require semen analysis to provide a specific answer. High-dose chemoradiotherapy and hematopoietic stem cell transplantation almost always cause permanent infertility in both genders, although some young women occasionally recover fertility.
Impaired immunity to infections	Hodgkin lymphoma and its treatment can lead to lifelong impairment of full immunity to infection. All patients should be given annual influenza immunization and pneumococcal immunization every 5 years. Patients whose spleen has been irradiated or removed should also be immunized against meningococcal types A and C and *Haemophilus influenza* type B. As for all adults, diphtheria and tetanus immunizations should be kept up-to-date.
Secondary neoplasms	Although uncommon, certain secondary neoplasms occur with increased frequency in patients who have been treated for Hodgkin lymphoma. These include acute myelogenous leukemia, thyroid, breast, lung, and upper gastrointestinal carcinoma and melanoma, and cervical carcinoma in situ. It is appropriate to screen for these neoplasms for the rest of the patient's life because they might have lengthy induction periods.

ABVD, Adriamycin, bleomycin, vinblastine, dacarbazine; *TSH,* thyroid-stimulating hormone.
From Abeloff MD: *Clinical oncology*, ed 3, Philadelphia, 2004, Saunders.

BASIC INFORMATION

DEFINITION

Hookworm is a parasitic infection of the intestine caused by the soil helminths *Necator americanus* and *Ancylostoma duodenale.*

SYNONYMS

Ground itch
Ancylostoma duodenale infection
Necator americanus infection

ICD-10CM CODES
B76.9 Hookworm disease, unspecified
B76.8 Other hookworm diseases

EPIDEMIOLOGY & DEMOGRAPHICS
INCIDENCE (IN U.S.):
- Varies greatly in different areas of the United States.
- Most common in rural areas of southeastern United States.
- Poor sanitation and increased rainfall increase incidence.

PREVALENCE (IN U.S.): Varies from 10% to 90% in regions where it is found.
PREDOMINANT AGE: Schoolchildren.

PHYSICAL FINDINGS & CLINICAL PRESENTATION
- Nonspecific abdominal complaints.
- Symptoms related to iron deficiency anemia depending on the amount of iron in the diet and worm burden (these organisms consume host's RBCs).
- Fatigue, tachycardia, dyspnea, and high-output failure.

- Hypoproteinemia and edema from loss of proteins into the intestinal tract.
- Unusual for pulmonary manifestations to occur when the larvae migrate through the lungs.
- Skin rash at sites of larval penetration in some individuals without prior exposure: ground itch.

ETIOLOGY

Two species can cause this disease: *N. americanus* and *A. duodenale. N. americanus* is the predominant cause of hookworm in the United States. They are soil nematodes (geohelminthic infections) that are acquired by skin contact (i.e., bare feet) with contaminated soils in moist, warm climate. Worldwide, over 700 million people are infected.
- Infection occurs via penetration of the skin by the larval form, with subsequent migration via the bloodstream to the alveoli, up the respiratory tract, then into the GI tract (Fig. 1H-58).
- *Ancylostoma* spp. infection can also occur via the oral route through ingestion of contaminated water supplies.
- Sharp mouth parts allow for attachment to intestinal mucosa.
- *Ancylostoma* spp. are more likely to cause iron deficiency anemia because they are larger and remove more blood daily from the bowel wall than the other hookworm species, *N. americanus.*

DIAGNOSIS

DIFFERENTIAL DIAGNOSIS
- Strongyloidiasis.
- Ascariasis.
- Other causes of iron deficiency anemia and malabsorption.

WORKUP

Examine stool for hookworm eggs. Shedding of eggs starts around 8 weeks after skin penetration in *N. americanum* infections and longer with *A. duodenale,* but eggs are indistinguishable between the two species.

LABORATORY TESTS

CBC to show hypochromic, microcytic anemia; possible mild eosinophilia and hypoalbuminemia.

IMAGING STUDIES

Chest x-ray: generally not helpful, occasionally shows opacities.

TREATMENT

NONPHARMACOLOGIC THERAPY
- Prevention of disease by not walking barefoot and by improving sanitary conditions.
- Vaccines are in development.

ACUTE GENERAL Rx
- Albendazole 400 mg once PO has become preferred treatment.
- Mebendazole 100 mg PO bid for 3 days or as a 500-mg single dose.
- Pyrantel pamoate 11 mg/kg (to max dose of 1 g) PO qd × 3 days.
- Iron supplementation may be helpful in patients with iron deficiency.

DISPOSITION

Easily treated.

REFERRAL

To gastroenterologist and infectious disease specialist if diagnosis uncertain.

PEARLS & CONSIDERATIONS

COMMENTS
- Appropriate disposal of human wastes is important in controlling the disease in areas with a high prevalence of hookworm infestation.
- Wearing shoes will avoid contact with contaminated soils, and the provision of safe water and sanitation for disposing human excreta is important in control of hookworm.

SUGGESTED READINGS
Available at www.expertconsult.com

EVIDENCE
Available at www.expertconsult.com

RELATED CONTENT
Hookworm Infection (Patient Information)

AUTHOR: **GLENN G. FORT, M.D., M.P.H.**

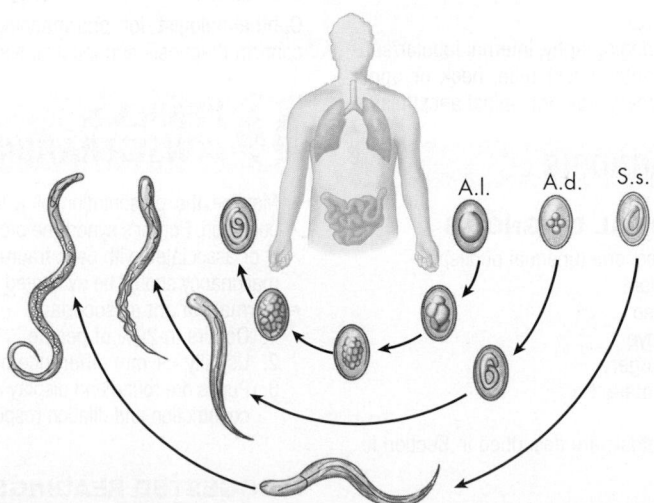

FIGURE 1H-58 Life cycle of intestinal nematodes with a migratory phase through the lungs. Eggs are passed with stools in *Ascaris lumbricoides (A.l.), Necator americanus,* or *Ancylostoma duodenale (A.d.),* or they hatch on their way out in *Strongyloides stercoralis (S.s.).* Ascaris eggs mature in soil, and humans are infected upon ingestion of these eggs. With hookworm and strongyloidiasis, humans are infected via skin penetration by filariform larvae. In all three infections, larvae pass through a migratory phase via the lungs before reaching maturity at their final habitat in the small intestine. (From Mandell GL et al: *Principles and practice of infectious diseases,* ed 7, Philadelphia, 2010, Churchill Livingstone.)

Diseases and Disorders

I

BASIC INFORMATION

DEFINITION
Horner's syndrome is the clinical triad of ipsilateral ptosis, miosis, and sometimes facial anhidrosis. Disruption of any of the three neurons in the oculosympathetic pathway (first-order, second-order, or third-order) can cause Horner's syndrome.

SYNONYMS
Oculosympathetic paresis
Raeder's paratrigeminal syndrome: Horner's syndrome of the third-order neuron associated with pain in the trigeminal nerve distribution

ICD-10CM CODES
G90.2 Horner's Syndrome

EPIDEMIOLOGY & DEMOGRAPHICS
Congenital or acquired.

PHYSICAL FINDINGS & CLINICAL PRESENTATION
- Ptosis is usually mild. It results from loss of sympathetic tone to Müller's muscle, which contributes approximately 2 mm of upper eyelid elevation. Weakness of the corresponding muscle in the lower eyelid causes it to elevate slightly. This combination causes narrowing of the palpebral fissure. Levator function of the eyelid is preserved.
- Miosis results from loss of sympathetic innervation to the iris dilator muscle (Fig. 1H-59). The affected pupil reacts normally to bright light and accommodation. Anisocoria is greater in dim light.
  1. Dilation lag: Horner's pupil dilates more slowly than the normal pupil when lights are dimmed (20 versus 5 sec) because it dilates passively as a result of relaxation of the iris sphincter.
- Presence of facial anhidrosis is variable and depends on the site of injury. It occurs with lesions affecting first-order or second-order neurons.
- Congenital Horner's syndrome may result in heterochromia. The affected eye has a lighter-colored iris.
- Acute cases may also present with conjunctival injection from the loss of sympathetic vasoconstriction.

FIGURE 1H-59 Horner's syndrome. The mild ptosis (1 to 2 mm) and the smaller pupil (in room light) can be seen on the affected right side. (From Palay D [ed]: *Ophthalmology for the primary care physician,* St Louis, 1997, Mosby.)

ETIOLOGY
Disruption of the ipsilateral sympathetic innervation to the eye and face. Lesions can damage any of the three neurons in the oculosympathetic pathway (Fig. E1H-60). First order neuron lesions are least common but are usually caused by pathology in the hypothalamus, brainstem, or cervicothoracic spinal cord. Second order neuron lesions are often caused by disease involving the cervicothoracic spinal cord, lung apex, or anterior neck. Third order neuron lesions are usually seen with disease in the internal carotid artery, skull base, cavernous sinus, or orbital apex. Location is often suggested by the presence of associated findings. Vascular disease and neoplasm must be considered.
Mechanical:
- Syringomyelia
- Trauma
- Tumors: benign, malignant head and neck cancers (thyroid, apical lung, mediastinal)
- Cervical rib
Vascular (ischemia, hemorrhage or arteriovenous malformation):
- Brainstem lesion: commonly occlusion of the posterior inferior cerebellar artery but other arteries may be responsible (vertebral; superior, middle or inferior lateral medullary arteries; superior or anterior inferior cerebellar arteries).
- Carotid artery aneurysm, dissection, arteritis: can also be from injury to other major vessels (internal carotid artery, subclavian artery, ascending aorta).
- Jugular venous ectasia.
- Cavernous sinus thrombosis.
- Cluster headache, migraine.
Miscellaneous:
- Idiopathic
- Congenital
- Demyelination (multiple sclerosis)
- Infection (apical tuberculosis, herpes zoster, Lyme disease)
- Myelitis
- Pneumothorax
- Iatrogenic (angiography, internal jugular/subclavian catheter, chest tube, neck or upper thoracic surgery, epidural spinal anesthesia)

DIAGNOSIS

DIFFERENTIAL DIAGNOSIS
Causes of anisocoria (unequal pupils):
- Normal variant
- Mydriatic use
- Prosthetic eye
- Prior eye surgery
- Unilateral cataract
- Iritis
Causes of ptosis are described in Section II.

WORKUP
History, physical examination, pharmacologic testing, imaging.

PHARMACOLOGIC TESTING
These medications may not be readily available. Pharmacologic testing should not delay evaluation in acute, painful, or traumatic cases or in patients with a history of malignancy.

- Topical cocaine test: confirms diagnosis (drops increase anisocoria by dilating normal pupil but not Horner's pupil).
- Topical apraclonidine test: confirms diagnosis (drops reverse anisocoria by causing dilation of Horner's pupil and constriction of normal pupil).
- Topical hydroxyamphetamine test: distinguishes first- and second-order neuron lesions from third-order sympathetic lesions (drops dilate normal pupil and first- or second-order Horner's pupil, but not third-order Horner's pupil). Testing must be delayed >48 hr after topical cocaine or apraclonidine testing. Topical phenylephrine may be used as an alternative (causes dilatation of pupil due to third-order neuron lesions).

IMAGING STUDIES
Results of pharmacologic testing as well as accompanying signs and symptoms should guide imaging:
- MRI brain: brainstem (diplopia, vertigo, ataxia, lateral medullary syndrome); cavernous sinus (eye movement abnormalities, sixth nerve palsy).
- MRI cervical and upper thoracic spinal cord: sensory changes/weakness of extremities, bowel/bladder dysfunction.
- MR or CT angiography (ultrasound is less sensitive): internal carotid artery dissection (acute Horner's syndrome with face or neck pain).
- CT chest and neck: evaluate lung apex, perivertebral areas, mediastinum if symptoms do not localize to the central nervous system; brachial plexus lesion (arm/hand pain or weakness).

Rx TREATMENT

- Treatment depends on underlying cause.
- Ptosis can be surgically corrected or treated with medication (phenylephrine drops).

REFERRAL
Ophthalmologist for pharmacologic testing to confirm diagnosis and localize lesion.

PEARLS & CONSIDERATIONS

- May be the presentation of a life-threatening condition. Horner's syndrome presenting acutely or associated with pain, trauma, or history of malignancy should be evaluated urgently.
- Normal variant anisocoria:
  1. Occurs in 20% of people
  2. Usually <1 mm difference between pupils
  3. Pupils are round and display a normal, brisk constriction and dilation response to light

SUGGESTED READINGS
Available at www.expertconsult.com

RELATED CONTENT
Horner's Syndrome (Patient Information)
Lung Neoplasms, Primary (Related Key Topic)

AUTHOR: **SUDEEP K. AULAKH, M.D.**

H

I

 BASIC INFORMATION

DEFINITION

Hot flashes are sudden onset of intense warmth that begins in the neck or face, or in the chest and progresses to the neck and face; often associated with profuse sweating, anxiety, and palpitations.

SYNONYMS

HFs
Vasomotor symptoms (VMSs)

ICD-10CM CODES
N95.1 Menopausal and female climacteric states
R23.2 Flushing

EPIDEMIOLOGY & DEMOGRAPHICS

- Hot flashes affect 75% of postmenopausal women.
- Most hot flashes begin 1 to 2 yr before menopause and may resolve after 2 yr. Average duration is 5 yr.
- 15% of women report duration of hot flashes >15 yr.
- Complementary therapies for hot flashes account for $34 billion in out-of-pocket spending in the U.S. annually.

PHYSICAL FINDINGS & CLINICAL PRESENTATION

- Profuse sweating and red blotching of skin may be noted during the vasomotor event.
- Palpitations and hyperreflexia may be present during the hot flash.
- Hot flashes typically last 1 to 5 min.
- Each hot flash is associated with increase in temperature, increased pulse rate, and increased blood flow into the hands and face.
- Hot flashes during sleep are common and are referred to as *night sweats*.
- There is considerable variation in the frequency of hot flashes. One third of women report more than 10 flashes per day.

ETIOLOGY

- Dysfunction of central thermoregulatory centers caused by changes in estrogen level at the time of menopause
- Tamoxifen use
- Chemotherapy-induced ovarian failure
- Androgen ablation therapy for prostate carcinoma

DIAGNOSIS

DIFFERENTIAL DIAGNOSIS

- Carcinoid syndrome
- Anxiety disorder.
- Idiopathic flushing
- Lymphoma (night sweats)
- Hyperthyroidism
- Hyperhidrosis

WORKUP

Evaluation of hot flashes is aimed at excluding the conditions listed in the differential diagnosis.

LABORATORY TESTS

- Follicle-stimulating hormone (FSH), luteinizing hormone, estradiol level. The serum FSH levels rather than estradiol levels are associated with greater severity of hot flashes in older postmenopausal women, suggesting that nonestrogen feedback systems may be important in modulating the severity of hot flashes. It is not necessary to obtain an FSH to make the diagnosis of menopausal status, however. An amenorrheic woman over age 50 with vasomotor symptoms is assumed to have made the menopausal transition and serum markers of menopause are not required to complete the diagnosis.
- Thyroid-stimulating hormone (TSH).

TREATMENT

NONPHARMACOLOGIC THERAPY

- Behavioral interventions such as relaxation training and paced respiration have been reported effective in reducing symptoms in some women.
- Avoidance of caffeine, alcohol, tobacco, and spicy foods may be beneficial.

GENERAL Rx

- Estrogen replacement therapy reduces hot flashes by 80% to 90%. Estrogen therapy, however, is contraindicated in many women, and others are fearful of its use. Potential risks and side effects should be considered before using estrogen in any patient. When using estrogen, it is best to use low dose (e.g., Prempro [conjugated equine estrogen 0.45 mg or 0.3 mg plus medroxyprogesterone 1.5 mg]). Femring is an intravaginal ring that is changed every 3 mo and approved to treat vasomotor symptoms in women who have had a hysterectomy. It provides both local and systemic estrogen.
- Megestrol acetate, a progestational agent, is a safer alternative to estrogen in women with a history of receptor-positive breast or uterine cancer and in men receiving androgen ablation therapy for prostate cancer. Usual dose is 20 mg bid.
- The antidepressant venlafaxine has been reported to be 60% effective in reducing hot flashes and represents an alternative treatment modality in women unable or unwilling to use estrogens. Starting dose is 37.5 mg qd, increased as tolerated up to a maximum of 300 mg/day. Other antidepressants such as desvenlafaxine and escitalopram have also been shown to be effective in reducing the number and severity of menopausal hot flashes. Trials have shown that paroxetine is also an effective agent for diminishing hot flashes in postmenopausal women and men receiving androgen ablation therapy.
- Duavee is a new FDA-approved treatment of moderate to severe vasomotor menopausal symptoms. It consists of a combination of conjugated estrogens and bazedoxifene, a new selective estrogen receptor modulator (SERM).
- The anticonvulsant gabapentin (300-1200 mg/day) represents another nonhormonal alternative in the treatment of hot flashes and can be used alone or in combination with venlafaxine.
- The antihypertensive clonidine is also somewhat effective in reducing the frequency of hot flashes in mild cases. Adverse effects include dry mouth, sedation, and dizziness.
- Vitamin E (800 IU/day) may be effective in patients with mild symptoms that do not interfere with sleep or daily function.
- Soy protein (use of soy extracts that contain plant-derived estrogens [phytoestrogens]) is often used; however, clinical trials have not shown clear efficacy.
- Several classes of herbal remedies are available to patients and are commonly used, generally without significant benefit. Frequently used agents are *Cimicifuga racemosa* (black cohosh, snakeroot, bugbane), *Angelica sinensis,* and evening primrose (evening star). Recent trials using the isopropanolic extract of black cohosh rootstock (Remifemin) did show some improvement in controlling menopausal symptoms. Such alternative medications may be used to treat mild to moderate symptoms, but it is possible that symptomatic improvements may derive in part from a placebo effect. Accupuncturists are the second most consulted therapists by menopausal women. Evidence of acupuncture efficacy as an HF treatment is conflicting. A recent randomized trial[1] revealed that Chinese medicine acupuncture was not superior to noninsertive sham acupucutre for women with moderately severe menopausal HFs.

SUGGESTED READINGS

Available at www.expertconsult.com

RELATED CONTENT

Hot Flashes (Patient Information)
Menopause (Related Key Topic)

AUTHOR: **FRED F. FERRI, M.D.**

[1] Ee C, et al.: Acupuncture for Menopausal Hot Flashes: A Randomized Trial, Ann Intern Med 164:146-154, 2016.

BASIC INFORMATION

DEFINITION
The human immunodeficiency virus (HIV) is a retrovirus that is responsible for causing acquired immunodeficiency syndrome (AIDS). HIV infection does not necessarily mean a person has AIDS.

SYNONYMS
AIDS: The result of progressive HIV infection in with which a person has a weakened immune system and meets specific diagnostic criteria (See "Acquired Immunodeficiency Syndrome" in Section I.)

ICD-10CM CODES
B20 Human immunodeficiency virus [HIV]

EPIDEMIOLOGY & DEMOGRAPHICS (IN U.S.)
- There are an estimated 1.2 million people infected with HIV in the United States (US), with approximately 1 out of 8 (12.8%) who do not know they are infected.
- In 2013, there were an estimated 47,352 new HIV infections, according to the CDC.
- Greatest incidence is in men who have sex with men (MSM) and racial minority populations.

PREDOMINANT RISK GROUPS:
- Gay, bisexual, and other MSM are the groups most affected by HIV.
- In 2010, MSM accounted for 63% of all new infections according to the CDC.
- HIV disproportionately affects MSM of younger age and black/African American and Hispanic background.
- Heterosexual transmission and injection drug use accounted for 25% and 8% of new HIV infections in 2010, respectively.

- Table 1H-38 summarizes risk factors associated with sexual transmission of HIV.

RACIAL DATA:
- In 2012, blacks/African Americans accounted for 47% of new HIV infections despite being 13% of the U.S. population.
- In 2012, Hispanics/Latinos accounted for 22% of new HIV infections despite being 17% of the U.S. population.

GENETICS
Familial Disposition:
Individuals with deletions in the *CCR5* gene are immune from infection with macrophage tropic virus (the predominant virus in sexual transmission). Other genetic variants may contribute to rapid progression or long-term control of the virus once infected. One in 300 individuals infected with HIV is an "elite controller," which means they are able to maintain a normal CD4 count and undetectable viral load through immune control.

Congenital Infection:
- 75% of HIV cases diagnosed in children younger than age 13 yr in 2010 were caused by peripartum infection, which may occur in utero, during delivery, or after delivery via breastfeeding.
- No specific congenital abnormalities are associated with HIV infection, although there is a higher risk of spontaneous abortion and low birth weight.

Neonatal Infection:
- May occur during delivery or via breastfeeding.
- Typically asymptomatic.

PHYSICAL FINDINGS & CLINICAL PRESENTATION
- Signs and symptoms are variable with stage of disease. "Stage 0" indicates a very early infection diagnosed when standard markers are converting from negative to positive.

- Acute HIV infection (0 to 3 months, usually within several weeks):
  1. Causes a self-limited mononucleosis-like illness in 50% to 80% of individuals, characterized by fever, sore throat, lymphadenopathy, headache, and a rash resembling roseola. Individuals may also be asymptomatic.
  2. In a minority of acute cases, aseptic meningitis, Bell's palsy, or peripheral neuropathy may occur.
  3. Rarely, opportunistic infections such as thrush or *Pneumocystis jiroveci* pneumonia (PJP) may occur.
- Chronic HIV infection is usually characterized by a prolonged asymptomatic phase followed by nonspecific symptoms of lymphadenopathy, fatigue, weight loss, diarrhea, and skin changes including seborrheic dermatitis, localized herpes zoster, and/or fungal infection.
- Advanced disease is characterized by AIDS-associated diseases, including infections and malignancies (see specific disorders).
- HIV infection in women may be associated with lower levels of viral load at comparable degrees of immunosuppression when compared with men. Furthermore, women may, on average, have higher CD4 counts at the time of HIV diagnosis.
- Another special consideration in women infected with HIV is the high incidence of human papillomavirus (HPV) co-infection and risk for cervical cancer. HIV-positive women should be screened for cervical cancer twice in the first year and then annually thereafter if pap smears are normal.
- Co-infection with HIV and hepatitis C is common because of similar transmission risk. Hepatitis C is most commonly transmitted by contaminated needles or blood exposure. Hepatitis C can be transmitted sexually, but the risk is low. Patients with HIV and hepatitis C progress faster to cirrhosis. Patients may already have signs of advanced liver disease at the time of diagnosis.

ETIOLOGY
- HIV is a single-stranded RNA retrovirus (Figure 1H-61) that is categorized as type 1 or 2.
- HIV-1 was derived from transmission of a simian immunodeficiency virus (SIV) from chimpanzees in Central Africa; HIV-2 was derived from an SIV found in sooty mangabey monkeys from West Africa.
- HIV-1 is the predominant pathogenic retrovirus in human populations; HIV-2 has limited distribution (primarily West Africa) and tends to progress less rapidly than HIV-1. HIV-2 should be considered in individuals from West Africa or whose sexual partners are from West Africa.
- HIV-1/2 are transmitted by sexual contact, shared needles, blood transfusion, or from mother to child during pregnancy, delivery, or breastfeeding.
- Primary target of infection: CD4 lymphocytes.

TABLE 1H-38 Risk Factors Associated with Sexual Transmission of HIV

Sexually transmitted infections
   Ulcerative or nonulcerative diseases
Genital tract inflammation
HIV disease
   Higher viral loads
   Lower CD4+ levels
   Acute HIV infection
   Lack of effective antiretroviral therapy
   Lack of heterozygosity or homozygosity for the inactivating 32-base pair deletion in the chemokine receptor gene *(CCR5)*
Anatomic factors
   Lack of circumcision
   Cervical ectopy
   Leukocytospermia
   ?Hormonal contraception
Sexual practices
   Receptive anal intercourse
   Sexual activity during menses
   Bleeding during intercourse (disruption of vaginal mucosa through trauma)
   Lack of barrier protection
HIV viral features
   Syncytium formation
   Certain viral clades

HIV, Human immunodeficiency virus.
From Bennett JE, Dolin R, Blaser MJ: *Mandell, Douglas, and Bennett's principles and practice of infectious diseases,* ed 8, Philadelphia, 2015, Saunders.

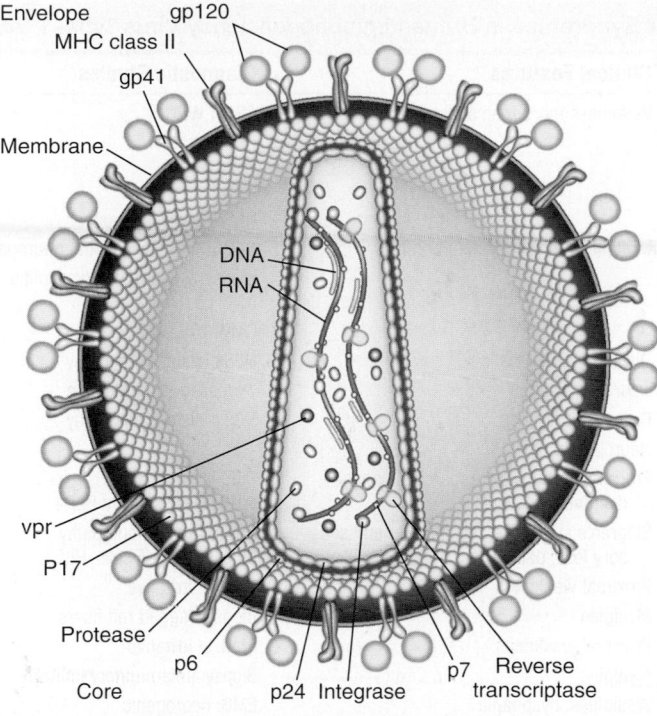

FIGURE 1H-61 Structure of the HIV-1 virion. The viral envelope is formed from the host cell membrane, into which the HIV-1 envelope proteins gp41 and gp120 have been inserted and may include several host cell proteins, most significantly the major histocompatibility complex class II proteins. The matrix between the envelope and the core is formed predominantly from gag protein p17. The core contains the viral RNA, closely associated with gag protein p7, in addition to RT and integrase. It has also been proven that virions contain complementary DNA, as shown, synthesized by the RT. The major structural proteins of the core are gag proteins p24 and p6. Also present within the virion are the protease and two cleavage products from the gag precursor protein (p1 and p2, not shown) of undetermined position within the virion. Viral protein R (Vpr) is also packaged in the virion and is thought to be localized within the core, as shown. (From Mandell GL et al: *Principles and practice of infectious diseases*, ed 7, Philadelphia, 2010, Saunders.)

Dx DIAGNOSIS

DIFFERENTIAL DIAGNOSIS

- Acute HIV infection: often diagnosed or confused with mononucleosis or other respiratory viral infections
- Late symptoms: similar to those produced by other wasting/chronic illnesses such as neoplasms, tuberculosis (TB), disseminated fungal infection (such as *Candida*), malabsorption, or depression
- HIV-related encephalopathy: confused with Alzheimer's disease or other causes of chronic dementia (cognitive impairment in HIV infection is described in another chapter in Section I); myelopathy and neuropathy possibly resembling other demyelinating diseases such as multiple sclerosis.
- Direct central nervous system (CNS) involvement: manifests as encephalopathy, myelopathy, or neuropathy in advanced cases. Table 1H-39 summarizes neuromuscular syndromes in HIV infection.
- Renal failure, rheumatologic disorders, thrombocytopenia, or cardiac abnormalities may be seen in association with HIV-1.

WORKUP

Since the debut of HIV/AIDS in the 1980s, diagnosis has been established by testing for antibodies to the virus. The CDC recommends routine testing for patients in all health care settings unless the patient declines (opt-out screening). This includes routine testing of pregnant women. It is also recommended that separate written consent should no longer be required, although by law this is being addressed on a state-by-state basis. Generally, all persons aged 13 to 64 should undergo HIV testing at least once, and more frequently (at least once a year) if sexually active.

- An FDA-approved at-home rapid HIV screening test is available. It uses swabs of oral fluids from upper and lower gums. A positive test requires confirmatory testing in the office.

LABORATORY TESTS

HIV antibodies are detected by a two-step technique:

- ELISA (enzyme-linked immunosorbent assay), which is a sensitive screening test.
- Confirmation of positive ELISA tests with more specific assays. The classic confirmatory test is the Western blot, but this is not commonly used anymore.
- Screening ELISA antibody tests will measure HIV-1 and HIV-2 antibodies. Confirmatory tests will generally differentiate between HIV-1 and HIV-2 as well. However, the viral load assays (HIV RNA PCR) are specific only for HIV-1.
- Fourth-generation antibody/antigen tests can detect the "p20" antigen, which is present early in HIV infection and can be used to diagnose HIV earlier than previous generations. An HIV RNA PCR should still be sent if acute HIV is suspected.

- Baseline viral resistance testing is recommended for all newly diagnosed patients with HIV to guide choice of antiretroviral therapy (ART).
- The CD4 count and HIV RNA polymerase chain reaction (PCR) should be measured in all patients.
- The CD4 count is a marker of current immune status. Table 1H-40 describes the World Health Organization (WHO) immunologic classification for established HIV infection.
- The HIV RNA PCR (viral load) is predictive of disease progression.
- Rapid serologic tests have been increasingly used and are useful in specific settings: occupational exposures, pregnant women in labor without previous testing, and patients in high seroprevalence areas (for immediate results). Specimens are either blood or saliva and results are given within 1 to 20 min. Although sensitivity is high (99%), false-positive tests are more common in low seroprevalence populations. Thus, all positive results must be confirmed with standard serology.
- Early during infection (i.e., acute HIV infection), standard antibody tests may be negative ("window period"). The standard for

TABLE 1H-39 Neuromuscular Syndromes in Human Immunodeficiency Virus Type–1 Infection

Diagnosis	Disease Stage	Clinical Features	Diagnostic Studies	Treatment
AIDP	Early > late	Weakness more than sensory loss	CSF: ↑ WBCs	Early: IVIG, steroids, plasmapheresis
CIDP			↑↑ Protein	Late: consider ganciclovir/foscarnet
			NCSs: demyelination	
MM	Early or late	Multiple painful mononeuropathies	NCSs: multifocal axonal neuropathy	Early: none
			Biopsy: inflammation/vasculitis	Late: steroids/cyclophosphamide
			CMV	Ganciclovir/foscarnet
Nucleoside	Any stage	Distal sensory loss	NCSs: distal axonopathy	Nucleoside withdrawal
Neuropathy		Neuropathic pain	Increased serum lactate	
DSPN	Late	Distal sensory loss	NCSs: distal axonopathy	NSAIDs, capsaicin
		Neuropathic pain		AED, tricyclics
PP	Late	Progressive flaccid paraparesis, urinary dysfunction, LS pain	CSF: increased WBCs (PMNs), CMV PCR+	Ganciclovir/foscarnet Cidofovir
DILS	Late	Sjögren's syndrome, distal motor and sensory loss, pain	NCSs: axonal neuropathy Biopsy: CD8+ T cells, HIV-1	Zidovudine/ART Steroids
Zidovudine	Any stage	Proximal weakness	EMG: ± irritative	Zidovudine withdrawal
Myopathy		Myalgias	Biopsy: ragged red fibers	
Polymyositis	Any stage	Proximal weakness	EMG: ± irritative	Steroids, IVIG
		Myalgias	Biopsy: inflammatory infiltrates	Immunosuppressants
ALS-like	Late	Weakness, dysphagia	EMG: neurogenic	ART

AED, Antiepileptic drug; *AIDP,* acute inflammatory demyelinating polyneuropathy; *ALS,* amyotrophic lateral sclerosis; *ART,* antiretroviral therapy; *CIDP,* chronic inflammatory demyelinating polyneuropathy; *CMV,* cytomegalovirus; *CSF,* cerebrospinal fluid; *DILS,* diffuse infiltrative lymphocytosis syndrome; *DSPN,* distal sensory polyneuropathy; *EMG,* electromyography; *HIV,* human immunodeficiency virus; *IVIG,* intravenous immunoglobulin; *LS,* lumbosacral; *MM,* mononeuritis multiplex; *NCS,* nerve conduction studies; *NSAID,* nonsteroidal anti-inflammatory drug; *PCR,* polymerase chain reaction; *PMNs,* polymorphonuclear leukocytes; *PP,* progressive polyradiculopathy; *WBCs,* white blood cells.
From Bennett JE, Dolin R, Blaser MJ: *Mandell, Douglas, and Bennett's principles and practice of infectious diseases,* ed 8, Philadelphia, 2015, Saunders.

TABLE 1H-40 World Health Organization Immunologic Classification for Established HIV Infection

HIV-Associated Immunodeficiency	Age-Related CD4 Values			
	<11 mo (% CD4+)	12-35 mo (% CD4+)	36-59 mo (% CD4+)	>5 yr (Absolute No./mm³ or % CD4+)
None or not significant	>35	>30	>25	>500
Mild	30-35	25-30	20-25	350-500
Advanced	25-29	20-24	15-19	200-349
Severe	<25	<20	<15	<200 or <15%

From Bennett JE, Dolin R, Blaser MJ: *Mandell, Douglas, and Bennett's principles and practice of infectious diseases,* ed 8, Philadelphia, 2015, Saunders.

diagnosing HIV during acute HIV infection is by testing for HIV RNA (viral load).

- In 2014, the CDC released a revised surveillance case definition for HIV infection. This information has been added in the EBM section of this topic. Table 1H-41 describes the WHO clinical staging of HIV/AIDS for adults and adolescents with confirmed HIV infection. Table 1H-42 compares the WHO and CDC staging systems.

Fig. 1H-62 describes the immunologic response to HIV infection.

 **TREATMENT**

NONPHARMACOLOGIC THERAPY
Maintenance of adequate nutrition

ACUTE GENERAL Rx
Acute management of opportunistic infections and malignancies (see AIDS-associated disorders, "*Pneumocystis jiroveci* Pneumonia," "Cryptococcosis," "Tuberculosis," "Cryptosporidiosis," "Toxoplasmosis," etc., elsewhere in this text).

CHRONIC Rx
All HIV-infected patients should be considered for ART regardless of CD4 cell count. The benefit of ART is well established in preventing progression to AIDS and associated comorbidities.

- Therapy is strongly recommended for all patients with symptomatic established HIV disease regardless of the CD4 count. Symptomatic HIV disease is defined as the

presence of any of the following: thrush, vaginal candidiasis, herpes zoster, peripheral neuropathy, bacillary angiomatosis, cervical dysplasia in situ, constitutional symptoms such as fever or diarrhea for more than 1 month, ITP, PID, or listeriosis.

- In asymptomatic individuals, ART is now recommended regardless of CD4 cell counts. The updated recommendations are due to the safety and benefit of newer antivirals in preventing AIDS and decreasing both morbidity and mortality. Earlier treatment may also help reduce transmission of the virus to others due to reductions in viral loads.

- ART generally consists of using a 3-drug regimen to treat HIV infection. Classes of antiretrovirals include:

TABLE 1H-41 World Health Organization Clinical Staging of HIV/AIDS for Adults and Adolescents With Confirmed HIV Infection

Clinical Stage 1

Asymptomatic

Persistent generalized lymphadenopathy

Clinical Stage 2

Moderate unexplained weight loss (<10% of presumed or measured body weight)*

Recurrent respiratory tract infections (e.g., sinusitis, tonsillitis, otitis media, pharyngitis)

Herpes zoster

Angular cheilitis

Recurrent oral ulceration

Papular pruritic eruptions

Seborrheic dermatitis

Fungal nail infections

Clinical Stage 3

Unexplained* severe weight loss (>10% of presumed or measured body weight)

Unexplained chronic diarrhea for longer than 1 month

Unexplained persistent fever (>37.6°C [99.7°F]), intermittent or constant, for longer than 1 month

Persistent oral candidiasis

Oral hairy leukoplakia

Pulmonary tuberculosis (current)

Severe bacterial infections (e.g., pneumonia, empyema, pyomyositis, bone or joint infection, meningitis, or bacteremia)

Acute necrotizing ulcerative stomatitis, gingivitis, or periodontitis

Unexplained anemia (<8 g/dL), neutropenia (<0.5 × 10⁹/L), or chronic thrombocytopenia (<50 × 10⁹/L)

Clinical Stage 4†

HIV wasting syndrome

Pneumocystis jirovecii

Recurrent severe bacterial pneumonia

Chronic herpes simplex infection (orolabial, genital or anorectal, longer than 1 month's duration, or visceral at any site)

Esophageal candidiasis (or candidiasis of trachea, bronchi, or lungs)

Extrapulmonary tuberculosis

Kaposi sarcoma

Cytomegalovirus infection (retinitis or infection of other organs)

Central nervous system toxoplasmosis

HIV encephalopathy

Extrapulmonary cryptococcosis, including meningitis

Disseminated nontuberculous mycobacterial infection

Progressive multifocal leukoencephalopathy

Chronic cryptosporidiosis (with diarrhea)

Chronic isosporiasis

Disseminated mycosis (coccidioidomycosis or histoplasmosis)

Recurrent nontyphoidal *Salmonella* bacteremia

Lymphoma (cerebral or B-cell non-Hodgkin's) or other solid HIV-associated tumors

Invasive cervical carcinoma

Atypical disseminated leishmaniasis

Symptomatic HIV-associated nephropathy or symptomatic HIV-associated cardiomyopathy

*Unexplained refers to when the condition is not explained by other causes.

†Some additional specific conditions can also be included in regional classifications (e.g., reactivation of American trypanosomiasis [meningoencephalitis or myocarditis]) in the World Health Organization region of the Americas and disseminated penicilliosis in Asia.

From Bennett JE, Dolin R, Blaser MJ: *Mandell, Douglas, and Bennett's principles and practice of infectious diseases,* ed 8, Philadelphia, 2015, Saunders.

1. Nucleoside/nucleotide reverse transcriptase inhibitor (NRTI): zidovudine (AZT), lamivudine (3TC), emtricitabine (FTC), tenofovir (TDF), abacavir (ABC), stavudine (D4T), or didanosine (DDI).
2. Protease inhibitors (PI): lopinavir/ritonavir, atazanavir, fosamprenavir, darunavir, saquinavir, amprenavir, tipranavir, nelfinavir, and indinavir. These PIs may be "boosted" by ritonavir to increase levels.
3. Non-nucleoside reverse transcriptase inhibitors (NNRTI): Nevirapine, efavirenz, etravirine, delavirdine, or rilpivirine.

4. Integrase Inhibitors (II): Raltegravir, elvitegravir, and dolutegravir.
5. Fusion Inhibitors: Enfuvirtide (T-20). This drug is administered through subcutaneous injections and is only used as part of a salvage regimen for individuals who have failed multiple other regimens.
6. CCR5 Inhibitors: Maraviroc. Before using this drug, a viral trophism assay should be checked to determine if the virus uses the CCR5 co-receptor to infect cells. If the virus uses the CXCR4 co-receptor, this drug will not be effective.

- Adding a fourth drug to the three-drug regimen does not improve viral suppression or outcomes and is not recommended. Treatment interruptions based upon CD4 responses appear harmful in recent comparative studies versus standard continuous treatment protocols and should be avoided. Antiretroviral regimens for initial therapy are summarized in Table 1H-44.
- Typical dosing regimen consists of two NRTIs and either a NNRTI, PI, or II. IIs are now the preferred third drug because of tolerability. Data support inclusion of lamivudine or emtricitabine as one of the two NRTIs.

TABLE 1H-42 Comparison of WHO and CDC Staging Systems*

WHO Stage[†]	WHO T-Lymphocyte Count and Percentage[‡]	CDC Stage[§]	CDC T-Lymphocyte Count and Percentage
Stage 1 (HIV infection)	CD4+ T-lymphocyte count of ≥500 cells/mm^3	Stage 1 (HIV infection)	CD4+ T-lymphocyte count of ≥500 cells/mm^3 or CD4+ T-lymphocyte percentage of ≥29
Stage 2 (HIV infection)	CD4+ T-lymphocyte count of 350-499 cells/mm^3	Stage 2 (HIV infection)	CD4+ T-lymphocyte count of 200-499 cells/mm^3 or CD4+ T-lymphocyte percentage of 14-28
Stage 3 (advanced HIV disease [AHD])	CD4+ T-lymphocyte count of 200-349 cells/mm^3	Stage 2 (HIV infection)	CD4+ T-lymphocyte count of 200-499 cells/mm^3 or CD4+ T-lymphocyte percentage of 14-28
Stage 4 (acquired immunodeficiency syndrome [AIDS])	CD4+ T-lymphocyte count of <200 cells/mm^3 or CD4+ T-lymphocyte percentage of <15	Stage 3 (AIDS)	CD4+ T-lymphocyte count of <200 cells/mm^3 or CD4+ T-lymphocyte percentage of <14

CDC, Centers for Disease Control and Prevention; *WHO*, World Health Organization.
*For reporting purposes only.
[†]Among adults and children aged ≥5 years.
[‡]Percentage applicable for stage 4 only.
[§]Among adults and adolescents (ages ≥13 years). CDC also includes a fourth stage, stage unknown; laboratory confirmation of HIV infection but no information on CD4+ T-lymphocyte count or percentage and no information on AIDS-defining conditions.
From Bennett JE , Dolin R, Blaser MJ: *Mandell, Douglas, and Bennett's Principles and Practice of Infectious Diseases*, ed 8, Philadelphia, 2015, Saunders.

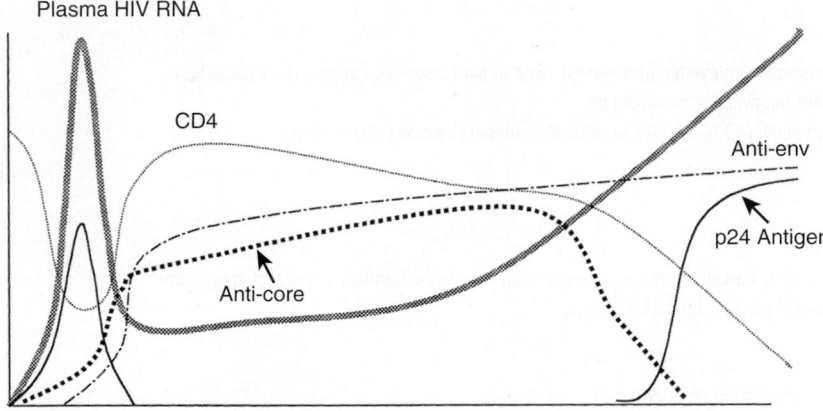

FIGURE 1H-62 Course of human immunodeficiency virus infection. (From Mandell GL [ed]: *Mandell, Douglas, and Bennett's principles and practice of infectious diseases*, ed 6, New York, 2005, Churchill Livingstone.)

Standard NRTIs include:
- Truvada (tenofovir/emtricitabine) 1 tablet once daily. Individuals with underlying renal dysfunction or requiring other nephrotoxic agents may be at increased risk of renal toxicity while taking tenofovir.
- Epzicom (abacavir/lamivudine) 1 tablet once daily. Abacavir may be associated with increased risk of myocardial infarction. Before using this drug, individuals should be checked for HLA-B*5701. Individuals with this allele are at higher risk of serious hypersensitivity reactions, and this drug should be avoided.
- Combivir (zidovudine/lamivudine) 1 tablet twice daily. Once widely prescribed; now rarely used due to lower efficacy compared with tenofovir-emtricitabine; zidovudine is associated with lipoatrophy and anemia, as well as GI and CNS side effects.

Standard Backbone Regimens include:
- IIs (These are now considered first line)
  1. Dolutegravir (50 mg once daily): The FDA has approved Triumeq, a fixed-dose combination of the integrase strand inhibitor dolutegravir and the NRTIs abacavir and lamivudine, for once-daily treatment of HIV-1 infection.
  2. Elvitegravir: Given with cobicistat (booster) and tenofovir/emtricitabine in a fixed-dose combination called Stribild.
  3. Raltegravir (400 mg twice a day).
- NNRTIs
  1. Efavirenz 600 mg daily: not recommended for women in the first trimester or those who are contemplating pregnancy..
  2. Rilpivirine: given with tenofovir and emtricitabine as part of a fixed-dose combination called Complera.
  3. Nevirapine 200 mg two times a day: avoid with CD4 count >250 in men and >350 cells per cubic millimeter in women because of the risk of hepatitis. The newer agent rilpivirine had higher virologic failures and should be considered an alternative agent.
  4. Etravirine 200 mg two times a day: This drug is generally used in patients for whom other regimens have failed. Etravirine retains activity in many patients that have developed resistance against efavirenz and nevirapine.

- PIs (ritonavir boosted)
  1. Lopinavir and ritonavir (200 mg/50 mg) 2 tablets twice a day (or 4 tablets once a day): most likely to cause diarrhea and has the greatest negative effect on triglyceride levels.
  2. Atazanavir and ritonavir (300 mg and 100 mg) 2 tablets a day: lower pill burden but use with caution with acid reducing agents—can alter absorption.
  3. Fosamprenavir and ritonavir (700 mg and 100 mg) 2 tablets twice a day (or 4 tablets once a day): cannot take fosamprenavir with sulfa allergy.
  4. Darunavir and ritonavir (800 mg and 100 mg a day). This is considered a preferred PI regimen within the DHHS guidelines.
  5. Saquinavir and ritonavir: Saquinavir is no longer recommended for initial treatment of any patient.
- All these drugs have their own unique, as well as class-specific, side effects and require careful follow-up to achieve optimal antiviral effects. Compliance with the drug regimen and tolerance of common side effects are critically

TABLE 1H-43 Prophylaxis to Prevent First Episode of HIV-related Opportunistic Disease

Pathogen	Indication	First Choice	Alternative
Pneumocystis jiroveci pneumonia (PJP, previously referred to as Pneumocystis carinii, PCP)	CD4+ count <200 cells/mm³ or oropharyngeal candidiasis CD4+ <14% or history of AIDS-defining illness CD4+ count >200 but <250 cells/mm³ if monitoring CD4+ count every 1-3 mo is not possible	Trimethoprim-sulfamethoxazole (TMP-SMX) double-strength PO daily; or single-strength daily	TMP-SMX 1 double-strength PO 3 times weekly; or Dapsone 100 mg PO daily or 50 mg PO bid; or Aerosolized pentamidine 300 mg via Respirgard II nebulizer every month; or Atovaquone 1500 mg PO daily
Toxoplasma gondii encephalitis	Toxoplasma IgG–positive patients with CD4+ count <100 cells/mm³ Seronegative patients receiving PCP prophylaxis not active against toxoplasmosis should have Toxoplasma serology retested if CD4+ count declines to <100 cells/mm³. Prophylaxis should be initiated if seroconversion occurred.	TMP-SMX, 1 double-strength PO daily	TMP-SMX 1 double-strength PO 3 times weekly; or TMP-SMX 1 single-strength PO daily; or Dapsone 50 mg PO daily + pyrimethamine 50 mg PO weekly + leucovorin 25 mg PO weekly; or Dapsone 200 mg PO weekly + pyrimethamine 75 mg PO weekly + leucovorin 25 mg PO weekly
Mycobacterium tuberculosis infection (TB) (treatment of latent TB infection or LTBI)	(1) Diagnostic test for LTBI, no evidence of active TB, and no prior history of treatment for active or latent TB (2) Diagnostic test for LTBI, but close contact with a person with infectious pulmonary TB and no evidence of active TB (3) A history of untreated or inadequately treated healed TB (i.e., old fibrotic lesions) regardless of diagnostic tests for LTBI and no evidence of active TB	Isoniazid (INH) 300 mg PO daily or 900 mg PO twice weekly for 9 mo—both plus pyridoxine 50 mg PO daily; or For persons exposed to drug-resistant TB, selection of drugs after consultation with public health authorities	Rifampin (RIF) 600 mg PO daily × 3-4 mo; or Rifabutin (RFB) 300 mg once daily for 4 mo. Be careful of drug interactions with these medications (PIs and NNRTIs).
Disseminated Mycobacterium avium complex (MAC) disease	CD4+ count <50 cells/mm³—after ruling out active MAC infection	Azithromycin 1200 mg PO once weekly; or Clarithromycin 500 mg PO bid; or Azithromycin 600 mg PO twice weekly	RFB 300 mg PO daily (dosage adjustment based on drug-drug interactions with antiretroviral therapy); rule out active TB before starting RFB
Streptococcus pneumoniae infection	CD4+ count >200 cells/mm³ and no receipt of pneumococcal vaccine in the past 5 yr CD4+ count <200 cells/mm³—vaccination can be offered In patients who received polysaccharide pneumococcal vaccination (PPV) when CD4+ count <200 cells/mm³ but has increased to >200 cells/mm³ in response to antiretroviral therapy	23-valent PPV 0.5 mL IM × 1 Revaccination every 5 yr may be considered	
Influenza A and B virus infection	All HIV-infected patients	Inactivated influenza vaccine 0.5 mL IM annually	
Histoplasma capsulatum infection	CD4+ count ≤150 cells/mm³ and at high risk because of occupational exposure or live in a community with a hyperendemic rate of histoplasmosis (>10 cases/100 patient-yr)	Itraconazole 200 mg PO daily	
Coccidioidomycosis	Positive IgM or IgG serologic test result in a patient from a disease-endemic area; and CD4+ count <250 cells/mm³	Fluconazole 400 mg PO daily Itraconazole 200 mg PO bid	
Varicella-zoster virus (VZV) infection	Pre-exposure prevention: Patients with CD4+ count ≥200 cells/mm³ who have not been vaccinated, have no history of varicella or herpes zoster, or who are seronegative for VZV Note: Routine VZV serologic testing in HIV-infected adults is not recommended. Postexposure—close contact with a person who has active varicella or herpes zoster For susceptible patients (those who have no history of vaccination or of either condition, or are known to be VZV seronegative)	Pre-exposure prevention: Primary varicella vaccination (Varivax), 2 doses (0.5 mL SC) administered 3 mo apart. If vaccination results in disease because of vaccine virus, treatment with acyclovir is recommended. Postexposure therapy: Varicella-zoster immune globulin (VariZIG) 125 IU per 10 kg (maximum of 625 IU) IM, administered within 96 hr after exposure to a person with active varicella or herpes zoster Note: As of June 2007, VariZIG can be obtained only under a treatment IND (1-800-843-7477, FFF Enterprises).	VZV-susceptible household contacts of susceptible HIV-infected persons should be vaccinated to prevent potential transmission of VZV to their HIV-infected contacts. Alternative postexposure therapy: Postexposure varicella vaccine (Varivax) 0.5 ml SC × 2 doses, 3 mo apart if CD4+ count >200 cells/mm³; or Preemptive acyclovir 800 mg PO 3×/day for 5 days These two alternatives have not been studied in the HIV population.
Human papillomavirus (HPV) infection	Women aged 11-26 yr. Men aged 11-21 yr	HPV quadrivalent vaccine 0.5 ml IM mo 0, 2, and 6	

TABLE 1H-43 Prophylaxis to Prevent First Episode of HIV-related Opportunistic Disease—cont'd

Pathogen	Indication	First Choice	Alternative
Hepatitis A virus (HAV) infection	HAV-susceptible patients with chronic liver disease or who are injection-drug users, or men who have sex with men. Certain specialists might delay vaccination until CD4+ count >200 cells/mm³.	Hepatitis A vaccine 1 ml IM × 2 doses—at 0 and 6-12 mo IgG antibody response should be assessed 1 mo after vaccination; nonresponders should be revaccinated	
Hepatitis B virus (HBV) infection	All HIV patients without evidence of prior exposure to HBV should be vaccinated with HBV vaccine, including patients with CD4+ count <200 cells/mm³. *Patients with isolated anti-HBc:* consider screening for HBV DNA before vaccination to rule out occult chronic HBV infection	Hepatitis B vaccine IM (Engerix-B 20 μg/mL or Recombivax HB 10 μg/ml) at 0, 1, and 6 mo Anti-HBs should be obtained 1 mo after completion of the vaccine series.	Some experts recommend vaccinating with 40-μg doses of either vaccine.
	Vaccine nonresponders: Defined as anti-HBs <10 IU/mL 1 mo after a vaccination series For patients with low CD4+ count at the time of first vaccination series, certain specialists might delay revaccination until after a sustained increase in CD4+ count with antiretroviral therapy.	Revaccinate with a second vaccine series.	Some experts recommend revaccinating with 40-μg doses of either vaccine.

Modified from Centers for Disease Control and Prevention. Guidelines for prevention and treatment of opportunistic infections in HIV-infected adults and adolescents: Recommendations from CDC, the National Institutes of Health, and the HIV Medicine Association of the Infectious Disease Society of America, *MMWR Morb Mortal Wkly Rep* 58(RR-4), 2009.

TABLE 1H-44 What Antiretroviral Regimen to Choose for Initial Therapy

Preferred Regimens	Comments
Integrase inhibitor-based regimen RAL + TDF/FTC Dolutegravir + TDF/FTC Dolutegravir/ABC/3TC Elvitegravir/cobicistat/TDF/FTC PI-based regimen DRV/r (once daily) + TDF/FTC Preferred regimen for pregnant women LPV/r (twice daily) + ZDV/3TC	

Alternative Regimens	Comments
NNRTI-based regimens (in alphabetical order) EFV/TDF/FTC EFV + ABC/3TC RPV/TDF/FTC RPV + ABC/3TC PI-based regimens (in alphabetical order) ATV/r + ABC/3TC ATV/r + TDF/FTC DRV + ABC/3TC FPV/r (once or twice daily) + either ABC/3TC or TDF/FTC LPV/r (once or twice daily) + either [(ABC or ZDV)/3TC] or TDF/FTC Integrase inhibitor-based regimens RAL + ABC/3TC	These regimens are now preferred. EFV should not be used during the first trimester of pregnancy or in women trying to conceive. NVP should not be used in patients with moderate to severe hepatic impairment (Child-Pugh B or C) Should not be used in women with pre-treatment CD4 >250 cells/mm³ or men with CD4 >400 cells/mm³ ABC should not be used in patients who test positive for HLA-B*5701 Use with caution in patients with high risk of cardiovascular disease or with pretreatment HIV RNA >100,000 copies/mL Once-daily LPV/r is not recommended in pregnant women.

Acceptable Regimens
EFV + AZT/3TC
NVP + TDF/FTC or ABC/3TC or AZT/3TC
RPV + AZT/3TC
ATV + ABC/3TC or AZT/3TC
ATV/r + AZT/3TC
DRV/r + AZT/3TC
FPV/r + AZT/3TC
LPV/r + AZT/3TC
RAL + AZT/3TC
MVC + AZT/3TC or TDF/FTC or ABC/3TC

3TC, Lamivudine; *ABC,* abacavir; *ATV,* atazanavir; *ddI,* didanosine; *DRV,* darunavir; *EFV,* efavirenz; *FPV,* fosamprenavir; *FTC,* emtricitabine; *INSTI,* integrase strand transfer inhibitor; *LPV,* lopinavir; *MRV,* maraviroc; *NNRTI,* nonnucleoside reverse transcriptase inhibitor; *NRTI,* nucleos(t)ide reverse transcriptase inhibitor; *NVP,* nevirapine; *PI,* protease inhibitor; *r,* low dose ritonavir; *RAL,* raltegravir; *RPV,* rilpivirine; *SQV,* saquinavir; *TDF,* tenofovir; *ZDV,* zidovudine.The following combinations in the recommended list are available as fixed-dose combination formulations: ABC/3TC, EFV/TDF/FTC, LPV/r, TDF/FTC, RPV/TDF/FTC, and ZDV/3TC.

Modified from Panel on Antiretroviral Guidelines for Adults and Adolescents. Guidelines for the use of antiretroviral agents in HIV-1–infected adults and adolescents. Department of Health and Human Services 1-161, 2012. http://www.aidsinfo.nih.gov/ContentFiles/AdultandAdolescentGL.pdf.

important to maintain drug efficacy. Antiviral response should be monitored by baseline HIV viral load and CD4 count and repeat measurement at 2 and 4 weeks into treatment and then periodically (every 3-6 months) to ensure viral suppression.

- All patients should have genotypic resistance testing upon entry into medical care and before initiation of ART.
- In experienced patients, an antiretroviral regimen should be constructed based on past antiretroviral use and the results of genotypic or phenotypic testing.
- The FDA has recently approved Genvoya, a fixed dose combination of elvitegravir, cobicistat, emtricitabine, and tenofovir alafenamide as a first line treatment for HIV-1 infection in patients ≥12 years old.
- Patients with a CD4 count <200/mm^3 should be given preventive therapy for

PJP (see "*Pneumocystis jiroveci [P. carinii]* Pneumonia").

- Evaluation of chronic diarrhea in patients with HIV is described in the AIDS topic in Section I.
- Criteria for discontinuing and restarting opportunistic infection prophylaxis for adults and adolescents with HIV infection is described in Table 1H-45.
- HIV infection in a pregnant woman poses special challenges and considerations. Appropriate and timely ART given to mother and newborn has been shown to dramatically reduce the risk of perinatal transmission of HIV. The goal of therapy is to achieve an undetectable viral load. For HIV-infected pregnant women who are already receiving ART: (1) Continue therapy if suppressing viral replication, but avoid use of efavirenz in the first trimester (substitution is recommended

in the first trimester); (2) If viremia on therapy, genotypic testing is recommended; (3) Nevirapine should be continued, regardless of CD4 count, if there is viral suppression. For HIV-infected pregnant women who have never received ART: (1) Women who require ART for their own health should start on ART in the first trimester. Most antiretrovirals are safe in pregnancy, however, efavirenz should be avoided because of teratogenicity (Class D), DDI and D4T should be avoided (potential of lactic acidosis), and some protease inhibitors may be dose-altered in pregnancy. Nevirapine should not be initiated in an antiretroviral-naive pregnant patient with CD4 counts >250 cells/mm^3 because of the risk of hepatotoxicity. (2) Women who do not need ART for their own health should also initiate three-drug therapy, but may do so at the end of the first trimester.

Diseases and Disorders

I

TABLE 1H-45 Criteria for Discontinuing and Restarting Opportunistic Infection Prophylaxis for Adults and Adolescents with Human Immunodeficiency Virus Infection

Opportunistic Infection	Criteria for Discontinuing Primary Prophylaxis	Criteria for Restarting Primary Prophylaxis	Criteria for Discontinuing Secondary Prophylaxis/Chronic Maintenance Therapy	Criteria for Restarting Secondary Prophylaxis/Chronic Maintenance Therapy
Pneumocystis pneumonia (PJP)	CD4$^+$ count >200 cells/mm^3 for >3 mo in response to ART	CD4$^+$ count <200 cells/mm^3	CD4$^+$ count increased from <200 cells/mm^3 to >200 cells/mm^3 for ≥3 mo in response to ART. If PJP is diagnosed when CD4$^+$ count >200 cells/mm^3, prophylaxis should probably be continued for life regardless of CD4$^+$ count rise in response to ART.	CD4$^+$ count <200 cells/mm^3, or if PCP recurred at a CD4$^+$ count >200 cells/mm^3
Toxoplasma gondii encephalitis (TE)	CD4$^+$ count >200 cells/mm^3 for >3 mo in response to ART	CD4$^+$ count <100-200 cells/mm^3	Successfully completed initial therapy, remain asymptomatic of signs and symptoms of TE, and CD4$^+$ count >200 cells/mm^3 for >6 mo in response to ART	CD4$^+$ count <200 cells/mm^3
Microsporidiosis	Not applicable	Not applicable	No signs and symptoms of non-ocular microsporidiosis and CD4$^+$ count >200 cells/mm^3 for >6 mo in response to ART. Patients with ocular microsporidiosis should be on therapy indefinitely regardless of CD4$^+$ count.	No recommendation
Disseminated *Mycobacterium avium* complex (MAC) disease	CD4$^+$ count >100 cells/mm^3 for ≥3 mo in response to ART	CD4$^+$ count <50 cells/mm^3	If fulfill the following criteria Completed ≥12 mo therapy, and No signs and symptoms of MAC, and Have sustained (≥6 mo) CD4$^+$ count >100 cells/mm^3 in response to ART	CD4$^+$ count <100 cells/mm^3
Bartonellosis	Not applicable	Not applicable	If fulfill the following criteria Received 3-4 mo of treatment CD4$^+$ count >200 cells/mm^3 for ≥6 mo Certain specialists would discontinue therapy only if *Bartonella* titers have also decreased by fourfold.	No recommendation
Mucosal candidiasis	Not applicable	Not applicable	If used, reasonable to discontinue when CD4$^+$ count >200 cells/mm^3	No recommendation
Cryptococcal meningitis	Not applicable	Not applicable	If fulfill the following criteria Completed course of initial therapy Remain asymptomatic of cryptococcosis CD4$^+$ count ≥200 cells/mm^3 for >6 mo in response to ART Certain specialists would perform a lumbar puncture to determine if cerebrospinal fluid is culture and antigen negative before stopping therapy.	CD4$^+$ count <200 cells/mm^3
Histoplasma capsulatum infection	If used, CD4$^+$ count >150 cells/mm^3 for 6 mo on ART	For patients at high risk for acquiring histoplasmosis, restart at CD4$^+$ count ≤150 cells/mm^3.	If fulfill the following criteria Received itraconazole for ≥1 yr Negative blood cultures CD4$^+$ count >150 cells/mm^3 for ≥6 mo in response to ART Serum *Histoplasma* antigen <2 units	CD4$^+$ count ≤150 cells/mm^3
Coccidioidomycosis	If used, CD4$^+$ count ≥250 cells/mm^3 for ≥6 mo	If used, restart at CD4$^+$ count <250 cells/mm^3	**Only for patients with focal coccidioidal pneumonia:** Clinically responded to ≥12 mo of antifungal therapy CD4$^+$ count >250 cells/mm^3 Receiving ART Suppressive therapy should be continued indefinitely, even with increase in CD4$^+$ count on ART for patients with diffuse pulmonary, disseminated, or meningeal diseases.	No recommendation

TABLE 1H-45 Criteria for Discontinuing and Restarting Opportunistic Infection Prophylaxis for Adults and Adolescents with Human Immunodeficiency Virus Infection—cont'd

Opportunistic Infection	Criteria for Discontinuing Primary Prophylaxis	Criteria for Restarting Primary Prophylaxis	Criteria for Discontinuing Secondary Prophylaxis/Chronic Maintenance Therapy	Criteria for Restarting Secondary Prophylaxis/Chronic Maintenance Therapy
Cytomegalovirus retinitis	Not applicable	Not applicable	$CD4^+$ count >100 cells/mm³ for >3-6 mo in response to ART. Therapy should be discontinued only after consultation with an ophthalmologist, taking into account magnitude and duration of $CD4^+$ count increase, anatomic location of the lesions, vision in the contralateral eye, and the feasibility of regular ophthalmologic monitoring. Routine (every 3 mo) ophthalmologic follow-up is recommended for early detection of relapse or immune restoration uveitis.	$CD4^+$ count <100 cells/mm³
Isospora belli infection	Not applicable	Not applicable	Sustained increase in $CD4^+$ count to >200 cells/mm³ for >6 mo in response to ART and without evidence of *I. belli* infection	No recommendation

Modified from Centers for Disease Control and Prevention. Guidelines for prevention and treatment of opportunistic infections in HIV-infected adults and adolescents. Recommendations from CDC, the National Institutes of Health, and the HIV Medicine Association of the Infectious Disease Society of America. *MMWR Morb Mortal Wkly Rep* 58(RR-4), 2009.

- Zidovudine (AZT) is recommended as a component of ART.
- Therapy should continue through the baby's birth. Zidovudine is given intravenously at the time of labor, regardless of whether it is an existing component of her three-drug regimen. In women with viral loads persistently >1000 copies/ml despite appropriate ART, cesarean section may further lower risk of transmission. Zidovudine (AZT) should also be given to the newborn for the first 6 weeks of life, and mothers should completely avoid nursing.

DISPOSITION
- Ongoing care consisting of frequent medical evaluations and monitoring of CD4 counts and HIV viral loads.
- Long-term care focused on providing up-to-date ART and prophylaxis of PJP and other opportunistic infections, as well as early detection of complications.
- Ongoing assessment for cardiovascular risk and other primary prevention interventions.
- Screening for hepatitis A, B, and C. Treatment when indicated. Drugs such as tenofovir and lamivudine have activity against both HIV and hepatitis B and may be used in patients with co-infection.
- Vaccinations including hepatitis A and B (when susceptible), Pneumovax, tetanus/diphtheria/pertussis, and influenza. Box 1H-9 summarizes vaccinations in HIV-positive adults.
- Yearly screening for other sexually transmitted infections (chlamydia, gonorrhea, syphilis).
- Consideration of AIDS (lymphomas, HPV) and non-AIDS related (screening for general population, age-specific cancers).

REFERRAL
To a physician knowledgeable and experienced in the management of HIV infection and its complications.

PREVENTION:
- Truvada may be used as preexposure prophylaxis (PrEP). Individuals who are HIV negative may take Truvada once a day to prevent HIV infection. PrEP has been demonstrated to be effective in MSM, heterosexuals, and injection drug users. Individuals on PrEP should be monitored every 3 months for renal dysfunction, HIV status, and adherence.
- Post-exposure prophylaxis (PEP) is an effective prevention intervention for individuals exposed to HIV infection, either occupationally or through a sexual exposure. PEP should be taken within 72 hours of an exposure and continued for 28 days. Baseline HIV status, renal function, hepatitis B/C, and liver function should be assessed. The recommended first-line regimen is raltegravir and Truvada.

ⓘ PEARLS & CONSIDERATIONS

COMMENTS
- HIV chemoprophylaxis after occupational exposure is described in Section V.
- Analysis of the impact of ART indicates that ART has saved at least 3 million years of life since the introduction into medicine more than 20 years ago.
- ART should be initiated in all HIV-infected individuals regardless of CD4 cell counts.
- Trials involving antiretroviral chemoprophylaxis before exposure for the prevention of HIV acquisition in MSM have shown that oral tenofovir disoproxil fumarate (FTC-TDF) provides protection against acquisition of HIV infection. This is known as *pre-exposure prophylaxis (PrEP)*. Detected blood levels strongly correlated with the prophylactic effect.
- ART in combination with avoidance of breast-feeding and elective cesarean section in women with viremia reduces risk for mother-to-child transmission.

BOX 1H-9 Vaccination in HIV-Positive Adults

Generally Avoid
- VZV
- BCG
- Oral polio
- Oral typhoid

Avoid if CD4+ Cells <200
- Yellow fever
- Measles

Give Routinely
- Tetanus/diphtheria (or Tdap)
- Hepatitis B
- *Streptococcus pneumoniae*
- Hib
- Influenza, yearly
- Hepatitis A

Give if Indicated for Travel
- Typhoid Vi
- Meningococcal
- Polio, IPV
- Rabies
- Japanese encephalitis
- Tick-borne encephalitis

From Auerbach P: *Wilderness medicine, expert consult* Premium Edition—Enhanced Online Features and Print, Philadelphia, 2012, Saunders.

 **EVIDENCE**

Available at www.expertconsult.com
SUGGESTED READINGS
Available at www.expertconsult.com

RELATED CONTENT
Human Immunodeficiency Virus (HIV) Infection (Patient Information)
Acquired Immunodeficiency Syndrome (Related Key Topic)

AUTHOR: **PHILIP A. CHAN, M.D., M.S.**

BASIC INFORMATION

DEFINITION

Huntington's disease is an autosomal dominant neurodegenerative disorder characterized by involuntary movements, psychiatric disturbance, and cognitive decline.

SYNONYMS

Huntington's chorea

ICD-10CM CODES
G10 Huntington's disease

EPIDEMIOLOGY & DEMOGRAPHICS

PEAK INCIDENCE: Late 30s and 40s, with onsets from ages 2 to 70 yr
PREVALENCE (IN U.S.): 4.1 to 8.4 cases/100,000 persons. Most common neurodegenerative cause of generalized chorea
PREDOMINANT SEX: Female = male
PREDOMINANT AGE: Adulthood
GENETICS: Autosomal dominant

PHYSICAL FINDINGS & CLINICAL PRESENTATION

- Chorea: irregular, rapid, flowing, nonstereotyped involuntary movements. When there is a writhing quality, it is referred to as choreoathetosis. Chorea is present early on and tends to decrease in end stages of disease.
- Dancelike, lurching gait, often caused by chorea.
- Westphal variant: cognitive dysfunction, bradykinesia, and rigidity. This variant is more commonly seen in juvenile-onset Huntington's.
- Oculomotor abnormalities are common early on and include increased latency of response and insuppressible eye blinking.
- Psychiatric disorders (can be present early on): depression is commonly seen as well as obsessive-compulsive behaviors and aggression associated with impaired impulse control.

ETIOLOGY

- Trinucleotide repeat disorder
- The responsible gene is the Huntington gene located on chromosome 4. Its function is not known.

DIAGNOSIS

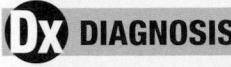

DIFFERENTIAL DIAGNOSIS

- Drug-induced chorea: dopamine, stimulants, anticonvulsants, antidepressants, and oral contraceptives have all been known to cause chorea.
- Sydenham's chorea: decreased incidence with decline of rheumatic fever.
- Benign hereditary chorea: autosomal dominant with onset in childhood; non-progressive and without associated dementia or behavioral problems.
- Senile chorea: possibly vascular in origin.
- Wilson's disease: autosomal recessive; tremor, dysarthria, and dystonia are more common presentations than chorea. A total of 95% of patients with neurologic manifestations will have Kayser-Fleischer rings.
- Postinfectious.
- Systemic lupus erythematosus: can be the presenting feature of lupus (rare).
- Chorea gravidarum: presents during first 4 to 5 mo of pregnancy and resolves after delivery.
- Paraneoplastic: seen most commonly in small-cell lung cancer and lymphoma.

WORKUP

Onset of symptoms in an individual with an established family history requires no additional investigation.

LABORATORY TESTS

- Genetic testing for CAG repeats
- If genetic tests are normal, obtain complete blood count with smear, erythrocyte sedimentation rate, electrolytes, serum ceruloplasmin, 24-hr urinary copper excretion, TFTs, antinuclear antibody, liver function tests, HIV, and ASO titer. Consider paraneoplastic markers.

IMAGING STUDIES

CT scan or MRI scan will show atrophy, most notably in the caudate and putamen. The cortex is involved to a lesser extent. A normal scan does not exclude the diagnosis.

TREATMENT

NONPHARMACOLOGIC THERAPY

- Supportive counseling
- Physical and occupational therapy
- Home health care
- Genetic counseling

CHRONIC Rx

- Chorea does not need to be treated unless it is disabling.
- Tetrabenazine (TBZ) is approved by the FDA for the symptomatic treatment of chorea seen in Huntington's disease. It is a reversible inhibitor of the vesicle monoamine transporter type 2 (VMAT-2). It inhibits primarily dopamine and to a lesser degree serotonin and norepinephrine. Side effects include parkinsonism and severe depression.
- Neuroleptics, typical or atypical, can be used for symptomatic management of neuropsychiatric issues and chorea at low doses (e.g., haloperidol 1 to 10 mg/day).
- Amantadine (up to 300 to 400 mg divided tid).
- Depression with suicidal ideation is common; may improve with tricyclic antidepressants or SSRI

DISPOSITION

Relentless course of variable duration leading to progressive disability and death

REFERRAL

- Should refer to psychiatry and neurology for treatment of mood disorders and movement disorders
- Genetic counseling

PEARLS & CONSIDERATIONS

- Suicide rate is fivefold that of the general population.
- Generational transmission is often associated with the phenomenon of "anticipation" with disease starting at an earlier age in a child because of increased repeat length compared with that of the parent.
- The number of repeats does correlate with age of onset but does not clearly correlate with disease severity. Interpretation of number of repeats is still difficult at this time; therefore it is debatable whether to disclose this information to patients.

SUGGESTED READINGS

Available at www.expertconsult.com

RELATED CONTENT

Huntington's Disease (Patient Information)

AUTHOR: **FARIHA ZAHEER, M.D.**

BASIC INFORMATION

DEFINITION
A hydrocele is a fluid collection in a serous scrotal space, usually between the layers of the tunica vaginalis (Fig. 1H-63). A hydrocele that fills with fluid from the peritoneum is termed *communicating*. This is distinguished from a *noncommunicating* hydrocele by history of variation in size throughout the day and palpation of a thickened cord above the testicle on the affected side. A communicating hydrocele is a small inguinal hernia in which fluid, but not peritoneal structures, traverses the processus vaginalis. In noncommunicating hydrocele, the processus vaginalis was obliterated during development. An abdominoscrotal hydrocele is a rare variant of a hydrocele in which there is a large, tense hydrocele that extends into the lower abdominal cavity.

ICD-10CM CODES
N43.3 Hydrocele, unspecified
N43 Hydrocele and spermatocele
N43.0 Encysted hydrocele
N43.1 Infected hydrocele
N43.2 Other hydrocele
P83.5 Congenital hydrocele

PHYSICAL FINDINGS & CLINICAL PRESENTATION
Symptoms:
- Scrotal enlargement
- Scrotal heaviness or discomfort radiating to the inguinal area
- Back pain

Physical findings:
- Most hydroceles are smooth and nontender. Scrotal distention may make it difficult to palpate the testis, but it is important to palpate the testis because some young men develop a hydrocele in association with a testis tumor
- Transillumination of the scrotum confirms the fluid-filled nature of the mass

ETIOLOGY
Hydroceles may occur as a congenital abnormality in which the processus vaginalis fails to close. In this case an inguinal hernia is virtually always associated with the malformation. Congenital hydroceles are most common in infants (1%-2% of neonates have hydroceles) and children. In adults, hydroceles are more frequently caused by infection, tumor, or trauma. Infection of the epididymis often results in the development of a secondary hydrocele. Tropical infections such as filariasis may produce hydroceles.

DIAGNOSIS

DIFFERENTIAL DIAGNOSIS
- Spermatocele
- Inguinoscrotal hernia
- Testicular tumor
- Varicocele
- Epididymitis

IMAGING STUDIES
Scrotal ultrasound is useful to rule out a testicular tumor as the cause of the hydrocele (Fig. 1H-64). The acute development of a hydrocele might be associated with the onset of epididymitis, testicular tumor, trauma, and torsion of a testicular appendage. An ultrasound of the scrotum may provide important diagnostic information.

TREATMENT
- No treatment if asymptomatic and testis is believed to be normal. Most congenital hydroceles resolve by 12 months of age following reabsorption of the hydrocele fluid.
- Surgical repair should be considered if the hydrocele is tense and large. Communicating hydroceles should be repaired in the same manner as an indirect hernia. The indications for repair of a noncommunicating hydrocele include failure to resolve and increase in size to one that is large and tense.
- Surgical correction is similar to a herniorrhaphy: an inguinal incision is made, the spermatic cord is identified, the hydrocele fluid is drained, and a high ligation of the processus vaginalis is performed.

PEARLS & CONSIDERATIONS
- The long-term risk of a communicating hydrocele is the development of an inguinal hernia.
- An inguinal hernia/hydrocele is likely if compression of the fluid-filled mass completely reduces the hydrocele.

SUGGESTED READINGS
Available at www.expertconsult.com

RELATED CONTENT
Hydrocele (Patient Information)

AUTHOR: **FRED F. FERRI, M.D.**

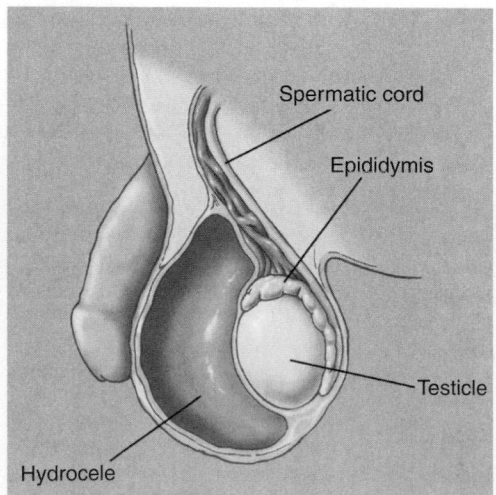

FIGURE 1H-63 Schematic representation of the testicle, epididymis, spermatic cord, and a hydrocele. (From Lipshultz LI et al: *Urology and the primary care practitioner,* ed 3, Philadelphia, 2008, Elsevier.)

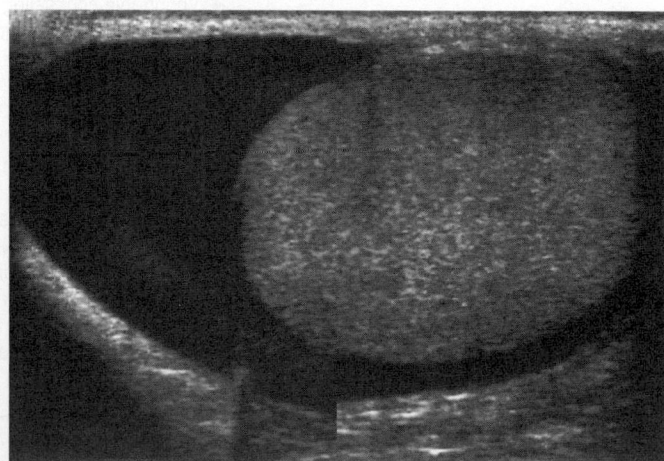

FIGURE 1H-64 Longitudinal ultrasound view of normal testis and moderate hydrocele. (From Grainger RG et al [eds.]: *Grainger & Allison's diagnostic radiology,* ed 4, London, 2001, Harcourt.)

BASIC INFORMATION

DEFINITION

Normal pressure hydrocephalus (NPH) is a syndrome of symptomatic hydrocephalus in the setting of normal cerebrospinal fluid (CSF) pressure. The classic clinical triad of NPH includes gait disturbance, cognitive decline, and incontinence.

SYNONYMS

Occult hydrocephalus
Extraventricular obstructive hydrocephalus
Chronic hydrocephalus

ICD-10CM CODES
G91.2 Normal pressure hydrocephalus
G91.8 Other hydrocephalus

EPIDEMIOLOGY & DEMOGRAPHICS

INCIDENCE: The exact incidence is not known. In one study the incidence was found to be 5.5 per 100,000, but it may account for up to 5% of dementia in the U.S. Hospital discharge data suggest approximately 11,500 now cases diagnosed annually (may be overestimated). The prevalence of NPH may be as high as 14% among extended care facility patients.
PREDOMINANT SEX: Males = females
PREDOMINANT AGE: NPH is more common with increasing age.

PHYSICAL FINDINGS & CLINICAL PRESENTATION

- Gait difficulty: patients often have difficulty initiating ambulation, and the gait may be broad based and shuffling, with the appearance that the feet are stuck to the floor ("magnetic gait" or "frontal gait disorder").
- Cognitive decline: mental slowing, forgetfulness and inattention typically without agnosia, aphasia, or other cortical disturbances.
- Incontinence: initially may have urinary urgency; incontinence later develops. Fecal incontinence also occasionally occurs.
- Gegenhalten (paratonia) or other frontal lobe signs may be seen.

ETIOLOGY

- Approximately 50% of cases are idiopathic; the remaining cases have a variety of causes, including prior subarachnoid hemorrhage, meningitis, head trauma, or intracranial surgery.
- Symptoms are presumed to result from stretching of sacral motor and limbic fibers that lie near the ventricles as dilation occurs.

Dx DIAGNOSIS

DIFFERENTIAL DIAGNOSIS

- Alzheimer's disease with extrapyramidal features
- Cognitive impairment in the setting of Parkinson's disease or parkinsonism-plus syndromes
- Diffuse Lewy body disease
- Frontotemporal dementia
- Cervical spondylosis with cord compromise in the setting of degenerative dementia
- Multi-infarct dementia
- HIV dementia

WORKUP

- Large-volume lumbar puncture:
  1. Mental status testing and time to walk a prespecified distance (usually 25 feet) are measured, followed by removal of 40 to 50 ml of CSF.
  2. Retest of mental status and timed walking are done later (sometimes at 1 and 4 hr). Patients who have significant improvement in gait or mental status may have a better surgical outcome; those with mild or negative response can have variable outcomes.
  3. Opening and closing pressure are measured; if pressure is elevated, alternative causes must be considered. Higher *normal* pressure may predict a good outcome from CSF shunting.
- Measurement of CSF outflow resistance by an infusion test or CSF pressure monitoring is sometimes used to help predict surgical outcome. External lumbar drainage (ELD) is being used more commonly.

LABORATORY TESTS

- CSF should be sent for routine fluid analysis to exclude other pathologies.
- CSF biomarkers may be useful in excluding Alzheimer's disease.
- The CSF protein lipocalin-type prostaglandin D synthase (L-PGDS) is being studied as a potential diagnostic biomarker in idiopathic NPH.

IMAGING STUDIES

- CT scan or MRI can be used to document ventriculomegaly. The distinguishing feature of NPH is ventricular enlargement out of proportion to sulcal atrophy (Fig. E1H-65), and typically the frontal horn ratio exceeds 0.50. An algorithm for evaluation of patients with enlarged ventricles is described in Fig. E1H-66.
- MRI has advantages over CT, including better ability to visualize structures in the posterior fossa, visualize transependymal CSF flow (seen as periventricular hyperintensity), and document extent of white matter lesions. On MRI a flow void in the aqueduct and third ventricle ("jet sign"), thinning and elevation of the corpus callosum on sagittal images, rounding of the frontal horns, and a narrow CSF space at the high convexity/midline areas relative to Sylvian fissure size may be seen.
- Isotope cisternography and dynamic MRI studies have not been shown to be superior in predicting shunt outcome.

Rx TREATMENT

There is no evidence that NPH can be effectively treated with medications.

NONPHARMACOLOGIC THERAPY

Response to ventriculoperitoneal shunting is variable. Some patients (variable depending on series reported) show significant improvement from shunting; however, effectiveness of shunting has never been demonstrated in a randomized-controlled trial. Gait is most likely to improve.

Factors that may predict positive outcome with surgery:
- NPH caused by prior trauma, subarachnoid hemorrhage, or meningitis
- History of mild impairment in cognition <2 yr duration
- Onset of gait abnormality before cognitive decline
- Imaging demonstrates hydrocephalus without sulcal enlargement, including normal-sized sylvian fissures and cortical sulci, and absent or mild white matter lesions.
- Transependymal CSF flow visualized on MRI
- Large-volume tap or ELD produces dramatic but temporary relief of symptoms
- High *normal* opening pressure

Factors that may predict negative outcome with surgery:
- Extensive white matter lesions or diffuse cerebral atrophy on MRI
- Moderate to severe cognitive impairment
- Onset of cognitive impairment before gait disorder
- History of alcohol abuse

ACUTE GENERAL Rx

Shunting in selected patients

DISPOSITION

Symptoms of NPH may progress over time. Prompt diagnosis may improve chances for treatment success.

REFERRAL

To neurologist for initial evaluation, including lumbar puncture, followed by neurosurgeon for shunting in appropriate patients

PEARLS & CONSIDERATIONS

Each of the cardinal symptoms of NPH is commonly seen in the elderly and occurs in multiple disease processes; therefore differential diagnoses should always be considered carefully.

CAUTION

Shunt complications, including subdural or intracerebral hematoma, may occur in 30% to 40% of patients.

SUGGESTED READINGS

Available at www.expertconsult.com

RELATED CONTENT

Normal Pressure Hydrocephalus (Patient Information)

AUTHOR: **TAMARA G. FONG, M.D., PH.D.**

ⓘ BASIC INFORMATION

DEFINITION

Hydronephrosis is dilation of the collecting system of the kidneys (renal pelvis and/or calyces). This can be due to obstruction of the kidney but may also be present without obstruction of urine flow.

SYNONYMS

Pelviectasis
Caliectasis
Pelvocaliectasis

ICD-10CM CODES

N13.1	Hydronephrosis with ureteral stricture, not elsewhere classified
N13.2	Hydronephrosis with renal and ureteral calculous obstruction
N13.30	Unspecified hydronephrosis
N13.39	Other hydronephrosis
N13.5	Crossing vessel and stricture of ureter without hydronephrosis
Q62.0	Congenital hydronephrosis

EPIDEMIOLOGY & DEMOGRAPHICS

Hydronephrosis in children is often caused by congenital and structural abnormalities of the kidneys and ureters, such as ureteropelvic junction obstruction (UPJ) and vesicoureteral reflux (VUR). Adults tend to develop hydronephrosis as a result of obstruction of one or kidneys, usually caused by stones, tumors, infections, and trauma.

Based on autopsy series, the prevalence of hydronephrosis is 2% to 3%.

CLINICAL PRESENTATION

HISTORY: Presentation may be quite variable and is related to the presence and chronicity of obstruction. Patients with hydronephrosis but without obstruction to urine flow are asymptomatic, and the condition is detected on imaging for other reasons.

When obstruction is rapid in onset, pain will often be severe. Pain is usually present along the flank with radiation toward the ipsilateral groin or lower abdominal quadrant. Nausea and vomiting are frequent. When obstruction is subacute to chronic, symptoms may be vague and less intense.

Urinary symptoms are often absent unless an associated condition (a distal ureteral calculus, for instance) produces these issues. In patients with a solitary or functionally solitary kidney, obstruction may cause oliguria or anuria.

PHYSICAL EXAMINATION: Examination in hydronephrosis is typically not helpful, although complete assessment of the patient is still warranted.

Special attention to the blood pressure, flank, and abdominal exam and genitourinary exam/rectal exam is indicated.

Palpable abdominal masses are rare, except in children with massive hydronephrosis. Costovertebral angle tenderness is not a particularly helpful finding.

Complete genitourinary and pelvic exams must be performed on patients with urologic complaints or demonstration by an imaging study of hydronephrosis.

If incomplete emptying of the bladder is a concern, residual urine volume can be evaluated indirectly by bedside ultrasonography or directly by catheterization.

ETIOLOGY

Hydronephrosis can be caused by extrinsic or intrinsic factors relative to the ureter. Causes can also be grouped as congenital or acquired.

- Extrinsic to urinary tract:
  1. Gravid uterus
  2. Retroperitoneal fibrosis or tumor (e.g., lymphoma)
  3. Aortic aneurysm
  4. Uterine fibroids
  5. Trauma (surgical or nonsurgical)
  6. Pelvic inflammatory disease
  7. Pelvic malignancies (e.g., prostate, colorectal, cervical, uterine, bladder)
  8. Iatrogenic injuries (pelvic surgery)
  Intrinsic:
- Extrarenal pelvis—not obstructed
- Ureteropelvic junction narrowing
- Ureterovesical junction narrowing
- Ureterocele
- Bladder neck obstruction
- Urethral valve
- Urethral stricture
- Meatal stenosis
- Intrinsic to urinary tract:
  1. Calculi
  2. Inflammation
  3. Trauma
  4. Sloughed papillae
  5. Ureteral tumor
  6. Blood clots
  7. Prostatic hypertrophy or cancer
  8. Bladder cancer
  9. Urethral stricture
  10. Phimosis

Ⓓⓧ DIAGNOSIS

DIFFERENTIAL DIAGNOSIS

Extrarenal pelvis: not obstructed and often confused for obstruction
- Urinary stones
- Neoplastic disease: kidney, ureter, bladder, urethra
- Prostatic hyperplasia
- Neurologic disease
- Urinary reflux
- Urinary tract infection
- Medication effects
- Trauma
- Congenital abnormality of urinary tract
- Urinary retention
- Retroperitoneal fibrosis
- Urinary trauma
- Iatrogenic injuries

LABORATORY TESTS

- Evaluation of kidney function by blood urea nitrogen and creatinine (usually implies bilat-

eral obstruction or unilateral obstruction of a solitary kidney).
- Electrolyte abnormalities including hypo- or hypernatremia, hyperkalemia, or distal renal tubular acidosis.
- Urinalysis and sediment examination may reveal white blood cells, red blood cells, or bacteria in the appropriate setting (e.g., infection, stones). Often the sediment is normal in obstructive renal disease.

IMAGING STUDIES

- Ultrasound evaluation of kidneys, bladder volume, as well as contour of collecting system and ureters (Fig. 1H-67). Ultrasound is >90% sensitive and specific for hydronephrosis.
- Abdominal CT scan without intravenous contrast medium provides excellent localization of the site of obstruction (Fig. 1H-68), especially if a ureteral calculus is the cause of obstruction. If kidney function is normal, CT urography (without and then with contrast and delayed images of the ureters, provides excellent anatomic information).

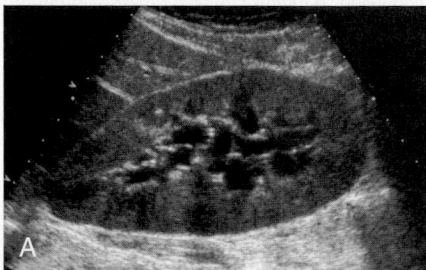
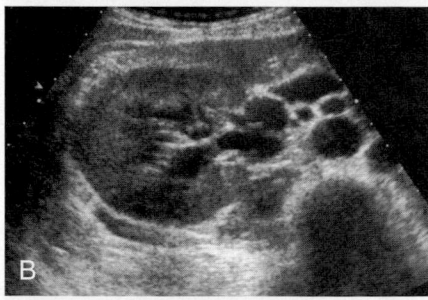
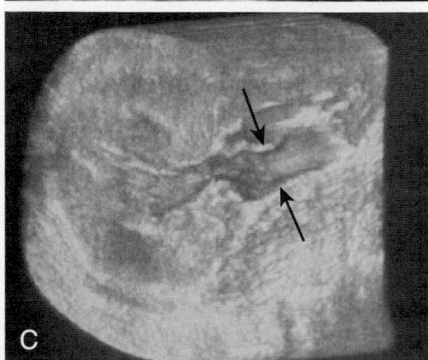

FIGURE 1H-67 Renal ultrasound study demonstrating hydronephrosis. A, Sagittal image. **B,** Transverse image. **C,** Transverse three-dimensional surface-rendered image; *arrows* indicate the dilated proximal ureter. (From Floege J et al: *Comprehensive clinical nephrology*, ed 4, Philadelphia, 2010, Saunders.)

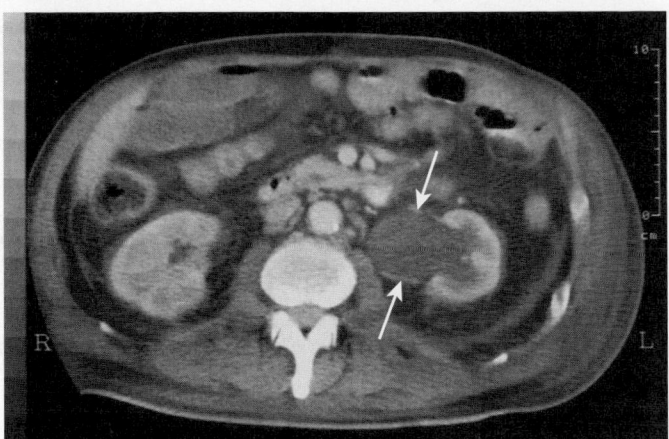

FIGURE 1H-68 CT scan of the abdomen showing a grossly hydronephrotic kidney on the left. *Arrows* mark dilated renal pelvis. Dilated loops of small bowel are seen in the right hypochondrium. Sequential sections demonstrated that the ureter was dilated along its length and that there was a pelvic mass, which was responsible for both bowel and left ureteric obstruction. The mass was subsequently shown to be arising from a carcinoma of the colon. (From Johnson RJ, Feehally J: *Comprehensive clinical nephrology,* ed 2, St Louis, 2000, Mosby.)

- MRI is an alternative to CT. Impaired renal function may preclude gadolinium administration. MRI provides good detail but cannot directly detect a stone and is cumbersome, time consuming, and expensive. MRI is considered after other tests have not yielded information.
- Antegrade or retrograde ureterograms further delineate the point of obstruction after obstruction is diagnosed.
- Voiding cystourethrogram can diagnose vesicoureteral reflux and bladder neck or urethral obstructions.
- Diuretic renography is a functional radioisotopic test and provides differential function of each kidney.

 **TREATMENT**

- Surgical treatment is required if urinary tract obstruction is associated with urinary tract infection, acute kidney injury, or uncontrollable pain.

- Ureteral stenting to decompress one or both kidneys and is preferred when obstruction is acute.
- Percutaneous nephrostomy tubes: longstanding obstruction, high likelihood of ureteral stent placement, or urinary drainage when a retrograde approach is not possible or fails.

ACUTE GENERAL Rx

Analgesics, antiemetics, and fluids for treatment of pain, nausea, and vomiting

DISPOSITION

Prompt treatment of infections and relief of obstruction prevent loss of kidney function. Chronic bilateral obstruction, often from benign prostatic hypertrophy, may cause chronic kidney disease.

REFERRAL

- Urology for timely diagnostic and/or therapeutic procedures
- Oncologist if a neoplasm is diagnosed
- Gynecologist if pregnancy or female pelvic anatomy is involved

PEARLS & CONSIDERATIONS

COMMENTS

- Hydronephrosis is not a primary disorder, and an underlying etiology must be sought.
- Children often have congenital causes; adults usually have acquired intrinsic or extrinsic causes.
- The extrarenal pelvis does not represent obstruction. This anatomical variant is diagnosed without specialty consultation by a diuretic renogram, CT urogram, or MR urogram.

PREVENTION

Timely and appropriate management of acute kidney obstruction prevents long-term kidney damage. Hydronephrosis may persist after relief of the obstructing cause.

SUGGESTED READINGS

Available at www.expertconsult.com

RELATED CONTENT

Hydronephrosis (Patient Information)

AUTHOR: **PETER L. STEINBERG, M.D.**

BASIC INFORMATION

DEFINITION

Hypercholesterolemia refers to a blood cholesterol measurement ≥200 mg/dl.

SYNONYMS

Hypercholesteremia
Dyslipidemia
Type II familial hyperlipoproteinemia

ICD-10CM CODES

E78.0 Pure hypercholesterolemia

EPIDEMIOLOGY & DEMOGRAPHICS

- Over 105 million (37%) adults in the U.S. have total blood cholesterol levels higher than 200 mg/dl. Of this group, more than 36 million adults have extremely high-risk cholesterol levels over 240 mg/dl (13%).
- For men over the age of 20 years, approximately 48% of white men, 45% of black men, and 50% of Hispanic men have high blood cholesterol.
- For women over the age of 20, approximately 50% of white women, 42% of black women, and 50% of Hispanic women have hypercholesterolemia.
- Prevalence of hypercholesterolemia increases with increasing age.
- According to NHANES data for 2009-2010, about 47% of adults had at least one of three risk factors for cardiovascular disease—uncontrolled high blood pressure, uncontrolled high levels of low-density lipoproteins (LDL) cholesterol, or current smoking.

PHYSICAL FINDINGS & CLINICAL PRESENTATION

- A detailed medication history should be performed because some medications may affect lipid levels (e.g., thiazides, corticosteroids, beta-blockers, and estrogens).
- The physical examination should include measurements of BMI and BP, thyroid and liver assessments, and examining peripheral pulses including carotids for bruits.
- Physical findings, particularly in the familial forms may include
  1. Tendon xanthomas
  2. Xanthelasma
  3. Arcus corneae
  4. Arterial bruits (young adulthood)

ETIOLOGY

Primary:
- Genetics
- Obesity
- Dietary intake
Secondary:
- Hypothyroidism
- Diabetes mellitus
- Nephrotic syndrome
- Obstructive liver disease: Hepatoma, extrahepatic biliary obstruction, primary biliary cirrhosis
- Alcohol or tobacco use
- Dysgammaglobulinemia (multiple myeloma, SLE)
- Drugs: Oral contraceptives, progesterone, corticosteroids, thiazide diuretics, β-blockers, androgenic steroids, retinoic acid derivatives, protease inhibitors

DIAGNOSIS

DIFFERENTIAL DIAGNOSIS

- Always consider underlying secondary causes for the elevated cholesterol.
- Patients with very high LDL cholesterol usually have genetic forms of hypercholesterolemia (see *Hyperlipoproteinemia, Primary*). Early detection of these cases and family testing to identify similarly affected relatives is important.
- Metabolic syndrome:
  1. A constellation of lipid and nonlipid risk factors of a metabolic origin
  2. Diagnosed when three or more of the following are present: abdominal obesity (waist circumference >40 in in men and >35 in in women); fasting triglycerides >150 mg/dl; HDL <40 mg/dl in males and <50 mg/dl in females; systolic BP >130 mmHg and diastolic BP >85 mmHg; fasting glucose >110 mg/dl

WHO SHOULD BE SCREENED:

- AACE recommends screening of patients >20 yr of age for elevated cholesterol every 5 yr, males >45 yr and females >55 yr of age every 1-2 yr, and >65 yr of age every yr up to 75 yr of age regardless of CAD risk status. Patients above 75 yr of age with multiple CAD risk factors should still continue to get screened annually.
- The USPSTF supports routine screening for men aged >35 yr and women aged >45 yr by measurement of nonfasting total and HDL cholesterol alone.
- In 2010, the USPSTF recommended routine screening for overweight and obesity in persons aged <20 yr.
- In 2011, ACC/AHA recommended screening for hypertriglyceridemia by a nonfasting measurement. A nonfasting level of <200 mg/dl is commensurate with an optimal level of <100 mg/dl and no further testing is required. However, a nonfasting level of >200 mg/dl warrants further testing with a fasting lipid profile.

LABORATORY TESTS

- Obtain a fasting lipid profile.
- Perform a workup for secondary causes if clinically indicated such as TSH, metabolic profile, LFTs, and fasting glucose.

TREATMENT

NONPHARMACOLOGIC THERAPY

- First line of treatment: dietary therapy can result in 5% to 15% reduction in LDL cholesterol level.
- Composition of the **TLC diet**:
  1. Total fat 25% to 30% of total calories
  2. Polyunsaturated fat up to 10% of total calories

TABLE 1H-46   Risk Factors for Heart Disease

1. Cigarette smoking
2. Hypertension (BP ≤140/90 mm Hg or on medications)
3. Low HDL cholesterol (<40 mg/dl)*
4. Family history of premature CHD (<55 yr in first-degree male relative or <65 yr in first-degree female relative)
5. Age (men ≥45 yr, women ≥55 yr)

*HDL cholesterol >60 mg/dl counts as a negative risk factor; its presence removes one risk factor from the total count.

TABLE 1H-47   Atherosclerotic Cardiovascular Disease

1. Coronary heart disease: acute coronary syndromes, history of myocardial infarction, stable or unstable angina, coronary or other arterial revascularization
2. Stroke or transient ischemic attack
3. Peripheral arterial disease

3. Monounsaturated fat up to 20% of total calories
4. Saturated fats <7% of total calories
5. Carbohydrate 50% to 60% of total calories
6. Protein 15% of total calories
7. No more than 200 mg/day of cholesterol
8. Fiber 20 to 30 g/day
- Increased physical activity: encourage 30 min of moderately intense physical activity, four to six times a week (e.g., brisk walking, riding stationary bike, water aerobics)
- Maintenance of a healthy weight
- Avoidance of tobacco products
- Counseling on CAD risk factors (Table 1H-46)
- Plant-based diets (including stanol-containing margarines, oat bran, and nuts) have shown effectiveness in controlling lipids.

ACUTE GENERAL Rx

No acute treatment needed

CHRONIC Rx

- The current guidelines represent a substantial departure from previous recommendations, which were based on LDL levels.
- The new guidelines identify four high-risk groups that benefit from statin therapy:
  Patients with clinical ASCVD (atherosclerotic cardiovascular disease) (Table 1H-47)
  LDL ≥190 mg/dl
  DM aged 40-75 years and LDL 70-189 mg/dl
  Ten-year risk for ASCVD ≥7.5% and LDL 70-189 mg/dl
- The 10-year risk of ASCVD is calculated with the risk calculator available at http://my.americanheart.org/cvriskcalculator
- ASCVD events are reduced by using the maximum tolerated statin intensity in the above groups shown to benefit the most (Tables 1H-48 and 1H-49).

TABLE 1H-48 Statin Intensity Therapies

High Intensity (Decrease LDL-C ≥50%)	Moderate Intensity (Decrease LDL-C 30%-49%)
Atorvastatin 40-80 mg	Atorvastatin 10-20 mg
Rosuvastatin 20-40 mg	Rosuvastatin 5-10 mg
—	Simvastatin 20-40 mg
—	Pravastatin 40-80 mg
—	Lovastatin 40 mg
—	Fluvastatin XL 80 mg
—	Fluvastatin 40 mg bid
—	Pitavastatin 2-4 mg

LDL-C, Low-density lipoprotein cholesterol.
From Stone N et al: 2013 ACC/AHA guideline on the treatment of blood cholesterol to reduce atherosclerotic cardiovascular risk in adults: a report of the American College of Cardiology/American Heart Association Task Force on Practice Guidelines, *J Am Coll Cardiol* 63(25 Pt. B):2889, 2014.

TABLE 1H-49 Statin Benefit Groups and Recommended Therapy

Statin Benefit Group	High Intensity	Moderate Intensity	Additional Testing
Clinical ASCVD	Yes	Consider¹	None
Primary LDL-C >190 mg/dl	Yes	Consider†	None
Diabetes without ASCVD and 10-year risk ≥7.5%*	Yes	Consider†	None
Diabetes without ASCVD and 10-year risk <7.5%*	Consider‡	Yes	Case-by-case
Primary prevention and 10-year risk ≥7.5%*	Consider†	Yes	Case-by-case
Primary prevention and 10-year risk <7.5%*	Consider‡	Consider‡	Case-by-case

ASCVD, Atherosclerotic cardiovascular disease; *LDL-C*, low-density lipoprotein cholesterol.
*Based on Pooled Cohort Risk Equations.
†If age >75 years or not candidate for high intensity.
‡If abnormal high-sensitivity C-reactive protein, coronary artery calcium, ankle-brachial index, lifetime risk.
From Boyden TF et al: Implementing new guidelines in the management of blood cholesterol, *Am J Med* 127:705, 2014.

- Additional factors such as CRP >2 mg/l, primary LDL >160, genetic hyperlipidemias, family history of premature CHD, ABI <0.9, and CAD score >300 Agatston units may be used in patients who are not in one of four statin benefit groups and for whom a decision to initiate statin therapy is otherwise unclear.
- Percent reduction in LDL cholesterol is used as a guide to compliance and adherence to therapy but is not considered a treatment goal.
- Moderate-intensity statin therapy should be continued for individuals >75 years of age for secondary prevention. However, factors such as comorbidities, safety, and priorities of care should be considered before initiating statins for primary prevention of ASCVD.
- Adherence to lifestyle and to statin therapy should be reiterated with patients before the addition of a nonstatin drug.
- Nonstatin therapies do not provide acceptable ASCVD risk reduction benefits compared with their potential adverse effects in ASCVD prevention. (Table E1H-50) summarizes oral drugs affecting lipoprotein metabolism.
- PCSK9 (proprotein convertase subtilisin/kexin type 9) inhibitors (alirocumab [Praluent], evolocumab [Repatha]) are indicated as adjunct to diet and maximally tolerated statin therapy for the treatment of adults with heterozygous familial hypercholesterolemia or clinical atherosclerotic cardiovascular disease, who require additional lowering of LDL cholesterol. These medications are administered by subcutaneous injection and are expensive.
- High-risk patients with a suboptimal response to statins who are unable to tolerate a recommended intensity or who are completely statin intolerant may benefit from the addition of a nonstatin cholesterol-lowering agent.
- The management of metabolic syndrome includes weight reduction, increased physical activity, and treatment of hypertension, elevated triglycerides, and low HDL cholesterol.
- According to recent studies, each 40 mg/dl reduction in LDL cholesterol by statin therapy confers a 20% reduction in ASCVD. In other words, a relative risk reduction of 30% in ASCVD by moderate-intensity therapy and 45% by high-intensity therapy has been approximated.

DISPOSITION AND FOLLOW-UP

- Baseline LFT testing should be done before initiation of statin therapy and as clinically indicated thereafter.

- CK level monitoring is not recommended unless a patient reports muscle weakness or myalgias.
- Statin therapy should be monitored by repeating a lipid profile within 4 to 12 weeks after initiation of therapy.
- Counseling about behavioral lifestyle changes and risk factors for CHD should be provided at every follow-up visit.
- Adverse effects of statin-associated diabetes varies by statin intensity: 1 excess case of diabetes per 1000 treated individuals with moderate-intensity statin and 3 excess cases of diabetes per 1000 treated individuals with high-intensity statin per year has been reported. Myopathy and hemorrhagic stroke incidence is around 1 excess case per 10,000 treated individuals.
- Per new guidelines, those who develop diabetes during statin therapy should be advised to continue it to reduce their risk of ASCVD events and should adhere to a heart-healthy diet, engage in physical activity, cease tobacco use, and maintain a healthy body weight (Table E1H-50).

REFERRAL

Patients with rare lipid disorders, hyperlipoproteinemias, patients resistant to treatment, on complex regimens, and with evidence of disease progression despite treatment should be referred to a lipid specialist.

PEARLS & CONSIDERATIONS

COMMENTS

- The American Academy of Pediatrics (AAP) guideline (*Pediatrics* 122:198, 2008) recommends consideration toward pharmacologic treatment for children with LDL >190 mg/dl or >160 mg/dl if other risk factors are present.
- *HDL cholesterol efflux capacity* refers to the ability of HDL to accept cholesterol from macrophages, which is a key step in reverse cholesterol transport. It is inversely associated with the incidence of cardiovascular events and may be a useful biomarker when added to traditional risk factors.

EVIDENCE

Available at www.expertconsult.com

SUGGESTED READINGS

Available at www.expertconsult.com

RELATED CONTENT

High Cholesterol (Patient Information)
Hyperlipoproteinemia, Primary (Related Key Topic)

AUTHOR: **PRIYA BANSAL, M.D., M.P.H.**

Hypercoagulable State (PTG)

BASIC INFORMATION

DEFINITION

Hypercoagulable state is an inherited or acquired condition associated with an increased risk of thrombosis.

SYNONYMS

Thrombophilia

ICD-10CM CODES
D68.5 Primary thrombophilia
D68.6 Other thrombophilia
D68.8 Other specified coagulation defects
D68.9 Coagulation defect, unspecified

EPIDEMIOLOGY & DEMOGRAPHICS

INCIDENCE: See Table 1H-51.
PREVALENCE, PREDOMINANT SEX, AND AGE: Significant variations in the prevalence rates and thrombotic risks for thrombophilia are reported. This may reflect geographic variation in the prevalence of genetic defects, different populations, or the presence of other unidentified thrombophilic risk factors. When thrombosis occurs, it is often associated with an acquired risk factor (e.g., surgery, pregnancy, oral contraceptive [OC] use). Annual risk of thrombosis is <1%.
GENETICS:
- Most people with a genetic defect will not have thrombotic disease.
- Multiple genetic defects are not uncommon (1% to 2% prevalence in patients with idiopathic venous thromboembolism [VTE]); strong synergistic effect when multiple defects are present. Low risk of recurrent thrombosis in patients with a single genetic defect. Approximately half of patients with unprovoked thrombosis have an identifiable inherited thrombophilia.

RISK FACTORS: Family history of thrombosis, increasing age, tobacco use, immobility, surgery, prior history of DVT, pregnancy, hormone replacement therapy, trauma, connective tissue disease, underlying malignancy, medications (Megace, tamoxifen, birth control pills)

PHYSICAL FINDINGS & CLINICAL PRESENTATION

- Inherited thrombophilia is usually associated with VTE, most commonly deep vein thrombosis (DVT)

- Some acquired thrombophilias are associated with arterial thrombosis. Table E1H-52 describes sites of thrombosis according to coagulation defect.
- Pregnancy complications
- Medical conditions associated with increased risk of thrombosis

ETIOLOGY

See Table 1H-53. The differential diagnosis of the patient presenting with thrombosis or thrombotic diathesis is described in Section II. Figure E1H-69 describes components of thrombus formation and actions of various antithrombotic and thrombolytic agents.

- Thrombosis is often a multifactorial process with genetic, environmental, and acquired factors. Table 1H-54 describes causes of acquired deficiencies in antithrombin III, protein S, or protein C.
- Thrombotic risk increases with use of OCs or hormone replacement therapy (HRT) and during the pregnancy/postpartum period.
- Adverse pregnancy outcomes may be caused by thrombosis of the uteroplacental circulation.

DIAGNOSIS

DIFFERENTIAL DIAGNOSIS

INHERITED: Factor V Leiden (FVL) mutation:
- Autosomal-dominant mutation with low penetrance.
- Causes activated protein C resistance (APCR); 90% of APCR is caused by FVL mutation.
- Most common inherited thrombophilia; accounts for 40% to 50% of cases.
- OC use in heterozygous carriers is associated with an eightfold increased risk of VTE compared with noncarriers and a thirty-fivefold increased risk of VTE compared with noncarriers not using OCs.
- May be associated with cardiovascular disease in select high-risk subgroups.
Prothrombin G20210A mutation:
- Autosomal-dominant mutation with low penetrance.
- OC use in heterozygous carriers is associated with a sixteenfold increased risk of VTE compared with noncarriers not using OCs.
- May be associated with cardiovascular disease in select high-risk subgroups and young patients with ischemic stroke.

- Causes increased mRNA accumulation and protein synthesis, leading to elevated prothrombin plasma concentrations.
Protein C, protein S, antithrombin (AT) deficiency:
- Autosomal-dominant inheritance; many mutations identified for each of these conditions.
- Decreased level (type I deficiency) or abnormal function (type II deficiency).
- First episode of thrombosis is usually in young adults.
Protein C and protein S:
- Homozygous condition is very rare; usually associated with lethal thrombosis in infancy.
- Associated with warfarin-induced skin necrosis, which occurs secondary to depletion of vitamin

TABLE 1H-53 Potential Prothrombotic States

Congenital

Deficiency of anticoagulants
AT-III, protein C or protein S, plasminogen
Resistance to cofactor proteolysis
Factor V Leiden
High levels of procoagulants
Prothrombin 20210 mutation
Damage to endothelium

Acquired

Obstruction to flow
Indwelling lines
Pregnancy
Polycythemia/dehydration
Immobilization
Injury
Trauma, surgery, exercise
Inflammation
IBD, vasculitis, infection, Behçet syndrome
Hypercoagulability
Pregnancy
Malignancy
Antiphospholipid syndrome
Nephrotic syndrome
Oral contraceptives
L-Asparaginase

Rare Other Entities

Congenital
Dysfibrinogenemia
Acquired
Paroxysmal nocturnal hemoglobinuria
Thrombocythemia
Vascular grafts

AT-III, Antithrombin III; *IBD,* inflammatory bowel disease.
From Kliegman RM et al: *Nelson textbook of pediatrics,* ed 19, Philadelphia, 2011, Saunders.

TABLE 1H-51 Hypercoagulable Conditions

	Prevalence in General Population (%)	Prevalence in Population with Thrombosis (%)	A/V Events	Relative Risk of Thrombosis
FVL mutation	5% of whites; rare in nonwhites	12-40%	V	Heterozygous: 3-7; homozygous: 80
Prothrombin G20210A mutation	3% of whites; rare in nonwhites	6-18%	V	3
AT deficiency	0.02%	1-3%	V	20-50
PC deficiency	0.2-0.4%	3-5%	V	7-15
PS deficiency	0.03-0.1%	1-5%	V	5-11
Antiphospholipid antibody syndrome	1-2%	5-21%	V + A	2-11

A, Arterial; *AT,* antithrombin; *FVL,* factor V Leiden; *PC,* protein C; *PS,* protein S; *V,* venous.

TABLE 1H-54 Causes of Acquired Deficiencies in Antithrombin III, Protein C, or Protein S

Antithrombin III	Protein C	Protein S
Neonatal period	Neonatal period	Neonatal period
Pregnancy	Liver disease	Pregnancy
Liver disease	DIC	Liver disease
DIC	Chemotherapy (CMF)	DIC
Nephrotic syndrome	Acute thrombosis	Inflammatory states
Major surgery		Acute thrombosis
Acute thrombosis		
Treatment with:		
Heparin	Warfarin	Warfarin
L-Asparaginase	L-Asparaginase	L-Asparaginase
Estrogens		Estrogens

CMF, Cyclophosphamide, methotrexate, 5-fluorouracil; *DIC,* disseminated intravascular coagulation.
From Hoffman R et al: *Hematology, basic principles and practice,* ed 5, Philadelphia, 2009, Churchill Livingstone.

K–dependent anticoagulant factors sooner than procoagulant factors in the first few days of therapy.
ΛT deficiency:
- Most thrombogenic of the inherited thrombophilias; 50% lifetime risk of thrombosis.
- Homozygous condition is very rare, probably not compatible with normal fetal development.
- Arterial thrombosis can occur rarely.
- Can cause heparin resistance.

Elevated factor VIII level:
- May be an important risk factor for thrombosis in African-American population.
- Increased risk of recurrent thrombosis.
- Genetic etiology is suspected but not yet identified.

Other possible causes: Non-O blood group, dysfibrinogenemia, elevated thrombin-activatable fibrinolysis inhibitor, elevated factor IX and factor XI levels

ACQUIRED: Antiphospholipid antibody syndrome (APS):
- Most common cause of acquired thrombophilia.
- Can present as arterial or venous thrombosis, recurrent pregnancy loss, and adverse pregnancy outcomes.
- Thromboembolic events occur in up to 30% of population; high risk of recurrent thrombosis (up to 70% reported).
- See "Antiphospholipid Antibody Syndrome" for more information.

Conditions associated with increased risk of thrombosis:
- Prior thrombosis
- Trauma
- Medical illness: heart failure, respiratory failure, infection, diabetes mellitus, obesity, nephrotic syndrome, inflammatory bowel disease
- Chronic hemolysis–paroxysmal nocturnal hemoglobinuria, sickle cell anemia
- Pregnancy (sixfold increased risk of VTE), postpartum, OC use (fourfold increased risk, higher risk with third-generation OCs), transdermal contraceptive patch, HRT (twofold increased risk), tamoxifen, raloxifene
- Immobilization, travel
- Surgery (especially orthopedic), central venous catheters

- Hyperviscosity syndromes
- Myeloproliferative disorders
- Malignancy: disease or treatment related
- Heparin-induced thrombocytopenia and thrombosis
- Smoking

WORKUP
- History (presence of conditions or use of medications predisposing to thrombosis, family history of thrombosis), physical examination, laboratory tests, imaging studies.
- Age-appropriate cancer screening.
- No consensus exists regarding screening for thrombophilia; few cost-effectiveness or outcomes data are available. Screening laboratory evaluation for patients suspected of having a biologic defect predisposing to thrombosis is described in Box E1H-10. Thrombophilia screening is probably overused, as results usually don't change management.
- Thrombophilia screening is not recommended for primary prevention of VTE; some advocate testing prior to OC use or pregnancy in women with a strong family history of thrombosis or thrombophilia.
- Screening not recommended if VTE was associated with an identified risk factor. A possible exception is thrombosis associated with pregnancy, the postpartum period, or with OC use.
- Unprovoked VTE:
  1. Screen individuals for APCR, prothrombin G20210A mutation, protein C, protein S, AT deficiency, and APS if any of the following are present: <50 yr of age at first episode of thrombosis, family history of thrombosis, recurrent thrombosis, thrombosis in unusual anatomic location, life-threatening thrombotic event, warfarin-induced skin necrosis or thrombosis in pregnancy/postpartum
  2. Screen all others for APS.
- Arterial thrombosis: Screen for APS.
- Note: Routine screening for factor VIII level or hyperhomocysteinemia is not recommended.

TIMING OF WORKUP:
- Ideally >3 wk after discontinuation of anticoagulation (except for APS, which requires prolonged anticoagulation).

- Note: Acute thrombosis, anticoagulation, pregnancy, and many medical conditions can affect the results and must be considered in the timing and interpretation of the workup.

LABORATORY TESTS
- CBC with peripheral smear, electrolytes, calcium, creatinine, BUN and liver function tests, prothrombin time/partial thromboplastin time, prostate-specific antigen (in men aged >50 yr), urinalysis
- Note: Genetic counseling and written informed consent should be obtained before genetic testing. Abnormal nongenetic tests should be repeated after 6 wk to decrease false-positive results.
- APCR: APC-resistance assay (using factor V–deficient plasma). Presence of lupus anticoagulant causes false positives. Follow-up positive APCR assay with genetic test for FVL.
- Prothrombin G20210A mutation test.
- AT, protein C, and protein S deficiency: functional assays; if decreased perform antigenic assay to determine type of deficiency. Antigenic assays for protein S should measure free and total levels. In protein C and protein S deficiency, the functional assay may be falsely low in the presence of APCR or elevated factor VIII level and falsely high if lupus anticoagulant is present.
- APS: any of the following found on two occasions at least 12 wk apart: lupus anticoagulant, anticardiolipin antibodies, or anti–B$_2$-glycoprotein-I antibodies.

IMAGING STUDIES
Chest radiograph and other tests as appropriate to diagnose thrombosis and rule out associated conditions

 **TREATMENT**

NONPHARMACOLOGIC THERAPY
OC/HRT use and smoking should be avoided.

PROPHYLAXIS
- Prophylactic anticoagulation in high-risk situations.
- Patients with AT deficiency may benefit from antithrombin concentrates in high-risk situations.
- Pregnancy prophylaxis: timing and intensity of therapy is based on the patient's risk (genetic or acquired defect and clinical history). Women with thrombophilia and recurrent adverse pregnancy outcomes may benefit from prophylaxis with heparin (low-molecular-weight heparin most commonly used) and low-dose aspirin.

ACUTE GENERAL Rx
Initial therapy is the same as for individuals with and without thrombophilia, with exceptions for protein C and AT deficiency as detailed in the following.
Venous thrombosis:
- Begin low-molecular-weight heparin (LMWH) and warfarin simultaneously. Continue heparin

H

Diseases and Disorders

I

for at least 5 days and until international normalized ratio (INR) is therapeutic for 2 consecutive days; continue warfarin for at least 3 mo. Aim for INR of 2 to 3. Unfractionated heparin (UH) or fondaparinux (factor Xa inhibitor) may be used as alternatives to LMWH. LMWH is preferred over UH (except in patients with massive pulmonary embolism, increased risk of bleeding or renal failure) because of equivalent or superior effectiveness and a better safety profile.

- Novel oral anticoagulants such as the direct thrombin inhibitor and the direct Xa inhibitor have been FDA approved for treatment in acute DVT. They have been found to be noninferior to Coumadin, appear easier to use with fewer drug interactions, and have a trend towards less major bleeding but they still lack a reversal agent.
- Thrombophilia is not associated with a higher risk of recurrent VTE during warfarin therapy, with the exception of cancer patients in whom LMWH for 3 to 6 mo is associated with lower rates of recurrence than warfarin therapy.
- In pregnancy, anticoagulate with heparin throughout pregnancy and for at least 6 wk postpartum. Minimum duration of anticoagulation should be 6 mo. LMWH is preferred over UH. Warfarin may be used postpartum.
- Consider thrombolysis or thrombectomy in patients with massive pulmonary embolism or large proximal lower extremity DVT.

Protein C deficiency:
- Warfarin-induced skin necrosis: Discontinue warfarin, give vitamin K, and start heparin anticoagulation. Consider protein C replacement with protein C concentrate or fresh frozen plasma. Warfarin may be restarted at a low dose (2 mg daily for 3 days and increase by 2 to 3 mg daily until target INR is reached). Continue heparin for at least 5 days and until warfarin-induced anticoagulation is achieved.

AT deficiency:
- AT concentrates may be used if difficulty achieving anticoagulation (heparin resistance), severe thrombosis, or recurrent thrombosis despite adequate anticoagulation.

Arterial thrombosis:
- Anticoagulation and evaluation for thrombolysis or surgery.

CHRONIC Rx

- Optimal duration of anticoagulation remains unknown. Length of therapy may be individualized by assessing the risk of recurrence. Residual thrombosis (on ultrasonography)

or elevated D-dimer levels after completion of anticoagulation are associated with an increased risk of recurrence. With these findings, consider prolonging anticoagulation.

- Must consider risk and benefit; risk of major bleeding 2% to 3% annually in general population on anticoagulation but higher in the elderly (7% to 9% per year). Long-term anticoagulation is usually not indicated given the low risk of recurrent thrombosis for most conditions and the bleeding risk associated with anticoagulation.
- Indefinite anticoagulation considered if ≥2 spontaneous thromboses or spontaneous thrombosis associated with any of the following:
  1. Life-threatening thrombosis or thrombosis at an unusual site
  2. More than a single genetic defect
  3. Presence of AT deficiency or APS
- Patients with active cancer may benefit from indefinite anticoagulation.

DISPOSITION

Depends on underlying condition

REFERRAL

Hematology, maternal-fetal medicine, obstetric medicine

 **PEARLS & CONSIDERATIONS**

COMMENTS

- Warfarin therapy effectively reduces the risk of recurrent VTE; when therapy is discontinued VTE risk increases.
- Previous episode of VTE is a major risk factor for recurrence regardless of the presence of thrombophilia. Risk is greatest in the first 2 yr after thrombosis. 20% of all patients with unprovoked VTE have recurrence within 5 yr.
- Genetic risk factors for thrombosis in nonwhites remain largely unknown.
- Interpreting workup: many medical conditions cause acquired abnormalities.
  1. Acute thrombosis may be associated with lupus anticoagulant, increased anticardiolipin antibodies, and elevated factor VIII levels
  2. Heparin therapy: antithrombin levels decrease by up to 30%; can affect lupus anticoagulant testing
  3. Warfarin therapy: cannot measure protein C and protein S (levels and function decrease);

antithrombin levels may increase; can affect lupus anticoagulant testing
  4. Protein C, protein S, and antithrombin levels decrease with acute thrombosis (<2 wk), surgery, liver disease, disseminated intravascular coagulation, and chemotherapy. Protein C level also decreases with severe infection but levels increase with age and hyperlipidemia. Protein S and antithrombin levels also decrease with nephrotic syndrome, pregnancy, and estrogen therapy (HRT, OC)
  5. APCR is increased with pregnancy, estrogen therapy (HRT, OCs), and certain cancers; elevated factor VIII level and antiphospholipid antibodies can cause APCR

PREVENTION

Risk of postthrombotic syndrome decreases if compression stockings are worn for at least 1 year, starting in the first month after the DVT.

PATIENT & FAMILY EDUCATION

National Blood Clot Alliance
120 White Plains Road, Suite 100
Tarrytown, NY 10591
http://www.stoptheclot.org/contact.htm
National Collaborative Outreach Project of the Blood Clot Outreach Program at the Hemophilia and Thrombosis Center University of North Carolina at Chapel Hill
http://www.clotconnect.org/about-clot-connect/about
Factor V Leiden Resources
http://www.fvleiden.org/resources/index.html
APS Foundation of America, Inc.
P. O. Box 801
LaCrosse, WI 54602-0801
http://www.apsfa.org/

SUGGESTED READINGS

Available at www.expertconsult.com

RELATED CONTENT

Thrombophilia (Patient Information)
Antiphospholipid Syndrome (Related Key Topic)
Deep Vein Thrombosis (Related Key Topic)
Pulmonary Embolism (Related Key Topic)

AUTHORS: **JOHN L. REAGAN, M.D.,** and **ANDREW ROGERS, M.D.**

H

Diseases and Disorders

I

BASIC INFORMATION

DEFINITION

Hyperemesis gravidarum is a severe and persistent form of nausea and vomiting resulting in at least a 5% weight loss, dehydration, ketonuria, and electrolyte imbalance, with typical onset at 4 to 8 wk of pregnancy continuing through 14 to 16 wk of pregnancy.

ICD-10CM CODES
O21.0 Mild hyperemesis gravidarum
O21.1 Hyperemesis gravidarum with metabolic disturbance

EPIDEMIOLOGY & DEMOGRAPHICS

INCIDENCE: 0.5% to 2% of pregnancies
GENETICS: No genetic disposition
RISK FACTORS: Women with increased placental mass, including molar pregnancy or multiple gestation, family history or personal history of hyperemesis gravidarum, prior miscarriage, nulliparity, preexisting diabetes, hyperthyroid disorder, peptic ulceration or other gastrointestinal disorders, depression, and asthma. Female fetus increases the risk by 1.5-fold.

PHYSICAL FINDINGS & CLINICAL PRESENTATION

- Weight loss of more than 5% from pregravid weight
- Symptoms—nausea, vomiting, spitting, enhanced olfactory senses, food and/or fluid intolerance, lethargy
- Signs—dehydration, poor skin turgor, dry mucous membranes, ketonuria, anemia, tachycardia, hypotension
- Complications include inadequate caloric intake, nutritional deficiencies, dehydration, and electrolyte abnormalities including hyponatremia, hypocalcemia, hypokalemia, and in severe cases hypochloremic metabolic acidosis or Wernicke's encephalopathy from thiamine deficiency

ETIOLOGY

Unknown but likely multifactorial. Theories include gestational hyperestrogenemia, gastric dysrhythmias, and hyperthyroidism.

DIAGNOSIS

DIFFERENTIAL DIAGNOSIS

- Gastrointestinal conditions—gastroenteritis, gastroparesis, achalasia, biliary tract disease, hepatitis, intestinal obstruction, peptic ulcer disease, appendicitis
- Genitourinary tract conditions—pyelonephritis, uremia, ovarian torsion, kidney stones, degenerating uterine leiomyoma
- Metabolic disease—diabetic ketoacidosis, porphyria, Addison's disease, hyperthyroidism

- Neurologic conditions—pseudotumor cerebri, vestibular lesions, migraines, tumors of the central nervous system
- Miscellaneous—drug toxicity or intolerance, psychologic
- Pregnancy-related conditions—acute fatty liver of pregnancy, preeclampsia

WORKUP

Diagnosis is one of exclusion. History and physical examination along with laboratory tests to rule out other causes of vomiting should be performed.

LABORATORY TESTS

- Urinalysis may show elevated specific gravity, ketonuria, or proteinuria
- Liver enzymes (elevated but usually <300 U/L)
- Serum bilirubin (<4 mg/dl)
- Serum amylase or lipase (up to 5× greater than normal)
- BMP, may reveal hyponatremia, hypokalemia, low serum urea
- CBC
- Calcium
- TSH and free T4 (transient hyperthyroidism occurs in 2/3 of women with hyperemesis gravidarum; this is biochemical hyperthyroidism that usually resolves by 18 wk gestation; treatment should not be undertaken without evidence of intrinsic thyroid disease)

IMAGING STUDIES

- Ultrasound to evaluate for multiple gestation or molar pregnancy
- Right upper quadrant ultrasound to evaluate for biliary tract disease

TREATMENT

NONPHARMACOLOGIC THERAPY

- Reassurance and support
- Avoidance of foods and smells that trigger nausea
- Oral ginger root
- Small frequent dry meals
- Eating prior to getting out of bed

ACUTE GENERAL Rx

- Nothing by mouth
- Intravenous fluid and electrolyte replacement with vitamin supplementation
- Thiamine administration prior to giving dextrose to avoid Wernicke's encephalopathy
- Pyridoxine (vitamin B$_6$)
- Doxylamine 25 mg qhs
- Antiemetics, including promethazine, phenothiazines, metoclopramide, and ondansetron, have been shown to be generally safe and effective in improving pregnancy outcome
- Restart oral intake gradually no less than 48 hr after vomiting has stopped

CHRONIC Rx

- Nasogastric feedings are useful alternatives in severe cases
- Total parenteral nutrition may be necessary in life-threatening cases

COMPLEMENTARY AND ALTERNATIVE MEDICINE

- Supportive psychotherapy
- Acupuncture
- Acupressure with use of a wrist band

DISPOSITION

- Infants born to pregnancies complicated by hyperemesis are more likely to be premature and small for gestational age.
- Lower rates of miscarriage have also been documented when comparing pregnancies complicated by hyperemesis gravidarum vs. controls.

PEARLS & CONSIDERATIONS

COMMENTS

Nausea and vomiting in early pregnancy are associated with psychosocial morbidity.

PREVENTION

Taking a multivitamin from time of conception

SUGGESTED READINGS
Available at www.expertconsult.com

RELATED CONTENT
Hyperemesis Gravidarum (Patient Information)

AUTHOR: **ALISON PATTERSON, M.D.**

BASIC INFORMATION

DEFINITION

- Primary hyperlipoproteinemia is a group of genetic disorders of the lipid transport proteins in the blood that manifests as abnormally elevated levels of cholesterol, triglycerides, or both in the serum of affected patients.
- Usually defined as total cholesterol, LDL, triglycerides or lipoprotein A levels above 90th percentile or HDL or apo A-1 levels below the 10th percentile for the general population. Figure E1H-71 illustrates the structure of lipoproteins. Plasma lipoprotein composition is described in Table E1H-55.

SYNONYMS

Hyperlipidemia

ICD-10CM CODES
E78.0	Pure hypercholesterolemia
E78.2	Mixed hyperlipidemia
E78.1	Pure hyperglyceridemia
E78.4	Other hyperlipidemia
E78.3	Hyperchylomicronemia

EPIDEMIOLOGY & DEMOGRAPHICS

INCIDENCE: The most common types are lipoprotein A excess, hypertriglyceridemia, and combined hyperlipidemia.
- Incidence of heterozygous familial hypercholesterolemia: 1:500.
- Incidence of homozygous familial hypercholesterolemia: 1:1 million.
- Familial hypercholesterolemia: autosomal-dominant disorder.
- Familial combined hyperlipidemia: possibly an autosomal-dominant disorder.
- Multifactorial predilection: apparent in majority of affected individuals.

GENETICS:
- Familial lipoprotein lipase deficiency: autosomal recessive, resulting in an elevation in the plasma chylomicrons and triglycerides
- Familial apoprotein CII deficiency: autosomal recessive, resulting in increased serum chylomicrons, very-low-density lipoprotein (VLDL), and hypertriglyceridemia
- Familial type 3 hyperlipoproteinemia: single-gene defect requiring contributory factors to manifest
- Familial hypercholesterolemia: autosomal-dominant defect of the LDL receptor, resulting in an elevated serum cholesterol level and normal triglycerides
- Familial hypertriglyceridemia: common, autosomal-dominant defect resulting in elevated VLDL and triglycerides
- Multiple lipoprotein–type hyperlipidemia: autosomal dominant, manifesting as isolated hypercholesterolemia, isolated hypertriglyceridemia, or hyperlipidemia
- Polygenic hypercholesterolemia: multifactorial
- Polygenic hyperalphalipoproteinemia: autosomal dominant or polygenic, causing an elevated high-density lipoprotein
- A classification of lipoprotein disorders is described in Table 1H-56.

PHYSICAL FINDINGS & CLINICAL PRESENTATION

- Familial lipoprotein lipase deficiency: recurrent bouts of abdominal pain in infancy, eruptive xanthomas, hepatomegaly, splenomegaly, lipemia retinalis
- Familial apoprotein CII deficiency: occasional eruptive xanthomas
- Familial type 3 hyperlipoproteinemia: xanthoma striata palmaris or tuberoeruptive xanthomas, xanthelasmas, arterial bruits at a young age, gangrene of the lower extremities at a young age
- Familial hypercholesterolemia: tendon xanthomas, arcus corneae, xanthelasma
- Familial hypertriglyceridemia: associated obesity; eruptive xanthomas can develop with exacerbations

ETIOLOGY

- Genetic defects causing lipid abnormalities
- Environmental influences including diet, drugs, and alcohol intake

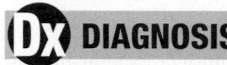

DIAGNOSIS

DIFFERENTIAL DIAGNOSIS

Secondary causes of hyperlipoproteinemias:
- Hypothyroidism
- Diabetes mellitus
- Pancreatitis
- Autoimmune hyperlipoproteinemia
- Nephrotic syndrome
- Biliary obstruction. Table 1H-57 describes the differential diagnosis of hyperlipidemia and dyslipidemia.

WORKUP

- Family history for premature cardiac disease
- Personal history of recurrent pancreatitis
- Detailed physical examination

LABORATORY TESTS:
- Standard lipid profile
- If normal, further testing with measurement of lipoprotein A, apo B, and apo A-1
- Lipoprotein electrophoresis and ultracentrifugation (for phenotypic classification)
- Workup for secondary causes: TSH, fasting glucose, liver function, renal function, urinary protein

TREATMENT

NONPHARMACOLOGIC THERAPY

- Cornerstone of treatment: dietary therapy
  1. TLC diet (therapeutic lifestyle changes): see "Hypercholesterolemia" topic
- Risk factor reduction includes smoking cessation, treatment of hypertension, exercise
- Familial lipoprotein lipase deficiency and familial apoprotein CII deficiency: fat-free diet
- Remainder of cases, except those with polygenic hyperalphalipoproteinemia: fat- and cholesterol-restricted diets
- Interventions to improve adherence are described in Table E1H-58

ACUTE GENERAL Rx

No acute treatment needed.

CHRONIC Rx

- Familial lipoprotein lipase deficiency, polygenic hyperalphalipoproteinemia, or familial apoprotein CII deficiency: no chronic drug therapy
- Familial type 3 hyperlipoproteinemia: usually responds well to secondary causes being treated and diet therapy; if not, fibric acids may be tried
- Familial hypercholesterolemia: HMG-CoA reductase inhibitors, bile acid sequestrants, or niacin. Alirocumab and evolocumab are subcutaneously injected PCSK9 (protein convertase subtilisin kexin type 9) inhibitors available as an adjunct diet and maximally tolerated statin therapy for adults with heterozygous familial hypercholesterolemia (HeFH).
- Familial hypertriglyceridemia: fibric acids (fenofibrate), niacin, omega-3 PUFA-containing fish oil capsules
- Multiple lipoprotein–type hyperlipidemia: drug therapy aimed at the predominant lipid abnormality noted
- Recent data suggest in patients with lipoprotein abnormalities that treatment goals should be based on non-HDL cholesterol rather than LDL cholesterol
- The FDA has approved mipomersen and lomitapide in patients with homozygous familial hypercholesterolemia already taking maximum doses of other lipid-lowering drugs. Both medicines are hepatotoxic and very expensive.
- Table E1H-59 describes the various medications used to treat hyperlipidemia.

DISPOSITION

- Those with polygenic hyperalphalipoproteinemia: excellent prognosis for longevity
- Those with familial hypercholesterolemia, familial type 3 hypercholesterolemia, or multiple lipoprotein–type hyperlipidemia: even with aggressive treatment, at high risk for accelerated atherosclerosis and coronary artery disease

PEARLS & CONSIDERATIONS

COMMENTS

- Patient information is available through the American Heart Association.
- Lipid-lowering drug therapy is recommended for children ≥10 yr whose LDL-C levels remain extremely elevated after 6 mo to 1 yr of dietary modification. Drug therapy also can be considered for children with LDL-C levels of ≥190 mg/dl.

SUGGESTED READINGS

Available at www.expertconsult.com

RELATED CONTENT

Hypercholesterolemia (Related Key Topic)

AUTHOR: **PRIYA BANSAL, M.D., M.P.H.**

TABLE 1H-56 Classification of Lipoprotein Disorders by Phenotypes, Genotypes, and Corresponding Clinical Manifestations

Phenotype (Frederickson Type)	Genotype	Elevated Cholesterol Type	Genetic Defect	Xanthomas	Other Clinical Manifestations
I (rare)	Familial hyperchylo-micronemia	Elevated chylomicrons	Familial lipoprotein lipase deficiency, Apo C-II deficiency	Eruptive skin xanthomas	Recurrent abdominal pain, hepato-splenomegaly
IIA	Familial hypercholes-terolemia	Elevated LDL	FHC, LDL receptor deficiency	Tendon xanthomas, xanthelasma, tuberous; planar palmar (homozygous)	Premature CAD, arcus corneae, arthritic symptoms
IIB	Familial combined hypercholester-olemia	Elevated LDL and VLDL	Reduced LDL receptor and increased apo B		
III (rare)	Familial dysbetalipopro-teinemia	Elevated IDL	Defective apo E2 synthesis	Tuberous, planar (palmar)	Premature CAD and peripheral vascular disease, male > female, obesity, abnormal glucose tolerance, hyperuricemia, aggravated by hypothyroidism, good response to therapy
IV	Familial hyperlipidema	Elevated VLDL	Increased VLDL production	None	CAD and peripheral vascular disease, obesity, abnormal glucose tolerance, hyperuricemia, arthritic
V (rare)	Endogenous hypertri-glyceridemia	Elevated VLDL, chylomicrons	Increased VLDL production and reduced LPL	Eruptive	

Apo, Apolipoprotein; *CAD,* coronary artery disease; *FHC,* familial hypercholesterolemia.
Modified from Graber MA: *The family practice handbook,* ed 4, St Louis, 2001, Mosby.

TABLE 1H-57 Differential Diagnosis of Hyperlipidemia and Dyslipidemia

Hypertriglyceridemia	Hypercholesterolemia	Increased Cholesterol and Triglycerides	Low HDL
Primary Disorders			
LPL deficiency	Familial hypercholesterolemia	Familial combined hyperlipidemia	Familial hypoalphalipoproteinemia
ApoCII deficiency	Familial defective apoB100	Dysbetalipoproteinemia	ApoAI mutations
Familial hypertriglyceridemia	Polygenic hypercholesterolemia	Diabetes mellitus	LCAT deficiency
Dysbetalipoproteinemia	Sitosterolemia	Hypothyroidism	ABCA1 deficiency
Secondary Disorders	Hypothyroidism	Glucocorticoids	Anabolic steroids
Diabetes mellitus	Obstructive liver disease	Immunosuppressives	Retinoids
Hypothyroidism	Nephrotic syndrome	Protease inhibitors	
High-carbohydrate diets	Thiazides	Nephrotic syndrome	
Renal failure		Lipodystrophies	
Obesity/insulin resistance			
Estrogens			
Ethanol			
β-Blockers			
Protease inhibitors			
Glucocorticoids			
Retinoids			
Bile acid–binding resins			
Antipsychotics			
Lipodystrophies			
Thiazides			

ABCA1, Adenosine triphosphate–binding cassette transporter 1; *apo,* apolipoprotein; *HDL,* high-density lipoprotein; *LCAT,* lecithin:cholesterol acyltransferase; *LPL,* lipoprotein lipase.
From Melmed S, Polonsky KS, Larsen PR, Kronenberg HM: *Williams textbook of endocrinology,* ed 12, Philadelphia, 2011, Saunders.

Hyperosmolar Hyperglycemic Syndrome

BASIC INFORMATION

DEFINITION

Hyperosmolar hyperglycemic syndrome (HHS) is characterized by severe hyperglycemia without ketosis, hyperosmolarity, intravascular volume depletion with water losses exceeding salt losses, and altered mental status. HHS is frequently complicated by multiple electrolyte and acid-base abnormalities. Symptoms result from hypertonicity and profound volume depletion.

SYNONYMS

Hyperosmolar coma
Nonketotic hyperosmolar syndrome
Hyperosmolar nonketotic state
HHS

ICD-10CM CODES

E08.00	Diabetes mellitus due to underlying condition with hyperosmolarity without nonketotic hyperglycemic-hyperosmolar coma (NKHHC)
E08.01	Diabetes mellitus due to underlying condition with hyperosmolarity with coma
E09.00	Drug or chemical induced diabetes mellitus with hyperosmolarity without nonketotic hyperglycemic-hyperosmolar coma (NKHHC)
E09.01	Drug or chemical induced diabetes mellitus with hyperosmolarity with coma
E11.00	Type 2 diabetes mellitus with hyperosmolarity without nonketotic hyperglycemic-hyperosmolar coma (NKHHC)
E11.01	Type 2 diabetes mellitus with hyperosmolarity with coma
E13.00	Other specified diabetes mellitus with hyperosmolarity without nonketotic hyperglycemic-hyperosmolar coma (NKHHC)
E13.01	Other specified diabetes mellitus with hyperosmolarity with coma

PHYSICAL FINDINGS & CLINICAL PRESENTATION

- Evidence of extreme volume depletion and dehydration (poor skin turgor, sunken eyeballs, dry mucous membranes)
- Neurologic defects (reversible hemiplegia, focal seizures)
- Orthostatic hypotension, tachycardia
- Evidence of precipitating factors (infection, myocardial ischemia, stroke)
- Suppressed mental status ranging from delirium to obtundation to coma (25% of patients)

ETIOLOGY

- Infections in up to 50% of cases (e.g., pneumonia, urinary tract infection, sepsis)
- New or previously unrecognized diabetes (30%)
- Noncompliance, dose reduction, or recent discontinuation of diabetic medication
- Stress (myocardial infarction, cerebrovascular accident)

- Drugs: diuretics (dehydration), phenytoin, diazoxide (impaired insulin secretion), glucocorticoids, chemotherapeutic agents, calcium channel blockers, total parenteral nutrition, substance abuse (alcohol, cocaine)

DIAGNOSIS

DIFFERENTIAL DIAGNOSIS

- Diabetic ketoacidosis
- Stroke
- Encephalitis
- Encephalopathy
- Myxedema coma

LABORATORY TESTS

- Hyperglycemia: serum glucose usually >600 mg/dl, serum/urine ketones absent or "small.
- CBC with differential, urinalysis, and blood and urine cultures should be performed to rule out infectious etiology.
- Hyperosmolarity: serum osmolarity usually >320 mOsm/L.
- Serum sodium: may be low, normal, or high. Because glucose draws fluid from the intracellular space, serum sodium concentration is relatively or absolutely lower than baseline. The serum sodium concentration may be normal, depressed, or elevated. In all cases, the patient is hypertonic with cellular water loss (dehydration). It is necessary to correct sodium for the serum glucose level. The corrected sodium can be obtained by increasing the serum sodium concentration by 2.4 mEq/dl for every 100 mg/dl increase in the serum glucose level over normal.
- Serum potassium: may be low, normal, or high; regardless of the initial serum level, the total body potassium deficit from urinary losses is approximately 5 to 15 mEq/kg.
- Serum bicarbonate: usually >15 mEq/L (mean, 17 mEq/L).
- Arterial pH: typically >7.30; serum bicarbonate and arterial pH may be lower if lactic acidosis is present.
- BUN: generally ranges from 60–90 mg/dl from severe dehydration and prerenal azotemia.
- Phosphorus: hypophosphatemia (average deficit, 70 to 140 mmol).
- Calcium: hypocalcemia (average deficit, 50 to 100 mEq).
- Magnesium: hypomagnesemia (average deficit is 50 to 100 mEq).
- ECG to rule out a concomitant myocardial infarction.

IMAGING STUDIES

- Chest radiography to rule out infectious process. The initial radiographs may be negative if the patient has significant volume depletion. Repeat chest radiography after 24 hours of volume repletion if pulmonary infection is suspected.
- The need for additional imaging, such as CT scans, is determined by biochemical or physical exam findings.

TREATMENT

ACUTE GENERAL Rx

- Vigorous fluid replacement: the volume and rate of fluid replacement are determined by renal and cardiac function. Slower infusion rate may be used initially in patients with compromised cardiovascular or renal status. Frequent clinical monitoring of fluid status is essential.
  - During the first hour, infuse 1000 ml of 0.9% normal saline (NS) to expand the intravascular fluid volume.
  - Infuse a second liter of 0.9% NS in the next hour if the patient hypotension persists.
  - Then, begin replacing the free water deficit with 0.45% NS at 250 to 500 mL/hr. Taper the 0.45% NS to replace the estimated fluid deficit over 24 to 36 hours.
  - When serum glucose is lowered to 300 mg/dl, change to 5% dextrose with 0.45% NS.
- Correct hyperglycemia: the goal is to decrease plasma glucose by 50 to 100 mg/dl/hr.
  - Vigorous IV volume repletion alone will decrease the serum glucose level by 80 mg/dl/hr. Insulin should not be administered until serum potassium is at least 3.3 mEq/L to prevent life-threatening hypokalemia.
  - A regular insulin IV bolus (0.1 units/kg of body weight) is followed by an insulin fusion of 0.1 units/kg/hr, and adjusted hourly until the serum glucose level approaches 300 mg/dl.
  - When serum glucose reaches 300 mg/dl, decrease insulin infusion to 0.02-0.05 units/kg/hr.
  - Avoid overly rapid glucose correction by insulin administration.
  - Maintain glucose at 250 to 300 mg/dL until mentally alert.
  - Before stopping IV insulin, administer subcutaneous insulin (dose depends on insulin sensitivity). Short- (regular) or rapid-acting (aspart, lispro, glulisine) subcutaneous insulins should be administered 1-2 hr before stopping IV insulin. Intermediate (NPH) or long-acting (glargine, detemir) subcutaneous insulins should be administered 2-4 hr before stopping IV insulin.
- Total daily insulin doses in insulin-naïve patients range from 0.5 to 0.8 units/kg/day. Approximately half this dose should be given as intermediate or long-acting insulin, and half as prandial insulin if the patient is eating.
- Potassium replacement: Monitor potassium every 2 hours until the patient has stabilized. Confirm adequate urine flow before initiating potassium (K) replacement. Rate of K replacement is based on initial potassium concentration. If K is <3.3 mEq/L, administer KCl 20–30 mEq/L of intravenous fluid (IVF) until K is >3.3 mEq/L. If K is 3.3-5.3 mEq/L, administer KCl at 10 to 30 mEq/L IVF to maintain a K of >4 mEq/L. If K >5.3 mEq/L, withhold potassium supplementation and check K every 2 hours. Continuous telemetric monitoring and hourly measurement of urinary output are recommended.

- Phosphate replacement: Replacement can be considered if serum phosphate is <2 mg/dl or there is evidence of a phosphate depletion syndrome such as rhabdomyolysis. In the absence of kidney failure, phosphate can be administered at a rate of 0.1 mmol/kg/hr (5-10 mmol/hr) to a maximum of 80 to 120 mmol in 24 hr.
- Magnesium replacement, in the absence of kidney failure, can be administered by the intramuscular route (0.05-0.10 mL/kg of 20% magnesium sulfate) or as an IV infusion (4-8 mL of 20% magnesium sulfate [0.08-0.16 mEq/kg]).

PEARLS & CONSIDERATIONS

COMMENTS
- The typical patient is an elderly or bed-confined diabetic with impaired ability to communicate thirst and who is evaluated after an interval of 1 to 2 weeks of prolonged osmotic diuresis.

SUGGESTED READINGS
Available at www.expertconsult.com

AUTHOR: **HILARY B. WHITLATCH, M.D.**

BASIC INFORMATION

DEFINITION

Hyperparathyroidism is an endocrine disorder caused by excessive secretion of parathyroid hormone (PTH) from the parathyroid glands. Autonomous production of PTH resulting in hypercalcemia defines primary hyperparathyroidism. Secondary hyperparathyroidism occurs when the parathyroid glands appropriately increase PTH production in response to low calcium or vitamin D states. Primary hyperparathyroidism is the focus of this section.

ICD-10CM CODES

E21.0	Primary hyperparathyroidism
E21.1	Secondary hyperparathyroidism, not elsewhere classified
E21.2	Other hyperparathyroidism
E21.3	Hyperparathyroidism, unspecified
N25.81	Secondary hyperparathyroidism of renal origin

EPIDEMIOLOGY & DEMOGRAPHICS

INCIDENCE: 4 cases per 100,000 persons per year. Although malignancy is the most common cause of hypercalcemia in hospitalized patients, primary hyperparathyroidism is the most common cause of hypercalcemia in the outpatient setting.
PREVALENCE: 3 cases/1000 persons
PREDOMINANT SEX AND AGE: Higher prevalence in women (female:male ratio 2:1) and older age (peaks in the seventh decade of life).

PHYSICAL FINDINGS & CLINICAL PRESENTATION

The majority of patients with primary hyperparathyroidism are asymptomatic. Diagnosis is usually considered in patients after an incidental discovery of hypercalcemia or during the evaluation for decreased bone mass. The development of symptoms varies with severity and rapidity of disease progression and reflects both the hypercalcemic and hyperparathyroid components of the disease process.

- Cardiovascular: hypertension, shortened QT interval, bradycardia, arrhythmia, valvular calcification, left ventricular hypertrophy, increased mean carotid intima-media thickness.
- GI: anorexia, nausea, vomiting, constipation, abdominal pain, peptic ulcer disease, pancreatitis
- GU: nephrolithiasis, nephrocalcinosis, renal insufficiency, polyuria, nocturia, nephrogenic diabetes insipidus, renal tubular acidosis
- Musculoskeletal: weakness, myopathy, bone pain, osteopenia, osteoporosis, gout, pseudogout, chondrocalcinosis, osteitis fibrosa cystica, subperiosteal bone resorption (Fig. 1H-72)
- CNS: confusion, anxiety, fatigue, lethargy, obtundation, depression, coma
- Other: pruritus, metastatic calcifications, band keratopathy

ETIOLOGY

- Most cases of primary hyperparathyroidism are sporadic, but hyperparathyroidism can be associated with rare familial conditions such as multiple endocrine neoplasia (MEN-1 and MEN-2). Mutations in certain genes have been linked to tumor development in both sporadic and familial cases such as hyperparathyroidism-jaw tumor syndrome. Higher prevalence of hyperparathyroidism is noted with head and neck irradiation, chronic low calcium or vitamin D status, and lithium therapy.
- Pathologic characteristics include adenoma (80%-85%), hyperplasia (10%-15%), or carcinomas (<1%-2%).

DIAGNOSIS

DIFFERENTIAL DIAGNOSIS

- Secondary hyperparathyroidism precipitated by conditions that result in hypocalcemia
  1. Renal calcium loss (i.e., medication: loop diuretics and hypercalcuria)
  2. Calcium deficiency
  3. Vitamin D deficiency
  4. Malabsorption
  5. Chronic kidney disease (most common)
  6. Pseudohypoparathyroidism (PTH resistance)
  7. Inhibition of bone resorption (i.e., bisphosphonates)
- Other causes of hypercalcemia include:
  1. Medications: thiazide diuretics, lithium therapy
  2. Vitamin D intoxication, milk-alkali syndrome
  3. Familial hypocalciuric hypercalcemia (FHH)

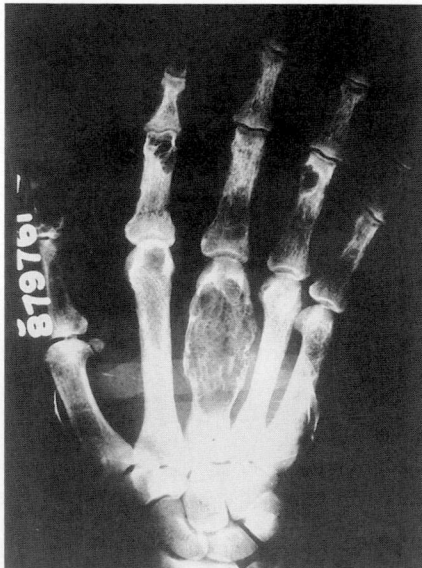

FIGURE 1H-72 Radiograph of hand from a patient with severe primary hyperparathyroidism. Note the dramatic remodeling associated with the intense region of high bone turnover in the third metacarpal, in addition to widespread evidence of subperiosteal and trabecular resorption. (Courtesy Fuller Albright Collection, Massachusetts General Hospital. From Larsen PR et al [eds]: *Williams textbook of endocrinology,* ed 10, Philadelphia, 2003, Saunders.)

4. Renal failure (tertiary hyperparathyroidism)
5. Granulomatous disorders (e.g., sarcoidosis)
6. Malignancy (e.g., lung cancer, lymphoma, multiple myeloma, bone metastasis)
7. Prolonged immobilization

WORK-UP

- Typically, primary hyperparathyroidism is confirmed with an elevated serum calcium and PTH level.
  1. Two measurements of serum calcium are required for the confirmation of hypercalcemia. Total calcium should be corrected for low albumin utilizing the formula: Corrected Calcium = Serum Calcium + 0.8 × 4 − serum albumin). If a reliable laboratory is available, ionized calcium should be considered especially in conditions associated with acid-base disturbances or low albumin states. Patients with primary hyperparathyroidism can also present with normal calcium levels. The most common reason for this finding is concomitant vitamin D deficiency and primary hyperparathyroidism.
  2. The serum intact PTH (iPTH) level is the single best test to evaluate the etiology of hypercalcemia. PTH is elevated or in the high normal range (i.e., inappropriately normal for an elevated calcium state) in primary hyperparathyroidism. PTH is decreased in most other conditions associated with elevated calcium.
- Other causes of hypercalcemia should be ruled out. These are typically associated with low PTH levels. Exceptions include lithium use and FHH.
  1. Review medication history to determine lithium, thiazide, vitamin D, or calcium intake.
  2. Check 24-hr urine calcium:creatinine to rule out FHH. Urine calcium is usually low in FHH. PTH can be normal or high in FHH.
  3. Consider PTH-related peptide (PTHrP) to evaluate hypercalcemia related to malignancies and vitamin D 1,25 to assess hypercalcemia secondary to granulomatous diseases or lymphomas.
  4. Multiple myeloma and bone metastasis can also result in a high calcium state and therefore must be appropriately evaluated.
- Rule out other causes of elevated PTH (i.e., secondary hyperparathyroidism). Serum calcium is typically low or low-normal in secondary hyperparathyroidism.
  1. Check calcium and 25 OH-vitamin D to rule out deficiency states.
  2. Check serum creatinine to assess renal function and 24-hr urine calcium and creatinine to evaluate renal loss

LABORATORY TESTS

- Serum calcium (ionized or corrected calcium): normal or elevated in primary hyperparathyroidism
- Serum phosphorus: low or low-normal in primary hyperparathyroidism.

- PTH: elevated or high normal in primary hyperparathyroidism
- 24-hr urine calcium and creatinine to evaluate risk for renal stones and to exclude FHH.
- Serum creatinine to assess GFR and renal status.
- PTHrP and 1,25 OH-vitamin D levels can be considered to rule out other causes of elevated calcium.
- Evaluation of 25 OH-vitamin D is recommended in all patients with hyperparathyroidism. Vitamin D deficiency can result in secondary hyperparathyroidism. Calcium levels are usually in the low-normal range in vitamin D deficiency.
- ECG may reveal shortening of the QT interval secondary to severe hypercalcemia (>12 mg/dl)

IMAGING STUDIES

- Parathyroid localization with technetium-99m sestamibi can identify potential adenomas to help with surgical planning.
- Parathyroid ultrasound is also used to localize the parathyroid adenoma.
- Bone mineral density of the spine, hip, and forearm (distal third) is recommended for all patients with hyperparathyroidism in order to assess the risk for osteoporosis and fragility fractures. Cortical bone loss (i.e., forearm or hip) is greater than trabecular bone loss (i.e., spine) in hyperparathyroidism.
- Renal ultrasound can be considered to assess asymptomatic renal stones.

Rx TREATMENT

Modality of treatment depends on disease progression and which patients are more likely to suffer end-organ effects of hyperparathyroidism or benefit the most from surgery.

- Surgery is the only definitive treatment for symptomatic primary hyperparathyroidism. Surgery can normalize calcium levels, decrease the risk for kidney stones, improve bone mineral density and fracture risk, and enhance quality of life measures.
  1. Indications for parathyroidectomy
     1. All patients younger than 50 yr
     2. Hypercalcemia (Ca >1 mg/dl above upper limit normal)
     3. Creatinine clearance <60 mL/min
     4. Osteoporosis (T-score <−2.5 or prior fragility fracture)
     5. Symptomatic hyperparathyroidism such as history of nephrolithiasis
  2. Surgical approaches include:
     1. Bilateral neck exploration under general anesthesia is the conventional surgical approach. An experienced endocrine surgeon cures >95% of patients undergoing bilateral neck exploration. Potential complications include transient and permanent hypocalcemia secondary to hypoparathyroidism and recurrent laryngeal nerve injury.

2. Minimally invasive parathyroidectomy performed by experienced surgeons is an excellent alternative to conventional surgery. It can be performed under cervical block anesthesia as an outpatient procedure with intraoperative monitoring of PTH before and after removal to document the expected fall after abnormal glands are removed.

- Ablation therapy (e.g., ethanol, angiographic, radiofrequency) can be considered in patients who are not surgical candidates. Limited data are available on efficacy and side effects. Repeat ablations may be required if hypercalcemia persists.
- Medical management
  1. Avoid medications that precipitate hypercalcemia (e.g., thiazide or lithium)
  2. Because inadequate calcium and vitamin D status stimulates PTH, it is not necessary to restrict calcium and vitamin D intake. Vitamin D replacement safely improves vitamin D level and decreases PTH level without significantly increasing serum calcium level and urinary calcium excretion.
  3. Encourage physical activity since immobilization increases bone resorption.
  4. Recommend adequate hydration (at least 2 L) to minimize the risk of nephrolithiasis.
- For patients who are not surgical candidates, pharmacologic options are available. Indications include symptomatic hyperparathyroidism or osteopenia associated with an increased fracture risk.
  1. Cinacalcet (Sensipar) is an oral calcimimetic agent that activates the calcium sensing receptor in the parathyroid gland. It decreases PTH production and subsequently serum calcium levels, without significant BMD changes. It is indicated for the treatment of secondary hyperparathyroidism associated with chronic kidney disease, for hypercalcemia associated with parathyroid carcinoma, and for the treatment of severe hypercalcemia in patients with primary hyperparathyroidism who are unable to undergo surgery.
  2. Agents that inhibit bone resorption such as bisphosphonates (e.g., alendronate, pamidronate, zoledronate), estrogens and selective estrogen receptor modulators (e.g., raloxifene) improve bone mineral density, and decrease calcium levels in patients with hyperparathyroidism. These agents should be considered when fracture reduction is the primary goal.
- Medical monitoring is recommended for asymptomatic primary hyperparathyroidism. The majority of patients do not manifest disease progression during observation. However, approximately 25% of asymptomatic patients require surgery over a 10-yr follow-up period.
  1. Indications for medical monitoring
     1. Clinically asymptomatic and >50 yr old

2. Serum calcium level only mildly elevated (<1 mg/dl above upper limit normal)
3. GFR >60 mL/min and no nephrolithiasis or nephrocalcinosis
4. No evidence of osteoporosis
5. Medically unfit for surgery or refusing surgery

- Symptoms should be assessed regularly. Serum calcium and creatinine should be checked yearly. Bone mineral density may be monitored every 2 yr.

ACUTE GENERAL Rx

Severe and/or symptomatic hypercalcemia may require hospitalization especially if serum calcium >12 mg/dl. Acute management of hypercalcemia includes:

- Vigorous hydration with IV normal saline (2-4 L/day). Fluid status must be monitored in patients with cardiac dysfunction or renal insufficiency in order to avoid fluid overload.
- Bisphosphonates can effectively decrease calcium levels. Zoledronate (4 mg IV over 15 min) or pamidronate (60-90 mg IV over 4 hr) are both effective. Onset of action is 24 to 48 hr.
- Calcitonin (4 units/kg IM/SC every 12 hr) may be used with bisphosphonates to achieve a more rapid reduction of calcium levels. Onset of action is within hours.

! PEARLS & CONSIDERATIONS

COMMENTS

- Parathyroidectomy should be considered for all patients with symptomatic hyperparathyroidism. If surgery is contraindicated or not desired, cinacalcet and bisphosphonates can be used.
- Asymptomatic patients can be monitored with serial calcium, creatinine, and bone mineral density measurements. Disease progression may result in surgery.
- Most patients can be managed medically by limiting factors that result in hypercalcemia (e.g., dehydration, immobilization, thiazide diuretics) and maintaining normal calcium and vitamin D intake.
- Patients with osteopenia and high fracture risk may require antiresorptive therapy such as bisphosphonates.

EBM EVIDENCE

Available at www.expertconsult.com

SUGGESTED READINGS
Available at www.expertconsult.com

RELATED CONTENT
Hyperparathyroidism (Patient Information)

AUTHOR: **VICKY CHENG, M.D.**

BASIC INFORMATION

DEFINITION

Hypersensitivity pneumonitis (HP) is a group of immunologically mediated pulmonary diseases, with or without systemic manifestations (e.g., fever, weight loss), caused by the inhalation of an antigen to which the patient is sensitized and hyperresponsive. Sensitization and exposure alone in the absence of symptoms do not define the disease.

SYNONYMS

HP - Extrinsic allergic alveolitis (EAA)
Some specific examples:
- ○ Bird fancier's lung
- ○ Farmer's lung
- ○ Malt worker's lung
- ○ "Ventilation" pneumonitis
- ○ Maple bark-stripper's lung
- ○ Sauna taker's lung
- ○ Hot tub lung

ICD-10CM CODES
J67.8 Hypersensitivity pneumonitis due to other organic dusts
J67.9 Hypersensitivity pneumonitis due to unspecified organic dust

EPIDEMIOLOGY & DEMOGRAPHICS

- Prevalence and incidence of HP vary considerably.
- Depend on definition and methods to establish diagnosis, intensity of exposure, environmental conditions, and genetic risk factors that remain poorly understood.
- More than 300 causative agents have been identified, and the number continues to grow.
- Causative agents in residential and occupational exposures include birds, mold, humidifiers, fountains, steam irons, dry sausage molds, moldy cheese, contaminated wood, biofilm contained within wind instruments (e.g., trombone, saxophone), and organic and inorganic chemicals, including metalworking fluids. A large series of patients with HP associated with down pillows, feather duvets, and down-upholstered furniture has been published. Likely several genes are involved that cause an exaggerated lung response to an offending agent. The major histocompatibility complex is the most studied thus far.
- A viral connection has been implicated that may enhance clinical exposure to an offending agent.

PHYSICAL FINDINGS & CLINICAL PRESENTATION

Vary depending on frequency and intensity of antigen exposure.
- Acute: fever, cough, malaise, and dyspnea 4 to 6 hr after an intense exposure, lasting 18 to 24 hr
- Subacute: insidious onset of productive cough, dyspnea on exertion, anorexia, and weight loss, usually from a heavy, sustained exposure

- Chronic: gradually progressive cough, dyspnea, malaise, and weight loss, usually from low-grade or recurrent exposure
- Physical examination: hypoxemia, cyanosis, crepitant rales, possible fever

ETIOLOGY

- Numerous environmental agents, often encountered in occupational settings.
- Common sources of antigens: "moldy" hay, silage, grain, or vegetables; bird droppings or feathers (including those found commonly in down pillows, blankets, and upholstered furniture); low-molecular-weight chemicals (e.g., isocyanates); pharmaceutical products.
- Fig. E1H-73 illustrates the pathogenesis of hypersensitivity pneumonitis.

(Dx) **DIAGNOSIS**

- Accurate diagnosis is important for differentiating HP from other interstitial lung diseases because the prognosis and treatment may differ.
- The clinical syndrome of acute HP is indistinguishable from an acute respiratory infection with a history of illness occurring within hours of exposure to an antigen.
- Need high index of suspicion.
- Detailed occupational and home exposure history is required.
- Lung biopsy is often necessary for diagnosis.

DIFFERENTIAL DIAGNOSIS

Acute Stages	Chronic Stages
Allergic bronchopulmonary aspergillosis	Idiopathic pulmonary fibrosis (IPF)
Pulmonary embolism	Bronchiectasis
Asthma	Chronic bronchitis
Aspiration pneumonia	Nonspecific interstitial pneumonia (NSIP)
Bacterial pneumonia	
Fungal or mycobacterial pneumonia	
Bronchiolitis obliterans–organizing pneumonia	Connective tissue–related lung disease
Eosinophilic pneumonia	Sarcoidosis
Churg-Strauss syndrome	
Wegener granulomatosis	

WORKUP

No single radiologic, physiologic, or immunologic test is specific for the diagnosis of HP. HP must be suspected in any patient presenting with cough, dyspnea, fever, and malaise. A thorough history focusing on potential exposures is essential. Table 1H-60 describes examples of occupational causes of HP.

Environmental and occupational history questions should ask about grain dusts, animal handling, food processing, cooling towers, fountains, metalworking fluids, symptom improvement away from exposure, pets (particularly birds), hobbies involving chemicals, feathers, or fur, organic dusts, presence of humidifiers, dehumidifiers, or hot tubs/saunas, leaking or

flooding indoors, visible fungal growth in living or working environment, feather pillows, bedding, or upholstered furniture.
Major criteria:
- History of symptoms compatible with HP that appear to worsen within hours after antigen exposure
- Confirmation of exposure to the offending agent by history, investigation of the environment, serum precipitin tests to potential agents (often referred to as a "hypersensitivity panel" by many labs), or bronchoalveolar lavage (BAL) antibody
- Compatible clinical symptoms, physical exam, and changes on chest radiograph or high-resolution CT (HRCT) of the chest
- BAL fluid lymphocytosis (if performed)
- Compatible histologic changes by lung biopsy (if performed): poorly formed graunulomas or mononuclear cell infiltrate
- Positive natural challenge (reproduction of symptoms and laboratory abnormalities after exposure to the suspected environment) or controlled inhalation challenge

Minor criteria:
- Basilar crackles
- Decreased diffusion capacity
- Arterial hypoxemia (either at rest or with exercise)

LABORATORY TESTS

- Routine laboratory tests do not make the diagnosis, but typically the erythrocyte sedimentation rate, C-reactive protein, lactate dehydrogenase, and leukocyte count are increased; elevated immunoglobulins IgG and IgM are nonspecific; rheumatoid factor (RF) and immune complexes are often positive; peripheral eosinophil count and serum IgE are generally normal.
- Lactate dehydrogenase (LDH) is increased and tends to decrease with improvement.
- Pulmonary function tests: restrictive ventilatory pattern is typically seen. Decreased FEV_1, decreased forced vital capacity, decreased total lung capacity, decreased diffusion capacity, and decreased static compliance.
- Arterial blood gases show mild hypoxemia (worsens with exercise).
- A-a gradient shows slight increase.
- Serum precipitin test for IgG antibodies against offending antigen detected in serum. It is sensitive but not specific for HP (asymptomatic patients may have IgG antibodies in serum). HP may also be present without a positive precipitin test.
- Skin testing: unclear if helpful. However, some believe it to be a safe, effective, and rapid procedure in the diagnosis and follow-up of patients with HP. Sensitivity is similar to that of the precipitin test but the specificity is higher.

IMAGING STUDIES

Chest x-ray: nonspecific; may be normal in early stage.
- Acute/subacute: bilateral interstitial and alveolar nodular infiltrates in a patchy or homogeneous distribution. Apices are often spared.

TABLE 1H-60 Examples of Occupational Causes of Hypersensitivity Pneumonitis

Occupation	Cause
Farmer	Thermophilic actinomycetes in moldy hay
Metal worker	Contamination of metal-working fluids with microorganisms such as *Mycobacteria immunogens* or fungi
Worker exposed to humidifiers	Contamination with microorganisms such as protozoa or fungi
Sugarcane worker	Moldy sugarcane (bagassosis)
Maple bark stripper	Fungi
Chicken or turkey worker	Avian proteins
Pharmaceutical worker	Penicillin
Food handler	Soybeans
Office worker	Microorganisms contaminating air conditioners or humidifiers
Swimming pool attendant	Fungal contamination in sprays around pool area
Animal worker	Rat proteins
Mushroom worker	Fungi
Wheat farmer or handler	Weevil-infested flour
Greenhouse worker	Fungi
Workers spraying urethane paint or adhesives/sealants (or less often, other workers using diisocyanate)	Methylene diphenyl diisocyanate, hexamethylene diisocyanate, toluene diisocyanates
Chemical worker using plastics, resins, paints	Trimellitic anhydride

From Goldman L, Schafer AI: *Goldman's Cecil medicine*, ed 24, Philadelphia, 2012, Saunders.

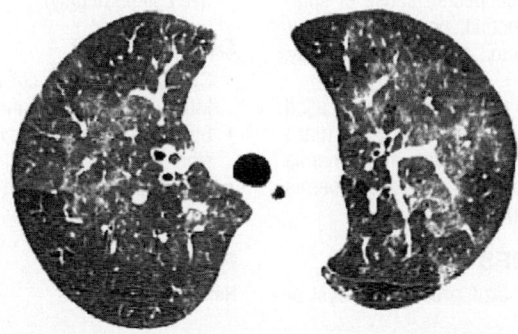

FIGURE 1H-74 In this patient with hypersensitivity pneumonitis, patchy ground-glass opacity is visible bilaterally. (From Mason RJ: *Murray & Nadel's textbook of respiratory medicine*, ed 5, Philadelphia, 2010, Saunders.)

- Chronic: diffuse reticulonodular infiltrates and fibrosis.
  High-resolution chest CT scan (Fig. 1H-74): no pathognomonic features but demonstrates airspace and interstitial patterns in the acute and subacute stage. The chronic stage reveals honeycombing and bronchiectasis.

 **TREATMENT**

NON-PHARMACOLOGIC THERAPY

Early recognition and avoidance of the causative antigen

ACUTE GENERAL Rx

- Glucocorticoids accelerate initial lung recovery but may have no effect long term (from a controlled study in farmer's lung). No prospective, randomized, placebo-controlled trials for other types of HP or subacute and chronic stages.

- Prednisone 0.5 to 1 mg/kg usually over 1 to 2 wk then tapered over 4 wk. Some patients, particularly those with subacute or chronic presentation, may require a longer course of therapy.

DISPOSITION/PROGNOSIS

Prognosis is generally better in patients with acute or subacute HP. Prognosis is worse in those with older age, desaturation during exercise, and findings of severe fibrosis by lung biopsy.
Acute: 4 to 48 hr
- Clinical: fever, chills, cough, hypoxia, malaise
- HRCT: ground-glass infiltrates
- Immunopathology: poorly formed, noncaseating granulomas or mononuclear cell infiltration in a peribronchial distribution, frequently with giant cells
- Prognosis: good

Subacute: weeks to 4 mo
- Clinical: dyspnea, cough, episodic flares
- HRCT: micronodules, air trapping
- Immunopathology: more well-formed, noncaseating granulomas, bronchiolitis, organizing pneumonia, and interstitial fibrosis
- Prognosis: good
Chronic: 4 mo to years
- Clinical: dyspnea, cough, fatigue, weight loss
- HRCT: fibrosis (possible), honeycombing, emphysema
- Immunopathology: granulomatous inflammation may be seen in addition to bronchiolitis obliterans (with or without organizing pneumonia) and honeycombing and fibrosis, lymphocytic infiltration, centrilobular and bridging fibrosis, neutrophil-mediated air space destruction, giant cells

REFERRAL

- Bronchoscopy: BAL provides useful supportive data in the diagnosis of HP. Usually reveals intense lymphocytosis (typically T cells >50%) of predominantly CD8+ suppressor cells. In the acute stage neutrophils predominate, but as the disease progresses to chronic form the ratio of CD4+ to CD8+ cells increases. When fibrosis is present the number of neutrophils increases.
- Lung biopsy: the histopathologic features of HP are distinctive but not pathognomonic. Bronchiolitis and interstitial pneumonitis with granuloma formation typically is seen. Variable degrees of interstitial fibrosis are seen in the chronic form. Chronic HP may be difficult to distinguish from IPF or NSIP pathologically.
- Laboratory inhalation challenge: testing to prove a direct relation between a suspected antigen and disease; extract of antigen is inhaled by nebulizer.

 **PEARLS & CONSIDERATIONS**

A clinical prediction rule using six features has high specificity and sensitivity for the diagnosis of acute and subacute HP:
- Exposure to a known offending agent
- Positive specific precipitating antibody
- Recurrent episodes of symptoms
- Inspiratory crackles
- Symptoms occurring 4 to 8 hr after exposure
- Weight loss
  HP occurs more frequently in smokers than nonsmokers (likely from an immunosuppressive effect).

SUGGESTED READINGS
Available at www.expertconsult.com

RELATED CONTENT
Hypersensitivity Pneumonitis (Patient Information)

AUTHORS: **MELISSA TUKEY, M.D., M.S.,** and **KRISTINA KRAMER, M.D.**

BASIC INFORMATION

DEFINITION

Hypersplenism is a syndrome characterized by splenomegaly, cytopenia (one or more of the following: anemia, thrombocytopenia, or leukopenia), and compensatory hyperplastic bone marrow. The cytopenias are correctable with splenectomy.

ICD-10CM CODES
D73.1 Hypersplenism

EPIDEMIOLOGY & DEMOGRAPHICS

Most often seen in patients with liver disease, hematologic malignancy, and infection

PHYSICAL FINDINGS & CLINICAL PRESENTATION

- Symptoms depend on the size of the spleen, rate of growth, and underlying disease.
- History: early satiety, abdominal discomfort or fullness, acute left upper quadrant (LUQ) pain (infarction, sequestration crisis), referred pain to left shoulder
- Physical examination: splenomegaly (normal spleen usually not palpable), LUQ tenderness, presence of a rub in LUQ (suggestive of splenic infarct), stigmata of cytopenias

ETIOLOGY

- Splenomegaly increases the proportion of blood channeled through the red pulp, causing inappropriate splenic pooling of both normal and abnormal blood cells. The size of the spleen determines the amount of cell sequestration. Up to 90% of platelets may be pooled in an enlarged spleen.
- Prolonged sequestration leads to increased destruction of RBCs. Platelets and white blood cells (WBCs) have about normal survival time even when sequestered and may be available if needed.
- Splenomegaly exacerbates cytopenias by dilution, possibly due to plasma volume expansion.

DIAGNOSIS

DIFFERENTIAL DIAGNOSIS

Hypersplenism can be caused by splenomegaly of almost any cause.
- Splenic congestion: cirrhosis (portal hypertension); congestive heart failure; portal, splenic, or hepatic vein thrombosis
- Hematologic causes: hemolytic anemia, spherocytosis, elliptocytosis, sickle cell anemia, thalassemia, extramedullary hematopoiesis, chronic transfusions, following use of granulocyte colony-stimulating factor
- Infections: viral (hepatitis, infectious mononucleosis, cytomegalovirus, HIV/AIDS), bacterial (abscess, endocarditis, sepsis, tuberculosis,

salmonella, brucella, Lyme's disease), parasitic (babesiosis, malaria, leishmaniasis, schistosomiasis, toxoplasmosis), fungal
- Malignancy: acute or chronic leukemia, lymphoma, histiocytosis, myeloproliferative diseases (polycythemia vera, essential thrombocythemia, myelofibrosis), metastatic tumors
- Inflammatory diseases: rheumatic fever, rheumatoid arthritis (Felty's syndrome), systemic lupus erythematosus, sarcoid, serum sickness
- Infiltrative diseases: amyloidosis, Gaucher's disease, Niemann-Pick disease, glycogen storage disease
- Anatomic abnormalities: cysts, hemangioma, hamartoma

WORKUP

History (including travel), physical examination, laboratory tests, imaging studies

LABORATORY TESTS

- CBC with differential: cytopenia, neutrophilia (infection)
- Peripheral smear: RBC and WBC morphology (abnormal cells may suggest infection, malignancy, bone marrow disease, rheumatologic disease), organisms (bacteria, malaria, babesiosis)
- Bone marrow aspiration/biopsy: hyperplasia of cytopenic cell lines; hematologic, infiltrative, or infectious disorders
- Tests to diagnose suspected cause of splenomegaly: liver function, hepatitis serology, HIV, rheumatoid factor, antinuclear antibody, tissue biopsy
- Note: red cell mass (^{51}Cr assay) may be used to assess severity of anemia. RBC mass measurement will differentiate true anemia (decrease in RBCs) from dilutional anemia (plasma volume expansion).

IMAGING STUDIES

- Ultrasound: splenic size, presence of cyst or abscess
- CT: estimate volume, obtain structural information: cyst, abscess, malignancy
- MRI: most useful for assessing vascular lesions and infections
- Nuclear medicine: liver-spleen scan: assess anatomy and function; may suggest presence of portal hypertension
- Consider other studies as suggested by history and examination: chest radiograph, echocardiogram, PET scan

TREATMENT

ACUTE GENERAL Rx

- Treat underlying disease
- Splenectomy is considered if:
  1. Indicated for the management of the underlying cause
  2. Persistent symptomatic disease (severe cytopenia) not responding to therapy
  3. Necessary for diagnosis

Risks:
- Infections (especially encapsulated organisms): risk greatest in the first 2 yr after splenectomy. Mortality rate from sepsis is fiftyfold greater in asplenic patients. Attempts to decrease risk include:
  1. Immunization with pneumococcal (PPSV23), meningococcal (2 doses), and *Haemophilus influenzae* vaccines at least 2 wk before splenectomy. Pneumococcal (PCV13) one-time vaccination either 8 wk before or >1 year after PPSV23 vaccination. Revaccination for pneumococcal (PPSV23) in 5 yr and again after 65 yr. Revaccination for meningococcal every 5 yr. Annual influenza vaccination.
  2. Prophylactic antibiotics after splenectomy in highest-risk patients.
  3. Patient education regarding the importance of rapid initiation of antibiotics at the first sign of infection.
- Thromboembolic complications.
- Possible increased risk of atherosclerotic heart disease and cancer.
- Splenectomy should not be performed if the spleen is the main site of hematopoiesis as a result of bone marrow failure (e.g., myelofibrosis).
- Other options include partial splenectomy, partial splenic embolization, radiofrequency ablation, portosystemic shunting (for congestive splenomegaly).

DISPOSITION

- Cytopenias usually correctable with splenectomy; normal cell counts in a few wk.
- Splenectomy may alleviate portal hypertension.
- Prognosis depends on the underlying disease.

REFERRAL

Hematology

PEARLS & CONSIDERATIONS

- Thrombocytopenia in hypersplenism is usually moderately severe (>50 × 10^9/L) and asymptomatic; severe thrombocytopenia (<20 × 10^9/L) suggests another diagnosis.

SUGGESTED READINGS
Available at www.expertconsult.com

RELATED CONTENT
Hypersplenism (Patient Information)
Felty's Syndrome (Related Key Topic)

AUTHOR: **SUDEEP K. AULAKH, M.D.**

BASIC INFORMATION

DEFINITION

Normal blood pressure (BP) in adults can be defined as systolic BP <120 mm Hg and diastolic BP <80 mm Hg. Prehypertension is defined as systolic BP between 120 and 139 mm Hg or diastolic between 80 and 89 mm Hg. Hypertension can be divided into stage 1: systolic BP from 140 to 159 mmHg or diastolic BP from 90 to 99 mm Hg and stage 2: systolic BP ≥160 mm Hg or diastolic BP ≥100 mm Hg. Measurements should be appropriately taken as described below.

SYNONYMS

Essential hypertension
Idiopathic hypertension
High BP

ICD-10CM CODES

I10	Essential (primary) hypertension
I15.0	Renovascular hypertension
I15.1	Hypertension secondary to other renal disorders
I15.2	Hypertension secondary to endocrine disorders
I15.8	Other secondary hypertension
I15.9	Secondary hypertension, unspecified
O10.919	Unspecified pre-existing hypertension complicating pregnancy, unspecified trimester
I67.4	Hypertensive encephalopathy

EPIDEMIOLOGY & DEMOGRAPHICS

- In the U.S., 50% of people age 60 to 69 yr and approximately 75% of people >70 yr of age are affected. Worldwide, it is estimated that 41% of people ages 35 to 70 yr have hypertension, and only 46.5% of them are aware of it.
- Peak prevalence increases with age and was highest among non-Hispanic black adults in the U.S.
- Hypertension is linked with a higher risk of heart attack, stroke, heart failure, and kidney disease.

PHYSICAL FINDINGS & CLINICAL PRESENTATION

Physical examination may be entirely within normal limits except for the presence of elevated BP. A proper initial physical examination on a hypertensive patient should include the following:

- The BP should be measured with an appropriately sized cuff (bladder of the cuff should cover at least two thirds of the circumference of the arm) and in both arms (the higher of the readings being used).
- The BP should be measured twice on each visit, and separated by at least 1 to 2 min to allow the return of trapped blood.
- The patient should be seated in a calm environment for at least 5 minutes with the arm

in which BP is measured rested on support level with the heart.
- Postural BP change should always be recorded in the elderly to diagnose postural hypotension. This is assessed by taking BP in supine (after 5 minute rest) and standing (after 2 minutes) positions. A drop of ≥20 mm Hg in systolic, a drop of ≥10 mm Hg diastolic BP, or symptoms of cerebral hypoperfusion is suggestive of postural (orthostatic) hypotension.
- A diagnosis of HTN may be established if the BP is markedly elevated (>180/110 mm Hg) or has evidence of end organ damage; otherwise such a diagnosis should wait until BP is found elevated on at least 3 visits, spaced over a period of weeks to months.
- Measure heart rate, height, weight, body mass index, and waist circumference.
- Physical examination should include searching for secondary causes, and sequelae of hypertension.
- Examine skin for the presence of café-au-lait spots (neurofibromatosis), uremic appearance (renal failure), and violaceous striae (Cushing's syndrome).
- Perform careful funduscopic examination; check for papilledema, retinal exudates, hemorrhages, arterial narrowing, arteriovenous compression.
- Examine neck for carotid bruits, distended neck veins, and enlarged thyroid gland.
- Perform extensive cardiopulmonary examination: check for a laterally displaced point of

maximal intensity, an S3 or S4, and valvular murmurs.
- Palpate abdomen for renal masses (pheochromocytoma, polycystic kidneys), and auscultate for bruit over the aorta and renal arteries.
- Examine arterial pulses (dilated or absent femoral pulses and BP greater in upper extremities than lower extremities suggest aortic coarctation).
- Look for truncal obesity (Cushing's syndrome) and pedal edema (congestive heart failure [CHF]).
- Table 1H-61 provides a guide to evaluation of identifiable causes of HTN. Fig. E1H-75 and Box E1H-12 describe the investigation of suspected endocrine causes of HTN.

ETIOLOGY

- Essential (primary) HTN (85%)
- Drug induced or drug related (5%)
  1. NSAIDs
  2. Oral contraceptives
  3. Corticosteroids
- Renal HTN (5%)
  1. Renal parenchymal disease (3%)
  2. Renovascular HTN (RVH) (<2%)
- Endocrine (<2%)
  1. Primary aldosteronism (at least 5%)
  2. Pheochromocytoma (0.2%)
  3. Cushing's syndrome and long-term steroid therapy (0.2%)
  4. Hyperparathyroidism or thyroid disease (0.2%)
- Coarctation of the aorta (0.2%)

TABLE 1H-61 Guide to Evaluation of Identifiable Causes of Hypertension

Suspected Diagnosis	Clinical Clues	Diagnostic Testing
Chronic kidney disease	Estimated GFR <60 ml/min/1.73 m² Urine albumin-to-creatinine ratio ≥30 mg/g	Renal sonography
Renovascular disease	New elevation in serum creatinine, marked elevation in serum creatinine with ACEI or ARB, drug-resistant hypertension, flash pulmonary edema, abdominal, or flank bruit	Renal sonography (atrophic kidney), CT or MR angiography, invasive angiography
Coarctation of the aorta	Arm pulses > leg pulses, arm BP > leg BP, chest bruits, rib notching on chest radiography	MR angiography, TEE, invasive angiography
Primary aldosteronism	Hypokalemia, drug-resistant hypertension	Plasma renin and aldosterone, 24-hr urine aldosterone and potassium after oral salt loading, adrenal vein sampling
Cushing's syndrome	Truncal obesity, wide and blanching purple striae, muscle weakness	1 mg dexamethasone-suppression test, urinary cortisol after dexamethasone, adrenal CT
Pheochromocytoma	Paroxysms of hypertension, palpitations, perspiration, and pallor; diabetes	Plasma metanephrines, 24-hr urinary metanephrines and catecholamines, abdominal CT or MR imaging
Obstructive sleep apnea	Loud snoring, large neck, obesity, somnolence	Polysomnography

ACEI, Angiotensin-converting enzyme inhibitor; *ARB*, angiotensin receptor blocker; *BP*, blood pressure; *CT*, computed tomography; *GFR*, glomerular filtration rate; *MR*, magnetic resonance; *TEE*, transesophageal echocardiography.
From Goldman L, Schafer AI: *Goldman's Cecil medicine,* ed 24, Philadelphia, 2012, Saunders.

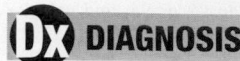 **DIAGNOSIS**

WORKUP

- The objective for the initial evaluation of HTN is to establish the diagnosis and stage of HTN.
- Gather office and nonoffice BP readings, assess presence of target organ damage (TOD), assess the level of global cardiovascular disease risk and produce a plan for individualized monitoring and therapy.
- Patient counseling and education should be prominent features of the initial evaluation.
- Pertinent history:
  1. Age of onset of HTN, previous antihypertensive therapy
  2. Family history of HTN, stroke, cardiovascular disease
- Diet, salt intake, caffeine, alcohol, drugs (e.g., oral contraceptives, NSAIDs, decongestants, steroids)
- Occupation, lifestyle, pain, socioeconomic status, psychologic factors
- Other cardiovascular risk factors: hyperlipidemia, obesity, diabetes mellitus
- Symptoms of secondary HTN:
  1. Headache, palpitations, excessive perspiration (possible pheochromocytoma)
  2. Weakness, polyuria (consider hyperaldosteronism)
  3. Claudication of lower extremities (seen with coarctation of aorta)
  4. Loud snoring, day-time somnolence, morning confusion (may warrant evaluation for sleep apnea)

LABORATORY TESTS

- Routine laboratory tests recommended before initiating therapy include:
  1. Urinalysis with microscopic evaluation; for signs of glomerulopathy
  2. Basic metabolic panel and calcium; for signs of kidney damage, hypokalemia (primary aldosteronism and Cushing's syndrome), hypercalcemia (hyperparathyroid).
  3. Complete blood count.
  4. Screening for coexisting diseases that may adversely affect prognosis; hemoglobin a1c or fasting glucose level, serum lipid panel.
  5. Optional tests include measurement of urinary albumin or albumin/creatinine ratio.
- Nonoffice (home, workplace, 24-hr ambulatory) BP determination to establish the pattern of HTN (sustained, "white coat," or "masked" HTN) in selected patients.
- Some general clinical clues for when to screen for secondary HTN include:
  1. Severe or resistant HTN.
  2. An acute rise in BP developing in a patient with previous stable BP.
  3. Age less than 30 yr, non-obese, non-black with no family history of HTN.
  4. Sudden onset or accelerated hypertension.
  5. Age of onset before puberty. If above is suspected, additional tests for secondary HTN should be done including renin, aldosterone, cortisol levels, 24-hr urine metanephrines, and serum catecholamines

IMAGING STUDIES

- ECG: check for presence of left ventricular hypertrophy (LVH) with strain pattern.
- Renal duplex ultrasonography, CT angiography or magnetic resonance angiography of the renal arteries in suspected renovascular hypertension (renal artery stenosis) may be considered.

Rx **TREATMENT**

NONPHARMACOLOGIC THERAPY

Lifestyle modifications (the initial treatment of hypertension should focus on lifestyle modifications):
- Weight loss if overweight (target BMI <25).
- Limit alcohol intake to 1 oz of ethanol per day (<2 drinks/day) in men or 0.5 oz (<1 drink/day) in women.
- Regular aerobic exercise (at least 30 min/day on most days).
- Reduce sodium intake to <100 mmol/day (<1.5 g of sodium/day).
- Maintain adequate dietary potassium (>3500 mg/day) intake in patients with normal kidney function.
- Smoking cessation.
- The BP reduction seen ranges from 2 to 20 mm Hg, most significant with substantial weight loss and the implementation of the Dietary Approaches to Stop Hypertension (DASH) eating plan, which relies on a diet high in fruits and vegetables, moderate in low-fat dairy products, and low in animal protein but with substantial amount of plant protein from legumes and nuts.

ACUTE GENERAL Rx

- Multiple recent consensus documents regarding blood pressure goals and when to initiate treatment have been published.
- According to AHA/ACC/CDC advisory algorithm, American Society of Hypertension/International Society of Hypertension (ASH/ISH), European Society of Hypertension and European Society of Cardiology (ESH/ESC), Canadian Hypertension Education Program (CHEP)[1]:
  ○ In patients age <80 yr old without diabetes or CKD or all ages with CKD, initiate therapy for BP ≥140/90 mm Hg (≥130/90 mm Hg in ESH/ESC). For patients ≥80 yr old without diabetes or CKD, initiate therapy for BP ≥150/90 mm Hg. For patients of all ages with diabetes, initiate therapy for BP ≥140/90 mm Hg (ASH/ISH), ≥140/85 mm Hg (ESH/ESC), and ≥130/80 mm Hg (CHEP).

- According to the writing group for JNC 8[2]:
  - In all patients, initiate pharmacologic treatment if diastolic BP is ≥90 mm Hg. In patients <60 years old, in diabetics, and in those with chronic kidney disease, pharmacologic treatment should be initiated for systolic BP ≥140 mm Hg, whereas in patients ≥60 years, the threshold for pharmacologic treatment for systolic BP has been raised to ≥150 mm Hg.
  - In the general non-black population, preferred initial agents are thiazide-type diuretics, angiotensin-converting enzyme inhibitors (ACEi), calcium channel blockers (CCBs), or angiotensin receptor blockers (ARBs). ACEi or ARBs are preferred initial agents in diabetics and those with CKD in this population.
  - Preferred initial agents in the black population (including diabetics) are thiazide-type diuretics or CCBs.
  - When selecting drugs, try to give once per day dosages to improve compliance. Also consider the cost of the medication, metabolic and subjective side effects, and drug-drug interactions.
  - All consensus guidelines agree that for patients <60 yr old without diabetes or CKD, target BP is <140/90 mm Hg, and for patients >80 yr old without diabetes or CKD, target BP is <150/90 mm Hg.
  - The major advantages and limitations of each class of drugs are described as follows:
    1. Thiazide diuretics:
       a. Advantages: inexpensive, once-daily dosing. Useful in edematous states, CHF, chronic renal disease, elderly patients (decreased incidence of hip fractures in elderly patients)
       b. Disadvantages: significant adverse metabolic effects (hypokalemia), increased risk of cardiac arrhythmias, sexual dysfunction, gout flares, possible adverse effects on lipids and glucose levels
    2. Beta-blockers:
       a. Advantages: ideal in hypertensive patients with ischemic heart disease or status post MI. Favored in hyperkinetic, young patients (resting tachycardia, wide pulse pressure, hyperdynamic heart) and stable CHF patients.
       b. Disadvantages: adverse effect on quality of life (increased incidence of fatigue, depression, impotence), bronchospasm, hypoglycemia, peripheral vascular disease, adverse effects on lipids, masking of signs and symptoms of hypoglycemia in diabetics.

---

[1]Salvo M et al: Reconciling multiple hypertension guidelines to promote effective clinical practice. *Ann Pharmacother* 48:1242-8 (2014).

[2]James PA et al: 2014 Evidence-based guidelines for the management of high blood pressure in adults. Report from the panel members appointed to the eighth Joint National Committee (JNC8), *JAMA* 311(5):507-520, 2014.

3. Calcium antagonists:
   a. Advantages: helpful in hypertensive patients with ischemic heart disease. Generally favorable effect on quality of life; can be used in patients with bronchospastic disorders, renal disease, peripheral vascular disease, metabolic disorders, and salt sensitivity. CCBs BP-lowering effect is independent of Na^+ intake.
   b. Disadvantages: diltiazem and verapamil should be avoided in patients with CHF due to systolic dysfunction because of their negative inotropic effects; pedal edema may occur with nifedipine and amlodipine; constipation can be severe in elderly patients receiving verapamil. CCB-related edema is positional in nature, it improves with lying position; additional strategies include switching CCB classes, reducing dosage, giving the medication later in the day, and adding a venodilator (nitrates, an ACE, or an ARB); diuretics may improve edema, but at the expense of a reduction in plasma volume.
4. ACE inhibitors:
   a. Advantages: first-line therapy for patients with left ventricular dysfunction, helpful in prevention of diabetic renal disease; effective in decreasing LVH, and remodeling.
   b. Disadvantages: dry cough is a frequent side effect (5% to 20% of patients); hyperkalemia may occur in patients with diabetes or severe renal insufficiency; hypotension may occur in volume-depleted patients; increased risk of renal failure in patients with renal artery stenosis; contraindicated in pregnancy.
5. ARBs:
   a. Advantages: well tolerated, favorable impact on quality of life; useful in patients unable to tolerate ACE inhibitors because of persistent cough and in CHF and diabetic patients; single daily dose. An episode of renal insufficiency with ACE inhibitors does not rule out future therapy with an ARB unless high-grade bilateral renal artery stenosis exists.
   b. Disadvantages: hypotension may occur in volume-depleted patients; hyperkalemia; risk of renal failure in renal artery stenosis; contraindicated in pregnancy.
6. Alpha-adrenergic blockers:
   a. Advantages: no adverse effect on blood lipids or insulin sensitivity; helpful in benign prostatic hypertrophy.
   b. Disadvantages: postural hypotension, sedation; syncope can be avoided by giving an initial low dose at bedtime. Generally considered third- or fourth-line agent.
7. Central alpha-antagonists:
   a. Oral clonidine mainstay of therapy for hypertensive urgencies because of the ease of administration and relative safety.
   b. Transdermal clonidine; useful in management of labile HTN, the hospitalized patient who cannot take medications by mouth, and patients subject to early morning BP surges. At equivalent doses, transdermal clonidine is more apt to precipitate salt and water retention than is the case with oral clonidine.
   c. Dose beyond 0.4 mg causes fatigue, sedation and dry mouth, salt and water retention, and rebound HTN upon abrupt termination of the medication.
8. Combined alpha- and beta-adrenergic receptor blockers:
   a. Labetalol, nebivolol, and carvedilol: Use is reserved to treat complicated hypertensive patient when an antihypertensive effect beyond beta-blockade is sought. IV labetalol is used for hypertensive emergencies. Carvedilol is shown to have less adverse effect on glycemic control than metoprolol and to reduce urinary protein excretion in hypertensive diabetic patients.
9. Direct-acting smooth muscle relaxant: Hydralazine
   a. Advantages: beneficial in black patients when used with isosorbide dinitrate.
   b. Disadvantages: may lead to reflex tachycardia, worsening ischemia (best used with nitrates), at higher doses or with renal failure can lead to a reversible drug-induced lupus.
10. Renin inhibitors: newest class of antihypertensives (Aliskiren):
    a. Advantages: generally well tolerated; once-daily dosing; can be used alone or in combination with other antihypertensive agents (avoid combining with ACEI or ARBs given increase of hyperkalemia)
    b. Disadvantages: contraindicated in pregnancy; should not be used in patients with impaired renal function; excessive cost; paucity of cardiovascular outcomes data showing benefit.

TREATMENT OF RENOVASCULAR HYPERTENSION: The therapeutic approach varies with the cause of the renovascular hypertension (RVH) (refer to "Renal Artery Stenosis" for additional information).
1. Young patients with fibromuscular dysplasia refractory to medical therapy can be treated with percutaneous transluminal renal angioplasty (PTRA).
2. Medical therapy is advisable in elderly patients with atheromatous RVH; useful agents are:
   a. Beta-blockers: highly effective in patients with elevated plasma renin
   b. ACE inhibitors: highly effective; however, should be avoided in patients with bilateral renal artery stenosis or with a solitary kidney and renal artery stenosis
   c. Diuretics: often used in combination with ACE inhibitors
3. Surgical revascularization: A recent trial revealed that renal-artery stenting does not confer a significant benefit with respect to the prevention of clinical events when added to comprehensive, multifactorial medical therapy in people with atherosclerotic renal-artery stenosis and hypertension or chronic kidney disease.[3]

HTN DURING PREGNANCY:
1. HTN complicates 5% to 12% of all pregnancies.
2. The American Obstetrical Committee defines BP of 130/80 mm Hg as the upper limit of normal at any time during pregnancy.
3. A rise of 30 mm Hg systolic or 15 mm Hg diastolic is also considered abnormal regardless of the absolute values obtained.
4. Hypertension during pregnancy can be from chronic HTN, gestational HTN, preeclampsia or preeclampsia superimposed on chronic HTN. It is important to distinguish the etiology because the risk to mother and fetus is much greater in preeclampsia.
5. Treatment of chronic HTN during pregnancy is as follows:
   a. Initial treatment with conservative measures (proper nutrition, limited physical activity).
   b. When drug therapy is necessary, initiation of methyldopa, hydralazine, labetalol, or atenolol is preferred. Table 1H-62 summarizes drugs used to treat hypertension in pregnancy.
   c. ACE inhibitors can cause fetal and neonatal complications; their use should be avoided in pregnancy.
   d. The safety of CCBs remains unclear.
   e. Diuretics should be used only if there is a specific reason for initiating and maintaining their use (e.g., HTN associated with severe fluid overload or left ventricular dysfunction).

MALIGNANT HTN, HYPERTENSIVE EMERGENCIES, AND HYPERTENSIVE URGENCIES:
Definitions:
1. Malignant HTN occurs with HTN when there are grades III and IV retinopathy (exudates, hemorrhages and papilledema).
   a. The rate of BP rise is a critical factor in the development of malignant HTN.
   b. Complications and mortality rates are much higher in malignant HTN compared to essential HTN.
   c. Requires immediate BP reduction (not necessarily into normal ranges) to prevent or limit target organ disease.

[3]Cooper CJ et al: Stenting and medical therapy for atherosclerotic renal-artery stenosis, N Engl J Med 370:13-22, 2014.

Diseases and Disorders

TABLE 1H-62 Drugs Used to Treat Hypertension in Pregnancy

Drug	Starting Dose	Maximum Dose	Comments
Acute Treatment of Severe Hypertension			
Hydralazine	5-10 mg IV every 20 min	20 mg*	Avoid in cases of tachycardia and persistent headaches
Labetalol	20-40 mg IV every 10-15 min	220 mg*	Avoid in women with asthma or congestive heart failure
Nifedipine	10-20 mg oral every 30 min	50 mg*	Avoid in case of tachycardia and palpitations
Long-Term Treatment of Hypertension			
Methyldopa	250 mg bid	4 g/day	
Labetalol	100 mg bid	2400 mg/day	
Nifedipine	10 mg bid	120 mg/day	
Thiazide diuretic	12.5 mg bid	50 mg/day	

*If desired blood pressure levels are not achieved, switch to another drug.
From Gabbe SG: *Obstetrics*, ed 6, Philadelphia, 2012, Saunders.

TABLE 1H-63 Parenteral Agents for Management of Hypertensive Emergencies

Agent	Dose	Onset of Action	Precautions
Parenteral Vasodilators			
Sodium nitroprusside	0.25-10 mcg/kg/min IV infusion	Immediate	Thiocyanate toxicity with prolonged use
Nitroglycerin	5-100 mcg/min IV infusion	2-5 min	Headache, tachycardia, tolerance
Nicardipine	5-15 mg/hr IV infusion	1-5 min	Protracted hypotension after prolonged use
Fenoldopam mesylate	0.1-0.3 mcg/kg/min IV infusion	1-5 min	Headache, tachycardia, increased intraocular pressure
Hydralazine	5-10 mg as IV bolus or 10-40 mg IM; repeat every 4-6 hr	10 min IV 20 min IM	Unpredictable and excessive falls in blood pressure; tachycardia, angina exacerbation
Enalaprilat	0.625-1.25 mg every 6 hr IV bolus	15-60 min	Unpredictable and excessive falls in blood pressure; acute renal failure in patients with bilateral renal artery stenosis
Parenteral Adrenergic Inhibitors			
Labetalol	20-80 mg as slow IV injection every 10 min, or 0.5-2.0 mg/min IV as infusion	5-10 min	Bronchospasm, heart block, orthostatic hypotension
Metoprolol	5 mg IV every 10 min for three doses	5-10 min	Bronchospasm, heart block, heart failure, exacerbation of cocaine-induced myocardial ischemia
Esmolol	500 mcg/kg IV over 3 min; then 25-100 mg/kg/min as IV infusion	1-5 min	Bronchospasm, heart block, heart failure
Phentolamine	5-10 mg IV bolus every 5-15 min	1-2 min	Tachycardia, orthostatic hypotension

IM, Intramuscular; *IV*, intravenous.
From Andreoli TE et al: *Andreoli and Carpenter's Cecil essentials of medicine*, ed 8, Philadelphia, 2010, Saunders.

2. Hypertensive emergencies is when the BP elevation causes evidence of impending or progressive organ dysfunction. It requires rapid lowering of BP to prevent end-organ damage.

3. Hypertensive urgencies are significant BP elevations without end-organ damage that should be corrected within 24 hrs of presentation.
   a. Patients are usually treated with oral antihypertensive medications.
   b. Most clinicians suggest lowering the BP to <160 mm Hg/<100 mm Hg or to a level no more than 30% lower than the patient's baseline BP.

Therapy: The choice of therapeutic agents varies with the cause. IV medications are preferred in hypertensive emergencies.

1. Nitroprusside is the drug of choice in hypertensive encephalopathy, HTN and intracranial bleeding, malignant HTN, HTN and heart failure, dissecting aortic aneurysm (used in combination with propranolol); its onset of action is immediate. Because it is metabolized to cyanide, patients should be carefully monitored for toxicity (mental status changes, acidemia).

2. Fenoldopam is a vasodilator agent useful for the short-term (up to 48 hr) management of severe HTN when rapid but quickly reversible reduction of BP is required. It should be avoided in patients with glaucoma.

3. Other commonly used agents are the IV CCBs nicardipine and clevidipine (useful for urgent treatment of HTN in the intensive care unit or operating room), the beta-blocker esmolol (useful in aortic dissection or postoperative HTN), labetalol (combined β-adrenergic and α-blocker useful in patients with coronary disease), phentolamine (useful for catecholamine-related emergencies), IV nitroglycerin (used in patients with cardiac ischemia and hypertensive crisis), and hydralazine (used for hypertensive emergencies in pregnancy).

4. Table 1H-63 describes parenteral agents for management of hypertensive emergencies. *The following are important points to remember when treating hypertensive emergencies:*
   a. Introduce a plan for long-term therapy at the time of the initial emergency treatment.
   b. Agents that reduce arterial pressure can cause the kidney to retain sodium and water; therefore the judicious administration of diuretics should accompany their use.
   c. The initial goal of antihypertensive therapy is not to achieve a normal BP, but rather to gradually reduce the BP; cerebral hypoperfusion may occur if the mean BP is lowered >40% in the initial 24 hr.

 **PEARLS & CONSIDERATIONS**

COMMENTS

- For patients with prehypertension, every 20/10 mm Hg increase in BP doubles the risk of cardiovascular events.
- Most patients will require at least two medications for BP control.
- If BP is greater than 20/10 mm Hg above goal, therapy should be initiated with two drugs.

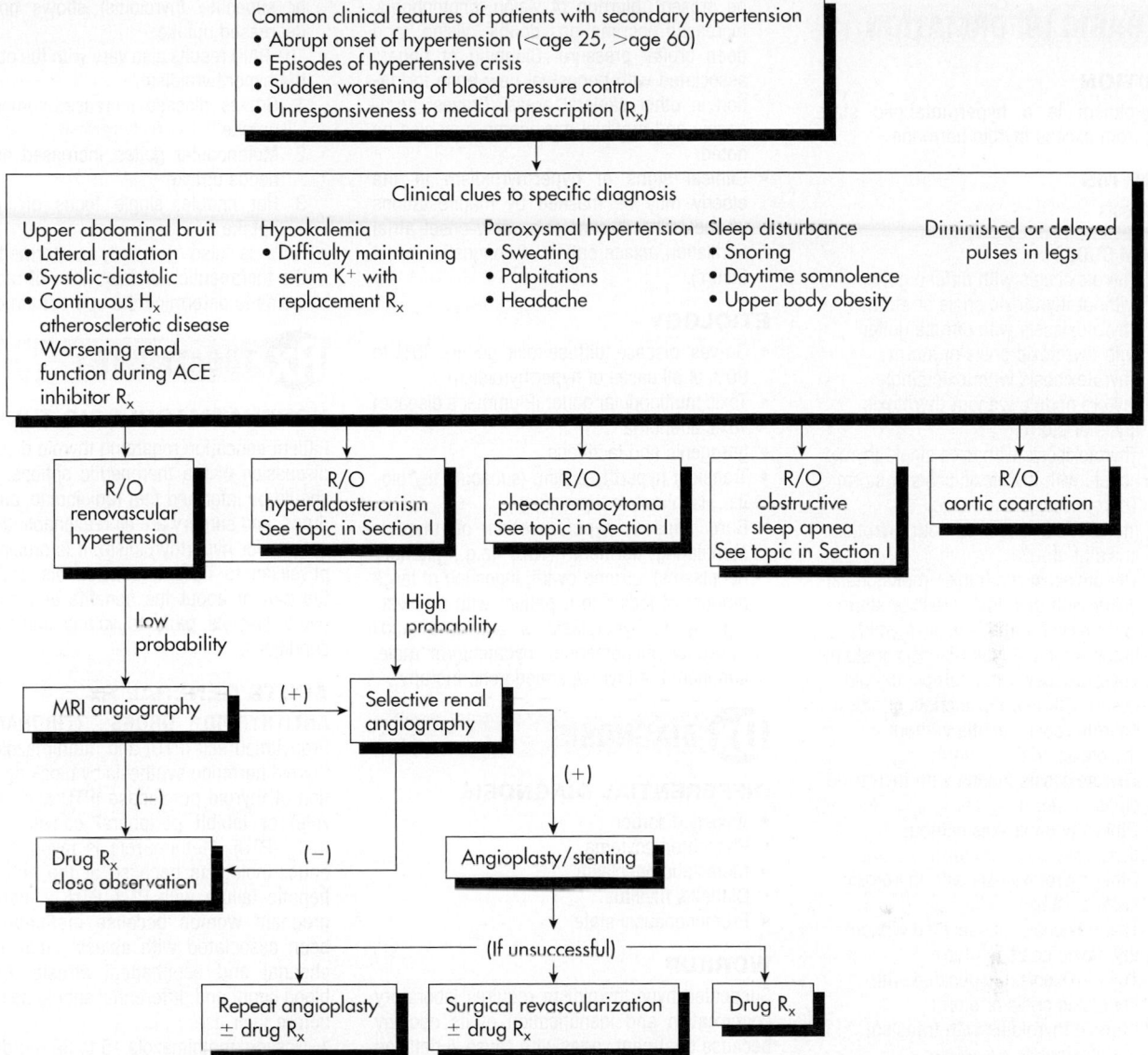

FIGURE 1H-77 Algorithm for identifying patients for evaluation of secondary causes of hypertension. *ACE,* Angiotensin-converting enzyme; *Hx,* history; *K,* potassium; *R/O,* rule out. (Modified from Goldman L, Ausiello D [eds]: *Cecil textbook of medicine,* ed 23, Philadelphia, 2008, Saunders.)

- Resistant HTN: HTN is considered resistant if the BP cannot be reduced below target levels in patients who are compliant with an optimal triple-drug regimen that includes a diuretic. Terms *refractory* and *resistant* are used interchangeably. Causes include pseudohypertension, measurement artifact, medication nonadherence, volume overload, and secondary HTN.
  1. Pseudohypertension in elderly: hardened and sclerotic artery is not compressible hence falsely elevates BP measurement artifact
  2. Measurement artifact: BP taken incorrectly (small cuff, improper support).
  Fig. E1H-76 describes an approach to patients with resistant HTN.

- Renal sympathetic denervation: A recent blinded trial did not show a significant reduction of systolic blood pressure in patients with resistant hypertension 6 mo after renal artery denervation as compared with a sham control.[4]
- Fig. 1H-77 describes an algorithm for evaluation of secondary causes of HTN.
- Barriers to BP control: system issues, provider issues; patient issues, and behavior issues. The rate at which physicians adopt recommended changes based on evidence-based findings can be quite slow and has been properly described as "clinical inertia."

- Indications for specialist referral for patients with HTN are described in Table E1H-64.

SUGGESTED READINGS
Available at www.expertconsult.com

RELATED CONTENT
High Blood Pressure (Patient Information)
High Blood Pressure–Child (Patient Information)
Renal Artery Stenosis (Related Key Topic)

AUTHORS: **TANIA B. BABAR, M.D.,** and **CRAIG L. BASMAN, M.D.**

[4]Bhatt DL et al: A controlled trial of renal denervation for resistant hypertension, *N Engl J Med* 370:1393-1401, 2014.

BASIC INFORMATION

DEFINITION
Hyperthyroidism is a hypermetabolic state resulting from excess thyroid hormone.

SYNONYMS
Thyrotoxicosis

ICD-10CM CODES
E05.00 Thyrotoxicosis with diffuse goiter without thyrotoxic crisis or storm
E05.01 Thyrotoxicosis with diffuse goiter with thyrotoxic crisis or storm
E05.10 Thyrotoxicosis with toxic single thyroid nodule without thyrotoxic crisis or storm
E05.11 Thyrotoxicosis with toxic single thyroid nodule with thyrotoxic crisis or storm
E05.20 Thyrotoxicosis with toxic multinodular goiter without thyrotoxic crisis or storm
E05.21 Thyrotoxicosis with toxic multinodular goiter with thyrotoxic crisis or storm
E05.30 Thyrotoxicosis from ectopic thyroid tissue without thyrotoxic crisis or storm
E05.31 Thyrotoxicosis from ectopic thyroid tissue with thyrotoxic crisis or storm
E05.40 Thyrotoxicosis factitia without thyrotoxic crisis or storm
E05.41 Thyrotoxicosis factitia with thyrotoxic crisis or storm
E05.80 Other thyrotoxicosis without thyrotoxic crisis or storm
E05.81 Other thyrotoxicosis with thyrotoxic crisis or storm
E05.90 Thyrotoxicosis, unspecified without thyrotoxic crisis or storm
E05.91 Thyrotoxicosis, unspecified with thyrotoxic crisis or storm
E06.2 Chronic thyroiditis with transient thyrotoxicosis

EPIDEMIOLOGY & DEMOGRAPHICS
INCIDENCE/PREVALENCE:
- Hyperthyroidism affects 2% of women and 0.2% of men in their lifetimes.
- Toxic multinodular goiter usually occurs in women >55 yr and is more common than Graves' disease in the elderly.

PHYSICAL FINDINGS & CLINICAL PRESENTATION
- Patients with hyperthyroidism generally present with tachycardia, tremor, hyperreflexia, anxiety, irritability, emotional lability, panic attacks, heat intolerance, sweating, increased appetite, diarrhea, weight loss, menstrual dysfunction (oligomenorrhea, amenorrhea). Presentation may be different in elderly patients (see the following).
- Patients with Graves' disease may present with exophthalmos, lid retraction, and lid lag (Graves' ophthalmopathy). The following signs and symptoms of ophthalmopathy may be present: blurring of vision, photophobia, increased lacrimation, double vision, and deep orbital pressure. Clubbing of fingers associated with periosteal new bone formation in other skeletal areas (Graves' acropachy) and pretibial myxedema may also be noted.
- Clinical signs of hyperthyroidism in the elderly may be masked by manifestations of coexisting disease (e.g., new-onset atrial fibrillation, exacerbation of congestive heart failure).

ETIOLOGY
- Graves' disease (diffuse toxic goiter): 80% to 90% of all cases of hyperthyroidism
- Toxic multinodular goiter (Plummer's disease)
- Toxic adenoma
- Iatrogenic and factitious
- Transient hyperthyroidism (subacute thyroiditis, Hashimoto's thyroiditis)
- Rare causes: hypersecretion of thyroid-stimulating hormone (TSH) (e.g., pituitary neoplasms), struma ovarii, ingestion of large amount of iodine in a patient with preexisting thyroid hyperplasia or adenoma (Jod-Basedow phenomenon), hydatidiform mole, carcinoma of thyroid, amiodarone therapy

DIAGNOSIS

DIFFERENTIAL DIAGNOSIS
- Anxiety disorder
- Pheochromocytoma
- Metastatic neoplasm
- Diabetes mellitus
- Premenopausal state

WORKUP
Suspected hyperthyroidism requires laboratory confirmation and identification of its etiology because treatment varies with cause. A detailed medical history will often provide clues to the diagnosis and etiology of the hyperthyroidism. Fig. E1H-78 describes a diagnostic approach to suspected hyperthyroidism.

LABORATORY TESTS
- Elevated free thyroxine (T_4)
- Elevated free triiodothyronine (T_3): generally not necessary for diagnosis
- Low TSH (unless hyperthyroidism is a result of the rare hypersecretion of TSH from a pituitary adenoma)
- Thyroid autoantibodies useful in selected cases to differentiate Graves' disease from toxic multinodular goiter (absent thyroid antibodies)

IMAGING STUDIES
- 24-hr radioactive iodine uptake (RAIU) is useful to distinguish hyperthyroidism from iatrogenic thyroid hormone synthesis (thyrotoxicosis factitia) and from thyroiditis.
- An overactive thyroid shows increased uptake, whereas a normal underactive thyroid (iatrogenic thyroid ingestion, painless or subacute thyroiditis) shows normal or decreased uptake.
- The RAIU results also vary with the etiology of the hyperthyroidism:
  1. Graves' disease: increased homogeneous uptake
  2. Multinodular goiter: increased heterogeneous uptake
  3. Hot nodule: single focus of increased uptake
- RAIU is also generally performed before the therapeutic administration of radioactive iodine to determine the appropriate dose.

TREATMENT

NONPHARMACOLOGIC THERAPY
Patient education regarding thyroid disease and discussion of the therapeutic options. Patients should be informed that radioiodine, antithyroid drugs, and surgery are all reasonable treatment options for hyperthyroidism. It is crucial for the physician to have a detailed discussion with the patient about the benefits and risks relative to lifestyle, patients' values, and coexisting conditions.

ACUTE GENERAL Rx
ANTITHYROID DRUGS (THIONAMIDES): Propylthiouracil (PTU) and methimazole inhibit thyroid hormone synthesis by blocking production of thyroid peroxidase (PTU and methimazole) or inhibit peripheral conversion of T_4 to T_3 (PTU). Methimazole is favored by most endocrinologists because of the potential for hepatic failure with PTU. PTU is preferred in pregnant women because methimazole has been associated with aplasia cutis and with choanal and esophageal atresia. Complete blood count and differential should be obtained before their use.
1. Dosage: methimazole 15 to 30 mg/day given as a single dose; PTU 50 to 100 mg PO q8h.
2. Antithyroid drugs can be used as the primary form of treatment or as adjunctive therapy before radioactive therapy or surgery or afterward if the hyperthyroidism recurs.
3. Side effects: skin rash (3% to 5% of patients), arthralgias, myalgias, granulocytopenia (0.5%). Rare side effects are aplastic anemia, hepatic necrosis from PTU, cholestatic jaundice from methimazole.
4. When antithyroid drugs are used as primary therapy, they are usually given for 6 to 18 mo; prolonged therapy may cause hypothyroidism. Monitor thyroid function every 2 mo for 6 mo, then less frequently.
5. The use of antithyroid drugs before radioiodine therapy is best reserved for patients in whom exacerbation of hyperthyroidism after radioactive iodine therapy is hazardous (e.g., elderly patients with coronary artery disease or significant coexisting morbidity). In these patients the antithyroid drug can be stopped 2 days before radioactive iodine therapy, resumed 2 days later, and continued for 4 to 6 wk.

RADIOIODINE THERAPY (RADIOACTIVE IODINE [RAI; ^{131}I]):

1. RAI is the treatment of choice for patients aged >21 yr and younger patients who have not achieved remission after 1 yr of antithyroid drug therapy. RAI is also used in hyperthyroidism caused by toxic adenoma or toxic multinodular goiter.
2. Contraindicated during pregnancy (can cause fetal hypothyroidism) and lactation. Pregnancy should be excluded in women of childbearing age before RAI is administered.
3. A single dose of RAI is effective in inducing a euthyroid state in nearly 80% of patients.
4. There is a high incidence of post-RAI hypothyroidism (>50% within first year and 2%/yr thereafter); these patients should be frequently evaluated for the onset of hypothyroidism (see "Chronic Rx").

SURGICAL THERAPY (SUBTOTAL THYROIDECTOMY):

1. Indicated in obstructing goiters, in any patient who refuses RAI and cannot be adequately managed with antithyroid medications (e.g., patients with toxic adenoma or toxic multinodular goiter), and in pregnant patients who cannot be adequately managed with antithyroid medication or develop side effects to them. Thyroidectomy can also be considered as primary therapy in refractory cases of amiodarone-induced hyperthyroidism. Thyroidectomy is not indicated for low RAIU hyperthyroidism.
2. Patients should be rendered euthyroid with antithyroid drugs before surgery.
3. Complications of surgery include hypothyroidism (28% to 43% after 10 yr), hypoparathyroidism, and vocal cord paralysis (1%).
4. Most patients should be started on replacement doses of levothyroxine (1.7 mcg/kg/day) before discharge from hospital.
5. Hyperthyroidism recurs after surgery in 10% to 15% of patients.

ADJUNCTIVE THERAPY: Propranolol alleviates the beta-adrenergic symptoms of hyperthyroidism; initial dose is 20 to 40 mg PO q6h; dosage is gradually increased until symptoms are controlled. Major contraindications to propranolol are congestive heart failure and bronchospasm. Diagnosis and treatment of thyrotoxic storm are also discussed in Section I.

CHRONIC Rx

- Patients undergoing treatment with antithyroid drugs should be seen every 1 to 3 mo until euthyroidism is achieved and every 3 to 4 mo while they remain on antithyroid therapy. After treatment is stopped, periodic monitoring of thyroid function tests with TSH is recommended every 3 mo for 1 yr, then every 6 mo for 1 yr, then annually.
- Orbital decompression surgery can be used to correct Graves' orbitopathy (Fig. E1H-79). The administration of the antioxidant selenium (100 mcg PO bid) has been recently reported as effective in improving quality of life, reducing ocular involvement, and slowing progression of the disease in patients with mild Graves' orbitopathy. Its mechanism of action is believed to be an effect on the oxygen free radicals and cytokines that play a pathogenic role in Graves' orbitopathy.

DISPOSITION

Successful treatment of hyperthyroidism requires lifelong monitoring for the onset of hypothyroidism or the recurrence of thyrotoxicosis.

REFERRAL

- Endocrinology referral is recommended at the time of initial diagnosis and during treatment.
- Surgical referral in selected patients (see "Surgical Therapy").
- Hospitalization of all patients with thyroid storm.

⚠ PEARLS & CONSIDERATIONS

COMMENTS

- Elderly hyperthyroid patients may have only subtle signs (weight loss, tachycardia, fine skin, brittle nails). This form is known as *apathetic hyperthyroidism* and manifests with lethargy rather than hyperkinetic activity. An enlarged thyroid gland may be absent. Coexisting medical disorders (most commonly cardiac disease) may also mask the symptoms. These patients often have unexplained congestive heart failure, worsening of angina, or new-onset atrial fibrillation resistant to treatment. See the entry "Graves' Disease"

for additional information on diagnosis and treatment.
- Subclinical hyperthyroidism is defined as a normal serum-free thyroxine and free triiodothyronine levels with a TSH level suppressed below the normal range and usually undetectable. These patients usually do not present with signs or symptoms of overt hyperthyroidism. Treatment options include observation or a therapeutic trial of low dose antithyroid agents for 6 mo to attempt to induce remission.
- *Thyrotoxic periodic paralysis (TPP)* is a hyperthyroidism-related hypokalemia and muscle-weakening condition resulting from a sudden shift of potassium into cells. Many patients do not have other symptoms of hyperthyroidism. Typical presentation involves an Asian adult male with acute fatigue and muscle weakness initially presenting in the lower extremities. Physical examination reveals decreased deep tendon reflexes, hypertension, and tachycardia. ECG often reveals U waves, high QRS voltage, and first-degree atrioventricular block. Additional laboratory testing reveals normal acid-base state, hypokalemia with low urinary potassium excretion (spot urinary potassium concentration <20 mEq/L from potassium shift into cells), hypophosphatemia, hypophostaturia, and hypercalciuria. Electromyography during attacks shows low-amplitude compound muscle action potential of the tested muscle. Therapy consists of cautious potassium supplementation (increased risk of rebound hyperkalemia). Use of nonselective beta-blockers (e.g., propranolol) to counteract hyperadrenergic activity, which may be causing TPP, may also be useful.

SUGGESTED READINGS

Available at www.expertconsult.com

RELATED CONTENT

Hyperthyroidism (Patient Information)
Graves' Disease (Related Key Topic)
Thyrotoxic Storm (Related Key Topic)

AUTHOR: **FRED F. FERRI, M.D.**

H

Diseases and Disorders

I

BASIC INFORMATION

DEFINITION
Hypertrophic osteoarthropathy (HOA) is a syndrome of clubbing of the digits, periostosis of long bones, abnormal proliferation of skin, and arthritis. Periostosis is usually involved with pain on palpation of the involved area. HOA may be primary or secondary to other underlying disease processes.

SYNONYMS
- Primary hypertrophic osteoarthropathy:
  1. Pachydermoperiostosis
  2. Idiopathic clubbing
  3. Touraine-Solente-Golé syndrome
- Secondary hypertrophic osteoarthropathy
- HOA

ICD-10CM CODES
M89.3	Hypertrophy of bone
M89.40	Other hypertrophic osteoarthropathy, unspecified site
M89.411	Other hypertrophic osteoarthropathy, right shoulder
M89.412	Other hypertrophic osteoarthropathy, left shoulder
M89.419	Other hypertrophic osteoarthropathy, unspecified shoulder
M89.421	Other hypertrophic osteoarthropathy, right upper arm
M89.422	Other hypertrophic osteoarthropathy, left upper arm
M89.429	Other hypertrophic osteoarthropathy, unspecified upper arm
M89.431	Other hypertrophic osteoarthropathy, right forearm
M89.432	Other hypertrophic osteoarthropathy, left forearm
M89.439	Other hypertrophic osteoarthropathy, unspecified forearm
M89.441	Other hypertrophic osteoarthropathy, right hand
M89.442	Other hypertrophic osteoarthropathy, left hand
M89.449	Other hypertrophic osteoarthropathy, unspecified hand
M89.451	Other hypertrophic osteoarthropathy, right thigh
M89.452	Other hypertrophic osteoarthropathy, left thigh
M89.459	Other hypertrophic osteoarthropathy, unspecified thigh
M89.461	Other hypertrophic osteoarthropathy, right lower leg
M89.462	Other hypertrophic osteoarthropathy, left lower leg
M89.469	Other hypertrophic osteoarthropathy, unspecified lower leg
M89.471	Other hypertrophic osteoarthropathy, right ankle and foot
M89.472	Other hypertrophic osteoarthropathy, left ankle and foot
M89.479	Other hypertrophic osteoarthropathy, unspecified ankle and foot
M89.48	Other hypertrophic osteoarthropathy, other site
M89.49	Other hypertrophic osteoarthropathy, multiple sites

EPIDEMIOLOGY & DEMOGRAPHICS
- Fig. 1H-80 provides a classification of HOA.
- Primary HOA is a familial autosomal-dominant disease affecting the age group between 1 and 20 years and is rare.
- There is a male/female ratio of 9:1 in occurrence.
- Secondary HOA is more common, typically occurs in adults 55 to 75 years of age. 80% to 90% of secondary HOA is associated with non–small cell lung cancer, most frequently adenocarcinoma; other associated illnesses include:
  1. Pulmonary: mesothelioma, bronchogenic carcinoma, lung abscesses, empyema, bronchiectasis, cystic fibrosis, pulmonary fibrosis, sarcoidosis, arteriovenous malformations
  2. Gastrointestinal: Carcinoma of esophagus or colon, biliary atresia, peptic ulcer disease, inflammatory bowel disease, hepatocellular carcinoma, liver cirrhosis, amebiasis, laxative abuse, achalasia.
  3. Cardiac: infective endocarditis, right-to-left cardiac shunts, aortic aneurysms, infected aortic bypass graft
  4. Hematologic: thalassemia, myelofibrosis, Hodgkin lymphoma
  5. Endocrine: thyroid acropachy, POEMS syndrome (polyneuropathy, organomegaly, endocrinopathy, M component, and skin changes)
  6. Connective tissue diseases
  7. Thymoma
  8. HIV infection
  9. Osteosarcoma
  10. Nasopharyngeal sarcoma

PHYSICAL FINDINGS & CLINICAL PRESENTATION
- Primary HOA typically presents with the insidious onset of clubbing of the hands (Fig. 1H-81) and feet, described as "spade-like." Finger clubbing is diagnosed by measurement of the digital index (Fig. 1H-82). Other signs and symptoms of HOA include:
  1. Joint pain and swelling
  2. Sensation of warmth or burning in the hands and feet

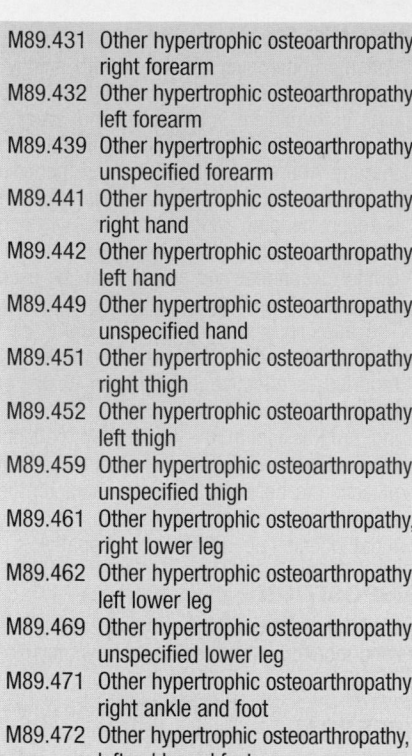

FIGURE 1H-80 Classification of hypertrophic osteoarthropathy. *AV,* Arteriovenous; *POEMS,* polyneuropathy, organomegaly, endocrinopathy, monoclonal proteins, and skin changes. (From Hochberg MC et al: *Rheumatology,* ed 5, St Louis, 2011, Mosby.)

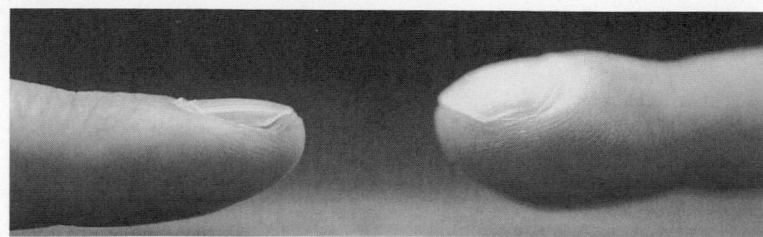

FIGURE 1H-81 Clubbing deformity. The finger on the right is clubbed compared with the normal finger shape on the left. (From Hochberg MC et al: *Rheumatology,* ed 5, St Louis, 2011, Mosby.)

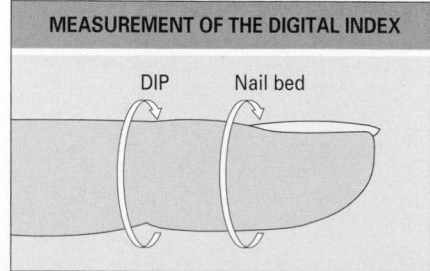

FIGURE 1H-82 The digital index. The perimeter of each of the 10 fingers is measured at the nail bed (NB) and at the distal interphalangeal joint (DIP). If the sum of the 10 NB:DIP ratios is more than 10, clubbing is probably present. (From Hochberg MC et al: *Rheumatology,* ed 5, St Louis, 2011, Mosby.)

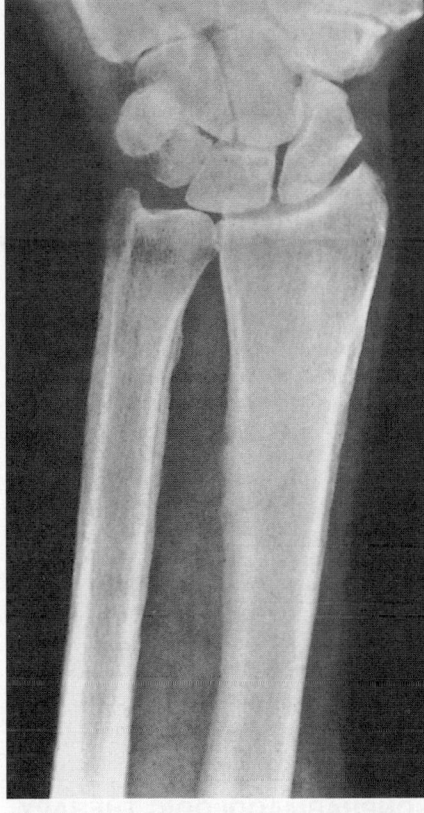

FIGURE 1H-83 Hypertrophic osteoarthropathy. Wrist radiograph showing periostosis at the distal ends of the radius and ulna. The coarse, layered appearance is most evident along the diaphyses. The relative sparing of the radial epiphyses is characteristic. (From Hochberg MC et al: *Rheumatology*, ed 5, St Louis, 2011, Mosby.)

3. Coarsening of facial features with grooves or depressions in the scalp, ptosis of the lids
4. Thickening of the arms and legs
5. Oily skin, diaphoresis, gynecomastia, and acne
6. Thin and shiny appearance of the skin around the nail bed
7. Nail convexity with nail "floating" sensation within the soft tissue is noticed on palpation of the base of the nail bed
8. Elephant legs: nonpitting soft tissue swelling with tenderness can be seen

- Secondary HOA patients may present with clinical symptoms before the underlying disorder can be detected. Signs and symptoms are similar to the previous symptoms in addition to findings related to the underlying disease (e.g., bronchogenic carcinoma, infective endocarditis).
- Patients presenting with painful joints prior to developing clubbing can be misdiagnosed as having inflammatory arthritis.

ETIOLOGY

The pathogenesis of HOA is not fully understood; current knowledge suggests that HOA results from the activation of one or more growth factors, such as vascular endothelial growth factor (VEGF) and platelet-derived growth factor, which are normally inactivated in the lungs and systemic circulation.

Dx DIAGNOSIS

Diagnosis is primarily clinical; radiographs and bone scans can help confirm the diagnosis.

DIFFERENTIAL DIAGNOSIS

Paget's disease, reactive arthritis, psoriatic arthritis, syphilitic periostosis, osteoarthritis, rheumatoid arthritis, osteomyelitis, scleromyxedema, and acromegaly.

WORKUP

HOA warrants an investigation into any associated illnesses.

LABORATORY TESTS

- Routine laboratory studies such as blood count, electrolytes, and urine studies are typically normal in primary and secondary HOA.
- Erythrocyte sedimentation rate is elevated in secondary HOA.
- Liver function tests may be abnormal in patients with secondary HOA from gastrointestinal pathology.
- Alkaline phosphatase may be elevated as a result of periostosis of long bones.
- Analysis of the synovial fluid from joint effusions reveals a low white blood cell count with normal viscosity, color, and complement levels.

IMAGING STUDIES

- Radiographs of the long bones show periosteal new bone formation (Fig. 1H-83).
- A chest radiograph should be obtained to rule out underlying lung cancer.
- Bone scan with technetium-99m reveals cortical uptake; SPECT/CT can increase specificity by excluding bony metastasis.
- Angiography findings may demonstrate hypervascularization of the finger pads.

Rx TREATMENT

ACUTE GENERAL Rx

- Treatment of primary HOA is symptomatic. Nonsteroidal antiinflammatory medications, corticosteroids, tamoxifen citrate, or retinoids can be used.
- Colchicine can be helpful for the pain due to subperiosteal new bone formation.
- Reconstructive surgery is indicated for correction of gross disfigurement.
- Case reports of infliximab use and arthroscopic synovectomy with some relief in primary HOA are present.
- Treatment of secondary HOA is to eradicate the underlying disease (e.g., antibiotics for infective endocarditis, surgery for bronchogenic carcinoma). Correction of heart malformation or removal of an underlying tumor is rapidly followed by regression of HOA.

CHRONIC Rx

In patients with secondary HOA refractory to NSAIDs and aspirin, octreotide (100 mcg subcutaneously twice daily) and bisphosphonates, including pamidronate (1 mg/kg intravenously to a maximum of 60 mg) and zolendronic acid, which inhibit VEGF expression, have significantly reduced pain.

Vagotomy has been tried with some success. However, the definitive treatment is to treat the underlying disease.

DISPOSITION

- Patients with primary HOA typically have symptoms of joint pain and swelling for the early part of their life. However, the disease becomes quiescent thereafter.
- Prognosis and disease course in patients with secondary HOA will depend on the underlying cause. The insidious development of clubbing suggests an infectious process, whereas the rapid progression of clubbing may suggest underlying malignancy.

REFERRAL

Referral should be made to rheumatology when the diagnosis of HOA is suspected and the cause remains unclear.

❗ PEARLS & CONSIDERATIONS

Some cases of primary HOA may later be found to be associated with an underlying disease such as patent ductus arteriosus, Crohn's disease, or myelofibrosis, in which case they become secondary.

COMMENTS

- Infections and intrathoracic malignancies are the most common causes of secondary HOA.
- The periostosis and the extent of involvement do not depend on the form of the disease (primary or secondary), but rather on its duration.
- HOA secondary to infection of an arterial graft has been reported.

SUGGESTED READINGS

Available at www.expertconsult.com

AUTHOR: **DURKHANI MAHBOOB, M.D.**

BASIC INFORMATION

DEFINITION

Hyperuricemia may be defined as serum uric acid >7.0 mg/dl in males or >6.0 mg/dl in females. Some persons who are normouricemic by this definition will have levels of uric acid that exceed the limit of solubility of uric acid in tissue. Data from the Framingham study indicate that hyperuricemia increased from 4.8% of the population in the early 1970s to 9.3% in the mid-1980s. Age is an important risk factor in the increasing incidence of hyperuricemia and gout. Women become hyperuricemic at an older age than men due to the uricosuric effect of estrogen. Most people with hyperuricemia are asymptomatic and will remain so; however, 20% of those with serum uric acid >9 mg/dl will develop gout in 5 yr. Hyperuricemia is strongly associated with gout, obesity, diabetes, hypertension, and cardiovascular disease but has not been proven to cause any of these conditions.

ASYMPTOMATIC HYPERURICEMIA

Definition: laboratory evidence of elevated serum uric acid without clinical disease known to be caused by hyperuricemia

ETIOLOGY

Overproduction of uric acid accounts for a minority of cases of hyperuricemia. Most cases are due to decreased renal clearance of uric acid and high dietary purine consumption. Fig. 1H-84 describes factors affecting urate balance. Table 1H-65 describes a classification of hyperuricemia and gout.

ICD-10CM CODES
E79.0 Hyperuricemia without signs of inflammatory arthritis and tophaceous disease

DIAGNOSIS

EVALUATION

The finding of hyperuricemia should prompt a thorough evaluation of potential causes and

TABLE 1H-65 Classification of Hyperuricemia and Gout

Impaired Uric Acid Excretion

Primary gout with decreased uric acid clearance
Secondary gout
Clinical conditions
Reduced glomerular filtration rate
Hypertension
Obesity
Systemic acidosis
Familial juvenile hyperuricemic nephropathy
Medullary cystic kidney disease
Lead nephropathy
Drugs
Diuretics
Ethanol
Low-dose salicylates (0.3-3.0 g/day)
Cyclosporine
Tacrolimus
Levodopa

Excessive Urate Production

Primary metabolic disorders
HPRT deficiency
PRPP synthetase overactivity
Glucose-6-phosphatase deficiency
Fructose-1-phosphate aldolase deficiency
Secondary causes
Clinical conditions
Myelo- and lymphoproliferative disorders
Obesity
Psoriasis
Glycogenoses III, V, VII
Drugs and dietary components
Nicotinic acid
Pancreatic extract
Cytotoxic drugs
Red meat, organ meat, shellfish
Alcoholic beverages (especially beer)
Fructose

HPRT, Hypoxanthine-guanine phosphoribosyltransferase; *PRPP,* phosphoribosyl pyrophosphate.
From Goldman L, Schafer AI: *Goldman's Cecil medicine,* ed 24, Philadelphia, 2012, Saunders.

related diseases. Fig. 1H-85 describes the evaluation of patients with hyperuricemia. If there is no clinical evidence of gout, nephrolithiasis, or acute kidney injury, the patient may be said to have asymptomatic hyperuricemia. Patients with hyperuricemia should be evaluated for potential causes of elevated uric acid including malignancy, renal insufficiency, toxins, lead toxicity, and dietary indiscretion. If a careful history and physical exam does not reveal an evident cause of persistent hyperuricemia, a 24-hr urine collection for uric acid and creatinine may be considered. Patients with urinary excretion of uric acid >800 mg/24 hr are likely to be overproducers of uric acid and should be investigated more thoroughly for the underlying cause of their hyperuricemia.

LABORATORY TESTS
- CBC with differential.
- BUN/creatinine.
- Urinalysis.
- Lipid profile.
- Consider 24-hr urine collection for uric acid.

TREATMENT

No specific therapy is indicated for most patients with asymptomatic hyperuricemia. Lifestyle and dietary modification are often advisable.

NONPHARMACOLOGIC THERAPY
- Weight loss
- Reduce alcohol intake, especially beer
- Reduce consumption of foods known to be high in purines such as red meat, organ meat, and high-fructose soft drinks.

PEARLS & CONSIDERATIONS

- Research in progress suggests there may be a causal relationship between hyperuricemia and early hypertension.
- Very high levels of serum uric acid may warrant treatment even if asymptomatic.
- Patients with hyperuricemia and a family history of gout should be followed closely for the development of gouty arthritis.
- Hyperuricemia in patients with gout (Fig. E1H-86) should almost always be treated with urate-lowering medication (see "Gout").
- The presence of gouty tophi or arthritis due to gout are absolute indications for urate-lowering therapy.

There is evidence suggesting that treatment of hyperuricemia slows the progression of chronic kidney disease in patients without gout. Recent studies have suggested that allopurinol use is associated with a reduced risk of myocardial infarction and reduction in all-cause mortality.

SUGGESTED READINGS
Available at www.expertconsult.com

RELATED CONTENT
Gout (Related Key Topic)

AUTHOR: **BERNARD ZIMMERMANN, M.D.**

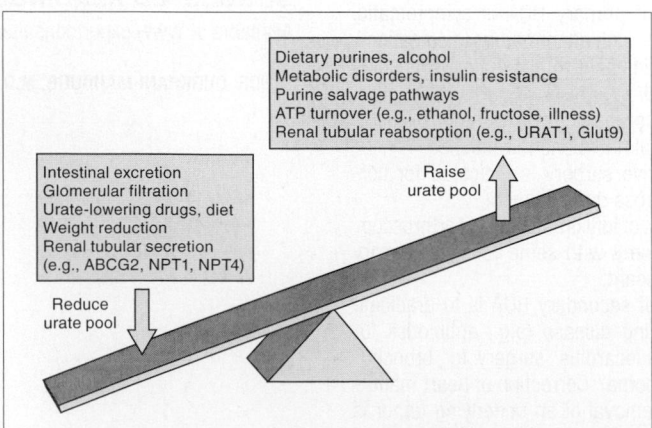

FIGURE 1H-84 Factors affecting urate balance. The systemic urate pool and the likelihood of gout are determined by the dynamic balance among dietary purines, endogenous synthesis and recycling, and disposal by the kidney and gut. (From Hochberg MC et al: *Rheumatology,* ed 5, St Louis, 2011, Mosby.)

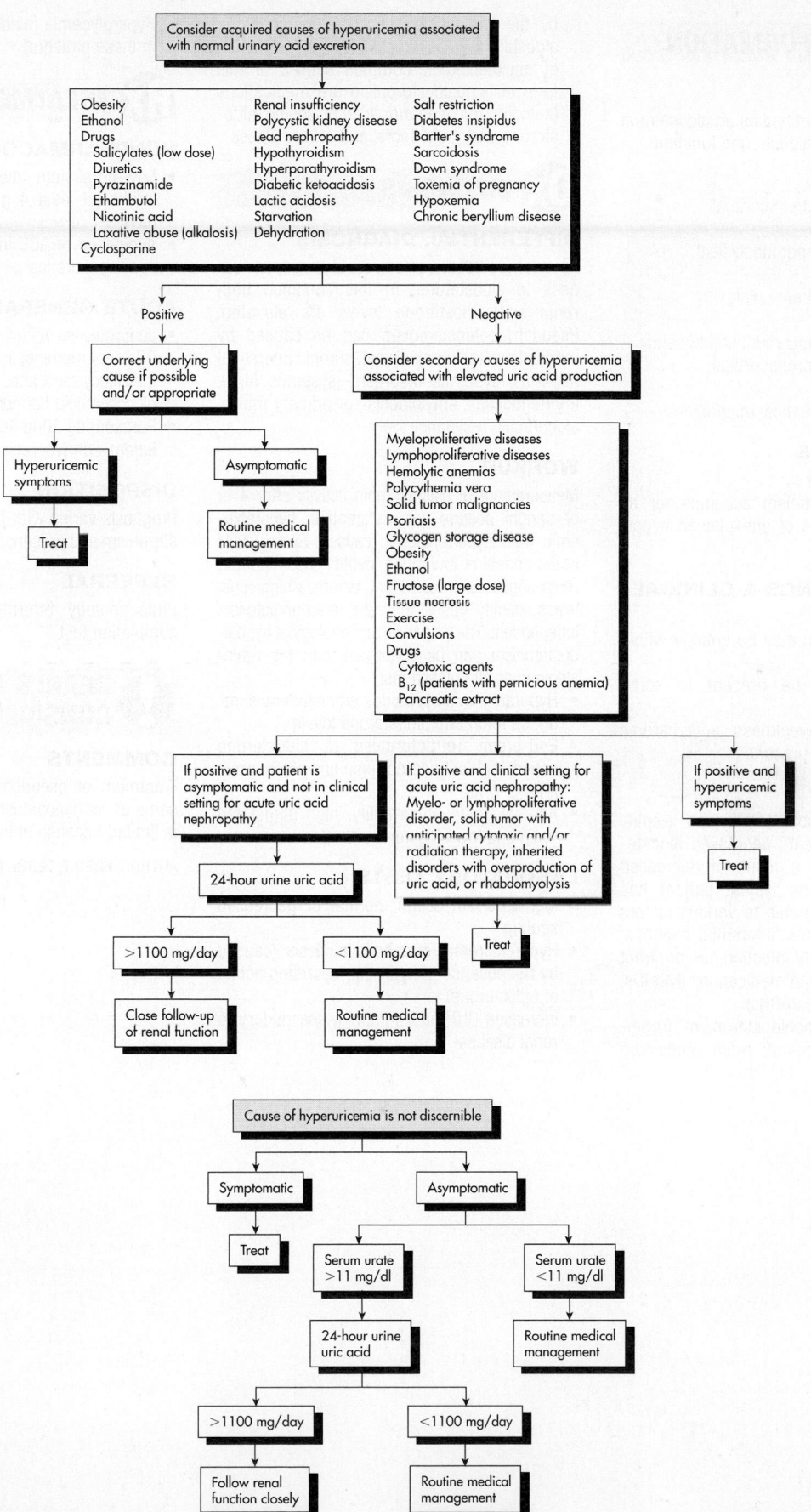

FIGURE 1H-85 Evaluation of patients with hyperuricemia. (From Harris ED et al, eds: *Kelley's textbook of rheumatology,* ed 7, Philadelphia, 2005, Saunders.)

 **BASIC INFORMATION**

DEFINITION

Hypoaldosteronism is defined as an aldosterone deficiency or impaired aldosterone function.

ICD-10CM CODES
E27.40 Unspecified adrenocortical insufficiency
E27.3 Drug-induced adrenocortical insufficiency
E27.9 Disorder of adrenal gland, unspecified
E27.1 Primary adrenocortical insufficiency
E27.40 Unspecified adrenocortical insufficiency
E27.49 Other adrenocortical insufficiency

EPIDEMIOLOGY & DEMOGRAPHICS

Selective hypoaldosteronism accounts for as many as 10% of cases of unexplained hyperkalemia.

PHYSICAL FINDINGS & CLINICAL PRESENTATION

- Physical examination may be entirely within normal limits.
- Hypertension may be present in some patients.
- Profound muscle weakness and cardiac arrhythmias may be present.

ETIOLOGY

- Hyporeninemic hypoaldosteronism (renin-angiotensin dependent): decreased aldosterone production as a result of decreased renin production; the typical patient has renal disease attributable to various factors (e.g., diabetes mellitus, interstitial nephritis, multiple myeloma, HIV infection, urinary tract obstruction, aging) and medications (NSAIDs, COX-2 inhibitors, ACEI/ARBs).
- Hyperreninemic hypoaldosteronism (renin-angiotensin independent): renin production by the kidneys is intact; the defect is in aldosterone biosynthesis or in the action of angiotensin II. Common causes of this form of hypoaldosteronism are medications (ketoconazole, heparin), lead poisoning, aldosterone enzyme defects, and severe illness.

 **DIAGNOSIS**

DIFFERENTIAL DIAGNOSIS

Pseudohypoaldosteronism: renal unresponsiveness to aldosterone. In this condition both renin and aldosterone levels are elevated. Pseudohypoaldosteronism can be caused by medications (spironolactone), chronic interstitial nephritis, systemic disorders (systemic lupus erythematosus, amyloidosis), or primary mineralocorticoid resistance.

WORKUP

Measurement of plasma renin activity after 4 hr of upright posture can differentiate hyporeninemic from hyperreninemic causes. Renin levels in the normal or low range identify cases that are renin-angiotensin dependent, whereas high renin levels identify cases that are renin-angiotensin independent. The diagnosis and etiology of hypoaldosteronism can be confirmed with the renin-aldosterone stimulation test:

- Hyporeninemic hypoaldosteronism: low stimulated renin and aldosterone levels
- End-organ refractoriness to aldosterone action: high stimulated renin and aldosterone levels
- Adrenal gland abnormality: high stimulated renin and low aldosterone levels

LABORATORY TESTS

- Increased potassium, normal or decreased sodium
- Hyperchloremic metabolic acidosis (caused by the absence of hydrogen-secreting action of aldosterone)
- Increased BUN and creatinine (secondary to renal disease)

- Hyperglycemia (diabetes mellitus is common in these patients)

TREATMENT

NONPHARMACOLOGIC THERAPY

- Low-potassium diet with liberal sodium intake (at least 4 g of sodium chloride per day)
- Avoidance of ACE inhibitors and potassium-sparing diuretics

ACUTE GENERAL Rx

- Judicious use of fludrocortisone (0.05 to 0.1 mg PO every morning) in patients with aldosterone deficiency associated with deficiency of adrenal glucocorticoid hormones
- Furosemide 20 to 40 mg qd to correct hyperkalemia of hyporeninemic hypoaldosteronism

DISPOSITION

Prognosis varies with the etiology of hypoaldosteronism and presence of associated disorders.

REFERRAL

Endocrinology referral for renin-aldosterone stimulation test

PEARLS & CONSIDERATIONS

COMMENTS

Treatment of pseudohypoaldosteronism is the same as for hypoaldosteronism; however, effect is limited because of impaired renal sensitivity.

AUTHOR: **FRED F. FERRI, M.D.**

H

I

BASIC INFORMATION

DEFINITION

Illness anxiety disorder (defined in DSM 5; previously hypochondriasis) is the preoccupation with the fear of having, or the idea that one has, a serious undiagnosed disease, despite a lack of significant corresponding somatic symptoms or medical evidence. Whether or not another medical diagnosis is present, the severity of health-related anxiety is clearly disproportionate to the individual's health status. Most medical literature explores the previously defined disorder hypochondriasis; it is unknown exactly how that evidence applies to illness anxiety disorder.

SYNONYMS

Hypochondriasis
Illness Anxiety Disorder

ICD-10CM CODES
F45.21 Hypochondriasis

EPIDEMIOLOGY & DEMOGRAPHICS

PREVALENCE: 1% to 5% (based on estimates of DSM-III and DSM-IV disorder hypochondriasis) but may be higher (3%-10%) in primary care outpatient settings
PREDOMINANT SEX: Equal frequency in men and women.
PREDOMINANT AGE: Onset at any age, but most commonly between ages 20 and 30 yr

GENETICS/RISK

No known genetic component. May be more common in less-educated individuals. A comorbid major mental disorder (e.g., generalized anxiety, obsessive-compulsive disorder, or depression) may affect over two-thirds of individuals with illness anxiety disorder; personality disorders and somatic symptom disorders may also be more common.

PHYSICAL FINDINGS & CLINICAL PRESENTATION

- Somatic symptoms or signs are not present or are only mild; the focus of anxiety is the suspected medical diagnosis itself (i.e., concern for illness rather than symptoms per se).
- Mild somatic symptoms, if present, often include nonpathologic physical signs or sensations (e.g., belching, orthostatic lightheadedness).
- High health anxiety persists despite reassuring clinical evaluation (though without the intensity of a delusion).
- Illness anxiety symptoms often correlate with psychosocial stressors.

- Illness preoccupation lasts at least 6 mo (the specific illness feared may vary).
- Disruption in health-related quality of life and/or social, occupational, or other important areas of functioning.
- Two presentation types: care-seeking (medical attention frequently sought) and care-avoidant (maladaptive avoidance of health care).
- No specific physical examination findings.

ETIOLOGY

Unknown neurobiologic etiology. Serious childhood illness or trauma may be associated with illness anxiety disorder in adulthood.

DIAGNOSIS

DIFFERENTIAL DIAGNOSIS

- Underlying medical condition
- Adjustment disorder (health-related anxiety in response to illness)
- Somatic symptom disorder (excessive distress related to somatic symptom[s])
- Body dysmorphic disorder (restricted to a circumscribed concern about appearance)
- Factitious disorder
- Malingering
- Generalized anxiety disorder with health concerns as one worry among others
- Major depressive disorder with health concerns occurring only during depressive episodes
- Psychosis, as may occur with depression and schizophrenia

WORKUP

- History, physical examination, age-appropriate screenings, and laboratory and imaging tests, as appropriate, to exclude underlying medical condition.
- Symptom measures (e.g., Health Anxiety Inventory) may be used for detection and monitoring of severity over time.
- Evaluation for other psychiatric disorders associated with illness anxiety such as depression and generalized anxiety.

TREATMENT

NONPHARMACOLOGIC THERAPY

- Psychotherapy, especially cognitive behavioral therapy (CBT), is the mainstay of treatment, with techniques to alter or restructure maladaptive thinking and behavior. Individual or group CBT, acceptance and commitment therapy (ACT), behavioral stress management, and mindfulness-based approaches have demonstrated success.

- Regularly scheduled brief medical appointments not contingent on symptoms
- Avoidance of repeated or non–medically indicated diagnostic testing, referrals, or treatments
- Limit on reading medical texts or websites
- Benign interventions (e.g., exercise, massage)

CHRONIC Rx

- Antidepressants may be helpful even in individuals without features of depression: placebo-controlled trials of fluoxetine and paroxetine suggest benefit.
- Treatment of comorbid psychiatric conditions, if present.

DISPOSITION

Waxing and waning course over decades; recovery rates between 30% and 85%. Positive prognostic factors include shorter duration of illness anxiety and lack of comorbid psychiatric disorder.

REFERRAL

Referral for CBT is the mainstay of treatment; referral to a psychiatrist may be needed in the case of comorbid psychiatric condition.

PEARLS & CONSIDERATIONS

- Psychotherapy and pharmacotherapy may be helpful treatment modalities for individuals open to treatment not directed at the perceived illness.
- In the updated DSM 5, hypochondriasis and related conditions were replaced by two new concepts: somatic symptom disorder (somatic symptoms present, with significant related distress) and illness anxiety disorder (somatic symptoms absent or minimal; concern focused on the idea of illness).

SUGGESTED READINGS
Available at www.expertconsult.com

RELATED CONTENT
Hypochondria (Patient Information)
Somatization Disorder (Patient Information)
Somatization Disorder (Related Key Topic)

AUTHOR: **LUCY KALANITHI, M.D., F.A.C.P.**

BASIC INFORMATION

DEFINITION

Male hypogonadism is a clinical syndrome involving subnormal testosterone levels and/or impaired sperm production due to dysfunction at one or both levels of the hypothalamic-pituitary-testicular axis.

SYNONYMS

Testicular dysfunction

ICD-10CM CODES
E29   Testicular dysfunction
E29.1   Testicular hypofunction
E29.8   Other testicular dysfunction
E29.9   Testicular dysfunction, unspecified
E23.0   Hypopituitarism
E23.1   Drug-induced hypopituitarism
E89.3   Postprocedural hypopituitarism

EPIDEMIOLOGY & DEMOGRAPHICS

INCIDENCE: Hypogonadism is the most common clinical disorder of the testis. Incidence is unclear due to the many possible underlying factors, nonspecificity of symptoms, and questions relating to the adequacy of a diagnostic serum total testosterone threshold.
PREVALENCE: Prevalence of hypogonadism increases with aging, obesity, diabetes mellitus, and other comorbidities. The average decrease in serum total testosterone levels in aging men is 1% to 2% per year. Prevalence rises to 23% among men in their 70s. However, in population-based surveys of community-dwelling middle-aged and older males, prevalence of hypogonadism is approximately 6%.
GENETICS: Genetic abnormalities underlie a number of hypogonadal disorders including Klinefelter syndrome, Noonan syndrome, hemochromatosis, Kallmann syndrome, and Prader-Willi syndrome.
RISK FACTORS: These are many and include genetic abnormalities; the aging process; pituitary and testicular lesions and disorders; medications; drug abuse; HIV disease; acute illnesses; chronic cardiac, hepatic, renal, and pulmonary diseases; cancer; ionizing radiation; chemotherapy; obesity; and malnutrition.

PHYSICAL FINDINGS & CLINICAL PRESENTATION

Sexual (specific)
- Decrease in frequency of erections
- Erectile dysfunction
- Decrease in libido
- Decreased fertility
- Small or shrinking testes
- Gynecomastia
- Diminished sexual hair
- Hot flushes and sweats

Neuropsychologic (less specific)
- Depression
- Inability to concentrate
- Diminished motivation and vitality
- Decrease in self-confidence
- Diminished energy and stamina
- Sleep disturbances

Physical features and findings
- Diminished capacity for physical activity
- Decrease in physical endurance and performance
- Diminished muscle mass and strength
- Increase in body fat
- Decrease or loss of axillary and pubic hair and decrease in shaving frequency
- Fine wrinkling over the lateral aspects of the face
- Breast enlargement with or without tenderness
- Change in consistency and decrease in size of testes
- Fragility fractures
- Anemia

ETIOLOGY

- The importance of a careful history and examination cannot be overstated to determine the etiology of possible hypogonadism. Primary hypogonadism is a result of a decrease in testicular testosterone secretion and/or a decrease in spermatogenesis with an associated increase in gonadotropin levels as in Klinefelter syndrome, cryptorchidism, and following orchitis, testicular trauma, chemotherapy, and irradiation.
- Secondary hypogonadism is due to hypothalamic-pituitary dysfunction, which results in a decrease in testosterone levels and/or spermatogenesis with gonadotropin levels that are subnormal or inappropriately within the normal range.
- Combined primary and secondary hypogonadism is a result of deficits at both the level of the hypothalamic-pituitary axis and testes with variable gonadotropin levels depending upon the predominance of the level of the defect.

DIAGNOSIS (FIG. 1H-87)

DIFFERENTIAL DIAGNOSIS

Hypogonadotropic or secondary hypogonadism
- Pituitary dysfunction—hypopituitarism, functioning or nonfunctioning pituitary tumor, lymphocytic hypophysitis, infiltrative disease as with sarcoidosis, hemochromatosis, and histiocytosis X
- Hyperprolactinemia—prolactinoma, medication-related, chronic kidney disease
- Genetic—Kallmann syndrome with anosmia, Prader-Willi syndrome with morbid obesity
- Acute and chronic illnesses, malnutrition, emotional disorders, HIV, sleep apnea, aging, malignancies, obesity, and renal, hepatic, pulmonary, and cardiac diseases
- Opioids, CNS—active medications, glucocorticoid excess, and GnRH analogues (androgen deprivation therapy)

Hypergonadotropic or primary hypogonadism
- Genetic—Klinefelter syndrome, Noonan syndrome, myotonic dystrophy
- Gonadal damage due to drugs, alcohol, radiation, chemotherapy, trauma
- Congenital anorchia (vanishing testis syndrome)
- Cryptorchidism

- Mumps orchitis, HIV orchitis
- Diabetes mellitus
- Hodgkin's disease
- Aging

Combined primary and secondary hypogonadism
- Hemochromatosis, sickle cell disease, thalassemia
- Alcoholism, glucocorticoid therapy, aging
- Chronic cardiac, hepatic, renal, pulmonary diseases, and HIV disease

WORKUP

- Determine the presence or absence of male hypogonadism on the basis of history, clinical manifestations and findings, and documentation of consistently low serum total testosterone levels and/or abnormal seminal fluid analysis.
- Morning serum total testosterone levels should be measured on at least 2 or 3 occasions for confirmation of diagnosis and when necessary followed by measurement of serum free or bioavailable testosterone.
- Serum FSH and LH levels are measured to determine whether hypogonadism is primary, secondary, or a result of combined defects of the hypothalamic-pituitary axis and testis. The case of testosterone deficiency should be definitively determined before initiation of testosterone replacement therapy.
- Hormonal assessment of gonadal status should not be done during an acute or subacute illness.

LABORATORY TESTS

- Serum total testosterone is tightly bound to sex hormone binding globulin (SHBG) and weakly bound to circulating albumin. 0.5% to 3% of serum total testosterone is unbound or free.
- Liquid chromatography tandem mass spectrometry assays for total serum testosterone are more accurate than immunoassays.
- Bioavailable testosterone refers to unbound testosterone plus the testosterone that is loosely bound to albumin.
- Free testosterone, if necessary, is best measured by equilibrium dialysis or centrifugal ultrafiltration.
- An SHBG measurement is helpful in determining the adequacy or normality of a serum total testosterone measurement. Conditions that lower SHBG include obesity, protein-losing states, androgens, hypothyroidism, and familial SHBG deficiency. Increases in SHBG occur in those with hyperthyroidism, hepatitis, cirrhosis, and HIV disease, aging, and by estrogens.
- The lower limit of normal for serum total testosterone in a healthy young male is approximately 240 to 280 ng/dl and a low-normal serum free testosterone in a young normal male is 9 pg/ml.
- Serum total testosterone levels can vary from day-to-day and there is a diurnal rhythm in young normal males with morning levels that are higher by approximately 20% to 25% as compared with levels in the afternoon.
- In elderly males, the diurnal rhythm is diminished with levels approximately 10% lower in the afternoon as compared with morning levels.

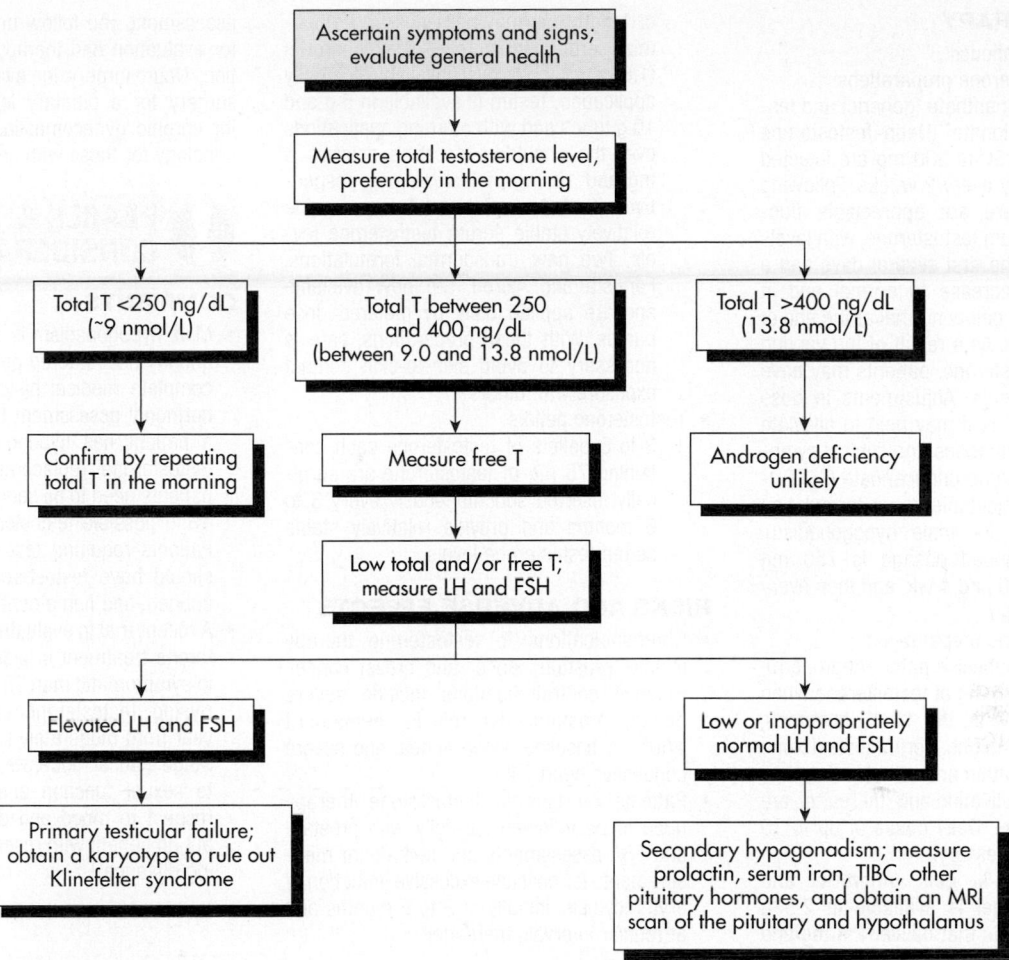

FIGURE 1H-87 Algorithm showing an approach for the diagnostic evaluation of adult men suspected of having androgen deficiency. (From Shalender B, Shehzad D: Diagnosis and treatment of hypogonadism in men, *Best Pract Res Clin Endocrin* 25(2):251-270, 2011.)

- Serum FSH and LH measurements are important in delineating primary, secondary, and combined hypogonadism.
- Hypogonadal symptoms are more likely to be seen in those with total serum testosterone level below the lower limit of values for young normal males. Serum total testosterone levels of <150 ng/dl are unequivocally low.
- Transient suppression of total serum testosterone may occur during acute illness, in males that are being treated with glucocorticoid, in those taking opiates or CNS-active medications, in those with malnutrition or poor eating habits, and during excessive physical exercise.
- Quantity and quality of sperm counts and activity can vary in a significant way for a variety of reasons. Therefore, in assessing fertility, seminal fluid analysis should be done on two or more occasions each separated by two or more weeks and on semen collected within an hour of ejaculation after more than two days of abstinence.
- Depending on the clinical picture and examination, other studies may be necessary including a karyotype analysis, for example, for Klinefelter syndrome, or serum prolac-

tin measurement for patients with possible hyperprolactinemia which may be drug-induced, related to a prolactinoma, or to chronic renal disease.

IMAGING STUDIES

- In males with severe androgen deficiency with low serum gonadotropin levels, increased serum prolactin levels, hypopituitarism, severe headaches, and visual defects, an MRI of the pituitary would be appropriate. In males with hypogonadism and a history of fractures, DXA measurements of spine and hip should be obtained to further delineate the status of the skeletal system.

Rx TREATMENT

- Testosterone replacement therapy is indicated when patients have symptoms and signs of hypogonadism and serum testosterone levels that are consistently subnormal with levels of <250 ng/dl. The goal of replacement therapy is to restore serum testosterone levels to within the normal range of values and to have a positive effect on the constel-

lation of hypogonadal symptoms and signs. Subnormal spermatogenesis, if present in such patients, is not affected by testosterone therapy. In patients with hypogonadotropic or secondary hypogonadism, chorionic gonadotropin and/or GnRH therapy can optimize spermatogenesis, whereas, generally in patients with primary hypogonadism, subnormal spermatogenesis and infertility are irreversible.

NONPHARMACOLOGIC THERAPY

- Weight reduction, especially when it appears to be a major factor underlying male hypogonadism.
- Discontinuation of anabolic steroids, CNS-active medications, and narcotic abuse.
- Surgery or radiation therapy for patients with a pituitary functioning or nonfunctioning tumor with visual field abnormality and headaches who are not candidates for further medical therapy or have been unsuccessfully treated with medication.
- Surgery indicated for chronic gynecomastia and, occasionally, in cases with recent-onset gynecomastia that has not responded to testosterone replacement therapy.

CHRONIC THERAPY

Testosterone formulations:

- Parenteral testosterone preparations:
  1. Testosterone enanthate (generic) and testosterone cypionate (Depo-Testosterone and generic) 150 to 200 mg are injected intramuscularly every 2 weeks. Following injections, there are appreciable fluctuations in serum testosterone, with levels rising within the first several days and a subsequent decrease to normal and in some cases to below normal at the end of the two weeks. As a result of the varying levels of testosterone, patients may have related symptoms. Adjustments in dose and dosing interval may help to alleviate the serum fluctuations and clinical symptoms. Testosterone undecanoate (AUEFD-ENDO) is an injectable depot formulation FDA-approved for male hypogonadism. The recommended dosage is 750 mg injected IM at 0 and 4 wk, and then every 10 wk thereafter.
- Topical testosterone preparations:
  1. Testosterone adhesive patch (Androderm) delivers 2.5 or 5 mg of testosterone when applied nightly to the back, abdomen, upper arms, or thighs. Serum testosterone levels rise to within normal range in a few hours after application and, thereafter, are relatively stable. Daily doses of up to 10 mg may be necessary.
  2. Testosterone 1% gels (AndroGel and Testim). Androgel is available in 2.5 g and 5 g gel units that deliver 2.5 mg and 5 mg of testosterone, respectively. The gel is applied daily in the morning by hand over the shoulder, upper arms, or abdomen. Adjustments in dose to 7.5 g or 10 g of gel may be necessary to optimize serum testosterone levels. AndroGel (1.62%) pump is also available for daily application. Testim is available in 5 g and 10 g tubes and with morning applications over the shoulders or arms delivers 5 mg and 10 mg of testosterone, respectively. Both AndroGel and Testim provide relatively stable serum testosterone levels. Two new transdermal formulations, Fortesta and Axiron, are now available and are applied daily by metered dose pumps. With these preparations, care is necessary to avoid skin-to-skin contact exposure with others.
- Testosterone pellets:
  1. 3 to 6 pellets of testosterone each containing 75 mg of testosterone are surgically inserted subcutaneously every 3 to 6 months and provide relatively stable serum testosterone levels.

RISKS AND ADVERSE EFFECTS

- Contraindications to testosterone therapy include prostate cancer and breast cancer. Relative contraindications include severe benign prostatic hyperplasia, hematocrit ≥50% at baseline, sleep apnea, and severe congestive heart failure.
- Patients on chronic testosterone therapy need to be followed carefully with prostate and PSA assessments and hematocrit measurements for possible excessive induction of erythrocytosis, initially at 3 to 6 months and at regular intervals thereafter.

REFERRAL

Endocrinology for full endocrine and metabolic assessment and therapy. Urology for further assessment and follow-up of the prostate and for evaluation and therapy of erectile dysfunction. Neurosurgery for evaluation and possible surgery for a pituitary lesion. Plastic surgery for chronic gynecomastia. Reproductive endocrinology for those with an infertility problem.

PEARLS & CONSIDERATIONS

COMMENTS

- Male hypogonadism is an important and frequently encountered problem that requires a complete medical history, examination, and hormonal assessment to determine whether a patient has hypogonadism and requires testosterone replacement therapy. Treated patients need to be seen on a regular basis to avoid possible testosterone adverse effects. Patients requiring testosterone replacement should have testosterone, prostate specific antigen, and hematocrit levels monitored.
- A recent trial to evaluate the effects of testosterone treatment in older men revealed that in symptomatic men 65 years of age or older, raising testosterone concentrations for 1 year from moderately low to the mid-normal range had a moderate benefit with respect to sexual function and some benefit with respect to mood and depressive symptoms but no benefit with respect to vitality or walking distance.[1]

AUTHOR: **JOSEPH R. TUCCI, M.D.**

[1]Snyder PJ, et al.: Effects of Testosterone Treatment in Older Men, *N Engl J Med* 374:611-624, 2016.

BASIC INFORMATION

DEFINITION

A decrease in parathyroid hormone (PTH) secretion or function results in hypoparathyroidism. In primary hypoparathyroidism, absence or dysfunction of the parathyroid gland results in inadequate PTH secretion and subsequent hypocalcemia and hyperphosphatemia. Surgical hypoparathyroidism is the most common etiology, followed by autoimmune disorders. Individuals with autoimmune polyglandular syndrome 1 typically present in childhood/adolescence with candidiasis, hypoparathyroidism, and adrenal insufficiency. Impaired function of PTH (i.e., PTH resistance) can also cause hypocalcemia and hyperphosphatemia, but the measured PTH level is elevated in this circumstance. A maternally transmitted mutation in the GNAS1 gene results in PTH resistance (i.e., pseudohypoparathyroidism). It is associated with characteristic features that include developmental delay, short stature, round facies, and short 4th metacarpal known as Albright's hereditary osteodystrophy (AHO). Paternal transmission manifests with AHO without PTH resistance (i.e., pseudopseudohypoparathyroidism; Table 1H-66). Secondary hypoparathyroidism, a condition in which PTH levels are low in response to hypercalcemic states, is discussed in Section IV (see hypercalcemia discussion in the "Calcium" topic).

ICD-10CM CODES
E20.0 Idiopathic hypoparathyroidism
E20.1 Pseudohypoparathyroidism
E20.8 Other hypoparathyroidism
E20.9 Hypoparathyroidism, unspecified
E89.2 Postprocedural hypoparathyroidism
P71.4 Transitory neonatal hypoparathyroidism

EPIDEMIOLOGY & DEMOGRAPHICS

The incidence and prevalence of primary hypoparathyroidism depends on the etiology of the condition. Postoperative hypoparathyroidism is the most common etiology and occurs in the setting of thyroid or parathyroid surgery. Transient hypoparathyroidism can be as high as 20% postoperatively but permanent dysfunction is less common (3%). Autoimmune disorders are the second most common cause of hypoparathyroidism in adults (female/male ratio of 1.4:1.0).

Autoimmune polyglandular syndrome type I is reported to have an incidence worldwide of 1:1,000,000. Other etiologies of hypoparathyroidism are very rare.

PHYSICAL FINDINGS & CLINICAL PRESENTATION

The symptoms of hypoparathyroidism are primarily related to hypocalcemia. The presentation of symptoms varies with the severity and duration of illness.
- Cardiovascular: prolonged QT intervals, QRS and ST segment changes, ventricular arrhythmias
- Musculoskeletal: muscle cramps, laryngospasm, osteomalacia (adults), rickets (children), weakened tooth enamel, osteosclerosis
- CNS: tetany (Chvostek's sign and Trousseau's sign), seizures, paresthesias, visual impairment from cataract formation, altered mental status, papilledema, and basal ganglia calcifications with longstanding disease
- GI: abdominal pain
- Renal: hypercalciuria and nephrolithiasis
- Other: dry scaly skin, brittle nails, dry hair

In addition to the hypocalcemia-related symptoms, syndromes associated with hypoparathyroidism can have distinct clinical findings. Conditions associated with hypoparathyroidism include:
- DiGeorge syndrome: dysmorphic facies, cleft palate
- Pseudohypoparathyroidism: developmental delay, short stature, round face, short 4th metacarpal (Albright's hereditary osteodystrophy)
- Hypoparathyroidism-retardation-dysmorphism syndrome: short stature, microcephaly, microphthalmia, small hands and feet, abnormal teeth
- Hypoparathyroidism-deafness-renal dysplasia syndrome: sensorineural deafness
- Autoimmune polyglandular syndrome type 1: mucocutaneous candidiasis and adrenal insufficiency

ETIOLOGY

There are several etiologies of hypoparathyroidism:
- Postoperative hypoparathyroidism: trauma during surgery to the neck.
- Developmental defects of the parathyroids
  1. Isolated hypoparathyroidism
  2. Branchial dysembryogenesis (DiGeorge's syndrome)

3. Hypoparathyroidism-retardation-dysmorphism syndrome
4. Hypoparathyroidism-deafness-renal dysplasia syndrome
5. Mitochondrial dysfunction associated with hypoparathyroidism
- Destruction of the parathyroids
  1. Autoimmune polyglandular syndrome type 1
  2. Radiation to the neck
  3. Infiltrative disease (e.g., metastatic carcinoma, Wilson's disease, hemochromatosis, thalassemia, granulomatous disease)
- Functional and secretory defects of the parathyroids
  1. Activating mutation of the calcium-sensing receptor alters the set point of the receptor and decreases PTH secretion
  2. Activating antibodies to calcium-sensing receptor alters the set point of the receptor and decreases PTH secretion
  3. PTH resistance (i.e., target organs unresponsive to PTH action)
     1. Pseudohypoparathyroidism (PHP): heterogeneous disorder presenting in childhood characterized by hypocalcemia, hyperphosphatemia, and elevated PTH levels. Table 1H-67 summarizes the various types of PHP.
     2. Hypermagnesemia and hypomagnesemia

DIAGNOSIS

DIFFERENTIAL DIAGNOSIS
- Secondary hypoparathyroidism as a result of hypercalcemia (discussed in the "Hypercalcemia" section)
- Other conditions associated with hypocalcemia. These conditions are usually associated with an elevated PTH hormone level.

WORKUP
- Serum calcium is usually low and phosphorus is elevated
  1. Two measurements of serum calcium are required for the confirmation of hypocalcemia. Total calcium should be corrected for low albumin utilizing the formula: Corrected Calcium = measured calcium + [(4 − albumin) × 0.8]. If a reliable laboratory is available, ionized calcium should be considered especially in conditions associated with acid-base disturbances or low albumin states.
  2. Serum phosphorus is usually high-normal or elevated in primary hypoparathyroidism.
- Serum intact PTH (iPTH) level is the single best test to evaluate the etiology of hypocalcemia. Typically, PTH is decreased in primary hypoparathyroidism and elevated in most other conditions associated with low calcium levels. However, PTH is also elevated in disorders associated with impaired PTH function (i.e., pseudohypoparathyroidism).

TABLE 1H-66 Types of Hypoparathyroidism

Type	Calcium	PO$_4$	PTH	Comments
Hypoparathyroidism	↓	↑	↓	Surgical removal (most common cause)
Pseudohypoparathyroidism	↓	↑	Ø↑	End-organ resistance to parathyroid hormone and Albright's hereditary osteodystrophy
Pseudo-pseudohypoparathyroidism	Normal	Normal	Normal	Only Albright's hereditary osteodystrophy

Adapted from Weissleder R et al: *Primer of diagnostic imaging*, ed 5, St Louis, 2011, Mosby.

TABLE 1H-67   Types of Pseudohypoparathyroidism (PHP)

Disorder	Urinary cAMP Response to PTH	Urinary PO₄ Response to PTH	Other Hormonal Resistance	AHO	Pathophysiology
PHP type 1A	Decreased	Decreased	Yes	Yes	Gₛα mutation
Pseudo-PHP	Normal	Normal	No	Yes	Gₛα mutation
PHP type 1B	Decreased	Decreased	No	No	*GNAS1* imprinting mutations
PHP type 1C	Decreased	Decreased	Yes	Yes	Gₛα activity normal
PHP type 2	Normal	Decreased	No	No	Vitamin D deficiency or myotonic dystrophy in some cases

AHO, Albright's hereditary osteodystrophy; *cAMP*, cyclic adenosine monophosphate; *GNAS1*, portion of the *GNAS* complex locus encoding Gₛα; *Gₛα*, α-subunit of the stimulatory G protein; *PO₄*, phosphate; *PTH*, parathyroid hormone.
From Melmed: *Williams textbook of endocrinology*, ed 12, Philadelphia, 2011, Saunders.

Genetic studies as indicated if medical or family history is suggestive.

LABORATORY TESTS

- Total and ionized calcium: low in hypoparathyroidism
- PTH: low in hypoparathyroidism and high in PTH resistance states like pseudohypoparathyroidism
- Phosphorus: high-normal or high in hypoparathyroidism
- Magnesium: both hypomagnesemia and hypermagnesemia can cause hypoparathyroidism
- ECG should be considered. Hypocalcemia associated with prolonged QT interval, rarely ST-segment elevations
- 24-hr urine for calcium to evaluate the risk for renal stones

 **TREATMENT**

NONPHARMACOLOGIC THERAPY

Parathyroid autotransplantation:

Hypoparathyroidism and subsequent hypocalcemia are common problems after neck exploration for total or near-total thyroidectomy or parathyroidectomy. In cases where there is concern for postoperative hypoparathyroidism, parathyroid autotransplantation of one or two parathyroid glands into the forearm or sternocleidomastoid muscle should be performed to prevent postoperative hypoparathyroidism.

PHARMACOLOGIC THERAPY

The mainstay of treatment for primary hypoparathyroidism is pharmacologic therapy with calcium and vitamin D supplementation. The goals of therapy are to control symptoms and minimize complications of therapy. The aim should be to achieve low-normal serum calcium (8.0-8.5 mg/dl), 24-hr urinary calcium <300 mg/day, and a calcium-phosphorus product <55.

- Vitamin D:
  1. There are several vitamin D preparations available on the market but the treatment of choice for patients with primary hypoparathyroidism is calcitriol. It is an active metabolite that does not require hydroxylation in the liver or kidney and therefore bypasses the PTH-mediated 1-α hydroxylation defect that occurs with hypoparathyroidism.
  2. Dose of 0.25 to 1 μg once or twice daily is usually required to correct hypocalcemia

and improve symptoms. Its maximal effect is seen after 10 hours and it lasts for 2 to 3 days.

- Calcium:
  1. Calcium carbonate or calcium citrates are common oral agents used for treatment of hypocalcemia associated with hypoparathyroidism. Calcium carbonate requires an acidic environment for effective absorption, and as a result, it must be taken with food. Its effectiveness is decreased with concomitant use of H₂ blockers or proton pump inhibitors. However, calcium carbonate is cheaper in cost than other calcium supplements and therefore it is first line in the management of hypocalcemia for some patients. The advantage of calcium citrate is that it does not require an acidic environment for effective absorption.
  2. Start with a dose of 500 to 1000 mg of elemental calcium tid and adjust the dose for a desired calcium in the low-normal range.
- Magnesium:
  1. Hypocalcemia is difficult to correct without normalizing magnesium levels.
  2. Magnesium sulfate IV 2 g over 20 min followed by 1 g/hr infusion can be considered in severe deficiency states. Milder deficiencies can be managed with oral magnesium 100 mg tid.
- Thiazide diuretics:
  1. Thiazide diuretics decrease urine calcium excretion and decrease kidney stones. They should be considered in individuals with urine calcium >250 mg/day.
- PTH replacement:
  1. Injectable synthetic human PTH (1-84) decreases urinary calcium excretion and maintains serum calcium in the normal range with reduced requirements for calcium and vitamin D supplementation.
  2. PTH (1-84, Natpara, an 84 amino acid single-chain polypeptide identical to native parathyroid hormone) is the first FDA approved for use in the treatment of hypoparathyroidism. The cost for a 4-week supply of Natpara exceeds $7000.

ACUTE GENERAL Rx

Severe and/or symptomatic hypocalcemia requires hospitalization. Acute management of hypocalcemia includes:

- Telemetry monitoring for arrhythmias associated with severe hypocalcemia
- IV infusion of calcium gluconate 10 mL of 10% solution to receive a bolus of 90 mg of elemental calcium followed by an infusion of 0.5 to 2 mg/kg/hr until calcium levels are in the low-normal range.

 **PEARLS & CONSIDERATIONS**

COMMENTS

- The mainstay of treatment for primary hypoparathyroidism is calcitriol and calcium supplementation to maintain a goal serum calcium level in the low-normal range. IV calcium should be considered if calcium <7.0 mg/dl. Magnesium levels should be assessed and appropriately replaced in all patients with hypocalcemia. Clinical trials are under way to evaluate the role of recombinant PTH for the treatment of primary hypoparathyroidism.
- In patients undergoing neck exploration, consideration should be given to the parathyroid glands. Autotransplantation of one or more parathyroid glands should be considered when appropriate to prevent postoperative hypoparathyroidism.

EBM **EVIDENCE**

Available at www.expertconsult.com

SUGGESTED READINGS
Available at www.expertconsult.com

AUTHOR: **VICKY CHENG, M.D.**

H

BASIC INFORMATION

DEFINITION

Hypopituitarism (from the Latin *pituita,* meaning "phlegm") is the deficiency of one or more of the hormones of the anterior or posterior pituitary gland resulting from diseases of the hypothalamus or pituitary gland. Panhypopituitarism indicates the loss of all the pituitary hormones but is often used in clinical practice to describe patients deficient in growth hormone (GH), gonadotropins, corticotropin, or thyrotropin in whom posterior pituitary function remains intact.

SYNONYMS

Panhypopituitarism
Pituitary insufficiency

ICD-10CM CODES
E23.0 Hypopituitarism
E23.0 Hypopituitarism
E23.1 Drug-induced hypopituitarism
E89.3 Postprocedural hypopituitarism

EPIDEMIOLOGY & DEMOGRAPHICS

Incidence of 4.2 cases per 100,000 persons

PHYSICAL FINDINGS & CLINICAL PRESENTATION

Symptoms depend on type of onset, number and severity of hormone deficiencies, their target organs, and age of onset.
- Mass effect of a pituitary tumor can cause headaches and visual disturbances (typically as bitemporal hemianopsia).
- Rhinorrhea.
- Corticotropin deficiency:
  1. Fatigue and weakness, no appetite, abdominal pain, nausea, vomiting, failure to thrive in children, and hyponatremia. If the onset is abrupt, hypotension and shock
- Thyrotropin deficiency:
  1. Fatigue and weakness, weight gain, cold intolerance, anemia, constipation
  2. Bradycardia, hung-up reflexes, pretibial edema, change in voice, and hair loss
- Gonadotropin deficiency:
  1. Loss of libido, erectile dysfunction, amenorrhea, hot flashes, dyspareunia, infertility, gynecomastia, decreased muscle mass, and anemia
- GH deficiency:
  1. Growth retardation in children
  2. Easy fatigue, hypoglycemia
  3. Lean mass is reduced and fat mass is increased, leading to obesity
  4. Decreased bone mineral density, increased low-density lipoprotein cholesterol, obesity, increased inflammatory cardiovascular markers (interleukin-6 and C-reactive protein)
- Hyperprolactinemia:
  1. Galactorrhea, hypogonadism, inability to lactate after delivery

2. Posterior pituitary (vasopressin; antidiuretic hormone [ADH] deficiency): diabetes insipidus with polyuria, polydipsia, nocturia, hypotension, and dehydration

ETIOLOGY

It can be congenital or acquired:
- Congenital: mutations in transcription factors produce multiple hormonal deficiencies. Mutations in genes produce single hormonal deficiency.
- Acquired: the result of destruction of pituitary cells caused by:
  1. Pituitary apoplexy: hemorrhage or infarction of the pituitary gland. Predisposing factors include diabetes mellitus, anticoagulation therapy, head trauma, and radiation therapy. Sheehan's syndrome: postpartum necrosis, a rare complication after pregnancy.
  2. Infiltrative disease, including sarcoidosis, hemachromatosis, histiocytosis X, Wegener's granulomatosis, lymphocytic hypophysitis, and infection of the pituitary (tuberculosis, mycosis, syphilis).
  3. Primary empty sella syndrome: flattening of the pituitary gland caused by extension of the subarachnoid space and filling of cerebrospinal fluid into the sella turcica.
  4. Pituitary tumors: classified by size (microadenomas, <10 mm; macroadenomas, >10 mm) and function. Prolactin secreting tumors and nonfunctioning tumors account for the majority of pituitary adenomas.
  5. Suprasellar tumors: craniopharyngiomas are the most common.

DIAGNOSIS

The diagnosis of hypopituitarism is suspected by clinical history and physical findings and is established by blood tests to confirm the presence of hormone deficiency.

DIFFERENTIAL DIAGNOSIS

The differential diagnosis is as outlined under "Etiology."

WORKUP

Includes baseline determination of each anterior pituitary hormone followed by dynamic provocative stimulation tests, radiograph imaging, and formal visual field testing. Table 1H-68 summarizes testing for assessment of anterior pituitary function.

LABORATORY TESTS
- Corticotropin deficiency:
  1. The presence of a 9:00 am cortisol level >20 mcg/dl or <4 mcg/dl usually confirms sufficiency or deficiency, respectively.
  2. Corticotropin stimulation test using 250 mcg of corticotropin given IV and measuring serum cortisol before and 30 and 60 min after administration. A normal

response is an increase in serum cortisol level >20 mcg/dl.
  3. With pituitary disease these test results may be indeterminate, and more dynamic testing such as an insulin-tolerance or metyrapone test may be necessary.
- Thyrotropin deficiency:
  1. Thyroid-stimulating hormone (TSH) and free T_4 measurements
  2. Primary hypothyroidism shows elevated TSH with low free T_4. Secondary hypothyroidism shows normal or low TSH with low free T_4 and low T_3 resin uptake.
- Gonadotropin deficiency:
  1. Follicle-stimulating hormone (FSH), luteinizing hormone (LH), estrogen, and testosterone measurements.
  2. In men, hypogonadotropic hypogonadism is seen with low testosterone levels and normal or low FSH and LH levels (ideally measured at 9:00 AM because of diurnal rhythm). Check free testosterone if patient is obese.
  3. In premenopausal women with amenorrhea, low estrogen with normal or low FSH and LH levels is typically seen.
- GH deficiency:
  1. Insulin-induced hypoglycemia stimulation test using 0.1 to 0.15 unit/kg regular insulin given IV and measuring GH 30, 60, and 120 min after administration. A normal response is a GH level >3 mcg/dl. This test is contraindicated in seizure disorder or ischemic heart disease.
  2. Combination of GH-releasing hormone plus arginine is an alternative test, with a diagnostic threshold of 9 mcg/L.
  3. Because the relation between serum insulinlike growth factor (IGF)-1 and GH levels blurs with age, a normal serum IGF-1 does not exclude the diagnosis in older adults.
- Hyperprolactinemia: prolactin levels may be elevated in prolactin-secreting pituitary adenomas.
- Vasopressin deficiency:
  1. Urinalysis shows low specific gravity.
  2. Urine osmolality is low.
  3. Serum osmolality is high.
  4. Fluid deprivation test over 18 hr with inability to concentrate the urine.
  5. Serum vasopressin level is low.
  6. Electrolytes may show hyponatremia and exclude hyperglycemia.

IMAGING STUDIES
- Imaging is the first step in identifying an underlying cause.
- MRI (Fig. 1H-88) is more sensitive than CT in visualizing the pituitary fossa, sella turcica, optic chiasm, pituitary stalk, and cavernous sinuses. It is also more sensitive in detecting pituitary microadenomas. CT with contrast can be used if MRI is not available.
- Surveillance scan at baseline and 12 mo thereafter depending on protocol and clinical symptoms.

TABLE 1H-68   Assessment of Anterior Pituitary Function

Test	Dose	Normal Response	Side Effects
ACTH			
Insulin tolerance	0.1-0.15 U/kg IV	Peak cortisol response >18 µg/dl, or ≥5µg/dl	Sweating, palpitation, tremor
Metyrapone	30 mg/kg PO at 11 P.M.	Peak 11-DOC ≥=7 µg/dl	Nausea, insomnia, adrenal crisis
		Peak cortisol ≤7 µg/dl	
		Peak ACTH >75 pg/ml	
CRH stimulation	100 µg IV	Peak ACTH ≥2-4-fold	Flushing
		Peak cortisol ≥20 µg/dl or ↑ ≥=7 µg/dl	
ACTH stimulation	250 µg IV or IM, or 1 µg IV	Peak cortisol ≥20 µg/dl	Rare
TSH			
Serum T₄ (free T₄)	200-500 µg IV	Peak TSH ≥2.5-fold, or ↑ ≥5-6 mU/L (females) or ≥2-3 mU/L (males)	Flushing, nausea, urge to micturate
Total T₃			
TSH—third-generation			
TRH stimulation			
PRL			
Serum PRL	200-500 µg IV	PRL ↑ ≥2.5-fold	Flushing, nausea, urge to micturate
TRH stimulation			
LH/FSH			
Serum LH and FSH	100 µg IV	Elevated in menopause and in men with primary testicular failure (otherwise normal) 300-900 ng/ml	Rare
Serum testosterone			
GnRH stimulation		LH ≥2-3-fold, or ↑ by 10 IU/L	
		FSH ≥1.5-2-fold, or ↑ ≥2 IU/L	
GH			
Insulin tolerance	0.1-0.15 U/kg	GH peak >5 µg/L	Sweating, palpitation, tremor
L-Arginine	Arginine 0.5 g/kg (maximum, 30 g) IV over 30-120 min	GH peak >0.4 µg/L	Nausea
Plus			
GHRH	GHRH 1-5 µg/kg	GH peak >4 µg/L	Flushing

ACTH, Adrenocorticotropic hormone; *CRH,* corticotropin-releasing hormone; *11-DOC,* 11-deoxycorticosterone; *FSH,* follicle-stimulating hormone; *GH,* growth hormone; *GHRH,* growth hormone–releasing hormone; *GnRH,* gonadotropin-releasing hormone; *LH,* luteinizing hormone; *PRL,* prolactin; *T₃,* triiodothyronine; *T₄,* thyroxine; *TSH,* thyroid-stimulating hormone; *TRH,* thyrotropin-releasing hormone.
From Melmed S, Polonsky KS, Larsen PR, Kronenberg HM: *Williams textbook of endocrinology,* ed 12, Philadelphia, 2011, Saunders, Elsevier Inc.

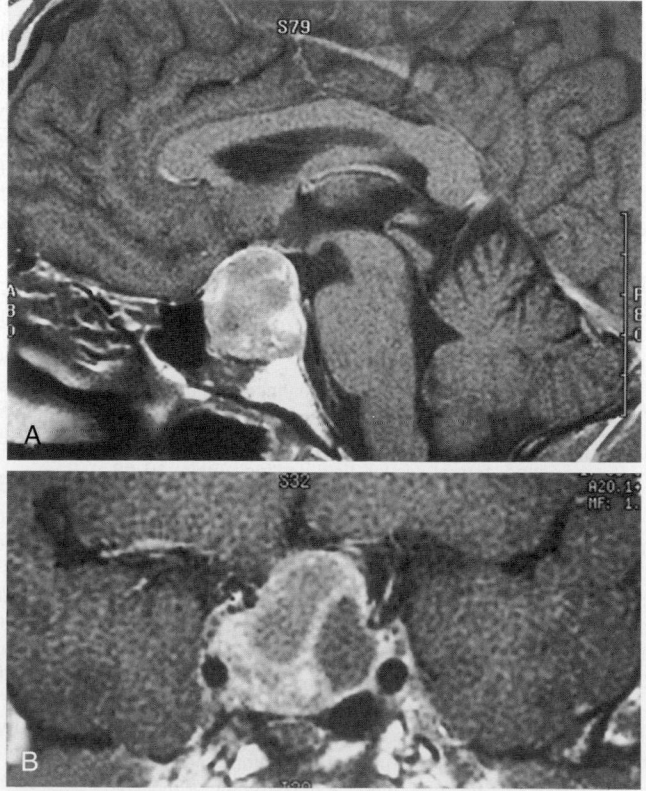

FIGURE 1H-88   T1-weighted gadolinium-enhanced MR of a pituitary adenoma. **(A)** Sagittal and **(B)** coronal images. (Courtesy of D. Thomas. From Bowling B: *Kanski's clinical ophthalmology,* ed 8, Philadelphia, 2016, Elsevier.)

 **TREATMENT**

Threefold: removing underlying cause (surgery or radiation), treating hormonal deficiencies, and addressing any other repercussions from deficiency. Table 1H-69 summarizes replacement therapy for adult hypopituitarism.

NONPHARMACOLOGIC THERAPY

- IV fluid resuscitation, correction of electrolyte and metabolic abnormalities with potassium bicarbonate, and oxygen therapy.
- Transsphenoidal surgery for tumors causing specific symptoms.
- Radiation or stereotactic radiosurgery ("gamma knife") for medically unresponsive, surgically unresectable tumors and tumors for which other modalities are contraindicated. It is both safe and effective for recurrent or residual pituitary adenomas.

TABLE 1H-69 Replacement Therapy for Adult Hypopituitarism*

Deficient Hormone

Treatment

Remarks

ACTH

Hydrocortisone: 10-20 mg/day in divided doses
Cortisone acetate: 15-25 mg/day in divided doses

TSH

L-Thyroxine: 0.05-0.2 mg/day according to T₄ levels

FSH/LH (in males)

Testosterone enanthate: 200 mg IM q2-3 wk
Testosterone skin patch: 2.5-5.0 mg/day (or up to 7.5 mg/day)
Testosterone gel: 3-6 g/day

For fertility: hCG three times weekly, or hCG + either FSH or menopausal gonadotropin or GnRH

FSH/LH (in females)

Conjugated estrogen: 0.3-0.625 mg/day
Micronized estradiol: 1 mg/day
Estradiol valerate: 2 mg
Piperazine estrone sulfate: 1.25 mg
Estradiol skin patch: 4-8 mg twice weekly

All of the estrogens are administered with progesterone or progestin sequentially or in combination if uterus is present

For fertility: Menopausal gonadotropin, and hCG, or GnRH

Growth hormone

Somatotropin (in adults): 0.2-1.0 mg/day SC
Somatotropin (in children): 0.02-0.05 mg/kg per day

Vasopressin

Intranasal desmopressin: 10-20 μg bid
Oral DDAVP: 300-600 μg/day, usually in divided doses

ACTH, Adrenocorticotropic hormone; *DDAVP,* desmopressin acetate; *FSH,* follicle-stimulating hormone; *GnRH,* gonadotropin-releasing hormone; *hCG,* human chorionic gonadotropin; *LH,* luteinizing hormone; *T4,* thyroxine; *TSH,* thyroid-stimulating hormone.

From Melmed S, Polonsky KS, Larsen PR, Kronenberg HM: *Williams textbook of endocrinology,* ed 12, Philadelphia, 2011, Saunders, Elsevier Inc.

ACUTE GENERAL Rx

Acute situations such as adrenal crisis or myxedema coma can occur in untreated hypopituitarism and should be treated accordingly with IV corticosteroids (e.g., hydrocortisone 100 to 250 mg bolus followed by hydrocortisone 100 mg IV q6h for 24 hr) and levothyroxine (e.g., 5 to 8 mcg/kg IV over 15 min, then 100 mcg IV q24h)

CHRONIC Rx

Treatment is lifelong:

- Adrenocorticotropic hormone (ACTH) deficiency: hydrocortisone 10 mg PO every morning and 5 mg PO every evening or prednisone 5 mg PO every morning and 2.5 mg PO every evening. Dexamethasone or prednisone is often preferred because of longer duration of action.
- LH and FSH deficiency:
  1. In men, testosterone enanthate or propionate 200 to 300 mg IM every 2 to 3 wk, or transdermal testosterone scrotal patches can be tried.
  2. In women who are not interested in fertility, conjugated estrogen 0.3 to 1.25 mg/day and held the last 5 to 7 days of each month with the addition of medroxyprogesterone 10 mg/day given during days 15 to 25 of the normal menstrual cycle. In those who have secondary hypogonadism and wish to become pregnant, pulsatile gonadotropic-releasing hormone may be of benefit.
- TSH deficiency: levothyroxine 0.05 to 0.15 mg/day.
- GH deficiency:
  1. GH replacement in children is universally accepted.
  2. GH replacement in adults is not generally recommended and requires careful consideration of each individual case. It may have effects on quality of life, body composition, bone density, and cardiovascular risk factors.
  3. Side effects of replacement include peripheral edema, arthralgia, and headaches.
  4. Usual GH dose is between 0.2 and 0.4 mg, determined by the age and gender of a patient and increments of 0.1 mg every 2 to 4 wk until serum IGF-1 is in the upper part of the normal range. Young adults and women taking estrogen require a higher dose.
- ADH deficiency:
  1. Desmopressin (DDAVP) 10 to 20 mcg by intranasal spray or 0.05 to 0.1 mg PO bid is used in patients with diabetes insipidus.
  2. Vasopressin: 5-10 U given IM or SC q6h.

DISPOSITION

- Hormone replacement therapy is adjusted according to serum hormone monitoring.
- If untreated can lead to adrenal crisis, severe hyponatremia and hypothyroidism, metabolic abnormalities, and death.
- Complications: visual deficit, adrenal crisis, susceptibility to infection and other stressors.

- Prognosis: stable patients have a favorable prognosis with replacement hormone therapy. Patients with acute decompensation are in critical condition with a high mortality rate.

REFERRAL

Consultation with an endocrinologist and neurosurgeon for surgical treatment

ⓘ PEARLS & CONSIDERATIONS

- All patients sustaining moderate to severe head injury should undergo assessment of anterior pituitary function during the acute phase and at 6 mo.
- IGF-1 can be used as a marker of GH deficiency.
- All tests of GH secretion are more likely to give false-positive results in obese patients.
- The GH axis is the most vulnerable to the effects of radiotherapy; doses as low as 18 Gy in children have caused GH deficiency.
- Sequence of hormonal disruption: GH secretion then gonadotropin secretion. TSH and adrenocorticotropic hormone secretion are somewhat resistant.
- Thyroxine supplementation increases the rate of cortisol metabolism and can lead to adrenal crisis, so corticosteroids should be replaced first.
- All patients receiving glucocorticoid replacement therapy should wear proper identification stating the need for this therapy.
- Stress doses of corticosteroids are indicated before surgery or for any medical emergency (e.g., sepsis, acute myocardial infarction).
- Antidiuretic hormone deficiency may be masked if there is ACTH deficiency with symptoms only appearing when cortisol has been replaced.

COMMENTS

- Mineralocorticoid replacement is not necessary in secondary adrenal insufficiency because the renin-angiotensin-aldosterone system is unaffected by pituitary failure.
- Patients with adult-acquired GH deficiency must meet at least two criteria before replacement therapy: a poor GH response to at least two standard stimuli and hypopituitarism from pituitary or hypothalamic damage. The criteria are different in children in whom GH is required for normal growth.
- Prevention of acute decompensation can be accomplished by reminding patients to increase the dose of hydrocortisone in response to stress.
- Medical therapy should precede surgical therapy.

SUGGESTED READINGS

Available at www.expertconsult.com

RELATED CONTENT

Hypopituitarism (Patient Information)

AUTHOR: **SHAHNAZ PUNJANI, M.D.**

BASIC INFORMATION

DEFINITION

Hypothermia is a rectal temperature <35° C (95.8° F). Accidental hypothermia is an unintentionally induced decrease in core temperature in the absence of preoptic anterior hypothalamic conditions.

ICD-10CM CODES
T68   Hypothermia
R68.0 Hypothermia, not associated with low
       environmental temperature

EPIDEMIOLOGY & DEMOGRAPHICS

- Hypothermia occurs most frequently in the following groups: alcoholics; homeless; learning-impaired; patients with cardiovascular, cerebrovascular, or pituitary disorders; those using sedatives or tranquilizers; and elderly patients.
- >700 persons in the United States die from hypothermia annually.

PHYSICAL FINDINGS & CLINICAL PRESENTATION

The clinical presentation varies with the severity of hypothermia. Shivering may be absent if body temperature is <33.3° C (92° F) or in patients taking phenothiazines.

Hypothermia may masquerade as cerebrovascular accident, ataxia, or slurred speech, or the patient may appear comatose or clinically dead. Signs of hypothermia are summarized in Box E1H-13.

Physiologic stages of hypothermia:
1. Stage HT I: Mild hypothermia (typical core temperature 32.2° to 35° C [90° to 95° F]): arrhythmias, ataxia
2. Stage HT II: Moderate hypothermia (core temperature 28° to 32.2° C [82.4° to 90° F]):
   a. Progressive decrease of level of consciousness, pulse, cardiac output, and respiration
   b. Fibrillation, dysrhythmias (increased susceptibility to ventricular tachycardia)
   c. Elimination of shivering mechanism for thermogenesis
3. Stage HT III: Severe hypothermia (core temperature ≤28° C to 24° C [82.4° F to 75° F]):
   a. Absence of reflexes or response to pain
   b. Decreased cerebral blood flow, decreased CO_2
   c. Increased risk of ventricular fibrillation or asystole
   d. Vital signs present
4. Stage IV: No vital signs (core temperature < 24° C [75° F])

ETIOLOGY

Exposure to cold temperatures for a prolonged period. Contributing factors include:
1. Drugs: ethanol, phenothiazines, sedative-hypnotics
2. Skin disorders: extensive burns, severe psoriasis, exfoliative dermatitis
3. Metabolic disorders: hypopituitarism, hypothyroidism, hypoadrenalism

4. Neurologic abnormalities: stroke, head trauma, acute spinal cord transection, impaired shivering
5. Other: lack of acclimatization, aggressive fluid resuscitation, sepsis, heat stroke treatment
6. Box E1H-14 summarizes factors predisposing to hypothermia

DIAGNOSIS

DIFFERENTIAL DIAGNOSIS

- It is crucial to determine an accurate core temperature measurement. Advantages and considerations of various methods to determine core temperature are summarized in Table 1H-70.
- Cerebrovascular accident
- Myxedema coma
- Drug intoxication
- Hypoglycemia

LABORATORY TESTS

1. Metabolic and respiratory acidosis are usually present.
   a. When blood cools, the arterial pH increases, oxygen tension (Po_2) increases, and the Pco_2 falls:
      (1) pH increases 0.008 U/° F (or 0.015 U/° C), causing a decrease in temperature.
      (2) Pao_2 increases 3.3%/° F, causing a decrease in temperature. Oxygenation considerations during hypothermia are described in Box 1H-15.
      (3) $Paco_2$ decreases 2.4%/° F, causing a decrease in temperature.
   b. Blood gas analyzers warm the blood to 37° C, increasing the partial pressure of dissolved gases, resulting in higher oxygen and carbon dioxide levels and a lower pH than the patient's actual values. Correction of arterial blood gases for temperature is unnecessary as a guide to therapy. The use of uncorrected values also permits reference to the standard acid–base nomograms.
2. A decrease in K^+ initially, then an increase in K^+ with increasing hypothermia; extreme hyperkalemia indicates a poor prognosis.
3. Hematocrit increases (caused by hemoconcentration), decreasing leukocytes and platelets (caused by splenic sequestration).
4. Blood viscosity, increased clotting time

TABLE 1H-70 Core Temperature Measurements

Type	Advantages	Considerations
Rectal	Convenient	Insert 15 cm (6 inches)
	Continuous monitoring	Lags during transition from cooling to rewarming
		Falsely elevated with peritoneal lavage
		Falsely low if probe is in cold feces or when lower extremities are frozen
Esophageal	Convenient	Insert 24 cm (9.5 inches) below larynx
	Continuous monitoring	Tracheal misplacement
		Aspiration
		Falsely elevated with heated inhalation
Tympanic	Approximates hypothalamic temperature via internal carotid artery	Probe: tympanic membrane perforation; canal hemorrhage Infrared: unreliable; cerumen effect
Bladder	Convenient	Unreliable
	Continuous monitoring	Falsely elevated with peritoneal lavage
		Falsely low with cold diuresis

From Auerbach P: *Wilderness medicine, expert consult* Premium Edition—Enhanced Online Features and Print, Philadelphia, 2012, Saunders.

BOX 1H-15 Oxygenation Considerations During Hypothermia

Detrimental Factors
Oxygen consumption increases with rise in temperature; caution if rapid rewarming; shivering also increases demand
Decreased temperature shifts oxyhemoglobin dissociation curve to the left
Ventilation-perfusion mismatch; atelectasis; decreased respiratory minute volume; bronchorrhea; decreased protective airway reflexes
Decreased tissue perfusion from vasoconstriction; increased viscosity
"Functional hemoglobin" concept: capability of hemoglobin to unload oxygen is lowered
Decreased thoracic elasticity and pulmonary compliance

Protective Factors
Reduction of oxygen consumption: 50% at 28° C (82.4° F); 75% at 22° C (71.6° F); 92% at 10° C (50° F)
Increased oxygen solubility in plasma
Decreased pH and increased $Paco_2$ shift oxyhemoglobin dissociation curve to right

From Auerbach P: *Wilderness medicine,* ed 4, St Louis, 2001, Mosby.

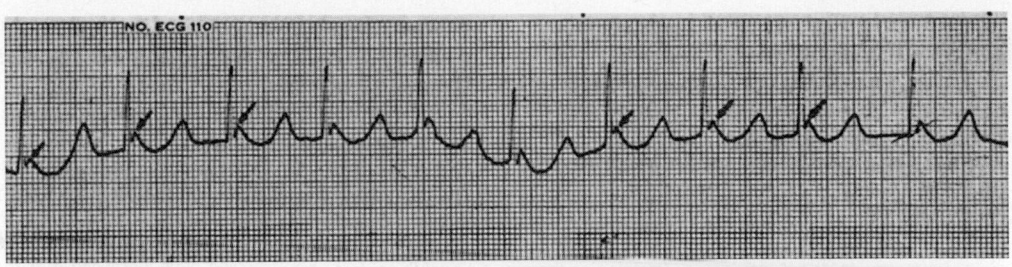

FIGURE 1H-90 Hypothermic J waves (Osborne waves) *(arrows)* **in an 80-year-old man with core temperature of 86° F (30° C).** These waves disappeared with rewarming. (From Morse CD, Rial WY: Emergency medicine. In Rakel RE [ed]: *Textbook of family practice,* ed 4, Philadelphia, 1990, Saunders.)

BOX 1H-16   Preparing Hypothermic Patients for Transport

1. The patient must be dry. Gently remove or cut off wet clothing, and replace it with dry clothing or a dry insulation system. Keep the patient horizontal, and do not allow exertion or massage of the extremities.
2. Stabilize injuries (i.e., the spine; place fractures in the correct anatomic position). Open wounds should be covered before packaging.
3. Initiate heated intravenous infusions (IVs) if feasible; bags can be placed under the patient's buttocks or in a compressor system. Administer a fluid challenge.
4. Active rewarming should be limited to heated inhalation and truncal heat. Insulate hot water bottles in stockings or mittens, and then place them in the patient's axillae and groin.
5. The patient should be wrapped. Begin building the wrap by placing a large plastic sheet on the available surface (floor, ground), and on it place an insulated sleeping pad. A layer of blankets, a sleeping bag, or bubble wrap insulating material is laid over the sleeping pad. The patient is then placed on the insulation. Heating bottles are put in place along with IVs, and the entire package is wrapped layer over layer, with the plastic as the final closure. The patient's face should be partially covered, but a tunnel should be created to allow access for breathing and monitoring.

From Auerbach P: *Wilderness medicine, Expert Consult premium edition—enhanced online features and print,* Philadelphia, 2012, Elsevier.

IMAGING STUDIES

- Chest x-ray: generally not helpful; may reveal evidence of aspiration (e.g., intoxicated patient with aspiration pneumonia)
- ECG: prolonged PR, QT, and QRS segments, depressed ST segments, inverted T waves, atrioventricular block, and hypothermic J waves (Osborne waves) may appear at temperatures less than 33.0° C (91.4° F); characterized by notching of the junction of the QRS complex and ST segments (Fig. 1H-90).

Rx TREATMENT

NONPHARMACOLOGIC THERAPY

- The first critical step in management of accidental hypothermia is initiating passive external rewarming by removing wet clothing and covering the patient with insulating material.
- Specific treatment of hypothermia varies with the following:
  1. Degree of hypothermia
  2. Existence of concomitant diseases (e.g., cardiovascular insufficiency)
  3. Patient's age and medical condition (e.g., elderly, debilitated patients vs. young, healthy patients)
- General measures:
  1. Secure an airway before warming all unconscious patients; precede endotracheal intubation with oxygenation (if possible)

to minimize the risk of arrhythmias during the procedure.
2. Peripheral vasoconstriction may impede placement of a peripheral intravenous catheter; consider femoral venous access as an alternative to the jugular or subclavian sites to avoid ventricular stimulation.
3. A Foley catheter should be inserted, and urinary output should be monitored and maintained >0.5 to 1 ml/kg/hr with intravascular volume replacement.
4. Box 1H-16 summarizes measures for preparing hypothermic patients for transport.

ACUTE GENERAL Rx

- Continuous ECG monitoring of patients is recommended. Ventricular arrhythmias can be treated with bretylium; lidocaine is generally ineffective, and procainamide is associated with an increased incidence of ventricular fibrillation in hypothermic patients.
- Correct severe acidosis and electrolyte abnormalities.
- Hypothyroidism, if present, should be promptly treated (see "Myxedema Coma").
- If clinical evidence suggests adrenal insufficiency, administer IV methylprednisolone.
  In patients unresponsive to verbal or noxious stimuli or with altered mental status, 100 mg of thiamine, 0.4 mg of naloxone, and 1 ampule of 50% dextrose may be given.

Warm (104° to 113° F [40° to 45° C]), humidified oxygen should also be given if available. Specific treatment:
1. Mild hypothermia (rectal temperature <32.3° C [90° F]): passive external rewarming is indicated. Place the patient in a warm room (temperature >21° C [69.8° F]), and cover with insulating material after gently removing wet clothing; recommended rewarming rates vary between 0.5° and 20° C/hr but should not exceed 0.55° C/hr in elderly persons.
2. Moderate to severe hypothermia:
   a. Active core rewarming
      (1) Delivery of heat by way of fluids: warm gastrointestinal irrigation (with saline enemas and by nasogastric tube); IV fluids (usually D_5NS without potassium) warmed to 104° to 107.6° F (40° to 42° C), peritoneal dialysis with dialysate heated to 40.5° to 42.5° C.
      (2) Inhalation of heated, humidified oxygen (warmed to 40° C [104° F]) increases core temperature by 1° C (1.8° F) per hr and decreases evaporative heat loss from respiration.
3. Active external rewarming: immersion in a bath of warm water (40° to 41° C); active external rewarming may produce shock because of excessive peripheral vasodilation. Ideal candidates are previously healthy, young patients with acute immersion hypothermia.
4. Extracorporeal blood warming with cardiopulmonary bypass appears to be an efficacious rewarming technique in young, otherwise healthy persons.
5. Patients with cardiac instability and those in cardiac arrest should be transported to a center capable of providing extracorporeal membrane oxygenation (ECMO) unless other conditions (e.g., trauma) require transport to a closer facility.

SUGGESTED READINGS
Available at www.expertconsult.com

RELATED CONTENT
Hypothermia (Patient Information)

AUTHOR: **FRED F. FERRI, M.D.**

BASIC INFORMATION

DEFINITION

Hypothyroidism is a disorder caused by the inadequate secretion of thyroid hormone.

SYNONYMS

Myxedema

ICD-10CM CODES

E03.9	Hypothyroidism, unspecified
E00.9	Congenital iodine-deficiency syndrome, unspecified
E89.0	Postprocedural hypothyroidism
E03.2	Hypothyroidism due to medicaments and other exogenous substances
E02	Subclinical iodine-deficiency hypothyroidism
E03.0	Congenital hypothyroidism with diffuse goiter
E03.1	Congenital hypothyroidism without goiter
E03.3	Postinfectious hypothyroidism
E03.8	Other specified hypothyroidism

EPIDEMIOLOGY & DEMOGRAPHICS

INCIDENCE/PREVALENCE: 1.5% to 2% of women and 0.2% of men. Overall, about 1 in 300 persons in the United States has hypothyroidism.

PREDOMINANT AGE: Incidence of hypothyroidism increases with age; among persons older than 60 yr, 6% of women and 2.5% of men have laboratory evidence of hypothyroidism (thyroid-stimulating hormone [TSH] more than twice normal level).

PHYSICAL FINDINGS & CLINICAL PRESENTATION

- Hypothyroid patients generally present with the following signs and symptoms: fatigue, lethargy, weakness, constipation, weight gain, cold intolerance, muscle weakness, slow speech, slow cerebration with poor memory.
- Skin: dry, coarse, thick, cool, sallow (yellow color caused by carotenemia); nonpitting edema in skin of eyelids and hands (myxedema) secondary to infiltration of subcutaneous tissues by a hydrophilic mucopolysaccharide substance. (Fig. E1H-91, *A* and *B*)
- Hair: brittle and coarse; loss of outer third of eyebrows.
- Facies: dulled expression, thickened tongue, thick and slow-moving lips.
- Thyroid gland: may or may not be palpable (depending on the cause of the hypothyroidism).
- Heart sounds: distant, possible pericardial effusion.
- Pulse: bradycardia.
- Neurologic: delayed relaxation phase of the deep tendon reflexes, cerebellar ataxia, hearing impairment, poor memory, peripheral neuropathies with paresthesia.
- Musculoskeletal: carpal tunnel syndrome, muscular stiffness, weakness.

ETIOLOGY

1. Primary hypothyroidism (thyroid gland dysfunction): the cause of >90% of the cases of hypothyroidism
   - Hashimoto's thyroiditis is the most common cause of hypothyroidism after age 8 yr
   - Idiopathic myxedema (nongoitrous form of Hashimoto's thyroiditis)
   - Previous treatment of hyperthyroidism (radioiodine therapy, subtotal thyroidectomy)
   - Subacute thyroiditis
   - Radiation therapy to the neck (usually for malignant disease)
   - Iodine deficiency or excess
   - Drugs (lithium, para-aminosalicylate, sulfonamides, phenylbutazone, amiodarone, thiourea)
   - Congenital (approximately one case per 4000 live births)
   - Prolonged treatment with iodides
2. Secondary hypothyroidism: pituitary dysfunction, postpartum necrosis, neoplasm, infiltrative disease causing deficiency of TSH
3. Tertiary hypothyroidism: hypothalamic disease (granuloma, neoplasm, or irradiation causing deficiency of thyrotropin-releasing hormone)
4. Tissue resistance to thyroid hormone: rare

DIAGNOSIS

DIFFERENTIAL DIAGNOSIS

- Depression
- Dementia from other causes
- Systemic disorders (e.g., nephrotic syndrome, congestive heart failure, amyloidosis)

LABORATORY TESTS

- Increased TSH: TSH may be normal if patient has secondary or tertiary hypothyroidism, is receiving dopamine or corticosteroids, or the level is obtained after severe illness
- Decreased free T_4
- Other common laboratory abnormalities: hyperlipidemia, hyponatremia, and anemia
- Increased antimicrosomal and antithyroglobulin antibody titers: useful when autoimmune thyroiditis is suspected as the cause of the hypothyroidism
- Fig. E1H-91, *C* describes a strategy for the laboratory evaluation of patients with suspected hypothyroidism

TREATMENT

NONPHARMACOLOGIC THERAPY

Patients should be educated regarding hypothyroidism and its possible complications. Patients should also be instructed about the need for lifelong treatment and monitoring of their thyroid abnormality.

ACUTE GENERAL Rx

Start replacement therapy with levothyroxine (L-thyroxine) 25 to 100 μg/day, depending on the patient's age and the severity of the disease. Physiologic combinations of L-thyroxine plus liothyronine do not offer any objective advantage over L-thyroxine alone. The levothyroxine dose may be

increased every 6 to 8 wk, depending on the clinical response and serum TSH level. Elderly patients and patients with coronary artery disease should be started with 12.5 to 25 μg/day (higher doses may precipitate angina). The average maintenance dose of levothyroxine is 1.7 μg/kg/day (100 to 150 μg/day in adults). The elderly may require <1 μg/kg/day, whereas children generally require higher doses (up to 3 to 4 μg/kg/day). Pregnant patients also have increased requirements. Estrogen therapy may also increase the need for thyroxine. Women with hypothyroidism should increase their levothyroxine dose by approximately 30% as soon as pregnancy is confirmed. Close monitoring of serum thyrotropin levels and adjustment of levothyroxine dose is recommended throughout pregnancy. Table E1H-71 summarizes conditions that alter levothyroxine requirements.

CHRONIC Rx

- Periodic monitoring of TSH level is an essential part of treatment. Patients should be evaluated initially with office visit and TSH levels every 6 to 8 wk until the patient is clinically euthyroid and the TSH level is normalized. The frequency of subsequent visits and TSH measurement can then be decreased to every 6 to 12 mo. Pregnant patients should be checked every trimester.
- For monitoring therapy in patients with central hypothyroidism, measurement of serum free thyroxine (free T_4 level) is appropriate and should be maintained in the upper half of the normal range.

REFERRAL

Admission to the hospital intensive care unit is recommended in all patients with myxedema coma. Additional information on the diagnosis and treatment of this life-threatening complication of hypothyroidism is available under "Myxedema Coma" in Section I.

PEARLS & CONSIDERATIONS

COMMENTS

Subclinical hypothyroidism occurs in as many as 15% of elderly patients and is characterized by an elevated serum TSH and a normal free T_4 level. Subclinical hypothyroidism is associated with an increased risk of coronary heart disease events and mortality, particularly in those with a TSH concentration of 10 mU/L or greater. Treatment is individualized. In general, replacement therapy is recommended for all patients with serum TSH >10 mU/L and with presence of goiter or thyroid autoantibodies.

EVIDENCE

Available at www.expertconsult.com

SUGGESTED READINGS

Available at www.expertconsult.com

RELATED CONTENT

Hypothyroidism (Patient Information)
Myxedema Coma (Related Key Topic)

AUTHOR: **FRED F. FERRI, M.D.**

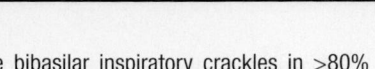

BASIC INFORMATION

DEFINITION

Idiopathic pulmonary fibrosis (IPF) is a specific form of chronic fibrosing interstitial pneumonia with histopathologic characteristics of usual interstitial pneumonia (UIP) occurring in the absence of an identifiable cause of lung injury. Clinically, it is characterized by progressive parenchymal scarring and loss of pulmonary function.

SYNONYMS

Cryptogenic fibrosing alveolitis
IPF
Pulmonary fibrosis
Usual interstitial pneumonia

ICD-10CM CODES
J84.112 Idiopathic pulmonary fibrosis

EPIDEMIOLOGY & DEMOGRAPHICS

- Incidence: 7-16 cases/100,000 persons worldwide. Clinically IPF affects >50,000 people in the U.S. and accounts for 20%-30% of interstitial lung diseases. It is the most common idiopathic interstitial pneumonia.
- Most commonly presents in 6th and 7th decades
- More common in men than women
- More common in current and past smokers
- Familial forms account for 3% to 25% of cases. Genetic variants: include mutations in surfactant protein C and telomerase as well as polymorphisms of the *MUC5B* gene.
- No distinct geographic distribution; no clear racial predilection

PHYSICAL FINDINGS & CLINICAL PRESENTATION

- Most present with gradual onset (>6 mo) of exertional dyspnea and nonproductive cough. Progressive dyspnea is usually the most prominent symptom. Cough affects up to 80% of patients with IPF, is frequently disabling, and lacks effective therapy.

- Fine bibasilar inspiratory crackles in >80% of patients, with progression upward as the disease advances.
- Clubbing is found in 25% to 50% of patients.
- Cyanosis and right heart failure (cor pulmonale) may occur late in the disease course.
- There are no extrapulmonary manifestations beyond clubbing and complications of right heart failure. Fever and wheezing are rare and suggest alternative diagnosis.
- Fig. 1I-2 is a chest radiograph showing diffuse bilateral lower lung predominant reticular opacities in a patient with IPF.

ETIOLOGY

- Unknown
- Cigarette smoking, environmental exposure, and microaspiration have been associated with IPF.
- Aberrant tissue repair and fibrosis are believed to play a greater role in the pathogenesis than generalized inflammation. Immune system activation and increased vascular permeability contribute to the underlying pathology.

DIAGNOSIS

DIFFERENTIAL DIAGNOSIS

- Sarcoidosis
- Drug-induced interstitial lung disease
- Pulmonary manifestations of collagen vascular diseases (e.g., rheumatoid arthritis [RA], systemic sclerosis)
- Hypersensitivity pneumonitis (HP)
- Occupational exposures (e.g., asbestos, silica) may cause pneumoconiosis that mimics IPF
- Other idiopathic interstitial pneumonias:
  1. Desquamative interstitial pneumonia (DIP)
  2. Respiratory bronchitis–interstitial lung disease (RB-ILD)
  3. Acute interstitial pneumonia (AIP)
  4. Nonspecific interstitial pneumonia (NSIP)
  5. Cryptogenic organizing pneumonia (COP)

WORKUP

- Almost all patients have abnormal chest radiograph at presentation, with bilateral reticular opacities most prominent in the periphery and lower lobes. Peripheral honeycombing may be seen.
- High-resolution CT scan (Fig. 1I-3) shows patchy peripheral reticular abnormalities with intralobular linear opacities, irregular septal thickening, subpleural honeycombing, and minimal, if any, ground-glass opacities.
- Pulmonary function testing shows restrictive pattern and reduced carbon monoxide diffusion into the lung.
- Six-minute walk test may show reduced exercise tolerance and/or exertional hypoxia.
- Laboratory abnormalities (nondiagnostic): mild anemia; increases in erythrocyte sedimentation rate, lactate dehydrogenase, C-reactive protein; low titer antinuclear antibody seen in up to 30% of patients.
- There is a limited role for bronchoalveolar lavage either in diagnosis or monitoring IPF.
- Gold standard for diagnosis is lung biopsy (open thoracotomy or video-assisted thoracoscopy). Hallmark features: heterogeneous distribution of parenchymal fibrosis against background of mild inflammation (UIP). In patients with characteristic chest CTs, lung biopsies can be avoided.
- When there is uncertainty, lung biopsy is critical to distinguish IPF from diseases with better prognosis and different treatment options.

TREATMENT

- Two newly FDA-approved oral therapies have proven efficacy in slowing disease progression.
- Pirfenidone is an antifibrotic medication without a known mechanism of action. It is taken three times a day. Its major side effects are nausea, abdominal discomfort, and photosensitivity. LFTs require periodic surveillance.

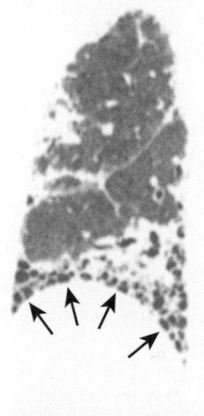 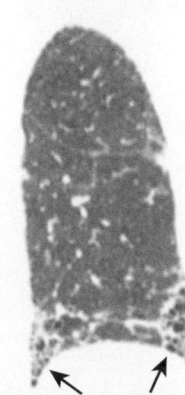

FIGURE 1I-3 Pulmonary fibrosis, honeycombing, and a usual interstitial pneumonia (UIP) pattern in idiopathic pulmonary fibrosis (IPF). Coronal high-resolution computed tomography reconstruction shows honeycombing (*arrows*) with a basal and subpleural predominance. This is typical of a UIP pattern. (Webb WR, Brant WE, Major NM: *Fundamentals of body CT*, ed 4, Philadelphia, 2015, Saunders.)

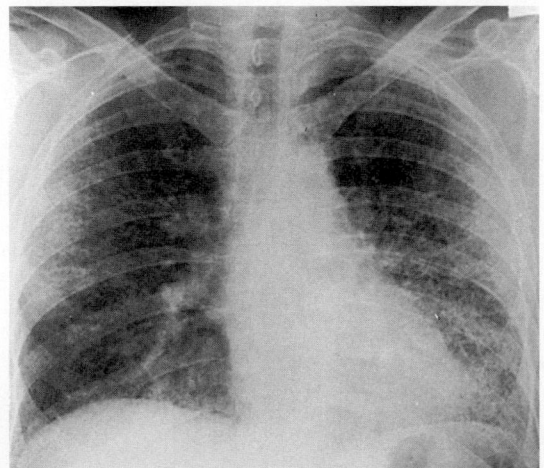

FIGURE 1I-2 Chest radiograph shows diffuse bilateral lower lung predominant reticular opacities in a patient with idiopathic pulmonary fibrosis (IPF). (From Mason RJ: *Murray & Nadel's textbook of respiratory medicine,* ed 5, Philadelphia, 2010, Saunders.)

Diseases and Disorders

- Nintedanib is a tyrosine kinase inhibitor taken twice daily. Its major side effect is diarrhea, which often resolves. LFTs also need to be followed.
- Additional new therapies are being investigated and are in phase I or II testing.
- In patients with advanced disease, treatment options include supportive care (pulmonary rehabilitation, supplemental oxygen, influenza and pneumococcal vaccination) and potential lung transplantation.
- Treatment of asymptomatic gastroesophageal reflux may be reasonable given association between pulmonary fibrosis and reflux or microaspiration.
- Lung transplantation is the only therapy shown to prolong survival in IPF. Posttransplant 5-yr survival for IPF patients is approximately 50% to 60%. Median survival time is longer after bilateral lung transplantation than single lung transplantation but is associated with more complications during the first year.
- Acute exacerbation of IPF, defined as worsening dyspnea (<1 mo), the presence of new opacities on radiograph, and the lack of evidence of infection, has a yearly incidence of 10% to 20%. Progressive respiratory failure may require mechanical ventilation. Treatment often includes high-dose corticosteroids and broad-spectrum antibiotics, although the efficacy of this approach is unproven and questionable.

DISPOSITION

- Spontaneous remissions do not occur.
- Natural history includes progressive loss of pulmonary function.
- There is an increased risk of lung cancer.
- Mean survival after the diagnosis of biopsy-confirmed IPF is 4 to 5 yr, although with new therapies available, survival is less defined.
- Respiratory failure is the most common cause of death.

REFERRAL

- To pulmonologist for review of abnormal chest imaging and establishing diagnosis
- Early referral for lung transplant

PEARLS & CONSIDERATIONS

- The course is progressive, with a high mortality rate. The most common cause of death in IPF is respiratory failure.
- Critical to differentiate IPF from other interstitial lung diseases because prognosis and response to treatment differ.

- Two new oral therapies shown to slow disease progression were recently approved. Additional novel treatments are being investigated.[1]

EVIDENCE

Available at www.expertconsult.com

SUGGESTED READINGS

Available at www.expertconsult.com

RELATED CONTENT

Idiopathic Pulmonary Fibrosis (Patient Information)

AUTHOR: **PETER LACAMERA, M.D.**

[1]Peljto AL et al: Association between the MUC5B promoter polymorphism and survival in patients with idiopathic pulmonary fibrosis, *JAMA* 309(21):2232-2239, 2013.

BASIC INFORMATION

DEFINITION

Immunoglobulin A (IgA) nephropathy is a proliferative glomerulonephritis associated with predominant deposition of IgA in the mesangium. The diagnostic hallmark of IgA nephropathy (IgAN) is predominance of IgA immune complex deposits, either alone or with IgG, IgM, or both in the glomerular mesangium, typically with complement component C3.

SYNONYM

Berger's disease
IgAN

ICD-10CM CODES
N02.8 IgA nephropathy
N02.1 IgA nephropathy with glomerular
      lesion, focal and segmental hyalinosis
      or sclerosis
N02.3 IgA nephropathy with glomerular
      lesion, mesangial proliferative (diffuse)
N02.5 IgA nephropathy with glomerular
      lesion, membrane proliferative (diffuse)

EPIDEMIOLOGY & DEMOGRAPHICS

INCIDENCE: IgAN is the most common primary glomerular disease worldwide. The annual incidence of IgAN in the United States is about 1 to 4 cases per 100,000 person-years, with a very low incidence in Africa and a higher incidence in East Asia. In Japan, the incidence is 10 times more frequent than in the United States. In Europe, there is a south-to-north increase in incidence, with populations in Nordic countries with higher risk than southern Europeans.

PREVALENCE: Prevalence data in the general population is demonstrated by one Finnish study that showed renal IgA deposition consistent with nephropathy in 1.3% of all autopsies. The prevalence rate by kidney biopsy is lower in the United States (20%) compared with Asian countries (40%). Lower rates could be biased by a conservative approach adopted by United States nephrologists who are reluctant to perform kidney biopsies in asymptomatic patients with minimal renal abnormalities.

PREDOMINANT SEX AND AGE: IgAN is most prevalent in the second and third decades of life with a male/female ratio of 2:1 in the United States.

GENETICS: Galactose-deficient IgA1 in the serum is a known heritable trait in diverse racial and ethnic groups and stems from a bone marrow defect. This disorder is characterized by galactose-deficient IgA1 mesangial deposits and its genetic predisposition is delineated by the 75% of IgAN patients who manifest elevated galactose-deficient IgA1 serum levels. Genome-wide association studies have identified multiple susceptibility loci.

RISK FACTORS: Disease development: IgAN is more common in males and has a higher association in Asians, whites, and Native Americans; it is rarely seen in African Americans.

Renal outcomes: Major risk factors and predictors of poor renal outcomes are older age, hypertension, proteinuria >1 g/day, and decreased GFR at diagnosis. Lower hemoglobin and albumin are also poor outcome risk factors. Renal histologic risk factors for poor renal outcomes include increased mesangial cellularity, segmental glomerulosclerosis, and tubular atrophy and interstitial fibrosis.

PHYSICAL FINDINGS & CLINICAL PRESENTATION

- Whereas 75% of children and young adults present with macroscopic hematuria often associated with upper respiratory infection or GI illness, older adults present primarily with microscopic hematuria, proteinuria, and hypertension.
- Loin pain may be associated with macroscopic hematuria (loin pain hematuria syndrome).
- Physical findings are usually unremarkable, except for hypertension in 20% to 30% of patients with chronic disease and edema in the 5% of patients with nephrotic range.
- Nephrotic range proteinuria is uncommon
- IgAN presents as acute kidney injury caused by hemoglobin toxicity from macroscopic hematuria in 5% of patients and as chronic kidney disease in 10% to 20% of patients.

ETIOLOGY

- Most cases are idiopathic. Henoch-Schönlein purpura may represent a vasculitic and systemic form of IgAN.
- Secondary causes of IgAN include hepatitis B; alcoholic cirrhosis; celiac disease; inflammatory bowel disease; psoriasis; sarcoidosis; cystic fibrosis; cancer of the lungs, larynx, or pancreas; HIV infection; systemic lupus erythematosus; rheumatoid arthritis; diabetic nephropathy; Sjögren's syndrome; and Reiter's syndrome.
- Fig. 1I-4 illustrates the pathogenesis of IgAN.

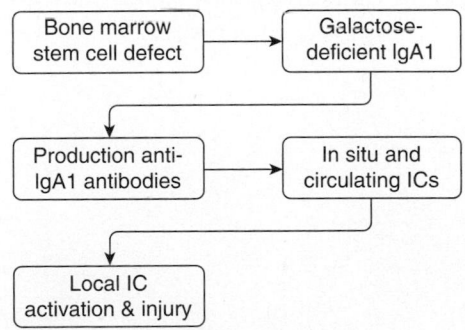

FIGURE 1I-4 Pathogenesis of IgA nephropathy.

DIAGNOSIS

DIFFERENTIAL DIAGNOSIS

The differential diagnosis includes the glomerular hematuric diseases.
- Henoch-Schönlein purpura.
- Hereditary nephritis.
- Thin glomerular basement membrane disease.
- Lupus nephritis.
- Vasculitis
- Poststreptococcal nephritis.
- Secondary causes associated with IgAN mentioned above.

WORKUP

- The diagnosis is suspected on the basis of clinical history and laboratory data. Episodes of gross hematuria with upper respiratory infections, urinalysis revealing worsening hematuria and RBC casts, and negative serologies for other causes of glomerulonephritis (e.g., lupus and vasculitis) are highly suspicious for the diagnosis. Although serum IgA levels are elevated in 50% of patients, testing sensitivity and specificity are low, and the diagnosis is confirmed by renal biopsy revealing mesangial IgA deposition.
- Prognosis is excellent with normal function and low proteinuria, so renal biopsy is restricted to patients with sustained proteinuria >1 g/day or worsening renal function

LABORATORY TESTS

- Urinalysis dipstick and sediment examination demonstrate protein, RBCs, and RBC casts.
- Serum creatinine may be elevated.
- Urine protein-to-creatinine ratios demonstrate degree of proteinuria.
- Serum IgA is elevated in only 50% of patients and has little clinical utility.

TREATMENT

Initially considered a benign disorder, IgAN is currently considered a common cause of kidney failure for which there is no specific treatment.

NONPHARMACOLOGIC THERAPY

- Moderate dietary protein restriction.
- Discourage smoking.

ACUTE AND CHRONIC GENERAL Rx

- Aggressive therapy for hypertension, preferably with angiotensin-converting enzyme inhibitors (ACEIs) or angiotensin II receptor blockers (ARBs). Goal blood pressure is <130/80 mm Hg if proteinuria is >1 g/day. Otherwise, 140/90 mmHg
- Patients with recurrent gross hematuria or isolated microscopic hematuria, no or minimal proteinuria (<1 g/day), normal blood pressure, and normal kidney function should only be monitored every 6 to 12 mo to assess disease progression. Fish oil should be considered.
- If bouts of recurrent macroscopic hematuria are associated with tonsillitis, tonsillectomy may benefit these patients, but this treatment modality is controversial.
- Patients with persistent proteinuria >1 g/day with or without hypertension are treated with ACEIs or ARBs. Glucocorticoid steroids are reserved for patients with persistent proteinuria >1 g/day despite ACEI and/or ARB administration and fish oil after 6 months.
- Patients with nephrotic syndrome, preserved kidney function, and minimal change in dis-

ease are treated with glucocorticoids for a 6-mo course.
- Patients with acute, severe kidney injury or rapidly progressive glomerulonephritis without chronic changes on biopsy are treated with glucocorticoids and cyclophosphamide for the initial 2-3 mo followed by glucocorticoids and azathioprine for 2 years as maintenance therapy.
- Patients with acute kidney injury require kidney biopsy to rule out acute tubular necrosis, which only needs supportive therapy, from crescentic IgAN, which needs aggressive medical management.
- Kidney transplantation is the treatment of choice for end-stage renal disease (ESRD). Although the recurrence rate of IgA in the transplanted kidney is 50%, allograft loss caused by recurrent IgAN is just 5%.
- Statins are indicated for all IgAN patients with dyslipidemia, hypertension, and other cardiovascular risks.
- Role of mycophenolate and plasmapheresis is undefined because of a lack of evidence.

COMPLEMENTARY & ALTERNATIVE MEDICINE

The role of fish oil is controversial. One large, randomized, placebo-controlled study showed benefit, but other small, randomized studies showed no benefit. The recommendation is if the patient has mild disease, leave it as an option for the patient, but an expert consensus group recommends fish oil along with ACEI/ARBs if proteinuria >1 g/day.

DISPOSITION/PROGNOSIS

- Complete remission occurs in <10% of patients.

- End-stage renal disease (ESRD) develops in 15% to 20% of patients within 10 years of onset and in 20% to 40% of patients within 20 years. Prognostic markers in IgAN are described in Box 1I-1.
- Poor prognostic indicators include hypertension, extent of renal insufficiency, extent of proteinuria, and certain histologic changes seen in renal biopsy (e.g., crescents, increased mesangial cells, glomerulosclerosis, and tubulointerstitial fibrosis or atrophy).
- Although not yet in commercial use, increased serum levels of glycan-specific IgG antibodies are predictive of risk of progression to ESRD or death, and increased serum levels of galactose-deficient IgA1 are correlated with risk of deterioration in kidney function.

REFERRAL

Patients with suspected IgAN are commonly referred to nephrologists for diagnosis and treatment, typically presenting with gross hematuria and urinalysis showing an active urinary sediment.

PEARLS & CONSIDERATIONS

COMMENTS

- Gross hematuria (red urine) is uncommon with intrinsic kidney disorders but is typically manifested in IgAN and cyst rupture in ADPKD.
- IgAN is not an entirely benign condition, even if microhematuria is the only clinical presentation, with up to 40% of patients reaching ESRD in 20 years.

BOX 1I-1 Prognostic Markers in IgA Nephropathy

Clinical
Poor prognosis
- Increasing age
- Severity of proteinuria
- Hypertension (increased systolic blood pressure)
- Renal impairment (decreased GFR)
- Decreased serum albumin
- Decreased hemoglobin
- Persistent microscopic hematuria

Good prognosis
- Recurrent macroscopic hematuria

Histopathologic (Oxford Classification)
Poor prognosis
- Increased mesangial cellularity
- Segmental glomerulosclerosis
- Tubular atrophy/interstitial fibrosis
- Crescents

No impact on prognosis
- Endocapillary hypercellularity

From Cancetta PA, et al: *Clin J Am Soc Nephrol* 9:617, 2014 and Jicheng L, et al: *Am J Kidney Dis* 62(5):891, 2013.

- Episodes of gross hematuria occurring with upper respiratory infections is a classic presentation for IgAN.

SUGGESTED READINGS

Available at www.expertconsult.com

AUTHOR: **PAUL S. KELLERMAN, M.D.**

BASIC INFORMATION

DEFINITION

Immune thrombocytopenic purpura (ITP) is an autoimmune disorder in which antibody-coated or immune complex–coated platelets are destroyed prematurely by the reticuloendothelial system, resulting in peripheral thrombocytopenia. In primary ITP the thrombocytopenia is isolated, whereas in secondary ITP the condition is associated with other disorders (e.g., SLE, HIV, CLL, lymphomas).

ICD-10CM CODES
D69.3 Immune thrombocytopenic purpura

EPIDEMIOLOGY & DEMOGRAPHICS

INCIDENCE: Primary ITP incidence is 10 in 100,000 adults, 5 in 100,000 children.
PREVALENCE: Five to 10 cases per 100,000 persons.
PREDOMINANT SEX: 72% of patients >10 yr are female; in children, males and females are affected equally.
PREDOMINANT AGE: Children ages 2 to 4 yr and young women (70% are < 40 yr).

PHYSICAL FINDINGS & CLINICAL PRESENTATION

The presentation of ITP is different in children and adults:
- Children generally present with sudden onset of bruising and petechiae from severe thrombocytopenia.
- In adults the presentation is insidious; a history of prolonged purpura may be present; many patients are diagnosed incidentally on the basis of automated laboratory tests that now routinely include platelet counts.
- The physical examination may be entirely normal.
- Patients with severe thrombocytopenia may have petechiae, purpura, epistaxis, or heme-positive stool from gastrointestinal bleeding. Life-threatening bleeding is uncommon and generally confined to patients with platelets <10,000 per cubic mm.
- Splenomegaly is unusual; its presence should alert to the possibility of other etiologies of thrombocytopenia.
- The presence of dysmorphic features (skeletal anomalies, auditory abnormalities) may indicate a congenital disorder as the cause of the thrombocytopenia.

ETIOLOGY

Increased platelet destruction caused by autoantibodies to platelet-membrane antigens. Hundreds of medications can cause thrombocytopenia. Drugs commonly implicated are quinidine, heparin, antibiotics (linezolid, vancomycin, sulfonamides, rifampin), platelet inhibitors (tirofiban, abciximab, eptifibatide), cimetidine, NSAIDs, thiazide diuretics, antirheumatic agents (gold salts, penicillamine), acetaminophen, and chemotherapeutic agents (cyclosporine, fludarabine, oxaliplatin).

DIAGNOSIS

DIFFERENTIAL DIAGNOSIS

- Falsely low platelet count (resulting from EDTA-dependent or cold-dependent agglutinins).
- Viral infections (e.g., HIV, hepatitis C, mononucleosis, rubella).
- Drug-induced (e.g., heparin, quinidine, sulfonamides).
- Hypersplenism resulting from liver disease.
- Myelodysplastic and lymphoproliferative disorders.
- Pregnancy, hypothyroidism.
- SLE, TTP, hemolytic-uremic syndrome.
- Congenital thrombocytopenia (e.g., Fanconi's syndrome, May-Hegglin anomaly, Bernard-Soulier syndrome)

LABORATORY TESTS

- Complete blood count, platelet count, and peripheral smear: platelets are decreased. The peripheral smear should show large platelets and no schistocytes (Fig. E1I-5). Red blood cells and white blood cells have a normal morphology. Unless the patient has been bleeding, the hemoglobin level and leukocyte count should be normal.
- Additional tests may be ordered to exclude other causes of the thrombocytopenia when clinically indicated (e.g., HIV, ANA, TSH [hypothyroidism and hyperthyroidism can cause thrombocytopenia], liver enzymes, Hep C ab).
- The direct assay for the measurement of platelet-bound antibodies has an estimated positive predictive value of 80% to 83%. A negative test cannot be used to rule out the diagnosis.

IMAGING STUDIES

CT scan of abdomen/pelvis in patients with splenomegaly to exclude other disorders causing thrombocytopenia

TREATMENT

NONPHARMACOLOGIC THERAPY

- Minimize activity to prevent injury or bruising (e.g., contact sports should be avoided).
- Stop any potentially offending drugs (see "Etiology"). Avoid medications that increase the risk of bleeding (e.g., aspirin and other NSAIDs).

ACUTE GENERAL Rx

- Treatment varies with the platelet count, patient's age, and bleeding status (Fig. I1-6).
- Observation and frequent monitoring of platelet count are needed in asymptomatic patients with platelet counts >30,000/mm^3.
- Oral prednisone 1 mg/kg/day in a tapering dose generally for 4 to 6 wk is the most common initial regimen. Methylprednisolone 30 mg/kg/day IV infused over a period of 20 to 30 min (maximum dose of 1 g/day for 2 or 3 days) plus IV immunoglobulin (1 g/kg/day for 2 or 3 days) and infusion of platelets should be given to patients with neurologic symptoms, internal bleeding, or those undergoing emergency surgery.
- Prednisone continued until the platelet count is normalized then slowly tapered off is indicated in adults with platelet counts <20,000/mm^3 and those who have counts <50,000/mm^3 and significant mucous membrane bleeding. Response rates range from 50% to 75%, and most responses occur within the first 3 wk. Oral dexamethasone at a dosage of 40 mg/day for 4 consecutive days has also been reported to induce a high response rate (85%). Continuation of corticosteroids is limited by long-term complications associated with its use (osteoporosis, weight gain, opportunistic infections, emotional lability)
- IV immunoglobulin (0.8 to 1.0 g/kg) is used in patients who have not responded to corticosteroids and often in pregnant patients. It rapidly increases platelet count in nearly 80% of patients, but its effect is transient. Anti-D immunoglobulin, a pooled IgG product derived from the plasma of Rh(D)-negative donors, is also effective. It can be given only to patients who are Rh(D) positive. Usual dose is 50 to 75 mcg/kg.
- Rituximab, a monoclonal antibody directed against the CD20 antigen, is used as a second-line agent. Usual dose is 375 mg/m^2 weekly × 4 wk.
- Splenectomy is considered second-line treatment and should be considered in adults with platelet count <20,000/mm^3 after 6 wk of medical treatment or after 6 mo if more than 10 to 20 mg of prednisone per day is required to maintain a platelet count >30,000/mm^3. In children, splenectomy is generally reserved for persistent thrombocytopenia (>1 yr) and clinically significant bleeding. Appropriate immunizations (pneumococcal vaccine in adults and children, *Haemophilus influenzae* vaccine, meningococcal vaccine in children) should be administered before splenectomy.
- Additional second-line agents are thrombopoietin receptor agonists, azathioprine, cyclosporin A, cyclophosphamide, danazol, dapsone, mycophenolate mofetil, and *Vinca* alkaloids. Romiplostim, a recombinant fusion protein, and the oral thrombopoietin-receptor agonist eltrombopag are effective in increasing platelet count in adult patients with chronic ITP refractory to corticosteroids and/or splenectomy. The American Society of Hematology guidelines revised in 2011 recommend the use of thrombopoietin-receptor agonists for adult patients with ITP at risk for bleeding, who have a contraindication to splenectomy, or do not have a response to at least one other therapy.
- Platelet transfusion is needed only in case of life-threatening hemorrhage.
- Third-line therapy for ITP consists of combination chemotherapy and hematopoietic stem cell transplantation.

Immune Thrombocytopenic Purpura (PTG)

DISPOSITION

- More than 80% of children have a complete remission within 8 wk.
- In adults, the course of the disease is chronic; only 5% of adults have spontaneous remission.

- The principal cause of death from ITP is intracranial hemorrhage (1% of children, 5% of adults).

SUGGESTED READINGS

Available at www.expertconsult.com

Immune Thrombocytopenic Purpura (Patient Information).

AUTHOR: **FRED F. FERRI, M.D.**

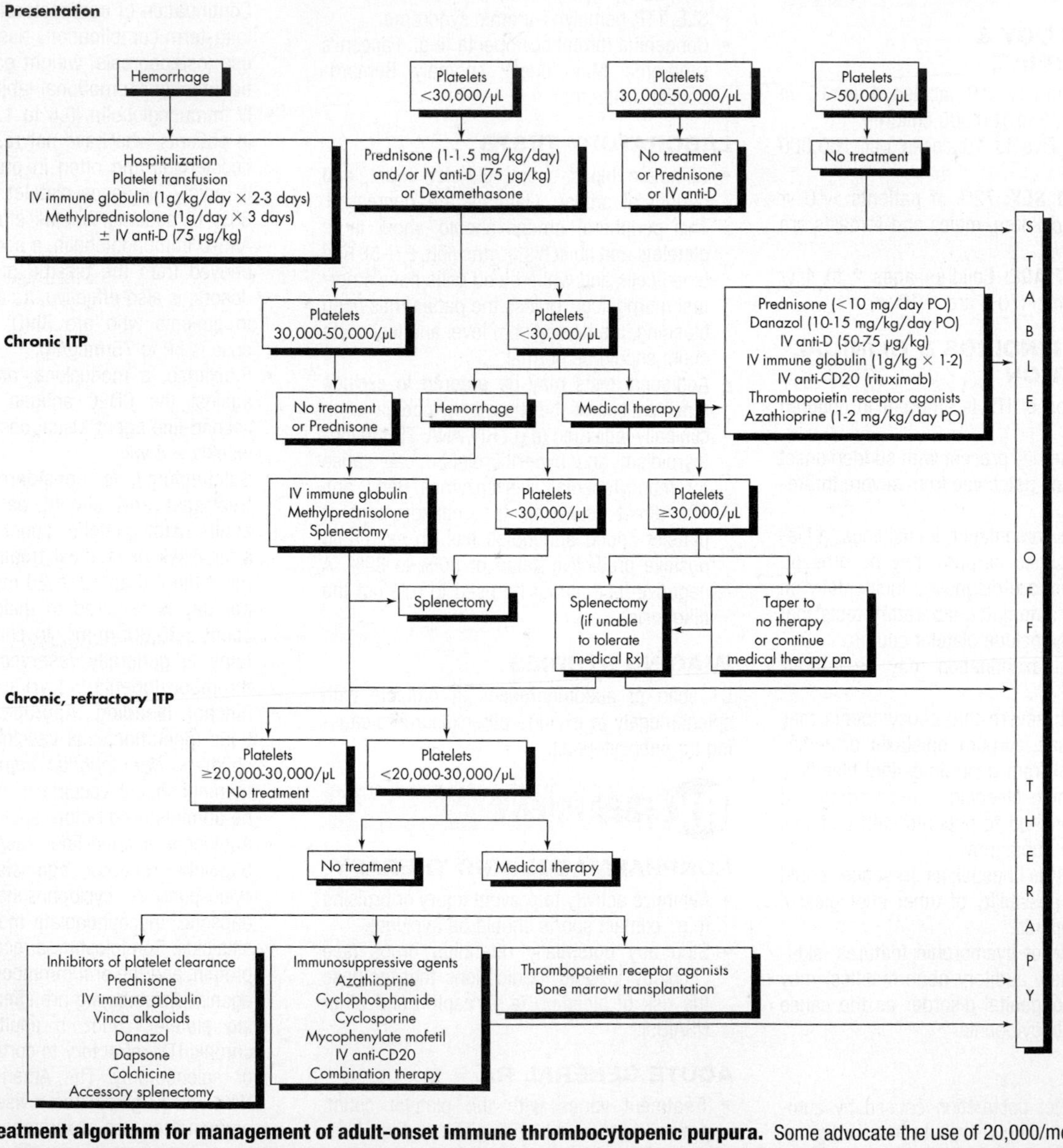

FIGURE 1I-6 Treatment algorithm for management of adult-onset immune thrombocytopenic purpura. Some advocate the use of 20,000/mcL as a guideline for therapy. The decision to treat patients with platelet counts lower than 50,000/mcL is based in part on evidence of bleeding, a history of bleeding, comorbid risk factors, lifestyle, and tolerance of therapy. There is no consensus as to duration of steroid therapy. The use of anti-D as initial therapy is appropriate only for Rh(D)-positive individuals who are not markedly anemic or hemolyzing. The goal of medical therapy is to attain a hemostatic platelet count, generally >20,000 to 30,000/mcL. The threshold for treatment depends on comorbid risk factors for bleeding and risk of trauma. Higher platelet counts may be appropriate for surgery or after trauma. Medications can be used individually, but combinations of azathioprine and danazol (or corticosteroids) may provide added benefit and allow lower doses to be used. Intravenous immunoglobulin (IVIG) and anti-D are generally reserved for severe thrombocytopenia unresponsive to oral agents. The decision to proceed to splenectomy depends on intensity of therapy required, tolerance to side effects, risk of surgery, and patient preference. IVIG and/or methylprednisolone may help to increase the platelet count immediately before splenectomy. Laparoscopic and open splenectomy have comparable outcomes. The decision to treat patients who have platelet counts lower than 20,000 to 30,000/mcL after splenectomy involves an assessment of the risk of hemorrhage versus the side effects of each form of therapy. (Modified from Hoffman R et al: *Hematology, basic principles and practice,* ed 5, Philadelphia, 2009, Churchill Livingstone.)

BASIC INFORMATION

DEFINITION

Impetigo is a superficial skin infection generally caused by *Staphylococcus aureus* and/or *Streptococcus* spp.

Common presentations are bullous impetigo (generally caused by staphylococcal disease) and nonbullous impetigo (from streptococcal infection and possible staphylococcal infection); the bullous form is caused by an epidermolytic toxin produced at the site of infection.

SYNONYMS

Impetigo vulgaris
Pyoderma
Impetigo contagiosa
Bullous impetigo

ICD-10CM CODES
L01.00 Impetigo, unspecified
L01.01 Non-bullous impetigo
L01.02 Bockhart's impetigo
L01.03 Bullous impetigo
L01.09 Other impetigo

EPIDEMIOLOGY & DEMOGRAPHICS

Impetigo is the most common bacterial skin infection in children 2 to 5 yr of age. Bullous impetigo accounts for 30% of cases and nonbullous for 70% of cases. Impetigo is most common in temperate zones, mostly during the summer in hot, humid weather. Common sources for children are dirty fingers, pets, and other children in school or day care centers. Impetigo often complicates insect bites, pediculosis, scabies, eczema, and poison ivy.

- Bullous impetigo is most common in infants and children. The nonbullous form is most common in children ages 2 to 5 yr with poor hygiene in warm climates.
- The overall incidence of acute nephritis with impetigo varies between 2% and 5%.

PHYSICAL FINDINGS & CLINICAL PRESENTATION

- Nonbullous impetigo begins as a single red macule or papule that quickly becomes a vesicle. Rupture of the vesicle produces an

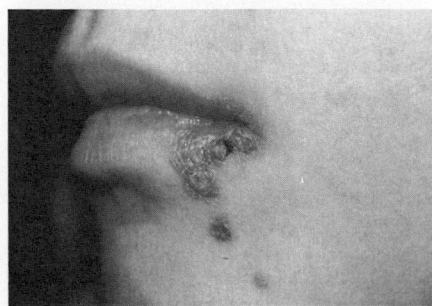

FIGURE 1I-7 Multiple crusted and oozing lesions of impetigo. (From Kliegman RM et al: *Nelson textbook of pediatrics*, ed 19, Philadelphia, 2011, Saunders.)

erosion of which the contents dry to form honey-colored crusts. Multiple lesions with golden yellow crusts and weeping areas are often found on the skin around the nose, mouth (Figure 1I-7), and limbs.
- Bullous impetigo is manifested by the presence of vesicles that enlarge rapidly to form bullae with contents that vary from clear to cloudy. There is subsequent collapse of the center of the bullae; the peripheral areas may retain fluid, and a honey-colored crust may appear in the center. As the lesions enlarge and become contiguous with the others, a scaling border replaces the fluid-filled rim; there is minimal erythema surrounding the lesions.
- Regional lymphadenopathy is most common with nonbullous impetigo.
- Constitutional symptoms are generally absent.

ETIOLOGY

- *S. aureus* coagulase positive is the dominant microorganism (50%–70% of cases).
- *S. pyogenes* (group A β-hemolytic streptococci): M-T serotypes of this organism associated with acute nephritis are 2, 49, 55, 57, and 60. Group B Steptococci are associated with newborn impetigo.

DIAGNOSIS

DIFFERENTIAL DIAGNOSIS

- Atopic dermatitis.
- Herpes simplex infection.
- Ecthyma.
- Folliculitis.
- Dermatitis herpetiformis.
- Insect bites.
- Scabies, pediculosis.
- Tinea corporis, cutaneous candidiasis.
- Pemphigus vulgaris and bullous pemphigoid.
- Chickenpox.
- Thermal burns.
- Contact dermatitis.
- Steven Johnson syndrome, Sweet syndrome.

WORKUP

Diagnosis is clinical.

LABORATORY TESTS

- Generally not necessary.
- Gram stain and culture and sensitivity to confirm the diagnosis when the clinical presentation is unclear.
- Sedimentation rate parallel to activity of the disease.
- Increased anti-DNAse B and antihyaluronidase.
- Urinalysis revealing hematuria with erythrocyte casts and proteinuria in patients with acute nephritis (most frequently occurring in children between ages 2 and 4 yr in the southern part of the United States).
- If recurrent staphylococcal impetigo develops, a culture of the anterior nares should be done to rule out a carrier state.

TREATMENT

NONPHARMACOLOGIC THERAPY

Remove crusts by soaking with wet cloth compresses (crusts block the penetration of antibacterial creams).

GENERAL Rx

- Application of 2% mupirocin ointment tid for 10 days or retapamulin 1% applied bid for 5 days to the affected area or until all lesions have cleared.
- Oral antibiotics are used in severe cases: commonly used agents are dicloxacillin 250 mg qid for 7 to 10 days, cephalexin 250 mg qid for 7 to 10 days, azithromycin 500 mg on day 1, 250 mg on days 2 through 5, amoxicillin/clavulanate 500 mg q8h.
- Impetigo can be prevented by prompt application of mupirocin or triple-antibiotic ointment (bacitracin, Polysporin, and neomycin) to sites of skin trauma.
- Patients who are carriers of *S. aureus* in their nares should be treated with mupirocin ointment applied to their nares bid for 5 days or a 10-day course of rifampin, 600 mg/day, combined with dicloxacillin (for MSSA) or TMP-SMX (for MRSA).
- Fingernails should be kept short, and patients should be advised not to scratch any lesions to avoid spread of infection.

DISPOSITION

Most cases of impetigo resolve promptly with appropriate treatment. Both bullous and nonbullous forms of impetigo heal without scarring.

REFERRAL

Nephrology referral in patients with acute nephritis

PEARLS & CONSIDERATIONS

COMMENTS

- Patients should be instructed on use of antibacterial soaps and avoidance of sharing of towels and washcloths because impetigo is extremely contagious.
- Children attending day care should be removed until 48 to 72 hr after initiation of antibiotic treatment.
- Bullous impetigo may be an early manifestation of HIV infection.

SUGGESTED READINGS

Available online at www.expertconsult.com

RELATED CONTENT

Impetigo (Patient Information)

AUTHOR: **FRED F. FERRI, M.D.**

Diseases and Disorders

BASIC INFORMATION

DEFINITION

Inclusion body myositis (IBM) is the most common myopathy with onset after the age of 50 yr. The idiopathic inflammatory myopathies include polymyositis (PM), dermatomyositis (DM), and inclusion body myositis and are associated with inflammatory movement of muscle fibers and recurrent weakness. Although classified among the inflammatory myopathies, its underlying pathophysiology has not yet been delineated.

SYNONYMS

IBM

ICD-10CM CODES
G72.41 Inclusion body myositis [IBM]

EPIDEMIOLOGY & DEMOGRAPHICS

INCIDENCE: 0.22 to 0.79 cases/100,000 persons; uncommon in Asians and African Americans
PREVALENCE: 0.5 to 7.1 cases/100,000 persons
PREDOMINANT SEX: Male/female ratio 1.3:1
PREDOMINANT AGE: 87% older than 50 yr
PEAK INCIDENCE: Seventh decade
RISK FACTORS: None known
GENETICS: Less than 10% of cases familial

PHYSICAL FINDINGS & CLINICAL PRESENTATION

- Insidious onset of slowly progressive proximal leg and distal arm weakness.
- Time to diagnosis from symptom onset often lags by years to a decade.
- Functional loss of strength in the legs most often precedes arm weakness.
- The cardinal clinical features include early weakness and atrophy of quadriceps muscles (difficulty climbing stairs, rising from chairs, and getting out of cars) along with wrist and finger flexor muscles (difficulty grasping, opening jars, and turning doorknobs). Ankle dorsiflexion weakness may also be prominent leading to foot drop and tripping.
- When examining strength, side to side asymmetries are seen in one or more muscle groups in the majority of patients. This stands in contrast to the symmetrical, proximal involvement of polymyositis and most muscular dystrophies.
- Dysphagia and/or mild facial weakness are present in over half of cases. Dysphagia may be the presenting symptom.
- Although sensory symptoms are usually lacking, one third have evidence for peripheral neuropathy on physical examination and/or electrodiagnostic testing.
- 10% to 15% of patients have concomitant autoimmune disorders such as systemic lupus erythematosus, Sjögren's syndrome, scleroderma, sarcoidosis, or thrombocytopenia. However, unlike polymyositis and dermatomyositis, IBM does not portend an increased risk of heart or lung disease nor cancer.

ETIOLOGY

The pathogenesis of IBM is not known. Inflammatory, degenerative, viral and prion etiologies have been postulated, but none substantiated.

 **DIAGNOSIS**

DIFFERENTIAL DIAGNOSIS

- Polymyositis (Table E1I-1)
- Dermatomyositis
- Amyotrophic lateral sclerosis
- Late-onset muscular dystrophies
- Acid maltase deficiency

WORKUP

- Thorough neurologic examination with emphasis on the motor exam is important.
- Nerve conduction studies should be performed to exclude other causes and EMG to document a myopathy.
- The diagnosis of definite IBM requires the following features on muscle biopsy (Fig. E1I-8): (1) inflammation, (2) inflammatory cells invading healthy muscle fibers, (3) vacuoles, and (4) amyloid deposits by Congo red staining, TDP-43 sarcoplasmic staining, or tubulofilaments on electron microscopy.

LABORATORY TESTS

Creatine kinase level (labs for collagen vascular diseases may be obtained after the diagnosis). A complete blood count and coagulation studies should be drawn in anticipation of the muscle biopsy.

IMAGING STUDIES

MRI may reveal atrophy and signal abnormalities in volar forearm muscle groups and quadriceps atrophy with relative preservation of the rectus femoris muscle.

 **TREATMENT**

NONPHARMACOLOGIC THERAPY

- Assistive devices for mobility such as canes, walkers, and wheelchairs are the mainstay of therapy.
- Occasionally knee orthoses or ankle-foot orthoses may improve and prolong ambulation.

ACUTE GENERAL Rx

None

CHRONIC Rx

- Experts have not found clinically significant improvement in functional strength with any pharmacologic therapy. Clinical trials of corticosteroids, methotrexate, intravenous immunoglobulin, anti-T lymphocyte globulin, etanercept, interferon β-1a, and oxandrolone have all failed to demonstrate functional improvements in limb strength.
- A short, small trial of a home exercise program demonstrated mild improvements in strength.
- IBM is generally refractory to therapy.

COMPLEMENTARY & ALTERNATIVE MEDICINE

Some patients choose to self-treat with creatine supplementation, coenzyme Q10, or lithium. There is no evidence supporting these treatments.

REFERRAL

- Patients with suspected IBM should be referred to a neurologist with subspecialty expertise in neuromuscular medicine.
- Physical therapy and occupational therapy consultations help the patient optimize ambulation and fine motor tasks, respectively.
- Speech therapy consultations can assist with symptomatic dysphagia.

PROGNOSIS

Life expectancy is not significantly altered in this late-onset, slowly progressive disorder. Some patients require wheelchair use 10 to 20 yr after disease onset.

 **PEARLS & CONSIDERATIONS**

COMMENTS

- In contrast to PM and DM, muscle weakness in IBM generally affects both distal and proximal muscles.
- A key to diagnosis rests in finding weakness of wrist and/or finger flexors (especially the deep finger flexors at the DIP joints) on examination.

PREVENTION

None known

PATIENT/FAMILY EDUCATION

Patient information and support groups can be found at: www.ninds.nih.gov/disorders/inclusion_body_myositis and http://www.myositis.org.

EBM EVIDENCE

Available at www.expertconsult.com

SUGGESTED READINGS

Available at www.expertconsult.com

AUTHOR: **MATTHEW P. WICKLUND, M.D.**

BASIC INFORMATION

DEFINITION

Fecal incontinence is defined as the involuntary loss of gas or liquid stool (minor incontinence) or the involuntary loss of solid stool (major incontinence).

SYNONYMS

Anal Incontinence
Accidental Bowel Leakage

ICD-10CM CODES
R15.9 Full incontinence of feces
F98.1 Encopresis not due to a substance or known physiological condition

EPIDEMIOLOGY & DEMOGRAPHICS

INCIDENCE: It affects 0.5% to 1.5% of the population younger than age 65, but >10% older than 65. More common in institutionalized patients.
PREVALENCE: Varies widely depending on definition used and population studied. Estimated 1/12 U.S. adults or about 18 million people. Prevalence increases with age and BMI in women.
PREDOMINANT SEX AND AGE: Slightly more common in females versus males and age >65
RISK FACTORS:
- History of urinary incontinence.
- Cognitive or behavioral dysfunction.
- Structural anorectal abnormalities (e.g., rectal prolapse, surgical trauma).
- Presence of neurologic, psychiatric disease (e.g., depression in females), or diabetes mellitus.
- Poor mobility, poor overall health, and age >70.
- Difficult childbirth with injuries to pelvic floor/obstetric injury.
- Fecal impaction from constipation or diarrhea.

PHYSICAL FINDINGS & CLINICAL PRESENTATION

- Should inspect perianal area and perform an internal digital rectal exam to evaluate for the presence of fecal material, prolapsing hemorrhoids, chemical dermatitis, scars, fistula or rectal prolapse.
- Assess for anocutaneous reflex. This may be elicited by stroking skin in each perianal quadrant (normal response is a brisk anal wink). Absent reflex is suggestive of nerve damage. Assess resting to squeezing anal tone by asking the patient to bear down.

Ask patient to strain to assess for rectal prolapse or excessive perianal descent.
ETIOLOGY:
- Usually multifactorial.
- Fecal impaction.
- Neurologic disorders:
  1. History of CVA.
  2. Multiple sclerosis.
  3. Spinal cord lesions.
  4. Diabetes mellitus.
- Anal trauma
  1. Anorectal surgery for hemorrhoids, fistula, and fissures.
  2. Vaginal delivery (anal sphincter tear, trauma to pudendal nerve).
  Radiation treatment.
- Idiopathic.

DIAGNOSIS

DIFFERENTIAL DIAGNOSIS

- Fecal encopresis.
- IBS.

WORKUP

- Requires detailed history taking that includes the onset and precipitating events, duration and severity, stool consistency and urgency. Important to evaluate for history of urinary incontinence, anorectal surgery or radiation, neurologic disorders, or prior vaginal deliveries and complete a thorough physical exam. Box E1I-2 describes a structured clinical approach to focal incontinence in older adults.
- Diagnostic workup includes anorectal manometry, endorectal ultrasound (simple and economical), MRI, proctosigmoidoscopy, defecography, pudendal nerve terminal latency, and anal electromyography (EMG).

TREATMENT

- Therapy is focused on three main approaches: medications, biofeedback, and surgery.
Medications focus on decreasing stool frequency and improving consistency, and include loperamide, diphenoxylate/atropine sulfate, methylcellulose, and anticholinergics (hyoscyamine). Phenylephrine gel may increase anal canal resting pressures.
- Solesta is a dextrananomer-hyaluronic gel that was FDA approved in 2011 for the treatment of fecal incontinence in adults who have failed conservative therapy. It consists of four 1 ml injections into the deep submucosal layer of the anal canal, about 5 mm above the dentate line. It is hypothesized that Solesta may narrow the anal canal and allow for better sphincter control.

NONPHARMACOLOGIC THERAPY

- Supportive therapy:
  1. Education, counseling, habit training.
  2. Dietary modifications (e.g., increased fiber and fluid intake, less caffeine).
  3. Modified Kegel exercises.
  4. Anal plugs (poorly tolerated).
- Biofeedback therapy:
Anal sphincter muscle training and strengthening.
- Surgery:
  1. Overlapping sphincteroplasty (most common).
  2. Anterior overlap repair (usually after obstetric trauma).
  3. Artificial anal sphincter.
  4. Colostomy (if intractable symptoms and/or failed all other therapies).
- Radiofrequency.
- Sacral nerve stimulation.
- Anal electrical stimulation.

REFERRAL

Colorectal surgery

PEARLS & CONSIDERATIONS

COMMENTS

The shame, embarrassment, and stigma associated with fecal and urinary incontinence pose significant barriers to seeking professional treatment, which results in many people who suffer from these conditions without help. Therefore, during routine office visits, asking all patients >70 yr about incontinence may be helpful.

PREVENTION

- Reduce constipation and avoid straining during bowel movements.
- Routine episiotomy is the most easily preventable risk factor for fecal incontinence in females.

PATIENT/FAMILY EDUCATION

http://digestive.niddk.nih.gov/ddiseases/pubs/fecalincontinence/index.aspx

SUGGESTED READINGS
Available at www.expertconsult.com

AUTHOR: **DAPHNE SCARAMANGAS-PLUMLEY, M.D.**

ⓘ BASIC INFORMATION

DEFINITION
Urinary incontinence is the involuntary loss of urine.

ICD-10CM CODES
R32   Unspecified urinary incontinence
N39.3   Stress incontinence (female) (male)
N39.46   Mixed incontinence
N39.49   Disorder of urinary system, unspecified
R39.81   Functional urinary incontinence

EPIDEMIOLOGY & DEMOGRAPHICS
INCIDENCE/PREVALENCE: In the general population between the ages of 15 and 64 yr, 1.5% to 5% of men and 10% to 25% of women have incontinence. In the nursing home population, 75% of the population has some degree of incontinence. Nearly 20% of children through the mid-teenage years have episodes of urinary incontinence.

CLINICAL, PSYCHOLOGICAL, & SOCIAL IMPACT
Fewer than 50% of the individuals with incontinence living in the community consult health care providers, preferring to suffer silently, turning to home remedies, commercially available absorbent materials, and supportive aids. As their condition worsens, they become depressed, sacrifice their independence, suffer from recurrent urinary tract infection and its sequelae, limit social interaction, refrain from sexual intimacy, and become homebound. In terms of costs, for all ages living in the community, it is estimated that $7 billion is spent for incontinence annually. With aging populations around the world, this cost is dramatically increasing every year.

MAJOR TYPES OF INCONTINENCE

- **Transient incontinence:** Incontinence occurring as a result or reaction to an acute medical problem affecting the lower urinary tract. Many of these problems can be reversed with treatment of the underlying problem.
- **Urge incontinence:** Involuntary loss of urine associated with an abrupt and strong desire to void. It is usually associated with involuntary detrusor contractions on urodynamic investigation. In neurologically impaired patients, the involuntary detrusor contraction is referred to as *detrusor hyperreflexia.* In neurologically normal patients, the involuntary contraction is called *detrusor instability.*
- **Stress incontinence** (Fig. 1I-9): The involuntary loss of urine with physical activities that increase abdominal pressure in the absence of a detrusor contraction or an overdistended bladder. Classification of stress incontinence:
  1. Type 0: Report of incontinence without demonstration of leakage.
  2. Type I: Incontinence in response to stress but with little descent of the bladder neck and urethra.
  3. Type II: Incontinence in response to stress with >2 cm descent of the bladder neck and urethra.
  4. Type III: Bladder neck and urethra wide open without bladder contraction; intrinsic sphincter deficiency; denervation of the urethra. The most common causes include urethral hypermobility and displacement of the bladder neck with exertion, intrinsic sphincter deficiency from failed antiincontinence surgery, prostatectomy, radiation, cord lesions, epispadias, and myelomeningocele.
- **Overflow incontinence:** Loss of urine resulting from overdistention of the bladder with resultant overflow or spilling of the urine. Causes include hypotonic-to-atonic bladder resulting from drug effect, fecal impaction, or neurologic conditions such as diabetes, spinal cord injury, surgery, or vitamin B_{12} deficiency. It is also caused by obstruction at the bladder neck and urethra. In this situation prostatism, prostatic cancer, urethral stenosis, antiincontinence surgery, pelvic prolapse, and detrusor-sphincter dyssynergia cause the incontinence.
- **Functional incontinence:** Involuntary loss of urine resulting from chronic impairments of physical and/or cognitive functioning. This is a diagnosis of exclusion. It consists of simply not getting to the toilet quickly enough due to significant mobility or cognitive impairment. The condition can sometimes be improved or cured by improving the patient's functional status, treating comorbidities, changing medications, and reducing environmental barriers.
- **Mixed stress and urge incontinence:** See Fig. 1I-9.
- **Sensory urgency incontinence:** Involuntary loss of urine as a result of decreased bladder compliance and increased intravesical pressures accompanied by severe urgency and bladder hypersensitivity without detrusor overactivity. This is seen with radiation cystitis, interstitial cystitis, eosinophilic cystitis, myelomeningocele, and radical pelvic surgery. Nephropathy can occur as a complication of this vesicoureteral reflux.
- **Sphincteric incontinence:**
  1. *Urethral hypermobility:* The basic abnormality is a weakness of pelvic floor support. Because of this weakness, during increases in abdominal pressure there is rotational descent of the vesical neck and proximal urethra. If the urethra opens concomitantly, stress urinary incontinence ensues. Urethral hypermobility is often present in women who are not incontinent. Its mere presence is not sufficient evidence to make the diagnosis of sphincteric abnormality unless incontinence is shown.
  2. *Intrinsic sphincter deficiency:* There is an intrinsic malfunction of the sphincter itself. It is characterized by an open vesical neck at rest and a low leak point pressure (<65 cm water). Urethral hypermobility and intrinsic sphincter deficiency may coexist in the same patient. Causes of intrinsic sphincter deficiency are previous pelvic surgery, antiincontinence surgery, urethral diverticulectomy, radical hysterectomy, abdominoperineal resection of the rectum, urethrotomy, Y-V plasty of the vesical neck, myelodysplasia, anterior spinal artery syndrome, lumbosacral disease, aging, and hyperestrogenism.

ⒹⓍ DIAGNOSIS

HISTORY
- History of present illness, psychosocial factors, congenital disorders, access issues for the physically challenged, neurologic disorders, and disorders pertinent to the urologic tract.

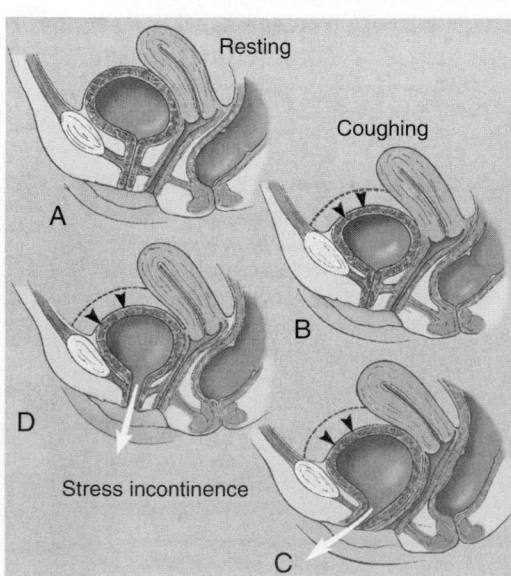

FIGURE 1I-9 A, Bladder and urethra in normal position. **B,** Intra-abdominal pressure transmitted to the bladder. **C,** Bladder and urethra in abnormal position with loss of support (hypermobile). **D,** Loss of urethral closure. (From Lipshultz LI et al. *Urology and the primary care practitioner,* ed 3, Philadelphia, 2008, Elsevier.)

I

- Review of prescription and nonprescription medications.
- Voiding diary to assess total voided volume, frequency of micturition, mean volume voided, largest single volume, diurnal distribution, nature and severity of incontinence.

WORKUP

- Physical examination including general examination, gait of the patient (neuromuscular deficits), estrogen status, vaginal examination to include the periurethral region, evaluation for cystocele, rectocele, and enterocele.
- Pelvic floor strength assessment.
- Rectal examination to assess sphincter tone and bulbocavernosus reflex.
- Neurologic examination.
- Postvoid residual check with bladder scan or catheter.

LABORATORY TESTS

Urinalysis, urine culture, urine cytology, blood urea nitrogen, creatinine.

IMAGING STUDIES

- Radiography: a KUB (kidney, ureter, and bladder) to assess bony skeleton.
- CT or intravenous pyelography (IVP) to rule out upper tract abnormalities, developmental anomalies, bladder configuration, and fistula.
- Renal ultrasound if contrast study is contraindicated.

SPECIALIZED STUDIES

Simple cystometrogram, complex urodynamics for leak point pressures and uroflowmetry, endoscopic evaluation, cystogram.

 **TREATMENT**

- The recommended approach to urinary incontinence is a stepped care plan, initiating with noninvasive behavioral modifications. In nonresponders, pharmacologic interventions and devices are tried next, and finally surgical intervention is done in those with persistent incontinence refractory to other therapies.
- Transient incontinence: treatment of underlying medical conditions and behavioral therapy to include habit training and timed voiding.
- Urge incontinence: anticholinergic and antimuscarinic agents (tolterodine, oxybutynin, trospium chloride, fesoterodine, darifenacin, solifenacin). Anticholinergics bind to muscarinic receptors in the bladder and relax detrusor smooth muscle but can cause dry mouth, constipation, confusion, and cognition abnormalities in the elderly. Other treatment modalities include biofeedback, Kegel exercises, and surgical removal of obstructing or other pathologic lesions. A recent trial comparing oral anticholinergic therapy and onabotulinum toxin A by injection shows similar reductions in the frequency of daily episodes of urgency urinary incontinence. The group receiving onabotulinum toxin A was less

likely to have dry mouth and more likely to have complete resolution of urgency urinary incontinence but higher rates of transient urinary retention and urinary tract infections. Mirabegron is a beta-3 adrenergic agonist recently FDA approved for overactive bladder. It is better tolerated than anticholinergic agents but has significant drug interactions and can cause urinary retention.

- Stress incontinence: pelvic floor muscle training (PFMT), Kegel exercises. Duloxetine improves incontinence rates and quality of life but does not cure incontinence. It can be tried if PFMT has been unsuccessful. PFMT is considered first-line therapy for stress incontinence and is also beneficial in mixed urge and stress incontinence. Midurethral-sling surgery is generally advocated when physiotherapy is unsuccessful. However, a recent trial[1] revealed that for women with stress incontinence, initial midurethral-sling surgery, compared with initial physiotherapy, results in higher rates of subjective improvement and subjective and objective cure at 1 year.
  1. Cystourethropexy (see Table E1I-2): (archaic) Burch procedure, Raz procedure, Stamey-Raz procedure, Gittes procedure, in situ transvaginal sling, pubovaginal sling with autologous or cadaver graft, laparoscopic Burch procedure, laparoscopic sling, tension-free vaginal tape.
  2. For intrinsic sphincter deficiency: bulking agents (e.g., collagen), sling, and artificial sphincter.
- Overflow incontinence: surgical removal of any obstructing lesions, clean intermittent catheterization, indwelling catheter.
- Functional incontinence: behavioral training to include habit training and timed voiding, incontinence undergarments and pads, external collecting devices, environmental manipulation.
- Mixed urgency and stress incontinence: PFMT and use of measures recommended in the management of stress and urge incontinence.

TABLE 1I-3 Transient Causes of Urinary Incontinence (DIAPPERS)

D	Delirium/confusional state
I	Infection—urinary (symptomatic)
A	Atrophic urethritis/vaginitis
P	Pharmaceuticals (diuretics, and so on)
P	Psychological, especially depression
E	Endocrine (hypercalcemia, hypokalemia, glycosuria)
R	Restricted mobility
S	Stool impaction

From Floege J et al. *Comprehensive clinical nephrology*, ed 4, Philadelphia, 2010, Saunders.

[1]Labrie J et al: Surgery versus physiotherapy for stress urinary incontinence, *N Engl J Med* 369:1124-1133, 2013.

- Sensory urgency: bladder relaxants (e.g., anticholinergics, muscle relaxants, and tricyclic antidepressants), behavior therapy to include habit training and timed voiding, cystoscopy and hydrodilation.
- Sphincteric deficiency: urethral bulking agents, sling procedure, artificial sphincter, mechanical clamp, external collection devices.
- Botox (onabotulinum toxin A injection; Allergan) has been approved for the treatment of urinary incontinence in patients with neurologic conditions (e.g., spinal cord injury) and those with multiple sclerosis who have overactive bladder.

 **PEARLS & CONSIDERATIONS**

COMMENTS

- Weight loss and exercise are helpful for urinary incontinence in obese women. Overweight and obese women with urinary incontinence also have a high prevalence of monthly fecal incontinence (16% found to be associated with low dietary fiber intake after adjustment for other known risk factors for fecal incontinence).
- Transient causes of urinary incontinence in the elderly are described in Table 1I-3.
- Other forms of incontinence:
  1. Nocturnal enuresis (ICD-9CM code: 788.3): can be caused by sphincter abnormalities and detrusor overactivity; can occur as idiopathic, neurogenic, and with outlet obstruction
  2. Postvoid dribble (ICD-9CM code: 599.2): a postsphincteric collection of urine seen with urethral diverticulum; can be idiopathic.
  3. Extraurethral incontinence: enterovesical (ICD-9CM codes: 596.1 and 596.2), urethral (ICD-9CM code: 599.1); also known as *fistula*.
- Conditions that predispose to surgical failure: advanced age, postmenopausal state, hysterectomy, prior failed incontinence surgery, concurrent detrusor instability, abnormal perineal electromyography, pelvic radiation

EBM **EVIDENCE**

Available at www.expertconsult.com

SUGGESTED READINGS

Available at www.expertconsult.com.

RELATED CONTENT

Urinary Incontinence (Patient Information)
Pelvic Organ Prolapse (Related Key Topic)

AUTHOR: **RUBEN ALVERO, M.D.**

Diseases and Disorders

I

BASIC INFORMATION

DEFINITION

Infertility in a reproductive age couple is the inability to conceive after adequate coital attempts have been made for ≥1 yr. In couples in which the female partner is >35 yr of age, an evaluation is justified after 6 mo without successful pregnancy.

SYNONYM

Sterility

ICD-10CM CODES

N46	Male infertility
N46.8	Other male infertility
N46.9	Male infertility, unspecified
N97.0	Female infertility associated with anovulation
N97.1	Female infertility of tubal origin
N97.2	Female infertility of uterine origin
N97.8	Female infertility of other origin
N97.9	Female infertility, unspecified
O09.00	Supervision of pregnancy with history of infertility, unspecified trimester
O09.01	Supervision of pregnancy with history of infertility, first trimester
O09.02	Supervision of pregnancy with history of infertility, second trimester
O09.03	Supervision of pregnancy with history of infertility, third trimester
Z31.81	Encounter for male factor infertility in female patient

EPIDEMIOLOGY & DEMOGRAPHICS

PEAK INCIDENCE: The incidence of infertility increases with age. Subtle decreases in female fertility start as early as age 30. The rate of infertility increases dramatically after age 37 and spontaneous pregnancies become extremely uncommon as women reach the mid-40s. There is also a more subtle but still detectable decrease in male fertility that can also start as early as age 30.
PREVALENCE: One in eight reproductive age couples experience infertility. This prevalence is consistent in all developed countries and there is evidence that it is historically stable.
PREDOMINANT SEX AND AGE: By definition this is a diagnosis of reproductive age couples. Infertility increases with aging in both males and females but more dramatically in women. Male factor is responsible in ~40% of couples and the female factor is responsible in ~40% of couples. The remainder of the cases are either combined male and female or unexplained infertility, meaning a clear cause is not identified.
RISK FACTORS: Aging is among the most common of risk factors, predominantly among females. Women are increasingly deferring pregnancy as a result of careers, which is likely associated with the increasing prevalence in certain sectors of the population. Sexually transmitted disease with chlamydia and gonorrhea is associated with pelvic inflammatory disease, which frequently results in tubal factor infertility. Extremes of

weight, especially overweight, are associated with ovulatory dysfunction. Male factor infertility is most commonly idiopathic, although trauma, infection, varicocele, and exposure to environmental toxins may be associated with compromise of semen parameters. Smoking is the most common lifestyle choice that impairs fertility.

PHYSICAL FINDINGS & CLINICAL PRESENTATION

- Age (both partners), but especially important in the female
- Previous fertility, particularly if no pregnancy has occurred in another relationship despite absence of contraception (both partners).
- Absence of secondary sexual characteristics (both partners).
- Irregular or absent menstruation (female).
- Hirsutism, acne, and alopecia suggestive of hyperandrogenism (female).
- Pelvic exam suggestive of uterine abnormality such as fibroids (female).
- Trauma or torsion of the testes (male).
- Small, firm testes (male).

ETIOLOGY

- Advanced age, especially female
- Pelvic inflammatory disease (results in tubal factor infertility)
- Endometriosis (results in tubal factor infertility)
- Female anatomic (uterine fibroids, polyps, intrauterine adhesions)
- Oligoovulation, most frequently due to polycystic ovarian syndrome (PCOS)
- Idiopathic, both male and female

Dx DIAGNOSIS

DIFFERENTIAL DIAGNOSIS

- Recurrent spontaneous abortion
- Ineffective attempts at natural conception
- Sterility due to previous permanent sterilization procedure

WORKUP

- The components of evaluation depend greatly on whether the female patient is reliably ovulating based on history (regular menses, premenstrual molimina such as breast tenderness) and laboratory testing (midluteal progesterone, basal body temperature testing, urinary LH predictor kits, mid-cycle ovulatory pain [Mittelschmerz], cervical mucus testing). Box E1I-3 and Fig. E1I-10 describe an approach to infertility diagnosis and management.
- Where the menstrual cycle is important in testing, the first day is defined as the first day of full menstrual flow.
- If the female patient does not appear to be ovulating, testing should consist of:
  1. TSH.
  2. Prolactin.
  3. Total testosterone/free testosterone (to assess for PCOS).
  4. Transvaginal pelvic ultrasound to assess for polycystic-appearing ovaries.
  5. 17-Hydroxyprogesterone (to assess for cryptic congenital adrenal hyperplasia).
  6. 2-hr glucose tolerance testing (if the patient has PCOS).
  7. FSH/estradiol/anti-müllerian hormone on the second or third day of the menstrual cycle (if present).
  8. Lipid panel (if the patient has PCOS, secondary to overlap with metabolic syndrome).
  9. Liver function test (if the patient has PCOS, in case treatment with insulin-sensitizing agents indicated).
  10. BUN/creatinine (if the patient has PCOS, in case treatment with insulin-sensitizing agents indicated).
  11. Semen analysis in the male partner.
  12. Hysterosalpingogram (especially if the history suggests previous pelvic infection).
- If the female patient appears to be ovulating, testing should consist of:
  1. Semen analysis in the male partner.
  2. Hysterosalpingogram (Fig. 1I-11).
  3. Mid-luteal progesterone, urinary LH predictor kits (to assess for ovulation).

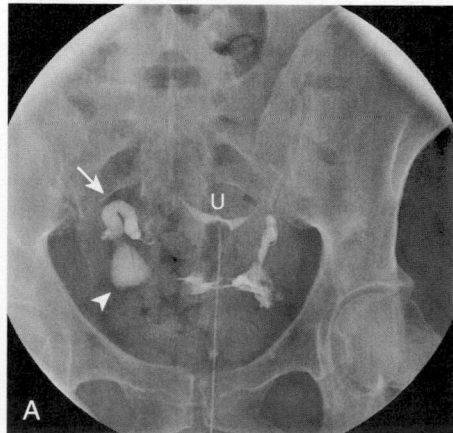
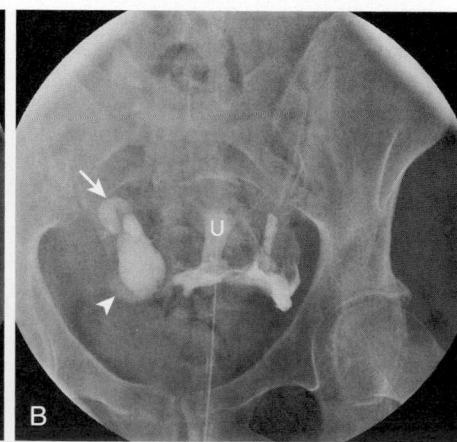

FIGURE 1I-11 Hysterosalpingogram spot radiographs early **(A)** and late **(B)** demonstrate a rounded collection of contrast material *(arrowhead)* adjacent to the dilated ampullary portion of the right fallopian tube *(arrow),* caused by peritubal pelvic adhesions related to previous pelvic inflammatory disease. Normal patient left fallopian tube. *U,* Uterus. (From Fielding JR et al: *Gynecologic imaging,* Philadelphia, 2011, Saunders.)

4. FSH, estradiol, anti-müllerian hormone on day 2 to 3 of menstrual cycle (ovarian reserve testing).
5. Transvaginal pelvic ultrasound to assess for uterine anomalies and antral follicle count as a measure of ovarian reserve.

LABORATORY TESTS

- Semen analysis, using Kruger strict morphology after 2 to 3 days of abstinence (male).
- Day 2 or 3 FSH, estradiol, and anti-müllerian hormone as a measure of ovarian reserve (female).
- Mid-luteal progesterone (ideally 7 days after ovulatory surge). Given variability and absence of a reliable threshold, most practitioners use clinical criteria to diagnose ovulatory dysfunction.
- Urinary LH ovulatory kits.
- See "Workup" for evaluation of couples where the female partner is oligo- or anovulatory.

IMAGING STUDIES

- Hysterosalpingogram (between days 6 and 12 of the menstrual cycle).
- Day 2 or 3 transvaginal pelvic ultrasound to assess uterine abnormalities and to count the number of small antral follicles (2 to 9 mm) as a measure of ovarian reserve. If oligo- or anovulatory, to assess for polycystic-appearing ovary.
- Day 2 or 3 pelvic ultrasound assesses anatomic abnormalities and the number of antral ("resting") follicles; also a means of evaluating ovarian reserve.

 TREATMENT

Once the patient presents for evaluation, testing should be completed as quickly as possible, ideally within one menstrual cycle. The couple should follow up with the evaluating provider once all testing is completed and treatment initiated as abnormalities are found.

ACUTE GENERAL Rx

- Male infertility: referral to reproductive endocrinologist if semen analysis is abnormal or hyperprolactinemia is diagnosed. In patients with varicocele, there is insufficient evidence to suggest that corrective surgery will significantly improve birth rates.
- Mild male factor infertility may be treated with intrauterine insemination but more severe forms will usually require assisted reproductive technologies (ART) with intracytoplasmic sperm injection (ICSI) in the laboratory, where sperm is injected directly into the oocyte. ICSI use has increased from 36.4% in 1996 to 76.2% in 2012 with the largest increase among cycles without male factor infertility. Compared with conventional IVF, ICSI use is not associated with improved postfertilization reproductive outcomes, irrespective of male factor infertility diagnosis.[1]

- Tubal factor infertility may be treated surgically if mild and if the female patient is young and can afford the time to attempt pregnancy over multiple menstrual cycles. If the patient is older or if the tubal pathology is moderate to severe, the patient should use in vitro fertilization (IVF) to achieve pregnancy.
- Oligo- or anovulation should be treated with ovulation induction agents. Women with euestrogenic ovulatory dysfunction can be treated with Letrozole as a first-line agent, using 2.5 mg in the first cycle attempt and increasing the dose by 2.5 mg up to a maximum dose of 10 mg if the patient fails to ovulate. A recent multicenter trial found that aromatase inhibitors achieved higher live birth rates than clomiphene citrate. Clomiphene citrate has historically been used but very well done randomized controlled trial convincingly demonstrated that Letrozole is superior. Far less commonly, ovulatory dysfunction is the result of hypothalamic dysfunction. In these patients, once hypothalamic or pituitary abnormalities are excluded with MRI, ovulation can be achieved using injected gonadotropins.
- Uterine anatomic abnormalities such as submucous fibroids, polyps, or intrauterine adhesions should be corrected if they are identified. Fibroids that do not impact the uterine cavity probably do not interfere with fertility. Removal of intramural or subserosal fibroids is reserved for situations in which these cause excessive vaginal bleeding, pain, or pressure.
- Unexplained infertility can be treated empirically using superovulation with clomiphene citrate or gonadotropins combined with intrauterine insemination with partner's sperm. Most providers recommend using clomiphene citrate with insemination as a first-line superovulatory agent because it is inexpensive. After 3 to 4 such cycles, few pregnancies occur and the couple should be advised to become more aggressive. Controversy exists as to whether gonadotropins with insemination or IVF should be used after clomiphene citrate superovulation induction. There is evidence suggesting that moving to IVF in a *fast-track* fashion shortens the time interval to achieving pregnancy. A recent randomized trial[2] in women with unexplained infertility revealed ovarian stimulation with letrozole resulted in a significantly lower frequency of multiple gestation but also a lower frequency of live birth, as compared with gonadotropin but not as compared with clomiphene.

COMPLEMENTARY & ALTERNATIVE MEDICINE

Acupuncture is widely used by women being treated for infertility. Limited data suggest some benefit, with possible mechanisms of action including increasing blood flow to the uterus. Patients may additionally benefit from the stress relief that acupuncture provides.

DISPOSITION

- Most couples will achieve a pregnancy, provided that they are willing to use aggressive techniques, including ART such as IVF and gamete donation.
- Adoption is also a worthwhile and viable possibility for couples that cannot conceive. These couples should be ready to take on some challenges, such as limited availability of adoptable children, as well as related financial and bureaucratic hurdles.

REFERRAL

Couples should be referred to a reproductive endocrinologist once the complexity of treatment exceeds the comfort level of the provider, whether a family physician, internist, or general gynecologist. Complex ovulation and superovulation induction and ART are usually managed by a board-certified reproductive endocrinologist.

 **PEARLS & CONSIDERATIONS**

COMMENTS

- >2.6% of all live births in the United States currently are the result of IVF.
- The incidence of heterotopic pregnancy in patients who have undergone IVF is relatively common; identification of a patient with ultrasound-proved intrauterine pregnancy who used ART to conceive should NOT necessarily exclude the possibility of an ectopic gestation.

PREVENTION

- Techniques that reduce the incidence of pelvic inflammatory disease, such as condom use, can reduce pelvic adhesions that are associated with tubal factor infertility.
- Women can be made aware of the fact that delaying pregnancy into the later reproductive years can reduce the chances for successful pregnancy.

PATIENT & FAMILY EDUCATION

Patient support groups such as *Resolve* (www.resolve.org) are available to help couples during evaluation and treatment of infertility, which can be extraordinarily stressful.

EBM **EVIDENCE**

Available at www.expertconsult.com

SUGGESTED READINGS

Available at www.expertconsult.com

RELATED CONTENT

Infertility (Patient Information)
Amenorrhea (Related Key Topic)
Pelvic Inflammatory Disease (Related Key Topic)
Polycystic Ovary Syndrome (Related Key Topic)

AUTHOR: **RUBEN ALVERO, M.D.**

[1]Boulet SL et al.: Trends in use of and reproductive outcomes associated with intracytoplasmic sperm injection, JAMA 313(3):255-263, 2015.

[2]Diamond MP, et al.: Letrozole, Gonadotropin, or Clomiphene for Unexplained Infertility, *N Engl J Med* 373:1230-1240, 2015.

Diseases and Disorders

 **BASIC INFORMATION**

DEFINITION

Inflammatory myopathies are idiopathic diseases of muscle characterized clinically by muscle weakness and pathologically by inflammation and muscle fiber breakdown. The four most common are dermatomyositis (DM), necrotizing autoimmune myositis, polymyositis (PM), and inclusion body myositis (IBM). See separate topic on "Inclusion Body Myositis" for details regarding the latter.

SYNONYMS

Idiopathic inflammatory myopathies
Myositis syndromes
Polymyositis
Dermatomyositis

ICD-10CM CODES
M33.90 Dermatopolymyositis, unspecified, organ involvement unspecified
M33.20 Polymyositis, organ involvement unspecified
M33.02 Juvenile dermatopolymyositis with myopathy
M33.12 Other dermatopolymyositis with myopathy
M33.22 Polymyositis with myopathy
M33.92 Dermatopolymyositis, unspecified with myopathy

EPIDEMIOLOGY & DEMOGRAPHICS

Inflammatory myopathies are the largest group of potentially treatable myopathies in children and adults.
DM:
• Occurs in children and in adults (bimodal age peak)
• Average age at diagnosis is 40 yr in adults. Age range in children: 5 to 14 yr
• More common in females than in males (2:1)
• Incidence 1:100,000
• Prevalence 1 to 10 cases/million in adults and 1 to 3.2 cases/million in children
• Up to one third of patients older than 50 with DM have an associated malignancy
PM:
• Occurs mostly in adults, very rare in children
• Average age at diagnosis >20 yr
• More common in females
• Least common inflammatory myopathy
• Exact incidence unknown

PHYSICAL FINDINGS & CLINICAL PRESENTATION

DM and PM:
• Most patients have a subacute onset over weeks to months.
• Pattern is typically symmetric proximal muscle weakness involving the proximal limbs (shoulder and pelvic girdles).
• Weakness of neck flexion and extension is common.
• Difficulty getting up from a chair, climbing stairs, reaching for objects above head, or combing hair.

• Distal muscle and ocular involvement is uncommon.
• Sensation is preserved.
• Reflexes may be preserved or diminished.
• Dysphagia and dysphonia result from involvement of striated muscle of the pharynx and proximal esophagus.
• Esophageal dysmotility is common in DM.
• Respiratory failure from associated pulmonary fibrosis.
• Cardiac conduction abnormalities can be seen with DM.
• Systemic autoimmune disease occurs frequently in PM, and rarely in DM.
• Skin findings in DM:
1. Heliotrope rash on the upper eyelids (Fig. 1I-12)
2. Erythematous rash on the face (see Fig. 1I-12)
3. May also involve the back and shoulders (shawl sign), neck and chest (V-shape), knees (Fig. 1I-13), and elbows
4. Photosensitivity
5. Gottron's papules (violaceous papules overlying dorsal interphalangeal or metacarpophalangeal areas, elbow or knee joints—Fig. 1I-14)
6. Nail cracking, thickening, and irregularity (Fig. 1I-15) with periungual telangiectasia (see Fig. 1I-14)

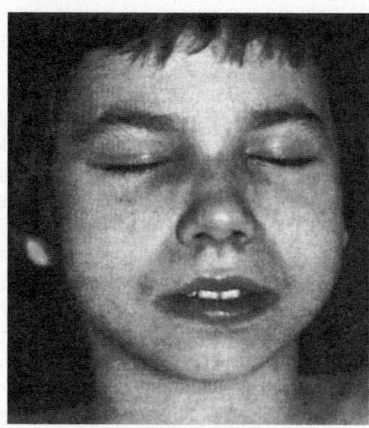

FIGURE 1I-12 The facial rash of juvenile dermatomyositis. There is erythema over the bridge of the nose and malar areas, with violaceous (heliotropic) discoloration of the upper eyelids. (From Behrman RE: *Nelson textbook of pediatrics,* ed 17, Philadelphia, 2004, Saunders.)

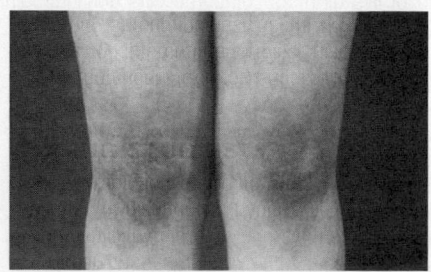

FIGURE 1I-13 Violaceous plaques on the knees in a patient with dermatomyositis (Gottron sign). (From Hochberg MC et al: *Rheumatology,* ed 5, St Louis, 2011, Mosby.)

7. Mechanic's hand: fissured, hyperpigmented, scaly, and hyperkeratotic; also associated with increased risk of interstitial lung disease

ETIOLOGY

DM: complex, immune-mediated microangiopathy. Adaptive immune response via humorally mediated complement attack
PM: unknown:
• Cell-mediated immune major histocompatibility-I (MHC-1) process directed against muscle fibers is likely, given biopsy features.
• A viral etiology has been proposed secondary to the presence of autoantibodies to histidyl transferase, anti-Jo-1, and signal recognition particle.

 **DIAGNOSIS**

• The diagnosis of each subtype of inflammatory myopathy is based on clinical history, pattern of muscle involvement, electromyographic findings, muscle biopsy, and presence of certain antibodies.
• Myopathic pattern of muscle weakness
• Characteristic rash in DM
• EMG shows myopathic (small-amplitude, short-duration, polyphasic) motor potentials with early recruitment

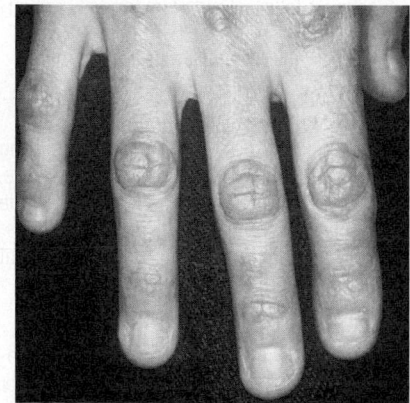

FIGURE 1I-14 Dermatomyositis (Gottron's papules). Note erythematous papules over joints and periungual telangiectasias. (From Noble J [ed]: *Textbook of primary care medicine,* ed 2, St Louis, 1996, Mosby.)

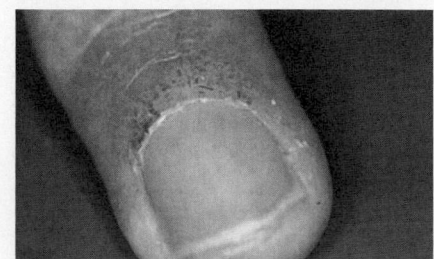

FIGURE 1I-15 Enlarged nailfold capillaries in a patient with dermatomyositis. (From Hochberg MC et al: *Rheumatology,* ed 5, St Louis, 2011, Mosby.)

TABLE 1I-5 Histologic Features of Idiopathic Inflammatory Myopathies

Feature	Dermatomyositis	Polymyositis	Inclusion Body Myositis
Necrosis of muscle fibers	+	+	+
Variation in fiber diameter	+	+	+
Regeneration of muscle fibers	+	+	+
Proliferation of connective tissue	+	+	+
Infiltration of mononuclear cells*	+	+	+
Perivascular and perimysial inflammation	+	–/+	–/+
Endomysial inflammation	–/+	+	+
Perifascicular atrophy	+	–	–
Abnormally dilated capillaries	+	–/+	–
Reduced capillary density	+	–/+	–
Deposition of complement on vessel walls	+	–/+	–
Microinfarcts	+	–	–
Invasion of non-necrotic fibers by cytotoxic T lymphocytes and macrophages	–	+	+
Expression of major histocompatibility complex class I on muscle fibers	–/+	+	+
Rimmed vacuoles with amyloid deposits and tubulofilaments†	–	–	+
Angulated or atrophic and hypertrophic fibers	–	–	+
Ragged red or cytochrome oxidase–negative fibers	–	–	+

*Inflammation is absent in a small proportion of polymyositis and dermatomyositis biopsies.
†Also seen in chronic neurogenic conditions and distal myopathies.
From Firestein GS et al: *Kelly's textbook of rheumatology,* ed 9, Philadelphia, 2013, Saunders, Elsevier.

- Majority of patients have "irritable" features (fibrillations and positive sharp waves) on EMG
- See "Laboratory Tests".
- Biopsy is required for diagnosis and should confirm inflammation before treatment is started. Table 1I-5 describes histologic features of idiopathic inflammatory myopathies. In idiopathic inflammatory myopathies, myopathic features (variation in fiber size, fiber splitting, fatty replacement of muscle tissue, and increased endomysial connective tissue) should be seen in addition to the following:
  1. DM: perifascicular atrophy, MAC deposition along capillaries
  2. PM: endomysial infiltrates composed of CD8+ T cells and macrophages invading nonnecrotic muscle fibers that express MHC-I antigen

DIFFERENTIAL DIAGNOSIS

- IBM
- Muscular dystrophies
- Amyloid myoneuropathy
- Amyotrophic lateral sclerosis
- Myasthenia gravis
- Eaton-Lambert syndrome
- Drug-induced myopathies (e.g., quinidine, NSAIDs, penicillamine, HMG CoA-reductase inhibitors)
- Diabetic amyotrophy
- Guillain-Barré syndrome
- Hyperthyroidism or hypothyroidism
- Lichen planus
- Amyopathic DM (rash without weakness)
- DM sine rash (weakness with characteristic biopsy, but no rash)
- Systemic lupus erythematosus (SLE)

- Contact atopic or seborrheic dermatitis
- Psoriasis

LABORATORY TESTS

- Creatine kinase (CK) is the most sensitive muscle enzyme test for muscle breakdown. It should be checked at onset, and serially monitored several times during treatment.
- CK is typically elevated (5-50x normal) in active PM.
- CK may be normal or only slightly elevated in DM.
- Aldolase, AST, ALT, alkaline phosphatase, and LDH may be elevated.
- Anti-Jo-1 antibodies are seen in myositis with associated interstitial lung disease but are not specific for either DM or PM.
- DM: Anti-MDA-5, anti-Mi-2, anti-TIF-1, and anti-NXP2 (implicated in cancer-associated dermatomyositis).
- PM: Antisynthetase antibodies (often seen in overlap myositis) associated with interstitial lung disease, arthritis, fever, and "mechanic's hands."
- Electrolytes, thyroid-stimulating hormone (TSH), Ca, and Mg should be evaluated to exclude other causes of weakness.
- Check ECG for cardiac involvement.

IMAGING STUDIES

- Chest x-ray is used to rule out pulmonary involvement. If suspicious for pulmonary interstitial disease, a high-resolution CT scan of the chest may be helpful.
- Video fluoroscopy or barium swallow study to look for upper esophageal dysfunction in patients with dysphagia and DM.

Rx TREATMENT

Goal: maintain function, minimize disease/iatrogenic sequelae

NONPHARMACOLOGIC THERAPY

- Sun-blocking agents with SPF 15 or greater for skin protection in patients with DM
- Physical therapy beneficial for gait training and increasing muscle tone and strength
- Occupational therapy assists with activities of daily living
- Speech therapy to monitor patients with swallowing dysfunction

ACUTE GENERAL Rx

- Corticosteroids are the mainstay of therapy. Start prednisone 1 to 2 mg/kg per day, up to a maximum dose of 100 mg/day. Continue until muscle strength improves or muscle enzymes have normalized for at least 4 wk. Begin tapering by 10 mg/mo until 60 mg/day, then slowly taper by 5 mg/mo. Consider every-other-day prednisone treatment at same dose (may decrease side effects).
- Consider IV immunoglobulin (IVIG) if patient fails to improve on prednisone, or muscle enzymes begin rising when tapering off prednisone. See "Chronic Rx" for specific dosage.
- Hydroxychloroquine can be used to treat the cutaneous lesions of DM.
- A treatment algorithm for adult patients with PM and DM is described in Fig. 1I-16.

CHRONIC Rx

- Chronic prednisone therapy may be needed for years, but other immunosuppressive ("steroid-sparing") agents may be added early to decrease long-term steroid side effects.
- Azathioprine 2 to 3 mg/kg per day tapered to 1 mg/kg per day once steroid is tapered to 15 mg/day. Reduce dosage monthly by 25-mg intervals. Maintenance dosage is 50 mg/day.
- Methotrexate 7.5 to 10 mg PO/wk, increased by 2.5 mg/wk to total of 25 mg/wk; consider IM dosing if PO is ineffective.
- IV immunoglobulin 2 g/kg total dose over 2 to 5 days.
- IV cyclophosphamide 1 g/M² monthly for 6 mo is preferred to oral dosing for refractory cases. However, oral dosing of cyclophosphamide is 1 to 3 mg/kg per day PO or 2 to 4 mg/kg per day in conjunction with prednisone.
- Cyclosporin A: initial dose 2.0 to 2.5 mg/kg bid; long-term maintenance is lowest effective dose.
- Mycophenolate mofetil 500 mg PO bid, titrate to 1500 mg PO bid over 1 to 2 mo.
- Hydroxychloroquine 200 mg PO daily; monitor for visual changes.

DISPOSITION

- 30% to 40% of patients achieve clinical remission with treatment.
- In patients with residual weakness, deficits typically remain stable over long-term follow-up.

Diseases and Disorders

I

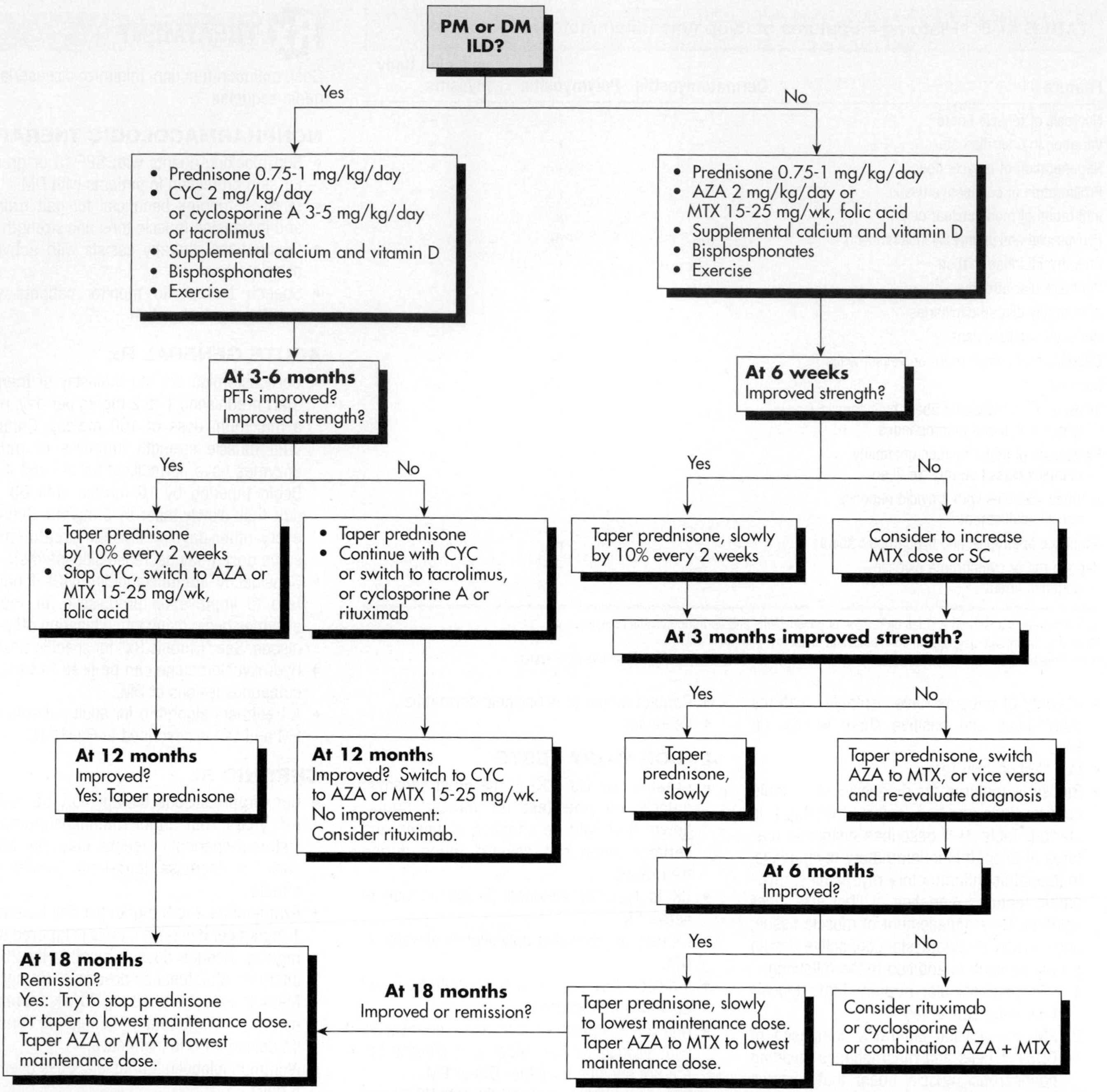

PM or DM ILD?

Yes →

- Prednisone 0.75-1 mg/kg/day
- CYC 2 mg/kg/day
  or cyclosporine A 3-5 mg/kg/day
  or tacrolimus
- Supplemental calcium and vitamin D
- Bisphosphonates
- Exercise

At 3-6 months
PFTs improved?
Improved strength?

Yes →

- Taper prednisone
  by 10% every 2 weeks
- Stop CYC, switch to AZA or
  MTX 15-25 mg/wk,
  folic acid

At 12 months
Improved?
Yes: Taper prednisone

At 18 months
Remission?
Yes: Try to stop prednisone
or taper to lowest maintenance dose.
Taper AZA or MTX to lowest
maintenance dose.

No →

- Taper prednisone
- Continue with CYC
  or switch to tacrolimus,
  or cyclosporine A or
  rituximab

At 12 months
Improved? Switch to CYC
to AZA or MTX 15-25 mg/wk.
No improvement:
Consider rituximab.

At 18 months
Improved or remission?

No →

- Prednisone 0.75-1 mg/kg/day
- AZA 2 mg/kg/day or
  MTX 15-25 mg/wk, folic acid
- Supplemental calcium and vitamin D
- Bisphosphonates
- Exercise

At 6 weeks
Improved strength?

Yes →
Taper prednisone, slowly
by 10% every 2 weeks

No →
Consider to increase
MTX dose or SC

At 3 months improved strength?

Yes →
Taper
prednisone,
slowly

No →
Taper prednisone, switch
AZA to MTX, or vice versa
and re-evaluate diagnosis

At 6 months
Improved?

Yes →
Taper prednisone, slowly
to lowest maintenance dose.
Taper AZA to MTX to lowest
maintenance dose.

No →
Consider rituximab
or cyclosporine A
or combination AZA + MTX

FIGURE 1I-16 Treatment algorithm for adult patients with polymyositis (PM) or dermatomyositis (DM). *AZA,* Azathioprine; *CYC,* cyclophosphamide; *ILD,* interstitial lung disease; *MTX,* methotrexate; *PFT,* pulmonary function test; *SC,* subcutaneous. (From Firestein GS et al: *Kelly's textbook of rheumatology,* ed 9, Philadelphia, 2013, Saunders, Elsevier.)

- 10% experience recurrent disease.
- Serum CK often returns to normal before symptoms improve.
- During exacerbations, enzymes may rise before clinical symptoms appear.
- Poor prognostic indicators include delay in diagnosis, older age, recalcitrant disease, malignancy, interstitial pulmonary fibrosis, dysphagia, leukocytosis, fever, and anorexia.
- Infection, malignancy, and cardiac and pulmonary dysfunction are the most common causes of death.
- With early treatment, 5- and 8-yr survival rates of 80% and 73%, respectively, have been reported.

REFERRAL

Neurology or rheumatology referral should be made to help establish the diagnosis and implement treatment.

PEARLS & CONSIDERATIONS

- Do not implement treatment before muscle biopsy.
- When assessing response to treatment, clinical muscle strength is more important than muscle enzyme tests.

- The concern for malignancies (ovary, lung, breast, GI) associated with DM is legitimate and merits screening in patients older than age 40 at time of diagnosis and every 2 to 3 yr thereafter.
- There does not appear to be any association between juvenile DM and malignancy.
- Overlap syndrome refers to patients with DM who also meet criteria for a connective tissue disorder (e.g., rheumatoid arthritis, scleroderma, SLE).
- In any patient taking steroids, closely monitor for:
  1. Diabetes or glucose intolerance (2-hour oral glucose tolerance test)
  2. Osteopenia/osteoporosis (DEXA scan q6mo)

3. Cataracts (yearly ophthalmologic appointment)
4. Hypertension
5. Psychiatric side effects including depression or psychosis
6. Poor sleep
7. Peptic ulcer disease (prescribe H_2 antagonist or proton pump inhibitor)

- Clinical and immune response features can be used for categorizing heterogeneous myositis syndromes and mutually exclusive and stable phenotypes and are useful for predicting clinical signs and symptoms, associated environmental and genetic risk factors, and responses to therapy and prognosis.

SUGGESTED READING

Available at www.expertconsult.com

RELATED CONTENT

Dermatomyositis and Polymyositis (Patient Information)
Inclusion Body Myositis (Related Key Topic)

AUTHOR: **GAVIN BROWN, M.D.**

BASIC INFORMATION

DEFINITION

Influenza is an acute febrile illness caused by infection with influenza type A or B virus. Seasonal influenza can include the H1N1 virus. A similar respiratory illness is severe acute respiratory syndrome (SARS) caused by a coronavirus called SARS-associated coronavirus (SARS-CoV). A new novel coronavirus was recognized in two patients in September 2012. This is a very different virus from the SARS agent; the two patients exhibited acute respiratory distress syndrome, renal failure, consumptive coagulopathy, and/or pericarditis. Now called the Middle East respiratory syndrome (MERS-CoV) virus, it has affected patients with connections to several Middle Eastern countries. Patients have fever and pneumonia requiring hospitalization. Transmission spread in 2015 to Korea and China, resulting in more than 185 cases. Dromedary camels and their milk are documented to harbor MERS-CoV.

SYNONYMS

Flu
Influenza-like illness (ILI)

ICD-10CM CODES
J11.00 Influenza due to other unidentified influenza virus with unspecified type of pneumonia
J12.9 Viral pneumonia, unspecified
J11.1 Influenza due to unidentified influenza virus with other respiratory manifestations

INFLUENZA EPIDEMIOLOGY & DEMOGRAPHICS

PEAK INCIDENCE: Winter outbreaks lasting 5 to 6 wk.
PREDOMINANT SEX: Male =female.
PREDOMINANT AGE: Attack rates are higher among children than adults, although children are less prone to develop pulmonary complications. During the 2014-2015 flu season, the highest hospitalization rate occurred with people 65 years and older (323/100,000)
INCIDENCE (IN U.S.): Annual incidence of influenza-related deaths is ~36,000 deaths/yr.

PHYSICAL FINDINGS & CLINICAL PRESENTATION

- "Classic flu" is characterized by abrupt onset of fever, headache, myalgias, anorexia, and malaise after a 1- to 2-day incubation period.
- Clinical syndromes are similar to those produced by other respiratory viruses, including pharyngitis, common colds, tracheobronchitis, bronchiolitis, and croup.
- Respiratory symptoms such as cough, sore throat, and nasal discharge are usually present at the onset of illness, but systemic symptoms predominate.
- Elderly patients may experience fever, weakness, and confusion without any respiratory complaints.

- Acute deterioration to status asthmaticus may occur in patients with asthma.
- Influenza pneumonia: rapidly progressive cough, dyspnea, and cyanosis may occur after typical flu onset. This may be caused by primary influenza pneumonia or secondary bacterial pneumonia (often pneumococcal or staphylococcal co-infection).
- For influenza A (H3N2v), children younger than 10 years lack immunity. People ≥65 years and those with morbid obesity are at high risk.

ETIOLOGY

- Variation in the surface antigens of the influenza virus, hemagglutinin (HA) and neuraminidase (NA), leading to infection with variants to which immunity is inadequate in the population at risk.
- Droplet transmission by small-particle aerosols and deposited on the respiratory tract epithelium.

 DIAGNOSIS

DIFFERENTIAL DIAGNOSIS

- Respiratory syncytial virus, adenovirus, parainfluenza virus infection.
- Secondary bacterial pneumonia or mixed bacterial-viral pneumonia.

WORKUP

- The accuracy of clinical diagnosis of influenza on the basis of symptoms alone is limited because symptoms from illness caused by other pathogens can overlap considerably with influenza. Diagnostic tests available for influenza include viral cultures, serology, rapid influenza diagnostic tests (RIDTs), reverse transcription-polymerase chain reaction (RT-PCR), and immunofluorescence assays.
- Virus isolation from nasal or throat swab or sputum specimens is the most rapid diagnostic method in the setting of acute illness.
- Specimens are placed into virus transport medium and processed by a reference laboratory.
- For serologic diagnosis:
  1. Paired serum specimens, acute and convalescent, the latter obtained 10 to 20 days later
  2. Fourfold rises or falls in the titer of antibodies (various techniques) considered diagnostic of recent infection
  3. Commercial rapid influenza diagnostic tests (RIDTs) are available. They can detect influenza virus antigens within 15 minutes of testing. Rapid flu test should be collected as early as possible, ideally within 4 days of onset. False-negative results are common during the flu season. A negative test result does NOT exclude diagnosis of influenza.
  4. Commercial RIDTs cannot determine if an H3N2 is a variant virus; when suspect H3N2v virus infection, send nasopharyn-

geal swab or aspirate in viral transport medium to state public health laboratory for rRT-PCR testing using CDC FLU rRT-PCR diagnostic panel assay.

LABORATORY TESTS

Septic syndrome presentation: CBC, ABG analysis, blood cultures

IMAGING STUDIES

- Chest x-ray examination when suspecting viral pneumonia: peribronchial and patchy interstitial infiltrates in multiple lobes with atelectasis. Table 1I-6 describes x-ray pulmonary findings based on virus type.
- Possible progression to diffuse interstitial pneumonitis.

 TREATMENT

NONPHARMACOLOGIC THERAPY

- Bed rest.
- Hydration.

ACUTE GENERAL Rx

- Supportive care: antipyretics; avoid use of aspirin in children because of the association with Reye's syndrome.
- Antibiotics if bacterial pneumonia is proved or suspected.
- Amantadine is NOT recommended due to resistant isolates.
- Neuraminidase inhibitors block release of virions from infected cells, resulting in shortened duration of symptoms and decrease in complications; effective against both influenza A and B, including A (H3N2v) for all hospitalized patients, those with severe and progressive illness, and high-risk patients with suspected or confirmed H3N2v.
  1. Zanamivir, administered via inhaler:
     For treatment, 10 mg (2 inhalations of 5 mg each) twice daily for 5 days.
     For prevention in households, 10 mg (2 inhalations of 5 mg each) once daily for 17 days.
     Not recommended in persons with underlying airways disease such as asthma or chronic obstructive pulmonary disease.
  2. Oseltamivir, administered orally:
     For treatment, 75 mg PO twice daily for 5 days.
     For prevention, 75 mg PO once daily for a minimum of 2 wk in an outbreak setting or 7 days after exposure for an adult.
  3. Emergency use authorization by the CDC for intravenous peramivir during the H1N1 pandemic was terminated in June 2010. Intravenous zanamivir is available in clinical trials or as an emergency investigational new drug.
- Placebo-controlled studies have suggested that antiviral therapy with any of the previously mentioned agents must ideally be initiated within 1 to 2 days of the onset of symptoms and reduces the duration of illness by ~1 day.

- Oseltamivir resistance developed on therapy in individuals with avian flu (H5N1) in Asia, and this is associated with poor outcome.
- Amantadine and rimantadine resistance are documented for novel (H1N1) influenza and H3N2 influenza virus.
- Systemic corticosteroids should not be routinely administered to patients with suspected or confirmed influenza, including H3N2v virus infection, except for patients on chronic corticosteroid therapy for COPD, asthma.

DISPOSITION

Patients are hospitalized if signs of pneumonia are present.

REFERRAL

Infectious disease and/or pulmonary consultation when influenza pneumonia is suspected.

PEARLS & CONSIDERATIONS

COMMENTS

- Prevention of influenza in patients at high risk is an important goal of primary care.
- Vaccines reduce the risk of infection and the severity of illness.
  1. Antigenic composition of the vaccine is updated annually. The northern hemisphere's 2015 to 2016 season trivalent vaccine includes A/Switzerland/9715293/2013 (H3N2)-like virus, influenza. A/California/7/2009(H1N1)-like virus, and one influenza B–like virus from the Yamagata lineage (B/Phuket/3073/2013-like). Quadrivalent vaccines contain these three antigens, plus an antigen from a second influenza B vaccine virus strain that is from the Victoria lineage (B/Brisbane/60/2008-like).
  2. Revaccination is recommended annually before onset of influenza activity in the community, even for those who received the vaccine in the previous season.
  3. Delaying vaccination to ensure persistence of vaccine-induced protection during flu season could result in missed opportunities to vaccinate.
  4. Seasonal influenza vaccine does not provide protection against the influenza

A (H3N2v) virus that is associated with agricultural fairs.
  5. Vaccination should be given at the start of the flu season (September-October) for all persons aged ≥6 mo. Vaccination is particularly important for persons who are at increased risk for severe complications from influenza. When vaccine supply is limited, vaccination efforts should focus on the following groups:
     a. All children aged 6 mo to 4 yr (59 mo).
     b. People 50 years and older.
     c. Adults and children with chronic cardiac (except hypertension) or pulmonary (including asthma), renal, hepatic, neurologic, hematologic or metabolic disease (including diabetes mellitus).
     d. Immunocompromised patients (including HIV-infected persons or patients immunosuppressed due to medications).
     e. Women who are or will be pregnant during the influenza season.
     f. Children aged 6 mo to 18 yr who are receiving long-term aspirin therapy.
     g. Residents of nursing homes and other long-term care facilities.
     h. American Indians/Alaska Natives.
     i. Persons who are morbidly obese (BMI ≥40).
     j. Health care workers (HCWs).
     k. Household contacts and caregivers of persons in the previous groups.
  6. Vaccination should be delayed for persons with moderate to severe acute febrile illness. Precautions include:
     a. Guillain-Barré syndrome within 6 wk following a previous dose of influenza vaccine.
     b. Moderate or severe acute illness with or without fever (for trivalent inactivated influenza vaccine).
  7. Contraindication to receiving vaccine is a previous severe allergic reaction to influenza vaccine.
  8. Special efforts should be made to vaccinate high-risk patients <65 yr, only 10% to 15% of whom are vaccinated each year.
  9. HCW vaccination minimizes transmission to patients and coworkers. Some

states mandate vaccination of HCWs; some healthcare facilities and other states require the wearing of face masks by unvaccinated HCWs during the influenza season, particularly when there is widespread flu.
  10. Vaccine efficacy varies by age and by type of circulating virus. Efficacy varies each year and has ranged from 23% to 60% overall efficacy during the past 5 seasons.
  11. Alternate vaccine formulations.
     a. Intradermal vaccine is available for injection into skin instead of muscle. This uses a smaller needle than the regular flu vaccine and might be preferred by adults aged 18 to 64 yr who do not like shots.
     b. Nasal spray, live-attenuated influenza vaccine (LAIV) is available for non-pregnant, healthy persons aged 2 to 49 yr. No preference is given to LAIV or inactivated influenza vaccine (IIV) for persons ages 2 to 49 years. Note: Give TIV if recipient has egg allergy or asthma or cares for immunosuppressed persons who require a protective environment.
     c. High-dose inactivated vaccine (60 micrograms hemagglutinin each flu strain) is available for persons ≥65 yr. Recent study concludes a significantly improved efficacy using high-dose vaccine.
     d. Thimerosal-free vaccine is available.
     e. IIV can be trivalent or quadrivalent, and egg-based or non-egg-based (cell culture or recombinant hemagglutinin).
     f. There is no preference for standard dose IIV, high dose IIV (age 65 or over) or intradermal IIV (ages 18-64).
     g. ACIP guidance for egg allergies:
        - If a person with egg allergy experiences only hives, then administer trivalent recombinant hemagglutinin influenza vaccine (RIV3) if ages 18 to 49, or IIV and observe for at least 30 minutes for reaction following vaccine.
        - If a person with egg allergy experiences other symptoms such as cardiovascular (e.g., hypotension),

TABLE 1I-6 Pulmonary Radiographic Findings Based on Virus Type

Virus	Centrilobular Nodules	Lobar Ground-Glass	Diffuse Ground-Glass	Thickened Interlobular Septa	Consolidation
Influenza	+++	+++	+		+
Epstein-Barr	+	+	+		+
Cytomegalovirus	++	++	++	+	+
Varicella-zoster	+++	+	+		
Herpes simplex	+	+++	+		+++
Measles	++	+	+		+
Hantavirus			+++	+	++
Adenovirus	++	+			+++

From Weissleder R et al: *Primer of diagnostic imaging*, ed 5, St Louis, 2011, Mosby.

respiratory distress (e.g., wheezing), gastrointestinal (e.g., nausea/vomiting), reaction requiring epinephrine or emergency medical attention, administer RIV3 if age 18 to 49, or refer to a physician with expertise in management of allergic conditions.

- If there is no known history of exposure to egg, but the person is suspected of having egg allergy, consult with a physician who has expertise in the management of allergies before vaccinating, or give RIV3 (if ages 18 to 49).
- Chemoprophylaxis:
  1. Table 1I-7 describes antiviral agents for influenza. Oseltamivir and zanamivir are recommended in the United States during the influenza season.
  2. Consider (after the current circulating strain of influenza has been shown to be sensitive):
     a. For high-risk patients in whom vaccination is contraindicated.
     b. When the available vaccine is known not to include the circulating strain.
     c. To provide added protection to immunosuppressed patients likely to have a diminished response to vaccination.
     d. In the setting of an outbreak, when immediate protection of unvaccinated or recently vaccinated patients at high risk of complications is desired.
  3. Chemoprophylaxis with antiviral drugs is not recommended for healthy persons exposed to seasonal influenza.
  4. Give for 2 wk in the case of late vaccination and for the duration of the flu season in all other patients.
  5. Treatment should not wait for laboratory confirmation of influenza.
  6. Do not give aspirin or aspirin-containing products to children with influenza-like illness due to the risk of Reye's syndrome.
- Other prevention strategies:
  1. Hand hygiene, cough etiquette (cover your cough), respiratory hygiene (use of tissues, facemasks for the ill and proper disposal).
  2. Seasonal flu personal protective equipment (PPE)—wear gloves and gowns as per universal/standard precautions. Per the CDC, wear a facemask, adhering to Droplet Precautions for 7 days after illness onset or until 24 hr after fever and respiratory symptoms are resolved, whichever is longer. Patient placement in a negative pressure room and N95 respirator for health care workers are recommended when conducting aerosol-generating procedures.
  3. For HPAI (H5N1, H7N9, H5N2, H5N8) per the CDC, wear eye protection, N95 respirator, gown, and gloves as for airborne and contact precautions.
  4. Management of ill health care workers—exclude from work until at least 24 hr after they no longer have a fever (without the use of fever-reducing medication). Extended exclusion time period when caring for severely immunocompromised patients.
  5. Standard cleaning and disinfection procedures.
- The Centers for Medicare and Medicaid Services plan to link healthcare worker vaccine acceptance with payment for performance.

SUGGESTED READINGS
Available at www.expertconsult.com

RELATED CONTENT
Influenza (Flu) (Patient Information)

AUTHOR: **MARLENE FISHMAN WOLPERT, M.P.H., C.I.C.**

TABLE 1I-7 Antiviral Agents for Influenza

	Amantadine	Rimantadine	Zanamivir	Oseltamivir
Protein target	M2	M2	Neuraminidase	Neuraminidase
Activity	A only (H1N1 and H3N2 are resistant)	A only (H1N1 and H3N2 are resistant)	A and B	A and B
Side effects	CNS (13%) GI (3%)	GI (6%)	? Bronchospasm	GI (9%)
Metabolism	None	Multiple (hepatic)	None	Hepatic
Excretion	Renal	Renal,+ others	Renal	Renal (tubular secretion)
Drug interactions	Antihistamines, anticholinergics	None	None	Probenecid (increased levels of oseltamivir)
Dose adjustments needed	≥65 yr old CrCl <50 ml/min	≥65 yr old CrCl <10 ml/min	None	CrCl <30 ml/min Severe liver dysfunction
Contraindications	Acute-angle glaucoma	Severe liver dysfunction	Underlying airway disease, asthma	
FDA-Approved Indications				
Therapy	Adults and children ≥1 yr old	Adults only	Adults and children ≥7 yr old	Adults and children ≥1 yr old*
Prophylaxis	Yes	Yes	Adults and children ≥5 yr old	Adults and children ≥13 yr old†

CrCl, Creatinine clearance; *FDA*, U.S. Food and Drug Administration; *GI*, gastrointestinal.
*FDA has authorized treatment of S-OIV (novel H1N1) virus with oseltamivir in children ≥3 mo of age.
†FDA has authorized prophylaxis for S-OIV (novel H1N1) virus with oseltamivir in children ≥1 yr.
From Mandell GL et al: *Principles and practice of infectious diseases*, ed 7, Philadelphia, 2010, Churchill Livingstone.

BASIC INFORMATION

DEFINITION

Insomnia is a disturbance of initiating or maintaining sleep. Restless, nonrestorative sleep may also be described as another specified insomnia. The disturbance occurs despite adequate circumstances and opportunity for sleep and is accompanied by significant distress or impairment in daytime functioning. In the new DSM-5, the diagnosis of primary insomnia has been replaced with **insomnia disorder** in order to avoid the distinction between primary and secondary forms of the disorder. This paradigm shift relates to widely accepted research in the field suggesting that there is a bidirectional and interactive relationship between insomnia and any coexisting medical and/or mental disorders. As such it suggests that insomnia is deserving of direct clinical attention that may be expected to have beneficial impact on both the insomnia and comorbid disorder as well.

SYNONYMS

Sleeplessness

Sleep disorder, sleep disturbance, dyssomnia (NOTE: The terms *sleep disorder, sleep disturbance,* and *dyssomnia* are generic and can refer to disorders of wakefulness [hypersomnia] or sleep-related behavior disorders [parasomnias])

Insomnia disorder

ICD-10CM CODES

F51.01	Primary insomnia
F51.02	Adjustment insomnia
F51.03	Paradoxical insomnia
F51.04	Psychophysiologic insomnia
F51.05	Insomnia due to other mental disorder
F51.09	Other insomnia not due to a substance or known physiological condition
G47.00	Insomnia, unspecified
G47.01	Insomnia due to medical condition
G47.09	Other insomnia
Z73.810	Behavioral insomnia of childhood, sleep-onset association type
Z73.811	Behavioral insomnia of childhood, limit setting type
Z73.812	Behavioral insomnia of childhood, combined type
Z73.819	Behavioral insomnia of childhood, unspecified type

EPIDEMIOLOGY & DEMOGRAPHICS

INCIDENCE (IN U.S.): 30% to 45% of adults experience insomnia per year.

PREVALENCE (IN U.S.): 1% to 15% of all adults and 25% of older adults develop persistent insomnia.

PREDOMINANT SEX: More common in women.

PREDOMINANT AGE: Transient insomnia can occur at any age; persistent insomnia is more common after age 60 yr.

GENETICS: Can run in families and may be genetically influenced. Circadian rhythm disorders and narcolepsy have been traced to specific genes.

PHYSICAL FINDINGS & CLINICAL PRESENTATION

- Difficulty falling asleep, difficulty staying asleep, or early morning awakening.
- Significant distress or impairment in daytime functioning such as fatigue or low energy, sleepiness, cognitive impairments, mood disturbances, or behavioral problems.
- Difficulty occurs despite adequate opportunity for sleep.
- Symptoms may be acute and self-limited, chronic but intermittent, or chronic and frequent.

ETIOLOGY

- Transient insomnia:
  1. Stress.
  2. Illness.
  3. Travel (across time zones).
  4. Environmental disruptions (noise, heat, cold, poor bedding, bed partners, unfamiliar surroundings, etc).
- Persistent insomnia:
  1. Mood and anxiety disorders (depression, hypomania/mania, PTSD).
  2. Psychophysiologic insomnia (conditioned arousal, extended sleep opportunity, sleep effort, poor sleep hygiene).
  3. Sleep-related breathing disorders (e.g., obstructive apnea and hypopnea, increased upper airway resistance).
  4. Chronobiologic (also known as circadian rhythm) disorder (delayed sleep phase, advanced sleep phase, shift work, non-24-hr sleep wake disorder secondary to blindness).
  5. Drug and alcohol abuse.
  6. Restless legs syndrome and periodic leg movements.
  7. Neurodegenerative (Alzheimer's disease, Parkinson's disease, etc).
  8. Medical (pain, GERD, nocturia, orthopnea, medications, etc).

DIAGNOSIS

Diagnostic and Statistical Manual of Mental Disorders (DSM-5) criteria for the diagnosis of insomnia disorder[1] is as follows:

- Dissatisfaction with sleep quantity or quality, with one or more of the following symptoms:
- Difficulty initiating sleep
- Difficulty maintaining sleep, characterized by frequent awakenings or trouble returning to sleep after awakenings
- Early-morning awakening with inability to return to sleep

[1] American Psychiatric Association: Diagnostic and statistical manual of mental disorders, 5th ed, American Psychiatric Publishing, Arlington, VA, 2013.

- The sleep disturbance causes clinically significant distress or impairment in daytime functioning, as evidenced by at least one of the following:
- Fatigue or low energy
- Daytime sleepiness
- Impaired attention, concentration, or memory
- Mood disturbance
- Behavioral difficulties
- Impaired occupational or academic function
- Impaired interpersonal or social function
- Negative effect on caregiver or family functioning
- The sleep difficulty occurs at least 3 nights per week, is present for at least 3 months, and occurs despite adequate opportunity for sleep

DIFFERENTIAL DIAGNOSIS

Insomnia disorder is only ruled out when the disorder is seen exclusively during other etiologies (see "Etiology"). It can be precipitated by a "primary" medical mental health, or other sleep-wake disorder, but continues as a comorbid condition even after the "primary disorder" has been treated.

WORKUP

- History (with bed partner interview, if possible).
- Sleep diary for 2 wk (Consider the Consensus Sleep Diary [Carney CE, et al. in Suggested Readings section]).
- Wrist actigraphy (detects gross limb movements and can distinguish wake from sleep states) and as an adjunct to a diary—provides some objective verification of the diary data.
- Validated sleep-quality rating scale (optional).
  1. Insomnia Severity Index.
  2. Pittsburgh Sleep Quality Index.
  3. Epworth Sleepiness Scale (see Daytime Sleepiness Test at http://www.sleepfoundation.org).

LABORATORY TESTS

- Evaluate for anemia (especially low ferritin level), uremia (for restless legs), thyroid function (if other signs present).
- Polysomnography (in home or in sleep laboratory) is not standard for but should be reserved for patients whose history suggests specific sleep-related breathing or movement disorders. It is indicated for symptoms suggestive of daytime sleepiness (obstructive sleep apnea, narcolepsy), nonrestorative sleep (periodic leg movements, chronic pain conditions), or sleep behavior suggesting parasomnia (somnambulism, REM sleep behavior).

IMAGING STUDIES

- Not generally helpful.
- Brain CT or MRI for severe daytime sleepiness or acute onset.

BOX 1I-4   Sleep Habits (Sleep Hygiene Measures) That May Improve Sleep

1. Reduce caffeine, alcohol, or tobacco late in the day or especially evening.
2. Avoid heavy meals at night, but consider a light snack before bed such as toast or a handful of nuts.
3. Increase daytime activity, but avoid exercise within 3-5 hours of bedtime.
4. Increase daytime exposure to natural light.
5. Reduce liquids in the last 4 hours before bedtime.
6. Consider white noise as background sound for the sleep environment.
7. Maintain regular bed and wake times.
8. Go to bed with calm mind; resolve arguments or set a time earlier in the day to review problems and perhaps write down plans, solutions, or things to do.
9. Keep light exposure in the middle of the night to a minimum when awake and attenuate morning light in the bedroom.
10. Avoid pets in the bed.

[1]American Psychiatric Association: *Diagnostic and statistical manual of mental disorders,* 5th ed, American Psychiatric Publishing, Arlington, VA, 2013.

 **TREATMENT**

NONPHARMACOLOGIC THERAPY

- Sleep hygiene measures (Box 1I-4) as a monotherapy are not very effective. More useful combined with procedures described next.
- Cognitive-behavioral therapy (CBT-I) has been shown to reduce time to fall asleep and time awake during the night, can reduce reliance on sleep medications, and has shown lasting effects after treatment has been discontinued.
- The standard components that comprise CBT-I are as follows:
  1. Stimulus Control, which addresses the conditioned cues that create arousal when attempting to sleep by restricting activity in bed to sleep and sex and not permitting sleep effort, worrying, watching TV, reading, etc., in bed (reconditioning of this type can take several days or weeks—patients should not come to expect positive changes on the first night)
  2. Sleep Restriction restricts sleep opportunity to the average amount of total sleep time the patient is getting as determined by baseline sleep diary data. Sleep time is increased incrementally, based on improving sleep efficiency. Note that restricted time in bed should never be <4.5 to 5 hr. For the elderly and infirm, average total sleep time plus 30 min is sometimes considered. For patients whose estimated average total sleep time is <4 hr, a diagnosis of paradoxical insomnia should be considered and CBT-I would be contraindicated.
  3. Cognitive Therapy targets unhelpful beliefs and worries about sleep, negative and unwanted thoughts, selective attention bias and monitoring, misperception of sleep and daytime deficits, and counterproductive safety behaviors that are thought to maintain insomnia.
  4. Sleep Hygiene is aimed at improving sleep habits (e.g., initiating or maintaining exercise, avoiding heavy meals at night, and decreasing or eliminating caffeine, nicotine, and alcohol intake). Environmental factors can also be addressed (e.g., using white noise and/or light attenuating bedroom). Caffeine sometimes can prove useful when used judiciously in the morning and early afternoon to combat the increased fatigue and somnolence that are produced early in therapy with sleep restriction and stimulus control. In addition, exercise contingently applied to daytime fatigue can also help to improve alertness during the day and increase sleep pressure at bedtime.
  5. Relaxation Exercises (e.g., progressive muscle relaxation, diaphragmatic breathing) may be good adjunctive therapy, especially in highly anxious patients, but are not thought to be essential in CBT-I. Increasingly, mindfulness-based practices are being effectively utilized alone and in combination with other elements of CBT-I. Mindfulness may help patients to adopt a more flexible and accepting stance toward insomnia.
- Circadian Rhythm Disturbances, such as in shift workers, many blind individuals who lack light-dark cycle to synchronize body clock, adolescents and young adults with delayed sleep phase syndrome, and jet lag can be treated with chronobiologic therapies such as chronotherapy, bright light exposure, melatonin, or melatonin agonists. However, the timing of these interventions can be critical to outcome and constitutes therapies that are very different from standard medical and/or behavioral treatment for insomnia.

ACUTE GENERAL Rx

- Benzodiazepine receptor agonists zolpidem 5 mg and zaleplon 5 mg for sleep-onset insomnia, and zolpidem continuous-release formulation 6.25 to 12.5 mg and eszopiclone 1 to 3 mg for maintenance insomnia.
- Suvorexant is an orexin receptor antagonist recently FDA approved for insomnia. Signaling of orexin neuropeptides sustains wakefulness. Suvorexant promotes sleep by blocking orexin neuropeptides from binding to their receptors. Most common side effect (10%) is next-day somnolence.
- Benzodiazepine sedative-hypnotics (e.g., temazepam 7.5 to 30 mg, triazolam 0.125 to 0.25 mg).
- A low-dose formulation (6 mg) of the tricyclic antidepressant doxepin, brand name Silenor, is also FDA approved for treatment of insomnia associated with sleep maintenance. This dose retains the hypnotic effect of doxepin without the typical tricyclic effects. A generic 10 mg/ml liquid formulation of doxepin is also available.
- In critical care: lorazepam 0.25 to 0.5 mg PO, SL, or IV as needed for sleep. In patients with acute delirium, haloperidol 0.25 to 0.5 mg IV as needed up to 2 mg/day may be less likely to worsen confusion.
- Melatonin agonist ramelteon 8 mg for sleep-onset insomnia when a mild agent without benzodiazepine side effects is desired.
- Avoid antihistamines except for occasional use.
- Optimize treatment of medical symptoms, especially pain.
- Most prescription and over-the-counter medications carry significant risk of adverse events and drug interactions, especially in the geriatric patient. Preferred pharmacotherapeutic agents in the elderly are zolpidem, zaleplon, eszopiclone, and ramelteon.

CHRONIC Rx

- Considerable research supports the efficacy of CBT-I, with acute treatment outcomes equivalent to pharmacotherapy, and better long-term outcomes and maintenance of treatment gains. Although there is limited availability of CBT-I specialists, especially in certain geographic areas, there are now online interactive evidence based self-help programs that can serve as an effective base for a stepped model of care. Patients who fail these attempts should still be encouraged to seek more tailored treatment with a specialist, especially when the insomnia is comorbid with other conditions.
- Three sedative-hypnotics—zolpidem continuous release, eszopiclone, and ramelteon—FDA approved for long-term use.
- Some evidence shows that benzodiazepines and benzodiazepine receptor agonists can be used for chronic insomnia on either intermittent or nightly use with moderate risk of tolerance and dependence but low risk of addiction.
- Sedating antidepressants (e.g., trazodone 25 to 150 mg, mirtazapine 7.5 to 30 mg, amitriptyline 25 to 50 mg, doxepin 10 mg) are in widespread use, with limited data on safety and efficacy. Amitriptyline should be avoided in older adults.
- Sedating antipsychotics (e.g., quetiapine 25 to 200 mg, olanzapine 2.5 to 10 mg at night) considered for severe mood or psychotic disorders associated with insomnia.

COMPLEMENTARY & ALTERNATIVE MEDICINE

Melatonin may shorten sleep-onset latency in some individuals. It may have more use in

the treatment of circadian rhythm disorders. Timing of administration in these types of cases requires careful consideration and would not be often administered at bedtime.

DISPOSITION

- Transient insomnia: usually self-limited. May require follow-up if stress-related or illness-related because of risk of depression or persistence. Prophylactic education regarding maladaptive sleep practices such as extending time in bed, and/or remaining in bed when unable to sleep, might be helpful in avoiding a more protracted course of insomnia.

  Persistent insomnia: Patients who respond well to CBT-I often continue to maintain gains at 1 and 2-yr follow-ups. Patients may need periodic follow-up to reinforce good sleep hygiene and stimulus control and for reevaluation of pharmacologic therapies. There is now a compelling amount of evidence that insomnia is associated with significant negative mental and health effects over time.

REFERRAL

- A referral to a behavioral medicine specialist may be required for CBT-I or for circadian rhythm disturbances (find a directory at http://www.behavioralsleep.org/findspecialist.aspx).
- Excessive daytime sleepiness not obviously caused by insomnia (e.g., narcolepsy, sleep-related breathing disorder).

- Nighttime behavior suggestive of a parasomnia (e.g., somnambulism, REM behavior disorder).
- Severe insomnia not responsive to basic interventions.

COMMENTS

CBT-I often results in worse sleep and more fatigue in the short run. Patients often respond to initial worsening of symptoms as a sign of failure; however, they should be encouraged to see this as an important piece of the therapy and to stay the course as new conditioned patterns begin to emerge, sleep efficiency improves, and total sleep time gradually increases. Patients should avoid compensating for lost sleep by extending sleep opportunity in the form of sleeping in or napping. Therefore, early treatment should focus on helping patients to manage daytime fatigue and sleepiness by engaging in activities that help patients stay awake and maintain set bed and wake times.

PREVENTION

It is estimated that 50% to 70% of individuals demonstrating the syndrome of insomnia (e.g., insomnia symptoms more than 3 days per week for a month along with deleterious daytime sequelae) are still syndromic 1 to 5 years later.

Therefore, early intervention with medication or education to prevent the development of maladaptive compensatory behaviors (e.g., napping, sleeping late, tossing and turning in bed, avoiding or decreasing daytime activity) may help to reduce the risk of developing persistent insomnia.

PATIENT & FAMILY EDUCATION

The National Sleep Foundation (http://www.sleepfoundation.org) is a comprehensive resource for health care providers and patients.

Available at www.expertconsult.com.

SUGGESTED READINGS

Available at www.expertconsult.com.

RELATED CONTENT

Sleep disorders (Algorithm in Section III)
Insomnia (Patient Information)

AUTHOR: **DONN POSNER, PH.D., C.B.S.M.**

Insulinoma

 BASIC INFORMATION

DEFINITION

Insulinoma is a pancreatic insulin-secreting tumor that leads to inappropriately elevated plasma insulin or proinsulin levels with suppression of hepatic glucose output and subsequent hypoglycemia, especially during periods of fasting.

ICD-10CM CODES

C25.4 Malignant neoplasm of endocrine pancreas
D13.7 Benign neoplasm of endocrine pancreas
D37.7 Neoplasm of uncertain or unknown behavior of other digestive organs (pancreas)

EPIDEMIOLOGY & DEMOGRAPHICS

INCIDENCE: One case per 250,000 persons annually. 90% of insulinomas are benign.
PREDOMINANT SEX AND AGE: Insulinomas occur in both sexes (approximately 60% in women) and at all ages. In a Mayo Clinic series, the median age at diagnosis was 50 yr in sporadic cases, but 23 yr in patients with multiple endocrine neoplasia, type 1 (MEN-1).

PHYSICAL FINDINGS & CLINICAL PRESENTATION

Symptoms typically occur in the morning before breakfast (i.e., fasting hypoglycemia as opposed to reactive hypoglycemia, which is not commonly associated with insulinoma).

Neuroglycopenic Symptoms	%
Various combinations of diplopia, blurred vision, sweating, palpitations, or weakness	85
Confusion or abnormal behavior	80
Unconsciousness or amnesia	53
Grand mal seizures	12
Adrenergic Symptoms	%
Sweating	43
Tremulousness	23
Hunger, nausea	12
Palpitations	10

ETIOLOGY, PATHOLOGY, PATHOPHYSIOLOGY

- Insulinomas are almost always solitary. Malignant insulinomas account for 5% of the total; they tend to be larger (6 cm). Metastases are usually to the liver (47%), regional lymph nodes (30%), or both.
- Insulinomas are evenly distributed in the head, body, and tail of the pancreas; ectopic insulinomas are rare (1% to 3%). Tumor size: 5% are ≤0.5 cm, 34% are 0.5 to 1 cm, 53% are 1 to 5 cm, and 8% are >5 cm.
- Histologic classification includes insulinoma in 86% of patients, adenomatosis in 5% to 15%, nesidioblastosis in 4%, and hyperplasia in 1%. Adenomatosis consists of multiple macroadenomas or microadenomas and occurs especially in patients with MEN-1. Nesidioblastosis is also a diffuse lesion in which islet cells form as buds on ductular structures.

 DIAGNOSIS

DIFFERENTIAL DIAGNOSIS (OF FASTING HYPOGLYCEMIA)

Hyperinsulinism:
- Insulinoma.
- Nonpancreatic tumors.
- Severe congestive heart failure.
- Severe renal insufficiency in non-insulin-dependent diabetes.

Hepatic enzyme deficiencies or decreased hepatic glucose output (primarily in infants and children):
- Glycogen storage diseases.
- Endocrine hypofunction.
- Hypopituitarism.
- Addison's disease.
- Liver failure.
- Alcohol abuse.
- Malnutrition.
  Exogenous agents:
- Sulfonylureas, biguanides.
- Insulin.
- Other drugs (aspirin, pentamidine).

Functional fasting hypoglycemia:
- Autoantibodies to insulin receptor or insulin.

LABORATORY TESTS

- An overnight fasting blood sugar level combined with a simultaneous plasma insulin, proinsulin, and/or C peptide level will establish the existence of fasting organic hypoglycemia in 60% of patients. Table E1I-8 describes biochemical patterns in patients with various causes of hyperinsulinemic hypoglycemia.
- If single overnight fasting glucose and insulin levels are nondiagnostic, a 72-hr fast is usually done with blood glucose and insulin levels determined at 2-to 4-hr intervals. A total of 75% of patients with insulinoma develop symptoms and a blood sugar level of <40 mg/dl by 24 hr, 92% to 98% develop these by 48 hr, and virtually all patients develop them by 72 hr. The test is considered positive for insulinoma if the plasma insulin/glucose ratio is more than 0.3. If at any point the patient becomes symptomatic, plasma insulin and glucose values should be obtained and IV glucose should be administered.
- The Endocrine Society guidelines for diagnosis of hypoglycemic disorders is based on glucose level <55 mg/dl (<3.1 mmol/L), elevated C-peptide level ≥0.61 ng/mL (≥0.2 nmol/L). Elevated insulin level ≥18 pmol/L, proinsulin level >5 pmol/L, and suppressed β-hydroxy-butyric acid level.
- An "amended" insulin-glucose ratio that accounts for the normal variation in insulin secretion according to prevailing glycemia has been shown to improve diagnostic accuracy of insulinomas. The "amended" insulin-glucose ratio is derived from the simple insulin-glucose ratio by subtracting 30 mg/dl (1.7 mmol/L) from the measured glucose concentrations.

IMAGING STUDIES

- Abdominal CT scan or MRI (Fig. E1I-17) detects half to two thirds of insulinomas (abdominal ultrasound is not effective); should be done only after laboratory tests for insulinoma have confirmed the diagnosis.
- Intraoperative ultrasound.
- Arteriography.
- Octreotide scan (Fig. E1I-18).

 TREATMENT

NONPHARMACOLOGIC THERAPY

- Enucleation of single insulinoma.
- Partial pancreatectomy for multiple adenomas.

ACUTE GENERAL Rx

- Carbohydrate administration.
- Diazoxide directly inhibits insulin release and has an extrapancreatic, hyperglycemic effect that enhances glycogenolysis.
- Lanreotide and octreotide (somatostatin analogues).
- Streptozotocin.

REFERRAL

To an endocrinologist and then to an endocrine surgeon.

SUGGESTED READINGS

Available at www.expertconsult.com.

RELATED CONTENT

Hypoglycemia (Algorithm in Section III)

AUTHOR: **FRED F. FERRI, M.D.**

 BASIC INFORMATION

DEFINITION

Multiple episodes of impulsive verbal or physical aggression out of proportion to perceived stressors or threats

ICD-10CM CODES
F63.81 Intermittent explosive disorder
F63.8 Other habit and impulse disorders
F63.9 Habit and impulse disorder, unspecified

EPIDEMIOLOGY & DEMOGRAPHICS

INCIDENCE: Unknown
PEAK INCIDENCE: Occurs earlier in life
PREVALENCE: Lifetime prevalence of 6%-7%
PREDOMINANT SEX AND AGE: Occurs more so in males and in people under the age of 50
GENETICS: Patients with intermittent explosive disorder (IED) are more likely to have first-degree relatives with the disorder. In addition, adoption and twin studies point to a >50% of the variance in aggression related to genetic factors.
RISK FACTORS: Prior history of violence, exposure to trauma, comorbid depression, anxiety, substance abuse or dependence, or cluster B personality disorders.

PHYSICAL FINDINGS & CLINICAL PRESENTATION

- Several episodes of verbal or physical aggression; the latter may include attacks on others or destruction of physical property.
- The aggression is out of proportion to any perceived stressors or threats.
- The aggression is impulsive.
- The aggression causes distress.
- The aggression is not accounted for by another disease process.
- The patient is at least 6 years of age.

ETIOLOGY

- Potentially an imbalance between aggression, originating from the amygdala and other limbic structures, and orbitofrontal and anterior cingulate cortices. This view is supported by multiple studies involving functional neuroimaging, specifically fMRI.
- From a neurochemical basis, a deficiency in the neurotransmitter serotonin appears involved. Serotonergic agents treat IED (see the following) and PET imaging shows a decrease in serotonergic innervation in the anterior cingulate cortex.

Dx DIAGNOSIS

DIFFERENTIAL DIAGNOSIS

- Psychiatrically, patients may suffer from mood, anxiety, psychotic, and personality disorders (primarily antisocial and borderline). In addition, patients may be under the effects of substances, or in withdrawal from them.
- Neuropsychiatrically, dementia, delirium, temporal lobe epilepsy, cardiovascular disease, multiple sclerosis, and brain lesions can all cause similar behavior.

- If delirium is expected, a wider, more systemic differential diagnosis should be explored.

WORKUP

- A thorough mental status exam should be performed. In addition, there should be careful consideration for other neuropsychiatric conditions if the history points in that direction.

LABORATORY TESTS

- Urine toxicology screen, as substance abuse is highly comorbid.
- Dementia workup when appropriate: CBC, head CT, Chem 7, B12, TSH, Folate, RPR.
- Delirium workup when appropriate; associated signs and symptoms may be helpful for guidance, especially in clinical settings.

IMAGING STUDIES

- Head CT or MRI, in cases where dementia, delirium, neurovascular disease, or brain lesions are expected. The appropriate test should be ordered depending on the particulars of the case (i.e., MRI to evaluate for MS).
- EEG is indicated to evaluate for seizure-related conditions.

 **TREATMENT (TABLE 1I-9)**

- Selective serotonin reuptake inhibitors (SSRIs) are considered first-line therapy. Multiple studies have been performed on fluoxetine, up to 60 mg per day, though it is not unreasonable to try other SSRIs given similar mechanisms of action. Cost, side effects, drug half-life, and drug-drug interactions need to be considered. Starting at 20 mg per day, and increasing by 10 mg every other week, for a total of a 12 week trial, is recommended.
- Unless there is a contraindication to SSRIs, AEDs should be considered second line, given their potential side effects and toxicities.
- Multiple large trials and meta-analyses also point to the efficacy of phenytoin, lamotrigine, topiramate, and valproate.
- Lithium has also shown to be helpful.

- See Table 1I-9 for details related to particular medications.

NONPHARMACOLOGIC THERAPY

- Cognitive-behavioral therapy has been shown to be helpful for patients with IED.
- Patients are taught to examine their thoughts in relation to stressful circumstances.
- Patients can be taught to examine their somatic sensations and change these through relaxation techniques.
- Relapse prevention is focused on helping patients avoid explosive behaviors in the future.

ACUTE GENERAL Rx

- See previous.

COMPLEMENTARY AND ALTERNATIVE MEDICINE

There is no evidence on the use of complementary or alternative medicine for this disorder.

REFERRAL

Referral to an outpatient mental health provider may be helpful.

PEARLS & CONSIDERATIONS

PREVENTION

No prevention measures have been identified.

PATIENT/FAMILY EDUCATION

Psychoeducation to the patient and family may be helpful, especially in helping to identify triggers and supporting the use of coping skills.

RELATED CONTENT

Abuse, Drug (Related Key Topic)
Attention Deficit-Hyperactivity Disorder (Related Key Topic)
Bipolar Disorder (Related Key Topic)
Conduct Disorder (Related Key Topic)
Personality Disorders (Related Key Topic)

AUTHOR: **ANTHONY GALLO, M.D.**

TABLE 1I-9 Medications for Intermittent Explosive Disorder

Medication	Starting Dose	Blood Level	Adverse Outcomes	Cautionary Notes
Fluoxetine	10 mg PO qAM	N/A	Mania, sexual dysfunction, SIADH.	Caution in patients with bipolar disorder.
Phenytoin	100 mg PO tid	10-20 mcg/ml	Hepatotoxicity, gingival hyperplasia.	Caution in patients with hepatic dysfunction.
Topiramate	50 mg daily	N/A	Sedation.	
Lamotrigine	25 mg daily	N/A	Rash, SJS.	Slow titration schedule.
Valproate	250 mg PO bid	75-125 mcg/ml	Hyperammonemia, pancreatitis, hepatic impairment.	Caution in patients with hepatic impairment.
Carbamazepine	200 mg PO bid	4-12 mcg/ml	Hepatic failure, SJS, blood dyscrasias, SIADH.	Caution in patients with hepatic impairment.
Lithium	300 mg PO bid	0.6-1.2 mEq/L	Hypothyroid, nephrotoxicity.	Caution in patients with renal impairment.

ℹ️ BASIC INFORMATION

DEFINITION

The International Continence Society defines interstitial cystitis (IC), otherwise known as painful bladder syndrome, as a clinical syndrome consisting of suprapubic pain related to bladder filling and accompanied by other symptoms such as increased daytime and nighttime frequency in the absence of proven infection or other obvious pathology. The American Urological Association defines interstitial cystitis/bladder pain syndrome (IC/BPS) as an unpleasant sensation perceived to be related to the urinary bladder that is associated with lower urinary tract symptoms >6 weeks' duration, in the absence of infection or other unidentifiable causes.

SYNONYMS

Interstitial cystitis/bladder pain syndrome (IC/BPS)
Painful bladder syndrome
Tic douloureux of bladder

ICD-10CM CODES
N30.1   Interstitial cystitis (chronic)
N30.9   Cystitis, unspecified
N30.10   Interstitial cystitis (chronic) without hematuria
N30.11   Interstitial cystitis (chronic) with hematuria

EPIDEMIOLOGY & DEMOGRAPHICS

INCIDENCE: 21 cases per 100,000 women and four cases per 100,000 men annually
PREVALENCE:
- 197 per 100,000 women and 41 per 100,000 men in the U.S.
- Because the disease is substantially underdiagnosed, it may actually affect one in five women and one in 20 men.
- More than 81% of women diagnosed with chronic pelvic pain and up to 84% of men initially diagnosed with chronic prostatitis actually have IC.
- More than 90% of patients diagnosed with overactive bladder who do not respond to anticholinergics are subsequently diagnosed with IC.

PREDOMINANT SEX AND AGE:
- White women constitute 95% of patients with IC.
- Female/male ratio of 5 to 10:1.
- Most prevalent in fourth and fifth decades of life.

PHYSICAL FINDINGS & CLINICAL PRESENTATION

- Urinary urgency, frequency (>8 in daytime), nocturia (>2 at night), and suprapubic pain are the most common symptoms.
- Suprapubic pain is worse with bladder filling or urinating and relieved after emptying.
- Dyspareunia.
- Symptoms lasting longer than 6 mo.
- Intensity of symptoms waxes and wanes.

- Insidious onset and worsens to the final stage within 5 to 15 yr.
- Exercise, stress, sexual activity, ejaculation, certain foods with high potassium and acids (beer, spices, bananas, tomatoes, chocolate, strawberries, artificial sweeteners, oranges, cranberries, caffeine), menstruation, prolonged sitting, and activation of allergies exacerbate the symptoms.
- Often associated with irritable bowel syndrome, migraine, endometriosis, skin sensitivities, multiple drug allergies, other allergies, vulvodynia, fibromyalgia, chronic fatigue syndrome, systemic lupus erythematosus, and mood disorders.
- Dysphoric mood.
- Lower abdominal tenderness.
- Tender prostate in digital rectal examination.
- Levator ani tenderness in female.
- Tenderness of anterior vaginal wall/bladder neck in female.

ETIOLOGY

Unknown. Fig. 1I-19 illustrates a hypothesis for etiologic cascade of painful bladder syndrome/interstitial cystitis.

🅳🆇 DIAGNOSIS

DIFFERENTIAL DIAGNOSIS

- Chronic pelvic pain
- Overactive bladder
- Recurrent urinary tract infection
- Endometriosis
- Pelvic adhesions
- Vulvar vestibulitis
- Vulvodynia
- Urethral pain syndrome
- Chronic nonbacterial prostatitis
- Frequent vaginitis
- Benign prostatic hyperplasia

WORKUP

- IC can be considered a diagnosis of exclusion when no known cause of painful bladder can be identified.
- There is no definite diagnostic test.
- Validated questionnaires such as Pelvic Pain and Urgency/Frequency scale (PUF), O'Leary-Sant symptoms and problem index, and Wisconsin IC scale. PUF is the most commonly used.

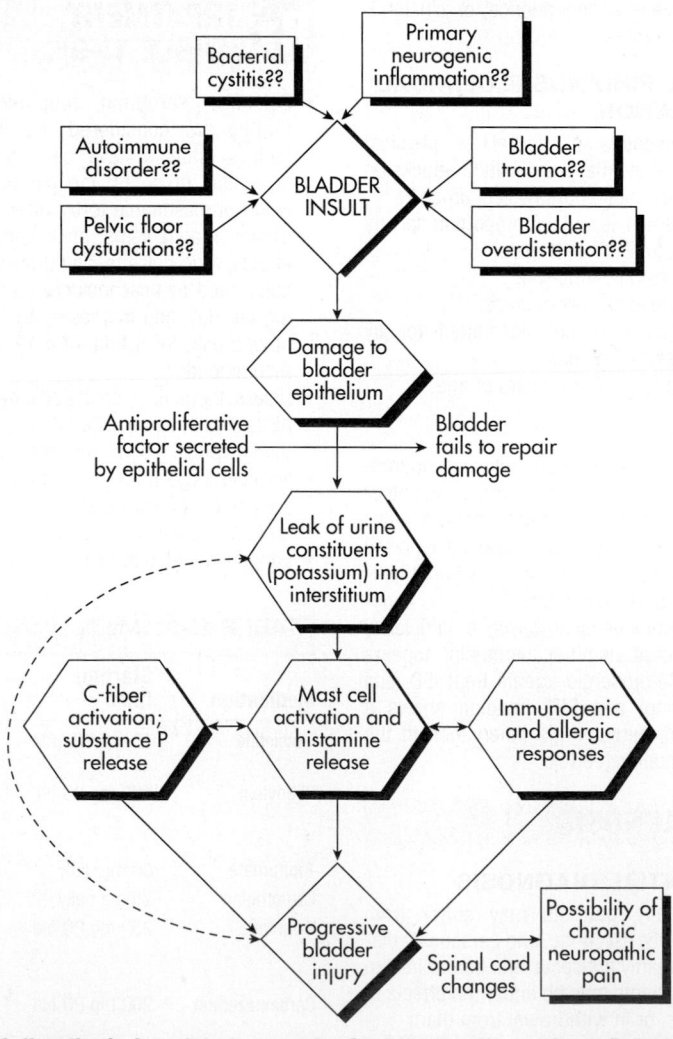

FIGURE 1I-19 Hypothesis for etiologic cascade of painful bladder syndrome/interstitial cystitis. (From Wein AJ: Painful bladder syndrome/interstitial cystitis and related disorders. In Wein AJ et al (eds): *Campbell-Walsh urology*, ed 11, Philadelphia, 2007, Elsevier.)

- Voiding diary shows low-volume (<100 ml) and high-frequency voiding pattern.
- National Institute of Diabetes and Diseases of the Kidney diagnostic criteria misses 60% of IC patients and is not clinically used anymore.
- Anesthetic bladder challenge: with this test the symptoms dissipate on instillation of an anesthetic cocktail into the bladder.
- Cystoscopy and hydrodistention under general anesthesia may show terminal hematuria, glomerulation, Hunner's ulcers, and small bladder capacity of less than 350 ml. Cystoscopy and/or urodynamic testing should be considered when the diagnosis is in doubt, but the tests are not necessary to confirm an IC/BPS diagnosis in uncomplicated cases.
- Bladder biopsy is not essential for diagnosis of IC.
- Parson's potassium sensitivity test (PST).
- Urodynamics are unnecessary in diagnosis of IC.

LABORATORY TESTS

- Urine analysis and culture.
- Urine cytology should be performed if microscopic or gross hematuria is present, or with other risk factors such as smoking, age >40 yr, and other bladder cancer risk factors.
- Culture of sexually transmitted diseases if clinically indicated. Nonbacteriuric patients with pyuria should be screened for *Chlamydia*.
- Urine biomarkers (e.g., antiproliferative factor) are promising but not ready for clinical use.

IMAGING STUDIES

CT or ultrasound of abdomen and pelvis may be considered to rule out other pathology.

 **TREATMENT**

- There is no consensus for optimal management.
- There is no cure for this disease.

NONPHARMACOLOGIC THERAPY

- Avoidance of activities associated with flare-ups
- Avoidance of smoking
- Dietary restriction, avoiding common irritants (e.g., coffee, citrus fruits)
- Physical therapy
- Exercise
- Behavioral therapy
- Bladder retraining
- Biofeedback
- Warm sitz bath, ice, heating pad
- Thiele massage (transrectal and transvaginal manual therapy of pelvic floor muscle) in presence of pelvic floor muscle tenderness and spasm
- Hydrodistention only gives temporary relief, so it is not commonly used anymore

ACUTE AND CHRONIC Rx

- A course of empiric antibiotics if not tried yet. Long-term oral antibiotics are not recommended.
- Oral therapy is tried first.
- Pentosan polysulfate sodium (Elmiron) is the only FDA-approved and most effective oral therapy.
- Most treatment takes 3 to 6 mo before maximum benefit is seen.
- Adjunct oral therapy includes tricyclic antidepressants (amitriptyline), cimetidine, antihistaminics (hydroxyzine, montelukast), neuroleptics (gabapentin, topiramate), analgesics (NSAIDs, opioid analgesics), and occasionally antimuscarinics.
- Oral therapies can be used in combination.
- Antihistaminics are preferred for patients with an allergy history or those who show mast cells in bladder biopsy.
- Oral prednisone is used in presence of Hunner's ulcers.
- Other drugs rarely used for IC are cyclosporin A, interleukin-10, imatinib, methotrexate, suplatast, misoprostol, and quercetin.
- Growth factor inhibitors, gene therapy, RDP 58, and vitamin B_3 analogue (BXL 628) may represent future therapies.
- Intravesical treatment is used when oral medications fail, for acute flare-ups, or before the oral medications take full effect.
- Dimethyl sulfoxide (DMSO), heparin, lidocaine, hyaluronic acid, capsaicin, botulinum toxin A, chondroitin sulfate, steroids, and Elmiron are drugs used for intravesical treatment.
- DMSO is the only FDA-approved intravesical treatment.
- DMSO is used less often now because of its side effects, specifically a garlic-like odor or taste on breath or skin that lasts 72 hr after treatment.
- Intravesical therapy typically involves mixture of heparin or Elmiron with lidocaine and sodium bicarbonate.
- Silver nitrate and Clorpactin have fallen out of favor.

SURGERY

- Major surgical intervention is not the mainstay of treatment.
- Patients whose condition is extreme and who are miserable may consider surgery if medications fail.
- Sacral neuromodulation (InterStim) is the current preferred surgical intervention.
- Laser ablation, fulguration, or resection is offered when Hunner's ulcers are seen in cystoscopy.
- Augmentation cystoplasty is not recommended.
- Cystourethrectomy with urinary diversion is rarely done.

COMPLEMENTARY & ALTERNATIVE MEDICINE

- Transcutaneous electric nerve stimulation
- Intravaginal electric nerve stimulation
- Acupuncture
- Urinary chelating agents such as Polycitra-K crystals, Urocit-K
- Prelief, an over-the-counter food additive
- Herbal remedies such as Algnot Plus, CystoProtek, Cysta-Q, aloe vera

DISPOSITION

- Close follow-up every month for 3 mo and every 3 mo thereafter.
- Voiding diary and symptom questionnaire are helpful to monitor response to treatment.

REFERRAL

- Urologist
- Pain specialist
- Physical therapist

⚠ PEARLS & CONSIDERATIONS

COMMENTS

- On average these patients see five physicians and endure irritating voiding symptoms for 5 yr before the disease is identified
- Besides symptom questionnaire and urine analysis, all other diagnostic tests are optional.
- PST is well tolerated.
- Negative cystoscopy does not rule out IC.

PREVENTION

Early identification and timely intervention improve patient outcome.

PATIENT & FAMILY EDUCATION

- IC support groups
- Interstitial Cystitis Association
- Interstitial Cystitis Network

SUGGESTED READINGS

Available at www.expertconsult.com

AUTHOR: **HEMANT K. SATPATHY, M.D.**

BASIC INFORMATION

DEFINITION

The interstitial lung diseases (ILDs) include more than 150 nonmalignant disorders, characterized by varying degrees of damage to the lung parenchyma or interstitium via inflammation and fibrosis. The term "ILD" can be confusing as processes affecting the alveolar space (e.g., pulmonary alveolar proteinosis) are also lumped under the title. A clinical classification of the interstitial lung diseases is summarized in Table 1I-10. The diseases can generally divided into three subgroups—those that are caused by an identifiable or suspected trigger, those that are associated with an underlying, more systemic disorder, and those that are idiopathic.

SYNONYMS

Interstitial pulmonary disease
ILD
Diffuse parenchymal lung disease (DPLD)
Interstitial pneumonia

ICD-10CM CODES

J84.17	Other interstitial pulmonary diseases with fibrosis in diseases classified elsewhere
J84.89	Other specified interstitial pulmonary diseases
J84.9	Interstitial pulmonary disease, unspecified
J84.115	Respiratory bronchiolitis interstitial lung disease
J84.848	Other interstitial lung diseases of childhood

EPIDEMIOLOGY & DEMOGRAPHICS

PREVALENCE: Varies with type of ILD. The most common ILDs are sarcoidosis, cryptogenic organizing pneumonia, and idiopathic pulmonary fibrosis. The prevalence of these syndromes varies widely across different populations as defined by age, gender, and race.

PREDOMINANT SEX & AGE: Some ILDs are more common in women, such as those resulting from connective tissue disorders. Lymphangiomyomatosis occurs exclusively in premenopausal women. ILD caused by occupational exposures are more common in men. Most ILDs occur in people >50 yr; however, sarcoidosis most often presents in younger populations.

RISK FACTORS: Although many ILDs are categorized as idiopathic, the most common identifiable risk factors include environmental exposures such as silicone, asbestos, or bird droppings; reactions to drugs such as chemotherapeutic agents, radiation therapy, cardiac medications, and finally some history of connective tissue disease such as rheumatoid arthritis or scleroderma.

PHYSICAL FINDINGS & CLINICAL PRESENTATION

- Shortness of breath (especially with exertion)
- Cough (dry)

TABLE 1I-10 Clinical Classification of the Interstitial Lung Diseases

Connective Tissue Diseases

Scleroderma
Polymyositis-dermatomyositis
Systemic lupus erythematosus
Rheumatoid arthritis
Mixed connective tissue disease
Ankylosing spondylitis

Treatment-Related or Drug-Induced Diseases

Antibiotics (nitrofurantoin, sulfasalazine)
Antiarrhythmics (amiodarone, tocainide, propranolol)
Anti-inflammatories (gold, penicillamine)
Anticonvulsants (dilantin)
Chemotherapeutic agents (mitomycin C, bleomycin, busulfan, cyclophosphamide, chlorambucil, methotrexate, azathioprine, BCNU [carmustine], procarbazine)
Therapeutic radiation
Oxygen toxicity
Narcotics

Primary and Idiopathic Diseases

Sarcoidosis
Primary pulmonary Langerhans cell histiocytosis (eosinophilic granuloma)
Amyloidosis
Pulmonary vasculitis
Gaucher's disease
Niemann-Pick disease
Hermansky-Pudlak syndrome
Neurofibromatosis
Lymphangioleiomyomatosis
Tuberous sclerosis
Idiopathic pulmonary fibrosis
Nonspecific interstitial pneumonia
Cryptogenic organizing pneumonia
Respiratory bronchiolitis ILD or desquamative interstitial pneumonia
Acute interstitial pneumonia
Lymphocytic interstitial pneumonia
Pleuroparenchymal fibroelastosis
Bone marrow transplantation
Eosinophilic pneumonia
Alveolar proteinosis
Alveolar microlithiasis
Metastatic calcification

Occupational and Environmental Diseases

Inorganic

Silicosis
Asbestosis
Hard-metal pneumoconiosis
Coal worker's pneumoconiosis
Berylliosis
Talc pneumoconiosis
Siderosis (arc welder)
Stannosis (tin)

Organic (hypersensitivity pneumonitis)

Bird breeder's lung
Farmer's lung

AIDS, Acquired immunodeficiency syndrome.
Modified from Mason, RJ: *Murray & Nadel's textbook of respiratory medicine*, 5th ed, Philadelphia, 2010, Saunders.

- Tachypnea
- Bibasilar end-inspiratory dry crackles
- Pulmonary hypertension
- Cyanosis, clubbing
  Hallmarks of ILD include a restrictive pattern and decreased diffusing capacity for carbon monoxide (DLCO) as demonstrated by pulmonary

function testing. The restrictive process can be the result of a number of factors depending on the type of ILD. Different types of ILD are characterized by varying degrees of acute inflammatory changes, which are potentially reversible, and fibrosis, which is largely irreversible.

- Specific changes may be seen:
  1. Granulomatous: accumulation of T lymphocytes, macrophages, and epithelioid cells into granulomas in lung parenchyma
  2. Inflammation and fibrosis: injury to epithelium causes inflammation; if chronic, inflammation spreads to interstitium and vascular areas

DIAGNOSIS

DIFFERENTIAL DIAGNOSIS

- Congestive heart failure
- Chronic renal failure
- Viral pneumonitis
- Pulmonary embolism
- Pulmonary hypertension
- Vasculitis
- Metastatic malignancy manifesting as lymphangitic carcinomatosis

WORKUP

- Well-defined patterns in pulmonary function tests are usually consistent with restrictive defect (decreased FVC, FRC, RV, and TLC) owing to decreased lung compliance caused by alveolar wall thickening as a result of inflammation and fibrosis. Diffusion capacity is usually reduced also because of inflammation and thickening of alveolar walls, though nonspecific. FEV_1/FVC is usually normal or increased because lung stiffness keeps small airways open, although some conditions (e.g., sarcoidosis) may result in air trapping.
- Bronchoscopy and bronchoalveolar lavage (BAL) may help identify type of ILD. However, their role in defining stage of disease and response to therapy is controversial. Histologic patterns in the interstitial lung diseases and their disease associations are summarized in Table 1I-11.
- If laboratory studies and imaging including HRCT fail in yielding a diagnosis, a surgical biopsy may be required.
- Fig. 1I-20 describes a diagnostic approach to occupational ILD.

LABORATORY TESTS

- ABGs may be normal or show respiratory alkalosis and widened Aa gradient.
- Blood tests for connective tissue diseases, such as antinuclear antibodies, anti-immunoglobulin antibodies (rheumatoid factors), LDH. Laboratory findings in the interstitial lung diseases are summarized in Table 1I-12.
- Serum precipitins confirm exposure if hypersensitivity pneumonitis is suspected.
- Antineutrophil cytoplasmic antibodies or anti-basement membrane antibodies if vasculitis is suspected.
- Angiotensin-converting enzyme testing (ACE levels) in sarcoidosis is of unclear value.

TABLE 1I-11 Histologic Patterns in the Interstitial Lung Diseases and Their Disease Associations

Histologic Patterns	Clinical Associations
Usual interstitial pneumonia	Idiopathic pulmonary fibrosis; connective tissue diseases (uncommon); asbestosis; chronic hypersensitivity pneumonitis; chronic aspiration pneumonia; chronic radiation pneumonitis; Hermansky-Pudlak syndrome
Nonspecific interstitial pneumonia	Idiopathic; connective tissue diseases; drugs; AIDS
Diffuse alveolar damage	Acute interstitial pneumonia (Hamman-Rich syndrome); acute respiratory distress syndrome (ARDS); drugs (cytotoxic agents, heroin, paraquat, ethchlorvynol, aspirin); toxic gas inhalation; radiation therapy; oxygen toxicity; connective tissue disease; infections
Organizing pneumonia	Cryptogenic organizing pneumonia; organizing stage of diffuse alveolar damage;; drugs (amiodarone, cocaine); infections; connective tissue diseases
Desquamative interstitial pneumonia/ respiratory bronchiolitis	Cigarette smoking; idiopathic DIP of childhood
Lymphocytic interstitial pneumonia	Idiopathic; hypogammaglobulinemia; autoimmune diseases, including Hashimoto's thyroiditis, lupus erythematosus, primary biliary cirrhosis, Sjögren's syndrome, myasthenia gravis, chronic active hepatitis; AIDS; allogeneic bone marrow transplantation
Eosinophilic pneumonia	Idiopathic acute and chronic; tropical filarial eosinophilia; parasitic infections; allergic bronchopulmonary aspergillosis; allergic granulomatosis of Churg and Strauss; hypereosinophilic syndrome; AIDS
Alveolar proteinosis	Pulmonary alveolar proteinosis; acute silicosis; aluminum dust; AIDS; myeloproliferative disorder
Diffuse alveolar hemorrhage	
With capillaritis	Wegener's granulomatosis; microscopic polyangiitis; systemic lupus erythematosus; polymyositis; scleroderma; rheumatoid arthritis; mixed connective tissue disease; lung transplantation; drugs (retinoic acid, propylthiouracil, Dilantin); Behçet's disease; cryoglobulinemia; Henoch-Schönlein purpura; pauci-immune glomerulonephritis; immune complex glomerulonephritis
Without capillaritis	Idiopathic pulmonary hemosiderosis; systemic lupus erythematosus; Goodpasture's syndrome; diffuse alveolar damage; pulmonary veno-occlusive disease; mitral stenosis; lymphangioleiomyomatosis
Amyloid deposition	Primary amyloidosis; multiple myeloma; lymphocytic interstitial pneumonia
Granuloma	Sarcoidosis; hypersensitivity pneumonitis; pulmonary Langerhans cell histiocytosis; silicosis; intravenous talcosis; berylliosis; lymphocytic interstitial pneumonia; infections

AIDS, Acquired immunodeficiency syndrome.
Modified from Mason, RJ: *Murray & Nadel's textbook of respiratory medicine*, 5th ed, Philadelphia, 2010, Saunders.

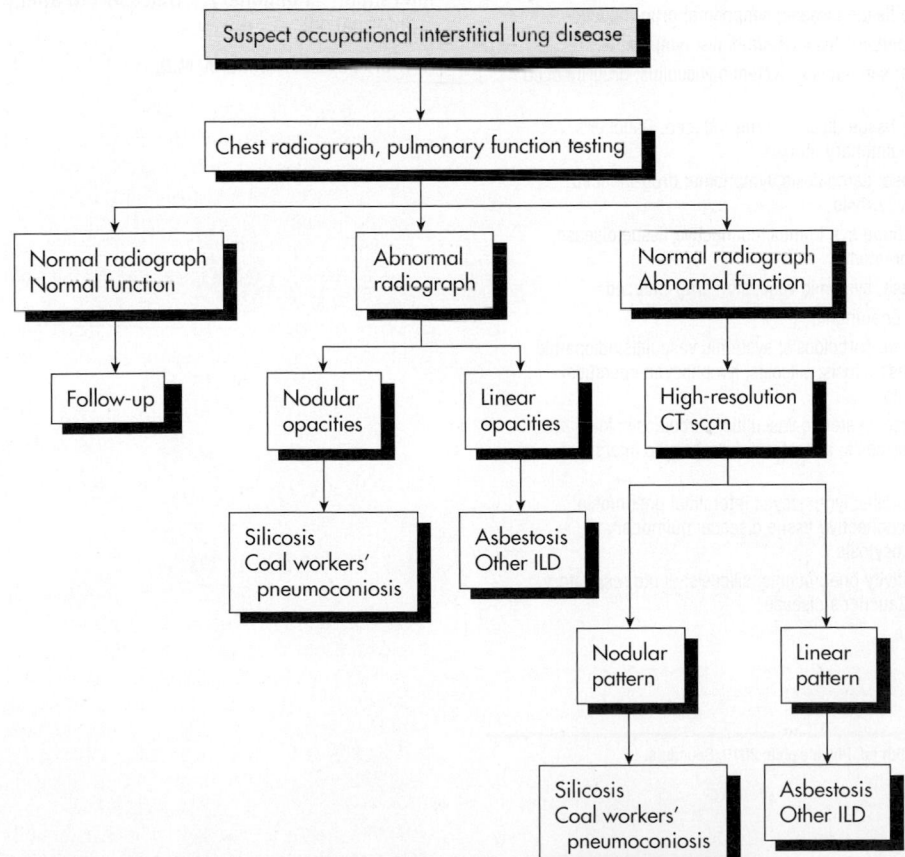

FIGURE 1I-20 Diagnostic approach to occupational interstitial lung disease (ILD). *CT,* Computed tomography. (From Goldman L, Ausiello D [eds]: *Goldman's Cecil textbook of medicine*, ed 23, Philadelphia, 2008, Saunders.)

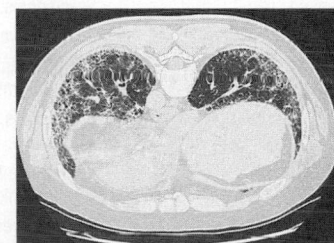

FIGURE 1I-21 High-resolution computed tomography scan of the chest shows fibrotic changes in a subpleural distribution with honeycombing consistent with usual interstitial pneumonia. (From Hochberg MC et al: *Rheumatology,* ed 5, St Louis, 2011, Mosby.)

IMAGING STUDIES

- Chest x-ray may be normal but commonly shows a bibasilar reticular pattern. Table 1I-13 summarizes radiographic features of the interstitial lung diseases.
- High-resolution CT (HRCT) (Fig. 1I-21) is the gold standard for evaluating parenchymal opacities seen on chest x-ray; it is also useful for determining potential biopsy sites.
- Echocardiography may be useful to evaluate cardiac function/dilation or to evaluate for pulmonary hypertension, which can complicate advanced ILDs.

 **TREATMENT**

NONPHARMACOLOGIC THERAPY

Avoidance of tobacco and occupational exposures

TABLE 1I-12 Radiographic Features of the Interstitial Lung Diseases

Feature	Diseases
Upper zone–predominant disease	Radiation pneumonitis; neurofibromatosis; chronic sarcoidosis; pulmonary Langerhans cell histiocytosis; silicosis; chronic hypersensitivity pneumonitis; chronic eosinophilic pneumonia; ankylosing spondylitis; nodular rheumatoid arthritis; berylliosis; drug-induced (amiodarone, gold, BCNU [carmustine]); radiation
Increased lung volumes	Lymphangioleiomyomatosis; chronic sarcoidosis; chronic pulmonary Langerhans cell histiocytosis; tuberous sclerosis; neurofibromatosis
Radiographic honeycomb lung	Idiopathic pulmonary fibrosis; connective tissue disease; asbestosis; drug-induced; lymphocytic interstitial pneumonia; chronic aspiration pneumonia; hemosiderosis; Hermansky-Pudlak syndrome; alveolar proteinosis
Pneumothorax	Pulmonary Langerhans cell histiocytosis; lymphangioleiomyomatosis; tuberous sclerosis; neurofibromatosis, IPF
Kerley's B lines	Lymphangitic carcinomatosis; lymphangioleiomyomatosis; left atrial hypertension (mitral valve disease, veno-occlusive disease); lymphoma; amyloidosis
Lymphadenopathy	Sarcoidosis; lymphoma; lymphangitic carcinomatosis; lymphoid interstitial pneumonia; berylliosis; amyloidosis; Gaucher's disease
Pleural disease	Lymphangitic carcinomatosis; connective tissue disease; asbestosis (pleural calcification); lymphangioleiomyomatosis (chylous effusion); drug-induced (nitrofurantoin, radiation); sarcoidosis
Eggshell calcification of lymph nodes	Silicosis; sarcoidosis; radiation

From Mason, RJ: *Murray & Nadel's textbook of respiratory medicine*, 5th ed, Philadelphia, 2010, Saunders.

TABLE 1I-13 Laboratory Findings in the Interstitial Lung Diseases

Finding	Diseases
Leukopenia	Sarcoidosis; connective tissue disease; lymphoma; drug-induced
Leukocytosis	Systemic vasculitis; hypersensitivity pneumonitis; lymphoma
Eosinophilia	Eosinophilic pneumonia; sarcoidosis; systemic vasculitis; drug-induced (sulfa, methotrexate)
Thrombocytopenia	Sarcoidosis; connective tissue disease; drug-induced; Gaucher's disease; idiopathic pulmonary fibrosis
Hemolytic anemia	Connective tissue disease; sarcoidosis; lymphoma; drug-induced; idiopathic pulmonary fibrosis
Normocytic anemia	Diffuse alveolar hemorrhage syndromes; connective tissue disease; lymphangitic carcinomatosis
Urinary sediment abnormalities	Connective tissue disease; systemic vasculitis; drug-induced
Hypogammaglobulinemia	Lymphocytic interstitial pneumonia
Hypergammaglobulinemia	Connective tissue disease; sarcoidosis; systemic vasculitis; idiopathic pulmonary fibrosis; asbestosis; silicosis; lymphocytic interstitial pneumonia; lymphoma
Serum autoantibodies	Connective tissue disease; systemic vasculitis; sarcoidosis; idiopathic pulmonary fibrosis; silicosis; asbestosis; lymphocytic interstitial pneumonia
Serum immune complexes	Idiopathic pulmonary fibrosis; lymphocytic interstitial pneumonia; systemic vasculitis; connective tissue disease; pulmonary Langerhans cell histiocytosis
Serum angiotensin-converting enzyme	Sarcoidosis; hypersensitivity pneumonitis; silicosis; acute respiratory distress syndrome; Gaucher's disease
Antibasement membrane antibody	Goodpasture's syndrome
Antineutrophil cytoplasmic antibody	Systemic vasculitis

From Mason, RJ: *Murray & Nadel's textbook of respiratory medicine*, 5th ed, Philadelphia, 2010, Saunders.

ACUTE GENERAL Rx

- Supplemental oxygen in patients with hypoxemia is helpful short and long term.
- Glucocorticoids are the mainstay of therapy for many of the ILDs. Patients should be continuously reevaluated after the initiation of treatment to gauge for response. If they are improved or stable, steroids may be tapered. If not, the same course may be maintained 4 additional wk. If patient's condition is unresponsive to steroids or declines as the steroids are tapered, may consider adding second agent (cyclophosphamide, azathioprine, mycophenolate, among other options).

CHRONIC GENERAL Rx

- Outpatient pulmonary rehabilitation may be of value.
- Lung transplantation may be considered in appropriate patients in severe stages of the disease.

REFERRAL

- Pulmonary referral for workup and management
- Surgical referral for biopsy

SUGGESTED READINGS
Available at www.expertconsult.com

RELATED CONTENT
Interstitial Pulmonary Disease (Patient Information)

AUTHOR: **PETER LACAMERA, M.D.**

BASIC INFORMATION

DEFINITION

Can be classified into two broad categories:
1. Acute interstitial nephritis (AIN): Decrease in renal function resulting from delayed hypersensitivity immune-mediated injury characterized histopathologically with edema and inflammation of the renal interstitium and tubules, classically sparing the glomeruli and blood vessels. Most often drug-induced.
2. Chronic interstitial nephritis: Represents a large and diverse group of disorders characterized by interstitial fibrosis with mononuclear leukocyte infiltration and tubular atrophy. It is a final common pathway of many chronic kidney diseases including chronic bacterial infections, obstruction, and high-grade vesicoureteral reflux. Histopathologically seen as atrophy and fibrosis of the renal interstitium.

SYNONYMS

Acute tubulointerstitial nephritis
Contracted kidney
Cirrhosis of the kidney
Granular kidney
Gouty kidney
Renal sclerosis
Chronic productive nephritis without exudation

ICD-10CM CODES
N05.9 Unspecified nephritic syndrome with unspecified morphologic changes
N17.2 Acute kidney failure with medullary necrosis
N05.8 Unspecified nephritic syndrome with other morphologic changes
N10 Acute tubulo-interstitial nephritis
N11.8 Other chronic tubulo-interstitial nephritis
N11.9 Chronic tubulo-interstitial nephritis, unspecified
N12 Tubulo-interstitial nephritis, not specified as acute or chronic

EPIDEMIOLOGY & DEMOGRAPHICS

PREVALENCE: Prevalence is significantly underestimated, and the incidence in the US remains unknown. Best available estimates come from measuring the incidence of unexpected AIN at autopsy (<1%), in unselected renal biopsies (1%-6%), and in renal biopsies selected for patients with acute renal failure (11%-15%). AIN may comprise 15% to 20% of all AKI cases.

PREDOMINANT SEX AND AGE: Older patients generally at higher risk given reduced glomerular filtration rates. Increasing prevalence in this population.

PEAK INCIDENCE: Median age at presentation is 65 yr.

RISK FACTORS: Risk of acute interstitial nephritis due to drugs (e.g., NSAIDs, penicillins, sulfa drugs) increases with volume depletion, underlying kidney disease, age >65 yr, congestive heart failure, and diabetes. Some autoimmune disorders are also risk factors.

PHYSICAL FINDINGS & CLINICAL PRESENTATION (FIG. 1I-22)

Classic triad of low-grade fever, maculopapular rash, and arthralgias is present in only 5% of cases of AIN. Patients may be asymptomatic or have symptoms such as fever, weight loss, fatigue, abdominal and flank pain, nausea, vomiting, altered mental status, myalgias, headache, oliguria, polyuria and/or nocturia, gross hematuria, nephrotic syndrome, tubulointerstitial nephritis and uveitis (TINU syndrome).

ETIOLOGY

- Drug-induced (70%) usually hypersensitivity reaction occurring about 15 days after exposure to the drug: antibiotics including penicillins, cephalosporins, sulfonamides, rifampin, ciprofloxacin, proton pump inhibitors, NSAIDs, H2 antagonists, anti-neoplastic agents, anticonvulsants, indinavir, 5-aminosalicylates, allopurinol. Up to 150 agents implicated
- Infection associated (15%) as a primary renal infection or complication of systemic infection
  1. Bacterial: *Corynebacterium diphtheriae, Legionella,* staphylococci, streptococci, *Yersinia*
  2. Viral: Cytomegalovirus, Epstein-Barr virus, hantaviruses, hepatitis C, herpes simplex virus, human immunodeficiency virus, mumps, polyomavirus, influenza A virus
  3. Other: *Mycobacterium, Mycoplasma, Rickettsia,* syphilis, toxoplasmosis
- Idiopathic (10%)
- Immune disorders: systemic lupus erythematosus, Sjögren's, granulomatosis with polyangiitis and other vasculitides, and autoimmune pancreatitis

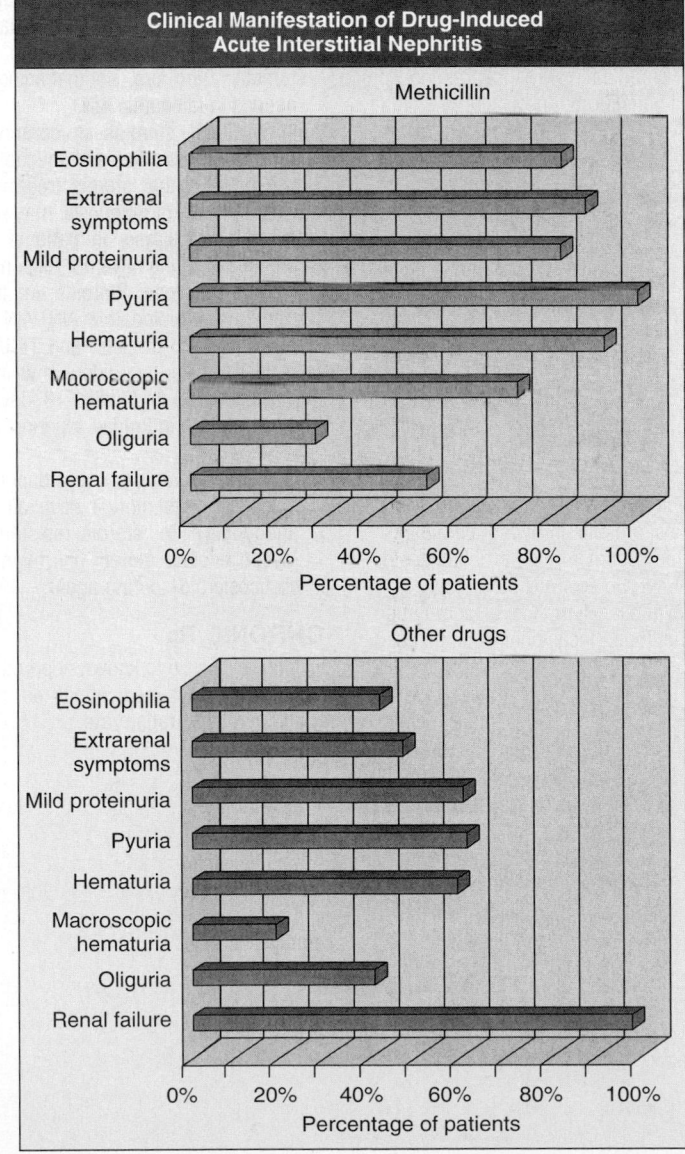

FIGURE 1I-22 Clinical manifestations of drug-induced acute interstitial nephritis. Data were pooled from different case reports, including 95 patients with methicillin-induced AIN and more than 200 patients with other drug-induced AIN. Patients with AIN associated with a nephrotic syndrome are not included. (From Floege J, Johnson RJ, Feehally J: *Comprehensive clinical nephrology*, ed 4, Philadelphia, 2010, Saunders.)

- Neoplastic disorders (multiple myeloma)
- Metabolic diseases (urate nephropathy, hypercalcemic nephropathy, hypokalemic nephropathy, oxalate nephropathy)
- Heavy metals (chronic form)
- Chronic urinary tract obstruction (chronic form)
- Sarcoidosis
- Other rare causes: IgG4 related tubulointerstitial nephritis, hypocomplementemic tubulointerstitial nephritis, DRESS syndrome

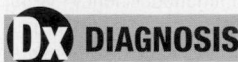 **DIAGNOSIS**

DIFFERENTIAL DIAGNOSIS

Any other causes of acute renal failure including acute tubular necrosis, glomerulonephritis, hypertensive nephrosclerosis, prerenal azotemia, obstructive nephropathy, renal vascular disease, and various electrolyte abnormalities

WORKUP

Medical history with focus on recent infection, illness, or new medication in the presence of acute to chronic onset of kidney failure; evaluation for underlying infection or insult

LABORATORY TESTS

- Urinalysis and microscopy: white blood cells, microhematuria, glucosuria, eosinophiluria (estimated sensitivity 60% and specificity 85%), proteinuria, phosphaturia, uricosuria, Beta 2 microglobinuria, WBC casts containing eosinophils are characteristic. Detection of eosinophiluria without pyuria is not helpful.
- Serum chemistry profile, rise in plasma creatinine temporally related to administration of offending drug, low serum phosphorus or urate level. Proximal renal tubular acidosis results in bicarbonaturia, and distal renal tubular acidosis results in hyperkalemia.
- Complete blood count with differential (eosinophilia occurs in 50% of AIN patients)
- DLST (drug induced lymphocyte stimulation tests): can be done. Occasionally can be used to identify offending drug in patients on multiple medications, but use may be limited due to expense, time delay, and low availability.

- Renal biopsy is the gold standard for diagnosis but is indicated only when diagnosis is unclear, removal of offending agent does not result in improvement, or steroid initiation is being considered.
- If drug-related AIN is not suspected, laboratory work up for infectious agents, vasculitis, and autoimmune disorders may be warranted based on the clinical context.

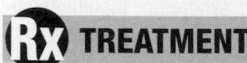 **TREATMENT**

NONPHARMACOLOGIC THERAPY

Largely supportive; removal of offending agent, if known, will resolve 60% of all cases.

ACUTE GENERAL Rx

- Correct fluid and electrolyte imbalances, maintain adequate hydration and urine output but avoid volume overload.
- Identify and treat infection as indicated.
- Avoid medications that impair renal blood flow.
- Uveitis in TINU syndrome may be asymptomatic; therefore, ophthalmologic exam is needed in idiopathic AIN.
- Initiation of steroids is controversial, but retrospective studies and anecdotal literature have shown that steroid treatment, started within 7 days of diagnosis, may reduce need for chronic dialysis in patients with drug-induced AIN who have not responded to drug withdrawal alone. Steroids are the basis of treatment in idiopathic AIN, AIN associated with systemic disease, and TINU. Dosing is typically pulsed steroids with IV methylprednisolone (250 mg daily ×3 days) followed by 0.5 to 1 mg/kg/day tapering over 4 to 6 weeks.
- Cyclophosphamide, cyclosporine, and mycophenolate mofetil have all been used anecdotally in steroid-resistant disease. Mycophenolate mofetil has been used as a corticosteroid-sparing agent.

CHRONIC Rx

- Limit exposure to known nephrotoxic agents.
- Renally adjust medications as indicated by glomerular filtration rate.

- Tight control of blood pressure, diabetes, and cholesterol to preserve kidney function as needed

DISPOSITION

With acute interstitial nephritis (AIN), 60% to 65% of patients will return to baseline. Partial recovery is seen in 10% to 20%, and irreversible damage in 5% to 10%. Relapse is common with reexposure to offending agents.

REFERRAL

Renal consultation is often necessary, especially if there is treatment-resistant disease, the diagnosis is unclear, or biopsy is required.

 **PEARLS & CONSIDERATIONS**

COMMENTS

Acute interstitial nephritis is most often due to drugs; 88% of the time, the drug was started in the past 30 days. In contrast to ATN, early AIN may be associated with polyuria with laboratory evidence of tubular dysfunction; therefore, a high index of suspicion in this clinical setting is essential to early diagnosis.

PREVENTION

Use known offending agents with care, especially in the elderly and those with known underlying kidney disease.

PATIENT/FAMILY EDUCATION

http://www.nlm.nih.gov/medlineplus/ency/article/000464.htm

SUGGESTED READINGS
Available at www.expertconsult.com

RELATED CONTENT
Interstitial Nephritis (Patient Information)

AUTHOR: **LIORA J. FARBER, M.D.**

BASIC INFORMATION

DEFINITION

Intraventricular conduction delay (IVCD) is a common clinical abnormality related to a conduction disturbance that occurs at various levels in the His-Purkinje system. This defect does not meet criteria for right bundle branch (RBBB), left bundle branch (LBBB), or hemifascicular block (Fig. 1I-23). It can be caused by anatomic abnormalities and the physiologic properties of cardiac tissue. It may occur between ventricles (interventricular), within Purkinje fibers or ventricular myocardium (intraventricular), or between layers of the myocardium (intramural). Parietal block occurs in the terminal Purkinje system and presents with prolonged QRS in leads V1 to V3 that exceeds significantly the QRS width from V4 to V6. This particular type of IVCD is associated with right ventricular arrhythmogenic dysplasia.

IVCD is defined by a QRS duration of >110 ms in adults, in children 8 to 16 yr of age >90 ms, and in children younger than 8 yr of age >80 ms in the ECG provided there is no criteria for either LBBB or RBBB. The conduction delay causing the prolonged QRS is considered to take place beyond the Purkinje's myocardial gates and arises from a slowing down in the cell-to-cell conduction.

SYNONYMS

IVCD
Nonspecific intraventricular conduction disturbance
Unspecified intraventricular conduction disturbance
Intraventricular conduction delay
Intraventricular block
Intraventricular conduction defect

ICD-10CM CODES

145.4 Non-specific intraventricular block
145.8 Other specified conduction disorders
145.9 Conduction disorder, unspecified

EPIDEMIOLOGY

- A Finnish Social Security Study, which consisted of 10,899 subjects with baseline ECGs, showed a prevalence of IVCD in 0.6% of the total population. 45.6% of subjects with a QRS duration ≥110 ms without evidence of cardiac disease or bundle branch block, had an increased risk of all cause mortality (relative risk [RR] 1.75, 95% CI, cardiac mortality (RR 1.87, 95% CI), and mortality due to arrhythmias (RR 2.90, 95% CI). The P values were .002, .04, and .007, respectively.
- IVCD has a consensus prevalence of 30% in patients with heart failure (HF) ranging between 14% and 47% in various studies.
- The reported prevalence in military aviators was similar to RBBB at 2:1000.

ETIOLOGY

Patients with IVCD are not a homogeneous group of patients and cannot be classified as such. A patient with IVCD secondary to dilated cardiomyopathy cannot be compared with a patient with IVCD secondary to LVH caused by hypertension or with patients with myocardial scarring secondary to myocardial infarction and other conditions. Therefore, the treatment for each patient has to be individualized and tailored to the underlying cause of the conduction defect.

The most common clinical conditions associated with IVCD are as follows:
- Coronary artery disease
- Infiltrative cardiomyopathy (CMO): amyloidosis, sarcoidosis, hemosiderosis, and so on
- Cardiomyopathies of other etiologies
- Left ventricular hypertrophy
- Endocarditis of the aortic valve
- Myocarditis
- Chagas disease (parasitic)
- Primary conduction diseases: Lenegre's disease, Lev disease
- Congenital anomalies
- Progressive systemic scleroderma
- Pulmonary embolism
- Cyclic antidepressants
- Hyperkalemia
- Hypothermia
- Intracardiac catheter manipulation

Antiarrhythmic drugs, class IA (e.g., procainamide, disopyramide, quinidine), and class IC (e.g., flecainide, encainide, and propafenone), amantadine, carbamazepine, cocaine, diphenhydramine, mesoridazine, and thioridazine. In addition, propoxyphene and propranolol can also cause IVCD by sodium channel blockade in older adults due to myocardial fibrosis caused by apoptosis.

Etiology can also be unknown in many cases.

PHYSICAL FINDINGS & CLINICAL PRESENTATION

IVCD per se is asymptomatic and is recognizable only with a 12 lead ECG.

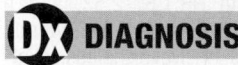

DIAGNOSIS

Intraventricular conduction delay (IVCD) is usually an incidental ECG finding. This defect does not meet criteria for RBBB, LBBB, or hemifascicular block.

DIFFERENTIAL DIAGNOSIS

- Unifascicular block
- Bifascicular block
- Wolff-Parkinson-White (WPW) pattern and variants
- LBBB
- RBBB

EVALUATION

The evaluation of the patient with IVCD should be oriented to discovering the cause of the ECG abnormality to implement appropriate therapy and counseling. Thorough history and physical exams must be performed to implement adequate laboratory and imaging testing based on the level of suspicion for the causes of IVCD listed earlier. Such tests could include but are not limited to:
- Standard laboratory testing appropriate for age, gender, and metabolic abnormalities
- Resting ECG
- Exercise ECG, with or without imaging
- Ambulatory ECG
- Echocardiogram
- Specialized studies based on known comorbidities and risk assessment or suspicion of them such as heart failure, myocardial infarction, cardiomyopathies, and so on

TREATMENT

The management goal of patients with IVCD should be the optimization of treatment for the underlying contributing conditions to the conduction defect. In selected patients at risk for sudden cardiac death (SCD) due to significant CAD or arrhythmogenic right ventricular dysplasia, appropriate referral should be made without delay.

Although cardiac resynchronization therapy (CRT) has been effective in reducing clinical events in patients with LBBB (LBBB and RBBB are independent predictors of increased risk of cardiac death in patients with HF), patients with IVCDs do not correlate with worsened prognosis nor clinical improvement of heart failure.

CRT offers no benefit for the management of patients with IVCD and in fact there may be an increased risk of ventricular tachycardia for this group of patients when receiving CRT or intracardiac defibrillator (ICD) devices.

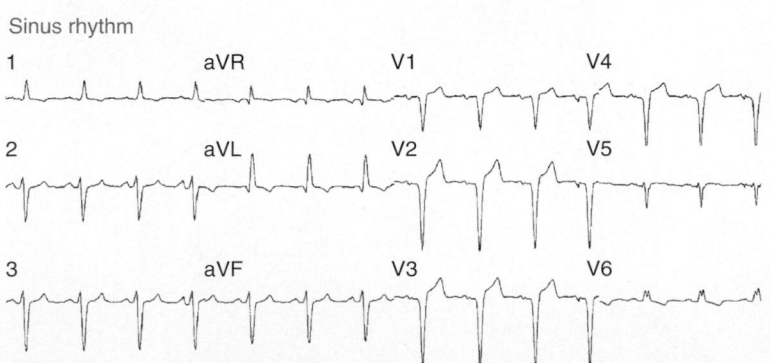

FIGURE 1I-23 Normal sinus rhythm baseline with intraventricular conduction delay resembling left bundle branch block (LBBB). (From Issa ZF: Clinical arrhythmology and electrophysiology: a companion to Braunwald's heart disease, ed 2, Philadelphia, 2012, Saunders.)

Strauss et al. have recently proposed that criteria for LBBB be changed to >140 ms in the male population and >130 ms in the female population for better guidance of device therapy.

PROGNOSIS

Different studies have shown that IVCD is associated with increased all-cause mortality with relative risk of (RR): 1.75-2.01, increased cardiac mortality with RR:1.87-2.53, and a markedly elevated risk of sudden arrhythmic death with RR: 2.9-3.11. Nevertheless, clinical correlation is needed because prognosis depends on underlying associated clinical conditions.

REFERRAL

Refer to a cardiologist if there is history of palpitations, dizziness, heart failure, myocardial infarction, or an abnormal cardiac exam.

PEARLS & CONSIDERATIONS

IVCD can be due to drugs such as Class I antiarrhythmic drugs.

IVCD can be a normal variant and is not always associated with cardiac pathology.

Clinical correlation (history and physical exam) is needed to identify associated cardiac abnormalities.

In patients with heart failure, cardiac resynchronization for IVCD does not influence prognosis or clinical improvement unless is associated with LBBB.

SUGGESTED READINGS

Available at www.expertconsult.com

AUTHORS: **JUAN A. ESCARFULLER, M.D.,** and **CLAUDIA SERRANO, M.D.**

BASIC INFORMATION

DEFINITION

Irritable bowel syndrome (IBS) is a chronic functional disorder manifested by alteration in bowel habits and recurrent abdominal pain and bloating. IBS is a symptom complex influenced by a variety of physiologic determinants from gut to brain and back. The ROME III criteria for diagnosis of IBS are:

- Recurrent abdominal pain or discomfort at least 3 days per month in the past 3 mo associated with ≥ two of the following:
  1. Pain is relieved or improved with defecation.
  2. Its onset is associated with a change in the frequency of bowel movement.
  3. Its onset is associated with a change in the form or appearance of the stool.
- The criteria must be fulfilled for at least the past 3 mo with symptom onset at least 6 mo before the diagnosis.

SYNONYMS

Irritable colon
Spastic colon
IBS

ICD-10CM CODES
K58   Irritable bowel syndrome
K58.9 Irritable bowel syndrome without diarrhea
K58.0 Irritable bowel syndrome with diarrhea

EPIDEMIOLOGY & DEMOGRAPHICS

- IBS is the most common functional bowel disorder. An estimated 15 million people in the United States have IBS.
- IBS occurs in 7% to 21% of the general population of industrialized countries and is responsible for >50% of gastrointestinal (GI) referrals. Worldwide adult prevalence is 12%. Incidence increases during adolescence and peaks in third and fourth decades of life.
- Female/male ratio is 2:1. Peak prevalence is from 20 to 39 years of age.
- Nearly 50% of patients have psychiatric abnormalities, with anxiety disorders being most common.

PHYSICAL FINDINGS & CLINICAL PRESENTATION

- The clinical presentation of IBS consists of abdominal pain and abnormalities of defecation, which may include loose stools, usually after meals and in the morning, alternating with episodes of constipation.
- Physical examination is generally normal.
- Nonspecific abdominal tenderness and distention may be present.

ETIOLOGY

- Unknown, believed to be multifactorial. Fig.1I-24 illustrates a biopsychological model of IBS pathophysiology.
- Associated pathophysiology includes altered GI motility, alteration in gut flora, and increased gut sensitivity
- Risk factors: anxiety, depression, personality disorders, history of childhood sexual abuse, and domestic abuse in women

DIAGNOSIS

Table 1I-14 summarizes the diagnostic criteria for IBS and Table 1I-15 subtypes IBS by predominant stool pattern.

DIFFERENTIAL DIAGNOSIS

- Inflammatory bowel disease (IBD)
- Diverticulitis
- Colon malignancy
- Endometriosis
- Peptic ulcer disease
- Biliary liver disease
- Chronic pancreatitis
- Constipation caused by medications (opiates, calcium channel blockers, anticholinergics)
- Diarrhea caused by medications (metformin, colchicine, proton pump inhibitors, antacids, antibiotics)
- Small-bowel overgrowth
- Celiac disease
- Parasites
- Lymphoma of GI tract

WORKUP

Diagnostic workup (Fig. E1I-25) is aimed primarily at excluding the conditions listed in the differential diagnoses. It is important to identify red flags of other diseases, such as weight loss, rectal bleeding, onset in patients >50 yr, fever, nocturnal pain, and family history of malignancy or IBD. Additional red flags include abnormal examination (e.g., mass, enlarged lymph nodes, stool positive for occult blood, muscle wasting) and abnormal laboratory values (anemia, leukocytosis, abnormal chemistry).

Common clinical criteria for diagnosis of IBS are >3 mo of symptoms, including abdominal pain that is relieved by a bowel movement, or pain accompanied by a change in bowel pattern, and abnormality in bowel movement 25% of the time, characterized by two of the following features:
- Abdominal distention
- Abnormal consistency
- Abnormal defecation (e.g., straining, sense of incomplete evacuation)
- Abnormal frequency
- Mucus with bowel movement

LABORATORY TESTS

- Blood work is generally normal. CBC is reasonable to evaluate for anemia. The presence of anemia should alert to the possibility of a colonic malignancy or IBD.
- Testing of stool for ova and parasites should be considered only in patients with chronic diarrhea. Evaluation of stool for *Clostridium difficile* may be helpful in patients with predominant diarrhea symptoms who have recently taken antibiotics.

IMAGING STUDIES

Imaging studies (e.g., flat and upright abdominal radiograph, small-bowel series, sonogram or CT of abdomen and pelvis) are normal and not necessary for diagnosis.

Lower endoscopy is generally normal except for the presence of some spasms. Colonoscopic imaging should be performed only in persons who have alarm features to rule out organic disease and in persons older than 50 yr to screen for colorectal cancer.

TREATMENT

NONPHARMACOLOGIC THERAPY

- Fig. 1I-26 illustrates the management of irritable bowel syndrome. The patient should be encouraged to maintain an adequate fiber intake and to eliminate foods that aggravate symptoms. Avoidance of caffeine, dairy products, fatty foods, and dietary excesses is also helpful.
- Cognitive-behavioral therapy is also recommended, particularly in younger patients because psychosocial stressors are important triggers of IBS. Reassurance and education about trigger avoidance and stress management are important.
- Importance of regular exercise and adequate fluid intake should be stressed.

GENERAL Rx

- The mainstay of treatment of IBS is a high-fiber diet. Fiber is helpful for relief of constipation but not for relief of pain. Because symptoms are chronic, the use of laxatives should generally be avoided.
- Soluble fiber (psyllium) is more effective in symptom relief than insoluble fiber (bran). Fiber supplementation with psyllium 1 tbsp bid or calcium polycarbophil (FiberCon) 2 tablets one to four times daily followed by 8 oz of water may be necessary in some patients.
- Patients should be instructed that there might be some increased bloating on initiation of fiber supplementation, which should resolve within 2 to 3 wk. It is important that patients take these fiber products on a regular basis and not only as needed. Fiber is not effective in patients with diarrhea-predominant IBS and may worsen symptoms in these patients.
- Patients who appear anxious can benefit from use of sedatives or selective serotonin reuptake inhibitors (SSRIs). Tricyclic antidepressants in low doses are also effective in some patients with diarrhea-predominant IBS.
- C-2 chloride channel activators: Lubiprostone (Amitiza) is a chloride channel activator that stimulates chloride-rich intestinal fluid secretion and accelerates small intestine and colonic transmit time. It may be effective in chronic constipation-predominant IBS unresponsive to conventional treatment. Usual dose is 8 to 24 mcg bid with food. Side effects include headache and nausea.
- Linaclotide (Linzess) is a guanylate cyclase-C (GC-C) agonist FDA approved for IBS with constipation. It stimulates secretion of chlo-

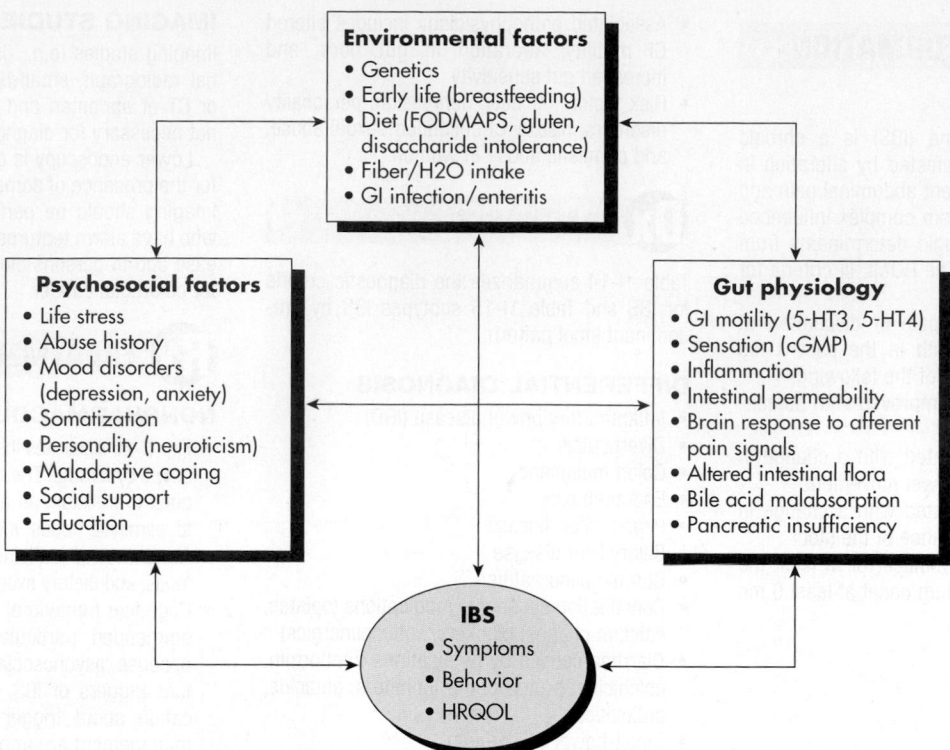

FIGURE 1I-24 A biopsychosocial model of irritable bowel syndrome pathophysiology. Irritable bowel syndrome is thought to be a multifactorial disorder, deriving from a potential multitude of etiopathogenic factors, including environmental, psychologic, and physiologic factors. This model highlights the complex, often bidirectional interplay of these factors in the experience of irritable bowel syndrome symptoms. *cGMP,* cyclic guanosine monophosphate; *5-HT3,*serotonin type 3; *5-HT4,*serotonin type 4; *FODMAPS,* fermentable oligosaccharides, disaccharides, monosaccharides, and polyols; *HRQOL,* health-related quality of life; *IBS,* irritable bowel syndrome. (Adapted from Sayuk GS, Gyawali CP: Irritable bowel syndrome: modern concepts and management options. *Am J Med* 128(8), 817-827, 2015.)

ride and bicarbonate into the intestinal lumen, mainly through activation of the CFTR ion channel, resulting in increased intestinal fluid and accelerated transit. Usual dose for IBS is 290 mcg 30 min before eating. The most common adverse effects are diarrhea, abdominal pain, flatulence, and abdominal distension.

- Eluxadoline (Viberzi) is a μ-opioid receptor agonist and Δ-opioid receptor antagonist FDA approved for IBS with diarrhea. It decreases muscle contractility, inhibits water and electrolyte secretion, and increases rectal sphincter tone. Usual dose is 100 mg PO bid taken with food.
- Loperamide is effective for diarrhea. Alosetron, a serotonin type-3 receptor antagonist previously withdrawn because of severe constipation and ischemic colitis, has been reintroduced with limited availability. It is indicated only for women with severe chronic diarrhea-predominant IBS unresponsive to conventional therapy and not caused by anatomic or metabolic abnormality. Starting dose is 1 mg qd.
- Alterations in gut flora have been identified as potentially contributing to IBS (84% of IBS patients have an abnormal lactulose breath test, suggesting small-intestinal bacterial overgrowth). Rifaximin, a gut-selective antibiotic, has been used in recent trials to eradi-

cate bacterial overgrowth (70% eradication rate). A dose of 400 mg tid for 10 days was reported effective in improving IBS symptoms up to 10 wk after discontinuation of therapy. Until additional evidence is available, use of rifaximin or other antibiotics in IBS should be reserved for patients with proven bacterial overgrowth.

- Antispasmodics-anticholinergics (e.g., dicyclomine, hyoscyamine) are often used, but efficacy data from clinical trials are inconclusive.
- Probiotics: Bifidobacteria and some combinations of probiotics have shown some limited efficacy. Lactobacilli do not appear to be effective for the treatment of IBS. Additional data showing efficacy is needed before probiotics can be endorsed for treatment of IBS.
- Antidepressants: SSRIs are more effective than placebo for relief of global IBS symptoms.

DISPOSITION
More than 60% of patients respond successfully to treatment over the initial 12 mo; however, IBS is a chronic, relapsing condition and requires prolonged therapy.

REFERRAL
GI referral is recommended in patients with rectal bleeding, fever, nocturnal diarrhea, anemia, weight

loss, or onset of symptoms >40 yr. Consultation is also necessary if specialized diagnostic procedures such as endoscopy are necessary.

! PEARLS & CONSIDERATIONS

COMMENTS
- Patients should be educated regarding maintenance of a high-fiber diet and elimination of stressors, which can precipitate attacks of IBS. They should be reassured that their condition does not lead to cancer.
- Recent drug efforts (alosetron, tegaserod) are aimed at serotonergic receptors in the gut because most of the serotonin in the body is found in the GI tract and is believed to be involved in the mediation of visceral sensation and motility.

EBM EVIDENCE

Available at www.expertconsult.com

- Cognitive-behavioral therapy is effective in the treatment of patients with IBS and should be considered as part of the armamentarium against this disorder.
- Some patients with IBS but without celiac disease show symptom improvement on a wheat-free diet. A 2- to 3-week trial of wheat

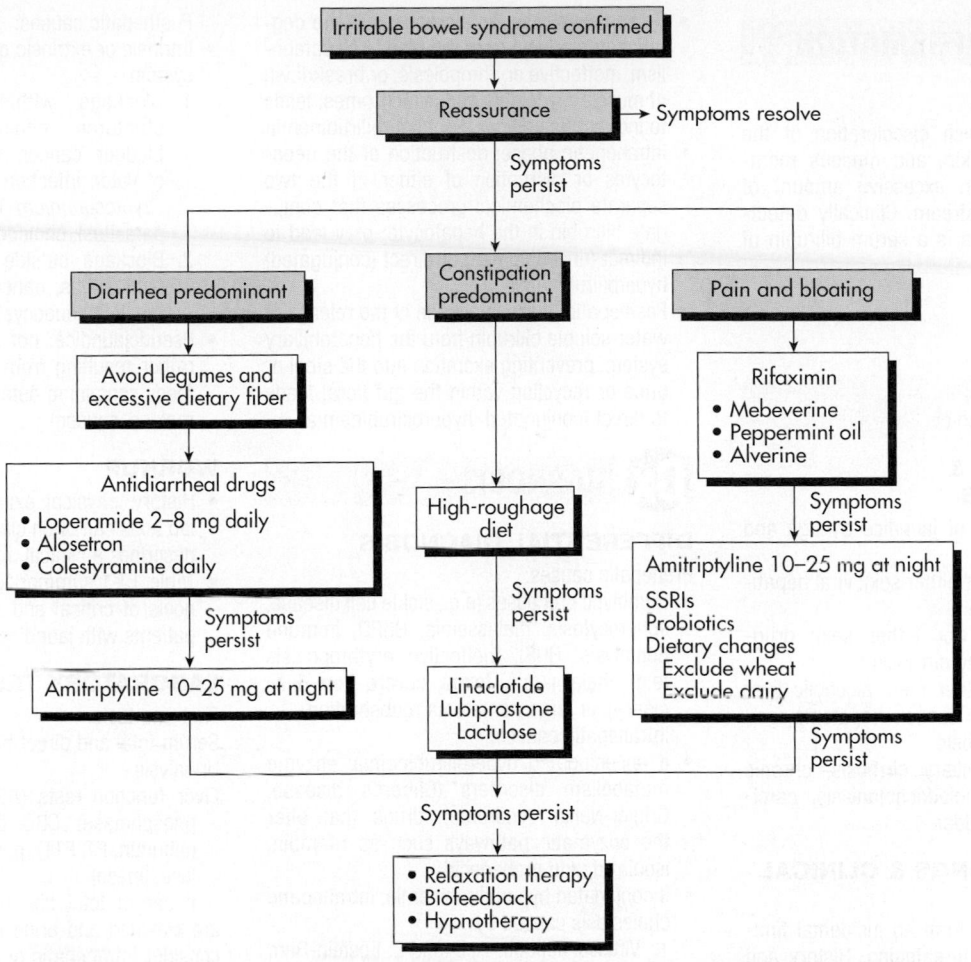

FIGURE 1I-26 Management of irritable bowel syndrome. (Modified from Palmer K.R., Ponman I.D.: ?? Alimentary tract and pancreatic disease. In Colledge N.R., Walker B.R., Ralston S.H.: *Davidson's principles and practice of medicine*, Philadelphia, 2010, Elsevier.)

TABLE 1I-14 Diagnostic Criteria* for Irritable Bowel Syndrome

Recurrent abdominal pain or discomfort[†] at least 3 d/mo in the previous 3 mo associated with ≥2 of the following:
1. Improvement with defecation
2. Onset associated with a change in frequency of stool
3. Onset associated with a change in form (appearance) of stool
4. Supporting symptoms (not required for diagnosis but helpful in confirming IBS presentation): (1) abnormal stool frequency (<3 bowel movements per week or >3 bowel movements per day), (2) abnormal stool form, (3) defecation straining, (4) urgency (feeling of incomplete evacuation), (5) passage of mucus, and (6) bloating.

IBS, Irritable bowel syndrome.
*Criteria fulfilled for the previous 3 mo with symptom onset at least 6 mo before diagnosis.
[†]Discomfort means an uncomfortable sensation not described as pain. In pathophysiology research and clinical trials, a pain or discomfort frequency of at least 2 d/wk during screening evaluation for subject eligibility.
Adapted from Sayuk GS, Gyawali CP: Irritable bowel syndrome: modern concepts and management options. *Am J Med* 128(8), 817-827, 2015.

TABLE 1I-15 Subtyping Irritable Bowel Syndrome by Predominant Stool Pattern

1. IBS with constipation—hard or lumpy stools* ≥25% and loose (mushy) or watery stools[†] ≥25% of bowel movements[‡]
2. IBS with diarrhea—loose (mushy) or watery stools[†] ≥25% and hard or lumpy stool* ≥25% of bowel movements[‡]
3. Mixed IBS—hard or lumpy stools* ≥25% and loose (mushy) or watery stools[†] ≥25% of bowel movements[‡]
4. Unsubtyped IBS—insufficient abnormality of stool consistency to meet criteria for IBS with constipation, diarrhea, or mixed[‡]

IBS, Irritable bowel syndrome.
*Bristol Stool Form Scale 1-2 (separate hard lumps like nuts [difficult to pass] or sausage-shaped but lumpy).
[†]Bristol Stool Form Scale 6-7 (fluffy pieces with ragged edges, a mushy stool or watery, no solid pieces, entirely liquid).
[‡]In the absence of use of antidiarrheals or laxatives.
Adapted from Sayuk GS, Gyawali CP: Irritable bowel syndrome: modern concepts and management options. *Am J Med* 128(8), 817-827, 2015.

---

avoidance may be reasonable in patients with treatment-resistant IBS.

SUGGESTED READINGS
Available at www.expertconsult.com

RELATED CONTENT
Irritable Bowel Syndrome (Patient Information)

AUTHOR: **FRED F. FERRI, M.D.**

Jaundice in the Adult Patient (ALG) (PTG)

BASIC INFORMATION

DEFINITION
Jaundice is a yellowish discoloration of the sclera (Fig. E1J-1), skin, and mucous membranes caused by an excessive amount of bilirubin in the bloodstream. Clinically detectable jaundice in adults is a serum bilirubin of 2.5 to 3 mg/dl.

SYNONYMS
Icterus

ICD-10CM CODES
R17 Unspecified jaundice

EPIDEMIOLOGY & DEMOGRAPHICS
The prevalent causes of jaundice by age and sex:
- Young adulthood (for either sex): viral hepatitis, Gilbert's disease
- Middle adulthood (for either sex): drug-induced hepatitis and cirrhosis
- Middle-aged and older men: alcoholic liver disease, pancreatic cancer, hepatoma, primary hemochromatosis
- Women: primary biliary cirrhosis, chronic active hepatitis, choledocholithiasis, carcinoma of the gallbladder

PHYSICAL FINDINGS & CLINICAL PRESENTATION
Presentation can vary from an incidental finding to acute and life threatening. History and physical examination give important clues to the underlying condition.
Key history of present illness findings:
- Duration of jaundice
- Associated symptoms: abdominal pain, fever, nausea, malaise, pruritus, chills, changes in urine and stool color, anorexia and/or weight loss
Key social history/exposure findings:
- Alcohol use, injection of illicit drugs, use of hepatotoxic medication or herbal products, blood transfusions, unprotected sex, ingestion of shellfish, travel, occupational exposure to toxins
Key past medical history findings:
- Prior abdominal/biliary surgery, prior episodes of jaundice, prior diagnosis of hepatitis B or C, inflammatory bowel disease
Key physical findings:
- Vital sign abnormalities: fever, hypotension, tachycardia
- Signs of acute disease: abdominal tenderness, splenomegaly, abdominal mass, encephalopathy, Murphy's sign
- Signs of chronic liver disease: palmar erythema, spider angiomas, bruising, gynecomastia, testicular atrophy, ascites, weight loss, Kayser-Fleischer rings (Wilson's), caput medusa, internal hemorrhoids, scleral icterus

ETIOLOGY
Disruption in any of the three phases of bilirubin metabolism can lead to jaundice:

- Prehepatic phase: an increase in heme degradation products from red blood cell catabolism, ineffective erythropoiesis, or breakdown of muscle myoglobin and cytochromes; leads to indirect (unconjugated) hyperbilirubinemia
- Intrahepatic phase: destruction of the hepatocytes or disruption of either of the two separate biochemical processes that conjugate bilirubin in the hepatocyte; may lead to indirect (unconjugated) or direct (conjugated) hyperbilirubinemia
- Posthepatic phase: blockage of the release of water-soluble bilirubin from the hepatobiliary system, preventing excretion into the stool or urine or recycling within the gut flora; leads to direct (conjugated) hyperbilirubinemia

DIAGNOSIS

DIFFERENTIAL DIAGNOSIS
Prehepatic causes:
- Hemolytic processes (e.g., sickle cell disease, spherocytosis, thalassemia, G6PD, immune hemolysis, HUS), ineffective erythropoiesis (e.g., thalassemia, folate, severe iron deficiency), or large hematoma reabsorption.
Intrahepatic causes:
- If unconjugated hyperbilirubinemia: enzyme metabolism disorders (Gilbert's disease, Crigler-Najjar syndrome), drugs that alter the enzymatic pathways such as rifampin, isoniazid, and probenecid.
- If conjugated hyperbilirubinemia: intrahepatic cholestasis caused by:
  1. Viruses: hepatitis A, B, and C; Epstein-Barr, hemorrhagic viruses (yellow fever, Ebola)
  2. Other infections: bacteria (leptospirosis, MAI), parasites (schistosomiasis, malaria, amebiasis), fungal (blastomyces, histoplasma)
  3. Alcohol: alcoholic hepatitis, alcoholic cirrhosis
  4. Autoimmune: primary biliary cirrhosis, primary sclerosing cholangitis, autoimmune hepatitis
  5. Hepatotoxic drug-induced: acetaminophen (most common), penicillins (most commonly Augmentin), chlorpromazine, steroids (estrogenic or anabolic), NSAIDs, valproic acid, some herbals such as kava, ma huang, and off-market weight loss supplements
  6. Hereditary/metabolic: sickle cell disease and other RBC dyscrasias, hemochromatosis, Wilson's disease, Dubin-Johnson and Rotor's syndromes, α-antitrypsin deficiency, glycogen storage disease, NASH (non-alcoholic steatohepatitis), porphyria, benign recurrent intrahepatic cholestasis
  7. Systemic disease: invading liver: sarcoidosis, amyloidosis, hemochromatosis, tuberculosis, *Mycobacterium avium intracellulare*
  8. Other: cirrhosis, sepsis, total parenteral nutrition, intrahepatic cholestasis of pregnancy, graft-versus-host disease, environmental toxins, benign postoperative state

Posthepatic causes:
- Intrinsic or extrinsic obstruction of the biliary system
  1. Blockage within hepatobiliary tree: strictures, cholangiocarcinoma, gallbladder cancer, carcinoma of ampulla of Vater, infection (e.g., cytomegalovirus, *Cryptosporidium* in patients with AIDS, parasites), choledocholithiasis
  2. Blockage outside of hepatobiliary tree: pancreatitis, pancreatic carcinoma, pancreatic pseudocyst, lymphoma
- Pseudojaundice: not related to bilirubin but rather resulting from excessive ingestion of foods containing beta carotene (e.g., carrots, melons, squash)

WORKUP
- History, physical examination, and first-line lab tests can often clarify diagnosis. Fig. 1J-2 describes a clinical approach to jaundice.
- Table 1J-1 summarizes the differential diagnosis of critical and emergent diagnoses in patients with jaundice.

LABORATORY TESTS
First-line tests:
Serum total and direct bilirubin
Urinalysis
Liver function tests (AST, ALT, GGTP, alkaline phosphatase), CBC, liver synthetic function (albumin, PT, PTT), pancreatic function (amylase, lipase)
If serum total bilirubin and direct bilirubin are elevated and urine is positive for bilirubin, consider intrahepatic or posthepatic process: If serum total bilirubin is elevated but direct bilirubin is normal (unconjugated hyperbilirubinemia) and urine is negative for bilirubin, consider prehepatic or intrahepatic processes.
- Additional tests if diagnosis unclear:
  1. Screen for hepatitis A, B, and C; if still unclear then consider following options based on H&P
  2. Other viruses: EBV, CMV
  3. Autoimmune disorders: antimitochondrial antibody (elevated in primary biliary cirrhosis); antismooth muscle antibody, ANA (elevated in autoimmune hepatitis); antinuclear cytoplasmic antibody (elevated in primary sclerosing cholangitis)
  4. Ceruloplasmin (elevated in Wilson's disease)
  5. Alpha-1 antitrypsin deficiency (elevated in cirrhosis and emphysema)
  6. Ferritin, Fe saturation (elevated in hemochromatosis)
  7. Blood smear (RBC dyscrasias)
- Diagnosis of exclusion: Gilbert's syndrome
Liver biopsy: essential in diagnosis of chronic hepatitis. Can be used for diagnosis of liver masses but carries a substantial risk.

IMAGING STUDIES
- Abdominal ultrasound: first-line study (Figs. E1J-3 and E1J-4) may be completed bedside, most sensitive for proximal biliary tract disease; presence of dilated ducts hints at an extrahepatic process

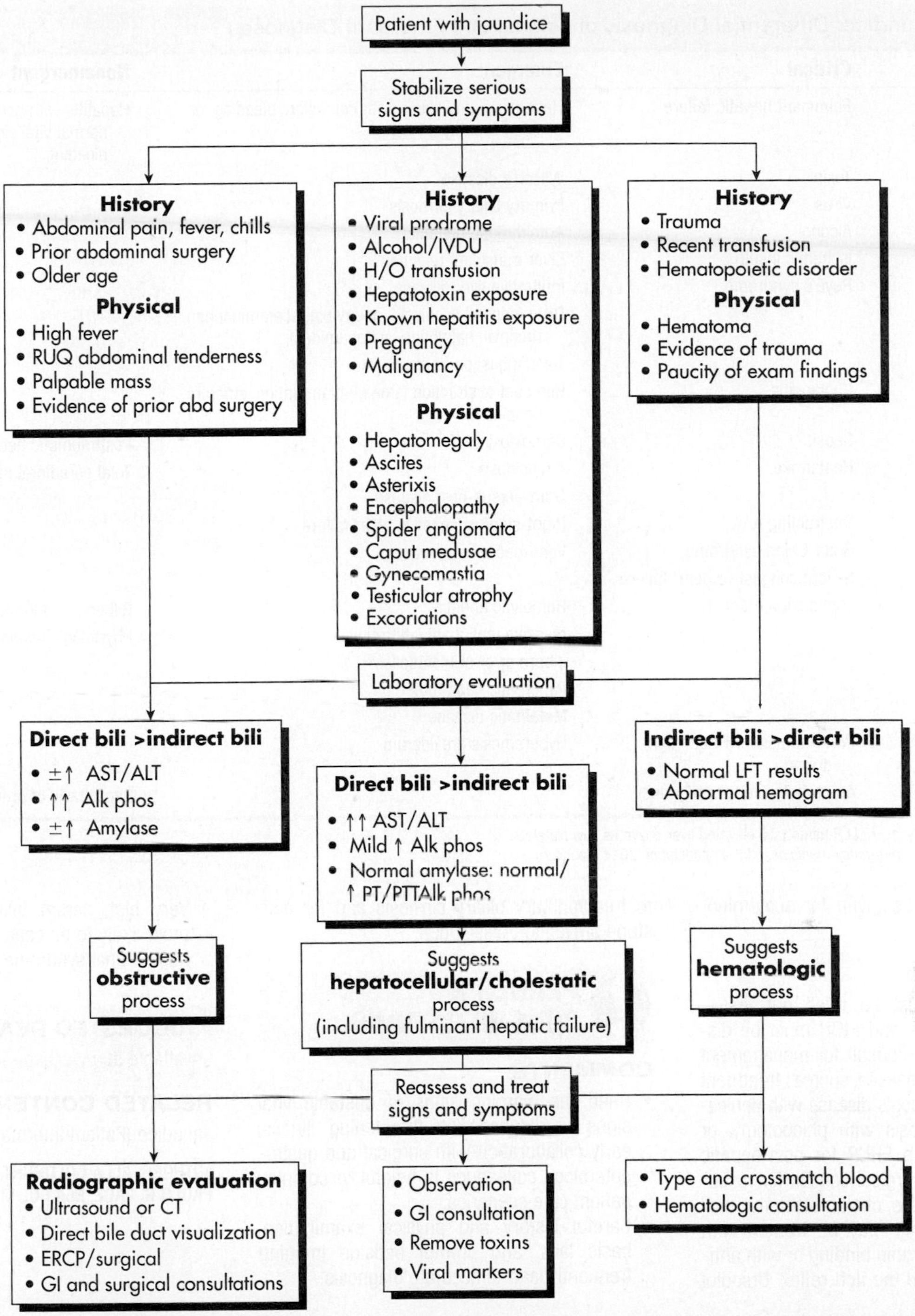

Patient with jaundice

Stabilize serious
signs and symptoms

History
- Abdominal pain, fever, chills
- Prior abdominal surgery
- Older age

Physical
- High fever
- RUQ abdominal tenderness
- Palpable mass
- Evidence of prior abd surgery

History
- Viral prodrome
- Alcohol/IVDU
- H/O transfusion
- Hepatotoxin exposure
- Known hepatitis exposure
- Pregnancy
- Malignancy

Physical
- Hepatomegaly
- Ascites
- Asterixis
- Encephalopathy
- Spider angiomata
- Caput medusae
- Gynecomastia
- Testicular atrophy
- Excoriations

History
- Trauma
- Recent transfusion
- Hematopoietic disorder

Physical
- Hematoma
- Evidence of trauma
- Paucity of exam findings

Laboratory evaluation

Direct bili >indirect bili
- ±↑ AST/ALT
- ↑↑ Alk phos
- ±↑ Amylase

Direct bili >indirect bili
- ↑↑ AST/ALT
- Mild ↑ Alk phos
- Normal amylase: normal/
  ↑ PT/PTTAlk phos

Indirect bili >direct bili
- Normal LFT results
- Abnormal hemogram

Suggests
obstructive
process

Suggests
hepatocellular/cholestatic
process
(including fulminant hepatic failure)

Suggests
hematologic
process

Reassess and treat
signs and symptoms

Radiographic evaluation
- Ultrasound or CT
- Direct bile duct visualization
- ERCP/surgical
- GI and surgical consultations

- Observation
- GI consultation
- Remove toxins
- Viral markers

- Type and crossmatch blood
- Hematologic consultation

FIGURE 1J-2 Management of the patient with jaundice. *Alk phos,* Alkaline phosphatase; *ALT,* alanine aminotransferase; *AST,* aspartate aminotransferase; *bili,* bilirubin; *CT,* computed tomography; *ERCP,* endoscopic retrograde cholangiopancreatography; *GI,* gastrointestinal; *H/O,* history of; *IVDU,* intravenous drug use; *LFT,* liver function test; *PT,* prothrombin time; *PTT,* partial thromboplastin time; *RUQ,* right upper quadrant. (From Marx A.J. et al: *Rosen's emergency medicine: concepts and clinical practice,* ed 7, Philadelphia, 2010, Elsevier)

- Abdominal CT: often necessary to elucidate more information on liver, pancreas, and distal biliary system
- Endoscopic retrograde cholangiopancreatography: rarely necessary for diagnostics. Refer to GI consultant
- Percutaneous transhepatic cholangiography: rarely necessary for diagnostics. Refer to GI or surgical consultant
- Magnetic resonance cholangiopancreatography: noninvasive visualization of bile and pancreatic ducts. Refer to GI consultant.

- Endoscopic ultrasound: used for characterization and, if needed, biopsy of any focal lesions found within biliary tree and/or pancreas. Refer to GI consultant

Rx TREATMENT

NONPHARMACOLOGIC THERAPY

Depends on underlying cause of the jaundice and clinical stability of the patient. Generally, obstructive causes require surgical treatment, while nonobstructive causes require medical treatment.

ACUTE GENERAL Rx

Acute, life-threatening illness (e.g., cholecystitis or ascending cholangitis) requires prompt diagnosis with basic labs and bedside diagnostics, with early surgical and GI consultation in conjunction. Suspicious medications should be stopped. Initiate medical management of symptoms with analgesia, IV fluids, correction of coagulopathies, and consideration of antibiotics.

Table 1J-1 Jaundice: Differential Diagnosis of Critical and Emergent Diagnoses

System	Critical	Emergent	Nonemergent
Hepatic	Fulminant hepatic failure	Hepatitis of any cause with confusion, bleeding, or coagulopathy	Hepatitis with normal mental status, normal vital signs, and no active bleeding
	Toxin	Wilson's disease	
	Virus	Primary biliary cirrhosis	
	Alcohol	Autoimmune hepatitis	
	Ischemic insult	Liver transplant rejection	
	Reye's syndrome	Infiltrative liver disease	
		Drug induced (isoniazid, phenytoin, acetaminophen, ritonavir, halothane, sulfonamides)	
		Toxin ingestion or exposure	
Biliary	Cholangitis	Bile duct obstruction (stone, inflammation, stricture, neoplasm)	
Systemic	Sepsis	Sarcoidosis	Posttraumatic hematoma resorption
	Heatstroke	Amyloidosis	Total parenteral nutrition
		Graft-versus-host disease	
Cardiovascular	Obstructing AAA	Right-sided congestive heart failure	
	Budd-Chiari syndrome	Veno-occlusive disease	
	Severe congestive heart failure		
Hematologic-oncologic	Transfusion reaction	Hemolytic anemia	Gilbert's syndrome
		Massive malignant infiltration	Physiologic neonatal jaundice
		Inborn error of metabolism	
		Pancreatic head tumor	
		Metastatic disease	
Reproductive	Preeclampsia or HELLP syndrome	Hyperemesis gravidarum	
	Acute fatty liver of pregnancy		Cholestasis of pregnancy

AAA, Abdominal aortic aneurysm; *HELLP,* hemolysis, elevated liver enzymes, low platelets.
From Marx JA, et al: *Rosen's emergency medicine,* ed 8, Philadelphia, 2014, Saunders.

N-Acetylcysteine can be given for acetaminophen overdose.

CHRONIC Rx

Reversible causes must be ruled out first—suspicious medications and EtOH must be discontinued. Consider GI consult for management of many intrahepatic diseases, such as treatment of hepatitis B or C, Wilson's disease with penicillamine, hemochromatosis with phlebotomy, or for stent insertion with ERCP for post-hepatic obstruction. Consider surgical consult for resection of pancreatic masses, cholecystectomy, etc.

Symptomatic pruritus may be treated with cholestyramine for bilirubin binding or with antihistamines to decrease the itch reflex. Ursodiol to treat primary biliary cirrhosis and for gallstone prevention/dissolution.

PEARLS & CONSIDERATIONS

COMMENTS

- Heed the warning signs of unstable vital signs to diagnose life-threatening illness; early collaboration with surgical and gastroenterology colleagues is helpful in complex patient care scenarios.
- Careful history and physical examination, basic labs, and prompt bedside imaging frequently lead to accurate diagnosis.

- Very high serum bilirubin (>15 mg/dl) is most likely to be seen in cirrhosis. Watch for hepatorenal syndrome in these patients.

SUGGESTED READINGS
Available at www.expertconsult.com

RELATED CONTENT
Jaundice (Patient Information)

AUTHORS: **ALLA GOLDBURT, M.D.,** and **PAOLO G. PACE, M.A.SC., M.D**

BASIC INFORMATION

DEFINITION

Juvenile idiopathic arthritis (JIA), previously referred to as juvenile rheumatoid arthritis (JRA), is a diverse spectrum of chronic arthritides, involving ≥1 joints for at least 6 weeks in a patient ≤16 yr of age. Other causes of arthritis must be excluded.

SYNONYMS

JIA
Juvenile rheumatoid arthritis
Still's disease (specifically systemic JIA)

ICD-10CM CODES

M08.00 Unspecified juvenile rheumatoid arthritis of unspecified site
M08.29 Juvenile rheumatoid arthritis with systemic onset, multiple sites
M08.40 Pauciarticular juvenile rheumatoid arthritis, unspecified site
M08.09 Unspecified juvenile rheumatoid arthritis, multiple sites
M08.20 Juvenile rheumatoid arthritis with systemic onset, unspecified site

EPIDEMIOLOGY & DEMOGRAPHICS

PREVALENCE: About 1 per 1000 children in the U.S.; more common in children of European ancestry

PHYSICAL FINDINGS & CLINICAL PRESENTATION

JIA is subdivided into seven categories based on the 2001 International League of Associations for Rheumatology (ILAR) classification criteria (summarized in Table 1J-2).
Systemic onset JIA (4%-17%)
  Arthritis in ≥1 joints with or preceded by fever of at least 2-wk duration that is quotidian (once daily) for at least 3 days and associated with at least one of the following: (1) evanescent erythematous rash (Fig. E1J-5); (2) generalized lymphadenopathy; (3) hepatomegaly, splenomegaly, or both; and (4) serositis.
Oligoarticular JIA (Fig. E1J-6) (27%-56%)
  Arthritis in <4 joints in the first 6 mo of disease. There are two subtypes:
    Persistent: ≤4 joints throughout the disease course.
    Extended: ≤4 joints during the first 6 mo extending to >4 joints after 6 mo.
Polyarthritis, rheumatoid factor (RF) negative (11%-28%)
  Arthritis in >5 joints during first 6 mo of the disease with negative RF.
Polyarthritis, RF positive (2%-7%)
  Arthritis involves ≥5 joints during first 6 mo of the disease with positive RF on at least two tests run 3 mo apart.
Anti–cyclic citrullinated (CCP) antibodies may also be present.

Most similar to adult rheumatoid arthritis; most likely to progress.
Psoriatic arthritis (2%-11%)
  Psoriasis and arthritis or psoriasis and ≥2 of the following:
    Dactylitis, nail pitting, onycholysis, and psoriasis in a first-degree relative.
Enthesitis-related arthritis (3%-11%)
  Arthritis or enthesitis and ≥2 of the following:
    Sacroiliac tenderness, positive HLA-B27, male age >6 yr, acute anterior uveitis, or first-degree relative with HLA-B27-associated disease
Undifferentiated arthritis (11%-21%)
  Fulfills criteria in ≥2 categories above, or none of them

ETIOLOGY

Influenced by both genetic and environmental factors

 DIAGNOSIS

DIFFERENTIAL DIAGNOSIS

- Infection: viral (parvovirus, toxic synovitis) or bacterial (Lyme, osteomyelitis, septic joints)
- Inflammation: lupus, serum sickness, inflammatory bowel disease
- Reactive: post-streptococcal, rheumatic fever
- Malignancy: leukemia, bone tumors

TABLE 1J-2 Overview of the Main Features of the Subtypes of Juvenile Idiopathic Arthritis

ILAR Subtype	Peak Age of Onset (yr)	Female: Male; % of All JIA	Arthritis Pattern	Extraarticular Features	Investigations	Notes on Therapy
Systemic arthritis	2-4	1:1; ~10% of JIA cases	Polyarticular, often knees, wrists, and ankles; also fingers, neck, and hips	Daily fever; evanescent rash; pericarditis; pleuritis	Anemia; WBC↑↑; ESR↑↑; CRP↑↑; ferritin;↑ platelets↑↑ (normal or ↑ in MAS)	Less responsive to standard treatment with MTX and anti-TNF agents; consider IL-1Ra in resistant cases
Oligoarthritis	>6	4:1; 50%-60% of JIA (but ethnic variation)	Knees ++; ankles, fingers +	Uveitis in ~30%	ANA positive in 60%; other tests usually normal; may have mildly ↑ ESR/CRP	NSAIDs and intraarticular steroids; occasionally require MTX
Polyarthritis, RF negative	6-7	3:1; 30% of JIA cases	Symmetric or asymmetric; small and large joints; cervical spine; TMJ	Uveitis in ~10%	ANA positive in 40%; RF negative; ESR ↑ or; ↑↑ CRP↑/normal; mild anemia	Standard therapy with MTX and NSAIDs, then if nonresponsive, anti-TNF agents or other biologics
Polyarthritis, RF positive	9-12	9:1; >10% of JIA cases	Aggressive symmetric polyarthritis	Rheumatoid nodules in 10%; low-grade fever	RF positive; ESR ↑↑; CRP ↑/normal; mild anemia	Long-term remission unlikely; early aggressive therapy is warranted
Psoriatic arthritis	7-10	2:1; >10% of JIA cases	Asymmetric arthritis of small or medium sized joints	Uveitis in 10%; psoriasis in 50%	ANA positive in 50%; ESR ↑; CRP ↑/normal; mild anemia	NSAIDs and intraarticular steroids; second-line agents less commonly
Enthesitis-related arthritis	9-12	1:7; 10% of JIA cases	Predominantly lower limb joints affected; sometimes axial skeleton (but less than adult AS)	Acute anterior uveitis; association with reactive arthritis and IBD	80% HLA-B27[1]	NSAIDs and intraarticular steroids; consider sulfasalazine as alternative to MTX

ANA, Antinuclear antibody; *AS,* ankylosing spondylitis; *CRP,* C-reactive protein; *ESR,* erythrocyte sedimentation rate; *IBD,* inflammatory bowel disease; *ILAR,* International League of Associations for Rheumatology; *IL-1Ra,* interleukin-1 receptor antagonist; *JIA,* juvenile idiopathic arthritis; *MAS,* macrophage activation syndrome; *MTX,* methotrexate; *NSAID,* nonsteroidal anti-inflammatory drug; *RF,* rheumatoid factor; *TMJ,* temporomandibular joint; *TNF,* tumor necrosis factor; *WBC,* white blood cell count.
From Firestein G et al: *Kelley's textbook of rheumatology,* ed 9, Philadelphia, 2013, Saunders.

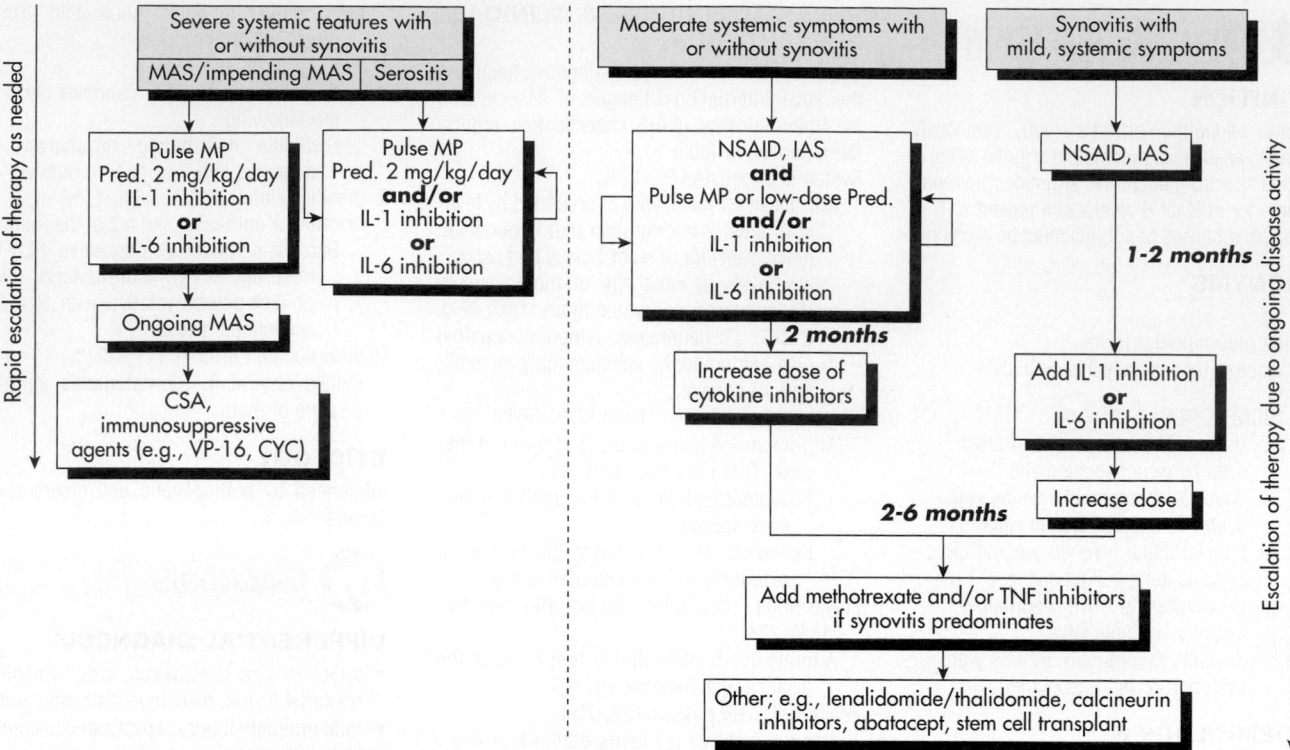

FIGURE 1J-9 Systemic juvenile idiopathic arthritis treatment algorithm. The treatment goal is remission of disease activity, both systemic and articular, and is stratified by severity of disease. Algorithm is divided into severe systemic disease manifestations (macrophage activation syndrome [MAS], serositis) or synovitis with milder systemic disease. Currently there is significant variability in practice regarding using corticosteroid as initial systemic therapy or moving directly to inflammatory cytokine inhibitors. At the time of this writing, interleukin (IL)-1 inhibition and IL-6 inhibition are currently in trials, and more information is likely to be available in the future. *CSA,* cyclosporine A; *CYC,* cyclophosphamide; *IAS,* intraarticular steroid; *MP,* methylprednisolone; *NSAID,* nonsteroidal anti-inflammatory drug; *Pred.,* prednisone; *TNF,* tumor necrosis factor. (From Firestein GS et al: *Kelly's textbook of rheumatology,* ed 9, Philadelphia, 2013, Saunders.)

LABORATORY TESTS

- There is no single diagnostic test. Other causes of arthritis must be excluded.
- Elevated sedimentation rate and C-reactive protein
- Mild anemia, leukocytosis
- Rheumatoid factor: rarely positive in children
- Antinuclear antibodies: elevation associated with ocular complications
- Pancytopenia, lab results consistent with a consumptive coagulopathy, and elevated liver enzymes are indicative of macrophage activation syndrome in systemic JIA. Bone marrow biopsy is needed to confirm diagnosis.

IMAGING STUDIES

- Radiographs show soft tissue swelling and periarticular osteopenia early in the disease (Fig. E1J-7).
- Joint destruction (Fig. E1J-8) is less frequent, but bony erosion and cyst formation may be present.

Rx TREATMENT

NONPHARMACOLOGIC THERAPY

Collaboration among the patient's pediatrician, pediatric rheumatologist, orthopedist, and physical therapists yields the best outcome. The goal is complete remission.
- Physical and occupational therapy.
- Education regarding diet and weight management (Fig. 1J-9).

CHRONIC GENERAL Rx

- NSAIDs, used as monotherapy or in conjunction with intraarticular steroids
- DMARDs: methotrexate, leflunomide, sulfasalazine
  - Required by two-thirds of children
  - Axial involvement is less responsive to methotrexate.
- Biologics: improve morbidity associated with JIA
  1. Tumor necrosis factor antagonists such as etanercept and adalimumab.
  2. T-cell modulator, abatacept, is approved for patients with polyarticular JIA who have not responded to anti-TNF therapy.
  3. IL-1 and IL-6 antagonists, anakinra and tocilizumab, respectively, offer promising results in patients with systemic JIA.
- Systemic corticosteroids should be limited when possible.

DISPOSITION

- 50% continue to have active disease into adulthood.
- 70% to 85% regain normal function.
- Macrophage activation syndrome is a life-threatening complication in systemic JIA.
- Oligoarticular JIA patients with positive ANA are at the highest risk for blindness due to chronic iridocyclitis and require frequent ophthalmologic monitoring.
- Systemic and localized growth disturbance can lead to growth failure and leg length discrepancies.

REFERRAL

- Early rheumatology consultation.
- Ophthalmology consultation at diagnosis and at least annually.
- Children age <7 years, with + ANA are at the highest risk for iritis, and require screening every 3 to 4 months.

! PEARLS & CONSIDERATIONS

COMMENTS

The FDA surveillance system for spontaneous adverse event reporting (SERS) has recently reported a warning for risk of malignancy related to anti-TNF agents in the pediatric population. However, baseline risk of malignancy in children with JIA is unknown and the SERS reporting system has limitations, including incomplete adverse event reporting. Initiation of anti-TNF therapy should be a decision made between families and pediatric rheumatologists.

SUGGESTED READINGS

Available at www.expertconsult.com

RELATED CONTENT

Juvenile Rheumatoid Arthritis (Patient Information)

AUTHOR: **MICHELLE C. MACIAG, M.D.**

 **BASIC INFORMATION**

DEFINITION

Kaposi's sarcoma (KS) is a vascular neoplasm most frequently occurring in AIDS patients. It can be divided into the following four subsets:

1. Classic KS: most frequently found in elderly Eastern European and Mediterranean males. It consists initially of violaceous macules and papules with subsequent development of plaques and red-purple nodules. Growth is slow, and most of the patients die of unrelated causes.
2. Epidemic or AIDS-related KS: most frequently occurs in homosexual men. Lesions are generally multifocal and widespread (Fig. E1K-1). Lymphadenopathy may be associated.
3. Endemic KS: usually affects African children and adults. An aggressive lymphadenopathic form affects African children in particular.
4. Immunosuppression-associated, or transplantation-associated, KS: usually associated with chemotherapy.

SYNONYM

KS

ICD-10CM CODES
C46.0   Kaposi's sarcoma of skin
C46.1   Kaposi's sarcoma of soft tissue
C46.2   Kaposi's sarcoma of palate
C46.3   Kaposi's sarcoma of lymph nodes
C46.4   Kaposi's sarcoma of gastrointestinal sites
C46.50 Kaposi's sarcoma of unspecified lung
C46.51 Kaposi's sarcoma of right lung
C46.52 Kaposi's sarcoma of left lung
C46.7   Kaposi's sarcoma of other sites
C46.9   Kaposi's sarcoma, unspecified

EPIDEMIOLOGY & DEMOGRAPHICS

- AIDS-related KS affects >35% of AIDS cases.
- Highest incidence is in homosexual men.

PHYSICAL FINDINGS & CLINICAL PRESENTATION

- AIDS-related KS: multifocal and widespread red-purple (Fig. 1K-4) or dark plaques (Fig. E1K-3) and/or nodules on cutaneous or mucosal surfaces (Fig. E1K-1).
- Generalized lymphadenopathy at the time of diagnosis is present in >50% of patients with AIDS-related KS; the initial lesions have a rust-colored appearance; subsequent progression to red or purple nodules or plaques occurs (Fig. E1K-2).
- Most frequently affected areas are the face, trunk, oral cavity, and upper and lower extremities.
- The GI tract is the most frequent site of internal involvement in classic KS.

- In AIDS-associated KS, 25% of patients have cutaneous involvement alone, whereas 29% have visceral lesions only (lymph nodes 50%, GI tract 50%, lungs 37%).

ETIOLOGY

A herpesvirus (HHV-8, KS-associated herpesvirus KSHV) has been isolated from patients with most forms of KS and is believed to be the causative agent. It can be transmitted sexually (homosexual or heterosexual activities) and by other forms of nonsexual contact such as maternal-infant transmission (common in African countries).

 **DIAGNOSIS**

DIFFERENTIAL DIAGNOSIS

- Stasis dermatitis.
- Pyogenic granuloma.
- Capillary hemangiomas.
- Granulation tissue.
- Postinflammatory hyperpigmentation.
- Cutaneous lymphoma.
- Melanoma.
- Dermatofibroma.
- Hematoma.
- Prurigo nodularis.

The differential diagnosis of cutaneous lesions in patients with HIV infection is described in Section II.

WORKUP

Diagnosis can generally be made on clinical appearance; tissue biopsy will confirm diagnosis.

LABORATORY TESTS

HIV in patients suspected of AIDS.

 **TREATMENT**

NONPHARMACOLOGIC THERAPY

Observation is a reasonable option in patients with slowly progressive disease.

GENERAL Rx

- All types of KS are radiosensitive. Radiation therapy is effective in non-AIDS KS and for

large tumor masses that interfere with normal function.
- Excisional biopsy often provides adequate treatment for single lesions and resected recurrences in classic KS.
- Liquid nitrogen cryotherapy can result in complete response in 80% of lesions.
- Interlesional chemotherapy with vinblastine is useful for nodular lesions >1 cm in diameter. Intralesional injection of interferon alfa-2b has also been reported as effective and well tolerated.
- HIV treatment is patients with HIV-related KS.
- Liposomal anthracyclines and paclitaxel are FDA approved as first-line and second-line monotherapy for advanced KS.
- Sirolimus (rapamycin), an immunosuppressive drug, is effective in inhibiting the progression of dermal KS in kidney transplant recipients.
- Alitretinoin gel (Panretin) for local lesions.

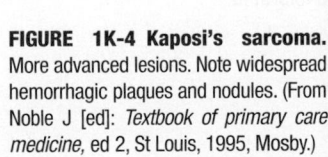 **PEARLS & CONSIDERATIONS**

COMMENTS

- Immunosuppression-associated KS usually regresses with the cessation, reduction, or modification of immunosuppression therapy in most patients. Similarly, in HIV patients KS responds concurrently with the decrease in serum HIV RNA and increase in the CD4 count.
- Kaposi sarcoma is associated with an increased risk of developing secondary malignancies (lymphomas, leukemia, myeloma).

SUGGESTED READINGS
Available at www.expertconsult.com

RELATED CONTENT
Kaposi's Sarcoma (Patient Information)
AIDS (Related Key Topic)

AUTHOR: **FRED F. FERRI, M.D.**

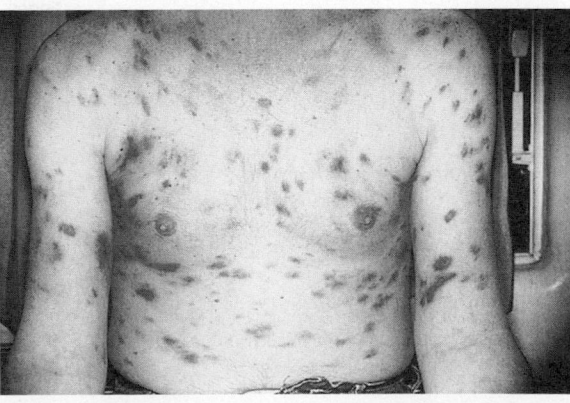

FIGURE 1K-4 Kaposi's sarcoma. More advanced lesions. Note widespread hemorrhagic plaques and nodules. (From Noble J [ed]: *Textbook of primary care medicine,* ed 2, St Louis, 1995, Mosby.)

BASIC INFORMATION

DEFINITION

Labyrinthitis is a peripheral vestibulopathy characterized by acute onset of vertigo usually associated with nausea and vomiting. It may be associated with hearing loss. It may be either serous or purulent.

SYNONYMS

Acute labyrinthitis
Acute vestibular neuronopathy
Vestibular neuronitis
Viral neurolabyrinthitis

ICD-10CM CODES

H81.23 Vestibular neuronitis, bilateral
H83.09 Labyrinthitis, unspecified ear
H83.01 Labyrinthitis, right ear
H83.02 Labyrinthitis, left ear
H83.03 Labyrinthitis, bilateral

EPIDEMIOLOGY & DEMOGRAPHICS

INCIDENCE (IN U.S.): Most common cause of prolonged spontaneous vertigo associated with nausea at any age
PREDOMINANT AGE: Any

CLINICAL PRESENTATION

- Vertigo, nausea, and vomiting with onset over several hours.
- Symptoms usually peak within 24 hr, then resolve gradually over several weeks.
- During the first day, the patient usually has difficulty focusing the eyes because of spontaneous nystagmus.
- Usually has benign course, with complete recovery within 1 to 3 mo, although older patients may have intractable dizziness that persists for many months.

PHYSICAL FINDINGS

- Nystagmus
- Nausea
- Vomiting
- Vertigo worsening with head movement
- Abnormal caloric ENG tests
- May have hearing loss in the affected ear
- Normal otoscopic exam typically
- Normal neurologic exam; may have signs of vestibular loss, such as a positive head thrust test

ETIOLOGY

Symptoms often preceded for 1 to 2 wk by a viral-like illness. It may be either bacterial or viral, and be either tympanogenic (i.e., resulting from spread of infection into the inner ear from the middle ear, antrum, or petrous apex), meningogenic, or hematogenic from encephalitis or brain abscess. The round window membrane is considered the most likely pathway of inflammatory mediators from the middle to the inner ear that subsequently give rise to labyrinthitis.

 DIAGNOSIS

DIFFERENTIAL DIAGNOSIS

- Acute labyrinthine ischemia (vascular insufficiency)
- Other forms of labyrinthitis (bacterial and syphilitic)
- Labyrinthine fistula
- Benign positional vertigo
- Meniere's syndrome
- Cholesteatoma
- Drug induced
- Eighth nerve tumor
- Head trauma
- Vertebrobasilar stroke

WORKUP

- Otoscopic examination
- Neurologic examination, with close attention to cranial nerves
- Bedside test of vestibular function, that is, head thrust or head heave test
- Audiogram if symptoms accompanied by hearing loss
- Caloric test if presentation is atypical

LABORATORY TESTS

- Routine laboratory tests are generally not helpful.
- If there is a history of significant emesis, check electrolytes, BUN, and creatinine.

IMAGING STUDIES

- Imaging studies are usually not necessary.
- Contrasted MRI may show enhancement of bony labyrinth. MRI of the brain with and without contrast with fine cuts through the internal auditory canal is indicated if there is an abnormal cranial nerve exam or suspicion of eighth nerve tumor.
- Head CT with fine cuts through temporal bones is indicated if there is a history of trauma or suspicion of cholesteatoma.

 TREATMENT

NONPHARMACOLOGIC THERAPY

- Reassurance.
- Initial bed rest, then encourage increase in activity as tolerated.

ACUTE GENERAL Rx

- Phenergan or other antiemetics are typically effective.
- Vestibular suppressant: meclizine 12.5 to 25 mg qid is often used. Scopolamine patch is also effective.
- Methylprednisolone 100 mg per day for 3 days, with slow taper over 3 wk.
- Valacyclovir has not been shown to be helpful.

CHRONIC Rx

No specific chronic therapy

DISPOSITION

Usually does not require hospital admission unless the patient is unable to tolerate oral intake of liquids.

REFERRAL

- Refer if symptoms persist or neurologic abnormalities are present.
- Consider vestibular rehabilitation, particularly in the elderly.

PEARLS & CONSIDERATIONS

COMMENTS

Labyrinthitis is a term that usually implies peripheral vestibulopathy associated with hearing loss. The term *vestibular neuronitis* is typically used when hearing is not affected. Despite this technical distinction, many physicians use these terms interchangeably.

SUGGESTED READINGS

Available at www.expertconsult.com

RELATED CONTENT

Labyrinthitis (Patient Information)
Vestibular Neuronitis (Related Key Topic)
Benign Paroxysmal Positional Vertigo (Related Key Topic)

AUTHOR: **SHARON S. HARTMAN POLENSEK, M.D., PH.D.**

BASIC INFORMATION

DEFINITION

Lactic acidosis (LA is a life-threatening condition characterized by accumulation of lactate, especially L-lactate, in the body. It represents an imbalance of lactate overproduction or underutilization usually resulting from tissue hypoperfusion and hypoxia (type A LA), or caused by toxins or medication-induced cellular toxicity (type B LA).

SYNONYMS

Lactic acidosis
Hyperlactatemia
LA

ICD-10CM CODES
E87.2 Acidosis

RISK FACTORS

- Sepsis
- Liver disease
- Severe anemia
- Severe trauma
- Advanced heart failure
- Cardiogenic shock
- Hypovolemic shock
- Diabetes mellitus
- Seizures
- Vigorous exercise
- Cocaine
- Medications (metformin, salicylates, beta-2 agonists, propofol, nucleoside reverse-transcriptase inhibitors)
- Thiamine deficiency
- Pheochromocytoma

PHYSICAL FINDINGS & CLINICAL PRESENTATION

- Shock, dehydration (tachycardia, decreased skin turgor, decreased urine output, hypotension, dry mucous membranes)
- Possible clues or precipitating factors (sepsis, bleeding, intoxication)
- Altered mental status
- Nausea, vomiting, abdominal pain
- Weakness, lethargy
- Tachypnea, rapid shallow berating caused by acidosis (Kussmaul's breathing)

ETIOLOGY

- Type A, related to tissue hypoperfusion or hypoxia, is probably the most common cause of LA.
  - Sepsis leading to systemic hypotension and microcirculation dysfunction leading to decreased extraction of oxygen and lactate clearance by the peripheral tissues
  - Shock: cardiogenic, hemorrhagic and obstructive shock; LA in those conditions is believed to be related to decreased clearance
  - Regional ischemia, such as acute mesenteric ischemia
  - Burns
- Type B: related to toxins, medications and liver dysfunction, alcoholism, malignancy
  - Metformin: patients who are at increased risk of L.A are those who are taking metformin and have renal or hepatic dysfunction, cardiac dysfunction, or those who overdose on the medication
  - Cyanide poisoning, beta^2 agonist excessive use, thiamine deficiency
  - Seizure

D-lactic acidosis is a rare type of LA that is associated with short bowel syndrome and bacterial overgrowth.

DIAGNOSIS

DIFFERENTIAL DIAGNOSIS

- Alcoholic ketoacidosis
- Uremic acidosis
- Diabetic ketoacidosis
- Fulminant hepatic failure

WORKUP

- Laboratory measurement of lactic acid to confirm diagnosis and assess for precipitating factors
- Identification of triggering conditions such as infections (blood cultures, urine cultures, chest radiographs), blood drug and toxins level (alcohol, metformin, cyanide); liver and kidney function tests (hepatitis, acute kidney insufficiency)

LABORATORY TESTS

- Normal lactate level is 2.0 to 2.5 meq/l.
- LA is defined by serum lactate concentration > 4 meq/L. An elevated blood lactate level is essential for confirmation of the diagnosis.
- Arterial blood gas analysis demonstrates metabolic acidosis usually with PH <7.3 and PCO$_2$ <40.
- Serum chemistries:
  - Low serum bicarbonate <15 meq/L
  - Large anion gap (AG) metabolic acidosis: AG >12 usually caused by lactate accumulation. A normal AG does not rule out lactic acidosis. Correction of the AG for the effect of serum albumin can improve its sensitivity.
  - Calculate AG: $AG = NA^+ - (Cl^- + HCO_3^-)$.
  - Mixed metabolic disturbances might demonstrate more than only AG acidosis, especially in patients with vomiting, diarrhea, and acute kidney injury.

IMAGING STUDIES

- Chest radiography is helpful if chest infection is suspected as a cause of sepsis or cardiogenic or obstructive shock is suspected.
- Abdominal CT scan or ultrasound might aid to the diagnosis if abdominal pain, regional ischemia, or liver failure is suspected as a cause of the lactic acidosis.

TREATMENT

NONPHARMACOLOGIC THERAPY

- The cornerstone of L.A treatment is reversing the causative condition.
- Continuous monitoring for patients with LA is warranted, including monitoring of mental status, urine output, and vital signs.
- Lactate levels should be checked every 2 to 6 hr.
- Surgery in the case of regional tissue ischemia or trauma with shock.
- Cardiac assist devices in the case of cardiogenic shock.
- Hemodialysis for drugs or toxins removal (i.e., metformin-induced LA).

ACUTE GENERAL Rx

Pharmacologic treatment consists of:
- Resuscitating the intravascular component with IV crystalloid or colloid solution fluids in cases of shock.
- Sodium bicarbonate IV infusion should be considered only if pH <7.1 and serum bicarbonate level is less than 6 meq/L. Infusion of 1-2 meq/L of sodium bicarbonate in a bolus form repeated every 30-60 min if the pH is less than 7.1
- Vasopressor therapy is cases of shock might be required; increasing doses of vasopressor might be needed as the acidosis can blunt the effect of catecholamines. Norepinephrine is generally preferred over dopamine as the initial vasopressor in most types of shock.
- Optimize oxygen delivery: When an inotrope is indicated to improve cardiac output, dobutamine is usually the preferred agent.

DISPOSITION

- Septic shock and lactic acid level > 4 meq/L is associated with a 28% mortality rate.
- There is a clear correlation with increasing lactate level and increased mortality.

REFERRAL

- In general, patients with LA should be admitted to the intensive care unit for close monitoring, frequent lactate, chemistries, and arterial blood gas analysis.

PEARLS & CONSIDERATIONS

COMMENTS

- Hemodialysis is not an effective way of clearing lactate or reversing LA, especially in cases of overproduction and tissue hypoxemia; it could be of value in cases of drug- and toxin-induced LA for removal of the offending agent.

PREVENTION

- Aggressive treatment of shock
- Avoidance of metformin in high-risk populations such as patients older than 85 yr and patients with kidney or liver impairment
- Early use of antibiotics in patients with sepsis

RELATED CONTENT

Diabetic Ketoacidosis (Related Key Topic)

SUGGESTED READINGS

Available at www.expertconsult.com

AUTHOR: **AHMAD M. ISMAIL, M.D.**

BASIC INFORMATION

DEFINITION

Lactose intolerance is the insufficient concentration of lactase enzyme, leading to fermentation of malabsorbed lactose by intestinal bacteria with subsequent production of intestinal gas and various organic acids, manifesting clinically with diarrhea, abdominal pain, flatulence, or bloating after lactose intake. *Lactose malabsorption* occurs when a substantial amount of lactose is not absorbed in the intestine. *Lactase deficiency* is defined as brush-border lactase activity that is markedly reduced relative to the activity observed in infants.

SYNONYMS

Lactase deficiency
Milk intolerance Carbohydrate malabsorption

ICD-10CM CODES
E73.9 Lactose intolerance, unspecified
E73.8 Other lactose intolerance

EPIDEMIOLOGY & DEMOGRAPHICS

- Nearly 50 million people in the United States have partial or complete lactose intolerance. There are racial differences, with <25% of white adults being lactose intolerant but >85% of Asian Americans and >60% of African Americans having some form of lactose intolerance.
- There are geographic variations: highest in Asians (up to 90%), lowest in northern Europeans (approximately 10%), intermediate in southern Europeans and Middle Eastern populations (up to 40%).

PHYSICAL FINDINGS & CLINICAL PRESENTATION

- Abdominal tenderness and cramping, bloating, flatulence.
- Diarrhea.
- Symptoms are directly related to the osmotic pressure of substrate in the colon and occur approximately 2 hr after ingestion of lactose.
- Physical examination: may be entirely within normal limits.

ETIOLOGY

- Before it can be absorbed, lactose is cleared to glucose and galactose by the enzyme lactase in the brush border of the small intestine. If the amount of lactase is marginal or its expression is left, lactose intolerance will results.
- Congenital lactase deficiency: common in premature infants; rare in term infants and generally inherited as a chromosomal recessive trait.
- Secondary lactose intolerance: usually a result of injury of the intestinal mucosa (Crohn's disease, viral gastroenteritis, AIDS enteropathy, cryptosporidiosis, Whipple's disease, sprue)

 **DIAGNOSIS**

DIFFERENTIAL DIAGNOSIS

- Inflammatory bowel disease.
- Irritable bowel syndrome.
- Pancreatic insufficiency.
- Nontropical and tropical sprue.
- Cystic fibrosis.
- Diverticular disease.
- Bowel neoplasm.
- Laxative abuse.
- Celiac disease.
- Parasitic disease (e.g., giardiasis).
- Viral or bacterial infections.

WORKUP

- A detailed dietary history is essential in the evaluation of patients with suspected carbohydrate malabsorption.
- The diagnosis can usually be made on the basis of the history and improvement with dietary manipulation.
- Diagnostic workup may include confirming the diagnosis with hydrogen breath test and excluding other conditions listed in the differential diagnosis that may also coexist with lactase deficiency.

LABORATORY TESTS

- Lactose breath hydrogen test: a rise in breath hydrogen >20 ppm within 90 min of ingestion of 50 g of lactose is positive for lactase deficiency. This test is positive in 90% of patients with lactose malabsorption. Common causes of false-negative results are recent use of oral antibiotics or recent high colonic enema.
- The lactose tolerance test is an older and less accurate testing modality (20% rate of false-positive and false-negative results). The patient is administered an oral dose of 1 to 1.5 g of lactose/kg body weight. Serial measurement of blood glucose level on an hourly basis for 3 hr is then performed. The test is considered positive if the patient develops intestinal symptoms and the blood glucose level rises <20 mg/dl above the fasting baseline level.
- Diarrhea associated with lactase deficiency is osmotic in nature with an osmotic gap and a pH <6.5.

IMAGING STUDIES

Imaging studies are generally not indicated. A small bowel series may be useful in patients with significant malabsorption.

Rx **TREATMENT**

NONPHARMACOLOGIC THERAPY

Management consists of reducing lactose exposure by avoiding milk and milk-containing products or using milk in which the lactose has been prehydrolyzed with lactase. A lactose-free diet generally results in prompt resolution of symptoms. Lactose is primarily found in dairy products but may be present as an ingredient or component of common foods and beverages. Possible sources of lactose include breads, candies, cold cuts, dessert mixes, cream soups, bologna, commercial sauces and gravies, chocolate, drink mixes, salad dressings, and medications. Labels should be read carefully to identify sources of lactose.

ACUTE GENERAL Rx

- Addition of lactase enzyme supplement (Lactaid tablets, Dairy Ease) before the ingestion of milk products may prevent symptoms in some patients. However, it is not effective for all lactose-intolerant patients.
- Lactose-intolerant patients must ensure adequate calcium intake. Calcium supplementation is recommended to prevent osteoporosis.

CHRONIC Rx

Patient education regarding foods high in lactose, such as milk, cottage cheese, or ice cream, is recommended.

DISPOSITION

Clinical improvement with restriction or elimination of milk products.

REFERRAL

GI referral for endoscopic procedures if concomitant GI disorders are suspected.

! **PEARLS & CONSIDERATIONS**

COMMENTS

- There is great variability in signs and symptoms in patients with lactose intolerance depending on the degree of lactase deficiency. Most individuals with presumed lactose malabsorption can tolerate 12 to 15 g of lactose or up to 12 oz of milk daily without symptoms.
- Nondairy synthetic drinks (e.g., Coffee-Mate) and use of rice milk are well tolerated.

SUGGESTED READINGS
Available at www.expertconsult.com

RELATED CONTENT
Lactose Intolerance (Patient Information)

AUTHOR: **FRED F. FERRI, M.D.**

 BASIC INFORMATION

DEFINITION

Laryngitis is an acute or chronic inflammation of the laryngeal mucous membranes.

SYNONYMS

Lower respiratory tract infection

ICD-10CM CODES
J04.0 Acute laryngitis
J37.0 Chronic laryngitis

EPIDEMIOLOGY & DEMOGRAPHICS

It is a common illness worldwide in both genders and all age groups, but the diagnosis is imprecise and, therefore, statistics are not readily available with respect to incidence and prevalence.

PHYSICAL FINDINGS & CLINICAL PRESENTATION

ACUTE LARYNGITIS:

- Clinical syndrome characterized by the onset of hoarseness, voice breaks, or episodes of aphonia; may also have accompanying sore throat, cough, nasal congestion, and rhinorrhea.
- Usually associated with viral upper respiratory infection.
- Larynx with diffuse erythema, edema, and vascular engorgement of the vocal folds, and occasionally mucosal ulceration.
- In young children subglottis is often affected, resulting in airway narrowing with marked hoarseness, inspiratory stridor, dyspnea, and restlessness.
- Respiratory compromise rare in adults.

CHRONIC LARYNGITIS: Characterized by hoarseness or dysphonia persisting for longer than 2 wk.

ETIOLOGY

ACUTE LARYNGITIS:

- Most often caused by viruses so treatment consists of supportive measures as outlined in "Nonpharmacologic Therapy" section.
- Studies evaluating the use of antibiotics (erythromycin, penicillin) in acute laryngitis failed to show objective clinical benefit over placebo so they are not routinely recommended. Antibiotics and other antimicrobials may be indicated in cases in which specific treatable pathogens are identified.
- Avoid decongestants because of their drying effect.
- Guaifenesin may be a useful adjunct as a mucolytic agent.
- In gastroesophageal reflux disease (GERD)-associated laryngitis use acid-suppressive therapy (H_2 blockers, proton pump inhibitors) and nocturnal antireflux precautions.

CHRONIC LARYNGITIS:

- Results from any of the following: tuberculosis, usually through bronchogenic spread; leprosy, from nasopharyngeal or oropha-

ryngeal spread; syphilis, in secondary and tertiary stages; rhinoscleroma, extending from the nose and nasopharynx; actinomycosis; cryptococcosis; histoplasmosis; blastomycosis; paracoccidiomycosis; coccidiosis; candidiasis; aspergillosis; sporotrichosis; rhinosporidiosis; parasitic infections including leishmaniasis and *Clinostomum* infection following raw fresh-water fish ingestion.
- Noninfectious causes of both acute and chronic laryngitis include malignancy, voice abuse (singers), GERD, and chemical or environmental irritants such as cigarettes and allergens. Other causes of inflammatory or granulomatous lesions of the larynx include relapsing polychondritis, Wegener's granulomatosis, and sarcoidosis.

 **DIAGNOSIS**

DIFFERENTIAL DIAGNOSIS

- Young children with signs of airway obstruction:
  1. Supraglottitis (epiglottitis).
  2. Laryngotracheobronchitis.
  3. Tracheitis.
  4. Foreign body aspiration.
- Adults with persistent hoarseness, consider noninfectious causes of laryngitis as listed previously.

WORKUP

- History and physical examination: diagnosis is usually apparent.
- Laryngoscopy for severe or persistent cases.
- Laryngeal cultures should be performed if a cause other than acute viral infection is suspected.
- Imaging not indicated unless there is evidence of airway compromise. Obtain plain radiographs of neck, anteroposterior and lateral views, to differentiate laryngitis from acute laryngotracheobronchitis or supraglottitis.

Rx TREATMENT

NONPHARMACOLOGIC THERAPY

- Rest the voice.
- Use an air humidifier.
- Ensure adequate hydration. Avoid alcohol and caffeine because of their diuretic effect.

ACUTE GENERAL Rx

- Antibiotics and other antimicrobials should generally not be used. They are indicated only when a specific pathogen is isolated; commonly employed antibacterial agents are macrolides; clarithromycin 500 mg by mouth bid for 5 to 7 days or azithromycin 500 mg followed by 250 mg once daily for 4 to 5 days if the cause of laryngitis is found to be *Mycoplasma pneumoniae* or *Chlamydophila pneumoniae* (the new name for what was formerly known as *Chlamydia pneumoniae*).
- Avoid decongestants because of their drying effect.

- Guaifenesin may be a useful adjunct as a mucolytic agent.
- In GERD-associated laryngitis use acid-suppressive therapy (H_2 blockers, proton pump inhibitors) and nocturnal antireflux precautions.

DISPOSITION

Uncomplicated laryngitis is usually benign, with gradual resolution of symptoms.

REFERRAL

- If symptoms persist for >2 wk, refer to otolaryngologist for laryngoscopy.
- Consider referral to gastroenterologist if GERD is suspected.

PEARLS & CONSIDERATIONS

- Most cases of uncomplicated acute laryngitis are viral in origin, and antibacterial agents should not be routinely administered.
- A recent Cochrane analysis in 2013 found no evidence for the use of empiric antibiotics in adults with laryngitis.
- The most difficult clinical challenge is often convincing patients with acute laryngitis that they do not need and will not benefit from antibacterial agents.

SUGGESTED READINGS

Available at www.expertconsult.com

RELATED CONTENT

Laryngitis (Patient Information)

AUTHOR: **GLENN G. FORT, M.D., M.P.H.**

BASIC INFORMATION

DEFINITION

Lead is a potent, pervasive neurotoxicant. Lead poisoning refers to multisystem abnormalities resulting from excessive lead exposure.

SYNONYM

Plumbism

ICD-10CM CODES

T56.0 X1A	Toxic effect of lead and its compounds, accidental (unintentional), initial encounter
T56.0X1D	Toxic effect of lead and its compounds, accidental (unintentional), subsequent encounter
T56.0X1S	Toxic effect of lead and its compounds, accidental (unintentional), sequela
T56.0X2A	Toxic effect of lead and its compounds, intentional self-harm, initial encounter
T56.0X2D	Toxic effect of lead and its compounds, intentional self-harm, subsequent encounter
T56.0X2S	Toxic effect of lead and its compounds, intentional self-harm, sequela
T56.0X3A	Toxic effect of lead and its compounds, assault, initial encounter
T56.0X3D	Toxic effect of lead and its compounds, assault, subsequent encounter
T56.0X3S	Toxic effect of lead and its compounds, assault, sequela
T56.0X4A	Toxic effect of lead and its compounds, undetermined, initial encounter
T56.0X4D	Toxic effect of lead and its compounds, undetermined, subsequent encounter
T56.0X4S	Toxic effect of lead and its compounds, undetermined, sequela

EPIDEMIOLOGY & DEMOGRAPHICS

- Lead poisoning is most common in children ages 1 to 5 yr (17,000 cases/100,000 persons). The highest rates are among blacks, those with low income, and urban children.
- In 1991 the Centers for Disease Control and Prevention (CDC) lowered the definition of a safe blood lead level to <10 mcg/dl of whole blood (a blood lead level of 25 mcg/dl was considered acceptable before 1991).
- It is estimated that >15% of preschoolers in the United States have a blood lead level >15 mcg/dl.

PHYSICAL FINDINGS & CLINICAL PRESENTATION

- Findings vary with the degree of toxicity (Table 1L-1). Examination may be normal in patients with mild toxicity.
- Myalgias, irritability, headache, and general fatigue may be present initially.
- Abdominal cramping, constipation, weight loss, tremor, paresthesias and peripheral neuritis, seizures, and coma may occur with severe toxicity.
- Motor neuropathy is common in children with lead poisoning; learning disorders are also frequent.

ETIOLOGY

Chronic, repeated exposure to paint containing lead, plumbing, storage of batteries, pottery, or lead soldering. Concentration of lead is generally highest in lead-based paint on exterior surfaces. Among interior surfaces, windows are most likely to have the highest lead content.

DIAGNOSIS

DIFFERENTIAL DIAGNOSIS

- Polyneuropathies from other sources.
- Anxiety disorder, attention deficit disorder.
- Malabsorption, acute abdomen.
- Iron-deficiency anemia.

WORKUP

Laboratory screening: all U.S. children should be considered to be at risk for lead poisoning and should be screened routinely starting at age 1 yr for low-risk children and age 6 mo for high-risk children.

LABORATORY TESTS

- Venous blood lead level: normal level, <5 mcg/dl; levels of 50 to 70 mcg/dl, indicative of moderate toxicity; levels >70 mcg/dl, associated with severe poisoning.
- Mild anemia with basophilic stippling on peripheral smear.
- Elevated zinc protoporphyrin levels or free erythrocyte protoporphyrin level.
- An increased body burden of lead with previous high-level exposure in patients with occupational lead poisoning can be demonstrated by measuring the excretion of lead in urine after premedication with calcium ethylenediamine tetraacetic acid (EDTA) or another chelating agent.

IMAGING STUDIES

- Imaging studies are generally not necessary.
- A plain abdominal film can visualize lead particles in the gut.
- "Lead lines" may be noted on x-ray films of long bones.

 TREATMENT

NONPHARMACOLOGIC THERAPY

- Provide adequate amounts of calcium, iron, zinc, and protein in patient's diet.
- Family education on sources of lead exposure and potential adverse health effects.

ACUTE GENERAL Rx

- The use of chelation in cases of acute lead poisoning is guided by the patient's clinical status and the blood lead level (BLL). For children with blood levels of 10 to 19 mcg/dl, the CDC recommends nonpharmacologic interventions (see "Nonpharmacologic Therapy").
- For children with blood levels between 20 and 44 mcg/dl, the CDC recommendations include case management by a qualified social worker, clinical management, environmental assessment, and lead hazard control. Chelation therapy should be considered in children with refractory blood lead levels.

Chelation therapy (Table 1L-2) is indicated in children with blood lead levels >45 mcg/dl:

- Succimer (DMSA) 10 mg/kg PO q8h for 5 days then q12h for 2 wk can be used in patients with levels between 45 and 70 mcg/dl.
- Edetate calcium disodium (EDTA) and dimercaprol (BAL) are effective in patients with severe toxicity.
- Use of both EDTA and DMSA is indicated in children with blood levels >70 mcg/dl.
- d-Penicillamine (Cuprimine) can also be used for lead poisoning, but it is not FDA approved for this condition.

CHRONIC Rx

- Reduce exposure, remove any potential lead sources.
- Correct iron deficiency and any other nutritional deficiencies.
- Recheck blood lead level 7 to 21 days after chelation therapy.

DISPOSITION

Patients with mild to moderate toxicity generally improve without any residual deficits. The presence of encephalopathy at diagnosis is a poor prognostic sign. Residual neurologic deficits may persist in these patients. Chelation therapy seems to slow the progression of renal insufficiency in patients with mildly elevated body lead burden.

REFERRAL

If exposure to lead is work related, it should be reported to the Office of the United States Occupational Safety and Health Administration (OSHA). Follow-up testing is mandatory in all patients after an abnormal screening blood lead level.

PEARLS & CONSIDERATIONS

COMMENTS

- Even blood lead concentrations as low as 5-10 mcg/dl are inversely associated with children's IQ scores at age 3 and 5 yr.
- Screening of household members of affected individuals is recommended.
- In children with blood lead levels of >45 mg/dl, treatment with succimer does not improve scores on tests of cognition, behavior, or neuropsychological function.
- Lead toxicity may delay growth and pubertal development in girls.
- Low-level environmental lead exposure may accelerate progressive renal insufficiency in patients without diabetes who have chronic

renal disease. Repeated chelation therapy may improve renal function and slow the progression of renal failure.

SUGGESTED READINGS
Available at www.expertconsult.com.

RELATED CONTENT
Lead Poisoning (Patient Information)
AUTHOR: **FRED F. FERRI, M.D.**

TABLE 1L-1 Serum Lead Levels and Symptoms

Level (µg/dL)	Symptoms	
	Adults	**Children**
10	None	Decreased IQ
		Decreased hearing
		Decreased growth
20	Increased protoporphyrin	Decreased nerve conduction velocity
	No symptoms	Increased protoporphyrin
30	Increased blood pressure	Decreased vitamin D metabolism
	Decreased hearing	
40	Peripheral neuropathies	Decreased hemoglobin synthesis
	Nephropathy	
	Infertility (men)	
50	Decreased hemoglobin synthesis	Lead colic
70	Anemia	Anemia
		Encephalopathy
		Nephropathy
100	Encephalopathy	Death

From Marx JA, et al: *Rosen's emergency medicine*, ed 8, Philadelphia, 2014, Saunders.

TABLE 1L-2 Chelators*

Chelator	Dose	Indications	Contraindications
Deferoxamine	15 mg/kg/hr up to 24 hr (titrate up slowly because of hypotension)	Iron level >500 g/dL or systemic symptoms	
Dimercaprol (British anti-Lewisite [BAL])	Lead encephalopathy: 75 mg/m² deep IM injection every 4 hr for 5 days in children or 4 mg/kg every 4 hr for adults Arsenic (severe): no established regimen; consider 3 mg/kg IM every 4 hr for 48 hr; then twice daily for 7-10 days Mercury: 5 mg/kg IM first; then 2.5 mg/kg every 12-24 hr	Lead level >70 g/dL or encephalopathy Arsenic: symptomatic patient with known exposure Mercury: inorganic	Peanut allergy Organic mercury poisoning
CaNa₂EDTA	1500 mg/m²/day continuous IV infusion 50 mg/kg/day or 1000 mg/m²/day in 2-4 divided doses for up to 5 days if less severe symptoms	Lead: given after first dose of BAL for blood lead level above 70 g/dL or encephalopathy	
Succimer (DMSA)	10 mg/kg q8h × 5 days; then q12h for 14 days	Lead level of 45-69 g/dL Arsenic: if tolerated orally for subacute and chronic toxicity Mercury: acute and chronic	
D-Penicillamine	25 mg/kg q6h × 5 days	Lead level of 45-69 g/dL, succimer not tolerated Arsenic: only if BAL and DMSA are unavailable Mercury: if BAL and DMSA are unavailable or not tolerated	Penicillin allergy
DMPS (investigational)	5 mg/kg/dose IM q6-8h day 1, q8-12h day 2, q12-24h day 3 and until 24-hr urine is <50 µg/L	Lead (chronic) Arsenic Mercury	

IM, Intramuscular; *IV*, intravenous.
*Indications for chelation and dosing regimens may change. Consult with a toxicologist or poison control center for the most up-to-date recommendations.
From Marx JA et al: *Rosen's emergency medicine*, ed 8, Philadelphia, 2014, Saunders.

BASIC INFORMATION

DEFINITION

Legg-Calvé-Perthes disease (LCPD) is characterized by circulatory compromise of the immature proximal femoral head leading to avascular necrosis. The classification of LCPD is outlined in Fig. 1L-1.

SYNONYMS

Perthes disease
Coxa plana
Capital femoral osteochondrosis
Osteonecrosis of the proximal femoral epiphysis
LCPD

ICD-9CM CODES
732.1 Perthes' disease
ICD-10CM CODES
M91.10 Juvenile osteochondrosis of head of femur [Legg-Calvé-Perthes], unspecified leg

EPIDEMIOLOGY & DEMOGRAPHICS

PREVALENCE: One case in 1300 children. More common in Caucasians.
INCIDENCE: One in 1200 children, younger than 15 years of age.
PREDOMINANT SEX: Male/female ratio of 4:1.
PREDOMINANT AGE: 4 to 10 yr.

PHYSICAL FINDINGS & CLINICAL PRESENTATION

- Initial symptom: usually a mildly painful limp.
- Pain may be referred down the inner aspect of the thigh to the knee.
- Positive roll test: with the patient in the supine position, rolling of the affected extremity into internal and external rotation elicits guarding, with limited range of motion.
- Pain at the extremes of movement and tenderness over anterior hip join.
- No history of trauma.
- Condition is bilateral in 10% to 20% of patients.

ETIOLOGY

Unknown.

DIAGNOSIS

DIFFERENTIAL DIAGNOSIS

Unilateral Disease
- Transient synovitis.
- Sickle cell disease.
- Septic arthritis.
- Neoplasm.
- Spondyloepiphyseal dysplasia tarda.

BILATERAL DISEASE

- Multiple epiphyseal dysplasia (MED).
- Sickle cell disease.
- Juvenile idiopathic arthritis.

WORKUP

Diagnosis is usually based on the physical findings and radiographic evaluation.

IMAGING STUDIES

- MRI most sensitive for early LCPD
- Plain roentgenography (anteroposterior and frog-leg lateral x-rays) (Fig. 1L-2) will show late changes.
- Technetium bone scanning may help confirm the diagnosis in early cases.

TREATMENT

ACUTE GENERAL Rx

- Non-weight bearing followed by bracing
- Bracing may be required for 2 to 3 years in a small percent of patients.
- NSAIDs for pain control.
- Range-of-motion physical therapy exercises.
- Surgical therapy in refractory cases: tenotomy, various osteotomies.

DISPOSITION

- Prognosis depends on age of patient and degree of involvement of the femoral head at onset.
- In patients younger than 6 yr, outcome is generally positive regardless of treatment.
- Patients over the age of 8 yr at onset often have poorer outcomes. Females tend to do worse than males in this age group.
- A few patients eventually develop degenerative arthritis.

REFERRAL

Referral to pediatric orthopedist when diagnosis is suspected.

PEARLS & CONSIDERATIONS

Both the etiology and treatment of LCPD remain controversial. Treatment recommendations vary widely and continue to evolve. Children >6 to 8 yr at age of onset may benefit from early surgical intervention.

SUGGESTED READINGS

Available at www.expertconsult.com.

RELATED CONTENT

Legg-Calvé-Perthes Disease (Patient Information)

AUTHOR: **MATTHEW J. STANISHEWSKI, D.O.**

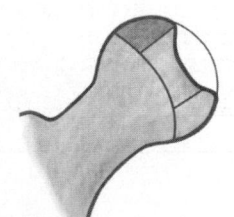
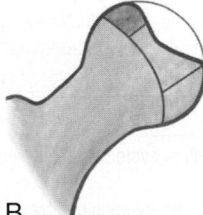
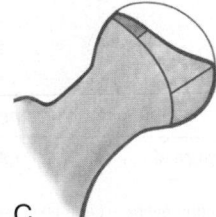

A   B   C

FIGURE 1L-1 Lateral pillar classification for Legg-Calvé-Perthes disease. A, There is no involvement of the lateral pillar. **B,** >50% of the lateral pillar height is maintained. **C,** <50% of the lateral pillar height is maintained. (From Kliegman RM et al: *Nelson textbook of pediatrics,* ed 19, Philadelphia, 2011, Saunders.)

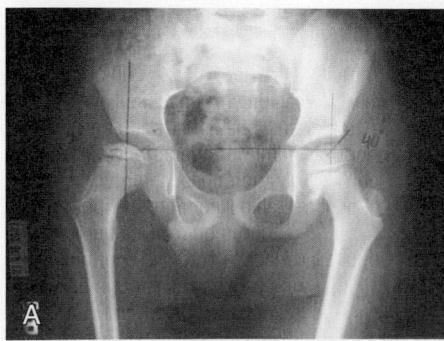
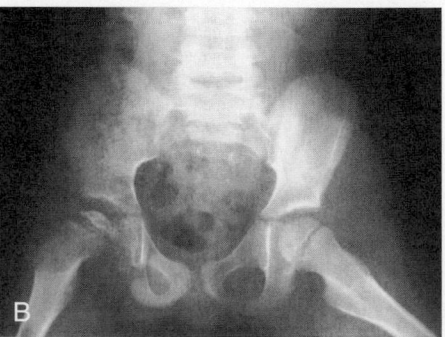

FIGURE 1L-2 A, Anteroposterior radiograph of the pelvis shows epiphyseal fragmentation in the right hip, characteristic of the fragmentation phase of Legg-Calvé-Perthes disease. **B,** The frog-leg lateral view demonstrates subchondral fracture, increased density of the femoral head, and some collapse. (From Kliegman RM et al: *Nelson textbook of pediatrics,* ed 19, Philadelphia, 2011, Saunders.)

L

Diseases
and Disorders

BASIC INFORMATION

DEFINITION

Acute lymphoblastic leukemia (ALL) is a malignancy of precursor B or T lymphocytes (lymphoblasts) characterized by uncontrolled proliferation of malignant lymphocytic cells with replacement of normal bone marrow elements and bone marrow failure. Lymphoblastic lymphoma is diagnosed when the disease presents in extramedullary sites (most commonly as mediastinal mass in T cell disease) *and* less than 25% of the bone marrow is involved.

SYNONYMS

Acute lymphocytic leukemia
Acute lymphoblastic leukemia
ALL

ICD-10CM CODES
C91.00 Acute lymphoblastic leukemia not having achieved remission
C91.01 Acute lymphoblastic leukemia, in remission
C91.02 Acute lymphoblastic leukemia, in relapse

EPIDEMIOLOGY & DEMOGRAPHICS

- ALL is primarily a disease of children (peak incidence occurring at 3-5 years of age).
- Overall incidence is 4.5 cases per 100,000 persons per year; 60% are under age 20. It is the most common malignancy of childhood. (SEER database accessed 11/26/15)
- Incidence varies according to race and ethnic group: 14.8 cases per million for blacks, 35.6 cases per million for whites, and 40.9 cases per million for Hispanics.
- Male:female ratio is 55% to 45%.

PHYSICAL FINDINGS & CLINICAL PRESENTATION

- Findings consistent with bone marrow failure and peripheral cytopenias– pallor, bruising, petechiae.
- Lymphadenopathy or hepatosplenomegaly.
- Fever (disease related or infectious), bone pain, weakness, weight loss, mental status changes, and neurologic findings associated with CNS involvement (if present).
- T cell lymphoblastic lymphoma is usually associated with a mediastinal mass.
- Table 1L-4 summarizes the clinical presentation of acute lymphoblastic leukemia.

ETIOLOGY

- Most cases are sporadic without established risk factors.
- Ionizing radiation exposure appears to be a risk factor.
- Down's syndrome (trisomy 21) is associated with an approximately 3% risk of developing leukemia by age 30, predominantly ALL. ALL may be seen with other hereditary premalignancy syndromes (e.g. ataxia-telangiectasia)

DIAGNOSIS

DIFFERENTIAL DIAGNOSIS

- Disorders associated with lymphocytosis in adults (e.g. chronic lymphocytic leukemia, mantle cell lymphoma) and adolescents (e.g. infectious mononucleosis).
- Disorders associated with circulating blasts or blastlike cells such as acute myeloid leukemia, prolymphocytic leukemia, blastoid mantle cell lymphoma, and Burkitt's lymphoma (mature B-cell leukemia/lymphoma).
- Lymphoblastic lymphoma.
- Aplastic anemia; ALL may present without circulating leukemia cells and only manifestation of bone marrow failure.
- Infectious mononucleosis.

WORKUP

- Identification of circulating abnormal cell population by flow cytometry. "Special stain" cytochemstries are sometimes available sooner, but are not specific—ALL should be negative for myeloperoxidase and chloroacetate esterase.
- Bone marrow examination (Fig. 1L-8).
- Flow cytometry to identify abnormal cell populations. CD19 identifies most precursor B-cells and terminal deoxynucleotidyltransferase (TdT), CD34, and *absence* of surface immunoglobulin establishes immature B-cell phenotype in most cases. Cytoplasmic CD3 and CD7 establishes immature T cell lineage in most cases. Aberrant myeloid markers (CD13, CD33) can be seen.
- Genetic studies important treatment categories, of which the most important is Philadelphia chromosome positive (Ph+) vs. Philadelphia chromosome negative (Ph–) disease, as these are treated differently. Ph status can be determined rapidly by polymerase chain reaction (PCR) or fluorescence *in situ* hybridization (FISH) and should be available within 24 to 48 hours of diagnosis. The WHO classification recognizes genetic variants of ALL as distinct syndromes (Table 1L-5), and the clinical

significance of common abnormalities is outlined in Table 1L-6.
- Genetic profiling for "Ph-like" ALL (genetic profile similar to Ph+ disease, but no BCR/ABL abnormality) or IKZF1 (IKAROS) mutations may provide additional prognostic information, but may not be uniformly available.
- Lumbar puncture is usually done at diagnosis, if practical, to assess for CNS involvement.

LABORATORY TESTS

- Complete blood count reveals normochromic, normocytic anemia, thrombocytopenia.
- Peripheral smear will usually reveal lymphoblasts.
- Initial blood work should also include assessment for basic organ function (creatinine, bilirubin), blood glucose (glucocorticoids are part of therapy) and spontaneous tumor lysis syndrome (K+, Ca++, PO_4++, uric acid).
- Coagulation studies prior to lumbar puncture.
- Evaluation for leukemia as outlined previously.

IMAGING STUDIES

- Chest x-ray to evaluate for the presence of mediastinal mass.
- CT for symptomatic complaints. Be cautious about contrast dye exposure in patients with evidence of spontaneous tumor lysis syndrome to avoid further renal injury.

TREATMENT

ACUTE GENERAL Rx

- Survival of children with ALL has improved from 10% to 90% in the last 40 years and is a major success story of modern medical science and research. Adults have fared less well, but cure rates have also improved to about 50% to 60% in standard risk patients and has been about 70% in younger (under 40 years) patients in recent trials.
- B cell and T cell disease are treated with the same protocols, with roughly identical outcomes in the current generation of therapy.

TABLE 1L-4 Clinical Presentation of Acute Lymphoblastic Leukemia

Symptoms and Signs	Etiology	Management
Fever	Disease or infection	Always conduct fever workup and provide broad antimicrobial coverage until infectious etiology is ruled out
Fatigue, pallor	Anemia (ALL infiltrating BM)	RBC transfusion (slow if anemia is severe; avoid in hyperleukocytosis)
Petechiae, bruising, bleeding	Thrombocytopenia (ALL infiltrating BM)	Transfuse with platelets
Pain	Leukemia infiltrating bones or joints or expanding BM cavity	Establish diagnosis and start chemotherapy
Respiratory distress, superior vena cava syndrome	Mediastinal mass	Avoid sedation in the presence of tracheal compression; establish diagnosis as soon as possible and start chemotherapy

ALL, Acute lymphoblastic leukemia; *BM,* bone marrow; *RBC,* red blood cell. From Hoffman R: *Hematology, basic principles and practice,* 6th ed, Philadelphia, 2013, Saunders.

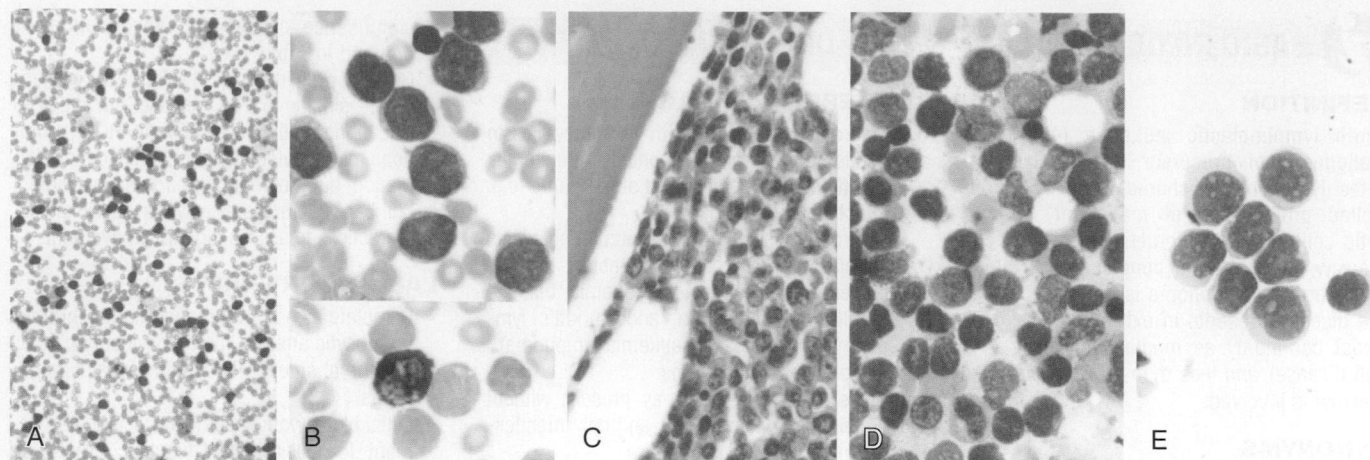

FIGURE 1L-8 Acute lymphoblastic leukemia: peripheral blood, bone marrow biopsy and aspirate, and cerebral spinal fluid. The illustration is from a 37-year-old male who presented with a WBC of 170,000/L and over 90% blasts with lymphoid morphology (**A** and **B,** *top*). An initial myeloperoxidase reaction (**B,** bottom) showed the blasts to be negative (positive cell is a segmented neutrophil that serves as an internal control). The bone marrow was packed with blasts as seen on the biopsy and aspirated material (**C** and **D**). The blasts were immunophenotyped by flow cytometry and were shown to be precursor-B lymphoblasts with the following phenotype: CD34+, HLA–DR+, TdT+, CD19+, CDI0+, cyCD79A+, cyIgM–, and sIg–. Cytogenetic studies illustrated the t(9;22), and molecular analysis revealed the p190 *BCR/ABL*. A spinal tap showed a WBC count of 120/L with an RBC count of 37/L. The differential showed 80% blasts. The morphology of the blasts on the cytospin of the cerebrospinal fluid (**E**) is somewhat altered by the preparation. Note the absence of significant red blood cells in the specimen. Given the high number of blasts in the peripheral blood, a more traumatic tap would have made it difficult to distinguish between central nervous system disease and contamination of the cerebrospinal fluid specimen by blood. (From Hoffman R et al: *Hematology, basic principles and practice,* ed 5, Philadelphia, 2009, Churchill Livingstone.)

Table 1L-5 WHO Classification of Precursor Lymphoid Neoplasms

B-lymphoblastic leukemia/lymphoma, not otherwise specified.

B-lymphoblastic leukemia/lymphoma with recurrent cytogenetic abnormalities

    B-lymphoblastic leukemia/lymphoma with t(9;22)(q34;q11.2); *BCR-ABL1*

    B-lymphoblastic leukemia/lymphoma with t(v*;11q23) *MLL* rearranged.

    B-lymphoblastic leukemia/lymphoma with t(12;21)(p13;q22); *TEL-AML1 (ETV6-RUNX1)*

    B-lymphoblastic leukemia/lymphoma with hyperdiploidy

    B-lymphoblastic leukemia/lymphoma with hypodiploidy

    B-lymphoblastic leukemia/lymphoma with t(5;14)(q32;q32); *IL3-IGH*

    B-lymphoblastic leukemia/lymphoma with t(1;19)(q23;p13.3); *EZA-PBX1 (TCF3-PBX-1)*

T-lymphoblastic leukemia/lymphoma.

v*, Variable gene partners.
From Vardiman JW et al, Blood 114 (5)937-951 (2009).

Table 1L-6 More Common Recurrent Cytogenetic Abnormalities in B-Lymphoblastic Leukemia/Lymphoma

Abnormality	Clinical Relevance
t(9;22)(q34;q11.2); *BCR-ABL1*	Incidence approximately 3% in children, 25% in adults; requires therapy with tyrosine kinase inhibitors.
t(v*;11q23) *MLL* rearranged.	Most common variant is t(4;11); often presents with very high WBC; confers worse prognosis; rare in adults; common in infant leukemia.
t(12;21)(p13;q22); *TEL-AML1*	Common in children (20%-30%); rare in adults; confers improved prognosis.
Hyperdiploidy	Seen in about 25% of children, less in adults; confers favorable prognosis.
Hypodiploidy	Uncommon; confers worse prognosis.
t(5;14)(q32;q32); *IL3-IGH*	Rare; commonly associated with eosinophilia; T cell disease, ? neutral prognostically
t(1;19)(q23;p13.3);	Incidence approximatey 5%; intermediate/favorable in children, intermediate/poor in adults.

v*, Variable gene partners. Many of these disorders also have distinct immunophenotypes by flow cytometry. Additional molecular abnormalities of recently defined relevance include mutations of IKZF1, which encodes a lymphoid transcription factor IKAROS, is associated with high relapse rates and gene expression profile similar to BCR-ABL1 translocated disease. Gene expression profiling has identified a subgroup of "Philadelphia chromosome-like" ALL with a gene expression similar to BCR-ABL1 translocation associated disease, which confers worse prognosis, but which may identify new opportunities for target therapies.

- Numerous protocols have been used in the North America, Europe and Asia for Ph-ALL and the specific protocol is likely to be determined by institution/physician familiarity and access to clinical trials (participation strongly recommended), among other factors.
- In the 1990's and early 2000's, it was noted that adolescents and young adult (AYA) patients had better outcomes on pediatric trials than adult trials. Consequently, this group (currently defined as age 15-39) is now often (especially younger AYA's) treated on pediatric protocols by pediatric services or on adult "pediatric inspired" protocols.
- Immediate therapy for treatment urgencies/emergencies
- Hyperleukocytic leukemia (WBC > 100,000/mcl) is uncommon in ALL and lymphocyte counts of 100,000 may be well tolerated. Prednisone and vincristine usually offer rapid cytoreduction and leukapheresis is rarely (but sometimes) required.
- Spontaneous tumor lysis is common in ALL and should be managed with vigorous hydration, allopurinol and rasburicase for elevated uric acid. This is discussed in more detail in AML chapter. Tumor lysis monitoring will be necessary at the start of therapy (every 6-8 hour K+, Ca++, PO_4++, uric acid, creatinine) for 24 to 72 hours.
- Therapy for Ph- negative ALL generally has four components:
  1. Induction therapy, typically with corticosteroids, cyclophosphamide (some regimens), vincristine, an anthracycline (doxorubicin or daunorubicin usually) and asparaginase. The CD20 directed antibody rituximab has been added to some protocols when high expression of CD20 is present on the blasts.

Table 1L-7 Risk Factors for Treatment Failure in Recent ALL trials

t(v*;11q23) *MLL* rearranged.

Hypodiploidy

Minimal residual disease after remission or consolidation*

Philadelphia chromosome like genomic signature (in Ph- ALL)[†]

*Measured variously after induction or consolidation therapy.
[†]Standardized testing for this is still in development, but it may have important treatment implications. Note also that many historic risk factors (e.g T-cell vs B-cell disease) have not been independent risk factors in current trials.
Roberts KG, et al Targetable kinase-activating lesions in Ph-like acute lymphoblastic leukemia, N Engl J Med 371 15(11):1005-1010, 2014.

2. Consolidation therapy is high dose therapy aimed at preventing relapse after remission has been obtained.

3. Maintenance therapy is low intensity outpatient therapy that is continued for 2-3 years after completion of consolidation. Prednisone, monthly vincristine ("Oncovin"), methotrexate and oral 6-mercaptopurine (POMP) are commonly used.

4. Central nervous system (CNS) prophylaxis is required since roughly two thirds of patients relapsed in the CNS in early trials This is usually done with intrathecal therapy (methotrexate, cytarabine and hydrocortisone)administered by lumbar puncture or sometimes ommaya reservoir. Because of increased toxicity, cranial radiation is reserved for patients with high risk features, such as active CNS disease at diagnosis.

- The use of allogeneic bone marrow transplant in first remission of ALL is controversial because of improving results with current non transplant therapies. It is usually recommended for patients in whom the likelihood of cure is considered less than 50% to 60% with chemotherapy alone, if practical by age and donor availability. Autologous bone marrow transplant is rarely used in Ph- ALL.

- Risk factors for treatment failure in recent protocols are outlined in Table 1L-7.

- Therapy of Ph+ ALL consists of a tyrosine kinase inhibitor (imatinib, dasatinib, nilotinib, ponatinib have been used) with chemotherapy.
  - 2 year survival has been reported as 50% to 65%, with various regimens, typically using allogeneic bone marrow transplant as consolidation if possible.
  - Low intensity induction (ie. without myelosuppressive chemotherapy) with dasatinib and prednisone or imatinib, vincristine and prednisone have resulted remission rates of 100% and 98% and may allow for less toxicity and hospitalization at diagnosis.

- Therapy of relapsed disease
  - Allogeneic bone marrow transplant will cure some patients with relapsed disease if a second remission can be obtained, but cure rates remain low in this setting.
  - Blinatumomab is a bispecific antibody that binds CD19 and CD3, redirecting T cells to leukemia cells, with approximately 40% of relapsed patients having remission.

- Chimeric antigen receptor T-cell (CAR-T) therapy, a form of targeted immunotherapy, has yielded remission rates of 70% to 90% in relapsed patients but currently has limited availability.

- Survivorship
  - Survivors of childhood and adult ALL are increasingly been seen in primary care practices; as of 2006 there were estimated > 50,000 survivors, likely increasing by about 2000+ per year.
  - Long term complications of ALL therapy include secondary malignancy from chemotherapy (usually in first 5-10 years) or from radiation (if given, no plateau in risk, congestive heart failure from anthracycline therapy (often manifesting 20-30 years after treatment), osteopenia and avascular necrosis from glucocorticoid therapy, obesity and neurocognitive defects. A recent review summarizes current recommendations and guidelines are accessible online (http://www.survivorshipguidelines.org/pdf/LTFUGuidelines_40.pdf, http://www.sign.ac.uk/pdf/sign132.pdf)

SUGGESTED READINGS

Available at www.expertconsult.com

RELATED CONTENT

Acute Lymphocytic Leukemia (ALL) (Patient Information)

AUTHOR: **PETER RINTELS, M.D.**

BASIC INFORMATION

DEFINITION

Acute myelogenous leukemia (AML) is a malignancy of hematopoetic progenitor cells that would normally give rise to mature myeloid granulocytes. Strictly speaking, AML is a subset of acute non-lymphocytic leukemia (ANLL), broadly distinguishing these diseases from the biologically distinct leukemias of lymphocytic origin and including leukemias involving the spectrum of myeloid stem cells, including precursors of granulocytes, monocytes, erythrocytes and megakaryocytes. Acute promyelocytic leukemia is a distinct leukemia syndrome that is part of the ANLL spectrum, but which has very different treatment implications. ANLL is characterized by maturation failure of myeloid progenitors, excessive numbers of immature progenitors ("blasts") and various degrees of bone marrow failure (neutropenia, thrombocytopenia, anemia).

SYNONYMS

Acute nonlymphocytic leukemia (ANLL)
Acute myeloid leukemia (AML)

ICD-10CM CODES

C92.60 Acute myeloid leukemia with 11q23-abnormality not having achieved remission
C92.61 Acute myeloid leukemia with 11q23-abnormality in remission
C92.62 Acute myeloid leukemia with 11q23-abnormality in relapse

C92.90 Myeloid leukemia, unspecified, not having achieved remission
C92.91 Myeloid leukemia, unspecified in remission
C92.92 Myeloid leukemia, unspecified in relapse
C92.A0 Acute myeloid leukemia with multilineage dysplasia, not having achieved remission
C92.A1 Acute myeloid leukemia with multilineage dysplasia, in remission
C92.A2 Acute myeloid leukemia with multilineage dysplasia, in relapse
C92.Z0 Other myeloid leukemia not having achieved remission
C92.Z1 Other myeloid leukemia, in remission
C92.Z2 Other myeloid leukemia, in relapse
C92.00 Acute myeloblastic leukemia, not having achieved remission
C92.01 Acute myeloblastic leukemia, in remission
C92.02 Acute myeloblastic leukemia, in relapse

EPIDEMIOLOGY & DEMOGRAPHICS

- AML incidence rises with age:
  - Incidence 20 to 55 years old: 1 to 3/100,000 persons/year.
  - Incidence 65 to 80 years old: 11 to 20/100,000 persons/year.
- Annual incidence is 4 cases/100,000 persons/year.
- Males slightly > females; European ancestry slightly > African ancestry.

PHYSICAL FINDINGS & CLINICAL PRESENTATION

Symptoms/Exam Findings:
- Complications of bone marrow failure:
  - Thrombocytopenia associated bleeding.
  - Fatigue and shortness of breath associated with anemia.
  - Infection associated with neutropenia.
- Complications of leukocytosis (hyperleukocytic leukemia, WBC > 100,000/mcl)
  - Retinal hemorrhage with visual symptoms.
  - Headache and intracranial bleeding.
  - Respiratory symptoms from pulmonary involvement.
- Systemic symptoms
  - Fatigue, fever (usually infectious, rarely tumor), bone pain (more common in ALL).
- Hemorrhagic complications of disseminated intravascular coagulation (DIC), especially with APML)
- Physical exam will reflect consequences of cytopenias (bruising from thrombocytopenia, pallor from anemia). Enlarged lymph nodes and enlarged liver and spleen are rare. Exam is often normal.
- Rarely disease will present as skin lesions (leukemia cutis) or mass lesions (granulocytic sarcoma).
- Gum hypertrophy and organ/skin involvement is more common in monocytic leukemia.

ETIOLOGY

- Environmental/exposure related: Benzene (best documented), organic solvents (including gasoline), cigarettes smoking (≥20 pack

---

BOX 1L-1 Stepwise Algorithm for Diagnosis and Classification of Acute Myelogenous Leukemia Using Cytomorphology, Cytochemistry, Immunophenotyping, Cytogenetics, and Molecular Cytogenetics

The criteria are based on Wright-Giemsa–stained blood and marrow smears and biopsy. The percentage of blast cells separates acute myeloid leukemia (AML) from myelodysplastic syndrome (MDS). The World Health Organization (WHO) classification defines AML as greater than 20% blasts in the marrow or blood. The next step is to define the blast population by immunophenotyping and/or immunohistochemistry. The initial evaluation separates AML from ALL. A history of exposure to prior cytotoxic chemotherapy or agents associated with AML defines the leukemia as *therapy-related acute myeloid leukemia* (t-AML). The WHO recognizes the unique clinical and biologic features of the therapy-related leukemias (t-AML). This subtype results from prior exposure to cytotoxic chemotherapy and/or radiation therapy. A majority of patients will have clonal cytogenetic abnormalities and now account for more than 40% of all patients with AML. The WHO recognizes two types of t-AML based on the type of prior exposure or treatment: alkylating agent–related AML and topoisomerase II inhibitor–related AML. The WHO classification defines major subgroups of AML that manifest recurring cytogenetic abnormalities. As a group, these AMLs have chromosomal translocations that result in the production of chimeric proteins, which are pivotal in the leukemogenic process. The genetic abnormalities define a specific biology, clinical course, and prognosis and therefore it is important to classify them separately. In this group of patients, the diagnosis is defined by the cytogenetic abnormality independent of the percentage of blasts. There are four recurrent translocations in this group. The diagnosis is

defined by the cytogenetic abnormalities and is not dependent on the number of blasts: (a) AML with t(8;21)(q22;q22), (AML1/ETO) (RUNX/CBFA2T1); (b) AML with abnormal bone marrow eosinophils and inv16(p13;q22) or t(16;16)(p13;q22), (CBFB/MYH11); (c) acute promyelocytic leukemia: AML with t(15;17)(q22;q21)(PML/RARA) or t(11;17)(q23;q12) (PLZF/RARA) or t(5;17)(q23;q12)(NPM/RARA), or t(11;17)(q13;q12) (NuMA/RARA); and (d) AML with 11q23 (MLL) abnormalities. If multilineage dysplasia is present, then the leukemia is classified as *acute leukemia with multilineage dysplasia*.

AML with multilineage dysplasia is characterized by the presence of 20% or more blasts in the marrow and dysplasia in at least 50% of the cells of at least two of the three main hemopoietic lines. The leukemia may occur de novo or after a preceding myelodysplastic, myeloproliferative, or overlap myelodysplastic/myeloproliferative syndrome unrelated to prior exposure to chemotherapy. If such a syndrome preceded the development of acute leukemia, the AML is best designated as AML "evolving from a myelodysplastic syndrome." When a leukemia fails to satisfy the cytogenetic, morphologic, or clinical criteria for the newly defined subgroups, it is classified as AML not otherwise categorized. The *not otherwise categorized* designation essentially applies the original FAB classification with some modifications, namely, acute promyelocytic leukemia (M3) is no longer included; a pure erythroleukemia has been distinguished from erythroleukemia, acute erythroid/myeloid type; and acute basophilic leukemia (very rare) has been added, as is a rare entity termed acute panmyelosis with myelofibrosis and the solid tumor myeloid sarcoma.

CD, Cluster designation; *MPO*, myeloperoxidase; *NEC*, nonerythroid cells; *NSE*, nonspecific esterase; *PAS*, periodic acid–Schiff; *SBB*, Sudan black B; *TdT*, terminal deoxynucleotidyl transferase; *TNC*, total nucleated cells.
From Hoffman R et al: *Hematology, basic principles and practice,* ed 5, Philadelphia, 2009, Churchill Livingstone.

year 1.34 relative risk), obesity, best documented in women.
- Hereditary disorders: Numerous, including Fanconi anemia, Bloom syndrome, Schwachman Diamond syndrome, Diamond Blackfan anemia, among others.
- Therapy related:
  - Alkylator (e.g. melphalan, busulfan, cisplatin) related: typical latency 5 to 7 years, associated with chromosome 5 and 7 abnormalities..
  - Topoisomerase II inhibitor (e.g. etoposide, doxorubicin): typical latency 1-3 years, associated with 11q23 (mixed lineage leukemia (MLL) gene) rearrangements.
- Radiation exposures (therapeutic – generally low risk), occupational.
- Antecedent hematologic disorders: Myelodysplasia, myeloproliferative disorders, aplastic anemia.

 DIAGNOSIS

DIFFERENTIAL DIAGNOSIS

- Disorders that can present with circulating blasts or cells with blast like appearance:
  - Acute myeloid leukemia/acute lymphocytic leukemia.
  - Myelodysplasia (up to 20% circulating blasts, if ≥ 20% = AML).
  - Primary myelofibrosis.
  - Chronic myeloid leukemia
  - Blastoid variant of mantle cell lymphoma.
  - Prolymphocytic leukemia
  - Blastic plasmacytoid dendritic cell neoplasm.
  - Atypical lymphocytes of Epstein Barr virus and other viral syndromes.

LABORATORY TESTS

- Complete blood counts and blood smear evaluation. Note that morphologic evaluation of blasts may suggest myeloid or lymphoid origin, but flow cytometry or cytochemistries (often faster) are needed to confirm. Auer rods equal myeloid origin.
- LDH is commonly elevated. Other biochemistries to assess organ function (creatinine, liver enzymes) and spontaneous tumor lysis syndrome (uric acid, potassium phosphate, calcium).
- Coagulation studies to assess DIC (always present in APML, but can be present in **all** forms of acute leukemia, especially acute monocytic leukemia.
- HLA typing for possible bone marrow transplant and platelet support.
- Cytochemical stains –
  - Myeloperoxidase can be performed in minutes, + in myeloid origin leukemia.
  - Alpha naphthyl acetate esterase ("non-specific esterase") stains mainly monocytic cells.
- Flow cytometry on blood and/or bone marrow (see Table 1L-8)
- Cytogenetic studies, ideally on bone marrow, but can be done on peripheral blood. Fluorescence in situ hybridization (FISH) is

Table 1L-8   Flow Cytometry Markers Used For Diagnosis of ANLL

Precursor stage	CD34, CD38, CD117, CD133, HLA-DR
Granulocytic (myeloid) markers	CD13, CD15 CD16, CD33, CD65, cytoplasmic myeloperoxidase
Monocytic markers	CD11c, CD14, CD64, CD4, CD11b, CD36, NG2 homologue
Megakaryocytic markers	CD41 (glycoprotein IIb/IIIa), CD61 (glycoprotein IIIa), CD42 glycoprotein 1b
Erythroid markers	CD235 (glycophorin A)

Adapted from Doehner H et al, Diagnosis and management of acute myeloid leukemia in adults, recommendations from an international expert panel, on behalf of the European LeukemiaNet, *Blood* 115: 453-474, 2010.

often used as an adjunct to conventional chromosome analysis.
- Molecular studies to further stratify risk groups and prognosis (see Table 1L-9).
- Formal diagnosis of acute nonlymphocytic leukemia is established if the marrow blast percentage is ≥ 20%, unless t(8;21), inv(16), t(16;16) or t(15;17) are present, in which case the percentage of blasts may be lower.
  - Myeloperoxidase (MPO) staining of 3% of blasts establishes myeloid lineage, but MPO may be negative in some AML cases diagnosed by flow cytometry.
  - Specific criteria exist for diagnosing other forms of ANLL, mainly to distinguish from myelodysplasia. The WHO AML classification is outlined in Table 1L-10.
  - Cytogenetic risk categories in AML are described in Table 1L-11. Bone marrow findings are described in Fig. E1L-9.

IMAGING STUDIES

- Imaging studies are typically directed to evaluating specific complaints.
- Echocardiogram or MUGA is usually needed to verify adequate cardiac function to tolerate anthracycline (usually daunorubicin) therapy, with left ventricular ejection fraction (LVEF) of > 50% typically considered acceptable.

TREATMENT

ACUTE GENERAL Rx

- Therapy of AML typically has three components:
  - Immediate therapy to correct metabolic, infectious, or hyperleukocytic emergencies (if needed).
  - Induction therapy, which is therapy of active disease intended to obtain remission and restore normal bone marrow function. Remission is defined as blasts <5% in the bone marrow, absolute neutrophils (ANC) of > 1000/mcl, platelets > 100,000/mcl and transfusion independence.
  - Consolidation therapy, typically some form of intensive chemotherapy or stem cell transplant therapy intended to prevent relapse.
- Hyperleukocytic symptoms are most typically seen with WBC > 100,000/mcl.
- Leukapheresis requires catheter placement and pheresis, but spares tumor lysis.

- Rapid cytoreduction with chemotherapy (cytarabine, hydroxyurea 3 grams orally) often adequate and easier, but risks of acute tumor lysis. Optimal management is therefore individualized.
- Tumor lysis syndrome (TLS) is associated with rise in uric acid, potassium and phosphate (with reciprocal fall in calcium) levels as well as renal failure.
- Mainstay of therapy is vigorous hydration possibly with furosemide to maintain urine output > 100 ml/m²/hour. Urinary alkalinization is controversial, usually not helpful.
- Allopurinol up to 600 mg PO or IV, adjusted for renal failure) for hyperuricemia.
- Rasburicase (0.05-0.2 mg/kg) lowers uric acid rapidly (hours) with single dose in TLS emergency; avoid in patients with G6PD deficiency.
- Induction chemotherapy typically consists of daunorubicin 60 or 90 mg/m2 IV for 3 days and cytarabine (Ara-C) 100 or 200 mg/m²/day as continuous infusion for 7 days ("7+3").
- Success rates are 60% to 80% and have been better in recent trials. Other agents used have included etoposide, idarubicin, and fludarabine, among others. Bone marrow examination is commonly performed at day 14 to assess adequacy of response with additional therapy given for large amounts of persisting disease.
- Consolidation therapy is controversial. Cytarabine 3 gm/m² for six doses was used for many years, but intermediate doses (1000-1500 mg/m²) for six doses appears equally effective and less toxic. Doses above 1000 mg/m² are poorly tolerated in patients over 60 yr because of cerebellar toxicity.
- For "favorable" risk disease, consolidation with chemotherapy alone with 2 to 4 cycles of intermediate/high dose cytarabine is typically given with long term survival of 60% to 70%.
- For intermediate risk and unfavorable risk disease, first remission allogeneic stem cell-marrow transplant is often recommended if a donor is available. If not, chemotherapy consolidation chemotherapy is offered, although the optimal therapy and schedule, especially for unfavorable disease, is uncertain.
- The role of autologous stem cell marrow transplant is controversial, with some evidence of a decrease in relapse rates after chemotherapy, but no clear benefit in overall survival.

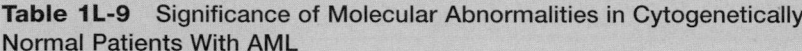

Table 1L-9 Significance of Molecular Abnormalities in Cytogenetically Normal Patients With AML

Molecular profile	Patients	4 year overall survival
Mutant CEBPA	67	62%
Mutant NPM, without FLT-3 ITD	150	60%
FLT-3 ITD present	164	24%
FLT-3 ITD absent, wild type NPM, wild type CEBPA (triple negative leukemia)	69	33%

CEBPA, CCAAT/enhancer binding protein α gene; *FLT-3 ITD*, fms-related tyrosine kinase gene internal tandem duplication; *NPM*, nucleophosmin gene.

Improved prognosis in patients with CEBPA mutations is limited to patients who lack FLT-3 ITD and have double mutations. CEBPA mutations are seen in approximately 6% to 10% of AML cases, NPM mutations in 25% to 35% (more common in cytogenetically normal cases) and FLT-3 ITD in approximately 20% to 30% of cases.

Data from Schlenk RF, et al: *N Engl J Med* 358: 1909-18, 2008, and Green CL, et al: *J Clin Oncol* 28: 2739-47, 2010.

TABLE 1L-10 Classification of Acute Myeloid Leukemia According to the Revised World Health Organization Classification (2008)

Category	Subtype/Definition
AML with recurrent cytogenetic abnormalities	t(8;21)(q22;q22); RUNX1-RUNX1T1* inv(16)(p13.1q22); CBFB-MYH11* t(16;16)(p13.1q22); CBFB-MYH11* t(15;17)(q22;q12); PML-RARA* t(9;11)(p22;q23); MLLT3-MLL t(6;9)(p23;q34); DEK-Nup214 inv(3)(q21q26.2); RPN1-EVI1 t(3;3)(q21;q26.2); RPN1-EVI1 t(1;22)(p13q13); RBM15-MKL1
AML with MDS-related changes	Morphologic features of MDS, or Prior history of MDS or MDS/MPN, or MDS-related karyotype, and None of the recurrent genetic abnormalities above
Therapy-related myeloid neoplasms	Late complications of cytotoxic chemotherapy (alkylating agents, topoisomerase II inhibitors) and/or ionizing radiation therapy†
AML, not otherwise specified	AML with minimal differentiation AML without maturation AML with maturation Acute myelomonocytic leukemia Acute monoblastic/monocytic leukemia Acute erythroid leukemia Acute megakaryoblastic leukemia Acute basophilic leukemia Acute panmyelosis with myelofibrosis
Myeloid sarcoma	
Myeloid proliferations related to Down syndrome	Transient abnormal myelopoiesis Myeloid leukemia associated with Down syndrome
Blastic plasmacytoid dendritic cell neoplasm	
Acute leukemia of ambiguous lineage	Acute undifferentiated leukemia Mixed-phenotype acute leukemia with t(9;22) (q34;q11.2); BCR-ABL1 t(v;11q23); MLL rearranged Mixed-phenotype acute leukemia, B/myeloid, NOS Mixed-phenotype acute leukemia, T/myeloid, NOS
Provisional entities	AML with mutated NPM1 AML with mutated CEBPA NK-cell lymphoblastic leukemia/lymphoma

AML, Acute myeloid leukemia; *MDS*, myelodysplastic syndrome; *MPN*, myeloproliferative neoplasm; *NK*, natural killer.
*Diagnosis of AML regardless of percentage of blasts.
†Excluded are patients with AML who have transformed from MPN.
From Hoffman R: *Hematology, basic principles and practice*, 6th ed, Philadelphia, 2013, Saunders.

- Allogeneic stem cell transplant is offered to patients with relapsed disease if a second remission can be obtained.
- Relapses after bone marrow transplant can sometimes be managed with donor lymphocyte infusions, adjustment of immune suppression to increase the graft vs. leukemia effect, and chemotherapy. In general, outcomes are poor with post-transplant relapses.

- Treatment of older patients (>60 yr) is problematic, with cure rates of 10% to 15%. Older patients do worse because they are more likely to have high risk features and less likely to tolerate therapy. Options for these patients include:
  - Standard induction therapy is reasonable for patients likely to tolerate it. Even in the absence of cure, quality of life is excellent in remission. Patients over 80 yr do not usually benefit, although this has been reconsidered recently. Some form of consolidation is usually given, with presumed greater benefit in "favorable" risk disease. The optimal regimen is not known.
  - Hypomethylating agents—decitabine and azacytidine—may be considered in patients unlikely to tolerate induction therapy, especially in the setting of low blast count (20%-30% bone marrow blasts) leukemia.
  - Low dose cytarabine (20 mg/m^2 twice daily or 40 mg/m^2 daily for 10 days subcutaneously) has shown survival benefit over hydroxyurea in low/intermediate risk patients.
  - Oral hydroxyurea dosed to counts and cytopenias.
  - Best supportive care.
  - Reduced intensity allogeneic stem cell transplant has yielded cure rates of 20% to 40% of highly selected patients, typically ages 60 to 75, and is an option for some.
- Acute Promyelocytic Leukemia (APML)
  APML is a distinct leukemia syndrome with very different treatment implications. Cure rates greater than 95% have been seen in current protocols in the absence of high risk features. It is associated with t(15;17), which translocates the PML gene to retinoic acid receptor α (PML-RARa). Uncommon variants are t(11;17) and t(5;17).
  - Risk groups in APML receiving anthracycline and retinoic acid therapy:

High risk:	WBC >10,000/mcl
Intermediate risk:	WBC ≤10,000/mcl, platelets ≤ 40,000/mcl.
Low Risk:	WBC ≤10,000/mcl, platelets > 40,000/mcl.

  - Patients in low and intermediate risk groups (WBC ≤10,000) had a two year event free survival of 97% using all transretinoic acid (ATRA) and arsenic trioxide (AsO$_3$) therapy in a recent trial.
  - Patients in the high risk group had approximately 75% 5 year survival using anthracycline (idarubicin) and ATRA therapy.
- APML is a medical emergency because of the high risk of bleeding complications.
  - All patients with APML have DIC, caused by overexpression of annexin II, (which increases generation of plasmin, degrading fibrin), elastases (which degrade fibrinogen and fibrinolytic inhibitors), and increased endothelial tissue plasminogen activator release.

Table 1L-11 European LeukemiaNet Defined Cytogenetic and Molecular Abnormalities Relevant to Prognosis in AML

Favorable	t(8;21)(q22;q22)*
	inv (16)(p13.1;q22) or t(16;16) (p13.1;q22) *
	Normal karyotype with mutated NPM1 and absent FLT-3 ITD
	Normal karyotype and mutated CEBPA
Intermediate-1	Normal karyotype and mutated NPM1 and FLT3-ITD
	Normal karyotype with wild type NPM1 and FLT3-ITD
	Normal karyotype without FLT3-ITD
Intermediate-2	t(9;11)(p22;q23)
	Cytogenetic abnormalities not classified as favorable or adverse
Adverse	Complex (3 or more abnormalities, unless associated with a known favorable abnormality),
	inv(3)(q21;q26.2) or t(3;3)(q21;q26.2);
	t(6;9)(p23;q34)
	t(variable;11)(variable;q23) (MLL gene rearrangement),
	-5 or del (5q);
	-7;
	abnormal (17p)

*AML associated with t(8;21)(q22;q22), inv (16)(p13.1;q22) or t(16;16) (p13.1;q22) are referred to core binding factor (CBF) leukemias. CBF is a modulator of DNA transcription that is affected by these mutations. Favorable risk groups have had 5 year survivals of about 60%, intermediate risk of approximately 25% to 30% and unfavorable risk of less than 5% in clinical trials from the 1990s.

Adapted from Doehner H et al, Diagnosis and management of acute myeloid leukemia in adults, recommendations from an international expert panel, on behalf of the European LeukemiaNet., *Blood* 115: 453-474, 2010.

- Early death due to hemorrhage is seen in 5% to 17% of newly diagnosed APML patients, usually intracranial or pulmonary. Risk factors include elevated WBC, increased age, and elevated creatinine.
- Retinoic acid rapidly stabilizes the coagulopathy of APML; consideration should be given to starting this immediately for suspected cases.
- Cryoprecipitate (usual dose 10 bags) to raise the fibrinogen level to 150 mg/dl and platelet transfusion to raise the count to >50,000//mcl should be given as needed.
- Unfractionated heparin may paradoxically stop bleeding in APML by inhibiting DIC, but is rarely used in the retinoic acid treatment era.

- Diagnosis of APML
  - Rapid diagnosis is essential due to treatment implications, Tests commonly available in 24 to 48 hours depending on local availability
  - Polymerase chain reaction for PML/RARa
  - FISH for t(15;17) or variants
  - Flow cytometry is typically distinct with lack of HLA-DR and CD34; CD13, CD33 and CD64 are usually positive
- Therapy of APML
  - Emergency measures to stabilize coagulapathy as outlined previously
  - Patients with WBC ≤10,000 (low/intermediate risk) are treated with retinoic acid and arsenic trioxide ("differentiation therapy")
  - Optimal therapy of higher risk patients is less well defined and may include anthracyclines (commonly idarubicin, also

daunorubicin) to lower WBC and decrease risk of differentiation syndrome
  - Maintenance therapy for 2 years is given in some APML protocols
- Differentiation syndrome (DS) is a potentially fatal complication of therapy with retinoic acid and arsenic trioxide. It is associated with fever, interstitial pulmonary infiltrates, peripheral edema, pleural and pericardial effusions and renal failure; it is commonly associated with rising WBC seen in patients on differentiation therapy.
  - Therapy for suspected differentiation syndrome is dexamethasone 10 mg/m^2 every 12 hr. Stopping retinoic acid and arsenic is appropriate for inadequate response to dexamethasone.
  - Prophylaxis for differentiation syndrome with dexamethasone 2.5 mg/m^2 every 12 hr has been suggested for WBC >5000 or creatinine > 1.4 mg/dl.

PEARLS & CONSIDERATIONS

- The diagnosis of acute myeloid leukemia or variants is often, but not always, a medical emergency requiring rapid clinical and laboratory assessment by appropriate expertise.
- APML is a distinct clinical entity with a high cure rate with current protocols, but requires intensive supportive care at the time of diagnosis.

SUGGESTED READINGS
Available at www.expertconsult.com

RELATED CONTENT
Acute Myelogenous Leukemia (Patient Information)

AUTHOR: **PETER RINTELS, M.D.**

BASIC INFORMATION

DEFINITION

Chronic lymphocytic leukemia (CLL) is a lymphoproliferative disorder characterized by proliferation and accumulation of mature-appearing neoplastic B-cells.

SYNONYMS

CLL

ICD-10-CM CODES

C91.10 Chronic lymphocytic leukemia of B-cell type not having achieved remission
C91.11 Chronic lymphocytic leukemia of B-cell type in remission
C91.12 Chronic lymphocytic leukemia of B-cell type in relapse

EPIDEMIOLOGY & DEMOGRAPHICS

- Most frequent form of leukemia in Western countries (14,620 new cases and 4650 deaths annually in the U.S.). Incidence rate is 4.5 per 100,000 person-years, and increases to 13 cases per 100,000 at age 65. It is more common in Caucasians and in those with a family history of CLL or other lymphoid malignancy.
- Generally occurs in elderly patients (70% of diagnoses are made in patients >65 yr of age). Median age at diagnosis in the U.S. is 71years.
- Male/female ratio of 2:1.
- CLL accounts for 0.9% of all cancers and 11% of all hematologic neoplasms.
- May be preceded by monoclonal B-cell lymphocytosis—a premalignant, asymptomatic condition with less than 5000 /mm³ CLL-like cells circulating in the blood

PHYSICAL FINDINGS & CLINICAL PRESENTATION

- At presentation most patients are asymptomatic. Many cases are diagnosed on the basis of incidental laboratory results.
- Symptoms include fatigue, recurrent infections (pneumonia, herpes zoster), enlarging lymph nodes
- B symptoms (fever, weight loss, and drenching night sweats) in 10% of patients at initial presentation
- Small diffuse lymphadenopathy and splenomegaly are typical findings on clinical examination, but they may be absent in a majority of patients at diagnosis
- A minority of CLL patients (~1%-10%) may develop autoimmune hemolytic anemia or immune thrombocytopenia at diagnosis or during the course of the disease.
- At a rate of 1% per year, CLL patients may experience a transformation of their disease into an aggressive lymphoma (Richter's transformation), characterized by a rapidly growing nodal mass, elevated LDH, and constitutional symptoms

ETIOLOGY

The etiology of CLL remains largely unknown, although accumulation of genetic defects causing resistance to apoptosis and chronic stimulation of the B-cell receptor by autoantigens or undefined microorganisms have been implicated.

DIAGNOSIS

- The diagnosis of CLL requires presence of >5000/mm³ clonal B-cells, for >3 months, with a characteristic immunophenotype on flow cytometry, which is essential for diagnosis
- CLL cells are typically positive for CD5, CD19, CD23 and weakly positive for CD20, while they are negative for CD10, Cyclin D1, and CD103. In some cases, molecular studies for CLL-specific chromosomal alterations (deletion of chromosome 13q, 11q, 17p or trisomy 12) may be helpful.
- Table 1L-12 describes the evaluation of CLL patients at diagnosis.

DIFFERENTIAL DIAGNOSIS

- Few acute infections with lymphocytosis (mononucleosis, pertussis)
- Other lymphoproliferative disorders that involve blood (can be distinguished using flow cytometry): follicular lymphoma, mantle cell lymphoma, splenic marginal zone lymphoma, prolymphocytic leukemia, adult T-cell lymphoma/leukemia, hairy cell leukemia.
- Acute lymphocytic leukemia can be differentiated by presence of lymphoblasts rather than mature lymphocytes
- Persistent polyclonal B-cell lymphocytosis: a rare, benign condition affecting (predominantly female) middle-aged smokers

LABORATORY TESTS

- Complete blood count demonstrates lymphocytosis with mature lymphocytes and characteristic "smudge cells" on the peripheral smear (Fig. 1L-10); anemia and thrombocytopenia may be present in more advanced cases.
- Bone marrow examination is **not** indicated in most cases, except when differentiation between autoimmune cytopenias and marrow infiltration by CLL is difficult.
- Hypogammaglobulinemia and elevated lactate dehydrogenase may be present at the time of diagnosis.
- Cytogenetic evaluation (using fluorescent *in situ* hybridization, FISH) is essential for prognostic assessment and optimal treatment selection (Table 1L-13).
- Other prognostic markers include: mutational status of the immunoglobulin heavy chain variable region (*IGHV*, unmutated gene with >98% homology indicates poor prognosis), presence of CD38 or ZAP-70 (also associated with poor prognosis). Additional mutation analysis is gaining importance for identifying patients with worse prognosis (mutations in *TP53, NOTCH1, SF3B1* and *BIRC3* genes)

TABLE 1L-12 Evaluation of Chronic Lymphocytic Leukemia (CLL) Patients at Diagnosis

History

B-symptom and fatigue assessment
Infectious history assessment
Occupational assessment for chemical exposure
Familial history of CLL and lymphoproliferative disorders
Preventive interventions for infections and secondary cancers

Physical Exam with attention to lymph nodes, spleen, liver and Waldeyer's ring

Laboratory Assessment—Essential

Complete blood count with differential
Morphology assessment of lymphocytes
Kidney and liver function tests, lactate dehydrogenase
Flow cytometry assessment to confirm immunophenotype of CLL
FISH analysis for del 17, del 11q, del 13 and trisomy 12
Hepatitis B screening prior to immunochemotherapy

Selected Tests Under Certain Circumstances

IgV$_H$ mutational analysis
Serum immunoglobulins
Serum b$_2$Microglobulin levels
Direct antiglobulin test (DAT), reticulocyte count if anemia present
CT scan of chest, abdomen and pelvis if there is a clinical concern for symptomatic adenopathy, or prior to chemotherapy
PET scan and/or biopsy if large nodal mass with suspected Richter's transformation present
Bone marrow aspirate and biopsy if unexplained cytopenias present
Familial counseling if first-degree relative with CLL

Teaching

Varicella zoster identification instruction
Skin cancer identification
Disease education (Leukemia and Lymphoma Society, CLL Topics, ACOR)

From Hoffmann R et al: *Hematology: basic principles and practice*, ed 6, Philadelphia, 2013, Elsevier.

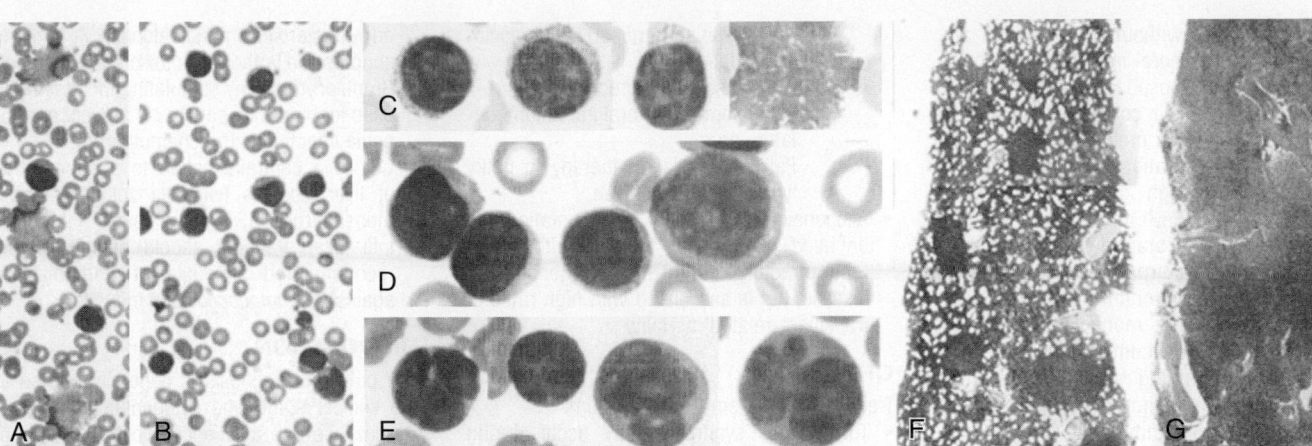

FIGURE 1L-10 Chronic lymphocytic leukemia. Peripheral blood smear **(A-E)** typically shows mature lymphocytes slightly larger than the red cells, with small amount of cytoplasm. Smudge cells **(F,G)**, which are artifacts resulting from fragility of the CLL cells, are typically seen.

TABLE 1L-13 Prognosis of Patients With CLL at the Time of Diagnosis, Stratified by Cytogenetic Risk Group

Cytogenetic alteration	Risk group	Percent of patients (some may overlap)	Median time to first chemotherapy	Median survival
Deletion 13q	Favorable	40%-60%	8 yr	11 yr
None	Intermediate	<20%	4 yr	9 yr
Trisomy 12	Intermediate	15%-30%	3 yr	9 yr
Deletion 11q	High	15%-20%	1 yr	7 yr
Deletion 17p	Ultra-high	~10%	<1 yr	3 yr

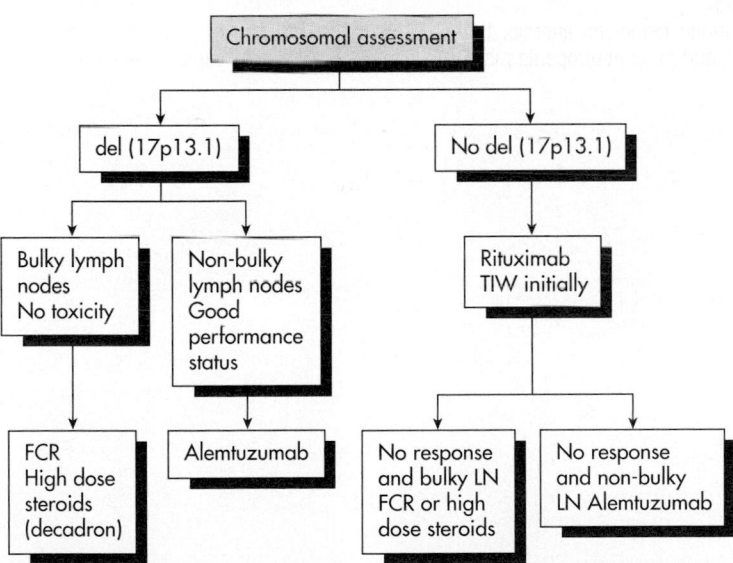

FIGURE 1L-11 Algorithm to treatment approach in chronic lymphocytic leukemia.

STAGING: Staging reflects the clinical burden of disease and aids assessment of prognosis and treatment decision-making. The historical staging systems by Rai and Binet remain in clinical use. They use **only** physical examination and the CBC (i.e,. no scans). The modified Rai system distinguishes three risk groups:

- Low risk (lymphocytosis alone, or Stage 0)
- Intermediate risk (presence of lymphadenopathy, hepatomegaly or splenomegaly, formerly Stage I/II)

- High risk (presence of anemia with hemoglobin <11 g/dL, or thrombocytopenia with platelet count <100,000/mm³, formerly stage III/IV).

The Binet system divides CLL into three stages:
- Stage A: involvement of <3 nodal areas (counting separately cervical, axillary, or inguinal lymph nodes, spleen, and liver).
- Stage B: three or more areas involved.
- Stage C: presence of anemia (hemoglobin <10 g/dl) or thrombocytopenia (<100,000/mm³), independent of the areas involved.

With either system, survival exceeds 10 years from diagnosis for the low-risk/stage A, is about 7 years for intermediate group/stage B and is <4 years for high-risk/stage C group, although these estimates are rapidly evolving.

IMAGING STUDIES

Imaging studies (CT or PET/CT scans) are not necessary for asymptomatic patients at diagnosis. They are obtained in case of clinical concerns for bulky internal adenopathy, Richter's transformation, or prior to starting chemotherapy.

Rx TREATMENT

- At present, there is no standard curative therapy for CLL, so treatment is only instituted for progressive or symptomatic disease with a goal of symptom relief and prolongation of life.
- "Watchful waiting" (i.e., observation without therapy) is the optimal strategy for all early stage, asymptomatic patients outside of clinical trials because early chemotherapy provides no survival or quality-of-life benefit.
- Chemotherapy is the standard of care for patients with symptoms related to disease, bulky adenopathy, rapidly increasing lymphocyte count, or progressive cytopenias (except for autoimmune cytopenias, which can be treated without chemotherapy)

ACUTE GENERAL Rx

- The initial chemotherapy is chosen depending on the patient's age, comorbidities, and CLL cytogenetics (Fig. 1L-11).
- Most older (>70 yr) patients receive combinations of one cytotoxic chemotherapy drug with (or without) an anti-CD20 monoclonal antibody: bendamustine +/- rituximab (typically, 6 monthly cycles), chlorambucil +/- obinatuzumab or ofatumumab, or fludarabine +/- rituximab. With these regimens, a vast majority (>80%) of patients achieve at least a partial remission, with median progression-free survival of about 2 to 4 years.
- Patients with significant comorbidities are offered a less intense regimen of oral chlorambucil with obinatuzumab or ofatumumab.

L

- Younger patients without comorbidities are often offered a more intense regimen of fludarabine, cyclophosphamide and rituximab (FCR), which results in complete remission in 72% of cases and in prolonged (>10 years) remission in some patients
- CLL with ultra-high cytogenetic profile (deletion 17p, *TP53* mutation) does not respond well to standard immunoche-motherapy and alternative agents (B-cell receptor complex inhibitors ibrutinib or idelalisib, anti-CD52 monoclonal antibody alemtuzumab) are recommended
- Regimens containing alkylating agents (chlorambucil, bendamustine, cyclophos-phamide) are recommended for patients with deletion 11q
- Recurrent CLL is often characterized by acquired deletion or mutation of the *TP53* gene and should be ideally treated in a clinical trial. It can also be treated with a variety of agents:
  - Anti-CD20 monoclonal antibodies: ofatumumab, obinatuzumab, ritux-imab, alone or in combination with chemotherapy; purine analogues (fludarabine, pentostatin); alkylating agents (bendamustine, cyclophos-phamide, CHOP-like combinations)
  - B-cell receptor complex inhibitors: ibrutinib and idelalisib. These novel oral agents are characterized by relatively good tolerance, high rate of durable responses, occasional persistent lymphocytosis, and extremely high cost of therapy

  - Alemtuzumab (anti-CD52 monoclonal antibody)
  - High-dose methylprednisolone
  - Lenalidomide (an oral immunomodulatory drug)
  - Palliative radiation therapy to bulky lymph nodes or spleen.
- Allogeneic bone marrow transplantation can be used for younger patients with recurrent, refractory, or ultra-high cytogenetic risk disease, but is associated with high rates of transplant-related mortality

CHRONIC Rx
Treatment of systemic complications:
- Tumor lysis syndrome may occur during initial or subsequent chemotherapy, but is extremely unlikely without it in CLL.
- CLL patients are at increased risk of solid tumors and should adhere to age-appropriate screening modalities; skin cancers, including melanoma, are particularly common.
- Hypogammaglobulinemia is frequent in CLL and may cause recurrent infections, particularly pneumonias. Immunoglobulin supplementation (250 mg/kg IV every 4 wk) may prevent infections but has no effect on the course of CLL.
- Patients after chemoimmunotherapy are at risk for, and often ultimately succumb to, opportunistic infections. Herpes zoster and *Pneumocystis jirovecii* prophylaxis is used during and after some chemoimmunotherapy regimens.
- Autoimmune hemolytic anemia, thrombocytopenia, and (rare) neutropenia may be treated with steroids, immunoglobulin, or immune suppression without cytotoxic chemotherapy
- Granulocyte colony stimulating factor is often used for older CLL patients to prevent neutropenia infections after chemotherapy.
- CLL is a contraindication to administration of live vaccines (varicella zoster, mumps/measles/rubella, yellow fever, intranasal influenza). Patients should adhere to the recommended schedule of immunization against *Pneumococcus* and influenza.

DISPOSITION
The patient's prognosis is generally related to the clinical stage and cytogenetic risk. Most patients die due to infectious complications of therapy for refractory disease after several lines of treatment. Histologic transformation to an aggressive lymphoma is also associated with high mortality. Palliative treatment should be offered to patients who are no longer benefitting from aggressive therapy to avoid pervasive and futile treatment with distressing complications.

SUGGESTED READINGS
Available at www.expertconsult.com.

RELATED CONTENT
Chronic Lymphocytic Leukemia (Patient Information)

AUTHOR: **ADAM J. OLSZEWSKI, M.D.**

BASIC INFORMATION

DEFINITION

Chronic myelogenous leukemia (CML) is a malignant clonal stem disease. Its hallmark is the Philadelphia chromosome, an acquired cytogenetic abnormality arising out of the reciprocal translocation of long arms of the *ABL* and *BCR* genes on chromosomes 9 and 22, resulting in the *BCR:ABL* fusion oncogene. CML, is characterized by abnormal myeloid proliferation and accumulation of immature granulocytes. CML manifests with a chronic phase (CP-CML) lasting months to years, which evolves into an advanced phase (AP-CML) characterized by poor response to therapy, worsening anemia, or decreased platelet count; this phase then evolves into a terminal blast phase (BP) resulting in acute leukemia (70% myeloid and approximately 30% lymphoid subtype). The WHO criteria for accelerated and blast phases of CML are described in Table 1L-14.

SYNONYMS

CML
Chronic granulocytic leukemia
Chronic myeloid leukemia

ICD-10CM CODES
C92.10 Chronic myeloid leukemia, BCR/ABL-positive, not having achieved remission
C92.11 Chronic myeloid leukemia, BCR/ABL-positive, in remission
C92.12 Chronic myeloid leukemia, BCR/ABL-positive, in relapse

EPIDEMIOLOGY & DEMOGRAPHICS

- The median age for CML presentation is usually in the mid-50 year range. It accounts for 15% to 20% of adult leukemias.
- Incidence is 1 to 2 cases per 100,000 people annually.

PHYSICAL FINDINGS & CLINICAL PRESENTATION

- Up to 50% patients are asymptomatic, with diagnosis based on abnormal blood counts.
- In chronic phase, symptomatic patients can have fatigue, weight loss, and left abdomen pain, and examination can reveal splenomegaly. Occasionally, a very high WBC count may lead to hyperviscosity-related symptoms.
- Patients in accelerated phase are usually symptomatic with fevers, sweats, weight loss, abdomen pain and progressive splenomegaly.
- Patients in blast phase in addition can have bone pain; symptoms of anemia, infectious complications and bleeding are also present.

ETIOLOGY

The etiology of CML is unclear though radiation exposure has been linked in its development.

TABLE 1L-14	WHO Criteria for Accelerated and Blast Phases of CML
Accelerated phase	Diagnosis can be made if one or more of the following is present: Blasts 10%-19% of peripheral blood white cells or bone marrow cells Peripheral blood basophils at least 20% Persistent thrombocytopenia (<100 × 10⁹/L) unrelated to therapy, or persistent thrombocytosis (>1000 × 10⁹/L) unresponsive to therapy Increasing spleen size and increasing WBC count unresponsive to therapy Cytogenetic evidence of clonal evolution (i.e., the appearance of an additional genetic abnormality that was not present in the initial specimen at the time of diagnosis of chronic phase CML) Megakaryocytic proliferation in sizable sheets and clusters, associated with marked reticulin or collagen fibrosis, and/or severe granulocytic dysplasia, should be considered as suggestive of CML-AP. (These findings have not yet been analyzed in large clinical studies; thus it is not clear whether they are independent criteria for accelerated phase. They often occur simultaneously with one or more of the other features listed.)
Blast crisis	Diagnosis can be made if one or more of following is present: Blasts 30% or more of peripheral blood white cells or bone marrow cells Extramedullary blast proliferation Large foci or clusters of blasts in bone marrow biopsy

From Hoffman R: *Hematology, basic principles and practice,* 6th ed, Philadelphia, 2013 Saunders.

 DIAGNOSIS

DIFFERENTIAL DIAGNOSIS

- Splenic lymphoma.
- Myeloproliferative syndrome.
- Chronic neutrophilic leukemia.
- Essential thrombocythemia.

LABORATORY TESTS

- CBC showing left-shifted myeloid cells, with broad spectrum and also can be accompanied by thrombocytosis.
- Median leukocyte count of 100,000/micro liter with classic "myelocyte bulge" (more myelocytes than the more mature metamyelocytes seen on the blood smear.
- Bone marrow biopsy demonstrates hypercellularity with granulocytic hyperplasia, increased ratio of myeloid cells to erythroid cells, and increased megakaryocytes (Fig. 1L-12).
- Bone marrow cytogenetics demonstrated the 9:22 translocation (Philadelphia chromosome) in >95% of patients (Fig. 1L-13).
- Leukocyte alkaline phosphatase is markedly decreased (unlike other myeloproliferative disorders).
- *BCR-ABL* fusion transcripts can be measured using quantitative RT-PCR technology using either peripheral blood or bone marrow; serial peripheral blood monitoring of transcript level is utilized at 3-month intervals to determine molecular remission status.

RISK STRATIFICATION

- Chronic phase CML patients can be stratified into low, intermediate, or high-risk criteria using the Sokal or Hasford criteria; more recently, the EUTOS score can be used to stratify patients into low or high-risk strata
- Patients developing secondary mutations have variable response to second-line therapies; the T315I mutation is typically associated with resistance and is treated with allogeneic stem cell transplantation

IMAGING STUDIES

Ultrasound or CT scan of abdomen can be done.

TREATMENT

Treatment with a potential to either cure CML or prolong long-term survival should be used according to the phase of the disease.

- Chronic phase: the therapeutic approach involves the use of either a first-generation (imatinib) or second-generation (dasatinib, nilotinib) oral tyrosine kinase inhibitor (TKI). The large majority of patients obtain hematologic and cytogenetic remissions; major molecular remissions are observed in 25% to 60% cases. Patients who lose their response or develop mutations can be treated with newer third-generation drugs (bosutinib, ponatinib).
- Accelerated phase: patients are initially treated with second-generation TKIs but ultimately require allogeneic stem cell transplantation.
- Blast phase: patients are initially treated with conventional induction chemotherapy as per the type of evolved acute leukemia and then subsequently undergo allogeneic stem cell transplantation.
- Symptomatic hyperleukocytosis can be treated with leukapheresis and hydroxyurea; allopurinol should be started to prevent urate nephropathy after the rapid lysis of the leukemia cells.
- Interferon-alfa is active in early chronic phase patients but has been replaced by the oral TKIs.

DISPOSITION

- Median survival for patients with chronic phase CML undergoing therapy with current TKIs is estimated to last 25+ years.
- Median survivals for patients with accelerated and blast phase CML are 5 years and 7 to 11 months, respectively.

REFERRAL

- To hematology physician.

BASIC INFORMATION

DEFINITION

Lichen planus (LP) refers to an idiopathic inflammatory disease manifesting with a papular skin eruption characteristically found over the flexor surfaces of the extremities, genitalia, and mucous membranes.

SYNONYMS

Lichen
Lichen planus et atrophicus
LP

ICD-10CM CODES
L43   Lichen planus
L43.0   Hypertrophic lichen planus
L43.1   Bullous lichen planus
L43.9   Lichen planus, unspecified
L43.8   Other lichen planus

EPIDEMIOLOGY & DEMOGRAPHICS

INCIDENCE: One in every 100 new patients seen in dermatology clinics in the United States is diagnosed with LP.
PREVALENCE: 440 cases/100,000 persons
PREDOMINANT SEX: Found equally between males and females (1:1).
PREDOMINANT AGE: Usually found in people between the ages of 30 and 60 yr.
PREDISPOSING FACTORS:
1. Associated with other autoimmune disorders (e.g., primary biliary cirrhosis, myasthenia gravis, ulcerative colitis, diabetes).
2. Associated with hepatitis C infection.
3. Drug-induced form affects any area of the body surface (e.g., beta-blocker, methyldopa, penicillamine, quinidine, nonsteroidal anti-inflammatory drugs, angiotensin-converting enzyme inhibitors, sulfonylurea agents).

PHYSICAL FINDINGS & CLINICAL PRESENTATION

The clinical presentation varies depending on the area involved.
History:
- Usually starts on an extremity and may remain localized or spread to involve other areas over a 1- to 4-mo period.
- Pruritic.

Physical findings:
- Anatomic distribution:
  1. Flexor surface of wrists, forearms, shins, and upper thighs.
  2. Neck and back area.
  3. Nails (5%-10% of patients).
  4. Scalp (lichen planopilaris).
  5. Oral mucosa, buccal mucosa, tongue, gingiva, and lips; oral lichen planus can cause extensive desquamative gingivitis.
  6. Vulva, penis (Fig. E1L-19).

Genital mucosa:
- Lesion configuration:
  1. Linear.
  2. Annular (more common).
  3. Reticular pattern noted on oral mucosa and genital area.

- Lesion morphology:
  1. Papules most common presentation (flat, smooth, shiny) (Fig. 1L-18)
  2. Hypertrophic
  3. Follicular
  4. Vesicular
- Color:
  1. Dark red, bluish red, purplish-violaceous color is noted in cutaneous LP.
  2. Individual lesions characteristically have white lines visible (Wickham's striae) (Fig. E1L-20).
  3. Oral and genital LP has a reticular network of white lines that may be raised or annular in appearance.
- Scalp lesions may result in alopecia.

ETIOLOGY

Lichen planus is characterized by an immunologic reaction mediated by CD8+ T cells. These cells induce keratinocytes to undergo apoptosis. Although the inflammatory reaction is believed to be autoimmune, the antigen targeted by these effector T lymphocytes is unknown.

DIAGNOSIS

- Clinical history and physical findings usually establish the diagnosis of LP.
- Skin biopsy (deep shave or punch biopsy of the most developed lesion) can be performed to confirm the diagnosis.

DIFFERENTIAL DIAGNOSIS

- Drug eruption, psoriasis, Bowen's disease, leukoplakia, candidiasis, lupus rash, secondary syphilis, seborrheic dermatitis, chronic graft vs. host disease.

WORKUP

If the diagnosis is questionable, a skin biopsy is performed.

LABORATORY TESTS

Laboratory tests are not specific for the diagnosis of LP. Lipid panels screening is useful since increases in serum triglycerides and decreases in HDL cholesterol are common in patients with LP.

IMAGING STUDIES

Imaging studies are not helpful in diagnosing LP.

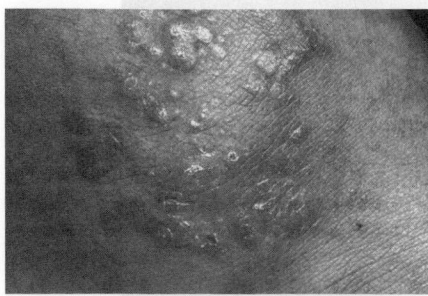

FIGURE 1L-18 Flat-topped, purple polygonal papules of the lichen planus. (From Morelli JG: Diseases of the epidermis. In Kliegman RM et al [eds]: *Nelson textbook of pediatrics,* ed 19, Philadelphia, 2011, Saunders.)

TREATMENT

NONPHARMACOLOGIC THERAPY

- Avoid scratching.
- Use mild soaps and emollients after bathing to prevent dryness.

GENERAL Rx

For cutaneous LP:
- Topical steroids (e.g., triamcinolone acetonide 0.1%, fluocinonide 0.05%, clobetasol propionate 0.05% cream or ointment) with occlusion used twice daily.
- Acitretin 30 mg/day PO for 8 wk.
- Systemic prednisone 30 to 60 mg/day as a starting dose and tapered to 15 to 20 mg/day maintenance for 6 wk can be used for widespread lesions.
- Intradermal steroid triamcinolone acetonide 5 mg/mL can be tried for thick hyperkeratotic lesions.
- Hydroxyzine 25 mg PO q6h can be used for pruritus.
- Phototherapy: PUVA or narrow-band ultraviolet B therapy: 2 or 3 times per week, for a total of 12 sessions (i.e., one cycle).

For oral LP:
- Topical steroid fluocinonide in an adhesive base used six times/day for 9 wk.
- Topical calcineurin in steroid-unresponsive cases.
- Topical or systemic retinoids 0.1% retinoic acid in an adhesive base or gel.
- Etretinate 75 mg/day for 2 mo.

DISPOSITION

- Spontaneous remissions of cutaneous LP occur in >65% of cases within the first year.
- Spontaneous remission of oral LP usually occurs by 5 yr.
- Approximately 10% to 20% of patients will have recurrence.

REFERRAL

To dermatologist if diagnosis is unclear

PEARLS & CONSIDERATIONS

COMMENTS

- LP can be remembered as purple, planar, pruritic, polygonal, papules, and plaques (six P's).
- Lesions can develop at the site of prior skin injury (Koebner's phenomenon).
- Although there is an increased risk of squamous cell carcinoma in chronic lesions of mucosal LP, transformation to skin cancer is uncommon.

SUGGESTED READINGS
Available at www.expertconsult.com

RELATED CONTENT
Lichen Planus (Patient Information)

AUTHOR: **TANYA ALI, M.D.**

L

BASIC INFORMATION

DEFINITION

Lichen sclerosus (LS) is a chronic inflammatory condition of the skin usually affecting the vulva, penis, perianal area, and groin.

SYNONYMS

Lichen sclerosus et atrophicus
Kraurosis vulvae
Balanitis xerotica obliterans
LS

ICD-10CM CODES
L90.0 Lichen sclerosus et atrophicus

EPIDEMIOLOGY & DEMOGRAPHICS

- Most common in postmenopausal women and men between ages 40 and 60 yr.
- More common in females (female/male ratio of 5:1). It affects 1.7% of the general adult female population.
- Can occur in children (usually prepubertal girls with involvement of the vulva and perineum).

PHYSICAL FINDINGS & CLINICAL PRESENTATION

- Erythema may be the only initial sign. A characteristic finding is the presence of ivory-white atrophic lesions on the involved area.
- Close inspection of the affected area will reveal the presence of white-to-brown follicular plugs on the surface (dells).
- When the genitals are involved, the white, parchment-like skin assumes an hourglass configuration around the introital and perianal area ("keyhole" distribution; Fig. 1L-21). Inflammation, subepithelial hemorrhages, and chronic ulceration may develop.
- In males, lesions are atrophic and may be hypopigmented or depigmented, resembling vitiligo. Phymosis and paraphymosis are common complications in uncircumcised males with LS.
- Lesions may be surrounded by an erythematous to violaceous halo.

- Dyspareunia, genital bleeding, and anal bleeding are common.
- Pruritis may be a prominent symptom.

ETIOLOGY

Unknown. There may be an autoimmune association and a genetic familial component.

DIAGNOSIS

DIFFERENTIAL DIAGNOSIS

- Localized scleroderma (morphea).
- Cutaneous discoid lupus erythematosus.
- Atrophic lichen planus.
- Psoriasis.
- Lichen simplex chronicus.
- Vulvar intraepithelial neoplasm.
- Extramammary Paget's disease.

WORKUP

Diagnosis is based on close examination of the lesions for the presence of ivory-white atrophic lesions and typical location.

LABORATORY TESTS

- Punch or deep shave biopsy can be used to confirm the diagnosis.
- Autoantibodies to extracellular matrix protein 1 (ECM-1) are present in 80% of LS patients and the ECM-1 titer correlates with disease activity.

TREATMENT

NONPHARMACOLOGIC THERAPY

- Attention to hygiene and elimination of irritants or excessive bathing with harsh soaps.
- Cyrotherapy and photodynamic therapy can be used in refractory cases.

GENERAL Rx

- Application of clobetasol propionate 0.05% topically bid for up to 4 wk is usually effective. Repeat courses of corticosteroids may be necessary because of the chronic nature of this disorder. Continual application of topical steroids may lead to atrophy of the vulva.

- There is no substantial evidence that use of topical sex hormones (e.g., topical testosterone [2%]) is effective in genital lichen sclerosus.
- Lubricants (e.g., Nutraplus cream) are useful to soothe dry tissues.
- Hydroxyzine 25 mg at bedtime is effective in decreasing nocturnal itching.
- Use of intralesional steroids, etretinate, and surgical management is usually reserved for refractory cases.

DISPOSITION

- The disease persists in approximately one third of patients.
- Most prepubertal girls improve spontaneously at menarche.
- Squamous cell carcinoma can develop within the lesions in 3% to 10% of older patients; therefore periodic examination and biopsy of suspicious areas are indicated.

PEARLS & CONSIDERATIONS

COMMENTS

- Prepubertal lichen sclerosus may be confused with sexual abuse in prepubertal girls and may lead to false accusations and investigations.
- Pregnancy leads to improvement and often complete resolution of lesions, suggesting a hormonal component to etiology of lesions.
- Lichen sclerosus of the vulva (kraurosis vulvae) usually occurs after menopause and is generally chronic. It can be painful and interfere with sexual activity.
- Lichen sclerosus of the penis (balanitis xerotica obliterans) is seen more commonly in uncircumcised males. It affects the glans and prepuce and may lead to stricture if it encroaches into the urinary meatus.

SUGGESTED READINGS
Available at www.expertconsult.com

RELATED CONTENT
Lichen Sclerosus (Patient Information)

AUTHOR: **FRED F. FERRI, M.D.**

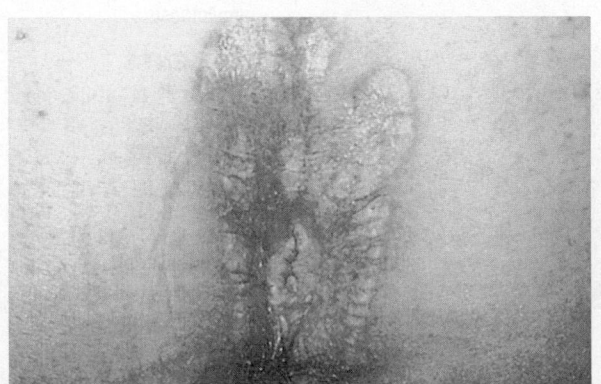

FIGURE 1L-21 Lichen sclerosus. Perianal area is thinned and chalk white (keyhole distribution). (Courtesy Department of Dermatology, University of North Carolina at Chapel Hill. From Goldstein BG, Goldstein AO: *Practical dermatology,* ed 2, St Louis, 1997, Mosby.)

BASIC INFORMATION

DEFINITION
Lichen simplex chronicus is neurodermatitis manifesting with localized areas of thickened, hyperplastic scaly skin due to prolonged and severe scratching in patients with no underlying dermatologic condition.

SYNONYMS
Neurodermatitis from rubbing
Circumscribed neurodermatitis

ICD-10CM CODES
L28.0 Lichen simplex chronicus

EPIDEMIOLOGY & DEMOGRAPHICS
PEAK INCIDENCE: Between 35 and 50 yr old.
PREVALENCE: Increased in patients with underlying anxiety disorders.
PREDOMINANT SEX AND AGE:
- Sex: Females > males (2:1).
- Age: Adults over 60.
RISK FACTORS: Anxiety disorders, dry skin, insect bites.

PHYSICAL FINDINGS & CLINICAL PRESENTATION
- Patients present with profound pruritus and localized scaly plaques with accentuated skin markings said to resemble tree bark (Fig. 1L-22).
- Lichenified circumscribed plaques. Trauma from rubbing and scratching accounts for persistence of the plaque.
- Commonly involved areas include hands and wrists (Fig. 1L-23), back and sides of neck, anterior tibias, anogenital areas, the scalp, the upper eyelid, the orifice of both ears, and ankles.

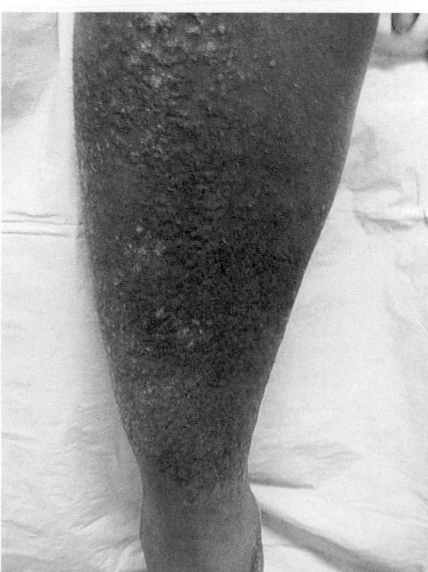

FIGURE 1L-22 Lichenified skin of the lower extremity caused by habitual rubbing. The confluence of multiple scaling papules has formed a large plaque of palpably thickened skin. (From Ferri FF et al: *Ferri's fast facts in dermatology,* Philadelphia, 2010, Saunders.)

ETIOLOGY
- Neurodermatitis due to long-term chronic rubbing and scratching more vigorously than a normal pain threshold would allow, resulting in thickened and leathery skin.
- Common triggers are excess dryness of skin, heat, sweat, and psychological stress. It can also accompany other conditions such as the fungal infections candidiasis or tinea cruris, or psoriasis, lichen sclerosus, and neoplasia, leading to squamous cell hyperplasia.
- Other causes include atrophic dermatitis and insect bites. Rare cases have shown links to lithium use, hair dye containing PPD, and long-term exposure to vehicle pollution.

DIAGNOSIS

DIFFERENTIAL DIAGNOSIS
- Lichen planus.
- Psoriasis.
- Atopic dermatitis.
- Insect bite.
- Nummular eczema.
- Contact dermatitis.
- Stasis dermatitis.

WORKUP
Patient history and skin examination. Skin biopsy when diagnosis is unclear or persistent symptoms.

LABORATORY TESTS
- Not generally necessary.
- Biopsy reveals hyperkeratosis, acanthosis, and mild to moderate lymphohistiocytic inflammatory infiltrate with prominent lichenification.

TREATMENT

NONPHARMACOLOGIC THERAPY
- Patient education is essential to break the itch-scratch cycle and facilitate treatment of any underlying dermatitis.
- Psychotherapy.

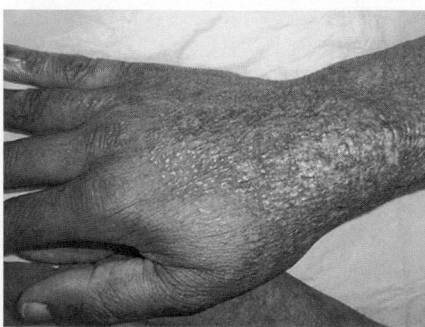

FIGURE 1L-23 Long-standing pruritus and scratching resulted in this thickened, hyperpigmented skin on the wrist consisting of numerous 1- to 2-mm papules. This "follicular" pattern is more common in African Americans. (From Ferri FF et al: *Ferri's fast facts in dermatology,* Philadelphia, 2010, Saunders.)

ACUTE GENERAL Rx
- Cessation of pruritus is the goal. Antihistamine hydroxyzine 25 mg at bedtime is effective in decreasing nocturnal itching.
- High-potency topical corticosteroids can be used initially but not indefinitely because of potential for steroid-induced atrophy.
- Steroid-containing tape may be effective in providing both occlusion and antiinflammatory effect.
- Intralesional corticosteroids.
- Anxiolytics, SSRIs.
- Oral doxepin (an antidepressant and anxiolytic).
- Mirtazapine.
- Tropical calcineurin inhibitor for vulvar lichenification.
Cyclosporin A
  Topical tacrolimus, 0.1% ointment, can be used for sensitive skin, face.
Botulinum intradermal injections.
  Alitretinoin, 30 mg daily for 3 mo, has shown some clinical improvement in case studies but needs further investigation as a potential rx.

CHRONIC Rx
Constant irritation of the skin must be avoided. Keeping skin moisturized, a covering to prevent scratching, or nail filing may be necessary.

DISPOSITION
Psychological intervention improves recovery. Regular follow-up visits facilitate long-term management.

REFERRAL
Refer to a psychologist for psychological evaluation and consultation, and a dermatologist in resistant cases.

PEARLS & CONSIDERATIONS

- Significant scratching may occur during nocturnal hours.
- The involved area is always at a site that is easily reached for scratching.
- Chronic scratching can also cause keratinocyte necrosis and the development of amyloid in the papillary dermis, called lichen amyloidosis.

COMMENTS
Patients may be at increased risk for scarring of the skin, changes in skin pigmentation, and bacterial and fungal infections of the involved skin.

PREVENTION
Prevent future incidences by continued therapy, stress management, and avoidance of common triggers and accompanying conditions.

SUGGESTED READINGS
Available at www.expertconsult.com

AUTHORS: **FRED F. FERRI, M.D.,** and
HEATHER FERRI, D.O.

 BASIC INFORMATION

DEFINITION

Listeriosis is a systemic infection caused by the gram-positive aerobic bacterium *Listeria monocytogenes.*

SYNONYMS

Listerial infection
Granulomatosis infantisepticum

ICD-10CM CODES
A32.0   Cutaneous listeriosis
A32.81 Oculoglandular listeriosis
A32.89 Other forms of listeriosis
A32.9   Listeriosis, unspecified
P37.2   Neonatal (disseminated) listeriosis

EPIDEMIOLOGY & DEMOGRAPHICS

INCIDENCE (IN U.S.):
- *Listeria* meningitis: about 0.7 cases/100,000 persons (fourth most common cause of community-acquired bacterial meningitis in adults)
- In pregnant women: 3.0 cases per 100,000 population
- In general population: 0.29 confirmed cases per 100,000 persons in 2009-2011 in the United States, but 1.3 per 100,000 cases in persons over the age of 65

PREDOMINANT SEX: Pregnant women are more susceptible to *Listeria* bacteremia, accounting for up to one third of reported cases.

PREDOMINANT AGE:
- Pregnant women
- Immunocompromised patients of any age
- Elderly patients are susceptible even in the absence of recognized immunocompromised states

GENETICS: Congenital infection:
- With transplacental transmission, syndrome termed *granulomatosis infantisepticum* in neonate
- Characterized by disseminated abscesses in multiple organs, skin lesions, and conjunctivitis
- Mortality: 33% to 100%

Neonatal infection:
- Infant becoming ill after 3 days of age; mother invariably asymptomatic
- Clinical picture of sepsis of unknown origin

PHYSICAL FINDINGS & CLINICAL PRESENTATION

Infections in pregnancy
1. More common in third trimester
2. Usually present with fever and chills without localizing symptoms or signs of infection
Meningoencephalitis
1. More common in neonates and immunocompromised patients, but up to 30% of adults have no underlying condition
2. In neonates: poor appetite with or without fever possibly the only presenting signs
3. In adults: presentation often subacute, with low-grade fever and personality change as only signs

4. Focal neurologic signs seen without demonstrable brain abscess on CT scan
Cerebritis/rhombencephalitis
1. Headache and fever may be only presenting complaints
2. Progressive cranial nerve palsies, hemiparesis, seizures, depressed level of consciousness, cerebellar signs, respiratory insufficiency may also be seen
Focal infections
1. Ocular infections (purulent conjunctivitis) and skin lesions (granulomatosis infantisepticum) as a result of inadvertent inoculation by laboratory and veterinary personnel
2. Others: arthritis, prosthetic joint infections, peritonitis, osteomyelitis, organ abscesses, cholecystitis

ETIOLOGY

- Direct invasion of skin and eye has been documented, but mechanism of GI entry is unclear.
- Organism's intracellular life cycle explanatory of:
  1. Importance of cell-mediated immunity in host defense
  2. Increased infection in neonates, pregnant women, and immunocompromised hosts

 **DIAGNOSIS**

DIFFERENTIAL DIAGNOSIS

- Meningitis caused by other bacteria, mycobacteria, or fungi
- CNS sarcoidosis
- Brain neoplasm or abscess
- Tuberculous and fungal (especially cryptococcal) meningitis
- Cerebral toxoplasmosis
- Lyme disease
- Sarcoidosis

WORKUP

Dictated by age, end-organ involvement, and immune status

LABORATORY TESTS

- Cultures of blood and other appropriate body fluids
- Variable CSF findings, but neutrophils usually predominate
- Organisms uncommonly seen on Gram stain and may be difficult to identify morphologically
- Monoclonal antibodies, polymerase chain reaction, and DNA probe techniques to detect *Listeria* in foods

IMAGING STUDIES

- If focal cerebral involvement suspected: CT scan or MRI
- MRI most sensitive for evaluation of brainstem and cerebellum

TREATMENT

Empiric therapy should be administered when diagnosis is suspected because overall mortality is 23%.

ACUTE GENERAL Rx

- Drugs of choice:
  1. IV ampicillin 2 g IV q 4 hr for adults. Children: 300 mg/kg per day IV in 4 to 6 divided doses. Infants 8 days to 1 month: 150 to 200 mg/kg per day divided in four doses. For infants ≤7 days: 100 mg/kg per day divided in two doses for infants weighing <2000 g and 150 mg/kg per day divided in three doses for infants weighing more than 2000 g.
  2. IV penicillin 12 to 24 million U/day in divided doses.
- Continuation of therapy for 2 weeks for bacteremia; 2 to 4 weeks for meningitis.
- Alternative (if penicillin allergic): trimethoprim/sulfamethoxazole or vancomycin.
- Gentamicin IV added to provide synergy in meningitis or endocarditis patients of any age.

CHRONIC Rx

Relapses reported, especially in immunocompromised hosts, after 2 wk of therapy.

DISPOSITION

Long-term follow-up of immunodeficiency state.

REFERRAL

Infectious disease consultation for all patients.

PEARLS & CONSIDERATIONS

COMMENTS

- Foodborne cases (1600 cases occur annually with a mortality rate of 16%) have been linked to various products: coleslaw, soft cheeses, unpasteurized milk and milk products, vegetables, undercooked chicken, hot dogs, luncheon meats, refrigerated smoked seafood, and so on.
- Complete decontamination of food products is difficult because *Listeria* is resistant to pasteurization and refrigeration.

SUGGESTED READINGS
Available at www.expertconsult.com

RELATED CONTENT
Listeriosis (Patient Information)

AUTHOR: **GLENN G. FORT, M.D., M.P.H.**

BASIC INFORMATION

DEFINITION
Liver abscess is a necrotic infection of the liver usually classified as pyogenic or amebic.

SYNONYMS
Pyogenic hepatic abscess
Amebic hepatic abscess

ICD-10CM CODES
K75.0 Abscess of liver

EPIDEMIOLOGY & DEMOGRAPHICS
INCIDENCE: Incidence of pyogenic liver abscess is 2.3 cases per 100,000 population.
PREVALANCE (WORLDWIDE): Amebic liver abscess is more common than pyogenic liver abscess.
PREVALENCE (IN U.S.): Pyogenic liver abscess is more common than amebic liver abscess.
PREDOMINANT SEX AND AGE: More common in men than women; male/female ratio of 2:1; most common in fourth to sixth decades of life.

PHYSICAL FINDINGS & CLINICAL PRESENTATION
- Fever, chills, and sweats
- Weakness/malaise
- Anorexia with weight loss
- Nausea, vomiting, and diarrhea
- Cough with pleuritic chest pain
- Right upper quadrant abdominal pain
- Hepatomegaly
- Splenomegaly
- Jaundice
- Pleural effusions, rales, and friction rubs may be present
- Most abscesses occur on the right lobe of the liver

ETIOLOGY
- Pyogenic liver abscess is usually polymicrobial (*Klebsiella pneumoniae* [43%], *Escherichia coli* [33%], *Streptococcus* spp. [37%], *Pseudomonas aeruginosa*, *Proteus* spp., *Bacteroides* spp. [24%], *Fusobacterium* spp., *Actinomyces* spp., gram-positive anaerobes, and *Staphylococcus aureus*).
- Pyogenic liver abscess occurs from:
  1. Biliary disease with cholangitis (accounts for approximately 40%-60%).
  2. Gallbladder disease with contiguous spread to the liver.
  3. Diverticulitis or appendicitis with spread via the portal circulation.
  4. Hematogenous spread via the hepatic artery, though uncommon; if a solitary organism is isolated, a distant source of hematogenous seeding should be sought.
  5. Penetrating wounds.
  6. Cryptogenic.
  7. Infection by way of portal system (portal pyemia).
  8. No causes found in approximately half of cases.
  9. Incidence increased in patients with diabetes and metastatic cancer.
  10. Table 1L-16 summarizes underlying etiology and bacteriology of liver abscesses.
- Amebic hepatic abscess is caused by the parasite *Entamoeba histolytica*. Amebiasis is usually due to fecal-oral contamination and invades the intestinal mucosa, gaining entry into the portal system to reach the liver. Amebic abscess occurs in 3% to 7% of patients with amebiasis.
Box 1L-2 describes pearls for amebic liver abscesses. The abscess is usually solitary (85%) and in the right lobe (72%).

DIAGNOSIS

The diagnosis of liver abscess requires a high index of suspicion after a detailed history and physical examination. Imaging studies and microbiologic, serologic, and percutaneous techniques (e.g., aspiration) confirm the presence of a liver abscess.

DIFFERENTIAL DIAGNOSIS
- Cholangitis
- Cholecystitis
- Diverticulitis
- Appendicitis
- Perforated viscus
- Mesentery ischemia
- Pulmonary embolism
- Pancreatitis

WORKUP
- The workup of a liver abscess should focus on differentiating between amebic and pyogenic causes.
- Features suggesting an amebic cause include travel to an endemic area, single abscess rather than multiple abscesses, subacute onset of symptoms, and absence of conditions predisposing to pyogenic liver abscess, as highlighted under "Etiology."
- Laboratory studies are not specific but are useful as adjunctive tests.
- Imaging studies cannot differentiate between the two, and bacteriologic cultures may be sterile in 50% of the cases.

LABORATORY TESTS
- Complete blood count: leukocytosis
- Liver function tests: alkaline phosphatase is most commonly elevated (95%-100%); aspartate transaminase (AST) and alanine transaminase (ALT) elevated in 50% of cases; elevated bilirubin (28%-30%); decreased albumin
- Prothrombin time (INR): prolonged (70%)
- Blood cultures: positive in 50% of cases
- Aspiration (50% sterile)
- Stool samples for *E. histolytica* trophozoites (positive in 10%-15% of amebic liver abscess cases)
- Serologic testing for *E. histolytica* should be done on all patients, but it is important to remember that it does not differentiate acute from old infections.

IMAGING STUDIES
- Ultrasound (80%-100% sensitivity in detecting abscesses) shows round or oval hypoechogenic mass (Fig. 1L-24, *A*).
- CT scan is more sensitive in detecting hepatic abscesses and contiguous organ extension and is the imaging study of choice (Fig. 1L-24, *B*, and Fig. 1L-25).
- Chest x-ray: abnormal in 50% of the cases, may reveal elevated right hemidiaphragm, subdiaphragmatic air-fluid levels, pleural effusions, and consolidating infiltrates.

TABLE 1L-16 Underlying Etiology and Bacteriology

Etiology	Bacteriology
Biliary, benign	*Escherichia coli* *Klebsiella* spp. *Enterococcus*
Biliary, malignant	*Pseudomonas* spp. Multiply resistant GN aerobes VRE Yeast
Diverticulitis/ appendicitis	GN aerobes *Bacteroides fragilis*
Severe cholecystitis	See Biliary, benign *Clostridium perfringens* *Bacteroides* spp.
Subcutaneous abscess	*Staphylococcus* spp. MRSA
Endocarditis	*Enterococcus* spp. *Staphyloccus* spp.
Cryptogenic	Anaerobes

GN, Gram-negative.
From Cameron, JL, Cameron AM: *Current surgical therapy*, ed 10, Philadelphia, 2011, Saunders.

BOX 1L-2 Pearls for Amebic Liver Abscesses

- Only 10%-20% of patients with amebic liver abscess have a history of diarrhea.
- Treat the intestinal infection to prevent relapse of amebic liver abscess. Failure to use luminal amebicidal agents after metronidazole in cases of amebic abscess results in a 10% relapse rate.
- Failure to show response to antiamebic medication requires evaluation for polymicrobial infection with bacteria.
- Amebic abscess usually responds clinically to antimicrobial therapy in 3 to 7 days, although imaging takes several months to show resolution.
- Percutaneous drainage is rarely required.

From Cameron, JL, Cameron AM: *Current surgical therapy*, ed 10, Philadelphia, 2011, Saunders.

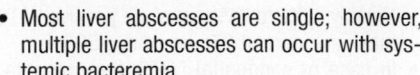

- Most liver abscesses are single; however, multiple liver abscesses can occur with systemic bacteremia.

 **TREATMENT**

NONPHARMACOLOGIC THERAPY

- The management of pyogenic liver abscess differs from that of amebic liver abscess.
- Medical management is the cornerstone of therapy in amebic liver abscess, whereas early intervention in the form of surgical therapy or catheter drainage and parenteral antibiotics is the rule in pyogenic liver abscess.

ACUTE GENERAL Rx

- Percutaneous drainage under CT or ultrasound guidance is essential in the treatment of pyogenic liver abscesses.
- Aspiration of hepatic amebic abscesses is not required unless there is no response to treatment or a pyogenic cause is being considered.
- Empiric broad-spectrum antibiotics are recommended initially until culture results are available. Common choices include:
  1. Metronidazole (500 mg IV q8h) plus ceftriaxone or levofloxacin.
  2. Monotherapy with a beta-lactam/beta-lactamase inhibitor, such as piperacillin/tazobactam (4.5 g q6h), ticarcillin-clavulanate (3.1 g q4h), or ampicillin-sulbactam (3 g q6h).
  3. Monotherapy with a carbapenem, such as imipenem (500 mg IV q6h), meropenem (1 g q8h), or ertapenem (1 g daily).
  4. Duration of antibiotic treatment is usually 4 to 6 wk with IV antibiotics used for the first 1 to 2 wk or until a favorable clinical response, followed thereafter with oral antibiotics (e.g., metronidazole 500 mg PO q8h plus ciprofloxacin 500 mg PO q12h).
  5. Third-generation cephalosporins should not be used as single agents for empiric therapy because of risk of the emergence of beta-lactamase-producing bacteria.
- Antibiotic coverage for amebic liver abscesses includes:
  1. Tissue agent: metronidazole 750 mg PO tid for 10 days
  2. Luminal agent: after therapy with tissue agent treatment with any luminal agent is required even if the stool is negative, such as paromomycin for 10 days or diiodohydroxyquin for 20 days.

CHRONIC Rx

- If fever persists for 2 wk despite percutaneous drainage and antibiotic therapy as outlined under "Acute General Rx," or if there is failure of aspiration or failure of percutaneous drainage, surgery is indicated.
- In patients not responding to intravenous antibiotics and percutaneous drainage, hepatic artery antibiotic infusion can be considered.
- In patients with evidence of metastatic disease that is causing biliary obstruction, a gastroenterology consultation for endoscopic retrograde cholangiopancreatography and stenting should be considered.

DISPOSITION

- Most patients with pyogenic liver abscesses defervesce within 2 wk of treatment with antibiotics and drainage.
- No randomized controlled studies have evaluated the optimal duration of antibiotic therapy for pyogenic liver abscess. Typical duration of antibiotic therapy is at least 4 to 6 wk.
- Pyogenic liver abscess cure rates using percutaneous drainage and antibiotics have been reported to be between 88% and 100%.
- Mortality rate of untreated pyogenic liver abscess is nearly 100%.
- Most patients with amebic liver abscesses defervesce within 4 to 5 days of treatment.
- Amebic liver abscess mortality rate is <1% unless complications occur (see "Comments").
- Follow-up imaging should be used to monitor response to therapy; continue treatment until CT scan shows complete or near-complete resolution of cavity.

REFERRAL

Infectious disease, gastroenterology, interventional radiology, and general surgical consultations are recommended in any patient with hepatic abscess.

 **PEARLS AND CONSIDERATIONS**

COMMENTS

- Complications of pyogenic and amebic liver abscesses include:
  1. Pleuropulmonary extension, resulting in empyema, abscess, and fistula formation
  2. Peritonitis
  3. Purulent pericarditis
  4. Sepsis
- Amebic liver abscesses complicate amebic colitis in nearly 10% of cases.

SUGGESTED READINGS

Available at www.expertconsult.com

RELATED CONTENT

Liver Abscess (Patient Information)

AUTHOR: **TANYA ALI, M.D.**

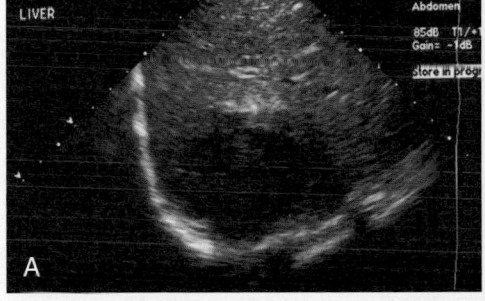
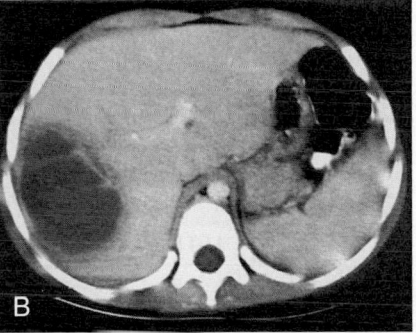

FIGURE 1L-24 A, Amebic abscess. Sonogram demonstrates a hypoechogenic mass in the right lobe of the liver with a more hypoechoic surrounding rim. **B,** CT scan demonstrates a low-attenuation mass in the right lobe of the liver with a prominent halo. (From Kuhn JP et al: *Caffrey's pediatric diagnostic imaging*, vol 2, ed 10, Philadelphia, 2004, Mosby.)

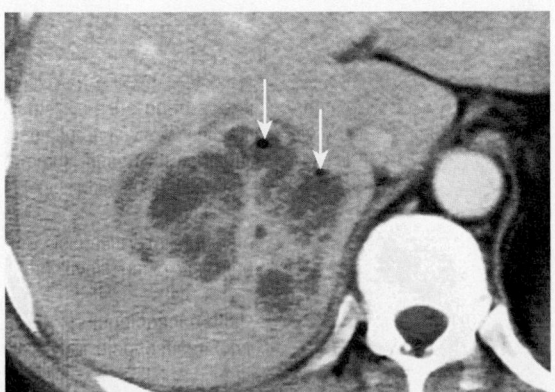

FIGURE 1L-25 ta Pyogenic liver abscess. A liver abscess containing *Escherichia coli* has irregular septations and contains a few bubbles of air (*arrows*). Because of the multiple loculations, this abscess did not respond to a percutaneous catheter for drainage and required surgical debridement. (Webb WR, Brant WE, Major NM: *Fundamentals of body CT*, ed 4, Philadelphia, 2015, Saunders.)

BASIC INFORMATION

DEFINITION

Long QT syndrome (LQTS) is a disorder of myocardial repolarization characterized by a prolongation of the QT interval on the ECG associated with an increased risk of developing life-threatening ventricular arrhythmias, most commonly torsades de pointes (a specific type of polymorphic ventricular tachycardia), which may lead to ventricular fibrillation and sudden cardiac death (SCD). This syndrome may be either genetic or acquired.

SYNONYMS

LQTS
Congenital forms:
  Jervell and Lange-Nielsen syndrome (associated with deafness)
  Romano-Ward syndrome (associated with normal hearing)

ICD-10CM CODES
I45.81 Long QT syndrome

EPIDEMIOLOGY & DEMOGRAPHICS

- Congenital LQTS is thought to account for >3000 deaths in childhood per year in the United States.
- Prevalence is felt to be 1:2000 of apparently healthy white young births. It may be higher because this is based on genetic testing of infants in whom the QTc was in excess of 470 and 460 milliseconds, respectively (Schwartz, 2009).
- Presence of LQTS has been shown in all racial groups. Review of data from the US portion of the international LQTS registry found a lower incidence but higher severity of QT prolongation among African Americans. These findings could be in part attributable to socioeconomic factors. (Fugate 2010)
- Incidence of LQTS is thought to be between 1:2500 and 1:10,000 in the general population, although it has been difficult to estimate due to incomplete penetrance. Congenital form associated with deafness is autosomal recessive (Jervell and Lange Nielsen syndrome) and is less common than the autosomal dominant form as well as more severe.
- Congenital form associated with normal hearing (Romano-Ward syndrome) is autosomal dominant. Although inheritance of LQTS is autosomal dominant, female predominance has often been observed and has been attributed to an increased susceptibility to cardiac arrhythmias in women. LQTS is more likely to express itself before puberty in males and after puberty in females.
- At least 15 different LQTS genes have been identified to date. LQTS is more common in women than in men.
- Mortality rate is estimated to be about 1% per year.
- Genetic mutations in the congenital LQTS are described in Table 1L-17. Common types of LQTS are described in Table 1L-18.

PHYSICAL FINDINGS & CLINICAL PRESENTATION

- Many episodes are stress mediated.
- Palpitations, presyncope.
- Syncope caused by ventricular tachycardia.
- SCD.
- Seizure.
- Family history of LQTS, but a family history of SCD has not been proved to be a risk factor for SCD in patients with LQTS.
- Abnormal ECG (prolonged QT) in asymptomatic relatives of known case.
- Prolonged QTc interval on ECG (QTc should be >460 ms in women and >440 ms in men).
- Notably, 20% to 25% genotype positive LQTS may have normal QTc on resting ECG.
- In case of congenital LQTS, the presentation of syncope or SCD is typically triggered by exercise and swimming in LQT1 patients, in LQT2 patients by emotion, pregnancy, or noise, and patients with LQT3 are at highest risk of events when at rest or asleep.

ETIOLOGY

- Cardiac repolarization abnormality.
- Congenital cause (hundreds of mutations on more than 10 genes have been identified).

TABLE 1L-17 Genetic Mutations in Congenital Long QT Syndrome

		Location	Gene	Current	Effect
Romano-Ward syndrome (autosomal-dominant inheritance)	LQT1	11p15.5	KCNQ1 (K+ channel)	I_{Ks}	↓ Function ↓ Repolarization
	LQT2	7q35-36	KCNH2 (K+ channel)	I_{Kr}	↓ Function ↓ Repolarization
	LQT3	3q21-24	SCN5A (Na+ channel)	I_{Na}	↑ Function ↑ Depolarization
	LQT4	4q25-27	ANK2	Unknown	Unknown
	LQT5	21q22	KCNE1 (K+ channel, sub-unit minK)	I_{Ks}	↓ Function ↓ Repolarization
Jervell and Lange-Nielsen syndrome (autosomal-recessive inheritance)		11p15.5	KvLQT1 (K+ channel)	I_{Ks}	↓ Function ↓ Repolarization
		21q22	KCNE 1 (K+ channel, sub-unit minK)	I_{Ks}	↓ Function ↓ Repolarization

From Crawford MH et al (eds): *Cardiology*, ed 2, St Louis, 2004, Mosby.

TABLE 1L-18 Common Types of Long QT (LQT) Syndrome

	LQT1	LQT2	LQT3
Pathophysiology			
Gene	KCNQ1 (KvLQT1)	KCNH2 (HERG)	SCN5A
Protein	$K_v7.1$	$K_v11.1$	$Na_v1.5$
Ionic current	Decreased I_{Ks}	Decreased I_{Kr}	Increased late I_{Na}
Clinical Presentation			
Incidence of cardiac events	63%	46%	18%
Incidence of SCD	4%	4%	4%
Arrhythmia triggers	Emotional/physical stress (swimming, diving)	Emotional stress, arousal (alarm clock, telephone), rest	Sleep/rest
ECG	Broad-based T wave	Low-amplitude, bifid T wave	Long isoelectric ST segment
QT response to exercise	Attenuated QTc shortening and an exaggerated QTc prolongation during early and peak exercise	Normal QT during exercise but with exaggerated QT hysteresis	Supernormal QT shortening
Management			
Exercise restriction	+++	++	?
Response to beta blockers	+++	+++	?
Potassium supplement	+	++	+
Left cervicothoracic sympathectomy	++	++	++
Response to mexiletine	+	+	++

From Issa Z et al: *Clinical arrhythmology and electrophysiology,* ed 2, Philadelphia, 2012, Saunders.

- Most of the gene mutations affect function of ion channels leading to prolonged repolarization (i.e., sodium and potassium channels resulting in either increased Na^+ influx or decreased K^+ efflux). These mutations prolong depolarization and predispose the patient to torsades de pointes.
- Acquired causes:
  1. Drugs: dofetilide, ibutilide, bepridil, quinidine, procainamide, sotalol, amiodarone, ranolazine, disopyramide, phenothiazines and antiemetic agents (droperidol, domperidone), tricyclic antidepressants, antipsychotics (quetiapine, ziprasidone, iloperidone), citalopram, antihistamines, quinolones, azithromycin, astemizole or cisapride given with ketoconazole or erythromycin, clarithromycin, and antimalarials, particularly among patients with asthma or those using potassium-lowering medications; also common in patients receiving methadone.
  2. Hypokalemia, hypomagnesemia, hypocalcemia (especially in patients with malabsorption syndrome).
  3. Liquid protein diet.
  4. Central nervous system lesions.
  5. Ischemia.
  6. Hypothyroidism.

Dx DIAGNOSIS

DIFFERENTIAL DIAGNOSIS

See "Syncope." Brugada's syndrome, arrhythmogenic right ventricular dysplasia, and LQTS are major causes of genetic sudden death syndromes (Fig. 1L-26).

Diagnostic criteria for the congenital LQTS as per 2013 HRS Guidelines:

LQTS is diagnosed:

a. In the presence of an LQTS risk score ≥3.5 in the absence of a secondary cause for QT prolongation and/or

b. In the presence of an unequivocally pathogenic mutation in one of the LQTS genes or

c. In the presence of a QT interval corrected for heart rate using Bazett's formula (QTc) ≥500 ms in repeated 12-lead electrocardiogram (ECG) and in the absence of a secondary cause for QT prolongation.

d. LQTS can be diagnosed in the presence of a QTc between 480 and 499 ms in repeated 12-lead ECGs in a patient with unexplained syncope in the absence of a secondary cause for QT prolongation and in the absence of a pathogenic mutation.

LQTS Risk Score (Schwartz 2011):

ECG Criteria

QTc >480 ms	3 points
QTc 460-480 ms	2 points
QTc 450-460 ms (males)	1 point
QTc 4th minute of recovery from exercise stress test >480 ms	1 point
Torsades de pointes	2 points
T-wave alternans	1 point
Notched T wave in three leads	1 point
Bradycardia	0.5 point

History

Syncope with stress	2 points
Syncope without stress	1 point
Congenital deafness	0.5 point
Definite family history of long QT	1 point
Unexplained cardiac death in first-degree relative <30 yr	0.5 point

Total score: 1 point: low probability of LQTS. 1.5 to 3 points: intermediate probability of LQTS. ≥ 3.5 points high probability.

WORKUP

Cardiology referral is recommended for all cases.

Genetic analysis is an essential step for risk stratification of patients with congenital prolonged QT and is important for identification of potential mutation carriers within the proband family. There is evidence for gene-specific triggers of events and therapeutic efficacy. Molecular screening should become part of the routine clinical management of LQTS.

In relatives of known patients with LQTS or in young patients with syncope:

- Stress test may prolong the QT interval or cause T-wave alternans.
- Valsalva maneuver: may prolong the QT interval or cause T-wave alternans.
- Prolonged ECG monitoring with various stimulations aimed at increasing catecholamines and assess for QT prolongation (perform in a setting that can provide resuscitation with α- and β-antagonists readily available).
- Epinephrine-induced prolongation of the QT interval (epinephrine infusion QT stress test)
- Genetic analysis
  1. *LQT1* locus of *KCNQ1* potassium channel gene.
  2. *LQT2* locus of *KCNH2* potassium channel gene.
  3. *LQT3* locus of *SCN5A* sodium channel gene.
  4. These three variants account for >90% of all genotyped LQTS patients, whereas the remaining genes are responsible for a minority of cases.
- Risk stratification for each genetic variant on the basis of gender and QTc: groups are defined on the basis of the probability of the first cardiac event (syncope, cardiac arrest, or sudden death) before the age of 40 years or before therapy. Specific mutations, depending on type, location, and degree, may confer a high risk even if the ECG abnormalities are mild. Clinically, QT interval duration was the strongest predictor of risk for cardiac events; a QTc exceeding 500 ms identifies patients with the highest risk.
  1. High risk (>50% of cardiac event): QTc ≥ 500 ms and LQT1 or LQT2, or male with LQT3.
  2. Moderate risk (30%-50%): QTc <500 ms in male with LQT3 or in female with LQT2 or LQT3, and female with LQT3 with QTc ≥500 ms.
  3. Low risk (<30%): QTc <500 ms and LQT1 or male LQT2 with QTc <500 ms.

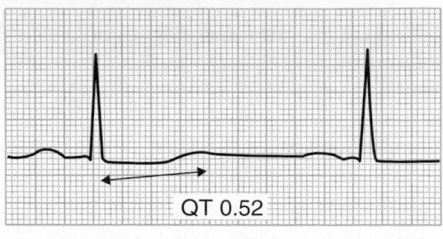

A

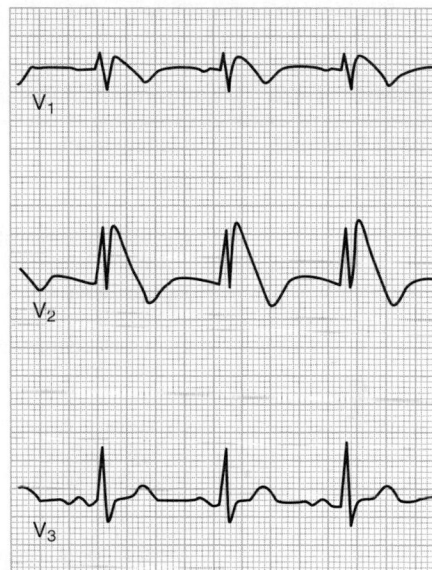

B

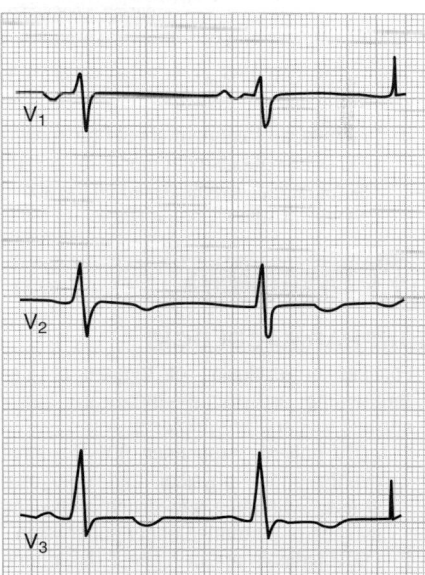

C

FIGURE 1L-26 Sinus rhythm electrocardiogram findings in three genetic sudden death syndromes. A, QT prolongation during sinus rhythm in a patient with long QT syndrome. **B,** ST elevation in V_1 and V_2 in a patient with Brugada's syndrome. **C,** T wave inversion in V_1-V_3 in a patient with arrhythmogenic right ventricular dysplasia. (From Goldman L, Schafer AI: *Goldman's Cecil medicine,* ed 24, Philadelphia, 2012, Saunders.)

TABLE 1L-19 Cardiac Event Risk Stratification Scheme Based on Genes, Gender, and QTc

Genetic Subtype	QTc <500 ms		QTc ≥550 ms	
	Male	Female	Male	Female
LQT1	Low	Low	High	High
LQT2	Low	Intermediate	High	High
LQT3	Intermediate	Intermediate	High	Intermediate

Probability of the first cardiac event (syncope, cardiac arrest, or sudden death) before the age of 40 years or before therapy. High = >50%, Intermediate = 30%-50%, Low = <30%.

TABLE 1L-20 Management of Patients with Long QT Syndrome

Type of Syndrome	Management	Indication
Congenital	Beta-blockers	Asymptomatic patients, symptomatic patients (who do not have bronchospasm)
	Cervicothoracic sympathectomy	Refractory symptoms, especially in pediatric patients
	Cardiac pacing	Refractory symptoms associated with bradycardia, pauses
	Implantable cardioverter-defibrillator	Cardiac arrest, refractory syncope, prophylaxis for moderate- to high-risk patients for cardiac events
Acquired	Elimination of causative drug or condition	All patients
	Magnesium sulfate	Nonsustained ventricular tachycardia, torsades de pointes (even with a normal serum magnesium concentration)
	Administration of potassium (to keep serum K+ >4.5 mEq/L)	Serum K+ <4.5 mEq/L
	Maneuvers to increase heart rate (cardiac pacing, isoproterenol)	Bradycardia, arrhythmias refractory to magnesium sulfate

K+, Potassium.
Adapted from Crawford MH et al (eds): *Cardiology*, ed 2, St Louis, 2004, Mosby.

4. Prophylactic treatment should be considered in all patients with moderate or high risk for cardiac events based on the above risk stratification scheme (Table 1L-19).

Rx TREATMENT

NONPHARMACOLOGIC

- Focuses on exclusion of triggers of life-threatening arrhythmia—there are gene-specific triggers for symptoms:
  1. *LQT1* patients experience 90% of lethal events under physical and emotional stress. Swimming and diving should be avoided or performed under supervision.
  2. *LQT2* patients are at highest risk during arousal or emotions, also during sleep and at rest but not at all during exercise; avoid sudden or excessive acoustic stimuli, especially during sleep (e.g., avoid telephone and/or alarm clock in the proximity)—as opposed to *LQT3* patients, in whom 80% of the events occur at rest or while asleep.
- Previously, all patient with LQTS have been instructed to avoid competitive sports. More recently, low risk, genetically confirmed LQTS

with borderline QTc prolongation, without prior cardiac symptoms and no familial history of SCD are thought to be safe to participate in competitive sports where AED and BLS personnel is available.

- Implantation of an implantable cardioverter-defibrillator (ICD) is recommended according to the ACC/AHA guidelines for patients with a good functional status for more than 1 yr and the following conditions (Table 1L-20):
  1. Survivors of cardiac arrest (class 1).
  2. Patients with syncope or ventricular tachycardia while receiving β-blockers (class IIa).
  3. Prophylaxis of SCD with use of β-blocker in patients with characteristics that suggest high risk (such as *LQT2* and *LQT3*, *QTc >500 ms*) (class IIb).

PHARMACOLOGIC

- With few exceptions (mostly borderline QTc and *LQT1* males aged >25 to 30 yr), all mutation carriers should be treated because of the risk of SCD during first cardiac event. All symptomatic patients should be treated as well.
- Beta-blockers an initial therapy of choice—there are differential responses to β-blocker

therapy among different genetic variants; especially effective among LQT1 patients. Studies showed the efficacy of β-blockers with an overall mortality <2% over a mean follow-up exceeding 5 yr.

- In patients with LQT3, mexiletine shortens the QTc and can be given with a β-blocker.
- In the 20% to 30% of patients who continue to have symptoms on a β-blocker, the main options are either left cardiac sympathetic denervation (LCSD) or the prophylactic implantation of an ICD.
- In patients with frequent ICD shocks or in those with high risk for SCD where ICD placement cannot be performed, cardiac pacing and/or LCSD may be indicated.
- In patients with recurrent syncope and/or aborted cardiac arrest despite combined ICD and β-blocker, LCSD as adjunctive therapy can be performed.
- Correctable factors including electrolyte disorder—hypokalemia and hypomagnesemia—and avoidance of precipitating drugs that may further prolong the QT interval is mandatory. A complete list of drugs that can potentially prolong QT may be found at www.qtdrugs.org.
- For patients with acquired form and torsades de pointes, IV magnesium and atrial or ventricular pacing are initial choices.
- Table 1L-20 summarizes management of patients with LQTS.

PROGNOSIS

In carefully treated patients, mortality is around 0.5% to 1% over 20 years.

The timing and frequency of syncope, QTc prolongation, and gender are predictive of risk for aborted cardiac arrest and SCD during adolescence. Higher risk is present in those with one or two or more episodes of syncope in the last 10 yr compared with those with no syncopal episodes, those with QTc >530 ms, and males aged 10 to 12 yr.

! PEARLS & CONSIDERATIONS

COMMENTS

Family history should be assessed for a history of sudden death and other deaths that may have occurred as manifestations of LQTS (e.g., sudden infant death, drowning, and loss of consciousness while driving).

SUGGESTED READINGS

Available at www.expertconsult.com

RELATED CONTENT

Long QT Syndrome (Patient Information)
Torsades de Pointes (Related Key Topic)

AUTHORS: **SIMON GRINGUT, M.D.**, and **BARRY FINE, M.D., Ph.D.**

Diseases
and Disorders

I

BASIC INFORMATION

DEFINITION

A lung abscess is an infection of the lung parenchyma resulting in a necrotic cavity containing pus.

SYNONYMS

Pulmonary abscess

ICD-10CM CODES

J85.1 Abscess of lung with pneumonia
J85.2 Abscess of lung without pneumonia
A06.5 Amebic lung abscess

EPIDEMIOLOGY & DEMOGRAPHICS

INCIDENCE: Has decreased over the last 30 years as a result of antibiotic therapy.

- Lung abscess in patients age 50 and over is associated with primary lung neoplasia in 30% of the cases.
- Lung abscesses commonly coexist with empyemas.

RISK FACTORS (SEE TABLE 1L-25):

1. Alcohol-related problems
2. Seizure disorders
3. Cerebrovascular disorders with dysphagia
4. Drug abuse
5. Esophageal disorders (e.g., scleroderma, esophageal carcinoma, etc.)
6. Poor oral hygiene
7. Obstructive malignant lung disease
8. Bronchiectasis

PHYSICAL FINDINGS & CLINICAL PRESENTATION

- Symptoms are generally insidious and prolonged, occurring for weeks to months
- Fever, chills, and sweats
- Cough
- Sputum production (purulent with foul odor)
- Pleuritic chest pain
- Hemoptysis
- Dyspnea
- Malaise, fatigue, and weakness
- Tachycardia and tachypnea
- Dullness to percussion, whispered pectoriloquy, and bronchophony
- Amphoric breath sounds (low-pitched sound of air moving across a large open cavity)

ETIOLOGY

- The most important factor predisposing to lung abscess is aspiration.
- Following aspiration as a major predisposing factor is periodontal disease.
- Lung abscess is rare in an edentulous person.
- Approximately 90% of lung abscesses are caused by anaerobic microorganisms (peptostreptococci, microaerophilic streptococci such as *Streptococcus milleri, Bacteroides* species, *Fusobacterium nucleatum, Prevotella*). Pulmonary actinomycosis will also generate lung abscess.
- In most cases anaerobic infection is mixed with aerobic or facultative anaerobic organisms (*S. aureus, E. coli, K. pneumoniae, P. aeruginosa*).
- Parasitic organisms including *Paragonimus westermani* and *Entamoeba histolytica*.
- Fungi including *Aspergillus, Cryptococcus, Histoplasma, Blastomyces,* and *Coccidioides* spp.
- Immunocompromised hosts may become infected with *Aspergillus,* mycobacteria, *Nocardia, Legionella micdadei,* and *Rhodococcus equi.*
- Lung necrosis caused by community strains of MRSA (USA 300 strain) in young adults or adolescents after acute influenza was initially reported in 2002 and can be quite fulminant.

DIAGNOSIS

Lung abscess may be primary or secondary.
- *Primary lung abscess* refers to infection from normal host organisms within the lung (e.g., aspiration, pneumonia).
- Secondary lung abscess results from other preexisting conditions (e.g., endocarditis, underlying lung cancer, pulmonary emboli).
Lung abscess may be acute or chronic.
- Acute lung abscess is present if symptoms are of less than 4 to 6 wk.
- Chronic lung abscess is present if symptoms last longer than 6 wk.

DIFFERENTIAL DIAGNOSIS

The differential diagnosis is similar to that for cavitary lung lesions:
- Bacterial (anaerobic, aerobic, infected bulla, empyema, actinomycosis, tuberculosis)

- Fungal (histoplasmosis, coccidioidomycosis, blastomycosis, aspergillosis, cryptococcosis, zygomycetes)
- Parasitic (amebiasis, echinococcosis)
- Malignancy (primary lung carcinoma, metastatic lung disease, lymphoma, Hodgkin's disease)
- Granulomatosis with polyangiitis, sarcoidosis, endocarditis, and septic pulmonary emboli

WORKUP

- The workup of a patient with lung abscess attempts to elicit a primary or a secondary cause.
- Blood tests are not specific in diagnosing lung abscesses.
- Most diagnoses are made from imaging studies; however, to diagnose a specific cause bacteriologic studies are needed.

LABORATORY TESTS

- CBC with leukocytosis
- Bacteriologic studies
  1. Sputum Gram stain and culture (commonly contaminated by oral flora)
  2. Percutaneous transtracheal aspiration
  3. Percutaneous transthoracic aspiration
  4. Fiberoptic bronchoscopy using bronchial brushings or bronchoalveolar lavage is the most widely used intervention when trying to obtain diagnostic bacteriologic cultures
- Blood cultures on some occasions (<30%) may be positive
- If an empyema is present, obtaining empyema fluid via thoracentesis may isolate the organism

IMAGING STUDIES

- Chest x-ray makes the diagnosis of lung abscess showing the cavitary lesion with an air-fluid level.
- Lung abscesses are most commonly found in the posterior segment of the right upper lobe.
- Chest CT scan can localize and size the lesion and assist in differentiating lung abscesses from other pathologic processes (e.g., tumor, empyema, infected bulla, etc.) (Fig. 1L-29).

TREATMENT

NONPHARMACOLOGIC THERAPY

- Oxygen therapy
- Postural drainage
- Respiratory therapy maneuvers

ACUTE GENERAL Rx

Piperacillin/tazobactam 3.375 g IV q6h in aspiration pneumonia with lung abscess

- Ceftriaxone 1 g IV q24h plus metronidazole 1 g IV q12h
- Clindamycin is more effective for anaerobic lung abscess than penicillin alone. Dose: 600 mg IV q8h until improved, then 300 to 600 mg PO q6h.

TABLE 1L-25   Risk Factors for Aspiration Pneumonia and Lung Abscess

Increased bacterial inoculum	Periodontal disease, gingivitis, tonsillar or dental abscess, drugs that decrease gastric acidity
Impairment of consciousness	Drugs, alcohol, general anesthesia, metabolic encephalopathy, coma, shock, cerebrovascular accident, cardiopulmonary arrest, seizures, surgery, trauma
Impaired cough and gag reflexes	Vocal cord paralysis, intratracheal anesthesia, endotracheal tube, tracheostomy, myopathy, myelopathy, other neurologic disorders
Impairment of esophageal function	Diverticula, achalasia, strictures, disorders of gastrointestinal motility, neoplasm, tracheoesophageal fistula, pseudobulbar palsy
Emesis	Nasogastric tube, gastric dilation, ileus, intestinal obstruction

From Cohen J, Powderly WG: *Infectious diseases,* ed 2, St Louis, 2004, Mosby.

- Penicillin 1 to 2 million units IV q4h until improvement (afebrile, decreased phlegm production), followed by penicillin VK 500 mg PO q6h for 2 to 3 weeks but often up to 6 to 8 weeks) can be given with metronidazole doses of 7.5 mg/kg IV q6h followed by PO 500 mg bid to qid dosing as an alternative to clindamycin.
- Penicillin should not be used alone because many mouth flora anaerobes now produce penicillinase enzymes. Metronidazole should not be used alone because it is not active against microaerophilic streptococci and some anaerobic cocci.
- Other alternatives are ampicillin/sulbactam and carbapenems such as ertapenem and meropenem.

CHRONIC Rx

- Bronchoscopy to assist with drainage and/or diagnosis is indicated in patients who fail to respond to antibiotics or if there is suspected underlying malignancy.

- Surgery is indicated on rare occasions (<10%) in patients with complications of lung abscess (see "Comments").

DISPOSITION

- More than 95% of patients are cured with the use of antibiotics alone.
- Complications of lung abscesses include:
  1. Empyema
  2. Massive hemoptysis
  3. Pneumothorax
  4. Bronchopleural fistula
  5. Hepatobronchial fistula
  6. Brain abscess
  7. Bronchiectasis
- Mortality is low in community-acquired lung abscess (2.5%).
- Hospital-acquired lung abscess carries a high mortality rate (65%).

REFERRAL

If lung abscess is present, consultation with pulmonary and infectious disease specialist is recommended.

PEARLS & CONSIDERATIONS

COMMENTS

- Refractory cases are usually the result of:
  1. Large cavity size (>6 cm)
  2. Recurrent aspiration
  3. Thick-walled cavities
  4. Underlying lung carcinoma
  5. Empyema formation
- Necrotizing pneumonia is similar to a lung abscess but differs in size (<2 cm in diameter) and number (usually multiple suppurative cavitary lesions).

SUGGESTED READINGS

Available at www.expertconsult.com

RELATED CONTENT

Lung Abscess (Patient Information)

AUTHOR: **GLENN G. FORT, M.D., M.P.H.**

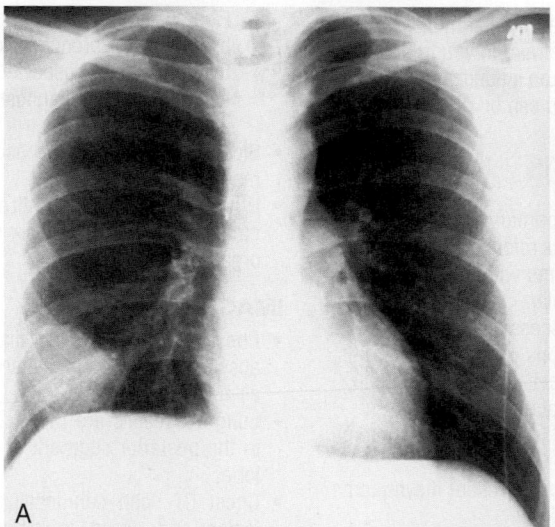
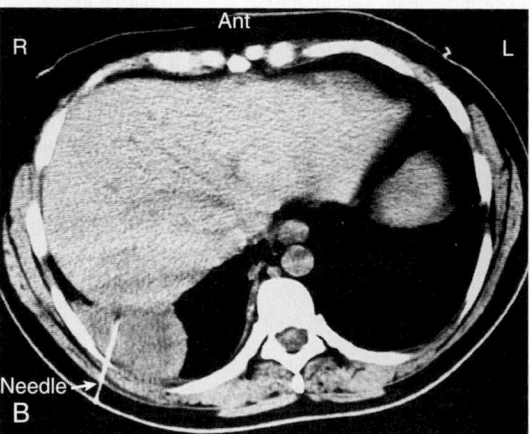

FIGURE 1L-29 Lung abscess. On a chest radiograph, a lung abscess may look to be a solid rounded lesion **(A),** or, if it has a connection with the bronchus, there may be an air-fluid level in a thick-walled cavitary lesion. CT scanning **(B)** can be used to localize the lesion and to place a needle for drainage and aspiration of contents for culture. (From Mettler FA [ed]: *Primary care radiology,* Philadelphia, 2000, Saunders.)

BASIC INFORMATION

DEFINITION

A primary lung neoplasm is a malignancy arising from lung tissue. The major types are non-small cell lung cancer (NSCLC; squamous cell carcinoma, adenocarcinoma, and large cell carcinoma) and small cell lung cancer (SCLC). However, the crucial issue in the diagnosis of lung cancer is the distinction between SCLC and NSCLC because the prognosis and therapeutic approaches are very different.

ADENOCARCINOMA: Represent 35% to 40% of lung carcinomas; frequently located in mid-lung and periphery; initial metastases are to lymphatics; frequently associated with peripheral scars; adenocarcinoma is described as preinvasive, minimally invasive, or invasive

SQUAMOUS CELL (EPIDERMOID): Represent 20% to 30% of lung cancers; central location; metastasis by local invasion; frequent cavitation and obstructive phenomena

SMALL CELL (OAT CELL): Represent 15% to 20% of lung carcinomas; central location; metastasis through lymphatics; associated with lesion of the short arm of chromosome 3; high cavitation rate

LARGE CELL: Represent 10% to 15% of lung carcinomas; frequently located in the periphery; metastasis to central nervous system and mediastinum; rapid growth rate with early metastasis

LEPIDIC-PREDOMINANT PATTERN (BRONCHOALVEOLAR): Represent 5% of lung carcinomas; frequently located in the periphery; may be bilateral; initial metastasis through lymphatic, hematogenous, and local invasion; no correlation with cigarette smoking; cavitation rare

SYNONYMS

Lung cancer

ICD-10CM CODES
C34.10 Malignant neoplasm of upper lobe, unspecified bronchus or lung
C34.11 Malignant neoplasm of upper lobe, right bronchus or lung
C34.12 Malignant neoplasm of upper lobe, left bronchus or lung
C34.2   Malignant neoplasm of middle lobe, bronchus or lung
C34.30 Malignant neoplasm of lower lobe, unspecified bronchus or lung
C34.31 Malignant neoplasm of lower lobe, right bronchus or lung
C34.32 Malignant neoplasm of lower lobe, left bronchus or lung
C34.80 Malignant neoplasm of overlapping sites of unspecified bronchus and lung
C34.81 Malignant neoplasm of overlapping sites of right bronchus and lung
C34.82 Malignant neoplasm of overlapping sites of left bronchus and lung
C34.90 Malignant neoplasm of unspecified part of unspecified bronchus or lung
C34.91 Malignant neoplasm of unspecified part of right bronchus or lung
C34.92 Malignant neoplasm of unspecified part of left bronchus or lung

EPIDEMIOLOGY & DEMOGRAPHICS

- Lung cancer is responsible for >30% of cancer deaths in males and >25% of cancer deaths in females. It has been the most common cancer in the world since 1985 and is the leading cause of cancer-related death.
- Tobacco smoke is implicated in 90% of cases; second-hand smoke is responsible for approximately 20% of cases.
- There will be an estimated 221,000 new cases of lung cancer and 158,000 deaths from lung cancer in 2015 in the U.S.
- Among women there has been a 600% increase in incidence of lung cancer during the past 80 years. The rates of death among women with lung cancer in the U.S. are the highest in the world.

PHYSICAL FINDINGS & CLINICAL PRESENTATION

- Weight loss, fatigue, fever, anorexia, dysphagia
- Cough, hemoptysis, dyspnea, wheezing
- Chest, shoulder, and bone pain
- Paraneoplastic syndromes (see Table 1L-26):
  1. **Lambert-Eaton myasthenic syndrome:** myopathy involving proximal muscle groups
  2. Endocrine manifestations: hypercalcemia, ectopic adrenocorticotropic hormone secretion, syndrome of inappropriate excretion of adrenocorticotropic hormone (SIADH)
  3. Neurologic: subacute cerebellar degeneration, peripheral neuropathy, cortical degeneration
  4. Musculoskeletal: polymyositis, clubbing, hypertrophic pulmonary osteoarthropathy
  5. Hematologic or vascular: migratory thrombophlebitis, marantic thrombosis, anemia, thrombocytosis, or thrombocytopenia
  6. Cutaneous: acanthosis nigricans, dermatomyositis
- Pleural effusion (10% of patients), recurrent pneumonias (from obstruction), localized wheezing
- **Superior vena cava syndrome:**
  1. Obstruction of venous return of the superior vena cava is most commonly caused by bronchogenic carcinoma or metastasis to paratracheal nodes.
  2. The patient usually reports headache, nausea, dizziness, visual changes, syncope, and respiratory distress.
  3. Physical examination reveals distention of thoracic and neck veins, edema of face and upper extremities, facial plethora, and cyanosis.
- **Horner's syndrome:** constricted pupil, ptosis, facial anhidrosis caused by spinal cord damage between C8 and T1 as a result of a superior sulcus tumor (bronchogenic carcinoma of the extreme lung apex)
- **Pancoast tumor:** a superior sulcus tumor associated with ipsilateral Horner's syndrome and shoulder pain

ETIOLOGY

- Tobacco abuse; the chance of developing lung cancer for a 40-pack-year persistent smoker is 20 times that of someone who never smoked
- Environmental agents (e.g., radon) and industrial agents (e.g., ionizing radiation, asbestos, nickel, uranium, vinyl chloride, chromium, arsenic, coal dust)
- Lung cancer susceptibility and risk increased in inherited cancer syndromes caused by germ-line mutations in p53, retinoblastoma, and germ-line mutation in the epidermal growth factor receptor (EGFR) gene.

TABLE 1L-26 Paraneoplastic Syndromes Associated with Bronchogenic Carcinoma

Syndrome	Cell Type	Mechanism
Hypertrophic pulmonary osteoarthropathy and clubbing	All except small cell	Unknown
Hyponatremia	Small cell most common; may be any type	SIADH, ectopic antidiuretic hormone production by tumor
Hypercalcemia	Usually squamous cell	Bone metastases, osteoclast-activating factor, parathyroid hormone–like hormone, prostaglandins
Cushing's syndrome	Usually small cell	Ectopic ACTH production
Lambert-Eaton myasthenic syndrome	Usually small cell	Voltage-sensitive calcium channel antibodies in >75%; affects presynaptic neuronal calcium channel activity
Other neuromyopathic disorders	Small cell most common; may be any type	Antineuronal nuclear antibodies, also known as anti-Hu; others unknown
Thrombophlebitis	All types	Unknown

ACTH, Adrenocorticotropic hormone; *SIADH,* syndrome of inappropriate secretion of antidiuretic hormone.
From Andreoli TE et al: *Andreoli and Carpenter's Cecil essentials of medicine,* ed 8, Philadelphia, 2010, Saunders.

Diseases and Disorders

DIAGNOSIS

DIFFERENTIAL DIAGNOSIS

- Pneumonia
- Tuberculosis (TB)
- Metastatic carcinoma to the lung
- Lung abscess
- Granulomatous disease
- Carcinoid tumor
- Sarcoidosis
- Benign lesions that simulate thoracic malignancy:
  1. Lobar atelectasis: pneumonia, chronic inflammatory disease, allergic bronchopulmonary aspergillosis
  2. Multiple pulmonary nodules: septic emboli, Wegener's granulomatosis, sarcoidosis, rheumatoid nodules, fungal disease, multiple pulmonary atrioventricular fistulas
  3. Mediastinal adenopathy: sarcoidosis, lymphoma, primary TB, fungal disease, silicosis, pneumoconiosis, drug-induced (e.g., phenytoin, trimethadione)
  4. Pleural effusion: congestive heart failure, pneumonia with parapneumonic effusion, TB, viral pneumonitis, ascites, pancreatitis, collagen-vascular disease

WORKUP

The workup generally includes chest CT, positron-emission tomographic (PET) scan, and tissue biopsy. Lab tests include CBC, serum chemistry studies. Diagnosis and staging of lung cancer should be performed simultaneously to minimize invasive testing.

LABORATORY TESTS

Various modalities are available to obtain a tissue diagnosis:

- Biopsy of any suspicious lymph nodes (e.g., supraclavicular or mediastinal node)
- Flexible fiberoptic bronchoscopy: brush and biopsy specimens are obtained from any visualized endobronchial lesions. The use of a gene-expression classifier improves the diagnostic performance of bronchoscopy for the detection of lung cancer. Trials have shown that the gene-expression classifier has a high sensitivity across different lesion sizes, locations, stages, and cell type of lung cancer. The combination of the classifier plus bronchoscopy has a sensitivity of >85%. In intermediate-risk patients with a non-diagnostic bronchoscopic examination, a negative classifier score provides support for a more conservative diagnostic approach.[1]
- Transbronchial needle aspiration: done with a special needle passed through the bronchoscope; this technique is useful to sample mediastinal masses or paratracheal lymph nodes
- Transthoracic fine-needle aspiration biopsy with fluoroscopic or CT scan guidance to evaluate peripheral pulmonary nodules
- Endobronchial ultrasound (EBUS) guided biopsy and staging can be used to evaluate suspected mediastinal and hilar nodes

[1]Silvestri GA et al: A bronchial genomic classifier for the diagnostic evaluation of lung cancer, *N Engl J Med* 373:243-251, 2015.

- Mediastinoscopy and anteromedial sternotomy in suspected tumor involvement of the mediastinum
- Pleural biopsy in patients with pleural effusion
- Thoracentesis of pleural effusion and cytologic evaluation of the obtained fluid: may confirm diagnosis

IMAGING STUDIES

- Chest x-ray (Fig. 1L-30): The radiographic presentation often varies with the cell type. Pleural effusion, lobar atelectasis, and mediastinal adenopathy can accompany any cell types.
- CT scan of chest (Fig. 1L-31) is performed to evaluate mediastinal and pleural extension of suspected lung neoplasms. The chest CT should include liver and adrenal glands (common sites of metastases). CT or MRI of brain should be considered in a patient presenting with neurologic symptoms (e.g., headaches, vision disturbances).
- PET with ^{18}F-fluorodeoxyglucose (^{18}FDG-PET) (Fig. 1L-32) is superior to CT in detecting mediastinal and distant metastases in NSCLC. It is useful for preoperative staging of NSCLC.
- The use of PET-CT for preoperative staging of NSCLC reduces both the total number of thoracotomies and the number of futile thoracotomies.

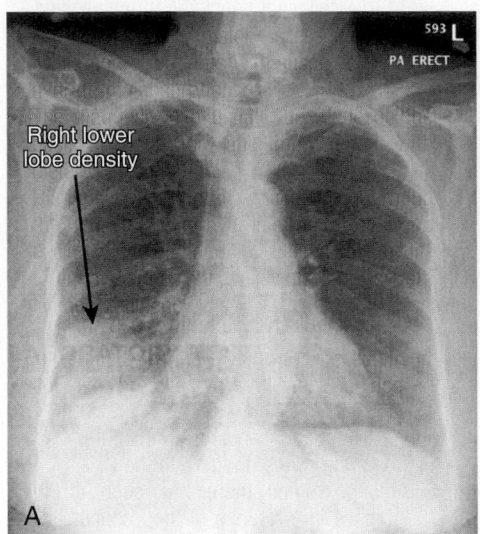
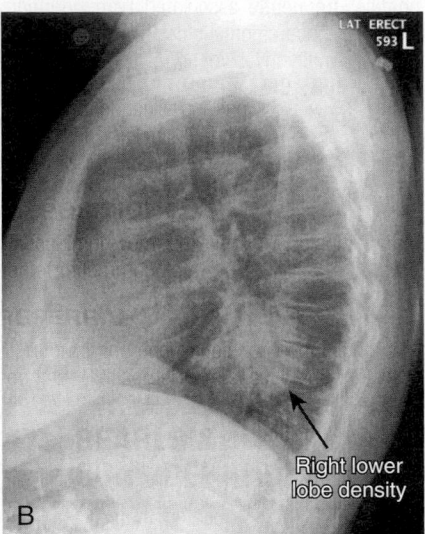

FIGURE 1L-30 Lung neoplasm, primary. Lung mass presenting with hemoptysis. **A,** Posterior-anterior (PA) chest x-ray. **B,** Lateral chest x-ray. This 83-year-old female presented with hemoptysis of a quarter-sized clot. Her posterior-anterior chest x-ray shows a rounded right lower lobe density. On the lateral view, this is visible in the retrocardiac space. This density measures 7.6 cm in diameter. Pneumonia, neoplasm, or abscess could have this appearance on chest x-ray. Computed tomography was performed to further delineate the pathology (see Fig. 1L-31). (From Broder JS: *Diagnostic imaging for the emergency physician,* Philadelphia, 2011, Saunders.)

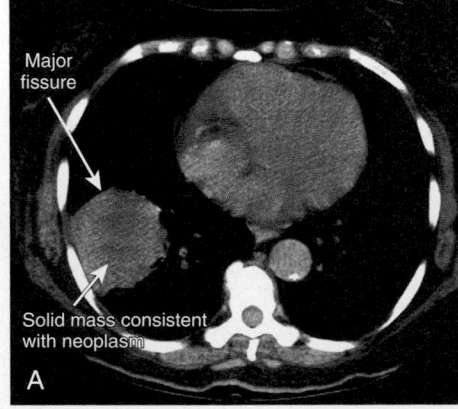
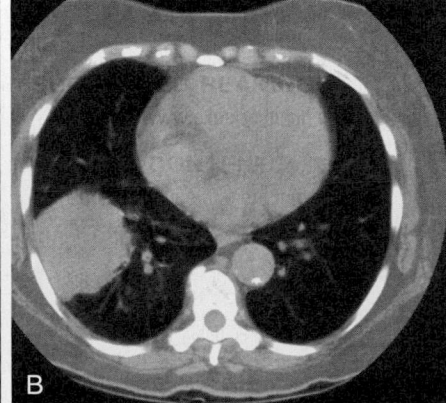

FIGURE 1L-31 Lung neoplasm, primary. Lung mass presenting with hemoptysis. Same patient as in Fig. 1L-30. Noncontrast computed tomography was performed (contrast was withheld as a consequence of the patient's renal dysfunction) and shows a 6 by 6 cm round lesion abutting the oblique fissure (also called the major fissure) and lateral chest wall. **A,** Soft tissue windows. **B,** Lung windows. On soft tissue windows, the center appears slightly darker, indicating lower density that may represent central necrosis. If IV contrast had been given, an area of necrosis would have failed to enhance. Infection or infarction is technically possible, but a pulmonary neoplasm is the most likely explanation for this lesion. Biopsy showed this to be a moderately differentiated squamous cell carcinoma. (From Broder JS: *Diagnostic imaging for the emergency physician,* Philadelphia, 2011, Saunders.)

STAGING

After confirmation of diagnosis, patients should undergo staging:

1. The TNM staging system is used for NSCLC. In this system, stage I (N0 [no lymph node involvement]) and stage II (N1 [spread to ipsilateral bronchopulmonary or hilar lymph nodes]) include localized tumors for which surgical resection is the preferred treatment. Stage III is subdivided into IIIA (potentially resectable) and IIIB (unresectable). Stage IV indicates metastatic disease.
2. In patients with SCLC, a more practical accepted staging system is the one developed by the Veterans Administration Lung Cancer Study Group. This system contains two stages:
   a. Limited-stage disease: confined to the regional lymph nodes and to one hemithorax (excluding pleural surfaces), which can be included in a single radiation portal
   b. Extensive-stage disease: spread beyond the confines of limited-stage disease
3. Pretreatment staging procedures for lung cancer patients, in addition to complete history and physical examination, generally include the following tests:
   a. Chest radiograph (posteroanterior and lateral), ECG
   b. Laboratory evaluation: complete blood count, complete metabolic panel, arterial blood gases, pulse oximetry.

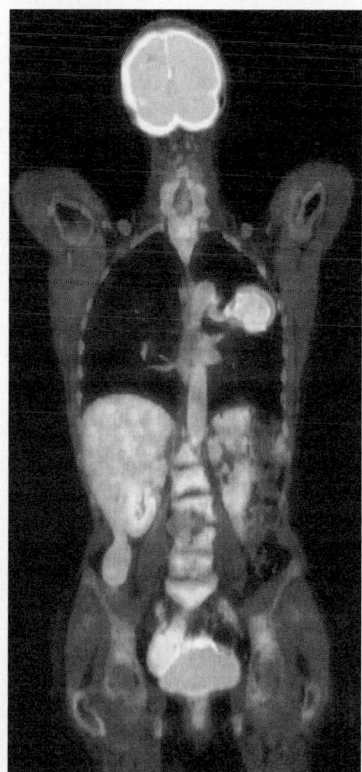

FIGURE 1L-32 Whole-body coronal [^{18}F]fluoro-2-deoxy-d-glucose positron emission tomography computed tomography (^{18}FDG-PET-CT) shows intense left upper lobe tracer accumulation (*arrow*) in a patient with bronchogenic carcinoma. Note normal high tracer activity within the brain (*arrowheads*). (From Mason, RJ: *Murray & Nadel's textbook of respiratory medicine*, 5th ed, Philadelphia, 2010, Saunders.)

c. Pulmonary function studies
d. CT scan of chest and PET scan: trials have shown a 51% relative reduction in futile thoracotomies for patients with suspected NSCLC who undergo preoperative assessment with PET with the tracer ^{18}FDG-PET in addition to conventional workup
e. Mediastinoscopy or anterior mediastinotomy in patients being considered for possible curative lung resection
f. Biopsy of any accessible suspect lesions
g. CT scan of liver and brain; radionuclide scans of bone in all patients with small cell carcinoma of the lung and patients with NSCLC neoplasms suspected of involving these organs
h. Bone marrow aspiration and biopsy only in selected patients with small cell carcinoma of the lung. In the absence of an increased lactate dehydrogenase or cytopenias, routine bone marrow examination is not recommended
i. Newer technologies in preoperative staging include endoscopic bronchial ultrasonography and esophageal ultrasonography to guide biopsies; however, cervical mediastinoscopy is standard criterion in preoperative nodal staging (sensitivity >93%, specificity >95%)

RX TREATMENT

NONPHARMACOLOGIC THERAPY

- Nutritional support
- Avoidance of tobacco and other substances toxic to the lungs
- Supplemental oxygen

ACUTE GENERAL Rx

NON–SMALL CELL CARCINOMA:

- Surgical resection is the best hope for cure in patients with operable NSCLC (stage I or II when the patient is a surgical candidate). Lobectomy is the best standard surgical approach. Lesser resections may be necessary in patients with marginal pulmonary reserve. Video-assisted thoracic surgery (VATS) is helpful in decreasing morbidity and shortening hospital stay.
  1. Surgical resection is indicated in patients with limited disease (not involving mediastinal nodes, ribs, pleura, or distant sites). This represents approximately 15% to 30% of diagnosed cases. Stereotactic ablative radiotherapy is a reasonable option for patients with localized NSCLC who are too frail for surgical correction.
  2. Preoperative evaluation includes review of cardiac status and evaluation of pulmonary function. Pneumonectomy is possible if the patient has a preoperative FEV_1 = 2 L or if the maximal voluntary ventilation is >50% of predicted capacity. Individuals with FEV_1 >1.5 L are suitable for lobectomy without further evaluation unless there is evidence of interstitial lung disease or undue dyspnea on exertion. In that case, carbon dioxide diffusion in

the lung (DLCO) should be measured. If the DLCO is <80% predicted normal, the individual is not clearly operable.
  3. Conventional radiotherapy fails to durably control the primary lung tumor in nearly 70% of patients and 2-yr survival is less than 40%. Stereotactic body radiation (SBRT) uses several highly focused radiation beams to deliver high doses in 3 to 5 fractions and appears to be more effective than conventional radiotherapy, with a local control rate equivalent to that with surgery in inoperable early stage lung cancer.
  4. Preoperative chemotherapy should be considered in patients with more advanced disease (stage IIIA) who are being considered for surgery because it increases the median survival time in patients with NSCLC compared with the use of surgery alone.
  5. Postoperative adjuvant chemotherapy with cisplatin plus vinorelbine significantly increases 5-yr survival (69% vs. 54%) in patients with completely resected stage II-IIIA NSCLC.

- Treatment of unresectable NSCLC:
  1. Radiotherapy alone used primarily for treatment of central nervous system and skeletal metastases, superior vena cava syndrome. Thoracic radiotherapy in combination with chemotherapy is standard therapy for unresectable stage 3 disease.
  2. Chemotherapy is the mainstay of treatment for advanced stage IIIB-IV NSCLC. Initial stratification is done based on pathology (squamous vs. non-squamous cancers) and presence of driver mutations (e.g. EGFR, ALK, and ROS1 mutations in adenocarcinomas). A platinum-based doublet regimen is recommended for fit patients, and single agents are offered to elderly patients and those with poor performance status. Various combination regimens are available with platinum plus pemetrexed preferred for non-squamous cancers while other for squamous cancers other doublets such as paclitaxel plus carboplatin, cisplatin plus vinorelbine, gemcitabine plus cisplatin, and cisplatin plus docetaxel are utilized with none being clearly superior to the others. The addition of bevacizumab to paclitaxel plus carboplatin results in significant survival benefit in nonsquamous cancers. Recent trials comparing nivolumab (a fully human IgG-4 PD-1 immune-checkpoint inhibitor antibody that disrupts PD-1 mediated signaling and restores antitumor immunity) versus docetaxel in advanced squamous cell and nonsquamous cell NSCLC revealed that among patients with advanced nonsquamous cell NSCLC that had progressed during or after platinum-based chemotherapy, overall survival was longer with nivolumab than with docetaxel.[2]

---

[2]Borghaei H, et al: Nivolumab versus docetaxel in advanced nonsquamous/non-small-cell lung cancer, *N Engl J Med* 373:1627-1631, 2015.

Among patients with advanced, previously treated squamous NSCLC, overall survival, response rate, and progression-free survival were significantly better with nivolumab than with docetaxel, regardless of PD-L1 expression level.[3] Maintenance chemotherapy is also associated with a survival benefit in responding patients.

3. Tyrosine kinase inhibitors targeting activating mutations are of use in patients whose adenocarcinomas harbor either EGFR, ALK, or ROS1 mutations. Gefitinib, erlotinib, and afatinib are oral EGFR inhibitors which have showed impressive responses and improvements in median overall survival to the range of 30 months. (These mutations are more common in adenocarcinomas found in patients who are never or light smokers and in Asian patients. Oncogenic fusion genes consisting of EML4 and anaplastic lymphoma kinase (ALK) are present in 4% to 5% of adenocarcinomas and can be treated with inhibitors crizotinib or ceritinib. Approximately 2% of adenocarcinomas have genetic rearrangements involving the ROS1 proto-oncogenic receptor tyrosine kinase (ROS1). Recent trials have shown that crizotimb has marked antitumor activity in these patients.

4. The use of immunotherapy specifically antibody directed to PDL1 receptor has been shown to improve survival in relapsed patients with both squamous and non-squamous cancers.

5. The addition of chemotherapy to radiotherapy improves survival in patients with locally advanced, unresectable (stages IIIA-IIIB) NSCLC.

---

[3]Brahmer J, et al: Nivolumab versus docetaxel in advanced squamous cell, non-small-cell lung cancer, *N Engl J Med* 373:123-135, 2015.

6. Early initiation of palliative care focusing on management of symptoms, psychosocial support, and assistance with decision making in patients with metastatic NSCLC leads to improved quality of life, longer survival, and less use of aggressive end-of-life care.

SMALL CELL LUNG CANCER:
- Limited-stage disease: standard treatments include thoracic radiotherapy and chemotherapy (cisplatin and etoposide).
- Extensive-stage disease: standard treatments include combination chemotherapy (platinum plus etoposide or irinotecan and platinum).
- Prophylactic cranial irradiation for patients in complete remission to decrease the risk of central nervous system metastasis.
- Despite high initial response rates, most patients eventually relapse. Topotecan or irinotecan may be an option for these patients.

DISPOSITION
- The 5-yr survival of patients with NSCLC when the disease is resectable is approximately 30%.
- Median survival time in patients with limited-stage disease and SCLC is 15 mo; in patients with extensive stage disease, it is 9 mo. Among patients with metastatic NSCLC, early palliative care results in longer survival and significant improvements in both quality of life and mood.

❗ PEARLS & CONSIDERATIONS
- CT screening with use of low-dose computed tomography (LDCT) for detection of lung cancer among persons with a heavy history of smoking increases the percentage of lung cancer cases that are diagnosed in

stage 1 and reduces mortality from lung cancer. The National Lung Screening Trial (NLST) showed that lung cancer screening with LDCT resulted in a 20% reduction in lung cancer mortality. New guidelines recommend annual LDCT for those who are current or former smokers aged 55 to 74. Screening should be discontinued once a person has not smoked for 15 years or develops a health problem that substantially limits life expectancy or the ability or willingness to have curative lung surgery.[4]

EVIDENCE

Available at www.expertconsult.com

SUGGESTED READINGS
Available at www.expertconsult.com

RELATED CONTENT
Lung Cancer (Patient Information)
Lung Cancer Screening (Patient Information)
Horner Syndrome (Related Key Topic)
Lambert-Eaton Myasthenic Syndrome (Related Key Topic)
Paraneoplastic Syndromes (Related Key Topic)
Superior Vena Cava Syndrome (Related Key Topic)

AUTHOR: **BHARTI RATHORE, M.D.**

---

[4]Moyer VA, on behalf of US Preventive Services Task Force: Screening for lung cancer: U.S. Preventive Services Task Force recommendation statement, *Ann Intern Med* 160:330-338, 2014.

BASIC INFORMATION

DEFINITION

Lyme disease is a multisystem inflammatory disorder caused by the transmission of a spirochete, *Borrelia burgdorferi*. Lyme disease is spread by the bite of infected *Ixodes* ticks, taking 36 to 48 hr for a tick to feed and transmit the infecting organism *B. burgdorferi* to the host.

SYNONYMS

Bannworth's syndrome (Europe)
Acrodermatitis chronica atrophicans

ICD-10CM CODES
A69.20 Lyme disease, unspecified
A69.21 Meningitis due to Lyme disease
A69.22 Other neurologic disorders in Lyme disease
A69.23 Arthritis due to Lyme disease
A69.29 Other conditions associated with Lyme disease

EPIDEMIOLOGY & DEMOGRAPHICS

INCIDENCE (IN U.S.): In the United States, 4.4 cases/100,000 persons; it is the most common vector-borne infection in the U.S., with more than 30,000 new cases reported each year. 90% of cases are found in: Massachusetts, Connecticut, Rhode Island, New York, New Jersey, Pennsylvania, Minnesota, Wisconsin, and California. The disease also occurs in Europe and Asia with a different *Ixodes* tick vector.
PEAK INCIDENCE: May to November.
PREDOMINANT SEX: Male = female.
PREDOMINANT AGE: Median age of 28 yr.

PHYSICAL FINDINGS & CLINICAL PRESENTATION

Lyme disease may present in the following stages:
- *Early localized stage (incubation period 3-30 days):* early Lyme disease, erythema migrans (EM); skin rash, often at site of tick bite (the CDC has defined EM rash as an expanding red macule or papule that must reach at least 5 cm in size, with or without central clearing); target lesions from ECM can be found in 60% to 80% of localized infections; possible fever, myalgias 3 to 32 days after tick bite.
- *Early disseminated stage (incubation period 3-6 weeks):* days to weeks later; multiorgan system involvement, including CNS with aseptic meningitis–type picture or Bell's palsy, joints (arthritis or arthralgias), cardiac including varying degrees of heart block; related to dissemination of spirochete
- *Late stage (incubation period months to years):* mo to yr after tick exposure; affects central and peripheral nervous system, cardiac, joints

Common presenting signs and symptoms include:
- EM (Fig. 1L-33). Most patients with EM (about 80%) have a single lesion but the bacteria can disseminate hematogenously to other sites in the skin and result in often smaller erythema migrans lesions.
- Lymphadenopathy, neck pains, pharyngeal erythema, myalgias, hepatosplenomegaly.
- Patients will complain of malaise, fatigue, lethargy, headache, fever/chills, neck pain, myalgias, back pain.

ETIOLOGY

B. burgdorferi transmitted from bite of an *Ixodes* tick (mostly in the nymph stage, but can also be from adult ticks). Human infection occurs through inoculation of spirochetes in infected saliva and usually requires tick attachment for more than 36 hours.

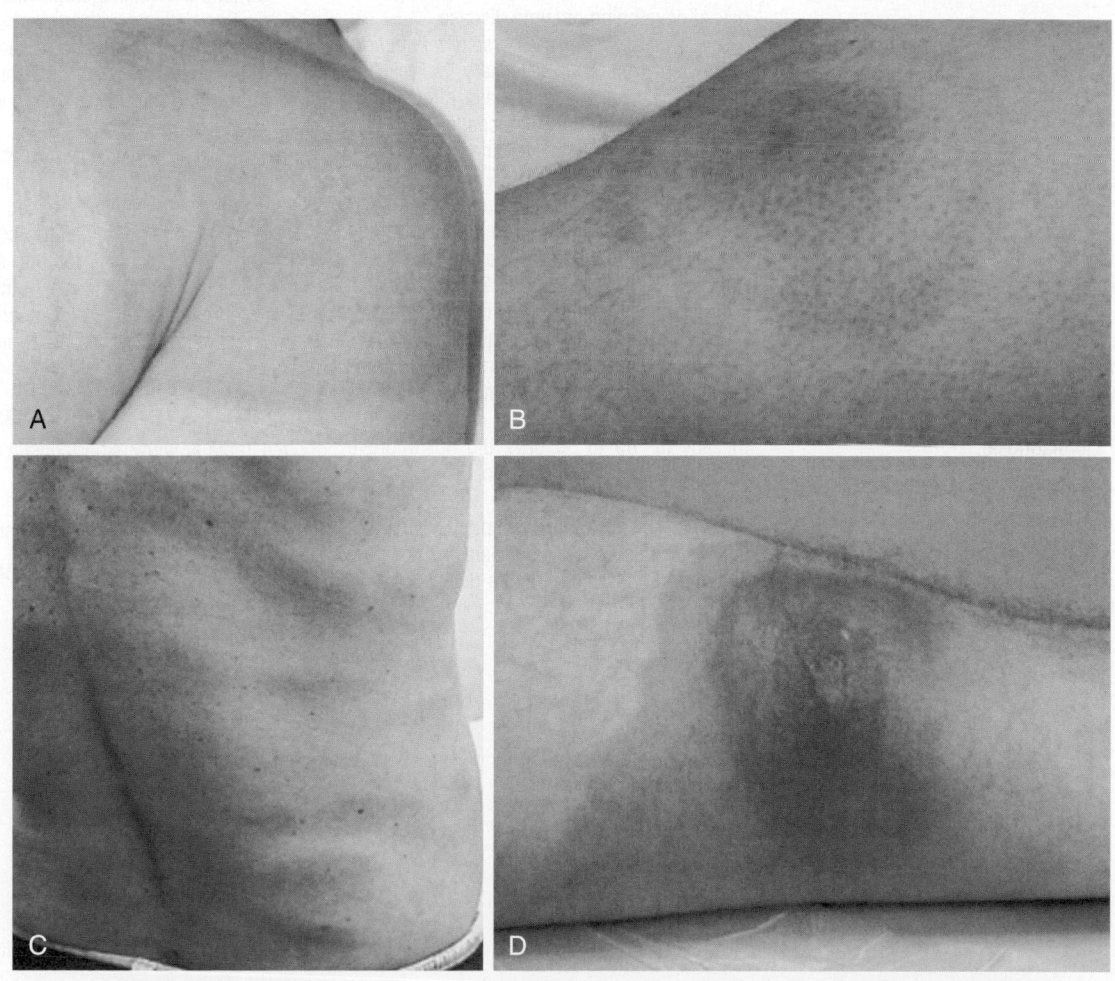

FIGURE 1L-33 Erythema migrans rash of Lyme disease. A, Typical macular lesion on left shoulder. **B,** Bull's eye lesion on lateral thigh with central punctum. **C,** Multiple lesions on back. **D,** Lesion with vesicular center on posterior thigh. (Courtesy Juan Salazar, MD, University of Connecticut Health Center.)

TABLE 1L-27 Criteria for Western Blot Interpretation in the Serologic Confirmation of Lyme Disease

Duration of Disease	Isotype Tested	Criteria for Positive Test
First month of infection	IgM	2 of the following 3 bands are present: 23 kD (OspC), 39 kD (BmpA), and 41 kD (Fla)
After first month of infection	IgG	5 of 10 bands are present: 18 kD, 21 kD, 28 kD, 30 kD, 39 kD, 41 kD, 45 kD, 58 kD (not GroEL), 66 kD, and 93 kD

Modified from Centers for Disease Control and Prevention: Recommendations for test performance and interpretation from the Second National Conference on Serologic Diagnosis of Lyme Disease, *MMWR Morb Mortal Wkly Rep* 44:590–591, 1995.

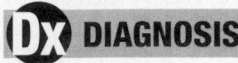 DIAGNOSIS

Clinical presentation, exposure to ticks in endemic area, and diagnostic testing for antibody response to *B. burgdorferi*. Serologic testing at early stages is usually negative; therefore, in early stage, documentation of erythema migrans lesion with a compatible epidemiologic history is sufficient for diagnosis, and laboratory testing is not indicated.

DIFFERENTIAL DIAGNOSIS
- Chronic fatigue/fibromyalgia.
- Acute viral illnesses.
- Babesiosis.
- Ehrlichiosis.

WORKUP
- ELISA testing and if positive or equivocal then followed by a Western blot IgM and IgG (Table 1L-27). A Western blot IgM assay is positive if 2 of 3 bands present. The Western blot IgG is positive if 5 of 10 bands present.
- An alternative serologic test is the VlsE C6 ELISA, which detects an IgG response earlier.
- Early disease often difficult to diagnose serologically secondary to slow immune response
- Culturing of skin lesions (EM) and polymerase chain reaction (PCR) of synovial fluid or CSF can also give the diagnosis.

IMAGING STUDIES
- ECG
- Echocardiogram if conduction abnormalities are present with cardiac involvement.
- CT scan, MRI of head for CNS involvement.

 TREATMENT

Early localized Lyme disease:
- Doxycycline 100 mg bid or amoxicillin 500 mg tid for 14 days (doxycycline offers the advantage of treating possible co-infection with *Anaplasma phagocytophilum;* however, it should be avoided in children >8 yr and pregnant females).
- Alternative treatments: cefuroxime axetil 500 mg bid for 14 to 21 days, azithromycin 500 mg PO for 7 to 10 days but should not be used as a first-line agent.
- A single dose of 200 mg doxycycline given within 72 hr of *Ixodes* tick bite can reduce the risk of developing of Lyme disease.

Early disseminated and late persistent infection:
- 28 days of treatment necessary; doxycycline and ceftriaxone appear equally effective for acute disseminated Lyme disease.
- Arthritis: 28 days of doxycycline or amoxicillin plus probenecid.
- Neurologic involvement requires parenteral antibiotics. Those who fail to respond should be treated with IV ceftriaxone or cefotaxime.
- Ceftriaxone 2 g/day IV for 21 to 28 days; alternative: cefotaxime 2 g q8h IV; alternative: penicillin G 5 million U qid.
- Cardiac involvement: IV ceftriaxone or cefotaxime plus cardiac monitoring.
- Prolonged treatment with IV or PO antibiotic therapy for up to 90 days did not improve symptoms more than placebo.

Post–Lyme disease syndrome:
- Presence of disabling symptoms such as fatigue, malaise, diffuse pains, and poor concentration, which may be due to an exuberant host inflammatory response

- Antibiotics are not indicated. Antibiotic treatment of patients with persistent unexplained symptoms despite previous antibiotic treatment of Lyme disease provides little, if any, benefit and carries significant risk.
- Supportive care

DISPOSITION
- The patient often needs careful follow-up and supportive care for the arthralgia-neuritis symptoms.
- Repeat episodes of EM in appropriately treated patients are due to reinfection and not to relapse.

REFERRAL
- To a neurologist if significant neurologic complications (meningitis, myelitis, ophthalmoplegia, Bell's palsy).
- To a cardiologist if the patient develops evidence of cardiac conduction disturbances or pericarditis.

! PEARLS & CONSIDERATIONS

- A physician diagnosis of classic EM in an endemic region of Lyme disease is sufficient to make a definitive diagnosis.
- In some patients with Lyme disease, nonspecific complaints such as headache, fatigue, and arthralgia may persist for months after appropriate (and ultimately successful) antibiotic treatment.
- There is no evidence of current or previous *Borrelia burgdorferi* infection in most patients evaluated at university-based Lyme disease referral centers. Psychiatric comorbidity and other psychological factors are prominent in the presentation and outcome of some patients who inaccurately ascribe longstanding symptoms to "chronic Lyme disease."

SUGGESTED READINGS
Available at www.expertconsult.com

RELATED CONTENT
Lyme Disease (Patient Information)

AUTHOR: **GLENN G. FORT, M.D., M.P.H.**

L

I

BASIC INFORMATION

DEFINITION

Lymphangitis refers to the inflammation of lymphatic vessels due to infectious or noninfectious causes. Infectious causes include bacteria, mycobacteria, viruses, fungi, and parasites.

SYNONYMS

Nodular lymphangitis
Sporotrichoid lymphangitis

ICD-10CM CODES
I89.1 Lymphangitis

EPIDEMIOLOGY & DEMOGRAPHICS

INCIDENCE (IN U.S.): Several hundred cases/yr of sporotrichoid lymphangitis; bacterial lymphangitis more common but not reported.

PHYSICAL FINDINGS & CLINICAL PRESENTATION

ACUTE LYMPHANGITIS:
- Commonly associated with a bacterial cellulitis.
- Usually develops after cutaneous inoculation of microorganisms into the lymphatic vessels through disrupted skin or as a result of spread from a distal infection.
- May or may not recognize a site of skin trauma (i.e., laceration, puncture, ulcer).
- In hours to days, distal appearance of erythema, edema, and tenderness, with linear erythematous streaks extending proximally to regional lymph nodes.
- Possible lymphadenitis and fever.
- Predisposition to group A streptococcal infection of the skin in those with uncontrolled diabetes mellitus, chronic lymphedema, and superficial fungal infections (e.g., tinea pedis).

SPOROTRICHOID OR NODULAR LYMPHANGITIS:
- Includes subcutaneous nodules that develop along the path of involved lymphatics.
- Most commonly results from inoculation of the skin of the hand.
- Usually preceded by well-defined episode of cutaneous inoculation or trauma.
- Lesions apparent from one to several weeks after inoculation.
- Initially, nodular or papular lesion; may ulcerate.
- May have frank pus or a serosanguineous discharge.

- Systemic complaints uncommon, but infection with certain microorganisms associated with fever, chills, myalgias, and headache.

ETIOLOGY

- Acute lymphangitis: usually associated with *Streptococcus pyogenes* (group A streptococcus), and to a lesser extent staphylococcus species, including community-acquired methicillin-resistant *S. aureus* (CA-MRSA).
- Nodular lymphangitis caused by one of several organisms.
  1. *Sporothrix schenckii* ("Rose gardener's disease").
     a. Most common recognized cause in the United States, usually in the Midwest.
     b. Found in soil and plant debris.
  2. *Nocardia brasiliensis:* found in soil.
  3. *Mycobacterium marinum:* associated with trauma related to water (e.g., aquariums, swimming pools, fish).
  4. *Leishmania brasiliensis.*
     a. Protozoal parasite transmitted to humans by sandflies, mostly to travelers in endemic areas.
     b. Small endemic focus in Texas.
  5. *Francisella tularensis.*
     a. Most often in Southern/Midwestern states (Arkansas, Missouri, Oklahoma).
     b. Associated with contact with infected mammals, (e.g., rabbits, squirrels) tick bites, and (rarely) water exposure.

DIAGNOSIS

DIFFERENTIAL DIAGNOSIS
- Nodular lymphangitis.
- Insect or snake bites.
- Filariasis.

WORKUP
- Acute lymphangitis: blood cultures.
- Nodular lymphangitis: various stains and cultures of drainage or biopsy specimens of inoculation sites to make definitive diagnosis.

LABORATORY TESTS
- WBCs possibly elevated with cellulitis.
- Eosinophilia common with helminthic infections.

TREATMENT

NONPHARMACOLOGIC THERAPY
Limb elevation.

ACUTE GENERAL Rx
- Penicillin possibly sufficient, but 1 wk of dicloxacillin or cephalexin 500 mg PO qid commonly used to ensure antistaphylococcal coverage; if CA-MRSA suspected, then use oral Bactrim DS one PO bid or clindamycin 300mg PO q6H. Reserve vancomycin 1 g IV every 12 hr for patients requiring IV therapy.
- If allergic to penicillin:
  1. Clindamycin 300 mg PO qid for 7 days *or*
  2. Erythromycin 500 mg PO qid for 7 days.
  3. Levofloxacin 500 mg PO daily or moxifloxacin 400 mg PO daily for 7 days.
- Nodular lymphangitis: specific therapy directed at etiologic agent.
- For superficial fungal infections: treatment may prevent recurrence of acute lymphangitis.

DISPOSITION
- Acute lymphangitis: usually resolves with therapy.
- Recurrent attacks: may lead to chronic lymphedema of limb, rarely resulting in elephantiasis nostras (nonfilarial elephantiasis).
- Nodular lymphangitis: usually responds to appropriate therapy.

REFERRAL
- If acute lymphangitis is more than a mild disease or if it involves the face.
- If nodular lymphangitis or filariasis is suspected.

PEARLS & CONSIDERATIONS

COMMENTS
- Outside of the United States, initial episodes of filariasis caused by *Brugia malayi* resemble acute lymphangitis.
- Chronic lymphedema or elephantiasis results from recurrent episodes.
- For chronic lymphedema, adherence to limb elevation, compression/support stockings, and adequate glycemic control (for patients with diabetes) all can reduce risk of acute lymphangitis.

SUGGESTED READINGS
Available at www.expertconsult.com

RELATED CONTENT
Lymphangitis (Patient Information)

AUTHOR: **RUSSELL J. MCCULLOH, M.D.**

BASIC INFORMATION

DEFINITION

A primary role of the lymphatic system is to transport proteins from the interstitium to the heart. When the transport capacity of the lymphatic system is reduced, proteins accumulate in the interstitium. Accumulated proteins attract water, which creates a high protein swelling in the subcutaneous tissues called lymphedema.

SYNONYMS

Elephantiasis

ICD-10CM CODES

I97.2   Postmastectomy lymphedema syndrome
I89.0   Lymphedema, not elsewhere classified
Q82.0   Hereditary lymphedema

EPIDEMIOLOGY & DEMOGRAPHICS

PRIMARY LYMPHEDEMA:
- Found in 1.1/100,000 people aged <20 yr.
- Females outnumber males 3.5:1.
- Incidence peaks between ages 12 and 16 (puberty).

SECONDARY LYMPHEDEMA: See specific etiology in the following.

PHYSICAL FINDINGS & CLINICAL PRESENTATION

Lymphedema is a slow onset, progressive disease characterized by an asymmetrical, inflammatory swelling, traveling distal to proximal, that can affect any body part including limbs, trunk, head/neck, and genitals (Fig. 1L-34). Box 1L-3 summarizes lymphedema staging from the International Society of Lymphology.

STAGE 0: LATENCY:
- Decreased lymphatic system transport capacity due to primary or secondary etiology.

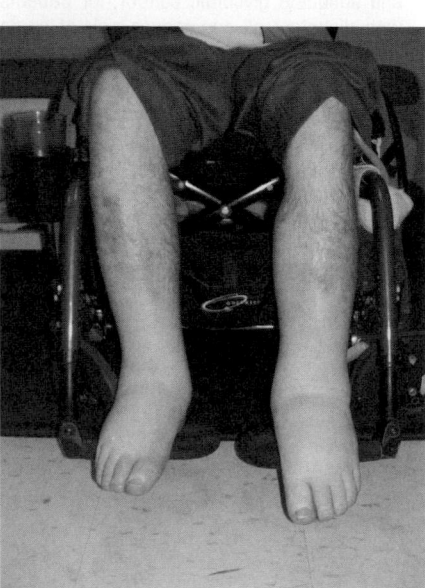

FIGURE 1L-34 Lymphedema before treatment.

- Subjective complaints of affected body part feeling heavy or achy.
- No objective findings, no apparent swelling.

STAGE I: REVERSIBLE:
- Edema is observable, soft, pitting and reversible with elevation.
- No secondary skin changes are present.

STAGE II: SPONTANEOUSLY IRREVERSIBLE:
- Skin becomes more firm/fibrotic, therefore less pitting.
- Edema does not reverse to normal with elevation.
- Possibility of infections (cellulitis), wounds, or weeping (lymphorrhea).

STAGE III: ELEPHANTIASIS:
- Skin becomes very firm/fibrotic, therefore nonpitting.
- Evidence of substantial skin changes (e.g., papillomas, lobules, *"peau d' orange"*).

ETIOLOGY: Lymphedema is caused by a reduction in lymphatic system transport and is classified into primary and secondary forms.

Primary Lymphedema.
- Occurs when the lymphatic system does not maturate properly during fetal development.
  1. Aplasia.
  2. Hypoplasia.
  3. Hyperplasia.
- Can be familial, genetic, or hereditary.
- Lymphedema congenital: symptoms present at birth.
- Lymphedema praecox: symptoms onset before the age of 35 (commonly during puberty).
- Lymphedema tardum: symptoms onset at the age of 35 or after.

Secondary Lymphedema.
- Occurs secondary to a disruption or obstruction of the lymphatic system caused by:
  1. Filariasis (#1 cause worldwide).
  2. Lymph node surgery/radiation due to cancer (#1 cause in the United States).

BOX 1L-3   Lymphedema Staging

Stage 0: Latent
- Impaired lymphatic function
- No evident edema; subclinical
- May last months or years before progression

Stage I: Spontaneously Reversible
- Early accumulation of protein-rich fluid
- Pitting edema
- Subsides with elevation

Stage II: Spontaneously Irreversible
- Accumulation of protein-rich fluid
- Pitting edema progresses to fibrosis
- Does not resolve with elevation alone

Stage III: Lymphostatic Elephantiasis
- Nonpitting
- Significant fibrosis
- Trophic skin changes

From International Society of Lymphology: The diagnosis and treatment of peripheral edema: 2009 consensus document of the International Society of Lymphology, *Lymphology* 42(2):51-60, 2009.

---

3. Other: chronic venous insufficiency (CVI), deep vein thrombosis (DVT), infection, surgery/trauma, lipedema, and obesity.

Dx DIAGNOSIS

- Lymphedema is primarily a clinical diagnosis made on the basis of past medical history and objective findings that distinguish it from other causes of chronic edema.
- A Stemmer's sign is often used to identify lymphedema (inability to pick up or pinch a fold of skin at the base of the second toe or finger).
- When physical examination is inconclusive, other available imaging tests can help make the diagnosis (see imaging studies below).

DIFFERENTIAL DIAGNOSIS

Other causes of edema that should be ruled out before treatment for lymphedema include cardiac, renal, hepatic, and thyroid dysfunction.

WORKUP

A detailed history and physical examination should help exclude most of the differential diagnoses.

LABORATORY TESTS

- Blood urea nitrogen, creatinine, liver function tests, albumin, urine analysis, and thyroid function tests are obtained to exclude possible systemic causes of edema.
- Genetic testing may be practical in defining a specific hereditary syndrome with a discrete gene mutation such as lymphedema distichiasis (*FOXC2*), Milroy's disease (*VEGFR-3*), Meige's disease, or Klippel-Trenaunay-Weber syndrome.

IMAGING STUDIES

- Lymphoscintigraphy: diagnostic image of choice for lymphedema (if needed).
- Indocyanine green (ICG) fluorescent lymphography: can now be used to identify sentinel nodes, to demonstrate superficial lymph channels and functional lymphatics, to indicate treatment pathways, and to confirm the effectiveness of therapeutic techniques.
- Magnetic resonance imaging (MRI): primarily used in tumor diagnosis.
- Duplex ultrasound: determines venous involvement in the edema.
- Computed axial tomography (CAT): distinguishes between fatty tissue and accumulations of protein-rich fluids.
- Lymphography: phased out in favor of less invasive techniques.

Rx TREATMENT

NONPHARMACOLOGIC THERAPY

- Complete decongestive therapy (CDT) is backed by longstanding research and experience as the primary treatment of choice for lymphedema in both children and adults (Fig. 1L-35). It should be delivered by a certified lymphedema therapist (CLT). CDT involves a two-phase treatment program:

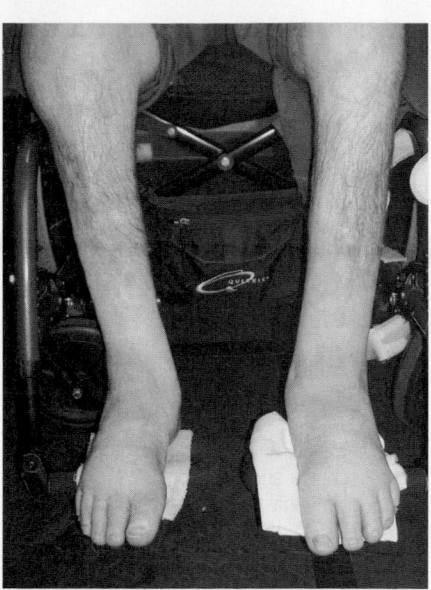

FIGURE 1L-35 Lymphedema after treatment.

1. Phase 1—Reduce tissue congestion of affected body part with daily treatments:
   1. Manual lymph drainage.
   2. Skin care.
   3. Compression wrapping of limb.
   4. Decongestive exercises.
2. Phase 2—Maintain decongestion with Home Maintenance Program:
   1. Daily use of elastic and inelastic compression garments that are properly fitted according to circumference and length to prevent lymphedema from returning.
   2. Compression is graduated; most of the compression is distal with decreasing compression in the stocking proximally.
   3. Different knits and compression classes are available for different stages of lymphedema.
   4. Choices of garments include below-the-knee stockings, thigh-high stockings, pantyhose, sleeves, bras, and truncal garments.

- Massage (or any modality that increases blood flow) can have negative effects on lymphedema by increasing vasodilation. Therefore it is contraindicated on the lymphedematous quadrants.
- Compression pumps have not been found to be effective in removing proteins from lymphedematous quadrants.
- Nutritional therapy (reducing the amount of proteins ingested) is ineffective in the treatment of lymphedema.

PHARMACOLOGIC THERAPY

No drugs have been shown to be beneficial in the treatment of lymphedema. Diuretics, in particular, have not been found to be effective in removing proteins from lymphedematous quadrants and may promote the development of volume depletion.

SURGERY

Surgery for lymphedema has been proven largely unsuccessful and should not be considered before CDT. Surgical procedures are divided into two types:
- Physiologic procedures: those performed to improve lymph node drainage (e.g., anastomoses of the lymph system with the venous system, lymph node transplant).
- Excisional or debulking procedures: those performed to excise the subcutaneous tissue (e.g., Charles' procedure, Thompson's procedure, the modified Homans' procedure, and liposuction). Liposuction-circumferential suction-assisted lipectomy represents a newly proposed method to reduce morbidity involved in the traditional excisional techniques.

! PEARLS & CONSIDERATIONS

- Lymphedema is a chronic, generally incurable but very manageable condition that requires lifelong care and attention along with psychosocial support.
- Children and adolescents (along with parents and adults) should be encouraged to pursue a normal life, participating in school activities and sports (preferably noncontact, such as swimming).
- Infections such as cellulitis should be treated promptly.
- If the etiology is filariasis caused by the parasites *Wuchereria bancrofti* or *Brugia malayi*, treatment is diethylcarbamazine citrate 5 mg/kg in divided doses for 3 wk.
- Patients with lymphedema commonly manifest psychiatric comorbidities as a result of their disease, such as anxiety, depression, adjustment problems, and difficulty in vocational, domestic, or social domains.
- Lymphedema can be complicated in rare cases by development of lymphangiosarcomata or other cutaneous malignancies.
- Gene therapy to develop new lymphangioses in the affected body parts is a potential clinical remedy in the future.

SUGGESTED READINGS

Available at www.expertconsult.com

RELATED CONTENT

Lymphedema (Patient Information)

AUTHORS: **FRANK G. FORT, M.D.,** and **KATHRYN TAYLOR ANILOWSKI, M.S., P.T., C.L.T.-L.A.N.A.**

BASIC INFORMATION

DEFINITION

Non-Hodgkin lymphoma (NHL) is a heterogeneous group of malignancies of the lymphoreticular system. There are approximately 40 different NHL subtypes.

SYNONYMS

NHL
Non-Hodgkin lymphoma

ICD-10CM CODES
C85.90 Non-Hodgkin lymphoma, unspecified, unspecified site
C85.91 Non-Hodgkin lymphoma, unspecified, lymph nodes of head, face, and neck
C85.92 Non-Hodgkin lymphoma, unspecified, intrathoracic lymph nodes
C85.93 Non-Hodgkin lymphoma, unspecified, intra-abdominal lymph nodes
C85.94 Non-Hodgkin lymphoma, unspecified, lymph nodes of axilla and upper limb
C85.95 Non-Hodgkin lymphoma, unspecified, lymph nodes of inguinal region and lower limb
C85.96 Non-Hodgkin lymphoma, unspecified, intrapelvic lymph nodes
C85.97 Non-Hodgkin lymphoma, unspecified, spleen
C85.98 Non-Hodgkin lymphoma, unspecified, lymph nodes of multiple sites
C85.99 Non-Hodgkin lymphoma, unspecified, extranodal and solid organ sites

EPIDEMIOLOGY

- Sixth most common neoplasm in the US (>50,000 new cases annually). Incidence increases with age; majority of patients are above 60 years of age.
- Diffuse large B-cell lymphoma (DLBCL) is the most common subtype (30% of the cases). Follicular lymphoma (FL) is the second most common subtype (25% of the cases).
- In patients with HIV, NHL is the most common tumor (followed by Kaposi sarcoma). DLBCL accounts for 80-90% of the cases of HIV-associated NHL.

PHYSICAL FINDINGS & CLINICAL PRESENTATION

- Patients often present with lymphadenopathy.
- Approximately one third of the NHL originate in extranodal sites, which can result in unusual presentations (e.g., gastrointestinal tract involvement can simulate peptic ulcer disease).
- Presence of B symptoms like unexplained weight loss, fever, fatigue, and night sweats are seen typically in aggressive or highly aggressive lymphomas.
- Aggressive lymphomas have acute or subacute presentation with increasing size of the mass and B symptoms.
- Indolent lymphomas have a more chronic course, with asymptomatic lymphadenopathy, and slowly progressive cytopenias.
- Hepatomegaly and splenomegaly may be present.
- Cough, dyspnea in pulmonary involvement.

DIAGNOSIS

DIFFERENTIAL DIAGNOSIS

- Hodgkin lymphoma.
- Viral infections.
- Metastatic carcinoma.
- Autoimmune conditions.
  A clinical algorithm for evaluation of lymphadenopathy is described in Section III. The differential diagnosis of lymphadenopathy is described in Section II.

WORKUP

Initial laboratory evaluation may reveal only mild anemia and elevated lactate dehydrogenase (LDH). In cases of highly aggressive NHL (e.g., Burkitt lymphoma), spontaneous tumor lysis syndrome (TLS) can be seen, which is characterized by hyperkalemia, hyperuricemia, hypocalcemia, hyperphosphatemia, and acidosis. TLS can be life threatening, and is considered a medical emergency. Acute management includes aggressive IV fluid repletion and rasburicase. Proper staging of NHL includes the following:

- A thorough history and physical examination.
- Excisional or incisional surgical biopsy is preferred. Image-guided core needle biopsies may be acceptable in patients without peripheral adenopathy. Fine needle aspirates are not adequate for precise lymphoma sub-classification. Laparoscopic lymph node biopsy or mediastinoscopy can be used on an outpatient basis for most patients with intraabdominal or mediastinal lymphoma, respectively.
- Tissue biopsy with histologic, immunophenotypic, and genetic studies interpretation.
- Routine laboratory evaluation (complete blood count, flow cytometry, ESR, urinalysis, LDH, blood urea nitrogen, creatinine, serum calcium, uric acid, liver function tests, serum protein electrophoresis.
- HIV and hepatitis B testing.
- Bone marrow evaluation (aspirate and biopsy) (Fig. E1L-36).
- CT scan of chest, abdomen and pelvis with IV contrast, if possible.
- Fluorine-18 fluorodeoxyglucose (FDG) positron emission tomography (PET) integrated with CT has emerged as a powerful tool for staging, response evaluation, and post-treatment surveillance in patients with aggressive subtypes of NHL.
- Depending on the histopathology (Table 1L-28), the results of the above studies and the planned therapy, some other tests may be performed.
- Lumbar puncture is needed in some patients with aggressive NHL, and most patients with HIV-associated NHL, to evaluate for CNS involvement by lymphoma.

CLASSIFICATION: For clinical approach, NHL is subdivided lymphomas into indolent, aggressive, and highly aggressive disease.
STAGING: The Ann Arbor staging system with Cotswold modification is described in Table 1L-29. Histopathology has greater therapeutic implications in NHL than in Hodgkin lymphoma. The frequency of indolent lymphomas among all lymphomas is described in Table 1L-30. The classification of aggressive lymphomas is described in Table 1L-31.

TREATMENT

ACUTE GENERAL Rx

The therapeutic regimen varies with specific lymphoma subtype and pathologic stage. Following are the commonly used therapeutic modalities:
INDOLENT NHL:
1. Deferment of therapy and careful observation in asymptomatic patients with low volume disease.
2. Local radiotherapy for stage I disease.
3. Rituximab, an anti-CD20 antibody, with or without chemotherapy is used in patients with symptomatic or progressive disease. Common chemotherapy agents added to rituximab are bendamustine and combination regimens such as cyclophosphamide, doxorubicin, vincristine, and prednisone.
4. The addition of rituximab to chemotherapy is generally well tolerated and has increased response and survival rates in these patients.
5. Second line chemotherapy or novel agents, such as lenalidomide or idelalisib are highly active in relapsed disease.
6. Stem cell transplantation (autologous or allogeneic) may confer long-term disease control in multiple relapsed or refractory disease.
7. *H. pylori*-associated gastric marginal zone lymphoma can be treated with a course of antibiotics. For persistent cases after eradication or *H. pylori* negative cases, radiotherapy is highly effective.
8. Table 1L-32 summarizes treatment strategies for indolent lymphomas.
AGGRESSIVE NHL: The most common intermediate-grade NHL is DLBCL. The addition of rituximab against CD20 B-cell lymphoma to the CHOP regimen (R-CHOP) increases the complete response rate and prolongs overall survival in patients with DLBCL without clinically significant increase in toxicity. R-CHOP has shown to be safe and effective in patients with HIV-associated NHL with CD4+ counts >50 cells/mm^3.

Most commonly regimens used in DLBCL include:
○ Three cycles of R-CHOP followed by involved-field radiotherapy or 6 cycles of R-CHOP alone are appropriate approaches in patients with localized DLBCL.
○ 6 cycles of R-CHOP with or without radiotherapy are appropriate in patients with advanced stage DLBCL.
○ Granulocyte-colony stimulating factor (e.g., filgrastim, pegfilgrastim) may be effective in reducing the risk of febrile neutropenia in patients over 65 years with aggressive lymphoma undergoing chemotherapy.

TABLE 1L-28 Histologic Features of Non-Hodgkin Lymphomas Involving Bone Marrow

Type of Lymphoma	Incidence of Involvement (%)	Pattern of Involvement*	Cytology	Comments
Small lymphocytic	85	FR, I, D	Small, mature lymphocytes; proliferation centers may be present	CD5+, CD19+ cells; paratrabecular infiltrates essentially rule out this diagnosis
Lymphoplasmacytic	80-100	FR, I, D, FP	Spectrum of cells from lymphocytes to plasma cells; immunoblasts may be present; Dutcher bodies common	Unlike SLL/CLL, occasional paratrabecular infiltrates may be present
Mantle cell	55-95	FR, I, D, FP	Small irregular lymphocytes; may be blastoid; rare cells with prominent nucleoli	CD5+, cyclin D1 positive; paratrabecular infiltrates may be present
Follicular	50-60	FP, D, FR, I	Small cleaved lymphocytes usually predominate; large cleaved or noncleaved cells may be present	CD10+; characteristically paratrabecular; neoplastic follicles may be apparent
Splenic marginal zone	73-100	FR, I, D, IS	Small lymphocytes with slightly irregular nuclei, condensed chromatin, and abundant cytoplasm	Intrasinusoidal infiltrates often prominent; reactive germinal centers may be present
Low-grade extranodal marginal zone	44	FR, P, I, IS	Small cells with condensed chromatin and scant to moderate amounts of cytoplasm; rare large cells may be admixed	Extent of bone marrow infiltration usually minimal
Nodal marginal zone	30-40	FR, I, P, D	Small cells with condensed chromatin and scant to moderate amounts of cytoplasm	
Diffuse large B cell	15-30	FR, D	Large cells with prominent nucleoli	Prominent component of T lymphocytes with or without histiocytes may be present; immunohistochemistry for B-cell antigens and other markers is essential in these cases; rare cases of large cell lymphoma are intravascular
Burkitt	35-60	I, D	Medium-sized cells with reticular chromatin, multiple small nucleoli, and basophilic cytoplasm; cytoplasmic vacuoles common	CD10+, c-MYC+; necrosis common; "starry sky" pattern may be seen
Peripheral T cell (unspecified)	80	FR, D	Polymorphic lymphoid population—nuclei often hyperchromatic and irregular; large cells with nucleoli may be present; prominent reactive cell component often intermixed with lymphoma cells	Vascularity and reticulin fibrosis frequently prominent
Anaplastic large cell	4-40	FR, I (scattered cells), D	Large cells with lobulated nuclei, prominent nucleoli, and abundant cytoplasm	Detection rate is higher with immunostaining for CD30 or ALK-1
Hepatosplenic T cell	100	IS	Medium-sized lymphocytes with dispersed chromatin	Lesions may be subtle; immunohistochemistry is often helpful
Lymphoblastic	50-60	I, D	Blastic cells with high mitotic rate	Identical to acute lymphoblastic leukemia
NK/T cell	0-25	I (scattered cells)	Variable size with pleomorphic nuclei	Immunostains or in situ hybridization (EBER) may be necessary to identify lymphoma cells in bone marrow sections

D, Diffuse; EBER, Epstein-Barr virus–encoded RNA; *FP,* focal paratrabecular; *FR,* focal random; *I,* interstitial; *IS,* intrasinusoidal; *NK,* natural killer; *P,* paratrabecular.
*Patterns may be mixed; the most common patterns are listed.
From Jaffe ES et al: *Hematopathology,* Philadelphia, 2011, Saunders.

TABLE 1L-29 Ann Arbor Staging System for Lymphomas

Stage*	Cotswold Modification of Ann Arbor Classification
I	Involvement of a single lymph node region or lymphoid structure
II	Involvement of two or more lymph node regions on the same side of the diaphragm (the mediastinum is considered a single site, whereas the hilar lymph nodes are considered bilaterally); the number of anatomic sites should be indicated by a subscript (e.g., II_3)
III	Involvement of lymph node regions on both sides of the diaphragm: III_1 (with or without involvement of splenic hilar, celiac, or portal nodes) and III_2 (with involvement of para-aortic, iliac, and mesenteric nodes)
IV	Involvement of one or more extranodal sites in addition to a site for which the designation E has been used

*All cases are subclassified to indicate the absence (A) or presence (B) of the systemic symptoms of significant fever (>38.0° C [100.4° F]), night sweats, and unexplained weight loss exceeding 10% of normal body weight within the previous 6 months. The clinical stage (CS) denotes the stage as determined by all diagnostic examinations and a single diagnostic biopsy only. In the Ann Arbor classification, the term pathologic stage (PS) is used if a second biopsy of any kind has been obtained, whether negative or positive. In the Cotswold modification, the PS is determined by laparotomy; X designates bulky disease (widening of the mediastinum by >one third or the presence of a nodal mass >10 cm), and E designates involvement of a single extranodal site that is contiguous or proximal to the known nodal site.
From Hoffmann R et al: *Hematology: basic principles and practice,* ed 5, Philadelphia, 2009, Churchill Livingstone.

TABLE 1L-30 Frequency of Indolent Lymphomas Among All Lymphomas in the World Health Organization Classification

Follicular lymphoma	22.1%
Extranodal marginal zone lymphoma of mucosa-associated lymphoid tissue type	7.6%
Small lymphocytic lymphoma/chronic lymphocytic leukemia	6.7%
Mantle cell	6.0%
Splenic marginal zone lymphoma	1.8%
Lymphoplasmacytic lymphoma	1.2%
Nodal marginal zone B-cell lymphoma (±monocytoid B cells)	1.0%

From Hoffman R et al: *Hematology: basic principles and practice*, ed 5, Philadelphia, 2009, Churchill Livingstone.

TABLE 1L-31 Classification of Aggressive Lymphomas

B-cell Neoplasms
Precursor B-cell lymphoma
Precursor B lymphoblastic leukemia/lymphoma
Mature B-cell lymphoma
Mantle cell lymphoma
Diffuse large B-cell lymphoma
Mediastinal (thymic) large B-cell lymphoma
Intravascular large B-cell lymphoma
Primary effusion lymphoma
Burkitt lymphoma
B-cell proliferations of uncertain malignant potential
Lymphomatoid granulomatosis
Posttransplant lymphoproliferative disorder, polymorphic

T-cell and NK-cell Neoplasms
Precursor T-cell
Precursor T lymphoblastic leukemia/lymphoma
Blastic NK cell lymphoma
Mature T-cell and NK-cell lymphoma
Adult T-cell leukemia/lymphoma
Extranodal NK/T cell lymphoma, nasal type
Hepatosplenic T-cell lymphoma
Peripheral T-cell lymphoma, unspecified
Angioimmunoblastic T-cell lymphoma
Anaplastic large cell lymphoma

NK, Natural killer.
From Hoffman R et al: *Hematology: basic principles and practice*, ed 5, Philadelphia, 2009, Churchill Livingstone.

TABLE 1L-32 Treatment Strategies for Indolent Lymphomas

Advanced Stage Disease
Watchful waiting
Alkylating agents
Purine analogs (rarely used)
Combination chemotherapy (e.g. CVP, CHOP)
Single agent rituximab
Chemoimmunotherapy (e.g. R-CVP, R-CHOP, R-bendamustine)
Idelalisib +/– rituximab
Lenalidomide +/– rituximab
High dose chemotherapy plus autologous stem cell transplantation
Reduced intensity conditioning allogeneic transplantation
Palliative radiotherapy
Localized Disease
Radiotherapy
Single agent rituximab

Adapted from Hoffman R et al: *Hematology: basic principles and practice*, ed 5, Philadelphia, 2009, Churchill Livingstone.

○ Treatment with high-dose chemotherapy and autologous bone marrow transplant: compared with conventional chemotherapy, increases overall survival in patients with chemotherapy-sensitive relapsed DLBCL.
○ Combination chemotherapy regimens for NHL are described in Table 1L-33.

HIGHLY AGGRESSIVE NHL: The most common high-grade NHL subtype is Burkitt lymphoma (BL). BL affects younger patients than DLBCL, and is common in HIV-infected individuals. Regimens more intensive than R-CHOP are needed to cure patients with high-grade NHL. The most commonly used multi-agent regimens include hyperCVAD or CODOX-M/IVAC, usually in combination with rituximab. The 5-year survival approximates 75%.

DISPOSITION

- Patients with indolent NHL in the rituximab era experience long survival despite the lack of curative potential of chemoimmunotherapy. Patients with aggressive NHL may achieve a cure with chemoimmunotherapy.
- Complete remission occurs in 35% to 50% of patients with aggressive NHL. Prognostic factors include the lymphoma subtype, age of patient, and extent of disease. Table E1L-34 describes the International Prognostic Index for aggressive lymphomas.
- Patients who present with HIV-related NHL and low CD4+ cell count have a poor prognosis (median duration of survival is 15-34 mo). Despite therapeutic advances, the management of HIV-associated lymphomas is challenging due to potential pharmacologic interactions and increased risk of infectious complications. It is important to optimize the CD4 cell count during treatment. Referral to an HIV oncologist is recommended.

SUGGESTED READINGS
Available at www.expertconsult.com

RELATED CONTENT
Non-Hodgkin's Lymphoma (Patient Information)

AUTHORS: **JORGE J. CASTILLO, M.D.,** and **ANN S. LACASCE, M.D.**

TABLE 1L-33 Combination Chemotherapy Regimens for Non-Hodgkin Lymphoma

Regimen	Dose	Days of Administration	Frequency
R-bendamustine			**Every 28 days**
Bendamustine	90 mg/m2 IV	1-2	
Rituximab	375 mg/m² IV	1	
R-CHOP			**Every 21 days**
Cyclophosphamide	750 mg/m² IV	1	
Doxorubicin	50 mg/m² IV	1	
Vincristine	1.4 mg/m² IV*	1	
Prednisone, fixed dose	100 mg PO	1-5	
Rituximab	375 mg/m² IV	1	
R-CVP			**Every 21 days**
Cyclophosphamide	1000 mg/m² IV	1	
Vincristine	1.4 mg/m² IV*	1	
Prednisone, fixed dose	100 mg PO	1-5	
Rituximab	375 mg/m² IV	1	

Adapted from Goldman L, Schafer AI: *Goldman's Cecil medicine,* ed 24, Philadelphia, 2012, Saunders.

L

I

BASIC INFORMATION

DEFINITION

Lynch syndrome is a hereditary predisposition to malignancy of the colon that is explained by a germline mutation in a DNA mismatch repair gene.

SYNONYMS

Hereditary non-polyposis colorectal cancer
HPNCC
Hereditary site-specific colon cancer

ICD-10CM CODES
C18.9 Malignant neoplasm of colon, unspecified

EPIDEMIOLOGY & DEMOGRAPHICS

The lifetime risk for developing colon cancer in the United States is approximately 6%. Up to 30% of colon cancer is inherited and 2% to 4% may be attributable to Lynch syndrome. The incidence of Lynch syndrome is estimated to be between 1:660 and 1:2000. Lynch syndrome is the most common form of hereditary colon cancer. The average age of diagnosis for Lynch syndrome is 45 years, although diagnosis can occur as early as the 20s or as late as the 70s.

RISK FACTORS: Family history of colon cancer or other hereditary non-polyposis colorectal cancer (HNPCC)-related cancers such as endometrial (up to 40% of women with Lynch syndrome may develop endometrial cancer), biliary tract, ovarian, stomach, upper urinary tract, or brain.

GENETICS: Autosomal-dominant inheritance pattern.

ETIOLOGY

Lynch syndrome is thought to be secondary to germline mutations in DNA mismatch repair genes. The predominant genes involved are *MSH2* and *MLH1*, which are tumor suppressor genes, although other genes have documented involvement (*PMS1, PMS2, MSH6,* and *EpCAM*). Mutations in these genes prevent repair of DNA mismatches during DNA replication. This is most prevalent in regions of DNA called microsatellites causing DNA microsatellite instability and leading to an increased risk for malignancy, especially colon cancer. *MSH6* mutations are associated with a markedly lower cancer risk than *MLH1* or *MSH2* mutations.

PHYSICAL FINDINGS & CLINICAL PRESENTATION

- Changes in bowel habits (prolonged constipation).
- Melena.
- Hematochezia.
- Abdominal pain.
- Unexplained weight loss.
- Decreased appetite.
- Right sided colon cancer (70%-85% of cases)

DIAGNOSIS

DIFFERENTIAL DIAGNOSIS

- Familial adenomatosis polyposis.
- Peutz-Jeghers syndrome.
- Juvenile polyposis.
- Nonhereditary colorectal cancer.
- Gardner syndrome.

WORKUP

If an individual presents with numerous adenomatous polyps or has multiple relatives with cancer at a young age, a family history complete with pedigree must be obtained. Clinical diagnosis of the Lynch syndrome can be made with the Amsterdam or Bethesda criteria.

- Revised Amsterdam (II) criteria (must meet all criteria):
  1. HNPCC-associated carrier diagnosis in at least three individuals in the family.
  2. One of the patients is a first-degree family member of two other patients.
  3. Involved patients occur in at least two successive generations with diagnosis of HNPCC.
  4. At least one diagnosis in family of HNPCC was made before age 50.
  5. The diagnoses are histologically confirmed.
  6. Familial adenomatous polyposis is excluded.
- Bethesda criteria (must meet all criteria):
  1. Colorectal cancer before age 50.
  2. Multiple colorectal cancers or other HNPCC-related cancers such as biliary tract, endometrial, stomach, or ovary.
  3. Colorectal cancer with microsatellite instability histology <60 years of age.
  4. Colorectal cancer or HNPCC-related cancer in first-degree relative <50 years of age.
  5. Colorectal cancer or HNPCC-related cancer in at least two first- or second-degree relatives, any age.
- If criteria for the Lynch syndrome are not met, no further analysis is necessary (although a genetic syndrome cannot be definitively excluded and genetic referral may be warranted).

LABORATORY TESTS

- If a patient meets criteria for Lynch syndrome, immunohistochemistry can be performed for the presence or absence of mismatch repair genes *MLH1, MSH2, MSH6,* and *PMS2*. Rarely, *MLH3* is identified.
- Microsatellite instability analysis should also be performed if criteria for Lynch syndrome are met.

 TREATMENT

- If the mutation has been identified in a family member, screening for this mutation can be performed via genetic testing. Informed consent must be obtained after a thorough explanation has been provided to each individual.

- Surveillance using colonoscopy can be performed in individuals who screen positive, while those who screen negative can be discharged. The mismatch repair gene that is mutated guides screening.
- According to the Netherlands Surveillance Protocol, for example, individuals with mutations in *MLH1, MSH2,* or *MSH6* should have colonoscopies every 1 to 2 yr starting at age 20 to 25 yr; urine cytology every 1 to 2 yr starting at age 30 to 35 yr; esophagogastroduodenoscopy every 1 to 2 yr starting at age 30 to 35 yr; and, in females, ultrasound of endometrium and CA-125 every 1 to 2 yr starting at age 30 to 35 yr.
- Aspirin may be protective against colorectal cancer in Lynch syndrome patients.

REFERRALS

- To gastroenterology for surveillance colonoscopies.
- To genetic counselor if patient satisfies Bethesda criteria.
- To psychologist as necessary for psychological support.

 PEARLS & CONSIDERATIONS

- Before genetic testing is instituted, informed consent must be obtained because consequences of this testing include the necessity of lifelong screenings such as colonoscopies.
- The risk of pancreatic cancer is increased in families with Lynch syndrome compared with the U.S. population.
- **Familial Colorectal Cancer Type X** refers to patients who meet the Amsterdam criteria for HPNCC but have no molecular evidence of a MMR deficiency. These patients have a lower risk of colon cancer and no increased risk of extracolonic cancer compared to those with Lynch syndrome.

PATIENT & FAMILY EDUCATION

- For information on local genetic counselors, visit the National Society of Genetic Counselors Web site at www.nsgc.org.
- For information on Lynch syndrome, visit www.mayoclinic.com/health/lynch-syndrome/DS00669.

EBM EVIDENCE

Available at www.expertconsult.com

SUGGESTED READINGS
Available at www.expertconsult.com

RELATED CONTENT
Colorectal Cancer (Related Key Topic)
Gardner's Syndrome (Related Key Topic)
Peutz-Jeghers Syndrome and other Polyposis Syndromes (Related Key Topic)

AUTHORS: **PAUL F. GEORGE, M.D.,** and **JOANNE M. SILVIA, M.D.**

BASIC INFORMATION

DEFINITION

Macular degeneration, usually referred to as *age-related macular degeneration* (ARMD), is an acquired degeneration of the retinal pigment epithelium and subsequently the neurosensory retina and choroid resulting in loss of central vision. The etiology is not known but a combination of genetic predisposition and certain risk factors plays an important role. Nonexudative (or "Dry") AMD is the most common but Exudative (or "Wet") AMD is the most visually devastating.

ICD-10CM CODES
H35.31 Nonexudative age-related macular degeneration
H35.32 Exudative age-related macular degeneration

EPIDEMIOLOGY & DEMOGRAPHICS

INCIDENCE (IN U.S.):
- Leading cause of irreversible blindness in people ≥50 yr in the developed world.
- Increases with age.
- In North America 15 million people currently have nonexudative AMD and 1.7 million have neovascular AMD. The overall prevalence is projected to increase by >50% by 2020.
- About 10% of patients with AMD have the neovascular form manifested by an often rapid decrease in central visual acuity caused by bleeding and scarring secondary to choroidal neovascularization.

PEAK INCIDENCE:
- Ages 75 to 80 yr
- Dramatically increases in incidence and prevalence with age until ~80% of people ≥75 yr have senile macular degeneration

PREVALENCE (IN U.S.):
- Varies, but ~5% of people >50 yr have some signs of macular degeneration.
- In the U.S., 25% of people over the age of 75 have macular degeneration

PREDOMINANT SEX: Males and females are affected equally (15% of white women >80 yr have severe AMD)

PREDOMINANT AGE: >50 yr

RISK FACTORS:
- Advancing age, especially over 70
- Genetic factors
- History of smoking within past 20 yr
- Dietary factors (low intake of antioxidants, zinc, and omega-3 fatty acids; high fat intake)
- Obesity
- White race

PHYSICAL FINDINGS & CLINICAL PRESENTATION
- Decreased central vision, distortion of vision (metamorphopsia), poor night vision
- Drusen, atrophy, macular hemorrhage, pigmentation, edema
- The most common abnormality seen in AMD is the presence of drusen, or yellowish deposits deep to the retina; this may be early in the course of disease

- Choroidal neovascular membrane (CNVM) develops with rapid change in vision due to leakage of exudative fluid and hemorrhage.

ETIOLOGY
- Genetics: 19 genes with mutations have been identified—dysregulation of the alternate complement system among other biochemical pathways.
- Pigmentary and vascular changes with exudate, edema, and scar tissue development
- Dry-type atrophy of the macula retinal pigment epithelium
- The main mediator of neovascularization in wet AMD is vascular endothelial growth factor (VEGF). It induces angiogenesis and increases inflammation and vascular permeability

DIAGNOSIS

DIFFERENTIAL DIAGNOSIS
- Central serous chorioretinopathy
- Pattern dystrophy of the retinal pigment epithelium
- Drug toxicity (hydroxychloroquine, deferoxamine)
- Hypertensive retinopathy
- Histoplasmosis and high myopia (less common causes of CNVM)
- Trauma with macular scar

WORKUP
- Complete eye examination, including visual field and fluorescein angiography
- Optical coherence tomography (OCT)

IMAGING STUDIES
- OCT
- Fluorescein angiography
- Fundus autofluorescence

TREATMENT

NONPHARMACOLOGIC THERAPY
- There is no laser treatment for dry AMD.
- Photodynamic treatment with verteporfin can be used in the rare case of exudative AMD that does not respond to intravitreal pharmacotherapy.
- Thermal laser (argon) for certain classic membranes (CNVM) is rarely used in the era of biologics

ACUTE GENERAL Rx
- The introduction of therapies blocking VEGF has dramatically changed the management of AMD and is now the standard of care in the management of neovascular AMD. Intravitreal injections of anti-VEGF agents (ranibizumab, bevacizumab and aflibercept) are first-line treatments for neovascular AMD. Intravitreal administration of ranibizumab, a humanized antibody fragment that neutralizes all active forms of VEGF A, was shown to stabilize or improve vision in 95% of patients compared to 65% of patients treated with verteporfin PDT. Aflibercept is a soluble protein that acts as a VEGF receptor decoy and is the most recently FDA-approved intravitreal therapy. Randomized controlled trials showed it

to be non-inferior to ranibizumab. Bevacizumab, a full-length monoclonal antibody to VEGF, is used off-label as intravitreal therapy. Its cost per intravitreal dose is significantly lower than that of ranibizumab and aflibercept. However, several comparative effectiveness trials have shown bevacizumab to be non-inferior to ranibizumab.
- A major concern regarding anti-VEGF treatment is the potential increased risk of stroke and cardiovascular disease but no study to date has shown an increased incidence due to intravitreal therapy.
- Laser photocoagulation therapy may be useful in patients with extrafoveal lesions but is no longer routinely recommended for wet AMD.

CHRONIC Rx
- Age Related Eye Disease Study 1 and 2 (AREDS): a large randomized controlled trial showed that supplementation with the antioxidant vitamins C (500 mg) and E (400 IU), beta carotene (15 mg), and the micronutrient zinc (80 mg zinc oxide and 2 mg cupric oxide to prevent zinc-induced anemia) in patients with intermediate nonexudative AMD resulted in a 25% risk reduction of progression to advanced AMD at 5 years.

DISPOSITION
- Follow closely by ophthalmologist, retinal specialist
- Frequency of follow-up determined by severity of disease
- Patients should self monitor with Amsler grid daily and report changes immediately
- Smoking cessation, sunglasses with UV A and B protection, diet high in green leafy vegetables and fish
- Most anti-VEGF treatment failures are due to missed follow-up visits. Patients should be reminded repeatedly to call if their vision worsens

PEARLS & CONSIDERATIONS

COMMENTS
- Recent trials with embryonic stem cell transplants have shown promise in macular degeneration.
- Statistically, the vision of only 1 of 10 affected persons can be saved, but the disease is so devastating that vigorous therapy should be considered in all patients.
- Vitamins with zinc and antioxidants may slow progression of AMD.
- Quitting smoking significantly reduces the risk of developing AMD.

EVIDENCE

Available at www.expertconsult.com

SUGGESTED READINGS
Available at www.expertconsult.com

RELATED CONTENT
Macular Degeneration (Patient Information)

AUTHOR: **ROBERT H. JANIGIAN, JR., M.D.**

BASIC INFORMATION

DEFINITION

Malabsorption is the diminished intestinal absorption of dietary nutrients. The majority of malabsorption is due to either congenital or acquired defects in the membrane transport system, absorption, and brush border processing in the intestinal epithelium.

SYNONYM

Maldigestion

ICD-10CM CODES

K90.9 Intestinal malabsorption, unspecified
K90.4 Malabsorption due to intolerance, not elsewhere classified
K90.89 Other intestinal malabsorption
K91.2 Postsurgical malabsorption, not elsewhere classified

EPIDEMIOLOGY & DEMOGRAPHICS

PREDOMINANT SEX AND AGE: More common in females with a mean age of 40
GENETICS:
• HLA-DQ2 present in 95% of Celiac Disease.
RISK FACTORS:
• Excessive alcohol consumption
• History of celiac disease
• History of IBD
• Intestinal surgery

PHYSICAL FINDINGS & CLINICAL PRESENTATION

• Most commonly nonspecific symptoms such as abdominal flatulence and distension are seen.
• Due to the osmotic load from maldigestion/malabsorption, watery diarrhea may be present. In the case of fat digestive disorder, steatorrhea ensues.
• Weight loss is very common but many patients are able to compensate by increased caloric load. Diffuse disease often has much more pronounced weight loss.
• Chronic protein malabsorption can cause hypoalbuminemia, leading to edema and ascites.
• Both microcytic and macrocytic anemia can result from micronutrient deficiency (iron/B12). These patient can be pale and present with fatigue.
• Bleeding disorders from vitamin K deficiency can lead to ecchymosis, melena, and hematuria.
• Vitamin D deficiency can lead to bone disorders. Secondary hyperparathyroidism can be a presenting feature.
• Electrolyte and vitamin deficiency can lead to neurologic disorders such as ataxia, weakness, and neuropathy, and may have positive Chvostek or trousseau sign.
• Disease specific dermatologic findings such as alopecia, pellagra, erythema nodosum, pyoderma gangrenosum, cheilosis, glossitis, and aphthous ulcers may be present.

ETIOLOGY

• Can be congenital or acquired
• Disease-specific etiology

DIFFERENTIAL DIAGNOSIS

• Crohn's disease
• Celiac disease
• Hartnup's disease
• Chronic pancreatitis
• Pancreatic insufficiency
• Cystic fibrosis
• Short bowel syndrome
• Neoplasm
• Abetalipoproteinemia
• Lactose intolerance
• Small intestine bacterial overgrowth
• Chronic atrophic gastritis
• Zollinger-Ellison syndrome
• Chronic cholestasis
• Cirrhosis

WORK-UP

• A detailed history including alcohol consumption, surgical history as well as autoimmune disease can help diagnose the underlying disease. It is important to screen for anemia and electrolyte abnormalities due to malabsorption.

LABORATORY TESTS

• CBC, serum iron, Vitamin B12, and folate to detect for anemia.
• Prothrombin time: elevated PT can suggest vitamin K deficiency.
• **Fat malabsorption:** The gold standard is the 72-hour stool fat collection. More than 6/g day in the stool is pathologic. This test can be cumbersome so other options are available. Sudan III stain and acid steatocrit tests are qualitative measures of steatorrhea. Serologic testing for celiac disease should be considered as well.
• **Carbohydrate malabsorption:** Carbohydrate malabsorption leads to fermentation of the undigested carbohydrates by intestinal bacteria.
• The urinary D-xylose test for carbohydrate absorption in the small intestine. After loading with D-xylose, urinary D-xylose levels are measured. Low levels suggest intestinal malabsorption.
• Lactose intolerance can be tested by the lactose tolerance test or the breath test. The lactose tolerance test measures blood glucose after lactose administration. Development of symptoms or inadequate increase in blood sugar is indicative of lactose intolerance. H_2/CO_2 breath tests using specific forms of carbohydrates can detect malabsorption as well.
• **Protein malabsorption:** Protein malabsorption is likely due to small intestinal bacterial overgrowth or protein gastroenteropathies. Alpha-1 antitrypsin clearance or 99mTc-albumin gamma camera scintigraphy may aid in this diagnosis.
• **Pancreatic insufficiency:** Fecal elastase and chymotrypsin levels can distinguish from pancreatic and intestinal causes.

• **Vitamin deficiency:** It is important to assess serum vitamin B12 and methymalonic acid levels. Schilling's test is rarely used but can be useful in some cases.
• **Bile acid malabsorption:** Quantitative stool bile acid measurement is the preferred method of diagnosis. SeHCAT test (selenium homocholic acid taurine test) is another option but less likely used.
• **Bacterial overgrowth:** This can be detected with endoscopic jejunal aspirate culture or a less invasive hydrogen breath test.

IMAGING STUDIES

• Abdominal US can identify thickened small bowel wall.
• Endoscopy for visualization and biopsy
• Small bowel follow through
• Abdominal CT/MRI
• ERCP/MRCP/EUS for identification of pancreatic abnormalities
• Capsule endoscopy

TREATMENT

Involves identification and treatment of the underlying illness, treatment of diarrhea, and nutritional repletion

NONPHARMACOLOGIC THERAPY

• A gluten-free diet in patients with celiac disease. Avoidance of lactose-containing product in lactose intolerance.
• Avoidance of caffeine and high sugar containing compounds has been found to decrease diarrhea in some cases.

ACUTE GENERAL Rx

• Control of the underlying disease should be primary goal
• It is also essential to control any volume and electrolyte abnormalities that might exist.

CHRONIC Rx

• Control of chronic diarrhea with loperamide or diphenoxylate with atropine should be one of the goals in a chronic malabsorptive state.
• Correction of volume and electrolyte disturbance with oral rehydration therapy should be made a priority.
• Bile acid conjugates can decrease steatorrhea in some cases.
• Pancreatic insufficiency is typically treated with a low-fat diet and exogenous pancreatic enzymes
• Teduglutide-homolog of GLP-2 has been shown to increase absorptive surface area in short bowel syndrome.
• Periodic DEXA scans are indicated in chronic malabsorption in the setting of vitamin D deficiency
• Oral supplementation with vitamins and minerals is important, sometimes requiring parenteral therapy

REFERRAL

- Gastroenterology consultation can help in diagnosis when initial laboratory testing is unclear.
- Nutrition consultation can help patients with diet modification to alleviate symptoms.

PEARLS & CONSIDERATIONS

COMMENTS

- Malabsorption should be considered a sign of an underlying disease.

- Treatment should focus on treating the underlying disorder.
- Nutrient and volume repletion should be priority in any treatment plan of malabsorption.

RELATED CONTENT

Section III Suspected Malabsorption (Algorithm)
Table 3-28 Tests for the Evaluation of Malabsorption
Celiac Disease (Related Key Topic)
Pancreatitis, Chronic (Related Key Topic)
Small Intestinal Bacterial Overgrowth (Related Key Topic)
Crohn's Disease (Related Key Topic)
Ulcerative Colitis (Related Key Topic)

Lactose Intolerance (Related Key Topic)
Short Bowel Syndrome (Related Key Topic)
Cystic Fibrosis (Related Key Topic)

SUGGESTED READINGS

Available at www.expertconsult.com

AUTHORS: **GEORGE CHOLANKERIL, M.D.,**
DIMITRI GITELMAKER, M.D., and
ALAN EPSTEIN, M.D.

BASIC INFORMATION

DEFINITION

Malaria is a protozoan disease caused by intraerythrocytic protozoa of the genus *Plasmodium* and transmitted by female *Anopheles* spp. mosquitoes. It is endemic throughout most of the tropics and is characterized by hectic fever and often presents with classic malarial paroxysm. Five species of genus *Plasmodium* usually infect humans (Table 1M-1):
- *P. falciparum*
- *P. vivax*
- *P. malariae*
- *P. ovale*
- *P. knowlesi*

SYNONYMS

Periodic fever
Tertian malaria
Quartan malaria
Tropical splenomegaly

ICD-10CM CODES
B54 Unspecified malaria
B50.9 *Plasmodium faluparum* malaria, unspecified
B51.9 *Plasmodium vivax* malaria without complications
B52.9 *Plasmodium malariae* malaria without complications
53.0 *Plasmodium ovale* malaria
B53.8 Other parasitologically confirmed malaria, not elsewhere classified

EPIDEMIOLOGY & DEMOGRAPHICS

Global:
- ~300 million cases a year in more than 100 countries
- Around 900,000 deaths per year, with more than 80% of the deaths occurring in children of sub-Saharan Africa
- 3 billion people live in malaria-endemic areas

U.S.:
- ~1500 cases reported to the CDC in the United States each year. In the majority of reported cases, U.S. civilians who acquired infection abroad had not adhered to a chemoprophylaxis regimen that was appropriate for the country in which they acquired malaria.
- More than 50% of the reported cases in the U.S. are *P. falciparum*. On average, there are six deaths per year in the United States.
- Most infections limited to:
  1. Immigrant population
  2. Returned travelers or troops from endemic area
- Occasionally, transmission through exposure to infected blood product or shared intravenous needles by users of injection drugs.
- Congenital transmission is possible.
- Local mosquito-borne transmission has been reported.
- Competent mosquito vectors are present.
  1. *A. albimanus* in eastern United States
  2. *A. freeborni* in western United States

Geographic distribution:
- *P. falciparum:* Sub-Saharan Africa, Papua New Guinea, Solomon Islands, Haiti, Indian subcontinent
- *P. vivax:* Central America, South America, North Africa, Middle East, Indian subcontinent
- *P. ovale:* West Africa
- *P. malariae:* worldwide

Parasite life cycle (Fig. 1M-1):
- Human infection begins when a female anopheline mosquito bites (only female anopheline mosquito takes blood meal) and inoculates plasmodial sporozoites into bloodstream. The bite usually occurs between dusk and dawn.
- The sporozoites then travel to liver and invade to hepatocytes.
- In the hepatocytes, the sporozoites mature to tissue schizont or become dormant hypnozoites.
- The tissue schizonts amplify the infection by producing a large number of merozoites (10,000 to 30,000).

- Each merozoite is capable of invading an RBC and can establish the asexual cycle of replication in RBCs.
- Asexual cycles produce and release 24 to 32 merozoites at the end of 48- or 72-hr *(P. malariae)* cycles.
- The hypnozoites are only found in relapsing malaria *P. vivax* or *P. ovale* and may remain dormant for up to 5 yr.
- Eventually some intraerythrocytic parasites develop into gametocytes. Male and female gametocytes are taken up by a female anopheline mosquito with a blood meal where they fertilize in the mosquito gut to produce a diploid zygote that matures to an ookinete; haploid sporozoites are generated that migrate to the salivary gland of the mosquito to infect another human.

PHYSICAL FINDINGS & CLINICAL PRESENTATION

- Fever is the hallmark of malaria, known as malarial paroxysm, initially daily until synchronization of infection after several wk, when fever may occur every other day (tertian) in *P. vivax*, *P. ovale*, or *P. falciparum* malaria or every third day (quartan) in *P. malariae* malaria. Table 1M-2 describes the WHO criteria for severe malaria.
- Classic malarial paroxysm characterized by
  1. Cold stage: abrupt onset of cold feeling associated with rigors, shakes.
  2. Hot stage: high fever (~40° C) associated with restlessness.
  3. Sweating stage: patient defervesces.
- Nonspecific symptoms are
  1. Headache.
  2. Cough.
  3. Myalgia.
  4. Vomiting.
  5. Diarrhea.
  6. Jaundice.
- *P. falciparum:*
  1. Most pathogenic of the four species.
  2. Rapidly progresses to high-level parasitemia.
  3. Important cause of the fatal malaria.

TABLE 1M-1 Features of the Five Species of Malaria Known to Cause Disease in Humans

	Plasmodium falciparum	Plasmodium vivax	Plasmodium ovale	Plasmodium malariae	Plasmodium knowlesi
Incubation period (days)	6-25	8-27	8-27	16-40	12
Asexual cycle (hours)	48 (tertian)	48 (tertian)	48 (tertian)	72 (quartan)	24 (tertian)
Relapse	No	Yes*	Yes*	No†	No
Chloroquine resistance	Yes‡	Rare§	No	No‖	No
Characteristic on thin blood film	Rings predominate, multiply infected RBCs, high parasitemia, rings with threadlike cytoplasm, double nuclei, banana-shaped gametocytes	Enlarged RBCs, Schüffner's dots, trophozoite cytoplasm ameboid, 12-24 merozoites in mature schizont	Oval RBCs with fringed edges, Schüffner's dots, trophozoite cytoplasm compact, 6-16 merozoites in mature schizont	Trophozoite cytoplasm compact (band forms), 6-12 merozoites in mature schizont, RBC unchanged	Similar to *P. malariae*, 8-10 merozoites in mature schizont, often in rosette pattern with central clump of pigment

*Relapses may appear months to years after initial infection due to dormant hypnozoites in the liver.
†Although relapse does not occur, *P. malariae* can produce persistent infections that remain below detectable limits in the blood for 20 to 30 years or more.
‡*P. falciparum* resistance to sulfadoxine/pyrimethamine, mefloquine, halofantrine, and artemisinin have also been reported in some areas, along with partial resistance to quinine and quinidine.
§*P. vivax* resistance to chloroquine now reported in some areas of Southeast Asia, Oceania, and South America.
‖Chloroquine-resistant *P. malariae* has also been reported in south Sumatra, Indonesia.
From Vincent JL et al: *Textbook of critical care*, ed 6, Philadelphia, 2011, Saunders.

4. Classic malarial paroxysm is usually absent.
5. Incubation period after exposure is 12 days (range: 9 to 60 days).
6. Cytoadherence and resetting of RBCs play central role in pathogenesis.
7. The sequestration of RBCs in vital organs leads to fatal complications.
8. Cerebral malaria is a feared complication.
9. Invades erythrocytes of all ages.
10. Lacks hypnozoites (intrahepatic stage), does not relapse.
11. Blood smear usually shows ring form only.
12. Pigment color is black.
13. Banana-shaped gametocytes; if seen in blood, smear is diagnostic.
14. Chloroquine resistance is widely present.

• *P. vivax:*
1. Known as tertian malaria: fever occurs every other day.
2. Duffy blood-group antigen FYA- or FYB-related receptor is needed for attachment to RBC.

3. FyFy phenotype (most West African) individuals are resistant to *P. vivax* malaria.
4. Incubation period after exposure is 14 days (range: 8 to 27 days).
5. Hypnozoites may cause relapse of infection after years.
6. Infects mainly reticulocytes.
7. Irregularly shaped large rings and trophozoites, enlarged RBCs, and Schüffner's dots are seen in peripheral blood smear (Fig. 1M-2).
8. Pigment color is yellow-brown.
9. *P. vivax* from Papua New Guinea have reduced sensitivity to chloroquine.
10. Primaquine is needed to eradicate the hypnozoites.

• *P. ovale:*
1. Also known as tertian malaria; fever occurs every other day.
2. Occurs mainly in tropical Africa.
3. Incubation period after exposure is 14 days (range: 8-27 days).
4. Hypnozoites may cause relapse of infection.
5. Infects mainly reticulocytes.
6. Infected RBC is seen as enlarged, oval shape containing large ring or trophozoites with Schüffner's dots.
7. Pigment color is dark brown.
8. Primaquine needed to eradicate the hypnozoites.
9. No chloroquine resistance has been encountered.

• *P. malariae:*
1. Known as quartan malaria; fever occurs every third day.
2. Common cause of chronic malarial infection.
3. May persist for 20 to 30 yr after leaving the endemic area.
4. Worldwide distribution.
5. Incubation period after exposure is 30 days (range: 16-60 days).
6. Lacks hypnozoites (intrahepatic stage).
7. May persist in blood for many years if treated inadequately.
8. Chronic infection may cause soluble immune-complex, resulting in nephritic syndrome.

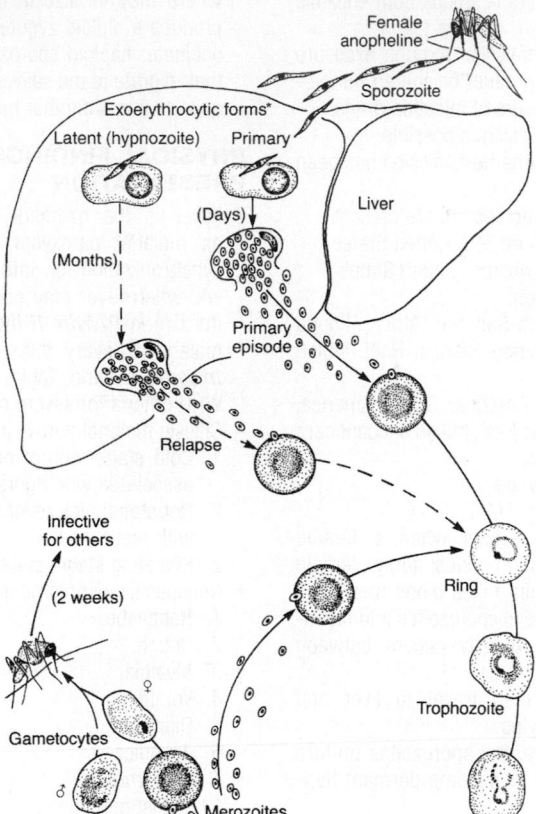

FIGURE 1M-1 Life cycle of plasmodia in humans. Exoerythrocytic forms are also called schizonts. (From Gorbach SL: *Infectious diseases,* ed 2, Philadelphia, 1998, Saunders.)

TABLE 1M-2 World Health Organization Criteria for Severe Malaria, 2000

Impaired consciousness
Prostration
Respiratory distress
Multiple seizures
Jaundice
Hemoglobinuria
Abnormal bleeding
Severe anemia
Circulatory collapse
Pulmonary edema

From Kliegman RM et al: *Nelson textbook of pediatrics,* ed 19, Philadelphia, 2011, Saunders.

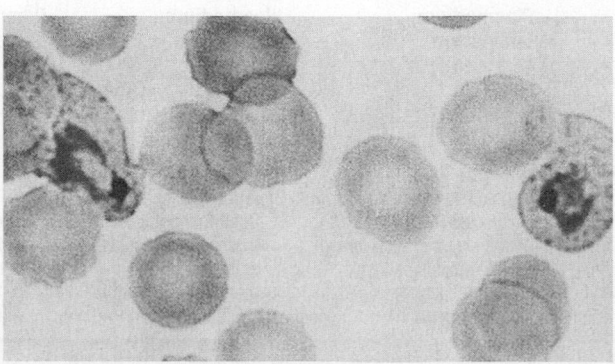

FIGURE 1M-2 Giemsa-stained blood smear in *Plasmodium vivax* malaria. Asexual parasites. Note that the parasites are large and ameboid; the infected erythrocytes are the largest cells in the field (because they are reticulocytes), and the erythrocytes contain numerous pink dots (Schüffner's dots) (×2000). (From Klippel JH et al [eds]: *Internal medicine,* ed 5, St Louis, 1998, Mosby.)

9. Infects mainly mature RBCs.
10. Band or rectangular forms of trophozoites are commonly seen in peripheral blood smear.
11. Pigment color is brown-black.

- Cerebral malaria:
  1. Feared complication of *P. falciparum* infection.
  2. Mortality is ~20%.
  3. Pathogenesis is poorly understood.
  4. Ischemia as a result of sequestration of parasites or cytokines induced by parasite toxin(s) is the key debate.
  5. Seizure and altered mental status leading to coma are cardinal manifestation.
  6. Hypoglycemia, lactic acidosis, and elevated circulating TNF-α may be present.
  7. CSF studies: no increase of WBC count or protein, raised lactate concentrate, and increased opening pressure, especially in children, may be present.

 **DIAGNOSIS**

DIFFERENTIAL DIAGNOSIS

- Typhoid fever
- Dengue fever
- Yellow fever
- Viral hepatitis
- Influenza
- Brucellosis
- UTI
- Leishmaniasis
- Trypanosomiasis
- Rickettsial diseases
- Leptospirosis

WORKUP

- Clinical diagnosis is notoriously inaccurate.
- Demonstration of malarial parasites in blood smear is essential.
- Newer molecular diagnostic techniques (polymerase chain reaction, rapid diagnostic tests) are promising.

LABORATORY TESTS

- The thick and thin blood film is required to identify malarial parasites. A Giemsa-stained film of the patient's peripheral blood should be examined for parasites as soon as possible.
- The thick smears are more sensitive and primarily used to detect the presence of parasites.
- The thin smears are used for species differentiation and parasite density estimation.
- A patient who is suspected of having malaria but who has no parasite seen in blood smears should have blood smears repeated every 12 to 24 hr for 3 consecutive days.

PREPARATION OF BLOOD SMEAR:

- Must be prepared from fresh blood obtained by pricking the fingers.
- The thin smear is fixed in methanol before staining.
- The thick smear is stained unfixed.
- The smear should be stained with a 3% Giemsa solution (pH of 7.2) for 30 to 45 min.

- The parasite density should be estimated by counting the percentage of RBCs infected, not the number of parasites, under an oil immersion lens on thin film.

COMMON ERRORS IN READING MALARIAL SMEARS:

- Platelets overlying an RBC
- Misreading artifacts as parasites
- Concern about missing a positive slide

MOLECULAR DIAGNOSIS OF MALARIA:

- Rapid diagnostic tests (RDT)
  1. Employ immunochromatographic lateral flow technology for antigen detection.
  2. Thus far only one RDT has been FDA approved: BinaxNOW Malaria test kit.
  3. This kit is based on antigens HRP-2 and aldolase.
  4. For *P. falciparum:* sensitivity 95% and specificity 94%.
  5. For *P. vivax:* sensitivity 69% and specificity 100%.
- Limitations of the BinaxNOW Malaria test:
  1. Not approved for mixed infections
  2. Should not be used for *P. malariae* and *P. ovale* as data are limited
  3. Positive test must be confirmed by microscopy
  4. Negative results require confirmation by thick and thin smears
  5. This test cannot be used to monitor therapy as antigen persists after the elimination of the parasite, causing false positives
- Other diagnostic tests available include:
  1. Tagged monoclonal antibodies for malaria antigen detection
  2. Nucleic acid amplification and detection: PCR can detect parasites down to a level of 1 to 5 parasites per microliter of blood. PCR can detect mixed species infection
  3. Fluorescence microscopy with acridine orange or other staining
  4. Dark field microscopy

Rx TREATMENT

NONPHARMACOLOGIC THERAPY

ANTIMOSQUITO MEASURES:

1. Eradication of mosquito breeding places by chemical spray
2. Use of mosquito nets properly in the endemic areas
3. Use of protective clothing
4. Use of insect spray (permethrin), mosquito coils, or repellents such as diethyltoluamide (DEET). For adults, DEET (30%-50%) is generally protective for at least 4 hr. For smaller children, use DEET at ≤20% concentration.

ACUTE GENERAL Rx

A definitive diagnosis of malaria is essential for specific antimalarial chemotherapy.

NON-FALCIPARUM MALARIA:

- Chloroquine 600 mg base (1000 mg chloroquine phosphate) PO loading dose, 6 hr later 300 mg base (500 mg salt), then 300 mg base (500 mg salt) daily for 2 days.

- In the case of *P. vivax* and *P. ovale,* treatment with primaquine 15 mg daily for 14 days is needed to eradicate the exoerythrocytic forms, especially the hypnozoites responsible for relapses.
- G6PD should be measured before primaquine is given. Primaquine is not recommended for those who are glucose-6-phosphate dehydrogenase deficient, because primaquine can cause hemolysis and even death in G6PD-deficient persons. Normal G6PD levels must be documented before using primaquine for either chemoprophylaxis or treatment.
- Chloroquine-resistant *P. vivax* has been documented; in that case, quinine is given.

FALCIPARUM MALARIA:

- Chloroquine can be used cautiously for falciparum malaria acquired in chloroquine-sensitive areas (chloroquine is more rapidly effective than quinine).
- Mainstay of treatment is oral quinine sulfate 10 mg (salt)/kg (usually 650 mg) q8h for 3 to 7 days + doxycycline 100 mg PO bid both for 7 days for adults. Pediatrics: quinine sulfate: 10 mg/kg PO tid plus clindamycin: 20 mg/kg per day divided in tid dose both for 7 days.
- Atovaquone-proguanil (Malarone): 250 mg atovaquone/100 mg proguanil: 4 adult tabs PO once a day for 3 days with food in adults or for pediatrics: pediatric tablets (62.5 mg atovaquone/25 mg proguanil) are used based on weight:
- 5 to 8 kg: 2 pediatric tabs PO once daily for 3 days
- 9 to 10 kg: 3 pediatric tabs PO once daily for 3 days
- 11 to 20 kg: 1 adult tab PO once daily for 3 days
- 21 to 30 kg: 2 adult tabs PO once daily for 3 days
- 31 to 40 kg: 3 adult tabs PO once daily for 3 days
- >40 kg: 4 adult tabs PO once daily for 3 days artemether-lumefantrine (Coartem) tablets: 4 tabs PO (at time zero and 8 hr later) then bid × 2 days for a total of six doses. For pediatrics:
- 5 to <15 kg: 1 tablet per dose
- 15 to <25 kg: 2 tablets per dose
- 25 to <35 kg: 3 tablets per dose
- >35 kg: 4 tablets per dose. The child should receive initial dose based on weight, then followed by second dose 8 hr later, then 1 dose PO bid for following 2 days

ALTERNATIVES:

- Quinine sulfate plus clindamycin 900 mg tid for 7 days in adults, or
- Mefloquine 750 mg PO then 500 mg PO 6 to 12 hr later in adults

NOTE: Parasitemia may paradoxically rise in the first 24 to 36 hr and is not an indication of treatment failure.

SEVERE FALCIPARUM MALARIA:

- It is a medical emergency; intensive care is preferred.
- Measurement of blood glucose, lactate, ABG is important.

- IV quinidine gluconate 10 mg salt/kg loading dose (maximum 600 mg) in NS; infuse slowly over 1 to 2 hr, followed by continuous infusion of 0.02 mg/kg/min until patient can swallow.
- Need to monitor ECG for observation of QT interval as can prolong. Also need to monitor blood pressure and glucose to avoid hypoglycemia.
- Alternatively, IV artesunate: 2.4 mg/kg IV first dose then at 12 and 24 hr followed by 2.4 mg/kg once daily. One recent study showed the superiority of parenteral artesunate over parenteral quinine in adults and children who could not take an oral medication.
- Plasmapheresis is an option for parasitemia >30% or in pregnant women and in elderly with severe malaria.

NOTE: WHO recommends IV artesunate as the treatment of choice for severe malaria in adults and children in area of low transmission. Data on children in high-transmission regions are limited, and WHO recommends treatment with artesunate, artemether, or quinine.

MULTIDRUG-RESISTANT MALARIA:
- Mefloquine 1250 mg as a single dose, or
- Halofantrine 500 mg every 6 hr for 3 doses, repeat same course after 1 wk
- Combination therapy usually preferred

DISPOSITION

RISK FACTORS FOR FATAL MALARIA:
- Failure to take chemoprophylaxis
- Delay in seeking medical care
- Misdiagnosis

COMPLICATIONS OF MALARIA:
- Anemia
- Acidosis
- Hypoglycemia
- Respiratory distress
- DIC
- Blackwater fever
- Renal failure
- Shock

REFERRAL

- To an infectious disease specialist or travel medicine expert for severe malaria complications
- To an intensive care specialist if severe cerebral malaria or other major organ failure develops
- All malaria cases are mandated to be reported to local and state health departments by health care providers or laboratory staff

❗ PEARLS & CONSIDERATIONS

HOST RESPONSE

- The specific immune response to malaria confers protection from high-level parasitemia and disease, but not from infection.
- Asymptomatic parasitemia without illness (premunition) is common among adults in endemic areas.
- Immunity is specific for both the species and the strain of infecting malarial parasites.

- Immunity to all strains is never achieved.
- Normal spleen function is an important host factor because of immunologic as well as filtering functions of the spleen.
- Both humoral and cellular immunity is necessary for protection.
- Polyclonal increase in serum level of IgG, IgM, and IgA occurs in immune individuals.
- Antibody to antigenically variant protein PfEMP1 is important for protection in case of *P. falciparum* malaria.
- Passively transferred IgG from immune individuals has been shown to be protective.
- Maternal antibody confers relative protection of infants from severe disease.
- Genetic disorders (sickle cell disease, thalassemia, and G6PD deficiency) confer protection from death because parasites are unable to grow efficiently in low-oxygen tensions, thus preventing high-level parasitemias.
- Individuals deficient of Duffy factor in RBCs are resistant to infection by *P. vivax*.
- Nonspecific defense mechanisms, such as cytokines (TNF-α, IL-1, -6, -8), also play an important role in protection, causing fever (temperatures of 40° C damage mature parasites) and other pathologic effects.

PREVENTION OF MALARIA: Medications are available for the prophylaxis of malaria and will vary depending on level of chloroquine resistance in a given area.

Areas free of chloroquine-resistant Falciparum malaria

Chloroquine 300 mg base (500 mg chloroquine phosphate) PO/wk. Start 1 wk prior to arrival in malaria area, then weekly while there and for 4 wk on leaving malaria area. Pediatric dose: 8.3 mg/kg (5 mg/kg base). Alternatives for adults include atovaquone-proguanil (Malarone): 1 adult tablet per day starting 1 to 2 days prior to arriving in malaria area, then daily while there and then for 7 days daily on leaving malaria area. For children, atovaquone-proguanil pediatric tablets based on weight:
11 to 20 kg 1 pediatric tablet
21 to 30 kg 2 pediatric tablets
31 to 40 kg 3 pediatric tablets
>40 kg 1 adult tablet

Areas with chloroquine-resistant Falciparum malaria
- Atovaquone-proguanil (Malarone): dosing as previously
- Mefloquine 250 mg (228 mg base) PO/wk, starting 1 wk before arriving in malaria area, weekly while there and then weekly for 4 wk on return. In children, mefloquine dose is based on weight:
- <15 kg 5 mg/kg
- to 19 kg ¼ adult dose
- to 30 kg ½ adult dose
- to 45 kg ¾ adult dose
- >45 kg adult dose
- Doxycycline 100 mg PO/day for adults and children aged >8. Start 1 to 2 days before travel, daily while in malaria area, and then daily for 4 wk on return.

SPECIAL CONSIDERATIONS:
- Long-term visitors or travelers
- Children aged <12 yr

- Immunocompromised host
- Pregnant women: chloroquine and mefloquine are safe in pregnancy but not atovaquone-proguanil. A recent trial revealed that the burden of malaria in pregnancy was significantly lower among adolescent girls or women who received intermittent preventive treatment with dihydroartemisinin-piperaquine than among those who received sulfadoxine-pyrimethamine, and monthly treatment with dihydroartemisinin-piperaquine was superior to three-dose dihydroartemisinin-piperaquine with regards to several outcomes.[1] Avoid doxycycline and primaquine.

VACCINATION:
- In 2015, Mosquirix (RTS,S): a recombinant protein-based vaccine, was approved in Europe to prevent malaria in babies in Africa. It showed an efficacy of about 30% in babies 6 to 12 weeks old and about 46% in babies 5 to 17 months old.
- New DNA-based vaccines are in development

MALARIA INFORMATION:
- CDC Travelers' Health Hotline (877) 394–8747; CDC Travelers' Health Fax (888) 232–3299
- CDC Malaria Epidemiology (770) 488–7788; internet: www.cdc.gov

SUGGESTED READINGS

Available at www.expertconsult.com

RELATED CONTENT

Malaria (Patient Information)

AUTHOR: **GLENN G. FORT, M.D., M.P.H.**

---

[1] Kakuru A, et al: Dihydroartemisinin-piperaquine for the prevention of malaria in pregnancy, *N Engl J Med* 374:928-939, 2016.

BASIC INFORMATION

DEFINITION

Malignant hyperthermia (MH) is a rare and life-threatening subclinical myopathy that can occur in genetically susceptible individuals after exposure to triggering agents, most commonly halogenated anesthetic gases, such as halothane, isoflurane, sevoflurane, and desflurane, or the depolarizing agent succinylcholine. These agents, given to susceptible individuals, often those with a genetic anomaly in the ryanodine or dihydropyridine receptor, may lead to excessive skeletal muscle contraction. Initial signs include rising end tidal carbon dioxide (PET CO$_2$) levels, tachycardia, and skeletal muscle rigidity. Mortality has recently been reported to be 1.4% to 5%, down from 70% in the past, likely due to monitoring for changes in PET CO2 and intraoperative temperature. Advanced age, muscularity, comorbidities, and disseminated intravascular coagulation (DIC) increase risk of death.

SYNONYMS

Malignant hyperthermia of anesthesia
Malignant hyperpyrexia
MH

ICD-10CM CODES
T88.3 Malignant hyperthermia due to anesthesia, initial encounter

EPIDEMIOLOGY & DEMOGRAPHICS

INCIDENCE: In the population as a whole undergoing general anesthesia, the incidence is approximately 1:100,000. It is widely believed that we fail to include a large number of unrecognized events, and that half of afflicted patients have had prior uneventful exposures to the same triggering agents. Children account for 42% to 52% of cases; however, any age may be affected.
GENETICS: Susceptibility to MH is due to mutation of the ryanodine receptor, less frequently the dihydropyridine (DHP) receptor, and sometimes both. Other clinical risk factors for susceptibility include central core myopathies and dystrophinopathies.
ETIOLOGY: Susceptibility to MH is inherited in an autosomal dominant fashion in 50% of cases, the rest presumed to be new mutations. At least 31 mutations on chromosome 19 are known to cause changes in the ryanodine receptor (RYR1) that result in the abnormalities of skeletal muscle calcium homeostasis and susceptibility to MH, with significant clinical variability due to incomplete penetrance and variable expressivity. In approximately 1% of cases, MH susceptibility is due to mutations of the gene on chromosome one coding for the dihydropyridine receptor.
PREVALENCE OF SUSCEPTIBILITY TO MALIGNANT HYPERTHERMIA: In the general population, 1:3000 are thought to carry a defective gene for the ryanodine receptor. However, the prevalence of susceptibility to MH (MHS) is estimated to be 1:2000. The difference is likely accounted for by other genetic abnormalities such as abnormalities of the DHP receptor and certain clinical risk factors (see risk factors in the following). In family cohorts of patients who are susceptible, the prevalence of susceptibility ranges from 1:200 to 1:5000 due to incomplete penetrance and variable expressivity.
GENETICS: Recently studied are four mutations in the RYR1 gene at the p Arg2508, which were found to have a crucial effect on the pathological conditions related to malignant hyperthermia. Of note, however, in a patient with known genetic susceptibility to MH, a history of uneventful anesthesia while using known triggering agents does not exclude the possibility of future MH crisis.
RISK FACTORS:
- Preoperatively, the patient and family history is used to evaluate the risk of MH crisis and the need for further testing. Patients with myopathies due to RYR1 abnormalities, such as central core myopathy, not true MH, should not receive succinylcholine or volatile anesthetics.
- Patients with dystrophinopathies such as Duchenne and Becker muscular dystrophy, enzymopathies of skeletal muscle such as McArdle's disease, or exercise- and heat-induced rhabdomyolysis, may develop rhabdomyolysis when exposed to these agents, and many authors deem it prudent to use only non-triggering agents. Other syndromes such as osteogenesis imperfecta, myotonia, and neuroleptic malignant syndrome are no longer felt to be associated with MHS.
PREDOMINANT AGE AND SEX: Male to female ratio of 2:1. Children account for up to half of cases.

PATHOPHYSIOLOGY
- In subjects genetically susceptible to dysregulated calcium release from the sarcoplasmic reticulum, administration of volatile anesthetic gases results in excessive release of sarcoplasmic Ca^{++}. Halothane will inhibit Ca^{++} reuptake resulting in unmitigated muscle contraction, increased aerobic and anaerobic metabolism, leading to CO2 production, elevated PET CO2, and tachycardia in patients unable to increase their alveolar minute volume.
- Hyperpyrexia results from hypermetabolism of skeletal muscle with an overwhelming amount of heat production resulting in the body's inability to dissipate this heat.

PHYSICAL FINDINGS & CLINICAL PRESENTATION
- Within minutes to hours after the triggering anesthetic is administered, the patient develops muscle rigidity, resulting in tachypnea and tachycardia. In the operating room, however, MH may be difficult to recognize because the latter signs are often attributed to inadequate sedation.
- Masseter muscle rigidity is common after initial induction of anesthesia; however, when prolonged, it may suggest MH.
- Hyperthermia or a rapidly increasing temperature from an anesthesia-induced hypothermic state is present in more than 50% of MH events. Hyperthermia is not always present early in MH crisis, and thus core body temperature is not a definitive inclusion factor in diagnosing MH at an early stage. Higher core body temperature correlates with morbidity, and in the OR, skin temperature underestimates core body temperature.
- The skin may initially be erythematous, progressing to a mottled, cyanotic appearance.
- Due to increased skeletal muscle metabolism, CO$_2$ production is increased, leading to elevated mixed venous and arterial pCO$_2$, and an elevated PET CO$_2$. Muscle injury with an elevated creatine kinase (CK) may lead to rhabdomyolysis and subsequent acute renal failure. Disseminated intravascular coagulation (DIC) may develop.
- Box 1M-1 summarizes the findings consistent with MH.

BOX 1M-1 Positive Findings Consistent with Malignant Hyperthermia (MH)

History of recent exposure to trigger agent, including volatile anesthetic agents or succinylcholine
Family or personal history of MH susceptibility
Total body rigidity
Masseter spasm
Inappropriately elevated (38.8° C) or rapidly increasing temperature (>1.5° C over 5 min)
Inappropriate tachypnea
Profuse sweating
Mottled, cyanotic skin
Dark urine, urine dipstick testing shows a positive result from blood without red cells in the sediment and no hemolysis
Unexplained, excessive bleeding
Unexplained ventricular tachycardia or fibrillation
Inappropriate hypercarbia (venous Paco$_2$ >65 mm Hg, arterial Paco$_2$ >55 mm Hg) if the patient is receiving positive-pressure ventilation or is spontaneously breathing with greater than normal minute ventilation
Arterial base excess more negative than −8 mEq/L
Arterial pH <7.25
Potassium concentration >6 mEq/L
Creatine kinase >10,000 IU/L

From Fuhrman BP et al: *Pediatric critical care,* ed 4, Philadelphia, 2011, Saunders.

BASIC INFORMATION

DEFINITION

A Mallory-Weiss tear (MWT) is a longitudinal mucosal laceration in the region of the gastro-esophageal junction.

SYNONYMS

Mallory-Weiss syndrome

ICD-10CM CODES
K22.6 Mallory-Weiss syndrome

EIDEMIOLOGY & DEMOGRAPHICS

- Accounts for 5% to 15% of cases of upper gastrointestinal (GI) bleeding
- Reported from early childhood to old age; the majority of patients are age 40 to 60 yr
- More common in males
- Alcohol use is present in 30% to 60%

PHYSICAL FINDINGS & CLINICAL PRESENTATION

- Vomiting, retching, or vigorous coughing will often, but not always, precede hematemesis.
- Patients may be clinically stable or present with tachycardia, hypotension, melena, hematochezia, epigastric pain, or back pain.
- Bleeding may be self-limited or severe.
- Tears may be seen in association with other upper GI tract lesions, including hiatal hernia (present in as many as 90% of patients), ulcers, and esophageal varices, particularly in alcoholics.

ETIOLOGY

- An acute increase in intraabdominal pressure is transmitted to the esophagus, resulting in mucosal laceration.
- Vomiting may be associated with alcohol use, cannabinoid use, ketoacidosis, ulcer disease, uremia, pancreatitis, chemotherapy, cholecystitis, pregnancy (in particular associated with hyperemesis gravidarum), myocardial infarction, or the postoperative period.
- Infrequently reported causes include chest wall trauma (including CPR), hiccups, coughing, seizures, lifting/straining, and labor and delivery.
- Tears may be iatrogenic, related to routine endoscopy (especially in struggling or retching patients, or in association with hiatal hernias), enteroscopy with or without overtubes, esophageal dilation, lower esophageal pneumatic disruption therapy for achalasia, endoscopic submucosal dissection, transesophageal echocardiography, or in association with polyethylene glycol electrolyte colonic lavage preparation.

DIAGNOSIS

DIFFERENTIAL DIAGNOSIS

- Esophageal or gastric varices
- Esophagitis or esophageal ulcers (peptic or pill-induced)
- Gastric erosions
- Gastric or duodenal ulcer
- Dieulafoy lesion
- Arteriovenous malformations
- Neoplasms (usually gastric)
- Boerhaave's syndrome

WORKUP

Endoscopy is the diagnostic method of choice.

LABORATORY TESTS

- Complete blood count, prothrombin time, partial thromboplastin time
- Electrolytes, blood urea nitrogen, creatinine, liver function tests, pregnancy test, tests to evaluate for predisposing conditions

IMAGING STUDIES

Upper GI series is usually not sensitive. Patients with concurrent chest pain, dyspnea, shock, or physical examination findings of crepitus or pleural effusion should have a chest radiograph or CT to exclude Boerhaave's syndrome.

TREATMENT

NONPHARMACOLOGIC THERAPY

- Supportive care
- Avoidance of aspirin, nonsteroidal antiinflammatory drugs, and anticoagulants

ACUTE GENERAL Rx

- Patients with active bleeding or hemodynamic instability require large-bore IVs, fluid resuscitation, and transfusion of blood products (red blood cells, fresh frozen plasma, and platelets) as appropriate.
- Nasogastric decompression and antiemetics may be considered.
- Endoscopic therapy for patients with active or ongoing hemorrhage (Fig. 1M-3). Therapeutic modalities include electrocoagulation, injection (e.g., 1:10,000 epinephrine, polidocanol), sclerotherapy (for bleeding associated with esophageal varices), band ligation, or endoscopic hemoclips (therapies may be used alone or in combination) (Fig. E1M-4).
- Arterial embolization in patients with active bleeding who are poor surgical candidates.

- Laparotomy, with gastrotomy and oversewing of the tear, is required in a small percentage of patients with uncontrolled bleeding.

CHRONIC Rx

- Healing will usually occur without specific therapy.
- H_2 blockers or proton pump inhibitors may be given to help facilitate healing but should not be used long term unless appropriate indications are present.

DISPOSITION

- Prognosis is good, with spontaneous cessation of bleeding in upwards of 90% of patients. Endoscopic features can guide treatment. Blatchford score <6 suggests no need for transfusion or endoscopic intervention.
- Delayed rebleeding is described in patients with high-risk stigmata (shock at initial presentation, spurting or oozing at initial endoscopy).
- Death has been reported in 3% to 12%, often in association with severe bleeding and underlying comorbid conditions such as advanced age, coagulopathy, elevated transaminases, thrombocytopenia, alcohol use, presentation with a very low hemoglobin level or melena, and multisystem organ failure.

REFERRAL

- Gastrointestinal referral for endoscopy
- Surgical referral for bleeding unresponsive to endoscopic treatment or in the setting of coexistent perforation

PEARLS & CONSIDERATIONS

Conditions predisposing to retching or vomiting should be identified and treated at presentation.

SUGGESTED READINGS

Available at www.expertconsult.com

RELATED CONTENT

Mallory-Weiss Tear (Patient Information)

AUTHOR: **HARLAN G. RICH, M.D.**

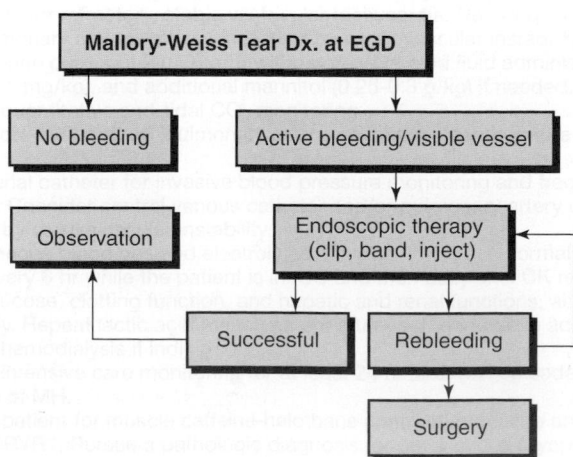

FIGURE 1M-3 Treatment algorithm for Mallory-Weiss tear. *EGD*, Esophagogastroduodenoscopy. (From Cameron JL, Cameron AM: *Current surgical therapy*, ed 10, Philadelphia, 2011, Saunders.)

M

 BASIC INFORMATION

DEFINITION

Marfan's syndrome (MFS) is an inherited disorder of connective tissue involving the skeleton, cardiovascular system, eyes, lungs, and central nervous system.

ICD-10CM CODES
Q87.40   Marfan's syndrome, unspecified
Q87.410 Marfan's syndrome with aortic dilation
Q87.418 Marfan's syndrome with other cardiovascular manifestations
Q87.42   Marfan's syndrome with ocular manifestations
Q87.43   Marfan's syndrome with skeletal manifestation

EPIDEMIOLOGY & DEMOGRAPHICS

PREVALENCE:
- One case per 10,000 persons.
- Both sexes are affected equally by this autosomal dominant syndrome.
- Approximately 30% of cases are a new mutation.

PHYSICAL FINDINGS & CLINICAL PRESENTATION

Diagnostic criteria for Marfan's syndrome (Table 1M-3):
- Skeleton: joint hypermobility (Fig. 1M-5), tall stature (Fig. 1M-6, A), pectus excavatum, reduced thoracic kyphosis, scoliosis, arachnodactyly (Fig. 1M-6, B), dolichostenomelia, pectus carinatum, and erosion of the lumbosacral vertebrae from dural ectasia*
- Eye: myopia, retinal detachment, elongated globe, ectopia lentis*
- Cardiovascular: mitral valve prolapse, endocarditis, arrhythmia, dilated mitral annulus, mitral regurgitation, tricuspid valve prolapse, aortic regurgitation, aortic dissection,* dilation of the aortic root*
- Pulmonary: apical blebs, spontaneous pneumothorax
- Skin and integument: inguinal hernias, incisional hernias, striae atrophicae
- Central nervous system: attention deficit disorder, hyperactivity, verbal-performance discrepancy, dural ectasia, anterior pelvic meningocele*

If the family history is positive for a close relative clearly affected by Marfan's syndrome, manifestations should be present in the skeleton and one of the other organ systems and the diagnosis confirmed by linkage analysis or mutation detection.

If the family history is negative or unknown, the patient should have manifestations in the skeleton, the cardiovascular system, and one other system and at least one of the manifestations indicated by an asterisk in the previous lists.

Manifestations are listed within each organ system in increasing specificity for Marfan's syndrome; although none is completely specific, those indicated by an asterisk are the most specific.

ETIOLOGY

Mutations in the gene that encodes fibrillin-1 (FBN_1), the major constituent of microfibrils, which form the frame for elastic fibers. All the manifestations of Marfan's syndrome can be explained by the defective microfibrils.

 DIAGNOSIS

DIFFERENTIAL DIAGNOSIS

Each of the clinical manifestations of the syndrome may have other causes; however, if the diagnostic criteria are met, the diagnosis is made.

WORKUP
- MFS diagnosis is made clinically, with genetic consultation if necessary
- Echocardiography to establish:
  1. Mitral valve prolapse
  2. Mitral regurgitation
  3. Tricuspid valve prolapse
  4. Aortic regurgitation
  5. Dilation of the aortic root
- Echocardiography should be repeated 6 months after initial diagnosis to evaluate for rate of aortic diameter enlargement
- Chest radiograph
- Transesophageal echocardiography, chest CT scan, chest MRI, or aortography for suspected aortic dissection
- Chest radiograph for pulmonary apical bullae
- Ophthalmologic examination by ophthalmologist
- Testing for FBN_1 mutations is available

 TREATMENT

- Regular cardiac and aorta monitoring by physical examination and echocardiography.

TABLE 1M-3   Diagnostic Criteria for Marfan's Syndrome

In the absence of a family history of MFS, a diagnosis can be reached in 1 of 4 scenarios:
Aortic diameter at Sinuses of Valsalva Z-score >2 AND Ectopia Lentis = MFS*
Aortic diameter at Sinuses of Valsalva Z-score ≥2 AND *FBN1* mutation = MFS
Aortic diameter at Sinuses of Valsalva Z-score ≥2 AND Systemic Score ≥7 = MFS*
Ectopia Lentis AND *FBN1* mutation known to associate with aortic aneurysm = MFS

In the absence of a family history of MFS, alternative diagnoses to MFS include:
Ectopia Lentis 6 Systemic Score AND *FBN1* mutation not known to associate with aortic aneurysm or no *FBN1* mutation = Ectopia Lentis syndrome
Aortic diameter at Sinuses of Valsalva Z-score >2 AND Systemic Score 2:5 (with at least one skeletal feature) without Ectopia Lentis = MASS phenotype
Mitral Valve Prolapse AND Aortic diameter at Sinuses of Valsalva Z-score <2 AND Systemic Score <5 without Ectopia Lentis = Mitral Valve Prolapse syndrome

In the presence of a family history of MFS, a diagnosis can be reached in 1 of 3 scenarios:
Ectopia Lentis AND Family History of MFS = MFS
Systemic Score ≥7 AND Family History of MFS = MFS*
Aortic diameter at Sinuses of Valsalva Z score ≥2 if older than 20 yr or ≥3 if younger than 20 yr AND Family History of MFS = MFS*

Scoring of Systemic Features (in points)†
Wrist AND thumb sign = 3 (wrist OR thumb sign = 1)
Pectus carinatum deformity = 2 (pectus excavatum or chest asymmetry = 1)
Hindfoot deformity = 2 (plain pes planus = 1)
Pneumothorax = 2
Dural ectasia = 2
Protrusio acetabuli = 2
Reduced US/LS AND increased arm/height AND no severe scoliosis = 1
Scoliosis or thoracolumbar kyphosis = 1
Reduced elbow extension = 1
Facial features (3/5) = 1 (dolichocephaly, enophthalmos, downslanting palpebral fissures, malar hypoplasia, retrognathia)
Skin striae = 1
Myopia >3 diopters = 1
Mitral valve prolapse (all types) = 1

Criteria for Causal *FBN1* Mutation
Mutation previously shown to segregate in a Marfan family
Any one of the following *de novo* mutations (with proven paternity and absence of disease in parents):
  Nonsense mutation
  In-frame and out-of-frame deletion/insertion
  Splice site mutations affecting canonical splice sequence or shown to alter splicing on mRNA/cDNA level
  Missense mutation affecting/creating cysteine residues
  Missense mutation affecting conserved residues of the EGF consensus sequence [(D/N)X(D/N)(E/Q)Xm(D/N)Xn(Y/F), with m and n representing variable number of residues; D, aspartic acid; N, asparagine; E, glutamic acid; Q, glutamine; Y, tyrosine; F, phenylalanine]
  Other missense mutations: segregation in family, if possible, + absence in 400 ethnically matched control chromosomes; if no family history, absence in 400 ethnically matched control chromosomes
Linkage of haplotype for n≥6 meioses to the *FBN1* locus

MFS, Marfan's syndrome; *US/LS*, upper segment/lower segment ratio.
*Without discriminating features of Shprintzen-Goldberg syndrome, Loeys-Dietz syndrome, or Ehlers-Danlos syndrome *and* after TGFBR1/2, collagen biochemistry, COL3A1 testing if indicated. Other conditions/genes will emerge with time.
†Maximum total: 20 points; score ≥7 indicates systemic involvement.
From Loeys BL et al: The revised Ghent nosology for the Marfan syndrome, *J Med Genet* 47:476-485, 2010.

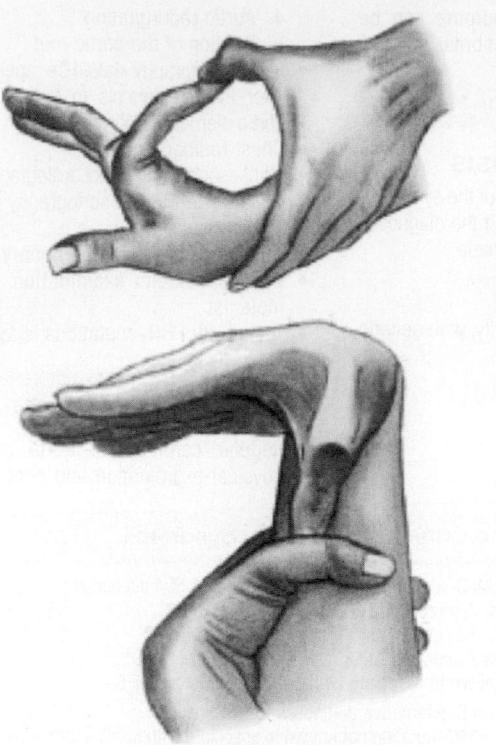

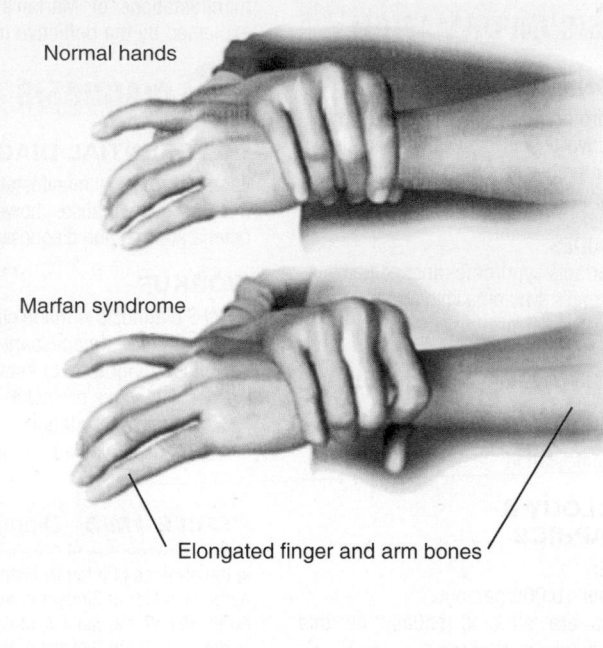

Normal hands

Marfan syndrome

Elongated finger and arm bones

FIGURE 1M-5 Marfan syndrome. The Steinberg test (thumb) and the Walker-Murdoch test (wrist) show arachnodactyly. (From Firestein GS et al: *Kelley's textbook of rheumatology,* ed 9, Philadelphia, 2013, Saunders, Elsevier.)

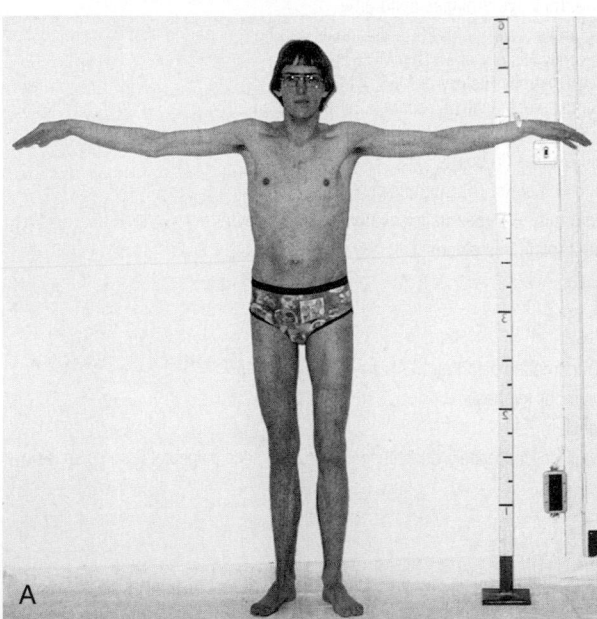

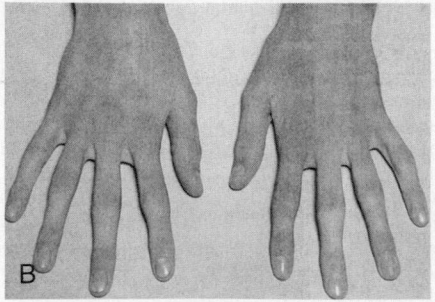

FIGURE 1M-6 A, Long limbs compared with the trunk. **B,** Arachnodactyly. (From Kanski JJ, Bowling B: *Clinical ophthalmology, a system approach,* ed 7, Philadelphia, 2010, Saunders.)

Surgical repair of the dilated aortic root/ascending aorta is generally performed when external diameter is ≥5 cm. Surgical repair may be performed earlier (at >4.0 cm diameter) in women contemplating pregnancy.

- Endocarditis prophylaxis.
- Restriction of contact sports, weight lifting, and overexertion.
- Beta-blockers are commonly prescribed to slow the rate of aortic root dilation. Patients with Marfan's syndrome and associated aneurysm should be receiving beta-blockers unless there is a contraindication to their use. Recent reports indicate that use of angiotensin receptor blockers significantly also slowed the rate of progressive aortic root dilation independent of hemodynamic effects. A recent trial among children and young adults with Marfan's syndrome who were randomly assigned to Losartan or Atenolol found no significant difference in the rate of aortic root dilation between the two treatment groups over a 3-year period.[1]
- Genetic counseling.
- Monitor aorta during pregnancy because of the increased risk of dissection.

SUGGESTED READINGS
Available at www.expertconsult.com

RELATED CONTENT
Marfan's Syndrome (Patient Information)

AUTHOR: **FRED F. FERRI, M.D.**

[1]Lacro RV, Sleeper LA, et al.: Atenolol versus Losartan in children and young adults with Marfan's syndrome, N Engl J Med 371:2061-71, 2014.

Diseases and Disorders

 BASIC INFORMATION

DEFINITION
Mastitis is local painful inflammation of the breast that may or may not be accompanied by infection, flulike symptoms, and abscess formation.

ICD-10CM CODES
N61	Inflammatory disorders of breast
O91.12	Abscess of breast associated with the puerperium
O91.22	Nonpurulent mastitis associated with the puerperium

EPIDEMIOLOGY & DEMOGRAPHICS
- In lactating mothers, typically occurs in first 3 mo postpartum (74%-95% of cases)
- When severe, mastitis can lead to a breast abscess (5%-11%) or septicemia
- Delayed diagnosis and treatment of lactational mastitis can lead to discontinuation of breastfeeding, breast tissue damage, recurrence
- In nonlactating women of childbearing age, often presents as granulomatous mastitis (GM)
- In older nonlactating women, often presents as periductal mastitis (PM) and is caused by inflamed milk ducts near the nipple
- Mastitis can also occur in infancy, when breast hypertrophy from maternal hormone leads to infection

PREVALENCE: Lactational mastitis occurs in up to 33% of mothers
PREDOMINANT SEX: Females
RISK FACTORS:
- Previous mastitis
- Milk stasis and missed feedings
- Cracked, fissured, or sore nipples
- Primiparity and infant attachment difficulties
- Cleft lip or palate or short frenulum in infant
- Use of manual breast pump
- Diabetes
- Breast implants
- Nipple piercings

PHYSICAL FINDINGS & CLINICAL PRESENTATION
- Warmth, redness, tenderness in breast
- Unilateral or bilateral
- Malaise, myalgias, fevers, chills
- Decreased milk output
- Breast is hard and swollen in a wedge-shaped area
- In PM, breast mass near nipple with retraction or discharge
- In GM, enlarged axillary lymph nodes or sinus tract formation

ETIOLOGY
- In lactational mastitis, milk stasis and irritation of the milk ducts due to local immune response to milk proteins.
  - Bacterial infection of subcutaneous tissue due to breaks in skin.

- Most commonly, *S. aureus;* less common, *S. epidermidis,* group A beta-hemolytic streptococci, *S. pneumoniae, E. coli, Candida albicans, M. tuberculosis.*
- GM results from inflammation with epithelioid histiocytes and multinucleated giant cells and can be caused by etiologies like tuberculosis, sarcoidosis, foreign body reaction, parasitic and mycotic infections, or idiopathic.
- Neonatal mastitis caused by *S. aureus* or gram-negative enteric bacteria.

 DIAGNOSIS

DIFFERENTIAL DIAGNOSIS
- Engorgement, plugged duct (see Table 1M-4)
- Breast abscess
- Inflammatory or other breast cancer (3% of women diagnosed with breast cancer are lactating)
- Mastitis as a symptom of hyperprolactinemia or galactorrhea
- GM can be manifestation of systemic disease (sarcoidosis, Wegener granulomatosis, GCA, polyarteritis nodosa, TB, syphilis)

WORKUP
- History and clinical exam with thorough breast exam and assessment of axillary nodes and nipple discharge are sufficient for diagnosis
- Recurrent mastitis should include workup for underlying breast disease

LABORATORY TESTS
- Simple lactational mastitis requires no milk culture or laboratory studies
- Obtain midstream sample of milk for culture and sensitivities in refractory mastitis or in MRSA-suspected cases
- CBC and blood cultures in toxic patients
- In abscess formation, culture of drainage or aspirate fluid
- Gram stain and culture indicated in infant mastitis

IMAGING STUDIES
- Not necessary unless refractory mastitis or abscess suspected
- Consider US to evaluate for abscess or mammogram when appropriate to exclude carcinoma

- In GM, mammogram and US-guided FNA are standard

 TREATMENT

NONPHARMACOLOGIC THERAPY
- Mainstay of therapy is effective milk removal through continued breastfeeding or pumping
- Consider referral to a certified lactation consultant to improve breastfeeding technique
- Warm compresses, increased fluid intake, good nutrition, and rest
- In abscess formation (10% of women who are treated for bacterial mastitis), surgical drainage or needle aspiration is necessary, followed by antibiotic therapy based on sensitivities of culture

ACUTE GENERAL Rx
- NSAIDs and analgesics (e.g., acetaminophen, ibuprofen). There is insufficient evidence to support or refute the effectiveness of antibiotic therapy. Common regimens include:
- No history of MRSA:
  1. Dicloxacillin 250 mg 4x/d for 7 d
  2. Cephalexin 500 mg 4x/d for 10-14 d
  3. Inpatient: nafcillin or oxacillin 2 g IV q4h
  4. Erythromycin may be used in patients allergic to penicillin
- Suspected MRSA or high-risk penicillin allergy:
  1. Trimethoprim/sulfamethoxazole 160 mg/800 mg 2x/d for 10 to 14 d; should not be used when breastfeeding healthy infants <2 mo or compromised infants
  2. Clindamycin 300 mg 4x/d for 10 to 14 d
  3. Inpatient: vancomycin 1 g IV q12h
- Oxytocin nasal spray if letdown reflex disturbed
- Consider treatment for candidal infection if bilateral symptoms and infant with thrush
  - Topical clotrimazole for mother and oral nystatin for infant, with careful washing of all pacifiers and nipples
  - If resistant to topical treatment, can consider oral fluconazole; however, data in breastfeeding are limited
- Infant mastitis typically treated in an inpatient setting with parenteral antibiotics based on results of Gram stain

TABLE 1M-4 Comparison of Findings of Engorgement, Plugged Duct, and Mastitis

Characteristics	Engorgement	Plugged Duct	Mastitis
Onset	Gradual, immediately	Gradual, after feedings	Sudden, after 10 days postpartum
Site	Bilateral	Unilateral	Usually unilateral
Swelling and heat	Generalized	May shift/little or no heat	Localized red, hot, and swollen
Body temperature	<38.4° C	<38.4° C	>38.4° C
Systemic symptoms	Feels well	Feels well	Flulike symptoms

From Lawrence RA, Lawrence RM: *Breastfeeding: a guide for the medical profession,* ed 5, St Louis, 1999, Mosby.

CHRONIC Rx

- No evidence proving benefit of prophylactic antibiotics to prevent lactational mastitis
- In GM, systemic corticosteroids or wide surgical resection

COMPLEMENTARY & ALTERNATIVE MEDICINE

- Complementary therapies not assessed in prospective studies: *Belladonna*, *Phytolacca*, *Chamomilla*, sulfur, *Bellis perennis*
- Several strains of lactobacilli have shown promise as probiotic agents that might be useful in treating mastitis, including *L. fermentum* and *L. salivarius*. These results should be replicated before this approach is adopted widely.

REFERRAL

Refer to surgeon for severe PM or significant lactational abscess that does not resolve with conservative measures

PEARLS & CONSIDERATIONS

COMMENTS

- 25% of breastfeeding mothers with 1 episode of mastitis stop breastfeeding.
- Increasing incidence of MRSA mastitis.
- Lactational mastitis is risk factor for vertical transmission of infections (i.e., HIV-1, CMV, measles, hepatitis B and C).
- When reassessing refractory nonlactational mastitis, the most important consideration is the possibility of cancer.
- Nonlactational mastitis can be a manifestation of systemic disease.
- GM mimics breast cancer both clinically and radiologically (>50% of reported cases are initially mistaken for carcinoma). This includes fine needle aspiration, which is sometimes interpreted as malignant.

RELATED CONTENT

Lactational Mastitis (Patient Information)
Abscess, Breast (Related Key Topic)
Fibrocystic Breast Disease (Related Key Topic)
Mastitis (Related Key Topic)

SUGGESTED READINGS

Available at www.expertconsult.com

AUTHORS: **MARY BETH SUTTER, M.D.,** and **ANDRE LEVCHENKO, Ph.D.**

BASIC INFORMATION

DEFINITION

- Pain in the breast
- Usually cyclic condition but may be noncyclic or extramammary

SYNONYMS

Mastalgia

ICD-10CM CODES

N64.4 Mastodynia

EPIDEMIOLOGY & DEMOGRAPHICS

- Mastodynia affects up to 70% of women at some time in their reproductive lives.
- Severe cyclic mastodynia lasting more than 5 days/mo and of sufficient intensity to interfere with sexual, physical, social, and work-related activities is reported among 30% of premenopausal women.
- Underlying fear of breast cancer is the reason most of these women seek medical consultation.
- One tenth of women with mastodynia require pain-relieving therapy.

PHYSICAL FINDINGS & CLINICAL PRESENTATION

- Usually the breasts are normal bilaterally
- Full, tender breasts
- Generalized breast nodularity without discrete lumps
- Chest wall tenderness: extramammary breast pain
- Distinguishing mammary from extramammary pain can be difficult
- With the patient lying on her side so that the breast tissue falls away from the chest wall, tenderness can then be reproduced by direct pressure over the offending site
- Cyclic mastodynia presents in the luteal phase of the menstrual cycle
- Women with cyclic mastodynia tend to have abdominal bloating, leg swelling, and other symptoms of premenstrual syndrome
- Noncyclic mastodynia, on the other hand, is unrelated to the menstrual cycle
- Extramammary breast pain simulates noncyclic mastodynia

ETIOLOGY

- Hormonal imbalance
- Abnormal lipid metabolism
- Premenstrual syndrome (20%)
- Fibrocystic breast disease
- Emotional abuse and anxiety
- Excessive caffeine intake
- Breast cancer (10%)
- Tietze syndrome (idiopathic costochondritis)

DIAGNOSIS

DIFFERENTIAL DIAGNOSIS

- See "Etiology."
- The majority of women with mastodynia have no underlying abnormality.

- Breast fullness and tenderness associated with hormonal changes fluctuate with the menstrual cycle.
- Similarly, breast nodularity, which may or may not be the result of fibrocystic breast disease, also fluctuates with the menstrual cycle.
- Discrete breast lumps need full evaluation to rule out malignancy.
- Tietze syndrome is usually unilateral and may be associated with chest wall swelling.

LABORATORY TESTS

Although hormonal imbalance and abnormal lipid metabolism have been implicated in the etiopathogenesis of mastodynia, there is no good evidence to support any consistent pattern of serum hormonal or lipid profile in women with mastodynia. These tests are therefore not recommended.

IMAGING STUDIES

- Mammography should be part of the baseline investigation if the woman is >35 yr.
- Ultrasound can be performed as needed; it is particularly helpful in the assessment of cystic breast lesions.
- In women <35 yr, imaging investigations are not helpful unless a lump has been palpated clinically. Consideration of family history for breast disease is important.
- There are no radiologic features associated with mastodynia: rather, radiologic investigations are performed to exclude the rare presence of a subclinical carcinoma.

TREATMENT

NONPHARMACOLOGIC THERAPY

- 85% of the women with mastodynia can be reassured after full clinical evaluation. In fact, reassurance can be considered first-line therapy for mastodynia since many women who present are concerned about significant pathology, especially cancer.
- The remaining 15% require some form of therapy in addition to reassurance.
- A firm, supportive brassiere designed for postpartum use is particularly helpful if mastodynia is associated with breast swelling.
- Follow a low-fat, high-carbohydrate diet.
- Reduce caffeine intake.

ACUTE GENERAL Rx

- Evening primrose oil, which contains gamma-linolenic acid, has been shown to have some effectiveness and is an acceptable treatment for mastodynia.
- Topical NSAID preparations may confer some benefit and can be prescribed for these women.
- Hormonal therapy is the mainstay of treatment and may include progesterone-only oral contraceptives or cyclic Provera.
- Danazol is the only drug approved by the FDA for the treatment of mastodynia. Danazol has some androgenic and peripheral antiestrogenic effects. Its efficacy is well established, with significant relief of mastodynia in 70% to 93% of cases.
  - Widespread use of danazol is limited because of its adverse side effects. These

include menstrual irregularities, depression, acne, hirsutism, and, in severe cases, voice deepening. Women taking danazol should be advised to use effective nonhormonal contraception because of the drug's potential adverse effects on the fetus.
  - The side effects of danazol can be significantly reduced by using a low dose (100 mg daily) and confining treatment to 2 wk preceding menstruation. However, alternatives should be explored.
- Tamoxifen, a synthetic antiestrogen, has also been shown to be effective in the treatment of mastodynia. Although effective in relieving symptoms, its use is extremely limited because of side effects. When used, it should be at a low dosage of 10 mg/day and duration should be limited to 6 mo at a time. In the U.S. this agent is not approved for use in women with mastodynia.
- Bromocriptine is a dopamine-receptor agonist whose primary action is inhibition of prolactin release. It has been used extensively in the treatment of severe cyclic mastodynia and is effective. Again, side effects such as headache and lightheadedness have limited its use.
- Lisuride maleate was recently found to be effective by one study.
- Other hormonal agents that have been reported to be effective in small studies cannot be recommended. Either they have unacceptable side effect profiles or their efficacy is not established. These agents include gestrinone, gonadotropin-releasing hormone analogues, progesterone, and hormone replacement therapy.

CHRONIC Rx

- Longstanding cases of mastodynia can be managed with intermittent low-dose danazol therapy to limit side effects. In between these courses of hormone, nonpharmacologic and nonhormonal therapy can be used.
- Severe, unremitting mastodynia that does not respond to medical treatment may require mastectomy; this is rare.

DISPOSITION

- Cyclic mastodynia resolves spontaneously in 20% to 30% of women.
- Up to 60% of women may develop recurrent symptoms 2 yr after treatment.
- Noncyclic mastodynia responds poorly to treatment but may resolve spontaneously in up to 50% of women.

SUGGESTED READINGS

Available at www.expertconsult.com

RELATED CONTENT

Breast Pain (Patient Information)
Abscess, Breast (Related Key Topic)
Fibrocystic Breast Disease (Related Key Topic)
Mastitis (Related Key Topic)

AUTHORS: **ALEXANDER B. OLAWAIYE, M.D.**, and **RUBEN ALVERO, M.D.**

BASIC INFORMATION

DEFINITION

Mastoiditis is inflammation of the mastoid process and air cells, a complication of otitis media.

SYNONYMS

Mastoid abscess

ICD-10CM CODES
H70.0 Acute mastoiditis
H40.1 Chronic mastoiditis
H70.8 Other mastoiditis and related
conditions
H70.9 Mastoiditis, unspecified

EPIDEMIOLOGY & DEMOGRAPHICS

INCIDENCE (IN U.S.): Since the introduction of antibiotic therapy and use of broad-spectrum antibiotics, there has been a marked decline in the incidence of acute mastoiditis.
PREDOMINANT SEX: More common in males
PREDOMINANT AGE: 2 mo to 18 yr
PEAK INCIDENCE: Early childhood

PHYSICAL FINDINGS & CLINICAL PRESENTATION

- Acute mastoiditis is usually a complication of acute otitis media.
- Most common presenting symptom is pain and tenderness in the postauricular region.
- Other signs or symptoms include:
  1. Fever
  2. Postauricular erythema and edema
  3. Protrusion of the pinna inferiorly and anteriorly
  4. Tympanic membrane usually intact with signs of acute otitis media
- Complications of acute mastoiditis include:
  1. Subperiosteal abscess (most common complication)
  2. Hearing loss
  3. Facial nerve palsy
  4. Labyrinthitis
  5. Intracranial complications such as hydrocephalus, meningitis, encephalitis, intracranial abscess, and lateral sinus thrombosis
- Chronic mastoiditis is characterized by chronic otorrhea and chronic tympanic membrane perforation.

ETIOLOGY

- Continuity exists between the middle air space and the mastoid cavity.
- Initial hyperemia and edema of the mucosal lining of the air cells result in accumulation of purulent exudate.

- Dissolution of calcium from bony septa and osteoclastic activity in the inflamed periosteum lead to bone necrosis and coalescence of air cells.
- Most common bacterial isolates are:
  1. *Streptococcus pneumoniae*
  2. *Streptococcus pyogenes*
  3. *Haemophilus influenzae*
  4. *Moraxella catarrhalis*
  5. *Staphylococcus aureus*
- Often, there are multiple organisms in chronic mastoiditis, with predominance of anaerobes and gram-negative bacteria.
- *Mycobacterium tuberculosis,* nontuberculous mycobacteria, *Aspergillus,* and *Rhodococcus equi* have been reported in cases of mastoiditis in severely immunocompromised individuals.

DIAGNOSIS

DIFFERENTIAL DIAGNOSIS

- Children
  1. Rhabdomyosarcoma
  2. Histiocytosis X
  3. Leukemia
  4. Kawasaki syndrome
- Adults
  1. Fulminant otitis externa
  2. Histiocytosis X
  3. Metastatic disease

WORKUP

A thorough history and physical examination are important in establishing diagnosis.

LABORATORY TESTS

- Fluid for Gram stain and culture may be obtained by myringotomy.
- If there is a perforation in the tympanic membrane with drainage, cultures of this may be taken after carefully cleaning the external canal.

IMAGING STUDIES

- Plain x-rays of the mastoid region may demonstrate clouding or opacification in areas of pneumatization.
- CT scan can demonstrate early involvement of bone (mastoiditis with bone destruction).
- MRI is more sensitive than CT scan in evaluating soft-tissue involvement and is useful in conjunction with CT scan to investigate other complications of mastoiditis.

TREATMENT

NONPHARMACOLOGIC THERAPY

Myringotomy, if the ear is not already draining

ACUTE GENERAL Rx

- Initiated with IV antibiotics directed against the common organisms *S. pneumoniae* and *H. influenzae.* Useful agents are amoxicillin/clavulanate, ceftriaxone, and cefotaxime. If the disease in the mastoid has had a prolonged course, coverage for *S. aureus* with gram-negative enteric bacilli may be considered for initial therapy until results of cultures become available. Add vancomycin if MRSA suspected or nafcillin/oxacillin if culture is positive for *S. aureus,* methicillin susceptible.
- Antibiotics continued until all signs of mastoiditis have resolved
- Directed against enteric gram-negative organisms and anaerobes in chronic mastoiditis
- Indications for mastoidectomy:
  1. Failure to improve after 72 hr of therapy
  2. Persistent fever
  3. Imminent or overt signs of intracranial complications
  4. Evidence of a subperiosteal abscess in the mastoid bone

DISPOSITION

Proceed with mastoidectomy when medical therapy fails.

REFERRAL

- To otorhinolaryngologist:
  1. If diagnosis is in doubt
  2. If aural complications present
  3. To evaluate for surgical intervention
- To neurosurgeon if intratemporal or intracranial extension of infection suspected
  1. Aural complications: bone destruction, subperiosteal abscess, petrositis, facial paralysis, labyrinthitis
  2. Intracranial complications: extradural abscess, lateral sinus thrombophlebitis or thrombosis, subdural abscess, meningitis, brain abscess, otitic hydrocephalus

PEARLS & CONSIDERATIONS

Mastoiditis is particularly difficult to eradicate because the mastoid air cells are poorly vascularized and difficult to drain.

SUGGESTED READINGS

Available at www.expertconsult.com

RELATED CONTENT

Mastoiditis (Patient Information)

AUTHOR: **GLENN G. FORT, M.D., M.P.H.**

BASIC INFORMATION

DEFINITION
Meckel diverticulum is an ileal diverticulum located 100 cm proximal to the cecum. It results from failure of the omphalomesenteric duct to obliterate completely (as it should by the eighth week of gestation).

SYNONYMS
MD

ICD-10CM CODES
Q43.0   Meckel's diverticulum (displaced) (hypertrophic)
C17.3   Meckel's diverticulum, malignant

EPIDEMIOLOGY & DEMOGRAPHICS
- Meckel diverticulum, based on autopsy studies and intraoperative evidence, occurs in 0.3% to 4% of the population and is the most prevalent congenital anomaly of the gastrointestinal (GI) tract. Complications occur more frequently in males.
- Most patients who develop symptoms are <10 yr.
- The lifetime risk of complications developing in a case of Meckel diverticulum is 4%.
- In adults, complications (small bowel obstruction [25%-40%], diverticulitis [20%]) are usually attributable to factors other than heterotopic mucosa.
- Tumors have rarely been reported in symptomatic Meckel diverticulum, with carcinoid being the most common type.

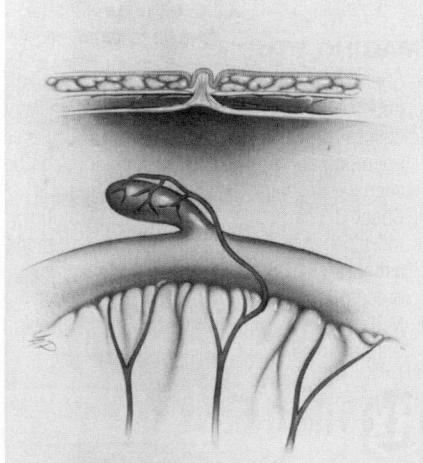

FIGURE 1M-10 Typical Meckel diverticulum located on the antimesenteric border. (From Kliegman RM et al: *Nelson textbook of pediatrics,* ed 19, Philadelphia, 2011, Saunders.)

PHYSICAL FINDINGS & CLINICAL PRESENTATION
- Painless lower GI bleeding (4%)
- Intestinal obstruction caused by intussusception, volvulus, herniation, or entrapment of a loop of bowel through a defect in the diverticular mesentery (6%)
- Meckel's diverticulitis mimics acute appendicitis (5%)
- Rare primary tumor arising from diverticulum (carcinoid, sarcoma, leiomyoma, adenocarcinoma)
- Asymptomatic (80%-95%)

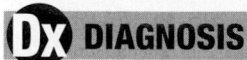

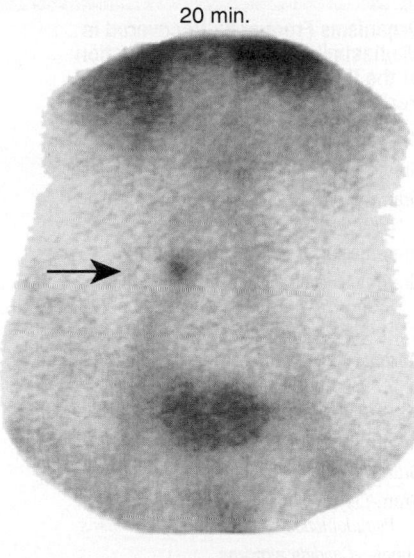

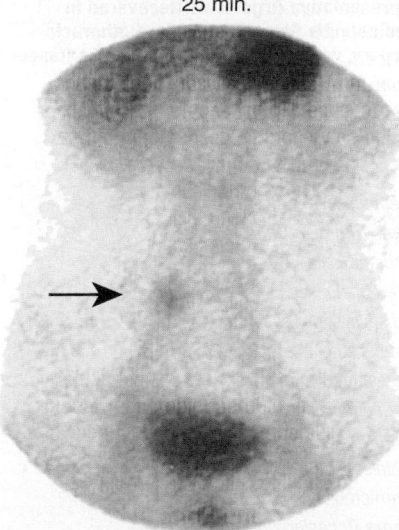

FIGURE 1M-11 Meckel scan demonstrating accumulation in the stomach superior bladder (inferior) and in the acid-secreting mucosa of a Meckel diverticulum. (From Kliegman RM et al: *Nelson textbook of pediatrics,* ed 19, Philadelphia, 2011, Saunders.)

ETIOLOGY & PATHOGENESIS
- As a remnant of the omphalomesenteric duct, Meckel diverticulum contains all layers of the intestinal wall and has its own mesentery and blood supply (branch of the superior mesenteric artery) (Fig. 1M-10).
- The majority of complicated cases of Meckel diverticulum contain ectopic mucosa (75% gastric, 15% pancreatic). It causes ulceration and bleeding of ileal mucosa adjacent to the acidic ectopic gastric secretions. Alkaline secretions of ectopic pancreatic tissue can also cause ulcerations.

(Dx) DIAGNOSIS

DIFFERENTIAL DIAGNOSIS
- Appendicitis
- Crohn's disease
- All causes of lower GI bleeding (polyp, colon cancer, arteriovenous malformation, diverticulosis, hemorrhoids)

WORKUP
- Diagnosis is often made intraoperatively when the preoperative diagnosis is appendicitis.
- Preoperative detection of symptomatic Meckel diverticulum requires a high index of suspicion.
- Meckel scan: In the case of GI bleeding of unknown source, a technetium scan will identify Meckel diverticulum (sensitivity: 85% in children, 62% in adults; specificity: 95% in children, 9% in adults) (Fig. 1M-11).
- In patients with suspected small-bowel obstruction, intussusception, or diverticulitis, a CT scan of the abdomen and pelvis is helpful.

(Rx) TREATMENT
- Surgical resection in symptomatic patients.
- There is controversy regarding the need to remove an incidentally found diverticulum, with most surgeons arguing in favor of resection.

SUGGESTED READINGS
Available at www.expertconsult.com

RELATED CONTENT
Meckel Diverticulum (Patient Information)

AUTHOR: **FRED F. FERRI, M.D.**

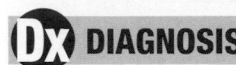 BASIC INFORMATION

DEFINITION

Mediastinitis is an infection involving the connective mediastinal tissue that fills the interpleural spaces and surrounds the mediastinal organs. It can be acute or chronic.

SYNONYMS

Fibrosing mediastinitis
Sclerosing mediastinitis
Granulomatous mediastinitis

ICD-10CM CODES

J98.5 Mediastinitis

EPIDEMIOLOGY

Acute mediastinitis occurs most frequently as a postoperative infection after a median sternotomy and can be a life-threatening infection. Most infections are bacterial in nature.

Chronic mediastinitis is a chronic form of infection in the mediastinum characterized by an invasive and compressive inflammatory infiltrate. It is mostly caused by fungi and some bacteria.

Incidence: Incidence of postoperative mediastinitis ranges from 0.4 to 5%.

Risk Factors:

Mediastinal infections have four possible sources:

- Direct contamination as seen in trauma or surgery (e.g., open heart, esophageal)
- Hematogenous or lymphatic spread
- Extension of infection from the neck or retroperitoneum
- Extension from the lung, pleura, or chest wall

PHYSICAL FINDINGS & CLINICAL PRESENTATION

- Patients with acute mediastinitis present with acute onset of fever, tachycardia, chest pain, dysphagia, or respiratory distress. There may be signs of sternal wound infection or cellulitis and/or crepitus and edema of the chest wall.
- Patients with chronic mediastinitis are mostly asymptomatic until symptoms develop related to invasion or obstructions of structures within the mediastinum or adjacent to the mediastinum, such as cough, dyspnea, wheezing, chest pain, dysphagia, or hemoptysis. Complications of chronic or sclerosing mediastinitis include:
  - Superior vena cava syndrome. Histoplasma is the most common nonmalignant cause of this syndrome, marked by edema of face, neck and torso; neck vein distention; and headache.
  - Pulmonary venous or arterial obstruction.
  - Esophageal obstruction, cor pulmonale, constructive pericarditis.
  - Thoracic duct obstruction.

ETIOLOGY (TABLE 1M-6)

Acute mediastinitis:

- Related to head and neck infections or esophageal perforation

- Anaerobic bacteria: *Peptostreptococci, Veillonella, Fusobacterium, Actinomyces, Prevotella, Eubacterium, Bacteroides*
- Aerobic bacteria: *Streptococcus, Staphylococcus, Corynebacterium, Moraxella,* enteric gram-negative rods
- Fungi: Candida albicans
- Related to cardiothoracic surgery
- Gram-positive bacteria: *Staphylococcus aureus, Staphylococcus epidermidis, Enterococcus, Streptococcus*

TABLE 1M-6   Microbiology of Mediastinitis

Organisms Frequently Recovered in Mediastinitis Secondary to Infection of the Head and Neck or Esophageal Perforation

Anaerobic

Gram-positive cocci—*Peptostreptococcus* spp.

Gram-positive bacilli—*Actinomyces, Eubacterium, Lactobacillus*

Gram-negative cocci—*Veillonella*

Gram-negative bacilli—*Bacteroides* spp., *Fusobacterium* spp., *Prevotella* spp., *Porphyromonas* spp.

Aerobic or Facultative

Gram-positive cocci—*Streptococcus* spp., *Staphylococcus* spp.

Gram-positive bacilli—*Corynebacterium*

Gram-negative cocci—*Moraxella*

Gram-negative bacilli—Enterobacteriaceae, *Pseudomonas* spp., *Eikenella corrodens*

Fungi—*Candida albicans*

Representative Organisms Recovered in Mediastinitis Secondary to Cardiothoracic Surgery, with Representative Rate and Range

Gram-Positive Cocci

Staphylococcus aureus, 25% (7.1%-66.7%)

Staphylococcus epidermidis, 30% (6%-45.5%)

Enterococcus spp., 10% (8%-18.8%)

Streptococcus spp., 2% (0%-18.2%)

Gram-Negative Bacilli

Escherichia coli, 5% (0%-12.5%)

Enterobacter spp., 10% (4%-21.4%)

Klebsiella spp., 3% (0%-21.1%)

Proteus spp., 2% (0%-7.1%)

Other Enterobacteriaceae, 2% (0%-20%)

Pseudomonas spp., 2% (0%-54%)

Fungi

C. albicans, <2 (0%-20.5%)

Polymicrobial, 10% (0%-40%)

Others Occasionally Reported

Acinetobacter, Salmonella spp., *Legionella* spp., *Bacteroides fragilis, Corynebacterium* spp., *Burkholderia cepacia, Mycoplasma hominis, Candida tropicalis, Aspergillus* spp., *Nocardia* spp., *Kluyvera, Gordonia sputi, Mycobacterium fortuitum, Mycobacterium chelonae, Rhodococcus bronchialis*

Other Unusual Causes of Mediastinitis

Anthrax, brucellosis, actinomycosis, paragonimiasis, *Streptococcus pneumonia*

From Bennett JE, Dolin R, Blaser MJ: *Mandell, Douglas, and Bennett's principles and practice of infectious diseases,* ed 8, Philadelphia, 2015, Saunders.

- Gram-negative bacteria: *Escherichia coli, Enterobacter, Klebsiella, Proteus, Pseudomonas,* other Enterobacteriaceae
- Fungi: *Candida albicans*

Chronic mediastinitis:

- *Histoplasma capsulatum,* a dimorphic fungus, is the most common and can cause mediastinal granuloma or fibrosing mediastinitis. A leakage of fungal antigens from lymph nodes into the mediastinal space is believed to cause a hypersensitivity reaction and subsequent exuberant fibrotic response.
- Other: *Mycobacterium tuberculosis, Nocardia,* actinomycosis, aspergillosis.

DX DIAGNOSIS

DIFFERENTIAL DIAGNOSIS

For chronic mediastinitis:

- Tumors that can also cause superior vena cava syndrome (e.g., Hodgkin and non-Hodgkin lymphomas, mesothelioma)
- Sarcoidosis
- Behçet syndrome
- Mediastinal fibrosis associated with radiation
- Silicosis

LABORATORY TESTS

- CBC with differential, C-reactive protein, and procalcitonin can point to bacterial infection
- Obtain cultures: aerobic and anaerobic bacteria and fungi, intraoperatively or of any purulent drainage
- Pathologic examination: distinguish between cancer and infection for chronic mediastinitis and allow for specific fungal stains on tissues

IMAGING STUDIES

- Chest x-ray: can show diffuse mediastinal widening or evidence of mediastinal abscess, including gas bubbles or fluid level. Pneumomediastinum or pneumothorax can be seen with esophageal perforation (Table 1M-7).
- Chest CT: can show the same as x-ray but is more sensitive in determining degree of mediastinal involvement and may guide drainage procedures for treatment or diagnosis.
- MRI may be superior to CT for sclerosing mediastinitis.

 TREATMENT

NONPHARMACOLOGIC THERAPY

Surgery remains the gold standard treatment of mediastinitis for optimal drainage and debridement.

- Open techniques: debridement of infected tissue and open packing of the wound with delayed closure or use of vacuum-assisted closure for acute mediastinitis
- Closed techniques: debridement of infected tissues, closure of the sternum, and postoperative irrigation through drainage tubes for acute mediastinitis

M

Diseases and Disorders

I

TABLE 1M-7 Risk Factors for Surgical Site Infection/Mediastinitis Post–cardiac Surgery

Preoperative Risk Factors	Operative Risk Factors	Postoperative Risk Factors
Increasing age	Emergent surgery	Need for reexploration
Diabetes	Heart transplant	Prolonged ICU stay
Staphylococcus aureus nasal colonization	Increasing complexity of surgery	Need for mechanical ventilation >48 hr
Previous sternotomy	Use of internal thoracic arteries in CABG	Lack of perioperative glucose control
COPD	Prolonged operative time	Placement of tracheostomy
Peripheral vascular disease	Hair removal by razor, not clippers	Postoperative myocardial infarction
Class 3-4 angina	Inappropriate timing of antibiotics	Receipt of multiple blood products
Renal failure requiring hemodialysis	Prolonged time on cardiopulmonary bypass	Postoperative low cardiac output state
History of endocarditis	High core temperature during bypass (>38° C)	
Cigarette smoking		
Low cardiac output		
Concurrent infection		
Prolonged preoperative hospitalization		
Preoperative use of a ventricular assist device		

CABG, Coronary artery bypass grafting; *COPD*, chronic obstructive pulmonary disease; *ICU*, intensive care unit.
From Bennett JE, Dolin R, Blaser MJ: *Mandell, Douglas, and Bennett's principles and practice of infectious diseases*, ed 8, Philadelphia, 2015, Saunders.

ACUTE GENERAL Rx

- Intravenous antibiotics: also a cornerstone of therapy but without surgery may fail. Broad-spectrum antibiotics should be used until cultures are finalized. Combination of piperacillin-tazobactam or meropenem plus vancomycin offers good initial coverage for acute mediastinitis. Other options include ciprofloxacin or cefepime for gram-negative rods, linezolid for gram-positive bacteria, metronidazole for anaerobic bacteria.
- Therapy is 2 to 3 weeks, but some cases may require 4 to 6 weeks.

CHRONIC Rx

- There is no definitive cure for chronic fibrosing or sclerosing mediastinitis. Antifungal agents and steroids generally do not work. The goal of therapy is to palliate symptoms by relieving airway, vascular, or esophageal obstruction. Surgery in patients with extensive fibrosis has high morbidity and mortality.

DISPOSITION

- Patients may need extensive wound care and possible vacuum-assisted closure and prolonged intravenous antibiotics.

REFERRAL

- Thoracic surgeon and/or head and neck surgeon for surgery and debridement
- Infectious diseases consultant for antibiotic selection and long-term management

 **PEARLS & CONSIDERATIONS**

COMMENTS

Histoplasma capsulatum is a dimorphic fungus found commonly in bird and bat fecal material and is most prevalent in the Ohio and Mississippi river valleys of the United States.

PREVENTION

Antibiotic prophylaxis should be given within 60 minutes before incision for surgeries requiring sternotomy. Options include cefazolin 1 g IV if <80 kg and 2 g if >80 kg, or cefuroxime 1.5 g IV. If the patient is penicillin allergic or has a history of methicillin-resistant *S. aureus* (MRSA) infection or surgery is to be done in a hospital where MRSA infection is common, use vancomycin 1 g IV.

SUGGESTED READINGS

Available online at www.expertconsult.com

AUTHOR: **GLENN G. FORT, M.D., M.P.H.**

BASIC INFORMATION

DEFINITION

Meigs' syndrome is characterized by the presence of a benign solid ovarian tumor associated with ascites and predominantly right hydrothorax that disappear after tumor removal.

ICD-10CM CODES
R18   Ascites
J91.8 Pleural effusion in other conditions classified elsewhere
R18.0 Malignant ascites
R18.8 Other ascites
C56.9 Malignant neoplasm of unspecified ovary

EPIDEMIOLOGY & DEMOGRAPHICS

- Occurs in <1% of ovarian fibromas (associated with approximately 0.004% of ovarian tumors)
- Most frequently encountered during middle age (average age, approximately 48 yr)

PHYSICAL FINDINGS & CLINICAL PRESENTATION

- Asymptomatic pelvic mass on bimanual examination
- Intermittent pelvic pain (intermittent torsion)
- Acute pelvic tenderness
- Acute abdominal tenderness
- Abdominal pelvic mass
- Abdominal bloating
- Fluid wave
- Shifting dullness
- "Puddle sign"
- Hyperresonance or flatness to chest percussion, absence of tactile and vocal fremitus
- Absent or loud bronchial breath sounds, rales, mediastinal displacement, tracheal shift
- Weight loss and emaciation

ETIOLOGY

- Not specifically known
- Usually associated with "edematous" fibromas (or other benign ovarian solid tumor) in excess of 10 cm
- Plausible that large fibroma with narrow stalk has inadequate lymphatic drainage; when coupled with intermittent torsion, results in backflow transudation into the peritoneal cavity; accumulated peritoneal ascites then pass to the right pleural cavity by the lymphatics (overloaded thoracic duct) or abdominal pleural commutation (i.e., foramen of Bochdalek)

DIAGNOSIS

DIFFERENTIAL DIAGNOSIS

- Abdominal ovarian malignancy
- Various gynecologic disorders:
  1. Uterus: endometrial tumor, sarcoma, leiomyoma ("pseudo-Meigs' syndrome")
  2. Fallopian tube: hydrosalpinx, granulomatous salpingitis, fallopian tube malignancy
  3. Ovary: benign, serous, mucinous, endometrioid, clear cell, Brenner tumor, granulosa, stromal, dysgerminoma, fibroma, metastatic tumor
- Nongynecologic (gastrointestinal tract or genitourinary tract tumor or pathology) causes of pelvic mass
  1. Ascites
  2. Portal vein obstruction
  3. Inferior vena cava obstruction
  4. Hypoproteinemia
  5. Thoracic duct obstruction
  6. Tuberculosis
  7. Amyloidosis
  8. Pancreatitis
  9. Neoplasm
  10. Ovarian hyperstimulation
  11. Pleural effusion
  12. Congestive heart failure
  13. Malignancy
  14. Collagen-vascular disease
  15. Pancreatitis
  16. Cirrhosis

WORKUP

- Clinical condition characterized by ovarian mass, ascites, and predominantly right-sided pleural effusion (the pleural effusion can also be left-sided in a small number of cases)
- Ovarian malignancy and the other causes (see "Differential Diagnosis") of pelvic mass, ascites, and pleural effusion to be considered
- History of early satiety, weight loss with increased abdominal girth, bloating, intermittent abdominal pain, dyspnea, nonproductive cough

LABORATORY TESTS

- Complete blood count to rule out inflammatory process
- Tumor markers (CA-125, hCG, AFP, CEA, LDH) to evaluate malignancy
- Chemical and liver function testing profile to evaluate metabolic or hepatic involvement
- Arterial blood gases if respiratory compromise

IMAGING STUDIES

- Pelvic sonography (color-flow Doppler evaluation of adnexal mass) initially to evaluate pelvic pathology (CT scan or MRI to further delineate neoplastic lesions [Fig. E1M-12])
- Chest x-ray

TREATMENT

NONPHARMACOLOGIC THERAPY

- Informed consent and proper preparation of patient for possible staging laparotomy (total abdominal hysterectomy and bilateral salpingo-oophorectomy, omentectomy, possible bowel resection, pelvic/periaortic lymphadenectomy)
- Bowel prep if considering pelvic malignancy

ACUTE GENERAL Rx

Depending on clinical presentation, size of pelvic mass, amount of ascites, and pleural effusion:
- If pelvic mass <10 cm with minimal ascites/pleural effusion: consider diagnostic laparoscopy (possible exploratory laparotomy) and salpingo-oophorectomy with removal of ovarian fibroma (tumor).
- If pelvic mass >10 cm with moderate/large amount ascites/pleural effusion: consider pleurocentesis if respiratory compromise (cytology: AFB) and exploratory laparotomy with salpingo-oophorectomy and removal of ovarian fibroma (tumor).
- Treat pelvic malignancy, gastrointestinal or genitourinary tumor as indicated.

CHRONIC Rx

- Resolution of ascites and right-sided pleural effusion after removal of ovarian fibroma
- No long-term follow-up for benign ovarian fibroma

DISPOSITION

Excellent progress and complete survival are expected.

REFERRAL

To gynecologist or gynecologic oncologist for evaluation and treatment, especially if malignancy considered or encountered

SUGGESTED READINGS
Available at www.expertconsult.com

AUTHOR: **RUBEN ALVERO, M.D.**

BASIC INFORMATION

DEFINITION

Melanoma is a skin neoplasm arising from the malignant degeneration of melanocytes. It is classically subdivided in four types:
1. Superficial spreading melanoma (70%) (Fig. 1M-13, *A*)
2. Nodular melanoma (15%-20%) (Fig. 1M-13, *B*)
3. Lentigo maligna melanoma (5%-10%)
4. Acral lentiginous melanoma (7%-10%)

SYNONYMS

Malignant melanoma
Cutaneous malignant melanoma

ICD-10CM CODES

C43.9	Malignant melanoma of skin, unspecified
C43.30	Malignant melanoma of unspecified part of face
C43.31	Malignant melanoma of nose
C43.4	Malignant melanoma of scalp and neck
C43.51	Malignant melanoma of anal skin
C43.52	Malignant melanoma of skin of breast
C43.59	Malignant melanoma of other part of trunk
C43.8	Malignant melanoma of overlapping sites of skin
D03.8	Melanoma in situ of other sites
D03.9	Melanoma in situ, unspecified

EPIDEMIOLOGY & DEMOGRAPHICS

- In 2015, an estimated 74,000 new cases and 10,000 deaths are expected in the United States and the estimated lifetime risk of the development of melanoma will be 1 in 50.
- Melanoma has doubled and tripled in incidence over the past 25 yr.
- Melanoma is much more common in whites (17.2 per 100,000 white men) than in African Americans (1 per 100,000 African American men). Increased risk of developing melanomas is found in patients with fair skin, red hair, light eyes, abundance of freckles, atypical moles or large amount of moles (>50). A personal history of any skin cancer or a family history of melanoma also increases the risk.
- Melanoma is the leading cause of death from skin cancer. Although it represents <10% of all skin-cancers, it accounts for at least 70% of deaths related to skin cancer.
- The median age at diagnosis is 53 yr.
- Superficial spreading melanoma occurs most often in young adults on sun exposed areas.
- Acral lentiginous melanoma is most often found in Asian Americans and African Americans and is not related to sun exposure.
- 8% to 10% of melanomas arise in people with a family history of the disease.

PHYSICAL FINDINGS & CLINICAL PRESENTATION

Variable depending on the subtype of melanoma:
- Superficial spreading melanoma is most often found on the lower legs, arms, and upper back. It may have a combination of many colors or may be uniformly brown or black.
- Nodular melanoma can be found anywhere on the body, but it most frequently occurs on the trunk on sun-exposed areas. It has a dark-brown or red-brown appearance and can be dome shaped or pedunculated. Lesions are frequently misdiagnosed because they may resemble a blood blister or hemangioma and may also be amelanotic.
- Lentigo maligna melanoma is generally found in older adults in areas continually exposed to the sun and frequently arising from lentigo maligna (Hutchinson's freckle) or melanoma in situ. It might have a complex pattern and variable shape; color is more uniform than in superficial spreading melanoma.
- Acral lentiginous melanoma frequently occurs on soles, subungual mucous membranes, and palms (sole of the foot is the most prevalent site). Unlike other types of melanoma, it has a similar incidence in all ethnic groups.
- The warning signs that the lesion may be a melanoma can be summarized with the ABCDE mnemonic:
  - **A:** Asymmetry (e.g., lesion is bisected and halves are not identical)
  - **B:** Border irregularity (uneven, ragged border)
  - **C:** Color variegation (presence of various shades of pigmentation)
  - **D:** Diameter enlargement (>6 mm)
  - **E:** Evolving (mole changing in size, shape, or color, or mole that differs visibly from surrounding moles ["ugly duckling" sign]) (Fig. 1M-14)

ETIOLOGY

- Ultraviolet light is the most important cause of malignant melanoma.
- There is a modest increase in melanoma risk in patients with small nondysplastic nevi and a much greater risk in those with dysplastic lesions.
- The *CDKN2A* gene, residing at the *9p21* locus, is often deleted in patients with familial melanoma.
- A mutated signal transduction molecule, v-raf murine sarcoma viral oncogene homolog B_1 (BRAF), has been identified in 50% to 70% of patients with melanoma.

DIAGNOSIS

DIFFERENTIAL DIAGNOSIS

- Dysplastic nevi
- Solar lentigo
- Vascular lesions
- Blue nevus
- Basal cell carcinoma
- Seborrheic keratosis

WORKUP

- Dermoscopy (use of an instrument that shines polarized light on skin surfaces and magnifies skin lesions) can increase the accuracy in diagnosing melanoma by 10% to 27%.
- Any suspicious lesion (Fig. 1M-15) should be biopsied. Perform excisional biopsy with elliptical excision that includes 1 to 2 mm of normal skin surrounding the lesion and extends to the subcutaneous tissue; incisional punch biopsy is sometimes necessary in surgically sensitive areas (e.g., digits, nose). It is essential that the size of the specimen be adequate to determine the histologic depth of penetration, which is known as the Breslow depth.
- Sentinel lymph node excision (SLNE) is probably the most important staging and potentially therapeutic procedure for patients with melanoma. It should be con-

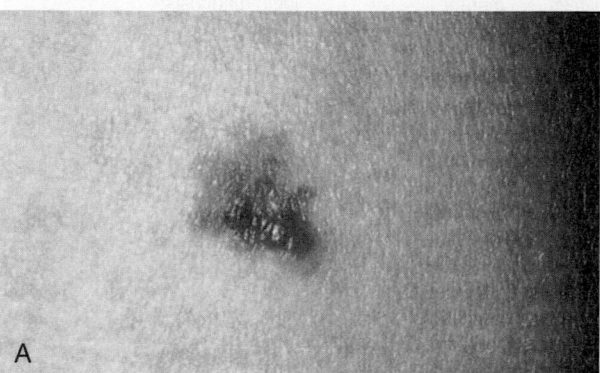
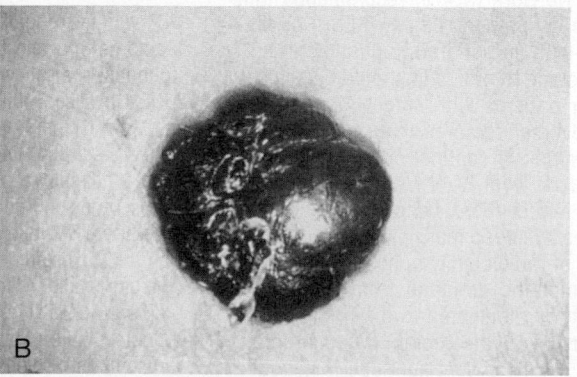

FIGURE 1M-13 A, Superficial spreading melanoma. **B,** Nodular melanoma. (From Abeloff MD [ed]: *Clinical oncology,* ed 3, New York, 2004, Churchill Livingstone.)

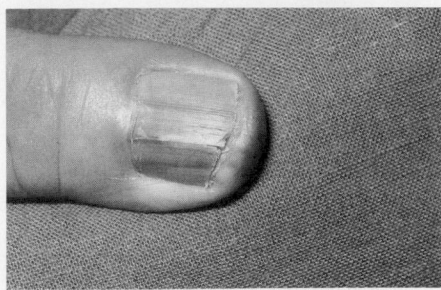

FIGURE 1M-14 Subungual melanoma with Hutchinson sign (pigment spreading from under the nail to involve the adjacent skin, usually of the proximal or lateral nail fold). These lesions are thought to emanate from the nail matrix. (From White GM, Cox NH [eds]: *Diseases of the skin, a color atlas and text,* ed 2, St Louis, 2006, Mosby.)

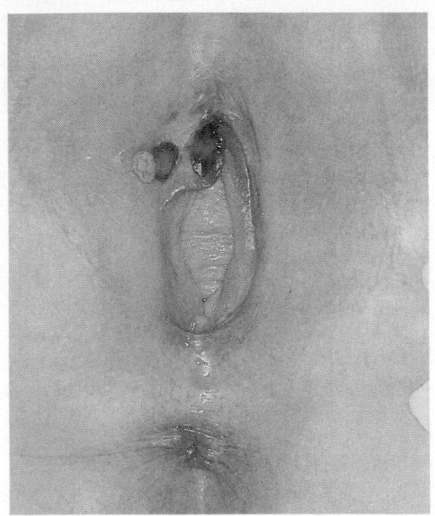

FIGURE 1M-15 Melanoma of the vulva. Benign nevi, vulva melanosis, and melanoma may occur in the vulvar region. Any suspicious pigmented lesion should be biopsied. The patient here is 75 years old. (Courtesy Paul Koonings, M.D. From White GM, Cox NH [eds]: *Diseases of the skin, a color atlas and text,* ed 2, St Louis, 2006, Mosby.)

sidered in patients with intermediate (1 to 4 mm) melanomas or high-risk skin tumors to obtain information regarding a patient's subclinical lymph node status with minimal morbidity. The National Comprehensive Cancer Network (NCCN) recommends that sentinel-lymph node biopsy (SLNB) be discussed with and offered to patients classified as stage IB or II, and should be considered for patients with stage IA melanoma and "adverse" features that might portend a higher risk of sentinel node involvement (e.g., Clark level IV or V, tumor thickness of 0.75 mm or more, lymphovascular invasion, positive deep margins). SLNB involves the use of radiologic lymphoscintigraphy to map lymphatic drainage from the site of the primary melanoma to the first sentinel lymph node in the region. When properly performed, if the sentinel node is negative the remaining lymph nodes in the region

will not have metastases in more than 98% of cases. If the sentinel nodes are negative, no additional regional surgery is recommended. The staging of intermediate thickness (1.2-3.5 mm) primary melanomas, according to the results of sentinel node biopsy, provides important prognostic information and identifies patients with nodal metastases whose survival can be prolonged by immediate lymphadenectomy.

- The staging system for melanoma adapted by the American Joint Committee on Cancer (AJCC) is as follows:

T classification	Thickness (mm)	Ulceration status/ mitoses
Tis	-	-
T1	≤1.00	a: no ulceration and mitoses <1/mm²
		b: with ulceration or mitoses ≥1/mm²
T2	1.01-2.00	a: no ulceration
		b: with ulceration
T3	2.01-4.00	a: no ulceration
		b: with ulceration
T4	≥4.00	a: no ulceration
		b: with ulceration
Regional nodes (N)	Number of nodes	Nodal metastatic mass
N0	0	None
N1	1	a: micrometastases
		b: macrometastases
N2	2-3	a: micrometastases
		b: macrometastases
N3	>4, or matted nodes, or in transit met(s)/ satellite(s) with metastatic nodes	a: micrometastases
		b: macrometastases
		c: in transit met(s)/ satellite(s) without metastatic nodes
Distant Metastases	M stage	
M0	No distant metastases	
M1a	Metastases to skin, subcutaneous tissue, distant nodes	
M1b	Metastases to lungs	
M1c	Metastases to any other visceral sites or to any site combined with elevated LDH	

Clinical Stage	TNM classification
Stage 0	TisN0M0
Stage I	A: T1aN0M0
	B: T1b-T2aN0M0
Stage II	A: T2b-T3aN0M0
	B: T3b-T4aN0M0
	C: T4bN0M0
Stage III	A: T(1-4)aN(1-2)aM0
	B: T(1-4)bN(1-2)aM0 or T(1-4)aN(1-2)bM0
	C: T(1-4)bN1bM0 or T(1-4) bN2b-cM0 or any TN3M0
Stage IV	Any M1 disease

LABORATORY TESTS

The pathology report should indicate the following:

- Tumor thickness (Breslow microstage).
- Tumor depth: the depth of invasion is the most important histologic prognostic parameter in evaluating the primary tumor.
- Mitotic rate: tabulated as mitoses per square millimeter in the dermal part of the tumor in which most mitoses are identified.
- Radial growth rates versus vertical growth rate: radial growth phase describes the growth of melanoma within the epidermis and along the dermal-epidermal junction.
- Tumor infiltrating lymphocytes have a strong predictive value in vertical growth phase melanomas and are defined as brisk, nonbrisk, or absent.
- Histologic regression: characterized by the absence of melanoma in the epidermis and dermis flanked on one or both sides by melanoma.
- Reverse-transcription polymerase chain reaction assay for tyrosine messenger RNA is a useful marker for the presence of melanoma cells. It is performed on sentinel lymph node biopsy and is useful for detection of submicroscopic metastases.
- Identification of somatic mutations in the gene encoding the serine-threonine protein kinase B-RAF (*BRAF*) which is found in approximately 50% to 70% of melanomas.

Rx TREATMENT

- Initial excision of the melanoma
- Reexcision of the involved area after histologic diagnosis:
  1. The margins of reexcision depend on the Breslow depth. For melanoma in situ with Breslow depth ≤2.0 mm, recommended surgical margin is 1 cm. If Breslow depth is ≤2.0 mm, margin should be 2 cm. For melanoma in situ, margin should be 5 mm.
  2. Low-risk or intermediate-risk tumors require excision of 1 to 3 cm.
  3. Melanomas of moderate thickness (0.9 to 2.0 mm) can be excised safely with 2-cm margins.
  4. A 1-cm margin of excision for melanoma with a poor prognosis (as defined by a tumor thickness ≥2 mm) is associated with a significantly greater risk of

M

Diseases
and Disorders

I

regional recurrence than is a 3-cm margin, but with a similar overall survival rate. Randomized clinical trials have also shown that radical surgery with 2 cm excision margins did not differ from that with 4 cm margins for survival in patients with cutaneous melanoma >2 mm thick.

- Lymph node dissection: recommended in all patients with enlarged lymph nodes. Lymph node evaluation is important in patients with melanoma 1 mm in depth because it determines the overall prognosis and need for therapeutic lymph node dissection or adjuvant treatment.
  1. Elective lymph node dissection remains controversial.
  2. It is indicated with positive sentinel node. It may be considered in those with a primary melanoma between 1 and 4 mm thick (especially in patients >60 yr).
- Adjuvant therapy with interferon alfa-2b is approved by the FDA for AJCC stages IIb- III melanoma; however, its statistical benefit remains modest. Peginterferon alfa-2b (which has a longer duration of action and can be given once a week compared to 3-5 times/week for standard interferon) has also been FDA approved for adjuvant treatment of stage III melanoma.
- Cytokines such as interferon alpha and high-dose interleukin-2 can be used in very selected cases in metastatic melanoma. Their use has been supplanted by the use of more modern therapeutic approaches.

- The use of immune checkpoint inhibitors has come to the forefront in the therapy of metastatic melanoma. Ipilimumab, an agent that blocks cytotoxic T-lymphocyte–associated antigen 4 to potentiate an antitumor T-cell response, has shown improved overall survival in patients with previously treated or untreated metastatic melanoma. Impressive and durable long term survival rates have been demonstrated in approximately 20% patient beyond 5 years. More recently, inhibitors of program death receptor (PD-1) and /or their ligands (PDL1/PDL2) have been found to provide impressive responses and improved survival in both relapsed and untreated patients with metastatic disease. The PD-1 inhibitors, nivolumab and pembrolizumab, have both been approved for the treatment of metastatic melanoma which has progressed or not responded after initial therapy with ipilimumab. Combined use of nivolumab and ipilimumab in previously untreated patients with BRAF V600 wild type unreactable or metastatic melanoma has been shown more effective than ipililmumab alone and may be a new option for first-line treatment of metastatic melanoma.
- In patients who carry the V600E *BRAF* mutation, the current approach involves the use of oral BRAF-inhibitors, with resultant improved rates of overall and progression-free survival in patients with previously untreated melanoma. Vcmurafenib is a selective BRAF inhibitor with a response rate of greater than 60% in patients with metastatic melanomas with V600

BRAF mutation. Oral selective MEK inhibitors (e.g., trametinib, cobimetinib) or combinations of these two receptor-inhibitors have showed improved survival outcomes when used together in this setting. Targeted therapy is useful in patients with rapidly growing melanoma with BRAF mutations, but resistance appears in almost all patients and median progression-free survival is 15 to 18 months.
- Patients with a history of melanoma should be followed up with skin examinations every 6 mo or sooner if patient detects any new lesions; the assessments usually consist of medical history, physical examination, laboratory values, and chest radiograph.

DISPOSITION

- Prognosis varies with the stage of the melanoma. The 5-yr survival related to thickness is as follows: <0.76 mm, 99% survival; 0.6 to 1.49 mm, 85%; 1.5 to 2.49 mm, 84%; 2.5 to 3.9 mm, 70%; >4 mm, 44%.
- The 5-yr survival in patients with distant metastasis is <10%.
- Treatment of advanced disease consists (in addition to surgical excision and lymph node dissection) of chemotherapy, immunotherapy, and radiation therapy.

RELATED CONTENT

Melanoma (Patient Information)

AUTHORS: **BHARTI RATHORE, M.D.**, and **FRED F. FERRI, M.D.**

BASIC INFORMATION

DEFINITION
Ménière's disease is a syndrome characterized by recurrent vertigo with fluctuating hearing loss, tinnitus, and fullness in the ear.

SYNONYMS
Endolymphatic hydrops
Lermoyez's syndrome
Idiopathic endolymphatic hydrops

ICD-10CM CODES
H81.09 Ménière's disease, unspecified ear
H81.01 Meniere's disease, right ear
H81.02 Meniere's disease, left ear
H81.03 Meniere's disease, bilateral

EPIDEMIOLOGY & DEMOGRAPHICS
INCIDENCE (IN U.S.): Varies between 4.3 and 15.3/100,000 persons
PREDOMINANT SEX: Female to male ratio of 1.3:1
PEAK INCIDENCE: Fourth to sixth decade of life

PHYSICAL FINDINGS & CLINICAL PRESENTATION
- Hearing may be unilaterally decreased.
- Pallor, sweating, and nausea may occur during a severe attack.
- Usually the patient develops a sensation of fullness and pressure along with decreased hearing and tinnitus in a single ear.
- The patient typically experiences severe vertigo, which peaks within minutes, then slowly subsides over hours.
- May see spontaneous nystagmus on examination.
- Persistent sense of disequilibrium for days is typical after an acute episode
- May have vestibulopathy demonstrable with a positive head thrust test.

ETIOLOGY
- Unknown; viral, autoimmune, and genetic causes have been suggested.
- Endolymphatic hydrops is the postmortem histologic hallmark. Recent research suggests that endolymphatic hydrops may create cytochemical changes that disturb endolymphatic fluid homeostasis, leading to spiral ganglion cell death.

DIAGNOSIS

Proposed guidelines by the American Academy of Otolaryngology-Head and Neck Surgery (AAO-HNS) for diagnosis of Ménière's disease:

DIFFERENTIAL DIAGNOSIS
- Acoustic neuroma
- Migrainous vertigo
- Multiple sclerosis
- Autoimmune inner ear syndrome
- Otitis media
- Vertebrobasilar disease
- Labyrinthitis

WORKUP
- Diagnosis is primarily made by history, although further diagnostic tests may help support the diagnosis. Guidelines to define Ménière's disease are described in Table 1M-8.
- Audiogram may show sensorineural hearing loss, with lower frequencies primarily affected. Hearing loss may recover either partially or completely after an attack. Recurrent attacks may lead to a persistent and progressive sensorineural hearing loss.
- Electronystagmography may show peripheral vestibular deficit.
- Electrocochleography (ECoG) records the summating potential and action potential of the eighth cranial nerve in response to auditory stimuli and may indicate significant endolymphatic hydrops if the ratio of summating potential to action potential (SP:AP) is greater than 0.35. Unfortunately, sensitivity and specificity of ECoG to diagnosis of Ménière's disease are low, due to their variability related to severity and chronicity of disease.
- More recently, the vestibular-evoked myogenic potential (VEMP), a short latency inhibitory potential of sternocleidomastoid muscle evoked by brief and loud monaural clicks or tone bursts, has been shown to be elevated or absent in some patients with Ménière's disease, reflecting impaired function of the saccule. However, this test also lacks significant sensitivity and specificity to Ménière's disease and has not yet been widely used in the clinical setting.

LABORATORY TESTS
No laboratory serologic test is specific for Ménière's disease. A thyroid panel, glucose, hemoglobin A1C, antinuclear antibodies, urinalysis, chemistry panel, Venereal Disease Research Laboratory (VDRL) Test, fluorescent treponemal antibody (FTA-ABS), Lyme disease antibodies, and allergy testing can be ordered to screen for other disorders such as thyroid or autoimmune diseases, diabetes, otorenal syndrome, syphilis, Lyme disease, and allergy-mediated Ménière's disease.

IMAGING STUDIES
- MRI to rule out acoustic neuroma, or other retrocochlear lesion, especially if cerebellar or CNS dysfunction is present
- Recent efforts have shown a role for MRI with intratympanic gadolinium.

TREATMENT

NONPHARMACOLOGIC THERAPY
Limit activity during attacks

ACUTE GENERAL Rx
- Prochlorperazine 5 to 10 mg PO q6h or 25 mg PO bid
- Promethazine 12.5 to 25 mg PO q4 to 6h
- Diazepam 5 to 10 mg IV/PO for acute attack
- Meclizine 25 mg q6h
- Scopolamine patch

CHRONIC Rx
- Diuretics such as hydrochlorothiazide or acetazolamide, salt restriction, and avoidance of caffeine are traditional.
- For refractory cases, intratympanic gentamicin injections to the affected ear, endolymphatic sac surgery

DISPOSITION
- Patients are usually followed by an otoneurologist or ENT specialist.
- Usual course of disease consists of alternating attacks and remissions.
- Majority of patients can be managed medically. Of patients, 10% to 30% will undergo surgical intervention for persistent incapacitating vertigo.

REFERRAL
To an otolaryngologist for surgical intervention if attacks persist despite medical therapy

SUGGESTED READINGS
Available at www.expertconsult.com

RELATED CONTENT
Ménière's Disease (Patient Information)

AUTHOR: **SHARON S. HARTMAN POLENSEK, M.D., PH.D.**

TABLE 1M-8 Guidelines to Define Ménière's Disease

Definition	Symptoms
Certain Ménière's disease	Definite Ménière's disease + histopathologic confirmation
Definite Ménière's disease	≥2 definitive spontaneous episodes of vertigo 20 min or longer Audiometrically documented hearing loss on at least one occasion Tinnitus or aural fullness in the treated ear Other causes excluded
Probable Ménière's disease	One definite episode of vertigo Audiometrically documented hearing loss on at least one occasion Tinnitus or aural fullness in the treated ear Other causes excluded
Possible Ménière's disease	Episodic vertigo without documented hearing loss, or sensorineural hearing loss (SNHL) fluctuating or fixed, with disequilibrium but nonepisodic Other causes excluded

 BASIC INFORMATION

DEFINITION
Meningiomas are generally slow-growing tumors arising from arachnoid cells of the arachnoid villi; 90% are benign.

ICD-10CM CODES
D32.0 Benign neoplasm of cerebral meninges

EPIDEMIOLOGY & DEMOGRAPHICS
INCIDENCE: 6/100,000 persons/yr; account for about one third of primary brain tumors and are the second most common brain tumor in adults; often underreported.

PREDOMINANT SEX AND AGE: Female/male ratio of almost 3:1 in the brain and up to 6:1 in the spinal cord; male = female in childhood

PEAK INCIDENCE: Males: sixth decade, females: seventh decade, incidence increases with age; rare in childhood

RISK FACTORS: Ionizing radiation results in increased incidence and a shorter latency period. Neurofibromatosis type 2 (NF2) is an autosomal dominant genetic disorder that predisposes to multiple intracranial tumors. Approximately half of all individuals with NF2 have meningiomas, most of which are intracranial. Studies have suggested a link between hormonal factors and development of meningioma. At present, there is no conclusive evidence to support a causal relationship with cell phone usage and subsequent development of meningioma.

GENETICS: Meningiomas may be isolated or found in association with other genetic diseases, such as neurofibromatosis type 2 and familial meningioma. Approximately half of meningiomas have allelic losses involving the NF2 and DAL-1 genes. Allelic losses of chromosomes 1p, 2p, 6q, 9q, 10q, 14q, 17p, and 18q may be associated with histologic progression.

TABLE 1M-9 Locations and Presentations of Meningiomas

Location	Presenting Manifestation
Parasagittal	Urinary incontinence, dementia, gradual paraparesis, seizures
Lateral convexity	Variable depending on structures compressed, including slow hemiparesis, speech abnormalities
Olfactory groove	Anosmia, visual disturbance, dementia, Foster-Kennedy syndrome
Suprasellar	Hormonal failure, bitemporal hemianopsia, optic atrophy
Sphenoid ridge	Extraocular nerve paresis, exostoses, proptosis, seizures

From Goetz CG, Pappert EJ: *Textbook of clinical neurology*, Philadelphia, 1999, Saunders.

PHYSICAL FINDINGS & CLINICAL PRESENTATION
- Neurologic symptoms vary with location and size (see Table 1M-9); meningiomas can arise from the dura at any site, although most commonly occur within the skull and at sites of dural reflection, such as the cerebral convexities and the falx. Other less common locations include the sphenoid wing, olfactory groove, and optic nerve sheath. Focal symptoms such as vision loss, hearing loss, or mental status change depend on the site of origin and the time course of growth.
- Most common presentation is with a focal or generalized seizure or gradually worsening neurologic deficit. Seizures are present preoperatively in 30% to 40%.
- Typically are slow growing and asymptomatic; many meningiomas are asymptomatic and/or discovered incidentally on a neuroimaging study or at autopsy.

ETIOLOGY
- Meningiomas are thought to arise from a multistep progression of genetic changes.
- Mutations of the NF2 gene on chromosome 22 are found in patients with neurofibromatosis type 2 and >50% of sporadic meningiomas. This gene is thought to act as a tumor suppressor gene; the protein product, merlin, is also involved in cytoskeletal organization.
- DAL-1 is another tumor suppressor gene, located on chromosome 18p, that has been identified in a subset of the approximately 40% of sporadic meningiomas with neither the NF2 gene mutations nor allelic loss of chromosome 22q.
- Cranial radiation may be responsible for some cases following an appropriate latency period from 10 to 20 yr. Meningiomas that result from radiation are generally more aggressive.
- The link with steroid hormones and their receptors is suggested by the increase in growth rate

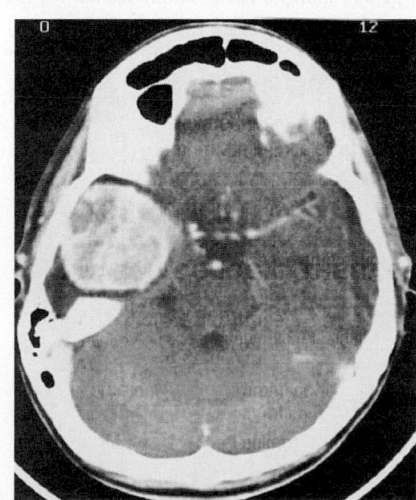

FIGURE 1M-16 Contrast-enhanced CT scan demonstrates a large contrast-enhancing right sphenoid wing meningioma. (From Specht N [ed]: *Practical guide to diagnostic imaging*, St Louis, 1998, Mosby.)

and/or development of meningiomas during pregnancy and increased incidence in women who use postmenopausal hormones or in association with breast carcinomas.

 DIAGNOSIS

DIFFERENTIAL DIAGNOSIS
Other well-circumscribed intracranial tumors that involve the dura or subdural space:
- Acoustic schwannoma (typically at the pontocerebellar junction)
- Ependymoma, lipoma, and metastases within spinal cord
- Metastatic disease from lymphoma/adenocarcinoma, inflammatory disease such as sarcoidosis and Wegener's granulomatosis, or infections such as tuberculosis

WORKUP
Imaging studies with CT or MRI, followed by surgical removal with histologic confirmation

LABORATORY TESTS
According to the World Health Organization (WHO) classification, there are nine benign histologic variants (account for 90% of all meningiomas) and four variants associated with increased recurrence and rates of metastasis. Ninety percent of meningiomas are classified as benign meningiomas or WHO grade I.

IMAGING STUDIES
- Cranial CT scanning or MRI can detect and determine the extent of meningiomas (Fig. 1M-16). CT can show hyperostosis and/or intratumoral calcifications. MRI (Fig. 1M-17) is the imaging modality of choice to demon-

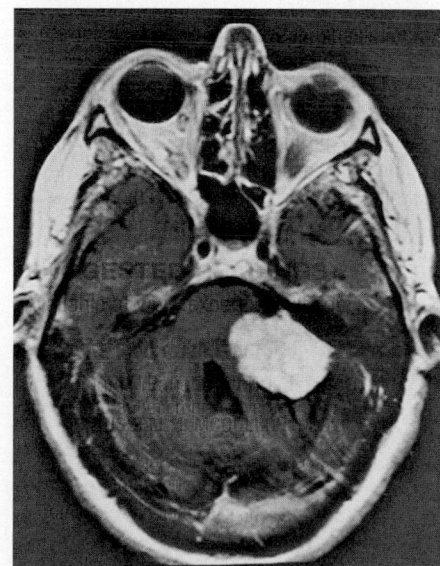

FIGURE 1M-17 MRI picture of a posterior fossa meningioma, demonstrated an extraaxial homogeneously contrast-enhanced mass arising from the tentorium and compressing the cerebellar hemisphere. (From Goetz CG, Pappert EJ: *Textbook of clinical neurology*, Philadelphia, 1999, Saunders.)

strate the dural origin of the tumor in most cases, with the characteristic "tail" sign.
- On nonenhanced scans, meningiomas typically are isodense or slightly hyperdense to brain and are homogeneous in appearance. They show homogeneous contrast enhancement; gadolinium can facilitate imaging of smaller additional lesions that are missed on unenhanced images.
- Indistinct margins, marked edema, mushroomlike projections from tumor, brain parenchymal infiltration, and heterogeneous enhancement are suggestive of more aggressive behavior.
- PET scan may help in predicting the aggressiveness of the tumor and the potential for recurrence, but it is not used routinely.

Rx TREATMENT

Primary management depends on signs or symptoms, age of patient, and location and size of tumor. Observation may be appropriate if tumors are discovered incidentally and/ or if growth is indolent and unlikely to cause symptoms.

PHARMACOLOGIC THERAPY
- Although a variety of chemotherapeutic agents have been studied, such as hydroxyurea, there is no established effective systemic therapy.
- Inhibition of hormone receptors, such as progesterone, estrogen, and androgen, has failed to demonstrate clinical benefit.
- Treatment with molecularly targeted approaches, such as angiogenesis inhibition, is currently under way.

NONPHARMACOLOGIC THERAPY
- The mainstay of treatment for meningiomas remains surgical removal. Complete resection is usually attempted, when feasible. After total excision, recurrence rates of 0% to 20% have been observed, while 20% to 50% of patients recur within 5 yr of a subtotal resection.

- Active surveillance to monitor for tumor recurrence is important.
- Radiation therapy is the only validated form of adjuvant therapy and may be beneficial in patients with incomplete resections or inoperable tumors. Stereotactic radiosurgery can provide local control with more limited toxicity.

ACUTE GENERAL Rx
- For lesions that cause significant mass effect, steroids are sometimes used to decrease brain edema.
- Anticonvulsants are used if the patient presents with seizures.

CHRONIC Rx
- Prophylactic use of anticonvulsants is not recommended in patients without a history of seizures.
- There is limited data on the efficacy of traditional chemotherapy, and the evidence is largely anecdotal. The most extensively evaluated agents are hydroxyurea, mifepristone (RU486), and interferon alfa-2b. Recently, somatostatin analogs have been evaluated in multicenter clinical trials.

DISPOSITION
- Estimated surgical mortality is 7%. Significant morbidity and mortality can be observed in meningiomas with otherwise favorable pathology secondary to unfavorable location (e.g., skull base).
- Long-term outcome varies, based on pathology, tumor grade, location, and completeness of resection.
- Most incidentally discovered meningiomas remain asymptomatic and have a slow rate of growth. Calcified tumors may be less likely to progress than noncalcified ones.
- Meningiomas may recur after surgical resection. In addition, some tumors show histologic progression to a higher grade. Features suggesting increased rate of recurrence include multiple allelic chromosomal losses,

local brain invasion, high rate of mitosis, and highly anaplastic features.

REFERRAL
- Neurosurgical consultation for all cases
- Neurology, radiation oncology, and oncology depending on presence of other sequelae and in setting of recurrence

PEARLS & CONSIDERATIONS

COMMENTS
- Many meningiomas are discovered incidentally; most are benign and remain asymptomatic. A first follow-up MRI should be performed 3 to 6 months after the tumor is identified to rule out an atypical meningioma with rapid growth.
- "Dural tail," which is thickening of the aura adjacent to the mass, is classic finding on neuroimaging studies.
- Individuals with neurofibromatosis type 2 are at high risk to develop meningiomas.

PATIENT & FAMILY EDUCATION
Meningioma mommas: www.meningiomamommas.org
Meningioma Support and Patient Information Group
National Brain Tumor Society
Meningioma Online Support Group: http://www.brainstrust.org/meningioma.htm

SUGGESTED READINGS
Available at www.expertconsult.com

RELATED CONTENT
Meningioma (Patient Information)

AUTHOR: **NICOLE J. ULLRICH, M.D., PH.D.**

BASIC INFORMATION

DEFINITION

Bacterial meningitis is an inflammation of meninges with increased intracranial pressure, and pleocytosis or increased WBCs in cerebrospinal fluid (CSF) secondary to bacteria in the pia-subarachnoid space and ventricles, leading to neurologic sequelae and abnormalities.

SYNONYMS

Spinal meningitis
Bacterial meningitis

ICD-10CM CODES
G00.9 Bacterial meningitis, unspecified
G00.8 Other bacterial meningitis
G01   Meningitis in bacterial diseases classified elsewhere

EPIDEMIOLOGY & DEMOGRAPHICS

INCIDENCE (IN U.S.): 1.3 to 2.0 cases/100,000 persons; 1.2 million cases per year in the world; 135,000 deaths annually worldwide. The rate of bacterial meningitis declined dramatically in the U.S. starting in the early 1990s with the introduction of the *Haemophilus influenzae* type b (Hib) vaccine and in 2000 with the introduction of the conjugate pneumococcal vaccine.

PREDOMINANT SEX: Male = female

PREDOMINANT AGE: All ages, neonate to geriatric

PHYSICAL FINDINGS & CLINICAL PRESENTATION

- Fever
- Headache
- Neck stiffness, nuchal rigidity, meningismus
- Altered mental state, lethargy
- Vomiting, nausea
- Photophobia
- Seizures
- Coma; lethargy, stupor
- Rash: petechial associated with meningococcal infection (Fig. 1M-18), purpura fulminans (Fig. 1M-19)
- Myalgia
- Cranial nerve abnormality (unilateral)
- Papilledema
- Dilated, nonreactive pupil(s)
- Posturing: decorticate/decerebrate
- Physical examination findings of Kernig's sign and Brudzinski's sign in adults with meningitis are often not helpful in determining meningeal inflammation

ETIOLOGY

The bacterial etiology of meningitis depends on the age of the patient. *Neisseria meningitidis* is now more common than *Haemophilus influenzae* as a cause of bacterial meningitis in children as well as adults, and streptococci are still common causes of bacterial meningitis. *H. influenzae* is the cause of >30% of cases of meningitis (usually in infants and children <6 yr of age). It is associated with sinusitis, otitis media.

- Neonates: group B streptococcus, gram-negative rods such as *E. coli, Listeria monocytogenes*

- Infants ≥1 mo and <3 mo: group B streptococci (40%), gram-negative rods (30%), *Streptococcus pneumoniae* (14%), and *Neisseria meningitidis* (12%)
- Infants ≥3 mo and <3 yr:
  1. *S. pneumoniae* (45%)
  2. *N. meningitidis* (34%)
  3. *S. agalactiae* (group B streptococci) (11%)
  4. *H. influenzae*
  5. *E. coli*
- Ages ≥3 yr and <10 yr:
  1. *S. pneumoniae* (47%)
  2. *N. meningitidis* (32%)
- Ages ≥10 yr and <19 yr:
  1. *N. meningitidis* (55%)
  2. *S. pneumoniae*
- Adults: *S. pneumoniae, N. meningitidis,* and *L. monocytogenes* (especially over age 50-60 or with cell-mediated immune deficiencies)
- People with HIV/AIDS are at increased risk for invasive meningococcal disease (IMD).

DIAGNOSIS

Diagnostic approach is based on patient presentation and physical examination (Fig. 1M-20). Lumbar puncture should be performed as soon as possible. Key elements to diagnosis are CSF evaluation and CT scan or MRI if the patient is in a coma or has focal neurologic deficits, pupillary abnormalities, or papilledema. Table 1M-10 describes tests of CSF in patients with suspected CNS infection.

DIFFERENTIAL DIAGNOSIS

- Endocarditis, bacteremia
- Intracranial tumor
- Lyme disease
- Brain abscess
- Partially treated bacterial meningitis
- Medications
- SLE
- Seizures
- Acute mononucleosis

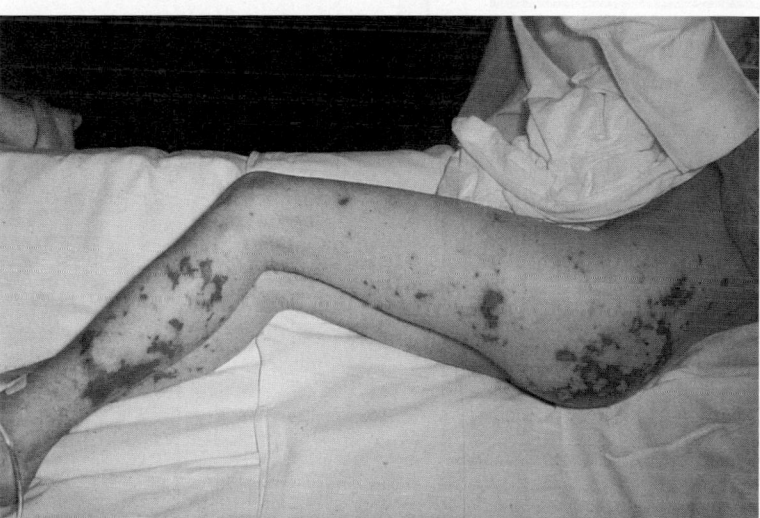

FIGURE 1M-18 Fully developed, almost pathognomonic hemorrhagic rash of meningococcal sepsis. (From Cohen J, Powderly WG: *Infectious diseases,* ed 2, St Louis, 2004, Mosby.)

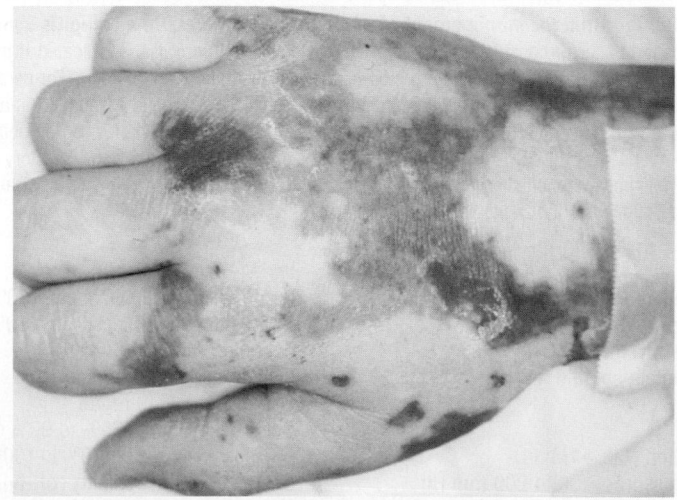

FIGURE 1M-19 Meningococcal purpura fulminans in overwhelming meningococcal meningitis. (From Adams JG et al: *Emergency medicine, clinical essentials,* ed 2, Philadelphia, 2013, Elsevier.)

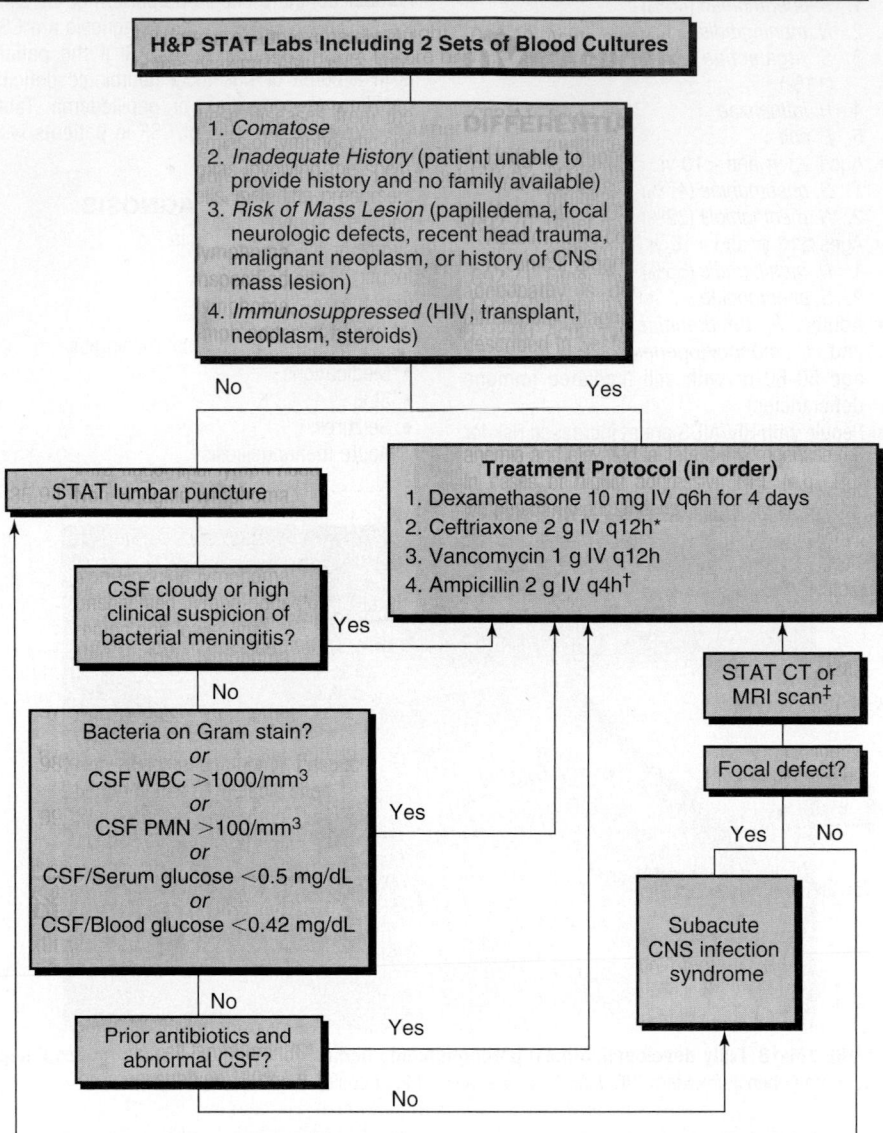

Management of Adults with Acute Meningitis Syndrome
(Fulminant course (<48 h) with fever, headache, usually with impaired sensorium and stiff neck. This protocol is not applicable if the dominant clinical impression is subarachnoid hemorrhage or acute psychosis.)

H&P STAT Labs Including 2 Sets of Blood Cultures

1. *Comatose*
2. *Inadequate History* (patient unable to provide history and no family available)
3. *Risk of Mass Lesion* (papilledema, focal neurologic defects, recent head trauma, malignant neoplasm, or history of CNS mass lesion)
4. *Immunosuppressed* (HIV, transplant, neoplasm, steroids)

No / Yes

STAT lumbar puncture

CSF cloudy or high clinical suspicion of bacterial meningitis?

Treatment Protocol (in order)
1. Dexamethasone 10 mg IV q6h for 4 days
2. Ceftriaxone 2 g IV q12h*
3. Vancomycin 1 g IV q12h
4. Ampicillin 2 g IV q4h†

STAT CT or MRI scan‡

Focal defect?

Yes / No

Bacteria on Gram stain?
or
CSF WBC >1000/mm³
or
CSF PMN >100/mm³
or
CSF/Serum glucose <0.5 mg/dL
or
CSF/Blood glucose <0.42 mg/dL

Yes

Subacute CNS infection syndrome

No

Prior antibiotics and abnormal CSF?

Yes

No

FIGURE 1M-20 Algorithm for management of adult patients with acute meningitis syndrome. *For severe cephalosporin allergy, consider meropenem or moxifloxacin. †Ampicillin is indicated if there is a history of alcoholism, organ transplant, malignancy, pregnancy, or age older than 50 years. For penicillin-allergic patients, an alternative is trimethoprim-sulfamethoxazole. ‡Consider magnetic resonance imaging *(MRI)* if the patient is known or suspected to have human immunodeficiency virus *(HIV)*, if it can be obtained rapidly. *CNS,* Central nervous system; *CSF,* cerebrospinal fluid; *CT,* computed tomography; *H&P,* history and physical examination; *PMN,* polymorphonuclear leukocyte; *WBC,* white blood cell. (From Vincent JL et al: *Textbook of critical care,* ed 6, Philadelphia, 2011, Saunders.)

- Other infectious meningitides
- Neuroleptic malignant syndrome
- Subdural empyema
- Rocky Mountain spotted fever

WORKUP

CSF examination (Table 1M-11):
- Opening pressure >100 to 200 mm Hg
- WBC usually >1000 WBC/mm³

- Neutrophilic predominance: >80%
- Gram stain of CSF: positive in 60% to 90% of patients
- CSF protein: >50 mg/dl
- CSF glucose: <40 mg/dl
- Culture: positive in 65% to 90% of cases
- CSF bacterial antigen: 50% to 100% sensitivity
- E-test for susceptibility of pneumococcal isolates

TABLE 1M-10 Tests of Cerebrospinal Fluid in Patients with Suspected Central Nervous System Infection

Routine Tests
White blood cell count with differential
Red blood cell count[a]
Glucose concentration[b]
Protein concentration
Gram stain
Bacterial culture

Selected Specific Tests Based on Clinical Suspicion
Viral culture[c]
Smears and culture for acid-fast bacilli
Venereal Disease Research Laboratory (VDRL)
India ink preparation
Cryptococcal polysaccharide antigen
Fungal culture
Antibody tests (IgM or IgG, or both)[d]
Nucleic acid amplification tests (e.g., polymerase chain reaction)[e]
Cytology[f]
Flow cytometry

---

[a]Should be checked in the first and last tubes; in patients with a traumatic tap, there should be a decrease in the number of red blood cells with continued flow of cerebrospinal fluid (CSF). See text for the formula for determining whether the numbers of CSF red blood cells and white blood cells are consistent with a traumatic tap.
[b]Compare with serum glucose drawn just before lumbar puncture.
[c]Yield of viral culture may be low.
[d]May be useful for specific causes of meningitis and encephalitis.
[e]Most useful for specific viral causes of encephalitis and causes of chronic meningitis.
[f]In patients with suspected malignancy.
From Bennett JE, Dolin R, Blaser MJ: *Mandell, Douglas, and Bennett's principles and practice of infectious diseases,* ed 8, Philadelphia, 2015, Saunders.)

LABORATORY TESTS

Blood culturing, WBC with differential, and CSF examination (see "Workup")

IMAGING STUDIES

- CT scan or MRI of head: necessary with increased intracranial pressure, coma, neurologic deficits
- Sinus CT: if sinusitis suspected

🆁🆇 TREATMENT

Empiric therapy is necessary with IV antibiotic treatment if patient has purulent CSF fluid at time of lumbar puncture, is asplenic, or has signs of DIC/sepsis pending Gram stain and culture results. Try to obtain blood and CSF cultures before starting antimicrobial therapy, but do not delay therapy if obtaining them is not possible. Therapy after Gram stain pending cultures is recommended for the following:
1. Neonates: ampicillin: 200 to 400 mg/kg per day divided q6 to 8 hr plus gentamicin: 7.5 mg/kg IV in 3 divided doses plus a

TABLE 1M-11 Typical Cerebrospinal Fluid Findings in Patients With Selected Infectious Causes of Meningitis

Cause of Meningitis	White Blood Cell Count (cells/mm³)	Primary Cell Type	Glucose (mg/dL)	Protein (mg/dL)
Viral	50-1000	Mononuclear[a]	>45	<200
Bacterial	1000-5000[b]	Neutrophilic[c]	<40[d]	100-500
Tuberculous	50-300	Mononuclear[e]	<45	50-300
Cryptococcal	20-500[f]	Mononuclear	<40	>45

[a]May be neutrophilic early in presentation.
[b]Range from <100 to >10,000 cells/mm³.
[c]About 10% of patients have cerebrospinal fluid (CSF) lymphocyte predominance.
[d]Should always be compared with a simultaneous serum glucose; ratio of CSF to serum glucose is ≤0.4 in most cases.
[e]May see a "therapeutic paradox," in which a mononuclear predominance becomes neutrophilic during antituberculous therapy.
[f]More than 75% of patients with acquired immunodeficiency syndrome have <20 cells/mm³.
From Bennett JE, Dolin R, Blaser MJ: *Mandell, Douglas, and Bennett's principles and practice of infectious diseases,* ed 8, Philadelphia, 2015, Saunders.

third-generation cephalosporin: cefotaxime or ceftriaxone

2. 1-23 months: vancomycin: 60 mg/kg per day IV (maximum up to 4 g/day) divided in 4 doses plus third-generation cephalosporin: ceftriaxone: 100 mg/kg (maximum dose 4 g/day) in 1 or 2 divided doses or cefotaxime: 300 mg/kg per day IV (maximum dose of 12 g/day) in 3 or 4 divided doses

3. Children: vancomycin: 60 mg/kg per day IV (maximum dose 4 g/day) in 4 divided doses plus third-generation cephalosporin: ceftriaxone 100 mg/kg per day IV (maximum 4 g/day) or cefotaxime: 300 mg/kg IV (maximum dose of 12 g/day) in 3 or 4 divided doses

4. Adults: vancomycin: 15-20 mg/kg IV every 8 to 12 hours plus third-generation cephalosporin: ceftriaxone: 2 g IV q12 hours or cefotaxime: 2 g IV q4 to 6 hr. For adults over 50 yr of age also add ampicillin 2 g IV every 4 hr to cover *Listeria*

5. Immunocompromised patients: vancomycin *plus* ampicillin *plus* either cefepime 2 g IV every 8 hr to cover *Pseudomonas* or meropenem 2 g IV q8 hr for adults, which also covers *Pseudomonas*

Use of corticosteroids in adults:

1. Dexamethasone 0.15 mg/kg q6h for first 4 days of therapy should be used for adults in developed countries with known or suspected bacterial meningitis. Decreased mortality and neurologic sequelae are seen with adjunct therapy. The benefit of dexamethasone is less clear in developing countries with high HIV prevalence and malnutrition or with delayed clinical presentations.

2. Dexamethasone also benefits children with Hib meningitis if given at the same time or before the first dose of the antibiotic: 0.15 mg/kg per dose q6 hr for 2 to 4 d. The use and benefit of corticosteroids in suspected or pneumococcal or meningococcal meningitis to prevent neurologic sequelae is not as clear and should be individualized after analysis of risk and benefits.

DISPOSITION

Bacterial meningitis is a reportable disease that needs to be reported to local health authorities. Droplet precautions should be used for first 24 hr of therapy for suspected or confirmed *N. meningitidis* infection.

REFERRAL

- To a neurologist if persistent neurologic sequelae develop after bacterial meningitis
- To an infectious disease consultant if a patient has recurrent bacterial meningitis; such patients deserve a workup for an anatomic (CSF dural leak) or immunologic defect (complement defect, hyposplenism, immunoglobulin deficiency)

 **PEARLS & CONSIDERATIONS**

COMMENTS

- Nosocomial bacterial meningitis may result from invasive procedures (e.g., placement of ventricular catheters, lumbar puncture, craniotomy, spinal anesthesia). Treatment of this different spectrum of microorganisms requires empirical antimicrobial therapy with vancomycin plus either cefepime, ceftazidime, or meropenem. In cases of basilar skull fracture, effective empirical antimicrobial therapy consists of vancomycin plus a third-generation cephalosporin.

- False-positive elevations of CSF where blood cell counts can be found after traumatic lumbar puncture or in patients with intracerebral or subarachnoid hemorrhage in which RBCs and WBCs are introduced into the subarachnoid space. In those instances, the following formula should be used as a correction factor for the true WBC count in the presence of CSF RBCs:

$$\text{Adjusted WBC in CSF} = \text{Actual WBC in CSF} - \frac{\text{WBC in blood} \times \text{RBC in CSF blood}}{\text{RBC in blood}}$$

In the previous equation, the amount being subtracted is the predicted CSF WBC that would occur if all the CSF WBCs were the result of blood contamination.[1]

- Prevention of meningitis can be achieved through chemoprophylaxis of close contacts (household members and anyone exposed to oral secretions).

- Effective medications are rifampin 10 mg/kg PO bid for 2 days or ceftriaxone 250 mg IM single dose in patients older than age 12; 125 mg IM if age 12 or younger.

- Ciprofloxacin 500 mg for prevention of *Neisseria* meningitis can be given to patients older than 18 yr who cannot tolerate rifampin to eradicate pharyngeal colonization.

- Menactra: a protein-conjugate vaccine against serogroup A, C, Y, W-135 capsular polysaccharides is available for adults (up to 55 yr) and children older than 2 yr.

ⒺBM **EVIDENCE**

Available at www.expertconsult.com

SUGGESTED READINGS

Available at www.expertconsult.com

RELATED CONTENT

Meningitis (Patient Information)
Viral Meningitis (Related Key Topic)
Fungal Meningitis (Related Key Topic)

AUTHOR: **GLENN G. FORT, M.D., M.P.H.**

[1]Bennett JE, et al: *Mandell, Douglas and Bennett's principles and practice of infectious diseases,* ed 8, Philadelphia, 2015, Saunders, p 1093.

Meningitis, Viral (PTG)

BASIC INFORMATION

DEFINITION

Viral meningitis is an acute febrile illness with signs and symptoms of meningeal irritation, usually with a lymphocytic pleocytosis of the cerebrospinal fluid (CSF) and negative CSF bacterial stains and cultures.

SYNONYMS

Aseptic meningitis
Viral meningitis

ICD-10CM CODES
A87.8 Other viral meningitis
A87.9 Viral meningitis, unspecified

EPIDEMIOLOGY & DEMOGRAPHICS (TABLE 1M-13)

INCIDENCE (IN U.S.): 11 cases/100,000 persons. Leads to 26,000 to 42,000 hospitalizations a year.
PREDOMINANT SEX: Male = female
GENETICS: Those with abnormal humoral immunity and agammaglobulinemia have associated difficulty with viral clearance.

PHYSICAL FINDINGS & CLINICAL PRESENTATION

- Fever
- Headache
- Nuchal rigidity
- Photophobia
- Myalgias
- Vomiting
- Rash

ETIOLOGY

- Enterovirus: 85% to 95% of all cases. Most common are coxsackie viruses and echoviruses

- Parechoviruses
- Mumps virus
- Measles
- Arboviruses from mosquitoes: EEE, West Nile, St Louis
- Herpes: HSV-1, HSV-2, VZV, HHV-6, and HHV-7
- Acute HIV
- Lymphocytic choriomeningitis virus
- Adenovirus
- CMV and EBV
- Other arthropod-borne viruses: Powassan virus
- Influenza A and B virus

DIAGNOSIS

The diagnostic approach is similar to that for bacterial meningitis (see "Meningitis, Bacterial"); the foremost need is to rule out bacterial meningitis with CSF evaluation. Presentation may be similar to that of meningitis with bacterial involvement.

DIFFERENTIAL DIAGNOSIS

- Bacterial meningitis
- Meningitis secondary to Lyme disease, TB, syphilis, amebiasis, leptospirosis
- Rickettsial illnesses: Rocky Mountain spotted fever
- Migraine headache
- Medications
- SLE
- Acute mononucleosis/Epstein-Barr virus
- Seizures
- Carcinomatous meningitis

WORKUP

CSF examination:
- Usually shows pleocytosis
- Lymphocytic predominance (neutrophils in early stages)
- Opening pressure: 200 to 250 mm Hg H_2O (≤250 mm/H_2O)

- WBC: 100 to 1000 mm^3
- Increased CSF protein (<200 mg/dl)
- Slightly decreased or normal CSF glucose (>45 mg/dl)
- Negative Gram stain, cultures, CIE, latex agglutination
- Viral cultures or serologic testing may be diagnostic
- Polymerase chain reaction for HSV or enterovirus (which could shorten duration of antibiotic treatment and hospitalization if bacterial meningitis was suspected)
- Antibody detection in CSF for diagnosis of West Nile virus meningitis

LABORATORY TESTS

CBC with differential, blood culturing, and CSF examination (see "Workup")

IMAGING STUDIES

CT scan or MRI: if cerebral edema, focal neurologic findings develop

TREATMENT

- No specific antiviral therapy for most viruses. Treatment is supportive unless HSV is detected, which would be treated with IV acyclovir: 10 mg/kg q8h in adults for 14 to 21 days. Up to 20 mg/kg q8h in children >12 yr.
- Empiric antibiotics may be given until CSF cultures exclude bacterial meningitis.

DISPOSITION

Viral meningitis is almost always an uncomplicated illness that will resolve; however, relapsing headache, myalgia, and weakness may occur for 2 to 3 wk after onset of symptoms.

PEARLS & CONSIDERATIONS

- Enteroviruses are the most common cause of viral meningitis and are transmitted by fecal-oral route and less commonly by the respiratory route. They are more common in summer and fall months. From 2000 to 2005, the most common serotypes were coxsackie viruses A9, B5, and B1 and echoviruses 6, 9, 13, 18, and 30.
- Herpes simplex type 2 (HSV-2) can be a cause of a primary episode of meningitis and also be a cause of recurrent episodes of lymphocytic meningitis. HSV-2 meningitis presents most often without a history of genital herpes or genital symptoms. Recurrent aseptic meningitis, also known as Mollaret's disease, is predominantly caused by HSV-2 infection.

SUGGESTED READINGS

Available at www.expertconsult.com

RELATED CONTENT

Meningitis (Patient Information)

AUTHOR: **GLENN G. FORT, M.D., M.P.H.**

TABLE 1M-13 Epidemiology of Acute Viral Meningitis

			Epidemiologic Factors*		
Season	Patient's Age (yr)	Patient's Sex	Risk Factor		Suggested Viral Agent
Summer-fall	Infant	—	Infected mother		Coxsackievirus B
	1-15	—	Swimming pools, closed communities		Enteroviruses
			Geographic area: California, southeastern United States		California serogroup virus
Winter	1-15	—	School exposure		Varicella virus, measles virus
		Male/female 3:1			Mumps virus
	16-21	—	College exposure		Measles virus
		Male/female 3:1 —			Mumps virus
					Epstein-Barr virus (mononucleosis)
	Any	—	Mice, rats, hamsters		Lymphocytic choriomeningitis virus
	Adults	—	Varicella-zoster		Varicella-zoster virus
Any	Any	—	Immunocompromise		Adenovirus
			Acquired immunodeficiency syndrome		Human immunodeficiency virus

*Epidemiologic factors are suggestive but should not be used to exclude diagnoses in individual cases.
From Gorbach SI: *Infectious diseases*, ed 2, Philadelphia, 1998, Saunders.

Diseases and Disorders

I

BASIC INFORMATION

DEFINITION

Menopause is the permanent cessation of menstrual periods for 1 yr after age 40 yr or permanent cessation of ovulation after lost ovarian activity. It is the reproductive stage of life marked by waxing and waning estrogen levels followed by decreasing ovarian function. Primary ovarian insufficiency (previously also referred to as premature ovarian failure) and no menstrual periods may also occur because of depletion of ovarian follicles before the age of 40 yr.

SYNONYMS

Change of life
Climacteric ovarian failure

ICD-10CM CODES
Z78.0	Asymptomatic menopausal state
N95.1	Menopausal and female climacteric states
N95.8	Other specified menopausal and perimenopausal disorders
E28.310	Symptomatic premature menopause
E28.319	Asymptomatic premature menopause

EPIDEMIOLOGY & DEMOGRAPHICS

- Average age of menopause in the United States is 51 yr.
- Age at which menopause occurs is primarily genetically determined.
- Smokers experience menopause an average of 1.5 yr earlier than nonsmokers.
- More than one third of a woman's life may be spent after menopause.
- Onset of perimenopause is usually in a woman's mid- to late-40s.
- Approximately 4000 women begin menopause each day.

PHYSICAL FINDINGS & CLINICAL PRESENTATION

- Atrophic vaginitis, which can cause burning, itching, bleeding, dyspareunia
- Either complete cessation of menses or a period of irregular cycles and diminished or heavier bleeding
- Osteoporosis
- Osteopenia/Psychological dysfunction:
  1. Anxiety
  2. Depression
  3. Insomnia
  4. Nervousness
  5. Irritability
  6. Inability to concentrate
- Sexual changes, decreased libido, dyspareunia
- Urinary incontinence
- Menopausal vasomotor symptoms (VMS, hot flashes, flushes), night sweats, cardiovascular disease, coronary artery disease, atherosclerosis, headaches, tiredness, and lethargy. A study from the University of Pennsylvania noted that the median duration of moderate-to-severe

hot flashes is 10.2 yr but that the length of hot flashes was largely dictated by how early these began in the perimenopause.

ETIOLOGY

- The most common etiology: physiologic, caused by depleted granulosa and theca cells that fail to react to endogenous gonadotropins, producing less estrogen; decreased negative feedback in the hypothalamic pituitary access, increased follicle-stimulating hormone (FSH), and increased luteinizing hormone (LH), which leads to stromal cells that continue to produce androgens as a result of the LH stimulation
- Surgical castration
- Family history of early menopause, cigarette smoking, blindness, abnormal chromosomal karyotype (Turner's syndrome, gonadal dysgenesis), precocious puberty, and left-handedness

DIAGNOSIS

DIFFERENTIAL DIAGNOSIS

- Asherman's syndrome
- Hypothalamic dysfunction
- Hypothyroidism
- Pituitary tumors
- Adrenal abnormalities
- Ovarian abnormalities
- Polycystic ovarian syndrome
- Pregnancy
- Ovarian neoplasm
- Tuberculosis of the endometrium

WORKUP

- If the clinical picture is highly suggestive of menopause, estrogen can be prescribed. If all symptoms resolve, then diagnosis has essentially been made. Before estrogen is prescribed, a complete history and physical examination are needed. If a patient has estrogen-dependent malignancy, unexplained abnormal uterine bleeding, history of thrombophlebitis, or acute liver disease, estrogen therapy is contraindicated.
- Progesterone challenge test: medroxyprogesterone 10 to 20 mg PO or progesterone 100 mg IM to induce withdrawal bleeding. If no withdrawal bleeding is obtained, a hypoestrogenic state is assumed to be present. This test is increasingly controversial, even if very commonly performed.
- Physical examination, height, weight, blood pressure, breast examination, and pelvic examination are needed.
- Assess risk for coronary artery disease, osteoporosis, cigarette smoking, personal history, history of breast cancer, liver disease, active coagulation disorder, or any unexplained vaginal bleeding.

LABORATORY TESTS

- FSH, LH, and estrogen levels: markedly elevated FSH and markedly depressed estrogen level constitute laboratory diagnosis of ovarian failure; LH only if polycystic ovarian

disease is to be ruled out in a younger patient. It is not necessary to obtain an FSH if the patient fulfills the clinical criteria for menopause. Similarly, since estradiol levels vary during the menstrual cycle, estradiol levels are rarely necessary or informative.
- TSH to rule out thyroid dysfunction and prolactin level if patient has symptoms of galactorrhea and if suspicion of pituitary adenoma exists
- A general chemistry profile to check for any systemic diseases
- Pap smear per standard guidelines, endometrial biopsy, or dilation and curettage in patients who have had irregular periods or intermenstrual or postmenopausal bleeding
- Mammogram as recommended by American Congress of Obstetricians and Gynecologists.

IMAGING STUDIES

- Per standard protocols, CT scan or MRI of sella if pituitary tumor is suspected
- Bone density studies if high-risk condition for osteoporosis exists
- Pelvic ultrasound to check endometrial stripe

TREATMENT

NONPHARMACOLOGIC THERAPY

- A balanced diet: low in fat, with total fat intake being <30% of calories; total calories sufficient to maintain body weight or produce weight loss if that is desired
- Avoidance of smoking and excessive alcohol or caffeine intake
- Exercise: weight-bearing exercise for osteoporosis prevention
- Kegel exercises for strengthening the pelvic floor
- Adequate calcium intake: 1500 mg elemental calcium qd is necessary to maintain zero calcium balance in postmenopausal women
- Change in the ambient temperature (may ameliorate hot flashes and reduce night sweats)
- Vitamin E
- Avoidance of caffeine, alcohol, and spicy foods if they trigger hot flashes
- Vaginal lubricants to help with the dyspareunia attributable to vaginal dryness (e.g., Replens, K-Y Jelly, or Gyne-Moistrin cream)

ACUTE GENERAL Rx

Vasomotor symptoms are best managed with systemic hormone therapy given in the lowest dose and for the shortest period possible. Estrogen replacement in symptomatic patients can be done in a variety of forms, including oral estrogen and transdermal estrogen patch. The lowest effective dose should be prescribed.
- Examples of oral estrogen include:
  1. Conjugated estrogens: start with 0.3 mg qd and increase to 1.25 mg qd depending on symptoms.
  2. Estradiol: start with 0.5 mg qd and increase to 2 mg qd.
  3. Esterified estrogens: start with 0.3 to 1.25 mg qd.

4. Estropipate: start with 0.625 to 2.5 mg qd.
5. Esterified estrogen/testosterone combination: give 1.25 mg and methyltestosterone 2.5 mg (Estratest) and esterified estrogen 0.625 mg and methyltestosterone 1.25 mg (Estratest HS [half-strength]). May improve sexual enjoyment and libido.

- If the patient has had a hysterectomy for benign disease, estrogen alone is sufficient. However, if she still has her uterus, progestin is necessary to prevent endometrial hyperplasia associated with unopposed estrogen, which is protective against endometrial cancer. Progestins can be prescribed as continual daily dose or cyclic fashion. Most commonly prescribed progestins include medroxyprogesterone acetate 2.5 mg, 5 mg, and 10 mg; Prometrium 100 mg, 200 mg, and 400 mg; and Aygestin 5 mg. Continuous hormone replacement therapy is preferred because after time the patient should be amenorrheic. Patients should be counseled that they may experience some irregular spotting for the first 6 to 9 mo after starting the hormone replacement therapy. Cyclic therapy will cause withdrawal bleeding.
- Combination oral preparations FemHRT, Prefest, Prempro, Activella, Premphase are commonly used. However, the U.S. Preventive Services Task Force recommends against the use of combined estrogen and progestin for the prevention of chronic conditions such as cardiovascular disease in postmenopausal women.
- Transdermal patches can be either estradiol (Estraderm, Vivelle, FemPatch) 0.025 to 0.1 mg applied twice weekly or Climara 0.025 to 0.1 mg used once a week. With these preparations, progesterone should be used in a similar fashion. Apply CombiPatch twice weekly (combination estrogen and progesterone) or Climara Pro once per week (one patch).
- Vaginal creams can be used; these should be reserved for local therapy of atrophic vaginitis. Systemic absorption does occur; however, blood levels are unpredictable. Usual dose 0.5 to 2 g intravaginally daily, cyclically 3 wk on 1 wk off. When symptoms improve, once to twice weekly is adequate maintenance.
- Vagifem estradiol vaginal tablets. Initial dosage: one Vagifem tablet, inserted vaginally, qd for 2 wk. Maintenance dose: one Vagifem tablet, inserted vaginally, twice weekly.
- Femring vaginal ring delivering the equivalent of 0.5 mg/day inserted every 3 mo or Estring 0.0075 mg/day.
- EstroGel 0.06% (estradiol gel) One Pump (1.25 g/day) applied to one arm from wrist to shoulder.
- The FDA contraindications to menopause hormone therapy include the following diseases

and disorders: active liver disease; current, past, or suspected breast cancer; active or recent anterior thromboembolic disease (angina, myocardial infarction); known or suspected estrogen-sensitive malignant conditions; known hypersensitivity to the active substance of the therapy or to any of the excipients; porphyria cutanea tarda; previous idiopathic or current venous thromboembolism; undiagnosed genital bleeding; untreated hypertension; untreated endometrial hyperplasia.
- For women in whom estrogen is contraindicated or for those who do not wish to take estrogen, the following regimens can be used:
  1. Serotonin reuptake inhibitors
  2. Depo-Provera 150 mg IM every month (may be helpful in alleviating hot flashes)
  3. Clonidine 0.05 to 0.15 mg PO qd (questionable efficacy) or transdermal clonidine patch
  4. Bellergal-S (questionable efficacy)
- Tibolone significantly improves vasomotor symptoms, libido, and vaginal lubrication. Not available in the U.S.

CHRONIC Rx

Hormone replacement therapy should be used only for the short term unless benefits outweigh the risks of long-term use. As a result of the results of the Women's Health Initiative (WHI), the FDA has instituted a "black box" warning on postmenopausal hormone replacement products suggesting that the lowest dose should be used for the shortest period of time. This necessitates a considered and nuanced counseling session with patients contemplating hormone replacement prior to the initiation of therapy and then on a periodic basis after that, usually at least a yearly basis.

DISPOSITION

If treated, the patient should have resolution of her symptoms and reduced incidence of osteoporosis. Lifelong medical supervision is necessary to monitor adequacy of treatment and prevention of complications. This should include annual Pap smears until the age of 65, pelvic examinations, breast examinations, mammography, and endometrial sampling of any type of abnormal bleeding. If untreated, the vasomotor symptoms will eventually disappear; however, this may take several years in a small percentage of women. Some women who are in their 80s have experienced hot flashes. Urogenital atrophy will continue to worsen. Osteoporosis and coronary artery disease risks will increase with every passing year.

REFERRAL

Most menopausal women are managed by their gynecologists. However, this condition can be managed adequately by the patient's primary

care physician who has an interest in treating menopausal women.

PEARLS & CONSIDERATIONS

COMMENTS

- Short-term risks of hormone replacement therapy (HRT) include an eighteenfold increased rise for cholecystitis, three-and-a-half-fold risk of a thrombocardiac event in the first year, and possible increased risk of stroke and myocardial infarction.
- Results of the WHI study found that for every 10,000 women taking HRT (combination of both estrogen and progesterone) for 1 yr (10,000 person-yr), seven more would have coronary events, eight would have more strokes, eight would have more pulmonary emboli, and eight would have earlier breast cancer than would 10,000 women taking placebo. Benefits of HRT were six fewer cases of colorectal cancer and five fewer hip fractures per 10,000 women.
- HRT should not be initiated or continued for the primary or secondary prevention of coronary heart disease.
- Estrogen-replacement therapy or HRT should only be prescribed for patients with sufficient menopausal symptoms that impact the patient's quality of life.
- Interestingly, women who start hormone therapy early in menopause may have cardiac and other benefits. A recent trial showed that oral estradiol therapy was associated with less progression of subclinical atherosclerosis (measured as change in carotid-artery intima media thickness [CIMT]) than with placebo when therapy was initiated within 6 years after menopause but not when it was initiated 10 or more years after menopause. Estradiol had no significant effect on cardiac CT measures of atherosclerosis in either postmenopause stratum.[1]

(EBM) EVIDENCE

Available at www.expertconsult.com

SUGGESTED READINGS

Available at www.expertconsult.com

RELATED CONTENT

Menopause (Patient Information)
Hot Flashes (Related Key Topic)
Osteoporosis (Related Key Topic)

AUTHOR: **RUBEN ALVERO, M.D.**

[1]Hodis HN, et al: Vascular effects of early versus late postmenopausal treatment with estradiol, *N Engl J Med* 374:1221-1231, 2016.

M

I

BASIC INFORMATION

DEFINITION

Menorrhagia is menstrual blood loss greater than 80 mL.

Metrorrhagia is bleeding between menses.

Polymenorrhea is bleeding that occurs more often than every 21 days.

Oligomenorrhea is bleeding less than every 35 days.

The new FIGO classification of abnormal uterine bleeding further defines abnormal bleeding by etiology. The acronym PALM-COEIN (polyp, adenomyosis, leiomyoma, malignancy or hyperplasia, coagulopathy, ovulatory dysfunction, endometrial, iatrogenic, or not yet classified) is now used to define abnormal uterine bleeding.

SYNONYMS

Abnormal uterine bleeding
Menometrorrhagia
Dysfunctional uterine bleeding

ICD-10CM CODES
N92.0 Excessive and frequent menstruation with regular cycle
N92.1 Excessive and frequent menstruation with irregular cycle
N92.4 Excessive bleeding in the premenopausal period
N92.2 Excessive menstruation at puberty
N92.6 Irregular menstruation, unspecified

EPIDEMIOLOGY & DEMOGRAPHICS

PREVALENCE: 30% of women in their lifetime; 5% of medical visits for women

PREDOMINANT SEX AND AGE: Female; peak in adolescence and perimenopausal periods

GENETICS: Von Willebrand disease; hereditary platelet dysfunction disorders; 20% of women at any age have underlying bleeding disorder

RISK FACTORS: Genetic predisposition, anticoagulation treatment, obesity

PHYSICAL FINDINGS & CLINICAL PRESENTATION

- History: age, age of menarche or menopause, menstrual bleeding patterns, severity of bleeding, pain, underlying medical conditions, surgical history, use of medications, signs and symptoms of hemostatic disorder including history of heavy bleeding since menarche, postpartum hemorrhage, surgery-related bleeding, bleeding from dental work, easy bruising, epistaxis, and frequent gum bleeding, family history of bleeding disorder
- Physical exam: general findings including excessive weight, signs of polycystic ovarian syndrome (PCOS) (hirsutism and acne), signs of thyroid disease (nodule), signs of insulin resistance (acanthosis nigricans), signs of bleeding disorder including petechiae, ecchymoses, pallor, swollen joints, pelvic examination including external, speculum, and bimanual exam

ETIOLOGY

- Pregnancy/miscarriage
- Endometrial polyps
- Adenomyosis
- Uterine leiomyoma
- Endometrial hyperplasia or carcinoma
- Coagulopathy, inherited or acquired
- Ovulatory dysfunction, most likely PCOS
- Endometrial
- Iatrogenic

DIAGNOSIS

DIFFERENTIAL DIAGNOSIS

Pregnancy, STD, PCOS, thyroid dysfunction, anovulation due to immature hypothalamic-pituitary-ovarian axis, perimenopausal transition, uterine pathology including endometrial hyperplasia or carcinoma, leiomyoma, adenomyosis, or endometrial polyp, von Willebrand's disease, platelet dysfunction disorder, iatrogenic due to medications including oral contraceptives or anticoagulants (warfarin)

WORKUP

- History
- Physical exam to evaluate for uterine pathology
- Laboratory, pathology, and imaging studies to determine etiology

LABORATORY TESTS

- Pregnancy test
- CBC with platelets to assess for anemia or platelet dysfunction
- TSH to assess for hypothyroidism or hyperthyroidism
- Chlamydia trachomatis testing if high risk for evaluation of pelvic infection
- Evaluation for cyclic menses
- Prothrombin time and partial thromboplastin time
- Testing for von Willebrand disease if clinically suspected (von Willebrand–ristocetin cofactor activity, von Willebrand factor antigen, and factor VIII)
- Endometrial sampling by endometrial biopsy or hysteroscopic sampling for women >45 yr or <45 yr with history of unopposed estrogen (PCOS, obesity), failed medical management, or persistent abnormal bleeding

IMAGING STUDIES

- Transvaginal ultrasound if abnormal exam or persistent symptoms
- Sonohysterography or hysteroscopy if ultrasound not adequate or suspicion for endometrial polyp or submucosal leiomyoma
- Transabdominal ultrasound in adolescents may be considered
- MRI not indicated initially

TREATMENT

NONPHARMACOLOGIC THERAPY

- Dilation and curettage
- Uterine artery embolization

- Hysteroscopic resection of uterine pathology including endometrial polyps and submucosal leiomyoma
- Endometrial ablation
- Hysterectomy

ACUTE GENERAL Rx

- Progestin
- Oral contraceptive pills
- Conjugated estrogens
- Surgical management if indicated including dilation and curettage, uterine artery embolization, or hysterectomy
- Hospitalization to maintain hemostasis and administer blood transfusion if severe menorrhagia

CHRONIC Rx

- Oral contraceptive pills. Can be used cyclically or continuously
- Levonorgestrel intrauterine device: high degree of efficacy
- Gonadotropin-releasing hormone agonist (goserelin)
- Nonsteroidal anti-inflammatory drugs
- Tranexamic acid, aminocaproic acid
- Danazol (significant side-effect profile requires justification for use; this is rare)
- Surgery for anatomic causes including resection of leiomyoma and hysterectomy
- Endometrial ablation if completed childbearing

REFERRAL

- If concern for uterine pathology as etiology for menorrhagia, referral to a gynecologist for surgical management indicated
- If endometrial sampling reveals endometrial hyperplasia or malignancy, referral to a gynecologist is indicated. Cyclic progestogen therapy is necessary with resampling. If endometrial hyperplasia associated with complex glands or atypia, consultation with gynecologic oncologist is important because of high degree of progression to malignancy.

PEARLS & CONSIDERATIONS

PREVENTION

Weight reduction
Intervention in women with chronic oligo-ovulation due to chronic exposure to unopposed estrogen.

EVIDENCE

Available at www.expertconsult.com

SUGGESTED READINGS

Available at www.expertconsult.com

RELATED CONTENT

Menorrhagia (Patient Information)
Dysfunctional Uterine Bleeding (Related Topic)

AUTHOR: **ERIN MEDLIN, M.D.**

BASIC INFORMATION

DEFINITION

Acute mesenteric lymphadenitis is a syndrome of acute right lower quadrant abdominal pain associated with mesenteric lymph node enlargement and a normal appendix.

SYNONYMS

Mesenteric lymphadenitis

ICD-10CM CODES

I88.0 Nonspecific mesenteric lymphadenitis

EPIDEMIOLOGY & DEMOGRAPHICS

- Incidence unknown
- Affects mostly children (<18 yr) with no sex preference
- When *Yersinia* enterocolitis is the cause, boys are more frequently involved

PHYSICAL FINDINGS & CLINICAL PRESENTATION

- Abdominal pain of variable severity (mild ache to severe colic) beginning in upper abdomen or right lower quadrant; eventually localizes in the right side but not in a precise location (unlike appendicitis)
- In *Yersinia* infection outbreaks (see Table E1M-14), symptoms include abdominal pain (84%), diarrhea (78%), fever (43%), anorexia (22%), nausea (13%), and vomiting (8%)
- Physical findings:
  1. Other lymphadenopathy (20% of cases)
  2. Right lower quadrant tenderness (site of maximal tenderness may vary from one examination to the next)
  3. Guarding (rare)
  4. Mild fever

ETIOLOGY & PATHOGENESIS

- Reactive hyperplasia of lymph nodes that drain the ileocecal region, similar to that seen in inflammatory or allergic conditions. One study reported that approximately two thirds of cases are secondary (reactive) and one third are primary (no demonstrable associated inflammatory process).
- *Yersinia enterocolitica, Y. pseudotuberculosis, Salmonella* species, *Escherichia coli,* and streptococci have been implicated in mesenteric adenitis. Clinical manifestations of yersiniosis are described in Table E1M-15.

DIAGNOSIS

In general, the diagnosis is made on exploration of the abdomen of a patient suspected of having acute appendicitis. On examination the appendix appears normal, and enlarged mesenteric lymph nodes are noted. Excision of an enlarged lymph node with culture and nodal histology may provide information regarding the etiology but is not routinely used.

DIFFERENTIAL DIAGNOSIS

- Acute appendicitis (5%-10% of patients admitted to hospitals with a diagnosis of appendicitis are discharged with a diagnosis of mesenteric adenitis)
- Crohn's disease
  Section II describes the differential diagnosis of right lower quadrant abdominal pain.

LABORATORY TESTS

- Complete blood count may show leukocytosis
- Abdominal sonography and CT scan with IV and oral contrast (Fig. 1M-24) may be useful
- Laparotomy if appendicitis is suspected

PROGNOSIS

Recurrent bouts are common; therefore if laparotomy is performed and a normal appendix is found, it should be removed.

SUGGESTED READINGS

Available at www.expertconsult.com

AUTHOR: **FRED F. FERRI, M.D.**

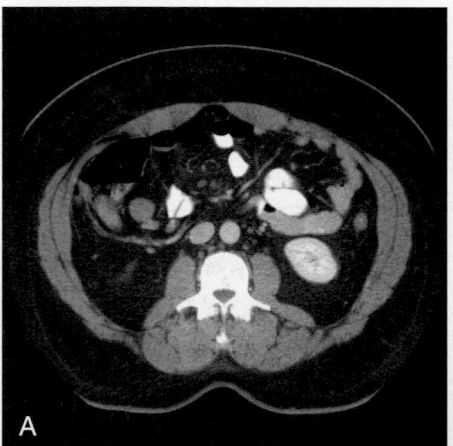
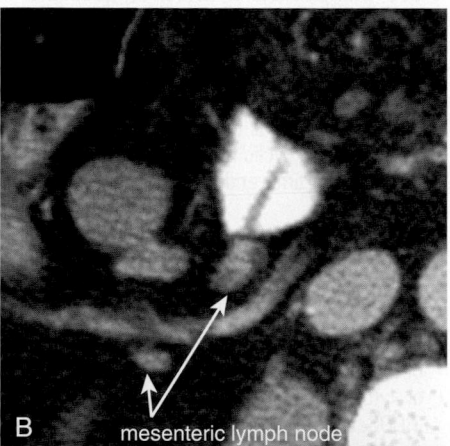
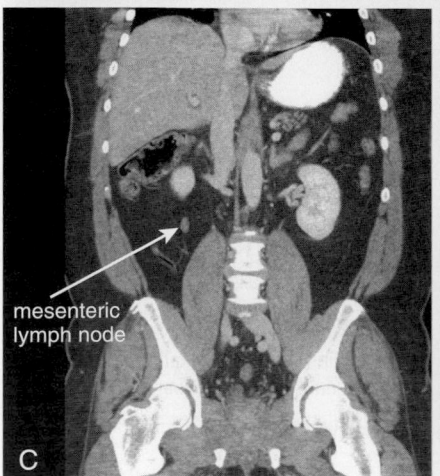
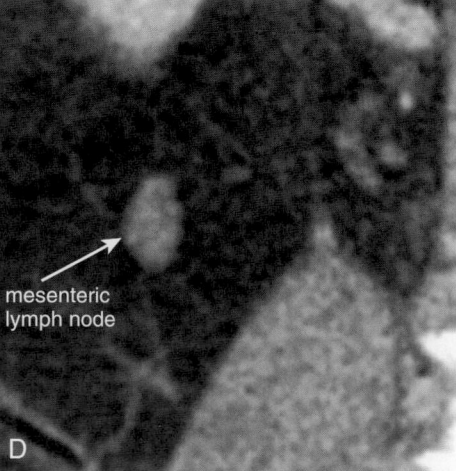

FIGURE 1M-24 Mesenteric adenitis, CT with IV and oral contrast, soft-tissue window. Mesenteric adenitis can mimic appendicitis in its clinical presentation. Enlarged lymph nodes are visible on CT. Lymph nodes have soft-tissue density and appear as discrete, rounded structures. On a single image they may appear similar to blood vessels or to the appendix, but on inspection of adjacent images it becomes clear that lymph nodes are rounded, not tubular like a blood vessel or the appendix. **A,** Axial image. **B,** Close-up from **A. C,** Coronal reconstruction. **D,** Close-up from **C.** (From Broder JS: *Diagnostic imaging for the emergency physician,* Philadelphia, 2011, Saunders.)

BASIC INFORMATION

DEFINITION

Acute mesenteric ischemia (AMI) is the sudden onset of intestinal hypoperfusion to all or part of the small bowel caused by emboli, arterial or venous thrombosis (Fig. E1M-25), or vasoconstriction from low-flow states.

SYNONYMS

Acute mesenteric ischemia
AMI

ICD-10CM CODES
K55.0 Acute vascular disorders of intestine

EPIDEMIOLOGY & DEMOGRAPHICS

INCIDENCE
- AMI accounts for 0.1% of hospital admissions.
- The incidence appears to be increasing. Factors for this include increased awareness among clinicians, the aging of the population, and improved intensive care, leading to longer survival of sicker patients. The mortality rate is 60% to 85%.

PREDOMINANT SEX AND AGE
- AMI caused by arterial embolism or thrombosis occurs more frequently in the elderly.
- AMI from mesenteric venous thrombosis often presents in younger age groups.

GENETICS: No specific genetic predisposition but may be related to underlying factors such as cardiac disease, atherosclerosis, and hypercoagulable states.

RISK FACTORS
- Advanced age, atherosclerosis, low cardiac output (especially atrial fibrillation), severe cardiac valvular disease, intraabdominal malignancy.
- In the subgroup of cases caused by venous thrombosis, risk factors include hypercoagulable states, portal hypertension, abdominal infection, blunt trauma, pancreatitis, and portal malignancy.
- Additional risk factors for AMI caused by nonocclusive mesenteric ischemia include recent cardiac surgery, dialysis, and cocaine use.
- Table 1M-16 summarizes risk factors for ischemic bowel disease.
- AMI may occur rarely in patients with no identifiable risk factors.

PHYSICAL FINDINGS & CLINICAL PRESENTATION
- The classic presentation is rapid onset of severe periumbilical pain "out of proportion to physical examination findings." An epigastric bruit may be present in some patients. Generally, patients with mesenteric venous thrombosis tend to present with a less abrupt onset of abdominal pain than those with acute arterial occlusion.
- Nausea and vomiting are commonly associated.
- Initial abdominal examination may be normal, with no rebound or guarding, or may include minimal distention or stool positive for occult blood.

- Later in the course the patient may present with gross distention, absence of bowel sounds, and peritoneal signs. In the elderly, mental status changes may occur.

ETIOLOGY
The pathophysiologic mechanisms that cause AMI include:
- Mesenteric arterial embolism (40% to 50% of cases of AMI): typically from the left atrium, left ventricle, or cardiac valves. The superior mesenteric artery is most commonly affected.
- Mesenteric arterial thrombosis: often in patients with prior progressive atherosclerotic stenoses, with superimposed abdominal trauma or infection. Thrombotic occlusion of previously stenotic mesenteric vessels accounts for 20% to 35% of cases of AMI.

- Mesenteric venous thrombosis may occur in the setting of hypercoagulable states (acquired or inherited), blunt trauma, abdominal infection, portal hypertension, pancreatitis, and portal malignancy.
- Nonocclusive mesenteric ischemia is caused by reduced intestinal perfusion, as seen with hypotension, hypovolemia, vasoconstricting drugs, and hemodialysis.
- Dissection or inflammation of the mesenteric artery accounts for less than 5% of cases of AMI.

DIAGNOSIS

DIFFERENTIAL DIAGNOSIS
Initially include other causes of abdominal pain of acute onset, including perforated peptic ulcer

Diseases and Disorders

I

TABLE 1M-16   Risk Factors for Ischemic Bowel Diseases*

Risk Factor	Arterial Thrombosis	Embolus	Mesenteric Vein Thrombosis	Nonobstructive Mesenteric Ischemia
Advanced age	+	+	+	+
Atherosclerosis	+			
Aortic dissection	+			
Low cardiac output	+	+		+
Congestive heart failure				+
Shock				+
Severe dehydration	+		+	
Cardiac arrhythmias, especially atrial fibrillation		+		+
Severe cardiac valvular disease		+		
Recent myocardial infarction	+			+
Intraabdominal malignancy			+	
Abdominal trauma			+	
Intraabdominal infection			+	
Intraabdominal inflammatory conditions			+	
Parasitic infection (ascariasis)			+	
Hypercoagulable states (venous thrombosis)			+	
Sickle cell anemia			+	
Recent cardiac surgery	+	+		+
Recent abdominal surgery			+	
Vascular aortic prosthetic grafts proximal to the superior mesenteric artery	+			
Hemodialysis				+
Vasculitis	+		+	
Pregnancy			+	
Decompression sickness			+	
Blast lung caused by systemic air embolism	+			
Drugs that cause constriction				
• Digitalis				+
• Cocaine				+
• Amphetamines				+
• Pseudoephedrine				+
• Vasopressin			+†	+
• Estrogen therapy			+	

*A plus sign (+) indicates that the factor is a risk for the disease subtype.
†Especially after sclerotherapy.
From Adams JG et al: *Emergency medicine, clinical essentials*, ed 2, Philadelphia, 2013, Elsevier.

and early appendicitis, as well as the varied causes of peritonitis.

WORKUP

- Early diagnosis is key. Treatment success is related to the duration of symptoms prior to diagnosis.
- Consider early laparotomy for diagnosis in cases with a high index of suspicion when imaging is not readily available.

LABORATORY TESTS

- Laboratory test results are nonspecific, especially early in the course. Elevated lactic acid, leukocytosis, acidosis, and elevated hematocrit from hemoconcentration can occur later in the course, often after progression to bowel necrosis has occurred, hence are not useful for early diagnosis.
- When a hypercoagulable state is suspected, workup may include proteins C and S, antithrombin III, and factor V Leiden. This will likely not affect the diagnosis of AMI but may help guide long-term therapy.
- Normal D-dimer testing may help rule out AMI. Elevated levels are nonspecific.

IMAGING STUDIES

- Biphasic contrast-enhanced CT is the preferred diagnostic mode (Fig. 1M-26). It is more easily available and has similar sensitivity to angiography, the prior gold standard test. Computed tomographic angiography (CTA) has 95% to 100% accuracy for the diagnosis of visceral ischemic syndromes and is also useful in detecting potential sources of emboli and other pathologic processes.

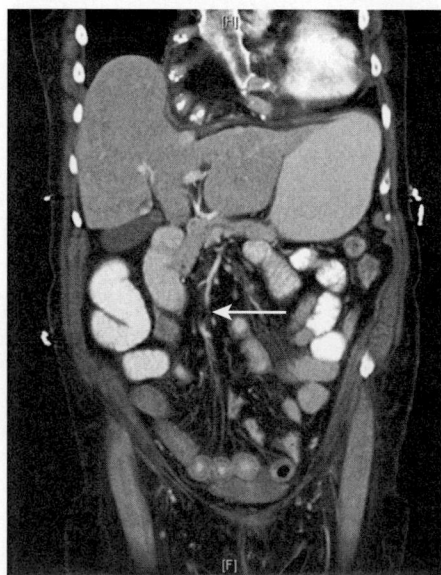

FIGURE 1M-26 Mesenteric ischemia, acute. CT after administration of oral and intravenous contrast in patient with embolism to superior mesenteric artery and ischemia of small bowel and right colon. *Arrow* points to embolus in superior mesenteric artery. (From Vincent JL et al: *Textbook of critical care,* ed 6, Philadelphia, 2011, Saunders.)

- Plain CT findings also are commonly nonspecific and more often found late in the course. Portal venous gas or intramural gas may be seen after the development of gangrene; in many cases, even at that advanced stage CT findings remain nonspecific.
- MR angiography (MRA) may be more useful in cases of mesenteric vein thrombosis causing AMI. It has also been found useful in monitoring the progress of patients with superior mesenteric venous thrombosis who are treated nonsurgically. MRA, however, takes longer than CTA to perform and can overestimate the degree of stenosis.
- Angiography may be considered if the diagnosis remains unclear after CT or MR imaging.
- Plain films are normal 25% of the time in the early stages. Suggestive findings may include ileus, bowel wall thickening, or intramural gas.
- Doppler ultrasound evaluation of intestinal blood flow is often limited by the presence of air-filled loops of bowel and is not an appropriate part of the diagnostic workup if AMI is the leading working diagnosis.

TREATMENT

- The goal of treatment is to restore blood flow to ischemic bowel as rapidly as possible before the occurrence of infarction.
- Treatment varies depending on etiology.

ACUTE GENERAL Rx

- Initial management should include hemodynamic monitoring and support, correction of acidosis, administration of broad-spectrum antibiotics, and gastric decompression by nasogastric tube.
- Vasoconstricting agents should be avoided.
- In the absence of active bleeding, the use of systemic anticoagulation is usually indicated. The optimal timing of initiation is unclear.

NONPHARMACOLOGIC THERAPY

- Signs of peritonitis mandate early laparotomy and resection of infarcted bowel.
- When workup is positive for major superior mesenteric artery (SMA) embolus, embolectomy is considered standard treatment in the absence of peritoneal signs. Depending on the location and degree of occlusion of the embolus, surgical revascularization, intraarterial infusion of thrombolytics or vasodilators, or systemic anticoagulation may be considered.
- In cases of SMA thrombosis, emergency surgical revascularization is the treatment of choice; stent placement may be a viable alternative.
- Angiography is needed to diagnose nonocclusive mesenteric ischemia before infarct and should be followed up by intraarterial vasodilator infusion. This approach has been shown to significantly reduce mortality rate in this situation.
- In patients with mesenteric vein thrombosis, treatment depends on the presence or absence of peritoneal signs. Laparotomy and resection of infarcted bowel is indicated in

more advanced cases. If there are no peritoneal signs, immediate anticoagulant therapy with heparin, and ultimately warfarin, may be adequate treatment.
- In general, percutaneous treatment with lytic therapy, balloon angioplasty, or stenting may be limited by the frequent presence of nonviable bowel, which would require laparotomy despite success with the percutaneous treatment.

CHRONIC Rx

In the subgroup of patients with mesenteric venous thrombosis, prevention of further thrombosis is indicated. The optimal duration of anticoagulation is unclear.

DISPOSITION

- Prognosis is best in AMI due to mesenteric venous thrombosis and after surgical treatment for acute arterial embolism. It remains poor in cases of arterial thrombosis and nonocclusive ischemia.
- With delayed diagnosis, intestinal infarction—resulting in perforation or gangrenous bowel, sepsis, shock, and death—is typical.

REFERRAL

- Early surgical consultation should be considered. There should be no delay with peritoneal signs.
- Surgery may be warranted for diagnostic purposes.

PEARLS & CONSIDERATIONS

COMMENTS

- The diagnosis of AMI should be considered in any patient with acute onset of abdominal pain out of proportion to physical findings, particularly in at-risk patients.
- Early diagnosis, before intestinal infarction occurs, is critical and correlates with improved survival rates.
- The use of endovascular procedures for AMI is becoming more common and may be most appropriate for patients with ischemia that is not severe and those who have severe coexisting conditions that place them at high risk for complications and death associated with open surgery.[1]

PREVENTION

Prevention of the underlying factors, most notably atherosclerotic disease

SUGGESTED READINGS

Available at www.expertconsult.com

RELATED CONTENT

Mesenteric Venous Thrombosis (Related Key Topic)

AUTHOR: **MARGARET TRYFOROS, M.D.**

[1]Clair DL, Beach JM: Mesenteric ischemia, *N Engl J Med* 374:959-968, 2016.

BASIC INFORMATION

DEFINITION

Mesenteric venous thrombosis (MVT) is a thrombotic occlusion of the mesenteric venous system involving major trunks or smaller branches and leading to intestinal infarction in its acute form.

ICD-10CM CODES
K55.0 Acute vascular disorders of intestine
K55.1 Chronic vascular disorders of intestine

EPIDEMIOLOGY & DEMOGRAPHICS

Between 5% and 15% of patients with acute mesenteric infarction have MVT. MVT is slightly more common in men than women. The typical age of occurrence is 50 to 60 yr. Table 1M-17 summarizes the incidence of ischemic bowel disease.

PHYSICAL FINDINGS & CLINICAL PRESENTATION

Acute MVT:
- Symptoms: abdominal pain in 90% of patients, typically out of proportion to the physical findings. Nausea and vomiting occur in 50% and gastrointestinal (GI) bleeding occurs in 50% (occult) and 15% (gross).
- Physical findings:
  1. Early: abdominal tenderness, decreased bowel sounds, abdominal distention
  2. Later: guarding and rebound tenderness, fever, septic shock
- Subacute MVT:
- Symptoms: nonspecific abdominal pain for weeks or months
- Physical findings: none
- Chronic MVT:
- Symptoms: upper GI hemorrhage from bleeding varices
- Physical findings: none other than signs of blood loss if significant

ETIOLOGY & PATHOGENESIS

Hypercoagulable states:
Peripheral deep venous thrombosis
Neoplasms
Antithrombin III, protein C, protein S deficiencies
Lupus anticoagulant (antiphospholipid antibody)
Oral contraceptive use, pregnancy
Polycythemia vera
Thrombocytosis
Paroxysmal nocturnal hemoglobinuria
Portal hypertension:
- Cirrhosis
- Inflammation:
- Pancreatitis
- Peritonitis (e.g., appendicitis, diverticulitis, perforated viscus)
- Inflammatory bowel disease
- Pelvic or intraabdominal abscess
- Intraabdominal cancer
- Postoperative state or trauma:
- Blunt abdominal trauma
- Postoperative states (abdominal surgery)

TABLE 1M-17 Incidence of Ischemic Bowel Diseases

Disease	Incidence (%)*
Superior mesenteric artery (SMA) embolism: • The SMA is susceptible to embolism because of large vessel caliber and a narrow angle of departure from the aorta. • The proximal SMA is most commonly obstructed within 6-8 cm of the aorta	50
Nonocclusive ischemia	25
SMA thrombosis	20
Mesenteric venous thrombosis	5

*Percentage of all cases of acute mesenteric ischemia.
From Adams JG et al: *Emergency medicine, clinical essentials*, ed 2, Philadelphia, 2013, Elsevier.

BOX 1M-3 Factors Associated with Mesenteric Venous Thrombosis

Hypercoagulable states
  Polycythemia vera
  Sickle cell disease
  Antithrombin III deficiency
  Protein C or S deficiency
  Malignancy
  Myeloproliferative disorders
  Estrogen therapy, oral contraceptive pills
  Pregnancy
Inflammatory conditions
  Pancreatitis
  Diverticulitis
  Appendicitis
  Cholangitis
Trauma
  Operative venous injury
  Postsplenectomy
  Blunt or abdominal trauma
Miscellaneous
  Congestive heart failure
  Renal failure
  Decompression sickness
  Portal hypertension

From Marx JA et al: *Rosen's emergency medicine*, ed 8, Philadelphia, 2014, Saunders.

- Box 1M-3 summarizes factors associated with mesenteric venous thrombosis
  Thrombosis may begin in small mesenteric branches (e.g., in hypercoagulable states) and propagate to the major venous mesenteric trunks or begin in large veins (e.g., in cirrhosis, intraabdominal cancer, surgery) and extend distally. If collateral drainage is inadequate, the intestine becomes congested, edematous, cyanotic, and hemorrhagic and eventually may infarct.

DIAGNOSIS

DIFFERENTIAL DIAGNOSIS

All other causes of abdominal pain (e.g., peritonitis, intestinal obstruction, pancreatitis, peptic ulcer disease, gastritis, inflammatory bowel disease, perforated viscus) are also to be considered in the differential diagnosis of GI hemorrhage.

WORKUP

Laboratory tests and imaging studies

LABORATORY TESTS

- Complete blood count: leukocytosis
- Electrolytes: metabolic acidosis (lactic) indicates bowel infarction
- Tests for hypercoagulable status

IMAGING STUDIES

- Computed tomographic angiography (CTA) is preferred imaging modality due to high accuracy (95%-100%). Use of two-phase imaging improves sensitivity for venous thrombosis
- Magnetic resonance angiography (MRA) can also be used; it avoids the risk of radiation and contrast material, but takes longer and may overestimate degree of stenosis
- Abdominal plain radiograph: ileus, ascites, bowel dilation, bowel wall thickening, loop separation, thumbprinting.

TREATMENT

- Anticoagulation with heparin or thrombolytic therapy. When medical treatment is unsuccessful, options include transhepatic and percutaneous mechanical thrombectomy, thrombolysis, and open intra-arterial thrombolysis
- Laparotomy if intestinal infarction is suspected
- Short ischemic segment: resection
- Long ischemic segment:
  1. Nonviable: resection or close
  2. Viable: intraarterial papaverine and/or thrombectomy followed by "second look" intervention

PROGNOSIS

- Mortality rate of acute MVT: 20% to 50%
- Recurrence rate: 15% to 25%

SUGGESTED READINGS

Available at www.expertconsult.com

RELATED CONTENT

Mesenteric Ischemia, Acute (Related Key Topic)

AUTHOR: **FRED F. FERRI, M.D.**

Diseases and Disorders

M

I

BASIC INFORMATION

DEFINITION

Malignant mesothelioma is a neoplasm that originates from the mesothelial surfaces of the pleural cavities (80%) or peritoneal cavities (20%).There are three major histologic subtypes: epithelial (most common), sarcomatous, and mixed (epithelial/sarcomatous).

ICD-10CM CODES
C45.0 Mesothelioma of pleura
C45.1 Mesothelioma of peritoneum
C45.2 Mesothelioma of pericardium
C45.7 Mesothelioma of other sites
C45.9 Mesothelioma, unspecified

EPIDEMIOLOGY & DEMOGRAPHICS

- Associated with asbestos exposure (all fiber types)
- About 2000 to 3000 new cases are diagnosed in the U.S. annually
- More common in men as a result of workplace asbestos exposure
- Incidence in the U.S. has leveled off due to lack of asbestos use and mining.
- Incidence of mesothelioma increases with age; median age at presentation is >70 years
- More than 8 million persons in the U.S. are currently at risk for mesothelioma because of prior asbestos exposure.

PHYSICAL FINDINGS & CLINICAL PRESENTATION

- Dyspnea
- Nonpleuritic chest pain
- Fever, weight loss, sweats, fatigue, loss of appetite
- Dysphagia, superior vena cava syndrome, Horner's syndrome in advanced stages
- Auscultation may reveal unilateral loss of breath sounds
- Dullness on percussion may be present

ETIOLOGY

- Asbestos exposure (>70% of patients)
- Other reported potentially causal factors include prior radiation therapy and extravasated Thorotrast, zeolite, and erionite fibers

DIAGNOSIS

DIFFERENTIAL DIAGNOSIS

Metastatic adenocarcinomas (from lung, breast, ovary, kidney, stomach, prostate)

WORKUP

- Staging evaluation (Fig. 1M-27) includes complete history (including occupational history), physical examination, and testing to determine potential operability (CT, bone scan, pulmonary function tests [PFTs])
- Thoracoscopy, pleuroscopy, and open-lung biopsy are useful in obtaining adequate tissue samples for diagnosis
- Pulmonary function tests

- PET-CT scan is performed only in patients considered candidates for surgery to determine respectability.
- Staging: the TNM system categories mesothelioma in stages I to IV similar to that used for non–small cell lung cancer

LABORATORY TESTS

- Diagnostic thoracentesis is generally insufficient for diagnosis because pleural effusions may only reveal atypical mesothelial cells.
- Immunohistochemistry is useful to distinguish adenocarcinoma from epithelial malignant mesothelioma (mesotheliomas are generally carcinoembryonic antigen negative and cytokeratin positive).
- Thrombocytosis and anemia may be found on initial laboratory evaluation.
- Serum osteopontin levels (when available) can also be used to distinguish persons with exposure to asbestos who do not have cancer from those with exposure to asbestos who have pleural mesothelioma.

IMAGING STUDIES

- Chest radiographs may reveal pleural plaques (Figs. 1M-28 and E1M-29) or calcifications in the diaphragm.
- CT scans of the chest and abdomen, bone scan, and PET scan are used to assess the stage of disease.

TREATMENT

GENERAL Rx

- Operable patient (epithelial type, no positive nodes, confined to pleura, adequate PFTs): the two surgical techniques for therapeutic intervention are decortication (pleurectomy) and extrapleural pneumonectomy. Postoperative chemotherapy with cisplatin and pemetrexed and subsequent external-beam radiation are used with limited success.
- Inoperable patient (disease too extensive, sarcomatous or mixed histology type, poor PFTs): supportive care with or without

radiation therapy for symptoms or supportive care plus chemotherapy. Combined modality therapies (surgery, radiation therapy, chemotherapy, and biologics) have also been used to reduce both local and distant recurrences. The combination of cisplatin and pemetrexed is used as front-line chemotherapy. More recently, a randomized trial has revealed the survival benefit of adding anti-angiogeneic agent bevacizumab in this setting to the standard chemotherapy regimen.
- Intrapleural instillation of cisplatin or biologics (e.g., interferons, interleukin-2) is generally limited to very early disease because it can only penetrate a very limited depth of the tumor and there is a propensity of the pleural space to become progressively obliterated with advancing disease.
- Radiation therapy is often used for palliation of local pain despite lack of trials to prove its utility.
- Obliteration of the pleural space (pleurodesis) with instillation of talc or tetracycline into the pleural cavity is done in the treatment of recurrent symptomatic pleural effusions.

DISPOSITION

Median survival is from 6 to 21 months for patients undergoing pleurectomy and ranges from 4 to 21 mo for extrapleural pneumonectomy. Survival is better for patients with the epithelial form, although overall median survival is approximately still 1 year.

PEARLS & CONSIDERATIONS

- Patients with early disease should be referred to treatment centers specializing in multidisciplinary therapy before attempts are made to obliterate the pleural space with pleurodesis.
- Patients with advanced or resected disease should be treated with appropriate combination chemotherapy as listed previously.

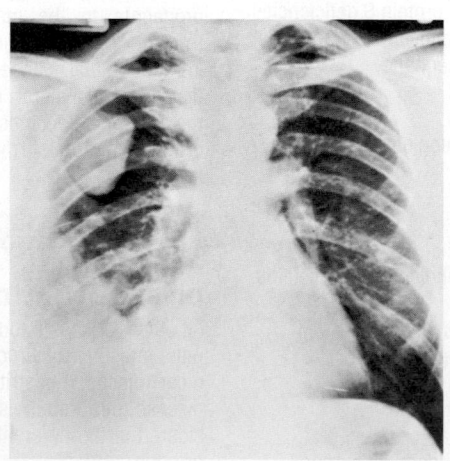

FIGURE 1M-28 Chest radiograph of patient with mesothelioma. Note several lobulated, pleural-based masses in right hemithorax accompanied by right pleural effusion. (From Weinberg SE et al: *Principles of pulmonary medicine*, ed 5, Philadelphia, 2008, Saunders.)

- Fibulin-3 may be useful as a blood and effusion biomarker for pleural mesothelioma. Recent data reveal that plasma fibulin-3 levels can distinguish healthy persons with exposure to asbestos from patients with mesothelioma. In conjunction with effusion fibulin-3 levels, plasma fibulin-3 levels can further differentiate mesothelioma effusions from other malignant and benign effusions.

SUGGESTED READINGS
Available at www.expertconsult.com

RELATED CONTENT
Mesothelioma (Patient Information)
Asbestosis (Related Key Topic)

AUTHOR: **BHARTI RATHORE, M.D.**

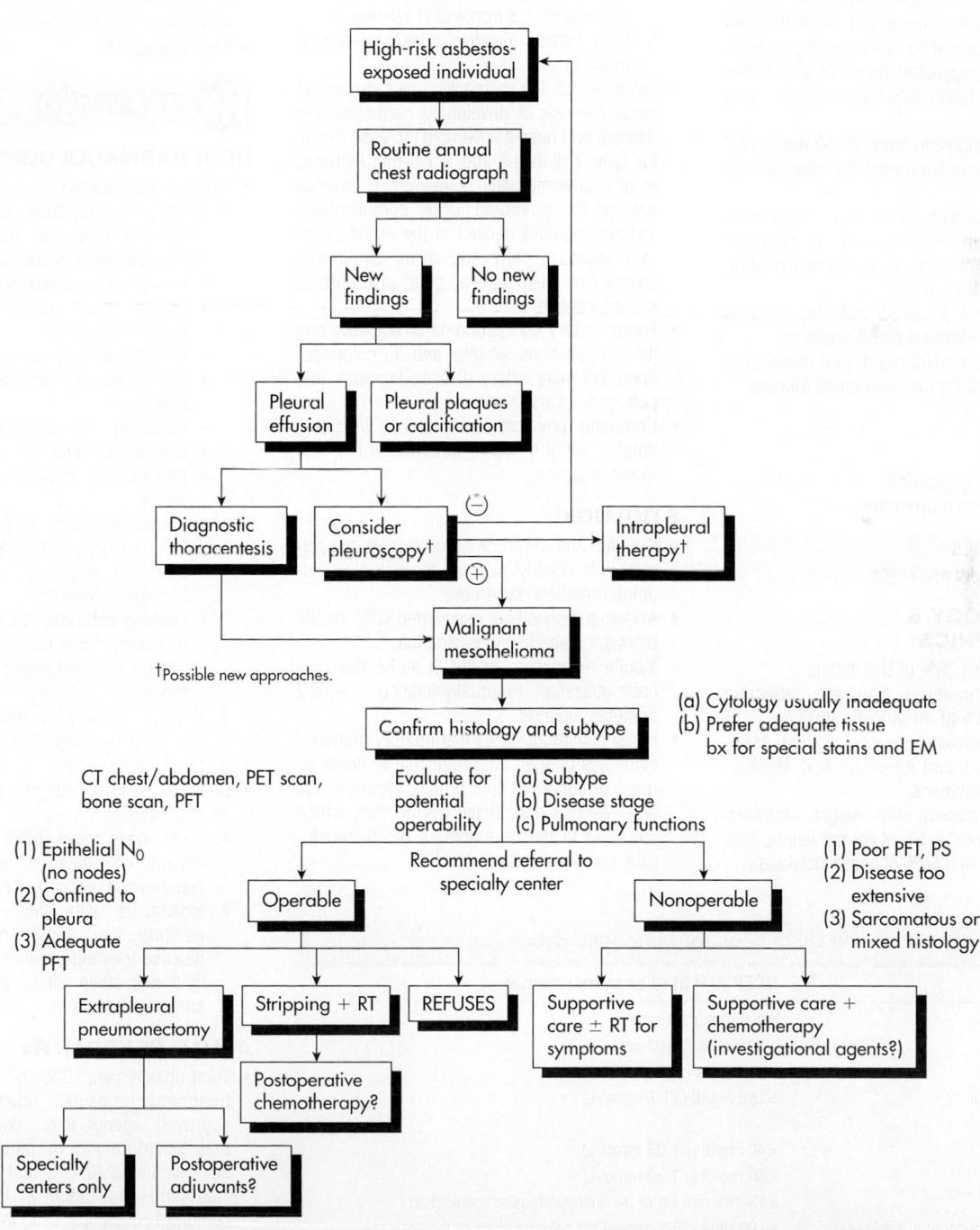

FIGURE 1M-27 Evaluation and treatment of mesothelioma. *bx,* Biopsy; *CT,* computed tomography; *EM,* electron microscopy; *PET,* positron emission tomography; *PFT,* pulmonary function test; *PS,* pleural sclerosis; *RT,* respiratory therapy. (From Abeloff MD: *Clinical oncology,* ed 3, New York, 2004, Churchill Livingstone.)

Metabolic Syndrome (PTG) (ALG)

BASIC INFORMATION

DEFINITION

Hyperglycemia, dyslipidemia, abdominal obesity, and hypertension are critical components of metabolic syndrome. Over the years, many definitions of the syndrome have been proposed and debated (see Table 1M-18). In 2009, a consensus statement from several organizations including the International Diabetes Federation (IDF) and American Heart Association defined "metabolic syndrome" as the presence of any three of the following criteria:

- Abdominal waist circumference >94 cm (37 in) in men and >80 cm (31 in) in women (the use of population- and country-specific definitions is suggested; however, until better data are available, IDF recommends using these cutoffs)
- Serum hypertriglyceridemia ≥150 mg/dl (1.7 mmol/L) or drug treatment for elevated triglycerides
- Serum high-density lipoprotein (HDL) cholesterol <40 mg/dl (1 mmol/L) in men and <50 mg/dl (1.3 mmol/L) in women or drug treatment for low HDL-C
- Blood pressure ≥130/85 mm Hg or drug treatment for elevated blood pressure
- Fasting glucose ≥100 mg/dl (5.6 mmol/L) or drug treatment for elevated blood glucose

SYNONYMS

Syndrome X
Insulin resistance syndrome
Obesity dyslipidemia syndrome

ICD-10CM CODES
E88.81 Metabolic syndrome

EPIDEMIOLOGY & DEMOGRAPHICS

- Affects close to 25% of U.S. adults
- Prevalence increases with age, affecting more than 40% of individuals >60 yr.
- Increasing prevalence among women, especially in the African American and Mexican American populations.
- Prevalence increases with weight. Metabolic syndrome is noted in 5% of normal weight, 22% of overweight, and 60% of obese individuals.

- Other risk factors include low socioeconomic status, lack of physical activity, high-carbohydrate diet, no alcohol intake, smoking, genetic predisposition, use of atypical antipsychotics, and postmenopausal status.

CLINICAL PRESENTATION

- Obesity, hypertension, dyslipidemia, and hyperglycemia as defined.
  1. Blood pressure: ≥130/85 mm Hg
  2. Abdominal obesity with waist circumference: >94 cm (37 in) in men and >80 cm (31 in) in women
  3. Triglycerides: ≥150 mg/dl (1.7 mmol/L)
  4. HDL: <40 mg/dl (1 mmol/L) in men and >50 mg/dl (1.3 mmol/L) in women
  5. High fasting glucose: ≥100 mg/dl (5.6 mmol/L)
- Patients with the metabolic syndrome are at twice the risk of developing cardiovascular disease and have a sevenfold increase in risk for type 2 diabetes and a 1.5-fold increase in all-cause mortality compared to patients without the syndrome. Other complications include cognitive decline in the elderly, fatty liver disease, polycystic ovary syndrome, obstructive sleep apnea, gout, and chronic kidney disease.
- Focus history on symptoms of diabetes and its complications, obesity and its complications, coronary artery disease (angina), and polycystic ovary syndrome.
- Complete physical examination, including height, weight, waist circumference, and blood pressure.

ETIOLOGY

- Genetic and environmental factors associated with obesity increase the risk of developing metabolic syndrome.
- Abdominal obesity is associated with insulin resistance and hyperinsulinemia.
- Insulin resistance results in ineffective glucose utilization, eventually leading to type 2 diabetes mellitus
- Hyperinsulinemia and inflammatory markers/cytokines play an important role in development of abnormal lipid profile, hypertension, and vascular endothelial dysfunction, which can lead to the development of atherosclerotic cardiovascular disease.

 DIAGNOSIS

DIFFERENTIAL DIAGNOSIS

- Other causes of weight gain or obesity (Cushing's syndrome, hypothyroidism)
- Other causes of hyperlipidemia (familial hyperlipidemia, hypothyroidism)
- Other causes of hypertension (Cushing's syndrome, hyperaldosteronism)
- Other forms of diabetes (type 1)

LABORATORY TESTS

- Fasting lipid profile (total cholesterol, low-density lipoprotein [LDL] cholesterol, HDL cholesterol, and triglycerides)
- Fasting glucose

Rx TREATMENT

NONPHARMACOLOGIC THERAPY

- Lifestyle modification:
  1. Dietary modifications aimed at weight loss. The American Heart Association (AHA) recommendations include
     - Consuming vegetables and fruits
     - Eating whole grains and high-fiber foods (≥30 g/day)
     - Eating fish twice weekly
     - Consuming lean animal and vegetable proteins
     - Reducing intake of sugary beverages
     - Minimizing sugar and sodium intake
     - Maintaining moderate to no alcohol intake
     - Consuming 50% to 55% of calories from carbohydrates, 15% to 20% of calories from protein, and 30% to 35% of calories from fat
     - Limiting saturated fat to less than 7% of energy, trans fat to less than 1% of energy, and cholesterol to less than 300 mg/day
  2. Physical activity of moderate intensity (i.e., brisk walking): 30 min daily
  3. Smoking cessation
- Consider bariatric surgery in the management of obesity:
  1. Body mass index (BMI) ≥40 kg/m² in patients who have not responded to diet and exercise (with or without drug therapy).
  2. Individuals with BMI >35 kg/m² and comorbidities (hypertension, impaired glucose tolerance, diabetes mellitus, dyslipidemia, sleep apnea) are also potential surgical candidates.

ACUTE GENERAL Rx

- Treat obesity (see "Obesity"): Pharmacologic treatment: consider orlistat and other approved agents (e.g., liraglutide, topiramate/phentermine) in patients who have not responded to diet and exercise if BMI >30 kg/m² or a BMI of 27 to 30 kg/m² with comorbid conditions. Drug therapy still needs to be in conjunction with diet and exercise.
- Treat hypertension (see "Hypertension"): Systolic blood pressures >140/90 mm Hg:

TABLE 1M-18 Common Definitions for Metabolic Syndrome

Criterion	NCEP ATP III (3 or more criteria)
Abdominal obesity	Waist circumference
Men	>40 inches (>102 cm)
Women	>35 inches (>88 cm)
Hypertriglyceridemia	>150 mg/dl (≥1.7 mmol/L)
Low HDL	
Men	<40 mg/dl (<1.03 mmol/L)
Women	<50 mg/dl (<1.30 mmol/L)
Hypertension	≥130/85 mm Hg or on antihypertensive medication
Impaired fasting glucose or diabetes	>100 mg/dl (5.6 mmol/L) or taking insulin or hypoglycemic medication

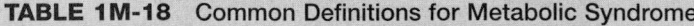

From Floege J et al: *Comprehensive clinical nephrology*, ed 4, Philadelphia, 2010, Saunders.

consider angiotensin-converting enzyme inhibitors or angiotensin II receptor blocker as first-line therapy.
- Treat hyperlipidemia: In the 2013 guidelines from the American College of Cardiology and American Heart Association (ACC/AHA), treatment goals for LDL-C and non-HDL-C are no longer recommended, and there are no guidelines for treating high triglyceride levels. The new guidelines specify four groups that merit intensive or moderately intensive statin therapy[1]:
  1. People with clinical atherosclerotic cardiovascular disease (ASCVD)
  2. People with LDL-C levels of ≥190 mg/dl
  3. People with diabetes, age 40 to 75
  4. People without diabetes, age 40 to 75 with LDL-C levels 70-190 mg/dl, and a 10-year ASCVD risk of 7.5% or higher as determined by the new risk calculator.[2]
- Treat diabetes:
  1. Goal HgAIC <7.0%
  2. Metformin as first-line therapy to improve insulin sensitivity
- Treat cardiovascular risk factors:

---

[1]Raymond C et al: New cholesterol guidelines: worth the wait? *Clev Clin J Med* 81:11-19, 2014.
[2]American Heart Association: *2013 Prevention Guideline Tools. CV risk calculator.* Available at http://my.americanheart.org/professional/statementsguidelines/preventionguidelines/preventionguidelines_VCM_subhomepage.jsp.

1. Consider aspirin. Aspirin should be started in patients with metabolic syndrome and an intermediate or elevated Framingham cardiovascular risk, if there are no contraindications.
2. Risk can be lowered with weight loss, exercise, smoking cessation, blood pressure control, diabetes management, and treatment of hyperlipidemia.

CHRONIC Rx
- Encourage lifestyle modification as discussed previously.
- Pharmacologic and surgical management to maintain therapeutic goals described above.

DISPOSITION
Weight loss can prevent disease progression. Appropriate treatment of obesity, hypertension, hyperlipidemia, and diabetes can improve morbidity and mortality rates.

REFERRAL
- To nutritionist for dietary counseling
- To weight loss and exercise programs
- To endocrinologist if difficulty reaching therapeutic goal and also to consider weight loss pharmacotherapy.
- To bariatric surgeon if patient meets surgical criteria (as noted previously)

! PEARLS & CONSIDERATIONS

PREVENTION
- Weight loss is essential for the prevention and treatment of metabolic syndrome.
- Recommend dietary modifications and moderate physical activity.
- Consider pharmacologic and surgical options in select individuals (as noted previously).

PATIENT & FAMILY EDUCATION
- Weight reduction programs, including Weight Watchers, Curves, etc.
- American Diabetes Association: http://www.diabetes.org
- Polycystic Ovarian Syndrome Association: http://www.pcosupport.org
- The Hormone Foundation: http://www.hormone.org

SUGGESTED READINGS
Available at www.expertconsult.com

RELATED CONTENT
Obesity (Related Key Topic)
Metabolic Syndrome (Patient Information)

AUTHOR: **HARIKRASHNA B. BHATT M.D.**

M

Diseases and Disorders

ⓘ BASIC INFORMATION

DEFINITION

An accidental or intentional ingestion of 1 g per kg methanol or ethylene glycol is considered lethal, although even small amounts can be toxic. Inhalational and dermal exposures rarely cause toxicity.

SYNONYMS

Antifreeze
Moonshine

ICD-10-CM CODES

T51.8   Toxic effect of alcohols
T51.1X1 Toxic effect of methanol
T51.1X2 Toxic effect of methanol, intentional self-harm
T52.8X1 Ethylene glycol poisoning

EPIDEMIOLOGY & DEMOGRAPHICS

INCIDENCE:

- In 2013, the American Association of Poison Control Centers reported 5956 and 1747 single-exposure cases of ethylene glycol and methanol poisoning, respectively
- Most cases are reported in adults older than 19 years and are predominantly men
- Accidental exposure is common in children, while alcoholism, polysubstance abuse, depression, and suicide are seen in adults

PHYSICAL FINDINGS & CLINICAL PRESENTATION

- Clinical manifestations depend on the quantity of ingestion, duration of time since ingestion, and whether co-ingestion of other substances occurs
- Early ingestion of either substances can mimic ethanol ingestion, with nausea, vomiting, inebriation, and CNS depression. Late effects include progressive CNS dysfunction, including seizure and coma, as well as respiratory and cardiopulmonary failure
- Visual symptoms ranging from blurry or snowy vision to complete visual loss and findings of papillary edema, afferent pupillary defect, retinal hyperemia, and Parkinson-like syndrome are indicative of methanol poisoning
- Abdominal pain, oliguria, hematuria, calcium oxalate crystalluria, tetany, cranial nerve palsy, and acute kidney injury suggest ethylene glycol toxicity

PATHOPHYSIOLOGY

- Toxicity of these alcohols is related to their metabolites rather than the parent compound
- Lethal dose for methanol is >15 to 30 mL and >1 to1.5 mL/kg for ethylene glycol
- Sequential metabolism by alcohol and aldehyde dehydrogenases converts methanol to formic acid and ethylene glycol to glycolic acid and oxalate, resulting in toxicity
- Figure 1M-31 depicts the pathways involved in methanol metabolism

- While methanol metabolites primarily cause retinal injury, ethylene glycol metabolites produce renal tubular injury and calcium oxalate stones
  1. Formic acid prevents oxygen utilization by mitochondria and causes organ dysfunction, including the retinal and optic neurons and the basal ganglia
  2. Oxalate forms calcium oxalate renal stones that are directly responsible for kidney injury

(Dx) DIAGNOSIS

DIFFERENTIAL DIAGNOSIS

- Other causes of a high anion gap metabolic acidosis include lactic acidosis, diabetic and alcoholic ketoacidosis, kidney failure (acute and chronic), early toluene toxicity, and salicylate intoxication
- Elevated plasma osmolal gap may be encountered in ethyl alcohol or isopropyl

alcohol ingestion and other serious illnesses like septic shock

EVALUATION AND WORKUP

- Diagnosis depends on history, clinical presentation, and laboratory abnormalities
- High anion gap metabolic acidosis (AG >12 mEq/L) with elevated plasma osmolal gap (>10 mOsm/kg; usually >25 mOsm/Kg) in an appropriate clinical setting should raise the suspicion of methanol or ethylene glycol ingestion.
- In either intoxication, an osmolal gap will initially be positive, but as the parent compound is converted to its metabolites, the osmolal gap will normalize and the serum anion gap will then become positive
- Serum methanol and ethylene glycol levels are elevated in their respective ingestions
- Acute kidney injury, hypocalcemia with prolonged QT interval, and calcium oxalate crystalluria are seen with ethylene glycol toxicity
- Wood's lamp fluorescence uses ultraviolet light to detect fluorescein contained in

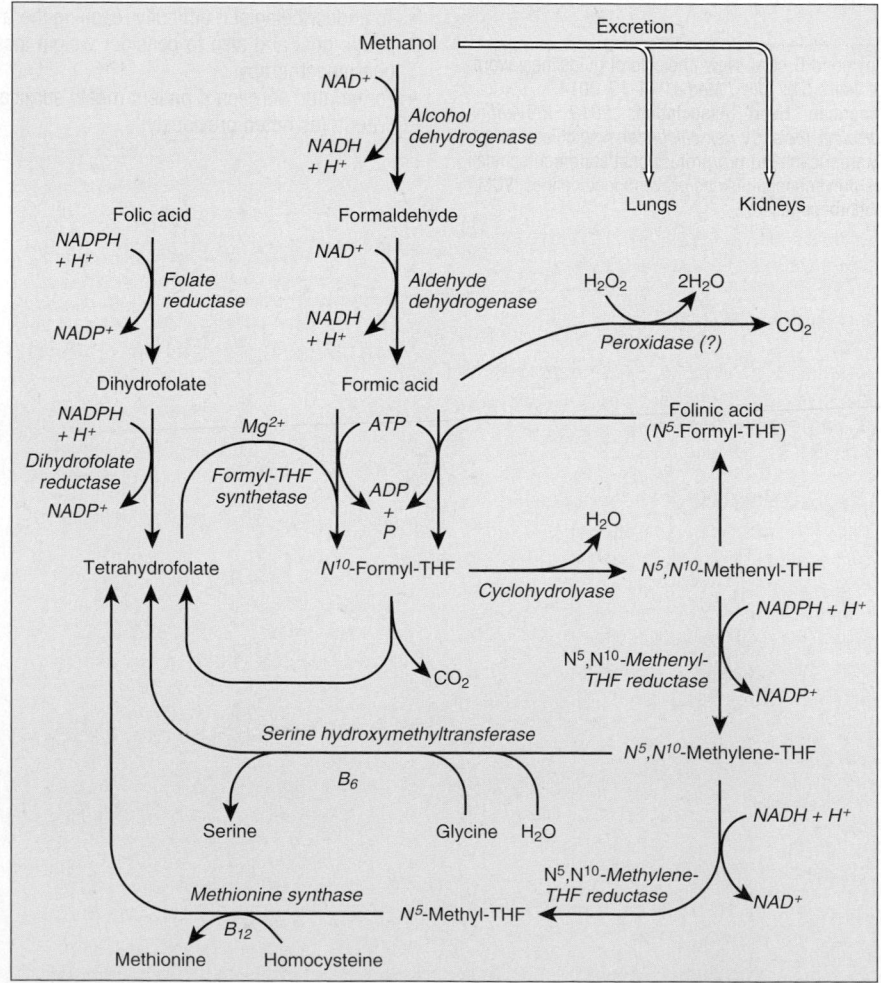

FIGURE 1M-31 Metabolic pathways involved in methanol metabolism, showing the role of folate derivatives as enzymatic cofactors operative in the elimination of formic acid. *ADP*, Adenosine diphosphate; *ATP*, adenosine triphosphate; *NAD+* and *NADH*, oxidized and reduced forms of nicotinamide adenine dinucleotide, respectively; *NADP+* and *NADPH*, oxidized and reduced forms of nicotinamide adenine dinucleotide phosphate, respectively; *THF*, tetrahydrofolate. (Adapted from Kruse JA. Methanol poisoning. *Intensive Care Med* 1992;18:391-7, with permission. From Vincent JL, Abraham E, Moore FA, Kochanek PM, Fink MP: *Textbook of critical care*, 6th ed, Philadelphia, 2011, Saunders.)

ethylene glycol preparations, but lacks sensitivity because not all preparations contain fluorescein. Fluorescence testing also lacks specificity due to a high rate of false positivity

LABORATORY TESTS

- Calculation of the anion gap and serum osmolal gap
  1. Anion gap determination: electrolytes and albumin
  2. Osmolal gap determination: measured and calculated serum osmolalities (sodium, BUN, glucose, ± ethanol)
- Arterial blood gas analysis, lactate, calcium, and creatine kinase
- Creatinine and urinalysis to evaluate presence of tubular injury and calcium oxalate crystals
- ECG to evaluate QT interval
- Toxicology screen with quantification: acetaminophen, salicylate, ethanol, methanol, ethylene glycol, and isopropyl alcohol

Rx TREATMENT

High index of suspicion and immediate recognition with early treatment remain crucial to reduce mortality. Box 1M-4 describes common commercial products that may contain ethylene glycol.

NONPHARMACOLOGIC THERAPY

- Establish airway, breathing, and circulation and advanced cardiac life support measures as required
- Rapid (within 60 minutes) gastric decontamination (charcoal and/or gastric lavage)
- Induction of vomiting is contraindicated even in conscious patients given the risks of development of central nervous system depression in these patients

ACUTE GENERAL Rx

- Principles of therapy include prevention of formation of toxic metabolites, correction of acidosis, and toxin removal
- Ethanol, a competitive substrate, and fomepizole, a competitive inhibitor of alcohol dehydrogenase, prevent formation of toxic metabolites of ethylene glycol and methanol

---

BOX 1M-4 Common Commercial Products That May Contain Ethylene Glycol

Paints and lacquers
Polishes and detergents
Inks
Cosmetics
Hydraulic brake fluids
Solar collector fluids
Car wash fluids

Data from Kruse JA: Methanol, ethylene glycol, and related intoxications. In Carlson RW, Geheb MA (eds): *Principles and practice of medical intensive care*, Philadelphia, 1993, Saunders.

- Fomepizole is preferred over ethanol given the increased incidence of adverse events with ethanol administration, its greater inhibition of alcohol dehydrogenase, and easier administration
- Intravenous isotonic fluids can facilitate urinary excretion; when acidosis is present (pH <7.3), isotonic bicarbonate should be utilized because reversal of acidosis helps prevent end-organ damage from toxic metabolites (goal pH, 7.35-7.45)
- Treatment with medications and/or hemodialysis is continued until the methanol or ethylene glycol concentration is <20 mg/dl
- Ethanol: dosing
  1. Target ethanol concentration is 100 to 200 mg/dl and requires close monitoring
  2. Loading dose: 800 mg/kg in a 10% solution of 5% dextrose in water will raise serum ethanol by 100 mg/dl
  3. Maintenance dose: infusion of 80 to 160 mg/kg/hr based on blood concentrations
- Fomepizole: indications for use
  1. Plasma concentration of methanol or ethylene glycol >20 mg/dl OR
  2. Documented ingestion with an osmolal gap >10 mOsm/L OR
  3. Suspected ingestion with at least two of the following criteria:
     A. Arterial pH <7.3
     B. Serum bicarbonate <20 mEq/L
     C. Osmolal gap >10 mOsm/L
     D. Urinary oxalate crystals in the case of ethylene glycol toxicity
- Fomepizole (4-methylpyrazole): dosing
  1. Loading dose: 15 mg/kg body weight
  2. Maintenance dose: 10 mg/kg body weight every 12 hr for 4 doses, then 15 mg/kg every 12 hr (if blood levels do not reach goal by 48 hr)
  3. During hemodialysis: Add 1–1.5 mg/kg/hr, or repeat loading dose every 4 hr
- The half-life of ethylene glycol and methanol increases with ethanol or fomepizole
- Hemodialysis should be considered in patients with significant metabolic acidosis (pH <7.15–7.20), kidney failure, visual abnormalities, electrolyte imbalances refractory to pharmacologic treatments, hemodynamic instability, seizures, coma, and serum concentrations as low as 20 mg/dl with acidosis or other end organ damage
- Duration of hemodialysis can be estimated using the formula: Time (hr) equals −V LN(5/A)/0.06 k, where V is the Watson total body water volume (L); A is the initial alcohol concentration (mmol/L); and k is 80% of the manufacturer's specified urea clearance (mL/min)
- Average duration of dialysis in studies was 8.4 ± 3.2 hr
  ▪ If blood concentration levels are not available, start by conducting an 8 hr intermittent hemodialysis session followed by 18 hr of continuous renal replacement therapy; adjust therapy afterward as clinically indicated
  ▪ Do not use heparin with dialysis as can increase risk of cerebral hemorrhage

---

ADJUNCTIVE Rx

- In ethylene glycol poisoning, thiamine and pyridoxine may decrease oxalic acid formation and direct metabolism to less toxic metabolites
- In methanol overdoses, folinic acid doses of 1 mg/kg given IV every 4 to 6 hr may increase formic acid metabolism
- Correct electrolyte abnormalities (hypocalcemia, etc.)
- Treat seizures

DISPOSITION

Transfer to a hospital with intensive care and hemodialysis capabilities should be entertained early in the course of intoxication

REFERRAL

- Regional poison center (toxicologist) and nephrology recommended to avoid treatment delays
- Ophthalmology for patients with visual symptoms
- Psychiatry if depression and suicidal ideation are present
- Detoxification centers for patients with substance abuse

PROGNOSIS

- Coma or seizures at presentation and prolonged severe acidosis correlate with increased mortality
- High osmolal gap and anion gap acidosis associate with high mortality
- Hyperglycemia may correlate with worse prognosis in methanol poisoning

⊘ PEARLS & CONSIDERATIONS

- Profound plasma osmolar gap or anion gap metabolic acidosis should raise suspicion for ethylene glycol and/or methanol ingestion. A high index of suspicion and early treatment are crucial to reducing mortality. The metabolites of methanol and ethylene glycol produce the clinical toxidrome
- Complaints of visual blurring, central scotomata, and blindness are consistent with methanol poisoning
- Calcium oxalate crystalluria, oliguria, and hematuria are consistent with ethylene glycol poisoning
- Fomepizole is preferred to ethanol due to complications associated with ethanol use
- Emergent hemodialysis is indicated with end organ damage and/or severe metabolic acidosis

SUGGESTED READINGS

Available at www.expertconsult.com

RELATED CONTENT

Algorithm for the management of acute poisoning (Algorithm, Section III)

AUTHORS: **NIKUNJKUMAR PATEL, M.D.,** and **ERIC S. KERNS, M.D.**

TABLE 1M-20 Names and Definitions of Vasculitis Adopted by the Chapel Hill Consensus Conference on the Nomenclature of Systemic Vasculitis

Name	
	Large-Vessel Vasculitis*
Giant cell (temporal arteritis)	Granulomatous arteritis of the aorta and its major branches, with a predilection for the extracranial branches of the carotid artery. Often involves the temporal artery. Usually occurs in patients older than 50 yr and often is associated with polymyalgia rheumatica
Takayasu's arteritis	Granulomatous inflammation of the aorta and its major branches. Usually occurs in patients younger than 50 yr
	Medium-Sized Vessel Vasculitis*
Polyarteritis nodosa (classic polyarteritis nodosa)	Necrotizing inflammation of medium-sized or small arteries without glomerulonephritis or vasculitis in arterioles, capillaries, or venules. Kawasaki's disease arteritis involving large, medium-sized, and small arteries and associated with mucocutaneous lymph node syndrome. Coronary arteries are often involved. Aorta and veins may be involved. Usually occurs in children
	Small-Vessel Vasculitis*
Wegener's granulomatosis†,‡	Granulomatous inflammation involving the respiratory tract and necrotizing vasculitis affecting small- to medium-sized vessels, e.g., capillaries, venules, arterioles, and arteries. Necrotizing glomerulonephritis is common
Churg-Strauss syndrome†,‡	Eosinophil-rich and granulomatous inflammation involving the respiratory tract and necrotizing vasculitis affecting small- to medium-sized vessels and associated with asthma and blood eosinophilia
Microscopic polyangiitis (microscopic polyarteritis)†,‡	Necrotizing vasculitis with few or no immune deposits affecting small vessels, e.g., capillaries, venules, or arterioles. Necrotizing arteritis involving small- and medium-sized arteries may be present. Necrotizing glomerulonephritis is very common. Pulmonary capillaritis often occurs
Henoch-Schönlein purpura‡	Vasculitis with immunoglobulin A–dominant immune deposits affecting small vessels, e.g., capillaries, venules, or arterioles. Typically involves the skin, gut, and glomeruli and is associated with arthralgias or arthritis
Essential cryoglobulinemic vasculitis‡	Vasculitis with cryoglobulin immune deposits affecting small vessels, e.g., capillaries, venules, or arterioles, and associated with cryoglobulins in serum. Skin and glomeruli are often involved
Cutaneous leukocytoclastic angiitis	Isolated cutaneous leukocytoclastic angiitis without systemic vasculitis or glomerulonephritis

*Large artery refers to the aorta and the largest branches directed toward major body regions (e.g., to the extremities and the head and neck); medium-sized artery refers to the main visceral arteries (e.g., renal, hepatic, coronary, and mesenteric arteries); and small artery refers to the distal arterial radicals that connect with arterioles (e.g., renal arcuate and interlobular arteries). Note that some small- and large-vessel vasculitides may involve medium-sized arteries; but large- and medium-sized vessel vasculitides do not involve vessels smaller than arteries.

†Strongly associated with antineutrophil cytoplasmic autoantibodies (ANCA).

‡May be accompanied by glomerulonephritis and can manifest as nephritis or pulmonary renal vasculitic syndrome.

From Runge MS, Greganti MA. Netter's internal medicine, ed 2 (Netter Clinical Science); Philadelphia, 2008, Saunders, p. 1053; Originally adapted from Jennette JC et al: Nomenclature of systemic vasculitides. Proposal of an international consensus conference. Arthritis Rheum 37(2):187-192, 1994.

CHRONIC Rx

Maintenance therapy

- Low-dose steroids, azathioprine, methotrexate, and rituximab have been demonstrated to be non-inferior to cyclophosphamide and can be used for maintenance therapy, although dosing intervals and duration of therapy are still being determined.

Prophylaxis for opportunistic infections like Pneumocystis carinii (jirovecii) pneumonia (PCP) is with low-dose sulfamethoxazole/trimethoprim given as one double-strength tablet three times weekly. Atovaquone is preferred in patients who are allergic to sulfonamides or who do not tolerate trimethoprim-sulfamethoxazole.

Relapse therapy

- Mild or non-life-threatening relapses while on maintenance therapy can be treated by increasing glucocorticoid dose or by adding azathioprine or methotrexate.
- In severe cases, treatment is the same as in remission induction; however, rituximab is often preferred over cyclophosphamide.

DISPOSITION

- Poor prognosis if untreated.
- Prompt diagnosis is important to permit initiation of therapy that may be life-saving and organ sparing.
- Renal failure and pulmonary involvement are the major causes of morbidity and mortality.
- With treatment, 2- to 5-yr survival rates are 74%.

REFERRAL

Nephrology consultation is needed for the diagnosis and management of renal disease.

Multiple specialists may be consulted depending on other organ system involvement.

PEARLS & CONSIDERATIONS

Relapse occurs in one third of the cases.

PCP occurs in 6% of the patients as a complication of immunosuppressive therapy.

SUGGESTED READINGS

Available at www.expertconsult.com

AUTHOR: **SYEDA M. SAYEED, M.D.**

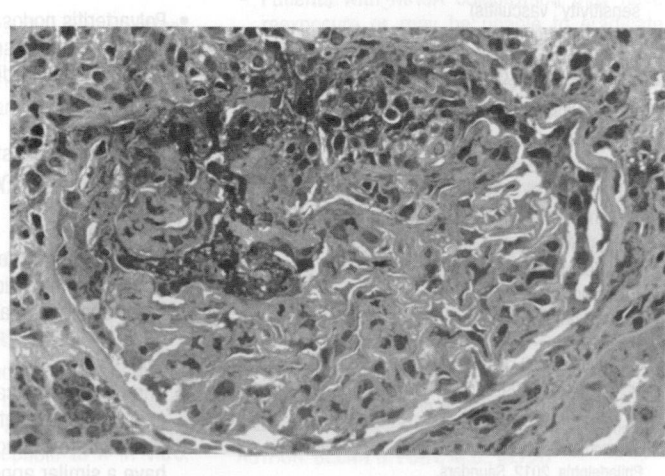

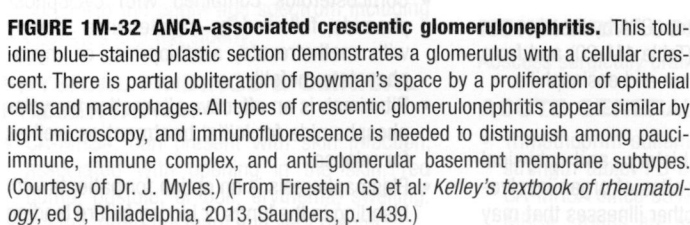

FIGURE 1M-32 ANCA-associated crescentic glomerulonephritis. This toluidine blue–stained plastic section demonstrates a glomerulus with a cellular crescent. There is partial obliteration of Bowman's space by a proliferation of epithelial cells and macrophages. All types of crescentic glomerulonephritis appear similar by light microscopy, and immunofluorescence is needed to distinguish among pauciimmune, immune complex, and anti–glomerular basement membrane subtypes. (Courtesy of Dr. J. Myles.) (From Firestein GS et al: Kelley's textbook of rheumatology, ed 9, Philadelphia, 2013, Saunders, p. 1439.)

BASIC INFORMATION

DEFINITION

Microsporidiosis is an infection caused by single-celled protozoan intracellular spore-forming organisms called Microsporidia. Recent evidence suggests a relationship between microsporidia and fungi. Infections occur more commonly in AIDS patients, travelers, children, organ transplant recipients, contact lens wearers, and the elderly.

SYNONYMS

Enterocytozoon bieneusi infection
Encephalitozoon species infections

ICD-10CM CODES
B60.8 Microsporidiosis
A07.8 Microsporidiosis, intestinal

EPIDEMIOLOGY & DEMOGRAPHICS

Microsporidia exist worldwide in the environment and can infect vertebrate and invertebrate hosts entering via ingestion or inhalation of spores.
PREVALENCE: One European study showed a prevalence of 5% to 8% in immunocompetent persons.

In a study of asymptomatic HIV patients, 15% had evidence of microsporidia on small bowel biopsy.
RISK FACTORS: Infections such as a nonbloody watery diarrhea and keratoconjunctivitis in contact lens wearers can occur in normal hosts, but immunocompromised hosts such as AIDS patients, organ transplant recipients, and bone marrow graft recipients are at greater risk for more severe disease and other organ involvement.

ETIOLOGY

- There are 1200 species of Microsporidia, but only 14 infect humans. The four most common are:
  1) *Enterocytozoon bieneusi*
  2) *Encephalitozoon intestinalis*
  3) *Encephalitozoon cuniculi*
  4) *Encephalitozoon hellem*
- These genotypes that infect humans have been identified in domestic, farm, and wild animals and thus may be a form of zoonotic disease.

PHYSICAL FINDINGS & CLINICAL PRESENTATION

Each species of microsporidia has different reported infections:
1) *Enterocytozoon bieneusi* can cause diarrhea, wasting syndrome, cholangitis, rhinitis, or bronchitis.

2) *Encephalitozoon intestinalis* can cause diarrhea, intestinal perforation, cholangitis, nephritis, and keratoconjunctivitis.
3) *Encephalitozoon cuniculi* can cause hepatitis, peritonitis, encephalitis, urethritis, prostatitis, nephritis, sinusitis, keratoconjunctivitis, cystitis, diarrhea, cellulitis, and disseminated infection.
4) *Encephalitozoon hellem* can cause keratoconjunctivitis, sinusitis, pneumonitis, nephritis, prostatitis, urethritis, cystitis, diarrhea, and disseminated infection.

DIAGNOSIS

DIFFERENTIAL DIAGNOSIS

- Other causes of watery nonbloody diarrhea: *Norovirus, Giardia, Cryptosporidia, Cyclospora,* and *Isospora belli*
- Other causes of keratoconjunctivitis: herpetic keratoconjunctivitis and acanthamoeba keratitis

WORKUP

Consists of the microscopic detection of microsporidia spores (1-2 mcm in diameter) in stool, body fluids, or tissue samples

LABORATORY TESTS

- Modified trichrome stain with light microscopy can be used on stool, urine, mucus, or tissues. Spores stain pink against a blue-green background.
- Fluorescent techniques: calcofluor white stain, Uvitex 2B, and Fungi-Fluor kit
- Indirect immunofluorescence
- Serology: detects IgM and IgG antibodies

TREATMENT

ACUTE GENERAL Rx

Treatment will depend on organism and site involved.
1) *Encephalitozoonidae* species:
   a) Intestinal or disseminated infection: albendazole 400 mg PO bid for 2 to 4 weeks depending on level of immunosuppression. Children: 15 mg/kg/day PO in divided doses.
   b) Keratoconjunctivitis: topical fumagillin 70 mcg/mL eye drops (2 drops every 2 hours for 4 days, then 2 drops 4 times a day). If associated with intestinal disease, add albendazole 400 mg PO bid for 2 to 4 weeks depending on degree of immunosuppression.
2) *Enterocytozoon bieneusi*: intestinal or disseminated disease—albendazole is not effective, but one can use fumagillin 20 mg PO tid (although this is not commercially available in the U.S.). Alternative: nitazoxanide 1 g PO bid for 60 days in AIDS patients.

CHRONIC Rx

Antimotility agents are useful to control diarrhea.

REFERRAL

- Infectious diseases physician for ART therapy if HIV+/AIDS
- Ophthalmologist if keratoconjunctivitis is suspected

PEARLS & CONSIDERATIONS

COMMENTS

- Microsporidia infections occur particularly in AIDS patients with CD4+ cell counts <50/ml.
- Microsporidia spores can remain active in the environment for prolonged periods of time (e.g., months).

PREVENTION

The most effective prevention in AIDS patients is to start ART to increase CD4+ count >100/ml; this will result in resolution of symptoms of enteric microsporidiosis (if already present) and serve as a prevention.

SUGGESTED READINGS
Available at www.expertconsult.com

AUTHOR: **GLENN G. FORT, M.D., M.P.H.**

BASIC INFORMATION

DEFINITION

Significant cognitive impairment in the absence of dementia with preserved activities of daily living (ADLs). Mild cognitive impairment (MCI) is an intermediate state between normal cognitive function and dementia. The main distinctions between MCI and mild dementia are that in the latter, more than one cognitive domain is invariably involved and substantial interference with daily life is evident.[1]

SYNONYMS

Cognitive impairment not dementia (CIND)
Dementia prodrome
Mild neurocognitive disorder
MCI

ICD-10CM CODES
G31.84 Mild cognitive impairment, so stated

EPIDEMIOLOGY & DEMOGRAPHICS

INCIDENCE:
- 12 to 15 cases per 1000 person-yr age ≥65
- 51 to 77 cases per 1000 person-yr age ≥75

PEAK INCIDENCE: In the elderly
PREVALENCE: 15% to 25% in those older than age 70.
PREDOMINANT SEX AND AGE: Male, age ≥75
GENETICS: *APOE4* genotype
- Various pathways result in amyloid accumulation and deposition in pre-Alzheimer's presenting as MCI.

RISK FACTORS: Male sex, age, lower socioeconomic status, lower educational level

CLINICAL PRESENTATION

- Subjective memory problems, preferably corroborated by another person.
- Preserved functional status (ADLs).
- Normal general thinking and reasoning skills.
- Subtypes of MCI include amnestic (mainly involves memory loss) vs. nonamnestic with involvement of other cognitive domains (single domain vs. multiple domains).
- Domains affected in MCI include memory, visuospatial skills, language, attention, and executive function.
- Altered sense of smell may be a clue to impending cognitive impairment and has been associated with progression of MCI to dementia.

ETIOLOGY

Neurodegenerative, vascular, traumatic, depression, or due to underlying medical condition

 **DIAGNOSIS**

DIFFERENTIAL DIAGNOSIS

- Delirium
- Dementia

- Depression
- "Reversible" cognitive impairment:
  1. Medication related (anticholinergics)
  2. Hypothyroidism
  3. Vitamin B_{12} deficiency
- Reversible CNS conditions
  1. Subdural hematoma
  2. Normal pressure hydrocephalus
  3. Metastatic disease

WORKUP

History
- Focus on cognitive deficits and impairment.
- Review all medications that may impact cognition (i.e., anticholinergics).
- Rule out depression and delirium.
- Perform functional assessment.

Physical exam
- Check blood pressure
- Neurologic exam to rule out reversible CNS causes of cognitive impairment
- Gait and balance assessment

Cognitive function testing:
Brief mental status testing using MOCA (Montreal Cognitive Assessment) or SLUMS (Saint Louis University Mental Status) for office screening followed by neuropsychological testing if appropriate for specific deficits in cognitive domains. MOCA may be a better tool in identifying and following MCI with higher sensitivity to monitor cognitive decline in longitudinal monitoring.

LABORATORY TESTS

- Complete blood count
- Comprehensive metabolic profile
- TSH
- Vitamin B_{12}
- Lipids
- At-risk groups should get consideration for rapid plasma reagin (RPR) and HIV evaluation.

IMAGING STUDIES

- CT imaging can detect most reversible CNS conditions leading to cognitive impairment.
- MRI further evaluates vascular, infectious, neoplastic, and inflammatory conditions.

 **TREATMENT**

- There is insufficient evidence to recommend use of cholinesterase inhibitors for MCI. They are not approved for treating MCI, have shown little efficacy in altering progression to dementia, and can have significant side effects.
- Consider treatment with these medications only if memory complaints appear to be affecting day-to-day quality of life in individual patients or in amnestic subtypes of MCI after risk-versus-benefit discussion with patient and family.

NONPHARMACOLOGIC THERAPY

- Role of cognitive rehabilitation to target specific deficits
- Caregiver education and counseling
- Physical and mental exercises to maintain cognition should be recommended

COMPLEMENTARY & ALTERNATIVE MEDICINE

No clear indications for antioxidants, and studies in humans are inconclusive.

DISPOSITION

- Progression to Alzheimer's at the rate of 5% to 15% per year
  1. Risk factors for progression to dementia include presence of vascular risk factors, significant cognitive impairment, depression, and presence of extrapyramidal signs.
- Mortality of those with MCI is twice that of those without MCI.
- Two- to threefold increase in risk of nursing home placement in those with MCI.

REFERRAL

Consider referral to a memory specialist if more than just memory is involved or for further evaluation of specific deficits.

 PEARLS & CONSIDERATIONS

COMMENTS

Patients with MCI usually report short-term memory concerns such as misplacing things, not remembering names of people, word-finding difficulties, forgetting day-to-day tasks, not being able to read a book, or not being able to follow a conversation.

MCI becomes clinically relevant when quality of life is affected such as problems making financial decisions and problems with personal day-to-day interactions.

Depression should be ruled out prior to making a diagnosis of MCI since it is highly prevalent in the elderly.

Anticholinergic medication use should be evaluated carefully prior to making a diagnosis of MCI.

PREVENTION

Patients with MCI should be counseled on strategies to prevent progression to dementia. They should remain physically and mentally active, have a well-balanced diet, continue activities that are socially engaging, reduce stress in their lives, and aggressively pursue treatment of vascular risk factors.

PATIENT & FAMILY EDUCATION

- Patients with MCI typically have poor retention and rapid loss of newly learned information.
- For additional information for patients, families, and clinicians: Alzheimer's Association (www.alzheimers.org)

SUGGESTED READINGS
Available at www.expertconsult.com

AUTHORS: **BIRJU B. PATEL, M.D.**, and **N. WILSON HOLLAND, M.D.**

[1]Knopman Ds, Petersen RC: Mild cognitive impairment and mild dementia: a clinical perspective, *Mayo Clin Proc* 89:1452, 2014.

BASIC INFORMATION

DEFINITION

Mitral regurgitation (MR) is retrograde blood flow into the left atrium resulting from an incompetent mitral valve. This condition can lead to left ventricular (LV) failure as well as increased left atrial and pulmonary pressures, with consequent pulmonary hypertension and right heart failure.

SYNONYMS

Mitral insufficiency
MR

ICD-10CM CODES
I34.0	Nonrheumatic mitral (valve) insufficiency
I05.1	Rheumatic mitral insufficiency
I05.9	Mitral valve disease, unspecified
I05.2	Rheumatic mitral stenosis with insufficiency
Q23.3	Congenital mitral insufficiency

EPIDEMIOLOGY & DEMOGRAPHICS

The incidence of MR has increased over the past 30 yr; however, this may be due to increasing availability of echocardiography and MR diagnosis rather than any real increase in the prevalence of this condition.

PHYSICAL FINDINGS & CLINICAL PRESENTATION

- Holosystolic, high-pitched, "blowing" murmur at apex with radiation to base, left axilla, or back; there is a poor correlation between the intensity of the systolic murmur and the degree of regurgitation. However, an early diastolic to mid-diastolic rumble (pseudomitral stenosis) suggests severe MR.
- The murmur of acute MR (e.g., from papillary muscle rupture) can be very soft or inaudible due to a large regurgitant volume entering a noncompliant left atrium, leading to an acute rise in left atrial pressure and thus lack of significant gradient for an audible murmur.
- Hyperdynamic apex, sometimes with palpable LV lift and apical thrill.
- Many patients with mild to moderate MR will remain asymptomatic and without evidence of hemodynamic compromise for years.
- Diminished S1, reflecting failure of valve leaflets to coapt completely, widely split S2 (decreased LV ejection time results in early A2) and presence of an S3
- Symptomatic patients with MR generally present with the following:
  1. Symptoms suggestive of heart failure (fatigue, dyspnea, orthopnea, paroxysmal nocturnal dyspnea, edema)
  2. Hemoptysis (caused by pulmonary hypertension)
  3. Atrial fibrillation

ETIOLOGY

Primary MR
- Idiopathic myxomatous degeneration of the mitral valve, mitral valve prolapse (most common cause of MR in industrialized countries)
- Papillary muscle dysfunction or rupture (typically as a result of an inferior wall myocardial infarction)
- Ruptured chordae tendineae
- Infective endocarditis
- Calcified mitral valve annulus
- Rheumatic valvulitis (may be combined with mitral stenosis; common in developing countries)
- Systemic lupus erythematosus (Libman-Sacks endocarditis)
- Drugs: fenfluramine, dexfenfluramine, pergolide, cabergoline
- Congenital cleft valve
- Ischemic mitral regurgitation due to papillary muscle dysfunction from multivessel CAD
Secondary MR
- Hypertrophic cardiomyopathy
- LV dilation (e.g., secondary to dilated cardiomyopathy)

DIAGNOSIS

DIFFERENTIAL DIAGNOSIS

- Hypertrophic cardiomyopathy
- Tricuspid regurgitation
- Aortic stenosis
- Aortic sclerosis
- Ventricular septal defect
- Atrial septal defect

WORKUP

- Diagnostic workup consists of echocardiography, ECG, and chest radiograph; cardiac catheterization sometimes needed to confirm severity of the disease.
- Recent studies suggest that in patients with severe asymptomatic MR and normal LV function, elevations of brain natriuretic peptide (BNP) >105 pg/ml have an independent and additive prognostic value that may identify patients at high risk and aid in the selection of patients for early surgery.

IMAGING STUDIES

- Echocardiography (Fig. 1M-34): dilated left atrium, hyperdynamic left ventricle (erratic motion of the leaflet is seen in patients with ruptured chordae tendineae); color flow Doppler will show evidence of MR. The most important aspect of the echocardiographic examination is the quantification of the severity of MR (Table 1M-22), LV systolic performance, and estimated right ventricular (RV) systolic pressure vena contracta width >0.6 cm, regurgitant volume >60 ml, regurgitant orifice area >0.40 cm^2 by PISA (proximal isovelocity surface area), and systolic pulmonary vein flow reversal are all echocardiographic criteria of severe MR.
- Chest x-ray:
  1. Left atrial enlargement, LV enlargement
  2. Possible pulmonary congestion, although most often normal

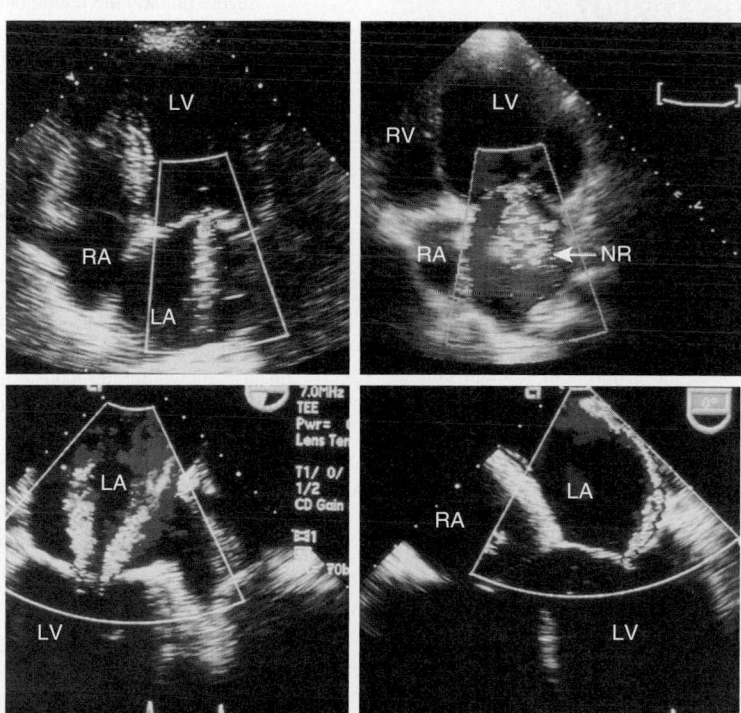

FIGURE 1M-34 Mitral regurgitation. Four panels depicting varying degrees of mitral regurgitation; the two *top panels* are apical four-chamber transthoracic views showing, on the *left,* mild mitral regurgitation and, on the *right,* moderate to severe mitral regurgitation. On the *left,* note the relatively narrow jet directed from the tips of the mitral valve toward the posterior left atrial wall. On the right, note the larger jet, filling approximately 40% of the left atrial cavity. The two *bottom panels* are transesophageal echocardiograms. On the *left,* note the mitral regurgitation occurring in two discrete jets and, on the *right,* the highly eccentric jet, which courses along the extreme lateral wall of the left atrium. *LA,* Left atrium; *LV,* left ventricle; *RA,* right atrium; *RV,* right ventricle. (From Zipes DP et al [eds]: *Braunwald's heart disease,* ed 7, Philadelphia, 2005, Saunders.)

TABLE 1M-22 Mitral Regurgitation Severity*

	(Mild)	II	III	IV (Severe)
MR = jet (%LA)	<15	15-30	35-50	>50
Spectral Doppler	Faint	—	—	Dense
Vena contracta	<3 mm	—	—	>6 mm
Pulmonary vein flow	S > D	—	—	Systolic reversed
RV (ml)	<30	30-44	45-59	≥60
ERO (cm²)	<0.2	0.2-0.29	0.3-0.39	≥0.40
PISA	Small	—	—	Large

*For some parameters, the observation is valid at the extremes of MR severity and there may be marked overlap in intermediate (grades II, III) MR. In these instances, no value is presented.
D, Antegrade flow in diastole; *ERO*, effective regurgitant orifice; *%LA*, percentage of left atrial area encompassed by the *MR* jet with color flow Doppler; *MR*, mitral regurgitation; *PISA*, proximal iso-velocity surface area; *RV*, regurgitant volume; *S*, antegrade flow in systole.
From Zipes DP et al (eds): *Braunwald's heart disease*, ed 7, Philadelphia, 2005, Saunders and the 2003 American Society of Echocardiography Guidelines.

- ECG:
  1. Left atrial enlargement
  2. LV hypertrophy
  3. Atrial fibrillation
- Cardiac catheterization: to confirm severity of MR, or to rule out presence of coronary artery disease in patients being evaluated for surgical replacement
- Can consider cardiac MRI in cases where echocardiography is limited or LV function/dimensions are borderline, or when clinical condition and echocardiographic findings are discordant.

 **TREATMENT**

NONPHARMACOLOGIC THERAPY

Salt restriction, surgical repair or replacement (see the following)

ACUTE GENERAL Rx

- Medical: medical therapy is primarily directed toward treatment of the source or its complications (e.g., atrial fibrillation, ischemic heart disease, infective endocarditis, hypertension, and heart failure).
  1. The utility of afterload reduction (to decrease the regurgitant fraction and to increase cardiac output) depends upon the etiology of MR and the administration of afterload reducers. In acute MR, intravenous nitroprusside has shown some utility. Long-term use of oral afterload reducers (e.g., ACE inhibitors or angiotensin receptor blockers [ARBs]) do not slow the progression of mitral regurgitation, and their use should be only for other indications such as hypertension and LV dysfunction.
  2. Control ventricular response only if atrial fibrillation with rapid ventricular response is present.
  3. Anticoagulants if atrial fibrillation occurs.
- Surgery: Surgery is the only definitive treatment for MR. Although no randomized trial of mitral valve repair vs. replacement exists, repair is favored over replacement in degenerative mitral valve disease due to its lower perioperative risk, improved event-free survival, freedom

from complications of prosthetic valves, and better postoperative LV function. It is a class I indication in patients with (Fig. 1M-35):
1. Acute severe MR
2. Symptomatic patients with severe primary MR despite optimal medical therapy and LVEF >30%, LV dilation, severe MR by echo criteria
3. Asymptomatic patients with severe MR but with evidence of declining LV function (EF 30% to 60%) or progressive dilation (LV at end-systole >40 mm)
   1. Concomitant mitral valve repair or MVR is indicated in patients with chronic severe primary MR undergoing cardiac surgery for other indications
- Surgery is a class IIa (reasonable) recommendation in:
1. Severe MR with new-onset atrial fibrillation, even if asymptomatic.
2. Asymptomatic severe MR with pulmonary hypertension (≥50 mm Hg at rest or ≥60 mm Hg during exercise).
3. Asymptomatic severe MR secondary to flail leaflet.
4. A recent study of early surgical intervention for severe MR secondary to a flail leaflet in patients with asymptomatic disease shows greater long-term survival and reduced rates of heart failure when compared with medical therapy alone.
   1. Asymptomatic severe MR with preserved LVEF (>60%) and size (<40 mm in end-systole) in whom the likelihood of successful repair without residual MR is >95% and operative mortality is <1%.
5. Surgery is a class IIb recommendation in symptomatic severe MR with severe LV dysfunction or dilatation (LVEF <30% or LV at end-systole >55 mm, respectively) in whom LV dysfunction is not the primary cause for the MR as well as functional MR where it is secondary to LV dysfunction, but in this group there should be NYHA Class III-IV symptoms.
- Quantitative grading of MR is a powerful predictor of the clinical outcome of asymptomatic MR. In general, patients with regurgitant orifice areas of ≥40 mm² should be consid-

ered for prompt surgery, whereas those with orifices between 20 and 39 mm² can be followed closely.
- Percutaneous mitral valve repair methods are currently being investigated, and the MitraClip device is now FDA approved for use in patients with significant symptomatic degenerative MR (>3+) who have too high a risk for surgery. The device is a catheter-delivered clip that grasps and approximates the edges of the mitral leaflets at the origin of the regurgitant jet. Early data have not demonstrated a significant efficacy in MR reduction compared with surgical replacement; however, it has been shown to improve NYHA functional class and quality of life measures.
- Ischemic MR has been a source of controversy. There has been recent debate as to whether moderate or greater MR should be fixed at the time of revascularization with CABG. A recent NEJM 2014 study looked at moderate ischemic MR and randomized patients to MV repair + CABG versus CABG alone. There was no increase in LV function improvement between groups and, while there was reduced incidence of moderate to severe MR following repair, there were increased number of untoward events like longer bypass time, longer hospitalizations, and more neurologic events. There was no difference in major adverse cardiac or cerebrovascular events deaths, readmissions, or quality of life at one year. Currently the evidence is not in favor of fixing moderate ischemic MR.

DISPOSITION

Prognosis is generally good unless there is significant impairment of left ventricular function or significantly elevated pulmonary artery pressures. Most patients remain asymptomatic for many years (average interval from diagnosis to onset of symptoms is 16 yr). In patients with chronic severe MR, MR is commonly progressive, with onset of other symptoms or left ventricular dysfunction within 6-10 yr. However surgery should be advised well before the onset of symptoms in case of worsening LVEF and LV systolic dimensions and presence of pulmonary hypertension or atrial fibrillation, all of which are poor prognostic signs.

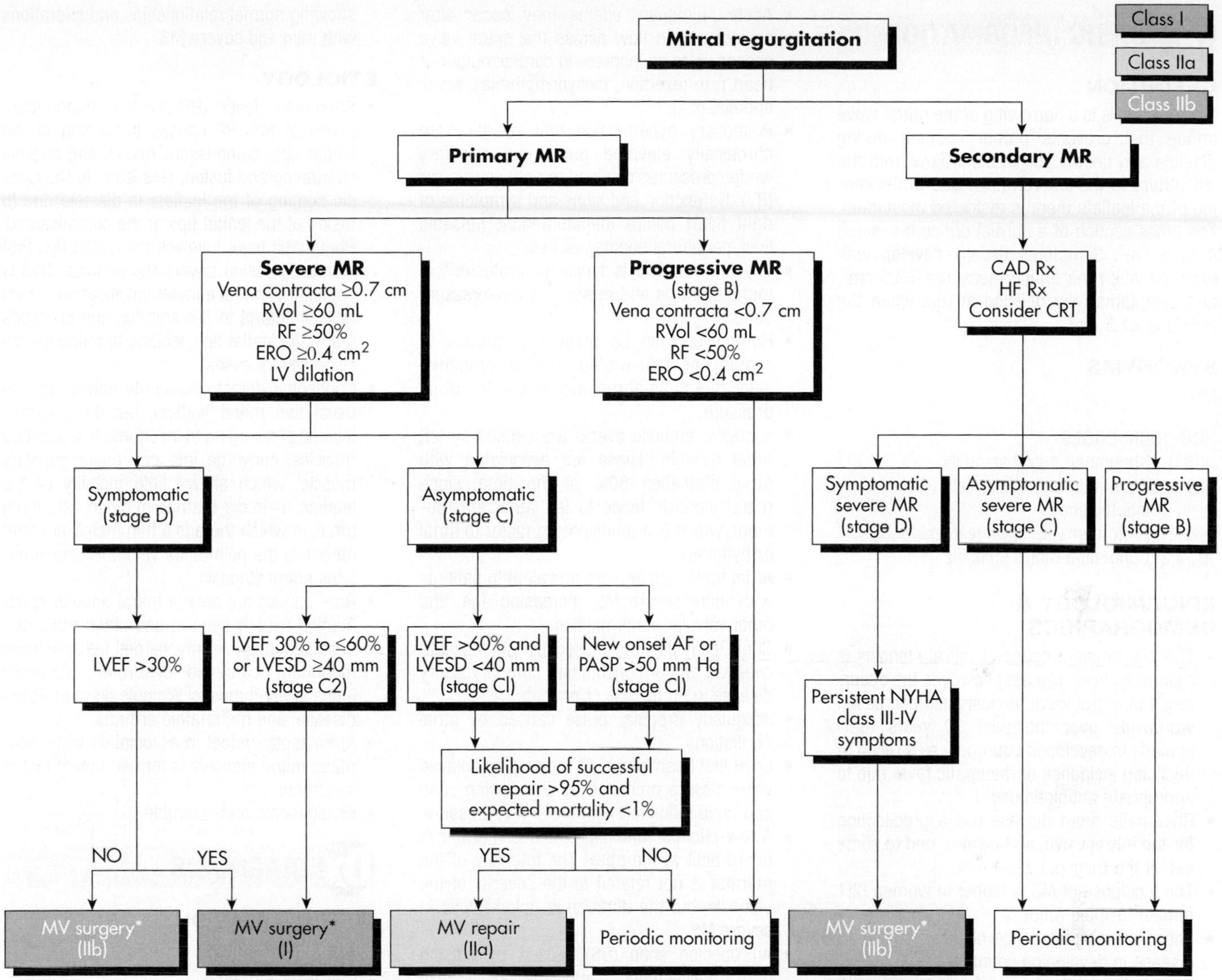

EBM PTG **Mitral Regurgitation** 803

Class I
Class IIa
Class IIb

M

Diseases
and Disorders

I

Mitral regurgitation

Primary MR

Secondary MR

Severe MR
Vena contracta ≥0.7 cm
RVol ≥60 mL
RF ≥50%
ERO ≥0.4 cm^2
LV dilation

Progressive MR
(stage B)
Vena contracta <0.7 cm
RVol <60 mL
RF <50%
ERO <0.4 cm^2

CAD Rx
HF Rx
Consider CRT

Symptomatic
(stage D)

Asymptomatic
(stage C)

Symptomatic
severe MR
(stage D)

Asymptomatic
severe MR
(stage C)

Progressive
MR
(stage B)

LVEF >30%

LVEF 30% to ≤60%
or LVESD ≥40 mm
(stage C2)

LVEF >60% and
LVESD <40 mm
(stage CI)

New onset AF or
PASP >50 mm Hg
(stage CI)

Persistent NYHA
class III-IV
symptoms

Likelihood of successful
repair >95% and
expected mortality <1%

NO   YES   YES   NO

MV surgery*
(IIb)

MV surgery*
(I)

MV repair
(IIa)

Periodic monitoring

MV surgery*
(IIb)

Periodic monitoring

FIGURE 1M-35 Indications for Surgery for MR. *Mitral valve repair is preferred over MVR when possible. *AF,* Atrial fibrillation; *CAD,* coronary artery disease; *CRT,* cardiac resynchronization therapy; *ERO,* effective regurgitant orifice; *HF,* heart failure; *LV,* left ventricular; *LVEF,* left ventricular ejection fraction; *LVESD,* left ventricular end-systolic dimension; *MR,* mitral regurgitation; *MV,* mitral valve; *MVR,* mitral valve replacement; *NYHA,* New York Heart Association; *PASP,* pulmonary artery systolic pressure; *RF,* regurgitant fraction; *RVol,* regurgitant volume; and *Rx,* therapy. (From Nishimura RA, et al. ACC/AHA guidelines for the management of patients with valvular heart disease. *J Am Coll Cardiol* 63(22):e57-e185, 2014.) http://dx.doi.org/10.1016/j.jacc.2014.02.536.)

REFERRAL

- Surgical referral in selected patients (see "Acute General Rx"). Emergency surgery is usually necessary in patients with acute MR caused by ruptured papillary muscle or chordae tendineae after myocardial infarction.
- Mitral valve repair can also be accomplished with percutaneous implantation of a MitraClip device in patients who are too high risk for surgery. The role of percutaneous repair of functional MR is still under active investigation.

PEARLS & CONSIDERATIONS

COMMENTS

- Although vasodilators and other agents should be used to treat hypertension in patients with severe mitral regurgitation, there is no evidence that they will delay the need for eventual valve surgery, which is the definitive treatment for severe MR.
- In 2007, the AHA guidelines for prevention of infectious endocarditis were revised and routine antibiotic prophylaxis to undergo dental or other invasive procedures is no longer recommended, unless the patient has prior endocarditis.

EBM **EVIDENCE**

Available at www.expertconsult.com

SUGGESTED READINGS

Available at www.expertconsult.com

RELATED CONTENT

Mitral Regurgitation (Patient Information)

AUTHOR: **SHALINE D. RAO, M.D.**

 BASIC INFORMATION

DEFINITION

Mitral stenosis is a narrowing of the mitral valve orifice that prevents proper opening during diastole and obstruction of blood flow from the left atrium to the left ventricle. Due to thickening of the leaflets there is restricted movement. The cross section of a normal orifice measures 4 to 6 cm². Symptoms usually develop with exercise when the orifice measures <2.5 cm², and symptoms may develop at rest when the orifice is <1.5 cm².

SYNONYMS

MS

ICD-10CM CODES
I05.0	Rheumatic mitral stenosis
I05.2	Rheumatic mitral stenosis with insufficiency
I34.2	Nonrheumatic mitral (valve) stenosis
Q23.2	Congenital mitral stenosis

EPIDEMIOLOGY & DEMOGRAPHICS

- The predominant cause of mitral stenosis is rheumatic heart disease; however, the occurrence of mitral valve stenosis has decreased worldwide over the past 30 years (particularly in developed countries) as a result of declining incidence of rheumatic fever due to appropriate antibiotic use.
- Rheumatic heart disease has a predilection for the mitral valve, aortic valve, and to some extent the tricuspid valve.
- The incidence of MS is higher in women (2:1 female-to-male ratio).
- There is high prevalence of rheumatic heart disease in developing countries.
- Outbreaks of rheumatic fever in the U.S. are due to increased virulence of a streptococcal strain or enhanced immigration from where rheumatic heart disease is prevalent.

PHYSICAL FINDINGS & CLINICAL PRESENTATION

- Dyspnea is the most common symptom along with fatigue and decreased exercise capacity. These symptoms occur due to an inability to increase cardiac output, especially with exercise, and elevated pulmonary capillary wedge pressures, with resultant increase in pulmonary artery pressures.
- The left ventricle is unaffected in pure MS; however, MS often coexists with mitral regurgitation and occasionally with aortic valve dysfunction, both of which can cause left ventricular dysfunction.
- "Mitral facies" which are pinkish-purple patches on the cheek due to low cardiac output and vasoconstriction, usually indicate severe MS.
- Paroxysmal nocturnal dyspnea (PND) and orthopnea secondary to elevated left atrial pressure may occur.

- Acute pulmonary edema may occur after an increase in flow across the mitral valve secondary to an increase in cardiac output or heart rate (exertion, tachyarrhythmias, fever, anemia, etc.).
- Pulmonary hypertension that results from chronically elevated pulmonary capillary wedge pressures can lead to right ventricular (RV) dysfunction and signs and symptoms of right heart failure (hepatomegaly, pulsatile liver, peripheral edema, ascites).
- The left ventricle is typically "protected" in mitral stenosis and exists in a low-pressure state.
- Hemoptysis can be present secondary to rupture of thin-walled dilated bronchial veins due to an abrupt increase in left atrial pressure.
- Systemic embolic events are caused by left atrial thrombi. These are associated with atrial fibrillation 80% of the time, since mitral stenosis leads to left atrial enlargement, which is a predisposing factor to atrial arrhythmias.
- Atrial fibrillation is more prevalent in patients with more severe MS, increasing age, and other valvular abnormalities.
- Chest pain can be caused by RV pressure overload and/or concomitant coronary artery disease in up to 15% of patients.
- Irregularly irregular pulse caused by atrial fibrillation.
- Loud first heart sound (S_1) caused by delayed valve closure preceded by an opening snap and rapid rising left ventricular (LV) pressure.
- A low-pitched rumbling diastolic murmur is heard best at the apex. The intensity of the murmur is not related to the severity of the stenosis, but the duration is holodiastolic in severe MS.
- An opening snap (OS) caused by tensing of the valve leaflets after the cusps have opened completely. The OS follows S_2 by 0.03 to 0.14 sec, and the shorter the S_2-OS interval, the more severe the MS, due to the increasing left atrial pressures.
- Prominent A wave on the pulmonary capillary wedge pressure tracing. This is analogous to the prominent A wave seen in systemic venous pressure tracings with tricuspid stenosis.
- A diastolic thrill may be palpable at the apex, especially with the patient in the left lateral recumbent position.
- An RV lift may be palpable at the left sternal border secondary to RV hypertrophy and pulmonary hypertension.
- An accentuated P_2 and/or a soft, early diastolic decrescendo murmur (Graham Steell murmur) caused by pulmonary regurgitation may be present in patients with pulmonary hypertension (not specific for mitral stenosis).
- Hoarseness due to the enlargement of the left atrium compressing the recurrent laryngeal nerve.
- Straightening of the left heart border seen on chest radiography indicative of left atrial enlargement.
- Fig. 1M-36 shows schematic representations of LV, aortic, and left atrial (LA) pressures,

showing normal relationships and alterations with mild and severe MS.

ETIOLOGY

- Rheumatic fever (RF) is the predominant cause of MS. RF causes thickening of the leaflet tips, commissure fusion, and chordal shortening and fusion. This leads to the classic doming of the leaflets in diastole due to fusion of the leaflet tips at the commissures. Rheumatic fever involves the leaflet tips first with progression toward the annulus. This is opposite of mitral annular calcification, which typically starts in the annulus and proceeds out to the leaflet tips, leading to mitral stenosis in severe cases.
- Congenital defect (parachute valve) has the usual two mitral leaflets, but the chordae, instead of diverging to insert into two papillary muscles, converge into one major papillary muscle, which allows little mobility of the leaflets, as in cor triatriatum (heart with three atria), in which there is a thin membrane that obstructs the pulmonary vein flow and simulates mitral stenosis.
- Rare causes are severe mitral annular calcification usually seen in end-stage renal disease patients, endomyocardial fibroelastosis, malignant carcinoid syndrome, systemic lupus erythematosus, Whipple disease, Fabry disease, and rheumatoid arthritis.
- Atrial septal defect in association with rheumatic mitral stenosis is termed Lutembacher syndrome.
- Medications: methysergide

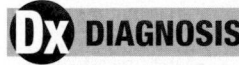 DIAGNOSIS

DIFFERENTIAL DIAGNOSIS

- Left atrial myxoma
- Ball valve thrombus
- Other valvular abnormalities (e.g., tricuspid stenosis, mitral regurgitation)
- Atrial septal defect

WORKUP

Physical examination and echocardiography

IMAGING STUDIES

- Echocardiography (Fig. 1M-37):
  1. Two-dimensional echocardiogram can measure valve area by direct planimetry or calculate it by the Doppler pressure half-time method (this may be inaccurate in patients with concomitant diastolic dysfunction or aortic insufficiency and in patients who have recently undergone mitral valvuloplasty) or the continuity equation can be used to calculate the valve area. A valve area less than 1 cm² is consistent with severe MS. The transmitral gradient can also be calculated. A mean gradient of >10 mm Hg indicates severe MS. 5 to 10 mm Hg is consistent with moderate MS, and 0 to 5 mm Hg is consistent with mild MS or no MS.
  2. Echocardiography will also show a markedly diminished E-to-F slope of the anterior

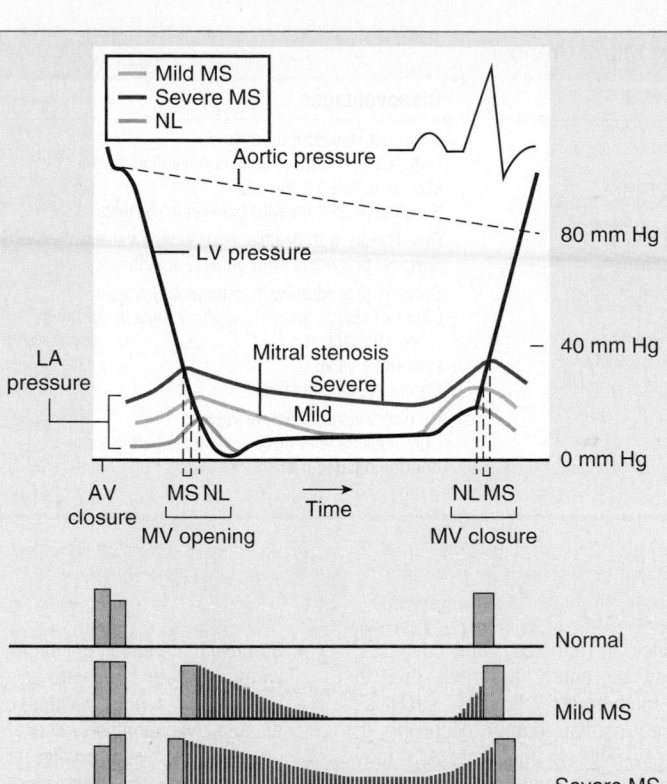

FIGURE 1M-36 Schematic representation of LV, aortic, and left atrial (LA) pressures, showing normal relationships and alterations with mild and severe MS. Corresponding classic auscultatory signs of MS are shown at the bottom. The higher left atrial v wave of severe MS causes earlier pressure crossover and earlier MV opening, leading to a shorter time interval between aortic valve (AV) closure and the opening snap (OS). The higher left atrial end-diastolic pressure with severe MS also results in later closure of the mitral valve. With severe MS, the diastolic rumble becomes longer and there is accentuation of the pulmonic component (P_2) of the second heart sound (S_2) in relation to the aortic component (A_2). (From Bonow R.O.: *Heart disease,* 9th ed, Philadelphia, 2012, Saunders.)

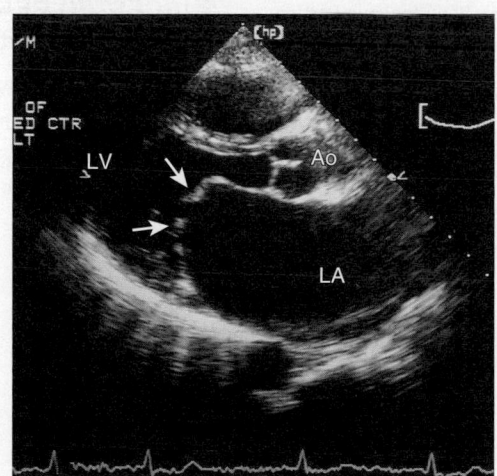

FIGURE 1M-37 Mitral stenosis. Parasternal long-axis view of a patient with mitral stenosis and a pliable noncalcified mitral valve leaflet. Note the "doming" motion of the mitral valve leaflets *(arrows).* Valves with these morphologic features are excellent candidates for percutaneous balloon valvotomy. *Ao,* Aorta; *LA,* left atrium; *LV,* left ventricle. (From Zipes DP et al [eds]: *Braunwald's heart disease,* ed 7, Philadelphia, 2005, Saunders.)

mitral valve leaflet during diastole; there is also fusion of the commissures, resulting in "doming" of the leaflets during diastole.
3. Grading of leaflet thickness, mobility, calcification, and subvalvular thickening (mitral valvuloplasty score) with a score of 0 to 4 for each characteristic can predict hemodynamic results and outcome of balloon mitral valvuloplasty (a low score of less than 8 is favorable for balloon valvuloplasty and a high score is unfavorable). A score above 8 would favor a surgical approach. In addition, mitral regurgitation that is greater than mild would preclude a balloon mitral valvuloplasty procedure.
4. Doppler echocardiography can be used to assess for pulmonary hypertension and to give an estimate of the pulmonary artery systolic pressure at rest and with exercise.
5. Patients with known mitral stenosis: a follow-up echocardiography is recommended to assess for pulmonary artery pressures and valve gradient (mitral valve area <1.0 cm² yearly, mitral valve area <1.5 cm² 1 to 2 yr, mitral valve area >1.5 cm² every 3 to 5 yr).
- Chest radiograph:
  1. Straightening of the left cardiac border caused by enlarged left atrium
  2. Left atrial enlargement on lateral chest radiograph
  3. Prominence of pulmonary arteries that indicates pulmonary hypertension
  4. Possible pulmonary congestion and edema (Kerley B lines)
- ECG:
  1. RV hypertrophy; right axis deviation caused by pulmonary hypertension
  2. Left atrial enlargement (broad, biphasic P waves in lead V1 and duration of P-waves >0.11 sec in lead II). This is termed "P-mitrale."
  3. Atrial fibrillation
- Cardiac catheterization:
  1. Allows the measurement of pulmonary artery pressure and transmitral pressure gradients at rest or with exercise (supine biking or raising weights with arms while lying supine).
  2. Allows the measurement of transmitral flow and calculation of the valve area.
  3. Is not routinely recommended for the evaluation of MS but is useful when the echocardiographic findings are nondiagnostic or discrepant with the clinical scenario.
  4. Cardiac catheterization in addition to echocardiography can be used to monitor the hemodynamics during a balloon mitral valvuloplasty procedure.

 **TREATMENT**

NONPHARMACOLOGIC THERAPY

Decrease level of activity in symptomatic patients and salt restriction if pulmonary congestion is present.

TABLE 1M-23 Approaches to Mechanical Relief of Mitral Stenosis

Approach	Advantages	Disadvantages
Closed surgical valvotomy	Inexpensive Relatively simple Good hemodynamic results in selected patients Good long-term outcome	No direct visualization of valve Only feasible with flexible, noncalcified valves Contraindicated if MR >2+ Surgical procedure with general anesthesia
Open surgical valvotomy	Visualization of valve allows directed valvotomy Concurrent annuloplasty for MR is feasible	Best results with flexible, noncalcified valves Surgical procedure with general anesthesia
Valve replacement	Feasible in all patients regardless of extent of valve calcification or severity of MR	Surgical procedure with general anesthesia Effect of loss of annular-papillary muscle continuity on LV function Prosthetic valve Chronic anticoagulation
Balloon mitral valvotomy	Percutaneous approach Local anesthesia Good hemodynamic results in selected patients Good long-term outcome	No direct visualization of valve Only feasible with flexible, noncalcified valves Contraindicated if MR >2+

LV, Left ventricular; *MR*, mitral regurgitation.
From Otto CM: *Valvular heart disease*, ed 2, Philadelphia, 2004, Saunders.

ACUTE GENERAL Rx

- Medical:
  1. Anticoagulation for the prevention of systemic embolic events in patients with MS and:
     1. Atrial fibrillation
     2. Prior embolic event
     3. Documented left atrial thrombus or left atrial appendage thrombus
     4. Severe mitral stenosis if associated with severe left atrial enlargement and spontaneous echo contrast indicating stagnant blood flow (class IIb indication)
  2. Ventricular rate control (to increase diastolic filling period) with beta-blockers, non-dihydropyridine calcium channel blockers, or digitalis and aggressive treatment of tachyarrhythmias.
  3. Treat congestive heart failure with loop diuretics and sodium restriction.
  4. Antibiotic prophylaxis to prevent recurrent rheumatic fever is usually not indicated unless presence of high-risk features such as prior endocarditis, prosthetic heart valves, valvulopathy of the transplanted heart, and certain cases of cyanotic congenital heart disease.

  5. Pregnancy in females with advanced MS may be poorly tolerated due to the hemodynamic changes such as increased cardiac output occurring in pregnancy. Mild to moderate MS may be tolerated in pregnancy with medical therapy alone.
- Table 1M-23 summarizes approaches to mechanical relief of mitral stenosis.
- Percutaneous balloon mitral valvotomy (BMV) is the therapy of choice for symptomatic patients with moderate to severe MS (valve area ≤ 1.5 cm^2) with a favorable valvuloplasty score, minimal or no mitral regurgitation and no left atrial thrombus. Balloon valvotomy is also indicated in asymptomatic patients with moderate to severe MS that has resulted in pulmonary artery pressures of 50 mm Hg at rest or 60 mm Hg with exercise. Percutaneous BMV is also considered the procedure of choice in pregnant women with rheumatic MS and in NYHA class III to IV heart failure and/or unresponsive to adequate medical treatment. In addition, it is a reasonable option for patients who are at high risk for surgery even when their valve morphology is not ideal (class IIa indication).

- Surgical intervention is indicated for patients with moderate to severe symptomatic MS when BMV is not available or is contraindicated (valvuloplasty score greater than or equal to 8) or the valve is calcified, MR that is more than mild, presence of left atrial thrombus and when the surgical risk is acceptable. The surgical approaches include closed mitral valvotomy, open valvotomy and repair (preferred), and mitral valve replacement when repair is not possible.

DISPOSITION

- Prognosis is generally good except in patients with chronic pulmonary hypertension.
- Operative mortality rates for mitral valve replacement are 1% to 5% at most institutions.

SUGGESTED READINGS
Available at www.expertconsult.com

RELATED CONTENT
Mitral Stenosis (Patient Information)

AUTHORS: **HARSHA V. GANGA, M.D.,** and **ARAVIND RAO KOKKIRALA, M.D.**

BASIC INFORMATION

DEFINITION
Mitral valve prolapse (MVP) is the bulging of one or both of the mitral valve leaflets ≥2 mm above the annular plane into the left atrium during systole. MVP syndrome refers to a constellation of MVP and associated symptoms (e.g., autonomic dysfunction, palpitations) or other physical abnormalities (e.g., pectus excavatum). Table 1M-24 describes a classification of mitral valve prolapse.

SYNONYMS
MVP
Mitral click murmur syndrome
Barlow's syndrome

ICD-10CM CODES
I34.1 Nonrheumatic mitral (valve) prolapse
I34.0 Nonrheumatic mitral (valve)
       insufficiency

EPIDEMIOLOGY & DEMOGRAPHICS
- MVP can be found by echocardiogram in 1% to 2.4% of the general population, with some studies suggesting that it is more common in women than in men.
- Increased incidence is seen with autoimmune thyroid disorders, Ehlers-Danlos syndrome, Marfan syndrome, osteogenesis imperfecta, pseudoxanthoma elasticum, pectus excavatum, anorexia nervosa, and bulimia.
- Compared to men, women with MVP have less posterior prolapse (22% vs. 31%), less flail (2% vs. 8%), more leaflet thickening (32% vs. 28%), and less frequent severe mitral regurgitation (MR) (10% vs. 23%).

TABLE 1M-24   Classification of Mitral Valve Prolapse

Mitral Valve Prolapse Syndrome
- Younger age (20-50 yr)
- Predominantly female
- Click or click-murmur on physical examination
- Thin leaflets with systolic displacement on echocardiography
- Associated with low blood pressure, orthostatic hypotension, palpitations
- Benign long-term course

Myxomatous Mitral Valve Disease
- Older age (40-70 yr)
- Predominantly male
- Thickened, redundant valve leaflets
- Mitral regurgitation on physical exam and echocardiography
- High likelihood of progressive disease requiring mitral valve surgery

Secondary Mitral Valve Prolapse
- Marfan syndrome
- Hypertrophic cardiomyopathy
- Ehlers-Danlos syndrome
- Other connective tissue diseases

Modified from Otto CM: *Valvular heart disease*, ed 2, Philadelphia, 2004, Saunders, p. 369.

- Although MVP is more common in women than men, men more often develop severe regurgitation requiring surgical intervention.

PHYSICAL FINDINGS & CLINICAL PRESENTATION
- Mid to late systolic click, heard best at the apex
- If regurgitation is present, a crescendo mid to late systolic murmur may be heard that worsens with standing and Valsalva's maneuver
- Timing of click within the cardiac cycle varies with loading conditions within the left ventricle (i.e., may occur earlier with standing or Valsalva and later with squatting or expiration)
- May be associated with small anteroposterior chest diameter, scoliosis, pectus excavatum, or low BMI.
- Most patients with MVP are asymptomatic; symptoms (if present) consist primarily of chest pain, palpitations, fatigue, dyspnea, or and anxiety
- Neurologic abnormalities (e.g., transient ischemic attack [TIA] or stroke) are rare
- A spectrum of arrhythmias, mainly paroxysmal supraventricular tachycardia and atrial and ventricular premature beats, etc., is also observed with mitral valve prolapse. There is also an increased association with Wolff-Parkinson-White syndrome and QT prolongation

ETIOLOGY
- Myxomatous degeneration of connective tissue within mitral valve, usually involving multiple leaflet segments. In contrast, fibroelastic deficiency of single leaflet segment develops in elderly patients.
- Congenital deformity of mitral valve and supportive structures
- Secondary to other disorders of connective tissue such as Ehlers-Danlos, Marfan, or pseudoxanthoma elasticum; association with other connective tissue disorders suggests MVP result of defective embryogenesis in cells of mesenchymal origin

DIAGNOSIS

DIFFERENTIAL DIAGNOSIS
- Other valvular abnormalities (especially mitral regurgitation [MR])
- Anxiety/panic disorders
- Pulmonary embolism
- Atypical chest pain

WORKUP
- Medical history and physical examination, with increased suspicion in patients with other findings of connective tissue disorder.
- Two- or three-dimensional echocardiography in patients with a systolic click or murmur on careful auscultation.
- Cardiac MRI is an emerging tool for the evaluation and diagnosis of MVP but has not yet been independently validated.

- ECG is most often normal but may show nonspecific ST-T wave changes, prolonged QT interval, or prominent Q waves.

IMAGING STUDIES
Echocardiography (Fig. 1M-38) shows one or more leaflets prolapsing >2 mm into the left atrium during systole in a long axis view. Mitral leaflets may be thickened (>5 mm). MR is typically present, though sometimes only during exertion. If moderate or severe MR is present, findings of dilated left atrium, LV dilation and/or dysfunction, and elevated estimated RV systolic pressures may also be present. There is an increased incidence of secundum-type atrial septal defects (ASDs) in patients with MVP, which may also be identified with echocardiography.

TREATMENT

NONPHARMACOLOGIC THERAPY
Avoidance of stimulants (e.g., caffeine, nicotine) in patients with palpitations. Sometimes, reassurance is sufficient to reduce the severity of symptoms in many patients.

ACUTE GENERAL Rx
β-blockers may be tried in symptomatic patients (e.g., palpitations, chest pain) to decrease the heart rate and contractility, thus potentially decreasing the stretch on the prolapsing valve leaflets.

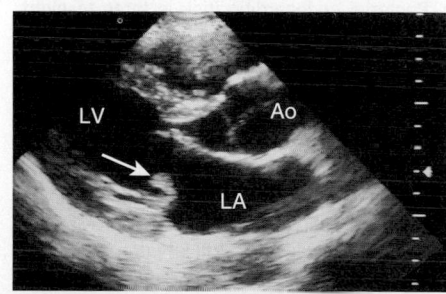

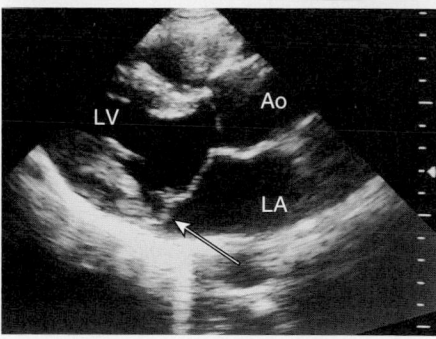

FIGURE 1M-38   Mitral valve prolapse. Parasternal long-axis view in diastole *(top)* and systole *(bottom)* in a patient with mitral valve prolapse and myxomatous changes. In the *upper panel,* note the open mitral valve and the diffuse thickening of the posterior mitral valve leaflet *(arrow).* The *lower panel* was recorded in systole. Note that both leaflets prolapse behind the plane of the mitral valve annulus. The prolapse of the posterior leaflet is somewhat more prominent *(arrow). Ao,* Aorta; *LA,* left atrium; *LV,* left ventricle. (From Zipes DP et al [eds]: *Braunwald's heart disease,* ed 7, Philadelphia, 2005, Saunders.)

TABLE 1M-25 Predictors of Clinical Outcome in Mitral Valve Prolapse

Predictor	Survival	Valve Surgery	Arrhythmias or Sudden Death	Endocarditis
Age	+++	+++	−	−
Gender	++	++	−	−
Leaflet thickness or redundancy	+++	+++	++++	++++
Severity of mitral regurgitation	++++	++++	++++	++++
Systolic click	+	−	−	−
Left ventricular dilation	+	++++	++	−
Left atrial dilation	−	++	+	−

Symbols indicate the relative predictive value of each variable for the listed clinical outcomes on a scale of no predictive value (−) to strongly predictive (++++).
From Bonow RO et al: *Braunwald's heart disease: a textbook of cardiovascular medicine*, Philadelphia, 2012, Saunders.

CHRONIC Rx

Monitoring for complications:

- Mitral regurgitation (most common complication); on rare occasion may occur acutely due to rupture of chordae tendineae.
- Routine echocardiographic monitoring is indicated at the following intervals with patients with evidence of mitral regurgitation:
  - Stage B with mild regurgitation—every 3 to 5 years
  - Stage B with moderate regurgitation—every 1 to 2 years
  - Stage C1 (asymptomatic severe MR without LV dysfunction)—every 6 to 12 months
- Bacterial endocarditis (risk is three to eight times that of the general population); higher risk in patients with regurgitation than without. However, routine antibiotic prophylaxis is not recommended.
- TIA or stroke caused by embolic phenomena (from fibrin and platelet thrombi) in patients with thickened leaflets; risk in young patients is <0.05% per year. If present, aspirin (75-325 mg) is indicated for secondary prevention.

- Cardiac arrhythmias (the vast majority are supraventricular and benign)
- Sudden death (rare); most often associated with acute flail leaflets or caused by ventricular arrhythmias associated with other structural heart disease
- The incidence of complications of MVP is very low (<1% per year) if mitral leaflet thickness is ≤0.5 mm, in young patients <45 yr, and in the absence of mitral systolic murmur or MR on Doppler echocardiography. Table 1M-25 describes predictors of clinical outcome in mitral valve prolapse.
- Risk factors that predict higher risk of complications are presence of moderate to severe MR, LV ejection fraction <50%, LA dimension >40 mm, age >50 years

SURGICAL REFERRAL

Surgical referral may be necessary in patients who develop progressive MR with surgical indications as per guidelines for valvular heart disease (see topic on mitral regurgitation).

 **PEARLS & CONSIDERATIONS**

COMMENTS

- Recent studies suggest that the prevalence of MVP and its propensity to cause symptoms and serious complications have been overestimated in the past.
- The relationship between MVP syndrome and sudden cardiac death is unclear, and the best evidence suggests that there is only a slight risk in subsets of patients with MVP who have severe MR, severe valvular deformity, complex ventricular arrhythmias, QT prolongation, and a history of syncope.
- Asymptomatic patients with MVP and mild or no MR can be evaluated clinically every 3 to 5 yr. High-risk patients (those with symptoms, arrhythmias, or significant regurgitation) should undergo a follow-up examination once a year.
- In 2007, the AHA guidelines for prevention of infectious endocarditis were revised and prophylactic antibiotics are no longer recommended for patients with MVP without previous endocarditis.

PATIENT & FAMILY EDUCATION

www.themitralvalve.org

SUGGESTED READINGS

Available at www.expertconsult.com

RELATED CONTENT

Mitral Valve Prolapse (Patient Information)

AUTHORS: **AMANDA C. DORAN, M.D., PH.D.,** and **JOHN V. WYLIE, M.D.**

BASIC INFORMATION

DEFINITION

Molar pregnancy is a premalignant gestational disorder. Molar pregnancies are classified as complete or partial based on morphologic and pathologic examination. Both complete and partial molar pregnancies have an abnormal placenta with enlargement and swelling of the chorionic villi and hyperplasia of the villous trophoblastic cells. Most molar pregnancies are complete and are characterized by generalized hydropic villous changes with no fetal tissue. Partial moles are characterized by a mixture of large hydropic villi and normal placental tissue and often have fetal tissue present. The risk of malignant sequelae (gestational trophoblastic neoplasia) for a complete mole is 18% to 29% and for a partial mole is 0% to 11%.

SYNONYMS

Hydatidiform mole
Gestational trophoblastic disease

ICD-10CM CODES
001.0 Classical hydatidiform mole
001.1 Incomplete and partial hydatidiform mole
001.9 Hydatidiform mole, unspecified

EPIDEMIOLOGY & DEMOGRAPHICS

INCIDENCE: 0.57 to 2/1000 pregnancies with wide regional variation
PREDOMINANT SEX AND AGE: Females of reproductive age, highest rates at extremes of reproductive ages
RISK FACTORS: Extremes of reproductive age (<21 and >40 yr), previous molar pregnancy, history of spontaneous abortion

PHYSICAL FINDINGS & CLINICAL PRESENTATION

Complete molar pregnancy:
- 80% to 90% present with vaginal bleeding at 6 to 16 wk gestational age
- 28% with uterine enlargement greater than expected for gestational age
- 8% with hyperemesis gravidarum
- 1% with gestational hypertension in the first or second trimester
- 15% with bilateral theca lutein cysts
- 15% will have a beta hCG >100,000 mIU/mL

Partial molar pregnancy:
- 90% present with an incomplete or missed abortion
- 75% present with vaginal bleeding
- <10% will have a beta hCG of >100,000 mIU/mL

ETIOLOGY

Complete molar pregnancy
- Fertilization of an oocyte with absent or inactive maternal chromosomes and duplication of paternal chromosomes (90% are 46, XX) or fertilization of an empty oocyte with 2 sperm (46, XY or XX)
- Uniform villous enlargement and no development of a fetus

Partial molar pregnancy
- Fertilization of a normal oocyte with 2 sperm (usually 69, XXY)
- Focal villous edema with identifiable fetus

DIAGNOSIS

DIFFERENTIAL DIAGNOSIS

Complete mole, partial mole, ectopic pregnancy, abortion (incomplete or spontaneous), normal intrauterine pregnancy

WORKUP
- Pelvic exam to evaluate for uterine size and bleeding
- Blood pressure to assess for gestational hypertension or preeclampsia (systolic blood pressure >140 or diastolic blood pressure >90)

- Fig. 1M-40 describes an algorithm for the diagnosis and management of molar pregnancy

LABORATORY TESTS
- Quantitative beta human chorionic growth hormone (beta hCG); significantly elevated levels >100,000 will raise suspicion for molar pregnancy
- Complete blood count (CBC) to assess for acute anemia from vaginal bleeding
- Comprehensive metabolic panel to evaluate for renal or liver disease
- TSH to evaluate for hyperthyroidism
- Urinalysis for proteinuria to evaluate for preeclampsia
- Type and screen to evaluate Rh and to prepare for surgery

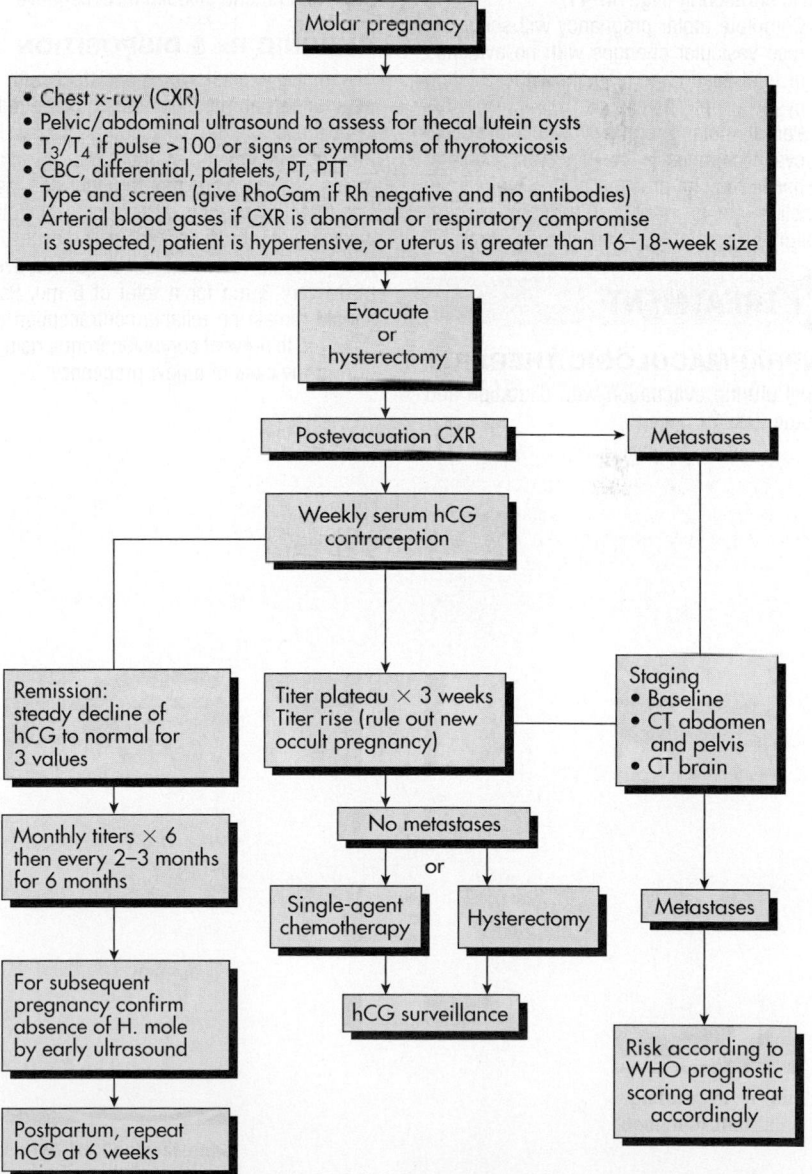

FIGURE 1M-40 Algorithm for the management of molar pregnancy. (From Copeland LJ: Gestational trophoblastic neoplasia. In Copeland LJ (ed): *Textbook of gynecology*, ed 2, Philadelphia, 2000, WB Saunders.) (From Gabbe SG: *Obstetrics*, ed 6, Philadelphia, 2012, WB Saunders.)

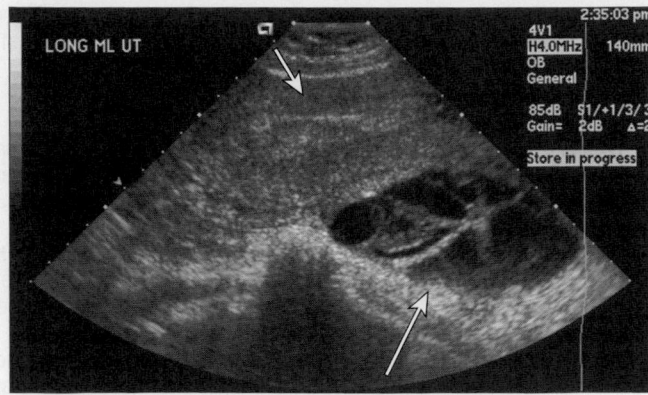

FIGURE 1M-41 Endovaginal ultrasound of the theca lutein cyst with early molar pregnancy. Note enlarged anechoic cystic spaces within the ovary *(arrows)*. (From Fielding JR et al: *Gynecology imaging,* Philadelphia, 2011, Saunders.)

IMAGING STUDIES

- Pelvic ultrasound (Fig. 1M-41)
  1. Complete molar pregnancy will show diffuse vesicular changes with no evidence of fetal tissue and may show theca lutein cysts
  2. Partial molar pregnancy will show focal cystic changes in the placenta and fetal tissue may be present
- Baseline chest x-ray to use for comparison if malignant trophoblastic disease develops

 **TREATMENT**

NONPHARMACOLOGIC THERAPY

Surgical uterine evacuation with dilatation and curettage (D&C)

ACUTE GENERAL Rx

D&C, Rh immune globulin if Rh negative

CHRONIC Rx & DISPOSITION

If pathology results are consistent with complete or partial mole, patients must be followed to evaluate for trophoblastic neoplasia. 15% to 20% of complete moles and 1% to 5% of partial moles will develop into trophoblastic neoplasia. Quantitative beta hCG should be followed weekly until three consecutive results show normal levels. After that, check quantitative beta hCG every 3 mo for a total of 6 mo. Patients should remain on reliable contraception during this time to prevent confusion from a rising beta hCG in the case of a new pregnancy.

REFERRAL

- If there is concern for a molar pregnancy, the patient should be managed by a gynecologist for uterine evacuation and follow-up.
- If there is a plateau or rise of the beta hCG during follow-up, the patient should be referred to a gynecologic oncologist for treatment with chemotherapy.

SUGGESTED READINGS

Available at www.expertconsult.com

RELATED CONTENT

Spontaneous Miscarriage (Related Key Topic)
Vaginal Bleeding During Pregnancy (Related Key Topic)

AUTHOR: **LAUREN ROTH, M.D.**

BASIC INFORMATION

DEFINITION
Molluscum contagiosum is a poxvirus infection characterized by discrete skin lesions with central umbilication.

SYNONYMS
MC

ICD-10CM CODES
B08.1 Molluscum contagiosum

EPIDEMIOLOGY & DEMOGRAPHICS
• Molluscum contagiosum spreads by autoinoculation, scratching, or touching a lesion.
• It usually occurs in young children. It is also common in sexually active adults and patients with HIV infection.
• Incubation period varies between 4 and 8 wk.
• Spontaneous resolution in immunocompetent patients can occur after several months.

PHYSICAL FINDINGS & CLINICAL PRESENTATION
• The individual lesion appears initially as a small (2-3 mm), flesh-colored, firm, smooth-surfaced papule with subsequent central umbilication. Lesions are frequently grouped (Fig. 1M-42). The size of each lesion generally varies from 2 to 6 mm in diameter.
• Typical distribution in children involves the face, extremities, and trunk. Mucous membranes are spared.
• Distribution in adults generally involves pubic and genital areas.

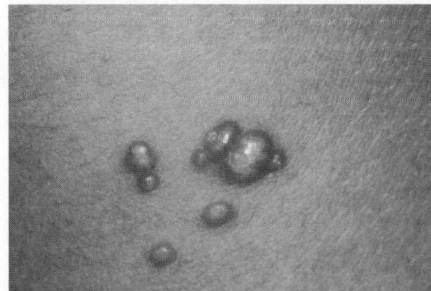

FIGURE 1M-42 Grouped molluscum. (From Kliegman RM et al: *Nelson textbook of pediatrics,* ed 19, Philadelphia, 2011, Saunders.)

• Erythema and scaling at the periphery of the lesions may be present as a result of scratching or hypersensitivity reaction.
• Lesions are not present on the palms and soles.

ETIOLOGY
Viral infection of epithelial cells caused by a poxvirus, molluscum contagiosum

DIAGNOSIS

Diagnosis is usually established by the clinical appearance of the lesions (distribution and central umbilication). A magnifying lens can be used to observe the central umbilication. If necessary, the diagnosis can be confirmed by removing a typical lesion with a curette and examining the content on a slide after adding potassium hydroxide and gentle heating. Staining with toluidine blue will identify viral inclusions.

DIFFERENTIAL DIAGNOSIS
• Verruca plana (flat warts): no central umbilication, not dome shaped, irregular surface, can involve palms and soles
• Herpes simplex: lesions become rapidly umbilicated
• Varicella: blisters and vesicles are present
• Folliculitis: no central umbilication, presence of hair piercing the pustule or papule
• Cutaneous cryptococcosis in AIDS patients: budding yeasts will be present on cytologic examination of the lesions
• Basal cell carcinoma: multiple lesions are absent
• Cellulitis

WORKUP
Careful examination of the papules

LABORATORY TESTS
Generally not indicated in children. Screening for other sexually transmitted diseases is recommended in all cases of genital molluscum contagiosum.

TREATMENT

GENERAL THERAPY
• Therapy is individualized depending on number of lesions, immune status, and patient's age and preference.

• Observation for spontaneous resolution is reasonable in patients with few, small, nonirritated, and nonspreading lesions. Genital lesions should be treated in all sexually active patients.
• Liquid nitrogen cryotherapy
• Carbon dioxide laser
• Curettage after pretreatment of the area with combination prilocaine 2.5% with lidocaine 2.5% cream (EMLA) for anesthesia is useful for treatment of a few lesions. Curettage should be avoided in cosmetically sensitive areas because scarring may develop.
• Treatments with liquid nitrogen therapy in combination with curettage are effective in older patients who do not object to some discomfort.
• Application of cantharidin 0.7% to individual lesions covered with clear tape will result in blistering over 24 hr and possible clearing without scarring. This medication should be avoided on facial lesions.
• Other treatment measures include use of imiquimod cream or tretinoin 0.025% gel or 0.1% cream at bedtime, daily use of salicylic acid (Occlusal) at bedtime, and use of laser therapy.
• Trichloroacetic acid peel generally repeated every 2 wk for several weeks is useful in immunocompromised patients with extensive lesions.

DISPOSITION
Most patients respond well to the therapeutic modalities listed previously. Spontaneous resolution can occur after 6 to 9 mo in some immunocompetent patients.

REFERRAL
To dermatology when diagnosis is in doubt or in patients with extensive lesions

PEARLS & CONSIDERATIONS

COMMENTS
Genital molluscum contagiosum in children may be indicative of sexual abuse.

RELATED CONTENT
Molluscum Contagiosum (Patient Information)

AUTHOR: **FRED F. FERRI, M.D.**

BASIC INFORMATION

DEFINITION

The plasma cell disorders are characterized by the monoclonal expansions of plasma cells that produce monoclonal immunoglobulin or immunoglobulin fragments. The term "monoclonal gammopathy of undetermined significance" (MGUS) is defined by the presence of a serum monoclonal (M) protein less than 3 g/dL and clonal plasma cells less than 10% in the bone marrow. In addition, there must be no evidence of end organ dysfunctions such as renal insufficiency, anemia, hypercalcemia, or bony lesions on skeletal surveys (Table 1M-27).

SYNONYMS

- MGUS
- Non-IgM MGUS
- IgM MGUS
- Light chain MGUS

ICD-10CM CODES
D47.2 Monoclonal gammopathy of undetermined significance (MGUS)

EPIDEMIOLOGY & DEMOGRAPHICS

INCIDENCE: In the U.S., the estimated age-adjusted incidence of MGUS is higher in men than in women. The annual incidence of MGUS in men is 120 per 100,000 population at age 50 yr and increases to 530 per 100,000 population at age 80 yr. The incidence for women is lower at 60 per 100,000 population at age 50 yr and 370 per 100,000 population at age 80 yr.
PREVALENCE: The prevalence of MGUS is associated with increased age, with approximately 1.5% of persons older than 50 yr of age and 3.0% of persons older than 70 yr of age have an elevated M protein level without end organ dysfunctions. Studies have shown that when first clinically recognized, MGUS is most likely to have been present undetected for a median duration of more than 10 yr. The prevalence of MGUS is also higher in African Americans. In one study from North Carolina, there was an almost threefold increase in prevalence among the African American population at 8.6% versus 3.6% among the Caucasian population.
PREDOMINANT SEX AND AGE: Median age of diagnosis is about 70 yr of age. Prevalence is higher in men than in women at any given age.
RISK FACTORS: Race (African American), older age, male sex, or exposure to pesticides. Also, shared environmental and/or genetic defects play an important role, since the relative risk of MGUS in relatives of mul-

tiple myeloma or MGUS patients is increased twofold to threefold. The risk of progression into multiple myeloma or related disorders is 1% per year.

PHYSICAL FINDINGS & CLINICAL PRESENTATION

- MGUS typically is detected after a routine blood test reveals an elevated total protein concentration and is a common finding in medical practice.
- Patients are asymptomatic.
- Physical exam is normal.

ETIOLOGY

- Unknown mechanism. The cause of malignant transformation of MGUS into multiple myeloma is still not well understood. The variety of factors include genetic changes, cytokine releases, and bone marrow angiogenesis, all of which may play a role in the progression of MGUS to multiple myeloma.
- Characterized by a rearrangement of immunoglobulin genes resulting in the production of a monoclonal protein.

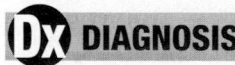 **DIAGNOSIS**

DIFFERENTIAL DIAGNOSIS

- Smoldering myeloma (Table E1M-28)
- Multiple myeloma
- Waldenström's agammaglobulinemic
- Secondary monoclonal gammopathies
  - Chronic liver disease
  - Rheumatologic diseases
  - Chronic myelomonocytic leukemia
  - Chronic neutrophilic leukemia
  - Lichen myxedematosus
- Pyoderma gangrenosum

LABORATORY TESTS

- Protein studies:
- Serum protein electrophoresis (Fig. E1M-43)
  - IgG most common, followed by IgM and IgA
- 24-hour urine protein excretion and urine electrophoresis
- Serum and urine immunofixation
- Determination of serum free light chain ratio (kappa and lambda free light chains)
- Hemoglobin
- Serum calcium and creatinine
- Examination of the bone marrow aspirate only when clinically indicated

IMAGING STUDIES

- Skeletal survey
- Bone mineral density resting at baseline (MGUS is associated with increased risk of osteoporosis)

 **TREATMENT**

1. Risk stratification
   - Low risk: serum M protein <1.5 g/dL, IgG subtype, normal genetics, free light chain ratio between 0.26 and 1.65. Absolute risk of progression (ARP) at 20 years is 5%.
   - Low-intermediate risk: any 1 factor abnormal. ARP at 20 years is 21%.
   - High-intermediate risk: any 2 factors abnormal. ARP at 20 years is 37%.
   - High risk: more than 3 factors abnormal. ARP at 20 years is 58%.
2. Follow-up by risk category
   - Patients with MGUS should be tested again within 4 to 6 mo from the time of first diagnosis to exclude evolving multiple myeloma. Those with low-risk MGUS can be followed up every 2 to 3 yr, whereas those with intermediate or high risk MGUS need to be followed up at least annually for life or until they develop a life-expectancy-threatening condition.
3. Reevaluation consists of:
   - serum protein–serum electrophoresis
   - 24-hour urine protein excretion
   - Hemoglobin
   - Serum creatinine and calcium
   - Careful history and physical examination to look for signs and symptoms known to evolve from MGUS

DISPOSITION

- Risk of myeloma at 25 yr is 30%.
- Annual risk of transformation to myeloma depends on type of M protein:
  - Immunoglobulin MGUS: 1% per year
  - Light-chain MGUS: 0.3% per year
- Risk of infection (bacterial and viral) is twofold compared with healthy controls
- Increased risk of mortality from bacterial infections

REFERRAL

To hematologist/oncologist for evaluation

! **PEARLS & CONSIDERATIONS**

- Approximately 55% of 70-yr-old patients diagnosed as having MGUS have had the condition for more than 10 yr.
- Most patients with MGUS should be monitored every 6 to 12 mo for signs and symptoms of progression.
- There is no indicated treatment.

SUGGESTED READINGS
Available at www.expertconsult.com

AUTHORS: **DONNY V. HUYNH, M.D.,** and **BHARTI RATHORE, M.D.**

TABLE 1M-27 Disease Definitions for the Monoclonal Gammopathies: MGUS and Related Disorders

Type of Monoclonal Gammopathy	Premalignancy with a Low Risk of Progression (1%-2% per year)	Premalignancy with a High Risk of Progression (10% per year)	Malignancy
IgG and IgA (non-IgM) monoclonal gammopathies*	**Non-IgM MGUS** All 3 criteria must be met: Serum monoclonal protein <3 g/dl Clonal bone marrow plasma cells <10%, and Absence of end-organ damage such as hypercalcemia, renal insufficiency, anemia, and bone lesions (CRAB) that can be attributed to the plasma cell proliferative disorder	**Smoldering multiple myeloma** Both criteria must be met: Serum monoclonal protein (IgG or IgA) ≥3 g/dl and/or clonal bone marrow plasma cells ≥10%, and Absence of end-organ damage such as lytic bone lesions, anemia, hypercalcemia, or renal failure that can be attributed to a plasma cell proliferative disorder	**Multiple myeloma** All 3 criteria must be met except as noted: Clonal bone marrow plasma cells ≥10% Presence of serum and/or urinary monoclonal protein (except in patients with true nonsecretory multiple myeloma), and Evidence of end-organ damage that can be attributed to the underlying plasma cell proliferative disorder, specifically Hypercalcemia: serum calcium >11.5 mg/dL or Renal insufficiency: serum creatinine >2 mg/dL or estimated creatinine clearance <40 mL/min Anemia: normochromic, normocytic with a hemoglobin value of >2 g/dL below the lower limit of normal or a hemoglobin value <10 g/dL Bone lesions: lytic lesions or severe osteopenia attributed to a plasma cell proliferative disorder or pathologic fractures
IgM monoclonal gammopathies	**IgM MGUS†** All 3 criteria must be met: Serum monoclonal protein <3 g/dl Clonal bone marrow lymphoplasmacytic cells <10%, and Absence of end-organ damage such as anemia, constitutional symptoms, hyperviscosity, lymphadenopathy, or hepatosplenomegaly that can be attributed to the underlying lymphoproliferative disorder	**Smoldering Waldenström macroglobulinemia** Both criteria must be met: Serum IgM monoclonal protein ≥3 g/dl and/or bone marrow lymphoplasmacytic infiltration ≥10%, and No evidence of anemia, constitutional symptoms, hyperviscosity, lymphadenopathy, or hepatosplenomegaly that can be attributed to the underlying lymphoproliferative disorder	**Waldenström macroglobulinemia** All criteria must be met: IgM monoclonal gammopathy (regardless of the size of the M-protein), and ≥10% bone marrow lymphoplasmacytic infiltration (usually intratrabecular) by small lymphocytes that exhibit plasmacytoid or plasma cell differentiation and a typical immunophenotype (e.g., surface IgM+, CD5+/–, CD10–, CD19+, CD20+, CD23–) that satisfactorily excludes other lymphoproliferative disorders including chronic lymphocytic leukemia and mantle cell lymphoma Evidence of anemia, constitutional symptoms, hyperviscosity, lymphadenopathy, or hepatosplenomegaly that can be attributed to the underlying lymphoproliferative disorder. **IgM myeloma** All criteria must be met: Symptomatic monoclonal plasma cell proliferative disorder characterized by a serum IgM monoclonal protein regardless of size Presence of 10% plasma cells on bone marrow biopsy Presence of lytic bone lesions related to the underlying plasma cell disorder and/or translocation t(11;14) on fluorescence in situ hybridization.
Light-chain monoclonal gammopathies	**Light-chain MGUS** All criteria must be met: Abnormal FLC ratio (<0.26 or >1.65) Increased level of the appropriate involved light-chain (increased kappa FLC in patients with ratio >1.65 and increased lambda FLC in patients with ratio <0.26) No immunoglobulin heavy-chain expression or immunofixation Clonal bone marrow plasma cells <10%, and Absence of end-organ damage such as hypercalcemia, renal insufficiency, anemia, and bone lesions (CRAB) that can be attributed to the plasma cell proliferative disorder	**Idiopathic Bence-Jones proteinuria** All criteria must be met: Urinary monoclonal protein or urine protein electrophoresis ≥500 mg/24 h and/or clonal bone marrow plasma cells ≥10% No immunoglobulin heavy-chain expression on immunofixation Absence of end-organ damage such as hypercalcemia, renal insufficiency, anemia, and bone lesions (CRAB) that can be attributed to the plasma cell proliferative disorder	**Light-chain multiple myeloma†** Same as multiple myeloma except no evidence of immunoglobulin heavy-chain expression

FLC, Free light chain; MGUS, monoclonal gammopathy of undetermined significance.

*Occasionally patients with IgD and IgE monoclonal gammopathies have been described and will be considered to be part of this category as well.

†Note that conventionally IgM MGUS is considered a subtype of MGUS, and similarly light-chain multiple myeloma is considered as a subtype of multiple myeloma. Unless specifically distinguished, when the terms MGUS and multiple myeloma are used in general, they include IgM MGUS and light-chain multiple myeloma, respectively.

From Rajkumar SV et al: Advances in the diagnosis, classification, risk stratification, and management of monoclonal gammopathy of undetermined significance: implications for recategorizing disease entities in the presence of evolving scientific evidence, *Mayo Clin Proc* 85(10):945-948, 2010.

M

Diseases and Disorders

BASIC INFORMATION

DEFINITION

Mononucleosis is a symptomatic infection most commonly caused by Epstein-Barr virus (EBV) and characterized by fever, tonsillar pharyngitis, and lymphadenopathy.

SYNONYMS

IM
Infectious mononucleosis (IM)
EBV

ICD-10CM CODES
B27 Infections mononucleosis
B27.0 Gamma herpesviral mononucleosis
B27.1 Cytomegaloviral mononucleosis
B27.8 Other infectious mononucleosis
B27.9 Infectious mononucleosis

EPIDEMIOLOGY & DEMOGRAPHICS

INCIDENCE (IN U.S.): 500 cases/100,000 persons/yr. Worldwide, approximately 95% of adults are infected with EBV at some point in life.
PREDOMINANT SEX: Incidence is the same, but occurs earlier in females.
PREDOMINANT AGE: Most common between the ages of 15 and 24 yr.

PHYSICAL FINDINGS & CLINICAL PRESENTATION

- Following an incubation period of 1 to 2 mo, a prodrome may occur, with fever, chills, malaise, and anorexia for several days. This is followed by the classic triad, which includes pharyngitis, fever, and adenopathy. Although fatigue and malaise may be prominent, pharyngitis is usually the most severe symptom. Tonsillitis with marked tonsillar exudates is common.
- Lymphadenopathy is most prominent in the cervical region but may be diffuse.
- Splenomegaly may occur, most commonly during the second wk of illness.
- Rash is uncommon but will occur in nearly all patients who receive ampicillin or amoxicillin.
- At times, IM can present as fever and adenopathy without pharyngitis. Although complications may be severe, they are uncommon and tend to resolve completely. Involvement of the hematologic, pulmonary, cardiac, or nervous system may occur; splenic rupture is rare. IM is usually a self-limited illness, but symptoms of malaise and fatigue may last months before resolving.
- Children are at the highest risk of airway obstruction. This is the most common cause of hospitalization from IM.

ETIOLOGY

The most common cause of IM is primary infection with EBV. Cytomegalovirus (CMV) can cause a similar disease syndrome, but CMV infection often occurs in infancy or early childhood and is minimally symptom-atic. Primary EBV infection during childhood also often causes few or no symptoms; persistent fatigue and recurrent/persistent fevers are the most common reasons parents bring symptomatic children to medical care. Infection during childhood is more common in lower socioeconomic groups. The frequency of IM in late adolescence is attributed to the onset of social contact between the sexes. Close personal contact is usually necessary for transmission. Transfer via saliva while kissing may be responsible for many cases. EBV can persist in the oropharynx of patients with IM for up to 18 mo. Transmission may also occur sexually as EBV can be isolated in cervical epithelial cells and male seminal fluid and can also be transmitted by blood transfusion.

DIAGNOSIS

DIFFERENTIAL DIAGNOSIS

- Heterophile-negative IM caused by cytomegalovirus (CMV)
- Bacterial and viral causes of pharyngitis
- Toxoplasmosis
- Acute retroviral syndrome of HIV, lymphoma

WORKUP

Initial testing consists of heterophile antibody (monospot) and CBC with differential. Fig. E1M-44 illustrates a diagnostic algorithm for EBV infection and IM.

LABORATORY TESTS

- A heterophile anitbody test is the best initial test for diagnosis of EBV infection (71% to 90% accuracy for diagnosing IM). However, the test has a 25% false negative rate in the first week of illness.
- Increased WBC is common, with a relative lymphocytosis and neutropenia. Atypical lymphocytes (Fig. E1M-45) are the hallmark of IM, but are not pathognomonic. Mild thrombocytopenia is common. A falling hematocrit may signal splenic rupture or severe immune-mediated hemolytic anemia. Elevated hepatocellular enzymes and cryoglobulins occur in many cases. Heterophile antibody, as measured by the monospot test, may be positive at presentation, or may appear later in the course of illness. A negative test should be repeated if clinical suspicion is high; negative results are common in patients symptomatic for <2 wk and children <4 yr. If this test remains negative for 8 wk, other causes of IM are likely. The monospot usually remains positive for 3 to 6 mo, but can last for 1 yr.
- In addition to the heterophile antibody, virus-specific antibodies may result in response to IM. Determination of these EBV-specific antibodies is rarely necessary to diagnose IM, although early diagnosis in monospot negative cases may be made by isolating IgM to the viral capsid antigen, which is usually positive during the acute illness.

IMAGING STUDIES

Chest x-ray may rarely show infiltrates. An elevated left hemidiaphragm may occur in cases of splenic rupture.

TREATMENT

NONPHARMACOLOGIC THERAPY

- Supportive rest is advocated by some, but effect on outcome is not clear.
- Splenectomy if rupture occurs; transfusions for severe anemia or thrombocytopenia

GENERAL Rx

- Pharmacologic therapy is not indicated in uncomplicated illness.
- The use of steroids (Fig. E1M-46) is suggested in patients who have severe thrombocytopenia or hemolytic anemia, or impending airway obstruction as a result of enlarged tonsils. Prednisone, 60 to 80 mg PO qid for 3 days, then tapered over 1 to 2 wk. Dexamethasone may also be used for severe tonsillar enlargement. There is no role for antiviral agents such as acyclovir in the management of IM.

CHRONIC Rx

A rare, chronic form of IM with persistent organ infection and inflammation has been described. This should not be confused with chronic fatigue syndrome, which is unrelated to EBV.

DISPOSITION

Eventual resolution of all symptoms is the rule.

PEARLS & CONSIDERATIONS

COMMENTS

- Contact sports should be avoided during the first month of illness, because splenic rupture can occur, even in the absence of clinically detectable splenomegaly.
- Between 30% and 75% of college freshmen are seronegative for EBV. Each year nearly 20% of susceptible persons become infected and up to 50% of these persons develop IM.

SUGGESTED READINGS
Available at www.expertconsult.com

RELATED CONTENT
Mononucleosis (Patient Information)
Epstein-Barr Virus Infection (Related Key Topic)

AUTHOR: **RUSSELL J. MCCULLOH, M.D.**

BASIC INFORMATION

DEFINITION

Morton neuroma is a common cause of forefoot pain that is caused by entrapment or thickening of one of the common plantar digital nerves leading to the toes. Morton neuroma manifests as pain in the plantar aspect of the forefoot, often localized between the metatarsal heads.

SYNONYMS

Morton metatarsalgia
Interdigital neuroma
Plantar neuroma
Metatarsal neuralgia
Morton's neuroma

ICD-10CM CODES
G57.6 Lesion of plantar nerve
G57.8 Other mononeuropathies of lower limb
G57.9 Mononeuropathy of lower limb, unspecified

EPIDEMIOLOGY & DEMOGRAPHICS

- Morton neuroma affects one of the common plantar digital nerves located at any of the four interspaces of the foot.
  1. It most commonly affects the third common plantar digital proper nerve, located in the third interspace.
  2. It occurs most frequently in patients who wear tight-fitting, high-heeled shoes.
- Morton neuroma is usually unilateral.
- The condition occurs most frequently in women.
- It usually presents between the fourth and sixth decade of life.

PHYSICAL FINDINGS & CLINICAL PRESENTATION

- Patients with Morton neuroma will present complaining of pain in the plantar aspect of the foot, typically localized between the metatarsal heads of the affected interspace.
- The pain may be described as stabbing, burning, tingling, or "electric" and may radiate to the digits.
- The pain is exacerbated by the use of tight-fitting shoes. Patients often feel as though they are walking on a marble.
- The pain can often be recreated by applying pressure at the plantar aspect of the inter space, starting just proximal to the metatarsal heads and proceeding distally.
- Mulder's sign: compression of the forefoot at the level of the metatarsophalangeal joints combined with plantar pressure at the affected interspace elicits a palpable "click."

ETIOLOGY

- Morton neuroma is considered to be an entrapment neuropathy of the affected common digital plantar nerve (Fig. 1M-47). The etiology remains obscure.
- The common plantar digital nerves are branches of the medial plantar nerve that course distally to supply the digits of the foot, passing just beneath the deep transverse intermetatarsal ligament. The third common plantar nerve is often supplied by a communicating branch of the lateral plantar nerve. This anatomic variation results in a thicker nerve that is more prone to trauma, a reason often cited to explain the prevalence of Morton neuroma in the third common plantar digital nerve.

- The deep transverse intermetatarsal ligament may also be implicated in the cause of a neuroma. If it is thickened or has aberrant bands, it may cause compression of the affected nerve.
- Soft tissue masses, such as a plantar lipoma, may also cause compression of the nerve against the ligament, leading to the formation of a neuroma.
- Histologic examination of resected Morton neuroma exhibits increased neural width, demyelination, intraneural fibrosis, and thickened endoneural capillaries.

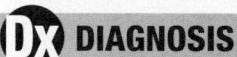 **DIAGNOSIS**

The diagnosis of Morton neuroma is primarily clinical. Laboratory tests and imaging modalities are generally not necessary.

DIFFERENTIAL DIAGNOSIS

- Peripheral neuropathy
- Tarsal tunnel syndrome
- Metatarsal stress fracture
- Freiberg's infraction
- Metatarsophalangeal joint capsulitis or bursal swelling
- Osteoarthritis
- Rheumatoid arthritis

WORKUP

Exclude other causes mentioned in "Differential Diagnosis."

IMAGING STUDIES

Weight bearing radiographs may be performed to exclude other pathologic conditions.
- MRI may be used to detect and localize a neuroma. The mass is best visualized on a T1-weighted image.
  1. MRI may be indicated to evaluate patients with recurrent neuromas and atypical symptoms. MRI can help distinguish a neuroma from intermetatarsal bursal swelling or synovitis in adjacent joints.
  2. Ultrasound imaging (Fig. 1M-48) can be used to visualize a neuroma. It will typically present as a hypoechoic mass.

Rx TREATMENT

NONPHARMACOLOGIC THERAPY

- Altering footwear is the first line of treatment.
- Wide shoes with a low heel are recommended.
- A metatarsal pad may also provide relief as it splays the metatarsal heads thereby decreasing the pressure on the neuroma.
- If adequate relief is noted with the above, then orthotics may also be considered.

ACUTE GENERAL Rx

- If conservative measures are unsuccessful, other treatment options include serial injections (Fig. 1M-49) with corticosteroids or a sclerosing agent. The sclerosing solution is commonly composed of bupivacaine and ethyl alcohol.

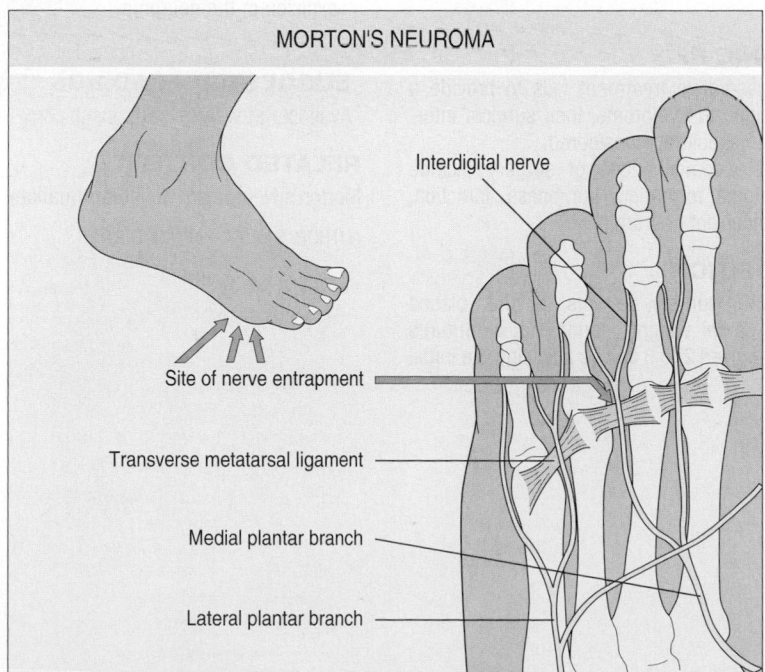

FIGURE 1M-47 Morton's neuroma. On the plantar surface of the foot, the interdigital nerve is compressed below the transverse metatarsal ligament and not between the metatarsal heads (plantar view). (From Hochberg MC et al: *Rheumatology*, ed 5, St Louis, 2011, Mosby.)

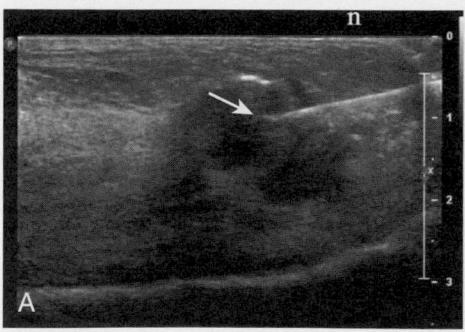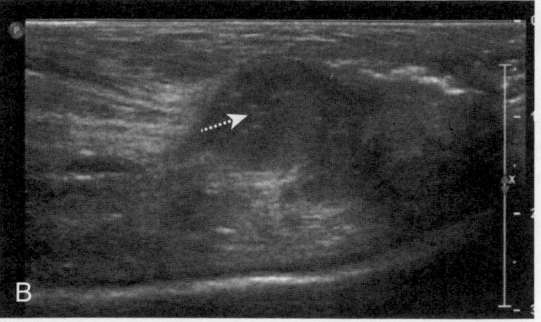

FIGURE 1M-48 Ultrasound-guided injection of a Morton neuroma in the third intermetatarsal space with steroid and anesthetic. Ultrasound image (**A**) shows the needle tip inside the Morton neuroma *(solid arrow)*. Ultrasound image (**B**) immediately following the injection shows multiple punctate echogenic foci within the Morton neuroma *(dashed arrow),* indicating successful injection of the steroid and anesthetic into the lesion. (From Pope TL et al: *Musculoskeletal imaging*, ed 2, Philadelphia, 2014, WB Saunders.)

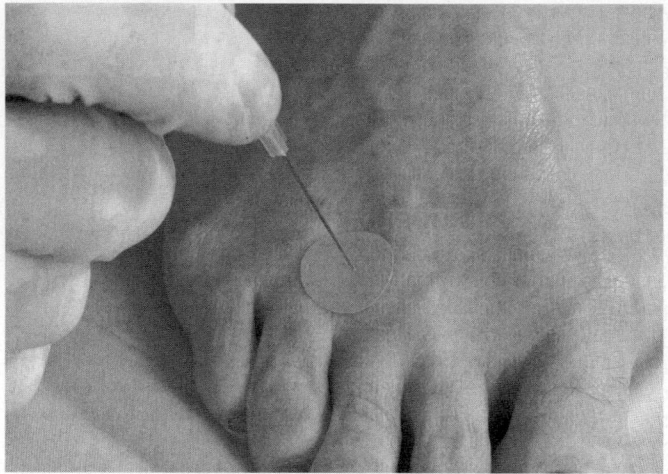

FIGURE 1M-49 Injection for interdigital (Morton) neuroma. The area is most easily injected from the dorsal aspect, usually between the metatarsal heads of the third and fourth toes. The area of tenderness is marked, the needle is inserted to 1 inch, and steroid with anesthetic is injected. (From Firestein GS et al: *Kelly's textbook of rheumatology,* ed 9, Philadelphia, 2013, Saunders.)

Recent trials[1] showed that corticosteroid injection is a reasonable temporizing intervention for some patients with Morton neuroma. Pain relief was, however, limited, and one third of steroid recipients underwent surgery at some point after 3 months.
- Nonsteroidal antiinflammatory agents may also provide relief.

[1]Thomson CE et al: Methylprednisolone injections for the treatment of Morton neuroma: a patient-blinded randomized trial, *J Bone Joint Surg Am* P5:790, 2013.

CHRONIC Rx
- If conservative treatment fails to provide a resolution to symptoms, then surgical intervention should be considered.
- Possible complications of surgery include hematoma formation, numbness, infection, and recurrent neuroma.

DISPOSITION
- Following surgery, patients are often placed on a partial weight-bearing status. Sutures are removed 2 to 3 weeks following the initial surgery. Patients generally return to their previous activity level in 4 to 6 weeks.
- Should a neuroma recur, a second surgical procedure may be performed.

REFERRAL
If surgery is being considered, a consultation with either a podiatrist or a foot and ankle specialized orthopedic surgeon is indicated.

 **PEARLS & CONSIDERATIONS**

COMMENTS
- Dr. Thomas G. Morton is given credit for describing this disorder in 1876.
- Morton neuroma may occur in any of the four interspaces of the foot but most commonly affects the third interspace.
- If conservative treatment and serial injections fail, surgery should be considered for the excision of the neuroma.

SUGGESTED READINGS
Available at www.expertconsult.com

RELATED CONTENT
Morton's Neuroma (Patient Information)

AUTHOR: **SARIKA PARIKH, D.P.M.**

 **BASIC INFORMATION**

DEFINITION

Motion sickness is a clinical syndrome associated with motion or perception of motion. Patients with motion sickness suffer perspiration, nausea, vomiting, increased salivation, and generalized malaise in response to movement.

SYNONYMS

Physiologic vertigo

ICD-10CM CODES
T75.3 Motion sickness

EPIDEMIOLOGY & DEMOGRAPHICS

INCIDENCE (IN U.S.): Common
PEAK INCIDENCE: Any age
PREVALENCE (IN U.S.): Common
PREDOMINANT SEX: Male = female
PREDOMINANT AGE: Any age
GENETICS: Not known to be genetic

PHYSICAL FINDINGS & CLINICAL PRESENTATION

- Vomiting
- Sweating
- Pallor

ETIOLOGY

- Motion (e.g., amusement rides, rides in automobiles or planes)

- Exacerbated by anxiety, fumes (e.g., industrial pollutants), visual stimuli
- Fig. 1M-50 describes a proposed neural pathway resulting in motion sickness

 **DIAGNOSIS**

DIFFERENTIAL DIAGNOSIS

- Acute labyrinthitis
- Gastroenteritis
- Metabolic disorders
- Viral syndrome

WORKUP

None necessary in routine case

 **TREATMENT**

NONPHARMACOLOGIC THERAPY

- Fixate on far object
- Cease motion
- Avoid reading
- Avoid alcohol

ACUTE GENERAL Rx

- Scopolamine patch is most effective. It should be applied to a hairless area behind the ear every 3 days prn. It should be applied >4 hr before antiemetic effect is required.
- Oral promethazine is effective but highly sedating.
- Over-the-counter oral preparations (e.g., Dramamine) are less effective.

- Meclizine 12.5 to 25 mg q6h may be effective but is very sedating.

CHRONIC Rx

- Rarely chronic
- Symptoms generally resolve completely with cessation of motion exposure.

DISPOSITION

Follow-up is not needed.

REFERRAL

If another diagnosis is suspected (e.g., purulent ear, fever, cranial nerve abnormalities)

PEARLS & CONSIDERATIONS

COMMENTS

- Many patients with migraine report having had severe motion sickness as a child.
- Improved ventilation, avoidance of large meals before travel, semirecumbent sitting, and avoidance of reading while in motion will minimize the risk of motion sickness.

SUGGESTED READINGS
Available at www.expertconsult.com

RELATED CONTENT
Motion Sickness (Patient Information)

AUTHOR: **FRED F. FERRI, M.D.**

Diseases and Disorders

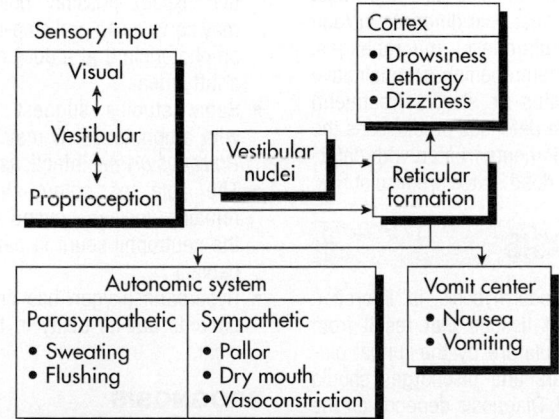

FIGURE 1M-50 Proposed neural pathway resulting in motion sickness. (From Kuhn S.M.: Motion sickness. In Keystone J.S., et al: *Travel medicine*, 2nd ed, Philadelphia, 2008, Elsevier, pp 435–440.)

BASIC INFORMATION

DEFINITION

Mucormycosis is a fungal infection by Zygomycetes fungi and includes species in the order Mucorales (*Rhizopus* sp., *Rhizomucor, Cunninghamella, Apophysomyces, Saksenaea, Absidia, Syncephalastrum, Cokeromyces, Mortierella*) and in the order Entomophthorales (*Conidiobolus* and *Basidiobolus*).

SYNONYMS

Zygomycosis

ICD-10CM CODES

B46.5 Mucormycosis, unspecified
B46.1 Rhinocerebral mucormycosis
B46.0 Pulmonary mucormycosis
B46.3 Cutaneous mucormycosis
B46.4 Disseminated mucormycosis

EPIDEMIOLOGY & DEMOGRAPHICS

- These fungi are ubiquitous in nature and can be found in soil and decaying vegetation. Infection is seen in association with underlying conditions, including diabetes mellitus especially with ketoacidosis, hematologic malignancies, stem cell or solid organ transplants, severe burns or trauma, treatment with deferoxamine or iron overload states, steroid treatment, immunodeficiency states (e.g., AIDS), injection drug use, and malnutrition. Immunocompetent hosts may become infected in tropical climates.
- The fungus gains entry to the body most commonly through the respiratory tract. The spores are deposited in the nasal turbinates and may be inhaled into the pulmonary alveoli. In cases of cutaneous mucormycosis, the spores are introduced directly into the skin lesion.
- After a tornado with winds >200 mph struck Joplin, Missouri, in May 2011, there were 13 confirmed cases of mucormycosis *(Apophysomyces trapeziformis),* including five deaths. While two patients had diabetes, none were immunocompromised. It was felt that the fungus entered through wounds sustained during the tornado. Wooden splinters were found in four patients.

PHYSICAL FINDINGS & CLINICAL PRESENTATION

- The most common presentation is rhinocerebral. Rhinocerebral-rhinoorbital-paranasal syndrome may present with fever, facial and orbital pain, headache, diplopia, loss of vision, facial or orbital cellulitis, facial anesthesia, cranial nerve dysfunction, black nasal discharge, epistaxis, and seizure. Physical findings in this situation include proptosis; chemosis; nasal, palatal, or pharyngeal necrotic ulcerations; and retinal infarction. Thrombosis of the cavernous sinus or internal carotid artery may occur. This form of mucormycosis is found most commonly in diabetics, primarily in the presence of acidosis, and in patients with leukemia and neu-

tropenia. Isolated CNS mucormycosis may result from hematogenous spread (can occur with injection drug users).
- Pulmonary mucormycosis can present with pneumonia, lung abscess, pulmonary infarction, pleurisy, pleural effusion, hemoptysis, chills, and fever. This form of mucormycosis is found most commonly in immunocompromised neutropenic hosts after chemotherapy for hematologic malignancies.
- Gastrointestinal zygomycosis presents with abdominal pain, diarrhea, gastrointestinal hemorrhage, ulcers, peritonitis, and bowel infarction. This form of mucormycosis is found most commonly in patients with extreme malnutrition and is believed to arise from ingestion of spores of the fungi.
- Cutaneous zygomycosis presents as nodular lesions (hematogenous seeding) or a wound infection. It primarily involves the epidermis and dermis after use of occlusive dressings that have not been properly sterilized.
- Cardiac mucormycosis is a form of endocarditis.
- Septic arthritis and osteomyelitis
- Brain abscess occurs most often from extension of the fungus from the nose or paranasal sinuses through adjacent bones in severely debilitated patients.
- Disseminated zygomycosis (rare but uniformly fatal)
- Physical findings depend on the location of the infection.

ETIOLOGY & PATHOGENESIS

The cause of mucormycosis is infection by a fungus of the Zygomycetes class (see "Definition"). Rhizopus and mucor species are the most common causes. Normal host defenses include leukocytes and pulmonary macrophages. Quantitative (e.g., neutropenia) or qualitative (e.g., diabetes mellitus or steroid treatment) disruption in the host defenses predisposes the patient to infection. Patients treated with deferoxamine for iron-overload states are also at risk.

DIAGNOSIS

The hallmark of mucormycosis is infarction and necrosis of host tissues that result from invasion of the vasculature by the fungal elements. Black eschars and discharges should be closely evaluated. Diagnosis depends on the demonstration of the organism in the tissue of a biopsy specimen.

DIFFERENTIAL DIAGNOSIS

- Infection of the sites described previously by other organisms (bacterial [including tuberculosis and leprosy], viral, fungal, or protozoan)
- Noninfectious tissue necrosis (e.g., neoplasia, vasculitis, degenerative) of the sites described previously

WORKUP

- Biopsy of infected tissue with direct-light microscopy examination establishes the diagnosis within minutes of the biopsy in

the case of nasopharyngeal infection. Fungal hyphae are broad (5- to 15-micron diameter) and irregularly branched and have rare septations, in contrast to molds such as *Aspergillus,* which are narrower, have regular branching, and have many septations.
- Bronchoalveolar lavage or bronchoscopy with biopsy for smear, culture, and histologic examination
- Radiographs and other imaging studies such as CT of symptomatic sites may be required before infection is suspected and tissue specimens are obtained.

TREATMENT

Aggressive correction of underlying disease (e.g., hyperglycemia, high steroid doses, use of immunosuppressive drugs) should be undertaken.

Standard therapy consists of aggressive surgical debridement of involved tissues and antifungal therapy. For invasive mucormycosis recommended treatment is with a lipid formulation of amphotericin B that allows higher doses with less nephrotoxicity. The start dose is 5 mg/kg of liposomal amphotericin B or amphotericin B lipid complex. Doses as high as 10 mg/kg have also been used.

Traditional amphotericin B given IV at a daily dose of 1.0 to 1.5 mg/kg infused over 2 to 4 hr daily for a total of 1 to 4 g can also still be used, but is associated with significant nephrotoxicity and adverse reactions such as fever, chills, myalgias, vomiting, and electrolyte disturbances.

- Other antifungals do not appear to be effective except possibly posaconazole, which may serve as an oral step-down therapy after amphotericin B at a dose of 400 mg bid with a fatty meal.
- Some studies suggest that caspofungin with amphotericin B may be synergistic for *Rhizopus oryzae* infections only.
- The role of colony-stimulating factors remains unclear, beyond that of increasing the neutrophil count in patients with neutropenia.
- Hyperbaric oxygen has been used in some patients but its utility in therapy is still not clear.

PROGNOSIS

- Sinus infection with no underlying disease: 75% survival
- Sinus infection with diabetes: 60% survival
- Sinus infection with renal disease: 25% survival

SUGGESTED READINGS

Available at www.expertconsult.com

AUTHOR: **GLENN G. FORT, M.D., M.P.H.**

 **BASIC INFORMATION**

DEFINITION

These are gram-negative bacteria that are resistant to at least one antimicrobial in three or more antimicrobial classes (antipseudomonal penicillins, third-generation cephalosporins, fluoroquinolones, carbapenems, and aminoglycosides).

SYNONYMS

CRE: carbapenem-resistant Enterobacteriaceae
ESBL: extended-spectrum beta-lactamases
MDR-GNB: multidrug-resistant gram-negative bacilli
MDRO: multidrug-resistant organisms
NDM-1: New Delhi metallo-beta-lactamase-1

ICD-10CM CODES
Z16.30 Resistance to unspecified antimicrobial drugs
Z16.10 Resistance to unspecified beta lactam antibiotics

EPIDEMIOLOGY & DEMOGRAPHICS

INCIDENCE: There is an increasing incidence of these bacteria in hospitals and long-term care facilities in the U.S. and around the world. ESBL bacteria were first discovered in Europe in 1984 and in the U.S. in 1988. CRE bacteria were first described in the late 1990s in the U.S. The NDM-1 bacteria were first noted in 2009 in Sweden in a patient from India.
PREDOMINANT SEX AND AGE: These bacteria can be seen in any age group. They may be more frequent in women due to increased risk of urinary tract sepsis.
RISK FACTORS: In general, these bacteria are more common in hospitals and long-term care facilities, but they are spread nosocomially through patient care and thus are now entering the community, where the incidence is also increasing. Specific risk factors include:
- Length of stay in the hospital
- Length of ICU stay
- Use of central line catheters
- Abdominal surgery
- Presence of gastrostomy or jejunostomy tube
- Prior administration of any antibiotic
- Prior residence in a long-term care facility
- Presence of indwelling urinary catheter

ETIOLOGY

- Several different classes of MDR-GNRs exist based on their resistance mechanism.
  1. ESBL: These bacteria contain enzymes that break open the beta-lactam ring of penicillins, cephalosporins, and aztreonam and thus inactivate antibiotics from those classes. Enzymes conferring resistance include:
     1. TEM beta-lactamases
     2. SHV beta-lactamases
     3. CTX-M beta lactamases
     4. OXA beta-lactamases
     5. These enzymes are plasmid-mediated and thus can spread from one gram-negative bacteria to another, causing outbreaks in a single institution.
  2. CRE: Enzymes conferring resistance include:
     1. Class A beta-lactamases: encoded on chromosomes or plasmids (e.g., *Klebsiella pneumoniae* carbapenamase [KPC], which has caused outbreaks in hospitals around the world)
     2. Class B: metallo-beta-lactamases (e.g., New Delhi metallo-beta-lactamase-1). Encoded on a mobile plasmid that can spread to other gram-negative bacteria.
     3. Class C and Class D beta-lactamases
- *Stenotrophomonas maltophilia*: MDR-GNR that acts as an opportunistic pathogen among mostly hospitalized patients with high morbidity and mortality. It has intrinsic or acquired resistance mechanisms to multiple antibiotic classes and has the ability to adhere to foreign materials and form a biofilm, which escapes host defenses.
- *Acinetobacter* sp. (e.g., *Acinetobacter baumannii*): strains have emerged that are resistant to all commercially available antibiotics. These bacteria have the capability to acquire diverse mechanisms of resistance including:
  1. AmpC beta-lactamases
  2. Beta-lactamases: serine and metallo-beta-lactamases

CLINICAL PRESENTATION

All these resistant bacteria have the capability of causing diverse infections, including
- Pneumonia
- Bacteremia
- Urinary tract sepsis
- Central line–associated infections
- Ventilator associated pneumonia (VAP)
- Surgical site infections
  VAP from *A. baumannii* now accounts for 8.4% of GNR pneumonias in the ICU.

 **DIAGNOSIS**

DIFFERENTIAL DIAGNOSIS

Other gram-negative rods such as:
- *Pseudomonas aeruginosa*
- *Klebsiella pneumoniae* that are not ESBL or CRE by resistance pattern
- *Morganella morgani*
- *Providencia, Proteus* sp., *Serratia*

WORKUP

Detection of ESBL and CRE bacteria can pose problems for the clinical microbiology laboratory:
1. To detect ESBL bacteria: automated systems such as Vitek use disk diffusion or broth dilution techniques, or double disk test or E-test strip with clavulanate
2. To detect CRE: modified Hodge test to detect carbapenamase-producing bacteria
3. In 2010, testing guidelines with respect to susceptibility involving several beta-lactam antibiotics were changed to better identify these bacteria via automated systems.

LABORATORY TESTS

Clinical testing is the same in infections from these resistant organisms as with nonresistant organisms:
- Cultures of any wounds, blood, sputum, urine, catheter tips
- CBC, liver function tests, urinalysis

IMAGING STUDIES

Studies depend on the clinical presentation but are similar to those for nonresistant bacteria causing infections.

Rx TREATMENT

Because of multidrug resistance, only a few reliable antibiotics are available to treat these infections.
1. ESBL bacteria: carbapenem antibiotics such as imipenem, meropenem, ertapenem, or the cephalosporin cefoxitin or tigecycline.
2. CRE bacteria: selection of antibiotic will depend on testing but tigecycline may be used clinically. Other alternatives include:
   1. IV colistin
   2. *Stenotrophomonas maltophilia:* only available agents are Bactrim (drug of choice), levaquin, and minocycline
   3. *A. baumannii:* will depend on susceptibility testing, but ampicillin-sulbactam, imipenem or meropenem, or tigecycline can be used for MDR strains. For pan-resistant strains, IV colistin ± rifampin can be used. Inhaled colistin can be used for pneumonia patients.

DISPOSITION

Morbidity and mortality can be quite high with infections from these MDR bacteria.
1. Nosocomial *Acinetobacter* pneumonia carries a mortality rate of 35% to 70%.
2. *Stenotrophomonas* infections carry a mortality rate of 21% to 69%.
3. ESBL infections carry a mortality rate of 3.7% despite therapy with carbapenem antibiotics.

REFERRAL

- Infectious diseases specialist for selection of best antibiotic choice and follow-up
- Microbiologist for specialized testing and interpretation of results
- Pulmonary specialist for severe forms of pneumonia
- Infection control officer to help prevent spread of these bacteria in an institution

SUGGESTED READINGS
Available at www.expertconsult.com

AUTHOR: **GLENN G. FORT, M.D., M.P.H.**

Multifocal Atrial Tachycardia

BASIC INFORMATION

DEFINITION

Multifocal atrial tachycardia (MAT) is a supraventricular, tachyarrhythmia (rate greater than 100 beats/min) with P waves having at least three or more different morphologies and irregular P-P intervals. An isoelectric baseline further differentiates MAT from atrial fibrillation or atrial flutter.

SYNONYMS

Chaotic atrial rhythm
Chronic atrial tachycardia
Repetitive multifocal paroxysmal atrial tachycardia
The term *wandering pacemaker* is used for a similar arrhythmia associated with a normal or slow heart rate (<100 beats/min).

ICD-10CM CODES
I47.1 Supraventricular tachycardia

EPIDEMIOLOGY & DEMOGRAPHICS

Estimated prevalence in hospitalized patients of 0.05% to 0.32%. Average age is 70s. Usually associated with underlying pulmonary disease with right atrial electromechanical delay. Chronic obstructive pulmonary disease (COPD) is present in approximately 55% of patients with MAT.

PHYSICAL FINDINGS & CLINICAL PRESENTATION

Symptoms:
- Palpitation
- Lightheadedness
- Syncope
- Symptoms of the underlying pulmonary disease
- Physical findings associated with the underlying pulmonary disease

ETIOLOGY

- Exact mechanism unknown
- Exacerbated by underlying pulmonary disease (COPD, hypoxia, pulmonary embolism, pneumonia), cardiac disease, hypercarbia, acidosis, electrolyte disturbances

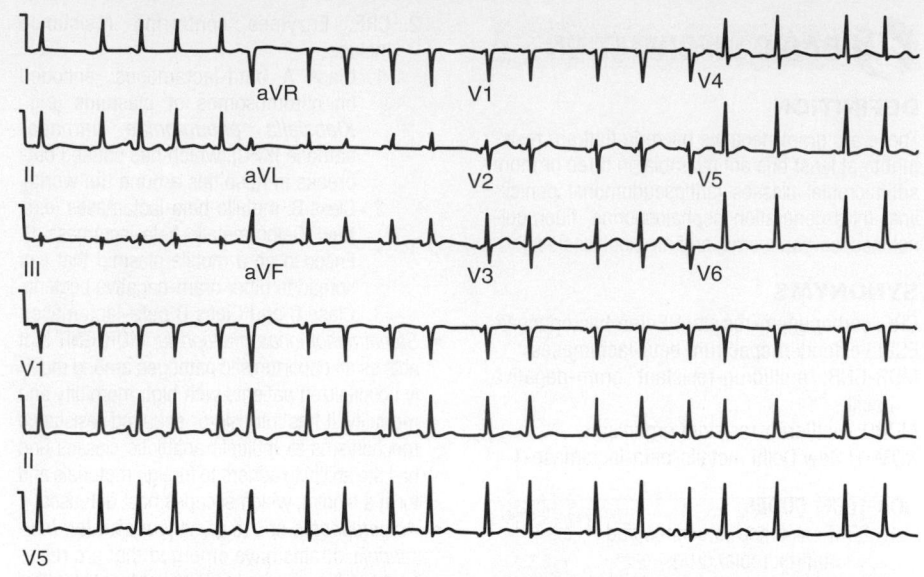

FIGURE 1M-41 Surface ECG of multifocal atrial tachycardia. Note the varying morphology of the P waves and the PR intervals. (From Issa Z et al: *Clinical arrhythmology and electrophysiology,* ed 2, Philadelphia, 2012, Saunders.)

DIAGNOSIS

DIFFERENTIAL DIAGNOSIS

- Atrial fibrillation
- Atrial flutter with variable AV conduction
- Sinus tachycardia
- Paroxysmal atrial tachycardia
- Extrasystole

WORKUP

- ECG (Fig. 1M-41)
- Chest x-ray
- Pulmonary function tests
- Electrolytes
- Arterial blood gases

TREATMENT

- Correction and/or improvement in the underlying pulmonary or metabolic dysfunction if possible and avoiding drugs such as digoxin, theophylline, etc.

- Electrolyte repletion, especially magnesium and potassium, to normal levels
- Calcium channel blockers—verapamil often used as first line in patients with preserved LV function
- β-blockers are typically contraindicated by obstructive lung disease or acute heart failure
- If the arrhythmia is asymptomatic, it can be left untreated
- Direct current cardioversion is ineffective
- No significant role for antiarrhythmics or catheter ablation
- In extreme cases of refractory MAT in symptomatic patients who cannot tolerate medical therapy or in MAT resistant to medical therapy, AV nodal ablation with pacemaker implantation has been performed.

SUGGESTED READINGS
Available at www.expertconsult.com

AUTHORS: **BARRY FINE, M.D., PH.D,** and **JOHN V. WYLIE, M.D.**

 BASIC INFORMATION

DEFINITION

Multiple myeloma (MM) is a plasma cell neoplasm characterized by clonal proliferation of malignant plasma cells in the bone marrow, monoclonal protein in the blood or urine, and associated end-organ dysfunction. Diagnostic criteria for the diagnosis of MM require the following:

1. Presence of ≥10% plasma cells on examination of the bone marrow (or biopsy of a tissue with monoclonal plasma cells).
2. Monoclonal protein in the serum or urine. Occasional patients without detectable monoclonal protein are considered to have nonsecretory myeloma.
3. Evidence of end-organ damage (*c*alcium elevation, *r*enal insufficiency, *a*nemia, or *b*one lesions [CRAB criteria]).

ICD-10CM CODES

C90.00 Multiple myeloma not having achieved remission
C90.01 Multiple myeloma in remission
C90.02 Multiple myeloma in relapse

EPIDEMIOLOGY & DEMOGRAPHICS

ANNUAL INCIDENCE:

- Five cases/100,000 persons (blacks affected twice as frequently as whites, males more than females)
- MM accounts for 10% of all hematologic cancers and is the most common primary bone malignancy.
- An estimated 26,850 new cases and 11,240 deaths will occur in 2015 in the United States.

PREDOMINANT AGE: Peak incidence is in the seventh decade at a median age of 70 yr.

PHYSICAL FINDINGS & CLINICAL PRESENTATION

The patient usually comes to medical attention because of one or more of the following:

- Bone pain (58%) commonly in the back and thorax or pathologic fractures (30%) caused by osteolytic lesions
- Anemia from bone marrow infiltration by plasma cells
- Recurrent infections as a result of impaired neutrophil function and deficiency of normal immunoglobulins (humoral deficiency)
- Nausea and vomiting caused by constipation and uremia
- Delirium resulting from hypercalcemia
- Neurologic complications, such as spinal cord or nerve root compression, blurred vision from hyperviscosity
- Purpura, epistaxis from thrombocytopenia
- Paresthesias, weight loss, generalized weakness

DX **DIAGNOSIS**

DIFFERENTIAL DIAGNOSIS

- Metastatic carcinoma to bone marrow

- Lymphoma, non-Hodgkin's
- Bone neoplasms (e.g., sarcoma)
- Monoclonal gammopathy of undetermined significance
- Primary amyloidosis
- Waldenström's macroglobulinemia
- Table 1M-29 compares diagnostic criteria for multiple myeloma variants and monoclonal gammopathy of unknown significance.

LABORATORY TESTS

- Normochromic, normocytic anemia; rouleaux formation on peripheral smear (Fig. 1M-52)
- Hypercalcemia is present in 15% of patients at diagnosis.
- Elevated blood urea nitrogen, creatinine, uric acid, and total protein

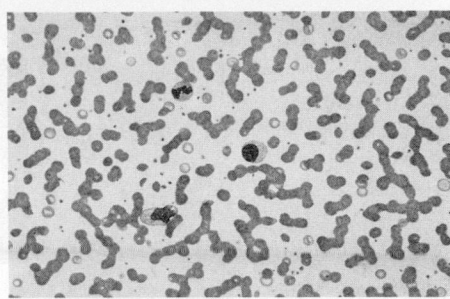

FIGURE 1M-52 Increased rouleaux formation is seen in this blood smear from a patient with a large M protein. Marked rouleaux formation is often a clue to the diagnosis of a plasma cell neoplasm, but may also be observed in other conditions (Wright-Giemsa stain). (From Jaffe ES et al: *Hematopathology,* Philadelphia, 2011, Saunders.)

TABLE 1M-29 Diagnostic Criteria for Multiple Myeloma, Myeloma Variants, and Monoclonal Gammopathy of Unknown Significance

Monoclonal Gammopathy of Undetermined Significance or Monoclonal Gammopathy, Unattributed/Unassociated

M protein in serum <30 g/L
Bone marrow clonal plasma cells <10%
No evidence of other B cell proliferative disorders
No myeloma-related organ or tissue impairment (no end-organ damage, including bone lesions)

Asymptomatic Myeloma (Smoldering Myeloma)

M protein in serum >30 g/L *or*
Bone marrow clonal plasma cell ≥10%
No related organ or tissue impairment (no end-organ damage, including bone lesions) or symptoms

Symptomatic Multiple Myeloma

M protein in serum or urine*
Bone marrow (clonal) plasma cells* or plasmacytoma
Related organ or tissue impairment (end-organ damage, including bone lesions)

Solitary Plasmacytoma of Bone

No M protein in serum or urine†
Single area of bone destruction caused by clonal plasma cells
Bone marrow not consistent with MM
Normal skeletal survey (and MRI of spine and pelvis if done)
No related organ or tissue impairment (no end-organ damage other than solitary bone lesion)†

Nonsecretory Myeloma

No M protein in serum or urine with immunofixation
Bone marrow clonal plasmacytosis ≥10% or plasmacytoma
Related organ or tissue impairment (end-organ damage, including bone lesions)

Extramedullary Plasmacytoma

No M protein in serum or urine†
Extramedullary tumor of clonal plasma cells
Normal bone marrow
Normal skeletal survey
No related organ or tissue impairment (end-organ damage including bone lesions)

Multiple Solitary Plasmacytomas (± Recurrent)

No M protein in serum or urine†
More than one localized area of bone destruction or extramedullary tumor of clonal plasma cells, which may be recurrent
Normal bone marrow
Normal skeletal survey and MRI of spine and pelvis if done
No related organ or tissue impairment (no end-organ damage other than the localized bone lesions)

Myeloma-Related Organ or Tissue Impairment (End-Organ Damage)

Calcium levels increased: serum calcium >0-25 mmol/L above the upper limit of normal or >2-75 mmol/L
Renal insufficiency: creatinine >173 mmol/L
Anemia: hemoglobin 2 g/dl below the lower limit of normal or hemoglobin <10 g/dl
Bone lesions: lytic lesions or osteoporosis with compression fractures (MRI or CT may clarify)
Other: symptomatic hyperviscosity, amyloidosis, recurrent bacterial infections (more than two episodes in 12 months)

*If flow cytometry is performed, most plasma cells (>90%) will show a neoplastic phenotype.
†A small M component may sometimes be present.
CT, Computed tomography; *MM,* multiple myeloma; *MRI,* magnetic resonance imaging.
From Hoffman R et al: *Hematology, basic principles and practice,* ed 6, Philadelphia, 2013, WB Saunders.

Diagnosis

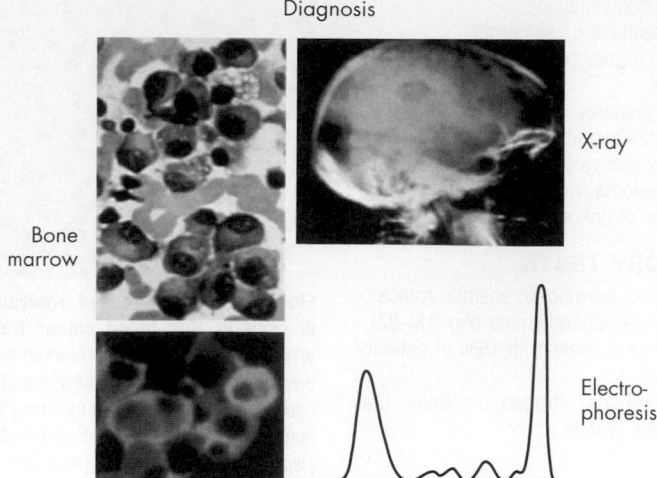

Bone marrow

X-ray

Electro-phoresis

FIGURE 1M-53 Common diagnostic features in multiple myeloma. Light chain-restricted plasma cells in a bone marrow aspirate; multiple lytic lesions in a skull radiograph; large monoclonal spike in the g-globulin area in serum electrophoresis. (From Hoffman R et al: *Hematology, basic principles and practice,* ed 5, Philadelphia, 2009, Churchill Livingstone.)

- Urine protein immunoelectrophoresis: proteinuria from overproduction and secretion of free monoclonal kappa or lambda chains (Bence Jones protein)
- Serum protein immunoelectrophoresis: monoclonal spike (M spike) on protein immunoelectrophoresis in approximately 75% of patients (Fig. 1M-53); decreased levels of normal immunoglobulins (Ig)
  1. The increased immunoglobulins are generally IgG (70%) and IgA (20%).
  2. Approximately 5% to 10% of patients have only increased light chains in the urine by electrophoresis (light chain MM).
  3. A small percentage (<2%) of patients have nonsecreting MM (no increase in immunoglobulins and no light chains in the urine) but have other evidence of the disease (e.g., positive bone marrow examination).
- Elevated serum free light chains (kappa or lambda types) with abnormally elevated or decreased kappa:lambda ratios suggestive of the presence of monoclonal light chain proteins.
- Hyponatremia, serum hyperviscosity (more common with production of IgA)
- Bone marrow examination: usually demonstrates nests or sheets of plasma cells, which comprise >20% of the bone marrow
- Serum beta-2 microglobulin is useful for prognosis because levels >8 mg/L indicate high tumor mass and aggressive disease.
- Elevated serum levels of lactate dehydrogenase at the time of diagnosis define a subgroup of myeloma patients with very poor prognosis.
- Nearly all patients with MM present with abnormal chromosomes identified by fluorescence in situ hybridization (FISH). High-risk patients (<25% of patients at diagnosis) are those with any of the following: deletion 17p, translocation 4:14, translocation 14:16, deletion 13q, or cytogenetic hypodiploidy.

IMAGING STUDIES

Radiograph films of painful areas often demonstrate punched-out lytic lesions or osteoporosis (Fig. 1M-53). MRI is the preferred technique for suspected spinal compression or soft tissue plasmacytomas. Bone scans may not be useful because MM lesions are not blastic.

STAGING

Table 1M-30 describes a historical multiple myeloma staging system. With use of newer tumor biology factors (see "Disposition") that can affect prognosis, along with tumor burden described in Table 1M-30 and patient-related factors, it is possible to classify patients in three risk groups (high, intermediate, and standard).

Rx TREATMENT

NONPHARMACOLOGIC THERAPY

- Prevention of renal failure with adequate hydration and avoidance of nephrotoxic agents and dye contrast studies

ACUTE GENERAL Rx

- Treatment strategy is mainly related to the identification of the determination of transplant-eligible patients (Fig. 1M-54).
- All patients should be considered for approximately 12 weeks of induction chemotherapy with triplet regimens such as the VRD regimen (dexamethasone, lenalidomide, and bortezomib) or the CyBorD regimen (cyclophosphamide, lenalidomide, dexamethasone). Upon demonstration of at least a very good response, patients can undergo stem cell mobilization and collection at that point.
- All patients with high-risk characteristics should be offered autologous stem cell transplant (ASCT) subsequently, provided they have adequate cardiac, pulmonary, and hepatic function. Currently, ASCT can be safely performed in most centers in fit patients up to age 75 years.

TABLE 1M-30 Durie-Salmon Multiple Myeloma Staging System

Stage	Criteria
I	All of the following: Hemoglobin >10 g/dl Serum calcium <12 mg/dl Normal bone radiograph or solitary lesion Low M-component production IgG level <5 g/dl IgA level <3 g/dl Urine light chain <4 g/24 hr
II	Fitting neither I nor III
III	One or more of the following: Hemoglobin <8.5 g/dl Serum calcium >12 mg/dl Advanced lytic bone lesions High M-component production IgG level >7 g/dl IgA level >5 g/dl Urine light chains >12 g/24 hr

Subclassification:
A Serum creatinine <2 mg/dl
B Serum creatinine <2 mg/dl

- It is unclear if all MM patients without high-risk features benefit from upfront ASCT. The duration of median improved survival with single ASCT is estimated to be 12 months. ASCT performed at relapse is also associated with improvement in overall survival.
- Patients should be offered maintenance chemotherapy with either lenalidomide or bortezomib after recovery from ASCT for at least 2 years but potentially indefinitely.
- Induction therapy in patients ineligible for transplantation (age >75 years, high comorbidity index, poor performance status) can be identical to that offered transplant-eligible patients. Alternatively, less aggressive regimens (doublet regimens or single agents) can be recommended, including the following:
  Melphalan, bortezomib, and prednisone
  Melphalan, lenalidomide, and prednisone
  Lenalidomide and dexamethasone
  Bortezomib and dexamethasone
- Therapy for relapsed and refractory myeloma can include second-generation proteasome inhibitors (carfilzomib), immunomodulatory drugs (thalidomide, pomalidomide), and steroids. More recently, elotuzumab, an antibody targeting signaling lymphocytic activation molecule F7 (SLAMF7) and Daratumumab, an antibody targeting CD38 antigen, have both showed responses and survival benefits in relapsed multiple myeloma and are expected to be approved in this setting.
- If the relapse occurs more than 6 months after conventional therapy is stopped, the initial chemotherapy regimen can be reinstituted.
- ASCT can be considered as salvage therapy in patients who had stem cells cryopreserved early in the course of the disease.
- Approximately 15% of patients with newly diagnosed MM are recognized incidentally and present without significant symptoms (asymptomatic MM, formerly known as

M

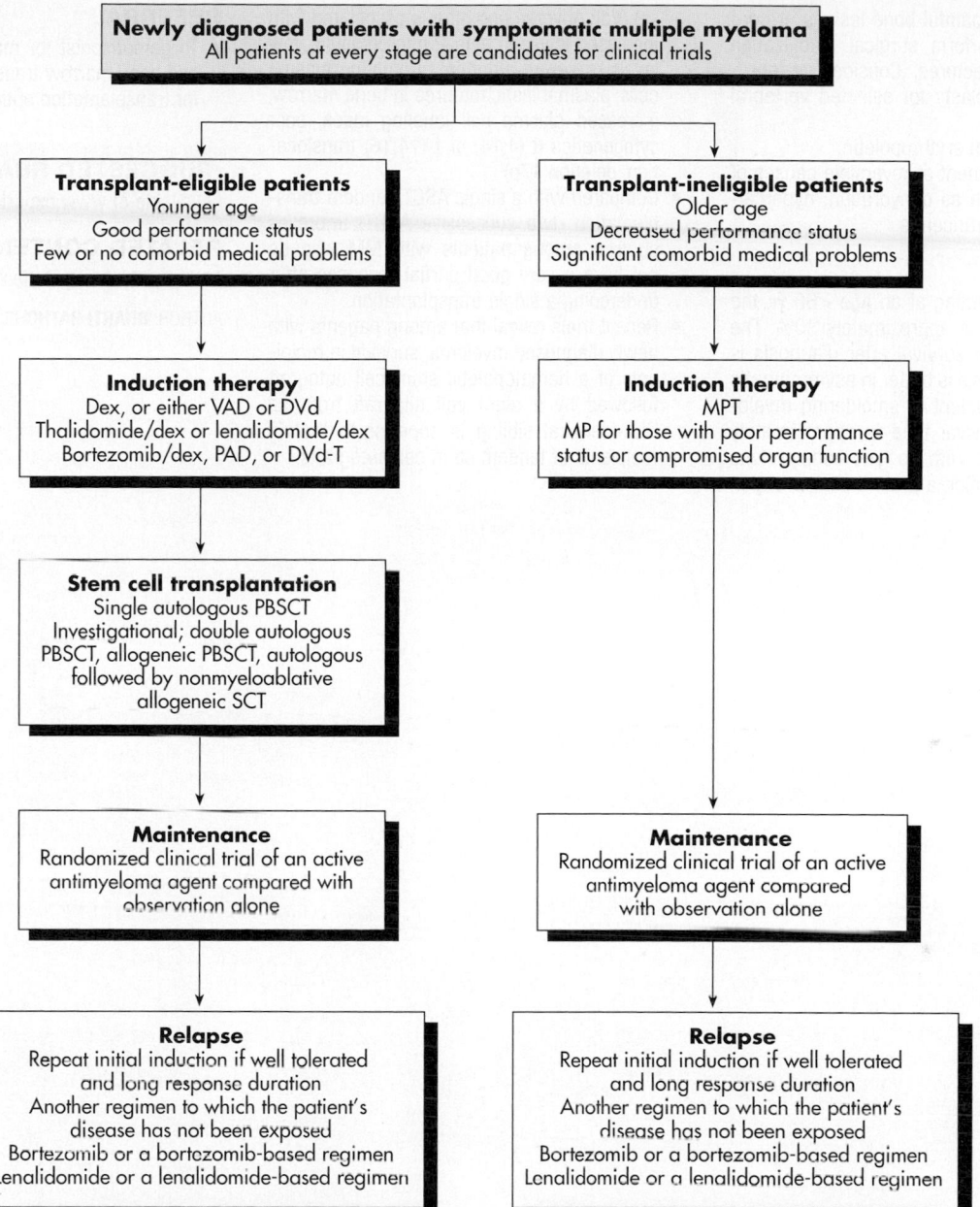

Newly diagnosed patients with symptomatic multiple myeloma
All patients at every stage are candidates for clinical trials

Transplant-eligible patients
Younger age
Good performance status
Few or no comorbid medical problems

Transplant-ineligible patients
Older age
Decreased performance status
Significant comorbid medical problems

Induction therapy
Dex, or either VAD or DVd
Thalidomide/dex or lenalidomide/dex
Bortezomib/dex, PAD, or DVd-T

Induction therapy
MPT
MP for those with poor performance
status or compromised organ function

Stem cell transplantation
Single autologous PBSCT
Investigational; double autologous
PBSCT, allogeneic PBSCT, autologous
followed by nonmyeloablative
allogeneic SCT

Maintenance
Randomized clinical trial of an active
antimyeloma agent compared with
observation alone

Maintenance
Randomized clinical trial of an active
antimyeloma agent compared
with observation alone

Relapse
Repeat initial induction if well tolerated
and long response duration
Another regimen to which the patient's
disease has not been exposed
Bortezomib or a bortezomib-based regimen
Lenalidomide or a lenalidomide-based regimen

Relapse
Repeat initial induction if well tolerated
and long response duration
Another regimen to which the patient's
disease has not been exposed
Bortezomib or a bortezomib-based regimen
Lenalidomide or a lenalidomide-based regimen

FIGURE 1M-54 A treatment algorithm for multiple myeloma. A treatment algorithm for patients who are
or are not suitable candidates for stem cell transplantation is presented. Further detail is provided in the text.
Dex, Dexamethasone; *DVd,* pegylated liposomal doxorubicin with vincristine and oral dexamethasone; *DVd-T,*
DVd with thalidomide; *MP,* melphalan and prednisone; *MPT,* melphalan and prednisone with thalidomide; *PAD,*
bortezomib with infusional doxorubicin and dexamethasone; *PBSCT,* peripheral blood stem cell transplantation;
SCT, stem cell transplantation; *VAD,* infusional doxorubicin and vincristine with oral dexamethasone. (Modified
from Runge MS, Greganti MA: *Netter's internal medicine,* Philadelphia, 2008, Saunders.)

smoldering myeloma). The rate of progression of smoldering MM to symptomatic disease is 10% per year for the initial
5 yr, decreasing to 5% for the next 5 yr, and
decreasing further to 1.5% per year thereafter. Observation alone is reasonable in these
patients because no survival advantage has
been demonstrated by treating them.
• An exception to this may be in high-risk
smoldering myeloma patients.[1] A recent

trial[2] has shown that early treatment with
lenalidomide plus dexamethasone of patients
with high-risk smoldering myeloma delays
progression to active disease and increases
overall survival.

CHRONIC Rx
• Promptly diagnose and treat infections.
Common bacterial agents are *Streptococcus
pneumoniae* and *Haemophilus influenzae.*

Prophylactic therapy against *Pneumocystis
jirovecii* with trimethoprim-sulfamethoxazole
must be considered in patients receiving
chemotherapy and high-dose corticosteroid
regimens. Vaccinate against *S. pneumoniae,*
influenza, and *H. influenzae.*
• Control hypercalcemia with IV fluids and
corticosteroids. Monthly infusions of the
bisphosphonate pamidronate or zoledronate
provide significant protection against skeletal complications and improve the quality of life of patients with advanced multiple
MM. Control pain with analgesics; radiation

[1]Kyle RA et al: Clinical course and prognosis of smoldering (asymptomatic) multiple myeloma, *N Engl J
Med* 356:2582-2590, 2007.

[2]Mateos MV et al: Lenalidomide plus dexamethasone
for high-risk smoldering multiple myeloma, *N Engl J
Med* 369:438-447, 2013.

therapy to treat painful bone lesions or cord compression. Perform surgical stabilization of pathologic fractures. Consider vertebroplasty or kyphoplasty for selected vertebral lesions.

- Treat anemia with erythropoietin.
- Aggressive treatment of reversible causes of renal failure such as dehydration, hypercalcemia, and hyperuricemia.

DISPOSITION

- In patients presenting at an age <60 yr, the 10-year survival is approximately 30%. The median length of survival after diagnosis is now 8 yr. Prognosis is better in asymptomatic patients with indolent or smoldering myeloma. Median survival time is approximately 10 yr in persons with no lytic bone lesions and a serum myeloma protein concentration <3 g/dl. Adverse outcome is associated with increased levels of beta-2 microglobulin, low levels of serum albumin, circulating plasma cells, plasmablastic features in bone marrow, increased plasma cell labeling index, poor cytogenetics (t (4;14) or t (14;16) translocation, deletion 17p)

- Compared with a single ASCT, tandem transplantation (two successive ASCT) improves survival among patients with MM who do not have a very good partial response after undergoing a single transplantation.
- Recent trials reveal that among patients with newly diagnosed myeloma, survival in recipients of a hematopoietic stem cell autograft followed by a stem cell allograft from an HLA-identical sibling is superior to that in recipients of tandem stem cell autografts.

REFERRAL

- To hematologist for management of disease and bone marrow transplant (BMT) specialist for transplantation options and management.

SUGGESTED READINGS

Available at www.expertconsult.com

RELATED CONTENT

Multiple Myeloma (Patient Information)

AUTHOR: **BHARTI RATHORE, M.D.**

BASIC INFORMATION

DEFINITION

Multiple sclerosis (MS) is a chronic predominantly autoimmune demyelinating disease of the central nervous system (CNS) characterized by subacute neurologic deficits correlating with CNS lesions separated in time and space, excluding other possible disease.
Subtypes include:

- Relapsing-remitting MS (RRMS) (82%): relapses followed by complete or near-complete recovery, 50% to 85% of which later transition to SPMS
- Secondary progressive MS (SPMS): progression of disability with few or no relapses
- Primary progressive MS (PPMS) (18%): progression from the onset, rare relapses
- Progressive relapsing or relapsing progressive courses can be incorporated into PPMS or SPMS respectively.
- Relapses are defined as a subacute onset of neurologic dysfunction that lasts for at least 24 hr due to inflammatory demyelination.

Classic rare MS variants include:

- Marburg variant: MRI reveals a tumorlike lesion with notable edema in one cerebral hemisphere. Pathology shows severe inflammation with necrosis: typically acute onset with a fulminant, often malignant, course. May also involve peripheral nerves.
- Balo's concentric sclerosis: Neuroimaging and pathology show alternating rings of myelination and demyelination resembling an onion bulb macroscopically and microscopically.
- Schilder's diffuse sclerosis: childhood onset with one to two large confluent lesions. Some cases were later found to be due to metabolic defects, and many have thus abandoned this disorder.
- Relapsing optic neuritis
- Neuromyelitis optica (Devic's disease): previously considered a variant, now classified as a distinct demyelinating disease. Lesions primarily involve the optic nerves and spinal cord. Most (75%) are aquaporin-4 receptor Ab positive.

SYNONYMS

MS
Disseminated sclerosis

ICD-10CM CODES
G35 Multiple sclerosis

EPIDEMIOLOGY & DEMOGRAPHICS

PEAK INCIDENCE: 20 to 40 yr in two thirds of patients; it is the most common permanently disabling disorder of the central nervous system in young adults; mean age of onset is 30 yr, range is infancy to 70 yr.
PREVALENCE: More common in people raised in northern latitudes and in certain genetic clusters. Prevalence per 10,000 varies from 20 in southern Europe to 150 to 180 in Canada,

northern United States, and northern Europe; and <10 in Asia, Central America, and most of Africa.
PREDOMINANT SEX & AGE: Female/male ratio is 2 to 3:1.
GENETICS: Frequency of MS in dizygotic twins and siblings is 3% to 5% and 20% to 40% in monozygotic twins. Most common associations include human leukocyte antigen classes I and II *(DRB1*1501, DQA1*0102, DQB1*0602)*, *(DRB1*0405-DQA1*0301-DQB1*0302* in Mediterranean population). A notable epigenetic interaction between vitamin D and the main MS-linked HLA-DRB1*1501 allele has been elucidated.

PHYSICAL FINDINGS & CLINICAL PRESENTATION

Findings depend on the location of the CNS lesion(s) and may include the following:

- Common: nonspecific complaints such as fatigue, blurred vision, diplopia, vertigo, falls, hemiparesis, paraparesis, monoparesis, numbness, paresthesias, ataxia, cognitive deficits, depression, sexual dysfunction, and urinary dysfunction
- Visual abnormalities: horizontal nystagmus, visual field defects, ***Marcus Gunn pupil*** (i.e., relative afferent papillary defect—normal direct and consensual light reflexes;

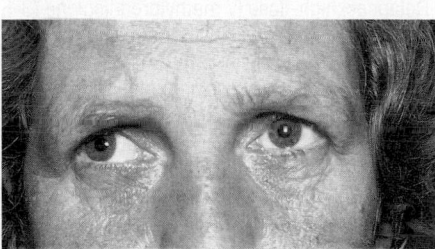

FIGURE 1M-55 Internuclear ophthalmoplegia may be an initial feature of brain stem involvement in multiple sclerosis. On lateral gaze to the right, adduction of the left eye is incomplete. On convergence, eye movement was normal. The lesion is in the left medial longitudinal bundle, between the nucleus in the pons and the third nerve nucleus on the opposite side. (From Forbes CD, Jackson WF. *Color atlas and text of clinical medicine,* ed 3, London, 2003, Mosby.)

however, when swinging flashlight from one eye to the other, direct light causes dilatation of pupil of affected eye), ***internuclear ophthalmoplegia*** (paresis of the adducting eye on conjugate lateral gaze with horizontal nystagmus of the abducting eye [Fig. 1M-55])

- Corticospinal tract(s) involvement: leads to upper motor neuron signs such as spasticity, hyperreflexia, clonus, extensor plantar responses, and upper motor neuron pattern of weakness
- Sensory loss: may include partial or full dermatomal loss of pain and temperature, loss of vibration (common) and position sense, or a thoracic band of sensory loss
- Ataxia: intention tremor, dysmetria, dysdiadochokinesis, titubation, inability to tandem gait
- Bladder dysfunction: detrusor hyperreflexia (urge incontinence), flaccidity (neurogenic bladder), and dyssynergia (bladder contracts against a closed sphincter)
- ***Lhermitte's sign:*** flexion of the neck elicits an electrical sensation extending down the spine and occasionally into the extremities
- ***Uhthoff's phenomenon:*** transient worsening of preexisting symptoms with small elevations in body temperature (e.g., during exercise or warm bathing)

ETIOLOGY

Remains unknown but multifactorial with evidence for autoimmunity (autoreactive T and B cells), environmental factors, and genetics (Mendelian and epigenetic). Environmental risk factors during childhood include certain viruses (e.g., Epstein-Barr virus and human herpes virus 6), low UV exposure, and month of birth (higher in spring). Other risk factors include low vitamin D level and smoking.

DX DIAGNOSIS

- MS: based on revised 2010 McDonald criteria (Table 1M-31)
- RRMS: see Table 1M-31)
- PPMS: insidious progression of disability with a positive CSF and either dissemination in both space and time *or* ongoing progression for at least 1 yr

TABLE 1M-31 Summary of Revised 2005-2010 McDonald Criteria for Diagnosis of Multiple Sclerosis

RRMS/Clinical Attacks	Clinical Lesions	Paraclinical Testing Needed
2	2	None
2	1	MRI dissemination in space *or* 2 MRI lesions consistent with MS plus positive CSF
1	2	MRI dissemination in time
1	1	MRI dissemination in space *or* 2 MRI lesions consistent with MS plus positive CSF and MRI dissemination in time

Evidence of clinical lesions by physical examination or evoked potentials.
CSF, Cerebrospinal fluid; *MRI,* magnetic resonance imaging; *MRI dissemination in space;* ≥1 T2 lesions in 2 of the 4 typical areas for MS lesions – periventricular, juxtacortical, infratentorial or spinal cord; *MRI dissemination in time,* a new lesion at follow-up MRI at any time, or presence of both an enhancing and nonenhancing lesion at any time.

DIFFERENTIAL DIAGNOSIS

- Autoimmune: acute disseminated encephalomyelitis (ADEM), postvaccination encephalomyelitis, Devic's disease
- Degenerative: subacute combined degeneration of the cord (vitamin B_{12} deficiency), amyotrophic lateral sclerosis, primary lateral sclerosis
- Infections: Lyme disease, neurosyphilis, HIV, tropical spastic paraparesis, progressive multifocal leukoencephalopathy, Whipple's disease
- Inflammatory: systemic lupus erythematosus, vasculitis, sarcoidosis, Sjögren's disease, Behçet's disease, celiac disease
- Inherited metabolic disorders: leukodystrophies
- Mitochondrial: Leber's hereditary optic neuropathy, mitochondrial encephalopathy, lactic acidosis, and strokelike episodes (MELAS)
- Neoplasms: CNS lymphoma, metastases
- Vascular: subcortical infarcts, Binswanger's disease

WORKUP

- Lumbar puncture for cases that are atypical or do not satisfy the diagnostic criteria for MS. Typical CSF abnormalities may include increased protein (less than 100 mg/dl), mild elevation of mononuclear white blood cells, and increased IgG synthesis rate. 70% of clinically definite MS (CDMS) have elevated CSF immunoglobulin (Ig) G index and 90% have oligoclonal bands. (Serum needs to be sent to lab simultaneously with CSF for both tests.) False-positive results with IgG index and rarely with positive OCBs can be seen in CNS infections, parainfections, vasculitis, and CNS lymphoma.
- Serum: complete blood count, ESR, chemistry panel, liver function tests, ANA, vitamin B_{12}, vitamin D.
- Consider collagen vascular serum tests, neuromyelitis optica IgG A, Lyme titre, ACE TSH, free T_4, anti-thyroglobulin A, very-long-chain fatty acids, arylsulfatase A.
- Consider optical coherence tomography or evoked potentials (visual, somatosensory and brain stem auditory evoked response).

IMAGING STUDIES

Head MRI ± gadolinium is recommended in all cases. Fig. 1M-56 illustrates imaging features of MS. MRI of the cervical spine can be helpful. MRI assesses acute and chronic lesions, and atrophy. A normal MRI of the brain does not conclusively exclude early MS.

 **TREATMENT**

NONPHARMACOLOGIC THERAPY

Patient education regarding disease characteristics, treatment options, risks and benefits of treatment, and prognosis. Often patients need intermittent rest periods on a daily basis and when physically active, and avoid exposure to heat, which typically worsens symptoms (not the disease).

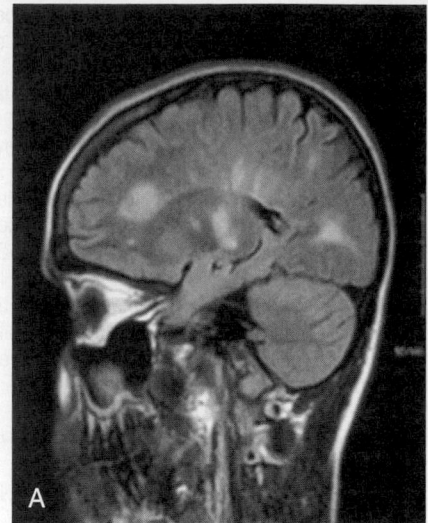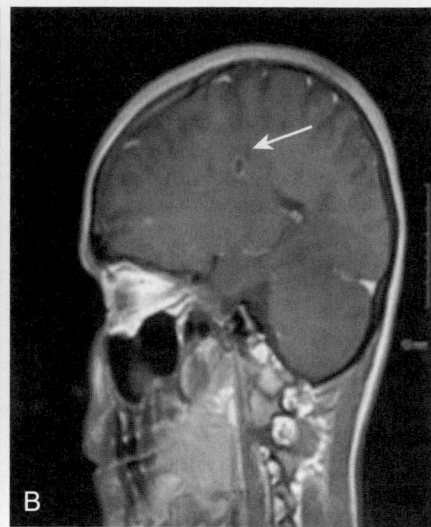

FIGURE 1M-56 Multiple sclerosis. A, Sagittal FLAIR image magnetic resonance scan shows multiple lesions in corpus callosum, "Dawson's fingers" (periventricular fingerlike lesions oriented towards the ventricles), along with ovoid and punctuate lesions in the deep white matter. **B,** Gadolinium-enhanced scan shows an enhancing lesion *(arrow)*.

Recommend physical therapy for new or worsening weakness, incoordination, or spasticity.

ACUTE GENERAL Rx

Relapses: high-dose IV methylprednisolone (3-5 days of 15 mg/kg/day, with a maximum of 1 g/day), often followed by a 7- to 10-day prednisone or methylprednisolone taper. High-dose corticosteroids do not alter the long-term course of disease. May consider IVIG, or plasmapheresis for refractory cases.

CHRONIC Rx

- FDA-approved therapies are only for relapsing MS; there are none yet approved for progressive MS.
- Disease-modifying injection therapy includes interferon beta-1a (IM Avonex, IM Plegridy, SC Rebif), interferon beta-1b (SC Betaseron, SC Extavia), and glatiramer acetate (SC Copaxone). Common side effects for interferons include flulike symptoms, liver toxicity, and leukopenia; CBC and LFTs (initially q1mo, then q3mo). Common side effects for Copaxone include injection site reactions and benign chest tightness; no serum studies are needed.
- Disease-modifying oral therapy: Consider baseline pregnancy test and infectious tests for all oral therapies, although not required by the FDA, such as VZV Ab, Lyme Ab, TB test, JC virus Ab, hepatitis Ab panel. Also review general risk of infections (hx UTIs, kidney stones, smoking, diabetes, bronchitis, disability, pulmonary function, and age). Typically monthly CBC and liver function tests for 6 mo then q3mo; pregnancy test.
  1. Fingolimod (Gilenya), a sphingosine-1-phosphate receptor modulator and lymphocyte sequester. Possible side effects: liver toxicity, bradycardia with first dose (requiring cardiac monitoring and ECG for

at least 8 hr after administration of first dose), arrhythmia, pancytopenia, macular edema (ophtho exam at baseline, 3 months, and thereafter for those with hx DM or uveitis), and reduced pulmonary function. Obtain VZV serology.
  2. Teriflunomide (Aubagio), reversible inhibitor of pyrimidine synthesis (enzyme dihydroorotate dehydrogenase). Possible side effects: diarrhea, abnormal liver function tests, nausea, and hair loss; pregnancy category X. Serum levels can be measured, and drug can be eliminated by charcoal or cholestyramine. Obtain TB test.
  3. Dimethyl fumarate (Tecfidera), mechanism includes inhibition of transcription of NF-KB. Frequent side effects include nausea, abdominal discomfort, and flushing—especially during the first month—and rarely leukopenia.
- Disease-modifying IV therapy:
  1. Natalizumab (Tysabri) is a monoclonal humanized Ab that binds integrin-α4 interfering with binding to VCAM-1. It has been associated with a *higher* risk of progressive multifocal leukoencephalopathy (JC virus) than other immunomodulatory therapies. Test for JC virus Ab at least annually (every 6 months if history of chemotherapy). If positive, PML is still rare, but risk increases with increased length of therapy, history of chemotherapy, and concomitant immunosuppressants.
  2. For rapidly progressive disability or frequent relapses on other maximum therapy, MS specialist may consider alemtuzumab, mitoxantrone, cyclophosphamide, or rituximab.
- Symptomatic therapy:
  - Dalfampridine (Ampyra) is a potassium channel blocker recently approved to improve walking speed in patients with MS.

- Treat spasticity with baclofen or tizanidine. Onabotulinum toxin type A injection for focal intractable spasticity. Intrathecal baclofen pump for generalized intractable spasticity. Acute worsening may be due to infections such as UTI, injury, recent surgery, or colder temperatures.
- Treat urge incontinence with anticholinergic/muscarinic therapy such as oxybutynin, tolterodine, or solifenacin. Treat urinary retention with tamsulosin. In both cases, rule out a bladder infection.
- Treat dysesthesias with gabapentin or oxcarbazepine.
- Fatigue: consider amantadine 100 mg bid, modafinil, stimulant, or fluoxetine.
- Tremor: clonazepam, carbamazepine, propranolol, or gabapentin.
- Depression and anxiety are common. Consider referring to both a counselor and psychiatrist.

DISPOSITION

Most patients have complete or near-complete recovery weeks to months after a relapse. Typically, 2 relapses occur in RRMS patient per year (75% will have >1 relapse). Although the rate of disease progression is highly variable, there is higher risk of greater long-term disability with higher relapse rate during the first 2-5 yr, poor recovery from initial relapses, older age of onset, involvement of multiple systems, male sex, African-American, and primary progressive disease.

REFERRAL

- Referral to neurologist is highly recommended. Referral to MS specialist should be considered in cases of poor response to therapy and/or if there is concern about complications of therapies.
- Consider referrals for physical, speech, and occupational therapy.
- Consider referral to urology if possible dyssynergia, or not responsive to treatment.

PEARLS & CONSIDERATIONS

- Clinically isolated syndrome (CIS): isolated demyelinating event and assessing risk of CDMS 1) in optic neuritis, if brain MRI is completely normal, there is 20% to 25% chance of CDMS over 15 yrs. 2) In CIS, if there are >2 T2 hyperintensities on brain MRI, there is 84% risk, and if there are >2 Gd + lesions there is a 96% risk of CDMS over 18 months.
- Pseudorelapses may occur with heat, fever, or infections (urinary tract infections common in patients with MS).
- Headache, fever, altered mental status, elevated CSF WBCs, or recurrent relapses over days to weeks, raises concern for CNS infection or ADEM.

 **EVIDENCE**

Available at www.expertconsult.com

SUGGESTED READINGS
Available at www.expertconsult.com

RELATED CONTENT
Multiple Sclerosis (Patient Information)

AUTHOR: **ALEXANDRA DEGENHARDT, M.D., M.M.Sc**

Multiple System Atrophy

 **BASIC INFORMATION**

DEFINITION

Multiple system atrophy (MSA) is an adult-onset (>30 years) fatal neurodegenerative disorder characterized by autonomic failure associated with Parkinsonism and/or cerebellar symptoms.

MSA is further subdivided into two main types:
- MSA-P (parkinsonism subtype), previously *Striatonigral degeneration*
- MSA-C (cerebellar subtype), previously *Olivopontocerebellar atrophy*

SYNONYMS

Atypical parkinsonism
Synculeinopathy
Shy-Drager syndrome
Olivopontocerebellar atrophy
Striatonigral degeneration

ICD-10CM CODES
G23.2 Striatonigral degeneration
G23.8 Olivopontocerebellar degeneration

EPIDEMIOLOGY AND INCIDENCE

INCIDENCE: Estimated mean incidence is 0.6 to 0.7 cases per 100,000 persons per year, with a range of 0.1 to 2.4 cases.

PREVALENCE:
- Estimated point prevalence is 4.4 cases per 100,000 patients.
- Rises to about 7.8 cases per 100,000 for age >40 years.
- Subtype distribution
  ○ MSA-P: 68% of cases
  ○ MSA-C: 32% of cases

PREDOMINANT SEX AND AGE:
- Male to female ratio is 1.3:1
- Mean age of onset is 57.8 years
- In Japan, the predominant subtype is MSA-C and mean survival is short.

GENETICS: Variants of *SNCA* gene (synuclein A gene, which makes alpha-synuclein) have been associated with higher risk of MSA; however, the exact mechanism is unknown.

RISK FACTORS: People with MSA perform some activities more often than the general population, such as drinking alcohol and tea, eating seafood, taking aspirin, and working in plant and machine operations. However, it is not clear if these behaviors are risk factors or coincidence.

PHYSICAL FINDINGS & CLINICAL PRESENTATION

- Parkinsonism: (see "Parkinson's Disease")
  ○ Tremor: Resting tremor in MSA is more likely to be a jerky tremor or myoclonic tremor. It is usually faster and symmetrical.
  ○ Rigidity: usually symmetric.
  ○ Postural instability: Seen early in the disease, usually within 1 to 3 years of onset, and is rapidly progressive, with patients being wheelchair dependent within 5 years. Falls are common early in MSA (within 3 years) and are more common in MSA-C.

- Dysautonomia:
  ○ Hallmark of MSA, present in both subtypes (99% of patients).
  ○ Orthostatic hypotension is symptomatic in 75% of the patients with lightheadedness or dizziness, especially in early morning and when quickly getting up after prolonged sitting. Drop in blood pressure of 30/15 mmHg within in 3 min of standing is required for diagnosis.
  ○ Erectile dysfunction is seen in 84% of males with MSA.
  ○ Cold hands or feet with red hand sign due to Raynaud's phenomenon.
  ○ Respiratory dysfunction with inspiratory stridor or sighs.
- Sleep apnea: more commonly obstructive sleep apnea. This results from airway obstruction and vocal cord restriction (in >50%). Nocturnal stridor and snoring and later daytime stridor are common.
- Urine incontinence (73% of patients).

ETIOLOGY

- Etiology of MSA is unclear. It is generally considered a sporadic disease. Many different models have been proposed, including environmental toxins such as formaldehyde, malathion, diazinon, benzene, hexane, ketone, and pesticides.
- MSA is a synucleinopathy; others include Parkinson's disease (PD) and Lewy body disease. Deposition of alpha synuclein is similar to Lewy body–like deposits, but is seen as glial cell inclusions and in different anatomical distribution than PD.

(Dx) DIAGNOSIS

- Definitive diagnosis of MSA requires pathological confirmation on autopsy.
- Possible and probable diagnoses of MSA are based on clinical findings (Table 1M-32).

DIFFERENTIAL DIAGNOSIS

- Progressive supranuclear palsy: Atypical Parkinsonism that presents with early falls and postural instability and can be differentiated by lack of tremors, supranuclear ocular palsy, lack of myoclonus, and, most important, less frequent dysautonomia.

- Parkinson's Disease: PD can develop mild dysautonomia and postural instability. Key in differentiation is timing of onset of these symptoms (much later for PD), levodopa responsiveness, asymmetry of PD, and much slower progression of PD.
- Corticobasal ganglionic degeneration: Atypical parkinsonism that can present with early falls and postural instability and can have myoclonus. Differentiated due to marked asymmetry of the disease, early and severe cognitive involvement, and presence of apraxia.
- Secondary parkinsonism: Usually lacks the presence of dysautonomia and may be more slowly progressive.
- Main differential diagnosis of MSA-C includes sporadic late-onset ataxias and autosomal dominant spinocerebellar ataxias (SCA).
- Fragile X associated tremor ataxia syndrome (FXTAS) must be distinguished from MSA and can be present up to 5% of adult-onset progressive cerebral ataxia.

WORK-UP

Autonomic failure early in disease can differentiate MSA and can be determined with:
- Thermoregulatory testing
- Thermal skin sweat test
- Tilt table test

LABORATORY TEST

- No routine laboratory tests are indicated.
- It is important to work up for secondary causes of parkinsonism and dysautonomia as appropriate.

IMAGING STUDIES

Some changes have been described on MRI of the brain in MSA, although they are not common or exclusive.
- Hot cross bun sign or T2 hyperintensity in a crosslike fashion in the *basis pontis*.
- T2 linear hyperintensities on the outer margin of the putamen.
- Middle cerebellar peduncle atrophy and infratentorial atrophy.
- CT is recommended for patients with contraindications to MRI.
- Ancillary neuroimaging tests include FDG-PET, transcranial ultrasonography, F-DOPA PET, ^{18}F-fluorodopamine PET, and ^{123}I-IBZM SPECT.

TABLE 1M-32 Diagnostic Criteria for MSA

Possible MSA	A sporadic, progressive, **adult (>30 yr)** onset disease characterized by • Parkinsonism or cerebellar syndrome • At least 1 feature of autonomic or urogenital dysfunction • At least 1 of the additional features	Additional Features: • Stridor • Babinski sign • Rapidly progressive parkinsonism • Poor response to levodopa • Postural instability within 3 yr • Cerebellar ataxia • Dysphagia within 5 yr • MRI changes suggestive of MSA
Probable MSA	A sporadic, progressive, **adult (>30 yr)** onset disease characterized by • Autonomic failure involving urinary dysfunction • Poorly levodopa-responsive parkinsonism or cerebellar dysfunction	
Definitive MSA	A sporadic, progressive, **adult (>30 yr)** onset disease pathologically confirmed by presence of high density glial cell inclusions in association with degenerative changes in striatonigral and olivopontocerebellar pathways.	

 **TREATMENT**

- Parkinsonism in MSA may respond to levodopa in 60% patients; however, <10% have an excellent response and the best response is usually seen at higher doses. This improvement is transient in >90% patients, usually 2 to 3 years on average.
- Parkinsonism in MSA does NOT respond to deep brain stimulation (DBS) surgery and is a diagnosis of exclusion for DBS surgery. Currently, there is no surgical treatment for parkinsonism in MSA.

NONPHARMACOLOGIC THERAPY

Most often, the initial treatment for orthostatic hypotension includes physical and supportive countermeasures to raise blood pressure, such as:
- Crossed leg stance with leaning against the wall
- Elastic stockings
- Correcting volume depletion and anemia
- Avoiding dehydration
- Liberal salt use

ACUTE GENERAL Rx

ORTHOSTATIC HYPOTENSION:

- Second FDA-approved medication for neurogenic orthostatic hypotension is *Droxidopa* (with midodrine being the only other medication).
- Recently approved Droxidopa is synthetic amino acid prodrug of norepinephrine that is orally bioavailable and has limited crossover through the blood-brain barrier and increases norepinephrine levels in brain.
- Other medications are used frequently to treat orthostatic hypotension (generally before Droxidopa), including mestinon, fludrocortisone, midodrine, and octreotide (Table 1M-33)

CHRONIC Rx

- Bladder dysfunction: Medication used includes oxybutynin, tolterodine, solifenacin, darifenacin, tamsulosin, prazosin, and moxysilate (specific antagonist of bladder α-adrenergic receptors), and use of botulinum toxin for bladder spasticity and urgency.
- Erectile dysfunction: Medication used includes sildenafil and tildenafil.
- Constipation: Medications include polyethylene glycol, bisacodyl, magnesium sulphate, macrogol, lubiprostone, and botulinum toxin. Long-term use of polyethylene glycol is safe in parkinsonian patients and is the recommended treatment of choice in PD.
- Sleep apnea: Usually treated with continuous positive airway pressure or bilevel positive airway pressure.

COMPLEMENTARY AND ALTERNATIVE MEDICINE

No evidence-based therapy. Patients with parkinsonism use *mucuna puriens* powder and fava beans. Both of them have levodopa in varying concentration and are not known to be any superior to *Sinemet*.

DISPOSITION

MSA is a relentlessly and rapidly progressive disabling disease. Mean survival in both subtypes is 7 to 9 years; sudden death and pneumonia are the two most common causes of death. Older age of onset and early autonomic dysfunction are predictive factors for rapid progression with shorter disease survival.

REFERRAL

- Neurology consultation is important to make the distinction between MSA and other causes of parkinsonism. Yearly evaluation for diagnosis may be needed. Reliability of diagnosis by a movement disorders expert is superior to that from a general neurologist (95% vs. 70%).
- Due to high incidence of nonmotor complications, a close coordination by different care providers is needed.

 **PEARLS AND CONSIDERATIONS**

Red flags for MSA in patient presenting with parkinsonism:
- Early postural instability, especially if wheelchair bound within 5 years.
- Rapid progression
- Abnormal postures, such as Pisa syndrome
- Severe bulbar dysfunction
- Respiratory dysfunction: inspiratory stridor or inspiratory signs
- Emotional lability

PATIENT/FAMILY EDUCATION

The Multiple System Atrophy Coalition supporting patients and caregivers: https://www.multiplesystematrophy.org

RELATED CONTENT

Parkinson's Disease (Related Key Topic)

SUGGESTED READING

Available at www.expertconsult.com

AUTHOR: **DANISH BHATTI, M.D.**

TABLE 1M-33   Medications for Orthostatic Hypotension in Parkinsonism

Medication	Mechanism of Action	Suggested Dosage	Common/Serious Side effects
Fludrocortisone*,† (9 alpha-Fluoro-17-Hydroxy-corticosterone)	A synthetic corticosteroid with mineralocorticoid effect on the kidney (inducing permease), enhancing Na+ reabsorption and increasing K+ excretion	0.1-0.5 mg per day	Acute withdrawal adrenal insufficiency, edema, hypokalemia, interaction with lithium and through CYP450
Midodrine*,† (2-amino-N-[dimethoxyphenyl-hydroxyethyl]-acetamide)	Midodrine is converted to active metabolite desgylmidodrine by deglycination reaction that selectively binds to and activates alpha-1-adrenergic receptors of vasculature	5-10 mg per day	Contraindicated in patients with severe organic heart disease, acute renal disease, urinary retention, pheochromocytoma, or thyrotoxicosis.
Droxidopa*,† (D,L Threo 3,4-Dihydroxy-phenylserine)	An orally active synthetic precursor of epinephrine that crosses blood-brain barrier and increases brain epinephrine levels	200-2000 mg per day	Headache, dizziness, and nausea. No significant known toxicity.
Mestinon† (Hydroxymethyl-pyridinium bromide dimethyl-carbamate)	Binds reversibly to acetyl-cholinesterase in PNS and increases ACH, leading to muscarinic effects of contraction of bronchial and intestinal smooth muscles, exocrine gland secretions, and nicotinic effect of skeletal muscle contraction.	120 to 660 mg per day in divided doses (usually QID)	Toxicity with confusion, ataxia, seizures; generalized weakness, fatigue and twitching, nausea, vomiting and cramps. Coma and death can occur. Antidote is atropine.
Octreotide‡ (pentaoxo-dithia-pentazacycloicosane-4-carboxamide)	A synthetic somatostatin analogue; even more potent inhibitor of growth hormone, glucagon, and insulin	100-1500 µg per day subcutaneously	Abdominal pain, decreased appetite, diarrhea

*Drug Warning: Potentially serious side effect of marked elevation of supine blood pressure.
†FDA Pregnancy Risk Category C
‡FDA Pregnancy Risk Category B
ACH, Acetylcholine; *CYP450*, Cytochrome P450; *PNS*, peripheral nervous system; *QID*, four times daily.

ℹ️ BASIC INFORMATION

DEFINITION

Mumps is an acute generalized viral infection that is usually characterized by nonsuppurative swelling and tenderness of one or both parotid glands. It is caused by mumps virus, a single-stranded RNA paramyxovirus, of which humans are the only natural host.

SYNONYMS

Viral parotitis
Parotitis

ICD-10CM CODES

B26.0 Mumps orchitis
B26.1 Mumps meningitis
B26.2 Mumps encephalitis
B26.3 Mumps pancreatitis
B26.81 Mumps hepatitis
B26.82 Mumps myocarditis
B26.83 Mumps nephritis
B26.84 Mumps polyneuropathy
B26.85 Mumps arthritis
B26.89 Other mumps complications
B26.9 Mumps without complication

EPIDEMIOLOGY & DEMOGRAPHICS

INCIDENCE (IN U.S.):
- About 300 infections/yr. Sporadic outbreaks still occur in schools, colleges, military posts, or summer camps started by an unvaccinated person.
- More than 150,000 cases/yr before licensure of mumps vaccine in 1967

PREDOMINANT SEX: Males = females
PREDOMINANT AGE: 75% of disease in teenage years
PEAK INCIDENCE: Late winter and early spring months
GENETICS: Congenital infection:
- First-trimester infection is associated with excessive fetal deaths.

- Second- and third-trimester infection is not associated with increased fetal mortality. Neonatal infection:
- Uncommon
- Uncommon in infants <1 yr because of passive immunity conferred by placental transfer of maternal antibody

PHYSICAL FINDINGS & CLINICAL PRESENTATION

- Prodromal period: includes low-grade fever, malaise, anorexia, and headache
- Parotid swelling (Fig. 1M-57) and tenderness; often the first signs of infection:
  1. Progresses over 2 to 3 days, then opposite side may become involved
  2. Unilateral parotitis in 25% of cases
  3. Considerable pain with parotid swelling, causing trismus and difficulty with mastication and pronunciation
  4. Pain exacerbated by eating or drinking citrus and other acidic foods
  5. Possible fever with parotid swelling, ranging up to 40° C
  6. Parotid swelling, usually resolving within 1 wk
- CNS involvement:
  1. May occur from 1 wk before to 2 wk after the onset of parotitis or even in its absence
  2. Meningitis:
     a. Occurs in 1% to 10% of patients with mumps parotitis
     b. Occurs three times more often in males than females
     c. Symptoms: headache, fever, nuchal rigidity, and vomiting
     d. Full recovery with no sequelae
  3. Encephalitis:
     a. May develop early, as a result of direct viral invasion of neurons, or late, around the second wk after onset of parotitis, and is a postinfectious demyelinating process.

b. Mumps accounted for only 0.5% of viral meningitis.
c. Symptoms: fever, alterations in the level of consciousness, possible seizures, paresis or paralysis, and aphasia. Fever can be quite high (40° to 41° C).
d. Cerebellitis and hydrocephalus are serious complications of mumps encephalitis.
e. May result in permanent sequelae or death.
4. Other rare neurologic complications include cerebellar ataxia, transverse myelitis, Guillain-Barré syndrome, and facial palsy.
- Epididymoorchitis:
  1. Most common extrasalivary gland complication of mumps in adult men
  2. Occurs in 38% of postpubertal males who have mumps
  3. Most often unilateral but is bilateral in 30% of males who develop this complication
  4. May precede development of parotitis and may be only manifestation of mumps
  5. Two thirds of cases develop during first week of parotitis
  6. Symptoms:
     a. Severe pain, swelling, and tenderness of the testes and scrotal erythema
     b. Fever and chills
  7. Some degree of testicular atrophy in 50% of cases, mo to yr later
  8. Sterility from bilateral orchitis is rare
- Involvement of pancreas and ovaries:
  1. Pancreas: abdominal pain, fever, and vomiting
  2. Ovaries: oophoritis
     a. Occurs in 5% of postpubertal women with mumps
     b. Symptoms include fever, nausea, vomiting, and lower abdominal pain
     c. May rarely result in decreased fertility and premature menopause
- Transient renal impairment: common and manifested by hematuria and polyuria
- Joint involvement:
  1. Migratory polyarthritis is most frequent
  2. Infrequently affects adults with mumps
  3. Occurs rarely in children
  4. Self-limited, with complete resolution
- Deafness:
  1. Most often unilateral, involving high frequencies; may rarely cause bilateral involvement
  2. Most patients recover
  3. Permanent unilateral deafness reported in 1 in 20,000 cases
  4. Labyrinthitis and end lymphatic hydrops also reported
- Myocardial involvement:
  1. Uncommon
  2. Rarely causes progressive and fulminant fatal myocarditis with dilated cardiomyopathy
  3. Refractory arrhythmia and congestive heart failure
  4. Coronary artery involvement

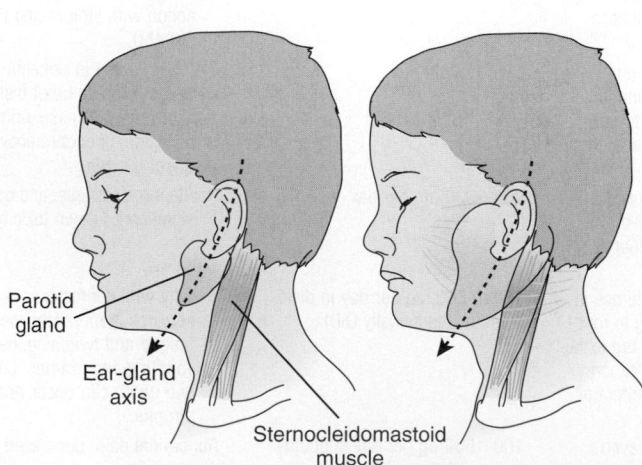

FIGURE 1M-57 Schematic drawing of a parotid gland infected with mumps *(right)* compared with a normal gland *(left)*. An imaginary line bisecting the long axis of the ear divides the parotid gland into two equal parts. These anatomic relationships are not altered in the enlarged gland. An enlarged cervical lymph node is usually posterior to the imaginary line. (From Mumps [epidemic parotitis]. In Krugman S et al [eds]: *Infectious diseases in children*, ed 6, St Louis, 1977, Mosby.)

(Figure labels: Parotid gland; Ear-gland axis; Sternocleidomastoid muscle)

- Eye involvement:
  1. Corneal endotheliitis following mumps parotitis

ETIOLOGY

- Virus is spread via direct contact, droplet nuclei, fomites, or oral or nasal secretions.
- Patients are contagious from 48 hr before to 9 days after parotid swelling.

 **DIAGNOSIS**

DIFFERENTIAL DIAGNOSIS

- Other viruses that may cause acute parotitis:
  1. Parainfluenza types 1 and 3
  2. Coxsackie viruses
  3. Influenza A
  4. Cytomegalovirus
- Suppurative parotitis:
  1. Most often caused by *Staphylococcus aureus*
  2. May be differentiated from mumps
     a. Extreme indurations, tenderness and erythema overlying the gland
     b. Ability to express pus from Stensen's duct or massage of parotid
- Other conditions that may occur with parotid enlargement or swelling:
  1. Sjögren's syndrome
  2. Leukemia
  3. Diabetes mellitus
  4. Uremia
  5. Malnutrition
  6. Cirrhosis
- Drugs that cause parotid swelling:
  1. Phenothiazines
  2. Phenylbutazone
  3. Thiouracil
  4. Iodides
- Conditions that cause unilateral swelling:
  1. Tumors
  2. Cysts
  3. Stones causing obstruction
  4. Strictures causing obstruction

WORKUP

- Diagnosis based on history of exposure and physical finding of parotid tenderness with mild to moderate constitutional symptoms.
- Diagnosis is confirmed by a variety of serologic tests or isolation of the virus.

LABORATORY TESTS

- Diagnosis is confirmed by a positive IgM mumps antibody or by fourfold rise between acute and convalescent sera by CF, ELISA, or neutralization tests. However, serologic mumps testing is particularly unhelpful in some vaccinated individuals who can have mumps without having the usual immunoglobulin M (IgM) spike. A polymerase chain reaction (PCR) assay is also available.
- Virus can be isolated from the saliva, usually from 2 to 3 days before to 4 to 5 days after the onset of parotitis. Researchers have shown that many cases labeled as "parotitis" are actually caused by other viruses (EB virus, human herpesvirus 6B, human parainfluenza virus).[1]
- Virus can be cultured from CSF in patients with meningitis during the first 3 days of meningeal findings. More rapid confirmation of mumps in the CSF is IgM antibody capture immunoassay and nested PCR assay.
- Virus can be detected in urine during the first 2 wk of infection.
- WBC:
  1. May be normal or possible mild leukopenia with a relative lymphocytosis
  2. Leukocytosis with left shift with extra–salivary gland involvement, such as meningitis, orchitis, or pancreatitis
- Serum amylase:
  1. Elevated in the presence of parotitis
  2. May remain elevated for 2 to 3 wk
  3. May be differentiated from mumps and parotids by isoenzyme analysis or serum pancreatic lipase
- Mumps meningitis:
  1. CSF WBCs from 10 to 2000 WBC/mm^3 with a predominance of lymphocytes
  2. In 20% to 25% of patients, predominance of polymorphonuclear cells
  3. CSF protein normal or mildly elevated
  4. CSF glucose low, <40 mg/dl, in 6% to 30% of patients

 **TREATMENT**

NONPHARMACOLOGIC THERAPY

- Supportive treatment
- Adequate hydration and nutrition

ACUTE GENERAL Rx

- Analgesics and antipyretics to relieve pain and fever
- Narcotic analgesics, along with bed rest, ice packs, and a testicular bridge, to relieve pain associated with mumps orchitis
- IV fluids for patients with frequent vomiting associated with mumps pancreatitis or meningitis

[1]Barshey AE et al: Viruses detected among sporadic cases of parotitis, United States 2009-2011, *J Infect Dis* 208:1979, 2013.

DISPOSITION

Most patients recover without incident.

REFERRAL

- To a neurologist if significant neurologic complications develop during or following mumps (myelitis, encephalitis, cranial nerve involvement, cerebellar ataxia, etc.)
- To a cardiologist if viral perimyocarditis develops
- To a urologist if orchitis develops

! PEARLS & CONSIDERATIONS

COMMENTS

Prevention:

- Attenuated live mumps virus vaccine has been available since 1967.
  1. Usually given in combination with measles and rubella vaccines (MMR)
  2. Should be given at 12 to 15 mo of age, and again at 5 to 12 yr
  3. Seroconversion in about 100% of infants given the vaccine
  4. Contraindicated in pregnant women and immunocompromised patients
  5. Patients with asymptomatic HIV infection and patients with symptomatic HIV infection, in the absence of severe immunosuppression, can safely receive mumps, measles, and rubella (MMR) vaccine
  6. Adverse events of vaccination include local pain, indurations, thrombocytopenic purpura, Guillain-Barré syndrome, and cerebellar ataxia
- The CDC and American Academy of Pediatrics (AAP) recommend that patients with mumps stay home from work or school for 5 days after onset of clinical symptoms.
- Because virus may be shed before the onset of parotid swelling, isolation possibly not of great value in limiting spread of infection. Use droplet precautions as per CDC and AAP.
- Mumps is an notifiable disease in all U.S. states.

SUGGESTED READINGS

Available at www.expertconsult.com

RELATED CONTENT

Mumps (Patient Information)

AUTHOR: **GLENN G. FORT, M.D., M.P.H.**

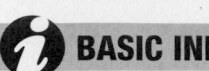

BASIC INFORMATION

DEFINITION

Muscular dystrophy (MD) refers to a heterogeneous group of inherited disorders resulting in characteristic patterns of muscle weakness, some with cardiac involvement. Only disorders with childhood or adult onset are considered here (i.e., excluding congenital myopathies).

ICD-10CM CODES
G71.0 Muscular dystrophy

EPIDEMIOLOGY & DEMOGRAPHICS

INCIDENCE:
- Most common childhood MD is Duchenne's muscular dystrophy (DMD) with an incidence of 1/3500 male births.
- Most common adult MD is myotonic dystrophy with an incidence as high as 1/8000.

GENETICS:
- **Dystrophinopathies:** X-linked recessive defect in dystrophin gene resulting in either absence (DMD) or reduced/defective (Becker's MD [BMD]) dystrophin (Fig. 1M-58)
- **Myotonic Dystrophy:** Autosomal dominant (AD) CTG trinucleotide repeat (see "Myotonia")
- **Limb-Girdle Muscular Dystrophy:** The majority are autosomal recessive, also autosomal dominant forms. Associated with deficiencies identified in multiple proteins (sarcoglycan, calpain, dystroglycan, and dysferlin may be most common; also may involve telethonin, lamin A/C, myotilin, and caveolin-3)
- **Emery-Dreifuss Muscular Dystrophy:** X-linked recessive defect in nuclear protein emerin or AR/AD defect in inner nuclear lamina proteins lamin A/C
- **Facioscapulohumeral Muscular Dystrophy:** AD; genetic mutation causes deletion of 3.3 kb repeat
- **Oculopharyngeal Muscular Dystrophy:** AD GCG trinucleotide repeat resulting in deficient mRNA transfer from nucleus

PHYSICAL FINDINGS & CLINICAL PRESENTATION
- **Dystrophinopathies:** Proximal arm and leg weakness with hypertrophic calf muscles

(Fig. 1M-59), delayed motor milestones, cognitive impairment, cardiac involvement, progressive course resulting in respiratory complications and respiratory failure
1. DMD (Fig. 1M-60) onset at 2 to 3 yr old, typically wheelchair-bound by 12 yr
2. BMD onset at 5 to 15 yr old, ambulatory beyond age 15
- **Myotonic Dystrophy:** Variable age of onset and severity manifesting as predominantly distal weakness with long face, percussion and grip myotonia, temporalis and masseter wasting, ptosis, hypersomnolence, cognitive impairment, and cardiac conduction defects. May be associated with frontal balding, cataracts, impaired glucose tolerance, and male infertility.
- **Limb-Girdle MD:** Phenotypically and genetically heterogenous characterized by proximal hip and shoulder girdle weakness, some genotypes featuring cardiac involvement
- **Emery-Dreifuss MD:** Early adulthood onset with predominantly humeroperoneal weakness, early contractures, and cardiac dysfunction
- **Facioscapulohumeral MD:** Onset typically in late childhood or adolescence with weakness mostly in face and shoulder girdle musculature and possible later, mild involvement of lower extremities
- **Oculopharyngeal MD:** Symptom onset typically in mid-adult life with ptosis, dysphagia, dysarthria, and proximal muscle weakness
- Table 1M-34 shows a classification of muscular dystrophies

 DIAGNOSIS

DIFFERENTIAL DIAGNOSIS

Myasthenia gravis, inflammatory myopathy, metabolic myopathy, endocrine myopathy, toxic myopathy, mitochondrial myopathy

WORKUP
- CK
- ECG, Holter monitor, echocardiography
- EMG
- Muscle biopsy with immunohistochemistry useful for diagnosis of dystrophinopathies and limb-girdle MD

- DNA analysis helpful if clinical suspicion is for myotonic, Emery-Dreifuss, facioscapulohumeral, and oculopharyngeal MDs
- Assessment of respiratory parameters, including forced vital capacity (FVC)

 TREATMENT

NONPHARMACOLOGIC THERAPY
- Genetic counseling
- Physical, occupational, respiratory, speech therapy as symptoms dictate
- Screening for sleep-disordered breathing with overnight polysomnogram (PSG) if clinically indicated
- Pacemaker placement may be necessary if cardiac conduction defect present

ACUTE GENERAL Rx
Prednisone may modestly prolong ambulation in DMD. A dose of 0.75 mg/kg/day may improve muscle strength and function over 6 months to 2 years. These short-term benefits must be weighed against the side effects of long-term steroid therapy.

CHRONIC Rx
Vigilance to avoid cardiac and respiratory complications, joint contractures

DISPOSITION
Variable course, because severity of phenotype is contingent upon both diagnosis and genotype

REFERRAL
- Surgical referral for correction of scoliosis or contractures may be necessary
- Assessment and follow-up in an MD specialty clinic

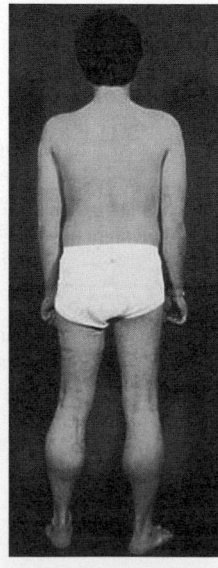

FIGURE 1M-59 Becker muscular dystrophy in a 24-year-old male. There is dystrophy of the shoulder girdle and calf pseudohypertrophy. (Courtesy Dr. R. Pascuzzi. From Libby PL et al: *Braunwald's heart disease: a textbook of cardiovascular medicine*, ed 8, Philadelphia, 2007, Saunders.)

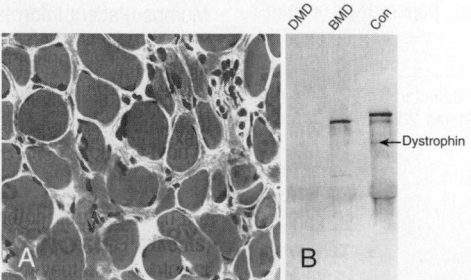

FIGURE 1M-58 A, Duchenne muscular dystrophy showing variation in muscle fiber size, increased endomysial connective tissue, and regenerating fibers. **B,** Western blot showing absence of dystrophin in DMD and altered dystrophin size in Becker muscular dystrophy (BMD) compared with control (Con). (Courtesy Dr. L. Kunkel, Children's Hospital, Boston. From Kumar V et al: *Robbins and Cotran pathologic basis of disease*, ed 7, Philadelphia, 2005, Saunders.)

FIGURE 1M-60 In Duchenne's muscular dystrophy, the patient will get up from the floor with Gower's maneuver. The boy will "walk up" his body with his hands as he rises. (From Remmel KS et al: *Handbook of symptom-oriented neurology*, ed 3, St Louis, 2002, Mosby.)

Diseases and Disorders

I

TABLE 1M-34 Classification of Muscular Dystrophies

Disease	Genetic Locus	Inheritance	Protein	Outcome
Duchenne/Becker		XR	Dystrophin	Lethal
Emery-Dreifuss		XR	Emerin, lamins A and C	40% lethality
Limb-Girdle Muscular Dystrophies				
LGMD 1A	5q31	AD	Myotilin	With LGMD, less-severe forms can emerge during the first three decades, leading to loss of ambulation after 30 yr of age. The most severe forms start at 3-5 yr of age and progress rapidly.
LGMD 1B	1q11-q21	AD	Laminin A/C	
LGMD 1C	3p35	AD	Caveolin	
LGMD 1D	6q23	AD	—	
LGMD 1E	7q	AD	—	
LGMD 1F	7q32	AD	—	
LGMD 1G	4p21	AD	—	
LGMD 2A	15q15.1-q21.1	AR	Calpain 3	
LGMD 2B	2p13	AR	Dysferlin	
LGMD 2C	13q12	AR	γ-Sarcoglycan	
LGMD 2D	17q12-q21.33	AR	α-Sarcoglycan	
LGMD 2E	4q12	AR	β-Sarcoglycan	
LGMD 2F	5q33-q34	AR	δ-Sarcoglycan	
LGMD 2G	17q11-q12	AR	Telethonin	
LGMD 2H	9q31-q34.1	AR	E3-Ubiquitin ligase (TRIM32)	
LGMD 2I	19q13.3	AR	Fukutin-related protein	
LGMD 2J	2q24.3	AR	Titin	
LGMD 2K	9q34	AR	Protein O-mannosyltransferase	
CMDs with CNS Involvement				
Fukuyama CMD	9q31	AR	Fukutin	LE, 11-16 yr
Walker-Warburg CMD	1p32	AR	O-Mannosyltransferase	LE, <3 yr
Muscle-eye-brain CMD	1p32-34	AR	O-MNAGAT	LE, 10-30 yr
CMDs without CNS Involvement				
Merosin-deficient classic type	6q2	AR	Merosin (laminin A₂)	Many patients never walk; others have an LGMD pattern
Merosin-positive classic type	4p16.3	AR	Selenoprotein N1, collagen VI α₂	Course stabilizes in late childhood; many continue to walk into adulthood
Integrin-deficient CMD	12q13	AR	Integrin α7	Presents early in infancy with hypotonia and delayed milestones
Other Dystrophies				
Facioscapulohumeral	4q35	AD	—	20% wheelchair bound
Oculopharyngeal	14q11.2-q13	AD/AR	Polyadenylate binding protein nuclear 1	Onset: ≈48 yr, 100% symptomatic by age 70
Myotonic dystrophy	19q13.3	AD	DMPK, CCHC-type zinc finger and CNBP	Onset: 50% show signs by age 20; variable severity

AD, Autosomal dominant; *AR*, autosomal recessive; *CCHC*, cysteine and histidine amino acid sequence in this class of zinc finger; *CMD*, congenital muscular dystrophy; *CNBP*, cellular nucleic acid–binding protein; *CNS*, central nervous system; *DMPK*, dystrophia myotonica-protein kinase; *LE*, life expectancy; *LGMD*, limb-girdle muscular dystrophy; *O-MNAGAT*, O-mannose β-1,2-*N*-acetylglucosaminyl transferase; *XR*, X chromosome related.
From Firestein G.S.: *Kelley's textbook of rheumatology*, ed 9, Philadelphia, 2013, Saunders.

 BASIC INFORMATION

DEFINITION

Mushroom poisoning is intoxication resulting from ingestion of poisonous mushrooms.

ICD-10CM CODES
T62.0X1A Toxic effect of ingested mushrooms, accidental (unintentional), initial encounter

EPIDEMIOLOGY & DEMOGRAPHICS

- 5% of all mushrooms are poisonous. Distinction between poisonous and edible mushrooms may be difficult even by experienced persons.
- Common poisonous species include *Amanita, Russula, Gyromitra,* and *Omphalotus* (see Table E1M-35).
- Identification of syndromes is more important than knowing the associated species (Table 1M-36).

PHYSICAL FINDINGS & CLINICAL PRESENTATION

- *Russula* causes confusion, delirium, visual disturbance, tachycardia, and diarrhea within a few hours of ingestion. Prognosis: spontaneous recovery (mortality rate >1%).

- *Amanita* and *Gyromitra* intoxication begins with symptoms of gastroenteritis (nausea, vomiting, diarrhea, and abdominal cramps) approximately 10 hr after ingestion. *Amanita* then causes cardiomyopathy and hepatic and renal failure. *Gyromitra* produces jaundice and seizures. Both mushrooms are associated with a 50% mortality rate.
- *Omphalotus* causes symptoms of gastroenteritis that subside spontaneously within 24 hr.

ETIOLOGY

- *Amanita* contains cytotoxic substances and isoxazoles that are gamma-aminobutyric acid neurotransmitter analogs.
- *Gyromitra* contains a pyridoxine antagonist that disrupts the gastrointestinal mucosa and causes hemolysis.
- *Russula* contains a cholinergic substance.

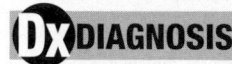 DIAGNOSIS

DIFFERENTIAL DIAGNOSIS

- Food poisoning
- Overdose of prescription or illegal drug
- Other intoxications
- See topic on specific organ failure (e.g., renal or hepatic failure) for differential diagnosis of those conditions

WORKUP

- History
- Inspection and identification of suspected mushrooms
- Mushroom or gastric content analysis (by thin-layer chromatography or radioimmunoassay)

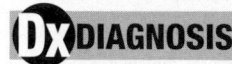 TREATMENT

- Gastric lavage
- Repeated administration of activated charcoal
- Penicillin G or silibinin can be used for *Amanita* mushroom intoxication. Silibinin interferes with hepatic uptake of alpha-amanitine. IV silibinin is not currently available in the U.S. Where available, it is given at a rate of 5 mg/kg IV over 1 hour, followed by 20 mg/kg/day. An oral form of silibinin is available in health food stores as an extract from milk thistle called silymarin. Dose is 1 g PO qid. IV benzyl penicillin reduces hepatocyte uptake of amatoxin.
- Supportive care as needed (may require respiratory assistance, hemodialysis, or emergency liver transplantation)

RELATED CONTENT

Mushroom Poisoning (Patient Information)

AUTHOR: **FRED F. FERRI, M.D.**

TABLE 1M-36 Mushroom Poisoning Syndromes

Syndrome	Commonly Implicated Mushrooms	Toxins
Short Incubation		
Delirium, restlessness	*Amanita muscaria, Amanita pantherina*	Ibotenic acid, muscimol
Parasympathetic hyperactivity	*Inocybe* spp., *Clitocybe* spp., *Boletus* spp.	Muscarine
Hallucinations, somnolence, dysphoria	*Psilocybe* spp., *Panaeolus* spp., *Conocybe* spp.	Psilocybin
Disulfiram reaction	*Coprinus atramentarius*	Coprine
Gastroenteritis	Many	Various uncharacterized irritants
Long Incubation		
Gastroenteritis, hepatorenal failure	*Amanita phalloides, Amanita virosa,* and other *Amanitia; Galerina, Cortinarius,* and *Lepiota* spp.	Cyclopeptides (i.e., amatoxins, phallotoxins)
Gastroenteritis, muscle cramping, hepatic failure, hemolysis, seizures, coma	*Gyromitra* spp.	Gyromitrin
Gastroenteritis, acute renal failure (temporary)	*Amanita smithiana*	Allenic norleucine
Gastroenteritis, acute renal failure (often irreversible)	*Cortinarius* spp.	Orellanine

From Bennett JE et al: *Mandell, Douglas, and Bennett's principles and practice of infectious diseases,* ed 8, Philadelphia, 2015, WB Saunders.

BASIC INFORMATION

DEFINITION

Myasthenia gravis (MG) is an autoimmune disorder that affects postsynaptic neuromuscular transmission classically mediated by antibodies directed against the nicotinic acetylcholine receptor (AChR) of the neuromuscular junction, resulting in a decrease in functional postsynaptic ACh receptors and consequent weakness. More recently, antibodies against muscle-specific tyrosine kinase (MuSK) have been described, which impact both pre- and postsynaptic function of the neuromuscular junction.

ICD-10CM CODES
G70.00 Myasthenia gravis without (acute) exacerbation
G70.01 Myasthenia gravis with (acute) exacerbation
P94.0   Transient neonatal myasthenia gravis

EPIDEMIOLOGY & DEMOGRAPHICS

INCIDENCE (IN U.S.): 10 to 20 cases annually per 1 million persons. It is the most common disorder of neuromuscular junction transmission.
PEAK INCIDENCE: Female, second to third decades; male, sixth to eighth decades
PREVALENCE (IN U.S.): One per 20,000 persons
PREDOMINANT SEX: Females are affected more often than males (3:2) in adults; they are equally affected in the elderly
GENETICS: Increased frequency of HLA-B8, DR3

PHYSICAL FINDINGS & CLINICAL PRESENTATION

- The hallmark of MG is fluctuating weakness worsened with exercise and improved with rest.
- Generalized weakness involving proximal muscles, diaphragm, and neck extensors is common.
- Weakness is confined to eyelids and extraocular muscles in approximately 15% of patients.
- Bulbar symptoms of ptosis, diplopia, dysarthria, and dysphagia are common.
- Reflexes, sensation, and coordination are normal.

ETIOLOGY

Antibody-mediated decrease in nicotinic AChR in the postsynaptic neuromuscular junction resulting in defective neuromuscular transmission and subsequent muscle weakness and fatigue. MuSK antibodies have been recognized since 2001 and present with a similar syndrome to AchR MG although they may have more bulbar weakness, proximal muscle atrophy, and either lack of or paradoxical response to pyridostigmine.

DIAGNOSIS

DIFFERENTIAL DIAGNOSIS

Lambert-Eaton myasthenic syndrome, botulism, medication-induced myasthenia, chronic progressive external ophthalmoplegia, congenital myasthenic syndromes, thyroid disease, basilar meningitis, intracranial mass lesion with cranial neuropathy, Miller-Fisher variant of Guillain-Barré syndrome

WORKUP

- Edrophonium (Tensilon) test (Fig. E1M-61): useful in MG patients with ocular symptoms. Cardiac monitoring and atropine ready at the bedside are essential. Patients with MG may also have a positive ice test (Fig. E1M-62).
- Repetitive nerve stimulation: successive stimulation shows decrement of muscle action potential in clinically weak muscle; may be negative in up to 50%.
- Single-fiber electromyography: highly sensitive; abnormal in up to 95% of patients.
- Serum AChR antibodies found in up to 90% of patients.
- A subset of patients with seronegative MG may have MuSK antibodies.

ADDITIONAL TESTS

- Spirometry to document pulmonary function
- CT scan or MRI with contrast of anterior chest to look for thymoma or residual thymic tissue
- Thyroid-stimulating hormone, free T_4 to rule out thyroid disease

TREATMENT

NONPHARMACOLOGIC THERAPY

- Patient education to facilitate recognition of worsening symptoms and impress need for medical evaluation at onset of clinical deterioration
- Avoidance of selected drugs known to provoke exacerbations of MG (beta-blockers, aminoglycoside and quinolone antibiotics, penicillamine, interferons, class I antiarrhythmics [procainamide, quinidine, etc.])
- Prompt treatment of infections, diet modification, and speech evaluation with dysphagia

ACUTE GENERAL Rx

- Symptomatic treatment with acetylcholinesterase inhibitors:
  1. Pyridostigmine 30 to 60 mg PO q4 to 6h initially; onset of effects is 30 min, duration 4 hr. May be titrated up to 120 mg every 4 hr. GI upset is not uncommon with higher doses and may respond to hyoscyamine.
- Immunosuppressive treatment with corticosteroids, azathioprine, mycophenolate mofetil, cyclosporine for long-term disease-modifying therapy

1. Prednisone initiated at 15 to 20 mg qd titrate by 5-mg increments to effect or
2. dose of 1 mg/kg/day with improvement in 2 to 4 wk and maximal response by 3 to 6 mo
3. Azathioprine initiated at 50 mg qd titrated to 2 to 3 mg/kg/day with clinical effect in 6 to 12 mo
4. Cyclosporine initiated at 5 mg/kg/day with clinical effect within 1 to 2 mo
- Plasmapheresis and IV immunoglobulin are short-term options for immunotherapy during an exacerbation. There is no significant difference in efficacy between IVIG and plasmapheresis.
- Mechanical ventilation is lifesaving in setting of a myasthenic crisis. Consider elective intubation if forced vital capacity <15 ml/kg, maximal expiratory pressure <40 cm H_2O, or negative inspiratory pressure <25 cm H_2O.

SURGICAL Rx

- In thymomatous MG, thymectomy is indicated in all patients. If the tumor cannot be surgically resected, chemotherapy can be considered for prevention of local invasion and symptom relief.
- For nonthymomatous autoimmune MG, thymectomy is an option in select patients, typically <40 yr.

DISPOSITION

Course of disease is highly variable. Mortality rate has decreased from 75% to 4.5% over past 4 decades.

REFERRAL

Surgical referral for thymectomy in selected cases (see "Surgical Rx")

PEARLS & CONSIDERATIONS

- Sustained upward or lateral gaze and arm abduction for 120 sec may be necessary to elicit subtle signs on examination.
- Myasthenic patients can worsen rapidly and warrant close, careful observation during an exacerbation.

SUGGESTED READINGS

Available at www.expertconsult.com

RELATED CONTENT

Myasthenia Gravis (Patient Information)

AUTHOR: **TAYLOR HARRISON, M.D.**

Myelodysplastic Syndrome PTG

BASIC INFORMATION

DEFINITION

Myelodysplastic syndromes (MDS) are a group of acquired clonal disorders affecting hematopoietic stem cells that is characterized by altered differentiation and proliferation. Patients present with peripheral blood cytopenias and morphologic abnormalities but have a hypercellular bone marrow upon examination. The increased marrow cellularity reflects ineffective hematopoiesis with inadequate maturation resulting in cytopenias.

CLASSIFICATION

- Several classification systems have been developed as our understanding of MDS has evolved. In 1982, the French-American-British (FAB) classification included refractory anemia, refractory anemia with ringed sideroblasts, refractory anemia with excess blasts, chronic myelomonocytic leukemia, and refractory anemia with excess blasts in transformation.
- In 1999, the World Health Organization (WHO) modified the FAB by incorporating newer morphologic insights and cytogenetic findings. It reduced the blast percentage for the diagnosis of acute myeloid leukemia to 20%, added refractory cytopenia with multilineage dysplasia, refractory cytopenia with multilineage dysplasia and ringed sideroblasts, refined refractory anemia with excessive blasts into types 1 and 2, and added unclassified MDS, and MDS associated with isolated del(5q).
- In 2008, the WHO further modified the classification by subcategorizing MDS into six categories.

SYNONYMS

MDS
Preleukemia

ICD-10CM CODES

D46.9 Myelodysplastic syndrome, unspecified
D46.C Myelodysplastic syndrome with isolated del(5q) chromosomal abnormality
D46.Z Other myelodysplastic syndromes

EPIDEMIOLOGY & DEMOGRAPHICS

INCIDENCE (IN U.S.): Approximately 80 cases/100,000 persons per yr. An estimated 30,000 new cases are diagnosed annually in the U.S.
PREDOMINANT AGE: More common in elderly patients; median age >65 yr

PHYSICAL FINDINGS & CLINICAL PRESENTATION

- Patients often present with fatigue due to anemia and also with thrombocytopenia and leukopenia.
- Skin pallor, mucosal bleeding, and ecchymosis may be present.
- Fever, infection, and dyspnea are common.

ETIOLOGY

Exposure to radiation, chemotherapeutic agents, benzene, or other organic compounds is associated with myelodysplasia. Table 1M-38 describes predisposing factors and epidemiologic associations of patients with MDS. Up to 40 genes are mutated in MDS with 90% of patients having at least one mutation and a median of two to three mutations detected per patient. These mutations affect specific functional pathways and can be subcategorized into those that affect spliceosome machinery, DNA methylation, chromatin modification, transcription factors, kinase signaling pathways, and DNA repair pathways.

DIAGNOSIS

DIFFERENTIAL DIAGNOSIS

- Hereditary dysplasias (e.g., Fanconi's anemia, Diamond-Blackfan syndrome)
- Vitamin B_{12}/folate deficiency
- Exposure to toxins (drugs, alcohol, chemotherapy)
- Renal failure
- Irradiation
- Autoimmune disease
- Paroxysmal nocturnal hemoglobinuria

WORKUP

Diagnostic workup (Fig. 1M-68) includes laboratory evaluation (Table E1M-39) and bone marrow examination (Fig. E1M-69). Cytogenetic analysis (Box E1M-5) by conventional metaphase karyotyping or by MDS FISH assessment should be performed in patients with MDS. Physical examination, medical history, and laboratory tests aiding in diagnosis of MDS are described in Table 1M-40.

 TREATMENT

NONPHARMACOLOGIC THERAPY

- Red blood cell transfusions in patients with severe symptomatic anemia
- Platelet transfusions in patients with severe thrombocytopenia or those with bleeding episodes

ACUTE GENERAL Rx

- The initial focus of MDS therapy relates to stratification of patients into low, intermediate, and high-risk states using well-defined and validated risk stratification systems. The original International Prognostic Scoring System (IPSS) incorporated cytopenias, cytogenetics, and blast percentage and is still clinically used. More classification systems have been proposed, and the revised IPSS (IPSS-R) has been created from an evaluation of more than 7000 patients. The IPSS-R utilizes a five-tier risk grouping and accounts for the degree of cytopenias as well as discrimination of bone marrow blast percentage and has 15 cytogenetic subtypes.
- Low-risk patients are treated with supportive care or growth factors.
- Poor-risk patients are treated with hypomethylating agents along with supportive care.

TABLE 1M-38 Predisposing Factors and Epidemiologic Associations of Patients with Myelodysplastic Syndrome

Heritable

Constitutional Genetic Disorders

Trisomy 8 mosaicism
Familial monosomy 7
Down syndrome (trisomy 21)
Neurofibromatosis 1
Germ cell tumors [embryonal dysgenesis del(12p)]

Congenital Neutropenia

Kostmann syndrome
Shwachman-Diamond syndrome

DNA Repair Deficiencies

Fanconi anemia
Ataxia-telangiectasia
Bloom syndrome
Xeroderma pigmentosum
Pharmacogenomic polymorphisms (GSTq1-null)

Acquired

Senescence

Mutagen Exposure

Alkylator therapy (chlorambucil, cyclophosphamide, melphalan, N-mustards)
Topoisomerase II inhibitors (anthracyclines)
β Emitters (32p)
Autologous stem cell transplantation
Environmental/occupational (benzene)
Tobacco
Aplastic anemia
Paroxysmal nocturnal hemoglobinuria

From Hoffman R et al: *Hematology, basic principles and practice*, ed 5, Philadelphia, 2009, Churchill Livingstone.

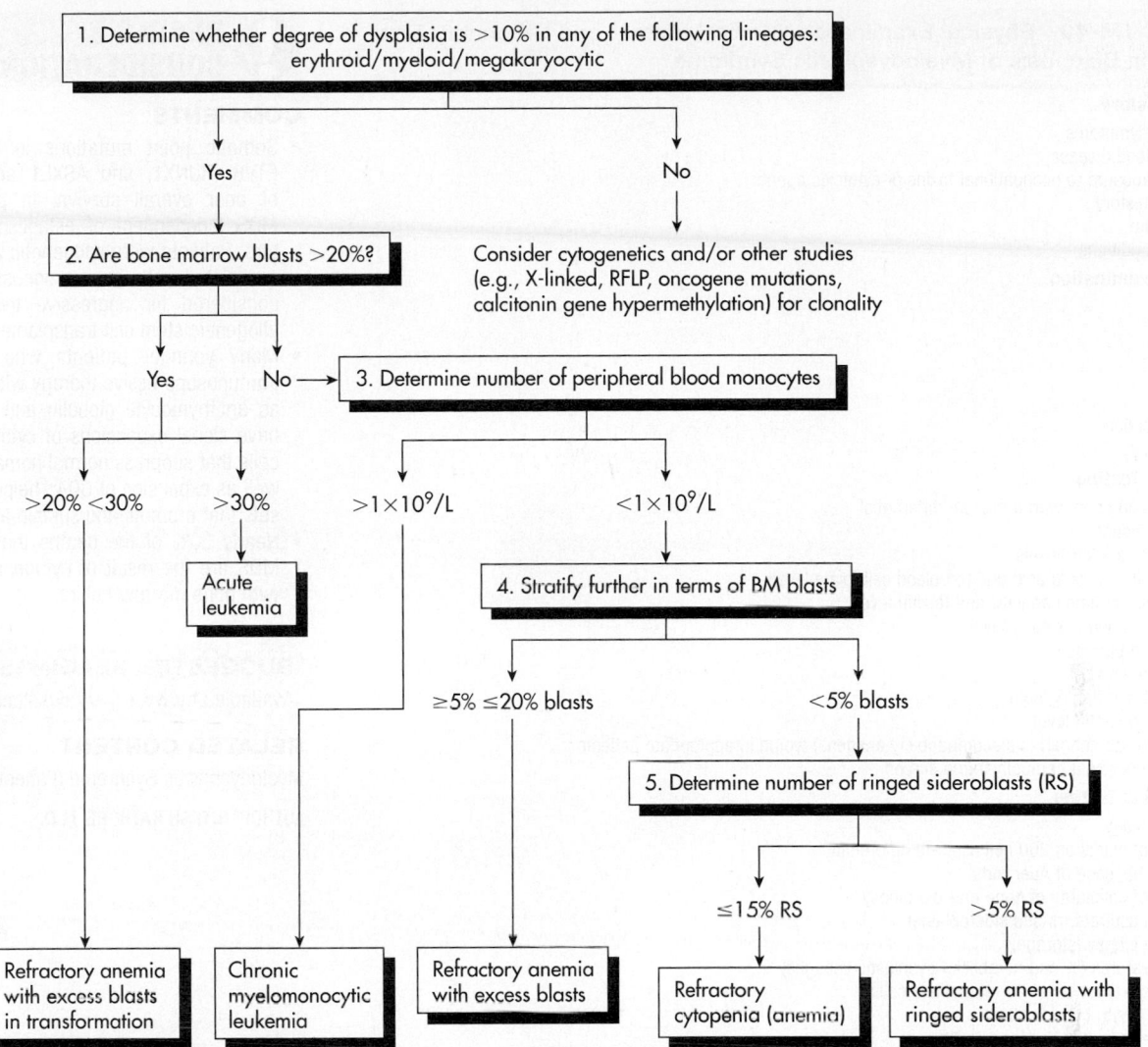

1. Determine whether degree of dysplasia is >10% in any of the following lineages: erythroid/myeloid/megakaryocytic

Yes — 2. Are bone marrow blasts >20%?

No — Consider cytogenetics and/or other studies (e.g., X-linked, RFLP, oncogene mutations, calcitonin gene hypermethylation) for clonality

Yes / No → 3. Determine number of peripheral blood monocytes

>20% <30% / >30% — Acute leukemia

>1×10⁹/L / <1×10⁹/L

4. Stratify further in terms of BM blasts

≥5% ≤20% blasts / <5% blasts

5. Determine number of ringed sideroblasts (RS)

≤15% RS / >5% RS

Refractory anemia with excess blasts in transformation | Chronic myelomonocytic leukemia | Refractory anemia with excess blasts | Refractory cytopenia (anemia) | Refractory anemia with ringed sideroblasts

FIGURE 1M-68 Myelodysplastic syndrome. *BM blasts,* Bone marrow blastocyst; *RFLP,* restriction fragment length polymorphism. (From Abeloff MD: *Clinical oncology,* ed 3, New York, 2004, Churchill Livingstone.)

- Appropriate patients are offered allogeneic stem cell transplantation (Fig. 1M-70) as a potentially curative option with high-volume centers treating patients <80 years old.
- Erythropoietin (10,000 to 40,000 units/week) or pegylated erythropoietin (200 to 500 mg every 1-3 weeks) is used in patients with symptomatic anemia. Responses with increase in hemoglobin and decreased transfusion requirements are achieved typically in patients who have serum erythropoietin levels <500 U/L and adequate iron stores.
- DNA methyltransferase inhibitors: Azacitidine, a pyrimidine nucleoside analogue of cytidine, has been shown to improve the quality of life for patients with MDS and probably prolong survival. Decitabine, another nucleoside analogue, has also been FDA approved for patients with MDS. These agents may also be useful in preventing the transition of MDS to AML.
- Immunomodulators: Lenalidomide, a novel analogue of thalidomide, has demonstrated hematologic activity in patients with low-rise MDS who have no response to erythropoietin or who are unlikely to benefit from conventional therapy. Lenalidomide can also reduce transfusion requirements and reverse cytologic and cytogenetic abnormalities in patients who have MDS with the 5q31 deletion.
- Results of chemotherapy are generally disappointing. Combination chemotherapy regimens (e.g., cytarabine plus daunorubicin) that are used to treat acute myeloid leukemias generally induce a complete response in only a minority of patients, and the average duration of response is <1 yr.
- The use of myeloid growth factors (granulocyte colony-stimulating factor [G-CSF], granulocyte-macrophage colony-stimulating factor [GM-CSF]) is reserved for patients with severe neutropenias and high infection risk. Additionally, these CSFs can provide a synergistic effect when used in combination with erythropoietin in terms of improvement in the hemoglobin levels.

CHRONIC Rx

Monitor for infections, bleeding, and complications of anemia. Supportive measures include blood transfusions and erythropoietin for anemia and antibiotics to treat opportunistic infections. Iron overload from frequent transfusions may require iron chelation therapy.

DISPOSITION

- Long-term remission rates in young patients with allogeneic stem cell transplantation approach 40% to 50%.
- The risk of transformation to acute myelogenous leukemia varies with the percentage of blasts in the bone marrow.
- According to the International Myelodysplastic Syndrome Risk Analysis Workshop, the most important variables in disease outcome are the specific cytogenetic abnormalities, the percentage of blasts in the bone marrow, and the number of hematopoietic lineages involved in the cytopenias.

REFERRAL

- Hematology referral for all patients with MDS
- Bone marrow transplant physician for evaluation for stem cell transplant eligibility as a potentially curative modality

TABLE 1M-40 Physical Examination, Medical History, and Laboratory Tests Aiding in Diagnosis of Myelodysplastic Syndrome

Medical History

Duration of symptoms
History of blood disease
History of exposure to occupational toxins or cytotoxic agents
Medication history
Alcohol intake
Comorbid conditions

Physical Examination

Pallor
Petechiae
Purpura
Bruising
Tachypnea
Signs of infection
Splenomegaly

Laboratory Testing

Complete blood count with a manual differential
Reticulocyte count
Vitamin B_{12} and folate levels
Consider methylmalonic acid and red blood cell folate levels
Iron, total iron-binding capacity, and ferritin level
Thyroid-stimulating hormone level
Lactate dehydrogenase
Antinuclear antibody
Coombs test and haptoglobin
Serum erythropoietin level
Human leukocyte antigen (histocompatibility antigens) typing in appropriate patients
Paroxysmal nocturnal hemoglobinuria screen

Bone Marrow Testing

Hematopathology
Percentage of blasts on 200 cell aspirate differential
Presence or absence of Auer rods
Percentage of cellularity of bone marrow biopsy
Iron stain on aspirate (ringed sideroblasts)
Iron stain on biopsy (storage)
Dysplastic features (% and number of dysplastic lineages)
Cytogenetics (karyotype of 20 metaphase cells)
Fluorescent in situ hybridization
Flow cytometry (not useful for quantitation)

From Hoffman R et al: *Hematology, basic principles and practice,* ed 5, Philadelphia, 2009, Churchill Livingstone.

PEARLS & CONSIDERATIONS

COMMENTS

- Somatic point mutations in TP53, EZH2, ETV6, RUNX1, and ASXL1 are predictors of poor overall survival in patients with MDS independent of established risk factors. Patients with cytogenetic abnormalities associated with poor prognosis should be considered for aggressive treatment with allogeneic stem cell transplantation.
- Many younger patients who respond to immunosuppressive therapy with drugs such as antithymocyte globulin and cyclosporine have clonal expansions of cytotoxic CD8$^+$ T cells that suppress normal hematopoiesis, as well as expansion of CD4$^+$ helper T-cell subsets that promote and sustain autoimmunity.
- Nearly 50% of the deaths that result from MDS are the result of cytopenia associated with bone marrow failure.

SUGGESTED READINGS

Available at www.expertconsult.com

RELATED CONTENT

Myelodysplastic Syndrome (Patient Information)

AUTHOR: **RITESH RATHORE, M.D.**

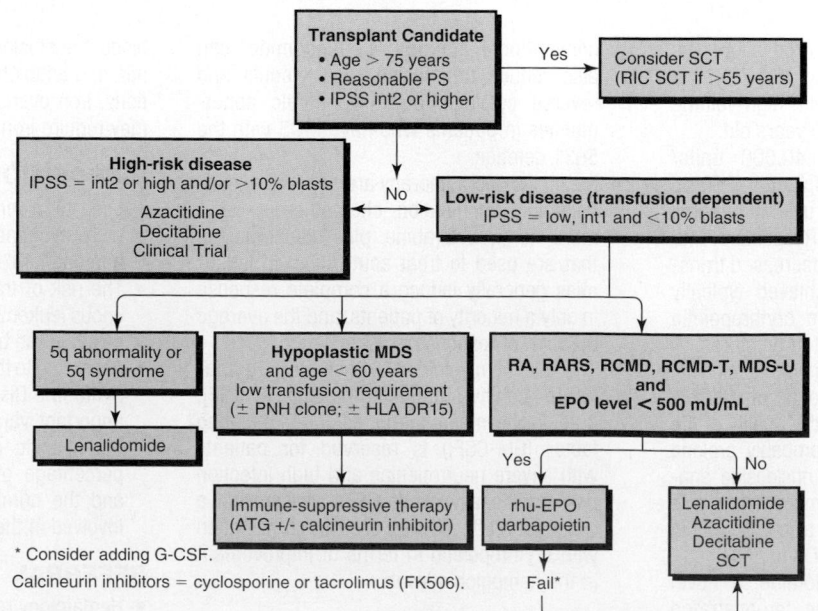

FIGURE 1M-70 Algorithm for management of a patient with myelodysplastic syndrome. *PNH,* Paroxysmal nocturnal hemoglobinuria; *PS,* performance status; *RIC,* reduced-intensity conditioning regimen; *SCT,* stem cell transplant. (From Hoffman R et al: *Hematology: basic principles and practice,* ed 5, Philadelphia, 2009, Churchill Livingstone.)

 **BASIC INFORMATION**

DEFINITION

Myocardial infarction (MI) is a clinical syndrome characterized by symptoms of myocardial ischemia, persistent electrocardiographic (ECG) changes, and release of biomarkers of myocardial necrosis resulting from an insufficient supply of oxygenated blood to an area of the heart. According to the European Society of Cardiology/American College of Cardiology, either one of the following criteria for acute evolving or recent MI satisfies the diagnosis:

1. Detection of the rise and/or fall of cardiac biomarker values (preferably cTn) with at least 1 value above the 99th percentile and with at least 1 of the following:
2. Symptoms of ischemia
3. New, or presumed new, significant ST-T changes or new LBBB. New ST elevation at the J point in at least 2 contiguous leads of ≥2 mm (0.2 mV) in men or ≥1.5 mm (0.15 mV) in women in leads V2–V3 and/or of ≥1 mm (0.1 mV) in other contiguous chest leads or the limb leads
4. Development of pathologic Q waves in the ECG
5. Imaging evidence of new loss of viable myocardium or a new regional wall motion abnormality
6. Identification of an intracoronary thrombus by angiography or autopsy
   ○ Pathologic findings of acute MI

MI may be classified as ST-segment elevation MI (STEMI) and non–ST-segment elevation MI [NSTEMI]) depending on the ECG findings on MI presentation. This entry primarily focuses on STEMI. For a discussion of NSTEMI, see "Acute Coronary Syndromes."

The *European Heart Journal* and the *Journal of the American College of Cardiology* published a new definition of acute MI that includes 5 subtypes of acute MI, imaging tests supporting the diagnosis, and biomarker thresholds after percutaneous coronary intervention (PCI) or coronary artery bypass grafting (CABG) in 2012.

- Type 1: Spontaneous MI related to ischemia due to a primary coronary event such as plaque erosion and/or rupture, fissuring, or dissection.
- Type 2: MI secondary to ischemia other than coronary artery disease, due to either increased oxygen demand or decreased supply (e.g., coronary endothelial dysfunction, coronary artery spasm, coronary embolism, anemia, arrhythmias, respiratory failure, hypertension with/without LVH, or hypotension). Also in critically ill patients or in patients undergoing major non-cardiac surgery, elevated values of cardiac biomarkers may appear due to the direct toxic effects of endogenous or exogenous high circulating catecholamine levels.
- Type 3: Sudden unexpected cardiac death, including cardiac arrest, often with symptoms suggestive of myocardial ischemia, accompanied by presumed new ST elevation, new left bundle branch block, or evidence of fresh thrombus in a coronary artery by angiography and/or at autopsy, or death occurring before blood samples could be obtained or at a time before the appearance of cardiac biomarkers in the blood.

- Type 4a: MI associated with percutaneous coronary intervention. Elevation of cTn >5× percentile of upper reference limit (URL) in patients with normal baseline value, or a rise of cTN >20% if the baseline values are stable and are stable or falling. In addition to either symptoms of ischemia, new ischemic ECG changes or new LBBB, or angiographic loss of a patent coronary artery, persistent slow or no-flow, or embolization, or imaging of new wall motion abnormality.
- Type 4b: MI associated with stent thrombosis as documented by angiography or at autopsy in the setting of myocardial ischemia and with a rise/fall of cardiac biomarker values.
- Type 5: MI associated with coronary artery bypass grafting. Elevation of cardiac biomarker values >10× 99% URL in patients with normal baseline cTn values, in addition to either new pathological Q waves or new LBBB, or new native coronary artery occlusion or imaging of new abnormal wall motion abnormality.

SYNONYMS

MI
Myocardial infarction
ST-elevation MI
Heart attack
Acute myocardial infarction
AMI
Coronary thrombosis
Coronary occlusion

ICD-10CM CODES

I21.01	ST elevation (STEMI) myocardial infarction involving left main coronary artery
I21.02	ST elevation (STEMI) myocardial infarction involving left anterior descending coronary artery
I21.09	ST elevation (STEMI) myocardial infarction involving other coronary artery of anterior wall
I21.11	ST elevation (STEMI) myocardial infarction involving right coronary artery
I21.19	ST elevation (STEMI) myocardial infarction involving other coronary artery of inferior wall
I21.21	ST elevation (STEMI) myocardial infarction involving left circumflex coronary artery
I21.29	ST elevation (STEMI) myocardial infarction involving other sites
I21.3	ST elevation (STEMI) myocardial infarction of unspecified site
I21.4	Non-ST elevation (NSTEMI) myocardial infarction
I22.0	Subsequent ST elevation (STEMI) myocardial infarction of anterior wall
I22.1	Subsequent ST elevation (STEMI) myocardial infarction of inferior wall
I22.2	Subsequent non-ST elevation (NSTEMI) myocardial infarction
I22.8	Subsequent ST elevation (STEMI) myocardial infarction of other sites
I22.9	Subsequent ST elevation (STEMI) myocardial infarction of unspecified site

EPIDEMIOLOGY & DEMOGRAPHICS

INCIDENCE/PREVALENCE (IN U.S.):

- In 2009, around 683,000 patients were discharged from U.S. hospitals with a diagnosis of acute coronary syndrome (ACS). Community incidence rates as well as mortality rates from STEMI have declined over the past decade, whereas those for NSTEMI have increased. At present, STEMI comprises approximately 30% to 40% of MI presentations. In-hospital mortality (approximately 5%-6%) and 1-year mortality (approximately 7%-18%). The most common cause of death in adults over the age of 40 is myocardial infarction. A heart attack takes the life of >1,500,000 people each year just in the United States.
- Modifiable risk factors such as hypertension, diabetes, and cigarette smoking have decreased from 2002 to 2009, except for hyperlipidemia, which has shown no significant change. Obesity has increased from 33% to 37.4%.
- Patients with first acute MI were found to have an almost threefold increase in cigarette smoking from 2002 to 2009. Cigarette smoking is associated with endothelial dysfunction, prothrombotic defects, and increased oxidative stress.
- It is more prevalent in males between the ages of 45 and 65 yr; no predominant sex after the age of 65
- Women comprised 30% of STEMI patients. They experience more lethal and severe first acute MIs than men regardless of comorbidity, previous angina, or age. Being a woman constituted a strong independent predictor of failure to receive reperfusion therapy, have longer reperfusion times, be less often given the standard of care treatment within 24 hours of presentation, and have higher risk for bleeding with antithrombotic therapy.
- At least one fourth of all MIs are clinically unrecognized. Approximately 23% of patients with STEMI in the U.S. have diabetes mellitus, and three quarters of all deaths among patients with diabetes mellitus are related to coronary artery disease. Diabetes mellitus is associated with higher short- and long-term mortality after STEMI. In the CRUSADE trial, 7% of eligible patients did not receive reperfusion therapy. The most important factor for not providing reperfusion therapy in eligible patients was increasing age.

PHYSICAL FINDINGS & CLINICAL PRESENTATION

Clinical presentation: Myocardial infarction is usually based on a history of substernal pressure type chest pain radiated to the neck, lower jaw, left arm or mid-back lasting 20 min or more that is not completely relieved by sublingual nitroglycerin. The pain may not be severe. Some patients may present with atypical symptoms such as nausea/vomiting, shortness of breath, fatigue, palpitations, and diaphoresis. The elderly in particular may present with dizziness, or syncope. The patients who tend to present with atypical symptoms are more likely to be women, diabetic patients, or elderly patients and less frequently receive reperfusion therapy and other evidence-based therapies than patients with a typical chest pain presentation. Records show that up to 30% of patients with STEMI present with atypical symptoms.

Physical findings:
- Skin may be diaphoretic and exhibit pallor (because of decreased oxygen).
- Rales may be present at the bases of lungs (indicative of heart failure [HF]).
- Cardiac auscultation may reveal an apical systolic murmur caused by mitral regurgitation from papillary muscle dysfunction; S_3 or S_4 may also be present.
- Up to 10% of patients may present with acute pulmonary edema and/or cardiogenic shock.
- Physical examination may be completely normal.

ETIOLOGY
- Coronary atherosclerosis and plaque rupture
- Coronary artery spasm
- Coronary embolism (caused by infective endocarditis, rheumatic heart disease, intracavitary thrombus, atrial fibrillation)
- Periarteritis and other coronary artery inflammatory diseases
- Dissection into coronary arteries (aneurysmal or iatrogenic)
- Calcium supplementation may promote vascular calcification. Studies have shown that calcium supplementation (but not dietary calcium intake) is associated with elevated risk for MI.
- MI with normal coronaries: more frequent in younger patients and cocaine addicts. The risk of acute MI is increased by a factor of 24

during the 60 min after the use of cocaine in persons who are otherwise at relatively low risk. Most patients with cocaine-related MI are young, nonwhite, male cigarette smokers without other risk factors for coronary heart disease and who have a history of repeated cocaine use. Blood and urine toxicology screen for cocaine is recommended in all young patients who present with acute MI.
- Hypercoagulable states, increased blood viscosity (polycythemia vera and autoimmune diseases such as systemic lupus, antiphospholipid syndrome)

(Dx) DIAGNOSIS

DIFFERENTIAL DIAGNOSIS
The various causes of myocardial ischemia are described along with the differential diagnosis of chest pain.

LABORATORY TESTS
- Electrocardiogram (Fig. 1M-71): a 12-lead ECG should be performed and shown to an experienced emergency physician within 10 min of ED arrival for all patients with chest discomfort (or anginal equivalent) or other symptoms suggestive of STEMI. If the initial ECG is not diagnostic for STEMI but the patient remains symptomatic and there is a high clinical suspicion for STEMI, serial ECGs at 5- to 10-minute intervals or continuous 12-lead ST-segment monitoring should be performed to detect the potential development of ST elevation. In patients with inferior STEMI, right-sided ECG leads should be obtained to look for ST elevation suggestive of right ventricular (RV) infarction. The joint

ESC/ACCF/AHA committee for the definition of MI established the definition for the diagnosis of ST-elevation MI, which is considered to be present when there is an ST-segment elevation in two contiguous leads, ≥2 mm for men and ≥1.5 mm for women in precordial leads and/or ≥1 mm in limb leads. ST-segment elevation is measured at 0.08 sec after the J point (the junction between the end of the QRS and the beginning of the ST segment). In addition, ST depression in >2 precordial leads (V1–V4) may indicate transmural posterior injury; multilead ST depression with coexistent ST elevation in lead aVR has been described in patients with left main or proximal left anterior descending artery occlusion.
- New or presumably new LBBB at presentation occurs infrequently, may interfere with ST-elevation analysis, and should not be considered diagnostic of acute myocardial infarction (MI) in isolation.
- ECG findings alone, without laboratory results, are sufficient to diagnose STEMI; therefore, treatment should not be delayed until biomarkers are available.
- Cardiac troponin levels: Cardiac-specific troponin T (cTnT) and cardiac-specific troponin I (cTnI) are generally indicative of myocardial injury with increases in serum levels of >99th percentile of a normal reference population. Detection of a rise and fall pattern of the measurements is essential to the diagnosis of AMI. The rise may occur relatively early after muscle damage (3-6 hr), peak at 12 to 16 hr, and may be present for several days after MI (up to 7 days for cTnI and more than 14 days for cTnT). cTnT or cTnI tests can be falsely positive for myocardial infarction in patients

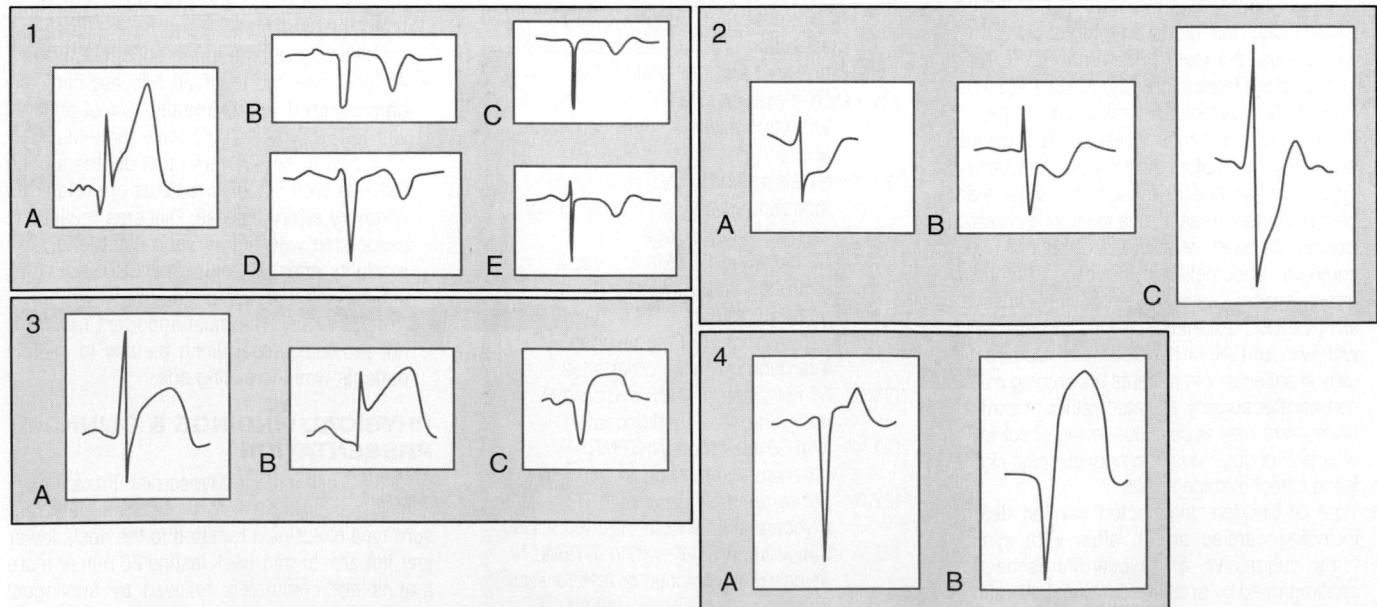

FIGURE 1M-71 Electrocardiographic findings of acute myocardial infarction (AMI). 1, T-wave abnormalities of AMI. *A,* Prominent "hyperacute" T wave. *B-E,* T-wave inversions of non-ST-segment elevation MI (NSTEMI). **2,** ST-segment depression. *A,* Flat. *B,* Downsloping. *C,* Upsloping. **3,** ST-segment elevation. *A,* Convex ST-segment elevation. *B,* Obliquely straight ST-segment elevation. *C,* Convex ST-segment elevation. **4,** Pathologic Q waves. *A,* Pathologic Q wave of completed myocardial infarction. *B,* Simultaneous ST-segment elevation with pathologic Q wave 2 hours into the course of ST-segment elevation MI (STEMI). (From Vincent JL et al: *Textbook of critical care,* ed 6, Philadelphia, 2011, Saunders.)

with renal failure, heart failure, myocarditis, aortic dissection, and pulmonary embolism. Recently, highly sensitive troponin assays (hs-cTnI, hs-cTnT) have also been developed to facilitate an early diagnosis of AMI. Most patients can be diagnosed with AMI within the first 2 to 3 hours of presentation. However, an initial negative high-sensitivity troponin at the time of presentation is not sensitive enough to completely rule out AMI. MI can be excluded in most patients by 6 hours of presentation, and guidelines suggest serial samples be obtained every 3 to 6 hours after an initial sample if there is a high degree of suspicion for AMI.

- CK-MB isoenzyme is also a useful marker for MI if troponin levels are not available. It is released in the circulation in amounts that correlate with the size of the infarct. An increased CK-MB value for the diagnosis of MI is defined as a measurement above the 99th percentile of the upper reference limit. CK-MB can be detected within 3 to 8 hr of the onset of chest pain, peak at 12 to 24 hr, and return to baseline levels within 24 to 48 hr. Troponin, however, is the preferred marker for the diagnosis of myocardial necrosis because of its increased sensitivity and specificity as compared to CK-MB. This preference was recommended by the 2007 Joint ESC/ACCF/AHA Task Force for the Definition of Myocardial Infarction. Because troponins need 7 to 14 days to be cleared by the kidneys, they are not sensitive enough to detect a recurrent MI within days from the initial MI. Therefore, CK-MB isoenzyme can be useful in such circumstances.

IMAGING STUDIES

Imaging studies such as a high-quality portable chest x-ray, transthoracic echocardiography, and a contrast chest CT scan should be used to differentiate STEMI from aortic dissection, pulmonary embolism, and other intrathoracic causes of chest pain (i.e., pneumonia and pneumothorax) in patients for whom this distinction is initially unclear, or to assess for complications of AMI such as pulmonary edema. Transthoracic echocardiography may provide evidence of focal wall motion abnormalities and facilitate triage in patients with ECG findings that are difficult to interpret.

RISK ASSESSMENT

Several risk assessment models are available. In the TIMI risk score for STEMI, the mean 30-day mortality was 6.7%. It is composed of eight baseline variables. The risk score showed a >40-fold graded increase in mortality, with scores ranging from 0 to >8 (P <0.0001); 30-day mortality was 0.1% among patients with a score of 0, 2.25 with a score of 5, and >8.8% among patients with a score of 8 or greater. The variables are divided between historical, exam, and presentation:
Historical:
1) Age 65 to 74 (2 points), >75 (3 points),
2) Diabetes/HTN or angina (1 point).
Exam:
3) SBP <100 mm Hg (3 points),

4) Heart rate >100 bpm (2 points),
5) Killip 2 to 4 (2 points),
6) Weight <67 kg (1 point).
Presentation:
7) Anterior ST elevation or LBBB (1 point),
8) Time to reperfusion >4 hr (1 point).
The higher the score, the higher the 30-day mortality rate. Risk assessment is a continuous process that should be repeated throughout hospitalization and at time of discharge.

 **TREATMENT**

NONPHARMACOLOGIC THERAPY

- Limit patient's activity: bed rest with bedside commode for the initial 12 to 24 hr. If the patient remains stable, gradually increase activity.
- Diet: nothing by mouth until stable, then clear liquids as tolerated to advance gradually to a diet tailored to the patient's comorbidities (i.e., diabetes, hypertension, heart failure, hyperlipidemia, renal failure, COPD, etc.).
- Patient education to decrease the risk of subsequent cardiac events, counseling on smoking cessation, dietary restrictions, regular exercise, and medication compliance should be initiated when the patient is medically stable.

ACUTE GENERAL Rx

- Fig. 1M-72 shows a treatment algorithm for STEMI. Assessment and treatment algorithm for non-ST-segment MI is described in Fig. 1M-73. Rationale of the treatment of a patient with STEMI is based on "time is muscle." Therefore, all communities should create and maintain a regional system of STEMI care that includes assessment and continuous quality improvement of EMS and hospital-based activities. A 12-lead ECG must be done by EMS personnel at the site of first medical contact (FMC).
- Reperfusion therapy should be administered to all eligible patients with STEMI with symptom onset within 12 hours. Indications for primary angioplasty and comparison with fibrinolytic therapy are described in Table 1M-41. Primary PCI (Fig. E1M-74) is the recommended method of reperfusion when it can be performed in a timely fashion by experienced operators with an ideal FMC-to-device time system goal of 90 minutes or less.
- In the absence of contraindications, fibrinolytic therapy (Table 1M-42) should be administered to patients with STEMI at non-PCI-capable hospitals when the anticipated FMC-to-device time at a PCI-capable hospital exceeds 120 minutes because of unavoidable delays. It should be administered within 30 minutes of hospital arrival.
- PCI is superior to thrombolytic therapy and is the standard of care. It is effective and generally results in more favorable outcomes than thrombolytic therapy.
- Primary PCI should be performed in patients with STEMI and persistent ischemic symptoms and who have contraindications to fibrinolytic therapy, irrespective of the time delay

from FMC, or in patients with cardiogenic shock or acute severe HF irrespective of time delay from myocardial infarction (MI) onset. Coronary stents (drug-eluting or bare-metal) are useful in patients with STEMI.

- For patients presenting to a non–PCI-capable hospital, rapid assessment should be done of 1) the time from onset of symptoms, 2) the risk of complications related to STEMI, 3) the risk of bleeding with fibrinolysis, 4) the presence of shock or severe HF, and 5) the time required for transfer to a PCI-capable hospital and a decision about administration of fibrinolytic therapy reached. Because the effectiveness of thrombolytics is time dependent, these agents should ideally be administered either in the field or within 30 min of the patient's arrival to the emergency department (door-to-needle time).
- Fibrinolytics therapy: if tissue plasminogen activator (t-PA) or reteplase is used, anticoagulants, such as heparin, are given to increase the likelihood of patency in the infarct-related artery for 48 hr and preferably for the duration of the index hospitalization, up to 8 days. In patients receiving fibrinolysis for STEMI, treatment with enoxaparin is superior to treatment with unfractionated heparin for 48 hr but is associated with an increase in major bleeding episodes. In patients receiving streptokinase or APSAC, heparin after thrombolysis is not indicated because it does not offer any additional benefit and can result in increased bleeding complications. Tenecteplase and reteplase are comparable with accelerated infusion recombinant t-PA in terms of efficacy and safety but are more convenient because they are administered by bolus injection. Lanoplase and heparin bolus plus infusion are as effective as tPA with regard to mortality rate, but the rate of intracranial hemorrhage is significantly higher.
- Absolute contraindications to thrombolytic therapy (Table 1M-43) include history of intracranial hemorrhage, known intracranial malignant neoplasm or arteriovenous malformation, ischemic stroke within 3 months (except acute ischemic stroke within 4.5 h), suspected aortic dissection, active bleeding or bleeding diathesis (except menses), significant closed head or facial trauma within 3 months, intracranial or intraspinal surgery within 2 months, or severe uncontrolled hypertension (unresponsive to therapy). For streptokinase, this applies to prior treatment within 6 months.
- Relative contraindications: history of chronic severe, poorly controlled hypertension, SBP >180 mm Hg, DBP >110 mm Hg, history of prior ischemic stroke more than 3 months, dementia, known intracranial pathology, traumatic or prolonged CPR (>10 minutes), major surgery <3 weeks, recent internal bleeding within 2 to 4 weeks, noncompressible vascular punctures, pregnancy, active peptic ulcer, oral anticoagulant therapy. After the administration of thrombolytics, immediate transfer to a PCI-capable facility is advisable without waiting for lytic results.

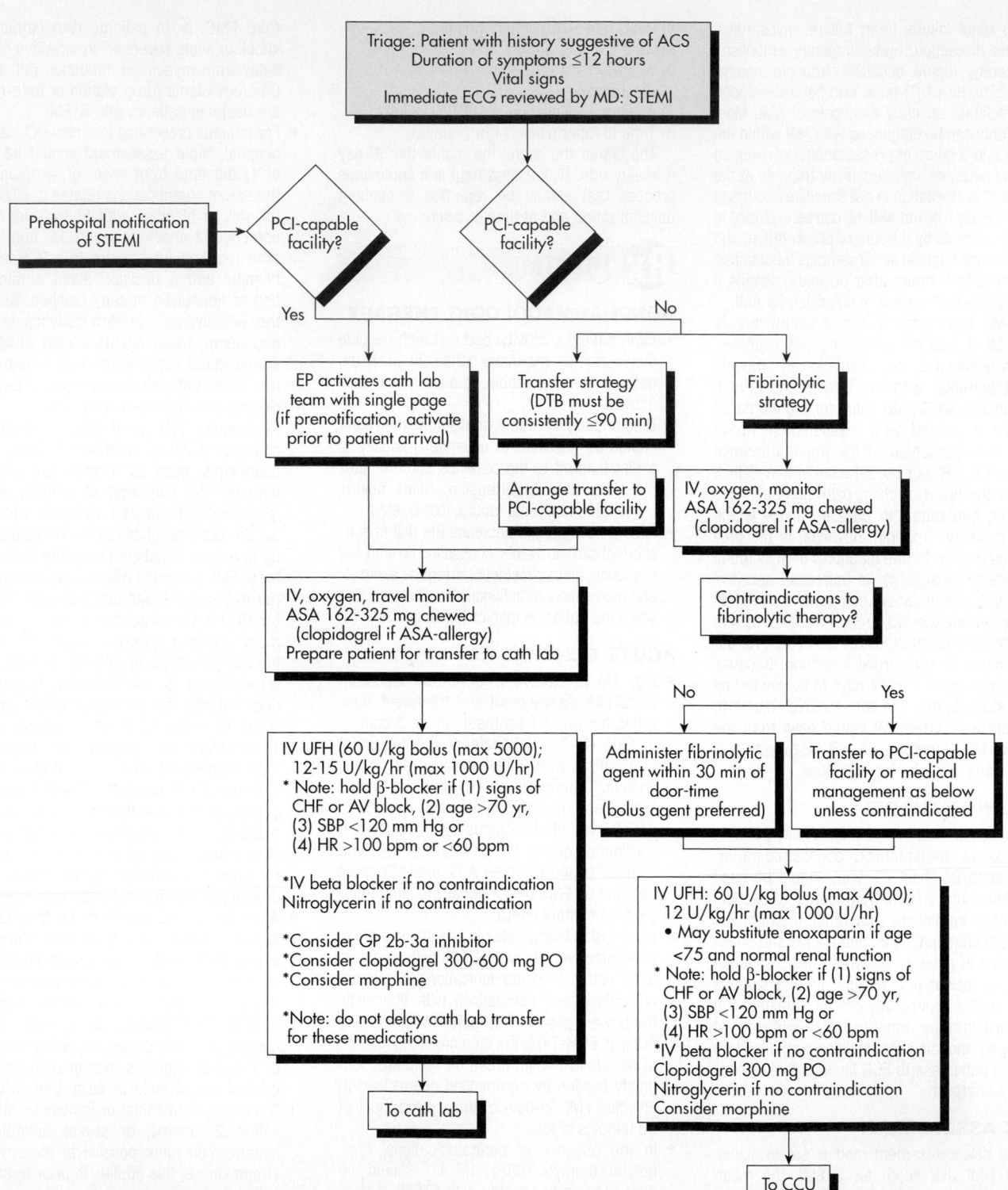

FIGURE 1M-72 Assessment and treatment algorithm for ST-segment elevation myocardial infarction (STEMI). *ACS*, Acute coronary syndrome; *ASA*, acetyl-salicylic acid; *AV*, atrioventricular; *bpm*, beats per minute; *cath lab*, catheterization laboratory; *CCU*, cardiac care unit; *CHF*, congestive heart failure; *DTB*, door-to-balloon time; *ECG*, electrocardiogram; *EP*, emergency physician; *GP*, glycoprotein; *HR*, heart rate; *IV*, intravenous/intravenous line; *PCI*, percutaneous coronary intervention; *PO*, orally; *SBP*, systolic blood pressure; *UFH*, unfractionated heparin. (From Adams JG et al: *Emergency medicine, clinical essentials*, ed 2, Philadelphia, 2013, Elsevier.)

- Transfer to a PCI-capable hospital: immediate transfer for STEMI patients who develop cardiogenic shock or acute severe HF, irrespective of the time delay from MI onset. Urgent transfer if the patient demonstrates evidence of failed reperfusion or reocclusion after fibrinolytic therapy.

- Coronary angiography should not be performed within the first 2 to 3 hours after administration of fibrinolytic therapy. Coronary artery bypass graft (CABG): urgent CABG is indicated in patients with STEMI and coronary anatomy not amenable to PCI who have ongoing or recurrent ischemia, cardio-

genic shock, severe HF, or other high-risk features. CABG is recommended in patients with STEMI at time of operative repair of mechanical defects.

- Therapeutic hypothermia should be started as soon as possible in comatose patients with STEMI and out-of-hospital cardiac

M

I

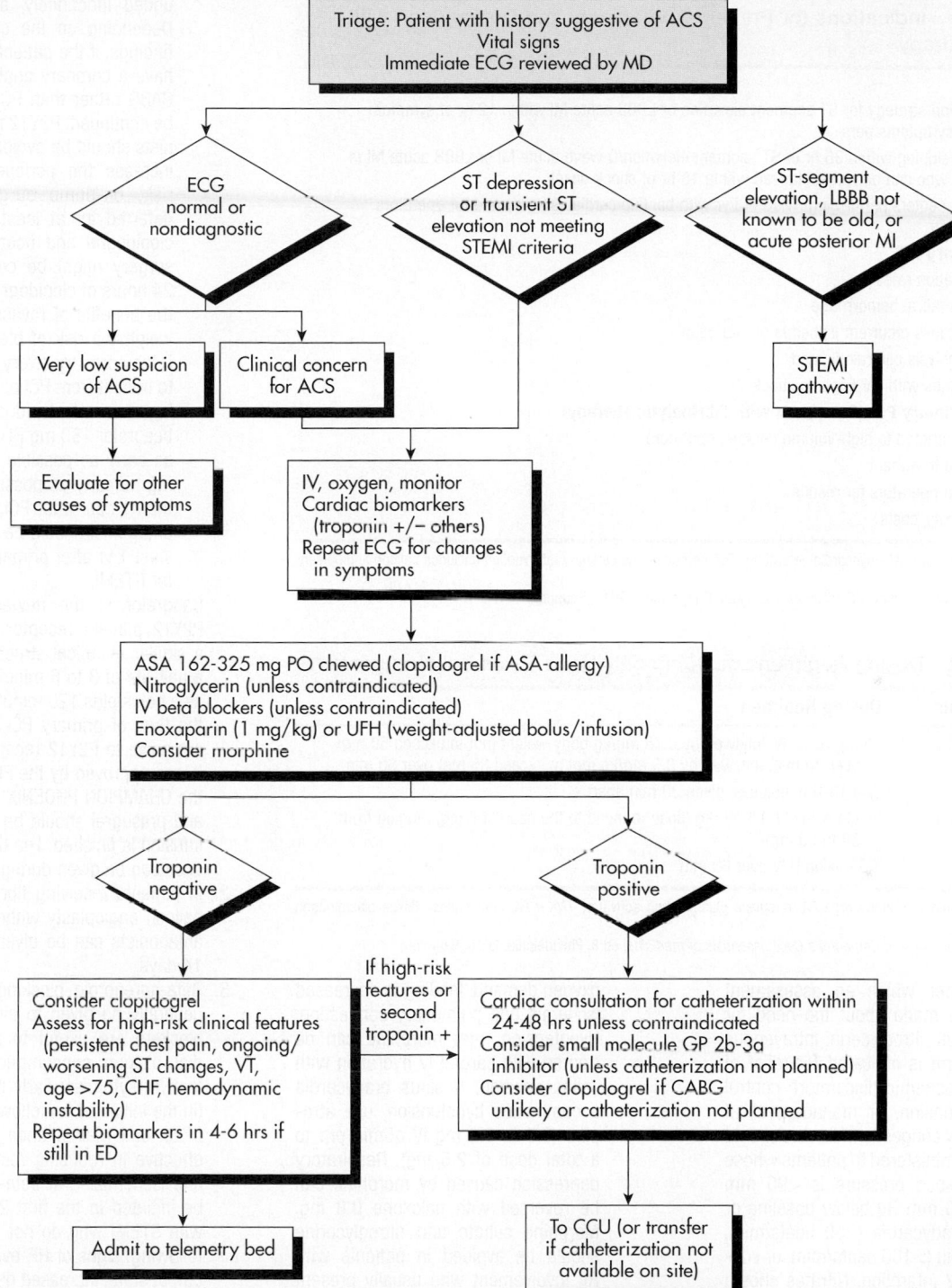

FIGURE 1M-73 Assessment and treatment algorithm for non–ST-segment elevation myocardial infarction. *ACS,* Acute coronary syndrome; *ASA,* acetylsalicylic acid; *CABG,* coronary artery bypass grafting; *CCU,* cardiac care unit; *CHF,* congestive heart failure; *ED,* emergency department; *ECG,* electrocardiogram; *GP,* glycoprotein; *IV,* intravenous/intravenous line; *LBBB,* left bundle branch block; *MI,* myocardial infarction; *STEMI,* ST-segment elevation myocardial infarction; *UFH,* unfractionated heparin; *VT,* ventricular tachycardia. (From Adams JG et al: *Emergency medicine, clinical essentials,* ed 2, Philadelphia, 2013, Elsevier.)

arrest caused by ventricular fibrillation (VF) or pulseless ventricular tachycardia, including patients who undergo primary PCI.

- Immediate angiography and PCI when indicated should be performed in resuscitated out-of-hospital patients.
- The use of mechanical circulatory support is reasonable in patients with STEMI who

are hemodynamically unstable and require urgent CABG.

- Until the catheterization team is ready or fibrinolytics are administered, medical therapy should be initiated immediately in the emergency department. This includes:
  1. Routine measures
     a. Oxygen: supplemental oxygen should be administered to patients with arte-

rial oxygen desaturation (SaO_2 less than 90%).

  b. Nitroglycerin: increase oxygen supply by reducing coronary vasospasm and decrease oxygen consumption by reducing ventricular preload. Patients with ongoing ischemic discomfort should receive sublingual nitroglycerin every 5 minutes for a total of 3

TABLE 1M-42 Dosing Regimens of Commonly Used Thrombolytic Agents

Thrombolytic Agents	Dosing Regimen
t-PA (alteplase)	15 mg bolus IV, followed by 0.75 mg/kg body weight (not to exceed 50 mg) over 30 min, followed by 0.5 mg/kg (not to exceed 35 mg) over 60 min
r-PA (reteplase)	Two 10-U IV boluses, given 30 min apart
TNK–t-PA (tenecteplase)	Single bolus IV 0.5 mg/kg (dose rounded to the nearest 5 mg, ranging from 30 to 50 mg)
Streptokinase	1.5 million U IV over 60 min

IV, Intravenous; *PA,* plasminogen activator; *r-PA,* reteplase plasminogen activator; *TNK–t-PA,* tenecteplase tissue plasminogen activator; *U,* units.
From Andreoli TE et al: *Andreoli and Carpenter's Cecil essentials of medicine,* ed 8, Philadelphia, 2010, Saunders.

doses, after which an assessment should be made about the need for intravenous nitroglycerin. Intravenous nitroglycerin is indicated for relief of ongoing ischemic discomfort, control of hypertension, or management of pulmonary congestion. Nitrates should not be administered to patients whose systolic blood pressure is <90 mm Hg or ≥30 mm Hg below baseline or severe bradycardia (<50 beats/min), tachycardia (>100 beats/min), or suspected RV infarction. Nitrates should not be administered to patients who have received a phosphodiesterase inhibitor for erectile dysfunction within the last 24 hr (48 hr for tadalafil).

c. Adequate analgesia: morphine sulfate 2 to 4 mg IV initially with increments of 2 to 8 mg IV at 5- to 10-min intervals can be given for severe pain unrelieved by nitroglycerin. Morphine can reduce the catecholamine surge caused by anxiety and pain, particularly in patients with anterior myocardial infarctions, which in turn can reduce heart rate and PCWP, the increased cardiac workload and

oxygen demand, leading to decreased ischemia and pulmonary congestion. Hypotension from morphine can be treated with careful IV hydration with saline solution. If sinus bradycardia accompanies hypotension, use atropine (0.5 to 1.0 mg IV q5min prn to a total dose of 2.5 mg). Respiratory depression caused by morphine can be reversed with naloxone 0.8 mg. Morphine sulfate and nitroglycerine should be avoided in patients with RV involvement who usually present with bradycardia and hypotension. Pain management in these cases should be provided preferentially with meperidine 25-50 mg intravenously q 4h, in combination with phenergan 12.5 mg to prevent nausea and/or vomiting. Blood pressure support with normal saline solution is of critical importance to maintain adequate hemodynamics until optimal revascularization is accomplished.

d. Aspirin 162 to 325 mg PO should be crushed and chewed to enhance drug absorption and delivery. It should be given as soon as possible and con-

tinued indefinitely, at 81 mg daily. Depending on the clinical and ECG findings, if the patient is suspected to have a coronary anatomy that needs CABG rather than PCI, aspirin should be continued. P2Y12 receptor antagonists should be avoided because they increase the perioperative bleeding risk; on-pump surgery should be deferred for at least 24 hours after clopidogrel and ticagrelor. Off-pump surgery might be considered within 24 hours of clopidogrel or ticagrelor if the benefits of revascularization outweigh the risk of bleeding. However, if the coronary artery disease is likely to benefit from PCI alone, then a loading dose of clopidogrel 600 mg or ticagrelor 180 mg PO should be given as early as possible or prasugrel 60 mg as early as possible and no later than 1 hour after PCI. P2Y12 receptor antagonist should be continued for at least 1 yr after primary PCI with stent for STEMI.

Cangrelor is the newest direct-acting P2Y12 platelet receptor inhibitor. It has a similar chemical structure to ATP, with a half-life of 3 to 6 minutes. It is given IV as a bolus plus 120 minutes of infusion at the time of primary PCI in patients who are naïve to P2Y12 receptor antagonists. It was approved by the FDA in 2015 after the CHAMPION PHOENIX trial. Clopidogrel and prasugrel should be started after its infusion is finished. The ticagrelor loading dose can be given during the infusion.

2. In patients receiving fibrinolytics only or balloon angioplasty without stent, P2Y12 antagonists can be given for as little as 14 days.

3. Beta-adrenergic blocking agents should generally be given to all patients. Beta-blockers are useful to reduce myocardial oxygen consumption and prevent tachyarrhythmias. Early IV beta blockage (in the initial 24 hr) followed by institution of an oral maintenance regimen is also effective in reducing recurrent infarction and ischemia. Oral beta-blockers should be initiated in the first 24 hr in patients with STEMI who do not have any of the following: signs of HF, evidence of a low-output state, increased risk for cardiogenic shock, or other contraindications for its use (bradycardia, PR interval more than 0.24 seconds, second- or third-degree heart block, active asthma, or reactive airways disease).

They should be continued during and after hospitalization for all patients with STEMI and with no contraindications to their use for at least 2 yr. Patients with initial contraindications to the use of beta-blockers in the first 24 hr after STEMI should be reevaluated to determine their subsequent eligibility. It is reasonable to administer intravenous beta-blockers at the time of presentation to patients with

TABLE 1M-43 Contraindications to Thrombolytic Therapy in Acute Myocardial Infarction

Absolute

Suspected aortic dissection
Active bleeding*
Any prior cerebral hemorrhage
Intracranial neoplasm
Cerebral aneurysm or arteriovenous malformation
Ischemic cerebrovascular accident within 3 mo

Relative

Bleeding diathesis, coagulopathy, or anticoagulant use
Major surgery within 3 wk
Puncture of a noncompressible vessel, internal bleeding, or head or major body trauma within previous 2 wk
Nonhemorrhagic stroke or gastrointestinal hemorrhage within 6 mo
Proliferative retinopathy
Active peptic ulcer disease
History of chronic, severe, poorly controlled hypertension
Severe uncontrolled hypertension on presentation (systolic blood pressure >180 mm Hg or diastolic blood pressure >110 mm Hg)
Traumatic or prolonged (>10 min) cardiopulmonary resuscitation
Pregnancy

*Does not include menstrual bleeding.
From Andreoli TE et al: *Andreoli and Carpenter's Cecil essentials of medicine*, ed 8, Philadelphia, 2010, Saunders.

STEMI and no contraindications to their use who are hypertensive or have ongoing ischemia.

4. Anticoagulation therapy: STEMI is due to plaque rupture exposing the underlying collagen platelets that are activated and the coagulation cascade is initiated. IV unfractionated heparin, bivalirudin, subcutaneous enoxaparin or fondaparinux can be used. In patients at high risk of bleeding, use of bivalirudin is reasonable. Anticoagulation therapy is usually continued for 48 hours after administration of lytic therapy unless streptokinase or APSAC is used.

5. In patients with acute MI, treatment with drug-eluting stents is associated with decreased 2-yr mortality rates and a reduction in the need for repeated revascularization procedures compared with treatment including bare-metal stents.

6. Gp IIb/IIIa inhibitors in the era of DAPT therapy and primary PCI have failed to show benefit with "upstream" treatment. Abciximab might be useful in the presence of large thrombus burden during primary PCI. For patients receiving bivalirudin as the primary anticoagulant, routine adjunctive use of GP IIb/IIIa inhibitors is not recommended but may be considered as adjunctive or "bail-out" therapy in selected cases.

CHRONIC Rx

- Discharge medications in all patients with MI (unless contraindicated) should include antiischemic medications (e.g., nitroglycerin, beta-blocker), lipid-lowering agents, and antiplatelet therapy (aspirin and/or P2Y12 antagonists).
- Aspirin, 81 mg PO daily, but should be continued indefinitely unless not tolerated (e.g., GI bleed). Clopidogrel 75 mg PO daily; ticagrelor, 90 mg bid, or prasugrel, 10 mg PO daily, can

be combined with aspirin and should be continued without interruption for a minimum of 30 days after bare-metal stent placement or for 12 months after drug-eluting stent placement; however, aspirin should be continued indefinitely. Combining P2Y12 antagonists with aspirin reduces risk for repeat myocardial infarction and stent thrombosis. If there is an elective surgical intervention pending, it is recommended to defer the surgery until completion of the full course of the P2Y12 antagonist treatment.

- Angiotensin-converting enzyme inhibitors (ACEIs) should be started within the first 24 hours of STEMI to all patients having STEMI with anterior infarction, pulmonary congestion, or LV EF <40%, in the absence of hypotension. They reduce LV dysfunction and dilation and slow the progression to HF during and after acute MI. Angiotensin receptor blockers, ARBs, should be given to patients who have indication but are intolerant of ACEIs. IV formulations of ACEIs should not be given within the first 24 hours of STEMI due to risk of hypotension. ARBs offer no advantage over ACEIs and should be considered only in patients who are intolerant to ACEIs.
  1. Commonly used ACEIs are ramipril 2.5 mg PO bid, captopril 12.5 mg PO bid, enalapril 2.5 mg PO bid, and lisinopril 2.5-5 mg PO qd initially, with subsequent titration as needed. Ramipril is associated with a lower mortality rate than most ACEIs.
  2. ACEIs may be stopped in patients without complications and no evidence of LV dysfunction after 6 to 8 weeks.
  3. ACEIs should be continued indefinitely in patients with impaired LV function (EF <40%) or clinical HF.
- Long-term aldosterone antagonist therapy should be prescribed for post-STEMI patients without significant renal dysfunction (creatinine ≤2.5 mg/dl in men and ≤2.0 mg/dl in women) or hyperkalemia who are already

taking an ACEI, a beta-blocker, and have LV EF <40% with symptomatic HF or diabetes.
- Statins should be started as early as possible in all patients with STEMI regardless of lipid panel, not only for their lipid-lowering effects, but also their anti-inflammatory properties (JUPITER trial), which can stabilize the ruptured plaque. Atorvastatin 80 mg can be used (PROVE IT-TIMI 22 and MIRACL trials). Fasting lipid panel should be checked during the first 24 hr of hospital course, and the intensive therapy can be stepped down if appropriate. Goal LDL cholesterol is <70 mg/dl. Consider addition of fenofibrate or niacin if triglycerides are significantly elevated. Recent data showed no improvement in outcome with increasing HDL cholesterol therapy using niacin; therefore its use to decrease HDL cholesterol is questionable.

COMPLICATIONS OF STEMI

Cardiogenic shock: emergent revascularization with either PCI or CABG is the recommended treatment.

Sustained ventricular tachycardia: implantable cardioverter-defibrillator therapy (ICD) is indicated before discharge in patients who develop sustained ventricular tachycardia/ventricular fibrillation more than 48 hr after STEMI, provided the arrhythmia is not due to transient or reversible ischemia, reinfarction, or metabolic abnormalities.

Pacing in STEMI: temporary pacing is indicated for symptomatic bradyarrhythmias unresponsive to medical treatment and after revascularization. AV block and bradyarrhythmias in the setting of inferior wall MI are usually transient, will not require long-term pacing, and usually resolve within 2 to 4 weeks of the event. On the contrary, AV block and bradyarrhythmias or new LBBB in the presence of an anterior wall MI is usually a sign of severe disruption of the bundle of His and often requires a permanent pacemaker.

Pericarditis after STEMI: aspirin is recommended for treatment of pericarditis after STEMI. Glucocorticoids and nonsteroidal anti-inflammatory drugs are potentially harmful for treatment of pericarditis after STEMI.

EVALUATION OF POST-MI PATIENTS:

- Noninvasive testing for ischemia should be performed before discharge to assess the presence and extent of inducible ischemia in patients with STEMI who have not had coronary angiography and do not have high-risk clinical features for which coronary angiography would be warranted. It might be considered before discharge to evaluate the functional significance of a noninfarct artery stenosis previously identified at angiography and/or before discharge to guide the postdischarge exercise prescription.
- Assessment of LV function: LV ejection fraction should be measured in all patients with STEMI.

Echocardiography to rule out presence of mural thrombi in patients suspected of having an extensive infarction (more common with anterior wall MI); contrast echocardiography is added if mural thrombus is suspected.

1. Assessment of risk for sudden cardiac death: Patients with an initially reduced LV ejection fraction, <40%, who are possible candidates for implantable cardioverter-defibrillator therapy should undergo reevaluation of LV ejection fraction at 90 days (or 42 days if no revascularization was performed). ICD is recommended when LVEF remains <35% in the presence of NYHA class II or III heart failure, or in patients with LVEF <30% regardless of symptoms, if the life expectancy is >1 yr.

- Cardiac rehabilitation/secondary prevention programs are recommended for patients with STEMI
- Lifestyle risk factors modification

DISPOSITION

The prognosis after MI depends on multiple factors:

- New bundle branch block, Mobitz II second-degree block, and third-degree heart block adversely affect outcome.
- Size of infarct: the larger it is, the higher the post-MI mortality rate. Significant myocardial stunning with subsequent improvement of ventricular function occurs in most patients after anterior MI. A lower level of creatine kinase, an estimate of the extent of necrosis, is independently predictive of recovery of function.
- Site of infarct: inferior wall MI carries a better prognosis than anterior wall MI; however, patients with inferior wall MI and right ventricular involvement have a high risk for arrhythmic complications and cardiogenic shock.
- Ejection fraction after MI: the lower the LV ejection fraction, the higher the mortality rate after MI. The risk of death is higher in the first 30 days after MI among patients with LV dysfunction, HF, or both.
- Presence of post-MI angina indicates a high mortality rate.

- Performance on low-level exercise test: the presence of ST-segment changes during the test is a predictor of high mortality rate during the first year.
- Presence of pericarditis during the acute phase of MI increases mortality rate at 1 yr.
- Type A behavior (competitive drive, ambitiousness, hostility) is associated with a lower mortality rate after symptomatic MI.
- The Killip classification is an independent predictor of all-cause 30-day mortality:
  1. Killip class I includes individuals with no clinical signs of HF. Mortality rate is 6%.
  2. Killip class II includes individuals with rales or crackles in the lungs, S_3 gallop, and elevated jugular venous pressure. Mortality rate is 17%.
  3. Killip class III describes individuals with frank acute pulmonary edema. Mortality rate is 38%.
  4. Killip class IV describes individuals in cardiogenic shock or hypotension (measured as systolic blood pressure <90 mm Hg) and evidence of peripheral vasoconstriction (oliguria, cyanosis, or sweating). Mortality rate is 67%.
- Self-reported moderate alcohol consumption in the year before acute MI is associated with reduced 1-yr mortality rate.
- Discharge medication in patients with MI should include lipid-lowering agents. Statins may also lower vascular inflammation and damage by mechanisms other than reduction of low-density lipoprotein cholesterol. Early initiation of statin treatment in patients with acute MI is associated with reduced 1-yr mortality rate.
- Additional poor prognostic factors include cigarette smoking, history of hypertension or prior MI, presence of ST-segment depression in acute MI, older age, diabetes mellitus, and female sex (especially women >50 yr). Lammintausta and Fonarrow reported that single men and women who live alone have a 60% to 70% greater risk of a heart attack. Furthermore, the study showed >160% increase in the risk of sudden death in these

groups when compared to people who are married or live with family.

- Renal disease, even mild, as assessed by the estimated glomerular filtration rate, is a major risk factor for cardiovascular complications after MI.
- Although black patients with MI have worse outcomes than their white counterparts, these differences did not persist after adjustment for patient factors and site of care.

PEARLS & CONSIDERATIONS

COMMENTS

- Approximately 1.5 million patients undergo PCI in the United States each year. Depending on local practices and the diagnostic criteria used, 5% to 30% of these patients have evidence of a periprocedural MI.
- The 12-lead ECG has low sensitivity for the detection of MI if the culprit lesion is in the left circumflex artery (LCX). If the initial 12-lead ECG is not diagnostic and high clinical suspicion for acute coronary syndrome exists it is reasonable to obtain additional posterior chest leads (V_7 to V_9) to detect LCX occlusion.

SUGGESTED READINGS

Available at www.expertconsult.com

RELATED CONTENT

Heart Attack (Patient Information)
Acute Coronary Syndrome (Related Key Topic)
Angina Pectoris (Related Key Topic)

AUTHORS: **CLAUDIA SERRANO, M.D.,** and **JUAN A. ESCARFULLER, M.D.**

 BASIC INFORMATION

DEFINITION

Myocarditis broadly refers to inflammation of the heart muscle. This may result from exposure to discrete external antigens such as viruses, bacteria, parasites, and drugs or from internal triggers such as autoimmune conditions.

ICD-10CM CODES
I40.0	Infective myocarditis
I40.1	Isolated myocarditis
I40.8	Other acute myocarditis
I40.9	Acute myocarditis, unspecified
A39.52	Meningococcal myocarditis
B26.82	Mumps myocarditis
B33.22	Viral myocarditis
B58.81	Toxoplasma myocarditis
D86.85	Sarcoid myocarditis
I01.2	Acute rheumatic myocarditis
I09.0	Rheumatic myocarditis
I41	Myocarditis in diseases classified elsewhere
I51.4	Myocarditis, unspecified

EPIDEMIOLOGY & DEMOGRAPHICS

- The incidence of focal myocarditis reported at autopsy is 1% to 9% in asymptomatic patients and 50% in patients infected with HIV.
- Myocarditis is a major cause of sudden unexpected death (as high as 8% to 9%) in young adults <40 years of age, especially in cases of idiopathic dilated cardiomyopathy, where myocarditis may account for 10% to 40% of the cases overall.

PHYSICAL FINDINGS & CLINICAL PRESENTATION

- Persistent tachycardia out of proportion to fever
- Faint S_1, S_3, and S_4 gallops on auscultation
- Murmur of functional mitral regurgitation and functional tricuspid regurgitation caused by severe left ventricular and right ventricular dilatation
- Pericardial friction rub if associated with pericarditis as in the clinical syndrome of myopericarditis
- Chest pain, especially pleuritic and positional, when the pericardium is involved
- Presyncope or syncope secondary to ventricular arrhythmias
- Non-specific viral prodrome and fatigue
- Congestive heart failure (CHF) symptoms that usually manifest with fatigue and decreased exercise capacity
- If myocarditis is severe and diffuse and rapid in evolution, it can present with acute CHF symptoms leading to cardiogenic shock and death
- Signs of biventricular failure (hypotension, hepatomegaly, peripheral edema, distention of neck veins, S_3 sounds, and pulmonary edema)
- Patients may present with a history of recent flulike syndrome (fever, arthralgias, malaise); children often have a more fulminant presentation than adults. Difficulty breathing is the most common presentation of pediatric myocarditis

- The most common presentations are dyspnea (72% of patients), chest pain (32%), and arrhythmias (18%), which include sinus tachycardia, and atrial and ventricular premature contractions
- Acute coronary syndrome, which can occur due to local coronary spasm and inflammation, and can present on ECG as acute injury pattern or ischemic changes
- Sudden cardiac death from ventricular tachycardia/ventricular fibrillation mediated by inflammation and/or scar, which sets up a re-entry mediated pathway for ventricular arrhythmias

ETIOLOGY

- Infection
  1. Viral (adenovirus, parvovirus B19, hepatitis C virus [HCV], Coxsackie B virus, cytomegalovirus, enterovirus, poliovirus, mumps, HIV, and Epstein-Barr virus, etc.). Viruses are the most common cause of myocarditis in developed countries. In the 1980s and 1990s, enteroviruses were frequently associated with myocarditis and dilated cardiomyopathy. In the past 10 years, however, other viruses such as adenovirus, HCV, parvovirus B19, and herpesvirus 6 (HH6) have emerged as the significant pathogens.
  2. Bacterial (*Staphylococcus aureus, Clostridium perfringens,* diphtheria, Mycoplasma and any severe bacterial infection)
  3. Mycotic (*Candida, Mucor, Aspergillus, Blastomyces, Histoplasma*)
  4. Parasitic (*Trypanosoma cruzi*—most common worldwide, *Trichinella, Echinococcus, Amoeba, Toxoplasma*)
  5. Rickettsia rickettsii
  6. Spirochetal (*Borrelia burgdorferi*–Lyme carditis)
- Rheumatic fever
- Systemic lupus erythematosus
- Wegener's granulomatosis
- Giant cell arteritis and Takayasu's arteritis
- Drugs (e.g., cocaine, emetine, doxorubicin, sulfonamides, isoniazid, methyldopa, amphotericin B, tetracycline, phenylbutazone, lithium, 5-fluorouracil, phenothiazines, interferon-alfa, tricyclic antidepressants, cyclophosphamides, smallpox vaccination)
- Toxins (carbon monoxide, ethanol, diphtheria toxin, lead, arsenicals)
- Systemic and collagen-vascular disease (scleroderma, sarcoidosis, celiac disease, Sjögren's syndrome, Kawasaki syndrome, etc.)
- Radiation
- Postpartum status
- Post stem cell transplantation
- Hypersensitivity reactions from insect bites, such as bee and wasp bites; from snake bites; and from tetanus toxoid

Dx **DIAGNOSIS (TABLE 1M-44)**

DIFFERENTIAL DIAGNOSIS

- Ischemic cardiomyopathy and other, nonischemic cardiomyopathies

- Acute coronary syndromes
- Valvulopathies
- Infiltrative diseases of the myocardium, such as sarcoidosis, amyloidosis, hemochromatosis, and Chagas' disease.

The differential diagnosis of chest pain is described in Section II.

WORKUP

- Medical history: the clinical presentation of myocarditis is nonspecific and can consist of fatigue, palpitations, dyspnea, precordial discomfort, and myalgias.
- Diagnostic workup includes chest x-ray examination, ECG, laboratory evaluation, echocardiogram, cardiac catheterization, cardiac MRI with late gadolinium enhancement, and endomyocardial biopsy (in selected patients on the basis of the likelihood of finding specific treatable disorders such as giant cell myocarditis). Of note, endomyocardial biopsy has a sensitivity of only 10% to 35% using standard histologic criteria. This is due to variability in interpretation and sampling error.

LABORATORY TESTS

- Elevated cardiac troponin is suggestive of myocarditis in patients with clinically suspected myocarditis. Troponin I specificity is 89%; sensitivity is 34% to 53%. A normal level does not rule out the diagnosis.
- Increased creatine kinase (CK) (with elevated MB fraction, lactate dehydrogenase), and aspartate aminotransferase from myocardial necrosis.
- Elevation of cardiac troponin I or T is more common than CK-MB elevation in patients with biopsy-proven myocarditis.
- The elevations of cardiac troponin I were correlated with a short duration (typically less than 1 mo) of CHF symptoms, indicating that the majority of myocardial necrosis occurs early in the disease course.
- Persistent elevations of cardiac biomarkers are indicative of ongoing myocardial necrosis.
- BNP or NT-proBNP is recommended if patient has heart failure symptoms.
- Increased erythrocyte sedimentation rate (nonspecific but may be of value in following the progress of the disease and the response to therapy).
- Increased white blood cell count, again, nonspecific (increased eosinophils if parasitic infection).
- Viral titers (acute and convalescent).
- Cold agglutinin titer, antistreptolysin O titer, blood cultures.
- Lyme disease antibody titer.
- RPR, VDRL.

IMAGING STUDIES

- Chest x-ray: enlargement of cardiac silhouette with or without pulmonary congestion may be present
- ECG: sinus tachycardia with nonspecific ST-T wave changes unless there is concomitant pericarditis in which the ECG changes are more specific; intraventricular conduction defects and bundle branch blocks are

TABLE 1M-44 Expanded Criteria for Diagnosis of Myocarditis

Suggestive of myocarditis:	2 positive categories
Compatible with myocarditis:	3 positive categories
High probability of being myocarditis:	all 4 categories positive

(Any matching feature in category = positive for category)

Category I: Clinical Symptoms

Clinical heart failure
Fever
Viral prodrome
Fatigue
Dyspnea on exertion
Chest pain
Palpitations
Presyncope or syncope

Category II: Evidence of Cardiac Structural or Functional Perturbation *in the Absence* of Regional Coronary Ischemia

Echocardiography evidence
Regional wall motion abnormalities
Cardiac dilation
Regional cardiac hypertrophy
Troponin release
High sensitivity (>0.1 ng/mL)
Positive indium In 111 antimyosin scintigraphy
and
Normal coronary angiography *or*
Absence of reversible ischemia by coronary distribution on perfusion scan

Category III: Cardiac Magnetic Resonance Imaging

Increased myocardial T2 signal on inversion recovery sequence
Delayed contrast enhancement after gadolinium-DTPA infusion

Category IV: Myocardial Biopsy—Pathologic or Molecular Analysis

Pathology findings compatible with Dallas criteria
Presence of viral genome by polymerase chain reaction or in situ hybridization

DTPA, Diethylenetriamine penta-acetic acid.
From Bonow R.O., et al.: *Heart disease,* 9th ed, Philadelphia, 2012, Saunders.

---

uncommon in typical viral myocarditis but are common manifestations in cardiac sarcoid and idiopathic giant cell myocarditis.

1. Lyme disease and diphtheria can cause varying degrees of heart block.
2. Changes mimicking acute myocardial infarction (ST elevations and Q waves) can occur with focal necrosis from myocarditis.

- Echocardiogram:
  1. The most useful test in detecting decreased ventricular function in suspected myocarditis even when subclinical.
  2. Acute severe myocarditis is associated with systolic dysfunction with decreased ejection fraction.
  3. Dilated and hypokinetic chambers
  4. The systolic dysfunction is generally global but may be regional or segmental as in the case of focal myocarditis.
  5. Abnormal tissue Doppler signal can provide additional evidence for the presence of myocarditis.
  6. The echocardiogram can also be helpful with diagnosing coexisting pericardial involvement.
  7. The spheroid dysfunctional ventricle in acute myocarditis tends to remodel to the more normal elliptical shape over several months.
- Cardiac catheterization and angiography:
  1. To rule out coronary artery disease and valvular disease. Coronary angiography is

most commonly normal with no evidence of coronary artery disease.
2. A right ventricular endomyocardial biopsy can confirm the diagnosis, although a negative biopsy result does not exclude myocarditis owing to the low sensitivity of this test. Recent studies have shown that myocardial biopsy may be unnecessary because immunosuppression therapy based on biopsy results is generally ineffective. However, if idiopathic giant cell myocarditis is suspected, biopsy can confirm this diagnosis, and immunosuppression therapy is often helpful in this patient cohort.

- Cardiac MRI (Fig. 1M-75):
  1. Can be used to detect myocardial edema and myocyte injury in myocarditis.
  2. Increased focal or global signal intensity can be used to calculate an edema ratio.
  3. Late gadolinium enhancement (LGE) and the presence of increased focal and global myocardial contrast enhancement relative to skeletal muscle.
  4. Any combination of two of the above has a sensitivity and specificity of 76% and 96%, with 85% diagnostic accuracy, and is probably the gold standard for diagnosis of myocarditis, as opposed to routine biopsy.
  5. Cardiac MRI has demonstrated that myocarditis tends to start as a focal process and becomes a more global process over time, with the extent of myocardial

enhancement correlating with clinical status and left ventricular function.
6. Some viral pathogens have focal involvement of the myocardium. Parvovirus B19 involves the subepicardial lateral wall of the left ventricle. HHV6 and especially the combination of HHV6/parvovirus B19 tend to involve the septum and present with more acute and chronic heart failure symptoms.
7. The pattern of LGE is different from that in ischemic cardiomyopathy. LGE in myocarditis tends to involve the epicardium with variable extension into the midmyocardium and sparing of the endocardium. This is in contrast to ischemic injury, which involves endocardium first with extension outward.

- Indium-111-labeled antimyosin antibody scintigraphy is positive in myocarditis with a sensitivity of up to 65%.

 **TREATMENT**

NONPHARMACOLOGIC THERAPY

- Supportive care is the first line of therapy for patients with myocarditis.
- Restrict physical activity (to decrease cardiac work). Bed rest is advisable during viremia.
- Avoid use of heavy alcohol and use of nonsteroidal antiinflammatory drugs.

ACUTE GENERAL Rx

- Treat underlying cause (e.g., use specific antibiotics for bacterial infection).
- Treat congestive heart failure (CHF) with diuretics, angiotensin-converting enzyme inhibitors (ACE inhibitors), and salt restriction. A beta-blocker may be added once clinical stability has been achieved. Digoxin should be used with caution and only at low doses.
- Patients who are left with an LVEF ≤35% despite optimal medical therapy for 3-9 mo, and who have good functional status with prognosis >1 yr, will benefit from primary prevention therapy with implantable cardioverter-defibrillator (ICD) implantation as in patients with ischemic cardiomyopathy and other nonischemic cardiomyopathies.
- Antiarrhythmics if needed for ventricular arrhythmias. ICD implantation for secondary prevention in patients who have life-threatening ventricular arrhythmias and have good functional status with prognosis >1 yr.
- In patients with chronic CHF from myocarditis, only ACE inhibitors, beta-blockers, and possibly aldosterone receptor antagonists will decrease their mortality in the long term (as with all CHF etiologies).
- Provide anticoagulation to prevent thromboembolism in atrial fibrillation, in severe left ventricular dysfunction with an EF <20%, and in patients with severe segmental wall motion abnormality of the apex.
- Inotropes or mechanical assist devices such as intra-aortic balloon pumps, Impella device, and left ventricular assist device (LVAD) if

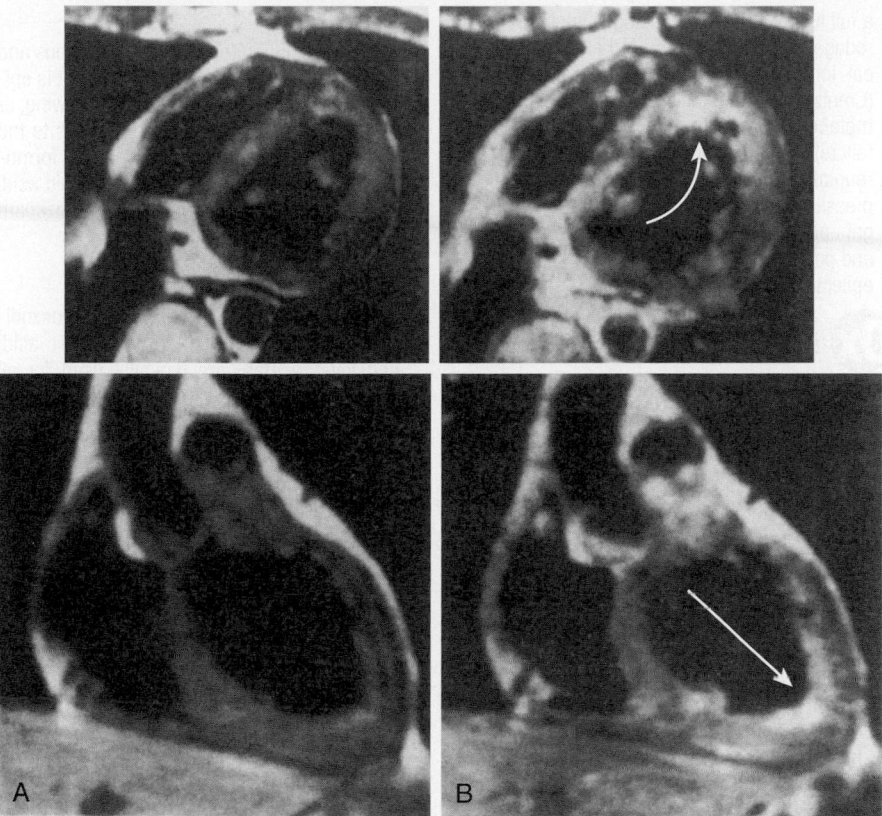

FIGURE 1M-75 A, Precontrast T1-weighted transaxial *(upper)* and coronal *(lower)* magnetic resonance images through the left ventricle in a patient with myocarditis. **B,** Postcontrast magnetic resonance images at the same levels after contrast injection. Note enhancement of the myocardial signal in the septum and apical region *(arrows).* (From Zipes DP et al [eds]: *Braunwald's heart disease,* ed 7, Philadelphia, 2005, Saunders.)

severe heart failure or if cardiogenic shock persists despite medical therapy.
- Cardiac transplantation in patients with chronic or acute fulminant myocarditis with intractable cardiomyopathy and persistent CHF.
- Corticosteroid use is contraindicated in early infectious myocarditis; it may be justified in only selected patients with intractable CHF, severe systemic toxicity, and severe life-threatening arrhythmias.
- Immunosuppressive drugs (prednisone with cyclosporine/cytoxan or azathioprine) do not have any significant effect on the prognosis of myocarditis and should not be used in the routine treatment of patients with myocarditis. Immunosuppression may have a role in the treatment of myocarditis from systemic autoimmune disease (e.g., lupus, scleroderma), in idiopathic giant cell myocarditis, sarcoidosis, or myocarditis caused by hypersensitivity reactions, or in severe hemodynamic compromise.
- In patients with ongoing viral genomic expression, preliminary data suggest that treatment with interferons may improve both symptoms and left ventricular function when compared with standard heart failure therapy.
- IV immunoglobulins have been studied, but because of lack of efficacy data, at present there is no indication for their use except in some pediatric cases or those refractory to immunosuppressive therapy.
- A treatment algorithm for patients with myocarditis is described in Fig. 1M-76.

DISPOSITION
- Most patients with acute myocarditis and mild cardiac involvement have a partial or a full clinical recovery. In some cases, however, the process may continue subclinically with eventual progression to a cardiomyopathy. Therefore all patients with myocarditis should be followed up at least initially at intervals of 1 to 3 mo. Of those with advanced cardiac dysfunction, one third will have residual cardiac dysfunction and 25% may progress to cardiac transplantation or death.
- Prognosis is best for patients with fulminant lymphocytic myocarditis (severe hemodynamic compromise, rapid onset of symptoms, or high fever). These patients tend to have complete recovery with total resolution of myocarditis on repeat biopsy.
- In contrast, patients with giant cell myocarditis have an extremely poor prognosis with a median survival of <6 mo, and most require cardiac transplantation.

REFERRAL

Consider heart transplant if intractable CHF develops.

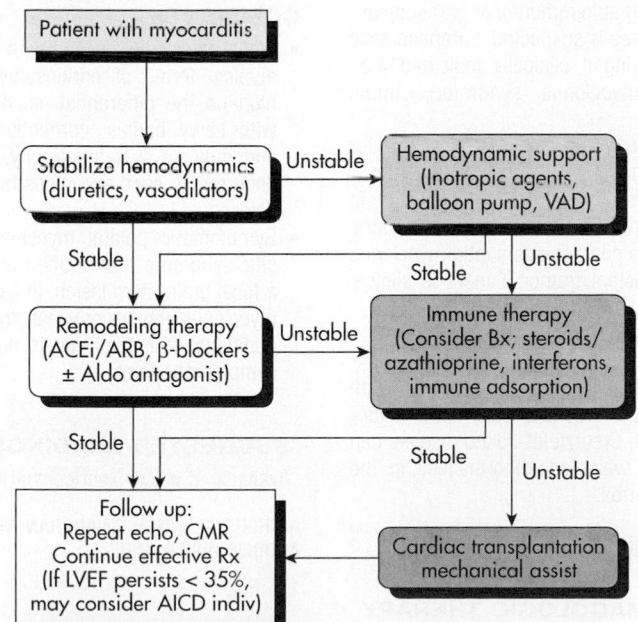

FIGURE 1M-76 Treatment algorithms for patients with myocarditis, depending on hemodynamic stability and response to general supportive and remodeling treatment regimen at each step. All patients should have aggressive support and appropriate follow-up. Immune therapy at present is still mainly to support those who have failed to improve spontaneously. *ACEi,* Angiotensin-converting enzyme inhibitors; *AICD,* automatic implantable cardioverter-defibrillator; *Aldo,* aldosterone; *ARB,* angiotensin receptor blockers; *Bx,* biopsy; *CMR,* cardiac magnetic resonance; *indiv,* based on individual assessment of risk versus benefit; *LVEF,* left ventricular ejection fraction; *VAD,* ventricular assist device. (From Bonow RO et al: *Heart disease,* ed 9, Philadelphia, 2012, Saunders.)

SUGGESTED READINGS

Available at www.expertconsult.com

RELATED CONTENT

Myocarditis (Patient Information)

AUTHORS: **HARSHA V. GANGA, M.D.,** and **ARAVIND RAO KOKKIRALA, M.D.**

BASIC INFORMATION

DEFINITION

Myoclonus is defined as a sudden, brief (<500 ms), and involuntary movement of the extremities, face, and/or trunk. Positive myoclonus is caused by excessive muscle contraction, whereas negative myoclonus is due to a transient loss of postural tone (e.g., asterixis). Myoclonus can be seen in a wide variety of neurologic and systemic disorders.

ICD-10CM CODES
G25.3 Myoclonus

EPIDEMIOLOGY & DEMOGRAPHICS

INCIDENCE: 1.3/100,000 persons
PREVALENCE: 8.6/100,000 persons
PREDOMINANT SEX AND AGE: No gender preference; age at onset varies by the etiology of the myoclonus
GENETICS: Varies by etiology, can be hereditary or sporadic

PHYSICAL FINDINGS & CLINICAL PRESENTATION

- Clinically, myoclonus can be classified by its distribution: focal (only one body part involved), multifocal, segmental (spread to adjacent body parts), axial (muscles innervated by one or several spinal levels), or generalized. It can occur at rest, with maintaining a posture, with action, or with an external stimulus (reflex myoclonus).
- Myoclonus can be due to involvement of the cerebral cortex, brain stem, spinal cord, or peripheral nerve. The causal location may not always influence the characteristics of the myoclonus.
- Negative myoclonus is typically seen in postural muscles of the limbs, causing a bobbing appearance. Asterixis is a form of negative myoclonus.

ETIOLOGY

- The causes of myoclonus are numerous and can be grouped into the categories of physiologic, essential, epileptic, and symptomatic.
- Physiologic myoclonus is a normal phenomenon and includes sleep (hypnic) jerks, hiccups (singultus), and exercise-induced myoclonus.
- Essential myoclonus occurs in the absence of other neurologic symptoms and is usually autosomal dominant. When dystonia is present, it is called myoclonus-dystonia. The myoclonus is often responsive to alcohol in this condition.
- In epileptic myoclonus, seizures dominate the clinical picture. Syndromes include infantile spasms and juvenile myoclonic epilepsy among others.
- Symptomatic or secondary myoclonus comprises myoclonus in the setting of an underlying neurologic disorder or other precipitant. The number of secondary causes prevents giving a full list, but common etiologies include neurodegenerative diseases (Alzheimer's, atypical forms of parkinsonism), CNS infections (Creutzfeldt-Jakob disease, viral encephalitis), metabolic derangements (uremia, hepatic failure), and drug-induced (selective serotonin reuptake inhibitors [SSRIs], tricyclic antidepressants [TCAs], lithium, stimulants, opioids, gabapentin), autoimmune, paraneoplastic, and post-hypoxic etiologies (myoclonic status epilepticus, Lance-Adams syndrome).

DIAGNOSIS

DIFFERENTIAL DIAGNOSIS

- Tremor: a rhythmic oscillation around a point; slower than myoclonus
- Tic: a rapid, patterned movement that, unlike myoclonus, may be briefly suppressed voluntarily or may be accompanied by a premonitory urge
- Dystonia: patterned contractions of agonist/antagonist muscles causing twisting or pulling; slower than myoclonus
- Chorea: typically slower, more complex writhing, patterned movements
- Psychogenic myoclonus: variable in duration and location, distractible, or entrainable

LABORATORY TESTS

- Evaluate for metabolic precipitants (renal and hepatic function, Mg, Ca, thyroid studies, ammonia)
- Toxicology screen (amphetamines, cocaine, opiates/opioids)
- Lumbar puncture if an infectious, inflammatory (including autoimmune), or paraneoplastic CNS process is suspected. Paraneoplastic antibody testing if clinically indicated (i.e., opsoclonus-myoclonus syndrome, limbic encephalitis)
- Electroencephalography (EEG) to evaluate for epileptic/cortical myoclonus
- Electromyography (EMG) may be useful in patients with mixed movement disorders, particularly to characterize subtle myoclonus from a coexistent tremor if there is clinical uncertainty

IMAGING STUDIES

MRI of the brain with and without gadolinium can evaluate for a structural lesion if the myoclonus is cortical. Creutzfeldt-Jakob disease can show diffusion weighted abnormalities in the striatum and cortex.

TREATMENT

NONPHARMACOLOGIC THERAPY

- Treatment should be directed toward correcting the underlying cause if it is reversible (e.g., hepatic or renal failure).
- Carefully remove or decrease potentially causative medications.

ACUTE Rx

Following evaluation for systemic infections and metabolic derangements, myoclonus that is epileptic; interferes with respiration, swallowing, or walking; or causes other severe distress to the patient may be managed acutely with IV formulation antiepileptic drugs such as valproic acid, levetiracetam, or benzodiazepines (lorazepam or midazolam).

CHRONIC Rx

- Clonazepam (preferred over other benzodiazepines for its long half-life), valproic acid, and levetiracetam are typically used for all forms of myoclonus, and often combinations of these medications are more effective.
- If dystonia is present (myoclonus-dystonia), a trial of levodopa is worthwhile although only rarely effective. Anticholinergics may also help dystonia. Botulinum toxin is used for focal dystonia.
- Peripheral focal myoclonus (e.g., hemifacial spasm) can also be helped by botulinum toxin.

DISPOSITION

The ultimate prognosis depends on the etiology of the myoclonus.

REFERRAL

Referral to a general neurologist or movement disorders center is appropriate.

PEARLS & CONSIDERATIONS

COMMENTS

- When myoclonus is seen with parkinsonism, atypical forms of parkinsonism should be high on the differential, such as dementia with Lewy bodies, corticobasal syndrome, and multiple system atrophy. Myoclonus is only rarely seen in idiopathic Parkinson's disease.
- Symptomatic palatal myoclonus is a specific syndrome that is often associated with a focal brain-stem lesion. In essential palatal myoclonus (no lesion), ear "clicking" is an additional symptom that is not seen in the symptomatic form.

SUGGESTED READINGS
Available at www.expertconsult.com

AUTHORS: **JENNIFER E. VAUGHAN, M.D.,** and **ANDREW DUKER, M.D.**

BASIC INFORMATION

DEFINITION

- Myofascial pain syndrome is myalgia characterized by trigger point.
- Trigger point: Trigger points are discrete, focal, hyperirritable spots located in a taut band of skeletal muscle. They produce pain locally and in a referred pattern. Muscle involvement is asymmetric and focal.

SYNONYMS

- Chronic myofascial pain (CMP)

ICD-10CM CODES
M79.1 Myalgia, myofascial pain syndrome

EPIDEMIOLOGY & DEMOGRAPHICS

- Myofascial pain syndrome is a common painful muscle disorder which can affect any sex at any age. About 85% of the general population at some point suffered from it during their lifetime. It also coexists with other chronic pain conditions.

PHYSICAL FINDINGS & CLINICAL PRESENTATION

- Regional body pain and stiffness; often muscles responsible for body posture are affected. Neck, upper back, and lower back muscles are commonly involved. The most commonly affected muscles are trapezius, scalene, infraspinatus, subscapularis, levator scapulae, piriformis, tensor fasciae latae, iliopsoas, gluteus, and quadratus lumborum. Pain is present at rest and with muscle movement.
- Table 1M-45 lists some distinguishing features of myofascial pain and fibromyalgia.
- Limited range of motion and pain-related weakness of affected muscle.
- Twitch response: Brisk contraction of a taut band of skeletal muscle fibers elicited by snapping palpation of a trigger point in that band producing a taut band.
- One or more trigger points asymmetrical location.
- Referred pain from a trigger point to a zone of reference, but not following dermatomal distribution.
- Resolution of the symptoms with lidocaine injection of the trigger point

ETIOLOGY

- Etiology is unknown. There are several proposed histopathologic mechanisms to account for the development of trigger points, but they are lacking scientific evidence. Most researchers agree that acute trauma or repetitive microtrauma may lead to the development of a trigger point.
- Fig. 1M-77 lists causes of myofascial pain and dysfunction.
- Lack of exercise, prolonged poor posture, vitamin deficiencies, sleep disturbances, and

TABLE 1M-45 Distinguishing Features of Myofascial Pain and Fibromyalgia

	Myofascial Pain	Fibromyalgia
Age distribution	20-40 yr	20-50 yr
Gender distribution	Mainly women	Mainly women
Distribution of pain	Localized; usually unilateral	Generalized; bilaterally symmetric
Tender points	Few	Multiple
Trigger points	Uncommon	Common
Fatigue	Localized muscle fatigue	Generalized fatigue
Sleep disturbance	Common	Common

From Firestein GS, et al: *Kelley's textbook of rheumatology*, ed 9, Philadelphia, 2013, Saunders.

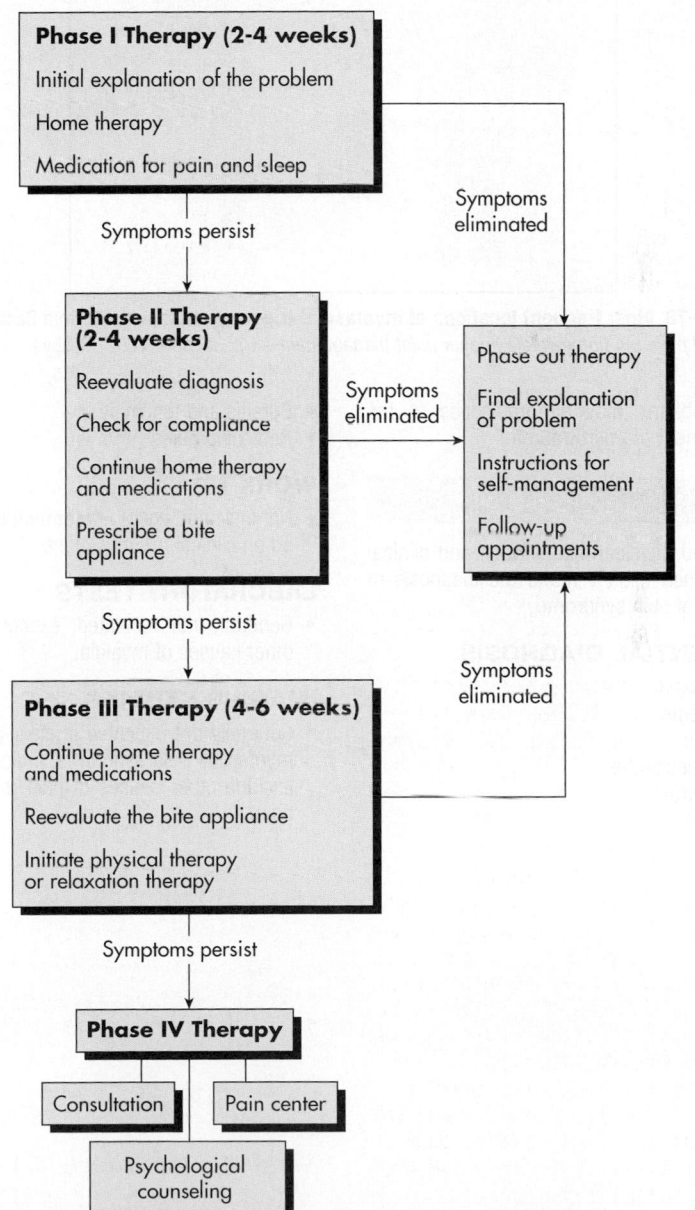

FIGURE 1M-77 Management of myofascial pain and dysfunction. Treatments are divided into four phases. If the symptoms are eliminated in any of the first three phases, the ongoing therapy is gradually phased out, and the patient is instructed in continued self-management of the condition. (Modified from Laskin DM, Block S: Diagnosis and treatment of myofascial pain dysfunction [MPD] syndrome, *J Prosthet Dent* 56:75–84, 1986.)

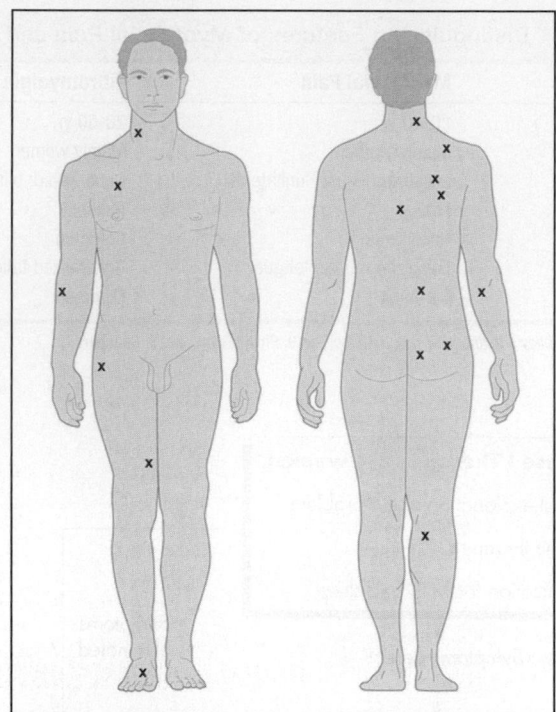

FIGURE 1M-78 Most frequent locations of myofascial trigger points. (Adapted from Rachlin E, Rachlin I: *Myofascial pain and fibromyalgia: trigger point management*, ed 2, St Louis, 2002, Mosby.)

joint problems may all predispose to the development of microtrauma.

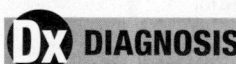 **DIAGNOSIS**

- A detailed physical examination and clinical presentation usually make the diagnosis of myofascial pain syndrome.

DIFFERENTIAL DIAGNOSIS

- Fibromyalgia
- Polymyositis
- Migraine
- Tension headache
- Muscle strain
- Bursitis and tendinitis
- Radiculopathies

WORK-UP

- Not indicated usually, treatment can be started on clinical grounds alone.

LABORATORY TESTS

- Generally not indicated, except to exclude other causes of myalgia.

IMAGING STUDIES

- Generally not indicated in clear-cut cases of myofascial pain syndrome. Indicated only to exclude other causes of pain (e.g., referred pain).

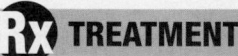 **TREATMENT**

- Spray and stretch therapy: involves passive stretching of the affected muscle. Position patient for maximum decrease in muscle tension, identify trigger points and mark them. Apply vapocoolant spray over entire length of the affected muscle. Passively stretch muscle by applying gentle pressure.
- Physical therapy: TENS unit, ultrasound, massage therapy, myofascial release technique.
- Invasive technique: Trigger point injection with 1% lidocaine is the most commonly used technique.
- NSAIDS and muscle relaxants: short-term use
- Fig. 1M-78 shows the management of myofascial pain and dysfunction.

REFERRAL

An interventional pain management referral is made if trigger point injection is indicated. To physical therapist for increasing ROM and massage therapy.

 **PEARLS & CONSIDERATIONS**

- Trigger point is commonly misdiagnosed as tender point, which is characteristic finding of fibromyalgia.
  Tender point: characterized as non-palpable nodule with symmetric and multiple locations. Tender points are located close to muscle attachment, usually not associated with specific muscle activity. Lacking twitch response and relief of symptoms with localized lidocaine injection.

SUGGESTED READINGS

Available at www.expertconsult.com

AUTHORS: **UZMA NASIR, M.D.,** and **SYEDA M. SAYEED, M.D.**

Diseases and Disorders

 **BASIC INFORMATION**

DEFINITION

Myotonia is a type of muscular dystrophy in which relaxation of a muscle after contraction is delayed or prolonged. The most common type of muscular dystrophy with myotonia is myotonic dystrophy. The nondystrophic myotonias (NDMs) are rare disorders (prevalence 1:100,000) caused by mutations in skeletal muscle chloride and sodium channels with the common clinical feature of myotonia without muscle wasting.

SYNONYMS

Myotonic dystrophy

ICD-10CM CODES
G71.1	Myotonic disorders
M62.89	Other specified disorders of muscle
M62.40	Contracture of muscle, unspecified site
G71.12	Myotonia congenita
G71.14	Drug induced myotonia

EPIDEMIOLOGY & DEMOGRAPHICS

- Three to five cases/100,000 persons
- Genetic disorder inherited as an autosomal-dominant illness
- Symptoms usually manifest during adolescence or early adulthood. Cases of infantile myotonic dystrophy have been described.

PHYSICAL FINDINGS & CLINICAL PRESENTATION

- Usual first symptom is distal extremity weakness sometimes associated with muscle stiffness, cramps, or difficulty relaxing grasp.
- Weakness spreads to eventually involve all muscle groups. Flexor neck muscle weakness and masseter and temporal wasting are often prominent features, as is dysarthria.
- Percussion of a muscle produces a slow contraction followed by prolonged relaxation. The myotonic reflex is best tested by percussing the thenar muscles and observing a slow flexion followed by slow relaxation of the thumb.
- As the disease progresses, generalized weakness becomes more pronounced and myotonia becomes less evident.
- Extramuscular involvement:
- Mental retardation of variable severity (may be absent)
- Frontal baldness (Fig. 1M-79)
- Cataracts
- Diabetes mellitus
- Hypogonadism
- Adrenal failure
- Cardiomyopathy
- Infantile myotonic dystrophy presents as neonatal extreme hypotonia with "shark mouth" deformity (upper lip forming an inverted V).

ETIOLOGY & PATHOGENESIS

Genetic disorder encoded on chromosome 19 leading to sustained firing of the muscle membrane, causing prolonged muscle contraction. Myotonic dystrophy 1 (the more common form) is caused by an expanded CTG repeat within the noncoding 3′ untranslated region of the myotonic dystrophy protein kinase *(DMPK)* gene. The less common form (myotonic dystrophy 2) is caused by an expanded CCTG repeat in the first intron of the zinc finger protein 9 *(ZNF9)* gene.

 **DIAGNOSIS**

DIFFERENTIAL DIAGNOSIS

The disease is limited to muscles and causes hypertrophy and stiffness after rest. Muscle function normalizes with exercise. There is no weakness. Symptoms are exacerbated by exposure to cold.

- Myotonia congenita (Thomsen's disease)
- May be autosomal dominant or recessive (two distinct varieties)
- Paramyotonia congenita (autosomal-dominant disease): weakness and stiffness of facial muscles and distal upper extremities, especially or exclusively on cold exposure
- Muscular dystrophies
- Inflammatory myopathies (polymyositis)
- Metabolic muscle diseases
- Myasthenic syndromes
- Motor neuron disease

WORKUP

- History and physical examination usually sufficient
- Muscle enzymes usually abnormal (creatine phosphokinase, aldolase, aspartate aminotransferase)
- Electromyography: typical myotonic "dive bomber" bursts
- Muscle biopsy: type I fiber atrophy, ring fibers, increased central nucleation

RX TREATMENT

- Phenytoin
- Quinine
- Quinidine
- Procainamide
- Acetazolamide
- Genetic counseling
- Assistive devices, orthotics
- In recent trials,[1] the use of mexiletine resulted in improvement of patient-reported stiffness in patients with nondystrophic myotonias.

DISPOSITION

- In myotonic dystrophy, death is usually caused by the wasting of skeletal muscle and defects in cardiac function.
- Among patients with myotonic dystrophy type 1, an invasive strategy based on systemic electrophysiological studies and prophylactic permanent pacing is associated with longer survival than a non-invasive strategy.[2]

REFERRAL

To neurologist

SUGGESTED READINGS
Available at www.expertconsult.com

AUTHOR: **FRED F. FERRI, M.D.**

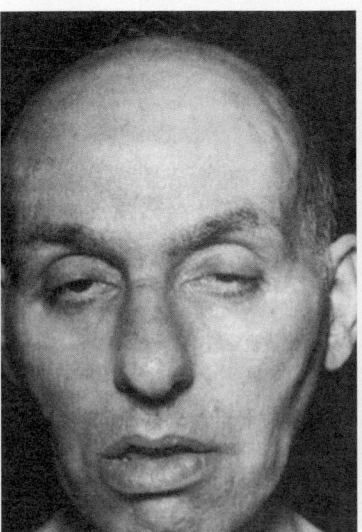
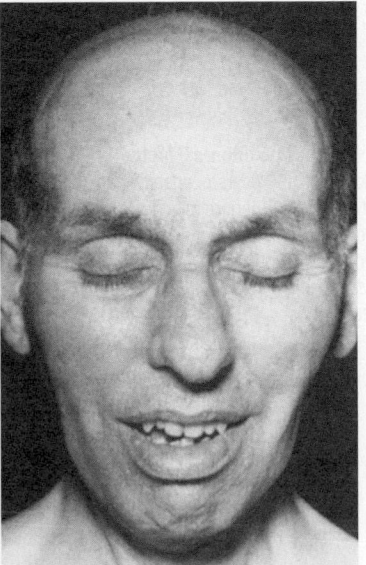

FIGURE 1M-79 Myotonic dystrophy with typical myopathic facies, frontal balding, and sunken cheeks. (From Dubowitz V: *Muscle disorders in childhood,* London, 1995, Saunders.)

[1]Statland JM et al: Mexiletine for symptoms and signs of myotonia in nondystrophic myotonia, *JAMA* 308(13): 1357-1365, 2012.
[2]Wahbi K et al: Electrophysiological study with prophylactic pacing and survival in adults with myotonic dystrophy and conduction system disease, *JAMA* 307(12):1292-1301, 2012.

BASIC INFORMATION

DEFINITION

Myxedema coma is a rare life-threatening complication of hypothyroidism characterized by profound lethargy or coma and usually accompanied by hypothermia.

ICD-10CM CODES
E03.5 Myxedema coma
E03.8 Other specified hypothyroidism
E03.9 Hypothyroidism, unspecified

PHYSICAL FINDINGS & CLINICAL PRESENTATION

- Mental obtundation, profound lethargy or coma
- Hypothermia (rectal temperature <35° C [95° F]); often missed by using ordinary thermometers graduated only to 34.5° C or because the mercury is not shaken below 36° C
- Bradycardia, hypotension (attributable to circulatory collapse)
- Delayed relaxation phase of deep tendon reflexes, areflexia
- Myxedema facies (Fig. 1M-80)
- Alopecia, macroglossia, ptosis, periorbital edema, nonpitting edema, doughy skin
- Bladder dystonia and distention
- Pleural, pericardial, and peritoneal effusions

ETIOLOGY

Decompensation of hypothyroidism from:
- Sepsis
- Exposure to cold weather
- Central nervous system depressants (sedatives, narcotics, antidepressants)
- Trauma, surgery
- Stroke, congestive heart failure, burns
- Intravascular volume contraction (GI blood loss, diuretic use)
- Myocardial infarction
- Metabolic derangements

DIAGNOSIS

DIFFERENTIAL DIAGNOSIS

- Severe depression, primary psychosis
- Drug overdose
- Cerebrovascular accident, liver failure, renal failure
- Hypoglycemia, CO_2 narcosis, encephalitis

WORKUP

Diagnosis of hypothyroidism and exclusion of contributing factors (e.g., sepsis, cerebrovascular accident) with laboratory and radiographic studies (see "Laboratory Tests")

LABORATORY TESTS

- Serum TSH and T_4 levels should be tested immediately. Results reveal markedly increased thyroid-stimulating hormone (if primary hypothyroidism), decreased serum free T_4
- Complete blood count with differential, urine and blood cultures to rule out infectious process
- Electrolytes, blood urea nitrogen, creatinine, liver function tests, calcium, glucose
- Arterial blood gases to rule out hypoxemia and carbon dioxide retention
- Stat cortisol level to rule out concomitant adrenal insufficiency prior to initiation of thyroid hormone replacement
- Elevated CPK may be present
- Hyperlipidemia is common

IMAGING STUDIES

- CT scan of head in suspected cerebrovascular accident
- Chest x-ray to rule out infectious process

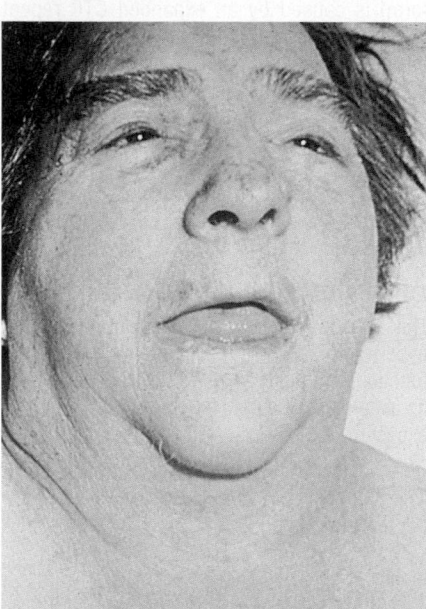

FIGURE 1M-80 Myxedema facies Note dull, puffy, yellowed skin; coarse, sparse hair; temporal loss of eyebrows; periorbital edema; prominent tongue. (Courtesy Paul W. Ladenson, M.D., The Johns Hopkins University and Hospital, Baltimore. In Seidel HM [ed]: *Mosby's guide to physical examination,* ed 5, St Louis, 2004, Mosby.)

TREATMENT

NONPHARMACOLOGIC THERAPY

- Prevent further heat loss; cover the patient but avoid external rewarming because it may produce vascular collapse. Consider warmed IV fluids.
- Support respiratory function; intubation and mechanical ventilation may be required.
- Monitor patient in the intensive care unit.

ACUTE GENERAL Rx

- Give levothyroxine 5 to 8 mcg/kg (200 to 500 mcg) IV infused over 15 min, then 50 to 100 mcg IV q24h until transition to an oral formulation is possible.
- Glucocorticoids should also be empirically administered until coexistent adrenal insufficiency can be ruled out. Hydrocortisone hemisuccinate 100 mg IV bolus is initially given, followed by 100 mg IV q8h until initial plasma cortisol level is confirmed normal.
- IV hydration with D_5NS is used to correct hypotension and hypoglycemia (if present); avoid overhydration and possible water intoxication because clearance of free water is impaired in these patients.
- Rule out and treat precipitating factors (e.g., antibiotics in suspected sepsis).

CHRONIC Rx

Refer to "Hypothyroidism" in Section I.

DISPOSITION

Mortality rate in myxedema coma is 20% to 25% despite aggressive therapy.

REFERRAL

Endocrinology consultation

PEARLS & CONSIDERATIONS

COMMENTS

If the diagnosis is suspected, initiate treatment immediately without waiting for confirming laboratory results.

RELATED CONTENT

Hypothyroidism (Patient Information)
Hypothyroidism (Related Key Topic)

AUTHOR: **FRED F. FERRI, M.D.**

Diseases and Disorders

I

BASIC INFORMATION

DEFINITION

Narcolepsy is a chronic neurologic sleep disorder characterized by excessive daytime sleepiness and dysregulation of rapid eye movement (REM) sleep. It is the second most common cause of disabling daytime sleepiness after obstructive sleep apnea. Symptoms of REM sleep dysregulation include cataplexy, sleep paralysis, and hallucinations during transition between wake and sleep. Difficulty sleeping with either frequent awakenings or disrupted sleep may also occur.

SYNONYMS

Hypersomnia of central origin
Narcolepsy with cataplexy
Narcolepsy-cataplexy syndrome
Narcolepsy with hypocretin deficiency
Gélineau syndrome

ICD-10CM CODES
G47.419 Narcolepsy without cataplexy
G47.411 Narcolepsy with cataplexy

EPIDEMIOLOGY & DEMOGRAPHICS

INCIDENCE: 0.74/100,000 persons/yr
PREVALENCE: 1 in 2,000 people
PREDOMINANT SEX: Males and females are equally affected.
AGE OF ONSET: Peak 15 to 30 yr (range, 10-55 yr)
GENETICS:
- Associated with human leukocyte antigen (HLA) subtypes, specifically, *DQB1*0602*, which is present in 95% of patients with cataplexy and 96% of patients with hypocretin deficiency.
- Risk of narcolepsy increases 20 to 40 times if a family member is affected.
- Monozygotic twin concordance rate is 17% to 36%, thus indicating an incomplete penetrance and suggesting an environmental factor in the disease process.

RISK FACTORS: Anesthesia, head injury, history of meningitis or encephalitis, family history of narcolepsy, tumor, vascular malformations, stroke, and obesity.

PHYSICAL FINDINGS & CLINICAL PRESENTATION

- Overwhelming urge to sleep with chronic hypersomnia may occur during the day.
- Cataplexy occurs in 60% to 100% of patients with narcolepsy and is reported as a partial or complete loss of voluntary muscle control with preserved consciousness that is precipitated by a strong emotion, more commonly with laughter. This is the most specific symptom and is considered pathognomonic for narcolepsy.
- Hypnagogic (wake to sleep) or hypnopompic (sleep to wake) hallucinations have been reported in 60% to 80% of patients with narcolepsy.
- Sleep paralysis, defined as loss of muscle tone during the transition between sleep

and wakefulness, occurs in 60% to 80% of patients with narcolepsy. It may occur with hallucinations and can be interrupted by sensory stimuli.
- Only about one third of patients will have all four symptoms: chronic daytime sleepiness, cataplexy, hypnagogic hallucinations, and sleep paralysis.
- Fragmented sleep is seen in 60% to 80% of narcolepsy patients and can often be mistaken for insomnia or other intrinsic sleep disorder.
- Other symptoms that have been reported in narcolepsy include automatic behavior or semipurposeful movements in 40% of patients and memory disturbance in 50% of patients.

ETIOLOGY

The loss of hypocretin/orexin signaling, genetic factors, and brain lesions are presently identified factors in the development of narcolepsy.
HYPOCRETIN/OREXIN:
- Loss of hypocretin-1 and hypocretin-2 (also known as orexin-A and orexin-B) producing neurons in the lateral hypothalamus.
- Human cerebrospinal fluid (CSF) levels of hypocretin-1 are low to undetectable in narcoleptics with cataplexy.
- Narcolepsy without cataplexy may have a different cause because CSF hypocretin levels are usually normal in those patients, so there may be a completely separate mechanism in these patients, or it may result from less extensive loss of hypocretin neurons or impaired signaling.

SECONDARY ETIOLOGIES:
- Tumors, vascular malformations, and strokes have all been reported to cause secondary narcolepsy.
- Direct injury to the hypocretin neurons or their projections is the most likely cause of secondary narcolepsy due to central nervous system lesions.
- Narcolepsy has been reported in genetic syndromes, including Prader-Willi syndrome and Niemann-Pick disease type C, as well as paraneoplastic syndromes.

Dx DIAGNOSIS

DIFFERENTIAL DIAGNOSIS

Excessive daytime somnolence:
- Autism
- Autosomal dominant cerebellar ataxia, deafness, and narcolepsy
- Behaviorally induced insufficient sleep syndrome
- Central or obstructive sleep apnea (sleep-disordered breathing)
- Circadian rhythm disorder
- Depression
- Diencephalic lesions
- Drug or alcohol abuse
- Hypothyroidism
- Idiopathic hypersomnia with long or short sleep time
- Inadequate sleep hygiene

- Insufficient sleep
- Increased intracranial pressure
Insomnia
- Kleine-Levin syndrome
- Medication effect
- Menstrual-related hypersomnia
- Posttraumatic narcolepsy
- Seizures
- Sleep fragmentation (multiple causes)
Cataplexy:
- Seizures
- Periodic paralysis
- Cardiovascular insufficiency
- Psychogenic (multiple causes)
- Lesions of the hypothalamus or brain stem

WORKUP

- Because persistent sleepiness can occur with many conditions, it is important to rule out other sleep disorders.
- Narcolepsy is often diagnosed by clinical history. The Epworth Sleepiness Scale is very useful in determining the degree of excessive daytime sleepiness (Table 1N-1).
- The diagnosis of narcolepsy can be made if there is a clear history of cataplexy in the setting of excessive daytime somnolence, without need for further diagnostic testing. Sleep laboratory testing or possibly laboratory testing is required if these symptoms do not exist.
- The medical history should include questions regarding severity of daytime hypersomnia while also evaluating for sleep-disordered breathing, transient muscle weakness triggered by emotion, hallucinations while falling asleep or upon awakening, and inability to move after awakening. The clinical evaluation should also address symptoms of seizures and paraneoplastic disorders while also asking about previous stroke or genetic disorders. A detailed family history is imperative. Hypothalamic dysfunction such as unexplained weight gain, endocrine abnormalities, circadian dysrhythmias, and autonomic nervous system problems may provide useful insight.
- A thorough examination including a detailed neurologic examination should be performed.
- Nocturnal polysomnography followed by a multiple sleep latency test (MSLT) remains the gold standard for the diagnosis of narcolepsy. A drug screen should also be performed to rule out pharmacologic modulations of sleep.

LABORATORY TESTS

HLA subtyping and CSF hypocretin/orexin levels may be attempted in suspected cases of narcolepsy. CSF hypocretin/orexin analysis is primarily a research tool. CSF hypocretin levels below 110 pg/mL are indicative of narcolepsy, but normal or high CSF hypocretin levels do not exclude the diagnosis.

Rx TREATMENT

Narcolepsy can be treated with a combination of behavioral and pharmacologic approaches.

NONPHARMACOLOGIC THERAPY

Avoidance of over-the-counter drugs and illicit drugs, optimal sleep hygiene and scheduled daily naps, and psychosocial support can be used for symptoms of excessive daytime somnolence. However, nonpharmacologic therapy is typically not sufficient for treatment of narcolepsy alone but is often used as adjunct therapy with medications.

PHARMACOLOGIC THERAPY

For excessive daytime somnolence:

- Sodium oxybate: a central nervous system depressant that can be used for the treatment of cataplexy and REM-related symptoms
- Modafinil 200 to 600 mg PO every morning or divided bid
- Armodafinil 150 or 250 mg PO as a single dose in the morning
- Methylphenidate 5 to 15 mg PO bid to tid
- Methylphenidate SR 18 to 54 mg PO every morning or divided bid
- Dextroamphetamine 10 to 60 mg PO qd
- Eldepryl 5 mg PO bid
  For cataplexy:
- Sodium oxybate: a central nervous system depressant that can be used for the treatment of cataplexy and REM-related symptoms

- Fluoxetine 20 mg PO qd initially
- Sertraline 25 mg PO qd initially
- Venlafaxine 25 mg PO qd initially
- Clomipramine 25 mg/day initially
- Protriptyline 5 mg tid initially
- Imipramine 25 to 50 mg/day initially
- Desipramine 10 mg bid initially

DISPOSITION

This is a chronic sleep disorder that may worsen for the first few years and then persist for life.

REFERRAL

Because of the complexity of this disorder and its ever-changing management and treatment, patients should be referred to centers or programs with highly trained sleep specialists with expertise caring for these patients, especially if sodium oxybate (Xyrem) therapy is needed.

PEARLS & CONSIDERATIONS

Many narcoleptics report the onset of symptoms beginning in childhood to early adulthood with a long delay of actual diagnosis on the order of 10 to 15 yr. Typically, excessive daytime sleepiness is the initial symptom followed by REM dysregulation (e.g., cataplexy, sleep paralysis, hypnagogic hallucinations). Patients with narcolepsy also have higher than expected incidence of other sleep disorders, including obstructive sleep apnea, periodic limb movements of sleep, and REM sleep behavior disorder.

COMMENTS

Narcolepsy is a rare disorder that is underdiagnosed. The average time from onset of symptoms to diagnosis is 5 to 15 years. Cataplexy is specific for narcolepsy, but other symptoms of REM dysregulation, including sleep paralysis and hypnagogic or hypnopompic hallucinations, can occur even in normal patients. Sleep-onset REM or REM periods on an MSLT may occur as a result of sleep deprivation or withdrawal from REM-suppressing drugs.

SUGGESTED READINGS

Available at www.expertconsult.com

RELATED CONTENT

Narcolepsy (Patient Information)

AUTHOR: **DON HAYES, JR., M.D., M.S.**

TABLE 1N-1 Epworth Sleepiness Scale

How likely are you to doze off or fall asleep in the following situations, in contrast to just feeling tired? This refers to your usual way of life in recent time. Even if you have not done some of these things recently, try to work out how they would have affected you. Use the following scale to choose the most appropriate number for each situation.

0 = would never doze
1 = slight chance of dozing
2 = moderate chance of dozing
3 = high chance of dozing

Situation	Chance of Dozing
Sitting and reading	
Watching TV	
Sitting and inactive in a public place (theater or meeting)	
As a passenger in a car for an hour without a break	
Lying down to rest in the afternoon when circumstances permit	
Sitting and talking to someone	
Sitting quietly after lunch (without alcohol)	
In a car, while stopped for a few minutes in traffic	
Total	

From Johns MW: A new method for measuring daytime sleepiness: the Epworth Sleepiness Scale, *Sleep* 14:540-545, 1991.

BASIC INFORMATION

DEFINITION

Necrotizing fasciitis (NF) is a rapidly spreading bacterial infection of the deep fascia, with associated inflammation, leading to necrosis of subcutaneous tissue planes. This infection can occur in wounds from trauma or surgical wounds or can be spontaneous or idiopathic. There are two clinical types, both of which carry a high rate of morbidity and mortality.

SYNONYMS

NF
Soft tissue gangrene
Flesh-eating bacteria
Fournier's gangrene
Hemolytic streptococcal gangrene

ICD-10CM CODES
M72.6 Necrotizing fasciitis

EPIDEMIOLOGY & DEMOGRAPHICS

PREDOMINANT SEX: Male > female.
PREDOMINANT AGE: 6 to 50 yr; less common in children.

EPIDEMIOLOGY

Invasive group A *Streptococcus* infection occurs at a rate of 3.5 cases per 100,000 persons, with a case fatality rate of around 24%.

PHYSICAL FINDINGS & CLINICAL PRESENTATION

CLINICAL TYPES OF NECROTIZING FASCIITIS:

- Type I necrotizing fasciitis: at least one anaerobic species is isolated in conjunction with one or more facultative anaerobic species, such as streptococci (not group A), *and* members of the Enterobacteriaceae
- Anaerobic bacteria, most commonly *Bacteroides* or *Peptostreptococcus* spp.
- Enterobacteriaceae: *Escherichia coli*, *Klebsiella* spp., *Proteus* spp., *Enterobacter* spp.
- Usually associated with diabetes or peripheral vascular disease
- Example of type I: Fournier's gangrene of the perineum
- Type II necrotizing fasciitis: Group A *Streptococcus* is isolated alone or in combination with other bacteria, most likely *Staphylococcus aureus*. Also known as hemolytic streptococcal gangrene
  1. Example of type II: Invasive group A *Streptococcus*, associated with virulence factors type 1 and type 3 M protein

EXAMPLES OF NECROTIZING FASCIITIS:

- Fournier's gangrene: Aggressive type I infection of the perineum usually caused by penetration of the gastrointestinal or urethral mucosa by enteric organisms. It can rapidly spread to involve the scrotum, penis, and abdominal wall or gluteal muscles, causing gangrene.
- Clostridial cellulitis: Caused by *Clostridium perfringens* associated by local trauma or surgery and crepitus caused by gas production; generally noted in the skin, with deeper tissues generally spared.

PHYSICAL FINDINGS

Minor skin trauma, toxic-appearing patient:

- Open skin wound.
- Severe pain at injury or surgical site.
- Fever, confusion, weakness, diarrhea.
- Early skin erythema, quickly spreading in hours to days.
- Skin redness changes to purple discoloration.
- Gangrenous skin changes may develop.
- Loosening of skin and subcutaneous skin in association with deep fascial necrosis (Fig. 1N-1). "Woody" induration and crepitus of involved area are characteristics.
- Muscle involvement, thrombosis of blood vessels, and myonecrosis may develop.
- Bullae and gas formation at site.

ETIOLOGY

- NF usually arises from skin damage or trauma. Risk is increased with presence of comorbidities (DM, cancer, liver disease, immunosuppression).
- Polymicrobial: mixture of anaerobes and aerobic enteric gram-negative rods.
- Group A streptococci *(S. pyogenes)*.
- *S. aureus.*
- *C. perfringens.*
- *Bacteroides fragilis.*
- *Vibrio vulnificus.*
- Methicillin-resistant *S. aureus* (MRSA), especially community-acquired MRSA.

 **DIAGNOSIS**

DIFFERENTIAL DIAGNOSIS

- Cellulitis.
- Pyomyositis.
- Gas gangrene.
- A classification of necrotizing skin, soft-tissue, and muscle infections is described in Table 1N-2.

WORKUP

- Diagnosis of necrotizing fasciitis generally requires incision and probing. In patients with necrotizing fasciitis, there is no resistance to probing subcutaneously and there is fascial plane involvement.
- Laboratory tests:
  1. Complete blood cell count (CBC) with differential (leukocytosis, anemia), elevated CRP ($\geq$15 mg/dL), hyponatremia (sodium <135 mEq/L), elevated creatinine (>1.6 mg/dL), hyperglycemia (glucose >180 mg/dL)
  2. Cultures of skin, soft tissue, or debrided tissue, aerobically and anaerobically. Blood cultures are positive in 60% of patients with type II infections and 20% with type I infections.
- Imaging:
  1. Radiographs show subcutaneous gas in fascial planes (Fig. 1N-2).
  2. Computed tomography (CT)/magnetic resonance imaging (MRI) may be helpful because they can detect gas in the tissues.

Rx TREATMENT

- Aggressive surgical debridement of involved necrotic tissues is essential as soon as possible to reduce mortality.
- Fasciotomies of extremities may be necessary.
- Empiric antibiotic treatment:

Type I: Piperacillin/tazobactam; carbapenems such as imipenem, meropenem, or doripenem; and third-generation cephalosporin + metronidazole or aminoglycoside + clindamycin are reasonable choices pending cultures. It is important to always have anaerobic coverage.

Type II: For group A *Streptococcus*, give intravenous (IV) penicillin G, 4 million U q4h in patients who weigh >60 kg with clindamycin, 600 to 900 mg IV q8h.
  1. Clindamycin has the added effect of suppressing toxin production. If MRSA is suspected, add vancomycin, daptomycin, or linezolid.
- Intravenous gammaglobulin (IVIG): 1 g/kg on day 1 and 0.5 g/kg on days 2 and 3 neutralizes circulating streptococcal toxins and has been shown beneficial in severe forms of invasive group A streptococcal infections, although data not definitive.

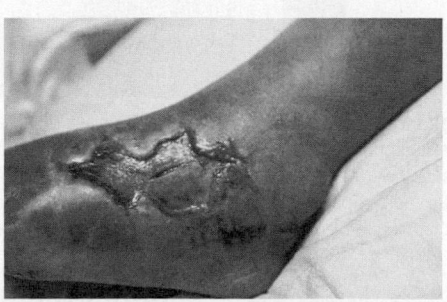

FIGURE 1N-1 Necrotizing fasciitis The so-called flesh-eating bacteria, group A β-hemolytic Streptococcus, can cause significant tissue destruction rapidly. This 32-year-old woman had pain, erythema, and swelling of the foot followed by necrotic ulceration over a week. There was no history of trauma. (Courtesy Roger Bitar, MD. From White GM, Cox NH [eds]: *Diseases of the skin, a color atlas and text,* ed 2, St Louis, 2006, Mosby.)

TABLE 1N-2 Classification of Necrotizing Skin, Soft-Tissue, and Muscle Infections

Disease	Bacteriology	Comments
Necrotizing Cellulitis		
Clostridial cellulitis	*Clostridium perfringens*	Local trauma, recent surgery; fascial/deep muscle spared
Nonclostridial cellulitis	Mixed: *Escherichia coli, Enterobacter, Peptostreptococcus* spp., *Bacteroides fragilis*	Diabetes mellitus predisposes; produces foul odor
Meleney's synergistic gangrene	*Staphylococcus aureus,* microaerophilic streptococci	Rare infection; postoperative; slowly expanding, indolent, ulceration in superficial fascia
Synergistic necrotizing cellulitis	Mixed aerobic and anaerobic, including *B. fragilis, Peptostreptococcus* spp.	Diabetes mellitus predisposes; variant of necrotizing fasciitis type I; involves skin, muscle, fat, and fascia
Necrotizing Fasciitis		
Type I	Mixed aerobic and anaerobic; staphylococci, *B. fragilis, E. coli,* group A streptococci, *Peptostreptococcus* spp., *Prevotella, Porphyromonas* spp., *Clostridium* spp.	Usually requires a breach in the mucous membrane layer either through surgery or penetrating injuries or from chronic medical conditions such as diabetes, peripheral vascular disease, malignancy, and anal fissures
Type II	Group A streptococci	Increasing in frequency and severity since 1985; very high mortality; often begins at site of nonpenetrating minor trauma such as a bruise or muscle strain but often no identified precursor
		Predisposing factors: blunt/penetrating trauma, varicella (chickenpox), intravenous drug abuse, surgical procedures, childbirth, nonsteroidal antiinflammatory drug use
Myonecrosis		
Clostridial myonecrosis	*Clostridium* spp.	Predisposing factors: deep/penetrating injury, bowel and biliary tract surgery, improperly performed abortion and retained placenta, prolonged rupture of the membranes, and intrauterine fetal demise or missed abortion in postpartum patients. Recurrent gas gangrene occurs at sites of previous gas gangrene.
Streptococcal myonecrosis	Streptococci	
Special Type of Necrotizing Soft-Tissue Infection		
Fournier's gangrene	Polymicrobial, with *E. coli* the predominant aerobe and *Bacteroides* the predominant anaerobe. Other microflora: *Proteus, Staphylococcus, Enterococcus,* aerobic and anaerobic *Streptococcus, Pseudomonas, Klebsiella,* and *Clostridium*	Necrosis of the scrotum or perineum that starts with scrotal pain and erythema and rapidly spreads onto anterior abdominal wall and gluteal muscle. It is more often seen in diabetics and can be associated with trauma.

From Vincent JL et al: *Textbook of critical care,* ed 6, Philadelphia, 2011, Saunders.

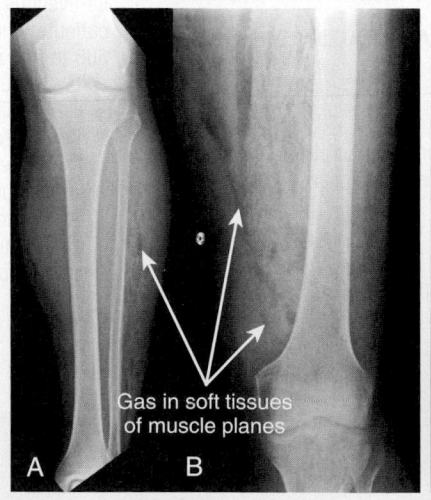
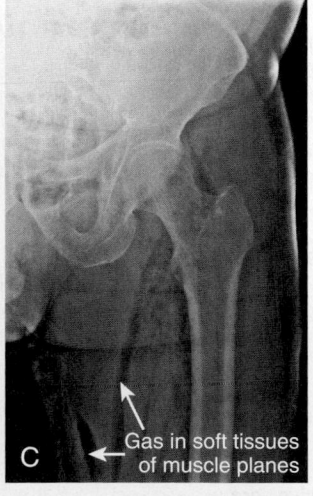

FIGURE 1N-2 Necrotizing fasciitis This 71-year-old man with aplastic anemia presented with fevers to 38.9° C, leg weakness, and extreme leg pain. Initially, the patient was thought to have neuropathic pain and weakness, possibly indicating spinal disease such as epidural abscess. He rapidly developed crepitus of his legs. Radiographs of the patient's legs were obtained, followed by noncontrast CT. **A,** Anterior-posterior (AP) tibia and fibula. **B,** AP femur. **C,** AP hip. Air is seen dissecting in muscle planes of the legs. On radiograph, air appears black. Given the wide distribution of air, a focal abscess is unlikely, and necrotizing fasciitis with gas-producing organisms should be suspected. (From Broder JS: *Diagnostic imaging for the emergency physician,* Philadelphia, 2011, Saunders.)

- For vibrio vulnificus use doxycycline plus ceftazidime, for aeromonas hydrophila use doxycycline plus ciprofloxacin.
- Hyperbaric oxygen evaluation as an adjunct to surgery and IV antibiotics.

SUGGESTED READINGS
Available at www.expertconsult.com

AUTHOR: **GLENN G. FORT, M.D., M.P.H.**

 **BASIC INFORMATION**

DEFINITION

Multiorgan systemic fibrosis related to gadolinium-based contrast exposure

SYNONYMS

Nephrogenic fibrosing dermopathy
Gadolinium-associated nephrogenic systemic fibrosis

ICD-10CM CODES
M35.5 Multifocal fibrosclerosis

EPIDEMIOLOGY & DEMOGRAPHICS

INCIDENCE: 1.6% to 4.6%
PREDOMINANT SEX AND AGE: No predilection for sex, often seen in middle age but can involve all age groups
RISK FACTORS: Linear, nonionically charged gadolinium-based contrast agents, including gadodiamide (Omniscan) and gadoversetamide (OptiMARK), along with linear, ionically charged gadopentetate (Magnevist) exposure, provide high risk among patients with severe renal dysfunction (Stage 4/GFR <30 mL/min per 1.73 m^2 or worse), including dialysis patients, with the highest risk in patients on peritoneal dialysis or acute kidney injury (AKI), particularly hepatorenal in origin. Proinflammatory states including major surgery, thrombotic events, infection, and malignancy as well as high-dose erythropoietin use in this population are associated with higher risk of nephrogenic systemic fibrosis. Higher than standard dose of gadolinium-based contrast agent is also associated with elevated risk of NSF.

PHYSICAL FINDINGS & CLINICAL PRESENTATION

- History of gadolinium-based contrast media in a patient with renal dysfunction (GFR <30 mL/min) or AKI, particularly in those patients with proinflammatory states.
- Presentation time varies from day of exposure to several months later, with a median of 11.5 days to up to 8 years after exposure being reported.
- Major criteria include pruritic, erythematous plaques with induration, and joint contractures.
- Minor criteria include superficial plaque, scleral plaques in patients less than 45 years old, and dermal papules.
- Skin presentations typically are symmetric and involve the extremities and trunk, generally sparing the face (Fig. 1N-3). Fibrosis can be extradermal, leading to multiorgan dysfunction. For example, fibrosis can lead

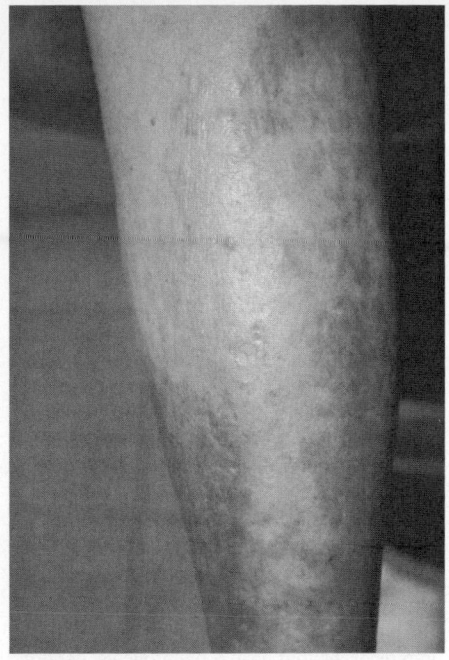

FIGURE 1N-3 Red-brown, shiny plaques indicate deeper skin involvement with nephrogenic systemic fibrosis. (From Girardi M: Nephrogenic systemic fibrosis: a dermatologist's perspective, *J Am Coll Radiol* 5(1):40-44, 2008.)

to respiratory failure from muscular involvement of the diaphragm. It can also affect the eyes and blood vessels.

ETIOLOGY

- Pathophysiology remains unclear, but current postulation is that free gadolinium ions deposit in the tissues after being displaced from the chelating agent and binding to anions, forming insoluble salts. Displacement of gadolinium from its chelating agent is postulated to occur more readily in proinflammatory states, allowing the gadolinium to enter the extravascular space. In renal failure, when the duration of gadolinium exposure is highest due to a decreased clearance of gadolinium, tissue deposition is higher. Deposition leads to fibrocyte recruitment and further contribution to the proinflammatory states, leading to further tissue injury and fibrocyte recruitment and ultimately tissue fibrosis.

 **DIAGNOSIS**

DIFFERENTIAL DIAGNOSIS

- Scleroderma

WORKUP

- Skin biopsy

LABORATORY TESTS

- None

IMAGING STUDIES

- None

Rx TREATMENT

No current effective treatment. There are no randomized clinical trials available. Case reports implementing corticosteroids, plasmapheresis, thalidomide, and methotrexate suggest little to no benefit, whereas case reports implementing photopheresis and sodium thiosulfate have shown modest benefit. Hemodialysis can effectively remove gadolinium contrast media, but no current evidence demonstrates that immediate hemodialysis is protective against development of nephrogenic systemic fibrosis. It is reasonable to perform dialysis following gadolinium contrast exposure in patients currently on dialysis. Resolution of renal dysfunction typically also results in the resolution of NSF.

REFERRAL

- Dermatology for biopsy

PEARLS & CONSIDERATIONS

COMMENTS

Given the lack of treatment modalities, prevention of this disease by avoidance of gadolinium-based contrast administration is best among patients with advanced CKD. All patients intended to receive gadolinium-based contrast for renal dysfunction should be screened.

PREVENTION

Unless essential diagnostic information is needed from a gadolinium-based contrast medium, these studies should be avoided in patients with a GFR less than 30 mL per minute per 1.73 m^2 or with AKI. Caution should also be used in children under 1 year and in pregnant women.

SUGGESTED READINGS
Available at www.expertconsult.com

PATIENT/FAMILY EDUCATION
Information on gadolinium-based contrast agents: http://www.fda.gov/Drugs/DrugSafety/PostmarketDrugSafetyInformationforPatientsandProviders/ucm142882.htm

AUTHORS: **NIKUNJKUMAR PATEL, M.D.,** and **SUSIE L. HU, M.D.**

BASIC INFORMATION

DEFINITION

Nephrotic syndrome is characterized by heavy proteinuria (usually defined as >3.5 g/24 hr), hypoalbuminemia, hyperlipidemia, lipiduria, and edema. Nephrotic-range proteinuria can have many causes that share a common mechanism of glomerular injury leading to proteinuria. Patients with this degree of proteinuria may or may not have the other features of the syndrome.

ICD-10CM CODES
N04.9 Nephrotic syndrome with unspecified morphologic changes
N04.0 Nephrotic syndrome with minor glomerular abnormality
N04.1 Nephrotic syndrome with focal and segmental glomerular lesions
N04.2 Nephrotic syndrome with diffuse membranous glomerulonephritis
N04.3 Nephrotic syndrome with diffuse mesangial proliferative glomerulonephritis
N04.4 Nephrotic syndrome with diffuse endocapillary proliferative glomerulonephritis
N04.5 Nephrotic syndrome with diffuse mesangiocapillary glomerulonephritis
N04.6 Nephrotic syndrome with dense deposit disease
N04.7 Nephrotic syndrome with diffuse crescentic glomerulonephritis
N04.8 Nephrotic syndrome with other morphologic changes

EPIDEMIOLOGY & DEMOGRAPHICS

- Among children (especially those less than 6 years of age), the most common causes of nephrotic syndrome are:
  A) Minimal change disease (75% of pediatric cases)
  B) FSGS (7%-20% of cases)

- Among adults, FSGS has now become the most common primary cause of nephrotic-range proteinuria. Membranous nephropathy is now the second most common primary cause of nephrotic syndrome. FSGS is more common in persons of African ancestry, whereas membranous nephropathy is seen more commonly in Caucasians. Overall, diabetic nephropathy remains the most common cause of nephrotic-range proteinuria.

PHYSICAL FINDINGS & CLINICAL PRESENTATION

- Patients usually present with severe lower extremity, periorbital edema, and weight gain.
- Ascites and anasarca can occur.
- Hypercoagulability (i.e., pulmonary embolism [PE]) and risk of infection (i.e., pneumococcal infection) are potential clinical manifestations.

ETIOLOGY

Glomerular diseases have often been grouped into diseases that have a nephrotic vs. nephritic presentation. This artificial delineation has traditionally implied that diseases associated with the "nephritic syndromes" are often associated with subnephrotic proteinuria, a fact that can cause diagnostic confusion, as any glomerular disease can present with nephrotic-range proteinuria. It is better to think of these diseases as having either a noninflammatory sediment (proteinuria alone with no casts or cellular elements) vs. an inflammatory sediment (i.e., those with RBC casts and/or dysmorphic RBCs in conjunction with proteinuria). Figure 1N-4 details this breakdown. In this chapter, we focus on those primary diseases that present with a noninflammatory sediment (namely, minimal change disease, focal segmental glomerulosclerosis, membranous nephropathy, and amyloidosis) as well as on a primary disease with an inflammatory sediment that often has nephrotic-range proteinuria (MPGN). Workup of so-called

"nephritic syndrome" as noted by worsening GFR in the setting of proteinuria and hematuria is detailed elsewhere. Important points regarding the most common etiologies of nephrotic syndrome are detailed below and in Table 1N-4.

- Minimal change disease: characterized by a bland urine sediment and abrupt onset of disease and equally abrupt remission. Proteinuria can be massive (>20 g daily). NSAID use, lithium, viral infections, and lymphoma have all been associated with secondary forms of MCD.
- FSGS: either primary or secondary. Primary FSGS denotes an idiopathic cause that is usually severe and requires immunosuppressive therapy. It is more prevalent in persons of African ancestry. Secondary FSGS refers to FSGS caused by a known etiology (e.g., heroin, sickle cell disease, scarring of any kind from prior injury, obesity, low nephron mass, HIV, etc.). Clinically, primary FSGS is more commonly associated with heavy proteinuria and nephrotic syndrome. By contrast, most cases of secondary FSGS are associated with lower levels of proteinuria (often subnephrotic), higher albumin levels, and less significant edema (HIV-associated nephropathy is an important exception in that it is associated with heavy proteinuria and rapid progression if not treated). Distinguishing between the two types is important for therapy (see the following).
- Membranous nephropathy: Membranous nephropathy can also be either primary or secondary. Primary membranous nephropathy is due to in situ deposition of antibody against a glomerular antigen (in at least 70% of cases the epitope has been found to be phospholipase A2 receptor). Proteinuria can be massive. Secondary membranous nephropathy is often due to infection (hepatitis B, malaria, schistosomiasis, syphilis), autoimmune disease (lupus), medications (gold), and malignancies. Distinguishing between the two subtypes is important for management (see the following).

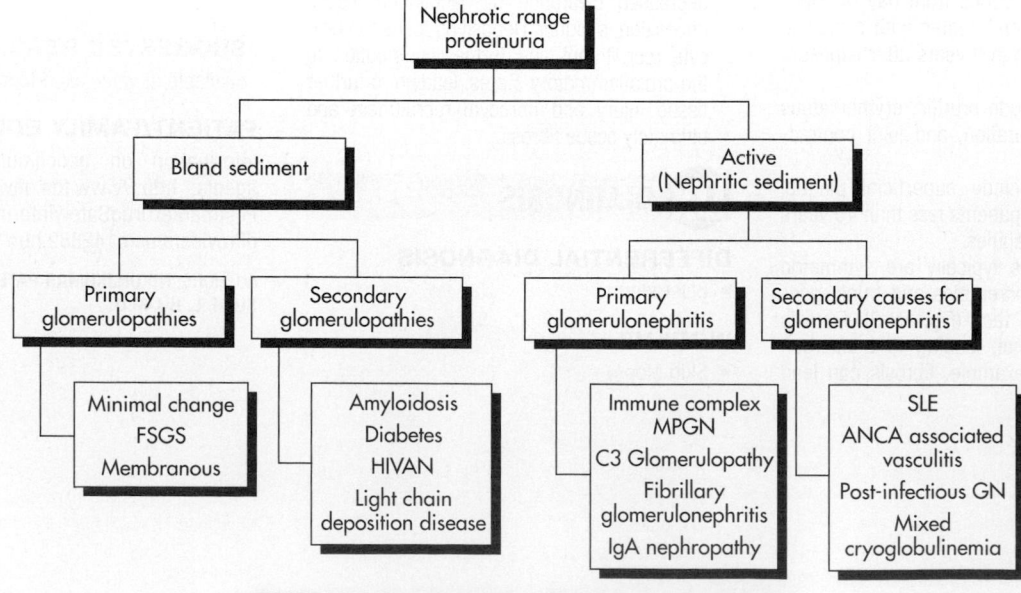

FIGURE 1N-4 An approach to nephrotic-range proteinuria

TABLE 1N-4 Important clinical, serological, and pathological features of selected diseases causing nephrotic syndrome

Disease	Important Clinical Features	Serological Features	Pathological Features
Minimal change disease	Explosive onset with heavy proteinuria and rapid remission with therapy. True steroid resistance is rare and should prompt rebiopsy to rule out FSGS	Complements are normal	LM shows completely normal kidney architecture IF: Normal EM: Diffuse podocyte effacement
Primary FSGS	Often heavier proteinuria and low serum albumin and edema. Tip lesion subtype and collapsing FSGS often have more explosive onset. Sediment usually bland, but RBCs can be seen. Usually no casts.	Complements are normal.	Light Microscopy: Only one glomerulus need show features of FSGS to make diagnosis. IF: Often devoid of immunoglobulin, although IgM can be seen EM: Often has diffuse podocyte effacement
Secondary FSGS	Proteinuria is often subnephrotic, or if nephrotic, serum albumin levels are maintained. Minimal edema.	HIV and parvovirus infection can cause phenotype identical to idiopathic collapsing FSGS.	LM: Often shows evidence of glomerulomegaly EM: Foot process effacement is more patchy.
Primary membranous nephropathy	Often seen in older Caucasian patients. More likely than other forms of nephrotic syndrome to be associated with thrombotic complications Sediment: bland. RBCs can be found, although RBC casts are usually found.	Serum antiphospholipase A2 receptor antibodies are found in 70% of patients with idiopathic primary membranous nephropathy. Antineutral endopeptidase antibodies are found in a minority of others.	LM: Characterized by thickening of the GBM; "spikes" can be seen on silver stain. IF: C3 and IgG noted in granular pattern. Newer techniques now stain for antiphospholipase A2 receptor antibody *in situ*. EM: Associated with subepithelial deposits
Secondary membranous nephropathy	Associated with **malignancy,** lupus, syphilis, hepatitis B and C, medications (gold, captopril, penicillamine, etc.).	Notable for the absence of antiphospholipase A2 antibodies ANA, hepatitis B, HCV serologies are helpful. RPR can be sent in context of appropriate history.	Morphology is exactly the same except when examined by EM. On high power, one sees both subendothelial and mesangial deposits in addition to classic subepithelial deposits.
Amyloidosis	Often found with massive proteinuria. Kidney size is enlarged. Bland sediment	UPEP, SPEP, serum free light chains may be positive. The UPEP will show glomerular proteinuria, which can help differentiate from myeloma kidney.	LM: Often notable for nodular pattern. Diagnosis can be made by staining using Congo red or thioflavin T. IF: antibody use can differentiate AA from AL amyloid EM shows characteristic, random 10-nm fibrils
Diabetes	Often associated with nephrotic-range proteinuria in the setting of retinopathy. Kidney sizes are preserved.	No specific serologic tests are positive.	LM: Nodular pattern often seen, thickened GBM
MPGN	Often associated with nephrotic-range proteinuria with a "nephritic" sediment RBC casts often seen along with dysmorphic RBC	Both C3 and C4 are often low in immune complex MPGN. Immune complex GN warrants checking SPEP, UPEP, as gammopathy is associated with MPGN. Hepatitis B, HCV, ANA, and cryoglobulins are also warranted. C3 alone is low in dense deposit disease and C3 glomerulonephritis, which may prompt specific tests for complement dysregulation.	The key point here is to look at the IF. If immunofluorescence shows both immunoglobulin and complement deposition, the diagnosis is immune complex MGPN. If only complement, the diagnosis is most likely C3 glomerulopathy (either dense deposit disease or C3 glomerulonephritis).

- Amyloidosis: Often due to overproduction of a light chain (AL amyloid) or due to a chronic inflammatory state (AA amyloid). Kidney size is often enlarged, and proteinuria can be massive. Congo red staining defines the diagnosis.
- Diabetic nephropathy: Often characterized by slowly progressive proteinuria in the face of retinopathy and preserved kidney size. The strength of correlation between retinopathy, proteinuria, and diabetic nephropathy is very strong in type 1 diabetic patients, and biopsy is not usually undertaken. The relationship is not as strong in type 2 diabetic patients, and the absence of retinopathy does not preclude a diagnosis of diabetic nephropathy.

MPGN: This is usually due to the deposition of immune complexes in conjunction with complement or activation of the alternative complement cascade without immune complexes (i.e., C3 glomerulopathy). Common immune complex causes

are from infections (hepatitis C), autoimmune diseases (SLE), or dysproteinemias (monoclonal gammopathies). Distinguishing between these possibilities guides therapy. Urinary sediment is often active with dysmorphic RBCs and RBC casts and is also associated with heavy proteinuria.

DX DIAGNOSIS

DIFFERENTIAL DIAGNOSIS

- Other states that present with edema (CHF, cirrhosis, protein-losing enteropathy, severe malnutrition)
- Glomerulonephritis (those diseases commonly associated with an inflammatory urinary sediment and inflammation of the glomerulus)
- Mimickers of glomerulonephritis (malignant HTN, preeclampsia, antiphospholipid syndrome)

WORKUP

- Evaluation should begin by looking at rate of change of serum creatinine, quantification of proteinuria by 24-hour collection, and manual examination of the urinary sediment.
- Bland urinary sediment and proteinuria >3.5 g/24 hr should prompt nephrology consultation.
- Serologic tests of use may be a UPEP, SPEP, HIV, hepatitis B surface antigen, hepatitis C virus (HCV) antibody, and antinuclear antibody (ANA). As urinary sediment examination is not 100% sensitive in ruling out an inflammatory process, C3 and C4 can be checked, as complement levels are often low in many inflammatory glomerulonephritides and are low in MPGN. Low complement levels may change the nature of the differential prior to biopsy.
- Ultimately, given that clinical acumen cannot reliably distinguish between various etiologies, a renal biopsy is usually required,

TABLE 1N-5 Important Definitions in Dealing With Treatment of Primary Nephrotic Syndrome

	Adults	Children
Definition		
Complete Remission	Reduction in proteinuria to <0.3 g/24 hours	<4 mg m-2h-1 on at least 3 occasions within 7 days and serum albumin >3.5 g/dl
Partial Remission	Reduction in proteinuria between 0.3 g/24 hour and 3.5 g daily with ≥50% decrease in proteinuria from baseline	Disappearance of edema, increase in serum albumin >3.5 g/dl and persistent proteinuria >4 mg m-2h-1 or >100 mg m-2day-1
*Relapse	Increase in proteinuria to >3.5 g daily after one month of complete or partial remission	Urine dipstick 3+ or proteinuria >40 mg/m²/hour occurring on 3 days within 1 week.
*Steroid Dependent	Two consecutive relapses occurring during therapy or within 14 days of completing therapy	Two relapses of proteinuria within 14 days after stopping or during alternate-day steroid therapy
*Steroid Resistant	Persistence of proteinuria without significant reduction despite prednisone therapy at 1 mg/kg for 16 weeks	Persistence of proteinuria despite prednisone therapy at 60 mg/m² for 4 weeks.

*These definitions only truly apply to diseases such as minimal change disease and FSGS.
Adapted from Cattran DC et al: Cyclosporine in idiopathic glomerular disease associated with the nephrotic syndrome: workshop recommendations, *Kidney Int* 72(12):1429-1447, 2007, and *KDIGO clinical practice guidelines for glomerulonephritis.*

except in very young children where there is a very high likelihood of minimal change disease, or in adults if contraindications are present (coagulopathy).
- Patients should also have a renal ultrasound to document the presence of two kidneys prior to attempting biopsy as well as documenting kidney size.

 TREATMENT

NONIMMUNOSUPPRESSIVE THERAPY
- Control of proteinuria is key to mitigating risk of progression. ACE-I or ARB should be titrated upwards (except in MCD, where it is not usually given due to complete response). Dual ACE-I and ARB use together is controversial given the higher risk of hyperkalemia.
- For patients with proteinuria above 1 g daily, goal BP should be 125/75 or less.
- With the exception of MCD, all patients with nephrotic-range proteinuria and hyperlipidemia should be treated with statins if tolerated.
- Although some patients with nephrotic syndrome are hypercoagulable (particularly patients with membranous nephropathy), the role of prophylactic anticoagulation is not well defined and is controversial. For patients with membranous nephropathy and serum albumin levels <2.0 g/dl, anticoagulation can be considered if bleeding risk is low.
- Patients should be placed on a low sodium diet (<2 grams daily) along with diuretics.
- Diuretic resistance is common (from gut wall edema and hypoalbuminemia). More bioavailable diuretics (bumetanide, torsemide) may be of benefit, along with use of thiazide diuretics.

- To prevent "diuretic braking," diuretics should be dosed at least on a bid basis.

IMMUNOSUPPRESSIVE THERAPY
In general, immunosuppressive therapy is dictated by the identified disorder. Important terms in dealing with the management of nephrotic-range proteinuria due to primary glomerular diseases are listed in Table 1N-5. First-line therapies for each disease are highlighted in the following.
- MCD: First-line therapy in adults is prednisone (1 mg/kg up to 80 mg for minimum of 4 weeks and maximum of 16 weeks with taper over 6 months if response noted). Second-line options include use of cyclophosphamide and/or cyclosporine.
- FSGS: Primary FSGS is often treated with high-dose prednisone (maximum 80 mg daily in adults) for 6 months. Alternative regimens include low-dose prednisone with cyclosporine. Treatment of secondary FSGS is based on halting the underlying cause and nonspecific therapy with blockade of the renin angiotensin system. Immunosuppression is avoided.
- Membranous nephropathy: Suggested first-line therapy for primary membranous nephropathy involves the Ponticelli protocol for 6 months (intravenous methylprednisolone 1 g/day⁻ for 3 days, then oral prednisone 0.4 mg/kg daily for the remainder of the month for months 1, 3, and 5 and oral cyclophosphamide 1.5-2.5 mg/kg daily on months 2, 4, and 6). Alternative therapy includes low-dose prednisone along with cyclosporine or tacrolimus alone for at least one year. Rituximab may become more commonly used as first-line therapy in the coming

years. Therapy for secondary membranous nephropathy is directed at the underlying cause (malignancy, SLE, etc.).
- Treatment of amyloidosis, diabetes, and MPGN is directed toward the underlying disorder. In rapidly progressive HCV-related MPGN, immunosuppressive therapy with the rituximab or glucocorticosteroids and cyclophosphamide can be administered in addition to treating HCV.

REFERRAL
Nephrology consultation is recommended in all cases of nephrotic syndrome.

❗ PEARLS & CONSIDERATIONS
- Proteinuria >2 g daily generally implies glomerular disease unless multiple myeloma is present. UPEP delineates the character of proteins excreted as tubular, glomerular, or overflow.
- Massive proteinuria (>10 g daily) is rarely seen with inflammatory diseases and usually indicates minimal change disease, FSGS, membranous nephropathy, or amyloidosis.
- Quantification of proteinuria should occur with a 24-hour urine collection initially along with a measure of creatinine excretion to document validity of the collection. Spot collections have not been validated for heavy proteinuria or in patients with rapidly changing creatinine values. A "spot" urine protein:creatinine ratio taken from the 24-hour collection defines the relationship between spot and "true" collections to monitor response to therapy.
- Most noninflammatory processes progress slowly. If a sediment without red blood cell casts is detected with a rapidly increasing serum creatinine and heavy proteinuria, the differential is relatively narrow:
  1. Minimal change disease and AIN as seen with NSAID use
  2. Nephrotic syndrome associated with ATN from hypovolemia
  3. Bilateral renal vein thrombosis superimposed on nephrotic syndrome
  4. Myeloma cast nephropathy
  5. Collapsing FSGS/HIVAN

SUGGESTED READINGS
Available at www.expertconsult.com.

RELATED CONTENT
Nephrotic Syndrome (Patient Information)

AUTHOR: **SANJEEV R. SHAH, M.D.**

Diseases and Disorders

I

BASIC INFORMATION

DEFINITION

Neuroblastomas are tumors of postganglionic sympathetic neurons that typically originate in the adrenal medulla or the sympathetic chain/ganglion. Often present at birth, but not diagnosed until later, when the child shows symptoms of the disease. They are almost exclusively a disease of childhood.

ICD-10CM CODES
C74.90 Malignant neoplasm of unspecified part of unspecified adrenal gland

EPIDEMIOLOGY & DEMOGRAPHICS

INCIDENCE (IN U.S.): 8%-10% of all solid tumors of childhood (third most common childhood cancer, after leukemia and brain tumors); 10.54 cases per 1 million per year in children younger than 15 years
PREDOMINANT SEX: Male/female ratio of 1:1.3
PEAK AGE: Early childhood. Mean age of onset is 18 mo; 33% onset by 1 year; 75% onset by 5 year; 97% by 10 year. In rare cases, neuroblastoma can be discovered by fetal ultrasound.
GENETICS: Germline deletion at the 1p36 or 11q14-23 locus is associated with neuroblastoma, and the same deletions are found somatically in sporadic neuroblastomas. Amplification of N-MYC (2p23), which encodes a nuclear transcription factor in the basic helix-loop-helix leucine zipper family. The prevalence of N-myc amplification is about 22% in neuroblastoma and is associated with advanced-stage disease and poor prognosis. There is a small subset with an autosomal dominant pattern of inheritance. Somatic recurrent mutations (ATRX gene) in tumors from patients with stage 4 neuroblastoma correlate with age at diagnosis and telomere length in children and young adults.

PHYSICAL FINDINGS & CLINICAL PRESENTATION

- The most common presentation of neuroblastoma is an abdominal mass. Neuroblastomas can arise anywhere along the sympathetic nervous system. The most common primary site is the adrenal gland (40%), followed by a mass in the abdomen (25%), thorax (15%), neck (5%), and pelvis (5%). In approximately 1% of cases a primary site cannot be identified. 70% to 80% of children have regional lymph node involvement or distant metastases to bone marrow, cortical bone, orbits, liver, and skin at time of presentation.
- Spinal cord/paraspinal: can present with localized back pain, signs of cord compression—paraplegia or stool/urine retention, abdominal mass, pain, or constipation.
- Watery diarrhea on rare occasions as result of secretion of vasoactive intestinal peptide (VIP) or due to protein losing enteropathy secondary to intestinal lymphangiectasia. Horner's syndrome (ptosis, miosis, anhidrosis) if it involves the stellate ganglion.

- Thoracic: difficulty breathing, dysphagia, infections, chronic cough
- Secondary symptoms referable to metastatic disease: fatigue, chronic pain (typically bony pain), pancytopenia, periorbital ecchymosis, proptosis, anorexia, weight loss, unexplained fever, multiple subcutaneous bluish nodules, irritability
- Paraneoplastic syndromes:
- **O**psoclonus-myoclonus syndrome (OMS) is described as "dancing eyes, dancing feet," which manifest as myoclonic jerks and chaotic eye movements in all directions. This may be initial presentation before tumor diagnosis; present in 1% to 3% of patients with neuroblastoma; of all patients with opsoclonus-myoclonus, approximately 50% have an underlying neuroblastoma. Patients who present with this syndrome must be evaluated for neuroblastoma; when present, the neuroblastoma often has more favorable biologic features.
  1. Progressive cerebellar ataxia.

DIAGNOSIS

WORKUP

- Careful general physical examination to look for mass
- Biopsy and resection of tumor when possible

LABORATORY TESTS

- Complete blood count, coagulation studies, erythrocyte sedimentation rate.
- 24-hour urine for catecholamines: homovanillic acid (HVA) and vanillylmandelic acid (VMA) are secreted by up to 90% of tumors.
- Nonspecific serum markers such as neuron-specific enolase, lactate dehydrogenase, and ferritin.
- Bone marrow biopsy and aspirate: karyotype, DNA index, N-MYC copy number.
- Minimum criteria for diagnosis are based on international consensus panel and require one of the following: (1) unequivocal pathologic diagnosis made from tumor tissue or (2) combination of bone marrow aspirate with unequivocal tumor cells and increased levels of serum or urinary catecholamine metabolites, as described above.
- Genetic/biologic variables have been studied in children with neuroblastoma, in particular the histology, aneuploidy of tumor DNA, and amplification of the N-MYC oncogene within tumor tissue, because treatment decisions may be based on these factors.
  ○ Hyperdiploid DNA is associated with favorable prognosis, especially in infants.
  ○ N-MYC amplification is associated with poor prognosis, regardless of patient age, likely due to association with deletion of chromosome 1p and gain of chromosome 17q.
  ○ Other biologic factors studied include profile of GABAergic receptors, expression of neurotrophin receptors, level of telomerase RNA and serum ferritin and lactate dehydrogenase.

IMAGING STUDIES

- Chest x-ray, abdominal plain film, skeletal survey, abdominal and renal/bladder ultrasound
- CT scan or MRI of the chest and abdomen to provide information about regional lymph nodes, vessel invasion, and distant metastases (Fig. 1N-5)
- Body scan with ^{131}I-MIBG (meta-iodobenzyl-guanidine), which is taken up by neuroblasts and is sensitive to metastases in the bone and soft tissue (64% of patients will develop thyroid dysfunction).
- Bone scan with Tc-99 MDP to visualize lytic bone lesions and metastases
- Urine catecholamines: elevated in 90% to 95% of patients with neuroblastomas
STAGING (staged according to the International Neuroblastoma Staging System [INSS])

I.	Confined to single organ
IIA.	Localized tumor with incomplete gross resection; ipsilateral lymph nodes negative
IIB.	Localized tumor with or without incomplete gross resection; ipsilateral lymph nodes positive
III.	Extension across midline, with or without lymph node involvement
IV.	Distant metastases to lymph nodes, bone, bone marrow, liver, skin, and/or other organs
IVs.	Localized primary tumor with dissemination limited to skin, liver, or bone marrow; limited to infants <18 months of age

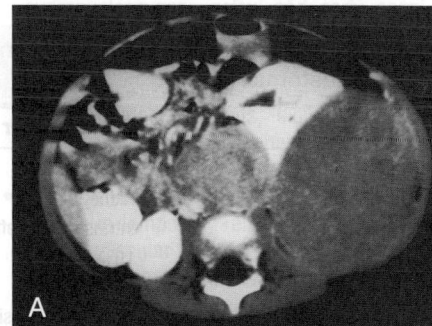
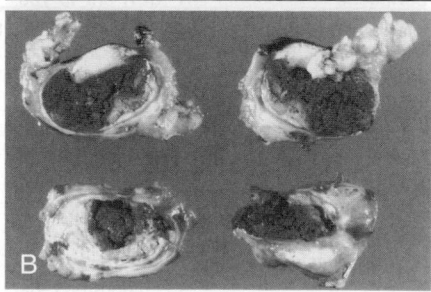

FIGURE 1N-5 Computed tomographic scan (A) shows adrenal neuroblastoma at diagnosis. Serial sections through adrenal neuroblastoma **(B)** show tumor with large areas of diffuse hemorrhage and calcification. (From Abeloff MD [ed]: *Clinical oncology*, ed 3, Philadelphia, 2004, Saunders.)

logic signs such as seizure or hemiparesis. Cognitive presentation may be variable but may include difficulty with complex attention, executive dysfunction or deficits in learning and memory. Associated findings include disturbances in emotional function and personality change. The features of major or mild NCD due to TBI vary by age of patient and specifics of the injury as well as other factors, such as premorbid functioning of the patient.

- Substance/medication induced: An NCD that persists beyond the duration of intoxication and acute withdrawal from a substance that is known to be capable of causing the observed impairments. NCD due to alcohol frequently manifests with memory, learning, and executive impairments. Neurocognitive disorders due to alcohol include Wernicke encephalopathy and Korsakoff syndrome. Wernicke syndrome is an acute neurologic disorder caused by thiamine deficiency manifesting with a clinic triad of encephalopathy, oculomotor dysfunction, and gait ataxia. Korsakoff syndrome is a late manifestation of Wernicke syndrome manifesting with dense anterograde and retrograde amnesia. MRI may show mammillary body atrophy. Major or mild NCD may be induced by medication or combinations of medications, including those with sedating and pain-ameliorating properties and those with anticholinergic properties. Particular attention should be paid to review of medications in any patient with major or mild NCD, especially those in the geriatric population.
- HIV infection: Neurocognitive deficits may show a subcortical pattern with prominent impairment of executive function with slowed processing speed and difficulty with learning new information.
- Prion disease: Neurocognitive deficits occur rapidly, typically over six months. In some variants, prominent psychiatric symptoms such as depression and anxiety may occur prior to neurocognitive deficits. Ataxia, myoclonus, chorea, and a prominent startle reflex are typically present.
- Huntington's disease: Early prominent changes in processing speed, organization, and planning rather than learning and memory are common. Behavior changes, changes in mood, anxiety, obsessive-compulsive symptoms, irritability, and apathy often precede motor symptoms.
- Other medical conditions: Many medical conditions can cause NCDs. Examples include structural brain lesions such as primary or secondary brain tumors, subdural hematomas or those seen in normal pressure hydrocephalus, hypoxia, infectious causes, endocrine conditions, immune disorders, and metabolic conditions. The temporal association between the onset or exacerbation of the medical condition and the development of the cognitive deficit supports the diagnosis.

Dx DIAGNOSIS

DIFFERENTIAL DIAGNOSIS

Etiology of major or mild NCD is assessed by taking a detailed history from the patient, family members, or other informants, complete physical examination, and ancillary tests, including neuropsychological testing and imaging studies. In some cases, the diagnosis remains unclear, while in other cases, the diagnosis is uncertain early on and becomes clear as the disease progresses. For any patient with a major or mild NCD, the initial differential includes each of the etiologies discussed in this chapter; however, this can often be narrowed by appropriate examination and investigation.

LABORATORY TESTS & IMAGING STUDIES

In all major and mild NCDs, careful history from patient and in most cases, from family and other reliable sources is essential. Detailed physical examination and neuropsychological testing and neuroimaging are indicated. In some cases, serology and lab testing, including B12 and TSH levels, are useful or diagnostic. Biomarkers and genetic screening tests are diagnostic in some cases. Particular attention should be paid to rule out underlying medical causes of the major or mild NCD.

Alzheimer's disease: Detailed history and physical examination including neuropsychological testing often points to the diagnosis. MRI may show hippocampal and temporoparietal cortical atrophy. PET scan may reveal hypometabolism in temporoparietal regions. Cerebrospinal fluid biomarkers include elevated total tau and phosphorylated tau levels with reduced amyloid beta-42. *APOE* testing may support diagnosis in patients with *APOE4* variant. For early onset, autosomal dominant inheritance mutation in *APP, PSEN1,* or *PSEN2* may be detected.

Frontotemporal disorder: In cases with early onset behavior or language disorders, an MRI or CT scan may show atrophy in frontal lobes and/or corresponding parts of anterior or inferior temporal lobes either bilaterally or asymmetrically. Functional imaging may show hypoperfusion in the corresponding regions. In familial cases, genetic mutations in genes encoding the microtubule-associated protein tau and the granulin gene may confirm the diagnosis.

Lewy body disease: Sleep study may help to confirm a diagnosis of REM sleep behavior disorder. Nuclear medicine testing including SPECT or PET may show low striatal dopamine transporter uptake.

Parkinson's disease: Abnormal dopamine transporter scans are supportive of the diagnosis.

Vascular disorder: Neurologic assessment often reveals a history of stroke or TIA. MRI or CT scan may show significant parenchymal injury attributed to cerebrovascular disease.

TBI: May be associated with abnormal CT or MRI scan showing petechial hemorrhages, subdural or subarachnoid hemorrhage, or evidence of contusion.

Prion disease: May be suspected in patients with appropriate clinical presentation, including rapidly progressive course. MRI may show gray matter hyperintensities in the subcortical region, particularly in the putamen and head of caudate nuclei. EEG reveals periodic synchronous biphasic or triphasic sharp waves complexes. CSF biomarkers including 14-3-3, S100 protein, or neuron-specific enolase is suggestive, though not diagnostic.

Huntington's disease: Genetic testing for CAG repeat is diagnostic.

Rx TREATMENT

- Initial treatment is directed to the underlying etiology.
- Treatment of memory disturbance may be indicated in some causes of major or mild NCDs, such as those caused by Alzheimer's disease.
- Treatment both acutely and chronically is often supportive and aimed at ameliorating behavior and other neuropsychiatric disturbances that may be present.
- Behavioral treatments should be considered first line for most behavior manifestations. Pharmacologic treatments for behavior disturbance have a limited role in improving overall quality of life for most causes of major or minor NCD, although they may have short-term efficacy in acute circumstances.
- Pharmacologic and cognitive behavior treatment may be helpful for associated psychiatric symptoms such as mood disorders, psychosis, and anxiety.
- Patient safety, including risks associated with driving, wandering, and cooking should be addressed early in the course of the illness.
- Family education and support may help reduce the need for a skilled nursing facility and reduce caregiver stress and burnout.
- Cognitive rehabilitation to promote recovery may be helpful.
- Supervised living may ensure appropriate long-term care in late stages of progressive illness.

! PEARLS & CONSIDERATIONS

- The core features of NCDs are an acquired cognitive decline that is based on both concern on the part of the individual, a knowledgeable informant, or the clinician, and performance on objective assessment that falls below the expected level or has been observed to decline.
- The distinction between major and mild NCD is inherently arbitrary. Precise thresholds are difficulty to determine, necessitating careful history taking and observation as well as integration of all clinical data.

- The strongest risk factor for major and mild NCDs is age, primarily because age increases the risk of neurodegenerative and cerebrovascular disease.

SUGGESTED READINGS

Available at www.expertconsult.com

RELATED TOPICS

Alzheimer's Disease
Delirium
Human Immunodeficiency Virus
Huntington's Disease
Parkinson's Disease
Progressive Supranuclear Palsy
Traumatic Brain Injury
Wernicke-Korsakoff Syndrome

AUTHOR: **MICHAEL FRIEDMAN, M.D.**

BASIC INFORMATION

DEFINITION

Neurofibromatosis (NF) is an autosomal-dominant disorder affecting bone, the nervous system, soft tissue, and skin. There are three major subtypes of NF disorders: NF type 1 (NF1), NF type 2 (NF2), and schwannomatosis. Schwannomatosis has only recently been recognized as a distinct disorder; currently very little is known about it.

SYNONYMS

NF1: von Recklinghausen disease, peripheral NF
NF2: bilateral acoustic neurofibromatosis, central NF

ICD-10CM CODES
Q85.00 Neurofibromatosis, unspecified
Q85.01 Neurofibromatosis, type 1
Q85.02 Neurofibromatosis, type 2

EPIDEMIOLOGY & DEMOGRAPHICS

- Incidence of NF1 (one case/3000 live births), NF2 (one case/25,000 live births).
- Prevalence of NF1 (one case/5000 persons), NF2 (one case/210,000 persons).
- NF1 and NF2 are autosomal dominant; approximately 50% of cases have no family history.
- The two disorders affect approximately 100,000 people in the United States.
- Affects males and females equally.
- NF1 may be associated with optic gliomas, astrocytomas, spinal neurofibromas, pheochromocytomas, and chronic myeloid leukemia.
- NF2 may be associated with meningiomas, spinal schwannomas, and cataracts.
- For schwannomatosis, the incidence is one per 30,000 persons, and the disease is mostly sporadic in nature.

PHYSICAL FINDINGS & CLINICAL PRESENTATION

- Common features of NF1 include:
  1. Café-au-lait macules (100% of children by age 2 yr).
     a. Hyperpigmented skin lesions (Fig. 1N-6) occurring anywhere on the body except the face, palms, and soles.
     b. Appear early in life and increase in size and number during puberty.
     c. Are focal or diffuse.
  2. Axillary and inguinal freckling (70%).
  3. Multiple neurofibromas (Figs. 1N-7 and 1N-8) can be soft or firm; three subtypes:
     a. Cutaneous: circumscribed, not specific for NF1.
     b. Subcutaneous: circumscribed, not specific for NF1.
     c. Plexiform: noncircumscribed, thick and irregular; can cause disfigurement of supportive structures and specific for NF1.
  4. Lisch nodule (small hamartoma of the iris) found in >90% of adult cases.

5. Visual defects possibly related to optic gliomas (2% to 5%).
6. Neurodevelopment problems such as learning disability and mental retardation (30% to 40%).
7. Skeletal disorders, including long bone dysplasia, pseudoarthrosis, scoliosis, short stature, and decreased bone mineral density.
- Common features of NF2 include:
  1. Hearing loss and tinnitus related to bilateral acoustic neuromas (>90% of adults).
  2. Cataracts (81%).
  3. Headache.
  4. Unsteady gait.
  5. Cutaneous and subcutaneous neurofibromas but fewer than in NF1.
  6. Café-au-lait macules (1%).
- Common features of schwannomatosis include painful multiple schwannomas of the spinal, peripheral, or cranial nerves *except* the vestibular nerve.

ETIOLOGY

- NF1 is caused by DNA mutations located on the long arm of chromosome 17 responsible for encoding the protein neurofibromin.
- NF2 is caused by DNA mutations located in the middle of the long arm of chromosome 22 responsible for encoding the protein merlin, which is a potent inhibitor of glioma growth.
- Both proteins are speculated to act as tumor suppressors.
- The etiology of schwannomatosis remains unclear; however, biallelic NF2 mutations are found in the schwannomas but nowhere else, suggesting that they are secondary mutations.

Dx DIAGNOSIS

- NF1 is diagnosed if the person has two or more of the following features:
  1. Six or more café-au-lait macules >5 mm in prepubertal patients and >15 mm in postpubertal patients.
  2. Two or more neurofibromas of any type or one plexiform neurofibroma.
  3. Axillary or inguinal freckling.
  4. Optic glioma.
  5. Two or more Lisch nodules (iris hamartomas).
  6. Sphenoid wing dysplasia or cortical thinning of long bones, with or without pseudoarthrosis.
  7. A first-degree relative (parent, sibling, or child) with NF1 based on the previous criteria.
- NF2 is diagnosed if the person has either of the following two criteria:
  1. Bilateral eighth nerve masses seen by appropriate imaging studies (e.g., CT, MRI).
  2. A first-degree relative with NF2 and either a unilateral eighth nerve mass or two of the following: neurofibroma, meningioma, glioma, schwannoma, or juvenile posterior subcapsular lenticular opacity.
- Schwannomatosis is diagnosed in an individual >30 yr having either of the following two criteria:
  1. Two nonintradermal schwannomas, no vestibular tumor found on MRI scan, no NF2 mutation.
  2. One nonvestibular schwannoma and a first-degree relative fitting the above criteria.

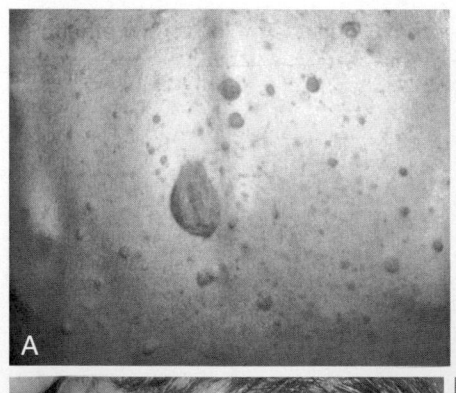
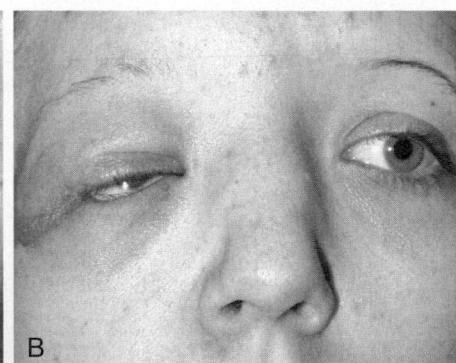
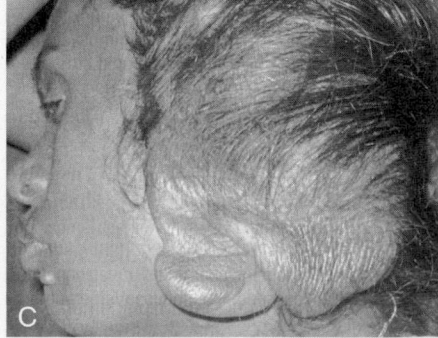
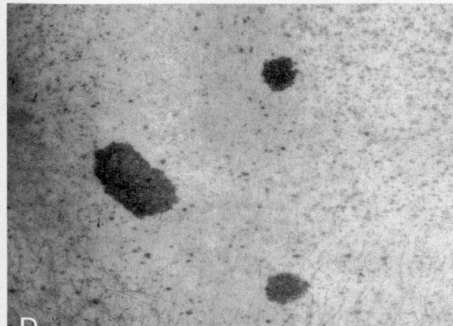

FIGURE 1N-6 Systemic features of NF1. A, Discrete neurofibromas. **B,** Nodular plexiform neurofibroma of the eyelid. **C,** Elephantiasis nervosa. **D,** Cafe-au-lait spots. (**C** courtesy S. Kumar Puri.; From Kanski JJ.; Bowling B. *Clinical ophthalmology, a systematic approach.* ed 7, Philadelphia, 2010, Saunders.)

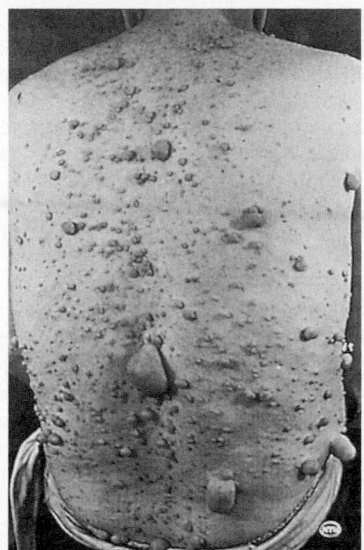

FIGURE 1N-7 Nodules. Solid, large (>1 cm), deep-seated mass in dermal or subcutaneous tissues. These nodules are neurofibromas in a patient with neurofibromatosis. (From Goldman L.; Ausiello D. [eds]: *Cecil textbook of medicine,* ed 22, Philadelphia, 2004, Saunders.)

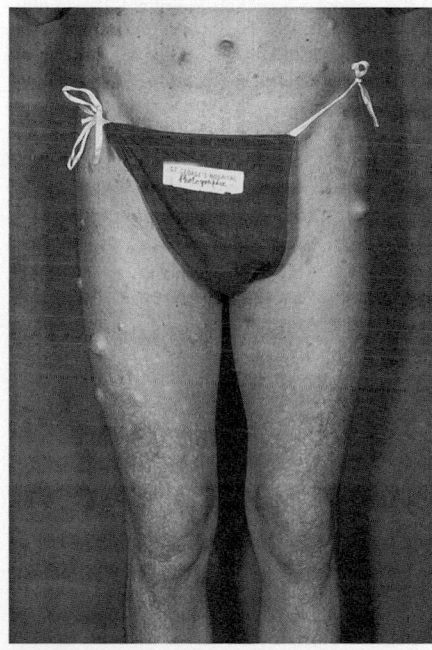

FIGURE 1N-8 Type 1 neurofibromatosis: wide-spread cutaneous neurofibromata are a prominent feature of the classical variant. (Courtesy of R.A. Marsde.; M.D. St George's Hospital, London. From McKee PH, Calonje E, Granter SR [eds]: *Pathology of the skin with clinical correlations,* ed 3, St Louis, 2005, Mosby.)

DIFFERENTIAL DIAGNOSIS

- Abdominal NF.
- Myxoid lipoma.
- Nodular fasciitis.
- Fibrous histiocytoma.
- Segmental NF.

WORKUP

The diagnosis of NF is usually self-evident. Workup is dictated by clinical symptoms in NF1 and usually includes MRI evaluation of the head and spine in NF2 and schwannomatosis. In fact, if NF2 is suspected but no vestibular nerve schwannomas are found, the diagnosis points to schwannomatosis.

LABORATORY TESTS

- Genetic testing is possible in individuals who desire prenatal diagnosis for NF1. There is no single standard test and multiple tests are required. Results can only tell if an individual is affected but cannot predict the severity of the disease due to variable expression.
- In NF2, linkage analysis testing provides a >99% certainty the individual has NF2.

IMAGING STUDIES

- MRI with gadolinium is the imaging study of choice in both NF1 and NF2 patients. MRI increases detection of optic gliomas, tumors of the spine, acoustic neuromas, and "bright spots" believed to represent hamartomas.
- MRI of the spine is recommended in all patients diagnosed with NF2 to exclude intramedullary tumors.

OTHER TESTS

- Wood lamp examination may be useful in patients with very pale skin for visualizing café-au-lait spots.
- Slit-lamp examination is recommended for children >6 yr to confirm the presence of Lisch nodules and subcapsular opacity.

Rx TREATMENT

Treatment is directed primarily at symptoms and complications of NF1 and NF2. As for schwannomatosis, resection should be reserved for tumors that are symptomatic or threaten to cause spinal cord compression.

NONPHARMACOLOGIC THERAPY

- Counseling addressing prognosis and genetic, psychological, and social issues.
- Hearing testing and speech pathology evaluation.

ACUTE GENERAL Rx

- Surgery is usually not done on skin tumors unless cosmetically requested or if suspicion of malignant transformation exists.
- Surgery may be indicated for spinal or cranial neurofibromas, gliomas, or meningiomas.
- Acoustic neuromas can be treated by surgical excision.

CHRONIC Rx

- Radiation may be indicated in optic nerve gliomas and patients whose central nervous system tumors show radiographic progression.
- Stereotactic radiosurgery with a gamma knife may be an alternative approach to surgery for acoustic neuromas.

DISPOSITION

- Prognosis varies according to the severity of involvement.
- There is no cure for NF.

REFERRAL

A multidisciplinary team of consultants is needed in patients with NF, including neurosurgeon, otolaryngologist, dermatologist, neurologist, audiologist, speech pathologist, geneticist, and neuropsychologist.

! PEARLS & CONSIDERATIONS

- Friedrich Daniel von Recklinghausen first reported his cases in 1882, although there had been similar accounts dating back to the 1600s.
- A high SPRED1 mutation detection rate has been identified in NF1 mutation-negative families with an autosomal dominant phenotype of CALMs with or without freckling and no other NF1 features.

COMMENTS

For additional information and patient resources, refer to the National Neurofibromatosis Foundation (www.nf.org) or Neurofibromatosis Inc. (www.nfinc.org).

SUGGESTED READINGS

Available at www.expertconsult.com

RELATED CONTENT

Neurofibromatosis Type 1 (Patient Information)
Neurofibromatosis Type 2 (Patient Information)

AUTHOR: **MARK F. BRADY, M.D., M.P.H., M.M.S.**

 BASIC INFORMATION

DEFINITION

Neuroleptic malignant syndrome (NMS) is a disorder characterized by hyperthermia, muscular rigidity, autonomic dysfunction, and depressed/fluctuating levels of arousal that evolve over 24 to 72 hr. This occurs as an idiosyncratic adverse reaction to medications that affect the central dopaminergic system, usually D2 receptors blockade.

SYNONYMS

NMS

ICD-10CM CODES
G21.0 Malignant neuroleptic syndrome

EPIDEMIOLOGY & DEMOGRAPHICS

INCIDENCE (IN U.S.): 0.07% to 0.15% annual incidence in psychiatric population.
PREDOMINANT SEX: More than two thirds of patients are male.
PREDOMINANT AGE: Young and middle-aged adults
PREDISPOSING FACTORS:
- History of intake of dopamine antagonists, e.g., antipsychotics

PHYSICAL FINDINGS & CLINICAL PRESENTATION

- Syndrome typically begins abruptly while the patient is taking therapeutic (not toxic) dosages of neuroleptics and reaches maximum severity within 72 hr.
- Severe muscle rigidity (hypertonia, cogwheeling, or "lead pipe" rigidity)
- Hyperthermia (38.6° to 42.3° C, usually <40° C)
- Autonomic symptoms: diaphoresis, dysphagia, sialorrhea, skin pallor, urinary incontinence
- Tachycardia, tachypnea
- Labile blood pressure (hypertension or postural hypotension)
- Agitation, catatonia, fluctuating consciousness, obtundation

ETIOLOGY

- Exact etiology is unknown, but it has been suggested that sudden and marked dopamine receptor blockade in nigrostriatal, hypothalamic, mesolimbic, and mesocortical pathways leads to clinical manifestations seen in NMS.
- Neuroleptic drugs have different potencies for inducing NMS:
  1. Typical neuroleptics: high potency, haloperidol; medium potency, chlorpromazine, fluphenazine; low potency, levomepromazine, loxapine
  2. Atypical neuroleptics: low potency, risperidone, olanzapine, clozapine, quetiapine

DX DIAGNOSIS

DIFFERENTIAL DIAGNOSIS

- Heatstroke, drug-induced states and overdose (Ecstasy abuse, phencyclidine), thyrotoxicosis, pheochromocytoma, serotonin syndrome
- Malignant hyperthermia, catatonia, acute psychosis with agitation
- CNS or systemic infections, including sepsis
- Table E1N-7 summarizes the differential diagnosis of neuroleptic malignant syndrome.

WORKUP

Careful drug history. There is a significant overlap in the features of NMS and serotonin syndrome. The major difference is the presence of hyperreflexia and myoclonus with serotonin syndrome.

LABORATORY TESTS

- Elevated creatine phosphokinase (CPK) (sensitivity 0.71)
- Urinary myoglobin
- Leukocytosis, usually 10,000 to 40,000/mm³
- Electrolytes and renal function
- Blood gases
- Drug levels

 TREATMENT

NONPHARMACOLOGIC THERAPY

- Stop all neuroleptic drugs and reinstitute any recently discontinued dopaminergic agonists.
- Respiratory support; nutritional support in cases with dysphagia or comatose.
- Careful fluid balance monitoring with adequate hydration (intravenous in severe cases).
- Active cooling (cooling blanket and antipyretics).
- Skilled nursing care is necessary to prevent decubitus ulcers in bed-confined patients.

ACUTE GENERAL Rx

- Bromocriptine, a dopamine receptor agonist, is the mainstay of therapy for patients with NMS. Initial doses of 2.5 to 10 mg are given IV q8h and are increased by 5 mg/day until clinical improvement is seen. The drug should be continued for at least 10 days after the syndrome has been controlled and then tapered slowly.
- Dantrolene therapy can inhibit the excessive muscle contractions that generate myoglobinemia. Initially, patients can be given 0.25 mg/kg IV q6-12h, followed by a maintenance dose up to 3 mg/kg/day. After 2 to 3 days, patients may be given the drug orally (25 to 600 mg/day in divided doses). Oral dantrolene therapy (50 to 600 mg/day) may be continued for several days afterward.
- Amantadine, an NMDA receptor antagonist with possible dopaminergic properties, administered orally at doses of 100 to 200 mg PO bid, has also been shown to reduce mortality in comparison to supportive therapy alone.
- IV benzodiazepines (e.g., diazepam 2 to 10 mg, with total daily dose of 10 to 60 mg) to relax muscles and control agitation.
- Electroconvulsive therapy with neuromuscular blockage in pharmacologically refractory cases. Succinylcholine should not be used because it may cause hyperkalemia and cardiac arrhythmias in patients with rhabdomyolysis or dysautonomia.

CHRONIC Rx

- Respiratory care, nutritional support, and physical therapy may be required in more severe cases.
- Appropriate therapy would be required in patients with persistent neuropsychiatric sequelae of NMS (e.g., antidepressants for depression, cognitive behavioral therapy for cognitive deficits, rehabilitation for contractures).

DISPOSITION

- Mortality rate is currently 5% to 10% despite therapeutic measures. Serious sequelae may occur in a further 20%. Complete recovery occurs in >70% of patients. Causes of death include cardiac arrhythmias, myocardial infarction, renal failure secondary to rhabdomyolysis, seizures, pulmonary edema, and bronchopneumonia.
- Factors adversely affecting mortality are development of renal failure and core temperature >104° F (40° C).
- Late neuropsychiatric sequelae.
- Monitor closely for future complications of pharmacologic therapy.

REFERRAL

If the patient's condition is critical, it is preferable to treat the patient in a medical/neurologic ICU.

PEARLS & CONSIDERATIONS

COMMENTS

- Early detection and diagnosis lead to a more favorable outcome. Refer to recent consensus diagnostic criteria as a guide. Treatment is a medical emergency.
- Sudden withdrawal from dopaminergic agents (such as those used in Parkinson's disease) may lead to "levodopa withdrawal syndrome" that presents with similar clinical manifestations.

SUGGESTED READINGS

Available at www.expertconsult.com

AUTHOR: **FARIHA ZAHEER, M.D.**

 BASIC INFORMATION

DEFINITION

Neuropathic pain is not itself a disease, but rather a symptom that is associated with multiple different diseases. Thus it is not enough to define its presence without searching for a cause. It is defined as the sensation derived from the abnormal discharges of impaired or injured neural structures in either the peripheral or central nervous system. Descriptors include:

- Hyperesthesia: heightened sensitivity to non-painful stimuli (e.g., light touch)
- Hyperalgesia: heightened sensitivity to painful stimuli (e.g., pinprick), or reduced threshold to feel pain
- Allodynia: pain provoked by a stimulus that is not normally painful

SYNONYMS

Neuralgia

ICD-10CM CODES

G58.0 Intercostal neuropathy
G58.7 Mononeuritis multiplex
G58.8 Other specified mononeuropathies
G58.9 Mononeuropathy, unspecified
G60.0 Hereditary sensory and motor neuropathy
G61.9 Inflammatory polyneuropathy, unspecified
G62.0 Drug-induced polyneuropathy
G62.1 Alcoholic polyneuropathy
G62.9 Polyneuropathy, unspecified
G63.2 Diabetic polyneuropathy
G63.5 Polyneuropathy in systemic connective tissue disease
G63.8 Polyneuropathy in other diseases classified elsewhere

EPIDEMIOLOGY & DEMOGRAPHICS

- Estimates of the prevalence of neuropathic pain in the general population range from 1.6% to 8.2%.
- Demographics vary widely depending on etiology, for example:
  1. Postherpetic neuralgia: affects elderly, pain seen in almost 100% of cases
  2. AIDS: 30% of patients affected
  3. Diabetes mellitus: 20% to 24% affected (prevalence rates vary, increasing with longer disease duration)
  4. Fabry disease: affects mostly children, pain in 81% to 90% of patients

PHYSICAL FINDINGS & CLINICAL PRESENTATION

- History: localize the disease with questions
  1. Quality (description) of neuropathic pain: burning, hot or cold, "icy hot," "pins and needles," stinging, lancinating, sharp, shooting
  2. Distribution of symptoms may aid in localization (i.e., "stocking-glove" symptoms in generalized neuropathy, numbness in a peripheral nerve territory in focal neuropathy)

3. Generalized small fiber neuropathy: dysesthesias without numbness common, but many etiologies (e.g., diabetes) cause both small and large fiber dysfunction
4. Large fiber neuropathy (LFPN): coexisting numbness, hyporeflexia, or weakness may be seen, usually worse distally
5. Nerve root: coexisting neck or low back pain that radiates along a specific dermatome; most common cause is structural compression
6. Spinal cord symptoms: coexisting spasticity, bowel or bladder involvement, sensory level
7. Prior history of thalamic stroke in central thalamic pain syndrome (Dejerine-Roussy syndrome)
8. Family history may suggest a genetic cause
- Examination: see Table 1N-8. Table 1N-9 describes joint involvement in neuropathic arthropathy. Fig. 1N-9 illustrates a diagnostic approach to neuropathic pain. Fig. 1N-10 shows a neuropathic ankle.

ETIOLOGY & LABORATORY EVALUATION (TABLE 1N-10)

- Metabolic: diabetes mellitus; malnutrition and alcoholism; vitamin B_{12} deficiency; thiamine deficiency; porphyria; Fabry's disease
- Inflammatory: immune vasculitides (lupus, Sjögren's syndrome, polyarteritis nodosa, etc.), acute inflammatory demyelinating polyneuropathy (classically presents with ascending weakness and numbness, although pain is also a common feature), chronic inflammatory demyelinating polyneuropathy, sarcoid, multiple sclerosis
- Infiltrative: amyloidosis, paraproteinemias (e.g., monoclonal gammopathy of uncertain significance [MGUS])
- Infectious: postviral (brachial neuritis), HIV/AIDS, HSV, varicella-zoster virus (VZV; postherpetic neuralgia), Lyme disease, leprosy (thickened nerves and skin lesions), syphilis
- Neoplastic and paraneoplastic-carcinomatous infiltration of nerve/nerve root, anti-Hu
- Drugs/toxins: history of exposure to alcohol, chemotherapeutic agents (paclitaxel, vincristine), isoniazid, metronidazole, or heavy metals (thallium, arsenic)

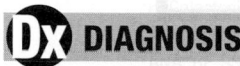 DIAGNOSIS

LABORATORY TESTS

- Fasting blood glucose (FBG)
- 2-hour oral glucose tolerance test (OGTT)
- Vitamin B_1 level
- If B_{12} level normal: serum methylmalonic acid and homocysteine levels
- Serum erythrocyte sedimentation rate (ESR), ANA, SS-A and SS-B, c-ANCA, p-ANCA
- RPR or FTA-ABS
- Serum ACE level (sarcoid)

TABLE 1N-8   Examination

Exam Finding	Localization
Pinprick/temperature loss alone	Small fibers only
Pinprick/temperature loss + vibratory/proprioceptive loss	Small and large fibers
Sensory loss and motor dysfunction worse distally than proximal	Large fiber neuropathy
Sensory loss and motor dysfunction along single nerve distribution	Single nerve
Sensory loss and motor dysfunction along multiple single nerves	Multiple mononeuropathies (i.e., mononeuropathy multiplex)
Motor and sensory loss involving multiple nerves belonging to specific region of brachial or lumbar plexus	Plexopathy
Sensory loss along dermatome with multiple myotomal muscles affected	Nerve root lesion
Asymmetric sensory loss without weakness and pseudoathetosis	Dorsal root ganglion
Vibratory/proprioceptive loss without pinprick/temperature loss	Dorsal column dysfunction (from compressive lesion, B_{12} deficiency, or tabes dorsalis from neurosyphilis)
Sensory level with weakness below the level of lesion and long tract signs (spasticity/Babinski's sign)	Spinal cord lesion
Hemisensory hyperalgesia	Contralateral thalamus

TABLE 1N-9   Joint Involvement in Neuropathic Arthropathy

Disease	Site of Involvement
Diabetes mellitus	Midtarsal, metatarsophalangeal, tarsometatarsal
Syringomyelia	Shoulder, elbow, wrist
Amyloidosis	Knee, ankle
Congenital sensory neuropathy	Knee, ankle, intertarsal, metatarsophalangeal
Tabes dorsalis	Knee, hip, ankle
Leprosy	Tarsal, tarsometatarsal

From Hochberg MC et al: *Rheumatology*, ed 5, St Louis, 2011, Mosby.

BASIC INFORMATION

DEFINITION

Any disorder affecting the peripheral nervous system, including nerve roots, plexuses, and individual peripheral nerves, that has a genetic basis of inheritance and has been or is capable of being transmitted along generations.

There are many different types of hereditary peripheral neuropathies, including Dejerine-Sottas disease, inherited metabolic neuropathies, hereditary sensory and autonomic neuropathies (HSANs), and hereditary motor neuropathies. Most disorders are diagnosed in infancy or childhood; as such, adult clinicians rarely see these patients. For this reason, this chapter discusses only the hereditary motor and sensory neuropathies that an adult clinician might encounter.

SYNONYMS

Charcot-Marie-Tooth (CMT) disease, a.k.a. hereditary motor-sensory neuropathy (HMSN)
Hereditary neuropathy with liability to pressure-sensitive palsies (HNPP)

ICD-10CM CODES
G60.0 Hereditary motor and sensory neuropathy
G60.8 Other hereditary and idiopathic neuropathies
G60.9 Hereditary and idiopathic neuropathy, unspecified

EPIDEMIOLOGY & DEMOGRAPHICS

All CMT: approximately 30 per 100,000
- CMT type 1 (demyelinating pathophysiology): 1 in 2500
- CMT type 2 (axonal pathophysiology): 7 in 1000
- CMT type 4 and CMT-X: rare (either axonal or demyelinating pathophysiology)
  HNPP: 2 to 5 per 100,000

PHYSICAL FINDINGS & CLINICAL PRESENTATION

CMT: Highly variable
- Age at onset earlier for CMT-1 than CMT-2, but both may present from childhood to old age.
- Severely affected patients have severe distal weakness and muscle atrophy with hand (prominently affecting interossei) and foot deformities (pes cavus, high arched feet, hammer toes).
- Mildly affected patients may have only foot deformity (pes cavus) with little or no weakness/sensory loss.
- Legs can be affected greater than arms, and patients will complain of gait abnormalities (steppage), which cause them to trip and fall.
- Sensory complaints (paresthesias, numbness, dysesthesia) are uncommon despite physical findings of impaired sensation.
- Decreased or absent reflexes.
- Some patients may have postural tremor of the upper limbs.
HNPP (a.k.a. tomaculous neuropathy):
- Age at onset is commonly adolescence.

- Disorder is characterized by recurrent entrapment of peripheral nerves with accompanying signs and symptoms (paresthesias and/or weakness in anatomic distributions). Most common are:
  1. Median nerve at the wrist (carpal tunnel syndrome)
  2. Ulnar nerve at the elbow (cubital tunnel syndrome)
  3. Painless brachial plexopathies
  4. Lateral femoral cutaneous nerve (meralgia paresthetica)
  5. Peroneal nerve at the fibular head
- May be associated with a generalized polyneuropathy.

ETIOLOGY

CMT: more than 30 subgroups have been identified and have various chromosomal abnormalities.
- Most common mutation is PMP-22 duplication, giving rise to CMT 1A demyelinating phenotype.
- Other mutations include P0 (demyelinating) and neurofilament light chain mutations (demyelinating or axonal phenotype)—see the following.
- Updated information may be available at http://www.neuro.wustl.edu/neuromuscular. HNPP: deletion of chromosome 17p11.2–12.

DIAGNOSIS

DIFFERENTIAL DIAGNOSIS

CMT: other genetic, metabolic, and multisystem disorders including:
- Spinocerebellar ataxias
- Friedreich's ataxia
- Leukodystrophies
- Refsum's disease (elevated serum phytanic acid)
- Distal spinal muscular atrophies and distal myopathies, which can present with pes cavus and other foot deformities
- Chronic inflammatory demyelinating polyneuropathy (CIDP)
HNPP:
- Hereditary neuralgic amyotrophy (HNA), which typically is painful rather than painless. In addition, in HNA, there is no evidence of generalized polyneuropathy.
- Multifocal motor neuropathy with conduction block (MMNCB)—autoimmune-mediated pure motor neuropathy
- Neuropathy associated with renal failure
- Lead neuropathy
- Neuropathy relating to paraproteinemia (demyelinating pathophysiology)

EVALUATION

CMT
- History of gradual onset symptoms is important to distinguish CMT from other forms of neuropathy.
- Detailed family history with *pedigree* is essential. Consider examination of multiple family members.
- History should evaluate for potential heavy metal exposure.

- History of dysesthesias is uncommon and should prompt search for acquired neuropathy or other inherited neuropathies (e.g., Fabry's disease).
HNPP: genetic testing after identification of multiple entrapment neuropathies on EMG and nerve conduction studies

LABORATORY TESTS

- Neurophysiology: electromyography (EMG) and nerve conduction studies (NCSs) must be done first to determine type of pathophysiology: demyelinating or axonal. This will guide genetic testing.
- NCSs in CMT-1 will reveal demyelinating physiology characterized by very slow conduction velocities (around 15 to 30 m/s) with prolonged distal latencies. Inherited demyelinating disorders can be distinguished from acquired demyelinating disorders (e.g., chronic inflammatory demyelinating polyneuropathy or CIDP) by the presence of conduction block in the latter.
- In HNPP, diffusely prolonged distal latencies with superimposed entrapment neuropathies at common sites will be seen on NCSs.
- EMG will reveal reinnervation characterized by long-duration, large-amplitude, polyphasic motor unit potentials (MUPs) with decreased MUP recruitment.
- Genetic tests are available for some CMT subtypes:
  1. CMT-1A: chromosome 17p11-PMP-22 duplication
  2. CMT-1B: chromosome 1q22-P0 mutation
  3. CMT-2E: chromosome 8p21-neurofilament light chain (NF-L) point mutation
  4. CMT-X: connexin 32 mutations
  5. HNPP: chromosome 17p11 deletion, which includes the PMP-22 gene
- Serum and 24-hour urine levels of heavy metals (arsenic, lead, etc.)
- SPEP, UPEP, immunofixation (for paraprotein).
- Anti-GM1 antibody (positive in ~50% of patients with MMNCB).
- Lumbar puncture may reveal elevated CSF protein in CIDP.
- Peripheral nerve biopsy:
  1. Demyelination with "onion bulb formation." Tomaculae, or focal thickening of myelin sheaths, is seen in HNPP
  2. Generally not indicated unless diagnosis is uncertain

IMAGING STUDIES

- Spine plain films: for evaluation of scoliosis.
- MRI: indicated if dissociative sensory loss (dorsal column dysfunction with intact spinothalamic tract function) or if upper motor neuron findings (spasticity, Babinski's sign, clonus, increased tendon reflexes) are present.
- Exclusion of involvement of brain or spinal cord compressive lesions causing arm or leg weakness.
- Some inherited peripheral demyelinating disorders (i.e., CMT-X) are associated with intracerebral white matter abnormalities on MRI.

- Exclusion of structural, infectious, or inflammatory nerve root pathology.

 **TREATMENT**

There is no known cure for any of these disorders. Management is supportive.

NONPHARMACOLOGIC THERAPY

- Physical therapy (PT) and occupational therapy (OT) to provide assistance with gait and coordination.
- PT and OT might provide walking aid such as ankle foot orthosis (AFO), cane, walker, or wheelchair depending on the severity of the neuropathy.
- Wrist splints for superimposed carpal tunnel syndrome.
- Elbow pads (Heelbo Pads) to cushion the ulnar nerve at the elbow.
- Heel-cord strengthening.
- Stretching exercises.
- Analgesics for pain associated with foot deformity.
- Surgical correction of foot deformities by orthopedic surgeons if indicated.

Vincristine may worsen existing neuropathy (important for oncologist to know if patient develops cancer requiring chemotherapy).

SURGICAL TREATMENT

- Patients with HNPP should probably not undergo surgical decompression of the median nerve at the wrist or the ulnar nerve at the elbow; these nerves are sensitive

to manipulation. Poor results have been reported with ulnar nerve transposition.
- Anesthesiologists should be aware of HNPP diagnosis in patients undergoing surgery to prevent compression neuropathies from occurring during surgical procedures.

GENETIC COUNSELING

Must be routinely done for patient and family when diagnosis is established. Many aspects of the patient and family's life are affected, including:

- Future progeny of patient and/or patient's parents or children
- Psychosocial aspects including social functioning, marriage, employment
- Financial needs
- Medical and life insurability

PROGNOSIS

- CMT: slowly progressive, and patients often remain ambulatory until late in life. Life expectancy is normal. Patients with respiratory involvement (i.e., phrenic nerve involvement with diaphragm paresis) may have shorter life expectancy.
- HNPP: benign prognosis.

DISPOSITION

Outpatient care. Routine follow-up appointments should be done initially every 6 mo, and then every 1 to 2 yr.

REFERRAL

- Neurology and/or neuromuscular disease specialist
- Podiatry for recurrent foot problems, including appropriate arches

 **PEARLS & CONSIDERATIONS**

PATIENT & FAMILY EDUCATION

Patients can benefit from use of Muscular Dystrophy Association (MDA) resources.

SUGGESTED READINGS

Available at www.expertconsult.com

RELATED CONTENT

Fig. 1N-9 Neuropathic pain, diagnostic approach (Algorithm, Section III)
Charcot-Marie-Tooth Disease (Related Key Topic)

AUTHOR: **GAVIN BROWN, M.D.**

Diseases and Disorders

I

BASIC INFORMATION

DEFINITION

Nonalcoholic fatty liver disease (NAFLD) is a spectrum of diseases based on histopathologic findings and representing a morphologic rather than a clinical diagnosis. It is liver disease occurring in patients who do not abuse alcohol and manifesting histologically by mononuclear cells and/or polymorphonuclear cells, hepatocyte ballooning, and spotty necrosis. Nonalcoholic steatohepatitis (NASH) is a subset of NAFLD. A diagnosis of NAFLD is contingent on the following factors:

1. Alcohol consumption in amounts less than those considered hepatotoxic.
2. Absence of serologic evidence of other hepatic diseases or disorders.
3. Liver biopsy showing predominant macrovesicular steatosis or steatohepatitis.

SYNONYMS

Nonalcoholic steatohepatitis (NASH)
NAFLD
Fatty liver hepatitis
Diabetes hepatitis
Alcohol-like liver disease
Laënnec's disease

ICD-10CM CODES
K76.0 Fatty (change of) liver, not elsewhere classified

EPIDEMIOLOGY & DEMOGRAPHICS

- NAFLD affects 20% to 30% of the general population.
- Increased prevalence in obese persons (57% to 74%), type 2 diabetes mellitus, and hyperlipidemia (primarily hypertriglyceridemia).
- Most common cause of abnormal liver test results in adults in the United States (accounts for up to 90% of cases of asymptomatic ALT elevations).
- 30 million obese adults have steatosis; 8.6 million may have steatohepatitis.
- There is a 3:1 female-to-male predominance.
- Approximately 20% of patients with NAFLD have NASH.

PHYSICAL FINDINGS & CLINICAL PRESENTATION

- Most patients are asymptomatic.
- Patients may report a sensation of fullness or discomfort on the right side of the upper abdomen.
- Nonspecific complaints of fatigue or malaise may be reported.
- Hepatomegaly is generally the only positive finding on physical examination.
- Acanthosis nigricans may be found in children.

ETIOLOGY

- Insulin resistance is the most reproducible factor in the development of NAFLD. High baseline and continuously increasing fasting insulin levels are independent determinants for future development of NFLD.
- Risk factors are obesity (especially truncal obesity), diabetes mellitus, hyperlipidemia.

DIAGNOSIS

DIFFERENTIAL DIAGNOSIS

- Alcohol-induced liver disease (a daily alcohol intake of 20 g in females and 30 g in males [three 12-oz beers or 12 oz of wine] may be enough to cause alcohol-induced liver disease).
- Viral hepatitis.
- Autoimmune hepatitis.
- Toxin- or drug-induced liver disease.

WORKUP

Diagnosis is usually suspected on the basis of hepatomegaly, asymptomatic elevations of transaminases, or "fatty liver" on sonogram of abdomen in obese patients with little or no alcohol use. Liver biopsy will confirm diagnosis and provide prognostic information. It should be considered in patients with suspected advanced liver fibrosis (presence of obesity or type 2 diabetes, AST/ALT ratio 1, age 45 yr).

LABORATORY TESTS

- Elevated ALT, AST: AST/ALT ratio is usually <1, but can increase as fibrosis advances. In advanced fibrosis AST to ALT ratio is >1 and platelet count is low.
- Negative serology for infectious hepatitis; generally normal GGTP and serum alkaline phosphatase.
- Hyperlipidemia (primarily hypertriglyceridemia) may be present.
- Elevated glucose levels may be present.
- Prolonged prothrombin time, hypoalbuminemia, and elevated bilirubin may be present in advanced stages.
- Elevated serum ferritin and increased transferrin saturation may be found in up to 10% of patients; however, hepatic iron index and hepatic iron level are normal.
- Liver biopsy may show a wide spectrum of liver damage, ranging from simple steatosis to advanced fibrosis and cirrhosis.

IMAGING STUDIES

- Ultrasound generally reveals diffuse increase in echogenicity as compared with that of the kidneys; CT scan reveals diffuse low-density hepatic parenchyma.
- Occasionally patients may have focal rather than diffuse steatosis, which may be misinterpreted as a liver mass on ultrasound or CT (Fig. E1N-14); use of MRI in these cases will identify focal fatty infiltration.
- Ultrasound elastography (Fibroscan) can also be used to evaluate hepatic fibrosis.

TREATMENT

NONPHARMACOLOGIC THERAPY

- Weight reduction in all obese patients. The American Gastroenterological Association recommends that the initial target weight loss be 10% of baseline weight at a rate of 1 to 2 lb (0.45 to 0.90 kg) per week.
- Increase physical activity.
- Alcohol has a deleterious effect on NAFLD and should be avoided.

GENERAL Rx

- No medications have been proved to directly improve liver damage from NAFLD.
- Medications to control hyperlipidemia (e.g., fenofibrates for elevated triglycerides) and hyperglycemia (e.g., metformin) can lead to improvement in abnormal liver test results.
- Pioglitazone therapy (30 mg/day) and vitamin E (800 IU/day) provide modest benefits in NASH.

DISPOSITION

- Patients with pure steatosis on liver biopsy generally have a relatively benign course.
- The presence of steatohepatitis or advanced fibrosis on liver biopsy is associated with a worse prognosis.

REFERRAL

- Liver transplantation should be considered in patients with decompensated, end-stage disease; however, in these patients there may be a recurrence of NAFLD posttransplantation.

PEARLS & CONSIDERATIONS

COMMENTS

- NAFLD is closely associated with metabolic disorders, even in nonobese, nondiabetic subjects. It can be considered an early predictor of metabolic disorders, particularly in the normal-weight population. The presence of metabolic syndrome is a strong predictor of NAFLD.
- NAFLD is associated with an increased risk of incident cardiovascular disease that is independent of the risk conferred by traditional risk factors and components of the metabolic syndrome.
- 10% of patients with NASH have progression to advanced fibrosis. Most common in patients older than 50, ALT > twice normal, BMI >28, triglycerides >150 mg/dL.
- Statins are not contraindicated in patients with NASH.

EVIDENCE

Available at www.expertconsult.com

SUGGESTED READINGS
Available at www.expertconsult.com

RELATED CONTENT
Fatty Liver (Patient Information)

AUTHOR: **FRED F. FERRI, M.D.**

 BASIC INFORMATION

DEFINITION

Obesity refers to having an excess amount of body fat in relation to lean body mass, or a body mass index (BMI) of ≥30 kg/m². Overweight is defined as BMI of 25 to 29.9 kg/m² and morbid obesity refers to adults with a BMI ≥40 kg/m². BMI is used as a surrogate measure of obesity. Abdominal obesity is defined as waist circumference >102 cm (40 inches) in men and >88 cm (35 inches) in women.

ICD-10CM CODES
E66.9	Obesity, unspecified
E66.01	Morbid (severe) obesity due to excess calories
E66.09	Other obesity due to excess calories
E66.1	Drug-induced obesity
E66.2	Morbid (severe) obesity with alveolar hypoventilation
E66.8	Other obesity
O99.210	Obesity complicating pregnancy, unspecified trimester
O99.211	Obesity complicating pregnancy, first trimester
O99.212	Obesity complicating pregnancy, second trimester
O99.213	Obesity complicating pregnancy, third trimester
O99.214	Obesity complicating childbirth
O99.215	Obesity complicating the puerperium

EPIDEMIOLOGY & DEMOGRAPHICS
- The World Health Organization first recognized obesity as a worldwide epidemic in 1997. As of 2005, 1.6 billion adults worldwide were classified as overweight, 400 million of whom were obese. It is predicted that the combination of overweight and obesity will soon eclipse public health issues such as malnutrition and infectious diseases as the most significant cause of poor health.
- Worldwide, data from the Global Burden of Disease Study from 1980 to 2013 indicate the prevalence of adult obesity has increased from 28.8% to 36.9% in men and 29.8% to 38% in women. The prevalence of children and adolescent obesity has also substantially increased.
- Based on U.S. National Health and Nutrition Examination (NHANES) data from 2009 to 2010, the prevalence of obesity in the United States was 35.7%. By 2015, it is estimated that two in every five adults and one in every four children in the United States will be obese.
- Based on U.S. NHANES data from 2011 to 2012 the prevalence of abdominal obesity was 54%. Abdominal obesity is closely associated with increased disease risk.
- The present cost of obesity in the U.S. population is estimated at $100 billion annually. Approximately two thirds of people living in the United States are overweight, which is the highest percentage in the world (Marie Ng, 2014).

- For persons with a BMI ≥30 kg/m², all-cause mortality is increased by 50% to 100% above that of persons with BMI in the range of 20 to 25 kg/m².
- Obesity is an independent risk factor for cardiovascular disease (CVD), type 2 diabetes, hypertension, cancer (particularly colon, prostate, breast, and gynecologic malignancies), sleep apnea, degenerative joint disease, thromboembolic disorders, digestive tract diseases (gallstones), and dermatologic disorders.
- Significant morbidity and risk of death are projected to begin in young adulthood, resulting in >100,000 excess cases of CHD by 2035, even with the most modest projection of future obesity.
- When children enter kindergarten, 12.4% are obese, and another 14.9% are overweight. Data show that incident obesity between the ages of 5 and 14 years is more likely to have occurred at younger ages.[1]
- Obesity in adolescence is significantly associated with increased risk of incident severe obesity in adulthood, with variations by sex and race/ethnicity. Overweight or obese adults who were obese as children have increased risk of type 2 DM, dyslipidemia, hypertension, and carotid artery atherosclerosis.
- Obesity is a major preventable cause of death and disability in the United States (the other is tobacco).
- Extensive data indicate that weight loss can reverse or arrest the harmful effects of obesity.
- In 2013 nearly 180,000 bariatric surgery procedures were performed in the U.S. Of these procedures 42% were laparoscopic sleeve gastrectomy, 34% were Roux-en-Y gastric bypass, and 15% were laparoscopic adjustable gastric banding.

PHYSICAL FINDINGS & CLINICAL PRESENTATION
- Physical examination should assess the degree and distribution of body fat, signs of secondary causes of obesity, and obesity-related comorbidities.
- Increased waist circumference is apparent. Excess abdominal fat is clinically defined as a waist circumference >40 inches (>102 cm) in men and >35 inches (>88 cm) in women (in Asian men and women, >36 inches and >33 inches, respectively).
- Symptoms associated with hypertension, coronary artery disease (CAD), and diabetes (e.g., polyuria, polydipsia, acanthosis nigricans, retinopathy, and neuropathy) may be present.
- Obesity is associated with cardiac hypertrophy, diastolic dysfunction, and decreased aortic compliance, which are independent predictors of cardiovascular risk.
- Joint pain and swelling are associated with degenerative joint disease secondary to obesity.
- The physical exam and ECG often underestimate the presence and extent of cardiac dysfunction in obese patients. Jugular venous

[1]Cunningham SA et al: Incidence of childhood obesity in the United States, *N Engl J Med*, 370:403-411, 2014.

distention and hepatojugular reflux may not be seen and heart sounds are frequently distant.
- A large quantity of fluid is present in the interstitial space of adipose tissue, as the interstitial space is ~10% of the tissue wet weight. This excess fluid in this compartment if redistributed into the circulation, can have negative repercussions in obese individuals with heart failure. Obese individuals have higher cardiac output and a lower total peripheral resistance than do lean individuals, and obesity is associated with persistence of elevated cardiac filling pressure during exercise.
- Obesity predisposes to heart failure through several different mechanisms: increased total blood volume, increased cardiac output, LVH, left ventricular diastolic dysfunction, and adipositas cordis (excessive epicardial fat and fatty infiltration of the myocardium).

ETIOLOGY
- The pathophysiology of obesity is complex and poorly understood, but includes social, nutritional, physiologic, psychological, and genetic factors.
- Environmental factors such as a sedentary lifestyle and chronic ingestion of excess calories can cause obesity.
- Obesity may be related to genetic factors, which are thought to be polygenic. Genetic studies with adopted children have demonstrated that they have similar BMIs to their biologic parents but not their adoptive parents. Twin studies also demonstrate a genetic influence on BMI.
- Secondary causes of obesity can result from medications (antipsychotics, steroids, and protease inhibitors being common ones) and neuroendocrine disorders (like Cushing's syndrome and hypothyroidism).

(Dx) **DIAGNOSIS**
- BMI will establish the diagnosis of obesity. BMI is defined as the adult's weight in kilograms divided by the square of his or her height—and is closely correlated with total body fat content.
- BMI values can categorize patients into three classes of obesity:
  1. Class I (mild): BMI of 30.0 to 34.9 kg/m²
  2. Class II (moderate): BMI of 35.0 to 39.9 kg/m²
  3. Class III (severe): BMI of ≥40 kg/m²
- Although BMI is commonly used to define obesity, it is not a highly accurate indicator of body fat composition in children, who are undergoing rapid changes in height, or in bodybuilders or athletes who have large amounts of muscle tissue.
- Waist circumference or waist-hip ratio is indicative of visceral adipose tissue/intraabdominal fat, which may be more deleterious than overall overweight or obesity.

DIFFERENTIAL DIAGNOSIS
It is important to evaluate obese patients for secondary medical causes of obesity. Hypothalamic disorders, hypothyroidism, Cushing's syndrome,

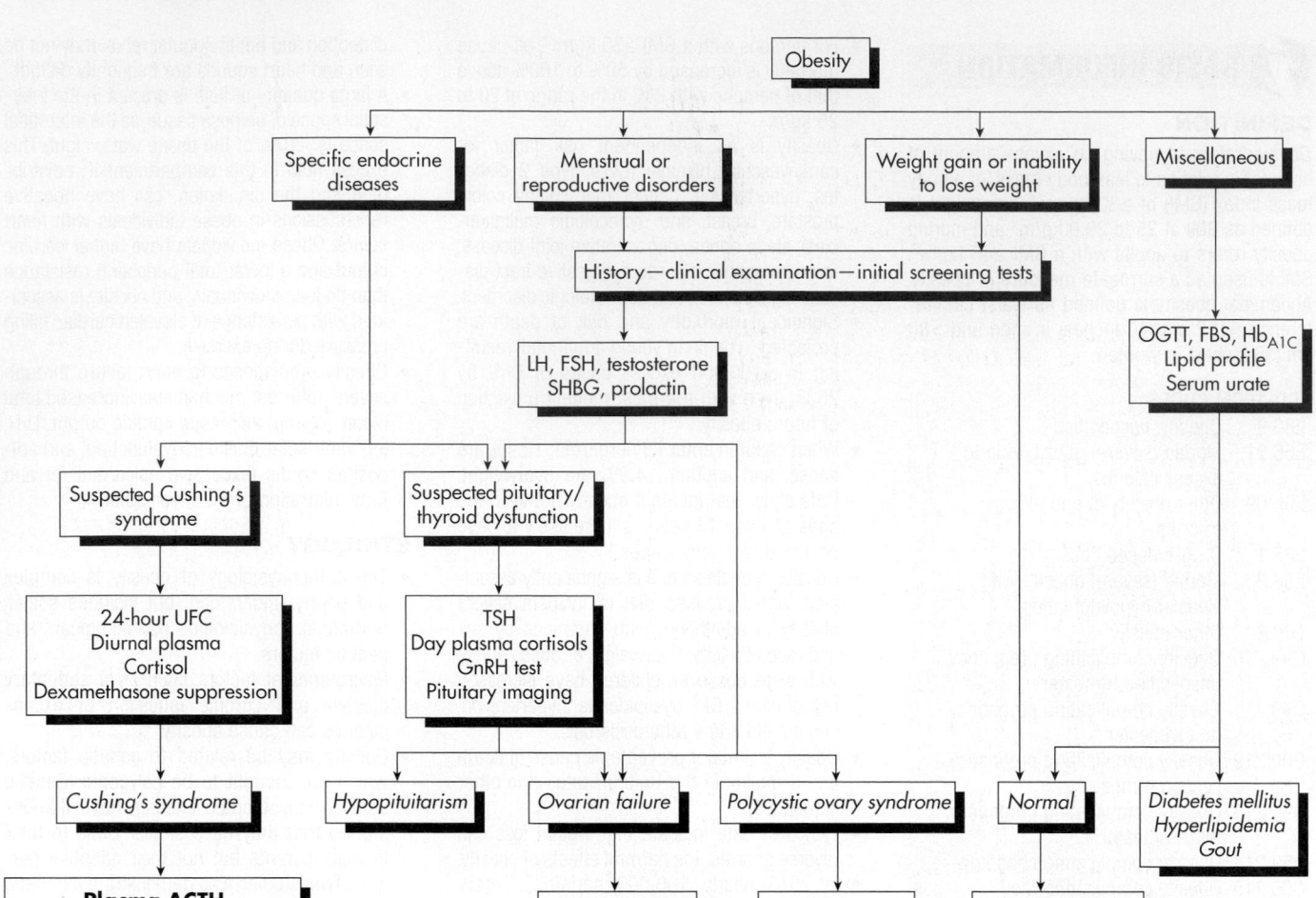

FIGURE 10-1 Endocrine evaluation of obesity. *ACTH,* Adrenocorticotropic hormone; *CRF,* corticotropin-releasing factor; *FBS,* fasting blood sugar; *FSH,* follicle-stimulating hormone; *Hb*$_{A1C}$ glycohemoglobin; *LH,* luteinizing hormone; *OGTT,* oral glucose tolerance test; *SHBG,* sex hormone-binding globulin; *UFC,* urinary free cortisol. (Modified from Besser CM, Thorner MO: *Comprehensive clinical endocrinology,* ed 3, St Louis, 2002, Mosby.)

insulinoma, depression, and drugs (corticosteroids, antidepressants, second-generation antipsychotics, sulfonylureas, and HIV protease inhibitors) can cause obesity. In children, certain genetic conditions, such as Prader-Willi syndrome, are associated with obesity.

WORKUP

History should be obtained regarding weight change, family history of obesity, and eating and exercise behavior. Assessment for eating disorders and depression should be made. Attention should be directed to the use of nutritional supplements, over-the-counter medications, hormones, diuretics, and laxatives. The workup of an obese patient typically requires laboratory work to assess for risks and complications as well as to rule out underlying causative medical conditions. Fig. 10-1 describes the evaluation of patients with suspected endocrine cause of obesity.

LABORATORY TESTS

- Obese patients should be assessed for medical consequences of their obesity by screening for metabolic syndrome. This includes measurement of fasting lipid profile, blood pressure, and waist circumference, and screening for diabetes or prediabetes (oral glucose tolerance test, fasting glucose, or hemoglobin A1C).
- Polycythemia might warrant screening for sleep apnea. Liver function tests should be obtained to screen for hepatic steatosis.
- In the proper clinical setting, thyroid function studies and dexamethasone suppression testing will exclude hypothyroidism and Cushing's syndrome as underlying causes of obesity. If insulinoma is suspected, the patient will need to undergo a 72-hour fast to confirm hypoglycemia with inappropriate insulin secretion.
- Obesity is associated with changes in the ECG, including a reduction in voltage and nonspecific ST-T changes that may interfere with diagnosis of left ventricular hypertrophy (LVH) or CAD.

IMAGING STUDIES

- Several methods are available for determining or calculating total body fat but offer no significant advantage over the BMI. These include measurement of total body water, total body potassium, bioelectrical impedance, and dual-energy x-ray absorptiometry.
- Buoyancy testing is an accurate method for determining total body fat composition.

OTHER STUDIES

Obesity increases the risk of obstructive sleep apnea, which, in turn, increases the risks of hypertension, cardiac arrhythmias, CVD, stroke, and heart failure. Therefore one should have a low threshold to screen obese patients for obstructive sleep apnea via sleep study/polysomnography.

℞ TREATMENT

The National Heart, Lung, and Blood Institute (NHLBI) developed guidelines for selecting treatment strategies for overweight and obese patients based on BMI and comorbidities. They recommend a combination of dietary management, physical activity management, and behavior therapy for anyone with a BMI ≥25 or with a high-risk waist circumference and two or more obesity-associated comorbidities. Pharmacotherapy should be

TABLE 10-1 Weight-Loss Treatment Guidelines from the National Heart, Lung, and Blood Institute*

	BMI				
Treatment	25.0-26.9	27.0-29.9	30.0-34.9	35.0-39.9	>40.0
Diet, physical activity, behavioral therapy, or all three	Yes	Yes	Yes	Yes	Yes
Pharmacotherapy†		In patients with obesity-related diseases.	Yes	Yes	Yes
Surgery‡				In patients with obesity-related diseases.	Yes

*Data are from www.nhlbi.nih.gov/guidelines/obesity/ob_home.htm. These guidelines are generally consistent with those from the American Heart Association, the American Medical Association, the American Diabetic Association, the Obesity Society (Practical Guide), the American Diabetes Association, the American Academy of Family Physicians, the American College of Sports Medicine, and the American Cancer Society. *BMI* denotes body mass index, calculated as the weight in kilograms divided by the square of the height in meters.
†Pharmacotherapy should be considered only in patients who are not able to achieve adequate weight loss with available conventional lifestyle modifications and who have no absolute contraindications for drug therapy.
‡Bariatric surgery should be considered only in patients who are unable to lose weight with available conventional therapy and who have no absolute contraindications for surgery.

considered for patients with a BMI ≥30 or ≥27 with comorbidities.

Bariatric surgery is indicated for patients with a BMI ≥35 with comorbidities and for any patient with a BMI ≥40 (Table 10-1).

NONPHARMACOLOGIC THERAPY

- The cornerstones for weight management and reduction are calorie restriction, exercise, and behavioral modification. Assessment of patient's willingness to make changes must be evaluated, as treatment is more likely to succeed in motivated patients.
- The NHLBI guidelines recommend an initial diet to produce a calorie deficit of 500 to 1000 kcal/day. This has been shown to reduce total body weight by an average of 8% over 3 to 12 mo.
- These guidelines recommend the use of a food diary to focus on dietary substitutes.
- Thirty minutes of moderate-intensity activity on 5 or more days of the week results in health benefits for obese individuals. Moreover, several studies indicate that 60 to 80 min of moderate to vigorous physical activity may provide additional benefit.
- Increased physical activity without caloric restriction (minimal or no weight loss) can reduce abdominal (visceral) adipose tissue and improve insulin resistance.
- The key features of the standard behavioral modification program include goal setting, self-monitoring, stimulus control (modification of one's environment to enhance behaviors that will support weight management), cognitive restructuring (increased awareness of perceptions of oneself and one's weight), and prevention of relapse (weight regain).
- Mammalian sleep is closely integrated with the regulation of energy balance. Trials have shown that the amount of human sleep contributes to the maintenance of fat-free body mass at times of decreased energy intake. Lack of sufficient sleep may compromise the efficacy of typical

dietary interventions for weight loss and related metabolic risk reduction.

ACUTE GENERAL Rx

- According to the NHLBI *Guidelines on the Identification, Evaluation, and Treatment of Overweight and Obesity in Adults* and the U.S. Food and Drug Administration (FDA), pharmacotherapy is indicated for:
  1. Obese patients with a BMI ≥30.
  2. Overweight patients with a BMI of ≥27 and concomitant obesity-related risk factors or diseases, such as hypertension, diabetes, or dyslipidemia.
- Pharmacologic treatment options include:
  1. Gastrointestinal lipase inhibitors: Orlistat is the only drug available for long-term treatment of obesity. It blocks the digestion and absorption of ingested dietary fat. It is a reversible inhibitor of pancreatic, gastric, and carboxyl ester lipases and phospholipase A2, which are required for the hydrolysis of dietary fat in the gastrointestinal tract. Side effects include flatulence, fecal incontinence, cramps, and oily spotting. There can also be impairment of absorption of fat-soluble vitamins (A, D, E, K) and beta-carotene. Oxalate-associated acute kidney injury and rare severe liver injury have also been reported.
  2. C serotonin agonists: Lorcaserin is a selective serotonin agonist that acts centrally to reduce appetite, aiding weight loss. Adverse effects include headache, upper respiratory infections, dizziness, and nausea. While there is little evidence of serotonin-associated cardiac valvular disease or pulmonary hypertension (as seen with nonselective serotonergic agonists fenfluramine and dexfenfluramine), long-term data is currently limited.
  3. Sympathomimetic medications: Phentermine and diethylpropion are currently approved for short-term treatment

of obesity. They reduce food intake by causing early satiety. Side effects include increased blood pressure and increased pulse. They are Schedule IV drugs with a potential for abuse. Other sympathomimetic drugs that have been removed from the market due to concerns about cardiovascular safety are sibutramine, phenylpropanolamine, and ephedrine.
4. Antidepressants: While not FDA-approved for treatment of obesity alone, bupropion and fluoxetine are antidepressants that have been associated with modest weight loss. The FDA has recently approved a fixed-dose combination of bupropion with the opioid receptor antagonist naltrexone. It is called Contrave and approved for use as an adjunct to diet and exercise in patients with BMI ≥30 kg/m² or a BMI ≥27 kg/m² and one or more weight-related comorbidities (e.g., diabetes, hypertension, dyslipidemia).
5. Antiepileptic drugs: Zonisamide and topiramate (also used in migraine therapy) have been associated with weight loss in clinical trials but are not currently FDA-approved for treatment of obesity alone.
6. Diabetes drugs: While not FDA-approved for treatment of obesity alone, metformin, pramlintide (synthetic human amylin), and glucagon-like polypeptide-1 agonists (GLP-1) (exenatide) have been associated with weight loss in the treatment of individuals with diabetes. The GLP-1 receptor agonist liraglutide (Victoza) is now FDA approved at a higher dose as Saxenda for chronic weight management in adults with BMI ≥30 or a BMI ≥27 with a weight-related comorbidity such as hypertension, dyslipidemia, or diabetes.

CHRONIC Rx

- According to the NHLBI guidelines, surgical intervention is an option for selected patients with clinically severe obesity (a BMI ≥40 or a BMI ≥35 with comorbid conditions), when patients are at high risk for obesity-associated morbidity or death, and when less invasive methods of weight loss have failed.
- Eligible patients should also be at an acceptable risk for surgery, well informed, and motivated.
- Bariatric surgery for weight loss falls into one of three general categories:
- Restrictive surgeries limit the amount of food the stomach can hold and slow the rate of gastric emptying. These include vertical banded gastroplasty and laparoscopic adjustable silicone gastric banding LAGB [Fig. E10-2]). Band slippage is the most common LAGB complication. Other potential complications include port or tubing malfunction, stomal obstruction, band erosion, pouch dilatation, and port infection. Gastric necrosis of the stomach wall is a rarer late complication that results from ischemia caused by a combination of gastric prolapse—the part of the stomach below the band herniates up through the device (Fig. E10-3)—and pressure from the band. Gastric bypass has

better outcomes than gastric band procedures for long-term weight loss, type 2 diabetes control and remission, hypertension, and hyperlipidemia. These procedures have benefits that include: lower perioperative mortality rate, a quicker recovery period, and no malabsorption issues. However, they are not as effective as gastric bypass for weight reduction and comorbidity improvement.

1. Malabsorptive surgeries reduce nutrient absorption by shortening the length of small intestine. These include jejunoileal bypass and the duodenal switch operation (DS).
2. Restrictive malabsorptive bypass procedures combine the elements of gastric restriction and selective malabsorption. These include Roux-en-Y gastric bypass (considered the gold standard because of its high level of effectiveness and durability) and biliopancreatic diversion. These procedures have higher rates of comorbidity improvement than restrictive surgeries, but can be complicated by malabsorption and nutritional deficiencies

- Compared with usual care, bariatric surgery is associated with reduced number of cardiovascular deaths and lower incidence of cardiovascular events in obese adults. A study on bariatric surgery patients demonstrated a significant reduction in long-term cardiovascular events. Ten-year follow-up estimated relative risk reductions ranging from 18% to 79% according to the Framingham risk score and 8% to 62% with the PROCAM risk score.
- A recent long-term observational study of obese patients with type 2 diabetes showed that bariatric surgery was associated with higher diabetes remission rates and fewer complications than usual care (Sjostrom et al, 2014). Remission of type 2 DM occurs in 60% to 80% of patients two years after surgery and persists in about 30% of patients 15 years after Roux-en-Y gastric bypass.
- Liposuction is removal of fat by aspiration after injection of physiologic saline. This technique reduces the subcutaneous fat but has failed to improve insulin sensitivity or risk factors for CHD.

DISPOSITION

- The incidence of venous thromboembolism in the upper tertile of BMI was 2.42 times that of the lowest BMI tertile. Obese patients have a higher incidence of postoperative thromboembolic events when undergoing noncardiac surgery.
- Obesity may be associated with higher rates of postoperative pulmonary complications and poor wound healing.
- Weight-stable obese subjects have an increased risk of arrhythmias and sudden death even in the absence of cardiac dysfunction.
- Obesity and the cardiac autonomic nervous system are intrinsically related. A 10% increase in body weight is associated with a decline in parasympathetic tone accompanied by a rise in mean heart rate. Conversely, a 10% weight loss in severely obese patients

is associated with significant improvement in autonomic nervous system cardiac modulation, including decreased heart rate and increased heart rate variability.

- Postmortem Determinants of Atherosclerosis in Youth (PDAY) study data provided convincing evidence that obesity in adolescents and young adults accelerates the progression of atherosclerosis decades before the appearance of clinical manifestations.
- Obesity accelerates the progression of native coronary atherosclerosis and after coronary artery bypass grafting.
- In older adults, obesity is associated with protection against hip fracture, but this protective effect on bone status does not offset the extensive array of potential adverse effects on conditions common in the older population.

REFERRAL

- Obesity is commonly seen in the primary care setting. If pharmacologic therapy is considered, consultation with physicians specializing in obesity and experienced with the use of the drug is recommended. In addition, consultation with nutritionists and behavioral therapists is helpful. A consultation with general surgery is indicated in patients being considered for surgical intervention.
- Recent trials have shown that among adolescents, use of gastric banding compared with lifestyle intervention results in a greater percentage achieving a loss of 50% of excess weight corrected for age. There were associated benefits to health and quality of life.

⚠ PEARLS & CONSIDERATIONS

COMMENTS

- Enhanced weight-loss counseling helps about one third of obese patients achieve long-term, clinically meaningful weight loss.
- The NHLBI launched the Obesity Education Initiative in January 1991. The overall purpose of the initiative is to help reduce the prevalence of overweight along with the prevalence of physical inactivity to reduce the risk of CHD and overall morbidity and mortality rates from CHD.
- The American Medical Association, in association with the Robert Wood Johnson Foundation and the U.S. Department of Health and Human Services, produced a primer for the assessment and management of adult obesity. The primer consists of 10 booklets that offer practical recommendations for addressing adult obesity in the primary care setting and is available free of charge at: http://www.amaassn.org/ama/pub/physician-resources.
- A recent study on BMI and all-cause mortality in a large prospective study suggests that optimal BMI range is between 20 and 24.9 (Patel AV, 2014).
- Recent research indicates that brown adipose tissue represents a natural target for the modulation of energy expenditure. The

presence of brown adipose tissue in humans may be quantified with the use of ^{18}F-FDG PET-CT. The amount of brown adipose tissue is inversely correlated with BMI, suggesting a potential role of brown adipose tissue in adult human metabolism.

- Obesity, glucose intolerance, and hypertension in childhood are strongly associated with increased rates of premature death from endogenous causes in this population.
- Recent trials have shown that among persons living in a controlled setting, calories alone account for the increase in fat. Protein affected energy expenditure and storage of lean body mass, but not body fat storage.
- There have been no evidence-based studies supporting combination medical therapy for weight loss.
- Data are lacking for the role of pharmacotherapy and bariatric surgery in the elderly population.

PREVENTION

- Prevention of overweight and obesity involves both increasing physical activity and dietary modification to reduce caloric intake.
- There is compelling evidence that prevention of weight regain in formerly obese individuals requires 60 to 90 min of moderate-intensity activity or lesser amounts of vigorous intensity activity.
- Moderate-intensity activity of approximately 45 to 60 min per day, or 1.7 physical activity level (PAL), is required to prevent the transition to overweight or obesity. For children, even more activity time is recommended.
- Clinicians can help guide patients to develop personalized eating plans and help them recognize the contributions of fat, concentrated carbohydrates, and large portion sizes.
- Clinicians must work with patients to modify other risk factors such as tobacco use, high glycemic intake, and elevated blood pressure to prevent the long-term chronic disease sequelae of obesity.
- Regular screening of body weight and BMI measurements at routine office visits can help identify early weight gain.

PATIENT & FAMILY EDUCATION

Information can be obtained on the American Obesity Association website (http://www.obesity.org) and the American Medical Association website (http://www.ama-assn.org).

 **EVIDENCE**

Available at www.expertconsult.com

SUGGESTED READINGS
Available at www.expertconsult.com

RELATED CONTENT
Obesity, Female (Patient Information)
Obesity, Male (Patient Information)
Obesity, Child (Patient Information)

AUTHOR: **CRAIG L. BASMAN, M.D.**

Diseases and Disorders

I

BASIC INFORMATION

DEFINITION
Obsessive-compulsive disorder (OCD) is characterized by obsessions (recurrent and persistent thoughts, urges, or images experienced as intrusive and unwanted) and/or compulsions (repetitive behaviors or mental acts performed in response to obsessions, or according to rules that must be applied rigidly) that are time-consuming (e.g., >1 hr/day) or cause marked impairment or distress. The symptoms are usually perceived as excessive and unreasonable.

SYNONYMS
OCD

ICD-10CM CODES
F42   Obsessive-compulsive disorder
F60.5 Obsessive-compulsive personality
       disorder

EPIDEMIOLOGY & DEMOGRAPHICS
PEAK INCIDENCE: Mean age at onset is 19.6 yr.
12-MONTH PREVALENCE: 1.2% of adults in the United States, international prevalence estimates are similar (1.1% to 1.8%)
PREDOMINANT SEX: Approximately equal distribution between sexes
PREDOMINANT AGE:
- Modal age of onset for females is between 20 and 29 yr.
- Modal age of onset for males is between 6 and 15 yr.

DISEASE COURSE:
- Condition is chronic with waxing and waning pattern.
- Symptoms typically worsen with stress.
- 15% show progressive deterioration, whereas 5% show an episodic course with little impairment between episodes.

GENETICS:
- OCD is a multifactorial familial condition that involves both polygenic and environmental risk factors.
- Rate of concordance is higher in monozygotic (57%) compared with dizygotic (27%) twins.
- Rate of disorder is also much higher in first-degree relatives of individuals with OCD and Tourette's disorder than in the general population.

PHYSICAL FINDINGS & CLINICAL PRESENTATION
- Persistent and recurrent intrusive and ego-dystonic obsessive ideas, thoughts, urges, or images that are perceived as alien and beyond one's control.
- Frequent experiencing of obsessions related to contamination (e.g., when using the telephone), excessive doubt (e.g., was the door locked?), organization (the need for a particular order), violent impulses (e.g., to yell obscenities in church), or intrusive sexual imagery.
- Compulsive behaviors (e.g., repeated hand washing, checking, rearranging) or mental rituals (e.g., counting, repeating phrases)

meant to temporarily ameliorate anxiety caused by obsessions.
- Obsessions and compulsions almost always accompanied by high anxiety and subjective distress. Both are usually seen as excessive and unreasonable.

ETIOLOGY
- Strong evidence of cortico-striato-thalamo-cortical circuit dysfunction.
- OCD onset may be temporally associated with infectious illness of CNS (e.g., Von Economo's encephalitis, Sydenham's chorea).
- OCD may follow head trauma or other premorbid neurologic condition, including birth hypoxia and Tourette's syndrome.
- Serotonergic, dopaminergic, and glutamatergic systems believed important in some ritualistic instinctual behaviors, with dysfunction of these pathways possibly giving rise to OCD.

DIAGNOSIS

DIFFERENTIAL DIAGNOSIS
- Obsessive-compulsive personality disorder (OCPD) is a maladaptive personality style defined by excessive rigidity, need for order and control, preoccupation with details, and excessive perfectionism. Unlike OCD, OCPD is ego-syntonic.
- Other psychiatric disorders in which obsessive or intrusive thoughts occur (e.g., body dysmorphic disorder, eating disorders, hypochondriasis, phobias, posttraumatic stress disorder).
- Impulse control disorders (e.g., trichotillomania [hair-pulling disorder], excoriation [skin-picking] disorder, pathologic gambling disorder, compulsive shopping, kleptomania, paraphilias/sexual compulsions).
- Neurologic disorders with repetitive behaviors (e.g., Tourette's syndrome, Sydenham's chorea, torticollis, autism).
- Delusions or psychosis, which may be mistaken for obsessive thoughts; unlike OCD, these individuals do not believe their obsessions are unreal and may likely meet criteria for another psychotic spectrum disorder that fully accounts for the obsessions (e.g., schizophrenia).

WORKUP
- Careful history leading to diagnosis.
- In adolescents and children: psychological testing to reveal learning disabilities.
  Screen for presence of past or current tic disorder, and ascertain degree of insight (good or fair, poor, absent/delusional) into OCD beliefs.

TREATMENT

NONPHARMACOLOGIC THERAPY
- Treatment will help ~50% of patients achieve partial remission within the first 6 mo.
- Cognitive-behavioral therapy (CBT), especially exposure/response prevention, is successful in up to 70% of patients, but nearly 25% drop out of treatment because of the initial anxiety the exposures create. Best results

are found for contamination obsessions and washing compulsions.

GENERAL Rx
- Antidepressants with serotonin reuptake blockade, including clomipramine, fluvoxamine, fluoxetine, paroxetine, sertraline, citalopram and escitalopram, venlafaxine, and duloxetine; optimal dosages are typically at the high end of the prescription range. Risk/benefit/alternatives discussion is crucial (e.g., dose-related risk of QT interval prolongation with serotonin reuptake inhibitors in general and clomipramine, citalopram, and escitalopram in particular).
- Clonazepam may be helpful in patients with extreme anxiety.
- Most improve with treatment, but few become symptom-free. No response in 15% of patients.
- Likely indefinite treatment. Relapse is common if medications are discontinued.
- Recent studies suggest that combination CBT and pharmacotherapy yields superior outcomes. More severe symptoms warrant combination therapy.
- Patients who do not respond to first-line treatments and those with comorbid psychosis and/or tic disorders may benefit from augmentation with a first- or second-generation antipsychotic medication (e.g., haloperidol, olanzapine, risperidone).
- Neurosurgical intervention (e.g., cingulotomy, deep brain stimulation) is reserved for the most severely symptomatic and treatment-resistant cases.

DISPOSITION
- Most mild to moderate cases can be managed on a regular outpatient basis. Treatment should typically start with SSRI monotherapy with regular follow-up to assess treatment response and side-effect management. Dose should be increased to maximum tolerated.
- Patient and family education may help improve medical adherence and support.

 PEARLS & CONSIDERATIONS

Patients with OCD typically have insight regarding the irrationality of their obsessions and compulsions but lack the ability to control them. This may cause intense shame and avoidance of medical care unless patient education and support are provided. Screen for OCD, especially among patients who present with "depression" or "anxiety."

SUGGESTED READINGS
Available at www.expertconsult.com

RELATED CONTENT
Obsessive-Compulsive Disorder (OCD) (Patient Information)

AUTHOR: **AGUSTIN G. YIP, M.D., PH.D.**

ℹ️ BASIC INFORMATION

DEFINITION

The term *ocular foreign body* refers to a foreign body on the surface of the corneal or conjunctival epithelium.

ICD-10CM CODES

T15   Foreign body on external eye
T15.0 Foreign body in cornea
T15.1 Foreign body in conjunctival sac
T15.8 Foreign body in other and multiple parts of external eye
T15.9 Foreign body on external eye, part unspecified

EPIDEMIOLOGY & DEMOGRAPHICS

INCIDENCE (IN U.S.): Universal, with a predominance in active people
PEAK INCIDENCE: Childhood through active adult years
PREDOMINANT SEX: Perhaps slightly more common in men
PREDOMINANT AGE: Childhood through active adult years

PHYSICAL FINDINGS & CLINICAL PRESENTATION

- Pain with foreign body sensation is the most common symptom.
- Causes of most common foreign bodies:
  1. Grinding (Fig. 10-4)
  2. Drilling
  3. Auto repair
  4. Airborne particles, such as blown by fans

Dx DIAGNOSIS

DIFFERENTIAL DIAGNOSIS

- History of corneal foreign body seen
- Hemorrhage, loss of vision
- Distorted anterior chamber, soft eye
- Corneal abrasion
- Corneal ulceration or laceration
- Glaucoma
- Herpes ulcers
- Infection
- Other keratitis
- Intraocular foreign body

WORKUP

- Fluorescein stain, slit-lamp examination if no foreign body is found
- Ultrasound examination
- Plain radiographs

LABORATORY TESTS

Intraocular pressure to make certain that eye has not been penetrated

IMAGING STUDIES

Occasionally, MRI of the orbits to identify foreign bodies not found by other means. Do not perform MRI if suspect metallic foreign body. Plain radiographs and ultrasound are sufficient.

Rx TREATMENT

NONPHARMACOLOGIC THERAPY

- Remove foreign body
- Treat infection
- Repair eye if ruptured
- Treat corneal abrasion or injury

ACUTE GENERAL Rx

- Saline irrigation
- Removal of foreign body with moist cotton-tipped applicator after instillation of topical anesthetic drops
- Use burr or more aggressive treatment if needed
- Cycloplegics, antibiotics, and pressure dressing after removal of foreign body
- Repair corneal laceration or damaged eye

DISPOSITION

If symptoms persist 24 hr after examination, refer to an ophthalmologist.

REFERRAL

To ophthalmology within 24 hr if patient not completely comfortable

❗ PEARLS & CONSIDERATIONS

COMMENTS

- Make sure foreign body is not intraocular (inside eye).
- Alkaline or acidic chemical foreign bodies can be dangerous; pH test must be performed if either of these is suspected (for all chemical foreign bodies).

SUGGESTED READINGS

Available at www.expertconsult.com

RELATED CONTENT

Corneal Foreign Body (Patient Information)

AUTHOR: **R. SCOTT HOFFMAN, M.D.**

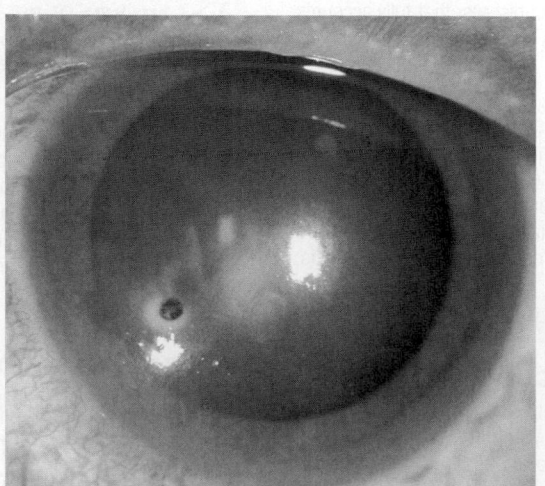

FIGURE 10-4 A small iron foreign body may be seen on external examination. (Courtesy Department of Dermatology, University of North Carolina at Chapel Hill. In Goldstein GB, Goldstein AO: *Practical dermatology,* ed 2, St Louis, 1997, Mosby.)

 BASIC INFORMATION

DEFINITION

Onychomycosis is defined as a persistent fungal infection affecting the toenails and fingernails.

SYNONYMS

Tinea unguium
Ringworm of the nails

ICD-10CM CODES

B35.1 Tinea unguium

EPIDEMIOLOGY & DEMOGRAPHICS

- Onychomycosis is most commonly found in people between the ages of 40 and 60 yr.
- Onychomycosis rarely occurs before puberty.
- Incidence: 20 to 100 cases/1000 population.
- Toenail infection is 4 to 6 times more common than fingernail infection.

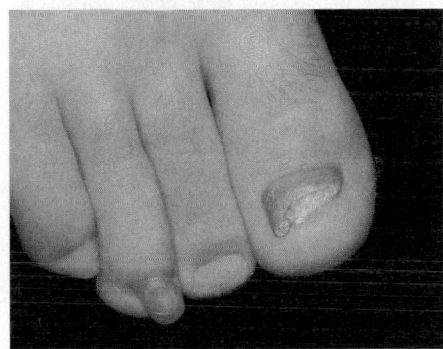

FIGURE 10-5 Distal subungual onychomycosis in a 5-year-old. Note how heavily infected nails occur adjacent to totally normal nails. Cutting back the big toe's nail plate has revealed the friable subungual debris. This material is the most desirable for culture. (From White GM, Cox NH [eds]: *Diseases of the skin, a color atlas and text*, ed 2, St Louis, 2006, Mosby.)

- Onychomycosis affects men more often than women.
- Occurs more frequently in patients with diabetes, peripheral vascular disease, and any conditions resulting in the suppression of the immune system.
- Occlusive footwear, physical exercise followed by communal showering, and incompletely drying the feet predispose the individual to developing onychomycosis.

PHYSICAL FINDINGS & CLINICAL PRESENTATION

- Onychomycosis causes nails to become thick, brittle, hard, distorted, and discolored (yellow to brown color) (Fig. 10-5). Eventually, the nail may loosen, separate from the nail bed, and fall off (Fig. 10-6).
- Onychomycosis is frequently associated with tinea pedis (athlete's foot).

ETIOLOGY

- The most common causes of onychomycosis are dermatophyte, yeast, and nondermatophyte molds.
- The dermatophyte *Trichophyton rubrum* accounts for 80% of all nail infections caused by fungus.
- *Trichophyton interdigitale* and *Trichophyton mentagrophytes* are other fungi causing onychomycosis.
- The yeast *Candida albicans* is responsible for 5% of the cases of onychomycosis and tends to involve fingernails more than toenails.
- Nondermatophyte molds *Scopulariopsis brevicaulis* and *Aspergillus niger*, although rare, can also cause onychomycosis.
- Onychomycosis is classified according to the clinical pattern of nail bed involvement. The main types are:
  1. Distal and lateral subungual onychomycosis (DLSO)
  2. Superficial onychomycosis
  3. Proximal subungual onychomycosis
  4. Endonyx onychomycosis
  5. Total dystrophic onychomycosis

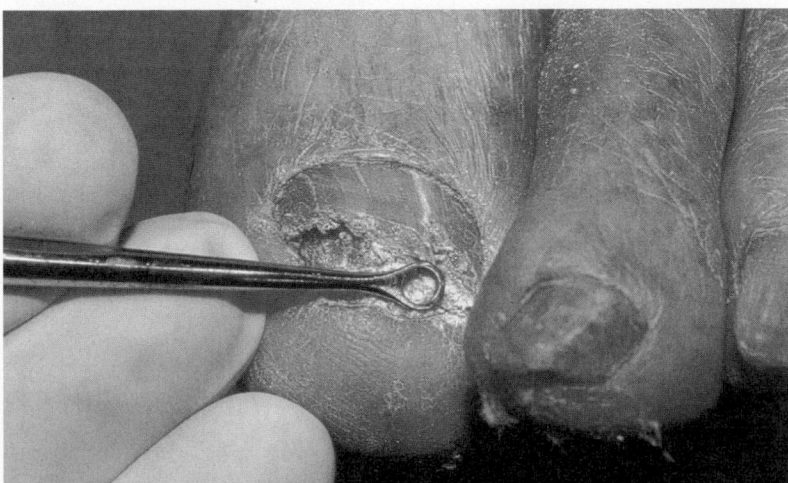

FIGURE 10-6 Collection of nail for culture. The subungual debris is the most valuable material for culture. After the nail is cut back, a curette may be used. Clippings of the nail may be added to the culture. (From White GM, Cox NH [eds]: *Diseases of the skin, a color atlas and text*, ed 2, St Louis, 2006, Mosby.)

 **DIAGNOSIS**

The diagnosis of onychomycosis is based on the clinical nail findings and confirmed by direct microscopy and culture.

DIFFERENTIAL DIAGNOSIS

- Psoriasis
- Contact dermatitis
- Lichen planus
- Subungual keratosis
- Paronychia
- Infection (e.g., *Pseudomonas*)
- Trauma
- Peripheral vascular disease
- Yellow nail syndrome

WORKUP

The workup of suspected onychomycosis is directed at confirming the diagnosis of onychomycosis by visualizing hyphae under the microscope by KOH prep or by culturing the organism. Although the standard for the diagnosis of fungal nail disease is a positive result on microscopic examination and culture of nail clippings with subungual debris or from surface debris in superficial white onychomycosis, treatment is often prescribed in the absence of confirmatory findings.

LABORATORY TESTS

- KOH prep: specificity is high but sensitivity is variable
- Fungal cultures on Sabouraud medium: culture may take 4 to 6 wk
- Dermatophyte test medium (DTM): an alternative to Sabouraud's that takes only 3 to 7 days and can be done in office setting. A color change indicates dermatophyte growth.
- Nail plate biopsy with periodic acid–Schiff (PAS) stain
- Blood tests are not specific in the diagnosis of onychomycosis and therefore not useful

IMAGING STUDIES

- Imaging studies are not very specific in making the diagnosis of onychomycosis and not useful.
- If an infection is present and osteomyelitis is a consideration, an x-ray of the specific area and a bone scan may help establish the diagnosis.

CLASSIFICATION

- The Onychomycosis Severity Index (OSI) is a new classification system for grading the severity of onychomycosis.
- The OSI score is obtained by multiplying the score for the area of involvement (range, 0-5) by the score for the proximity of the disease to the matrix (range, 1-5). Ten points are added for the presence of a longitudinal streak or a patch (dermatophytoma) or for >2 mm of subungual hyperkeratosis.
- Mild onychomycosis corresponds to a score of 1 to 5; moderate to a score of 6 to 15; severe to a score of 16 to 35.

O

 **TREATMENT**

NONPHARMACOLOGIC THERAPY

- Surgical removal of the nail plate is a treatment option; however, the relapse rate is high.
- Prevention of reinfection by wearing properly fitted shoes, avoiding public showers, and keeping feet and nails clean and dry.
- Short-pulse laser therapy is fungicidal and is a newer treatment modality for onychomycosis. Most patients will require 2 to 4 treatments, each lasting 15 to 30 minutes. Laser therapy is useful in patients with contraindications to oral agents. It is, however, expensive ($250-$1000 per treatment) and not covered by most insurance plans.

ACUTE GENERAL Rx

- Topical antifungal creams are used for early superficial nail infections.
  1. Miconazole 2% cream applied over the nail plate bid
  2. Clotrimazole 1% cream bid
  3. Ciclopirox: topical antifungal nail lacquer can be used for moderate onychomycosis that spares the lunula. Success rate <10%
  4. Efinaconazole 10% topical solution is modestly effective in treating toenail onychomycosis due to *Trichophyton rubrum* and/or *Trichophyton mentagrophytes*. Dosage is 1 drop (2 drops for big toenail) once daily for 48 weeks. Tavaborole 5% is a topical oxaborole also FDA approved for toenail onychomycosis. Cost and formulary are limiting factors with these agents.
  5. Tavaborole 5% solution is an oxaborole antifungal drug approved for topical treatment of toenail onychomycosis due to trichophyton rubrum or trychophyton mentagrophytes. It is applied to affected toenails once daily for 48 weeks. It is mod-

estly effective but much more expensive than topical ciclopirox 8% nail lacquer.
- Oral agents.
  1. Terbinafine
     a. For toenails: 250 mg/day for 3 mo
     b. For fingernails: 250 mg/day for 6 wk
  2. Itraconazole
     a. For toenails: 200 mg PO daily for 3 mo
     b. For fingernails: 200 mg PO daily for 6 wk
  3. Fluconazole: not as effective as terbinafine or itraconazole
     a. For toenails: 150 to 300 mg once weekly for 18 to 26 wk
     b. For fingernails: 150 to 300 mg once weekly for 12 to 16 wk
- All oral agents used for onychomycosis require periodic monitoring of liver function blood tests. Patients should be advised to watch for symptoms of drug-induced hepatitis (anorexia, fatigue, nausea, right upper quadrant pain) while taking these oral antifungal agents. They should stop their medication and contact their physician immediately if symptoms occur.
- Itraconazole is contraindicated in patients taking cisapride, astemizole, triazolam, midazolam, and terfenadine. Statins should be discontinued during itraconazole therapy. Itraconazole requires gastric acidity for absorption; patients should be advised not to take oral antacids, H_2 blockers, or proton pump inhibitors while taking itraconazole.
- Fluconazole is contraindicated in patients taking cisapride and terfenadine.
- Oral antifungal agents should not be initiated during pregnancy.

DISPOSITION

- Spontaneous remission of onychomycosis is rare.
- A disease-free toenail is reported to occur in approximately 25% to 50% of patients treated with the oral antifungal agents mentioned previously.

REFERRAL

- Podiatry consultation is indicated in diabetic patients for proper instruction in foot care, footwear, and nail debridement or surgical removal of the toenail.
- Dermatology consultation is indicated in patients refractory to treatment or if another diagnosis is considered (e.g., psoriasis).

⚠ PEARLS & CONSIDERATIONS

COMMENTS

- The growth of fungus on an infected nail typically begins at the end of the nail and spreads under the nail plate to infect the nail bed as well.
- Carefully consider the informational insert regarding drug-drug interactions and contraindications before initiating oral antifungal agents.
- Meta-analysis showed cure rates with the oral agents as follows: terbinafine (about 75%), itraconazole (60%-65%), and fluconazole (about 50%).

SUGGESTED READINGS
Available at www.expertconsult.com

RELATED CONTENT
Nail Fungus (Patient Information)
Ringworm (Patient Information)

AUTHOR: **GLENN G. FORT, M.D., M.P.H.**

Diseases
and Disorders

I

BASIC INFORMATION

DEFINITION

- Opioid addiction/dependence is defined as a cluster of cognitive, behavioral, and physiologic symptoms in which the individual continues use of opiates despite significant opiate-induced problems. Opiate dependence is a chronic, relapsing disorder characterized by repeated self-administration that usually results in opiate tolerance, withdrawal, and compulsive drug use. Tolerance is the need to increase dose to achieve the same effect. Dependence may occur with or without the physiologic symptoms of tolerance and withdrawal.
- There are four stages of addiction:
  1. Stage I, acute drug effects: rewarding effects of drug result from neurobiologic changes in response to the acute drug use. Duration varies from hours to days.
  2. Stage II, transformation to addiction: associated with changes in neuronal function that accumulate with repeated administration and diminish over days or weeks after discontinuation of drug use.
  3. Stage III, relapse after extended periods of abstinence: precipitated by an incubation of cue-induced craving (people, places, and things as triggers) and priming (relapse precipitated by drug exposure).
  4. Stage IV, end-stage addiction: vulnerability to relapse endures for years and results from prolonged changes at the cellular level.
- Pseudoaddiction: undertreatment of pain resulting in "opiate-seeking" behaviors such as "doctor shopping" and multiple emergency department visits. These behaviors disappear with adequate treatment of pain.

SYNONYMS

Opiate addiction
Opiate abuse
Narcotic addiction
Narcotic abuse

ICD-10CM CODES
F11.10 Opioid abuse, uncomplicated
F11.120 Opioid abuse with intoxication, uncomplicated
F11.121 Opioid abuse with intoxication delirium
F11.122 Opioid abuse with intoxication with perceptual disturbance
F11.129 Opioid abuse with intoxication, unspecified
F11.14 Opioid abuse with opioid-induced mood disorder
F11.150 Opioid abuse with opioid-induced psychotic disorder with delusions
F11.151 Opioid abuse with opioid-induced psychotic disorder with hallucinations
F11.159 Opioid abuse with opioid-induced psychotic disorder, unspecified
F11.181 Opioid abuse with opioid-induced sexual dysfunction
F11.182 Opioid abuse with opioid-induced sleep disorder
F11.188 Opioid abuse with other opioid-induced disorder
F11.19 Opioid abuse with unspecified opioid-induced disorder

EPIDEMIOLOGY & DEMOGRAPHICS

INCIDENCE: There are 980,000 opiate addicts in the United States; less than one third are in treatment.
PREVALENCE:
- In 2014, 10.3 million persons reported using prescription opioids non-medically.
- Emergency department visits involving misuse or abuse of prescription opioids increased 153% between 2004 and 2011.
- Admissions to substance-abuse treatment programs linked to prescription opioids more than quadrupled between 2002 and 2012.
- The percentage of eighth-, tenth-, and twelfth-graders who have used heroin has more than doubled since the late 1990s. This increase has largely been attributed to decreased price and increased purity in the last decade.

PREDOMINANT SEX: Males abuse opiates more commonly than females, with a male/female ratio of 3:1 for heroin and 1.5:1 for prescription opiates.
PEAK INCIDENCE: The majority of new abusers of opiates are <26 yr.
RISK FACTORS:
- Family history
- Prior history of addiction
- Psychiatric disorders
GENETICS:
- Genetic epidemiologic studies suggest a high degree of heritable vulnerability for opiate dependence.
- Gene polymorphism for dopamine receptor/transporters, opioid receptors, serotonin receptors/transporters, proenkephalin, and catechol-O-methyltransferase all appear to be associated with vulnerability to opiate dependence. Future interventions for opiate dependence may include medications identified through genetic research.

PHYSICAL FINDINGS & CLINICAL PRESENTATION

- Physical examination is often noncontributory.
- Small-sized pupils may be the only observable sign of use because only mild tolerance develops for miosis.
- Scars or tracks from chronic IV use may be visible over the veins of the arms, hands, ankles, neck, and breasts.
- Inflamed nasal mucosa or respiratory wheezing may be apparent in patients who are snorting heroin or OxyContin.
- Patients in withdrawal may have more dramatic findings such as tachycardia, hypertension, fever, piloerection (goose flesh), mydriasis, lacrimation, central nervous system (CNS) arousal, irritability, and repeated yawning. In patients with sympathetic overactivity and panic attacks, use of CNS stimulants, such as amphetamines or cocaine, should also be ruled out.

- Although gastrointestinal symptoms of nausea, vomiting, and abdominal pain are common in opiate withdrawal, other causes such as gastroenteritis, pancreatitis, peptic ulcer disease, and intestinal obstruction need to be ruled out.
- The history may provide relevant information in making the diagnosis. Significant findings may include:
  1. A long history of opiate self-administration, typically by the IV or intranasal route but sometimes through smoking as well.
  2. Polysubstance use. Intoxication by drugs other than narcotics (e.g., benzodiazepines, barbiturates) should be ruled out in unconscious patients.
  3. A high incidence of non-opiate-related psychiatric disorders (>80%).
  4. History of problems at work, school, or relationships associated with drug use.
  5. History of legal problems associated with drug use, such as arrest for possession, robbery, or prostitution.
  6. History of interpersonal violence (as perpetrator or victim).
  7. History of physical problems such as skin infections, phlebitis, endocarditis, or liver diseases attributable to acetaminophen toxicity (Vicodin/Percocet) or viral hepatitis. Hepatitis C is the most prevalent blood-borne pathogen. It is present in approximately 90% of opiate-dependent people and is often spread by sharing IV drug paraphernalia or snorting devices. There is also a higher incidence of HIV infection.

ETIOLOGY

Opioid dependence is a biopsychosocial disorder. Pharmacologic, social, genetic, and psychodynamic factors interact to influence abusive behaviors. Pharmacologic factors are especially prominent in opiate addiction because these drugs are strong reinforcing agents because of their euphoric effects and their ability to reduce anxiety and increase self-esteem and the patient's subjective feelings of improved ability to cope with daily challenges.

DIAGNOSIS

DIFFERENTIAL DIAGNOSIS

- Psychiatric disorders (e.g., anxiety, depression, bipolar disorder).
- Acute medical illness (e.g., hypoglycemia, seizure disorder, sepsis, renal or hepatic insufficiency) may mimic opiate withdrawal symptoms.

WORKUP

The history is the most important part of the workup. Useful screening tools are the CAGE-AID (Table 10-2), the DAST-10 (Table 10-3), and the CRAFFT (Table 10-4). The CAGE-AID has a sensitivity of 70% and a specificity of 85% when two questions are answered in the affir-

TABLE 10-2   CAGE-AID

1. Have you ever tried to **C**ut down on your alcohol or drug use?
2. Do you get **A**nnoyed when people comment about your drinking or drug use?
3. Do you feel **G**uilty about things you have done while drinking or using drugs?
4. Do you need an **E**ye-opener to get started in the morning?

Two or more questions answered in the affirmative require further assessment. *AID*, adapted to include drugs.
From Bowman S, Eiserman J, Beletsky, L, Stancliff S: Reducing the health consequences of opioid addiction in primary care, *Am J Med* 126, 565-571, 2013.

TABLE 10-3   Drug Abuse Screening Test (DAST-10)

1. Have you used drugs other than those required for medical reasons?
1. Do you abuse more than one drug at a time?
1. Are you unable to stop using drugs when you want to?
1. Have you ever had blackouts or flashbacks as a result of drug use?
1. Do you ever feel bad or guilty about your drug use?
1. Does your spouse (or parents) ever complain about your involvement with drugs?
1. Have you neglected your family because of your use of drugs?
1. Have you engaged in illegal activities in order to obtain drugs?
1. Have you ever experienced withdrawal symptoms (felt sick) when you stopped taking drugs?
1. Have you had medical problems as a result of your drug use (e.g., memory loss, hepatitis, convulsions, bleeding)?

Two or more questions answered in the affirmative require further assessment.
From Bowman S, Eiserman J, Beletsky, L, Stancliff S: Reducing the health consequences of opioid addiction in primary care, *Am J Med* (2013) 126, 565-571.

mative. The DAST-10 can discriminate between current users versus former users. The CRAFFT is a useful screening tool for adolescents. A CRAFFT score of 2 or higher is optimal for identifying any problem (sensitivity 76%, specificity 94%), any disorder (sensitivity 80%, specificity 86%), and drug dependence (sensitivity 92%, specificity 80%).

- Observation of opiate withdrawal is indicative of opiate addiction.
- Observation of purposeful behaviors such as complaints and manipulations directed at getting more drugs and anxiety during withdrawal is suggestive of opiate addiction.
- Screen blood and urine for opiate metabolites.
- Screen for communicable diseases: HIV, hepatitis B and hepatitis C, tuberculosis.
- Screen for endocarditis in patients with newly diagnosed murmurs.

LABORATORY TESTS
- Urine and serum toxicology screen
- Complete blood count

TABLE 10-4   CRAFFT Screening Tool for Adolescents

1. Have you ever ridden in a **C**ar driven by someone (including yourself) who was high or had been using alcohol or drugs?
1. Do you ever use alcohol or drugs to **R**elax, feel better about yourself, or fit in?
1. Do you ever use alcohol or drugs while you are by yourself **A**lone?
1. Do you ever **F**orget things you did while using alcohol or drugs?
1. Do your **F**amily or Friends ever tell you that you should cut down on your drinking or drug use?
1. Have you ever gotten into **T**rouble while you were using alcohol or drugs?

Two or more questions answered in the affirmative require further assessment.
From Bowman S, Eiserman J, Beletsky, L, Stancliff S: Reducing the health consequences of opioid addiction in primary care, *Am J Med* 126, 565-571, 2013.

- Chemistries (alanine aminotransferase, aspartate aminotransferase, serum creatinine): elevated liver function test (LFT) results may be from viral hepatitis or acetaminophen toxicity
- Hepatitis screen: if hepatitis C antibody positive, follow up with hepatitis C polymerase chain reaction (viral load) even in patients with normal LFTs
- HIV
- PPD

IMAGING STUDIES
Generally not helpful in routine diagnosis and treatment. Consider echocardiography in patients with heart murmurs and liver sonography or CT scan in patients with elevated LFTs or who are positive for hepatitis C or B (increased risk of hepatocellular carcinoma).

🆁🅇 TREATMENT

NONPHARMACOLOGIC THERAPY
- Brief counseling interventions during a visit with their primary care physician or OB/GYN have proved efficacious in motivating patients for treatment.
- Therapeutic communities (residential).
- 12-step or other self-help groups (e.g., Alcoholics Anonymous, Narcotics Anonymous).
- Relapse prevention (counseling).
- Opioid prevention education (Table 10-5)

ACUTE Rx
- Medical withdrawal (not overdosed).
- Short- (30 days) or long-term (30 to 180 days) protocols.
- Buprenorphine (opioid partial agonist) or methadone (opioid agonist) is initiated in tapering doses.
- Clonidine 0.1 mg bid to tid can be used to minimize autonomic symptoms (sweating) and craving.
- Nonsteroidal antiinflammatory drugs for body and muscle aches.

TABLE 10-5   Basic Components of Opioid Overdose Prevention Education Curriculum

1. Know the signs of an opioid overdose (e.g., unresponsive, limp, slow, shallow breathing, pale or clammy, finger nails or lips turning blue, gurgling)
1. Call 911
1. Administer rescue breathing
1. Administer naloxone if no response and Emergency Medical Services have not yet arrived
1. Stay with the person until help arrives

From Bowman S, Eiserman J, Beletsky, L, Stancliff S: Reducing the health consequences of opioid addiction in primary care, *Am J Med* 126, 565-571, 2013.

- The anticholinergic dicyclomine can be used to minimize gastrointestinal hyperactivity.
- Nonbenzodiazepine hypnotics, low-dose atypical antipsychotics (e.g., quetiapine), or low-dose tricyclic antidepressants are effective for promoting adequate sleep.

CHRONIC Rx
Opioid antagonist treatment:
- Naltrexone: does not stabilize neuronal circuitry like partial or full opioid agonists and generally results in poor outcomes, much like Antabuse for alcohol.
- Opioid partial agonist therapy: buprenorphine.
- Opioid agonist therapy: methadone.

NOTE: Buprenorphine and methadone are both metabolized by the cytochrome P450 3a4 and 2d6 I isoenzyme pathways. Prescribers should be aware of multiple possible drug interactions.

PATIENT SELECTION FOR BUPRENORPHINE OR METHADONE
- Appropriate patients for buprenorphine office-based treatment:
  1. Patients interested (highly motivated) in treatment
  2. Have no major contraindications (see following)
  3. Can be expected to be reasonably compliant with treatment
  4. Understand the benefits and risks of buprenorphine treatment
  5. Willing to follow safety precautions
- Less likely to be appropriate for office-based treatment:
  1. Have comorbid dependence on benzodiazepines or other CNS depressants (including ethylene alcohol)
  2. Have significant untreated psychiatric comorbidities
  3. Have active or chronic suicidal or homicidal ideation or attempts
  4. Have multiple previous treatments with frequent relapses
  5. Have poor response to previous treatment with buprenorphine
  6. Have significant medical complications (e.g., hepatic insufficiency, bacterial endocarditis, active tuberculosis)

- Methadone maintenance: narcotic treatment program (clinic setting) indications
- Evidence of opiate addiction >1 yr
- Two failed previous treatment attempts
- Patients not appropriate for office-based treatment
- Eligible without active "use" if prior methadone maintenance patient within previous 2 mo
- Pregnancy

DISPOSITION

- Opioid addiction is a chronic, relapsing disease.
- High rate of relapse after "detox."
- Relapse potential after medically supervised withdrawal from methadone:
  1. 90% after 1 yr stable in treatment
  2. 80% after 3 yr stable in treatment
  3. 70% after 5 yr stable in treatment
- Postmarketing surveillance indicates that the diversion and abuse of prescription opioid medications increased between 2002 and 2010 and plateaued or decreased between 2011 and 2013. These findings suggest that the United States may be making progress in controlling the abuse of opioid analgesics.[1]

[1]Dart RC et al.: Trends in opioid analgesic abuse and mortality in the United States, *N Engl J Med* 372:241-248, 2015.

REFERRAL

Refer to addiction medicine specialist or narcotic treatment program when the neurobiologic disease of opioid addiction is identified.

 **PEARLS & CONSIDERATIONS**

COMMENTS

- Methadone maintenance is the gold standard for the pregnant opiate-addicted patient regardless of the duration of the addiction or prior treatment attempts. Detoxification is contraindicated during pregnancy.
- Breastfeeding is encouraged in mothers on methadone maintenance. The American Academy of Pediatrics statement regarding "Transfer of Drugs and Other Chemicals into Human Milk" has placed methadone into the "usually compatible with breastfeeding" group based on the assumption that maternal urine is monitored to detect use of illicit drugs. The U.S. Department of Health and Human Services also recommends that mothers on methadone be encouraged to breastfeed.
- When a physician identifies a patient as a "drug seeker," it is imperative that the

physician avoid abruptly stopping the opiate prescription because this will often result in the patient's buying the drugs illegally. These patients should be counseled and referred for treatment.
- Patients on methadone or buprenorphine who have pain resulting from an acute injury will need pain medication in addition to their daily dose of methadone or buprenorphine. They will require higher than usual doses of pain medications because of opiate receptor blockade attributable to their methadone or buprenorphine use.
- Opiate-dependent patients have a lower pain threshold resulting from hyperalgesia caused by the long-term use of opiates.

PREVENTION

Education is the hallmark of prevention.
- School drug prevention education programs.
- Educate children about their family medical history, including diseases of addiction.
- Address childhood psychiatric disorders to prevent self-medicating.

PATIENT & FAMILY EDUCATION

- Stigma of addictions and treatment often interferes with good treatment.
- Family needs to be educated so they can support the patient's efforts.
- Encourage family meeting with addiction specialist, counselor.
- Recommend support groups for family members. Table 10-6 identifies organizations providing referral information for patients. Recommendations for integrating risk reduction strategies for addressing opioid misuse in the primary care setting are summarized in Table 10-7.

SUGGESTED READINGS
Available at www.expertconsult.com

RELATED CONTENT
Drug Abuse (Patient Information)

AUTHOR: **FRED F. FERRI, M.D.**

TABLE 10-6 Organizations Providing Referral Information for Patients

Organization	Resources/Website
Substance Abuse and Mental Health Services Administration (SAMHSA)	Opioid treatment program directory: http://dpt2.samhsa.gov/treatment/
Physicians who provide buprenorphine	Buprenorphine physician and treatment program locator: http://buprenorphine.samhsa.gov/bwns_locator/
Pain Action	Chronic pain management materials for patients: www.painaction.org
Substance abuse treatment facilities	Substance Abuse treatment facility locator: http://dasis3.samhsa.gov/
Harm Reduction Coalition	Local risk reduction resources and programs, overdose prevention education, and naloxone prescribing information: http://www.harmreduction.org/
Narcotics Anonymous (NA)	General information and meeting information for NA, a 12-step program modeled after Alcoholics Anonymous: www.na.org

From Bowman S, Eiserman J, Beletsky, L, Stancliff S: Reducing the health consequences of opioid addiction in primary care, *Am J Med* 126, 565-571, 2013.

TABLE 10-7 Recommendations for Integrating Risk Reduction Strategies for Addressing Opioid Misuse in the Primary Care Setting

Risk Reduction Tools	Type of Client	Delivery Recommendations
Brief substance abuse screening	All clients, particularly those individuals prescribed opioid medications or with a history of substance abuse problems.	Administer CAGE-AID* or similar screening tool as part of routine treatment.
Motivational interviewing	Clients who have identified opioid use or abuse.	Standard procedure may be delivered by primary care provider or other clinic staff.
Comprehensive tools for safer injections, including safer injection education	Clients who have reported, or are suspected of injection drug use. Tools should be available to all patients, not only those identified as drug users.	Resources (including educational materials, syringes, alcohol wipes, etc.) distributed and discussed by the primary care provider or other clinic staff.
Naloxone prescription and distribution	Targeting individuals using illicit or prescribed opioids, including individuals prescribed opioids.	Discussion, prescription of naloxone by the primary care provider; additional education may be delivered by other clinic staff.
Buprenorphine prescription	Targeting individuals using illicit or prescribed opioids, seeking medication assisted treatment.	Discussion and prescription by the primary care provider.

*For a full definition of CAGE-AID, see Table 10-2.
From Bowman S, Eiserman J, Beletsky, L, Stancliff S: Reducing the health consequences of opioid addiction in primary care, *Am J Med* 126, 565-571, 2013.

BASIC INFORMATION

DEFINITION

- *Optic atrophy* refers to the degeneration of axons of the optic nerve.
- It is a sign indicative of optic nerve insult rather than a distinct disease entity.

SYNONYMS

Unilateral/bilateral optic atrophy

ICD-10CM CODES
H47.2 Optic atrophy

EPIDEMIOLOGY & DEMOGRAPHICS

PREDOMINANT SEX: Depends on etiology
PREDOMINANT AGE: Variable
PEAK INCIDENCE: Varies depending on cause

PHYSICAL FINDINGS & CLINICAL PRESENTATION

- Optic atrophy is identified weeks to months after an initial insult such as optic neuritis, trauma, or ischemia. Frequently, it is noted by the physician during a routine eye exam.
- Asymmetry of disc color is often first subtle finding.
- Temporal part of optic disc is pale initially (Fig. 10-7); later, the entire disc becomes pale/white.
- Optic disc pallor occurs 4 to 6 wk after optic nerve insult.
- Unilateral lesion produces a relative afferent pupillary defect (RAPD): swing flashlight eye to eye; abnormal pupil dilates to direct light.
- Decreased visual acuity, blurred vision, visual field deficits (e.g., central scotoma), abnormal color vision (e.g., red desaturation).

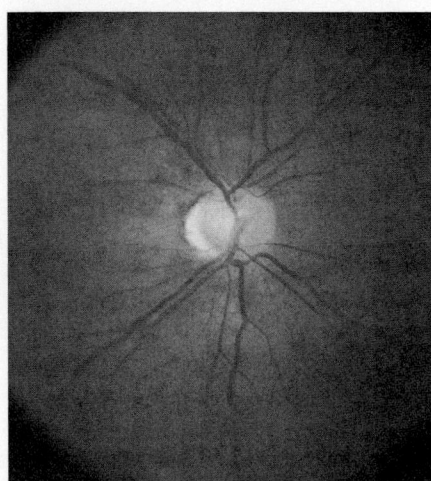

FIGURE 10-7 Optic atrophy. Patient's right eye shows atrophy. (Courtesy John W. Payne, M.D., The Wilmer Ophthalmological Institute, The Johns Hopkins University and Hospital, Baltimore. From Seidel HM [ed]: *Mosby's guide to physical examination*, ed 4, St Louis, 1999, Mosby.)

ETIOLOGY

- Optic neuritis—MS, sarcoidosis, Devic's disease, infections (syphilis, CMV, HIV, Lyme disease)
- Vascular—ischemic optic neuropathy, central retinal artery occlusion, temporal arteritis
- Compression—pituitary tumor, meningioma, thyroid eye disease
- Hereditary—Leber's hereditary optic neuropathy
- Nutritional, toxic, and metabolic—amiodarone, isoniazid, B_{12} deficiency, tobacco, alcohol
- Trauma
- Glaucoma (end-stage disease)

DIAGNOSIS

DIFFERENTIAL DIAGNOSIS

- Optic disc anomalies such as myelinated nerve fibers, "blonde" fundus

WORKUP

- A detailed history to identify onset and course, exposure to risk factors such as toxic/nutritional factors, detailed family history, and associated findings such as headache, eye pain, proptosis, or neurologic deficits
- Ophthalmic examination to document deficits of visual acuity, color vision, contrast sensitivity, and visual fields must be performed. Relative afferent pupillary defect (RAPD) on swinging flashlight examination is sine qua non for unilateral optic nerve disease and must be documented. Absence indicates retinal disease or bilateral lesions.
- General examination and neurologic examination can provide clues to an underlying cause.
- Pertinent laboratory testing as noted below; genetic studies with a genetic consultation can be obtained in cases with a suggestive history. Lumbar puncture should be obtained in patients with unexplained optic atrophy especially with neurologic deficits.
- In the absence of an obvious cause, contrasted MRI of brain and orbits should be obtained to evaluate for demyelinating lesions and compressive lesions of the anterior visual pathways.

LABORATORY TESTS

- Depends on suspected cause: none for trauma, tumor, or MS
- Serum B_{12}, serology for syphilis
- Autoimmune diseases: ESR, ANA, ACE, aquaporin-4 antibodies

IMAGING STUDIES

- MRI of the brain with contrast, fat suppression, and special (thin) cuts through orbits is necessary to identify compressive lesions in all patients with unexplained optic atrophy; especially important in patients with positive predictive factors for abnormal imaging (e.g., young age, progression, bilateral findings).
- If sarcoid is suspected, order chest x-ray and/or chest CT.

TREATMENT

ACUTE GENERAL Rx

Treat the underlying cause—discontinue identifiable toxins, use B_{12} replacement, neurosurgical intervention is necessary if tumor is found; consider IV steroids if there is evidence for active demyelinating disease.

CHRONIC Rx

The optic nerve does not regenerate, although symptoms often improve.

DISPOSITION

- Visual loss usually occurs over weeks to months.
- Appointment with neurologist or ophthalmologist

REFERRAL

Depends on the underlying disease process

PEARLS & CONSIDERATIONS

COMMENTS

- An experienced clinician should be able to identify pale optic discs and an RAPD.
- Pupillary dilation with mydriatic agents (e.g., tropicamide) may be necessary to optimize funduscopic examination.
- Patient education material can be obtained from the National Eye Institute, Department of Health and Human Services, 9000 Rockville Pike, Bethesda, MD 20892.

SUGGESTED READINGS
Available at www.expertconsult.com

AUTHOR: **SACHIN KEDAR, M.B.B.S., M.D.**

BASIC INFORMATION

DEFINITION

Optic neuritis is an inflammation of the optic nerve resulting in impaired visual function.

SYNONYMS

Optic papillitis
Retrobulbar neuritis

ICD-10CM CODES
H46.9 Unspecified optic neuritis
H46.8 Other optic neuritis

EPIDEMIOLOGY & DEMOGRAPHICS

INCIDENCE (IN U.S.): 1 to 5/100,000 person(s) per year; rates vary according to incidence of multiple sclerosis (MS)
PREVALENCE (IN U.S.): Common in patients with MS
PREDOMINANT SEX: Female/male ratio: 1.8:1
PEAK INCIDENCE: 20 to 49 yr, mean 30
GENETICS: Unknown. If due to MS, it is more common in patients with certain HLA blood types and in monozygotic twins of affected siblings.

PHYSICAL FINDINGS & CLINICAL PRESENTATION

- Presentation with acute or subacute (days) visual loss, often accompanied by periocular tenderness that worsens with eye movements.
- **Marcus Gunn pupil** (relative afferent pupillary defect [RAPD]): direct and consensual response are normal; however, when flashlight is swung from eye to eye, the affected eye's pupil dilates to direct light.
- Decreased visual acuity
- Unilateral visual field abnormalities—often a central scotoma (Fig. E10-8)
- Color desaturation; red is most often affected
- Normal orbit and fundus 66% cases; in 33% there is disc edema (Fig. 10-9), uveitis, or periphlebitis.
- May have movement or light-induced phosphenes (flashes of light lasting 1 to 2 sec).

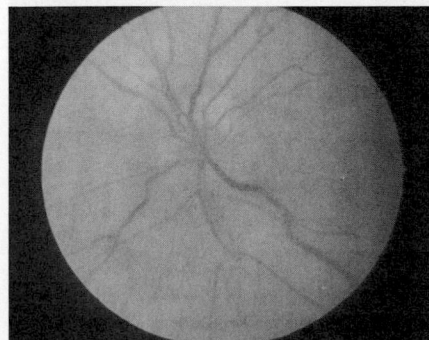

FIGURE 10-9 A case of optic neuritis. The optic disc edema seen here is often not present. Note the otherwise normal fundus. (Courtesy of J. Barton, M.D., Beth Israel Deaconess Medical Center, Boston.)

- Uhthoff's phenomenon (benign exercise- or heat-induced deterioration of vision) is seen in some. Vision may also worsen in bright sunlight.
- Over time the optic disc may atrophy and become pale.

ETIOLOGY

An inflammatory response associated with an infection or autoimmune disease (such as collagen vascular disease, granulomatous disease, MS, or neuromyelitis optica).

DIAGNOSIS

Consistent clinical presentation and exclusion of alternate ocular pathology, infection, and CNS mass lesions. Classic triad includes loss of vision, retroorbital pain, and dyschromatopsia. 70% of cases are unilateral and 30% bilateral.

DIFFERENTIAL DIAGNOSIS

For optic neuritis
- Inflammatory: MS, neuromyelitis optica (NMO), sarcoidosis, lupus, Sjögren's, Behçet's, postinfectious, postvaccination, neuroretinitis, acute disseminated encephalomyelitis, paraneoplastic, autoimmune optic neuropathy
- Infectious: syphilis, TB, Lyme disease, *Bartonella,* HIV, CMV, herpes, helminths, chickenpox, Q fever, periorbital infections, *Toxocara* sp.
- Ischemic: anterior and posterior ischemic optic neuropathies, diabetic papillopathy, branch or central retinal artery or vein occlusion
- Drugs and toxins: arsenic, methanol, ethambutol, cyclosporine, etc.
- Mitochondrial: Leber's hereditary optic neuropathy, other mitochondrial

WORKUP

A thorough neurologic examination; recommend dilated ophthalmoscopy.

LABORATORY TESTS

Acute optic neuritis is a clinical diagnosis based on presentation with classical features: acute, painful unilateral loss of vision associated with RAPD in a young person with no other apparent causes such as trauma. In atypical cases additional studies may be considered.
- CBC, ANA, ACE, ESR
- Consider HIV Ab, Lyme titer, RPR, other autoimmune or infectious causes
- Bilateral or recurrent ON: NMO IgG; paraneoplastic CRMP-5-IgG

IMAGING STUDIES

- MRI of the brain and orbits (thin section fat-suppressed T_2-weighted) ± gadolinium to look for compressive and infiltrative causes and assess the risk to develop MS. Often enhancement of the optic nerve is seen.
- Consider using optical coherence tomography to follow optic nerve atrophy objectively longitudinally.

TREATMENT

NONPHARMACOLOGIC THERAPY

Assure patient that in most cases there is near complete recovery of vision.

ACUTE Rx

Treat if the visual loss is severe or if there is an abnormal MRI (higher risk of MS). Treatment is with methylprednisolone (MP) 250 mg IV every 6 hr (or 1 g IV daily) for 3 days followed by an oral prednisone taper of 11 days.

CHRONIC Rx

Depends on underlying cause. Disease-modifying treatment when increased risk of developing MS or neuromyelitis optica. See topic "Multiple Sclerosis."

DISPOSITION

Most often vision is worst at the end of week 1, followed by recovery over months. In the Optic Neuritis Treatment Trial (ONTT), 90% had 20/40 or better vision at 1 yr and 3% had 20/200 or worse. Of initial 20/200 or worse cases, only 5% remained in that group at 6 mo.

REFERRAL

- To neurologist for other neurologic signs and to assess risk of developing MS. In ONTT (Optic Neuritis Treatment Trial), risk of MS >15 yr was 72% with ≥1 lesion(s) on MRI, and 25% with a normal MRI
- To ophthalmologist when atypical features or slowly progressive; urgently when other ocular pathology is present or if vision worsens or does not improve after several wk, or pain is severe

PEARLS & CONSIDERATIONS

- Bilateral optic neuritis suggests a systemic inflammatory disorder, infection, NMO, or paraneoplastic, but can also occur in MS.
- Acute bilateral loss of vision with a severe headache or diplopia should raise concern for pituitary apoplexy and/or giant cell arteritis.

EVIDENCE

Available at www.expertconsult.com

SUGGESTED READINGS

Available at www.expertconsult.com

RELATED CONTENT

Idiopathic Intracranial Hypertension (Related Key Topic)
Multiple Sclerosis (Related Key Topic)

AUTHOR: **SACHIN KEDAR, M.B.B.S., M.D.**

Oral Cancer  EBM PTG

BASIC INFORMATION

DEFINITION

Oral cancers refer to malignant transformation of the oral tissues usually preceded by a process of sequential dysplastic changes leading to the development of squamous carcinoma. Oral squamous cell cancers (OSCC) include oral cavity cancers (lip, floor of mouth, buccal mucosa, anterior tongue, gingivae, hard palate, retromolar trigone), oropharynx cancers (base of tongue, tonsils, soft palate, pharyngeal walls), and hypopharynx cancers (pyriform sinus, postcricoid area, posterior pharyngeal wall)

SYNONYMS

Head and neck cancer
Oral malignant neoplasm

ICD-10CM CODES
C01	Malignant neoplasm of base of tongue
C03	Malignant neoplasm of gum
C04	Malignant neoplasm of floor of mouth
C05	Malignant neoplasm of palate
C06	Malignant neoplasm of other and unspecified parts of mouth
C09	Malignant neoplasm of tonsil
C10	Malignant neoplasm of oropharynx
C11	Malignant neoplasm of nasopharynx
C12	Malignant neoplasm of piriform sinus
C13	Malignant neoplasm of hypopharynx
C14	Malignant neoplasm of other and ill-defined sites of lip, oral cavity and larynx
C14.0	Malignant neoplasm of pharynx, unspecified
C14.2	Malignant neoplasm of Waldeyer's ring
C14.8	Malignant neoplasm of overlapping sites of lip, oral cavity and pharynx

EPIDEMIOLOGY & DEMOGRAPHICS

INCIDENCE & PREVALENCE: OSCC comprise the sixth most common cancer in the world. An estimated 530,000 cases are diagnosed annually around the globe, and the rates have been rising, particularly in young people and among minorities. In 2015, it is estimated that approximately 45,780 new cases and 8650 deaths occurred in the U.S. The incidence of oral cancers linked to alcohol and tobacco use has been declining in the U.S., whereas those linked to human papillomavirus (HPV), primarily HPV type 16, are on the rise, especially for cancers located in the tonsils and base of tongue. In developed countries across the world, HPV is increasingly implicated in the growing incidence of oral cancer. In Asian countries where chewing betel nut is customary, oral cancer accounts for up to 40% of cancers in some regions. Squamous cell carcinoma is the most common malignancy that occurs in the oral cavity. Minor salivary gland cancers, lymphomas, and sarcomas are less common.

PREDOMINANT SEX & AGE::
- Male:female ratio is 2.5:1 in the U.S.
- Black males have a higher early incidence in the 50- to 60-yr age group, but with increasing age, white men predominate.

GENETICS: The genes that are critically altered in OSCC include *TP53*, the retinoblastoma family, *p16* and cyclin *D1*. The *TP53*, *CCND1*, and *CDKN2A* genes are established cancer genes in HPV-negative cancers. *TP53* and the genes encoding the Rb family are established cancer genes in HPV-positive cancers. Signaling pathways that are involved in the pathogenesis of

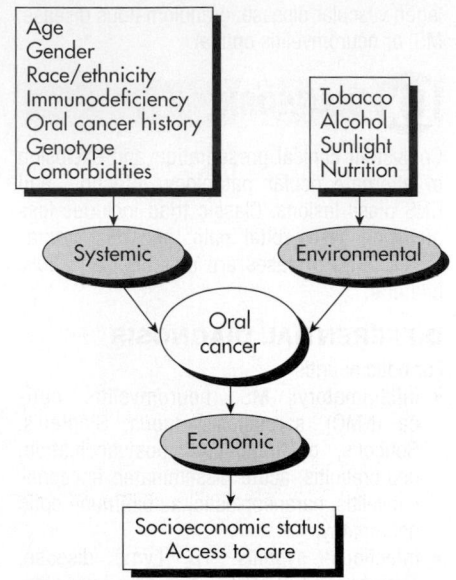

FIGURE 10-10 Risk model for oral cancer. Oral cancer is a multifactorial disease process that includes systemic, environmental, and economic effects. The interplay of these variables ultimately leads to the incidence of this disease. The multifactorial nature of oral cancer should be addressed in the assessment of a patient's risk. (From Jones DL, Rankin KV: Oral cancer and associated risk factors. In Cappelli D Mobley C (eds): *Prevention in clinical oral health care,* St. Louis, 2008, Elsevier, pp 68–77.)

oral cancers include that of the human epidermal receptor (HER) family, vascular endothelial growth factor (VEGF) receptor, and signal transducer and activator of transcription 3 (STAT 3). The tumor suppressor gene *TP53* is frequently mutated in HPV-negative tumors.

RISK FACTORS (FIG. 10-10):
- Tobacco use of any kind
- HPV infection (primarily types 16 and 18)
- Alcohol
- Immune deficiency
- Radiation
- Betel nut consumption
- Solar radiation

PHYSICAL FINDINGS & CLINICAL PRESENTATION

- Specific patient complaints may include the following: oral ulcers or mass, choking, difficulty breathing, dysphagia, odynophagia, voice hoarseness, globus sensation, otalgia, ear or nose stuffiness, hemoptysis, trismus, neck mass, and pain in the head/neck region.
- Generalized symptoms and signs may include weight loss, fatigue, anorexia, altered mood, and sleep.
- Clinically, oral cancers can present as:
  1. Erythroplakia (flat red patch); can mimic inflammatory or traumatic lesions
  2. Leukoplakia (white patch; Fig. 10-11)
  3. Raised lesion
  4. Ulcerated lesion
  5. Warty lesion or growth

DIAGNOSIS

DIFFERENTIAL DIAGNOSIS
- Oral leukoplakia
- Invasive fungal infections
- Chancre of early syphilis and gumma of tertiary syphilis

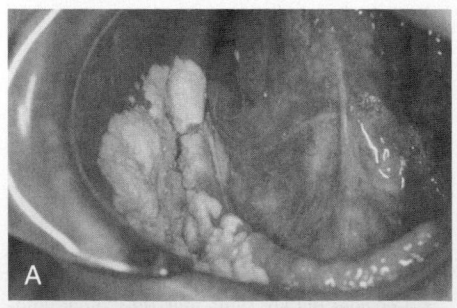
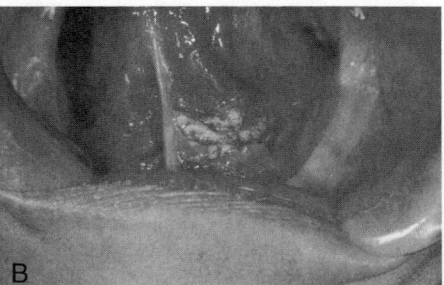
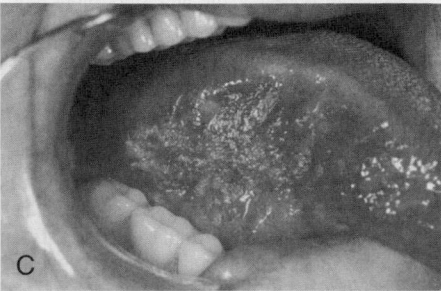

FIGURE 10-11 Squamous cell carcinoma of the oral mucosa. A, Leukoplakia. **B,** Invasive carcinoma of the floor of the mouth. **C,** Invasive carcinoma of the tongue. (Courtesy G. Putnam. In White GM, Cox NH [eds]: *Diseases of the skin: a color atlas and text,* ed 2, St Louis, 2006, Mosby.)

O

Diseases
and Disorders

I

- Chronic ulcer
- Metastatic or locally invading cancers from sinuses or other sites of the body

PATIENT WORKUP

- Primary workup includes either biopsy or fine-needle aspiration (FNA) of the presenting lesion or suspected neck lymph node for histopathologic analysis. HPV assessment with p16 immunohistochemical staining and confirmatory in situ hybridization (ISH) testing is performed when indicated for oropharynx primary tumors.
- Detailed examination of the oral cavity, pharynx, larynx, neck, ears, nose, and cranial nerves should be performed.
- Laryngoscopy and examination under anesthesia are commonly performed.
- Pretreatment evaluation of tumor size, the extent of invasion, and the presence or absence of regional lymph node metastases is critical for planning treatment.
- Laboratory workup can include complete blood count, chemistries including electrolytes, renal panel, liver panel, glucose, and thyroid function.
- Staging workup includes CT or MRI imaging of the head and neck and a chest x-ray. If locoregional or advanced disease is a consideration, the PET scan is typically completed.
- The TNM system is used for staging of OSCC and is subdivided according to primary tumor sites: 1. lip and oral cavity, 2. pharynx.

 **TREATMENT**

- Surgery, radiation therapy, and chemotherapy are treatment modalities involved in the treatment plan for OSCC.
- The use of supportive and special therapeutic modalities such as nutritional therapy including feeding gastrostomy, speech and swallowing therapy, reconstructive surgery, and speech prosthesis may be required often.
- For treatment purposes OSCC are classified as early (T1 or T2 lesions), locoregional (T3-4 or any N), or metastatic (M1) stages. Site-specific TNM staging is done as per the primary tumor site (e.g., oral cavity, oropharynx, hypopharynx, etc.)

- After staging completion, the initial treatment considerations include:
  1. Determination of primary tumor resectability (resectable vs. unresectable)
  2. Management of neck nodes
  3. Intent of radiation therapy (curative vs. palliative)
  4. Need for organ preservation
  5. Need for reconstructive surgery
  6. Need for chemotherapy
  7. HPV status of tumor
- Localized tumors (stage I or II) can be approached by initial surgical resection or definitive radiotherapy. Loco-regionally advanced tumors (stage III and localized IV) that are resectable are typically approached by upfront surgery followed by adjuvant radiation and/or chemotherapy. Unresectable patients are typically treated with definitive chemotherapy and radiotherapy. Patients with distant metastatic disease are treated with systemic chemotherapy, while locally recurrent tumors can be approached with either surgery or chemotherapy or both.
- Surgery is typically associated with less morbidity than radiation therapy. Surgical therapy traditionally involved wide-exposure approaches (mandibulotomy, transpharyngeal access). Newer surgical techniques allow tumor resection through the mouth. Recently, transoral robotic surgery (TORS) has been developed to improve access to oropharyngeal squamous cell carcinomas with excellent oncologic outcomes.
  1. Acute surgical complications can include infection, bleeding, aspiration, wound breakdown, fistula, and flap loss.
  2. Surgical procedures can cause functional deficits in speech and swallowing, but these adverse effects can be minimized by appropriate reconstruction and prostheses.
- Definitive radiation therapy is reserved for patients who cannot tolerate surgery or for whom surgical resection would result in particularly severe functional impairment.
  1. Radiation therapy can include external beam radiation and brachytherapy.
  2. Radiation therapy side effects include mucositis, skin reaction, loss of taste, dysphagia, dental caries and decay, and xerostomia.
  3. Late complications can include skin and soft tissue atrophy and fibrosis, osteoradionecrosis, and trismus.

- Systemic chemotherapy can be administered alone or in combination with radiotherapy, depending on the disease stage. Agents typically used include cisplatin, carboplatin, 5-fluorouracil, taxanes, methotrexate, and the epidermal growth factor receptor (EGFR) antibody cetuximab.
  1. For locally advanced OSCC, the combination of cisplatin and radiotherapy is the regimen of choice.
  2. For metastatic or recurrent OSCC, combination chemotherapy regimens plus the use of EGFR antibody has shown improvement in overall survival.

DISPOSITION

- Prognosis depends on the staging and resectability of the primary tumor as well as on patient performance status.
- Tumor HPV status is a strong and independent prognostic factor for survival among patients with oropharyngeal cancer.

REFERRAL

Referral to multidisciplinary head and neck cancer team consisting of ENT or head/neck surgeon, radiation oncologist, and medical oncologist.

PEARLS & CONSIDERATIONS

COMMENTS

- Oral and pharyngeal cancer is the sixth most common cancer globally.
- Biopsy is the key for diagnosis.
- Posttreatment surveillance is important.

PREVENTION

- Encourage patients to stop using any type of tobacco and drinking alcohol.
- Examine oral cavities at annual checkups and work up suspicious lesions.

SUGGESTED READINGS

Available at www.expertconsult.com

RELATED CONTENT

Mouth Cancer (Patient Information)

AUTHOR: **RITESH RATHORE, M.D.**

BASIC INFORMATION

DEFINITION

Orchitis is an inflammatory process (usually infectious) involving the testicles. Infection may be viral or bacterial and can be associated with infection of other male sex organs (prostate, epididymis, or bladder) or lower urogenital tract or sexually transmitted diseases often via hematogenous spread. Common causes are:
- Viral: mumps—20% postpubertal; coxsackie B virus
- Bacterial: pyogenic via spread from involving epididymis; bacteria include *Escherichia coli, Klebsiella pneumoniae, P. aeruginosa, Staphylococcus, Streptococcus* or *Rickettsia, Brucella* spp.
- Other:
  1. Viral—HIV-associated, CMV
  2. Fungi
     1. Cryptococcosis
     2. Histoplasmosis
     3. *Candida*
     4. Blastomycosis
     5. Syphilis
  3. *Mycobacterium tuberculosis* and *M. leprae*
  4. Parasitic causes: toxoplasmosis, filariasis, schistosomiasis
- Table 10-8 describes a classification of epididymitis and orchitis based on etiology.

SYNONYMS

Epididymo-orchitis
Testicular infection
Testicular inflammation

ICD-10CM CODES
N45.9 Orchitis, epididymitis, and epididymo-orchitis without abscess
A54.1 Gonococcal orchitis
A56.1 Chlamydial orchitis
N51.1 Mumps orchitis

EPIDEMIOLOGY & DEMOGRAPHICS

PREDOMINANT SEX: Male
PREDOMINANT ORGANISM: The leading cause of viral orchitis is mumps. The mumps virus rarely causes orchitis in prepubertal males but involves one or both testicles in nearly 30% of postpubertal males.

PHYSICAL FINDINGS & CLINICAL PRESENTATION
- Testicular pain, unilateral or bilateral swelling
- May have associated epididymitis, prostatitis, fever, scrotal edema, erythema, cellulitis
- Inguinal lymphadenopathy
- Acute hydrocele (bacterial)
- Rare development: abscess formation, pyocele of scrotum, testicular infarction
- Spermatic cord tenderness may be present
- Granulomatous

DIAGNOSIS

Clinical presentation as described previously with possible history of acute viral illness or concomitant epididymitis.

DIFFERENTIAL DIAGNOSIS
- Epididymo-orchitis-gonococcal
- Autoimmune disease
- Vasculitis
- Epididymitis
- Mumps, with or without parotitis
- Neoplasm
- Hematoma
- Spermatic cord torsion

LABORATORY TESTS
- CBC with differential
- Urinalysis
- Viral titer—mumps
- Urine culture
- Ultrasound of testicle to rule out abscess

IMAGING STUDIES
Ultrasound if abscess suspected

TREATMENT

- Dependent on cause
- Viral (mumps): observation; bed rest, ice packs, analgesics, and a scrotal sling for support may provide some relief of discomfort that accompanies mumps orchitis
- Bacterial: empiric antibiotic treatment with parenteral antibiotic treatment until pathogen identified: ceftriaxone (250 mg IM once) plus doxycycline (100 mg PO bid for 10 days), in men <35 yr old to cover *Neisseria gonorrhoeae* and *Chlamydia trachomatis.* In homosexual men or men >35 yr old: levofloxacin

500 to 750 mg IV/PO qd for 10 to 14 days *or* ampicillin-sulbactam *or* third-generation cephalosporin or ticarcillin-clavulanate.
- Surgery for abscess, pyogenic process

DISPOSITION
Follow-up for evidence of recurrence, hypogonadism, and infertility may be needed with bilateral orchitis.

REFERRAL
- To a urologist if surgical drainage is needed
- To an endocrinologist if hypogonadism develops
- To a fertility specialist if infertility develops

PEARLS & CONSIDERATIONS

Consider tuberculous orchitis if symptoms fail to respond to standard antibacterial therapy, even in the absence of chest radiographic evidence of pulmonary tuberculosis.

SUGGESTED READINGS
Available at www.expertconsult.com

RELATED CONTENT
Orchitis (Patient Information)
Epididymitis (Related Key Topic)
Mumps (Related Key Topic)

AUTHOR: **GLENN G. FORT, M.D., M.P.H.**

TABLE 10-8 Classification of Epididymitis and Orchitis

Acute Epididymitis or Epididymoorchitis	Granulomatous Epididymitis or Orchitis	Viral Orchitis
Neisseria gonorrhoeae	*Mycobacterium tuberculosis*	Mumps
Chlamydia trachomatis	*Treponema pallidum*	Enteroviruses
Escherichia coli		
Streptococcus pneumoniae		
Klebsiella spp.	*Brucella* spp.	
Salmonella spp.	Sarcoid	
Other urinary tract pathogens	Fungal	
Idiopathic	Parasitic	
	Idiopathic	

From Cohen J, Powderly WG: *Infectious diseases,* ed 2, St Louis, 2004, Mosby.

 BASIC INFORMATION

DEFINITION

Orthostatic hypotension (OH) is defined as the presence of at least one of the following: a decrease in systolic blood pressure by ≥20 mm Hg or a decrease in diastolic blood pressure by ≥10 mm Hg within 3 min of standing. It is a physical sign that requires further investigation to discern its underlying etiology.

SYNONYMS

Postural hypotension

ICD-10CM CODES
I95.1 Orthostatic hypotension

EPIDEMIOLOGY & DEMOGRAPHICS

- The incidence of OH is increased in older people and in those with diseases associated with autonomic dysfunction (e.g., Parkinson disease, diabetes mellitus).
- OH may cause up to 30% of all syncopal events in the elderly, and OH is associated with an increased risk of heart failure among those aged 45 to 55 yr and an increased risk of cardiovascular disease and all-cause mortality among those aged 55 yr and older.
- There is emerging evidence of an association between orthostatic hypotension and cognitive dysfunction among older adults.

PHYSICAL FINDINGS & CLINICAL PRESENTATION

- Symptoms may include dizziness, light-headedness, syncope, visual and auditory disturbances, weakness, diaphoresis, pallor, and nausea. OH may also be asymptomatic, especially in older hypertensive patients.
- Associated with increased autonomic activity during meals (from increased splanchnic blood flow), exercise, and hot weather.
- Supine and nocturnal hypertension in patients with OH may indicate an underlying autonomic dysfunction.

ETIOLOGY

- The assumption of an upright posture results in the pooling of approximately 500 mL of blood in the lower extremities due to gravity and decreased venous return, decreased cardiac output, and decreased arterial pressure. The consequent increase in sympathetic tone due to increased carotid baroreceptor activity causes arterial and venous constriction as well as positive inotropic and chronotropic effects, thereby limiting the fall in upright blood pressure. Peripheral vasoconstriction is also mediated by increased activity of the renin-angiotensin system and decreased activity of atrial natriuretic factor.
- Impairment of the baroreceptor reflex, as in central or peripheral autonomic dysfunction and aging, may cause OH because decreased

blood pressure cannot be counteracted by the aforementioned regulatory mechanisms.

 **DIAGNOSIS**

DIFFERENTIAL DIAGNOSIS

Common:
- Medications: antihypertensives, antidepressants (tricyclics), antipsychotics (phenothiazines), alcohol, narcotics, barbiturates, insulin, nitrates, PDE-5 inhibitors, alpha-adrenergic antagonists
- Reduced intravascular volume (hemorrhage, dehydration, hyperglycemia, hypoalbuminemia)
- Postprandial effect (especially in the elderly)
- Vasovagal syncope
- Deconditioning
- Central autonomic dysfunction (Parkinson's disease)
- Peripheral autonomic dysfunction (diabetes mellitus, Guillain-Barré syndrome)

Uncommon:
- Central autonomic dysfunction (Shy-Drager syndrome)
- Postganglionic autonomic dysfunction: impaired norepinephrine release
- Autoimmune autonomic dysfunction: nicotinic acetylcholine receptor autoantibodies
- Paraneoplastic autonomic dysfunction: anti-Hu antibodies (in small-cell lung cancer)
- Postural tachycardia syndrome (POTS): usually occurs in young women; an abnormally large increase in heart rate is observed in the upright position caused by increased venous pooling from autonomic dysfunction of the lower extremities, but blood pressure is not affected because of an excess of plasma norepinephrine
- Impaired cardiac output (myocardial infarction, aortic stenosis, arrhythmias)
- Cerebrovascular accident
- Adrenal insufficiency
- Deconditioning
- Carotid sinus hypersensitivity
- Anxiety, panic attacks
- Seizures
- Sepsis
- Idiopathic

WORKUP

- Measure supine blood pressure after the patient has been resting comfortably. The duration of time that the patient should spend supine and standing when measuring orthostatic hypotension is controversial. Limited evidence supports having the patient remain supine for 5 to 10 minutes before obtaining the supine blood pressure, followed by blood pressure measurement within 1 minute of standing and again after 3 minutes of standing. The blood pressure cuff must be held at the level of the right atrium; holding the cuff below this level will result in a 5 to 10 mm Hg underestimation of blood pressure.
- Thorough neurologic examination should be performed.
- Rule out treatable causes (e.g., medications, volume depletion).

LABORATORY TESTS

- Hemoglobin and hematocrit
- Consider when treatable causes of OH have been ruled out:
  1. Blood pressure and heart rate monitoring with a tilt table test
  2. Plasma norepinephrine measurements (to distinguish postganglionic from preganglionic autonomic dysfunction)
  3. Other methods, which use the Valsalva maneuver or measure sweating as indirect means of evaluating the autonomic nervous system

IMAGING STUDIES

None

Rx TREATMENT

NONPHARMACOLOGIC THERAPY

- Patient education (leg crossing, prolonged sitting before first standing in the morning, avoid excessive straining and hot baths)
- High-salt diet (e.g., bouillon cubes); caution if history of heart failure
- Liberal fluid intake
- Take needed antihypertensive medications at different times of the day
- Raise the head of the bed at night
- Compression stockings (to include splanchnic circulation)
- Multiple low-carbohydrate meals to avoid postprandial OH
- Avoid large carbohydrate loads and excess alcohol consumption

ACUTE GENERAL Rx

- Correction of volume status
- Review medication list and attempt to eliminate those potentially contributing to OH

CHRONIC Rx

- Fludrocortisone: 0.1 mg/day (may combine with an alpha-1 agonist to lower the dose of each); monitor for electrolyte disturbances and supine hypertension
- Midodrine (alpha-1 agonist): 10 mg three times a day; monitor for supine hypertension
- Erythropoietin (consider if anemic)
- Caffeine (for postprandial hypotension)

OTHER TREATMENTS

- Pyridostigmine (enhances renal sodium reabsorption): 0.2 to 0.6 mg/day (not FDA-approved for this indication)
- Octreotide: 300 to 600 mg/day (not FDA-approved for this indication)
- Indomethacin (prostaglandin inhibitor)
- DDAVP (experimental)
- Droxidopa (used for patients with autonomic dysfunction to increase the availability of norepinephrine) has been FDA approved for treatment of adults with symptomatic neurogenic orthostatic hypotension caused by primary autonomic failure or nondiabetic autonomic neuropathy

 PEARLS & CONSIDERATIONS

COMMENTS

- The presence of OH should always trigger a search for an underlying etiology.
- OH is diagnosed by observing changes in blood pressure, not heart rate.
- Volume depletion should cause an increased heart rate on standing; a lack of heart rate response in this setting suggests autonomic dysfunction.
- Pharmacotherapy with mineralocorticoids may require concomitant potassium replenishment and monitoring for hypertension.
- Evidence to support the efficacy of pharmacologic interventions to treat OH, including midodrine, is limited.
- The etiology of OH is often multifactorial in older patients, but increased susceptibility to volume depletion due to decreased baroreceptor reflexes frequently contributes.
- Evidence suggests that nursing home residents with more stringent SBP control (<140 mm Hg) have a lower risk of OH than nursing home residents with less stringent SBP control.
- The physical examination of patients with dizziness, gait disturbance, and/or falls should include an assessment for OH.
- Because OH may be asymptomatic, physical examination of those at risk must include assessment of blood pressure in both the supine and upright positions.

SUGGESTED READINGS

Available at www.expertconsult.com

AUTHOR: **TIMOTHY W. FARRELL, M.D., A.G.S.F.**

BASIC INFORMATION

DEFINITION

Osgood-Schlatter disease is painful swelling of the growing tibial tuberosity in adolescents.

SYNONYMS

Juvenile osteochondrosis

ICD-10CM CODES

M92.40 Juvenile osteochondrosis of patella, unspecified knee

EPIDEMIOLOGY & DEMOGRAPHICS

PREVALENCE: 4 cases/100 adolescents.
PREDOMINANT SEX: Male/female ratio of 3:1.
PREDOMINANT AGE: Males: age 12 to 15 years, females: age 8 to 12 years.

PHYSICAL FINDINGS & CLINICAL PRESENTATION

- Gradual onset of pain and swelling of the tibial tubercle.
- Worsening of pain after athletic activity.
- Reproduction of pain with resisted knee extension.

ETIOLOGY

- Repetitive microtrauma and avulsion of the developing ossification center of the tibial tuberosity.
- Anatomic variants such as patella alta.

DIAGNOSIS

DIFFERENTIAL DIAGNOSIS

- Stress fracture of the proximal tibia.
- Hoffa disease.
- Sinding-Larsen-Johansson syndrome.
- Patellar tendinitis.

WORKUP

- The diagnosis of Osgood-Schlatter disease is generally made on clinical grounds.
- Imaging may be indicated to exclude fracture or bony tumors.

IMAGING STUDIES

- Lateral x-rays may show separation and fragmentation of the upper tibial epiphysis (Fig. 10-12).
- Musculoskeletal ultrasound (Fig. 10-13) can also be used and may be helpful in evaluating soft tissue, tendons, and noncalcified cartilage.

TREATMENT

NONPHARMACOLOGIC THERAPY

- Activity modification with increased periods of rest.
- Physical therapy.

ACUTE GENERAL Rx

- Ice, especially after exercise.
- Nonsteroidal antiinflammatory drugs.
- Quadriceps stretching exercises.

DISPOSITION

- Condition usually heals when the epiphysis closes.
- 90% of patients respond to conservative treatment.
- Recent studies have shown promising results with the use of hyperosmolar dextrose injections in recalcitrant disease.
- Surgery is rarely needed in the treatment of Osgood-Schlatter disease, but can be used for relief of persistent symptoms in which patients have separated ossicles or an abnormally ossified tibial tuberosity.

REFERRAL

Orthopedic consultation is recommended when symptoms persist >6 to 8 weeks with conservative treatment.

PEARLS & CONSIDERATIONS

COMMENTS

Larsen-Johansson disease is a similar disorder. While the diagnosis of Osgood-Schlatter disease is clinical, imaging may be needed to rule out infection, fracture, and malignancy.

SUGGESTED READINGS

Available at www.expertconsult.com

RELATED CONTENT

Osgood-Schlatter Disease (Patient Information)

AUTHOR: **AMY L. LUNDHOLM, D.O.**

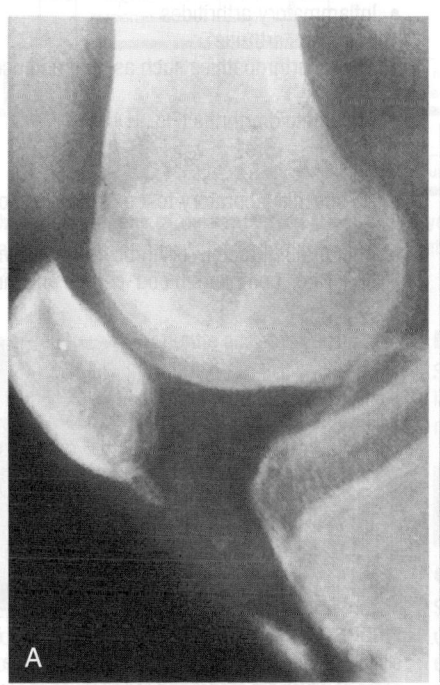
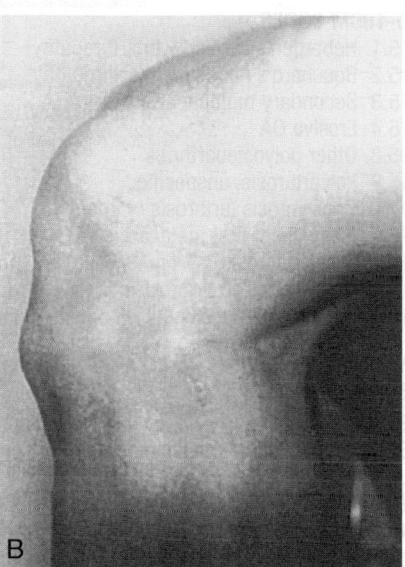

FIGURE 10-12 A, Radiograph of Osgood-Schlatter disease demonstrating thickening of patella tendon, fragmentation of the tibial tubercle, and soft tissue swelling. **B,** Clinical picture of bony prominence anteriorly at the tibial tubercle. (From Scuderi G [ed]: *Sports medicine: principles of primary care*, St Louis, 1997, Mosby.)

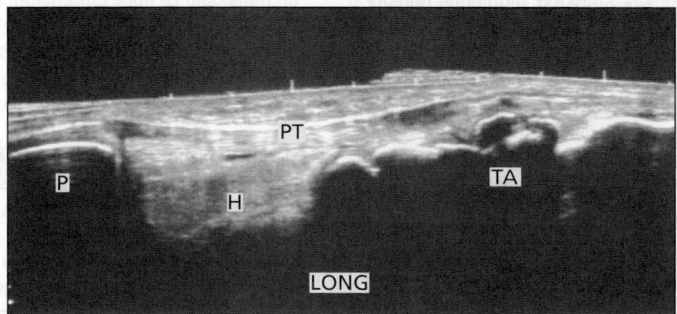

FIGURE 10-13 EFOV of a patient with Osgood-Schlatter disease in the long axis with a knee in extension showing irregularity and fragmentation of the distal tibial apophysis. *P,* Patella; TA, tibial apophysis, PT, patella tendon, H, Hoffa's fat. (From McNally E: *Practical musculoskeletal ultrasound*, ed 1, New York, 2005, Churchill Livingstone, p. 146.)

 BASIC INFORMATION

DEFINITION
Osteochondritis dissecans (OCD) refers to a localized necrosis of the bone with detachment of the overlying subchondral bone and cartilage. The suffix "-itis" is a misnomer, as the disease does not involve inflammation.

SYNONYMS
Osteochondrosis

Avascular necrosis (AVN), aseptic necrosis, ischemic necrosis—AVN and OCD have the same pathophysiology; AVN is a more generic term, whereas OCD is used specifically when a detached fragment of bone and/or cartilage is seen on imaging.

ICD-10CM CODES
M93.20	Osteochondritis dissecans of unspecified site
M93.211	Osteochondritis dissecans, right shoulder
M93.212	Osteochondritis dissecans, left shoulder
M93.219	Osteochondritis dissecans, unspecified shoulder
M93.221	Osteochondritis dissecans, right elbow
M93.222	Osteochondritis dissecans, left elbow
M93.229	Osteochondritis dissecans, unspecified elbow
M93.231	Osteochondritis dissecans, right wrist
M93.232	Osteochondritis dissecans, left wrist
M93.239	Osteochondritis dissecans, unspecified wrist
M93.241	Osteochondritis dissecans, joints of right hand
M93.242	Osteochondritis dissecans, joints of left hand
M93.249	Osteochondritis dissecans, joints of unspecified hand
M93.251	Osteochondritis dissecans, right hip
M93.252	Osteochondritis dissecans, left hip
M93.259	Osteochondritis dissecans, unspecified hip
M93.261	Osteochondritis dissecans, right knee
M93.262	Osteochondritis dissecans, left knee
M93.269	Osteochondritis dissecans, unspecified knee
M93.271	Osteochondritis dissecans, right ankle and joints of right foot
M93.272	Osteochondritis dissecans, left ankle and joints of left foot
M93.279	Osteochondritis dissecans, unspecified ankle and joints of foot
M93.28	Osteochondritis dissecans other site
M93.29	Osteochondritis dissecans multiple sites

ETIOLOGY & PATHOPHYSIOLOGY
- While the cause remains unknown, predisposing factors have been identified, including genetic predisposition, repetitive microtrauma, and single trauma followed by bone ischemia. The sequence of events likely entails bone injury, hypovascularization with defective repair, bone necrosis with structural collapse, and detachment of the overlying subchondral bone and cartilage.
- OCD is seen more often in children and adolescents and is more commonly associated with repetitive trauma and sports.

EPIDEMIOLOGY & DEMOGRAPHICS
PREVALENCE: 2 cases/10,000 persons.
PREDOMINANT SEX: Male/female ratio of 3:1.
PREDOMINANT AGE: Typically between 10 and 20 years of age.

CLINICAL PRESENTATION & PHYSICAL FINDINGS
- OCD most commonly affects the knee (75%) followed by the elbow (6%) and the ankle (4%); the other joints are affected in 15% of cases.
- Early lesions cause nonspecific pain with activity.
- As the disease progresses, stiffness and intermittent swelling occurs.
- Range of motion is usually intact in the knees.
- If a loose fragment becomes detached, it can cause locking or catching.
- Physical exam reveals tenderness at the site of the lesion; crepitus may also be present.
- When the knee is involved a positive Wilson sign can sometimes be found (pain with knee extension and internal rotation). Antalgic gait and limp can occur in chronic cases.
- Rare asymptomatic cases have been reported.

DX DIAGNOSIS

DIFFERENTIAL DIAGNOSIS
- Knee: torn meniscus, patellofemoral syndrome, medial plica syndrome, stress fracture.
- Elbow: Panner's disease, Little League elbow, epicondyle fracture, epicondylitis.
- Talus: ankle sprain, os trigonum tarsal coalition.

IMAGING STUDIES
- X-rays including "tunnel views" are the initial test of choice.
- Early, small lesions can look normal or show only increased subchondral bone density.
- The defining lesion of OCD is seen on x-ray as a subchondral bone fragment surrounded by a radiolucent, crescent-shaped line (Fig. 10-19).
- MRI (Fig. 10-20) is the most sensitive test (91%) and is useful to identify OCD in symptomatic patients with normal x-rays.
- Contrast is used to evaluate blood supply to the affected fragment, evaluating stability.

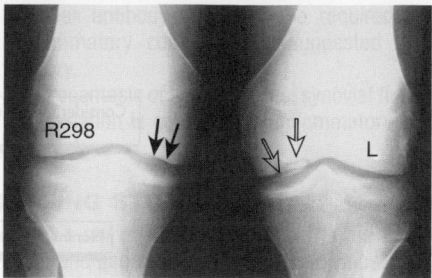

FIGURE 10-19 Bilateral, asymmetrical osteochondritis dissecans with a healed right lesion (black arrows) and an unhealed, unstable left lesion (open arrows) in a 17-year-old tennis player. (From DeLee D, Drez D [eds]: DeLee and Drez's orthopaedic sports medicine, ed 2, Philadelphia, 2003, Saunders.)

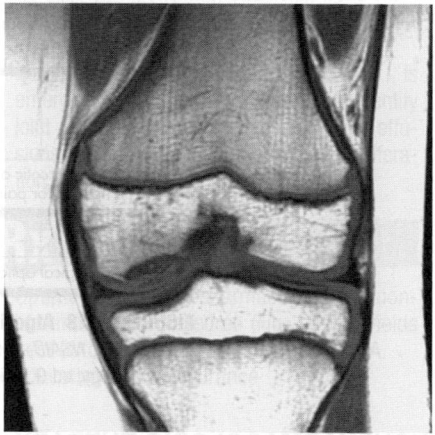

FIGURE 10-20 Osteochondritis dissecans (OCD). A coronal MRI of an OCD lesion of the medial femoral condyle. (From Frontera WR: Clinical sports medicine: medical management and rehabilitation, Philadelphia, 2006, Saunders.)

Rx TREATMENT

ACUTE GENERAL Rx
- Conservative management: usually indicated in juvenile OCD without an intraarticular foreign body and for adult patients who have a small, stable fragment.
- Non–weight bearing and immobilization for 4 to 6 weeks; physical therapy once healing starts.
- Surgery: indicated for juvenile OCD with a loose body and in cases that fail to improve after 4 to 6 months of conservative management; also indicated in adults with OCD.

DISPOSITION & PROGNOSIS
- Office follow-ups are initially frequent, every 2 weeks.
- X-ray changes should be monitored every 6 weeks while immobilized.
- Return to activity can be attempted once the patient is pain free and has an intact active full range of motion; it usually takes from 3 to 6 months.
- Once complete healing occurs, joint function usually returns to normal.
- Complete healing is frequent in skeletally immature children with small lesions (95%),

but in adults with larger lesions complete healing is less common (50%).

REFERRAL

- Orthopedic consultation for most symptomatic children and adults with OCD for staging and management options.
- Surgical options include arthroscopic drilling, fixation with Kirschner wires, special screws, and chondrocyte transplantation.

PEARLS & CONSIDERATIONS

COMMENTS

- Although inflammation is suggested by the name, it has not been shown to be of significance in this disorder. *Osteochondral lesion* or *osteochondrosis dissecans* may be

more appropriate terms to describe these disorders.
- Repetitive trauma with ischemic necrosis is the most likely cause.
- The condition is often bilateral, especially in the knee, which could suggest the possibility of an endocrine or genetic basis.
- This condition should always be considered in the patient whose "sprained ankle" does not improve over the usual course of treatment.

SUGGESTED READINGS

Available at www.expertconsult.com

RELATED CONTENT

Osteochondritis Dissecans (Patient Information)

AUTHOR: **DAN A. CRISTESCU, M.D.**

ℹ️ BASIC INFORMATION

DEFINITION

Osteoporosis is characterized by a progressive decrease in bone mass that results in increased bone fragility and a higher fracture risk. The various types are as follows:

PRIMARY OSTEOPOROSIS: Affects 80% of women and 60% of men with osteoporosis.

- Idiopathic osteoporosis: unknown pathogenesis; may occur in children and young adults
- Type I osteoporosis: may occur in postmenopausal women (ages 51-75); characterized by accelerated and disproportionate trabecular bone loss and associated with vertebral body and distal forearm fractures (estrogen withdrawal effect)
- Type II osteoporosis (involutional): occurs in both men and women aged >70 yr; characterized by both trabecular and cortical bone loss and associated with fractures of the proximal humerus and tibia, femoral neck, and pelvis

SECONDARY OSTEOPOROSIS: Affects 20% of women and 40% of men with osteoporosis; osteoporosis that exists as a common feature of another disease process, heritable disorder of connective tissue, or drug side effect (see "Differential Diagnosis")

ICD-10CM CODES
M81.0	Age-related osteoporosis without current pathological fracture
M81.4	Drug-induced osteoporosis
M81.5	Idiopathic osteoporosis
M81.6	Localized osteoporosis

EPIDEMIOLOGY & DEMOGRAPHICS

PREVALENCE (IN U.S.)
- <25 million men and women
- Twice as common in women
- Results in 1.5 million fractures annually (70% women)
- Osteoporosis-related fractures in 50% of women and 20% of men aged >65 yr
- Results: institutionalization, death, and costs in excess of $10 billion annually

RISK FACTORS
- Age: each decade after 40 yr associated with a fivefold increased risk

- Genetics:
  1. Ethnicity (white/Asian are affected more often than blacks, with Polynesians affected the least)
  2. Gender (females affected more often than males)
  3. Family history (hip fracture in first-degree relative)
- Environmental factors: poor nutrition, calcium deficiency, physical inactivity, medication (chronic corticosteroid use [>3 mo], PPIs, aromatase inhibitors, anticonvulsants, anticoagulants, SSRIs), tobacco use, alcohol use (>3 drinks/day), traumatic injury, high caffeine intake
- Chronic disease states: estrogen deficiency, androgen deficiency, hyperthyroidism, inflammatory bowel disease, diabetes mellitus, hypercortisolism, cirrhosis, malabsorption, gastrectomy, multiple myeloma

PHYSICAL FINDINGS & CLINICAL PRESENTATION
- Most commonly silent with no signs and symptoms
- Insidious and progressive development of dorsal kyphosis *(dowager's hump)*, loss of height, and skeletal pain typically associated with fracture; other physical findings related to other conditions with associated increased risk for osteoporosis (see "Risk Factors")

ETIOLOGY
- Primary osteoporosis: multifactorial, resulting from a combination of factors including nutrition, peak bone mass, genetics, level of physical activity, age of menopause (spontaneous vs. surgical), and estrogen status
- Secondary osteoporosis: associated decrease in bone mass resulting from an identified cause, including endocrinopathies, hypogonadism, hyperthyroidism, hyperparathyroidism, Cushing's syndrome, hyperprolactinemia, acromegaly, diabetes mellitus, gastrointestinal disease, malabsorption, primary biliary cirrhosis, gastrectomy, malnutrition (including anorexia nervosa), and medications (corticosteroids, PPIs, rosiglitazone, pioglitazone)
- Clinical risk factors used in WHO FRAX 10-year fracture risk calculator are summarized in Table 10-11

🇩ₓ DIAGNOSIS

DIFFERENTIAL DIAGNOSIS
- Malignancy (multiple myeloma, lymphoma, leukemia, metastatic carcinoma)
- Primary hyperparathyroidism
- Osteomalacia
- Paget's disease
- Osteogenesis imperfecta: types I, III, and IV (see also "Epidemiology & Demographics" and "Etiology")

WORKUP
- History and physical examination (20% of women with type I osteoporosis have associated secondary cause), with appropriate evaluation for identified risk factors and secondary causes
- Diagnosis of osteoporosis made by bone mineral density (BMD) determination (BMD should ideally evaluate the hip, spine, and wrist)
  1. Dual-energy x-ray absorptiometry (DEXA) is the gold standard for screening and monitoring changes in BMD due to excellent precision, widespread availability, low cost, and minimal radiation exposure. DEXA (Fig. 10-23) is indicated in all women 65 years and older and in postmenopausal women younger than 65 years of age who are at risk for fracture (e.g., weight <127 lbs, parental history of hip fracture, use of medications that cause bone loss, smoking, alcoholism, rheumatoid arthritis, or presence of diseases that cause bone loss). Causes of erroneous bone mineral density measures by DXA in the lumbar spine are summarized in Table 10-12.
- Recommendations as to when to repeat bone density testing should be based on initial T scores (Fig. 10-24). Data from the Study of Osteoporotic Fractures indicates

TABLE 10-12 Causes of Erroneous Bone Mineral Density Measures by DXA in the Lumbar Spine

Overestimation of Bone Mineral Density

Extraneous calcification (lymph nodes, aorta)
Degenerative disk and spine disease (osteophytes)
Ankylosing spondylitis
Vertebral fracture
Sclerotic metastases
Vertebral hemangioma
Overlying metal artifacts (navel rings)
Surgical interventions (metallic rods, spinal fusion)
Vertebroplasty
Paget disease
Treatment with strontium ranelate

Underestimation of Bone Mineral Density

Laminectomy

From Pope TL, Bloem HL, Beltran J, Morrison WB, Wilson DJ: *Musculoskeletal imaging*, ed 2, Philadelphia, 2014, Saunders.

TABLE 10-11 1994 WHO Criteria for the Diagnosis of Osteoporosis Based on the Measurement of Bone Density and T Score Equivalent Cut Points

Diagnostic Category	Standard Deviations Below the Young-Adult Mean	T Score
Normal	≤1 SD	Equal to or better than −1
Osteopenia (low bone mass)	Between 1 and 2.5 SD	Between −1 and −2.5
Osteoporosis	≥2.5 SD	Equal to or poorer than −2.5
Severe (established) osteoporosis	≥2.5 SD + a fragility fracture	Equal to or poorer than −2.5 + a fragility fracture

From Hochberg MC et al: *Rheumatology*, ed 5, St Louis, 2011, Mosby.

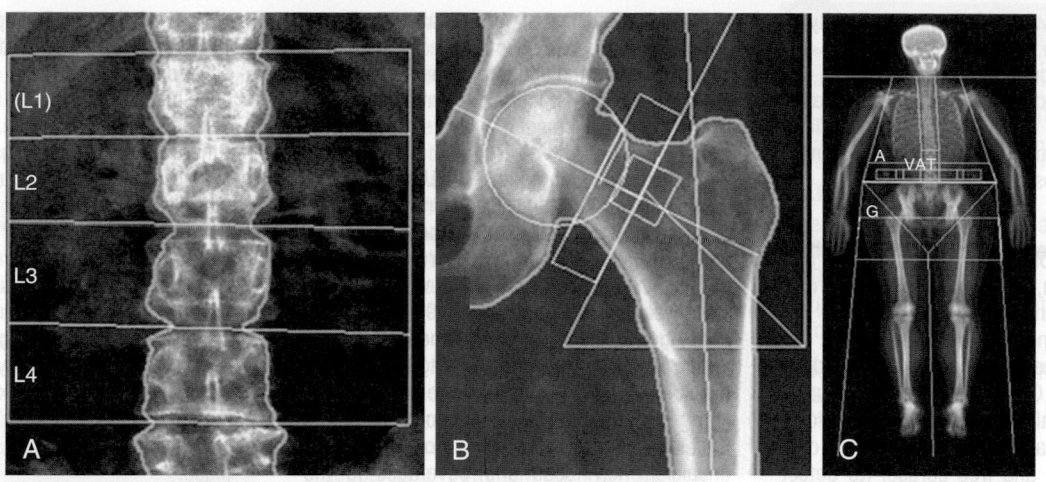

FIGURE 10-23 Dual-energy X-ray absorptiometry (DXA) provides "areal" bone mineral density (BMD) (g/cm^2) and is currently the gold standard for diagnosis of osteoporosis by bone densitometry (World Health Organization definition T score −2.5 or below) in (**A**) posteroanterior lumbar spine (L1-4) or (**B**) hip (femoral neck or total). **C,** DXA of the whole body can provide information on total and regional BMD and body composition (fat and muscle mass). Recent additional parameters measured are android A/gynoid G ratio and visceral adipose tissue (VAT). (Pope TL, Bloem HL, Beltran J, Morrison WB, Wilson DJ: *Musculoskeletal imaging,* ed 2, Philadelphia, 2014, Saunders.)

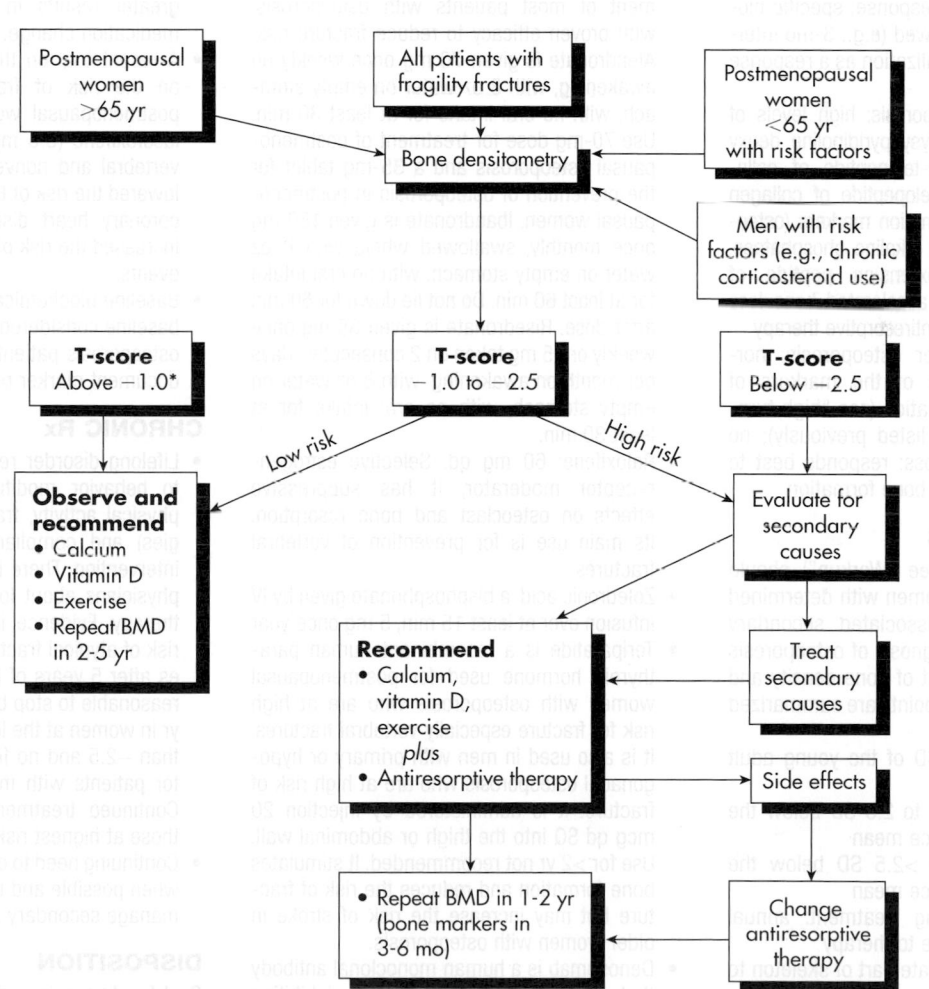

*Patients with fragility fractures and a T-score above −1.0 should be evaluated for other causes of pathologic fracture.

FIGURE 10-24 Diagnosis and management of osteoporosis. The diagram outlines an approach based largely on evidence from studies of postmenopausal white women, with dual-energy x-ray absorptiometry used to measure bone mineral density *(BMD).* Its application to other populations, including patients with secondary osteoporosis and other methods of assessing BMD, is not established. (Modified from Larsen PR et al: *Williams textbook of endocrinology,* ed 11, Philadelphia, 2008, Saunders.)

BASIC INFORMATION

DEFINITION

Otitis externa refers to a variety of conditions causing inflammation and/or infection of the external auditory canal (and/or auricle and tympanic membrane). There are six subgroups of otitis externa:

1. Acute localized otitis externa (furunculosis)
2. Acute diffuse bacterial otitis externa (i.e., "swimmer's ear")
3. Chronic otitis externa
4. Eczematous otitis externa
5. Fungal otitis externa (otomycosis)
6. Invasive or necrotizing (malignant) otitis externa (Fig. 10-25)

SYNONYMS

See "Definition."

ICD-10CM CODES
H60.90 Unspecified otitis externa, unspecified ear
H60.2   Malignant otitis externa
H60.3   Other infective otitis externa
H60.5   Acute otitis externa, non-infective
H60.8   Other otitis externa

EPIDEMIOLOGY & DEMOGRAPHICS

INCIDENCE (IN U.S.):
- Among the most common disorders
- Affects 3% to 10% of patients seeking otologic care

PREVALENCE (IN U.S.):
- Diffuse otitis externa is most often seen in swimmers and in hot, humid climates, conditions that lead to water retention in the ear canal. In the United States, 44% of AOE-related healthcare visits occur June to August.
- Necrotizing otitis externa is more common in elderly, diabetics, and immunocompromised patients.

PREDOMINANT SEX: None
PREDOMINANT AGE:
- Occurs at all ages
- Necrotizing otitis externa: typically occurs in elderly: mean age >65 yr

PHYSICAL FINDINGS & CLINICAL PRESENTATION

The two most common symptoms are otalgia, ranging from pruritus to severe pain exacerbated by motion (e.g., chewing), and otorrhea. Patients may also experience aural fullness and hearing loss as a result of swelling with occlusion of the canal. More intense symptoms may occur with bacterial otitis externa, with or without fever, and lymphadenopathy (anterior to tragus). Findings unique to specific forms of the infection include:

- Acute localized otitis externa (furunculosis):
  1. Occurs from infected hair follicles, usually in the outer third of the ear canal, forming pustules and furuncles
  2. Furuncles are superficial and pointing or deep and diffuse
- Impetigo:
  1. In contrast to furunculosis, this is a superficial spreading infection of the ear canal that may also involve the concha and the auricle
  2. Begins as a small blister that ruptures, releasing straw-colored fluid that dries as a golden crust
- Erysipelas:
  1. Caused by group A *Streptococcus*
  2. May involve the concha and canal
  3. May involve the dermis and deeper tissues
  4. Area of cellulitis, often with severe pain
  5. Fever, chills, malaise
  6. Regional adenopathy
- Eczematous or seborrheic otitis externa:
  1. Stems from a variety of dermatologic problems that can involve the external auditory canal

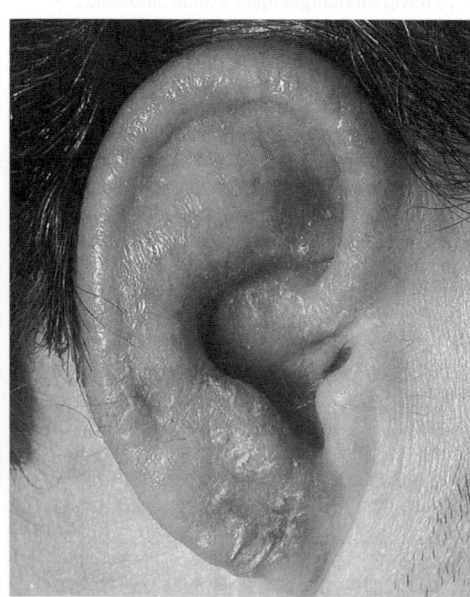

FIGURE 10-25 Malignant external otitis. Severe infection of the ear has occurred after months of chronic inflammation of the pinna. (From Habif TP: *Clinical dermatology: a color guide to diagnosis and therapy*, ed 3, St Louis, 1996, Mosby.)

2. Severe itching, erythema, scaling, crusting, and fissuring possible
- Acute diffuse otitis externa (swimmer's ear):
  1. Begins with itching and a feeling of pressure and fullness in the ear that becomes increasingly tender and painful
  2. Mild erythema and edema of the external auditory canal, which may cause narrowing and occlusion of the canal, leading to hearing loss
  3. Minimal serous secretions, which may become profuse and purulent
  4. Tympanic membrane may appear dull and infected
  5. Usually absence of systemic symptoms such as fever, chills
- Otomycosis:
  1. Chronic superficial infection of the ear canal and tympanic membrane
  2. In primary fungal infection, major symptom is intense itching
  3. In secondary infection (fungal infection superimposed on bacterial infection), major symptom is pain
  4. Fungal growth of variety of colors
- Chronic otitis externa:
  1. Dry and atrophic canal
  2. Typically lack of cerumen
  3. Itching, often severe, and mild discomfort rather than pain
  4. Occasionally mucopurulent discharge
  5. With time, thickening of the walls of the canal, causing narrowing of the lumen
- Necrotizing otitis externa (also known as malignant otitis externa). Typically seen in older patients with diabetes or in patients who are immunocompromised.
  1. Redness, swelling, and tenderness of the ear canal
  2. Classic finding of granulation tissue on the floor of the canal and the bone–cartilage junction
  3. Small ulceration of necrotic soft tissue at bone–cartilage junction
  4. Most common symptoms: pain (often severe) and otorrhea
  5. Lessening of purulent drainage as infection advances
  6. Facial nerve palsy often the first and only cranial nerve defect
  7. Possible involvement of other cranial nerves

ETIOLOGY
- Acute localized otitis externa: *Staphylococcus aureus*
- Impetigo:
  1. *S. aureus* including MRSA
  2. *Streptococcus pyogenes*
- Erysipelas: *S. pyogenes*
- Eczematous otitis externa:
  1. Seborrheic dermatitis
  2. Atopic dermatitis
  3. Psoriasis
  4. Neurodermatitis
  5. Lupus erythematosus

- Acute diffuse otitis externa:
  1. Swimming
  2. Hot, humid climates
  3. Tightly fitting hearing aids
  4. Use of ear plugs
  5. *Pseudomonas aeruginosa*
  6. *S. aureus* including MRSA
- Otomycosis:
  1. Prolonged use of topical antibiotics and steroid preparations
  2. Uncontrolled diabetes mellitus can contribute to risk
  3. *Aspergillus* (80% to 90%)
  4. *Candida*
- Chronic otitis externa: persistent low-grade infection and inflammation
- Necrotizing otitis externa (NOE):
  1. Complication of persistent otitis externa
  2. Extends through Santorini's fissures, small apertures at the bone-cartilage junction of the canal, into the mastoid and along the base of the skull
  3. *P. aeruginosa*

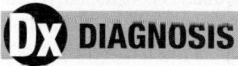 **DIAGNOSIS**

DIFFERENTIAL DIAGNOSIS

- Acute otitis media
- Bullous myringitis
- Mastoiditis
- Foreign bodies
- Neoplasms
- Contact dermatitis
- Eczema
- Ramsey-Hunt syndrome
- Seborrhea
- Otomycosis
- Referred pain

WORKUP

Thorough history and physical examination

LABORATORY TESTS

- Cultures from the canal are usually not necessary unless the condition does not respond to treatment.
- Leukocyte count normal or mildly elevated.
- Erythrocyte sedimentation rate is often quite elevated in malignant otitis externa.

IMAGING STUDIES

- CT scan is the best technique for defining bone involvement and extent of disease in malignant otitis externa.
- MRI is slightly more sensitive in evaluation of soft tissue changes and intracranial extension of infection.
- Gallium scans are more specific than bone scans in diagnosing NOE.
- Follow-up scans are helpful in determining efficacy of treatment.

NOTE: Expert opinion supports history and physical examination as the best means of diagnosis. Persistent pain that is constant and severe should raise the question of NOE (particularly in the elderly, diabetics, and immunocompromised patients).

 **TREATMENT**

NONPHARMACOLOGIC THERAPY

- Cleansing and debridement of the ear canal with cotton swabs and hydrogen peroxide or other antiseptic solution allows a more thorough examination of the ear.
- If the canal lumen is edematous and too narrow to allow adequate cleansing, a cotton wick or gauze strip inserted into the canal serves as a conduit for topical medications to be drawn into the canal. Usually remove wick after 2 days.
- Local heat is useful in treating deep furunculosis.
- Incision and drainage is indicated in treatment of superficial pointing furunculosis.

ACUTE GENERAL Rx

Topical medications:

- An acidifying agent such as 2% acetic acid (Vosol) inhibits growth of bacteria and fungi
- Topical antibiotics (in the form of otic or ophthalmic solutions) or antifungals, often in combination with an acidifying agent and a steroid preparation
- The following are some of the available preparations:
  1. Neomycin otic solutions and suspensions:
     a. With polymyxin-B-hydrocortisone (Cortisporin)
     b. With hydrocortisone-thonzonium (Coly-Mycin S)
  2. Polymyxin-B-hydrocortisone (Otobiotic)
  3. Quinolone otic solutions:
     a. Ofloxacin 0.3% solution (Floxin Otic)
     b. Ciprofloxacin 0.3% with hydrocortisone (Cipro HC)
  4. Quinolone ophthalmic solutions:
     a. Ofloxacin 0.3% (Ocuflox)
     b. Ciprofloxacin 0.3% (Ciloxan)
  5. Aminoglycoside ophthalmic solutions:
     a. Gentamicin sulfate 0.3% (Garamycin)
     b. Tobramycin sulfate 0.3% (Tobrex)
     c. Tobramycin 0.3% and dexamethasone 0.1% (TobraDex)
  6. Chloramphenicol 0.5% otic solution or 0.25% ophthalmic solution (Chloromycetin)
  7. Gentian violet (methylrosaniline chloride 1%, 2%)
  8. Antifungals:
     a. Amphotericin B 3% (Fungizone lotion)
     b. Clotrimazole 1% solution (Lotrimin)
     c. Tolnaftate 1% (Tinactin)
- Topical preparations should be applied qid (bid for quinolones, antifungals), generally for 3 days after cessation of symptoms (average 10 to 14 days total)

Systemic antibiotics:

- Reserved for when the infection has spread beyond the ear canal
- Treatment usually for 10 days with ciprofloxacin 750 mg q12h or ofloxacin 400 mg q12h, or with antistaphylococcal agent (e.g., dicloxacillin or cephalexin 500 mg q6h). Use Bactrim or clindamycin when MRSA suspected or cultured at one DS twice a day instead

of cephalexin or dicloxacillin. For malignant otitis externa (due to *Pseudomonas aeruginosa* in >90% of cases), effective agents are imipenem-cilastatin 0.5 g IV q6h or ciprofloxacin 400 mg IV q12h or 750 mg PO q12h or cefepime 2 g q12h.

Treatment for NOE:

- Requires prolonged therapy up to 3 mo; whether to use oral parenteral therapy based on clinical judgment
- Oral quinolones, ciprofloxacin 750 mg q12h or ofloxacin 400 mg q12h may be appropriate initial therapy or used to shorten the course of IV therapy
- Intravenous antipseudomonals with or without aminoglycosides are also appropriate
- Local debridement

Pain control:

- May require NSAIDs or opioids
- Topical corticosteroids to reduce swelling and inflammation

CHRONIC Rx

- Patients prone to recurrent infections should try to identify and avoid precipitants to infection.
- Swimmers should try tight-fitting ear plugs or tight-fitting bathing caps and remove all excess water from the ears after swimming.
- Treat underlying systemic diseases and dermatologic conditions that predispose to infection.

DISPOSITION

Inadequate treatment of otitis externa may lead to NOE and mastoiditis.

REFERRAL

To an otolaryngologist:

- NOE
- Treatment failure
- Severe pain

PEARLS & CONSIDERATIONS

Otitis externa varies in severity from a mild irritation of the external acoustic canal (swimmer's ear) that resolves spontaneously by simply removing the offending agent (stay out of fresh water or wear ear plugs when swimming) to a life-threatening infection with the risk of intracranial extension, gram-negative bacterial meningitis, and severe neurologic impairment with multiple cranial neuropathy. Do not miss severe malignant otitis externa in patients who are diabetic or immunocompromised.

SUGGESTED READINGS

Available at www.expertconsult.com

RELATED CONTENT

Otitis Externa (Patient Information)

AUTHOR: **RUSSELL J. MCCULLOH, M.D.**

BASIC INFORMATION

DEFINITION
Otitis media is the rapid onset of signs and symptoms of inflammation in the middle ear.

SYNONYMS
Acute suppurative otitis media
Purulent otitis media
Acute otitis media
AOM

ICD-10CM CODES
H65.0 Acute serous otitis media
H65.1 Other acute nonsuppurative otitis media
H65.9 Nonsuppurative otitis media, unspecified
H65.2 Chronic serous otitis media
H65.3 Chronic mucoid otitis media
H65.6 Other chronic nonsuppurative otitis media
H66.0 Acute suppurative otitis media
H66.4 Suppurative otitis media, unspecified
H66.9 Otitis media, unspecified
H66.1 Chronic tubotympanic suppurative otitis media
H66.2 Chronic atticoantral suppurative otitis media

EPIDEMIOLOGY & DEMOGRAPHICS
INCIDENCE (IN U.S.):
- Affects patients of all ages but is largely a disease of infants and young children.
- Affects approximately 80% of all children by age 5 yr.
- Occurs three or more times in one third of all children by age 3 yr.
- Costs associated with otitis media exceed $5 billion, with 40% of the costs occurring from patients ages 1 to 3
- From 1995 to 2006, 80% of children diagnosed with otitis media received an antibiotic at initial visit.
- Nearly 1 in 14 children prescribed an antibiotic for AOM experiences an adverse drug event (e.g., nausea, vomiting, rash, etc.) due to antibiotic use.

PEAK INCIDENCE:
- Between 9 and 15 mo
- Second peak between ages 4 and 6 yr
- Fall, winter, early spring (coincident with peak respiratory virus prevalence in the community)

PREDOMINANT SEX: Males

PREDOMINANT AGE:
- 47% to 60% of all children have their first episode of otitis media during their first year of life and 80% by their fifth birthday.
- Incidence of infection declines with age; seen infrequently in adults.

GENETICS: Familial disposition:
- Native Americans
- Eskimos
- Australian aborigines
- Those with a strong family history
- Immune globulin G (IgG) or subclass deficiencies Congenital infection: high incidence in children born with cleft palates and other craniofacial abnormalities

Other risk factors:
- Day care attendance
- Limited or lack of breastfeeding
- Tobacco smoke exposure

PHYSICAL FINDINGS & CLINICAL PRESENTATION
- Moderate to severe bulging of the tympanic membrane
- Fluid in the middle ear along with signs and symptoms of local inflammation (Figs. 10-26 and 10-27).
  1. Erythema with diminished light reflex
- As infection progresses, middle ear exudation occurs (exudative phase); the exudate rapidly changes from serous to purulent (suppurative phase).
  1. Retraction and poor motility of the tympanic membrane, which then becomes bulging and convex
- At any time during the suppurative phase the tympanic membrane may rupture, releasing the middle ear contents (otorrhea).
- Erythema of the tympanic membrane without other abnormalities is not a diagnostic criterion for acute otitis media (AOM) because it may occur with any inflammation of the upper respiratory tract, crying, or nose blowing.

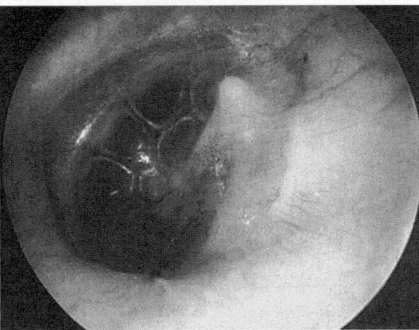

FIGURE 10-26 Otitis media with effusion of left ear. Retracted eardrum, prominent short process of malleus, and air bubbles seen anteriorly through the tympanic membrane. (From Behrman RE: *Nelson textbook of pediatrics,* ed 16, Philadelphia, 1996, Saunders.)

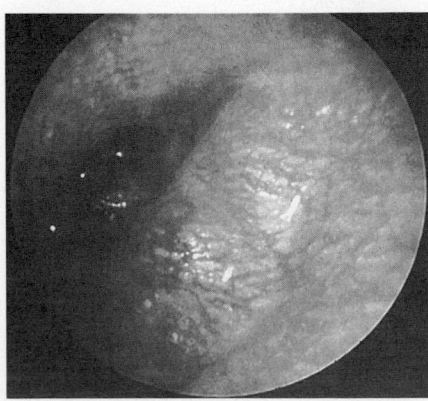

FIGURE 10-27 Acute left otitis media. (From Behrman RE: *Nelson textbook of pediatrics,* ed 16, Philadelphia, 1996, Saunders.)

- Symptoms:
  1. Rapid- or recent-onset otalgia, ranging from slight discomfort to severe, spreading to the temporal region
  2. Ear stuffiness and hearing loss may precede or follow otalgia
  3. Otorrhea if tympanic membrane has ruptured
  4. Vertigo, nystagmus, tinnitus, fever, lethargy, irritability, nausea, vomiting, anorexia
- After an episode of AOM:
  1. Persistence of effusion for weeks or months (called secretory, serous, or nonsuppurative otitis media)
  2. Fever and otalgia usually absent
  3. Hearing loss possible (10 to 50 dB, with predominant involvement of the low frequencies)

ETIOLOGY
- Most common etiologic factor is a viral upper respiratory tract infection, which causes inflammation and dysfunction of the eustachian tube and transient aspiration of nasopharyngeal secretions into the middle ear. Bacterial colonization from the nasopharynx in conjunction with eustachian tube dysfunction leads to infection.
- May occasionally develop as a result of hematogenous spread or by direct invasion from the nasopharynx.
- Conjugated pneumococcal vaccination of children has resulted in decreases in *Streptococcus pneumoniae* causing AOM.
- Most common bacterial pathogens:
  1. *S. pneumoniae* causes 30% to 40% of cases and is the least likely of the major pathogens to resolve without treatment
  2. *Haemophilus influenzae* causes up to 50% of cases
  3. *Moraxella catarrhalis* causes 10% to 20% of cases
  4. Of increasing importance, infection caused by penicillin-nonsusceptible *S. pneumoniae* (MIC >0.1 mg/ml), ranging from 8% to 34%. About 50% of PNSSP isolates are penicillin-intermediate (MIC 0.1 to 2.0 mg/ml)
- Viral pathogens:
  1. Respiratory syncytial virus
  2. Rhinovirus
  3. Adenovirus
  4. Influenza
- Others:
  1. *Mycoplasma pneumoniae*
  2. *Chlamydia trachomatis*

DIAGNOSIS

DIFFERENTIAL DIAGNOSIS
- Otitis externa
- Otitis media with effusion (OME)
- Referred pain
  1. Mouth
  2. Nasopharynx
  3. Tonsils
  4. Other parts of the upper respiratory tract
- Section II describes the differential diagnosis of earache

WORKUP

Thorough otoscopic examination. Adequate visualization of the tympanic membrane may require removal of cerumen and debris.

- Tympanometry
  1. Measures compliance of the tympanic membrane and middle ear pressure
  2. Detects the presence of fluid
- Acoustic reflectometry
  1. Measures sound waves reflected from the middle ear
  2. Useful in infants >3 mo
  3. Increased reflected sound correlated with the presence of effusion
  4. Tympanometry and acoustic reflectometry are useful in detection of middle ear effusion but do not provide information regarding infection/inflammation

LABORATORY TESTS

- Tympanocentesis
  1. Not necessary in most cases because the microbiology of middle ear effusions has been shown to be quite consistent
  2. May be indicated in:
     a. Highly toxic patients
     b. Patients who do not respond to treatment in 48 to 72 hr
     c. Immunocompromised patients
- Cultures of the nasopharynx: sensitive but not specific
- Blood counts (generally not necessary): usually show a leukocytosis with polymorphonuclear elevation
- Plain mastoid radiographs: generally not indicated; will reveal haziness in the periantral cells that may extend to entire mastoid
- CT or MRI may be indicated if serious complications suspected (meningitis, brain abscess, severe mastoiditis)

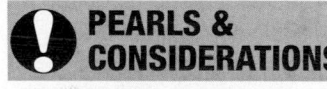

Rx TREATMENT

ACUTE GENERAL Rx

Hydration, avoidance of irritants (e.g., tobacco smoke), nasal systemic decongestants, cool mist humidifier
Antimicrobials:
NOTE: Most uncomplicated cases of AOM resolve spontaneously, without complications. Studies have demonstrated limited therapeutic benefit from antibiotic therapy. Watchful waiting is appropriate for children who look well, can be comforted with supportive care, and are old enough to easily evaluate. Children <24 mo with bilateral AOM should receive antibiotic therapy. Children with severe signs or symptoms (moderate or severe otalgia or otalgia for ≥48 hr or temperature ≥39°C) should also receive antibiotic therapy. When opting to use antibiotic therapy:

- Amoxicillin remains the drug of choice for first-line treatment of uncomplicated AOM despite increasing prevalence of drug-resistant *S. pneumoniae.*

- Treatment failure is defined by lack of clinical improvement of signs or symptoms after 3 days of therapy.
- With treatment failure, in the absence of an identified etiologic pathogen, therapy should be redirected to cover:
  1. Drug-resistant *S. pneumoniae*
  2. β-lactamase–producing strains of *H. influenzae* and *M. catarrhalis*
- Agents fulfilling these criteria include amoxicillin/clavulanate, second-generation (e.g., cefuroxime axetil, cefaclor) or third-generation cephalosporins (e.g., oral cefdinir or cefpodoxime or IM ceftriaxone). Do not use cefaclor, cefixime, loracarbef, and ceftibuten given limited activity against pneumococci.
- TMP/SMX and macrolides have been used as first- and second-line agents, but pneumococcal resistance to these agents is rising (up to 25% resistance to TMP/SMX and up to 10% resistance to erythromycin).
- Cross-resistance between these drugs and the β-lactams exists; therefore patients who do not respond to amoxicillin are more likely to have infections resistant to TMP/SMX and macrolides.
- Fluoroquinolones are not indicated as first- or second-line therapy for AOM and should be avoided in young children due to risks of musculoskeletal effects and lack of dosing guidance.
- Treatment should be modified according to cultures and sensitivities when available.
- Generally treatment course is 10 days for children <2 yr and those with severe symptoms, 7 days for children age 2 to 5 yr, and 5 to 7 days for children ≥6 yr.
- Follow up should be tailored to clinical improvement and concern for neurocognitive development delays in at-risk children. Standard follow-up of all cases is no longer required.
- Antibiotic prophylaxis to reduce the frequency of AOM episodes in children with recurrent AOM is not recommended.
  NOTE: Effusions may persist for 8 wk or longer in many cases of adequately treated otitis media.

SURGICAL Rx

- No evidence to support the routine use of myringotomy, but in severe cases it provides prompt pain relief and accelerates resolution of infection.
- Purulent secretions retained in the middle ear can lead to increased pressure that may lead to spread of infection to contiguous areas. Myringotomy to decompress the middle ear is sometimes necessary to avoid complications.
- Complications include mastoiditis, facial nerve paralysis, labyrinthitis, meningitis, and brain abscess.
- Other procedures used for drainage of the middle ear include insertion of a ventilation tube and/or simple mastoidectomy.

CHRONIC Rx

- Myringotomy and tympanostomy tube placement for persistent or recurrent middle ear effusion unresponsive to medical therapy for ≥3 mo if bilateral or ≥6 mo if unilateral.
- Adenoidectomy, with or without tonsillectomy, often advocated for treatment of recurrent otitis media, although indications for this procedure are controversial.
- Long-term complications include tympanic membrane perforations, cholesteatoma, tympanosclerosis, ossicular necrosis, toxic or suppurative labyrinthitis, hearing loss, and intracranial suppuration.

DISPOSITION

Patients can be treated at home as outpatients with the rare exception of patients with evidence of local suppurative complications (e.g., meningitis, acute mastoiditis, brain abscess, cavernous sinus, or lateral vein thrombosis).

REFERRAL

- To otorhinolaryngologist if:
  1. Medical treatment failure
  2. Diagnosis uncertain: adults with one or more episodes of otitis media should be referred for ear-nose-throat evaluation to rule out underlying process (e.g., malignancy)
  3. Any of the above-mentioned acute and chronic complications

! PEARLS & CONSIDERATIONS

COMMENTS

- Otoscopic findings are critical for accurate AOM diagnosis. AOM microbiology has changed with use of pneumococcal conjugate vaccine (PCV13). Antibiotics are modestly more effective than no treatment but cause adverse effects in 4% to 10% of children. Most antibiotics have comparable clinical success.
Prevention:
- Multiple component conjugate vaccines have helped decrease recurrent episodes of AOM
- Breastfeed and bottle-feed infants in an upright position
- Avoidance of irritants (e.g., tobacco smoke)

EBM EVIDENCE

SUGGESTED READINGS

Available at www.expertconsult.com

AUTHOR: **RUSSELL J. MCCULLOH, M.D.**

 BASIC INFORMATION

DEFINITION

Ovarian tumors can be benign, requiring operative intervention but not recurring or metastasizing; malignant, recurring, metastasizing, and having decreased survival; or borderline, having a small risk of recurrence or metastases and generally having a good prognosis. An emerging concept is the possibility that many ovarian cancers have origins on nonovarian tissues such as distal fallopian tube and endometriotic implants.

SYNONYMS

Epithelial ovarian cancer
Germ cell tumor
Sex cord stromal tumor
Ovarian tumor of low malignant potential

ICD-10CM CODES

C56.9 Malignant neoplasm of unspecified ovary
C56.1 Malignant neoplasm of right ovary
C56.2 Malignant neoplasm of left ovary

EPIDEMIOLOGY & DEMOGRAPHICS

INCIDENCE: 12.9 to 15.1 cases/100,000 persons; ~25,000 new cases annually. Lifetime risk for developing ovarian cancer is 1.4%. It is the leading cause of gynecologic cancer-related deaths.
PREVALENCE: Median age of 63 yr; peaks at age 75 to 79 yr (54/100,000)
RISK FACTORS: Low parity, delayed childbearing, smoking, polycystic ovary syndrome, endometriosis, use of talc on the perineum (unlikely), high-fat diet, fertility drugs (unlikely), Lynch II syndrome (nonpolyposis colon cancer, endometrial cancer, breast cancer, and ovarian cancer clusters in first- and second-degree relatives), breast-ovarian familial cancer syndrome, site-specific familial ovarian cancer. Factors that decrease the risk of ovarian cancer include previous pregnancy, oral contraceptive pill use, hystorectomy, tubal ligation.

GENETICS: The greatest risk factors of ovarian cancer are a family history and associated genetic syndromes. Familial susceptibility has been shown with the *BRCA1* gene located on 17q12 to 21. This correlates with breast-ovarian cancer syndrome.

PHYSICAL FINDINGS & CLINICAL PRESENTATION

- 60% present with advanced disease
- Abdominal fullness, early satiety, dyspepsia
- Pelvic pain, back pain, constipation
- Pelvic or abdominal mass
- Lymphadenopathy (inguinal)
- Sister Mary Joseph nodule (umbilical mass)

ETIOLOGY

- Can be inherited as site-specific familial ovarian cancer (two or more first-degree relatives have ovarian cancer)
- Breast-ovarian cancer syndrome (clusters of breast and ovarian cancer among first- and second-degree relatives)
- Lynch syndrome
- No family history and unknown etiology in the majority of ovarian cancer cases

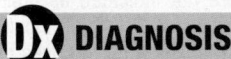 DIAGNOSIS

DIFFERENTIAL DIAGNOSIS

- Primary peritoneal cancer mesothelioma
- Benign ovarian tumor
- Functional ovarian cyst
- Endometriosis
- Ovarian torsion
- Pelvic kidney
- Pedunculated uterine fibroid
- Primary cancer from breast, gastrointestinal tract, or other pelvic organ metastasized to the ovary

WORKUP

- Definitive diagnosis made at laparotomy; epithelial ovarian cancer most common type of ovarian cancer (95% of ovarian cancer)

- Careful physical and history, including family history
- Exclusion of nongynecologic etiologies
- Observation of small cystic masses in premenopausal women for regression for 2 mo
- FIGO classification of ovarian carcinoma is described in Table 10-14.

LABORATORY TESTS

- Complete blood count
- Chemistry profile
- CA-125 or lysophosphatidic acid level. Use of these tests for annual screening is controversial, and most experts warn against universal screening with this marker. Only about 50% of early-stage ovarian cancers will be associated with elevated CA-125. Additionally, false elevations may occur with uterine leiomyoma, endometriosis, pregnancy, and intraabdominal infections. The PLCO cancer screening trial revealed that annual screening based on CA-125 and vaginal ultrasound is ineffective and diagnostic follow-up of false positives resulted in 15% serious complication rate.
- Consider: human chorionic gonadotropin, inhibin, alpha-fetoprotein, neuron-specific enolase, and lactate dehydrogenase in patients at risk for germ cell tumors.
- A panel of 3 serum biomarkers (apolipoprotein A-1 [ApoA-1], transthyretin [TTR], and transferrin [TF]) has been reported useful in distinguishing normal samples from early-stage ovarian cancer with a sensitivity of 84% and normal samples from late-stage ovarian cancer with a sensitivity of 97%.
- *BRCA1/2* testing is recommended for all women with ovarian cancer.

IMAGING STUDIES

- Ultrasound
- Chest x-ray
- CT or MRI of abdomen and pelvis help evaluate extent of disease (Fig. 10-29)
- Mammogram

TABLE 10-14   FIGO Classification of Ovarian Carcinoma

Stage I	Growth limited to the ovaries:
	Stage IA: Growth limited to one ovary, no ascites and no tumor present on the external surface; capsule intact
	Stage IB: Growth limited to both ovaries, no ascites and no tumor present on the external surface; capsule intact
	Stage IC: Stage 1A or 1B where there is tumor on the surface of either ovary; or with ruptured capsules or with ascites containing malignant cells or positive peritoneal washings. Surgical spillage of a malignant cyst upgrades the patient to IC, although it is unlikely that this event affects prognosis.
Stage II	Growth involving one or both ovaries with pelvic extension:
	Stage IIA: Extension and/or metastases to the uterus and tubes
	Stage IIB: Extension to other pelvic tissues
	Stage IIC: Stage IIA or IIB with tumor on the surface of either ovary or positive peritoneal washings or malignant ascites
Stage III	Growth involving one or both ovaries with peritoneal implants outside the pelvis or positive retroperitoneal or inguinal lymph nodes:
	Stage IIIA: Microscopic seeding of abdominal peritoneal surfaces
	Stage IIIB: Macroscopic disease outside the pelvis less than 2 cm in diameter
	Stage IIIC: Abdominal implants greater than 2 cm and/or positive nodes
Stage IV	Growth involving one or both ovaries with distant metastases including parenchymal (but not superficial) liver metastases and pleural effusions containing malignant cells

From Symonds EM, Symonds IM: *Essential obstetrics and gynaecology*, ed 4, London, 2004, Churchill Livingstone.

TREATMENT

NONPHARMACOLOGIC THERAPY

Virtually all cases of ovarian cancer involve surgical exploration. This includes:

- Abdominal cytology
- Total abdominal hysterectomy and bilateral salpingo-oophorectomy (except in early stages in which fertility preservation is an issue)
- Omentectomy
- Diaphragm sampling
- Selective lymphadenectomy (pelvic and paraaortic nodes)
- Primary cytoreduction with a goal of residual tumor diameter <<2 cm
- Bowel surgery, splenectomy if needed to obtain optimal (<<2 cm) cytoreduction
- Conventional treatment includes surgical debulking (cytoreduction) followed by chemotherapy. However, patients with low-grade, well-differentiated stage I ovarian cancer do not benefit from adjuvant chemotherapy.

ACUTE GENERAL Rx

- Optimal cytoreduction is generally followed by chemotherapy (except in some early-stage disease [stage I without high-risk features is treated with surgery alone]).
- Cisplatin-based combination chemotherapy is used for stage II or greater, 6-mo treatment. Compared with IV paclitaxel plus cisplatin, IV paclitaxel plus intraperitoneal cisplatin and paclitaxel improves survival rates in patients with optimally debulked stage III ovarian cancer.
- Chemotherapy regimens continue to change as research continues. Bevacizumab, a humanized antivascular endothelial growth factor monoclonal antibody, has been shown to be effective in improving progression-free survival in women with ovarian cancer. Trials using bevacizumab during and up to 10 months after carboplatin and paclitaxel chemotherapy have shown prolongation of the median progression-free survival by about 4 months in patients with advanced epithelial ovarian cancer. Olaparib, an oral polymerase inhibitor, has shown antitumor activity in patients with high-grade serous ovarian cancer with or without BRCA1 and BRCA2 germline mutations. Trials have shown that olaparib as maintenance treatment significantly improved progression-free survival among patients with platinum-sensitive, relapsed high-grade serous ovarian cancer.

- Second-look surgery when chemotherapy is complete generally is no longer recommended because this procedure has not been shown to improve survival.
- Recent trials have shown that neoadjuvant chemotherapy followed by interval debulking surgery is not inferior to debulking surgery followed by chemotherapy as a treatment option for patients with bulky stage IIIC or IV ovarian carcinoma. Complete resection of all macroscopic disease, whether performed as primary treatment or after neoadjuvant chemotherapy, remains the objective whenever cytoreductive surgery is performed.

CHRONIC Rx

- If CA-125 elevated, may have recurrent disease
- Physical and pelvic examinations every 3 mo for 2 yr, every 4 mo during third year, then every 6 mo

- Routine monitoring of CA-125 at every visit does not improve survival and should be reserved for addressing specific clinical concerns
- Yearly Pap smear

DISPOSITION

- Overall 5-yr survival rates remain low because of the preponderance of late-stage disease:
  1. Stage I and II: 80% to 100%
  2. Stage III: 15% to 20%
  3. Stage IV: 5%
- Younger patients (<50 yr) in all stages have a considerably better 5-yr survival than older patients (40% vs. 15%).
- Among women with high-grade serous ovarian cancer, BRCA2 mutation, but not BRCA1 deficiency, is associated with improved survival, improved chemotherapy response, and genome instability compared with BRCA wild-type.
- Among patients with invasive epithelial ovarian cancer (EOC), having a germline mutation in BRCA1 or BRCA2 is associated with improved 5-yr overall survival. BRCA2 carriers have the best prognosis.

COMMENTS

- The U.S. Preventive Services Task Force has concluded that current evidence does not show any mortality benefit to routine screening for ovarian cancer with transvaginal ultrasonography or single-threshold serum CA-125 testing and that the harms of such screening are at least moderate.
- Patients at high risk for developing ovarian cancer (BRCA1/BRCA2 gene mutation, hereditary nonpolyposis colorectal cancer syndrome) should consider prophylactic salpingo-oophorectomy after childbearing is complete. Prophylactic bilateral salpingo-oophorectomy reduces ovarian cancer by 80%. If surgery is declined, the National Comprehensive Cancer Network guidelines recommend intensive surveillance with pelvic and abdominal sonogram and serum CA-125 every 6 mo starting at age 35 or 10 yr earlier than cancer diagnosis in family member.

EBM EVIDENCE

Available at www.expertconsult.com

SUGGESTED READINGS

Available at www.expertconsult.com

RELATED CONTENT

Ovarian Cancer (Patient Information)
Ovarian Neoplasm, Benign (Related Key Topic)

AUTHOR: RUBEN ALVERO, M.D.

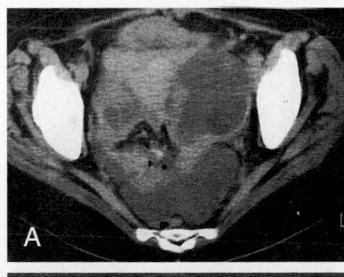
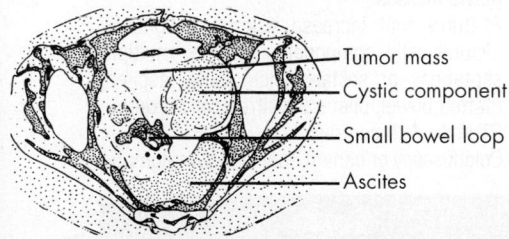
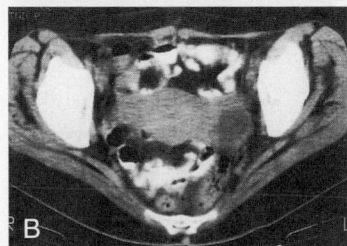
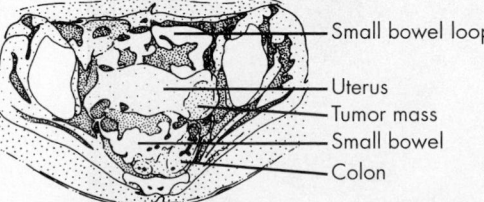

Tumor mass
Cystic component
Small bowel loop
Ascites

Small bowel loop
Uterus
Tumor mass
Small bowel
Colon

FIGURE 10-29 Response to chemotherapy. A 51-year-old woman presented with a rapid increase in abdominal girth. **A,** On CT scan, she was found to have a 12 x 8 cm ovarian mass with a cystic component; peritoneal involvement was extensive, and 6 L of ascites was removed. Pathologic examination showed a poorly differentiated tumor. The tumor was not resectable, and she was treated with combination chemotherapy. After one cycle of therapy, her abdomen returned to normal size. **B,** A CT scan reveals only a small residual ovarian mass. Surgery after four cycles of chemotherapy showed no gross or microscopic tumor. She received four more cycles of chemotherapy but relapsed 1 year later with abdominal metastases. (From Skarin AT: *Atlas of diagnostic oncology*, ed 3, St Louis, 2003, Mosby.)

Diseases and Disorders

BASIC INFORMATION

DEFINITION

Benign ovarian neoplasms are often clinically indistinguishable from their malignant counterparts. Therefore, all persistent adnexal masses must be considered malignant until proven otherwise. Nonneoplastic tumors include:
- Germinal inclusion cyst
- Follicle cyst
- Corpus luteum cyst
- Pregnancy luteoma
- Theca lutein cysts
- Sclerocystic ovaries
- Endometrioma
  Neoplastic tumors derived from coelomic epithelium include:
- Cystic tumors: serous cystadenoma, mucinous cystadenoma, mixed forms
- Tumors with stromal overgrowth: fibroma, adenofibroma, Brenner tumor
  Tumors derived from germ cells are dermoids (benign cystic teratomas).

ICD-10CM CODES
D27.9 Benign neoplasm of unspecified ovary
D27.0 Benign neoplasm of right ovary
D27.1 Benign neoplasm of left ovary

EPIDEMIOLOGY & DEMOGRAPHICS
- **Reproductive years:**
  1. Most common benign ovarian neoplasms: serous cystadenoma and benign cystic teratoma
  2. Most common adnexal mass: functional cyst
  3. Risk of malignancy increases after age 40 yr.
- **Infants:** adnexal masses are usually follicular cysts attributable to maternal hormone stimulation that regress during first few months of life.
- **Childhood:**
  1. Adnexal masses are rare
  2. 8% malignant
  3. Almost always dysgerminomas or teratomas (germ cell origin)
  4. Frequency of malignancy inversely correlated with age
- **Adolescence:**
  1. Most common adnexal mass is a functional cyst.
  2. Most common neoplastic ovarian tumor is a benign cystic teratoma.
  3. Solid/cystic adnexal tumors are rare and almost always dysgerminomas or malignant teratomas.

PHYSICAL FINDINGS & CLINICAL PRESENTATION
- Usually asymptomatic
- Pelvic pain or pressure
- Dyspareunia
- Abdominal pain ranging from mild to severe peritoneal irritation
- Increasing abdominal girth or distention
- Adnexal mass ot pelvic examination
- Children: abdominal or rectal mass

ETIOLOGY
- Physiologic
- Endometriosis
- Unknown

DIAGNOSIS

DIFFERENTIAL DIAGNOSIS
- Ovarian torsion
- Malignancy: ovary, fallopian tube, colon
- Uterine fibroid
- Diverticular abscess, diverticulitis
- Appendiceal abscess, appendicitis (especially in children)
- Tubo-ovarian abscess
- Paraovarian cyst
- Distended bladder
- Pelvic kidney
- Ectopic pregnancy
- Retroperitoneal cyst or neoplasm

WORKUP
- Complete history and physical examination
- Pelvic or rectovaginal examination to reveal firm, irregular, mobile mass
- Laparoscopy or laparotomy to establish diagnosis

LABORATORY TESTS
- Pregnancy test
- Serum tumor markers:
  1. Cancer antigen 125 (CA-125)
  2. Alpha-fetoprotein (endodermal sinus tumor, immature teratoma)
  3. Beta-human chorionic gonadotropin
  4. Lactate dehydrogenase (dysgerminoma)

IMAGING STUDIES
Ultrasound (Fig. 10-30):
- May differentiate adnexal mass from other pelvic masses
- Features that increase risk of malignancy include solid component, papillae, multiple septations or solitary thick septa, ascites, matted bowel, bilaterality, irregular borders
- CT scan with contrast
- Colonoscopy or barium enema, if symptomatic

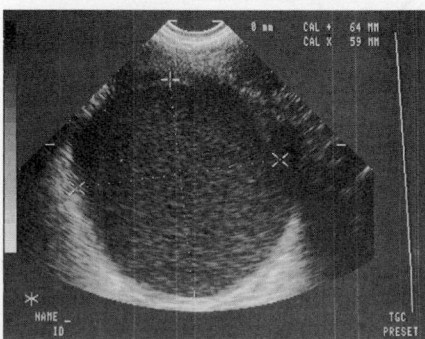

FIGURE 10-30 Ultrasonogram reveals a cyst 6.5 cm across, which was found at laparotomy to be an endometrioma full of altered blood, the so-called chocolate cyst. This may cause cyclical or chronic pelvic pain. (From Greer IA et al: *Mosby's color atlas and text of obstetrics and gynecology,* London, 2000, Harcourt.)

TREATMENT

NONPHARMACOLOGIC THERAPY
Repeat pelvic examination, typically with transvaginal pelvic ultrasound, for premenopausal women in 4 to 6 wk to rule out persistent cyst.

ACUTE GENERAL Rx
Indications for surgery:
- Postmenopausal or premenarchal palpable adnexal mass
- Adnexal mass with suspicious ultrasound features
- Premenopausal woman with persistent cyst >5 cm
- Any adnexal mass >8 cm
- Suspected torsion or rupture

CHRONIC Rx
- Depends on diagnosis
- Possible suppression of formation of new cysts by oral contraceptives

DISPOSITION
Depends on diagnosis

REFERRAL
- If malignancy suspected
- If surgery required

SUGGESTED READINGS
Available at www.expertconsult.com

RELATED CONTENT
Ovarian Cysts (Patient Information)

AUTHOR: **RUBEN ALVERO, M.D.**

BASIC INFORMATION

DEFINITION

Over the counter (OTC) medications are pharmacologic agents that patients can buy without a physician's prescription. They come in different forms, such as pills, creams, ointments, patches, or drops.

SYNONYMS

Medications without a prescription

ICD-10 CM Codes:

V22.1 Supervision of otherwise normal pregnancy

EPIDEMIOLOGY AND DEMOGRAPHICS

INCIDENCE: More than 90% of women take some form of OTC medications in pregnancy
PEAK INCIDENCE: Majority of use occurs in winter and spring due to common respiratory illnesses

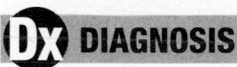

DIAGNOSIS

WORK-UP

At the initial prenatal visit, a full history and physical should be performed. Patients should be asked regarding all prescription and OTC medication use, along with herbals and supplements in order to ensure that no harmful or dangerous substances are being used.

COUNSELING

Despite their availability, certain OTC medications can have significant side effects, interact with other medications, and can be toxic when exceeding recommended doses. Patients should therefore be cautious and aware of these issues when taking OTC medications.

PEARLS AND CONSIDERATIONS

COMMENTS

- OTC medications are most commonly used for treatment of cough/cold, allergies, gastrointestinal issues, skin rashes/lesions, and pain relief.
- In general, pregnant women are excluded from clinical trials to determine drug safety, and the majority of information regarding fetal effects results from animal studies. Due to this lack of information, many OTC medications are not rated as category A according to the FDA risk classification system (Table 10-15).
- Certain medications are considered to be safe in pregnancy due to widespread use with no well known association with teratogenicity (Table 10-16), whereas others have been known to have a causal relationship with adverse effects in pregnancy (Table 10-17).
- The most sensitive period during a pregnancy is the first trimester due to organogenesis. Therefore, any medications that are not absolutely essential should be avoided during this time.

Table 10-15 FDA Pregnancy Risk Classification System

Category	Definition
Category A	Adequate and well-controlled studies have failed to demonstrate a risk to the fetus in any trimester of pregnancy.
Category B	Animal reproduction studies have failed to demonstrate a risk to the fetus and there are no adequate and well-controlled studies in pregnant women.
Category C	Animal reproduction studies have shown an adverse effect of the fetus and there are no adequate and well-controlled studied in human. However, potential benefits may warrant use of the drug in pregnant women despite potential risks.
Category D	There is positive evidence of human fetal risk based on adverse reaction data from investigational or marketing experience or studies in humans. However, potential benefits may warrant use of the drug in pregnant women despite potential risks.
Category X	Studies in animals or humans have demonstrated fetal abnormalities, and there is positive evidence of human fetal risk based on available data. Risks involved in use of this drug in pregnant women clearly outweigh potential benefits.

Table 10-16 OTC Medications Considered to Be Relatively Safe in Pregnancy*

Drug Name	Drug Class	FDA Risk Classification
Folic acid	Dietary supplement	A
Pseudoephedrine	Decongestant	B
Cetirizine	Antihistamine	B
Diphenhydramine	Antihistamine	B
Ranitidine	Antihistamine	B
Dimenhydrinate	Antiemetic	B
Loperamide	Anti-diarrheal	C
Hydrocortisone (topical)	Corticosteroid	C
Dextromethorphan	Antitussive	C
Docusate sodium	Stool softener	C
Omeprazole	Proton pump inhibitor	C
Calcium carbonate	Antacid	C
Simethicone	Antiflatulent	C

*Despite claims to the relative "safety" of these products, there remain questions about their risk in pregnancy. For example, psuedoephedrine use was considered low risk based on older cohort studies but newer data show some association with birth defects such as hemifacial microsomia, small intestinal atresia, and gastroschisis.

Table 10-17 OTC Medications to Use With Caution in Pregnancy

Drug Name	Drug Class	FDA Risk Classification	Safety Concerns
Aspirin	Salicylate	B	Associated with neonatal hemorrhage and increased perinatal mortality. Can be used in specific situations, such as maternal clotting disorders or history of pre-eclampsia
Guaifenesin	Expectorant	C	Possible increased risk of neural tube defects if used in the first trimester, but otherwise considered safe in pregnancy
Caffeine	Stimulant	C	Associated with spontaneous abortion in high doses; use with caution
Ibuprofen, Naproxen	NSAID	D	Associated with oligohydramnios, premature closure of ductus arteriosus in third trimester, and fetal nephrotoxicity
Nicotine	Stimulant	D	Associated with intrauterine growth restriction and preterm birth; however, nicotine replacement is preferable to smoking in pregnancy

PATIENT/FAMILY EDUCATION

Patients should be referred to the CDC website (http://www.cdc.gov/pregnancy/meds) for information regarding the use of specific medications.

SUGGESTED READINGS

Available at www.expertconsult.com

AUTHOR: **AAKRITI CARRUBBA, M.D.**

Diseases and Disorders

BASIC INFORMATION

DEFINITION
Paget's disease of bone is a focal disorder of chaotic bone remodeling with increased osteoblastic and osteoclastic activity that results in disorganized woven and lamellar bone in one or more skeletal sites. The end result is bone of poor quality that is enlarged, hypervascular, and susceptible to deformation and fracture.

SYNONYMS
Osteitis deformans

ICD-10CM CODES
M88.9	Osteitis deformans of unspecified bone
M88.0	Osteitis deformans of skull
M88.1	Osteitis deformans of vertebrae
M88.869	Osteitis deformans of unspecified lower leg
M88.89	Osteitis deformans of multiple sites
M90.60	Osteitis deformans in neoplastic diseases, unspecified site
M90.679	Osteitis deformans in neoplastic diseases, unspecified ankle and foot
M90.68	Osteitis deformans in neoplastic diseases, other site
M90.69	Osteitis deformans in neoplastic diseases, multiple sites

EPIDEMIOLOGY & DEMOGRAPHICS
Epidemiologic data suggest an origin of Paget's disease in Great Britain spreading to other areas by English colonists beginning in the seventeenth century. Highest prevalence occurs in Eastern and Western Europe and in those who have emigrated to New Zealand, Australia, South Africa, and North America. Paget's is rarely seen in Japanese, Chinese, Asian Indians, sub-Saharan Africans, and Middle Eastern Arabs.

Most commonly diagnosed in those aged >50 yr and rare before 40 yr.

Prevalence estimates of up to 3% of population aged >50 yr and up to 10% in those aged >90 yr.
PREDOMINANT SEX: Variable preponderance of males.
PREDOMINANT AGE: Middle or advanced years.
FAMILIAL INCIDENCE: Common, family history positive in up to 40% of cases.

PHYSICAL FINDINGS & CLINICAL PRESENTATION
- Most common sites of involvement: pelvis (70%), lumbar spine (53%), sacrum, femur (55%), skull (42%), tibia (30%) (Fig. E1P-1), humerus, scapula.
- Uncommon: hand, foot, fibula.
- Lesions in one (monostotic) or more bones (polyostotic).
- Gradual progression of disease in affected bone(s) with rare appearance at new site(s).
- Many patients are asymptomatic, but up to 40% of patients who come to medical attention present with bone pain.
- Symptoms and signs include bone and articular pain often related to secondary arthritis, bone deformities and enlargement,

increased warmth over pagetic bone, skull enlargement, nerve entrapment or compression syndromes, cranial nerve deficits especially deafness, spinal cord compression and vascular steal syndromes, fissure fractures, fractures, and neoplastic degeneration.

ETIOLOGY
Etiology remains unknown

Extensive epidemiologic and laboratory data are in keeping with potential role of paramyxoviral infection of osteoclasts in a genetically susceptible individual with or without documented genetic mutations.

Dx DIAGNOSIS

Diagnosis is often suspected in asymptomatic patients with isolated elevation of alkaline phosphatase without evidence of liver disease.

DIFFERENTIAL DIAGNOSIS
- Osteosclerosis
- Hyperphosphatasia
- Familial expansile osteolysis
- Fibrous dysplasia
- Skeletal neoplasm (primary or metastatic)
- Osteomalacia with secondary hyperparathyroidism

LABORATORY TESTS
- Increase in serum alkaline phosphatase or bone-specific alkaline phosphatase
- Increase in urine NTx/creatinine ratio or plasma CTx
- Bone biopsy may be necessary to rule out sarcomatous degeneration or metastatic disease

IMAGING STUDIES (FIG. E1P-2)
Bone scintigraphy is the most sensitive test for delineating the extent and site of pagetic lesions but nonspecific in that areas of uptake may be related to arthritis or metastatic lesions. Radiographs (Fig. 1P-3) will further delineate characteristic pagetic changes.

Rx TREATMENT

Indications for therapy include extensive or symptomatic disease; neurologic complications; involvement of weight-bearing bones, skull, vertebrae, and other areas of critical involvement, for example, in proximity to joints; and prevention of excess bleeding from an orthopedic procedure on pagetic bone.

NONPHARMACOLOGIC THERAPY
- Optimization of calcium and vitamin D intake and appropriate guidance regarding ambulatory needs.
- Orthopedic stabilization may be required for patients with pseudofractures.

SPECIFIC THERAPY
Bisphosphonates are the mainstay of therapy and include oral alendronate or risedronate and intravenous pamidronate or zoledronic acid.
- SC salmon calcitonin when bisphosphonates are not tolerated or are contraindicated as in those with GFR of <35 mL/min
- Acetaminophen, aspirin, and nonsteroidal drugs for relief of pain

DISPOSITION
- Without treatment, progression of disease is common
- With treatment, remissions of varying duration in most patients. Bisphosphonates can normalize bone turnover in a high proportion of patients, but evidence that long-term suppression of bone turnover prevents complications or improves the clinical outcome is currently inconclusive.
- Careful and regular clinical and biochemical follow-up at 3- to 6-month intervals with necessity of retreatment in patients with continued pagetic activity or reactivation
- With first ever intravenous dose of pamidronate or zoledronic acid, patients may experience a flu-like syndrome for several days that may be prevented with acetaminophen

SUGGESTED READINGS
Available at www.expertconsult.com

RELATED CONTENT
Paget's Disease of Bone (Patient Information)

AUTHOR: **JOSEPH R. TUCCI, M.D.**

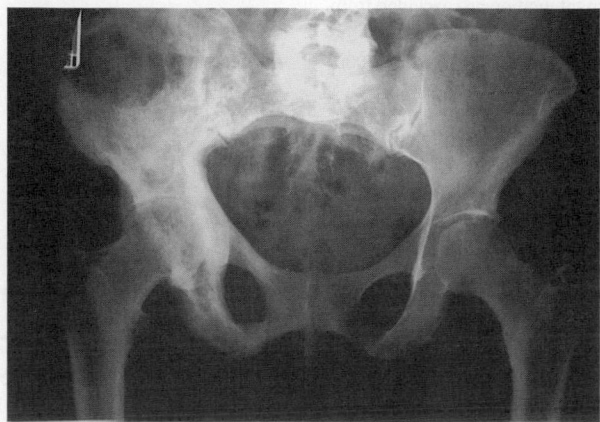

FIGURE 1P-3 Paget's disease of the bone. Frontal radiograph of the pelvis shows marked prominence of the trabeculae in the right ilium, ischium, and pubic bones, with small lytic areas identified as compatible with the later stages of Paget's disease. (From Specht N [ed]: *Practical guide to diagnostic imaging,* St Louis, 1998, Mosby.)

BASIC INFORMATION

DEFINITION

Paget's disease of the breast is a malignant disease that presents itself as a scaly, sore, eroding, bleeding ulcer of the nipple. It represents an extension of a ductal adenocarcinoma of the breast. Microscopically, typical large clear cells (Paget's cells) with pale and abundant cytoplasm and hyperchromatic nuclei with prominent nucleoli are found in the epidermal layer. Paget's disease is more often associated with primary invasive or in situ carcinoma of the breast.

ICD-10CM CODES

C50.0	Malignant neoplasm of nipple and areola
C50.011	Malignant neoplasm of nipple and areola, right female breast
C50.012	Malignant neoplasm of nipple and areola, left female breast
C50.019	Malignant neoplasm of nipple and areola, unspecified female breast
C50.021	Malignant neoplasm of nipple and areola, right male breast
C50.022	Malignant neoplasm of nipple and areola, left male breast
C50.029	Malignant neoplasm of nipple and areola, unspecified male breast

EPIDEMIOLOGY & DEMOGRAPHICS

- Not common
- Found in one in 100 to 200 breast cancer patients

PHYSICAL FINDINGS & CLINICAL PRESENTATION

- Variable; most often reveals an erythematous, irregularly bordered plaque on the nipple.
- Itching or burning nipple and/or reported lump
- Very minimal scaly lesion that may bleed when scales are lifted
- Typical ulcer located on nipple with serous fluid weeping or small amount of bleeding coming from it (Fig. 1P-4)
- Palpable carcinoma in the breast of some patients

ETIOLOGY

- Exact origin unknown
- Possibly migration of either in situ or invasive carcinoma cells in breast to nipple skin to produce Paget's disease

DIAGNOSIS

DIFFERENTIAL DIAGNOSIS

- Chronic dermatitis
- Florid papillomatosis of the nipple or nipple adenoma
- Eczema

WORKUP

- Clinically apparent
- Careful breast examination with diagnosis in mind
- Palpable mass or mammographic lesions in 60% to 70% of patients

A clinical algorithm for the evaluation of nipple discharge is described in Section III, "Breast, Nipple Discharge Evaluation."

LABORATORY TESTS

Biopsy of nipple lesion

IMAGING STUDIES

Mammograms to search for possible primary carcinoma

TREATMENT

NONPHARMACOLOGIC THERAPY

- Fewer patients:
  1. Paget's disease of nipple only finding when mammographically negative breast
  2. Consideration of wide excision of nipple with or without radiation
- Other patients: additional invasive or in situ carcinoma recognized
- Either modified mastectomy or breast conservation treatment
- Presence of underlying in situ or invasive carcinoma in mastectomy specimen of majority of patients

ACUTE GENERAL Rx

Systemic adjuvant therapy depending on extent of invasive carcinoma found

DISPOSITION

- Parallel prognosis to that of breast cancer patient without Paget's disease
- Regular follow-up as in other invasive or in situ carcinoma patients

REFERRAL

At outset, all suspicious nipple lesions should be referred for evaluation and treatment.

SUGGESTED READINGS

Available at www.expertconsult.com

RELATED CONTENT

Paget's Disease of the Breast (Patient Information)
Breast Cancer (Related Key Topic)

AUTHOR: **RUBEN ALVERO, M.D.**

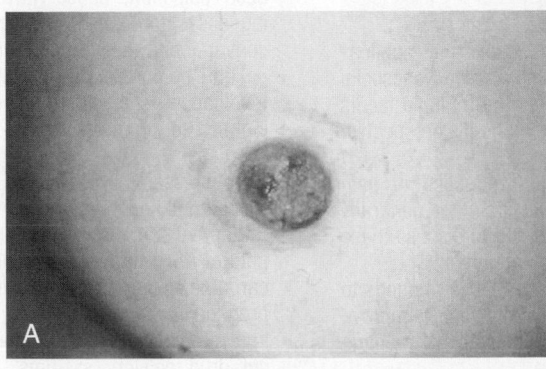
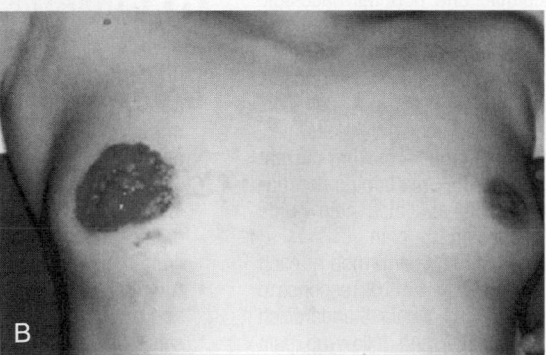

FIGURE 1P-4 A and **B,** Paget's disease of the nipple. (Courtesy Sehwan Han, M.D.)

BASIC INFORMATION

DEFINITION

Chronic pain is pain that persists for longer than the expected time frame or that is associated with progressive, nonmalignant disease. Pain is an unpleasant sensory and emotional experience associated with actual or potential tissue damage or described in terms of such damage. The perception of pain is influenced by physiologic, psychological, and social factors.

SYNONYMS

Nonmalignant chronic pain
Pain management

ICD-10CM CODES
G89.4	Chronic pain syndrome
G89.29	Other chronic pain
G89.21	Chronic pain due to trauma
G89.22	Chronic post-thoracotomy pain
G89.28	Other chronic postprocedural pain
G89.3	Neoplasm related pain (acute) (chronic)

EPIDEMIOLOGY & DEMOGRAPHICS

Estimates of the prevalence of chronic pain in the United States vary widely. Data from one national survey (1999-2002 National Health and Nutrition Examination Survey [NHANES]) reported a prevalence of chronic regional and widespread pain of 11% and 3.6%, respectively, while the National Center for Health Statistics estimates that 32.8% of the U.S. population suffers from some form of chronic pain. Chronic pain is the third leading cause of physical impairment in the United States, and related costs are estimated to be tens of billions annually. Patients with chronic pain may also experience changes in mood, depression, sleep disturbances, fatigue, and decreased overall physical functioning.

CLINICAL PRESENTATION

- History: comprehensive patient assessment, including history of present illness (cause of pain, location, timing, characteristics, exacerbating/relieving factors, triggers), past therapies (pharmacologic and nonpharmacologic and outcomes of these therapies), medical history, family and social history, psychiatric history (including history of depression, anxiety, abuse, and/or other psychological disorders), substance use history, allergies, sleep patterns and disturbances, and current medications. Social supports, coping mechanisms, and spirituality can also help guide development of a treatment plan.
- Pain assessment should be performed at each visit; includes pain intensity (1 to 10), response to medication, and attributes of pain. Standardized templates for both initial and follow-up pain assessment have been developed by various organizations. The Brief Pain Inventory is an example of a widely used assessment tool. In addition, a functional assessment should be performed. Tools such as the Functional Ability

Questionnaire (FAQ5) can guide the clinician in determining a patient's functional status. Lastly, consider assessment of a patient's risk for substance abuse.
- Physical examination: directed at systems affected by pain (often musculoskeletal) and neurologic examination.
- Look for contributing factors (e.g., comorbidities, lifestyle factors) and barriers to effective care (e.g., behavioral, social, insurance)

ETIOLOGY

Chronic pain can generally be categorized as originating from one of five etiologies: musculoskeletal, neuropathic, inflammatory, mechanical, or mixed. Chronic pain may include such diagnoses as headache, low back pain, previous trauma, arthritis, neurogenic (e.g., trigeminal neuralgia), psychogenic (related to depression or anxiety), fibromyalgia, reflex sympathetic dystrophy, myofascial pain syndrome, phantom limb pain, idiopathic, or unknown.

Dx **DIAGNOSIS**

DIFFERENTIAL DIAGNOSIS

- Depends on etiology (musculoskeletal, neuropathic, inflammatory, mechanical, or mixed)
- Depression and anxiety disorders can be both a cause and a result of chronic pain, so temporal association of these disorders is important.

WORKUP

- Workup should be directed at identifying the source of pain
- Laboratory testing, imaging studies, and/or electromyographic studies should be used when etiology of chronic pain is unknown or unclear, when comorbidities are suspected, and as the history and physical examination direct.
- Consider use of random urine drug screens or other tests to screen for presence of illegal drugs, unreported prescribed medications, or alcohol use.

Rx **TREATMENT**

- Studies increasingly support the application of a multidisciplinary, biopsychosocial approach that addresses the multiple facets of pain and includes the patient's perspective and goals.
- Therapeutic goal is the reduction of pain (elimination of chronic pain is generally unlikely and providers need to discuss these limitations with patients at outset).
- A written care plan that includes methods to address the patient's personal goals, improve sleep, increase physical activity, manage stress, and reduce pain.

NONPHARMACOLOGIC THERAPY

- Exercise (recommended for all patients and tailored to individual abilities and needs)

- Modalities: heat therapy, cold therapy, transcutaneous electrical nerve stimulation (TENS) units, manipulative therapy, cognitive behavioral therapy, psychological counseling, and physical therapy
- Electrostimulation therapy: TENS units
- Behavioral therapies: cognitive behavioral therapy, hypnosis, biofeedback, relaxation therapy
- Music therapy (in conjunction with other types of therapy)
- Surgery

ACUTE GENERAL Rx

- Short-acting antiinflammatory and analgesic medications (e.g., acetaminophen/NSAIDs/opioids). Avoid use of NSAIDs in patients with hypertension, CHF, or any type of CKD.
- Topical analgesics (lidocaine, NSAIDs, capsaicin)
- Trigger point or joint injections (immediate anesthetic plus long-acting corticosteroids)
- Epidural steroid injections
- Nerve blocks

CHRONIC Rx

- Pain management with long-acting pharmacologic agents is considered a key aspect of therapy but is often underused. Fig. 1P-5 illustrates a strategy for pharmacologic management of pain using the World Health Organization (WHO) analgesic ladder. Fig. E1P-6 describes another algorithm for pain management.
- Long-acting NSAIDs. Table 1P-1 describes adjuvant analgesic drugs for chronic pain.
- Sustained-release opioids (used for moderate to severe pain that has failed other therapeutic interventions): oxycodone, morphine SR, methadone (use with caution), or fentanyl patch; short-acting opioids can be used in conjunction with these agents for management of breakthrough pain. Conversion to a long-acting opioid should be based on an equianalgesic conversion. Opioids are rarely beneficial in the treatment of inflammatory or mechanical pain and are not indicated for treatment of headaches (http://www.acpinternist.org/archives/2008/01/extra/pain_charts.pdf).
- Table 1P-2 provides guidelines for opioid dose selection, conservative initial starting doses for opioid-naïve individuals, and conversion ratios for opioid rotation in patients on chronic opioids. Titration of these medications should not exceed the equivalent of 100 mg morphine/day to avoid risk of overdose.
- Antidepressants (tricyclic and selective serotonin reuptake inhibitor)
- Anticonvulsant medications particularly helpful for neuropathic conditions (e.g., carbamazepine, valproic acid, gabapentin, pregabalin)
- Implantable methods, epidural and intrathecal drug delivery systems, dorsal column stimulators
- Treatment of insomnia and sleep disorders to reduce pain with standard sleep-inducing agents (trazodone, antihistamines)

P

Diseases and Disorders

I

WHO ANALGESIC LADDER

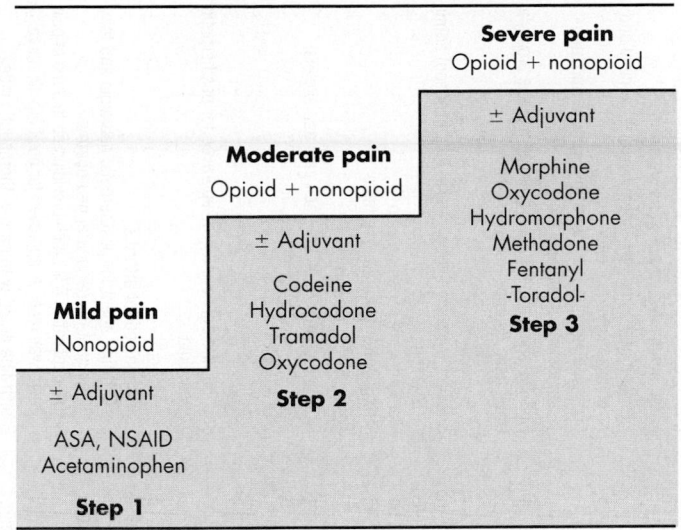

Severe pain
Opioid + nonopioid

± Adjuvant

Morphine
Oxycodone
Hydromorphone
Methadone
Fentanyl
-Toradol-

Step 3

Moderate pain
Opioid + nonopioid

± Adjuvant

Codeine
Hydrocodone
Tramadol
Oxycodone

Step 2

Mild pain
Nonopioid

± Adjuvant

ASA, NSAID
Acetaminophen

Step 1

• Advance up the ladder if pain persists

FIGURE 1P-5 Strategy for pharmacologic management of pain using the World Health Organization (WHO) analgesic ladder. Multiagent therapy is usually required for optimal pain management. Patients with mild pain should be started on a nonopioid analgesic, and those with moderate pain on a step 2 opioid. Many patients can benefit from the addition of a nonopioid to the opioid (e.g., for bone pain) or an adjuvant agent to the opioid (e.g., for neuropathic pain). If this combination does not produce adequate relief or the patient has severe pain, step 3 opioids should be started initially. Toradol (ketorolac) is a nonsteroidal antiinflammatory drug *(NSAID)* with the pain-relieving potency of a step 3 opioid. Many patients can benefit from the addition of nonopioid analgesics or adjuvants, if indicated. *ASA,* Aspirin. (From Hoffman R et al: *Hematology, basic principles and practice,* ed 5, Philadelphia, 2009, Churchill Livingstone.)

COMPLEMENTARY & ALTERNATIVE MEDICINE

Acupuncture and massage (evidence-based for some indications). Acupuncture is most likely to benefit patients with low back pain, neck pain, chronic idiopathic or tension headache, migraine, and knee osteoarthritis.

REFERRAL

- Pain medicine specialist or multidisciplinary pain clinic: useful when primary therapies fail, in patients with complex pain conditions, or for invasive therapies
- Consider referral to an addiction specialist if patient has a history of substance abuse or addiction
- Psychiatry/psychological services for counseling, if needed

❗ PEARLS & CONSIDERATIONS

- Patient consent should be obtained in the form of a written treatment agreement before initiating treatment. This agreement should outline the goals of therapy, use of a single provider or treatment team and a single pharmacy, limitations on dose and number of prescribed medications, prohibition on use with alcohol or sedating medications, keeping medication safe and secure, prohibition on selling or sharing medication, limitations on refills, compliance with all components of the treatment plan, the role of drug screening, and consequences of nonadherence.
- Follow-up assessment should occur every 1 to 6 mo and include a complete pain assessment (see earlier), review of the type of long-acting analgesic used and dosage, use of breakthrough analgesics, side effects and their management, use of nonpharmacologic therapies, and adjunct medication use.

COMMENTS

- Medication dependence and addiction should not be confused. Most patients receiving chronic opioid therapy can become dependent on these medications for pain relief but opioid addiction does not occur. Patients exhibiting signs of addiction often will seek escalating doses of medication, request refills of prescriptions earlier than planned, and engage in drug-seeking activities (e.g., emergency department visits between prescriptions, seeking multiple prescriptions).
- Side effects need not preclude use of opioid medications and should be anticipated. Antiemetics can aid in controlling nausea. Constipation can be managed with stool softeners and laxatives.
- The emphasis of comprehensive pain management for non–cancer-related chronic pain has led to a fourfold increase in prescribing of opioid medications in the United States. This increase in opiate use has also led to a rise in the misuse and abuse of these medications. Providers should proceed with caution before initiating pain management with opiate medications and should familiarize themselves with processes and tools for pain assessment and medication management. Forty-two states have developed prescription drug monitoring programs (PDMPs) to assist providers in identifying issues of abuse, polypharmacy, and misuse of controlled substances.

PATIENT & FAMILY EDUCATION

National Pain Foundation (http://www.pain connection.org)
American Pain Foundation (http://www.pain foundation.org)
National Institutes of Health (http://www.nih.gov)

SUGGESTED READINGS

Available at www.expertconsult.com

RELATED CONTENT

Pain Medications (Patient Information)

AUTHOR: **ANNGENE G. ANTHONY, M.D., M.P.H.**

TABLE 1P-1 Adjuvant Analgesic Drugs for Chronic Pain

Drug	Dosage	Indications	Adverse Effects	Comments
Tricyclic Antidepressants				
Amitriptyline, imipramine, desipramine, nortriptyline	10-150 mg/day	Peripheral neuropathy, postherpetic neuralgia, other types of peripheral neuropathic pain, central pain, facial pain, fibromyalgia, headache prophylaxis, irritable bowel syndrome, and chronic low back pain with or without radiculopathy	Sedation, dry mouth, confusion, weight gain, constipation, urinary retention, ataxia, cardiac conduction delay (QTc prolongation)	First-line agents for neuropathic pain and headache prophylaxis Secondary amine drugs (e.g., nortriptyline) have fewer side effects than tertiary amines (e.g., amitriptyline) Contraindicated in glaucoma
Serotonin-Norepinephrine Reuptake Inhibitors				
Venlafaxine	75-225 mg/day	Peripheral neuropathy, headache prophylaxis	Sedation, dry mouth, constipation, ataxia, hypertension, hyperhidrosis	Dose adjustment in patients with renal dysfunction
Duloxetine	60-120 mg/day	Peripheral neuropathy, fibromyalgia, chronic back pain	Sedation, dry mouth, constipation, hyperhidrosis	U.S. Food and Drug Administration (FDA)-approved for fibromyalgia and diabetic neuropathy Contraindicated in glaucoma
Anticonvulsants				
Gabapentin	600-3600 mg/day	Peripheral neuropathy, postherpetic neuralgia, other types of peripheral neuropathic pain, central pain, pelvic pain, headache prophylaxis, radiculopathy, chronic postsurgical pain	Sedation, weight gain, dry mouth, ataxia, edema	First-line agent for neuropathic pain FDA-approved for postherpetic neuralgia Effective preemptively for postoperative pain
Pregabalin	150-600 mg/day	Peripheral neuropathy, postherpetic neuralgia, central pain, fibromyalgia	Sedation, weight gain, dry mouth, ataxia, edema	First-line agent for neuropathic pain FDA-approved for diabetic neuropathy, postherpetic neuralgia, fibromyalgia Effective preemptively for postoperative pain Same mechanism of action as gabapentin
Carbamazepine	200-1600 mg/day	Facial neuralgias, diabetic neuropathy	Sedation, ataxia, diplopia, hyponatremia, agranulocytosis, diarrhea, aplastic anemia, hepatotoxicity, Stevens-Johnson syndrome	First-line agent and FDA-approved for trigeminal and glossopharyngeal neuralgia Contraindicated in patients with porphyria and atrio-ventricular conduction block
Topiramate	50-400 mg/day	Headache prophylaxis, chronic low back pain with or without radiculopathy	Sedation, ataxia, diplopia, weight loss, diarrhea, metabolic acidosis, kidney stones	First-line agent and FDA-approved for migraine prophylaxis Often used as appetite suppressant
Corticosteroids (Systemic)				
Prednisone	5-60 mg/day	Inflammatory arthritis, other inflammatory pain conditions (e.g., inflammatory bowel disease), traumatic nerve injury, complex regional pain syndrome	Myriad psychiatric, gastrointestinal, neurologic, and cardiac side effects; immunosuppression, weakness, edema, weight gain, elevated glucose, poor wound healing, others	Stronger evidence supports local (i.e., injection) administration More effective for acute pain Strong anti-inflammatory effects
Miscellaneous				
Muscle relaxants	Variable depending on drug	Skeletal muscle spasm, acute spinal pain, temporomandibular disorder Baclofen effective for spasticity, dystonia, and trigeminal neuralgia	Sedation, ataxia, blurred vision, confusion, asthenia, xerostomia and other gastrointestinal effects, palpitations	First-line agents for acute back pain and skeletal muscle spasm
Lidocaine patch	1-3 patches every 12 hr	Postherpetic neuropathy, peripheral neuropathy, other types of neuropathic and possibly myofascial pain associated with allodynia	Minimal systemic side effects when applied appropriately	Second-line agent and FDA-approved for postherpetic neuralgia
Capsaicin cream	0.025% applied three or four times per day	Postherpetic neuralgia, peripheral neuropathy and other types of neuropathic pain, chronic postsurgical pain, arthritis, and other musculoskeletal conditions	Burning on application Minimal systemic side effects when applied appropriately	FDA-approved for arthritis Second-line agent for postherpetic neuralgia and third-line agent for peripheral neuropathy Single application 8% patch providing up to 3 mo of pain relief was recently approved for postherpetic neuralgia
Cannabinoids	Variable depending on drug and delivery route	Strongest evidence is for multiple sclerosis May be effective for peripheral neuropathy and other types of neuropathic pain spasticity	Myriad psychiatric, neurologic, and cardiac effects; xerostomia, abdominal pain, and other gastrointestinal effects	Fourth-line agent with narrow therapeutic index Modest analgesic effect comparable to codeine

From Goldman L, Schafer AI: *Goldman's Cecil medicine*, ed 24, Philadelphia, 2012, Saunders.

TABLE 1P-2 Guidelines for Opioid Dose Selection, Conservative Initial Starting Doses for Opioid-Naïve Individuals, and Conversion Ratios for Opioid Rotation in Patients on Chronic Opioids

Opioid Naïve	Morphine SR	Codeine	Oxycodone	Hydrocodone	Hydromorphone	Methadone	Fentanyl	Oxymorphone
Initial dose and range in opioid-naïve patient (starting dose range for repeated dosing)*	15 mg (15-30 mg q 8-12h)	30 mg (15-60 mg q 4-6h)	5 mg (5-15 mg q 4-6h)	5 mg (5-10 mg q 4-6h)	2 mg (2-4 mg q 4-6h)	2.5 mg q 6-12h	NA	5 mg q 4-6h

Opioid Tolerant Converting from:	Morphine PO	Codeine	Oxycodone	Hydrocodone	Hydromorphone	Methadone	Fentanyl	Oxymorphone
Morphine IM 10 mg (the gold standard for opioid comparisons)	20-30 mg	60-90 mg†	5 mg	5-10 mg q 4-6h	2 mg	2.5 mg	25-µg patch/72 hr	5 mg (the gold standard for opioid comparisons)
Morphine SR 30 mg PO q 8-12h, 60-90 mg/24h		30-90 mg q 4h	3-45 mg/24 hr oxycodone, approx 50% of morphine dose	30-45 mg/24 hr	12-18 mg/24 hr	24-hr dose morphine 30-90 mg 4:1 conversion 90-300 mg 8:1 conversion >300 mg 12:1	25-mcg patch/72 hr	5 mg q 12h ER
Codeine 30-60 mg q 4h	15-30 mg q 3-4h		5-7.5 mg q 4h	5-10 mg q 4h	12 mg/24 hr	2.5 mg q 8-12h	12.5-µg patch/72 hr	2.5-5 mg q 4-6h IR
Oxycodone 5 mg q 3-4h	10 mg	30-60 mg q 3-4h		5-10 mg q 4h	12 mg/24 hr	2.5 mg q 8-12h	25-µg patch/72 hr	5 mg q 4-6h IR
Hydrocodone 10 mg q 3-4h	15 mg	30-60 mg q 3-4h	5 mg q 3-4h		12 mg/24 hr		12.5-µg patch/72 hr	2.5-5 mg q 4-6h IR
Hydromorphone 2 mg q 4h	10 mg		5 mg	5-10 mg q 4h		2.5 mg q 8-12h	25-µg patch/72 hr	5 mg q 4-6h IR
Methadone 5 mg q 8h	20 mg SR q 8h		10 mg q 3-4h		4 mg q 4-6h		25-µg patch/72 hr	5 mg q 12h ER
Fentanyl 25 µg/hr patch	90 mg morphine per 24 hr (1 µg to 4 mg morphine)					5 mg q 8-12h		5 mg q12h ER
Oxymorphone ER 5 mg q 12h	15 mg SR q 12h		5 mg q 8-12h	10 mg q 4-6h	12 mg/24 hr	5 mg q 8-12h	25-µg patch/72 hr	

Note: Recommended starting doses are low and should be titrated upward slowly to minimize adverse effects. Limitations of equianalgesic tables exist because they are based on single-dose studies in opioid-naïve individuals. Convert opioid 1 to morphine equivalents and calculate dose of opioid 2 according to conversion ratio then reduce the calculated dose for opioid 2 by 1/3 to 1/2 to ensure safety of the 24-hr total daily dose. Rescue dose is 10% to 20% of daily opioid dose given every 3 to 4 hr as needed. Titration upward for unrelieved pain should be by 25% to 30% of the current 24-hr dose, adjusted by daily amount of rescue medications needed over a several-week period. Equivalent or equianalgesic doses for the different opioid preparations vary in different publications. ER, Extended release; IR, immediate release.

*Conservative low equianalgesic starting doses for opioid-naïve individuals adapted from published recommendations.
†Doses above 1.5 mg/kg not recommended because of increase in side effects.
From Hochberg MC et al: Rheumatology, ed 5, St Louis, 2011, Mosby.

P

Diseases and Disorders

I

BASIC INFORMATION

DEFINITION
Pancreatic cancer is an adenocarcinoma derived from pancreatic duct epithelium.

ICD-10CM CODES
C25.9 Malignant neoplasm of pancreas, unspecified
C25.0 Malignant neoplasm of head of pancreas
C25.1 Malignant neoplasm of body of pancreas
C25.2 Malignant neoplasm of tail of pancreas
C25.3 Malignant neoplasm of pancreatic duct

EPIDEMIOLOGY & DEMOGRAPHICS
INCIDENCE: In the U.S., it is estimated that there will be 49,000 new cases and 45,500 deaths in 2015. It is the fourth leading cause of cancer-related death in the U.S. The majority of patients present with advanced disease, and less than 20% of patients present with potentially resectable tumors.
PREDOMINANT SEX: Male/female ratio of 2:1
PREDOMINANT AGE: Median age at diagnosis is 71 years

PHYSICAL FINDINGS & CLINICAL PRESENTATION
Presenting symptoms are generally related to location:
Jaundice (60%-70% of pancreatic cancers are located in the head of the pancreas)
Abdominal pain: generally dull upper abdominal pain or vague abdominal discomfort
Weight loss
Anorexia/change in taste, asthenia
Nausea
Uncommonly: depression, gastrointestinal bleeding, acute pancreatitis (from obstruction of the pancreatic duct), back pain
Trousseau syndrome (hypercoagulability in the setting of malignancy) may be initial presentation in some patients.
Physical findings:
Icterus
Cachexia, temporal wasting
Ascites, peripheral lymphadenopathy, hepatomegaly
Excoriations from scratching pruritic skin

ETIOLOGY
Unknown, but several conditions have been associated with pancreatic cancer:
• Smoking
• Alcoholism
• Genetics: 5% to 10% of patients have a family history of the disease
• Genetic syndromes and associated genes: Hereditary pancreatitis (*PRSS1*, *SPINK1*), Peutz-Jeghers syndrome (*STK11[LKB1]*), familial atypical multiple mole and melanoma syndrome (*p16*), hereditary breast and ovarian cancer syndromes (*BRACA1*, *BRACA2*, *PALB2*), ataxia telangiectasia (*ATM*), Li-Fraumeni syndrome (*P53*)

• Gallstones
• Diabetes mellitus (present in at least 50% of patients with pancreatic cancer)
• Chronic pancreatitis
• Diet rich in animal fat
• Occupational exposure: oil refining, paper manufacturing, chemical industry
• Overweight or obesity during early adulthood is associated with a greater risk of pancreatic cancer and a younger age of disease onset. Obesity at an older age is associated with a lower overall survival in patients with pancreatic cancer.
• Possible increased risk for certain type-2 diabetes medications (GLP-1 receptor agonists and DPP-4 inhibitors). However, recent trials have failed to confirm increased risk.

DIAGNOSIS

DIFFERENTIAL DIAGNOSIS
• Common duct cholelithiasis
• Cholangiocarcinoma
• Common duct stricture
• Sclerosing cholangitis
• Primary biliary cirrhosis
• Autoimmune pancreatitis
• Drug-induced cholestasis (e.g., phenothiazines)
• Other pancreatic tumors (islet cell tumor, cystadenocarcinoma, epidermoid carcinoma, sarcomas, lymphomas)

WORKUP
Initial laboratory testing includes complete blood count, serum chemistries. The bile duct antigen CA 19-9 is not used as a screening test but can be utilized as a modality for detecting recurrence and for therapeutic monitoring in patients undergoing therapy.

Routine Laboratory Tests	% Abnormal
Alkaline phosphatase	80
Bilirubin	55
Total protein	15

Routine Laboratory Tests	% Abnormal
Amylase	15
Hemoglobin	60

IMAGING STUDIES
Multidetector helical CT with IV administration of contrast is the imaging procedure of choice for initial evaluation. Endoscopic ultrasonography is useful when the diagnosis is strongly suspected and tissue is required for diagnostic purposes. Fine-needle aspiration biopsy combined with endoscopic ultrasonography is the preferred modality for evaluation of cystic or mass lesions to determine malignancy. Endoscopic retrograde cholangiopancreatography (ERCP) is useful in patients with jaundice needing an endoscopic stent to relieve obstruction.

Noninvasive Imaging	% Abnormal
Abdominal ultrasonography	60
Abdominal CT scan (with contrast) (Fig. 1P-7)	90
Abdominal MRI scan	90
Invasive Imaging	
ERCP	90
CT scan or ultrasonography-guided needle aspiration cytology	90-95

STAGING FOR PANCREATIC CANCER
PRIMARY TUMOR (T):
TX Primary tumor cannot be assessed
T0 No evidence of primary tumor
T1 Tumor <2 cm
T2 Tumor >2 cm, confined to the pancreas
T3 Tumor extends locally beyond the pancreas
T4 Tumor involves celiac or superior mesenteric arteries

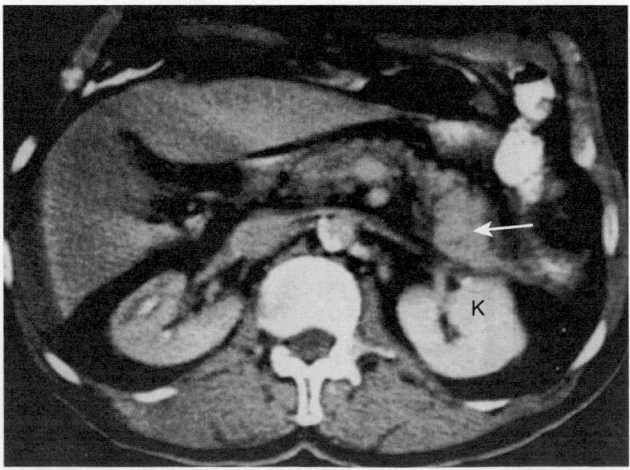

FIGURE 1P-7 CT scan of a patient with adenocarcinoma of the body and tail of the pancreas. The tumor *(arrow)* is seen anterior and adjacent to the left kidney *(K)*. At operation, the tumor was invading Gerota's fascia. (From Sabiston D: *Textbook of surgery,* ed 17, Philadelphia, 2005, Saunders.)

LYMPH NODES (N):

NX   Regional lymph nodes cannot be
      assessed
N0   No regional lymph node metastasis
N1   Regional lymph node metastasis

DISTANT METASTASES (M):

MX   Presence of distant metastasis
      cannot be assessed
M0   No distant metastasis
M1   Distant metastasis

STAGING GROUPS:

IA   T1, N0, M0
IB   T2, N0, M0
IIA   T3, N0, M0
IIB   T1-3, N1, M0
III   T4, N0-1, M0
IV   T1-4, N0-1, M1

A clinical/radiographic staging system for adenocarcinoma of the pancreatic head and uncinate process is described in Table 1P-3.

TREATMENT

SURGERY FOR RESECTABLE DISEASE

Curative cephalic pancreatoduodenectomy (Whipple's procedure) for tumors in the head and neck of the pancreas is appropriate for only 10% to 20% of patients whose lesion is <5 cm, solitary, and without locoregional invasion. Surgical mortality rate can be up to 5%. Tumors in the body or tail of the pancreas are removed by means of a distal pancreatectomy, which often includes a splenectomy. Due to the complexity of surgery and risk for significant morbidity and mortality, current guidelines recommend that pancreatic resections be carried out in centers that perform at least 15 to 20 cases annually. In addition, a recent review concluded that high-volume institutions are associated with higher negative-margin status and higher 5-year survival rates, and that patients are more likely to receive multimodality therapy at these centers.

Adjuvant chemotherapy has been demonstrated to improve postoperative survival in multiple randomized trials and is considered the standard approach currently. The use of 5-fluorouracil (5-FU) or gemcitabine for a period of 6 months is currently recommended, with median survival in the 21-month range expected for patients with a complete resection. The use of adjuvant radiotherapy in this setting is controversial and is best limited to patients with poor risk features, margin-positive surgery, or with multiple nodal or extranodal tumor involvement. An emerging strategy is the use of neoadjuvant preoperative treatment using chemotherapy combined with radiotherapy in patients with resectable pancreatic cancer. Palliative therapeutic ERCP with metal or plastic stents is performed for biliary decompression.

CHEMOTHERAPY

In patients with advanced disease, accepted approaches can include the administration of gemcitabine alone or combined with the oral EGFR inhibitor erlotinib. More recently, a combination therapy regimen consisting of oxaliplatin, irinotecan, fluorouracil, and leucovorin (FOLFIRINOX) offers increased median survival in metastatic pancreatic cancer when compared to gemcitabine (11.1 mo versus 6.8 mo) but at the cost of increased toxicity. A second trial revealed that in patients with metastatic pancreatic cancer, the combination of nab-paclitaxel plus gemcitabine significantly improved overall survival, but rates of peripheral neuropathy and myelosuppression were increased.

- Poor survival outcomes are seen in patients with poor performance status, significant weight loss, and with liver metastases.
  - External-beam radiotherapy is effective for palliation of pain.
  - Combined chemotherapy and radiotherapy can be utilized in the case of patients with locally advanced but unresectable cases and confers a modest improvement in median overall survival.

DISPOSITION

- Adjuvant chemotherapy has a significant survival benefit in patients with resected pancreatic cancer.
- Recent trials have shown that adjuvant postoperative chemotherapy with gemcitabine or 5-FU significantly delays the development of recurrent disease after complete resection of pancreatic cancer. Pancreatic cancer is the most lethal common cancer because it is usually diagnosed at an advanced stage and is resistant to therapy. Median survival for locally unresectable disease is about 14 to 16 months, while the median survival for metastatic disease is 10 to 12 months.

PEARLS & CONSIDERATIONS

COMMENTS

- The U.S. Preventive Services Task Force (USPSTF) recommends against routine screening for pancreatic cancer in asymptomatic adults by abdominal palpation, ultrasonography, or serologic markers. The USPSTF found no evidence that screening for pancreatic cancer is effective in reducing mortality rates. There is potential for significant harm because of the low prevalence of pancreatic cancer, limited accuracy of available screening tests, invasive nature of diagnostic tests, and poor outcome of treatment. Alcohol consumption, specifically liquor consumption of three or more drinks per day, increases pancreatic cancer mortality independent of smoking.
- Patients should be referred for pancreatic cancer surgery only to medical centers that perform at least 15 to 20 cases a year, given the superior outcomes in higher-volume centers.
- Adjuvant chemotherapy with either a gemcitabine or 5-fluoruracil (5-FU) regimen for 6 months is proven to improve survival and should be recommended in all patients with a maintained performance status after surgical resection. The role of radiotherapy in the adjuvant setting is best restricted to patients with disease that is high risk for local recurrence.

RELATED CONTENT

Pancreatic Cancer (Patient Information)

AUTHOR: **RITESH RATHORE, M.D.**

TABLE 1P-3 Clinical/Radiographic Staging System for Adenocarcinoma of the Pancreatic Head and Uncinate Process

Clinical Stage	>AJCC Stage	TUMOR-VESSEL RELATIONSHIP ON COMPUTED TOMOGRAPHY			
		SMA	Celiac Axis	CHA*	SMV-PV
Resectable (all four are required to be resectable)†	I/II	Normal tissue plane between tumor and vessel	Normal tissue plane between tumor and vessel	Normal tissue plane between tumor and vessel	Patent (may include tumor abutment or encasement)
Borderline resectable (only one of the four required)	III	Abutment	Abutment	Abutment or short segment encasement	May have short segment occlusion if reconstruction possible
Locally advanced (only one of the four required)	III	Encasement	Encasement	Extensive encasement with no technical option for reconstruction	Occluded with no technical option for reconstruction

AJCC, American Joint Commission for Cancer; *CHA*, common hepatic artery; *SMV–PV,* superior mesenteric vein–portal vein confluence. Abutment refers to ≤180 degrees or ≤50% of the vessel circumference; encasement is <180 degrees or <50% of the vessel circumference.

*Assumes normal vascular anatomy; for example, encasement of the CHA is not a limitation in performing PD when there is an uninvolved replaced right hepatic artery arising from the superior mesenteric artery.

†Assumes the technical ability to resect and reconstruct the SMV, PV, or SMV-PV confluence when necessary. Others would consider tumor-vein abutment/encasement, which results in deformity of the vein as borderline resectable.

From Cameron JL, Cameron AM: *Current surgical therapy,* ed 10, Philadelphia, 2011, Saunders.

BASIC INFORMATION

DEFINITION

- Acute pancreatitis is an inflammatory process of the pancreas with intrapancreatic activation of enzymes that may also involve peripancreatic tissue and/or remote organ systems.
- Commonly used scoring systems for acute pancreatitis are described in Table 1P-4.

The **Revised Atlanta Criteria**[1] use early prognostic signs, organ failure, and local complications to define disease severity:

1. Mild pancreatitis: no organ failure, no local or systemic complications, pancreatitis typically resolves in first week
2. Moderate pancreatitis: transient organ failure (≤48 hours) *or* local complications (e.g., pancreatic necrosis, peripancreatic fluid collections, peripancreatic necrosis) *or* exacerbation of comorbid disease
3. Severe pancreatitis: persistent organ failure (>48 hours)

The **BALI Score**[2] evaluates only four variables:
1. BUN ≥25 mg/dL
2. Age ≥65 years
3. LDH ≥300 U/L
4. Interleukin-6 level ≥300 pg/mL

These measurements are taken at admission and at 48 hours. Mortality is >25% for a score of 3 and exceeds 50% with a score of 4.

Severe acute pancreatitis (SAP) is diagnosed by the presence of any of the following criteria:

1. Organ failure with one or more of the following: shock (systolic blood pressure <90 mm Hg), pulmonary insufficiency (Pao_2 ≤60 mm Hg), renal failure (serum creatinine >2 mg/dl after rehydration), and gastrointestinal bleeding (>500 mL/24 hr)
2. Local complications such as necrosis, pseudocyst, or abscess
3. At least three of Ranson's criteria (see below) *or*
4. At least eight of the Acute Physiology and Chronic Health Evaluation II (APACHE II) criteria

ICD-10CM Codes
K85.0 Idiopathic acute pancreatitis
K85.1 Biliary acute pancreatitis
K85.2 Alcohol induced acute pancreatitis
K 85.3 Drug induced pancreatitis
K85.6 Other acute pancreatitis
K85.9 Acute pancreatitis, unspecified

EPIDEMIOLOGY & DEMOGRAPHICS

- There are >240,000 cases of acute pancreatitis reported annually in the United States, with nearly 50% due to gallstone disease.
- Acute pancreatitis is most often secondary to biliary tract disease and alcohol. The rate of pancreatitis continues to rise and ranges from 10 to 45 cases/100,000 in Western countries.
- Incidence in urban areas is twice that of rural areas (20/100,000 persons in urban areas).
- 20% of patients have necrotizing pancreatitis; the remainder have interstitial, or edematous, pancreatitis.
- Acute pancreatitis accounts for >220,000 hospital admissions in the United States each year.

PHYSICAL FINDINGS & CLINICAL PRESENTATION

- Epigastric tenderness and guarding, often radiating to the back; pain usually developing suddenly, reaching peak intensity within 10 to 30 min, severe and lasting several hours without relief
- Hypoactive bowel sounds (from ileus)
- Tachycardia, shock (from decreased intravascular volume)
- Confusion (from metabolic disturbances)
- Fever
- Tachycardia, decreased breath sounds (atelectasis, pleural effusions, acute respiratory distress syndrome [ARDS])
- Jaundice (from obstruction or compression of biliary tract)
- Ascites (from tear in pancreatic duct, leaking pseudocyst)
- Palpable abdominal mass (pseudocyst, phlegmon, abscess, carcinoma)
- Evidence of hypocalcemia (Chvostek's sign, Trousseau's sign)
- Evidence of intraabdominal bleeding (hemorrhagic pancreatitis):
  1. Gray-blue discoloration around the umbilicus *(Cullen's sign)*
  2. Bluish discoloration involving the flanks *(Grey Turner's sign)*
- Tender subcutaneous nodules (caused by subcutaneous fat necrosis)

ETIOLOGY

- In >90% of cases: biliary tract disease (calculi or sludge) or alcohol, most common after 5 to 10 yr of heavy drinking
- Drugs (e.g., thiazides, furosemide, corticosteroids, tetracycline, estrogens, valproic acid, metronidazole, azathioprine, methyldopa, pentamidine, ethacrynic acid, procainamide, amiodarone, sulindac, nitrofurantoin, angiotensin-converting enzyme inhibitors, danazol, cimetidine, piroxicam, gold, ranitidine, sulfasalazine, isoniazid, acetaminophen, cisplatin, didanosine, opiates, erythromycin, metformin, GLP-1 receptor agonists, incretin mimetics)
- Abdominal trauma

TABLE 1P-4 Commonly Used Scoring Systems: Advantages and Disadvantages

System	Scoring	Advantages	Disadvantages
Ranson's criteria on admission: 1. Age >55 yr 2. WBC >16 × 10⁹/L 3. LDH >350 U/L 4. AST >250 U/L 5. Glucose >200 mg/dl During initial 48 hr: 1. Hgb falls below 10 mg/dl 2. BUN rises by >5 mg/dl 3. Ca <8 mg/dl 4. Pao₂ <60 mm Hg 5. Base deficit >4 mEq/L 6. Fluid sequestration >6 L	1 point for each factor listed; score >3 indicates SAP	Well known, relatively easy to calculate	Requires 48 hr to complete evaluation
APACHE II*	Score >8 predicts SAP	Can be calculated within 24 hr of admission	Requires large dataset for processing
BISAP 1. BUN >25 mg/dl 2. Altered mental status 3. Presence of SIRS 4. Age >60 yr 5. Pleural effusions	1 point for each factor listed; score >3 indicates SAP	Ease of use, available within 24 hr of admission	Significantly lower sensitivity than either Ranson's or APACHE II; results in greater likelihood of missing severe AP
CTSI	Based on radiographic data	Excellent predictor of local complications; can show infected pancreatic necrosis	Requires 72 to 96 hr, making it a poor test for guiding decisions at admission

APACHE, Acute Physiology and Chronic Health Evaluation; *AST*, aspartate aminotransferase; *BISAP*, Bedside Index for Severity in Acute Pancreatitis; *BUN*, blood urea nitrogen; *Ca*, serum calcium; *CTSI*, Computed Tomography Severity Index; *Hgb*, hemoglobin; *LDH*, lactate dehydrogenase; *SAP*, severe acute pancreatitis; *SIRS*, systemic inflammatory response syndrome; *WBC*, white blood cell count.
*Based on diverse variables, including age, physiology, and long-term health; equation available at www.sfar.org/scores2/apache22.html#calcul. Adding body mass index (BMI) to APACHE II (the APACHE O score) increases discrimination (1 point added for BMI 26-30; 2 points for BMI >30).
Modified from Cameron JL, Cameron AM: *Current surgical therapy*, ed 10, Philadelphia, 2011, Saunders.

[1]Banks PA et al.; Acute Pancreatitis Classification Working Group: Classification of acute pancreatitis-2012: revision of the Atlanta classification and definitions by international consensus, *Gut* 62(1):102-111, 2013.
[2]Spitzer AL et al.: Applying Ockham's razor to pancreatitis prognostication: a four-variable predictive model, *Ann Surg* 243(3):380-388, 2006.

- Surgery
- Endoscopic retrograde cholangiopancreatography (ERCP)
- Infections (predominantly viral infections)
- Peptic ulcer (penetrating duodenal ulcer)
- Pancreas divisum (congenital failure to fuse of dorsal or ventral pancreas)
- Idiopathic
- Pregnancy
- Vascular (vasculitis, ischemic)
- Hypolipoproteinemia (types I, IV, and V)
- Hypercalcemia
- Pancreatic carcinoma (primary or metastatic)
- Renal failure
- Hereditary pancreatitis
- Occupational exposure to chemicals: methanol, cobalt, zinc, mercuric chloride, creosol, lead, organophosphates, chlorinated naphthalenes
- Others: scorpion bite, obstruction at ampulla region (neoplasm, duodenal diverticula, Crohn's disease), hypotensive shock, autoimmune pancreatitis

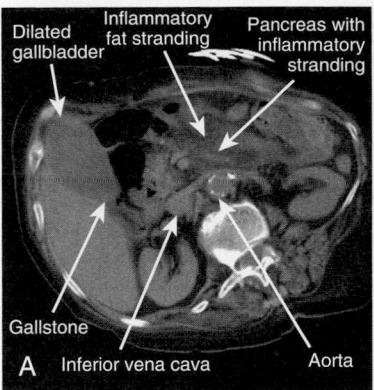
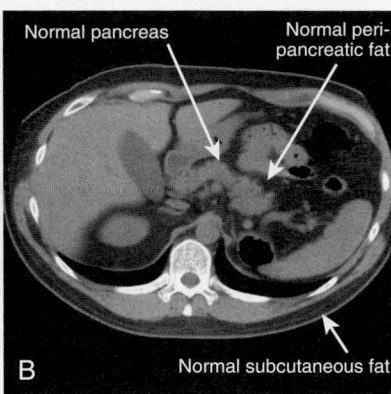

FIGURE 1P-8 Gallstone pancreatitis and normal pancreas for comparison, axial CT without contrast. A, Gallstone pancreatitis CT. A dilated gallbladder is visible with a hyperdense dependent lesion consistent with a gallstone. The region of the pancreas shows significant inflammatory stranding. In this patient, the pancreas lies just anterior to the left renal vein, which can be seen crossing anterior to the aorta and entering the inferior vena cava. **B,** A normal pancreas is visible. This pancreas is surrounded by uninflamed fat, which is dark (nearly black). Compare this normal fat with normal subcutaneous fat. (From Broder JS: *Diagnostic imaging for the emergency physician,* Philadelphia, 2011, Saunders.)

Dx DIAGNOSIS

DIFFERENTIAL DIAGNOSIS

- PUD
- Acute cholangitis, biliary colic
- High intestinal obstruction
- Early acute appendicitis
- Mesenteric vascular obstruction
- DKA
- Pneumonia (basilar)
- Myocardial infarction (inferior wall)
- Renal colic
- Ruptured or dissecting aortic aneurysm
- Mesenteric ischemia

LABORATORY TESTS

Pancreatic enzymes:

Amylase is increased, usually elevated in the initial 3 to 5 days of acute pancreatitis. Isoamylase determinations (separation of pancreatic cell isoenzyme components of amylase) are useful in excluding occasional cases of salivary hyperamylasemia. The use of isoamylase rather than total serum amylase reduces the risk of erroneously diagnosing pancreatitis and is preferred by some as initial biochemical test in patients suspected of having acute pancreatitis.

Urinary amylase determinations are useful to diagnose acute pancreatitis in patients with lipemic serum, to rule out elevated serum amylase caused by macroamylasemia, and to diagnose acute pancreatitis in patients whose serum amylase is normal.

Serum lipase levels are elevated in acute pancreatitis; the elevation is less transient than serum amylase; concomitant evaluation of serum amylase and lipase increases diagnostic accuracy of acute pancreatitis. An elevated lipase/amylase ratio is suggestive of alcoholic pancreatitis.

Elevated serum trypsin levels are diagnostic of pancreatitis (in absence of renal failure).

Serum C-reactive protein at 48 hr is an excellent laboratory marker of severity.

Rapid measurement of urinary trypsinogen-2 (if available) is useful in the emergency department as a screening test for acute pancreatitis in patients with abdominal pain; a negative dipstick test for urinary trypsinogen-2 rules out acute pancreatitis with a high degree of probability, whereas a positive test indicates need for further evaluation.

Interleukin-6 level: worse prognosis with level ≥300 pg/mL.

ADDITIONAL TESTS

- Complete blood count: reveals leukocytosis; hematocrit (Hct) may be initially increased as a result of hemoconcentration; decreased Hct may indicate hemorrhage or hemolysis.
- Blood urea nitrogen (BUN) is increased because of dehydration. Serial BUN measurements are the most valuable lab test for predicting mortality during the initial 48 hr.
- Elevation of serum glucose in a previously normal patient correlates with the degree of pancreatic malfunction and may be related to increased release of glycogen, catecholamines, and glucocorticoid release and decreased insulin release.
- Liver profile: aspartate aminotransferase (AST) and lactate dehydrogenase (LDH) are increased as a result of tissue necrosis; bilirubin and alkaline phosphatase may be increased from common bile duct obstruction. A threefold or greater rise in serum alanine aminotransferase concentrations is an excellent indicator (95% probability) of biliary pancreatitis.
- Serum calcium is decreased as a result of saponification, precipitation, and decreased parathyroid hormone response.
- Arterial blood gases: Pao$_2$ may be decreased as a result of ARDS, pleural effusion(s); pH may be decreased as a result of lactic acidosis, respiratory acidosis, and renal insufficiency.
- Serum electrolytes: potassium may be increased from acidosis or renal insufficiency; sodium may be increased from dehydration.

IMAGING STUDIES

- Abdominal plain films are useful initially to distinguish other conditions that may mimic pancreatitis (perforated viscus). They may reveal localized ileus (sentinel loop), pancreatic calcifications (chronic pancreatitis), blurring of left psoas shadow, dilation of transverse colon, calcified gallstones.
- Chest x-ray may reveal elevation of one or both diaphragms, pleural effusions, basilar infiltrates, or platelike atelectasis.
- Abdominal ultrasonography is useful in detecting gallstones (sensitivity of 60%-70% for detecting stones associated with pancreatitis). Its availability and noninvasive nature make it the initial imaging study of choice; its major limitation is the presence of distended bowel loops overlying the pancreas.
- CT scan (Fig. 1P-8) is less sensitive than ultrasound in identifying gallstones and exposes the patient to risk of contrast-induced nephropathy. It is, however, superior to ultrasonography in identifying pancreatitis and defining its extent, and it also plays a role in diagnosing pseudocysts (they appear as a well-defined area surrounded by a high-density capsule); gastrointestinal fistulation or infection of a pseudocyst can also be identified by the presence of gas within the pseudocyst. Sequential contrast-enhanced CT is useful for detection of pancreatic necrosis. The severity of pancreatitis can also be graded by CT scan (Table 1P-5). (A = normal pancreas, B = enlarged pancreas [1 point], C = pancreatic and/or peripancreatic inflammation [2 points], D = single peripancreatic collection [3 points], E = at least two peripancreatic collections and/or retroperitoneal air [4 points]. Percentage of pancreatic necrosis <30% [2 points], 30% to 50% [4 points], >50% [6 points]. The CT severity index is calculated by adding grade points to points assigned for percentage of necrosis.
- Magnetic resonance cholangiopancreatography (MRCP) has >90% sensitivity for

TABLE 1P-5   Computed Tomography Severity Index Score for Pancreatitis*

Grade[†]	CT Findings	Score
A	Normal pancreas	0
B	Focal or diffuse enlargement of the pancreas, contour irregularities, heterogeneous attenuation, no peripancreatic inflammation	1
C	Grade B plus peripancreatic inflammation	2
D	Grade C plus a single fluid collection	3
E	Grade C plus multiple fluid collections or gas	4

Percent Necrosis Present on Ct	Score
0	0
<33	2
33-50	4
>50	6

*Severity Index Score = Grade score + Percent necrosis score. Maximum score = 10; severe disease = 6 or higher.
[†]Severity of the acute inflammatory process.
From Adams JG et al: *Emergency medicine, clinical essentials*, ed 2, Philadelphia, 2013, Elsevier.

choledocholithiasis and can identify other anatomic abnormalities.

- Endoscopic ultrasonography (EUS) is a minimally invasive test that provides high-resolution imaging of the pancreas. It is useful to identify anatomic abnormalities of the pancreas and has good sensitivity and specificity for small gallstones (≤5 mm).
- ERCP indications: useful to perform biliary sphincterotomy and stone removal in the presence of a retained bile duct stone seen on imaging. The role and timing of ERCP in patients with acute biliary pancreatitis has been controversial. Guidelines from the American College of Gastroenterology suggest that urgent ERCP (within 24 hr of admission) is indicated in patients with biliary pancreatitis who have concurrent acute cholangitis, but it is not needed in most patients who do not have evidence of ongoing biliary obstruction.[3,4]

Rx TREATMENT

NONPHARMACOLOGIC THERAPY
- Bowel rest with avoidance of liquids or solids during the acute illness
- Avoidance of alcohol and any drugs associated with pancreatitis

ACUTE GENERAL Rx
GENERAL MEASURES:
- Assess severity of pancreatitis (see Table 1P-4).
- Maintain adequate intravascular volume with vigorous IV hydration. Aggressive fluid resuscitation (250-500 mL/hr) with isotonic crystalloids is critical in managing acute pancreatitis.
- Patient should remain NPO until clinically improved, stable, and hungry. Enteral feedings are preferred over total parenteral nutrition. Enteral nutrition reduces mortality, multiple organ failure, systemic infections, and

operative interventions more than total parenteral nutrition does in patients with acute pancreatitis. Parenteral nutrition may be necessary in patients who do not tolerate enteral feeding or in whom an adequate infusion rate cannot be reached within 2 to 4 days. Early enteral feeding through a nasogastric (NG) feeding tube is often used instead of an oral diet, but evidence to support this strategy is limited. A recent trial did not show superiority of early NG tube feeding, as compared to oral diet after 72 hours, in reducing the rate of infection or death in patients with acute pancreatitis at high risk for complications.[5]
- Nasogastric suction is useful only in severe pancreatitis to decompress the abdomen in patients with ileus.
- Control pain: IV morphine or fentanyl. Meperidine and hydromorphone are also commonly used narcotics for pain control.
- Correct metabolic abnormalities (e.g., replace calcium and magnesium as necessary).

SPECIFIC MEASURES:
- Pancreatic or peripancreatic infection develops in 40% to 70% of patients with pancreatic necrosis. However, IV antibiotics should not be used prophylactically for all cases of pancreatitis; their use is justified if the patient has evidence of septicemia, pancreatic abscess, or pancreatitis caused by biliary calculi. Their use should generally be limited to 5 to 7 days to prevent development of fungal superinfection. Appropriate empiric antibiotic therapy should cover:
  1. *Bacteroides fragilis* and other anaerobes (cefotetan, cefoxitin, metronidazole, or clindamycin plus aminoglycoside)
  2. *Enterococcus* (ampicillin)
- Surgical therapy has a limited role in acute pancreatitis; it is indicated in the following:
  1. Gallstone-induced pancreatitis: cholecystectomy when acute pancreatitis subsides. However, randomized trials have shown that patients with mild gallstone

pancreatitis can undergo cholecystectomy safely during the first 48 hr of hospitalization.
  2. Perforated peptic ulcer.
  3. Necrotizing pancreatitis with infected necrotic tissue is associated with an elevated rate of complications and increased risk of death. Traditional treatment has been open necrosectomy; surgical necrosectomy induces a proinflammatory response and is associated with a high complication rate. Recent trials have shown that a step-up approach consisting of percutaneous drainage followed, if necessary, by minimally invasive retroperitoneal necrosectomy may have a lower rate of complications and death. Endoscopic transgastric necrosectomy, a form of natural orifice transluminal endoscopic surgery, has been shown in recent trials to be effective in reducing the proinflammatory response as well as reducing complications.
- Identification and treatment of complications:
  1. **Pseudocyst:** round or spheroid collection of fluid, tissue, pancreatic enzymes, and blood.
     1. Diagnosed by CT scan or sonography.
     2. Treatment: Pancreatic pseudocysts can be drained surgically or endoscopically. The endoscopic approach is preferable when the patient's anatomy is suitable and an experienced endoscopist is available. CT scan or ultrasound-guided percutaneous drainage (with a pigtail catheter left in place for continuous drainage) can be used, but the recurrence rate is high; the conservative approach is to reevaluate the pseudocyst (with CT scan or sonography) after 6 to 7 wk and surgically drain it if the pseudocyst has not decreased in size.
     3. Generally, pseudocysts <5 cm in diameter are reabsorbed without intervention, whereas those >5 cm require surgical intervention after the wall has matured.
  2. **Phlegmon:** represents pancreatic edema. It can be diagnosed by CT scan or sonography. Treatment is supportive because it usually resolves spontaneously.
  3. **Pancreatic abscess:** diagnosed by CT scan (presence of bubbles in the retroperitoneum); Gram staining and cultures of fluid obtained from guided percutaneous aspiration usually identify bacterial organism. Therapy is surgical (or catheter) drainage and IV antibiotics (imipenem-cilastatin is the drug of choice).
  4. **Pancreatic ascites:** usually caused by leaking of pseudocyst or tear in pancreatic duct. Paracentesis reveals very high amylase and lipase levels in the pancreatic fluid; ERCP may demonstrate the lesion. Treatment is surgical correction if exudative ascites from severe pancreatitis does not resolve spontaneously.

[3]Fogel EL, Sherman S: ERCP for gallstone pancreatitis, *N Engl J Med* 370:150-157, 2014.
[4]Tenner S et al: American College of Gastroenterology guidelines: management of acute pancreatitis, *Am J Gastroenterol* 108:1400-1415, 2013.
[5]Bakker OJ et al.: Early versus on-demand nasogastric tube feeding in acute pancreatitis, *N Engl J Med* 371:1983-1993, 2014.

TABLE 1P-6 Prognostic Criteria for Acute Pancreatitis

Ranson Criteria*	Simplified Glasgow Criteria†	Computed Tomography Criteria‡
On admission: Age >55 yr	*Within 48 hr of admission:* Age >55 yr	Normal
WBC >16,000/μL	WBC >15,000/μL	Enlargement
AST >250 U/L LDH >350 U/L	LDH >600 U/L	Pancreatic inflammation
Glucose >200 mg/dl	Glucose >180 mg/dl	Single fluid collection
48 hr after admission:	Albumin <3.2 g/dl	Multiple fluid collection
Hematocrit decrease by >10	Ca²⁺ <8 mg/dl	
BUN increase by >5 mg/dl	Arterial Po₂ <60 mm Hg	
Ca²⁺ <8 mg/dl	BUN >45 mg/dl	
Arterial Po₂ <60 mm Hg		
Base deficit >4 mEq/L		
Fluid sequestration >6 L		

AST, Aspartate aminotransferase; *BUN,* blood urea nitrogen; *LDH,* lactate dehydrogenase; *WBC,* white blood cells.
*Three or more Ranson's criteria predict a complicated clinical course. Data from Ranson JH et al: Prognostic signs and nonoperative peritoneal lavage in acute pancreatitis, *Surg Gynecol Obstet* 143:209-219, 1976.
†Data from Blamey SL et al: Prognostic factors in acute pancreatitis, *Gut* 25:1340, 1984.
‡Grades A and B represent mild disease with no risk of infection or death. Grade C represents moderately severe disease with a minimal likelihood of infection and essentially no risk of mortality. Grades D and E represent severe pancreatitis with an infection rate of 30% to 50% and mortality rate of 15%. Data from Balthazar EJ et al: Acute pancreatitis value of CT in establishing prognosis, *Radiology* 174:331, 1990.
From Goldman L, Ausiello D (eds): *Cecil textbook of medicine,* ed 24, Philadelphia, 2012, Saunders.

5. Gastrointestinal bleeding: caused by alcoholic gastritis, bleeding varices, stress ulceration, or disseminated intravascular coagulation (DIC).
6. Renal failure: caused by hypovolemia, resulting in oliguria or anuria, cortical or tubular necrosis (shock, DIC), or thrombosis of renal artery or vein.
7. Hypoxia: caused by ARDS, pleural effusion, or atelectasis.

THERAPY OF UNCOMMON FORMS OF PANCREATITIS

1. **Autoimmune pancreatitis (AIP):** Fibroinflammatory disease characterized by an IgG4 lymphoplasmacytic infiltrate. It is a variant of chronic pancreatitis and it has been associated with other autoimmune disorders (e.g., primary sclerosing cholangitis, Sjögren syndrome). The inflammatory process is generally responsive to corticosteroid therapy. Older men aged 60 to 70 years are primarily affected. Patients present with abdominal pain, weight loss, anorexia, and obstructive jaundice. Immunoglobulin G₄ levels are elevated. Radiographically on CT, the pancreas is diffusely enlarged, with a characteristic smooth, capsule-like rim ("sausage pancreas"). Type II autoimmune hepatitis (idiopathic duct-centric chronic pancreatitis) is associated with inflammatory bowel disease and not related to IgG4 cell deposition.

2. **Hypertriglyceridemic pancreatitis (HTGP):** Beneficial results have been reported with early (within 48 hr) initiation of apheresis with IV heparin and insulin in addition to conventional treatment modalities for acute pancreatitis when there is concomitant hyperglycemia with severe acute pancreatitis.

DISPOSITION

Prognosis varies with the severity of pancreatitis; overall mortality rate in acute pancreatitis is 5% to 10%. Prognostic criteria for acute pancreatitis are described in Table 1P-6.

REFERRAL

- Hospitalization is indicated in moderate to severe cases of pancreatitis.
- Surgical consultation is needed in suspected gallstone pancreatitis, perforated peptic ulcer, or presence of necrotic or infected foci. Acute pancreatitis can generally be attributed to gallstones when patients have both abnormal liver enzymes and gallstones (or sludge) on imaging. Such patients should consider cholecystectomy prior to discharge to prevent recurrent pancreatitis.
- Gastroenterology consultation in severe or recurrent pancreatitis, when ERCP is needed for gallstone pancreatitis, or when the cause of pancreatitis is unclear.

 **PEARLS & CONSIDERATIONS**

- Acute pancreatitis is the most common major complication of ERCP. NSAIDs are potent inhibitors of phospholipase A₂, cyclooxygenase, and neutrophil-endothelial interactions, which play an important role in the pathogenesis of acute pancreatitis. Preliminary trials show that among patients at high risk for post-ERCP pancreatitis, rectal indomethacin (given as two 50-mg indomethacin suppositories administered immediately after ERCP) significantly reduced the incidence of post-ERCP pancreatitis.
- Pancreatic stent placement decreases the risk of post-ERCP pancreatitis.
- Statins reduce risk for pancreatitis in adults. Fibrates do not affect risk for pancreatitis.
- Diabetes mellitus may develop from extensive pancreatic necrosis.

 **EVIDENCE**

Available at www.expertconsult.com

SUGGESTED READINGS
Available at www.expertconsult.com

RELATED CONTENT
Acute Pancreatitis (Patient Information)

AUTHOR: **FRED F. FERRI, M.D.**

BASIC INFORMATION

DEFINITION

Chronic pancreatitis is a recurrent or persistent inflammatory process of the pancreas characterized by chronic pain and by pancreatic exocrine and/or endocrine insufficiency. It is classified anatomically as either large-duct disease or small-duct (minimal change) disease.

ICD-10CM CODES
K86.1 Other chronic pancreatitis
K86.0 Alcohol-induced chronic pancreatitis

EPIDEMIOLOGY & DEMOGRAPHICS

- Chronic pancreatitis occurs in approximately five to 10 per 100,000 persons in industrialized countries.
- Average age at diagnosis is 35 to 55 yr; male/female ratio is 5:1.

PHYSICAL FINDINGS & CLINICAL PRESENTATION

- Persistent or recurrent epigastric and left upper quadrant pain that may radiate to the back
- Tenderness over the pancreas, muscle guarding
- Significant weight loss
- Bulky, foul-smelling stools, greasy in appearance
- Epigastric mass (10% of patients)
- Jaundice (5%-10% of patients)

ETIOLOGY

- Chronic alcoholism (most common cause)
- Obstruction (ampullary stenosis, tumor, trauma [with pancreatic duct stricture], pancreas divisum, annular pancreas)
- Tobacco
- Hereditary pancreatitis
- Severe malnutrition
- Idiopathic
- Untreated hyperparathyroidism (hypercalcemia)
- Mutations of the cystic fibrosis transmembrane conductance regulator *(CFTR)* gene and the TF genotype
- Other genetic mutations (Cationic trypsinogen gene, chemotrypsinogen C gene, calcium-sensing receptor gene, claudin-2 gene, serine protease inhibitor, kazal type 1 gene)
- ***Autoimmune pancreatitis (AIP):*** (5% of chronic pancreatitis cases): presents clinically with jaundice (63% of patients) and abdominal pain (35%). CT may reveal diffusely enlarged pancreas, enhanced peripheral rim of hypoattenuation "halo," and low-attenuation mass in head of pancreas. Laboratory values reveal elevated serum immunoglobulin (Ig) G4, elevated serum Ig or gamma-globulin level, presence of antilactoferrin antibody (ALA), anticarbonic anhydrase (ACA) II level, anti-smooth-muscle antibody (ASMA), or antinuclear antibody (ANA).
- ***Sclerosing pancreatitis:*** a form of chronic pancreatitis characterized by infrequent attacks of abdominal pain, irregular narrowing of the pancreatic duct, and swelling of the pancreatic parenchyma; patients have high levels of serum immunoglobulins (IgG4). Chronic sclerosing pancreatitis is also known as *autoimmune pancreatitis.*

DIAGNOSIS

DIFFERENTIAL DIAGNOSIS

- Pancreatic cancer
- Peptic ulcer disease
- Cholelithiasis with biliary obstruction
- Malabsorption from other etiologies
- Recurrent acute pancreatitis
- Renal insufficiency
- Intestinal ischemia or infarction
- Other: Crohn's disease, gastroparesis, inflammatory bowel disease

WORKUP

Medical history with focus on alcohol use, laboratory tests, diagnostic imaging

LABORATORY TESTS

- Serum amylase and lipase may be elevated (normal amylase levels, however, do not exclude the diagnosis).
- Hyperglycemia, glycosuria, hyperbilirubinemia, and elevated serum alkaline phosphatase may also be present.
- 72-hr fecal fat determination (rarely performed) reveals excess fecal fat. Fecal elastase test requires only 20 g of stool.
- Secretin stimulation test is the best test for diagnosing pancreatic exocrine insufficiency.
- Lipid panel: significantly elevated triglycerides can cause pancreatitis.
- Serum calcium: hyperparathyroidism is a rare cause of chronic pancreatitis.
- Elevated levels of serum IgG4 are found in sclerosing pancreatitis and AIP.
- Elevated serum Ig or gamma-globulin level, presence of ALA, ACA II level, ASMA, or ANA in AIP.

IMAGING STUDIES

- Plain abdominal radiographs (Fig. E1P-9) may reveal pancreatic calcifications (95% specific for chronic pancreatitis).
- Ultrasound of abdomen may reveal duct dilation, pseudocyst, calcification, and presence of ascites.
- Contrast-enhanced CT scan of abdomen is the initial modality of choice. It is useful to detect calcifications (Fig. E1P-10), evaluate for ductal dilation (Fig. E1P-11), and rule out pancreatic cancer.
- Endoscopic retrograde cholangiopancreatography (ERCP) had been traditionally used to evaluate for the presence of dilated ducts, strictures, pseudocysts, and intraductal stones. However, for the evaluation of pancreatic parenchyma and duct system newer, less invasive modalities such as magnetic resonance cholangiopancreatography and endoscopic ultrasonography (EUS) are preferred. EUS (Fig. E1P-12) has a sensitivity of 97% and a specificity of 60% for chronic pancreatitis and a very low complication rate. Fine-needle aspiration biopsy combined with EUS is the preferred modality for evaluation of cystic or mass lesions to determine malignancy.

TREATMENT

NONPHARMACOLOGIC THERAPY

- Avoidance of alcohol and tobacco
- Frequent, small-volume, low-fat meals

ACUTE GENERAL Rx

- Avoidance of narcotics if possible (simple analgesics or NSAIDs can be used). Fig. E1P-13 describes an approach to the patient with painful chronic pancreatitis.
- Treatment of steatorrhea with pancreatic supplements (e.g., Pancrease, Creon, pancrelipase titrated prn based on the amount of steatorrhea and patient's weight loss). All non–enteric-coated enzymes should be used with acid-suppressing medications. Proton pump inhibitors and H_2 blockers reduce inactivation of the enzymes from gastric acid.
- Antioxidants (vitamin A, selenium, vitamin E) may be helpful for pain control in chronic pancreatitis.
- Percutaneous or via EUS celiac plexus blockade with corticosteroids or neurolysis with ethanol may provide temporary pain relief.
- Treatment of complications (e.g., type 1 diabetes mellitus).
- Glucocorticoid therapy in patients with AIP and sclerosing pancreatitis can induce clinical remission and significantly decrease serum concentrations of IgG4, immune complexes, and the IgG4 subclass of immune complexes.

CHRONIC Rx

- Surgical intervention may be necessary to eliminate biliary tract disease and improve flow of bile into the duodenum by eliminating obstruction of pancreatic duct.
- ERCP with endoscopic sphincterectomy and stone extraction is useful in selected patients.
- Transduodenal sphincteroplasty or pancreaticojejunostomy in selected patients. Surgery should also be considered in patients with intractable pain.
- Percutaneous or EUS-guided celiac plexus blockade using glucocorticoids is effective in providing short-term pain relief in nearly half of patients.

DISPOSITION

- Long-term survival is poor (50% of patients die within 10 yr from chronic pancreatitis or malignancy).
- Prognosis is best in patients with recurrent acute pancreatitis resulting from cholelithiasis, hyperparathyroidism, or stenosis of the sphincter of Oddi.

REFERRAL

Gastrointestinal referral for ERCP, surgical referral in selected patients (see "Chronic Rx")

SUGGESTED READINGS
Available at www.expertconsult.com

RELATED CONTENT
Chronic Pancreatitis (Patient Information)
Pancreatitis, Acute (Related Key Topic)

AUTHOR: **FRED F. FERRI, M.D.**

BASIC INFORMATION

DEFINITION

- A **panic attack** is a relatively brief, sudden episode of intense fear or apprehension, often associated with a sense of impending doom and various uncomfortable and disquieting physical symptoms. Panic attacks may be uncued ("out of the blue") or cued (i.e., triggered by a particular object or situation). Panic attacks may be present in a variety of different anxiety-related disorders (e.g., phobias, social anxiety, obsessive-compulsive disorder). Table 1P-7 describes criteria for diagnosis of panic attack.
- **Panic disorder** is diagnosed at least after two uncued panic attacks have occurred followed by at least 1 mo (or more) of significant concern about future attacks, worry about their implications, or a major change in behavior related to these attacks. The criteria for diagnosis of panic disorder is summarized in Table 1P-8. **Agoraphobia** is anxiety about, and avoidance of, places or situations in which the ability to escape is perceived to be limited or embarrassing or in which help might not be available in the event of having a panic attack.

SYNONYMS

Anxiety attacks
Fear attacks
Ataque de nervios

ICD-10CM CODES
F41.0 Panic disorder
F40.0 Agoraphobia

EPIDEMIOLOGY & DEMOGRAPHICS

INCIDENCE (IN U.S.): 1% 1-mo incidence of panic attacks

TABLE 1P-7 Criteria for Diagnosis of a Panic Attack

A discrete period of intense fear or discomfort, in which ≥4 of the following symptoms developed abruptly and reached a peak within 10 min
- Palpitations, pounding heart, or accelerated heart rate
- Sweating
- Trembling or shaking
- Sensations of shortness of breath or being smothered
- Feeling of choking
- Chest pain or discomfort
- Nausea or abdominal distress
- Feeling dizzy, unsteady, light-headed, or faint
- Derealization (feelings of unreality) or depersonalization (being detached from oneself)
- Fear of losing control or going crazy
- Paresthesias (numbness or tingling sensations)
- Chills or hot flashes

From Kliegman RM et al: *Nelson essentials of pediatrics*, ed 5, Philadelphia, 2006, Saunders.

PREVALENCE (IN U.S.):
- 15% to 20% lifetime prevalence of one or more panic attacks.
- Panic disorder is much more uncommon, with a lifetime prevalence of 1.5% to 3.5%; chronicity of condition reflected by a similar 1-yr prevalence rate of 1% to 2%.
- Agoraphobia is relatively rare; 0.3% to 1% lifetime prevalence; 30% to 50% of patients diagnosed with panic disorder also have agoraphobia.
- Lower rates of panic disorder are reported among Latinos, African Americans, Caribbean blacks, and Asian Americans (DSM 5)
- Lower estimates for Asian, African, and Latin American countries (0.1%-0.8%) (DSM 5)

PEAK INCIDENCE:
- Chronic condition with a waxing and waning course.
- Bimodal incidence peaks noted, with the first peak between ages 15 and 24 yr and second peak between ages 35 and 44 yr.

PREDOMINANT SEX:
- Women more commonly affected (>85% of clinical population).
- Panic disorder twice as common in women.
- Panic disorder with agoraphobia three times as common in women.

PREDOMINANT AGE:
- Age of onset is typically late adolescence to mid-30s. Onset earlier in males (24 yr) than females (28 yr).
- Onset after age 45 yr is rare and should raise suspicion of different etiology.

GENETICS:
- Risk of developing panic disorder in first-degree relatives of individuals with panic disorder is four to seven times that of general population.
- Findings in twin studies: approximately 60% of contributing factors to panic are genetic.

PHYSICAL FINDINGS & CLINICAL PRESENTATION

Panic disorder
- Present either with a panic attack or with fear and anxiety related to anticipation of a future panic attack or its implications.
- Typical presentation: unexpected, untriggered periods of intense anxiety and fear with associated physiologic changes (e.g., palpitations, sweating, tremulousness, shortness of breath, chest pain, gastrointestinal distress, faintness, derealization, paresthesia). This is accompanied by associated fears of dying, heart attack, stroke, passing out, losing control, or losing one's mind. Panic attacks are often described as "the most terrifying" episode an individual has experienced.
- Emergency or physician visits often occasioned by physical symptoms such as chest

TABLE 1P-8 Criteria for Diagnosis of Panic Disorder

1. Recurrent unexpected panic attacks with associated worry or behavior change
2. Not due to effects of a drug, medication, or medical condition

pain, dizziness, or difficulty breathing. Thirty percent of patients presenting with chest pain have panic disorder.

Agoraphobia:
- Rare complaints to physician. May manifest in missed office visits or tardiness. Patients may request home visits or telephone care.
- Activities usually self-limited by avoiding public situations where the patient believes he or she might experience a panic attack and would be unable to exit readily, such as the following:
  1. Crowded public areas (stores, public transportation, flying, church)
  2. Individual interactions (hairdresser, dentist, neighborhood meetings)
  3. Driving (especially if alone, far from home over bridges, through tunnels, on highways or on isolated roads)
- On exposure to or anticipation of exposure to feared situations, significant anxiety occurs. Anxiety may generate somatic symptoms that trigger a full-blown panic attack. Patients believe that escape from these situations reduces the alarming symptoms, thus reinforcing future avoidance. In actuality, symptom relief stems from adrenaline breaking down in the body after approximately 20 minutes.

ETIOLOGY

Hypotheses (NOTE: There are sufficient data to support each model. Models are not mutually exclusive.)
1. Central dyscontrol of autonomic arousal (typically localized to the locus ceruleus); similar symptoms may be chemically induced with yohimbine, caffeine, or cholecystokinin.
2. Cognitive overreaction (i.e., "catastrophic misinterpretation") to relatively mild or benign physiologic cues that then triggers a genuine autonomic cascade and further misinterpretations.
3. Dysfunction of a central suffocation alarm mechanism; some signs of compensated respiratory alkalosis. Can be experimentally induced with sodium lactate or carbon dioxide.

RISK FACTORS

1. Temperamental. Negative affect and anxiety sensitivity are risk factors for the onset of panic attacks. Severe separation anxiety in childhood may precede the panic disorder.
2. Environmental. Sexual and physical abuse in childhood is common in panic disorder. Most panic sufferers are able to identify a coalescence of stressors preceding their first panic attack.
3. Genetic and physiological. Although the exact genes are unknown, it is believed that multiple genes contribute to the vulnerability to panic attacks.

DIAGNOSIS

DIFFERENTIAL DIAGNOSIS

Medical conditions:
- Endocrinopathies:
  1. Hyperthyroidism
  2. Hyperparathyroidism
  3. Pheochromocytoma
  4. Carcinoid tumor

- Cardiac and respiratory diseases:
  1. Arrhythmias
  2. Myocardial infarction
  3. Chronic obstructive pulmonary disease
  4. Asthma
  5. Mitral valve prolapse
- Metabolic:
  1. Hypoglycemia
  2. Electrolyte imbalances
  3. Porphyria
- Seizure disorders
- Psychiatric disorders (NOTE: Panic attacks are common in a variety of psychiatric disorders. Panic disorder could be conceptualized as a phobia of the somatic sensations or situations that have become paired with panic attacks.)
  1. Phobias (e.g., specific phobia or social phobia). Note that fear of going on a plane because of crashing would be a specific phobia, whereas fear of going on a plane because one is then trapped and worries about panic is more suggestive of panic disorder with agoraphobia.
  2. Obsessive-compulsive disorder (cued by exposure to the object of the obsession)
  3. Posttraumatic stress disorder (cued by recall of a stressor)
  4. Generalized anxiety disorder (cued by excessive worry)
- Therapeutic (theophylline, steroids) and recreational (cocaine, amphetamine, caffeine, diet pills) drugs and drug withdrawal (alcohol, cannabis, barbiturates, benzodiazepines)

WORKUP

- Emergency presentation: cardiac, respiratory, or neurologic symptoms
- History and physical examination to rule out a concomitant medical or substance-related condition

NOTE: Panic disorder and agoraphobia are not diagnoses of exclusion, but exclusion of other conditions is usually required.

LABORATORY TESTS

- Thyroid profile
- Electrolyte measures, including calcium
- Toxicology screen
- ECG
- Acute cases: possible monitoring and cardiac enzymes to rule out arrhythmia or ischemia

IMAGING STUDIES

- For temporal lobe dysfunction (e.g., temporal lesions or as ictal or interictal manifestation of temporal lobe seizures): brain CT scan or MRI or an electroencephalogram in some patients
- Holter monitor to rule out occult or episodic arrhythmias
- Chest x-ray, arterial blood gases, or pulmonary function tests if respiratory compromise suspected

 **TREATMENT**

NONPHARMACOLOGIC THERAPY

Cognitive-behavioral therapy (CBT), in particular Panic Controlled Treatment, is generally very effective, with strongest results for cognitive restructuring (i.e., challenging catastrophic misinterpretations of somatic symptoms), in vivo or imaginal exposures (i.e., exposure to panic triggers in a controlled graded hierarchical fashion from least to most difficult with the goal of habituation and extinction of the fear response), and interoceptive exposures (i.e., repeated recreation and management of feared somatic sensations via activities such as chair spinning, straw breathing, and hyperventilation). CBT effect sizes are equal to or larger than for pharmacotherapy, attrition rates are lower, and relapse rates are lower. Treatment may take several sessions spread over weeks and may require referral to a behavioral specialist.

Traditionally, exposure therapy has relied upon a "desensitization paradigm" (i.e., habituation), in which the goal is to continue exposing an individual to a feared stimulus until the fear is no longer present (e.g., having a person with panic disorder remain in a shopping mall until anxiety has subsided). The assumption has been that habituation is the active ingredient in learning/fear reduction.

New research by Michelle G. Craske, PhD., suggests that fear habituation itself is not a predictor or mediator of outcomes when treating anxiety disorders. Craske theorizes that fear reduction during a prolonged exposure does not ensure that a person will not re-experience fear when encountering the feared stimulus in the future (e.g., reducing one's fear in a shopping mall does not ensure that one will not experience fear in other shopping malls). Rather, she suggests that strengthening "inhibitory learning' is the central mechanism of action for fear reduction.

Inhibitory learning acts as a competitor to the original fear; therefore, the stronger an exposure, the better it will compete with the original fear and the less likely the original fear will return. Several strategies can be employed to strengthen inhibitory learning. The goal is to violate expectations about the fear a person is going to experience.

The most effective manner to strengthen inhibitory learning is to find ways to surprise a person by violating an expectation multiple times in a single exposure. For example, if a person with panic disorder is conducting an in vivo exposure, combining it with an interoceptive exposure will be more effective (e.g., going to a shopping mall and hyperventilating at the same time).

Because of the element of surprise offered by inhibitory learning, cognitive restructuring occurs following an exposure rather than before it. Practicing cognitive restructuring prior to an exposure has been found to actually weaken an exposure. Craske suggests that varying the contexts of an exposure as much as possible is the most effective way to reduce anxiety (e.g., multiple shopping malls, multiple interoceptive exposures). Recent research suggests that an Internet-based mindfulness treatment program might be an effective approach for treating anxiety disorders.

ACUTE GENERAL Rx

- Benzodiazepines, particularly alprazolam: highly effective in the acute setting although long-term use is contraindicated for effective outcome.
- Low-dose alprazolam for patients with rare panic attacks and asymptomatic periods (0.25 to 0.5 mg PO or sublingually prn).
- Start patient on selective serotonin reuptake inhibitor (SSRI) or similar agent and taper patient off benzodiazepine by wk 2 to 3.

CHRONIC Rx

- Preferred pharmacologic agents: antidepressants with a significant serotonin reuptake inhibitory action. Generally start at low dose and titrate upward. Minimum treatment duration is 6 to 8 mo, but many patients need to take medications indefinitely.
  1. SSRIs: paroxetine (10-60 mg/day), sertraline (50-200 mg/day), citalopram (20-60 mg/day), escitalopram (5-30 mg/day), and fluoxetine (5-60 mg/day)
  2. Imipramine (100-300 mg/day)
  3. Venlafaxine (75-225 mg/day)
- Combination CBT plus SSRI has shown good long-term effects and is somewhat better than antidepressants or CBT alone. Combination CBT plus benzodiazepine does not provide any added benefit and may undermine CBT (interoceptive and in-vivo exposures may be less effective if the benzodiazepine is completely controlling the anxiety).

DISPOSITION

- Typical course is chronic but with significant waxing and waning (common to have long periods of remission).
- Presence of agoraphobia associated with a more chronic course.
- Findings with long-term follow-up studies: 6 to 10 yr after treatment some 30% are in remission, 40% to 50% have improved with residual symptoms, and the remainder are either unchanged or worse.

REFERRAL

- If patients do not respond to an SSRI
- Cognitive-behavioral therapy is the preferred treatment.

 **PEARLS & CONSIDERATIONS**

- Patient and family education is an important first step in the management of panic disorder. Education provides more adaptive explanations for the benign somatic sensations paired with panic. Presentation of genetic information and explanation of the benign nature of the physiology of each of the symptoms the patient experiences serve as a good start to allay fears and reduce stigma.
- Resumption of avoided activities or situations is a positive prognostic sign and may promote further therapeutic gains.

SUGGESTED READINGS

Available at www.expertconsult.com

RELATED CONTENT

Panic Disorder (Patient Information)

AUTHOR: **JEFFREY P. WINCZE, PH.D.**

 BASIC INFORMATION

DEFINITION
Panniculitis refers to inflammation of subcutaneous fat. Most cases are found in association with a systemic disease. Panniculitis can be separated into groups based on histopathologic characteristics. Panniculitis is classified into lobular or septal panniculitis based on whether the inflammation is seen in the fat lobules or septae, respectively. It can be further classified based on whether the inflammation is found with or without vasculitis (Table 1P-9) and by predominant cell type.

SYNONYMS
None

ICD-10CM CODES
M79.3	Unspecified panniculitis
M5400	Panniculitis affecting regions of neck and back, site unspecified
M5401	Panniculitis affecting regions of neck and back, occipito-atlanto-axial region
M5402	Panniculitis affecting regions of neck and back, cervical region
M54.03	Panniculitis affecting regions of neck and back, cervicothoracic region
M54.04	Panniculitis affecting regions of neck and back, thoracic region
M54.05	Panniculitis affecting regions of neck and back, thoracolumbar region
M54.06	Panniculitis affecting regions of neck and back, lumbar region
M54.07	Panniculitis affecting regions of neck and back, lumbosacral region
M54.08	Panniculitis affecting regions of neck and back, sacral and sacrococcygeal region
M54.09	Panniculitis affecting regions, neck and back, multiple sites in spine

EPIDEMIOLOGY & DEMOGRAPHICS
The epidemiology of the various panniculitides varies with each disease process. The most common panniculitis is erythema nodosum (refer to chapter on erythema nodosum). Another common panniculitis seen in the clinical setting is lipodermatosclerosis (LDS), which is usually seen in young, overweight females with associated venous insufficiency.

PHYSICAL FINDINGS & CLINICAL PRESENTATION
- Skin lesions can appear as nonspecific areas of erythema or erythematous nodules and/or plaques. The nodules can be palpated beneath the dermis. Ulceration, atrophy, and sclerosis can be associated clinical features of these lesions.
- The lesions are frequently painful and tender to palpation.
- Associated constitutional symptoms such as low-grade fevers, malaise, fatigue, myalgias, and arthralgias may be present.
- These skin findings usually are found on the lower limbs; however, the location of these lesions can vary with each specific panniculitis, that is, erythema nodosum is found on the pretibial areas of the lower extremities (Fig. 1P-14), erythema induratum occurs on the calf, and lupus panniculitis occurs on the upper arms, shoulders, and face.
- Skin findings tend to evolve as the types of inflammatory cells change over the course of a few days.

ETIOLOGY
Panniculitis can be either primary/idiopathic or secondary. Common secondary etiologies can be classified into the following broad categories:
- Infections: bacterial (streptococci), mycobacterial, fungal, parasitic, and viral.
- Inflammatory/connective tissue disease: erythema nodosum, erythema induratum, lipodermatosclerosis, lupus panniculitis, cutaneous polyarteritis nodosa, dermatomyositis-associated panniculitis.
- Malignancy: subcutaneous panniculitis-like type T cell lymphoma.
- Pancreatic disease: pancreatic panniculitis, which is associated with pancreatitis or pancreatic carcinoma.
- Immunodeficiency states: alpha-1 antitrypsin deficiency panniculitis, which is associated with pulmonary and hepatic disease.
- Trauma: cold panniculitis (due to exposure to the cold), traumatic panniculitis, and factitial panniculitis (due to injection of medication or foreign substances into the subcutaneous fat).
- Deposition: calciphylaxis, gout.

Panniculitis can be a sign of an underlying systemic disease. Lupus panniculitis can occur alone or may present before or after the onset of either discoid lupus erythematosus or systemic lupus erythematosus.

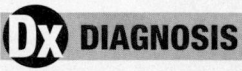 DIAGNOSIS

DIFFERENTIAL DIAGNOSIS
- The skin lesions of panniculitis need to be distinguished from other skin lesions that may manifest similarly, such as insect bites, thrombophlebitis, and cellulitis.
- Disorders affecting the deep dermis or fascia (i.e., plaque morphea, eosinophilic fasciitis), benign or malignant tumors manifesting as subcutaneous nodules, and nodules with deep bruising may have similar clinical findings and be difficult to distinguish from panniculitis.

WORKUP
- Diagnosis of panniculitis depends on a thorough history and physical examination, evaluation of patient's risk factors, skin lesion appearance and distribution, as well as any associated clinical findings.
- If the diagnosis is unclear or needs to be confirmed, a deep skin biopsy should be performed. The preferred biopsy is an excisional biopsy, but a large 6- to 8-mm punch biopsy may be sufficient.

Although the above often establishes a diagnosis, there are times when it is difficult to accurately diagnose a specific panniculitis. Different forms of panniculitides have similar clinical findings while others are rare, complicating the presentation. Biopsy specimens may be too superficial to assess for the involvement of the subcutaneous fat or to assess for the

---

TABLE 1P-9   Classification of Panniculitis

I. Without prominent vasculitis
  A. Septal inflammation
    1. Lymphocytic and mixed: erythema nodosum and variants.
    2. Granulomatous: palisaded granulomatous diseases, sarcoidosis, subcutaneous infection: tuberculosis, syphilis.
    3. Sclerotic: scleroderma, eosinophilic fasciitis, lipodermatosclerosis, toxins.
  B. Lobular inflammation
    1. Neutrophilic: infection, ruptured folliculitis and cysts, pancreatic fat necrosis.
    2. Lymphocytic: lupus panniculitis, poststeroid panniculitis, lymphoma/leukemia.
    3. Macrophagic: histiocytic cytophagic panniculitis.
    4. Granulomatous: erythema induratum/nodular vasculitis, palisaded granulomatous diseases, sarcoidosis, Crohn's disease.
    5. Mixed inflammation with many foam cells: α1-antitrypsin deficiency, traumatic fat necrosis.
    6. Eosinophilic: eosinophilic panniculitis, arthropod bites, parasites.
    7. Enzymatic fat necrosis: pancreatic enzyme panniculitis.
    8. Crystal deposits: scleredema neonatorum, subcutaneous fat necrosis of the newborn, gout, oxalosis.
    9. Embryonic fat pattern: lipoatrophy, lipodystrophy.
II. With prominent vasculitis (septal or lobular)
  A. Neutrophilic: leukocytoclastic vasculitis, subcutaneous polyarteritis nodosa, thrombophlebitis, ENL.
  B. Lymphocytic: nodular vasculitis, perniosis, angiocentric lymphomas.
  C. Granulomatous: nodular vasculitis/erythema induratum, ENL, granulomatosis with polyangiitis, Churg-Strauss allergic granulomatosis.
III. Mixed patterns

ENL, Erythema nodosum leprosum
From Lee L, Werth V: The skin and rheumatic diseases: panniculitis. In Firestein G et al (eds): *Kelley's textbook of rheumatology,* ed 9, Philadelphia, 2013, Elsevier Saunders, p. 611.

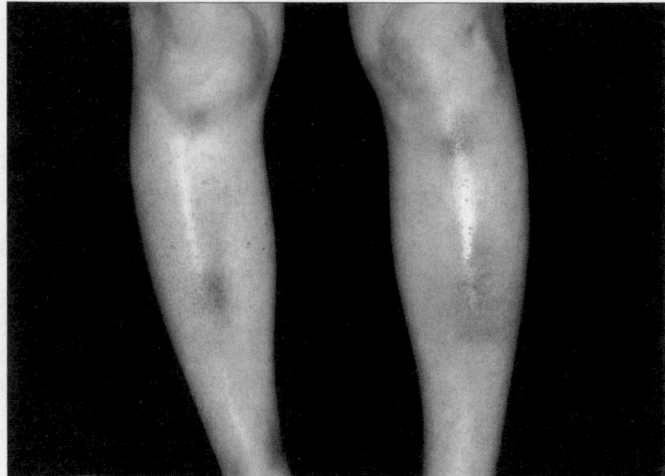

FIGURE 1P-14 Erythema nodosum secondary to acute sarcoidosis. (From Hochberg MC et al: *Rheumatology*, ed 5, St Louis, 2011, Mosby.)

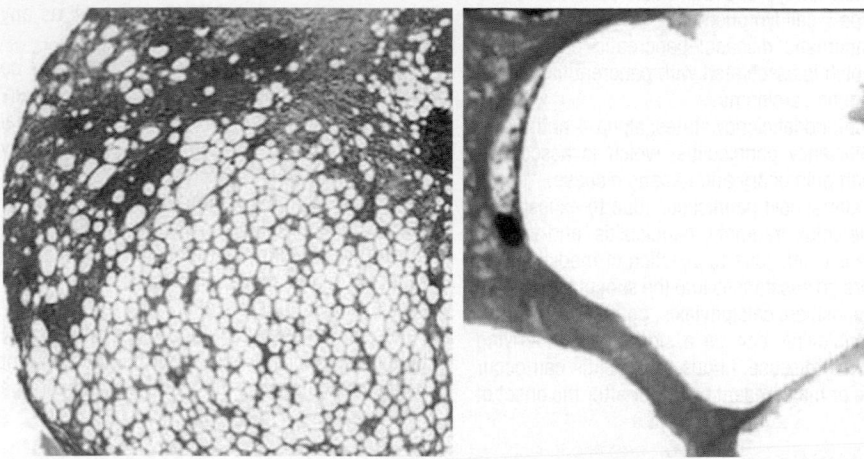

FIGURE 1P-15 Mixed lobular and septal panniculitis. (From Hochberg MC et al [eds]: Callen JP and Requena L: Cutaneous vasculitis and panniculitis. In *Rheumatology*, ed 6, Philadelphia, 2015, Elsevier Mosby, pp 1350.)

presence of vasculitis. Inflammation of the subcutaneous fat is a changing process, with varying histologic findings as well as physical characteristics of skin lesions based on the stage of evolution. Cellular infiltrates may not be confined to one location in the subcutaneous fat, and may overlap between septa and lobules (Figure 1P-15).

LABORATORY TESTS

Depending on the suspected underlying disorder, the following workup may be considered:
- Throat swab for rapid streptococcal screen, ASO titer, CBC, PPD, chest radiograph, tissue cultures, and histologic stains for organisms
- Amylase, lipase
- Serum alpha-1 antitrypsin level

- ESR, CRP
- Laboratory evaluation for possible connective tissue disease
- Further special studies of biopsy sample if malignancy is suspected

IMAGING STUDIES

- Chest radiography.
- Ankle-brachial index for assessment of peripheral vascular disease.
- Further imaging based on clinical suspicion of disease (i.e., CT scan of abdomen for pancreatitis).

 **TREATMENT**

Treatment of panniculitis is toward treatment of the underlying etiology. Any suspected medications should be discontinued. Appropriate antibiotics to treat underlying infections should be prescribed.

NONPHARMACOLOGIC THERAPY

- Leg elevation, bed rest
- Support stockings

ACUTE GENERAL Rx

- Nonsteroidal antiinflammatory medications (NSAIDs)
- Oral corticosteroids

CHRONIC Rx

- Oral potassium iodide (300-900 mg per day)
- Oral corticosteroids
- Colchicine
- Hydroxychloroquine
- Immunosuppressive medications

REFERRAL

- Dermatology for biopsy of skin lesions
- Specific specialists based on underlying etiology

SUGGESTED READINGS

Available online at www.expertconsult.com

RELATED CONTENT

Erythema Nodosum (Related Key Topic)

AUTHOR: **JOANNE SZCZYGIEL CUNHA, M.D.**

 BASIC INFORMATION

DEFINITION
Paraneoplastic syndromes are a large group of syndromes caused by hormonal, immunologic, or other soluble factors due to the presence of a malignancy. Findings and symptoms are specific to each syndrome. Paraneoplastic syndromes affect multiple organ systems, but predominantly the central and peripheral nervous systems, endocrine system, kidneys, and skin.

ICD-10CM CODES
G13.0 Paraneoplastic neuromyopathy and neuropathy
G13.1 Other systemic atrophy primarily affecting central nervous system in neoplastic disease
E83.5 Disorders of calcium metabolism
E73.1 Lambert-Eaton syndrome
E73.2 Other myasthenic syndromes in neoplastic disease

EPIDEMIOLOGY & DEMOGRAPHICS
- Paraneoplastic syndromes may affect as many as 8% of cancer patients.
- See Table 1P-10 for epidemiology of each syndrome.

PHYSICAL FINDINGS & CLINICAL PRESENTATION
Hypercalcemia of malignancy
- Nausea/vomiting
- Constipation
- Abdominal pain
- Hypertension
- Anorexia
- Fatigue
- Altered mental status (from confusion to coma)
- Depression/anxiety
- Renal failure

SIADH
- Headache
- Weakness
- Anorexia
- Nausea
- Vomiting
- Memory impairment, irritability, restlessness
- Mental status changes may progress to obtundation or coma if hyponatremia is <125 mEq/L.

Cushing's syndrome
- Rapid weight gain
- Muscle weakness
- Generalized edema
- Centripetal fat distribution, progressing to obesity; limbs are often spared or wasted
- Hypertension
- Characteristic "moon facies" due to accumulation of fat deposition in the cheeks
- Skin atrophy, easy bruising, and purple abdominal striae due to skin fragility
- Hyperpigmentation, notably in sun-exposed areas
- Menstrual irregularity, mild hirsutism in women

Limbic encephalitis (LE)
- Slow progression of mood, psychiatric changes
- Hallucinations
- Short-term memory loss
- If hypothalamus is involved, may develop hyperthermia or somnolence.
- Two thirds develop multifocal nervous system involvement.

Paraneoplastic Thrombocytosis
- Thrombosis
- Nausea
- Vomiting
- Paresthesias

Paraneoplastic Erythrocytosis
- Erythroderma
- Post-shower (aquagenic) pruritus
- Plethora

Paraneoplastic cerebellar degeneration (PCD)
- May develop prodrome of dizziness, nausea, vomiting.
- Ataxia
- Diplopia
- Dysphagia
- Dysarthria
Paraneoplastic glomerulonephritis
- Renal failure
- Oliguria or anuria
- Malaise
- Nausea or vomiting

Lambert-Eaton myasthenic syndrome (LEMS)
- Gradual onset of pelvic girdle and lower-extremity weakness, progressing in caudo-cranial direction
- Hyporeflexia
- Fatigue
- Mild bulbar dysfunction
- Dysautonomia, especially erectile dysfunction

Myasthenia gravis (MG)
- Ocular symptoms: ptosis and diplopia
- Weakness of facial muscles, notably with fatigable chewing
- Lower-extremity weakness that starts distally and progresses proximally
- May progress to involve muscles of respiration and respiratory crisis

Paraneoplastic dermatologic and rheumatologic syndromes
- Acanthosis nigricans
- Dermatomyositis (DM)
- Erythroderma
- Hypertrophic osteoarthropathy
- Leukocytoclastic vasculitis
- Paraneoplastic pemphigus (PNP)
- Polymyalgia rheumatica (PMR)
- Sweet syndrome (acute febrile neutrophilic dermatosis)

ETIOLOGY
Paraneoplastic endocrine syndromes (PES) are due to tumor production of hormones or peptides that lead to metabolic derangements:
Hypercalcemia of malignancy:
Humoral hypercalcemia of malignancy (HHM): 80% of hypercalcemia of malignancy cases. Most commonly due to production of parathyroid hormone–related peptide (PTHrP) in lung and breast cancer (also seen in renal, bladder, and ovarian cancer). More rarely, can see 1,25-dihydroxyvitamin D production

---

TABLE 1P-10 Epidemiology of Each Paraneoplastic Syndrome

Condition	Prevalence	Risk Factors
Hypercalcemia of malignancy	Up to 10%-20% of all cancer patients	Squamous cell cancers (lung, head, and neck), breast, kidney, bladder, and ovarian cancers, lymphoma
Syndrome of inappropriate antidiuretic hormone (SIADH)	Up to 1%-2% of all cancer patients	
	Found in 10%-45% of SCLC patients	SCLC
Cushing's syndrome	Approximately 2% in all cancer patients (50% of these are SCLC)	SCLC
		Pituitary adenoma, benign and malignant adrenal tumors, carcinoid tumors
Limbic encephalitis (LE)	Less than 1%	SCLC
		Testicular germ cell tumor
		Breast cancer
		Ovarian teratoma
Paraneoplastic cerebellar degeneration	Less than 1%	SCLC
		Hodgkin's lymphoma
		Breast cancer
Lambert-Eaton myasthenic syndrome (LEMS)	3% of SCLC patients	SCLC, prostate cancer, lymphoma
Paraneoplastic thrombocytosis	5%-20% of patients with solid tumors	Lung, colorectal, mesothelioma
Paraneoplastic erythrocytosis	4% of patients	Renal cell carcinoma, breast cancer
Paraneoplastic glomerulonephritis	2%-4% of patients	Hodgkin's lymphoma, thymoma, prostate cancer
Myasthenia gravis (MG)	15% of thymoma patients	Thymoma

SCLC, Small cell lung cancer.

from increased 1α-hydroxylase activity in Hodgkin and non-Hodgkin lymphomas or ectopic production of parathyroid hormone (PTH) by the tumor.

Osteolytic activity: 20% of hypercalcemia of malignancy cases. Tumor cells metastasize, infiltrate bone, and produce local factors that stimulate osteoclast activation.

SIADH: production of antidiuretic hormone (arginine vasopressin, atrial natriuretic peptide) by tumor cells. Due to ectopic ADH production, patients will demonstrate dilute serum in the face of concentrated urine.

Cushing's syndrome: ectopic ACTH promotes excess production of cortisol and other glucocorticoids from the adrenal glands, which do not respond to normal HPA feedback.

Paraneoplastic neurologic syndromes (PNS) are due to immune cross-reactivity between tumor cells and components of the nervous system. Tumor-directed antibodies (onconeural antibodies) are produced by the patient in response to a developing cancer. These onconeural antibodies and associated onconeural antigen-specific T lymphocytes inadvertently attack components of the nervous system because of antigenic similarity.

Paraneoplastic Erythrocytosis: mediated by inappropriate production of erythropoietin (EPO) and associated with a mutation in the Von Hippel-Lindau gene, commonly seen with renal cell carcinoma.

Paraneoplastic Thrombocytosis: mediated by inflammatory cytokines, in particular IL-6, as well as elevated acute phase reactants ESR and CRP. Elevated thrombopoietin levels may also be seen.

Paraneoplastic Glomerulonephritis: marked by new renal failure in the setting of newly diagnosed malignancy and is not due to direct metastatic involvement of the kidneys or genitourinary system. Diseases include minimal change disease, rapidly progressive glomerulonephritis, focal segmental glomerulonephritis, IgA nephropathy.

LE, PCD, LEMS, MG: cross-reactive autoantibodies against various components of the central and peripheral nervous system

 DIAGNOSIS

DIFFERENTIAL DIAGNOSIS

Hypercalcemia of malignancy: primary hyperparathyroidism, familial hypocalciuric hypercalcemia, excess calcium intake, vitamin D toxicity, thiazide diuretics. It is important to differentiate between HHM and osteolytic causes of malignancy-associated hypercalcemia because prognosis and response to treatment differ.

SIADH: hypovolemic hyponatremia, volume overload, reset osmostat, psychogenic polydipsia.

Cushing's syndrome: excess glucocorticoid administration, pituitary adenoma, benign or malignant adrenal tumors.

Paraneoplastic Thrombocytosis: reactive thrombocytosis from iron deficiency anemia or inflammation.

Paraneoplastic Erythrocytosis: polycythemia vera, secondary polycythemia from smoking, high-affinity hemoglobinopathies, or chronic hypoxia.

Paraneoplastic Glomerulonephritis: renal failure from intrinsic injury from nephrotoxic agents (e.g., chemotherapy), postrenal failure from bladder obstruction, or rarely direct metastatic invasion from a primary tumor.

LE, PCD, LEMS, MG: multiple sclerosis, stroke, meningitis, encephalitis

WORKUP

- History and physical examination. Box 1P-1 summarizes the evaluation and diagnosis of paraneoplastic syndromes.
- Age-appropriate cancer screening
- CT chest, PET in the paraneoplastic neurologic syndromes (PNS)
- EEG, EMG

LABORATORY TESTS

Hypercalcemia of malignancy
- Serum calcium and albumin levels to measure corrected calcium (HHM more common when serum Ca^{2+} >13 mg/dL)
- Ionized serum calcium
- PTH (low to normal)
- PTHrP (elevated)
- $1,25(OH)_2D$ levels (if the above values are inconclusive)

SIADH
- Serum and urine sodium (serum sodium <135 mEq/L or urine sodium >40 mEq/L)
- Serum and urine osmolality (serum osm <280 mOsm/kg of water and/or urine osm >100 mOsm/kg of water)

Cushing's syndrome
- High-dose dexamethasone suppression: 2 mg dexamethasone by mouth every 6 hr for 72 hr, with measurement of urinary 17-hydroxycorticosteroid at 9 A.M. and midnight days 2 and 3
- Low-dose dexamethasone suppression: 1 mg dexamethasone given with measurement of morning serum cortisol
- Dexamethasone suppression test distinguishes pituitary vs. ectopic source of ACTH

- Potassium and glucose should be monitored closely due to increased risk of hypokalemia and hyperglycemia
- **LE:** Anti-Hu, Anti-Ma2, Anti-CRMP5, Anti-GAD, anti-amphiphysin, CSF analysis, Anti-NMDAR, Anti-SOX2, Anti-SOXB1
- **PCD:** Anti-Yo, Anti-Hu, Anti-Ma, Anti-Ri, Anti-VGCC, Anti-mGluR1, CSF analysis, Anti Tr/Anti-DNER
- **LEMS:** Anti-VGCC (P/Q), CSF analysis
- **MG:** Anti-AchR, Anti-MuSk, CSF analysis
- **Paraneoplastic thrombocytosis:** CBC, liver panel, iron panel, inflammatory markers, ESR, CRP
- **Paraneoplastic erythrocytosis:** CBC, EPO level
- **Paraneoplastic glomerulonephritis:** BMP, urinalysis, urine protein to creatinine ratio, 24-hour urine protein collection, urine sediment analysis

IMAGING STUDIES

Hypercalcemia of malignancy: CT imaging to evaluate for breast lesion, lung mass, or lymphadenopathy

SIADH: CT imaging to evaluate for brain or lung mass

Cushing's syndrome: CT scan, MRI, or octreotide scan

LE, PCD, LEMS, MG: CT chest, FDG-PET scan, MRI

Paraneoplastic erythrocytosis: CT renal mass protocol or renal ultrasound to evaluate for renal cell carcinoma

(Rx) TREATMENT

NONPHARMACOLOGIC THERAPY

Hypercalcemia of malignancy
- Treatment of underlying malignancy, either surgical resection or chemotherapy/radiation of identified tumors
- Fluid resuscitation, typically 1 L bolus followed by 200 to 300 mL/hr to achieve euvolemia; followed by maintenance hydration

SIADH
- Surgical resection of identified tumors
- Fluid restriction

BOX 1P-1 Evaluation and Diagnosis of Paraneoplastic Syndromes

- Characterize abnormality; obtain laboratory studies and biopsy as necessary.
- Carefully elicit any additional symptoms and signs.
- Eliminate common causes.
- If there is no obvious etiology, consider a paraneoplastic syndrome.
- If findings are consistent with a known syndrome, screen for underlying malignancy.
- If signs and symptoms are consistent with a known paraneoplastic syndrome, undertake a search for an unknown primary cancer or recurrence or progression of a known primary tumor.
- Screening should include a careful physical examination with breast, gynecologic, and prostate evaluations; basic hematology, chemistry, and urine studies; chest radiograph; and mammogram.
- Computed tomography (CT) of the abdomen and pelvis or positron emission tomography CT scan is indicated if there are any suspicious symptoms, signs, or laboratory abnormalities. Antibody testing for paraneoplastic neurologic syndromes and/or skin biopsy should be performed as indicated.
- Consider treatment of cancer and/or appropriate palliative treatment, including immunosuppressive therapy for paraneoplastic symptoms when possible.

Cushing's syndrome
- Surgical resection of identified tumors

LE, PCD, LEMS, MG
- IVIG
- Plasma exchange
- Prednisone and tacrolimus being studied

ACUTE GENERAL Rx

Hypercalcemia of malignancy
- Furosemide intravenously once euvolemia has been reached, although clinical efficacy is debatable
- Bisphosphonates, either pamidronate or zole-dronic acid intravenous infusions (treatment side effects are renal dysfunction and osteonecrosis of the jaw).
- Calcitonin weight-based dosing, although tachyphylaxis occurs after 48 hours of administration
- Corticosteroids in cases of myeloma and lymphoma
- Hemodialysis in severe cases

SIADH
- If urine sodium is >308 mOsm/kg and patient develops seizure or obtundation, then sodium replacement with hypertonic saline (3%) is indicated
- Sodium should not be corrected at a rate faster than 9 mEq/L in any 24-hour period or faster than 18 mEq/L in any 48-hour period to decrease chances of osmotic demyelination syndrome

Cushing's syndrome
- Management of volume status and blood pressure with diuretics and antihypertensive agents

CHRONIC Rx
- Chronic treatment is centered on treatment of the underlying malignancy.

Hypercalcemia of malignancy
- Bisphosphonate therapy every 4 weeks In cases of bone metastasis

- Chronic calcitonin use can be considered

SIADH
- Demeclocycline and vasopressin receptor antagonists (vaptans; conivaptan and tolvaptan, although both are approved for initial administration in hospitalized patients only)
- Cessation of any possible causative medications
- Maintain adequate dietary protein and salt intake

Cushing's syndrome: inhibition of steroid production with ketoconazole, mitotane, metyrapone, aminoglutethimide

LE/PCD: Glucocorticoids, cyclophosphamide, rituximab

LEMS: 3,4-diaminopyridine, pyridostigmine, azathioprine

MG: Pyridostigmine, azathioprine, cyclosporin A, tacrolimus, mycophenolate, rituximab

Paraneoplastic thrombocytosis: consider prophylactic low-molecular-weight heparin or aspirin if no contraindications exist.

DISPOSITION
Specific to each condition; however, humoral hypercalcemia of malignancy carries a poor overall prognosis with 30-day mortality of 50%.

REFERRAL
Oncology, endocrinology, neurology, nephrology

⚠ PEARLS & CONSIDERATIONS

COMMENTS
- Signs or symptoms of a paraneoplastic syndrome may manifest prior to the identification of a malignancy.
- If paraneoplastic syndrome is suspected, a thorough workup for a tumor is indicated.
- With treatment of the primary tumor, the clinical effects of hypercalcemia of malignancy,

SIADH, and Cushing's syndrome may improve or resolve.
- Recovery from paraneoplastic anti-NMDAR encephalitis due to ovarian cancer has been reported after salpingo-oophorectomy.
- The effects of the neurologic paraneoplastic syndromes can be long-term, due to permanent CNS or PNS damage. In neurologic paraneoplastic syndromes, tumor detection can be difficult, since the immune system, which is causing the syndrome, is also keeping the tumor in check.

PREVENTION
- Smoking cessation
- Age-appropriate cancer screening

PATIENT & FAMILY EDUCATION
In conditions with autoimmune etiology (LE, PCD, LEMS, MG), symptoms may not improve even If tumor is identified and treated, as damage to the nervous system may be sustained or permanent.

SUGGESTED READINGS
Available at www.expertconsult.com

AUTHORS: **WILLIAM M. RAFELSON, M.D., M.B.A.,** and **JOHN L. REAGAN, M.D.**

BASIC INFORMATION

DEFINITION
Idiopathic Parkinson's disease (PD) is a progressive neurodegenerative disorder characterized clinically by rigidity, tremor, postural instability, and slowness of movement (bradykinesia).

SYNONYMS
Paralysis agitans

ICD-10CM CODES
G20   Parkinson's disease
G21.11 Neuroleptic induced parkinsonism
G21.1 Other drug-induced secondary parkinsonism
G21.2 Secondary parkinsonism due to other external agents
G21.3 Postencephalitic parkinsonism
G21.4 Vascular parkinsonism
G21.8 Other secondary parkinsonism
G21.9 Secondary parkinsonism, unspecified

EPIDEMIOLOGY & DEMOGRAPHICS
PREVALENCE:
- Affects more than 1 million people in North America. It is the second most common neurodegenerative disease worldwide.
- In age group <40 yr, <5/100,000 are affected.
- In those aged >70 yr, 700/100,000 are affected.
- Highest incidence in whites, lowest incidence in Asians and African Americans

PHYSICAL FINDINGS & CLINICAL PRESENTATION
- Tremor (Fig. 1P-16)—typically a resting tremor with a frequency of 4 to 6 Hz that is often first noted in the hand as a pill-rolling tremor (thumb and forefinger). Can also involve the leg and lip. Tremor improves with purposeful movement. Usually starts asymmetrically.
- Rigidity—increased muscle tone that persists throughout the range of passive movement of a joint. This, too, is usually asymmetric at onset.
- Akinesia/bradykinesia—slowness in initiating movement
- Postural instability—tested by "pull test." Ask patient to stand in place with back to examiner. Examiner pulls patient back by the shoulders, and proper response would be to take no steps back or very few steps back without falling. Retropulsion is a positive test as is falling straight back. This is not usually severe early on. If falls and postural reflexes are greatly impaired early on, then consider other disorders.
- Masked facies (hypomimia)—face seems expressionless, giving the appearance of depression. Decreased blink; often there is excess drooling.
- Gait disturbance
- Stooped posture, decreased arm swing
- Difficulty initiating the first step; small shuffling steps that increase in speed (festinating gait). Steps become progressively faster and shorter while the trunk inclines further forward.
- Other complaints and findings early on include handwriting becoming smaller (micrographia), and voice becoming softer and often "gruffer" (hypophonia).

ETIOLOGY
- Unknown
- Most cases are sporadic, with age being the most common risk factor, although there is probably a combination of both environmental and genetic factors contributing to disease expression. There are rare familial forms with at least seven different genes identified; these include the parkin gene, which is a significant cause of early-onset autosomal recessive PD and LRRK2, which is the most common cause of familial and sporadic parkinsonism.

DIAGNOSIS
A clinical diagnosis can be made based on a comprehensive history and physical examination. The four cardinal signs used to diagnose PD are (mnemonic = TRAP):
1. **T**remor (resting, typically 4-6 Hz)
2. **R**igidity, of the cogwheel type
3. **A**kinesia/bradykinesia—slowness of movement
4. **P**ostural instability—failure of postural "righting" reflexes leading to poor balance and falls
One need not demonstrate all four cardinal signs to make a presumptive diagnosis of PD and begin treatment.

DIFFERENTIAL DIAGNOSIS
- Multiple system atrophy—distinguishing features include autonomic dysfunction (including urinary incontinence, orthostatic hypotension, and erectile dysfunction), parkinsonism, cerebellar signs, and normal cognition.
- Diffuse Lewy body disease—parkinsonism with concomitant dementia: patients often have early hallucinations and fluctuations in level of alertness and mental status.
- Corticobasal degeneration—often begins asymmetrically with apraxia, cortical sensory loss in one limb, and sometimes alien limb phenomenon.
- Progressive supranuclear palsy—tends to have axial rigidity greater than appendicular (limb) rigidity. These patients have early and severe postural instability. Hallmark is supranuclear gaze palsy that usually involves vertical gaze (especially downward) before horizontal.
- Essential tremor—bilateral postural and action tremor
- Secondary (acquired) parkinsonism
  1. Iatrogenic—any of the neuroleptics and antipsychotics. The high-potency D_2-blocker neuroleptics are most likely to cause parkinsonism. Quetiapine is an atypical antipsychotic with lower risk of causing parkinsonism. Metoclopramide can also cause parkinsonism. Abuse of methamphetamine has been recently linked to risk of PD.
  2. Postinfectious parkinsonism—von Economo's encephalitis
  3. Parkinson's pugilistica—after repeated head trauma
  4. Toxins (e.g., MPTP, manganese, carbon monoxide)
  5. Cerebrovascular disease "vascular parkinsonism" (basal ganglia infarcts); often lower limbs (especially gait) affected more than upper extremities

WORKUP
1. Identification of clinical signs and symptoms associated with PD (see "Physical Findings") and elimination of conditions that may mimic it with a comprehensive history and physical examination
2. Routine genetic testing is not recommended.

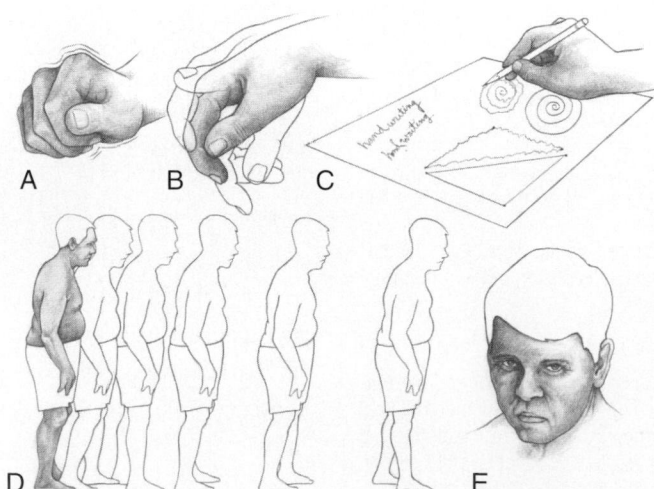

FIGURE 1P-16 The parkinsonian syndrome. A, The "pill-rolling" tremor. **B,** Tremor that can worsen with emotional stress. **C,** Handwriting abnormalities, which include micrographia. **D,** Typical posture and gait, which becomes faster (festination). **E,** Lack of facial expression as well as "stare" from decreased blinking. (From Remmel KS et al: *Handbook of symptom oriented neurology,* ed 3, St Louis, 2002, Mosby.)

IMAGING STUDIES

Computed tomographic (CT) scan has almost no role in investigations. Magnetic resonance imaging (MRI) of the head may sometimes distinguish between idiopathic PD and other conditions that present with signs of parkinsonism (see "Differential Diagnosis").

Rx TREATMENT

NONPHARMACOLOGIC THERAPY

- Physical therapy, patient education and reassurance, treatment of associated conditions (e.g., depression) are important. A safe, practical, and reasonable exercise regimen must be encouraged, individualized to the patient's access to resources and motivation. Recent trials reveal that t'ai chi training is effective in reducing balance impairment and falls and improving functional capacity.
- Avoidance of drugs that can induce or worsen parkinsonism: neuroleptics (especially high potency), certain antiemetics (prochlorperazine, trimethobenzamide), metoclopramide, nonselective MAO inhibitors (may induce hypertensive crisis), reserpine, methyldopa

ACUTE GENERAL Rx

- There continues to be controversy whether levodopa or dopamine agonists should be the initial treatment. In younger patients, agonists are usually the drug of choice; in patients >70 yr, levodopa is typically the preferred initial therapy.
- It is appropriate to initiate pharmacotherapy when required by symptoms; prior practice of waiting for limitation of ADLs is now outdated. Fig. E1P-17 describes an approach to patients with parkinsonism.
- Motor complications do develop during the course of the disease and likely reflect the combination of disease progression together with the side effects of dopaminergic medications.

CHRONIC Rx

- Levodopa therapy
  1. Cornerstone of symptomatic therapy—should be used with a peripheral dopa decarboxylase inhibitor (carbidopa) to minimize side effects (nausea, lightheadedness, postural hypotension). The combination of the two drugs is marketed under the trade name Sinemet. Levodopa therapy has been found to reduce morbidity and mortality in PD patients.
  2. Usual starting dose is 25/100 mg (carbidopa/levodopa) tid 1 hr before (or after) meals.
  3. Controlled-release preparations (e.g., Sinemet CR) are available, but their use should be deferred to a neurologist.
  4. Stalevo (combination Sinemet and entacapone, a COMT inhibitor). Useful for patients with motor fluctuations (wearing off); has no role in treating early patients with PD.
- Dopamine receptor agonists (ropinirole and pramipexole) are not as potent as levodopa, but they are often used as initial treatment in younger patients to attempt to delay the onset of complications (dyskinesias, motor fluctuations) associated with levodopa therapy. These medications are more expensive than levodopa. In general, they cause more side effects than levodopa, including nausea, vomiting, light-headedness, peripheral edema, confusion, and somnolence. They can also cause impulse control behaviors such as hypersexuality, binge eating, and compulsive shopping and gambling. Presence of these must be assessed at each visit.
  1. Ropinirole: initial dose is 0.25 mg tid
  2. Pramipexole: initial dose is 0.125 mg tid
- MAO-B inhibitors can be used as monotherapy early in the disease or as adjunctive therapy in later stages; they have been shown to have milder symptomatic benefit than dopamine agonists or levodopa. They are well tolerated and easy to titrate. Concurrent use of stimulants and sympathomimetics should be avoided. Certain food restrictions may apply.
  1. Rasagiline: initial dose is 0.5 mg qd, then 1 mg daily. A recent study, ADAGIO, suggests that 1 mg rasagiline may have disease-modifying benefits, but results must be interpreted with caution.
  2. Selegiline: Usual dose, 5 mg bid with breakfast and lunch. Has amphetamine byproduct so has mild stimulant-like effects, which can be beneficial in some patients.
- Amantadine (unclear mechanism of action, but reported to modulate the dopamine and glutamate systems in the CNS) can be used alone early in the disease. It is especially useful in the treatment of dyskinesias. Dosage is 100 mg tid (titrate q week from 100 mg qd). Must adjust for elderly and renal impairment. The most notable side effect, especially in the elderly, is confusion.
- Anticholinergic agents are only helpful in treating tremor and drooling in patients with PD. Potential side effects include constipation, urinary retention, memory impairment, and hallucinations. They should be avoided in the elderly.
  1. Trihexyphenidyl: initial dose, 1 mg PO tid
  2. Benztropine: usual dose, 0.5 to 1 mg qd or bid

SURGICAL OPTIONS

- Pallidal (globus pallidus interna) and subthalamic deep-brain stimulation (subthalamic nucleus) are currently the surgical options of choice for patients with advanced PD; similar improvement in motor function and adverse effects have been reported after either procedure. Compared with ablative procedures, DBS has the advantage of being reversible and adjustable. Thalamic DBS may be useful for refractory tremor. It improves the cardinal motor symptoms, extends medication "on" time, and reduces motor fluctuations during the day. In general, patients are likely to benefit from this therapy if they show a clear response to levodopa. Therefore, when considering DBS, patients should be evaluated for motor response to levodopa by stopping levodopa overnight and evaluating motor response before and after a dose of levodopa.
- Surgery is often limited to patients with disabling, medically refractory problems, and patients must still have a good response to L-dopa to undergo surgery. Yet for many patients, earlier stimulation might provide an improved motor benefit before disability from other symptoms has occurred and should be considered at an earlier stage of PD. DBS results in decreased dyskinesias, fluctuations, rigidity, and tremor.

DISPOSITION

PD usually follows a slowly progressive course leading to disability over the course of several years. However, every patient will progress individually, and patients should be reassured that this diagnosis does not, by definition, result in being either wheelchair- or bed-bound.

REFERRAL

- Neurology consultation is recommended at initial diagnosis of PD.
- Exercise is important for all patients with PD.
- Participation in outpatient physical therapy program is recommended for patients with moderate to advanced disease.

ⓘ PEARLS & CONSIDERATIONS

- Asymmetry of symptoms at onset is very useful in distinguishing PD from other causes of parkinsonism.
- Although resting tremor is a common presenting symptom, up to 25% of patients with idiopathic PD do not have classic resting tremor.

EBM EVIDENCE

Available at www.expertconsult.com

SUGGESTED READINGS

Available at www.expertconsult.com

RELATED CONTENT

Parkinson's Disease (Patient Information)

AUTHOR: **U. SHIVRAJ SOHUR, M.D., PH.D.**

ⓘ BASIC INFORMATION

DEFINITION

Paronychia is a localized superficial infection or abscess of the lateral and proximal nail fold. Paronychia may be acute or chronic.

SYNONYMS

Nail bed infection
Nail bed abscess

ICD-10CM CODES
L03.019 Cellulitis of unspecified finger

EPIDEMIOLOGY & DEMOGRAPHICS

- Acute paronychia affects males and females equally.
- Chronic paronychia is more common in females than males (9:1).
- Acute paronychia most often occurs in children.
- Chronic paronychia usually presents in the fifth or sixth decade of life.
- Paronychia is the most common infection of the hand.

PHYSICAL FINDINGS & CLINICAL PRESENTATION

- Acute paronychia usually presents with the sudden onset of redness, swelling, and pain with abscess or cellulitis formation in the nail fold. Fluid with purulence is often present.
- Chronic paronychia is insidious, presenting with mild swelling and erythema of the nail folds.
- Acute paronychia usually involves only one finger.
- Chronic paronychia may involve more than one finger.
- Acute paronychia usually involves the thumb.
- Chronic paronychia commonly involves the middle finger.

ETIOLOGY

- Any disruption of the seal between the proximal nail fold and the nail plate can cause paronychial infections.
- Acute paronychia is almost always bacterial in origin (e.g., methicillin-sensitive *Staphylococcus aureus* [most common, but also consider MRSA], *Streptococcus pyogenes*, *Enterococcus faecalis*, *Proteus* and *Pseudomonas* species, and anaerobes).
- Chronic paronychia is commonly caused by *Candida albicans* (70%), with bacterial organisms accounting for the remaining 30%.
- Trauma, nail biting, hangnails, diabetes, and long-term exposure to water are common predisposing features of paronychia.

ⓓₓ DIAGNOSIS

The diagnosis of paronychia is self-evident on physical examination.

DIFFERENTIAL DIAGNOSIS

- Herpetic whitlow caused by herpes simplex
- Pyogenic granuloma
- Viral warts
- Ganglions
- Squamous cell carcinoma

WORKUP

A workup is usually not pursued unless there is treatment failure.

LABORATORY TESTS

- Gram stain and culture any purulent drainage.
- Potassium hydroxide mount may show pseudohyphae.

IMAGING STUDIES

Radiographs of the digit if concerned about osteomyelitis.

ⓇX TREATMENT

NONPHARMACOLOGIC THERAPY

- For acute paronychia without purulent drainage, warm soaks tid or qid are helpful. If pus is present, surgical drainage is required (Fig. 1P-18).
- For chronic paronychia, avoid frequent immersion in water or exposure to moisture.

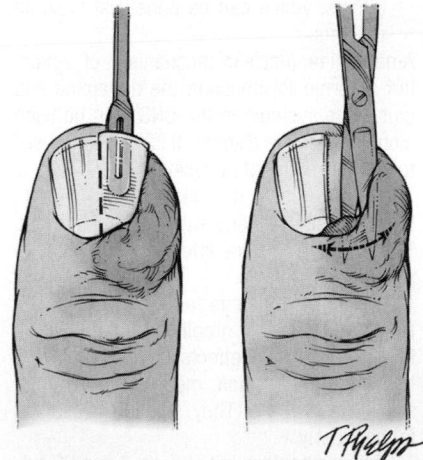

FIGURE 1P-18 Surgical drainage of acute paronychia. The lateral nail on the affected side is gently elevated from the nail bed, and a longitudinal strip of nail is removed. If this does not decompress the infection adequately, the margins of the nail fold are opened gently to drain the adjacent soft tissues. (From Cameron JL, Cameron AM: *Current surgical therapy,* ed 10, Philadelphia, 2011, Saunders.)

ACUTE GENERAL Rx

- Trimethoprim-sulfamethoxazole DS 1 PO bid for 7 days is usually the antibiotic of choice for acute paronychia.
- Alternative antibiotic choices include dicloxacillin 500 mg qid, cephalexin 500 mg qid, clindamycin, and amoxicillin-clavulanate potassium.
- Surgical drainage is indicated if purulent discharge is noted.
- A No. 11 blade scalpel is used to lift the lateral perionychium and proximal eponychium off the nail, facilitating drainage.
- If the pus is located beneath the nail, the lateral edge of the nail can be lifted off the nail bed and excised.

CHRONIC Rx

- If no fungal organism is found, tincture of iodine (2 drops bid) helps keep the nail and skin dry.
- Chronic paronychia caused by *Candida albicans* is treated with topical antifungal agents (e.g., miconazole or ketoconazole applied tid).
- Unresponsive cases may be treated with itraconazole or fluconazole, but this should be done in consultation with dermatology and/or infectious disease.
- Surgery may be needed in refractory cases.

DISPOSITION

- Most acute paronychias with appropriate treatment resolve within 7 to 10 days.
- Osteomyelitis is a potential complication of paronychia.
- Untreated chronic paronychia leads to thickening and discoloration with eventual nail loss.

REFERRAL

Chronic paronychia refractory to topical medical therapy is best referred to dermatology and/or infectious disease. A hand surgeon is consulted if abscess drainage or surgery is being considered.

❗ PEARLS & CONSIDERATIONS

COMMENTS

The gastrointestinal tract, including the mouth and bowel, and the genitourinary tract in women are the usual sources of *C. albicans* in chronic paronychia.

SUGGESTED READINGS
Available at www.expertconsult.com

RELATED CONTENT
Paronychia (Patient Information)

AUTHOR: **GLENN G. FORT, M.D., M.P.H.**

BASIC INFORMATION

DEFINITION

Patent ductus arteriosus (PDA) is a persistence of the fetal communication between the descending aorta and main pulmonary artery. It is a derivative of the sixth aortic arch. This connection allows for blood to bypass the fetal lungs (which are not participating in gas exchange) and be directed into the descending aorta to supply structures below this region. It usually closes soon after birth under the physiologic effects of elevated oxygen level. Defects can range in size from so small as to be undetectable to large enough to cause volume loading of the left ventricle and pulmonary hypertension.

SYNONYMS

PDA

ICD-10CM CODES
Q25.0 Patent ductus arteriosus

EPIDEMIOLOGY & DEMOGRAPHICS

- Prevalence is 2.9 per 10000 live births. Incidence has increased dramatically due to improved survival of premature infants (especially those born <30 weeks' gestation).
- Female predominance 2:1
- Increased incidence in congenital rubella and with associated cyanotic congenital heart disease

PHYSICAL FINDINGS & CLINICAL PRESENTATION

- Loud machinery-like murmur appreciated over the left scapula and in the left infraclavicular area in patients with left to right shunting (Fig. 1P-21)
  ○ Widened pulse pressure
- Apex beat is displaced and volume loaded and the precordium is active
- Increased jugular venous pressure (with RV failure)
  ○ Where the defect has resulted in irreversible pulmonary hypertension, there is no murmur, and cyanosis and clubbing, particularly of the feet (differential cyanosis) will be present
- Exertional dyspnea and fatigue
- Patients with small defects: generally asymptomatic
- Fig. 1P-20 shows the anatomy of patent ductus arteriosus.

DIAGNOSIS

DIFFERENTIAL DIAGNOSIS

- Rule out other causes of continuous murmurs such as aortopulmonary shunts or window, coronary fistula, ruptured sinus of Valsalva aneurysm, and mixed aortic stenosis and regurgitation
- Coarctation of the aorta will have a murmur over the scapula but arm-leg pressure gradient and hypertension.
  ○ In patients with Eisenmenger syndrome, consider ASD and VSD in the differential diagnosis

WORKUP

- ECG:
  1. When the defect is large enough to cause left-sided volume overload there may be LA enlargement, LV hypertrophy
  2. When pulmonary hypertension has occurred, right-axis deviation, RVH and P pulmonale may be present
- Chest x-ray
- Echocardiography (Fig. 1P-22)
- Cardiac magnetic resonance imaging (MRI), or CT
- Cardiac catheterization

IMAGING STUDIES

- Chest x-ray: cardiomegaly, left heart enlargement, increased pulmonary vascular pattern
- Echocardiography with Doppler flow studies is generally diagnostic. The parasternal and suprasternal views can show the presence of the PDA, the size of the defect, and the direction of shunting. Echocardiography can also show the effect of the PDA on left heart chamber sizes and measure the pulmonary:systemic shunt ratio (Qp:Qs) and determine if pulmonary hypertension has developed.
- Transesophageal echocardiography is modestly helpful, especially when patients have poor acoustic windows
- Cardiac MRI and CT: may be useful if echo is not diagnostic; the PDA may be directly visualized and its morphology described with either technique. MRI is gold standard for assessing LV size and function, and it can determine whether the left-sided chambers are enlarged and establish the degree of shunting using phase contrast imaging to determine the Qp:Qs noninvasively. MRI is also useful to assess for associated lesions; cardiac CT can offer similar information at the price of radiation exposure
- Cardiac catheterization: Left- and right-heart catheterization can be used when the diagnosis remains in doubt. It can also help to estimate the degree of left to right shunting, establish right-sided pressures, demonstrate the PDA morphology, and attempt closure where technically feasible
- PDAs are classified based on the amount of left-to-right shunting:
  ○ Small: Qp:Qs <1.5:1
  ○ Moderate: Qp:Qs 1.5 – 2.2:1
  ○ Large: Qp:Qs >2.2:1

TREATMENT

NONPHARMACOLOGIC THERAPY

- NSAIDs (e.g., indomethacin, ibuprofen) may be used to cause PDA closure in the premature infant; the mechanism of action is by inhibition of local prostaglandin synthesis, which is necessary for the duct to remain open in many cases. These are ineffective in term infants and older patients.
- Antibiotic prophylaxis is only recommended where there has been previous endocarditis
- Where there is volume overload, patients can be treated with diuretics and digoxin until formal device or surgical closure can be performed
- In older patients with secondary pulmonary hypertension, pulmonary vasodilators can be extremely helpful in improving symptoms and mortality and potentially allowing safe closure of the defect

GENERAL Rx

- Closure of a PDA is considered if there is evidence for volume overload or signs of pulmonary hypertension where the pulmonary

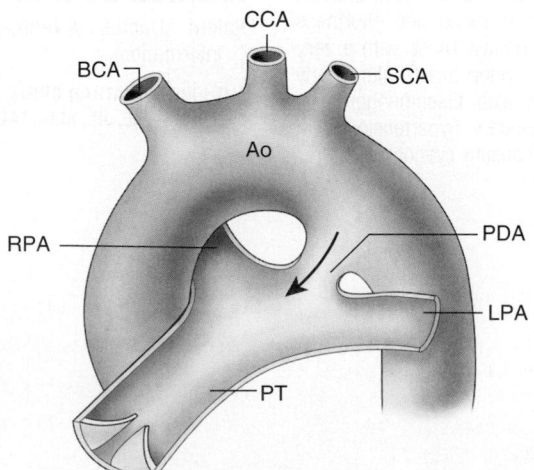

FIGURE 1P-20 Anatomy of a patent ductus arteriosus. Note the relationships among the position of the ductus, left subclavian artery, and pulmonary artery bifurcation. *Ao,* Aorta; *BCA,* brachiocephalic; *CCA,* common carotid artery; *LPA,* left pulmonary artery; *PDA,* patent ductus arteriosus; *PT,* pulmonary trunk; *RPA,* right pulmonary artery; *SCA,* subclavian artery. (From Perloff JK, ed. *Clinical recognition of congenital heart disease,* ed 4, Philadelphia, 1994, Saunders.)

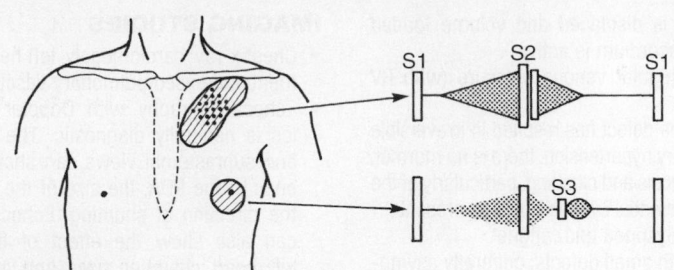

FIGURE 1P-21 Cardiac findings of patent ductus arteriosus. A systolic thrill may be present in the area shown by dots. (Park MK: *Park's pediatric cardiology for practitioners,* ed 6, Philadelphia, 2014, WB Saunders.)

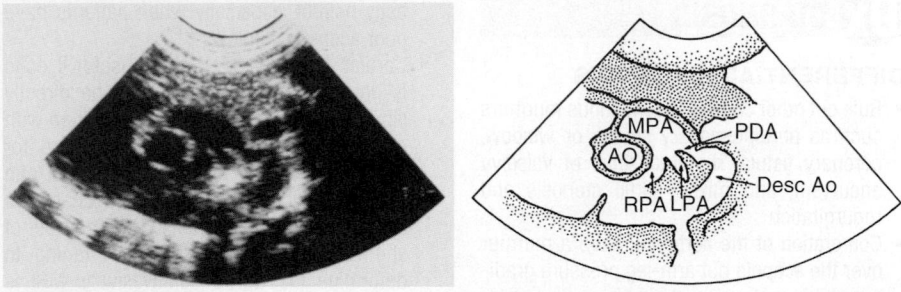

FIGURE 1P-22 Parasternal short-axis view demonstrating patent ductus arteriosus (PDA) that connects the main pulmonary artery (MPA) and the descending aorta (Desc Ao). *AO,* Aorta; *LPA,* left pulmonary artery; *RPA,* right pulmonary artery. (Park MK: *Park's pediatric cardiology for practitioners,* ed 6, Philadelphia, 2014, WB Saunders.)

pressures have not become excessively high. Additionally, because >95% of PDAs can successfully be closed percutaneously with a low rate of complications, many advocate closing a PDA when there is the presence of an audible murmur. The chief indication for this "prophylactic closure" is the low but non-zero incidence of infective endocarditis in this condition, although there is no clear evidence to support this procedure and controversy remains.
- In patients with pulmonary hypertension, treatment with pulmonary vasodilators should be considered prior to closure.
- Device closure is possible in >95% of cases, and various devices are available for these defects. Use of different types depends on morphology of the defect
- Surgical closure may be performed when a patient is undergoing cardiac surgery for other reasons or when the PDA is not suitable for device closure, such as in the case of very large defects or when the child is too small (<6 kg)
- Closure is not indicated in patients with severe pulmonary hypertension, as these patients may require right-to-left shunting to maintain cardiac output.

DISPOSITION
- Long-term outcome depends on the size of the lesion and the associated degree of left-to-right shunting. Defects with a small shunt generally do very well, apart from the possibility of endocarditis. Those with moderate shunts may develop left atrial and left ventricular volume overload and shortness of breath or arrhythmias. Those with a very large shunt may develop heart failure early then go on to develop Eisenmenger syndrome (fixed pulmonary hypertension with reversal of shunt causing cyanosis) if unrepaired.

- Endocarditis is uncommon and usually occurs at the site where the high-velocity jet lesion enters the PA but generally can be treated medically
- Basic preoperative assessment for patients with adult congenital heart disease (ACHD) should include systemic arterial oximetry, an ECG, chest radiograph, TTE, and blood tests for full blood count and coagulation screen.
- Intracardiac shunts are considered of moderate risk for preoperative evaluation for noncardiac procedure. High-risk features include severe systolic dysfunction (EF <35%), severe pulmonary hypertension (whether primary or secondary), cyanotic heart disease, or severe left-side outlet obstruction.
- Clinical follow-up is recommended for adult patients to exclude residual deficits, pulmonary hypertension and LV dilation and dysfunction, and atrial arrhythmias.
- Infective endocarditis prophylaxis for dental procedures:
  1. Prophylaxis is not indicated for an unrepaired PDA.
  2. Prophylaxis is indicated for a repaired PDA in the first 6 months following the repair or where prosthetic material is present and there is a residual defect.
- The estrogen-containing oral contraceptive pill is not recommended in ACHD patients at risk of thromboembolism, such as those with cyanosis related to an intracardiac shunt, atrial fibrillation, severe PAH, or Fontan repair.
- Women with a repaired PDA generally can undergo pregnancy and delivery normally. Those with an unrepaired defect of a size that would ordinarily be repaired are recommended to undergo repair before becoming pregnant.

SUGGESTED READINGS
Available at www.expertconsult.com

RELATED CONTENT
Patent Ductus Arteriosus (PDA) (Patient Information)

AUTHORS: **JONATHAN GINNS, M.D.,** and **JOHN V. WYLIE, JR., M.D., FACC**

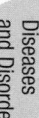

ⓘ BASIC INFORMATION

DEFINITION

Pediculosis is lice infestation. Human beings can be infested with three kinds of lice: *Pediculus capitis* (head louse), *Pediculus corporis* (body louse), and *Phthirus pubis* (pubic, or crab, louse). Lice feed on human blood and deposit their eggs (nits) on the hair shafts (head lice and pubic lice) and along the seams of clothing (body lice). Nits generally hatch within 7 to 10 days. Lice are obligate human parasites and cannot survive away from their hosts for longer than 7 to 10 days.

SYNONYMS

Lice

ICD-10CM CODES
B85.2 Pediculosis, unspecificd
B85.0 Pediculosis due to Pediculus humanus capitis
B85.1 Pediculosis due to Pcdiculus humanus corporis
B85.4 Mixed pediculosis and phthiriasis
Z20.7 Contact with and (suspected) exposure to pediculosis, acariasis and other infestations

EPIDEMIOLOGY & DEMOGRAPHICS

- There are 6 to 12 million cases of head lice in the United States yearly. The estimated annual direct and indirect cost of head louse infestation in the United States is $1 billion.
- Lice infestation of the scalp is most common in children (girls affected more often than boys).
- Infestation of the eyelashes is most frequently seen in children and may indicate sexual abuse.
- The chance of acquiring pubic lice from one sexual exposure with an infcsted partner is >90% (most contagious STD known).
- Body lice is most common in conditions of poor hygiene.

PHYSICAL FINDINGS & CLINICAL PRESENTATION

- Pruritus with excoriation may be caused by hypersensitivity reaction, inflammation from saliva, and fecal material from the lice.

FIGURE 1P-25 Body louse, *Pediculus humanus var. corporis*, as it was obtaining a blood meal from human host. (Courtesy Public Health Image Library, Centers for Disease Control and Prevention. From Vincent JL et al: *Textbook of critical care*, ed 6, Philadelphia, 2011, Saunders.)

- Nits can be identified by examining hair shafts.
- The presence of nits on clothes is indicative of body lice.
- Lymphadenopathy may be present (cervical adenopathy with head lice, inguinal lymphadenopathy with pubic lice).
- Head lice is most frequently found in the back of the head and neck, behind the ears.
- Scratching can result in pustules and crusting.
- Pubic lice may affect the hair around the anus.

ETIOLOGY

Lice are transmitted by close personal contact or use of contaminated objects (e.g., combs, clothing, bed linen, hats).

Ⓓ DIAGNOSIS

DIFFERENTIAL DIAGNOSIS

- Seborrheic dermatitis
- Scabies
- Eczema
- Other: pilar casts, trichonodosis (knotted hair), monilethrix

WORKUP

Diagnosis is made by seeing the lice (Fig. 1P-25) or their nits. Combing hair with a fine-toothed comb is recommended because visual inspection of the hair and scalp may miss more than 50% of infestations.

LABORATORY TESTS

Wood's light examination is useful to screen a large number of children: live nits fluoresce, empty nits have a gray fluorescence, nits with unborn louse reveal white fluorescence.

Ⓡ TREATMENT

NONPHARMACOLOGIC THERAPY

- Patients with body lice should discard infested clothes and improve their hygiene.
- Combing out nits is a widely recommended but unproven adjunctive therapy.
- Personal items such as combs and brushes should be soaked in hot water for 15 to 30 min.
- Close contacts and household members should also be examined for the presence of lice.

ACUTE GENERAL Rx

The following products are available for treatment of lice:
- Permethrin: available over the counter (1% permethrin [Nix]) or by prescription (5% permethrin [Elimite]); should be applied to the hair and scalp and rinsed out after 10 min. A repeat application 7 days later is generally not necessary in patients with head lice. It can be applied to clean, dry hair and left on overnight (8 to 14 hours) under a shower cap. Resistance to permethrin is now widcspread.

- Malathion, an organophosphate, is effective in head lice. It is available by prescription. Use should be avoided in children ≤2 yr. It is not commonly used because of its objectionable odor, fear of flammability, and prolonged application time (8 to 12 hr).
- Spinosad (Natroba) is a newer FDA-approved product for head lice. It is a topical suspension applied to dry hair for 10 min, then rinsed. It may be repeated 7 days later if necessary. It is more effective than permethrin but also much more expensive. It is safe in pregnancy (category B—no evidence of risk in humans).
- Benzyl alcohol lotion, 5% (Ulesfia) can be used for treatment of head lice in patients >6 mo old. The lotion is applied to dry hair and left on for 10 min. Treatment must be repeated after 7 days because the drug is not ovicidal.
- Eyelash infestation can be treated with the application of petroleum jelly rubbed into the eyelashes three times a day for 5 to 7 days. The application of baby shampoo to the eyelashes and brows three or four times a day for 5 days is also effective. The use of fluorescein drops applied to the lids and eyelashes is also toxic to lice.
- In patients who have previously not responded to treatment or in whom resistance with 1% permethrin cream rinse occurs, a 10-day course of trimethoprim-sulfamethoxazole (TMP-SMX) 8 mg/kg/day in divided doses is an effective treatment for head lice infestation, especially for eyelash infestations with *Phthirus pubis*.
- Ivermectin, an antiparasitic drug, given as an oral dose of 400 mcg/kg of body weight on days 1 and 8, is effective for head lice resistant to other treatments (currently not FDA approved for pediculosis). Ivermectin 0.5% lotion is FDA approved as a single-use topical treatment for head lice in patients 6 mo or older. Cost is more than $200 for 4 oz.

❗ PEARLS & CONSIDERATIONS

COMMENTS

- Patients with pubic lice should notify their sexual contacts. Sex partners within the last month should be treated.
- Parents of patients should also be educated that head lice infestation (unlike body lice) does not indicate poor hygiene.

SUGGESTED READINGS
Available at www.expertconsult.com

RELATED CONTENT
Lice (Patient Information)

AUTHOR: **FRED F. FERRI, M.D.**

BASIC INFORMATION

DEFINITION

Pelvic abscess is an acute or chronic infection, most commonly involving the pelvic viscera. Treatment and possible cure require directed therapy that will involve antibiotic therapy and, if medical therapy fails, subsequent surgical therapy. There are four categories based on etiologic factors:

- Ascending infection, spreading from cervix through endometrial cavity to adnexa, forming a tubo-ovarian complex
- Infection occurring in the puerperium, which spreads to the adnexa from the endometrium or myometrium by a hematogenous or lymphatic route
- Abscess complicating pelvic surgery
- Involvement of the pelvic viscera as a result of spread from contiguous organs, such as appendicitis or diverticulitis

SYNONYMS

Tubo-ovarian abscess (TOA)
Vaginal cuff abscess

ICD-10CM CODES
N70.93	Salpingitis and oophoritis, unspecified
N70.0	Acute salpingitis and oophoritis
N70.1	Chronic salpingitis and oophoritis
K63.0	Abscess of intestine
K65.1	Peritoneal abscess
K68.11	Postprocedural retroperitoneal abscess
K68.12	Psoas muscle abscess
K68.19	Other retroperitoneal abscess

EPIDEMIOLOGY & DEMOGRAPHICS

INCIDENCE:
- 34% of hospitalized patients with pelvic inflammatory disease
- 1% to 2% of patients undergoing hysterectomy, most with vaginal approach
- Peak incidence third to fourth decade

RISK FACTORS: Same risk factors as for pelvic inflammatory disease, although in 30% to 50% of patients there is no prior history of salpingitis before abscess forms.

PHYSICAL FINDINGS & CLINICAL PRESENTATION

- Abdominal or pelvic pain (90%)
- Fever or chills (50%)
- Abnormal bleeding (21%)
- Vaginal discharge (28%)
- Nausea (26%)
- Up to 60% to 80% present in the absence of fever or leukocytosis; absence of these findings should not exclude diagnosis

ETIOLOGY

- Mixed flora of anaerobes, aerobes, and facultative anaerobes, such as *Escherichia coli*, *Bacteroides fragilis*, *Prevotella* spp., aerobic streptococci, and *Peptococcus* and *Peptostreptococcus* spp.

- *Neisseria gonorrhoeae* and *Chlamydia* are the major etiologic bacteria in cervicitis and salpingitis but are rarely found in abscess cavity cultures.
- In elderly patients consider diverticular disease.

DIAGNOSIS

DIFFERENTIAL DIAGNOSIS

- Pelvic neoplasms, such as ovarian tumors and leiomyomas.
- Inflammatory masses involving adjacent bowel or omentum, such as ruptured appendicitis or diverticulitis.
- Pelvic hematomas, as may occur after cesarean section or hysterectomy.
- Section III describes the diagnostic approach to patients with a pelvic mass; the differential diagnosis of pelvic mass is described in Section II.
- The differential diagnosis of pelvic pain is described in Section II.
- Sonogram or CT scan: commonly used due to associated pain and guarding, resulting in a suboptimal abdominal or pelvic examination, and to characterize anatomic abnormalities such as an adnexal mass.
- Most common cause of preventable death: physician delay in diagnosis.

LABORATORY TESTS

- CBC with differential
- Aerobic as well as anaerobic cultures of cervix, blood, urine, sputum, peritoneal cavity (if entered), and abscess cavity before starting antibiotics
- Pregnancy test in patients of reproductive age

IMAGING STUDIES

- Sonogram: noninvasive, inexpensive study to confirm diagnosis, estimate size of abscess, and monitor response to therapy; sensitivity >90%
- CT scan: used for both diagnosis and therapy (CT-guided drainage) (Fig. E1P-26)
  1. Useful where sonogram provides insufficient information, as with intraabdominal abscesses
  2. Success rate with CT-guided abscess drainage: unilocular, 90%; multilocular, 40%

TREATMENT

Major concerns:
1. Desire for future fertility
2. Likelihood of rupture of abscess, with resulting peritonitis, septic shock, and morbid sequelae

ACUTE GENERAL Rx

- Clinical quandary is whether patient requires immediate laparoscopic surgery (uncertain diagnosis or suspicion of rupture) or management with IV antibiotics, reserving surgery for

those with inadequate clinical response (e.g., 48 to 72 hr of therapy, with persistent fever or leukocytosis, increasing size of mass, or suspicion of rupture)
- Surgery indicated in poor response to medical therapy. Early surgery may be needed in those with large adnexal masses (>8 cm), or in immunocompromised patients
- Antibiotic combinations:
  1. Clindamycin 900 mg IV q8h or metronidazole 500 mg IV q6-8h plus gentamicin either 5 to 7 mg/kg q24h or 1.5 mg/kg q8h
  2. Alternatives: ampicillin-sulbactam 3 g IV q6h or cefoxitin 2 g IV q6h or cefotetan 2 g IV q12h plus doxycycline 100 mg IV q12h
- During medical management, high index of suspicion for acute rupture, such as acute worsening of abdominal pain or new-onset tachycardia and hypotension, mandating immediate surgical intervention after patient stabilization
- Surgical options:
  1. Laparoscopy with drainage and irrigation
  2. Transvaginal colpotomy (abscess must be midline, dissect rectovaginal septum, and be adherent to vaginal fornix)
  3. Laparotomy, including total abdominal hysterectomy with bilateral salpingo-oophorectomy or unilateral salpingo-oophorectomy
  4. Evidence of ruptured tubo-ovarian abscess is a surgical emergency

DISPOSITION

- Of patients treated with medical therapy, response in 75%, with a 50% pregnancy rate. Pregnancy rate decreases with recurrent episodes.
- No response in 30% to 40%; can be treated with either CT-guided drainage or surgical intervention, keeping in mind that unilateral adnexectomy may give equal chance of cure versus hysterectomy, yet preserve reproductive potential.

REFERRAL

If patient has a tubo-ovarian abscess, refer to gynecologist.

PEARLS & CONSIDERATIONS

COMMENTS

If *Actinomyces* species is isolated from culture, treatment with penicillin is required for an extended period (6 wk-3 mo).

SUGGESTED READINGS

Available at www.expertconsult.com

RELATED CONTENT

Pelvic Inflammatory Disease (Related Key Topic)
Pelvic Abscess (Patient Information)

AUTHOR: **RUBEN ALVERO, M.D.**

 BASIC INFORMATION

DEFINITION

Pelvic inflammatory disease (PID) is a polymicrobial infection of the upper female genital tract, including a combination of any of the following:
- Endometritis, salpingitis, tubo-ovarian abscess, or pelvic peritonitis
- Resulting from an ascending lower genital tract infection
- Not related to obstetric or surgical intervention
- Clinically, PID can be classified as acute (≤30 days duration), subclinical, and chronic (>30 days duration)

SYNONYMS

PID
Adnexitis
Pyosalpinx
Salpingitis
Tubo-ovarian abscess

ICD-10CM CODES

A54.24 Gonococcal female pelvic inflammatory disease
A56.11 Chlamydial female pelvic inflammatory disease
N73.8   Other specified female pelvic inflammatory diseases
N73.9   Female pelvic inflammatory disease, unspecified
N74   Female pelvic inflammatory disorders in diseases classified elsewhere
A54.2   Gonococcal pelviperitonitis and other gonococcal genitourinary infections
A56.1   Chlamydial infection of pelviperitoneum and other genitourinary organs
N73.9   Female pelvic inflammatory disease, unspecified
A18.17 Tuberculous female pelvic inflammatory disease

EPIDEMIOLOGY & DEMOGRAPHICS

INCIDENCE/PREVALENCE:
- Estimated 600,000 to 1 million cases annually (U.S.), affecting primarily young, sexually active women
- Diagnosed in 2% to 5% of women seen in sexually transmitted disease clinics
- Very common cause of female infertility and ectopic pregnancy

RISK FACTORS:
- Adolescent sexually active females <<20 yr
- Previous episode of gonococcal PID
- Multiple sexual partners

PHYSICAL FINDINGS & CLINICAL PRESENTATION
- Lower abdominal pain
- Abnormal vaginal discharge
- Abnormal uterine bleeding
- Dysuria
- Dyspareunia
- Nausea and vomiting (suggestive of peritonitis)
- Fever
- Right upper quadrant tenderness (perihepatitis): 5% of PID cases
- Cervical motion tenderness and adnexal tenderness
- Adnexal mass

ETIOLOGY
- *Chlamydia trachomatis*
- *Neisseria gonorrhoeae*
- Polymicrobial infection: *Bacteroides fragilis, Escherichia coli, Gardnerella vaginalis, Haemophilus influenzae, Mycoplasma hominis, Ureaplasma urealyticum*
- *Mycobacterium tuberculosis* (an important cause in developing countries)
- Cytomegalovirus (CMV)
- Over 85% of cases are due to sexually transmitted cervical pathogens or bacterial vaginosis-associated microbes, and approximately 15% are due to respiratory or enteric organisms that have colonized the lower genital tract

 **DIAGNOSIS**

DIFFERENTIAL DIAGNOSIS
- Ectopic pregnancy
- Appendicitis
- Ruptured ovarian cyst
- Endometriosis
- Urinary tract infection (cystitis or pyelonephritis)
- Renal calculus
- Adnexal torsion
- Proctocolitis

WORKUP
Diagnostic considerations:
- Clinical diagnosis is difficult and imprecise. The spectrum of disease ranges from asymptomatic to life-threatening tubo-ovarian abscess. PID should be suspected in at-risk patients who present with pelvic or lower abdominal pain.
- Clinical diagnosis of symptomatic PID has a positive predictive value of 65% to 90% compared with laparoscopy as the standard.
- No single historical, physical, or laboratory finding is both sensitive and specific for the diagnosis of PID.
- Empiric treatment for PID should be initiated in sexually active young women and other women at risk for STDs if they are experiencing pelvic or lower abdominal pain, if no cause for the illness other than PID can be identified, and if one or more of the following minimum criteria are present on pelvic examination:
  1. Uterine tenderness
  2. Adnexal tenderness
  3. Cervical motion tenderness
- The requirement that all three minimum criteria be present before the initiation of empiric treatment could result in insufficient sensitivity for the diagnosis of PID. The presence of signs of lower genital tract inflammation (predominance of leukocytes in vaginal secretions), in addition to one of the three minimum criteria, increases the specificity of the diagnosis.
- Additional criteria to increase the specificity of the diagnosis of PID in women with severe clinical signs:
  1. Oral temperature >>38.3° C (101° F)
  2. Abnormal cervical or vaginal discharge
  3. Elevated erythrocyte sedimentation rate (ESR)
  4. Elevated C-reactive protein
  5. Laboratory documentation of cervical infection with *N. gonorrhoeae* or *C. trachomatis*
- Presence of abundant numbers of WBCs on saline microscopy of vaginal fluid.
- Definitive criteria for diagnosing PID warranted in selected cases:
  1. Laparoscopic abnormalities consistent with PID
  2. Histopathologic evidence of endometritis on biopsy. Endometrial biopsy is warranted in women undergoing laparoscopy who do not have visual evidence of salpingitis because endometritis is the only sign of PID in some women
  3. Transvaginal sonography or other imaging techniques showing thickened fluid-filled tubes with or without free pelvic fluid or tubo-ovarian complex

LABORATORY TESTS
- Leukocytosis
- Elevated acute phase reactants: ESR >15 mm/hr, C-reactive protein
- Gram stain of endocervical exudate: >30 polymorphonuclear cells per high-power field correlates with chlamydial or gonococcal infection
- Endocervical cultures for *N. gonorrhoeae* and *C. trachomatis*
- Fallopian tube aspirate or peritoneal exudate culture if laparoscopy performed
- Human chorionic gonadotropin to rule out ectopic pregnancy
- All women who receive a diagnosis of acute PID should be tested for HIV, as well as gonorrhea and chlamydia, using nucleic amplification tests (NAATs)

IMAGING STUDIES
- Transvaginal ultrasound to look for adnexal mass has sensitivity for PID of 81%, specificity of 78%, and accuracy of 80%.
- MRI has sensitivity for PID of 95%, specificity of 89%, and accuracy of 93%. It is useful for establishing the diagnosis of PID and detecting other processes responsible for the symptoms. Disadvantages are its higher cost and limited availability.
- CT scan (Fig. 1P-27).

TREATMENT

NONPHARMACOLOGIC THERAPY
- Most patients are treated as outpatients.

- Criteria for hospitalization (CDC, 2006) as follows:
  1. Surgical emergencies such as appendicitis cannot be excluded
  2. Tubo-ovarian abscess
  3. Pregnant patient
  4. Patient is immunodeficient
  5. Severe illness, nausea, or vomiting precluding outpatient management
  6. Patient unable to follow or tolerate outpatient regimens
  7. No clinical response to outpatient therapy

ACUTE GENERAL Rx

Regimens for treatment of PID should also be effective against *N. gonorrhoeae* and *C. trachomatis* because endocervical screening for these organisms does not rule out upper reproductive tract infections.

INPATIENT REGIMENS: Recommended parenteral regimen A

- Cefotetan 2 g IV q12h *OR*
  Cefoxitin 2 g IV q6h *PLUS*
  Doxycycline 100 mg PO or IV q12h *OR*
- Clindamycin 900 mg IV q8h PLUS
  Gentamicin loading dose IV or IM (2 mg/kg of body weight), followed by a maintenance dose (1.5 mg/kg) q8h. Single daily dosing (3 to 5 mg/kg) can be substituted.

Alternative parenteral regimens

- Ampicillin/sulbactam 3 g IV q6h *PLUS*
  Doxycycline 100 mg PO or IV q12h

OUTPATIENT REGIMENS: Recommended intramuscular/oral regimens

- Ceftriaxone 250 mg IM in a single dose *PLUS*
- Doxycycline 100 mg PO bid for 14 days
  WITH or WITHOUT
  Metronidazole 500 mg PO bid for 14 days *OR*
- Cefoxitin 2 g IM in a single dose and probenecid, 1 g PO administered concurrently in a single dose *PLUS*
  Doxycycline 100 mg PO bid for 14 days
  WITH or WITHOUT
  Metronidazole 500 mg PO bid for 14 days *OR*
- Cefoxitin 2 gm IM in a single dose and Probenecid 1 gm orally given at the same time *PLUS*
  Doxycycline 100 mg PO bid for 14 days
  WITH or WITHOUT
  Metronidazole 500 mg PO bid for 14 days *OR* other third-generation cephalosporin (ceftizoxime or cefotaxime) PLUS
  Doxycycline 100 mg orally bid for 14 days
  WITH or WITHOUT
- Metronidazole 500 mg orally twice a day for 14 days.

CHRONIC Rx

Hospitalized patients receiving IV therapy:
1. Significant clinical improvement is characterized by defervescence, decreased abdominal tenderness, and decreased uterine, adnexal, and cervical motion tenderness within 3 to 5 days.
2. If no clinical improvement occurs, further diagnostic workup is necessary, including possible surgical intervention.

DISPOSITION

- Long-term sequelae of PID: recurrent PID, chronic pelvic pain, ectopic pregnancy, infertility, Fitz-Hugh-Curtis syndrome (Fig. 1P-28)
- Risk of tubal infertility related to episodes of PID: first episode, 8%; second episode, 20%; third episode, 40%
- Essential to evaluate and treat male sex partners

REFERRAL

If there is no clinical improvement with outpatient therapy observed within 72 hr, patient should be hospitalized and gynecology consult requested.

 **PEARLS & CONSIDERATIONS**

COMMENTS

- Maintain a low threshold for the diagnosis of PID.
- Women with documented chlamydial or gonococcal infections have a high rate of reinfection within 6 mo of treatment. Repeat testing of all women who have been diagnosed with chlamydia or gonorrhea is recommended 3 to 6 mo after treatment, regardless of whether their sex partners were treated.
- All women diagnosed with acute PID should be offered HIV testing.
- Male sex partners of women with PID should be examined and treated if they had sexual contact with the patient during 60 days preceding the patient's onset of symptoms. If a patient's last sexual intercourse was >60 days before onset of symptoms or diagnosis, the patient's most recent sex partner should be treated.
- Patients should be instructed to abstain from sexual intercourse until therapy is completed and until they and their sex partners no longer have symptoms.

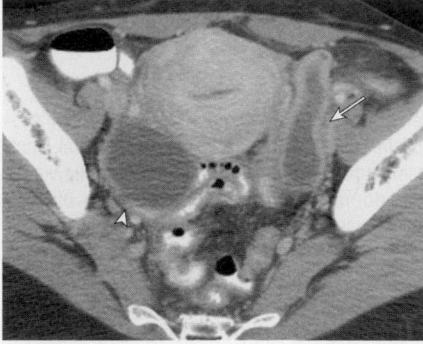

FIGURE 1P-27 Pelvic inflammatory disease with pyosalpinx in a 26-yr-old patient. Computed tomographic image through pelvis shows cystic tubular structure with thick enhancing walls *(arrow)* lateral to the uterus, which, in absence of oral contrast, could be mistaken for a loop of small bowel. (From Fielding JR et al: *Gynecologic imaging,* Philadelphia, 2011, WB Saunders.)

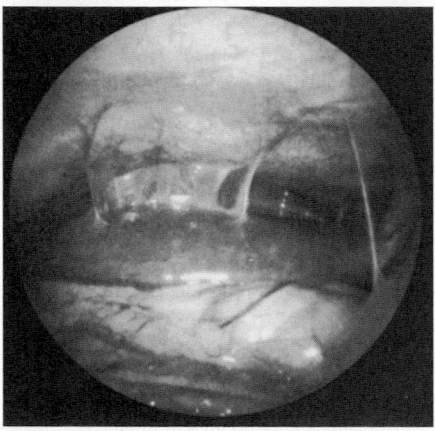

FIGURE 1P-28 "Violin string" adhesions are visualized in this patient with Fitz-Hugh-Curtis syndrome. (From Copeland LJ: *Textbook of gynecology,* ed 2, Philadelphia, 2000, WB Saunders.)

SUGGESTED READINGS
Available at www.expertconsult.com

RELATED CONTENT
Pelvic Inflammatory Disease (Patient Information)
Abscess, Pelvic (Related Key Topic)
Chlamydia Genital Infections (Related Key Topic)
Gonorrhea (Related Key Topic)

AUTHOR: **RUBEN ALVERO, M.D.**

BASIC INFORMATION

DEFINITION

Pelvic organ prolapse (POP) or *uterine prolapse* refers to the protrusion of the uterus into or out of the vaginal canal. In a first-degree uterine prolapse, the cervix is visible when the perineum is depressed. In a second-degree uterine prolapse, the uterine cervix has prolapsed through the vaginal introitus, with the fundus remaining within the pelvis proper. In a third-degree uterine prolapse (i.e., complete uterine prolapse, uterine procidentia), the entire uterus is outside the introitus. Table 1P-13 compares the various types of prolapse.

SYNONYMS

Genital prolapse
Uterine descensus
Uterine prolapse
POP

ICD-10CM CODES
N81.4	Uterovaginal prolapse, unspecified
N81.5	Vaginal enterocele
N81.6	Rectocele
N81.I8	Other female genital prolapse
N81.2	Incomplete uterovaginal prolapse
N81.82	Incompetence or weakening of pubocervical tissue

EPIDEMIOLOGY & DEMOGRAPHICS

PREVALENCE: Most prevalent in postmenopausal multiparous women.
RISK FACTORS:
- Pregnancy, especially POP symptoms during pregnancy
- Labor
- Vaginal childbirth
- Obesity
- Chronic coughing
- Constipation
- Pelvic tumors
- Ascites
- Strenuous physical exertion, especially during pregnancy
- Maternal history of prolapse
- Caucasian race
GENETICS: Increased incidence in women with spina bifida occulta.

PHYSICAL FINDINGS & CLINICAL PRESENTATION

- Pelvic pressure
- Bearing-down sensation
- Bilateral groin pain
- Sacral backache
- Coital difficulty
- Protrusion from vagina
- Spotting
- Ulceration
- Bleeding
- Examination of patient in lithotomy, sitting, and standing positions and before, during, and after a maximum Valsalva effort

- Erosion or ulceration of the cervix possible in the most dependent area of the protrusion

ETIOLOGY

- Vaginal childbirth and chronic increases in intraabdominal pressure leading to detachments, lacerations, and denervations of the vaginal support system
- Further weakening of pelvic support system by hypoestrogenic atrophy
- Direct injury to the levator ani, neurologic injury from stretching of the pudendal nerves
- Some cases from congenital or inherited weaknesses within the pelvic support system
- Neonatal uterine prolapse mostly coexistent with congenital spinal defects

DIAGNOSIS

DIFFERENTIAL DIAGNOSIS

- Occasionally, elongated cervix; body of the uterus remains undescended.
- Diagnosis is based on history and physical examination. Currently there is only one genital tract prolapse classification system that has attained international acceptance and recognition: the patient pelvic organ

prolapse quantification (POP-Q) (Boxes 1P-2 and 1P-3).

WORKUP

- If erosion or ulceration of the cervix is present, a Pap smear followed by a cervical biopsy should be performed if indicated.
- If urinary symptoms are significant, further urodynamic workup is indicated, looking for concurrent cystourethrocele, cystocele, enterocele, or rectocele.

LABORATORY TESTS

Urine culture

IMAGING STUDIES

Ultrasound if concurrent fibroids need further evaluation, CT or MRI (Fig. 1P-29) in symptomatic patients with unclear diagnosis

TREATMENT

NONPHARMACOLOGIC THERAPY

- Prophylactic measures
  1. Diagnosis and treatment of chronic respiratory and metabolic disorders
  2. Correction of constipation

TABLE 1P-13 Types of Genital Prolapse

Original Position of Organs	Prolapse	Symptoms (in addition to the general symptoms of discomfort, dragging, the feeling of a "lump," and, rarely, coital problems)
Anterior	Urethrocele Cystocele	Urinary symptoms (stress incontinence, urinary frequency)
Central	Cervix/uterus: 1st, 2nd, and 3rd degree Procidentia	Bleeding and/or discharge from ulceration in association with procidentia
Posterior	Rectocele Enterocele	Bowel symptoms, particularly the feeling of incomplete evacuation and sometimes having to press the posterior wall backwards to pass stool

From Drife J, Magowan B: *Clinical obstetrics and gynaecology,* Philadelphia, 2004, WB Saunders.

BOX 1P-2 Staging of Pelvic Organ Prolapse Based on POP-Q Examination

Stage 0	No prolapse.
Stage I	Most distal prolapse >1 cm above hymenal ring.
Stage II	Most distal point is ≤1 cm above hymenal ring.
Stage III	Most distal point is >1 cm below the hymenal ring but not farther than 2 cm less than the total vaginal length (TVL) (i.e., ≥1 cm but ≤ [TVL − 2] cm).
Stage IV	Complete vaginal eversion.

From Pemberton J (ed): *The pelvic floor,* Philadelphia, 2002, WB Saunders.

BOX 1P-3 Points of Reference for POP-Q

Point A: 3 cm above the hymen on anterior vaginal wall (Aa) or posterior vaginal wall (Ap). Point Aa roughly corresponds with the urethrovesical junction.
Point B: The lowest extent of the segment of vagina between point A and the apex of the vagina. Unlike point A, it is not fixed but will be the same as A if point A is the most protruding point. In maximal prolapse it will be the same as point C.
Point C: The most distal part of the cervix or vaginal vault.
Point D: The posterior fornix, which is omitted in women with prior hysterectomy.
Genital hiatus: From midline external urethral meatus to inferior hymenal ring.
Perineal body: From inferior hymenal ring to middle of anal orifice.
Vaginal length: This should be measured without undue stretching of the vagina.

From Pemberton J (ed): *The pelvic floor,* Philadelphia, 2002, WB Saunders.

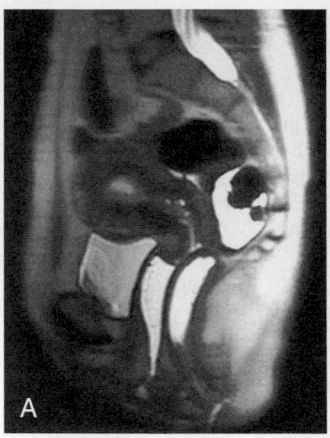 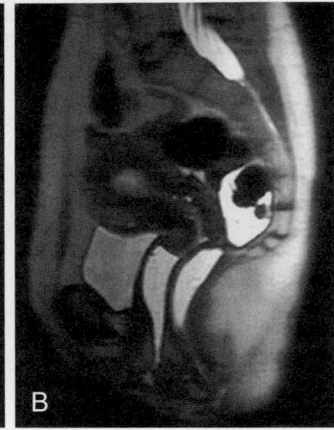 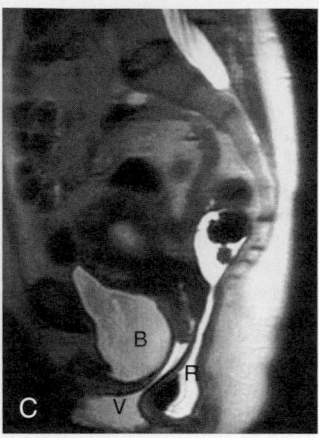

FIGURE 1P-29 A, Moderate global pelvic prolapse in a woman with stress urinary incontinence, pelvic heaviness, and constipation after three vaginal deliveries. At rest, all viscera are normally situated in the pelvis. **B,** With Kegel contraction, note that all viscera remain normally situated in the pelvis. **C,** With maximal strain, bladder *(B)*, vagina *(V)*, and rectum *(R)* are well below the pelvic floor. (From Fielding JR et al: *Gynecologic imaging,* Philadelphia, 2011, WB Saunders.)

3. Weight control, nutrition, and smoking cessation counseling
4. Pelvic muscle exercises
- Supportive pessary therapy
  1. Ring-type pessary useful for first- or second-degree prolapse
  2. Gellhorn pessary preferred for more advanced prolapse
  3. Use of pessaries in conjunction with continuous hormone replacement therapy, unless contraindicated
  4. Perineorrhaphy under local anesthesia possibly needed to support the pessary if the vaginal outlet is very relaxed

ACUTE GENERAL Rx
- Patients who are only infrequently symptomatic: insertion of a tampon or diaphragm for temporary relief when prolonged standing is anticipated
- Neonatal uterine prolapse: simple digital reduction or the use of a small pessary

CHRONIC Rx
- Hormone replacement therapy at the time of menopause helps preserve tissue strength, maintain elasticity of the vagina, and promote the durability of surgical repairs.
- Gold standard for therapy is vaginal hysterectomy.
- Vaginal apex should be well suspended, but a prophylactic sacrospinous ligament fixation is not routinely required.
- If occult enterocele present, McCall culdoplasty is performed.
- If vaginal approach to hysterectomy is contraindicated, abdominal hysterectomy is performed; vaginal apex likewise well supported. Use of laparoscopically assisted approaches, including robotically assisted approaches, is increasing. Questions do exist as to whether the robotic approach is cost-effective for this indication.
- Colpocleisis is considered for the elderly patient who is sexually inactive and is a high-risk patient from a surgical point of view; can

be done rapidly under local anesthesia with mild sedation if necessary.
- For symptomatic women who desire childbearing: management with pessaries or pelvic muscle exercises is recommended; if surgical correction is required, transvaginal sacrospinous fixation is the preferred method. Concern for breakdown of the repair due to pregnancy and childbirth exists, however.
- Other surgical options are sling operations and sacral cervicopexy.
- Trials have shown that as compared with anterior colporrhaphy, use of a standardized, trocar-guided mesh kit for cystocele repair results in higher short-term rates of successful treatment but also in higher rates of surgical complications and postoperative adverse events.
- Women without stress incontinence undergoing vaginal surgery for POP are at risk for postoperative urinary incontinence. Use of a prophylactic midurethral sling inserted during vaginal prolapse surgery has been shown to result in a lower rate of urinary incontinence at 3 and 12 months but a higher rate of adverse events (UTIs, major bleeding complications, incomplete bladder emptying).

DISPOSITION
If untreated, uterine prolapse progressively worsens.

REFERRAL
To a gynecologist/urologist if pessary fitting or surgical intervention is needed

⚠ PEARLS & CONSIDERATIONS

COMMENTS
- More than 300,000 surgeries are performed annually in the United States for pelvic organ prolapse
- Surgery contraindicated in mild or asymptomatic uterine prolapse because the patient

will seldom benefit from the operation although exposed to its risks. The Optimal Randomized Trial compared the sacrospinous ligament fixation (SSLF) and uterosacral ligament suspension (ULS) surgical approaches to correct apical prolapse and also whether perioperative behavioral therapy with pelvic floor muscle training (BPMT) improved outcomes of prolapse surgery. The trial showed that two years after vaginal surgery for prolapse and stress urinary incontinence, neither ULS or SSLF was significantly superior to the other for anatomic, functional, or adverse event outcomes. Perioperative BPMT did not improve urinary symptoms at 6 mo or prolapse outcomes at 2 yr.[1]

SUGGESTED READINGS
Available at www.expertconsult.com

RELATED CONTENT
Pelvic Organ Prolapse (Patient Information)
Uterine Prolapse (Patient Information)
Incontinence, Urinary (Related Key Topic)

AUTHOR: **RUBEN ALVERO, M.D.**

[1]Barber MD et al: Comparison of 2 transvaginal surgical approaches and perioperative behavioral therapy for apical vaginal prolapse, the Optimal Randomized Trial, *JAMA* 311(10):1023-1034, 2014

BASIC INFORMATION

DEFINITION

- *Pemphigus* refers to a group of rare, potentially fatal, chronic, autoimmune blistering diseases of the skin and mucous membranes
- Pemphigus has four main subtypes:
  1. Pemphigus vulgaris (PV) (most common) (Fig. 1P-30)
     1. Pemphigus vegetans, a rare clinical variant of PV
  2. Pemphigus foliaceus (PF)
     1. Pemphigus erythematosus, a variant of PF
  3. Paraneoplastic pemphigus
  4. Immunoglobulin (Ig) A pemphigus

SYNONYMS

Pemphigus
PV
Fogo selvagem: endemic pemphigus foliaceus
Senear-Usher syndrome: pemphigus erythematosus

ICD-10CM CODES
L10.0 Pemphigus vulgaris

EPIDEMIOLOGY & DEMOGRAPHICS

- Incidence is approximately one case per 100,000 persons and varies substantially by geographic region.
- More common in Ashkenazi Jews and people of Middle Eastern descent.
- Typically occurs in the fourth and fifth decades of life, although range of ages affected is broad and it may occur in the very young or elderly.
- No gender predilection

PHYSICAL FINDINGS & CLINICAL PRESENTATION

- History:
  1. Multiple oropharyngeal ulcerations and erosions typically occur first (60% of cases), which can then be followed by a more generalized bullous eruption involving the skin within several weeks or months

2. Blisters are fragile and rupture easily, leaving painful erosions and ulcerations that may be the predominant clinical finding
3. Pain associated with oral mucosal blistering often results in dysphagia and hoarseness
4. Not commonly pruritic
- Physical findings:
  1. Anatomic distribution
     a. Oral mucosa
     b. Can also involve the pharynx, larynx, vagina, penis, anus, and conjunctival mucosa
     c. Generalized cutaneous involvement (Figs. 1P-31 and 1P-32)
  2. Lesion configuration
     a. Any stratified squamous epithelial surfaces can become involved
  3. Lesion morphology
     a. Flaccid bullae and vesicles. The **"bulla-spread phenomenon" (Asboe-Hansen sign)** Is elicted by pressure on an intact bulla, gently forcing the fluid to spread under the adjacent skin

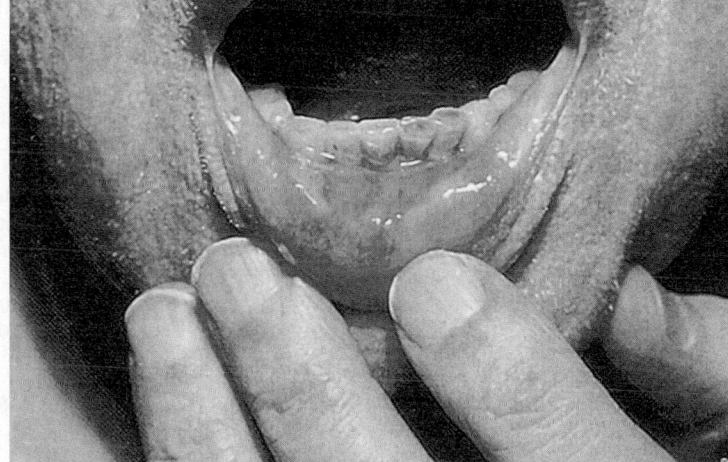

FIGURE 1P-30 Pemphigus vulgaris with oral lesions and no intact bullae. (Courtesy Department of Dermatology, University of North Carolina at Chapel Hill. From Goldstein BG, Goldstein AO: *Practical dermatology,* ed 2, St Louis, 1997, Mosby.)

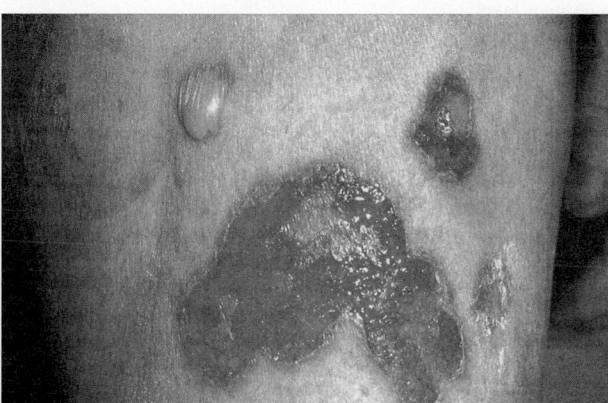

FIGURE 1P-31 Pemphigus vulgaris; extensive erosions and blisters are present on the shin. (Courtesy R. A. Marsden, M.D., St. George's Hospital, London. From McKee PH et al [eds]: *Pathology of the skin with clinical correlations,* ed 3, St Louis, 2005, Mosby.)

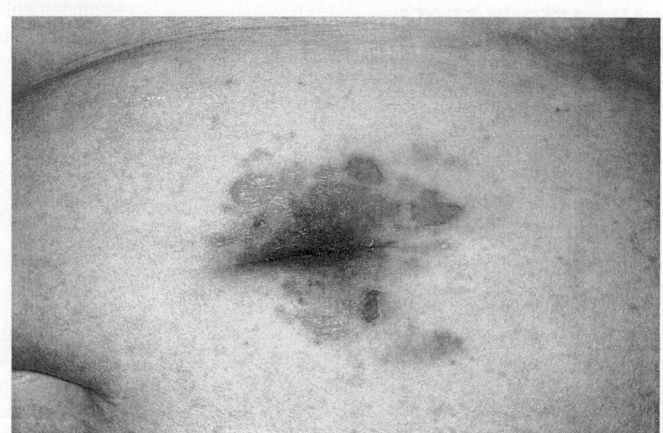

FIGURE 1P-32 Pemphigus vulgaris: umbilical lesions showing intact blisters as well as raw erosions. (Courtesy R. A. Marsden, M.D., St. George's Hospital, London. From McKee PH et al [eds]: *Pathology of the skin with clinical correlations,* ed 3, St Louis, 2005, Mosby.)

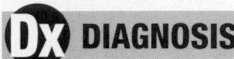
b. Erosion with crusting commonly occurs

4. Positive **Nikolsky sign:** when the clinician applies lateral pressure to normal-appearing skin at the periphery of active lesions, separation of the superficial epidermis occurs

ETIOLOGY

Autoimmune disease caused by autoantibodies against the cell surface of keratinocytes. The predominant antibody in PV is directed against desmoglein 3; in PF it is directed against desmoglein 1.

DIAGNOSIS

The diagnosis of pemphigus vulgaris should be suspected in patients with painful oral erosions and flaccid bullae or erosions on the skin. The diagnosis is confirmed by histology, immunofluorescence pattern of perilesional skin, indirect immunofluorescence (IIF) testing of serum, or ELISA testing for anti-desmoglein 1 (Dsg1) and anti-Dsg3 autoantibodies.

DIFFERENTIAL DIAGNOSIS

- Bullous pemphigoid (Table 1P-14)
- Cicatricial pemphigoid
- Behçet's syndrome
- Erythema multiforme
- Hailey-Hailey disease
- Aphthous stomatitis
- Bullous lupus erythematosus
- Drug eruptions
- Dermatitis herpetiformis
- Epidermolysis bullosa acquisita
- IgA pemphigus
- Paraneoplastic pemphigus
- Pemphigus foliaceus

WORKUP

Skin biopsy is diagnostic; specimens should be sent for routine histochemical staining and direct immunofluorescence. Certain laboratory values may also be useful in establishing the diagnosis of pemphigus.

LABORATORY TESTS

- Skin biopsy reveals intraepidermal vesicles, also called *acantholysis* (loss of cell adhesion between the epidermal cells).

- Indirect immunofluorescence may detect circulating autoantibodies.
- Direct immunofluorescence studies of perilesional skin demonstrate IgG directed against keratinocyte surfaces in the epidermis.

TREATMENT

NONPHARMACOLOGIC THERAPY

- Mild soaps and emollients to skin
- Burow's solution may be useful for weeping erosions.
- When there are extensive raw surfaces, daily baths are helpful in removing the thickened crusts and reducing foul odor.
- Soft diet and viscous lidocaine can be used in patients with oral lesions.
- A mixture of equal parts of simethicone (Maalox), elixir of diphenhydramine, and viscous lidocaine is also effective.

ACUTE GENERAL Rx

- For localized disease, topical steroids may be effective. Silver sulfadiazine (silvadene) 1% can be used as a topical antimicrobial agent.
- For generalized disease, systemic corticosteroids (prednisone) are the mainstay of therapy and often work rapidly to halt blistering.
  1. Initial dose of prednisone is usually 1 mg/kg/day, then tapered over weeks as blistering decreases.
  2. Steroid-sparing immunosuppressive therapies are often initiated simultaneously with prednisone to minimize the side effects of prolonged corticosteroid therapy.

CHRONIC Rx

- Adjuvant therapy such as immunosuppressants, anti-inflammatories, chemotherapeutic agents, and biologics are useful for disease control and to shorten the length of treatment with oral steroids; treatment duration and dosing are determined by clinical response:
  1. Mycophenolate mofetil (MMF) 1 to 1.5 g twice/day: usually chosen as steroid-sparing agent
  2. Azathioprine is less expensive than MMF and can be used when cost is an overriding issue

- Refractory disease:
  1. IV Ig
  2. Rituximab (anti-CD20 monoclonal antibody)
  3. Plasmapheresis

DISPOSITION

- Medication is continued until clinical disease is suppressed and pemphigus antibody disappears from serum. A negative DIF test once the antibody is no longer present is predictive of sustained remission.
- Before the use of oral corticosteroids, pemphigus was usually a fatal disease with most patients dying within 5 yr of diagnosis.
- Combined corticosteroids and adjuvant therapy have decreased mortality rates to <10%.
- Death generally occurs from sepsis or complications related to medical therapy.

REFERRAL

Dermatology
Otolaryngology

PEARLS & CONSIDERATIONS

COMMENTS

- PV, unlike bullous pemphigoid, is a disease of middle-aged persons.
- Early diagnosis of pemphigus is important to initiate prompt treatment.
- Oral corticosteroids have many substantial side effects, and patients should be monitored for osteoporosis, hypertension, and diabetes. Supplementation with vitamin D and biphosphonates should be considered for osteoporosis prevention and treatment.

SUGGESTED READINGS

Available at www.expertconsult.com

RELATED CONTENT

Pemphigus Vulgaris (Patient Information)

AUTHORS: **JESSICA CORWIN, M.D., M.P.H.,** and **KACHIU C. LEE, M.D., M.P.H.**

TABLE 1P-14 Differentiation of Pemphigus Vulgaris and Bullous Pemphigoid

Characteristics	Pemphigus Vulgaris	Bullous Pemphigoid
Age	Usually occurs in middle-aged persons	>60 yr
Site	Oral mucosa, face, chest, groin	Flexural areas, groin, axilla; less often involving mucosal surfaces
Findings	Flaccid bullae and erosions, intraepidermal blisters, IgG autoantibodies against keratinocyte surfaces	Intact bullae, subepidermal blisters, IgG autoantibodies against hemidesmosomal antigens
Treatment	Prednisone 1 mg/kg/day with adjuvant immunosuppressant agents; refractory disease may require intravenous immunoglobulin, plasmapheresis, or rituximab	Prednisone 1 mg/kg/day with adjuvant immunosuppressant therapy; localized disease may be controlled with topical steroids
Prognosis	>90% respond; steroid side effects significant	>90% respond; remissions and recurrences common

BASIC INFORMATION

DEFINITION

Peptic ulcer disease (PUD) is an ulceration in the stomach or duodenum resulting from an imbalance between mucosal protective factors and various mucosal damaging mechanisms (see "Etiology").

SYNONYMS

PUD
Duodenal ulcer (DU)
Gastric ulcer (GU)

ICD-10CM CODES

K25.3 Acute gastric ulcer without hemorrhage or perforation
K25.7 Chronic gastric ulcer without hemorrhage or perforation
K26.3 Acute duodenal ulcer without hemorrhage or perforation
K26.7 Chronic duodenal ulcer without hemorrhage or perforation
K27.0 Acute peptic ulcer, site unspecified, with hemorrhage
K27.1 Acute peptic ulcer, site unspecified, with perforation
K27.2 Acute peptic ulcer, site unspecified, with both hemorrhage and perforation
K27.3 Acute peptic ulcer, site unspecified, without hemorrhage or perforation
K27.4 Chronic or unspecified peptic ulcer, site unspecified, with hemorrhage
K27.5 Chronic or unspecified peptic ulcer, site unspecified, with perforation
K27.6 Chronic or unspecified peptic ulcer, site unspecified, with both hemorrhage and perforation
K27.7 Chronic peptic ulcer, site unspecified, without hemorrhage or perforation

K27.9 Peptic ulcer, site unspecified, unspecified as acute or chronic, without hemorrhage or perforation
P78.82 Peptic ulcer of newborn
Z87.11 Personal history of peptic ulcer disease

EPIDEMIOLOGY & DEMOGRAPHICS

• Incidence: 250,000 to 500,000 (200,000 to 400,000 duodenal; 50,000 to 100,000 gastric) annually; duodenal ulcer/gastric ulcer ratio is 4:1.
• Anatomic location: <90% of duodenal ulcers occur in the first portion of the duodenum; gastric ulcers occur most frequently in the lesser curvature near the incisura angularis.

PHYSICAL FINDINGS & CLINICAL PRESENTATION

• Physical examination is often unremarkable.
• Patient may have epigastric tenderness, tachycardia, pallor, hypotension (from acute or chronic blood loss), nausea and vomiting (if pyloric channel is obstructed), boardlike abdomen and rebound tenderness (if perforated), and hematemesis or melena (with a bleeding ulcer). Box 1P-4 describes key symptoms and signs of peptic ulcer.

ETIOLOGY

Often multifactorial. The following are common mucosal damaging factors:
• *Helicobacter pylori* infection. *H. pylori* is the major cause of PUD. It is found in more than 70% of patients with duodenal ulcers and gastric ulcers in the United States. Rates are much higher (>90%) in other parts of the world. Eradication of *H. pylori* markedly reduces peptic ulcer recurrence.

• Medications (NSAIDs, glucocorticoids). Risk factors for development of NSAID-related ulcers are described in Table 1P-15.
• Incompetent pylorus or lower esophageal sphincter
• Bile acids
• Impaired proximal duodenal bicarbonate secretion
• Decreased blood flow to gastric mucosa
• Acid secreted by parietal cells and pepsin secreted as pepsinogen by chief cells
• Cigarette smoking
• Alcohol

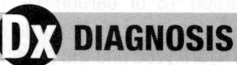 DIAGNOSIS

DIFFERENTIAL DIAGNOSIS

• Gastroesophageal reflux disease
• Cholelithiasis syndrome
• Pancreatitis
• Gastritis
• Nonulcer dyspepsia
• Neoplasm (gastric carcinoma, lymphoma, pancreatic carcinoma)
• Angina pectoris, myocardial infarction, pericarditis
• Dissecting aneurysm
• Other: high small-bowel obstruction, pneumonia, subphrenic abscess, early appendicitis

WORKUP

Comprehensive history and physical exam to exclude other diagnoses. Diagnostic modalities include endoscopy or upper GI series. Endoscopy is preferred and remains the gold standard for diagnosis of PUD. The presence of a mucosal break ≥5 mm in the stomach or duodenum confirms the diagnosis.

LABORATORY TESTS

• Routine laboratory evaluation is usually unremarkable.
• Anemia may be present in patients with significant GI bleeding.
• *H. pylori* testing by endoscopic biopsy, urea breath test, stool antigen test (*H. pylori* stool antigen), or specific antibody test is recommended:

BOX 1P-4 Key Symptoms and Signs of Peptic Ulcer

Uncomplicated Ulcer
No symptoms ("silent ulcer" in up to 40% of cases)
Epigastric pain
Pain may radiate to the back, thorax, other parts of abdomen (cephalad most likely, caudad least likely)
Pain may be nocturnal (most specific), "painful hunger" relieved by food, or continuous (least specific)
Nausea
Vomiting
Heartburn (mimics or associated with gastroesophageal reflux)

Complicated Ulcer
Acute perforation
Severe abdominal pain
Shock
Abdominal boardlike rigidity (and rebound and other signs of peritoneal irritation)
Free intraperitoneal air
Hemorrhage
Hematemesis and/or melena
Hemodynamic changes, anemia
Previous history of ulcer symptoms (80%)
Gastric outlet obstruction
Satiation, inability to ingest food, eructation
Nausea, vomiting (and related disturbances)
Weight loss

From Goldman L, Schafer AI: *Goldman's Cecil medicine*, ed 24, Philadelphia, 2012, Saunders.

TABLE 1P-15 Risk Factors for Development of NSAID-Related Ulcers

Definite
Advanced age
History of ulcer
Concomitant corticosteroid therapy
Concomitant anticoagulation therapy
High doses of NSAIDs
Serious systemic disorders

Possible
Concomitant infection with *Helicobacter pylori*
Cigarette smoking
Consumption of alcohol

NSAIDs, Nonsteroidal antiinflammatory drugs.
From Andreoli TE et al: *Andreoli and Carpenter's Cecil essentials of medicine*, ed 8, Philadelphia, 2010, Saunders.

 **BASIC INFORMATION**

DEFINITION

Peritonitis refers to the acute onset of severe abdominal pain caused by peritoneal inflammation.

Secondary peritonitis is a localized (abscess) or diffuse peritonitis originating from a defect in abdominal viscus.

SYNONYMS

Acute abdomen
Surgical abdomen

ICD-10CM CODES
K65.0	Generalized (acute) peritonitis
K65.8	Other peritonitis
K65.9	Peritonitis, unspecified
A18.31	Tuberculous peritonitis
A54.85	Gonococcal peritonitis
A74.81	Chlamydial peritonitis
K35.2	Acute appendicitis with generalized peritonitis
K35.3	Acute appendicitis with localized peritonitis
K65.2	Spontaneous bacterial peritonitis
N73.3	Female acute pelvic peritonitis
N73.4	Female chronic pelvic peritonitis
N73.5	Female pelvic peritonitis, unspecified
P78.1	Other neonatal peritonitis

EPIDEMIOLOGY & DEMOGRAPHICS

Common presentation as a result of diverse etiologies; for example, 5% to 10% of the population has acute appendicitis at some point in their lives.

PHYSICAL FINDINGS & CLINICAL PRESENTATION

- Acute abdominal pain
- Abdominal distention and ascites
- Abdominal rigidity, rebound, and guarding
- Fever, chills
- Exacerbation with movement
- Anorexia, nausea, and vomiting
- Constipation
- Decreased bowel sounds
- Hypotension and tachycardia
- Tachypnea, dyspnea

ETIOLOGY

- Microbiology: most common is gram-negative bacteria (*Escherichia coli, Enterobacter, Klebsiella, Proteus*), gram-positive bacteria (enterococci, streptococci, staphylococci), anaerobic bacteria (*Bacteroides, Clostridium*), and fungi

- Acute perforation peritonitis: gastrointestinal perforation, intestinal ischemia, pelvic peritonitis, and other forms
- Postoperative peritonitis: anastomotic leak, accidental perforation, and devascularization
- Posttraumatic peritonitis: after blunt or penetrating abdominal trauma

Dx DIAGNOSIS

DIFFERENTIAL DIAGNOSIS

- Postoperative: abscess, sepsis, bowel obstruction, injury to internal organs
- Gastrointestinal: perforated viscus, appendicitis, inflammatory bowel disease, infectious colitis, diverticulitis, acute cholecystitis, peptic ulcer perforation, pancreatitis, bowel obstruction
- Gynecologic: ruptured ectopic pregnancy, pelvic inflammatory disease, ruptured hemorrhagic ovarian cyst, ovarian torsion, degenerating leiomyoma
- Urologic: nephrolithiasis, interstitial cystitis
- Miscellaneous: abdominal trauma, penetrating wounds, infections caused by intraperitoneal dialysis

WORKUP

- Acute peritonitis is mainly a clinical diagnosis based on patient history and physical examination.
- Laboratory and imaging studies (see "Laboratory Tests") assist in determining the need for and type of intervention.
- If patient is hemodynamically unstable, immediate diagnostic laparotomy should be performed in lieu of adjuvant diagnostic studies.

LABORATORY TESTS

- Complete blood count: leukocytosis, left shift, anemia
- SMA7: electrolyte imbalances, kidney dysfunction
- Liver function tests: ascites from liver disease, cholelithiasis
- Amylase: pancreatitis
- Blood cultures: bacteremia, sepsis
- Peritoneal cultures: infectious etiology
- Blood gas: respiratory versus metabolic acidosis
- Ascitic fluid analysis: exudate versus transudate
- Urinalysis and culture: urinary tract infection
- Cervical cultures for gonorrhea and *Chlamydia*
- Urine/serum human chorionic gonadotropin

IMAGING STUDIES

- Abdominal series: free air from perforation, small or large bowel dilation from obstruction, identification of fecalith
- Chest x-ray examination: elevated diaphragm, pneumonia
- Pelvic/abdominal ultrasound: abscess formation, abdominal mass, intrauterine versus ectopic pregnancy, identify free fluid suggestive of hemorrhage or ascites
- CT: mass, ascites

Rx TREATMENT

NONPHARMACOLOGIC THERAPY

- IV hydration to correct dehydration, hypovolemia
- Blood transfusion to correct anemia from hemorrhage
- Nasogastric decompression, especially if obstruction is present
- Oxygen: intubation if necessary
- Bed rest

ACUTE GENERAL Rx

- Surgery to correct underlying pathology, such as controlling hemorrhage, correcting perforation, draining abscess
- Broad-spectrum antibiotics to cover both gram-negative aerobic and gram-negative anaerobic bacteria:
  1. Mild-moderate disease: piperacillin-tazobactam 3.375 g IV q6h or 4.5 g IV q8h *or* ticarcillin-clavulanate 3.1 g IV q6h. Alternative agents are ciprofloxacin 400 mg IV q12h or levofloxacin 750 mg IV q24h *plus* metronidazole 1 g IV q12h.
  2. Severe life-threatening disease: imipenem 500 mg IV q6h or meropenem 1 g IV q8h. Alternative agents are ampicillin *plus* metronidazole *plus* ciprofloxacin.
- Pain control: morphine or meperidine as needed (hold until diagnosis confirmed)

DISPOSITION

Depends on etiology of peritonitis, age of patient, coexisting medical disease, and duration of process before presentation

REFERRAL

Surgical consultation is required in all cases of acute peritonitis.

SUGGESTED READINGS
Available at www.expertconsult.com

AUTHOR: **RUBEN ALVERO, M.D.**

BASIC INFORMATION

DEFINITION

Spontaneous bacterial peritonitis (SBP) is an inflammatory reaction of the peritoneum secondary to the presence of bacteria or other microorganisms. More specifically, SBP is defined as an ascitic fluid infection without an evident intraabdominal surgically treatable source occurring primarily in patients with advanced cirrhosis of the liver.

SYNONYMS

Primary peritonitis
SBP

ICD-10CM CODES
K65.2 Spontaneous bacterial peritonitis

EPIDEMIOLOGY & DEMOGRAPHICS

PREVALENCE: The prevalence of SBP in cirrhotic patients admitted to the hospital has been estimated at 10% to 30%.
PREDOMINANT SEX: Males affected more often than females.

PHYSICAL FINDINGS & CLINICAL PRESENTATION

- Acute fever with accompanying abdominal pain/ascites, nausea, vomiting, diarrhea.
- In cirrhotic patients, presentation may be subtle with a low-grade temperature (100° F) with or without abdominal abnormalities.
- In patients with ascites, a heightened degree of awareness is necessary for detection
- Jaundice and encephalopathy.
- Deterioration of mental status and/or renal function.

ETIOLOGY

- *Escherichia coli.*
- *Klebsiella pneumoniae.*
- *Streptococcus pneumoniae.*
- *Streptococcus* and *Enterococcus* spp.
- *Staphylococcus aureus.*
- Anaerobic pathogens: *Bacteroides, Clostridium* organisms.
- Other: fungal, mycobacterial, viral.

DIAGNOSIS

The diagnosis of SBP is established by a positive ascitic fluid bacterial culture and an elevated ascitic fluid absolute polymorphonuclear leukocyte count ($\geq$250 cells/mm³).

DIFFERENTIAL DIAGNOSIS

- Appendicitis (in children).
- Perforated peptic ulcer.
- Secondary bacterial peritonitis.
- Peritoneal abscess.
- Splenic, hepatic, or pancreatic abscess.
- Cholecystitis.
- Cholangitis.

WORKUP

Paracentesis and ascitic fluid analysis will confirm diagnosis (see "Laboratory Tests").

LABORATORY TESTS

Ascitic fluid analysis reveals the following:
- Cell count with an absolute polymorphonuclear cell count >250/mm³.
- Presence of bacteria on Gram stain.
- pH <7.31.
- Lactic acid >32 mg/dl.
- Protein <1 g/dl.
- Glucose >50 mg/dl.
- Lactate dehydrogenase <225 mU/mL.
- Positive culture of peritoneal fluid.
- Measurement of the serum/ascites/albumin gradient: The serum/ascites/albumin gradient indirectly measures portal pressure. The albumin concentration of ascitic fluid and serum must be obtained on the same day. The ascitic fluid value is subtracted from the serum value to obtain the gradient. If the difference (not a ratio) is >1.1 g/dl, the patient has portal hypertension, with 97% accuracy. If the difference is <1.1 g/dl, portal hypertension is not present. The majority of patients with SBP have portal hypertension as a result of cirrhosis.

IMAGING STUDIES

- Abdominal ultrasound: if there is clinical difficulty in performing paracentesis.
- CT scan: to rule out secondary peritonitis (if indicated) and to exclude abscess, mass.

 TREATMENT

ACUTE GENERAL Rx

- Cefotaxime (2 g IV q8h) or ceftriaxone (2 g IV q24h) or ticarcillin-clavulanate or piperacillin-tazobactam. Continue therapy for 7 days. Repeat diagnostic paracentesis can be done at day 2. Repeat paracentesis at 48 hr will demonstrate a significant decrease in polymorphonuclear count in patients with SBP. If ascites PMN count decreases by at least 25% at day 2, IV therapy can be switched to PO (levofloxacin 250 mg PO bid) to complete 7 days of therapy.
- IV albumin (1.5 g/kg of body weight upon initial diagnosis and 1 g/kg of albumin on day 3) if BUN >30 mg/dL, serum creatinine >1 mg/dl, bilirubin >4 mg/dL.

PROPHYLAXIS

- Ciprofloxacin 500 mg PO qd or levofloxacin 250 mg PO qd.
- Alternative therapy: TMP-SMX one double-strength tablet PO qd.
- Prophylaxis should be continued until disappearance of ascites or until liver transplantation.

DISPOSITION

- The overall mortality rate from an episode of SBP is 20%, and following an episode, the 1-year mortality rate approaches 70%.

REFERRAL

- To a gastroenterologist for management of ascites and prevention of recurrent SBP.
- To an infectious disease specialist for management of difficult-to-treat infections, antibiotic-resistant bacterial infections, or antibiotic drug intolerance.

PEARLS & CONSIDERATIONS

COMMENTS

- Renal failure is a major cause of morbidity in cirrhotic patients with SBP. The use of IV albumin (1.5 g/kg at the time of diagnosis and 1 g/kg on day 3) may lower the rate of renal failure and mortality in patients with SBP.
- The criteria for the diagnosis of SBP require that abdominal paracentesis be performed and ascitic fluid be analyzed before a diagnosis of SBP can be made.
- Culturing ascitic fluid as if it were blood (with bedside inoculation of at least 10 mL of ascitic fluid directly into blood culture bottles at the bedside) has been shown to significantly increase the culture positivity of the ascitic fluid in the 80% to 100% range.
- Avoid therapeutic paracenteses during active infection.
- Positive blood cultures in an individual with ascites require exclusion of a peritoneal source by paracentesis.
- Follow-up paracentesis is indicated only in selected cases (worsening clinical status, nosocomial SBP, infection with atypical organism, recent β-lactam exposure).

SUGGESTED READINGS
Available at www.expertconsult.com

AUTHOR: **GLENN G. FORT, M.D., M.P.H.**

BASIC INFORMATION

DEFINITION
Peritonsillar abscess is an acute infection located between the capsule of the palatine tonsil and the superior constrictor muscle of the pharynx.

SYNONYMS
Quinsy, PTA

ICD-10CM CODES
J36 Peritonsillar abscess

EPIDEMIOLOGY & DEMOGRAPHICS
INCIDENCE (IN U.S.): 30:100,000/yr for ages 5 to 59. For adolescents, the incidence is 40:100,000/yr. It is the most common deep infection of the head and neck in children and adolescents, accounting for at least 50% of cases.
PEAK INCIDENCE: Bimodal frequency during the year, with highest occurrence from November to December and April to May.
PREVALENCE: 45,000 cases/yr in the United States
PREDOMINANT SEX: Male > female
PREDOMINANT AGE: Highest incidence is adults aged 20 to 40 yr.
RISK FACTORS: Smoking, periodontal disease, oropharyngeal or dental infection, male gender

PHYSICAL FINDINGS & CLINICAL PRESENTATION
- There is often a delay of 2 to 5 days between abscess formation and local and systemic symptoms
- Sore throat, which may be severe and unilateral
- Dysphagia and odynophagia
- Otalgia on the side of abscess
- Foul-smelling breath
- Facial swelling
- Drooling
- Headache
- Fever
- Trismus: the examination of the pharynx can be limited by trismus
- Hoarseness, muffled voice (also called "hot potato voice")
- Tender submandibular and anterior cervical lymph nodes
- Tonsillar hypertrophy with likely peritonsillar edema
- Contralateral deflection of the uvula: the distinguishing feature of peritonsillar abscess is inferior medial displacement of the infected tonsil with contralateral deviation of the uvula (Fig. 1P-42)
- Stridor

ETIOLOGY
- Peritonsillar abscess is usually a complication of tonsillitis or acute bacterial pharyngitis caused by blockage of salivary ducts. Tonsillitis → peritonsillar cellulitis → peritonsillar abscess

- Group A β-hemolytic *Streptococcus* is the most common bacterial cause, accounting for 15% to 30% of cases in children and 5% to 10% of cases in adults.
- Less common aerobic causes are *Staphylococcus aureus, Haemophilus influenzae, Neisseria* species.
- The most common anaerobic organism is *Fusobacterium.*

DIAGNOSIS

DIFFERENTIAL DIAGNOSIS
- Hypertrophic tonsillitis
- Infectious mononucleosis
- Peritonsillar cellulitis
- Retropharyngeal abscess
- Epiglottitis
- Dental abscess (retromolar)
- Lymphoma
- Ludwig's angina
- Tubercular granuloma
- Cervical adenitis
- Diptheria
- Foreign body
- Neoplasm

WORKUP
- Based on history and physical exam. Aspiration of pus established diagnosis of peritonsillar abscess
- Consider additional testing if presentation is less clear.

LABORATORY TESTS
- Consider rapid strep antigen testing and/or pharyngeal culture and sensitivity.
- Aspiration of the abscess for culture and sensitivity (see "Treatment" for role of aspiration in tx)
- Consider lab testing for mononucleosis (patients with peritonsillar abscess have a 20% incidence of mononucleosis)

IMAGING STUDIES
- Consider ultrasound, CT scan (Fig. 1P-41), or MRI to help differentiate abscess from cellulitis or mass when diagnosis is unclear.
- Intraoral ultrasound may improve diagnosis and aspiration of PTA compared with visual inspection in adult patients.
- MRI provides better soft-tissue differentiation than CT.

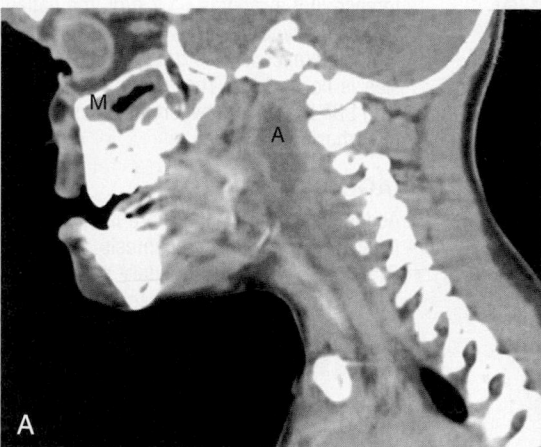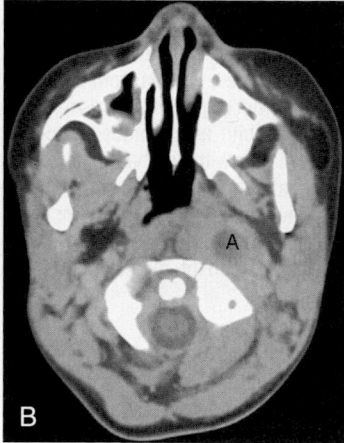

FIGURE 1P-41 CT of parapharyngeal abscess in a 3-yr-old child. A, Sagittal section demonstrating parapharyngeal abscess *(A)* and mucosal swelling *(M)* in the maxillary sinus. **B,** Coronal section of parapharyngeal abscess *(A)*. (From Kliegman RM et al: *Nelson textbook of pediatrics,* ed 19, Philadelphia, 2011, Saunders.)

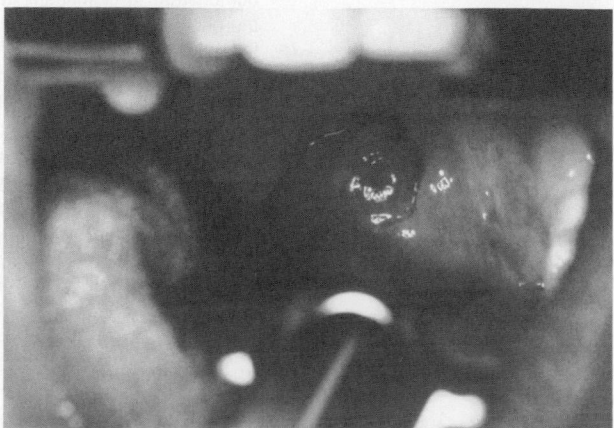

FIGURE 1P-42 Peritonsillar abscess with uvular displacement to the right. (Marx JA et al: *Rosen's emergency medicine,* ed 8, Philadelphia, 2014, WB Saunders.)

TREATMENT

NONPHARMACOLOGIC THERAPY

- Drainage of the abscess by needle aspiration or by surgical incision and drainage. Intraoral ultrasound-guided needle aspiration is a useful adjunct in the presence of trismus

ACUTE GENERAL Rx

- Aspiration or surgical drainage AND antibiotics for 10 to 14 days
- Initial antibiotics should cover group A *Streptococcus* and anaerobes
- Intravenous
  1. Piperacillin/tazobactam or ticarcillin/clavulanate. If penicillin allergic, use IV clindamycin (600-900 mg IV q8h).
  2. Ampicillin-sulbactam 3 g q6h
  3. Penicillin G 10 million units q6h AND metronidazole 500 mg q6h (may use clindamycin 900 mg q8h if penicillin allergic)
- OR oral
  1. Amoxicillin-clavulanic acid 875 mg twice daily
  2. Penicillin VK 500 mg 4 times daily AND metronidazole 500 mg 4 times daily
  3. Clindamycin 600 mg twice daily or 300 mg 4 times daily
- Selection of antibiotics should be guided by culture and sensitivity of the organism Consulting local antimicrobial guidelines for resistance profiles is also advisable for empiric coverage before culture results are available.

CHRONIC Rx

- Tonsillectomy can be considered 3 to 6 mo after diagnosis of peritonsillar abscess with or without the diagnosis of recurrent tonsillitis.
- Though rare, in adults and children with an acute case of peritonsillar abscess and a history of recurrent pharyngitis or previous peritonsillar abscess, a specialist may recommend a *quinsy or hot tonsillectomy*, an immediate removal of the tonsils after starting IV antibiotics.

DISPOSITION

- Successful treatment is defined by symptomatic improvement in sore throat, fever, and/or tonsillar swelling within 24 hr of intervention.
- Treatment failure is defined by lack of symptomatic improvement or worsening despite 24 hr of antimicrobial therapy (with or without surgical drainage).

REFERRAL

- Consider ENT or diagnostic radiology for drainage of abscess.
- Consider ENT for tonsillectomy if criteria are met.

PEARLS & CONSIDERATIONS

COMMENTS

- Risk for a recurrence is immediate (within 4 days) and long term (2 to 3 yr).
- Most recurrences occur shortly after the initial presentation, suggesting continued infection rather than recurrence.

- Overall recurrence rate is 10% to 15%.
- Supportive treatment for pain control and hydration. Newer reports suggest a single dose of dexamethasone (10 mg) administered following needle aspiration will reduce pain at 24 hours as compared with placebo (see "Suggested Readings").

PREVENTION

- Adequate treatment of peritonsillar abscess.
- Up to 30% of patients with peritonsillar abscess meet criteria for tonsillectomy.

PATIENT/FAMILY EDUCATION

Advise family members to call with any trouble breathing, swallowing, or talking.

SUGGESTED READINGS

Available at www.expertconsult.com

AUTHORS: **PETER J. SELL, D.O.,** and **AMITY RUBEOR, D.O.**

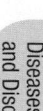

Diseases and Disorders

BASIC INFORMATION

DEFINITION

Pertussis is a prolonged bacterial infection of the upper respiratory tract characterized by paroxysms of an intense cough.

SYNONYMS

Whooping cough

ICD-10CM CODES

A37.90 Whooping cough, unspecified species without pneumonia
A37.00 Whooping cough due to Bordetella pertussis without pneumonia
A37.01 Whooping cough due to Bordetella pertussis with pneumonia
A37.10 Whooping cough due to Bordetella parapertussis without pneumonia
A37.11 Whooping cough due to Bordetella parapertussis with pneumonia
A37.80 Whooping cough due to other Bordetella species without pneumonia
A37.81 Whooping cough due to other Bordetella species with pneumonia
A37.90 Whooping cough, unspecified species without pneumonia
A37.91 Whooping cough, unspecified species with pneumonia

EPIDEMIOLOGY

INCIDENCE (IN U.S.): Case reports from 2014 were 28,660, including nine deaths, predominantly in infants younger than 3 months of age. This total is essentially unchanged from 2013 (28,639 cases) and is less than the 48,277 cases reported in 2012, the highest rate reported since 1955. In 2014, there was a pertussis epidemic in California with nearly 10,000 cases reported (26 cases/100,000). Highest incidence was among infants younger than 1 year (174.6 cases/100,000), although rates appear to be increasing in adolescents 13 to 15 years of age.
PEAK INCIDENCE:
- Childhood
- Usually affects children aged <1 yr
- Increasing infections seen in adolescence
PREDOMINANT AGE:
- 50% in children aged <1 yr
- 20% in children aged >15 yr
- Classically an infection of infants and young children, pertussis is often overlooked as a cause of chronic cough in adults. However, a resurgence of pertussis has been observed in recent years, with nearly 50% of all cases identified in adolescents and adults, likely due to waning immunity and decreased effectiveness of acellular vaccines in early childhood compared to older, whole-cell-derived vaccines.

PHYSICAL FINDINGS & CLINICAL PRESENTATION

- Infection is characterized by 3 phases: catarrhal, paroxysmal, and convalescent

- Catarrhal phase: Usually begins with a 1- to 2-wk prodrome that resembles a common cold. This phase may be mild or absent in adolescents and adults given partial immunity from prior immunization
- After this initial phase, increased production of mucus occurs. Excessive lacrimation and conjunctival infection should heighten the suspicion for pertussis
- Paroxysmal phase: Increased mucus production is followed by an intense, paroxysmal cough, ending with gasps and an inspiratory whoop
- In some children, apnea, cyanosis and anoxia are noted; posttussive gagging and vomiting are characteristic of pertussis
- Cases can be severe and life-threatening in young infants, particularly children <6 months old
- When prolonged, frank exhaustion and even apnea occur. The paroxysmal phase lasts from 2 wk to 2 mo
- Convalescent phase: Lasts over 2 months and is characterized by cough of decreasing severity

ETIOLOGY

Bordetella pertussis, a gram-negative rod that adheres to human cilia and respiratory epithelia

DIAGNOSIS

DIFFERENTIAL DIAGNOSIS

- Croup
- Epiglottitis
- Foreign body aspiration
- Bacterial pneumonia
- Viral pneumonia

WORKUP

Pertussis is often overlooked as a cause of chronic cough, especially in adolescents and adults. The presence of posttussive emesis and/or inspiratory whoop increases the likelihood of pertussis but only modestly. Therefore, clinicians must use their overall impression in pursuing the diagnosis.
- Enzyme-linked immunosorbent assay for detection of antibody to pertussis. Polymerase chain reaction (PCR) is the most sensitive method for rapid detection of pertussis. PCR testing should be used only to confirm a diagnosis in persons with signs and symptoms consistent with pertussis. PCR testing sensitivity declines and is unlikely to be positive after 1 month of infection. PCR testing after 5 days of treatment with antibiotics can cause false-negative results and is generally not recommended
- Blood cultures in hospitalized patients
- Chest x-ray
- Culture of bacteria, usually from nasopharynx by aspiration or by swabbing the posterior nasopharynx with a polyester-tipped, rayon-tipped, or nylon-flocked swab
- Immunofluorescent staining of nasopharyngeal secretions

- Serologic tests for immunoglobulin G (IgG) or A (IgA) are available. A twofold increase between acute and convalescent sera is considered proof of seroconversion. A single elevated IgG or IgA titer is considered diagnostic when no acute serum is available. Can be useful for diagnosis later in illness.

LABORATORY TESTS

Complete blood count, which usually demonstrates marked lymphocytosis:
- Up to 18,000 white blood cells
- 70% to 80% lymphocytes

IMAGING STUDIES

Chest x-ray examination is of value if secondary bacterial pneumonia is suspected.

TREATMENT

ACUTE GENERAL Rx

- Intensive supportive care:
  1. Adequate hydration
  2. Control of secretions
  3. Maintenance of airway
- Antibiotics (Table 1P-17) are indicated even though their ability to alter the course of the disease is controversial.
  1. Azithromycin 500 mg on day 1, followed by 250 mg for days 2 to 5. Erythromycin 50 mg/kg/day for 14 days. Recent literature reports indicate that a 7-day treatment regimen may be as effective as a 14-day course of erythromycin. TMP/SMX 320/1600 mg per day in divided doses can be used in patients with allergy or intolerance to macrolides.
  2. Although unproved, dexamethasone 1 mg/kg/day in four doses for severe, life-threatening paroxysms.
  3. Ceftriaxone 75 mg/kg/day in two doses for broad coverage of secondary bacterial pneumonias.
  4. Close observation of infants <6 months old as risk for apnea is high in this age group.
- Vaccination is successful in preventing the disease: universal vaccination is advised for all children and adults. The Advisory Committee on Immunization Practices (ACIP) updated Tdap recommendations to include a single dose of Tdap vaccine in place of routine Td for adults age 19-64 yr and a single-dose Tdap for adults 65 yr and older who have or will have close contact with an infant (>12 mo). The ACIP also recommends that all pregnant women receive a dose of Tdap with every pregnancy, preferably during weeks 27 to 36 of gestation.
- Azithromycin, clarithromycin, or erythromycin is recommended for all household contacts and should be given to all persons at high risk of severe disease from pertussis and who were in contact with a pertussis case within 21 days of cough onset: TMP/SMX in two oral doses per day for those intolerant to macrolides.

P

TABLE 1P-17 Recommended Antimicrobial Treatment and Postexposure Prophylaxis for Pertussis, by Age Group

	PRIMARY AGENTS		ALTERNATE AGENT*	
Age Group	Azithromycin	Erythromycin	Clarithromycin	TMP-SMZ
<1 mo	Recommended agent, 10 mg/kg/day in a single dose for 5 days (only limited safety data available)	Not preferred. Erythromycin is substantially associated with infantile hypertrophic pyloric stenosis. Use if azithromycin is unavailable; 40-50 mg/kg/day in 4 divided doses for 14 days	Not recommended (safety data unavailable)	Contraindicated for infants aged <2 mo (risk for kernicterus)
1-5 mo	10 mg/kg/day in a single dose for 5 days	40-50 mg/kg/day in four divided doses for 14 days	15 mg/kg/day in two divided doses for 7 days	Contraindicated at age <2 mo. For infants aged ≥2 mo: TMP 8 mg/kg/day plus SMZ 40 mg/kg/day in two divided doses for 14 days
Infants aged ≥6 mo and children	10 mg/kg in a single dose on day 1 (maximum 500 mg), then 5 mg/kg/day (maximum 250 mg) on days 2-5	40 mg/kg/day (maximum 1-2 g/day) in four divided doses for 14 days	15 mg/kg/day in 2 divided doses (maximum 1 g/day) for 7 days	TMP 8 mg/kg/day plus SMZ 40 mg/kg/day in two divided doses for 14 days
Adolescents and adults	500 mg in a single dose on day 1 then 250 mg/day on days 2-5	2 g/day in four divided doses for 14 days	1 g/day in two divided doses for 7 days	TMP 320 mg/day, SMZ 1600 mg/day in two divided doses for 14 days

*Trimethoprim-sulfamethoxazole (TMP-SMZ) can be used as an alternative agent to macrolides in patients aged ≥2 mo who are allergic to macrolides, who cannot tolerate macrolides, or who are infected with a rare macrolide-resistant strain of *Bordetella pertussis*.
From Centers for Disease Control and Prevention: Recommended antimicrobial agents for treatment and postexposure prophylaxis of pertussis: 2005 CDC guidelines, *MMWR Morbid Mortal Wkly Rep* 54:1-16, 2005.

Diseases and Disorders

I

DISPOSITION

Close attention to accepted vaccination schedules is the best prevention.

REFERRAL

To intensive care setting for life-threatening infections:
- Pulmonologist
- Infectious disease specialist

 **PEARLS & CONSIDERATIONS**

- The diagnosis of pertussis in a young child is easily recognized, but in adults pertussis can be a subtle diagnosis and is often missed.

The tip-off is often a persistent, hacking, and productive cough with minor or no fever in a previously healthy person that lasts <2 wk.
- Approximately 11% of pertussis cases in the pediatric population are attributable to vaccine refusal, dispelling the myth that herd immunity protects children whose parents refuse pertussis vaccine.

 **EVIDENCE**

Available at www.expertconsult.com

SUGGESTED READINGS

Available at www.expertconsult.com

RELATED CONTENT

Pertussis (Patient Information)

AUTHOR: **RUSSELL J. MCCULLOH, M.D.**

BASIC INFORMATION

DEFINITION

- A hamartomatous polyp is a benign intestinal growth that may contain all components of the intestinal mucosa. In gastrointestinal polyposis, multiple such polyps coexist within the intestinal tract, and associated manifestations are usually also present.
- Juvenile polyps are benign polyps composed of cystic dilatations of glandular structures within the fibroblastic stroma of the lamina propria. They may cause bleeding or intussusception.
- Commonly recognized syndromes are Peutz-Jeghers syndrome, juvenile polyposis syndrome, Cowden's disease, Bannayan-Ruvalcaba-Riley syndrome, and Cronkhite-Canada syndrome. Other, lesser known inherited hamartomatous polyposis syndromes are hereditary mixed polyposis syndrome, intestinal ganglioneuromatosis and neurofibromatosis (variant of von Recklinghausen's syndrome), Devon family syndrome, basal cell nevus syndrome, and tuberous sclerosis (may involve gastrointestinal tract). Table 1P-18 describes general features of some inherited colorectal cancer syndromes.

ICD-10CM CODES
D12.6 Colon, unspecified (adenomatosis of colon, hereditary polyposis)

EPIDEMIOLOGY

- Colonic adenomas, the precursors of nearly all colorectal cancers, are found in nearly 40% of patients by age 60 yr.
- 25% of men and 15% of women who undergo colonoscopy are found to have one or more adenomas.
- Detection of any adenoma in patients <60 yr confers an increased risk of colorectal cancer (by a factor of 2.6) in their first-degree relatives.

PHYSICAL FINDINGS & CLINICAL PRESENTATION

PEUTZ-JEGHERS SYNDROME (PJS):

- Transmission: autosomal dominant with incomplete penetrance. The syndrome is caused in the majority of patients by a germline mutation of the *STK11/LKB1* tumor suppression gene on chromosome 19P13.
- Disease expression:
  1. Stomach, small and large intestinal hamartomas with bands of smooth muscle in the lamina propria
  2. Pigmented lesions around mouth (lips and buccal mucosa [Fig. 1P-44]), nose, hands, feet, genitals, and perineal areas
  3. Ovarian tumors
  4. Sertoli cell testicular tumors
  5. Airway polyps
  6. Pancreatic cancer
  7. Breast cancer
  8. Urinary tract polyps
- Cumulative lifetime cancer risk
  1. Colon cancer: 39%
  2. Stomach cancer: 29%
  3. Small intestine cancer: 13%
  4. Pancreatic cancer: 36%
  5. Breast cancer: 54%
  6. Ovarian cancer: 10%
  7. Sertoli cell tumor: 9%
  8. Overall cancer risk: 93%
- Clinical manifestation:
  1. Gastrointestinal, small-bowel obstruction, intussusception, gastrointestinal bleeding
  2. See chapters on relevant malignancies for their signs and symptoms

DIAGNOSIS:

The diagnosis of PJS is made with any of four major criteria:
1. Two or more histologically confirmed PJS polyps
2. Any number of PJS polyps and a family history of PJS
3. Characteristic mucocutaneous pigmentation and a family history of PJS, or
4. Any number of PJS polyps and characteristic mucocutaneous pigmentation

JUVENILE POLYPOSIS SYNDROME:

- Transmission: autosomal dominant
- Disease expression
  1. Solitary juvenile polyps numbering 10 or more in the rectum or throughout the gastrointestinal tract; the polyps are smooth and covered with normal epithelium
  2. Various congenital abnormalities coexist in 20%
- Cumulative cancer risk is increased (may be as high as 50%)
- Clinical manifestation
  1. Intestinal obstruction
  2. Intussusception
  3. Gastrointestinal bleeding

COWDEN'S DISEASE:

- Transmission: autosomal dominant, rare
- Disease expression
  1. Juvenile intestinal polyposis
  2. Orocutaneous hamartomas
  3. Fibrocystic breast disease and breast cancer
  4. Goiter and thyroid cancer
  5. Facial tricholemmomas (papules) in 83%
- Cumulative cancer risk
  1. Gastrointestinal: same as general population
  2. Thyroid: 3% to 10%
  3. Breast: 25% to 50%

BANNAYAN-RUVALCABA-RILEY SYNDROME:

- Transmission: autosomal dominant, rare
- Disease expression
  1. Juvenile intestinal polyposis
  2. Macrocephaly
  3. Developmental delay
  4. Penile pigmented spots
  5. Cumulative cancer risk unknown

CRONKHITE-CANADA SYNDROME:

- Transmission: acquired
- Age of onset: midlife

TABLE 1P-18 General Features of Some Inherited Colorectal Cancer Syndromes

Syndrome	Polyp Histology	Polyp Distribution	Age of Onset	Risk of Colon Cancer	Genetic Lesion	Clinical Manifestations	Associated Lesions
Familial adenomatous polyposis (Fig. 1P-43)	Adenoma	Large intestine, duodenum	16 yr (range, 8-34 yr)	100%	5q (*APC* gene)	Rectal bleeding, abdominal pain, bowel obstruction	Desmoids, CHRPE
Peutz-Jeghers syndrome	Hamartoma	Large and small intestine	First decade	Slightly above average	19p (*STK11* gene)	Possible rectal bleeding, abdominal pain, intussusception	Orocutaneous melanin pigment spots, other tumors
MUTYH-associated polyposis	Adenoma	Large intestine, duodenum	45-50 yr (range, 13-60 yr)	75% (range, 50%-100%)	1p (*MYH* gene)	Rectal bleeding, abdominal pain, bowel obstruction	CHRPE, osteomas
Juvenile polyposis	Hamartoma (rarely adenoma)	Large and small intestine	First decade	≈9%	PTEN, SMAD4, BMPR1	Possible rectal bleeding, abdominal pain, intussusception	Pulmonary AVMs
Hereditary nonpolyposis colon cancer	Adenoma	Large intestine	40 yr (range, 18-65 yr)	30%	Mismatch repair genes*	Rectal bleeding, abdominal pain, bowel obstruction	Other tumors (e.g., ovary, uterus, pancreas, stomach)

AVM, Arteriovenous malformation; *CHRPE*, congenital hypertrophy of the retinal pigment epithelium; *MUTYH*, mutY homolog (*Escherichia coli*).
*Including *hMSH2*, *hMSH3*, *hMSH6*, *hMLH1*, *hPMS1*, and *hPMS2*.
From Goldman L, Schafer AI: *Goldman's Cecil medicine*, ed 24, Philadelphia, 2012, Saunders.

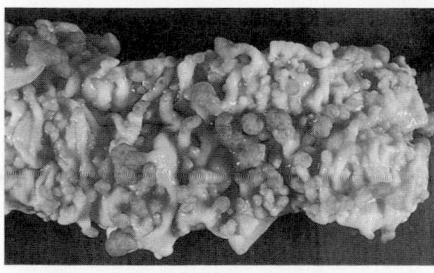

FIGURE 1P-43 Familial adenomatous polyposis. This disorder is marked by the development of hundreds of large bowel adenomas, as seen in this segment of large bowel, which is covered with adenomas of various sizes. It usually arises in the second and third decades. (From Skarin AT: *Atlas of diagnostic oncology*, 4th ed, St Louis, 2010, Mosby, 2010.)

- Disease expression
  1. Diffuse gastrointestinal juvenile polyposis (50%-95% of cases)
  2. Chronic diarrhea and protein-losing enteropathy (the entire intestinal mucosa may be inflamed), which leads to abdominal pain, weight loss, and various complications of malnutrition
  3. Dystrophic nails
  4. Alopecia
  5. Hyperpigmentation
- Cumulative cancer risk: same as the average population

 **DIAGNOSIS**

Diagnosis is suggested in many cases by family history and confirmed by colonoscopy and physical findings described previously.

 **TREATMENT**

GENERAL Rx/SURVEILLANCE

Peutz-Jeghers syndrome:
- Colonoscopies with polypectomies and upper endoscopy every 2 to 3 years beginning in teen years
- MRI or endoscopic ultrasound of the pancreas every 1 to 2 years beginning at age 30
- Screening for breast cancer, testicular cancer, possibly ovarian cancer
- Surveillance of small bowel with capsule endoscopy or CT or magnetic resonance

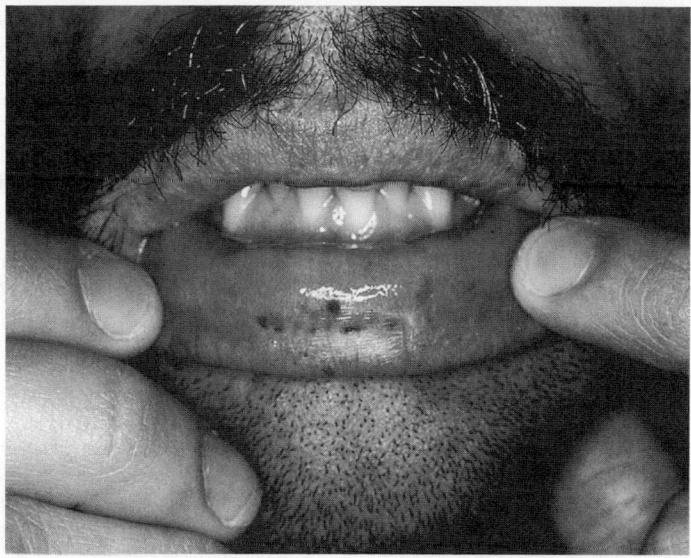

FIGURE 1P-44 Peutz-Jeghers syndrome, macular pigmentation of lower lip. (James WD et al: *Andrews' diseases of the skin*, ed 12, Philadelphia, 2016, WB Saunders.)

enterography every 2 to 3 years starting at age 8 to 10 years.

Juvenile polyposis syndrome:
- Colonoscopies with polypectomies and upper endoscopy every 2 to 3 years beginning at age 15
- Total colectomy if numerous polyps
- Esophagogastroscopics and polypectomies

Cowden's disease:
- Rigorous breast cancer screening or prophylactic simple bilateral mastectomy with reconstruction.

Cronkhite-Canada syndrome:
- Progressive malabsorption syndrome is the hallmark of this syndrome, and no specific treatment exists. Enteral or parenteral feeding is the cornerstone of management and can result in remission.
- Other syndromes
  - Serrated polyposis syndrome: colonoscopy yearly
  - PTEN hamartoma tumor syndrome: Colonoscopy every 5 years beginning at age 35

DISPOSITION
- The screening of first-degree relatives of patients with colonic adenomas detected before 60 yr of age is controversial. Some recommend

beginning colonoscopic screening at age 40 yr or 10 yr younger than the age at diagnosis of the youngest person in the family with an adenoma.
- Recommended interval between colonoscopies from the U.S. Consensus Guidelines for Colonoscopic Surveillance after Polypectomy are as follows:
  1. 10 yr for small, rectal hyperplastic polyps
  2. 5 to 10 yr for one to two low-risk adenomas (tubular adenomas <1 cm)
  3. 3 yr for low-risk adenomas or any high-risk adenoma (large [≥1 cm] or histologically advanced adenomas [tubulovillous or villous adenomas or villous adenomas and those with high-grade dysplasia])
  4. <3 yr for presence of >10 adenomas
  5. 2 to 6 mo for inadequately removed adenomas

SUGGESTED READINGS
Available at www.expertconsult.com

RELATED CONTENT
Peutz-Jeghers Syndrome (Patient Information)
Familial Adenomatous Polyposis and Gardner Syndrome (Related Key Topic)

AUTHOR: **FRED F. FERRI, M.D.**

Diseases and Disorders

 **BASIC INFORMATION**

DEFINITION

Peyronie's disease is an abnormal curvature and shortening of the penis during an erection. This is caused by scarring of the tunica albuginea of the corpora cavernosa.

SYNONYMS

Plastic induration of the penis
Penile fibromatosis

ICD-10CM CODES
N48.6 Induratio penis plastica

EPIDEMIOLOGY & DEMOGRAPHICS

- Peyronie's disease occurs in approximately 1% of men.
- It is commonly seen between the ages of 45 and 60 yr.
- A genetic predisposition has been suggested.
- There are no incidence and prevalence data available in the literature.

PHYSICAL FINDINGS & CLINICAL PRESENTATION

- Painful erections
- Tenderness over the scar tissue area
- Erectile dysfunction
- Curvature of the erected penis interfering with penetration
- Dupuytren's contracture is a commonly associated finding in patients with Peyronie's disease

ETIOLOGY

- Specific cause is unknown. It is believed that scar tissue forms on either the dorsal or ventral midline surface of the penile shaft. The scar restricts expansion at the involved site, causing the penis to bend or curve in one direction.
- The precipitating factor appears to be trauma from repetitive microvascular injury caused by vigorous sexual intercourse, accidents, or prior surgeries (e.g., transurethral or radical prostatectomy, cystoscopy).

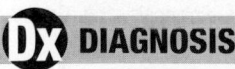 **DIAGNOSIS**

Diagnosis is based on the clinical findings.

DIFFERENTIAL DIAGNOSIS

- The history differentiates congenital from acquired curvatures of the penis.
- Other causes of erectile dysfunction must be excluded, including metabolic, diabetic, thyroid, and renal causes, in addition to hypogonadism and hyperprolactinemia.

WORKUP

History and physical examination alone will usually establish the diagnosis of Peyronie's disease.

LABORATORY TESTS

There are no specific blood tests to diagnose Peyronie's disease. Electrolytes, blood urea nitrogen, creatinine, glucose, thyroid function tests (thyroid-stimulating hormone, T_3U, T_4), testosterone, and prolactin levels are blood tests to exclude other medical causes of erectile dysfunction.

IMAGING STUDIES

Imaging studies are not specific.

 **TREATMENT**

NONPHARMACOLOGIC THERAPY

A conservative approach of reassurance and observation is taken at first because the disease process may be self-limiting.

ACUTE GENERAL Rx

Although not substantiated by direct randomized, controlled clinical trials, the following treatment modalities have been tried:
- Vitamin E 400 mg bid.
- Paraaminobenzoic acid 12 g/day.
- Colchicine 0.6 mg bid for 2 to 3 wk.
- Fexofenadine 60 mg bid for 3 mo.
- Steroid injection into the scar tissue.
- Collagenase injection into the scar tissue.
- Radiation to the scar tissue area.
- Extracorporeal shockwave therapy (ESWT): Current evidence on the safety, but not the efficacy, of ESWT appears adequate. From comparative studies, the main benefits of ESWT were the alleviation of pain and reduction of angulation of the penis. In one comparative study, 10 of 20 patients receiving ESWT had a decrease in the curvature of at least 30%. Case series evidence also suggested some improvement of sexual performance.
- Other medications that can be helpful include verapamil, tamoxifen, and interferon.

CHRONIC Rx

In patients who have progressed to intractable pain with erection or erectile dysfunction, surgical treatment with excision of the plaque and skin grafting may be indicated.

DISPOSITION

Peyronie's disease evolves slowly and in some cases can resolve on its own. Waiting for 1 yr before proceeding with surgical attempts is recommended.

REFERRAL

A urologic consultation is recommended in patients with progressive symptoms and erectile dysfunction.

 **PEARLS & CONSIDERATIONS**

COMMENTS

- Peyronie's disease is not commonly seen in younger patients because they are able to sustain intracorporeal pressures high enough to stretch the scar tissue, preventing it from deforming the penis during erection.
- Trauma from buckling of the erected penis is thought to be the precipitant cause of scar formation and Peyronie's disease. It is found more often in men who are sexually very active and vigorous, having sexual intercourse daily or almost daily.
- Sexual positions with the woman being on top or thrusting the penis into the anterior vaginal wall are thought to increase the chances of developing Peyronie's disease.

SUGGESTED READINGS

Available at www.expertconsult.com

RELATED CONTENT

Peyronie's Disease (Patient Information)

AUTHOR: **TANYA ALI, M.D.**

Diseases
and Disorders

I

BASIC INFORMATION

DEFINITION

Inflammation of the pharynx or tonsils

SYNONYMS

Sore throat
Group A streptococci (GAS)

ICD-10CM CODES
J02.9 Acute pharyngitis, unspecified
J03.0 Acute tonsillitis
J03.9 Acute tonsillitis, unspecified
J04.0 Acute laryngitis

EPIDEMIOLOGY & DEMOGRAPHICS

Acute pharyngitis accounts for 1.3% of outpatient visits to health care providers in the United States.
PEAK INCIDENCE: Late winter/early spring (GAS infections)
PREDOMINANT SEX: Females = males
PREDOMINANT AGE:
- All ages affected
- Streptococcal pharyngitis most common among school-age children (5-15 yr of age). GAS are responsible for 5% to 15% of cases of pharyngitis in adults and 20% to 30% of cases in children (5-15 yr of age).

PHYSICAL FINDINGS & CLINICAL PRESENTATION

- Pharynx:
  1. May appear normal to severely erythematous
  2. Tonsillar hypertrophy and exudates commonly seen but do not indicate etiology
- Viral infection:
  1. Rhinorrhea
  2. Conjunctivitis
  3. Cough
- Bacterial infection, especially GAS:
  1. High fever
  2. Systemic signs of infection
- Herpes simplex or enterovirus infection: vesicles
- Streptococcal infection:
  1. Rare complications:
     a. Scarlet fever
     b. Rheumatic fever
     c. Acute glomerulonephritis
  2. Extension of infection: tonsillar, parapharyngeal, or retropharyngeal abscess presenting with severe pain, high fever, trismus
- Streptococcal tonsillitis is manifested as acute onset of fever, headache, neck pain, odynophagia, sore throat, otalgia, red tongue with enlargement of papillae, sore throat, red swollen uvula, and tender anterior cervical adenitis.
- Peritonsillar abscess (accumulation of pus between the tonsil and its capsule) is the most common complication of acute tonsillitis. Clinical signs include deformed posterior pharynx, medial displacement of the uvula, trismus, and muffled voice (hot-potato voice).
- Table 1P-19 describes seven danger signs in patients with sore throat.

ETIOLOGY

- Viruses:
  1. Respiratory syncytial virus
  2. Influenza A and B
  3. Epstein-Barr virus
  4. Adenovirus
  5. Herpes simplex
- Bacteria:
  1. GAS: *Streptococcus pyogenes.* β-Hemolytic GAS are the most common cause of acute tonsillitis.
  2. *Neisseria gonorrhoeae*
  3. *Fusobacterium necrophorum* (10% of pharyngitis): highest incidence in patients aged 15 to 30 years
- Other organisms:
  1. *Mycoplasma pneumoniae*
  2. *Chlamydophila pneumoniae*
  3. *Arcanobacterium haemolyticum*

DIAGNOSIS

DIFFERENTIAL DIAGNOSIS

- Sore throat associated with granulocytopenia, thyroiditis
- Tonsillar hypertrophy associated with lymphoma
- Section II describes the differential diagnosis of sore throat.

WORKUP

The Centor criteria to identify patients at risk for GAS consists of (1) fever subjective or measured >38.1° C (100.5° F), (2) absence of cough, (3) tonsillar exudates, (4) tender anterior cervical lymphadenopathy. Patients with ≤1 criteria are at low risk and do not need additional testing. The McIsaac criteria adds 1 point for ages 3 to 14 and subtracts a point for ages ≥45 yr.
- Rapid streptococcal antigen test (culture should be performed if rapid test negative)
- Throat swab for culture to exclude *S. pyogenes, N. gonorrhoeae* (requires specific transport medium) in selected cases

LABORATORY TESTS

- Bloodwork is only rarely necessary
- Complete blood count with differential
  1. May help support diagnosis of bacterial infection when diagnosis is unclear
  2. Streptococcal infection suggested by leukocytosis >15,000/mm^3
- Viral cultures, serologic studies rarely needed
- Monospot if diagnosis is unclear

TABLE 1P-19 Seven Danger Signs in Patients with Sore Throat

1. Persistence of symptoms longer than 1 wk without improvement
2. Respiratory difficulty, particularly stridor
3. Difficulty in handling secretions
4. Difficulty in swallowing
5. Severe pain in the absence of erythema
6. A palpable mass
7. Blood, even in small amounts, in the pharynx or ear

From Andreoli TE et al: *Andreoli and Carpenter's Cecil essentials of medicine,* ed 8, Philadelphia, 2010, Saunders.

IMAGING STUDIES

Seldom indicated. If necessary to distinguish between tonsillitis and peritonsillar abscess, CT or MRI of the neck can be done.

TREATMENT

NONPHARMACOLOGIC THERAPY

- Fluids
- Salt water gargles

ACUTE GENERAL Rx

- Analgesics: aspirin (adults) or acetaminophen or ibuprofen (adults and children)
- If streptococcal infection proven or suspected:
  1. Penicillin V 500 mg PO bid for 10 days or benzathine penicillin 1.2 million U IM once (adults). Children: penicillin V 250 mg bid or tid
  2. Erythromycin 500 mg PO bid or 250 mg qid for 10 days or azithromycin if penicillin allergic
- If gonococcal infection proven or suspected: ceftriaxone 250 mg IM once.
- Amoxicillin 500 mg tid for 10 days is the primary antibiotic treatment of streptococcal tonsillitis. Macrolides or clindamycin can be used in penicillin-allergic patients.
- Treatment of peritonsillar abscess is drainage through needle or incision.

CHRONIC Rx

- Recurrent streptococcal infections are common and may represent reinfection from other household members, including pets.
- There is no conclusive evidence from randomized clinical trials that tonsillectomy is superior to antibiotic therapy for recurrent tonsillitis in adults.
- Tonsillopharyngitis is generally managed in an outpatient setting with follow-up arranged in 1 to 2 wk. Admission to the hospital is indicated for local suppurative complications (peritonsillar abscess; lateral pharyngeal or posterior pharyngeal abscess; impending airway closure; or inability to swallow food, medications, or water).

REFERRAL

- To otolaryngologist:
  1. If peritonsillar or other abscess is suspected
  2. If tonsillar hypertrophy persists

SUGGESTED READINGS
Available at www.expertconsult.com

RELATED CONTENT
Sore Throat (Patient Information)
Strep Throat (Patient Information)
Tonsillitis (Patient Information)

AUTHOR: **GLENN G. FORT, M.D., M.P.H.**

BASIC INFORMATION

DEFINITION

Pheochromocytomas are catecholamine-producing tumors that originate from chromaffin cells of the adrenergic system. They generally secrete both norepinephrine and epinephrine, but norepinephrine is usually the predominant amine.

SYNONYMS

Paraganglioma

ICD-10CM CODES
C74.9 Malignant neoplasm of adrenal gland, unspecified
C75.9 Malignant neoplasm of endocrine gland, unspecified
E27.5 Adrenomedullary hyperfunction

EPIDEMIOLOGY & DEMOGRAPHICS

- Incidence: 0.05% of population; peak incidence in 30s and 40s.
- Approximately 25% of patients with apparently sporadic pheochromocytoma may be carriers of mutations.
- Approximately 25% of pheochromocytomas are familial and associated with genetic disorders (Table 1P-20). Pheochromocytoma is a feature of two disorders with an autosomal-dominant pattern of inheritance:
  1. Multiple endocrine neoplasia (MEN) type 2
  2. Von Hippel-Lindau disease: angioma of the retina, hemangioblastoma of the central nervous system, renal cell carcinoma, pancreatic cysts, and epididymal cystoadenoma

- Pheochromocytomas occur in 5% of patients with neurofibromatosis type 1.

PHYSICAL FINDINGS & CLINICAL PRESENTATION

- Hypertension: can be sustained (55%) or paroxysmal (45%).
- Headache (80%): usually paroxysmal in nature and described as "pounding" and severe.
- Palpitations (70%): can be present with or without tachycardia.
- Hyperhidrosis (60%): most evident during paroxysmal attacks of hypertension.
- Physical examination may be entirely normal if done in a symptom-free interval; during a paroxysm the patient may demonstrate marked increase in both systolic and diastolic pressure, profuse sweating, visual disturbances (caused by hypertensive retinopathy), dilated pupils (from catecholamine excess), paresthesias in the lower extremities (caused by severe vasoconstriction), tremor, tachycardia.
- Orthostatic hypotension is common among patients with pheochromocytoma due to reduction of blood volume and desensitization of adrenergic receptors by the chronic excess of catecholamines.

ETIOLOGY

- Catecholamine-producing tumors that are usually located in the adrenal medulla.
- Specific mutations of the RET protooncogene cause familial predisposition to pheochromocytoma in MEN 2.
- Mutations in the von Hippel-Lindau tumor suppressor gene (*VHL* gene) cause familial disposition to pheochromocytoma in von Hippel-Lindau disease.
- Recently identified genes for succinate dehydrogenase subunit D *(SDHD)* and succinate dehydrogenase subunit B *(SDHB)* predispose carriers to pheochromocytoma and globus tumors.

DIAGNOSIS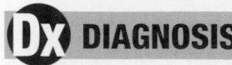

DIFFERENTIAL DIAGNOSIS

- Anxiety disorder
- Thyrotoxicosis
- Amphetamine or cocaine abuse
- Carcinoid
- Essential hypertension

WORKUP

Laboratory evaluation and imaging studies to locate the neoplasm (Fig. 1P-45). Misdiagnosis of pheochromocytoma is not uncommon. Correct interpretation of biochemical tests and imaging is crucial to a correct diagnosis.

LABORATORY TESTS

- Although there is no consensus on the best test, plasma-free metanephrines have been suggested as the test of first choice for excluding the tumor. Elevated plasma concentrations of normetanephrines or metanephrine have a sensitivity of up to 100%, but the specificity is markedly lower (85%).
- 24-hr urine collection for metanephrines (90% sensitivity, 95% specificity) will also show increased metanephrines; the accuracy of the 24-hr urinary levels for metanephrines can be improved by indexing urinary metanephrine levels by urine creatinine levels.

TABLE 1P-20 Autosomal Dominant Syndromes Associated with Pheochromocytoma and Paraganglioma

Syndrome	Gene	Gene Locus	Protein Product	Protein Function	Gene Mechanism	Typical Tumor Location
SDHD (familial paraganglioma type 1)*	*SDHD*	11q23	SDH D subunit	ATP production	Tumor suppressor	Skull base and neck; occasionally adrenal medulla, mediastinum, abdomen, pelvis
Familial paraganglioma type 2*	*SDHAF2*	11q13.1	Flavination cofactor	ATP production	Tumor suppressor	Skull base and neck; occasionally abdomen and pelvis
SDHC (familial paraganglioma type 3)	*SDHC*	1q21	SDH C subunit	ATP production	Tumor suppressor	Skull base and neck
SDHB (familial paraganglioma type 4)	*SDHB*	1p36.1-35	SDH B subunit	ATP production	Tumor suppressor	Abdomen, pelvis and mediastinum; rarely adrenal medulla, skull base, and neck
MEN1	*MEN1*	11q13	Menin	Transcription regulation	Tumor suppressor	Adrenal medulla
MEN2A and MEN2B	*RET*	10q11.2	RET	Tyrosine kinase receptor	Protooncogene	Adrenal medulla, bilaterally
Neurofibromatosis type 1	*NF1*	17q11.2	Neurofibromin	GTP hydrolysis	Tumor suppressor	Adrenal-periadrenal
von Hippel-Lindau disease	*VHL*	3p25-26	VHL	Transcription elongation suppression	Tumor suppressor	Adrenal medulla, bilaterally; occasionally paraganglioma
Familial pheochromocytoma	*FP/TMEM127*	2q11	Transmembrane protein	Regulation of the mTORC1 signaling complex	Tumor suppressor	Adrenal medulla

ATP, Adenosine triphosphate; *GTP,* guanosine triphosphate; *MEN,* multiple endocrine neoplasia; *SDH,* succinate dehydrogenase.
*Associated with maternal imprinting.
From Melmed S: *Williams textbook of endocrinology,* ed 12, Philadelphia, 2011, Saunders, Elsevier.

IMAGING STUDIES

- Abdominal CT scan (Fig. E1P-46) with and without contrast (88% sensitivity) is useful in locating pheochromocytomas >0.5 inch in diameter (90% to 95% accurate).
- MRI with contrast: pheochromocytomas demonstrate a distinctive MRI appearance (up to 100% sensitivity); MRI may become the diagnostic imaging modality of choice.
- Scintigraphy with 131 or 1-123 I-MIBG (up to 100% sensitivity) (Fig. E1P-46): this norepinephrine analog localizes in adrenergic tissue; it is particularly useful in locating extraadrenal pheochromocytomas.
- 6-[^{18}F]Fluorodopamine positron emission tomography is reserved for cases in which clinical symptoms and signs suggest pheochromocytoma and results of biochemical tests are positive but conventional imaging studies cannot locate the tumor. It is also used for identification of metastatic disease.

Rx TREATMENT

GENERAL Rx

Laparoscopic adrenalectomy (surgical resection for both benign and malignant disease):

1. Preoperative stabilization with combination of alpha-adrenergic blocking agents (phenoxybenzamine, prazosin, doxazosin, or terazosin), beta-blocker, and liberal fluid and salt intake starting 10 to 14 days before surgery. Beta-blockers should be avoided until patients receive adequate alpha-adrenergic blockade for several days to avoid hypertensive crisis due to unopposed alpha stimulation. Amlodipine or verapamil can be added to beta-blockers if blood pressure control is still inadequate. Table E1P-21 describes orally administered drugs to treat pheochromocytoma.
2. Hypertensive crisis preoperatively and intraoperatively can be controlled with nitroprusside. Table E1P-22 summarizes intravenously administered drugs used to treat pheochromocytoma.

! PEARLS & CONSIDERATIONS

COMMENTS

- Obtaining a detailed family history is important because 25% of pheochromocytomas are familial.
- Screening for pheochromocytoma should be considered in patients with any of the following:
  1. Malignant hypertension
  2. Poor response to antihypertensive therapy
  3. Paradoxical hypertensive response
  4. Hypertension during induction of anesthesia, parturition, surgery, or thyrotropin-releasing hormone testing
  5. Hypertension associated with imipramine or desipramine
  6. Neurofibromatosis (increased incidence of pheochromocytoma)
- All patients with pheochromocytoma should be screened for MEN-2 and von Hippel-Lindau disease with the pentagastrin test, serum parathyroid hormone, ophthalmoscopy, MRI of the brain, CT scan of the kidneys and pancreas, and ultrasonography of the testes.
- In patients with pheochromocytoma, routine analysis for mutations of *RET, VHL, SDHD,* and *SDHB* is indicated to identify pheochromocytoma-associated syndromes.

SUGGESTED READINGS

Available at www.expertconsult.com

RELATED CONTENT

Pheochromocytoma (Patient Information)
Hypertension (Related Key Topic)

AUTHORS: **MARK F. BRADY, M.D., M.P.H., M.M.S.,** and **FRED F. FERRI, M.D.**

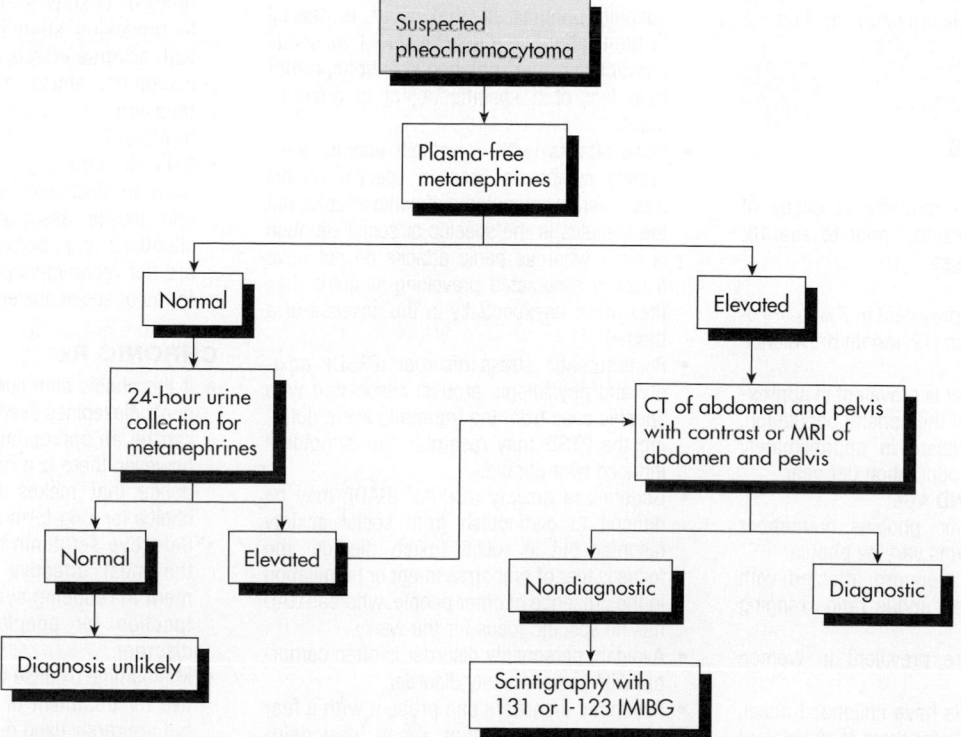

FIGURE 1P-45 Pheochromocytoma. *CT,* Computed tomography; *IMIBG,* iodine metaiodobenzyl guanidine; *MRI,* magnetic resonance imaging.

BASIC INFORMATION

DEFINITION

Specific phobias are anxiety disorders characterized by an excessive, persistent fear elicited by a specific object or situation that is then avoided or tolerated with intense distress. The provoking stimulus may be a specific object, such as an animal or insect; natural environments, such as heights or water; or a specific situation, such as the sight of blood, the receipt of an injection, or being in a tunnel or on a bridge. Social anxiety disorder (formerly named social phobia) is a specific, separately diagnosed disorder characterized by a fear of being embarrassed, humiliated, or rejected in social or performance situations. Agoraphobia also is a separately diagnosed disorder, characterized by an intense anxiety about being in a place or situation from which they would not be able to escape in the event of a panic attack or panic-like symptoms. Such situations include being in enclosed/crowded spaces or being more than a certain distance from home alone. If agoraphobia is present in individuals with panic disorder, both diagnoses are given.

SYNONYMS

Simple phobia (obsolete name for specific phobia)
Phobias named for the provoking stimulus, such as arachnophobia (fear of spiders) and acrophobia (fear of heights)

> **Specific phobias are codes:**
> **ICD-10CM**
> F40.1 Social phobias
> F40.2 Specific phobias
> F40.8 Other phobic anxiety disorders
> F40.9 Phobic anxiety disorder, unspecified
> **Agoraphobia:**
> **ICD-10CM**
> F40.00

EPIDEMIOLOGY & DEMOGRAPHICS

PEAK INCIDENCE: The majority of cases of specific phobia tend to onset prior to age 10; median onset is from ages 7-10.
PREVALENCE (IN U.S.):
- Specific phobias are prevalent in 7% to 9% of the general population (12-month prevalence rate).
- Social anxiety disorder is prevalent in approximately 7% to 13% of the general population.
- Agoraphobia is prevalent in approximately 1.7% of the general population per year.
PREDOMINANT SEX AND AGE:
- Females with specific phobias outnumber males 2:1, though rates vary by phobia.
- More women than men are affected with social anxiety disorder (odds ratios ranging from 1.5-2.2).
- Agoraphobia is more prevalent in women than men (2:1).
- Most specific phobias have childhood onset, although it is possible for them to develop at any age.

- Situational phobias tend to have a later age of onset compared to natural environment, animal, or blood-injection phobias.
- Onset of social anxiety disorder usually occurs in the mid-teens, with onset after age 25 being unusual; this disorder is generally lifelong.
- Onset of agoraphobia typically occurs in late adolescence or early adulthood; two thirds of cases onset prior to age 35.
GENETICS: Specific phobia and social anxiety disorder are more common in first-degree relatives.

PHYSICAL FINDINGS & CLINICAL PRESENTATION

- When approaching the phobic stimulus, the experience of extreme anxiety is often accompanied by autonomic symptoms such as tachycardia, tremor, and diaphoresis; depersonalization may occur. In blood or injection phobias, symptoms are often followed by a parasympathetic response that can cause vasovagal syncope.
- Specific phobias frequently occur with other anxiety disorders.

ETIOLOGY

There is no clear etiology and likely is a combination of factors including temperamental (e.g., behavioral inhibition, neuroticism), environmental (e.g., negative encounters with the feared stimulus, parental overprotection), and genetic.

 DIAGNOSIS

DIFFERENTIAL DIAGNOSIS

- Social anxiety disorder is distinguished from specific phobias in that what is feared is humiliation or embarrassment in social interaction or performance situations, rather than fear of a specific object or environment.
- Panic attacks (with or without agoraphobia): anxiety symptoms seen in specific phobia may resemble symptoms of panic attacks, but the stimulus in the specific or social situation is clear, whereas panic attacks do not have a clearly associated provoking stimulus (i.e., they occur unexpectedly in the absence of a trigger).
- Posttraumatic stress disorder (PTSD): anxiety and physiologic arousal associated with specific cues from the traumatic event defining the PTSD may resemble the symptoms induced by a phobia.
- Generalized anxiety disorder (GAD): may be difficult to distinguish from social anxiety disorder, but in social anxiety disorder the focus is fear of embarrassment or humiliation in the presence of other people, whereas GAD has no specific focus for the worry.
- Avoidant personality disorder is often comorbid with social anxiety disorder.
- Psychotic disorders can present with a fear of being in public that arises from delusions.

WORKUP

- History: usually diagnostic. This should include information about other medical disorders, medications, any history of past trauma, and substance abuse. Fig. 1P-47 describes a diagnostic decision tree for specific phobias.
- Physical examination: to confirm absence of cardiovascular abnormalities such as arrhythmias or evidence of endocrinologic reasons for hyperarousal such as an enlarged or tender thyroid gland.

LABORATORY TESTS

No specific laboratory tests are indicated.

IMAGING STUDIES

No specific imaging studies are recommended.

Rx TREATMENT

NONPHARMACOLOGIC THERAPY

- Cognitive-behavioral therapy (CBT) and exposure-based treatments have been effective for treating specific phobia and social anxiety disorder in controlled trials and are considered an appropriate first-line treatment.
- Behavioral treatments sometimes involve relaxation training, often paired with visualization and progressive desensitization.
- Success rates in treating specific phobias are higher when the phobia is not complicated by other anxiety disorders.

ACUTE GENERAL Rx

- Although benzodiazepines provide rapid relief of anxiety associated with exposure to provoking stimuli, they are associated with adverse effects including somnolence, accidents, abuse, and dependence, and thus are not recommended as a first-line treatment.
- Beta-blockers (e.g., propranolol) have been used to decrease autonomic hyperarousal and tremor associated with performance situations (e.g., before public speaking), but are not recommended for more generalized forms of social anxiety disorder.

CHRONIC Rx

- If the phobic stimulus is rarely encountered, benzodiazepines used on an as-needed basis can be an appropriate long-term treatment; however, there is a risk of abuse and dependence that makes them a less desirable choice for long-term treatment.
- Selective serotonin reuptake inhibitors are the most effective pharmacologic treatment in reducing symptoms and improving function for people with social anxiety disorder.
- Monoamine oxidase inhibitors are also effective for treatment of social anxiety disorder, but are rarely used due to dietary restrictions and adverse effects.

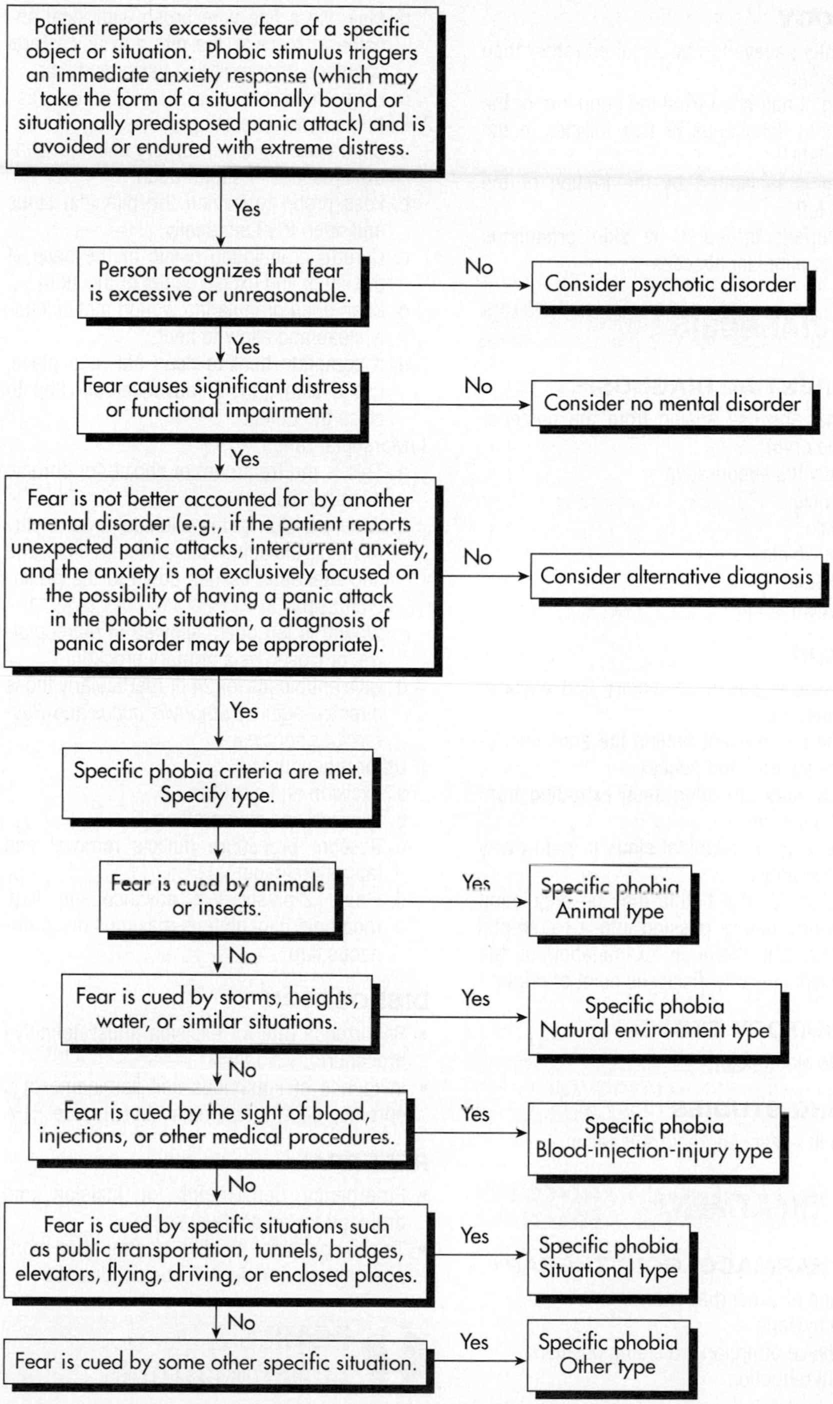

Diagnostic Decision Tree

Patient reports excessive fear of a specific object or situation. Phobic stimulus triggers an immediate anxiety response (which may take the form of a situationally bound or situationally predisposed panic attack) and is avoided or endured with extreme distress.

↓ Yes

Person recognizes that fear is excessive or unreasonable. → No → **Consider psychotic disorder**

↓ Yes

Fear causes significant distress or functional impairment. → No → **Consider no mental disorder**

↓ Yes

Fear is not better accounted for by another mental disorder (e.g., if the patient reports unexpected panic attacks, intercurrent anxiety, and the anxiety is not exclusively focused on the possibility of having a panic attack in the phobic situation, a diagnosis of panic disorder may be appropriate). → No → **Consider alternative diagnosis**

↓ Yes

Specific phobia criteria are met. Specify type.

↓

Fear is cued by animals or insects. → Yes → **Specific phobia Animal type**

↓ No

Fear is cued by storms, heights, water, or similar situations. → Yes → **Specific phobia Natural environment type**

↓ No

Fear is cued by the sight of blood, injections, or other medical procedures. → Yes → **Specific phobia Blood-injection-injury type**

↓ No

Fear is cued by specific situations such as public transportation, tunnels, bridges, elevators, flying, driving, or enclosed places. → Yes → **Specific phobia Situational type**

↓ No

Fear is cued by some other specific situation. → Yes → **Specific phobia Other type**

FIGURE 1P-47 Specific phobia: diagnostic decision tree. (From Lieberman, K: Social and specific phobias. In Lieberman K. (ed.): *Psychiatry behavioral science and clinical essentials: a companion to Tasman,* Philadelphia, 2000, Saunders, p. 368-378.)

COMPLEMENTARY & ALTERNATIVE MEDICINE

No definitive evidence supports complementary or alternative medicines in the treatment of phobic disorders.

DISPOSITION

Phobic disorders are generally present for life, although outpatient-based treatment may effectively reduce symptoms.

REFERRAL

Recommended for confirmation of diagnosis and for evaluation for psychotherapy and other treatment modalities.

! PEARLS & CONSIDERATIONS

People with social anxiety disorder often have low self-esteem and fear being scrutinized by others such that they avoid or are fearful of any situation in which others may assess or evaluate them directly or indirectly. More than half are concurrently affected by another anxiety disorder, and alcohol and other substance dependence is common because these patients often use substances to mask their anxiety.

SUGGESTED READINGS

Available at www.expertconsult.com

RELATED CONTENT

Phobias (Patient Information)
Panic Disorder, With or Without Agoraphobia (Related Key Topic)
Posttraumatic Stress Disorder (Related Key Topic)
Social Anxiety Disorder (Related Key Topic)

AUTHOR: **KRISTY L. DALRYMPLE, PH.D.**

 BASIC INFORMATION

DEFINITION

From the Latin words *pilus,* meaning "hair," and *nidus,* meaning "nest."

A *pilonidal sinus* is a short tract that extends from the skin surface and most likely represents a distended hair follicle. It is most commonly found in the intergluteal fold sacrococcygeal region, but it can also occur in the interdigital area, umbilicus, chest wall, and scalp. An *acute pilonidal abscess,* which consists of pus and a wall of edematous fat, results from rupture of an infected follicle into fat. A *chronic pilonidal abscess* results when an infected follicle ruptures directly into surrounding tissues; the wall of a chronic pilonidal abscess consists of fibrous tissue. A *pilonidal cyst* develops from a chronic abscess of long duration as a thin and flat lining of epithelium grows into the cavity from the skin surface.

SYNONYMS

Jeep disease
Pilonidal sinus
Pilonidal cyst

ICD-10CM CODES
L05   Pilonidal cyst
L05.0 Pilonidal cyst with abscess
L05.9 Pilonidal cysts without abscess

EPIDEMIOLOGY & DEMOGRAPHICS

INCIDENCE: 26 cases per 100,000 persons
PREDOMINANT SEX: Males are more commonly affected than females (2.2:1).
AVERAGE AGE OF PRESENTATION: 21 yr
RISK FACTORS:
- Male sex
- Caucasian race
- Family predisposition
- Obesity
- Sedentary lifestyle
- Occupation requiring prolonged sitting
- Local hirsutism
- Poor hygiene
- Increased sweat activity

PHYSICAL FINDINGS & CLINICAL PRESENTATION

- May manifest as asymptomatic pits or pores in the natal cleft (Fig. E1P-48)
- Tenderness after physical activity or prolonged sitting
- Acute pilonidal abscess in 20% of patients with pilonidal disease
- Presents as a hot, tender, fluctuant swelling just lateral to the midline over the sacrum that may exude pus through the midline pit
- Chronic pilonidal abscess in 80% of patients with pilonidal disease
- Acute suppuration, tenderness, swelling, and heat
- Infrequently, systemic reaction: occasionally fever, leukocytosis, and malaise

ETIOLOGY

- Currently believed to be acquired rather than congenital.
- Drilling of hair shed from the perineum or the head into sebaceous or hair follicles in the natal cleft.
- Drilling is facilitated by the friction of the natal cleft.
- Subsequent infection by skin organisms leads to pilonidal abscess.

 DIAGNOSIS

DIFFERENTIAL DIAGNOSIS

- Perianal abscess arising from the posterior midline crypt
- Hidradenitis suppurativa
- Carbuncle
- Furuncle
- Osteomyelitis
- Anal fistula
- Coccygeal sinus

WORKUP

- Diagnosis is based on history and physical examination.
- Midline pits present behind the anus overlying the sacrum and coccyx.
- Broken hairs are often seen extruding from the midline pits.
- Insert probe in pilonidal sinus in path away from the anus.
- Complicated anal fistula may be angulating posteriorly before passing into a retrorectal abscess, but thorough examination of the anal cavity usually discloses point of origin.

LABORATORY TESTS

Complete blood count

IMAGING STUDIES

CT scan in advanced, recurrent cases

 TREATMENT

NONPHARMACOLOGIC THERAPY

Prevention of exacerbations:
1. Local hygiene
2. Avoidance of prolonged sitting position
3. Weight reduction

ACUTE GENERAL Rx

- Procedure of choice for first-episode acute abscess: simple incision and drainage in an outpatient setting. Box E1P-5 describes surgical options for the treatment of pilonidal sinus.
- Cure rate of 76% after 18 mo
- Antibiotics: generally not indicated unless the patient has a medical condition such as rheumatic heart disease or is immunosuppressed

CHRONIC Rx

Elective treatment of pilonidal disease:
1. Minimal surgery:
   a. Remove hair from midline pits and shave buttocks.

b. May use a fine wire brush with local anesthesia to clear the pits and any lateral openings of granulation tissue and hair.
   c. Keep area clean.
2. Fistulotomy and curettage:
   a. Used when minimal surgery does not control episodes of suppuration
   b. Pass probe to outline the pilonidal sinus and open tract surgically
   c. Curette granulation tissue at the base of the sinus and excise edges of the skin
   d. Keep open granulating wound meticulously clean and allow to heal
   e. If complete healing does not take place, use a skin graft or advancement flap to close the defect
3. Marsupialization:
   a. This is the treatment of choice for chronic pilonidal disease.
   b. Wide excision of the pilonidal area is performed, including all affected skin and subcutaneous tissues down to the presacral fascia.
   c. Wound is left open, allowed to marsupialize, or closed as a primary procedure.
   d. Give antibiotics for 24 hr (particularly those directed against *Staphylococcus* and *Bacteroides* species).
4. Other procedures:
   a. Excision and closure
   b. Excision and skin grafting
   c. Bascom procedure (follicle removal and lateral drainage)
   d. Flaps: *Z*-plasty, V-Y advancement flap, rhomboid flap, gluteus maximus myocutaneous flap

DISPOSITION

- Recurrence rate for excision (most definitive procedure): 1% to 6%
- Incidence of squamous cell carcinoma in a chronic, recurrent pilonidal sinus is rare <1%

REFERRAL

- Emergency department for incision and drainage for an acute abscess
- To a surgeon for elective treatment or management of chronic or recurrent disease

 PEARLS & CONSIDERATIONS

COMMENTS

Because of significant associated morbidity, the elective surgical procedures outlined are performed only after the potential risks versus benefits are carefully weighed.

SUGGESTED READINGS
Available at www.expertconsult.com

RELATED CONTENT
Pilonidal Cyst (Patient Information)

AUTHOR: **RUBEN ALVERO, M.D.**

P

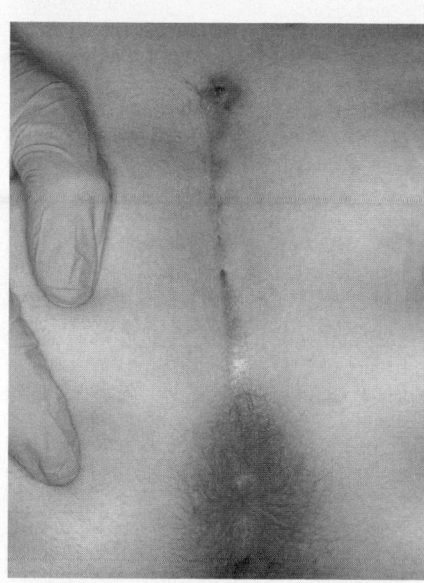

FIGURE E1P-48 Midline pits in the gluteal cleft represent a classic finding of pilonidal disease. (From Cameron JL, Cameron AM: *Current surgical therapy*, ed 19, Philadelphia, 2011, Saunders.)

BOX E1P-5   Surgical Options for the Treatment of Pilonidal Sinus

Midline Approach
Sinus excision: open vs. marsupialization vs. closure

Unroofing and Curettage
Asymmetric or oblique excision
Karydakis procedure
Bascom: open vs. closure
Cleft
Flaps
Rhomboid
V-Y advancement
Z-plasty
Gluteal myocutaneous

Others
Phenolization
Vacuum-assisted closure

From Cameron JL, Cameron AM: *Current surgical therapy,* ed 10, Philadelphia, 2011, Saunders.

BASIC INFORMATION

DEFINITION

Pinworms are a noninvasive infestation of the intestinal tract by *Enterobius vermicularis,* a helminth of the nematode family. It is a small (1 cm in length), white, thread-like roundworm that typically inhabits the cecum, appendix, and adjacent areas of the ileum and ascending colon.

SYNONYMS

Enterobiasis
Oxyuriasis

ICD-10CM CODES

B80 Enterobiasis

EPIDEMIOLOGY & DEMOGRAPHICS

- Most common intestinal nematode; approximately 30,000 cases annually in the United States.
- Worldwide distribution, but most common in temperate climates.
- The prevalence of pinworm infection is lowest in infants and reaches highest infection rate in school-age children (ages 5-14 yr).
- Eggs are infective within 6 hr of oviposition and may remain so for 20 days.
- Clusters are found in families, institutionalized persons, and homosexual men.

PHYSICAL FINDINGS & CLINICAL PRESENTATION

- Most infested persons are asymptomatic.
- Perianal itching is the most common reported symptom, with scratching leading to excoriation and sometimes secondary infection.
- The vagina may become infested with pinworms.
- Rarely insomnia, irritability, anorexia, and weight loss are described.
- Granulomas have been described in various organs resulting from worms wandering outside the intestines and dying there.

ETIOLOGY & PATHOGENESIS

- *E. vermicularis* is highly prevalent throughout the world, particularly in countries of the temperate zone. Human beings are the only host for this worm. Infestation is by fecal-oral route; ingested eggs hatch in the stomach and the larvae migrate to the colon, where they mature. Gravid female worms containing an average of 10,000 ova migrate to the perianal skin at night, lay their eggs there, and die. The eggs embryonate within 6 hr and cause itching; scratching causes egg deposition under fingernails, from which they can contaminate food or lead to autoreinfection. Ova may also be airborne and collect in dust that may be on the floor or on furniture.
- *E. vermicularis* may be transmitted between sexual partners, especially those engaging in oral-anal sex.

DIAGNOSIS

DIFFERENTIAL DIAGNOSIS

- Perianal itching related to poor hygiene
- Hemorrhoidal disease and anal fissures
- Perineal yeast/fungal infections
  Section II describes the causes of pruritus ani.

WORKUP

Identification of adult worms or eggs. *E. vermicularis* ova are ovoid but flattened on one side and measure approximately 56 × 27 micrometers (Fig. 1P-49). The eggs can be identified on transparent tape placed on the perianal skin on awakening. (NOTE: Five consecutive negative tests rule out the diagnosis.) A single examination detects 50% of infections, three examinations detect 90%, and five examinations detect 99%.

TREATMENT

- Single dose of mebendazole (100 mg) with a repeat dose given after 2 wk results in cure rates of 90% to 100%.
- Single dose of albendazole (400 mg) with a second dose given 2 wk later is also highly effective.
- Pyrantel pamoate (11 mg/kg up to 1 g) can prevent against *E. vermicularis.* It is available as a suspension and has minimal toxicity (mild transient gastrointestinal symptoms, headache, drowsiness). A repeat dose after 2 wk is recommended because of the frequency of reinfection and autoinfection.
- Other infected family members, classmates, or residents of long-term care facilities should be treated at the same time as the index case.

PEARLS & CONSIDERATIONS

- Eosinophilia is not observed in most cases because tissue invasion does not occur.
- Good hand hygiene is the most effective method of prevention.
- Frequent changing of underclothes, bed clothes, and bed sheets is helpful to decrease risk of autoinfection.
- Personal hygiene and cleanliness are crucial. Fingernails should be cut short and scrubbed frequently.

SUGGESTED READINGS

Available at www.expertconsult.com

RELATED CONTENT

Pinworms (Patient Information)

AUTHOR: **FRED F. FERRI, M.D.**

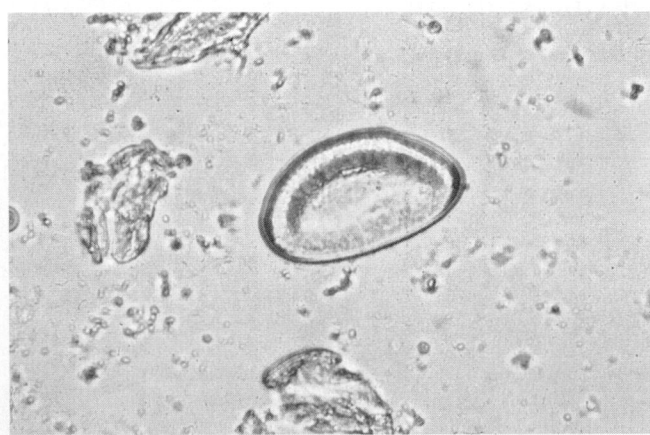

FIGURE 1P-49 Enterobius vermicularis embryonated egg. Note larva inside (40 × 10 μm). (From Gorbach SL et al [eds]: *Infectious diseases,* ed 2, Philadelphia, 1998, Saunders.)

BASIC INFORMATION

DEFINITION

Piriformis syndrome is a form of low back pain caused by prolonged or excessive contraction of the piriformis muscle and characterized by pain and instability. The pain is usually present in the hip, groin, buttock, coccyx, and distal part of the lower extremity.

SYNONYMS

- Deep gluteal syndrome
- Pelvic outlet syndrome
- Infrapiriform foramen syndrome
- Wallet sciatica
- Pocket sciatica

ICD-10CM CODES
S74.00 Injury of sciatic nerve at hip and thigh level

EPIDEMIOLOGY & DEMOGRAPHICS

- Women are affected more than men.
- It occurs in middle-aged patients (mean age of about 38).
- Incidence of piriformis syndrome has been estimated at 2.4 million/yr.
- Female-to-male incidence ratio is 6:1.
- About 6% of patients with sciatica have piriformis syndrome.

PHYSICAL FINDING & CLINICAL PRESENTATION

CLINICAL PRESENTATION: Patients with piriformis syndrome may present the following symptoms:
- Gluteal pain (97.9% of cases) which may:
  1. Be chronic
  2. Radiate to the distal part of the lower extremities
  3. Worsen with squatting or walking
- Rectal pain (worse during defecation)
- Hip movements (especially adduction and internal rotation) cause pain
- Labia majora or scrotal pain
- Dyspareunia in women
- Disturbances of potency in men
- Pain and discomfort on sitting

PHYSICAL FINDINGS:
- Piriformis syndrome is a diagnosis of exclusion.
- There are no neurologic deficits in patients with piriformis syndrome.
- There is tenderness over the gluteal area.
- Gluteal atrophy may be present.
- Sacroiliac tenderness.
- Shortening of the limb on the affected side.
- Other signs used in diagnosing piriformis syndrome include:
  1. *Lasègue sign*—Extension of the knee with the hip flexed to 90 degrees produces pain in the vicinity of the greater sciatic notch.
  2. *Pace sign*—Resisted abduction-external rotation of the thigh causes pain and weakness on the affected side.
  3. *Freiberg sign*—With the patient in the supine position, passive internal rotation of the extended thigh causes pain.
  4. Pain in the back when the patients lies with the painful side up and involved leg flexed.

ETIOLOGY

1. Trauma to the buttocks/gluteal region.
2. Spinal stenosis.
3. Anatomic variations of the division of the sciatic nerve.
4. As the sciatic nerve passes through the greater sciatic foramen, it is in close proximity to the piriformis muscle (Fig. 1P-50). Pain results from compression of the sciatic nerve by the piriformis muscle.
5. Laminectomy.
6. Intragluteal injection.
7. Hypertrophy and spasm of the piriformis muscle.
8. Excessive exercise
9. Leg length discrepancy (leading to altered biomechanics causing stretching and shortening of piriformis muscle)

 DIAGNOSIS

DIFFERENTIAL DIAGNOSIS

1. Lumbosacral disc or spine injury (lumbar radiculopathy)
2. Sacroiliac joint injury/inflammation (sacroiliitis)
3. Hamstring injury
4. Sciatic nerve entrapment
5. Paraspinal muscle spasm
6. Herniated intervertebral disc
7. Unrecognized pelvic fracture
8. Iliac vein thrombosis
9. Postlaminectomy syndrome
10. Undiagnosed nephrolithiasis
11. Trochanteric bursitis

WORKUP

Usually involves imaging studies
- Computed tomography scan:
  1. Used to identify spinal stenosis
  2. May show a large mass anterior to the piriformis muscle
- Magnetic resonance imaging:
  1. May show an enlarged piriformis muscle on T_1- or T_2-weighted images
  2. Asymmetry in piriformis muscle size between symptomatic and asymptomatic sides (Fig. 1P-51)
- Electromyogram (EMG):
  1. Normal EMG findings in the gluteus minimus, gluteus medius, and tensor fasciae latae muscles
  2. Abnormal EMG findings in the gluteus maximus and piriformis muscles

℞ TREATMENT

Sciatica due to piriformis syndrome is usually treated conservatively. Treatment modalities include physical therapy, lifestyle modalities, medications, and psychotherapy.

TREATMENT DURING ACUTE PHASE

- Stop offending activities
- Start physical therapy (PT) and occupational therapy treatment
  a) PT
    1. The basic PT treatment is **stretching** and **manual therapy.**
    2. PT modalities are most beneficial when used in conjunction with stretching exercise.
    3. Ultrasound and/or moist heat is recommended before stretching.

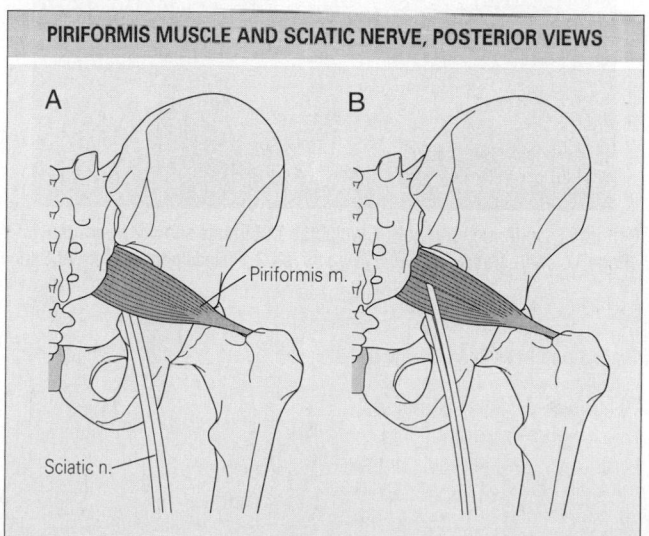

PIRIFORMIS MUSCLE AND SCIATIC NERVE, POSTERIOR VIEWS

A   B

Piriformis m.

Sciatic n.

FIGURE 1P-50 Piriformis muscle and sciatic nerve, posterior views. The piriformis muscle arises from the anterior surface of the sacrum and the gluteal surface of the ilium and crosses the greater sciatic foramen to insert onto the superior border of the greater trochanter. **A,** In most instances, the sciatic nerve passes along the anterior surface of the piriformis muscle and exits the pelvis below the piriformis muscle, passing posteriorly along its inferior border. **B,** In some individuals, a portion of the sciatic nerve passes through the piriformis muscle. Other anatomic variants have been described. (From Hochberg MC et al: *Rheumatology,* ed 5, St Louis, 2011, Mosby.)

4. Massage of the lumbosacral and gluteal areas reduces muscle tightness and sciatic nerve irritation.
5. Cold pack and/or electrical stimulation may be applied after exercise.

b) Occupational therapy. Advise patients to:
1. Avoid sitting for prolonged periods.
2. Make frequent stops when driving to get up and stretch.

c) Surgical intervention. This is considered only when medical treatment fails and symptoms become intractable and/or disabling. Indications for surgical intervention include hematoma, abscess, neoplasm, compression of the nerve by gluteal vein varicosities. Response to surgical treatment is often disappointing. Promising results include:
1. Piriformis tendon release
2. Sciatic neurolysis

d) Other treatment modalities
- Local injection of anesthetics into trigger points
- Botulinum toxin injection
- Nonsteroidal antiinflammatory drugs and opiates
- Transrectal message

TREATMENT DURING RECOVERY PHASE

- Start gradual strengthening activities for the piriformis and gluteal muscles.
- Continue therapeutic modalities.
- Start light sport-specific activities and functional training if patient is asymptomatic.
- Some athletes may consider changing their footwear to avoid additional stress on the piriformis muscle.

TREATMENT DURING MAINTENANCE PHASE

- Continue performing a home exercise program for increasing flexibility and strength.
- Athletes may increase their training volume as tolerated.
- Compliance to a daily stretching program is crucial to avoid recurrence of this syndrome.

REFERRAL

- Physical therapist: to instruct patients about stretching and pain-relieving maneuvers
- Orthopedic: when diagnosis is in doubt, the patient failed conservative treatment, and surgical evaluation is needed
- Neurologist: for EMG studies

PEARLS & CONSIDERATIONS

COMMENTS

Athletes may return to play when:
1. They are pain free with full range of motion.
2. They have full strength in the affected side.

PREVENTION

To prevent the recurrence of pain:
1. Avoid risk factors.
2. Continue stretching exercises.
3. Correction of biomechanical deficiencies

SUGGESTED READINGS

Available at www.expertconsult.com

AUTHOR: **DANIEL K. ASIEDU, M.D., PH.D.**

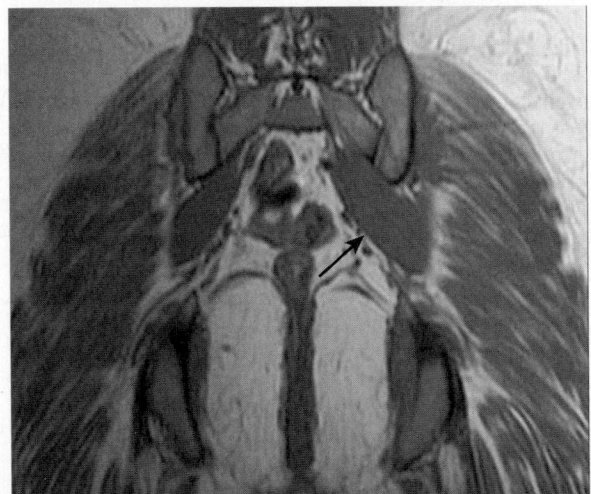

FIGURE 1P-51 Piriformis syndrome. Coronal T1-weighted MR image shows hypertrophy of the left piriformis muscle *(arrows)*. (Pope TL et al: *Musculoskeletal imaging*, ed 2, Philadelphia, 2014, WB Saunders.)

BASIC INFORMATION

DEFINITION

Pituitary adenoma is a benign neoplasm of the anterior lobe of the pituitary that causes symptoms, either by excess secretion of hormones or by a local mass effect as the tumor impinges on other, nearby structures (e.g., optic chiasm, hypothalamus, pituitary stalk). Pituitary adenomas are classified by their size, function, and features that characterize their appearance. Microadenomas are <10 mm in size, and macroadenomas are ≥10 mm in size.

- *Acromegaly* is the disease state characterized by a pituitary adenoma that secretes growth hormone (GH).
- A *prolactinoma* secretes prolactin (PRL).
- *Cushing's disease* is a disease state of hypersecretion of adrenocorticotropic hormone (ACTH).
- *Thyrotropin-secreting pituitary adenomas* secrete primarily thyroid-stimulating hormone (TSH).
- *Nonsecretory pituitary adenomas* are those in which the neoplasm is a space-occupying lesion whose secretory products do not cause a specific disease state.

ICD-10CM CODES
D35.2 Benign neoplasm of pituitary gland

EPIDEMIOLOGY & DEMOGRAPHICS

CLASSIFICATION (BY HORMONE SECRETED):
- PRL only: 35%.
- No hormone: 30%.
- GH only: 20%.
- PRL and GH: 7%.
- ACTH: 7%.
- Luteinizing hormone (LH), follicle-stimulating hormone (FSH), TSH: 1%.

PREVALENCE/INCIDENCE:
- Pituitary adenomas: up to 10% to 15% of all intracranial neoplasms; 3% to 27% at autopsy series.
- Prolactinomas: up to 20% in women with unexplained primary or secondary amenorrhea.
- GH-secreting pituitary adenoma: 50 to 60 cases per 1 million persons.
- Thyrotropin-secreting pituitary adenoma: 2.8% of pituitary adenomas with a slight female/male predominance of 1.7:1
- Corticotropin-secreting pituitary adenomas: female/male predominance of 8:1 but overall rare diagnosis.

PHYSICAL FINDINGS & CLINICAL PRESENTATION

PROLACTINOMAS:
- Females:
  1. Galactorrhea.
  2. Amenorrhea.
  3. Oligomenorrhea with anovulation.
  4. Infertility.
  5. Estrogen deficiency and associated osteopenia.
  6. Decreased vaginal lubrication.
- Males:
  1. Large tumors more common as a result of delayed diagnosis.
  2. Possible impotence, decreased libido, or hypogonadism.
  3. Galactorrhea rare because males lack the estrogen-dependent breast growth and differentiation.

GH-SECRETING PITUITARY ADENOMA: ACROMEGALY:
- Coarse facial features.
- Oily skin.
- Prognathism.
- Carpal tunnel syndrome.
- Osteoarthritis.
- History of increased hat, glove, or shoe size.
- Decreased exercise capacity.
- Visual field deficits.
- Diabetes mellitus.

CORTICOTROPIN-SECRETING PITUITARY ADENOMA: CUSHING'S DISEASE:
- Usually present when the tumor is small (1 to 2 mm).
- 50% of the tumors <<5 mm.
- Other symptoms:
  1. Truncal obesity.
  2. Round facies (moon face).
  3. Dorsocervical fat accumulation (buffalo hump).
  4. Hirsutism.
  5. Acne.
  6. Menstrual disorders.
  7. Hypertension.
  8. Striae.
  9. Bruising.
  10. Thin skin.
  11. Hyperglycemia.

THYROTROPIN-SECRETING PITUITARY ADENOMA:
- In males, larger, more invasive, and more rapidly growing tumors that present later in life.
- Other symptoms: thyrotoxicosis, goiter, visual impairment.

NONSECRETORY PITUITARY ADENOMAS (ENDOCRINE INACTIVE PITUITARY ADENOMA):
- Usually large at the time of diagnosis.
- Symptoms:
  1. Bitemporal hemianopsia as a result of compression of the optic chiasm.
  2. Hypopituitarism from compression of the pituitary gland.
  3. Hypogonadism in men and in premenopausal women.
  4. Cranial nerve deficits caused by extension into the cavernous sinus.
  5. Hydrocephalus from extension into the third ventricle, compressing the foramen of Monro.
  6. Diabetes insipidus resulting from compression of the hypothalamus or pituitary stalk (a rare complication).

ETIOLOGY
Benign neoplasms of epithelial origin

DIAGNOSIS

DIFFERENTIAL DIAGNOSIS
PROLACTINOMA:
- Pregnancy.
- Postpartum puerperium.
- Primary hypothyroidism.
- Breast disease.
- Breast stimulation.
- Drug ingestion (especially phenothiazines, antidepressants, haloperidol, methyldopa, reserpine, opiates, amphetamines, and cimetidine).
- Chronic renal failure.
- Liver disease.
- Polycystic ovarian disease.
- Chest wall disorders.
- Spinal cord lesions.
- Previous cranial irradiation.

ACROMEGALY: Ectopic production of GH-releasing hormone from a carcinoid or other neuroendocrine tumor

CUSHING'S DISEASE:
- Diseases that cause ectopic sources of ACTH overproduction (including small-cell carcinoma of the lung, bronchial carcinoid, intestinal carcinoid, pancreatic islet cell tumor, medullary thyroid carcinoma, or pheochromocytoma).
- Adrenal adenomas, adrenal carcinoma.
- Nelson's syndrome.

THYROTROPIN-SECRETING PITUITARY ADENOMAS: Primary hypothyroidism.

NONSECRETORY PITUITARY ADENOMA: Nonneoplastic mass lesions of various etiologies (e.g., infectious, granulomatous).

WORKUP
Screening tests for functional pituitary adenomas are described in Table 1P-23.

PROLACTINOMA: First step: measurement of basal PRL levels (practitioners should be aware of discriminatory values in their own institutions).
- Elevated PRL levels are correlated with tumor size.
- Level >200 ng/mL indicates likely prolactinoma, with levels of 100 to 200 ng/mL being equivocal and possibly associated with medications or other sources.
- Basal PRL levels between 20 and 100 suggest a microadenoma as well as other conditions such as psychotropic drug ingestion, recent breast examination, and even a recent meal.
- Basal level <<20 ng/mL is usually considered normal. Each laboratory should develop its own normative values, however, and practitioner should refer to these values.
- Threshold level for obtaining imaging such as MRI should be developed by individual providers depending on the level of specificity and sensitivity desired.

ACROMEGALY:
- First screening tests are the measurement of the serum insulin-like growth factor I level, postprandial serum GH, and TRH stimulation test.

TABLE 1P-23 Screening Tests for Functional Pituitary Adenomas

Disorder	Test	Comments
Acromegaly	IGF1 OGTT with GH obtained at 0, 30, and 60 min.	Interpret IGF1 relative to age- and gender-matched controls. Normal subjects should suppress GH to <1 µg/L.
Prolactinoma	Serum PRL level.	A level >500 µg/L is pathognomonic for macroprolactinoma. If >200 µg/L, prolactinoma is likely.*
Cushing's disease	24-hr UFC Nighttime salivary cortisol dexamethasone (1 mg) at 11 PM and fasting plasma cortisol measured at 8 AM ACTH assay	Ensure that urine collection is total and accurate by measuring urinary creatinine. Free salivary cortisol reflects circadian rhythm, and elevated levels may indicate Cushing's disease. Normal subjects suppress to <1.8 µg/dL. Distinguishes adrenal adenoma from ectopic ACTH or Cushing's disease.
TSH-secreting tumor	TSH measurement Free T_4 by dialysis Total T_3.	If T_4 or T_3 is elevated and TSH is measurable or elevated, a TSH-secreting tumor may be present.

ACTH, adrenocorticotropic hormone; *GH*, growth hormone; *IGF1*, insulin-like growth factor type 1; *OGTT*, oral glucose tolerance test; *PRL*, prolactin; *T3*, triiodothyronine; *T4*, thyroxine; *TSH*, thyroid-stimulating hormone; *UFC*, urinary free cortisol.
*Risperidone may result in prolactin levels >200 µg/L.
From Melmed S et al: *Williams textbook of endocrinology,* ed 12, Philadelphia, 2011, WB Saunders.

- Follow with an oral glucose tolerance test.
- Failure to suppress serum GH to <2 ng/mL with an oral load of 100 g glucose is considered conclusive.
- A GH-releasing hormone level >300 ng/mL is indicative of an ectopic source of GH.

CUSHING'S DISEASE:
- Normal or slightly elevated corticotropin levels ranging from 20 to 200 pg/mL; normal is 10 to 50 pg/mL (normative data should be developed by each institution for its population).
- Level <<10 pg/mL usually indicates an autonomously secreting adrenal tumor.
- Level >>200 pg/mL suggests an ectopic corticotropin-secreting neoplasm.
- Cushing's disease can be assessed by absence of cortisol suppression with the low-dose dexamethasone test but with the presence of cortisol suppression after the high-dose test. As a method to distinguish Cushing's disease from an ectopic source of ACTH, this test is robust.
- 24-hr urine collection should demonstrate an increased level of cortisol excretion.

THYROTROPIN-SECRETING PITUITARY ADENOMA:
- Highly sensitive thyrotropin assays, which evaluate the presence of thyrotoxicosis, are one way to detect a thyrotropin-secreting tumor.
- Free alpha subunit is secreted by >80% of tumors, with the ratio of the alpha subunit to thyrotropin <1.
- With central resistance to thyroid hormone, ratio is <1, and the sella is normal.
- Laboratory tests show elevated serum levels of both T_3 and T_4.

NONSECRETORY PITUITARY ADENOMA:
- Visual field testing.
- Assessment of the pituitary and organ function to determine if there is hypopituitarism or hypersecretion of hormones (even if the effects of hypersecretion are subclinical).
- TRH to provoke secretion of FSH, LH, and LH-beta-subunit; will not elicit response in normal persons.

- Exclusion of Klinefelter's syndrome in patient with longstanding primary hypogonadism, elevated gonadotropin levels, and enlargement of the sella.

IMAGING STUDIES
Study of choice: MRI of the pituitary (Fig. E1P-52) and hypothalamus.
- When evaluating Cushing's disease, small size at the onset of symptoms noted.
- MRI, in this case, only 60% sensitive at best and may yield false-positive results.
- CT scan only when MRI is unavailable or is otherwise contraindicated.

(Rx) TREATMENT

NONPHARMACOLOGIC THERAPY
SURGERY:
- Selective transsphenoidal resection of the adenoma (Table 1P-24) is the treatment of choice for acromegaly, Cushing's disease, and thyrotropin-secreting pituitary adenomas, all of which tend to be microadenomas at the time of onset of symptoms.
- Macroadenomas, such as the nonsecretory pituitary adenoma, may also be surgically removed, but risk of recurrence is greater with these tumors and adjunctive therapy such as irradiation may also be necessary.
- Bilateral adrenalectomy has been performed in patients with Cushing's disease after failure of other therapies; complications requiring lifelong hormone replacement or Nelson's syndrome (rapid enlargement of pituitary tumor due to adrenal resection) may occur.

RADIOTHERAPY:
- Radiotherapy is used primarily as adjuvant treatment. It is reserved for patients who have not responded to surgical treatment and who still have symptoms of the adenoma.
- Used with varying degrees of success in all the different pituitary adenomas.
- Radiotherapy complications include long-term hypopituitarism (40% of patients) and secondary neoplasms (1.5% of patients).

TABLE 1P-24 Transsphenoidal Pituitary Surgery

Primary Indications
General

Visual tract or central nervous system compression arising from within sella
Relief of compressive hypopituitarism by presenting, residual, or recurrent tumor tissue
Tumor recurrence after surgery or irradiation
Pituitary hemorrhage
Cerebrospinal fluid leak
Resistance to medical therapy
Intolerance of medical therapy
Personal choice
Desire for immediate pregnancy with macroadenoma
Requirement for diagnostic tissue histology

Specific

Acromegaly
Cushing's disease
Clinically nonfunctioning macroadenoma
Prolactinoma
Nelson's syndrome
TSH-secreting adenoma

Side Effects
Transient

Diabetes insipidus
Cerebrospinal fluid leak and rhinorrhea
Inappropriate ADH secretion
Arachnoiditis
Meningitis
Postoperative psychosis
Local hematoma
Arterial wall damage
Epistaxis
Local abscess
Pulmonary embolism
Narcolepsy

Permanent (up to 10%)

Diabetes insipidus
Total or partial hypopituitarism
Visual loss
Inappropriate ADH secretion
Vascular occlusion
CNS damage: oculomotor palsy, hemiparesis, encephalopathy
Nasal septum perforation

Surgery-Related Mortality (up to 1%)

Brain, hypothalamic
Vascular damage
Postoperative meningitis
Cerebrospinal fluid leak
Pneumocephalus
Acute cardiopulmonary disease
Anesthesia-related
Seizure

ADH, Antidiuretic hormone; *CNS,* central nervous system; *TSH,* thyroid-stimulating hormone.
From Melmed S et al: *Williams textbook of endocrinology,* ed 12, Philadelphia, 2011, WB Saunders.

ACUTE GENERAL Rx
PROLACTINOMA:
- Bromocriptine, a dopamine analogue, is generally given orally in divided doses of 1.5 to 10 mg. Cabergoline is given once or twice weekly. It is better tolerated and more effective than bromocriptine for tumor shrinkage but more expensive.

- Side effects include orthostatic hypotension, nausea, and dizziness; avoided by beginning with low-dose therapy.
- Other compounds include pergolide mesylate, a long-acting ergot derivative with dopaminergic properties, as well as other nonergot derivatives.

ACROMEGALY:

- Somatostatin analogues: octreotide, lanreotide administered as monthly injections.
- Cabergoline or bromocriptine can also be used. They have modest activity but can be administered orally and are less expensive than somatostatin analogues.
- Pegvisomant can also be used to normalize IGF-1 levels.

CUSHING'S DISEASE:

- Ketoconazole, which inhibits the cytochrome P-450 enzymes involved in steroid biosynthesis, is effective in managing mild to moderate disease in daily oral doses of 600 to 1200 mg.
- Metyrapone and aminoglutethimide can be used to control hypersecretion of cortisol but are generally used when preparing a patient for surgery or while waiting for a response to radiotherapy.

THYROTROPIN-SECRETING PITUITARY ADENOMA:

- Ablative therapy with either radioactive iodide or surgery is indicated.
- Treatment directed to the thyroid alone may accelerate growth of the pituitary adenoma.
- Octreotide has been shown to be effective in doses similar to those used for acromegaly.

NONSECRETORY PITUITARY ADENOMA:

- There is no role for medical therapy at this time.
- Surgery and radiotherapy may be indicated. An algorithm for the management of nonfunctioning pituitary adenomas is described in Fig. 1P-53.

CHRONIC Rx

For all pituitary adenomas:

- Careful follow-up is important. Patients undergoing transsphenoidal microsurgical resection should be seen in 4 to 6 wk to ensure that the adenoma has been completely removed and that the endocrine hypersecretion is resolved.

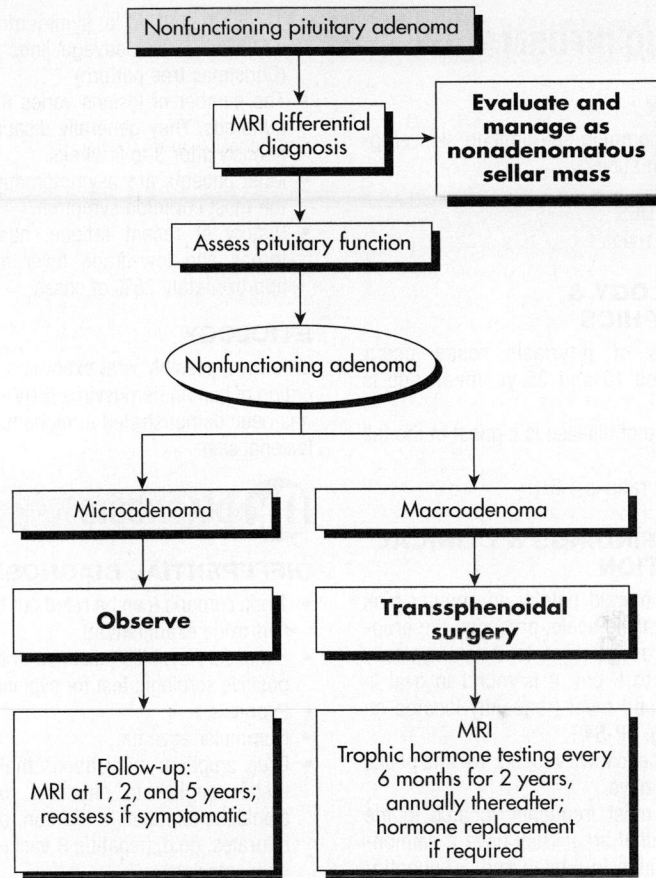

FIGURE 1P-53 Management of nonfunctioning pituitary adenomas. Skilled interpretation of magnetic resonance images is crucial to diagnosing a nonadenomatous mass such as a meningioma, aneurysm, or other sellar lesion. (From Melmed S et al: *Williams textbook of endocrinology*, ed 12, Philadelphia, 2011, WB Saunders.)

- If there is good clinical response, patient should be monitored yearly for recurrence and to follow the level of the hypersecreted hormone.
- Patients who have undergone irradiation should have close follow-up with backup medical therapy because response to radiotherapy may be delayed; incidence of hypopituitarism also increases with time.

SUGGESTED READINGS

Available at www.expertconsult.com

RELATED CONTENT

Evaluation of suspected pituitary tumor (Algorithm, Section III)
Pituitary Adenoma (Patient Information)
Acromegaly (Related Key Topic)
Amenorrhea (Related Key Topic)
Cushing's Disease and Syndrome (Related Key Topic)
Galactorrhea (Related Key Topic)
Prolactinoma (Related Key Topic)

AUTHOR: **RUBEN ALVERO, M.D.**

BASIC INFORMATION

DEFINITION

Pityriasis is a common self-limiting skin eruption of unknown etiology.

ICD-10CM CODES
L42 Pityriasis rosea

EPIDEMIOLOGY & DEMOGRAPHICS

- Most cases of pityriasis rosea occur between ages 10 and 35 yr; mean age is 23 yr.
- The incidence of disease is highest in the fall and spring.
- Female/male ratio is 1.5:1.

PHYSICAL FINDINGS & CLINICAL PRESENTATION

- Initial lesion (herald patch), an annular pink patch with trailing scale, precedes the eruption by approximately 1 to 2 wk; typically measures 3 to 6 cm; it is round to oval in appearance and most frequently located on the trunk (Fig. 1P-54).
- Eruptive phase follows within 2 wk and peaks after 7 to 14 days.
- Lesions are most frequently located in the lower abdominal area. They have a salmon-pink appearance in whites and a hyperpigmented appearance in blacks.
- Most lesions are 4 to 5 mm in diameter; center has a "cigarette paper" appearance; border has a characteristic ring of scale (collarette). When stretched across the long axis, the scales tend to fold across the lines of stretch, the so-called "hanging curtain sign."

- Lesions occur in a symmetric distribution and follow the cleavage lines of the trunk (Christmas tree pattern).
- The number of lesions varies from a few to hundreds. They generally disappear spontaneously after 3 to 8 weeks.
- Most patients are asymptomatic; pruritus is the most common symptom.
- History of recent fatigue, headache, sore throat, and low-grade fever is present in approximately 25% of cases.

ETIOLOGY

Unknown, possibly viral exanthem. Active replication of human herpesvirus (HHV)-6 and HHV-7 has been demonstrated in mononuclear cells of lesional skin.

DIAGNOSIS

DIFFERENTIAL DIAGNOSIS

- Tinea corporis (can be ruled out by potassium hydroxide examination).
- Secondary syphilis (absence of herald patch, positive serologic test for syphilis).
- Psoriasis.
- Nummular eczema.
- Drug eruption: medications that may cause rashes similar to pityriasis rosea include clonidine, captopril, interferon, bismuth, barbiturates, gold, hepatitis B vaccine, and imatinib mesylate.
- Other viral exanthem.
- Seborrheic dermatitis.
- Eczema.
- Lichen planus.
- Tinea versicolor (the lesions are more brown and the borders are not as ovoid).
- Erythema migrans.

WORKUP

Presence of herald lesion and characteristic rash are diagnostic. Skin biopsy is generally reserved for atypical cases.

LABORATORY TESTS

Generally not necessary; serologic test for syphilis if clinically indicated.

TREATMENT

NONPHARMACOLOGIC THERAPY

The disease is self-limited and generally does not require any therapeutic intervention.

ACUTE GENERAL Rx

- Use calamine lotion or oral antihistamines in patients with significant pruritus. Corticosteroid lotions or creams also provide some relief from itching.
- Use prednisone tapered over 2 wk in patients with severe pruritus.
- Direct sun exposure or use of ultraviolet light within the first week of eruption is beneficial in decreasing the severity of disease.
- One small trial showed improvement of rash and pruritis with erythromycin 250 mg qid for 2 weeks.

DISPOSITION

- Spontaneous complete resolution of the rash within 4 to 8 wk.
- Recurrence rare (<2% of cases).

PEARLS & CONSIDERATIONS

COMMENTS

Reassure patient that the disease is not contagious and its course is benign.

SUGGESTED READINGS
Available at www.expertconsult.com

RELATED CONTENT
Pityriasis Rosea (Patient Information)

AUTHOR: **FRED F. FERRI, M.D.**

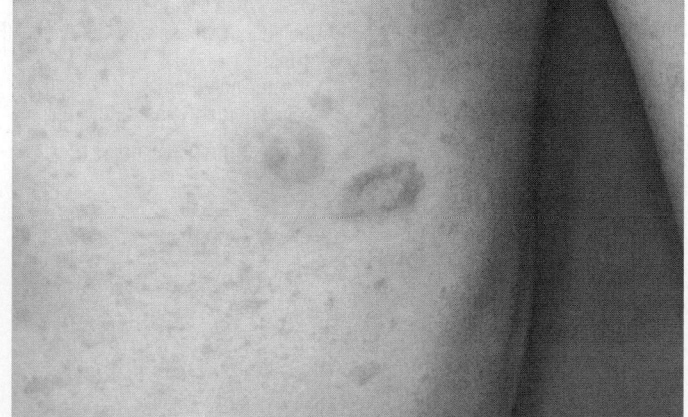

FIGURE 1P-54 Herald patch and surrounding pityriasis rosea. (From Kliegman RM et al: *Nelson textbook of pediatrics,* ed 19, Philadelphia, 2011, Saunders.)

BASIC INFORMATION

DEFINITION

Placenta previa is the implantation of the placenta over the internal os. Four degrees of this abnormality (Fig. 1P-55) have been traditionally defined; however, the accurate localization of the placental edge in relation to the discrete point of the internal os with transvaginal sonography makes the following terms outmoded:
1. Total placenta previa: the internal os is covered completely.
2. Partial placenta previa: the internal os is partially covered.
3. Marginal placenta previa: the edge of the placenta is at the margin of the internal os.
4. Low-lying placenta: the placenta is implanted in the lower uterine segment and, although its edge does not reach the internal os, is in close proximity to it.

ICD-10CMCODES
044   Placenta previa
044.0 Placenta previa specified as without hemorrhage
044.1 Placenta previa specified as with hemorrhage

EPIDEMIOLOGY & DEMOGRAPHICS

INCIDENCE: 0.26% to 0.7% of pregnancies
RISK FACTORS:
- Previous cesarean delivery (after one cesarean delivery, the risk is 1% to 4%; after four or more, the risk approaches 10%).
- Multiparity has also been associated with placenta previa.
- Smoking and cocaine use.
- Previous myomectomy or Asherman syndrome.
- Multiple gestation.
- Abnormal or large placenta.

PHYSICAL FINDINGS & CLINICAL PRESENTATION

The classic presentation of placenta previa is painless vaginal bleeding, usually in the second or third trimester. Uterine contractions may or may not be present. On physical examination, the uterus is soft and pain free. The fetus is often in breech, transverse lie, or high. Fetal distress is usually not present.

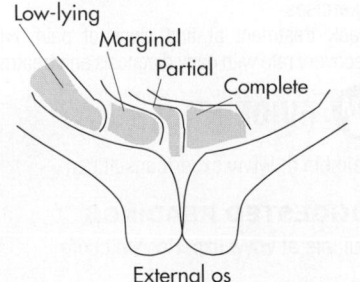

FIGURE 1P-55 Depiction of degrees of placenta previa. (From Weissleder R et al: *Primer of diagnostic imaging,* St Louis, 2007, Mosby.)

DIAGNOSIS

DIFFERENTIAL DIAGNOSIS
- Placenta accreta
- Placenta percreta
- Placenta Increta
- Vasa previa
- Abruptio placentae
- Vaginal or cervical trauma
- Labor
- Local malignancy

WORKUP
- Do *not* perform a digital vaginal examination.
- The diagnosis of placenta previa can seldom be firmly established by physical examination alone. A speculum examination in a hospital setting to exclude any local bleeding may be performed.
- This diagnosis should not be dismissed until thorough evaluation, including sonography, has completely excluded its presence.

LABORATORY TESTS
- A complete blood count can be used to monitor hemoglobin and hematocrit.
- A Kleihauer-Betke preparation of maternal blood in all Rh-negative women and Rh-immune globulin when indicated

IMAGING STUDIES
- The simplest and safest method of placental localization is transabdominal sonography with confirmatory imaging by transvaginal ultrasonography (TVS). Transabdominal ultrasound alone is inaccurate in the diagnosis of placenta previa and should be used only as a screening tool. TVS (Fig. E1P-56) has become the gold standard for the diagnosis of placenta previa. It is safe even in the presence of active bleeding. A distance of ≤20 mm from placental edge to interior cervical os is becoming a new criterion for performing term cesarean delivery in women with placenta previa.
- MRI has also been effective in detecting placenta previa, although sonography remains the preferred method.

TREATMENT

NONPHARMACOLOGIC THERAPY
- In preterm pregnancies with no active bleeding, close observation and expectant management are indicated. In those with active bleeding, conservative management, including blood transfusions for severe bleeds, is appropriate. The woman should stay in the hospital for at least 48 hr after the bleeding has stopped.
- Bed rest, preferably in a hospital setting, should be prescribed.

ACUTE GENERAL Rx
- Initial assessment for signs of maternal hemodynamic compromise or hemorrhagic shock; large-bore IV access with crystalloid fluid resuscitation

- Assess fetal status and gestational age by sonogram and continuous fetal heart rate monitoring
- Cross-matched blood should be made available during bleeding episodes; if the hemorrhage is severe, cesarean delivery is indicated despite fetal immaturity
- Tocolytic therapy may be considered in those women in preterm labor, as well as the administration of corticosteroids to enhance fetal lung maturity

CHRONIC Rx
- Cesarean delivery is necessary in nearly all cases of placenta previa.
- Uncontrollable hemorrhage after placental removal should be anticipated as a result of the poorly contractile nature of the lower uterine segment. The need for hysterectomy to control bleeding should be discussed with the patient before delivery.

DISPOSITION

Because of the unpredictable nature of placenta previa, not all women with placenta previa can be treated expectantly.

REFERRAL

Affected women and their families should be aware of all signs and symptoms that would necessitate immediate transport to the hospital. The possibility of hysterectomy should also be discussed early during pregnancy.

PEARLS & CONSIDERATIONS

COMMENTS

Third-trimester measurement of the distance from the placental edge to the internal cervical os by TVS commonly is used to gauge the likelihood of need for cesarean section. The decision to offer women with a placenta that is situated 11 to 20 mm away a trial of labor remains controversial. Recent reports by Vergani et al indicate that more than two thirds of women with a placental edge to cervical os distance of >10 mm fewer than 28 days before delivery can deliver vaginally without increased risk of hemorrhage.

SUGGESTED READINGS
Available at www.expertconsult.com

RELATED CONTENT
Placenta Previa (Patient Information)
Vaginal Bleeding During Pregnancy (Related Key Topic)

AUTHORS: **SONYA S. ABDEL-RAZEQ, M.D.,** and **RUBEN ALVERO, M.D.**

BASIC INFORMATION

DEFINITION

The plantar fascia arises from the calcaneal tuberosity and has various attachments as it travels longitudinally along the foot to the digits (Fig. 1P-57). The plantar fascia acts as a tension band supporting the medial longitudinal arch of the foot. Plantar fasciitis describes the local inflammation and subsequent pain occurring at the insertion at the medial calcaneal tuberosity or along the course of the fascial band.

SYNONYMS

Heel pain syndrome

ICD-10CMCODES
M72.2   Plantar fascial fibromatosis
M77.30 Calcaneal spur, unspecified foot
M77.31 Calcaneal spur, right foot
M77.32 Calcaneal spur, left foot

EPIDEMIOLOGY & DEMOGRAPHICS

INCIDENCE: Plantar fasciitis affects >1 million persons/yr in the United States. Two thirds of patients will seek care from their primary care physician for this condition. It is one of the most common causes of heel pain in adults.
PREDOMINANT SEX: Females slightly greater than males, studies vary.
PREDOMINANT AGE: Commonly middle aged; any age group possible.
RISK FACTORS: Weight gain, obesity (present in 90% of patients), increased activity, change in activity type, prolonged standing, hard surfaces, trauma, certain activities (see "Etiology").

PHYSICAL FINDINGS & CLINICAL PRESENTATION

- Pain is localized to the heel or along the course of the plantar fascia.
- Pain is greatest upon first steps in the morning and upon standing after rest (poststatic dyskinesia).
- Symptoms may improve throughout the day or with ambulation, but may persist or increase with prolonged standing.
- Pain may be elicited with ankle dorsiflexion and simultaneous subtalar eversion.

- Often exquisitely tender upon palpation of the medial calcaneal tuberosity.
- May have localized or medial heel edema.

ETIOLOGY

- Any factor that increases the tension at the insertion of the fascia on the medial calcaneal tuberosity, creating local inflammation. Evidence suggests that plantar spurs are secondary rather than an etiology; these are an incidental finding in about 30% of asymptomatic patients.
- Achilles/ankle equinus or pseudoequinus.
- Active STJ/rearfoot pronation, such as with calcaneal or forefoot varus.
- A strain of the fascia or dorsiflexory force of the forefoot on the midfoot or vice versa. Example: jumping from a height, sprinting from starting blocks, reaching on a ladder.

DIAGNOSIS

DIFFERENTIAL DIAGNOSIS

- Calcaneal fracture, including traumatic or stress fracture, or bone bruise. Caution: If the patient has jumped from a height, calcaneal fracture is often missed on x-ray.
- Tarsal tunnel syndrome.
- Calcaneal osteomyelitis.
- Bone cyst or bone tumor.
- Posterior tibial tendon dysfunction (often misdiagnosed as plantar fasciitis).
- Flexor hallucis longus tendonitis (also often misdiagnosed as plantar fasciitis).
- Plantar fascial fibromatosis (thickening/soft tissue mass along the plantar fascial band).
- Systemic cause: gout, Paget's disease of the bone, psoriasis, Reiter's syndrome, etc.
- Rupture of the plantar fascia.

STUDIES

- Weight-bearing x-rays: rule out tumor or trauma (lateral, oblique, calcaneal axial views).
- MRI/bone scan to rule out stress fracture (can take two weeks to show on x-ray).
- MRI or ultrasound if suspected plantar fascial fibromatosis.
- May need to rule out tarsal tunnel syndrome with nerve conduction studies.

TREATMENT

- Supportive lace-up sneakers with firm, cushioned sole. Avoid flexible sneakers!
- Ice, stretching exercises, NSAIDs, limit activity.
- Low-dye strapping/taping.
- Injection (Fig. 1P-58): Although corticosteroid injection is often used, evidence supporting this treatment is limited. Trials have shown that pain improvement after steroid injection is slightly faster than placebo. Benefits are likely to be short lived.
- Custom orthotics will limit subtalar joint overpronation and other faulty biomechanics.
- Add heel cushion to orthotics if acute pain/inflammation.
- Heel lifts if the etiology is Achilles equinus or pseudoequinus.
- Night splints maintain ankle dorsiflexion overnight.
- Severe cases may require a cast or cast walker for 4 to 6 weeks.
- Recalcitrant cases may require surgical endoscopic or open fasciotomy.
- Extracorporeal shock-wave therapy (ESWT): Focal high-intensity ESWT without local anesthesia may be a reasonable alternative to surgery in patients resistant to conservative management.

DISPOSITION

Cases that are treated early and acute cases with sudden onset have a higher likelihood of resolving completely. Chronic recalcitrant cases may require surgery.

REFERRAL

- For biomechanical exam or surgical consult (podiatric/orthopedic foot/ankle surgeon).
- Physical therapy is often beneficial when first-line therapy fails.

! PEARLS & CONSIDERATIONS

COMMENTS

Caution: common, seemingly simple diagnosis. Do not overlook differential diagnosis.

PREVENTION

- Avoid shoes with bendable/flexible soles and shoes without laces/straps.
- Maintain foot/ankle flexibility with stretching exercises.
- Seek treatment at first signs of pain. Faster recovery rate with early diagnosis and treatment.

EBM EVIDENCE

Available at www.expertconsult.com

SUGGESTED READINGS

Available at www.expertconsult.com

RELATED CONTENT

Plantar Fasciitis (Patient Information)

AUTHOR: **BROOKE E. KEELEY, D.P.M.**

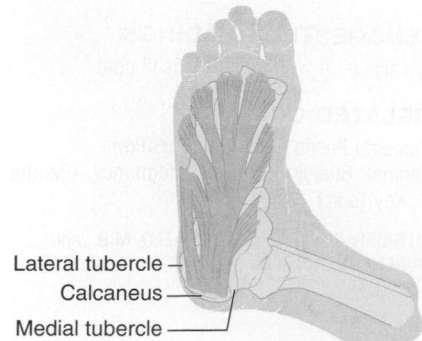

Lateral tubercle
Calcaneus
Medial tubercle

FIGURE 1P-57 Plantar view of origin and insertion of plantar fascia. (From Frontera WR: *Essentials of physical medicine and rehabilitation,* ed 2, Philadelphia, 2008, Saunders.)

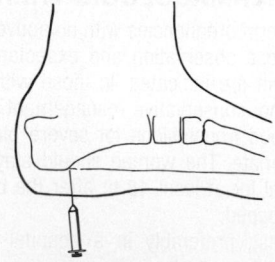

FIGURE 1P-58 Injection site for plantar fasciitis. Injection should be through the sole into the area of maximum tenderness. A 25- or 27-gauge needle should be used and the medication injected slowly because some pain may occur. The total volume should be no >1.5 ml. (From Mercier L: *Practical orthopedics,* ed 5, St Louis, 2002, Mosby.)

 BASIC INFORMATION

DEFINITION

Pleurisy refers to the inflammation of the parietal pleura. This inflammation results in pleuritic chest pain that is characteristically worsened with respiration or movement.

SYNONYMS

Pleuritis

ICD-10CM CODES

R09.1 Pleurisy

EPIDEMIOLOGY & DEMOGRAPHICS

INCIDENCE: One of the most common causes of pleuritic chest pain is viral pleurisy. However, there are a variety of disorders that may result in pleurisy. Infectious diseases, rheumatologic disorders, thromboembolic events, and trauma may all lead to pleural inflammation. Therefore, the incidence of pleurisy varies in accordance with the underlying etiology.

PHYSICAL FINDINGS & CLINICAL PRESENTATION

- The defining characteristic of pleurisy is chest pain that worsens with respiration, coughing, or sneezing.
- Pleuritic chest pain is typically described as sharp or stabbing. However, pleuritic chest pain may also be described as dull pain, burning pain, or a "catch" while breathing.
- Movements of the trunk or chest wall may exacerbate pain. Patients with pleurisy may locate the position of minimal discomfort and remain still in that position.
- Dyspnea may be associated with pleurisy.
- Physical exam may be remarkable for a pleural friction rub.
- Decreased breath sounds, rales, or egophony may be appreciated if pneumonia is the underlying etiology of the patient's pleurisy.

ETIOLOGY

- Pleurisy is caused by inflammation of the parietal pleura. The visceral pleura is not innervated by nociceptors. However, injury or inflammation at the periphery of the lung parenchyma often results in inflammation of the overlying parietal pleura. The parietal pleura, which lines the rib cage and the lateral portion of each hemidiaphragm, is innervated by intercostal nerves; therefore pain is localized to the cutaneous distribution of those nerves (over the chest wall). The parietal pleura of the central diaphragm is innervated by fibers that travel with the phrenic nerve; therefore pain associated with inflammation in this area is referred to the ipsilateral shoulder or neck.
- Various underlying etiologies may result in pleurisy, including:
  1. Thromboembolism (pulmonary embolism).
  2. Viral infection (coxsackieviruses, respiratory syncytial virus [RSV], cytomegalovirus [CMV], adenovirus, Epstein-Barr virus [EBV], parainfluenza, influenza).
  3. Bacterial infection (pneumonia or tuberculous pleuritis).
  4. Fungal infection (coccidioidomycosis, histoplasmosis).
  5. Rheumatologic disease (rheumatoid arthritis, systemic lupus erythematosus [SLE]).
  6. Medications.
  7. Malignancy of the lung or pleura.
  8. Trauma (rib fracture).
  9. Hereditary (familial Mediterranean fever, sickle cell disease).

Dx DIAGNOSIS

DIFFERENTIAL DIAGNOSIS

- Cardiac: myocardial infarction, ischemia, pericarditis.
- Intraabdominal process: pancreatitis, cholecystitis.
- Thromboembolic: pulmonary embolism, infarction of lung parenchyma.
- Traumatic/mechanical: rib fracture or pneumothorax.
- Viral infection: viral infections may lead to epidemic pleurodynia (also known as Bornholm's disease). Implicated viruses include coxsackieviruses, RSV, CMV, adenovirus, EBV, parainfluenza, influenza. Of note, viral pleurisy is a diagnosis of exclusion.
- Bacterial infection: pneumonia or tuberculous pleurisy.
- Fungal infection: coccidioidomycosis, histoplasmosis.
- Rheumatologic disease: rheumatoid arthritis, SLE.
- Medications: drug-induced lupus.
- Hereditary causes: familial Mediterranean fever, sickle cell disease.
- Malignancy: malignancy affecting the lung or pleura.
- Uremia.

WORKUP

- A thorough history and physical exam of all patients presenting with pleuritic chest pain should be taken. The time course of the patient's symptoms can provide valuable diagnostic clues. Acute onset of symptoms is suggestive of traumatic injuries, spontaneous pneumothorax, pulmonary embolism, or myocardial infarction. Subacute onset of symptoms suggests a potential infectious, rheumatologic, or medication-induced cause. Viral pleurisy is often associated with prodromal symptoms of upper respiratory infection. Chronic or recurrent symptoms suggest a potential malignant, tuberculous, or hereditary cause.
- Chest x-ray to evaluate for pneumonia, pneumothorax, or pleural effusion.
- ECG to evaluate for infarction, ischemia, or pericarditis.
- Evaluation for pulmonary embolism should be undertaken if clinical suspicion exists.

LABORATORY TESTS

- Laboratory testing varies based on suspected underlying etiology. Consider CBC, Chem 7, and D-Dimer testing depending on clinical presentation.
- If a pleural effusion is present, diagnostic thoracentesis may provide valuable diagnostic clues to the underlying etiology.

IMAGING STUDIES

- Chest x-ray
- ECG.
- CT chest in selected patients.

Rx TREATMENT

- Treatment of pleurisy consists of pain control as well as treating the underlying condition.
- NSAIDs are the preferred first-line agent to control pain associated with pleurisy. Human studies have been limited to trials using indomethacin for pain control, although an NSAID class effect is presumed.
- Indomethacin 50 mg orally up to three times a day has been found to be effective in relieving pain and is associated with an improvement in mechanical lung function.

SUGGESTED READINGS

Available at www.expertconsult.com

AUTHOR: **CHAKRAVARTHY REDDY, M.D.**

BASIC INFORMATION

DEFINITION

Aspiration pneumonia is a vague term that refers to pulmonary abnormalities following abnormal entry of endogenous or exogenous substances in the lower airways. It is generally classified as:

- Aspiration (chemical pneumonitis)
- Primary bacterial aspiration pneumonia
- Secondary bacterial infection of chemical pneumonitis

ICD-10CM CODES
J69.0 Pneumonitis due to inhalation of food and vomit

EPIDEMIOLOGY & DEMOGRAPHICS

INCIDENCE (IN U.S.):
- Few reliable data.
- 20% to 35% of all pneumonias.
- 5% to 15% of all community-acquired pneumonias.

PEAK INCIDENCE: Elderly patients in hospitals or nursing homes.

PREVALENCE (IN U.S.): Unknown (unreliable data).

PREDOMINANT SEX: Males and females affected equally.

PREDOMINANT AGE: Elderly.

PHYSICAL FINDINGS & CLINICAL PRESENTATION

- Shortness of breath, tachypnea, cough, sputum, fever after vomiting, or difficulty swallowing.
- Rales, rhonchi, often diffusely throughout lung.

ETIOLOGY

Complex interaction of etiologies, ranging from chemical (often acid) pneumonitis after aspiration of sterile gastric contents (generally not requiring antibiotic treatment) to bacterial aspiration.

COMMUNITY-ACQUIRED ASPIRATION PNEUMONIA:

- Generally results from predominantly anaerobic mouth bacteria (anaerobic and microaerophilic streptococci, fusobacteria, gram-positive anaerobic nonspore-forming rods), *Bacteroides* species (*melaninogenicus, intermedius, oralis, ureolyticus*), *Haemophilus influenzae,* and *Streptococcus pneumoniae*
- Rarely caused by *Bacteroides fragilis* (of uncertain validity in published studies) or *Eikenella corrodens*
- High-risk groups: the elderly; alcoholics; IV drug users; patients who are obtunded; stroke victims; and those with esophageal disorders, seizures, poor dentition, or recent dental manipulations.

HOSPITAL-ACQUIRED ASPIRATION PNEUMONIA:

- Often occurs among elderly patients and others with diminished gag reflex; those with nasogastric tubes, intestinal obstruction, or ventilator support; and especially those exposed to contaminated nebulizers or unsterile suctioning.
- High-risk groups: seriously ill hospitalized patients (especially patients with coma, acidosis, alcoholism, uremia, diabetes mellitus, nasogastric intubation, or recent antimicrobial therapy, who are frequently colonized with aerobic gram-negative rods); patients undergoing anesthesia; those with strokes, dementia, or swallowing disorders; the elderly; and those receiving antacids or H_2 blockers (but not sucralfate).
- Hypoxic patients receiving concentrated O_2 have diminished ciliary activity, encouraging aspiration.
- Causative organisms:
  1. Anaerobes listed above, although in many studies gram-negative aerobes (60%) and gram-positive aerobes (20%) predominate.
  2. *E. coli, P. aeruginosa, S. aureus* including MRSA, *Klebsiella, Enterobacter, Serratia, Proteus* spp., *H. influenzae, S. pneumoniae, Legionella,* and *Acinetobacter* spp. (sporadic pneumonias) in two thirds of cases.
  3. Fungi, including *Candida albicans,* in <1%.

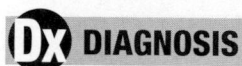 **DIAGNOSIS**

DIFFERENTIAL DIAGNOSIS

- Other necrotizing or cavitary pneumonias (especially tuberculosis, gram-negative pneumonias).
- See "Pulmonary Tuberculosis."

WORKUP

- Chest x-ray.
- Complete blood count (CBC), blood cultures.
- Sputum Gram stain and culture.
- Consideration of tracheal aspirate.

LABORATORY TESTS

- CBC: leukocytosis often present.
- Sputum Gram stain.
  1. Often useful when carefully prepared immediately after obtaining suctioned or expectorated specimen, examined by experienced observer.
  2. Only specimens with multiple white blood cells and rare or absent epithelial cells should be examined.
  3. Unlike nonaspiration pneumonias (e.g., pneumococcal), multiple organisms may be present.
  4. Long, slender rods suggest anaerobes.
  5. Sputum from pneumonia caused by acid aspiration may be devoid of organisms.
  6. Cultures should be interpreted in light of morphology of visualized organisms.

IMAGING STUDIES

- Chest x-ray often reveals bilateral, diffuse, patchy infiltrates and posterior segment upper lobes. Chemical pneumonitis typically affects the most dependent regions of the lungs.
- Aspiration pneumonia of several days' or longer duration may reveal necrosis (especially community-acquired anaerobic pneumonias) and even cavitation with air-fluid levels, indicating lung abscess.

TREATMENT

NONPHARMACOLOGIC THERAPY

- Airway management to prevent repeated aspiration.
- Ventilatory support if necessary.

ACUTE GENERAL Rx

Acute aspiration of acidic gastric contents without bacteria may not require antibiotic therapy; consult infectious disease or pulmonary expert.

- Community-acquired anaerobic aspiration pneumonia: clindamycin (600 mg IV twice daily followed by 300 mg q6h orally). Intravenous penicillin G (1 to 2 million U q4 to 6h) can also still be used. Alternative oral agents include: amoxicillin-clavulanate (875 mg orally twice daily), amoxicillin plus metronidazole or oral moxifloxacin (400 mg orally once daily). Do not use metronidazole alone, as this is associated with high failure rates.
- Nursing home aspirations: levofloxacin 500 to 750 mg qd or piperacillin-tazobactam 3.375 g q6h or ceftazidime 2 g q8h ± vancomycin if MRSA suspected or known.
- Hospital-acquired aspiration pneumonia:
  1. Piperacillin-tazobactam 3.375 g IV q6h, or cefoxitin 2 g IV q8h ± vancomycin IV to cover MRSA. Alternative agents are ceftriaxone 1 g IV q24h plus metronidazole 500 mg IV q6h or 1 g IV q12h.
  2. Knowledge of resident flora in the microenvironment of the aspiration within the hospital is crucial to intelligent antibiotic selection; consult infection control nurses or hospital epidemiologist.
  3. Confirmed *Pseudomonas* pneumonia should be treated with antipseudomonal beta-lactam agent plus an aminoglycoside until antimicrobial sensitivities confirm that less toxic agents may replace the aminoglycoside.
  4. Do not use metronidazole alone for anaerobes.

DISPOSITION

Repeat chest x-ray in 6 to 8 wk in most patients.

REFERRAL

For consultation with infectious disease and/or pulmonary experts for patients with respiratory distress, hypoxia, ventilatory support, pneumonia in more than one lobe, or necrosis or cavitation on x-ray examination or for those not responding to antibiotic therapy within 2 to 3 days.

SUGGESTED READINGS
Available at www.expertconsult.com

RELATED CONTENT
Aspiration Pneumonia (Patient Information)

AUTHOR: **GLENN G. FORT, M.D., M.P.H.**

Diseases and Disorders

 **BASIC INFORMATION**

DEFINITION

Bacterial pneumonia is an infection involving the lung parenchyma.

SYNONYMS

Community-acquired pneumonia
CAP

ICD-10CM CODES

J15.9	Unspecified bacterial pneumonia
J69.0	Pneumonitis due to inhalation of food and vomit
J15.9	Unspecified bacterial pneumonia
J13	Pneumonia due to *Streptococcus pneumoniae*
J15.1	Pneumonia due to *Pseudomonas*
J15.20	Pneumonia due to staphylococcus, unspecified
J15.0	Pneumonia due to *Klebsiella pneumoniae*
J14	Pneumonia due to *Haemophilus influenzae*
J15.211	Pneumonia due to methicillin-susceptible Staphylococcus aureus
J15.212	Pneumonia due to methicillin-resistant Staphylococcus aureus
J15.6	Pneumonia due to other aerobic Gram-negative bacteria
J15.7	Pneumonia due to Mycoplasma pneumoniae

EPIDEMIOLOGY & DEMOGRAPHICS

- The incidence of community-acquired pneumonia (CAP) is 1 in 100 persons. CAP is the most common infectious cause of death in the U.S.
- The incidence of health care facility–acquired pneumonia (HCAP) is 8 cases per 1000 persons annually.
- Primary care physicians see an average of 10 cases of pneumonia annually.
- Hospitalization rate for pneumonia is 15% to 20%. Incidence is highest among the oldest adults.
- Most cases of pneumonia occur in the winter and in elderly patients.

PHYSICAL FINDINGS & CLINICAL PRESENTATION

- Fever, tachypnea, chills, tachycardia, cough
- Presentation varies with the cause of pneumonia, the patient's age, and the clinical situation:
  1. Patients with streptococcal pneumonia usually present with high fever, shaking chills, pleuritic chest pain, cough, and copious production of rusty-appearing purulent sputum. Pleurisy and parapneumonic effusions are also common. Potential complications include bacteremia, empyema, and distant infections (e.g., meningitis).
  2. *Mycoplasma pneumoniae:* insidious onset; headache; dry, paroxysmal cough that is worse at night; myalgias; malaise;

sore throat; extrapulmonary manifestations (e.g., erythema multiforme, aseptic meningitis, urticaria, erythema nodosum) may be present.
  3. *Chlamydia pneumoniae:* persistent, nonproductive cough, low-grade fever, headache, sore throat.
  4. *Legionella pneumophila:* high fever, mild cough, mental status change, myalgias, diarrhea, respiratory failure.
  5. MRSA pneumonia: often preceded by influenza, may present with shock and respiratory failure.
  6. Elderly or immunocompromised hosts with pneumonia may initially present with only minimal symptoms (e.g., low-grade fever, confusion); respiratory and nonrespiratory symptoms are less commonly reported by older patients with pneumonia.
  7. In general, auscultation of patients with pneumonia reveals crackles and diminished breath sounds.
  8. Percussion dullness is present if the patient has pleural effusion.
  9. The clinical impression of pneumonia has an overall sensitivity of 70% to 90%; specificity ranges from 40% to 70%.

ETIOLOGY

- *Streptococcus pneumoniae* (20%-60% of CAP cases): incidence has been declining due to widespread use of pneumococcal vaccination
- *Haemophilus influenzae* (3%-10% of CAP cases)
- *L. pneumophila* (1%-5% of adult pneumonias) (2%-8% of CAP cases)
- *Klebsiella, Pseudomonas, Escherichia coli*
- *Staphylococcus aureus* (3%-5% of CAP cases)
- Atypical organisms such as *M. pneumoniae, C. pneumoniae,* and *L. pneumophila* implicated in up to 40% of cases of CAP
- Pneumococcal infection responsible for 50% to 75% of CAPs. Influenza infection is one of the important predisposing factors to *S. pneumoniae* and *S. aureus* pneumonia; gram-negative organisms cause >80% of nosocomial pneumonias
- Predisposing factors:
  1. Chronic obstructive pulmonary disease: *H. influenzae, S. pneumoniae, Legionella, Moraxella catarrhalis*
  2. Seizures: aspiration pneumonia
  3. Compromised hosts: *Legionella,* gram-negative organisms
  4. Alcoholism: *Klebsiella, S. pneumoniae, H. influenzae*
  5. HIV: *S. pneumoniae*
  6. IV drug addicts with right-sided bacterial endocarditis: *S. aureus*
  7. Older patient with comorbid diseases: *C. pneumoniae*

 **DIAGNOSIS**

DIFFERENTIAL DIAGNOSIS

- Viral pneumonias: Viral pneumonias/pneumonitis are on the rise. Several viruses alone or in combination can cause pneu-

monias in adults. Influenza is the predominant virus, but respiratory syncytial virus (RSV), parainfluenza viruses, adenoviruses, rhinoviruses, coronaviruses, and human metapneumovirus are all possible etiologies. The diagnosis is based on clinical suspicion, negative bacterial workup, and/or respiratory cultures, serologies, or rapid PCR testing.
- Exacerbation of chronic bronchitis
- Pulmonary embolism or infarction
- Lung neoplasm
- Bronchiolitis
- Sarcoidosis
- Hypersensitivity pneumonitis
- Pulmonary edema
- Drug-induced lung injury
- Fungal pneumonias
- Parasitic pneumonias
- Atypical pneumonia
- Tuberculosis

WORKUP

Laboratory evaluation and chest x-ray. Table 1P-25 summarizes diagnostic testing for CAP. Useful tools for assessing severity of illness are the *CURB-65* (see "Disposition") and *Pneumonia Severity Index.* Poor prognostic indicators are hypotension (SBP <90 or DBP <60), respiratory rate >30/min, hyperpyrexia (>40° C), or hypothermia (<35° C). None of these indices is as valuable as clinical judgment of the physician.

- Laboratory TestsComplete blood count with differential; white blood cell count is elevated, usually with left shift
- Blood cultures (hospitalized patients only): positive in approximately 20% of cases of pneumococcal pneumonia
- Pneumococcal urinary antigen test can be used to detect the C-polysaccharide antigen of *S. pneumoniae.* It is a useful tool in the treatment of hospitalized adult patients with CAP.
- Direct immunofluorescent examination of sputum when suspecting *Legionella* (e.g., direct fluorescent antibody stain is a highly specific and rapid test for detecting legionellae in clinical specimen) or urine *Legionella* antigen test
- Serologic testing for HIV in selected patients
- Serum electrolytes (hyponatremia in suspected *Legionella* pneumonia), BUN, creatinine
- Serum procalcitonin level: May be helpful to distinguish pneumonia from heart failure in patients presenting to the emergency department with acute dyspnea. The procalcitonin level is significantly higher in patients with pneumonia than in those without.[1]
- Pulse oximetry or arterial blood gases: hypoxemia with partial pressure of oxygen <60 mm Hg while the patient is breathing room air, a standard criterion for hospital admission

[1]Alba GA, et al: Diagnostic and prognostic utility of procalcitonin in patients presenting to the emergency department with dyspnea, *Am J Med* 129:96, 2016.

TABLE 1P-25 Diagnostic Testing for Community-Acquired Pneumonia (CAP)

Test	Sensitivity	Specificity	Comment
Chest radiograph	65%-85%	85%-95%	CT is more sensitive to infiltrates. Recommended for all patients.
Computed tomography	Gold standard	Not infection specific	Should not be done routinely but helpful to identify cavitation and loculated pleural fluid. Recommended in the evaluation of nonresponding patients.
Blood cultures	10%-20%	High when positive	Usually shows pneumococcus (in 50%-80% of positive samples) and defines antibiotic susceptibility. Recommended in patients with severe CAP, particularly if not on antibiotic therapy at the time of testing.
Sputum Gram stain	40%-100% depending on criteria	0%-100% depending on criteria	Can correlate with sputum culture to define predominant organism and can be used to identify unsuspected pathogens. Recommended if sputum culture is obtained. May not be able to narrow empirical therapy choices.
Sputum culture			Use if suspect drug-resistant or unusual pathogen, but positive result cannot separate colonization from infection. Obtain via tracheal aspirate in all intubated patients.
Oximetry or arterial blood gas			Both define severity of infection, need for oxygen; if hypercarbia is suspected, a blood gas sample is needed. Recommended in severe CAP.
Serologic testing for *Legionella*, *Chlamydia pneumoniae*, *Mycobacterium pneumoniae*, viruses			Accurate, but usually requires acute and convalescent titers collected 4-6 wk apart. Not routinely recommended.
Legionella urinary antigen	50%-80%		Specific to serogroup 1, but the best acute diagnostic test for *Legionella*.
Pneumococcal urinary antigen	70%-100%	80%	False positives if recent pneumococcal infection. Can increase sensitivity with concentrated urine.
Serum procalcitonin			Not a routine test, but if done, should be measured with the highly sensitive Kryptor assay. May help guide duration of therapy and need for ICU admission.

From Vincent JL et al: *Textbook of critical care*, ed 6, Philadelphia, 2011, Saunders

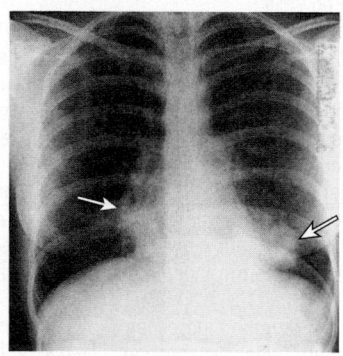

FIGURE 1P-59 *Streptococcus pneumoniae* pneumonia, bilateral lower zone consolidation (*arrows*). Although pneumococcal pneumonia is typically unifocal, multifocal involvement is not uncommon. (From Grainger RG et al: *Grainger and Allison's diagnostic radiology*, ed 4, London, 2001, Harcourt.)

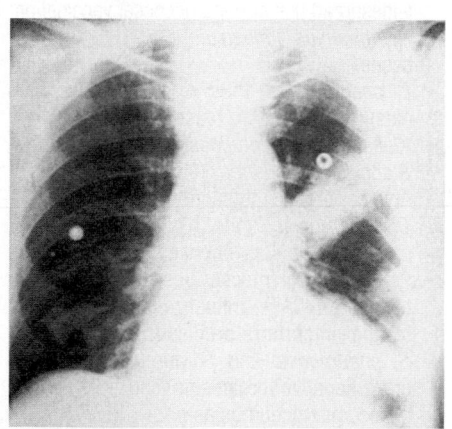

FIGURE 1P-60 Multilobar involvement occurring with *Legionella pneumophila* pneumonia. (From Mason RJ: *Murray & Nadel's textbook of respiratory medicine*, 5th ed, Philadelphia, 2010, Saunders.)

IMAGING STUDIES

Chest x-ray (Fig. 1P-59): findings vary with the stage and type of pneumonia and the hydration of the patient:

- Classically, pneumococcal pneumonia presents with a segmental lobe infiltrate.
- Diffuse infiltrates on chest x-ray can be seen with *L. pneumophila* (Fig. 1P-60), *M. pneumoniae*, viral pneumonias, *P. jirovecii (carinii)*, miliary tuberculosis, aspiration, aspergillosis.
- An initial chest x-ray is also useful to rule out the presence of any complications (pneumothorax, empyema, abscesses).

(Rx) TREATMENT

NONPHARMACOLOGIC THERAPY

- Avoidance of tobacco use
- Oxygen to maintain partial oxygen pressure in arterial blood >60 mm Hg
- IV hydration, correction of dehydration
- Assisted ventilation in patients with significant respiratory failure

ACUTE GENERAL Rx

- Initial antibiotic therapy should be based on clinical, radiographic, and laboratory evaluation.

- Macrolides (azithromycin or clarithromycin) or levofloxacin is recommended for empiric outpatient treatment of CAP. Box E1P-6 summarizes empirical therapy regimens for severe CAP. Cefotaxime or a beta-lactam/ beta-lactamase inhibitor can be added in patients with more severe presentation who insist on outpatient therapy. Duration of treatment ranges from 7 to 14 days. The treatment of choice in suspected *Legionella* pneumonia is either a quinolone (e.g., moxifloxacin) or a macrolide (e.g., azithromycin) antibiotic.
- In the hospital setting, patients admitted to the general ward can be treated empirically with a second- or third-generation cephalosporin (ceftriaxone, ceftizoxime, cefotaxime, or cefuroxime) plus a macrolide (azithromycin or clarithromycin) or doxycycline. An antipseudomonal quinolone (levofloxacin or moxifloxacin) can be substituted in place of the macrolide or doxycycline.
- Empiric therapy in ICU patients: IV beta-lactam (ceftriaxone, cefotaxime, ampicillin-sulbactam) plus an IV quinolone (levofloxacin, moxifloxacin) or IV azithromycin.
- In hospitalized patients at risk for *P. aeruginosa* infection, empiric treatment should consist of an antipseudomonal beta-lactam (meropenem, doripenem, imipenem, or piperacillin-tazobactam) plus an aminoglycoside plus an antipseudomonal quinolone.
- In patients with suspected methicillin-resistant *S. aureus*, vancomycin or linezolid is effective.

- Steroids: A metaanalysis published in 2015 by Siemieniuk et al showed that in hospitalized adults with CAP, systemic steroid therapy may reduce mortality, the need for mechanical ventilation, and length of hospital stay. Based on those results and several other supportive studies, corticosteroids (i.e., methylprednisolone 0.5 mg/kg IV q12h for 5 days) are recommended by several experts in hospitalized adult patients presenting with severe CAP, as long as no major contraindications for steroid usage are present.

CHRONIC Rx

Parapneumonic effusion and empyema can be managed with chest tube placement for drainage. Instillation of fibrinolytic agents (streptokinase, urokinase, or, more commonly, tissue plasminogen activator (TP) with Dnase (i.e., dornase alfa) by chest tube may facilitate the drainage of effusions not responding to chest tube drainage alone. A thoracoscopic debridement or a surgical decortication may be necessary in resistant cases.

DISPOSITION

- Most patients respond well to antibiotic therapy. Risk factors for a poor outcome from CAP are summarized in Box 1P-7.
- Indications for hospital admission are:
  1. Hypoxemia (oxygen saturation <90% while patient is breathing room air)
  2. Hemodynamic instability
  3. Inability to tolerate medications
  4. Active coexisting condition requiring hospitalization. A criterion often used to determine hospital admission is known as the "CURB-65": **C**onfusion, **B**UN >19.6 mg/dl, **R**espiratory rate >30 breaths/min, systolic **B**P <90 mg Hg, and diastolic BP ≤60 mm Hg, age ≥**65**. Patients are generally admitted to the hospital if they fulfill 2 or more criteria and to the ICU if they have 3 or more criteria

---

BOX 1P-7 Risk Factors for a Poor Outcome from Community-Acquired Pneumonia

Patient-Related Factors
- Male sex
- Absence of pleuritic chest pain
- Nonclassic clinical presentation
- Neoplastic illness
- Neurologic illness
- Age >65 years
- Family history of severe pneumonia or death from sepsis

Abnormal Physical Findings
- Respiratory rate >30 breaths/min on admission
- Systolic (<90 mm Hg) or diastolic (<60 mm Hg) hypotension
- Tachycardia (>125 beats/min)
- High fever (>40° C) or afebrile
- Confusion

Laboratory Abnormalities
- Blood urea nitrogen >19.6 mg/dl
- Leukocytosis or leukopenia (<4000/mm^3)
- Multilobar radiographic abnormalities
- Rapidly progressive radiographic abnormalities during therapy
- Bacteremia
- Hyponatremia (<130 mmol/L)
- Multiple organ failure
- Respiratory failure
- Hypoalbuminemia
- Thrombocytopenia (<100,000/mm^3)
- Arterial pH <7.35
- Pleural effusion

Pathogen-Related Factors
- High-risk organisms:
  ○ Type III pneumococcus, *Staphylococcus aureus,* gram-negative bacilli (including *Pseudomonas aeruginosa*), aspiration organisms, severe acute respiratory syndrome
- Possibly high levels of penicillin resistance (minimal inhibitory concentration of at least 4 mg/L) in pneumococcus

Therapy-Related Factors
- Delay in initial antibiotic therapy (more than 4-6 hours)
- Initial therapy with inappropriate antibiotic therapy
- Failure to have a clinical response to empirical therapy within 72 hours

From Vincent JL et al: *Textbook of critical care,* ed 6, Philadelphia, 2011, Saunders.

! PEARLS & CONSIDERATIONS

COMMENTS

- Use of gastric acid suppressive therapy (H$_2$ receptor antagonists, proton pump inhibitors [PPIs]) has been associated with an increased risk of CAP. It appears that PPI therapy started within the previous 30 days is associated with an increased risk for CAP, whereas longer-term current use is not.
- Causes of slowly resolving or nonresolving pneumonia:
  1. Difficult to treat infections: viral pneumonia, *Legionella,* pneumococci or staphylococci with impaired host response, tuberculosis, fungi
  2. Neoplasm: lung, lymphoma, metastasis
  3. Congestive heart failure
  4. Pulmonary embolism
  5. Immunologic or idiopathic: Wegener granulomatosis, pulmonary eosinophilic syndromes, systemic lupus erythematosus
  6. Drug toxicity (e.g., amiodarone)
- If patients with pneumonia are not doing well, repeat films should be taken promptly. In those with complete clinical recovery, it is reasonable to wait 6 to 8 wk before repeating the radiograph to document clearing of the infiltrate. The benefit of routine radiography after pneumonia has been questioned due to the low 1 yr incidence of lung cancer. Opponents propose a selective approach limiting follow-up chest x-ray to middle-aged and older adults.
- Prevention: Older adults should receive sequentially the 23-valent pneumococcal polysaccharides vaccine (PPSV23) and the pneumococcal conjugated vaccine (PCV13). The ACIP recommends giving the PCV13 first to be followed after a year by the PPSV23. This recommendation includes patients younger than 65 years with some defined risk factors (end-stage renal disease, sickle cell disease, congenital or acquired asplenia, HIV infection, congenital or acquired immunodeficiency, nephrotic syndrome, leukemia, lymphoma, Hodgkin's disease, generalized malignancy, iatrogenic immunosuppression, solid organ transplant, multiple myeloma, CSF leak, cochlear implant).
- Prevention: In season, patients should also receive influenza vaccination.

EBM EVIDENCE

Available at www.expertconsult.com

SUGGESTED READINGS

Available at www.expertconsult.com

RELATED CONTENT

Bacterial Pneumonia (Patient Information)

AUTHOR: **NAIM AOUN, M.D.**

BASIC INFORMATION

DEFINITION

Mycoplasma pneumonia is an infection of the lung parenchyma caused by a small bacterium, *Mycoplasma pneumoniae*.

SYNONYMS

Primary atypical pneumonia
Eaton's pneumonia
Walking pneumonia

ICD-10CM CODES

J15.7 Pneumonia due to *Mycoplasma pneumoniae*

EPIDEMIOLOGY & DEMOGRAPHICS

INCIDENCE (IN U.S.):
- It is a frequent cause of community-acquired pneumonia. CDC estimates 2 million cases a yr with 100,000 pneumonia-related hospitalizations.
- Many cases probably resolve without coming to medical attention.
- Incidence is estimated at one case per 1000 persons annually.
- Incidence is estimated to at least triple every (approximately) 5 yr during epidemics.

PEAK INCIDENCE:
- Some increased incidence in fall to early winter.
- Seems more prevalent in temperate climates.

PREVALENCE (IN U.S.):
- Estimated to be present in one in every five patients hospitalized for pneumonia (generally a self-limited disease, so its true prevalence is unknown).
- Estimated to cause 7% of all cases of pneumonia and approximately half the cases in those aged 5 to 20 yr.

PREDOMINANT SEX: Equal distribution

PREDOMINANT AGE:
- Most commonly affected: school-age children and young adults (ages 5-20 yr).
- Occurs in older adults as well, especially with household exposure to a young child.
- More severe infections in affected elderly patients.

GENETICS: Familial disposition:
- None known.
- May be more severe in patients with sickle cell anemia.

Neonatal infection: severe respiratory distress, sometimes requiring intubation, attributed to this disease in infants.

PHYSICAL FINDINGS & CLINICAL PRESENTATION

- Nonexudative pharyngitis (common).
- Headache, otalgia common.
- Fever may be mild or not present.
- Rhonchi or rales without evidence of consolidation (common) in lower lung zones.
- Associated with bullous myringitis (nonspecific finding; perhaps no more frequently than in other pneumonias).
- Skin rashes in up to one fourth of patients
  1. Morbilliform.
  2. Urticaria.
  3. Erythema nodosum (unusual).
  4. Erythema multiforme (unusual).
  5. Stevens-Johnson syndrome (rare).
- Muscle tenderness (<50% of the patients).
- On examination (and confirmed with testing):
  1. Mononeuritis or polyneuritis.
  2. Transverse myelitis.
  3. Cranial nerve palsies.
  4. Meningoencephalitis.
- Lymphadenopathy and splenomegaly.
- Conjunctivitis.
- Table 1P-26 summarizes the clinical manifestations of *Mycoplasma pneumoniae*.

ETIOLOGY

Infection is spread person-to-person via respiratory droplets or secretions with an incubation period of 1 to 4 wk.

DIAGNOSIS

DIFFERENTIAL DIAGNOSIS

- *Chlamydia* (now known as *Chlamydophila*) *pneumoniae*.
- *Chlamydophila psittaci*.
- *Legionella* spp.
- *Coxiella burnetii*.
- Several viral agents.
- Q fever.
- *Streptococcus pneumoniae*.
- Pulmonary embolism or infarction.

WORKUP

- Chest x-ray.
- Thorough history and physical examination.

- Laboratory tests.
- Evaluation guided by symptoms and findings.

LABORATORY TESTS

- White blood cells (WBCs):
  1. WBC count >10,000/mm^3 in approximately one fourth of patients.
  2. Differential count nonspecific.
  3. Leukopenia rare.
- Cold agglutinins:
  1. Detected in approximately half of the patients.
  2. Also may be found in:
     a. Lymphoproliferative diseases.
     b. Influenza.
     c. Mononucleosis.
     d. Adenovirus infections.
     e. Occasionally, Legionnaires' disease.
  3. Titers typically >1:64.
     a. May be detectable with bedside testing.
     b. Appear between days 5 and 10 of the illness (so may be demonstrable when patient is first examined) and disappear within 1 mo.
- Complement fixation testing assay specific for mycoplasma antigens of paired sera (fourfold rise) or a single titer ≥1:32 in patients with pneumonia and a compatible history:
  1. Considered diagnostic in the appropriate clinical setting.
  2. Other assays include ELISA, antigen capture-enzyme immunoassay, and PCR.
- Culture of the organism from specimens.
  1. Only truly specific test for infection.
  2. Technically difficult and done reliably by few laboratories.
  3. May require weeks to get results.
- Sputum
  1. Often no sputum produced for laboratory testing.
  2. When present, Gram-stained specimens show polymorphonuclear cells without organisms.
- Infection occasionally complicated by pancreatitis or glomerulitis.
- Disseminated intravascular coagulation is a rare complication.
- Electrocardiographic evidence of pericarditis or myocarditis may be present.

IMAGING STUDIES

- Predilection for lower lobe involvement (upper lobes involved in less than a fourth), with radiographic abnormalities frequently out of proportion to those on physical examination (Fig. 1P-61).
- Small pleural effusions in approximately 30% of patients.
- Large effusions: rare.
- Infiltrates: patchy, unilateral, and with a segmental distribution, although multilobar involvement may be seen.
- Evidence of hilar adenopathy on chest radiographs in 20% to 25%.
- Rare cases reported:
  1. Associated lung abscess.
  2. Residual pneumatoceles.

TABLE 1P-26 Clinical Manifestations of *Mycoplasma Pneumoniae* Infection

Respiratory tract	Pharyngitis, laryngitis, acute bronchitis, bronchopneumonia
Skin and mucosa	Maculopapular and vesicular exanthema, urticaria, purpura, erythema nodosum, erythema multiforme, Stevens-Johnson syndrome
Central nervous system	Meningitis, meningoencephalitis, acute psychosis, cerebellitis, Guillain-Barré syndrome?
Parenchymatous organs	Pancreatitis, diabetes mellitus, nonspecific reactive hepatitis, subacute thyroiditis?
Miscellaneous	Hemorrhagic bullous myringitis, hemolytic anemia, pericarditis, thromboembolism?

Some association remains uncertain.
From Cohen J, Powderly WG: *Infectious diseases*, ed 2, St Louis, 2004, Mosby.

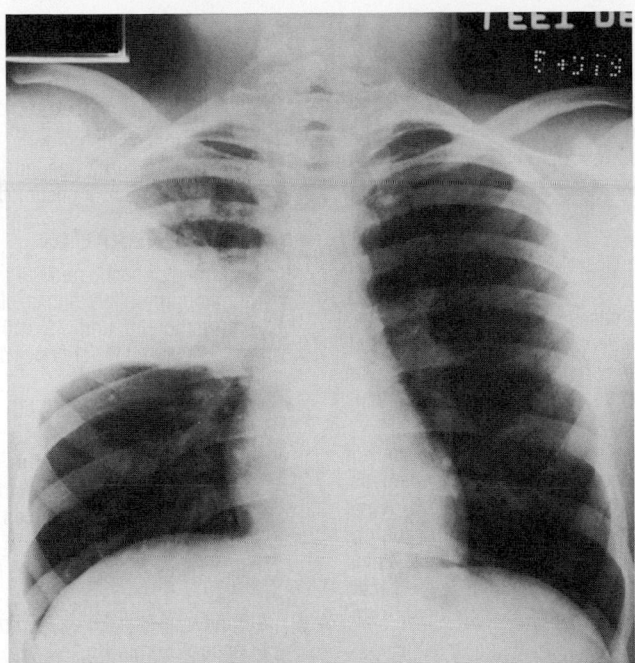

FIGURE 1P-61 Localized airspace opacification resulting from *Mycoplasma pneumoniae*. (From Specht N [ed]: *Practical guide to diagnostic imaging,* St Louis, 1998, Mosby.)

3. Lobar collapse.
4. Hyperlucent lung syndrome.

Rx TREATMENT

ACUTE GENERAL Rx

- Therapy: azithromycin 500 mg qd × 3 or 500 mg initially, then 250 mg daily for 4 days for adults. For children: 10 mg/kg in one dose on first day, then 5 mg/kg in one dose for 4 days or clarithromycin: 500 mg bid for 10 days in adults, 15 mg/kg per day in two divided doses for 10 days in children. Alternatives include erythromycin (500 mg qid) for adults or 30 to 40 mg/kg per day in four divided doses in children or doxycycline: 2 to 4 mg/kg per day in one or two divided doses for 10 days, maximum daily dose: 100 to 200 mg, but this agent cannot be used in young children or women of childbearing age. Respiratory fluoroquinolones such as Levaquin or moxifloxacin are alternative agents for treatment in adults but should not be used in young children.
- Therapy shortens the duration and severity of symptoms and may hasten radiographic clearing, but the disease is self-limiting.

CHRONIC Rx

- Effective antimicrobial therapy does not eliminate the organism from the respiratory secretions, which may be positive for weeks.
- Serum antibody response does not necessarily provide lifelong immunity.
- Chronic symptoms do not occur, although clinical relapses may occur 7 to 10 days after the initial response and may be associated with new areas of infiltration.

DISPOSITION

- Clinical improvement is almost universal within 10 days.
- Infiltrates generally clear within 5 to 8 wk.
- Rare deaths are likely attributable to underlying medical diseases.
- Person-to-person spread can be minimized by avoiding open coughing, especially in enclosed areas.

REFERRAL

- Not responding to treatment.
- Severe infection.
- Severe extrapulmonary manifestations.
- Multilobe involvement accompanied by respiratory embarrassment (very rare).

⊘ PEARLS & CONSIDERATIONS

COMMENTS

X-ray resolution complete by 8 wk in approximately 90% of patients.

SUGGESTED READINGS

Available at www.expertconsult.com

RELATED CONTENT

Mycoplasma Pneumonia (Patient Information)

AUTHOR: **GLENN G. FORT, M.D., M.P.H.**

BASIC INFORMATION

DEFINITION

Pneumocystis jiroveci pneumonia (PJP) is a serious respiratory infection caused by the fungal pathogen *P. jiroveci* (formerly known as *P. carinii*).

SYNONYMS

PCP
PJP

ICD-10CM CODES
B59 Pneumocystosis

EPIDEMIOLOGY & DEMOGRAPHICS

INCIDENCE (IN U.S.):
- Seen primarily in the setting of acquired immunodeficiency syndrome (AIDS).
- Approximately 95% of cases occur in HIV infected individuals with CD4 counts <200/mm³.
- Also seen in other immunocompromised patients with severe cell-mediated immune deficiency (congenital T-cell deficiency, acute leukemia, lymphoma, bone marrow or organ transplant deficiency).
- May be associated with glucocorticoid use (usually higher than 20 mg/day).
- Rituximab use has been associated with PJP in HIV-negative patients, most of whom had hematologic cancers.

PEAK INCIDENCE: Age 20 to 40 years (parallel to AIDS epidemic).
PREDOMINANT SEX: Equal incidence when adjusted for HIV status.
PREDOMINANT AGE:
- 20 to 40 years
GENETICS: Neonatal infection:
- Most frequent opportunistic infection among HIV-infected children, occurring in approximately 30%.
- Neonatal occurrence unusual.

PHYSICAL FINDINGS & CLINICAL PRESENTATION

- Fever, cough, shortness of breath present in almost all cases. May be subacute or insidious.
- Lungs frequently clear to auscultation, although rales occasionally present.
- Cyanosis and pronounced tachypnea in severe cases.
- Hemoptysis unusual.
- Spontaneous pneumothorax.

ETIOLOGY

- *P. jiroveci* (formerly *P. carinii*) recently reclassified as a fungal organism (previously classified as a protozoan) (Fig. E1P-62).
- Reactivation of dormant infection.
- Extrapulmonary involvement rare but possible.

DIAGNOSIS

DIFFERENTIAL DIAGNOSIS

- Other opportunistic respiratory infections:
  1. Tuberculosis
  2. Histoplasmosis
  3. Cryptococcosis

- Nonopportunistic infections:
  1. Bacterial pneumonia
  2. Viral pneumonia
  3. Mycoplasmal pneumonia
  4. Legionellosis
- Occurs almost exclusively in the setting of profound depression of cellular immunity.

WORKUP

- Chest x-ray (Fig. 1P-63) or chest CT (Fig. 1P-64).
- Arterial blood gases.
- Because *Pneumocystis* cannot be cultured, diagnosis relies on detection of the organism by colorimetric or immunofluorescent stains or PCR.
- Cannot be cultured. Sputum examination for cysts of PJP and to exclude other pathogens.
- Bronchoscopy with bronchoalveolar lavage or lung biopsy for diagnosis if sputum examination is negative or equivocal. Stains such as Gomori methenamine silver stain or toluidine blue O are used to identify the organism.
- Fig. E1P-65 describes an algorithm for the diagnostic evaluation and management of patients with suspected *Pneumocystis* pneumonia.

LABORATORY TESTS

- Arterial blood gas monitoring.
- Elevated lactate dehydrogenase in majority of cases.
- HIV antibody test and CD4 cell count if cause of underlying immune deficiency state is unclear.
- Beta-D-glucan testing may be positive (92% sensitivity, 86% specificity).

IMAGING STUDIES

- PJP may appear as diffuse, unilateral, bilateral, or interstitial infiltrates on chest x-ray or CT. Imaging may be normal in up to one quarter of individuals. Pneumothoraces may also occur.

TREATMENT

NONPHARMACOLOGIC THERAPY

- Supplemental oxygen.
- Ventilatory support if needed.
- Prompt thoracotomy if pneumothorax develops.

ACUTE GENERAL Rx

For confirmed or suspected PJP:
- Trimethoprim-sulfamethoxazole (15-20 mg/kg trimethoprim and 75-100 mg/kg sulfamethoxazole qd) PO or IV per day divided and given q6 to 8h.
- Pentamidine (4 mg/kg IV qd) (severe cases with a contraindication to trimethoprim/sulfamethoxazole). Careful monitoring is required, can cause nephrotoxicity, numerous electrolyte disturbances, and cardiac arrhythmias.
- Either regimen with prednisone (40 mg PO bid):
  1. If arterial oxygen pressure <70 mm Hg.
  2. If arterial-alveolar oxygen pressure difference >35 mm Hg.
  3. Dose tapered to 20 mg bid after 5 days and 20 mg qd after 10 days.
- Therapy continued for 3 weeks.
- Alternative therapies available for patients unable to tolerate conventional therapy:
  1. Dapsone/trimethoprim
  2. Clindamycin/primaquine
  3. Atovaquone
- Table 1P-27 summarizes causes of deterioration in an HIV-infected patient receiving treatment for PJP.

CHRONIC Rx

- After completion of therapy, prophylaxis should be maintained with trimethoprim-sulfamethoxazole (one single-strength tablet PO qd or double-strength three times weekly) until the CD4 cell count is >200 for three months.

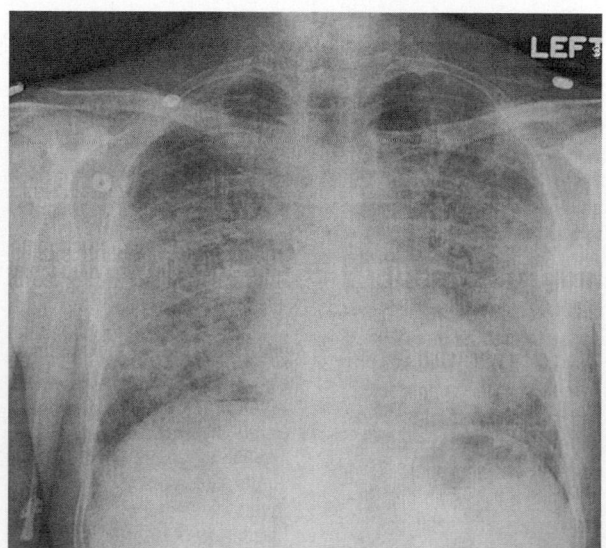

FIGURE 1P-63 Chest radiograph showing diffuse interstitial infiltrate in a patient with *Pneumocystis jiroveci* pneumonia. (From Firestein GS et al [eds]: *Kelly's textbook of rheumatology,* ed 9, Philadelphia, 2013, Saunders.)

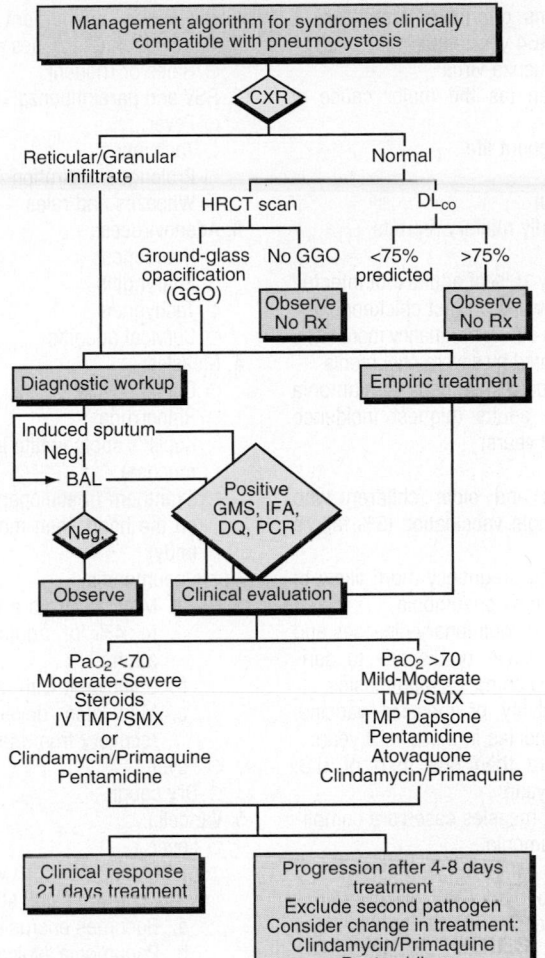

• Patients intolerant of this therapy should be treated with dapsone (100 mg PO qd) or atovaquone (1500 mg PO qd).
• Inhaled pentamidine (300 mg monthly by standardized nebulizer) is less effective and is reserved for patients intolerant to other forms of prophylaxis.

DISPOSITION

After completion of therapy, long-term ambulatory follow-up is mandatory to provide secondary prevention of PJP (see "Chronic Rx" previously) and management of the underlying immunodeficiency syndrome.

REFERRAL

• To pulmonologist for bronchoscopy if diagnosis cannot be confirmed by sputum examination.
• To an infectious disease specialist if case is severe or difficult to manage.

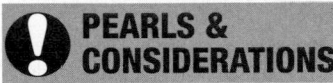

PEARLS & CONSIDERATIONS

COMMENTS

• All patients, especially those with severe infection or intolerant of conventional therapy, should be followed by a physician experienced in the management of PJP and, if appropriate, in the long-term management of HIV infection or other underlying disease.
• Severe and life-threatening hypoglycemia may occur 1 or 2 weeks after start of IV pentamidine. Monitor closely and advise the patient of symptoms of hypoglycemia.

SUGGESTED READINGS

Available at www.expertconsult.com

RELATED CONTENT

Pneumocystis Pneumonia (Patient Information)

AUTHOR: **PHILIP A. CHAN, M.D., M.S.**

FIGURE 1P-65 Algorithm for the diagnostic evaluation and management of patients with suspected *Pneumocystis* pneumonia. *BAL*, Bronchoalveolar lavage; *CXR*, chest x-ray; *DL_{CO}*, single-breath diffusing capacity for carbon monoxide; *DQ*, Diff-Quik (stain); *GGO*, ground-glass opacities; *GMS*, Gomori methenamine silver (stain); *HRCT*, high-resolution computed tomography; *IFA*, immunofluorescent antibody (stain); *IV*, intravenous; *PCR*, polymerase chain reaction, *Rx*, treatment; *TMP/SMX*, trimethoprim-sulfamethoxazole. (Bennett et al: *Mandell, Douglas, and Bennett's principles and practice of infectious diseases*, ed 8, Philadelphia, 2015, WB Saunders.)

TABLE 1P-27 Causes of Deterioration in an HIV-Infected Person Receiving Treatment for PJP

Etiology	Explanation
Severe Progressive PCP	
Iatrogenic	Pulmonary edema due to IV fluid overload when giving TMP-SMX IRIS following early initiation of ART
Side effects of therapy	Anemia (e.g., caused by TMP-SMX), methemoglobinemia (e.g., caused by dapsone, primaquine)
Inadequate therapy	Incorrect dosage or route of administration Adjuvant glucocorticoids not given for treatment of moderate or severe PCP
Postbronchoscopy	Sedation Pneumothorax
Pneumothorax	Spontaneous Associated with intubation and positive pressure ventilation
Copathology in lung	Bacterial infection Pulmonary Kaposi sarcoma Intercurrent pulmonary embolism
Wrong diagnosis	Empiric diagnosis of PCP, and correct diagnosis is another pathology (e.g., bacterial pneumonia)

ART, Antiretroviral therapy; *HIV*, human immunodeficiency virus; *IRIS*, immune reconstitution inflammatory syndrome; *IV*, intravenous; *PJP*, *Pneumocystis jiroveci* pneumonia; *TMP-SMX*, trimethoprim-sulfamethoxazole.(Bennett JE et al: *Mandell, Douglas, and Bennett's principles and practice of infectious diseases*, ed 8, Philadelphia, 2015, WB Saunders.)

Diseases and Disorders

 BASIC INFORMATION

DEFINITION

Viral pneumonia is infection of the pulmonary parenchyma caused by any of a large number of viral agents. The most important viruses are discussed.

SYNONYMS

Viral pneumonia
Nonbacterial pneumonia
Atypical pneumonia

ICD-10CM CODES
J12.9   Viral pneumonia, unspecified
J12.89 Other viral pneumonia

EPIDEMIOLOGY & DEMOGRAPHICS

INCIDENCE (IN U.S.):
- Influenza virus:
  1. 10% to 20% of population in temperate zones infected during 1 to 2 month epidemics occurring yearly during winter months.
  2. Up to 50% infected during pandemics.
  3. Secondary bacterial pneumonia develops in small percentage of infected persons.
- Incidence of other important viral pathogens that cause pneumonias is not known precisely.

PEAK INCIDENCE:
- Influenza:
  1. Winter months for influenza A
  2. Year round for influenza B
  3. Peak of pneumonia seen weeks into the outbreak of infection
- Respiratory syncytial virus (RSV) and parainfluenza virus:
  1. Winter and spring
- Adenovirus:
  1. Endemic (miliary)
- Varicella:
  1. Spring in temperate zones
- Measles:
  1. Year round
- Cytomegalovirus (CMV):
  1. Year round

PREVALENCE (IN U.S.):
- Often related to immune status of the population or presence of an epidemic
- Normal hosts (estimates):
  1. 86% of cases of pneumonia resulting in hospitalization in American adults
  2. 16% of pediatric pneumonias managed as outpatients
  3. 49% of hospitalized infants with pneumonia
- Important problem in hosts with impaired immunity

PREDOMINANT SEX:
- None generally
- Male sex may predispose to more severe respiratory disease in RSV infection

PREDOMINANT AGE:
- Influenza:
  1. Overall incidence greatest at age 5 years
  2. Lower with increasing age
  3. The most serious sequelae in those with chronic medical illnesses, especially cardiopulmonary disease
  4. Hospitalizations greatest in infants and adults aged >64 years
- RSV and parainfluenza virus:
  1. Young children (as the major cause of pneumonia)
  2. Occurs throughout life
- Adenoviruses:
  1. Young children
  2. Adults, primarily military recruits
- Varicella:
  1. Approximately 16% of adults (not infected in childhood) who contract chickenpox
  2. Acute varicella during pregnancy more likely to be complicated by severe pneumonia
  3. 90% of reported varicella pneumonia cases are in adults (highest incidence ages 20 to 60 years)
- Measles:
  1. Young adults and older children who received a single vaccination (5% failure rate)
  2. Measles during pregnancy more likely to be complicated by pneumonia
  3. Underlying cardiopulmonary diseases and immunosuppression predispose to serious pneumonia complicating measles
  4. Before availability of measles vaccine, 90% of pneumonias in those <10 years
  5. Currently more than one third of U.S. patients >14 years
  6. 3% to 50% of measles cases are complicated by pneumonia
- CMV:
  1. Neonatal through adult
  2. Immunosuppression is key predisposing factor

GENETICS: Familial disposition:
- Close contact, not genetics, is important in acquisition
- Congenital anomalies and immunosuppression worsen course of RSV pneumonia
Congenital infection:
- CMV is the most common intrauterine infection in the U.S.
- Pneumonia occurs occasionally in infants with symptomatic congenital infection.
Neonatal infection:
- Severe RSV pneumonia
- Adenovirus pneumonia
  1. 5% to 20% mortality rate
  2. Can lead to residual restrictive or obstructive functional abnormalities
- "Varicella neonatorum"
  1. Disseminated visceral disease including pneumonia
  2. May develop in neonates whose mothers develop peripartum chickenpox
- CMV pneumonia
  1. Generally fatal
  2. Associated with severe cerebral damage in this population

PHYSICAL FINDINGS & CLINICAL PRESENTATION

1. Influenza:
   - Fever, cough, or sore throat (referred to as influenza-like illness [ILI])
   - Uncomfortable or lethargic appearance
   - Prominent dry cough (rarely hemoptysis)
   - Flushed integument and erythematous mucous membranes
   - Rales or rhonchi
2. RSV and parainfluenza:
   - Fever
   - Tachypnea
   - Prolonged expiration
   - Wheezes and rales
3. Adenoviruses:
   - Hoarseness
   - Pharyngitis
   - Tachypnea
   - Cervical adenitis
4. Measles:
   - Conjunctivitis
   - Rhinorrhea
   - Koplik's spots (white lesions on the buccal mucosa)
   - Exanthem (maculopapular rash that starts on the head, then moves down to rest of body)
   - Pneumonitis
     a. May occur as a complication in 3% to 4% of adolescents and young adults
     b. Coincident with rash
     c. May also develop after apparent recovery from measles
   - Fever
   - Dry cough
5. Varicella:
   - Fever
   - Maculopapular or vesicular rash (all lesions at the same stage)
     a. Becomes encrusted
     b. Pneumonia typical 1 to 6 days after rash appears
     c. Pneumonia (Fig. E1P-66) accompanied by cough and occasionally hemoptysis
   - Few auscultatory abnormalities noted on examination of the lungs
6. CMV:
   - Fever
   - Paroxysmal cough
   - Occasional hemoptysis
   - Diffuse adenopathy when pneumonia occurs after transfusion

ETIOLOGY

Viral infection can lead to pneumonia in both immunocompetent and immunocompromised hosts.

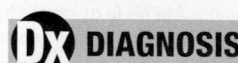 DIAGNOSIS

DIFFERENTIAL DIAGNOSIS

- Bacterial pneumonia, which frequently complicates (i.e., can follow or be simultaneous with) viral pneumonia
- Other causes of atypical pneumonia:
  1. *Mycoplasma* spp.
  2. *Chlamydia* spp.
  3. *Coxiella* spp.
  4. Legionnaires' disease
- Acute respiratory distress syndrome (ARDS)
- Physical findings and associated hypoxemia confused with pulmonary emboli

WORKUP

- Information about the current prevalent strain of influenza virus can be obtained from local health departments or from the Centers for Disease Control and Prevention.
- Influenza and other viruses may be cultured from respiratory secretions during the initial few days of the illness (special media and techniques necessary).
- Respiratory viral panels that use PCR-based assays to test for a variety of viruses are extremely sensitive and are becoming the test of choice.
- Rapid flu tests have a 50% sensitivity in diagnosing influenza (a negative test does not mean the patient does not have influenza).
- Measles and adenovirus pneumonia are usually diagnosed clinically and can be confirmed with serology.
- CMV may be grown in culture or PCR amplified from bronchoalveolar lavage samples. An algorithm for the workup and management of suspected severe influenza pneumonia in the critical care unit is described in Fig. E1P-67. Open lung biopsy is required for a definite diagnosis of CMV pneumonia.

LABORATORY TESTS

- Sputum Gram stain (usually produced in scanty amounts) typically shows few polymorphonuclear leukocytes and few bacteria.
- White blood cell count may vary from leukopenic to modest elevation, usually without a leftward shift.
- Disseminated intravascular coagulation occasionally complicates adenovirus type 7 pneumonia.
- Multinucleated giant cells on Tzanck preparation of an unroofed vesicular lesion are useful in diagnosing varicella in a patient with an infiltrate (also found in herpes simplex).
- Severe immunosuppression is associated with symptomatic CMV pneumonia (usually reactivation of latent infection or in previously seronegative recipients from the donor).
- Hypoxemia may be profound.
- Cultures may be helpful in identifying superinfecting bacterial pathogens.
- When they occur, parapneumonic pleural effusions are exudative.

IMAGING STUDIES

- Chest radiographs may demonstrate a spectrum of findings from ill-defined, patchy, or generalized interstitial infiltrates, which can be associated with ARDS.
- A localized dense alveolar infiltrate suggests a superimposed bacterial pneumonia.
- Small calcified nodules may develop as a radiographic residual of varicella pneumonia.

 **TREATMENT**

NONPHARMACOLOGIC THERAPY

General:
- Measures to diminish person-to-person transmission
- Modified bed rest

- Maintenance of adequate hydration
- Possible ventilatory support for severe pneumonia or ARDS

Influenza:
- Yearly prophylactic strain-specific influenza vaccination (only subvirion vaccine should be used in children <13 years) can be given to prevent infection.
- Live, attenuated influenza vaccines administered by nose drops as effective as injected inactivated viral vaccines.

RSV:
- Isolation techniques are important in limiting spread of RSV infections.
- Immunoglobulins with a high RSV-neutralizing antibody titer are beneficial in treatment.

Adenoviruses:
- Intestinal inoculation of respiratory adenoviruses has been used to successfully immunize military recruits.
- Although they produce no disease in recipients, the viruses may be shed chronically and may infect others at a later date.
- These vaccines are not available for civilian populations.

Varicella:
- Live, attenuated varicella vaccine has been successfully used in clinical trials.
- Varicella-zoster immune globulin should be administered within 4 days of exposure to prevent or modify the disease in susceptible persons.
- Nonimmunized persons exposed to varicella are potentially infectious between 10 and 21 days after exposure.

Measles:
- Effective measles vaccine is available.
  1. The vaccine should be administered at age 15 months.
  2. A second dose should be administered at the time of school entry.
- Live, attenuated vaccine or gamma-globulin can prevent measles in unvaccinated persons if administered early after exposure.
- Vitamin A given PO for 2 days reduces morbidity and mortality rates from measles in exposed children.

Severe acute respiratory syndrome (SARS)-associated coronaviruses:
- No vaccine currently available.
- Supportive care: ribavirin ineffective, use of steroids or interferon-alpha of unclear value.

ACUTE GENERAL Rx

- **General:** Administer appropriate antibiotics for bacterial superinfections.
- **Influenza:**
  1. Amantadine and rimantadine for influenza A (not active against influenza B). Early use can speed recovery from small airway dysfunction, but whether it influences the development or course of pneumonia is uncertain.
  2. The neuraminidase inhibitors oseltamivir and zanamivir are effective if given in the first 48 hours of symptoms of influenza; their efficacy in established influenza pneumonia is unclear.
  3. Aerosolized ribavirin or amantadine may have a role in treating severe influenza pneumonia, but they have not been approved for this indication.
- **RSV and parainfluenza:**
  1. Ribavirin aerosol is effective for severe RSV pneumonia.
  2. There is no approved antiviral therapy for parainfluenza virus pneumonia.
- **Adenoviruses:** no effective agent; some case reports of cidofovir use but unproved.
- **Varicella:**
  1. Varicella pneumonia can be treated with IV acyclovir.
  2. Adults who develop chickenpox should be considered for acyclovir treatment, which may prevent the development of pneumonia.
- **Measles:** no effective antimeasles agent.
- **CMV:**
  1. Acyclovir can prevent CMV infection in renal transplant recipients.
  2. Ganciclovir and foscarnet, with or without CMV hyperimmune globulin, show promise in the treatment of serious CMV infection, including pneumonia, in compromised hosts.

DISPOSITION

- Supportive therapy is useful.
- Death is possible during acute illness.
- Residual functional abnormalities may be persistent or develop into or predispose to chronic respiratory diseases in later life.
- Morbidity and mortality rates after most viral pneumonias are increased by bacterial superinfection.

REFERRAL

- Uncertainty about the diagnosis in a compromised host.
- Symptoms or findings are progressive.
- Severe respiratory compromise, diffuse infiltrates, or the development of ARDS.

PEARLS & CONSIDERATIONS

COMMENTS

- Influenza spreads by close contact and by small droplets transmitted by cough.
- RSV is effectively transmitted by fomites and by direct contact (little by aerosol).
- Varicella is transmitted by direct contact or by aerosol.
- Of the three major forms of parainfluenza viruses (types 1 to 3), type 3 is the most common cause of viral pneumonia; types 1 and 2 primarily cause laryngotracheitis.
- Recent evidence indicates that a newly discovered virus known as metapneumovirus is a common cause of upper respiratory infections worldwide; this virus can cause pneumonia.

SUGGESTED READINGS
Available at www.expertconsult.com

RELATED CONTENT
Legionnaires' Disease (Patient Information)
Viral Pneumonia (Patient Information)

AUTHOR: **PHILIP A. CHAN, M.D., M.S.**

Diseases and Disorders

P

 BASIC INFORMATION

DEFINITION

A spontaneous pneumothorax (SP) is defined as air in the pleural space, collapsing the lung without a precipitating event. This can be primary SP (otherwise healthy people without any obvious underlying lung disease) or secondary SP (with underlying lung disease).

SYNONYMS

Primary spontaneous pneumothorax
Secondary spontaneous pneumothorax

ICD-10CM CODES

J93.0	Spontaneous tension pneumothorax
J93.11	Primary spontaneous pneumothorax
J93.12	Secondary spontaneous pneumothorax
J93.81	Chronic pneumothorax
J93.83	Other pneumothorax
J93.9	Pneumothorax, unspecified
J95.811	Postprocedural pneumothorax
P25.1	Pneumothorax originating in the perinatal period
S27.0XXA	Traumatic pneumothorax, initial encounter
S27.0XXD	Traumatic pneumothorax, subsequent encounter
S27.0XXS	Traumatic pneumothorax, sequela

EPIDEMIOLOGY & DEMOGRAPHICS

- Approximately 20,000 new cases of SP occur each year in the United States.
- SP is more common in men than women (6:1).
- Incidence of primary SP is 7.4 per 100,000 in men and 1.2 per 100,000 in women.

- Incidence of secondary SP is 6.3 per 100,000 in men and 2.0 per 100,000 in women.
- SP is commonly seen in tall, thin young men aged 20 to 40 yr.
- Risk factors include smoking, family history, Marfan's syndrome, homocystinuria, and thoracic endometriosis.
- Anorexia nervosa is thought to be a risk factor due to pulmonary parenchymal consequences of malnutrition.

PHYSICAL FINDINGS & CLINICAL PRESENTATION

- Sudden onset of pleuritic chest pain (90%), usually at rest and no relationship between the onset of pneumothorax and physical activity, which often becomes dull after a few hours.
- Pain is usually unilateral and can be sharp and agonizing and associated with considerable apprehension.
- Dyspnea (80%), which often resolves within 24 hr, despite persistence of pneumothorax.
- Cough (10%).
- Asymptomatic (5%); may take up to 7 days to come to medical attention.
- Tachycardia.
- Hypoxemia.
- Hypercapnia is rare because the alveolar ventilation is maintained by the contralateral lung.
- Decreased chest excursion on the affected side.
- Diminished breath sounds.
- Subcutaneous emphysema may be present.
- Hyperresonance on percussion.

ETIOLOGY

- In primary SP, rupture of small blebs and bullae, usually located near the apex of the upper lobes, is a common cause.

- In secondary SP, chronic obstructive pulmonary disease is the most common cause, but it can also be associated with pneumonia, bronchogenic carcinoma, mesothelioma, sarcoidosis, tuberculosis, cystic fibrosis, and many other lung diseases (Fig. 1P-68).

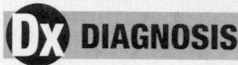 **DIAGNOSIS**

Established by the chest x-ray (Fig. 1P-69).

DIFFERENTIAL DIAGNOSIS

- Pleurisy.
- Pulmonary embolism.
- Myocardial infarction.
- Pericarditis.
- Asthma.
- Pneumonia.

WORKUP

CXR

LABORATORY TESTS

Arterial blood gases may show hypoxemia and hypocapnia as a result of hyperventilation.

IMAGING STUDIES

- SP is usually confirmed by upright CXR:
  1. A white visceral pleural line. The absence of vessel markings peripheral to this line helps differentiate from mimicking conditions such as an overlying skin fold. A lateral width of 1 cm corresponds to 27% pneumothorax, and 2 cm occupies 49% of the hemithorax.
  2. The left lateral decubitus position is the most sensitive and the supine position the least sensitive. Inspiratory and expiratory films have equal sensitivities.
  3. As little as 50 mL of air can be detected on upright film.

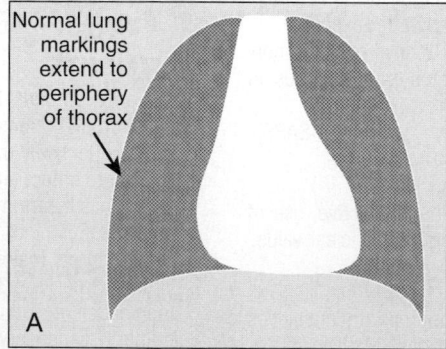
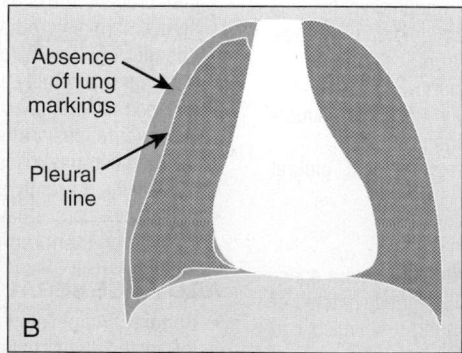

FIGURE 1P-68 Pneumothorax. A, Schematic of normal lung. **B,** Schematic of pneumothorax. Pneumothoraces can range in size from tiny to massive. Because of the variability in their size and location, pneumothoraces can be difficult to detect on chest x-ray. For example, a pneumothorax that is anterior or posterior rather than lateral may be hidden on frontal chest x-ray, particularly one taken in the supine position. An upright chest x-ray should be obtained if possible. An expiratory film is thought to be more sensitive, because the lung and thorax decrease in size during expiration, but air trapped in the pleural space remains the same size and thus appears relatively larger. Subtle pneumothoraces may not be visible on chest x-ray. In some cases, subcutaneous air may be the only visible clue to underlying lung injury. CT is extremely sensitive for pneumothorax, although controversy remains over the proper management of pneumothoraces seen only on CT. Ultrasound is also thought to be more sensitive than chest x-ray for detection of pneumothorax, although, again, the management of pneumothorax seen only on ultrasound is uncertain because this is a relatively newly described method of detection. The chest x-ray findings of pneumothorax include a lack of the normal lung markings, which should be visible to the periphery of the chest wall. Sometimes a line marking the boundary of the lung and visceral pleura is visible, although this can be confused with ribs and with the medial margin of the scapula. Depending on the degree of pneumothorax and lung collapse, the lung parenchyma may appear denser than the opposite side. In extreme cases of tension pneumothorax, the pressure exerted by the air in the pleural space may begin to displace other structures, including the diaphragm and mediastinum. In tension pneumothorax, the hyperinflated hemithorax may also have abnormally positioned ribs, with a position more horizontal than usual. (From Broder JS: *Diagnostic imaging for the emergency physician,* Philadelphia, 2011, Saunders.)

- Tension pneumothorax (Fig. 1P-70) is a medical emergency and should be suspected when the patient is hemodynamically unstable or with contralateral tracheal and mediastinal deviation and ipsilateral flattening or inversion of the diaphragm on the CXR (Fig. E1P-71).

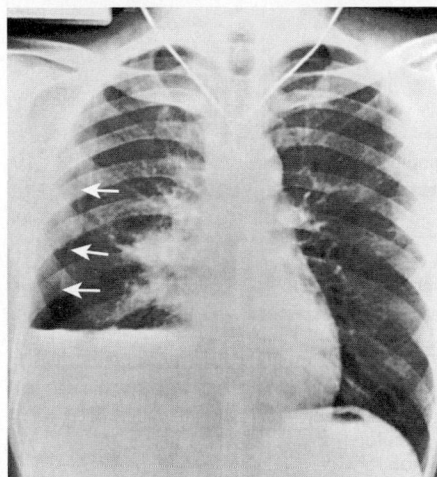

FIGURE 1P-69 Chest radiograph shows right hydropneumothorax. Horizontal line in lower right hemithorax is interface between air and liquid in pleural space. *Arrows* point to visceral pleura above level of effusion. There is air in pleural space between visceral pleura and chest wall. (From Weinberg SE et al: *Principles of pulmonary medicine,* ed 5, Philadelphia, 2008, Saunders.)

- CT scan is considered acceptable for a patient with recurrent pneumothorax or persistent air leak, and for planning surgery.

Rx TREATMENT

INITIAL MANAGEMENT

- 100% oxygen administration reduces the partial pressure of nitrogen in pleural capillaries, consequently quadrupling the rate of pneumothorax absorption, and should be administered to all patients with pneumothorax.
- Further treatment is based on the size of the pneumothorax.
  1. If the pneumothorax is small (<2 cm between lung and chest wall on CXR) and the patient is asymptomatic, the patient can be treated with observation alone. Repeat imaging should be performed to ensure stability/resorption of the pneumothorax.
  2. If the pneumothorax is large (>2 cm), or if the patient is symptomatic with chest pain and dyspnea, initial management should focus on removing air from the pleural space. Needle aspiration is the treatment of choice in the clinically stable patient.
- Needle aspiration can be done at the bedside using a large-bore angiocatheter needle or commercially available catheter aspiration kit. The needle is introduced in the second intercostal space midclavicular line. The catheter is left in place and attached to a three-way stopcock and a large syringe. Air is aspirated until resistance is met or the patient experiences significant coughing. Repeat CXR is done immediately after aspiration and again in 4 to 24 hr to document reexpansion of the lung. If the pneumothorax fails to resolve with aspiration, repeated aspiration is reasonable for primary spontaneous pneumothorax.
- If there is improvement but not complete resolution of pneumothorax after the aspiration, the catheter can be attached to a Heimlich (one-way) valve to allow further lung expansion. Some stable patients can be discharged home with this device in place if close follow-up monitoring can be obtained. Chest tube insertion has been recommended for patients with primary SP who are unsuccessful in controlling symptoms by simple aspiration or catheter aspiration. Most patients can be managed with small chest tubes (<12 Fr). The chest tube can be connected to a water seal device, with or without suction, and left in position until the pneumothorax has resolved.
- An algorithmic approach to the treatment of primary spontaneous pneumothorax is outlined in Fig. 1P-72.

PREVENTION

- Approximately 25% to 50% of patients with primary SP with have a recurrence within 1 yr.
- Prevention of spontaneous pneumothorax is surgical intervention or instillation of sclerosing agents through a chest tube.
- Indication for the surgical intervention is second ipsilateral SP, first contralateral SP, simultaneous bilateral SP, persistent air leak (>5-7 days), failure of lung reexpansion by the chest tube, and professions at risk (e.g., pilots, divers).
- The current recommended surgical approach is the use of video-assisted thoracoscopy (VATS) with bullectomy and pleurodesis. Surgical chemical pleurodesis is best achieved with sterile talc. The overall recurrence rate is estimated at <5% after VATS.
- Instillation of a sclerosing agent through a chest tube: doxycycline and talc slurry are the preferred agents; minocycline is considered to be an acceptable agent. The recurrence rates for the instillation of sclerosing agents (minocycline 5 mg/kg in 50 ml of normal saline or doxycycline 500 mg in 50 ml of normal saline) are higher than for VATS-guided therapy (<25%). Therefore this mode of therapy should be reserved for patients who are poor surgical candidates.

DISPOSITION

- Smoking cessation should be advised.
- Death from primary SP is uncommon. In patients with secondary SP and chronic obstructive pulmonary disease, mortality rates range from 1% to 16%.

FIGURE 1P-70 Tension pneumothorax. On this PA chest radiograph, the left hemithorax is very dark or lucent because the left lung has collapsed completely *(white arrows)*. The tension pneumothorax can be identified by the fact that the mediastinal contents, including the heart, are shifted toward the right *(black arrows)*, and the left hemidiaphragm is flattened and depressed. (From Mettler FA et al: *Primary care radiology,* Philadelphia, 2000, Elsevier.)

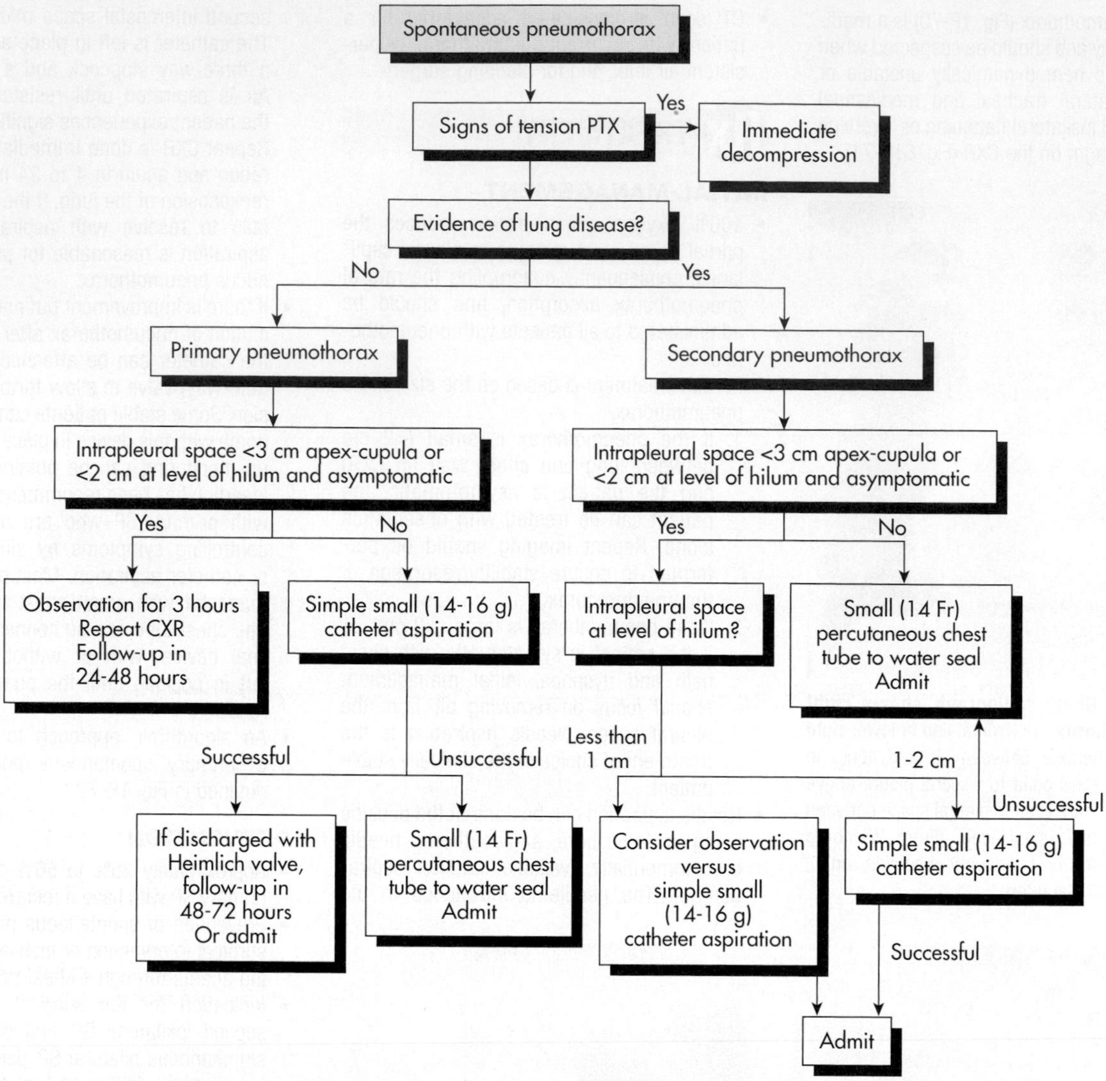

Spontaneous pneumothorax

↓

Signs of tension PTX → **Yes** → Immediate decompression

↓

Evidence of lung disease?

No ← → **Yes**

Primary pneumothorax | Secondary pneumothorax

Intrapleural space <3 cm apex-cupula or <2 cm at level of hilum and asymptomatic | Intrapleural space <3 cm apex-cupula or <2 cm at level of hilum and asymptomatic

Yes — **No** | **Yes** — **No**

Observation for 3 hours Repeat CXR Follow-up in 24-48 hours | Simple small (14-16 g) catheter aspiration | Intrapleural space at level of hilum? | Small (14 Fr) percutaneous chest tube to water seal Admit

Successful — **Unsuccessful** | **Less than 1 cm** — **1-2 cm**

If discharged with Heimlich valve, follow-up in 48-72 hours Or admit | Small (14 Fr) percutaneous chest tube to water seal Admit | Consider observation versus simple small (14-16 g) catheter aspiration | Simple small (14-16 g) catheter aspiration

Unsuccessful

Successful

Admit

FIGURE 1P-72 Algorithmic approach to the treatment of primary spontaneous pneumothorax. *CXR,* Chest radiograph. (From Adams JG et al: *Emergency medicine: clinical essentials,* ed 2, Philadelphia, 2013, Elsevier.)

REFERRAL

A pulmonary specialist and surgical consultation are recommended.

⚠ PEARLS & CONSIDERATIONS

- The rate of pleural air absorption is approximately 1.25% of the volume of the hemithorax per day. Therefore the interval for complete resolution of pneumothorax with observation can be estimated.
- Catamenial pneumothorax is a rare condition characterized by recurrent SP coinciding with the onset of menses. It usually affects the right lung and is believed to be caused by endometriosis with involvement of the diaphragm and/or pleura. It is believed to be hormonally related, and treatment is aimed at endometrial suppression.

COMMENTS

- Patients with AIDS and *Pneumocystis jiroveci* infection have a high incidence of SP. Treatment typically requires chest tube placement and either thoracoscopy or open thoracotomy.

EBM EVIDENCE

Available at www.expertconsult.com

SUGGESTED READINGS

Available at www.expertconsult.com

RELATED CONTENT

Pneumothorax (Patient Information)

AUTHOR: **HISASHI TSUKADA, M.D., Ph.D.**

P

 **BASIC INFORMATION**

DEFINITION

Poison ivy dermatitis is a contact dermatitis caused by exposure to urushiol, the oil of plants of the genus *Toxicodendron,* which includes poison ivy, poison oak, and poison sumac.

SYNONYMS

Rhus dermatitis
Toxicodendron dermatitis

ICD-10CM CODES
L23.7 Allergic contact dermatitis due to plants, except food

EPIDEMIOLOGY & DEMOGRAPHICS

INCIDENCE: Affects 10 million to 40 million Americans annually.
PEAK INCIDENCE: More frequent in months when outdoor activity is more common.
PREVALENCE: From 50% to 75% of the adult population is clinically sensitive to these plants. Sensitivity rates are lower in urban areas. (Tolerance is found in 10%-15% of the population.)
PREDOMINANT SEX AND AGE: Sensitization occurs most commonly between ages 8 and 14 yr. Sensitivity wanes with age, especially in individuals with limited exposure or prior mild reactions.
GENETICS: There is believed to be a genetic susceptibility to sensitivity; however, the rash occurs in all ethnicities and skin types.
RISK FACTORS: Firefighters, forestry workers, farmers, and outdoor workers in general as well as those who participate in outdoor recreation. These plants are indigenous to the United States, Canada, and Mexico, and cases are most common in these areas.

PHYSICAL FINDINGS & CLINICAL PRESENTATION

- Patients typically present with intense pruritus and rash. The patient may not be aware of exposure to the plant.
- Symptoms typically peak from 1 to 14 days after exposure depending on the degree of exposure and thickness of affected skin.
- Dermatitis may initially present as erythema and may develop into papules, vesicles, and bullae.
- Lesions may be found in the classic linear configuration, typically in exposed areas likely to have been in contact with plants (Fig. E1P-73). Atypical appearance or location of dermatitis is more common with secondary exposure, such as through pets or infected tools or clothing.
- Face and genital involvement may present with significant edema.
- Inhalation of urushiol aerosolized by fire can cause significant respiratory tract inflammation.

This can be a particular occupational hazard of forest firefighters.
- Postinflammatory hyperpigmentation may occur, more commonly in dark skin types. This usually resolves with treatment.

ETIOLOGY

- Initial contact with oil of plants in this genus, which is released with damage to plant parts, causes a classic T-lymphocyte–mediated delayed-type allergic reaction.
- Subsequent exposures cause a cell-mediated cytotoxic immune response.

 **DIAGNOSIS**

DIFFERENTIAL DIAGNOSIS

- Allergic contact dermatitis from other plants or nonplant substances.
- Irritant contact dermatitis.
- Nummular dermatitis.
- Arthropod reactions, including scabies and bedbug bites.

WORKUP

Typically not needed. Diagnosis is based on characteristic rash and possibly history of exposure.

Rx TREATMENT

Prevention is the most effective treatment.

NONPHARMACOLOGIC THERAPY

- After known exposure, patients should remove contaminated clothing and wash the skin gently with soap and water. Washing after appearance of dermatitis does not prevent further lesions.
- Calamine lotion, cool compresses, baking soda, or colloidal oatmeal baths may provide symptomatic relief.
- Keep nails short and clean to help prevent secondary bacterial infection.
- Exposed clothing, as well as tools, pets, and equipment, should be washed with soap and water to prevent secondary exposure.

ACUTE GENERAL Rx

- Topical steroids are generally not helpful. They may be effective for symptom management in mild, early cases with erythema and pruritus but no vesiculation.
- Topical antibiotics should be avoided.
- Use of antihistamines for associated pruritus may be effective, but this has not been extensively studied.
- Systemic corticosteroids offer significant relief in moderate to severe *Rhus* dermatitis, including generalized rash or severe facial or genital involvement.
- Effective dosing of oral prednisone is 1 mg/kg/day over 7 to 10 days (maximum 60 mg initial dose), with tapering over an additional 7 to 10 days.

- Inadequate doses or too-rapid tapering of systemic steroids may cause symptom rebound.
- IM treatment with long-acting triamcinolone suspension may be considered for patients intolerant of oral therapy.

CHRONIC Rx

- Recurrence may be caused by repeated exposure to fomites, including contaminated clothing, equipment, or pets.
- Secondary bacterial infection of the skin is the most common complication of *Rhus* dermatitis. Staph and strep are the most common pathogens, but MRSA must be considered.

DISPOSITION

Untreated *Rhus* dermatitis will resolve in 1 to 3 weeks.

REFERRAL

Refer to dermatology if there is diagnostic confusion.

! **PEARLS & CONSIDERATIONS**

PREVENTION

- Patients should be educated regarding identification and avoidance as well as washing to remove the oil after known exposure.
- Total avoidance of the plants may not be practical.
- The use of barrier creams applied before exposure to prevent dermatitis may be of some benefit, particularly in potential occupational (therefore predictable) exposure.
- Products available for postexposure prophylaxis are effective; however, equal efficacy may be obtained from less expensive liquid dishwashing soap.
- Desensitization has not been found to be effective.

PATIENT & FAMILY EDUCATION

- "Leaves of three, let it be," is a helpful reminder for patients.
- Patient education material, including access to photographs of the leaves of these plants in a variety of seasons and conditions, may be useful.

SUGGESTED READINGS
Available at www.expertconsult.com

RELATED CONTENT
Poison Ivy (Patient Information)
Contact Dermatitis (Related Key Topic)

AUTHOR: **MARGARET TRYFOROS, M.D.**

Polycystic Kidney Disease (PTG)

BASIC INFORMATION

DEFINITION

Autosomal dominant polycystic kidney disease (ADPKD) is a systemic inherited disorder due to mutations in either the PKD1 or PKD2 gene. These mutations lead to cyst formation and growth in multiple organs including kidneys, liver, and pancreas. ADPKD is also associated with multiple gastrointestinal and cardiovascular abnormalities. It is the most common inherited kidney disease, and its prevalence is more common than that of Huntington's disease, hemophilia, sickle cell disease, cystic fibrosis, myotonic dystrophy, and Down syndrome combined.

SYNONYMS

Adult Polycystic Kidney Disease
Polycystic Kidney Disease

ICD-10CM CODES

Q61.3	Polycystic kidney, unspecified
Q61.2	Polycystic kidney, adult type
Q61.19	Other polycystic kidney, infantile type
Z82.71	Family history of polycystic kidney

EPIDEMIOLOGY & DEMOGRAPHICS

- Most common single genetic cause of chronic kidney disease (CKD)
- Mendelian dominant disorder
- Affects all ethnic groups equally worldwide
- Approximately 85 percent of ADPKD individuals have a mutation on chromosome 16 (PKD1 locus), and 15% have a mutation located on chromosome 4 in the PKD2 gene.
- Each child of an affected parent has a 50% chance of inheriting the mutated gene.
- The disease has 100% penetrance and does not skip generations.

INCIDENCE:

- Between 1 in 400 and 1000 live births in the U.S.

GENETICS: ADPKD is caused by a mutation in the PKD1 gene located on the short arm of chromosome 16, which lies next to the TSC2 gene. The gene encoding polycystin-1 (PC1) plays a vital role in cell-cell and cell-matrix interactions and primary ciliary function. Mutations in PKD1 lead to an alteration in the differentiation of epithelial cells and the abnormal phenotypic expressions characteristic of ADPKD.

- ADPKD is less commonly caused by a mutation in the PKD2 gene located on chromosome 4. PKD2 encodes the protein polycystin-2 (PC2), which is involved in intracellular calcium signaling. PKD2 patients typically have milder disease with later onset of end-stage renal disease (ESRD), death, and hypertension. Polycystin 1 and 2 form a single functional complex through interactions of their intracellular carboxy termini. Consequently, a mutation of either PKD1 or PKD2 results in a similar phenotype.

CLINICAL PRESENTATION

ADPKD is a systemic disorder, and symptoms relate primarily to the kidney cyst burden and extra kidney involvement, including polycystic liver disease and vascular complications. Total kidney volume (TKV) and cyst volume in ADPKD increase exponentially over time in patients with ADPKD.

RENAL MANIFESTATIONS

Many patients with ADPKD are asymptomatic. The diagnosis is established by either the identification of an afflicted family member, asymptomatic screening (approximately 40%), or renal imaging performed for another reason. Patients may present with gross hematuria, flank mass/pain, polyuria/nocturia, fever due to a kidney or lower urinary tract infection, nephrolithiasis, or blood pressure elevation. All of these complications are manifested through increased cyst burden or TKV.

Gross hematuria occurs in 35% to 50% of patients with ADPKD and is associated with increased TKV. Hematuria is also caused by rupture of a cyst into the collecting system or is secondary to nephrolithiasis. Nephrolithiasis occurs in approximately 27% of ADPKD patients and is due in part to low levels of urinary citrate. Kidney stones may present as flank pain or hematuria, which is commonly microscopic.

Polyuria, nocturia, and increased thirst in ADPKD occur from impaired urinary concentrating ability and increases in circulating vasopressin levels.

Proteinuria is not a common feature of ADPKD and is usually less than 1 g/day. However , the presence of detectable proteinuria and microalbuminuria is correlated with increased TKV and more severe kidney disease.

Urinary tract infections are common in patients with PKD but do not appear to be more common than in the general population. Renal cyst infections are specific to ADPKD, and patients typically present with localized flank pain, fevers, and nausea and vomiting, similar to pyelonephritis.

Flank Pain: Acute flank pain can be caused by a kidney stone, kidney or liver cyst rupture, or hemorrhage. Chronic pain is typically due to enlarged kidneys, either unilaterally or bilaterally.

CARDIAC MANIFESTATIONS

Hypertension occurs in 60% of patients with ADPKD prior to any substantial decline in kidney function and appears earlier in males than in females. Hypertension in ADPKD is due to upregulation of renin-angiotensin-aldosterone system (RAAS). Hypertension is a predictor of worse renal outcome and is associated with cardiovascular morbidity and mortality. Cardiac valvular abnormalities occur in 25% to 30% of patients and include mitral valve prolapse and aortic regurgitation.

EXTRARENAL MANIFESTATIONS

1. The prevalence of intracranial aneurysms (ICA) in ADPKD is approximately 5% and increases to as high as 20% in patients with a first-degree relative with a known intracranial aneurysm rupture.
2. Rupture of an ICA is a serious complication of PKD and may produce significant permanent morbidity or death. Routine screening for ICA is recommended for patients with a family history of ICA or intracerebral bleed, or for patients with warning symptoms such as a sentinel headache .
3. In addition to kidney cysts, cysts can develop in the liver, pancreas, and seminal vesicles. Hepatic cysts are common and occur in up to ~85% of ADPKD patients by the age of 30 years. Hepatic cysts represent the most common extrarenal manifestation of ADPKD. Liver cystic disease is typically asymptomatic and develops slightly later than kidney cysts in ADPKD. However, hepatic cysts can cause serious complications including pain, infection, bleeding, and biliary obstruction. Liver cysts continue to grow and expand after patients reach ESRD.
4. Colonic diverticula and abdominal or inguinal hernias occur more frequently in ADPKD patients.

Seminal vesical cysts have been reported to occur in up to 40% of men with ADPKD but are not associated with changes in fertility.

NATURAL HISTORY

- Patients with PKD1 mutations have faster disease progression than patients with PKD2 mutations, and the median age of onset of ESRD is 54 years in PKD1 patients and 74 years in PKD2 patients.
- Other clinical risk factors associated with progressive kidney disease in ADPKD include male sex, onset of hypertension before 35 years of age, early onset of gross hematuria, presence of proteinuria or microalbuminuria, increased urinary sodium excretion, and increased low-density lipoprotein cholesterol (LDL) levels. However, all of these risk factors are mediated through cyst burden or TKV.
- Data from the Consortium of Radiologic Imaging studies of Polycystic Kidney Disease (CRISP) indicate that the decline in renal blood flow and the increases in TKV and cyst volume are strong predictors of future renal functional decline and progression to CKD stage 3. Baseline height-adjusted TKV (htTKV) of 600 mL/min predicts the risk of developing stage 3 CKD within 8 years.

DIAGNOSIS

Ultrasound of the kidneys is the most commonly used imaging modality for screening and diagnosis and is inexpensive, readily available, noninvasive, and free of radiation. CT and MRI are also used but typically in the setting of acute complications. CT scan and MRI are more sensitive than ultrasound, as they can detect cysts less than 1 cm in size.

The following diagnostic criteria are used for diagnosis of ADPKD in asymptomatic individuals who are at risk of developing ADPKD (i.e., those with positive family history of ADPKD):

1. Individuals 15 to 39 years of age: At least three unilateral or bilateral kidney cysts.
2. Individuals 40 to 59 years of age: At least two cysts in each kidney.
3. Individuals older than 60 years of age: At least four cysts in each kidney.

With no family history of ADPKD, there is no definitive number of cysts and/or cyst location that provides an unequivocal diagnosis. The diagnosis is strongly suspected when multiple and bilateral kidney cysts are present along with hepatic cysts.

Genetic testing can be done to diagnose ADPKD when imaging results are equivocal and when a definitive diagnosis is required in a young individual such as a potential living donor.

DIFFERENTIAL DIAGNOSIS

- Multiple benign simple cysts
- Autosomal-recessive PKD
- Familial juvenile nephronophthisis
- Medullary cystic or UMOD (uromodulin) disease
- Medullary sponge kidney
- Tuberous sclerosis
- von Hippel-Lindau syndrome
- Acquired cystic kidney disease

LABORATORY TESTS

- Hemoglobin and hematocrit may be elevated because of increased erythropoietin production but are typically similar to levels in other patients with CKD.
- Urinalysis can show microscopic hematuria and proteinuria (seldom >1 g/24 hr).
- With decreased kidney function, blood urea nitrogen and creatinine are elevated.
- Platelet counts can be mildly reduced in patients with extensive polycystic liver disease.
- Metabolic acidosis, hyperparathyroidism, and hyperphosphatemia are all associated with CKD in ADPKD.

Rx TREATMENT

NONPHARMACOLOGIC THERAPY

- Restriction of dietary salt (<2 g sodium/24 h) and calories is recommended.
- Cyclic adenosine monophosphate (cAMP) contributes to cyst formation and growth in ADPKD. Vasopressin stimulates the production of cAMP. Increasing water intake to greater than 3 L/day can suppress vasopressin. Increasing water intake is recommended in all ADPKD patients with preserved renal function. However, in patients with CKD, serum sodium should be monitored.

ACUTE GENERAL Rx

- The treatment of gross hematuria is typically supportive with bed rest, hydration, and analgesics. Antihypertensive medications should be stopped during this time.
- Extracorporeal shock wave lithotripsy (ESWL) has been used in patients with small obstructing kidney stones (<2 cm in diameter) in the renal pelvis or calyces. Percutaneous nephrolithotomy is another potential option.
- Infections are treated with antibiotics that penetrate cysts such as fluoroquinolones, Bactrim, vancomycin, and chloramphenicol.

CHRONIC GENERAL Rx

- Data from the HALT PKD trial showed that in young individuals with preserved kidney function, strict BP control of <110/75 mm Hg was associated with slower increase in TKV, reduced urinary albumin excretion, and a greater reduction of left ventricular mass index.
- For all ADPKD patients, the goal BP is <130/80 mm Hg. For young, healthy patients with ADPKD and with intact kidney function, the goal BP target can be <110/75 mm Hg.
- ACE inhibitors or angiotensin receptor blockers are the first drug of choice for treatment of hypertension.
- Hyperlipidemia should be aggressively treated with LDL targets less than 80 mg/dl.
- Pretransplant unilateral or bilateral nephrectomy is recommended only in select patients with recurrent infections, significant kidney enlargement causing limitation of daily activities, and malnutrition.
- For patients with ESRD, peritoneal or hemodialysis can be used as a bridge to kidney transplantation.

New therapies impacting cyst growth:
- A number of compounds that impact the cyst growth are being tested in ADPKD.
- Vasopressin receptor antagonist tolvaptan was shown to significantly decrease the kidney volume in a phase 3 double-blind, placebo-controlled randomized trial involving patients with PKD and preserved renal function. Further trials are being planned to test the safety and efficacy of tolvaptan.
- A small trial involving a somatostatin analogue, octreotide long-acting repeatable depot (octreotide-LAR), showed that there was significantly less increase in TKV in the octreotide group compared to placebo.

REFERRAL

- Patients with ADPKD should be referred at time of diagnosis to a nephrologist for ongoing care if possible. Urology can also be consulted in patients with nephrolithiasis for recurrent episodes of gross hematuria, or the consideration for nephrectomy before transplantation.

Genetic counseling should be offered if patients plan to start a family or are considering having their children screened. Individuals at risk for ADPKD should undergo pretest and posttest counseling if they are found to have ADPKD.

 **PEARLS & CONSIDERATIONS**

- ADPKD is the most common single genetic cause of CKD.
- TKV increases exponentially over time, and the increase in TKV is a strong predictor of future renal function decline.
- Increasing water intake to >3L/day is recommended in patients with ADPKD and preserved renal function.
- Strict blood pressure control is recommended in all patients with ADPKD.

 **EVIDENCE**

Available at www.expertconsult.com

SUGGESTED READINGS
Available at www.expertconsult.com

RELATED CONTENT
Polycystic Kidney Disease (Patient Information)

AUTHORS: **BHARATHI REDDY, M.D.,** **APARNA SHARMA, M.D.,** and **ARLENE CHAPMAN, M.D.**

P

Diseases and Disorders

I

BASIC INFORMATION

DEFINITION

Polycystic ovary syndrome (PCOS) is characterized by an accumulation of incompletely developed follicles in the ovaries due to anovulation and associated with ovarian androgen production. In its complete form, it is associated with polycystic ovaries, amenorrhea, hirsutism, and obesity. Criteria for PCOS according to published definitions are described in Table 1P-29.

SYNONYMS

Stein-Leventhal syndrome
PCOS

ICD-10CM CODES
E28.2 Polycystic ovarian syndrome

EPIDEMIOLOGY & DEMOGRAPHICS

- 6% to 25% of reproductive-age women (most common endocrine disorder in this population).
- Symptoms usually begin around the time of menarche, and the diagnosis is often made during adolescence or young adulthood.
- Increased risk of endometrial and ovarian cancers.
- PCOS is the most common cause of anovulatory infertility

PHYSICAL FINDINGS & CLINICAL PRESENTATION

- Oligomenorrhea or amenorrhea.
- Dysfunctional uterine bleeding.
- Infertility.
- Hirsutism.
- Acne, alopecia, acanthosis nigricans (Fig. 1P-75).
- Obesity (40% only), predominantly abdominal obesity.
- Insulin resistance (type 2 diabetes mellitus).
- Hypertension.

ETIOLOGY & PATHOGENESIS

Elevated serum luteinizing hormone (LH) concentrations and an increased serum LH/follicle-stimulating hormone (FSH) ratio result either from an increased gonadotropin-releasing hormone hypothalamic secretion or less likely from a primary pituitary abnormality. This results in dysregulation of androgen secretion and increased intraovarian androgen, the effect of which in the ovary is follicular atresia, maturation arrest, polycystic ovaries, and anovulation. Hyperinsulinemia is a contributing factor to ovarian hyperandrogenism, independent of LH excess. A role for insulin growth factor (IGF) receptors has been postulated for the association of PCOS and diabetes. Fig. 1P-76 illustrates the pathologic mechanisms in PCOS.

DIAGNOSIS

The diagnosis of PCOS excludes secondary causes (androgen-producing neoplasm, hyperprolactinemia, adult-onset congenital adrenal hyperplasia).
Clinical:

- The symptoms, signs, and biochemical features of PCOS vary greatly among women and may change over time.
- PCOS is the most common cause of chronic anovulation with estrogen present. A positive progesterone withdrawal test establishes the presence of estrogen. Medroxyprogesterone (Provera) 10 mg qd is administered for 5 days and bleeding occurs if estrogen is present.
- The presence of oligomenorrhea, hirsutism, obesity, and documented polycystic ovaries establishes the diagnosis.

DIFFERENTIAL DIAGNOSIS

Causes of amenorrhea:
- Primary (unusual in PCOS).
  1. Genetic disorder (Turner's syndrome).
  2. Anatomic abnormality (e.g., imperforate hymen).
- Secondary
  1. Pregnancy.
  2. Functional (cause unknown, anorexia nervosa, stress, excessive exercise, hyperthyroidism, less commonly hypothyroidism, adrenal dysfunction, pituitary dysfunction, severe systemic illness, drugs such as oral contraceptives, estrogens, or dopamine agonists).
  3. 1.3. Abnormalities of the genital tract (uterine tumor, endometrial scarring, ovarian tumor).

LABORATORY TESTS

- Glucose tolerance test at the initial presentation and every 2 yr thereafter (rule out diabetes mellitus). Impaired glucose tolerance is very common, occurring in approximately 30% of women with PCOS.
- Fasting lipid panel (rule out dyslipidemia), alanine aminotransferase, aspartate aminotransferase (rule out hepatic steatosis).
- Elevated LH/FSH ratio >2.5.
- Prolactin level elevation in 25%.
- Elevated androgens (testosterone [free and total levels], DHEA-S) (rule out androgen-secreting tumor).
- Other: thyroid-stimulating hormone (rule out hypothyroidism), 17-hydroxyprogesterone (rule out congenital adrenal hyperplasia), 24-hr urine for cortisol and creatinine (rule out Cushing's syndrome).
- TSH
- Table 1P-30 summarizes laboratory testing to exclude other causes of ovulatory dysfunction and hyperandrogenism.

IMAGING STUDIES

Pelvic ultrasound (Fig. 1P-77) (or CT scan) reveals the presence of twofold to fivefold ovarian enlargement with a thickened tunica albuginea, thecal hyperplasia, and 20 or more subcapsular follicles from 1 to 15 mm in diameter (Fig. 1P-78). It is important to note that having polycystic ovaries alone does not make the diagnosis of PCOS because 20% of women with polycystic ovaries have no symptoms.

TREATMENT

The goal is to interrupt the self-perpetuating abnormal hormone cycle:

TABLE 1P-29 Criteria for Polycystic Ovary Syndrome According to Published Definitions

	NICHD/NIH/1990	Rotterdam 2003	AE-PCOS/2009
Diagnostic criteria	Requires simultaneous presence of: Clinical and/or biochemical hyperandrogenism Menstrual dysfunction	Requires the presence of at least two criteria: Clinical and/or biochemical hyperandrogenism Ovulatory dysfunction PCOM	Requires the presence of: Hyperandrogenism and/or hyperandrogenemia Ovarian dysfunction: oligoovulation or anovulation and/or polycystic ovaries
Exclusion criteria	Congenital adrenal hyperplasia, androgen-secreting tumors, Cushing's syndrome, and hyperprolactinemia	Congenital adrenal hyperplasia, androgen-secreting tumors, and Cushing's syndrome	21-hydroxylase-deficient nonclassic adrenal hyperplasia, androgen-secreting neoplasms, androgenic–anabolic drug use or abuse, the hyperandrogenic-insulin resistance-acanthosis nigricans syndrome, thyroid dysfunction, and hyperprolactinemia
Clinical traits	Hirsutism, acne, and alopecia	Hirsutism, acne, and androgenic alopecia	Hirsutism
PCOM	Not included	At least one ovary showing either: Twelve or more follicles of 2-9 mm in diameter Ovarian volume, 10 mL	At least one ovary showing either: Twelve or more follicles of 2-9 mm in diameter Ovarian volume, 10 mL

AE-PCOS, Androgen Excess and PCOS Society; *NICHD/NIH,* National Institute for Child Health and Human Development/National Institutes of Health; *PCOM,* polycystic ovarian morphology.
From Fielding JR et al: *Gynecologic imaging,* Philadelphia, 2011, Saunders.

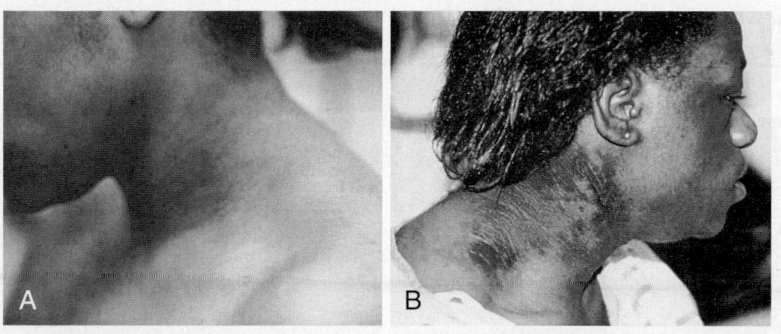

FIGURE 1P-75 Acanthosis nigricans. A, Moderate acanthosis nigricans (i.e., darkening and thickening of skin) at the lateral lower fold of the neck. Notice facial hirsutism (sideburns) in the same patient. **B,** Severe acanthosis nigricans in another patient with severe insulin resistance. (**B,** Courtesy of Dr. R. Ann Word, Dallas, Texas. From Melmed S et al: *Williams textbook of endocrinology,* ed 12, Philadelphia, 2011, Saunders.)

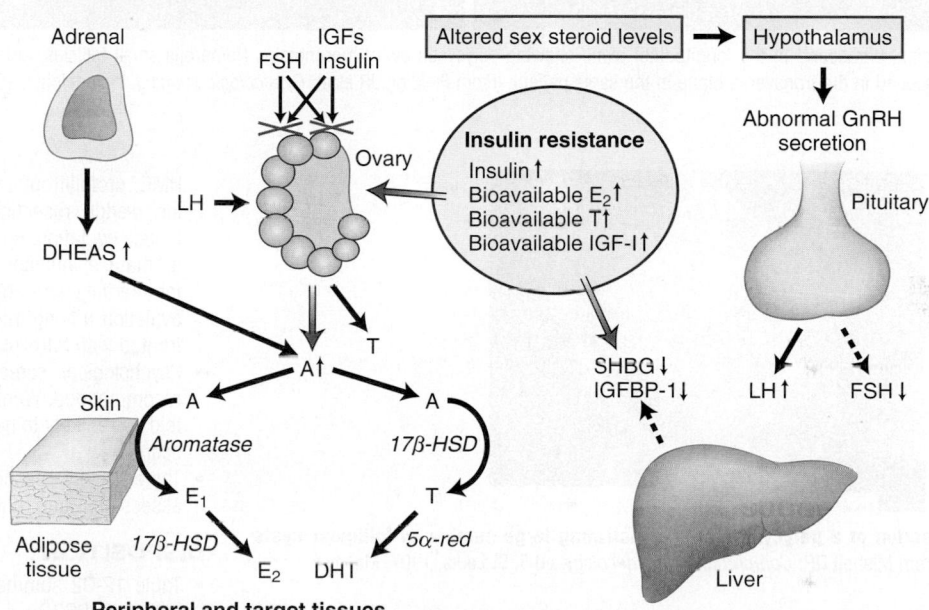

Peripheral and target tissues

FIGURE 1P-76 Pathologic mechanisms in polycystic ovary syndrome (PCOS). A deficient in vivo response of the ovarian follicle to physiologic quantities of follicle-stimulating hormone (*FSH*), possibly because of an impaired interaction between signaling pathways associated with FSH and insulin-like growth factors (*IGFs*) or insulin, may be an important defect responsible for anovulation in PCOS. Insulin resistance associated with increased circulating and tissue levels of insulin and bioavailable estradiol (*E$_2$*), testosterone (*T*), and IGF1 gives rise to abnormal hormone production in a number of tissues. Oversecretion of luteinizing hormone (*LH*) and decreased output of FSH by the pituitary, decreased production of sex hormone–binding globulin (*SHBG*) and IGF-binding protein 1 (*IGFBP-1*) in the liver, increased adrenal secretion of dehydroepiandrosterone sulfate (*DHEAS*), and increased ovarian secretion of androstenedione (*A*) all contribute to the feed-forward cycle that maintains anovulation and androgen excess in PCOS. Excessive amounts of E$_2$ and T arise primarily from the conversion of A in peripheral and target tissues. T is converted to the potent steroids estradiol or DHT (dihydrotestosterone). Reductive 17β-hydroxysteroid dehydrogenase (17β-HSD) enzyme activity may be conferred by protein products of several genes with overlapping functions; 5α-reductase (5α-red) is encoded by at least two genes, and aromatase is encoded by a single gene. *GnRH,* Gonadotropin-releasing hormone. (From Melmed S et al: *Williams textbook of endocrinology,* ed 12, Philadelphia, 2011, Saunders.)

TABLE 1P-30   Laboratory Testing to Exclude Other Causes of Ovulatory Dysfunction and Hyperandrogenism

Lab	Evaluation for:	Comment
Total and/or bioavailable testosterone	Androgen-secreting tumor	Measure if there are symptoms concerning for an androgen-secreting tumor or if biochemical evidence of hyperandrogenism is needed to make the diagnosis of polycystic ovary syndrome. Rapid progression or a total testosterone >200 ng/dl should prompt a workup for an androgen-secreting tumor.
Dehydroepiandrosterone sulfate	Androgen-secreting tumor	Measure if there are symptoms concerning for an androgen-secreting tumor. Although modest elevations in dehydroepiandrosterone sulfate can be seen in polycystic ovary syndrome, rapid progression or greater elevations should prompt a workup for an adrenal androgen-secreting tumor.
Morning 17-hydroxyprogesterone	Late-onset congenital adrenal hyperplasia	This disorder is caused by a partial adrenal enzyme defect that leads to impaired cortisol production, compensatory elevation in adrenocorticotropic hormone, and subsequent excess androgen production. Symptoms may mimic polycystic ovary syndrome. Normal values <200 ng/dl. If higher than this, adrenocorticotropic hormone stimulation test recommended.
24-hour urine for cortisol and creatinine; dexamethasone suppression test; salivary cortisol	Cushing's syndrome	Consider ruling out Cushing's syndrome in women with an abrupt change in menstrual pattern, later-onset hirsutism, or other evidence of cortisol excess such as hypertension, facial plethora, supraclavicular fullness, hyperpigmented striae, and fragile skin.
Prolactin	Hyperprolactinemia	May be accompanied by galactorrhea. Consider ruling this out in all women with irregular menstrual cycles.
Thyroid function studies	Hyper- or hypo-thyroidism	Consider ruling out thyroid dysfunction in all women with irregular menstrual cycles.

*Data from Setji and Brown, adapted with kind permission of Springer Science+Business Media.[1]
From Setji TL, Brown AJ: Polycystic ovary syndrome: Update on diagnosis and treatment, *Am J Med* 127:912-919, 2014.

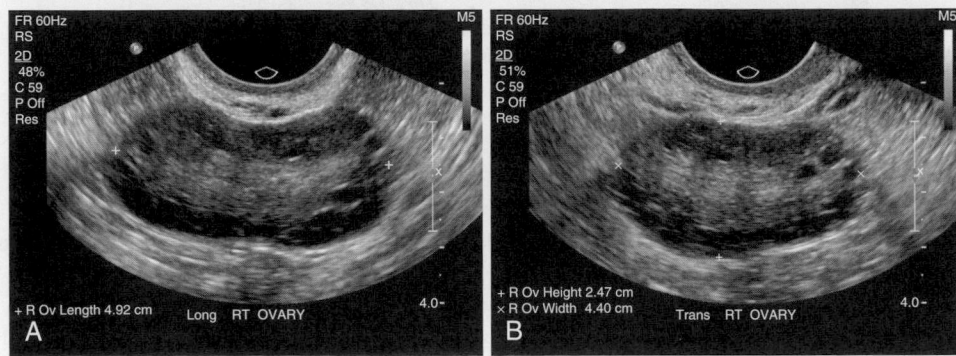

FIGURE 1P-77 A, Transvaginal ultrasound in the longitudinal plane showing polycystic ovary morphology. Numerous small follicles surround an echogenic central stroma. **B,** Transvaginal ultrasound in the transverse plane in the same patient. (From Fielding JR et al: *Gynecologic imaging,* Philadelphia, 2011, Saunders.)

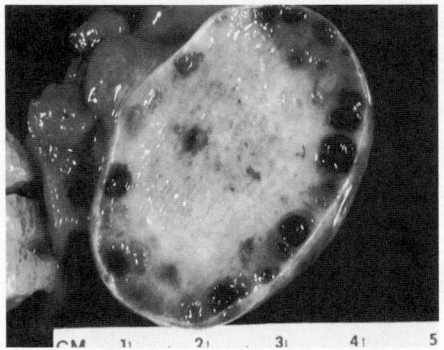

FIGURE 1P-78 Sagittal section of a polycystic ovary illustrating large number of follicular cysts and thickened stroma. (From Mishell DR: *Comprehensive gynecology,* ed 3, St Louis, 1997, Mosby.)

- Reduction of ovarian androgen secretion by laparoscopic ovarian wedge resection. Laparoscopic ovarian surgery (laparoscopic ovarian drilling [LOD]) is a useful alternative that does not trigger ovarian hyperstimulation.
- Reduction of ovarian androgen secretion by using oral contraceptives or LH-releasing hormone (LHRH) analogs.
- Weight reduction for all obese women with PCOS. Loss of abdominal fat seems to be crucial to restore ovulation.
- FSH stimulation with clomiphene HMG or pulsatile LHRH.

- Urofollitropin (pure FSH) administration.
- Metformin improves ovulation, insulin sensitivity, and possibly hyperandrogenemia.
Choice of treatment:
- The management of hirsutism without risking pregnancy includes oral contraceptives, glucocorticoids, LHRH analogs, or spironolactone (an antiandrogen). Finasteride and flutamide may be similarly effective in reducing hirsutism as spironolactone.
- Pregnancy can be achieved with clomiphene (alone or with glucocorticoids, human chorionic gonadotropin, or bromocriptine), HMG, urofollitropin, pulsatile LHRH, or ovarian wedge resection. Metformin may also induce ovulation. Recent trials comparing the aromatase inhibitor letrozole to clomiphene for infertility have shown higher live-birth and ovulation among infertile women with PCOS treated with letrozole.
- Psychological screening for depression is recommended. Women with PCOS are four-fold more likely to have abnormal depression scores.
- Table 1P-31 describes a mnemonic for assessment and management of PCOS.

DISPOSITION
- Table 1P-32 summarizes metabolic complications in PCOS.

SUGGESTED READINGS
Available at www.expertconsult.com

RELATED CONTENT
Polycystic Ovarian Syndrome (Patient Information)

AUTHOR: **FRED F. FERRI, M.D.**

TABLE 1P-31 MY PCOS: Mnemonic for Assessment and Management of Polycystic Ovary Syndrome (PCOS)

	Assessment	Management
<u>M</u>etabolic	2-hour glucose tolerance test with 75 grams oral glucose, measuring serum glucose at time 0 and 120 min. Lipid profile Liver function tests (if other risk factors for nonalcoholic fatty liver disease)	Lifestyle intervention: diet, exercise, and weight loss (if overweight or obese) Metformin for abnormal glucose tolerance not controlled with lifestyle Statin therapy if patient meets criteria (Adult Treatment Panel-III or American College of Cardiology/American Heart Association guidelines)
C<u>y</u>cle control	Ask about menstrual pattern; normal cycle length is 28 days (range 21-35)	If amenorrhea for 3 months or more, induce withdrawal bleed with progesterone (after negative pregnancy test) Hormonal therapy Examples: • Estrogen-containing oral contraceptives (monthly cycling, seasonal cycling, continuous use) • Vaginal ring • Patch • Progestin-only pill (smokers, hypertension) • Progestin-eluting intrauterine device (Mirena®) • Progesterone prn to induce withdrawal bleeding (medroxyprogesterone acetate 10 mg daily for 10-14 days, micronized progesterone 400 mg daily for 10-14 days) Metformin (second-line therapy)
<u>P</u>sychosocial	Screen for depression, disordered eating Affirm that polycystic ovary syndrome is an important medical issue; provide nonjudgmental support Discuss stress management Reinforce self-care behaviors	Mental health referral and/or antidepressant therapy may be warranted if depression or disordered eating is identified
<u>C</u>osmetic	Ferriman-Gallwey score as guide to assess hirsutism Evaluate for acne and male pattern hair loss Serum androgen levels if uncertain about degree of hirsutism or atypical symptoms	Estrogen-containing hormonal contraception Antiandrogens such as spironolactone or finasteride. Teratogenic; only use with contraception) Cyproterone acetate (not available in the U.S.) Eflornithine hydrochloride 13.9% cream Laser or electrolysis Topical treatment for acne Minoxidil 2.5% or 5% for male pattern hair loss
<u>O</u>vulation and fertility	Counsel that fertility is reduced in polycystic ovary syndrome, but patients typically not infertile Assess fertility goals	If subfertility is an issue, consider referral to Reproductive Endocrine for possible clomiphene citrate therapy Metformin has limited role
<u>S</u>leep apnea	Screen for sleep apnea: daytime somnolence, morning headache, reflux symptoms, snoring, observed interrupted breathing	Refer for sleep study Continuous positive airway pressure therapy recommended if sleep apnea diagnosed

*Data from Setji and Brown, adapted with kind permission of Springer Science+Business Media.[1]
PCOS, Polycystic ovary syndrome.
From Setji TL, Brown AJ: Polycystic ovary syndrome: Update on diagnosis and treatment, *Am J Med* 127:912-919, 2014.

TABLE 1P-32 Metabolic Complications in Polycystic Ovary Syndrome

Abnormal Glucose Tolerance (Impaired Glucose Tolerance or Type 2 Diabetes)	30% of obese polycystic ovary syndrome women have impaired glucose tolerance, and 10% have type 2 diabetes by age 40. In thin women with polycystic ovary syndrome, 10% have impaired glucose tolerance, and 1.5% have type 2 diabetes.
Obesity	Prevalence of obesity varies considerably in women with polycystic ovary syndrome. Previously, prevalence rates of obesity were estimated based on populations of women with polycystic ovary syndrome seeking care. A recent study comparing patients presenting for care in a polycystic ovary syndrome clinic with an unselected population evaluated during a preemployment physical suggests that obesity and overweight may not be more common in polycystic ovary syndrome. In that study, 63.7% of polycystic ovary syndrome clinic patients were obese, compared with 28% of unselected women with polycystic ovary syndrome identified during screening, and 28% of nonpolycystic ovary syndrome controls. Polycystic ovary syndrome symptoms, including hyperandrogenism and oligo-ovulation, are exacerbated by obesity.
Metabolic Syndrome	33%-50% of U.S. women with polycystic ovary syndrome have metabolic syndrome compared to only 12% in a similarly aged National Health and Nutrition Examination Survey population. In contrast, only 8.2% of women with polycystic ovary syndrome in Italy met criteria for metabolic syndrome. Thus, metabolic syndrome varies by geographic location, a finding likely related to different body mass index, though other causes including genetics and diet could also be playing a part.
High blood pressure	Data have been conflicting, but a large Kaiser Permanente study demonstrated that hypertension or elevated blood pressure was more than twice as common in women with polycystic ovary syndrome (27% vs. 12%).
Dyslipidemia	Dyslipidemia is more prevalent in women with polycystic ovary syndrome compared to controls (15% vs. 6%). In a metaanalysis, triglyceride values were 26 mg/dl higher (95% CI 17-35), low-density lipoprotein cholesterol was 12 mg/dl higher (95% CI 10-16), and high-density lipoprotein-cholesterol was 6 mg/dl lower (95% CI 4-9) in women with polycystic ovary syndrome compared with controls. Women with polycystic ovary syndrome also have higher concentrations and proportions of small, dense low-density lipoprotein cholesterol.
Nonalcoholic fatty liver disease and nonalcoholic steatohepatitis	Nonalcoholic fatty liver disease and nonalcoholic steatohepatitis have recently been recognized as a potential complication in women with polycystic ovary syndrome. Prevalence of fatty liver disease in polycystic ovary syndrome women has been estimated to be 15%-55%, depending on the diagnostic parameter used (level of serum alanine aminotransferase or ultrasound). Individuals that may be at higher risk of nonalcoholic fatty liver disease including nonalcoholic steatohepatitis include those with metabolic syndrome, insulin resistance, and possibly hyperandrogenemia.
Cardiovascular disease	Many studies demonstrate abnormal surrogate markers of cardiovascular disease in women with polycystic ovary syndrome. However, data regarding cardiovascular disease risk are conflicting with some studies suggesting an increased risk in women with polycystic ovary syndrome, whereas other studies have not found this difference in cardiovascular risk. While it is important to recognize and treat cardiovascular risk factors in this population, further research of cardiovascular risk and complications is still needed to clarify the long-term risk.

CI, Confidence interval.

From Setji TL, Brown AJ: Polycystic ovary syndrome: Update on diagnosis and treatment, *Am J Med* 127:912-919, 2014.

 **BASIC INFORMATION**

DEFINITION

Polycythemia vera is a disorder of the myeloid/erythroid stem cell resulting in erythropoietin-independent proliferation of erythrocytes.

SYNONYMS

PV
Primary polycythemia
Vaquez disease

ICD-10CM CODES
D45 Polycythemia vera

EPIDEMIOLOGY & DEMOGRAPHICS

INCIDENCE: 1 case per 100,000 persons. Occurs most commonly in patients aged 50 to 75 years. Mean age at onset is 60 yr; men are affected more often than are women.

PHYSICAL FINDINGS & CLINICAL PRESENTATION

Polycythemia vera has a latent, proliferative, and spent phase. The patient generally comes to medical attention because of symptoms associated with increased blood volume and viscosity or impaired platelet function:

- Impaired cerebral circulation resulting in headache, vertigo, blurred vision, dizziness, transient ischemic attack, cerebrovascular accident
- Fatigue, poor exercise tolerance
- Pruritus, particularly after bathing (caused by overproduction of histamine)
- Bleeding: epistaxis, upper gastrointestinal bleeding (increased incidence of peptic ulcer disease)
- Abdominal discomfort from splenomegaly; hepatomegaly may be present
- Hyperuricemia may result in nephrolithiasis and gouty arthritis
- Nearly 20% of patients experience arterial or venous thrombosis as their initial symptom. Hepatic brain thrombosis or portal vein thrombosis should raise suspicion for PV.

The physical examination may reveal:
- Facial plethora, congestion of oral mucosa, ruddy complexion
- Enlargement and tortuosity of retinal veins
- Splenomegaly (found in >75% of patients)

 **DIAGNOSIS**

DIFFERENTIAL DIAGNOSIS

Smoking:
- Polycythemia is caused by increased carboxyhemoglobin, resulting in left shift in the hemoglobin (Hgb) dissociation curve.
- Laboratory evaluation shows increased hematocrit (Hct), RBC mass, erythropoietin level, and carboxyhemoglobin.
- Splenomegaly is not present on physical examination.

Hypoxemia (secondary polycythemia):
- Living for prolonged periods at high altitudes, pulmonary fibrosis, congenital cardiac lesions with right-to-left shunts.

- Laboratory evaluation shows decreased arterial oxygen saturation and elevated erythropoietin level.
- Splenomegaly is not present on physical examination.

Erythropoietin-producing states:
- Renal cell carcinoma, hepatoma, cerebral hemangioma, uterine fibroids, polycystic kidneys.
- The erythropoietin level is elevated in these patients, and the arterial oxygen saturation is normal.
- Splenomegaly may be present with metastatic neoplasms.

Stress polycythemia (Gaisböck's syndrome, relative polycythemia):
- Laboratory evaluation demonstrates normal RBC mass, arterial oxygen saturation, and erythropoietin level; plasma volume is decreased.
- Splenomegaly is not present on physical examination.

Hemoglobinopathies associated with high oxygen affinity:
- An abnormal oxyhemoglobin-dissociation curve (P50) is present.

WORKUP

PV is suspected when the hemoglobin level exceeds 18.5 g/dl in men or 16.5 g/dl in women after secondary causes have been excluded. Recent developments in molecular biology have identified a single, acquired point mutation in the Janus kinase 2 *(JAK2)* gene in the majority of patients with polycythemia vera and other pH-negative myeloproliferative disorders. The *JAK2* mutation is found in >95% of patients with polycythemia vera and can be used for diagnostic purposes. Testing for the *JAK2 V617F* mutation with polymerase chain reaction assay is now available. In patients with high hematocrit (>52% in men or >48% in women) and in the absence of coexisting secondary erythrocytosis, the presence of the *JAK2* mutation is sufficient for the diagnosis of polycythemia vera.

The World Health Organization diagnostic criteria for polycythemia vera are described in Table 1P-33.

LABORATORY TESTS

- Elevated RBC count (>6 million/mm³), elevated Hgb (>18 g/dl in men, >16 g/dl in women), elevated Hct (<54% in men, <49% in women)
- Increased white blood cell count (often with basophilia; basophilia is a strong predictor of PV instead of a reactive state); thrombocytosis is found in the majority of patients
- Elevated leukocyte alkaline phosphatase, serum vitamin B_{12} (due to increased levels of transcobalamin III produced in proliferating leukocytes), and uric acid levels (due to DNA turnover in the marrow)
- Low serum erythropoietin level
- Peripheral blood smear: may reveal basophils or immature myeloid forms
- Bone marrow aspiration revealing RBC hyperplasia (Fig. E1P-79) and absent iron stores

 **TREATMENT**

NONPHARMACOLOGIC THERAPY

Phlebotomy to keep Hct >45% in men and >42% in women is the mainstay of therapy. Phlebotomy, however, has no effect on the development of myelofibrosis.

ACUTE GENERAL Rx

- Add aspirin in patients younger than 60 years without prior thromboembolic event.
- Hydroxyurea can be used in conjunction with phlebotomy in patients older than 60 years to decrease the incidence of thrombotic events.
- Interferon-alpha-2b is also effective in controlling RBC values without significant side effects.
- Box 1P-8 describes an algorithm for management of patients with polycythemia vera.
- Recent trials have shown that ruxolitinib, a Janus kinase (JAK) 1 and 2 inhibitor was superior to standard therapy in controlling the hematocrit, reducing the spleen volume and improving symptoms associated with polycythemia vera.

TABLE 1P-33 World Health Organization 2008 Diagnostic Criteria for Polycythemia Vera

Major Criteria

1. Hemoglobin (Hgb) >18.5 g/dl (men), >16.5 (women); *or* Hgb or hematocrit (Hct) >99% reference range for age, sex, or altitude of residence; *or* Hgb >17 g/dl (men), >15 g/dl (women) if associated with a sustained increase of ≥2 g/dl from baseline that cannot be attributed to correction of iron deficiency; *or* elevated red cell mass (>25% above mean normal predicted value)

2. Presence of *JAK2 V617F* or similar mutation

Minor Criteria

1. Bone marrow trilineage myeloproliferation
2. Subnormal serum erythropoietin level
3. Endogenous erythroid colony formation in vitro

Either both major criteria and one minor criterion *or* the first major criterion and two minor criteria must be met for diagnosis of polycythemia vera.

From Andreoli TE et al: *Andreoli and Carpenter's Cecil essentials of medicine,* ed 8, Philadelphia, 2010, Saunders.

BOX 1P-8 *Algorithm for Management of Patients with Polycythemia Vera*

Low-risk young patients (age <60 years) and no history of thrombosis, platelet count <1.5 × 10^6 mm^3
Phlebotomy + low-dose aspirin (81 mg/day) to maintain hematocrit lower than 45% in males and lower than 42% in females. Aspirin should not be used in patients with histories of a hemorrhagic episode or with extreme thrombocytosis (>1.5 × 10^6 mm^3) or acquired von Willebrand syndrome.

↓

Thrombosis or hemorrhage
Systemic symptoms
Severe pruritus refractory to histamine antagonists
Painful splenomegaly

↓

Hydroxyurea 15-20 mg/kg (unless younger than 40 years, pregnant, intolerant to hydroxyurea; consider pegylated INF)

↓

Pegylated INF 45 to 180 μg/wk or INF (3 × 10^6 units three times a week; alter dose depending on response and toxicity). Consider the use of pegylated INF, which can be administered once weekly.

↓

If platelet control is inadequate or patient cannot tolerate interferon, one option is the use of anagrelide. However, the use of this drug is controversial. In this case, supplemental phlebotomy is required to maintain hematocrit lower than 45% in males and lower than 42% in females, and the use of hydroxyurea should be considered, especially if patient continues to have thrombotic episodes.

↓

If the patient has increasing splenomegaly, systemic symptoms, or repeated thromboses despite adequate dose of hydroxyurea (2-3 g/day), start busulfan, 4 to 6 mg/day orally for 4 to 8 weeks. It should be mentioned that the sequential use of hydroxyurea and busulfan may be associated with an increased risk of leukemia. Supplemental phlebotomy may be required.

Painful splenomegaly

↓

Splenectomy + continued systemic therapy

↓

High-risk patients (age >60 years), previous thrombosis, platelet count >1.5 × 10^6 mm^3
Phlebotomy to hematocrit of 42% in females and 45% in males
Aspirin (81 mg/day) to be given only in patients with platelet counts <1.5 × 10^6 mm^2
Myelosuppressive therapy with hydroxyurea 30 mg/kg orally for 1 week
Then 15 to 20 mg/kg

↓

If patient continues to have thrombotic episodes and has extreme thrombocytosis or cannot tolerate hydroxyurea
Consider pegylated INF 45 to 180 μg/wk or add busulfan 4 to 6 mg/d orally for 4 to 8 weeks.
If on busulfan, stop when blood counts are normalized or platelet count is lower than 300,000 mm^3.
Occasional supplemental phlebotomy if hematocrit is >42% in females and greater than 45% in males; when patient relapses (patient is symptomatic), initiate busulfan therapy again at same dose.

Patient age >70 years
Phlebotomy + low-dose aspirin + hydroxyurea

↓

No response or poor compliance
Busulfan 4 to 6 mg/day orally for 4 to 8 weeks. Stop when blood counts are normalized or platelet count is lower than 300,000 mm^3.

From Hoffman R.: *Hematology, basic principles and practice*, 6th ed, Philadelphia, 2013, Saunders.

CHRONIC Rx

- Patient education regarding need for lifelong monitoring and treatment.
- Adjunctive therapy: treatment of pruritus with antihistamines, control of significant hyperuricemia with allopurinol, reduction of gastric hyperacidity with antacids of H_2 blockers, low-dose aspirin to treat vasomotor symptoms in patients without bleeding diathesis. Low-dose aspirin can safely prevent thrombotic complications in patients with polycythemia vera and should be given to all patients in absence of contraindications.

DISPOSITION

- The median survival time without treatment is 6 to 18 mo after diagnosis; phlebotomy extends the average survival time to 12 yr.
- Patients with polycythemia vera with a hematocrit <45% have a significantly lower rate of cardiovascular death and major thrombosis than those with hematocrit of 45% to 50%.
- Prognosis is worse in patients >60 yr and those with a history of thrombosis.

SUGGESTED READINGS
Available at www.expertconsult.com

RELATED CONTENT
Polycythemia Vera (Patient Information)

AUTHOR: **FRED F. FERRI, M.D.**

Diseases
and Disorders

I

 **BASIC INFORMATION**

DEFINITION

Polymyalgia rheumatica (PMR) is an inflammatory condition characterized by neck, shoulder girdle, and pelvic girdle muscle pain and stiffness of at least four weeks' duration. PMR can occur alone or in conjunction with giant cell arteritis (GCA).

SYNONYMS

Anarthritic rheumatoid syndrome
PMR

ICD-10CM CODES
M35.3 Polymyalgia rheumatica

EPIDEMIOLOGY & DEMOGRAPHICS

PREVALENCE: 60 to 80/100,000; Scandinavian and Northern European populations are high risk.
PREDOMINANT SEX: Female/male ratio of 2:1.
PREDOMINANT AGE: Age greater than 50 years with peak between seventh and eight decade. Unlikely in those less than 50 years old.

PHYSICAL FINDINGS & CLINICAL PRESENTATION

- Typically, abrupt onset of muscle pain, symmetric myalgias, and stiffness.
- Neck, shoulders, lower back, hips, thighs, and occasionally trunk and arms are involved. Shoulders are usually affected first.
- Patients often note severe pain and stiffness during the night, with difficulty rising and dressing.
- Constitutional symptoms of fatigue, malaise, weight loss, loss of appetite, and depression may accompany pain and stiffness.
- Physical exam shows passive range of motion is preserved, strength testing is normal; subdeltoid and subacromial bursitis most prominent finding, minimal joint synovitis.
- Fever, chills, night sweats, visual disturbances, headaches, or jaw claudication should raise suspicion of giant cell arteritis and be further evaluated.

ETIOLOGY

Appears related to the presence of HLA-D4 haplotype, which is associated with global activation of the innate immune system and circulating monocytes that produce IL-1 and IL-6, leading to inflammation.

Dx DIAGNOSIS

DIFFERENTIAL DIAGNOSIS

See Box 1P-9.

WORKUP

- Initial laboratory evaluation: ESR, CRP, CBC, CPK.
- ESR >40 in majority of patients.
- CBC may show a normocytic, normochromic anemia and thrombocytosis.
- Clinical diagnosis: Symptoms of stiffness, aching, pain, increased ESR and CRP
- An algorithm for diagnosing polymyalgia rheumatica without giant cell arteritis is described in Fig. 1P-80.

- Table 1P-34 describes diagnostic criteria for PMR.

Rx TREATMENT

ACUTE GENERAL Rx

- Prednisone 15 to 20 mg/day with dramatic improvement in symptoms in 24 to 48 hrs.
- Initial prednisone dose should be maintained for 4 to 8 weeks.
- Steroid dose may be reduced by 20% every month if patient remains symptom free.
- ESR and CRP should be monitored for disease activity and steroid dose adjustment.
- When dose reaches 10 mg/day, taper slowly. Flares, typical during tapering, can be managed by increasing prednisone by 10% to 20%.
- A proton pump inhibitor should be initiated with glucocorticoids.
- Attention should be paid to bone health. Calcium and vitamin D supplementation should be started early and bisphosphonates used if indicated by bone density measurement.

! PEARLS & CONSIDERATIONS

Patients with PMR should be monitored carefully for the development of giant cell arteritis. Patients who have incomplete response to treatment with prednisone or have an evolving pattern of pain and swelling should be

reevaluated for the possibility of a different diagnosis.

SUGGESTED READINGS

Available at www.expertconsult.com

RELATED CONTENT

Polymyalgia Rheumatica (PMR) (Patient Information)
Giant Cell Arteritis (Related Key Topic)
Vasculitis, Systemic (Related Key Topic)

AUTHOR: **ALISHA LAKHANI, M.D., M.P.H.**

BOX 1P-9   Differential Diagnosis of Polymyalgia Rheumatica

Rheumatoid arthritis
Rotator cuff syndrome
Osteoarthritis of shoulder and hip joints
Fibromyalgia
Polymyositis/dermatomyositis
Spondyloarthritis
Systemic lupus erythematosus
Vasculitides
Paraneoplastic myalgias
Infection-associated myalgias
RS3PE (remitting seronegative symmetric synovitis and pitting edema)
Parkinson's disease
Hypothyroidism

From Hochberg M: *Rheumatology,* ed 4, Philadelphia, 2007, Mosby.

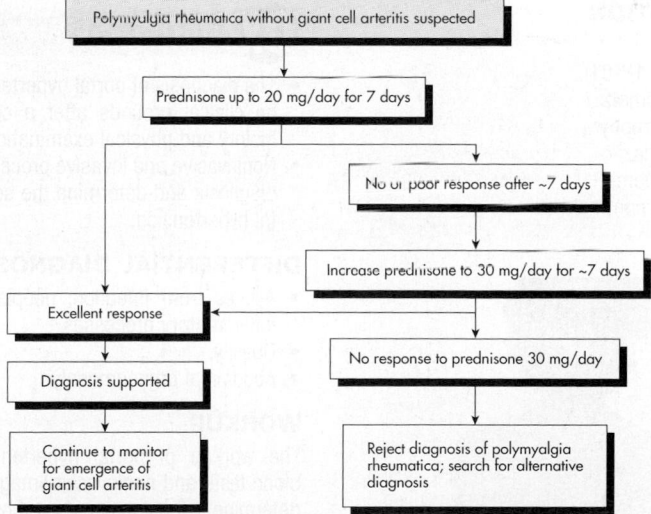

FIGURE 1P-80 Algorithm for diagnosing polymyalgia rheumatica without giant cell arteritis. (From Firestein GS et al: *Kelly's textbook of rheumatology,* ed 9, Philadelphia, 2013, Saunders.)

TABLE 1P-34   Polymyalgia Rheumatica: Diagnostic Criteria

Chuang et al 1982	Healey 1984
• Age of onset = 50 yr or older • Erythrocyte sedimentation rate >40 mm/h • Bilateral aching and stiffness for =1 mo and involving two of the following areas: neck or torso, shoulders or proximal regions of the arms, and hips or proximal aspects of the thighs • Exclusion of all other diagnoses causing PMR-like symptoms	• Age of onset = 50 yr or older • Erythrocyte sedimentation rate >40 mm/h • Pain persisting =1 mo and involving two of the following areas: neck, shoulders, and pelvic girdle • Absence of other diseases capable of causing the musculoskeletal symptoms • Morning stiffness lasting >1 hr • Rapid response to prednisone (=20 mg/day)??

From Hochberg M: *Rheumatology,* ed 4, Philadelphia, 2007, Mosby.

BASIC INFORMATION

DEFINITION
Clinically significant portal hypertension is defined as a portal vein pressure >10 mm Hg, most commonly attributable to liver disease.

SYNONYMS
None

ICD-10CM CODES
K76.6 Portal hypertension

EPIDEMIOLOGY & DEMOGRAPHICS
- Incidence of portal hypertension is not known.
- Cirrhosis is the most common cause of portal hypertension in the United States.
- Portal hypertension is developed by >90% of patients with cirrhosis.
- Alcoholic and viral liver diseases are the most common causes of cirrhosis and portal hypertension in the United States.
- Schistosomiasis is the main cause of portal hypertension outside the United States.
- Esophageal varices may appear when portal vein pressure rises to >10 mm Hg.
- Variceal hemorrhage is the most serious complication of portal hypertension and may occur when portal pressures rise >12 mm Hg.

PHYSICAL FINDINGS & CLINICAL PRESENTATION
- Jaundice.
- Ascites (Fig. 1P-81).
- Spider angiomata.
- Testicular atrophy.
- Gynecomastia.
- Palmar erythema.
- Dupuytren's contracture.

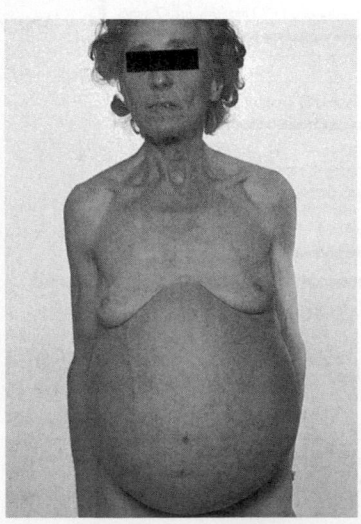

FIGURE 1P-81 Ascites secondary to portal hypertension. Note the dilated collateral vein running up the right side of the abdomen. (From Forbes A et al [eds]: *Atlas of clinical gastroenterology,* ed 3, Oxford, 2005, Mosby.)

- Asterixis (with advanced liver failure).
- Irritability, encephalopathy.
- Splenomegaly.
- Dilated veins in the anterior abdominal wall.
- Venous pattern on the flanks.
- Caput medusae (tortuous collateral veins around the umbilicus).
- Hemorrhoids.
- Hematemesis.
- Melena.
- Pruritus.

ETIOLOGY
Pathophysiologically caused by:
1. Conditions resulting in an increased resistance to flow.
   - **Prehepatic** (e.g., portal vein thrombosis, splenic vein thrombosis, congenital stenosis).
   - **Hepatic** (e.g., cirrhosis, alcoholic liver disease, primary biliary cirrhosis, schistosomiasis).
   - **Posthepatic** (e.g., Budd-Chiari syndrome, constrictive pericarditis, inferior vena cava obstruction, cor pulmonale, tricuspid regurgitation).
2. Conditions leading to increase in portal blood flow.
   - Splanchnic arterial vasodilation accompanying portal hypertension, mediated by local release of nitric oxide.
   - Arterial-portal venous fistulae.

Table 1P-35 summarizes the etiology of portal hypertension.

DIAGNOSIS

- The diagnosis of portal hypertension is made on clinical grounds after a comprehensive history and physical examination.
- Noninvasive and invasive procedures confirm diagnosis and determine the severity of portal hypertension.

DIFFERENTIAL DIAGNOSIS
- Ascites from infection, neoplasm, or other inflammatory processes.
- Obesity.
- Abdominal organomegaly.

WORKUP
The workup of portal hypertension includes blood tests and noninvasive imaging studies to determine if the cause of portal hypertension is prehepatic, hepatic, or posthepatic. Ascitic fluid analysis is a key part of the diagnosis.

LABORATORY TESTS
- Complete blood count with platelets.
- Liver function tests with serum albumin.
- Prothrombin and partial thromboplastin times.
- Hepatitis B surface antigen and antibody.
- Hepatitis C antibody.
- In selected cases: iron, total iron-binding capacity, and ferritin; antinuclear antibody, anti–smooth muscle antibodies, antimitochondrial antibody, ceruloplasmin, alpha-1 antitrypsin.

- Ascitic fluid analysis: a serum-ascites albumin gradient ≥1.1 mg/dl suggests portal hypertension. Polymorphonuclear cells ≥250 cells/mL or positive Gram stain or culture suggest complicating spontaneous bacterial peritonitis (SBP).

IMAGING STUDIES
- Duplex-Doppler ultrasound is effective in screening for portal hypertension.
- Less commonly, CT/MRI/MRA scanning (Figs. 1P-82 and E1P-83) or liver-spleen nuclear medicine scanning can be used if the results from ultrasound are equivocal.
- Upper endoscopy is the most reliable test documenting the presence of esophageal varices.

TREATMENT

The treatment of portal hypertension is complex and involves measures to reduce the hypertension directly, minimize volume overload, correct underlying disorders, and prevent complications (most notably SBP and variceal bleeding).

NONPHARMACOLOGIC THERAPY
Dietary sodium restriction to generally 2000 mg/day forms the basis of therapy to limit fluid overload.

ACUTE GENERAL Rx
- For tense ascites, serial large-volume paracentesis (LVP) is generally recommended. The use of albumin infusion (8 to 10 g/L of ascites fluid removed) during LVP >5 L has been shown to reduce the incidence of postparacentesis circulatory dysfunction, although its use remains somewhat controversial.
- IV diuretics, typically furosemide and spironolactone, are used to achieve natriuresis and net negative salt and water balance. Renal function and serum electrolytes are monitored frequently, with transition to an oral regimen for long-term therapy.
- SBP is treated with IV antibiotics directed against enteric bacteria.
- Acute variceal hemorrhage is treated with crystalloid and blood product resuscitation, IV octreotide, terlipressin/vasopressin or somatostatin, and urgent upper endoscopy, often with sclerotherapy or band ligation. Patients with acute variceal hemorrhage should receive antibiotic prophylaxis against SBP.
- Traditionally, a transjugular intrahepatic portosystemic shunt (TIPS) or surgical shunt placement may be considered in patients not responding to above measures. However, recent data show early TIPS placement improved outcomes in acute variceal hemorrhage.

CHRONIC Rx
- Dietary sodium restriction in combination with diuretics: the typical ratio of furosemide 40 mg to spironolactone 100 mg retains normal serum potassium levels in most patients.

TABLE 1P-35 Etiology of Portal Hypertension

Condition	Site of Increased Resistance	FHVP	WHVP	HVPG	SPP	Liver Disease
Cirrhosis	Intrahepatic sinusoidal	Normal	Increased	Increased	Increased	Yes
Alcoholic hepatitis	Intrahepatic sinusoidal	Normal	Increased	Increased	Increased	Yes
Extrahepatic portal, splenic, or mesenteric vein thrombosis	Extrahepatic presinusoidal	Normal	Normal	Normal	Increased	No
Early primary biliary cirrhosis, PSC, sarcoid, schistosomiasis, congestive heart failure, noncirrhotic portal fibrosis, NRH	Intrahepatic presinusoidal	Normal	Normal/?raised	Normal/?raised	Increased	No
Hemochromatosis, peliosis, infiltrative disease, acute fatty liver of pregnancy	Intrahepatic sinusoidal hypertension	Normal	Increased	Increased	Increased	Yes
Veno-occlusive disease, posttransplant rejection	Intrahepatic postsinusoidal hypertension	Normal	?Increased	?Decreased	Increased	Yes
Budd-Chiari syndrome (noncirrhotic)	Extrahepatic postsinusoidal hypertension	Increased	Increased	Normal	Increased	Depends on severity
Constrictive pericarditis, inferior vena cava obstruction, congenital inferior vena cava web, right heart failure	Extrahepatic postsinusoidal hypertension	Increased	Increased	Normal	Increased	Depends on severity

FHVP, Free hepatic venous pressure; *HVPG,* hepatic venous pressure gradient; *SPP,* systolic pulse pressure; *WHVP,* wedged hepatic venous pressure.
From Vincent JL et al: *Textbook of critical care,* ed 6, Philadelphia, 2011, Saunders.

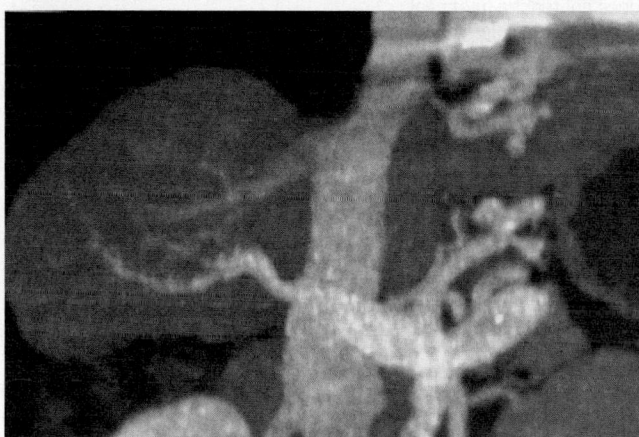

FIGURE 1P-82 MR angiography showing portal hypertension with collaterals. The shrunken liver and collateral are obvious. (From Forbes A et al [eds]: *Atlas of clinical gastroenterology,* ed 3, St Louis, 2005, Mosby.)

- Nonselective beta-blockers (propranolol and nadolol) in dosages sufficient to reduce the resting heart rate by 25% have been shown to be effective in primary prophylaxis for first-time variceal bleeding and for preventing recurrent variceal bleeding. Dosages are usually given bid and decreased if heart rate falls to <55 beats/min or systolic blood pressure drops to <90 mm Hg. The addition of a long-acting nitrate (e.g., isosorbide-5-mononitrate) has been shown to improve portal hemodynamics. Findings of a prospective trial of beta-blockers to prevent the formation of varices were negative. The combination of beta-blockade plus endoscopic esophageal variceal banding is superior to either intervention alone.
- Intermittent LVP may be needed in "diuretic resistant" patients.

- Patients with prior SBP merit lifelong antibiotics for secondary prevention.
- Abstinence from alcohol or treatment for hepatitis B or hepatitis C. Vaccination for hepatitis A and B as appropriate.
- Hepatic transplantation is an option in selected patients.

DISPOSITION
- The most common complication associated with portal hypertension is variceal bleeding. The risk of bleeding from varices is approximately 15% at 1 yr.
- Development of the hepatorenal syndrome (HRS) is associated with high near-term mortality. In particular, HRS may complicate SBP, which emphasizes the importance of making the diagnosis of SBP and instituting appropriate prophylaxis.

REFERRAL
Consultation with a gastroenterologist is recommended in all patients with portal hypertension to screen for esophageal varices.

PEARLS & CONSIDERATIONS

Splanchnic arterial vasodilation is increasingly recognized as an important component of the pathophysiology of portal hypertension and ascites. There may be vasodilation in other capillary beds as well; of note, pulmonary arteriolar vasodilation can create a significant shunt fraction and resultant hypoxemia in the absence of chest radiograph or CT chest evidence of parenchymal disease. The diagnosis is suspected when otherwise unexplained hypoxia arises in a patient with cirrhosis, along with platypnea (dyspnea worse when sitting upright) and orthodeoxia (desaturation with upright posture). The diagnosis is confirmed by echocardiography with agitated saline, in which there is delayed appearance of bubbles in the left heart after injection into a peripheral vein.

COMMENTS
Portal hypertension and its complications carry significant morbidity and mortality rates. Emphasize ethanol abstinence, provide vaccinations and prophylactic therapy where indicated, and consider early referral to a specialist for assistance with management and consideration for hepatic transplantation.

SUGGESTED READINGS
Available at www.expertconsult.com

AUTHOR: **MEL L. ANDERSON, M.D.**

BASIC INFORMATION

DEFINITION

Portal vein thrombosis (PVT) is thrombotic occlusion of the portal vein. The thrombus can also involve segments of the mesenteric veins and/or the splenic vein.

SYNONYMS

Pylethrombosis
PVT

ICD-10CM CODES
I81 Portal vein thrombosis

EPIDEMIOLOGY & DEMOGRAPHICS

- Occurs with equal frequency in children (peak age: 6 yr) and adults (peak age: 40 yr)
- Occurs in 8% to 25% of patients with decompensated cirrhosis

PHYSICAL FINDINGS & CLINICAL PRESENTATION

- Acute PVT may present with sudden onset of fever and abdominal pain (when there is mesenteric extension).
- Upper gastrointestinal hemorrhage (hematemesis and/or melena) caused by esophageal varices.

ETIOLOGY & PATHOPHYSIOLOGY

In children: umbilical sepsis (pathophysiology unknown). In adults:
1. Hypercoagulable states:
   - Antiphospholipid syndrome.
   - Neoplasm (common cause).
   - Paroxysmal nocturnal hemoglobinuria.
   - Myeloproliferative diseases.
   - Oral contraceptives.
   - Polycythemia vera.
   - Pregnancy.
   - Protein S or C deficiency.
   - Sickle cell disease.
   - Thrombocytosis.
2. Inflammatory diseases:
   - Crohn's disease.
   - Pancreatitis.
   - Ulcerative colitis.
3. Complications of medical intervention:
   - Ambulatory dialysis.
   - Chemoembolization.
   - Liver transplantation.
   - Partial hepatectomy.
   - Sclerotherapy.
   - Splenectomy.
   - Transjugular intrahepatic portosystemic shunt.
4. Infections:
   - Appendicitis.

- Diverticulitis.
- Cholecystitis.
5. Miscellaneous:
   - Cirrhosis (common cause).
   - Bladder cancer.

Pathophysiology: PVT results in portal hypertension, leading to esophageal and gastrointestinal varices. The liver sustained by the hepatic artery maintains normal function.

Dx DIAGNOSIS

DIFFERENTIAL DIAGNOSIS

Causes of upper gastrointestinal hemorrhage and abdominal pain are described in Section II.

WORKUP

- Abdominal ultrasound with Doppler (Fig. 1P-84) or MRI may show the PVT. Abdominal ultrasound color Doppler imaging has a 98% negative predictive value and is considered the imaging modality of choice in diagnosing PVT.
- Determination of underlying cirrhosis of the liver should be the foremost step. It is crucial to differentiate acute from chronic PVT because chronic PVT does not require treatment.
- Esophagogastroscopy typically shows esophageal varices.
- Laboratory evaluation for hypercoagulable state is not cost-effective in patients with cirrhosis.

Rx TREATMENT

- Anticoagulation data on thrombolytic therapy are inconclusive and there is no formal recommendation for or against anticoagulation in acute PVT. However, anticoagulation is generally recommended for patients with extension of PVT into the superior mesenteric vein to prevent intestinal infarction. In patients with chronic PVT and concomitant cirrhosis, long-term anticoagulation is generally not recommended.
- Variceal sclerotherapy or banding.
- Surgical mesocaval or splenorenal shunt.
- The roles of thrombolysis and transjugular intrahepatic portosystemic shunt continue to evolve.

REFERRAL

- To surgeon to rule out intestinal infarction.
- To gastroenterologist.

SUGGESTED READINGS

Available at www.expertconsult.com

AUTHOR: **FRED F. FERRI, M.D.**

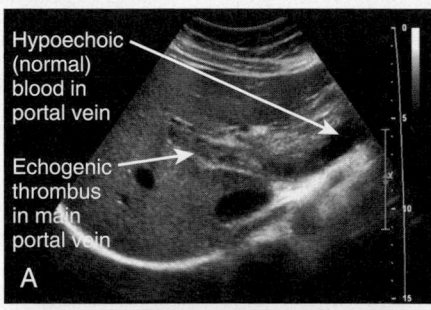

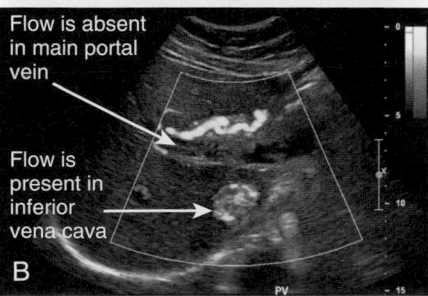

FIGURE 1P-84 Portal vein thrombosis: ultrasound. This 22-year-old female, 2 months postpartum, presented with 1 week of right upper quadrant pain. Ultrasound was performed to evaluate for suspected cholecystitis or symptomatic cholelithiasis. Instead, portal vein thrombosis was discovered. The postpartum state is a risk factor for this condition. Hypercoagulable states and inflammatory or neoplastic abdominal conditions, including pancreatitis and abdominal malignancies, also can result in portal vein thrombosis. **A,** Ultrasound gray scale image showing thrombus in the main portal vein. **B,** Doppler ultrasound showing no flow within the portal vein. (From Broder JS: *Diagnostic imaging for the emergency physician*, Philadelphia, 2011, Saunders.)

 BASIC INFORMATION

DEFINITION

Postconcussive syndrome (PCS) refers to persistent neurologic, cognitive, and psychological symptoms that result from traumatic brain injury (TBI). There is no consensus regarding the duration of symptoms to make the diagnosis, but symptoms usually manifest or significantly worsen within a few days following head trauma and persist for weeks to months. PCS can also follow moderate and severe brain injury, although it is more commonly associated with mild brain injury or concussion. Concussion is an acute trauma-induced alteration of mental function lasting <24 hr, with or without preceding loss of consciousness.

SYNONYMS

PCS
Postconcussion syndrome
Posttraumatic nervous instability or brain injury
Postcontusion syndrome or encephalopathy
Status post commotio cerebri

ICD-10CM CODES
F07.81 Postconcussional syndrome

EPIDEMIOLOGY & DEMOGRAPHICS

- Incidence is approximately 27 cases per 100,000 persons/year
- From 30% to 80% of patients with mild to moderate brain injury will experience some symptoms of PCS.
- Usually reported in the young, ages 20 to 30 yr.
- Risk factors include female sex, low socioeconomic status, previous TBI, severe bodily injury from TBI, headaches, and unsettled court cases.

PHYSICAL FINDINGS & CLINICAL PRESENTATION

- Usually present without focal neurologic deficits on examination.
- Symptoms start within a few days to weeks after the head injury and usually persist after 3 mo.
- Can be divided into early and late or persistent (>6 mo).
- 15% of patients will have persistent symptoms 1 yr later.
- Symptoms include (at least three of the following after TBI to meet ICD-10 criteria):
  1. Headache (usually of fronto-occipital location and showing characteristics of tension or migraine headache). The International Headache Society suggests that coding and attribution of headaches with characteristics of primary headaches but in the setting of an inciting event should be attributed to the event, unless there was a known history of the headache and the inciting event was seen as aggravating/initiating the preexisting migraine/tension headache.
  2. Fatigue
  3. Dizziness and/or vertigo
  4. Impaired memory
  5. Difficulty in concentrating
  6. Insomnia
  7. Irritability
  8. Lowered tolerance of stress, emotion, or alcohol
- Other associated symptoms: noise sensitivity, neck pain, nondermatomal paresthesias, interference with social role functioning.

ETIOLOGY

- Caused by TBI from events such as falls, motor vehicle accidents, military injuries, and contact sports.
- Postmortem findings reveal diffuse axonal injury as the primary pathologic finding along with small petechial hemorrhages and local edema.
- The primary injury triggers a slew of pathophysiological changes at the cellular level secondary to the axonal stretching and injury, leading to alterations in membrane and intracellular physiology, thereby affecting neurotransmission. These changes are believed to be a factor in determining whether the outcome will be an apparent normal recovery or persistent postconcussion symptoms.
- A psychogenic origin has been suggested by a number of empiric and clinical observations; however, limitations in methodology and differing definitions preclude firm conclusions. Prior history of anxiety is a strong risk factor for occurrence of PCS.

DIAGNOSIS

A careful history, a nonfocal neurologic examination, and normal neurologic testing will usually establish the diagnosis.

DIFFERENTIAL DIAGNOSIS

- Headache (dissection of the vertebral artery, occipital neuralgia)
- Epidural hematoma
- Subdural hematoma
- Skull fracture
- Cervical spine disk disease
- Whiplash
- Cerebrovascular accident
- Depression
- Anxiety

WORKUP

To exclude other causes of neurologic symptoms after TBI:
- Normal results of electroencephalography
- Normal evoked potentials
- Neuropsychological testing, which often reveals difficulties in concentration, memory, language, and executive function

LABORATORY TESTS

Various biomarkers in blood and cerebrospinal fluid and genetic testing have been proposed and studied in patients with TBI, but these tests are not specific and are not routinely used.

IMAGING STUDIES

- There is no imaging modality to diagnose PCS. PCS is primarily a clinical diagnosis.
- 10% of CT scans of the head following mild TBI are abnormal, showing mild subarachnoid hemorrhage, subdural hemorrhage, or contusions.
- MRI of the head after an mTBI is abnormal in 30% of patients with normal CT scans and may show irregular brain contours or old cerebral contusions.
- Recent improvements in imaging modalities, including diffuse tensor imaging (DTI) and susceptibility weighted imaging (SWI) in MRI, functional MRI (fMRI), and metabolic imaging such as magnetic resonance spectroscopy (MRS), positron emission tomography (PET), and single-photon emission computed tomography (SPECT) imaging, appear to be promising in elucidating the underlying pathophysiology of TBI and PCS, although they have not found a major role in clinical practice yet.
- None of the imaging modalities have been able to predict the occurrence of PCS in patients with mild TBI

TREATMENT

Must be recognized as a physiologic and psychological problem and treated accordingly.

GENERAL Rx

- Must be individualized to the patient's particular symptoms.
- Simple and early reassurance is often the major treatment.
- Symptoms are often refractory to treatment
- Supportive care may include the use of non-narcotic analgesics and antiemetics.
- Pain management.
- Amitriptyline has been widely used for posttraumatic tension-type headaches as well as for nonspecific symptoms such as irritability, dizziness, insomnia, and depression.
- Posttraumatic migraine-type headaches can be treated with a trial of propranolol or amitriptyline alone or in combination.
- Depression can be treated with selective serotonin reuptake inhibitors but may not respond as well when compared with patients without PCS who have depression.
- Some patients may be admitted for severe symptoms; most can be managed as outpatients.
- There may be a role for cognitive behavioral therapy in treating symptoms.

NONPHARMACOLOGIC THERAPY

- Early psychological intervention and cognitive rehabilitation are key for full recovery.
- Physical and occupational therapy.
- Avoidance of alcohol, narcotics, and sleep deprivation.
- Explanation of symptoms and expectations, combined with early follow-up with reassurance, may hasten resolution of symptoms.

DISPOSITION

- Most patients improve after mild TBI without any residual deficits within 3 months.

- Although good improvement is typically seen within the first 6 mo, patients can continue to show improvement for up to 12-18 mo.
- Patients with very severe brain injuries (low Glasgow Coma Scale [GCS] score) and prolonged anterograde amnesia are at increased risk of development of some degree of permanent cognitive and personality disturbance.
- Predictors for the development of persistent PCS include:
  1. Female sex
  2. Ongoing litigation (conflicting studies)
  3. Low socioeconomic status
  4. Prior headaches
  5. Prior TBI
  6. Prior psychiatric illnesses such as anxiety

REFERRAL

Early consultations with psychologists, psychiatrists, neurologists, and rehabilitation specialists in an outpatient setting may be beneficial.

ⓘ PEARLS & CONSIDERATIONS

- PCS starts within a few days after the injury.
- Recognizing depression and treating pain symptoms early in the course may help prevent the development of persistent PCS (>1 yr).
- The severity of the trauma does not clearly predict the risk of PCS.
- The severity of brain injury is usually documented by initial GCS score, duration of loss of consciousness, and duration of amnesia; however, there is a move toward tests of function, such as neuropsychological testing or fMRI.

COMMENTS

- Attempts to determine how much of a role psychological and/or neurologic factors play in the PCS are important but very difficult.

- No medication at hospital discharge has been proved to change the natural course of the disease.

SUGGESTED READINGS

Available at www.expertconsult.com

RELATED CONTENT

Post-concussion Syndrome (Patient Information)

AUTHOR: **PRASHANTH KRISHNAMOHAN, M.B.B.S, M.D.**

 **BASIC INFORMATION**

DEFINITION

- Postherpetic neuralgia (PHN) is a pain syndrome that results as a complication of herpes zoster (HZ). HZ, also known as shingles, is a painful vesicular eruption in a dermatomal distribution. HZ is caused by the reactivation of varicella zoster virus (VZV) in someone with a known history of varicella. PHN is pain and/or dysesthesia that persist for 3 or more months at the site of resolved HZ.

ICD 10-CM CODES
B02.29 Other postherpetic nervous system involvement

EPIDEMIOLOGY & DEMOGRAPHICS

INCIDENCE: PHN occurs in approximately 9% to 34 % of HZ patients. It is the most frequent chronic complication of herpes zoster and the most common neuropathic pain resulting from infection. In one study, at age 60 years, approximately 60% of patients with HZ developed PHN, and at age 70 years, 75% developed PHN. In another study, the incidence of PHN at 9 years post-HZ eruption was 21%.

PEAK INCIDENCE: Unknown

PREDOMINANT SEX AND AGE:
- PHN occurs equally in males and females.
- The likelihood of developing PHN significantly increases with advancing age.

GENETICS:
- Family history of HZ is considered a risk factor for HZ, with higher risk if multiple family members have had HZ.

RISK FACTORS:
- Advanced age
- Greater severity of HZ prodromal pain
- Greater severity of pain during acute HZ eruption
- Location—specifically ophthalmic (V1) location and brachial plexus

PHYSICAL FINDINGS & CLINICAL PRESENTATION

- HZ typically presents as a painful vesicular eruption in a dermatomal distribution. Rarely, HZ can occur subclinically with dermatomal pain in the absence of a rash.
- PHN is pain that continues for 3 months at the dermatomal site of the resolved HZ. The pain may be described as burning, stabbing, shooting, or shock-like.
- Patients may note an amplified response to stimuli at the site of PHN, with increased pain response (hyperalgesia), pain to typically non-noxious stimuli (allodynia), or focal changes in autonomic function (e.g., increased sweating).
- Physical examination should include a comparison of sensory function in the affected dermatome with that on the contralateral side.

ETIOLOGY

- PHN is associated with damage and scarring to the dorsal root ganglion secondary to inflammation related to active herpes zoster infection.

 **DIAGNOSIS**

DIFFERENTIAL DIAGNOSIS

Zoster sine herpete (subclinical HZ without skin eruption)

℞ TREATMENT

ACUTE GENERAL Rx

- Administration of acyclovir or valacyclovir within 72 hours of HZ onset is thought to help reduce the likelihood of developing PNH. However, one Cochrane review paper found no difference with acyclovir administration.
- A single published study supports the use of amitriptyline (25 mg daily) as an adjunct to an antiviral agent in acute HZ to decrease the incidence of PHN and the pain associated with subsequent PHN.
- A suggestive non-controlled study with co-administration of valacyclovir and gabapentin during acute HZ reduced the incidence of PHN as well.
- Corticosteroids do NOT prevent PHN.

CHRONIC Rx
TOPICAL TREATMENTS:
- Lidocaine 5% patches may be used for mild pain.
- Capsaicin 0.075% cream (although little reported efficacy) 5 times per day.
- Capsaicin 8% patch has greater efficacy, but overall analgesia may be minimal at best, with 1/3 of patients unable to tolerate the agent due to burning, stinging, and erythema. However, a single 60-minute treatment with high concentration capsaicin patch was found in one study to reduce PHN for up to 12 weeks regardless of concomitant systemic neuropathic pain medication use.

ORAL TREATMENTS: First line:
- Gabapentinoids (gabapentin, pregabalin) are the only FDA-approved therapy for PHN and are some of the most commonly used first-line therapies for chronic PHN pain. Dosing includes gabapentin 300 mg 3 times a day (titrating up to max 3600 mg/day) and pregabalin 75 mg nightly (titrating up to 300 mg twice daily).
- Tricyclic antidepressants such as amitriptyline (25 mg/day, increased 25 mg every night to a maximum of 75 mg/night), desipramine (10-25 mg/day, increased every 3 days as needed to a maximum of 150 mg/day) and nortriptyline (10-25 mg/day increased by 25 mg/day weekly as needed to maximum of 75 mg day) are another first line treatment. These medications have a delayed onset of action and may not work as well in patients with certain types of pain, such as burning pain or allodynia. They have a considerable side effect profile. Their use in elderly patients should be carefully considered. The serotonin-norepinephrine reuptake inhibitor duloxetine is also commonly used in resistant cases with mixed results.
- A recent study showed the combination of gabapentin and nortriptyline was more effi-

cacious than either drug as monotherapy for neuropathic pain.

Second Line:
- Opiates (e.g., controlled-release oxycodone): the side effects, the possibility of misuse, and the potential for abuse must be weighed.

Other Modalities:
- Dorsal root entry zone (DREZ) lesions have been used with an improvement rate of 20% in long-term studies.
- For recalcitrant cases, epidural corticosteroids and nerve blocks, botulinum toxin, and cryotherapy
- Fig. 1P-85 describes a treatment algorithm for HZ and PHN.

COMPLEMENTARY AND ALTERNATIVE MEDICINE:
- Acupuncture
  - Studies on acupuncture and PHN pain have had varying results; however, the only randomized control study showed no significant difference in pain reduction between control and treatment groups.

❗ PEARLS & CONSIDERATIONS

COMMENTS

- Careful consideration of treatment side effects and drug interactions is needed.
- The natural history of PHN is slow resolution, and most individuals respond to medical therapy. However, a subtype of patients may develop severe, long-lasting pain that is recalcitrant to medical therapy.
- In a questionnaire study of 385 adults age >65 years old with persistent acute pain, the mean duration of PHN is 3.3 years.

PREVENTION

- Vaccination
  - A live-attenuated VZV vaccine (Zostavax®) is effective in reducing the risk for both HZ and PHN (11 and 43 needed to vaccinate to prevent a case of HZ or PHN, respectively), with the main benefit being the reduction of morbidity caused by PHN. Vaccination reduces the risk of PHN by 67% in patients >60 years old.
  - FDA-approved 50 and older; currently, the CDC recommends at age 60 regardless of history of chicken pox.
  - Data still insufficient regarding long-term prevention of HZ and PHN given efficacy likely wanes over time.

PATIENT/FAMILY EDUCATION

The only well-documented means of preventing PHN is the prevention of herpes zoster, of which vaccination has the only proven efficacy. Patients should understand both the benefits and the potential adverse effects of treatment. They should be informed that pain relief will likely not be immediate; frequent reassessment may be needed and drug doses should be increased as necessary.

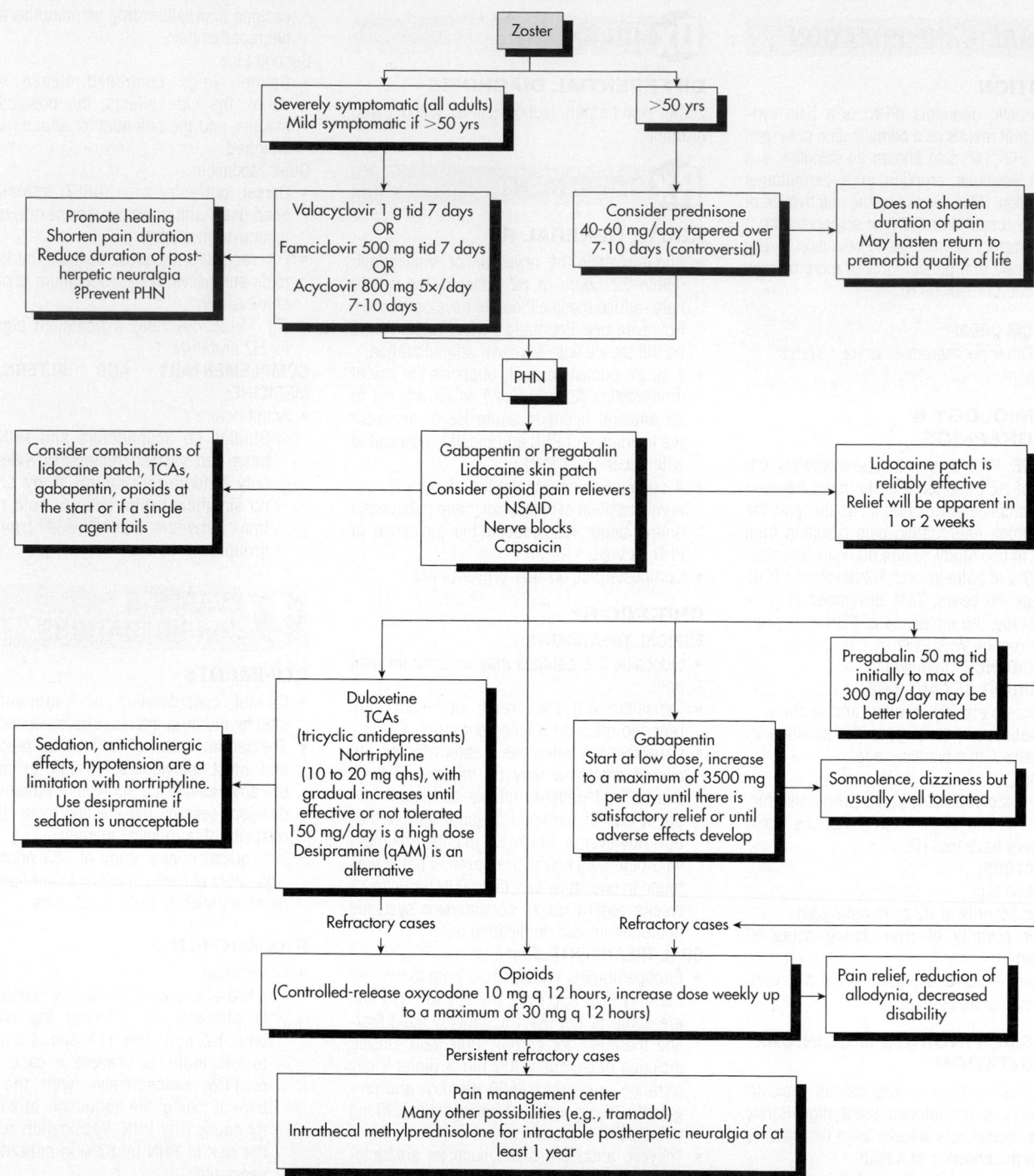

FIGURE 1P-85 Treatment of herpes zoster and postherpetic neuralgia. *NSAID,* Nonsteroidal antiin-flammatory drug; *PHN,* postherpetic neuralgia. (Modified from Habif TA: *Clinical dermatology,* ed 4, St Louis, 2004, Mosby.)

RELATED CONTENT

Herpes Zoster (Related Key Topic)
Peripheral Neuropathy

SUGGESTED READINGS

Available at www.expertconsult.com

AUTHORS: **EMILY Z. HEJAZI, M.D., M.S.,** and
LISA K. PAPPAS-TAFFER, M.D.

BASIC INFORMATION

DEFINITION

Major or minor depressive episodes occurring within 3 to 12 months of delivery

SYNONYMS

Postpartum blues
Postpartum depression
Postpartum psychosis

ICD-10CM CODES
F53: includes postpartum depression and postpartum psychosis
O90.6: includes postpartum blues, postpartum dysphoria and sadness

EPIDEMIOLOGY & DEMOGRAPHICS

INCIDENCE: Approximately half a million women in the United States are affected annually by postpartum depression.
PREVALENCE: Perinatal depression affects 1 in 7 women
GENETICS: A family history of mood disorders is a risk factor for postpartum depression
RISK FACTORS: Risk factors include depression or anxiety during pregnancy, traumatic birth experiences, stressful life events during pregnancy or the postpartum period, infant NICU admission or preterm delivery, poor social support, history of depression, and problems with breastfeeding.

PHYSICAL FINDINGS & CLINICAL PRESENTATION

Patients present with depressed or irritable mood, decreased interest in activities, appetite and sleep changes, weight changes, decreased energy, excessive guilt or feelings of worthlessness, psychomotor agitation or retardation, and possibly suicidal/homicidal ideation. The diagnosis of major depressive episode requires that symptoms be present nearly every day for two weeks and that the woman experiences a decline from a previous level of functioning.

ETIOLOGY

The decline in reproductive hormones following delivery is believed to contribute to the development of postpartum depression in some women. In addition, women with a history of depression, stressful life events, and a family history of mood disorders have an increased risk of both depression and postpartum depression.

DIAGNOSIS

DIFFERENTIAL DIAGNOSIS
- Hyperthyroid
- Hypothyroid
- Postpartum blues: syndrome with weepiness and sadness usually occurring shortly after delivery and resolving by 10 days postpartum.
- Postpartum psychosis: usually occurs between 1 to 2 weeks post-delivery and is characterized by extreme disorganization of thought, hallucinations, and bizarre behavior. It requires rapid intervention as there is a real risk of suicide or infanticide
- Bipolar disorder

WORK-UP
- History and physical examination
- Screening all postpartum women with a screening instrument such as the Edinburgh Postnatal Depression Scale (specific to the postpartum period and takes less than 5 minutes to complete) or the Patient Health Questionnaire 9
- In any patient with postpartum depression, screening for bipolar disorder

LABORATORY TESTS
There are no diagnostic laboratory tests.

IMAGING STUDIES
None

TREATMENT

NONPHARMACOLOGIC THERAPY
- Psychotherapy: studies have shown psychotherapy to be equally effective to fluoxetine.

ACUTE GENERAL Rx
- Therapy with a selective serotonin reuptake inhibitor should be considered as first-line treatment because of low risk of toxic effects with overdose and ease of dosing. However, if patient has had good success with another medication in the past, then it is appropriate to restart that medication. Start at half the recommended dose and increase after 4 days, with gradual up-titration until therapeutic effects are seen.
- A single medication is favored over multiple medications in order to decrease exposure to the fetus/neonate.
- Sertraline is the first-line selective serotonin reuptake inhibitor recommended for breastfeeding mothers secondary to existing evidence suggesting little risk for infants. There is, however, no evidence of adverse infant effects from mothers taking sertraline, paroxetine or fluvoxamine. Fluoxetine may be present in higher levels in breast milk and breastfed infants.
- Tricyclic antidepressants do not appear to pass in significant amounts into breastfeeding infants and their use appears to be safe. Data regarding atypical antidepressants and breastfeeding is limited.

CHRONIC Rx
- Medical therapy should be continued until at least 6 months after remission.
- Long-term therapy should be considered for women with a history of 3 or more episodes of depression.

DISPOSITION
- Without treatment, the duration of postpartum depression averages seven months.

- Fifteen percent to 85% of women will experience at least one relapse after completing medical therapy.

REFERRAL
- Consider referral to psychiatrist if a patient demonstrates no improvement after six weeks of drug therapy or experiences a relapse.
- Prompt or urgent referral to psychiatrist is indicated if a patient has signs/symptoms of postpartum psychosis, bipolar disorder, or expresses suicidal/homicidal ideation.

PEARLS & CONSIDERATIONS

COMMENTS
- Depression and anxiety both during and after pregnancy can have negative effects not only on the mother but also on her fetus, new baby, and family. Low birth weight, decreased fetal growth, increased NICU admission rates, increased neonate crying, and decreased developmental scores have been seen with these disorders when untreated. In addition, depression is associated with increased smoking, alcohol, and drug use, which can have negative effects on the infant and family. These factors should be taken into account when counseling women about medical therapy.
- Selective serotonin reuptake inhibitors do pass through breast milk but are present in very small quantities compared with the transplacental exposure infants receive in utero. Adverse infant effects are extremely rare; however, long-term data is lacking.

PREVENTION
In a patient with a history of postpartum depression, recurrence risk is approximately 25%. These patients should be screened for depression both during and after pregnancy. It is reasonable to initiate prophylactic therapy in patients with a history of depression, and they should have close postpartum follow-up for early identification of depressive episodes.

PATIENT/FAMILY EDUCATION
National Women's Health Information Center: www.womenshealth.gov
Postpartum Support International: www.postpartum.net
Center for Disease Control and Prevention: http://www.cdc.gov/reproductivehealth/depression/

RELATED CONTENT
Depression, Major (Related Key Topic)

SUGGESTED READINGS
Available at www.expertconsult.com

AUTHOR: **CLAIRE SCHULTZ, M.D.**

BASIC INFORMATION

DEFINITION

Postpartum hemorrhage (PPH) is classically defined as estimated blood loss >500 mL after a vaginal birth or >1000 mL after a cesarean section. Primary PPH is hemorrhage within the first 24 hr after delivery. Secondary PPH is hemorrhage after 24 hr and within 6 to 12 wk.

SYNONYMS

Obstetric hemorrhage

ICD-10CM CODES
072.1 Other immediate postpartum hemorrhage
072.2 Delayed and secondary postpartum hemorrhage

EPIDEMIOLOGY & DEMOGRAPHICS

INCIDENCE: 4% to 6%
PREDOMINANT SEX AND AGE: Female of reproductive age
RISK FACTORS: Prolonged labor, augmented labor, rapid labor, history of PPH, episiotomy, preeclampsia, multiple gestation, macrosomic infant, operative delivery, chorioamnionitis, bleeding dyscrasia, Asian or Hispanic ethnicity

PHYSICAL FINDINGS & CLINICAL PRESENTATION (TABLE 1P-36)

- Bleeding is generally brisk at time of delivery.
- Examination findings include boggy uterus with continued passage of clot or blood with fundal pressure.
- Objective findings can also include hypotension, tachycardia, and oliguria with substantial blood loss.

ETIOLOGY

- Primary: uterine atony (>80%), retained placenta, coagulopathies, lacerations
- Secondary: subinvolution of placental site, retained products, infection, coagulopathies

DIAGNOSIS

WORKUP

- Bladder should be emptied
- Bimanual examination to evaluate for atony; massage if it is present
- Examination to verify that no lacerations are present, including cervical examination with necessary lighting and retractors
- Ultrasonography at bedside to evaluate for retained tissue or clot
- Examination to verify that placenta is intact

LABORATORY TESTS

Significant hemorrhage can lead to disseminated intravascular coagulation (DIC). If DIC is suspected, complete blood count and coagulation panels should be ordered. Similarly, if coagulopathy is suspected, evaluation of clotting factors should be ordered.

IMAGING STUDIES

Ultrasonography can be used to scan for retained products, including clot or placenta. It can be performed to assess the need for more invasive measures, such as instrumentation or a manual sweep.

TREATMENT

Medical management with uterotonics is generally the first line of treatment:
- Oxytocin (IV, 10-40 units diluted into IV solution, or 10 units IM); often given prophylactically immediately after delivery
- Methergine (IM, 0.2 mg)
- Hemabate (IM, 0.25 mg)
- Misoprostol (800-1000 mcg rectally)

NONPHARMACOLOGIC THERAPY

Secondary management includes the following:
- Packing with gauze, Foley catheter, or tamponade balloon
- Uterine curettage for suspected retained products
- Uterine artery embolization
- Surgical management with laparotomy
  1. Hypogastric artery ligation
  2. Bilateral uterine artery ligation (O'Leary sutures)
  3. B-lynch sutures
  4. Hysterectomy

ACUTE GENERAL Rx

- Uterotonics, surgical management, embolization, blood transfusion. Fig. 1P-86 outlines the management of postpartum hemorrhage.
- Table 1P-37 describes therapeutic response to initial fluid resuscitation. Dosing regimen for oxytocic drugs is summarized in Table 1P-38. Blood product replacement is described in Box 1P-10.

CHRONIC Rx

For anemia: ferrous sulfate supplementation to support new red blood cell production

---

TABLE 1P-36 Presentation of Symptoms in Postpartum Hemorrhage

% Blood loss (mL)	Systolic blood pressure (mm Hg)	Signs and symptoms
10-15 (500-1000)	Normal	Tachycardia, palpitations, dizziness
15-25 (1000-1500)	Low-normal	Tachycardia, weakness, diaphoresis
25-35 (1500-2000)	70-80	Restlessness, pallor, oliguria
35-45 (2000-3000)	50-70	Collapse, air hunger, anuria

From Vincent JL et al: *Textbook of critical care,* ed 6, Philadelphia, 2011, WB Saunders.

TABLE 1P-37 Therapeutic Response to Initial Fluid Resuscitation

Response	Description	Follow-up treatment
Rapid response	<20% of blood volume lost	No additional fluids or blood are needed.
Transient response	20%-40% of blood volume lost; responds to initial fluid bolus but later has worsening vital signs	Continue fluids and consider blood transfusions.
Minimal or no response	Ongoing severe hemorrhage with >40% blood volume lost	Continue aggressive fluid and blood product replacements.

From Vincent JL et al: *Textbook of critical care,* ed 6, Philadelphia, 2011, WB Saunders.

TABLE 1P-38 Dosing Regimens for Oxytocic Drugs

Drug	Regimens
Oxytocin (Pitocin)	5-unit IV bolus
	Add 20-40 units oxytocin to 1 L of fluids
	10 units intramyometrially
Methylergonovine (Methergine)	0.2 mg IM every 2-4 hr
Ergonovine (Ergotrate Maleate)	100-125 mcg IM or intramyometrially every 2-4 hr
	200-250 mcg IM
	Total dose 1.25 mg
Carboprost (Hemabate)	250 mcg IM or intramyometrially every 15-90 min
	Total dose 2 mg
Misoprostol	800 mcg PR or 800 mcg of sublingual misoprostol

IM, Intramuscular; *IV,* intravenous; *PR,* per rectum.
From Vincent JL et al: *Textbook of critical care,* ed 6, Philadelphia, 2011, WB Saunders.

DISPOSITION

- The patient should be closely watched for at least 24 hr after a postpartum hemorrhage. Laboratory findings should be monitored to follow trends on the Hunt and Hess scale. Vital signs should be monitored for evidence of hemodynamic stability and appropriate response to anemia.
- Morbidity can include shock, acute respiratory distress syndrome, Sheehan's syndrome, and loss of fertility.

REFERRAL

During the course of a postpartum hemorrhage, the anesthesiology department should be notified and adequate nursing should be available. Early considerations should be made to notify obstetricians. If bleeding is brisk or estimated blood loss is considerable, preparation should be made for transfusion of blood products, including drawing blood for typing and notifying the blood bank.

SUGGESTED READINGS

Available at www.expertconsult.com

AUTHOR: **LEO HAN, M.D.**

Diseases and Disorders

BOX 1P-10   Blood Product Replacement

Cross-matched blood
Type-specific or "saline cross-matched" blood
Compatible ABO and Rh blood types
Rh-negative blood is preferable.
Warm the blood, if possible, especially if the rate of infusion is >100 ml/min or if the total volume transfused is high; cold blood is associated with an increased incidence of arrhythmias and paradoxical hypotension.
Administer calcium if blood is transfused rapidly at >100 ml/min because of binding of calcium by anticoagulants in banked blood.
Give 6-10 units fresh frozen plasma (FFP) for every 10 units of packed red blood cell transfusions.
Give 10-12 units of platelets if the platelet count decreases to <50 × 109/L.
Cryoprecipitate can be given to replace fibrinogen in addition to the FFP.
Consider 60-120 mcg/kg intravenous bolus injection of recombinant activated factor VII (rFVIIa).

From Vincent JL et al: *Textbook of critical care,* ed 6, Philadelphia, 2011, WB Saunders.

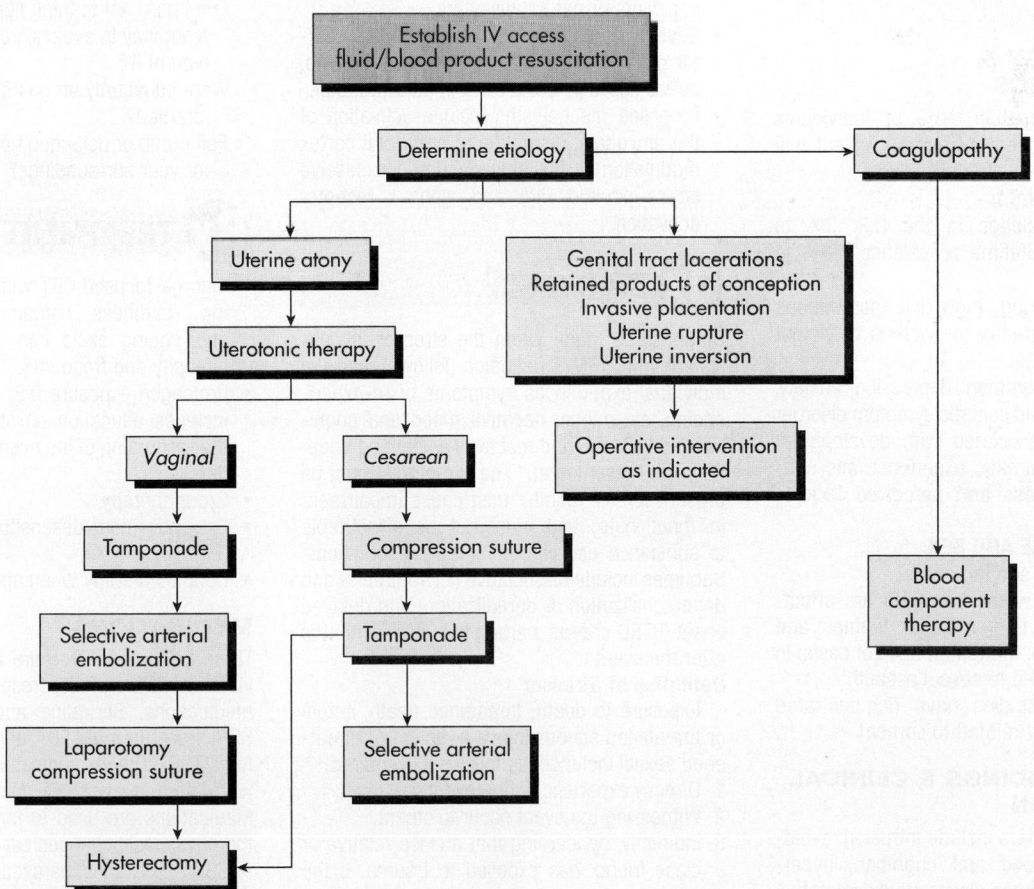

FIGURE 1P-86 Management of postpartum hemorrhage. (From Gabbe SG: *Obstetrics,* ed 6, Philadelphia, 2012, WB Saunders.)

 **BASIC INFORMATION**

DEFINITION

Posttraumatic stress disorder (PTSD) develops in some people after witnessing or experiencing a traumatic event that involves actual or threatened injury to self or others. Symptoms continue longer than a month after the event or have delayed onset and include: intrusive thoughts, nightmares, flashbacks, avoidance of things associated with the trauma, hypervigilance, sleep disturbance, and negative changes in mood and cognition. These symptoms cause distress and a decline in interpersonal, social, and occupational functioning. People with PTSD may feel numb or irritable, may be easily startled or frightened, and sometimes isolate themselves from others. They are at risk for comorbid psychiatric illness, substance abuse, and suicide.

SYNONYMS (HISTORICAL)

Soldier's heart
Effort syndrome
Shell shock
Concentration camp syndrome

ICD-10CM CODES
F43.10 Post-traumatic stress disorder, unspecified
F43.11 Post-traumatic stress disorder, acute
F43.12 Post-traumatic stress disorder, chronic

EPIDEMIOLOGY & DEMOGRAPHICS

INCIDENCE: Fewer than 10% of individuals who have experienced a traumatic event will develop PTSD.
PREVALENCE (IN U.S.):
- 12-month prevalence in the U.S. 3% to 6%. Estimated lifetime prevalence 7.8% to 12.3%.
- Prevalence among high-risk populations (e.g., combat veterans or victims of violent crimes) up to 58%.
- Comorbidity is common: depression, anxiety, substance use, and somatic symptom disorder
- Factors most associated with development are previous traumatic experience and subsequent life stress and perceived lack of social support
PREDOMINANT AGE AND SEX:
- No predisposing age factors.
- Twice as many women as men are affected (prevalence 10%-14% for women and 5%-6% for men). More than 50% of cases in women are related to sexual assault.
GENETICS: Twin studies have demonstrated genetic vulnerability related to combat.

PHYSICAL FINDINGS & CLINICAL PRESENTATION

Core symptom clusters include intrusion, avoidance, negative mood and cognition, hyperarousal, and sometimes dissociative symptoms. Individuals present with different variations of these symptoms. Symptoms must occur for >1 month and result in significant distress and functional impairment.
Key PTSD symptoms:
1. Distressing memories or dreams of the event. Note: Children older than 6 may express this symptom in repetitive play.
2. Flashbacks.
3. Intense distress after reminders of the event.
4. Avoidance due to trauma-related thoughts or feelings.
5. Persistent negative trauma-related emotions.
6. Feeling detached.
7. Aggressive or reckless behavior.
8. Hypervigilance.
9. Problems with concentration or sleep.
10. Depersonalization.

ETIOLOGY

- Common types of trauma: violent personal assault, natural disaster, military combat, rape, motor vehicle accident, childhood abuse and neglect, critical illness or hospitalization in ICU, severe physical injury, diagnosis of life-threatening illness.
- Risk factors: previous trauma, initial severity of reaction to event, psychiatric history, childhood abuse or neglect, poor social support, gender, age.
- Interpersonal violence is more likely to cause PTSD than events such as motor vehicle accidents or natural disasters.
- Severity of physical injury is a weaker predictor of PTSD than the psychological distress; stress duration is the most important factor.
- Proposed mechanisms include activation of the amygdala, disruption of prefrontal cortex modulation of the amygdala, and excessive stress-induced HPA and alpha-1 receptor activation.

DX DIAGNOSIS

Diagnosis is made when the stressor is consistent with DSM 5 definition (follows), and the individual experiences symptoms of re-experiencing, avoidance, negative mood and cognition, and arousal and reactivity as defined under "Clinical Presentation." The symptoms must be present for >1 month, must cause impairment in functioning, and must not be attributable to substance use or other medical conditions. Subtypes include dissociative (PTSD criteria and depersonalization or derealization) and delayed onset (PTSD criteria starting at least six months after the event.)
Definition of Stressor
Exposure to death, threatened death, actual or threatened serious injury, or actual or threatened sexual violence, as follows: (1 required)
1. Directly experiencing the event.
2. Witnessing the event occur to others.
3. Indirectly, by learning that a close relative or close friend was exposed to trauma. If the event involved actual or threatened death, it must have been violent or accidental.

Repeated or extreme indirect exposure to aversive details of the event(s), usually in the course of professional duties (e.g., first responders collecting body parts; professionals repeatedly exposed to details of child abuse).

DIFFERENTIAL DIAGNOSIS

- Adjustment disorders: precipitating stress is less catastrophic and psychological reaction is less specific.
- Mood disorder: depression or bipolar
- Anxiety disorder
Borderline personality disorder
- Somatic symptom or conversion disorder (functional neurological symptom disorder)
- Psychotic disorder
- Traumatic brain injury

WORKUP

- Among self-report questionnaires and structured diagnostic instruments, the best validated is the Posttraumatic Diagnostic Scale.
- Laboratory and imaging are not clinically useful.
- Primary care PTSD (PC-PTSD) screen recommended by the Veterans Administration. "Yes" answers to three of four of the questions is a positive screen:
In your life, have you ever had any experience that was so frightening, horrible, or upsetting that, in the past month, you:
Have had nightmares about it or thought about it when you did not want to?
Tried hard not to think about it or went out of your way to avoid situations that reminded you of it?
Were constantly on guard, watchful, or easily startled?
Felt numb or detached from others, activities, or your surroundings?

RX TREATMENT

- Trauma-focused CBT with sensitivity to pacing, readiness, containment, dissociation, and coping skills can decrease symptom intensity and frequency.
- Prolonged exposure (PE), a type of CBT that includes education on stress response and the recounting of the event, including sensory details.
- Group therapy.
- Eye movement desensitization reprocessing (EMDR).
- Couples therapy when appropriate.

MEDICATIONS

There is no definitive cure for PTSD, and individuals have varying responses to different medications. Sertraline and paroxetine, both SSRIs, are the only FDA-approved medications for PTSD. Other medication use is off-label with differing levels of evidence to support use. Medications are used to target symptoms and the physiologic changes associated with PTSD.
- SSRIs: sertraline, paroxetine, fluoxetine
- SNRIs: venlafaxine, duloxetine
- Other antidepressants: mirtazapine

- Alpha-adrenergic receptor blockers: Prazosin may decrease nightmares; guanfacine may be helpful in treating arousal symptoms
- Atypical antipsychotics have had mixed results in clinical trials. Risperidone been shown to be effective in some studies. Other antipsychotics are sometimes used off-label to target individual patient symptoms such as paranoia, extreme anxiety, or angry outbursts
- Ketamine: A recent clinical trial of intravenous ketamine infusion at 0.5 mg/kg showed PTSD symptom reduction at 24 hours

ACUTE GENERAL Rx

- Immediate postincident debriefing may worsen outcome.
- A brief course of benzodiazepines may be helpful acutely but has not been shown to decrease development of core symptoms.
- Beta-adrenergic blockers may be helpful if given within hours after the trauma to disrupt the physiologic stress response.
- Sedating antidepressants or sleep aids may be helpful for initial insomnia.

COMPLEMENTARY & ALTERNATIVE APPROACHES

Acupuncture has been shown to be effective in decreasing symptoms of PTSD.

DISPOSITION

- Recovery rates are highest in the first 12 mo after onset.
- Average duration of symptoms is 36 mo for those who undergo treatment and 64 mo for those never treated.
- 50% chance of remission at 2 yr; 50% have chronic symptoms.
- Predictors of chronic course include previous trauma, premorbid psychiatric function, panic reaction at time of event, prolonged terror, or dissociation at time of event.

REFERRAL

Because early intervention improves outcome, refer to psychiatry as soon as diagnosis made.

PEARLS & CONSIDERATIONS

- PTSD can be associated with suicidal ideation and attempts.
- PTSD can be associated with aggressive and violent behavior.
- Traumatic medical experiences such as being in the ICU, myocardial infarction, or an emergent cesarean section can cause PTSD.

- Individuals with PTSD are at risk for comorbid psychiatric disorder, including substance abuse.
- Among combat veterans of recent wars, there is a 41% co-occurrence with mild TBI.
- PTSD may vary culturally and present as culturally specific syndromes and idioms of distress.

Treatment can be effective even if it begins years after the traumatic event occurred.

SUGGESTED READINGS
Available at www.expertconsult.com

RELATED CONTENT
Posttraumatic Stress Disorder (PTSD) (Patient Information)

AUTHOR: **KAILA COMPTON, M.D., Ph.D.**

BASIC INFORMATION

DEFINITION
Precocious puberty is defined as sexual development occurring before age 8 yr in females and 9 yr in males.

SYNONYMS
Pubertas praecox

ICD-10CM CODES
E30.1 Precocious puberty

EPIDEMIOLOGY & DEMOGRAPHICS
INCIDENCE: Estimated to be between 1 in 5000 to 1 in 10,000.
PREDOMINANT SEX: Females are affected more often than males for the idiopathic variant; for other causes, dependent on the underlying etiology.
GENETICS: The genetics for some of the etiologies of precocious puberty is known. Deficiency of *MKRN3* causes central precocious puberty in humans.

PHYSICAL FINDINGS & CLINICAL PRESENTATION
- In females: breast development, pubic hair development, accelerated growth, menarche.
- In males: increase in testicular volume and penile length, pubic hair development, accelerated growth, muscular development, acne, change in voice, penile erections.

ETIOLOGY
- Idiopathic or true: diagnosis of exclusion.
- Central nervous system (CNS) pathology: tumors, hydrocephalus, ventricular cysts, benign lesions.
- Severe hypothyroidism.
- Posttraumatic head injury.
- Genetic disorders: neurofibromatosis, tuberous sclerosis, McCune-Albright syndrome, congenital adrenal hyperplasia.
- Gonadal tumors.
- Nongonadal tumors: hepatoblastoma.
- Exposure to exogenous sex steroids.

DIAGNOSIS

DIFFERENTIAL DIAGNOSIS
- Most common diagnoses to consider: premature thelarche and premature adrenarche.
- Gonadotropin hormone-releasing hormone (GnRH)-dependent precocious puberty: idiopathic, CNS tumors, hypothalamic hamartomas, neurofibromatosis, tuberous sclerosis, hydrocephalus, status after acute head injury, ventricular cysts, status after CNS infection.
- GnRH-independent precocious puberty: congenital adrenal hyperplasia, adrenocortical tumors (males), McCune-Albright syndrome (females), gonadal tumors, ectopic human chorionic gonadotropin (hCG)-secreting tumors (chorioblastoma, hepatoblastoma), exposure to exogenous sex steroids, severe hypothyroidism.
- Table 1P-39 summarizes the differential diagnosis of sexual precocity.

WORKUP
Thorough history and physical examination are essential to determine if the patient has true precocious puberty. Particular attention should be paid to growth, development, order of appearance of the secondary sexual characteristics, pubertal development in family members, medications, neurologic symptoms, Tanner staging, abdominal and neurologic examination. Flowcharts for diagnosing sexual precocity in females and males are shown in Figs. 1P-88 and 1P-89.

LABORATORY TESTS
- GnRH testing will help determine if dependent or independent cause.
- Sex hormone studies: luteinizing hormone, follicle-stimulating hormone, hCG, testosterone (males), estrogen (females). Levels of sex steroids should be determined in the morning, with use of assays that have detection limits adapted to pediatric values. In girls, serum estradiol levels are highly variable and have a rather low sensitivity for the diagnosis of precocious puberty.
- Free T_4, thyroid-stimulating hormone (TSH)

IMAGING STUDIES
- CT scan or MRI of the brain to evaluate for CNS pathology.
- Consideration of pelvic ultrasound in female patients to evaluate for ovarian cysts or tumors.
- Abdominal imaging with CT scan if intraabdominal pathology suspected.

TREATMENT

NONPHARMACOLOGIC THERAPY
- Good communication with the parents is essential to care.
- Psychological support for the child may be needed with regard to self-image and problems with peer acceptance.

ACUTE GENERAL Rx
There is no acute therapy for precocious puberty.

CHRONIC Rx
Therapy depends on the etiology of precocious puberty. For the treatment of central or gonadotropin-dependent precocious puberty depot GnRH agonists (leuprorelin, leuprolide, triptorelin, goserelin, histrelin, buserelin) are effective.
- Leuprolide is given 0.25 to 0.3 mg/kg with a 7.5 mg minimum IM every 4 wk. Local side effects include pain, erythema, and inflammatory reactions. Other side effects include headaches and menopausal-like symptoms (asthenia, hot flashes).
- For other CNS lesions and extragonadal tumors, therapy is dependent on the type of lesion, location of the lesion, and the overall prognosis of the underlying problem.
- For severe hypothyroidism, treatment with thyroid hormone will result in regression of the sexual development. The child will subsequently undergo appropriate pubertal development later in life.
- For familial male gonadotropin-independent precocious puberty, the androgen-synthesis inhibitor ketoconazole can be used at doses of 600 mg/day divided tid, or a combination of the aromatase inhibitors testolactone or anastrozole and spironolactone can be used.

DISPOSITION
- For true precocious puberty and some CNS lesions, long-term outcome is usually very good. When drug therapy is instituted, it is continued until a time when further pubertal development is appropriate. It is then discontinued, allowing the child to progress through puberty.
- For other cases, long-term outcomes depend on the prognosis of the underlying cause.

REFERRAL
- Initial workup can be instituted by the primary care provider.
- Referral to an endocrinologist is indicated for most children because they will need long-term management, monitoring, and treatment.
- Attention to the emotional needs of the child is important.

SUGGESTED READINGS
Available at www.expertconsult.com

RELATED CONTENT
Precocious Puberty (Patient Information)

AUTHOR: **RUBEN ALVERO, M.D.**

TABLE 1P-39   Differential Diagnosis of Sexual Precocity

	Plasma Gonadotropins	LH Response to GnRH	Serum Sex Steroid Concentration	Gonadal Size	Miscellaneous
Gonadotropin-Dependent					
True precocious puberty	Prominent LH pulses (premature reactivation of GnRH pulse generator)	Pubertal LH response initially during sleep	Pubertal values of testosterone or estradiol	Normal pubertal testicular enlargement or ovarian and uterine enlargement	MRI of brain to rule out CNS tumor or other abnormality; skeletal survey for McCune-Albright syndrome (by US)
Incomplete Sexual Precocity (Pituitary Gonadotropin-Independent)					
Males					
Chorionic gonadotropin-secreting tumor in males	High hCG, low LH	Prepubertal LH response	Pubertal value of testosterone	Slight to moderate uniform enlargement of testes	Hepatomegaly suggests hepatoblastoma; CT scan of brain if chorionic gonadotropin-secreting CNS tumor suspected
Leydig cell tumor in males	Suppressed	No LH response	Very high testosterone	Irregular, asymmetric enlargement of testes	
Familial testotoxicosis	Suppressed	No LH response	Pubertal values of testosterone	Testes symmetric and >2.5 cm but smaller than expected for pubertal development; spermatogenesis occurs	Familial; probably sex-limited, autosomal dominant trait
Virilizing congenital adrenal hyperplasia	Prepubertal	Prepubertal LH response	Elevated 17-OHP in CYP21 deficiency or elevated 11-deoxycortisol in CYP11B1 deficiency	Testes prepubertal	Autosomal recessive, may be congenital or late-onset form, may have salt loss in CYP21 deficiency or hypertension in CYP11B1 deficiency
Virilizing adrenal tumor	Prepubertal	Prepubertal LH response	High DHEAS and androstenedione values	Testes prepubertal	CT, MRI, or US of abdomen
Premature adrenarche	Prepubertal	Prepubertal LH response	Prepubertal testosterone, DHEAS, or urinary 17-ketosteroid values appropriate for pubic hair stage 2	Testes prepubertal	Onset usually after 6 yr of age; more frequent in CNS-injured children
Females					
Granulosa cell tumor (follicular cysts may present similarly)	Suppressed	Prepubertal LH response	Very high estradiol	Ovarian enlargement on physical examination, CT, or US	Tumors often palpable on physical examination
Follicular cyst	Suppressed	Prepubertal LH response	Prepubertal to very high estradiol	Ovarian enlargement on physical examination, CT, or US	Single or recurrent episodes of menses and/or breast development; exclude McCune-Albright syndrome
Feminizing adrenal tumor	Suppressed	Prepubertal LH response	High estradiol and DHEAS values	Ovaries prepubertal	Unilateral adrenal mass
Premature thelarche	Prepubertal	Prepubertal LH, pubertal	Prepubertal or early estradiol response	Ovaries prepubertal	Onset usually before 3 yr of age
Premature adrenarche	Prepubertal	Prepubertal LH response	Prepubertal estradiol; DHEAS or urinary 17-ketosteroid values appropriate for pubic hair stage 2	Ovaries prepubertal	Onset usually after 6 yr of age; more frequent in brain-injured children
Late-onset virilizing congenital adrenal hyperplasia	Prepubertal	Prepubertal LH response	Elevated 17-OHP in basal or corticotropin-stimulated state	Ovaries prepubertal	Autosomal recessive
In Both Sexes					
McCune-Albright syndrome	Suppressed	Suppressed	Sex steroid pubertal or higher	Ovarian (on US); slight testicular enlargement	Skeletal survey for polyostotic fibrous dysplasia and skin, examination for café au lait spots
Primary hypothyroidism	LH prepubertal; FSH may be slightly elevated	Prepubertal FSH may be increased	Estradiol may be pubertal	Testicular enlargement; ovaries cystic	TSH and prolactin elevated; T$_4$ low

CNS, Central nervous system; *CT*, computed tomography; *CYP*, P450 cytochrome isoenzyme; *DHEAS*, dehydroepiandrosterone sulfate; *GnRH*, gonadotropin-releasing hormone; *hCG*, human chorionic gonadotropin; *LH*, luteinizing hormone; *17-OHP*, 17-hydroxyprogesterone; *T$_4$*, thyroxine; *TSH*, thyrotropin; *US*, ultrasonography.
From Melmed S et al: *Williams textbook of endocrinology*, ed 12, Philadelphia, 2011, WB Saunders.

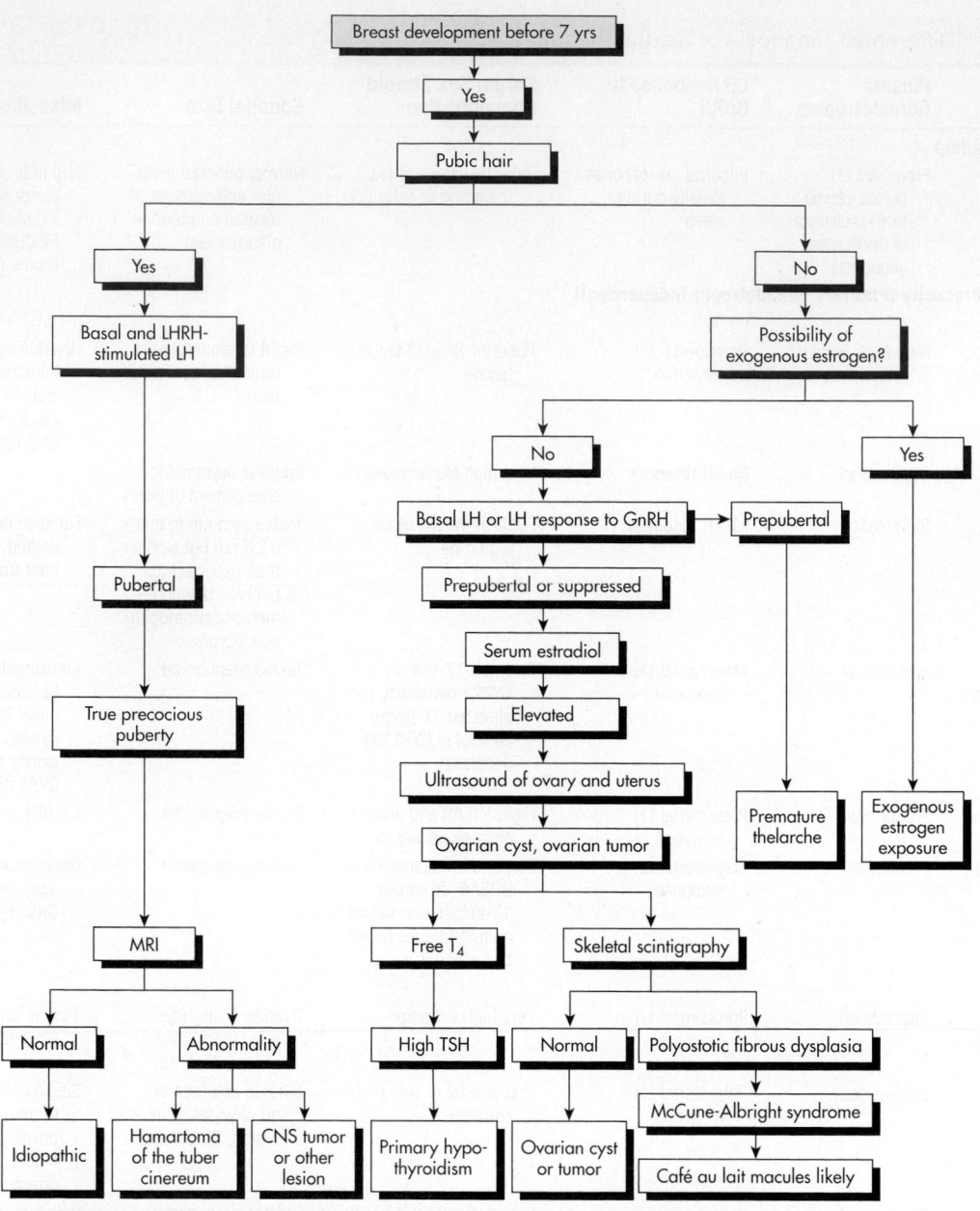

FIGURE 1P-88 Flowchart for diagnosing sexual precocity in girls. *CNS*, Central nervous system; *FSH*, follicle-stimulating hormone; *LH*, luteinizing hormone; T₄, thyroxine; *TSH*, thyroid-stimulating hormone. (From Melmed S et al: *Williams textbook of endocrinology*, ed 3, Philadelphia, 2011, WB Saunders.)

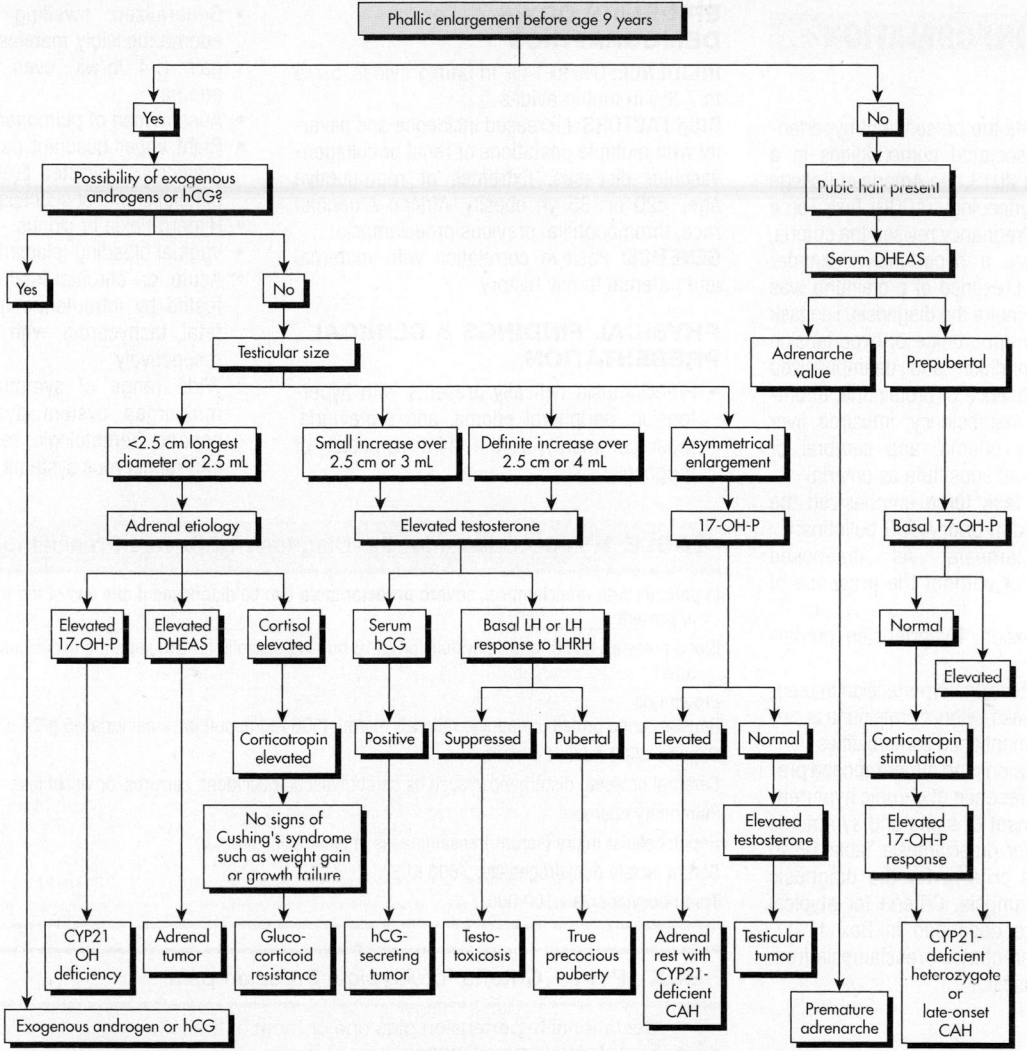

FIGURE 1P-89 Flowchart for diagnosing sexual precocity in a phenotypic male. *CAH*, Congenital adrenal hyperplasia; *DHEAS*, dehydroepiandrosterone sulfate; *hCG*, human chorionic gonadotropin; *17-OH-P*, 17-hydroxyprogesterone. (From Melmed S et al. *Williams textbook of endocrinology*, ed 12, Philadelphia, 2011, WB Saunders.)

BASIC INFORMATION

DEFINITION

Preeclampsia involves the presence of hypertension with other associated comorbidities in a pregnant woman. In 2013, the American College of Obstetrics and Gynecology (ACOG) Task Force on Hypertension in Pregnancy revised the criteria, making preeclampsia a hypertensive disorder and one where the presence of proteinuria was no longer needed to make the diagnosis. The task force reinforced the importance of hypertension as a necessary condition and deemphasized proteinuria. In the absence of proteinuria, thrombocytopenia, renal insufficiency, impaired liver function, pulmonary edema, and cerebral or visual symptoms could substitute as criteria.

Additionally, the task force emphasized the categories employed in prior ACOG bulletins:
1. Preeclampsia/eclampsia: As diagnosed previously, with or without the presence of proteinuria
2. Chronic hypertension: Hypertension predating pregnancy
3. Gestational hypertension: Hypertension in pregnancy after 20 weeks without proteinuria or any of the previously mentioned comorbidities
4. Chronic hypertension with superimposed preeclampsia: The presence of chronic hypertension with new onset of signs and symptoms meeting criteria for preeclampsia Table 1P-40 summarizes the criteria for the diagnosis of severe preeclampsia. Criteria for atypical preeclampsia are described in Box 1P-11. Table 1P-41 differentiates preeclampsia from chronic hypertension.

SYNONYMS

Pregnancy-induced hypertension
Toxemia of pregnancy

ICD-10CM CODES

O11.1	Pre-existing hypertension with pre-eclampsia, first trimester
O11.2	Pre-existing hypertension with pre-eclampsia, second trimester
O11.3	Pre-existing hypertension with pre-eclampsia, third trimester
O11.9	Pre-existing hypertension with pre-eclampsia, unspecified trimester
O14.00	Mild to moderate pre-eclampsia, unspecified trimester
O14.02	Mild to moderate pre-eclampsia, second trimester
O14.03	Mild to moderate pre-eclampsia, third trimester
O14.10	Severe pre-eclampsia, unspecified trimester
O14.12	Severe pre-eclampsia, second trimester
O14.13	Severe pre-eclampsia, third trimester
O14.90	Unspecified pre-eclampsia, unspecified trimester
O14.92	Unspecified pre-eclampsia, second trimester
O14.93	Unspecified pre-eclampsia, third trimester

EPIDEMIOLOGY & DEMOGRAPHICS

INCIDENCE: 0% to 14% in primigravidas, 5.7% to 7.3% in multigravidas
RISK FACTORS: Increased incidence and severity with multiple gestations or renal or collagen-vascular diseases. Extremes of reproductive age, <20 or>35 yr, obesity, African American race, thrombophilia, previous preeclampsia.
GENETICS: Positive correlation with maternal and paternal family history

PHYSICAL FINDINGS & CLINICAL PRESENTATION

- Preeclampsia typically presents with hypertension, peripheral edema, and proteinuria, most commonly in the third semester of pregnancy.
- Generalized swelling or nondependent edema, possibly manifested by rapid weight gain (>4 lb/wk) even in the absence of edema
- Auscultation of pulmonary rales
- Right upper quadrant pain (HELLP syndrome [hemolysis, elevated liver enzymes, and low platelet count] or subcapsular liver hematoma)
- Hyperreflexia or clonus
- Vaginal bleeding (placental abruption)
- Acute or chronic fetal compromise manifested by intrauterine growth restriction or fetal tachycardia with late decelerations, respectively
- Wide range of symptoms attributable to multiorgan system dysfunction, involving hepatic, hematologic, renal, pulmonary, and central nervous systems

---

TABLE 1P-40 Criteria for the Diagnosis of Severe Preeclampsia

In patients with preeclampsia, **severe preeclampsia** can be diagnosed if any one of the following criteria is present:

Blood pressure ≥160 mm Hg systolic or ≥110 mm Hg diastolic on two separate occasions at least 6 hours apart

Proteinuria

Random urine protein:creatinine ratio ≥5 mg/mL (500 mg/mmol) *or* proteinuria ≥5 g/24 h

Oliguria <500 mL in 24 hours

Cerebral or visual disturbances such as cerebrovascular accident, seizures, or visual loss

Pulmonary edema

Hepatocellular injury (serum transaminases at least twice normal)

Serum lactate dehydrogenase: >600 IU/L

Thrombocytopenia <100,000

BOX 1P-11 Criteria for Atypical Preeclampsia

- Gestational hypertension plus one or more of the following:
- Symptoms of preeclampsia
- Hemolysis
- Thrombocytopenia (<100,000/mm^3)
- Elevated liver enzymes: two times the upper limit of the normal value for aspartate transaminase (AST) and alanine transaminase (ALT)
- Gestational proteinuria plus one or more of the following:
  - Symptoms of preeclampsia
  - Hemolysis
  - Thrombocytopenia
  - Elevated liver enzymes
  - Early signs and symptoms of preeclampsia-eclampsia at <20 weeks
  - Late postpartum preeclampsia-eclampsia (>48 hours postpartum)

From Gabbe SG: *Obstetrics*, ed 6, Philadelphia, 2012, WB Saunders.

TABLE 1P-41 Differences Between Preeclampsia and Chronic Hypertension

Feature	Preeclampsia	Chronic Hypertension
Age (yr)	Young (<20)	Older (>30)
Parity	Primigravida	Multigravida
Onset	After 20 wk of pregnancy	Before 20 wk of pregnancy
Weight gain and edema	Sudden	Gradual
Systolic blood pressure	<160 mm Hg	>160 mm Hg
Funduscopic findings	Spasm, edema	Arteriovenous nicking, exudates
Left ventricular hypertrophy	Rare	More common
Proteinuria	Present	Absent
Plasma uric acid	Increased	Normal
Blood pressure after delivery	Normal	Elevated

- Possibility of severe disease despite "normal" blood pressure readings, so a high index of suspicion must be maintained in high-risk situations

ETIOLOGY

- Exact etiology or toxic substance is unknown
- Theories:
  1. Imbalance between thromboxane A_2 (vasoconstrictor and platelet aggregator) and prostacyclin (vasodilator)
  2. Abnormal trophoblastic invasion of spiral arteries
  3. Increased sensitivity to angiotensin II by the muscular walls of the arteries
  4. Excess circulating soluble fms-like tyrosine kinase 1 (*sFlt1*), which binds placental growth factor (PlGF) and vascular endothelial growth factor (VEGF), may have a pathogenic role
- Potential secondary effects of the metabolic, inflammatory endothelial alternatives in preeclampsia are described in Table 1P-42.

Dx DIAGNOSIS

DIFFERENTIAL DIAGNOSIS

- Acute fatty liver of pregnancy
- Appendicitis
- Diabetic ketoacidosis
- Gallbladder disease
- Gastroenteritis
- Glomerulonephritis
- Hemolytic-uremic syndrome
- Hepatic encephalopathy
- Hyperemesis gravidarum
- Idiopathic thrombocytopenia
- Thrombotic thrombocytopenic purpura
- Nephrolithiasis
- Pyelonephritis
- Peptic ulcer disease
- Systemic lupus erythematosus
- Viral hepatitis

WORKUP

- Two blood pressure measurements with the patient in lateral recumbent position at least 4 hr apart, with an absolute pressure 140 mm Hg systolic or 90 mm Hg diastolic. A single blood pressure greater than or equal to systolic 160 mm Hg or greater than or equal to 110 mm Hg diastolic. Hypertension can thus be confirmed in brief period to allow for immediate treatment of the blood pressure.
  - Evaluation for proteinuria: >>Greater than or equal to 300 mg per 24-hour urine collection
  - Protein/creatinine ratio greater than or equal to 0.3
  - 1+ on dipstick ONLY IF OTHER METHODS NOT AVAILABLE
- In the absence of proteinuria, preeclampsia may be diagnosed with new onset of hypertension and one of the following:
  - Platelet count less than 100,000/mL
  - Serum creatinine concentrations greater than 1.1 mg/dL, or doubling of serum Cr levels in the absence of other renal disease
  - Elevated serum liver transaminases to twice the normal concentration
  - Pulmonary edema
  - Cerebral or visual symptoms
- Because of the insidious nature of the disease with potential for multiple organ involvement, as well as its prevalence, complete evaluation for preeclampsia in any pregnant patient presenting with central nervous system derangement or gastrointestinal symptoms after 20 wk of gestation
- Evaluation for associated conditions such as disseminated intravascular coagulation, hepatic dysfunction, or subcapsular hematoma
- Fig. 1P-90 outlines a management plan for patients with severe preeclampsia

TABLE 1P-42 Potential Secondary Effects of the Metabolic, Inflammatory Endothelial Alternatives in Preeclampsia

CVS	Increased peripheral resistance leading to hypertension Increased vascular permeability and reduced maternal plasma volume
Lungs	Laryngeal and pulmonary edema
Renal	Glomerular damage leading to proteinuria, hypoproteinemia, and reduced oncotic pressure, which further exacerbates the hypovolemia. May develop acute renal failure ± cortical necrosis
Clotting	Hypercoagulability, with increased fibrin formation and increased fibrinolysis, i.e., disseminated intravascular coagulation
Liver	HELLP syndrome Hepatic rupture
CNS	Thrombosis and fibrinoid necrosis of the cerebral arterioles Eclampsia (convulsions), cerebral hemorrhage, and cerebral edema
Fetus	Impaired uteroplacental circulation, potentially leading to FGR, hypoxemia, and intrauterine death

CVS, Cardiovascular system; *CNS,* central nervous system; *FGR,* fetal growth restriction; *HELLP,* hemolysis, elevated liver enzymes, low platelets.
From Drife J, Magowan B: *Clinical obstetrics and gynecology,* Philadelphia, 2004, WB Saunders.

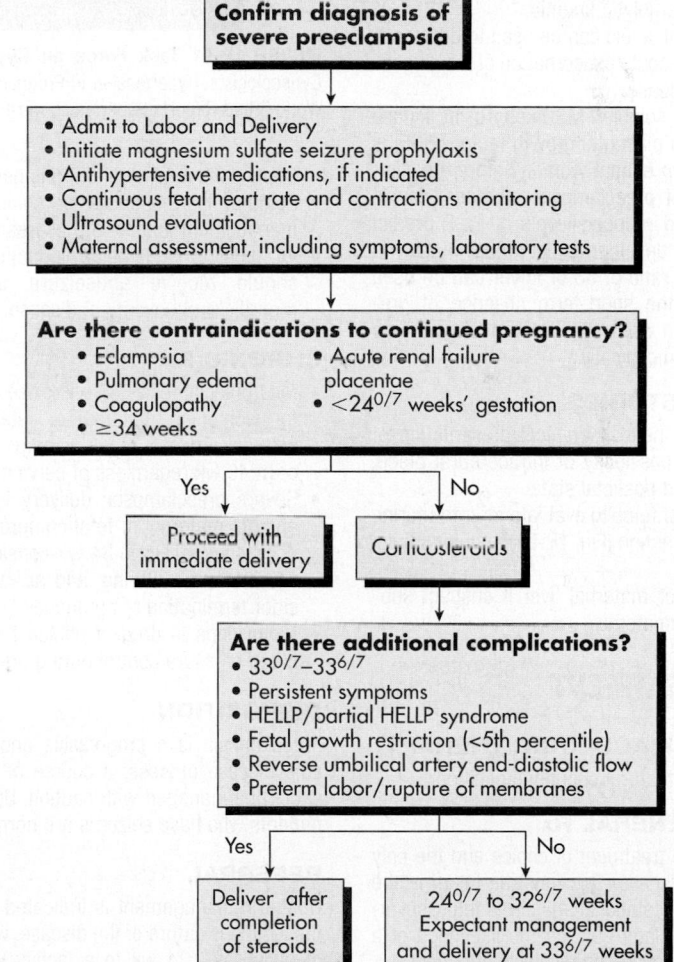

FIGURE 1P-90 Management plan for patients with severe preeclampsia. (From Gabbe SG: *Obstetrics,* ed 6, Philadelphia, 2012, WB Saunders.)

LABORATORY TESTS

- High-risk patients: baseline assessment of renal function (24-hr urine collection for protein and creatinine clearance), platelets, blood urea nitrogen, creatinine, liver function tests (LFTs), and uric acid should be obtained at the first prenatal visit.
- Complete blood count (hemoglobin, hematocrit, platelets) may show signs of volume contraction or HELLP syndrome.
- LFTs (aspartate aminotransferase, alanine aminotransferase, lactate dehydrogenase) are useful in evaluation for HELLP syndrome or to exclude important differentials.
- Hyperuricemia or increased creatinine may indicate decreasing renal function.
- Prothrombin time, partial thromboplastin time, and fibrinogen should be checked to rule out disseminated intravascular coagulation.
- Peripheral smear may demonstrate microangiopathic hemolytic anemia.
- Complement levels can be used to differentiate from an acute exacerbation of a collagen-vascular disease.
- The ratio of soluble FMS-like tyrosine kinase 1 (sFlt-1) to placental growth factor (PlGF) is elevated in pregnant women before the clinical onset of preeclampsia. Increased levels of *sFlt1* and reduced levels of PlGF predict subsequent development of preeclampsia. An sFlt-1:PlGR ratio of 38 or lower can be used to predict the short-term absence of preeclampsia in women in whom the syndrome is suspected clinically.[1]

IMAGING STUDIES

- CT scan of head if atypical presentation of eclampsia, possibility of intracerebral bleed, or prolonged postictal state
- Sonogram of fetus to evaluate for intrauterine growth restriction (Fig. 1P-91), amniotic fluid, placenta
- Sonogram of maternal liver if suspect subcapsular hematoma

 **TREATMENT**

NONPHARMACOLOGIC THERAPY

Bed rest in left lateral decubitus position

ACUTE GENERAL Rx

Delivery is the treatment of choice and the only cure for the disease. This must be taken in the context of the gestational age of the fetus, severity of the preeclampsia, and the likelihood of a successful induction and reliability of patient.

- Administer magnesium sulfate 6 g IV loading dose, with 2 to 3 g maintenance or phenytoin at 10 to 15 mg/kg loading dose, then 200 mg IV q8h starting 12 hr after loading dose.
- Hydralazine 10 mg IV, labetalol hydrochloride 20 to 40 mg IV, nifedipine 20 mg SL can be used for acute blood pressure control.

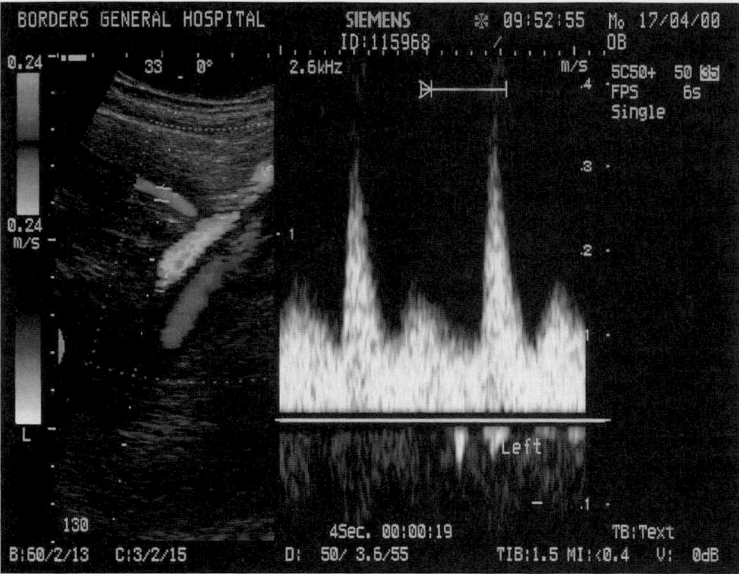

FIGURE 1P-91 Task Force on Hypertension in Pregnancy. American College of Obstetricians and Gynecologists. Hypertension in Pregnancy. http://www.acog.org/Resources-And-Publications/Task-Force-and-Work-Group-Reports/Hypertension-in-Pregnancy, November 2013.

- Continuous fetal monitoring is needed.
- Epidural is anesthesia of choice for pain management in labor or cesarean section.
- All patients undergoing induction of labor should receive antiseizure medications regardless of severity of disease.

CHRONIC Rx

- Mild preeclampsia<37 wk: close observation for worsening maternal or fetal condition, with delivery at >37 wk with favorable cervix or at 40 wk regardless of cervical status.
- Severe preeclampsia: delivery in the presence of maternal or fetal compromise, labor, or >34 wk; at 28 to 34 wk consider steroids with close monitoring, and at <24 wk consider termination of pregnancy.
- Methyldopa is drug of choice for long-term blood pressure control during pregnancy.

DISPOSITION

Preeclampsia is a progressive and unpredictable disease process; a course of expectancy should be managed with caution. Up to 20% of patients who have seizures are normotensive.

REFERRAL

Obstetric management is indicated because of the insidious nature of the disease, with transfer of all cases <34 wk to a facility with a level three nursery.

 **PEARLS & CONSIDERATIONS**

COMMENTS

- Low-dose aspirin, beginning as early as the second trimester, decreases the risk of preeclampsia, preterm birth, and intrauterine growth retardation in women who are at high risk of preeclampsia.

The American College of Obstetricians and Gynecologists (ACOG) recommends low-dose aspirin beginning in the late first trimester for women with a history of early-onset preeclampsia and preterm delivery at <34 weeks' gestation or preeclampsia in more than one prior pregnancy. The U.S. Preventive Services Task Force (USPSTF) recommends the use of low-dose aspirin (81 mg/day) as preventive medication after 12 weeks of gestation in women who are at high risk for preeclampsia.

- Calcium supplementation 1500 mg qd should also be considered in high-risk patients beginning after the first trimester to decrease the risk of recurrence.
- Although the absolute risk of end-stage renal disease (ESRD) in women who have had preeclampsia is low, preeclampsia is a marker for an increased risk of subsequent ESRD.
- The development of preeclampsia may be one of the earliest identifiable risk markers for potential future cardiovascular disease in women. It has been shown that women who develop preeclampsia have a higher incidence of cardiovascular risk factors including components of the metabolic syndrome within 1 yr of delivery.

SUGGESTED READINGS
Available at www.expertconsult.com

RELATED CONTENT
Preeclampsia (Patient Information)
Eclampsia (Related Key Topic)
Hypertension (Related Key Topic)

AUTHOR: **RUBEN ALVERO, M.D.**

[1]Zeisler H et al: Predictive value of the sFlt-1:PlGF ratio in women with suspected preeclampsia, *N Engl J Med* 374:13–22, 2016.

 BASIC INFORMATION

DEFINITION

Premature labor is defined as regular contractions that result in cervical dilation or effacement prior to 37 wk gestation.

SYNONYMS

Preterm labor

ICD-10CM CODES
060.0 Preterm labor without delivery
060.1 Preterm spontaneous labor with preterm delivery
060.2 Preterm spontaneous labor with term delivery

EPIDEMIOLOGY & DEMOGRAPHICS

INCIDENCE: The incidence of preterm births in the U.S. has increased over the past two decades from 9.5% in 1981 to 12.7% in 2006. Between 40% and 45% of these births follow spontaneous preterm labor; either the remaining preterm births result from preterm premature rupture of membranes (PPROM), or they occur secondary to maternal or fetal indications.

PREDOMINANT SEX AND AGE: Pregnant women at the extremes of reproductive age (<<17 yr and >>35 yr) are at greatest risk.

GENETICS: A genetic component has been suggested. Women with sisters who have had preterm births and women with grandparents who were born preterm may be at increased risk for having preterm deliveries themselves. Single-nucleotide polymorphisms have also been associated with preterm labor.

RISK FACTORS: Risk factors for premature labor include a prior preterm delivery, intrauterine infection, systemic or genital tract infections, interpregnancy interval (<6 mo), short cervical length (<25 to 30 mm), low pre-pregnancy BMI (<19.8 kg/m^2), age <17 yr or >35 yr), a history of elective pregnancy termination, history of prior stillbirth, African-American ethnicity, vaginal bleeding, polyhydramnios or oligohydramnios, multiple gestation, structural abnormalities of the uterus, history of cervical cone biopsy or loop electrocautery excision, in vitro fertilization or ovulation induction, tobacco use, heavy alcohol consumption, cocaine use, heroin use, and psychological or social stress.

PHYSICAL FINDINGS & CLINICAL PRESENTATION

Presenting symptoms include increased pelvic pressure, abdominal cramping or contractions, increased vaginal discharge, vaginal spotting, or leakage of fluid.

ETIOLOGY

Causes of premature labor are varied and often difficult to determine. Premature labor may be secondary to infection, systemic illness, trauma, anatomic abnormalities (i.e., uterine anomaly such as lateral fusion defects like unicornuate or bicornuate uterus), or a combination of factors. It is thought that cervical ripening is the most common first step to premature labor or delivery. Subsequently, decidual-membrane activation occurs, as do contractions (Box 1P-12).

 **DIAGNOSIS**

DIFFERENTIAL DIAGNOSIS

The differential should include premature labor, preterm rupture of membranes, preterm contractions (contractions prior to 37 wk gestation that do not result in cervical change), and abdominal pain or cramping secondary to other medical conditions. There are many conditions that may cause preterm contractions or premature labor. These include:
- Infection
  1. Chorioamnionitis
  2. Genital tract infections, including bacterial vaginosis, gonorrhea, chlamydia
  3. Urinary tract infections, including pyelonephritis, cystitis, or asymptomatic bacteriuria
  4. Gastroenteritis
- Trauma
- Placental abruption
- Illicit drug use
- Preterm premature rupture of membranes
- Appendicitis
- Nephrolithiasis
- Pancreatitis
- Cholelithiasis

WORKUP

- History and physical exam to rule out trauma, abuse, other causes of abdominal pain, and infection

- Fetal heart rate monitoring and tocometry to determine fetal status and contraction frequency
- Speculum exam to visually assess the cervix and assess for rupture of membranes, bleeding, infection, or advanced cervical dilation
  1. If the patient is <<35 wk gestation, a Fetal Fibronectin (FFN) test should be collected prior to performing a digital exam or transvaginal ultrasound. A FFN test can help predict preterm delivery if the patient has a cervical length on transvaginal ultrasound of <<30 mm.
- Digital exam to determine cervical dilation and effacement, and fetal station

LABORATORY TESTS

- CBC
- Urine analysis and culture
- Urine toxicology screen
- Collect tests for GBS, gonorrhea, and *Chlamydia*
- Perform a wet prep for yeast, bacterial vaginosis, and *Trichomonas*
- Fetal fibronectin
- Consider PT, PTT, INR, CMP, amylase, and lipase
- Amniocentesis may be performed if an intraamniotic infection is suspected

IMAGING STUDIES

A formal ultrasound is indicated to determine estimated fetal weight, fetal presentation, amniotic fluid volume, placental location and appearance, and cervical length.

RX TREATMENT

Patients with premature labor should be delivered promptly when an intraamniotic infection

---

BOX 1P-12 Factors Linked to Preterm Labor

Demographic and Psychosocial
Extremes of age (>40 yr, teenagers)
Lower socioeconomic status
Tobacco use
Cocaine abuse
Prolonged standing (occupation)
Psychosocial stressors

Reproductive and Gynecologic
Prior preterm delivery
Diethylstilbestrol exposure
Multiple gestations
Anatomic endometrial cavity anomalies
Cervical incompetence
Low pregnancy weight gain
First-trimester vaginal bleeding
Placental abruption or previa

Surgical
Prior reproductive organ surgery
Prior paraendometrial surgery other than genitourinary (appendectomy)

Infectious
Urinary tract infections
Nonuterine infections
Genital tract infections (bacterial vaginosis)

From Marx JA et al: *Rosen's emergency medicine: concepts and clinical practice*, ed 7, Philadelphia, 2010, Elsevier.

is suspected or when they have cervical dilation >5 cm, a persistently nonreassuring fetal heart rate tracing, intrauterine growth restriction, or vaginal bleeding concerning for placental abruption.

NONPHARMACOLOGIC THERAPY

- Smoking cessation
- Bedrest, activity restriction, and pelvic rest are often recommended, but there are insufficient data to support this practice.

ACUTE GENERAL Rx

- Antenatal administration of corticosteroids between 24 wk and 33 6/7 wk gestation is recommended for women at risk of preterm delivery to prevent neonatal respiratory distress syndrome and decrease the incidence of intraventricular hemorrhage and necrotizing enterocolitis.
- Numerous tocolytic agents have been used in an attempt to inhibit contractions (Box 1P-13). Although efficacy is unclear, they can be utilized during an observation period in an effort to prolong gestation for administration of steroids or to transfer the mother to a facility capable of caring for preterm infants. This, of course, assumes there are no maternal or fetal medical contraindications to use of tocolytic drugs and no indications for rapid delivery. The most commonly used tocolytics are beta-mimetics (terbutaline), magnesium sulfate, calcium channel blockers (nifedipine), or prostaglandin synthetase inhibitors (indomethacin, ketorolac, sulindac).

- Routine antibiotic use has failed to show benefit in the absence of a known infection. But all mothers in preterm labor (without a documented negative group B strep culture) should be given antibiotics to prevent neonatal infection.

CHRONIC Rx

- Patients with a history of prior spontaneous preterm birth may be candidates for prophylactic use of 17 alpha-hydroxyprogesterone

---

BOX 1P-13 Commonly Used Tocolytic Agents

Magnesium sulfate
    4-6 g IV bolus over 30 min
    2-4 g/hr IV infusion
Terbutaline
    5-10 mg PO q4-6h
    0.25-0.5 mg SC q30 min-6 h
    10-80 µg/min IV
Ritodrine[1]
    10 mg PO q2-4 h
    5-10 mg IM q2-4 h
    50-350 µg/min IV
Isoxsuprine
    20 mg PO q4-6 h
    0.05-0.5 mg/min IV

[1] Ritodrine is currently discontinued in the U.S.
IV, Intravenously; *PO*, orally; *SC*, subcutaneously.
From Marx JA et al: *Rosen's emergency medicine: concepts and clinical practice,* ed 7, Philadelphia, 2010, Elsevier.

caproate between 16 wk and 36 wk gestation.
- Patients with a history of preterm birth and short cervix may also be candidates for prophylactic or rescue cerclage.
- There is no evidence supporting the use of maintenance tocolytic therapy.

REFERRAL

- Women who present in preterm labor should be referred to an obstetrician and transferred to a facility with a neonatal intensive care unit.
- For women who present for prenatal care with a history of preterm delivery, early referral to an obstetrician is also recommended.

 **EVIDENCE**

Available at www.expertconsult.com

SUGGESTED READINGS
Available at www.expertconsult.com

RELATED CONTENT
Abruptio Placentae (Related Key Topic)
Breech Birth (Related Key Topic)

AUTHOR: **LAUREN MAY, M.D.**

BASIC INFORMATION

DEFINITION
Premature rupture of membranes (PROM) is defined as rupture of membranes at term before the onset of labor.

SYNONYMS
Preterm premature rupture of membranes (prior to 37 weeks)
PROM

ICD-10CM CODES
042 Premature rupture of membranes

EPIDEMIOLOGY & DEMOGRAPHICS
INCIDENCE: Affects approximately 8% of all pregnancies.
RISK FACTORS: Intraamniotic infection, low socioeconomic status, second and third trimester bleeding, low body mass index, nutritional deficiencies, connective tissue disorders, maternal cigarette use, cervical conization or cerclage, short cervix, pulmonary disease in pregnancy, uterine overdistension, amniocentesis, prior history of PROM, prior history of preterm delivery.

PHYSICAL FINDINGS & CLINICAL PRESENTATION
- Patients will classically present complaining of leakage or gush of fluid from the vagina. Patients may also present with contractions and vaginal bleeding. Additional symptoms can include fever, chills or abdominal pain if there is concurrent infection. Ultrasound will often demonstrate oligohydramnios.

ETIOLOGY
- Premature rupture of membranes at term may occur due to physiologic changes in addition to uterine contractions causing shearing forces. Although there are many risk factors for PROM, it often occurs in the absence of any known risk factor.

DIAGNOSIS

DIFFERENTIAL DIAGNOSIS
Differential diagnosis includes leakage of urine or vaginal discharge.

WORKUP
- Sterile speculum examination demonstrating pooling of fluid in posterior fornix, visualization of fluid coming out of the cervix during Valsalva maneuver, basic vaginal pH, and characteristic ferning pattern of vaginal fluid that is dried on a microscope.
- Care should be taken to avoid any procedure that may introduce infection, so digital examination should be avoided unless patient is in active labor or delivery is imminently planned. This is of particular importance in preterm PROM.

- Fig. 1P-92 shows initial assessment and management of women with premature rupture of the membranes.

LABORATORY TESTS
- pH test: sample vaginal fluid from posterior fornix. Normal vaginal pH is 4.5 to 6.0. pH of amniotic fluid is 7.1 to 7.3. False positive test can occur in presence of blood or semen, antiseptic of bacterial vaginosis.
- Microscopy: visualization of ferning of vaginal fluid allowed to dry on the microscope slide. False positive test can occur if cervical mucus is sampled.
- Commercially available tests: AmniSure and other tests are available and demonstrate good sensitivity and specificity; however, per the American College of Obstetrics and Gynecology, these should be considered ancillary to standard evaluation.

IMAGING STUDIES
- Abdominal ultrasound: evaluation of amniotic fluid volume either by maximum vertical pocket or amniotic fluid index. Oligohydramnios or low fluid volume in itself should not be considered diagnostic of PROM.

- Amniotic fluid dye test: This is considered the gold standard in diagnosis of PROM, used in clinical scenario of suspected preterm PROM with equivocal testing. Indigo carmine dye is injected via ultrasound guidance into the amniotic sac, and diagnosis made if blue dye passes into vagina.

TREATMENT

NONPHARMACOLOGIC THERAPY
- All patients with PROM should have prompt evaluation of gestational age, fetal well-being via NST monitoring, and fetal presentation. In a patient with evidence of intraamniotic infection or fetal distress, prompt delivery is recommended. Close monitoring and consideration of delivery is recommended if there is concern for placental abruption.
- Collect swab for evaluation of GBS status.

ACUTE GENERAL Rx
Term PROM:
- Any patient diagnosed with PROM at term should proceed toward delivery. Induction of labor has been shown to decrease time to

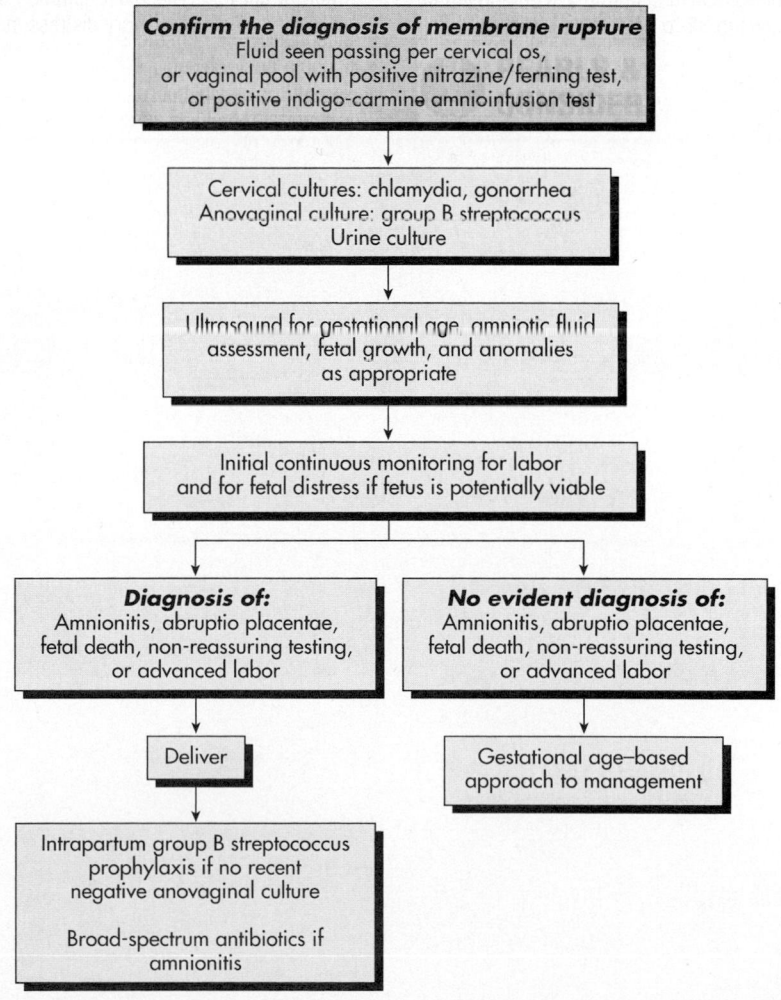

FIGURE 1P-92 Initial assessment and management of women with preterm premature rupture of the membranes. (From Mercer BM: Preterm premature rupture of the membranes: diagnosis and management. *Clin Perinatol* 31:765, 2004.)

Within the figure:

Confirm the diagnosis of membrane rupture
Fluid seen passing per cervical os, or vaginal pool with positive nitrazine/ferning test, or positive indigo-carmine amnioinfusion test

↓

Cervical cultures: chlamydia, gonorrhea
Anovaginal culture: group B streptococcus
Urine culture

↓

Ultrasound for gestational age, amniotic fluid assessment, fetal growth, and anomalies as appropriate

↓

Initial continuous monitoring for labor and for fetal distress if fetus is potentially viable

Diagnosis of:
Amnionitis, abruptio placentae, fetal death, non-reassuring testing, or advanced labor

No evident diagnosis of:
Amnionitis, abruptio placentae, fetal death, non-reassuring testing, or advanced labor

Deliver

Gestational age–based approach to management

Intrapartum group B streptococcus prophylaxis if no recent negative anovaginal culture

Broad-spectrum antibiotics if amnionitis

delivery, risk of chorioamnionitis, endometritis, and NICU admissions, with no increase in rate of operative delivery.

- A period of expectant management can be offered in select patients who decline induction and have been appropriately counseled.
- Routine induction agents may be used. The most researched agents for induction in setting of PROM include oxytocin and prostaglandins. Oxytocin has been shown to be associated with lower rates of chorioamnionitis.
- GBS prophylaxis should be provided in GBS positive individuals or individuals with GBS unknown status and concurrent risk factors

Preterm PROM:

- 34 weeks or above: Clinician should proceed toward delivery as in term patients
- 24 to 34 weeks:
  1. Administration of betamethasone for fetal lung maturity
  2. Administration of prophylactic antibiotics to prolong latency period, consisting of 7-day course of parenteral and oral therapy. Current guidelines recommend ampicillin or amoxicillin and erythromycin.
  3. Expectant management until 34 weeks, unless fetal lung maturity is demonstrated between 32 to 34 weeks.
  4. Magnesium sulfate administration if delivery is imminent and <32 weeks
  5. GBS prophylaxis in setting of GBS unknown/GBS positive if delivery is expected.

CHRONIC Rx

- Hospitalization with expectant management is recommended for all patients with preterm PROM. Ongoing maternal and fetal surveillance in a hospital setting allows for quick recognition of infection, labor, or fetal compromise secondary to cord compression.

DISPOSITION

- Most women with preterm PROM will proceed to deliver within one week despite medical interventions. Latency period is generally longer when PROM occurs at an earlier gestational age.
- Clinical chorioamnionitis develops in 13% to 16% of preterm PROM. This risk is increased with earlier PROM as well as with an increase in the number of digital vaginal examinations.
- Complications of preterm PROM are related mostly to complications of prematurity, and decrease with increasing gestational age at time of delivery. The most common complications include respiratory distress, neonatal

infection, intraventricular hemorrhage, and necrotizing enterocolitis.
- There is a 1% to 2% risk of antenatal demise in the setting of preterm PROM.

REFERRAL

- Consultation with an Ob-Gyn is recommended in the setting of preterm PROM.

 **PEARLS & CONSIDERATIONS**

PREVENTION

- Patients with a history of preterm delivery (with or without PROM) may benefit from administration of progesterone supplementation in future singleton pregnancy starting at 16 to 24 weeks to prevent preterm delivery.

SUGGESTED READINGS

Available at www.expertconsult.com

RELATED CONTENT

Premature Labor (Related Key Topic)
Abruptio Placentae (Related Key Topic)

AUTHOR: **CLAIRE SCHULTZ, M.D.**

(i) BASIC INFORMATION

DEFINITION

Premenstrual syndrome (PMS) is a cyclic recurrence during the luteal phase of the menstrual cycle of somatic, affective, and behavioral disturbances that are of sufficient severity to affect interpersonal relationships adversely or interfere with normal activities.

SYNONYM

PMS

ICD-10CM CODES

N94.3 Premenstrual tension syndrome

EPIDEMIOLOGY & DEMOGRAPHICS

- PMS is believed to be extremely prevalent, intermittently affecting approximately one third of all premenopausal women.
- Severe cases occur in approximately 2% to 10% of women with PMS.
- Those seeking treatment for PMS are usually in their 30s or 40s.
- The natural history of PMS has not been clearly elucidated.

PHYSICAL FINDINGS & CLINICAL PRESENTATION

- Diverse and potentially disabling symptoms. Table 1P-43 summarizes common symptoms of cyclic PMS.
- Associated with >150 psychological, physical, and behavioral symptoms
- Most frequent reason for seeking treatment: emotional symptoms
- Most common emotional symptoms: depression, irritability, anxiety, labile moods, anger, crying easily, sadness, extreme sensitivity, nervous tension
- Most common physical symptoms: headache, bloating, cramps, breast tenderness, migraines, fatigue, weight gain, aches and pains, palpitations
- Most common behavior symptom: food cravings

- Other behavioral symptoms: increased appetite, increased alcohol intake, decreased motivation, decreased efficiency, avoidance of activities, staying home, sleep changes, libido changes, forgetfulness, decreased concentration

ETIOLOGY

- Etiology remains obscure.
- Because of the multifactorial, multiorgan nature of PMS, a single etiologic cause is unlikely.

(Dx) DIAGNOSIS

DIFFERENTIAL DIAGNOSIS

- A diagnosis of exclusion, so other medical or psychological disorders should be ruled out.
- Most common disorders: depression or anxiety, thyroid disease.

WORKUP

- History
- Physical examination
- Laboratory studies to rule out alternative diagnosis
- If no alternative diagnosis confirms diagnosis of PMS, basal body temperature charting is used to determine if the patient is ovulating:
  1. If she is not ovulating, it is not PMS.
  2. If she is ovulating, symptoms should be charted for at least two cycles to determine if the symptoms occur in the luteal phase.
  3. If symptoms are not occurring in the luteal phase, it is not PMS and further investigation is needed.
     a. If symptoms occur in the follicular phase, patient has premenstrual exacerbation of another condition.
     b. If symptoms do not occur in the follicular phase, diagnosis of PMS is confirmed.

LABORATORY TESTS

- None available to specifically confirm the diagnosis of PMS
- Thyroid function tests to rule out thyroid disease

(Rx) TREATMENT

NONPHARMACOLOGIC THERAPY

- Individualization of the treatment plan to maximize therapeutic response. Fig. 1P-93 describes a summary of treatment approaches to PMS.
- Psychosocial intervention:
  1. Education
  2. Stress management
  3. Environmental changes
  4. Adequate rest and sleep
  5. Regular exercise
- Nutritional recommendations:
  1. Regularly eaten, well-balanced meals
  2. Adequate amounts of protein, fiber, and complex carbohydrates; low fat
  3. Avoidance of foods that are high in salt and simple sugars; may promote water retention, weight gain, and physical discomfort
  4. Avoidance of caffeine-containing beverages; stimulant effects of caffeine may worsen tension, irritability, and insomnia
  5. Avoidance of alcohol and illicit drugs; may worsen emotional lability
  6. Calcium supplementation (1000 mg/day for women 19 to 50 yr, 1300 mg/day for girls 14 to 18 yr) to reduce the physical and emotional symptoms
  7. Magnesium (360 mg/day) to reduce water retention and the negative effect associated with PMS
  8. Pyridoxine (vitamin B_6) 50 mg bid to improve depression, fatigue, irritability, and natural diuretic ability; neurotoxicity observed at higher dosages

ACUTE GENERAL Rx

Suppression of ovulation:
- Oral contraceptives: one pill per day
- Progestin-only oral contraceptive: one pill per day
- Oral micronized progesterone: 100 mg every morning and 200 mg every evening on days 17 through 28 of menstrual cycle
- Progestin suppository: 200 to 400 mg bid on days 17 through 28 of menstrual cycle
- Oral contraceptive containing drospirenone/ethinyl estradiol: very effective in decreasing physical symptoms
- Medroxyprogesterone: 150 mg IM q3mo
- Levonorgestrel implants: surgical insertion every 5 yr
- Transdermal estradiol: one or two 100-µg patches every 3 days
- Danazol: 100 to 200 mg/day (ovulation not suppressed at this dose); has significant side-effect profile
- Gonadotropin-releasing hormone (GnRH) agonists: daily by intranasal spray or monthly by depot injection; profound hypoestrogenism, concerns for osteoporosis and vasomotor symptoms

Suppression of physical symptoms:
- Spironolactone: 25 to 50 mg bid on days 14 through 28 of menstrual cycle
- Mefenamic acid

TABLE 1P-43   Common Symptoms of Cyclic Premenstrual Syndrome

Somatic Symptoms

Abdominal bloating	Constipation or diarrhea
Acne	Headache
Alcohol intolerance	Peripheral edema
Breast engorgement and tenderness	Weight gain
Clumsiness	

Emotional and Mental Symptoms

Anxiety	Insomnia
Change in libido	Irritability
Depression	Lethargy
Fatigue	Mood swings
Food cravings (especially salt and sugar)	Panic attacks
Hostility	Paranoia
Inability to concentrate	Violence toward self and others
Increased appetite	Withdrawal from others

From Goldman L, Schafer AI: *Goldman's Cecil medicine,* ed 24, Philadelphia, 2012, WB Saunders.

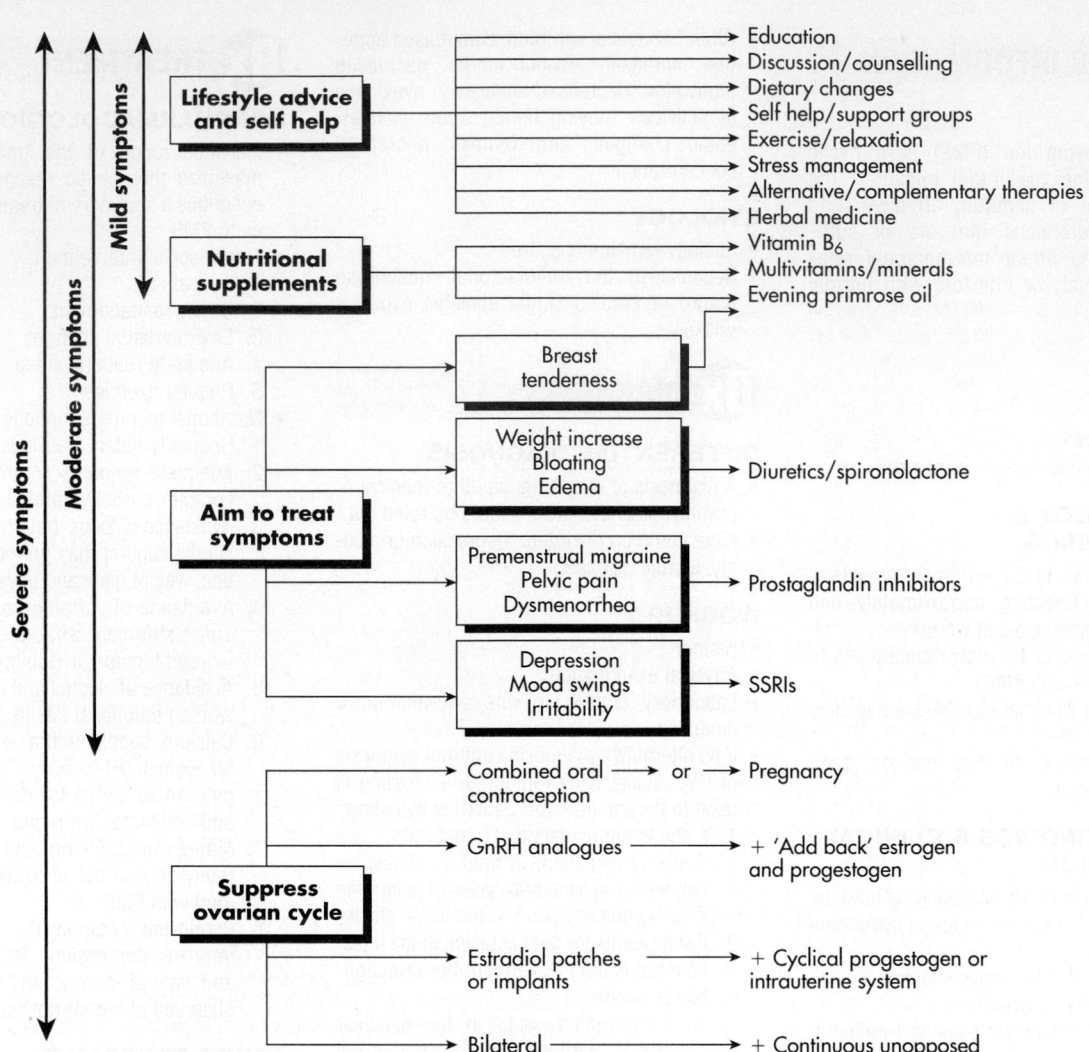

FIGURE 1P-93 Summary of treatment approaches to PMS. (Modified from Andrews G: Premenstrual syndrome. In Andrews G. (ed): *Women's sexual health*, Oxford, 2005, Elsevier.)

1. For fluid retention: 250 mg tid on days 24 through 28 of cycle
2. For pain: 500 mg tid on days 19 through 28 of cycle
- Bromocriptine: 5 mg/day on days 10 through 26 of cycle
- Danazol: 200 mg/day on days 19 through 28 of cycle
- Naproxen: 550 mg bid on days 17 through 28 of cycle, Naprosyn-500 mg bid on days 17 through 28 of cycle

Suppression of psychological symptoms:
- Nortriptyline: 50 to 125 mg/day
- Fluoxetine: 20 mg/day or 90 mg weekly (this medication has indications for premenstrual dysphoric disorder)
- Buspirone: 10 mg bid or tid on days 16 through 28 of cycle, then taper drug
- Alprazolam: 25 mg tid on days 16 through 28 of cycle, then taper drug
- Clonidine: 0.1 mg bid
- Naltrexone: 0.25 mg/day on days 9 through 18 of cycle
- Atenolol: 50 mg/day

- Paroxetine: 20 mg/day
- Sertraline: 50 to 100 mg/day
- Nefazodone: initial dosage 100 mg bid; after 1 wk increase to 150 mg bid
- Propranolol: 20 to 40 mg bid
- Verapamil: 100 to 320 mg qd

CHRONIC Rx

- Therapy is largely trial and error, with the goal of providing effective treatment with the safest and most simple therapy. Provider should initially attempt to ameliorate the most pronounced symptom(s).
- For severe intractable PMS: bilateral oophorectomy; give trial of GnRH therapy or danazol before surgery (bilateral oophorectomy should be exceedingly rare).
- Estrogen replacement therapy recommended postoperatively to reduce the risk of osteoporosis, heart disease, and genitourinary atrophy.

DISPOSITION

Improved symptoms in 90% of women over time

REFERRAL

- For counseling with a psychologist or psychiatrist if underlying psychiatric disorder is discovered (cognitive-behavioral therapy)
- To a gynecologist if surgical therapy is contemplated

SUGGESTED READINGS

Available at www.expertconsult.com

RELATED CONTENT

Premenstrual Syndrome (Patient Information)
Dysmenorrhea (Related Key Topic)
Premenstrual Dysphoric Disorder (Related Key Topic)

AUTHOR: **RUBEN ALVERO, M.D.**

 **BASIC INFORMATION**

DEFINITION

Preoperative evaluation is the clinical risk evaluation for patients undergoing surgery. It is an overall assessment of patient's health and surgery's risk. The goal of the assessment is not to "clear" the patient for the surgery, because there is always some level of risk, but to provide accurate preoperative risk stratification and implement possible risk reduction strategies. Preoperative evaluation should also include functional assessment and determine social support. It also provides an opportunity for discussion and helps to alleviate patient's anxiety before surgery.

SYNONYMS

Preoperative evaluation and risk reduction
Risk reduction in patients undergoing invasive procedures
Preoperative clearance

ICD-10CM CODES
Z01.810 Encounter for preprocedural cardiovascular examination
Z01.811 Encounter for preprocedural respiratory examination
Z01.818 Encounter for other preprocedural examination
Z01.812 Encounter for preprocedural laboratory examination

EPIDEMIOLOGY & DEMOGRAPHICS

The number of outpatient surgical procedures performed in the United States has been gradually increasing over the years. By the end of 2010, outpatient procedures accounted for more than 50% of all surgeries compared with less than 33% in 2000. (U.S. Surgical Procedure Volumes Report #A626, February 2012).

Some studies have shown the benefits of preoperative testing while others have shown no added benefit. Lack of added benefit has been particularly true for otherwise healthy individuals: the prevalence of significant unrecognized disease and the predictive value of tests are both low for this population—leading to an excess of false-positive tests.

In a trial of 1061 ambulatory surgical patients randomly assigned to preoperative testing or no testing, there was no difference in perioperative adverse events or events within 30 days of the surgery (Chung F et al., 2009).

Certain risk factors do exist that may be helpful: The nature and extent of surgery appear to play a role, as do increasing age, exercise capacity, and certain medications. Additionally, patients with certain preexisting conditions such as diabetes may benefit from adjustments to their insulin preoperatively, for instance. The primary care physician may be best suited to adjust medications. Box 1P-14 describes stratification of risk of common noncardiac surgical procedures.

Preoperative evaluation offers an excellent opportunity to reach out to patients about other preventive, screening, and routine health care issues as well. The primary care physician is uniquely poised to provide an accurate assessment and risk stratification of patients and to develop care plans for follow-up. This information can then be used to help surgeons counsel patients and guide patients' decision making.

PEAK INCIDENCE: When there are adverse consequences from surgery, cardiovascular complications account for the majority of morbidity and mortality in patients. Perioperative MIs (PMI) is one of the most important predictors of short- and long-term morbidity and mortality associated with surgery. The highest incidence of PMI is in the first 3 to 5 days after surgery.

PHYSICAL FINDINGS & CLINICAL PRESENTATION

The history, physical, and other studies need to assess the risks for myocardial infarction, arrhythmias, heart failure, endocarditis, stroke, venous thrombosis and pulmonary embolism, prolonged mechanical ventilation and respiratory failure, hemorrhage, diabetic acidosis, renal or hepatic failure, and infection.

WORKUP (FIG. 1P-94)

HISTORY: A thorough medical history is the most valuable tool. Assess the urgency of the surgical procedure. A conversation with the surgical team is helpful for urgent and emergent procedures.

Some standard screening questionnaires have been adapted to help identify patients who would benefit from formal preoperative evaluation.

- Age is important to consider because age is often associated with an increasing number

of comorbidities, which are in turn associated with an increase in perioperative risk.
- All patients should be asked about their exercise capacity before surgery. One way to assess functional capacity is in metabolic equivalents (METS) (*Circulation,* 2009) (Table 1P-44). Studies have shown that those who have a low exercise capacity have twice as much risk for postoperative complications compared to those who have high exercise capacity.
- Evaluate for evidence of active cardiac conditions: unstable angina, recent MI (<30 days), significant arrhythmia, decompensated CHF, and severe valvular disease.
- Other medical conditions and risk factors:
  1. Stable CAD, compensated CHF, HTN
  2. Chronic lung diseases
  3. Obstructive sleep apnea (preoperative screening [STOP-Bang, Berlin scores] in all patients)
  4. Other medical comorbidities: CVA, diabetes mellitus (DM), CKD, liver diseases
  5. Personal or family history of anesthetic complications
  6. Personal or family history of hypercoagulable states or bleeding disorders
  7. Medications such as anticoagulants, antiplatelets, NSAIDs, and oral hypoglycemic agents
  8. Smoking
  9. Alcohol
     1. Obesity
     2. Pregnancy
- Consider further testing based on above risk factors. The decision to order preoperative tests should be guided by the patient's clinical history, comorbidities, and physical examination findings. Cardiac evaluation algorithm for noncardiac surgery is described later (Fleisher et al, 2007).

In August 2014, The American College of Cardiology and American Heart Associated (ACC/AHA) updated their guidelines.[1] These new guidelines classify the urgency of surgery in 4 categories:
- Emergency (necessary within 6 hours)
- Urgent (necessary within 6-24 hours)
- Time-sensitive (can delay 1-6 weeks)
- Elective (can delay up to 1 year)

Surgical risk based on surgical and patient characteristics is either low (<1% risk of major adverse cardiac events) or high (≥1% risk of major adverse cardiac events). The intermediate risk category has been eliminated. Examples of high-risk procedures include vascular surgery, orthopedic surgery, intraperitoneal and intrathoracic surgery, head and neck surgery, and prostate surgery. Ambulatory surgery, endoscopic procedures, and cataract surgery are considered low risk. The Revised Cardiac Risk Index (RCRI) is based on the following 6 factors, each worth a point: high-risk surgery, ischemic heart disease, heart failure, stroke or TIA, diabetes requiring

[1]Fleisher LA et al: 2014 ACC/AHA guideline on perioperative cardiovascular evaluation and management of patients undergoing noncardiac surgery: a report of the American College of Cardiology/American Heart Association Task Force on practice guidelines, *J Am Coll Cardiol* 64:e77-e137, 2014.

BOX 1P-14	Stratification of Risk of Common Noncardiac Surgical Procedures	
High risk (>5%)	Emergent and urgent major operations, especially in the elderly
	Aortic and noncarotid major vascular surgery
	Surgery associated with large fluid status change or blood loss
Intermediate risk (1%-5%)	Head and neck surgery
	Carotid endarterectomy surgery
	Major thoracic surgery
	Major abdominal surgery
	Orthopedic surgery
	Prostate surgery
Low risk (<1%)	Eye and skin surgery
	Endoscopy
	Breast
	Ambulatory procedure

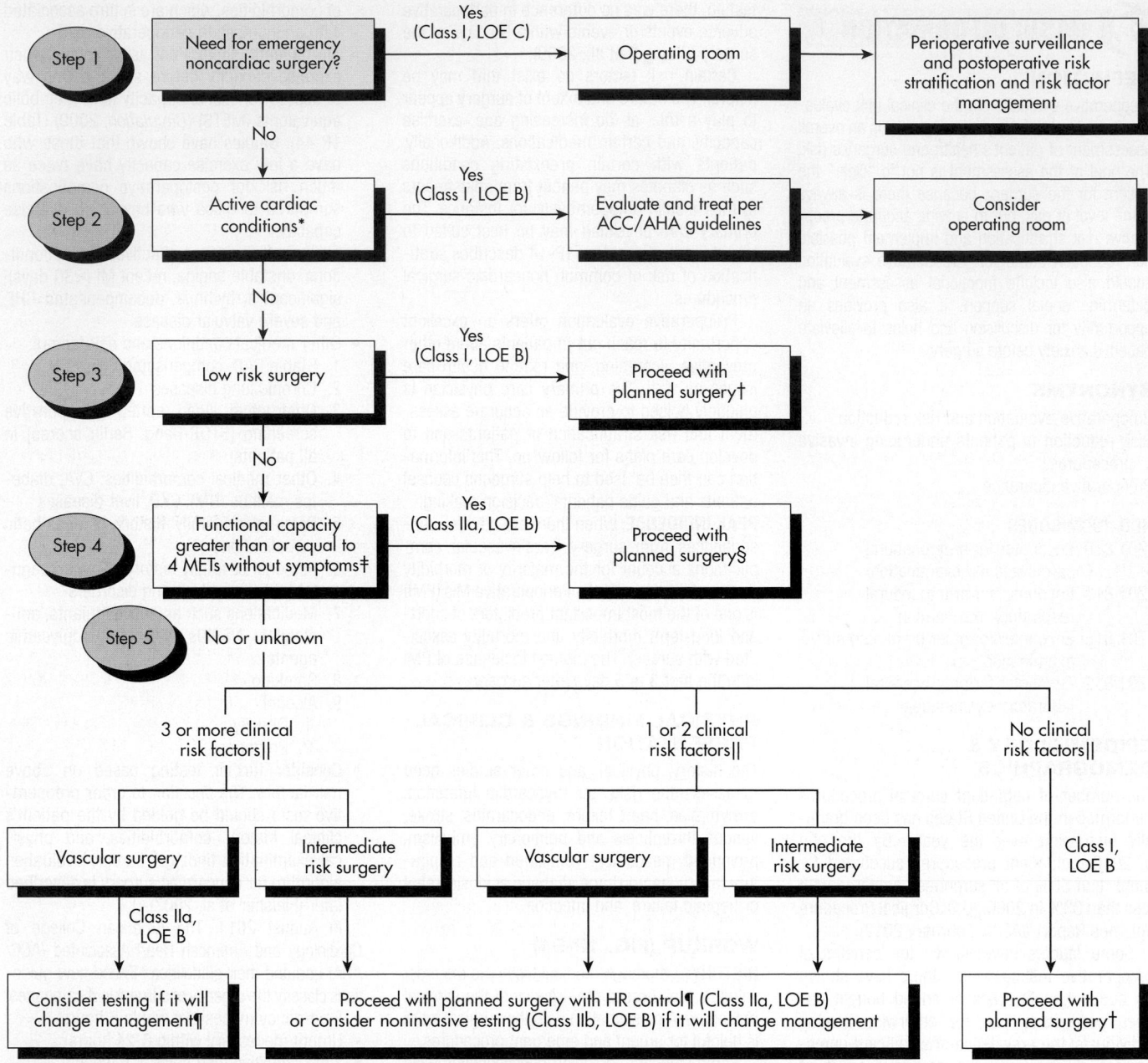

FIGURE 1P-94 Stepwise approach to preoperative cardiac assessment. Cardiac evaluation and care algorithm for noncardiac surgery based on active clinical conditions, known cardiovascular disease, or cardiac risk factors for patients 50 years of age or older. (Adapted from Fleisher LA et al: ACC/AHA 2007 Guidelines on perioperative cardiovascular evaluation and care for noncardiac surgery, *Circulation* 116: e418-e500, 2007.)

TABLE 1P-44 Functional Capacity (Metabolic Equivalents)

<4 Mets	4-10 Mets	>10 Mets
Daily living activities	Heavy housework	Strenuous exercise
Walking (2 mph)	Walking up a hill	Skiing
Walk 1-2 blocks	Walking (4 mph)	Tennis (single)
	Cycling	
	Golf	
	Tennis (double)	

(1 MET: energy expenditure of 70-kg man sitting quietly)

Adapted from Fleisher LA et al: ACC/AHA 2007 Guidelines on perioperative cardiovascular evaluation and care for noncardiac surgery, *Circulation* 116:e418-e500, 2007.

insulin, and renal insufficiency (serum creatinine >2.0 mg/dL). A patient with a RCRI score 0 to 1 is considered to be at low risk; a value of 2 or above is high risk.

PHYSICAL EXAMINATION

- Vital signs: blood pressure, heart rate and rhythm, rate and ease of respirations, and temperature.
- Cardiovascular exam. Auscultate heart to check for heart murmurs, pathologic heart sounds, and ventricular systolic or diastolic dysfunction.
- Respiratory exam. Auscultate lungs for crackles, wheezes, decreased breath sounds.
- Vascular exam. Examine for carotid, abdominal, and femoral bruits.
- Integumentary exam. Check for evidence of venous stasis in lower extremities, petechiae, and unusual bruises.
- Mental status. Conduct a mini-mental exam.

LABORATORY TESTS & IMAGING STUDIES

- Determine the patient's age, height, weight.
- Routine laboratory studies are not necessary unless there is a specific medical indication (*Anesthesiology*, 2002). Testing need not be repeated if results are recently available, unless there has been a change in clinical status.
  1. Low-risk procedures do not require routine basic metabolic panel, blood glucose, liver function, hemostasis evaluation, or a urine analysis.
  2. For intermediate- and high-risk procedures as well as in the setting of diabetes, cardiac, or renal disease, obtain a complete blood count.
  3. A CBC is recommended for all patients older than age 65 undergoing major surgery as well as anyone undergoing a surgery with expected large amounts of blood loss.
  4. Fasting glucose is recommended for all patients age >45 yr. Coagulation studies are only needed for patients with personal or family history of bleeding or thrombophilia and for those taking anticoagulants.
  5. Urine hCG is recommended for all women of childbearing age.
- Electrocardiogram: routine ECG is not recommended. The 2007 ACC/AHA guidelines do recommend resting 12 leads ECG for patients with:
  1. At least one clinical risk factor for those who are undergoing vascular surgery (class I, level of evidence (LOE) B)
  2. Known cardiovascular disease, peripheral arterial disease, and cerebrovascular disease for patients scheduled for intermediate-risk surgery (class I, LOE C)
  3. No clinical risk factors for patients scheduled to undergo vascular surgery (class IIa, LOE B)
  4. At least one clinical risk factor for patients who are undergoing intermediate-risk surgery (class IIb LOE B)

- Echocardiography: indicated only if new signs and symptoms of CHF or new cardiac murmurs on physical examination.
- Exercise or pharmacologic stress testing: only indicated for evaluation of the potentially high-risk patients: for patients scheduled to undergo vascular surgery with 3 or more clinical risk factors and poor functional capacity (<4 METS) if it will change management (class IIa) (Fleisher et al, 2007).
- Chest x-ray: routine CXR is not recommended. It is indicated for patients >50 years of age undergoing high-risk procedures (American College of Physicians [ACP] recommendations) and patients with new respiratory symptoms, suspected congestive heart failure, or valvular heart disease.
- Pulmonary function tests: It is only recommended for patients undergoing lung resection surgery but can be considered in:
  1. Patients with COPD or asthma, only if clinical evaluation cannot determine if they are at their best baseline.
  2. Patients with dyspnea or exercise intolerance that remains unexplained after clinical evaluation.
- Arterial blood gas: should be obtained only when clinically significant (to determine if lung disease is compensated).

Rx TREATMENT

- Beta blockers: While routine administration of perioperative beta-blockers was advocated for many years, conflicting evidence currently exists regarding their efficacy. While confirming a decrease in cardiac events with aggressive preoperative beta-blockade, the POISE trial (extended-release metoprolol beginning on the day of surgery) showed an increase in mortality and stroke risk (*Lancet*, 2008). On the other hand, DECREASE IV (fluvastatin + bisoprolol) demonstrated a cardioprotective effect of perioperative beta-blocker use without increased incidence in perioperative stroke or mortality (Dunkelgrun M et al, 2009). For now, the only class I indication for perioperative beta-blockers is the continuation of a beta-blocker in patients who are already taking it. In addition, several class IIa recommendations exist for patients with CAD and multiple clinical risk factors who are undergoing intermediate- to high-risk surgery and especially vascular surgery. In these situations, beta-blockers should be started at least 1 wk before surgery with careful dose titration to avoid frank bradycardia or hypotension.
- Statins: decrease cardiovascular events in patients undergoing vascular surgery (*N Engl J Med*, 2009).
- Aspirin: continuation of aspirin should be considered in patients who were previously taking aspirin (Class IIa, LOE B). For surgeries where increased bleeding could result in significant morbidity (e.g., neurosurgery) or when the risk of stopping aspirin is minimal, aspirin should be stopped 7 days or more

before surgery. Aspirin can be restarted on the first postoperative day as long as adequate hemostasis has been achieved.
- Adenosine diphosphate (ADP) antagonists (ticlopidine, clopidogrel, prasugrel): in patients with recently placed stents, elective surgical procedures should be delayed (minimum 3 wk for bare metal stents [BMS] and 3 mo for drug-eluting stents [DES]) while the patient is undergoing dual antiplatelet therapy. For procedures that must be performed, continuation of aspirin therapy is recommended. A short-term discontinuation of anti-ADP therapy while aspirin is continued may be relatively safe (*Circulation*, 2009).
- Anticoagulation therapy: patients taking warfarin who have a high risk of thromboembolism should be bridged with low-molecular-weight heparin (LMWH) (with the last dose 24 h before surgery) or unfractionated heparin (UFH) (with drip stopped 4 hr before surgery). Resumption of bridging therapy within 24 hr is safe for minor procedures but is associated with unacceptable, high bleeding rates in patients undergoing major surgery (Dunn et al, 2007). Therefore, it is recommended to wait 48 to 72 hr postoperatively to resume bridging therapy in patients who had major surgery. Another alternative regimen is to resume warfarin 12 to 24 hr postoperatively without any bridging therapy (Douketis et al, 2008).
- NSAIDs: NSAID therapy is almost never necessary, and it should be stopped before surgery (5-10 days prior).
- Pacemakers and defibrillators: consultation with an electrophysiologist is recommended. Pacemaker should be reprogrammed to an asynchronous mode (VOO, DOO), and defibrillation function must be set off to avoid unintentional discharge during surgery (electrocauterization).
- Smoking: smoking cessation is recommended at least 8 wk before surgery.
- Chronic obstructive pulmonary disease (COPD): COPD therapy should be optimized. Steroids and maximal bronchodilator therapy are reasonable for patients who are not at their best baseline.
- Hypertension: SBP <180 mm Hg and DBP <110 mm Hg are generally considered acceptable. In case of elective surgery, though, it is better to postpone it to allow for better BP control.
- Diabetes mellitus:
  1. Type I DM: scheduled basal insulin should be given the night before surgery or the morning of surgery. Continuous insulin infusion with glucose infusions might be necessary during prolonged procedures.
  2. In type II DM with oral therapy: short-acting sulfonylureas and other oral agents should be held the same day. Metformin and long-acting sulfonylureas should be held one day prior, and metformin should be kept on hold for 48 hr postoperatively. Short-acting insulin sliding scale should be used for blood glucose control meanwhile.

3. In insulin-dependent type II DM: 50% to 100% of the basal insulin should be given depending on whether the patient will be able to eat postoperatively. During major procedures, patients may need an insulin drip and D5% infusion.

4. Currently, a blood glucose level <180 mg/dl postoperatively is considered appropriate. Aggressive blood glucose control (81-108 mg/dl vs. <180 mg/dl) showed a slight increase in risks in both surgical and medical critical care patients. (NICE-SUGAR Study Investigators, 2009).

- Liver disease: nonoperative alternative should be strongly recommended in patients with advanced cirrhosis. If surgery is deemed necessary, optimize preoperative status: correct coagulopathy, thrombocytopenia, volume status, electrolytes, ascites, and encephalopathy.

- End-stage renal disease: achieve euvolemia and correct electrolytes. Patients receiving hemodialysis should undergo dialysis the day before surgery. In patients with a prior history of uremic bleeding, desmopressin administration should be considered.

- Corticosteroid management and adrenal insufficiency: in patients taking exogenous steroids, continuation of the same steroid regimen is reasonable. In those with chronic adrenal insufficiency, steroid supplementa-

tion is generally recommended with the dose titrated to the level of stress of the surgical procedure.

PEARLS & CONSIDERATIONS

COMMENTS

Although most individuals will not require any significant preoperative testing, certain conditions will require further workup.

- Ischemic heart disease
  1. If patient has angina, determine frequency, precipitating factors, response to rest and nitroglycerin
  2. If patient has had prior cardiac catheterizations or coronary revascularizations, obtain previous records
- Dysrhythmias and pacemakers
  1. Examine current and prior ECGs for high-grade atrioventricular block, symptomatic ventricular arrhythmias, and supraventricular tachycardias at uncontrolled rates.
  2. If patient has a pacemaker, establish the type and mode, date of implantation, and when it was last interrogated.
- Valvular and congenital heart disease
  1. Look for signs of severe valvular heart disease on last echocardiographic evaluations.

- Cerebrovascular disease
  1. Inquire about prior carotid artery ultrasounds
- Venous thromboembolism
  1. Determine results of studies for thrombophilia (factor V Leiden mutation, lupus anticoagulant, antithrombin III, protein C or S).
- Tools for cardiac risk assessment:
  1. http://www.statcoder.com
  2. http://www.infopoems.com

PATIENT & FAMILY EDUCATION

Advise patients that their preoperative evaluation visit with their PCP is another opportunity for them to bring up concerns or get questions answered about their upcoming procedure.

EVIDENCE

Available at www.expertconsult.com

SUGGESTED READINGS

Available at www.expertconsult.com

AUTHORS: **PRIYA SARIN GUPTA, M.D., M.P.H.,** and **TONY ABDO, M.D.**

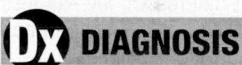 BASIC INFORMATION

DEFINITION

Pressure ulcers are soft tissue lesions resulting from compression, shearing forces, friction, and moisture that usually occur over bony prominences and external surfaces over an extended period of time.

SYNONYMS

Decubitus ulcers
Pressure sores
Bedsores
Decubiti

ICD-10CM CODES

L89   Pressure ulcers
Subcategories of codes determined by stage and location of ulcer
L89.153 Example: Stage 3 ulcer of sacral area
L98.491 Non-pressure chronic ulcer of skin of other sites limited to breakdown of skin
L98.492 Non-pressure chronic ulcer of skin of other sites with fat layer exposed
L98.493 Non-pressure chronic ulcer of skin of other sites with necrosis of muscle
L98.494 Non-pressure chronic ulcer of skin of other sites with necrosis of bone
L98.499 Non-pressure chronic ulcer of skin of other sites with unspecified severity

EPIDEMIOLOGY & DEMOGRAPHICS

- The incidence of pressure ulcers varies by clinical setting.
- An estimated 2.5 million cases of pressure ulcers are treated each year in acute care facilities across the United States.
- Occurs in all health care settings to include hospitals, nursing homes, and residential homes. The reported rates on admission in a nursing home range from 10% to 35%. Its incidence rate is highest in institutions with lower staffing levels of registered nurses and certified nursing assistants, reflecting emphasis on health care resources more than medical decision making.

- Associated with impaired quality of life with significant morbidity and mortality. One-year mortality rate roughly approaches 40%.
- Pain occurs in two-thirds of patients with stage II or greater pressure ulcers.
- Complicated by cellulitis, osteomyelitis, abscesses, sepsis, sinus tracts, heterotrophic calcification, systemic amyloidosis, and squamous cell cancer.

CLINICAL PRESENTATION

There are a number of staging systems that have been developed and utilized to describe the stages of pressure ulcers. The most commonly used system is the National Pressure Ulcer Advisory Panel (NPUAP). The European Pressure Advisory Panel recommends similar stages except for the presence of suspected deep tissue injury and unstageable ulcers.

The National Pressure Ulcer Advisory Panel (NPUAP) outlined the staging system of pressure ulcers as follows:

Stage I: Nonblanchable redness in a localized area usually over a bony prominence. Darkly pigmented skin may not have the obvious blanching but its color may appear different from the surrounding area.

Stage II: Partial-thickness dermal loss. It presents as a shallow lesion, with no slough or bruising. May also present as an intact or ruptured serum-filled blister. This does not include skin tears, tape burns, perineal dermatitis, maceration, or excoriation.

Stage III: Full-thickness dermal loss involving damage or necrosis of subcutaneous tissue that may extend down to, but not through, underlying fascia, muscle, bone, or tendon. There may be undermining and tunneling. Slough may be present. Stage 3 ulcers can be shallow in areas without subcutaneous tissue, which includes the bridge of the nose, ear, occiput, and the malleolus.

Stage IV: Full-thickness skin loss with exposed muscle, bone, or other supporting structures (e.g., tendons, joint capsule, or cartilage). Slough or eschar may be present. These ulcers often include undermining and tunneling (Fig. 1P-95).

Deep tissue injury: Purple or maroon localized area of discolored, intact skin or blood-filled

or thin blister over a dark wound bed due to damage of underlying tissue from pressure and/or shear.

Unstageable: Full-thickness tissue loss with the base of the ulcer covered by slough (green, brown, tan, gray, yellow) or eschar (tan, brown, or black) on the wound bed.

Mucosal pressure ulcers are not staged.

PATHOGENESIS

The development of pressure ulcers is a complex process that requires the application of external forces to intact skin. Pressure ulcers are soft tissue injuries caused by constant, unrelieved pressure in tissues overlying bony prominences. In general, the four major external factors include pressure, friction, shearing forces (gravity effect on friction), and moisture. Risk factors include immobility, incontinence, malnutrition, compromised skin perfusion, sensory loss, and concurrent medical illnesses. A number of neurologic and non-neurologic diseases may contribute, lead to, or exacerbate the development of pressure ulcers. However, further studies need to be performed to identify whether these are independent predictors.

DX DIAGNOSIS

DIFFERENTIAL DIAGNOSIS

- Venous insufficiency ulcers
- Arterio-occlusive ulcers
- Diabetic ulcers
- Neuropathic ulcers
- Skin cancer
- Cellulitis
- Kennedy ulcers (rapidly progressing unpreventable ulcers that occur at the end of life)
- Incontinence-associated dermatitis
- Perineal dermatitis

DIAGNOSTIC WORK-UP

Evaluate ulcer characteristics, including stage, appearance, location, and size (documented on a clock face, with the patient's head at 12 o'clock and feet at 6 o'clock). For stages III and IV, describe the wound bed (epithelialization, granulation tissue, necrotic tissue, eschar); presence of exudates, including type and amount; depth and wound edges (undermining, sinus tracts, tunneling, or fistulas); signs of infection (purulent drainage, odor, surrounding cellulitis); and pain. In addition, pressure ulcer risk factors and causes should be reassessed.

LABORATORY TESTS

- Directed at identifying causes or risk factors or any complications arising from the pressure ulcer (e.g., abscess or osteomyelitis).
- Cultures of wound bed are not believed to be helpful and should be avoided. Deep tissue biopsy is the gold standard if a culture is indicated.
- Markers for malnutrition include prealbumin, albumin, transferrin, lymphocyte count, and total cholesterol level.
- Complete blood count if systemic infection is suspected.

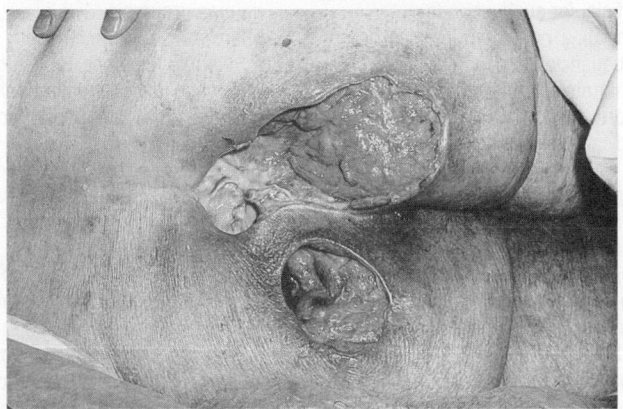

FIGURE 1P-95 Natural debridement of pressure injury at 2 weeks. (From Tallis R, Fillit H: *Brockelhurst's textbook of geriatric medicine and gerontology*, ed 6, London, 2003, Churchill Livingstone.)

IMAGING STUDIES

- Ultrasound not proven to be effective.
- Plain radiographs, MRI, and bone scan may help identify osteomyelitis when clinically suspected.
- A comparison study of 44 patients scheduled for open biopsy did not show MRI to have superior diagnostic benefit over plain radiography.

 **PREVENTION & TREATMENT**

Conduct a structured risk assessment:
- Identify high-risk patients using standardized risk assessment scales and risk prediction tools (e.g., Braden and Norton in the US, and Waterlow scale in the UK).
- Schedule skin inspection and good skin care for high-risk patients.
- Focus on controlling moisture and temperature
  1. Minimize prolonged skin exposure to moisture, urine, or stool.
  2. Treat dry, cracked skin.
- Use repositioning and pressure-reducing devices (e.g., foam mattresses, low–air loss beds, pillows, or foam wedges when in bed or in a chair).
  1. Patient repositioning (based on individual tissue tolerance):
     A recent multicenter trial demonstrated no difference in pressure ulcer formation in high-risk nursing home patients turned at 2-, 3-, and 4-hour intervals when on a high-density foam mattress.
  2. Bed surface

Air-fluidized beds
a. Two RCTs found that use of air-fluidized beds contributed to the healing of a greater number of ulcers after 15 days compared with standard care.
b. Systematic review revealed no differences in rate of pressure ulcer healing with use of either alternating-pressure mattresses or low–air loss beds compared with standard care.

Pressure-relieving overlays
One RCT demonstrated that a viscoelastic pad on the operating table significantly reduced incidence of postoperative pressure ulcers compared with a standard operating table.

Foam alternatives
a. Forty-one RCTs demonstrated that patients lying on standard hospital mattresses are more likely to develop pressure ulcers than those patients lying on higher specification foam mattresses.
   ○ Use adequate support surfaces while in bed or in a chair to prevent "bottoming out" (defined as less than 1 inch between patient and support surface; measured by putting hand under support surface and feeling thickness to patient).
   ○ Recent systematic review of pressure ulcer prevention strategies showed poor methodology in most studies. Use of support surfaces, repositioning, optimized nutrition, and sacral skin moisturizing was most appropriate.

The 2010 consensus statement from the National Pressure Ulcer Advisory Panel established that some pressure ulcers are unavoidable in situations where pressure cannot be relieved and perfusion cannot be improved. The 2014 consensus identified risk factors in specific situations that may lead to the development of unavoidable pressure ulcers. These include: impaired tissue oxygenation/cardiovascular instability, hypovolemia, sepsis, anasarca, peripheral vascular disease: venous/arterial, sensory impairment, immobility, end of life skin failure, multi-organ failure.

NON-PHARMACOLOGIC THERAPY

- Pressure ulcers should be cleaned at each dressing change
- Avoid agents that are cytotoxic to epithelial cells (e.g., iodine, iodophor, sodium hypochlorite, hydrogen peroxide, acetic acid, alcohol).
- Wound irrigation should not exceed 15 psi and is best done with an 18-gauge angiocatheter. Necrotic tissue should be debrided quickly because it delays wound healing and increases risk of infection.
  ○ Do not debride hard, dry, stable eschar on heels or ischemic limbs.
- No single dressing or product is superior; should be used to keep ulcer bed moist and protect it from urine/stool. Silver dressings (which are felt to be antimicrobial), topical phenytoin, and growth factors should be limited to difficult-to-heal wounds, chronic ulcers, and extensive burns given their extra cost and limited scientific validation. Reduce pressure by using foam mattress, dynamic support surface (e.g., low–air loss bed), and frequent repositioning (e.g., every 2 hours or, in cases of poor perfusion, more frequently).
- Hyperbaric oxygen, ultrasound, ultraviolet, electromagnetic therapy, and low-energy radiation either are ineffective or have not been extensively evaluated for efficacy.
- Negative pressure devices (VAC devices) may help in wounds that have significant drainage. They also may improve healing by promoting angiogenesis, improving tissue perfusion, and decreasing bacterial count. Calcium alginate and foam dressings may also be beneficial for such wounds.
- Although correcting poor nutrition has been shown to be beneficial, a recent large investigation demonstrated that feeding tube insertion did not prevent or heal pressure ulcers, but increased the risk for developing a pressure ulcer.
- Minimize or promptly remove urinary and/or fecal contamination.
- Use a standardized assessment tool to monitor wound healing on a weekly basis. Examples of monitoring scales include the Pressure Sore Status Tool (PSST) and Pressure Ulcer Scale for Healing (PUSH) in addition to the NPUAP staging system.
- No RCTs have compared debridement versus NO debridement in the treatment of pressure ulcers.

○ Thirty-two RCTs have compared different debridement agents, but there is insufficient evidence to promote the use of one particular agent.
○ One RCT demonstrated ulcers treated with collagenase healed significantly more quickly than those treated with hydrocolloid.
○ One RCT comparing honey-treated dressing with dressing soaked with saline showed faster healing times with the honey-treated group.
○ A meta-analysis and one RCT found significant benefit in rates of healing with use of hydrocolloid dressings versus traditional saline gauze dressings but not over other forms such as hydrogels, foam dressings, or collagenase.
- No benefit was found with nutritional and vitamin supplements, artificial nutrition, or ultrasound therapy.

ACUTE GENERAL Rx

- Management of pressure ulcers is directed by the staging of the ulcer.
- The cornerstone of therapy involves the use of appropriate wound dressings, pressure-reducing devices, treatment of infection, debridement, and surgical consultation when appropriate.
- All pressure ulcers are colonized with bacteria. Clinically evident infections should be assessed with culture and treated appropriately with topical and systemic antibiotics.
- Adjunctive therapies such as electrical stimulation, negative pressure wound therapy, therapeutic ultrasound, hyperbaric oxygen, topical oxygen, and application of growth factors to the wound are being investigated.
- Pain medications are necessary because pressure ulcers are often painful. One study found that excruciating pain was more prevalent in nursing home residents with pressure ulcers. Local factors that may be contributing to pain such as ischemia, infection, or breakdown of surrounding skin should be properly addressed.

CHRONIC Rx

- Continue vigilance with pressure reduction because pressure ulcers can recur with minimal trauma.
- There are no randomized trials available to identify whether repositioning makes a difference in the healing rates of pressure ulcers or what the optimal repositioning regimen should be.
- Consider radiologic evaluation for infected ulcer bed, occult osteomyelitis, or abscess.

COMPLEMENTARY & ALTERNATIVE MEDICINE

Vitamin C, zinc, and multivitamin supplements may be beneficial for patients with nutritional deficiencies. However, their efficacy has not been conclusively demonstrated. Anabolic steroids are sometimes recommended in patients with weight loss and protein depletion. However, the evidence is not conclusive as of yet.

P

DISPOSITION

- When systematic risk assessments are done and preventive measures are followed, most pressure ulcers can be prevented. Most ulcers heal when appropriate management strategies are followed.
- Stage IV ulcers in high-risk patients (e.g., paraplegics) can take months or years to heal.

REFERRAL

- Physical and occupational therapists to improve bed and chair mobility
- Wounds with necrotic tissue need referral to persons trained in sharp debridement
- To plastic surgeons for operative repair for large stage III or IV ulcers that do not respond to optimal care
- To a specialty wound center for non-healing ulcers

PEARLS & CONSIDERATIONS

COMMENTS

- Up to 10% of older persons will have a pressure ulcer.
- Because 70% of pressure ulcers occur in older persons, the approach should be similar to other multifactorial geriatric syndromes with a multidisciplinary team approach. Identify and reduce all modifiable risk factors for pressure ulcers.
- Treat the pain associated with pressure ulcers.
- Proper skin care, use of support surfaces, mobilization, and attention to nutrition are key for prevention and treatment.
- Clinical studies have not revealed if any one dressing product is superior.

- Non-healing ulcers require assessment for debridement, infection, abscess, and/or referral to a wound center.

PATIENT & FAMILY EDUCATION

- Educate patient and family members on the risk factors for pressure ulcers.
- Encourage mobility and adequate nutritional intake and avoid bed rest.

SUGGESTED READINGS
Available at www.expertconsult.com

RELATED CONTENT
Bed Sores (Patient Information)

AUTHORS: **MARY-BETH WELESKO, M.S., A.P.R.N.-B.C., W.C.C.,** and **NOEL S.C. JAVIER, M.D.**

Diseases and Disorders

BASIC INFORMATION

DEFINITION

Priapism is the persistent, usually painful erection associated or unassociated with sexual stimulation. There are two major forms: low-flow (veno-occlusive) priapism and high-flow priapism (associated with increased arterial inflow without increased venous outflow resistance).

ICD-10CM CODES
N48.30 Priapism, unspecified
N48.31 Priapism due to trauma
N48.32 Priapism due to disease classified elsewhere
N48.33 Priapism, drug-induced
N48.39 Other priapism

EPIDEMIOLOGY & DEMOGRAPHICS

- Peak incidence is seen from ages 5 to 10 yr and 20 to 50 yr.
- In the younger group, priapism is often associated with sickle cell disease or neoplasm. In the older group it is often caused by pharmacologic agents.
- Low-flow (veno-occlusive priapism [type I]) is much more common than high-flow (type II).

PHYSICAL FINDINGS & CLINICAL PRESENTATION

- In idiopathic priapism the initial erection is associated with prolonged sexual excitement. Previous transient episodes are frequently reported. The erection involves the corpora cavernosa alone. Detumescence does not occur spontaneously.
- In secondary priapism, sexual excitement need not be involved. Otherwise the clinical picture is the same as in idiopathic priapism.
- Table 1P-45 compares normal erection and priapism.

ETIOLOGY

Idiopathic: prolonged sexual arousal
Secondary or associated causes:
- Sickle cell disease
- Diabetes
- Leukemia (especially chronic myelogenous leukemia)
- Solid tumor (malignant) penile infiltration
- Spinal cord injury
- Perineal or penile trauma
- Iatrogenic
- Total parenteral nutrition, which includes a fat emulsion
- Hyperosmolar IV contrast
- Spinal or general anesthesia
- Anticoagulant therapy
- Phenothiazines
- Trazodone
- Intracorporeal injection therapy for impotence
- Phosphodiesterase type 5 inhibitors (e.g., sildenafil [Viagra], tadalafil [Cialis], vardenafil [Levitra])

PATHOPHYSIOLOGY

- Low-flow priapism: prolonged erection leads to edema of the cavernosal trabeculae, resulting in a sequence of stasis, thrombosis, venous occlusion, fibrosis, scarring, and possibly impotence.
- High-flow priapism: cavernosal artery rupture leading to an arteriocavernous fistula.

DIAGNOSIS

WORKUP

None if the associated underlying causes are known to be present. Otherwise they should be ruled out. Low-flow priapism can be distinguished from high-flow priapism by obtaining a corporeal blood gas value. A PO_2 <30 mm Hg, PCO_2 >60 mm Hg, and a pH <7.25 are consistent with low-flow priapism. High-flow priapism can be confirmed by a perineal Doppler ultrasound or arteriography (useful to identify arterial-lacunar fistula).

TREATMENT

Goal: achieve detumescence with preservation of potency.
1. Medical therapies:
   - Ice packs
   - Ice water enemas
   - Hot water enemas
   - Pressure dressing
   - Sedatives
   - Analgesics
   - Antispasmodic/anticholinergic drugs
   - Estrogens
   - Anticoagulants
   - Procaine
   - Amyl nitrite
   - Local or general anesthesia
   - Ketamine (1 mg/lb)
2. In the patient with sickle cell disease: intravenous hydration, alkalinization, transfusion or exchange transfusion, oxygen.
3. Corporeal irrigation with normal saline may be used for low-flow priapism. The midshaft of the penis can be injected with a small-gauge butterfly needle and irrigated with 10 to 20 ml of normal saline, followed by an intracorporeal injection of an alpha-adrenergic agonist every 5 min until detumescence. Commonly

used intracavernous vasoconstrictor agents are epinephrine (10 to 20 mcg), phenylephrine (250 to 500 mcg), and ephedrine (50 to 100 mg). It is mandatory to monitor the patient's blood pressure and pulse when using alpha-adrenergic agonists.
4. Surgery:
   - Cavernospongiosum shunt
   - Glans-cavernosum shunt
   - Cavernosaphenous shunt
   - In the less common situation of high-flow priapism (diagnosed by the finding of bright red arterial blood on aspiration), arterial embolization or surgical ligation is recommended.

PROGNOSIS

Impotence is associated with the duration of priapism, with 36 hr being an important threshold.

REFERRAL

To urologist

EVIDENCE

Available at www.expertconsult.com

RELATED CONTENT

Priapism (Patient Information)

AUTHOR: **FRED F. FERRI, M.D.**

TABLE 1P-45 Comparison of Normal Erection and Priapism

Factor	Normal Erection	Priapism
Portion of penis involved	Corpora cavernosa and corpus spongiosum and glans	Corpora cavernosa
Cause	Vasodilatation of penile arteries	Obstruction of venous outflow Disturbance of neuroarterial mechanism (imbalance between it and adrenergic activity) Increased viscosity
Sexual desire	Present	Absent
Pain	Absent	Present
Duration	Minutes to hours	Hours to days

From Nseyo UO (ed): *Urology for primary care physicians*, Philadelphia, 1999, Saunders.

BASIC INFORMATION

DEFINITION

Primary biliary cirrhosis (PBC) is a chronic, variably progressive cholestatic liver disease most often affecting women and characterized by destruction of the small intrahepatic bile ducts leading to portal inflammation, fibrosis, cirrhosis, and ultimately, liver failure.

SYNONYMS

Biliary cirrhosis
Nonsuppurative destructive cholangitis
Autoimmune cholangiopathy PBC

ICD-10CM CODES
K74.3 Primary biliary cirrhosis

EPIDEMIOLOGY & DEMOGRAPHICS
INCIDENCE:
- PBC affects all races and accounts for up to 2% of deaths from cirrhosis worldwide.
- Annual incidence rates range from 0.7 to 49 cases per million.

PREVALENCE: Prevalence is greatest in the U.K., Scandinavia, Canada, and the U.S. and varies tremendously by geographic areas, ranging from 6.7 to 402 cases per million. Disease burden seems to be increasing, which may be a result of better detection rather than true rise in disease incidence.

PREDOMINANT SEX: Female to male ratio of up to 10:1.

PREDOMINANT AGE: Onset typically occurs between the ages of 30 and 65 yr, and it is uncommon before age 25 yr.

PREDOMINANT RACE: Predominantly Caucasian but can be seen in other races.

GENETICS:
- Although there are no clearly identified genetic factors associated with PBC, there is a clear familial occurrence. Prevalence among first-degree relatives is 5% to 6%, and 1% to 6% of all patients have at least one affected family member. The concordance rate among monozygotic twins is 63%.
- Up to 84% of patients with PBC have at least one other autoimmune disorder, such as thyroiditis, Sjögren's syndrome, rheumatoid arthritis, Raynaud's phenomenon, scleroderma, systemic lupus erythematosus, pernicious anemia, or autoimmune thrombocytopenia purpura. A variant form of PBC exists as an overlap syndrome with autoimmune hepatitis (AIH).
- PBC is closely associated with a greater risk of hepatocellular carcinoma as well as an overall greater risk of cancer.

ETIOLOGY
- Although the cause of PBC remains unknown, it is believed to require both a genetic susceptibility as well as an environmental trigger, ultimately leading to the modification of mitochondrial proteins triggering a persistent T lymphocyte–mediated attack on intralobular bile duct epithelial cells.

- PBC is associated with the DRB1*04, *08, *14 family of alleles, but there is a great deal of variation among ethnicities.
- Possible environmental triggers include cigarette smoking, urinary tract infections, reproductive hormone replacement, nail polish, and toxic waste sites (particularly exposure to halogenated hydrocarbons), as well as xenobiotics in animal models of PBC.
- Recent studies have identified a group of autoantigens collectively known as the "M2 subtype" of autoantigens that play a major role in the early pathogenesis of PBC. These are peptides within the mitochondrial membrane that share structural homology. The enzyme complex subunit (PDC-E2) is one of the key autoantigens in this group. Patients with PBC have a tenfold increased concentration of cytotoxic $CD8^+$ lymphocytes recognizing this peptide in their livers compared with their blood, and most antimitochondrial antibodies (AMAs), which are the serologic hallmark of this disease, react to the PDC-E2 subunit. In addition, bile duct epithelial cells handle PDC-E2 in a unique way that exposes them to immune-mediated attack by PDC-E2–oriented cytotoxic T cells. Future therapies may be specific immunomodulation directed at these peptides.
- In addition to the T lymphocyte–mediated direct destruction of small bile ducts, secondary damage to hepatocytes results from the chronic accumulation of bile acids.

PHYSICAL FINDINGS & CLINICAL PRESENTATION
Clinical stages:
- Asymptomatic
- Symptomatic
- Cirrhotic
- Hepatic failure

Symptoms:
- 50% to 60% of patients may be asymptomatic; 40% to 100% of these patients will develop symptoms, and nearly 25% of symptomatic patients at diagnosis will progress to liver failure within 10 yr without treatment.
- Fatigue (20%-85% of patients) and pruritus (20%-75% of patients) are the usual presenting symptoms.
- Fatigue can be chronic and correlated with daytime somnolence and autonomic dysfunction.
- Pruritus is worse at night with constricting, coarse garments, and in association with dry skin and hot, humid weather. The cause is unknown; it is no longer believed to be a result of the retention of bile acids in skin. Pruritus may first occur during pregnancy but is distinguished from pruritus of pregnancy because it persists into the postpartum period and beyond.
- Other common symptoms include dyslipidemia (>75%), sicca symptoms (70%), jaundice (10%-60%), xanthomas (15%-50%), osteoporosis (35%), scleroderma-like lesions (15%), unexplained right upper quadrant pain (10%), thyroiditis (10%), and manifestations of portal hypertension.

- Musculoskeletal complaints caused by inflammatory arthropathy in 40% to 70% of patients: 5% to 10% experience development of chronic rheumatoid arthritis, and 10% experience development of "arthritis of PBC."
- Steatorrhea may be seen in advanced disease.

Physical Examination:
- Variable: Findings depend on stage of disease at time of presentation; patients at the early stage may be completely unaffected.
- Excoriations may be present.
- Hepatomegaly (70%) and splenomegaly (initially 35%) may be present in more advanced disease.
- Xanthomas and jaundice appear in advanced disease. Kayser-Fleischer rings are rare and result from copper retention. Hyperpigmentation of the skin due to melanin deposition may be present.
- Late physical findings mirror those of cirrhosis: spider nevi, temporal and proximal limb wasting, ascites, palmar erythema, gynecomastia, loss of chest or axillary hair, and edema.

DIAGNOSIS

The diagnosis of PBC can be established when two of the following three criteria are met.
- Positive serum AMA, titer >1:40
- Biochemical evidence of cholestasis (mainly alkaline phosphatase elevation ≥1.5 times the upper limit of normal)
- Characteristic liver histology: nonsuppurative destructive cholangitis and destruction of interlobular bile ducts

DIFFERENTIAL DIAGNOSIS
- Drug-induced cholestasis
- PBC-AIH overlap syndrome: reported in almost 10% of adults with AIH or PBC; transition from stable PBC to AIH and vice versa also seen
- Other etiologies of chronic liver disease and cirrhosis, such as alcoholic cirrhosis, chronic viral hepatitis, primary sclerosing cholangitis, AIH, sarcoidosis, hepatic amyloidosis, chemical/toxin-induced cirrhosis, other hereditary or familial disorders (e.g., cystic fibrosis, α-1-antitrypsin deficiency)
- Biliary obstruction

WORKUP
History, physical examination, laboratory evaluation, liver biopsy

LABORATORY TESTS
- AMAs found in 95% of patients with PBC and are 90% specific.
- Antinuclear antibodies (ANAs) and AMAs found in approximately 50% of patients. In approximately 5% of patients, AMAs are absent or present only in low titer (AMA-negative PBC). Nearly all of these patients have ANA or AMAs, or both.
- Cholestatic pattern of liver biochemical markers; markedly increased alkaline phosphatase (of hepatic origin).
- γ-Glutamyl transpeptidase is increased.

- Serum IgM levels are increased (lower in AMA-negative PBC).
- Bilirubin level is normal early on and increases with disease progression (direct and indirect) in 60% of patients. Increased serum bilirubin level is a poor prognostic sign.
- Aminotransferase level may be normal and, if increased, is rarely more than five times the upper limit of normal.
- Markedly increased serum lipids in more than 50% of patients. Total cholesterol may exceed 1000 mg/dl. No increased risk for death from atherosclerosis seen, possibly because of high levels of LP-X, an anti-atherogenic low-density lipoprotein particle, very-high-density lipoprotein levels, and low serum levels of lipoprotein(a).
- Percutaneous liver biopsy confirms or rules out the diagnosis, allows staging, but is not essential to make diagnosis or to initiate medical therapy in patients with typical liver chemistry and positive AMA test.
- Histology is not uniform, so histologic stage is based on the most advanced lesion present.
  1. Stage I: Lymphocytic infiltration of the epithelial cells of the small bile ducts with granuloma-like lesions, limited to portal triads (bridging fibrosis)
  2. Stage II: Extension of inflammatory cells to periportal parenchyma, invasion by foamy macrophages, and development of biliary piecemeal necrosis
  3. Stage III: Fibrous septa link portal triads
  4. Stage IV: Frank cirrhosis; hyaline deposits and accumulation of stainable copper are also seen

IMAGING STUDIES

If history, physical examination, blood tests, and liver biopsy are all consistent with PBC, neither imaging nor cholangiography is necessary (Fig. E1P-96).

PROGNOSIS

- Median survival was 10 yr but may be getting longer with earlier diagnosis and initiation of treatment.
- Mean time of progression from stage I or II disease to cirrhosis with no medical treatment is 4 to 6 yr.
- Neither presence nor total titer level of AMAs predicts survival, disease progression, or response to therapy.
- Prognostic laboratory measures: Serum bilirubin is the best predictor of survival and the most heavily weighted factor in prognostic models.
- Response to ursodiol therapy can be prognostic: Patients with a decrease in alkaline phosphatase level of at least 40% or to the reference range after 1 yr of treatment with ursodeoxycholic acid (UDCA) may have a prognosis similar to an age-matched healthy population. Similarly, the Mayo Risk score, a predictor of short-term survival probability (http://www.mayoclinic.org/gi-rst/mayomodel1.html), can also reliably predict life expectancy when calculated after 6 mo of ursodiol therapy.

- Poorer prognosis exists with jaundice, advanced histologic stage, advanced age, edema, coagulopathy, and ascites.

🅡🅧 TREATMENT

- Treatment is according to the clinical stage of the disease.
- Asymptomatic stage: Follow bilirubin every 3 mo. Once liver function test results become abnormal, begin UDCA at 13 to 15 mg/kg/day in a twice-daily divided dose regardless of histologic stage. Side effects may include headaches, dizziness, diarrhea or constipation, dyspepsia, nausea, weight gain of approximately 5 lbs during the first 1 to 2 yr, back pain, and upper respiratory infections. Watch for interactions with cholestyramine and other bile-acid sequestrants, as well as antacids, which may interfere with UDCA absorption. Efficacy is best if started during stage I or II disease but should be started at any stage of disease. Lifelong therapy is currently recommended, but benefits are still observed if therapy is interrupted and restarted.
- Treatment also includes treatment of associated conditions such as pruritus, osteoporosis, increased low-density lipoprotein level, malabsorption, vitamin deficiencies, anemia, hypothyroidism, and any eventual complications of cirrhosis.
- 33% of patients will not respond to medical therapy and will proceed to liver transplantation, which is the only definitive treatment for this disease.

ACUTE GENERAL Rx

- Symptomatic stage: Goals of treatment are resolution of pruritus, decrease of alkaline phosphatase levels, and delay of progression to liver failure.
- Ursodiol can significantly improve bilirubin and alkaline phosphatase levels, prolong survival without liver transplantation, and delay progression of liver fibrosis and development of portal hypertension.
- The addition of colchicine, methotrexate, or fibrates has not been found to be of benefit to mortality or time to liver transplantation in controlled trials.
- Prednisone, azathioprine, penicillamine, and cyclosporine are no longer used because of limited efficacy and significant toxicity.
- For the pruritus of PBC, cholestyramine resin (4 g/dose; maximum, 16 g/day) reduces pruritus in most patients but must be given at least 5 hrs before ursodiol to avoid reducing the efficacy of that drug. Antihistamines at bedtime help nighttime symptoms. Rifampin (150-300 mg bid) or oral opiate antagonists such as naltrexone (12.5-50 mg daily) can be used for pruritus refractory to bile acid sequestrants. Intractable pruritus can be an indication for liver transplantation.

CHRONIC Rx

- Liver function tests should be checked every 3 to 6 mo.

- Management of sicca syndrome: Artificial tears can be used initially for dry eyes. Saliva substitutes can be used for xerostomia and dysphagia; pilocarpine or cevimeline can be used for refractory cases. Moisturizers and lubricants can be given for vaginal dryness.
- Treatment/Prevention of osteopenia/osteoporosis: Patients with PBC should be provided 1000 to 1500 mg calcium daily in divided doses and 1000 IU of vitamin D daily in the diet and as supplements if needed. Bone densitometry should be done every 1 to 3 yr. Alendronate (70 mg weekly) should be considered if patients are osteopenic in the absence of acid reflux or known varices.
- Hyperlipidemia is common in patients with cholestatic liver disease. Statins are safe in patients who may need treatment even if liver chemistry is abnormal.
- Vitamin A, K, and E deficiencies can be clinically important in advanced cases and respond to oral replacement.
- Upper endoscopy to assess for varices should be done every 2 to 3 yr in patients with cirrhosis or Mayo risk score >4.1. Nonselective beta-blockers or endoscopic banding can be considered for prevention of variceal hemorrhage.
- Regular screening for hepatocellular carcinoma with ultrasound and α-fetoprotein every 6 to 12 mo is recommended for patients with cirrhosis.
- Liver transplantation is the only effective treatment for patients with liver failure. Indications for transplantation include hepatic decompensation (ascites, encephalopathy, jaundice), hepatocellular carcinoma fulfilling Milan criteria (see "Hepatocellular Carcinoma"), and intractable pruritus.
- The outcome of liver transplantation for patients with PBC is more favorable than that of nearly all other liver disease categories. The survival rates are 85% to 90% and 80% to 85% at 1 and 5 yr, respectively. Although recurrent disease may develop in 30% of patients after liver transplantation over 10 yr, patient and graft survival is usually not affected.

DISPOSITION

Definitive treatment requires liver transplantation; survival is 7 to 16 yr depending on symptoms at time of diagnosis.

REFERRAL

Gastroenterology and/or hepatology for treatment, evaluation for liver transplantation, and management of portal hypertension

SUGGESTED READINGS
Available at www.expertconsult.com

RELATED CONTENT
Primary Biliary Cirrhosis (PBC) (Patient Information)

AUTHORS: **JEANETTE G. SMITH, M.D.,** and **NICOLETTE RODRIGUEZ, B.A.**

Primary immunodeficiency diseases (PIDDs) are a collection of >200 rare disorders involving the absence or malfunction of integral parts of the immune system. The etiologies of PIDDs are not communicable in the infectious sense, but vertically transmissible via transfer of inherited genetic defects. Although some defects affect a single part of the immune system, others cause multicomponent breakdown of combined innate and cellular immune responses and suggest the interplay of epigenetic influences. To be considered a PIDD, the cause must not be secondary to another disease, drug/chemical, or environmental exposure. Primary immunodeficiency disease onset may occur at birth, as most do, or at any subsequent developmental stage and may affect anyone, with only specific regard to gender or ethnicity.

SYNONYMS
PID
PIDD
PI

ICD-10CM CODES
D84.9 Immunodeficiency, unspecified
D80.5 Immunodeficiency with increased immunoglobulin M [IgM]
D80.9 Immunodeficiency with predominantly antibody defects, unspecified
D81.0 Severe combined immunodeficiency [SCID] with reticular dysgenesis
D81.1 Severe combined immunodeficiency [SCID] with low T- and B-cell numbers
D81.2 Severe combined immunodeficiency [SCID] with low or normal B-cell numbers

D81.9 Combined immunodeficiency, unspecified
D82.2 Immunodeficiency with short-limbed stature
D82.3 Immunodeficiency following hereditary defective response to Epstein-Barr virus
D82.8 Immunodeficiency associated with other specified major defects
D82.9 Immunodeficiency associated with major defect, unspecified
D83.0 Common variable immunodeficiency with predominant abnormalities of B-cell numbers and function
D83.1 Common variable immunodeficiency with predominant immunoregulatory T-cell disorders
D83.2 Common variable immunodeficiency with autoantibodies to B- or T-cells
D83.9 Common variable immunodeficiency, unspecified

EPIDEMIOLOGY & DEMOGRAPHICS
Overall about 1:500 are born with and 1:1200 currently live with a PIDD, these numbers generally exclude the milder forms of immunodeficiency (e.g., IgA deficiency). The predilection for age and gender varies according to the specific disorder.

PHYSICAL FINDINGS & CLINICAL PRESENTATION
The history, signs, and symptoms depend on the precise genetic disorder. Recurrent, persistent, or unusual infections, as well as developmental delay or congenital anomalies, are among the most common attributes present when consid-

ering a primary immunodeficiency as a potential diagnosis.

ETIOLOGY
• Inherited

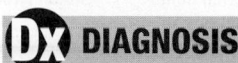 DIAGNOSIS

The International Union of Immunological Societies (IUSIS) PID expert committee has set forth a PID classification system that is updated every other year. The PIDs are grouped into 8 categories, based on the primary mechanism of each disease. Due to the complexity of the classification system in clarifying a PID case and the reasoning that most PIDs will present in nonimmunological fields of medicine, a phenotype-based algorithmic approach highlighting the clinical and biological characteristics of a particular PID has been synthesized to aid in diagnosis.
• Combined T-cell and B-cell immunodeficiencies
• Well-defined syndromes with immunodeficiency (Table 1P-46)
• Predominantly antibody deficiencies (Table 1P-47)
• Disease of immune dysregulation
• Congenital defects of phagocyte number, function, or both
• Defects of innate immunity
• Auto-inflammatory disorders
• Complement deficiencies (Table 1P-48)

DIFFERENTIAL DIAGNOSIS
• Secondary immunodeficiency, primary infections

TABLE 1P-46 Antibody and B-Cell Deficiencies

Disease	Functional Deficiencies	Mechanism of Defect
Agammaglobulinemia		
X-linked	Decrease in all serum Ig isotypes; reduced B-cell numbers	Pre-B receptor checkpoint defect; Btk mutation
Autosomal recessive forms	Decrease in all serum Ig isotypes; reduced B-cell numbers	Pre-B receptor checkpoint defect; mutations in IgM heavy chain (μ), surrogate light chains, Igα, BLNK
Hypogammaglobulinemia, Isotype Defects		
Selective IgA deficiency	Decreased IgA; may be associated with increased susceptibility to bacterial infections and protozoa such as *Giardia lamblia*	*TACI* mutations in some patients
Selective IgG2 deficiency	Increased susceptibility to bacterial infections	Small subset has deletion in IgG2 locus
Common variable immunodeficiency	Hypogammaglobulinemia; normal or decreased B-cell numbers	*ICOS* and *TACI* mutations in some patients
ICF syndrome	Hypogammaglobulinemia; occasional mild T-cell defects	*DNMT3B* mutations
Hyper-IgM Syndromes		
X-linked	Defects in helper T-cell–mediated B-cell, macrophage, and dendritic cell activation; defects in somatic mutation, class switching, and germinal center formation; defective cell-mediated immunity	*CD40L* mutations
Autosomal recessive with cell-mediated immune defects	Defects in helper T-cell–mediated B-cell, macrophage, and dendritic cell activation; defects in somatic mutation, class switching, and germinal center formation; defective cell-mediated immunity	*CD40, NEMO* mutations
Autosomal recessive with antibody defect only	Defects in somatic mutation and isotype switching	*AID, UNG* mutations

AID, Activation-induced cytidine deaminase; *BLNK*, B-cell linker; *DNMT3B*, DNA methyltransferase 3B; *ICF*, immunodeficiencies, centromeric instability, and facial anomalies; *Ig*, immunoglobulin; *ICOS*, inducible costimulator; *NEMO*, NF-κB essential modulator; *TACI*, transmembrane activator and calcium modulator and cyclophilin ligand interactor; *UNG*, uracil N-glycosylase.
From Adkinson NF, et al: *Middleton's allergy principles and practice*, ed 8, Philadelphia, 2014, WB Saunders.

TABLE 1P-47 Predominant Antibody Deficiencies

	Disease	Mode of Inheritance/Genetic Locus	Clinical Features
Severe reduction in all serum immunoglobulin isotypes with absent B-cells	Bruton tyrosine kinase deficiency	XL/Xq21.3-22	Severe bacterial infections (especially of the respiratory tract), absent lymphoid tissue
	μ heavy chain deficiency	AR/14q32.3	Severe bacterial infections
	λ5 deficiency	AR/22q11.21	Severe bacterial infections
	Igα deficiency	AR/19q13.2	Severe bacterial infections
	Igβ deficiency	AR/17q23	Severe bacterial infections
	BLNK deficiency	AR/10q23.2	Severe bacterial infections
	Thymoma with immunodeficiency (Good syndrome)	None	Recurrent infection with encapsulated bacteria and diarrhea, autoimmune phenomena
	Myelodysplasia	Variable/monosomy 7, trisomy 8, dyskeratosis congenita	Recurrent infections and pancytopenia
Severe reduction in at least two serum immunoglobulin isotypes with low or normal B-cell numbers	Common variable immunodeficiency syndromes TACI alterations BAFFR alterations MSH5 alterations	≈10% with family history AR or AD AD and AR/17p11.2 AR/22q13 Unk/6p22.1-p21.3	Recurrent respiratory tract infections leading to chronic sinusitis, hearing loss, bronchiectasis, autoimmune disease, lymphoproliferation, malignancy (especially non-Hodgkin lymphoma and gastric carcinoma)
	ICOS deficiency	AR/2q33	Recurrent infections
	CD19 deficiency	AR/16p11.2	Recurrent infections
	X-linked lymphoproliferative disease (mutation in SH2 domain protein 1A)	XL/Xq25-q26	Fulminant infection with EBV, lymphoma, dysgammaglobulinemia
Severe reduction in serum IgG and IgA with increased IgM and normal B-cell numbers (disorders of immunoglobulin class switching)	CD40 ligand deficiency	XL/Xq26.3-Xq27.1	Recurrent infections with bacteria and opportunistic pathogens, neutropenia, autoimmune disease
	CD40 deficiency	AR/20q11-20q13.2	Recurrent infections with bacteria and opportunistic pathogens, neutropenia, autoimmune disease
	NF-κB essential modulator (NEMO) hypomorphic mutations	XL/Xq28	Recurrent infections with bacteria and opportunistic pathogens, neutropenia, autoimmune disease
	AID deficiency	AR/12p13	Recurrent bacterial infections and diarrhea, marked enlargement of lymphoid organs
	UNG deficiency	AR/12q23-q24.1	Recurrent bacterial infections and diarrhea, marked enlargement of lymphoid organs
Isotype or light-chain deficiencies with normal B-cell numbers	Ig heavy-chain deficiency	AR/14q32	Most patients are healthy
	κ-chain deficiency	AR/2p11.2	Most patients are healthy
	Isolated IgG subclass deficiency	Variable/unknown	Most patients are healthy
	IgA deficiency associated with IgG subclass deficiency	Variable/unknown	Most patients are healthy
	Selective IgA deficiency	Variable/unknown	Most patients asymptomatic, but increased prevalence of infections, autoimmune disease, atopy, and celiac disease
Specific antibody deficiency with normal immunoglobulin level and B-cell number	Inability to make antibodies to specific antigens	Variable/unknown	Recurrent sinopulmonary infection, bronchiectasis, diarrhea, autoimmune disease
Transient hypogammaglobulinemia of infancy	IgG and IgA deficiency	Variable/unknown	More likely to be male (60%-80%), mild infections and diarrhea, atopy

AID, Activation-induced cytidine deaminase; *BAFF-R,* B-cell–activating factor receptor; *BLNK,* B linker; *EBV,* Epstein-Barr virus; *ICOS,* inducible T-cell costimulator; *Igα,* immunoglobulin-associated α; *Igβ,* immunoglobulin-associated β; *λ5,* immunoglobulin lambda-like polypeptide; *MSH5,* mutS homolog 5; *NF-κB,* nuclear factor kappa-B; *TACI,* transmembrane activator and CAML-interactor; *UNG,* uracil DNA glycosylase.

From Hoffman R: *Hematology, basic principles and practice,* ed 6, Philadelphia, 2013, Saunders.

WORK-UP

- A thorough history detailing the type, location, and frequency of the infections, as well as any physical exam findings that may indicate recurrent or persistent infections (e.g., scarred tympanic membranes) is essential in the initial characterization of the suspect immunodeficiency.

LABORATORY TESTS

- Screening Tests
  - Complete blood count with a manual differential: the most important test upon initial evaluation is whether lymphocyte, neutrophil, or platelet counts are normal.
  - Quantitative immunoglobulin levels (IgG, IgA, IgM, IgE): The specimen should be processed at a CLIA (Clinical Laboratories Improvement Act)-approved laboratory and be evaluated within the context of the patient's age and clinical presentation.
  - Vaccine responsive antibody quantification: Important to the evaluation of an antibody deficiency disorder is evaluating whether there are truly low serum immunoglobulin responses to both polysaccharide- and protein-based vaccines. Table E1P-49 describes antibody specificities commonly used in flow cytometry for immunodeficiency assessment.

- Any further investigation should defer to an immunologist for guidance based on history, symptoms, and clinical presentation and may involve a more precise analysis of immunoglobulin subtypes, T and B lymphocytic subsets, cell surface markers, complement levels, and gene sequencing.

Rx TREATMENT

Treatment depends highly on the specific immunodeficiency and should always include primary treatment and prophylaxis of the offending infectious agents. Education on the necessary precautions to minimize potential infections is crucial. A systematic consideration of the appropriate vaccinations is key to avoid any unnecessary infections or complications. Specific PIDDs carry the risk of malignancies and require regular screenings.

Immunoglobulin replacement is standard treatment for most primary immunodeficiencies to reduce the incidence of serious bacterial infections. Available immunoglobulin G products include Hyquia, Gammagard liquid, Gamune XC, and Hizentra. The newest FDA-approved product is Hyquia. It contains human immune globulin 10% with recombinant hyaluronidase. It is administered subcutaneously every 3 to 4 weeks. It has dosing advantages compared to other immune globulin subcutaneous (IGSC) products, but may be more difficult to self-administer because of the need to give hyaluronidase first. The risk of immunogenicity with chronic exposure to recombinant human hyaluronidase is a concern, and its safety in children has not been established.[1]

NONPHARMACOLOGIC THERAPY

Surgical intervention may be necessary for specific congenital malformations and possibly if malignancy is identified. In the case of a severe combined immune deficiency, patient bone marrow transplantation may be a therapeutic option.

PATIENT/FAMILY EDUCATION

- Due to the nature of primary immunodeficiencies, affecting both the patient and family members, genetic counseling is key to comprehensive patient care. Although immunologists are well versed in the genetic inheritance of the PIDDs, referral to a genetic counselor is often advised.

SUGGESTED READINGS

Available at www.expertconsult.com

Author: **KEVIN V. PLUMLEY, M.D., M.P.H.,** and **STEVEN M. SEPE, M.D., PH.D.**

[1]The medical letter on drugs and therapeutics, 57(1476):121-122.

TABLE 1P-48 Inherited Complement Deficiencies

Deficiency	Chromosomal Location	Number of Cases Reported	Clinical Features; Diagnostic Strategy
C1q	1	10-100	SLE, infections; CH50 near zero
C1r/c	12	10-100	SLE, infections; CH50 near zero
C4	6	10-100	SLE, infections; CH50 near zero
C2	6	Many	SLE, infections, some asymptomatic; CH50 near zero
C3	19	10-100	Infections frequent and severe, glomerulonephritis; CH50 near zero
Factor D	19	<10	*Neisseria*; AH50 near zero
Factor B	6	<10	*Neisseria*; AH50 near zero
Properdin	X	>100	*Neisseria*; AH50 diminished
MBL	10	Millions	Most asymptomatic infections, SLE; CH50 normal, MBL assay required
C5	9	10-100	*Neisseria*; CH50 near zero
C6	5	>100	*Neisseria*; CH50 near zero
C7	5	>100	*Neisseria*; CH50 near zero
C8	1 and 9	>100	*Neisseria*; CH50 near zero
C9	5	Many	*Neisseria*; CH50 diminished
Factor I	4	10-100	*Neisseria*, HUS; C3 may be diminished, many require mutation analysis
Factor H	1	10-100	*Neisseria*, HUS; C3 may be diminished, many require mutation analysis
MCP	1	<10	HUS; mutation analysis required
C1 inhibitor	11	Many	Angioedema; C1 antigen and functional levels
CR3/CR4	16	>100	Leukocyte adhesion deficiency, very severe systemic infections, lack of pus; flow cytometry
CD59	11	<10	Paroxysmal nocturnal hemoglobinuria; flow cytometry

AH50, Serum dilution that lyses 50% of a red cell suspension; *CH50,* serum dilution that lyses 50% of a red cell suspension; *HUS,* hemolytic uremic syndrome; *MBL,* mannose-binding lectin; *MCP,* membrane cofactor protein; *SLE,* systemic lupus erythematosus.

From Adkinson NF, et al: *Middleton's allergy principles and practice,* ed 8, Philadelphia, 2014, WB Saunders.

BASIC INFORMATION

DEFINITION

- Women younger than 40 yr of age with amenorrhea, oligomenorrhea, or dysfunctional uterine bleeding for 4 mo or more along with follicle stimulating hormone (FSH) levels in the menopausal range meet diagnostic criteria for primary ovarian insufficiency.
- Menopause younger than the age of 40 yr.

SYNONYMS

Hypergonadotropic hypogonadism
Premature ovarian failure
Premature menopause
Gonadal dysgenesis

ICD-10CM CODES
E28.3	Primary ovarian failure
E28.9	Ovarian dysfunction, unspecified
E28.310	Symptomatic premature menopause
E28.39	Other primary ovarian failure

EPIDEMIOLOGY & DEMOGRAPHICS

INCIDENCE: Affects 1% to 4% of the female population in the U.S.
PREDOMINANT AGE: 1:250 incident cases by age 35 and 1:100 by age 40

PHYSICAL FINDINGS & CLINICAL PRESENTATION

- The most common presentation is disturbance in menstrual pattern due to intermittent ovarian function.
- Between 5% and 30% of affected women have another affected female relative.
- Between 10% and 30% of affected women already have a concurrent autoimmune condition, the most common of which is hypothyroidism.
- Symptoms of estrogen deficiency include hot flashes, night sweats, poor concentration, drying of the vagina, and infertility.
- Physical exam may reveal stigmata of an autoimmune condition such as vitiligo, thyroid enlargement, or Turner's syndrome (webbed neck, short stature, and high-arched palate).

ETIOLOGY (SEE TABLE 1P-52)

Idiopathic in 95% of cases

DIAGNOSIS

DIFFERENTIAL DIAGNOSIS

- Pregnancy
- Causes of secondary amenorrhea include eating disorder, exercise, drugs, sarcoidosis, polycystic ovarian disease, hypothalamic amenorrhea, hyperprolactinemia/prolactinoma, and Cushing's disease.

WORKUP

- After pregnancy is ruled out, the initial evaluation should include the measurement of serum prolactin, FSH, and thyrotropin (TSH) levels.
- If the FSH level is in the menopausal range (>40 ulU/mL by radioimmunoassay), the test should be repeated in 1 month along with a serum estradiol measurement to confirm the diagnosis of primary ovarian insufficiency.

LABORATORY TESTS

Once a diagnosis of premature ovarian failure is made, other evaluations include:
- Autoimmune disorders, adrenal insufficiency (seen in 3% of cases): serum anti-adrenal and anti-21 hydroxylase antibodies should be measured.
- Hypothyroidism: serum TSH, T_4, and anti-TPO antibodies
- All cases should be screened for osteoporosis by DXA for bone mineral density.
- A karyotype analysis should be performed for all patients to look for chromosomal defects including Turner's variant or deletions of the X chromosome.
- Permutations for the fragile X syndrome (*FMR1* gene) should be checked for as well.

IMAGING STUDIES

Pelvic ultrasound has no proven benefit in the management of these patients.

TREATMENT

NONPHARMACOLOGIC THERAPY

Counseling or patient support group should be offered to all women with low self-esteem and depression due to the psychological scar left by the diagnosis.

ACUTE GENERAL Rx

- Physiologic estrogen and progestin replacement is reasonable in the cases of young women until they reach the age of natural menopause.
- A dose of 100 mcg of estradiol per day, administered by transdermal patch, achieves average estradiol level observed in normal menstruating women and effectively treats symptoms.
- Cyclic medroxyprogesterone at a dose of 10 mg per day for 12 days each month is the preferred progestin to provide protection against endometrial cancer.

TABLE 1P-52 Mechanisms and Causes of Primary Ovarian Insufficiency

Accelerated Follicular Depletion

Genetic: Turner's syndrome, fragile X premutations, galactosemia
Toxic: Chemotherapy, radiation, infections such as mumps or cytomegalovirus
Autoimmune: Polyglandular failure, hypothyroidism, Addison's disease, vitiligo, myasthenia gravis

Abnormal Follicular Stimulation

Gonadotropin receptor function: follicle stimulating hormone/luteinizing hormone receptor mutation
Enzyme defects: Aromatase deficiency
Luteinized follicles

- Pregnancy may occur while a woman is taking estrogen and progesterone therapy and the therapy should be stopped immediately if the pregnancy test is found to be positive.

CHRONIC Rx

- Intake of 1200 mg of elemental calcium and 800 units of vitamin D_3 per day should be encouraged to prevent bone loss. A serum 25-hydroxyvitamin D level of 30 ng per ml or higher should be maintained.
- Patients with positive tests for adrenal antibodies should be evaluated annually for adrenal insufficiency by corticotropin stimulation test.
- Patients who wish to avoid pregnancy should use a barrier method or an IUD.
- Options for parenthood include adoption, foster parenthood, egg donation, and embryo donation.

DISPOSITION

Women with the known diagnosis should be encouraged to maintain a lifestyle that optimizes bone and cardiovascular health, including regular weight-bearing exercises, adequate intake of calcium (1200 mg daily) and vitamin D (800 IU daily), healthy diet to prevent obesity, and screening for cardiovascular risk factors.

REFERRAL

Referral to gynecologist and reproductive endocrinologist may be helpful in patients who decide to pursue parenthood.

PEARLS & CONSIDERATIONS

COMMENTS

- Common etiologies should be ruled out, including chromosomal abnormalities, fragile X premutations, and autoimmune causes.
- Management directed at symptom resolution and bone protection primarily, but should include psychosocial support for women facing this devastating diagnosis.

PREVENTION

Early diagnosis of primary ovarian insufficiency important for osteoporosis prevention and possibly prevention of coronary artery disease.

PATIENT & FAMILY EDUCATION

www.pofsupport.org
poi.nichd.nih.gov

SUGGESTED READINGS
Available at www.expertconsult.com

AUTHOR: **PRIYA BANSAL, M.D., M.P.H.**

BASIC INFORMATION

DEFINITION

Primary sclerosing cholangitis (PSC) is a chronic progressive cholestatic liver disease characterized by segmental fibrosing and inflammation of intrahepatic and extrahepatic bile ducts complicated by recurrent cholangitis, cholangiocarcinoma (CCA), cirrhosis, and portal hypertension.

SYNONYMS

Chronic obliterative cholangitis
Fibrosing cholangitis
Stenosing cholangitis
PSC

ICD-10CM CODES
K83.0 Cholangitis
K83.0 Disease of biliary tract, unspecified

EPIDEMIOLOGY & DEMOGRAPHICS

- The incidence and prevalence of PSC are 0.9 to 1.3 cases and 8.5 to 16.2 cases per 100,000 population, respectively.
- About 65% of patients with PSC are men.
- Mean age of presentation is 30 to 40 yr.
- 60% to 80% of patients with PSC also have inflammatory bowel disease (IBD). 4% to 5% of patients with ulcerative colitis (UC) will develop PSC. PSC is an independent risk factor for developing colon cancer in patients with IBD.
- PSC can coexist with other autoimmune liver diseases. Autoimmune hepatitis (AIH) and PSC overlap syndrome can be seen in young adults and children.
- Cholangiocarcinoma is present in 1% to 2% of PSC patients at diagnosis. The lifetime risk is 5% to 10%.
- The median survival from time of diagnosis is 10 to 15 yr without liver transplantation.

PHYSICAL FINDINGS & CLINICAL PRESENTATION

- Most patients are asymptomatic (15%-40%) at the time of diagnosis with normal physical findings. However, many patients will have abnormal liver tests and a known diagnosis of IBD.
- More than 75% of asymptomatic patients develop symptoms, the most common of which are nonspecific pruritus (70%) and fatigue (70%). Physical findings of symptomatic patients may reveal jaundice, skin excoriation and hyperpigmentation from scratching, hepatosplenomegaly, and xanthelasma. Other symptoms include abdominal discomfort, steatorrhea, jaundice, and weight loss, which are concerning for advanced PSC, sepsis, or mechanical obstruction (i.e., cholangitis), and malignancy (i.e., cholangiocarcinoma).
- Patients can also present with advanced liver disease and decompensated cirrhosis (i.e., ascites, spontaneous bacterial peritonitis, hepatic encephalopathy, and variceal

hemorrhage) or hepatic failure. In patients with cirrhosis, physical findings may reveal a shrunken nodular liver and evidence of portal hypertension.

ETIOLOGY

- The cause of PSC is unknown, but the most likely mechanism is immunologic priming in a genetically susceptible patient causing phenotypic expression of PSC.
- Genetic and immunologic factors are supported by reports of familial occurrence of this disorder and increased frequency of HLA B8 and DR3. Genome-wide association studies have discovered novel loci associated with PSC, but the functional aspects of these genes are still unknown.
- Portosystemic inflammation caused by translocation of the gut microbiota is an increasing area of research. The close association with UC and PSC may be secondary to gut-activated T lymphocytes in IBD causing portal inflammation because of overlapping adhesion molecules in the gut and liver.

DIAGNOSIS

Diagnosis is based on characteristic cholangiographic findings in combination with clinical, biochemical, and in some cases histologic features. It is increasingly common to diagnose PSC based on imaging with magnetic resonance cholangiopancreatography (MRCP). Liver biopsy is now rarely used to diagnose disease. Table 1P-53 describes staging of PSC.

DIFFERENTIAL DIAGNOSIS

- Surgical biliary trauma
- Ischemic cholangitis
- Intraarterial chemotherapy (5-FU/floxuridine)
- AIDS-related cholangiopathy
- Choledocholithiasis
- Recurrent pyogenic cholangitis
- Cholangiocarcinoma
- IgG4-associated cholangitis (IAC)
- Diffuse intrahepatic metastasis
- Histiocytosis X

TABLE 1P-53 Staging of Primary Sclerosing Cholangitis

Stage	Description
I—Portal	Portal edema, inflammation, ductal proliferation; abnormalities do not extend beyond the limiting plate
II—Periportal	Periportal fibrosis with or without inflammation extending beyond the limiting plate
III—Septal	Septal fibrosis, bridging necrosis, or both
IV—Cirrhotic	Biliary cirrhosis

From Cameron JL, Cameron AM: *Current surgical therapy*, ed 10, Philadelphia, 2011, Saunders.

WORKUP

History, physical examination, laboratory evaluation, imaging studies, and possible liver biopsy

LABORATORY TESTS

- Serum biochemical tests usually indicate cholestasis with predominant elevation in the serum alkaline phosphatase (three to ten times the upper limit of normal). However, this value can vary and be normal during the disease course. Serum aminotransferase levels are elevated in the majority of patients (two to three times the upper limits of normal). Serum bilirubin is usually normal at the time of diagnosis unless patient has advanced stricturing disease.
- A wide range of autoantibodies can be detected in patients with PSC; however, they are nonspecific for PSC, including the perinuclear antineutrophil cytoplasmic antibody (pANCA), autoantibodies such as antinuclear antibody (ANA), and anti-smooth muscle antibody (ASMA). Anti-mitochondrial antibody (AMA), which is characteristic of primary biliary cirrhosis, is *NOT* found in PSC and can be helpful in excluding PSC. Serum IgG levels are useful in the diagnosis of PSC-AIH overlap syndrome and IAC with autoimmune pancreatitis. In particular, elevated levels of IgG4 are found in 10% to 20% of PSC patients, with a subset of these patients displaying features of autoimmune pancreatitis. PSC patients with elevated IgG4 seem to respond to corticosteroid therapy, and hence all patients with PSC should be tested once for IgG4.

IMAGING STUDIES

- Cholangiography, with MRCP or ERCP, is considered to be the gold standard for the diagnosis of PSC. Characteristic findings reveal segmental fibrosis of bile ducts with saccular dilatation of normal intervening areas resulting in a "beads-on-a-string" appearance (Fig. 1P-99).

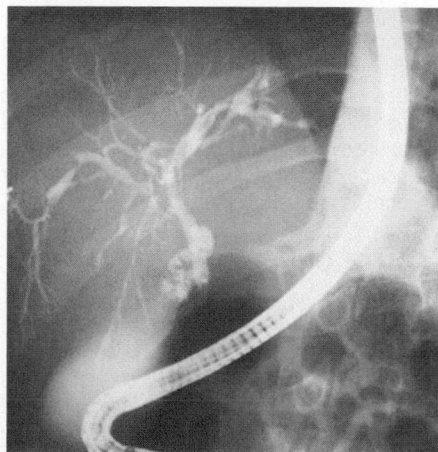

FIGURE 1P-99 A 29-year-old male patient who was diagnosed with PSC 5 years previously. Both the intra- and extrahepatic bile ducts are involved at cholangiography. (From Parlak E et al: An endoscopic finding in patients with primary sclerosing cholangitis: retraction of the main duodenal papilla into the duodenum wall, *Gastrointest Endosc* 65[3]:535, 2007.)

- Magnetic resonance cholangiopancreatography (MRCP) has an overall diagnostic accuracy rate of 90%. It is the first imaging modality of choice when PSC is suspected because endoscopic retrograde cholangiopancreatography (ERCP) can be associated with serious complications (i.e., pancreatitis and cholangitis).
- Liver biopsy is not necessary for the diagnosis of PSC in patients with typical cholangiographic findings, except for small duct PSC, which makes up 5% of patients with PSC. Biopsies are subject to sample variation, and the typical "onion skin"–type periductal fibrosis finding is rare. Liver biopsy may help in the diagnosis of PSC-AIH overlap syndrome, small-duct PSC (normal cholangiogram), or IAC.

Ⓡ🆇 TREATMENT

- No medical therapy has been established to be effective in halting the disease progression of PSC.
- Ursodeoxycholic acid (UDCA) has shown variable benefit in randomized controlled trials. Although biochemical improvement has been seen with UCDA, there has been no proven benefit on survival. In two trials, high-dose UCDA (28-30 mg/kg/day) was associated with colorectal dysplasia, liver transplantation, and varices. Therefore, high-dose UDCA is *NOT* universally recommended as medical therapy in patients with PSC. A trial of medium- or low-dose UDCA ~20 mg/kg/day is used by some clinicians, since some trials have shown biochemical response.
- Oral vancomycin may show clinical and biochemical response in pediatric patients, but no randomized clinical trial has been performed.
- Management of PSC patients is aimed at symptom relief and management of complications from PSC (i.e., obstruction/strictures).
- The use of corticosteroids and other immunosuppressive agents is not recommended in patients with PSC alone; however, it is recommended in patients with PSC-AIH overlap syndrome or elevated IgG4.
- Use of tumor necrosis factor inhibitors has been ineffective in PSC. Other monoclonal antibody therapies targeting lymphocyte trafficking, tyrosine kinase signaling, and liver fibrosis are being studied.

ACUTE GENERAL Rx

- With mild pruritus, skin emollients and antihistamines are recommended as the first-line treatment. With moderate or severe pruritus, bile acid sequestrants (i.e., cholestyramine 16 g/day) are the preferred choice for the initial management of pruritus. Alternative agents for pruritus refractory to bile acid sequestrants include rifampicin 150 to 300 mg twice daily, naltrexone 50 mg daily, sertraline 75 to 100 mg daily, or phenobarbital 90 mg at bedtime.

- Patients who present with increasing serum bilirubin and/or worsening pruritus, progressive bile duct dilatation on imaging studies, or cholangitis need to be evaluated for dominant strictures with imaging. A dominant stricture is a stenosis >1.5 mm in the common bile duct or ≥1 mm in the hepatic duct.
- ERCP with brushings, cytology, and fluorescent in situ hybridization (FISH) is recommended to evaluate dominant strictures for cholangiocarcinoma. Once malignancy is excluded, balloon dilatation with or without stenting is recommended to treat symptoms. Routine stenting is not required, but short-term stenting may be helpful in patients with severe stricture. If ERCP is unsuccessful, percutaneous cholangiopancreatography with stenting should be considered.
- In noncirrhotic patients with dominant strictures refractory to endoscopic or percutaneous management, surgery should be considered, although this may complicate future liver transplantation surgery.
- Antibiotic usage is recommended in patients with dominant strictures/obstructions both acutely and for long-term prophylaxis in patients with recurrent cholangitis.

CHRONIC Rx

- Avoidance of alcohol and vaccination against hepatitis A and B are advised.
- Patients with PSC are at risk for osteoporosis and osteopenia. At time of diagnosis, a DEXA scan is recommended and should be repeated in 2 to 4 yr. Calcium (1000 to 1500 mg) and vitamin D 600 to 800 IU daily are recommended for patients with osteopenia, and the addition of bisphosphonate is recommended in patients with osteoporosis.
- Patients with newly diagnosed PSC should have a full colonoscopy with biopsies to exclude concurrent IBD and for surveillance of colorectal cancer. In patients with IBD, continued surveillance colonoscopy with biopsies, or chromoendoscopy, at 1- to 2-yr intervals is recommended. In patients without IBD, a suggested 3- to 5-yr surveillance interval has been recommended due to an increased risk of colorectal cancer.
- Cholangiocarcinoma (CCA) development is common in PSC. PSC patients with biochemical or symptomatic deterioration should be evaluated for CCA. Surveillance for CCA with annual MRCP and CA19-9 has been recommended by some authorities. Abnormal values should prompt further investigation of dominant strictures with ERCP. Although CA19-9 may detect CCA, even high levels (>129 U/mL) may lack specificity since one-third of patients did not have CCA after 30 months of follow up. These differences may in part be due to genotypic differences in *FUT2/3* alleles that affect expression of CA19-9.
- Annual transabdominal ultrasound is recommended due to the increased risk of gallbladder malignancy. If masses or polyps >8 mm

are detected, cholecystectomy should be performed.
- Patients with cirrhosis are recommended to have gastroesophageal variceal and hepatocellular carcinoma (HCC) surveillance at regular intervals.
- With advanced disease, fat-soluble vitamin deficiencies such as A, E, and D should be assessed.
- In cases of HCC and CCA, depending on underlying liver disease, resection versus liver transplantation would be required.

DISPOSITION

Liver transplantation is the only effective treatment for patients with end-stage liver disease, portal hypertension, liver failure, and recurrent or intractable bacterial cholangitis. Survival is excellent, with 90% and 80% survival rates at 1 and 5 yr, respectively. The recurrence of PSC after transplant is reportedly 5% to 20%. Transplant referral is warranted when MELD exceeds 14 or greater, or with worsening cholangitis or intractable pruritus.

REFERRAL

Gastroenterology and/or hepatology for treatment of PSC, management of its complications, surveillance of associated malignancy, and evaluation for liver transplantation.

❗ PEARLS & CONSIDERATIONS

- Management of PSC targets symptom relief, complications of PSC, cirrhosis, early carcinoma detection, and timely referral for liver transplantation.
- High-dose UDCA is not universally recommended for treatment of PSC.
- Patients are at increased risk for the development of colorectal cancer, gallbladder cancer, and cholangiocarcinoma and need surveillance.
- Patients with PSC and ulcerative colitis have more common right-sided colon involvement and greater risk of pouchitis after colectomy with an ileal pount-anal anastomosis.
- In patients with cirrhosis, surveillance for gastroesophageal varices and HCC is recommended.
- Liver transplant remains the only definitive therapy for complications of PSC.

SUGGESTED READINGS

Available at www.expertconsult.com

RELATED CONTENT

Ulcerative Colitis (Related Key Topic)

AUTHORS: **CHARLES WANG, M.D.**, and **AMANDA PRESSMAN, M.D.**

 BASIC INFORMATION

DEFINITION

Progressive supranuclear palsy (PSP) is an atypical parkinsonian syndrome characterized by supranuclear gaze impairment, prominent and early postural instability with falls, axial greater than appendicular rigidity, and poor or absent response to levodopa.

SYNONYMS

Steele-Richardson-Olszewski syndrome
Progressive supranuclear ophthalmoplegia PSP

ICD-10CM CODES

G23.1 Progressive supranuclear ophthalmoplegia
G23.9 Degenerative disease of basal ganglia, unspecified

EPIDEMIOLOGY & DEMOGRAPHICS

INCIDENCE: 1.1 per 100,000 (5.3 per 100,000 over age 50)
PREVALENCE: 4.9 per 100,000 (6.4 per 100,000 age-adjusted)
PREDOMINANT SEX AND AGE: Slight male predominance; mean age onset 65 yr, very uncommon for onset <50 yr
GENETICS: Familial cases have been reported only rarely. The vast majority of cases are sporadic.

PHYSICAL FINDINGS & CLINICAL PRESENTATION

Tremorless parkinsonism is the general clinical presentation, and differentiation from idiopathic Parkinson's disease can be challenging early in the disease course. However, there are certain symptoms that can serve as "red flags" to consider PSP:

- Early postural instability and retropulsion leads to frequent falls; falls within the first year of onset of symptoms is typically the rule.
- Supranuclear gaze palsy is often preceded by slowing of vertical saccades; square wave jerks may be present; blepharospasm is common.
- Dystonia of the frontalis and procerus muscles gives the PSP patient a "surprised" or "frightened" expression as opposed to the hypomimia of Parkinson's disease (Fig. 1P-100).
- Speech is typically strained, spastic, hypernasal, with a low-pitched dysarthria.
- Pseudobulbar affect and "emotional incontinence" can be seen, with easy crying or laughter.
- Early cognitive impairment, most commonly with apathy, disinhibition, and anxiety.

ETIOLOGY

PSP is caused by neuronal degeneration of nuclei in the brain stem and basal ganglia as a result of abnormal tau protein accumulation in tufted astrocytes and neurofibrillary tangles.

 DIAGNOSIS

DIFFERENTIAL DIAGNOSIS

- Parkinson's disease: responds more robustly to levodopa, progresses more slowly, and lacks "red flag" symptoms listed previously.
- Corticobasal degeneration: also a tauopathy like PSP, but parkinsonism is associated with prominent asymmetric dystonia, cortical sensory signs such as astereognosis, apraxia, and sometimes an "alien hand" syndrome.
- Multiple system atrophy: distinguished by dysautonomia (particularly orthostatic hypotension), cerebellar ataxia, and inspiratory stridor.
- Dementia with Lewy bodies: A syndrome of coinciding dementia and parkinsonism, visual hallucinations, and fluctuating mental status.

WORKUP

- PSP is a clinical diagnosis, best made by a neurologist familiar with the disorder, such as a movement disorders specialist.
- A robust response to levodopa may lead consideration away from PSP.
- Brain MRI (see the following) can be helpful.

LABORATORY TESTS

There are no diagnostic laboratory tests.

IMAGING STUDIES

- Dorsal midbrain atrophy is commonly seen on MRI and is referred to as the "hummingbird sign" due to the elongated beak appearance seen on the midsagittal plane.
- Dopamine transporter imaging (DaTScan with [^{123}I]β-CIT SPECT) shows reduced uptake in PSP and is therefore not useful in differentiating PSP from Parkinson's disease or other causes of parkinsonism.

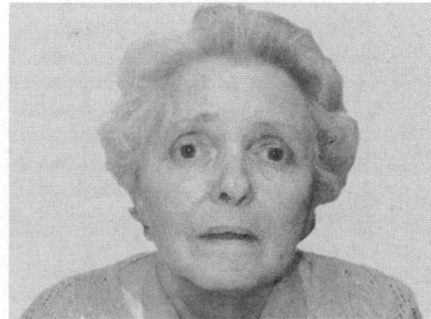

FIGURE 1P-100 A patient with progressive supranuclear palsy with staring expression, frontalis overactivity, and retrocollis. She is wearing a neck sling for a fractured wrist sustained in a fall. (From Burn D, Lees A: Progressive supranuclear palsy: where are we now? *Lancet Neurol* 1:359, 2002.)

TREATMENT

NONPHARMACOLOGIC THERAPY

- Physical and occupational therapy are essential for avoiding the morbidity associated with frequent falls. Assistive devices such as a walker or wheelchair should be encouraged.
- Dysphagia is a common finding that should be monitored closely in conjunction with a speech therapist.
- Prisms may be helpful to compensate for misalignment and diplopia resulting from the eye movement abnormalities; however, benefits, if noted, tend to be short-lived as the disease progresses.

CHRONIC Rx

- Although classically felt to be unresponsive to levodopa, there is often a transient but meaningful response to higher doses of levodopa (1200 mg/day). The poor response to levodopa is most likely due to the loss of postsynaptic dopamine receptors.
- Anticholinergic medications should be avoided.
- Blepharospasm can be effectively treated with botulinum toxin injections.

DISPOSITION

Median latency from symptom onset to wheelchair-bound state is 5 yr and to death is 7 yr in PSP-Richardson syndrome. Lifespan improves to 10 to 12 yr in the PSP-parkinsonism and PSP-pure akinesia with gait freezing phenotypes.

REFERRAL

Referral to a general neurologist or movement disorders center is appropriate.

PEARLS & CONSIDERATIONS

COMMENTS

Consider PSP in a parkinsonian patient with the onset of falls within 1 yr of diagnosis, vertical eye movement abnormalities, early cognitive impairment, pseudobulbar affect, frontonasal dystonia, or poor response to levodopa.

PATIENT & FAMILY EDUCATION

Patient and caregiver information and resources can be found through CurePSP at www.psp.org.

SUGGESTED READINGS

Available at www.expertconsult.com

AUTHOR: **ANDREW DUKER, M.D.,** and **JENNIFER E. VAUGHAN, M.D.**

BASIC INFORMATION

DEFINITION

Prolactinomas are monoclonal tumors that secrete prolactin.

ICD-10CM CODES
D35.2   Benign neoplasm of pituitary gland
E22.8   Other hyperfunction of pituitary gland

EPIDEMIOLOGY & DEMOGRAPHICS

INCIDENCE: Most common pituitary tumor; nearly 30% of all pituitary adenomas secrete enough prolactin to cause hyperprolactinemia.
PREDOMINANT SEX: Microadenomas are more common in women; macroadenomas are found more frequently in men.

PHYSICAL FINDINGS & CLINICAL PRESENTATION

- Men: decreased facial and body hair, infertility, small testicles; may also have decreased libido, erectile dysfunction, and delayed puberty (caused by decreased testosterone as a result of inhibition of gonadotropin secretion).
- Women: physical examination may be normal; history may reveal amenorrhea, galactorrhea (Fig. E1P-101), oligomenorrhea, and anovulation.
- Both sexes: visual field defects and headache may occur depending on size of tumor and its expansion.

ETIOLOGY

Prolactin-secreting pituitary adenomas: microadenomas (<10 mm diameter) or macroadenomas (>10 mm diameter). No risk factors have been identified for sporadic prolactinomas. Rarely prolactinomas can be part of multiple endocrine neoplasia (MEN) type 1 syndrome.

DIAGNOSIS

DIFFERENTIAL DIAGNOSIS

Secretion of prolactin is under tonic inhibitory control by hypothalamic dopamine. Hyperprolactinemia may be caused by the following:

- Drugs: risperidone, phenothiazines, methyldopa, reserpine, monoamine oxidase inhibitors, androgens, progesterone, cimetidine, tricyclic antidepressants, haloperidol, meprobamate, chlordiazepoxide, estrogens, narcotics, metoclopramide, verapamil, amoxapine, cocaine, oral contraceptives
- Hepatic cirrhosis, renal failure, primary hypothyroidism
- Ectopic prolactin-secreting tumors (hypernephroma, bronchogenic carcinoma)
- Infiltrating diseases of the pituitary (sarcoidosis, histiocytosis)
- Head trauma, chest wall injury, spinal cord injury
- Polycystic ovary disease, pregnancy, nipple stimulation
- Idiopathic hyperprolactinemia, stress, exercise

WORKUP

- The diagnosis of prolactinoma is established by demonstration of an elevated serum prolactin level (after exclusion of other causes of hyperprolactinemia) and radiographic evidence of a pituitary adenoma.
  1. Normal mean prolactin levels are 8 ng/mL in women and 5 ng/mL in men.
  2. Prolactin levels >100 ng/mL are suspicious for prolactinomas. Most macroprolactinomas raise prolactin levels >250 ng/mL and levels >300 ng/mL are virtually diagnostic of prolactinomas.
  3. Prolactin levels can vary with time of day, stress, sleep cycle, and meals. More accurate measurements can be obtained 2 to 3 hr after awakening, preprandially, and when patient is not distressed.
  4. Serial measurements are recommended in patients with mild prolactin elevations.
- TSH, free T_4, BUN, Creat, ALT, AST are useful tests. Pregnancy test in all women of childbearing age.
- All patients with prolactinomas should undergo visual field testing. Serial evaluation is recommended, particularly during pregnancy in patients with macroadenomas.

IMAGING STUDIES

- MRI with gadolinium enhancement is the procedure of choice in the radiographic evaluation of pituitary disease.
- In absence of MRI, a radiographic diagnosis is best accomplished with a high-resolution CT scanner and special coronal cuts through the pituitary region.

TREATMENT

NONPHARMACOLOGIC THERAPY

Pregnancy and breastfeeding should be avoided because they can encourage tumor growth.

ACUTE GENERAL Rx

- Management of prolactinomas depends on their size and encroachment on the optic chiasm and other vital structures, the presence or absence of gonadal dysfunction, and the patient's desires regarding fertility. Patients with microprolactinomas without sumptoms of hypogonadism do not require treatment. Fig. 1P-102 describes a management algorithm for prolactinomas.
- Medical therapy is preferred when fertility is an important consideration. Prolactinomas are treated with the dopamine agonists (DA) bromocriptine and cabergoline.
  1. Bromocriptine: initial dose is 0.625 mg at bedtime for the first week. After 1 wk, add morning dose of 1.25 mg. Gradually increase dose by 1.25 mg/wk until dose of 5 to 10 mg/day is achieved. Bromocriptine decreases size of the tumor and generally lowers the prolactin level into the normal range when the initial serum prolactin is <500 ng/mL. Side effects of bromocriptine are nausea, constipation, dizziness,

and nasal stuffiness. Bromocriptine appears to be safe during pregnancy.
  2. Cabergoline is a longer-acting dopamine agonist that is more expensive but may be more effective and better tolerated than bromocriptine; initial dose is 0.25 mg twice weekly.
  3. After therapy is initiated, MRI should be repeated in 1 year for microprolactinomas if the prolactin level normalizes. For macroprolactinomas, MRI is repeated after 2 months and every 6 to 12 months until stable on serial studies.
- Transsphenoidal resection: option in an infertile patient who cannot tolerate bromocriptine or cabergoline or when medical therapy is ineffective. The success rate depends on the location of the tumor (entirely intrasellar), experience of the neurosurgeon, and size of the tumor (<10 mm in diameter); the recurrence rate may reach 80% within 5 yr. Possible complications of transsphenoidal surgery vary with experience and skill of the neurosurgeon and tumor anatomy and include transient diabetes insipidus, hypopituitarism, cerebrospinal fluid rhinorrhea, and infections (meningitis, wound infection).
- Pituitary irradiation is useful as adjunctive therapy of macroadenomas (>10 mm in diameter) and in patients with persistent hypersecretion after surgery. Potential complications include cranial nerve damage, radionecrosis, and cognitive abnormalities.
- Stereotactic radiosurgery (gamma knife) has become popular as a modality in the treatment of prolactinomas. A high dose of ionizing radiation is delivered to the tumor through multiple ports. Its advantage is minimal irradiation to surrounding tissues. Proximity of the tumor to the optic chiasm limits this therapeutic modality.

CHRONIC Rx

- Patients on medical therapy require periodic measurement of prolactin levels. An attempt to reduce the dose of bromocriptine or cabergoline can be made after the prolactin level has been normal for 2 yr. An MRI scan of the pituitary should be obtained to rule out tumor enlargement within 6 mo of initiation of tapering regimen.
- Evaluation and monitoring of pituitary function are recommended after transsphenoidal surgery.

DISPOSITION

- Transsphenoidal surgery will result in a cure in nearly 50% to 75% of patients with microadenomas and 10% to 20% of patients with macroadenomas.
- Nearly 20% of microprolactinomas resolve during long-term dopamine agonist treatment.

PEARLS & CONSIDERATIONS

COMMENTS

- Patients must be monitored for several years after surgery because up to 50% of microad-

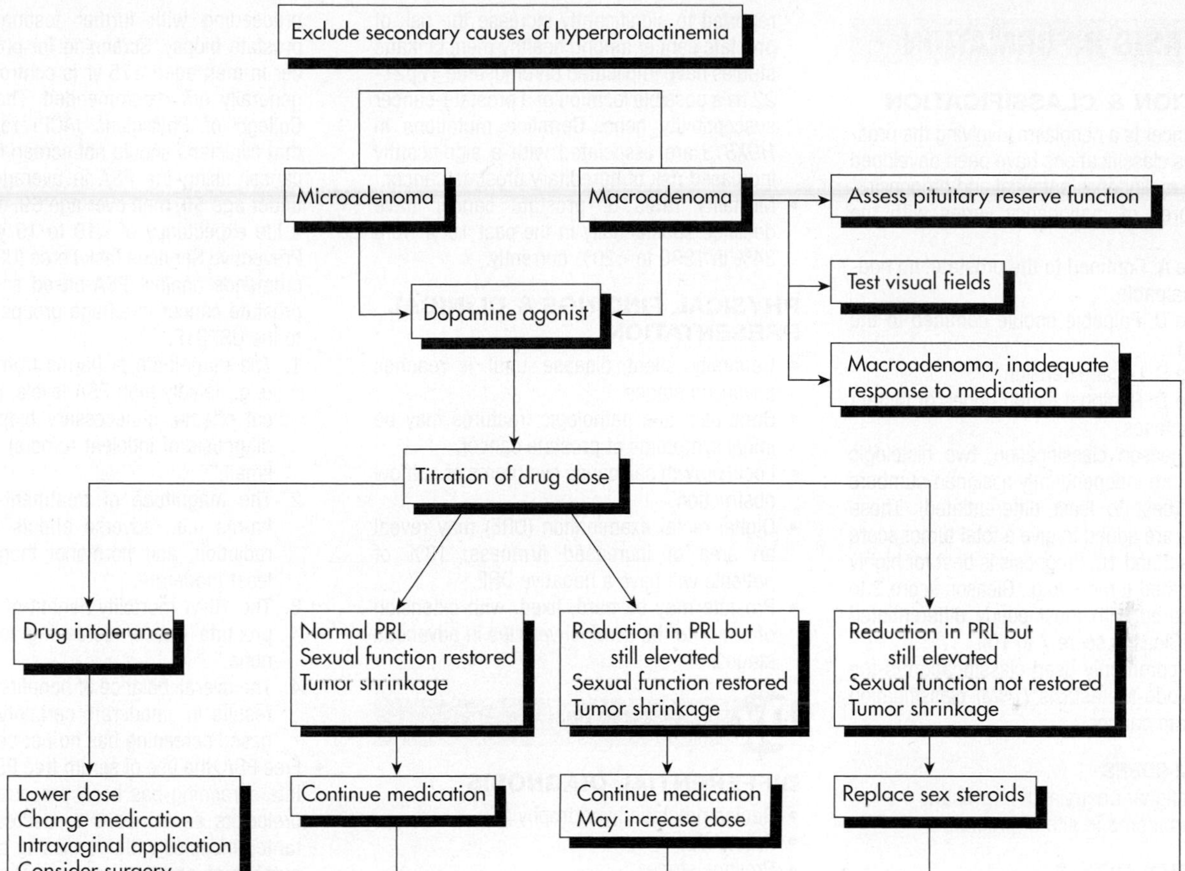

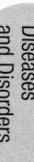

```
Exclude secondary causes of hyperprolactinemia
```

```
Microadenoma          Macroadenoma ──────► Assess pituitary reserve function
                                     ──────► Test visual fields
                                     ──────► Macroadenoma, inadequate
                                             response to medication
      └──► Dopamine agonist ◄──┘
```

```
Titration of drug dose
```

Drug intolerance	Normal PRL Sexual function restored Tumor shrinkage	Reduction in PRL but still elevated Sexual function restored Tumor shrinkage	Reduction in PRL but still elevated Sexual function not restored Tumor shrinkage
Lower dose Change medication Intravaginal application Consider surgery	Continue medication	Continue medication May increase dose	Replace sex steroids
	Monitor PRL levels Repeat MRI annually	Monitor PRL levels Repeat MRI annually	Monitor PRL levels Repeat MRI annually
No tumor shrinkage or visual field not improved	PRL not reduced No tumor shrinkage	PRL reduced Tumor not smaller	Desires pregnancy
Surgery	Increase dose or switch medication	Repeat MRI in 4 months	
	Surgery or radiotherapy rarely required for residual tumor	Surgery or radiotherapy rarely required for residual tumor	

FIGURE 1P-102 Prolactinoma management. After secondary causes of hyperprolactinemia have been excluded, subsequent management decisions are based on clinical imaging and biochemical criteria. *MRI,* Magnetic resonance imaging; *PRL,* prolactin. (Modified from Larsen PR et al: *Williams textbook of endocrinology,* ed 11, Philadelphia, 2008, Saunders.)

enomas and nearly 90% of macroadenomas can recur.
• Pituitary microadenomas are found in 10.9% of autopsies, and 44% of these microadenomas are prolactinomas.

EVIDENCE

Available at www.expertconsult.com

SUGGESTED READINGS

Available at www.expertconsult.com

RELATED CONTENT

Prolactinoma (Patient Information)

AUTHOR: **FRED F. FERRI, M.D.**

 **BASIC INFORMATION**

DEFINITION & CLASSIFICATION

Prostate cancer is a neoplasm involving the prostate. Various classifications have been developed to evaluate malignancy potential and prognosis.

- The degree of malignancy varies with the stage:
  1. Stage A: Confined to the prostate, no nodule palpable.
  2. Stage B: Palpable nodule confined to the gland.
  3. Stage C: Local extension.
  4. Stage D: Regional lymph nodes or distant metastases.
- In the Gleason classification, two histologic patterns are independently assigned numbers 1 to 5 (best to least differentiated). These numbers are added to give a total tumor score between 2 and 10. Prognosis is best for highly differentiated tumors (e.g., Gleason score 2 to 4) compared with most poorly differentiated tumors (Gleason score 7 to 10).
- Another commonly used classification is the Tumor-Node-Metastasis (TNM) classification of prostate cancer.

ICD-10CM CODES
C61   Malignant neoplasm of prostate
D07.5 Carcinoma in situ of prostate

EPIDEMIOLOGY & DEMOGRAPHICS

- Prostate cancer has surpassed lung cancer as the most common nonskin cancer in men.
- In the United States, more than 220,000 new cases are diagnosed yearly, and nearly 30,000 males die from prostate cancer each year (second leading cause of death from cancer in U.S. men).
- Incidence of prostate cancer increases with age: uncommon <50 yr; 80% of new cases are diagnosed in patients aged ≥65 yr. Widespread PSA testing has doubled the incidence of prostate cancer and the lifetime risk for prostate cancer to approximately 16%. Prostate cancer is also diagnosed earlier, and the incidence of clinically "silent" T1 tumors has increased from 17% in 1989 to 48% in 2001 since the advent of PSA screening. Currently, approximately 80% of prostate cancer cases are diagnosed as localized disease and only 4% as metastatic disease.
- Prostate cancer is found at autopsy in more than half of U.S. men older than 50 years but is the cause of death in only 3%.
- Average age at time of diagnosis is 72 yr.
- Blacks in the United States have the highest incidence of prostate cancer in the world (one in every nine males).
- Incidence is low in Asians.
- Approximately 9% of all prostate cancers may be familial. Obesity is a risk factor for prostate cancer. High-fat, low-fiber diet increases risk. High insulin levels may also increase the risk of prostate cancer. Dietary supplementation with vitamin E has been

reported to significantly increase the risk of prostate cancer among healthy men. Linkage studies have implicated chromosome 17p21-22 as a possible location of a prostate-cancer susceptibility gene. Germline mutations in *HOXB13* are associated with a significantly increased risk of hereditary prostate cancer.
- Mortality rates of prostate cancer have declined substantially in the past 15 yr from 34% in 1990 to <20% currently.

PHYSICAL FINDINGS & CLINICAL PRESENTATION

- Generally silent disease until it reaches advanced stages.
- Bone pain and pathologic fractures may be initial symptoms of prostate cancer.
- Local growth can cause symptoms of outflow obstruction.
- Digital rectal examination (DRE) may reveal an area of increased firmness; 10% of patients will have a negative DRE.
- Prostate may be hard, fixed, with extension of tumor to the seminal vesicles in advanced stages.

Dx DIAGNOSIS

DIFFERENTIAL DIAGNOSIS
- Benign prostatic hypertrophy
- Prostatitis
- Prostate stones

LABORATORY TESTS
- Fig. E1P-104 describes the assessment and treatment of patients with prostate cancer suspected on the grounds of a DRE and PSA. Measurement of prostate-specific antigen (PSA) is controversial in early diagnosis of prostate cancer. PSA screening is associated with psychological harm, and its potential benefits remain uncertain. In asymptomatic men with no history of prostate cancer, screening using PSA does not reduce all-cause mortality or death from prostate cancer. Normal PSA is found in >20% of patients with prostate cancer, whereas only 20% of men with PSA levels between 4 ng/mL and 10 ng/mL have prostate cancer. Most guidelines encourage a shared decision-making approach between patient and physician regarding PSA testing. Available evidence favors clinician discussion of the pros and cons of PSA screening with average-risk men aged 65 to 69 yr. Only men who express a definite preference for screening should have PSA testing. Rather than widespread annual PSA screening, a reasonable approach may be to focus on high-risk men (those with PSA levels ≥2 ng/mL at age 60). The American Cancer Society recommends offering the PSA test and DRE yearly to men aged ≥50 yr who have a life expectancy of at least 10 yr. Earlier testing, starting at age 40 to 45 yr, is recommended for men at high risk (e.g., blacks, men with family history of prostate cancer). An isolated elevation in PSA level should be confirmed several weeks later before

proceeding with further testing, including prostate biopsy. Screening for prostate cancer in men aged ≥75 yr is controversial and generally not recommended. The American College of Physicians (ACP) recommends that clinicians should not screen for prostate cancer using the PSA in average-risk men under age 50, men over age 69, or men with a life expectancy of <10 to 15 yr. The U.S. Preventive Services Task Force (USPSTF) recommends against PSA-based screening for prostate cancer in all age groups. According to the USPSTF:
1. The magnitude of harms from screening (e.g., falsely high PSA levels, psychological effects, unnecessary biopsies, overdiagnosis of indolent tumors) is "at least small."
2. The magnitude of treatment-associated harms (i.e., adverse effects of surgery, radiation, and hormonal therapy) is "at least moderate."
3. The 10-yr mortality benefit of PSA-based prostate cancer screening is "small to none."
4. The overall balance of benefits and harms results in "moderate certainty that PSA-based screening has no net benefit."
- Free PSA: the use of serum free PSA for prostate screening has been proposed by some urologists as a means to decrease unwarranted biopsies without missing a significant number of prostate cancers. This approach is based on the higher free PSA in men with benign prostatic hyperplasia and the higher protein-bound PSA levels in men with prostate cancer. For example, in men with total PSA levels of 4 to 10 ng/mL, the cancer probability is 0.25, but if the percentage of free PSA is ≤17%, the probability of cancer increases to 0.45.
- PSA velocity: the rate of increase of serum PSA over time (PSA velocity) can aid in the diagnosis of prostate cancer. A yearly PSA velocity >0.75 ng/mL increases the likelihood of later malignancy when total PSA is still within normal range. Proper interpretation of PSA velocity requires at least three PSA measurements over an 18-month period because most PSA variations are physiologic. Recent trials have cast a doubt on the value of PSA velocity by showing that adding PSA velocity as a trigger for biopsy did not improve predictive accuracy beyond that of using PSA threshold values alone.
- Age-adjusted PSA: there is evidence that the current threshold of 4.0 ng/mL is inadequate for younger men, because in a recent study 22% of men with PSA levels between 2.6 and 4.0 were found to have prostate cancer. The concept of age-related cutoffs remains controversial. Lowering the upper limit of normal for PSA would improve sensitivity but decrease specificity.
- Prostatic acid phosphatase can be used for evaluation of nonlocalized disease.
- Prostate cancer gene 3 *(PCA3)* is overexpressed in prostate cancer cell, and high levels are suggestive of prostate cancer.

Measurement of *PCA3* in urine specimens collected after digital exams is helpful to make decisions about prostate biopsy in men with elevated PSA.

- Transrectal biopsy and fine-needle aspiration of prostate can confirm the diagnosis. Indications for biopsy include an abnormal PSA level, an abnormal DRE, or a previous biopsy specimen that showed prostatic intraepithelial neoplasia or prostatic atypia. The number of cores taken is patient specific, typically including a minimum of 10 cores. Prostate volume negatively affects cancer detection rate (23% in glands >50 cm^3, 38% in glands <50 cm^3).

IMAGING STUDIES

- Bone scan is useful to evaluate bone metastasis (present or eventually develops in almost 80% of patients). However, according to the American Urological Association (AUA), the routine use of bone scanning is not required for staging of prostate cancer in asymptomatic men with clinically localized cancer if the PSA level is ≤20 ng/mL.
- CT scan, MRI, and transrectal ultrasonography may be useful in selected patients to assess extent of prostate cancer. High-resolution MRI with magnetic nanoparticles has been used for the detection of small and otherwise undetectable lymph node metastases in patients with prostate cancer. However, according to the AUA, transrectal ultrasonography adds little to the combination of PSA and DRE. Similarly, CT and MRI imaging are generally not indicated for cancer staging in men with clinically localized cancer and PSA <25 ng/mL. With regard to pelvic lymph node dissection in staging, the AUA states that it may not be required in patients with PSA levels <10 ng/mL and when PSA level is <20 ng/mL and the Gleason score is <6.

Rx TREATMENT

NONPHARMACOLOGIC THERAPY

Watchful waiting is reasonable in selected patients with early-stage (T-IA) and projected life expectancy <10 yr or in patients with focal and moderately differentiated carcinoma.

ACUTE GENERAL Rx

- Therapeutic approach varies with the following:
  1. Stage of the tumor.
  2. Patient's life expectancy.
  3. General medical condition.
  4. Patient's treatment preference (e.g., patient may be opposed to orchiectomy).
- The optimal treatment of clinically localized prostate cancer is unclear. It is important to remember that all forms of treatment have potential adverse effects. Management requires careful consideration of the potential benefits and harms of intervention, the patient's age, health status, and individual preferences.

1. Radical prostatectomy is generally performed in patients with localized prostate cancer and life expectancy >10 yr. Radical prostatectomy reduces disease-specific mortality, overall mortality, and the risks of metastasis and local progression. The absolute reduction in the risk of death after 10 yr is small, but the reductions in the risks of metastasis and local tumor progression are substantial. Postoperative complications of radical prostatectomy include urinary incontinence (10%-20% depending on degree of neurovascular bundle and urethral preservation, patient age, and correct mucosal apposition) and erectile dysfunction (percentage >50% and varies with patient age, preoperative erectile dysfunction, stage of tumor at time of surgery, and preservation of neurovascular bundle). Lower complication rates occur in hospitals that perform a large number of prostatectomies. Fewer men will have postsurgical erectile dysfunction after unilateral or bilateral nerve-sparing surgery. In men undergoing prostatectomy, robotic-assisted laparoscopic surgery represents an alternative to open retropubic radical prostatectomy. Despite advertisements that suggest that there are fewer complications after robotic surgery, recent data show that sexual dysfunction occurs postoperatively in about 88% of patients who have undergone robotic-assisted or conventional prostatectomy and that incontinence problems are more prevalent (33%) with robotic surgery than with open retropubic radical prostatectomy (RPP) (27%). Recent trials have shown that prostatectomy is preferred over "watchful waiting" in patients with localized prostate cancer detected by PSA if the PSA level is >10 ng/mL. In this subgroup, the 10-year mortality is 48.4% with prostatectomy versus 61.6% with watchful waiting. In men who have low-risk disease (PSA level <10 mcg/L, stage <T2a, Gleason score <3 + 3), and <6% risk for prostate cancer–specific death at 15 yr, watchful waiting (WW) and active surveillance (AS) are reasonable and underutilized options.

2. Radiation therapy (external-beam irradiation or brachytherapy with implantation of radioactive pellets [iodine-125 or palladium-103 seeds] into the prostate gland) represents an alternative in patients with localized prostate cancer, especially poor surgical candidates or patients with a high-grade malignancy. The efficacy of brachytherapy is comparable to external radiation. In patients receiving external-beam radiation, a total dose of 79.2 Gy (high dose) compared with a total dose of 70.2 Gy (conventional dose) has been reported to lower the risk of recurrence without increased risk of morbidity and mortality. Newer radiation treatments such as intensity-modulated radiation therapy (IMRT) and proton therapy are becoming increasingly popular and replacing the older technique of conformal radiation therapy over the past 10 years. Trials have shown that among patients with nonmetastatic prostate cancer, the use of IMRT compared with conformal therapy is associated with less gastrointestinal morbidity and fewer hip fractures but more erectile dysfunction; IMRT compared with proton therapy is associated with less GI morbidity. Patients with localized prostate cancer and high risk for extraprostatic disease and disease recurrence (e.g., Gleason score ≤7 with multiple positive biopsy cores and clinical stage T1b-T2b) may benefit (increased overall survival) with the addition of 6 mo of androgen suppression therapy to radiation therapy.

3. Watchful waiting is reasonable in patients who are too old or too ill to survive longer than 10 yr. If the cancer progresses to the point where it becomes symptomatic, palliation can be attempted with several methods. Conservative management is also reasonable for patients with Gleason score of 2 to 4 because these patients do not have a shortened life expectancy and treatment is associated with long-term side effects. Watchful waiting also appears to be safe in older men with less-aggressive disease. Individual preferences play a central role in the decision whether to treat or to pursue active surveillance.

- Patients with advanced disease and projected life expectancy <10 yr are candidates for radiation therapy and hormonal therapy (diethylstilbestrol, luteinizing hormone–releasing hormone analogs, antiandrogens, bilateral orchiectomy).
- Recommended treatment of patients with regional metastatic prostate cancer with projected life expectancy ≥10 yr includes radiation therapy and hormonal therapy.
- Prostate cancer is an androgen-receptor-dependent disease, and the blocking of androgen-receptor signaling is an effective treatment modality. Androgen deprivation therapy (ADT) is the mainstay of treatment for metastatic prostate cancer. Adverse effects of ADT include decreased libido, impotence, hot flashes, osteopenia with increased fracture risk, metabolic alterations, and changes in mood and cognition. Adjuvant treatment with luteinizing hormone-releasing hormone (LHRH) agonists (goserelin, leuprolide, or triptorelin) plus antiandrogens (flutamide, bicalutamide, or nilutamide), when started simultaneously with external-beam radiation, improves local control and survival in patients with locally advanced prostate cancer. Pamidronate inhibits osteoclast-mediated bone resorption and prevents bone loss in the hip and lumbar spine in men receiving treatment for prostate cancer. Gonadotropin-releasing hormone (GnRH) receptor antagonists can be used for rapid medical castration of men with advanced prostate cancer. Degarelix is an injectable

GnRH agonist useful to suppress testosterone in patients with prostate cancer who are not good candidates for LHRH agonists and refuse surgical castration. Assessment of bone density and treatment with once-weekly oral alendronate can prevent and improve the bone loss that occurs in men receiving ADT for prostate cancer.

- Docetaxel plus prednisone or docetaxel plus estramustine can be used in metastatic hormone–refractory prostate cancer. Newer treatments for hormone-refractory prostate cancer (castration-resistant cancer) include immunotherapy with sipuleucel and cabazitaxel, a microtubule inhibitor that interferes with cell mitosis and replication. Both agents can prolong survival but adverse effects can be severe and both agents are very expensive. Abiraterone is an oral agent that blocks biosynthesis of androgens by inhibiting CYP17, an enzyme required for androgen biosynthesis. It has been FDA approved for oral treatment, in combination with prednisone, of metastatic castration-resistant prostate cancer in patients previously treated with docetaxel.
- Enzalutamide is a newer nonsteroidal anti-androgen. Trials have shown it to be highly effective in extending survival in patients with metastatic castration-resistant prostate cancer. It can be used sequentially with other agents such as docetaxel, abiraterone, cabazitaxel, and immunotherapy. Radium-223, an alpha emitter, selectively targets bone metastases and has been found effective in improving survival in men with castration-resistant prostate cancer and bone metastases.
- The poly(adenosine diphosphate [ADP]-ribose) polymerase (PARP) inhibitor has shown a high response rate in patients whose prostate cancers were no longer responding to standard treatments and who had defects in DNA-repair genes.

CHRONIC Rx

- Patients should be monitored at 3- to 6-mo intervals with clinical examination and PSA for the first year, then every 6 mo for the second year, then yearly if stable. For patients who have undergone radical prostatectomy, a rising PSA level suggests evidence of residual or recurrent prostate cancer. Salvage radiotherapy may potentially cure patients with disease recurrence after radical prostatectomy.
- Chest radiography and bone scan should be performed yearly or sooner if patient develops symptoms.

DISPOSITION

- Prognosis varies with the stage of the disease and the Gleason classification (see "Definition"). For patients between ages 65 and 69 yr at diagnosis and a Gleason score of 2 to 4, the probability of dying from prostate cancer 15 yr after diagnosis is 0.06 and that of dying from other causes is 0.56. If the Gleason score is 7 to 10, the probability of dying from prostate cancer increases to 0.72 and from other causes varies from 0.25 to 0.36.
- The ploidy of the tumor also has prognostic value; prognosis is better with diploid tumor cells and worse with aneuploid tumor cells.
- For grade 1 tumors, the extended 10-yr, disease-specific survival is similar for patients with prostatectomy (94%), radiotherapy (90%), and conservative management (93%); survival rate is better with surgery than with radiotherapy or conservative management in patients with grade 2 or 3 localized prostate cancer.
- Expression of the gene *EZH2* has been identified as an important factor in the determination of the aggressiveness of prostate cancer. A recent study revealed that expression of the *EZH2* gene may be a better predictor of clinical failure than Gleason score, tumor stage, or surgical margin status. Testing for *EZH2* protein in prostate cancer tissue may be useful to determine prognosis and direct treatment.
- Preoperative PSA level and PSA velocity have prognostic significance. Men whose PSA level increases by >2.0 mcg/mL during the year before the diagnosis of cancer may have a relatively high risk of death from prostate cancer despite undergoing radical prostatectomy.

- Extraprostatic disease is detected at radical prostatectomy in 38% to 52% of patients and is associated with a risk of disease recurrence, progression, and death. In these patients, adjuvant radiotherapy results in significantly reduced risk of PSA relapse and disease recurrence; however, the improvements in metastases-free survival and overall survival are not statistically significant.
- The Prostate Cancer Prevention trial revealed that the use of 5-alpha-reductase inhibitors lowers the incidence of prostate cancer but also increases the incidence of high-grade tumors (Gleason score >7). It is possible that these agents delay diagnosis of prostate cancer by lowering PSA levels and decreasing prostate size. The trade-off inherent in using 5-alpha-reductase inhibitors for prostate cancer prevention is risk of one additional high-grade cancer in order to avert three or four lower-grade cancers. Based on these results, the FDA's Oncologic Drugs Advisory Committee concluded that finasteride and dutasteride do not have a favorable risk-benefit profile for chemoprevention of prostate cancer in healthy men.
- Patients undergoing prostatectomy are more likely to have urinary incontinence than those undergoing radiotherapy at 2 years and 5 years. However, at 15 years there are no significant relative differences in disease-specific functional outcomes among men undergoing prostatectomy or radiotherapy.

 **EVIDENCE**

Available at www.expertconsult.com

SUGGESTED READINGS
Available at www.expertconsult.com

RELATED CONTENT

Prostate Cancer (Patient Information)

AUTHOR: **FRED F. FERRI, M.D.**

BASIC INFORMATION

DEFINITION

Benign prostatic hyperplasia (BPH) is the benign growth of the prostate, generally originating in the periureteral and transition zones, with subsequent obstructive and irritative voiding symptoms.

SYNONYMS

Benign prostate hyperplasia
BPH
Prostatic hypertrophy

ICD-10CM CODES

N40.0 Enlarged prostate without lower urinary tract symptoms
N40.1 Enlarged prostate with lower urinary tract symptoms
N40.2 Nodular prostate without lower urinary tract symptoms
N40.3 Nodular prostate with lower urinary tract symptoms

EPIDEMIOLOGY & DEMOGRAPHICS

- 80% of men have evidence of BPH by age 80 yr.
- Medical and surgical intervention for problems caused by BPH is required in <20% of males by age 75 yr.
- Transurethral resection of the prostate (TURP) is the tenth most common operative procedure (<400,000/yr in U.S.).
- 10% to 30% of men with BPH have occult prostate cancer.

PHYSICAL FINDINGS & CLINICAL PRESENTATION

- Digital rectal examination (DRE) reveals enlargement of the prostate.
- Focal enlargement may be indicative of malignancy.
- There is poor correlation between size of prostate and symptoms (BPH may be asymptomatic if it does not encroach on the urethral lumen).
- Most patients with BPH report difficulty in initiating urination (hesitancy), decrease in caliber and force of stream, incomplete emptying of bladder often resulting in double voiding (need to urinate again a few minutes after voiding), postvoid "dribbling," and nocturia.

ETIOLOGY

Multifactorial; a functioning testicle is necessary for development of BPH (as evidenced by the absence in males who were castrated before puberty).

DIAGNOSIS

DIFFERENTIAL DIAGNOSIS

- Prostatitis
- Prostate cancer
- Strictures (urethral)
- Medications interfering with the muscle fibers in the prostate and also with bladder function
  - Opiates: impaired autonomic function
  - Decongestants: increased sphincter tone

- Antihistamines: decreased parasympathetic tone
- Tricyclic antidepressants: anticholinergic effects
- Neurogenic bladder
- Bladder cancer

WORKUP

Symptom assessment (use of American Urological Association [AUA] Symptom Index for BPH [Table 1P-54]), laboratory tests, and imaging studies. Fig. E1P-105 describes a diagnostic approach to patients with BPH.

LABORATORY TESTS

- Prostate-specific antigen (PSA): protease secreted by epithelial cells of the prostate; elevated in 30% to 50% of patients with BPH. Testing for PSA increases detection rate for prostate cancer and tends to detect cancer at an earlier stage. However, the PSA test does not discriminate well between patients with symptomatic BPH and those with prostate cancer, particularly if the cancer is pathologically localized and curable. The test may also trigger additional evaluation, including ultrasound biopsy of the prostate. Asymptomatic men with PSA levels >2 ng/mL do not need annual testing. According to the AUA, PSA testing and DRE should be offered to any asymptomatic man <50 yr with a life expectancy of 10 yr. PSA testing can also be offered at an earlier age in men at higher risk of prostatic cancer (e.g., first-degree relatives with prostate cancer; African American race).

TABLE 1P-54 International Prostate Symptom Score (I-PSS)

Symptom	SCORE						Total Score
	Not at All	Less Than 1 Time in 5	Less Than Half the Time	About Half the Time	More Than Half the Time	Almost Always	
Incomplete emptying: Over the past month, how often have you had a sensation of not emptying your bladder completely after you finished urinating?	0	1	2	3	4	5	
Frequency: Over the past month, how often have you had to urinate again <2 hr after you finished urinating?	0	1	2	3	4	5	
Intermittency: Over the past month, how often have you found you stopped and started again several times when you urinated?	0	1	2	3	4	5	
Urgency: Over the past month, how often have you found it difficult to postpone urination?	0	1	2	3	4	5	
Weak stream: Over the past month, how often have you had a weak urinary stream?	0	1	2	3	4	5	
Straining: Over the past month, how often have you had to push or strain to begin urination?	0	1	2	3	4	5	
	None	1 Time	2 Times	3 Times	4 Times	5 or More Times	
Nocturia: Over the past month, how many times did you most typically get up to urinate from the time you went to bed at night until the time you got up in the morning?	0	1	2	3	4	5	
Total I-PSS score =							

- Measurement of "free" PSA is useful to assess the probability of prostate cancer in patients with normal DRE and total PSA between 4 and 10 ng/mL. In these patients the global risk of prostate cancer is 25%. However, if the free PSA is >25%, the risk of prostate cancer decreases to 8%, whereas if the free PSA is <10%, the risk of cancer increases to 56%. Free PSA is also useful to evaluate the aggressiveness of prostate cancer. A low free PSA percentage generally indicates a high-grade cancer, whereas a high free PSA percentage is generally associated with a slower growing tumor.
- Elevated measurement of prostate cancer gene 3 (PCA3) in urine specimens collected after digital exam is helpful in deciding about prostate biopsy in men with elevated PSA (increased PCA3 = increased likelihood of prostate cancer).
- Urinalysis, urine culture, and sensitivity to rule out infection (if suspected).
- Blood urea nitrogen and creatinine to rule out postrenal insufficiency.

IMAGING STUDIES

- Transrectal ultrasound may be indicated in patients with palpable nodules or significant elevation of PSA. It is also useful to estimate prostate size. BPH may also be evident in suprapubic ultrasound and MRI.
- Uroflowmetry may be used to determine relative impact of obstruction on urine flow. Urethral pressure profile is useful to predict prostatic hypertrophy within the urethral lumen.
- Pressure flow studies, although invasive, are particularly helpful in patients whose history and/or examination suggest primary bladder dysfunction as a cause of symptoms of prostatism. They are also useful in patients for whom a distinction between prostatic obstruction and impaired detrusor contractility may affect the choice of therapy. However, pressure flow studies may not be useful in the workup of the usual patient with symptoms of prostatism.
- Postvoid residual urine measurement has not been proved useful in predicting the need for or response to treatment; it may be useful in monitoring the course of the disease in patients who elect nonsurgical treatment.
- Urethral cystoscopy is an option during later evaluation if invasive treatment is being planned.

Rx TREATMENT

NONPHARMACOLOGIC THERAPY

- Avoidance of caffeine or any other foods that may exacerbate symptoms
- Avoidance of medications that may exacerbate symptoms (e.g., most cold and allergy remedies)

GENERAL Rx

- Asymptomatic patients with prostate enlargement caused by BPH generally do not require treatment. Patients with mild to moderate

symptoms are candidates for pharmacologic treatment (see below). For patients who have specific complications from BPH, prostate surgery is usually the most appropriate form of treatment. However, surgery may result in significant complications (e.g., incontinence, infection).

- Alpha-blockers (e.g., tamsulosin, alfuzosin, doxazosin, prazosin, terazosin) relax smooth muscle of the bladder neck and prostate and can increase peak urinary flow rate. They have no effect on the size of the prostate. Alpha-1 blockers are useful in symptomatic patients to relieve symptoms of obstruction by causing relaxation of smooth muscle tone in the prostatic capsule, urethra, and bladder neck.
- Hormonal manipulation with finasteride, a 5-alpha-reductase inhibitor that blocks conversion of testosterone to dihydrotestosterone, can reduce the size of the prostate. Usual dose is 5 mg qd. Treatment requires ≥6 mo for maximal effect.
- Dutasteride is also a 5-alpha-reductase inhibitor useful to decrease prostate size and improve urinary flow. In addition to inhibiting the isoform of 5-alpha-reductase located in the prostate, the medication inhibits a second isoform and reduces dihydrotestosterone formation in the skin and liver. Usual dose is 0.5 mg qd.
- Tadalafil 2.5 to 5 mg qd has been FDA-approved to treat patients with signs and symptoms of BPH and patients with both ED and signs and symptoms of BPH. Tadalafil can potentiate the hypotensive effect of alpha-blockers and should not be used in combination with alpha-blockers.
- The dietary supplement saw palmetto is commonly used for relief of symptoms of BPH. Recent trials using 160 mg of saw palmetto bid did not improve symptoms of BPH. This contrasts with the positive findings of many previous studies. Trials with higher dose-ranging protocols are currently in progress.
- TURP is the most commonly used surgical procedure for BPH. It is recommended for patients unresponsive to medical therapy who have renal insufficiency, recurrent UTIs, bladder stones, or gross hematuria. Transurethral incision of the prostate (TUIP), a procedure almost equivalent in efficacy, is limited to patients whose estimated resection tissue weight would be 30 g or less. TUIP can be performed in an ambulatory setting or during a 1-day hospitalization. Open prostatectomy is typically performed on patients with very large prostates. A prostatic urethral lift implant (UroLift) is now available for BPH. It is placed transurethrally at the site of obstruction to open the urethra by compressing the obstructing prostatic lobes and holding them permanently retracted with suture-based implants.
- Laser therapy for BPH is a less invasive alternative to TURP; YAG laser enucleation has minimal effect on potency, libido, or patient satisfaction with his sex life and is associated with retrograde ejaculation. However, recent studies indicate that at least in the initial 7 mo after surgery, TURP is moderately

more effective than laser therapy in relieving symptoms of BPH.
- Transurethral needle ablation with radiofrequency to remove periurethral prostate tissue is being increasingly used in patients with prostate volume >60 mL and moderate symptoms. It has a low morbidity rate, but treatment failure is approximately 25% at 5 yr and <80% at 10 yr.
- Balloon dilation of the prostatic urethra is less effective than surgery for relieving symptoms but is associated with fewer complications. It is a reasonable treatment option for patients with smaller prostates and no middle lobe enlargement.
- Surgery need not be the treatment of last resort for most patients; that is, patients need not undergo other treatments for BPH before they can have surgery. However, recommending surgery on the grounds that a patient's surgical risk will "only increase with age" is generally inappropriate.

DISPOSITION

With appropriate therapy, symptoms improve or stabilize in <70% of patients with BPH.

REFERRAL

Urology referral for patients with severe or intolerable symptoms and for any patient suspected of having prostate cancer (10%-30% of men with BPH)

PEARLS & CONSIDERATIONS

COMMENTS

- Emerging technologies for treating BPH, including transurethral holmium laser enucleation, transurethral electrovaporization, and transurethral microwave thermotherapy of the prostate, appear promising; however, long-term effectiveness has not yet been demonstrated.
- The increase in the use of pharmacologic management has resulted in <30% reduction in the total number of TURP procedures.
- Combined drug therapy for BPH with an alpha-blocker and a 5-alpha-reductase inhibitor is superior to monotherapy with either agent.
- Saw palmetto extract is ineffective for BPH symptoms. Trials have shown that even at three times the standard dosing, saw palmetto extract had no greater effect than placebo on improving lower urinary symptoms associated with BPH.

Available at www.expertconsult.com

SUGGESTED READINGS
Available at www.expertconsult.com

RELATED CONTENT
Enlarged Prostate (Patient Information)

AUTHOR: **FRED F. FERRI, M.D.**

BASIC INFORMATION

DEFINITION

Prostatitis refers to inflammation of the prostate gland. There are four major categories:
1. Acute bacterial prostatitis (type I).
2. Chronic bacterial prostatitis (type II).
3. Chronic prostatitis/pelvic pain syndrome (CP/CPPS) (type III): subdivided into type IIIA (inflammatory) and IIIB (noninflammatory).
4. Asymptomatic inflammatory prostatitis (type IV).

ICD-10CM CODES
N41.0 Acute prostatitis
N41.1 Chronic prostatitis

EPIDEMIOLOGY & DEMOGRAPHICS

- 50% of men will have symptoms of prostatitis in their lifetime.
- Prostatitis accounts for >8% of visits to urologists and 1% of visits to primary care physicians.
- The prevalence of chronic bacterial prostatitis is 5% to 10%.
- CP/CPPS is the most common of the clinically defined prostatitis syndromes, with prevalence ranging from 9% to 12% of men.
- Acute bacterial prostatitis accounts for 10% of all cases of prostatitis.

PHYSICAL FINDINGS & CLINICAL PRESENTATION

1. Acute bacterial prostatitis:
   - Sudden or rapidly progressive onset of:
     1. Dysuria.
     2. Frequency.
     3. Urgency.
     4. Nocturia.
     5. Perineal pain that may radiate to the back, rectum, or penis.
   - Hematuria or a purulent urethral discharge may occur.
   - Occasionally urinary retention complicates the course.
   - Fever, chills, and signs of sepsis can also be part of the clinical picture.
   - On rectal examination the prostate is typically tender.
2. Chronic bacterial prostatitis:
   - Characterized by positive culture of expressed prostatic secretions. May cause symptoms such as suprapubic, low back, or perineal pain; mild urgency, frequency, and dysuria with urination; and possibly recurrent urinary tract infections.
   - May be asymptomatic when the infection is confined to the prostate.
   - May present as an increase in severity of baseline symptoms of benign prostatic hypertrophy (BPH).
   - When cystitis is also present, urinary frequency, urgency, and burning may be reported.
   - Hematuria may be a presenting complaint.
   - In elderly men, new onset of urinary incontinence may be noted.

3. CP/CPPS:
   - Presents similarly with pain in the pelvic region lasting >3 mo. Symptoms also can include pain in the suprapubic region, low back, penis, testes, or scrotum.
   - The symptoms can be of variable severity and may include lower urinary tract symptoms, sexual dysfunction, and reduced quality of life.

ETIOLOGY

1. Acute bacterial prostatitis:
   - Acute, usually gram-negative infection of the prostate gland. *E. coli* is the most commonly isolated organism.
     1. Generally associated with cystitis.
     2. Results from the ascent of bacteria into the urethra.
   - Occasionally the route of infection is hematogenous or a lymphatogenous spread of rectal bacteria.
   - Consider *Neisseria gonorrhoeae* or *Chlamydia trachomatis* in young patients (age <35 yr) with risk of sexually transmitted disease (STD).
2. Chronic bacterial prostatitis:
   - Often asymptomatic. *E. coli* is the most commonly isolated organism.
   - Exacerbation of symptoms of BPH caused by the same mechanism as in acute bacterial prostatitis.
3. CP/CPPS:
   - Type IIIA: refers to symptoms of prostatic inflammation associated with the presence of white blood cells in prostatic secretions with no identifiable bacterial organism.
   - *Chlamydia* infection may be etiologically implicated in some cases.
   - Type IIIB: refers to symptoms of prostatic inflammation with no or few white blood cells in the prostatic secretion.
   - Its cause is unknown. Spasm in the bladder neck or urethra may be responsible for the symptoms.

DIAGNOSIS

DIFFERENTIAL DIAGNOSIS

- BPH with lower urinary tract symptoms
- Prostate cancer
- Interstitial cystitis/bladder pain syndrome
- Pelvic floor dysfunction
- Bladder cancer
- Urolithiasis
- UTI
- Proctitis

WORKUP

- Rectal examination:
  1. Tender prostate most suggestive of acute bacterial prostatitis.
  2. Enlarged prostate common in chronic bacterial prostatitis.
  3. Normal prostate is consistent with chronic bacterial prostatitis and CP/CPPS.
- Expression of prostatic secretions by prostate massage is contraindicated in acute bacterial prostatitis but is appropriate in the other three situations.

LABORATORY TESTS

- Urinalysis.
- Urine culture and sensitivity.
- Bacterial localization studies can be performed but are cumbersome and impractical in most clinical settings.
- Cell count and culture of expressed prostatic secretions.
- Prostate-specific antigen (PSA) is not used to diagnose prostatitis and is not recommended unless a nodule is present on digital examination. A rapid rise over baseline should raise the possibility of prostatitis even in the absence of symptoms. In such cases, a follow-up PSA after treatment of prostatitis is appropriate.
- Complete blood count and blood cultures if fever, chills, or signs of sepsis exist.

TREATMENT

1. Acute bacterial prostatitis:
   - Uncomplicated (with risk of STD, age <35 yr): ceftriaxone 250 mg IM × 1 dose *or* cefixime 400 mg PO × 1 *then* doxycycline 100 mg bid × 10 days.
   - Uncomplicated with low risk of STD: levofloxacin 500 mg qd or ciprofloxacin 500 mg bid × 10 to 14 days.
2. Chronic bacterial prostatitis:
   - First-line choice is a quinolone (ciprofloxacin or levofloxacin) for 4 wk.
   - Trimethoprim-sulfamethoxazole (TMP-SMX) is second-line choice for 1 to 3 mo if the organism is sensitive. Tissue penetration for TMP-SMX is not as good as quinolones, and there is evidence of increasing uropathogenic resistance.
3. CP/CPPS:
   - No specific treatment. A brief course of NSAIDs may be tried until urine localization cultures are completed. Alfuzosin may reduce symptoms in men who have not received prior therapy with an alpha-blocker.
   - Recent trials have shown modest improvement with quinolones (possibly secondary to their anti-inflammatory and analgesic effects), but antibiotics are not generally effective and should be avoided in patients who are afebrile and have normal urinalysis results.

SUGGESTED READINGS
Available at www.expertconsult.com

RELATED CONTENT
Prostatitis (Patient Information)

AUTHOR: **FRED F. FERRI, M.D.**

BASIC INFORMATION

DEFINITION
Pruritus ani refers to an intense chronic itching of the anus and perianal skin.

SYNONYMS
Anal neurodermatitis

ICD-10CM CODES
L29.0 Pruritus ani

EPIDEMIOLOGY & DEMOGRAPHICS
- Any age can be affected.
- Occurs in 1% to 5% of the population.
- Male/female predominance of 4:1.

PHYSICAL FINDINGS & CLINICAL PRESENTATION
- Anal itching.
- Anal fissures.
- Hemorrhoids.
- Excoriations.
- Pinworms.
- Fecal incontinence.

ETIOLOGY
Anorectal diseases and fecal contamination:
- Diarrhea.
- Anal incontinence.
- Hemorrhoids.
- Fissures.
- Fistulae.
- Rectal prolapse.
- Malignancy: Bowen's disease, epidermoid cancer, perianal Paget's disease.

Infections:
- Fungal: candidiasis, dermatophytes.
- Parasitic: pinworms, scabies.
- Bacterial: *Staphylococcus aureus,* erythrasma.
- Lymphogranuloma venereum.
- Granuloma inguinale.
- Chancroid.
- Molluscum contagiosum.
- Trichomoniasis.
- Venereal: herpes, gonococcal syphilis, human papillomavirus.

Local irritants:
- Moisture, obesity, excessive perspiration.
- Soaps, hygiene products.

- Toilet paper: perfumed, dyed.
- Underwear: irritating fabrics, detergents.
- Anal creams, suppositories.
- Dietary: coffee, beer, acidic foods.
- Drugs: mineral oil, ascorbic acid, hydrocortisone sodium succinate, quinine, colchicine.

Dermatologic diseases:
- Psoriasis.
- Atopic dermatitis.
- Seborrheic dermatitis.
   Section II also describes the various causes of pruritus ani.

DIAGNOSIS

DIFFERENTIAL DIAGNOSIS
- Allergies.
- Anxiety.
- Dermatologic conditions.
- Infections.
- Parasites.
- Diabetes mellitus.
- Chronic liver disease.
- Neoplasia.
- Proctalgia fugax.

WORKUP
- Detailed history regarding bowel habits, hygiene, use of perfumed products, and medical history.
- Inspection of perianal area.
- Possible biopsy to exclude neoplasia.
- Microscopic inspection of scrapings.
- Colposcopy of perineum.

LABORATORY TESTS
- Chemistry profile.
- Urinalysis.
- Cultures.
- Stool for ova and parasites.
- Tape test.
- Glucose tolerance test, if necessary.

TREATMENT

NONPHARMACOLOGIC THERAPY
- Avoidance of tight, nonbreathable clothing and underclothing.
- Discontinuation or curtailment of coffee, beer, citrus fruits, tomatoes, chocolate,

and tea. Dietary modification is frequently recommended, although its effectiveness has not been established.
- Cleansing of anal area after bowel movements with a premoistened pad or tissue and avoidance of perfumes and dyes present in toilet paper and soaps.
- Avoidance of excessive perspiration.
- Aggressive management of fecal leakage or incontinence to avoid soiling of perianal skin.

ACUTE GENERAL Rx
- Minimization of frequent loose stools with antidiarrheals and fiber agents if appropriate.
- Use of a 1% hydrocortisone cream sparingly bid during the acute phase of pruritus ani but not for >2 wk to avoid atrophy.
- Protective ointments such as zinc oxide may be helpful.
- Treatment of predisposing factors, such as parasites, diabetes, liver disease, hemorrhoids, and other infections.

CHRONIC Rx
- Possible complications: excoriation and secondary bacterial infection; must be treated aggressively.
- Longstanding, intractable pruritus ani: good response to intracutaneous injections of methylene blue and other agents, steroid injection.

DISPOSITION
- Usually good results with total resolution of symptoms.
- In some, persistent and recurrent symptoms.

REFERRAL
To colorectal specialist if conservative measures fail or if patient experiences rectal bleeding or change in bowel movements.

SUGGESTED READINGS
Available at www.expertconsult.com

RELATED CONTENT
Anal Itching (Patient Information)
Hemorrhoids (Related Key Topic)

AUTHOR: **RUBEN ALVERO, M.D.**

ⓘ BASIC INFORMATION

DEFINITION

Pruritus vulvae refers to intense itching of the female external genitalia.

SYNONYMS

Vulvodynia

ICD-10CM CODES

L29.2 Pruritus vulvae
L29.3 Anogenital pruritus, unspecified

EPIDEMIOLOGY & DEMOGRAPHICS

- A female disorder that can affect women at any age.
- Young girls: infection is usually causative.
- Postmenopausal women: frequently affected because of hypoestrogenic state.

PHYSICAL FINDINGS & CLINICAL PRESENTATION

Constant, intense itching or burning of the vulva.

ETIOLOGY

- Approximately 50% of acute cases are caused by monilial infection or trichomoniasis.
- Other infectious causes are herpes simplex, condylomata acuminata, and molluscum contagiosum.
- Other causes:
  1. Infestations with scabies, pediculosis pubis, and pinworms.
  2. Dermatoses such as hypertrophic dystrophy, lichen sclerosus, lichen planus, and psoriasis.
  3. Neoplasms such as Bowen's disease, Paget's disease, and squamous cell carcinoma.
  4. Allergic or chemical dermatitis caused by dyes in clothing or toilet paper, detergents, contraceptive gels, vaginal medications, douches, or soaps.
  5. Vulvar or vaginal atrophy.
- Severe pruritus is probably caused by degeneration and inflammation of terminal nerve fibers.
- Most intense itching occurs with hyperplastic lesions.
- Children typically (75%) have nonspecific pruritus, lichen sclerosus, bacterial infections, yeast infection, or pinworm infestation.

ⒹⓍ DIAGNOSIS

DIFFERENTIAL DIAGNOSIS

- Vulvitis.
- Vaginitis.
- Lichen sclerosus.
- Squamous cell hyperplasia.
- Pinworms.
- Vulvar cancer.
- Syringoma of the vulva.

WORKUP

- Inspection of vulva, vagina, and perianal area for infection, fissures, ulcerations, induration, or thick plaques.
- Must rule out trichomoniasis, candidiasis, bacterial vaginosis, allergy, vitamin deficiencies, diabetes. Fig. 1P-106 describes a diagnostic approach to the diagnosis of vulvar pruritus.

LABORATORY TESTS

- Wet prep of saline and potassium hydroxide of vaginal discharge.
- Tape test to look for pinworms.
- Vaginal cultures.
- Biopsy when needed (punch biopsy commonly used).

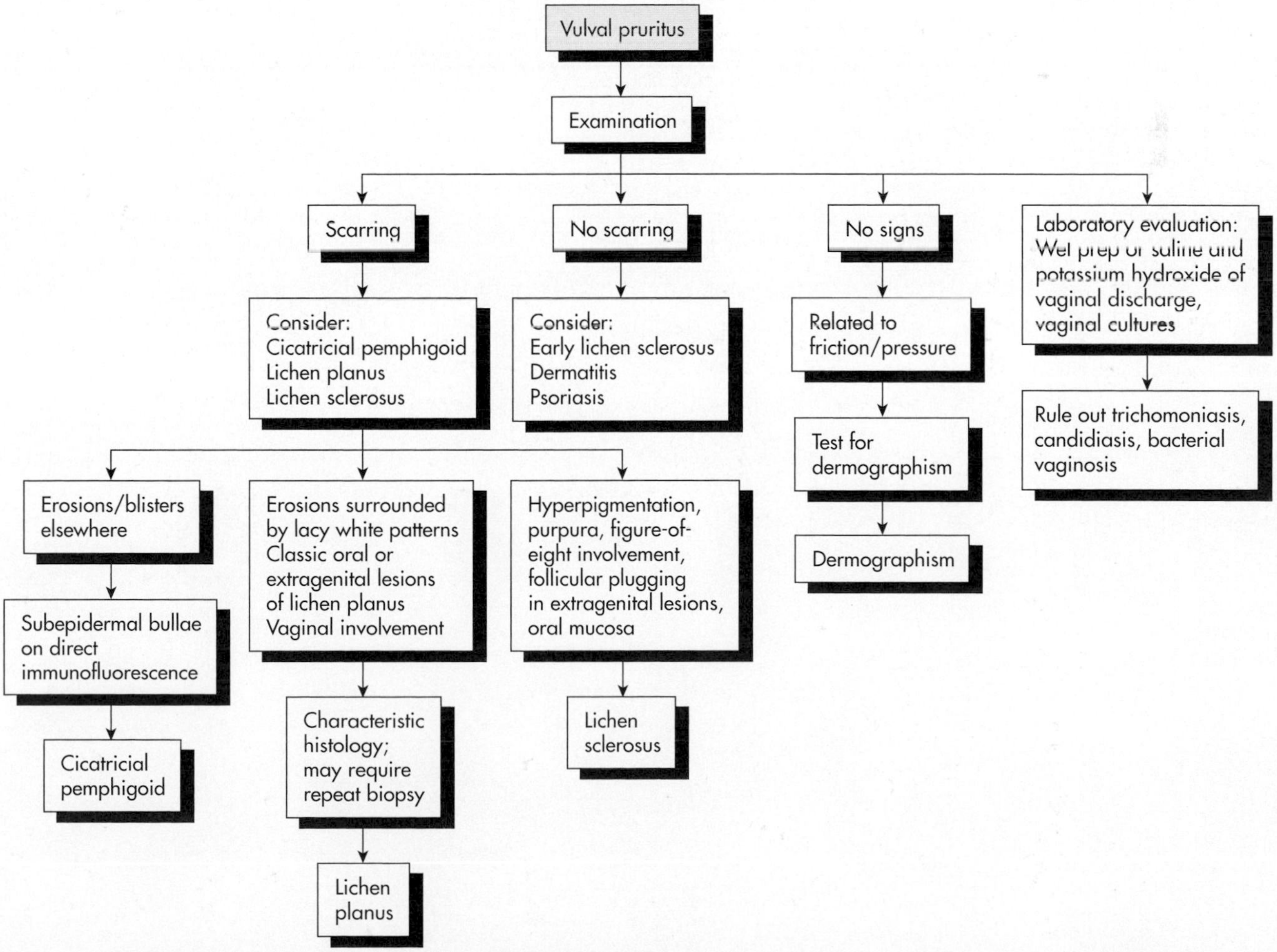

FIGURE 1P-106 Diagnosis of vulvar pruritus. (Modified from Bolognia JL et al , eds: *Dermatology,* ed 2, St Louis, 2008, Mosby.)

 **TREATMENT**

NONPHARMACOLOGIC THERAPY
- Keep vulva clean and dry.
- Wear white cotton panties.
- Avoid perfumes and body creams over vulvar area because they can cause irritation.
- Reduce stress.
- Apply wet dressings with aluminum acetate (Burow's) solution frequently.
- Sitz baths may be helpful.

ACUTE GENERAL Rx
Need to treat underlying problem:
- Yeast infection: any of the vaginal creams or difluconazole 150 mg one-time dose.
- Trichomoniasis or *Gardnerella vaginalis:* metronidazole 500 mg or 375 mg PO bid for 7 days.
- Urinary tract infection: treatment of specific organism.
- Estrogen replacement therapy if atrophy is the cause of pruritus.
- Pinworms: mebendazole 100 mg 1 tablet at diagnosis and repeated in 1 to 2 wk; also treat other members in family aged >2 yr.

- Squamous cell hyperplasia: local application of corticosteroids.
  1. One of the high- or medium-potency corticosteroids (0.025% or 0.01% fluocinolone acetonide or 0.01% triamcinolone acetonide) can be used to relieve itching.
  2. Rub into vulva bid or tid for 4 to 6 wk.
  3. Once itching is controlled, fluorinated steroid can be discontinued and patient can be switched to hydrocortisone preparation.
- Lichen sclerosus: topical 2% testosterone in petrolatum massaged into the vulvar tissue, bid or tid; clobetasol propionate gel 0.05% tid for 5 days is effective.
- Treatment with immune response modifiers.

CHRONIC Rx
- If not relieved by topical measures: intradermal injection of triamcinolone (10 mg/mL diluted 2:1 saline); 0.1 mL of the suspension injected at 1-cm intervals and tissue gently massaged.
- If symptoms still uncontrollable: SC injection of absolute alcohol 0.1 mL at 1-cm intervals.

DISPOSITION
Usually controlled with conservative measures and topical steroids.

REFERRAL
- To a gynecologist for further workup if conservative measures do not give relief.
- When burning rather than itching predominates, the patient should be evaluated for signs of sensory neuropathy.

SUGGESTED READINGS
Available at www.expertconsult.com

RELATED CONTENT
Lichen Sclerosus (Related Key Topic)
Vaginitis, Estrogen-Deficient (Related Key Topic)
Vaginitis, Fungal (Related Key Topic)
Vaginitis, Prepubescent (Related Key Topic)
Vaginitis, Trichomonas (Related Key Topic)

AUTHOR: **RUBEN ALVERO, M.D.**

P

 BASIC INFORMATION

DEFINITION

Calcium pyrophosphate dihydrate crystal deposition (CPPD) disease refers to the precipitation of calcium pyrophosphate dihydrate (CPP) in connective tissues that may be asymptomatic or may be associated with several clinical syndromes, including acute and chronic arthritis. CPP was formerly abbreviated and commonly referred to as "CPPD" because the dihydrate is necessary for crystallization, but the abbreviation is now reserved for "CPP deposition." Alternative names representing specific clinical or radiographic features of CPPD disease include pseudogout, chondrocalcinosis, and pyrophosphate arthropathy.

Pseudogout/acute CPP crystal arthritis is used to describe acute attacks of CPP crystal induced arthritis that clinically resembles the arthritis that is commonly encountered in urate gout. The term "acute CPP crystal arthritis" is now preferred in place of "pseudogout."

Chondrocalcinosis (CC) refers to radiographic calcification in hyaline cartilage and/or fibrocartilage and does not confirm the diagnosis of CPPD-related arthritis as it can be present in other types of crystal deposition diseases or be asymptomatic.

Pyrophosphate arthropathy is the term used for a chronic structural arthropathy related to CPPD deposition.

SYNONYMS

Calcium pyrophosphate dihydrate crystal deposition disease
CPP crystal deposition disease
Chondrocalcinosis
Pyrophosphate arthropathy

ICD-10CM CODES
M11.2 Other chondrocalcinosis
M11.9 Crystal arthropathy, unspecified
M11.8 Other specified crystal arthropathies
M11.1 Familial chondrocalcinosis

EPIDEMIOLOGY & DEMOGRAPHICS
PREVALENCE:
- The epidemiology of CPPD crystal deposition is described in Table 1P-55.
- Most linked with advancing age (average age of 70)

GENETICS: Associated with *ANKH* (ankylosis human) gene, which functions to transport inorganic pyrophosphate (PPi) out of cells. Familial mutations can increase extracellular PPi and lead to onset of CPPD disease in third or fourth decade of life.

PHYSICAL FINDINGS & CLINICAL PRESENTATION

- *Acute CPP crystal arthritis/pseudogout:* monoarticular attacks most commonly involve the knee but can be polyarticular. Patients, especially the elderly, can have systemic manifestations such as fever and altered mental status. Situations that may trigger acute CPPD crystal arthritis are described in Box E1P-16.

TABLE 1P-55 Epidemiology of Calcium Pyrophosphate Dihydrate Crystal Deposition

Age association	Rises with age
Sex distribution	(F:M) 1:1
Chondrocalcinosis prevalence	8.1% (age range 63 to 93)
Pyrophosphate arthropathy prevalence	3.4% (age range 40 to 89)
Geography	Appears ubiquitous
Genetic associations	Mutations of *ANKH* gene on chromosome 5p (CCAL2) and unknown genes on chromosome 8q (CCAL1)

From Hochberg MC et al: *Rheumatology*, ed 5, St Louis, 2011, Mosby.

- Asymptomatic disease ("asymptomatic CPPD")
- Pseudogout ("acute CPP crystal arthritis")
- Pseudo-RA ("chronic CPP crystal inflammatory arthritis"): symmetric polyarthritis
- Pseudo-OA, with or without superimposed acute attacks ("OA with CPPD")
- Pseudoneuropathic joint disease
- Crowned-dens syndrome caused by crystal deposition in the ligamentum flavum of the cervical spine either asymptomatic or causing acute neck pain
- "Pseudo-polymyalgia rheumatica (pseudo-PMR)": pain and stiffness in the neck and shoulder girdle mimicking PMR

ETIOLOGY
- Idiopathic
- Familial
- Trauma
- Hemochromatosis
- Metabolic and endocrine disorders: hyperparathyroidism, hypophosphatasia, hypomagnesemia, Gitelman syndrome, gout, ochronosis, acromegaly, Wilson's disease, familial hypocalciuric hypercalcemia, X-linked hypophosphatemic rickets

 DIAGNOSIS

DIFFERENTIAL DIAGNOSIS
- Gouty arthritis
- Septic arthritis
- RA
- PMR

Table 1P-56 describes metabolic diseases predisposing to CPPD disposition. Section II describes the differential diagnosis of acute monoarticular and oligoarticular arthritis and crystal-induced arthritides. An algorithm for evaluation and treatment of CPPD is shown in Fig. 1P-107.

LABORATORY TESTS
- Arthrocentesis with presence of weakly positive birefringent rhomboid-shaped crystals by compensated polarized light microscopy (Fig. E1P-108)

- Synovial fluid should always be analyzed for cell count with differential, crystals, Gram stain, and culture because acute CPP crystal arthritis/pseudogout and septic arthritis can coexist.
- Evaluate for possible metabolic cause, especially in younger patients aged <55 yr or patients with florid polyarticular disease. Box 1P-17 describes screening blood tests for metabolic diseases associated with CPPD crystal deposition.

IMAGING STUDIES
- Plain radiographs often reveal CC located parallel to subchondral bone.
  - Classic locations for CC include knee menisci (Fig. E1P-109), wrist triangular fibrocartilage, and symphysis pubis (Fig. 1P-110).
- Musculoskeletal ultrasound can detect deposition of CPP crystals within the hyaline cartilage and/or fibrocartilage. In contrast to urate crystal deposits in gout, CPP crystals often deposit within the substance of the hyaline cartilage, providing a means to distinguish CPP from urate deposition that occurs on the surface of the hyaline cartilage (Fig. E1P-111).

 TREATMENT

NONPHARMACOLOGIC THERAPY
General measures such as immobilization of inflamed joint

ACUTE GENERAL Rx
- Monoarticular pseudogout:
  1. Aspiration followed by corticosteroid injection (often superior to systemic treatment in the elderly)
- Polyarticular pseudogout:
  1. Oral corticosteroids or NSAIDs if not contraindicated

CHRONIC GENERAL Rx
Prophylaxis: daily low-dose colchicine 0.6 mg twice daily or once daily as tolerated
- Pseudo-RA or refractory disease: hydroxychloroquine or methotrexate
- Anakinra (Interleukin-1 receptor antagonist): treatment and prophylaxis of polyarticular acute CPP crystal arthritis unresponsive to oral corticosteroids
- Treat underlying metabolic disease

DISPOSITION
Structural joint damage may occasionally occur, requiring arthroplasty in rare cases.

REFERRAL
Rheumatology

! PEARLS & CONSIDERATIONS

COMMENTS
Acute CPP crystal arthritis/pseudogout attacks have been reported to occur in the setting of

TABLE 1P-56 Metabolic Diseases Predisposing to Calcium Pyrophosphate Dihydrate Deposition

	CC	Pseudogout	Chronic PA
Hemochromatosis	Yes	Yes	Yes
Hyperparathyroidism	Yes	Yes	No
Hypophosphatasia	Yes	Yes	No
Hypomagnesemia	Yes	Yes	No
Gout	Possibly	Possibly	No
Acromegaly	Possibly	No	No
Ochronosis	Yes	Yes	No
Familial hypocalciuric hypercalcemia	Possibly	No	No
X-linked hypophosphatemic rickets	Possibly	Possibly	Possibly

CC, Chondrocalcinosis; *PA,* pyrophosphate arthropathy.

surgical procedures, diuresis, bisphosphonate administration, and hyaluronate joint injections.

SUGGESTED READINGS

Available at www.expertconsult.com

RELATED CONTENT

Pseudogout (Patient Information)
Gout (Related Key Topic)

AUTHORS: **NICOLE B. YANG, M.D.,**, and **ANTHONY M. REGINATO, PH.D., M.D.**

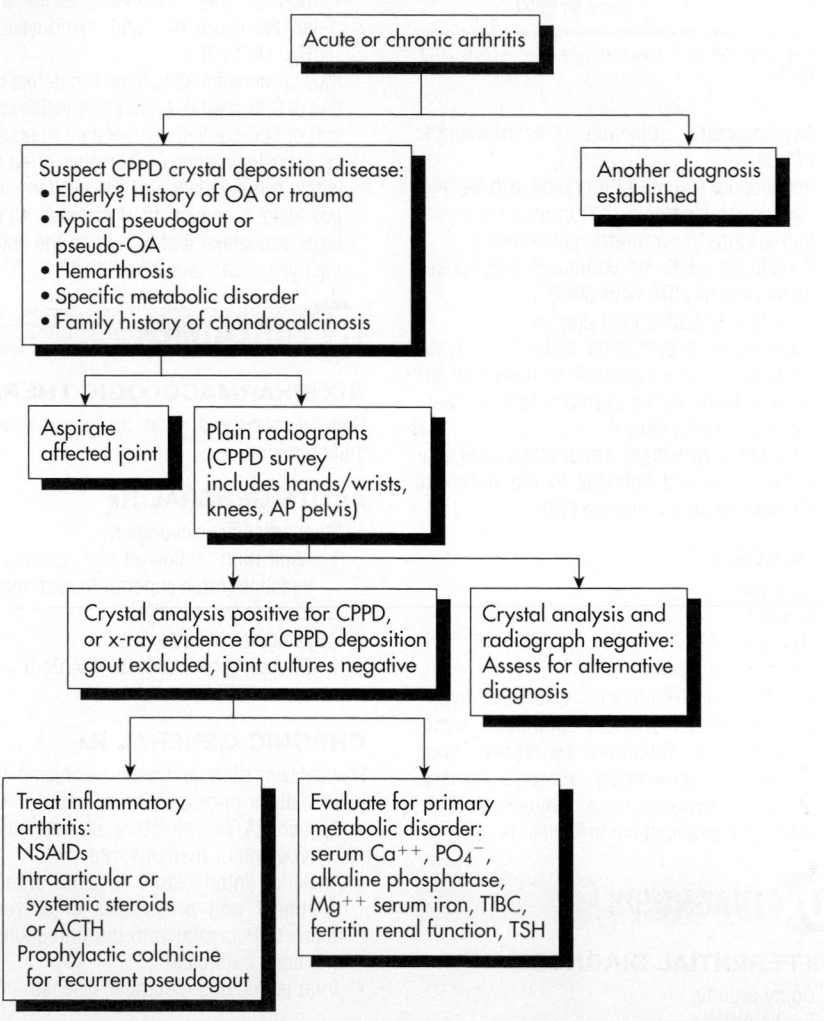

FIGURE 1P-107 Algorithm for evaluation and treatment of calcium pyrophosphate dihydrate disease. *ACTH,* Adrenocorticotropic hormone; *AP,* anteroposterior; *CPPD,* calcium pyrophosphate deposition; *NSAIDs,* nonsteroidal antiinflammatory drugs; *OA,* osteoarthritis; *TIBC,* total iron-binding capacity; *TSH,* thyroid-stimulating hormone. (From Harris ED et al: *Kelley's textbook of rheumatology,* ed 7, Philadelphia, 2005, Saunders.)

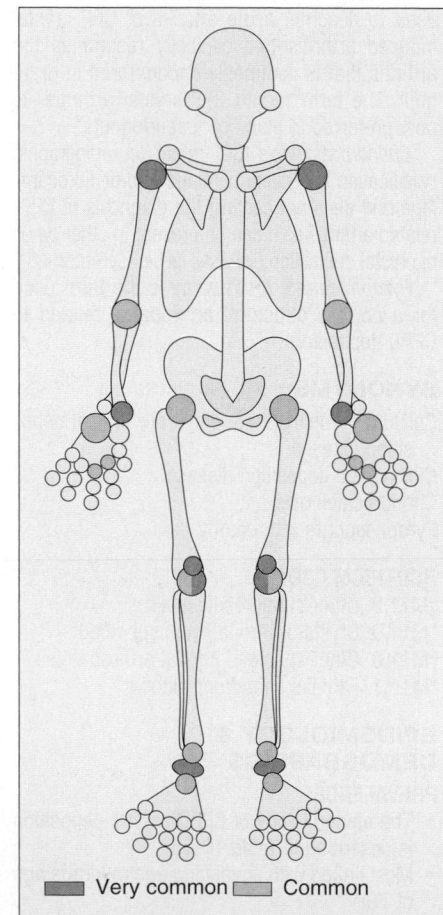

FIGURE 1P-110 Chronic arthropathy. Common sites of involvement of chronic pyrophosphate arthropathy. (From Hochberg MC et al: *Rheumatology,* ed 5, St Louis, 2011, Mosby.)

BOX 1P-17 Screening Blood Tests for Metabolic Diseases Associated with Calcium Pyrophosphate Dihydrate Crystal Deposition

Calcium
Alkaline phosphatase
Magnesium
Ferritin
Liver function
Thyroid-stimulating hormone

From Hochberg MC et al: *Rheumatology,* ed 5, St Louis, 2011, Mosby.

BASIC INFORMATION

DEFINITION

Psittacosis is a systemic infection caused by the bacterium *Chlamydophila psittaci* (formerly known as *Chlamydia psittaci*) and is predominantly transmitted by birds.

SYNONYMS

Ornithosis
Parrot pneumonia

ICD-10CM
A70 *Chlamydia psittaci* infections

EPIDEMIOLOGY & DEMOGRAPHICS

INCIDENCE (IN U.S.):
- Between 2000 and 2009 there were between 8 and 25 cases a year but only 4 cases in 2010.
- True incidence possibly higher because infections may be subclinical.
- Highest incidence among pet owners and people working with birds.

PEAK INCIDENCE: Age 30 to 60 yr.

PREVALENCE (IN U.S.):
- Low among humans.
- More than 130 avian species serve as hosts of the bacterium, and between 5% to 8% of birds carry the organism, including poultry, seagulls, and geese.
- Most human infections are from birds of the order Psittaformes, which includes cockatiels, parrots, cockatoos, and budgerigars.

PREDOMINANT SEX: Equal sex distribution.

PREDOMINANT AGE: More common in adults.

PHYSICAL FINDINGS & CLINICAL PRESENTATION

- Incubation period of 5 to 15 days.
- Subclinical infection.
- Onset abrupt or insidious.
- Most common symptoms:
  1. Fever.
  2. Myalgias.
  3. Chills.
  4. Cough.
- Most common clinical syndrome: atypical pneumonia with fever, headache, dry cough, and a chest radiograph more dramatically abnormal than the physical examination.
- Ranges from mild disease to respiratory failure and death, although this is extremely unusual.
- Other clinical presentations:
  1. Mononucleosis-like syndrome.
  2. Typhoidal form.
- Most frequent physical findings:
  1. Fever.
  2. Pharyngeal erythema.
  3. Rales.
  4. Hepatomegaly.
- Less common findings:
  1. Somnolence.
  2. Confusion.
  3. Relative bradycardia.
  4. Pleural rub.
  5. Adenopathy.
  6. Splenomegaly.
  7. Horder's spots (pink blanching maculopapular rash).
- Besides the lungs, other specific end-organ involvement:
  1. Pericarditis.
  2. Myocarditis.
  3. Endocarditis.
  4. Hepatitis
  5. Joints.
  6. Kidneys (glomerulonephritis).
  7. Central nervous system.

ETIOLOGY

- *C. psittaci* is an obligate intracellular bacterium.
- Infection is usually spread by the respiratory route from infected birds, by direct contact or aerosolization of dried feces or bird feather dust, and rarely from a bite.
- There is a history of exposure to birds in 85% of patients, mostly with birds as pets.
- Strains from turkeys and psittacine birds are most virulent for human beings.
- Cows, goats, and sheep are occasionally implicated.

DIAGNOSIS

DIFFERENTIAL DIAGNOSIS

- *Legionella.*
- *Mycoplasma.*
- *Chlamydophila pneumoniae.*
- Viral respiratory infections.
- Typhoid fever.
- Viral hepatitis.
- Aseptic meningitis.
- Mononucleosis.

WORKUP

- Complete blood count, renal and liver function tests.
- *Chlamydophila* serology.
- Chest x-ray.
- Special immunostaining of respiratory secretions.

LABORATORY TESTS

- White blood count is normal or slightly elevated.
- ESR and C-reactive protein are generally elevated.
- Mild liver function abnormalities are common (50%).
- Blood cultures are almost always negative.
- Studies on respiratory secretions:
  1. Direct immunofluorescent antibody of respiratory secretions with monoclonal antibodies to chlamydial antigens.
  2. *Chlamydophila* lipopolysaccharide antigen by enzyme immunoassay.
  3. Polymerase chain reaction.
- Serologic studies:
  1. Complement-fixing antibodies (CF).
  2. Microimmunofluorescence antibody test (MIF).
  3. Possible false-negative results and cross-reaction with other chlamydial species with both techniques.

IMAGING STUDIES

- Chest x-ray is abnormal in 50% to 90% with a variety of patterns.
- Pleural effusions are common.

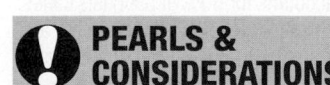

TREATMENT

NONPHARMACOLOGIC THERAPY

Oxygen supplementation as needed.

ACUTE GENERAL Rx

- Doxycycline (100 mg PO bid) for 10 to 14 days after fever declines *or*
- Tetracycline (500 mg PO qid).
- Macrolides such as erythromycin or azithromycin are considered second-line agents in adults but first-line agents in children.
- Quinolones such as ciprofloxacin and moxifloxacin are effective in vitro, but more studies are needed for clinical use.

CHRONIC Rx

In the rare cases of endocarditis, combination of heart valve replacement and prolonged antibiotic course may be the treatment of choice.

DISPOSITION

- Mortality rate is low (0.7%).
- Poor prognostic factors:
  1. Advanced age.
  2. Leukopenia.
  3. Severe hypoxemia.
  4. Renal failure.
  5. Confusion.
  6. Multilobe pulmonary involvement.
- Possible reinfection.

REFERRAL

- To infectious disease expert:
  1. Complicated atypical pneumonia or other end-organ involvement.
  2. Suspicion of an outbreak.
- To pulmonologist for diagnostic bronchoscopy.

PEARLS & CONSIDERATIONS

COMMENTS

- Hospitalized patients do not require specific isolation precautions.
- Any confirmed or suspected case of psittacosis should be reported to public health authorities.
- Recent evidence indicates that *C. psittaci* may be associated with induction of a rare form of lymphoma found in the ocular adnexa; case reports have described regression of ocular lymphoma with antibiotic treatment for *C. psittaci*.

SUGGESTED READINGS
Available at www.expertconsult.com

AUTHOR: **GLENN G. FORT, M.D., M.P.H.**

ⓘ BASIC INFORMATION

DEFINITION

Psoriasis is a chronic skin disorder characterized by excessive proliferation of keratinocytes, resulting in the formation of thickened scaly plaques, itching, and inflammatory changes of the epidermis and dermis. The various forms of psoriasis include guttate, pustular, and arthritis variants.

ICD-10CM CODES
L40	Psoriasis
L40.4	Guttate psoriasis
L40.1	Generalized pustular psoriasis
L40.8	Other psoriasis
L40.9	Psoriasis unspecified
L40.54	Psoriatic juvenile arthropathy
L40.0	Psoriasis vulgaris

EPIDEMIOLOGY & DEMOGRAPHICS

- Psoriasis affects 1% to 3% of the world's population. Most patients have limited psoriasis involving <5% of their body surface.
- There is a strong association between psoriasis and human leukocyte antigens (HLAs) B13, B17, and B27 (pustular psoriasis).
- Peak age of onset is bimodal (adolescents and at age 60 yr).
- Men and women are affected equally.

PHYSICAL FINDINGS & CLINICAL PRESENTATION

- Approximately 85% of patients with psoriasis have mild-to-moderate disease.
- The primary psoriatic lesion is an erythematous papule topped by a loosely adherent scale. Scraping the scale results in several bleeding points *(Auspitz sign).*
- Chronic plaque psoriasis generally manifests with symmetric, sharply demarcated, erythematous, silver-scaled patches affecting primarily the intergluteal folds, elbows, scalp, fingernails, toenails, and knees (Fig. 1P-112). This form accounts for 80% of psoriasis cases.
- Psoriasis can also develop at the site of any physical trauma (sunburn, scratching). This is known as *Koebner's phenomenon.*
- Nail involvement is common (pitting of the nail plate), resulting in hyperkeratosis, onychodystrophy with onycholysis.
- Pruritus is variable; soreness and bleeding may occur.
- Joint involvement can result in sacroiliitis and spondylitis.
- Guttate psoriasis is generally preceded by streptococcal pharyngitis and manifests with multiple droplike lesions on the extremities and the trunk.
- Adverse effect on psychological and social functioning, with affected persons often feeling stigmatized.

ETIOLOGY

- Unknown, but there is a strong genetic component and high heritability. There are at least nine chromosomal loci with linkage to psoriasis. These loci are called psoriasis

susceptibility 1 through 9 (PSORS1-PSORS9). PSORS1 locus in the major histocompatibility complex (MHC) region on chromosome 6 is considered the most important susceptibility locus and is believed to account for 35% to 50% of the heritability of the disease.
- Familial clustering (genetic transmission with a dominant mode with variable penetrants).
- One third of persons affected have a positive family history.
- A high prevalence of celiac disease has been noted in patients with psoriasis.

Ⓓ DIAGNOSIS

DIFFERENTIAL DIAGNOSIS

- Contact dermatitis.
- Atopic dermatitis.
- Stasis dermatitis.
- Tinea.
- Nummular dermatitis.
- Candidiasis.
- Mycosis fungoides.
- Cutaneous systemic lupus erythematosus.
- Secondary and tertiary syphilis.
- Drug eruption.
- Dermatomyositis (DM).
- Lupus erythematosus (LE).
- Seborrheic dermatitis.
- Pityarisis rosea.
- Lichen planus.

WORKUP

- Diagnosis is clinical. Blood work is rarely needed.
- Skin biopsy is rarely necessary.

LABORATORY TESTS

Generally not necessary for diagnosis.

Ⓡ TREATMENT

NONPHARMACOLOGIC THERAPY

- Sunbathing generally leads to improvement.
- Eliminate triggering factors (e.g., stress, certain medications [e.g., lithium, beta-blockers, antimalarials]). Severe emotional stress tends to aggravate psoriasis.
- Patients with psoriasis benefit from a daily bath in warm water followed by application of a cream or ointment moisturizer. Regular use of an emollient moisturizer limits evaporation of water from the skin and allows the stratum corneum to rehydrate itself.
- PUVA therapy (see "General Treatment").
- Local hyperthermia has been used successfully to clear psoriatic plaques, but relapse is common.
- Occlusive treatment with surgical tape or dressings is effective as monotherapy or in combination with topical medications.

GENERAL Rx

Therapeutic options vary according to the extent of disease. Approximately 70% to 80% of all patients can be treated adequately with topical therapy.

- Patients with limited disease (<20% of the body) can be treated with the following:
  1. Topical steroids: disadvantages are brief remissions, expense, and decreased effect with continued use. Salicylic acid can be compounded by pharmacist in concentrations of 2% to 10% and used in combination with a corticosteroid to decrease the amount of scale.
  2. Calcipotriene: a vitamin D analogue effective for moderate plaque psoriasis. Adults should comb the hair, apply solution to the lesions, and rub it in, avoiding uninvolved skin. Disadvantages include its cost and potential burning and skin irritation. It should not be used concurrently with salicylic acid because calcipotriene is inactivated by the acidic nature of salicylic acid. Taclonex ointment is a combination of calcipotriene and the high-potency corticosteroid betamethasone dipropionate. It is well tolerated and more effective than either agent used alone but also much more expensive.
  3. Tar products (Estar, LCD, Psorigel) can be used overnight and are most effective when combined with ultraviolet B (UVB) light (Goeckerman regimen).
  4. Anthralin: useful for chronic plaques; can result in purple-brown staining; best used with UVB light.
  5. Retinoids such as tazarotene 0.05%, 0.1% cream or gel, are effective in thinning plaques but are expensive and can cause irritation.
  6. Other useful measures include tape or occlusive dressing, UVB and lubricating agents, and interlesional steroids.
- Therapeutic options for persons with generalized disease (affecting >20% of the body) and for those with inadequate response to topical agents:
  1. UVB light exposure three times a week: this therapy does not require administration of a systemic drug (unlike psoralen plus ultraviolet A [PUVA]), but to be effective, it requires removal of scale with keratolytic agents and emollients.
  2. Oral PUVA administered two to three times weekly is effective for generalized disease. It is often considered in patients for whom narrow-band UVB therapy is ineffective. However, many PUVA treatments are required, necessitating frequent office visits, and it may be associated with phototoxicity, such as erythema and blistering, and increased risk of skin cancer.
- Systemic treatments include methotrexate 25 mg/wk for severe psoriasis. Etretinate (a synthetic retinoid) is most effective for palmar-plantar pustular psoriasis. Dose is 0.5 to 1 mg/kg/day. It can cause liver enzyme and lipid abnormalities and is teratogenic.
- Apremilast is a phosphodiesterase type-4 inhibitor used in moderate to severe plaque psoriasis. Side effects include diarrhea, nausea, headache, and worsening depression.
- Cyclosporine is also effective in severe psoriasis; however, relapses are common.

P

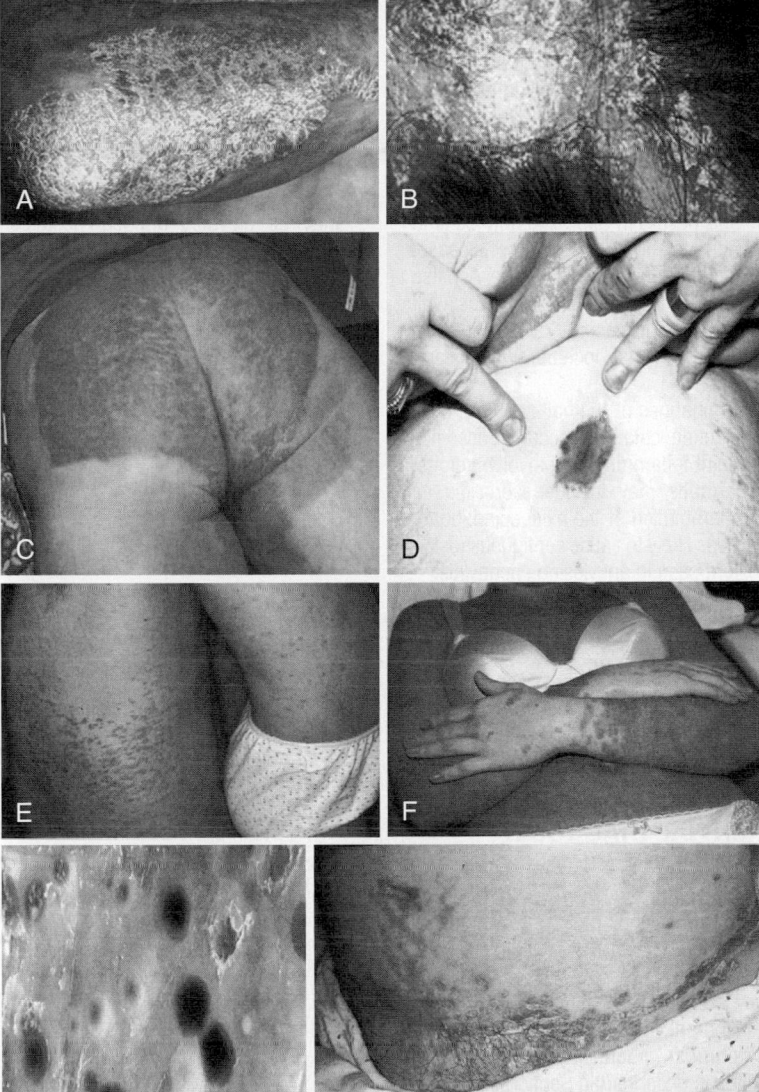

FIGURE 1P-112 Clinical phenotypes in psoriasis: plaque psoriasis (psoriasis vulgaris). A, At extensor surface of elbow and on scalp (**B**). **C,** Genital psoriasis. **D,** Inframammary and umbilical flexural psoriasis. **E,** Guttate psoriasis in a father and child. **F,** Erythrodermic psoriasis on the trunk and upper limbs. **G,** Pustular psoriasis on the foot. **H,** The Koebner phenomenon on a surgical abdominal wound. (From Firestein GS et al: *Kelly's textbook of rheumatology,* ed 9, Philadelphia, 2013, Saunders.)

- Chronic plaque psoriasis may be treated with alefacept, a recombinant protein that selectively targets T lymphocytes. Treatment with alefacept for 12 wk (0.025, 0.075, or 0.150 mg/kg of body weight IV weekly) may result in significant improvement. Some patients also demonstrate a sustained clinical response after the cessation of treatment. This medication is very expensive (a 12-wk course can cost >$8000).
- TNF inhibitors: Treatment with etanercept, a tumor necrosis factor (TNF) antagonist, for 24 wk can also lead to a reduction in severity of plaque psoriasis. Efalizumab, a humanized monoclonal antibody that inhibits the activation of T cells, has also been reported to produce significant improvement in plaque psoriasis treatment period. Adalimumab—a fully human, anti-TNF-alpha monoclonal antibody—has been reported to be effective for joint and skin manifestations of psoriasis.
- Newer biologic agents in patients with moderate to severe plaque psoriasis are ustekinumab (an interleukin-12 and interleukin-23 blocker), brodalumab and secukinumab anti–interleukin-17 receptor antibodies, and briakinumab, a monoclonal antibody against the p40 molecule shared by interleukin-12 and interleukin-23, which is overexpressed in psoriatic skin lesions. Secukinumab (Cosentyx) is the first IL-17A antagonist FDA-approved for moderate to severe plaque psoriasis.

DISPOSITION

The course of psoriasis is chronic, and the disease may be refractory to treatment.

REFERRAL

- Dermatology referral is recommended in all patients with generalized disease.
- Hospital admission may be necessary for severe diffuse or poorly responsive psoriasis. The Goeckerman regimen combines daily application of tar with UVB exposure and can result in prolonged remissions.

! PEARLS & CONSIDERATIONS

COMMENTS

Psoriasis is more emotionally than physically disabling for most patients. Counseling may be indicated, particularly when it affects younger patients.

 **EVIDENCE**

Available at www.expertconsult.com

SUGGESTED READINGS

Available at www.expertconsult.com

RELATED CONTENT

Psoriasis (Patient Information)
Psoriatic Arthritis (Related Key Topic)

AUTHOR: **FRED F. FERRI, M.D.**

ℹ️ BASIC INFORMATION

DEFINITION

Psoriatic arthritis (PsA) is an inflammatory arthropathy occurring in association with cutaneous psoriasis. It is often included in a class of disorders called the *seronegative spondyloarthropathies,* a family of diseases characterized by inflammation of the spine, peripheral joints, and entheses (sites of insertion of tendon into bone). Classifications of psoriatic arthritis are described in Table 1P-57.

ICD-10CM CODES
L40.5+ Arthropathic psoriasis
L40.54 Psoriatic juvenile arthropathy
L40.52 Psoriatic arthritis mutilans

EPIDEMIOLOGY & DEMOGRAPHICS

INCIDENCE: 6 per 100,000 per year in the general population.
PREVALENCE: 0.1% to 0.2% overall, variable estimates of 7% to 30% of patients with psoriasis (psoriasis incidence varies by population but overall estimated prevalence of 1% to 2% of general population)
PREDOMINANT SEX: Equal male/female distribution
PREDOMINANT AGE: Symptom onset generally age 30 to 55 yr.

PHYSICAL FINDINGS & CLINICAL PRESENTATION

- Arthritis, dactylitis, spondylitis, and enthesitis occur in the setting of known psoriasis.
- Joint symptoms predate skin psoriasis in about 15% of patients.
- Arthritis is inflammatory in nature, commonly characterized by prolonged morning stiffness, joint erythema, warmth, or swelling including joint effusions.
- Distribution of joint involvement follows five classically described patterns (Box 1P-18).
- Often more than one pattern will occur simultaneously and patterns can evolve over time

in an individual patient. Subtypes of psoriatic arthritis are described in Box 1P-18. The distal interphalangeal (DIP) joints and spine are each affected in 40 to 50 percent of cases.

- Dactylitis refers to diffuse swelling of a digit, either finger or toe, which is typically the result of inflammation in both small joints of the digit as well as associated digital tendons. Dactylitis is common in psoriatic arthritis and occurs in approximately 30% to 40% of patients during the course of disease.
- Enthesitis commonly occurs at the Achilles tendon insertion into the calcaneus as well as the insertion of the plantar fascia. Findings on physical exam may include swelling and tenderness.
- Dystrophic changes of the nails (pitting, onycholysis, leukonychia may occur in association with joint inflammation in involved digits.
- Spondyloarthritis may include sacroiliitis as well as inflammation of the axial spine, but is generally less likely to cause contiguous fusion to the extent seen in ankylosing spondylitis.
- Ocular inflammation including conjunctivitis and uveitis can also occur in some patients with PsA.

ETIOLOGY

Unknown.

Dx DIAGNOSIS

DIFFERENTIAL DIAGNOSIS

- Rheumatoid arthritis.
- Erosive osteoarthritis.
- Crystal arthritis including gout and pseudogout.
- Other seronegative spondyloarthropathies, including reactive arthritis, enteropathic arthritis, and ankylosing spondylitis.
- The differential diagnosis of spondyloarthropathies is described in Section III.

WORKUP

- Diagnosis generally made on clinical grounds based on history, exam, and radiographic findings given lack of specific lab findings.

An algorithm for the diagnosis of psoriatic arthritis is described in Fig. 1P-113.
- Early diagnosis may be difficult to establish when the arthritis develops before skin lesions appear.

LABORATORY TESTS

- No specific/diagnostic lab tests.
- Acute phase reactants such as ESR and CRP may be elevated although less commonly than in patients with rheumatoid arthritis.
- Anemia of chronic disease may be seen.
- RF, while generally negative, can be present in >10% of patients.
- *HLA B27* is significantly more common in patients with axial inflammation (note that *HLA B27* positivity is present in up to 8% of general population).
- Arthrocentesis of active joint generally demonstrates inflammatory synovial fluid and absence of crystals.

IMAGING STUDIES

- Radiographic findings (Fig. 1P-114) of involved joints may include soft tissue swelling, joint space narrowing, subluxation, erosive changes, and new bone formation such as periostitis and fusion.
- Severe digital erosive change with adjacent heterotopic bone formation may give rise to "pencil in cup" deformity seen in arthritis mutilans.

BOX 1P-18 Subtypes of Psoriatic Arthritis

Distal interphalangeal joint–predominant arthritis (10%) (Fig. 1P-115).
Symmetric polyarthritis–predominant arthritis (5%-20%).
Asymmetric oligoarthritis or monoarthritis (70%-80%).
Axial disease–predominant (spondylitis and/or sacroiliitis) (5%-20%).
Arthritis mutilans (rare).

From Hochberg MC et al: *Rheumatology,* ed 5, St Louis, 2011, Mosby.

TABLE 1P-57 Classifications of Psoriatic Arthritis

Moll and Wright	CLASSIFICATION CRITERIA FOR PSORIATIC ARTHRITIS (CASPAR)*		
	Points	Category	Description
Presence of psoriasis and: An inflammatory arthritis (peripheral arthritis and/or sacroiliitis or spondylitis) The (usual) absence of serologic tests for rheumatoid factor	2	Current psoriasis or personal or family history of psoriasis	Psoriatic skin or scalp disease confirmed by dermatologist or rheumatologist; history of psoriasis from patient, family physician, dermatologist, rheumatologist, or other qualified practitioner; patient-reported history of psoriasis in first- or second-degree relative
	1	Psoriatic nail dystrophy on current physical examination	Includes onycholysis, pitting, and hyperkeratosis
	1	Negative for rheumatoid factor	Enzyme-linked immunosorbent assay or nephelometry preferred (no latex) using local laboratory reference range
	1	Current dactylitis or history of dactylitis documented by a rheumatologist	Swelling of entire digit
	1	Radiographic evidence of juxtaarticular new bone formation	Ill-defined ossification near joint margins excluding osteophyte formation on plain radiographs of hand or foot

*Psoriatic arthritis is diagnosed when ≥3 points are assigned in the presence of inflammatory articular disease (joint, spine, or entheseal).
From Hochberg MC et al: Rheumatology, ed 5, St Louis, 2011, Mosby.

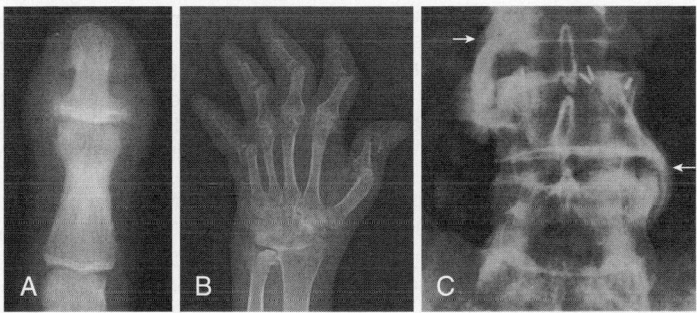

FIGURE 1P-113 Algorithm to be used in the diagnosis of individual patients presenting with possible psoriatic arthritis. Some patients may present with typical articular manifestations of psoriatic arthritis, but in the absence of skin or nail disease. They can be diagnosed as having definite psoriatic arthritis only when psoriasis subsequently develops. *ACPA,* Anticitrullinated protein antibody; *RF,* rheumatoid factor; *SpA,* spondyloarthropathy. (Firestein GS et al: *Kelly's textbook of rheumatology,* ed 9, Philadelphia, 2013, Saunders.)

FIGURE 1P-114 Psoriatic arthritis (x-ray). A, Distal interphalangeal joint with classic radiographic findings, including soft tissue swelling, bone erosions with accompanying bone proliferation, and lack of osteoporosis. **B,** Arthritis mutilans resulting from psoriatic arthritis with destructive changes and joint deformity of the hand and pancompartmental ankylosis of the wrist. **C,** Psoriatic spondylitis. Thick asymmetric paravertebral ossifications (*arrows*), which are characteristic of psoriatic spondylitis and reactive arthritis. (From Resnick D, Niwayama G: *Diagnosis of bone and joint disorders,* Philadelphia, 1988, WB Saunders.)

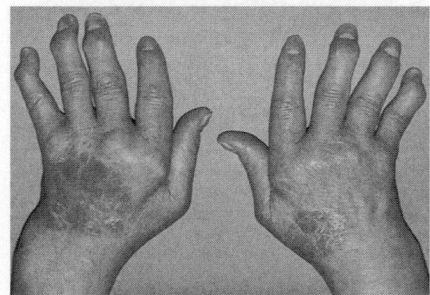

FIGURE 1P-115 The hands of a woman with symmetric polyarthritis. Initially this was indistinguishable from rheumatoid disease, but note the distal interphalangeal joint involvement, which is uncommon in rheumatoid arthritis, as well as the skin psoriasis. (From Klippel J et al [eds]: *Primary care rheumatology,* London, 1999, Mosby.)

- Findings in patients with spondylitis may include sacroiliitis and development of vertebral syndesmophytes that often bridge adjacent vertebral bodies.
- Musculoskeletal ultrasound may be helpful in the evaluation of an inflamed enthesis or joint.
- MRI may be helpful in the evaluation of sacroiliitis or spinal involvement.

 **TREATMENT**

ACUTE GENERAL Rx
- NSAIDs may be used for mild symptoms or limited involvement.
- Intraarticular corticosteroid injections can be used as adjunctive therapy in involved joints.

CHRONIC Rx
The choice of therapeutic agents in psoriatic arthritis depends on the types of clinical manifestations by an individual patient as not all agents are effective for all types of clinical manifestations. For example, inflammation at the enthesis and spine are not responsive to traditional oral disease-modifying agents such as methotrexate or leflunomide but are responsive to tumor necrosis factor (TNF) blocking agents such as infliximab, adalimumab, and etanercept.

- NSAIDs may be used for mild or limited disease
- In patients with several sites of active peripheral joint disease, elevated acute phase reactants, or with evidence of erosive changes on imaging, traditional DMARDs such as methotrexate, sulfasalazine, and leflunomide should be considered early in disease.
- In patients with peripheral arthritis who fail to respond to traditional DMARD therapy, additional therapy with a tumor necrosis factor (TNF) inhibitor should be considered. Current FDA-approved TNF inhibitors for psoriatic arthritis include etanercept, infliximab, adalimumab, golimumab, and certolizumab pegol.
- In patients with predominant axial disease not responsive to NSAIDs, anti-TNF therapy should be considered for initial disease-modifying therapy.
- Enthesitis and dactylitis are poorly responsive to oral DMARD therapy but like spondylitis will often respond to anti-TNF therapy.
- Ustekinumab, a human IgG monoclonal antibody that binds to the p40 subunit of interleukin-12 and -23 and is responsible for T-helper-17 inflammatory cell suppression effectively treats psoriasis and psoriatic arthritis and is FDA approved as an alternative biologic treatment for psoriatic arthritis. Recent trials involving brodalumab, an anti-IL17RA monoclonal antibody, have shown significantly improved response rates.
- New targeted therapeutics have recently been demonstrated to be effective in psoriatic arthritis and approved for use in psoriatic arthritis. These include ustekinumab, which is a biologic targeted inhibitor of IL12/23 previously found to be effective in psoriasis. Another agent recently approved is apremilast, which is an oral phosphodiesterase 4 (PDE 4) inhibitor that has been demonstrated to be effective in psoriatic arthritis. Secukinumab, (IL-17 inhibitor) and abatacept CTLA4-Ig), a selective T-cell costimulation modulator, are currently being studied for psoriatic arthritis

REFERRAL
Rheumatology for confirmation of diagnosis and management.

⊘ PEARLS & CONSIDERATIONS

- Patients frequently have a positive family history of psoriasis or psoriatic arthritis.
- Severity of skin psoriasis and activity of inflammatory arthritis are frequently discordant.

SUGGESTED READINGS
Available at www.expertconsult.com

RELATED CONTENT
Psoriatic Arthritis (Patient Information).

AUTHOR: **SYEDA M. SAYEED, M.D.**

BASIC INFORMATION

DEFINITION

Psychosis is a state in which external reality is distorted by delusions and/or hallucinations (a delusion is a fixed false idiosyncratic belief; a hallucination is a false auditory, visual, olfactory, tactile, or taste perception).

SYNONYMS

Psychosis is a key finding in many mental illnesses, such as brief psychotic disorder, delusional disorder, schizoaffective disorder, schizophrenia, schizophreniform disorder, or shared psychotic disorder. Psychosis can also present as part of the evolution of a mood disorder (depression and bipolar disorder), a sign of an underlying medical condition, or a manifestation of a toxic state, i.e., abuse of substances or withdrawal state.

ICD-10CM CODES

F09	Unspecified organic or symptomatic mental disorder.
F10.5	Psychotic disorder due to psychoactive substance use
F05	Delirium not induced by alcohol and other psychoactive substances.
F06.0	Organic hallucinosis.
F32.3	Major depressive disorder, single episode, severe with psychotic features.
F30.2 and F31.2	Manic episode with psychosis and bipolar affective disorder with psychosis.

EPIDEMIOLOGY & DEMOGRAPHICS

One-year prevalence: 4.5 per 1000. The (demographics of) psychosis depends on the underlying disorder.

PHYSICAL FINDINGS & CLINICAL PRESENTATION

History:
- Past and current medical history important to identify potential medical etiologies.
- Medication use.
- Use of illicit substances or alcohol.
- Identification of functional and social impairment.
- Behavior that is odd or unpredictable; patient may be acting based on misinterpretation of their reality or false perceptions (delusions or hallucinations).

Examination:
- Examine for symptoms of:
  1. Mood disorder: delusions or hallucinations are usually congruent with the mood (e.g., auditory hallucinations in a depressed patient may tell the patient what a terrible person he is).
  2. Altered or disorganized thought pattern: usually reflected in disorganized speech (including word salad, thought blocking, rhyming, clang associations).
  3. Lack of insight into problems
  4. Signs of Parkinson's disease, dementia.

ETIOLOGY

- Involves an interaction among:
  1. Dopaminergic overactivity (particularly in the mesolimbic, nigrostriatal, and mesocortical systems).
  2. Environmental, social, or childhood factors.
  3. Genetic predisposition.

DIAGNOSIS

WORKUP

- Evaluate for potential confounding factors. Fig. 1P-116 describes an algorithmic approach to evaluation of the psychotic patient.
- Underlying mental disorder: schizophrenia, major depression, brief psychotic disorder, delusional disorder, schizoaffective disorder, schizophreniform disorder.
- Underlying personality disorder: borderline, paranoid, schizoid, schizotypal.
- Underlying medical conditions: infections ranging from UTIs to HIV/AIDS, Parkinson's disease, Huntington's disease, leprosy, malaria, sarcoidosis, systemic lupus erythematosus, prion disease, hypoglycemia, postpartum state, cerebrovascular event, temporal lobe epilepsy, brain neoplasm.
- Medications: systemic steroids, anticonvulsants, antiparkinsonian medications, some chemotherapy, scopolamine.
- Underlying dementia: Alzheimer's disease, Lewy body dementia, vascular dementia.
- Illicit drugs (usually with chronic use; can be caused by intoxication or withdrawal): LSD, PCP, cocaine, gamma-hydroxybutyrate (GHB; withdrawal), alcohol, amphetamines, and marijuana. New substances of abuse (e.g., "bath salts," synthetic cannabinoids) may not be detected by current toxicology panels.
- Traumatic brain injury.
- Intensive care unit stay: hypoxia, decreased cardiac output, infection, medications, sleep deprivation, alteration of diurnal cycle, sensory deprivation or overload, pain.
- Emotional stress.

LABORATORY TESTS

Consider checking chemistry panel (calcium), complete blood count, UA, liver function tests, cortisol, HIV, rapid plasma reagin, thyroid-stimulating hormone, toxicology screen, lumbar puncture (LP).

IMAGING STUDIES

Consider chest x-ray (rule out sarcoid), electroencephalography, head CT or MRI.

TREATMENT

NONPHARMACOLOGIC THERAPY

- Cognitive-behavioral therapy.
- Social and behavioral skills training.
- Training for self-management of disease.
- Aforementioned strategies favored over psychoanalytic techniques given the relative inability for abstract thought and lack of insight in psychotic patients.
- Family intervention, including education and strategies to reduce emotional expression.
- Counseling for substance abuse.

ACUTE GENERAL Rx

- Antipsychotics, such as haloperidol and consider combining with anticholinergics like benztropine to reduce side effects if such arise; low doses should control first episode. Use with caution in elderly patients because adverse effects limit effectiveness. Second-generation antipsychotics are also useful starting with low doses. Alternative formulations are available; e.g., rapid injectable form or oral disintegrating tablets.
- Benzodiazepines if agitation is severe.
- Discontinue offending medication if present.

CHRONIC Rx

Second-generation antipsychotics may reduce the incidence of tardive dyskinesia but may increase incidence of metabolic disorders compared with first-generation antipsychotics. Multicenter trials showed similar efficacy between first and second generation. Consider economic, including insurance formulary, factors when selecting a maintenance regimen.

DISPOSITION

Prognosis varies according to etiology of psychosis. In general, the more severe and longer the psychotic episode, the worse the prognosis.

REFERRAL

Patient should be admitted for acute stabilization if actively psychotic to prevent harm to self and others as well as ensure administration of medications.

PEARLS & CONSIDERATIONS

- Delusions and/or hallucinations are hallmarks of psychosis.
- Rule out medical or drug causes of psychosis.
- Antipsychotics are the mainstay of acute and chronic treatment.
- Consider alternatives to antipsychotics in elderly or intellectually disabled patients (see "Nonpharmacologic Therapy").

SUGGESTED READINGS

Available at www.expertconsult.com

RELATED CONTENT

Psychosis (Patient Information)
Delirium (Related Key Topic)

AUTHORS: **ARNALDO A. BERGES, M.D.,** and **RICHARD J. GOLDBERG, M.D., M.S.**

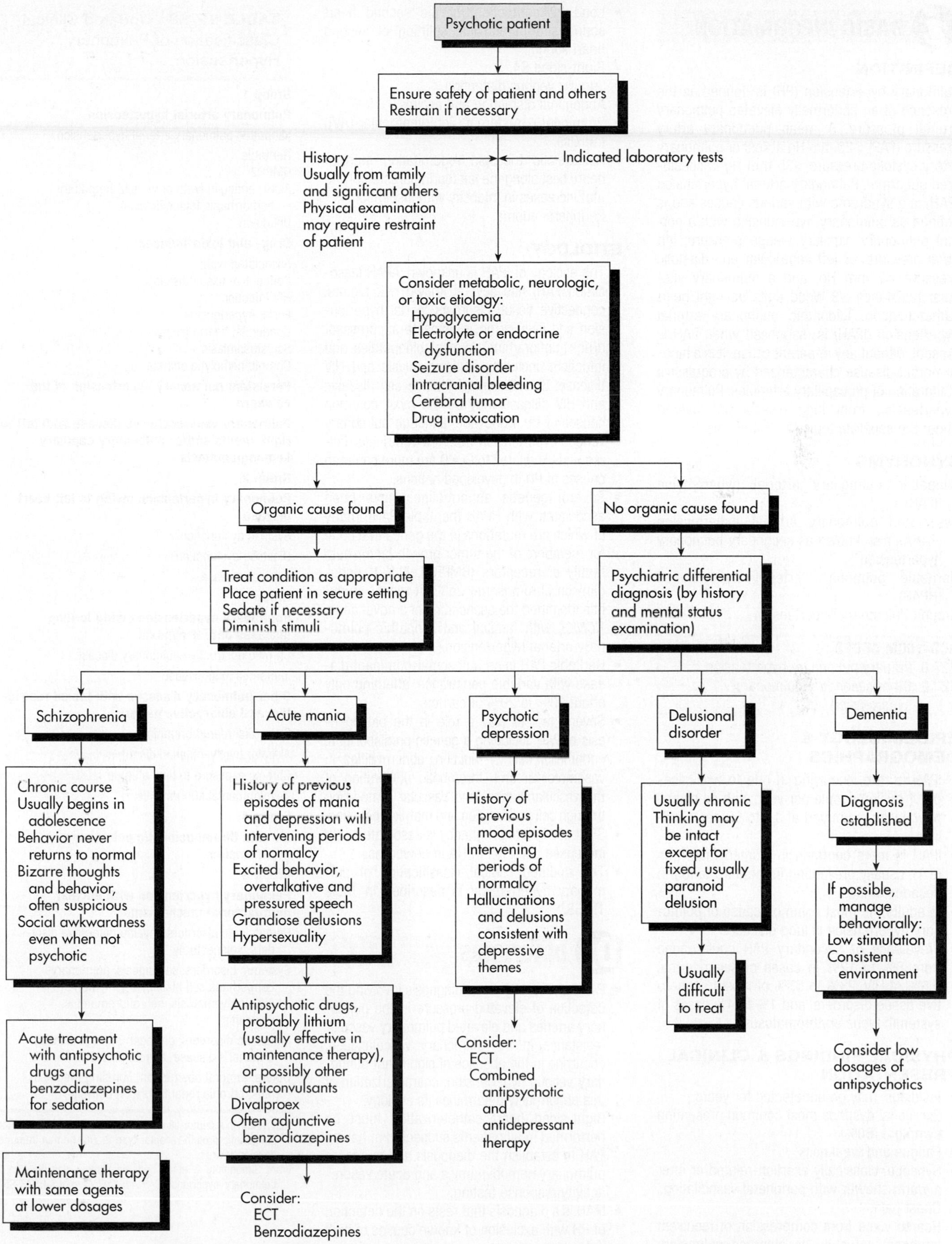

Psychotic patient

↓

Ensure safety of patient and others
Restrain if necessary

↓

History ——————→ ←—————— Indicated laboratory tests
Usually from family
and significant others
Physical examination
may require restraint
of patient

Consider metabolic, neurologic,
or toxic etiology:
  Hypoglycemia
  Electrolyte or endocrine
    dysfunction
  Seizure disorder
  Intracranial bleeding
  Cerebral tumor
  Drug intoxication

↓

Organic cause found | No organic cause found

Treat condition as appropriate
Place patient in secure setting
Sedate if necessary
Diminish stimuli

Psychiatric differential
diagnosis (by history
and mental status
examination)

Schizophrenia | **Acute mania** | **Psychotic depression** | **Delusional disorder** | **Dementia**

Chronic course
Usually begins in
  adolescence
Behavior never
  returns to normal
Bizarre thoughts
  and behavior,
  often suspicious
Social awkwardness
  even when not
  psychotic

History of previous
  episodes of mania
  and depression with
  intervening periods
  of normalcy
Excited behavior,
  overtalkative and
  pressured speech
Grandiose delusions
Hypersexuality

History of
  previous
  mood episodes
Intervening
  periods of
  normalcy
Hallucinations
  and delusions
  consistent with
  depressive
  themes

Usually chronic
Thinking may
  be intact
  except for
  fixed, usually
  paranoid
  delusion

Diagnosis
established

↓

Acute treatment
  with antipsychotic
  drugs and
  benzodiazepines
  for sedation

Antipsychotic drugs,
  probably lithium
  (usually effective in
  maintenance therapy),
  or possibly other
  anticonvulsants
Divalproex
Often adjunctive
  benzodiazepines

Consider:
ECT
Combined
  antipsychotic
  and
  antidepressant
  therapy

Usually
difficult
to treat

If possible,
  manage
  behaviorally:
Low stimulation
Consistent
  environment

↓

Maintenance therapy
  with same agents
  at lower dosages

Consider:
ECT
Benzodiazepines

Consider low
dosages of
antipsychotics

FIGURE 1P-116 Evaluation of psychotic patient. *ECT*, Electroconvulsive therapy. (Modified from Greene
HL et al [eds]: *Decision making in medicine*, ed 2, St Louis, 1998, Mosby.)

BASIC INFORMATION

DEFINITION

Pulmonary hypertension (PH) is defined as the presence of an abnormally elevated pulmonary arterial pressure. A mean pulmonary artery pressure (PAP) >25 mm Hg at rest or pulmonary artery systolic pressure >35 mm Hg is considered abnormal. Pulmonary arterial hypertension (PAH) is a syndrome with various causes and is defined as pulmonary hypertension with a normal pulmonary capillary wedge pressure, left atrial pressure, or left ventricular end diastolic pressure ≤5 mm Hg, and a pulmonary vascular resistance >3 Wood units on right heart catheterization. Idiopathic pulmonary arterial hypertension (IPAH) is diagnosed when PAH is present without any apparent cause. It is a highly morbid disease characterized by progressive obliteration of precapillary arterioles. Pulmonary hypertension from lung disease is covered under the separate topic Cor Pulmonale.

SYNONYMS

Idiopathic pulmonary arterial hypertension (IPAH)
Associated pulmonary arterial hypertension (PAHA), also known as secondary pulmonary hypertension
Heritable pulmonary arterial hypertension (HPAH)
Group I Pulmonary Hypertension

ICD-10CM CODES
I27.0 Primary pulmonary hypertension
I27.2 Other secondary pulmonary hypertension

EPIDEMIOLOGY & DEMOGRAPHICS

- IPAH is rare, occurring in one to two cases per 1 million people per year, with an overall prevalence estimated at 15 to 50 per 1 million.
- IPAH is more common in women than men (3:1), usually presenting in the third to fourth decades of life.
- In adults the most common cause of pulmonary hypertension is lung disease.
- Prevalence of secondary PAH could range from 8% to 12% in cases of scleroderma, 0.5% of HIV, 23% to 53% of mixed connective tissue disorders, and 1% to 4% cases of systemic lupus erythematosus.

PHYSICAL FINDINGS & CLINICAL PRESENTATION

- Insidious, may go undetected for years.
- Exertional dyspnea most common presenting symptom (60%).
- Fatigue and weakness.
- Syncope, classically exertion-related or after a warm shower with peripheral vasodilation.
- Chest pain.
- Hoarse voice from compression of recurrent laryngeal nerve by an enlarged pulmonary artery (Ortner's syndrome).

- Loud P2 component of the second heart sound and paradoxical splitting of second heart sound.
- Right-sided S4.
- Jugular venous distention.
- Abdominal distention and ascites.
- Prominent parasternal (right ventricular [RV]) impulse.
- Holosystolic tricuspid regurgitation murmur heard best along the left fourth parasternal line that increases in intensity with inspiration.
- Peripheral edema.

ETIOLOGY

- The etiology of IPAH is unknown. APAH (associated PAH) has several known risk factors: connective tissue disorders, portal hypertension and liver cirrhosis, appetite-suppressant drugs (fenfluramine), hemoglobinopathies, and infections including schistosomiasis and HIV disease. Schistosomiasis, sickle cell disease, and HIV disease may be the most common causes of PH worldwide, although pulmonary venous hypertension from left ventricular failure and PH related to COPD are more common causes of PH in developed nations.
- Several genetic abnormalities have been associated with HPAH (heritable PAH), many of which are mutations in the genes that code for members of the tumor growth factor-beta family of receptors (BMPR-II, ALK-1, endoglin) on chromosome 2q33. A recent study[1] has identified the association of a novel gene, *KCNK3*, with familial and idiopathic pulmonary arterial hypertension.
- Heritable PAH is an autosomal-dominant disease with variable penetrance, affecting only about 10% to 20% of carriers.
- Several factors play a role in the pathogenesis of PAH, including a genetic predisposition, endothelial cell dysfunction, abnormalities in vasomotor control, thrombotic obliteration of the vascular lumen, and vascular remodeling through cell proliferation and matrix production.
- SSRI use in late pregnancy is associated with increased persistent PHA in newborns.
- The updated clinical classification of pulmonary hypertension is described in Table 1P-58.

DIAGNOSIS

- PAH is a hemodynamic diagnosis involving the detection of elevated pressure in the pulmonary arteries and elevated pulmonary vascular resistance in the pulmonary vascular bed, occurring in the absence of significant pulmonary venous hypertension; characterization of this abnormality determines its etiology.
- Right-sided heart catheterization must be performed in all patients suspected of having PAH to establish the diagnosis and to assess pulmonary hemodynamics and acute vasoreactivity response testing.
- IPAH is a diagnosis that rests on the detection of PH with exclusion of known causes of high pulmonary arterial pressure.

TABLE 1P-58 Updated Clinical Classification of Pulmonary Hypertension

Group 1
Pulmonary arterial hypertension

Idiopathic pulmonary arterial hypertension
Heritable
BMPR2
ALK1, endoglin (with or without hereditary hemorrhagic telangiectasia)
Unknown

Drug- and toxin-induced

Associated with:
Connective tissue diseases
HIV infection
Portal hypertension
Congenital heart diseases
Schistosomiasis
Chronic hemolytic anemia

Persistent pulmonary hypertension of the newborn

Pulmonary veno-occlusive disease with left to right shunts and/or pulmonary capillary hemangiomatosis

Group 2
Pulmonary hypertension owing to left heart disease

Systolic dysfunction
Diastolic dysfunction
Valvular disease

Group 3
Pulmonary hypertension owing to lung diseases and/or hypoxia

Chronic obstructive pulmonary disease
Interstitial lung disease
Other pulmonary diseases with mixed restrictive and obstructive pattern
Sleep-disordered breathing
Alveolar hypoventilation disorders
Chronic exposure to high altitude
Developmental abnormalities

Group 4
Chronic thromboembolic pulmonary hypertension

Group 5
Pulmonary hypertension with unclear multifactorial mechanisms

Hematologic disorders: myeloproliferative disorders, splenectomy

Systemic disorders: sarcoidosis, pulmonary Langerhans cell histiocytosis: lymphangioleiomyomatosis, neurofibromatosis, vasculitis

Metabolic disorders: glycogen storage disease, Gaucher's disease, thyroid disorders

Others: tumoral obstruction, fibrosing mediastinitis, chronic renal failure on dialysis

ALK1, Activin receptor-like kinase type 1; *BMPR2*, bone morphogenetic protein receptor type 2; *HIV*, human immunodeficiency virus.
From Simonneau G et al: Updated clinical classification of pulmonary hypertension, *J Am Coll Cardiol* 54:S43-S54, 2009.

DIFFERENTIAL DIAGNOSIS

The differential diagnosis is as listed under "Etiology."

EVALUATION

- Consists of establishing the diagnosis and etiology.
- Echocardiography with Doppler technique can provide a noninvasive but limited estimation of systolic PAP. Common findings include tricuspid regurgitation, right heart enlargement, abnormal movement of septum and, rarely, pericardial effusion. However, the diagnosis of PH cannot be established by echocardiography alone, as echocardiography can overestimate or underestimate PAP.
- ECG shows RV enlargement, strain pattern, and right axis deviation.
- Chest radiograph (Fig. E1P-117) shows enlarged central pulmonary arteries and right heart enlargement. Chest radiography is abnormal in 90% of patients at diagnosis.
- A normal chest radiograph does not rule out the diagnosis. High-resolution computed tomography (CT) (Fig. E1P-118) can assist in the evaluation for emphysema or interstitial lung disease. Ventilation-perfusion lung scan has high sensitivity for chronic thromboembolic disease. The diagnosis should be confirmed by pulmonary angiography, which has high specificity.
- Pulmonary function tests may show obstructive (airway disease) and/or restrictive disease (parenchymal disease) depending on etiology. Diffusion capacity of carbon monoxide in the lung is reduced due to pulmonary vascular destruction in PAH.
- In asymptomatic patients the severity of pulmonary arterial hypertension (PAH) disease should be evaluated in a systematic and consistent manner, using a combination of World Health Organization (WHO) functional class (FC), exercise capacity, and echocardiographic, laboratory, and hemodynamic variables to inform therapeutic decisions.
- Symptomatic patients with PAH, in the absence of contraindications, should undergo acute vasoreactivity testing using a short-acting agent at a center with experience in the performance and interpretation of vasoreactivity testing.
- Right heart catheterization is required to assess pulmonary hemodynamics, exclude shunts and left heart disease, and perform acute vasoreactivity response testing.
- Screening for the presence of PAH with Doppler echocardiography is warranted in individuals with a known predisposing genetic mutation or first-degree relative with IPAH, connective tissue diseases (especially scleroderma), congenital heart disease with left-to-right shunt, or portal hypertension undergoing evaluation for orthotopic liver transplantation.
- Determining the degree of functional impairment, as assessed by the WHO functional classification system (Classes I-IV) and the 6-min walk test (6MWT), is a useful way to monitor disease progression and assess response to treatment.

LABORATORY TESTS

- Complete blood count is usually normal in PAH but may show secondary polycythemia.
- Arterial blood gases show low PO_2 and oxygen saturation.
- Overnight oximetry and/or sleep study to rule out sleep apnea or hypopnea.
- Other blood tests: antinuclear antibody (ANA), antineutrophil cytoplasmic antibodies (ANCA), anti-Scl-70, anticentromere, ribonucleoprotein antibody levels, and rheumatoid factor (RF) to screen for underlying connective tissue disease, HIV serology, liver function tests, and antiphospholipid antibodies.
- Brain natriuretic peptide (BNP) level can provide prognostic information, with elevation in BNP level being associated with increased mortality.
- Ventilation-perfusion lung scan has high sensitivity for chronic thromboembolic PAH. The diagnosis should be confirmed by pulmonary angiography, which has high specificity.

Rx TREATMENT

- Most of the evidence in management of PAH is limited to IPAH/HPAH. There is some evidence in treatment of PAHA associated with connective tissue disease, especially scleroderma, and congenital heart disease. The recommendations for treating PAH associated with other causes are limited to case studies and expert opinions.
- There is some evidence for the use of advanced therapies for sarcoidosis-associated PH. The heterogeneity of sarcoid-associated PH complicates the interpretation.

NONPHARMACOLOGIC THERAPY

- Oxygen therapy to improve alveolar oxygen flow in both idiopathic and secondary PH. Goal oxygen saturation >90%.
- Avoidance of vigorous exercise and pregnancy.

GENERAL TREATMENT:

1. Diuretics (e.g., furosemide 40-80 mg qd) improve dyspnea by reducing preload and peripheral edema. Avoid excessive diuresis in patients who are preload dependent.
2. Digoxin 0.25 mg qd has been used in patients with IPAH with inconclusive benefits.
3. Oral anticoagulation with warfarin is recommended especially for IPAH, as per a 1984 retrospective study by Fuster et al that showed improved long-term survival. This practice is supported by the high incidence of antemortem clots found in autopsy in the small pulmonary arteries and arterioles of patients with IPAH. Recommended goal for INR is lower at 1.5 to 2.5.

CHRONIC Rx

- Acute vasoreactivity response testing should be done in all patients at the time of right heart catheterization. Epoprostenol, adenosine, or nitric oxide is generally used to assess the response. A positive response is a fall in mean PAP of >10 mm Hg to a value of <40 mm Hg, with increased or unchanged cardiac output. Fewer than 10% of patients are responders in IPAH.

- The positive responders may benefit from treatment with calcium channel blockers (diltiazem, amlodipine, or nifedipine). Verapamil is not recommended because of its negative inotropic effects. All patients should be reassessed in 6 to 8 wk to demonstrate sustained benefit from the calcium channel blocker.
- Calcium channel blockers (CCBs) should not be used empirically to treat PAH in the absence of demonstrated acute vasoreactivity.

PROSTANOIDS

- These synthetic prostacyclin analogues act as potent vasodilators of pulmonary arteries and inhibitors of platelet aggregation. Ideal for class IV patients.
  1. Epoprostenol: IV formulation with very short half-life. Requires long-term IV access with associated risks of infection and thrombosis. Rapid tachyphylaxis with dose escalation is seen. Common side effects include jaw pain, abdominal cramping, and diarrhea. Limited evidence exists for use in secondary PAH patients.
  2. Treprostinil: IV and SQ formulation with longer half-life. Main disadvantage is pain at SQ pump site (no long-term evidence for IV formulation). Treprostinil is also available as a nebulized inhaled solution.
  3. Iloprost: aerosolized formulation with short half-life requiring 6 to 8 treatments/day.
  4. Beraprost: PO formulation. Not approved in the U.S.

GUANYLATE CYCLASE STIMULATORS

These are oral agents that are useful for class II and III patients
1. Riocigulat
   - Endothelin receptor antagonists (ERAs):
     1. These oral pulmonary vasodilators require monthly liver function tests, and often the response is delayed by weeks. Thus, it is not an ideal starting therapy for WHO class IV patients. It is effective in class II and III patients.
     2. Bosentan (nonselective endothelin A and B receptor blocker): Sitaxsentan and ambrisentan (selective endothelin A receptor blockers).
   - Macitentan: Recently FDA approved. Recommended dose is 10 mg/day. Cost of one month of treatment is >$6000.
   Phosphodiesterase (PDE-5) inhibitors:
These are oral agents that act by increasing the concentration of nitric oxide. Highly effective in WHO class II patients, both in IPAH and scleroderma-associated PAH.
Sildenafil is administered as 20 mg PO tid up to 80 mg PO tid.
   - Tadalafil dose is 40 mg once daily.
   - Guanylate cyclase (sGC) stimulators: Riociguat was recently FDA approved.
   Caveats to treatment depending on WHO class of symptoms are as follows:
According to consensus definition, patients with PAH who demonstrate acute vasoreactivity should be considered candidates for a trial of therapy with an oral calcium channel blocker

(CCB), except in the case of right heart failure or other contraindications.

CCBs should not be used empirically to treat PAH in the absence of demonstrated acute vasoreactivity, as described previously.

- For treatment-naive PAH patients with WHO functional class FC II or III symptoms who are not candidates for, or who have failed CCB therapy, monotherapy should be initiated with an approved ERA, phosphodiesterase-5 (PDE5) inhibitor, or the soluble guanylate cyclase stimulator riociguat.
- For treatment-naive PAH patients with WHO functional Class FC III symptoms who have evidence of rapid progression of their disease or other markers of a poor clinical prognosis, consideration of initial treatment with a parenteral prostanoid is recommended.
- For treatment-naive PAH patients in WHO class FC IV who are unable, or do not desire, to manage parenteral prostanoid therapy, treatment with an inhaled prostanoid in combination with an ERA is recommended.
- For WHO class FC III or IV PAH patients with unacceptable clinical status despite established PAH-specific monotherapy, addition of a second class of PAH therapy to improve exercise capacity is recommended. Such patients should be evaluated at centers with expertise in the evaluation and treatment of complex patients with PAH.
- Combination therapies: considered when there is no improvement or deterioration on monotherapy.
- Bosentan + inhaled iloprost (STEP trial) showed some benefit over monotherapy.
- IV epoprostenol + oral bosentan (BREATH-2 trial) did not show much difference.
- IV epoprostenol + oral sildenafil (PACES trial) showed benefit over monotherapy.

INVASIVE RX

Lung transplantation and heart-lung transplantation are other options in patients with end-stage class IV disease.

- Atrial septostomy may be performed as a bridge to transplant. The defect can be closed at the time of transplantation.
- Extracorporeal membrane oxygenation (ECMO) is also commonly used as a bridge to transplant. Atrial septostomy is recommended for individuals with a room air SaO_2 >90% who have severe right-sided heart failure (with refractory ascites) despite maximal diuretic therapy, or who have signs of impaired systemic blood flow (such as syncope) from reduced left heart filling.
- Lung transplant recipients with IPAH had survival rates of 73% at 1 yr, 55% at 3 yr, and 45% at 5 yr.

TREATMENT OF SECONDARY PAH, APAH:

- Directed toward cause. Some situations merit mention.
- PAH with uncorrected congenital heart disease: Eisenmenger's syndrome. Medical

treatment generally ineffective. Heart-lung transplantation required in most patients. PH may persist after surgical correction of congenital heart disease, and pulmonary vasodilators can be effective therapies in this patient population.

- PAH with scleroderma: selective pulmonary vasodilators are effective.
- PAH with lung disease or hypoxia: oxygen therapy, for hypoxemia, CPAP (for OSA), control of primary disease process.
- PAH with chronic thromboembolic disease: may consider pulmonary vasodilators after anticoagulation and pulmonary thromboendarterectomy (or if thromboendarterectomy is not an option) if continued symptoms and elevation in PVR and transpulmonary gradient.
- PAH with HIV: control of viral load by antiretroviral therapy.

FOLLOW-UP

Regular follow-up at 3-mo intervals with clinical assessment: WHO class and 6MWT, 6 to 12 mo objective assessment of RV function by ECG and cardiac catheterization studies.

DISPOSITION

- The 6MWT is predictive of survival in patients with idiopathic PAH. A baseline 6MWT <250 m is associated with a 50% risk of death at 2 yr. Drop in O_2 saturation >10% during the test increases mortality risk 2.9 times over a median follow-up of 26 mo.
- A BNP level ≥350 pg/mL at baseline evaluation is associated with a 25% risk of death at 2 yr.
- WHO class II and III patients with PAH have a mean survival of 3.5 yr.
- WHO class IV patients have a mean survival of 6 mo.
- As per the REVEAL (Registry to Evaluate Early and Long-term Pulmonary Arterial Hypertension Disease Management) risk score, poor prognostic signs include:
  1. Signs of RV failure.
  2. WHO functional class III or IV.
  3. Walk a distance of <165 meters in 6-min walk test.
  4. Peak VO2 <15 mL/min/kg in cardiopulmonary testing.
  5. Elevated BNP levels >180 pg/mL.
  6. Presence of pericardial effusion.
  7. TAPSE [tricuspid annular plane systolic excursion] <2 cm on echo of right ventricle.
  8. Right atrial pressure >20 mm Hg or pulmonary vascular resistance of >32 Wood units on right heart catheterization.
  9. Increased heart rate >92 or BP <109 mm Hg.
  10. Male gender >60 years of age.
  11. Concomitant renal dysfunction with estimated glomerular filtration rate ≤30/mL/min/m.
  12. Diffusion capacity of lung for carbon monoxide (DLCO) <33%.

REFERRAL

If the diagnosis of IPAH/HPAH is suspected, a consultation with a pulmonary specialist is recommended. PHA may require disease-specific consultations. Advanced cases need to be transferred to transplant centers.

! PEARLS & CONSIDERATIONS

- The exertional dyspnea of PAH is typically described by patients as being relentlessly progressive over several months to a year, often out of proportion to, or in the absence of, underlying heart or lung disease.
- Over 20% of patients in the Registry to Evaluate Early and Long-term PAH Disease Management had symptoms for more than 2 years before PAH was recognized. Consideration of the diagnosis of PAH in the differential diagnosis of unexplained dyspnea, especially in younger individuals, is essential.
- Chest x-ray may reveal evidence of interstitial fluid or fibrosis within the lungs in cases of secondary PH. IPAH is not associated with infiltrates on chest radiograph.

COMMENTS

- RV systolic pressure (RVSP) as estimated by echocardiography is not a good indicator of the presence of PAH because RVSP increases with age and body mass index. Athletically conditioned men also have a higher resting RVSP. Thus, these measurements can be misleading.
- Abrupt development of pulmonary edema during acute vasodilator testing suggests pulmonary venoocclusive disease or pulmonary capillary hemangiomatosis and is a contraindication to long-term vasodilator treatment.
- In advanced PAH, heart rate increase is the main compensatory mechanism and reflects increased sympathetic tone. A higher heart rate at rest is an important marker of prognosis and should be assessed at frequent intervals after initiation of treatment for PAH.

FUTURE DIRECTIONS

- Serotonin receptor modulators, platelet-derived growth factor, and Rho kinase inhibitors.
- Gene analysis to identify genes that determine individual disease susceptibility and help identify targeted therapy.

EBM EVIDENCE

Available at www.expertconsult.com

SUGGESTED READINGS
Available at www.expertconsult.com

RELATED CONTENT
Pulmonary Hypertension (Patient Information)

 AUTHOR: **RABIA ARSHAD, M.D.**

BASIC INFORMATION

DEFINITION

Acute cardiogenic pulmonary edema (ACPE) is a life-threatening condition that may occur when there is elevated left ventricular (LV) filling pressure related to systolic or diastolic LV dysfunction.

SYNONYMS

CPE
Cardiogenic pulmonary edema
Acute cardiogenic pulmonary edema
ACPE
Acute heart failure [AHF] with pulmonary edema

ICD-10CM CODES

I50.1 Left ventricular failure
J68.1 Pulmonary edema due to chemicals, gases, fumes and vapors
J81.0 Acute pulmonary edema
J81.1 Chronic pulmonary edema

EPIDEMIOLOGY & DEMOGRAPHICS

- Leading cause of hospitalization (6.5 million hospital days in the United States each year).
- In-hospital mortality rate is 10% to 20%, particularly when associated with acute MI.

PHYSICAL FINDINGS & CLINICAL PRESENTATION

- Dyspnea (exertional or at rest, paroxysmal nocturnal dyspnea, orthopnea).
- Cough and wheezing.
- Diaphoresis, perioral and peripheral cyanosis.
- Pink, frothy sputum.
- Moist, bilateral pulmonary rales are the most common findings and noted in up to 87% of the patients.
- Increased pulmonary second sound, S_3 gallon S3 gallop is present in up to one-third of the patients and correlates well with the degree of LV systolic dysfunction and BNP levels.
- Hypertension (unless in cardiogenic shock and hypotensive).
- Tachycardia.
- Bulging neck veins with elevated jugular venous pressure and positive hepatojugular reflex.
- Altered mental status or drowsiness due to hypoperfusion.
- Peripheral edema.
- Among these, S3 gallop and elevated JVP are the most specific signs for acute decompensated heart failure causing acute pulmonary edema.

ETIOLOGY

Increased pulmonary capillary pressure attributable to:

- Acute myocardial infarction.
- Exacerbation of chronic congestive heart failure due to arrhythmia, myocardial ischemia, poor dietary or medical compliance, use of concomitant nonsteroidal antiinflammatory drugs, calcium antagonists such as verapamil and diltiazem, excessive alcohol consumption, anemia, or inadequately treated hypertension.
- Valvular regurgitation (e.g., acute mitral regurgitation due to papillary muscle rupture).
- Ventricular septal defect.
- Severe myocardial ischemia causes left ventricular diastolic dysfunction prior to causing systolic dysfunction.
- Mitral stenosis, particularly with tachycardia.
- Bilateral renal artery stenosis.
- Postpartum cardiomyopathy.
- Other: cardiac tamponade, endocarditis, myocarditis, arrhythmias, hypertensive crisis, endocrine abnormalities such as thyrotoxicosis.

DIAGNOSIS

DIFFERENTIAL DIAGNOSIS

- Noncardiogenic pulmonary edema (see Fig. E1P-119).
- Viral pneumonitis and other pulmonary infections.
- Pulmonary embolism.
- Exacerbation of asthma.
- Exacerbation of chronic obstructive pulmonary disease.
- Sarcoidosis.
- Pulmonary fibrosis.
- Lymphangitic carcinomatosis.

LABORATORY TESTS

- Arterial blood gases (ABGs): respiratory and metabolic acidosis, decreased Pa_{O_2}, increased Pa_{CO_2}, low pH. (NOTE: The patient may initially show respiratory alkalosis as a result of hyperventilation in attempts to maintain Pa_{O_2}.)
- Measurement of plasma brain natriuretic peptide (elevated). The Breathing Not Properly [BNP] Multinational Study demonstrated that elevated BNP levels are able to distinguish dyspnea caused by heart failure from those caused by pulmonary disease. The BASEL study with nt-pro-BNP demonstrated similar results in patients presenting with acute dyspnea.
- Cardiac biomarkers: troponin I levels to evaluate for possible acute myocardial infarction.
- Basic chemistries: hyponatremia is common in chronic heart failure; evaluate renal function.

IMAGING STUDIES

- ECG:
  1. May have evidence of ischemia, arrhythmias, or LV hypertrophy (often seen in diastolic dysfunction).
- Chest x-ray (Fig. 1P-120):
  1. Bilateral interstitial and alveolar infiltrates is most common finding. Signs of chronic congestive heart failure: pulmonary congestion with Kerley B lines; fluffy perihilar infiltrates seen in the early stages.
  2. Pleural effusions.
  3. Enlarged cardiac silhouette.
- Echocardiogram:
  1. Useful to evaluate valvular abnormalities, diastolic versus systolic dysfunction.
  2. Can help differentiate cardiogenic versus noncardiogenic pulmonary edema by estimating pulmonary capillary wedge pressure using E/E' ratio, where E = early diastolic transmitral blood flow velocity and E' = early diastolic mitral annular tissue velocity.
- Right heart catheterization (RHC): May be used in selected patients such as those in shock or unclear hemodynamics. RHC in pulmonary edema will show increased pulmonary artery diastolic pressure and pulmonary capillary wedge pressure (PCWP) generally ≥25 mm Hg; low mixed venous oxyhemoglobin saturation. In the ESCAPE trial, use of RHC did not significantly affect in-hospital or 6 mo mortality or days of hospitalization compared with clinical assessment alone and was related to more adverse events.

TREATMENT

ACUTE GENERAL Rx

All the following steps can be performed concomitantly:

- 100% oxygen by face mask. Noninvasive ventilation (continuous positive airway pressure [CPAP]) or bilevel noninvasive positive-pressure ventilation [NPPV]) reduces dyspnea and corrects metabolic abnormalities more rapidly than does standard oxygen therapy, and may reduce the need for endotracheal intubation. Both CPAP and bilevel NPPV systems can improve oxygenation and lower carbon dioxide. Monitor ABGs; if marked hypoxemia or severe respiratory acidosis, intubate the patient and place on a mechanical ventilator. Positive pressure ventilation (invasive or noninvasive) decreases preload and afterload and reduces the work of breathing, while positive end expiratory pressure improves oxygenation.
- Pharmacologic preload reducers:
  1. Furosemide: 1 mg/kg IV bolus (typically 40-100 mg) to rapidly establish diuresis and decrease venous return through its venodilator action; may double the dose in 30 min if no effect. As per the DOSE trial (NEJM March 3, 2011), among patients with acute decompensated heart failure, there were no significant differences in patient global assessment of symptoms or in the change in renal function when diuretic therapy was administered by bolus as compared with continuous infusion or at a high dose as compared with a low dose
  2. Nitrates: particularly useful if the patient has concomitant chest pain or is hypertensive.
     a. Nitroglycerin: 150 to 600 mcg SL or nitroglycerin spray may be given immediately on arrival and repeated multiple times if the patient remains symptomatic and blood pressure remains stable.
     b. 2% nitroglycerin ointment: 1 to 3 inches out of the tube applied continuously; absorption may be erratic.
     c. IV nitroglycerin: 100 mg in 500 mL of D_5W solution; start at 6 mcg/min (2 mL/hr).

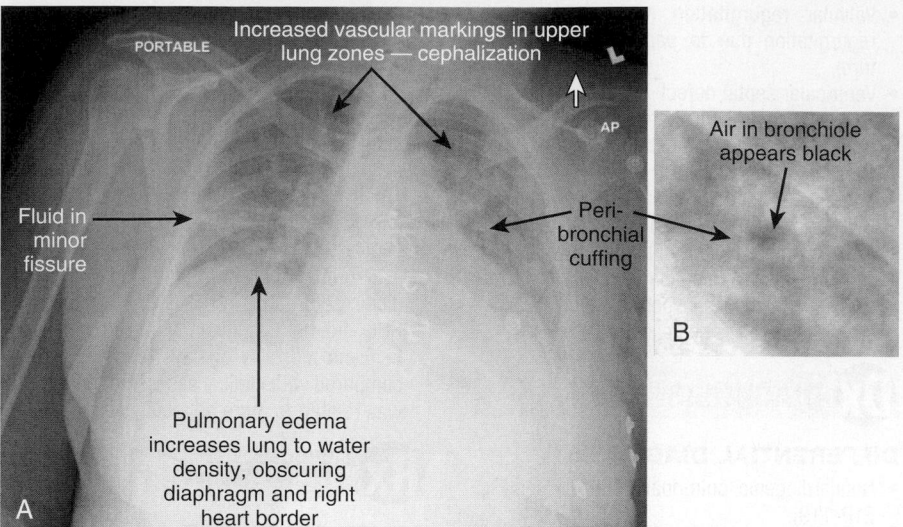

FIGURE 1P-120 **Pulmonary edema. A,** Anterior-posterior chest x-ray. **B,** Close-up from **A.** This 53-year-old female with end-stage renal disease missed dialysis and presented to the emergency department. Her examination demonstrated bilateral rales. Her x-ray shows mild cardiomegaly, bilateral interstitial opacities, and cephalization of the pulmonary vascular markings. The minor fissure appears thickened. These findings are consistent with pulmonary edema. In addition, peribronchial cuffing is present. As discussed elsewhere, this is a nonspecific thickening of the bronchial wall that can occur from edema in the setting of heart failure, asthma, viral illness, or even infections such as pertussis. The thickened wall appears white, whereas the air-filled bronchiole appears black and has a circular short-axis cross section. (From Broder JS: *Diagnostic imaging for the emergency physician,* Philadelphia, 2011, Saunders.)

3. Morphine: 2 to 4 mg IV, SC, or IM; may repeat q15min prn. It decreases venous return, anxiety, and systemic vascular resistance (naloxone should be available at bedside to reverse the effects of morphine if respiratory depression occurs). However, potential adverse effects of morphine administration may outweigh these physiologic benefits, and the role of morphine in treatment of ACPE has recently been questioned.
- Fluid and sodium restriction: Aggressive restriction of fluids (<800 cc/day) and salt (<800 mg/day) did not improve outcomes in a randomized trial and may be unnecessary.[1]
- Vasodilator therapy:
  1. Angiotensin-converting enzyme (ACE) inhibitors: captopril 25 mg PO tablet can be used for SL administration (placing a drop or two of water on the tablet and placing it under the tongue helps dissolve it); onset of action is <10 min, peak effect can be reached in 30 min. ACE inhibitors can also be given IV (e.g., enalapril at 1 mg IV given q2h prn). ACE-I is contraindicated in bilateral renal artery stenosis.

  2. Nitroprusside: useful for afterload reduction in hypertensive patients with decreased cardiac index (CI).
     a. Increases the CI and decreases LV filling pressure.
     b. Nitroprusside use in patients with acute myocardial infarction is controversial because it may increase ischemia by decreasing blood flow to the myocardium.
  3. Nesiritide (recombinant human BNP) causes potent vasodilation in the venous and arterial vessels, including coronary vasculature, produces significant reduction in venous and ventricular filling pressures, and mildly increases cardiac output. However, its high cost and potential safety concerns, including increased mortality, have limited its use.
  4. Seralaxin, an experimental drug, which is a recombinant form of relaxin-2, increases production of NO and binds to endothelial B receptor on endothelial cells causing vasodilation. It can be used effectively for pulmonary edema from both systolic and diastolic heart failure.[2]

- Inotropes:
  1. Dopamine and dobutamine: parenteral inotropic agent of choice in severe cases of cardiogenic pulmonary edema. It can be administered at a dosage of 2.5 to 10 mcg/kg/min IV. However, neither low-dose dopamine nor nesiritide improved diuresis or renal function when added to standard diuretics in ROSE-AHF trial.[3]
  2. IV phosphodiesterase inhibitors (amrinone, milrinone, and enoximone [not available in U.S.]) may be useful in refractory cases. Milrinone may be associated with increased hypotension and new atrial arrhythmias with increased mortality in patients with ischemia HF and should be used with caution.
- Levosimendan is a novel agent that increases myocardial contractility and produces peripheral vasodilation through calcium sensitization. In clinical trials such as REVIVE-II and SURVIVE, levosimendan has been shown to significantly increase cardiac output, reduce PCWP and afterload, and improve dyspnea compared with standard care. It has, however, been associated with increased atrial fibrillation and hypotension.
- Potential future therapies: Istaroxime, natriuretic peptides, adenosine antagonists, vasopressin antagonists, endothelin antagonists.
- Mechanical support:
  1. Intra-arterial balloon pump (IABP): decreases afterload
  2. Ultrafiltration/aquapheresis

(!) **PEARLS & CONSIDERATIONS**

COMMENTS

Accumulated evidence still favors the use of noninvasive ventilation, especially CPAP, in patients with ACPE, especially as this therapy reduces dyspnea and helps correct metabolic abnormalities more rapidly than standard oxygen therapy. The role of morphine in the treatment of ACPE has come into question. Also refer to section on Heart Failure.

(EBM) **EVIDENCE**

Available at www.expertconsult.com

SUGGESTED READINGS

Available at www.expertconsult.com

AUTHORS: **SUBASIT ACHARJI, M.D.,** and **MARC PAUL WAASE, M.D., PH.D.**

[1]Aliti GB, Rabelo ER, Clausell N, et al: Aggressive fluid and sodium restriction in acute decompensated heart failure: a randomized clinical trial. *JAMA* 173(12): 1058-1064, 2013.

[2]Filippatos G, Terrlink JR, Farmakis D, et al: Serelaxin in acute heart failure patients with preserved left ventricular ejection fraction: results from the RELAX-AHF trial. *Eur Heart J* 35(16):1041-1050, 2014.

[3]Chen HH, Anstrom KJ, Givertz MM: Low-dose dopamine or low-dose nesiritide in acute heart failure with renal dysfunction: the ROSE acute heart failure randomized trial. *JAMA* 310(23):2533-2543. 2013.

Diseases
and Disorders

I

 **BASIC INFORMATION**

DEFINITION

Pulmonary embolism (PE) refers to the lodging of a thrombus or other embolic material from a distant site in the pulmonary circulation. A classification of acute pulmonary embolism is described in Table 1P-59.

SYNONYMS

Pulmonary thromboembolism
PE

ICD-10CM CODES

I26	Pulmonary embolism
I26.01	Septic pulmonary embolism with acute cor pulmonale
I26.09	Other pulmonary embolism with acute cor pulmonale
I26.90	Septic pulmonary embolism without acute cor pulmonale
I26.99	Other pulmonary embolism without acute cor pulmonale
I27.82	Chronic pulmonary embolism
Z86.711	Personal history of pulmonary embolism

EPIDEMIOLOGY & DEMOGRAPHICS

- 650,000 cases of PE occur in the United States each year (increased incidence in women and with advanced age); annually, as many as 300,000 people in the United States die from acute PE, and the diagnosis is often not made until after autopsy. The incidence of PE is increasing with the increasing use of spiral CT scans, with a lower severity of illness and lower mortality, suggesting the increase is caused by earlier diagnosis.
- More than 90% of pulmonary emboli originate in the deep venous system of the lower extremities.
- Pulmonary thromboembolism is associated with >200,000 hospitalizations and nearly 30,000 deaths each yr in the United States.
- 8% to 10% of victims of PE die within the first hr.

PHYSICAL FINDINGS & CLINICAL PRESENTATION

- Most common symptom: dyspnea (82%-85%).
- Tachypnea (30%-60%).

- Cough (30%-40%)
- Wheezing (20%)
- Chest pain: may be nonpleuritic or pleuritic (infarction) (40%-49%).
- Syncope (massive PE) (10%-14%).
- Fever, diaphoresis, apprehension.
- Hemoptysis (2%).
- Evidence of DVT may be present (e.g., swelling and tenderness of extremities).
- Cardiac examination may reveal: tachycardia (23%), increased pulmonic component of S2, murmur of tricuspid insufficiency, right ventricular heave, right-sided S3.
- Pulmonary examination: may demonstrate rales, localized wheezing, friction rub.

ETIOLOGY

- Thrombus, fat, or other foreign material
- Risk factors for PE:
  1. Prolonged immobilization, reduced mobility.
  2. Postoperative state, major surgery.
  3. Trauma to lower extremities, immobilizer, or cast.
  4. Estrogen-containing birth control pills, hormone replacement therapy.
  5. Prior history of DVT or PE.
  6. CHF.
  7. Pregnancy and early puerperium.
  8. Visceral cancer (lung, pancreas, alimentary and genitourinary tracts).
  9. Spinal cord injury.
  10. Advanced age.
  11. Obesity.
  12. Hematologic disease (e.g., factor V Leiden mutation, antithrombin III deficiency, protein C deficiency, protein S deficiency, lupus anticoagulant, polycythemia vera, dysfibrinogenemia, paroxysmal nocturnal hemoglobinuria, acquired protein C resistance without factor V Leiden, G20210A prothrombin mutation).
  13. COPD, diabetes mellitus, acute medical illness.
  14. Prolonged air travel.
  15. Central venous catheterization.
  16. Autoimmune diseases (SLE, IBD, RA).

Dx DIAGNOSIS

DIFFERENTIAL DIAGNOSIS

- Myocardial infarction.
- Pericarditis.

- Pneumonia.
- Pneumothorax.
- Chest wall pain.
- GI abnormalities (e.g., peptic ulcer, esophageal rupture, gastritis.
- CHF
- Pleuritis.
- Anxiety disorder with hyperventilation.
- Pericardial tamponade.
- Dissection of aorta.
- Asthma.

WORKUP

- Clinical assessment alone is insufficient to diagnose or rule out PE. It is also important to remember that no single noninvasive test has both high sensitivity and high specificity for PE. Consequently, in addition to clinical assessment, most patients require an imaging test to diagnose PE. Figs. 1P-121 and 1P-122 are diagnostic algorithms for suspected PE. The Wells prediction rules can be used to estimate the probability of PE. Each of the following findings is assigned a score:
  1. Clinical signs/symptoms of deep vein thrombosis (score = 3.0).
  2. No alternate diagnosis as likely or more likely than PE (score = 3.0).
  3. Heart rate >100/min (score = 1.5).
  4. Immobilization or surgery in last 4 weeks (score = 1.5).
  5. Previous history of DVT or PE (score = 1.5).
  6. Hemoptysis (score = 1.0).
  7. Cancer actively treated within last 6 months (score = 1.0).
- The probability of PE is high if total score is >6, moderate if 2-6; and low if <2.
- The modified Wells score divides PE as likely (>4 points) or unlikely (<4 points).
- A low clinical probability of PE in association with a normal plasma D-dimer measurement essentially rules out PE, and further imaging is not needed. If clinical probability is intermediate or high, and/or the D-dimer measurement is abnormal, further workup with imaging is needed.
- CT pulmonary angiography (CTPA) (see Fig. 1P-123) is an excellent diagnostic modality (83% sensitivity and 96% specificity).
- V/Q scan is reserved for patients with clinically significant contrast allergies or renal insufficiency, or when CTPA is not available.
- Pulmonary angiogram (gold standard) can confirm the diagnosis, but is rarely used.
- Serial compressive duplex ultrasonography of lower extremities can be used in patients with "low-probability" lung scan and high clinical suspicion (see "Imaging Studies"). It is useful if positive; negative results do not exclude PE.

LABORATORY TESTS

- ABGs may reveal hypoxemia and respiratory alkalosis (decreased PaO_2 and $PaCO_2$ and increased pH); normal results do not rule out PE.
- Alveolar-arteriolar (A-a) oxygen gradient, a measure of the difference in oxygen concentration between alveoli and arterial blood,

---

TABLE 1P-59 Classification of Acute Pulmonary Embolism

Classification	Presentation	Therapy
Massive PE	Systolic blood pressure <90 mm Hg or poor tissue perfusion or multisystem organ failure plus right or left main pulmonary artery thrombus or "high clot burden"	Thrombolysis or embolectomy or inferior vena caval filter plus anticoagulation
Submassive PE	Hemodynamically stable but moderate or severe right ventricular dysfunction or enlargement	Addition of thrombolysis, embolectomy, or filter remains controversial
Small to moderate PE	Normal hemodynamics and normal right ventricular size and function	Anticoagulation

From Bonow RO et al: *Heart disease*, ed 9, Philadelphia, 2012 ,Saunders.

BASIC INFORMATION

DEFINITION

The quadrilateral space is formed by the long head of the triceps brachii muscle medially, the teres minor muscle superiorly, the teres major inferiorly, and the medial aspect of the humerus laterally (Fig. 1Q-2). The axillary nerve innervates the teres minor and deltoid muscles and the posterolateral cutaneous region of the shoulder and upper arm.

The quadrilateral space syndrome (QSS) is a rare neurovascular syndrome characterized by shoulder pain, paresthesias, and point tenderness in lateral aspect of quadrilateral space due to compression or mechanical injury of the axillary nerve in the quadrilateral space.

SYNONYM(S)

QSS
Lateral axillary hiatus syndrome
nQSS (neurogenic quadrilateral space syndrome)
vQSS (vascular quadrilateral space syndrome)

ICD-10CM CODES
Code varies with specific etiology of syndrome

EPIDEMIOLOGY & DEMOGRAPHICS

INCIDENCE: Rare in general population, more common in participants in sports that involve abduction and external rotation of upper extremities (baseball, volleyball, swimming, yoga) and in professional window cleaners

DOMINANT SEX: 7:1 male:female ratio, most likely due to traditional sex distribution in overhead or "throwing" athletics

RISK FACTORS

Professional athletes, window cleaners.
Physical Findings & Clinical Presentation
- Diffuse shoulder pain
- Diminished abduction and posterior
- Nondermatomal neuropathic pain
- Weakness and numbness in the shoulder, most commonly in posterior region
- Vascular manifestations may be present (thrombosis, digital or hand ischemia, decreased pulses, pallor)

ETIOLOGY

- Repetitive mechanical injury to the posterior circumflex humeral artery
- Proximal humeral head fractures and callus formations
- Anterior shoulder dislocation resulting in traction and compression
- Fibrous bands (posttraumatic) causing fixed structural impaction of the quadrilateral space
- Soft tissue and osseous tumors, paralabral cysts

DIAGNOSIS

DIFFERENTIAL DIAGNOSIS

- Anterior dislocation
- Proximal humeral fracture
- Brachial neuritis

- Parsonage-Turner syndrome
- Thrombosis or aneurysmal formation in more proximal branches of axillary artery

WORKUP

- Computed tomographic angiography (CTA)
- Digital subtraction angiography (DSA)
- Magnetic resonance angiography (MRA)
- Ultrasound (US)
- Electromyography (EMG): indicated primarily to rule out alternative diagnoses

LABORATORY TESTS

- None indicated

IMAGING STUDIES

- CTA, DSA, MRA: Fixed posterior circumflex humeral artery (PCHA) occlusion due to thrombosis with or without distal embolization
- MRI: Denervation edema (acute, increased T2 and STIR signal and size) or fatty atrophy (chronic) of the teres minor and/or deltoid muscle

TREATMENT

NONPHARMACOLOGIC THERAPY

- Physical therapy
- Limitation of inciting activities
- Surgical decompression (see the following)

ACUTE GENERAL Rx

- Nonsteroidal antiinflammatory drugs (NSAIDs)
- Neurolysis and excision of existing fibrous bands or space occupying lesions
- If fixed PCHA occlusion due to thrombosis: PCHA ligation with or without thrombolysis or surgical thromboembolectomy

CHRONIC Rx

- Postoperative PT
- Anticoagulation for 3 months in patients with PCHA thrombosis

COMPLEMENTARY & ALTERNATIVE MEDICINE

- None

DISPOSITION

- In most cases, return to full activity after several weeks

REFERRAL

- Vascular surgery, orthopedics, neurology

SUGGESTED READINGS
Available at www.expertconsult.com

AUTHOR: **FRED F. FERRI, M.D.**

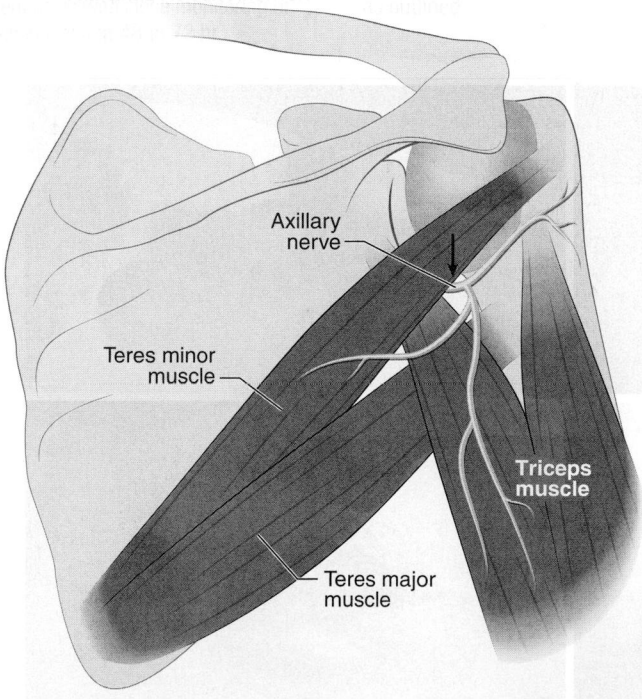
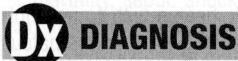

FIGURE 1Q-2 Drawing of the quadrilateral space. View from the posterior aspect of the scapula demonstrating the four margins of the space: the teres minor muscle superiorly (*Tm*), the teres major muscle inferiorly (*TM*), the medial aspect of the humerus laterally, and the triceps muscle medially (*TrM*). Note the axillary nerve passing though the quadrilateral space (*arrow*) and providing branches to the teres minor, triceps, and deltoid muscles. (From Pope TL, Bloem HL, Beltran J, Morrison WB, Wilson DJ: *Musculoskeletal imaging*, ed 2, Philadelphia, 2014, Saunders.)

BASIC INFORMATION

DEFINITION

Ramsay Hunt syndrome is a localized herpes zoster infection involving the seventh nerve and geniculate ganglia, resulting in hearing loss, vertigo, and facial nerve palsy.

SYNONYMS

Herpes zoster oticus
Geniculate herpes
Herpetic geniculate ganglionitis

ICD-10CM CODES
B02.21 Postherpetic geniculate ganglionitis

EPIDEMIOLOGY & DEMOGRAPHICS

PREDOMINANT SEX: Equal sex distribution
PREDOMINANT AGE:
- Increasingly common with advancing age
- Rare in childhood

PHYSICAL FINDINGS & CLINICAL PRESENTATION

- Characteristic vesicles:
  1. On pinna
  2. In external auditory canal (Fig. 1R-2)
  3. In distribution of the facial nerve and, occasionally, adjacent cranial nerves
- Facial paralysis on the involved side
- Auditory symptoms include mild to severe tinnitus, deafness, vertigo, and nystagmus.

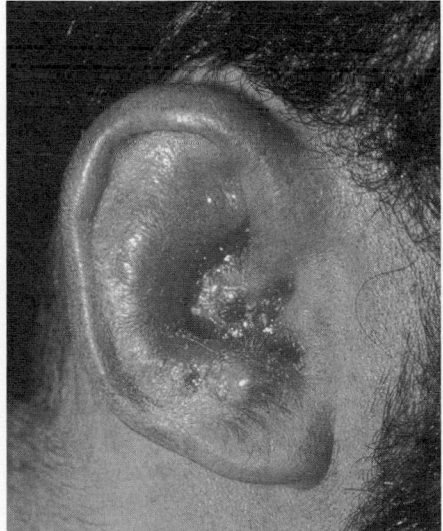

FIGURE 1R-2 Herpes zoster of the geniculate ganglion resulting in vesicles on the ear (as shown here) and tympanic membrane occurs in Ramsay Hunt syndrome. Both seventh and eighth cranial nerve functions may be affected. (From White GM, Cox NH [eds]: *Diseases of the skin: color atlas and text,* ed 2, St Louis, 2006, Mosby.)

ETIOLOGY

- Reactivation of dormant infection with varicella-zoster virus after primary varicella
- Herpetic inflammation of the geniculate ganglion is thought to be the cause of this syndrome.

DIAGNOSIS

- Usually made by recognition of the clinical features detailed previously
- Viral culture and/or microscopic examination of specimens taken from active vesicles

DIFFERENTIAL DIAGNOSIS

- Herpes simplex
- External otitis
- Impetigo
- Enteroviral infection
- Guillain-Barre syndrome
- Bell's palsy of other etiologies, such as Lyme Disease
- Acoustic neuroma (before appearance of skin lesions)
  The differential diagnosis of headache and facial pain is described in Section II.

WORKUP

If the diagnosis is in doubt, confirm varicella-zoster virus infection.

LABORATORY TESTS

- Generally not necessary
- Viral culture of specimens of vesicular fluid and scrapings of the vesicle base
- Tzanck preparation, which may reveal multinucleated giant cells
- Direct immunofluorescent staining of scrapings

IMAGING STUDIES

MRI may demonstrate enhancement of the facial and vestibulocochlear nerves before appearance of vesicles.

TREATMENT

ACUTE GENERAL Rx

- Use of corticosteroids is controversial.
- Acyclovir (800 mg PO five times qd for 10 days), famciclovir (500 mg tid for 7 days), or valacyclovir (1 g q8h for 7 days) may hasten healing.
- Use of prednisone (60 mg PO qd for 7 days or on a tapering regimen, 40 mg PO for 2 days, 30 mg for 7 days, followed by tapering course) is recommended by some authors but its use remains controversial.
- Analgesics should be used as indicated.

CHRONIC Rx

- Duloxetine and amitriptyline are effective in postherpetic pain.

- Other agents for postherpetic pain include gabapentin and pregabalin.
- Narcotic analgesics may occasionally be necessary.

DISPOSITION

Recurrences are unusual.

REFERRAL

To otolaryngologist: patients with persistent facial paralysis for potential surgical decompression of the facial nerve

PEARLS & CONSIDERATIONS

COMMENTS

Immunodeficiency states, particularly HIV infection, should be considered in:
- Younger patients
- Severe cases
- Patients with a history of specific risk behavior

SUGGESTED READINGS

Available at www.expertconsult.com

RELATED CONTENT

Ramsay Hunt Syndrome (Patient Information)

AUTHOR: **GLENN G. FORT, M.D., M.P.H.**

 **BASIC INFORMATION**

DEFINITION

Raynaud's phenomenon (RP) is a vasospastic disorder that causes an exaggerated response to cold temperatures and/or emotional stress, resulting in episodic digital ischemia. It presents as a cold-induced, symmetric, sharply demarcated white or blue discoloration of the distal fingers or toes, followed by erythema at a variable time after rewarming.

SYNONYMS

Primary Raynaud's phenomenon or Raynaud's disease
Secondary Raynaud's phenomenon

ICD-10CM CODES
I73.0   Raynaud's syndrome
I73.00 Raynaud's syndrome without gangrene
I73.01 Raynaud's syndrome with gangrene

EPIDEMIOLOGY & DEMOGRAPHICS

- RP is classified clinically into primary or secondary forms and affects approximately 3% to 5% of the general population, 15% of children younger than 12 yr, and less than 1% of adults older than 60 yr.
- Occurs more commonly in colder climates.
- Primary RP usually occurs between the ages of 12 and 25 yr.
- It is more likely to affect women than men (4:1).
- 5% to 15% of patients with primary Raynaud's phenomenon develop a secondary cause later in the course of the disease (mostly a connective tissue disorder).
- Secondary RP tends to begin after age 35 to 40 yr.
- Secondary RP occurs in more than 90% of patients with scleroderma and in approximately 30% of patients with systemic lupus erythematosus or Sjögren's syndrome.

PHYSICAL FINDINGS & CLINICAL PRESENTATION

- The typical manifestation of RP is the biphasic color response of the digits to cold exposure and rewarming, which may or may not be accompanied by pain. RP most often affects the hand (Fig. 1R-3).
  1. White (pallor) or blue (cyanotic) discoloration of the digit(s) resulting from vasospasm on cold or vibration exposure.
  2. Red (rubor) with or without pain and paresthesia when vasospasm resolves and blood returns to the digit.
- Color changes can sometimes be induced by placing the hand in an ice bath, although this is not recommended as a diagnostic maneuver because responses may be inconsistent even in patients with definite RP.
- Color changes are well delineated, symmetric, and usually bilateral, involving the fingers and toes. The index, middle, and ring fingers are commonly involved and the thumb infre-

quently; however, if the thumb is involved, that suggests secondary causes of RP.
- Fingertips are most often involved, but feet, ears, nose, tongue, and nipples can also be affected.
- Patients with RP may exhibit a violaceous or reticular pattern of skin of arms and legs, sometimes with regular, unbroken circles (livedo reticularis).
- Duration of attacks can range from seconds to hours and averages 15 to 20 min.
- Chronic skin changes resulting from repeated attacks may include skin thickening and brittle nails. Ulcerations and, rarely, gangrene may occur.
- Physical examination should also include examination for symptoms associated with autoimmune disease, such as fever, rash, arthritis, dry eyes, dry mouth, myalgias, or cardiopulmonary abnormalities.

ETIOLOGY

- Primary RP can also be called idiopathic Raynaud's phenomenon, primary Raynaud's syndrome, or Raynaud's disease. It occurs in the absence of any associated disease.
- With primary RP, the possibility that another first-degree family member is affected is reported as approximately 25%.
- Secondary RP is associated with an underlying pathologic condition or disorder, use of certain drugs, or related occupation. Secondary RP is associated with:
  1. CREST syndrome (calcinosis, RP, esophageal involvement, sclerodactyly, and telangiectasia)
  2. Scleroderma, Sjögren's syndrome, mixed connective tissue disease, polymyositis, and dermatomyositis
  3. Primary pulmonary hypertension
  4. Systemic lupus erythematosus, arteritis
  5. Rheumatoid arthritis
  6. Thromboangiitis obliterans (Buerger's disease)
  7. Drugs (beta-blockers, ergotamine, methysergide, vinblastine, bleomycin, oral contraceptives, nicotine, clonidine, cocaine, caffeine, vinyl chloride, tegafur, interferon alfa, interferon beta)
  8. Hematologic disorders (polycythemia, cryoglobulinemia, cold agglutinins, paraproteinemia, cryofibrinogenemia)

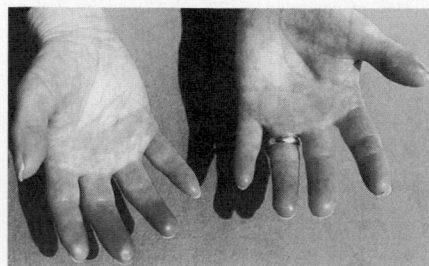

FIGURE 1R-3 Raynaud's phenomenon. Sharply demarcated cyanosis of the fingers with proximal venular congestion (livedo reticularis) is seen. (From Klippel J et al [eds]: *Primary care rheumatology*, London, 1999, Mosby.)

9. Carpal tunnel syndrome
10. Use of tools that vibrate
11. Endocrine disorders (hypothyroidism, carcinoid syndrome, pheochromocytoma, metabolic syndrome)
12. Estrogen replacement therapy without progesterone
13. Hypercoagulable states, protein C, protein S, antithrombin III deficiency, factor V Leiden deficiency, and antiphospholipid syndrome
14. Poliomyelitis is a rare cause
15. Primary biliary cirrhosis
16. Vasospastic disorders (migraines, Prinzmetal angina)
17. Malignancies (angiocentric lymphoma, ovarian cancer)

Dx **DIAGNOSIS**

Clinical criteria:
- Definite RP: repeated episodes of biphasic color change on cold exposure
- Possible RP: Uniphasic color changes plus numbness or paresthesia on cold exposure
- No RP: No color change on cold exposure
The suggested criteria for primary RP are:
- Symmetric attacks
- Absence of tissue necrosis, ulceration, gangrene, or peripheral vascular disease
- Absence of a secondary cause on the basis of a patient's history and general physical examination
- Negative nail-fold capillary examination
- Negative test for antinuclear antibody (ANA)
- Normal erythrocyte sedimentation rate (ESR)
Secondary RP is suggested by the following findings:
- Onset of symptoms after age 30 yr
- Male gender
- Episodes that are painful, asymmetric, or associated with ischemic skin lesions
- Clinical features suggestive of a connective-tissue disease
- Elevated specific autoantibody tests and ESR
- Evidence of microvascular disease on microscopy of nail-fold capillaries

DIFFERENTIAL DIAGNOSIS

- Neurogenic thoracic outlet syndrome or carpal tunnel syndrome
- Frostbite or cold weather injury
- Medication reaction (ergotamine, chemotherapeutic agents)
- Atherosclerosis, thromboembolic disease
- Buerger's disease, embolic disease
- Acrocyanosis
- Livedo reticularis
- Injury from repetitive motion

WORKUP

- Fig. 1R-4 describes an approach to diagnosis of Raynaud's phenomenon. Once the diagnosis of RP is established, differentiating primary from secondary is helpful in treatment and prognosis.
- Patients who are younger when their symptoms occur, have a normal history and physical examination and normal nail-fold

Ask the following screening questions:
1. Are your fingers unusually sensitive to cold?
2. Do your fingers change color when they are exposed to cold temperature?
3. Do they turn white, blue, or both?

The diagnosis of Raynaud's phenomenon is confirmed by a positive response to all three questions

The diagnosis of Raynaud's phenomenon is excluded if the response to questions 2 and 3 is negative

Exclude potential causative or aggravating factors:
- **Occupational and environmental factors**
  Polyvinyl chloride, frostbite, hand-arm vibration, and hypothenar hammer syndrome
- **Drugs**
  Chemotherapeutic agents, interferon, estrogen, nicotine, narcotics, sympathomimetic agents, ergotamines, β-blockers (nonselective), clonidine
- **Neuropathy**
  Carpal tunnel syndrome

History of single-digit asymmetric attacks, absent peripheral pulses, asymmetry of blood pressure, or evidence of critical ischemia: patients should undergo arterial Doppler ultrasonography, MRI/MRA, or angiography.

Abnormal findings indicate presence of obstructive vascular disease:
- **Atherosclerosis**
- **Thromboangiitis obliterans**
- **Embolic disease**
- **Thoracic outlet syndrome**
- **Vasculitis**
- **Kimura's disease**

Symptoms or signs suggestive of systemic disease (myalgias, arthralgias, fever, weakness, weight loss, rash, arthritis, sicca syndrome, or symptoms of heart or lung disease) with or without abnormal nail-fold capillaries: patients should undergo the following studies:
- Complete blood count
- General blood chemical analyses
- Urinalysis
- Test for antinuclear antibodies
- Test for rheumatoid factor
- Test for disease-specific autoantibodies
- C3 and C4 complement levels

Patients with positive results have rheumatic disease:
- **Scleroderma**
- **Systemic lupus erythematosus**
- **Mixed connective tissue disease**
- **Dermatomyositis**
- **Polymyositis**
- **Sjögren's syndrome**
- **Vasculitis**
- **Antiphospholipid syndrome**
- **Undifferentiated CTD**

Normal medical history and physical examination (no digital lesions or gangrene, normal nail-fold capillaries): patients do not need to undergo specialized studies and can be considered to have **primary Raynaud's phenomenon**

Patients with negative results have **primary Raynaud's phenomenon**

Patients with negative results should undergo the following:
- Thyroid-function test
- Serum protein electrophoresis
- Test for cryoglobulins and cryofibrinogen

Patients with positive results have other systemic diseases:
- **Hypothyroidism**
- **Cancer**
- **Cold agglutinin syndrome**
- **POEMS syndrome**
- **Cryoglobulinemia**
- **Cryofibrinogenemia**
- **Hyperviscosity syndrome**

FIGURE 1R-4 Approach to diagnosis of Raynaud's phenomenon. *CTD,* Connective tissue disease; *MRA,* magnetic resonance angiography; *MRI,* magnetic resonance imaging; *POEMS,* polyneuropathy, organomegaly, endocrinopathy, monoclonal gammopathy, and skin changes. (From Firestein GS et al [eds]: *Kelly's textbook of rheumatology,* ed 9, Philadelphia, 2013, Saunders.)

capillaries, and have no history of digital Ischemic lesions can be considered as having primary RP. These patients can be monitored clinically without any further testing.
- If a secondary cause of RP is suspected, appropriate laboratory testing is recommended (see "Laboratory Tests"). Secondary RP has associated abnormal nail-fold microscopy.

LABORATORY TESTS
- CBC, serum electrolytes, blood urea nitrogen, creatinine, ESR, ANAs, VDRL antibody test, rheumatoid factor, and urinalysis should be included in the initial evaluation.
- If the history, physical examination, and initial laboratory tests suggest a possible secondary cause, specific serologic testing (e.g., anticentromere antibodies, anti-Scl 70, cryoglobulins, complement testing, and serum protein electrophoresis) may be indicated.
- Noninvasive vascular testing includes finger systolic blood pressures, segmental blood pressure measurements, cold recovery time (measure vasoconstrictor and vasodilator responses of finger to cold), fingertip thermography, and laser Doppler with thermal challenge (measures relative change in skin blood flow with ambient warming).

IMAGING STUDIES
- The diagnosis of RP should not be made on the basis of laboratory tests, and imaging studies should not replace a good history and physical examination.
- Duplex ultrasound can image the palmar arch and digital arteries for patency.
- Magnetic resonance angiography is useful for imaging larger arteries.
- Contrast angiography is the gold standard for arterial imaging.
- Nail-fold capillary microscopy can differentiate primary from secondary RP.
- Videomicroscopy and thermography are also useful for diagnosis of RP.

Rx TREATMENT

NONPHARMACOLOGIC THERAPY
- Avoid drugs that may precipitate RP (see "Etiology").
- Avoid cold exposure and sudden temperature shifts. Use warm gloves, hats, and garments during the winter months or before going into cold environments (e.g., air-conditioned rooms).
- Avoid stressful situations, and use relaxation techniques in preventing RP attacks.

ACUTE GENERAL Rx
- Acute measures to terminate an attack include rotating the arms in a windmill pattern, placing the hands under warm water or in a warm body fold such as the axilla, and the swing-arm maneuver.
- Medications are indicated in the treatment of RP if there are signs of critical ischemia or if the quality of life of the patient is affected to the degree that activities of normal living are no longer possible and preventive techniques do not work.

CHRONIC Rx
- Dihydropyridine calcium channel blockers (e.g., nifedipine, amlodipine, felodipine, nisoldipine, isradipine) are the most effective pharmacologic treatment for RP and are the drugs of choice.
- Nifedipine is most often prescribed at a dose of 10 to 20 mg 30 min before cold exposure. If symptoms occur with long duration, nifedipine XL 30 to 180 mg PO qd is often effective.
- Some potential therapeutic options include direct vasodilators such as nitroprusside, hydralazine, papaverine, minoxidil, niacin, and griseofulvin. Topical 1% nitroglycerin or topical I-arginine, ethyl nicotinate, hexyl

nicotinate, thurfyl salicylate may also be useful, particularly if low blood pressure is a concern.

- Phosphodiesterase inhibitors (cilostazol, pentoxifylline, and sildenafil), angiotensin 2 receptor antagonists (losartan), and selective serotonin reuptake inhibitors (fluoxetine) have been used with some limited success.
- Alpha receptor antagonists such as prazosin and phenoxybenzamine have shown some effectiveness in treating RP.
- The prostaglandins, including inhaled iloprost, IV epoprostenol, alprostadil, and tadalafil, may be promising in severe RP. However, additional experience and controlled studies are needed.
- Antioxidants like zinc gluconate have been used to decrease tissue damage.
- *N*-Acetylcysteine and probucol have been shown to lead to improvement in RP.
- Anticoagulation with IV unfractionated heparin or subcutaneous low-molecular-weight heparin and addition of aspirin can be considered during the acute phase of a severe ischemic event. Aspirin (81 mg/day) therapy can be considered in all patients with secondary RP with a history of ischemic ulcers or thrombotic events; however, caution should be exercised because aspirin can theoretically worsen vasospasm by the inhibition of prostacyclin. Long-term anticoagulation with heparin or warfarin is not recommended unless there is evidence of a hypercoagulable state.

- Bypass surgery can be performed for severe RP associated with reconstructible arterial occlusive disease.
- Sympathectomy is available for unreconstructible occlusive disease or pure vasospastic disease refractory to medical treatment.
- Microsurgical revascularization of the hand and digital reconstruction may improve digital vascular perfusion and heal digital ulcers when proximal arterial occlusion is associated with digital vasospasm.
- Ischemic digital lesions should be treated with topical antibiotics and daily cleansing with soap and water. Digits that progress to dry gangrene should be permitted to undergo autoamputation. Surgical amputation is limited for intractable pain or deep tissue infection.

DISPOSITION

The prognosis of patients with RP depends on the etiology.

- Primary RP is fairly benign, usually remaining stable and controlled with nonpharmacologic medical treatment.
- Remission of primary RP can occur spontaneously.
- Patients with secondary RP, specifically those with scleroderma, CREST syndrome, or thromboangiitis obliterans, may develop severe ischemic digits with ulceration, gangrene, and autoamputation.

REFERRAL

- Rheumatology consult is indicated if secondary collagen vascular disease is diagnosed.
- Vascular surgery consult is indicated if ulcers, gangrene, or threatened digit loss is noted.

❗ PEARLS & CONSIDERATIONS

- Most patients with RP can be managed by a primary care provider.
- It is important to differentiate primary from secondary forms. Secondary forms may become manifest as far out as 10 yr from the diagnosis of RP. It is important to take immediate action during an attack, and patients are encouraged to:
  1. Keep warm
  2. Not use tobacco products
  3. Avoid aggravating medications
  4. Control stress
  5. Exercise
  6. Follow up with a physician

SUGGESTED READINGS

Available at www.expertconsult.com

RELATED CONTENT

Raynaud's Phenomenon (Patient Information)

AUTHORS: **SYEDA M. SAYEED, M.D.,** and **FRED F. FERRI, M.D.**

BASIC INFORMATION

DEFINITION

Reiter's syndrome is one of the seronegative spondyloarthropathies, so called because serum rheumatoid factor is not present in these forms of inflammatory arthritis. Its characteristic clinical trial consists of urithritis, conjunctivitis, and arthritis. Hans Reiter was a Nazi war criminal and many believe that he should no longer be given name recognition to designate this syndrome. There is an international consensus that the term *reactive arthritis* (ReA) should replace the name "Reiter's syndrome" to describe this constellation of signs and symptoms. Unfortunately, the original name is still associated with the syndrome. Reiter's syndrome is an asymmetric polyarthritis that affects mainly the lower extremities and is associated with one or more of the following:

- Urethritis
- Cervicitis
- Dysentery
- Inflammatory eye disease
- Mucocutaneous lesions

SYNONYMS

Reiter's disease
Reactive arthritis
Seronegative spondyloarthropathy

ICD-10CM CODES
M02.30 Reiter's disease, unspecified site

EPIDEMIOLOGY & DEMOGRAPHICS

INCIDENCE (IN U.S.): 0.0035% annually of men ≤50 yr
PEAK INCIDENCE: Most common in the third decade
PREDOMINANT SEX: Male
PREDOMINANT AGE: 20 to 40 yr
GENETICS: Familial disposition: strongly associated with HLA-B27 (63% to 96%)

PHYSICAL FINDINGS & CLINICAL PRESENTATION

- Polyarthritis
  1. Affecting the knee and ankle
  2. Commonly asymmetric
- Heel pain and Achilles tendinitis, especially at the insertion of the Achilles tendon
- Plantar fasciitis
- Large effusions
- Dactylitis, or "sausage toe"
- Urethritis
- Uveitis or conjunctivitis; uveitis can progress to blindness without treatment
- Keratoderma blennorrhagicum, circinate balanitis
  1. Hyperkeratotic lesions on soles of the feet (Fig. E1R-6), toes, penis (Fig. E1R-7), hands
  2. Closely resembles psoriasis
- Aortic regurgitation similar to that seen in ankylosing spondylitis

ETIOLOGY

- Epidemic Reiter's syndrome after outbreaks of dysentery has been well described.
- Genetically susceptible HLA-B27 individuals are at risk for developing Reiter's syndrome after infection with certain pathogens:
  1. *Salmonella*
  2. *Shigella*
  3. *Yersinia enterocolitica*
  4. *Chlamydia trachomatis*
- Symptom complex indistinguishable from Reiter's syndrome has been described in association with HIV infection.

DIAGNOSIS

DIFFERENTIAL DIAGNOSIS

- Ankylosing spondylitis
- Psoriatic arthritis
- Rheumatoid arthritis
- Gonococcal arthritis-tenosynovitis
- Rheumatic fever
- Serum sickness
- Gout
- Chronic mucocutaneous candidiasis

WORKUP

- X-ray examination of affected joints
- Synovial fluid examination and culture
- Careful examination of eyes and skin
- Cultures for gonococcus (urethral, cervical, stool)

LABORATORY TESTS

- Elevated but nonspecific erythrocyte sedimentation rate
- No specific laboratory tests to diagnose Reiter's syndrome
- Do not use HLA-B27 testing as a diagnostic tool

IMAGING STUDIES

Plain radiographs:
- Juxtaarticular osteopenia of affected joints
- Erosions and joint space narrowing in more advanced disease
- Periostitis and reactive new bone formation at the insertions of the Achilles tendon and the plantar fascia
- Sacroiliitis:
  1. Unilateral or bilateral
  2. Indistinguishable from ankylosing spondylitis
- Vertebral bridging osteophytes

TREATMENT

NONPHARMACOLOGIC THERAPY

Physical therapy to maintain range of motion of the spine and other joints

ACUTE GENERAL Rx

- Flares treated with nonsteroidal anti-inflammatory drugs such as indomethacin (25-50 mg PO tid). Refractory cases can be treated with methotrexate or infliximab.

- Mucocutaneous lesions are visually self-limited and clear with topical corticosteroids. Acitretin or cyclosporine can be used for refractory 84-inch lesions.
- Enteric or urethral infection should be treated with appropriate antibiotic coverage.
- Uveitis should be treated with steroid eye drops in consultation with an ophthalmologist.
- Achilles tendinitis and plantar fasciitis should be treated with injections of methylprednisolone (40-80 mg).
- Sulfasalazine (500-1000 mg PO bid, then titrate up to maximum 3 g/day) may be effective.
- Careful monitoring for the following is essential:
  1. Gastrointestinal toxicity
  2. Hypersensitivity
  3. Bone marrow suppression
- Persistent and uncontrolled disease should be managed with cytotoxic drugs (methotrexate, azathioprine) in consultation with a rheumatologist.

CHRONIC Rx

Chronic disease is best managed by a team approach with the collaboration of a rheumatologist or other experienced physician and physical therapist.

DISPOSITION

- Recurrences are frequent, even with treatment.
- Long-term sequelae:
  1. Persistent polyarthritis
  2. Chronic back pain
  3. Heel pain
  4. Progressive iridocyclitis
  5. Aortic regurgitation

REFERRAL

- To ophthalmologist if uveitis is suspected
- To rheumatologist if arthritis and tendinitis fail to improve rapidly after a course of nonsteroidal antiinflammatory drugs

PEARLS & CONSIDERATIONS

COMMENTS

- Infection with HIV is associated with particularly severe cases of Reiter's syndrome.
- HIV testing is recommended, especially if risk factors such as unprotected sexual activity or IV drug use are identified.

SUGGESTED READINGS
Available at www.expertconsult.com

RELATED CONTENT
Reiter's Syndrome (Patient Information)

AUTHOR: **GLENN G. FORT, M.D., M.P.H.**

 **BASIC INFORMATION**

DEFINITION

Renal abscess and perinephric abscess are a purulent complication of an underlying urinary infection of the ascending tract with an obstructed pyelonephritis. Predisposing factors include diabetes and renal stones. There is lobar necrosis with renal abscess and perirenal fat necrosis in perinephric abscess.

SYNONYMS

Intrarenal abscess
Perinephric abscess
Kidney abscess

ICD-10CM CODES
N15.1 Renal and perinephric abscess

EPIDEMIOLOGY & DEMOGRAPHICS

INCIDENCE: Ranges from 1 to 10 per 10,000 hospital admissions
PREDOMINANT SEX AND AGE: In one study median age was 59.8 years
RISK FACTORS: Diabetes and renal stones

PHYSICAL FINDINGS & CLINICAL PRESENTATION

- Symptoms include fever, flank pain, abdominal pain, and urinary frequency or dysuria.
- At times renal abscess can present insidiously in the elderly or persons with diabetes.

ETIOLOGY

These infections may be a complication of a urinary tract infection that ascends to the upper tract, usually due to gram-negative bacteria, or a complication of a bacteremia with hematogenous seeding to the kidney, usually secondary to a *Staphylococcus aureus* infection.

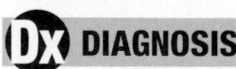 **DIAGNOSIS**

DIFFERENTIAL DIAGNOSIS

- Acute pyelonephritis with papillary necrosis
- Acute lobar nephronia: acute nonsuppurative renal infection
- Renal cell carcinoma
- Malakoplakia: rare granulomatous inflammatory disease seen with *Escherichia coli* infection
- Emphysematous pyelonephritis: gas formation within the renal parenchyma caused by infection by facultative anaerobes or *Candida* spp.

WORKUP

Combination of laboratory tests and imaging

LABORATORY TESTS

- Blood cultures, urine cultures, urinalysis, and CBC are basic tests.
- Elevated ESR or C-reactive protein may be marker for a deep-seated infection.

IMAGING STUDIES

- Ultrasound may show thick-walled fluid-filled cavity in renal parenchyma. A perinephric abscess is confined to the perinephric space by Gerota's fascia.
- CT with contrast is preferred over ultrasound for the diagnosis (Fig. 1R-8).
- MRI and nuclear scans are of limited value.

 **TREATMENT**

Antibiotic therapy and, when necessary, interventional radiology or surgical drainage procedure

NONPHARMACOLOGIC THERAPY

- Therapy for a renal abscess greater than 5 cm in diameter should be percutaneous drainage by CT- or US-guided therapy along with intravenous antibiotics.
- A perinephric abscess should be drained percutaneously with CT or US guidance.
- At times a nephrectomy may be required for severe cases, usually in diabetic patients.

ACUTE GENERAL Rx

A renal abscess less than 5 cm in diameter can be treated successfully with targeted intravenous therapy (92% success rate for abscess 3 to 5 cm in diameter). Antibiotic choices are based on culture results but initially should

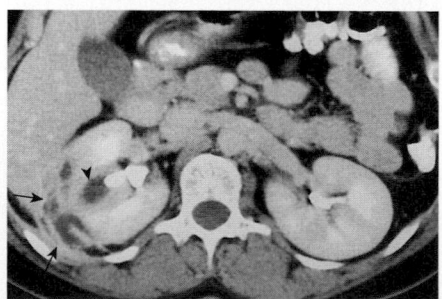

FIGURE 1R-8 Renal abscess. Contrast-enhanced CT scan shows an abscess in the medulla of the kidney *(arrowhead)* with penetration and extension into the perinephric space *(arrows)*. (Courtesy L. Towner.)

target gram-negative bacteria unless infection is secondary to staphylococcal bacteremia. Empiric antibiotic therapy in geographic areas where fluoroquinolone resistance rates are <10% consists of ciprofloxacin 400 mg IV loading dose. In areas with high fluoroquinolone resistance rates, ceftriaxone 1 g IV is appropriate. If perinephric abscess is associated with staphylococcal bacteremia, give IV nafcillin if methicillin-susceptible *Staphylococcus aureus* (MSSA) or vancomycin 1 g IV q12h if methicillin-resistant *S. aureus*.

CHRONIC Rx

Antibiotic therapy generally continues for 2 to 3 weeks, some of which can be completed with oral therapy.

DISPOSITION

Antibiotics such as trimethoprim-sulfamethoxazole and quinolone antibiotics penetrate well in the kidney and are ideal oral agents for therapy.

REFERRAL

Interventional radiology, urologic surgeon, and infectious diseases consult

! **PEARLS & CONSIDERATIONS**

COMMENTS

This diagnosis should be considered in patients who are being treated for pyelonephritis with appropriate antibiotics and fail to respond clinically after 5 days.

PREVENTION

Early and targeted therapy for urinary tract infections, especially in diabetic patients

SUGGESTED READINGS
Available at www.expertconsult.com

RELATED CONTENT
Pyelonephritis (Related Key Topic)
Urinary Tract Infection (Related Key Topic)

AUTHOR: **GLENN G. FORT, M.D., M.P.H.**

 **BASIC INFORMATION**

DEFINITION

Renal artery stenosis (RAS) is the progressive narrowing of the renal artery, which is most commonly due to atherosclerosis or fibromuscular dysplasia (FMD). RAS is an important, potentially reversible cause of hypertension, ischemic nephropathy, and destabilizing cardiac syndromes. RAS increases the risk of renal artery occlusion via progression of the severity of the stenosis.

SYNONYMS

RAS
Renovascular disease

ICD-10CM CODES
I70.1	Atherosclerosis of renal artery
I15.0	Renovascular hypertension
I77.9	Disorder of arteries and arterioles, unspecified
Q27.1	Congenital renal artery stenosis

EPIDEMIOLOGY & DEMOGRAPHICS

- RAS:
  1. Atherosclerotic RAS (ARAS) accounts for about 90% of cases. True prevalence is unknown.
     a. General population autopsy studies: 10%, 27% over 50 years; hypertensive patients: 0.2% to 5%.
     b. In the general population >65 years of age, the prevalence is 6.8% by Doppler ultrasound (5.5% of women, 9.1% of men, 6.7% of African Americans, and 6.9% of Caucasians). Of those with ARAS, 12% had bilateral disease.
     c. In patients with malignant hypertension, the prevalence is 43% in Caucasians and 7% in African Americans. In patients with mild hypertension, the prevalence is <1%.
     d. In patients with peripheral artery disease, the prevalence is 22% to 59%.
  2. FMD accounts for approximately 10% of chronic RAS. It is typically seen in younger women (81%). FMD was previously thought to be a disease of the young and healthy with few risk factors, but recent data suggest an average age of diagnosis of 54 years, and 26% have bilateral disease.

ETIOLOGY

RAS:
- Atherosclerosis: Atherosclerotic renal artery stenosis is a process similar to atherosclerosis in other vascular beds with similar risk factors: family history, smoking, diabetes, hypertension, and hyperlipidemia. ARAS most often involves the ostium and proximal third of the main renal artery.
- Fibromuscular dysplasia (FMD) (Fig. 1R-9): etiology unknown. Classified into three categories based on the layer of arterial wall affected:

medial (>90%), intimal (<10%), adventitial (<1%). FMD typically involves the distal main renal artery and intrarenal branches.

PATHOGENESIS

- Pathogenesis of fibromuscular dysplasia is unknown. Fibromuscular dysplasia involves abnormal constrictions and dilations of the renal artery, leading to a typical "string of beads" finding on angiography.
- The pathogenesis of atherosclerotic RAS is similar to that of atherosclerosis in other vascular beds.
- The pathogenesis of renovascular hypertension is related to the neurohormonal cascade resulting from renal ischemia. The macula densa of the kidney senses a decreased systemic blood pressure caused by the reduced blood flow through the stenotic artery. Renal hypoperfusion or ischemia produces an increase in plasma renin that converts angiotensin I to angiotensin II, producing vasoconstriction and aldosterone secretion, sodium retention, and potassium wasting. Hypertension results and can be self-sustaining, even in the case of unilateral RAS, because of hypertensive damage to the contralateral kidney.
- The pathogenesis of ischemic nephropathy is a topic of current debate. Whether renal dysfunction develops purely from persistent ischemia related to progressively narrowed vessels or from repetitive small ischemic insults and upregulation of inflammatory mediators is yet to be fully elucidated.
- "Flash" or sudden-onset pulmonary edema, a manifestation usually seen in bilateral ARAS, results from sodium and water retention

as well as upregulation of the sympathetic nervous system.

NATURAL HISTORY

- RAS caused by fibromuscular dysplasia rarely causes renal artery occlusion or ischemic nephropathy.
- ARAS rarely progresses to total occlusion. One study of serial ultrasounds of patients with RAS demonstrated that those with >60% stenosis progressed to total occlusion in 1 year in only 5% of cases; an additional 11% had progressed by 2 years.

PHYSICAL FINDINGS & CLINICAL PRESENTATION

Progressive RAS
- Renal artery stenosis should be considered in any Caucasian female aged <30 years with hypertension not attributed to any other cause, or in any patient aged >50 years with new-onset refractory hypertension, or with stable hypertension that has abruptly and significantly worsened.
- Renal artery stenosis most often presents as a clinically asymptomatic finding. Manifestations can include renovascular hypertension, ischemic nephropathy, or flash pulmonary edema.
- Flash pulmonary edema in the absence of cardiac disease most often indicates severe bilateral renal artery stenosis.
- Renovascular hypertension should be considered if blood pressure control remains suboptimal on a medication regimen that includes 3 maximally dosed medications, including a diuretic.

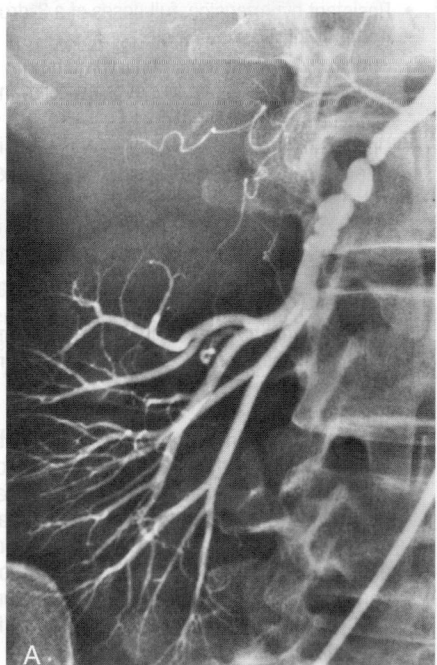
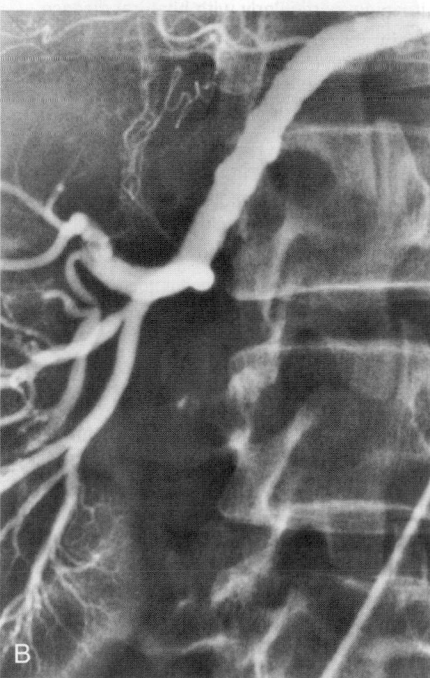

FIGURE 1R-9 Fibromuscular dysplasia. A, Selective renal arteriogram illustrating the beaded appearance of fibromuscular dysplasia with multiple webs characteristic of medial fibroplasia in a 39-yr-old woman. **B,** Selective injection of the same renal artery after technically successful percutaneous transluminal renal angioplasty. (Courtesy Michael McKusick, M.D., Mayo Clinic, Rochester, Minnesota. From Floege J et al: *Comprehensive clinical nephrology,* ed 4, Philadelphia, 2010, Saunders.)

NUCLEAR RENOGRAPHY (WITHOUT CAPTOPRIL):

- A noninvasive test conducted when renal atrophy is present to document differential kidney function. This can be useful when determining whether to revascularize an atrophic kidney or to remove it in renovascular hypertension. Atrophic kidneys with <20% differential renal function are unlikely contributors to ongoing worsening kidney function but may still contribute to renovascular hypertension.

Rx TREATMENT

ACUTE GENERAL Rx

RAS:

The treatment of renal artery stenosis must be targeted to the clinical presentation.

- Asymptomatic RAS requires no treatment.
- Patients with chronic hypertension in the setting of incidentally discovered RAS require only antihypertensive medical therapy.
- Patients in whom RVH is suspected should be initially treated with antihypertensive therapy, specifically medications that block the renin-angiotensin-aldosterone system. As discussed below, failure to control blood pressure on an aggressive regimen represents a reason to consider renal revascularization.
- Patients with ischemic nephropathy should be considered for intervention only if the renal function is rapidly declining or flash pulmonary edema develops in the setting of bilateral renal artery stenosis.

PHARMACOLOGIC THERAPY

- Because of the activation of the renin-angiotensin-aldosterone system in RAS, ACEIs or ARBs are recommended and well tolerated (92%) for the treatment of RVH. Kidney function should be monitored carefully when initiating or titrating these medications, particularly when bilateral RAS (78% tolerability) or unilateral stenosis with solitary kidney is present to avoid precipitating AKI.
- Diuretics should be considered in patients with congestive heart failure or flash pulmonary edema.
- Antiplatelet therapy and statin therapy in patients with atherosclerotic RAS

NONPHARMACOLOGIC THERAPY

- If either blood pressure cannot be controlled by medications alone, flash pulmonary edema occurs, or there is rapid decline in renal function, referral for renal angiography, angioplasty, and stenting may be indicated.
- Angioplasty without stenting is insufficient for atherosclerotic lesions due to a high failure rate of adequate dilation of the artery or a high rate of restenosis.
- Occasionally a kidney that has lost its function due to RAS may cause refractory hypertension. This situation would be discovered only by renal vein renin sampling in a patient with unilateral renal atrophy. In such cases,

nephrectomy of the atrophied kidney may be the best method to control blood pressure.

- Rarely is renal artery bypass required.
- If RAS is suspected as the cause of flash pulmonary edema or rapidly declining kidney function, bilateral disease is likely, and, if confirmed by angiography, both renal arteries should be stented.
- Hypertension is rarely cured with revascularization in patients with atherosclerotic RAS due to high background essential hypertension. The goal of intervention is to gain control of blood pressure and reduce the number of blood pressure medications.
- The ACC/AHA guidelines for clinical indications of renal artery revascularization in the presence of significant stenosis include:
  1. Accelerated, resistant, or malignant hypertension (class IIa)
  2. Hypertension with unilateral small kidney (class IIa)
  3. Hypertension with intolerance to medication (class IIa)
  4. Treatment of cardiac destabilization syndromes such as unexplained heart failure exacerbations or episodes of flash pulmonary edema (class I), and refractory or unstable angina (class IIa)
  5. Progressive chronic kidney disease with bilateral RAS or RAS associated with a solitary functioning kidney (class IIa)
- Many patients who meet these criteria will not demonstrate a beneficial response to renal revascularization; careful selection of patients for angiography and intervention must be made.
- Randomized, controlled trials (e.g., ASTRAL, CORAL, DRASTIC, and STAR) have shown no benefit to percutaneous therapy compared to medical therapy, with endpoints of blood pressure control, renal function, and cardiovascular events. However, these trials did have several inherent limitations.
  1. DRASTIC trial was a small angioplasty-only trial that showed no difference in blood pressure but did show decrease in daily doses of antihypertensive drugs and number of drugs in the intervention group. Cross-over was high from the medication arm to the intervention arm.
  2. The ASTRAL trial was a moderate-sized trial of stenting versus medication in e RAS that showed no difference in blood pressure control or the number of antihypertensives. RAS severity was only moderate in the study population, decreasing the likelihood of finding a positive result.
  3. CORAL is a large prospective multicenter trial comparing stenting versus medication in severe RAS (>60% stenosis); this study confirms that in patients with atherosclerotic renal-artery stenosis and hypertension, clinical outcomes are not improved by stenting, and renal artery stenting is futile in those patients. Again, RAS severity was moderate in many patients, potentially diluting the beneficial effects of intervention on those with severe RAS.

- With these limitations in mind, there is no prospective randomized controlled trial that has shown a benefit in any subgroup of patients with renal artery stenosis of revascularization over medical management. Therefore, it is recommended that the decision to refer a patient for revascularization be made by specialists who are practiced and skilled in handling hypertension and renal artery stenosis.

FIBROMUSCULAR DYSPLASIA

- Medical therapy should include an ACEI or ARB to control blood pressure unless severe bilateral disease is present (rare).
- RVH from fibromuscular dysplasia (FMD) is often cured by renal artery revascularization because many younger patients do not have background essential hypertension.
- In most cases, patients should be referred for renal artery angioplasty regardless of whether blood pressure can be controlled medically.
- Stenting is not appropriate in patients with FMD because angioplasty alone usually yields a durable result. In addition, recurrence of FMD is common, and the presence of stents may hinder additional interventions.
- Renal artery bypass may be necessary in patients whose FMD recurs multiple times or in whom angioplasty failed to yield an improvement in blood pressure.

DISPOSITION & REFERRAL

- Patients with uncontrolled hypertension on multiple agents should be referred for management by a hypertension specialist.
- Percutaneous intervention for atherosclerotic RAS must be reserved for selected patients until further data are available.

! PEARLS & CONSIDERATIONS

- Renal artery stenosis is most commonly an incidental finding and clinically silent.
- Renal artery stenosis may present as hypertension, renal dysfunction, or both, or flash pulmonary edema.
- Stenting is inappropriate for most patients with RAS. Consideration should be made only in high-risk patients and after consultation with a specialist in the field.
- The modality for the type of imaging should depend on the expertise of the institution.

SUGGESTED READINGS

Available at www.expertconsult.com

RELATED CONTENT

Renal Artery Stenosis (Patient Information)
Hypertension (Related Key Topic)

AUTHORS: **CHRIS W. PAN, M.D., M.B.A., M.S.,** and **PRANAV M. PATEL, M.D.**

BASIC INFORMATION

DEFINITION

Renal cell carcinoma is a primary carcinoma originating in the renal parenchyma from the malignant transformation of proximal renal tubular epithelial cells. Most renal cell cancers are of clear cell type; papillary tumors comprise 15% of renal cancers, and chromophobe cancers make up 10%.

SYNONYMS

Hypernephroma
Renal cell carcinoma (RCC)

ICD-10CM CODES

C64.9 Malignant neoplasm of kidney, except renal pelvis
C64.1 Malignant neoplasm of right kidney, except renal pelvis
C64.2 Malignant neoplasm of left kidney, except renal pelvis
C64.9 Malignant neoplasm of unspecified kidney, except renal pelvis
C65.9 Malignant neoplasm of renal pelvis

EPIDEMIOLOGY & DEMOGRAPHICS

INCIDENCE: In 2015, an estimated 61,500 new cases and 14,000 deaths were expected in the U.S. Two percent of cases of renal cancer are associated with inherited syndromes.
PREDOMINANT SEX: Male:female ratio is approximately 2:1.
PREDOMINANT AGE: Peak incidence is at age 50 to 70 years.

PHYSICAL FINDINGS & CLINICAL PRESENTATION

Patients are often asymptomatic until they have advanced disease. The classic presentation of RCC includes the triad of flank pain, hematuria, and a palpable abdominal mass, but currently this now represents an unusual presentation. Current presenting findings in RCC include:

Hematuria	50%-60%
Elevated erythrocyte sedimentation rate	50%-60%
Abdominal mass	25%-45%
Anemia	20%-40%
Flank pain	35%-40%
Hypertension	20%-40%
Weight loss	30%-35%
Fever	5%-15%
Hepatic dysfunction	10%-15%
Classic triad (hematuria, abdominal mass, flank pain)	5%-10%
Hypercalcemia	3%-6%
Erythrocytosis	3%-4%
Varicocele	2%-3%

ETIOLOGY

Hereditary forms:
- Familial renal carcinoma.
- Renal carcinoma associated with Von Hippel-Lindau disease.

- Hereditary papillary renal cell carcinoma.

Risk factors:
- Cigarette smoking.
- Obesity.
- Phenacetin-containing analgesics.
- Asbestos, lead, Thorotrast, and chromium exposure.
- Gasoline and other petroleum products.
- Role of the *VHL* gene on chromosome 3.

DIAGNOSIS

DIFFERENTIAL DIAGNOSIS

- Transitional cell carcinomas of the renal pelvis (8% of all renal cancers).
- Wilms' tumor.
- Other primary renal carcinomas and sarcomas.
- Renal cysts.
- Retroperitoneal tumors.

WORKUP

LABORATORY TESTS

- Urinalysis: hematuria.
- Complete blood count: anemia or erythrocytosis.
- Nonmetastatic hepatic dysfunction with elevated alkaline phosphatase, prolonged prothrombin time, and hypoalbuminemia.
- Hypercalcemia (caused by parathyroid-related protein).

IMAGING STUDIES

Nearly 50% of renal cancers are now detected because a renal mass is incidentally detected on radiographic evaluation.
- Renal ultrasound.
- Abdominal CT scan with contrast (Fig. 1R-13 and Fig. 1R-14); CT-guided biopsy is generally not necessary for diagnosis of solid masses >4 cm (high likelihood of cancer).
- MRI.
- Renal arteriogram.
- Intravenous pyelography.

STAGING

See Table 1R-4.

COMMON SITES OF METASTASES

Lung	50%-60%
Bone	30%-40%
Regional nodes	15%-30%
Main renal vein	15%-20%
Perirenal fat	10%-20%
Adrenal (ipsilateral)	10%-15%
Vena cava	10%-15%
Brain	10%-15%
Adjacent organs (colon, pancreas)	10%
Kidney (contralateral)	2%

TREATMENT

- Surgery
1. Surgical nephrectomy (open procedure or laparoscopic approach) is the only effective management for stages I, II, and some stage III tumors. Although radical nephrectomy had long been the standard treatment, retrospective studies have shown that partial rather than radical nephrectomy is associated with improved survival and is appropriate for patients with renal cell neoplasms <4 cm that are not adjacent to the renal pelvis or invading the vena cava.
2. Laparoscopic robotic-assisted nephrectomy is being progressively adopted in multiple centers, primarily for nephron-sparing surgery in the case of tumors <4 cm. Advantages of this approach include less blood loss, minimal effects on renal function, and similar oncologic outcomes. Disadvantages include increased costs and limitations in tumor size and locations eligible for robotic surgery.

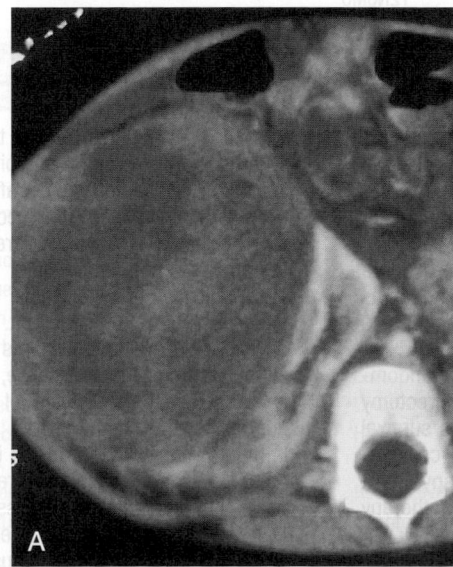
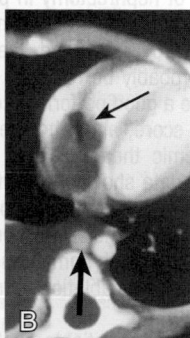

FIGURE 1R-13 Renal cell carcinoma. Ultrasound demonstrates a 17-mm hyperreflective mass in the left kidney with posterior shadowing. (From Grainger RG et al [eds]: *Grainger & Allison's diagnostic radiology,* ed 4, London, 2001, Harcourt.)

BASIC INFORMATION

DEFINITION
Renal vein thrombosis is the thrombotic occlusion of one or both renal veins.

ICD-10CM CODES
I82.3 Embolism and thrombosis of renal vein

EPIDEMIOLOGY & DEMOGRAPHICS
- Incidence unknown; probably an underdiagnosed condition.
- May occur at any age with no gender preference.
- Epidemiology tied to the underlying cause.

PHYSICAL FINDINGS & CLINICAL PRESENTATION
Acute bilateral renal vein thrombosis:
- Back and bilateral flank pain.
- Acute renal failure.

Acute unilateral renal vein thrombosis:
- Flank pain.
- Decline in renal function.
- Hematuria.
- Increase in the amount of proteinuria if associated with nephrotic syndrome.

Chronic unilateral renal vein thrombosis:
- May be silent.
- Pulmonary emboli and hemolysis.
- Back pain.
- Deep vein thrombosis in lower extremities.
- Edema.
- Glycosuria.
- Hyperchloremic acidosis.
- Left varicocele (if the left renal vein is thrombosed).
- Dilated abdominal veins.

ETIOLOGY & PATHOGENESIS
- Extrinsic compression by a tumor or retroperitoneal mass.
- Invasion of the renal vein or inferior vena cava by tumor (almost always renal cell cancer).
- Trauma.
- Hypercoagulable states.
- Dehydration.
- Glomerulopathies (membranous glomerulonephritis, crescentic glomerulonephritis, systemic lupus erythematosus, amyloidosis) especially in the presence of nephrotic syndrome when the serum albumin is <2 g/dl.

NOTE: For unknown reasons, diabetic nephropathy is not commonly associated with renal vein thrombosis even if the nephrotic syndrome is present.

A controversy has existed regarding whether the renal vein thrombosis association with nephrotic syndrome is a complication of nephrotic syndrome or whether renal vein thrombosis occurring in the setting of increased renal vein pressure (e.g., with congestive heart failure, constrictive pericarditis, or extrinsic compression) can independently cause proteinuria. Current evidence is that renal vein thrombosis does not cause nephrotic syndrome.

DIAGNOSIS

DIFFERENTIAL DIAGNOSIS
The diagnosis of renal vein thrombosis does not include any differential consideration. The differential diagnosis is that of proteinuria. Renal vein thrombosis should be considered if proteinuria worsens or if renal function worsens in a patient with glomerulonephritis. Renal vein thrombosis should also be considered in patients with pulmonary emboli and no lower-extremity deep vein thrombosis.

WORKUP
Clinical suspicion (see "Differential Diagnosis") and imaging studies.

IMAGING STUDIES
- Abdominal ultrasound.
- Abdominal MRI or CT with contrast (Fig. 1R-16).

- Renal arteriography (delayed films during venous phase).
- Selective renal vein venography (inferior venacavogram images should be obtained before advancing the catheter in the vena cava because clots, if present, could be dislodged).
- Renal biopsy may be indicated if evidence of nephritis is present (e.g., active urinary sediment).

TREATMENT

- Anticoagulation in acute renal vein thrombosis to prevent pulmonary emboli and in attempt to improve renal function and decrease proteinuria.
- Thrombolytic therapy or surgical thrombectomy has also been reported to be effective
- The value of anticoagulation in chronic renal vein thrombosis is dubious except in nephrotic patients with membranous glomerulonephritis with profound hypoalbuminemia where prolonged prophylactic anticoagulation may be of benefit even if renal vein thrombosis has not been documented.

PROGNOSIS
Probable worsening of the underlying glomerulonephritis by acute renal vein thrombosis; the effect of chronic renal vein thrombosis is unclear.

AUTHOR: **FRED F. FERRI, M.D.**

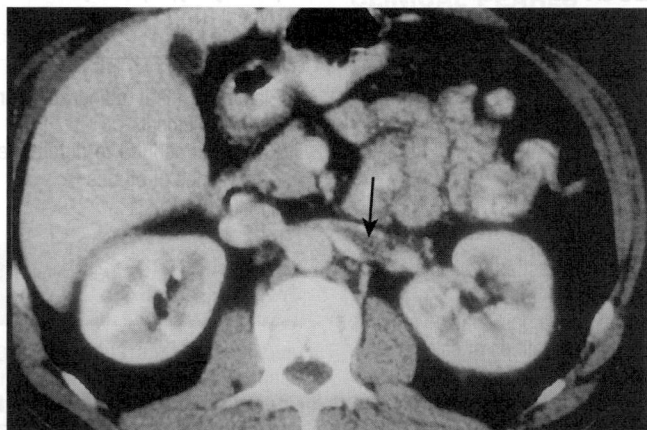

FIGURE 1R-16 Renal vein thrombus in a patient with nephritic syndrome. Contrast medium–enhanced CT at the level of the renal vein shows thrombus in the left renal vein *(arrow)*. (From Grainger R.G.; et al. [eds]: *Grainger & Allison's diagnostic radiology,* ed 4, Philadelphia, 2001, Churchill Livingstone.)

BASIC INFORMATION

DEFINITION

Restless legs syndrome (RLS) is an awake phenomenon consisting of an urge to move legs, usually associated with feeling of discomfort in legs.

SYNONYMS

RLS
Wittmaack-Ekbom syndrome

ICD-10CM CODES
G25.81 Restless legs syndrome

EPIDEMIOLOGY & DEMOGRAPHICS

PREVALENCE: Average prevalence rate is 1% to 29%. Prevalence estimates in Europe are around 10%, and 0.1% to 12% in East Asian population.
PEAK PREVALENCE: 10% in persons aged 30 to 79 and 19% in persons aged 80 or above.
PREDOMINANT SEX: Early-onset RLS is more common in females, with 2:1 female/male ratio.
PREDOMINANT AGE: Prevalence of RLS increases with age, and it is more commonly seen in elderly population.
GENETICS: Genetic basis of RLS has been reported, particularly in early-onset RLS.
- Autosomal dominant disorder
- Common among first-degree relatives
- RLS associated with certain sequences in chromosome 6p,12q, 14q, 9p, 20p, 2p, 16p
RISK FACTORS: Diabetes mellitus (most consistent risk factor for RLS), iron deficiency anemia (IDA), end-stage renal disease (ESRD) requiring hemodialysis, pregnancy, rheumatoid arthritis, Parkinson's disease, neuropathy, and myelopathy

CLASSIFICATION

- Primary RLS is without any obvious cause, with no associated disorder.
- Secondary RLS results from other medical conditions; the most frequently found associations are pregnancy, IDA, ESRD, and Parkinson disease.

PHYSICAL FINDINGS & CLINICAL PRESENTATION

- Wide spectrum of severity of clinical manifestations has been reported in RLS.

- Most common symptom is unpleasant sensations in legs ("dysesthesias"), reported as discomfort or "creepy-crawling" sensations, mostly bilateral. Arms are occasionally involved.
- There is an extreme urge to move legs and relief is sustained as long as the movement continues.
- Symptoms are worse at night or evening. Best sleep is usually early in the morning.

ETIOLOGY

The exact etiology remains unknown. Pharmacologic, pathologic, physiologic, and imaging studies have implicated dopaminergic pathways, brain iron metabolism, and endogenous opioid pathways.

DIAGNOSIS

DIFFERENTIAL DIAGNOSIS

- Periodic limb movement disorder (PLMD)
- Nocturnal leg cramps
- Painful peripheral neuropathy
- Akathisia
- Positional discomfort
- Volitional movements, foot tapping, leg rocking

WORKUP

- Diagnosis of RLS is based on established clinical criteria (Table 1R-6) and normal neurologic examination.
- Testing is done to determine possible cause of secondary RLS. All patients with RLS should be screened for iron deficiency.
- Polysomnography to document periodic limb movements during sleep
- Leg activity monitors to determine limb movements during sleep but they are unable to distinguish periodic limb movements from periodic movements associated with sleep apnea.
- Nerve conduction studies and electromyography for associated peripheral neuropathy

LABORATORY TESTS

- Iron status: serum ferritin, total iron binding capacity, percent saturation
- CBC for anemia in case of iron deficiency

- Metabolic panel: blood urea nitrogen and serum creatinine for renal insufficiency

IMAGING STUDIES

No imaging studies are required for diagnosis for RLS.

TREATMENT

Treatment options for RLS include:
- Dopaminergic agents, levodopa, and dopamine agonists help to ameliorate RLS symptoms, decrease periodic limb movements, and improve sleep. Dopamine agonists, pramipexole and ropinirole, are first-line agents in the treatment of RLS.
- Ritigotine patch (Neupro) is also effective and FDA-approved for moderate to severe RLS.
- Anticonvulsants, such as gabapentin, have been shown to be effective in multiple studies. A recent trial has shown that pregabalin is also effective and well tolerated for RLS.[1] Limited case reports reveal use of lamotrigine, Gabitril, and topiramate in patients who are intolerant to other agents.
- Opiates, mostly methadone, are generally reserved as last line of treatment.
- Iron replacement should be started in case of iron deficiency. Iron supplements are indicated even with low-normal ferritin levels (<45 ng/mL).

NONPHARMACOLOGIC THERAPY

- Avoidance of caffeine, alcohol, nicotine, and medications that exacerbate RLS (selective serotonin reuptake inhibitors, dopamine blocking agents, stimulants)
- Physical and mental activity
- Good sleep hygiene

ACUTE GENERAL Rx

Once the diagnosis of RLS is considered based on clinical criteria as mentioned in Table 1R-6 and causes impairment of quality of life, a dopamine agonist (bromocriptine, pramipexole, or ropinirole) should be started at low dose and then gradually tapered depending on tolerance. Dopaminergic medications have the potential to cause iatrogenic worsening (augmentation) of RLS with long-term treatment.

REFERRAL

Refer to neurologist if diagnosis is uncertain or an underlying disorder is suspected.

SUGGESTED READINGS
Available at www.expertconsult.com

RELATED CONTENT
Restless Legs Syndrome (Patient Information)

AUTHOR: **FARIHA ZAHEER, M.D.**

TABLE 1R-6 Diagnostic Criteria for Restless Legs Syndrome

Minimal Criteria
1. Desire to move the legs usually associated with paresthesias.
2. Motor restlessness, as characterized by floor pacing, leg rubbing, stretching, and flexing.
3. Worse at rest, with relief by activity.
4. Worse at night.

Additional Criteria
1. Sleep disturbances, as difficulty in sleep onset and maintaining sleep, daytime fatigue, or somnolence.
2. Involuntary movements, as periodic limb or leg movements in sleep and periodic or aperiodic limb movements while awake.
3. Neurologic examination is normal in idiopathic restless legs syndrome.
4. Clinical course may begin at any age but most severe in middle and older age.
5. Family history suggests autosomal dominant mode of inheritance in 1/3 of the cases.

From Stiansy K et al: Clinical symptomatology and treatment of restless leg syndrome and periodic limb movement disorder, *Sleep Med Rev* 6(4):253-265, 2002.

[1]Allen RP et al: Comparison of pregabalin with pramipexole for restless legs syndrome, *N Engl J Med* 370:621-631, 2014.

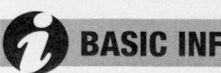
BASIC INFORMATION

DEFINITION

Retinal detachment is the separation of the neurosensory retina (NSR) from the retinal pigment epithelium (RPE). This results in the accumulation of subretinal fluid (SRF) in the potential space between the NSR and the RPE. The main types of retinal detachment are **rhegmatogenous** (caused by retinal tear with vitreous fluid passing through the defect), **tractional** (subretinal fluid caused by fibrous proliferation and pulling from vitreous gel), and **exudative** (accumulation of subretinal fluid due to inflammation or tumors).

ICD-10CM CODES

H33   Retinal detachment and breaks
H33.2 Serous retinal detachment
H33.5 Other retinal detachments
H33.0 Retinal detachment with retinal break

EPIDEMIOLOGY & DEMOGRAPHICS

INCIDENCE (IN U.S.):
- Annual incidence roughly 1 in 10,000
- Particularly common in patients with high myopia of 5 diopters or more
- Incidence 1% to 2% after cataract surgery

PEAK INCIDENCE: Incidence increases with increasing age or increasing myopia.

PREVALENCE (IN U.S.): Busy ophthalmologists may see one or two acute retinal detachments per month.

PREDOMINANT AGE:
- Most common age group is 40 to 70 years old.
- Peak age coincides with peak incidence of acute posterior vitreous detachment, as this is the most important cause of a retinal tear.
- Rare in children and almost always due to congenital ocular disorders (Stickler syndrome) or trauma.

RISK FACTORS:
- Myopia
- Lattice degeneration (peripheral retinal thinning)
- Previous ocular surgery–particularly cataract surgery
- Family history
- Ocular trauma
- Fluoroquinolones (controversial)
- Ocular inflammation (uveitis)
- Retinal vascular disease–particularly diabetic retinopathy
- Intraocular tumor (ocular or metastatic)

PHYSICAL FINDINGS & CLINICAL PRESENTATION

- Sudden onset of flashes of light and floaters associated with a peripheral shadow or curtain
- May progress rapidly over days to involve central vision
- Generally no pain unless associated with ocular inflammation
- Examination reveals elevation of retina and vessels associated with tears in the retina (Figs. 1R-17 and 1R-18) and/or hemorrhage in the vitreous

ETIOLOGY

- The overwhelming majority of retinal detachments are caused by a retinal tear or hole (rhegmatogenous) occurring after acute separation of the vitreous (posterior vitreous detachment [PVD]).
- Cataract surgery is thought to cause biochemical changes in the vitreous resulting in PVD.
- High myopia and lattice degeneration cause thin areas of the retina resulting in holes.
- Most common cause of traction RD is severe proliferative diabetic retinopathy resulting in fibrovascular proliferation with contraction of fibrous tissue and secondary detachment of retina.
- Ocular tumors and inflammation including posterior uveitis and scleritis are the most common causes of exudative retinal detachment.

 DIAGNOSIS

DIFFERENTIAL DIAGNOSIS

- Degenerative retinoschisis.
- Uveal effusion syndrome.
- Choroidal detachment.
- Hemorrhage.
- Tumors.

WORKUP

- Full eye examination with dilated fundus exam and retinal drawing to document tears and extent of detachment.
- Visual fields.
- Ultrasonography to show the retinal detachment or tumors beneath it.
- Medical workup only when inflammation or systemic disease considered.

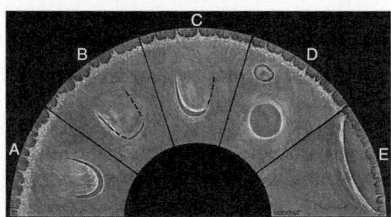

FIGURE 1R-17 Retinal tears. *A,* Complete U-shaped; *B,* linear; *C,* L-shaped; *D,* operculated; *E,* dialysis. (From Kanski JJ, Bowling B. *Clinical ophthalmology: a systematic approach,* ed 7, Philadelphia, 2010, Saunders.)

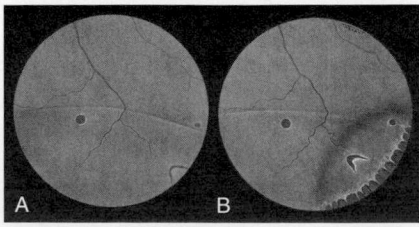

FIGURE 1R-18 Appearance of retinal breaks in detached retina. A, Without scleral indentation; **B,** with indentation. (From Kanski JJ, Bowling B. *Clinical ophthalmology: a systematic approach,* ed 7, Philadelphia, 2010, Saunders.)

LABORATORY TESTS

Usually not necessary unless exudative detachment is being considered.

IMAGING STUDIES

B scan ultrasonography (US) of the eye.

 TREATMENT

NONPHARMACOLOGIC THERAPY

Immediate surgery. The three principal methods for reattachment of the retina in patients with primary retinal detachment are scleral buckling, vitrectomy, and pneumatic retinopexy. There is a paucity of randomized trials comparing these procedures and the choice remains subjective. Some data suggest that vitrectomy may be preferable for detachment in pseudophakic eyes, whereas primary detachment in phakic eyes with complexity exceeding the original indications for pneumatic retinopexy may be treated with scleral buckling or vitrectomy.

ACUTE GENERAL Rx

- Early surgery to repair the detachment.
- Treatment of the underlying disorder.

CHRONIC Rx

Occasionally, steroids or other treatment of underlying inflammatory disease, if indicated.

DISPOSITION

- Immediately refer to an ophthalmologist.
- Early intervention improves outcomes.

REFERRAL

Immediately.

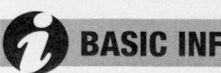 PEARLS & CONSIDERATIONS

COMMENTS

If treated early, most patients will recover a substantial portion of their vision.

SUGGESTED READINGS

Available at www.expertconsult.com

AUTHOR: **ROBERT H. JANIGIAN, M.D.**

BASIC INFORMATION

DEFINITION

Retinal hemorrhages occur as a result of rupture of the rich retinal capillary network. The location of the vascular pathology determines the type of hemorrhage and may aid in the differential diagnosis. Preretinal hemorrhage usually implies neovascularization or traction, intraretinal hemorrhage is caused by rupture of capillaries or aneurysms within the retina, and subretinal hemorrhage occurs when there is rupture of choroidal vessels or subretinal neovascularization. Retinal hemorrhages are abnormal, and causes should be sought (see "Etiology").

SYNONYMS

Retinal hemorrhage
Subretinal or preretinal hemorrhages
Splinter hemorrhage, dot and blot hemorrhages
Roth spots (small white centered blood, traditionally associated with endocarditis)

ICD-10CM CODES
H35.60   Retinal hemorrhage, unspecified eye
H35.61   Retinal hemorrhage, right eye
H35.62   Retinal hemorrhage, left eye
H35.63   Retinal hemorrhage, bilateral

EPIDEMIOLOGY & DEMOGRAPHICS

INCIDENCE (IN U.S.): Busy ophthalmologists see one or two cases a month.
PEAK INCIDENCE:
- In children: associated primarily with trauma and hematologic disorders (must consider shaken baby syndrome in every child with retinal hemorrhages), rare retinal vascular diseases of children (Coat's syndrome, Eale's disease).
- Associated with trauma, diabetes, vascular disease (hypertensive retinopathy, retinal vascular occlusions, sickle cell disease, anemia), macular degeneration, altitude changes (mountain climbing).
PREDOMINANT AGE: Usually vascular disease in older patients.

PHYSICAL FINDINGS & CLINICAL PRESENTATION

- Retinal hemorrhages in general do not cause loss of vision or ocular symptoms unless associated with other ocular pathology—symptoms, when present, are generally from the systemic cause.
- Ophthalmoscopy reveals hemorrhage within the retina, or on the nerve or subretinal area.

- Evidence of diabetes, hypertension, tumors, inflammation, macular degeneration, and drug use.

ETIOLOGY

- Vascular: diabetic retinopathy, hypertensive retinopathy, retinal vein occlusion, carotid occlusive disease, Valsalva retinopathy, radiation retinopathy, retinal macroaneurysm, ischemic optic neuropathy.
- Elevated intracranial pressure (hemorrhages generally located around or on optic nerve).
- Trauma.
- Inflammatory diseases: retinal vasculitis, lupus.
- Infectious: HIV retinopathy, endocarditis.
- Neoplastic: leukemia, vascular tumors of the retina, choroidal melanoma, metastatic tumors.
- Degenerative diseases: age-related macular degeneration, myopia, angioid streaks.
- Rapid changes in altitude (mountain climbing or scuba diving).
- Drugs: interferon, cocaine.

 DIAGNOSIS

DIFFERENTIAL DIAGNOSIS

- Evaluate patients for local and systemic diseases (diabetes is most common).
- Trauma in children or adults.
- Venous or arterial occlusion associated with atherosclerotic or heart disease may cause retinal hemorrhage.
- Rule out malignant melanoma, trauma, hypertensive or cardiovascular disease.
  1. Section II describes the differential diagnosis of acute painless loss of vision.

WORKUP

- Complete history and general physical examination, evaluate for trauma; look for systemic diseases and medication etiologies.
- Complete eye exam including dilated fundus exam.

LABORATORY TESTS

- Minimum: complete blood count, erythrocyte sedimentation rate, complete blood chemistries.
- Visual field testing.

IMAGING STUDIES

- Color photography and fluorescein angiography (assess for retinal vascular causes, vasculitis, macular degeneration).
- Ocular ultrasound if tumor is in differential.
- Carotid Doppler scan.
- Trauma: skull radiographs or head CT (evaluate for fractures).

 TREATMENT

NONPHARMACOLOGIC THERAPY

- Laser or treatment of underlying disorder.
- Carotid endarterectomy if indicated.

ACUTE GENERAL Rx

- Laser treatment may be indicated for certain retinal diseases (diabetic retinopathy, retinal vein occlusion, retinal macroaneurysm).
- Treatment may be indicated for wet macular degeneration or diabetic retinopathy (intravitreal injection).
- Treat underlying systemic disease.
- Repair any damage from trauma.

CHRONIC Rx

- Vitamin therapy: Age Related Eye Disease Study formulation for macular degeneration.
- Treatment will differ depending on various causes of bleeding.
- Treat medical problems (diabetes, hypertension, etc.).
- Encourage adequate control of underlying medical disorders.

DISPOSITION

If present, hemorrhage in the retina is generally considered abnormal; refer to ophthalmologist for evaluation.

REFERRAL

Immediate referral to an ophthalmologist, especially if there is a significant change in vision; early treatment significantly affects outcome.

⊘ PEARLS & CONSIDERATIONS

COMMENTS

- Vision may return substantially.
- Complete recovery of vision depends on cause.
- Chronic situations may have poor prognosis.

SUGGESTED READINGS
Available at www.expertconsult.com

RELATED CONTENT
Diabetic Retinopathy (Patient Information)

AUTHOR: **ROBERT H. JANIGIAN, M.D.**

BASIC INFORMATION

DEFINITION

Retinitis pigmentosa (RP) refers to a group of phenotypically variable and genetically diverse retinal dystrophies resulting in predominantly rod photoreceptor cell death. Subsequent cone and retinal pigment epithelial involvement can also be seen. The term "retinitis" is a misnomer as inflammation plays a very minor role in the pathology. Visual manifestations usually include night blindness (nyctalopia) and loss of peripheral vision.

ICD-10CM CODES
H35.5 Hereditary retinal dystrophy

EPIDEMIOLOGY & DEMOGRAPHICS

PEAK INCIDENCE:
- Autosomal recessive incidence: in the 20s
- Autosomal dominant form: in the 40s

PREVALENCE (IN U.S.):
- Approximately 1 in 4000 in the U.S. and 1 in 5000 worldwide.
- It is the most commonly encountered hereditary fundus dystrophy.

PREDOMINANT SEX: X-linked presents only in males, but there is no gender predilection with the other genetic varieties.

PREDOMINANT AGE: Onset usually in young adulthood but can present at any time from infancy up to 30s to 50s, depending on mode of inheritance.

GENETICS:
- Over 100 genetic loci have been mapped on more than 50 genes representing all inheritance patterns.
- 20% autosomal recessive.
- 10% to 20% autosomal dominant.
- 10% X-linked.
- Up to 40% have no family history and an unknown molecular genetic basis.

PHYSICAL FINDINGS & CLINICAL PRESENTATION

- Classic triad: bone spicule and pigment clumping in the mid periphery (Fig. E1R-19), "waxy pallor" of the optic nerve and arteriolar attenuation (Fig. E1R-20).
- Findings almost always bilateral but may be asymmetric.
- Other findings: depigmentation and atrophy of RPE, cataracts, and macular edema.
- Typical symptoms: decrease in night vision and peripheral vision. Patients typically lose night vision to a greater extent than they lose day vision, and they lose peripheral vision before losing central vision.

ETIOLOGY
RP may occur as an isolated sporadic disorder, or may be inherited as AD, AR, or XL. Gene mutations that cause RP generally affect the biological function of the photoreceptors and RPE. The end result is photoreceptor apoptosis and cell death. XL is the least common but most severe form, and may result in complete blindness by the third or fourth decade.

DIAGNOSIS

DIFFERENTIAL DIAGNOSIS

- Previous chorioretinitis: syphilis, CMV retinitis, rubella, diffuse unilateral subacute retinitis.
- Must consider other genetic disorders that cause retinal degeneration, including gyrate atrophy, choroideremia, Refsum disease, cone-rod dystrophy, cone dystrophy, and Leber congenital amaurosis.
- Toxic retinopathies (phenothiazines, chloroquine).

WORKUP

- Electrophysiologic studies (electroretinogram results are most important).
- Dark adaptation studies.
- Visual fields.
- Medication history.

LABORATORY TESTS

- Usually not necessary.
- VDRL if syphilis is a consideration.
- Consider other conditions that cause pigmentary degeneration of the retina: serum ornithine level or ornithine-lysine ratio (for gyrate atrophy of the retina and choroid) and serum phytanic acid level (for Refsum disease).

IMAGING STUDIES

- Color fundus photography
- Optical coherence tomography
- Fluorescein angiography

TREATMENT

CHRONIC Rx

- No proven therapy to prevent photoreceptor cell death.
- Nutritional and supplement therapy is controversial: high-dose vitamin A palmitate (15,000 IU) was shown to slow the decline of ERG response, but whether it translates to better visual prognosis is not clear.
- Docosahexaenoic acid (DHA), an omega-3 fatty acid thought to be important for photoreceptor function, has been evaluated in two clinical trials for its potential to slow vision

loss in RP, but neither study showed a clear benefit.
- Based on clinical trial results, some experts recommend a regimen of 15,000 IU of vitamin A palmitate daily, lutein 12 mg daily, and two portions of oily fish weekly.
- Use of UV-absorbing sunglasses and brimmed hats for protection from high levels of light exposure seems prudent.
- Drugs that may negatively impact RP include isotretinoin (Accutane), sildenafil (Viagra), and vitamin E.
- Cystoid macular edema should be treated with carbonic anhydrase inhibitors including topical dorzolamide and acetazolamide.
- Emerging therapies: Argus II retinal implant is a phototransducing chip that is surgically placed on the retinal surface and is FDA approved for RP patients with bare light perception or no light perception. Trials are under way using gene therapy targeted for specific gene mutations. Ciliary neurotrophic factor (CNTF) has been shown to slow retinal degeneration, and clinical trials are presently in progress.

DISPOSITION

- Reassurance that total blindness is rare; the overwhelming majority of patients maintain sight in one eye.
- Low vision evaluation.
- Annual comprehensive eye examination with visual fields and possibly ERG every 2 years.
- Liver function studies for those on high-dose vitamin A.

REFERRAL
To ophthalmologist to confirm diagnosis.

PEARLS & CONSIDERATIONS

COMMENTS

- Patient education material can be obtained from the Retinitis Pigmentosa Foundation Fighting Blindness, 1401 Mt. Royal Avenue, 4th Floor, Baltimore, MD 21217.
- Information regarding ongoing clinical trials for RP can be found at clinicaltrials.gov.

SUGGESTED READINGS
Available at www.expertconsult.com

RELATED CONTENT
Retinitis Pigmentosa (Patient Information)

AUTHOR: **ROBERT H. JANIGIAN, M.D.**

BASIC INFORMATION

DEFINITION

Retropharyngeal abscess is a soft tissue infection of the throat involving retropharyngeal space. The anatomic boundaries of the retropharyngeal space are the middle layer of the deep cervical fascia (abutting the posterior esophageal wall) anteriorly and the deep layer of the deep cervical fascia posteriorly (Fig. 1R-23). These two fasciae fuse inferiorly at the level between the first and second thoracic vertebrae.

ICD-10CM CODES
J39.0 Retropharyngeal and parapharyngeal abscess

EPIDEMIOLOGY & DEMOGRAPHICS

Retropharyngeal abscess occurs most commonly in children between the ages of 2 and 4 yr, analogous to suppurative cervical adenitis. This represents the peak age group for numerous viral upper respiratory tract infections and their attendant complications, acute otitis media and sinusitis. Retropharyngeal space infection is less common in older children and adults because the lymph nodes atrophy by the age of 3 to 4 yr.

PHYSICAL FINDINGS & CLINICAL PRESENTATION

- The onset of a retropharyngeal infection may be insidious, with little more than fever, irritability, drooling, a muffled voice (dysphonia), or possibly nuchal rigidity.
- The acute symptoms relate to pressure and inflammation produced by the abscess on either the airway or the upper digestive tract and pharynx. The patient may have intense dysphagia, drooling, and odynophagia, or there may be some element of respiratory

distress from edema and inflammation of the airway (stridor, tachypnea, or both).
- Unwillingness to move the neck because of discomfort is often a prominent presenting feature and should lead to consideration of retropharyngeal abscess if the child is febrile and irritable.
- Extension of the neck is usually affected more than flexion. This causes the patient to hold his or her neck stiffly or to present with torticollis.
- Trismus is unusual.
- On physical examination it may be possible to appreciate midline or unilateral swelling of the posterior pharyngeal wall. The mass may be fluctuant to the examining finger, and care must be taken to avoid rupture of the abscess into the upper airway.

Complications are numerous and could be fatal; these include airway obstruction, septicemia, thrombosis of the internal jugular vein, carotid artery rupture, and acute necrotizing mediastinitis. Aspiration with resultant pneumonia may complicate retropharyngeal abscess if rupture of the abscess occurs and empties into the airway. Infection can spread from one space in the neck to another.

The most dreaded complication is jugular vein suppurative thrombophlebitis (Lemierre's syndrome), in which the vessels of the carotid sheath become infected, leading to bacteremia and metastatic spread of infection to the lungs, brain, and mediastinum.

ETIOLOGY

- The retropharyngeal space comprises two chains of lymph nodes that drain the nasopharynx, adenoids, posterior paranasal sinuses, middle ear, and eustachian tube. Accordingly, suppurative infections in these areas may provide the seeds for infection for retropharyngeal abscess.

- The predominant bacterial species are *Streptococcus pyogenes* (group A *Streptococcus*), *Staphylococcus aureus*, and respiratory anaerobes (including *Fusobacteria, Prevotella,* and *Veillonella* species). *Haemophilus* species are also occasionally found.
- In young children, infection usually reaches this space by lymphatic spread from a septic focus in the pharynx or sinuses.
- In adults, infection may reach the retropharyngeal space from either local or distant sites. Penetrating trauma (e.g., from chicken bones or iatrogenic) is the usual source of local spread. More distant sources of infection include odontogenic sepsis and peritonsillar abscess (now a rare cause).

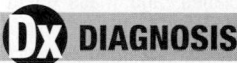

DIAGNOSIS

DIFFERENTIAL DIAGNOSIS
- Cervical osteomyelitis
- Pott's disease
- Meningitis
- Calcific tendonitis of the long muscle of the neck

IMAGING STUDIES

- A lateral neck film may be helpful in delineating the presence of a retropharyngeal abscess and may demonstrate cervical lordosis; the retropharyngeal space is considered widened and pathologic if it is greater than 7 mm at C2 or 14 mm at C6 (Fig. 1R-24).
  - There must be attention to technical issues when performing the study, especially in children. The film should be a perfect lateral, and the child must keep the neck in extension during inspiration to avoid a false thickening of the retropharyngeal space. Crying, particularly in infants, may also cause false thickening of the retropharyngeal space.

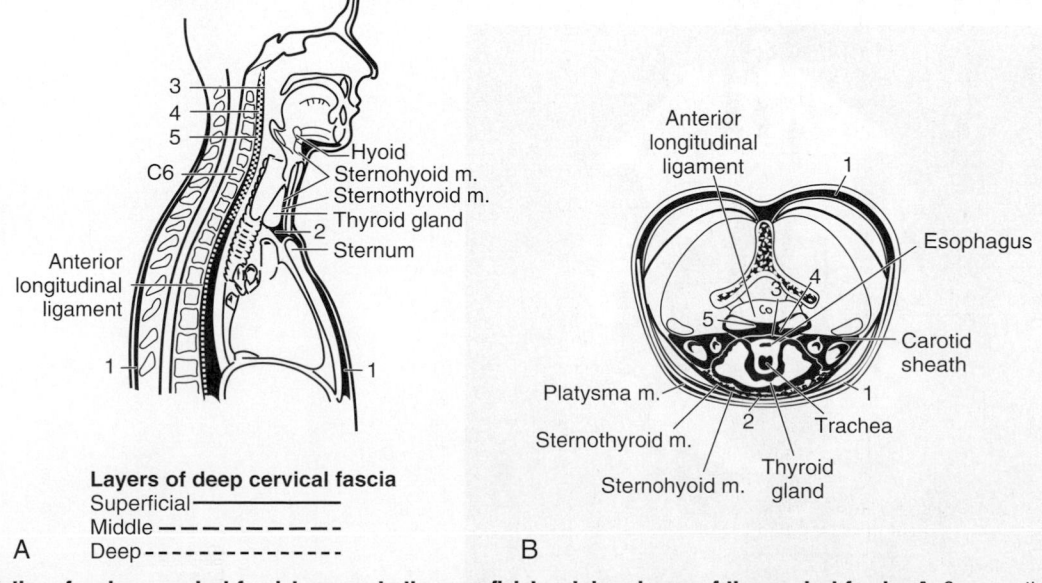

FIGURE 1R-23 Relation of various cervical fascial spaces to the superficial and deep layers of the cervical fascia. A, Cross section of the neck at the level of the thyroid isthmus. **B,** Coronal section in the suprahyoid region of the neck. *1,* Superficial space; *2,* pretracheal space; *3,* retropharyngeal space; *4,* "danger" space; *5,* prevertebral space.

- A CT scan of the neck is the best tool to identify abscesses in the retropharyngeal area, but it is not perfect. Both the sensitivity and specificity of the CT scan in predicting the presence of drainable purulent material are quite variable from study to study, ranging between 68% and 100%.
  - The CT scan provides more information than the plain radiograph because it can generally differentiate between retropharyngeal cellulitis and retropharyngeal abscess and can demonstrate extension of the retropharyngeal abscess to contiguous spaces in the neck. Findings on CT common to both cellulitis and abscess are a low-density core, soft tissue swelling, obliterated fat planes, and mass effect. The best differential finding on CT scan is "complete rim enhancement," which is indicative of abscess (Fig. 1R-25). The abscess may be seen as a mass impinging on the posterior pharyngeal wall.
- MRI of the neck is more sensitive than CT, and technetium scanning can be helpful

in detecting bone involvement. T2-weighted images may identify and localize areas of pus for drainage or aspiration. Gadolinium enhancement is important to accurately define the soft tissue component. Finally, MRI is useful for imaging vascular lesions, such as jugular thrombophlebitis.

TREATMENT

ACUTE GENERAL & CHRONIC Rx

- High-dose penicillin (2 million to 4 million units IV q4h) plus metronidazole (500 mg IV q8h) or ampicillin-sulbactam (50 mg/kg/dose IV q6h) or clindamycin (13 mg/kg/dose IV q8h) are effective antimicrobial selections. Parenteral treatment is maintained until the patient is afebrile and clinically improved. Antibiotics should be adjusted as culture data become available, and oral therapy is continued to complete at least a 14-day course.
- Surgical intervention has historically played a prominent role in the management of

retropharyngeal abscess in conjunction with antibiotic therapy. Drainage is indicated when there is a large hypodense area or when a patient has not responded to parenteral therapy alone.
- When the CT does not demonstrate a large hypodense area, a trial of antibiotic therapy without drainage is appropriate. Some investigators also support a trial of IV antibiotic therapy alone when small abscesses are identified by CT scans as long as there is no compromise of the airway.

PEARLS & CONSIDERATIONS

PREVENTION

The complications of deep neck infection in any space are numerous and potentially fatal. Early diagnosis, with prompt and appropriate management, is key to avoiding these complications.

AUTHOR: **RUBY K. SATPATHY, M.D.**

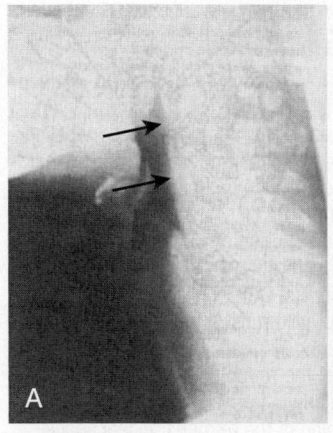
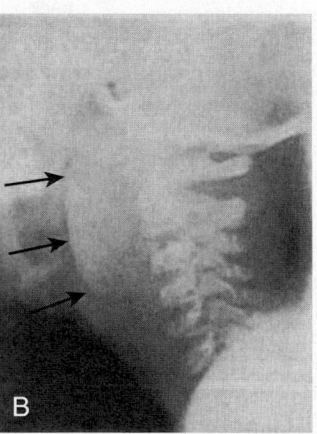

FIGURE 1R-24 Lateral radiographs of the neck show normal lateral cervical view **(A)** and expansion of the prevertebral soft tissues by a retropharyngeal abscess **(B).**

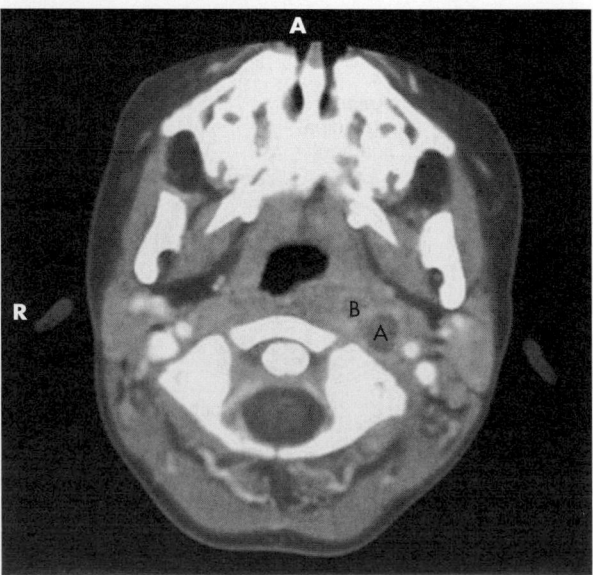

FIGURE 1R-25 CT scan of a retropharyngeal abscess (A and B) demonstrates a low-density core, soft tissue swelling, obliterated fat planes, mass effect, and rim enhancement.

BASIC INFORMATION

DEFINITION

Rh incompatibility occurs when a pregnant woman has Rh-negative blood and her baby has positive blood. This situation causes risk of isoimmunization.

ICD-10CM CODES
O36.0910 Maternal care for other rhesus isoimmunization, first trimester, not applicable or unspecified
T80.4 Rh incompatibility reaction
T80.4 Unspecified complication following infusion, transfusion, and therapeutic injection

EPIDEMIOLOGY & DEMOGRAPHICS

INCIDENCE:
- The absence of the D antigen (Rh negative blood type) occurs in 15% of whites, 7% of blacks, and less than 1% of the Native American and Asian populations. If the father's blood type is not known, the chance that an Rh − pregnant woman is bearing an Rh + fetus is approximately 60%.
- Of those pregnancies complicated by Rh incompatibility, the risk of maternal isoimmunization to the D antigen is approximately 8% for each ABO-compatible pregnancy if no prophylaxis is given.
- Maternal-fetal ABO incompatibility is somewhat protective against Rh isoimmunization.

GENETICS: Five major loci determine Rh status: C, D, E, c, e. The presence of the D antigen results in an Rh + individual, while its absence results in an Rh − individual. Of Rh + fathers, 45% are homozygotes, and 55% are heterozygotes. For homozygous Rh + fathers, the probability of an Rh + offspring is 100%. The probability for heterozygotes is approximately 50%.

RISK FACTORS:
- RhD-negative woman.
- Antepartum: fetal-to-maternal transfusion.
- Intrapartum: fetal-to-maternal transfusion, spontaneous abortion, ectopic pregnancy, abruptio placentae, abdominal trauma, chorionic villus sampling, amniocentesis, percutaneous umbilical blood sampling (PUBS), external cephalic version, manual removal of the placenta, therapeutic abortion, autologous blood product administration.
- Maternal history of hydrops or sensitization to RhD.

ETIOLOGY

The initial response to D antigen exposure is production of immunoglobulin (Ig) M (molecular weight 900,000) that does not cross the placenta.

With a repeated exposure, IgG (MW 160,000) is produced. Hemolysis in the fetus results once maternal IgG is present in the fetal circulation by crossing the placenta. This may produce erythroblastosis fetalis or hemolytic disease in the newborn, resulting in antepartum or neonatal death or neurologic damage to the fetus because of hyperbilirubinemia and kernicterus.

DIAGNOSIS

LABORATORY TESTS

ABO and Rh blood type and an antibody screen as part of the initial prenatal profile.
- If antibody screen negative:
  1. Repeat antibody screen at 28 wk gestation.
  2. Obtain neonatal blood type after delivery.
  3. If Rh incompatibility is confirmed by the neonatal blood type, a Kleihauer-Betke/ flow cytometry or rosette test should be performed to determine the amount of fetomaternal transfusion in the following high-risk circumstances: abruptio placentae, placenta previa, cesarean delivery, intrauterine manipulation, manual removal of the placenta.
- If anti-D antibody screen is positive:
  1. Maternal indirect Coombs test is needed to determine antibody titer.
  2. Determine paternal Rh status and zygosity.
  3. If father is heterozygous, PUBS or amniotic fluid is needed to determine fetal Rh status.

IMAGING STUDIES

Ultrasound evaluation may show subcutaneous edema, ascites, pleural effusion, pericardial effusion, or hepatomegaly. It can diagnose hydrops fetalis, but it cannot predict it.

Doppler ultrasound of middle cerebral artery can predict moderate to severe anemia.

TREATMENT

PREVENTION OF D ISOIMMUNIZATION

- 50 mcg of D immunoglobulin: after spontaneous or induced abortion or ectopic pregnancy <13 wk gestation.
- 300 mcg of D immunoglobulin (protects against 30 ml of fetal blood).
  1. After spontaneous or induced abortion >13 wk gestation, amniocentesis, chorionic villous sampling, PUBS, external cephalic version, or other intrauterine manipulation.
  2. As antepartum prophylaxis at 28 wk gestation. Maternal anti-D prophylaxis does not cause hemolysis in the fetus or newborn.

3. At 40 wk gestation or at delivery if the neonate is D- or Du-positive.
4. If Kleihauer-Betke or rosette test confirms >30 mL of fetal red blood in maternal circulation, additional D immunoglobulin is indicated. Confirm adequacy of therapy by a maternal indirect Coombs test 48 to 72 hr after Rh immune globulin is given.

MANAGEMENT OF D ISOIMMUNIZED PREGNANCIES

- Serial amniocentesis for assessment of amount of fetal bilirubin in fluid (OD_{450}) after 25 wk gestation with interpretation of the Delta OD_{450} according to criteria established by Liley.
- PUBS if ultrasonographic evidence of hydrops, rising zone II Delta OD_{450} values on amniocentesis, or maternal history of a severely affected child.
- Intrauterine exchange transfusion if severe anemia is documented remote from term.
- Initiation of steroids for lung maturation at 28 wk in severely affected pregnancies with delivery at lung maturity.
- Delivery as soon as lung maturation is achieved in mild to moderately affected pregnancies.

Fig. 1R-26 shows an algorithm for clinical management of a patient with red cell sensitization in the first affected pregnancy and Fig. 1R-27 shows an algorithm for clinical management of a patient with red cell sensitization and a previously affected fetus or infant.

DISPOSITION

Survival of nonhydropic infants is 90%. Of infants with hydrops, 82% survive.

REFERRAL

Refer all Rh isoimmunized pregnancies to a tertiary care center before 18 to 20 wk gestation.

SUGGESTED READINGS
Available at www.expertconsult.com

AUTHORS: **HUSSAIN NASERI, M.D.,** and **BHARTI RATHORE, M.D.**

Diseases and Disorders

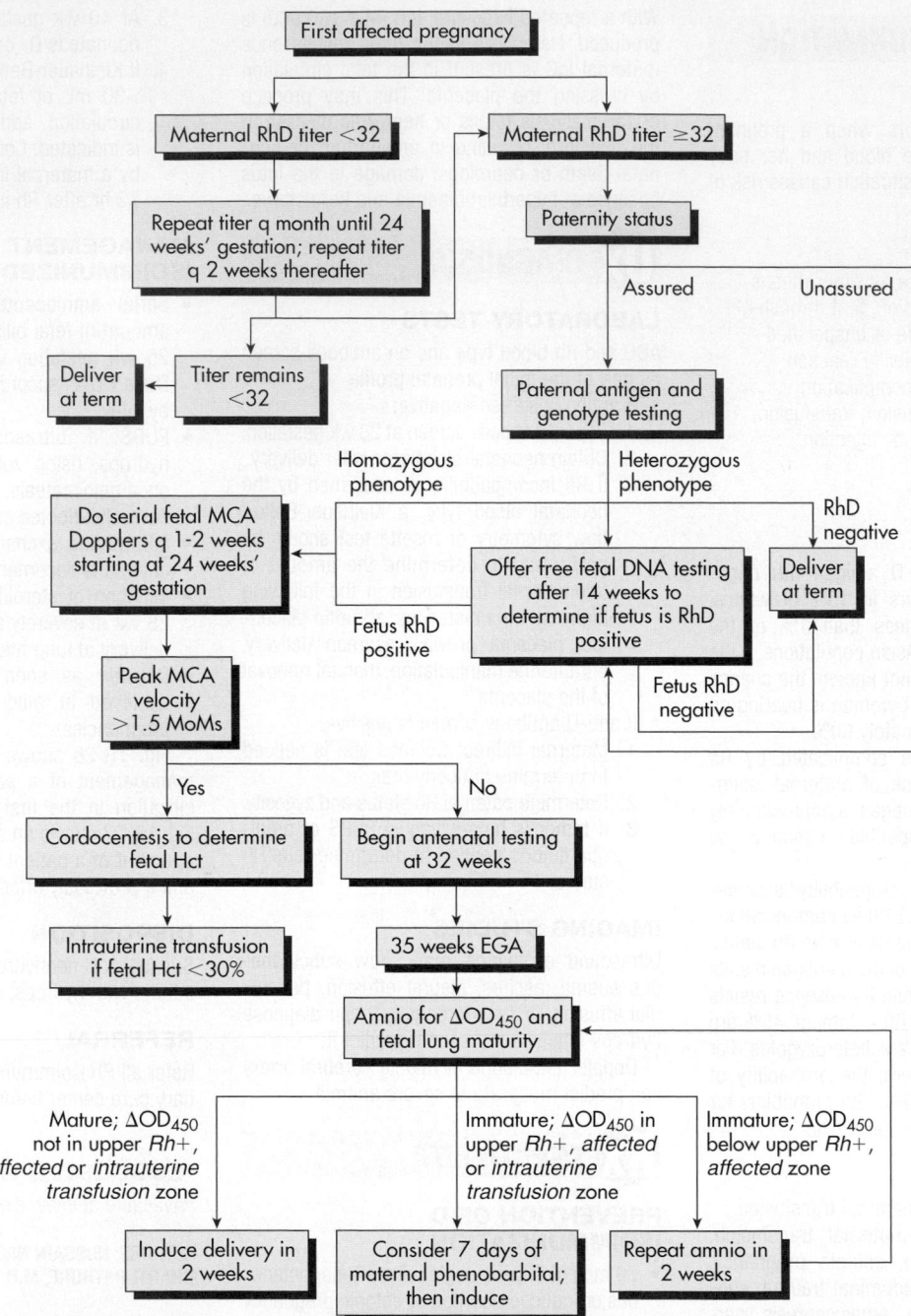

FIGURE 1R-26 Algorithm for clinical management of a patient with red cell sensitization in the first affected pregnancy. (From Gabbe SG: Obstetrics, ed 6, Philadelphia, 2012, Saunders.)

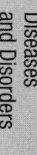

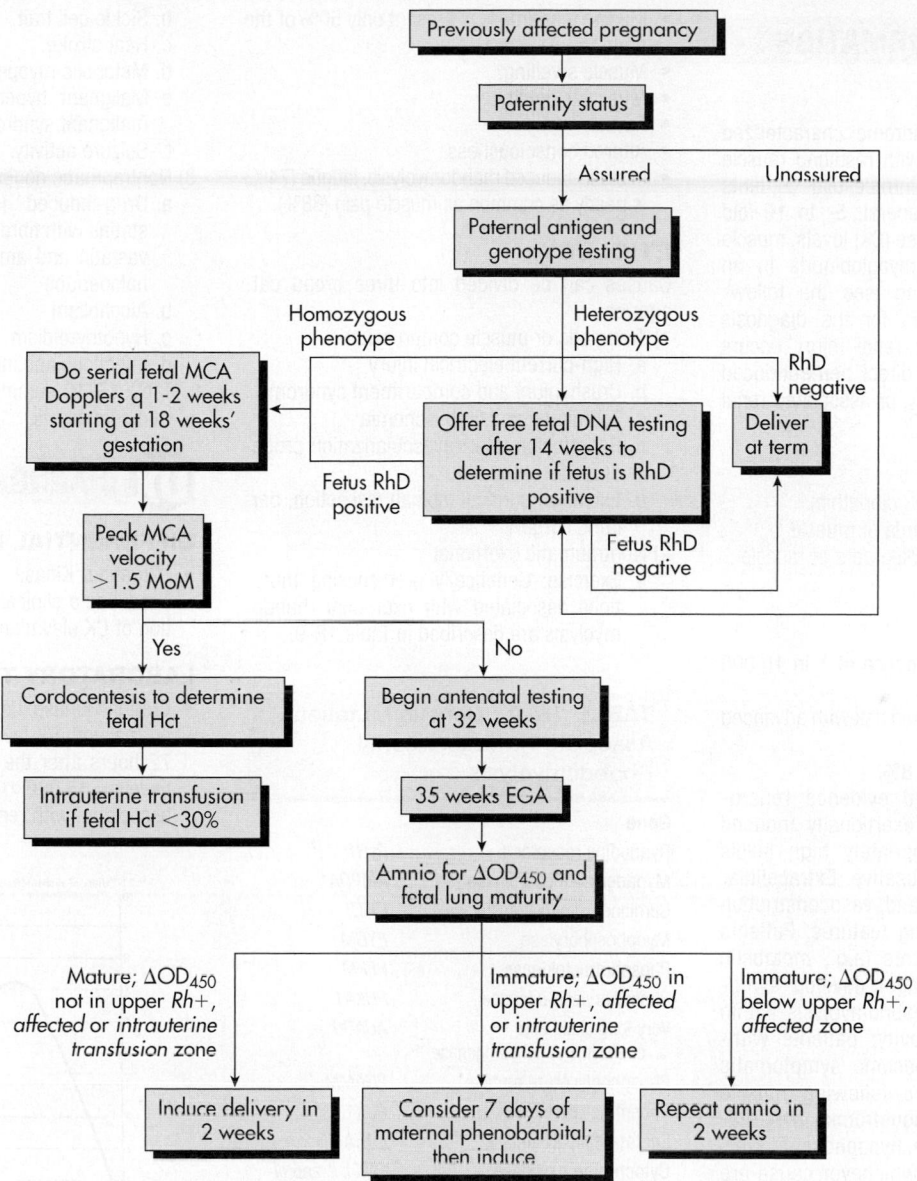

FIGURE 1R-27 Algorithm for clinical management of a patient with red cell sensitization and a previously affected fetus or infant. (From Gabbe SG; *Obstetrics,* 6 ed, Philadelphia, 2012, Saunders.)

BASIC INFORMATION

DEFINITION

Rhabdomyolysis is a syndrome characterized by striated muscle lysis with resulting muscle damage and leakage of intracellular contents into the circulation. In general, 5- to 10-fold elevations of creatine kinase (CK) levels, muscle pain, and presence of myoglobinuria in an appropriate clinical setting (see the following) are sufficient criteria for the diagnosis of rhabdomyolysis. Acute renal injury occurs from tubular obstruction, direct heme-induced proximal tubular cell injury, or associated renal vasoconstriction.

ICD-10CM CODES
M62.82 Rhabdomyolysis (idiopathic)
T79.6   Traumatic ischemia of muscle
M62.89 Other specified disorders of muscle

EPIDEMIOLOGY & DEMOGRAPHICS

PREDOMINANT AGE: Incidence of 1 in 10,000 in the U.S.
Rare in children. Increased risk with advanced age, i.e., >80 years
MORTALITY RATE: 5% to 8%.
ONSET: There is limited evidence regarding timing of onset of exertionally induced rhabdomyolysis. Inappropriately high levels of exercise are often causative. Extracellular fluid volume depletion and vasoconstriction are common predisposing features. Patients with increased risk factors (e.g., metabolic myopathies, advanced age) develop symptoms associated with rhabdomyolysis within 2 to 6 hours after activity; patients without such risk factors become symptomatic around 12 to 36 hours following muscle injury. Hypokalemia, hyponatremia, hypernatremia, hypomagnesemia, hypophosphatemia, and hypocalcemia from whichever cause are predisposing.

CK levels rise within 2 to 12 hours of the onset of muscle injury, peak generally by 24 to 72 hours, and decline 3 to 5 days after cessation of muscle injury. Peak CK concentrations may predict development of renal injury. In patients with rhabdomyolysis secondary to malignant hyperthermia, CK concentrations peak approximately 14 hours after acute episode.

Cholesterol-lowering therapy with "statin" agents is common, and rhabdomyolysis occurs infrequently with these medications, although myalgias are a frequent complaint. The average duration of statin therapy before the onset of myopathy is 6 months with symptom resolution, and normalization of serum CK concentrations occurs within days to weeks following drug discontinuation. The average time for onset of rhabdomyolysis after addition of fibrate to statin therapy is 32 days.

PHYSICAL FINDINGS & CLINICAL PRESENTATION

- Classic triad: 1) muscle pain, 2) weakness, and 3) dark urine from myoglobinuria.

- Muscle tenderness is present only 50% of the time.
- Muscle swelling.
- Muscular rigidity.
- Fever.
- Altered consciousness.
- In statin-induced rhabdomyolysis, fatigue (74%) is nearly as common as muscle pain (88%).

ETIOLOGY

Causes can be divided into three broad categories:
1) Traumatic or muscle compression
   a. High-current electrical injury
   b. Crush injury and compartment syndrome
   c. Tourniquet and limb ischemia
   d. Reperfusion after revascularization procedures for ischemia
   e. Extensive surgical (spinal) dissection, bariatric surgery
2) Nontraumatic exertional
   a. Exercise: Genetically predisposing mutations associated with exertional rhabdomyolysis are described in Table 1R-9.

TABLE 1R-9 Genetic Mutations Associated with Exertional Rhabdomyolysis

Gene	
Ryanodine receptor 1	RyR1
Myoadenylate deaminase	AMPDA1
Carnitine palmitoyltransferase II	CPT2
Myophosphorylase	PYGM
Phosphofructokinase	PFKM
Phosphorylase b kinase	PHKA1
Very long chain acyl coenzyme-A dehydrogenase	ACAD9
Phosphoglycerate mutase	PGAMM
Phosphoglycerate kinase	PGK1
Lactate dehydrogenase	LDHA
Cytochrome c oxidase	COX I, II, and III
Cytochrome b (complex III)	CYTB
Mitochondrial tRNA	Mt-tRNA
β-Sarcoglycan	SGCB

From Goldman L, Schafer AI: *Goldman's Cecil medicine*, ed 24, Philadelphia, 2012, Saunders.

   b. Sickle cell trait.
   c. Heat stroke.
   d. Metabolic myopathies.
   e. Malignant hyperthermia and neuroleptic malignant syndrome.
   f. Seizure activity.
3) Nontraumatic nonexertional
   a. Drug-induced (statins, combination of statins with fibrates, or erythromycin, simvastatin and amiodarone, amphetamines, haloperidol)
   b. Alcoholism
   c. Hypothyroidism
   d. Infectious and inflammatory myositis
   Table 1R-10 summarizes the various causes of rhabdomyolysis.

DIAGNOSIS

DIFFERENTIAL DIAGNOSIS

- "Creatine Kinase Elevation" in Section IV describes a clinical algorithm for the evaluation of CK elevation.

LABORATORY TESTS

- Creatine kinase: Usually 5× the upper limit of normal with CK levels typically peaking 24 to 72 hours after the initial insult (Fig. 1R-28). Levels >15,000 U/L are more likely to be associated with renal injury.

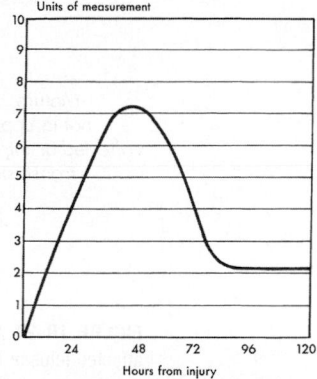

FIGURE 1R-28 Typical creatine kinase elimination curve. (From Rosen P [ed]: *Emergency medicine*, ed 4, St Louis, 1998, Mosby.)

TABLE 1R-10 Causes of Rhabdomyolysis

Muscle Injury/Ischemia	Trauma, Pressure Necrosis, Electric Shock, Burns, Acute Vascular Disease
Myofiber exhaustion	Seizures, excessive exercise, heat exhaustion
Toxins	Alcohol, cocaine, heroin, amphetamines, Ecstasy, phencyclidine, snakebite
Drugs	Statins, fibrates, zidovudine, neuroleptic malignant syndrome, azathioprine, theophylline, lithium, diuretics
Electrolyte disorders	Hypophosphatemia, hypokalemia, excess water shifts (hyperosmolality)
Infections	Viral (influenza, HIV, Coxsackievirus, Epstein-Barr virus), bacterial (*Legionella, Francisella, Streptococcus pneumoniae, Salmonella, Staphylococcus aureus*)
Familial	McArdle's disease, carnitine palmitoyl transferase deficiency, malignant hyperthermia
Other	Hypothyroidism, polymyositis, dermatomyositis

From Floege J et al: *Comprehensive clinical nephrology*, ed 4, Philadelphia, 2010, Saunders.

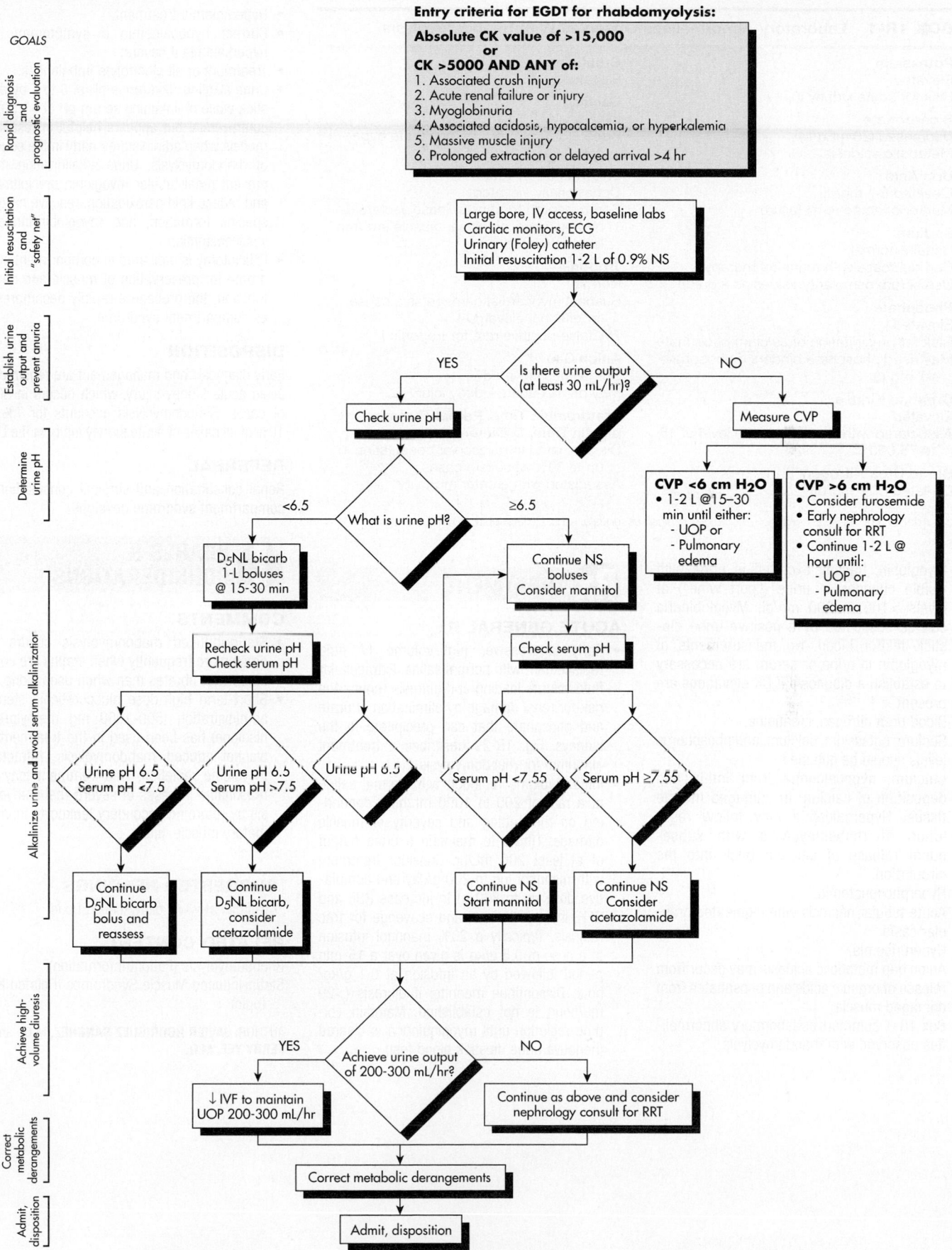

FIGURE 1R-29 Early goal-directed therapy for rhabdomyolysis. *CK,* Creatine kinase; *CVP,* central venous pressure; *D5NL bicarb,* 5% dextrose in normal sodium bicarbonate solution; *EGDT,* early goal-directed therapy; *IV,* intravenous; *IVF,* intravenous fluid; *NS,* normal saline; *RRT,* renal replacement therapy; *UOP,* urinary output. (From Adams JG et al: Emergency Medicine, Clinical Essentials, 2nd ed, Philadelphia, Elsevier 2013.)

BOX 1R-1 Laboratory Abnormalities Observed With Rhabdomyolysis

Potassium
Elevated
Risk for acute kidney injury

Bicarbonate
Decreased (20 mEq/L)
Metabolic acidosis

Uric Acid
Elevated (>7 mg/dl)
Marker of acute renal failure

Sodium
Usually normal
Can decrease with mannitol therapy
Use serum osmolarity values as a guide

Phosphate
Elevated
Risk for precipitation of calcium phosphate
May need phosphate binders if phosphate >7 mg/dl

Creatine Kinase
Elevated
Associated with creatine kinase level of 15 to 75,000

Blood Urea Nitrogen
Elevated (>20 mg/dl)

Creatinine
Elevated

Calcium
Initially low
Rebound phase may demonstrate hypercalcemia

Liver Function Tests
Occasionally elevated
Serum aspartate transaminase, lactate dehydrogenase, aldolase, muscle enzyme levels elevated

Troponin
Normal
Suspect myocardial damage as a cause (or effect) if elevated
7% false-positive rate for troponin I

Anion Gap
Sometimes elevated
May predict acute kidney injury

Prothrombin Time, Partial Thromboplastin Time, D-Dimer
Disseminated intravascular coagulation in up to 30% of severe cases
Associated with greater mortality

From Adams J.G.; et al. *Emergency medicine, clinical essentials,* ed 2, Philadelphia, 2013, Elsevier.

- Myoglobin: Rapidly excreted in urine with visible changes in urine ("port wine") at levels >100 to 300 mg/dl. Myoglobinuria can be suspected by a positive urine dipstick test for blood. No measurements of myoglobin in urine or serum are necessary to establish a diagnosis if CK elevations are present.
- Blood urea nitrogen, creatinine.
- Sodium, potassium, calcium, and phosphorus levels should be obtained.
- Calcium: hypocalcemia from influx and deposition of calcium in damaged muscle tissue. Hypercalcemia may follow resolution of rhabdomyolysis with subsequent release of calcium back into the circulation.
- Hyperphosphatemia.
- Acute tubular necrosis with pigmented granular casts.
- Hyperuricemia.
- Anion gap metabolic acidosis may occur from release of organic acids and phosphates from damaged muscle.
- Box 1R-1 summarizes laboratory abnormalities observed with rhabdomyolysis.

 **TREATMENT**

ACUTE GENERAL Rx

- Early, aggressive, high-volume IV fluid replacement with normal saline. Extracellular fluid volume loading and diuresis reduce the risk for renal damage by elimination of urate and phosphate that can precipitate in the kidneys. Fig. 1R-29 describes a treatment algorithm for rhabdomyolysis.
- Initiate volume repletion with normal saline at a rate of 200 to 1000 mL/hour depending on the setting and severity of muscle damage. Titrate to maintain a urine output of at least 200 mL/hr. Consider treatment with mannitol (up to 200 g/day and cumulative dose up to 800 g) to increase RBF and GFR, induce diuresis, and scavenge for free radicals. Typically a 20% mannitol infusion at a dose of 0.5 g/kg is given over a 15-min period followed by an infusion at 0.1 g/kg/ hour. Discontinue mannitol if diuresis (>20 mL/hour) is not established. Maintain volume repletion until myoglobinuria is cleared (negative urine dipstick blood test).

- Hyperkalemia treatment.
- Correct hypocalcemia if symptomatic or hyperkalemia if severe.
- Treatment of all electrolyte imbalances.
- Urine alkalinization (urine pH of 6 to 7 by dipstick while maintaining serum pH at ~7.50) is controversial but appears helpful in research models when administered early in the course of rhabdomyolysis. Urine alkalinization may prevent renal tubular myoglobin precipitation and reduce lipid peroxidation, reactive oxygen species formation, and myoglobin-induced vasoconstriction.
- Fasciotomy is indicated in compartment syndrome for preservation of muscle and nerve function; the procedure rapidly decompresses compartment syndrome.

DISPOSITION

Early diagnosis and management are required to avoid acute kidney injury, which occurs in 30% of cases. Rhabdomyolysis accounts for 7% to 10% of all cases of acute kidney injury in the U.S.

REFERRAL

Renal consultation and surgical consultation if compartment syndrome develops

⊘ PEARLS & CONSIDERATIONS

COMMENTS

- Statin-induced rhabdomyolysis occurs 12 times more frequently when statins are combined with fibrates than when used alone.
- Short-term high-dose glucocorticoid steroid administration (500-1000 mg methylprednisolone) has been used in the treatment of alcohol-induced rhabdomyolysis, refractory to volume repletion. This treatment may be reasonable in cases of severe rhabdomyolysis by retarding secondary leukocyte inflammatory muscle injury.

SUGGESTED READINGS

Available at www.expertconsult.com

RELATED CONTENT

Rhabdomyolysis (Patient Information)
Statin-Induced Muscle Syndromes (Related Key Topic)

AUTHOR: **JAVIER RODRIGUEZ SANCHEZ, M.D.,** and **JERRY YEE, M.D.**

BASIC INFORMATION

DEFINITION

Rheumatoid arthritis (RA) is a systemic auto-immune disease characterized by inflammatory polyarthritis which affects peripheral joints, especially the small joints of the hands and feet. It is a chronic, progressive disease in which untreated inflammation may lead to cartilage and bone erosions and joint destruction resulting in functional impairment.

ICD-10CM CODES

M06.9	Rheumatoid arthritis, unspecified
M05.10	Rheumatoid lung disease with rheumatoid arthritis of unspecified site
M05.20	Rheumatoid vasculitis with rheumatoid arthritis of unspecified site
M05.30	Rheumatoid heart disease with rheumatoid arthritis of unspecified site
M05.39	Rheumatoid heart disease with rheumatoid arthritis of multiple sites
M05.40	Rheumatoid myopathy with rheumatoid arthritis of unspecified site
M05.49	Rheumatoid myopathy with rheumatoid arthritis of multiple sites
M05.50	Rheumatoid polyneuropathy with rheumatoid arthritis of unspecified site
M05.59	Rheumatoid polyneuropathy with rheumatoid arthritis of multiple sites
M05.60	Rheumatoid arthritis of unspecified site with involvement of other organs and systems
M05.69	Rheumatoid arthritis of multiple sites with involvement of other organs and systems
M05.70	Rheumatoid arthritis with rheumatoid factor of unspecified site without organ or systems involvement
M05.79	Rheumatoid arthritis with rheumatoid factor of multiple sites without organ or systems involvement
M05.80	Other rheumatoid arthritis with rheumatoid factor of unspecified site

EPIDEMIOLOGY & DEMOGRAPHICS

INCIDENCE: Annual incidence in northern Europe and the United States 0.15 to 0.60 per 1000.
TYPICAL AGE AT DIAGNOSIS: Usually fourth or fifth decade. Steadily increases with age until the mid-70s.
PREVALENCE: 0.5% to 1.0% of the worldwide population, with different rates in different ethnic groups.
PREDOMINANT SEX: *Females > males (2-3:1).*
RISK FACTORS: Female gender, age, tobacco use, silica exposure, and obesity.

PHYSICAL FINDINGS & CLINICAL PRESENTATION

Initial presentation:
Pain, swelling, warmth in one or more peripheral joints, frequently with symmetric small joint involvement, often associated with >1 hour of morning stiffness and constitutional symptoms such as fatigue, malaise, low-grade fevers, and weight loss occurring over a period of weeks to months. A subset of patients can also present with acute onset polyarthritis instead of insidious symptoms.
Most common joints involved include metacarpophalangeal (MCP) joints, proximal interphalangeal (PIP) joints, and metatarsophalangeal (MTP) joints as well as wrists.
Other affected joints involved include elbows, shoulders, hips, knees, and ankles.
Distal interphalangeal (DIP) joints are spared.
Sacroiliac and vertebral joints are spared, except for the C1 and C2 articulations.
Chronic longstanding disease:
"Swan-neck" (DIP flexion and PIP hyperextension), "boutonniere" (DIP hyperextension and PIP flexion), and "Z-thumb" (MCP flexion and IP hyperextension) deformities (Fig. 1R-30), ulnar deviation and subluxation of the MCP joints (Fig. 1R-31) as well as radial deviation of the wrists.
C1-C2 (atlantoaxial) inflammation can lead to odontoid erosion and transverse ligament laxity/rupture, resulting in atlantoaxial subluxation and cord compression.

Joint damage of wrists, elbows, shoulders, hips, and knees can lead to severe osteoarthritis, necessitating joint surgery and/or replacement.
Extraarticular manifestations:
Secondary Sjögren's syndrome (~35%): immune-mediated inflammation of lacrimal and salivary glands, resulting in dry mouth (xerostomia) and eyes (keratoconjunctivitis sicca).
Rheumatoid nodules (25%): nontender, firm nodules on extensor surfaces and pressure points, usually in rheumatoid factor positive (RF+) disease. Histopathology demonstrates palisading histiocytes surrounding a central area of fibrinoid necrosis.
Felty's syndrome: RA with splenomegaly and leukopenia. Most patients are positive for HLA-DR4 and RF.
Pulmonary disease:
Pleural disease (exudative effusions, pleuritis).
Interstitial lung disease (up to 10% clinically significant).
Bronchiolitis obliterans.
Cryptogenic organizing pneumonia.
Pulmonary nodules. A combination of RA and pneumoconiosis is called Caplan syndrome.
Neuromuscular:
Entrapment neuropathy (carpal tunnel, tarsal tunnel, cubital tunnel most commonly involved).
Mononeuritis multiplex.
Peripheral neuropathy. Cervical myelopathy and cord compression in atlantoaxial subluxation.
Pachymeningitis (rare).
Vasculitis.
Cardiac disease:
Pericarditis (most common).
Myocarditis.
Valvular nodules.
There is an increased risk of cardiovascular disease compared to the general population, probably due to accelerated atherosclerosis from systemic inflammation.
Ocular disease:
Keratoconjunctivitis sicca (dry eye, without dry mouth) (10%).
Episcleritis, scleritis, scleral thinning, scleromalacia perforans, ulcerative keratitis.
Amyloidosis: occurs in longstanding, poorly controlled RA. Usually presents as nephrotic syndrome. Can affect heart, kidney, liver, spleen, intestines, and skin.
Osteoporosis.

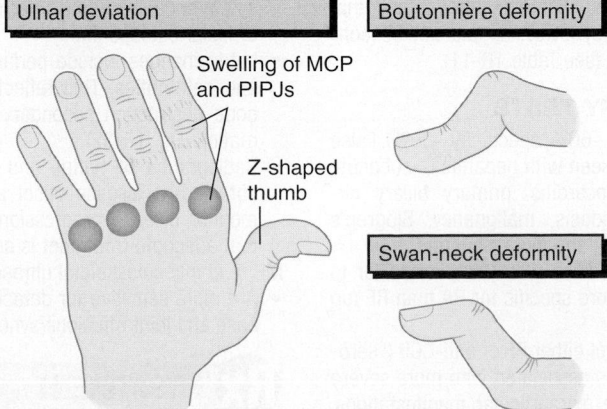

Ulnar deviation
Boutonnière deformity
Swelling of MCP and PIPJs
Z-shaped thumb
Swan-neck deformity

FIGURE 1R-30 Characteristic hand deformities in rheumatoid arthritis. *MCP,* Metacarpophalanges; *PIPJs,* proximal interphalangeal joints. (From Ballinger A: *Kumar & Clark's essentials of clinical medicine,* ed 6, Edinburgh, 2012, Saunders.)

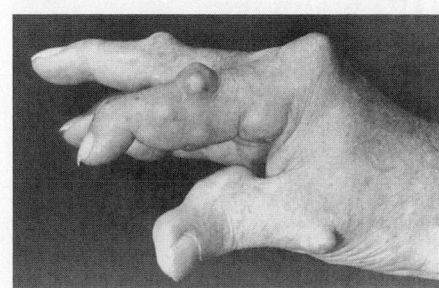

FIGURE 1R-31 Rheumatoid arthritis. Hand of a 60-year-old man with seropositive rheumatoid arthritis. There are fixed deformities and gross rheumatoid nodules. (From Canoso JJ: *Rheumatology in primary care,* Philadelphia, 1997, Saunders.)

ETIOLOGY

The exact cause of RA remains unknown despite extensive research. It is likely that a combination of genetic, hormonal, and environmental factors lead to aberrant immune activation and inflammatory response in the joint. A common genetic background plays a role in susceptibility to disease, as twins and first-degree relatives of RA patients are at increased risk of developing the disease compared to the general population. Patients with HLA-DR4, DR1, and DR14 alleles have increased susceptibility to RA; in particular, one amino acid sequence in the DR β chain, known as the shared epitope, is over-represented in these patients. Other identified genetic associations include polymorphisms in *PTPN22, PADI4, CTLA4, TRAF1-C5, STAT4, TNFAIP3*. Epigenetic factors are also likely to be involved. Multiple environmental factors have also been implicated as possible etiologic factors, including cigarette smoking, silica exposure, and low socioeconomic class. Infectious agents such as *P. gingivalis*, Epstein-Barr virus, and parvovirus B19 have also been reported as possible triggers.

Stages of disease development presumably include:

- Initiation of the innate immune response through toll-like receptor (TLR) activation by a stimulating signal.
- Perpetuation of inflammatory response through activation of the adaptive immune system. There is migration of inflammatory cells (autoreactive B and T cells, monocytes) into the joint space, activation of macrophage-like and fibroblast-like synoviocytes, and development of a "synovial pannus," a thickened synovial membrane.
- The pannus releases proinflammatory cytokines (TNF-α, IL-1, IL-6, IL-15, IL-17, IL-18) as well as proteases, which erode cartilage and bone. Bone erosions are caused mainly by osteoclasts, which express the receptor activator of NF-κB (RANK). TNF-α, IL-1, and IL-17 promote the expression of RANK ligand (RANKL) on T cells and fibroblast-like synoviocytes.
- Many of the new "biologic" disease-modifying antirheumatic drugs (DMARDs) are engineered to target these cytokines (see treatment section).

Ⓓ🅧 DIAGNOSIS

The American College of Rheumatology and the European League against Rheumatism developed new classification criteria for RA in 2010. These are based on a point system where patients with score ≥6/10 are considered to have "definite RA." Four variables constitute the new criteria:

1. The number and size of involved joints (0 to 5 points, with higher scores for a larger number of small joints affected).
2. Levels of rheumatoid factor (RF) and anti-cyclic citrullinated peptide (CCP) antibody (0 to 3 points, with a higher score for a high-titer positive RF or anti-CCP).

TABLE 1R-11 Factors Useful for Differentiating Early Rheumatoid Arthritis from Osteoarthritis

	Rheumatoid Arthritis	Osteoarthritis
Age at onset	Childhood and adults, peak incidence in 50s	Increases with age
Predisposing factors	Susceptibility epitopes (HLA-DR4, HLA-DR1, HLA-DR14)	Trauma
	Polymorphisms, epigenetic factors, infectious agents	Congenital abnormalities (e.g., shallow acetabulum)
	Smoking, silica exposure	
Early symptoms	Morning stiffness, pain, swelling	Pain increases through the day and with use
Joints involved	Wrists, MCP, PIP, and MTP joints; DIP joints are almost never involved.	DIP joints (Heberden's nodes), PIP joints (Bouchard's nodes), carpometacarpal joints, weight-bearing joints (hips, knees)
Physical findings	Soft tissue swelling, warmth	Bony osteophytes, minimal soft tissue swelling early on, crepitus
Radiologic findings	Periarticular osteopenia, marginal erosions	Subchondral sclerosis, osteophytes
Laboratory findings	Increased CRP, RF, and anti-CCP antibody, anemia, thrombocytosis	Normal

anti-CCP, anticitrullinated protein; *CRP-RF*, C-reactive protein-rheumatoid factor; *DIP*, distal interphalangeal joint; *MCP*, metacarpophalangeal joint; *MTP*, metatarsophalangeal joint; *PIP*, proximal interphalangeal joint.

3. Elevated erythrocyte sedimentation rate (ESR) or C-reactive protein (CRP) (1 point).
4. Symptom duration ≥6 weeks (1 point).

DIFFERENTIAL DIAGNOSIS

- Infectious causes: parvovirus B19, hepatitis B, hepatitis C, poststreptococcal reactive arthritis, acute rheumatic fever.
- Connective tissue diseases: systemic lupus erythematosus, scleroderma, mixed connective tissue disease, Sjögren's syndrome.
- Seronegative spondyloarthropathies.
- Calcium pyrophosphate deposition (CPPD or "pseudo-RA").
- Polyarticular gout.
- Polymyalgia rheumatica.
- Remitting seronegative symmetric synovitis with pitting edema (RS3PE) can resemble seronegative RA in elderly patients.
- Hemochromatosis.
- Paraneoplastic syndrome.
- Osteoarthritis, a degenerative arthritis that lacks prolonged morning stiffness and that usually lacks synovitis, should not be confused with RA (see Table 1R-11).

LABORATORY TESTS

- RF (sensitivity ~60%; specificity ~80%). False positives are seen with hepatitis C, subacute bacterial endocarditis, primary biliary cirrhosis, sarcoidosis, malignancy, Sjögren's syndrome, SLE, and increasing age.
- Anti-CCP antibodies. Sensitivity is similar to RF, but it is more specific for RA than RF (up to 95%-98%).
- The presence of either RF or anti-CCP ("sero-positive RA") is associated with more severe disease, more extraarticular manifestations, and worse prognosis.
- Elevated ESR and/or CRP. Will decline with treatment; thus can be used to monitor dis-

ease activity along with physical examination and clinical presentation.

- CBC with differential. Possible anemia of chronic disease and thrombocytosis.
- Hypoalbuminemia and hypergammaglobulinemia.
- ANA is present is 20% to 30% of patients. However, complement will usually be normal or increased, in contrast to patients with systemic lupus erythematosus. Many patients will have secondary Sjögren's syndrome (positive ANA with negative SSA and SSB).
- Inflammatory synovial fluid with >2000 PMNs. Of note, patients with RA have an increased risk of developing septic arthritis. Hence, synovial fluid with white blood cells >50,000 cells/mm³ is concerning for an infectious process and must always be ruled out.

IMAGING STUDIES

Plain radiography:

- Early changes include soft tissue swelling, symmetrical joint space narrowing, and periarticular osteopenia.
- Later changes include periarticular erosions and deformities. This reflects cartilage and bone destruction secondary to pannus formation (Fig. 1R-32).
- Radiographs of hands and feet should be obtained at disease onset and repeated to monitor disease progression and to ensure that adequate treatment is achieved.

MRI and musculoskeletal ultrasound:

- Are more sensitive for detecting erosive disease and joint effusions/synovitis.

Ⓡ🅧 TREATMENT

- Early identification and treatment of RA with DMARDs is crucial. More than half of patients

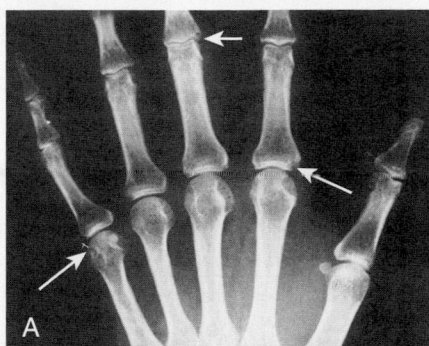

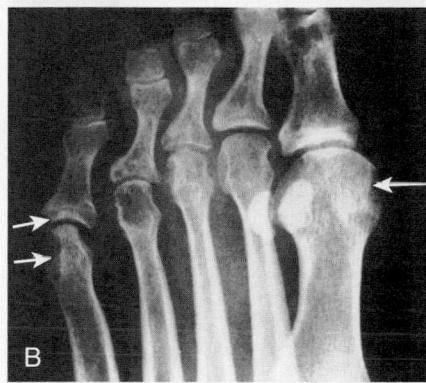

FIGURE 1R-32 Rheumatoid arthritis. A, Periarticular osteopenia and marginal erosions in metacarpophalangeal joints and a proximal interphalangeal joint *(arrows).* **B,** In the same patient, marginal erosions at metatarsal heads. (From Canoso JJ: *Rheumatology in primary care,* Philadelphia, 1997, Saunders.)

have radiographic joint damage within 2 years of disease onset, but early aggressive treatment with DMARDs and/or biologic agents is associated with decreased progression of synovitis and bone erosions, and with decreased disability. Fig. 1R-33 describes the American College of Rheumatology recommendations for treatment of rheumatoid arthritis. Goal of therapy is to "treat to a target" of low disease activity or remission.

ACUTE GENERAL Rx

- NSAIDs: can be used initially to relieve pain and mild inflammation, or used later in the disease course for additional control of mild pain. NSAIDs are not disease modifying.
- Corticosteroids: oral or intraarticular, frequently used initially to reduce inflammation rapidly until oral DMARD treatments take effect. They may also be used during acute flares or in low doses for additional control of inflammation. Corticosteroids have many side effects, including but not limited to weight gain, increased risk of diabetes, osteoporosis, and avascular necrosis.

CHRONIC Rx

DMARDs: Can be classified into "nonbiologic" and "biologic" treatments.

Nonbiologic DMARDs: most commonly used agents are methotrexate (MTX), hydroxychloroquine (HCQ), sulfasalazine (SSZ), and leflunomide (LEF). Most of these are associated with potential toxicity and require close monitoring. They are also slow-acting drugs that require >8 weeks to become fully effective.

MTX is the most commonly used DMARD worldwide for the treatment of RA. It is effective as monotherapy in only 30% of patients with RA.

"Triple therapy"—MTX, HCQ, and SSZ—has been shown to be superior to MTX alone.

Biologic DMARDs: newer biologically engineered therapies, which target cytokines and cells involved in the RA inflammatory response. Major side effects include an increased risk of severe infection, most notably reactivation of tuberculosis with anti-TNF agents. A negative PPD or interferon γ-release assay is a prerequisite to initiate therapy. Biologic DMARDs are most effective when used in combination with a nonbiologic DMARD, usually MTX.

The five approved tumor necrosis factor α inhibitors (TNFI) include infliximab, etanercept, adalimumab, certolizumab pegol, and golimumab.

Abatacept (CTLA-4Ig) is a recombinant protein that prevents costimulatory binding of antigen presenting cell to T cell, preventing T cell activation.

Tocilizumab (anti–IL-6) is a monoclonal antibody against the IL-6 receptor.

Tofacitinib (JAK3 inhibitor) inhibits the JAK-STAT intracellular signaling pathway, thus preventing the production of inflammatory mediators. The first oral biologic DMARD, it can be used as monotherapy or in combination with MTX.

Rituximab (anti-CD20) is a monoclonal antibody against the CD20 antigen on B lymphocytes.

Immunization, cardiovascular disease prevention (smoking cessation, blood pressure control, cholesterol control), and osteoporosis prevention (with calcium and vitamin D supplementation and bisphosphonate therapy) should be addressed in all RA patients.

DISPOSITION

- Remissions and exacerbations are common, but condition is chronically progressive in the majority of cases.
- Joint degeneration and deformity often lead to disability. Joint replacement is indicated for patients with severe joint damage whose symptoms are poorly controlled by medical management.
- Early and aggressive diagnosis and treatment are crucial in preventing or slowing joint destruction.

REFERRAL

- Early referral to rheumatologist.
- Orthopedic consultation for corrective surgery.

! PEARLS & CONSIDERATIONS

RA sometimes develops acutely in the postpartum patient; conversely, as high as 75% of pregnant RA patients will experience remission during pregnancy.

SUGGESTED READINGS
Available at www.expertconsult.com

RELATED CONTENT
Rheumatoid Arthritis (Patient Information)

AUTHOR: **EDITH GARNEAU, M.D.**

R

Diseases and Disorders

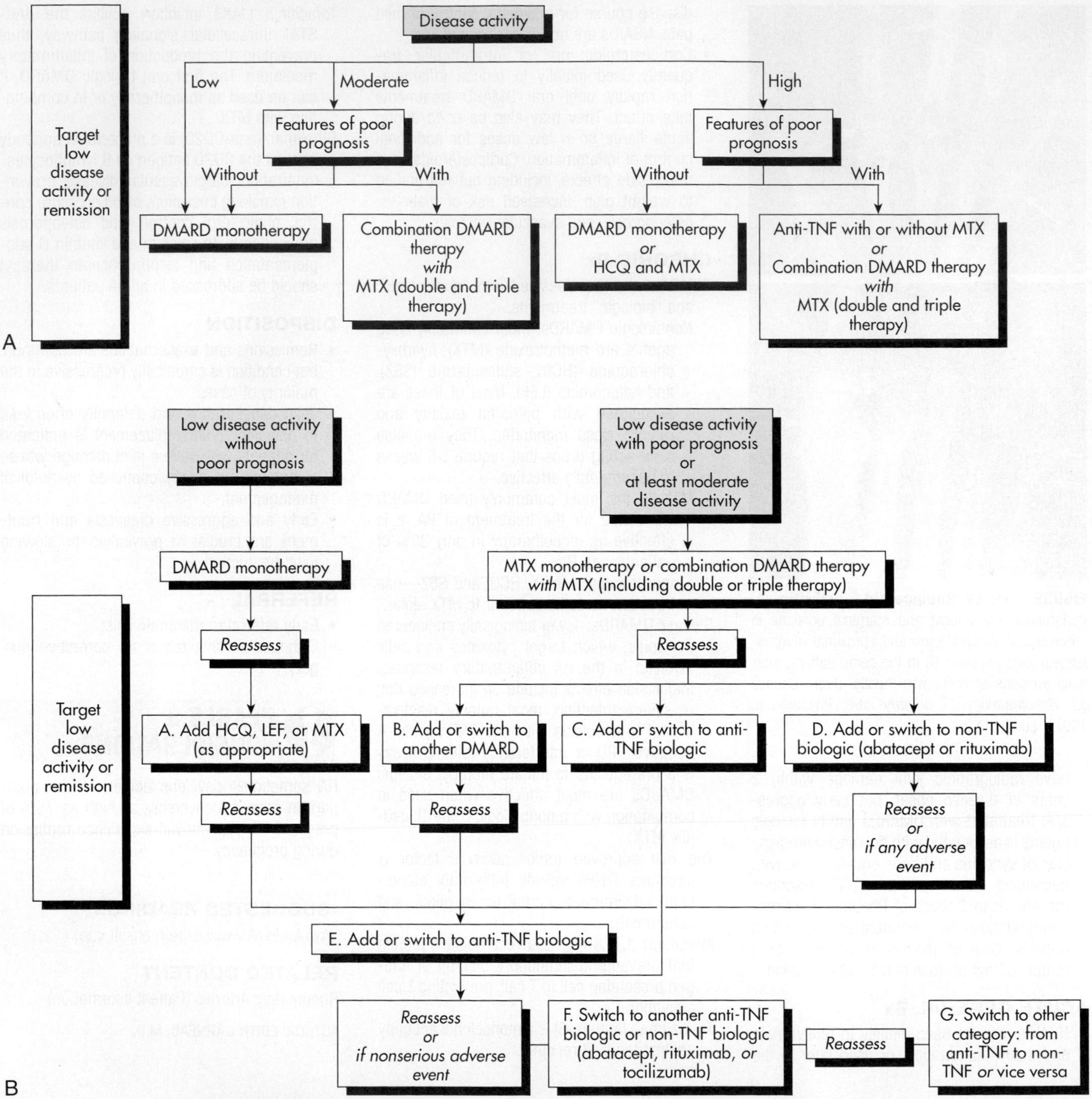

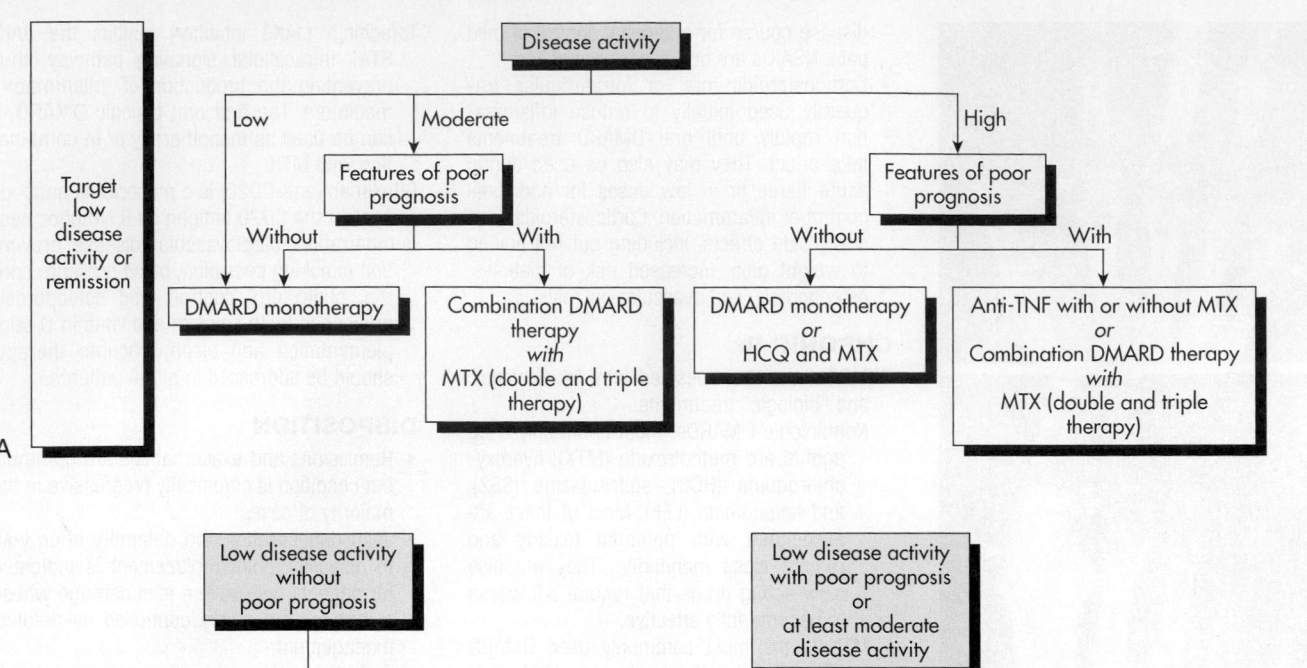

FIGURE 1R-33 **American College of Rheumatology recommendations for treatment of rheumatoid arthritis. A,** Early disease. **B,** Established disease. *DMARD,* Disease-modifying antirheumatic drug; *HCQ,* hydroxychloroquine; *LEF,* leflunomide; *MTX,* methotrexate; *TNF,* tumor necrosis factor. (From Firestein GS: et al. [eds]: *Kelly's textbook of rheumatology,* ed 9, Philadelphia, 2013, Saunders.)

BASIC INFORMATION

DEFINITION

Rocky Mountain spotted fever (RMSF) is a life-threatening, tick-borne febrile illness caused by infection with *Rickettsia rickettsii.* The infection occurs when *R. rickettsii* in the salivary glands of a vector tick is transmitted into the dermis, spreading and replicating in the cytoplasm of endothelial cells and eliciting widespread vasculitis and end-organ damage.

SYNONYMS

RMSF

ICD-10CM CODES
A77.0 Spotted fever due to Rickettsia rickettsii

EPIDEMIOLOGY & DEMOGRAPHICS

INCIDENCE: 0.18 to 0.32 cases per 100,000 person-years. Infections have been reported throughout the United States.

PREVALENCE: Most prevalent in the Southeast, followed by the South Central states, but seen anywhere (Fig. 1R-35). It has recently been reported in eastern Arizona, with common brown dog ticks *(Rhipicephalus sanguineus)* implicated as a vector of *R. rickettsii.*

PREDOMINANT SEX: Affects both genders equally.

PREDOMINANT AGE: Occurs at any age, but more likely in children ages 5 to 14 yr.

PHYSICAL FINDINGS & CLINICAL PRESENTATION

- Incubation: 2 to 14 days
- First symptoms: fever, headache, malaise, myalgias

Common History, Signs, or Symptoms	%
Tick bite	65
Fever	100
Rash	90
Rash on palms and soles (Fig. 1R-36)	80
Headache	90
Myalgia	75
Nausea or vomiting	60
Abdominal pain	40
Conjunctivitis	30
Edema	20
Pneumonitis	15
Any severe neurologic complication (including stupor, delirium, seizures, ataxia, papilledema, focal neurologic deficits, and coma)	30

- Rash: a petechial rash is the hallmark of RMSF
  1. Appears during first 3 days in 50%; by day 5, 80% have it. No rash in 10%.
  2. Initial appearance: blanching erythematous macules on wrists and ankles that then spread to trunk, palms, and soles (Fig. 1R-37). The rash involves palms and soles in more than 30% of cases and usually spares the face.
  3. Lesions may evolve into papules and eventually become nonblanching (petechiae or palpable purpura).
- Gastrointestinal symptoms:
  1. Nausea, vomiting, and abdominal pain are common.
  2. Occasionally may mimic an "acute abdomen" (e.g., appendicitis, cholecystitis).
  3. Mild hepatitis.
- Cardiopulmonary involvement:
  1. Interstitial pneumonitis.
  2. Myocarditis.

- Renal problems:
  1. Prerenal azotemia.
  2. Interstitial nephritis.
  3. Glomerulonephritis.
- Neurologic involvement:
  1. Encephalitis (confusion, lethargy, delirium).
  2. Ataxia.
  3. Convulsion.
  4. Cranial nerve palsy.
  5. Speech impediment.
  6. Hemiparesis or paraparesis.
  7. Spasticity.
- Fulminant RMSF:
  1. Early, widespread vascular necrosis leading to multisystem illness and death.

ETIOLOGY & PATHOGENESIS

- Infectious agent: *R. rickettsii* (an intracellular bacterium).
- Vector: dog tick and wood tick (vertical transmission exists in ticks, but horizontal transmission involving rodents represents an important reservoir for the agent). In the United States *R. rickettsii* is transmitted mainly by the American dog tick *(Dermacentor variabilis)* and the Rocky Mountain wood tick *(D. andersoni).*
- Pathogenesis: the spread of *R. rickettsii* is hematogenous with attachment to the vascular endothelium, causing a vasculitis. The manifestations of this illness are caused by increased vascular permeability.

DIAGNOSIS

DIFFERENTIAL DIAGNOSIS

Influenza A, enteroviral infection, typhoid fever, leptospirosis, infectious mononucleosis, viral hepatitis, sepsis, ehrlichiosis, gastroenteritis, acute abdomen, bronchitis, pneumonia, meningococcemia, disseminated gonococcal infection, secondary syphilis, bacterial endocarditis, toxic shock syndrome, scarlet fever, rheumatic fever, measles, rubella, typhus, rickettsialpox, Lyme disease, drug hypersensitivity reactions, idiopathic thrombocytopenic purpura, thrombotic thrombocytopenic

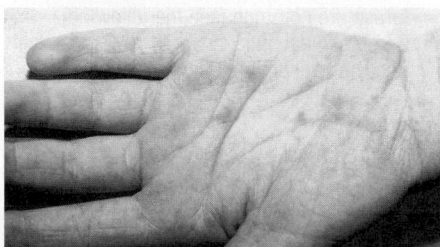

FIGURE 1R-36 Palmar rash associated with Rocky Mountain spotted fever. (From Walker DH, Raoult D: *Rickettsia rickettsii* and other spotted fever group rickettsiae [Rocky Mountain spotted fever and other spotted fevers]. In Mandell GL et al [eds]: *Principles and practice of infectious diseases,* ed 5, New York, 2000, Churchill Livingstone.)

FIGURE 1R-35 Spotted fever rickettsiosis. Number of reported cases, by county, United States, 2010. (From Centers for Disease Control and Prevention: Summary of notifiable diseases—United States, 2010, *MMWR Morb Mortal Wkly Rep* 59[53]:1-111, 2012.)

☐ 0 ▧ 1-14 ▨ ≥15

Diseases and Disorders

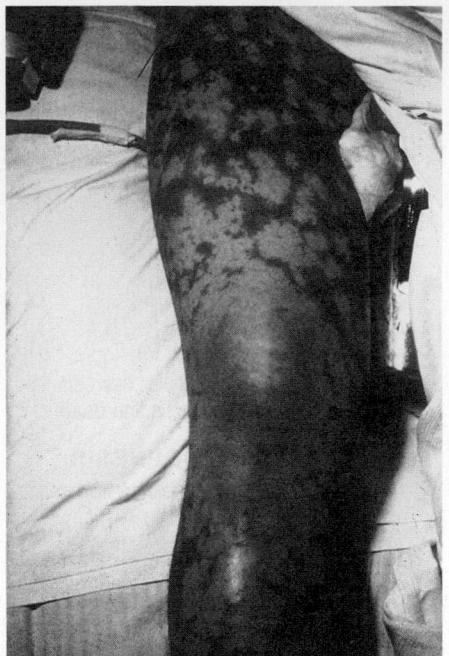

FIGURE 1R-37 Late appearance of rash: Rocky Mountain spotted fever manifesting on lower extremity. (Courtesy of Theodore Woodward, MD.) (From Marx JA et al: *Rosen's emergency medicine: concepts and clinical practice,* 7 ed, Philadelphia, 2010, Elsevier.)

purpura, Kawasaki disease, immune complex vasculitis, connective tissue disorders.

WORKUP

- Consider RMSF in any patient with an acute febrile illness with headache and myalgia, especially with an associated history of tick exposure. Absence of rash does not rule out the diagnosis.
- Ricketisial antibodies take several weeks to develop; therefore, serologic testing is of limited utility in acute illness.
- Box 1R-2 shows the diagnostic criteria for Rocky Mountain spotted fever.

LABORATORY TESTS

- Thrombocytopenia and elevated aminotransferase are common (see the following).
- Cerebrospinal fluid analysis reveals a lymphocyte-predominant pleocytosis.

Routine Tests	%
White cell count	
<10,000/mm³	72
>10% bands	69
Platelet count	
<150,000/mm³	52
<99,000/mm³	32
Serum sodium value <132 mEq/L	56

BOX 1R-2 Diagnostic Criteria for Rocky Mountain Spotted Fever

Laboratory Criteria
- Serologic evidence of a significant change in serum antibody titer reactive with *Rickettsia rickettsii* antigens between paired serum specimens, as measured by a standardized assay conducted in a commercial, state, or reference laboratory.
- Demonstration of *R. rickettsii* antigen in a clinical specimen by immunohistochemical methods.
- Detection of *R. rickettsii* DNA in a clinical specimen by the polymerase chain reaction (PCR) assay.
- Isolation of *R. rickettsii* from a clinical specimen in cell culture.
  For confirmed cases, a significant change in titer must be determined by the testing laboratory; examples of commonly used measures of significant change include, but are not limited to, a fourfold or greater change in antibody titer as determined by indirect immunofluorescent antibody (IFA) assay or an equivalent change in optical density measured by enzyme-linked immunosorbent assay (EIA or ELISA).

Case Classification (CDC Case Definition, 2004)
Confirmed: The patient has a clinically compatible illness that is laboratory confirmed.
Probable: The patient has a clinically compatible illness and serologic evidence of antibody reactive with *R. rickettsii* in a single serum sample at a titer considered indicative of current or past infection (cutoff titers are determined by individual laboratories).

CDC, Centers for Disease Control and Prevention.
From Diagnosis and management of tickborne rickettsial diseases: Rocky Mountain spotted fever, ehrlichioses, and anaplasmosis—United States. *MMWR Recomm Rep* 55(RR-4):18, 2006, and from Marx JA et al: *Rosen's emergency medicine: concepts and clinical practice,* 7 ed, Philadelphia, 2010, Elsevier.)

Routine Tests	%
Aspartate aminotransferase ≥2× normal	62
Alanine aminotransferase ≥2× normal	39
Bilirubin value >1.4 mg/dl	30
Cerebrospinal fluid	
Opening pressure ≥250 mm H₂O	14
Glucose value ≤50 mg/dl	8
Protein value ≥50 mg/dl	35
White cell count ≥5/mm³	38
Mononuclear cell predominance	46
Polymorphonuclear cell predominance	50

- Etiologic tests:
  1. Antibody titers to *R. rickettsii* (by indirect fluorescent antibody test). The diagnosis of RMSF requires a fourfold increase 2 wk apart and thus is not helpful in the care of the patients despite a sensitivity and specificity of near 100%.
  2. The only test that can provide a timely diagnosis is the immunohistologic demonstration of *R. rickettsii* in skin biopsy specimens.

Rx TREATMENT

- Oral or IV doxycycline, 200 mg/day in 2 divided doses for 7 days or for 2 days after defervescence.
- Chloramphenicol, 50 mg/kg/day in 4 divided doses; chloramphenicol may be preferred during pregnancy because of the effects of doxycycline on fetal bones and teeth; therapy continued for at least 2 days after defervescence.

PROGNOSIS

Fatality rate: 1% to 4% (five times greater if treatment is initiated after day 5 of illness, which is more likely in the absence of rash and during seasonal nonpeak tick activity). Long-term sequelae seen in patients who recover from severe RMSF: paraparesis, hearing loss; peripheral neuropathy; bladder and bowel incontinence; cerebellar, vestibular, and motor dysfunction; language disorders; limb amputation; and scrotal pain after cutaneous necrosis.

SUGGESTED READINGS
Available at www.expertconsult.com

RELATED CONTENT
Rocky Mountain Spotted Fever (Patient Information)

AUTHOR: **FRED F. FERRI, M.D.**

 **BASIC INFORMATION**

DEFINITION

Rosacea is a chronic skin disorder characterized by papules and pustules affecting the face and often associated with flushing and erythema.

SYNONYMS

Acne rosacea

ICD-10CM CODES
L71   Rosacea
L71.9 Rosacea unspecified
L71.1 Rhinophyma
L71.8 Other rosacea
L71.0 Perioral dermatitis

EPIDEMIOLOGY & DEMOGRAPHICS

- Rosacea occurs in 1 in 20 Americans.
- Onset often between ages 30 and 50 yr
- More common in people of Celtic origin; however, this disease may be overlooked in nonwhites because skin pigmentation results in atypical presentation.
- Female/male ratio of 3:1.

PHYSICAL FINDINGS & CLINICAL PRESENTATION

- Facial erythema, presence of papules, pustules, and telangiectasia.
- Excessive facial warmth and redness are the predominant presenting symptoms.
- Itching is generally absent.
- Comedones are absent (unlike acne).
- Women are more likely to show symptoms on the chin and cheeks, whereas in men the nose is commonly involved.
- Ocular findings (mild dryness and irritation with blepharitis, conjunctival injection, burning, stinging, tearing, eyelid inflammation, swelling, and redness) are present in 50% of patients.
Rosacea can be classified into four major subtypes:
1. Erythematotelangiectatic (vascular): erythema in central part of face, telangiectasia, flushing.
2. Papulopustular (inflammatory): presence of dome-shaped erythematous papules and small pustules, in addition to facial erythema, flushing, and telangiectasia.
3. Phymatosis (Fig. E1R-38): presence of thickened skin with prominent pores that may affect the nose (rhinophyma), chin (gnathophyma), forehead (metophyma), eyelids (blepharophyma), and ears (otophyma).
4. Ocular: conjunctival injection, sensation of foreign body in the eye, telangiectasia and erythema of lid margins, scaling.

ETIOLOGY

- Unknown but believed to involve the vasculature.
- Hot drinks, alcohol, and sun exposure may accentuate the erythema by causing vasodilation of the skin.
- Flare-ups may also result from reactions to medications (e.g., simvastatin, angiotensin-converting enzyme inhibitors, vasodilators, fluorinated corticosteroids), stress, extreme heat or cold, wind, humidity, strenuous exercise, spicy drinks, menstruation.

 **DIAGNOSIS**

DIFFERENTIAL DIAGNOSIS

- Drug eruption.
- Acne vulgaris.
- Contact dermatitis.
- Systemic lupus erythematosus.
- Carcinoid flush.
- Idiopathic facial flushing.
- Seborrheic dermatitis.
- Facial sarcoidosis.
- Photodermatitis.
- Mastocytosis.
- Perioral dermatitis.
- Granulomas of the skin.

WORKUP

Diagnosis is based on clinical findings. Distinguishing features between acne and rosacea are the presence of telangiectasia and deep diffuse erythema and absence of comedones in rosacea.

Rx **TREATMENT**

NONPHARMACOLOGIC THERAPY

- Avoid alcohol, excessive sun exposure, and hot drinks of any type.
- Use of mild, nondrying soap is recommended; local skin irritants should be avoided.
- Sunscreens are an important component of therapy and should be applied each morning.
- Daily circular massage for several minutes of the central portion of the face is helpful in decreasing lymphedema and inflammation in this area.
- Reassure patient that rosacea is completely unrelated to poor hygiene.
- Vascular laser surgery is effective for telangiectasia.
- Surgical options are available for telengiectasia and rhinophyma and include dermabrasion, laser ablation, heated scalpel, electrocautery, and radiofrequency electrosurgery.

GENERAL Rx

- Several classes of drugs are used in treatment of rosacea, including the metronidazole family, the tetracycline family, and azelaic acid.
- Vascular rosacea: topical therapy with metronidazole aqueous gel (MetroGel) applied bid is effective as initial therapy for mild cases. A new 1% formulation of metronidazole (Noritate) applied daily may improve patient compliance. Clindamycin lotion (Cleocin), sulfacetamide, or erythromycin 2% solution may also be effective. Brimonidine (Mirvaso) is a selective alpha$_2$-adrenergic receptor agonist FDA-approved as a gel preparation for topical treatment of adults with persistent facial erythema of rosacea.
- Pustular and ocular rosacea: systemic antibiotics (doxycycline 100 mg qd or tetracycline 250 mg qid until symptoms diminish, then taper off).

Minocycline 50 to 100 mg qd should be used only in resistant cases because this medication is expensive. Oral metronidazole (200 mg qd to bid) for 4 to 6 wk is also effective. A 1% cream formulation of the antiparasitic drug ivermectin (Soolantra) is effective for papulopustular rosacea with minimal adverse effects.
- Isotretinoin (Accutane) 0.5 to 1 mg/kg/day in two divided doses for 15 to 20 wk can be used for refractory papular and pustular rosacea; use of retinoids may, however, worsen erythema and telangiectasis.
- Erythema and flushing may respond to low-dose clonidine (0.05 mg bid).
- Treatment of phymatous rosacea: oral tetracyclines, oral isotretinoin, ablative/pulsed dye laser therapy, electrosurgery.
- Treatment of ocular rosacea: topical or oral tetracyclines, artificial tears, and/or lid cleansing for eyelid hygiene.

DISPOSITION

- Rosacea is often resistant to initial treatment and recurrent. Periods of remission and relapse are common.
- The progression of rosacea is variable. Typical stages include:
1. Facial flushing.
2. Erythema and/or edema and ocular symptoms.
3. Papules and pustules.
4. Rhinophyma.

 **PEARLS & CONSIDERATIONS**

COMMENTS

- The course of the disease is typically chronic, with remissions and relapses.
- Patients with resistant cases may have *Demodex folliculorum* mite infestation or tinea infection (diagnosis can be confirmed with potassium hydroxide examination); the role of *D. folliculorum* in rosacea is unclear. These mites can sometimes be found in large numbers in the lesions; however, their numbers do not generally decline with treatment.
- Rosacea can result in emotional and social stigmas, especially because many people associate rosacea and rhinophyma with alcohol abuse.
- Early consultation with an ophthalmologist is recommended in patients with suspected ocular involvement.

EBM **EVIDENCE**

Available at www.expertconsult.com

SUGGESTED READINGS
Available at www.expertconsult.com

RELATED CONTENT
Rosacea (Patient Information)

AUTHOR: **FRED F. FERRI, M.D.**

Diseases and Disorders

BASIC INFORMATION

DEFINITION

Roseola is a benign viral illness found in infants and characterized by high fevers that last 3 or 4 days, followed by defervescence, and development of a macular or maculopapular rash.

SYNONYMS

Exanthem subitum.
Sixth disease.
Roseola infantum.
Pseudorubella.
Human herpesvirus 6 (HHV-6), human herpesvirus 7 (HHV-7).

ICD-10CM CODES
B08.2 Exanthema subitum (sixth disease)

EPIDEMIOLOGY & DEMOGRAPHICS

- Nearly one third of all infants develop roseola before the age of 2 yr.
- Peak prevalence is between 7 and 13 mo.
- More than 90% of children older than 2 yr of age are seropositive for the virus causing roseola.
- Roseola is spread from person to person. It is not known how it is spread, but it must be very efficiently spread and presumably via the respiratory tract.
- There is no predilection for gender or time of year.
- Like other herpesviruses, HHV-6 induces a lifelong latent infection in humans.

PHYSICAL FINDINGS & CLINICAL PRESENTATION

- Typically the child develops a high fever, usually up to 104° F (40° C), that lasts for 3 to 5 days.
- Fever may be associated with a runny nose, irritability, and fatigue.
- A rash appears within 48 hr of defervescence; it begins on the neck or trunk and then spreads to the extremities, and persists for a few hours to 2 days.
- Faint pink maculopapular rash that blanches when palpated (Fig. E1R-39) and generally nonpruritic. The mucous membranes are spared.
- Other common findings: cervical and/or occipital adenopathy, erythematous tympanic membranes, anorexia.
- Nagayama spots: red papules on the soft palate or base of the uvula.
- Seizures.
- Less common: febrile seizures (≤6% of cases), cough, diarrhea, aseptic meningitis.

ETIOLOGY

- Roseola is usually caused by human herpesvirus-6 (HHV-6) in the great majority of cases but other causes include human herpesvirus-7, enteroviruses, adenoviruses, and parainfluenza virus type 1. A small percentage of children may have primary infection with HHV-7.
- The incubation period is between 5 and 15 days.

DIAGNOSIS

The diagnosis of roseola is usually made by the clinical presentation as stated previously. It can be confirmed serologically by indirect immunofluorescence assays, ELISA, neutralization assays, and immunoblot. Viral culture is the gold standard to document active viral replication but is expensive, time consuming, and available only in research laboratories.

DIFFERENTIAL DIAGNOSIS

- Rubeola (measles).
- Rubella.
- Fifth disease (erythema infectiosum) caused by parvovirus B19.
- Enteroviral infections.
- Drug eruption.
- Mononucleosis.
- All causes of fever (e.g., otitis media, pneumonia, and urinary tract infection).
- Meningitis.

WORKUP

- If unsure of the diagnosis of roseola in a febrile infant, a fever workup is done to rule out other infectious causes.
- The decision to proceed with a fever workup is a clinical judgment call.

LABORATORY TESTS

- CBC with differential usually shows relative neutropenia and mild atypical lymphocytosis.
- Erythrocyte sedimentation rate (ESR), blood cultures as indicated.
- Urinalysis and urine cultures.
- Stool cultures if diarrhea is present.
- Lumbar puncture if needed to rule out meningitis in patients with mental status changes.
- Commercial assays can be used to detect HHV-6-specific IgG antibody responses but IgM assays are not always reliable for acute infection.
- A PCR real-time assay is available to quantify viral DNA in blood and body fluids, but it is generally reserved to detect reactivation of virus in immunocompromised patients, such as hematopoietic stem cell transplant patients.

IMAGING STUDIES

Chest x-ray to rule out pneumonia.

TREATMENT

NONPHARMACOLOGIC THERAPY

- Supportive care.
- Maintain hydration by drinking clear fluids: water, fruit juice, lemonade, and so forth.
- Sponge bathe with lukewarm water if febrile.

ACUTE GENERAL Rx

- Acetaminophen 10 to 15 mg/kg per dose at 4-hr intervals for fever.
- Ibuprofen 5 to 10 mg/kg per dose at 6-hr intervals (maximal dose 600 mg).

CHRONIC Rx

Roseola is a viral disease that is short lasting; chronic treatment is usually not an issue.

DISPOSITION

- Roseola is generally a benign, self-limited disease that usually lasts approximately 1 wk.
- Complications, although rare, can occur and include:
  1. Febrile seizures.
  2. Meningitis.
  3. Encephalitis.
  4. Pneumonitis.
  5. Hepatitis.

REFERRAL

Subspecialty consultation is made with the appropriate discipline if any of the previously mentioned complications occur (e.g., neurology for seizures).

PEARLS & CONSIDERATIONS

COMMENTS

- A child with fever and rash should be excluded from day care.
- HHV-6 is named accordingly because it is the sixth herpesvirus discovered after herpes simplex 1 (HSV-1), HSV-2, cytomegalovirus (CMV), Epstein-Barr virus (EBV), and varicella-zoster virus (VZV).
- Roseola is called sixth disease because it represents the sixth childhood "exanthem"; the other five are measles, scarlet fever, rubella, Dukes disease, and erythema infectiosum.

SUGGESTED READINGS
Available at www.expertconsult.com

RELATED CONTENT
Roseola (Patient Information)

AUTHOR: **GLENN G. FORT, M.D., M.P.H.**

Diseases and Disorders

BASIC INFORMATION

DEFINITION

Salivary gland neoplasms are benign or malignant tumors of a salivary gland (parotid, submandibular, or sublingual).

SYNONYMS

These tumors are often named according to their histologic type (see "Diagnosis").

ICD-10CM CODES

C08.9 Malignant neoplasm of major salivary gland, unspecified
C07 Malignant neoplasm of parotid gland
C08.0 Malignant neoplasm of submandibular gland
C08.1 Malignant neoplasm of sublingual gland

EPIDEMIOLOGY & DEMOGRAPHICS

INCIDENCE: One to two cases per 100,000 person-years (1% of all head and neck tumors).
DISTRIBUTION:
- Parotid gland, 85% (80% are benign).
- Submandibular gland, 10% (55% are benign).
- Sublingual and minor glands, 5% (35% are benign).

PHYSICAL FINDINGS & CLINICAL PRESENTATION

- Parotid gland:
  1. Painless swelling overlying the masseter muscle (under the temporomandibular joint).
  2. Pain.
  3. Facial nerve palsy.
  4. Cervical lymph nodes.
  5. Mass in oral cavity.
- Submandibular gland: swelling under anterior portion of the mandible.
- Sublingual gland: intraoral swelling under the tongue, medial to the mandible.

 DIAGNOSIS

PATHOLOGY

HISTORY:
Benign Tumors
- Mixed tumor (usually parotid).
- Adenolymphoma (Warthin's tumor).
- Pleomorphic adenoma.
- Capillary hemangioma, lymphangioma (in children).
- Intraductal papilloma.
- Other (e.g., myoepithelioma, canalicular adenoma, basal cell adenoma).

MALIGNANT TUMORS

- Mucoepidermoid carcinoma (most common malignant tumor of the parotid gland).
- Adenoid cystic carcinoma.
- Adenocarcinoma.
- Malignant mixed tumor.
- Squamous cell carcinoma.
- Other.

STAGE (TNM):

T_0	No evidence of primary tumor
T_1	Tumor <2 cm
T_2	Tumor 2 to 4 cm
T_3	Tumor 4 to 6 cm
T_4	Tumor >6 cm

All subdivided into
- Without local extension.
- With local extension.

N_0	No lymph node metastasis
N_1	Single ipsilateral node <3 cm
N_2	Ipsilateral, contralateral, or bilateral node <6 cm
N_3	Any node >6 cm
M_0	No distant metastasis
M_1	Distant metastasis
Stage I	T_{1a} or $_{2a}N_0M_0$
Stage II	$T_{1b,2b,3a}$ N_0M_0
Stage III	$T_{3b,4a}$ N_0M_0 or any T except $_{4b}N_1M_0$
Stage IV	T_{4b} any N any M or any T $N_{2,3}M_0$ or any T, any N_1M_1

WORKUP

- Fine-needle aspiration. The sensitivity, specificity, and accuracy of parotid gland aspirates are approximately 92%, 100%, and 98%, respectively.
- Imaging by CT scan or MRI (Fig. 1S-1).
- Open biopsy (rarely indicated).

 TREATMENT

Malignant tumors:
- Surgery is the mainstay of treatment; gland resection and neck dissection if lymph nodes are involved.
- A lateral lobectomy with preservation of facial nerve should be considered for tumors confined to the superficial lobe of the parotid gland. Gross tumor should not be left in situ, but if the facial nerve is able to be preserved by "peeling" tumor off the nerve, it should be attempted, followed by radiation therapy for microscopic disease.
- Postoperative radiation is indicated for high-grade malignancies demonstrating extraglandular disease, perineural invasion, direct invasion of surrounding tissues, or regional metastases.
- Chemotherapy.
Benign tumors: surgery for tumor resection.

PROGNOSIS OF MALIGNANT TUMORS

Five-year survival rates:
- Mucoepidermoid carcinoma: 75% to 95%.
- Adenoid cystic carcinoma: 40% to 80%.
- Adenocarcinoma: 20% to 75%.
- Malignant mixed tumor: 35% to 75%.
- Squamous cell carcinoma: 25% to 60%.

 PEARLS & CONSIDERATIONS

COMMENTS

Salivary gland neoplasms most often present as slow-growing, well-circumscribed masses. Pain, rapid growth, nerve weakness, fixation to skin or underlying muscle, and paresthesias usually are indicative of malignancy.

EBM EVIDENCE

Available at www.expertconsult.com

SUGGESTED READING

Available at www.expertconsult.com

RELATED CONTENT

Salivary Gland Tumors (Patient Information)

AUTHOR: **FRED F. FERRI, M.D.**

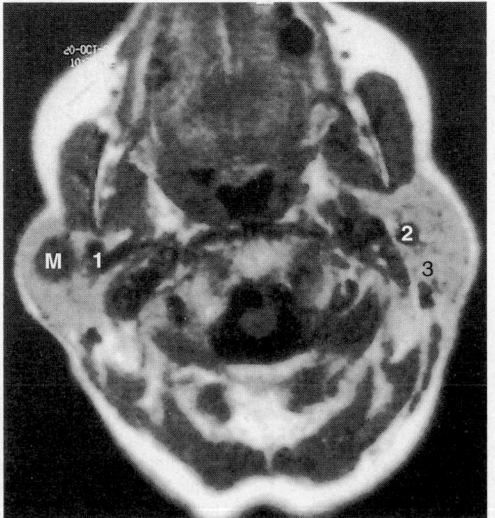

FIGURE 1S-1 Pleomorphic Adenoma of Parotid Gland. Pleomorphic adenoma in the right parotid (M) is a well-defined, low-signal intensity mass on the axial T_1-weighted MRI. Note displacement of the retromandibular vein **(1)** medially by the mass compared with the normal left retromandibular vein **(2)**. The left facial nerve **(3)** branching through the normal left parotid is seen. (From Skarin AT: *Atlas of diagnostic oncology*, ed 4, St Louis, 2010, Mosby.)

 **BASIC INFORMATION**

DEFINITION

Salmonellosis is an infection caused by one of several serotypes of a gram-negative bacillus of the genus *Salmonella*. Current *Salmonella* nomenclature is described in Table 1S-1.

SYNONYMS

Typhoid fever
Paratyphoid fever
Enteric fever

ICD-10CM CODES
A02.0 *Salmonella* enteritis
A02.1 *Salmonella* sepsis
A02.2 Localized *Salmonella* infections
A02.8 Other specified *Salmonella* infections
A0.9 *Salmonella* infection, unspecified

EPIDEMIOLOGY & DEMOGRAPHICS

INCIDENCE (IN U.S.):
- Epidemiologically, the clinical syndromes are divided into those that cause a typhoidal type of infection (systemic illness with fever and abdominal pain) such as *Salmonella typhi* and those that do not: nontyphoidal *Salmonella* infections (gastroenteritis) such as *S. enteritidis*, *S. newport*, and *S. typhimurium*.
- Estimated 1 million cases/yr of nontyphoidal salmonellosis in the United States (leading cause of foodborne illness in the U.S.). In 2009, contaminated peanut butter and peanut products caused a nationwide *Salmonella typhimurium* outbreak in 46 states, affecting more than 700 people.
- Largest outbreak of gastroenteritis syndrome (nontyphoidal): 200,000 who ingested contaminated milk.
- Approximately 500 cases of *Salmonella typhi* infection are reported each year, of which nearly 80% is associated with foreign travel.

PEAK INCIDENCE: Summer and fall.
PREDOMINANT AGE:
- <20 yr old.
- >70 yr old.
- Highest rates of infection in infants, especially neonates.

GENETICS:
Neonatal infection
- Highly susceptible to infection with nontyphoidal *Salmonella*.

PHYSICAL FINDINGS & CLINICAL PRESENTATION

- Infections
  1. Localized to GI tract (gastroenteritis).
  2. Systemic (typhoid fever).
  3. Localized outside of GI tract.
- **Gastroenteritis**
  1. Incubation period: 12 to 48 hr.
  2. Nausea, vomiting.
  3. Diarrhea, abdominal cramps.
  4. Fever.
  5. Bacteremia: occurs mostly in the immunocompromised host or those with underlying conditions, including HIV infection.
  6. Self-limited illness lasting 3 or 4 days.
  7. Colonization of GI tract persistent for months, especially in those treated with antibiotics.
- **Typhoid fever**
  1. Incubation period of few days to several wk.
  2. Prolonged fever, often with a stepwise-increasing temperature pattern.
  3. Myalgias.
  4. Headache, cough, sore throat.
  5. Malaise, anorexia.
  6. Abdominal pain.
  7. Hepatosplenomegaly.
  8. Diarrhea or constipation early in the course of illness.
  9. Rose spots (faint, maculopapular, blanching lesions) sometimes seen on chest or abdomen.
- Untreated disease
  1. Fever lasting 1 to 2 mo.
  2. Main complication: GI bleeding caused by perforation from ulceration of Peyer's patches in the ileum.
  3. Rare complications:
     a. Mental status changes.
     b. Shock.
  4. Relapse rate of approximately 10%.
- Infections outside GI tract
  1. Can occur in virtually any location.
  2. Usually occur in patients with underlying diseases.
  3. Endocarditis, endovascular infections are caused by seeding of atherosclerotic plaques or aneurysms.
  4. Hepatic or splenic abscesses in patients with underlying disease in these organs.
  5. Urinary tract infections in patients with renal TB or schistosomiasis.
  6. *Salmonellae* are a frequent cause of gram-negative meningitis in neonates.
  7. Osteomyelitis in children with hemoglobinopathies (particularly sickle cell disease).

ETIOLOGY

- More than 2000 serotypes of *Salmonella* exist, but only a few cause disease in humans. Host factors and conditions predisposing to the development of systemic disease with nontyphoidal *Salmonella* strains are described in Table 1S-2.
- Raw produce is an increasingly recognized vehicle for salmonellosis. In 2008 there was a large outbreak of *Salmonella* Saintpaul involving 1500 persons, of whom 21% were hospitalized and 2 died. It was due to contaminated jalapeno and serrano peppers. More recently outbreaks of human *Salmonella* infections have been increasingly associated with contact with live poultry.
- Some found only in humans are the cause of enteric fever.
  1. *S. typhi.*
  2. *S. paratyphi.*
- Some responsible for gastroenteritis and frequently isolated from raw meat and poultry and uncooked or undercooked eggs.
  1. *S. typhimurium.*
  2. S. enteritidis.
- *S. choleraesuis* is a prototype organism that causes extraintestinal nontyphoidal disease.
- Transmission generally via ingestion of contaminated food or drink.
- Outbreaks of gastroenteritis related to contaminated poultry, meat, and dairy products are common.
- Typhoid fever is a systemic illness caused by serotypes exclusive to humans.
  1. Acquisition by ingestion of food or water contaminated by other humans
  2. Most cases in the United States are:
     a. Acquired during foreign travel: 80% of cases.
     b. Acquired by ingestion of food prepared by chronic carriers, many of

---

TABLE 1S-2 Host Factors and Conditions Predisposing to the Development of Systemic Disease with Nontyphoidal *Salmonella* Strains

Neonates and young infants (≤3 mo of age)
HIV/AIDS
Other immunodeficiencies and chronic granulomatous disease
Immunosuppressive and corticosteroid therapies
Malignancies, especially leukemia and lymphoma
Hemolytic anemia, including sickle cell disease, malaria, and bartonellosis
Collagen vascular disease
Inflammatory bowel disease
Achlorhydria or use of antacid medications
Impaired intestinal motility
Schistosomiasis, malaria
Malnutrition

From Kliegman RM et al: *Nelson textbook of pediatrics*, ed 19, Philadelphia, 2011, Saunders.

TABLE 1S-1 *Salmonella* Nomenclature

Traditional Usage	Formal Name	CDC Designation
S. typhi	S. enterica* subsp. enterica ser. Typhi	S. ser. Typhi
S. dublin	S. enterica subsp. enterica ser. Dublin	S. ser. Dublin
S. typhimurium	S. enterica subsp. enterica ser. Typhimurium	S. ser. Typhimurium
S. choleraesuis	S. enterica subsp. enterica ser. Choleraesuis	S. ser. Choleraesuis
S. marina	S. enterica subsp. houtenae ser. Marina	S. ser. Marina

CDC, Centers for Disease Control and Prevention; *ser.*, serovar; *subsp.*, subspecies.
*Some authorities prefer *S. choleraesuis* or *S. enteritidis* rather than *S. enterica* to describe the species.
From Kliegman RM et al: *Nelson textbook of pediatrics*, ed 19, Philadelphia, 2011, Saunders.

S

whom have acquired the organism outside of the United States.

DIAGNOSIS

DIFFERENTIAL DIAGNOSIS
- Other causes of prolonged fever:
  1. Malaria.
  2. TB.
  3. Brucellosis.
  4. Amebic liver abscess.
- Other causes of gastroenteritis:
  1. Bacterial: *Shigella, Yersinia, Campylobacter* spp.
  2. Viral: Norwalk virus, rotavirus.
  3. Parasitic: *Entamoeba histolytica, Giardia lamblia.*
  4. Toxic: enterotoxigenic *E. coli, Clostridium difficile.*

WORKUP
- Typhoid fever
  1. Cultures of blood, stool, urine; repeat if initially negative.
  2. Blood cultures are more likely to be positive early in the course of illness.
  3. Stool and urine cultures are more commonly positive in the second and third wk of illness.
  4. Highest yield with bone marrow biopsy cultures: 90% positive.
  5. Serology using Widal's test Is helpful in retrospect, showing a fourfold increase in convalescent titers.
- Gastroenteritis: stool cultures.
- Extraintestinal localized infection:
  1. Blood cultures.
  2. Cultures from the site of infection.

LABORATORY TESTS
- Neutropenia is common.
- Transaminitis is possible.
- Culture to grow organism: blood, body fluids, biopsy specimens.

IMAGING STUDIES
- Not routinely indicated.
- Radiographs of bone may be suggestive of osteomyelitis (particularly in patients with sickle cell disease and bone infarctions).
- CT scan or sonogram of abdomen:
  1. May reveal hepatic or splenic abscesses or pleural involvement.
  2. May reveal aortic aneurysm.

TREATMENT

NONPHARMACOLOGIC THERAPY
Adequate hydration and electrolyte replacement in people with diarrhea.

ACUTE GENERAL Rx
Treatment decisions must consider the severity of infection and the risk for extraintestinal disease.
- Typhoid fever:
  1. Levofloxacin 750 mg PO/IV q24h or ciprofloxacin 500 mg PO bid or 400 mg IV bid for 7 to 10 days. Should not be used as first line in patients from South Asia due to resistance unless known to be susceptible.
  2. Ceftriaxone 2 g IV qd for 7 to 14 days or cefixime (20-30 mg/kg/day orally divided into q12h dosing for 7-14 days).
  3. Another alternative agent: azithromycin (1 g orally then 500 mg daily for 5-7 days)
  4. Children: see Table 1S-3. In general, quinolones are avoided in children unless a multidrug-resistant strain is involved due to concerns of possible cartilage damage. Another alternative for children: azithromycin (10-20 mg/kg to 1 g maximum once daily for 5-7 days)
  5. If tests show susceptibility, can also use amoxicillin or Bactrim in adults and children.
  6. Dexamethasone 3 mg IV initially, followed by 1 mg IV q6h for eight doses for patients with shock or mental status changes.
- Gastroenteritis:
  1. Usually not indicated for gastroenteritis alone because this illness usually self-limited.
  2. Treatment may prolong the carrier state and is discouraged for healthy patients <50 yr of age who have relatively mild disease.
  3. Prophylactic treatment for patients who are at high risk of developing complications from bacteremia (see Table 1S-3).
     a. Neonates.
     b. Patients with hemoglobinopathies.
     c. Patients with atherosclerosis.
     d. Patients with aneurysms.
     e. Patients with prosthetic devices.
     f. Immunocompromised patients.

CHRONIC Rx
- Carrier states are possible in those with typhoid fever.
- More common in people >60 yr of age and in people with gallstones.

- Usual site of colonization is the gallbladder.
- Treatment should be considered for those with persistently positive stool cultures and for food handlers.
- Suggested regimens for eradication of carrier state:
  1. Ciprofloxacin 500 mg PO bid for 4 wk.
  2. SMX/TMP 1 to 2 DS tabs PO bid for 6 wk (if susceptible).
  3. Amoxicillin 2 g PO q8h for 6 wk (if susceptible).
- Cholecystectomy may be required in carriers with gallstones who fail medical therapy, but this is rarely indicated for nontyphoidal salmonellosis currently.
- Prolonged course of oral therapy or lifetime suppression for patients with AIDS who have chronic infection.

DISPOSITION
- Typhoid fever
  1. Treated patients usually respond to therapy; small percentage of chronic carriers.
  2. Untreated patients may have serious complications.
- Gastroenteritis
  1. Usually self-limited.
  2. May be recurrent or persistent in AIDS patients.

REFERRAL
- If gastroenteritis is persistent or recurrent.
- If there is evidence of extraintestinal infection, typhoid fever, or chronic carriers.

 **PEARLS & CONSIDERATIONS**

COMMENTS
- Fluoroquinolones remain the most reliably effective class of antibiotics for empiric therapy despite increasing resistance. Fluoroquinolones should not be used in children or pregnant women.
- Infections should be reported to local health departments.
- Recent outbreaks in the United States have been traced back to raw tomatoes, peanut butter, pet turtles, and frozen pot pies.

 **EVIDENCE**

Available at www.expertconsult.com

SUGGESTED READINGS
Available at www.expertconsult.com

RELATED CONTENT
Salmonellosis (Patient Information)

AUTHOR: **GLENN G. FORT, M.D., M.P.H.**

TABLE 1S-3 Treatment of *Salmonella* Gastroenteritis

Organism and Indication	Dose and Duration of Treatment
Salmonella infections in infants <3 mo of age or immunocompromised persons (in addition to appropriate treatment for underlying disorder)	Cefotaxime 100-200 mg/kg/day every 6 hr for 5-14 days or Ceftriaxone 75 mg/kg/day once daily for 7 days or Ampicillin 100 mg/kg/day every 6 hr for 7 days or Cefixime 15 mg/kg/day for 7-10 days

From Kliegman RM et al: *Nelson textbook of pediatrics*, ed 19, Philadelphia, 2011, Saunders.

Diseases and Disorders

BASIC INFORMATION

DEFINITION

Sarcoidosis is a chronic multisystem granulomatous disease characterized histologically by the presence of nonspecific, noncaseating granulomas.

SYNONYMS

Boeck's sarcoid

ICD-10CM CODES

D86   Sarcoidosis
D86.0 Sarcoidosis of lung
D86.1 Sarcoidosis of lymph nodes
D86.2 Sarcoidosis of lung with sarcoidosis of lymph nodes
D86.3 Sarcoidosis of skin
D86.8 Sarcoidosis of other and combined sites
D86.9 Sarcoidosis, unspecified

EPIDEMIOLOGY & DEMOGRAPHICS

INCIDENCE (IN U.S.): Incidence is 11 in 100,000 in whites and 35 in 100,000 in blacks; presents most commonly in the winter and early spring. (The adjusted annual incidence among black Americans is roughly three times higher than among white Americans [35.5 cases/100,000, as compared with 10.9/100,000] and is likely more chronic and fatal in black Americans.)
PREDOMINANT SEX: Increased incidence in females.
PREDOMINANT AGE: 20 to 40 yr.
GENETICS: Familial clustering has been described. Having a first-degree relative with sarcoidosis increases the risk for disease five-fold (ACCESS study). There have been reports of association between sarcoidosis and gene products, specifically HLA class II antigens, encoded by HLA-DRB1 and DQB1 alleles.

PHYSICAL FINDINGS & CLINICAL PRESENTATION

- Clinical manifestations often vary with the stage of the disease and degree of organ involvement. Patients may be asymptomatic, but a chest radiograph may demonstrate findings consistent with sarcoidosis (see "Imaging Studies"). Nearly 50% of patients with sarcoidosis are diagnosed by incidental findings on chest radiograph. Thoracic involvement occurs in >90% of patients with sarcoidosis.
- Frequent manifestations:
  1. Pulmonary manifestations: dry, nonproductive cough; dyspnea; chest discomfort.
  2. Constitutional symptoms: fatigue, weight loss, anorexia, malaise, night sweats.
  3. Visual disturbances: blurred vision, ocular discomfort, conjunctivitis, iritis, uveitis (65% of patients).
  4. Dermatologic manifestations (30% of patients): erythema nodosum (10% of patients), macules, papules, subcutaneous nodules, hyperpigmentation, lupus

pernio (indurated violaceous lesions on the nose, lips, ears, and cheeks that can erode into underlying cartilage and bone) (Fig. 1S-2).
  5. Myocardial disturbances, arrhythmias, cardiomyopathy, various conduction abnormalities, and pericardial effusion. Cardiac sarcoidosis is much more common than clinically appreciated and is

found in up to 25% of patients in the United States.
  6. Splenomegaly, hepatomegaly.
  7. Rheumatologic manifestations: arthralgias have been reported in up to 40% of patients.
  8. **Löfgren's syndrome**, consisting of arthritis, erythema nodosum, and bilateral hilar adenopathy, occurs in 9% to 34% of patients.

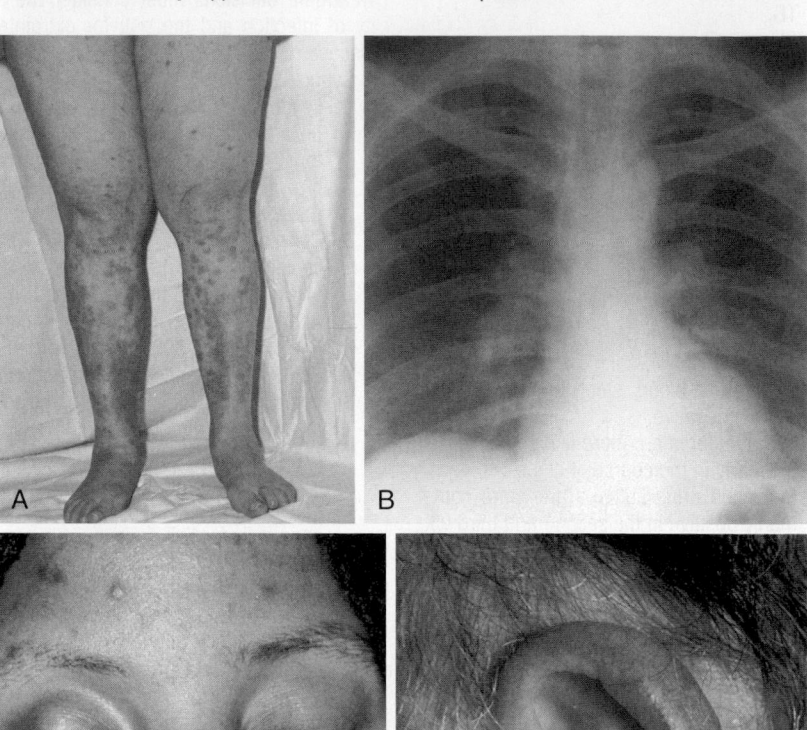

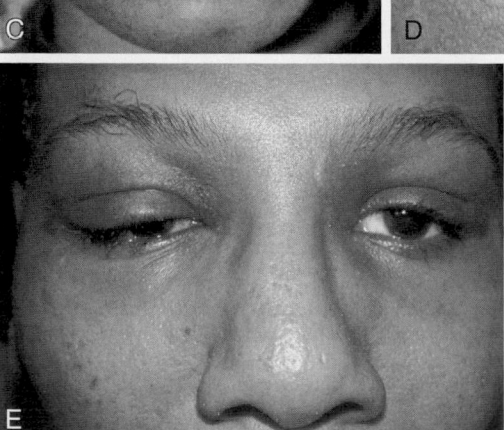

FIGURE 1S-2 Sarcoidosis. A, Erythema nodosum. **B,** Bilateral hilar lymphadenopathy. **C,** Seventh nerve palsy. **D,** Lupus pernio. **E,** Lacrimal gland enlargement. (**D** courtesy M.A. Mir. From Mir MA: *Atlas of clinical diagnosis*, Philadelphia, 2003, Saunders.)

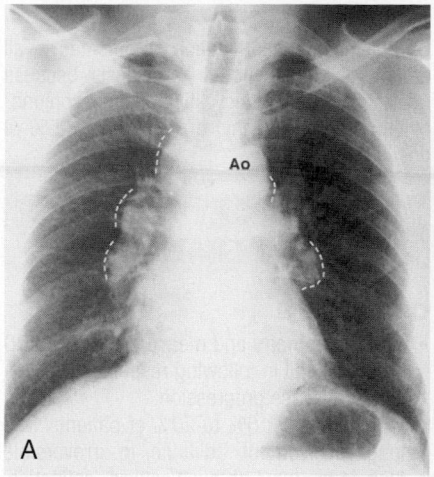

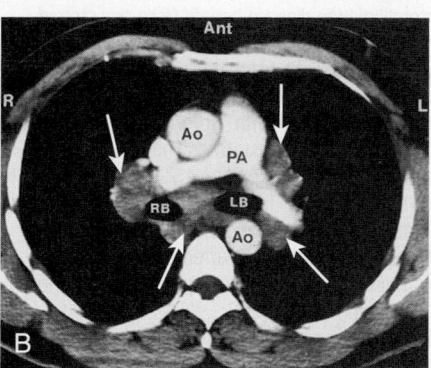

FIGURE 1S-3 Sarcoid. Marked lymphadenopathy *(dotted lines)* is seen in the region of both hila in the right paratracheal region **(A).** The transverse contrast-enhanced CT scan of the upper chest **(B)** clearly shows the ascending and descending aorta *(Ao)* as well as the pulmonary artery *(PA)* and superior vena cava. The right and left mainstem bronchus area is also seen. The arrows indicate the extensive lymphadenopathy. *LB,* Left bronchus; *RB,* right bronchus. (From Mettler FA [ed]: *Primary care radiology,* Philadelphia, 2000, Saunders.)

TABLE 1S-4   Indications for Use of Corticosteroids in Sarcoidosis

Disorder	Treatment
Iridocyclitis	Corticosteroid eye drops; local subconjunctival deposit of cortisone
Posterior uveitis	Oral prednisone
Pulmonary involvement	Steroids rarely recommended for stage I; typically used if infiltrate remains static or worsens over 3-mo period or the patient is symptomatic
Upper airway obstruction	Rare indication for intravenous steroids
Lupus pernio	Oral prednisone shrinks the disfiguring lesions
Hypercalcemia	Responds well to corticosteroids
Cardiac involvement	Corticosteroids usually recommended if patient has arrhythmias or conduction disturbances
Central nervous system involvement	Response is best in patients with acute symptoms
Lacrimal/salivary gland involvement	Corticosteroids recommended for disordered function, not gland swelling
Bone cysts	Corticosteroids recommended if symptomatic

From Andreoli TE (ed): *Cecil essentials of medicine,* ed 8, Philadelphia, 2010, Saunders.

9. Neurologic and other manifestations: cranial nerve palsies, diabetes insipidus, meningeal involvement, parotid enlargement, hypothalamic and pituitary lesions, peripheral adenopathy. Neurosarcoidosis is detected in up to 25% of patients and can occur in the absence of apparent disease elsewhere. The presence of anterior uveitis, parotiditis, fevers, and facial nerve palsy is known as **Heerfordt syndrome**.

ETIOLOGY

Unknown. A cardinal feature of sarcoidosis is the presence of CD4+ T cells that interact with antigen-presenting cells to initiate the formation and maintenance of granulomas. Multiple lines of evidence suggest that sarcoidosis may result from the interaction of multiple genes with environmental exposures or infection.

Dx DIAGNOSIS

DIFFERENTIAL DIAGNOSIS

- Tuberculosis.
- Lymphoma.
- Hodgkin's disease.
- Metastases.
- Pneumoconioses.
- Enlarged pulmonary arteries.
- Infectious mononucleosis.
- Lymphangitic carcinomatosis.
- Idiopathic hemosiderosis.
- Alveolar cell carcinoma.
- Pulmonary eosinophilia.
- Hypersensitivity pneumonitis.
- Fibrosing alveolitis.
- Collagen disorders.
- Parasitic infection.

Section II describes the differential diagnosis of granulomatous lung disease and a classification of granulomatous disorders.

WORKUP

- No pathognomonic diagnostic test exists for sarcoidosis, so the diagnosis remains one of exclusion. Workup is aimed at excluding critical organ involvement, determining extent and severity of disease, and excluding other disease. The presence of noncaseating granulomas does not establish the diagnosis, because conditions such as tuberculosis and malignancies, among others, can cause granulomas. A complete neurologic and ophthalmologic examination is mandatory. A complete occupational and environmental exposure history is recommended.
- Initial laboratory evaluation should include complete blood count, serum chemistries (alanine aminotransferase, aspartate aminotransferase, alkaline phosphatase, electrolytes, blood urea nitrogen, creatinine, serum calcium), urinalysis, 24-hour urinary excretion of calcium, CRP, ESR, and tuberculin skin test.
- Chest radiograph and ECG should also be obtained in all patients with sarcoidosis.
- Pulmonary function testing: spirometry, diffusion capacity of carbon monoxide–single breath.
- Biopsy should be done on accessible tissues suspected of sarcoid involvement (conjunctiva, skin, lymph nodes); bronchoscopy with transbronchial biopsy (85% diagnostic yield) is often performed in patients without any readily accessible site. Endobronchial ultrasound-guided fine-needle aspiration of intrathoracic lymph nodes also has high diagnostic yield and makes use of mediastinoscopy usually unnecessary. Among patients with suspected Stage I/II pulmonary sarcoidosis undergoing tissue confirmation, the use of endosonographic nodal aspiration compared with bronchoscopic biopsy resulted in greater diagnostic yield.

LABORATORY TESTS

Laboratory abnormalities:
- Hypergammaglobulinemia, anemia, leukopenia may be present.
- Liver function test abnormalities are common.
- Hypercalcemia (11% of patients), hypercalciuria (40% of patients; attributable to increased gastrointestinal absorption, abnormal vitamin D metabolism, and increased calcitriol production by sarcoid granuloma).
- Angiotensin-converting enzyme: elevated in approximately 60% of patients with sarcoidosis; nonspecific and generally not useful as a diagnostic tool and in following the course of the disease.

IMAGING STUDIES

- Chest radiograph (Fig. 1S-3): pulmonary sarcoidosis is classified based on radiographic pattern. Adenopathy of the hilar and paratracheal nodes is a frequent finding. Parenchymal changes may also be present, depending on the stage of the disease (stage 0, normal radiograph; stage I, bilateral hilar adenopathy; stage II, stage I plus pulmonary infiltrate; stage III, pulmonary infiltrate without adenopathy; stage IV, advanced fibrosis with evidence of "honeycombing," hilar retraction, bullae, cysts, and emphysema).

- Pulmonary function tests (spirometry and diffusing capacity of the lung for carbon dioxide): may be normal or may reveal a restrictive ventilatory defect with reduced forced vital capacity, reduced DLCO, or both.
- For patients without apparent lung involvement, ^{18}F-fluorodeoxyglucose positron emission tomography (FDG-PET) is useful in identifying sites for diagnostic biopsy.
- CT imaging is generally unnecessary for most patients with sarcoidosis. It is indicated when the chest radiograph is atypical for sarcoidosis or if the patient has hemoptysis.
- FDG-PET and MRI with gadolinium are useful in patients with suspected cardiac and neurologic involvement.
- Gallium-67 scan: represents an older testing modality. It will localize in areas of granulomatous infiltrates; however, it is not specific and not necessary. The "panda" sign (localization in the lacrimal and salivary glands, giving a "panda" appearance to the face) is suggestive of sarcoidosis.

℞ TREATMENT

GENERAL Rx
- Many patients with sarcoidosis will not require any treatment. In general, treatment should be instituted when organ function is threatened. Corticosteroids (Table 1S-4) are the mainstay of therapy when treatment is required (e.g., prednisone 40 mg qd for 8 to 12 wk with gradual tapering of the dose to 10 mg qod over 8 to 12 mo); corticosteroids should be considered in patients with severe symptoms (e.g., dyspnea, chest pain); hypercalcemia; ocular, central nervous system, or cardiac involvement; or progressive pulmonary disease. Patients with interstitial lung disease benefit from oral steroid therapy for 6 to 24 mo.
- A lack of benefit from steroid therapy may be due to the presence of irreversible fibrotic disease. Patients with progressive disease refractory to corticosteroids may be treated with methotrexate 7.5 to 15 mg once per week or another immunosuppressant such as azathioprine or mycophenolate mofetil.
- Hydroxychloroquine is effective for chronic disfiguring skin lesions, hypercalcemia, and neurologic involvement.
- Nonsteroidal antiinflammatory drugs are useful for musculoskeletal symptoms and erythema nodosum.
- Pulmonary rehabilitation in patients with significant respiratory insufficiency. Consider liver and lung transplantation in patients unresponsive to conventional treatment.
- Pulmonary hypertension is a dreaded complication of advanced pulmonary sarcoidosis. The prognosis for patients with sarcoidosis-associated pulmonary hypertension is not known.

DISPOSITION
- The majority of patients with sarcoidosis have spontaneous remission within 2 yr and do not require treatment. Their course can be followed by periodic clinical evaluation, chest radiographs, and pulmonary function tests.
- Blacks have increased rates of pulmonary involvement, a worse long-term prognosis, and more frequent relapses.
- Up to one third of patients have unrelenting disease, leading to clinically significant organ impairment. Adverse prognostic factors in sarcoidosis include age of onset >40 yr, cardiac involvement, neurosarcoidosis, progressive pulmonary fibrosis, chronic hypercalcemia, chronic uveitis, involvement of nasal mucosa, nephrocalcinosis, and presence of cystic bone lesions and lupus pernio.

REFERRAL
Ophthalmologic examination is indicated in all patients with suspected sarcoidosis because ocular findings (iridocyclitis, uveitis, conjunctivitis, and keratopathy) are found in ≥25% of documented cases.

 **PEARLS & CONSIDERATIONS**

COMMENTS
- Serial spirometry and measurement of DLCO can be useful in following response to therapy and disease progression.
- Approximately 15% to 20% of patients with lung involvement advance to irreversible lung impairment (bronchiectasis, cavitation, progressive fibrosis, pneumothorax, and respiratory failure). Death from pulmonary failure occurs in 5% to 7% of patients with sarcoidosis.
- Newer treatment approaches are aimed at targeting mechanisms involving CD4 type 1 helper T cells.
- The diagnosis of sarcoidosis should be reconsidered in the presence of atypical manifestations or persistent/progressive disease despite appropriate therapy.
- Diagnostic biopsy may not be necessary in most patients presenting with asymptomatic bilateral lympadenopathy (with no other evidence of malignancy), in those with Lofgren syndrome, or in those with Heerfordt syndrome.

SUGGESTED READINGS
Available at www.expertconsult.com

RELATED CONTENT
Sarcoidosis (Patient Information)

AUTHOR: **IMRANA QAWI, M.D.**

BASIC INFORMATION

DEFINITION

Sarcomas are heterogenous groups of malignant tumors of connective tissue, with more than 100 distinct entities. They show a wide range of differentiation—blood vessels (angiosarcoma), fat tissue (liposarcoma), and bone (osteosarcoma), among others. Sarcomas can be classified into two basic types: soft tissue sarcoma (STS) and primary bone sarcoma. Affecting virtually all tissues, they are more common in soft tissues, but 75% occur in the limbs. Sarcomas of bone are extremely rare. There are three histiogenic types: osteosarcoma, Ewing's sarcoma, and chondrosarcoma.

ICD-10CM CODES
C40 Malignant neoplasm of bone and articular cartilage of limbs
C41 Malignant neoplasm of bone and articular cartilage of other unspecified sites
C22.3 Angiosarcoma of liver
C49.9 Malignant neoplasm of connective and soft tissue, unspecified
C49.0 Malignant neoplasm of connective and soft tissue of head, face, and neck

EPIDEMIOLOGY & DEMOGRAPHICS

INCIDENCE: Soft tissue sarcoma: 30 cases per million per annum.
Sarcoma of bone: 8 cases per million per annum.
Soft tissue sarcoma can occur at any age.
- In the United States there are 7800 new cases per year.
- Incidence increases with age.
- Average age of diagnosis is 57 yr.
- Men and women are affected equally.
- Soft tissue sarcomas represent <1% of all newly diagnosed malignancies.
Sarcomas of bone represent 0.2% of all new cancers.
- About 2600 new cases in the United States each year.
Osteosarcoma and Ewing's sarcoma (the two most common bone tumors) occur predominantly during childhood and adolescence.

GENETICS
See "Etiology."
Physical Findings & Clinical Presentation
- Bone sarcomas. Clinical presentation usually includes:
  1. Pain—at rest or at night.
  2. Swelling or mass at the site.
  3. Pathologic fractures.
- Soft tissue sarcomas:
Present with painless mass (usually >5 cm).
Mass grows slowly for months or years.

ETIOLOGY
- Most sarcomas arise sporadically.
- Genetic predispositions:

1. Familial retinoblastoma (mutation of the *RBI* gene at 13q14) predisposes to osteosarcoma.
2. Neurofibromatosis type 1 (mutation of *NF1* gene at 17q11) predisposes to malignant peripheral nerve sheath tumor (malignant schwannomas and neurofibrosarcomas).
3. Diaphyseal aclasis (an autosomal inherited condition) is associated with increased risk of peripheral chondrosarcoma.
- Environmental causes:
1. Previous radiotherapy (e.g., for cervical or breast cancer): predisposes to sarcoma 4 to 10 yr after exposure.
2. Chronic lymphedema: associated with the development of angiosarcoma.
3. Exposure to chemicals (e.g., dioxins, phenoxyacetic herbicides, vinyl chloride increase the risk of hepatic angiosarcoma).
4. Viruses (e.g., human herpesvirus 8 plays a role in the development of Kaposi's sarcoma).
5. Foreign body (shrapnel, medical implants).

DIAGNOSIS

WORKUP
- Soft tissue sarcoma: any unexplained superficial soft tissue mass >5 cm, or any deep-seated soft tissue mass should be regarded as malignant until proven otherwise.
- Bone sarcoma: patients with unexplained bone pain, persistent bone tenderness, or nonmechanical bone pain (especially when it disturbs sleep or rest) have bone cancer until proven otherwise.
- Patients with suspected spontaneous fracture or recurrence of the fracture with minor trauma should be considered as having bone cancer.
- Referral to a sarcoma treatment center of all patients with a suspected sarcoma is recommended.

IMAGING STUDIES
- A chest spiral CT scan is compulsory for staging purposes. Chest spiral CT helps detect lung metastasis, since metastasis through blood to the lungs is the principal form of spread.
- Staging aids in estimating prognosis, survival, and plan management.
- The American Joint Committee on Cancer (AJCC) and International Union Against Cancer (IUCC) are widely used for staging classification.
- Soft tissue sarcoma.
- Magnetic resonance imaging (MRI) is the initial imaging modality of choice, especially for soft tissue sarcoma of the extremities, trunk, and head and neck. CT with IV contrast is also useful for diagnosis.
- Ultrasound is used to help differentiate between benign and suspicious lesions.
- Bone sarcoma.
- Radiograph (Fig. 1S-4) is the initial imaging of choice. It helps to rule out bone tumor, shows calcification, and reveals bone erosions. Fig. 1S-5 summarizes radiographic features that may help differentiate benign from malignant lesions.
- A multidisciplinary approach is essential. The team should include radiologist, surgeons, pathologist, medical oncologist, and radiation therapists.

BIOPSY
- In nearly all cases a biopsy is needed to establish a tissue diagnosis.
- Multiple core needle biopsies are usually done.
- An excisional biopsy may be used for superficial lesions <5 cm.
- In carefully selected cases an open biopsy may be done (rarely used because of its high complication rate).
- For difficult to palpate or necrotic soft sarcomas, ultrasound or computed tomography (CT)–guided biopsies are performed.
- Biopsy results are interpreted collaboratively by the specialist sarcoma pathologist, surgeon, and radiologist together.

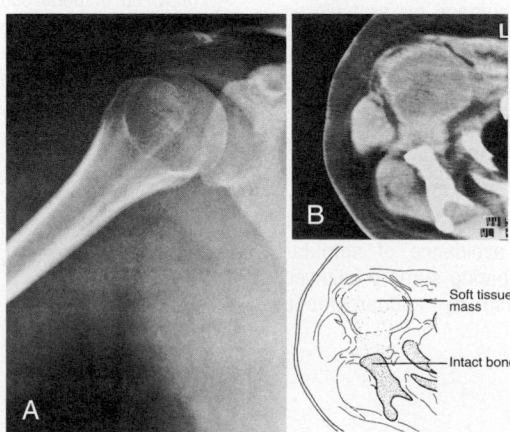

FIGURE 1S-4 Fibrosarcoma. A, Anteroposterior plain film of the shoulder of a 40-year-old woman with a history of an enlarging mass in the right axilla shows an ill-defined mass adjacent to the lateral border of the scapula. **B,** CT section with contrast enhancement shows the extent of the mass and the lack of bone involvement. The tumor proved to be a fibrosarcoma. (From Skarin AT: *Atlas of diagnostic oncology,* ed 3, St Louis, 2003, Mosby.)

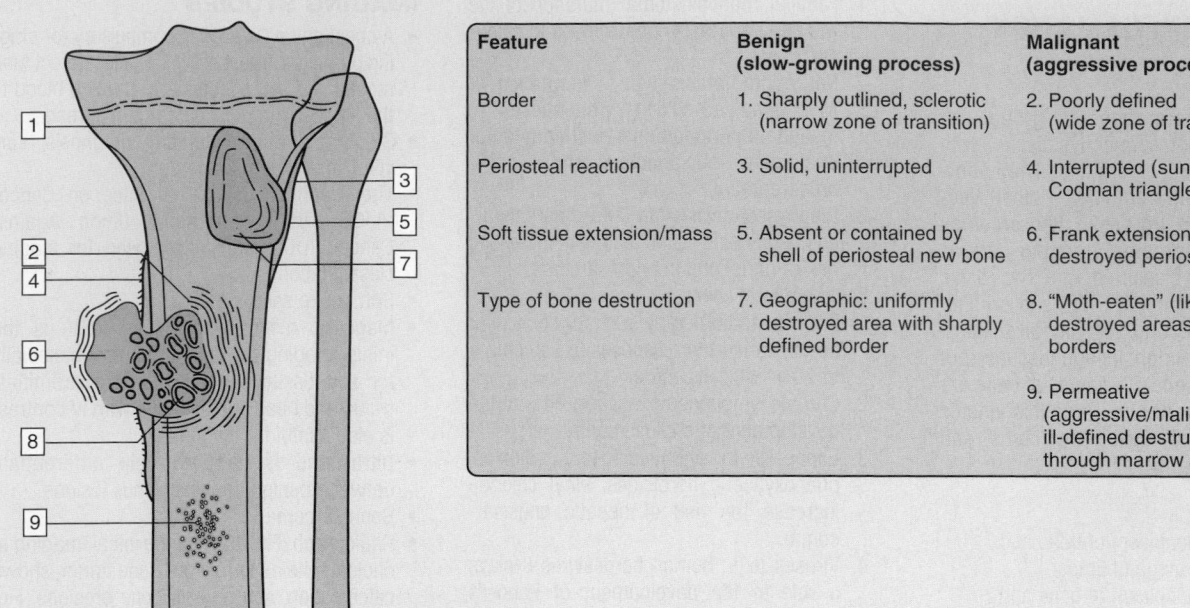

FIGURE 1S-5 Benign versus malignant bone lesions. The radiographic features illustrated may help differentiate benign from malignant lesions. (From Bullough PG, Vigorita VJ: *Atlas of orthopedic pathology*. Baltimore/New York, 1984, University Park Press/Gower Medical Publishing, in Skarin AT: *Atlas of diagnostic oncology*, 4 ed, St Louis, 2010, Mosby, 2010.)

HISTOLOGIC DIAGNOSIS

- Treatment planning is guided by a histologic diagnosis.
- Histologic diagnosis is made according to the World Health Organization (WHO) classification.
- WHO has defined >50 histologic subtypes of soft tissue sarcoma.
- Newer methods such as immunocytochemistry and cytogenetics can aid diagnosis. They identify tumor lineage.

Rx TREATMENT

Treatment depends on the extent of the disease and falls into several groups.

ACUTE GENERAL Rx

- Tumors treated by surgery: for example, in most adults soft tissue sarcoma and sarcoma of bone are not sensitive to chemotherapy.
  1. Surgery must be done by surgeon trained to treat this disease.
  2. Wide excision with negative margins is the standard surgical procedure.
  3. For bone sarcomas amputation has been the standard procedure. Recent advances permit the avoidance of amputation with limb-sparing surgery followed by reconstruction by endoprosthetic replacement.

- Chemotherapy followed by local therapy: for example, osteosarcoma.
  1. Early chemotherapy to reduce disseminated micrometastasis and tumor size.

Systemic chemotherapy regimens for advanced soft tissue sarcoma typically comprise multiple drugs such as the MAID regimen (mesna, doxorubicin, ifosfamide, dacarbazine) and the AIM regimen (doxorubicin, ifosfamide, mesna). Single-agent therapy with either doxorubicin or ifosfamide is also appropriate in the palliative setting. More recently, pazopanib, a tyrosine kinase inhibitor, has been approved in patients with metastatic or recurrent sarcoma. Trabectedin, an agent derived from a marine organism, has now been approved in metastatic or unresectable leiomyosarcoma or liposarcoma.

- Follow-up of bone sarcoma after treatment includes:
  1. Periodic monitoring with radiographs and other imaging modalities.
  2. CT scan of the chest.
  3. Bone scan.
- Follow-up of soft tissue sarcoma (extremities):
  1. Physical exam detects 97% of recurrence.
  2. Physical exam is done every 3 to 6 mo for 3 yr, then every 6 mo for the next 2 yr for stage II and III cancers, then annually.
  3. Imaging.
- Stage I: CXR every 6 to 12 mo.

- Stages II and III: image the primary site with MRI or CT.
- Chest x-ray or chest CT every 3 to 6 mo for 5 yr, then annually.

REFERRAL

- Sarcomas are relatively uncommon yet comprise a wide variety of different entities; as such, evaluation by multidisciplinary oncology teams with expertise in this field is recommended.
- Treatment and follow-up guidelines have been published by the National Comprehensive Cancer Network (www.nccn.org).

SUGGESTED READINGS

Available at www.expertconsult.com

AUTHOR: **DANIEL K. ASIEDU, M.D., PH.D.**

BASIC INFORMATION

DEFINITION

Scabies is a contagious disease caused by the mite *Sarcoptes scabici*.

ICD-10CM CODES
B86 Scabies

EPIDEMIOLOGY & DEMOGRAPHICS

- Scabies is generally acquired by sleeping with or in the bedding of infested individuals.
- It is generally associated with poor living conditions and is also common in hospitals and nursing homes.

PHYSICAL FINDINGS & CLINICAL PRESENTATION

- Primary lesions are caused when the female mite burrows within the stratum corneum, laying eggs within the tract she leaves behind; burrows (linear or serpiginous tracts, see Fig. E1S-6) end with a minute papule or vesicle.
- Primary lesions are most commonly found in the web spaces of the hands, wrists, buttocks, scrotum, penis, breasts, axillae, and knees. They are often confused with eczema (Fig. E1S-7).
- Secondary lesions result from scratching or infection.
- Intense pruritus, especially nocturnal, is common; it is caused by an acquired sensitivity to the mite or fecal pellets and is usually noted 1 to 4 wk after the primary infestation.
- Examination of the skin may reveal burrows, tiny vesicles, excoriations, inflammatory papules.

- Widespread and crusted lesions (Norwegian or crusted scabies) may be seen in elderly and immunocompromised patients (Fig. E1S-8). Pruritus may be mild or absent due to impaired host immune response.
- Table 1S-4 summarizes the different presenting forms of scabies.

ETIOLOGY

- Human scabies is caused by the mite *S. scabiei*, var. *hominis* (Fig. E1S-9). After impregnation on the skin surface, the gravid female burrows in the stratum corneum within 30 min and gradually extends the tract along the boundary with the stratum granulosum depositing 10 to 25 oval eggs in a 4- to 5-wk period. The eggs hatch in 3 to 5 days, and larvae move to the skin surface and mature in 2 to 3 wk, resuming the cycle.
- Clinical manifestations result from a delayed type IV hypersensitivity reaction to the mete, eggs, saliva, or scybala.

DIAGNOSIS

DIFFERENTIAL DIAGNOSIS

- Pediculosis.
- Atopic dermatitis.
- Flea bites.
- Seborrheic dermatitis.
- Dermatitis herpetiformis.
- Contact dermatitis.
- Nummular eczema.
- Syphilis.
- Other insect infestation.

WORKUP

Diagnosis is made on the clinical presentation and on the demonstration of mites, eggs, or mite feces.

LABORATORY TESTS

- Microscopic demonstration of the organism, feces, or eggs: a drop of mineral oil may be placed over the suspected lesion before removal; the scrapings are transferred directly to a glass slide; a drop of potassium hydroxide is added and a cover slip is applied.
- Skin biopsy is rarely necessary to make the diagnosis.

TREATMENT

NONPHARMACOLOGIC THERAPY

Clothing, underwear, and towels used in the 48 hr before treatment must be laundered.

ACUTE GENERAL Rx

- Permethrin 5% cream is usually effective with one treatment; it should be massaged into the skin from head to soles of feet and applied under fingernails and toenails (it's best if applied in the evening and left overnight to maximize exposure); remove 8 to 14 hr later by washing. Repeat in 1 to 2 wk. Permethrin is safe for children >2 mo old.
- A single dose (150-200 μg/kg in 6-mg tablets) of ivermectin, an antihelmintic agent, is also effective for the treatment of scabies. It is the best treatment for generalized crusted scabies. Three to seven doses of ivermectin given on days 1, 2, 8, 9, 15, 22, and 28 may be needed for crusted scabies.

TABLE 1S-4 Different Presenting Forms of Scabies

Presenting Forms of Scabies	Specific High-Risk Populations	Clinical Manifestations	Limited Differential Diagnoses
Classic scabies (scabies vulgaris)	Infants and children; sexually active adults; men who have sex with men	Intense generalized pruritus, worse at night; inflammatory pruritic papules localized to finger webs, flexor aspects of wrists, elbows, axillae, buttocks, genitalia, female breasts; lesions and pruritus spare the face, head, and neck; secondary lesions include eczematization, excoriation, impetigo	Dermatitis herpetiformis, drug reactions, eczema, pediculosis corporis, lichen planus, pityriasis rosea
Scalp scabies	Infants and children; institutionalized older adults; AIDS patients; patients with pre-existing crusted scabies	Atypical crusted papular lesions of the scalp, face, palms, and soles	Dermatomyositis, ringworm, seborrheic dermatitis
Crusted scabies (Norwegian scabies, scabies norvegica, scabies crustosa)	Institutionalized older adults; institutionalized developmentally disabled (Down syndrome); homeless, especially HIV-positive; all immunocompromised patients, particularly those with AIDS or positive for HIV or HTLV-1; transplant recipients; patients on prolonged systemic corticosteroids and chemotherapy	Psoriasiform hyperkeratotic papular lesions of the scalp, face, neck, hands, feet, with extensive nail involvement; eczematization and impetigo common	Contact dermatitis, drug reactions, eczema, erythroderma, ichthyosis, psoriasis
Nodular scabies	Sexually active adults; men who have sex with men; HIV-positive men > HIV-positive women	Violaceous pruritic nodules localized to male genitalia, groin, axillae, representing hypersensitivity reaction to mite antigens	Acropustulosis, atopic dermatitis, Darier's disease, lupus erythematosus, lymphomatoid papulosis, papular urticaria, necrotizing vasculitis, secondary syphilis

AIDS, Acquired immunodeficiency syndrome; *HIV*, human immunodeficiency virus; *HTLV-1*, human T cell lymphotropic virus type 1.
From Bennett JE et al: *Mandell, Douglas, and Bennett's principles and practice of infectious diseases*, ed 8, Philadelphia, 2015, WB Saunders.

Schizophrenia  EBM PTG

 BASIC INFORMATION

DEFINITION

Schizophrenia is a disorder that causes significant distortions in thinking, perception, speech, and behavior. Characteristics include psychosis, apathy, social withdrawal, and cognitive impairment, which result in significant social impairment.

SYNONYMS

Dementia praecox

ICD-10CM CODES
F20   Schizophrenia
F20.0 Paranoid schizophrenia
F20.1 Hebephrenic schizophrenia
F20.2 Catatonic schizophrenia
F20.3 Undifferentiated schizophrenia
F20.5 Residual schizophrenia
F20.6 Simple schizophrenia
F20.8 Other schizophrenia
F20.9 Schizophrenia, unspecified

EPIDEMIOLOGY & DEMOGRAPHICS

INCIDENCE: 0.2 per 1000.
PREVALENCE: 0.5%; lifetime prevalence risk, 0.4%.
PREDOMINANT SEX: Males have a more severe illness with earlier onset. Prevalence in males approximately 1.4 times higher.
PREDOMINANT AGE:
- Age of onset of psychotic symptoms is the early 20s for males and the late 20s for females.
- Age of onset of negative symptoms is usually earlier (i.e., the mid-teenage years).
PEAK INCIDENCE: Between ages of 16 and 30 yr.
GENETICS:
- Genetics accounts for 70% of risk; the remaining 30% associated with other factors such as urban environments, migration, or cannabis use.
- First-degree relatives have a 10 times greater chance of becoming schizophrenic.
- Discordant rates among identical twins are higher than expected with the simple inheritance pattern.
- Associations with several chromosomes have been described, but none has been replicated.
- Evidence exists that triplet nucleotide repeat expansion (e.g., such as that seen with Huntington's disease) may play a role in the inheritance of the disease.

PHYSICAL FINDINGS & CLINICAL PRESENTATION

- Schizophrenia is best defined as a dementing illness that begins early in life and that progresses slowly throughout the lifetime.
- Frequent structural brain imaging findings include the enlargement of the ventricular system, a loss of brain volume and cortical gray matter, and an alteration of the white matter tracts.
- The initial "negative" symptoms of adolescence (prodromal phase)—cognitive decline, social withdrawal and awkwardness, loss of motivation and pleasure, and loss of emotional expressiveness—begin after a period of normal development.
- During early adulthood, positive symptoms of psychosis and thought disturbance occur; psychotic symptoms then wax and wane throughout life. Treatment ameliorates positive symptoms, but generally does little for negative ones.
- The condition is also accompanied by cognitive impairment, including problems with attention and concentration, psychomotor speed, learning, memory, and executive functions (e.g., abstract thinking, problem solving, planning).
- Social and occupational dysfunction can be profound.

ETIOLOGY

- The basic determination of whether this is a degenerative or developmental condition has not been made.
- The major hypothesis is that abnormality of the mesocortical pathways produces the hypofrontality and the negative symptoms. This occurs along with a compensatory hyperactivation of the mesolimbic pathways, which produces the positive symptoms of psychosis.

 DIAGNOSIS

DIFFERENTIAL DIAGNOSIS

- Schizophrenia is diagnosed when an individual has experienced at least 6 mo (1 mo if using ICD-10 criteria) of hallucinations, delusions, thought disorders, catatonia, or negative symptoms (e.g., avolition, anhedonia, social isolation, affective flattening).
- Any medical condition, medicine, or substance that can affect brain homeostasis can cause psychosis; this is distinguished from schizophrenia by a relatively brief course and an alteration in mental status that suggests an underlying delirium.
- Other neurologic conditions that have psychosis as the initial presentation (e.g., Huntington's disease) need to be ruled out.
- Mood disorders with psychosis: these are indistinguishable from schizophrenia cross-sectionally but have a longitudinal course that includes full recovery.
- Delusional disorder involves nonbizarre delusions and lacks the thought disturbance, hallucinations, and negative symptoms of schizophrenia.
- Autism in the adult has an early age of onset and lacks significant hallucinations or delusions.

WORKUP

- History and physical examination to help determine whether the psychosis is primary or secondary.
- Neurologic examination to uncover the soft neurologic signs (e.g., clumsiness, cortical thumb, loss of fine motor movements) that are common with schizophrenia.

LABORATORY TESTS

- No laboratory tests are specific.
- Laboratory examinations (e.g., chemistry profile, blood count, sedimentation rate, toxicology screen, and urinalysis) are geared toward excluding a primary medical condition or toxic state. Note that new common drugs of abuse may not be detectable with regular screening tests.

IMAGING STUDIES

- CT or MRI of the brain during the initial workup; repeated if the course of the illness varies from what is expected.
- EEG may reveal slowing when psychosis is the result of an encephalopathy. Findings can be similar as a result of common medication use for treatment of psychosis.

Rx TREATMENT

NONPHARMACOLOGIC THERAPY

- Significant social support is required by most schizophrenic patients, but available support services are grossly inadequate. Schizophrenic patients constitute nearly one third of all homeless individuals and approximately 5% of the incarcerated population. They usually require help with basic social, occupational, and interaction skills.
- Family stress can precipitate relapse and re-hospitalization. Family interventions can reduce morbidity.
- Cognitive behavioral therapy can reduce the severity of both psychotic and negative symptoms.
- Illness management training for patients can increase medication adherence and reduce symptom distress.
- Integrated treatment that includes assertive community treatment, family involvement programs, and social skills training reduces the severity of both psychotic and negative symptoms, reduces comorbid substance misuse, reduces hospital days, increases adherence to treatment, and increases satisfaction with treatment.

ACUTE GENERAL Rx

- Acute psychosis is usually adequately controlled with antipsychotic agents.
- Few differences in effectiveness exist between first-generation antipsychotics (e.g., haloperidol, perphenazine, fluphenazine, chlorpromazine) and second-generation antipsychotics (e.g., risperidone, olanzapine, quetiapine, ziprasidone, aripiprazole, clozapine, lurasidone) for nonrefractory patients. First-generation antipsychotics are slightly more likely than second-generation antipsychotics to cause a parkinsonian state and eventual tardive dyskinesia (rate of tardive dyskinesia, 15%-30%). Antiparkinsonian drugs (e.g., benztropine, amantadine) are used to ameliorate the parkinsonism. Risperidone has been shown to be superior to haloperidol for the prevention of acute psychotic relapse.

- Sedatives (i.e., benzodiazepines and, to a lesser degree, barbiturates) can be used transiently if a patient is in an agitated state.

CHRONIC Rx

- Relapse prevention is a major goal of treatment. Noncompliance is common and leads to high relapse rates. Antipsychotic agents usually must be continued at the same doses that controlled psychosis. For noncompliant patients, long-acting injectable preparations given biweekly, monthly, or every three months can be used.
- Most patients frequently switch among antipsychotics; there is considerable individual variability with regard to antipsychotic response and vulnerability to specific adverse effects.
- Clozapine is more effective than other agents for treatment-refractory patients. However, it requires monitoring to prevent life-threatening adverse effects. Olanzapine may also be more effective than less expensive first-generation drugs but has substantial adverse metabolic effects. Lurasidone is a newer second-generation antipsychotic that appears to be better tolerated, but longer-term studies are needed.
- Neurocognitive improvement associated with antipsychotic treatment among patients with schizophrenia is small and does not differ between first-generation and second-generation antipsychotics.
- Antiparkinsonian agents may also need to be continued for the long term.
- Tardive dyskinesia (i.e., choreoathetoid movements of the muscles of tongue and face and occasionally of other muscle groups) can occur in as many as 30% of patients with the long-term use of neuroleptics.
- The negative symptoms of schizophrenia can resemble depression. In addition, depressive disorders may occur in schizophrenic patients. Antidepressant treatment of the negative symptoms is usually not effective. However, antidepressants can improve the symptoms of a comorbid depressive episode.

- Mood stabilizers (e.g., lithium, valproate, carbamazepine) are of little use unless the patient has a comorbid impulse control disorder.
- Substance abuse is a major problem for more than a third of schizophrenic patients. More than half of these patients smoke cigarettes. Unfortunately, these individuals do poorly in traditional substance abuse treatment programs. Specialized "dual-diagnosis" programs with highly structured aftercare are required.
- Specific antipsychotic medications have been associated with weight gain (i.e., olanzapine and clozapine) and QT prolongation. Hyperlipidemia and diabetes mellitus are associated with second-generation antipsychotics, and hyperprolactinemia is associated with first-generation antipsychotics. (Risperidone, a second-generation antipsychotic, can also produce hyperprolactinemia.) Clozapine is associated with agranulocytosis and a decrease in intestinal motility. Metabolic status and weight should be screened before the start of treatment and at regular intervals.
- Patients with schizophrenia have a higher lifetime incidence of suicide, with 20% attempting on one or more occasions and 5% to 6% completing suicide. Comorbid use of substances and hopelessness are associated risk factors. Clozapine has shown the ability to decrease the incidence of suicidal attempts in schizophrenia patients.
- Several 1st and 2nd generation antipsychotics are available in long-acting injectable preparations that may be helpful in addressing issues of poor compliance or difficulty when treatment needs to be supervised.

DISPOSITION

- The positive symptoms of as many as 20% to 30% of schizophrenic patients do not respond to available treatments. A much higher fraction of patients experience relapse as a result of poor compliance.
- Negative symptoms are responsible for the 50% to 70% of patients in whom deterioration in occupational and social function continues.

- Approximately 10% of schizophrenic patients will complete suicide.
- The course of the illness is most strongly predicted by the level of social development attained at the onset of psychosis.
- Schizophrenic patients die 12 to 15 years sooner than the average population, mostly as a result of physical causes related to a lack of access to health care or as a result of health risk factors (e.g., smoking, obesity).

REFERRAL

- If hospitalization is required.
- If patient is noncompliant.
- If patient is resistant to treatment.

 **PEARLS & CONSIDERATIONS**

- Rule out delirium caused by medical conditions, medications, or substance abuse before diagnosing an individual's psychotic behavior as schizophrenia.
- All antipsychotic medications have high discontinuation rates in chronic schizophrenia treatment. Olanzapine and clozapine may be more effective than other antipsychotics for chronic treatment, but they have significant side effects.
- Significant social support is required for most patients with schizophrenia. Nonpharmacologic therapy should be used in conjunction with pharmacotherapy.

SUGGESTED READINGS

Available at www.expertconsult.com

RELATED CONTENT

Schizophrenia (Patient Information)

AUTHORS: **ARNALDO A. BERGES, M.D.,** and **RICHARD J. GOLDBERG, M.D., M.S.**

BASIC INFORMATION

DEFINITION

Scleritis is inflammation of the sclera (the fibrous layer of the eye underlying the conjunctiva and episclera). It is characterized by edema and cellular infiltration of the entire thickness of the sclera. Classification of immune:

1. Anterior nonnecrotizing scleritis: can be subdivided into diffuse or nodular.
2. Anterior necrotizing scleritis with inflammation: can be subdivided into vasoocclusive, granulomatous, or surgically induced. Aggressive form of scleritis. Average age of onset is 60 yr. Bilateral in 60% of patients.
3. Scleromalacia perforans: typically affects elderly women with longstanding rheumatoid arthritis.
4. Posterior scleritis: involves the deeper tissues of the eye and is potentially blinding. Age of onset is often under 40 yr. Bilateral in 35% of cases.

SYNONYMS

Anterior scleritis
Diffuse nodular, necrotizing scleritis
Scleromalacia perforans
Scleral melt syndrome

ICD-10CM CODES
H15.0 Scleritis
H15.1 Episcleritis

EPIDEMIOLOGY & DEMOGRAPHICS

PEAK INCIDENCE: Increases with increasing age.
INCIDENCE (IN U.S.): Busy ophthalmologists may see one or two cases a year
PREVALENCE (IN U.S.): Relatively rare.
PREDOMINANT SEX: 61% women.
PREDOMINANT AGE: 52 yr.

PHYSICAL FINDINGS & CLINICAL PRESENTATION

- Deep, boring (dull) eye pain that may awaken patient from sleep.
- Photophobia.
- Tearing.
- Painful eye movements.
- Globe is tender to touch.
- Conjunctival injection (Fig. 1S-13).
- Thinning of the sclera.
- An underlying systemic autoimmune disease is found in >50% of patients. Most common rheumatic problem is rheumatoid arthritis. Most patients with systemic disease are diagnosed before development of scleritis.

ETIOLOGY

- Inflammatory (seen with rheumatoid arthritis, granulomatosis with polyangiitis [Wegener granulomatosis], relapsing polychondritis, polyarteritis nodosa), lupus, sarcoidosis.
- Allergic.
- Infectious scleritis (herpes zoster, tuberculosis, Lyme disease, syphilis, *Pseudomonas aeruginosa, Nocardia,* leprosy) is uncommon, accounting for 4% to 18% of cases
- Approximately 50% of patients with scleritis have an underlying systemic disease (vasculitis, infectious disease).

DIAGNOSIS

DIFFERENTIAL DIAGNOSIS

Most common causes are rheumatoid arthritis and other collagen-vascular diseases.

- Occasionally there are allergic, infectious, or traumatic causes.
- Conjunctivitis, iritis, and episcleritis should be considered in the differential diagnosis. Patients with episcleritis generally have less pain and vision is unaffected.

WORKUP

- Eye examination.
- Visual field examination.
- Workup for autoimmune disease (e.g., vasculitis, collagen vascular diseases)

LABORATORY TESTS

Rheumatoid factor, antinuclear antibody, erythrocyte sedimentation rate, ANCA (c-ANCA, p-ANCA), antiphospholipid antibodies, may be useful for underlying etiology.

IMAGING STUDIES

Usually not necessary; CT scan of orbit may be useful in selected patients for collagen vascular disease or vasculitis.

TREATMENT

NONPHARMACOLOGIC THERAPY

- Bandage lenses.
- Surgery if thinning of the sclera is severe to prevent eye rupture.

ACUTE GENERAL Rx

Immunotherapy:

- Steroids (topical, periocular, and systemic).
- Cycloplegic drops.
- Nonsteroidal antiinflammatory drugs (topical and systemic); systemic more effective than topical.
- Cytotoxic agents (cyclophosphamide, azathioprine, mycophenolate mofetil, methotrexate).
- Immune modulators (cyclosporin, tacrolimus).
- Specific antibodies (infliximab, rituximab).

CHRONIC Rx

- Systemic corticosteroids can be given for the underlying disease.
- Local steroids may be helpful.
- Control underlying disease.

DISPOSITION

Urgent referral to ophthalmologist because this disorder can be a sight-threatening condition.

REFERRAL

Should be managed by ophthalmologist; complications of scleritis can be severe, including scleral melt, inflammation, corneal involvement.

PEARLS & CONSIDERATIONS

COMMENTS

Necrotizing scleritis can be an ominous diagnosis because these patients often have other severe underlying debilitating vasculitic disease processes.

SUGGESTED READINGS
Available at www.expertconsult.com

AUTHOR: **R. SCOTT HOFFMAN, M.D.**

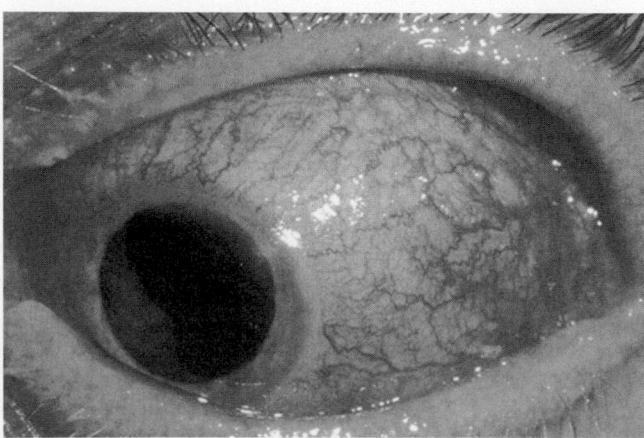

FIGURE 1S-13 In diffuse anterior scleritis, widespread injection of the conjunctival and deep episcleral vessels occurs. (From Palay D [ed]: *Ophthalmology for the primary care physician,* St Louis, 1997, Mosby.)

BASIC INFORMATION

DEFINITION

Scleroderma or systemic sclerosis (SSc) is a term used to describe a connective tissue disorder that is characterized by thickening and fibrosis of the skin. It is divided into two forms: localized scleroderma and systemic sclerosis. Skin thickening without any organ involvement is known as localized scleroderma and includes three subset conditions (see Box 1S-1). Systemic sclerosis includes skin fibrosis along with variable severe involvement of diverse internal organs. It is further divided into two major subgroups: (1) limited cutaneous SSc (lcSSc), which involves skin thickening of the face, neck, and distal to the elbows and knees; and (2) diffuse cutaneous SSc (dcSSc), which affects the skin in a more generalized distribution including the proximal and distal extremities, face, neck, and trunk. Table 1S-6 compares localized scleroderma and SSc.

SYNONYMS

Systemic sclerosis

Morphea applies to localized scleroderma that affects only the skin

Scleredema is a disease of the skin that is distinct from scleroderma

ICD-10CM CODES

M34.0 Progressive systemic sclerosis
M34.1 CREST syndrome
M34.2 Systemic sclerosis induced by drug and chemical

BOX 1S-1   Classification of Scleroderma

I. Localized scleroderma
   A. Morphea
   B. Linear scleroderma
   C. Scleroderma en coup de sabre
II. Systemic sclerosis
   A. Limited cutaneous systemic sclerosis
   B. Diffuse cutaneous systemic sclerosis

From Hochberg MC et al: *Rheumatology,* ed 5, St Louis, 2011, Mosby.

M34.81 Systemic sclerosis with lung involvement
M34.82 Systemic sclerosis with myopathy
M34.83 Systemic sclerosis with polyneuropathy
M34.89 Other systemic sclerosis
M34.9 Systemic sclerosis, unspecified
L94.0 Localized scleroderma (morphea)
L94.1 Linear scleroderma

EPIDEMIOLOGY & DEMOGRAPHICS

Incidence and prevalence of SSc varies between studies due to variations between geographic regions and time periods.
INCIDENCE: There are an estimated 2.3 to 22.8 cases per 1 million persons per year, but many mild cases go unrecognized.
PREVALENCE: 50 to 300 cases per 1 million persons.
PREDOMINANT SEX: Female/male ratio of 4:1.
PREDOMINANT AGE: 30 to 50 years old
DISTRIBUTION: Worldwide
Physical Findings & Clinical Presentation
PHYSICAL FINDINGS:
1. Skin
   ○ Initial presentation of puffy hands and fingers may occur in some patients.
   ○ Tightening of the skin begins on the hands and then progresses to the forearms, face, and neck. The skin is shiny, taut, and sometimes red, with loss of creases and hair. Skin thickening involving the fingers or toes is known as sclerodactyly (Fig. 1S-14). Skin involvement in scleroderma is classified as lcSSc or dcSSc, depending on the distribution of the skin thickening (see previously) (Fig. E1S-15). Fig. 1S-16 illustrates the method used to semiquantify skin thickness in scleroderma.
   ○ Skin tightening may limit movement by causing flexion contractures of the fingers, wrists, and elbows. Perioral skin tightening (Fig. E1S-17) results in decreased oral aperture, furrowing around the lips, and dry membranes.
   ○ Pigmentary skin changes (hypo- or hyper-pigmentation) may occur.

   ○ Telangiectasias (dilated capillaries) may be seen on face, hands, mucous membranes (Fig. E1S-17) and trunk.
   ○ Subcutaneous calcinosis.
   ○ In dsSSc patients, the skin fibrosis can soften to normal skin (occurring two years after onset of skin manifestation), and joint mobility can improve.
   ○ Skin atrophy and thinning can also occur in the late stages of SSc.
2. Musculoskeletal
   ○ Arthralgias and swelling
   ○ Symmetric inflammatory arthritis
   ○ Myalgias
   ○ Myopathy
   ○ Tendon friction rubs (physical exam finding of a palpable rub felt over tendon sheaths–fingers, wrists, elbows, knees, and/or ankles)
3. Gastrointestinal involvement
   ○ Esophageal dysmotility with heartburn
   ○ Esophageal stricture with dysphagia and odynophagia
   ○ Delayed gastric emptying
   ○ Gastrointestinal bleeding from mucosal telangiectasias, gastric antral vascular ectasias, or gastritis
   ○ Small bowel dysmotility with abdominal cramps, bloating, and diarrhea
   ○ Colon dysmotility with constipation
   ○ Intestinal bacterial overgrowth resulting in irregular bowel movements (diarrhea alternating with constipation)
   ○ Pseudoobstruction (functional ileus)
   ○ Primary biliary cirrhosis (see "Primary Biliary Cirrhosis" in Section I)
4. Pulmonary
   ○ Interstitial lung disease (ILD): pulmonary fibrosis with symptoms of dyspnea and nonproductive cough as well as fine inspiratory crackles on examination. Seen in both lcSSc and dcSSC, but it is more common and severe in dcSSC.
   Pulmonary arterial hypertension (PAH): presenting with dyspnea and/or fatigue. Can be identified in both lcSSc and dcSSc, but it is more commonly seen in lcSSc.
5. Cardiac
   ○ Pericarditis or pericardial effusion
   ○ Myositis or myocardial fibrosis that can lead to congestive heart failure or arrhythmias
   ○ Left or right systolic or diastolic dysfunction

TABLE 1S-6   Comparison of Localized Scleroderma and Systemic Sclerosis

Feature	Localized Scleroderma/ Morphea	Systemic Sclerosis
Skin findings	Patches or linear distribution of thickened skin	Sclerodactyly ± proximal skin thickening
Raynaud's phenomenon	Absent	Present
Digital ischemic changes	Absent	Usually present (digital pitting scars or ulcers, loss of fingerpad substance)
Internal organ disease	Absent	Present
Antinuclear antibody	Positive in ≥50% of cases	Positive in ≥85% of cases
Scleroderma-specific auto-antibodies*	Negative	Positive in 60% of cases
Biopsy—histologic findings	Dermal fibrosis	Dermal fibrosis

*Scleroderma-specific antibodies include antibodies to centromere, topoisomerase-1 (Scl 70), and RNA polymerase III.
From Hochberg MC et al: *Rheumatology,* ed 5, St Louis, 2011, Mosby.

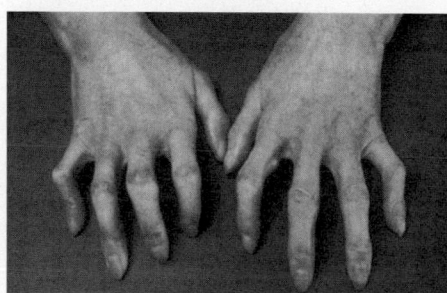

FIGURE 1S-14 Sclerodactyly in a patient with systemic sclerosis. (From Hochberg MC et al: *Rheumatology,* ed 5, St Louis, 2011, Mosby.)

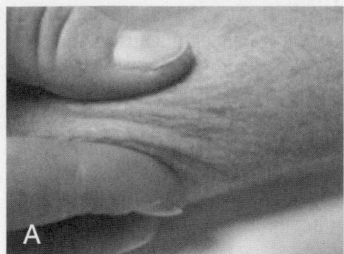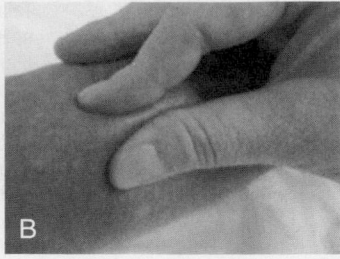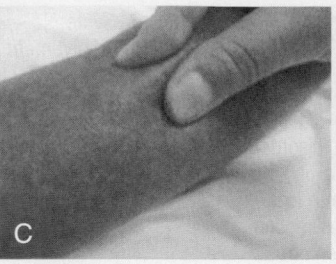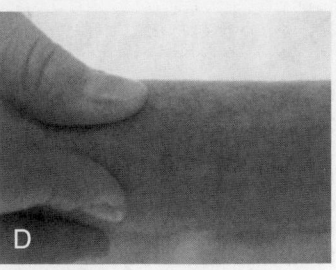

FIGURE 1S-16 Method used to semi-quantify skin thickness in scleroderma. The modified Rodnan skin score is obtained by clinical palpation of 17 different body areas (fingers, hands, forearms, upper arms, chest, abdomen, thighs, lower legs, and feet) and subjective averaging of the thickness of each specific site: 0 = normal **(A)**; 1 = mild **(B)**; 2 = moderate **(C)**; and 3 = severe **(D)**. The maximum score is 51. (From Firestein GS et al: *Kelly's textbook of rheumatology,* ed 9, Philadelphia, 2013, Saunders.)

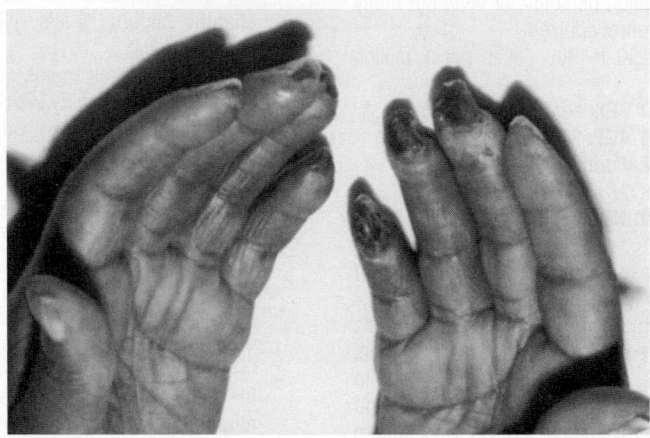

FIGURE 1S-18 Digital gangrene on the fingertips of a patient with scleroderma. (From Hochberg MC et al: *Rheumatology*, ed 5, St Louis, 2011, Mosby.)

6. Renal
   - Rapidly progressive renal failure also known as scleroderma renal crisis (SRC): new-onset hypertension, anemia with schistocytes on peripheral blood smear, thrombocytopenia and renal insufficiency with active urinary sediment and proteinuria
7. Vascular
   - Raynaud phenomenon (RP) – vasospasm of the fingers with exposure to cold, resulting in color changes of the digits along with numbness/tingling and pain or discomfort.
   - Complications of this vascular involvement include: digital pitted scars or ulcers (Fig. 1S-18), nonreversible ischemic changes with impending tissue loss, dry gangrene, and autoamputation.
   - Nailfold capillary abnormalities: seen with nailfold capillaroscopy, including capillary dilatation, avascularity, or "drop out" of capillaries.
8. Other organ involvement
   - Hypothyroidism
   - Erectile dysfunction
   - Sjögren's syndrome
   - Entrapment neuropathies
   - Depression

CLINICAL PRESENTATION:
- Raynaud's phenomenon: initial complaint in 70% of patients (NOTE: The prevalence of Raynaud's phenomenon is 5% to 10% in the general population; most cases do not progress to scleroderma)
- Finger or hand swelling that is sometimes associated with carpal tunnel syndrome
- Arthralgias/arthritis
- Internal organ involvement

LcSSc (previously known as CREST syndrome):
   - Calcinosis, Raynaud's syndrome, Esophageal dysmotility, Sclerodactyly Telangiectasias—skin fibrosis is limited to the distal extremities. This acronym is now considered obsolete by many because it does not accurately reflect the burden of internal organ involvement.

ETIOLOGY

The etiology of this condition is unknown, but genetic and environmental factors (infectious agents, occupational exposures, drugs) contribute to the manifestation of the disease. Genetic profiles show clustering of different alleles according to the subtype of SSc.

Pathologically, small- and medium-sized arteries become injured, leading to fibrin deposition and ultimately luminal occlusion, causing chronic tissue hypoxia. There is also an abnormal selection of fibroblasts and aberrant control of connective tissue synthesis by fibroblasts and other cells. This fibrosis occurs in different organs, causing dysfunction and eventual failure. Although there are characteristic autoantibodies detected, it is not clear that they directly participate in the pathogenesis of the disease.

(Dx) DIAGNOSIS

The American College of Rheumatology (ACR) and European League Against Rheumatism (EULAR) have created criteria as a guide in diagnosing and classifying SSc. These include a scoring system for both clinical and laboratory findings (sclerodactyly, fingertip lesions, telangiectasias, abnormal nailfold capillaries, Raynaud's phenomenon, PAH/ILD, and SSc-related autoantibodies).

DIFFERENTIAL DIAGNOSIS
DERMATOLOGIC:
- Scleredema
- Amyloidosis
- Porphyria cutanea tarda
- Eosinophilic fasciitis
- Reflex sympathetic dystrophy
- Nephrogenic systemic fibrosis
SYSTEMIC:
- Idiopathic pulmonary fibrosis
- Primary pulmonary hypertension
- Primary biliary cirrhosis
- Cardiomyopathies
- Gastrointestinal dysmotility problems
- Systemic lupus erythematosus and overlap syndromes

WORKUP

Laboratory tests and imaging studies

LABORATORY TESTS
- Antinuclear antibodies (ANA): nucleolar (more common), homogeneous, or speckled patterns.
- Rheumatoid factor positive in 20% of patients.
- Routine biochemistry tests may indicate specific organ involvement (e.g., liver, kidney, muscle).

The following extractable nuclear antigens are either present or absent in SSc:
- Anticentromere antibodies: generally positive in one third of patients with lcSSc.
- Anti-Scl-70 antibody: positive in 40% of patients with dcSSc and has an increased risk of developing ILD.
- Anti-RNA polymerase III antibody: portends a worse prognosis and extensive skin fibrosis and increases risk of developing SRC.

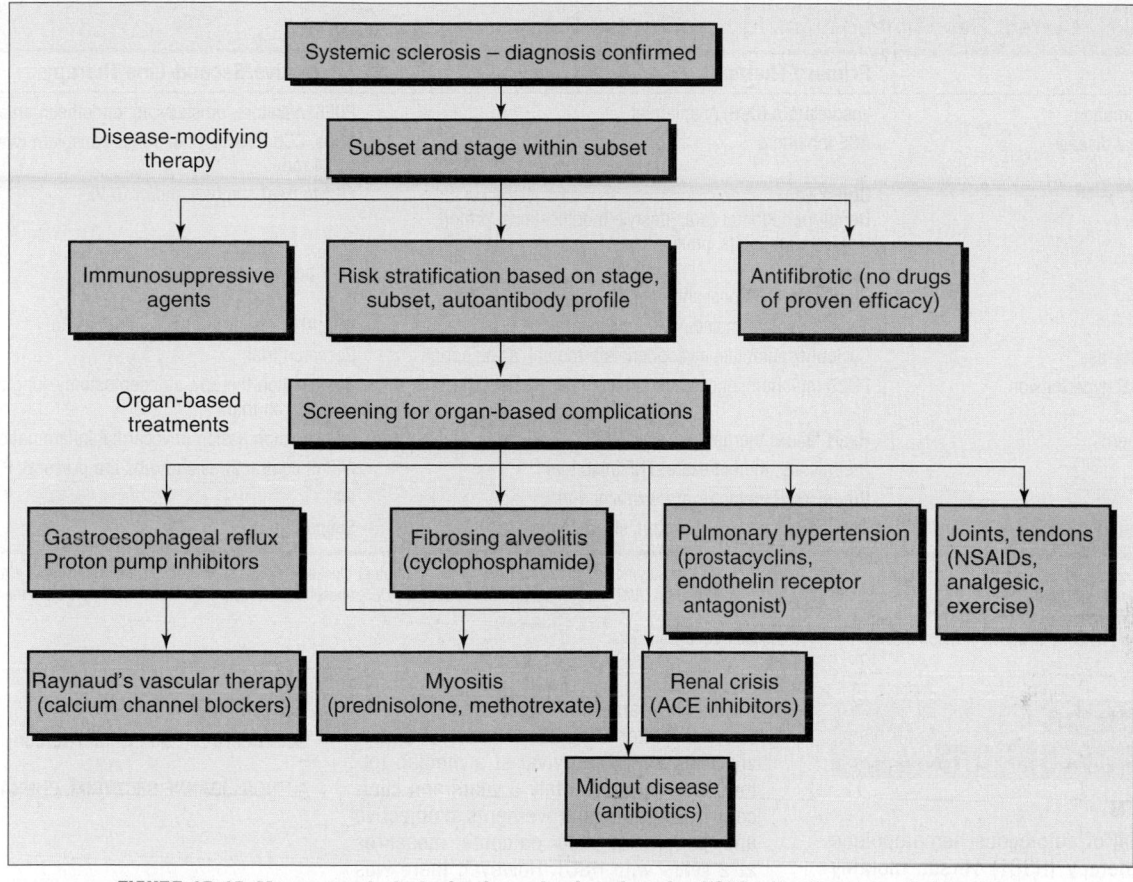

FIGURE 1S-19 Management strategies in systemic sclerosis. *NSAIDs,* Nonsteroidal antiinflammatory drugs. (From Hochberg MC et al: *Rheumatology,* ed 5, St Louis, 2011, Mosby.)

- Autoantibodies against ribonucleoprotein (anti-RNP): positive in 20% of patients.
- Negative antibody to native DNA
- Negative anti-smooth muscle antibody

IMAGING AND OTHER STUDIES

1. Arthritis: joint radiographs
2. Gastrointestinal
   - Endoscopy (diagnostic procedure of choice; may be therapeutic)
   - Cine-esophagography (in rare circumstances)
   - Barium swallow (occasionally indicated)
   - Esophageal manometry (almost never necessary)
3. Pulmonary
   - Chest x-ray
   - Pulmonary function tests (especially single-breath diffusion capacity for carbon monoxide)
   - Thoracic high-resolution computed tomography (HRCT) scan
   - Bronchoscopy with biopsy
   - Bronchoalveolar lavage
4. Cardiac
   - ECG
   - Ambulatory (Holter) ECG monitoring
   - Echocardiography
   - Cardiac catheterization
5. Kidney: renal biopsy
6. Skin: skin biopsy
7. Vascular: nailfold capillaroscopy

🅁🅇 TREATMENT

Currently, there is no disease-modifying therapy available for SSc. Generally, the internal organ involvement of the disease is treatable. Fig. 1S-19 illustrates management strategies in SSc. Immunosuppressive agents are used in individual patients. Prednisone should be used with extreme caution, especially in doses >20 mg/day. Table 1S-7 summarizes current recommendations for treatment of scleroderma.

1. Raynaud's syndrome:
   - Keep hands and body warm
   - Avoid smoking
   - Calcium channel blockers (i.e., long-acting dihydropyridines)
   - Peripheral α1-adrenergic blockers
   - Angiotensin II receptor blockers
   - Pentoxifylline
   - Phosphodiesterase inhibitors
   - Stellate ganglion blockades
   - Digital sympathectomy
2. Arthralgias: nonsteroidal antiinflammatory drugs or low-dose corticosteroids (5-10 mg of prednisone per day)
3. Myositis: methotrexate or azathioprine with low-dose corticosteroids
4. Skin: for extensive skin fibrosis, immuno-modulatory drugs have been used such as methotrexate, mycophenolate mofetil and cyclophosphamide, but have not been proved to be beneficial

5. Esophageal reflux
   - H$_2$-receptor blockers
   - Proton pump inhibitors
6. Interstitial lung disease
   - Cyclophosphamide for symptomatic scleroderma-related ILD
   - Mycophenolate mofetil and rituximab have been reported to be beneficial but are still being studied in clinical trials
   - Lung transplantation for patients with advanced pulmonary involvement
7. Pulmonary hypertension
   - Oxygen
   - Diuretics (with caution)
   - Prostacyclins (epoprostenol, iloprost, treprostinil)
   - Endothelin-1 receptor inhibitors (bosentan, ambrisentan)
   Phosphodiesterase 5 inhibitors (sildenafil, tadalafil)
8. Renal involvement
   - Angiotensin-converting enzyme inhibitors
   - Dialysis
   - Renal transplantation

REFERRAL

Rheumatology consultation is indicated. Consider pulmonary, cardiology, or gastrointestinal consultations depending on organ involvement.

TABLE 1S-7 Current Recommendations for Treatment of Scleroderma

Manifestation	Primary Therapy	Alternative/Second-Line Therapy
Raynaud's phenomenon	Vasodilators (CCB) Antiplatelet	PDE5 inhibitors, prostacyclin, endothelin antagonists
Hypertensive renal disease	ACE inhibitors	ARBs, CCB, prostacyclin, renal transplant (wait at least 24 mo)
GI involvement	**Upper GI** Dental/periodontal care, lifestyle modifications, proton pump inhibitors, prokinetics	EGD to treat stenosis and/or GAVE
	Lower GI Probiotics, rotational antibiotics	Total parenteral nutrition
Skin	Mycophenolate mofetil, cyclophosphamide	IVIG, ATG, research trial (severe cases)
Interstitial lung disease	Cyclophosphamide, mycophenolate mofetil, azathioprine	Research trial
Pulmonary arterial hypertension	PDE5 inhibitors, endothelin antagonists, prostacyclin	Combination therapy, atrioseptostomy, lung transplant, research trial
Cardiac involvement	Heart failure therapy, diuretics, CCB	Immunosuppression (myocardial inflammation)
Joints	Prednisone, methotrexate, TNF inhibitors	IVIG (if contractures and rubs are present), PT/OT
Muscles	Prednisone, methotrexate, azathioprine	IVIG
Psychosocial	Antidepressants, pain control, sleep control	Support group

ACE, Angiotensin-converting enzyme; *ARBs,* angiotensin receptor blockers; *ATG,* antithymocyte globulin; *CCB,* calcium channel blockers; *EGD,* esophagogastroduodenoscopy; *GAVE,* gastric antral vascular ectasia; *GI,* gastrointestinal; *HSCT,* hematopoietic stem cell transplantation; *IVIG,* intravenous immunoglobulin; *PDE5,* phosphodiesterase-5 inhibitor; *PT/OT,* physical therapy/occupational therapy; *TNF,* tumor necrosis factor.

From Firestein GS et al: *Kelly's textbook of rheumatology,* ed 9, Philadelphia, 2013, Saunders.

 **PEARLS & CONSIDERATIONS**

COMMENTS

- A recent trial of autologous hematopoietic stem cell therapy (HSCT) versus monthly cyclophosphamide in patients with early diffuse cutaneous systemic sclerosis showed better long-term event-free survival and overall survival at a median follow-up of approximately 6 years and clinically meaningful improvements in objective and patient-reported outcome measures at 2 years with HSCT. However, there was greater treatment-related mortality.

RELATED CONTENT

Scleroderma (Patient Information)

AUTHOR: **JOANNE SZCZYGIEL CUNHA, M.D.**

BASIC INFORMATION

DEFINITION

Scoliosis is a lateral curvature of the spine in the upright position, usually 10 degrees or greater. Scoliosis may be classified as either structural (fixed, nonflexible) or nonstructural (flexible, correctable).

ICD-10CM CODES
M41	Scoliosis
M41.0	Infantile idiopathic scoliosis
M41.1	Juvenile idiopathic scoliosis
M41.3	Thoracogenic scoliosis
M41.20	Other idiopathic scoliosis, site unspecified
M41.80	Other forms of scoliosis, site unspecified
Q67.5	Congenital deformity of spine
M41.40	Neuromuscular scoliosis, site unspecified

EPIDEMIOLOGY & DEMOGRAPHICS (IDIOPATHIC FORM)

PREDOMINANT SEX: The incidence of scoliosis is the same in males and females; however, females have up to a 10-fold greater risk of curve progression.

PREVALENCE: Four cases per 1000 persons. Idiopathic scoliosis is present in 2% to 4% of adolescents.

PREDOMINANT AGE:
- Onset variable.
- Most curves found in adolescents (age ≥11 yr).

PHYSICAL FINDINGS & CLINICAL PRESENTATION

- Record patient age (in years plus months) and height.
- Perform neurologic examination to rule out neuromuscular disease.
- Inspect the shoulders and iliac crests to determine if they are level.
- Palpate the spinous processes to determine their alignment.

- Have the patient bend forward symmetrically at the waist with the arms hanging free (Adams' position); observe from the back or front to detect abnormal spine rotation (Fig. 1S-20).

ETIOLOGY

- 90% unknown, usually referred to as *idiopathic* (genetic).
- Congenital spine deformity.
- Neuromuscular disease.
- Leg-length inequality.
- Local inflammation or infection.
- Acute pain (disk disease).
- Chronic degenerative disk disease with asymmetric disk narrowing.
  Curves of an idiopathic nature or those accompanying congenital deformity or neuromuscular disease are associated with structural changes. The nonstructural types (leg-length discrepancy, inflammation, or acute pain) disappear when the offending disorder is corrected.

 DIAGNOSIS

WORKUP

- Curvatures associated with congenital spine abnormalities, neuromuscular disease, and other less common forms of scoliosis can usually be identified by history or associated radiographic or physical findings.
- The diagnosis of scoliosis is suspected on the basis of physical examination and confirmed by radiography performed while the patient is in a standing position. Physical examination with the Adams' forward bend test and scoliometer measurement can identify scoliosis and the radiologic testing for Cobb angle measurement can confirm the diagnosis. The Risser grade measures ossification. It consists of 5 grades ranging from 25% ossification in grade 1 to fusion of ossified epiphysis to the iliac wing in grade 5. Scoliosis screening is described in Fig. 1S-21.

IMAGING STUDIES

- Diagnosis of idiopathic scoliosis is confirmed by a standing roentgenogram of the spine.

- Severity of the curve is measured in degrees, usually by the Cobb method (Fig. 1S-22).
- MRI is usually not indicated unless there is pain, a neurologic deficit, or a left thoracic curve (which is often associated with an underlying spinal disorder).

℞ TREATMENT

ACUTE GENERAL Rx

- Treatment or correction of cause if curve is nonstructural.
- Early detection is key in treating genetic curve.
- Regular observation for curves <20 degrees.
- Bracing for idiopathic curves of 25 to 45 degrees in patients with an immature skeleton to prevent progression.
- Surgery for idiopathic curves >45 degrees in patients with an immature skeleton.

DISPOSITION

- The larger the curve at detection, the greater the chance of progression.
- Progression is more common in young children who are beginning their growth spurt.
- Curves in females are more likely to progress.
- Curves <20 degrees will improve spontaneously >50% of the time.
- Failure to diagnose and treat these curves may allow progressive deformity, pain, and cardiopulmonary compromise to develop.
- Spinal deformities >50 degrees in adults may progress and eventually become painful.
- There is no difference in the rate of back pain in the general population and patients with adolescent idiopathic scoliosis.

REFERRAL

For orthopedic consultation if structural curve is present.

❗ PEARLS & CONSIDERATIONS

COMMENTS

- Congenital scoliosis has a high incidence of cardiac and urinary tract abnormalities.
- Bracing is not intended to completely straighten the idiopathic curve. It may improve the curvature, but is mainly used to stabilize and prevent progression.
- The initial Cobb angle magnitude (≥25 degrees) is the most important predictor of long-term curve progression.

SUGGESTED READINGS
Available at www.expertconsult.com

RELATED CONTENT
Scoliosis (Patient Information)

AUTHOR: **FRED F. FERRI, M.D.**

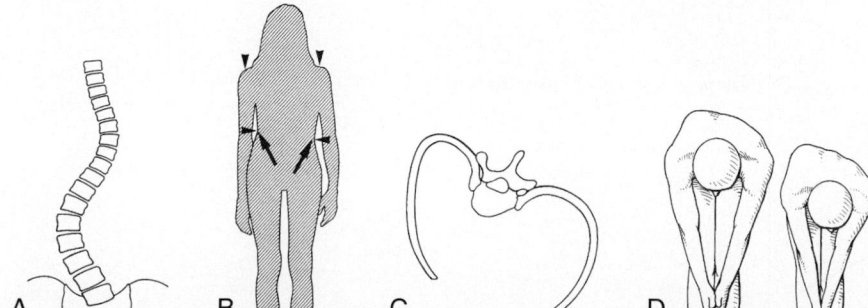

FIGURE 1S-20 Structural changes in idiopathic scoliosis. A, As curvature increases, alterations in body configuration develop in both the primary and compensatory curve regions. **B,** Asymmetries of shoulder height, waistline, and the elbow-to-flank distance are common findings. **C,** Vertebral rotation and associated posterior displacement of the ribs on the convex side of the curve are responsible for the characteristic deformity of the chest wall in scoliosis patients. **D,** In the school screening examination for scoliosis, the patient bends forward at the waist. Rib asymmetry of even a small degree is obvious. (From Scoles PV: Spinal deformity in childhood and adolescence. In Behrman RE, Vaughn VC III [eds]: *Nelson textbook of pediatrics,* ed 5, Philadelphia, 1989, Saunders.)

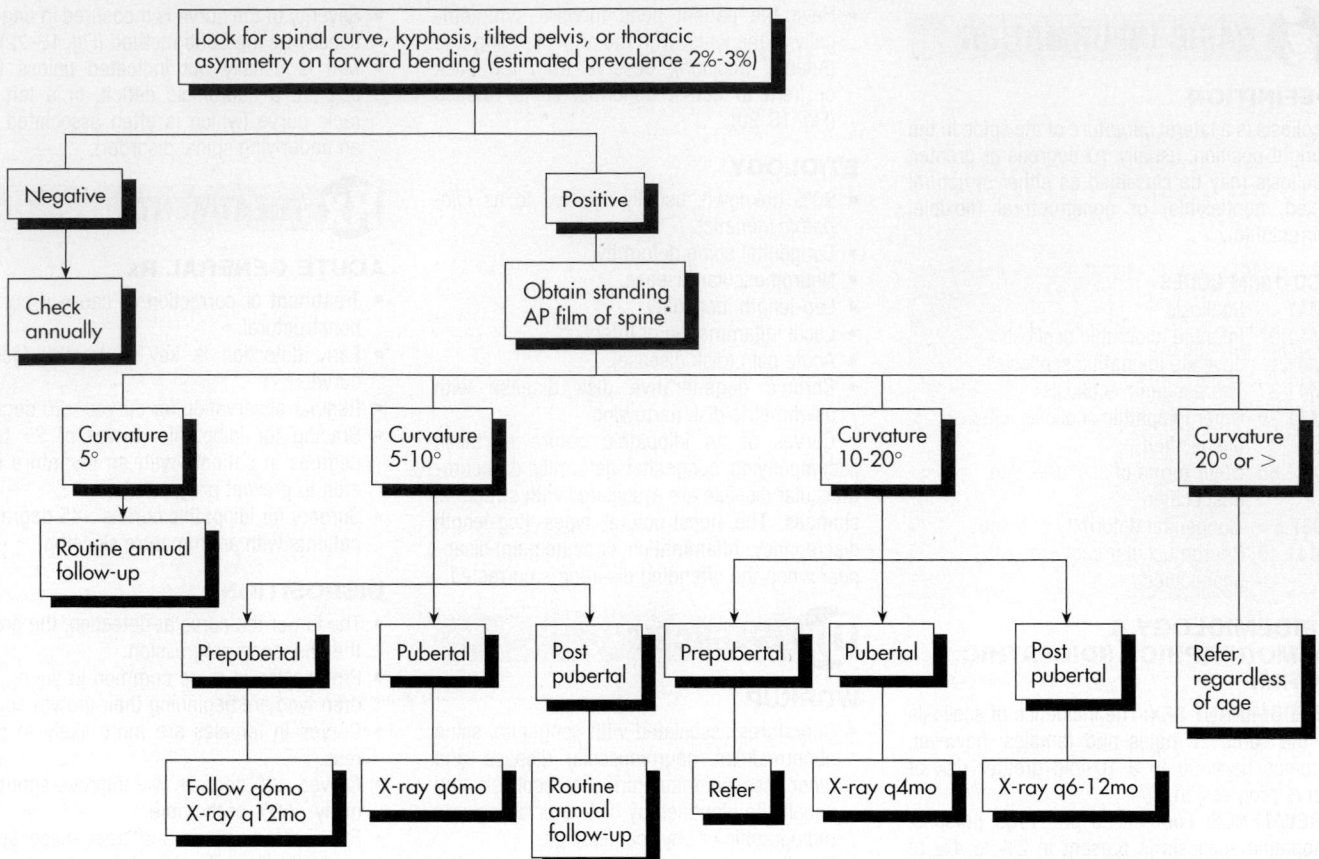

FIGURE 1S-21 Scoliosis screening and follow-up. *AP,* Anteroposterior. (From Driscoll C [ed]: *The family practice desk reference,* ed 3, St Louis, 1996, Mosby.)

*Cobb method of angle measurement.

1. Find the lowest vertebra whose bottom tilts toward concavity of curve.
2. Erect a perpendicular line from extension of bottom surface.
3. Find highest vertebra as in #1 and erect perpendicular from extension of top surface.
4. Measure intersecting angle = angle of scoliosis.

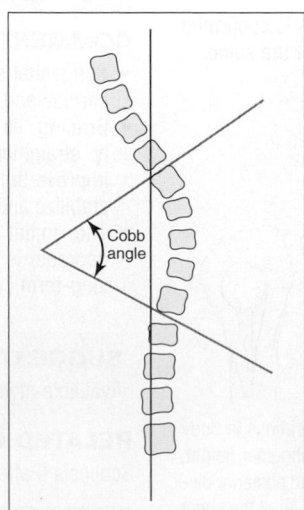

FIGURE 1S-22 Cobb angle. This is measured using the superior and inferior end plates of the most tilted vertebrae at the end of each curve. (From Tschudy MM, Arcara KM: *The Harriet Lane handbook,* ed 19, Philadelphia, 2012, Mosby.)

BASIC INFORMATION

DEFINITION

Recurrent depressive episodes during autumn and winter alternating with nondepressive episodes during spring and summer (less frequently, recurring depressive episodes during spring and summer, alternate with nondepressive episodes during autumn and winter). Patients with seasonal affective disorder (SAD) have experienced two episodes of major depression in the past 2 yr that demonstrate the temporal seasonal relations and have had no nonseasonal episodes over this period. Furthermore, seasonal depressive episodes substantially outnumber nonseasonal depressive episodes throughout the individual's lifetime.

SYNONYMS

SAD
Seasonal depression
Winter depression
Wintertime blues

ICD-10CM CODES
F33   Recurrent depressive disorder
F33.0 Recurrent depressive disorder, current episode, mild
F33.1 Recurrent depressive disorder, moderate
F33.2 Recurrent depressive disorder, severe without psychotic symptoms
F33.3 Recurrent depressive disorder, severe with psychotic symptoms
F33.4 Recurrent depressive disorder, currently in remission
F33.9 Recurrent depressive disorder, unspecified

EPIDEMIOLOGY & DEMOGRAPHICS

- Climate, genetic vulnerability, and psychological and sociocultural factors all play a role. The risk of seasonal mood swings is clearly associated with northern latitudes. The prevalence of SAD is estimated to be 0.5% to 1.5% in northern European populations, but up to 10% to 20% of these populations report milder, recurrent episodes consistent with subsyndromal SAD. In the United States, it is estimated that about 5% of the population experiences SAD.
- As with other depressive disorders, women are affected disproportionately.
- Younger age, as well as greater familiarity with SAD, is associated with increased prevalence.

PHYSICAL FINDINGS & CLINICAL PRESENTATION

- The symptoms of SAD can be identical to those of other depressive episodes, but tend to include features associated with atypical major depression, including low energy, oversleeping, irritability, weight gain, and overeating. The onset of neurovegetative symptoms often precedes the onset of cognitive and affective symptoms.
- Average duration is 5 mo, generally beginning in November.

ETIOLOGY

- Explanations focus on diathesis-stress models. An interaction between biologic and cognitive-affective factors appears to contribute to SAD. Retinal sensitivity anomalies and emotional reactivity to light stimuli, genetic variables predisposing to seasonal shift in sleep patterns in response to shorter photoperiod, circadian rhythm disturbance, and irregularities in melatonin, serotonin, and melatonin-serotonin interaction have been identified as potential risk factors. Shorter photoperiod and decrease in sunlight are hypothesized to be the triggers.
- Several neurotransmitters implicated, including dopamine, serotonin, and norepinephrine.
- Cognitive risk factors include elevated rumination and negative cognitions related to the winter season and its impact on one's mood.
- Low activity and exercise levels, which are also implicated in nonseasonal depression, have been shown in some studies to characterize SAD.
- Patients with nonseasonal depression and/or anxiety may also show symptom exacerbations during the winter months.

 DIAGNOSIS

Diagnostic workup similar to that for major depression.

DIFFERENTIAL DIAGNOSIS

- Major depressive disorder.
- Minor depression or adjustment disorder.
- Bipolar affective disorder.
- Evaluate for substance use (especially alcohol).
- Medical illness or medications that may contribute to depression (e.g., endocrine disorders, neurologic disease).

WORKUP

- As with major depression, consider medical etiologies and rule out as indicated by the presenting signs and symptoms. Consider endocrine evaluation, especially thyroid function; sleep studies and a toxicology screen might be considered.
- Structured Interview Guide for the Hamilton Depression Rating Scale–Seasonal Affective Disorders Version (SIGH-SAD) used in research settings.
- In patients with major depressive disorder treated longitudinally, the routine use of depression scales to monitor outcome can help identify seasonal fluctuations of symptoms. Self-report scales to assess seasonal fluctuations in depressive symptoms have been developed but are not routinely used in clinical settings.

LABORATORY TESTS

As directed by presenting symptoms.

IMAGING STUDIES

Generally not indicated.

TREATMENT

NONPHARMACOLOGIC THERAPY

- Phototherapy presupposes that artificial light at a similar strength to natural sunlight will prevent the biologic changes that mediate SAD.
- Many studies have demonstrated efficacy of light therapy in individuals with SAD. Recent studies indicate that light therapy may also be efficacious with various subtypes of depression, including both melancholic and atypical, and for individuals with nonseasonal depression, though more research is needed.
- Light therapy may be used as a first-line treatment; choice of light therapy versus medication or psychotherapy depends on various factors, however, including severity of symptoms and suicidality, prior response to medication or light therapy, feasibility, and patient preference.
- Some studies showing retinal sensitivity anomalies in SAD normalize following phototherapy.
- Phototherapy tends to use 2500 to 10,000 lux delivered by a commercial light box or a portable head-mounted unit. Phototherapy is recommended to begin within 2 wk of the start of symptoms and continue through the winter months. Patients are instructed to sit ~18 in from the light box for 30 min up to several hours once or twice per day for a minimum of 1 wk.
- A recent meta-analysis demonstrated efficacy of high-density negative ions in reducing depressive severity, although further research is needed to determine whether efficacy is comparable to light therapy.
- Small trials have demonstrated the efficacy of cognitive-behavioral therapy tailored specifically for SAD, either alone or with possible additive effects to light therapy. CBT for SAD appears to operate through distinct mechanisms than light therapy (e.g., reducing rumination and negative SAD-related cognitions). Patients with elevated cognitive symptoms of depression may benefit from CBT or combined CBT with light therapy over light therapy alone, but further research is needed.

PHARMACOLOGIC THERAPY

Bupropion effective in preventing recurrence.

ACUTE GENERAL Rx

Necessary if patient is suicidal.

CHRONIC Rx

- Growing support for use of SSRIs for SAD (e.g., fluoxetine, sertraline), although more research is needed.
- Preliminary studies demonstrated efficacy of novel antidepressants that act on melatonin (i.e., agomelatine), but further research is needed.

DISPOSITION

Psychiatric referral may be helpful to confirm diagnosis. Recommended for high-risk and suicidal patients.

REFERRAL

For active suicidal ideation, psychosis, symptoms suggestive of bipolar disorder.

 **PEARLS & CONSIDERATIONS**

Patients with SAD may present with a complaint of overeating, particularly food high in carbohydrates.

SUGGESTED READINGS

Available at www.expertconsult.com

RELATED CONTENT

Seasonal Affective Disorder (SAD) (Patient Information)

AUTHORS: **MARK ZIMMERMAN, M.D.**, and **CATHERINE D'AVANZATO, PH.D.**

BASIC INFORMATION

DEFINITION

Seborrheic dermatitis (SD) is a common, inflammatory skin condition characterized by a mild to severe rash with scaling and erythema that occurs in areas of the skin rich in sebaceous glands.

SYNONYMS

SD
Dandruff
Cradle cap (Fig. 1S-23)
Sebopsoriasis
Seborrheic eczema
Pityriasis capitis
Seborrhea

ICD-10CM CODES
L21.9 Seborrheic dermatitis, unspecified
L21.1 Seborrheic infantile dermatitis
L21.8 Other seborrheic dermatitis

EPIDEMIOLOGY & DEMOGRAPHICS

PREVALENCE: Affects 3% to 5% of otherwise healthy adults.
PREDOMINANT SEX AND AGE: Can occur from infancy through old age, with peak incidence in adolescents and young adults and increasing again after age 50 yr. More common in men than women.
RISK FACTORS: More common in patients with HIV/AIDS, Parkinson's disease, other neurologic disorders, mood disorders, chronic alcoholic pancreatitis, hepatitis, cancer, and genetic disorders (e.g., Down syndrome). Occurs more often during winter season.

PHYSICAL FINDINGS & CLINICAL PRESENTATION

- Mild, greasy scaling of the scalp and nasolabial folds (Fig. 1S-24), postauricular skin, beard area, eyebrows, trunk, and sometimes the central face. Blepharitis, otitis externa, and coexisting acne vulgaris or pityriasis may also be present. Itching and stinging of lesions can occur. Increased occurrence during times of stress or sleep deprivation.
- The scale often has a yellow, greasy appearance.

ETIOLOGY

- Fungal infections of the *Malassezia* species have been associated with SD, and the skin changes are thought to result from an inflammatory response to malassezia yeast.
- Altered immune function may play a role. Patients with SD may show upregulation of interferon (IFN)-α, expressed interleukin-6 (IL-6), expressed IL-1β, and IL-4.

DIAGNOSIS

DIFFERENTIAL DIAGNOSIS

- Atopic dermatitis.
- Candidiasis.
- Dermatophytosis.

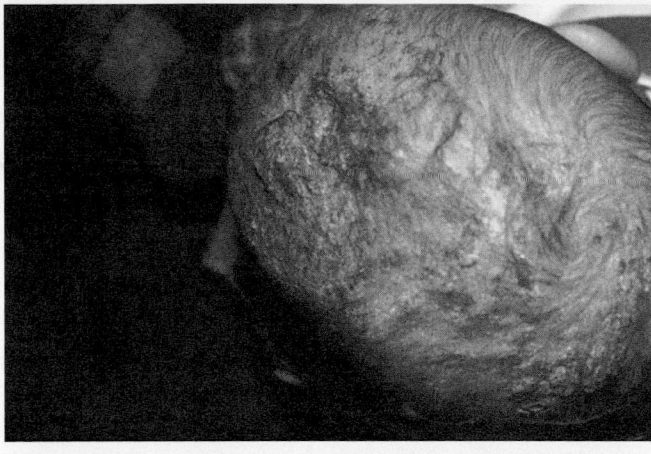

FIGURE 1S-23 Cradle cap in an infant. (From Kliegman RM et al: *Nelson textbook of pediatrics,* ed 19, Philadelphia, 2011, Saunders.)

- Impetigo.
- Psoriasis.
- Rosacea.
- Systemic lupus erythematosus.
- Tinea infection.
- Contact dermatitis.
- Nummular dermatitis.

WORKUP

- Diagnosis usually based on clinical identification of lesions.
- Skin biopsies can be performed, if warranted, to distinguish SD from similar disorders

LABORATORY TESTS

- Microscopic examination with special stains can be used to determine if yeast cells are present in keratinocytes.
- HIV testing

TREATMENT

NONPHARMACOLOGIC THERAPY

- Patient education that SD is a chronic condition and treatment is aimed at resolving lesions but does not prevent recurrence.
- General recommendations: wash skin regularly, soften and remove scales, and apply moisturizing emollients after washing.
- Scale removal can be accomplished through the application of mineral or olive oil and removed with a comb or brush after 1 hr.

ACUTE GENERAL Rx

- Topical steroids: can be in the form of shampoos, creams, or ointments. Can be used alone or in more severe SD with antifungals.
- Antifungals (e.g., Nizoral, selenium sulfide, ketoconazole [the most evidence for effectiveness among antifungals], ciclopirox, fluconazole). Reserve oral antifungal therapy for patients with widespread SD or SD that is refractory to topical therapy. Itraconazole 200 mg/day for 7 days is a sample oral regimen.

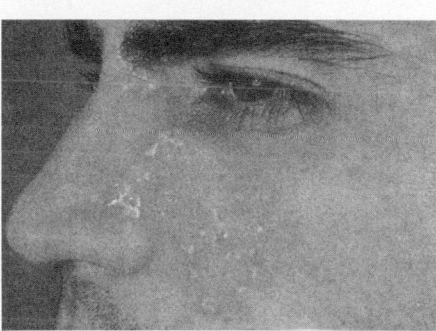

FIGURE 1S-24 Seborrheic dermatitis. (From Swartz MH: *Textbook of physical diagnosis,* ed 7, Philadelphia, 2014, Saunders, 2014.)

- Calcineurin inhibitors (e.g., tacrolimus ointment, pimecrolimus cream): good when face and ears are affected.
- Keratolytics (e.g., tar, salicylic acid, zinc pyrithione).
- Treatment of any secondary bacterial infection with oral antibiotics.

CHRONIC Rx

Recalcitrant SD: topical azole combined with desonide regimen (limit use to 2 wk), pimecrolimus cream.

COMPLEMENTARY & ALTERNATIVE MEDICINE

Tea tree oil (melaleuca oil).

REFERRAL

Consider referral to dermatology for recalcitrant cases or uncertain diagnosis

PEARLS & CONSIDERATIONS

- Use a combination of topical steroids and antifungal cream for severe SD.
- Limit use of steroids to 2-wk course of treatment due to risk of cutaneous atrophy and telangiectasias.

- SD of the scalp can be treated with an antifungal (e.g., 2% ketoconazole) or keratolytic shampoo. Limit use of antifungal shampoos to twice a week to prevent drying of the scalp. Alternate the use of antifungal shampoos with a moisturizing shampoo.
- In patients with widespread SD, consider testing for HIV infection.

SUGGESTED READINGS
Available at www.expertconsult.com

RELATED CONTENT
Seborrheic Dermatitis (Patient Information)

AUTHOR: **ANNGENE G. ANTHONY, M.D., M.P.H.**

 **BASIC INFORMATION**

DEFINITION

Absence seizures are a type of generalized seizures, characterized by brief episodes of staring with impairment of consciousness (absence). They usually last a few seconds, up to 20 to 30 sec. The onset and the end of the seizures are sudden. Usually the patients are not aware of them and resume the activity they were doing before the seizure. The electroencephalogram signature of absence seizures consists of a generalized 3-Hz spike and slow wave discharges.

SYNONYMS

Childhood absence epilepsy
Petit mal epilepsy
Absence seizures

ICD-10CM CODES

G40.309 Generalized idiopathic epilepsy and epileptic syndromes, not intractable, without status epilepticus
G40.009 Localization-related (focal) (partial) idiopathic epilepsy and epileptic syndromes with seizures of localized onset, not intractable, without status epilepticus
G40.019 Localization-related (focal) (partial) idiopathic epilepsy and epileptic syndromes with seizures of localized onset, intractable, without status epilepticus
G40.109 Localization-related (focal) (partial) symptomatic epilepsy and epileptic syndromes with simple partial seizures, not intractable, without status epilepticus
G40.119 Localization-related (focal) (partial) symptomatic epilepsy and epileptic syndromes with simple partial seizures, intractable, without status epilepticus
G40.209 Localization-related (focal) (partial) symptomatic epilepsy and epileptic syndromes with complex partial seizures, not intractable, without status epilepticus
G40.219 Localization-related (focal) (partial) symptomatic epilepsy and epileptic syndromes with complex partial seizures, intractable, without status epilepticus

EPIDEMIOLOGY & DEMOGRAPHICS

INCIDENCE: 1 to 10 cases per 100,000 population.
PEAK INCIDENCE: 6 to 7 yr.
PREVALENCE: Represents up to 18% of all pediatric epilepsy syndromes.
PREDOMINANT SEX AND AGE: More common in girls than in boys, absences typically begin between 4 and 8 yr.

PHYSICAL FINDINGS & CLINICAL PRESENTATION

- Patients with absence seizures usually have normal physical and neurologic examinations.
- During the seizures, the patients are unresponsive and can have motor phenomena (automatisms, eye blinks, mouth and hand movements).
- Absence seizures are not associated with postictal confusion.
- They may be triggered by hyperventilation associated with activity.
- Tonic clonic seizures are not usually a feature of this syndrome. If this is the case, other etiologies should be investigated, such as juvenile absence epilepsy, juvenile myoclonic epilepsy, complex partial seizures, etc.

ETIOLOGY

Genetic.

 **DIAGNOSIS**

DIFFERENTIAL DIAGNOSIS

- Juvenile absence epilepsy.
- Juvenile myoclonic epilepsy.
- Complex partial seizures.
- Nonepileptic spells comprised of staring.

WORKUP

- EEG with hyperventilation and photic stimulation is crucial in the diagnosis.
- Ambulatory EEG and video EEG are recommended for patients with diagnostic uncertainty.

LABORATORY TESTS

No specific studies needed.

IMAGING STUDIES

- MRI of the brain should be performed in all epilepsy patients, especially if the EEG does not show the typical characteristic of absence seizures (3-Hz spike and slow wave discharges).
- CT scans of the head should be avoided in children due to unnecessary exposure to radiation and low yield of the test except when MRI cannot be obtained.

 **TREATMENT**

The medication of choice based on the best current evidence available is ethosuximide, followed by valproic acid and lamotrigine.

NONPHARMACOLOGIC THERAPY

Not applicable.

GENERAL Rx

- Ethosuximide: initial dose: 10 mg/kg/day; then after 7 days, 20 mg/kg.
- Valproic acid (Depakote): initial dose: 5 to 10 mg/kg/day (divided bid), maximum dose 60 mg/kg/day
- Lamotrigine: dose for patients on no other antiepileptic drugs. Wk 1 and 2: 0.3 mg/kg/day. Wk 3 and 4: 0.6 mg/kg/day. Wk 5 onward: increase every 1 to 2 wk by 0.6 mg/kg/day.

Maintenance: 4.5 to 7.5 mg/kg/day. Warning: should be used with caution due to the potential for toxicity and Stevens-Johnson syndrome. Patients on other antiepileptic drugs can also have severe adverse reactions.

CHRONIC Rx

- Children with recurrent seizures require chronic treatment.
- If children are seizure free for a period of 1 to 2 yr, a trial on no medications should be considered; children, unlike adults, can "outgrow" seizures.

COMPLEMENTARY & ALTERNATIVE MEDICINE

Not applicable.

DISPOSITION

- Response to treatment is excellent.
- Absence seizures tend to remit in teenage years.
- Epilepsy can be considered as resolved once 10 years have elapsed since the last event, including 5 years free from medications.

REFERRAL

Patients with epilepsy and seizures should be referred for a consultation by a neurologist, preferably one specializing in epilepsy.

PEARLS & CONSIDERATIONS

COMMENTS

- Absence seizures can be present in other epilepsy syndromes.
- Valproic acid should be avoided in girls and women with childbearing potential due to the risk of teratogenicity.
- Carbamazepine and phenytoin should be avoided in the treatment of absence seizures, since these medications may worsen seizures and could provoke absence status epilepticus.
- All women of childbearing age taking antiepileptic drugs should take folic acid supplementation (1-4 mg/day) for the prevention of neural tube defects.

PREVENTION

Sleep deprivation and alcohol consumption should be avoided.

PATIENT & FAMILY EDUCATION

- Patients with ongoing seizures are forbidden to drive; check state regulations and laws regarding driving and epilepsy.

SUGGESTED READINGS

Available at www.expertconsult.com

RELATED CONTENT

Absence Seizures (Patient Information)

AUTHOR: PATRICIO SEBASTIAN ESPINOSA, M.D., M.P.H.

BASIC INFORMATION

DEFINITION

Febrile seizures are seizures that occur in febrile children (fever of at least 100.4° F [38° C]) between the ages of 6 and 60 months in the absence of infection of the central nervous system (CNS), metabolic disturbance, or history of neonatal seizures or a previous unprovoked seizures. Febrile seizures are subdivided into 2 categories: simple and complex. Simple febrile seizures last <15 min, are generalized (without a focal component), and occur once in a 24-hr period, whereas complex febrile seizures are prolonged (>15 min), show focal neurologic signs, or occur more than once in 24 hr.

SYNONYMS

Febrile convulsions
Febrile seizures

ICD-10CM CODES
R56.0 Febrile convulsions

EPIDEMIOLOGY & DEMOGRAPHICS

INCIDENCE: Febrile seizures are the most common seizures of childhood. 2% to 5% of children will have a febrile seizure by age 60 mo. Simple febrile seizures represent 65% to 90% of febrile seizures.
PREDOMINANT SEX AND AGE: Slightly more common in boys than girls.
PEAK INCIDENCE: 6 to 60 mo
PREVALENCE: Represents up to 18% of all pediatric epilepsy syndromes

PHYSICAL FINDINGS & CLINICAL PRESENTATION

- Children with febrile seizures have normal physical and neurologic examinations.
- Viral illnesses are the predominant cause of febrile seizures.

ETIOLOGY

- Viral infections are a common cause of fever that triggers febrile seizures.
- Febrile seizures tend to occur in families. Although clear evidence exists for a genetic basis of febrile seizures, the mode of inheritance is unknown.
- Febrile seizures are likely multifactorial with genetic and environmental factors.

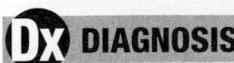 DIAGNOSIS

DIFFERENTIAL DIAGNOSIS

- CNS infection (i.e., meningitis).
- Epilepsy.

WORKUP

- It is important to first investigate whether an underlying infection exists. Fig. 1S-25 describes guidelines for febrile seizure evaluation.
- In patients with simple self-limited febrile seizures with rapid return to consciousness and a normal neurologic examination, further workup is not routinely recommended.
- In patients with complex febrile seizures, laboratory workup and brain imaging are recommended.
- EEG is not routinely recommended in the evaluation of a neurologically healthy child with simple partial seizures.

LABORATORY TESTS

- Routine blood workup (CBC with differential, CMP, electrolytes), blood and urine cultures are often performed, but there is no evidence that these tests are necessary for identifying the cause of a simple febrile seizure.
- CSF analysis: lumbar puncture guidelines (American Academy of Pediatrics).
- Lumbar puncture should be performed in children with febrile seizures and signs and symptoms of meningitis (e.g., neck stiffness, Kernig sign, Brudzinski sign), or if the patient history or examination suggests the presence of meningitis or intracranial infection.
- In infants 6 to 12 months of age with febrile seizures, lumbar puncture is an option if they have not received the recommended *Haemophilus influenza* type b (Hib) or pneumococcal vaccinations, or if their immunization status is unknown.
- Lumbar puncture is also considered an option in children with febrile seizures pretreated with antibiotics.

IMAGING STUDIES

- MRI of the brain is not required in the routine evaluation of patients with simple febrile seizures.
- Imaging of the brain should be considered in children with complex febrile seizures and in children with focal neurologic deficits.
- CT scans of the head should be avoided in children, if possible, due to exposure to radiation and the relative low yield of the test compared with MRI. CT scans of the head are reserved for neurologic emergencies and are adjusted for weight in children.

 TREATMENT

Febrile seizures do not usually require antiepileptic drug treatment.

NONPHARMACOLOGIC THERAPY
Not applicable

GENERAL Rx
Symptomatic treatment of fever.

CHRONIC Rx
No chronic treatment for febrile seizures is recommended.

COMPLEMENTARY & ALTERNATIVE MEDICINE
Not applicable.

DISPOSITION

- Treatment is not recommended.
- Febrile seizures should stop by age 60 months.
- Risk of recurrence in the first 2 years after an initial febrile seizure is 15% to 70%.

REFERRAL

Patients with recurrent febrile seizures need to be referred for a consultation by a pediatric neurologist.

❗ PEARLS & CONSIDERATIONS

COMMENTS

- It is crucial to find out the etiology of the fever and to treat it appropriately.
- Patient with seizures and fever after age 60 mo are not classified as febrile seizures.

PREVENTION

Antipyretics do not reduce the recurrence risk of febrile seizures. However, fever should be treated and worked up independently of the diagnosis of febrile seizures.

PATIENT & FAMILY EDUCATION

- Children with febrile seizures do not need antiepileptic drug treatment.
- Patient education and information can be obtained at the Epilepsy Foundation: www.epilepsyfoundation.org. Parents should be reassured that children without underlying developmental problems will usually not have lasting neurologic effects from febrile seizures.

SUGGESTED READINGS
Available at www.expertconsult.com

RELATED CONTENT
Fever Seizures (Patient Information)

AUTHOR: **PATRICIO SEBASTIAN ESPINOSA, M.D., M.P.H.**

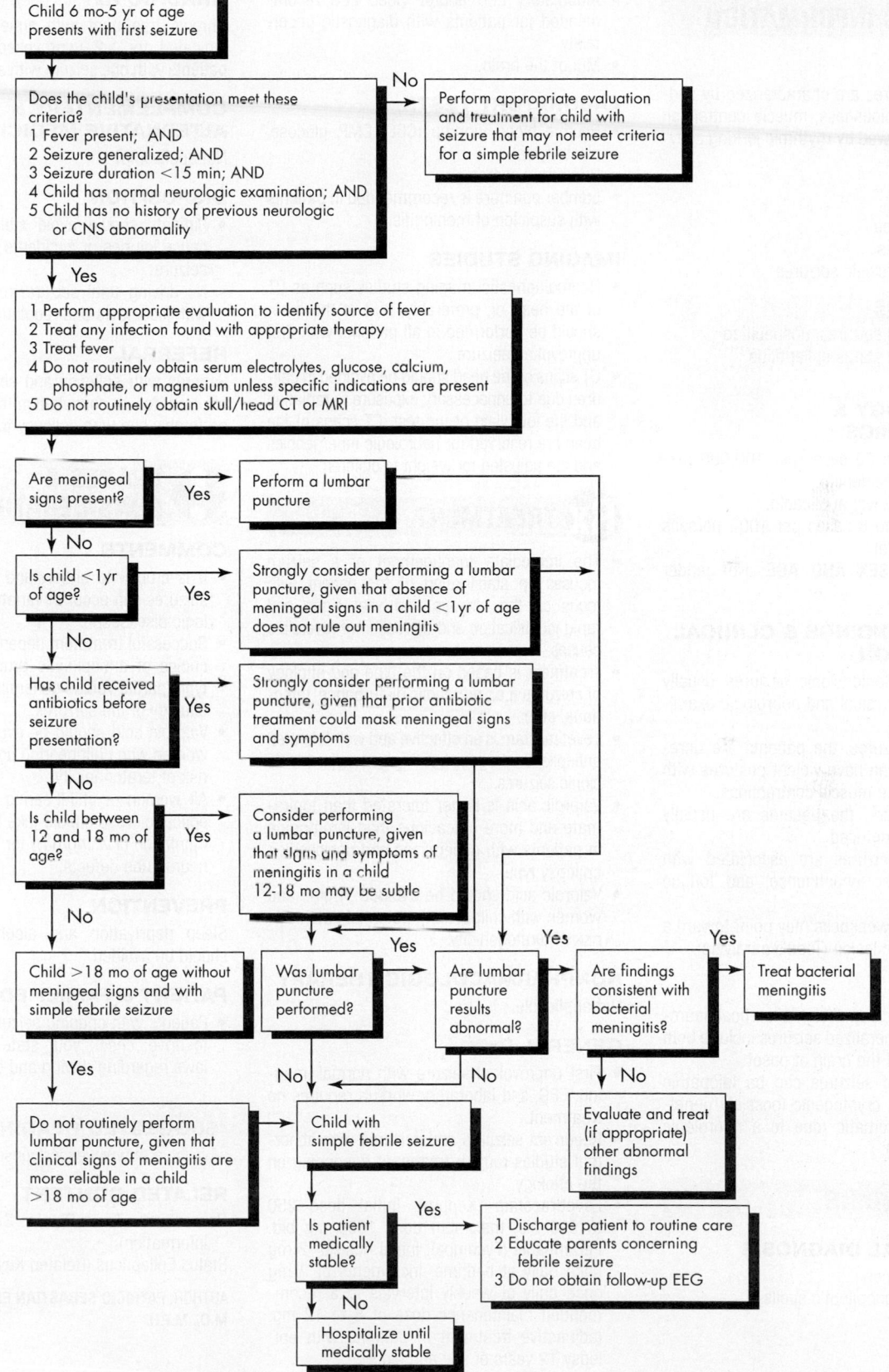

FIGURE 1S-25 Guidelines for febrile seizure evaluation. (From Custer JW, Rau RE: *The Harriet Lane handbook,* ed 18, St Louis, 2009, Mosby.)

Seizures, Generalized Tonic Clonic (PTG)

BASIC INFORMATION

DEFINITION

Tonic clonic seizures are characterized by sudden loss of consciousness, muscle contraction (tonic phase) followed by rhythmic jerking activity (clonic phase).

SYNONYMS

Convulsive seizures
Grand mal seizures
Generalized tonic clonic seizures

ICD-10CM CODES

G40.6 Grand mal seizures, unspecified
G41.0 Grand mal status epilepticus

EPIDEMIOLOGY & DEMOGRAPHICS

INCIDENCE: 30 to 50 cases per 100,000 person-yr (epilepsy incidence).
PEAK INCIDENCE: Not applicable.
PREVALENCE: 5 to 8 cases per 1000 persons (epilepsy incidence).
PREDOMINANT SEX AND AGE: No gender preference.

PHYSICAL FINDINGS & CLINICAL PRESENTATION

- Patients with tonic clonic seizures usually have normal physical and neurologic examinations.
- During the seizures, the patients are unresponsive and can have violent postures with severe repetitive muscle contractions.
- After the seizure, the patients are usually lethargic and confused.
- Tonic clonic seizures are associated with injuries, bladder incontinence, and tongue biting.
- Focal postictal weakness may point toward a focal neurologic lesion (Todd's paralysis).

ETIOLOGY

- Seizures are a cardinal sign of cortical neurologic injury. Generalized seizures include both hemispheres of the brain at onset.
- The etiology of seizures can be idiopathic (likely genetic), cryptogenic (possibly genetic), and symptomatic (due to a neurologic injury/infection).

DIAGNOSIS

DIFFERENTIAL DIAGNOSIS

- Convulsive syncope.
- Psychogenic nonepileptic spells.
- EPI
- TIA
- Vertigo

WORKUP

- EEG. An EEG can help confirm the presence of epilepsy but cannot be used to exclude the diagnosis.

- Ambulatory EEG and/or video EEG recommended for patients with diagnostic uncertainty.
- MRI of the brain.

LABORATORY TESTS

- Routine blood workup (CBC, CMP, glucose, electrolytes).
- Urine drug screen.
- Lumbar puncture is recommended in patients with suspicion of meningitis.

IMAGING STUDIES

- Neurodiagnostic imaging studies such as CT of the head or, preferably, MRI of the brain should be performed in all patients with first unprovoked seizure.
- CT scans of the head should be avoided in children due to unnecessary exposure to radiation and the low yield of the test. CT scans of the head are reserved for neurologic emergencies and are adjusted for weight in children.

 TREATMENT

- The immediate management of a seizure focuses on stabilization of the patient with focus on the airways and vital signs and rapid identification and correction of reversible causes.
- Treatment is based on the type and etiology of seizures (i.e., metabolic disturbance, infectious, etc.).
- Levetiracetam is an effective and well-tolerated antiepileptic drug for treating generalized tonic clonic seizures.
- Valproic acid is better tolerated than topiramate and more efficacious than lamotrigine in patients with generalized and unclassified epilepsy types.
- Valproic acid should be avoided in girls and women with childbearing potential due to the risk of teratogenicity.

NONPHARMACOLOGIC THERAPY

Not applicable.

GENERAL Rx

- First unprovoked seizure with normal imaging, EEG, and laboratory workup requires no treatment.
- Recurrent seizures and seizures with abnormal studies require treatment depending on the etiology.
- Levetiracetam (Keppra): Initial dose 250 to 500 bid, maximum dose 1500 mg bid. Perampanel (Fycompa): Initial dose of 2 mg once daily at bedtime, increments of 2 mg once daily at weekly intervals to a recommended maintenance dose of 8 to 12 mg. (adjunctive treatment in patients with epilepsy 12 years of age and older).
- Valproic acid (Depakote): Initial dose: 10 to 15 mg/kg/day (divided bid), maximum dose 60 mg/kg/day.

CHRONIC Rx

Chronic treatment with antiepileptic drugs is indicated for ≥2 unprovoked seizures or in patients with one seizure with abnormal workup.

COMPLEMENTARY & ALTERNATIVE MEDICINE

Not applicable.

DISPOSITION

- Patients should avoid situations that may cause injuries or accidents in the event of a seizure.
- No driving until seizure-free in accordance with local laws and regulations.

REFERRAL

Patients with epilepsy and seizures should be referred for a consultation by a neurologist, preferably one with epilepsy training.

PEARLS & CONSIDERATIONS

COMMENTS

- It is crucial to understand that tonic clonic seizures can occur in variety of acute neurologic diseases.
- Successful treatment depends on the correct choice of antiepileptic drugs based on the type (partial versus generalized in onset) and etiology of the seizures.
- Valproic acid should be avoided in girls and women with childbearing potential due to the risk of teratogenicity.
- All women of childbearing age taking antiepileptic drugs should take folic acid supplementation (1-4 mg/day) for the prevention of neural tube defects.

PREVENTION

Sleep deprivation and alcohol consumption should be avoided.

PATIENT & FAMILY EDUCATION

- Patients with ongoing seizures are forbidden to drive; check your state regulations and laws regarding driving and epilepsy.

SUGGESTED READINGS

Available at www.expertconsult.com

RELATED CONTENT

Generalized Tonic-Clonic Seizures (Patient Information)
Status Epilepticus (Related Key Topic)

AUTHOR: **PATRICIO SEBASTIAN ESPINOSA, M.D., M.P.H.**

S

Diseases
and Disorders

 BASIC INFORMATION

DEFINITION

Partial seizures are characterized by focal cortical discharges that provoke seizure symptoms related to the area of the brain involved. Simple partial seizures do not cause impairment of consciousness. However, partial seizures can evolve into complex partial and/or tonic clonic seizures.

SYNONYMS

Simple partial seizures
Focal seizures
Partial seizures

ICD-10CM CODES
G40.0   Localization-related (focal) (partial) idiopathic epilepsy and epileptic syndromes with seizures of localized onset
G40.109 Localization-related (focal) (partial) symptomatic epilepsy and epileptic syndromes with simple partial seizures, not intractable, without status epilepticus

EPIDEMIOLOGY & DEMOGRAPHICS

INCIDENCE: 30 to 50 cases per 100,000 person yr
PREVALENCE: 5 to 8 cases per 1000 persons
PREDOMINANT SEX AND AGE: No gender preference

PHYSICAL FINDINGS & CLINICAL PRESENTATION

- Patients with partial seizures usually have normal physical and neurologic examinations unless the focal seizures are due to a structural abnormality such as a stroke, where the patient will have a neurologic exam consistent with the area of CNS structural damage.
- During partial seizures the patients are conscious, unless there is spread of the epileptic focus causing secondary generalization and unresponsiveness. A focal seizure can evolve to a generalized tonic clonic seizure. Clues to this progression include a subjective aura before the onset of convulsion, unilateral shaking, and head turning to one side (versive head turning).
- Patients with partial seizures can experience postictal weakness/paralysis that usually resolves within 24 hr (Todd's paralysis). However, focal neurologic deficits may also be indicative of a structural brain lesion.
- Manifestations of complex partial seizures may include automatisms (semipurposeful behaviors) such as fumbling of fingers or lip smacking.

ETIOLOGY

- Seizures in general are a cardinal sign of cortical neurologic injury.
- The etiology of partial seizures can be idiopathic (likely genetic), cryptogenic (unknown, possibly genetic), and symptomatic (due to a neurologic injury).

- Frequent causes of partial seizures are tumor, stroke, CNS infections (cysticercosis, abscesses), arteriovenous malformations (AVMs), traumatic brain injury, cortical malformations, and others.

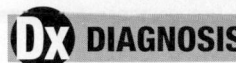 DIAGNOSIS

DIFFERENTIAL DIAGNOSIS

- Transient ischemic attack.
- Movement disorders.
- Psychogenic nonepileptic spells.
- Migraines.

WORKUP

- EEG.
- Ambulatory EEG and/or video EEG recommended for patients with diagnostic uncertainty.

LABORATORY TESTS

Routine blood workup (CBC, CMP, glucose, electrolytes) may be considered in appropriate clinical situations.

IMAGING STUDIES

- In the acute setting, a CT scan of the head is high yield to rule out space-occupying lesions.
- MRI of the brain with a defined epilepsy protocol should be performed in all patients with recurrent seizures.
- CT scans of the head should be avoided in children if possible, unless in an emergency setting.

Rx TREATMENT

- Carbamazepine traditionally has been the standard initial drug treatment for partial seizures. Lacosamide is indicated as monotherapy or adjunctive therapy in patients with partial-onset seizures. The initial recommended dose is 50 mg twice daily; increase at weekly intervals by 50 mg twice daily, up to a recommended maintenance dose of 100 to 200 mg twice daily. An alternate loading dose schedule: 200 mg PO/IV as a single dose, followed 12 hr later by starting 100 mg PO/IV bid × 1 week; then increase dose at weekly intervals by 50 mg bid, up to a recommended dose of 150 to 200 mg bid.
- Lamotrigine and levetiracetam are effective and well-tolerated antiepileptic drugs for treating partial seizures.
- Other antiepileptic drugs (e.g., perampanel, oxcarbazepine, ezogabine) may be used by an epilepsy specialist in specific cases.
- Surgical treatments (e.g., temporal lobectomy in mesial temporal sclerosis) may be indicated in refractory cases of partial seizures.

GENERAL Rx

- After a first unprovoked seizure with normal examination, imaging, and EEG, no treatment may be necessary.

- Recurrent seizures and seizures with abnormal studies require treatment in the form of medicines, consideration of surgery, or with approved medical devices.

DISPOSITION

- Response to treatment often depends on the etiology of the partial seizures.
- 47% of patients become seizure free with monotherapy and 67% with polytherapy.
- Patients who do not respond to three drugs should be referred to an Epilepsy Center for consideration of surgical treatment.
- No driving until seizure free in accordance with local laws and regulations.

REFERRAL

Patients with epilepsy and seizures should be referred for a consultation by a neurologist, preferably one with a special interest in epilepsy.

PEARLS & CONSIDERATIONS

COMMENTS

- It is crucial to understand that partial seizures can be due to a variety of neurologic diseases.
- Successful treatment depends on the correct choice of antiepileptic drugs based on patient's gender and comorbidities.
- Valproic acid should be avoided in girls and women with childbearing potential due to the risk of teratogenicity.
- All women in childbearing age taking antiepileptic drugs should take folic acid supplementation (1-4 mg/day) for the prevention of neural tube defects.

PREVENTION

- Sleep deprivation and alcohol consumption should be avoided.
- Drug compliance is compulsory to prevent seizure recurrence.

PATIENT & FAMILY EDUCATION

- Patient education and information can be obtained at the Epilepsy Foundation: www.epilepsyfoundation.org.
- Patients with ongoing seizures are forbidden to drive; check your state regulations and laws regarding driving and epilepsy.
- Patients should be counseled on general seizure precautions such as swimming, bathing, and heights.

SUGGESTED READINGS
Available at www.expertconsult.com

RELATED CONTENT
Partial Motor Seizures (Patient Information)

AUTHOR: **PATRICIO SEBASTIAN ESPINOSA, M.D., M.P.H.**

BASIC INFORMATION

DEFINITION

Sepsis is an exaggerated inflammatory response to an infectious stimulus. It is generally caused by generalized bacterial or fungal infection and characterized by evidence of infection, fever or hypothermia, hypotension, and evidence of end-organ compromise. The Sepsis Definitions Task Force has recently updated definitions for sepsis and septic shock. A major change in the new definitions is the elimination of mention of SIRS*. According to the new definitions, sepsis is now defined as evidence of infection plus life-threatening organ dysfunction, clinically characterized by an acute change in 2 points or greater in the SOFA score**. The new clinical criteria for septic shock include sepsis with fluid, unresponsive hypotension, serum lactate level greater than 2 mmol/L, and the need for vasopressors to maintain mean arterial pressure of 65 mm Hg or greater.[1,2]

SYNONYMS

Septicemia
Sepsis syndrome
Severe sepsis
Systemic inflammatory response syndrome
Septic shock

ICD-10CM CODES
A41.9   Sepsis, unspecified organism
A41.50 Gram-negative sepsis, unspecified

---

*SIRS (Systemic Inflammatory Response Syndrome): Variables in SIRS criteria include respiratory rate (breaths/min), white blood cell count (10^9/L), hands (%), heart rate (beats/min), temperature (°C), and arterial carbon dioxide tension (mm Hg). Score range is 0-4.

**SOFA (Sequential [Sepsis-Related] Organ Failure Assessment): Variables in SOFA criteria include PaO_2/FIO_2 ratio, Glasgow Coma Scale score, mean arterial pressure (mm Hg), administration of vasopressors with type/dose/rate of infusion, serum creatinine (mg/dL) or urine output (mL/d), bilirubin (mg/dL), and platelet count (10^9/L). Score range is 0-24.

[1]Abraham E: New Definitions for Sepsis and Septic Shock: Continuing Evolution but With Much Still to Be Done, *JAMA* 315(8):757-759, 2016.

[2]Shankar-Hari M, et al.: Developing a New Definition and Assessing New Clinical Criteria for Septic Shock: For the Third International Consensus Definitions for Sepsis and Septic Shock (Sepsis-3), *JAMA* 315(8):775-787, 2016.

A41.2   Sepsis due to unspecified *Staphylococcus*
A41.4   Sepsis due to anaerobes
A41.51 Sepsis due to *Escherichia coli* [E. coli]
A41.52 Sepsis due to Pseudomonas
A54.86 Gonococcal sepsis
B37.7   Candidal sepsis
A32.7   Listerial sepsis
A40.0   Sepsis due to streptococcus, group A
A40.1   Sepsis due to streptococcus, group B
A40.3   Sepsis due to Streptococcus pneumoniae
A40.8   Other streptococcal sepsis
A40.9   Streptococcal sepsis, unspecified
A41.01 Sepsis due to Methicillin susceptible *Staphylococcus aureus*
A41.02 Sepsis due to Methicillin resistant *Staphylococcus aureus*

EPIDEMIOLOGY & DEMOGRAPHICS

INCIDENCE (IN U.S.):
- Exact incidence is unknown.
- Approximately 750,000 cases of severe sepsis occur among hospitalized patients each year in the United States.
- Complicates a minority of bacteremia cases and may occur in the absence of documented bacteremia.

PREDOMINANT SEX: Males slightly more commonly affected than females.

PREDOMINANT AGE:
- Neonatal period.
- Patients >65 yr of age account for 60% of all cases of severe sepsis.

GENETICS:
- Familial disposition: a great variety of congenital immunodeficiency states and other inherited disorders may predispose to septicemia.
- Neonatal infection: incidence is high in neonatal period.

PHYSICAL FINDINGS & CLINICAL PRESENTATION

- Fever or hypothermia.
- Hypotension.
- Tachycardia.
- Tachypnea.
- Altered mental status.
- Bleeding diathesis.

- Skin rashes.
- Symptoms that reflect primary site of infection: urinary tract, GI tract, CNS, respiratory tract.
- Table 1S-8 describes some clinical signs and symptoms of sepsis.

ETIOLOGY

- Disseminated infection with a great variety of bacteria:
  - A. Gram-negative bacteria.
    1. *Escherichia coli*.
    2. *Klebsiella* spp.
    3. *Pseudomonas aeruginosa*.
    4. *Proteus* spp.
    5. *Neisseria meningitides*.
  - B. Gram-positive bacteria.
    1. *Staphylococcus aureus* (including MRSA).
    2. *Streptococcus* spp.
    3. *Enterococcus* spp.
- Less common infections:
  1. Fungal.
  2. Viral.
  3. Rickettsial.
  4. Parasitic.
- Sepsis is a complex dysregulation of both inflammation and coagulation. There is activation of coagulation, inflammatory cytokines, complement, and kinin cascades with release of a variety of vasoactive endogenous mediators.
- Predisposing host factors:
  1. General medical condition.
  2. Extremes of age.
  3. Immunosuppressive therapy.
  4. Recent surgery.
  5. Granulocytopenia.
  6. Hyposplenism.
  7. Diabetes.
  8. Instrumentation.

DIAGNOSIS

DIFFERENTIAL DIAGNOSIS
- Cardiogenic shock.
- Acute pancreatitis.
- Pulmonary embolism.
- Systemic vasculitis.
- Toxic ingestion.
- Exposure-induced hypothermia.
- Fulminant hepatic failure.
- Collagen-vascular diseases.

TABLE 1S-8 Clinical Signs and Symptoms of Sepsis

Infection	General	Inflammatory	Hemodynamic	Tissue Perfusion
Documented or suspected	Temperature >38°C or <36°C Heart rate >90 beats/min Respiratory rate ≥20 breaths/min Altered mental status Hyperglycemia Third spacing of fluid	WBC count <4000 or >12,000 cells/mcL or ≥10% bands	Hypotension: systolic blood pressure <90 mm Hg MAP <70 mm Hg SVo_2 >70 CI >3.5 L/min/m²	Hypoxemia: (Pao_2/Fio_2 <300) Acute oliguria (urine output <0.5 mL/kg/hr) Coagulopathy Abnormal liver function tests Platelet count <100,000 cells/μL Lactic acidosis Skin mottling

CI, Cardiac index; *MAP*, mean arterial pressure; *SVo2*, mixed venous oxygen saturation; *WBC*, white blood cell.
From Cameron JL, Cameron AM: *Current surgical therapy*, ed 10, Philadelphia, 2011, Saunders.

WORKUP

- Evaluation should focus on identifying a specific pathogen and localizing the site of primary infection.
- Hemodynamic, metabolic, coagulation disorders should be carefully characterized.
- Intensive monitoring, including the use of central venous catheters.

LABORATORY TESTS

- Cultures of blood and examination and culture of sputum, urine, wound drainage, stool, and CSF, depending on the presenting signs and symptoms for each patient.
- CBC with differential, coagulation profile.
- Routine chemistries, LFTs.
- ABGs, lactic acid level; procalcitonin can be useful as a marker of bacterial infection as a cause of the sepsis.
- Urinalysis.

IMAGING STUDIES

- Chest x-ray.
- Other radiographic and radioisotope procedures according to suspected site of primary infection.

TREATMENT

NONPHARMACOLOGIC THERAPY

- Tissue oxygenation: mixed venous oxygen saturation maintained >70% if possible; early mechanical ventilation with low title volume (6 mL/kg predicted body weight) to protect lung parenchyma from overstretching and "volutrauma."
- Focal infection should be drained if possible, and potentially infected catheters should be removed.

ACUTE GENERAL Rx

- Blood pressure support, rapid IV fluid resuscitation and vasopressors (Fig. 1S-27), if needed, with the goal of reestablishing a mean arterial blood pressure >65 mm Hg; reduction in blood lactate and improved mixed venous oxygen saturation >70% within 6 hr of recognition of septic shock is associated with improved survival. If possible, measure vena cava oxygen saturation (ScvO$_2$) to assess adequacy of resuscitation. If the ScvO$_2$ is <70%, consider packed red blood cell transfusion to achieve Hct >30%. Start inotropic agents (dobutamine) if ScvO$_2$ is <70% despite transfusion and adequate fluid resuscitation.

1. IV hydration; crystalloids are as effective as colloids as resuscitation fluids, give 30 mL/kg IV if fluid depletion is suspected. Most patients need 4 to 6 L of fluid in the first 6 hours. Trials have shown that resuscitation with balanced crystalloids or albumin compared with other fluids seems to be associated with reduced mortality and that albumin replacement in addition to crystalloids alone does not improve the rate of survival at 28 and 90 days.
2. Therapy with vasopressors (e.g., norepinephrine, epinephrine, vasopressin) if mean arterial blood pressure of >65 mm Hg cannot be maintained by hydration alone. A recent trial comparing low-dose vasopressin with norepinephrine revealed that low-dose vasopressin did not reduce mortality rates as compared with norepinephrine among patients with septic shock who were treated with catecholamine vasopressors.
- Correction of acidosis by improving the tissue perfusion, not by giving bicarbonate
   1. Mechanical ventilation as needed.
- Antibiotics
   1. Directed at the most likely sources of infection. Table 1S-9 describes initial antibiotic recommendations for septic patients.
   2. Should generally provide broad coverage of gram-positive and gram-negative bacteria (or fungi if clinically indicated).
   3. Antibiotics should be administered within 1 hr of the diagnosis of septic shock—this is a medical emergency.
   4. The role of corticosteroids in the acute management of septicemia has long been debated. Previous trials had shown that corticosteroid therapy improved hemodynamic outcomes in patients with severe septic shock. Patients with relative adrenal insufficiency may benefit from low-dose therapy with hydrocortisone (200 mg IV by continuous infusion for 7 days). Recent trials, however, revealed that hydrocortisone did not improve survival or reversal of shock, either overall or in patients who did not have a response to corticotropin, although hydrocortisone hastened reversal of shock in patients in whom shock was reversed. Until definitive data are available, the decision to administer corticosteroids for septic shock should be based on the individual patient's severity of illness versus risk of corticosteroid

administration. The corticotropin (ACTH) stimulation test is not helpful and should not be used to determine the need for corticosteroid in these patients.
- Blood transfusion: A lower hemoglobin threshold is preferred. Trials have shown that among patients with septic shock, mortality at 90 days and rates of ischemic events and use of life support is similar among those assigned to blood transfusion at a higher hemoglobin threshold (hemoglobin level of 9 g/dL or less) and those assigned to blood transfusion at a lower threshold (hemoglobin level of 7 g/dL or less).

CHRONIC Rx

- Adjust antibiotic therapy on the basis of culture results.
- In general, continue antibiotic therapy for a minimum of 7 to 10 days.
- If hyperglycemia develops during treatment start continuous insulin IV infusion, maintain blood glucose in the 110 to 180 mg/dl level, and avoid insulin-induced hypoglycemia.

DISPOSITION

All patients with sepsis should be hospitalized and given access to intensive monitoring and nursing care.

REFERRAL

- To infectious diseases expert.
- To physician experienced in critical care.

PEARLS & CONSIDERATIONS

COMMENTS

- Mortality rises quickly if antibiotic therapy is not instituted promptly (preferably within 1 hr of onset of shock) and metabolic derangements are not treated aggressively.
- Human recombinant activated protein C (drotrecogin alfa activated) was taken off the market as a treatment for sepsis after follow up studies showed no added benefit to standard sepsis care.

SUGGESTED READINGS

Available at www.expertconsult.com

AUTHORS: **GLENN G. FORT, M.D., M.P.H.,** and **FRED F. FERRI, M.D.**

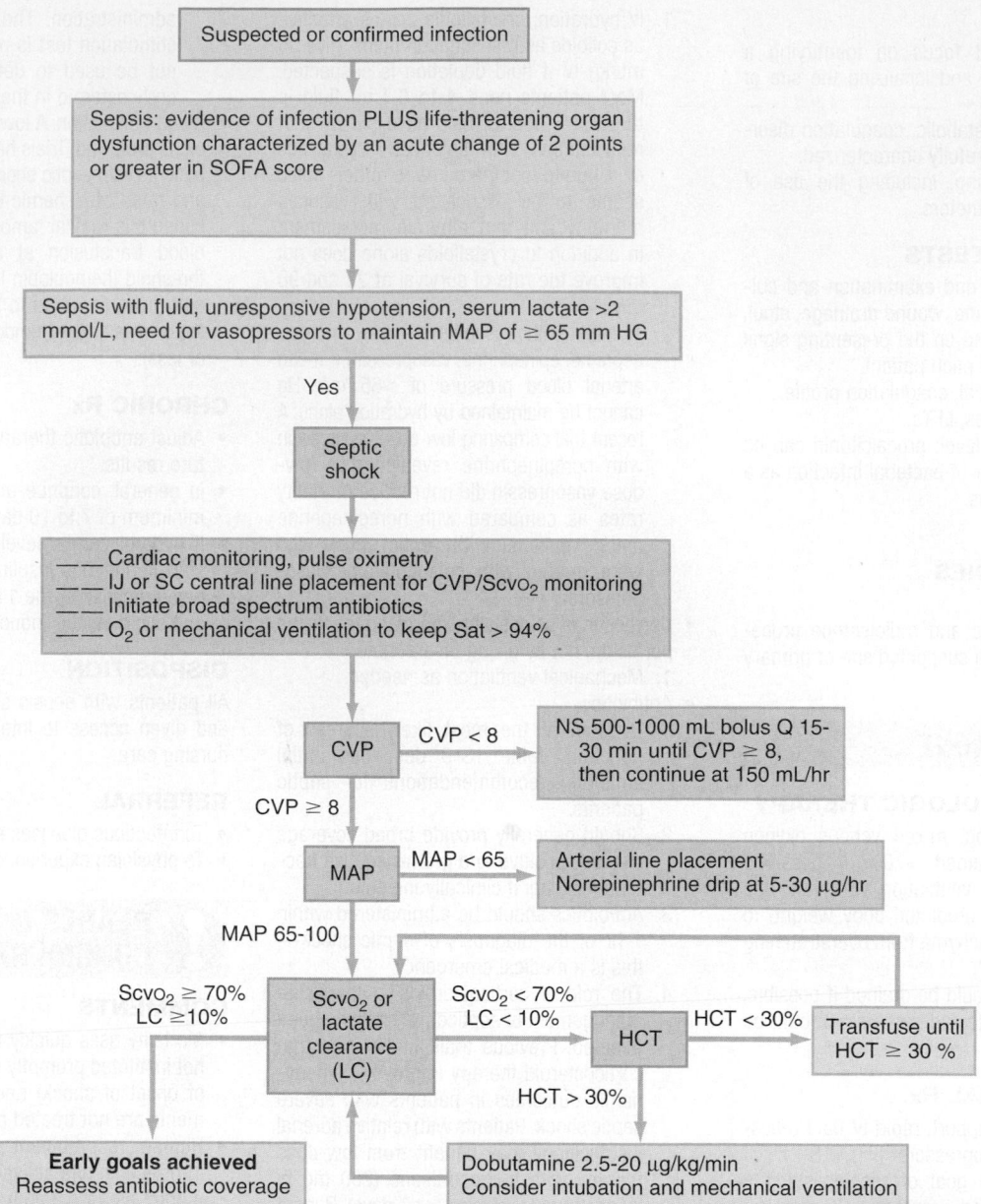

FIGURE 1S-27 Flow diagram outlining the protocol for quantitative resuscitation in treatment of patients with severe sepsis or septic shock. This protocol outlines specific hemodynamic and physiologic parameters the clinician should seek to achieve within the first 6 hr of care. This protocol is focused on resuscitation and should be used in conjunction with standard clinical care for patients with suspected infection, such as appropriate diagnostic studies to determine the focus of infection and appropriate antimicrobial agents to treat the infection. *CVP,* Central venous pressure; *HCT,* hematocrit; *ICU,* intensive care unit; *IJ,* internal jugular; *MAP,* mean arterial pressure; *NS,* normal saline; *Paco$_2$,* partial pressure of carbon dioxide, arterial; *Sat,* peripheral oxygen saturation; *SBP,* systolic blood pressure; *SC,* subclavian; *Scvo$_2$,* central venous oxygen saturation; *SOFA score,* sequential (sepsis-related) organ failure assessment score. (Modified from Bennett JE, et al.: *Mandell, Douglas, and Bennett's Principles and Practice of Infectious Diseases,* ed 8, Philadelphia, 2015, WB Saunders.)

S

TABLE 1S-9 Empirical Antibiotic Options for Patients With Severe Sepsis or Septic Shock

	Suspected Source				
	Lung	**Abdomen**	**Skin/Soft Tissue**	**Urinary Tract**	**Source Uncertain**
Major Community-Acquired Pathogens	*Streptococcus pneumoniae* *Haemophilus influenzae* *Legionella* *Chlamydia pneumoniae*	*Escherichia coli* *Bacteroides fragilis*	*Streptococcus pyogenes* *Staphylococcus aureus* Polymicrobial	*E. coli* *Klebsiella* species *Enterobacter* species *Proteus* spp. Enterococci	
Empirical Antibiotic Therapy	Moxifloxacin *or* levofloxacin *or* azithromycin *plus* cefotaxime *or* ceftazidime *or* cefepime *or* piperacillin-tazobactam	Imipenem *or* meropenem *or* doripenem *or* piperacillin-tazobactam ± aminoglycoside If biliary source: piperacillin-tazobactam, ampicillin-sulbactam, *or* ceftriaxone with metronidazole	Vancomycin *or* daptomycin *plus either* imipenem *or* meropenem *or* piperacillin-tazobactam; ± clindamycin (see text)	Ciprofloxacin *or* levofloxacin (if gram-positive cocci, use ampicillin *or* vancomycin ± gentamicin)	Vancomycin *plus either* doripenem *or* ertapenem *or* imipenem *or* meropenem
Major Commensal or Nosocomial Microorganisms	Aerobic gram-negative bacilli	Aerobic gram-negative rods Anaerobes *Candida* spp.	*Staphylococcus aureus* (? MRSA) Aerobic gram-negative rods	Aerobic gram-negative rods Enterococci	Consider MDRO if in area of high prevalence. Consider echinocandin if neutropenic or indwelling intravascular catheter
Empirical Antibiotic Therapy	Imipenem *or* meropenem *or* doripenem *or* cefepime (if *Acinetobacter baumannii* or carbapenem-resistant *Klebsiella* in ICU, add colistin)	Imipenem *or* meropenem ± aminoglycoside (consider echinocandin)	Vancomycin *or* daptomycin *plus* imipenem-cilastatin *or* meropenem *or* cefepime, ± clindamycin	Vancomycin *plus* imipenem *or* meropenem *or* cefepime	Cefepime *plus* vancomycin ± caspofungin

Dosages for intravenous administration (normal renal function):
*Imipenem-cilastatin, 0.5-1.0g q6-8h
*Meropenem, 1-2g q8h
*Doripenem, 0.5g q8h
Piperacillin-tazobactam, 3.375g q4h or 4.5g q6h
Vancomycin, load 25-30mg/kg, then 15-20 q8-12h
Cefepime, 1-2g q8h
Levofloxacin, 750mg q24h
Ciprofloxacin, 400mg q8-12h
Moxifloxacin, 400mg qd
Ceftriaxone, 2g q24h
Caspofungin, 70mg, followed by 50mg q24h

Colistin: loading dose = 5mg/kg body weight. For maintenance dosing, see University of California, Los Angeles Dosing Protocol: www.infectiousdiseases-ucla-affiliated.org/Intranet/FILES/ColistinDosing.pdf
ICU, Intensive care unit; *MDRO*, multidrug-resistant organisms; *MRSA*, methicillin-resistant *Staphylococcus aureus*.
For MDRO, resistance usually includes carbapenems.
*Carbapenems are less susceptible to extended-spectrum β-lactamases; base choice on local resistance pattern.
From Bennett JE et al: *Mandell, Douglas, and Bennett's principles and practice of infectious diseases,* ed 8, Philadelphia, 2015, WB Saunders.

BASIC INFORMATION

DEFINITION

Septic arthritis is a highly destructive form of joint disease most often caused by hematogenous spread of organisms from a distant site of infection. Direct penetration of the joint as a result of trauma or surgery and spread from adjacent osteomyelitis may also cause bacterial arthritis. Any joint in the body may be affected.

SYNONYMS

Infectious arthritis
Bacterial arthritis
Pyogenic arthritis

ICD-10CM CODES
M00.9 Pyogenic arthritis, unspecified

EPIDEMIOLOGY & DEMOGRAPHICS

INCIDENCE (IN U.S.): Unknown.
PREVALENCE (IN U.S.): Unknown.
PREDOMINANT SEX: Gonococcal arthritis in females.
PREDOMINANT AGE: Gonococcal arthritis in sexually active adults.
PEAK INCIDENCE:
- Gonococcal arthritis: young adults.
- Other bacterial causes: all ages.

PHYSICAL FINDINGS & CLINICAL PRESENTATION

- Hallmark: acute onset of monoarticular joint pain, erythema, heat, and immobility.
- Limited range of motion of the joint.
- Effusion, with varying degrees of erythema and increased warmth around the joint.
- Single joint affected in 80% to 90% of cases of nongonococcal arthritis.
- Gonococcal dermatitis-arthritis syndrome.
  1. Typical pattern is a migratory polyarthritis or tenosynovitis.
  2. Small pustules on the trunk or extremities.
- Febrile patient at presentation.
- Most commonly affected joints in adult: knee and hip, but any joint may be involved; in children: hip.

ETIOLOGY

- Bacteria spread from another locus of infection.
  1. Highly vascular synovium is invaded by hematogenously spread bacteria.
  2. WBC enzymes cause necrosis of synovium, cartilage, and bone.
  3. Extensive joint destruction is rapid if infection is not treated with appropriate IV antibiotics and drainage of necrotic material.
- Predisposing factors: rheumatoid arthritis, prosthetic joints, advanced age, immunodeficiency (HIV, DM, immunosuppressive drugs), gout, sexual activity (gonococcal arthritis), skin infections, cutaneous ulcers (contiguous spread), recent joint surgery, recent intraarticular infection. Fig. E1S-28

illustrates routes by which bacteria can reach the joint.
- The most common nongonococcal organisms are staphylococci (40%), streptococci (28%), and gram-negative bacilli (19%). Less common are mycobacteria (8%), gram-negative cocci (3%), anaerobes (1%), and gram-positive bacilli (1%).
- Staphylococci (*S. aureus* and coagulase-negative staphylococcal species) account for >50% of prosthetic-hip and prosthetic-knee infections. *S. aureus* is very common in patients with rheumatoid arthritis.

DIAGNOSIS

DIFFERENTIAL DIAGNOSIS

- Gout.
- Pseudogout.
- Trauma.
- Hemarthrosis.
- Rheumatic fever.
- Adult or juvenile rheumatoid arthritis.
- Spondyloarthropathies such as reactive arthritis (Reiter's syndrome).
- Osteomyelitis.
- Viral arthritides.
- Septic bursitis.
- Lyme disease caused by *Borrelia burgdorferi*.

WORKUP

- Joint aspiration, Gram stain, and culture of the synovial fluid. Fig. 1S-29 describes an algorithm for synovial fluid analysis in septic arthritis.
- Immediate arthrocentesis before other studies are undertaken or antibiotics instituted. Synovial fluid should be evaluated at bedside and then sent for lab evaluation.

LABORATORY TESTS

- Joint fluid analysis.
  1. Synovial fluid leukocyte count is usually elevated >50,000 cells/mm³ with > 80% polymorphonuclear cells.
  2. Counts are highly variable, with similar findings in gout, pseudogout, or rheumatoid arthritis. Lower WBC counts can occur in joint replacement, disseminated gonococcal disease, and peripheral leukopenia.
  3. Synovial fluid glucose or protein is not helpful because results are not specific for septic arthritis. The differential diagnosis of synovial fluid abnormalities is described in Section IV.
  4. PCR testing: useful for detection of uncommon organisms (e.g., Lyme disease).
  5. Crystal analysis: septic arthritis can coexist with crystal arthropathy; therefore, the presence of crystals does not preclude a diagnosis of septic arthritis.
- Blood cultures: positive in 25% to 50% of patients with septic arthritis.
- Culture of possible extraarticular sources of infection.
- Elevated peripheral WBC count, ESR (nonspecific), C-reactive protein (CRP) (nonspecific).

When elevated, ESR and CRP may be useful to monitor therapeutic response.
- If gonococcus is suspected, perform nucleic acid amplification tests (NAATs) on synovial fluid.

IMAGING STUDIES

- Radiograph of the affected joint (Fig. E1S-30): useful to rule out osteomyelitis, fractures, chondrocalcinosis, or inflammatory arthritis.
- MRI: findings that suggest an acute intraarticular infection include the combination of bony erosions with marrow edema.
- CT scan: useful for early diagnosis of infections of the spine, hips, and sternoclavicular and sacroiliac joints.
- Ultrasound: can be useful for detecting effusions in joints that are more difficult to examine (e.g., hip).

 TREATMENT

NONPHARMACOLOGIC THERAPY

- Affected joints aspirated daily to remove necrotic material and to follow serial WBC counts and cultures.
- If no resolution with IV antibiotics and closed drainage: open debridement and lavage, particularly in nongonococcal infections.
- Prevention of contractures:
  1. After acute stage of inflammation, range-of-motion exercises of the affected joint.
  2. Physical therapy helpful.

ACUTE GENERAL Rx

- IV antibiotics immediately after joint aspiration and Gram stain of the synovial fluid. Empiric antibiotic therapy (Table E1S-10) is based on organism found on Gram stain of synovial fluid:
  1. Gram-positive cocci: vancomycin: 15 to 20 mg/kg IV q8 to 12h. Keep trough levels at 15 to 20 mcg/mL.
  2. Gram-negative cocci: ceftriaxone: 1 to 2 g IV q day in adults (children: 50 to 100 mg/kg IV q day).
  3. Gram-negative rods: ceftriaxone, cefepime: 1 to 2 g IV q8 to 12 h in adults (children: 100-150 mg/kg/day divided in q8h dosing), piperacillin-tazobactam: 4-5 g q6h. Aztreonam or fluoroquinolones can be used in patients with allergy to penicillin or cephalosporins.
  4. Negative Gram stain: vancomycin plus either cefepime or a carbapenem such as meropenem: 1 g IV q8h in adults (children: 60 mg/kg/day divided in q8h dosing) or ertapenem.

SUGGESTED READINGS
Available at www.expertconsult.com

RELATED CONTENT
Septic Arthritis (Patient Information)

AUTHOR: **GLENN G. FORT, M.D., M.P.H.**

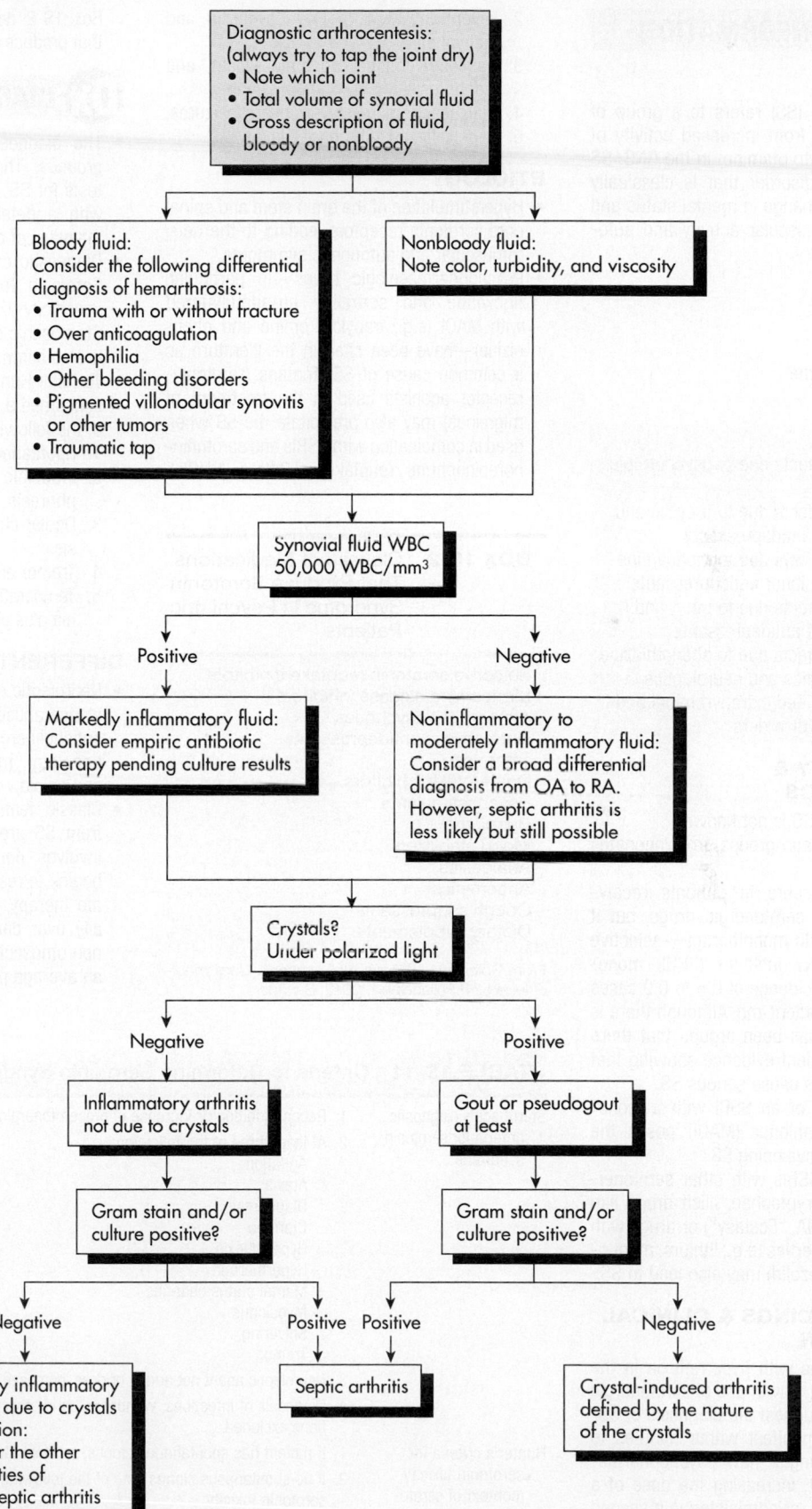

FIGURE 1S-29 Algorithm for synovial fluid analysis in septic arthritis. *OA,* Osteoarthritis; *RA,* rheumatoid arthritis; *WBC,* white blood cell count. (From Harris ED et al [eds]: *Kelley's textbook of rheumatology,* ed 7, Philadelphia, 2005, Saunders.)

 BASIC INFORMATION

DEFINITION

Serotonin syndrome (SS) refers to a group of symptoms resulting from increased activity of serotonin (5-hydroxytryptamine) in the CNS. SS is a drug-induced disorder that is classically characterized by a change in mental status and alteration in neuromuscular activity and autonomic function.

SYNONYMS

SS
Hyperserotonemia
Serotonergic syndrome
Serotonin toxicity

ICD-10CM CODES

Y49	Adverse effects due to psychotropic drugs
Y49.0	Adverse effects due to tricyclic and tetracyclic antidepressants
Y49.1	Adverse effects due to monoamino-oxidase-inhibitor antidepressants
Y49.2	Adverse effects due to other and unspecified antidepressants
Y49.3	Adverse effects due to phenothiazine antipsychotics and neuroleptics
G25.89	Other specified extrapyramidal and movement disorders

EPIDEMIOLOGY & DEMOGRAPHICS

- The incidence of SS is not known.
- SS is seen in all age groups, from neonates to elderly.
- SS classically occurs in patients receiving two or more serotonergic drugs, but it can also occur with monotherapy—selective serotonin reuptake inhibitor (SSRI) monotherapy has an incidence of 0.5 to 0.9 cases of SS per 1000 patient-mo. Although there is an FDA alert, it has been argued that there is a lack of sufficient evidence showing that SSRIs and triptans cause serious SS.
- Concomitant use of an SSRI with a monoamine oxidase inhibitor (MAOI) poses the greatest risk of developing SS.
- Combination of SSRIs with other serotonergic drugs (e.g., tryptophan, illicit drugs like cocaine and MDMA, "Ecstasy") or drugs with serotonergic properties (e.g., lithium, meperidine, triptans, linezolid) may also lead to SS.

PHYSICAL FINDINGS & CLINICAL PRESENTATION

- Findings of clonus with hyperreflexia in the setting of recent (<5 wk) use of serotonergic agents strongly suggest the diagnosis of SS.
- Symptoms can manifest within minutes to hours after starting a new psychopharmacologic treatment, increasing the dose of a serotonergic drug, or administering a second serotonergic drug.
- Clonus (inducible, spontaneous, and ocular) is the key finding in establishing a diagnosis of SS.
- Other pertinent findings include:
  1. Confusion, agitation, hypomania.

2. Fever >38° C (100° F), tachycardia, and tachypnea.
3. Nausea, vomiting, abdominal pain, and diaphoresis.
4. Diarrhea, tremors, shivering, and seizures.
5. Hyperreflexia and muscle rigidity.

ETIOLOGY

- Hyperstimulation of the brain stem and spinal cord serotonin receptors leading to the neuromuscular and autonomic symptoms.
- Psychopharmacologic drugs—in particular, fluoxetine and sertraline co-administered with MAOI (e.g., tranylcypromine and phenelzine)—have been cited in the literature as a common cause of SS. Triptans (serotonin-receptor agonists used in the treatment of migraines) may also precipitate the SS when used in combination with SSRIs and serotonin-norepinephrine reuptake inhibitors (SNRIs).

BOX 1S-2 **Classes of Medications That Produce Serotonin Syndrome in Psychiatric Patients**

Selective serotonin reuptake inhibitors
Monoamine oxidase inhibitors
Atypical antipsychotics
Heterocyclic antidepressants
Trazodone
Dual-uptake inhibitors
Psychostimulants
Buspirone
Mood stabilizers
Analgesics
Antiemetics
Cough suppressants
Dietary supplements

From Goldman L, Schafer AI: *Goldman's Cecil medicine*, ed 24, Philadelphia, 2012, Saunders.

Box 1S-2 describes classes of medications that produce SS in psychiatric patients.

DIAGNOSIS

- The diagnosis of SS is made on clinical grounds. There are no specific laboratory tests for SS. A high index of suspicion along with a detailed medication history is the mainstay of diagnosis.
- Diagnostic criteria: most accurate is Hunter Serotonin Toxicity Criteria (sensitivity 84%, specificity 97%, confirmation by toxicologist). Sternbach's diagnostic criteria (Table 1S-11) is also commonly used.
- To fulfill Hunter criteria a patient must have consumed a serotonergic drug and have one of the following:
  1. Spontaneous clonus.
  2. Inducible clonus plus agitation or diaphoresis.
  3. Ocular clonus plus agitation or diaphoresis.
  4. Tremor and hyperreflexia.
  5. Temperature >38° C (100° F) plus hypertonia plus ocular clonus or inducible clonus.

DIFFERENTIAL DIAGNOSIS

- Neuroleptic malignant syndrome (NMS), substance abuse (e.g., cocaine, amphetamines), anticholinergic toxicity, thyroid storm, infection (e.g., meningitis, encephalitis), alcohol and opioid withdrawal.
- Classic features in differentiation of NMS from SS are that SS develops over 24 hr, involves neuromuscular hyperactivity, and begins to resolve within 24 hr with appropriate therapy, whereas NMS develops gradually over days to weeks, involves sluggish neuromuscular response, and resolves over an average period of 1 wk to 10 days.

TABLE 1S-11 Criteria to Determine Serotonin Syndrome and Toxicity

Sternbach's diagnostic criteria for serotonin syndrome	1. Recent addition or increase of proserotonergic medication
	2. At least three of the following:
	○ Agitation
	○ Ataxia
	○ Diaphoresis
	○ Diarrhea
	○ Hyperreflexia
	○ Hyperthermia
	○ Mental status changes
	○ Myoclonus
	○ Shivering
	○ Tremor
	3. Neuroleptic agent not added or dose increased before the onset of symptoms
	4. Diagnosis of infections, withdrawal, and other poisoning or metabolic disruptions excluded
Hunter's criteria for serotonin toxicity (context of serotonergic medications)	1. If patient has spontaneous clonus, serotonin toxicity present
	2. If no spontaneous clonus, one of the following needed for a diagnosis of serotonin toxicity:
	○ Inducible clonus *and* agitation *or* diaphoresis
	○ Ocular clonus *and* agitation *or* diaphoresis
	○ Tremor *and* hyperreflexia
	○ Temperature >38° C *and* ocular clonus *or* inducible clonus

From Adams JG et al: *Emergency medicine, clinical essentials*, ed 2, Philadelphia, 2013, Elsevier.

WORKUP

- Because SS is a clinical diagnosis, there is no laboratory test that confirms the diagnosis, and serum serotonin concentration does not correlate with clinical picture. Other causes are described in "Differential Diagnosis." Thus, all patients should have blood tests and diagnostic imaging studies to rule out infectious, toxic, and metabolic causes.
- Additional laboratory tests are performed to exclude complicating features of SS (e.g., renal failure secondary to rhabdomyolysis).

LABORATORY TESTS

- CBC with differential to rule out sepsis.
- Electrolytes, BUN, and creatinine to rule out acidosis and renal failure.
- Blood and urine toxicology screen.
- Thyroid function tests.
- Creatine-phosphokinase (CPK) with isoenzymes.
- Urine and blood cultures.
- ECG because ventricular rhythm disturbance is a potentially fatal complication.

IMAGING STUDIES

Imaging studies are not specific in the diagnosis of SS and are only ordered to exclude other causes with similar clinical presentations as SS.

Rx TREATMENT

- Once a diagnosis of SS is established, appropriate consultation with a medical toxicologist, clinical pharmacologist, and/or poison control center should be sought.
- Management includes:
  1. Discontinue use of all potential precipitating drugs.
  2. Provide supportive management.
  3. Control agitation.
  4. Administer serotonin antagonists.
  5. Control autonomic instability.
  6. Control hyperthermia.
  7. Reassess the need to resume the use of the serotonergic agent once the symptoms have resolved.

NONPHARMACOLOGIC THERAPY

- Discontinuation of the drug is the mainstay of therapy.
- Treatment is supportive: maintaining oxygenation and blood pressure and monitoring respiratory status. Hypotensive patients may require both IV fluids and vasopressor therapy.
- Patients who are severely hyperthermic with temperatures >41° C (106° F) should be given IV sedation, paralyzed, and intubated. Cooling blankets can be used for patients with mild to moderate hyperthermia. There is no role for acetaminophen here.
- Intubation is recommended for patients unable to protect their airways as a result of mental status changes or seizures.

ACUTE GENERAL Rx

- Benzodiazepines for control of agitation are preferred to physical restraints.
  1. Lorazepam 1 to 2 mg IV every 30 min has been used effectively in treating agitation, muscle rigidity, myoclonus, and seizure complications.
  2. Diazepam is an alternative choice.
- Blood pressure management with short-acting agents such as esmolol and nitroprusside.
- Serotonin antagonists should be titrated to clinical effectiveness in patients for whom nonpharmacologic therapy and benzodiazepines are not achieving adequate response, although substantial and rigorous data are lacking.
  1. Cyproheptadine 4 mg tablet or 2 mg/5 mL syrup is given 12 mg initially followed by 2 mg every 2 hr until therapeutic response is achieved in adults (up to 32 mg/day); children ages 7 to 14 should receive 4 mg every 6 hr (up to 16 mg/day), children ages 2 to 6 should receive 2 mg every 6 hr (up to 12 mg/day), and children younger than 2 yr should receive a maximum of 0.25 mg/kg/day as 0.06 mg/kg every 6 hr.
  2. Atypical antipsychotic agents with serotonin antagonist properties (e.g., olanzapine 10 mg SL) have been tried with some success.

3. Chlorpromazine 50 to 100 mg IM may be considered in severe cases.

CHRONIC Rx

For patients not requiring hospital admission, cyproheptadine and lorazepam can be given in an oral dose on a prn basis with close follow-up.

DISPOSITION

- SS is a potentially life-threatening condition if not recognized early, although it does exist on a spectrum.
- Prompt diagnosis and withdrawal of the medication result in improvement of symptoms within 24 hr.
- Seizures, rhabdomyolysis, hyperthermia, ventricular arrhythmia, respiratory arrest, and coma are all complicating features of SS.

REFERRAL

All cases of SS secondary to psychotropic medications should be referred to a psychiatrist.

PREVENTION

Modify prescription practices by avoiding multidrug regimens.

PEARLS & CONSIDERATIONS

The combined use of SSRIs and MAOIs is contraindicated.

COMMENTS

- The use of SSRIs and other serotonergic agents is not an absolute contraindication; however, prompt withdrawal of the medication is recommended if any symptoms suggesting SS occur.
- SS is usually found in patients being treated for depression, bipolar disorders, obsessive-compulsive disorder, attention-deficit disorder, and Parkinson's disease.

SUGGESTED READINGS

Available at www.expertconsult.com

AUTHOR: **MARK F. BRADY, M.D., M.P.H., M.M.S.**

 **BASIC INFORMATION**

DEFINITION

Shaken baby syndrome is a potentially life-threatening and severe form of abuse in which an infant or child is violently shaken. Intracranial injury is caused by rapid acceleration and rotation of the cranium (sometimes associated with impact on a solid object which leads to rapid angular deceleration). The classic injury pattern associated with shaking includes diffuse subdural hemorrhage, retinal hemorrhages, and diffuse brain injury (Fig. E1S-33). The diagnosis is often difficult to make because the clinical manifestations are nonspecific, perpetrators are unlikely to report a history of trauma, and there may be little to no external signs of injury.

SYNONYMS

Shaken infant syndrome
Abusive head trauma
Nonaccidental head injury

ICD-10CM CODES
T74.1	Physical abuse
T74.4	Shaken infant syndrome, initial encounter
T74.4XXD	Shaken infant syndrome, subsequent encounter
T74.4XXS	Shaken infant syndrome, sequela

EPIDEMIOLOGY & DEMOGRAPHICS

INCIDENCE: Most common cause of death or serious neurologic injury resulting from child abuse. It is specific to infancy, when children have unique anatomic features. A population-based study conducted in the United States showed an incidence of abusive head trauma in children <2 yr of 17 per 100,000 persons with a higher incidence in the first year of life compared to the second. Population-based studies in Europe show similar incidence in the first yr.

PEAK INCIDENCE: Shaken babies are typically younger than 1 yr; with median age of 4 mo.

PREVALENCE: ~25% of clinically diagnosed babies with shaken baby syndrome die, and ~80% of the remaining suffer lifelong neurologic damage.

PREDOMINANT SEX: About 60% of identified victims of shaking injury are male. Children of families who live at or below the poverty level are at an increased risk for these injuries as well as any type of child abuse.

RISK FACTORS: History of abuse, history of domestic violence, low socioeconomic status, perinatal illness, incessant crying, and family dysfunction. The perpetrators in 65% to 90% of cases are males and are most commonly the father.

PHYSICAL FINDINGS & CLINICAL PRESENTATION

In several retrospective series, no history of a traumatic event was offered in 64% to 97% of cases. One study of 364 children with shaken baby syndrome found that 40% had no signs of external injury on initial evaluation. Majority will have an abnormal neurologic examination. Generally present with nonspecific symptoms (i.e., seizures, failure to thrive, vomiting associated with lethargy or drowsiness, decreased feeding, hypothermia, bradycardia, hypertension or hypotension, respiratory irregularities, apnea, coma or death). Retinal and cranial hemorrhages and brain injury are hallmarks of the syndrome. Other signs of abuse such as skull fractures, occult fractures (particularly of ribs and long bone diaphysis), abdominal injury and hearing loss, may be present.

ETIOLOGY

Angular deceleration forces cause primary parenchymal injury including traumatic axonal injury. Neuropathology and imaging techniques have established the cause of brain injury as hypoxic ischemic encephalopathy.

 **DIAGNOSIS**

DIFFERENTIAL DIAGNOSIS

Head trauma from other etiology vs. infection vs. bleeding disorder vs. other etiology

WORKUP

Imaging of the brain, skeletal survey

LABORATORY TESTS

CBC, chemistry, coagulation study, lumbar puncture if meningitis is considered

IMAGING STUDIES

Initial study of unenhanced CT scan and skeletal survey. MRI should be done as follow up in patients with abnormal CT findings and is indicated for infants who are asymptomatic but require neuroimaging after finding noncranial injuries.

 **TREATMENT**

Treatment focused on targeting specific injuries and also on prevention of future injuries.

NONPHARMACOLOGIC THERAPY

Admission to a hospital for observation.

ACUTE GENERAL Rx

Supportive care and interventions as dictated by the clinical, laboratory, and imaging findings

CHRONIC Rx

Counseling, working with the child's school to optimize academic development

REFERRAL

Neurologist and neurosurgery (if needed)

 **PEARLS & CONSIDERATIONS**

PREVENTION

The National Center on Shaken Baby Syndrome offers a prevention program. Additionally, researchers like Harvey Karp have suggested ideas.

PATIENT & FAMILY EDUCATION

Shaken baby syndrome can result in lifelong, irreversible injuries. Prevention is a key component. Infants crying most commonly leads to shaking. Therefore the National Center on Shaken Baby Syndrome offers a prevention program, the **Period of Purple Crying,** which seeks to help parents and other caregivers understand crying in normal infants. By defining and describing the sometimes inconsolable infant crying that can sometimes cause stress, anger, and frustration in parents and caregivers, the program hopes to educate and empower people to prevent abusive head trauma.

Another method that may help is one suggested by author Dr. Harvey Karp's "five S's":
1. Shushing: use "white noise" or rhythmic sounds that mimic the constant whir of noise in the womb.
2. Side/stomach positioning: place the baby on the left side to help digestion.
3. Sucking: let the baby breast-feed or bottle-feed, or give the baby a pacifier or finger to suck on.
4. Swaddling: wrap the baby up snugly in a blanket to help him or her feel more secure.
5. Swinging gently: rock in a chair, use an infant swing, or take a car ride to help duplicate the constant motion the baby felt in the womb.

EBM EVIDENCE

Available at www.expertconsult.com

SUGGESTED READINGS

Available at www.expertconsult.com

AUTHORS: **PRIYA SARIN GUPTA, M.D, M.P.H., LEANNA R. GARBUS, O.M.S. III,** and **POOJA VERMA, M.D.**

Diseases
and Disorders

I

 BASIC INFORMATION

DEFINITION

Shigellosis is an inflammatory disease of the bowel caused by one of four species of *Shigella*. It is the third most common cause of diarrhea in the United States after *Salmonella* and *Campylobacter* and the most common cause of bacillary dysentery in the United States.

SYNONYMS

Bacillary dysentery

ICD-10CM CODES
A03.9 Shigellosis, unspecified
A03.0 Shigellosis due to Shigella dysenteriae
A03.1 Shigellosis due to Shigella flexneri
A03.2 Shigellosis due to Shigella boydii
A03.3 Shigellosis due to Shigella sonnei
A03.8 Other shigellosis

EPIDEMIOLOGY & DEMOGRAPHICS

INCIDENCE (IN U.S.): 6.59 cases per 100,000 population with approximately 450,000 cases/yr
PREDOMINANT SEX: Male homosexuals at increased risk.
PREDOMINANT AGE: Shigellosis predominantly affects children with 28 cases per 100,000 population in children <4 yr old and 25.67 cases per 100,000 population in children aged 4 to 11.
PEAK INCIDENCE: Summer.
GENETICS: Neonatal infection: rare but severe.

PHYSICAL FINDINGS & CLINICAL PRESENTATION

- Possibly asymptomatic, but incubation period can range from 1 to 7 days with an average of 3 days.
- Mild illness that is usually self-limited, resolving in a few days.
- High fever.
- Watery diarrhea. Dysentery (abdominal cramps, tenesmus, and numerous, small-volume stools with blood, mucus, and pus).
- Descending intestinal tract illness, reflecting infection of small bowel first and then the colon.
- Severe disease is more common in children and elderly and outside of the United States.
- Complications of severe illness:
  1. Seizures.
  2. Megacolon.
  3. Intestinal perforation.
  4. Death.
- Extraintestinal manifestations are uncommon (reactive arthritis in up to 3% of patients).

- Bacteremia is more common in children; in adults it has been described in patients with AIDS, the elderly, and diabetics.
- Hemolytic-uremic syndrome (HUS): can be caused by *S. dysenteriae* 1.
- Reactive arthritis, sometimes as part of Reiter's syndrome following *S. flexneri* infection.

ETIOLOGY

- *Shigella:* gram-negative rod bacteria that are less susceptible to stomach acid and thus as few as 10 to 100 bacteria can cause disease. The bacteria invade colonic tissue and cause inflammation.
  1. *S. flexneri.*
  2. *S. dysenteriae.*
  3. *S. sonnei.*
  4. *S. boydii.*
- *S. sonnei* is the most commonly isolated species in the United States (over 75% of cases), and it usually causes a mild watery diarrhea.
- Direct person-to-person transmission is thought to be the most common route. Outbreaks among men who have sex with men have occurred because of direct or indirect oral-anal contact.
- Contaminated food or water may transmit disease.
- Outbreaks have occurred in day care centers, a community wading pool frequented by toddlers, and residential institutions.

 DIAGNOSIS

DIFFERENTIAL DIAGNOSIS

- May mimic other bacterial gastroenteritis, such as *Clostridium difficile*, *Salmonella*, *Campylobacter*, and *Yersinia*.
- Dysentery can also be caused by *Entamoeba histolytica*.
- Bloody diarrhea may resemble disease caused by invasive *E. coli* (IEC).
- Hemolytic-uremic syndrome caused by enterohemorrhagic *E. coli* (O157:H7).

LABORATORY TESTS

- The diagnosis is established by bacterial stool culture.
- Stool should be cultured from fresh samples, because the yield is increased by processing the specimen soon after passage. The best yield is from the mucoid part of the stool.
- Serology is available but rarely useful.
- Polymerase chain reaction (PCR) is available but due to cost used mainly for outbreak investigations.
- Fecal leukocyte preparation may show WBCs.
- Total WBCs may be low, normal, or high. Leukemoid reactions can occur in children.

- Blood cultures should be obtained in patients with severe disease or sepsis syndromes.

IMAGING STUDIES

Abdominal radiographs may suggest megacolon or perforation in rare, severe cases.

 TREATMENT

NONPHARMACOLOGIC THERAPY

- Adequate hydration.
- Electrolyte replacement.

ACUTE GENERAL Rx

Antibiotics recommend in all patients with positive stool cultures:
- To shorten course of illness.
- To limit transmission of illness.
- For adults: Pending susceptibilities, ciprofloxacin 750 mg PO bid for 3 days or levofloxacin 500 to 750 mg q day for 3 days should be used. An alternative is azithromycin 500 mg q day for 3 days.
- For children: IV ceftriaxone (50 mg/kg/day) for 5 days in cases of severe disease. For oral therapy, can use cefixime: 8 mg/kg/day as single daily dose or divided q12h for 5 days *or* azithromycin: 10 mg/kg/day in a single daily dose for 3 days. A short course of an oral quinolone can also be used safely although they are not approved for children.

DISPOSITION

- Most disease is self-limited and resolves without treatment.
- Severe illness may be fatal.

REFERRAL

For severe illness or complications.

PEARLS & CONSIDERATIONS

COMMENTS

- Shigella is one cause of "gay bowel syndrome."
- Illness is worsened by agents that decrease intestinal motility.
- Food handlers, child care providers, and health care workers should have a negative stool culture documented following treatment.

SUGGESTED READINGS
Available at www.expertconsult.com

RELATED CONTENT
Shigellosis (Patient Information)

AUTHOR: **GLENN G. FORT, M.D., M.P.H.**

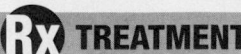

 BASIC INFORMATION

DEFINITION

Short bowel syndrome (SBS) is a malabsorption syndrome that results from extensive small intestinal resection or congenital causes (Table 1S-13).

SYNONYMS

Short bowel
SBS

ICD-10CM CODES
K91.2 Postsurgical malabsorption, not
        elsewhere classified

EPIDEMIOLOGY & DEMOGRAPHICS

- Parallels Crohn's disease (see "Crohn's Disease" in Section I), which is the most common cause of the syndrome in adults.
- In children, two thirds of short bowels are related to congenital abnormalities (intestinal atresia, gastroschisis, volvulus, aganglionosis) and one third are related to necrotizing enterocolitis.
- Prevalence: 10,000 to 20,000 cases are estimated to exist in the United States.

PHYSICAL FINDINGS & CLINICAL PRESENTATION

- Diarrhea and steatorrhea
- Weight loss
- Anemia related to iron or vitamin B_{12} absorption
- Bleeding diathesis related to vitamin K malabsorption
- Osteoporosis/osteomalacia related to vitamin D and calcium malabsorption
- Hyponatremia, hypokalemia
- Hypovolemia
- Other macronutrient or micronutrient deficiency states

ETIOLOGY

- Extensive bowel resection for treatment of the conditions mentioned previously (see "Epidemiology"). SBS typically does not occur until less than 200 cm of healthy small intestine remains. Risk for SBS is decreased if colon is intact.

TABLE 1S-13 Causes of Short Bowel Syndrome

Congenital
Congenital short bowel syndrome
Multiple atresias
Gastroschisis
Bowel resection
Necrotizing enterocolitis
Volvulus with or without malrotation
Long-segment Hirschsprung disease
Meconium peritonitis
Crohn's disease
Trauma

From Kliegman RM et al: *Nelson textbook of pediatrics*, ed 19, Philadelphia, 2011, Saunders.

- Congenital (Table 1S-13).
  The human intestine is 3 to 8 m in length. Removal of up to half of the small intestine produces no disruption in nutrient absorption, and most patients can maintain nutritional balance on oral feeding if they have more than 100 cm (3 ft) of jejunum. Similarly, 100 cm of intact jejunum can maintain a normal water, sodium, and potassium balance under normal circumstances. The presence of an intact colon can compensate for some small intestine loss.
  Site-specific functions:
- Calcium, magnesium, phosphorus, iron, and vitamins are absorbed in the duodenum and proximal jejunum.
- Vitamin B_{12} and bile acids are absorbed in the ileum. The resection of more than 60 cm of ileum results in vitamin B_{12} malabsorption. The loss of more than 100 cm results in fat malabsorption (from the loss of bile acids).
- The loss of gastrointestinal endocrine hormones can affect intestinal motility.
- Intestinal bacterial overgrowth may also occur, especially if the ileocecal valve is lost.

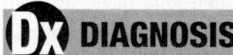 **DIAGNOSIS**

Presence of macronutrient and/or micronutrient loss in a patient with a known history of bowel resection

DIFFERENTIAL DIAGNOSIS

Because the history of significant bowel resection is typically known, there is no differential diagnosis. If that history is not known, all causes of weight loss, malabsorption, and diarrhea must be considered.

TABLE 1S-14 Management Strategies for Short Bowel Syndrome

1. Acute phase
   a. Treat postoperative complications
   b. Maintain full support via the parenteral route
   c. Initiate low-rate trophic enteral feeds
   d. Document amount and site of remaining bowel and underlying disease
2. Early adaptation (up to 1 yr postsurgery)
   a. Increase enteral nutrition to tolerance; supplement with glutamine
   b. Achieve permanent parenteral access, if indicated
   c. Maximize antiperistaltic agents
   d. Octreotide for high-output ostomy or fistula
   e. Dietary counseling
   f. Clinical trials of trophic growth factors
3. Long-term adaptation (>1 yr postsurgery)
   a. Recruit bypassed bowel
   b. Bowel-lengthening procedure (Bianchi or STEP)
   c. Monitor for development of TPN-associated complications, and refer for transplant before recurrent sepsis, thrombosis, or end-stage liver disease

From Cameron JL, Cameron AM: *Current surgical therapy*, ed 10, Philadelphia, 2011, Saunders.

 **TREATMENT**

Extensive small bowel resection with colectomy (<100 cm of jejunum)
- Rx: long-term total parenteral nutrition (TPN). Some patients can switch to oral intake after 1 to 2 yr of TPN. In jejunostomy patients, excessive fluid loss can be reduced with H_2 blockers, proton pump inhibitors, or octreotide. Micronutrients are supplemented.

Extensive small bowel resection with partial colectomy (usually patients with Crohn's disease)
- Rx: oral intake alone is possible in all patients with >100 cm of jejunum. In addition to vitamin B_{12} deficiency, these patients often have diarrhea. Consider lactose malabsorption and bacterial overgrowth treated, respectively, with lactose restriction and antibiotics (tetracycline 250 mg tid or metronidazole 500 mg tid for 2 wk). Nonspecific antidiarrheal agents may also be indicated (e.g., Imodium or codeine). The patient must be monitored for micronutrient losses.
- Table 1S-14 summarizes management strategies for SBS. Intestinal transplantation is performed mostly in children at selective centers.
- FDA-approved medications for SBS in patients receiving nutritional support are:
  1. Recombinant growth hormone somatropin (Zorbtive): effective in increasing weight and reducing parenteral nutrition volume. These effects do not persist when the drug is stopped.
  2. Teduglutide (Gattex), a recombinant DNA analog of glucagon-like peptide-2. It promotes mucosal growth in the small bowel through stimulation of crypt cell proliferation and inhibition of enterocyte apoptosis. This drug may have to be continued indefinitely for effects to persist.

COMPLICATIONS
- Oxalate kidney stones
- Cholesterol gallstones
- D-Lactic acidosis

PROGNOSIS
- Directly dependent on the extent of the bowel resection and in the case of Crohn's disease by the underlying illness
- Whether the colon remains in continuity with the small bowel is an important factor in the patient's ability to adapt after significant small bowel resection.

EBM **EVIDENCE**

Available at www.expertconsult.com

RELATED CONTENT

Short Bowel Syndrome (Patient Information)
Malabsorption (Related Key Topic)

AUTHOR: **FRED F. FERRI, M.D.**

DEFINITION

Short QT syndrome (SQTS) is a genetically inherited disorder of cardiac repolarization characterized by a severely shortened QT interval on the ECG, leading to atrial and ventricular arrhythmias and sudden cardiac death in affected individuals. This is a primary electrical disorder and patients have structurally normal hearts.

SYNONYMS

SQTS

ICD 10CM CODES
I45.89 Other specified conduction disorders

EPIDEMIOLOGY AND DEMOGRAPHICS

- Unknown; disease described for the first time only in 2000 (Gussak et al., 2000)
- This is primarily because, while there is near-unanimity on what constitutes the upper limit of a normal QT interval, no such consensus exists about the lower limit. In most (but not all) cases of the SQTS, the QT or QTc (corrected QT interval) has been <360 msec; however, there are many individuals with that QT interval who are clinically unaffected. Consequently, the incidence and prevalence is unknown, especially given the extremely small number of individuals diagnosed with the syndrome.
- Genetics: the disease is genetically heterogeneous and transmitted in an autosomal dominant fashion. So far, six variants have been identified. Three represent gain of function mutations, and three represent loss of function mutations. SQT1 is the most common variant described, due to a mutation in the cardiac ion channel KCNH2(HERG).

PHYSICAL FINDINGS AND CLINICAL PRESENTATION

- Seen across all age groups, though most patients are children or young adults.
- Syncope and cardiac arrest are the most common presenting features. Syncope is likely due to ventricular arrhythmias. Sudden death can happen with exercise as well as at rest. Cardiac arrest is often the first manifestation of the disease with a peak incidence in the first year of life.
- Atrial fibrillation and flutter are well described as being part of the syndrome.
- A significant percentage of patients are asymptomatic

ETIOLOGY

- Cardiac repolarization abnormality
- Genetic channelopathy transmitted via autosomal dominant mode, caused by missense mutations on genes (six identified so far)
- Mutations cause an increase in net outward current from either a reduction in inward depolarizing currents INa or ICa or augmentation of outward repolarizing currents I to I K1, I K-ATP, I ACh, I Kr or I Ks. The resultant shortening of the action potential causes a shortening of the effective refractory period, with subsequent increased susceptibility of both atrial and ventricular muscle to premature depolarizations that lead to AF and VF.
- Acquired causes—see "Differential Diagnosis"

Dx DIAGNOSIS

- The differential diagnosis of a short QT includes various conditions such as hyperkalemia, hypercalcemia, acidosis, digitalis toxicity, effect of acetylcholine or epinephrine, sinus tachycardia, or hyperthermia. All these are possible causes of an acquired short QT interval that must be ruled out before a diagnosis of SQTS can be entertained.
- It must be remembered that merely having a short QT on the surface ECG does not confer a diagnosis of SQTS. The clinical history, including family history and genetic testing, are included in the criterion necessary to establish a diagnosis of SQTS, and are invaluable in making the diagnosis (Table 1S-15).

WORK-UP

- Evaluation of any survivor of sudden death starts with a detailed history and physical examination, with particular emphasis on family history. Many patients with SQTS have unexplained syncope or palpitations prior to resuscitated sudden death. Atrial fibrillation is common in SQTS patients and a family history of lone AF should also be sought, in addition to resuscitated VF arrest.
- Physical examination is mostly normal in patients with SQTS.

- ECG findings in SQTS include not only an abnormally short QT interval (usually <360 msec), but usually also a short or even absent ST interval, with the T-wave appearing to emanate directly from the S-wave. T-waves are usually any combination of tall, narrow, and symmetric, with a prolonged Tpeak-Tend ratio (Fig. 1S-34). Another feature to look for is the lack of adaptation of the QT interval to the heart rate (diminished rate dependence) as a result of which the corrected QT interval can be misleading; therefore, QT measurement on resting ECG in SQTS is more accurate with heart rate as close to 60 as possible.
- Echocardiogram and cardiac MRI should be performed to confirm a lack of structural heart disease.
- Holter recordings and stress tests can document a lack of variation of the QT interval in relation to the RR cycle; this is an important aspect of establishing the diagnosis. The QT interval shortens only slightly with increasing heart rates, so the QT and QTc values approach normal levels during faster heart rates. The QT fails to lengthen at slower heart rates.
- At electrophysiology study, the atrial and ventricular refractory periods are usually very short (140-200 msec at a CL of 400-600 msec). Sustained atrial fibrillation or flutter with rapid ventricular rates is often induced with programmed stimulation in the atrium. The inducibility of VF in SQTS patients at EPS is about 60%. EPS has a role in adding to the diagnosis by demonstrating short A and V refractory periods (also seen in other channelopathies such as Brugada syndrome), but given its low sensitivity it cannot be used for risk stratification.

TABLE 1S-15 SQTS Diagnostic Criteria

	Points
QT$_c$, msec	
<370	1
<350	2
<330	3
Jpoint-Tpeak interval <120 msec	1
Clinical history	
History of sudden cardiac arrest	2
Documented polymorphic VT or VF	2
Unexplained syncope	1
Atrial fibrillation	1
Family history	
First- or second-degree relative with high-probability SQTS	2
First- or second-degree relative with autopsy-negative sudden cardiac death	1
Sudden infant death syndrome	1
Genotype	
Genotype positive	2
Mutation of undetermined significance in a culprit gene	1

VF, ventricular fibrillation; *VT*, ventricular tachycardia.
A minimum of 1 point must be obtained in the electrocardiographic section in order to obtain additional points.
High-probability SQTS: ≥4 points; intermediate-probability SQTS; 3 points, low-probability SQTS: ≤2 points. Electrocardiogram: must be recorded in the absence of modifiers known to shorten the QT. Jpoint-Tpeak interval must be measured in the precordial lead with the greatest amplitude T-wave. Clinical history: events must occur in the absence of an identifiable etiology, including structural heart disease. Points can only be received for 1 of cardiac arrest, documented polymorphic VT, or unexplained syncope. Family history: points can only be received once in this section.
Adapted from Gollob MH, Redpath CJ, Roberts JD: The short QT syndrome: proposed diagnostic criteria, *J Am Coll Cardiol* 57(7):802-812, 2011. http://dx.doi.org/10.1016/j.jacc.2010.09.048)

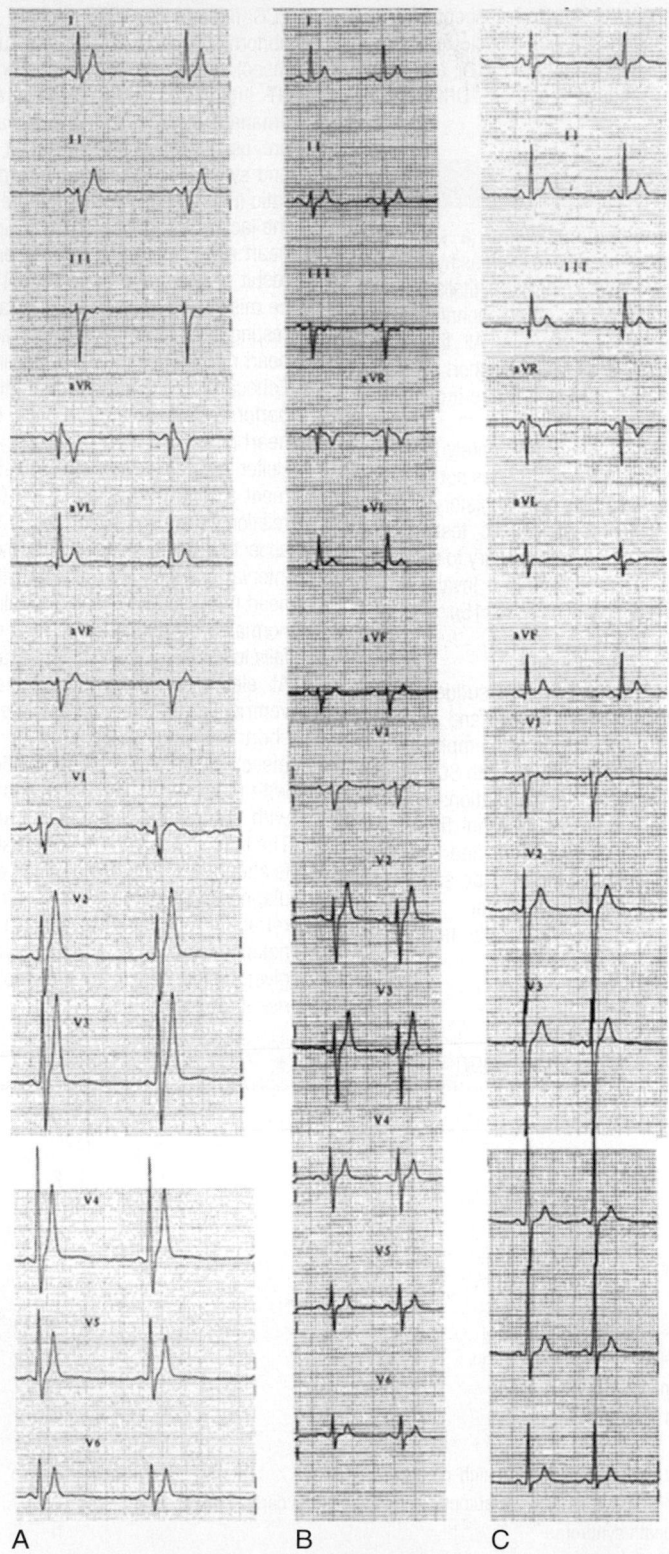

FIGURE 1S-34 Twelve-lead ECG (25 mm/s paper speed) of family 1 patients. A, Patient 1 (IV, 3): sinus rhythm, heart rate 52 beats per minute (bpm); left-axis deviation, QT 280 msec. **B,** Patient 2 (IV, 2): sinus rhythm, heart rate 96 bpm; left-axis deviation, QT 220 msec. **C,** Patient 3 (V, 1): sinus rhythm with mean heart rate 92 bpm, QT 260 msec. (Adapted with permission from Gaita F et al: Short QT syndrome: a familial cause of death, *Circulation* 108:965-970, 2003.)

LABORATORY TESTS

Genetic testing is recommended for all patients in whom a diagnosis of SQTS is suspected. This is especially true if they have a clinical or family history of syncope or sudden death.

 **TREATMENT**

- There is no significant clinical data on how to approach patients with an isolated short QT interval but no family or clinical history or genotype criterion (low and intermediate probability of SQTS). Risk stratification of these patients is not possible at this time; however, they should be referred to an electrophysiologist with expertise on this topic for comprehensive testing, including genetic testing.
- Patients with QT <330 msec and one criterion from clinical/family history or genetic testing fall in the high probability category of SQTS and hence a higher risk subgroup for sudden cardiac death. An ICD implant is recommended in this group for secondary and possibly also primary prevention against sudden cardiac death.
- SQTS is a highly lethal disease and survivors of cardiac arrest are at high risk for subsequent events. ICD implantation is strongly recommended in this group.
- A peculiar issue in patients with SQTS implanted with an ICD is double counting of peaked T-waves that are closely coupled to the QRS complex. This often leads to inappropriate ICD shocks. Most ICDs have programming modifications that can be turned on to get around this problem.
- Pharmacologic therapy is usually only advised in patients with multiple and frequent appropriate ICD shocks.
- However, they may be the mainstay of therapy in patients in whom an ICD cannot be implanted for various reasons, including in children in whom technical challenges are significant.
- While many drugs, such as flecainide, sotalol, ibutilide, hydroquinone, and amiodarone, have been used in an attempt to increase the QT interval, most of the available data favor hydroquinidine as the drug of choice across all forms of the SQTS.

REFERRAL

Consultation with an electrophysiologist is strongly recommended if SQTS is suspected.

 **PEARLS AND CONSIDERATIONS**

- SQTS is a rare genetic syndrome causing arrhythmias and sudden death.
- Should be suspected in patients with QT interval <360 msec presenting with syncope, sudden cardiac death, or atrial fibrillation and a family history of the same.

AUTHOR: **JOYDEEP GHOSH, M.D.**

Diseases and Disorders

BASIC INFORMATION

DEFINITION

Sialadenitis is an inflammation of the salivary glands.

ICD-10CM CODES
K11.20 Sialadenitis, unspecified

EPIDEMIOLOGY & DEMOGRAPHICS

Parotid or submandibular glands are most frequently affected (Fig. 1S-37).

PHYSICAL FINDINGS & CLINICAL PRESENTATION

- Pain and swelling of the affected salivary gland.
- Increased pain with meals.
- Erythema and localized tenderness at the duct opening.
- Massage may express purulent discharge from duct orifice.
- Induration and pitting of the skin, with involvement of the masseteric and submandibular spatial planes in severe cases.

ETIOLOGY

- Ductal obstruction is generally from a mucus plug caused by stasis of saliva with increased viscosity with subsequent stasis and infection.
- Acute suppurative sialadenitis is a bacterial infection of the salivary gland. Most frequent infecting organisms are *Staphylococcus aureus* (50%-90% of cases), streptococcal species, *Haemophilus influenzae, Pseudomonas, Enterobacter, Klebsiella, Enterococcus, Proteus,* and *Candida* spp.
- Sjögren's syndrome, diabetes mellitus, hypothyroidism, renal failure, trauma, radiation therapy, chemotherapy, dehydration, and chronic illness are predisposing factors.
- Mumps is the most common cause of non-suppurative acute sialadenitis. Majority of cases (>80%) occur in children younger than 15 years.

DIAGNOSIS

DIFFERENTIAL DIAGNOSIS

- Salivary gland neoplasm.
- Ductal stricture.
- Sialolithiasis.
- Decreased salivary secretion as a result of medications (e.g., amitriptyline, diphenhydramine, anticholinergics).

WORKUP

- Generally not necessary. Fig. 1S-38 describes a diagnostic algorithm.
- Ultrasound or CT scan in patients not responding to medical treatment.

LABORATORY TESTS

- Generally not indicated.
- Complete blood count with differential to possibly reveal leukocytosis with left shift.

IMAGING STUDIES

- Ultrasound or CT scan may be needed in patients not responding to medical therapy.
- Sialography should not be performed during the acute phase.

TREATMENT

NONPHARMACOLOGIC THERAPY

- Massage of the gland: may express pus and relieve some of the pressure.
- Rehydration.
- Warm compresses.
- Oral cavity irrigations.
- Administration of sialagogues such as lemon drops or vitamin C lozenges.

ACUTE GENERAL Rx

- Amoxicillin-clavulanate 500 to 875 mg or cefuroxime 250 to 500 mg bid should be given for 10 days. Clindamycin is an alternative choice in patients allergic to penicillin.
- IV antibiotics (e.g., cefoxitin, nafcillin) can be given in severe cases.

DISPOSITION

Complete recovery unless the patient has underlying obstruction (e.g., ductal stricture, tumor, or stone)

REFERRAL

- To ear-nose-throat specialist for nonresolving cases despite appropriate antibiotic therapy.
- For salivary gland incision and drainage, which may be necessary in resistant cases.

PEARLS & CONSIDERATIONS

COMMENTS

Prevention of dehydration will decrease the risk of sialadenitis.

SUGGESTED READINGS
Available at www.expertconsult.com

RELATED CONTENT

Salivary Gland Inflammation (Patient Information)
Sialolithiasis (Related Key Topic)
Salivary Gland Neoplasm (Related Key Topic)

AUTHOR: **FRED F. FERRI, M.D.**

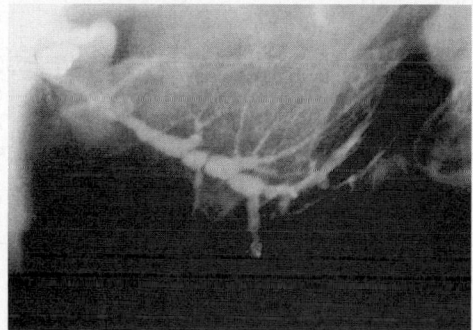

FIGURE 1S-37 Sialogram of patient with chronic sialadenitis showing sausage link–like patterns and massive duct dilation. (From Blitzer CE et al: Sialadenitis. In Johnson JT, Yu VL [eds]: *Infectious diseases and antimicrobial therapy of the ears, nose, and throat,* Philadelphia, 1997, Saunders.)

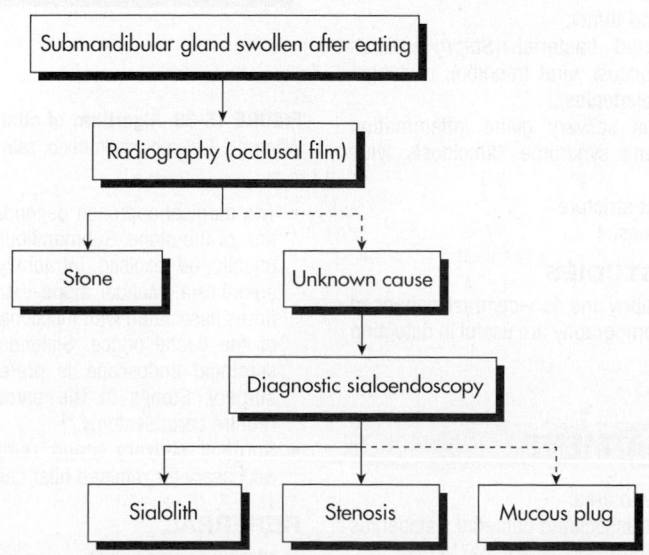

FIGURE 1S-38 Diagnostic algorithm. (From C.-Q. Yu et al.: Selective management of obstructive submandibular sialadenitis, Br J Oral Maxillofacial Surg 46(1): 46–49, 2008.)

BASIC INFORMATION

DEFINITION

Sialolithiasis is the existence of hardened intraluminal deposits in the ductal system of a salivary gland.

SYNONYMS

Salivary gland stone
Salivary calculus

ICD-10CM CODES
K11.5 Sialolithiasis

EPIDEMIOLOGY & DEMOGRAPHICS

Affects patients mostly in the fifth to eighth decades and occurs most commonly in the submandibular gland (80%); only 14% are located in a parotid gland.

PHYSICAL FINDINGS & CLINICAL PRESENTATION

- Symptoms: colicky postprandial pain and swelling of a salivary gland. Tends to have a remitting/relapsing course.
- Signs: swelling and tenderness of a salivary gland. The stone may be felt by palpation of the floor of the mouth (Fig. 1S-37).

ETIOLOGY

- The cause is unknown. Contributing factors include saliva stagnation, sialadenitis (inflammation of a salivary gland), ductal inflammation, or injury (Fig. 1S-38).
- Salivary calculus composition is mainly calcium phosphate and carbonate, often combined with small proportions of magnesium, zinc, ammonium salts, and organic materials or debris.

DIAGNOSIS

DIFFERENTIAL DIAGNOSIS

- Lymphadenitis.
- Salivary gland tumor.
- Salivary gland bacterial (*Staphylococcus* or *Streptococcus*), viral (mumps), or fungal infection (sialadenitis).
- Noninfectious salivary gland inflammation (e.g., Sjögren's syndrome, sarcoidosis, lymphoma).
- Salivary duct stricture.
- Dental abscess.

IMAGING STUDIES

- Ultrasonography and non–contrast-enhanced computed tomography are useful in detecting the stone.
- Sialography.

TREATMENT

- Warm soaks to area.
- Antibiotics if associated bacterial sialadenitis is present.
- Bland diet; avoid citrus fruit and spices.

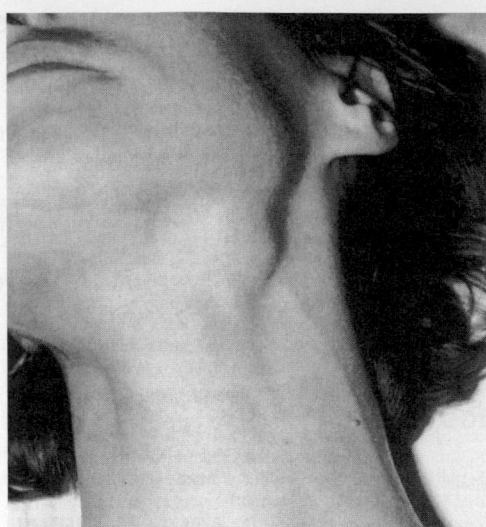

FIGURE 1S-37 Patient with large calculus and obstruction of the left submandibular gland. (From Blitzer CE et al: Sialadenitis. In Johnson JT, Yu VL [eds]: *Infectious diseases and antimicrobial therapy of the ears, nose, and throat,* Philadelphia, 1997, Saunders.)

Formation of Sialolith

Confounding
- Inflammation
- Infection
- Bacteria

Physical gland changes
- Gland injury
- Metaplasia of ductal epithelium
- Epithelium exfoliation
- Ductal nidus foreign body
- Ductal obstruction

Salivary component changes
- Medication
- Salivary stasis
- Decrease in saliva production
- Calcium deposition
- Decrease in pH

Organic components
- Bacteria
- Exfoliated epithelial cell

Inorganic components
- Calcium
- Phosphate

Histological | **Heterogenous** | **Homogenous**

Chemical component structure

Chemical component structure
Hydroxyapatite $Ca_{10}(PO_4)(OH)_2$
Whitlockite $Ca_3(PO_4)_2$
Brushite $CaHPO_4 \cdot 2H_2O$

FIGURE 1S-38 Algorithm of clinical findings and pathogenesis of sialolithiasis. (From Lee L.T. and Wong Y.K. Sialolithiasis in minor salivary glands. J Oral Maxillofac Surg 2010.)

- The surgical approach depends on the location of the stone. Submandibular stones can usually be excised intraorally under local anesthesia. Manual stone extraction sometimes associated with incisional enlargement of the ductal orifice. Sialendoscopy with a semirigid endoscope is preferred to open surgery. Stones in the parotid duct may require parotidectomy.
- Surgical salivary gland removal may be necessary for retained hilar calculi.

REFERRAL

To otorhinolaryngologist.

RELATED CONTENT

Salivary Gland Stones (Patient Information)
Sialoadenitis (Related Key Topic)
Primary Gland Neoplasm (Related Key Topic)

SUGGESTED READINGS

Available at www.expertconsult.com

AUTHOR: FRED F. FERRI, M.D.

BASIC INFORMATION

DEFINITION

- Sickle cell disease (SCD) is a hemoglobinopathy characterized by the production of hemoglobin S caused by substitution of the amino acid valine for glutamic acid in the sixth position of the gamma-globin chain. When exposed to lower oxygen tension, red blood cells (RBCs) assume a sickle shape, resulting in stasis of RBCs in capillaries. Painful crises are caused by ischemic tissue injury resulting from obstruction of blood flow produced by sickled erythrocytes. Vasoocclusive crises are the main reason for hospital admission of children with sickle cell disease.
- Patients with SCD include those who are homozygous for sickle cell hemoglobin (HbSS), also called sickle cell anemia (SCA) and those with one sickle hemoglobin gene plus a gene from another abnormal hemoglobin type (e.g., HbSβ±thalassemia, HbSC).

SYNONYMS

Sickle cell anemia
SCA
SCD
Hemoglobin S disease

ICD-10CM CODES
D57.1	Sickle-cell disease without crisis
D57.20	Sickle-cell/Hb-C disease without crisis
D57.211	Sickle-cell/Hb-C disease with acute chest syndrome
D57.212	Sickle-cell/Hb-C disease with splenic sequestration
D57.219	Sickle-cell/Hb-C disease with crisis, unspecified
D57.3	Sickle-cell trait
D57.40	Sickle-cell thalassemia without crisis
D57.411	Sickle-cell thalassemia with acute chest syndrome
D57.412	Sickle-cell thalassemia with splenic sequestration
D57.419	Sickle-cell thalassemia with crisis, unspecified
D57.80	Other sickle-cell disorders without crisis
D57.811	Other sickle-cell disorders with acute chest syndrome
D57.812	Other sickle-cell disorders with splenic sequestration
D57.819	Other sickle-cell disorders with crisis, unspecified

EPIDEMIOLOGY & DEMOGRAPHICS

- Sickle cell hemoglobin S is transmitted by an autosomal-recessive gene. In African Americans, the incidence of sickle cell anemia at birth is 1 in 600 and the incidence of all genotypes of sickle cell disease is 1 in 300.
- Sickle cell trait occurs in approximately 300 million people worldwide, with the highest prevalence of approximately 30% to 40% in sub-Saharan Africa. In the United States, it is found in nearly 10% of black Americans.
- It is estimated that 2000 babies are born with sickle cell disease in the United States each year.
- There is no predominant sex.

PHYSICAL FINDINGS & CLINICAL PRESENTATION

- Physical examination is variable depending on the degree of anemia and presence of acute vasoocclusive syndromes or neurologic, cardiovascular, genitourinary, and musculoskeletal complications. Pain in adults with sickle cell disease is the rule rather than the exception and is far more prevalent and severe than reported in older large-scale surveys.
- There is no clinical laboratory finding that is pathognomonic of painful crisis of sickle cell disease. The diagnosis of a painful episode is made solely on the basis of the medical therapy and physical examination.
- Bones are the most common site of pain. Dactylitis, or hand-foot syndrome (acute, painful swelling of the hands and feet), is the first manifestation of sickle cell disease in many infants. Irritability and refusal to walk are other common symptoms. After infancy, musculoskeletal pain can be symmetric, asymmetric, or migratory, and it may or may not be associated with swelling, low-grade fever, redness, or warmth.
- In both children and adults, sickle vasoocclusive episodes are difficult to distinguish from osteomyelitis, septic arthritis, synovitis, rheumatic fever, or gout.
- When abdominal or visceral pain is present, care should be taken to exclude sequestration syndromes (spleen, liver) or the possibility of an acute condition such as appendicitis, pancreatitis, cholecystitis, urinary tract infection, pelvic inflammatory disease, or malignancy.
- Pneumonia develops during the course of 20% of painful events and can present as chest and abdominal pain. In adults chest pain may be a result of vasoocclusion in the ribs and often precedes a pulmonary event. The lower back is also a frequent site of painful crisis in adults.
- The acute chest syndrome manifests with chest pain, fever, wheezing, tachypnea, and cough. Chest radiograph may reveal pulmonary infiltrates. Common causes include infection (Mycoplasma, Chlamydia, viruses), infarction, and fat embolism.
- Musculoskeletal and skin abnormalities seen in sickle cell anemia include leg ulcers (particularly on the malleoli) and limb-girdle deformities caused by avascular necrosis of the femoral and humeral heads. Osteonecrosis of the heads of the femur and humerus is found in nearly 50% of adults with sickle cell disease.
- Endocrine abnormalities include delayed sexual maturation and late physical maturation, especially evident in boys.
- Neurologic abnormalities on examination may include seizures and altered mental status. Strokes occur in about 10% of children and adults with sickle cell anemia and approximately 35% of children with sickle cell anemia have cerebrovascular disease.
- Infections, particularly involving Salmonella, Mycoplasma, and Streptococcus, are relatively common.
- Severe splenomegaly as a result of sequestration often occurs in children before splenic atrophy.

DIAGNOSIS

DIFFERENTIAL DIAGNOSIS

- Thalassemia
- Iron-deficiency anemia, leukemia
- The differential diagnosis of patients presenting with a painful crisis is discussed in "Physical Findings"

WORKUP

- Screening of all newborns regardless of racial background is performed in the United States. Screening can be performed with sodium metabisulfite reduction test (Sickledex test).
- Hemoglobin electrophoresis will also confirm the diagnosis and is useful to identify hemoglobin variants such as fetal hemoglobin and hemoglobin A_2.
- Sickle cell disease encompasses genotypes associated with hemolysis and vasoocclusive crisis. Hemoglobin electrophoresis results, mean corpuscular volume, erythrocyte morphology, and degree of anemia can be used to differentiate among the sickle cell syndromes.
- For prenatal diagnosis, initial step is identification of parenteral globin gene mutation by DNA-based testing. If positive, then DNA-based testing of chorionic villus sampling or amniotic fluid cells is performed.

LABORATORY TESTS

- Anemia (resulting from chronic hemolysis), reticulocytosis, leukocytosis, and thrombocytosis are common.
- Elevations of bilirubin and lactate dehydrogenase are also common.
- Peripheral blood smear may reveal sickle cells, target cells, poikilocytosis, and hypochromia (Fig. 1S-40).

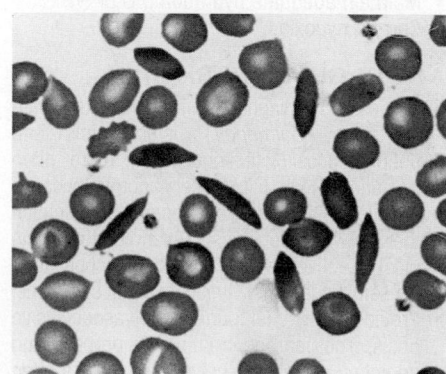

FIGURE 1S-40 Photomicrograph of peripheral blood smear with sickle cells, typical of sickle cell anemia. (From Andreoli TE [ed]: *Cecil essentials of medicine*, ed 4, Philadelphia, 1997, Saunders.)

- Elevated blood urea nitrogen and creatinine may be present in patients with progressive renal insufficiency.
- Urinalysis may reveal hematuria and proteinuria. Patients with SCD should be screened for microalbuminuria and proteinuria with spot urine testing by 10 yr of age.

IMAGING STUDIES

- Chest x-ray is useful in patients presenting with chest syndrome. Cardiomegaly may be present on chest x-ray.
- MRI or bone scan is useful to rule out suspected osteomyelitis (usually the result of *Salmonella*).
- CT scan or MRI of brain is not indicated in asymptomatic adults and children with SCD but is often needed in patients with neurologic complications such as transient ischemic attack, cerebrovascular accident, seizures, or altered mental status.
- Transcranial Doppler ultrasonography (TCD) is a useful commodity to identify children with sickle cell anemia who are at risk for stroke. There should be an annual screening starting at age 2 until age 16. Patients determined to be at risk (transcranial Doppler velocity ≥200 cm/s) should be enrolled in long-term transfusion programs. These are effective in reducing risk of stroke by >90%. In adults magnetic resonance angiography (MRA) can be used instead of TCD to identify those at risk for stroke.
- Doppler echocardiography may be helpful in diagnosing pulmonary hypertension but has a low positive predictive value. Screening for vasculopathy is done by estimating the tricuspid regurgitant jet velocity (TRV). Elevated values are predictive of early mortality. The prevalence of pulmonary hypertension when right heart catheterization is performed is approximately 6% in adults with sickle cell disease.

🆁🆇 TREATMENT

NONPHARMACOLOGIC THERAPY

- Patients should be instructed to avoid conditions that may precipitate sickling crisis, such as hypoxia, infections, acidosis, and dehydration.
- Maintain adequate hydration (PO or IV).
- Correct hypoxia.

ACUTE GENERAL Rx

- Aggressively diagnose and treat suspected infections (*Salmonella* osteomyelitis and pneumococcal infections occur more often in patients with sickle cell anemia because of splenic infarcts and atrophy). Combination therapy with a cephalosporin and erythromycin plus incentive spirometry and bronchodilators is useful in patients with acute chest syndrome.
- Provide pain relief during the vasoocclusive crisis. The fear of creating or perpetuating addiction or being deceived by patients often causes physicians to prescribe subtherapeutic dosages of opioids. However, available evidence suggests that the prevalence of drug addiction among patients with sickle cell anemia is no higher than in the overall U.S.

population. Medications should be administered on a fixed time schedule with a dosing interval that does not extend beyond the duration of the desired pharmacologic effect.

1. Meperidine is contraindicated in patients with renal dysfunction or central nervous system disease because its metabolite, normeperidine (which is excreted by the kidneys), can cause seizures.
2. Narcotics (e.g., morphine 0.1 mg/kg IV q3-4h or 0.3 mg/kg PO q4h) should be given on a fixed schedule (not prn for pain), with rescue dosing for breakthrough pain as needed.
3. Except when contraindications exist, concomitant use of nonsteroidal anti-inflammatory drugs should be standard treatment.
4. Nurses should be instructed not to give narcotics if the patient is heavily sedated or respirations are depressed.
5. When the patient shows signs of improvement, narcotic drugs should be tapered gradually to prevent withdrawal syndrome. It is advisable to observe the patient on oral pain relief medications for 12 to 24 hr before discharge from the hospital.
6. Analgesic medications should be used in combination with psychological, behavioral, and physical modalities in the management of sickle cell disease.
   - Incentive spirometry is recommended in patients hospitalized for a vasoocclusive crisis.
- Aggressively diagnose and treat any potential complications (e.g., septic necrosis of the femoral head, priapism, bony infarcts, and acute chest syndrome).
- Overall strategies for the management of acute chest syndrome are described in Table 1S-16.
- Hydroxurea (15 mg/kg body weight per day in patients with normal creatinine clearance)

increases hemoglobin F levels and reduces the incidence of vasoocclusive complications. It is generally well tolerated. Side effects consist primarily of mild, reversible neutropenia. There is strong evidence to support use of hydroxyurea therapy in patients 9 mo and older to decrease the frequency of vasoocclusive crises and acute chest syndrome. Hydroxyurea therapy is also strongly recommended for adults with three or more vasoocclusive crises during any 12-month period, with SCD pain or chronic anemia interfering with daily activities, or with severe or recurrent episodes of acute chest syndrome. It should be avoided in patients with existing leukopenia, thrombocytopenia, or severe hypoplastic anemia. It is indicated for adults with sickle cell anemia who have moderate to severe disease, typically those with three or more acute painful crises or episodes of the acute chest syndrome in the previous year.
- Replace folic acid (1 mg PO qd) due to loss from increased utilization of folic acid stores due to chronic hemolysis. Sickle cell patients also often have mineral and vitamin deficiencies (calcium, zinc, and vitamins A, C, D, and E) and may need vitamin and nutritional supplementation.

CHRONIC Rx

- Guidelines for prompt management of fever, infections, pain, and specific complications should be reviewed.
- Genetic counseling is recommended in all cases.
- Silent cerebral infarcts are the most common neurologic injury in children with sickle cell anemia and are associated with the recurrence of an infarct (stroke or silent cerebral infarct) and impaired cognition. A recent trial revealed that regular blood-transfusion therapy significantly reduced the incidence of cerebral infarct in children

---

TABLE 1S-16 Overall Strategies for the Management of Acute Chest Syndrome

Prevention

Incentive spirometry and periodic ambulation in patients admitted for vasoocclusive crises, surgery, or febrile episodes

Watchful waiting in any hospitalized child or adult with sickle cell disease (pulse oximetry monitoring and frequent respiratory assessments)

Avoidance of overhydration

Intense education and optimum care of patients who have sickle cell anemia and asthma

Diagnostic Testing and Laboratory Monitoring

Blood cultures

Nasopharyngeal samples for viral culture (respiratory syncytial virus, influenza)

Blood counts every day and appropriate chemistries

Continuous pulse oximetry

Chest radiographs

Treatment

Blood transfusion (simple or exchange)

Supplemental O_2 for drop in pulse oximetry by 4% over baseline, or values <90%

Empirical antibiotics (cephalosporin and macrolide)

Continued respiratory therapy (incentive spirometry and chest physiotherapy as necessary)

Bronchodilators and steroids for patients with asthma

Optimum pain control and fluid management

From Kliegman RM et al: *Nelson textbook of pediatrics*, ed 19, Philadelphia, 2011, Saunders.

with sickle cell anemia. Additional research is required before these results can be translated into medical practice to develop a balance between stroke prevention and avoidance of unnecessary transfusions. Exchange transfusions may be necessary for patients with acute neurologic signs, in aplastic crisis, or undergoing surgery. The target hemoglobin level is 10 to 11 g/dl (hematocrit 30%). Transfusing to a higher Hb/Hct should be avoided due to associated hyperviscosity if there is a substantial portion of HbS in the blood. Indications for transfusion in sickle cell disease are described in Table 1S-17. Serum ferritin level should be monitored quarterly. Iron overload due to blood transfusions (transfusional hemosiderosis) can be treated with chelating agents (deferoxamine [SC infusion], deferasirox [PO], and deferiprone [PO]).

- Angiotensin-converting enzyme inhibitor therapy is recommended for microalbuminuria in adults with SCD.
- Children and adults with proliferative sickle cell retinopathy should be referred to specialists for consideration of laser photocoagulation.
- Allogeneic stem cell transplantation can be curative in young patients with symptomatic sickle cell disease; however, the death rate from the procedure is nearly 10%, the marrow recipients are likely to be infertile, and there is an undefined risk of chemotherapy-induced malignancy. Myeloablative stem cell transplantation is generally limited to children under age 16 with severe disease.
- Penicillin V 125 mg PO bid should be administered by age 2 mo and increased to 250 mg bid by age 3 yr. Penicillin prophylaxis can be discontinued after age 5 yr except in children who have had splenectomy.
- Table 1S-18 summarizes disease-modifying treatments to consider.

REFERRAL

- Hospitalization is generally recommended for most crises and complications.
- Psychosocial counseling and support structures should be developed.
- At least yearly evaluation by a hematologist competent in sickle cell anemia is recommended in all patients with sickle cell anemia. Children with transcranial doppler ultrasonography >170 cm per second should be referred to a subspecialist with expertise in long-term transfusion therapy for stroke prevention.
- Referral to a nephrologist if proteinuria is detected (>300 mg/24 h).
- Patients with pulmonary hypertension should follow up with a cardiologist and a pulmonologist.
- Referral to an ophtalmologist for an annual dilated retinal examination beginning at 10 yr of age. Persons with normal dilated retinal exam should be rescreened at 1- to 2-yr intervals.

TABLE 1S-17 Indications for Transfusion in Sickle Cell Disease

	Duration	Consensus	Method	Goal*
Stroke, acute	Single	+	Ex	HbS <30%
Stroke, ongoing care	Chronic	+	Either	HbS <30%
High-velocity transcranial Doppler	Chronic	+	Either	HbS <30%
ACS, initial episode	Single	+	Dir > Ex	Hgb 10
ACS, recurrent	6-12 mo	+	Either	
Pulmonary hypertension	Chronic	+	Either	
Multiorgan failure	Single	+	Ex	
Major surgery	Single	+	Dir	Hgb 10
Acute anemia	Single	+	Dir	
Recurrent spleen sequestration	Chronic	+		
Sepsis/meningitis	Single	+	Dir	
Severe chronic pain	6-12 mo	+		
Congestive heart failure	Chronic	+		
Silent infarct with abnormal neuropsychology	Chronic	−		
Pregnancy		−		
Anemia/renal failure	Chronic	−		
Leg ulcers	6-12 mo	−		
Severe growth delay		−		
Severe eye disease		−		
Priapism		−		

ACS, Acute chest syndrome; *Dir*, direct; *Ex*, exchange; *Hb*, hemoglobin type; *Hgb*, hemoglobin concentration; +, consensus reached; −, consensus not reached.
*Goal of transfusion if a consensus has been reached.
From Fuhrman BP et al: *Pediatric critical care*, ed 4, Philadelphia, 2011, Saunders.

TABLE 1S-18 Disease-Modifying Treatments to Consider*

Robust clinical data	Penicillin prophylaxis
	Streptococcus pneumoniae vaccination
	Hydroxyurea
	Chronic exchange transfusion
	Iron chelation for chronic iron overload[†]
Limited clinical data	Folate supplementation[‡]
	Haemophilus influenzae vaccination
	Influenza vaccination
	Erythropoietin
	Phlebotomy
Experimental	Hb F reactivation with decitabine, histone deacetylase inhibitors, or imids
	Erythropoietin for chronic relative reticulocytopenia
	Nutritional supplements and antioxidants (e.g., glutamine, zinc, multivitamins)
	N-acetylcysteine

Hb F, Fetal hemoglobin.
*See text for specific indications and limitations.
[†]Best data from thalassemia patient experience.
[‡]Risks minimal (however, can mask vitamin B_{12} deficiency). Therefore, it is generally done.
From Hoffman R: Hematology, basic principles and practice, ed 6, Philadelphia, 2013, Saunders.

❗ PEARLS & CONSIDERATIONS

COMMENTS

- Pain in adults with sickle cell disease is the rule rather than the exception and needs to be treated appropriately.
- Patients and their families should receive genetic counseling and should be made aware of the difference between sickle cell trait and sickle cell disease.
- Regular immunizations and pneumococcal vaccination are recommended. The prophylactic administration of penicillin soon after birth and the timely administration of pneumococcal and *Haemophilus influenzae* type b vaccines have resulted in a significant decline in the incidence of these infections. The heptavalent conjugated pneumococcal

vaccine (Prevan) should be administered from 2 mo of age. The 23-valent unconjugated pneumococcal vaccine is given from age 2 yr and can be boosted once 3 yr later. Influenza vaccination can be given after 6 mo of age.

- Patients should be instructed on a well-balanced diet and appropriate folic acid supplementation.
- The presence of dactylitis, Hb 7, or leukocytosis in the absence of infection during the first 2 yr of life indicates a higher risk of severe sickle cell disease later in life.
- Among patients with sickle cell disease, acute chest syndrome is commonly precipitated by fat embolism and infection, especially community-acquired pneumonia. Among older patients and those with neurologic symptoms, the syndrome often progresses to respiratory failure.
- Poloxamer 188, a nonionic surfactant with hemorheologic and antithrombotic properties, has been reported to produce a significant but relatively small decrease in the duration of painful episodes and an increase in the proportion of patients who achieved resolution of the symptoms. A more significant effect was observed in patients who received concomitant hydroxyurea.
- Pulmonary hypertension is a complication of chronic hemolysis and is associated with a high risk of death. It can be detected by Doppler echocardiography in more than 30% of adult patients with sickle cell disease. Cardiac catheterization will confirm the diagnosis. It is resistant to hydroxyurea therapy.
- Neurocognitive brain dysfunction is common in sickle cell disease. Trials have shown that compared with healthy controls, adults with sickle cell disease have a poorer cognitive performance, which is associated with anemia and age.
- Among patients with sickle cell disease hospitalized with vasoocclusive pain crisis, the use of inhaled nitric oxide compared with placebo did not improve time to crisis resolution.
- The average life span of individuals with sickle cell trait is similar to that of the general population. However, it is associated with a higher incidence of renal medullary cancer.

SUGGESTED READINGS
Available at www.expertconsult.com

RELATED CONTENT
Sickle Cell Anemia (Patient Information)

AUTHOR: **FRED F. FERRI, M.D.**

 BASIC INFORMATION

DEFINITION

Sinus node dysfunction is a group of cardiac rhythm disturbances characterized by abnormalities of the sinus node, including (1) chronic, inappropriate bradycardia; (2) sinus pauses, arrest, or exit block; (3) sinoatrial exit block; and (4) alternating sinus bradycardia with paroxysmal supraventricular tachyarrhythmias (frequently atrial fibrillation) known as tachycardia-bradycardia syndrome. When sinus node dysfunction is associated with symptoms, it is called sick sinus syndrome (SSS).

SYNONYMS

Sinus pause
Sinus arrest
Tachycardia-bradycardia syndrome
Sinoatrial exit block
SSS
Bradycardia-tachycardia syndrome

ICD-10CM CODES
I49.5 Sick sinus syndrome

EPIDEMIOLOGY & DEMOGRAPHICS

- In children: associated with congenital and acquired heart disease, particularly after cardiac surgery.
- In adults: it is primarily a disease of the elderly secondary to idiopathic degenerative disease. A recent population study has suggested that white race, increased BMI, prolonged baseline QRS or right bundle branch block, HTN, or other cardiovascular diseases are associated with increased incidence of sick sinus syndrome.

PHYSICAL FINDINGS & CLINICAL PRESENTATION

- Light-headedness, syncope, presyncope, palpitations. Other manifestations include dyspnea on exertion and worsening angina.
- Physical examination may be normal or reveal abnormalities (e.g., signs of congestive heart failure, heart murmurs, or gallop sounds) associated with the underlying heart disease.

ETIOLOGY

- Sinus node fibrosis is the primary etiology, which may also affect the atrioventricular node, the His bundle, or its branches.
- Polypharmacy should be considered, and obtaining an accurate medicine list is essential.
- In addition, acute coronary syndromes, diseases of the SA nodal artery, inflammatory and infiltrative diseases such as hemochromatosis, amyloidosis, collagen vascular diseases (SLE and scleroderma), epicardial and pericardial diseases, medications (beta-blockers, calcium channel blockers, methyldopa, cimetidine, clonidine, lithium and antiarrhythmics), trauma following cardiac surgery, hypothyroidism, hypothermia, hypoxia, sepsis, muscular dystrophies (myotonic dystrophy, Friedreich ataxia), infectious etiologies such as Lyme disease, increased intracranial pressure.

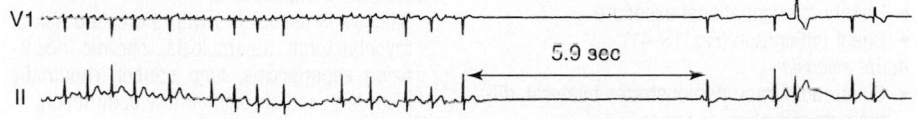

FIGURE 1S-39 Tachycardia-bradycardia syndrome. Two surface ECG leads show atrial fibrillation that spontaneously terminates followed by a 5.9-second pause before sinus rhythm resumes. The patient became light-headed during this period. (From Issa Z et al: *Clinical arrhythmology and electrophysiology*, ed 2, Philadelphia, 2012, Saunders.)

 **DIAGNOSIS**

DIFFERENTIAL DIAGNOSIS

- Bradycardia: atrioventricular block
- Tachycardia: atrial fibrillation or atrial flutter
- Sinus tachycardia
- Medication toxicity

WORKUP

- ECG (Fig. 1S-39)
- Ambulatory cardiac rhythm monitoring
- 24-hour ambulatory ECG (Holter) with diary to correlate symptoms to findings
- Event recorder or a loop recorder if symptoms are less frequent
- Exercise stress testing to evaluate the severity of chronotropic incompetence
- Electrophysiologic testing, including sinus nodal recovery time and sinoatrial conduction time

TREATMENT

- Permanent pacemaker placement is primarily indicated if bradycardia is symptomatic. Indications for permanent pacemaker in sinus node dysfunction are described in Table 1S-19.
- In tachycardia-bradycardia syndrome, drug treatment is indicated for tachycardia, primarily with AV node blocking agents after placement of the permanent pacemaker.

REFERRAL
To cardiologist

SUGGESTED READINGS
Available at www.expertconsult.com

AUTHORS: **AMANDA C. DORAN, M.D., PH.D.,** and **DANIEL R. FRISCH, M.D.**

Diseases and Disorders

S

TABLE 1S-19   Indications for Permanent Pacing in Sinus Node Dysfunction

Class	Indications
I	• Sinus node dysfunction with documented symptomatic bradycardia or sinus pauses • Symptomatic sinus bradycardia that is iatrogenic and will occur as a consequence of essential long-term therapy of a type and dose of drugs for which there are no acceptable alternatives. • Symptomatic chronotropic incompetence.
IIa	• Sinus node dysfunction, occurring spontaneously or as a result of necessary drug therapy, with a heart rate of less than 40 beats/min when a clear association between significant symptoms consistent with bradycardia has not been documented. • Unexplained syncope when sinus abnormalities are observed or provoked with electrophysiologic study.
IIb	• A chronic heart rate of less than 40 beats/min, while awake, in the minimally symptomatic patient.
III	• Sinus node dysfunction in asymptomatic patients, including those in whom substantial sinus bradycardia (heart rate of less than 40 beats/min) is a consequence of long-term drug treatment. • Sinus node dysfunction in which symptoms suggestive of bradycardia are clearly documented as not associated with a slow heart rate. • Symptomatic bradycardia associated with nonessential drug therapy.

ACC, American College of Cardiology; *AHA*, American Heart Association; *HRA*, Heart Rhythm Society.
Adapted from ACC/AHA/HRS 2008 revised guidelines.

BASIC INFORMATION

DEFINITION

Silicosis is a lung disease attributable to the inhalation of silica (silicon dioxide) in crystalline form (quartz) or in cristobalite or tridymite forms.

SYNONYMS

Pneumoconiosis caused by silica

ICD-10CM CODES
J62.8 Pneumoconiosis due to other dust containing silica

EPIDEMIOLOGY & DEMOGRAPHICS

- Occupational disease affecting men and women involved in gathering, milling, processing, or using silica-containing rock or sand. Jobs that can lead to silicosis are described in Box 1S-6.
- An estimated 200,000 miners and 1.7 million others have experienced an occupational exposure to silica.

PHYSICAL FINDINGS & CLINICAL PRESENTATION

- There are three patterns of silicosis: acute, chronic, and accelerated.
- Simple silicosis may be asymptomatic with the only manifestation being an abnormal chest radiograph.
- Acute silicosis is also known as silicoproteinosis. Develops several weeks to <5 years after silica exposure. Presents with rapid onset of cough, weight loss, fatigue, and pleuritic chest pain.
- Chronic silicosis will present with cough, dyspnea, and sputum production in 35% of the cases. It is the most common clinical presentation, and onset is after decades of repeated exposure.
- Accelerated silicosis may have an initial asymptomatic phase followed by increasing frequency of symptoms parallel with worsening radiographic abnormalities. Develops <10 years after initial high-level exposure.

BOX 1S-6   Jobs That Can Lead to Silicosis

Mining: surface or underground mining (tunneling)
Milling: ground silica for abrasives and filler
Quarrying
Sandblasting (e.g., of buildings, preparing steel for painting)
Pottery; ceramic or clay work
Grinding, polishing using silica wheels
Stone work
Foundry work: grinding, molding, chipping
Refractory brick work
Glass making: to polish and as an abrasive
Boiler work: cleaning boilers
Manufacture of abrasives

From Goldman L, Schafer AI: *Goldman's Cecil medicine*, ed 24, Philadelphia, 2012, Saunders.

ETIOLOGY

- Silica particles are ingested by alveolar macrophages, which in turn release oxidants causing cell injury and cell death, attract fibroblasts, and activate lymphocytes, increasing immunoglobulins in the alveolar space.
- Hyperplasia of alveolar epithelial cells occurs.
- Collagen accumulates in the interstitium.
- Neutrophils also accumulate and secrete proteolytic enzymes, which leads to tissue destruction and emphysema.
- Silica dust may be carcinogenic (not proven).
- Exposure to silicosis predisposes to tuberculosis.
- Some patients develop rheumatoid silicotic pulmonary nodules and may have arthritic symptoms of rheumatoid arthritis (Caplan's syndrome). Scleroderma has also been associated with silicosis.

DIAGNOSIS

DIFFERENTIAL DIAGNOSIS

- Other pneumoconiosis, berylliosis, hard metal disease, asbestosis
- Sarcoidosis
- Tuberculosis
- Interstitial lung disease
- Hypersensitivity pneumonitis
- Lung cancer
- Langerhans' cell granulomatosis (histiocytosis X)
- Granulomatous pulmonary vasculitis

WORKUP

- History of occupational exposure
- Chest radiograph (Fig. 1S-41)

Acute silicosis:
- Chest radiograph demonstrates bilateral, diffuse ground-glass opacities.
- Chest CT demonstrates diffuse nodular and patchy consolidative opacities.
- Milky and lipoproteinaceous effluent is seen on bronchoalveolar lavage (BAL).
- Lung biopsy is not necessary in the setting of a definite exposure history.

- Exclusion of other causes like pulmonary edema, alveolar hemorrhage, and pulmonary alveolar proteinosis is necessary.

Chronic silicosis:
- Chest radiographic demonstrates multiple small, rounded opacities (<10 cm in diameter) distributed in the upper lung zones.
- Progressive massive fibrosis (PMF) refers to coalescence of the nodules of chronic silicosis with calcified hilar adenopathy.
- Pulmonary function tests (PFT) shows mixed obstructive and restrictive defect.
- High resolution CT scan (HRCT), bronchoscopy, and lung biopsies have limited diagnostic role unless atypical radiographic features are noted.

Accelerated silicosis
- Radiographic pattern is that of simple silicosis, although development of radiographic abnormalities is more rapid. This has greater risk for PMF.

TREATMENT

- Treatment is symptomatic (supplemental O_2 for hypoxemia, bronchodilators, antibiotics for infections).
- Prevention (industrial hygiene).
- Smoking cessation.
- Supportive measures (oxygen, bronchodilators).
- Vaccination against influenza and pneumococcus.
- Whole-lung lavage may have a role in acute silicoproteinosis.
- Treatment of associated tuberculosis if present.
- Consider lung transplant for patients who develop chronic respiratory failure.

Associated Complications
- Silicosis is associated with increased risk of mycobacterial tuberculosis, chronic necrotizing aspergillosis, lung cancer, rheumatic disorders, and chronic airflow obstruction.

RELATED CONTENT

Silicosis (Patient Information)

AUTHORS: **MICHAEL AGUSTIN, M.D.,** and **SAMAAN RAFEQ, M.D.**

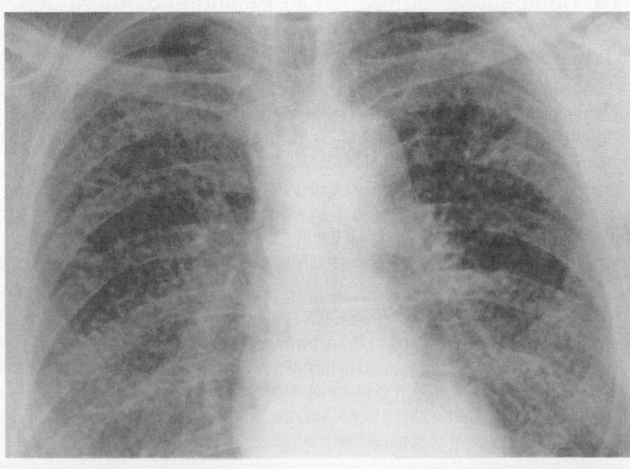

FIGURE 1S-41 Simple silicosis. There are multiple small (2- to 4-mm) nodules distributed throughout the lungs, with an upper lobe predominance. (From McLoud TC: *Thoracic radiology: the requisites,* St Louis, 1998, Mosby.)

BASIC INFORMATION

DEFINITION

Sinusitis is inflammation of the mucous membranes lining one or more of the paranasal sinuses. The various presentations are:
- Acute sinusitis: infection lasting <4 wk, with complete resolution of symptoms.
- Subacute infection: lasts from 4 to 12 wk, with complete resolution of symptoms.
- Recurrent acute infection: episodes of acute infection lasting <30 days, with resolution of symptoms, which recur at intervals at least 10 days apart.
- Chronic sinusitis: inflammation of the sinosinal cavities lasting >12 wk, with persistent upper respiratory symptoms. It accounts for 1% to 2% of total physcian encounters.
- Acute bacterial sinusitis superimposed on chronic sinusitis: new symptoms that occur in patients with residual symptoms from prior infection(s). With treatment, the new symptoms resolve but the residual ones do not.

SYNONYMS

Rhinosinusitis: sinusitis is almost always accompanied by inflammation of the nasal mucosa; thus it is now the preferred term.

ICD-10CM CODES
J32.9	Chronic sinusitis, unspecified
J01.90	Acute sinusitis, unspecified
J01.00	Acute maxillary sinusitis, unspecified
J01.01	Acute recurrent maxillary sinusitis
J01.10	Acute frontal sinusitis, unspecified
J01.11	Acute recurrent frontal sinusitis
J01.20	Acute ethmoidal sinusitis, unspecified
J01.21	Acute recurrent ethmoidal sinusitis
J01.30	Acute sphenoidal sinusitis, unspecified
J01.31	Acute recurrent sphenoidal sinusitis
J01.80	Other acute sinusitis
J01.81	Other acute recurrent sinusitis
J01.91	Acute recurrent sinusitis, unspecified
J32.0	Chronic maxillary sinusitis
J32.1	Chronic frontal sinusitis
J32.2	Chronic ethmoidal sinusitis
J32.3	Chronic sphenoidal sinusitis
J32.8	Other chronic sinusitis

EPIDEMIOLOGY & DEMOGRAPHICS

INCIDENCE (IN U.S.): Seems to correlate with the incidence of upper respiratory tract infections and higher in women than men; 30 million cases a year in the United States.

PEAK INCIDENCE:
- Fall, winter, spring: September through March
- In adults: greatest incidence between 45 and 74 years of age
- Approximately 6% to 7% of children presenting with respiratory symptoms have acute sinusitis.

PHYSICAL FINDINGS & CLINICAL PRESENTATION

- Patients often give a history of a recent upper respiratory illness with some improvement, then a relapse.
- Mucopurulent secretions in the nasal passage:
  1. Purulent nasal and postnasal discharge lasting 7 to 10 days
  2. Facial tightness, pressure, or pain
  3. Nasal obstruction
  4. Headache
  5. Decreased sense of smell
  6. Purulent pharyngeal secretions, brought up with cough, often worse at night
- Erythema, swelling, and tenderness over the infected sinus in a small proportion of patients:
  1. Diagnosis cannot be excluded by the absence of such findings.
  2. These findings are not common, and do not correlate with number of positive sinus aspirates.
- Intermittent low-grade fever in about half of adults with acute bacterial sinusitis.
- Toothache is a common complaint when the maxillary sinus is involved.
- Periorbital cellulitis and excessive tearing with ethmoid sinusitis:
  1. Orbital extension of infection: chemosis, proptosis, impaired extraocular movements
- Characteristics of acute sinusitis in children with upper respiratory tract infections:
  1. Persistence of symptoms
  2. Cough
  3. Bad breath
- Symptoms of chronic sinusitis (may or may not be present):
  1. Nasal or postnasal discharge
  2. Fever
  3. Facial pain or pressure
  4. Headache
- Nosocomial sinusitis is typically seen in patients with nasogastric tubes or nasotracheal intubation.

ETIOLOGY

- Each of the four paranasal sinuses is connected to the nasal cavity by narrow tubes (ostia), 1 to 3 mm in diameter; these drain directly into the nose through the turbinates. The sinuses are lined with a ciliated mucous membrane (mucoperiosteum).
- Acute viral infection:
  1. Infection with the common cold or influenza
  2. Mucosal edema and sinus inflammation
  3. Decreased drainage of thick secretions/obstruction of the sinus ostia
  4. Subsequent entrapment of bacteria
     a. Multiplication of bacteria
     b. Secondary bacterial infection
- Other predisposing factors:
  1. Tumors
  2. Polyps
  3. Foreign bodies
  4. Congenital choanal atresia
  5. Other entities that cause obstruction of sinus drainage
  6. Allergies
  7. Asthma
- Dental infections lead to maxillary sinusitis.
- Viruses recovered alone or in combination with bacteria (in 16% of cases):
  1. Rhinovirus
  2. Coronavirus
  3. Adenovirus
  4. Parainfluenza virus
  5. Respiratory syncytial virus
- The principal bacterial pathogens in sinusitis are *Streptococcus pneumoniae*, nontypable *Haemophilus influenzae*, and *Moraxella catarrhalis*.
- In the remainder of cases *Streptococcus pyogenes, Staphylococcus aureus,* beta-hemolytic streptococci, and mixed anaerobic infections (*Peptostreptococcus, Fusobacterium, Bacteroides, Prevotella* spp.) are found.
- Infection is polymicrobial in about one third of cases.
- Anaerobic infections are seen more often in cases of chronic sinusitis and in cases associated with dental infection; anaerobes are unlikely pathogens in sinusitis in children.
- Fungal pathogens are isolated with increasing frequency in immunocompromised patients but remain uncommon pathogens in the paranasal sinuses. Fungal pathogens include: *Phaeohyphomycosis, Aspergillus, Pseudallescheria, Sporothrix,* and *Zygomycetes* spp.
- Nosocomial infections: occur in patients with nasogastric tubes, nasotracheal intubation, cystic fibrosis, and immunocompromised state.
  1. *S. aureus* (including MRSA)
  2. *Pseudomonas aeruginosa*
  3. *Klebsiella pneumoniae*
  4. *Enterobacter* spp.
  5. *Proteus mirabilis*
- Organisms typically isolated in chronic sinusitis:
  1. *S. aureus*
  2. *S. pneumoniae*
  3. *H. influenzae*
  4. *P. aeruginosa*
  5. *Anaerobes*

DIAGNOSIS

DIFFERENTIAL DIAGNOSIS

- Temporomandibular joint disease
- Migraine headache
- Cluster headache
- Dental infection
- Trigeminal neuralgia
- Allergic rhinitis
- Drugs (cocaine, decongestant overuse)
- Gastroesophageal reflux disease
- Wegener granulomatosis
- Cystic fibrosis

WORKUP

- The diagnosis is generally based on clinical signs and symptoms (purulent rhinorrhea and facial pain). Radiologic tests and cultures are not recommended initially and should be considered only when treatment is ineffective and sinusitis persists.
- In the normal healthy host, the paranasal sinuses should be sterile. Although the contiguous structures are colonized with bacteria and likely contaminate the sinuses, the mucociliary lining functions to remove these bacteria.
- Gold standard for diagnosis: recovery of bacteria in high-density $\geq 10^4$ colony-forming

units/ml from a paranasal sinus, in the setting of a patient with history of upper respiratory infection and symptoms persisting for 7 to 10 days. Sinus aspiration is the best method for obtaining cultures; however, it must be performed by an otorhinolaryngologist and is not practical for the primary care practitioner. Therefore, most diagnoses are based on the clinical history and presentation, possibly supported by radiologic evaluations.

1. Overall, standard radiographs are of limited use in diagnosis, although negative films are strong evidence against the diagnosis
2. CT scans:
   a. Much more sensitive than plain radiographs in detecting acute changes and disease in the sinuses
   b. Recommended for patients requiring surgical intervention, including sinus aspiration; it is a useful adjunct to guide therapy
3. Transillumination:
   a. Used for diagnosis of frontal and maxillary sinusitis
   b. Absence of light transmission indicates that sinus is filled with fluid
   c. Dullness (decreased light transmission) is less helpful in diagnosing infection
4. Endoscopy:
   a. Used to visualize secretions coming from the ostia of infected sinuses
   b. Culture collection via endoscopy often contaminated by nasal flora; not nearly as good as sinus puncture
5. Sinus puncture:
   a. Gold standard for collecting sinus cultures
   b. Generally reserved for treatment failures, suspected intracranial extension, and nosocomial sinusitis

 **TREATMENT**

NONPHARMACOLOGIC THERAPY

To help promote sinus drainage:
- Air humidification with vaporizers (for steam) or humidifiers (for a cool mist)
- Application of hot, wet towel over the face
- Sipping hot beverages
- Hydration

ACUTE GENERAL Rx

- Sinus drainage:
  1. Nasal vasoconstrictors, such as phenylephrine nose drops, 0.25% or 0.5%
  2. Topical decongestants should not be used for more than a few days because of the risk of rebound congestion
  3. Systemic decongestants
  4. Corticosteroids: Nasal or systemic corticosteroids, such as nasal beclomethasone. Oral corticosteroids combined with antibiotics may be associated with modest benefit for short-term relief of symptoms in adults with severe symptoms of acute sinusitis compared with antibiotics alone.

Oral corticosteroids as monotherapy are not associated with improved clinical outcomes in adults with clinically diagnosed acute sinusitis.[1]
5. Nasal irrigation, with hypertonic or normal saline (saline may act as a mild vasoconstrictor of nasal blood flow)
6. Use of antihistamines has no proven benefit, and the drying effect on the mucous membranes may cause crusting, which blocks the ostia, thus interfering with sinus drainage
- Analgesics, antipyretics

Antimicrobial therapy:
- Most cases of acute sinusitis have a viral cause and will resolve within 2 wk without antibiotics.
- Current treatment recommendations favor symptomatic treatment for those with mild symptoms. Physicians grossly overprescribe antibiotics for presumed bacterial sinusitis despite a much higher prevalence of viral infections.
- Antibiotics should not be prescribed for mild to moderate sinusitis within the first week of illness. They should be reserved for those with severe symptoms who meet the criteria for diagnosis of sinusitis.
- Antibiotic therapy is usually empiric, targeting the common pathogens:
  1. First-line antibiotics in children include amoxicillin or amoxicillin/clavulanate. For adults amoxicillin/clavulanate or doxycycline is first-line agent, with quinolones (levofloxacin or moxifloxacin) reserved as second-line agents unless patient is penicillin allergic.
  2. Second-line antibiotics include the newer macrolides: clarithromycin, and oral cephalosporins: cefuroxime axetil, cefprozil, cefaclor, loracarbef, but high rate of resistance of *S. pneumoniae* is a concern with these agents as is *H. influenzae* resistance with TMP-SMX and azithromycin such that they should no longer be used as first-line agents.
  3. For patients with uncomplicated acute sinusitis, the less expensive first-line agents appear to be as effective as the costlier second-line agents.
- Hospitalization and IV antibiotics may be required for more severe infection and those with suspected intracranial complications. Broader-spectrum antibiotic coverage may be indicated in severe cases, to cover for MRSA, *Pseudomonas*, and fungal pathogens.
- Duration of therapy generally 5 to 7 days in adults rather than 10 to 14 days as recommended in the past.

Optimal duration of treatment in children varies from 10 to 28 days.

Surgery:
- Surgical drainage indicated
  1. If intracranial or orbital complications suspected
  2. Many cases of frontal and sphenoid sinusitis
  3. Chronic sinusitis recalcitrant to medical therapy

- Surgical debridement imperative in the treatment of fungal sinusitis

Complications:
- Untreated, sinusitis may lead to a number of serious, life-threatening complications.
- Intracranial complications include meningitis, brain abscess, and epidural and subdural empyema.
- Intracranial sequelae are more common with frontal and ethmoid infections.
- Extracranial complications include orbital cellulitis, blindness, orbital abscess, osteomyelitis.
- Extracranial sequelae are more commonly seen with ethmoid sinusitis.

CHRONIC Rx

- Chronic sinusitis: Evidence supports daily high-volume saline irrigation with topical corticosteroid therapy at a first line therapy for chronic sinusitis. A short course of systemic corticosteroids (1-3 wk), short course of doxycycline (3 wk), or a leukotriene antagonist may be considered in patients with nasal polyps. A prolonged course (3 mo) of macrolide antibiotic may be considered for patients without polyps.[2]
- Surgical intervention may be necessary in nonresponders

REFERRAL

- To infectious disease specialist if failure to respond to initial therapy
- To otorhinolaryngologist for:
  1. Failure to respond to therapy
  2. Suspected fungal infection
  3. Suspected intracranial or orbital complications

ⓘ PEARLS & CONSIDERATIONS

- Recurrent sinusitis is usually related to anatomic defects, poor drainage, or immunocompromised states; such patients deserve a thorough workup by an ENT specialist and/or an infectious disease specialist.
- Nosocomial sinusitis from obstruction by nasotracheal or nasogastric tubes is not uncommon and can be difficult to recognize in patients in the critical care units.

SUGGESTED READINGS

Available at www.expertconsult.com

RELATED CONTENT

Sinusitis (Patient Information)

AUTHOR: **GLENN G. FORT, M.D., M.P.H.**

[1] Venekamp RP, et al.: Systemic corticosteroid therapy for acute sinusitis, *JAMA* 313(12):1258-1259, 2015.
[2] Rudmik L, Soler ZM: Medical Therapies for Adult Chronic Sinusitis: A Systematic Review, *JAMA* 314(9):926-939, 2015.

BASIC INFORMATION

DEFINITION

Sjögren's syndrome (SS) is an autoimmune disorder that targets exocrine glands. It is characterized by lymphocytic and plasma cell infiltration and destruction of salivary and lacrimal glands with subsequent diminished lacrimal and salivary gland secretions. It occurs in both primary and secondary forms.
- Primary: dry mouth (xerostomia) and dry eyes (xerophthalmia) develop as isolated entities.
- Secondary: associated with other autoimmune connective tissue diseases.

SYNONYMS

Sicca syndrome
Sicca complex

ICD-10CM CODES
M35.00 Sicca syndrome, unspecified
M35.01 Sicca syndrome with keratoconjunctivitis
M35.02 Sicca syndrome with lung involvement
M35.03 Sicca syndrome with myopathy
M35.04 Sicca syndrome with tubulointerstitial nephropathy
M35.09 Sicca syndrome with other organ involvement

EPIDEMIOLOGY & DEMOGRAPHICS

INCIDENCE: 3.9 per 100,000
PREVALENCE: Prevalence is 0.2% to 2.7% of population; secondary SS is also common and can affect up to 19% of patients with systemic lupus erythematosus (SLE) and 26% to 31% of rheumatoid arthritis (RA) and scleroderma patients.
PREDOMINANT SEX: Female/male ratio is approximately 10:1
PREDOMINANT AGE: Peak incidence is in the fourth and fifth decade, but SS can occur in all ages.
RISK FACTOR: Seen in all races/ethnicities, but more common in Caucasians.

PHYSICAL FINDINGS & CLINICAL PRESENTATION

- Diagnosis of SS is based on the presence of at least two of three objective diagnostic tests below:
  1. Positive serum levels of anti-SS-A/Ro and/or anti-SS-B/La or a positive rheumatoid factor and antinuclear antibody (ANA) titer of at least 1:320.
  2. Salivary gland biopsy exhibiting focal sites of inflammation. One or more sites of inflammation per 4 mm^2 is considered to be positive.
  3. Keratoconjunctivitis sicca with ocular staining score of three or more (the dissipation rate of a specialized dye that is applied to the tear film that bathes the surface of the eye; a score of three or more is considered to be positive).
- Dry mouth with dry lips (cheilosis), erythema of tongue (Fig. 1S-42) and other mucosal surfaces, carious teeth
- Dry eyes (conjunctival injection, corneal ulceration, blurred vision, decreased luster, enlargement of lacrimal glands, and irregularity of the corneal light reflex)
- Salivary gland enlargement and dysfunction, with subsequent difficulty in chewing and swallowing food and in speaking without frequent water intake, thickened saliva, and burning sensation in mouth
- Leukocytoclastic vasculitis may be present.
- Skin ulceration, photosensitivity, and allergic drug eruptions
- Extraglandular involvement occurs in 50% of patients. There are multiple systemic manifestations associated with SS, which include the following:
  1. Dyspareunia and pruritus can occur secondary to vaginal dryness.
  2. Pulmonary involvement includes interstitial lung disease (e.g., NSIP), chronic obstructive pulmonary disease, lymphocytic interstitial pneumonitis, fibrosis, and xerotrachea.
  3. Gastrointestinal conditions such as celiac disease, esophageal dysmotility, type I

autoimmune hepatitis, primary biliary cirrhosis, and pancreatitis can occur.
  4. Renal manifestations include renal tubular acidosis, Fanconi syndrome, glomerulonephritis, and interstitial nephritis.
  5. Neurologic involvement including peripheral neuropathy and trigeminal neuropathy.
  6. Musculoskeletal symptoms including arthralgias and polymyopathy.
  7. Hematologic conditions such as lymphoma and pancytopenia. Nearly 5% of patients develop B-cell lymphoma.
  8. RA and other connective tissue diseases are present in secondary SS.
  9. Autoimmune thyroiditis may be observed in patients with SS.

ETIOLOGY

Sjögren's syndrome is an autoimmune disorder of unclear etiology. It is associated with certain HLA-DQ and HLA-DR alleles. It has been postulated that viral agents (e.g., hepatitis C and Epstein-Barr virus) may trigger the clinical manifestations.

DIAGNOSIS

DIFFERENTIAL DIAGNOSIS
- Medication-related dryness (e.g., anticholinergics, antihistamines)
- Age-related exocrine gland dysfunction
- Mouth breathing
- Anxiety
- HIV infection
- Hepatitis C infection
- Diabetes mellitus
- Chronic sialadenitis
- Acromegaly
- Type V hyperlipidemia
- Graft-versus-host disease
- Other: sarcoidosis, primary salivary hypofunction, radiation injury, amyloidosis
- IgG4-related disease
- Ocular herpetic lesions, blepharitis, corneal abrasions
- An algorithm for the diagnosis of SS is provided in Fig. 1S-43.

WORKUP

Workup involves ocular and oral examination and laboratory and radiographic testing to demonstrate the following criteria for diagnosis of primary and secondary SS.
PRIMARY:
- Symptoms and objective signs of ocular dryness:
  1. Schirmer's test (Fig. 1S-44): <5 mm wetting per 5 min
  2. Positive rose-bengal or fluorescein staining of cornea and conjunctiva to demonstrate keratoconjunctivitis sicca
  3. Tear breakup time and tear osmolality measured after instillation of fluorescein
- Symptoms and objective signs of dry mouth:
  1. Decreased parotid flow using Lashley cups or other methods

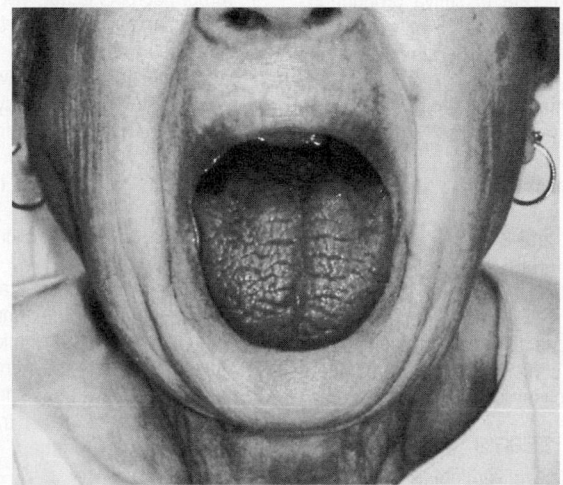

FIGURE 1S-42 "Crocodile tongue" in a patient with Sjögren's syndrome. (From Noble J: *Primary care medicine,* ed 3, St Louis, 2001, Mosby.)

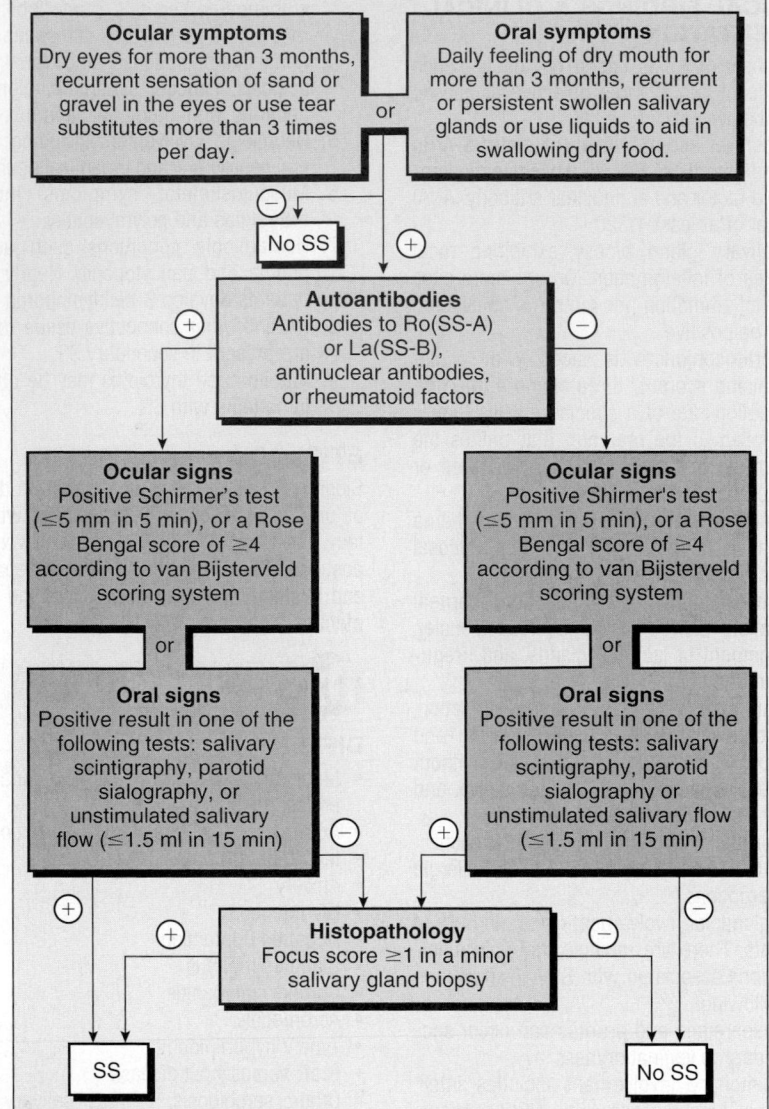

FIGURE 1S-43 Suggested algorithm for the diagnosis of Sjögren's syndrome. Exclusion criteria include hepatitis C or human immunodeficiency virus infection, sarcoidosis, graft-versus-host disease, preexisting lymphoma, previous head or neck irradiation, and use of anticholinergic drugs. (From Hochberg MC et al: *Rheumatology,* ed 5, St Louis, 2011, Mosby.)

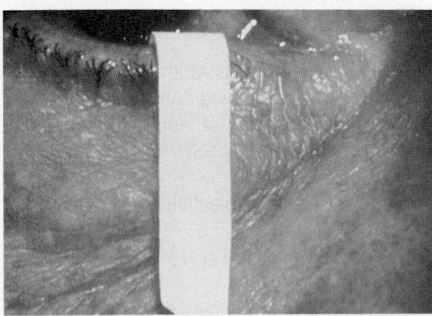

FIGURE 1S-44 Schirmer test in a patient with Sjögren's syndrome. Wetting of less than 5 mm/5 min of the filter paper strip is shown. (From Hochberg MC et al: *Rheumatology,* ed 5, St Louis, 2011, Mosby.)

2. Abnormal biopsy result of minor salivary gland (focus score >1 based on average of four assessable lobules)

3. Assessment of rate of saliva production in which collection of ≤1.5 mL after two expectorations 15 min apart is considered positive

- Evidence of systemic autoimmune disorder:
  1. Elevated rheumatoid factor (70%-90% of patients)
  2. Elevated titer of ANA >1:320 (80% of patients)
  3. Presence of anti-SS-A (Ro) (>60% of patients) or anti-SS-B (La) antibodies (40% of patients)

SECONDARY:
- Characteristic signs and symptoms of SS
- Clinical features sufficient to allow a diagnosis of RA, SLE, polymyositis, or scleroderma

LABORATORY TESTS
- Positive ANA (80% of patients) with autoantibodies anti-SS-A and anti-SS-B may be present.

- Additional laboratory abnormalities may include elevated erythrocyte sedimentation rate, anemia (normochromic, normocytic), abnormal liver function studies, elevated serum beta$_2$ microglobulin levels, rheumatoid factor, hypergammaglobulinemia, antibodies to double–stranded DNA in cases with proteinuria, serum C3 and C4, and cryoglobulins (30% of patients).
- A definite diagnosis of SS can be made with a salivary gland biopsy showing focal lymphocytic sialadenitis with focus score of 1 per 4 mm^2 of glandular tissue.

Rx TREATMENT

NONPHARMACOLOGIC THERAPY
- Adequate fluid replacement. Ameliorate skin dryness by gently blotting dry after bathing, leaving a small amount of moisture, and then applying a moisturizer.
- Increased environmental moisture by using humidifiers
- Proper oral hygiene (daily topical fluoride use, antimicrobial mouth rinses, and stabilization of oral cavity pH) to reduce the incidence of caries.
- Sugar-free chewing gum and sour lemon lozenges to stimulate salivary secretion.
- Periodic dental and ophthalmologic evaluations to screen for complications

GENERAL Rx
- Use artificial tears frequently.
- The muscarinic agonist pilocarpine (5 mg PO qid) is useful to improve dryness.
- Cyclosporine 0.05% ophthalmic emulsion may also be useful for dry eyes.
- Cevimeline, a cholinergic agent with muscarinic agonist activity, 30 mg PO tid is effective for the treatment of dry mouth in patients with SS.
- Hydroxychloroquine alone or in conjunction with methotrexate may be useful for arthralgias and cutaneous manifestations.
- Oral cyclosporine only improves the symptoms of subjective dryness.
- Tumor necrosis factor (TNF) antagonists have not shown benefit in short-duration placebo-controlled trials.
- Rituximab (RTX) has shown some improvement in oral dry mouth symptoms, relieving marked salivary and lacrimal gland swelling in a retrospective review and showing possible reduced fatigue in a randomized clinical trial.
- Propionic acid gel can be used for vaginal dryness.
- Systemic manifestations are treated according to symptoms and complications.
- Cyclophosphamide, azathioprine, and mycophenolate mofetil are generally reserved for life-threatening extraglandular manifestations.
- Fig. 1S-45 describes a treatment algorithm for Sjögren's syndrome.

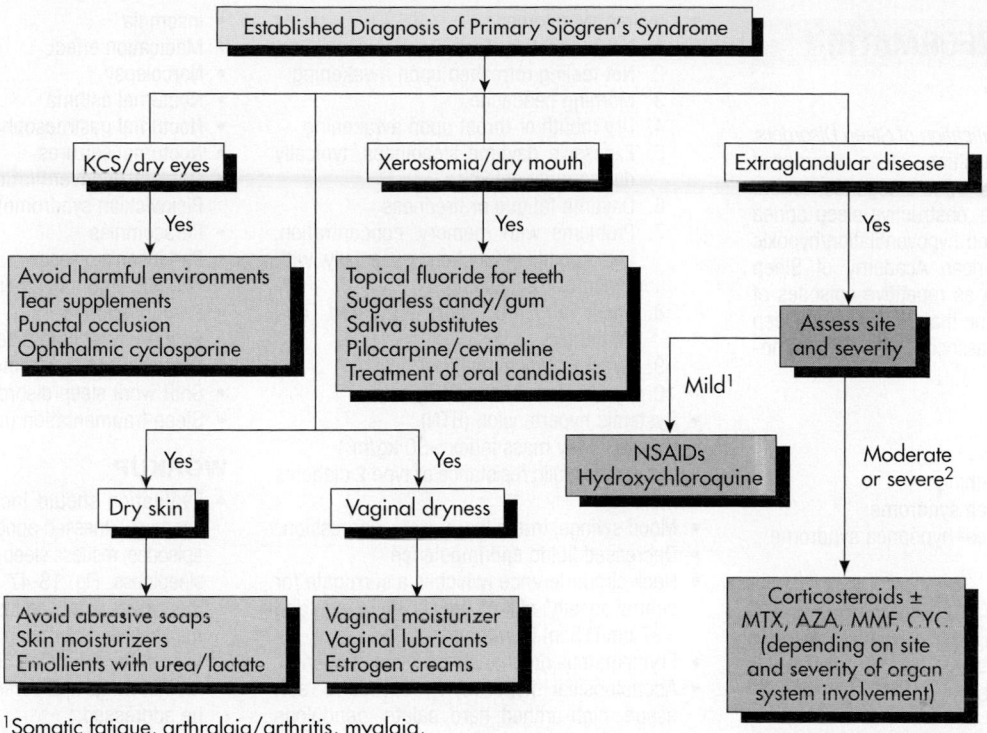

FIGURE 1S-45 **Treatment algorithm for Sjögren's syndrome.** The treatment of Sjögren's syndrome usually requires a multidisciplinary approach involving rheumatologists, ophthalmologists, dentists/oral surgeons, otolaryngologists, and other subspecialists, depending on the extent of extraglandular disease. In all cases, it is prudent to minimize the use of medications that can exacerbate the symptoms of dryness, such as antihistamines, antidepressants, muscle relaxers, and other drugs with anticholinergic properties. The treatment of extraglandular disease is individualized according to the site and severity of organ system involvement. The approaches indicated in the algorithm for the treatment of extraglandular disease are not supported by evidence from randomized, controlled trials, but rather from expert opinion based on retrospective case series and clinical experience. *AZA,* Azathioprine; *CNS,* central nervous system; *CYC,* cyclophosphamide; *KCS,* keratoconjunctivitis sicca; *LIP,* lymphocytic interstitial pneumonitis; *MMF,* mycophenolate mofetil; *MTX,* methotrexate; *NSAIDs,* nonsteroidal antiinflammatory drugs; *NSIP,* nonspecific interstitial pneumonitis; *PNS,* peripheral nervous system. (From Firestein GS et al: *Kelly's textbook of rheumatology,* ed 9, Philadelphia, 2013, Saunders.)

REFERRAL
- Rheumatology referral is generally indicated.
- Referral should be made to an oncologist when lymphoma is suspected.

 **PEARLS & CONSIDERATIONS**

COMMENTS
- Unusual presentations of SS may occur in association with polymyalgia rheumatica, chronic fatigue syndrome, fever of unknown origin, and inflammatory myositis.

- The most serious complication of primary SS is the development of non-Hodgkin's lymphoma and other lymphoproliferative disorders, which occur at a 10- to 44-fold increased rate as compared to age-matched controls.

 EVIDENCE

Available at www.expertconsult.com

SUGGESTED READINGS
Available at www.expertconsult.com

RELATED CONTENT
Sjögren's Syndrome (Patient Information)

AUTHOR: **NICOLE B. YANG, M.D.**

BASIC INFORMATION

DEFINITION

The *International Classification of Sleep Disorders, Second Edition,* classifies sleep-disordered breathing disorders into three categories: central sleep apnea syndrome, obstructive sleep apnea (OSA), and sleep-related hypoventilation/hypoxic syndromes. The American Academy of Sleep Disorders defines OSA as repetitive episodes of upper airway obstruction that occur during sleep and that are typically associated with oxyhemoglobin desaturations.

SYNONYMS

Sleep apnea syndrome
Sleep-disordered breathing
Obstructive sleep apnea syndrome
Obstructive sleep apnea–hypopnea syndrome
OSA

ICD-10CM CODES
G47.30 Sleep apnea, unspecified
G47.31 Primary central sleep apnea
G47.33 Obstructive sleep apnea (adult) (pediatric)
G47.37 Central sleep apnea in conditions classified elsewhere
G47.39 Other sleep apnea
P28.3   Primary sleep apnea of newborn

EPIDEMIOLOGY & DEMOGRAPHICS

OSA is a common disease in the U.S. Data from the Wisconsin Cohort Study indicated that the current prevalence of moderate to severe sleep-disordered breathing (apnea-hypopnea index, measured as events/hour, ≥15) is 10% among 30- to 49-year-old men; 17% among 50- to 70-year-old men; 3% among 30- to 49-year-old women; and 9% among 50- to 70-year-old women.[1] The prevalence of OSA with associated excessive daytime somnolence is approximately 3% to 7% in adult men and 2% to 5% in adult women.[2] The prevalence is higher in obese and hypertensive patients. ~2% of children have OSA[3], which develops more commonly between the ages of 2 to 8 yr when adenotonsillar size is largest relative to upper airway. Risk factors include obesity and craniofacial and upper airway soft tissue abnormalities, retrognathia, and potential risk factors include heredity, current tobacco smoking, nasal congestion, and diabetes.

PHYSICAL FINDINGS & CLINICAL PRESENTATION

- Nocturnal symptoms, including nocturia and angina pectoris
- Snoring that can be loud, habitual, and bothersome to others
- Witnessed apneas that often interrupt snoring and end with a snort
- Gasping, choking, or smothering sensations that arouse the patient from sleep
- Restless sleep associated with frequent arousals
- Daytime symptoms:
  1. Nonrestorative sleep
  2. Not feeling refreshed upon awakening
  3. Morning headache
  4. Dry mouth or throat upon awakening
  5. Excessive daytime sleepiness, typically during quiet activities
  6. Daytime fatigue or tiredness
  7. Problems with memory, concentration, and cognitive function, especially with executive functioning
  8. Easily angered, short tempered, and inattentive
  9. Hyperactivity in children
  10. Symptoms of fibromyalgia
- Systemic hypertension (HTN)
- Obesity (body mass index >30 kg/m^2)
- History of insulin resistance or type 2 diabetes mellitus
- Mood swings, irritability, anxiety, depression
- Decreased libido and impotence
- Neck circumference (which is a surrogate for central obesity) of >43 cm (17 in) in men and >37 cm (15 in) in women
- Erythematous oropharynx because of snoring.
- Adenotonsillar hypertrophy, excessive soft tissue, high-arched hard palate, pendulous uvula, prominent tongue, large degree of overjet, and retrognathia or micrognathia can be present.
- Narrowing of lateral airway walls is independent predictor of OSA in men but not women.
- Craniofacial skeletal abnormalities can lead to OSA, particularly among children and non-obese adults.
- A positive family history increases an individual's risk with each additional close family member with OSA.

ETIOLOGY

- Narrowing of upper airway as a result of obesity or increased peripharyngeal fat deposition, retrognathia and/or micrognathia, adenotonsillar hypertrophy, macroglossia, or neuromuscular weakness
- Upper airway muscular weakness as a result of neuromuscular disorders, primary CNS disorders (e.g., stroke), or metabolic disorders
- Other diseases associated with the development of OSA (e.g., hypothyroidism, acromegaly)

DIAGNOSIS

DIFFERENTIAL DIAGNOSIS

- Anemia
- Anxiety or panic disorder
- Behaviorally induced insufficient sleep syndrome
- Cardiac or heart disease
- Central sleep apnea
- Circadian rhythm disorder
- Depression
- Drug or alcohol abuse
- Gastroesophageal reflux
- Hypothyroidism
- Idiopathic hypersomnia with long or short sleep time
- Inadequate sleep hygiene
- Insomnia
- Medication effect
- Narcolepsy
- Nocturnal asthma
- Nocturnal gastroesophageal reflux
- Nocturnal seizures
- Obesity-hypoventilation syndrome (i.e., Pickwickian syndrome)
- Parasomnias
- Parkinson's disease
- Periodic limb movement disorder
- Primary snoring
- Pulmonary or lung disease
- Restless legs syndrome
- Shift work sleep disorder
- Sleep fragmentation (multiple causes)

WORKUP

- Evaluation should include questions about snoring, witnessed apneas, gasping or choking episodes, restless sleep, and excessive daytime sleepiness. Fig. 1S-47 describes the Epworth Sleepiness Scale, an instrument that evaluates the likelihood of dozing in eight different situations in the preceding 30 days.
- Mood swings and personality changes should be addressed.
- Job performance and difficulty driving or previous motor vehicle accidents related to excessive daytime sleepiness should be discussed.
- Additional concerns include morning dry mouth/throat, morning headaches, alcohol intake, weight gain, mood or personality changes.
- A thorough drug history should include muscle relaxants and sedatives.
- A family history should target any family members with OSA.
- Physical exam is frequently normal in patients with OSA except for the presence of obesity, enlarged neck circumference, and HTN.
- OSA is confirmed by nocturnal polysomnography (PSG), which is the gold standard for diagnosis. The PSG (Fig. 1S-46) should be performed during the patient's typical sleeping hours; it should include all stages of sleep as well as sleep in the supine position.
- The severity of the OSA is determined by the apnea-hypopnea index (AHI) (Table 1S-20), which is derived from the total number of apneas and hypopneas divided by the total sleep time.
- Recommended severity cutoff levels for the AHI in adult patients are as follows:
  1. Mild: 5 to 15 episodes/hr (with symptoms)
  2. Moderate: 15 to 30 episodes per hr
  3. Severe: >30 episodes per hr
- In children, the cutoff values for severity are lower than adult values
- Criteria for the treatment of mild OSA often require symptoms, including excessive daytime sleepiness, cardiovascular disease, HTN, and mood swings.
- In-home respiratory monitoring may be effective alternative to PSG for evaluation of OSA.

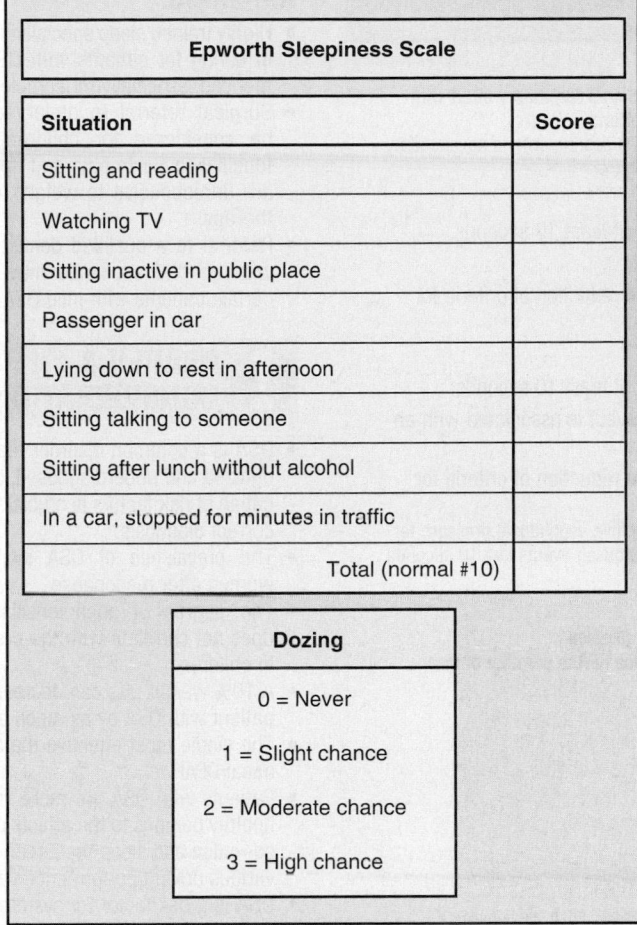

Epworth Sleepiness Scale	
Situation	**Score**
Sitting and reading	
Watching TV	
Sitting inactive in public place	
Passenger in car	
Lying down to rest in afternoon	
Sitting talking to someone	
Sitting after lunch without alcohol	
In a car, stopped for minutes in traffic	
Total (normal #10)	

Dozing
0 = Never
1 = Slight chance
2 = Moderate chance
3 = High chance

FIGURE 1S-47 The Epworth Sleepiness Scale. This instrument asks patients about their likelihood of dozing in eight different situations over the past month. (From Mason RJ et al: *Murray and Nadel's textbook of respiratory medicine,* ed 5, Philadelphia, 2010, WB Saunders.)

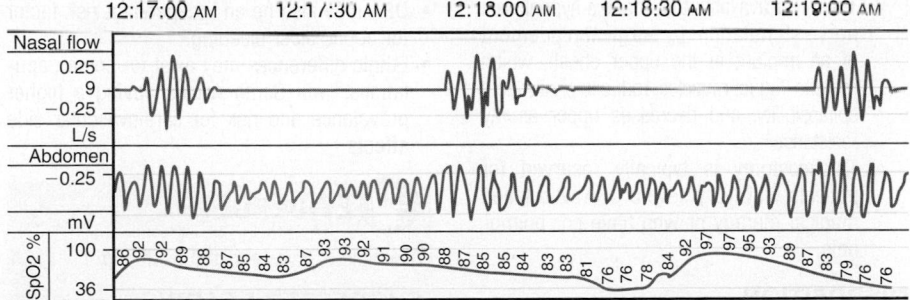

FIGURE 1S-46 Polysomnographic tracing of a patient with obstructive sleep apnea during two minutes of non–rapid eye movement sleep. Displayed are airflow in the upper airway ("nasal flow"), recorded with a nasal pressure transducer; respiratory effort ("abdomen"), recorded by inductance plethysmography; and oxygen saturation of hemoglobin (SpO$_2$), recorded with pulse oximetry. (From Goldman L, Schafer AI: *Goldman's Cecil medicine,* ed 24, Philadelphia, 2012, WB Saunders.)

LABORATORY TESTS

- Arterial blood gas testing should be performed if a patient has suspected pulmonary HTN or cor pulmonale to rule out daytime hypoxemia or hypercapnia.
- Thyroid-stimulating hormone level should be obtained if hypothyroidism is suspected.
- Fasting glucose level is recommended because OSA increases the risk of developing diabetes independent of other risk factors.
- CBC is helpful to look for anemia; iron studies if anemia is detected and ferritin level if concomitant RLS is present.
- Pulmonary function testing if pulmonary disorder is suspected or to assess severity of neuromuscular disease, if present.
- ECG or echocardiogram is indicated if a cardiac disorder (e.g., arrhythmia, pulmonary HTN) is suspected.

IMAGING STUDIES

- Plain radiography of the neck can be helpful to assess the soft tissues of patients with suspected anatomic abnormalities.
- Chest x-ray if pulmonary disease is suspected.

Rx TREATMENT

NONPHARMACOLOGIC THERAPY

- Behavioral modifications:
  1. Weight loss in overweight and obese patients. Weight loss is effective for reducing the severity of OSA, and if significant, it may potentially allow some patients to discontinue continuous positive airway pressure (CPAP) therapy.
  2. Weight loss with bariatric surgery may improve OSA in some patients, but its definitive role remains unclear. In a recent trial in obese patients with OSA, the use of bariatric surgery compared with conventional weight loss therapy did not result in a statistically greater reduction in AHI despite major differences in weight loss.
  3. Exercise without weight loss may improve OSA.
  4. Avoid alcohol for 4 to 6 hr before bedtime.
  5. Avoid muscle relaxants and sedating medications.
  6. Sleep hygiene training, especially avoiding sleep deprivation
  7. Avoid or eliminate supine sleeping positions.
  8. Avoid medications that may worsen OSA.
- Medical treatment:
  1. CPAP is the primary therapy for OSA. It delivers a constant airway pressure that acts as a pneumatic splint that relieves the upper airway obstruction.
  2. Other methods of delivering positive pressure include:
  3. Bilevel positive airway pressure (BiPAP), which delivers a preset inspiratory and expiratory airway pressure.
  4. Auto titrating positive airway pressure (APAP), which increases or decreases the level of pressure in response to change in airflow, a vibratory snore, or change in circuit pressure.
  5. Adaptive servo ventilation provides a varying amount of inspiratory pressure superimposed on a low level of CPAP.
  6. Oral appliance constructed by a reputable and qualified dentist may be effective for the treatment of mild OSA in certain patients, especially those with retrognathia. Mandibular advancement devices (MADs) are a good alternative to CPAP in patients who are unable to tolerate CPAP. Trials have shown that although CPAP is more effective than MADs in reducing AHI (4.5 vs 11 events/h, respectively), self-reported adherence with use of MADs is higher (6.5 vs 5.2h/night for CPAP use). There was no overall difference between MADs and CPAP with respect to improve-

TABLE 1S-20 Definitions*

Events

Apnea: Cessation of breathing lasting 10 seconds or longer. Obstructive: continued respiratory effort with paradoxical motion of rib cage and abdomen; central: absent respiratory effort.

Hypopnea: Different definitions used. Two alternative definitions are part of the scoring criteria advanced by the American Academy of Sleep Medicine:

1. Score a hypopnea if all of the following are present:
   a. Nasal pressure signal excursions; drop ≥30% of baseline for at least 10 seconds.
   b. There is a ≥4% desaturation from pre-event baseline.
   c. At least 90% of the event's duration must meet the amplitude reduction of criteria for hypopnea.
2. Score a hypopnea if all of the following are present:
   a. Nasal pressure signal excursions; drop ≥50% of baseline for at least 10 seconds.
   b. There is a ≥3% desaturation from pre-event baseline *or* the event is associated with an arousal. (The latter does not require a desaturation.)
   c. At least 90% of the event's duration must meet the amplitude reduction of criteria for hypopnea.

Respiratory Effort–Related Arousal (RERA): Pattern of progressively more negative esophageal pressure terminated by a sudden change in pressure to a less negative level and an arousal; events last 10 seconds or longer.

Metrics of Severity

Apnea-Hypopnea Index: Average number of apneas plus hypopneas per hour of sleep.
Respiratory Disturbance Index: Average number of apneas plus hypopneas plus RERAs per hour of sleep.

Consensus Definitions of Severity

Normal: <5 episodes/h
Mild sleep apnea: ≥5 and <15 episodes/h
Moderate sleep apnea: ≥15 and <30 episodes/h
Severe sleep apnea: ≥30 episodes/h

Concept of Sleep Apnea Syndrome

Sleep-disordered breathing with complaint of excessive sleepiness.

*See also American Academy of Sleep Medicine.
From Mason RJ et al: *Murray and Nadel's textbook of respiratory medicine*, ed 5, Philadelphia, 2010, WB Saunders.)

ment in blood pressure, daytime sleepiness, or quality of life.

7. Optimal treatment of allergic rhinitis is needed; nasal irrigation with saline followed by nasal corticosteroids is often helpful.
8. Symptoms of excessive daytime sleepiness may linger and require further investigation or medical therapy.
9. Patients should be considered for surgery if multiple attempts at CPAP therapy have failed and if an oral appliance is not an option. If the patient opts for surgery, ensure that it is performed by a reputable and qualified otolaryngologist and is based on the location of airway collapse.

- Surgical treatment
  ○ Surgery is done to correct specific anatomic areas of narrowing: nasal, pharyngeal, and tongue base/hypopharynx
  ○ Adenotonsillectomy is often curative for children with OSA.
  ○ Nasal septoplasty/turbinectomy should be considered for patients with nasoseptal deformities.
  ○ Uvulopalatopharyngoplasty, which involves resection of the uvula and the soft palate,

is effective for a small number of patients. However, predicting which patients will benefit is difficult.
  ○ The latest available treatment is hypoglossal nerve stimulation (by surgical placement of an implant in the upper chest), which recruits lingual muscles, reduces pharyngeal collapsibility, and decreases upper airway resistance[4]
  ○ Tracheostomy is typically reserved for patients with very severe OSA who failed medical therapy or who have cor pulmonale.

DISPOSITION

- The short-term prognosis for excessive daytime sleepiness and snoring is good to excellent with the regular use of nasal CPAP, but no studies have been performed to address the long-term effects in a large population of patients.
- Residual symptoms of excessive daytime sleepiness can occur in some patients with OSA despite regular CPAP use. This has led the FDA to approve modafinil for the management of residual sleepiness.

REFERRAL

- Highly trained sleep specialists with expertise in caring for patients with OSA are recommended, especially for complex cases.
- Surgical referral to otolaryngology should be considered for children with adenotonsillar hypertrophy and for adults who are unresponsive to weight loss and CPAP therapy.
- Referral to a qualified dentist for treatment with an oral appliance may be useful for certain patients with mild OSA.

① PEARLS & CONSIDERATIONS

- OSA is a common disorder that is underrecognized and underdiagnosed, so the identification of risk factors is crucial for making the correct diagnosis.
- The prevalence of OSA increases among women after menopause.
- The degree of adenotonsillar hypertrophy does not correlate with the presence of OSA in children.
- A 10% weight loss can decrease the AHI of a patient with OSA by as much as 50%.
- The single most effective therapy for OSA is nasal CPAP.
- Patients with OSA are more vulnerable than healthy persons to the effects of alcohol consumption and sleep restriction with regard to various driving performance variables.
- OSA is a risk factor for systemic and pulmonary hypertension, stroke, atrial fibrillation, and coronary artery disease. In patients with untreated HTN and OSA, the use of CPAP results in small but statistically significant reductions in blood pressure.
- OSA may also be an independent risk factor for peptic ulcer bleeding.
- Ethnic differences may exist for some populations, with South Asians having a higher prevalence and risk for cardiovascular side effects.

EBM EVIDENCE

Available at www.expertconsult.com

SUGGESTED READINGS

Available at www.expertconsult.com

RELATED CONTENT

Sleep Apnea (Patient Information)

AUTHORS: **GRACE PAUL, M.D.**, and **DON HAYES, JR., M.D., M.S.**

ℹ️ BASIC INFORMATION

DEFINITION

Slipped capital femoral epiphysis (SCFE) is characterized by displacement of the capital femoral epiphysis (femoral head) posteriorly on the metaphysis (femoral neck) at the level of the physis (growth plate). It commonly presents with hip or knee pain and an abnormal gait.

- Typically unilateral, but bilateral in about one-third of cases.
- Classified as stable when the child is able to walk and bear weight, or unstable when the child is not. In both cases, the child should remain non–weight-bearing pending orthopedic evaluation.

SYNONYMS

Slipped capital femoral epiphysis, nontraumatic
Slipped upper femoral epiphysis
Slipped upper femoral epiphysis, nontraumatic
SCFE

ICD-10CM CODES
M93.003	Unspecified slipped upper femoral epiphysis (nontraumatic), unspecified hip
M93.001	Unspecified slipped upper femoral epiphysis (nontraumatic), right hip
M93.002	Unspecified slipped upper femoral epiphysis (nontraumatic), left hip
M93.011	Acute slipped upper femoral epiphysis (nontraumatic), right hip
M93.012	Acute slipped upper femoral epiphysis (nontraumatic), left hip
M93.013	Acute slipped upper femoral epiphysis (nontraumatic), unspecified hip
M93.021	Chronic slipped upper femoral epiphysis (nontraumatic), right hip
M93.022	Chronic slipped upper femoral epiphysis (nontraumatic), left hip
M93.023	Chronic slipped upper femoral epiphysis (nontraumatic), unspecified hip
M93.031	Acute on chronic slipped upper femoral epiphysis (nontraumatic), right hip
M93.032	Acute on chronic slipped upper femoral epiphysis (nontraumatic), left hip
M93.033	Acute on chronic slipped upper femoral epiphysis (nontraumatic), unspecified hip

EPIDEMIOLOGY & DEMOGRAPHICS

INCIDENCE: The incidence is 13.35 cases per 100,000 in boys and 8.07 cases per 100,000 in girls.
PEAK INCIDENCE: Average age at diagnosis is 13.5 years for boys and 12 years for girls.
PREVALENCE: 10.8 cases per 100,000 children
GENETICS: More commonly seen in blacks and Hispanic populations; no strong evidence of genetic predisposition
RISK FACTORS: Obesity is by far the greatest risk factor.

PHYSICAL FINDINGS & CLINICAL PRESENTATION

- Commonly presents with pain in the knee, hip, groin, or thigh and altered gait.
- On physical exam, may note limited range of motion of the affected hip on internal rotation. The involved hip typically will go into obligatory external rotation if passively flexed up to 90 degrees.
- The slip occurs at the weakest part of the physeal plate and results in the displacement of the head from the metaphysis, giving the characteristic "ice cream falling off the cone" appearance on radiographs.

ETIOLOGY

- SCFE occurs when shearing forces at the femoral head exceed the strength of the capital femoral physis. This most commonly occurs during the preadolescent growth spurt.
- Multifactorial: Predisposing factors include obesity, trauma, history of radiation exposure, and endocrine/metabolic disorders.
- Obesity: Of children diagnosed with SCFE, 63% are at the 90th percentile for weight or higher.
- Endocrine disorders: Consider an underlying endocrinopathy in thin patients who are <8 years old or >15. Hypothyroidism, hypogonadism, panhypopituitarism, or growth hormone deficiency may be identified. Some authors recommend a screening TSH/T4 and bone age assessment at the time of diagnosis.

🅓🅧 DIAGNOSIS

DIFFERENTIAL DIAGNOSIS

- Stress fracture or apophyseal avulsion fracture
- Avascular necrosis (Legg-Calvé-Perthes disease)
- Hip apophysitis
- Transient synovitis
- Septic arthritis or osteomyelitis
- Adductor muscle strain (groin pull)

WORKUP

- Diagnosis is based on physical examination and radiologic findings.
- Laboratory testing can be done to look for secondary causes.

LABORATORY TESTS

Consider renal, endocrine (growth hormone and thyroid function) tests, especially in patients less than 10 years of age who are not obese.

IMAGING STUDIES

- Obtain bilateral hip radiographs with both AP and frog-leg lateral views. Plain radiographs are both sensitive and specific enough to make the diagnosis.
- Widening, irregularity, and lucency of the physis may be noted.
- If the radiograph is normal but suspicion remains high, MRI may be diagnostic. MRI is also helpful in diagnosing complications of SCFE, such as osteonecrosis.

℞ TREATMENT

- At diagnosis, or when suspicious for SCFE, place the child on non–weight-bearing crutches or in a wheelchair pending further evaluation.
- The initial goals of treatment are to prevent slip progression and avoid complications.
- Surgical management is required, and orthopedic referral is imperative. The gold standard procedure is insertion of a single cannulated screw at the center of the epiphysis. In acute SCFE, a second screw may be required to confer greater stability to an unstable joint.

NONPHARMACOLOGIC THERAPY

- The standard treatment for SCFE is surgery.
- The standard surgical procedure of stable SCFE is in situ fixation with a single screw.
- Prophylactic treatment of the contralateral hip in SCFE is not recommended in most patients.

DISPOSITION

- SCFE is a common preadolescent disorder in which early diagnosis and proper management can prevent future complications such as osteonecrosis and chondrolysis.
- Osteonecrosis/avascular necrosis occurs in up to 60% of unstable SCFE; associated factors include overreduction of unstable SCFE, reduction of stable SCFE, pin penetration of posterior quadrant, and multiplicity of pins. Bone scan or MRI is helpful in making the diagnosis.
- Chondrolysis: acute dissolution of articular cartilage and narrowing of the joint space. The patient presents with pain, joint stiffness, and decreased range of motion in all directions. It is characteristically seen as a complication of surgery but occurs in about 10% of cases of untreated SCFE.

❗ PEARLS & CONSIDERATIONS

- Physicians should consider SCFE when a child between the ages of 10 to 15 years presents with limping and groin, hip, thigh, or knee pain. About one third of cases are bilateral.
- Physical exam usually shows decreased internal rotation of the hip and obligatory external rotation.
- Radiography to evaluate for SCFE should include anteroposterior and lateral views of the hips. Obtain frog-lateral views for suspected stable SCFE and true lateral views for unstable SCFE.
- The standard treatment of stable SCFE is in situ fixation with a single screw.

EBM EVIDENCE

Available at www.expertconsult.com

SUGGESTED READINGS

Available at www.expertconsult.com

RELATED CONTENT

Slipped Femoral Epiphysis (Patient Information)

AUTHOR: **MICHELLE C. MACIAG, M.D.**

🛈 BASIC INFORMATION

DEFINITION

- Mechanical obstruction means the blockage of the intestinal lumen, preventing the passage of luminal contents through the gut tube.
- This may be either:
  a) Simple obstruction: in which the lumen may be *partially* or *completely blocked* but with intact intestinal blood flow
  b) Strangulated obstruction
    1. This is a surgical emergency.
    2. Usually the obstruction is complete, blood flow to the obstructed segment is cut off, and tissue necrosis and gangrene may occur.

ICD-10CM CODES
K56.6 Other and unspecified intestinal obstruction
K56.9 Ileus, unspecified
K56.5 Intestinal adhesions (bands) with obstruction
K56.4 Other impaction of intestine
K56.3 Gallstone ileus
K56.2 Volvulus
K5.1 Intussusception
K56 Paralytic ileus and intestinal obstruction

EPIDEMIOLOGY & DEMOGRAPHICS

- The most frequently encountered surgical disorder of the small intestines is mechanical small bowel obstruction (SBO).
- 75% of all cases of small bowel obstruction are due to intraabdominal adhesion related to prior abdominal surgery, such as appendectomy, colorectal surgery, and gynecologic procedures.

PREDOMINANT SEX AND AGE: None

PHYSICAL FINDINGS & CLINICAL PRESENTATION

PHYSICAL FINDINGS: These may include:
- Abdominal distention, especially in distal bowel obstruction
- Hyperactive bowel sounds (an early occurrence)
- Hypoactive bowel sounds (late finding)
- Hernia
- Rectal examination may reveal
  1. Blood (suggestive of neoplasm or strangulation)
  2. Masses (may suggest obturator hernia)

CLINICAL PRESENTATION: There are four key symptoms: abdominal pain, vomiting, distention, and constipation
- Abdominal pain
  1. Often crampy; intermittent
  2. Constant pain (that is, change in pain's character) signifies serious complication
- Nausea
- Vomiting (bilious vomiting seen in proximal obstructions)
- Diarrhea (early finding)
- Constipation (a late finding)
- Fever, tachycardia, and peritoneal signs (these late findings may be seen with strangulation or intestinal ischemia)

- It is important to perform serial abdominal examinations to detect changes early.

ETIOLOGY

- Postoperative adhesions (may cause acute obstruction usually within one month of surgery; or chronic obstructions can occur years later)
- Incarcerated inguinal hernia
- Malignant tumor
- IBD
- Gallstone ileus
- Stricture
- Cystic fibrosis
- Volvulus
- In children consider pyloric stenosis, intussusception, congenital atresia

ⒹⓍ DIAGNOSIS

DIFFERENTIAL DIAGNOSIS
- Acute cholangitis
- Cholecystitis
- Gastroenteritis
- Inflammatory bowel disease
- Diverticulitis
- Endometriosis
- Mesenteric ischemia
- Pancreatitis
- Dysmenorrhea
- Ovarian torsion

WORKUP

- During the initial evaluation of patients with suspected SBO, the primary objectives are to gauge the degree of metabolic derangement and volume depletion and to assess the need for and expediency of surgery. As with many surgical conditions, determining the correct diagnosis and management strategy hinges on a focused yet thorough history and physical examination.

LABORATORY TESTS

- Laboratory abnormalities are not diagnostic of bowel obstruction but instead may indicate complications of obstruction. Essential laboratory tests include:
  1. Basic metabolic panel
  2. CBC: hemoconcentration, leukocytosis
  3. Urinalysis
  4. Serum amylase: may be elevated
  5. LDH
  6. Hepatic panel
  7. Type and cross-match (in anticipation of possible surgical intervention)

IMAGING STUDIES

- Initial radiographic evaluation begins with plain x-ray films of the abdomen (supine and upright) and an upright chest radiograph. An upright chest radiograph is of paramount importance to inspect for pneumoperitoneum and also for evidence of aspiration in a patient with a history of vomiting. A supine and upright plain abdominal x-ray in patients with suspected small bowel obstruction may show:
  1. Ladder-like pattern of dilated small bowel loops with air-fluid levels (Fig. 1S-48) indicating small bowel obstruction
  2. Accumulation of air and fluid proximal and clearance of fluid and air distal to the post of obstruction
- Enteroclysis (a fluoroscopic x-ray of the small intestine) is useful in detecting obstruction and can distinguish partial from complete blockage and adhesions from metastases.
- CT scan is the study of choice if the patient has fever, tachycardia, abdominal pain, and leukocytosis. It can reveal the etiology of the obstruction: abscess, inflammatory process, extra-luminal pathology, and/or metastases.
- CT can elucidate the cause, such as the presence of a mass (Fig. 1S-49) or a hernia with subsequent obstruction (Fig. 1S-50). In addition, CT has high sensitivity for detecting

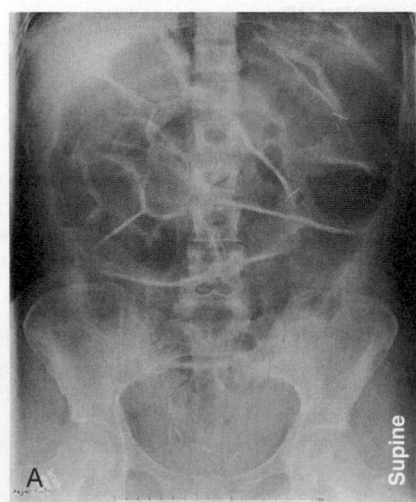
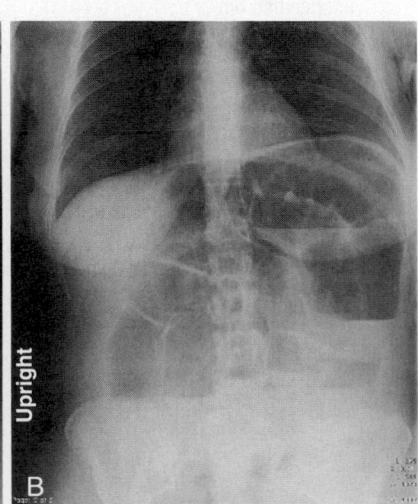

FIGURE 1S-48 A, Supine film showing dilated loops of small bowel in a patient with small bowel obstruction. **B,** Upright abdominal film revealing multiple air-fluid levels and small bowel dilation, consistent with a diagnosis of small bowel obstruction. (From Marx J: *Rosen's emergency medicine: concepts and clinical practice*, ed 6, Philadelphia, 2006, Saunders.)

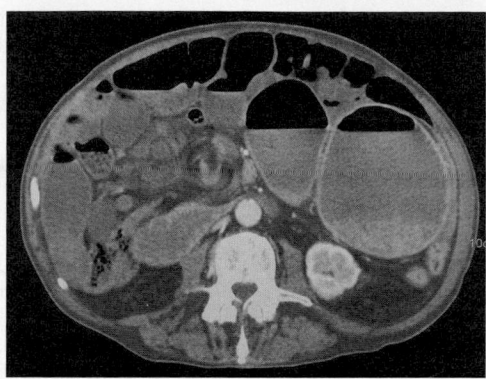

FIGURE 1S-49 CT scan of small bowel volvulus with notable mesenteric torsion. (From Cameron JL, Cameron AM: *Current surgical therapy*, ed 10, Philadelphia, 2011, Saunders.)

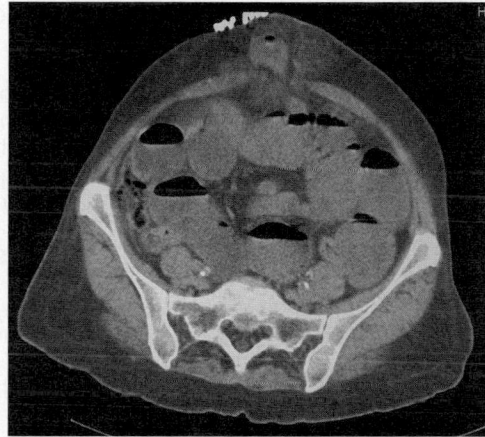

FIGURE 1S-50 CT scan of complete small bowel obstruction due to incisional hernia. (From Cameron IL, Cameron AM: *Current surgical therapy*, ed 10, Philadelphia, 2011, Saunders.)

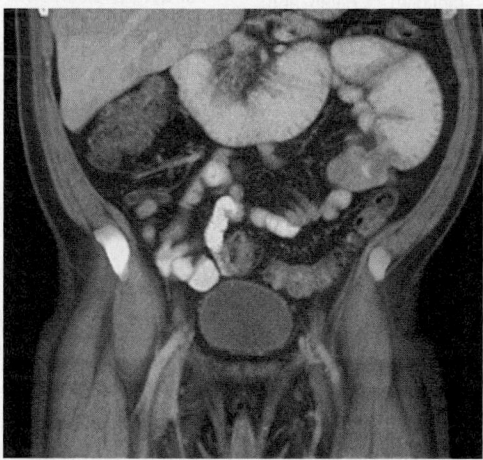

FIGURE 1S-51 Coronal image of CT scan showing mass in proximal small bowel with decompressed loops of small bowel distal to obstruction. (From Cameron JL, Cameron AM: *Current surgical therapy*, ed 10, Philadelphia, 2011, Saunders.)

strangulation and pneumoperitoneum indicative of a perforation and is particularly useful in the early postoperative setting to rule out ischemia, intraabdominal abscess, or morbidity as the underlying cause. It is also useful in patients with a history of malignancy to differentiate potentially recurrent disease from adhesions (Fig. 1S-51).

- CT enterography, in which intraluminal distention is achieved with administration of large volumes of oral contrast such as water-methylcellulose solution, can be useful. This modality is most often used to diagnose patients with Crohn's disease–related strictures, and its benefit is high-resolution imaging of the bowel wall; however, it is impractical in the patient with gastrointestinal (GI) distress who is nauseated and vomiting.

 **TREATMENT**

EMERGENCY ROOM CARE

- Vigorous fluid resuscitation and correction of electrolyte disorders underpin the initial therapeutic goals of both nonoperative and preoperative management strategies. Placing a Foley catheter to measure urinary output, establishing adequate intravenous access, and reassessing hemodynamic and electrolyte status are all essential in the initial management.
- Initial treatment consists of:
  1. Designate the patients nothing by mouth ("NPO")
  2. Fluid resuscitation (with isotonic Ringer's or normal saline solution)
  3. Bowel decompression (via nasogastric [NG] tube placement): a standard NG tube provides symptomatic relief, prevents added gas and fluid accumulation proximally, and enables the serial assessment of antegrade fluid movement.
  4. Pain management
  5. Antiemetic administration
  6. Surgical consultation: must be done early
  7. Antibiotic administration

NONSURGICAL INPATIENT CARE

- Continue NG suction.
- Provide adequate fluid.

  Patients with low-grade partial SBOs are prone to spontaneous resolution with conservative interventions such as bowel rest, NG decompression, and appropriate fluid resuscitation. For partial or simple obstructions resolution usually occurs within 72 hr.

SURGICAL CARE

More than 25% of inpatients admitted because of SBO will require an operation. Patients with complete or high-grade partial SBO are most likely to need surgery, with less than 20% successfully managed nonoperatively. Surgery is indicated in:

- Strangulated obstruction (which is a surgical emergency)
- Simple complete obstruction: after failed nonoperative care

AUTHOR: **DANIEL K. ASIEDU, M.D., PH.D.**

 **BASIC INFORMATION**

DEFINITION

Small bacterial overgrowth (SIBO) is the presence of excessive native and/or nonnative bacteria in the small intestine (bacterial count $>10^5$/mL) causing chronic diarrhea and malabsorption.

SYNONYM

Bacterial Overgrowth Syndrome
SIBO

ICD-10CM CODES
K90.4   Malabsorption due to intolerance, NEC
K90.89 Other intestinal malabsorption

EPIDEMIOLOGY & DEMOGRAPHICS

PREVALENCE: The prevalence of SIBO is varied based on the population studied and the diagnostic tests used. It has shown to be prevalent in up to 12.5% to 20% of the healthy population using glucose and lactulose breath test.
PREDOMINANT SEX AND AGE: SIBO affects predominantly the elderly population. The elderly population has decreased gastric secretion and hypomotility due to age-associated decline as well as increased use of motility-altering medications.
RISK FACTORS
- Advanced age is a known risk factor as there is thought to be an age-associated decline in GI motility.
- Patients with irritable bowel syndrome have a higher prevalence of SIBO compared to the general population. Initial studies have shown up to 65% to 80% of IBS patients with confirmed SIBO with an abnormal lactulose breath test.
- Other risk factors include UGI tract surgery, inflammatory bowel disease, chronic pancreatitis, immunodeficiency, liver disease and obesity.

PHYSICAL FINDINGS & CLINICAL PRESENTATION

- Patients will present with nonspecific findings, which include abdominal distension, bloating, and/or pain. Other common symptoms include diarrhea and subsequent weight loss and weakness.
- The severity of symptoms reflects the extent of bacterial overgrowth.
- Severe malabsorption can present as symptoms secondary to vitamin deficiencies. Fat-soluble vitamin deficiencies can present as night blindness (vitamin A), osteomalacia and hypocalcaemia (vitamin D), or prolonged bleeding (vitamin K). Bacterial overgrowth can affect vitamin B12 absorption in the ileum leading to neuropathies with sensory ataxia.

ETIOLOGY

Disorders that disrupt protective mechanisms against bacterial burden predispose patients to SIBO.
- Patients with structural or anatomical abnormalities are at greater risk. These include patients with small bowel diverticula, small intestinal strictures, surgical blind loops, ileocecal resections, or gastric resections (increasing common cause of SIBO).

- Motility disorders predispose to SIBO because of the ineffective clearance of bacteria from the proximal bowel into the colon. Examples of this include gastroparesis and small bowel dysmotility, both suggestive of poorly controlled diabetes. Long-standing celiac disease can also interfere with small bowel motility.
- It is thought that recent antibiotic use as well as antacid medication can alter the normal bacterial flora in the small intestine, contributing to SIBO.

 **DIAGNOSIS**

DIFFERENTIAL DIAGNOSIS

- Celiac disease
- Chronic pancreatitis
- Inflammatory bowel disease
- Irritable bowel syndrome
- Tropical sprue
- Whipple's disease
- Lactose intolerance

WORK-UP

- Diagnostic testing should include workup for diarrhea, anemia, and malabsorption. While endoscopy with jejunal aspirate and culture was a diagnostic tool of choice, its role is limited because of low specificity. While breath tests have their limitations as well, they are noninvasive and easy to perform.

LABORATORY TESTS

- Breath tests have become more commonplace in diagnosing SIBO. Typically fermenting bacteria reside in the colon. In SIBO, fermenting bacteria is present in the small intestine as well. A carbohydrate test dose (typically lactulose or glucose) is given and its byproduct (hydrogen) is measured as it is excreted in the breath. In SIBO, exhaled hydrogen concentrations rise early.
- Standard anemia workup is essential. CBC may suggest macrocytic anemia secondary to B12 deficiency.
- Nutritional status should be evaluated with albumin levels.
- Stool evaluation can aid in the diagnosis as well. An increase in fecal fat may be suggestive of SIBO. Stool WBC, culture, ova, and parasites should be ordered as well to rule out other infectious etiology.

IMAGING STUDIES

- Endoscopic evaluation of the small intestine can be useful in finding structural and motility causes of bacterial overgrowth such as diverticula and strictures. Small bowel biopsy may aid in the diagnosis of celiac disease as well.
- Jejunal aspirate cultures via endoscopy are considered a standard of diagnosis. Aspirate cultures that exceed 10^5 organisms/mL suggest the presence of SIBO.
- There are several limitations to jejunal aspirate cultures. Bacterial overgrowth is not uniform and may be in inaccessible areas to endoscopist and can easily be missed. Contamination from oropharyngeal flora can lead to false-positive tests. Also endoscopy is an invasive test

and other methods of testing such as a breath test may be a more practical initial approach.

 **TREATMENT**

The goal is to treat the underlying cause and treat the bacterial overgrowth with antibiotic therapy.

NONPHARMACOLOGIC THERAPY

- Structural disorders such as strictures, fistula and diverticula may require surgical intervention.

ACUTE GENERAL Rx

- 7- to 10-day course of antibiotic therapy with rifaximin, amoxicillin-clavulanate, or metronidazole and ciprofloxacin has been shown to be beneficial.
- Nutritional support with vitamin replacement and dietary modification (lactose-free diet).

CHRONIC Rx

- Recurrence is common after antibiotic therapy. These patients may require subsequent courses of antibiotic therapy.
- Avoid using antacid medication.
- Avoid drugs that reduce GI motility (opiods).
- Consider lactose-free diet if the response to antimicrobial agents is incomplete.

DISPOSITION

- Prognosis is dependent on underlying cause of SIBO. Although recurrence rate is high, antibiotic therapy remains the mainstay of therapy.

REFERRAL

- Gastroenterology consultation for small bowel evaluation.
- Surgical consultation with an underlying structural disorder.

! **PEARLS & CONSIDERATIONS**

COMMENTS

- SIBO is due to a disruption of protective mechanisms against bacterial burden
- Look for risk factors including UGI tract surgery, structural disorders, IBD, IBS, and disorders decreasing GI motility.
- Diagnosis can be made with hydrogen breath test or endoscopic jejunal aspirate culture.
- Treatment is with antibiotics.
- The combination of vitamin B12 deficiency (due to bacterial consumption) and an elevated serum folate level (due to bacterial production) is suggestive of SIBO.

RELATED CONTENT

Small Intestinal Bacterial Overgrowth (Patient Information)
Irritable Bowel Syndrome (Related Key Topic)
Malabsorption (Related Key Topic)

SUGGESTED READINGS
Available at www.expertconsult.com

AUTHOR: **GEORGE CHOLANKERIL, M.D.**

S

BASIC INFORMATION

DEFINITION

Somatization disorder has been replaced in DSM 5 with the diagnostic term *somatic symptom disorder*. In this condition, one or more somatic symptoms are distressing or disruptive of daily life. There are often disproportionate thoughts about the seriousness of one's symptoms, persistent anxiety about one's health, and excessive time and energy devoted to the symptoms. There is often a pattern of recurring multiple somatic complaints that begin before the age of 30 yr and persist over several years. Patients complain of multiple symptoms, but persistent pain is common. DSM 5 drops the term "unexplained by a medical condition" from the criteria.

SYNONYMS

Briquet's syndrome
Nonorganic physical symptoms
Medically unexplained symptoms
Functional somatic symptoms
Somatic symptom disorder
Somatic symptom and related disorders

ICD-10CM CODES
F45.0 Somatization disorder
F45.1 Undifferentiated somatoform disease

EPIDEMIOLOGY & DEMOGRAPHICS

PREVALENCE (IN U.S.): Lifetime rates of 0.25% to 2% in women, ≤0.2% in men
PEAK INCIDENCE: Typically before age 25 yr
PREDOMINANT SEX: Women are more commonly affected in the U.S. (10:1 ratio)
PREDOMINANT AGE: Onset occurs before age 30 yr and usually in adolescence.
GENETICS: In males, there is a high risk of associated substance abuse or antisocial personality disorder.

PHYSICAL FINDINGS & CLINICAL PRESENTATION

- Onset is characteristically in the teens; course is marked by frequent, often unexplained, and frequently disabling pain symptoms and physical complaints.
- Patient frequently undergoes multiple procedures and seeks treatment from multiple physicians. Symptom focus rotates periodically with new physicians sought for new complaints.
- Patient often has a comorbid psychiatric disorder, most commonly generalized anxiety, panic disorder, or depression.

ETIOLOGY

- Somatic symptoms may result from a heightened awareness of certain bodily sensations, combined with a tendency to interpret these sensations as indicative of a medical illness.
- Believed to be the physical expression of psychologic distress; there appears to be a biologic predisposition.
- May be more common in individuals without sufficient verbal or intellectual capacity to communicate psychologic distress, individuals with alexithymia (inability to describe emotional states), or individuals from cultural backgrounds that consider emotional distress as an undesirable quality.
- Some aspects of somatic symptom disorder possibly learned from somatizing parents.

DIAGNOSIS

DIFFERENTIAL DIAGNOSIS

- Psychologic factors affecting other medical conditions (ICD-10CM F45.1, DMS 5 316): psychologic or behavioral factors adversely affect the medical condition in various ways, such as influencing the course of the medical condition or interfering with treatment.
- Conversion disorder: an alteration or loss of voluntary motor or sensory function without demonstrable physical cause and related to a psychologic stress or a conflict. Findings provide evidence of incompatibility between the symptom and recognized neurologic or medical conditions.
- Factitious disorder (e.g., Munchausen's syndrome) and malingering: The psychologic basis of the complaints in somatization disorder is not conscious as it is in factitious disorder, in which the goal is to be in the patient role, or malingering, in which symptoms are also produced consciously but for some secondary gain like a monetary award in litigation or opioids.

WORKUP

- Rule out a general medical condition.
- If somatization is suspected on the basis of a history of repeated, multiple, unexplained complaints, restraint in ordering tests is recommended.

LABORATORY TESTS

No specific laboratory tests are required.

IMAGING STUDIES

No specific imaging studies are required.

TREATMENT

NONPHARMACOLOGIC THERAPY

- Legitimize patient's complaints.
- Minimize diagnostic investigation and symptomatic treatment. Only do invasive testing or procedures when there are clear-cut signs, not just symptom reports.
- Set attainable treatment goals. Patients may benefit from realizing that even though they cannot be cured, they will be cared for. This may help reassure them that they will continue to have a relationship with the caregiver.
- Treat coexisting psychiatric conditions such as depression and anxiety.

ACUTE GENERAL Rx

- At each visit do a brief physical examination focusing on the area of complaint.
- Gently praise increased functioning rather than focusing on symptoms.
- Explore recent life events and ask how the patient is handling these.
- Convey empathy with the patient's suffering and psychosocial difficulties.
- No specific pharmacologic therapy has been clearly proven effective, although a number of agents, including gabapentin and St. John's wort, have been useful in some studies.

CHRONIC Rx

- Provide one primary care practitioner to manage care.
- Avoid confronting the patient regarding the psychologic origin of symptoms.
- Ensure follow-up visits at regular intervals (e.g., 2- to 4-wk intervals that are not symptom contingent; maintain the regularity even if the symptoms improve so that the patient does not need new symptoms to continue the relationship).
- Avoid invasive or expensive diagnostic procedures unless there are clear signs of new illness, not just symptoms.
- Diagnose and treat mood or anxiety disorders.
- Cognitive behavior therapy groups have been helpful for patients with unexplained somatic symptoms and can dramatically improve functioning.

DISPOSITION

A chronic condition with frequent exacerbations

REFERRAL

If the patient is open to discussing psychologic issues, a referral for psychotherapy can be made.

PEARLS & CONSIDERATIONS

Patients with somatization disorder respond best to establishing a regular working relationship with a primary care provider. Avoiding confrontations about the origins of symptoms, investigating symptoms when related to actual signs of disease, and gently investigating concurrent stressors will help avoid most of the common problems with this population.

Patients with subsyndromal symptoms (i.e., failing to meet the full criteria but having three or more medically unexplained symptoms) may be just as challenging and chronic. They warrant approaches similar to those utilized for the full syndrome.

SUGGESTED READINGS

Available at www.expertconsult.com

RELATED CONTENT

Somatization Disorder (Patient Information)

AUTHOR: **STUART J. EISENDRATH, M.D.**

Diseases and Disorders

I

BASIC INFORMATION

DEFINITION
Spasticity is an exaggerated tone that displays a velocity-dependent increase in resistance of muscles to a passive stretch stimulus.

SYNONYMS
Hypertonicity

ICD-10CM CODES
M62.838 Other muscle spasm
G81.10 Spastic hemiplegia affecting unspecified side
R25.0 Abnormal head movements
R26.0 Ataxic gait
G81.10 Spastic hemiplegia affecting unspecified side
G83.9 Paralytic syndrome, unspecified
G80.9 Cerebral palsy, unspecified

EPIDEMIOLOGY & DEMOGRAPHICS
INCIDENCE: Spasticity affects between 47% and 70% of people with multiple sclerosis, 32% to 36% of those with spinal cord injury, approximately 20% of those with stroke, more than 90% with cerebral palsy, and approximately 50% of patients with traumatic brain injury.
PREDOMINANT SEX AND AGE: Spasticity is not affected by sex, race, or age group, nor is it more prevalent in any of those groups.
RISK FACTORS: Multiple sclerosis, stroke, spinal cord injury, cerebral palsy, traumatic brain injury

PHYSICAL FINDINGS & CLINICAL PRESENTATION
- Patient may present with impaired gait, impaired limb function, decreased mobility, or discomfort due to increased muscle tone.
- While increased tone may preserve strength in the affected muscles, function may be impaired, especially fine motor. Examine active and passive motion, reflexes, and functions:
  1. Strength may be normal or decreased. Isometric strength is typically greater than concentric strength.
  2. Tone may be variably increased to passive range of motion (modified Ashworth scale; see Table 1S-21).
  3. Reflexes are typically brisk.
  4. Patient may have accompanying extensor plantar signs, clonus, or spontaneous flexor spasms.
  5. Function may be impaired or enhanced due to increased tone.

TABLE 1S-21   Modified Ashworth Scale

0	No increase in muscle tone
1	Slight increase in muscle tone, manifested by a catch and release or by minimal resistance at the end range of motion when the part is moved in flexion or extension/abduction or adduction
1+	Slight increase in muscle tone, manifested by a catch, followed by minimal resistance throughout the remainder (less than half) of the range of motion
2	More marked increase in muscle tone through most of the range of motion, but the affected part is easily moved
3	Considerable increase in muscle tone, passive movement is difficult
4	Affected part is rigid in flexion or extension (abduction or adduction)

From Stein J: Spasticity. In Frontera WR et al (eds): *Essentials of physical medicine and rehabilitation,* ed 2, Philadelphia, 2008, Saunders.

ETIOLOGY
Upper motor neuron injury, most commonly due to multiple sclerosis, stroke, spinal cord injury, cerebral palsy, traumatic brain injury

DIAGNOSIS

DIFFERENTIAL DIAGNOSIS
Rigidity, clonus, dystonia, dyskinesia, myotonia, tetanus, muscle contracture, cramps

WORKUP
- A diagnosis is established clinically.
- Investigate reversible exacerbating causes of spasticity: underlying infection, bladder distention, bowel impaction, fracture, pain.

LABORATORY TESTS
Urinalysis, complete blood count, metabolic panel

IMAGING STUDIES
Chest x-ray, abdominal x-ray series, bladder ultrasound

TREATMENT

First treat reversible causes of spasticity (see "Workup"), then proceed to physical and pharmacologic therapeutics. Lastly, consider surgical intervention in severe, refractory cases.

NONPHARMACOLOGIC THERAPY
- Physical therapeutics include range of motion and muscle stretching, serial casting or orthotics, muscle cooling, electrical stimulation.

- Surgical procedures include tenotomy, tendon lengthening, and tendon transfers. More invasive surgical interventions include peripheral neurectomy, myelotomy, and rhizotomy.

ACUTE GENERAL Rx
- Oral medications: baclofen, tizanidine, diazepam, dantrolene (Table E1S-22)
- Other interventions: intrathecal baclofen, botulinum toxin intramuscular injections, chemical nerve blocks (with bupivacaine, phenol, or ethyl alcohol)

COMPLEMENTARY & ALTERNATIVE MEDICINE
EMG biofeedback

DISPOSITION
Typically nonprogressive, but medications may lose efficacy after long duration of use. Drug holidays (with use of alternate spasmolytic) may be beneficial.

REFERRAL
- Physicians: neurologist or physiatrist with expertise in botulinum toxin injection and/or intrathecal spasmolytic therapy is recommended when oral medications are ineffective or not tolerated.
- Physical and occupational therapy

PEARLS & CONSIDERATIONS

- Assess whether the spasms recently increased in severity or intensity (as would occur with reversible exacerbating causes).
- Consider whether patient's tone is beneficial or detrimental to patient's functionality or overall health status.
- Spasticity may assist posture and mobility, as well as maintain muscle mass and bone mineralization, reduce dependent edema, and prevent deep venous thromboses.
- Spasticity may impair patient's functionality, interfere with activities of daily living, interfere with sleep, and cause discomfort.
- Monitor liver function with dantrolene and tizanidine, as these drugs may cause hepatotoxicity.

SUGGESTED READINGS
Available at www.expertconsult.com

AUTHOR: SACHIN KEDAR, M.B.B.S., M.D.

 **BASIC INFORMATION**

DEFINITION

Spinal cord compression is characterized by the neurologic loss of function from compression of the spinal cord or cauda equina in the spinal canal. Fig. 1S-56 illustrates a schematic demarcation of levels of principal dermatomes shown as distinct segments. Lesions may develop gradually or acutely and be complete or incomplete. Incomplete lesions often present as distinct syndromes (Table 1S-23), as follows:

- Anterior cord syndrome
- Brown-Séquard syndrome
- Cauda equina syndrome
- Central cord syndrome
- Conus medullaris syndrome

ICD-10CM CODES
G83.81 Brown-Séquard syndrome
G83.4 Cauda equina syndrome
G95.81 Conus medullaris syndrome
Other lesions listed by site

EPIDEMIOLOGY

Spinal cord injury (SCI) occurs more commonly in males with a mean age of 38 years. Alcohol plays a major role in at least 25% of SCI.
INCIDENCE: 11,000 new cases/yr
PREVALENCE: 171,000 persons
COST (IN U.S.): >$5 billion/yr

RISK FACTORS: Underlying spinal disease can predispose to SCI:
- Cervical spondylosis
- Atlantoaxial instability
- Congenital conditions (tethered cord)
- Osteoporosis
- Ankylosing spondylitis
- Rheumatoid arthritis of the cervical spine

PHYSICAL FINDINGS & CLINICAL PRESENTATION

Clinical features reflect the amount of spinal cord involvement:
- Motor loss and sensory abnormalities
- Babinski testing usually positive
- Clonus
- Gradual compression, often presenting with progressive difficulty walking, clonus with weight bearing, and involuntary spasm; development of sensory symptoms; bladder dysfunction (late)
- *Central cord syndrome:* results in a variable quadriparesis. It is described as a motor impairment greater in upper than lower extremities, bladder dysfunction, and variable degree of sensory loss below the injury level. It occurs after mild trauma in the setting of preexisting cervical spondylosis and results in variable quadriplegia.
- *Anterior cord syndrome:* affects the anterior or ventral 2/3 of the spinal cord, sparing the dorsal columns. It is most commonly caused by a vascular injury to the anterior spinal artery. Physical manifestations are motor, pain, and temperature loss below the lesion.

- *Brown-Séquard syndrome:*
  1. Caused by injury to either half of the spinal cord and resulting in the loss of motor function, position, vibration, and light touch on the affected side
  2. Pain and temperature sense loss on the opposite side
- *Conus medullaris syndrome:* results in variable motor loss in the lower extremities with loss of bowel and bladder function
- *Cauda equina syndrome:* usual low back pain, weakness in both lower extremities, saddle anesthesia, and loss of voluntary bladder and bowel control

ETIOLOGY

- Trauma. Most SCIs result from high-speed motor vehicle accidents, falls, sports injuries, or violence.
- Tumor
- Infection
- Inflammatory processes
- Degenerative disk conditions with spinal stenosis
- Acute disk herniation
- Cystic abnormalities
- Ankylosing spondylitis
- Table 1S-24 summarizes physical examination findings associated with vertebral fractures and spinal cord injuries

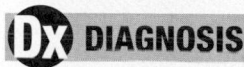 **DIAGNOSIS**

DIFFERENTIAL DIAGNOSIS

- See "Etiology."
- Section II describes the differential diagnosis of paraplegia.

WORKUP

- Spinal cord compression: emergent and requires immediate referral for radiographic and neurologic assessment.
- Mental status evaluation and CNS function should be included, as SCI might be associated with head trauma.
- The primary assessment of a patient with SCI follows the ABCD prioritization scheme.
- Airway management in a patient with suspected SCI dictates in-line immobilization of the spine at all times. Hyperextension of the neck is contraindicated. A jaw thrust must be used to open the airway, and required intubation must be done with the head/neck in a neutral position.
- Techniques to minimize spine movement include the use of log-roll movements and a back board for transfer and placement of a rigid cervical collar.
- Lab results are usually unremarkable; however, underlying infectious or inflammatory causes can be associated.

IMAGING STUDIES

- Depends on the suspected etiology.
- Neurologic signs and symptoms of SCI in the setting of normal plain x-rays should warrant further imaging studies.

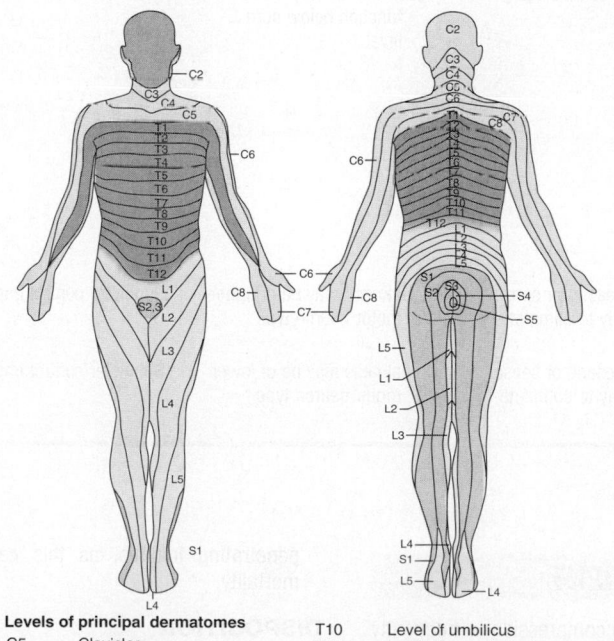

Levels of principal dermatomes

C5	Clavicles
C5,6,7	Lateral parts of upper limbs
C8, T1	Medial sides of upper limbs
C6	Thumb
C6,7,8	Hand
C8	Ring and little fingers
T4	Level of nipples
T10	Level of umbilicus
T12	Inguinal or groin regions
L1,2,3,4	Anterior and inner surfaces of lower limbs
L4,5 S1	Foot
L4	Medial side of great toe
S1,2, L5	Posterior and outer surfaces of lower limbs
S1	Lateral margin of foot and little toe
S2,3,4	Perineum

FIGURE 1S-56 Schematic demarcation of levels of principal dermatomes shown as distinct segments. There is actually considerable overlap between any two adjacent dermatomes. (From Goldman L, Schafer AI: *Goldman's Cecil medicine,* ed 24, Philadelphia, 2011, Saunders.)

TABLE 1S-23 Spinal Cord Syndromes

Syndrome	Sensory	Motor	Sphincter Involvement
Central cord syndrome	Variable	Upper extremity weakness, distal > proximal	Variable
Brown-Séquard syndrome	Ipsilateral position and vibration sense loss, Contralateral pain and temperature sensation loss	Motor loss ipsilateral to cord lesion	Variable
Anterior cord syndrome	Loss of pin and touch sensation Vibration, position sense preserved	Motor loss or weakness below cord level	Variable
Transverse cord syndrome—complete	Loss of sensation below level of cord injury	Loss of voluntary motor function below cord level	Sphincter control lost
Conus medullaris syndrome	Saddle anesthesia may be present, or sensory loss may range from patchy to complete transverse pattern	Weakness may be of upper motor neuron type	Sphincter control impaired
Cauda equina syndrome	Saddle anesthesia may be present, or sensory loss may range from patchy to complete transverse pattern	Weakness may be of lower motor neuron type	Sphincter control impaired

From Marx JA et al: *Rosen's emergency medicine*, ed 8, Philadelphia, 2014, WB Saunders.

- A complete set of cervical x-rays should include anteroposterior, lateral, and open-mouth odontoid views.
- After initial resuscitative efforts, fine-cut helical CT scans with coronal and sagittal reconstructions have replaced plain radiographs in most trauma centers as an initial evaluation in detecting spine fractures.
- MRI provides a detailed image of the spinal ligaments, intervertebral discs, and paraspinal soft tissues and is very sensitive for detecting epidural hematoma (Fig. 1S-57).

 **TREATMENT**

- Urgent surgical decompression is frequently indicated as soon as the etiology is established.
- Corticosteroids: Methylprednisolone reduces the amount of secondary injury that occurs after SCI and has become an important tool in the treatment of SCI by improving outcomes. Corticosteroids should not be used in patients with associated traumatic brain injury and

penetrating injuries, as this can increase mortality.

DISPOSITION

Indicators regarding prognosis:

- The greater the distal motor and sensory sparing, the greater the expected recovery.
- When a plateau of recovery is reached, no further improvement is expected.
- Rapid improvement is associated with enhanced long-term recovery. Patients with acute traumatic SCI need monitoring in the

TABLE 1S-24 Physical Examination Findings Associated with Vertebral Fractures and Spinal Cord Injuries

Injury	Physical Examination Area	Associated Findings
Vertebral fracture	Spine	Tenderness of the neck and/or back. Examine the entire spine because vertebral fractures may occur in multiples.
	Neurologic	See spinal cord injury below.
	Chest	*Thoracic spine fractures:* check for chest tenderness, unequal breath sounds, and arrhythmia, which are suggestive of an associated intrathoracic injury or myocardial contusion.
	Abdomen/pelvis	*Thoracolumbar and lumbar spine fractures:* check for abdominal or pelvic tenderness. For instance, up to 50% of patients with a transverse process fracture and 33% of patients with a Chance fracture have concurrent intraabdominal pathology. A transverse area of ecchymosis on the lower abdominal wall (seat belt sign) increases the chance of an abdominopelvic injury.
	Extremity	*Thoracolumbar and lumbar spine fractures:* check for calcaneal tenderness because 10% of calcaneal fractures are associated with a low thoracic or lumbar fracture. Mechanistically, these areas are fractured as a result of axial loading.
Spinal cord injury	Neurologic, motor (anterior column)	Assess motor function on a scale of 0 to 5. The *motor level* is defined as the most caudal segment with at least 3/5 strength. Injuries to the first eight cervical segments result in tetraplegia (previously known as quadriplegia); lesions below the T1 level result in paraplegia.
	Neurologic, sensory (spinothalamic tract)	Assess sensory function via pinprick and light touch on the following scale: 0 = absent; 1 = impaired; 2 = normal. The *sensory level* is defined as the most caudal segment of the spinal cord with normal sensory function. The highest intact sensory level should be marked on the patient's spine to monitor for progression.
	Neurologic, sensory (dorsal column)	Assess vibratory sensory function on a scale of 0 to 2 by using a tuning fork over bony prominences. Assess position sense (proprioception) by flexing and extending the great toe.
	Neurology, deep tendon reflex	On a scale of 0 to 4, assess the deep tendon reflexes in the upper (biceps, triceps) and lower (patellar, Achilles) extremities.
	Anogenital	Assess rectal tone, sacral sensation, signs of urinary or fecal retention or incontinence, and priapism. Also check the anogenital reflexes: an *anal wink* (S2-S4) is present if the anal sphincter contracts in response to stroking the perianal skin area. The *bulbocavernosus reflex* (S3-S4) is elicited by squeezing the glans penis or clitoris (or pulling on an inserted Foley catheter), which results in reflexive contraction of the anal sphincter.
	Head-to-toe examination	A spinal cord injury may mask a patient's ability to perceive and localize pain. Imaging of high-risk areas, such as the abdomen, and areas of bruising or swelling may be required to exclude occult injuries.

From Adams JG et al: *Emergency medicine, clinical essentials,* ed 2, Philadelphia, 2013, Elsevier.

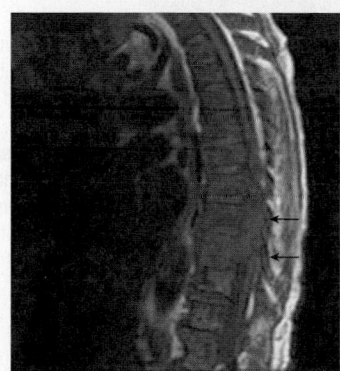

FIGURE 1S-57 Magnetic resonance image demonstrating compression of the thecal sac *(arrows).* (From Adams JG et al: *Emergency medicine, clinical essentials,* ed 2, Philadelphia, 2013, Elsevier.)

ICU and evaluation for potential life-threatening complications, including cardiovascular instability and respiratory failure.
- Prophylaxis against DVT and PE should always be provided.

REFERRAL
Immediate radiographic and neurologic referral for further evaluation and treatment in all suspected cases of spinal cord compression

SUGGESTED READINGS
Available at www.expertconsult.com

RELATED CONTENT
Spinal Stenosis (Patient Information)

AUTHORS: **DOUGLAS VON HERZEN, M.D.,** and **CATHERINE ELIAS NAJEM, M.D.**

BASIC INFORMATION

DEFINITION
A spinal epidural abscess (SEA) is a focal suppurative infection occurring in the spinal epidural space.

SYNONYM
SEA

ICD-10CM CODES
G06.1 Intraspinal abscess and granuloma

EPIDEMIOLOGY & DEMOGRAPHICS

INCIDENCE (IN U.S.):
- 2 to 25 cases/100,000 hospitalized patients/yr
- May be increasing over the past 3 decades

PREDOMINANT AGE
- Median age of onset approximately 50 yr (35 yr in intravenous drug users)
- Peak incidence in seventh and eighth decades of life

PHYSICAL FINDINGS & CLINICAL PRESENTATION
- The presentation of SEA can be nonspecific.
- Fever, malaise, and back pain are the most consistent early symptoms.
- Pain is often focal. It may initially be mild but can progress to become severe.
- As the disease progresses, root pain can occur, followed by motor weakness, sensory changes, bladder and bowel dysfunction, and paralysis.
- Physical findings may be limited to fever or spinal tenderness.
- The evolution to neurologic deficits can occur as quickly as a few hours, or over weeks to months.
- Once paralysis occurs, it may quickly become irreversible without the appropriate intervention.

ETIOLOGY
- Pyogenic bacteria account for the majority of cases in the United States. Immigrants from TB-endemic areas may present with tuberculous SEAs. Fungi and parasites can also cause this condition. The most common causative organism is *Staphylococcus aureus*. Gram-negative bacilli and anaerobes may be seen if the infection has a urinary or GI source.
- Most posterior SEAs are thought to originate from distant focus (e.g., skin and soft tissue infections), while anterior SEAs are commonly associated with diskitis or vertebral osteomyelitis. No source was found in approximately one third of cases.
- Associated predisposing conditions include diabetes mellitus, alcoholism, cancer, AIDS, and chronic renal failure, or following epidural anesthesia, spinal surgery or trauma, prolonged epidural catheter placement, paraspinal glucocorticoid or analgesic injections, accupuncture, or IV drug use. No predisposing condition is found in approximately 20% of patients.

- Damage to the spinal cord can be caused by direct compression of the spinal cord, vascular compromise, bacterial toxins, and inflammation.

DIAGNOSIS

DIFFERENTIAL DIAGNOSIS
- Herniated disk
- Vertebral osteomyelitis and diskitis
- Metastatic tumors
- Meningitis

LABORATORY TESTS
- WBC may be normal or elevated.
- ESR is usually elevated over 30 mm/hr.

- Blood cultures are positive in approximately 60% of patients with SEA.
- CSF cultures are positive in 19%, but lumbar puncture is unnecessary, and may be contraindicated.
- Once imaging is done, CT-guided aspiration or open biopsy should be done to determine causative organism. Abscess content culture is positive in 90% of patients.

IMAGING STUDIES
- MRI with gadolinium is the imaging modality of choice (Fig. 1S-58); CT scan with contrast may show the abscess (Fig. 1S-59) but is less sensitive than MRI.

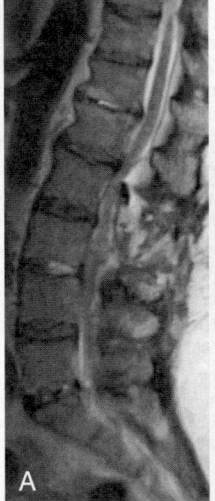
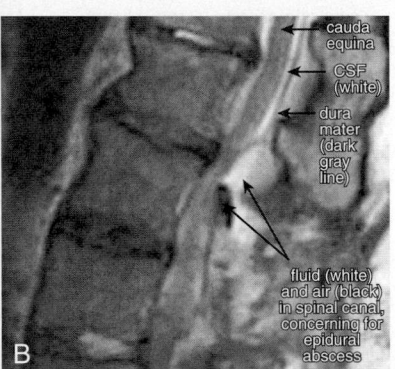

FIGURE 1S-58 Same patient as in Fig. 1S-59, in whom noncontrast computed tomography showed air in the spinal canal, concerning for epidural abscess. Magnetic resonance imaging (MRI) of the lumbar spine without contrast was performed, as the patient was in acute renal failure. **A,** This T₂-weighted sagittal MR image provides useful information even without gadolinium contrast. **B,** Close-up. On T₂-weighted MRI sequences, fluid including cerebrospinal fluid *(CSF)* appears white. Fat-containing tissues such as bone marrow and the spinal cord or cauda equina appear dark gray. Calcified bone appears nearly black due to an absence of resonating protons. Air appears completely black for the same reason. The midline sagittal image shows the cauda equina to be impinged upon by an epidural fluid collection containing air—an epidural abscess. The dura mater is visible as a thin, dark gray line parallel to the spinal cord. It is indented in the region of the epidural abscess. (From Broder JS: *Diagnostic imaging for the emergency physician,* Philadelphia, 2011, Saunders.)

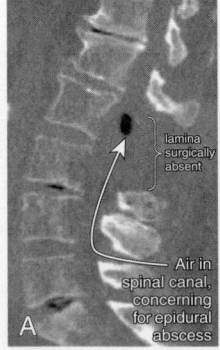
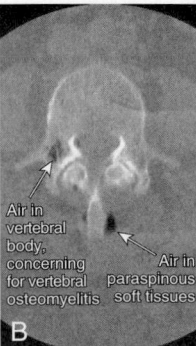
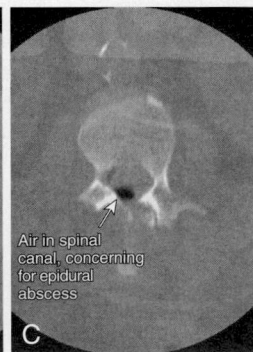

FIGURE 1S-59 This 67-year-old female presented with delirium and fever. Three months prior, she had undergone lumbar laminectomy, and her wound had been treated with a wound VAC dressing. Magnetic resonance imaging was not initially available, so noncontrast computed tomography (CT) was performed. Noncontrast CT is excellent at delineating air, which appears black on bone windows. **A,** The midsagittal view demonstrates air *(black)* in the spinal canal at the L2 and L3 levels. On the axial views **(B, C),** air is visible in the spinal canal, in paraspinal soft tissues, and within the vertebral body. These findings are concerning for a paraspinal infection that has developed into an epidural abscess with vertebral osteomyelitis. (From Broder JS: *Diagnostic imaging for the emergency physician,* Philadelphia, 2011, Saunders.)

- CT with myelography is more sensitive for cord compression.

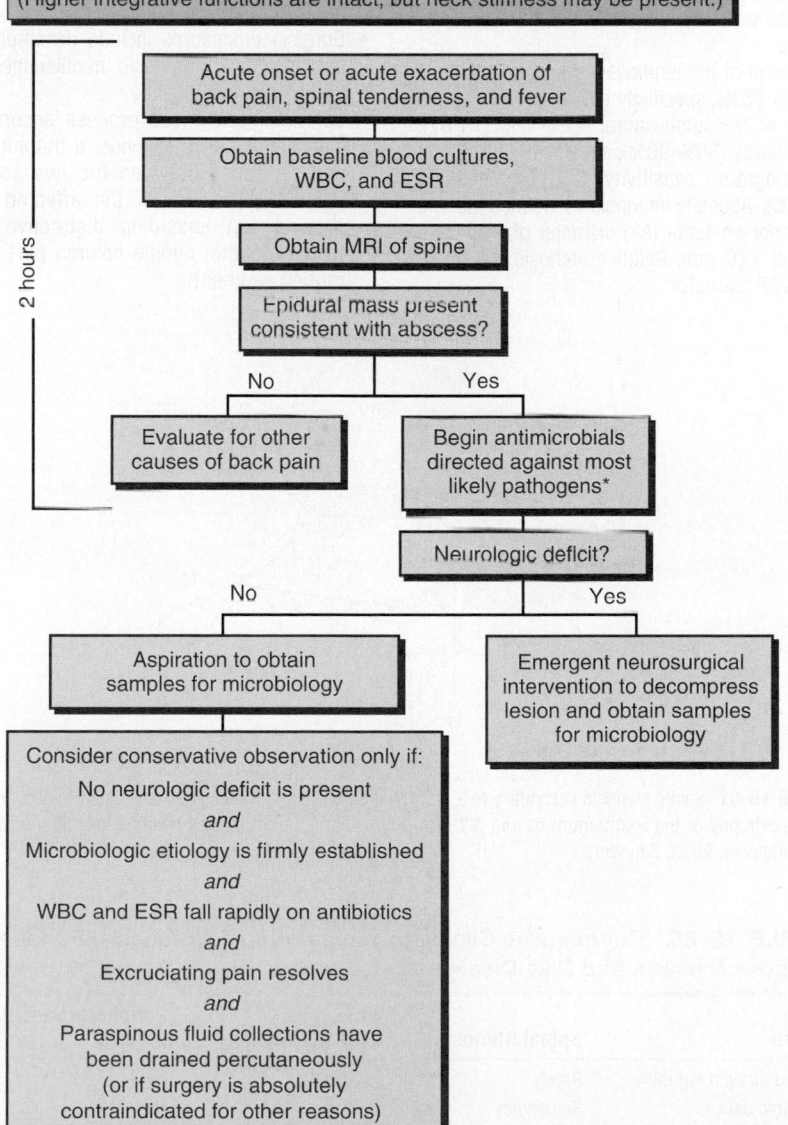

Rx TREATMENT

NONPHARMACOLOGIC THERAPY

- Surgical decompression is the mainstay of treatment. Decompression within the first 24 hr has been related to an improved prognosis.
- Nonsurgical treatment is effective in some patients, but failure rate may be excessive. This approach should not be considered and should only be attempted in the absence of signs of compressive myelopathy and with very careful follow-up.

ACUTE GENERAL Rx

- In addition to surgery, antibiotics directed at the most likely organism should be initiated. Fig. 1S-60 describes an algorithm for the management of patients with SEA.
- If the organism is unknown, broad coverage against staphylococci, streptococci, and gram-negative bacilli should be initiated. Empiric antimicrobial therapy typically includes vancomycin plus an antipseudomonal cephalosporin or carbapenem. The regimen can be adjusted according to culture results. Therapy should continue for at least 4 to 6 wk.

CHRONIC Rx

Neurologic deficits may remain despite aggressive treatment.

DISPOSITION

Irreversible paralysis and death can occur in up to 25% of patients.

REFERRAL

All cases should be referred to a neurosurgeon and an infectious disease specialist.

! PEARLS & CONSIDERATIONS

- It is critically important to recognize this process early; the prognosis is generally excellent if treatment is initiated while symptoms are localized and before evidence of myelopathy develops.
- The likelihood of success postsurgery is low in patients who have developed complete paralysis for longer than 36 hours.

SUGGESTED READINGS

Available at www.expertconsult.com

AUTHOR: **GLENN G. FORT, M.D., M.P.H.**

FIGURE 1S-60 Algorithm for the management of patients with spinal epidural abscess syndrome. If magnetic resonance imaging (MRI) cannot be performed, myelography, high-contrast computed tomography (CT), or CT-myelography may be an acceptable alternative to localize an epidural abscess. *If abscess drainage can be performed promptly, antimicrobial drugs may be withheld until specimens for microbial analysis are obtained. ESR, Erythrocyte sedimentation rate; WBC, white blood cell. (From Vincent JL et al: Textbook of critical care, ed 6, Philadelphia, 2011, Saunders.)

Diseases and Disorders

 BASIC INFORMATION

DEFINITION

Spinal stenosis is the pathologic condition caused by the compressing or narrowing of the spinal canal, nerve root canal, or intervertebral foramina at the lumbar region.

SYNONYMS

Central spinal stenosis
Lateral spinal stenosis
Spondylosis

ICD-10CM CODES

M48.06 Spinal stenosis, lumbar region

EPIDEMIOLOGY & DEMOGRAPHICS

More common between 50 and 60 yr of age

PHYSICAL FINDINGS & CLINICAL PRESENTATION

- Symptoms caused by direct mechanical compression or indirect vascular compression of the nerve roots or the cauda equina.
- Neurogenic claudication: leg, buttock, or back pain precipitated by walking and relieved by sitting.
- Pain may radiate down to ankles and is associated with numbness, tingling, and weakness.
- Taking a flexed posture reduces symptoms because it increases the available space in the lumbar spinal canal.
- Decreased lumbar extension.
- Normal peripheral pulses.
- Positive Romberg's sign (decreased proprioception).
- Wide-based gait.
- Reduced knee and ankle reflex.
- Urine incontinence.

ETIOLOGY

Spinal stenosis may be primary or secondary (Fig. 1S-61)
- Primary stenosis (congenital or developmental narrowing)
  1. Idiopathic
  2. Achondroplasia
  3. Morquio-Ullrich syndrome
- Secondary stenosis (acquired)
  1. Degenerative (hypertrophy of the articular processes, disk degeneration, ligamentum flavum hypertrophy, spondylolisthesis)
  2. Fracture/trauma
  3. Postoperative (postlaminectomy)
  4. Paget's disease
  5. Ankylosing spondylitis
  6. Tumors
  7. Acromegaly

 DIAGNOSIS

DIFFERENTIAL DIAGNOSIS

- Osteoarthritis of the knee or hip
- Acute cauda equina syndrome, resulting from compression by epidural abscess or tumors

- Pain and weakness caused by multiple myeloma or osteomyelitis
- Intermittent claudication—peripheral vascular disease
- Peripheral neuropathy such as that caused by a herniated nucleus pulposus
- Scoliosis or spondylolisthesis
- Rheumatoid diseases: ankylosing spondylitis, Reiter's syndrome, fibromyalgia
- Table 1S-25 compares clinical features of spinal stenosis, peripheral vascular disease, and disk disease.

WORKUP

History, physical examination, and specific imaging studies

IMAGING STUDIES

- Lumbar spine film sensitivity 66%, specificity 93%.
- Ultrasound of the spinal canal has also been used.
- CT scan of the lumbosacral spine: sensitivity (75%-85%), specificity (80%).
- MRI of the lumbosacral spine (Fig. 1S-62): sensitivity (80%-90%), specificity (95%).
- Myelogram: sensitivity (77%), specificity (72%). Absolute stenosis is defined as the anterior-posterior (AP) diameter of the spinal canal <10 mm. Relative stenosis: 10 to 12 mm AP diameter.

- Electromyography (EMG) and nerve conduction velocity (NCV) are additional studies particularly useful in differentiating peripheral neuropathy from lumbar spinal stenosis.

 TREATMENT

NONPHARMACOLOGIC THERAPY

- Physiotherapy
- Lumbar corsets
- Back exercises
- Abdominal muscle strengthening
- Aquatic exercises

ACUTE GENERAL Rx

- Surgery is indicated in patients with significant compression of nerve roots as determined by MRI or CT and incapacitating symptoms limiting activities of daily living or bladder and bowel incontinence.
- Surgical procedures include decompressive laminectomy, arthrodesis, hemilaminectomy, and medial facetectomy.
- Lumbar interspinous process decompression using X-STOP device: a titanium oval spacer placed between the two adjacent spinous processes of the affected level; provides an unloading distractive force to the stenotic middle column part of the motion segment.

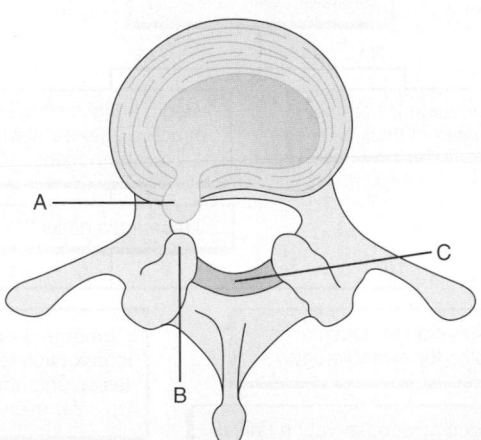

FIGURE 1S-61 Spinal stenosis secondary to a combination of disk herniation *(A)*, facet joint hypertrophy *(B)*, and hypertrophy of the ligamentum flavum *(C)*. (From Firestein GS et al: *Kelly's textbook of rheumatology*, ed 9, Philadelphia, 2013, Saunders.)

TABLE 1S-25 Comparative Clinical Features of Spinal Stenosis, Peripheral Vascular Disease, and Disc Disease

Feature	Spinal Stenosis	Disc Prolapse	Peripheral Vascular Disease
Reduced straight leg raise	Rarely	Usually	No
Neurologic deficit	Sometimes	Often	No
Leg pain on walking	Yes	Usually	Yes
Leg pain on sitting	No	Yes	No
Pain relief on standing still	No	No	Yes
Pain relief on sitting	Yes	No	Yes
Numbness/paresthesia	Yes	Yes	Sometimes

From Carr A, Hamilton W: *Orthopedics in primary care*, ed 2, Philadelphia, 2005, Butterworth-Heinemann.

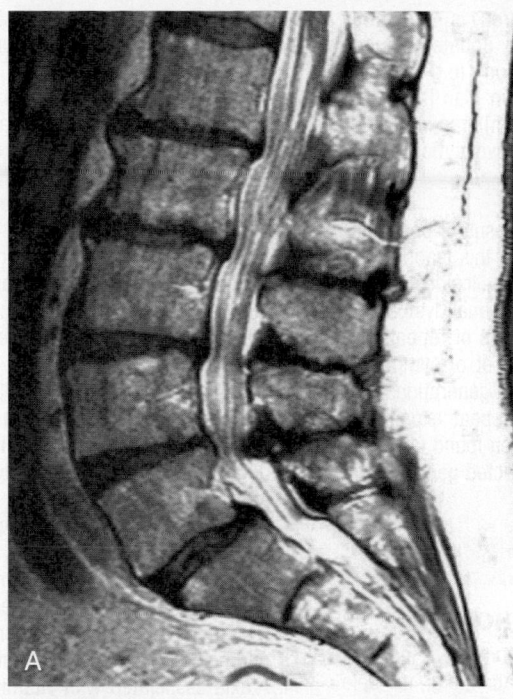
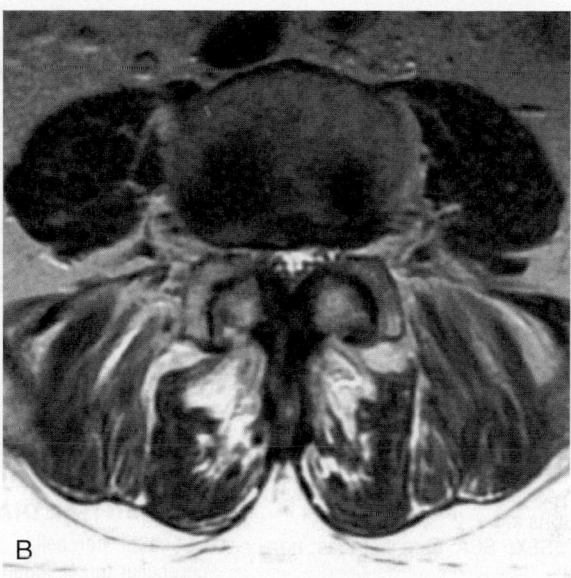

FIGURE 1S-62 Degenerative spinal stenosis. A, The sagittal T2-weighted magnetic resonance image shows decreased anteroposterior diameter of the neural canal at the L4-5 level due to redundancy of the ligamentum flavum. **B,** The axial image through the L4-5 disk shows decreased cross-sectional area of the thecal sac from hypertrophic changes of the facet joints posterolateral to the thecal sac. (Courtesy Dr. John Crues, University of California, San Diego.)

- There is little value in adding fusion to decompression surgery. For most patients, spinal stenosis surgery should be limited to decompression when no overt instability is present. Trials have shown that fusion for the treatment of spinal stenosis should be restricted to patients who have proven spinal instability, as confirmed on flexion-extension radiographs; vertebral destruction caused by trauma, tumors, infections, or spinal deformities, such as congenital spondylolisthesis or adult scoliosis.[1]

CHRONIC Rx

- Conservative therapy with NSAIDs (ibuprofen 800 mg PO tid, naproxen 500 mg PO bid) may be tried for symptomatic relief in addition to acetaminophen 1 g PO qid.
- Epidural glucocorticoid injections are widely used to treat symptoms of lumbar spinal stenosis; however, rigorous data are lacking regarding the effectiveness and safety

of these injections. A recent trial revealed that in the treatment of lumbar spinal stenosis, epidural injection of glucocorticoids plus lidocaine offered minimal or no short-term benefit as compared with epidural injection of lidocaine alone.

DISPOSITION

- Approximately 20% of patients having surgery require repeat surgery within 10 yr. Nearly one third of these patients continue to experience pain.
- The natural history of spinal stenosis is one of slow progression. Although not very common, cord compression with resultant bowel and bladder incontinence and paresis can occur.
- Operative treatment is more effective in reducing pain and disability than nonoperative treatment.

REFERRAL

- Patients who have spinal stenosis should be referred to an orthopedic surgeon specializing in back surgery or to a neurosurgeon.

- Pain clinic referrals should be made if surgery is contraindicated or if the patient does not want surgery.

! PEARLS & CONSIDERATIONS

COMMENTS

- Approximately one third of patients have coexisting peripheral vascular disease.
- The severity of cauda equina constriction is directly related to the walking ability and the pain intensity in the legs and back.
- Spinal stenosis is also a cause of chronic low back pain in the young.

SUGGESTED READINGS

Available at www.expertconsult.com

RELATED CONTENT

Spinal Stenosis (Patient Information)

AUTHOR: **JORGE A. VILLAFUERTE, M.D.**

[1]Peul WC, Moojen WA: Fusion for spinal stenosis, safeguard or superfluous surgical implant? *N Engl J Med* 374(15):1478-1479, 2016.

BASIC INFORMATION

DEFINITION

The spinocerebellar ataxias (SCAs) are a heterogeneous group of autosomal-dominant inherited genetic conditions that cause progressive ataxia and other neurologic symptoms.

SYNONYMS

Autosomal-dominant cerebellar ataxia (ADCA)
Machado-Joseph disease (eponym for SCA3; this may be the most common SCA)

> **ICD-10CM CODES**
> G11.9 Hereditary ataxia, unspecified
> G11.8 Other hereditary ataxias

EPIDEMIOLOGY & DEMOGRAPHICS

PREVALENCE: The prevalence of the condition is approximately 3 persons per 100,000. The most common SCAs are 1, 2, 3, 6, and 7.
PREDOMINANT SEX: SCA demonstrates no gender preference.
PREDOMINANT AGE: The age of onset is often during the 30s or 40s. However, this can be highly variable, even within family groups; SCAs can occur anytime from childhood to late adulthood.
GENETICS: All SCAs are inherited in an autosomal dominant fashion; however, reduced penetrance can be present.

PHYSICAL FINDINGS & CLINICAL PRESENTATION

- Chronically progressive cerebellar ataxia is the predominant symptom of all of the SCAs. It typically presents as a combination of balance and gait difficulty, limb incoordination, nystagmus, and dysarthria.
- More than 36 different genetic subtypes of SCA have been described to date. Although certain clinical characteristics are common to specific SCA subtypes, these conditions have significant overlap and variability; therefore, making a diagnosis based on the clinical presentation alone can be challenging and sometimes impossible without genetic testing. The more common SCAs may include the following distinguishing features in addition to ataxia:
  1. SCA1 can be characterized by nystagmus, spasticity, and neuropathy.
  2. SCA2 can be characterized by slow saccades, gaze palsy, neuropathy, and sometimes parkinsonism or dementia.
  3. SCA3, also known as Machado-Joseph disease (Fig. 1S-63), can be characterized by neuropathy, amyotrophy, parkinsonism, and dystonia.
  4. SCA6 is generally felt to be a pure cerebellar syndrome with ataxia and nystagmus (gaze evoked and downbeat) as well as a frequently later age of onset.
  5. SCA7 is characterized by dementia, vision loss caused by a pigmentary maculopathy, and spasticity.

6. Knowledge in this area is constantly expanding and being updated. Online sources of information (e.g., Online Mendelian Inheritance in Man [http://www.ncbi.nlm.nih.gov/omim]) can be invaluable for tracking new developments.

ETIOLOGY

Several of the SCAs are the result of polyglutamine CAG repeat expansions; this leads to the accumulation of mutant proteins inside neurons, which is thought to cause neuronal dysfunction and cell death. Higher numbers of repeats are correlated with an earlier onset of symptoms, and anticipation in subsequent generations may be present. Other types of repeat expansions and point mutations have been found with several SCAs; for others, the affected gene has not been identified.

DIAGNOSIS

DIFFERENTIAL DIAGNOSIS

- Structural cerebellar abnormality: includes cerebellar tumor, inflammation (e.g., multiple sclerosis), stroke, or hemorrhage; the time course for these causes is typically more acute or subacute than chronic.
- Endocrine dysfunction: hypothyroidism or hypoparathyroidism can uncommonly cause ataxia.
- Alcoholic cerebellar degeneration: caused by heavy alcohol use; gait ataxia predominates.
- Other toxin-induced ataxias: antiepileptic medications, lithium, heavy metals (lead, manganese, mercury, bismuth), and chemotherapeutic agents.
- Creutzfeldt-Jakob disease: rapidly progressive ataxia, dementia, and myoclonus.
- Paraneoplastic cerebellar degeneration: found in association with primary malignancies (e.g., small cell lung cancer, breast cancer); subacute-onset ataxia that progresses rapidly.
- Celiac disease: gluten-sensitive enteropathy with malabsorption may be associated with ataxia; autoantibodies such as antigliadin, anti-tissue transglutaminase (TTG), and/or IgA endomysial antibodies are typically present.
- Anti-glutamic acid decarboxylase (GAD) antibody-associated cerebellar ataxia: a rare autoimmune cause of late-onset ataxia that may be partially responsive to immunotherapy.
- Multiple system atrophy (MSA): cerebellar variant of this disorder causes ataxia; there is typically associated parkinsonism with some degree of autonomic dysfunction (e.g., orthostatic hypotension, urinary incontinence); brain MRI may reveal pontocerebellar atrophy.
- Friedreich's ataxia: autosomal recessive inheritance, generally younger age of onset (i.e., mean 15 yr of age), lower limb areflexia, and posterior column dysfunction.
- Ataxia associated with vitamin E deficiency: can be an autosomal recessive disorder or acquired; clinically resembles Friedreich's ataxia, with areflexia and loss of position sense.
- Ataxia telangiectasia: autosomal recessive inheritance, childhood onset, oculocutaneous telangiectasias, and immunodeficiency.
- Wilson's disease: can cause hepatic dysfunction, psychiatric symptoms, and a variety of movement disorders, including ataxia; particularly important to screen for this in patients who are young at onset because it is treatable.
- Dentatorubral-pallidoluysian atrophy (DRPLA): autosomal dominant like SCA but typically has ataxia with associated choreoathetosis,

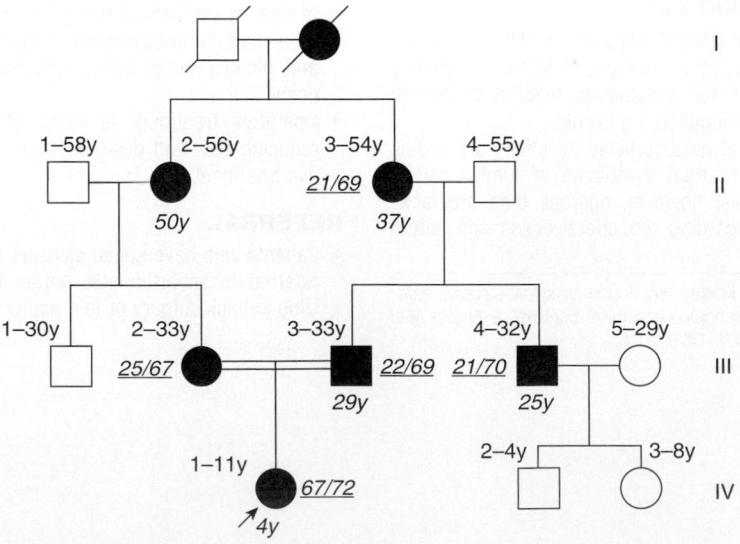

FIGURE 1S-63 Family pedigree of proband (IV-1). Age at onset of spinocerebellar ataxia type 3 symptoms is given beneath symbols (*italics*). Above symbols the actual age of the members of the family are given. If tested, the number of CAG repeat units of the *ATXN3* allele pair is also given (*underscored italics*). (From Daniel R. Carvalho et al.: *Homozygosity enhances severity in spinocerebellar ataxia type 3; Pediatric neurology*, Volume 38, Issue 4, April 2008, pp. 296–299.)

BOX 1S-9 Classification of Ataxia

Congenital Ataxias

Hereditary Ataxias

Autosomal Recessive Ataxias.
- Friedreich's ataxia
- Ataxia–telangiectasia
- Ataxia with oculomotor apraxia type 1
- Ataxia with oculomotor apraxia type 2
- Autosomal recessive spastic ataxia of Charlevoix-Saguenay
- Abetalipoproteinemia
- Ataxia with isolated vitamin E deficiency
- Refsum's disease
- Cerebrotendinous xanthomatosis
- Marinesco-Sjögren syndrome
- Autosomal recessive ataxia with known gene locus
- Early-onset cerebellar ataxia

X-Linked Ataxias
- Fragile X tremor ataxia syndrome

Autosomal Dominant Ataxias
- Spinocerebellar ataxias
- Dentatorubral-pallidoluysian atrophy
- Episodic ataxias

Nonhereditary Degenerative Ataxias
- Multiple system atrophy, cerebellar type
- Sporadic adult-onset ataxia of unknown etiology

Acquired Ataxias
- Alcoholic cerebellar degeneration
- Ataxia as a result of other toxic causes (e.g., antiepileptic medications, lithium, solvents)
- Paraneoplastic cerebellar degeneration (e.g., anti-Hu, anti-VGKC, anti-CV2)
- Other immune-mediated ataxias (e.g., gluten ataxia, ataxia associated with anti-glutamic acid decarboxylase antibodies)
- Acquired vitamin E deficiency
- Hypothyroidism
- Ataxia as a result of physical causes (e.g., heat stroke, hyperthermia)

From Goetz CG: *Textbook of clinical neurology*, ed 3, Philadelphia, 2007, Saunders.

myoclonus, epilepsy, and dementia; frequently grouped with the SCAs due to its shared pathogenic CAG repeat expansion.
- Fragile X–associated tremor/ataxia syndrome: premutation of the fragile X mutation gene; more common among males than females; late onset of ataxia (i.e., >50 yr), tremor, and sometimes parkinsonism; MRI often shows T2 hyperintensities in the middle cerebellar peduncle.
- Episodic ataxias: autosomal dominant, transient ataxia lasting seconds to days depending on the mutation; pediatric onset in most; ataxia may be responsive to acetazolamide.
- Spastic ataxias: distinguished by prominent, symmetric spasticity, particularly of the lower extremities. Most of these conditions have an autosomal recessive pattern of inheritance and include autosomal recessive spastic ataxia of Charlevoix-Saguenay (ARSACS), hereditary spastic paraplegia (HSP), and cerebrotendinous xanthomatosis.
- Box 1S-9 shows the classification of the various causes of ataxia.

LABORATORY TESTS
- Rule out acquired causes of ataxia, depending on the clinical scenario, with thyroid studies, toxicology screening, and the determination of the vitamin E level or presence of paraneoplastic antibodies.
- For pediatric patients, screen for ataxia telangiectasia with serum alpha-fetoprotein (AFP).
- Screen for Wilson's disease with ceruloplasmin and, if indicated, a 24-hour urinary copper determination.
- Genetic testing is commercially available for many but not all of the SCAs (SCA 1, 2, 3, 5, 6, 7, 8, 10, 12, 13, 14, 17, 28, DRPLA).

IMAGING STUDIES
- MRI of the brain should be performed to exclude structural abnormalities.
- Cerebellar or brain stem atrophy can be seen with several of the SCA subtypes.

 **TREATMENT**

NONPHARMACOLOGIC THERAPY
- Speech therapy for dysarthria and dysphagia.
- Physical therapy.
- Occupational therapy.

CHRONIC Rx
Treatment is symptomatic and supportive. In some cases, parkinsonism can respond to levodopa. Clonazepam can be helpful if tremor is prominent. Spasticity can be treated with baclofen or tizanidine. Focal spasticity or dystonia may benefit from botulinum toxin injections.

DISPOSITION
All SCA disorders are progressive, although the speed is variable from subtype to subtype and from patient to patient. On average, patients become wheelchair bound 15 yr after the onset of ataxia, and death can occur after 20 to 25 yr.

REFERRAL
Referral to a general neurologist or to a movement disorders center is appropriate.

⊘ PEARLS & CONSIDERATIONS

COMMENTS
- Genetic testing can have consequences for both the patient and the family. These issues should be discussed during the informed consent process. Patients who desire asymptomatic testing as a result of a relevant family history should undergo genetic counseling before testing.
- In symptomatic patients with a family history of dominantly inherited ataxia, the diagnostic process is relatively straightforward. Genetic testing that is directed toward likely mutations by phenotype and ethnic origin should be the first step rather than an extensive workup for other causes.

PATIENT & FAMILY EDUCATION
Patient educational materials, as well as contact information for support and advocacy groups, are available through the National Ataxia Foundation: http://www.ataxia.org

SUGGESTED READINGS
Available at www.expertconsult.com

AUTHOR: **ANDREW DUKER, M.D.,** and **JENNIFER E. VAUGHAN, M.D.**

 **BASIC INFORMATION**

DEFINITION

Spontaneous miscarriage is fetal loss before week 20 of pregnancy, calculated from the patient's last menstrual period or the delivery of a fetus weighing <500 g. Early loss is before menstrual week 12, whereas late loss refers to losses from weeks 12 to 20.

Miscarriage can also be classified as incomplete (partial passage of fetal tissue through partially dilated cervix), complete (spontaneous passage of all fetal tissue), threatened (uterine bleeding without cervical dilation or passage of tissue), inevitable (bleeding with cervical dilation without passage of fetal tissue), or missed abortion (intrauterine fetal demise without passage of tissue).

Recurrent miscarriage involves three or more spontaneous pregnancy losses before week 20. However, in actual practice, most reproductive experts consider two spontaneous pregnancy losses sufficient to initiate an evaluation for habitual or recurrent spontaneous abortion. The definition is somewhat variable depending on the source.

SYNONYMS

Spontaneous abortion
Miscarriage

ICD-10CM CODES
O03.9 Complete or unspecified spontaneous abortion without complication
O03.89 Complete or unspecified spontaneous abortion with other complications

EPIDEMIOLOGY & DEMOGRAPHICS

INCIDENCE: 5% to 20% of clinically recognized pregnancies; 80% of miscarriages occur in the first trimester. Recurrent miscarriage occurs in <1% of couples attempting to have children.

GENETICS

- Distribution of abnormal karyotypes: autosomal trisomy (50%), monosomy 45,X (20%), triploidy (15%), tetraploidy (10%), structural chromosomal abnormalities (5%).
- With two or more spontaneous miscarriages, a karyotype can be performed on the products of conception to evaluate for aneuploidy, which may be associated with a balanced translocation in one of the parents, and which has a substantially increased risk for abortion (depending on the actual type of translocation); if the pregnancy is carried to term, it has a 3% to 5% risk for an unbalanced karyotype. In patients with habitual abortion, evaluation for anatomic defects such as uterine septum and for antiphospholipid syndrome (lupus anticoagulant, beta 2 glycoprotein IgG/IgM, and anticardiolipin antibody) IgG/IgM should also be obtained.

RISK FACTORS

Vaginal bleeding, especially >3 d, carries with it a 15 to 20% chance of miscarriage. Diabetes should be controlled to reduce risk.

PHYSICAL FINDINGS & CLINICAL PRESENTATION

- Profuse bleeding and cramping have a higher association with miscarriage than bleeding without cramping, which is more consistent with a threatened miscarriage.
- Cervical dilation with history or finding of fetal tissue at cervical os may be present.
- In cases of missed abortion, uterine size may be smaller than menstrual dating, in contrast to molar gestation, where size may be greater than dates.

ETIOLOGY

- In a general overview the etiology can be classified in terms of maternal (environmental) and fetal (genetic) factors, with the majority of miscarriages being related to genetic or chromosomal causes.
- Causes: uterine anomalies (unicornuate uterus risk, 50%; bicornuate or septate uterus risk, 25%-30%); incompetent cervix (iatrogenic or congenital, associated with 20% of mid-trimester losses); diethylstilbestrol exposure in utero (T-shaped uterus); submucous leiomyomas; intrauterine adhesions or synechiae; luteal phase or progesterone deficiency; autoimmune disease such as anticardiolipin, beta 2 glycoprotein or lupus anticoagulant autoantibodies; uncontrolled diabetes mellitus. Rare or controversial causes include HLA associations between mother and father; infections such as tuberculosis, *Chlamydia,* and *Ureaplasma;* smoking and alcohol use; irradiation; and environmental toxins. Most of the literature is observational in nature, which may skew risk factor data.
- Use of fluconazole in pregnancy is associated with a statistically significant increased risk of spontaneous miscarriage.

 **DIAGNOSIS**

DIFFERENTIAL DIAGNOSIS

- Normal pregnancy
- Hydatidiform molar gestation
- Ectopic pregnancy
- Dysfunctional uterine bleeding
- Pathologic endometrial or cervical lesions

WORKUP

- All patients with bleeding in the first trimester should have an evaluation for possible ectopic pregnancy.
- If there are three early, prior pregnancy losses, a workup and treatment for recurrent miscarriage should begin before next conception. If there is a strong history for second-trimester loss, consideration for cerclage should be given if the history is consistent with incompetent cervix (e.g., painless cervical dilation).
- Most providers will initiate an evaluation for couples who have had 2 previous losses.
- One unexplained fetal loss beyond 10 wk or 1 birth before 34 wk because of preeclampsia should prompt an evaluation for antiphospholipid syndrome.

LABORATORY TESTS

- Type and antibody screen are used to evaluate the need for Rh immune globulin.
- Recurrent pregnancy loss: During the preconception period in patients with habitual abortion, hemoglobin A_{1c}, anticardiolipin antibody, lupus anticoagulant, 20210A beta 2 glycoprotein antibodies, karyotyping, and anatomic evaluation, hysterosalpingography, or saline ultrasonography to assess for uterine septum. With increasing age, oocyte quality is a factor, and some practitioners will perform day 3 of the menstrual cycle FSH and anti-müllerian hormone to assess for diminished ovarian reserve, septate uterus. Progesterone level <5 mg/dl suggests nonviable gestation vs. >25 mg/dl, which suggests a good prognosis.

IMAGING STUDIES

Transvaginal sonogram (preferred) can be used with menstrual dating and serum quantitative human chorionic gonadotropin to document pregnancy location, fetal heart presence, gestational sac size, and adnexal pathology.

 **TREATMENT**

NONPHARMACOLOGIC THERAPY

Depending on the patient's clinical status, desire to continue the pregnancy, and certainty of the diagnosis, expectant management can be considered. In pregnancies <6 wk or >14 wk, complete expulsion of fetal tissue usually occurs, and surgical intervention such as D&C can be avoided.

ACUTE GENERAL Rx

- Incomplete miscarriage between 6 and 14 wk can be associated with great blood loss; these patients should undergo D&C.
- In cases of missed abortion, if fetal demise has occurred >6 wk before or gestational age is >14 wk, there is an increased risk of hypofibrinogenemia with disseminated intravascular coagulation. Thus D&C or manual vacuum aspiration should be performed early in the disease course. Consider use of misoprostol (Cytotec) 200 mg PO q6h as an alternative approach if patient desires a less invasive approach.
- Rh-negative patients should be given RhoGAM 50 mcg IM to prevent Rh isoimmunization.

PEARLS & CONSIDERATIONS

Spontaneous pregnancy loss is recommended as a replacement for the term *abortion* and to acknowledge the emotional aspects of losing a pregnancy.

SUGGESTED READINGS

Available at www.expertconsult.com

RELATED CONTENT

Miscarriage (Patient Information)

AUTHOR: **RUBEN ALVERO, M.D.**

BASIC INFORMATION

DEFINITION

Squamous cell carcinoma (SCC) is a malignant tumor of the skin arising in the epithelium.

SYNONYMS

SCC
Skin cancer

ICD-10CM CODES

C44.5	Malignant neoplasm of skin of trunk
C44.4	Malignant neoplasm of skin of scalp and neck
D04	Carcinoma in situ of skin
C44.9	Malignant neoplasm of skin, unspecified
C44.0	Malignant neoplasm of skin of lip
C44.2	Malignant neoplasm of skin of ear and external auricular canal
C44.3	Malignant neoplasm of skin of other and unspecified parts of skin
C44.02	Squamous cell carcinoma of skin of lip
C44.121	Squamous cell carcinoma of skin of unspecified eyelid, including canthus
C44.122	Squamous cell carcinoma of skin of right eyelid, including canthus
C44.129	Squamous cell carcinoma of skin of left eyelid, including canthus
C44.221	Squamous cell carcinoma of skin of unspecified ear and external auricular canal
C44.222	Squamous cell carcinoma of skin of right ear and external auricular canal
C44.229	Squamous cell carcinoma of skin of left ear and external auricular canal
C44.320	Squamous cell carcinoma of skin of unspecified parts of face
C44.321	Squamous cell carcinoma of skin of nose
C44.329	Squamous cell carcinoma of skin of other parts of face
C44.42	Squamous cell carcinoma of skin of scalp and neck
C44.520	Squamous cell carcinoma of anal skin
C44.521	Squamous cell carcinoma of skin of breast
C44.529	Squamous cell carcinoma of skin of other part of trunk
C44.621	Squamous cell carcinoma of skin of unspecified upper limb, including shoulder
C44.622	Squamous cell carcinoma of skin of right upper limb, including shoulder
C44.629	Squamous cell carcinoma of skin of left upper limb, including shoulder
C44.721	Squamous cell carcinoma of skin of unspecified lower limb, including hip
C44.722	Squamous cell carcinoma of skin of right lower limb, including hip
C44.729	Squamous cell carcinoma of skin of left lower limb, including hip
C44.82	Squamous cell carcinoma of overlapping sites of skin

EPIDEMIOLOGY & DEMOGRAPHICS

- SCC is the second most common cutaneous malignancy, comprising 20% of all cases of nonmelanoma skin cancer.
- Incidence is highest in lower latitudes (e.g., southern Unites States, Australia).
- Male/female ratio is 2:1.
- Incidence increases with age and sun exposure.
- In black patients, SCC are 20% more common than basal cell carcinomas (BCC).
- Average age at diagnosis is 66 yr.

PHYSICAL FINDINGS & CLINICAL PRESENTATION

- SCC frequently begins at the site of actinic keratosis and commonly affects the scalp, neck region, back of hands, superior surface of the pinna, and the lip (Fig. 1S-65). On the lower lip, SCC often develops on actinic cheilitis. A history of smoking is a significant predisposing factor.
- The lesion may have a scaly, erythematous macule or plaque.
- Telangiectasia, central ulceration may also be present (Fig. 1S-66). The ulcer may be superficial and hidden by a crust. Removal of the crust may reveal a well-defined papillary base.
- Most SCCs present as exophytic lesions that grow over a period of months.
- Although most SCCs are relatively slow growing and nonaggressive, some (2%-5%) can exhibit rapid growth and metastases. Aggressive tumors are more common in immunocompromised patients and when arising from scars, burns, or prior injury (Marjolin's ulcer). Presence of SCC on ears, lips, or size >2 cm are high-risk features of SCC.

ETIOLOGY

Risk factors include ultraviolet B radiation, immunosuppression (kidney transplant recipients have a significantly increased risk), arsenic exposure, HPV infection, medications (azathioprine, sorafenib, tumor necrosis factor [TNF] inhibitors), sicoid LE, erosive lichen planus, chronic ulcers, prior radiation exposure, and tobacco abuse.

DIAGNOSIS

DIFFERENTIAL DIAGNOSIS

- Keratoacanthomas
- Actinic keratosis
- Amelanotic melanoma
- Basal cell carcinoma
- Benign tumors
- Healing traumatic wounds
- Spindle cell tumors
- Warts

WORKUP

Diagnosis is made by full-thickness skin biopsy (incisional or excisional).

TREATMENT

ACUTE GENERAL Rx

- Electrodesiccation and curettage for small SCCs (<2 cm in diameter), superficial tumors, and lesions located in extremity and trunk.
- Tumors thinner than 4 mm can be managed by simple local removal.
- Lesions between 4 and 8 mm thick or those with deep dermal invasion should be excised.
- Tumors penetrating the dermis can be treated with several modalities, including excision and Mohs' surgery, radiation therapy, and chemotherapy. Mohs' surgery is commonly used for lesions on the face.
- Metastatic SCC can be treated with cryotherapy and combination of chemotherapy using 13-*cis*-retinoic acid and interferon-alpha 2A.

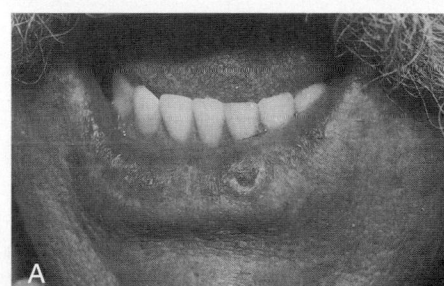
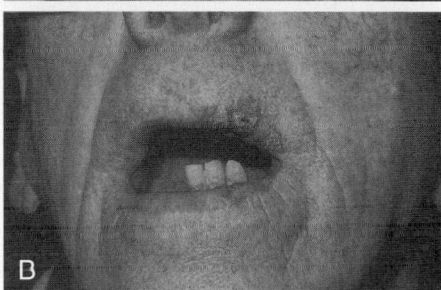

FIGURE 1S-65 Squamous cell carcinoma of the lip. The lower lip **(A)** is a relatively commonly affected site. Smoking is a risk factor for this site, and the prognosis is poorer compared to similar-sized lesions at other sun-exposed sites. Treatment is usually by wedge excision or with radiotherapy. By contrast, the upper lip margin **(B)** is a relatively uncommon site. The chronic trauma from the patient's only three teeth may have been relevant. (From White GM, Cox NH [eds]: *Diseases of the skin, a color atlas and text*, ed 2, St Louis, 2006, Mosby.)

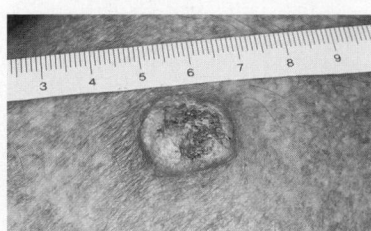

FIGURE 1S-66 Squamous cell carcinoma. Nodular hyperkeratotic lesion with central erosion. (From Noble J et al: *Textbook of primary care medicine*, ed 3, St Louis, 2001, Mosby.)

DISPOSITION

- Survival is related to size, location, degree of differentiation, immunologic status of the patient, depth of invasion, and presence of metastases. Risk factors for metastasis include lesions on the lip or ear, increasing lesion depth, and poor cell differentiation.
- Patients whose tumors penetrate through the dermis or exceed 8 mm in thickness are at risk of tumor recurrence.
- The most common metastatic locations are regional lymph nodes, liver, and lung.
- Tumors on the scalp, forehead, ears, nose, and lips also carry a higher risk.
- The rate of SCC metastasis from all skin sites ranges from 0.5% to 5.2%.
- SCCs originating in the lip and pinna metastasize in 10% to 20% of cases.
- Five-year survival for metastatic SCC is 34%.

REFERRAL

Oncology referral for metastatic SCC

⚠ PEARLS & CONSIDERATIONS

COMMENTS

- SCC arising in areas of prior radiation, thermal injury, and areas of chronic ulcers or chronic draining sinuses are more aggressive and have a higher frequency of metastasis than those originating in actinic damaged skin.
- Oral retinoids may be useful as a preventative strategy in patients with immunosuppression.
- Nicotinamide (500 mg bid, available over the counter) mitigates some of the deleterious effects of UV radiation and has been reported to lower the incidence of non-melanoma skin cancer (NMSCO) by 23%.[1]

EBM EVIDENCE

Available at www.expertconsult.com

SUGGESTED READINGS

Available at www.expertconsult.com

RELATED CONTENT

Squamous Cell Carcinoma (Patient Information)

AUTHOR: **FRED F. FERRI, M.D.**

[1]Chen AC, et al: A phase 3 randomized trial of nicotinamide for skin cancer chemoprevention, *N Engl J Med* 373:1618, 2015.

ⓘ BASIC INFORMATION

DEFINITION

Statin-induced muscle syndromes (SIMS) include myopathy, myalgia, myositis, and rhabdomyolysis. Definitions for these syndromes are inconsistent in the medical literature.

- Myopathy: a general term defined as any disease of muscles.
- Myalgia: muscle weakness or pain without serum creatinine kinase elevation.
- Myositis: muscle weakness or pain with an increased serum creatinine kinase level.
- Rhabdomyolysis: muscle weakness or pain and a marked serum creatinine kinase level usually greater than 10 times the upper limit of normal and serum creatinine elevation as well as signs of brown urine and elevated urine myoglobin. A rare **immune-mediated necrotizing myopathy (IMNM)**, also known as **statin-associated autoimmune myopathy**, has also been associated with the use of statins with symptoms persisting after discontinuation of the drug. This condition presents with symmetric proximal arm and leg weakness and severe elevations of muscle enzymes.

SYNONYMS

Statin-induced myopathies
Statin-induced myositis
Statin-induced myalgias
Statin-induced rhabdomyolysis
Statin-associated autoimmune myopathy

ICD-10CM CODES

M60.9	Myositis, unspecified
M62.82	Rhabdomyolysis
G72.2	Myopathy due to other toxic agents
G72.9	Myopathy, unspecified
G72.81	Critical illness myopathy
G72.89	Other specified myopathies
M60.89	Other myositis, multiple sites

EPIDEMIOLOGY & DEMOGRAPHICS

INCIDENCE: Risk of statin-induced rhabdomyolysis is 1.2 per 10,000 persons/yr. Rhabdomyolysis risk of death is 0.15 deaths per 1 million prescriptions. SIMS most commonly occur in people aged 51 to 75, which may reflect the pattern of statin use. Statin-associated autoimmune myopathy is extremely rare, occurring in 2 or 3 of every 100,000 patients treated with statins.
PEAK INCIDENCE: Patients on high-dose statins have a 0.9% incidence of statin-induced rhabdomyolysis.
PREVALENCE: The prevalence of statin-induced myalgias is about 1% to 5%, similar to placebo in clinical trials, although observational studies have suggested a prevalence of 10% or higher. Statins may cause elevated transaminases (ALT, AST) at a prevalence of 0.5% to 2.0% and rhabdomyolysis ~0.08%.
PREDOMINANT SEX AND AGE: The mean age of hospitalized patients with statin-induced myopathy or rhabdomyolysis was 64 yr. Slightly more common in women (56%).

GENETICS: Interpatient variability exists in the activity of the *CYP3A4* gene for the metabolism of simvastatin, atorvastatin, and lovastatin. Homozygous carriers of CYP2D6 (poor metabolizers) had a higher rate of discontinuation of simvastatin due to muscle syndromes compared with the CYP2D6 wild-type genotype; patients taking atorvastatin and having a muscle event were more likely to have the CYP2D6*4 allele. SLCO1B1 polymorphisms encode for the organic anion transport of statins into the liver cells. Some data exist on deficiencies in ubiquinone (coenzyme Q10) in patients with a mutation in the *COQ2* gene.
RISK FACTORS: Small body frame; age over 80 yr; women, particularly frail elderly women; patients taking multiple drugs, especially gemfibrozil, niacin, cyclosporine, itraconazole, ketoconazole, erythromycin, clarithromycin, verapamil, amiodarone; renal or liver impairment; pharmacogenetic variability; hypothyroidism; excessive alcohol intake; vigorous exercise; severe infections; excessive grapefruit juice ingestion; inherited defects of muscle metabolism such as carnitine palmityl transferase II deficiency, McArdle's disease, and myoadenylate deaminase deficiency; acquired myopathies such as postpoliomyelitis syndrome; lipophilic statins (simvastatin, atorvastatin, lovastatin); multiple conditions such as diabetes; and drugs of abuse (amphetamines, heroin, cocaine, phencyclidine).

PHYSICAL FINDINGS & CLINICAL PRESENTATION

- Myopathy can occur at any time, although it is more common within the first 4 weeks of therapy.
- Proximal generalized muscle aches, body aches, and pains, and may be mild or severe.
- Dark-colored urine
- Muscle cramps, spasms, tenderness, or stiffness
- Unusually tired or weak
- Nocturnal cramping
- Tendon pain

ETIOLOGY

- History of current statin use
- May be explained by one of three deficiencies of end products of the 3-hydroxy-3-methylglutaryl-coA reductase pathway: cell signaling and apoptosis, mitochondrial function and ubiquinone concentrations, and cholesterol concentrations and cell membrane integrity.
- The risk may be enhanced by drug interactions that interfere with hepatic metabolism and gut wall transport of interacting medications and by pharmacodynamic effects.
- Underlying metabolic muscle disorder may predispose a patient to develop myopathy.

Ⓓⓧ DIAGNOSIS

DIFFERENTIAL DIAGNOSIS

Bursitis, tendinitis, radiculopathy, osteoarthritis, muscle strain, myofascial pain, hypothyroidism, proton-pump inhibitor-induced polymyositis, viral illness, polymyositis, and polymyalgia rheumatica

WORKUP

Workup consists of a thorough history, including exercise history, urine color, medication history, and physical exam to palpate tenderness and obtain blood tests to evaluate muscle and kidney damage.

LABORATORY TESTS

If severe myopathy or rhabdomyolysis is suspected:
- Elevated CPK, positive serum myoglobin, elevated BUN, serum creatinine, AST, ALT, LDH, and potassium
- Urine creatinine, positive casts, and hemoglobin in urine with absence of red blood cells
- Consider electrocardiogram and assessment of calcium, phosphate, and uric acid.

If mild to moderate myopathy is suspected:
- Monitor TSH and CPK levels; CPK may only be elevated when sudden severe myopathy occurs.
- If the patient has brown or dark urine or elevated CPK, monitor BUN and serum creatinine.
- In statin-associated autoimmune myopathy, the creatine kinase level is usually ≥10 times the upper limit of normal. In these patients, muscle biopsy specimens will be positive for autoantibodies against HMG-CoA reductase.

IMAGING STUDIES

- Not recommended
- In statin-associated autoimmune myopathy, electromyography shows small-amplitude motor-unit potentials with increased spontaneous activity characteristic of an active myopathic process. Muscle edema is evident on MRI.[1]

ⓇⓍ TREATMENT

NONPHARMACOLOGIC THERAPY

- Treatment of rhabdomyolysis is generally supportive in nature (see "Rhabdomyolysis" topic).

ACUTE GENERAL Rx

- Stop statin therapy immediately if muscle symptoms occur. Check history, potential drug-drug interactions, CPK, TSH, renal function, hepatic function, and urinalysis.
- If patients have suspected rhabdomyolysis, they should be hospitalized and treated with supportive therapy and monitoring of complications.
- If CPK <10× the upper limit of normal without symptoms, continue statin therapy at the same or lower dosage
- If CPK <10× the upper limit of normal with intolerable symptoms, discontinue statin.
- If CPK >10× the upper limit of normal, discontinue statin.

---

[1]Mammen AL: Statin-associated autoimmune myopathy, *N Engl J Med* 374:664-669, 2016.

Box 1S-10 describes recommendations of the National Lipid Association Statin Safety Assessment Task Force regarding statin and muscle safety.

CHRONIC Rx

- After stopping the statin and symptom or CPK resolution, which may take up to 4 months, consider the same statin at a lower dosage or a different statin at an equivalent or lower dosage.
- When restarting therapy, consider statins such as low-dose rosuvastatin; pravastatin; and alternate-day dosing of rosuvastatin or atorvastatin.
- If patient had rhabdomyolysis secondary to statin therapy, consider nonstatin treatments.
- If the patient develops myopathy after a second trial of therapy, statin treatment should be permanently discontinued and nonstatin cholesterol-lowering therapy initiated.
- For IMNM (statin-associated autoimmune myopathy), immunosuppressive therapy with prednisone (1 mg per kilogram of body weight per day) and at least one agent (methotrexate, azathioprine, or mycophenolate mofetil) have been used. In resistant cases, IV immune globulin or another agent such as rituximab may be added.

COMPLEMENTARY & ALTERNATIVE MEDICINE

- The effect of coenzyme Q10 on reducing or preventing SIMS remains controversial. Given its safety, coenzyme Q10 can be recommended if the actions listed under "Chronic Rx" are insufficient to continue the use of the statin and if the muscle symptoms have been limited to myalgias. Use coenzyme Q10 with caution in patients taking warfarin, as its anticoagulant effect may be decreased.
- Observational studies have suggested an association between vitamin D deficiency and statin-induced myopathy. Data are conflicting. The effects of supplementing vitamin D in patients with statin myopathy are limited and cannot be recommended unless a vitamin D deficiency is present.

DISPOSITION

- Usually resolves within 1 wk up to 4 mo after discontinuing statin therapy.
- Once the patient has a full recovery, an alternative statin can be tried.
- Statins should not be restarted in IMNM.

REFERRAL

- If rhabdomyolysis is suspected, immediate referral for hospitalization is suggested.

 **PEARLS & CONSIDERATIONS**

COMMENTS

SIMS are usually mild and will resolve within a few wk after discontinuing statin therapy. However, such syndromes may progress to rhabdomyolysis.

PREVENTION

- Follow the 2013 AHA/ACC treatment guidelines to achieve the appropriate percent reduction in LDL cholesterol and limit the concomitant use of fibrates with statins.
- Discontinue statin therapy prior to and during surgical procedures.
- If patient requires a short-term therapy with an interacting medication such as an azole antifungal, temporarily discontinue statin therapy until interacting therapy is completed.
- If statin–fibric acid therapy is warranted, fenofibrate is preferred over gemfibrozil to decrease risk of myopathy.
- Baseline liver function testing before initiation of statin therapy and only if clinically indicated thereafter

PATIENT & FAMILY EDUCATION

- Inform patients to promptly report muscle weakness, unexpected muscle pain, or brownish urine.
- Ensure that the pharmacist and/or primary care physician checks for drug-drug interactions with every new prescription, including those from dentists and physicians from other specialties.
- Coenzyme Q10 may lessen milder muscle symptoms from statins, but patients should inform their physician and pharmacist if they decide to use this supplement.

BOX 1S-10 Recommendations to Health Care Professionals Regarding Statin and Muscle Safety

- Whenever muscle symptoms or an increased CK level is encountered in patients receiving statin therapy, health professionals should attempt to rule out other causes, because these are most likely to explain the findings. Other common causes include increased physical activity, trauma, falls, accidents, seizure, shaking chills, hypothyroidism, infections, carbon monoxide poisoning, polymyositis, dermatomyositis, alcohol abuse, and drug abuse (cocaine, amphetamines, heroin, or PCP).
- Obtaining a pretreatment, baseline CK level can be considered in patients who are at high risk of experiencing muscle toxicity (e.g., older patients or those combining a statin with an agent known to increase myotoxicity), but this is not routinely necessary in other patients.
- It is unnecessary to measure CK levels in asymptomatic patients during the course of statin therapy, because marked, clinically important CK elevations are rare and are usually related to physical exertion or other causes.
- Patients receiving statin therapy should be counseled about the increased risk of muscle symptoms, particularly if initiation of vigorous, sustained endurance exercise or a surgical operation is being contemplated; they should be advised to report such muscle symptoms to a health professional.
- Creatine kinase measurements should be obtained in symptomatic patients to help gauge the severity of muscle damage and facilitate decision of whether to continue therapy or alter doses.
- In patients who develop intolerable muscle symptoms with or without CK elevation and for whom other etiologies have been ruled out, the statin should be discontinued. Once symptoms disappear, the same or different statin at the same or a lower dose can be restarted to test the reproducibility of symptoms. Recurrence of symptoms with multiple statins and doses requires initiation of other lipid-altering therapy.
- In patients who develop tolerable muscle symptoms or have no symptoms but have a CK level <10 × ULN, statin therapy may be continued at the same or reduced doses and symptoms may be used as the clinical guide to stop or continue therapy.
- In patients who develop rhabdomyolysis (CK >10,000 IU/L or >10 × ULN with an elevation in serum creatinine or need for intravenous hydration therapy), statin therapy should be stopped. Intravenous hydration therapy in a hospital should be instituted if indicated for patients experiencing rhabdomyolysis. Once patients recover, risk vs. benefit of statin therapy should be carefully reconsidered.

CK, Creatine kinase; *PCP,* phencyclidine; *ULN,* upper limit of normal.
From McKenney JM et al: Final conclusions and recommendations of the National Lipid Association Statin Safety Assessment Task Force, *Am J Cardiol* 97(suppl 8A):89C-94C, 2006.

SUGGESTED READINGS
Available at www.expertconsult.com

RELATED CONTENT

Rhabdomyolysis (Related Key Topic)

AUTHORS: **LISA COHEN, PHARM.D.,** and **ANNE L. HUME, PHARM.D.**

 **BASIC INFORMATION**

DEFINITION

Status epilepticus is a medical neurologic emergency. It is historically defined as 30 min of continuous seizure activity or two or more seizures without full recovery of consciousness between seizures. However, in practice a continuous seizure that lasts >5 min is treated as status epilepticus.

SYNONYMS

Convulsive status epilepticus
Nonconvulsive status epilepticus

ICD-10CM CODES

G41 Status epilepticus
G40.301 Generalized idiopathic epilepsy and epileptic syndromes, not intractable, with status epilepticus

EPIDEMIOLOGY & DEMOGRAPHICS

INCIDENCE: 40 to 100 cases per 100,000 persons
PEAK INCIDENCE: It is most common among children younger than 1 yr and adults older than 60 yr.
PREDOMINANT SEX AND AGE: No gender preference

PHYSICAL FINDINGS & CLINICAL PRESENTATION

- Patients can present with repetitive tonic clonic movements of the body (convulsive status epilepticus); other patients are comatose and nonresponsive (nonconvulsive status epilepticus).
- Patients may also present with lethargy, intermittent confusion, and involuntary movements.

ETIOLOGY

- Status epilepticus can be the result of an acute neurologic injury, such as stroke, meningitis, brain tumor, etc.
- In patients with epilepsy, abrupt discontinuation of antiepileptic drugs can result in status epilepticus.
- See Table 1S-26 for causes of status epilepticus.

TABLE 1S-26 Causes of Status Epilepticus

- Stroke (ischemic/hemorrhagic)
- CNS infections
- Traumatic head injury
- CNS toxicity: certain medications, drugs, ethanol
- Brain tumors or other mass lesions
- Metabolic disturbances: hypoglycemia, hyponatremia
- Abrupt discontinuation of antiepileptic drugs in patient with epilepsy
- Cryptogenic

CNS, Central nervous system.

 **DIAGNOSIS**

DIFFERENTIAL DIAGNOSIS

- Convulsive syncope
- Encephalopathies: metabolic, infectious, toxic, etc.
- Nonepileptic spells

WORKUP

- ABCs
- ICU admission
- Emergent electroencephalogram (EEG)
- Continuous video EEG in refractory cases
- Investigation of the patient with status epilepticus is summarized in Box 1S-11.

LABORATORY TESTS

- Routine blood workup (CBC, CMP, glucose, electrolytes)
- Urine drug screen
- Lumbar puncture and CSF analysis in patients with suspected meningitis

IMAGING STUDIES

- Immediate CT scan of the head

- MRI of the brain should be performed once the patient is in a stable condition.

TREATMENT

- Patients with continuous seizure activity over 3 min need intravenous lorazepam 0.1 mg/kg at 2 mg/min (or diazepam 0.2 mg/kg at 5 mg/min only when lorazepam is not available).
- In the absence of intravenous access, intramuscular administration of midazolam 10 mg in an adult is a superior alternative.
- Failure of response to lorazepam or midazolam is referred to as established status epilepticus and should be followed by intravenous fosphenytoin 20 mg/kg (PE) at a rate not greater than 150 mg/min. An alternate to fosphenytoin is phenytoin 20 mg/kg IV at up to 50 mg/min as tolerated. Vital signs should be monitored during the infusion.
- If seizures continue, intravenous valproate, levetiracetam, phenobarbital, midazolam, and propofol are alternatives. Many of these drugs remain under investigation, and superiority of one agent is not established.

BOX 1S-11 Investigation of the Patient with Status Epilepticus

To Be Performed in All Patients with Status Epilepticus
Serum glucose, electrolytes, calcium, magnesium
Blood gas, serum osmolality
Toxicology screen (serum and urine)
Antiepileptic drug levels
Complete blood count (RBC, differential WBC, platelet count)
Liver enzymes, serum ammonium
Blood culture
Lumbar puncture, including:
  1. Opening pressure
  2. Cell count, Gram stain, smear for acid-fast bacilli
  3. Viral and bacterial cultures
  4. PCR for herpesvirus
EEG, preferably continuous monitoring with video
  1. To monitor for subtle or subclinical seizures
  2. To guide antiepileptic drug therapy
  3. To localize the epileptogenic brain region (focal slowing or epileptiform activity)

To Be Considered in Patients with Status Epilepticus
Structural neuroimaging (CT, MRI)
  1. To diagnose acute infarction, hemorrhage, vascular malformation, encephalitis, abscess, neurocysticercosis, neoplasm
  2. In nonlesional cases, may localize the epileptogenic zone by evidence of focal edema in the affected cortical region
  3. To assess the degree of cerebral edema and diagnose impending uncal or transtentorial herniation
  4. MR angiography may identify CNS vasculitis, especially in medium or large vessel disease
Functional neuroimaging (PET, SPECT)
  1. In nonlesional cases, may identify the epileptogenic zone
Cerebral angiography
  1. To identify small vessel CNS vasculitis, which may not be visible on MR angiography
Rheumatologic workup for vasculitides
ESR, C-reactive protein, rheumatoid factor, serum complement levels, antineutrophil cytoplasmic antibodies
Brain biopsy
  1. To diagnose cerebral vasculitis (granulomatous compared with nongranulomatous)
  2. To identify malformations of cortical development

CNS, Central nervous system; *CT,* computed tomography; *EEG,* electroencephalography; *ESR,* erythrocyte sedimentation rate; *MRI,* magnetic resonance imaging; *PCR,* polymerase chain reaction; *PET,* positron emission tomography; *RBC,* red blood cell; *SPECT,* single-photon emission computed tomography; *WBC,* white blood cell. From Fuhrman BP et al: *Pediatric critical care,* ed 4, Philadelphia, 2011, Saunders.

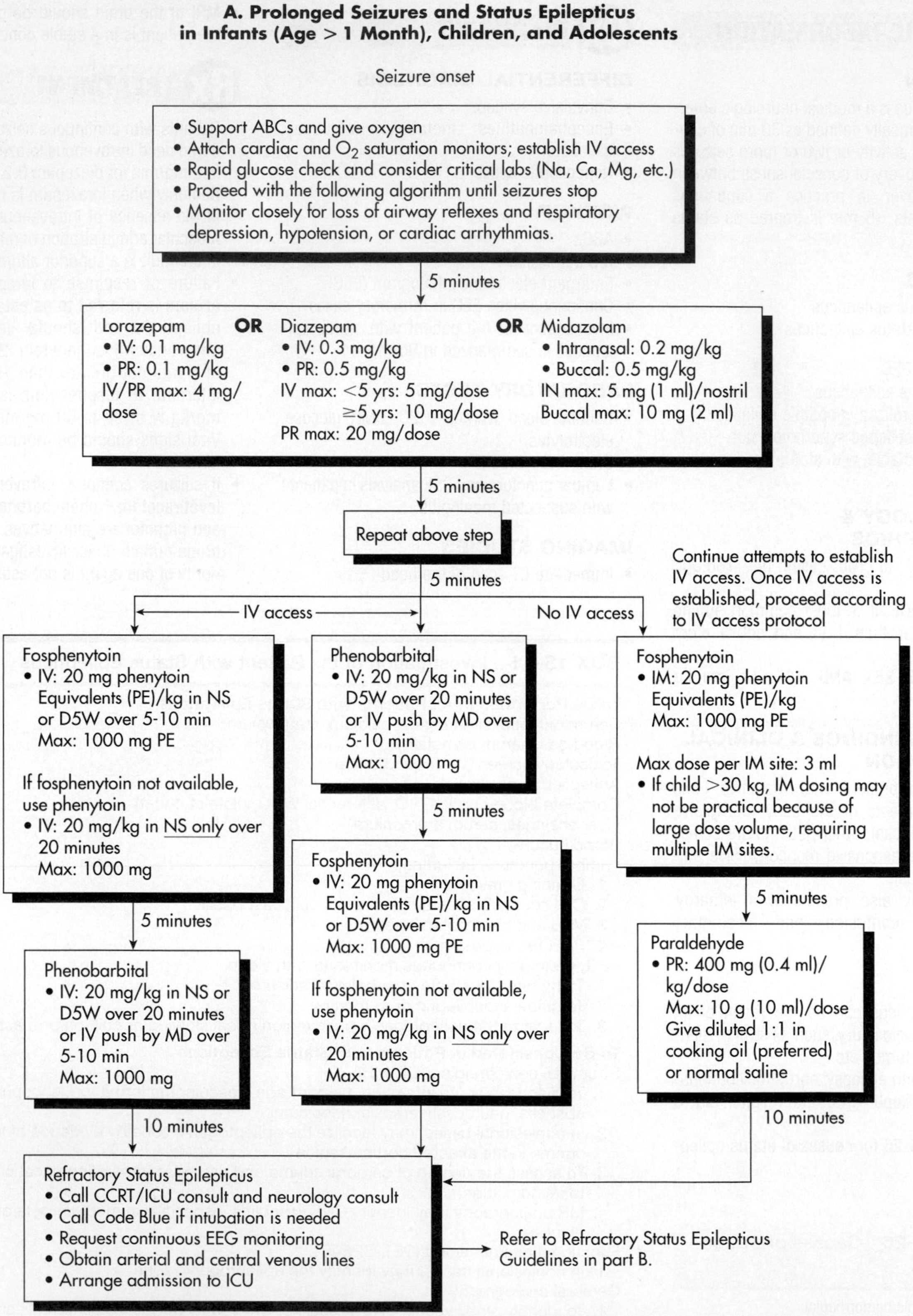

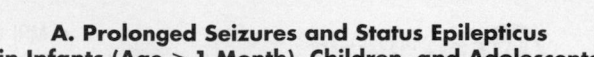

A. Prolonged Seizures and Status Epilepticus in Infants (Age > 1 Month), Children, and Adolescents

Seizure onset

- Support ABCs and give oxygen
- Attach cardiac and O_2 saturation monitors; establish IV access
- Rapid glucose check and consider critical labs (Na, Ca, Mg, etc.)
- Proceed with the following algorithm until seizures stop
- Monitor closely for loss of airway reflexes and respiratory depression, hypotension, or cardiac arrhythmias.

5 minutes

Lorazepam   **OR**
- IV: 0.1 mg/kg
- PR: 0.1 mg/kg
IV/PR max: 4 mg/dose

Diazepam   **OR**
- IV: 0.3 mg/kg
- PR: 0.5 mg/kg
IV max: <5 yrs: 5 mg/dose
         ≥5 yrs: 10 mg/dose
PR max: 20 mg/dose

Midazolam
- Intranasal: 0.2 mg/kg
- Buccal: 0.5 mg/kg
IN max: 5 mg (1 ml)/nostril
Buccal max: 10 mg (2 ml)

5 minutes

Repeat above step

5 minutes

IV access ←——————→ No IV access

Continue attempts to establish IV access. Once IV access is established, proceed according to IV access protocol

Fosphenytoin
- IV: 20 mg phenytoin Equivalents (PE)/kg in NS or D5W over 5-10 min
Max: 1000 mg PE

If fosphenytoin not available, use phenytoin
- IV: 20 mg/kg in NS only over 20 minutes
Max: 1000 mg

Phenobarbital
- IV: 20 mg/kg in NS or D5W over 20 minutes or IV push by MD over 5-10 min
Max: 1000 mg

Fosphenytoin
- IM: 20 mg phenytoin Equivalents (PE)/kg
Max: 1000 mg PE

Max dose per IM site: 3 ml
- If child >30 kg, IM dosing may not be practical because of large dose volume, requiring multiple IM sites.

5 minutes

Fosphenytoin
- IV: 20 mg phenytoin Equivalents (PE)/kg in NS or D5W over 5-10 min
Max: 1000 mg PE

If fosphenytoin not available, use phenytoin
- IV: 20 mg/kg in NS only over 20 minutes
Max: 1000 mg

5 minutes

5 minutes

Phenobarbital
- IV: 20 mg/kg in NS or D5W over 20 minutes or IV push by MD over 5-10 min
Max: 1000 mg

Paraldehyde
- PR: 400 mg (0.4 ml)/kg/dose
Max: 10 g (10 ml)/dose
Give diluted 1:1 in cooking oil (preferred) or normal saline

10 minutes

10 minutes

Refractory Status Epilepticus
- Call CCRT/ICU consult and neurology consult
- Call Code Blue if intubation is needed
- Request continuous EEG monitoring
- Obtain arterial and central venous lines
- Arrange admission to ICU

Refer to Refractory Status Epilepticus Guidelines in part B.

FIGURE 1S-67 Guidelines for the treatment of prolonged seizures and status epilepticus in infants (age >1 month), children, and adolescents. (From The Hospital for Sick Children, Toronto, Canada. In Fuhrman BP et al: *Pediatric critical care*, ed 4, Philadelphia, 2011, Saunders.)

**B. Refractory Status Epilepticus
in Infants (Age > 1 Month), Children, and Adolescents**

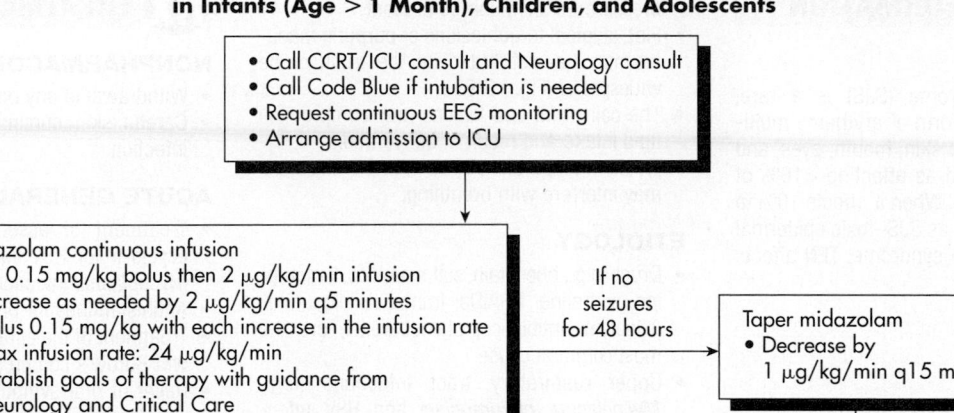

- Call CCRT/ICU consult and Neurology consult
- Call Code Blue if intubation is needed
- Request continuous EEG monitoring
- Arrange admission to ICU

Midazolam continuous infusion
- IV: 0.15 mg/kg bolus then 2 μg/kg/min infusion
- Increase as needed by 2 μg/kg/min q5 minutes
- Bolus 0.15 mg/kg with each increase in the infusion rate
- Max infusion rate: 24 μg/kg/min
- Establish goals of therapy with guidance from Neurology and Critical Care
- Maintain phenobarbital and phenytoin at therapeutic serum levels with maintenance doses

If no seizures for 48 hours →

Taper midazolam
- Decrease by 1 μg/kg/min q15 min

If seizures recur, reinstate midazolam for another 48 hours

If seizures persist ↓

Thiopental continuous infusion via CVL
- CVL: 2-4 mg/kg bolus then 2-4 mg/kg/hr
- Increase as needed by 1 mg/kg/hr every 30 minutes
- Bolus 2 mg/kg with each increase in the infusion rate
- Max infusion rate: 6 mg/kg/hr
- Establish goals of therapy with guidance from Neurology and Critical Care
- Discontinue midazolam and phenobarbital
- Maintain phenytoin at therapeutic serum levels
- Monitor thiopental levels

If no seizures for 48 hours →

Taper thiopental
- Decrease rate by 25% q3 hours
- Reinstitute phenobarbital while tapering

If seizures persist ← | → If seizures recur

Individualized therapy in consultation with Critical Care and Neurology

FIGURE 1S-67 (Continued)

- Fig. 1S-67 describes guidelines for the treatment of prolonged seizures and status epilepticus in infants (>1 mo), children, and adolescents and refractory status epilepticus.

NONPHARMACOLOGIC THERAPY
None

GENERAL Rx
It is important to find out the etiology of the status epilepticus (e.g., metabolic disturbance, infection). The appropriate treatment/understanding of the underlying cause of the status epilepticus will impact successful treatment.

CHRONIC Rx
- Chronic treatment of status epilepticus depends on underlying etiology.
- Patient with status epilepticus due to epilepsy will need chronic treatment.

COMPLEMENTARY & ALTERNATIVE MEDICINE
Not applicable

DISPOSITION
- Response to treatment depends on the etiology of the status epilepticus.

- When there is no CNS injury as a cause or result of the status epilepticus, the prognosis is good.
- No driving until seizure freedom in accordance with local laws and regulations.

REFERRAL
Status epilepticus is a neurologic emergency; therefore immediate inpatient neurologic consultation is warranted.

! **PEARLS & CONSIDERATIONS**

COMMENTS
- Status epilepticus is a medical emergency that carries a high risk of mortality. Mortality among patients who present in status epilepticus is 15% to 22%. Among those who survive, functional ability will decline in 25% of cases.
- Continuous video EEG is crucial in the treatment of these patients because some of them may not be clinically seizing (convulsing) but electrographically they may still have subclinical repetitive seizures or subclinical status epilepticus.

PREVENTION
Medication compliance is crucial in patients with epilepsy.

PATIENT & FAMILY EDUCATION
- Patients with epilepsy have normal lives.
- The goal of treatment is no seizures and no side effects to medications.
- Patient education and information can be obtained at the Epilepsy Foundation: www.epilepsyfoundation.org
- Pregnant women with epilepsy should visit the Antiepileptic Drug Pregnancy Registry website for information and assistance: www.massgeneral.org/aed
- Patients with ongoing seizures are forbidden from driving; check state regulations and laws regarding driving and epilepsy.

SUGGESTED READINGS
Available at www.expertconsult.com

AUTHOR: **PATRICIO SEBASTIAN ESPINOSA, M.D., M.P.H.**

ℹ️ BASIC INFORMATION

DEFINITION

Stevens-Johnson syndrome (SJS) is a rare, severe vesiculobullous form of erythema multiforme (EM) affecting the skin, mouth, eyes, and genitalia. SJS is defined as affecting <10% of body surface area (BSA). When it affects 10% to 30% of BSA, it is known as SJS–toxic epidermal necrolysis (TEN) overlap syndrome. TEN affects >30% of BSA.

SYNONYMS

SJS
Herpes iris
Febrile mucocutaneous syndrome

ICD-10CM CODES

L51.1 Stevens-Johnson syndrome

EPIDEMIOLOGY & DEMOGRAPHICS

- SJS affects predominantly children and young adults.
- Male/female ratio is 2:1.
- Prevalence: 1:100,000 for SJS and 1:1,000,000 for TEN

PHYSICAL FINDINGS & CLINICAL PRESENTATION

- The cutaneous eruption generally occurs within 8 wk of drug initiation and is generally preceded by vague, nonspecific symptoms of low-grade fever and fatigue (influenza-like symptoms) occurring 1 to 14 days before the skin lesions. Cough is often present. Fever may be high during the active stages.
- Enlarging red-purple macules or papules and bullae generally occur on the conjunctiva, mucous membranes of the mouth (Fig. 1S-68), nares, and genital regions. Lesions rapidly spread to their maximum extent usually within 2 days.
- Corneal ulcerations may result in blindness.
- Ulcerative stomatitis results in hemorrhagic crusting.
- Nikolsky sign (shearing off of epidermis with pressure on skin) can be present.
- Flat, atypical target lesions or purpuric maculae may be distributed on the trunk or be widespread (Fig. 1S-69).
- The pain from oral lesions may compromise fluid intake and result in dehydration.
- Thick, mucopurulent sputum and oral lesions may interfere with breathing.

ETIOLOGY

- Drugs (e.g., phenytoin, sulfonamides, lamotrigine, sertraline, NSAIDs, tramadol, allopurinol, β-lactam antibiotics, phenobarbital) are the most common cause.
- Upper respiratory tract infections (e.g., *Mycoplasma pneumoniae*) and HSV infections have also been implicated.

ⓇⓍ DIAGNOSIS

DIFFERENTIAL DIAGNOSIS

- Toxic erythema (drugs or infection)
- Pemphigus
- Pemphigoid
- Urticaria
- Hemorrhagic fevers
- Serum sickness
- *Staphylococcus* scalded-skin syndrome
- Behçet's syndrome

WORKUP

- Diagnosis is generally based on clinical presentation and characteristic appearance of the lesions.
- Skin biopsy is generally reserved for when classic lesions are absent and diagnosis is uncertain. Biopsy reveals epidermal necrolysis but cannot distinguish between SJS, TEN, and EM.

LABORATORY TESTS

CBC with differential, cultures in cases of suspected infection.

IMAGING STUDIES

Chest x-rays may show patchy changes in patients with pulmonary involvement.

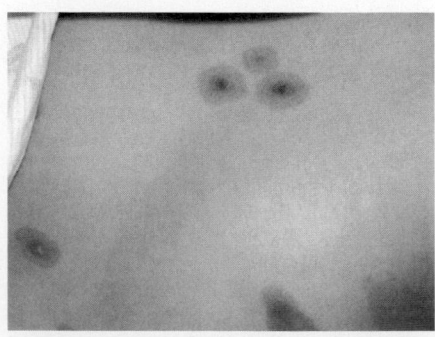

FIGURE 1S-68 Lip changes found in Stevens-Johnson syndrome associated with *Mycoplasma pneumoniae* infection. (From Kliegman RM et al: *Nelson textbook of pediatrics,* ed 19, Philadelphia, 2011, Saunders.)

FIGURE 1S-69 Classic erythema multiforme skin lesions found in Stevens-Johnson syndrome associated with *Mycoplasma pneumoniae* infection. (From Kliegman RM et al: *Nelson textbook of pediatrics,* ed 19, Philadelphia, 2011, Saunders.)

ⓇⓍ TREATMENT

NONPHARMACOLOGIC THERAPY

- Withdrawal of any potential drug precipitants
- Careful skin nursing to prevent secondary infection

ACUTE GENERAL Rx

- Treatment of associated conditions (e.g., acyclovir for HSV infection, azithromycin for *Mycoplasma* infection)
- Antihistamines for pruritus
- Treatment of the cutaneous blisters with cool, wet Burow's compresses
- Relief of oral symptoms by frequent rinsing with lidocaine (Xylocaine Viscous)
- Liquid or soft diet with plenty of fluids to ensure proper hydration
- Treatment of secondary infections with antibiotics
- Corticosteroids: use remains controversial and there is a clear risk of sepsis; they should be used only in severe cases early in the disease; when used, prednisone 20 to 30 mg bid until new lesions no longer appear, then rapidly tapered
- Topical steroids: may use to treat papules and plaques; however, should not be applied to eroded areas
- Vitamin A: may be used for lacrimal hyposecretion
- Consider IVIG in severe cases.

DISPOSITION

- Prognosis varies with severity of disease. It is generally good in patients with limited disease; however, mortality rate may approach 10% in patients with extensive involvement. A severity of illness score known as SCORETEN that incorporates increased glucose level (>252 mg/dL), increased BUN (>28 mg/dL), electrolytes (serum bicarbonate <20 mEq/L), age (>40 yr), immunosuppression (presence of cancer), involvement >10% of BSA, and increased heart rate (>120 beats/min) can be used to calculate mortality risk.
- Oral lesions may continue for several months.
- Scarring and corneal abnormalities may occur in 20% of patients.

REFERRAL

- Management of SIS is similar to those with extensive burns. Hospital admission in a unit used for burn care is recommended in severe cases.
- Urethral involvement may necessitate catheterization.
- Ocular involvement should be monitored by an ophthalmologist.

SUGGESTED READINGS

Available at www.expertconsult.com

RELATED CONTENT

Stevens-Johnson Syndrome (Patient Information)

AUTHOR: **FRED F. FERRI, M.D.**

S

 **BASIC INFORMATION**

DEFINITION

Stomatitis is inflammation involving the oral mucous membranes. Mucositis is inflammation and ulceration of the mucous membranes. It is most commonly seen in the mouth but can occur anywhere in the GI, genitourinary (GU), or respiratory tract. It is most often due to side effects of chemotherapy or radiation therapy (Fig. E1S-70) in cancer patients.

SYNONYMS

Heterogeneous grouping of unrelated illnesses, each with its own designation(s)

ICD-10CM CODES
K12	Stomatitis and related lesions
K12.1	Other forms of stomatitis
K13.0	Other and unspecified lesions of oral mucosa
K12.0	Recurrent oral aphthae
B37.0	Candidal stomatitis
A69.0	Necrotizing ulcerative stomatitis
B08.4	Enteroviral vesicular stomatitis with exanthem
B08.61	Bovine stomatitis
B37.0	Candidal stomatitis
K12.30	Oral mucositis (ulcerative), unspecified
K12.31	Oral mucositis (ulcerative) due to antineoplastic therapy
K12.32	Oral mucositis (ulcerative) due to other drugs
K12.33	Oral mucositis (ulcerative) due to radiation
K12.39	Other oral mucositis (ulcerative)

PHYSICAL FINDINGS & CLINICAL PRESENTATION

WHITE LESIONS:
- Candidiasis (thrush).
- Caused by yeast infection (*Candida albicans*).
- Examination: white, curdlike material (Fig. E1S-71) that when wiped off leaves a raw bleeding surface.
- Epidemiology: seen in the very young and the very old, those with immunodeficiency (AIDS, cancer), persons with diabetes, and patients treated with antibacterial agents.
- Other.
  1. Leukoedema: filmy opalescent-appearing mucosa, which can be reverted to normal appearance by stretching. This condition is benign.
  2. White sponge nevus: thick, white corrugated folds involving the buccal mucosa. Appears in childhood as an autosomal dominant trait. Benign condition.
  3. Darier's disease (keratosis follicularis): white papules on the gingivae, alveolar mucosa, and dorsal tongue. Skin lesions

also present (erythematous papules). Inherited as an autosomal dominant trait.
  4. Chemical injury: white sloughing mucosa.
  5. Nicotine stomatitis: whitened palate with red papules.
  6. Lichen planus: linear, reticular, slightly raised striae on buccal mucosa. Skin is involved by pruritic violaceous papules on forearms and inner thighs.
  7. Discoid lupus erythematosus: lesion resembles lichen planus.
  8. Leukoplakia: white lesions that cannot be scraped off; 20% are premalignant epithelial dysplasia or squamous cell carcinoma.
  9. Hairy leukoplakia: shaggy white surface that cannot be wiped off; seen in HIV infection, caused by Epstein-Barr virus.

RED LESIONS:
- Candidiasis may present with red lesions instead of the more frequent white. Median rhomboid glossitis is a chronic variant.
- Benign migratory glossitis (geographic tongue): area of atrophic depapillated mucosa surrounded by a keratotic border. Benign lesion, no treatment required.
- Hemangiomas.
- Histoplasmosis: ill-defined, irregular patch with a granulomatous surface, sometimes ulcerated.
- Allergy.
- Anemia: atrophic reddened glossal mucosa seen with pernicious anemia.
- Erythroplakia: red patch usually caused by epithelial dysplasia or squamous cell carcinoma.
- Burning tongue (glossopyrosis): normal examination; sometimes associated with denture trauma, anemia, diabetes, vitamin B_{12} deficiency, psychogenic problems.

DARK LESIONS (BROWN, BLUE, BLACK):
- Coated tongue: accumulation of keratin; harmless condition that can be treated by scraping.
- Melanotic lesions: freckles, lentigines, lentigo, melanoma, Peutz-Jeghers syndrome, Addison's disease.
- Varices.
- Kaposi's sarcoma: red or purple macules that enlarge to form tumors; seen in patients with AIDS.

RAISED LESIONS:
- Papilloma.
- Verruca vulgaris.
- Condyloma acuminatum.
- Fibroma.
- Epulis.
- Pyogenic granuloma.
- Mucocele.
- Retention cyst.

BLISTERS:
- Primary herpetic gingivostomatitis (Fig. E1S-72).
- Caused by herpes simplex virus type 1 or, less frequently, type 2.

- Course: day 1: malaise, fever, headache, sore throat, cervical lymphadenopathy; days 2 and 3: appearance of vesicles that develop into painful ulcers of 2 to 4 mm in diameter; duration of up to 2 wk.
- Recurrent intraoral herpes: rare; recurrences typically involve only the keratinized epithelium (lips).
- Pemphigus and pemphigoid.
- Hand-foot-mouth disease: caused by coxsackievirus group A.
- Erythema multiforme.
- Herpangina: caused by echovirus.
- Traumatic ulcer.
- Primary syphilis.
- Perlèche (or angular cheilitis).
- Recurrent aphthous stomatitis (canker sores): most common oral mucosa lesion; may be associated with many systemic diseases.
- Behçet's syndrome (aphthous ulcers, uveitis, genital ulcerations, arthritis, and aseptic meningitis).
- Reiter's syndrome (conjunctivitis, urethritis, and arthritis with occasional oral ulcerations).
- Unknown cause.

Course: solitary or multiple painful ulcers may develop simultaneously and heal over 10 to 14 days. The size of the lesions and the frequency of recurrences are variable.

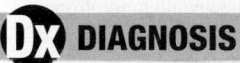 **DIAGNOSIS**

WORKUP
- White lesions: candidiasis (thrush) diagnosis: ovoid yeast and hyphae seen in scrapings treated with KOH culture.
- Blisters:
  1. Exfoliative cytology.
  2. Viral culture.
  3. Immunofluorescence for herpes antigen.

TREATMENT

White lesions: candidiasis (thrush) treatment:
- Topical with nystatin or clotrimazole.
- Systemic with ketoconazole or fluconazole.

Blisters:
- Supportive.
- Consider acyclovir.

Recurrent intraoral herpes/aphthous ulcerations: topical corticosteroids (dexamethasone ointment applied to the identified ulcer tid) or systemic steroids for severe cases.

SUGGESTED READINGS
Available at www.expertconsult.com

RELATED CONTENT
Stomatitis (Patient Information)

AUTHOR: **FRED F. FERRI, M.D.**

Diseases and Disorders

BASIC INFORMATION

DEFINITION

Strabismus is a condition of the eyes in which the visual axes of the eyes are not aligned. The misalignment may be constant or intermittent, and it may vary depending on the gaze direction (comitant or incomitant).

SYNONYMS

Esotropia
Exotropia
Heterotropia
Hypertropia
Hypotropia
Restrictive eye movement
Crossed eyes
Walleye
Squint
Lazy eye
Floating eye

ICD-10CM CODES

H50.9 Strabismus, unspecified
H50.0 Convergent concomitant strabismus
H50.1 Divergent concomitant strabismus
H50.2 Vertical strabismus
H50.3 Intermittent heterotropia
H50.4 Other and unspecified heterotropia
H50.0 Heterophoria
H50.6 Mechanical strabismus
H50.8 Other specified strabismus
H51.9 Unspecified disorder of binocular movement

EPIDEMIOLOGY & DEMOGRAPHICS

INCIDENCE (IN U.S.): 2% of the population
PEAK INCIDENCE: Childhood
PREDOMINANT SEX: None
PREDOMINANT AGE: Variable depending on type, but more common in childhood
GENETICS: Most childhood forms suggest polygenic inheritance patterns with variable penetrance, although certain types (i.e., accommodative esotropia) show a definite hereditary predisposition.

PHYSICAL FINDINGS & CLINICAL PRESENTATION

- Conjugate gaze loss with the eyes fixing independently
- Diplopia in acquired adult-onset strabismus
- Decreased range of eye movements in paralytic and restrictive forms
- Amblyopia (a decrease in best-corrected visual acuity in an otherwise structurally healthy eye) may occur with untreated strabismus with a childhood onset.

ETIOLOGY

Often obscure in childhood strabismus
- Many cases of esotropia are congenital.
- Accommodative esotropia occurs later, with the peak incidence between 2 to 4 years of age.
- Higher risk with neurologic disease, vision loss, or severe refractive errors.

- Orbital or ocular trauma
- Thyroid disorders or other orbital inflammatory disease

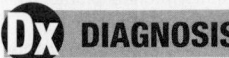

DIAGNOSIS

DIFFERENTIAL DIAGNOSIS

- Evaluation of eye position and movement
- Vision testing
- Refractive errors
- Central nervous system (CNS) tumors
- Orbital tumors
- Brain and CNS dysfunction
- Thyroid disease
- Myasthenia gravis

WORKUP

- Eye examination. Fig. E1S-73 illustrates diagnostic tests that help differentiate between common causes of strabismus. Strabismus is classified according to the type and magnitude of misalignment. Esotropia refers to an inward deviation of the nonfixing eye and exotropia to the

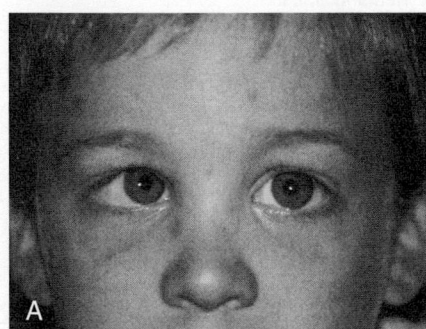

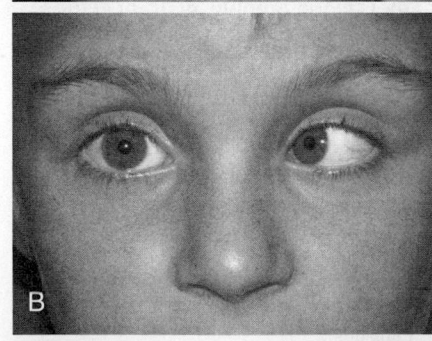

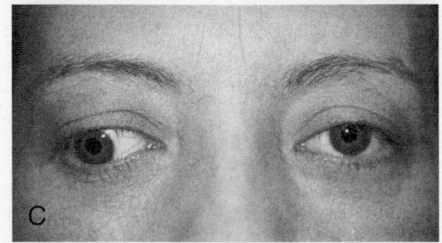

FIGURE 1S-74 Hirschberg test. A, The right corneal reflex is near the temporal border of the pupil, indicating an angle of about 15°. **B,** The left corneal reflex is at the limbus, indicating an angle of about 45°. **C,** The right corneal reflex is at the limbus in a divergent squint. (**A** courtesy J. Yanguela. From Kanski JJ, Bowling B: *Clinical ophthalmology, a systematic approach,* ed 7, Philadelphia, 2010, Saunders.)

outward deviation of the nonfixing eye. Hypertropia is a vertical deviation in which the nonfixing eye is higher, and hypotropia is a vertical deviation in which the nonfixing eye is lower.
- Measurement of deviation: the *Hirschberg test* (Fig. 1S-74) gives a rough estimate of the angle of a manifest strabismus and is especially useful in young or uncooperative patients or when fixation in the deviating eye is poor.
- Visual field testing
- MRI or CT to rule out tumors or other intracranial pathology in paralytic strabismus
- Thyroid function tests in acquired restrictive strabismus
- Myasthenia gravis workup in acquired, unstable strabismus

LABORATORY TESTS

Generally not needed

IMAGING STUDIES

Necessary only if other neurologic findings are found

TREATMENT

THERAPY

- Glasses
- Surgery
- Prisms
- Occlusion to relieve diplopia
- Orthoptic exercises
- Botulinum toxin

CHRONIC Rx

- Glasses
- Prisms
- Occluding devices for intractable diplopia caused by strabismus
- Botulinum toxin

DISPOSITION

Glasses, prisms, and/or surgery may reestablish normal or improved ocular alignment and recover binocular single vision.

REFERRAL

- Early for full evaluation and rehabilitation of functional and cosmetic ocular alignment
- To an ophthalmologist for management (usually)

SUGGESTED READINGS

Available at www.expertconsult.com

RELATED CONTENT

Strabismus (Patient Information)

AUTHORS: **DAVID ROBBINS TIEN, M.D.,** and **ALEXANDRA MEYER TIEN, M.D.**

 **BASIC INFORMATION**

DEFINITION

Ischemic stroke is the sudden onset of a focal neurologic deficit as a result of ischemia. Acute ischemic stroke may be defined as relating to the first few days after onset of neurologic symptoms. However, the purpose of this chapter is to help the provider make decisions regarding the acute stroke patient within the first several hours of symptoms; this is the crucial time for definitive treatment interventions.

SYNONYMS

Stroke
Brain attack
Cerebrovascular accident (this is a nonspecific term and should not be used.)

ICD-10CM CODES
I63	Cerebral infarction
I63.3	Cerebral infarction due to thrombosis of cerebral arteries
I63.4	Cerebral infarction due to embolism of cerebral arteries
I63.5	Cerebral infarction due to unspecified occlusion or stenosis of cerebral arteries
I63.6	Cerebral infarction due to cerebral venous thrombosis, nonpyogenic
I63.8	Other cerebral infarction
I63.9	Cerebral infarction, unspecified
I67.89	Other cerebrovascular disease

EPIDEMIOLOGY & DEMOGRAPHICS

INCIDENCE:
- ~800,000 new or recurrent strokes occur each year in the U.S.
- Stroke is the number five cause of death (130,000 deaths every year) and the leading cause of long-term disability in the U.S.

PREVALENCE: There are ~4.5 million stroke survivors in the U.S.

RISK FACTORS: Hypertension, dyslipidemia, diabetes mellitus, and smoking are the four major risk factors. Other risk factors include atrial fibrillation (most common cause of cardioembolic stroke), mechanical heart valve, patent foramen ovale, recent myocardial infarction, carotid stenosis, hypercoagulable states, subclinical atrial tachyarrhythmias without clinical atrial fibrillation, sickle cell disease, and obesity.

GENETICS: Multifactorial

PHYSICAL FINDINGS & CLINICAL PRESENTATION

Clinical presentation varies with the artery and region of CNS affected. Following are some common syndromic presentations. Please note that this list is not comprehensive and that all findings for a particular syndrome may not be listed here.
- Large- to medium-sized arteries:
  1. Left middle cerebral artery: right face, arm, and leg weakness and sensory loss with aphasia (expressive, receptive, or both); possible hemianopia
  2. Right middle cerebral artery: left face, arm, and leg weakness and sensory loss with hemineglect; possible hemianopia

3. Basilar artery: typically an acute loss of consciousness preceded by vertigo, nausea, vomiting, and diplopia; quadriparesis or quadriplegia may be seen, including "locked-in" syndrome
4. Posterior cerebral artery: unilateral hemianopia; blindness with anosognosia (Anton syndrome) if bilateral
5. Anterior cerebral artery: unilateral leg weakness and sensory loss
6. Cerebellum: ataxia (typically of the limbs), often with vertigo, nausea, and vomiting
- Small arteries (common lacunar syndromes)
  1. Lateral medullary (Wallenberg's) syndrome
  2. Posterior limb internal capsule

ETIOLOGY

Etiologies include atherosclerosis, cardioembolism, artery-to-artery embolism, small-vessel lipohyalinosis, arteritis, arterial dissection, and vasospasm.

 **DIAGNOSIS**

DIFFERENTIAL DIAGNOSIS

The differential diagnosis of acute ischemic stroke includes hemorrhagic stroke (intracerebral hemorrhage), seizure with postictal paralysis, migraine with hemiparesis, syncope, hypoglycemia, hypertensive encephalopathy, and conversion disorder.

LABORATORY TESTS

- Immediate (Box 1S-12): CBC, metabolic panel that includes blood glucose and renal function, PT/INR, aPTT, troponin I, and urinalysis. Blood glucose is the only test required before initiation of IV tPA.

- National Institutes of Health Stroke Scale: a brief, focused neurologic examination aimed at providing a numeric estimate of the severity of stroke; can be performed by any health care provider trained in its use; may increase the likelihood of the correct assessment of stroke
- ECG and telemetry monitoring
- Echocardiogram to look for potential cardiogenic source of embolism, infective endocarditis and intracardiac shunts

IMAGING STUDIES

- Immediate (Fig. 1S-75): computed tomography (CT) of the head without contrast to rule out hemorrhage.
- MRI of the brain with stroke protocol to assess the extent of stroke (because CT typically will not show an ischemic stroke for several hours), but it is rarely needed in the hyperacute setting to determine reperfusion strategy, although some newer techniques like diffusion and perfusion MR are being utilized for this purpose at some centers.
- Several other neuroimaging studies are useful during the early stages of acute stroke to assess whether there is a thrombus that is amenable to intervention (Table 1S-27).

Cross reference: see "Transient Ischemic Attack" for general workup, which is identical to that for ischemic stroke.

 **TREATMENT**

NONPHARMACOLOGIC THERAPY

GENERAL CONSIDERATIONS:
- Airway and breathing should be maintained.
- Supplemental oxygen should be provided to keep the oxygen saturation at ≥92%.

BOX 1S-12   Immediate Diagnostic Studies: Evaluation of a Patient With Suspected Acute Ischemic Stroke

All Patients
Noncontrast brain computed tomographic scan (magnetic resonance imaging, if available)
Blood glucose level[1]
Serum electrolyte and renal function tests
Electrocardiography
Markers of cardiac ischemia
Complete blood count, including platelet count[2]
Prothrombin time/international normalized ratio
Activated partial thromboplastin time
Oxygen saturation

Selected Patients
Hepatic function tests
Toxicology screen
Blood alcohol level
Pregnancy test
Arterial blood gas tests (if hypoxia is suspected)
Chest radiography (if lung disease is suspected)
Lumbar puncture (if subarachnoid hemorrhage is suspected and computed tomography scan is negative for blood)
Electroencephalogram (if seizures are suspected)

[1] Only test recommended before initiation of IV rtPA.
[2] Although it is desirable to know the results of these tests before giving a patient tissue plasminogen activator, thrombolytic therapy should not be delayed while awaiting the results unless (1) there is clinical suspicion of a bleeding abnormality or thrombocytopenia; (2) the patient has received heparin or warfarin; or (3) the patient's use of anticoagulants is not known.
From Christensen H et al: Abnormalities on ECG and telemetry predict stroke outcome at 3 months, *J Neurol Sci* 234:99-103, 2005.

S

Diseases and Disorders

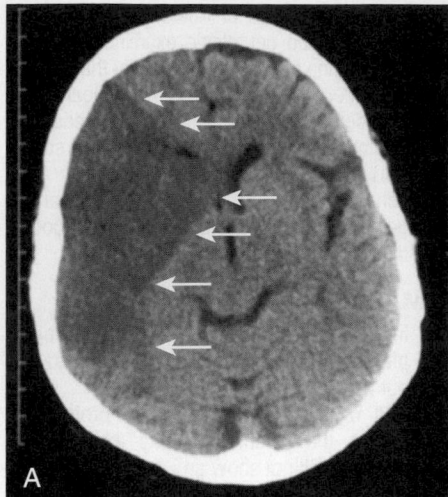 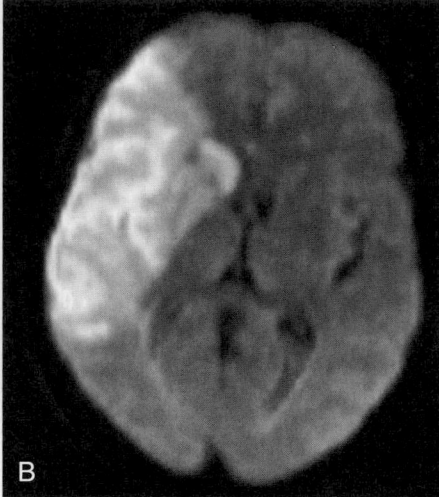

FIGURE 1S-75 Large right middle cerebral artery infarct on an unenhanced computed tomographic scan **(A)** and a diffusion-weighted magnetic resonance image **(B)**. There is a mass effect, and this patient is at risk for cerebral herniation syndromes.

TABLE 1S-27	Imaging Modalities for Stroke	
Imaging Modality	**Advantage**	**Disadvantage**
Cerebral catheter angiography	• Allows for the definitive assessment of cerebral circulation (gold standard) • Allows for the deployment of intra-arterial thrombolysis and thrombectomy devices if a thrombus is found • Allows for the assessment of collateral circulation	• Invasive (significant risks) • High cost • Not available at all facilities
Doppler studies	• Noninvasive • May be performed at the patient's bedside	• Can be limited by the patient's body habitus • Operator dependent
Magnetic resonance angiography	• Excellent view of the large arteries of the neck and brain • No contrast material needed	• Cannot be performed in patients who are critically ill, who are unable to tolerate supine positioning, who have a pacemaker or other ferromagnetic hardware, or who are claustrophobic
Magnetic resonance perfusion	• Assesses cerebral hemodynamics • May show ischemic penumbra (i.e., the area of the brain that may be saved by timely intervention)	• Not commonly available • Not well standardized
CT angiography	• Excellent view of the large arteries of the neck and brain • Similar to magnetic resonance angiography with regard to resolution	• Requires intravenous contrast
CT perfusion	• Assesses cerebral hemodynamics • May show ischemic penumbra (i.e., the area of the brain that may be saved by timely intervention)	• Challenging to interpret in some cases • Not routinely available at many facilities • Requires intravenous contrast

• Pneumatic compression devices or pharmacologic means should be applied to help prevent deep venous thromboses.
• Avoid any and all oral intake until swallowing is clearly unimpaired; this helps to avoid aspiration pneumonia.
• Early mobilization for rehabilitation is desirable.
• Consider neurosurgical intervention for craniectomy in select cases. Typical cases in which craniectomy may be performed

include cerebellar ischemia with compression of the brain stem and/or the fourth ventricle as well as large right middle cerebral artery ischemia. Available evidence suggests that it may be better to perform early hemicraniectomy (<48 hr) to achieve better outcomes. Decompressive hemicraniectomy has shown good benefit in terms of mortality but not much benefit in terms of disability and functional outcomes.

ACUTE GENERAL Rx
INTRAVENOUS THROMBOLYSIS:
• IV TPA is the only medical therapy approved by the U.S. FDA for the treatment of acute ischemic stroke. Clinical trials involving tenecteplase, a genetically engineered mutant TPA, have shown significantly better reperfusion and clinical outcomes than alteplase in patients with stroke who were selected on the basis of CT perfusion imaging but is still not approved for routine clinical use.
• The time window for administration is within 3 hr of symptom onset.
• There are strict criteria for the administration of IV TPA (see Box 1S-13).
• The protocol is weight based, with 90 mg being the maximum allowable dose.
• The risk of brain hemorrhage with IV TPA is about 5% in stroke patients.
• Recent data suggest that IV TPA can be administered safely and with benefit in select patients up to 4.5 hours after symptom onset. There are additional exclusion criteria if IV TPA is given beyond the 3-hr window.

IMMEDIATE CATHETER CEREBRAL ANGIOGRAPHY FOR ENDOVASCULAR INTERVENTION
(Figs. 1S-76 and 1S-77): Methods available:
• The Merci clot retrieval system, cleared by the FDA in 2004, was the first device for clot retrieval in acute stroke. However, recanalization rates were only modest, and poorly designed clinical trials failed to demonstrate improved outcomes over standard thrombolytic therapy. Subsequently, several new devices have been developed for mechanical clot retrieval with excellent recanalization rates. Multiple randomized clinical trials published in the last two to three years using these newer devices on a carefully selected patient population with large vessel occlusions in the anterior circulation have demonstrated improved neurologic outcomes with endovascular treatment.
• The American Heart Association/American Stroke Association recently published an update of its original guidelines on acute ischemic stroke, recommending endovascular treatment (Class I: Level A evidence) for highly selected patients.
• Intraarterial tissue plasminogen activator (TPA) is used routinely for up to 6 hr after the onset of symptoms, although it is not approved by the U.S. FDA for this purpose.
Pearls and caveats:
• Multimodal therapy (i.e., thrombectomy and intraarterial TPA) is sometimes performed.
• Endovascular treatment may be performed for select cases in which intravenous (IV) TPA has failed to recanalize an occluded artery.
• Endovascular intervention may be an option for cases in which there are systemic contraindications to IV TPA.
• Endovascular intervention is useful only for large, accessible thrombi. Therefore, if a

BOX 1S-13 Three-Hour Criteria for Tissue Plasminogen Activator (Alteplase [Activase]) Use in Patients with Thromboembolic Stroke

Criteria for considering TPA as a treatment option:
- Clinical presentation consistent with an ischemic stroke with clearly demonstrable neurological deficits
- Noncontrast CT head without evidence of hemorrhage
- Time since onset of symptoms (or last known normal if time of onset not known) clearly <3 hr (3-4.5 hr with additional exclusion criteria) before TPA administration would begin
- Age ≥18 years

Criteria for excluding TPA as a treatment option:
- Absolute exclusion criteria:
- Historic and clinical findings suggestive of subarachnoid hemorrhage, even if CT scan is normal
  1. Sudden, severe headache, often with a loss of consciousness at onset
  2. Vomiting
- Active internal bleeding, increased risk of bleeding, or known bleeding diathesis, including those resulting from:
  1. Recent use of warfarin with an INR of ≥1.7
  2. Use of heparin within 48 hr with a prolonged aPTT
  3. Current use of direct thrombin inhibitors or factor Xa inhibitors
  4. Platelet count of <100,000/mm³
  5. History of intracranial hemorrhage
  6. Known intracranial neoplasm, arteriovenous malformation or aneurysm
  7. Arterial puncture at a noncompressible site within the past 7 days
- Stroke, intracranial surgery, or head trauma within the previous 3 mo
- Systolic blood pressure >185 mm Hg or diastolic blood pressure >110 mm Hg that does not decrease below that range with treatment
- Blood glucose <50 mg/dl or >400 mg/dl
- CT findings:
  1. Evidence of intracranial hemorrhage
  2. Hypodensity or effacement of the sulci in one third of the territory of the middle cerebral artery

Relative exclusion criteria:
- Major surgery or serious trauma within the preceding 14 days
- Acute myocardial infarction (recent within the previous 3 months) or post–myocardial infarction pericarditis
- GI or GU bleeding within the past 21 days
- Seizure at stroke onset
- Rapidly improving neurologic signs or isolated mild neurologic deficits
- Patient who is pregnant or lactating

Additional exclusion criteria for administering IV tPA in the 3-4.5 hour window
- Age >80 years
- High stroke scale on presentation (NIHSS > 25)
- Current use of oral anticoagulants regardless of INR

Prior history of stroke and diabetes mellitus

aPTT, Activated partial thromboplastin time; *CT*, computed tomography; *GI*, gastrointestinal; *GU*, genitourinary; *INR*, international normalized ratio; *TPA*, tissue plasminogen activator.

Modified from Rakel RE [ed]: *Principles of family practice*, ed 6, Philadelphia, 2002, Saunders.

stroke patient is a candidate for IV TPA, then he or she should probably receive IV TPA.
- One can reasonably expect an endovascular recanalization rate of 60% in appropriate patients when used alone. Combining the Solitaire device with other endovascular approaches has shown recanalization rates close to 88% in recent studies (Solitaire).
- Complications can ensue from the endovascular procedure itself, including an intracerebral hemorrhage rate that is similar to that associated with IV TPA. A recent metaanalysis revealed that among patients with acute ischemic stroke, cardiovascular therapy with mechanical thrombectomy versus standard medical care with TPA was associated with improved functional outcomes and higher rates of angiographic revascularization, but no significant difference in symptomatic

intracranial hemorrhage or all-cause mortality at 90 days.[1]
- Endovascular intervention is typically available only at select large stroke centers.
- Some practitioners are making use of perfusion imaging (i.e., CT perfusion and magnetic resonance perfusion) to assess whether there is salvageable brain tissue before performing the procedure. In some cases, this may lead to a dramatic expansion of traditional time windows; this practice is currently being studied in clinical trials.
- Fever: Fever is harmful during acute stroke. Ascertaining and addressing the cause while

[1]Badhiwala JH, et al: Endovascular thrombectomy for acute ischemic stroke: A meta-analysis, *JAMA* 314(17):1832-1843, 2015.

lowering an elevated temperature is strongly advised.

HYPERTENSION: Elevated blood pressure is common during acute stroke, and it often subsides without specific therapy. In general, hypertension is not treated acutely unless it is extremely high (e.g., >220 mm Hg systolic blood pressure); there is evidence of organ damage caused by the hypertension; or thrombolysis is being considered, in which case the blood pressure needs to come down (if it can be safely accomplished) to <185/110 mm Hg. It is risky to severely decrease blood pressure in the presence of acute ischemic stroke as it can cause an extension of the stroke into the ischemic penumbra. A 15% to 25% decrease over the first 24 hours is recommended.

HYPOTENSION: The presence of systemic hypotension in acute ischemic stroke portends a poor outcome. The cause should be sought, and volume depletion should be corrected with normal saline. Cardiac arrhythmias should be treated. Induced hypertension with vasopressor agents may be useful for select cases with an ischemic penumbra that is at risk, but caution is strongly advised.

HYPOGLYCEMIA: Hypoglycemia can mimic stroke. Prompt assessment of serum glucose level and replacement as necessary are important.

HYPERGLYCEMIA: The presence of hyperglycemia worsens ischemic stroke outcome. Hyperglycemia should be managed aggressively.

ANTIPLATELET THERAPY: Oral or feeding tube administration of aspirin (325 mg/day) within 48 hours of stroke onset is advised to decrease the likelihood of a repeat ischemic stroke. Other oral antiplatelet regimens approved for secondary stroke prophylaxis (e.g., clopidogrel, aspirin plus extended-release dipyridamole) will also suffice and may be superior in the long term. In patients with acute ischemic stroke and atrial fibrillation, full dose anticoagulation with heparin infusion or low molecular weight heparin should be avoided in the acute setting, as this could potentially harm the patient by causing symptomatic intracranial hemorrhage and there is very little evidence to suggest any benefit.

DISPOSITION

Patients with acute ischemic stroke should be cared for in a stroke unit or an intensive care unit. Nurses with skills in stroke care and telemetry monitoring should be routine. Once the patient is stable and the workup is complete, rehabilitation should be arranged.

REFERRAL

Patients with acute ischemic stroke should be transported to a hospital in which providers are skilled in stroke care. Depending on the severity and duration of symptoms, the patient may qualify for immediate endovascular intervention at a comprehensive stroke center, even if he or she is not a candidate for IV TPA. If complications from brain edema develop, further evaluation by a neurosurgeon may be helpful during the acute phase.

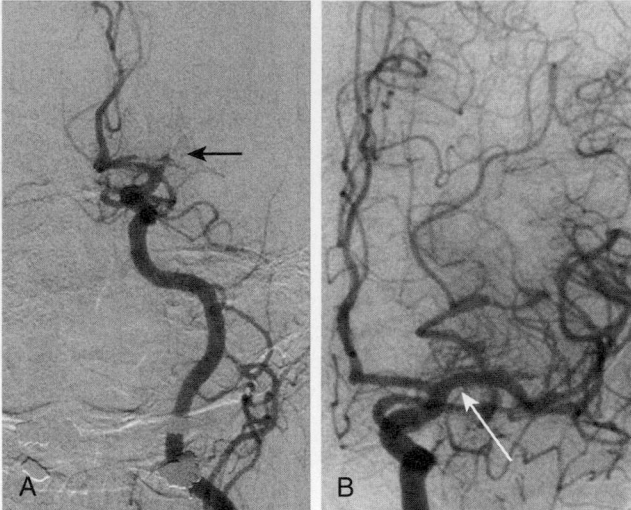

FIGURE 1S-76 A, A catheter angiogram showing left middle cerebral artery occlusion, which caused severe stroke symptoms for several hours. **B,** The artery was opened with the Merci clot retrieval system, and this resulted in normal flow.

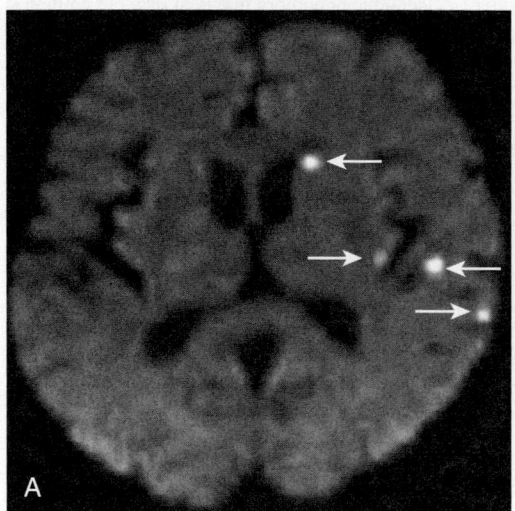

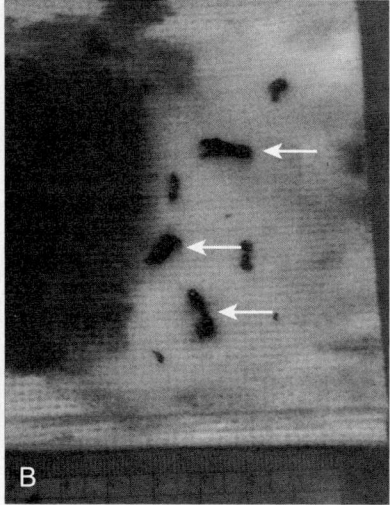

FIGURE 1S-77 A, A diffusion-weighted magnetic resonance image of the same patient as shown in previous figure, this time showing only mild left cerebral ischemia after intervention. The patient was clinically normal. **B,** Thrombi removed from the middle cerebral artery with the use of the Merci clot retrieval system.

PEARLS & CONSIDERATIONS

PREVENTION

- The prevention of acute ischemic stroke depends on the aggressive management of risk factors in individual patients.
- Cross reference: stroke, secondary prevention
- Paroxysmal atrial fibrillation is common in patients with cryptogenic stroke. A recent study found that noninvasive ambulatory ECG monitoring for 30 days significantly improved the detection of atrial fibrillation by a factor of >5 and nearly doubled the rate of anticoagulant treatment compared to the standard practice of short duration ECG monitoring

PATIENT & FAMILY EDUCATION

Patients and families need to be taught about ways to reduce the risk for recurrent stroke, including lifestyle modifications. Education about rehabilitation goals, when appropriate, should also be accomplished.

 EVIDENCE

Available at www.expertconsult.com

SUGGESTED READINGS

Available at www.expertconsult.com

RELATED CONTENT

Algorithm for the emergency evaluation of a patient with suspected stroke (Algorithm, Section III)
Stroke (Patient Information)

AUTHOR: **PRASHANTH KRISHNAMOHAN, M.B.B.S., M.D.**

 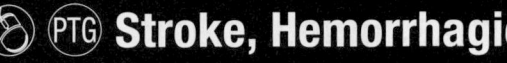

S

 BASIC INFORMATION

DEFINITION

Hemorrhagic stroke is the sudden onset of a focal neurologic deficit caused by hemorrhage into or around the brain.

SYNONYMS

Intracerebral hemorrhage (ICH)
Intracranial hemorrhage
Cerebrovascular attack (This is a nonspecific term and should not be used.)
The term *subarachnoid hemorrhage* refers to a specific location for hemorrhage, which commonly occurs as a result of a ruptured aneurysm. Please see "Subarachnoid Hemorrhage" for additional information.

ICD-10CM CODES

I61   Intracerebral hemorrhage
I61.0 Intracerebral hemorrhage in hemisphere, subcortical
I61.1 Intracerebral hemorrhage in hemisphere, cortical
I61.2 Intracerebral hemorrhage in hemisphere, unspecified
I61.3 Intracerebral hemorrhage in brainstem
I61.4 Intracerebral hemorrhage in cerebellum
I61.5 Intracerebral hemorrhage, intraventricular
I61.6 Intracerebral hemorrhage, multiple localized
I61.9 Nontraumatic intracerebral hemorrhage, unspecified

EPIDEMIOLOGY & DEMOGRAPHICS

INCIDENCE: There are approximately 800 to 1000 new or recurrent strokes per year in the United States, of which ~10% to 15% are hemorrhagic.
RISK FACTORS:
- Hypertension
- Anticoagulant use
- Thrombolysis
- Alcoholism
- Illicit drug use (e.g., cocaine)
- Cerebral amyloid angiopathy
GENETICS: Multifactorial

PHYSICAL FINDINGS & CLINICAL PRESENTATION

The presentation varies with the region of the brain that is affected. The following are common locations for hemorrhage:
- Basal ganglia
- Cerebellum
- Pons
- Lobar (i.e., amyloid angiopathy)
- The ICH score is a widely used grading scale for risk stratification. Parameters used to calculate the ICH score include Glasgow Coma Scale (GCS) (0 to 2 points) at presentation, patient age ≥80 (1 point), ICH volume ≥30 mL (1 point), presence of intraventricular blood (1 point), and infratentorial origin of blood (1 point). Scores range from 0 to 6 with a score of 0 conferring 0% mortality and a score of 6 with estimated 100% mortality.

ETIOLOGY

- Rupture of vessels
- Aneurysm
- Arteriovenous malformation
- Brain tumor
- Amyloid angiopathy

 DIAGNOSIS

DIFFERENTIAL DIAGNOSIS

- Ischemic stroke
- Seizure with postictal paralysis
- Syncope
- Migraine with hemiparesis
- Conversion disorder

LABORATORY TESTS

- CBC, metabolic panel including blood glucose and renal function, PT/INR, aPTT, urinalysis, and toxicology screens
- ECG and telemetry monitoring

IMAGING STUDIES

- Immediate: CT scanning of the head without contrast is highly sensitive for hemorrhage (Fig. 1S-78).
- CT or MR angiogram to rule out an underlying vascular malformation. CT spot sign on the CTA has been shown to be a reliable early predictor of hematoma expansion.
- MRI of the brain with a gradient echo sequence is also highly sensitive for hemorrhage, including intracerebral microhemorrhages that may not be visible with computed tomography scanning. MRI may also help to identify underlying brain tumors or vascular malformations, especially if the bleeding occurs at atypical sites.

 TREATMENT

NONPHARMACOLOGIC THERAPY

- Urgent neurosurgical evaluation is needed in many cases either for evacuation of the hematoma or for relieving raised intracranial pressure by procedures such as EVD placement or decompressive surgeries.
- Surgery should be performed promptly for cases of cerebellar hemorrhage of >3 cm when the patient is deteriorating clinically, showing brain stem edema or hydrocephalus.
- Surgery for lobar or deep brain clots may be considered for select cases, although the level of evidence for efficacy is not high.
- Recent innovative surgical techniques, such as instillation of thrombolytic agents for intraventricular hemorrhage and minimally invasive surgery for hematoma evacuation, appear to be promising. Clinical trials are currently in progress to assess whether these approaches improve mortality and neurologic outcomes.

ACUTE GENERAL Rx

The cornerstones of medical management of acute intracerebral hemorrhage include:
Control of hypertension
Correction of coagulopathy
Management of elevated intracranial pressure
Treatment of seizures
Hypertension (Box 1S-14): Blood pressure should be quickly lowered by 15% and then gradually and safely brought to the individual patient's target range. In theory, this may diminish the expansion of the hematoma. More aggressive control of SBP to 140 or less in the acute setting has been shown to be safe in clinical trials with slightly improved outcomes compared to less aggressive BP control (target SBP <180) and is currently recommended by the American Heart Association/American Stroke

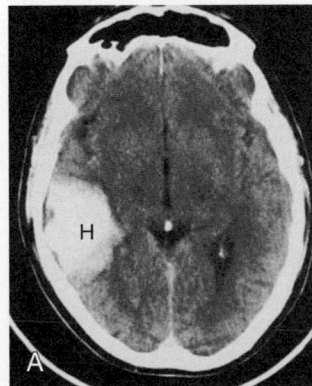 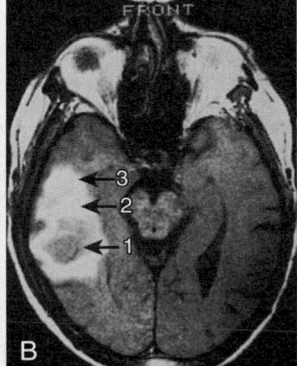 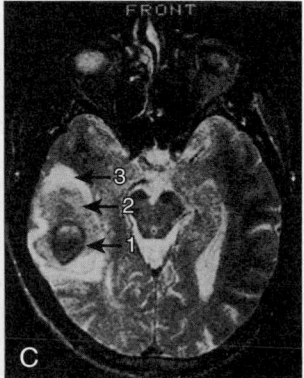

FIGURE 1S-78 Hemorrhage. Axial CT image **(A)** demonstrates a large area of acute hemorrhage *(H)* in right temporal lobe. T_1-weighted **(B)** and T_2-weighted **(C)** MRI scans demonstrate the hemorrhage in various stages of breakdown. Center of lesion is dark on T_1- and T_2-weighted images, indicating oxyhemoglobin *(1)*. Intermediate zone is bright on T_1-weighted image and gray on T_2-weighted image, indicating intracellular methemoglobin *(2)*. Outer rim is bright on both T_1- and T_2-weighted images, indicating hextracellular methemoglobin *(3)*. (From Vincent JL et al: *Textbook of critical care,* ed 6, Philadelphia, 2011, Saunders.)

BOX 1S-14   Suggested Recommended Guidelines for the Treatment of Elevated Blood Pressure in Patients with Spontaneous Intracerebral Hemorrhage

1. SBP of >200 mm Hg or MAP of >150 mm Hg: Consider the aggressive reduction of BP with continuous intravenous infusion, with BP monitoring every 5 min.
2. SBP of >180 mm Hg or MAP of >130 mm Hg with evidence or suspicion of elevated ICP: Consider ICP monitor and reducing BP with intermittent or continuous intravenous medications to keep cerebral perfusion pressure >60 to 80 mm Hg.
3. SBP of >180 mm Hg or MAP of >130 mm Hg without evidence or suspicion of elevated ICP: Consider a modest reduction of BP (e.g., MAP of 110 mm Hg or target blood pressure of 160/90 mm Hg) with intermittent or continuous intravenous medications, and clinically reexamine the patient every 15 min.

BP, Blood pressure; *ICP,* intracranial pressure; *MAP,* mean arterial pressure; *SBP,* systolic blood pressure.
Modified from Broderick J et al: Guidelines for the management of spontaneous intracerebral hemorrhage in adults: 2007 update, *Stroke* 38:2001-2023, 2007.

Association guidelines. Evidence suggests that a more sustained BP control with continuous IV medications might be more beneficial than using intermittent medications resulting in significant BP variability.

Correction of Coagulopathy

- Early hematoma expansion has been associated with poor outcome.
- Protamine sulfate is used to treat cases of heparin-induced intracerebral hemorrhage.
- Prothrombin concentrate complex (PCC) is now recommended for reversal of warfarin-associated ICH. FFP may also be used for this purpose, although it carries the disadvantage of administering more volume, potentially leading to complications such as pulmonary edema and slightly longer times to reversal of coagulopathy compared to PCC. Vitamin K should be administered IV along with flash-frozen plasma (FFP)/PCC for sustained effects. Routine use of recombinant factor VII concentrates is not recommended due to insufficient evidence and concern for increased risk of thromboembolic events.
- Idarucizumab (Praxbind) is a humanized monoclonal antibody fragment that can be used for urgent reversal of the anticoagulant effect of the direct thrombin inhibitor dabigatran (Pradaxa).
- Andexanet alfa, a recombinant modified human factor X2 decoy protein has been effective for reversion of the anticoagulant effect of apixaban (Eliquis) and rivaroxaban (Xarelto).
- Recommendations for thrombolytic-associated intracerebral hemorrhage treatment include the consideration of the infusion of platelets and cryoprecipitate.
- Hemostatic therapy has not been shown convincingly to improve outcomes, despite reducing hematoma expansion. Efforts are under way to identify patients at high risk of early hematoma expansion by using clinical and radiographic information to determine who may benefit from more aggressive hemostatic intervention.

Elevated intracranial pressure: this condition should be treated with a graded approach, which may include the elevation of the head of the bed, analgesia/sedation, hyperventilation, and osmotic therapy. In patients clinically suspected to have elevated ICP or with GCS <8, invasive monitoring of the ICP may be required. If conservative treatment fails to control ICP, EVD placement or other decompressive procedures like craniotomy need to be pursued.

Seizures: If seizures occur, they should be treated aggressively, including with intravenous medications, if needed. Although widely practiced, routine use of prophylactic antiepileptic medications is not recommended. Continuous EEG monitoring should be employed in patients with suspected seizures or unexplained low levels of consciousness.

Supportive Treatment:

- Hyperglycemia: a high blood glucose level predicts a worse outcome. Markedly elevated glucose levels should be lowered to <200 mg/dl.
- Antipyretics should be administered for fever in addition to searching for a cause of the fever.
- Care should be taken to avoid hypoxia. Airway and ventilatory management should happen early and concurrently with the primary management of ICH.
- Pneumatic compression devices should be applied to help prevent deep venous thrombosis. Chemical DVT prophylaxis can be started after 48 to 72 hours in most situations once the bleed has been determined to be stable.
- Early mobilization for rehabilitation is desirable.

DISPOSITION

For large hemorrhages or unstable patients, immediate referral to a stroke center

REFERRAL

Patients with hemorrhagic stroke should be transported to a hospital where providers are skilled in the treatment of stroke and cerebrovascular diseases including the availability of neurosurgery services and neurocritical care. Depending on the severity and duration of symptoms, the patient may require neurosurgical intervention.

❗ PEARLS & CONSIDERATIONS

- Outcomes are inversely correlated with hemorrhage size.
- Specific reversal agents may be useful for warfarin-, heparin-, or thrombolysis-associated hemorrhage.
- No procoagulant medications have yet been shown to be safe and effective for the mitigation of spontaneous intracerebral hemorrhage in placebo-controlled trials.

PREVENTION

- Prevention depends on the aggressive management of risk factors in individual patients, including hypertension, smoking, alcohol use, and cocaine use.
- Newer oral anticoagulants (NOACs) dabigatran, apixaban, rivaroxaban are uniformly associated with an overall reduced risk of iatrogenic intracerebral hemorrhage (ICH) when used for stroke prevention in atrial fibrillation. Any of the currently available NOACs can be considered first line for patients at high risk for ICH.[1]

PATIENT & FAMILY EDUCATION

Patients and families need to understand that most patients will not soon achieve functional independence and that rehabilitation will be a long process. Education about avoiding antithrombotic agents should be stressed as appropriate for individual circumstances.

SUGGESTED READINGS

Available at www.expertconsult.com

RELATED CONTENT

Stroke (Patient Information)

AUTHOR: **PRASHANTH KRISHNAMOHAN, M.B.B.S., M.D.**

---

[1]Chatterjee S et al.: New oral anticoagulants and the risk of intracranial hemorrhage: traditional and Bayesian meta-analysis and mixed treatment comparison of randomized trials of new oral anticoagulants in atrial fibrillation, *JAMA Neurol* 70(12):1486-1490, 2013.

BASIC INFORMATION

DEFINITION

Secondary prevention of stroke involves preventing the recurrence of a cerebral vascular ischemic or hemorrhagic stroke after a primary event. Now includes preventative treatments after a transient ischemic event (reversible symptoms with no MRI findings after 24 hours).

SYNONYMS

Brain attack
Stroke
Cerebral thrombosis
Cerebral hemorrhage
Brain infarct

ICD-10CM CODES

I65.2	Occlusion and stenosis of carotid artery
I65.0	Occlusion and stenosis of vertebral artery
I65.9	Occlusion and stenosis of unspecified precerebral artery
I66	Occlusion and stenosis of cerebral artery, not resulting in cerebral infarction
I65.1	Occlusion and stenosis of basilar artery

EPIDEMIOLOGY

Stroke is the third leading cause of death in the U.S. Each year, there are a total of 800,000 strokes, of which approximately 200,000 are recurrent strokes. Thus, secondary prevention of ischemic stroke remains good treatment strategy. Secondary prevention is specifically targeted toward modifiable risk factors.

RISK FACTORS: Age is the most important nonmodifiable risk factor. Modifiable risk factors include hypertension, hyperlipidemia, cigarette smoking, excessive alcohol consumption, physical inactivity, obesity (i.e., a body mass index of >25 kg/m^2), illegal drug use (amphetamines, cocaine), excessive alcohol use, and diabetes mellitus.

GENETICS: Multifactorial

PHYSICAL FINDINGS & CLINICAL PRESENTATION

- Stroke can have a varied presentation. Typically, the individual has a sudden definable loss of motor, sensory, visual, or cognitive functions that have a clear time of onset and that are noticed by others or by the individuals themselves.
- Physical findings such as weakness and/or numbness in one limb or on one side of the body, facial droop, visual field loss, or the inability to understand or communicate with others raises one's suspicion of a stroke event.

ETIOLOGY

- Strokes are broadly divided into ischemic or hemorrhagic (i.e., intraparenchymal or sub-arachnoid hemorrhage)
- Ischemic strokes can be caused by large-vessel atherosclerosis, cardioembolism such as in atrial fibrillation or cardiomyopathy, or small vessel disease such as lacunar stroke. Rare causes such as recreational drug use (e.g., cocaine abuse); arterial dissection; and hypercoagulable states need to be considered when ischemic stroke occurs in younger individuals.
- The most common cause of intracerebral hemorrhage is uncontrolled hypertension. Spontaneous rupture of a brain aneurysm causes subarachnoid hemorrhage.

DIAGNOSIS

DIFFERENTIAL DIAGNOSIS

- Seizure and postictal states
- Complicated migraine
- Hypoglycemia
- Brain tumor
- Somatization disorder

WORKUP

- Blood glucose level HBA1c
- APTT, PT/INR, CBC, and CMP
- Fasting lipid panel
- Hypercoagulability tests for young stroke patients with no obvious risk factors

IMAGING STUDIES

- Computed tomography scanning of the head without contrast can differentiate between ischemic and hemorrhagic stroke. MRI of the brain is a more specific test.
- Carotid ultrasound and transcranial Doppler are used to detect large-vessel atherosclerosis. Magnetic resonance and computed tomography angiography are good alternatives.
- Echocardiogram and ECG can be used to detect a cardioembolic source.

TREATMENT

The secondary prevention of stroke is targeted toward modifiable risk factors. These include lifestyle modifications such as appropriate diet, exercise, weight loss, and smoking cessation, avoidance of heavy alcohol use, and risk factor modification as listed below. All patients with noncardioembolic ischemic stroke or transient ischemic attack (TIA) should be on aspirin (50 to 325 mg/day), a combination of aspirin and extended-release dipyridamole, or clopidogrel. A consultation with a neurologist should be considered for young stroke patients and for patients with no obvious cause or with stroke from unusual causes (e.g., hypercoagulable states, dissections). Treatment with a combination of Plavix and aspirin in secondary stroke prevention when no other pressing medical conditions require their use is no longer recommended; this was published in the MATCH trial.

PREVENTING STROKE IN SPECIFIC CONDITIONS

Cardioembolic strokes as a result of atrial fibrillation (AF) have two first-line drug therapies: warfarin and dabigatran. Warfarin remains a first-line therapy with an international normalized ratio (INR) between 2.0 and 3.0. Dabigatran at a dosing regimen of 150 mg twice a day has efficacy equal to that of warfarin without the need for routine monitoring of INR. The U.S. Food and Drug Administration approved dabigatran for nonvalvular AF. Recently the newer antithrombotic agents such as rivaroxaban and apixaban have been introduced for nonvalvular AF. Expert consult by a neurologist is recommended before starting these newer agents. It is important to note that these agents do not have an effect on the PT/INR or APTT in cases where there is a bleed, and no standard effective reversal therapy is available.

1. For patients with contraindications to anticoagulants, aspirin (325 mg/day) is recommended. The Active-A trial suggested that a combination of aspirin and clopidogrel is slightly better than aspirin alone for those unable to tolerate warfarin.
2. Cardioembolic strokes as a result of a prosthetic metallic valve: anticoagulant therapy with warfarin is recommended with a goal INR between 2.5 and 3.5.
3. Strokes as a result of large-vessel atherosclerosis (i.e., symptomatic carotid stenosis): for patients with recent TIA or ischemic stroke within the last 6 months and ipsilateral severe (70%-99%) carotid artery stenosis, carotid endarterectomy (CEA) performed by a surgeon is recommended and results in a perioperative morbidity and mortality rate of <6%. For patients with recent TIA or ischemic stroke and ipsilateral moderate (50%-69%) carotid stenosis, CEA is recommended within 14 days of the event. When the degree of stenosis is <50%, there is no indication for CEA. Carotid stenting is not indicated except for cases in which surgery is high risk. Current trials are comparing carotid enterectomy versus carotid stenting. As of 2013, the Carotid Revascularization Endarterectomy Versus Stenting Trial (CREST) has shown no inferiority of stenting versus endarterectomy, and stenting may favor younger patients or those at higher surgical risk for complications.
4. Symptomatic intracranial atherosclerosis: treatment with aspirin has proven effective and just as efficacious as warfarin in both the WASID and WARSS studies. The utility of angioplasty and stenting in patients with symptomatic intracranial atherosclerosis is available at several stroke centers but remains investigational (Fig. 1S-79). In April 2011 the NINDS stopped enrollment into the symptomatic intracranial artery stenosis stenting trial (SAMMPRIS).
5. Patent foramen ovale (PFO): the American Academy of Neurology recommends medical therapy for stroke patients with PFO. Trials are under way to evaluate if endovascular PFO closure reduces the risk of recurrent transient ischemic attacks or strokes.
6. Intracerebral hemorrhage: for immediate management, please refer to the chapter on intracerebral hemorrhage. Antiplatelet agents should be held for 3 to 4 weeks and can be restarted if there is a compelling indication such as nonvalvular atrial fibrillation. The American Stroke Association/American Heart

Association 2010 guideline recommends avoiding long-term anticoagulation (e.g., warfarin, heparin) after spontaneous lobar intracerebral hemorrhage, but antiplatelet therapy (e.g., aspirin, clopidogrel, Aggrenox) may be considered in all cases of intracerebral hemorrhage where there is a definite indication. Consider a neurology consultation in these cases.

PREVENTING LONG-TERM COMPLICATIONS AFTER A STROKE

Evaluation by a physical, occupational, and speech therapist will reduce the long-term disability that can follow a stroke event. The American Stroke Association 2010 guideline recommends a multidisciplinary approach to rehabilitation. Studies have shown an improved survival and recovery. Home-based rehabilitation can be considered after discussion with the rehabilitation specialist.

RISK FACTOR MODIFICATION

1. Hypertension: antihypertensive treatment is recommended for both the prevention of recurrent stroke and the prevention of other vascular events in persons who have had an ischemic stroke or a TIA. Absolute target blood pressure level and reduction are uncertain and should be individualized. Blood pressure should be lowered gradually over a period of months to prevent cerebral hypoperfusion and extension of stroke. Lifestyle modifications as listed previously should be included as part of a comprehensive antihypertension treatment plan.
2. Diabetes: the goal for the hemoglobin A_{1c} level should be <7%. For type 2 diabetics, diet and exercise can prove very beneficial. Type 1 diabetics can also benefit from diet and compliance with their insulin regimen. Uncontrolled hyperglycemia can lead to acceleration of both intracranial and extracranial arteriosclerosis. Always consider consulting a diabetic educator.
3. Hyperlipidemia: for patients with ischemic stroke or TIA with elevated cholesterol levels, statin agents are recommended. The target goals for cholesterol lowering are an LDL-C level of <100 mg/dl and an LDL-C level of <70 mg/dl for very high-risk persons with multiple risk factors (e.g., both coronary artery disease and diabetes).
4. Cigarette smoking: absolute cessation is required. Try to offer pharmacologic therapy or counseling services to the patient. Secondhand tobacco exposure is just as dangerous, so inquire about secondhand exposure.
5. Obesity: weight reduction may be considered for all overweight ischemic stroke and TIA patients to maintain the goal of a body mass index of between 18.5 and 24.9 kg/m² and a waist circumference of <35 in for women and <40 in for men.
6. Excessive alcohol consumption: patients with ischemic stroke or TIA who are heavy drinkers should eliminate or reduce their consumption of alcohol. Light to moderate levels of no more than two drinks per day for men and one drink per day for nonpregnant women may be considered.

DISPOSITION

Secondary stroke prevention is a multifaceted approach of lifestyle modification and pharmacologic intervention that is aimed at preventing or limiting disability.

REFERRAL

For complicated recurrent strokes, a referral to a neurologist who specializes in stroke is recommended.

PEARLS & CONSIDERATIONS

The modification of risk factors is the best preventive measure for stroke. Lifestyle modification is a very important aspect of secondary stroke prevention. Always consider the patient's ability to afford the therapy and prescribed follow-up tests. Experience teaches us that patients sometimes will not let us know about their ability to afford therapies unless we inquire.

PREVENTION

Prevention is the goal of treatment, and compliance is the most important factor. Review risk factor reduction and pharmacologic therapy as previously discussed.

PATIENT/FAMILY EDUCATION

More information can be obtained from the following sources:
- American Heart Association, National Center, 7272 Greenville Avenue, Dallas, TX 75231
- American Stroke Association, 1-888-4-STROKE or 1-888-478-7653
- H.O.P.E. for Stroke, 250 Duck Pond Drive, Wantagh, NY 11793, 516-804-8495

EBM EVIDENCE

Available at www.expertconsult.com

SUGGESTED READINGS

Available at www.expertconsult.com

RELATED CONTENT

Stroke (Patient Information)
Transient Ischemic Attack (Related Key Topic)

AUTHOR: **NAWAZ HACK, M.D.**

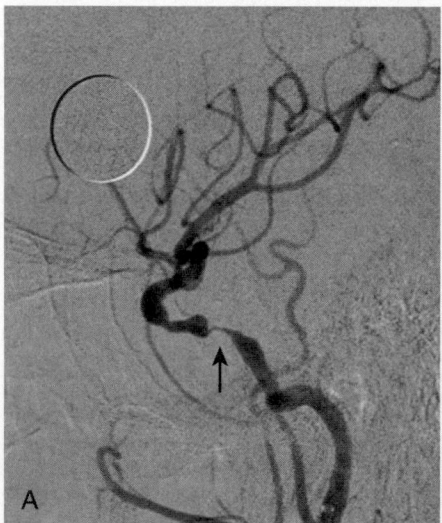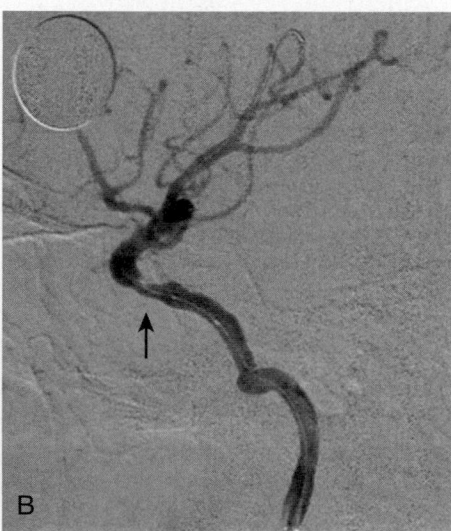

FIGURE 1S-79 A, Intracranial high-grade symptomatic stenosis. **B,** This patient failed aggressive medical therapy and responded only to angioplasty and stenting.

S

 **BASIC INFORMATION**

DEFINITION

Stuttering is a problem of speech fluency, usually starting in early childhood. Stuttered speech is broken by repetitions, prolongations or abnormal stoppages of sounds, syllables, or words.

SYNONYMS

Childhood-Onset Fluency Disorder

ICD-10CM CODES
F80.81 Stuttering

EPIDEMIOLOGY & DEMOGRAPHICS

INCIDENCE: Approximately 5% of children have stuttered 6 months or more. About 1% of the population is affected by stuttering at any given time.
PREDOMINANT SEX AND AGE: During childhood, twice as many boys stutter as girls. More girls than boys outgrow stuttering, which results in four times as many men stuttering as women.
GENETICS: Studies show higher rates of stuttering within families of those who stutter and a higher concordance for stuttering in identical twins compared to fraternal twins.
RISK FACTORS: Presence of other speech or language disorder, family history of stuttering, onset after 3.5 years of age, male sex, and stuttering over 6 months in duration.

PHYSICAL FINDINGS & CLINICAL PRESENTATION

- Stuttering usually presents between the ages of 2 and 5, when normal language development begins and children are transitioning from using simple phrases to more complex sentences. Stuttered speech is characterized by at least one of the following: repetitions (for for for example), prolongations (fffffor example), interjections, broken words, audible or silent blocking, and circumlocutions (word substitutions to bypass difficult words).
- If stuttering is left untreated, it can lead to significant impairment in academic, social, and occupational spheres. Affected individuals show fear and embarrassment around speech and may avoid speaking in some situations. Compensatory maladaptive behaviors may also develop such as eyelid closing, involuntary movements, and some physical tension around the mouth during speech.
- Differentiating stuttering from normal developmental dysfluency is important. Normal dysfluency occurs in many children, is self-limited, and does not need treatment. It is characterized by occasional stuttering events (once every 10 sentences) and brief stuttering events (<0.5 second). The child does not seem concerned about the dysfluency and the disrupted speech tends to come and go based on whether the child is tired, excited, or talking about new or complex topics. Stuttering, in comparison, is defined by more frequent (>3%-10% of speech) and longer stuttering events (>0.5 second). Also, the repetitions are greater in number ("for for for for for example" as opposed to "for for for example") and the prolongations are longer ("Forrrrrrrrrrrrrrrr example" as opposed to "Forrrrr example").

ETIOLOGY

- Findings in twin studies consistently demonstrate strong phenotype inheritance in identical twins.
- Researchers at present are utilizing genome-wide association study (GWAS) and functional genome-wide association study (fGWAS) techniques to better understand specific genetic variations that are associated with stuttering. One research group found that susceptibility to nonsyndromic stuttering is associated with variations in genes governing lysosomal metabolism. Another group found that variations in genes which govern zinc and glucose mitigated neurological functions are associated with stuttering. Findings from both research groups have not been confirmed or replicated.
- Stuttering might be related to abnormal elevations of cerebral dopamine activity.
- Brain imaging studies show distinct differences in sensorimotor integration centers in the brains of those who stutter compared to controls.
- Although parents do not cause their child's stuttering, a critical, impatient, or interrupting speech environment can lead to worsening stuttered speech.

 DIAGNOSIS

DIFFERENTIAL DIAGNOSIS

Stuttering is classified as developmental, neurogenic, or psychogenic.

Developmental stuttering, known simply as stuttering, is the most common form of speech dysfluency and usually presents in the preschool years.

Neurogenic stuttering, by contrast, is much less common and can result from a traumatic brain injury, infection, or cerebrovascular accident. Psychogenic stuttering is much less common than developmental stuttering, too, but it, like neurogenic stuttering, has an identifiable precipitant, which most often takes the form of an emotional stressor/injury as opposed to a physical injury.

Psychogenic stuttering can be differentiated from developmental stuttering because those affected with it are usually not overly concerned about their dysfluency. Additionally, unlike developmental stuttering, psychogenic stuttering does not improve when the affected individual sings or recites something in a chorus, or when the auditory processing of his own voice is blocked, i.e., with ear plugs or when music is played in headphones. Differentiating neurogenic stuttering from developmental and psychogenic stuttering can be more challenging, especially in cases where no clear history exists or no visual evidence is available. Similar to individuals with psychogenic stuttering, some

with neurogenic stuttering do not notice their stuttered speech and thus can appear unconcerned about it. Other times, affected individuals do notice their speech dysfluency and are troubled by it, as is the case in developmental stuttering. Adding to the complexity is the fact that a history of developmental stuttering is a risk factor for the emergence of neurogenic stuttering; that is, successfully treated developmental stuttering can reemerge after a brain injury.

WORKUP

- The clinical interview should include assessment of symptoms (onset, context, quality, frequency, duration, etc.) and impact on academic, social, or occupational spheres. A developmental history and family history of stuttering should be obtained, as well as assessing for family discord or recent emotional stressors. One should also try to assess parental response to the child's stuttering (intrusive/critical/anxious vs. accepting/patient/calm).
- A full physical exam should be conducted with special attention to the mental status exam and neurologic exam.
- No laboratory tests or imaging studies are indicated unless neurogenic stuttering is suspected.
- Evaluation by an audiologist for a formal hearing assessment to rule out hearing loss or discrimination disorder may be beneficial in some cases.

TREATMENT

NONPHARMACOLOGIC THERAPY

- Typically, the treatment of choice for stuttering is Speech and Language Therapy (SALT). Medications are not a first-line treatment.
- SALT consists of varying combinations of the following treatment modalities: fluency-shaping mechanisms, stuttering modification, delayed auditory feedback devices, and the Lidcombe approach (parental use of operant conditioning techniques). Current research is focusing on what elements in SALT are specifically accounting for treatment response.
- The above therapies help the child reduce fear about stuttering and produce speech more easily. The child is helped to speak slower and without increased physical tension and struggle. Families are encouraged to create an atmosphere of acceptance and calm for their child to speak and to model slower speech.

ACUTE GENERAL Rx

- There have been no large-scale pharmacologic treatment trials for stuttering. Smaller-scale trials and case studies have been conducted with a variety of agents, including clonidine, antipsychotics, and GABA-A partial agonists. Clonidine was found to be ineffective in reducing speech dysfluency. Weaker studies involving antipsychotic medications have found some positive effects, but almost all of these studies have serious methodologic problems and the associated side-effect profile makes using these agents for the long-term treatment of stuttering prohibitive. In some instances (e.g., a TBI patient with resulting neurogenic stuttering and psychosis), an antipsychotic might work well. A recent double-blind, randomized, placebo-controlled study of the GABA-A partial agonist pagoclone showed a modest reduction in speech dysfluency in adults.

- Case reports of deep brain stimulation of the ventral intermediate nucleus of the thalamus have shown some reduction in speech dysfluency in adults with severe stuttering.

DISPOSITION

Although the natural rate of recovery from stuttering is thought to be as high as 88%, evidence shows that the best treatment results occur when children are referred early.

REFERRAL

Those with severe stuttering should be referred immediately to a speech-language pathologist for further evaluation and treatment. Those with mild stuttering should be referred if stuttering continues for longer than 6 weeks or if there is significant concern by the parent or child.

SUGGESTED READINGS

Available at www.expertconsult.com

AUTHOR: **JAMISON ROGERS, M.D.**

BASIC INFORMATION

DEFINITION

A hordeolum is an acute inflammatory process affecting the eyelid and arising from the meibomian (posterior) or Zeis (anterior) glands. It is most often infectious and usually caused by *Staphylococcus aureus*. When infection involves the meibomian glands, it is called meibomianitis.

SYNONYMS

Hordeolum
Meibomianitis

ICD-10CM CODES

H00.011 Hordeolum externum right upper eyelid
H00.012 Hordeolum externum right lower eyelid
H00.013 Hordeolum externum right eye, unspecified eyelid
H00.014 Hordeolum externum left upper eyelid
H00.015 Hordeolum externum left lower eyelid
H00.016 Hordeolum externum left eye, unspecified eyelid
H00.019 Hordeolum externum unspecified eye, unspecified eyelid
H00.021 Hordeolum internum right upper eyelid
H00.022 Hordeolum internum right lower eyelid
H00.023 Hordeolum internum right eye, unspecified eyelid
H00.024 Hordeolum internum left upper eyelid
H00.025 Hordeolum internum left lower eyelid
H00.026 Hordeolum internum left eye, unspecified eyelid
H00.029 Hordeolum internum unspecified eye, unspecified eyelid

EPIDEMIOLOGY & DEMOGRAPHICS

INCIDENCE (IN U.S.): Unknown.
PREVALENCE (IN U.S.): Unknown.
PREDOMINANT SEX: No gender predilection.
PREDOMINANT AGE: May occur at any age.
NEONATAL INFECTION: Rare in the neonatal period.
PEAK INCIDENCE: May occur at any age.

PHYSICAL FINDINGS & CLINICAL PRESENTATION

- Abrupt onset with pain and erythema of the eyelid.
- Localized, tender mass in the eyelid (Fig. 1S-82).

- May be associated with blepharitis.
- External hordeolum: points toward the skin surface of the lid and may spontaneously drain.
- Internal hordeolum: can point toward the conjunctival side of the lid and may cause conjunctival inflammation.

ETIOLOGY

- 75% to 95% of cases are caused by *S. aureus*.
- Occasional cases are caused by *Streptococcus pneumoniae*, other streptococci, gram-negative enteric organisms, or mixed bacterial flora.

DIAGNOSIS

DIFFERENTIAL DIAGNOSIS

- Eyelid abscess.
- Chalazion.
- Allergy or contact dermatitis with conjunctival edema.
- Acute dacryocystitis.
- Herpes simplex infection.
- Cellulitis of the eyelid.

LABORATORY TESTS

- Generally, none are necessary.
- If incision and drainage are performed, specimens should be sent for bacterial culture.

TREATMENT

NONPHARMACOLOGIC THERAPY

External stye (eyelash follicle): Usually responds to warm compresses and will drain spontaneously.

ACUTE GENERAL Rx

- Systemic antibiotics generally not necessary.
- For internal stye, use hot packs *plus* oral dicloxacillin 500 mg qid × 7 days. If suspecting

MRSA, use trimethoprim-sulfamethoxazole DS bid in place of dicloxacillin. In patients with hospital-acquired infection, consider linezolid 600 mg PO bid.
- For external stye, topical erythromycin ophthalmic ointment applied to the lid margins two to four times daily until resolution may be helpful in some cases.
- Incision and drainage: rarely needed but should be considered for progressive infections.

DISPOSITION

- Usually sporadic occurrence.
- Possible relapse if resolution is not complete.

REFERRAL

- For evaluation by an ophthalmologist if visual acuity or ocular movement is affected or if the diagnosis is in doubt.
- For surgical drainage if necessary.

PEARLS & CONSIDERATIONS

COMMENTS

Seborrheic dermatitis may coexist with hordeolum.

SUGGESTED READINGS

Available at www.expertconsult.com

RELATED CONTENT

Chalazion (Patient Information)
Stye (Hordeolum) (Patient Information)

AUTHOR: **GLENN G. FORT, M.D., M.P.H.**

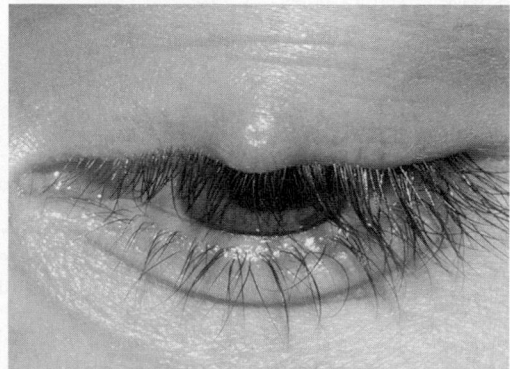

FIGURE 1S-82 External stye. (From Palay D [ed]: *Ophthalmology for the primary care physician*, St Louis, 1997, Mosby.)

BASIC INFORMATION

DEFINITION

Subarachnoid hemorrhage (SAH) is defined as hemorrhage into the subarachnoid space surrounding the brain. This can be nontraumatic or traumatic in nature. Here we will focus upon nontraumatic subarachnoid hemorrhage. Box 1S-15 describes the Hunt and Hess clinical classification of patients presenting with aneurysmal SAH.

SYNONYMS

Subarachnoid bleed
SAH

ICD-10CM CODES

I60	Subarachnoid hemorrhage
I60.1	Subarachnoid hemorrhage from middle cerebral artery
I60.2	Subarachnoid hemorrhage from anterior communicating artery
I60.3	Subarachnoid hemorrhage from posterior communicating artery
I60.4	Subarachnoid hemorrhage from basilar artery
I60.5	Subarachnoid hemorrhage from vertebral artery
I60.7	Subarachnoid hemorrhage from intracranial artery, unspecified

EPIDEMIOLOGY & DEMOGRAPHICS

INCIDENCE: Nontraumatic: 6 to 8 cases/100,000 persons per yr
PREDOMINANT SEX: Women aged >55 yr were found to have a 25% greater risk of developing SAH compared with men of the same age.
PREDOMINANT AGE: The mean age at onset is 55 yr.
PEAK INCIDENCE: Most aneurysmal SAH occurs in people who are between the ages of 55 and 60 yr.
GENETICS:
- First-degree relatives have a 5 to 12 times greater risk of developing SAH compared with the general population.
- Autosomal dominant polycystic kidney disease is known to be associated with cerebral aneurysms in 8% of cases; screening is recommended in families with this condition in which one family member has experienced a ruptured aneurysm.
- Collagen vascular diseases such as Marfan syndrome, Ehler Danlos syndrome have also been implicated in the formation of aneurysms.
RISK FACTORS: Although genetics seem to play a factor in SAH, lifestyle factors are more important for determining overall risk. These risk factors include smoking, hypertension, oral contraception, pregnancy, and amphetamine/cocaine use.

PHYSICAL FINDINGS & CLINICAL PRESENTATION

- The primary symptom is a sudden, severe headache in 97% of cases. This is classically described as the "worst headache of my life" and also called a thunderclap headache. This headache may be associated with nausea/vomiting, neck pain, seizure, or complete loss of consciousness.
- 30% to 60% of patients report a history of headaches during the weeks preceding the actual hemorrhage event. These are most likely sentinel bleeds that represent microhemorrhages.
- Altered mental status and coma may result from the direct effect (hemorrhagic mass effect), but more likely is the result of acutely increased intracranial pressure.
- A posterior communication aneurysm may present as oculomotor (cranial nerve III) palsy, even in a nonruptured setting.
- Table E1S-28 describes the World Federation of Neurologic Surgeons clinical classification of SAH.

ETIOLOGY

- Trauma is the most common cause of SAH; a ruptured aneurysm is the most common cause of spontaneous SAH (75%-80% of spontaneous SAH).
- Idiopathic SAH, also known as angiogram-negative SAH, accounts for 5% to 20% of spontaneous SAH. In these cases, no angiographic cause of the hemorrhage is found. This entity is also known as benign perimesencephalic SAH and is thought to occur due to rupture of venous plexus in the cisterns surrounding the brain stem.
- Other causes of spontaneous SAH include arteriovenous malformations, bleeding into preexisting tumors, vasculitis, and cerebral artery dissection.
- Cocaine abuse, sickle cell anemia, coagulopathies, and pituitary apoplexy can also result in SAH.

DIAGNOSIS

DIFFERENTIAL DIAGNOSIS

- Intracerebral hemorrhage as a result of trauma, intratumoral bleed, stroke with hemorrhagic conversion, venous hemorrhage associated with venous sinus thrombosis, mycotic aneurysm rupture.
- Other causes: thunderclap headaches such as idiopathic thunderclap headache, migraine headache, sexual headache, cough headache, exertional headache, secondary causes including, but not limited to, pituitary apoplexy or acute hydrocephalus

WORKUP

IMAGING STUDIES:
- Computed tomography (CT) of the head (Fig. 1S-83) shows hemorrhage in more than 95% of cases, especially during the acute phase (i.e., 24-48 hr) after the onset of bleeding. Box 1S-16 describes the Fisher grade of SAH on initial CT (Fisher III being associated with highest risk of vasospasm). About 3% to 5% of SAH may be missed on initial CT of the head. MRI head, specifically FLAIR sequence, is helpful in detecting subarachnoid blood if clinically suspected.
- Lumbar puncture should be performed in all cases of suspected SAH with "normal CT of the head." The following suggest SAH:
  1. An RBC count of more than $100,000/m^3$ in tubes 1 AND 4. This is to differentiate from a traumatic tap in which there will be a drop in RBC count from tube 1 to 4.
  2. Presence of xanthochromia or bilirubin in the cerebrospinal fluid.
  3. SAH can also be excluded by the following two criteria: CSF RBC count $< 2000 \times 10^6/L$ and no xanthochromia.

BOX 1S-15 **Hunt and Hess Clinical Classification of Subarachnoid Hemorrhage**

I	Asymptomatic or mild headache and neck stiffness
II	Moderate to severe headache and neck stiffness ± cranial nerve palsy
III	Mild focal deficit, lethargy, or confusion
IV	Stupor, moderate to severe hemiparesis
V	Deep coma, extensor posturing

From Vincent JL et al: Textbook of critical care, ed 6, Philadelphia, 2011, Saunders.

BOX 1S-16 **Fisher Grade of Subarachnoid Hemorrhage on Initial Computed Tomography**

1	No blood detected
2	Diffuse or vertical layers <1 mm thick
3	Localized subarachnoid clot and/or vertical layers ≥1 mm thick
4	Intraparenchymal or intraventricular clot with diffuse or no SAH
Modified Fisher CT Rating Scale	
1	Minimal or diffuse thin SAH without IVH
2	Minimal or thin SAH with IVH
3	Thick cisternal clot without IVH
4	Thick cisternal clot with IVH

CT, Computed tomography; IVH, intraventricular hemorrhage; SAH, subarachnoid hemorrhage.
From Vincent JL et al: Textbook of critical care, ed 6, Philadelphia, 2011, Saunders.

- CT angiogram
- Digital subtraction angiography with 3D processing when indicated is the gold standard for diagnosis of etiology in subarachnoid hemorrhage.

LABORATORY TESTS

- Basic laboratory values, including CBC, chemistry panel, prothrombin time, partial thromboplastin time, and platelet count
- Serum troponin to evaluate for severe cardiac stress; elevated troponins indicate cardiac ischemia secondary to catecholamine surge and is associated with poor outcome.
- Patients with SAH are prone to developing cerebral salt wasting, resulting in hyponatremia. Sodium levels should be monitored frequently.

 **TREATMENT**

NONPHARMACOLOGIC THERAPY

- Airway, breathing, and circulation
- Once stabilized, good neurologic exam
- Cerebrospinal fluid drainage may be required for patients who develop hydrocephalus and increased intracranial pressure. It is also recommended for patients with Hunt and Hess grade 3 or higher.

ACUTE GENERAL Rx

- Critical care management: initial management strategies are geared toward stabilizing the patient and preventing re-hemorrhage and hydrocephalus. Rehemorrhage is associated with very high mortality rates.
- Blood pressure control: Tight blood pressure control is paramount, before securing the aneurysm to protect against rerupture. This can be done with the use of antihypertensive infusions such as nicardipine infusion. A systolic blood pressure of less than 140 mm Hg is recommended. Placement of arterial line is recommended. After securing of the aneurysm, liberalization of blood pressure parameters is the standard.

- Pain control: using short-acting and less-sedating medications (e.g., codeine, low-dose morphine).
- Seizures occur in about 3% of patients during the acute phase; use of prophylactic antiepileptics is controversial and not recommended, but patients presenting with seizures should be treated appropriately with anticonvulsants.
- Vasospasm: cerebral vasospasm is a morbid complication leading to cerebral ischemia, disability, and death after SAH. It typically develops between day 4 and 14 (but may occur up to day 21) after the hemorrhage, and it reaches a peak on day 6 to 8. Treatment strategies include:
  1. "Triple H" therapy—*H*ypertension, *H*ypervolemia, and *H*emodilution—was originally described to maintain cerebral perfusion. However, its efficacy has been questioned in treating vasospasm. Rather, current medical therapy for vasospasm focuses upon hypertension, with typical mean arterial pressure goals of 90 to 100 (after aneurysm is secured), and euvolemia instead of hypervolemia, as the latter was found to lead to significant cardiopulmonary and hemodynamic complications.
  2. Nimodipine: has been shown to improve outcomes if it is administered between days 4 and 21 after the hemorrhage, even if it does not significantly reduce the amount of vasospasm detected on angiography.
  3. Statins are no longer recommended for vasospasm prevention.
  4. Intraarterial therapies such as intraarterial calcium channel blockers and balloon angioplasty may be employed as needed.
- In cases of aneurysmal SAH, treatment focuses on occlusion/exclusion of the aneurysm to prevent rebleeding. The most common treatment methods are:
  1. Microsurgical clipping: performed through a craniotomy by placing a clip around the neck of the aneurysm.
  2. Endovascular coiling: performed via digital subtraction angiography; it consists of deploying platinum coils inside the

aneurysm or stents in the parent artery to cause thrombosis of the aneurysmal sac. Most aneurysms are currently treated endovascularly.

CHRONIC Rx

- Management of reversible risk factors mentioned above (smoking, hypertension, drug use).
- Management of neurologic disability through physical therapy and rehabilitation.

DISPOSITION

- SAH is often associated with a poor outcome with a death rate between 30% and 40%; 10% to 15% of patients die before they reach the hospital.
- Almost half of those who survive hospitalization have cognitive impairments or disability that affect their lifestyles.

REFERRAL

Patients should be managed in a cerebrovascular center that maintains capacity to perform open surgical and endovascular procedures, with a critical care unit experienced in caring for neurosurgical patients.

 **PEARLS & CONSIDERATIONS**

COMMENTS

- "Thunderclap" headaches should be considered SAH till proven otherwise and evaluated by CT of the head with/without LP. MRI FLAIR sequence is also a helpful modality.
- All SAH should be managed in a critical care setting (preferably neurocritical care unit) with neurosurgical care available.
- Measures to prevent rebleeding include adequate control of blood pressure and aneurysm treatment with the use of coiling or clipping.

PREVENTION

Controlling some of the modifiable risk factors, including smoking and blood pressure, may help to decrease the risk of aneurysmal rupture.

PATIENT & FAMILY EDUCATION

- SAH is a devastating condition, with most survivors developing significant neurologic or cognitive deficits. A good support system and an adequate physical and cognitive rehabilitation program may prove useful to survivors.
- Screening may be useful for patients with two or three first-degree relatives with SAH.

 EVIDENCE

Available at www.expertconsult.com

SUGGESTED READINGS

Available at www.expertconsult.com

RELATED CONTENT

Subarachnoid Hemorrhage (Patient Information)

AUTHORS: **FARHAN A. MIRZA, M.B.B.S.,** and **JUSTIN F. FRASER, M.D.**

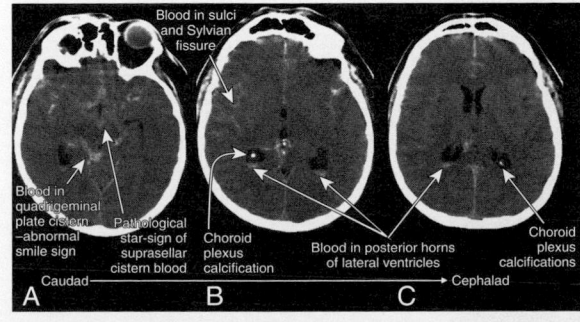

FIGURE 1S-83 Subarachnoid hemorrhage (SAH), noncontrast CT, brain windows. Acute SAH appears white on noncontrast computed tomography (CT) brain windows. **A** through **C,** nonconsecutive axial slices, progressing from caudad to cephalad. In this case of diffuse SAH, note the presence of subarachnoid blood filling the sulci, as well as extending into the cisterns, Sylvian fissures, and even lateral ventricles. In **A,** blood *(white)* fills the suprasellar cistern. This star-shaped structure is normally filled with CSF *(black).* The quadrigeminal plate cistern is normally a smile-shaped black crescent, filled with CSF, but in this case is filled with blood. Extremely bright calcifications in the choroid plexus of the posterior horns of the lateral ventricles are common, normal findings—do not mistake these for hemorrhage. Note their similarity in density to bone of the calvarium. (From Broder JS: *Diagnostic imaging for the emergency physician,* Philadelphia, 2011, Saunders.)

 **BASIC INFORMATION**

DEFINITION

Subclavian steal syndrome is an occlusion or severe stenosis of the proximal subclavian artery leading to decreased antegrade flow or retrograde flow in the ipsilateral vertebral artery and neurologic symptoms referable to the posterior circulation.

SYNONYMS

Proximal subclavian (or innominate) artery stenosis or occlusion

ICD-10CM CODES
G45.8 Other transient cerebral ischemic attacks and related syndromes

EPIDEMIOLOGY & DEMOGRAPHICS

- Similar to that of other manifestations of atherosclerosis (coronary artery disease, cerebrovascular disease, or peripheral vascular disease)
- Affects middle-aged persons (men somewhat younger than women on average) with arteriosclerotic risk factors, including family history, smoking, diabetes mellitus, hyperlipidemia, hypertension, and sedentary lifestyle

PHYSICAL FINDINGS & CLINICAL PRESENTATION

Symptoms:
- Many patients are asymptomatic.
- Upper-extremity ischemic symptoms: fatigue, exercise-related aching, coolness, numbness of the involved upper extremity.

- Neurologic symptoms are reported by 25% of patients with known unilateral subclavian steal. These include brief spells of:
1. Vertigo
2. Diplopia
3. Decreased vision
4. Oscillopsia
5. Gait unsteadiness
These spells are only occasionally provoked by exercising the ischemic upper extremity (classic subclavian steal). Left subclavian steal is more common than right, but the latter is more serious.
- Posterior circulation stroke related to subclavian steal is rare.
- Innominate artery stenosis can cause decreased right carotid artery flow and cerebrovascular symptoms of the anterior cerebral circulation, but this is uncommon.

Physical findings:
- Delayed and smaller volume pulse (wrist or antecubital) in the affected upper extremity
- Lower blood pressure in the affected upper extremity
- Supraclavicular bruit
NOTE: Inflating a blood pressure cuff will increase the bruit if it originates from a vertebral artery stenosis and decrease the bruit if it originates from a subclavian artery stenosis.

ETIOLOGY & PATHOGENESIS

Etiology:
- Atherosclerosis
- Arteritis (Takayasu's disease and temporal arteritis)
- Embolism to the subclavian or innominate artery
- Cervical rib
- Long-term use of a crutch

- Occupational (baseball pitchers and cricket bowlers)
Pathogenesis: the vertebral artery originates from the subclavian artery. For subclavian steal to occur, the occlusion must be proximal to the takeoff of the vertebral artery. On the right side, only a small distance separates the bifurcation of the innominate artery and the takeoff of the vertebral artery, explaining why the condition occurs less commonly on the right side. Occlusion of the innominate artery must affect right carotid artery flow.

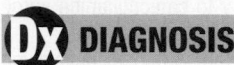 **DIAGNOSIS**

The carotid arteries should be evaluated at least noninvasively in all cases.

DIFFERENTIAL DIAGNOSIS

- Posterior circulation transient ischemic attack or stroke
- Upper-extremity ischemia
1. Distal subclavian artery stenosis or occlusion
2. Raynaud's syndrome
3. Thoracic outlet syndrome

WORKUP

- Noninvasive upper-extremity arterial flow studies
- Doppler sonography of the vertebral, subclavian, and innominate arteries
- Arteriography, magnetic resonance arteriogram (Fig. 1S-84)

 **TREATMENT**

- In most patients the disease is benign and requires no treatment other than atherosclerosis risk factor modification and aspirin. Symptoms tend to improve over time as collateral circulation develops.
- Vascular surgical reconstruction requires a thoracotomy; it may be indicated in innominate artery stenosis or when upper-extremity ischemia is incapacitating.

AUTHOR: **FRED F. FERRI, M.D.**

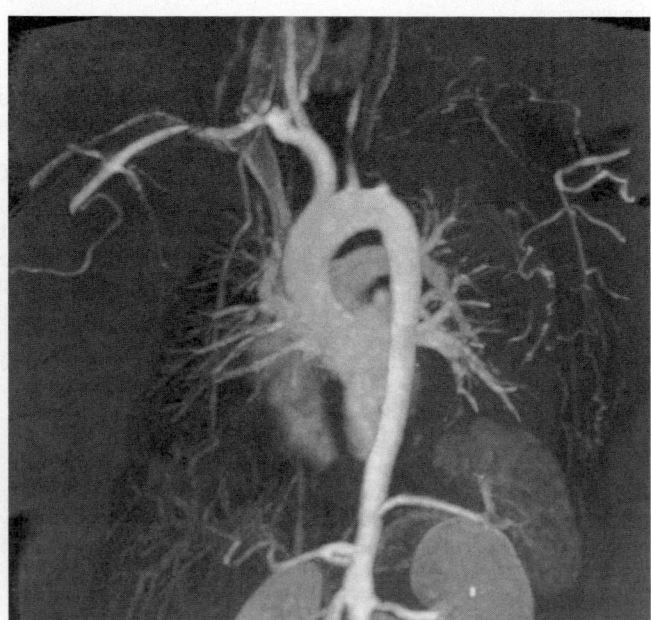

FIGURE 1S-84 Magnetic resonance arteriogram demonstrating diffuse moderate stenosis of the proximal left common carotid and proximal occlusion of the left subclavian artery coming off the aortic arch with development of an extensive collateral network. (From Hochberg MC et al: *Rheumatology,* ed 5, St Louis, 2011, Mosby.)

BASIC INFORMATION

DEFINITION

A subdural hematoma (SDH) is a collection of blood or blood products between the arachnoidal layer and the dura or meningeal layer surrounding the brain. Subdural hematomas can be acute (ASDH) or chronic (CSDH) and vary significantly in presentation and treatment.

SYNONYMS

Subdural hemorrhage

ICD-10CM CODES
S06.5   Traumatic subdural hemorrhage
I62.03   Chronic subdural hematoma
I62.01   Acute subdural hematoma

EPIDEMIOLOGY & DEMOGRAPHICS
INCIDENCE:
- The exact incidence of ASDH is unknown, but it is commonly seen in patients with head injury.
- CSDH is most common in the elderly with an estimated incidence of 1.72 to 13.1 per 100,000.

PREVALENCE: Unknown
PREDOMINANT AGE AND SEX:
- Peak incidence of CSDH is in the eighth decade and is notably higher in males.
- ASDHs usually present in the trauma setting and can happen in all age groups. In particular, shaken baby syndrome can be associated with SDH in the infant population.

RISK FACTORS:
- Trauma and antithrombotic therapy are the most common risk factors for ASDH and CSDH.
- Brain atrophy secondary to advanced age and alcoholism are common risk factors, especially with the coagulopathy/thrombocytopenia seen in chronic alcoholics.
- Intracranial hypotension associated with CSF shunts or leaks is uncommon but can result in acute or chronic SDH.

PHYSICAL FINDINGS & CLINICAL PRESENTATION

Symptoms vary on the basis of acuity, size, and location. Acute traumatic SDHs are often seen in traumatic brain injury patients, and their Glasgow Coma Scale may vary according to the extent of brain injury, size of hematoma, and associated compression. When associated with a midline shift (i.e., >5 mm), they can cause signs of cerebral herniation (e.g., ipsilateral pupil dilation, contralateral weakness) requiring prompt surgical evacuation.
- Patients with CSDH may present with diverse nonspecific symptoms such as headaches, confusion, aphasia, hemiparesis, TIA-like symptoms, and seizures.

ETIOLOGY

SDH is usually the result of shearing and tearing of a bridging vein between the brain parenchyma and the dura mater. Other causes of bleeding into the subdural space include contusion, extension of parenchymal hemorrhage. In the setting of spontaneous SDH, other vascular abnormalities, such as AV malformation, aneurysm, and dural AV fistula, should be kept in mind.

DIAGNOSIS

DIFFERENTIAL DIAGNOSIS
CSF hygromas, abscesses, and tumor infiltrations

WORKUP
- Clinical assessment: patient history, including medications, specifically anticoagulants/antiplatelets; alcohol abuse; recent trauma; cancer; and recent bacterial infections
- Neurologic examination: Glasgow Coma Scale, cranial nerves, motor/sensory exam CT head

LABORATORY TESTS
Assessment of the patient's coagulation status including CBC with platelet count, prothrombin time, partial thromboplastin time and liver function test (especially with a history of alcoholism or liver failure)

IMAGING STUDIES
CT head (Fig. 1S-85): demonstrates the classic crescentic collection between the brain and inner table. For comatose and trauma patients, include a cervical spine CT scan. ASDH is usually hyperdense, whereas a CSDH is usually hypodense on noncontrast CT. Contrast is only needed if there are concerns about tumor or infection.

TREATMENT

- Correction of underlying coagulopathy, if present (e.g., Coumadin/ASA/clopidogrel reversal)
- Admission for overnight monitoring in the setting of acute SDH

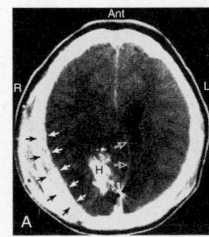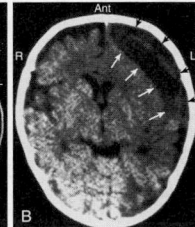

FIGURE 1S-85 A, Noncontrast CT scan of an acute subdural hematoma shows a crescentic area of increased density in the right posterior parietal region between the brain and the skull (*black and white arrows*). An area of intraparenchymal hemorrhage (*H*) is also seen. **B,** A chronic subdural hematoma for a different patient is shown. There is an area of decreased density in the left frontoparietal region (*arrows*) that effaces the sulci, compresses the anterior horn of the left lateral ventricle, and shifts the midline somewhat to the right. (From Mettler FA [ed]: *Primary care radiology,* Philadelphia, 2000, Saunders.)

- The majority of SDH can be managed without surgery in awake patients with normal neurologic examinations.
- Medical management of CSDH using antifibrinolytic therapy with tranexamic acid 650 mg per day is showing promising results. Studies will continue to evaluate its efficacy as a medical therapy for SDH.

NONPHARMACOLOGIC THERAPY
Surgical treatment is indicated in:
- ASDHs measuring >10 mm in thickness with a midline shift >5 mm on CT scan and a compromised neurologic status should most often be evacuated.
- In CSDH with a mass effect, a clear change in the neurologic examination from baseline, and/or enlargement of the hematoma size, evacuation via craniotomy or burr hole should be considered.

DISPOSITION
Depending on the size and location of the SDH and the examination of the patient, observation can range from the ICU to outpatient management. When observation of the patient is considered, clinical examinations should be serially performed. Patient baseline and follow-up clinical examinations are more important than CT scan findings.

REFERRAL
Neurosurgical and operative consultation should be made available.

PEARLS & CONSIDERATIONS

COMMENTS
- Many elderly patients have small CSDHs or hygromas. Unless these are associated with seizures or clinical or radiographic progression, they are usually not emergent and usually do not require neurosurgical intervention. Recurrence after surgical management for CSDH is common.
- SDHs in elderly patients can have a mixed hyperdense and hypodense appearance on noncontrast CT scan; this is suggestive of subdural membranes and chronic components.

PATIENT & FAMILY EDUCATION
Individuals with SDHs are at higher risk for seizure, so surveillance is important.

RELATED CONTENT
Subdural Hematoma (Patient Information)

AUTHOR: **FARHAN A. MIRZA, M.B.B.S.,** and **JUSTIN F. FRASER, M.D.**

BASIC INFORMATION

DEFINITION

Superior vena cava (SVC) syndrome is a set of symptoms that results when a mediastinal mass compresses the SVC or the veins that drain into it, resulting in obstruction of blood flow from the head, neck, upper torso, or extremities to the right atrium.

SYNONYM

SVC

ICD-10CM CODES

I87.1	Compression of vein
S25.20XA	Unspecified injury of superior vena cava, initial encounter
S25.29XA	Other specified injury of superior vena cava, initial encounter

EPIDEMIOLOGY & DEMOGRAPHICS

- SVC syndrome occurs in 15,000 persons in the United States every year.
- More than 50% of patients present with SVC at the initial manifestation of a previously undiagnosed malignancy.
- Mirrors lung cancer (especially small cell carcinoma) and lymphoma (see "Lung Neoplasm" and "Lymphoma" in Section I).

PHYSICAL FINDINGS & CLINICAL PRESENTATION

The pathophysiology of the syndrome involves the increased pressure in the venous system

draining into the SVC, producing edema of the head, neck, and upper extremities. Symptoms develop over a period of 2 wk in one third of patients and include:

- Shortness of breath
- Chest pain

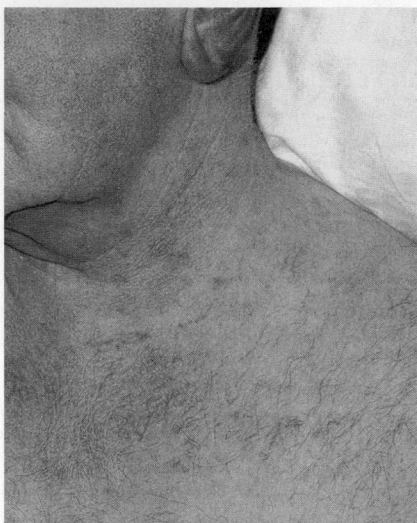

FIGURE 1S-86 Superior vena cava obstruction causing dilated veins and plethora of the upper trunk and neck in a patient with bronchial carcinoma. Patients with superior vena cava obstruction are occasionally referred to dermatologists with suspected contact allergy (eyelid swelling) or angioedema (facial or hand swelling). (From White GM, Cox NH [eds]: *Diseases of the skin, a color atlas and text*, ed 2, St Louis, 2006, Mosby.)

- Cough
- Dysphagia, hoarseness, stridor
- Headache
- Syncope
- Visual trouble

Signs:
- Chest wall vein distention (Fig. 1S-86)
- Neck vein distention
- Facial edema, facial plethora
- Upper-extremity swelling
- Cyanosis

ETIOLOGY

- Lung cancer (65% of all cases, of which half are small cell lung cancer)
- Lymphoma (15%)
- Thymoma
- Tuberculosis
- Goiter
- Aortic aneurysm (arteriosclerotic or syphilitic)
- SVC thrombosis
  1. Primary: associated with a central venous catheter
  2. Secondary: as a complication of SVC syndrome associated with one of the abovementioned causes
- Inflammatory process, fibrosing mediastinitis
- Fig. 1S-87 illustrates the anatomy of superior vena cava syndrome. Table 1S-30 summarizes common malignancies associated with SVC syndrome in adults.

Dx DIAGNOSIS

CT scan of the chest with contrast (Fig. 1S-88) is the most useful diagnostic study. MRI is

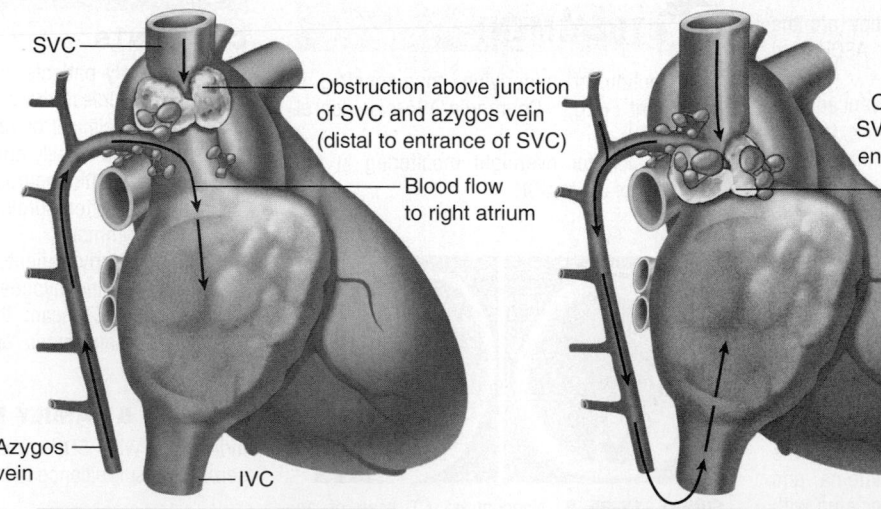

SVC

Obstruction above junction of SVC and azygos vein (distal to entrance of SVC)

Obstruction in SVC (proximal to entrance of SVC)

Blood flow to right atrium

Azygos vein

IVC

Manifestations of supra-azygos SVC obstruction
- Distended arm and neck veins
- Edema of neck, face, and arms
- Congested mucous membranes (mouth)
- Dilated, tortuous vessels on upper chest and back

Manifestations of infra-azygos SVC obstruction
- More severe symptoms but all of the features for obstruction distal to entrance of SVC
- Dilation of collateral vessels on anterior and posterior abdominal wall with downward blood flow into IVC, then back to heart

A

B

FIGURE 1S-87 Anatomy of superior vena cava (SVC) syndrome. Lymph nodes may obstruct blood return above the entrance of the azygos vein **(A)**, resulting in edema of the face, neck, and arms and distended veins in the neck and arms and over the upper chest. Obstruction below the return of the azygos vein **(B)** results in retrograde flow through the azygos through collateral veins to the inferior vena cava (IVC), with all the symptoms and signs in **A** plus dilation of the veins over the abdomen as well. (Modified from Skatin AT (ed): *Atlas of diagnostic oncology*, ed 3, Philadelphia, 2003, Elsevier.)

TABLE 1S-30 Malignancies Associated with Superior Vena Cava (SVC) Syndrome in Adults*

Neoplastic Diagnosis	Percentage of SVC	Percentage of Disease-Associated SVC
Lung cancer, stage 3B or 4:	48-81	
Small cell lung cancer		15-45
Squamous cell cancer		20-25
Adenocarcinoma		5-25
Large cell carcinoma		4-30
Lymphoma:	2-21	
Diffuse large cell lymphoma		64
Lymphoblastic lymphoma		33
Breast cancer	11	

*Include lung cancer, lymphomas, and metastases from other solid tumors. 75% to 85% of patients with SVC have neoplastic disease.

From Zipes DP et al (eds): *Braunwald's heart disease,* ed 7, Philadelphia, 2005, Saunders.

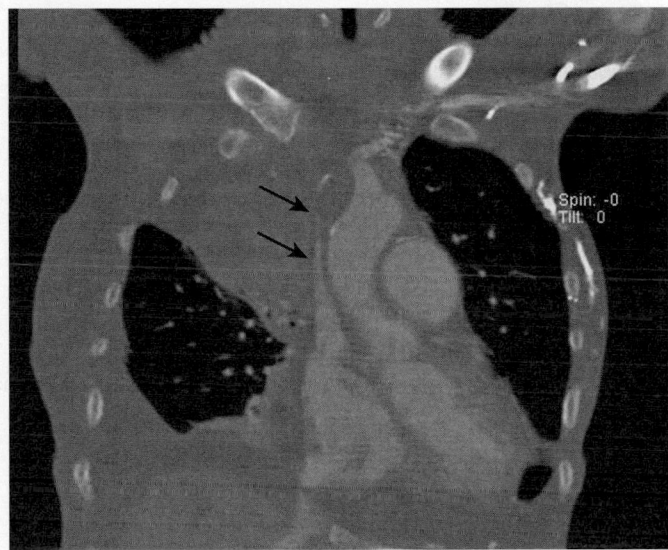

FIGURE 1S-88 Computed tomography scan showing blockage of the superior vena cava *(arrows).* (From Adams JG et al: *Emergency medicine, clinical essentials,* ed 2, Philadelphia, 2013, Elsevier.)

usually adequate to establish the diagnosis of SVC obstruction and to assist in the differential diagnosis of probable cause.

DIFFERENTIAL DIAGNOSIS

The syndrome is characteristic enough to exclude other diagnoses. The differential diagnosis concerns the underlying etiologies listed above.

WORKUP

- Chest radiograph (mediastinal widening, pleural effusion)
- Chest CT with contrast or MRI (in patient who cannot tolerate contrast medium)
- Venography: warranted only when an intervention (e.g., stent or surgery) is planned
- Percutaneous needle biopsy, endobronchial ultrasound-guided needle biopsy, or mediastinoscopy are usually the initial diagnostic modalities used to establish a histologic diagnosis

RX TREATMENT

- Tissue diagnosis is usually needed before commencing therapy. EBUS is now considered the first step in evaluation. Mediastinoscopy would be considered if EBUS is nondiagnostic or there is high clinical suspicion for lymphoma.
- Management is guided by the severity of the symptoms and the underlying etiology.
- Emergency empiric radiation is indicated in critical situations such as respiratory failure or central nervous system signs associated with increased intracranial pressure.
- Treatment of the underlying malignancy:
  1. Radiotherapy: the majority of tumors causing SVC syndrome are sensitive to radiotherapy
  2. Systemic chemotherapy
- Anticoagulant or fibrinolytic therapy in patients who do not respond to cancer treatment within a week or if an obstructing thrombus has been documented.
- Loop diuretics are often used, but their effect is limited.
- Upright positioning and fluid restriction until collateral channels develop and allow for clinical regression are useful modalities for SVC syndrome secondary to benign disease.
- Steroids (dexamethasone 4 mg q6h) may be useful in reducing the tumor burden in lymphoma and thymoma after definitive diagnosis is made.
- Percutaneous self-expandable stents that can be placed under local anesthesia with radiologic manipulation are useful in the treatment of SVC syndrome to bypass the obstruction, especially in cases associated with malignant tumors.
- Surgical bypass grafting is infrequently used to treat SVC syndrome.

REFERRAL

To a thoracic surgeon, pulmonary specialist, or oncologist

AUTHOR: **GAETANE MICHAUD, M.D.**

 **BASIC INFORMATION**

DEFINITION

Supraventricular tachycardia (SVT) is a group of rapid regular tachyarrhythmia. There are three major categories of SVT
1. Atrial Tachycardia: an arrhythmia that originates from the atrium and does not involve the AV node. This is usually a focal arrhythmia. In some, the underlying mechanism may be reentry, either with a small circuit (microreentry) or a large circuit (macroreentry).
2. AV nodal reentrant tachycardia (AVNRT);
3. AV reentrant tachycardia (AVRT) (Figure 1S-89). The latter two are reentrant arrhythmia that always involve the AV node as part of the circuit (Figure 1S-89).

Other forms of arrhythmia that involve the atria, such as atrial fibrillation and atrial flutter, have distinct electrocardiographic features and will not be discussed here. Rare forms of SVT such as inappropriate sinus tachycardia, sinus mode reentry tachycardia, and junctional tachycardia are beyond the scope of this chapter.

SYNONYMS

SVT
Paroxysmal Supraventricular tachycardia (SVT)

ICD-10CM CODES
I47.1 Supraventricular tachycardia

EPIDEMIOLOGY & DEMOGRAPHICS

SVT is most commonly diagnosed between the ages of 12 and 30. SVT occurs most commonly in patients with no prior cardiac conditions. AVNRT is the most common type of SVT in both genders and at all ages. It occurs most commonly in young women. AVRT is the second most common SVT, and it is typically diagnosed in younger patients as compared to the age of patients with AVNRT. AT is more commonly associated with structural heart disease.

PHYSICAL FINDINGS & CLINICAL PRESENTATION

- Patients may be either symptomatic or asymptomatic.

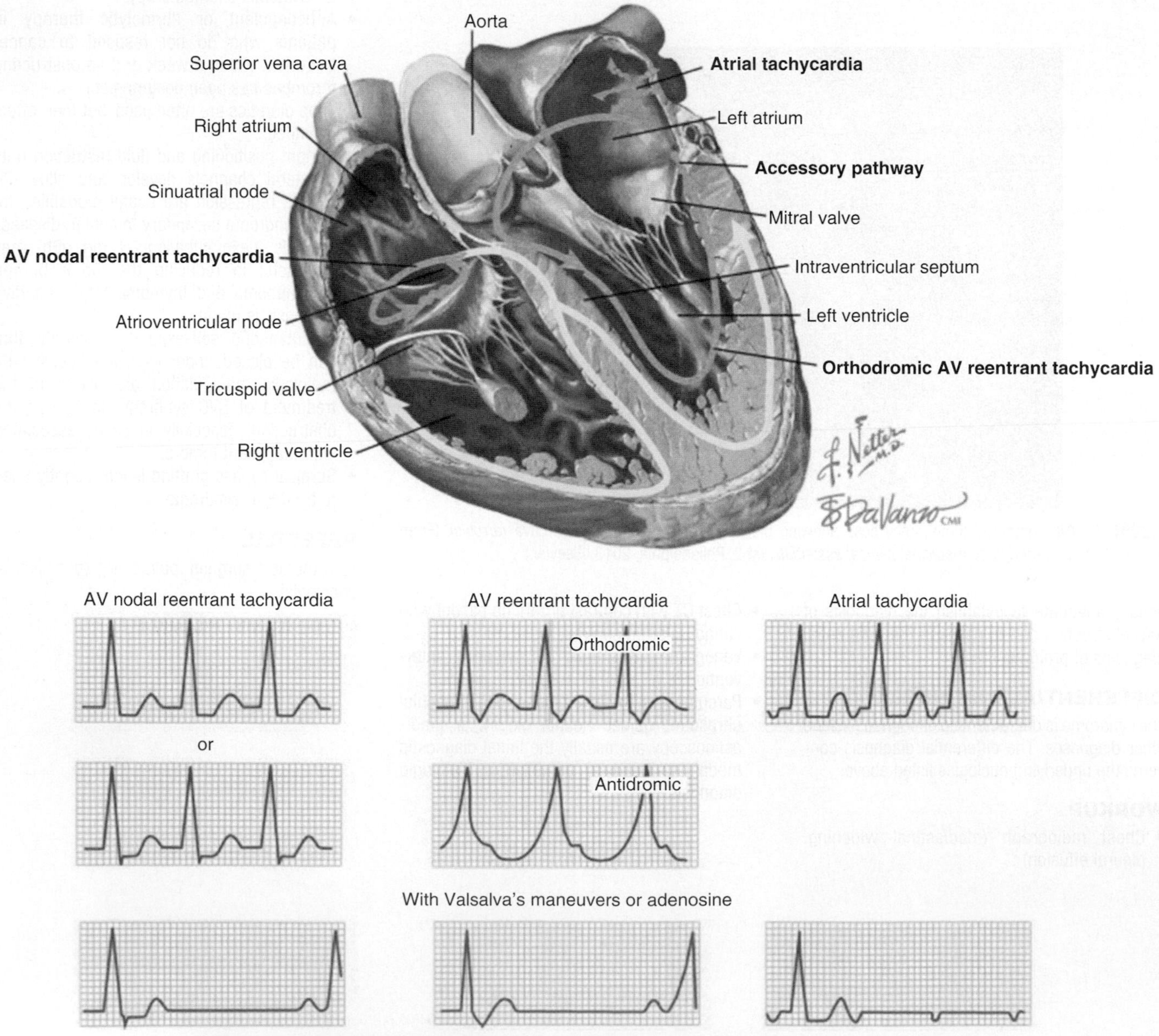

Aorta
Superior vena cava
Right atrium
Sinuatrial node
AV nodal reentrant tachycardia
Atrioventricular node
Tricuspid valve
Right ventricle

Atrial tachycardia
Left atrium
Accessory pathway
Mitral valve
Intraventricular septum
Left ventricle
Orthodromic AV reentrant tachycardia

AV nodal reentrant tachycardia

or

AV reentrant tachycardia

Orthodromic

Antidromic

With Valsalva's maneuvers or adenosine

Atrial tachycardia

FIGURE 1S-89 Typical electrocardiographic recordings and anatomic representation of the common supraventricular tachycardias. *AV,* Atrioventricular. From *Netter's cardiology,* ed 2, 2010, WB Saunders, an imprint of Elsevier Inc. Adapted from Delacretaz E: Clinical practice: supraventricular tachycardia, *N Engl J Med* 354:1039–1051, 2006.

- Patient may be aware of "fast" heartbeat (palpitations), may complain of weakness, dyspnea, dizziness, chest pain, presyncope or, rarely, syncope.
- Patients with AVNRT may complain of neck pounding during the episode due to simultaneous contraction of the atrial and ventricles with closed AV valves and hence sharp increase in atrial and neck venous pressure.
- In some cases the episodes can be triggered by physical activity or psychological stress, but in others there may not be an obvious trigger. In patients with AVNRT, sometimes the arrhythmia is reproducibly initiated when bending forward to pick up an item from the floor.
- Hemodynamic status during the arrhythmia may vary and depend on the patient's comorbidities and presence of underlying structural heart disease. Usually, patients are hemodynamically stable.
- Physical examination is most commonly normal and unrevealing, except rapid regular heart rate and occasionally hypotension.

ETIOLOGY (SEE FIGURE 1S-89)

- AVNRT—Dual electrical pathways within the AV node. In typical AVNRT the anterograde limb conducts slowly (slow pathway) and the retrograde limb has fast conduction properties (fast pathway), and vice versa in atypical AVNRT.
- AVRT is accessory pathway mediated, either orthodromic (antegrade through the AV node and retrograde through the accessory pathway) or antidromic (antegrade through the accessory pathway and retrograde through the AV node). In the case of antidromic tachycardia, the QRS will be wide and fully preexcited. In some patients the presence of accessory pathway is not evident on the baseline ECG (concealed accessory pathway), while in others it is manifest in the baseline ECG, presenting the typical features of the Wolff-Parkinson-White syndrome.
- Atrial fibrillation and atrial flutter are covered in separate chapters.
- Paroxysmal atrial tachycardia and multifocal atrial tachycardia—abnormal automaticity of atrial tissue or triggered activity. In some cases (especially in patients who underwent previous cardiac surgery such as valve replacement or ASD closure), the underlying mechanism is macroreentrant AT.

Dx DIAGNOSIS AND DIFFERENTIAL DIAGNOSIS

The diagnosis of SVT relies principally on the 12-lead ECG. Every patient should have a 12-lead ECG done. Typically patients with SVT will present with a narrow complex QRS tachycardia with a ventricular rate faster than 100 beats per minute (bpm) and typically faster than 130-150 (bpm).

- P wave morphology can be useful in discriminating rhythms. P waves with a similar axis to the sinus node can be atrial tachycardias and sinus tachycardias. P waves with retrograde depolarization of the atria (seen as inverted in the inferior leads) can be seen in AVNRT, AVRT, and atrial tachycardia. Sawtooth P waves are indicative of classical counterclockwise typical type I flutter, and an absence of P waves with irregular R-R intervals points to atrial fibrillation. Variable (>3) morphologies of P wave are suggestive of multifocal atrial tachycardia. Wide QRS complex (>0.12 sec) with initial slurring (delta wave) during sinus rhythm and short PR (<0.12 sec) is characteristic of Wolff-Parkinson-White (WPW) syndrome.

In AVNRT, due to the small size of the circuit within the AV node and the fast retrograde conduction, there is simultaneous depolarization of the ventricles and atria, thus making the P wave "buried" in the QRS and therefore not visible or inscribed very close to the QRS at the final part of the QRS complex, and sometimes creating a "pseudo terminal S wave" usually seen in leads II, III, and aVF and "pseudo terminal R waves" at the end of the QRS in V1 and aVR (Figure 1S-89).

In orthodromic AVRT, the P wave is usually visible close after the QRS due to the rapid conduction properties of the accessory pathway (short RP tachycardia). In AT, the P wave is usually noticed farther away after the QRS (long RP tachycardia) (Figure 1S-89).

Other diagnostic maneuvers that may assist in the differential diagnosis are vagal maneuvers (such as carotid sinus massage or giving IV AV nodal blocking agents such as adenosine or verapamil) to produce AV nodal conduction block. This will terminate reentrant arrhythmia dependent on the AV node—AVNRT and AVRT—but not AT, which will continue, albeit with nonconducted P waves.

Other arrhythmias that present with narrow complex tachycardia like PSVT are:
1. Fascicular VT.
2. Junctional tachycardias.
3. Artifact such as with Parkinson's.

SVT can conduct with bundle branch block (BBB) and wide QRS due to preexisting BBB on the baseline ECG or due to aberrant conduction (rate-dependent BBB). When a patient presents with wide QRS tachycardia, VT must be excluded first. Features to distinguish SVT from ventricular tachycardia are outlined in Table 1S-31.

WORKUP

- Electrocardiography.
- Echocardiography to exclude structural heart disease
- Thyroid function tests
- Complete blood count to exclude anemia or infection as a causative factor
- In most cases the workup will be negative, with no underlying cardiac or systemic pathology and no clear triggers for an acute episode.
- Holter or event monitor to document the arrhythmias if they are paroxysmal and not documented yet.

Rx TREATMENT

NONPHARMACOLOGIC THERAPY

If the patient is hemodynamically unstable, prompt synchronized cardioversion with an external defibrillator using 50 to 100 J should be performed.

If the patient is stable, Valsalva maneuver in the supine position is the most effective way to terminate most types of SVT; carotid sinus massage (after excluding occlusive carotid disease and murmurs over the carotid arteries) is also commonly used to elicit vagal efferent impulses. These are effective in terminating AVRT, AVNRT, and some types of atrial tachycardia, but in the case of sinus tachycardia, atrial flutter, and atrial fibrillation, they only transiently slow down AV conduction without terminating the actual tachycardia.

PHARMACOLOGIC THERAPY

- Adenosine is useful for treatment of orthodromic AVRT and AVNRT and can uncover the underlying rhythm in paroxysmal atrial tachycardia; it is the first choice of therapy for treatment of almost all episodes of SVT unresponsive to vagal maneuvers. The dose

TABLE 1S-31 Features That May Differentiate Ventricular Tachycardia from Supraventricular Tachycardia with Aberrancy

Helpful Features	Implications
Positive QRS concordance	Diagnostic of VT
Presence of AV dissociation, capture beats, or fusion beats	Diagnostic of VT
Atypical RBBB (monophasic R, QR, RS, or triphasic QRS in V$_1$; R:S ratio <1, QS or QR, monophasic R in V$_6$)	Suggests VT
Atypical LBBB (R >30 min or R to S [nadir or notch] >60 min in V$_1$ or V$_2$; R:S ratio <1, QS or QR in V$_6$)	Suggests VT
Shift of axis from baseline	Suggests VT
History of CAD	Suggests VT
QRS during tachycardia identical to QRS during sinus rhythm	Suggests SVT
Termination with adenosine	Suggests SVT

AV, Atrioventricular; *CAD*, coronary artery disease; *LBBB*, left bundle branch block; *RBBB*, right bundle branch block; *SVT*, supraventricular tachycardia; *VT*, ventricular tachycardia.

From Andreoli TG et al (eds): *Andreoli and Carpenter's Cecil essentials of medicine*, ed 8, Philadelphia, 2010, Saunders.

is 6 mg given as a rapid IV bolus; tachycardia is usually terminated within a few seconds. If this fails, may repeat with 12 mg IV bolus. Contraindications are second or third degree atrioventricular block, WPW with atrial fibrillation, sick sinus syndrome, and chronic use of drugs such as dipyridamole, theophylline, or aminophylline and heart transplant. Adenosine may cause bronchospasm in asthmatics.

- Verapamil 5 to 10 mg IV is given over 5 min; if no effect, may repeat in 30 min.
  1. Verapamil should be used cautiously in patients with SVT associated with hypotension.
  2. Slow injection of calcium chloride (10 ml of a 10% solution given over 5 to 8 min before verapamil administration) decreases the hypotensive effect without compromising its antiarrhythmic effect.
- Metoprolol (IV 5 mg/2 min up to 15 mg) or esmolol (500 µg/kg IV bolus, then 50 µg/kg/min) may be effective in the treatment of SVT.
- IV digoxin (0.75 to 1 mg slow IV loading in increments of 0.25 mg over several hours) if other agents are not effective.
  1. Digoxin, beta-blockers, and calcium-channel blockers should be avoided in patients with pre-excitation syndrome and antidromic AVRT or atrial fibrillation to avoid increased conduction through the accessory pathway.
- A recent trial comparing "standard valsalva" (patient placed in a semirecumbent [45-degree] position and directed to strain to 40 mm Hg pressure for 15 seconds by forced expiration and to stay in the semi-recumbent position for 60 seconds) to "modified valsalva" (patient asked to strain in the same way in the semi-recumbent position, but immediately afterword asked to lay flat and raise their legs to 45 degrees for 15 seconds) found that the modified valsalva was more effective than the standard valsalva maneuver for restoring sinus rhythm in patients with supraventricular tachycardia.[1]

CHRONIC TREATMENT

The goal is prevention of recurrent episodes. In patients with infrequent and minimally symptomatic episodes without preexcitation, providing treatment is optional only during acute episodes. In patients with recurrent symptomatic episodes, regular treatment with beta-blockers, nondihydropyridines, or calcium channel blockers can be performed; if these fail, class Ic antiarrhythmics are an option. It is also possible to treat patients who have infrequent symptomatic episodes with a "pill in the pocket" strategy with either beta-blockers or other antiarrhythmic. Patients who fail antiarrhythmic therapy, develop side effects due to medications, or refuse medical therapy should be referred for catheter ablation. This is a highly effective mode of treatment with low risk of complications.

DISPOSITION

Most patients respond well with resolution of the SVT upon treatment (see "Acute General Rx"). Some patients may need chronic AV blocking agents for recurrence.

REFERRAL

Radiofrequency ablation (RFA) is the procedure of choice in symptomatic patients who are refractory to medical therapy especially in AVRT, AVNRT, and atrial flutter. RFA has high efficacy rates (single procedure success is 93.2%), low all-cause mortality (0.1%), and low adverse events (2.9%). Despite high reported success rates, RFA appears to be underused in clinical practice.

❗ PEARLS & CONSIDERATIONS

SUGGESTED READINGS
Available at www.expertconsult.com

RELATED CONTENT
Supraventricular Tachycardia (Patient Information)
AUTHORS: **MOTI HAIM, M.D.,** and **YUVAL KONSTANTINO, M.D.**

---

[1]Appelbaum A, et al.: Revert trial collaborators: postural modification to the standard valsalva maneuver for emergency treatment of supraventricular tachycardias (REVERT): a randomized controlled trial, *Lancet* 386:1747-1753, 2015.

 **BASIC INFORMATION**

DEFINITION

Syncope is the transient loss of consciousness with spontaneous recovery that results from an acute global reduction in cerebral blood flow. There are 3 major types: neurally mediated, orthostatic, and cardiac. Syncope is a symptom, and the goal is to distinguish lethal causes from benign causes of transient loss of consciousness.

ICD-10CM CODES
R55 Syncope and collapse

EPIDEMIOLOGY & DEMOGRAPHICS

- Syncope accounts for 3% to 5% of emergency department visits.
- 30% of the adult population will experience at least one syncopal episode during their lifetimes.
- Incidence of syncope is highest in elderly men and young women.
- 15% of children and adolescents experience syncope; less than 5% have cardiac causes.

PHYSICAL FINDINGS & CLINICAL PRESENTATION

- Blood pressure: if low, consider orthostatic hypotension; if unequal in both arms (difference >20 mm Hg), consider subclavian steal or dissecting aneurysm. (NOTE: Blood pressure [BP] and heart rate should be recorded in the supine and standing positions, waiting at least 5 minutes between each position.) If there is a drop in BP but no change in heart rate (HR), the patient may be taking a beta-blocker or may have an autonomic neuropathy.
- Pulse: if patient has tachycardia, bradycardia, or irregular rhythm, consider arrhythmia.
- Heart: if there are murmurs present, consider syncope attributable to left ventricular outflow obstruction (aortic stenosis or idiopathic hypertrophic subaortic stenosis); if there are jugular venous distention and distal heart sounds, consider cardiac tamponade.
- Carotid sinus pressure: can be diagnostic if it reproduces symptoms and other causes are excluded; a pause >3 sec or a systolic BP drop >50 mm Hg without symptoms or <30 mm Hg with symptoms when sinus pressure is applied separately on each side for <5 sec is considered abnormal. This test should be avoided in patients with carotid bruits or cerebrovascular disease. ECG monitoring, IV access, and bedside atropine should be available when carotid sinus pressure is applied.

ETIOLOGY

- Neurally mediated syncope: most common type, accounting for two-thirds of cases. It includes vasovagal, situational, carotid hypersensitivity, and postexertional syncope.
  1. Psychophysiologic (emotional upset, panic disorders, hysteria, hyperventilation)
  2. Visceral reflex (micturition, defecation, food ingestion, coughing, ventricular contraction, glossopharyngeal neuralgia)
  3. Carotid sinus pressure
  4. Reduction of venous return caused by Valsalva maneuver
- Orthostatic hypotension (10% of cases)
  1. Hypovolemia
  2. Vasodilator medications
  3. Autonomic neuropathy (diabetes, amyloid, Parkinson's disease, multisystem atrophy)
  4. Pheochromocytoma
  5. Carcinoid syndrome
- Cardiac (10%-20%)
  1. Reduced cardiac output
     a. Left ventricular outflow obstruction (aortic stenosis, hypertrophic cardiomyopathy)
     b. Obstruction to pulmonary flow (pulmonary embolism, pulmonic stenosis, primary pulmonary hypertension)
     c. Myocardial infarct with pump failure
     d. Cardiac tamponade
     e. Mitral stenosis
     f. Reduction of venous return (atrial myxoma, valve thrombus)
     g. Beta-blocker therapy
  2. Arrhythmias or asystole
     a. Extreme tachycardia (>160-180 beats/min)
     b. Severe bradycardia (<30-40 beats/min)
     c. Sick sinus syndrome
     d. Atrioventricular block (second or third degree)
     e. Ventricular tachycardia or fibrillation
     f. Long QT syndrome
     g. Pacemaker malfunction
     h. Psychotropic medications and beta-blockers

Dx DIAGNOSIS

DIFFERENTIAL DIAGNOSIS

1. Seizure (see "Workup")
2. Vertebrobasilar transient ischemic attack (TIA) usually manifests as diplopia, vertigo, or ataxia but not loss of consciousness. Isolated episodes of transient loss of consciousness (TLOC) without accompanying neurologic symptoms are unlikely to be TIAs.
3. Recreational drugs or alcohol.
4. Functional causes, such as stress and somatoform disorders.
5. Sleep disorders, such as sleep attacks and narcolepsy, are also in the differential for TLOC.
6. Head trauma.

WORKUP

The history is crucial to diagnosing the cause of syncope and may suggest a diagnosis that can be evaluated with directed testing. History is also important to determine other etiologies for TLOC, such as seizure. Fig. E1S-90 describes an algorithm for syncope evaluation.
- Sudden LOC: consider cardiac arrhythmias.
- Gradual LOC: consider orthostatic hypotension, vasodepressor syncope, hypoglycemia.
- History of aura before LOC or prolonged confusion (>1 min), amnesia, or lethargy after LOC suggests seizure rather than syncope.
- Patient's activity at the time of syncope:
  1. Micturition, coughing, defecation: consider syncope caused by decreased venous return.
  2. Turning head or while shaving: consider carotid sinus syndrome.
  3. Physical exertion in a patient with murmur: consider aortic stenosis.
  4. Arm exercise: consider subclavian steal syndrome.
  5. Assuming an upright position: consider orthostatic hypotension.
- Associated events:
  1. Chest pain: consider myocardial infarction, pulmonary embolism.
  2. Palpitations: consider arrhythmias.
  3. Incontinence (urine or fecal) and tongue biting are associated with seizure or syncope.
  4. Brief, transient shaking after LOC may represent myoclonus from global cerebral hypoperfusion and not seizures. However, sustained tonic/clonic muscle action is more suggestive of seizure.
  5. Focal neurologic symptoms or signs point to a neurologic event such as a seizure with residual deficits (e.g., Todd's paralysis) or cerebral ischemic injury.
  6. Psychologic stress: syncope may be vasovagal.
- Review current medications, particularly antihypertensive and psychotropic drugs.
- All patients presenting with syncope require electrocardiography, orthostatic vital signs, and QT interval monitoring.

LABORATORY TESTS

Routine blood tests rarely yield diagnostically useful information and should be done only if they are specifically suggested by the results of the history and physical examination. Box E1S-17 describes possibly useful tests. The following are commonly ordered tests:
- Pregnancy test in women of childbearing age
- Complete blood count to look for anemia and signs of infection
- Electrolytes, blood urea nitrogen, creatinine, magnesium, and calcium to look for electrolyte abnormalities and evaluate fluid status
- Serum glucose level
- Cardiac troponins, especially if the patient gives a history of chest pain before the syncopal episode
- Drug and alcohol levels with suspected toxicity

IMAGING STUDIES

- ECG to rule out arrhythmias; may be diagnostic in 5% to 10% of patients.
- Echocardiography.
- If seizure is suspected, CT scan and/or MRI of the head and electroencephalogram may be useful.
- If head trauma or neurologic signs on examination, CT or MRI may be helpful.

- If arrhythmias are suspected, a 24-hr Holter monitor or admission to a telemetry unit is appropriate. In general, Holter monitoring is rarely useful, revealing a cause for syncope in <3% of cases. Loop recorders that can be activated after syncopal episode to retrieve information about the cardiac rhythm during the preceding 4 min add considerable diagnostic yield in patients with unexplained syncope.
- Implantable cardiac monitors that function as permanent loop recorders or implantable cardioverter-defibrillators, which are placed subcutaneously in the pectoral region with the patient under local anesthesia, are useful in patients with cardiac syncope.
- Electrophysiologic studies may be indicated in patients with structural heart disease and/or recurrent syncope.

TILT-TABLE TESTING

- Useful to support a diagnosis of neurally mediated syncope. Patients age >50 yr should have stress testing before tilt-table testing. Positive results would preclude tilt-table testing.
- Indicated in patients with recurrent episodes of unexplained syncope as well as patients in high-risk occupations (e.g., pilots, bus drivers) (Fig. 1S-91). The test is also useful for identifying patients with prominent bradycardic response who may benefit from implantation of a permanent pacemaker. The test is contraindicated in patients with recent stroke, MI, and severe coronary or carotid disease.
- It is performed by keeping the patient strapped in an upright posture on a tilt table with footboard support. The angle of the tilt table varies from 60 to 80 degrees. The duration of upright posture during tilt-table testing varies from 25 to 45 min.
- The hallmark of neurally mediated syncope is severe hypotension associated with a paradoxic bradycardia triggered by a specific stimulus. The diagnosis of neurally mediated

syncope is likely if upright tilt testing reproduces these hemodynamic changes in <15 min and causes presyncope or syncope.

PSYCHIATRIC EVALUATION

- May be indicated in young patients without heart disease who have frequently recurring transient loss of consciousness and other somatic symptoms.
- Generalized anxiety disorder, pain disorder, and major depression predispose patients to neurally mediated reactions and may result in syncope.

 TREATMENT

NONPHARMACOLOGIC THERAPY

- Ensure proper hydration; consider compression stockings and salt tablets in appropriate patients.
- Eliminate medications that may induce hypotension.

ACUTE GENERAL Rx

- Varies with the underlying etiology of syncope (e.g., pacemaker in patients with syncope resulting from complete heart block).
- Syncope caused by orthostatic hypotension is treated with volume replacement in patients with intravascular volume depletion. Also consider midodrine to promote venous return by adrenergic-mediated vasoconstriction and Florinef for its mineralocorticoid effects to increase intravascular volume.

DISPOSITION

Prognosis varies with the age of the patient and the etiology of the syncope. In general:

- Benign prognosis (very low 1-yr morbidity rate) in patients:
  1. Age <30 yr and having noncardiac syncope

  2. Age <70 yr and having vasovagal or psychogenic syncope or syncope of unknown cause
- Poor prognosis (high mortality and morbidity rates) in patients with cardiac syncope, with presenting systolic BP <90 mm Hg.
- Patients with the following risk factors have a higher 1-yr mortality rate: abnormal ECG, history of ventricular arrhythmia, history of congestive heart failure.

REFERRAL

Hospital admission in elderly patients without prior history of syncope or unknown etiology of their syncope and in any patients suspected of having cardiac syncope, with presenting systolic BP <90 mm Hg.

PEARLS & CONSIDERATIONS

COMMENTS

- Section III, "Palpitations, Dizziness, and/or Syncope," describes an algorithmic approach to the patient.
- The etiology of syncope is identified in <50% of cases during the initial evaluation.
- A thorough history and physical examination are the most productive means of establishing a diagnosis in patients with syncope.

EBM EVIDENCE

Available at www.expertconsult.com

SUGGESTED READINGS

Available at www.expertconsult.com

RELATED CONTENT

Syncope (Patient Information)

AUTHOR: **TZU-CHING (TEDDY) WU, M.D., M.P.H.**

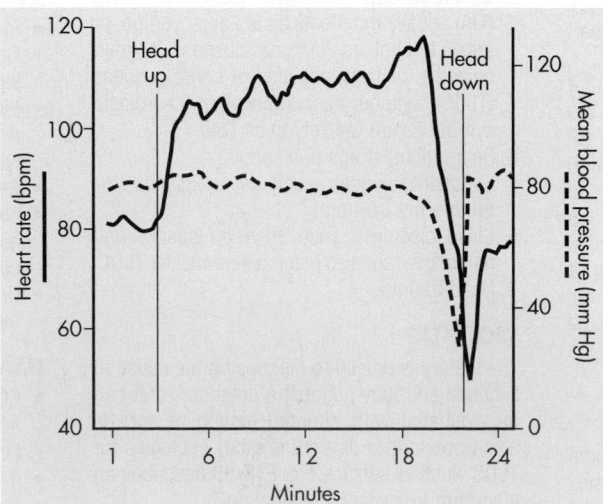

FIGURE 1S-91 Head-up tilt test performed on an 18-year-old woman with a history of syncope associated with pain, preceded by a prodrome of dizziness, graying vision, and diaphoresis. A similar prodrome preceded syncope during the test. Note the precipitous and nearly simultaneous decline of heart rate and blood pressure after an initial rise in heart rate. Vital signs returned to normal rapidly after the head was lowered. (Courtesy Robert F. Sprung, University of Utah. In Goldman L, Ausiello D [eds]: *Cecil textbook of medicine,* ed 22, Philadelphia, 2004, Saunders.)

BASIC INFORMATION

DEFINITION

The expected, osmotically driven, and "appropriate" physiologic response to serum (or plasma) hypotonicity is inhibition of hypothalamic osmoreceptors, which suppresses antidiuretic hormone release and increases excretion of dilute urine. A decrease in total body water (TBW) that is proportionately greater than accompanying decreases of total body cation corrects serum sodium (S_{Na}) (mEq/L) toward normal. The syndrome of inappropriate antidiuresis (SIAD) is defined by the occurrence of "inappropriately" concentrated urine in patients with hypotonic hyponatremia and normal extracellular fluid volume (ECFV). The S_{Na} is closely approximated by the following equation:

$$S_{Na} = \frac{TBNa_e + TBK_e}{TBW}$$

where $TBNa_e$ and TBK_e represent total body exchangeable sodium and potassium respectively (mEq), and TBW represents total body water (L).

Hyponatremia results from either loss of cation (numerator) or an increase of TBW (denominator), or both. In SIAD, an expanded TBW in the presence of normal bodily potassium and sodium content produces hyponatremia. The severity of hyponatremia associated with SIAD depends on the severity of the urinary dilution defect and on the intake of fluids that are electrolyte-free. Hemodynamic stimuli known to stimulate ADH release preclude a diagnosis of SIAD and include decreased ECFV (decreased TBNa), hypotension, and decreased effective arterial blood volume (EABV). This latter group manifests an increased ECFV with increased TBNa and includes congestive heart failure, nephrotic syndrome, cirrhosis, and other circumstances of significant "third spacing" of salt and water.

The earlier term syndrome of inappropriate antidiuretic hormone (SIADH) has been discarded by some because 10% to 15% of such patients have suppressed or undetectable serum ADH concentrations, although the remainder demonstrate nonosmotic stimulation of ADH. The group with suppressed ADH is postulated to have either increased sensitivity of renal collecting duct principal cells to ADH, secretion of other ADH-like peptides, and/or changes in renal hemodynamics resulting in decreased distal delivery of sodium and water despite normal systemic hemodynamics. Moreover, establishing a diagnosis of SIAD does not entail measuring ADH levels or demonstrating high serum ADH concentrations. Patients with hypothyroidism and adrenal insufficiency are excluded from the definition of SIAD, although they otherwise fulfill the diagnostic criteria (normal ECFV, hyponatremia, concentrated urine, and elevated levels or response to ADH). Finally, some include the use of drugs that inhibit free water excretion as a category of SIAD. Others consider this circumstance a separate diagnostic entity. The diagnosis also cannot be made in patients with acute or chronic kidney disease or recent use of loop diuretics. However, thiazide-induced hyponatremia *is* considered a form of SIAD or SIAD-type physiology.

SYNONYMS

SIADH
Syndrome of inappropriate antidiuretic hormone secretion
Syndrome of inappropriate ADH release
Inappropriate secretion of antidiuretic hormone

ICD 10-CM CODE(S)
E22.2 Syndrome of inappropriate secretion of antidiuretic hormone

EPIDEMIOLOGY & DEMOGRAPHICS

INCIDENCE: Hyponatremia occurs in 15% to 20% of hospitalized patients, of whom ~50% have SIAD. Overall hyponatremia at hospital admission is associated with a multivariate-adjusted odds ratio of in-hospital mortality of 1.47 (1.33-1.62). The effect is significant regardless of the severity of the hyponatremia and persists at one and five years of follow-up.

PHYSICAL FINDINGS & CLINICAL PRESENTATION

- Clinically, the ECF volume is normal. Hemodynamic stability is present, and edema, ascites, large pleural effusions, and other evidence of third-spacing are absent.
- Manifestations of the precipitating cause or underlying disease may be evident (e.g., fever and delirium following the use of 3,4-methylenedioxy-methamphetamine [MDMA, ecstasy]), stigmata of alcoholism or malnutrition, fever and/or localizing symptoms related to pneumonia or other pulmonary disease, occurrence in the setting of marathon running or other extreme endurance exercise, or headaches and visual field defects from an intracranial mass).
- Delirium, lethargy, and seizures may be present if hyponatremia occurs rapidly (within < 24 hours). Neurologic abnormalities such as ataxia, mood changes, and proximal muscle weakness may be subtle in chronic hyponatremia, even if relatively severe (defined as S_{Na} <120 mEq/L).
- Diminished reflexes and extensor plantar responses may occur with severe hyponatremia.

ETIOLOGY

- Drugs: Thiazide diuretics and SSRI antidepressants are the two most common causes of drug-related hyponatremia. Others include narcotic analgesics, carbamazepine, phenothiazines, tricyclic antidepressants, MDMA (ecstasy), nicotine, clofibrate, haloperidol, NSAIDs, nicotine, MAO inhibitors, chlorpropamide, vasopressin, desmopressin, oxytocin, chemotherapeutic agents (vincristine, vinblastine, cyclophosphamide).
- Neoplasms: lung, oropharynx, stomach, duodenum, pancreas, brain, thymus, bladder, prostate, endometrium, mesothelioma, lymphoma, Ewing's sarcoma
- Pulmonary disorders: pneumonia, aspergillosis, pulmonary abscess, TB, bronchiectasis, emphysema, cystic fibrosis, status asthmaticus, respiratory failure associated with positive-pressure breathing
- Intracranial pathology: trauma, neoplasms, infections (meningitis, encephalitis, brain abscess), hemorrhage, hydrocephalus, multiple sclerosis, Guillain-Barré syndrome
- Postoperative period: surgical stress, positive pressure ventilation, anesthetic agents
- Other: acute intermittent porphyria, psychosis, delirium tremens, general anesthesia, endurance exercise
- Table 1S-32 summarizes common etiologies of the syndrome of inappropriate antidiuresis.

DIFFERENTIAL DIAGNOSIS

- Solute-limited water excretion ("tea and toast" diet, beer-drinker's potomania)
- Hyponatremia associated with subclinical hypovolemia
- Primary polydipsia
- Endocrine disorders (hypothyroidism, adrenal insufficiency)
- Hypokalemia (due to decreased TBK_c)
- Hypertonic hyponatremia (hyperglycemia, iatrogenic administration of mannitol, sorbitol, glycine)
- Reset osmostat
- Hyponatremia associated with subclinical heart or liver disease
- Factitious ("pseudohyponatremia") (extreme hyperproteinemia or hyperlipidemia)

WORKUP

- Normal ECFV by history and physical examination. No history of large-volume electrolyte and/or fluid losses. No generalized edema, ascites, or large pleural effusions.
- Laboratory evaluation (see "Laboratory Tests") is consistent with excessive ADH secretion or sensitivity in the absence of osmotic or hemodynamic stimuli for ADH secretion. Rarely, a water loading test is conducted, or plasma arginine vasopressin measurement is done.
- Normal thyroid, adrenal, and cardiac function.
- No recent or concurrent use of loop diuretics.
- Failure to correct hyponatremia after 0.9% saline infusion.
- Correction of hyponatremia through fluid restriction alone is possible but unlikely because low urine volumes severely limit urinary free water loss.
- Diagnostic criteria for SIADH are described in Table 1S-33.

LABORATORY TEST(S)

- SNa < lower limit of normal
- Decreased serum osmolality (<275 mOsm/kg)
- Urine osmolality >100 mOsm/kg with plasma hypotonicity

TABLE 1S-32 Common Etiologies of the Syndrome of Inappropriate Antidiuretic Hormone Secretion (SIADH)

Tumors

Pulmonary/mediastinal (bronchogenic carcinoma, mesothelioma, thymoma)

Extrapulmonary (duodenal carcinoma, pancreatic carcinoma, ureteral/prostate carcinoma, uterine carcinoma, nasopharyngeal carcinoma, leukemia)

Central Nervous System Disorders

Mass lesions (tumors, brain abscesses, subdural hematoma)

Inflammatory diseases (encephalitis, meningitis, systemic lupus erythematosus, acute intermittent porphyria, multiple sclerosis)

Degenerative/demyelinating diseases (Guillain-Barré syndrome, spinal cord lesions)

Miscellaneous (subarachnoid hemorrhage, head trauma, acute psychosis, delirium tremens, pituitary stalk section, transsphenoidal adenomectomy, hydrocephalus)

Drug-Related

Stimulated release of AVP (nicotine, phenothiazines, tricyclics)

Direct renal effects and/or potentiation of AVP antidiuretic effects (desmopressin, oxytocin, prostaglandin synthesis inhibitors)

Mixed or uncertain actions (ACE inhibitors, carbamazepine and oxcarbazepine, chlorpropamide, clofibrate, clozapine, cyclophosphamide, 3,4-methylenedioxymethamphetamine ["Ecstasy"], omeprazole; serotonin reuptake inhibitors, vincristine)

Pulmonary

Infections (tuberculosis, acute bacterial and viral pneumonia, aspergillosis, empyema)

Mechanical/ventilatory causes (acute respiratory failure, COPD, positive-pressure ventilation)

Other Causes

Acquired immunodeficiency syndrome (AIDS) and AIDS-related complex

Prolonged strenuous exercise (marathon, triathlon, ultramarathon, hot-weather hiking)

Senile atrophy

Idiopathic

From Melmed S: *Williams textbook of endocrinology,* ed 12, Philadelphia, 2011, Saunders.
ACE, Angiotensin-converting enzyme; *AVP,* arginine vasopressin; *COPD,* chronic obstructive pulmonary disease.

TABLE 1S-33 Diagnostic Criteria for the Syndrome of Inappropriate Antidiuretic Hormone Release.

Essential Diagnostic Criteria

Decreased extracellular fluid effective osmolality (<270 mOsm/kg)

Inappropriate urinary concentration (>100 mOsm/kg)

Clinical normovolemia

Elevated urinary sodium concentration under conditions of normal salt and water intake

Absence of adrenal, thyroid, or pituitary insufficiency

Absence of chronic kidney disease

Absence of diuretic use

Supplemental Criteria

Abnormal water loading test (inability to excrete at least 90% of a 20-ml/kg water load in 4 hours and/or failure to dilute urine osmolality to <100 mOsm/kg)

Plasma vasopressin level inappropriately elevated relative to the plasma osmolality

No significant correction of SNa with volume expansion, but improvement after fluid restriction

From Floege J et al: *Comprehensive clinical nephrology,* ed 4, Philadelphia, 2010, Saunders.

- Urinary sodium usually >40 mEq/L with normal dietary salt intake
- Normal or low BUN, creatinine
- Normal TSH
- Decreased uric acid

IMAGING STUDIES

Not routinely required for diagnosis of SIAD. In relevant clinical circumstances, imaging may be required to facilitate a structural cause of SIAD.

℞ TREATMENT

NONPHARMACOLOGIC THERAPY

If there is a need for urgent correction, therapies are required that increase urinary free water loss despite the persistent increases in ADH level or effect. With mild SIAD, reasonable degrees of fluid restriction (10-15 mL/kg/day) combined with increased solute loads (diets that are high in protein, sodium chloride, and potassium chloride) may increase free water clearance sufficiently until an underlying cause is determined or until definitive therapy is initiated.

ACUTE GENERAL Rx
PHARMACOLOGIC THERAPY

Rate of Correction. All patients with moderate to severe hyponatremia warrant intense serial monitoring of S_{Na}, and urine volume and chemistry (osmolality, K, and Na) during the initial 48 hours of admission and during active therapy to make sure that recommended rates of correction are achieved but not exceeded. The level of nursing intensity may require the resources of an ICU or step-down unit, even if patients are minimally symptomatic. The vast majority of patients with SIAD have chronic hyponatremia (developing over a period of greater than

24 hours) that is associated with mild symptoms because adequate time for cerebral compensation has elapsed. In this case the most important therapeutic principle is to avoid rapid rates of correction that can cause severe neurologic injury due to osmotic demyelination syndrome. In patients with chronic hyponatremia (duration > 24 hours), S_{Na} should not be corrected faster than 6 mEq/L/day. If the patient truly has SIAD, free water loss and rate of change of S_{Na} during conservative therapy or 0.9% infusion should be low, and predictable during administration of hypertonic saline. If, however, the patient has unrecognized volume contraction that is repaired by NaCl infusion, or if the underlying cause of SIAD resolves rapidly, then a simultaneous aquaresis (water diuresis) may occur with unexpectedly rapid rates of correction.

In the minority of patients with acute hyponatremia (duration <24 hours), excessive rates of correction are of minimal concern, and the goal is to repair the hyponatremia rapidly enough to prevent or reduce the severity of acute cerebral edema. In this circumstance the serum sodium should be increased by 4 to 6 mEq/L within the first three hours if symptoms are mild-moderate and within the first one hour if symptoms are severe (seizures, coma, obtundation).

Acute Hyponatremia. The rapid correction of serum sodium mandated in acute hyponatremia requires the use of hypertonic saline, despite the patient's normal TBNa, as total body sodium (see earlier equation) can be increased more rapidly than TBW (see earlier equation) can be decreased. Infusion of each 1 ml/kg body weight of 3% saline infusion (513 mEq/L) increases the serum sodium level by approximately 1 mEq/L. Rates of correction may be higher if there is unrecognized ECFV contraction that is repaired by the NaCl infusion, with a resulting rapid aquaresis. The infusion volume and rate should reflect the therapy goals outlined previously. Furosemide 20 to 40 mg IV may be a useful adjuvant by increasing urinary loss of free water as infused sodium is excreted and by helping to prevent symptomatic increases in ECFV.

Chronic Hyponatremia. The goal of therapy in chronic hyponatremia due to SIAD is to restore TBW to normal while maintaining already-normal quantities of TBK_e and $TBNa_e$. This is accomplished by estimating the patient's TBW and then calculating the 24-hour free water loss required to attain the selected target S_{Na} (see "Rates of Correction"). A general rule of thumb is to assume that ratio of TBW (L)/ weight (kg) is about 5% higher than the normonatremic baseline in SIAD patients in mild-moderate hyponatremia. The following example demonstrates the calculations needed to determine the target TBW and free water loss required to yield the desired S_{Na} target after 24 hours of therapy for chronic hyponatremia:

Example 1: A 70-year-old woman taking chlorthalidone and an SSRI who develops a serum sodium of 120 mEq/L.

24 hour Target S_{Na} = Current S_{Na} + 6 mEq/L = 126 mEq/L

Current weight 70 kg

Assumed usual percent TBW 50%

Approximate current percent TBW = 50% + 5% = 55%

Current TBW = 0.55 × 70 kg = 38.5 L

Current TBNa + TBK = (38.5 L × 120 mEq/L) = 4620 mEq

Target TBW (at 24 hours) = 4620 mEq/(126 mEq/L) = 36.6 L

Target net free water loss = Current TBW − Target TBW = 1.9 L

Target total urine free water excretion (with allowance for 1 L oral fluid intake) = 2.9 L

Furosemide and Saline Strategy. The classical method is to increase urinary volume and electrolyte-free water loss via furosemide-induced diuresis, which also restricts urine tonicity (i.e., total of urinary [Na] + [K] concentrations) volume and limit urine tonicity (concentrations of urinary Na and K) to approximately 75 mEq/L. Urinary losses of Na and K are then replaced in higher concentrations than that excreted to effect net electrolyte-free water loss. The following table illustrates the urine output and replacement solution volumes required in Patient 1 to achieve the target S_{Na}.

Target Total Furosemide-Induced Urinary Free Water Excretion = 2.9 L

(Urine Na + K = 75 mEq/L)

Replacement Solutions	Cation mEq/L	Net Free Water Loss/L urine	Target Urine Output (L)
0.9% Saline	154	1 − (75/154) = 0.5	2.9/0.5 = 5.8
3% Saline	513	1 − (75/513) = 0.85	2.9/0.85 = 3.4

Periodic monitoring of S_{Na}, urine volume, and urine chemistries (osmolarity, sodium, and potassium) is critical to ensure that urine volumes do not exceed targets and that SNa is correcting as predicted.

Use of Direct Vasopressin Receptor Antagonists. Conivaptan (20 mg IV × 1 followed by continuous IV infusion of 20 to 40 mg/day for 2-4 days) and tolvaptan (15-60 mg/day PO, titrated daily from 15 mg as needed) are selective type 2 vasopressin receptor (V_2) antagonists. Compared to the use of furosemide and NaCl infusions, their use is relatively straightforward and convenient for patients and medical personnel. Urinary electrolyte losses are minimal, meaning that their dosing can be titrated to produce urine output equal to the actual targeted urine free water loss. Therapeutic effects occur relatively quickly, enabling relatively rapid evaluation and titration of dosing for inpatients provided that S_{Na} and urine output are closely monitored. While the cost of the medications is considerable, the savings of just one hospital day offsets the cost of the medication.

CHRONIC Rx

- When SIAD is chronic fluid restriction (ideally < 15 mL/kg) may be needed indefinitely in conjunction with high dietary electrolyte and protein content that increases obligatory free water losses through solute diuresis.
- NaCl tablets and protein powders serve the same purpose. Monthly monitoring of electrolytes is recommended in patients with chronic SIAD.
- Demeclocycline 300 to 600 mg PO twice daily. Contraindicated in hepatic disease.

DISPOSITION

- Mortality exceeding 40% has been reported in patients with S_{Na} <110 mEq/L.
- Hospital readmission rates are common in chronic SIAD when an underlying cause(s) cannot be eliminated, especially if patients are unwilling or unable to restrict their fluid intake and follow dietary recommendations.
- Growing evidence suggests that even mild to moderate chronic hyponatremia has been associated with bone loss, falls, and increased fracture risk, especially in elderly patients.

REFERRAL

Urgent emergency department evaluation and hospital admission are appropriate for moderate to severe hyponatremia due to SIAD, especially if it is acute or symptomatic, or if therapy is being initiated. Because of the high risk of complications from overly aggressive or ineffective treatment, referral to a nephrologist, endocrinologist, or critical care physician is recommended.

SUGGESTED READING

Available at www.expertconsult.com

RELATED CONTENT

Syndrome of Inappropriate Secretion of Antidiuretic Hormone (Patient Information)

AUTHOR: **MARK D. FABER, M.D.**

ℹ️ BASIC INFORMATION

DEFINITION

Syphilis is a systemic sexually transmitted treponemal disease, with acute and chronic manifestations, characterized by primary skin lesions; secondary eruption involving skin and mucous membranes; long periods of latency; and late lesions of the skin, bone, viscera, central nervous system, and cardiovascular system.

SYNONYMS

Lues

ICD-10CM CODES
A51.0 Primary genital syphilis
A51.1 Primary anal syphilis
A51.2 Primary syphilis of other sites
A51.3 Secondary syphilis of skin and
 mucous membranes
A51.4 Other secondary syphilis
A51.5 Early syphilis, unspecified
A52 Late syphilis
A52.0 Cardiovascular syphilis
A52.1 Symptomatic neurosyphilis
A52.3 Asymptomatic neurosyphilis
A52.3 Neurosyphilis, unspecified
A53.9 Syphilis, unspecified

EPIDEMIOLOGY & DEMOGRAPHICS

- Widespread, primarily involving ages 20 to 35 yr. Racial differences in incidence are related to social factors. Usually more prevalent in urban areas. Estimated annual incidence of more than 55,000 cases in the U.S. Rates reached historic lows in the U.S. in 2000 but began increasing among males in 2001, and increase has continued. Rates are disproportionately higher among black and Hispanic men who have sex with men (MSM) compared with white MSM and among young MSM.
- Communicability is indefinite and variable. Communicable during primary, secondary, and latent mucocutaneous lesions in up to first 4 yr of latency. Most probable congenital transmission occurs in early maternal syphilis. Adequate penicillin treatment ends infectivity within 24 to 48 hr.

PHYSICAL FINDINGS & CLINICAL PRESENTATION

PRIMARY SYPHILIS: Characteristic lesion is a painless chancre on genitalia, mouth, or anus (Fig. 1S-92); atypical primary lesions may occur. Usually appears 3 wk after exposure and may spontaneously involute.
SECONDARY SYPHILIS:
- Localized or diffuse mucocutaneous lesions and generalized lymphadenopathy. It is common to have constitutional symptoms, flulike symptoms. May begin approximately 4 to 6 wk after appearance of primary lesion. Manifestations may resolve in 1 wk to 12 mo.

- 60% to 80% of patients have maculopapular lesions on their palms and soles.
- Condylomata lata intertriginous papules form at areas of friction and moisture, such as the vulva.
- 21% to 58% have mucocutaneous or mucosal lesions (pharyngitis, tonsillitis, "mucous patch" lesion on oral and genital mucosa).

EARLY LATENT (≤1 YR): Generally asymptomatic. Latent syphilis is defined as syphilis characterized by seroreactivity without other evidence of primary, secondary, or tertiary disease. Because latent syphilis is not transmitted sexually, the objective of diagnosing and treating persons in this stage is to prevent complications and transmission from a pregnant woman to her fetus.

LATE LATENT (>1 YR):
- Characterized by gummas (nodular, ulcerative lesions) that can involve the skin, mucous membranes, skeletal system, and viscera.
- Manifestations of cardiovascular syphilis include aortitis, aneurysm, or aortic regurgitation.
- Neurosyphilis may be asymptomatic or symptomatic. Tabes dorsalis, meningovascular syphilis, general paralysis, or insanity may occur. Iritis, choroidoretinitis, and leukoplakia may also occur.

ETIOLOGY

- *Treponema pallidum,* a spirochete
- Spread by sexual intercourse or by intrauterine transfer

Ⓓ DIAGNOSIS

DIFFERENTIAL DIAGNOSIS

- Other genitoulcerative diseases such as herpes, chancroid (see Section II)
- See Section III for a clinical algorithm for the evaluation of genital ulcer disease

WORKUP

Confirmation is primarily through laboratory diagnosis. An algorithm for interpretation of reactive serologic tests for syphilis is described in Fig. E1S-93.
- A presumptive diagnosis of syphilis requires use of two tests: a nontreponemal test (i.e., venereal disease research laboratory [VDRL] or rapid plasma reagin [RPR]) and a treponemal test (i.e., fluorescent treponemal antibody absorbed [FTA-ABS] tests, the *T. pallidum* passive particle agglutination [TP-PA] assay, various enzyme immunoassays [EIAs], chemiluminescence immunoassays, immunoblots, or rapid treponemal assays).
- The diagnosis of neurosyphilis depends on a combination of cerebrospinal fluid (CSF) tests (CSF cell count or protein and a reactive CSF-VDRL) in the presence of reactive serologic test results and neurologic signs and symptoms. Among persons with HIV infection, CSF leukocyte count usually is elevated (>5 WBC/mm³). Using a higher cutoff (>20 WBC/mm³) might improve the specificity of neurosyphilis diagnosis.

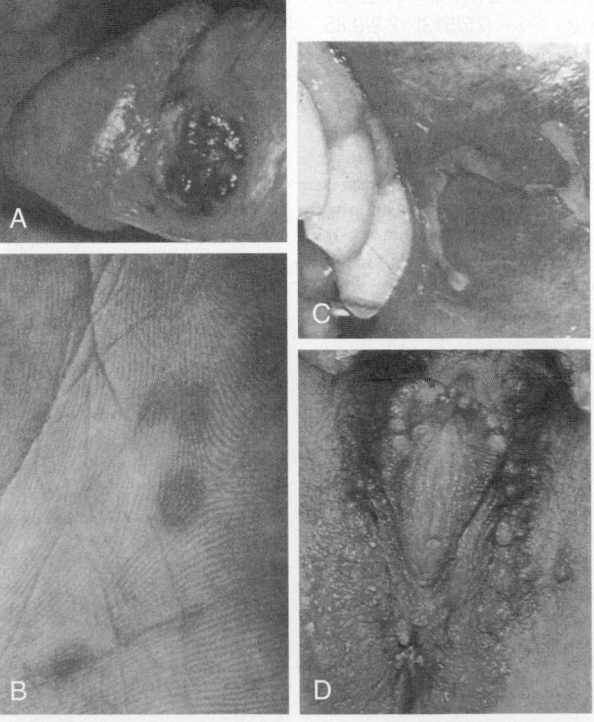

FIGURE 1S-92 Syphilis lesions. A, Chancre in primary syphilis. **B,** Palmar lesions of a coppery color in secondary syphilis. **C,** Mucous patch in secondary syphilis. **D,** Condylomata lata in secondary syphilis. (**A, C,** and **D** from Forbes CD, Jackson WF: *Color atlas and text of clinical medicine,* ed 3, London, 2003, Mosby. **B** from Habif TP et al: *Skin disease: diagnosis and treatment,* St Louis, 2001, Mosby.)

LABORATORY TESTS

- Dark-field microscopy of fluid from lesion to look for treponeme is the definitive method for diagnosis of early syphilis.
- Serologic testing, both nontreponemal (VDRL, RPR) and treponemal (FTA, MHA). Many labs now screen patients for syphilis with automated treponemal antibody immunoassays and then confirm positive results with nontreponemal tests. The use of only one type of serologic test is insufficient for diagnosis because each type of test has limitations, including the possibility of false-positive test results in persons without syphilis. False-positive nontreponemal test results can be associated with various medical conditions unrelated to syphilis, including autoimmune conditions, older age, and injection-drug use; therefore, persons with a reactive nontreponemal test should receive a treponemal test to confirm the diagnosis of syphilis. Positive results on both treponemal and nontreponemal testing indicate new untreated syphilis. When the nontreponemal test is negative despite a positive screen, an additional treponemal screen may be helpful. Trials have shown that two positive treponemal screens help identify a population with likely prior or current syphilis, and treatment of these patients may be justifiable.
- In patients with neurosyphilis, serologic criteria for response to therapy is a fourfold or greater decrease in VDRL titer over 6 to 12 months.
- Lumbar puncture (LP) for cerebrospinal fluid VDRL (CSF-VDRL) in patients with evidence of latent syphilis. When reactive in the absence of substantial contamination of CSF with blood, it is considered diagnostic of neurosyphilis. The Centers for Disease Control and Prevention indications for LP are neurologic symptoms, treatment failure, any eye or ear involvement, or evidence of active syphilis (aortitis, gumma, iritis).
- HIV testing in all patients.

TREATMENT

ACUTE GENERAL Rx

- Early (primary and secondary): penicillin G benzathine 2.4 million U IM. Recommended regimen for infants and children is benzathine penicillin G 50,000 units/kg IM, up to the adult dose of 2.4 million units in a single dose. Doxycycline 100 mg bid × 14 days might be effective in nonpregnant penicillin-allergic patients. Azithromycin 2

g PO × 1 dose should not be used as first-line treatment for syphilis and should be used with caution and only when treatment with penicillin or doxycycline is not feasible. Azithromycin should not be used in MSM, persons with HIV, or pregnant women. Careful clinical and serologic follow-up of persons receiving any alternative therapy is essential. Persons with a penicillin allergy whose compliance with therapy or follow-up cannot be ensured should be desensitized and treated with benzathine penicillin.
- Early latent syphilis in adults: penicillin G 2.4 million units IM in a single dose.
- Late latent syphilis or latent syphilis of unknown duration in adults: penicillin G benzathine 2.4 million U IM q wk × 3 wk. Doxycycline 100 mg PO bid × 4 wk is an acceptable alternative in nonpregnant patients allergic to penicillin.
- Tertiary syphilis (refers to gummas and cardiovascular syphilis but not to neurosyphilis): penicillin G benzathine 2.4 million U IM q wk × 3 wk (total dose of 7.2 million units).
- Neurosyphilis: aqueous crystalline penicillin G 18 to 24 million U/day, administered as 3 to 4 million U IV q4h or continuous infusion for 10 to 14 days. An alternative regimen consists of procaine penicillin 2.4 million U IM/day plus probenecid 500 mg PO qid, both for 10 to 14 days.
- Congenital syphilis: aqueous crystalline penicillin G 50,000 U/kg/dose IV q12h × first 7 days of life and q8h after that for a total of 10 days or procaine penicillin G 50,000 U/kg/dose IM/day × 10 days.
- Primary and secondary syphilis among persons with HIV infection: benzathine penicillin G 2.4 million units IM in a single dose.
- Early latent syphilis among persons with HIV infection: benzathine penicillin G 2.4 million units IM in a single dose.
- Late latent syphilis among persons with HIV infection: benzathine penicillin G 2.4 million units IM weekly for 3 wk.

DISPOSITION

- Repeat quantitative nontreponemal tests at 3, 6, and 12 mo. Pregnancy requires monthly tests until delivery.
- If a fourfold increase in titer occurs, if initial high titer fails to drop by fourfold within a year, or signs persist, retreatment may be indicated. Because treatment failure may be the result of unrecognized CNS infection, CSF examination can be considered in such situations. For retreatment, weekly infections of benzathine penicillin G 2.4 million units IM for

3 wk is recommended, unless CSF examination indicates that neurosyphilis is present.
- Pregnant women without a fourfold drop in titer in a 3-mo period need to be retreated.
- Cases should be reported to local or state health department for referral, follow-up, and partner notification.

REFERRAL

- Pregnant and possible congenital syphilis
- Pregnant and allergic to penicillin, with need to be desensitized
- Late latent syphilis with serious central nervous system, cardiovascular, or other organ system compromise

! PEARLS & CONSIDERATIONS

- Jarisch-Herxheimer reaction (fever, myalgia, tachycardia, hypotension) may occur within 24 hr of treatment.
- One third of untreated patients develop central nervous system and/or cardiovascular sequelae.
- Up to 80% of those treated during late stages remain seropositive indefinitely.
- Treponemal tests remain positive even after adequate therapy.
- Male circumcision does not decrease the incidence of syphilis (unlike HIV, HSV-2, and HPV infection).
- Partner notification and treatment:
  1. Persons who are exposed within 90 days preceding the diagnosis of primary, secondary, or early latent syphilis in a sex partner might be infected even if seronegative; therefore, such persons should be treated presumptively.
  2. Persons who were exposed ≥90 days before the diagnosis of syphilis in a sex partner should be treated presumptively if serologic test results are not available immediately and the opportunity for follow-up is uncertain.

SUGGESTED READINGS
Available at www.expertconsult.com

RELATED CONTENT
Syphilis (Patient Information)
Tabes Dorsalis (Related Key Topic)

AUTHOR: **RUBEN ALVERO, M.D.**

BASIC INFORMATION

DEFINITION

- Systemic lupus erythematosus (SLE) is a chronic inflammatory disorder characterized by autoantibody production responsible for antibody-mediated and immune complex deposition tissue damage. SLE involves multiple organs and systems and has heterogeneous disease patterns. Relapses and remissions are a common feature.

SYNONYMS

SLE, lupus

ICD-10CM CODES

M32	Systemic lupus erythematosus
M32.0	Drug-induced systemic lupus erythematosus
M32.8	Other forms of systemic lupus erythematosus
M32.9	Systemic lupus erythematosus, unspecified
M32.10	Systemic lupus erythematosus, organ or system involvement unspecified
M32.11	Endocarditis in systemic lupus erythematosus
M32.12	Pericarditis in systemic lupus erythematosus
M32.13	Lung involvement in systemic lupus erythematosus
M32.14	Glomerular disease in systemic lupus erythematosus
M32.15	Tubulo-interstitial nephropathy in systemic lupus erythematosus
M32.19	Other organ or system involvement in systemic lupus erythematosus

EPIDEMIOLOGY & DEMOGRAPHICS

INCIDENCE: Varies across gender, race/ethnic groups, and geography from 20 to 70 cases per 100,000 persons. Prevalence higher among African Americans, Asian Americans, and Hispanics. There are an estimated 350,000 people with SLE in the U.S.

PREDOMINANT SEX: Female/male ratio is 9:1. The ratio is highest in reproductive age group, and about half of that in patients younger than 16 and older than 55.

PREDOMINANT AGE: Mean age at diagnosis is 31.

PHYSICAL FINDINGS & CLINICAL PRESENTATION

- Constitutional: unexplained fever (rare in active SLE), fatigue (80% to 100% patients), malaise (see Table 1S-34).
- Mucocutaneous lesions (more than 80% of patients): Acute (associated with + Ro antibody): malar rash sparing nasolabial folds (acute cutaneous lupus) (Fig. 1S-96); annular or papulosquamous rash (subacute cutaneous lupus) (Fig. 1S-97); Chronic: raised erythematous patches with subsequent edematous plaques and adherent scales (discoid cutaneous lupus), lupus profundus, lupus tumidus (Fig. 1S-98); alopecia, photosensitivity, nasal,

TABLE 1S-34 Potential Clinical Manifestations of Systemic Lupus Erythematosus

Target Organ	Potential Clinical Manifestations
Constitutional	Fatigue, anorexia, weight loss, fever, lymphadenopathy
Musculoskeletal	Arthritis, myositis, arthralgias, myalgias, avascular necrosis, osteoporosis
Skin	Malar rash, discoid rash, photosensitive rash, cutaneous vasculitis, livedo reticularis, periungual capillary abnormalities, Raynaud's phenomenon, alopecia, oral and nasal ulcers
Renal	Hypertension, proteinuria, hematuria, edema, nephrotic syndrome, renal failure
Cardiovascular	Pericarditis, myocarditis, conduction system abnormalities, Libman-Sacks endocarditis
Neurologic	Seizures, psychosis, cerebritis, stroke, transverse myelitis, depression, cognitive impairment, headaches, pseudotumor, peripheral neuropathy, chorea, optic neuritis, cranial nerve palsies
Pulmonary	Pleuritis, interstitial lung disease, pulmonary hemorrhage, pulmonary hypertension, pulmonary embolism
Hematologic	Immune-mediated cytopenias (hemolytic anemia, thrombocytopenia or leukopenia), anemia of chronic inflammation, hypercoagulability, thrombocytopenic thrombotic microangiopathy
Gastroenterology	Hepatosplenomegaly, pancreatitis, vasculitis affecting bowel, protein-losing enteropathy
Ocular	Retinal vasculitis, scleritis, episcleritis, papilledema

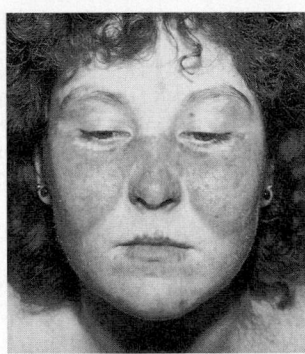

FIGURE 1S-96 Acute cutaneous lupus erythematosus (LE) (systemic LE). The classic butterfly rash occurs in 10% to 50% of patients with acute LE. (From Habif TP: *Clinical dermatology: a color guide to diagnosis and therapy*, ed 3, St Louis, 1996, Mosby.)

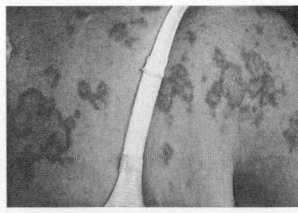

FIGURE 1S-97 Subacute cutaneous lupus. (From Hochberg MC et al: *Rheumatology*, ed 4, St Louis, 2008, Mosby.)

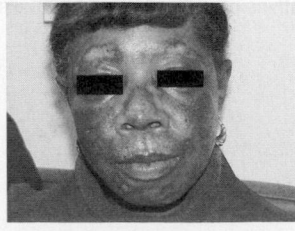

FIGURE 1S-98 Discoid lupus erythematosus. (From Firestein GS et al: *Kelley's textbook of rheumatology*, ed 8, Philadelphia, 2008, Saunders.)

or oropharyngeal ulcerations (classically painless, but discoid lesions may be painful); Raynaud's phenomenon; leukocytoclastic vasculitis, chilblains; livedo reticularis or livedo racemosa (secondary to antiphospholipid antibody syndrome); skin biopsy hallmark: interface dermatitis.
- Musculoskeletal (about 90% of lupus patients): arthralgias are more common than true arthritis, but nonerosive deforming arthritis is not rare; myositis.
- Cardiac: pericardial rub (pericarditis) is most common; valvular heart disease: valve nodules and thickening (Libman-Sacks endocarditis); congestive heart failure, myocarditis, premature atherosclerotic heart disease.
- Pulmonary: pleuritis (most common), acute or chronic pneumonitis, diffuse alveolar hemorrhage, pulmonary hypertension.
- Gastrointestinal: dysphagia, mesenteric vasculitis, peritonitis, pancreatitis, hepatitis.
- Neuropsychiatric: headache, psychosis, seizure, acute confusional states, peripheral or cranial neuropathy, transverse myelitis, stroke (may be associated with antiphospholipid syndrome), cognitive dysfunction.
- Hematologic (about 50% of lupus patients): anemia (hemolytic, anemia of chronic disease, aplastic anemia), thrombocytopenia, leukopenia, lymphadenopathy, secondary antiphospholipid antibody syndrome.
- Renal: acute renal failure, proteinuria, nephritic syndrome, nephrotic syndrome.

ETIOLOGY

Lupus may develop in genetically susceptible individuals, triggered by endogenous and exogenous factors. SLE susceptibility involves MHC class II polymorphism with commonly observed association with HLA-DR-2, DR3, DR4, and DR8. SLE is also associated with inherited deficiencies of C1q, C2, C4a, others. There is predilection for familial clustering of SLE with risk in monozygotic twins—about

25% to 50%—and 5% in dizygotic twins. Environmental factors such as UV light, Epstein-Barr virus infection, and tobacco smoking may have a triggering role. Autoantibody production is the hallmark of disease development and diagnosis of SLE. Evidence supports the improper processing of nuclear proteins and nucleic acid from cell death. Impairments in neutrophil cell death via a process termed NET-osis (nuclear extracellular trap) contribute to the accumulation of nuclear debris. This, in turn, can lead to the presentation of self-nuclear material to plasmacytoid dendritic cells. Plasmacytoid dendritic cells propagate antibody and immune complex production via a type I interferon-dependent mechanism.

 **DIAGNOSIS**

DIFFERENTIAL DIAGNOSIS
- Rheumatoid arthritis, mixed connective tissue disease, systemic vasculitis
- Neoplastic disorder
- Hematologic malignancy, paraneoplastic syndrome
- Systemic infection
- Other: thrombotic thrombocytopenic purpura/hemolytic uremic syndrome, primary antiphospholipid antibody syndrome

EVALUATION
The diagnosis of SLE is suspected when any four or more of the following 1997 American College of Rheumatology (ACR) criteria (sensitivity 86%, specificity 93%) are present. These criteria were developed for research purposes, and diagnosis should be made on clinical grounds. The 2012 Systemic Lupus International Collaborating Clinics (SLICC) Classification Criteria (sensitivity 94%, specificity 92%) is also a validated tool for the diagnosis of SLE.

1997 ACR Criteria
- Malar rash
- Discoid rash
- Photosensitivity (recurrence of unusual skin rash in sun-exposed areas)
- Oral or nasopharyngeal painless ulceration, observed by physician
- Arthritis (nonerosive)
- Serositis (pleuritis, pericarditis)
- Renal disorder (persistent proteinuria >0.5 g/day, or ≥3+ on dipstick if quantification not performed; cellular casts)
- Neurologic disorder (seizures, psychosis [in absence of offending drugs or metabolic derangement])
- Hematologic disorder:
  1. Hemolytic anemia with reticulocytosis
  2. Leukopenia (<4000/mm³ total on two or more occasions)
  3. Lymphopenia (<1500/mm³ on two or more occasions)
  4. Thrombocytopenia (<100,000/mm³ in the absence of offending drugs)
- Immunologic disorder:
  1. Anti–double-stranded DNA antibody (anti-dsDNA)

2. Anti-Smith antibody (anti-Sm)
3. Antiphospholipid antibodies (anticardiolipin IgM or IgG, lupus anticoagulant, anti-beta-2 glycoprotein IgM or IgG, or false-positive fluorescent treponemal antibody absorption test or *Treponema pallidum* immobilization for 6 months)
- Antinuclear antibody (ANA): an abnormal titer of ANA by immunofluorescence or equivalent assay at any time in the absence of drugs known to be associated with drug-induced lupus syndrome

2012 SLICC Criteria
SLE can be diagnosed if:
I. Biopsy-proven nephritis with either ANA or anti-dsDNA antibodies
II. *or*
III. Patient satisfies four clinical criteria, requiring at least one clinical and at least one immunologic criterion
IV. Clinical Criteria
  1. Acute cutaneous lupus (malar rash, bullous lupus, toxic epidermal necrolysis, photosensitive lupus rash, maculopapular lupus, subacute cutaneous lupus)
  2. Chronic cutaneous lupus (discoid, hypertrophic verrucous, panniculitis, mucosal lupus, lupus tumidus, chilblains lupus, lichen planus)
  3. Oral ulcers or nasal ulcers
  4. Nonscarring alopecia
  5. Synovitis (more than two joints or inflammatory arthralgias of more than two joints)
  6. Serositis (pleurisy for more than 1 day, pericardial pain for more than 1 day)
  7. Renal (>500 mg proteinuria/24 hours) or RBC casts)
  8. Neurologic (seizures, psychosis, mononeuritis multiplex, myelitis, peripheral or cranial neuropathy, acute confusional state)
  9. Hemolytic anemia
  10. Lymphopenia (<1000/mm³ at least once)
  11. Thrombocytopenia (<100,000/mm³ at least once)
V. Immunologic Criteria
  1. ANA
  2. Anti-dsDNA (>2× laboratory reference range)
  3. Anti-Smith
  4. Antiphospholipid antibodies (lupus anticoagulant, RPR, anti-cardiolipin IgA, IgG, IgM, anti-β2 glycoprotein IgA, IgG, IgM)
  5. Low complement
  6. Direct Coombs test in the absence of hemolytic anemia

LABORATORY TESTS
Suggested initial laboratory evaluation of suspected SLE:
  ANA
- Complete blood count with differential, blood urea nitrogen and serum creatinine, urinalysis, ESR, PTT, complements (C3, C4)

Consider additional laboratory testing in a patient with strong suspicion for systemic lupus:
- Anti-dsDNA, anti-Smith, anti-SSA, anti-SSB, anti-RNP antibodies. Table 1S-35 summarizes autoantibodies and clinical significance in SLE.
- Lupus anticoagulant, RPR, anticardiolipin antibodies, anti-beta-2 glycoprotein antibodies especially in patients with thrombotic events or recurrent miscarriages
- Urinalysis for RBC, cellular casts
- Random spot urine protein: urine creatinine ratio, 24-hour urine protein collection if proteinuria; >0.5 or >500 mg/24 hours is abnormal, respectively.
  Direct Coombs test

IMAGING STUDIES
- Chest x-ray for evaluation of pulmonary involvement (pleural effusion, pulmonary infiltrates)
- Electrocardiogram for chest pain
- Echocardiogram if murmur, evidence of new or unexplained congestive heart failure, or suspected pericarditis

TABLE 1S-35 Autoantibodies and Clinical Significance in Systemic Lupus Erythematosus (SLE)

Autoantibody	Prevalence in SLE	Clinical Significance
Antinuclear Antibody		
Anti-dsDNA	60%	95% specificity for SLE; fluctuates with disease activity; associated with glomerulonephritis
Anti-Smith	20%-30%	99% specificity for SLE; associated with anti-U1RNP antibodies
Anti-U1RNP	30%	Antibody associated with mixed connective tissue disease and lower frequency of glomerulonephritis
Anti-Ro/SSA	30%	Associated with Sjögren's syndrome, photosensitivity, SCLE, neonatal lupus, congenital heart block
Anti-La/SSB	20%	Associated with Sjögren's syndrome, SCLE, neonatal lupus, congenital heart block, anti-Ro/SSA
Antihistone	70%	Also associated with drug-induced lupus
Antiphospholipid	30%	Associated with arterial and venous thrombosis, pregnancy morbidity

SCLE, Subacute cutaneous lupus erythematosus.
From Firestein GS et al: *Kelley's textbook of rheumatology,* ed 9, Philadelphia, 2013, Saunders.

S

Diseases and Disorders

 **TREATMENT**

NONPHARMACOLOGIC THERAPY

- Avoidance of sunlight and use of high-SPF sunscreen (>35).
- Screening and counseling for modifiable cardiovascular risk factors such as cigarette smoking and uncontrolled HTN.
- Counseling for pregnancy planning for patients of childbearing age.
- Calcium and vitamin D supplementation for prevention of early osteoporosis.

GENERAL Rx

- Treatment should be targeted toward the involved organ(s).
- Limited and defined courses of corticosteroids are useful for a variety of SLE symptoms. Steroid therapy should be restricted to acute or subacute control of symptoms, due to the increased cardiovascular risk and increased organ damage associated with chronic steroid use.
- Consider checking G6PD in certain ethnic groups more predisposed to antimalarial-induced hemolytic anemia.
- Hydroxychloroquine has best evidence for reducing flares, organ damage, lipids, thrombosis; improving survival, augmenting action of mycophenolate mofetil (MMF) in lupus nephritis, and preventing seizures. Additional useful medications are listed in the following:
- Methotrexate or azathioprine is used as steroid-sparing drugs. Indications for immunosuppressive therapy in SLE are described in Tables 1S-36 and 1S-37.
- Joint pain and mild serositis are generally well controlled with nonsteroidal anti-inflammatory drugs or low-dose corticosteroids. Hydroxychloroquine and methotrexate are also

effective for arthritis. Leflunomide and rituximab may be considered for difficult arthritis.
- Cutaneous manifestations
  1. Topical or intradermal corticosteroids are helpful for individual discoid lesions, especially in the scalp.
  2. Hydroxychloroquine alone or in combination with quinacrine and/or chloroquine could be considered for refractory skin disease.
- Hematologic manifestations
  1. Corticosteroids are first-line therapy.
  2. Azathioprine can be used for thrombocytopenia or hemolytic anemia. Check for TPMT genetic mutation before the first use.
  3. Intravenous immunoglobulin (IVIG) or rituximab may be considered for severe leukopenia, autoimmune hemolytic anemia, or autoimmune thrombocytopenia.
- Central nervous system manifestations.
  1. Headaches are treated symptomatically. Most headaches will not be SLE-related and should be treated accordingly.
  2. Anticonvulsants and antipsychotics may be indicated.
  3. Standard therapy for other neuropsychiatric SLE symptoms is not established.
- Renal disease (Class III, IV or IV/V with cellular crescents lupus nephritis; see Table 1S-38). INDUCTION: 6-month treatment
  1. The typical treatment induction period is 6 months. The use of intravenous cyclophosphamide (CYC) with corticosteroids given at monthly intervals is more effective in preserving renal function than is treatment with glucocorticoids alone. Low-dose "Euro-Lupus" protocol may be equally efficacious and less toxic for certain populations (e.g., Caucasians) than high-dose regimen. MMF is considered

equivalent to CYC based on high-quality studies, with better tolerability and fertility profile. MMF may be preferred in African Americans and Hispanics. MMF or azathioprine is a good option for treatment maintenance.
Severe nonrenal organ disease:
  1. Evidence from systematic randomized controlled trials for nonrenal lupus treatment is comparatively limited.
  2. High-dose intravenous CYC is used as induction treatment. Azathioprine or MMF may be used as maintenance.
  3. IVIG may be considered in severe disease especially when concomitant infection is present.
  4. Plasmapheresis or plasma exchange may be considered in critical situation: first-line therapy in Guillain-Barre syndrome, TTP, second line for SLE-related hemolytic anemia, cerebritis, and DAH. Infectious complications are common.
- New therapy
  1. Belimumab (decreases activation of B cells): When used in addition to standard therapy, patients on belimumab showed improvement in cutaneous and musculoskeletal disease. Belimumab-treated patients had decreased SLE activity, a reduced time to disease flare, and lower glucocorticoid exposure. Safety data were good. Patients with CNS or serious kidney disease were excluded.
  2. Abatacept (downregulates T cell activation): limited data about improvement in arthritis, fatigue, sleep if added to routine therapy. Interest in studying the molecule in lupus nephritis is ongoing; limited study data are not positive.
Rituximab (anti-CD 20 monoclonal antibody, targets B cells): randomized controlled trials for rituximab as an adjunct induction agent were negative in terms of both renal and nonrenal outcomes.

DISPOSITION

- Most patients with SLE experience remissions and exacerbations.
- Five-year survival rate has improved to more than 90% in patients with newly diagnosed SLE since the advent of potent immunosuppressive therapy. The 15-year survival rate is now 85%.
- Early death related to SLE activity and infections; late death due to CVD.
- Lupus nephritis progression rate to ESRD in 10% to 30% within 15 years.
- African Americans, Asian Americans, and Hispanic Americans in general have a worse prognosis. The leading cause of death in SLE patients in developed countries is premature atherosclerosis. The quality of life for many SLE patients is poor due to fatigue, chronic pain, and cognitive impairment.

TABLE 1S-36 Indications for Immunosuppressive Therapy in Systemic Lupus Erythematosus

General Indications

Involvement of major organs or extensive involvement of nonmajor organs (skin) refractory to other agents, or both

Failure to respond to or inability to taper corticosteroids to acceptable doses for long-term use

Specific Organ Involvement

Renal

Proliferative or membranous nephritis (nephritic or nephritic syndrome), or both

Hematologic

Severe thrombocytopenia (platelets <20,000/mm^3)

Thrombotic thrombocytopenic purpura–like syndrome

Severe hemolytic or aplastic anemia, or immune neutropenia not responding to glucocorticoids

Pulmonary

Lupus pneumonitis or alveolar hemorrhage, or both

Cardiac

Myocarditis with depressed left ventricular function, pericarditis with impending tamponade

Gastrointestinal

Abdominal vasculitis

Nervous system

Transverse myelitis, cerebritis, optic neuritis, psychosis refractory to corticosteroids, mononeuritis multiplex, severe peripheral neuropathy

From Firestein GS et al: *Kelly's textbook of rheumatology,* ed 9, Philadelphia, 2013, Saunders.

TABLE 1S-37 Recommended Immunosuppressive Therapy for Major Organ Involvement in Systemic Lupus Erythematosus

Disease Severity	Induction Therapy	Maintenance Therapy
Mild	High-dose GC (0.5-1 mg/kg/day prednisone ×4-6 wk, tapered to 0.125 mg/kg every other day within 3 mo) alone or in combination with AZA (1-2 mg/kg/day)	Low-dose GC (prednisone ≤0.125 mg/kg on alternative days) alone or with AZA (1-2 mg/kg/day)
	If no remission within 3 mo, treat as moderately severe	Consider further gradual tapering at the end of each year of remission
Moderate	MMF (2 g/day) (or AZA) with GC as above; if no remission after the first 6-12 mo, treat as severe	MMF tapered to 1.5 g/day for 6-12 mo and then to 1 g/day; consider further tapering at the end of each year in remission. Alternative: AZA (1-2 mg/kg/day)
Severe	Pulse IV-CYC alone or in combination with pulse IV-MP for the first 6 mo (background GC 0.5 mg/kg/day for 4 wk, then taper)	Quarterly pulses of IV-CYC for at least 1 year beyond remission
	If no response, consider adding RTX or switch to MMF	Alternative: AZA (1-2 mg/kg/day), MMF (1-2 g/day)

AZA, Azathioprine; *CYC,* cyclophosphamide; *GC,* glucocorticoid; *IV,* intravenous; *MMF,* mycophenolate mofetil; *MP,* methylprednisolone; *RTX,* rituximab.
From Firestein GS et al: *Kelley's textbook of rheumatology,* ed 9, Philadelphia, 2013, Saunders.

TABLE 1S-38 Severity of Lupus Nephritis*

Proliferative Disease

Mild	Type III without severe histologic features (e.g., crescents, fibrinoid necrosis); low chronicity index (i.e., ≤3); normal renal function; nonnephrotic-range proteinuria
Moderately severe	Mild disease as defined above with partial or no response after the initial induction therapy or delayed remission (>12 months), or
	Focal proliferative nephritis with adverse histologic features or reproducible increase of at least 30% in serum creatinine levels, or
	Diffuse proliferative nephritis (class IV) without adverse histologic features
Severe	Moderately severe as defined above but not remitting after 6 to 12 months of therapy, or
	Proliferative disease with impaired renal function and fibrinoid necrosis or crescents in >25% of glomeruli, or
	Mixed membranous and proliferative nephritis, or
	Proliferative nephritis with high chronicity alone or in combination with high activity (chronicity index >4 or chronicity index >3 and activity index >10), or
	Rapidly progressive glomerulonephritis (doubling of serum creatinine within 2 to 3 months)

Membranous Nephropathy

Mild	Nonnephrotic-range proteinuria with normal renal function
Moderate	Nephrotic-range proteinuria with normal renal function at presentation
Severe	Nephrotic-range proteinuria with impaired renal function at presentation (at least 30% increase in serum creatinine)

*Concomitant therapy with corticosteroids or other immunosuppressive drugs may modify urinary sediment and/or histologic findings and should be taken into consideration.
From Hochberg MC et al: *Rheumatology,* ed 5, St Louis, 2011, Mosby.

REFERRAL

- Rheumatology consultation for all patients with SLE
- Hematology consultation for patients with significant hematologic abnormalities (e.g., severe hemolytic anemia or thrombocytopenia)
- Nephrology consultation in patients with proteinuria and/or suspected renal involvement
- Dermatology consultation for patients with unexplained or unusual skin rash
- Cardiology consultation for patients with lupus carditis, arrhythmias

! PEARLS & CONSIDERATIONS

- Arthritis in SLE often has no prolonged morning stiffness and is not erosive on x-rays; reversible joint deformities in lupus are termed Jaccoud's arthropathy.
- Myocardial infarction is 50 times more common in young female patients than in age-matched control group.
- Prevent adverse effects of medications: consider prophylaxis for infections and appropriate vaccinations, ensure yearly Pap and other cancer screening as clinically indicated; for patients taking CYC, intervention to preserve bladder and fertility should be considered; manage bone health.

EBM EVIDENCE

Available at www.expertconsult.com

SUGGESTED READINGS
Available at www.expertconsult.com

RELATED CONTENT
Systemic Lupus Erythematosus (Patient Information)

AUTHOR: **KATARZYNA GILEK-SEIBERT, M.D., RH.M.S.U.S.**

 **BASIC INFORMATION**

DEFINITION

Takayasu's arteritis is a rare type of chronic idiopathic systemic granulomatous large-vessel vasculitis that primarily affects the aorta and its main branches. It often presents as a pulseless disease caused by widespread arterial stenosis.

SYNONYMS

Pulseless disease
Aortitis syndrome
Aortic arch arteritis
Nonspecific aortoarteritis

ICD-10CM CODES
M31.4 Aortic arch syndrome [Takayasu]

EPIDEMIOLOGY & DEMOGRAPHICS

Takayasu's arteritis is the third most common childhood vasculitis worldwide, although it is relatively uncommon in Europe and North America. Most cases have been reported in Japan, China, India, and Mexico. There is typically a considerable delay to diagnosis in Western populations as opposed to Asian countries, owing in large part to the increased incidence in Asia.
INCIDENCE: Incidence in the United States is 2.6/1 million persons.
PREDOMINANT SEX AND AGE: The female/male ratio is 8:1. The age of onset is usually between 10 and 40 yr of age, with three quarters of patients presenting between the age of 10 and 20 years old.

PHYSICAL FINDINGS & CLINICAL PRESENTATION

According to the clinical manifestations, Takayasu's arteritis can be divided into five groups:
  Type I: Cerebral ischemic type
  Type II: Hypertensive type
  Type III: Limb ischemic type
  Type IV: Aneurysm type
  Type V: Cardiopulmonary vascular and visceral vascular type
- Takayasu's arteritis is typically divided into systemic and occlusive stages, with the occlusive stage characterized by ischemia and symptoms from arterial occlusion. Table 1T-1 summarizes common symptoms and signs in Takayasu's arteritis.
- The systemic stage of Takayasu's arteritis manifests as nonspecific inflammatory symptoms, including the following:
  1. Low-grade fever
  2. Malaise
  3. Weight loss
  4. Fatigue
  5. Arthralgia and myalgia
- The occlusive stage of Takayasu's arteritis may progress to stenosis or aneurysm of the aorta and its primary branches, and may manifest as a variety of clinical signs and symptoms, such as:
  1. Arm or leg claudication, weakness, and numbness
  2. Amaurosis fugax, diplopia, headache, orthostasis, vertigo, memory loss, trouble thinking, or syncope
  3. Angina or myocardial infarction
  4. Vascular bruits of the carotid artery, subclavian artery, and aorta
  5. Discrepancy of blood pressures between the upper extremities, typically of ≥10 mm Hg
  6. Diminished or absent pulses, ischemic ulcerations, or gangrene in advanced disease
  7. Hypertension
  8. Retinopathy
  9. Aortic insufficiency as a result of aortic root dilatation and aneurysm formation
  10. Weakness of the arterial walls may give rise to localized aneurysms/dissection.

ETIOLOGY

- The cause of Takayasu's arteritis is poorly understood. Cell-mediated mechanisms (cytotoxic T cell, macrophage, natural killer cells, and others) are thought to be important to the pathogenesis. Positive associations with HLA-B52, HLA-B39, and HLA-B67 have been identified, suggesting an immunogenetic component.
- Cytokines (such as tumor necrosis factor-alpha [TNF-α], interleukin-6 [IL-6], and interferon-gamma [IFN-γ]), a variety of chemokines, and other proteins (including perforin and matrix metalloproteinases) are involved in induction and amplification of the inflammatory response and tissue injury. Infiltration by inflammatory cells (lymphocytes, macrophages, and multinucleated giant cells) into the vasa vasorum and media of the large elastic arteries (Fig. E1T-2) leads to production of matrix metalloproteinases (MMP), which cause destruction of elastic fibers in the arterial wall, neovascularization, and other inflammatory changes. An intermediate stage, driven in part by TNF-alpha, leads to mucopolysaccharide deposition and proliferation of fibroblasts and smooth muscle cells causing intimal hypertrophy. With chronic disease, inflammatory lesions progress to either thick fibrotic calcified narrowings (≥90% of cases) or aneurysms if fibrosis is insufficient and the arterial wall is instead thinned and dilated (≥25% of cases).
- Infection, in particular, tuberculosis, has been implicated in the pathogenesis of Takayasu's disease with several studies reporting an increased incidence of caseating granulomas in Takayasu patients. Additional immunologic studies lend support to a pathogenic role of CD4 and CD8 T-cells in this patient population.

TABLE 1T-1 Common Symptoms and Signs (%) in Takayasu's Arteritis

Symptom/Sign	Study					
	Japan (n = 52)	India (n = 106)	China (n = 530)	Korea (n = 129)	USA (n = 60)	Mexico (n = 107)
Fatigue/constitutional	27%	—	—	34%	43%	78%
Weight loss	—	9%	—	11%	20%	22%
Musculoskeletal	6%	5%	—	—	53%	53%
Claudication	13%	—	25%	21%	90%	29%
Headache	31%	44%	—	60%	42%	57%
Visual changes	6%	12%	10%	20%	30%	8%
Syncope/dizziness	40%	26%	14%	36%	35%	13%
Palpitations	23%	19%	—	23%	10%	43%
Dyspnea	21%	26%	11%	42%	—	72%
Carotidynia	21%	—	—	2%	32%	—
Hypertension	33%	77%	60%	40%	35%	72%
Bruit	—	35%	58%	37%	80%	94%
Decreased pulses	62%	—	37%	55%	60%	96%
Asymmetric blood pressure	—	—	—	—	47%	

From Hochberg MC et al: *Rheumatology*, ed 5, St Louis, 2011, Mosby.

TABLE 1T-2 Pathologic Characteristics of Selected Forms of Vasculitis

	Takayasu's Arteritis	Polyarteritis Nodosa	Wegener's Granulomatosis	Churg-Strauss Syndrome	Henoch-Schönlein Purpura	Cutaneous Leukocytoclastic Angiitis
Vessels involved	Elastic (large) or muscle (medium-sized) arteries	Medium-sized and small muscle arteries	Small arteries and veins; sometimes medium-sized vessels	Small arteries and veins; sometimes medium-sized vessels	Capillaries, venules, arterioles	Capillaries, venules, arterioles
Organ involvement	Aorta, aortic arch and major branches, pulmonary arteries	Skin, peripheral nerve, gastrointestinal tract, other viscera	Upper respiratory tract, lungs, kidneys, skin, eyes	Upper respiratory tract, lungs, heart, peripheral nerves	Skin, joints, gastrointestinal tract, kidneys	Skin, joints
Type of vasculitis and inflammatory cells	Granulomatous with some giant cells; fibrosis in chronic stages	Necrotizing, with mixed cellular infiltrate	Necrotizing or granulomatous (or both); mixed cellular infiltrate plus occasional eosinophils	Necrotizing or granulomatous (or both); prominent eosinophils and other mixed infiltrate	Leukocytoclastic, with some lymphocytes and variable eosinophils; IgA deposits in affected tissues	Leukocytoclastic, with occasional eosinophils

From Goldman L, Schafer AI: *Goldman's Cecil medicine*, ed 24, Philadelphia, 2012, Saunders.

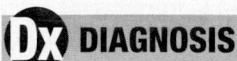 **DIAGNOSIS**

Diagnostic criteria for Takayasu's arteritis were established by the American College of Rheumatology in 1990. A diagnosis is made if at least three of the six criteria are present; this results in a sensitivity of 91% and specificity of 98%. The criteria are:

- Age of disease onset <40 yr
- Claudication of the extremities
- Decreased brachial artery pulse
- Systolic blood pressure difference ≥10 mm Hg between left and right arms
- Bruit over one or both of the subclavian arteries or the abdominal aorta
- Abnormal arteriogram, not related to arteriosclerosis or fibromuscular dysplasia

DIFFERENTIAL DIAGNOSIS

Table 1T-2 describes pathologic characteristics of selected forms of vasculitis. Other causes of inflammatory arteritis must be excluded:

- Temporal arteritis (giant cell arteritis)
- Syphilis
- Tuberculosis
- Systemic lupus erythematosus
- Rheumatoid arthritis
- Buerger's disease
- Behçet's disease
- Marfan syndrome
- Ehlers-Danlos syndrome
- Cogan's syndrome
- Kawasaki disease
- Spondyloarthropathies

WORKUP

Any young patient with findings of absent pulses and loud bruits merits a workup for Takayasu's arteritis. The workup generally includes blood testing to look for signs of inflammation as well as imaging studies. An angiogram continues to be the diagnostic gold standard; however, due to advances in noninvasive vascular imaging, modalities such as magnetic resonance and computed tomography angiography (MRA and CTA), ultrasound, and FDG-PET are commonly used for diagnosis as well as in serial monitoring of disease activity.

LABORATORY TESTS

- Erythrocyte sedimentation rate (ESR) and serum C-reactive protein levels are usually elevated, but can be normal even in the setting of active vasculitis.
- A CBC may reveal a normal or elevated white blood cell count as well as anemia.
- Immunologic studies may include elevated immunoglobulins (IgG and IgA) and complement components (C3 and C4).
- Hypercoagulation and increase in platelet aggregation
- Recent studies have attempted to establish a link between elevated levels of various interleukins and other inflammatory markers and active disease.

IMAGING STUDIES

- Imaging of the entire aorta and major branch vessels using angiography, CTA or MRA
- CTA can detect changes in the vessel wall and provide an accurate representation of luminal diameters.
- Cardiovascular magnetic resonance (CMR) provides information on vessel lumen and wall thickening, cardiac morphology and function, and myocardial tissue characterization.
- Angiography (Fig. 1T-3) can show the narrowing of the aorta and its branches, aneurysm formation, poststenotic dilation, and the development of any collateral circulation. Angiographic findings are classified into five types:
  1. Type I: lesions that involve only branches of the aortic arch
  2. Type IIa: lesions that involve the ascending aorta, the aortic arch, and its branches

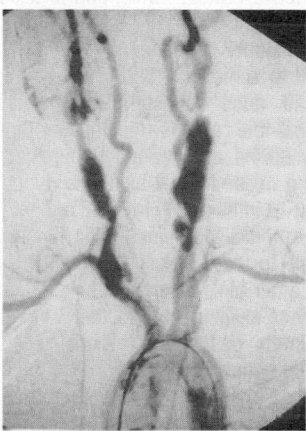

FIGURE 1T-3 Angiogram of a child with Takayasu's arteritis that shows massive bilateral carotid dilation, stenosis, and poststenotic dilation. (From Behrman RE: *Nelson textbook of pediatrics*, ed 16, Philadelphia, 2000, Saunders.)

  3. Type IIb: lesions from IIa plus the thoracic descending aorta
  4. Type III: lesions that involve the thoracic descending aorta, abdominal aorta, and/or renal arteries
  5. Type IV: lesions that involve the abdominal aorta and/or renal arteries
  6. Type V: lesions that involve the entire aorta and its branches
- Chest radiography: pathologic changes of the aorta are often visible, with areas of alternating stenosis and dilation seen. Segmental calcification outlining areas of aortic narrowing is characteristic of Takayasu's disease.
- Ultrasound: carotid, thoracic, and abdominal ultrasound are useful adjunctive imaging studies to diagnose the occlusive disease that results from Takayasu's arteritis. The addition of Doppler is helpful to assess blood flow and absent pulses.

- Positron emission tomography using radioisotope fluorodeoxyglucose (FDG-PET) as a marker for tissue with high glucose uptake has shown promising results in terms of specificity and sensitivity.

Rx TREATMENT

- To date there have been no controlled clinical trials evaluating the efficacy or safety of different agents in the acute or chronic treatment of Takayasu's arteritis.

ACUTE GENERAL Rx

- High-dose glucocorticoids are first-line therapy for suppressing systemic symptoms and stopping disease progression. Prednisone (40-60 mg PO daily or 1 mg/kg/day) can be used for 3 months or intravenous steroids can be administered initially.
- Patients are monitored for symptoms and the ESR is followed. Attempts to taper prednisone can be made with resolution of constitutional symptoms, significant decline in the ESR and C-reactive protein levels, and in accordance with imaging studies.
- The majority of patients require a second agent to achieve and sustain remission with steroid dose reduction. Commonly used second-line agents include methotrexate, azathioprine, and cyclophosphamide.
- Strong observational evidence supports use of TNF-α inhibitors in treating patients refractory to initial therapies and in those patients unable to taper steroids. Limited experience with other biologic agents, including the IL-6 inhibitor tocilizumab and the B-cell inhibitor rituximab, has shown promising results in certain patient groups.

CHRONIC Rx

Patients with Takayasu's arteritis are monitored closely for signs of relapse and disease complications with clinical assessment, inflammatory biomarkers (e.g., ESR and CRP), and imaging.

Multiple indexes exist for the assessment of disease activity, including the NIH criteria for active disease, the Disease Extent Index-Takayasu (DEI-Tak), and the Indian Takayasu's Arteritis Score (ITAS).

- Treatment of hypertension in these patients can be difficult, especially since typically there is concurrent glucocorticoid therapy and there is the potential for renovascular hypertension. Special monitoring should be employed when using ACE inhibitors due to the high frequency of renal artery stenosis in this population.
- Percutaneous angioplasty or bypass grafts should be considered for irreversible arterial stenoses with severe ischemia (cardiac or cerebral), severe hypertension in renal artery stenosis, or aneurysmal enlargement with risk of rupture. Five-year arterial complication rate after surgical or endovascular revascularization is 44%; the likelihood of complications increases sevenfold when inflammation is present at the time of revascularization.
- There have been positive data regarding drug-eluting stents, and in particular sirolimus-covered stents, likely related to the synergistic effect of its antiproliferative and immunosuppressive properties.
- Studies of coronary artery angioplasty and stenting in this population are limited, due to a high frequency of coronary lesions that are near the ostia; a large number of these patients have surgical interventions as opposed to percutaneous interventions.
- Aortic regurgitation may require valve replacement or repair by surgery, although the need to manipulate friable tissue can lead to complications such as valvular detachment after replacement.

DISPOSITION

- Immunosuppressant therapy may achieve clinical remission.
- No studies have proved that treatment results in regression of stenosis, although there are limited case reports describing the return of pulses with treatment.
- With the addition of a second agent for patients with treatment resistance or relapse, 50% remission has been seen.
- Quality of life is comparable to that of patients with rheumatoid arthritis or ankylosing spondylitis.
- Mortality results are mixed, with high rates in reports from Asia and lower rates in studies performed in the United States (2%). In the absence of major complications (MI, stroke, severe HTN, heart failure, aneurysm), 5-year survival rates reach 95%. In the presence of major complications, 5-year survival is 50% to 70%.

- Death can occur suddenly from a ruptured aneurysm, a myocardial infarction, or a cerebrovascular accident.

Pregnancy: Patients with Takayasu's arteritis are generally advised against pregnancy, as it can seriously affect both the mother and the child. Heart failure, embolism, and thrombosis are common complications during pregnancy. If a pregnant woman is diagnosed with the disease, oxytocin should be injected to the corpus uteri directly (when needed), and the intravenous route should be avoided. It is important to maintain the mother's blood pressure in a stable range and to avoid fluctuations in hemodynamics. Also vaginal delivery should be avoided, and cesarean section should be adopted.

REFERRAL

Whenever the diagnosis of vasculitis is suspected, a rheumatology consultation is appropriate. Vascular surgery and cardiology consultations are recommended for any evidence of carotid, peripheral, or coronary artery disease or if a large abdominal aneurysm is found.

! PEARLS & CONSIDERATIONS

With long-term glucocorticoid use, consider measures to protect against bone loss. Bisphosphonates have been studied prospectively with corticosteroid use in this fashion; remember to ensure adequate dietary calcium and vitamin D intake as well.

COMMENTS

The long-term prognosis of patients with treated Takayasu's disease varies by geography, and 10-yr survival ranges from 80% to 96%.

SUGGESTED READINGS

Available at www.expertconsult.com

RELATED CONTENT

Vasculitis (Related Key Topic)

AUTHORS: **IHAB ALOMARI, M.D.,** and **PRANAV M. PATEL, M.D.**

BASIC INFORMATION

DEFINITION

Takotsubo cardiomyopathy, also known as stress cardiomyopathy (SC), is a syndrome characterized by transient systolic dysfunction and ballooning of the apical and/or mid segments of the left ventricle (LV) that mimics acute myocardial infarction (MI) but in the absence of obstructive coronary artery disease with acute ECG changes including ST segment elevation or depression, in the absence of recent head trauma, intracranial hemorrhage, pheochromocytoma, myocarditis, or hypertrophic cardiomyopathy. Typically, but not always, it is preceded by severe illness or intense emotional, physical, or psychological stress. Initially described in the 1990s in Japan, on left ventriculography this irreversible cardiomyopathy has a distinctive shape similar to a *tako-tsubo* pot with a narrow neck and round bottom, used by fishermen to trap octopi.

SYNONYMS

Stress cardiomyopathy (SC)
Left ventricular apical ballooning syndrome (LVABS)
Broken heart syndrome

ICD-10CM CODES
I51.81 Takotsubo syndrome

EPIDEMIOLOGY & DEMOGRAPHICS

INCIDENCE: Uncertain, although increasingly reported. The recurrence rate is 11.4% over 4 yr after initial presentation. Occurs mostly in summer; fewest cases in winter.
PREVALENCE: Studies suggest that it comprises 0.7% to 2.5% of cases presenting with acute coronary syndrome (ACS).
PREDOMINANT SEX AND AGE: Postmenopausal women (90%) are predominantly affected. Mean age 66.8 years
RISK FACTORS: Frequently, but not always, triggered by severe medical illness or intense emotional or physical stress (death of loved ones, domestic abuse, fierce arguments, financial hardships, etc.)

PHYSICAL FINDINGS & CLINICAL PRESENTATION

- Acute substernal chest pain, dyspnea, syncope, shock, electrocardiographic (ECG) changes, or elevated cardiac biomarkers; similar to an acute MI.
- Heart failure, a frequent complication (30%) of takotsubo, is seen mostly in patients with other comorbidities and poor functional class. Recovery of function within a few days or weeks after admission is typical. In one experimental study, resolution was described as immediate after injection of adenosine.

Overall prognosis is no longer thought to be benign:
- Even short-term LV dysfunction can lead to thromboembolic phenomena. Anticoagulation is recommended for certain patients.
- Serious in-hospital complications requiring mechanical support are seen as frequently as with ACS patients.

ETIOLOGY

Not well understood. Hypotheses include excessive catecholamine release, coronary artery spasm, and/or microvascular disease. Unknown why women are more commonly affected or why the apex and/or mid cavity are affected. Fig. 1T-4 depicts the interplay among triggers, pathogenic factors, and predisposing factors in SC.

Several mechanisms have been advocated for acute and reversible coronary microvascular dysfunction:
- Acute microvascular spasm.
- Excessive sympathetic stimulation may induce myocardial metabolic impairment and stunning. Neurogenic stunned myocardium caused by an acute cardiac autonomic dysfunction.
- Coronary artery disease with aborted myocardial infarction. Transient coronary occlusion by a fast-dissolving clot. Spontaneous reperfusion.

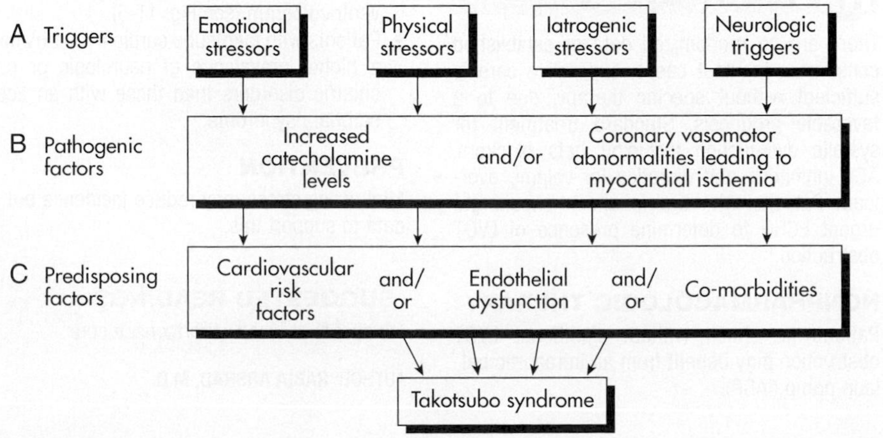

- Occurrence in postmenopausal women may support the hypothesis of stress-mediated vasoconstriction enhanced by estrogen depletion
- Studies have documented elevated plasma norepinephrine and epinephrine levels in Takotsubo cardiomyopathy.
- Increased serum concentrations of catecholamines have been shown to generate direct myocyte injury. Oxidation of catecholamines results in the formation of highly toxic substances and free radicals, causing intracellular calcium overload and myocardial cell damage. The typical histologic signs of catecholamine toxicity, which are described as focal, mononuclear, inflammatory areas of fibrotic response and characteristic contraction bands, are also reported to be present in takotsubo cardiomyopathy.
- Several studies have indicated that beta-adrenoceptor stimulation is associated with alteration in gene expression of Ca^{2+}-regulatory proteins, which are crucial for contractile function.
- More recently, a catecholamine disorder of glucose metabolism has been suggested on the basis of decreased LV apical ^{18}F-fluorodeoxyglucose uptake on positron emission PET scanning.
- Increased beta-adrenoreceptors in the apex and increased surface area of the apex due to trabeculations have also been proposed.

DIAGNOSIS

Mayo Clinic proposed criteria (2008) for diagnosis of SC: All 4 criteria required to make diagnosis.
- Transient hypokinesis, akinesis, or dyskinesis in the left ventricular mid segments with or without apical involvement (Fig. 1T-5); regional wall motion abnormalities (RWMA) that extend beyond a single epicardial vascular distribution; and frequently, but not always, a stressful trigger.
- Absence of obstructive coronary disease or angiographic evidence of acute plaque rupture.
- New ECG abnormalities (ST-segment elevation and/or T-wave inversion) or modest elevation in cardiac troponins. Ogura and associates reported that the absence of reciprocal changes, the absence of abnormal Q wave, and the sum of ST-segment elevation in leads V4–6 more than the sum of ST-segment elevation in leads V1-3 identified takotsubo cardiomyopathy with a high sensitivity and specificity. Kosuge and associates recently reported that the combination of the presence of ST-segment depression in lead aVR and the absence of ST-segment elevation in lead V1 also showed a high sensitivity and specificity for diagnosing takotsubo cardiomyopathy. Q-T dispersion is more common in Takotsubo.
- Absence of pheochromocytoma or myocarditis.

A Triggers	Emotional stressors	Physical stressors	Iatrogenic stressors	Neurologic triggers

B Pathogenic factors	Increased catecholamine levels	and/or	Coronary vasomotor abnormalities leading to myocardial ischemia

C Predisposing factors	Cardiovascular risk factors	and/or	Endothelial dysfunction	and/or	Co-morbidities

Takotsubo syndrome

FIGURE 1T-4 The interplay among triggers, pathogenic factors, and predisposing factors in Takotsubo disease. (From Pelliccia F et al: Takotsubo syndrome (stress cardiomyopathy): an intriguing clinical condition in search of its identity, *Am J Med* 127:699-704, 2014.)

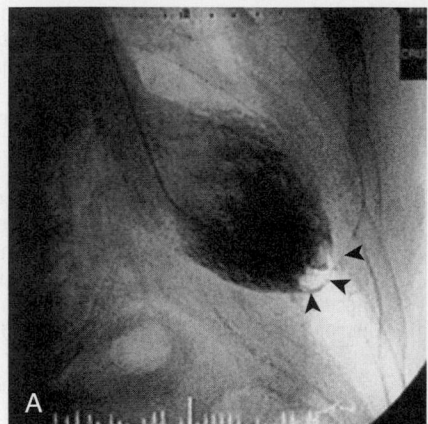
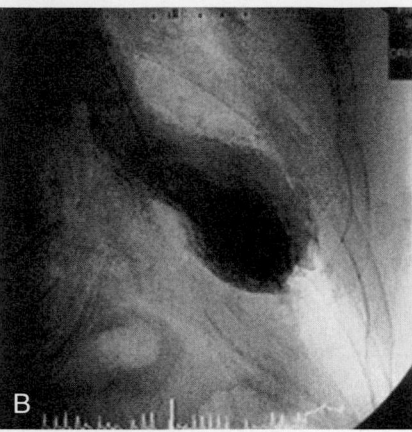

FIGURE 1T-5 A and **B,** Left ventriculogram showing apical ballooning characteristic of stress-induced cardiomyopathy. (From Mitsuma W et al: *JACC* 51(1): cover, 2008.)

- An inverted takotsubo pattern—mid ventricular ballooning with sparing of the basal and apical segments—atypical variant.
- The RWMA of the right ventricle is present in 30% of patients who tend to develop CHF and who have a poor outcome.

DIFFERENTIAL DIAGNOSIS
- Acute MI
- Cardiac syndrome X
- Prinzmetal's angina
- Myocarditis
- Cocaine abuse

WORKUP
- This should be suspected in postmenopausal women who present with ACS after intense stress.
- Cardiology consult should be immediately obtained.
- Significant CAD should be ruled out as an etiology of the cardiomyopathy, usually by coronary catheterization.

LABORATORY TESTS
- Cardiac biomarkers are often elevated, but typically less than MI. Beta natriuretic peptide (BNP) levels are also commonly elevated.
- Histopathologic findings include interstitial infiltrates of mononuclear lymphocytes and macrophages with fibrosis and contraction band necrosis. These findings are different from coagulation necrosis seen in typical atherosclerotic epicardial artery occlusion and myocardial infarction.

IMAGING STUDIES
- Typically diagnosed in the catheterization lab during left ventriculography, although echocardiography (ECHO) can also show the characteristic apical ballooning. Contrast ECHO is quite useful to exclude apical thrombus. Cardiovascular MRI at the time of initial clinical presentation may provide relevant func-

tional and tissue information that might aid in the establishment of the diagnosis of SC.
- Cardiac magnetic imaging (CMR) features helpful in diagnosis: absence of late gadolinium enhancement (LGE) in contrast to MI and consistent with myocardial viability.

COMPLICATIONS
- Approximately 20% include cardiogenic shock, heart failure, arrhythmias, intraventricular thrombus formation (incidence 2.5%), acute clinically significant mitral regurgitation, LV outflow tract (LVOT) obstruction, free wall rupture, and even death. An LV apical thrombus carries a great risk of cerebrovascular accident and distant embolization during the recovery phase.
- Risk score to predict likelihood of acute HF based on three variables: age >70 years, presence of physical stressor, and LV ejection fraction <40%.
- Prognosis is worse for males.
- Although overall prognosis is good, arrhythmic risk is increasingly being recognized. Vulnerable populations include patients with a QTc >500 msec.

Rx TREATMENT

There are no randomized data or established consensus. In most cases, supportive care is sufficient without specific therapy, due to a favorable prognosis. Standard treatment for systolic dysfunction including beta blockers, ACE inhibitors, and diuretics for volume overload. Patients who are in shock should get urgent ECHO to determine presence of LVOT obstruction.

NONPHARMACOLOGIC THERAPY
Patients in shock without significant LVOT obstruction may benefit from an intraaortic balloon pump (IABP).

ACUTE GENERAL Rx
- Patients who are hemodynamically stable should be started on a beta-blocker, ACE inhibitor, and diuretic if needed.
- Patients who are in shock and with significant LVOT obstruction may benefit from cautious fluid resuscitation (if no significant pulmonary congestion), and use of beta-blockers (can improve hemodynamics by resolution of the obstruction). The use of IABP in this case is controversial due to the potential worsening of LVOT obstruction.
- Patients with systolic anterior motion (SAM) of the anterior mitral valve leaflet or LVOT obstruction should not be exposed to inotropic agents even if they are in shock.

CHRONIC Rx
- Continued medical therapy and repeat ECHO (in 4-6 wk) to ensure normalization of systolic function (most patients normalize by this time).
- Duration of medical therapy is debatable. A period of 3 to 6 mo has been suggested.
- Three months of anticoagulation is suggested if an intraventricular thrombus is detected.
- Recently published data could not find the protective effect of β-blockers in preventing the occurrence or recurrence of SC.
- Ace inhibition is associated with increased survival.

DISPOSITION
Carries a favorable prognosis compared to STEMI or NSTEMI; in-hospital mortality is approximately 2%.

REFERRAL
Follow-up with a cardiologist is suggested.

❗ PEARLS & CONSIDERATIONS

COMMENTS
- The term *takotsubo* is the Japanese name for an octopus trap (*tako-tsubo*), which has a similar shape of the LV in systole during a left ventriculogram (see Fig. 1T-5).
- Patients with takotsubo cardiomyopathy have a higher prevalence of neurologic or psychiatric disorders than those with an acute coronary syndrome.

PREVENTION
Minimizing stress may reduce incidence but no data to support this.

SUGGESTED READINGS

Available at www.expertconsult.com

AUTHOR: **RABIA ARSHAD, M.D.**

BASIC INFORMATION

DEFINITION

Four species of adult tapeworm (cestodes) may infect humans as the definitive host: *Taenia saginata* (beef tapeworm), *Taenia solium* (pork tapeworm), *Diphyllobothrium latum* (fish tapeworm), and *Hymenolepis nana*. In addition, several tapeworms (*T. solium, T. crassiceps, T. multiceps*) can infect human tissue in their larval form, resulting in cysticercosis, and others infect in their intermediate forms, resulting in hydatid disease (see "Echinococcosis" in Section I). Table 1T-3 describes common cestode parasites of humans, their typical vectors, and their usual symptoms.

SYNONYMS

Cysticercosis (larval infection by *T. solium*)

ICD-10CM CODES
B68.0 *Taenia solium* taeniasis
B68.1 *Taenia saginata* taeniasis
B68.9 Taeniasis unspecified
B70.0 Diphyllobothriasis
B71.9 Cestode infection, unspecified

EPIDEMIOLOGY & DEMOGRAPHICS

INCIDENCE (IN U.S.):
- Diagnosed primarily in immigrants, particularly those from Latin America and Southeast Asia
- Varies widely by country of origin and dietary practices

PREVALENCE (IN U.S.):
- *T. saginata*: <0.1%
- *D. latum*: <0.05%
- *T. solium*: <0.1%
- *H. nana*: sporadic, often in setting of outbreak

PREDOMINANT SEX: Equal sex distribution
PREDOMINANT AGE:
- *T. saginata, T. solium, D. latum*: 20 to 39 yr of age

- *H. nana* in setting of institution outbreaks: children

PHYSICAL FINDINGS & CLINICAL PRESENTATION

Adult worms
1. Attach to bowel mucosa via suckers, hooks, or grooves depending on species
2. Feed and grow, producing digestive/body/reproductive segments called proglottids
3. Cause minimal or no symptoms or sequelae but occasionally can cause nausea, anorexia, or epigastric pain.

Cysticercosis: larval infection by *T. solium*
1. Mass lesions of brain (neurocysticercosis), soft tissue, viscera
2. Neurocysticercosis may cause seizures, hydrocephalus (due to ventricle obstruction)

Prolonged infection with *D. latum*
1. Vitamin B$_{12}$ deficiency
2. Megaloblastic anemia

ETIOLOGY

TAPEWORM:
- Adult worms consist of a head (scolex), neck, and hundreds or thousands of proglottids. Each proglottid contains male and female reproductive organs, including eggs.
- Adult worm resides in small or large bowel; proglottids and eggs are passed in stool.
- *T. saginata* may produce up to 100,000 eggs/proglottid and *T. solium* up to 50,000 eggs/proglottid.
- Eggs are ingested by the animal intermediate host (Fig. 1T-6).
- Eggs hatch into larvae.
- Larvae perforate the host intestinal wall and disseminate into skeletal muscle, brain, viscera.
- Develop into cysticerci (scolex inside a cyst) over several weeks
- Humans eat infected beef *(T. saginata)*, pork *(T. solium)*, or fish *(D. latum)*.

- Larval scolex attaches to intestinal wall and mature into adults within the GI lumen.
- *H. nana* infection is acquired by ingesting eggs in human or rodent feces.

CYSTICERCOSIS:
- Humans ingest eggs of *T. solium* in food contaminated with human feces that contain the eggs.
- Eggs hatch into larvae in gut and cross intestinal wall.
- Larvae disseminate widely through tissues (particularly soft tissue and CNS) forming cystic lesions containing either viable or nonviable larvae.

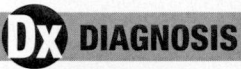 **DIAGNOSIS**

WORKUP

- Stool examination for eggs or proglottids (tapeworm)
  1. Eggs of *Taenia* spp. cannot be differentiated by microscopy, but the species can be identified through examination of the proglottids in stool.
  2. Eggs of *Taenia* spp. are round and measure 30 to 40 micrometers.
- Cerebral CT scan (neurocysticercosis)
- Serum antibody (neurocysticercosis) with high sensitivity with multiple cysts (94%) but low with a single cyst or calcified cysts (as low as 28%)
- CBC may show eosinophilia

IMAGING STUDIES

- Tapeworm: incidental finding on upper GI series
- Neurocysticercosis:
  1. Cerebral cysts are readily demonstrated by CT scan or MRI.
  2. Calcified lesions are an incidental finding

TABLE 1T-3 Common Cestode Parasites of Humans, Their Typical Vectors, and Their Usual Symptoms

Parasite Species	Developmental Stage Found in Humans	Common Name	Transmission Source	Symptoms Associated with Infection
Diphyllobothrium latum	Tapeworm	Fish tapeworm	Plerocercoid cysts in freshwater fish	Usually minimal; with prolonged or heavy infection, vitamin B$_{12}$ deficiency
Hymenolepis nana	Tapeworm, cysticercoids	Dwarf tapeworm	Infected humans	Mild abdominal discomfort
Taenia saginata	Tapeworm	Beef tapeworm	Cysts in beef	Abdominal discomfort, proglottid migration
Taenia solium	Tapeworm	Pork tapeworm	Cysticerci in pork	Minimal
Taenia solium (Cysticercus cellulosae)	Cysticerci	Cysticercosis	Eggs from infected humans	Local inflammation, mass effect; if in central nervous system, seizures, hydrocephalus, arachnoiditis
Echinococcus granulosus	Larval cysts	Hydatid cyst disease	Eggs from infected dogs	Mass effect leading to pain, obstruction of adjacent organs; less commonly, secondary bacterial infection, distal spread of daughter cysts
Echinococcus multilocularis	Larval cysts	Alveolar cyst disease	Eggs from infected canines	Local invasion and mass effect leading to organ dysfunction; distal metastasis possible
Taenia multiceps	Larval cysts	Coenurosis, bladder worm	Eggs from infected dogs	Local inflammation and mass effect
Spirometra mansonoides	Larval cysts	Sparganosis	Cysts from infected copepods, frogs, snakes	Local inflammation and mass effect

(Bennett JE et al: *Mandell, Douglas, and Bennett's principles and practice of infectious diseases,* ed 8, Philadelphia, 2015, WB Saunders.)

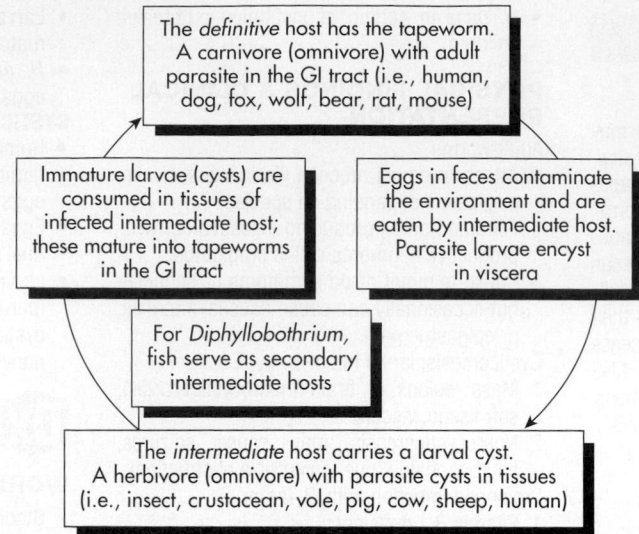

The *definitive* host has the tapeworm. A carnivore (omnivore) with adult parasite in the GI tract (i.e., human, dog, fox, wolf, bear, rat, mouse)

Immature larvae (cysts) are consumed in tissues of infected intermediate host; these mature into tapeworms in the GI tract

Eggs in feces contaminate the environment and are eaten by intermediate host. Parasite larvae encyst in viscera

For *Diphyllobothrium*, fish serve as secondary intermediate hosts

The *intermediate* host carries a larval cyst. A herbivore (omnivore) with parasite cysts in tissues (i.e., insect, crustacean, vole, pig, cow, sheep, human)

FIGURE 1T-6 Cestode parasites alternate larval and adult stages in two different hosts. *GI*, Gastrointestinal. (Bennett JE et al: *Mandell, Douglas, and Bennett's principles and practice of infectious diseases*, ed 8, Philadelphia, 2015, WB Saunders.)

 TREATMENT

ACUTE GENERAL Rx

- All adults and children with intestinal tapeworm infections should be treated with a single oral dose of praziquantel.
  1. *T. solium:* 5 to 10 mg/kg
  2. *T. saginata:* 5 to 10 mg/kg
  3. *D. latum:* 5 to 10 mg/kg
  4. *H. nana:* 25 mg/kg and a repeat dose 7 to 10 days later if heavy infection
- Praziquantel acts by causing changes in the teguments of the worms, allowing increased permeability to calcium ions, which then accumulate inside worm and cause paralysis.
- Repeat stool screening at 1 and 3 mo to confirm cure.
- Can use purgatives adjunctively to hasten clearance of deceased worms from intestine
- An alternative therapy to praziquantel for tapeworm infections is niclosamide, 2 g PO once for adults and 1 g for children 11 to 34 kg and 1.5 g for children over 34 kg.
- Therapy that may be considered for symptomatic cysticercosis:
  1. May regress spontaneously (i.e., no treatment)

2. Surgery, especially in cases of ventricular obstruction (neurocysticercosis)
3. Albendazole 10 to 15 mg/kg/day PO divided in two doses for 8 days
4. Praziquantel 50 to 100 mg/kg/day PO for 15 to 30 days divided in three doses
5. Use of steroids in neurocysticercosis may reduce CNS inflammation and increase levels of albendazole in CNS.
- Therapy contraindicated with:
  1. Ocular infections
  2. Cerebral infections in which local inflammation caused by destruction of the parasite may cause significant damage/inflammation
- Adjunctive antiepileptics may be necessary for neurocysticercosis

CHRONIC Rx

- Retreatment if required
- Avoidance of undercooked pork, meat, or fish
- Cysticercosis: proper hand washing, proper disposal of human waste

DISPOSITION

- Neurologic follow-up for patients with neurocysticercosis

- Ophthalmologic follow-up for patients with ocular involvement

REFERRAL

Patients treated for neurocysticercosis should be evaluated by a physician experienced in managing this infection, if possible.

❗ PEARLS & CONSIDERATIONS

COMMENTS

T. solium is the most dangerous of the tapeworms because of the potential for cysticercosis by means of autoinfection.

SUGGESTED READINGS

 Available at www.expertconsult.com

RELATED CONTENT

Tapeworm Infection (Patient Information)
Cysticercosis (Related Key Topic)

AUTHORS: **RUSSELL J. MCCULLOH, M.D.**

 **BASIC INFORMATION**

DEFINITION

Tardive dyskinesia (TD) is a syndrome of involuntary movements associated with the long-term use of antipsychotic medication, particularly first-generation antipsychotics. Patients exhibit rapid, repetitive, stereotypic movements that mostly involve the oral, lingual, trunk, and limb areas.

SYNONYMS

Orofacial dyskinesia
Tardive syndrome
TD

ICD-10CM CODES
G24.01 Drug induced subacute dyskinesia

EPIDEMIOLOGY & DEMOGRAPHICS

- The disorder is caused by dopamine-blocking antipsychotics (e.g., haloperidol) and antiemetics (e.g., metoclopramide, prochlorperazine, and promethazine).
- With first-generation antipsychotics, at least 20% of patients are affected with TD, and ~5% are expected to develop TD with each year of antipsychotic treatment.
- The incidence of TD with second-generation antipsychotics is reduced only by about one third. With the increasing use of these medications, TD remains a serious problem.
- Risk increases with the duration of antipsychotic treatment, in female and in elderly patients, in patients with brain damage or dementia, with concurrent anticholinergic use, and in patients with nonschizophrenia diagnoses.

PHYSICAL FINDINGS & CLINICAL PRESENTATION

- TD is classically described as a chronic condition of insidious onset, but symptoms are variable over time and may even improve despite continued antipsychotic therapy.
- The condition typically appears with the reduction or withdrawal of the antipsychotic medications.
- TD classically involves stereotypic movements of the mouth and tongue, including lip smacking and puckering, tongue twisting and protrusion, and facial grimacing.
- TD may also involve slow, writhing movements of the trunk or choreoathetotic movements of the fingers and toes.
- The involuntary mouth movements associated with TD may be suppressed by voluntary actions (e.g., putting food in the mouth, talking).
- Variants of TD with similar treatment include tardive dystonia (e.g., torticollis, blepharospasm), tardive myoclonus, tardive akathisia, and tardive tics.

ETIOLOGY

TD is caused by chronic exposure to dopamine receptor antagonists that is thought to result in the upregulation of dopamine receptors in the basal ganglia as well as damage to striatal cholinergic neurons. Dysfunction of striatal GABAergic interneurons has also been implicated. It has been proposed that dopamine receptor hypersensitivity and neurodegenerative changes might cause altered synaptic plasticity of excitatory synapses onto striatal interneurons, resulting in an imbalance between the direct and indirect basal ganglia pathways.

 **DIAGNOSIS**

DIFFERENTIAL DIAGNOSIS

- Acute extrapyramidal symptoms (e.g., short-term withdrawal dyskinesias, parkinsonism, akathisia)
- Basal ganglia movement disorders (e.g., Huntington's chorea, Tourette's syndrome, levodopa-induced dyskinesia in Parkinson's disease, Wilson's disease)
- Autoimmune diseases (Sydenham's chorea, multiple sclerosis)
- Other causes of neurologic damage (e.g., lead or mercury toxicity, HIV, neurosyphilis, head injury, neurodegeneration from illicit substances)
- Mannerisms associated with disorganized type or catatonic type schizophrenia
- Hyperthyroidism-induced choreoathetosis
- Edentulous dyskinesias and improperly fitted dentures
- Rabbit syndrome (a rare variant of extrapyramidal symptoms with rapid vertical orofacial movements without tongue involvement); may respond to anticholinergic agents

WORKUP

TD is a diagnosis of exclusion, with emphasis on a complete neuropsychiatric and medication history and a thorough physical examination.

IMAGING STUDIES

Standard brain imaging is normal in patients with TD.

Rx **TREATMENT**

ACUTE GENERAL Rx

- Treatment is predicated on prevention: limit the indications for antipsychotics; use the lowest effective dose; discontinue the drugs, when feasible; and monitor patients frequently. Anticholinergic medications may worsen symptoms.
- Switch to second-generation antipsychotics, if possible.

CHRONIC Rx

- If continued antipsychotic treatment is needed, switching to clozapine or quetiapine is the preferred initial treatment.
- For mild to moderate TD, clonazepam, amantadine, propranolol, levetiracetam, zonisamide, vitamin B_6, and gingko biloba may be helpful, although controlled trial evidence remains weak.
- For severe or persistent TD, tetrabenazine, a centrally acting synaptic dopamine depleter, is becoming a first-line treatment option. The prodrug of an isomer of tetrabenazine, valbenazine, was recently granted breakthrough drug status by the FDA.
- For disabling TD, deep brain stimulation of the subthalamic nucleus or internal globus pallidus seems to provide significant symptom reduction without exacerbation of psychiatric symptoms.
- TD is potentially irreversible in nearly two thirds of patients; thus, patients undergoing long term treatment with dopamine receptor-blocking medications require frequent monitoring and aggressive management at the onset of TD symptoms.

REFERRAL

Movement disorder specialist consultation if symptoms are severe

! **PEARLS & CONSIDERATIONS**

- After removal of the causative medication, symptoms of tardive dyskinesia can take months to resolve or may become permanent (higher risk in elderly, female sex, prolonged use, and higher dose of causative medication).
- First-generation antipsychotics should be resumed to treat TD in the absence of active psychosis only as a last resort for persistent, disabling, and treatment-resistant TD.
- Avoid anticholinergic medications (e.g., benztropine), which may exacerbate TD symptoms.
- Recent evidence suggests increased overall mortality among patients with TD, which highlights the need for referral for more aggressive specialized interventions.

SUGGESTED READINGS
Available at www.expertconsult.com

RELATED CONTENT
Tardive Dyskinesia (Patient Information)

AUTHOR: **JOHN A. GRAY, M.D., PH.D.**

BASIC INFORMATION

DEFINITION

Temporomandibular joint (TMJ) syndrome refers to a group of disorders leading to symptoms of the TMJ. Temporomandibular joint disorders (TMD) can be classified as intraarticular (within the joint) or extraarticular (involving the surrounding musculature).

SYNONYMS

Temporomandibular dysfunction
Painful temporomandibular joint
TMJ
Temporomandibular disorders (TMD)

ICD-10CM CODES
N26.60 Temporomandibular joint disorder, unspecified

EPIDEMIOLOGY & DEMOGRAPHICS

- 15% of the population have TMJ disorders.
- Females are affected more often than males (4:1 ratio).
- Occurs between the second and fourth decades of life.
- Usually unilateral, affecting either side with equal frequency.

PHYSICAL FINDINGS & CLINICAL PRESENTATION

- Often unilateral pain in the muscles of mastication, usually described as a "dull" ache
- Otalgia
- Odontalgia
- Headaches (frontal, temporal, retro-orbital)
- Tinnitus
- Dizziness
- Clicking or popping sounds with movement of the TMJ
- Joint locking
- Application of mild anterior pressure with a finger placed posteriorly to each tragus may result in tenderness, clicking, or crepitus.
- Limited range of motion of the TMJ
- Symptoms usually appear in association with a stressful life event

ETIOLOGY

- Multifactorial, encompassing local anatomic anomalies to systemic disease processes
- Myofascial pain-dysfunction syndrome: the most common cause of TMJ syndrome and results from teeth grinding and clenching the jaw (bruxism)
- Internal TMJ derangement: abnormal connection of the articular disk to the mandibular condyle
- Degenerative joint disease
- Rheumatoid arthritis
- Gouty arthritis
- Pseudogout
- Ankylosing spondylitis
- Trauma
- Prior surgery (orthodontic, intraarticular steroid injection)
- Tumors

DIAGNOSIS

Can be made based on history and physical examination in most cases.

DIFFERENTIAL DIAGNOSIS

Includes the list provided above. Myofascial pain-dysfunction syndrome, internal TMJ derangement, and degenerative joint disease represent >90% of all causes of TMJ syndrome. Others not mentioned include dental problems such as dental caries, loss of posterior teeth support, and Eagle's syndrome (stylohyoid syndrome, carotidynia, and trigeminal neuralgia). Alternative diagnoses such as otitis, mastoiditis, salivary gland disorders, migraine headache, sinusitis, posthepatic neuralgia, trigeminal neuralgia, glossopharyngeal neuralgia, and giant cell arteritis should always be excluded.

WORKUP

The diagnosis is based largely on history and physical examination findings. Radiographic imaging evaluation is used to exclude anatomic or systemic causes of disease when conservative management has failed.

LABORATORY TESTS

Laboratory examination is not very helpful.

IMAGING STUDIES

- Plain radiographs: the most common views are the panoramic, transorbital, and transpharyngeal in both opened and closed positions.
- Arthrography is helpful in looking for meniscus involvement but is seldom performed anymore.
- CT scan is highly accurate in diagnosing meniscal and osseous derangements of the TMJ.
- MRI is the procedure of choice and has replaced arthrography in cases of disabling pain or if locking occurs. It is used to determine disc position and morphology along with degenerative bony changes.

TREATMENT

NONPHARMACOLOGIC THERAPY

- Soft diet to rest the muscles of mastication
- Heat 15 to 20 min 4 to 6 times per day
- Massage of the masseter and temporalis muscles
- Formed splints or bite appliances to reduce compression of retrodiscal tissue (Fig. E1T-10)
- Range-of-motion exercises
- Cognitive-behavioral therapy and biofeedback have been shown to reduce pain.
- Acupuncture

ACUTE GENERAL Rx

- Nonsteroidal antiinflammatory drugs: ibuprofen 800 PO mg tid PRN, naproxen 500 mg PO bid prn, titrated to relieve symptoms
- Muscle relaxants at bedtime: diazepam 2.5 to 5 mg PO tid PRN or amitriptyline 5 to 100 mg PO qd PRN

- In degenerative joint disease of the TMJ, intraarticular steroid injection can be tried
- Botulism toxin injections into the masticatory muscles
- Arthrocentesis with joint lavage and lysis of adhesions (Fig. E1T-11)
- In patients with pain and clicking in the TMJ that is unresponsive to nonsurgical treatment, the disc should be repositioned arthroscopically or by open surgery (discoplasty) (see "Chronic Rx")

CHRONIC Rx

- Most of the above treatments are used for myofascial pain-dysfunction syndrome; however, they can be applied to other causes of TMJ syndrome. Surgery is usually a measure of last resort in patients who do not respond to nonpharmacologic and acute general treatment.
- Surgical procedures include:
  1. Meniscoplasty
  2. Meniscectomy
  3. Subcondylar osteotomy
  4. TMJ reconstruction

DISPOSITION

The course depends on the underlying etiology; however, less than 5% of adults with temporomandibular symptoms develop chronic symptoms.

REFERRAL

All patients with TMJ syndrome refractory to conservative nonpharmacologic and acute therapy should be referred to a periodontist, oral maxillofacial surgeon, or ear-nose-throat surgeon.

PEARLS & CONSIDERATIONS

Patients with rheumatoid arthritis involving the TMJ usually have bilateral involvement.

COMMENTS

Frequently, emotional stress initiates the myofascial pain-dysfunction, which accounts for 85% of all cases of TMJ syndrome.

SUGGESTED READINGS
Available at www.expertconsult.com

RELATED CONTENT
Temporomandibular Joint (TMJ) Syndrome (Patient Information)

AUTHORS: **RYAN W. ZUZEK, M.D.,** and **DOUGLAS BURTT, M.D.**

 **BASIC INFORMATION**

DEFINITION

Testicular neoplasms are primary cancers originating in a testis.

SYNONYMS

Testis tumor
Testicular neoplasms

ICD-10CM CODES

C62.00 Malignant neoplasm of unspecified undescended testis
C62.01 Malignant neoplasm of undescended right testis
C62.02 Malignant neoplasm of undescended left testis
C62.10 Malignant neoplasm of unspecified descended testis
C62.11 Malignant neoplasm of descended right testis
C62.12 Malignant neoplasm of descended left testis
D40.10 Neoplasm of uncertain behavior of unspecified testis
D40.11 Neoplasm of uncertain behavior of right testis
D40.12 Neoplasm of uncertain behavior of left testis

EPIDEMIOLOGY & DEMOGRAPHICS

INCIDENCE: 5.4 cases per 100,000 men annually. White men have the highest incidence at 6.3 cases/100,000 men. Testicular cancer is the most common cancer diagnosis in men between 15 and 35 yr. The incidence has been gradually increasing since 1975.
PREVALENCE: 1% to 2% of all cancers in males.
PREDOMINANT AGE: Can occur in any age but most common in young adults; average age for embryonal cell carcinoma: 30 yr; average age for seminoma: 36 yr.

PHYSICAL FINDINGS & CLINICAL PRESENTATION

- Testicular cancer typically presents as a painless mass in the testis. Any mass within the testicle should be considered cancer until proven otherwise. It may be found by the patient, who brings it to the attention of a physician, or it may be found by a physician on a routine examination.
- Symptoms other than scrotal or testicular swelling are typically absent unless the cancer has metastasized (10% of patients at diagnosis). Occasionally a patient may report scrotal fullness or heaviness. About 10% of patients present with acute pain. Back pain secondary to enlarged retroperitoneal lymph nodes can occur. Gynecomastia from tumors that secrete beta-human chorionic gonadotropin (hCG) is found in 5% of men with testicular cancer.
- Testicular palpation should be performed with two hands. Transillumination may distinguish a solid mass (e.g., cancer) and a fluid-filled lesion (e.g., hydrocele or spermatocele). The mass is nontender; indeed, it is less sensitive than a normal testicle.

ETIOLOGY, CLASSIFICATION, & PATHOLOGY

- Cryptorchidism (undescended testes) is a major risk factor even if corrected by orchiopexy; however, treatment of undescended testis before puberty decreases the risk of testicular cancer from fivefold to twofold. Other risk factors are family history (risk is 8 to 10 times as high in a brother of a person with testicular cancer), genetic disorders (Down's syndrome, testicular dysgenesis syndrome), Klinefelter's syndrome, infertility, tobacco use, and white race (risk is highest among whites and lowest among blacks).
- Classification: testicular cancers can be classified as pure seminomas or nonseminomatous germ cell tumors (embryonic carcinoma, choriocarcinoma, yolk sac carcinoma, teratoma).
- Pathology: germ cell tumors account for >95% of testicular cancers.

Cell Type	Frequency (%)
Seminoma	42
Embryonal cell carcinoma	26
Teratocarcinoma	26
Teratoma	5
Choriocarcinoma	1

- Other rare types:
  1. Yolk sac carcinoma.
  2. Mixed germ cell tumors.
  3. Carcinoid tumor.
  4. Sertoli cell tumors.
  5. Leydig cell tumors.
  6. Lymphoma.
  7. Metastatic cancer to the testes.
- TNM staging system for testicular cancer
  1. T_0: No apparent primary.
  2. T_1: Testis only (excludes rete testis).
  3. T_2: Beyond the tunica albuginea.
  4. T_3: Rete testis or epididymal involvement.
  5. T_4: Spermatic cord.
     1. Spermatic cord.
     2. Scrotum.
- N_0: No nodal involvement.
- N_1: Ipsilateral regional nodal involvement.
- N_2: Contralateral or bilateral abdominal or groin nodes.
- N_3: Palpable abdominal nodes or fixed groin nodes.
- N_4: Juxtaregional nodes.
- M_0: No distant metastases.
- M_1: Distant metastases present.

The clinical stages consist of stage I, with tumor confined to the testis; stage II, with positive regional lymph nodes; and stage III, with metastases. Figure 1T-12 shows the clinical staging of testicular cancer.

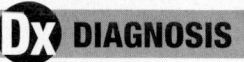 **DIAGNOSIS**

DIFFERENTIAL DIAGNOSIS

- Spermatocele.
- Varicocele.
- Hydrocele.
- Epididymitis/orchitis.
- Epidermoid cyst of the testicle.
- Epididymis tumors.
- Inguinal hernia.
- Hematocele or testicular rupture.
- Torsion of testicular appendage.
- Skin cancer.

WORKUP

Physical examination, laboratory tests, and imaging studies (see Section III, "Testicular Mass"). A radical inguinal orchiectomy is diagnostic and therapeutic. Immunohistochemical analysis is used to determine the histologic composition of the tumor. Staging involves CT of chest, abdomen, and pelvis and measurement of beta subunit of human chorionic gonadotropins (β-hCG), alpha-fetoprotein, and lactate dehydrogenase.

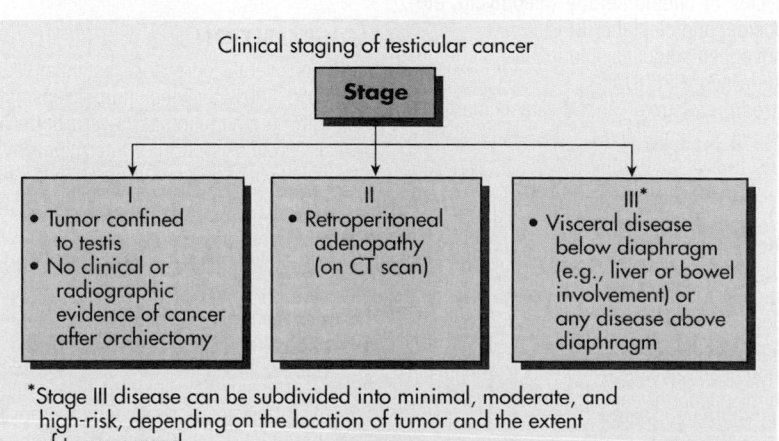

FIGURE 1T-12 Clinical Staging of Testicular Cancer. The AJCC TNM staging system is less commonly used, because it is based upon histologic evaluation of the orchidectomy specimen and retroperitoneal periaortic lymph node dissection. Because the latter may not be performed in every patient, the clinical staging system is generally more practical. (From Skarin AT. *Atlas of diagnostic oncology*, ed 4, St Louis, 2010, Mosby.)

LABORATORY TESTS

- Serum hCG: elevated in approximately 20% of patients with pure seminomas.
- Serum alpha-fetoprotein (AFP): elevated in nonseminoma tumors, never elevated in patients with pure seminomas.
  One or both of these tumor markers will be elevated in 70% of cases of testicular cancer.
- Serum lactate dehydrogenase (LDH) level: elevated with rapid turnover of malignant cells.
- Testicular biopsy contraindicated.

IMAGING STUDIES

- Testicular ultrasound.
- CT scan of chest, pelvis, and abdomen.
- MRI of the brain in patients with neurologic symptoms.
- PET scan is not recommended (frequent false positives).

(Rx) TREATMENT

- Seminoma
  1. Stage I: Most patients with clinical stage 1 are cured with orchiectomy. Radical orchiectomy plus one cycle of single agent carboplatin chemotherapy or radiation therapy (RT) to the para-aortic lymph nodes was the standard of treatment for many years but has been eliminated in many instances and most patients are treated with active surveillance post orchiectomy. More relapses are associated with surveil-lance (20% vs. 4% with radiotherapy or chemotherapy), but long-term survival approaches 100% irrespective of initial option chosen.[1]
  2. Stage IIA or IIB: RT or cisplatin-based chemotherapy (e.g., cisplatin, bleomycin, etoposide).
- Nonseminoma
  1. Stage IA: radical orchiectomy plus nerve sparing retroperitoneal lymph node dis-section (RPLND).
  2. Stage IB: Same as stage IA plus two cycles of chemotherapy (bleomycin, eto-poside, and cisplatin [BEP]).
  3. Advanced stages: cisplatin-based chemo-therapy or RPLND.
- Posttreatment surveillance for testicular can-cer survivors (annually).
  1. Fertility assessment.
  2. Physical examination and skin exam-ination (increased risk of dysplastic nevi).
  3. Testicular examination (3%-4% risk of second testicular cancer).
  4. Serum tumor markers (hCG, AFP).
  5. Abdominal and pelvic CT every 3 to 4 months for 2 years, every 6 to 12 months in third and fourth year, and annually thereafter.

[1]Hanna NH, Einhorn LH: Testicular cancer, discoveries and updates, *N Engl J Med* 371:2005-2016, 2014.

TABLE 1T-4 International Germ Cell Consensus Criteria for Testicular Cancer

Nonseminoma	Seminoma
Good Prognosis	
Testis/retroperitoneal primary	Any primary site
And	*And*
No nonpulmonary visceral metastases	No nonpulmonary visceral metastases
And	*And*
Good markers—all of	Normal AFP, any hCG, any LDH
• AFP < 1000 ng/mL and	
• hCG < 5000 IU/L (1000 ng/mL) and	
• LDH < 1.5 × upper limit of normal	
58% of nonseminomas	90% of seminomas
5-year PFS 89%	5-year PFS 82%
5-year survival 92%	5-year survival 86%
Intermediate Prognosis	
Testis/retroperitoneal primary	Any primary site
And	*And*
No nonpulmonary visceral metastases	Nonpulmonary visceral metastases
And	*And*
Intermediate markers—any of	Normal AFP, any hCG, any LDH
• AFP ≥ 1000 and ≤ 10,000 ng/mL or	
• hCG ≥ 5000 IU/L and ≤ 50,000 IU/L or	
• LDH ≥ 1.5 × normal and ≤ 10 × normal	
28% of nonseminomas	10% of seminomas
5-year PFS 75%	5-year PFS 67%
5-year survival 80%	5-year survival 72%
Poor Prognosis	
Mediastinal primary	No patients classified as
Or	poor prognosis
Nonpulmonary visceral metastases	
Or	
Poor markers—any of	
• AFP > 10,000 ng/mL or	
• hCG > 50,000 IU/L (10,000 ng/mL) or	
• LDH > 10 × upper limit of normal	
16% of nonseminomas	
5-year PFS 41%	
5-year survival 48%	

AFP, α-fetoprotein; *hCG,* human chorionic gonadotrophin; *LDH,* lactate dehydrogenase; *PFS,* progression-free survival.
From Skarin AT. *Atlas of diagnostic oncology,* ed 4, St Louis, 2010, Mosby.

DISPOSITION

- The overall cure for testicular cancer is >95% (80% for metastatic disease). Patients with pure seminomas have a better progno-sis. Prognosis can be determined by criteria established by the International Germ Cell Consensus Criteria (Table 1T-4). Because treatment produces favorable outcomes even in advanced stages, the U.S. Preventive Services Task Force recommends against screening asymptomatic men for testicu-lar cancer. There is also an increased risk for metabolic syndrome (insulin resistance, hypertension, dyslipidemia, abdominal obe-sity) after radiation or chemotherapy.
- Therapeutic radiation and chemotherapy are risk factors for cancers of thyroid, lymphoma, kidney, pancreas, stomach, and leukemia. There is also an increased risk for metabolic syndrome (insulin resistance, hypertension, dyslipidemia, abdominal obesity) after radia-tion or chemotherapy.

(EBM) EVIDENCE

Available at www.expertconsult.com

SUGGESTED READINGS

Available at www.expertconsult.com

RELATED CONTENT

Testicular Cancer (Patient Information)

AUTHOR: **FRED F. FERRI, M.D.**

 **BASIC INFORMATION**

DEFINITION

Testicular torsion is a twisting of the spermatic cord leading to cessation of testicular blood flow, ischemia, and infarction if left untreated.

SYNONYMS

Spermatic cord torsion

ICD-10CM CODES
N44.03 Torsion of testis, unspecified

EPIDEMIOLOGY & DEMOGRAPHICS

INCIDENCE: Affects one in 4000 males aged <25 yr
PREDOMINANT AGE: Two thirds of all cases occur between the ages of 12 and 18 yr, but may occur at any age, including antenatally.

PHYSICAL FINDINGS & CLINICAL PRESENTATION

- Typical sequence is sudden onset of hemiscrotal pain, then swelling, nausea, and vomiting without fever or urinary symptoms.
- Physical examination may reveal a tender firm testis, high-riding testis, horizontal lie of testis, absent cremasteric reflex, and no pain with elevation of testis. Absence of the cremasteric reflex (stroking or pinching the medial thigh normally causes contraction of the cremaster muscle and elevation of the testis) is the most sensitive physical finding.
- Painless testicular swelling occurs in 10%.
- One out of three patients reports previous episodes of spontaneously remitting scrotal pain.

- In the neonate, testicular torsion should be presumed in patients with a painless, discolored hemiscrotal swelling.
- In rare cases, torsion may involve an undescended testicle. In such situations an empty hemiscrotum is palpated together with a tender lump in the inguinal area.

ETIOLOGY

- There are two types of testicular torsion: extravaginal, caused by nonadherence of the tunica vaginalis to the dartos layer, and intravaginal, caused by malrotation of the spermatic cord with the tunica vaginalis. Intravaginal torsion accounts for 90% of cases.
- Torsion usually occurs in the absence of any precipitating events. Trauma accounts for <10% of cases.

 **DIAGNOSIS**

Diagnosis is made mainly by clinical suspicion (Table 1T-5). Color Doppler ultrasound evaluation or a nuclear testicular scan (Fig. 1T-13) may help with the diagnosis. Ultrasonography will show absent or decreased blood flow; scintigraphy reveals decreased perfusion on symptomatic side.

DIFFERENTIAL DIAGNOSIS

See Fig. 1T-14.
- Torsion of the testicular appendages (appendix testis)
- Testicular tumor
- Epididymitis
- Incarcerated inguinoscrotal hernia
- Orchitis

- Spermatocele
- Hydrocele, varicocele

WORKUP

The diagnosis is usually based on history and physical examination.

IMAGING STUDIES

- Radionuclide scrotal scanning (technetium-99m): cold testicle
- Doppler ultrasonic stethoscope (Doppler flowmetry)

Rx TREATMENT

Surgical derotation of the spermatic cord followed by bilateral testicular fixation with nonabsorbable sutures. If the affected testis is nonviable, orchiectomy of the affected testis and orchiopexy of the contralateral side are performed. Attempts at manual detorsion should not delay surgical consultation.

PROGNOSIS

- The degree of ischemia depends on the duration of torsion and the degree of rotation of the spermatic cord.
- There is an 80% testicular salvage rate if detorsion occurs within 12 hr of onset.
- After 24 hr, irreversible testicular infarction is expected.
- Because the contralateral testes can be affected (immunologic process), when treatment is delayed and return of blood flow does not occur after detorsion, some recommend orchiectomy of the infarcted testicle.

TABLE 1T-5 Differentiation of Testicular Torsion, Epididymitis, and Appendage Torsion

	Testicular Torsion	Epididymitis*	Appendage Torsion
Historical Features			
Age	Peak incidence in neonatal and adolescent groups but may occur at any age	Primarily adolescents and adults but may occur at any age	Typically prepubertal boys
Risk factors	Undescended testicle (neonate), rapid increase in testicular size (adolescent), failure of previous orchiopexy	Sexual activity or promiscuity, GU anomalies, GU instrumentation	Presence of appendages
Pain onset	Sudden	Gradual	Gradual or sudden
Previous episodes of similar pain	Possible (spontaneous detorsion)	Unlikely	Occasional
History of trauma	Possible	Possible	Possible
Nausea, vomiting	More likely	Less likely	Less likely
Dysuria	Less likely	More likely	Less likely
Physical Findings			
Fever	Less likely	More likely, particularly with advanced disease (epididymoorchitis)	Less likely
Location of swelling and tenderness	Testicle, progressing to diffuse hemiscrotal involvement	Epididymis, progressing to diffuse hemiscrotal involvement	Localized to head of affected testicle or epididymis
Cremasteric reflex	Testicular torsion less likely if present	May be present or absent	May be present or absent
Testicle position	High-riding testicle, transverse alignment	Normal position, vertical alignment	Normal position, vertical alignment
Pyuria	Less likely	More likely	Less likely

GU, Genitourinary.
*Including epididymoorchitis.
From Adams JG et al: *Emergency medicine, clinical essentials,* ed 2, Philadelphia, 2013, Elsevier.

REFERRAL

To urologist

⚠ PEARLS & CONSIDERATIONS

- Manual detorsion by external rotation of the testis toward the thigh can be attempted for adolescent intravaginal torsion if an operating facility is not readily available.
- Extravaginal torsion is diagnosed in the newborn. Intravaginal torsion can occur at any age but is usually diagnosed in males ages 12 to 18 yr.

SUGGESTED READINGS

Available at www.expertconsult.com

RELATED CONTENT

Testicular Torsion (Patient Information)

AUTHOR: **FRED F. FERRI, M.D.**

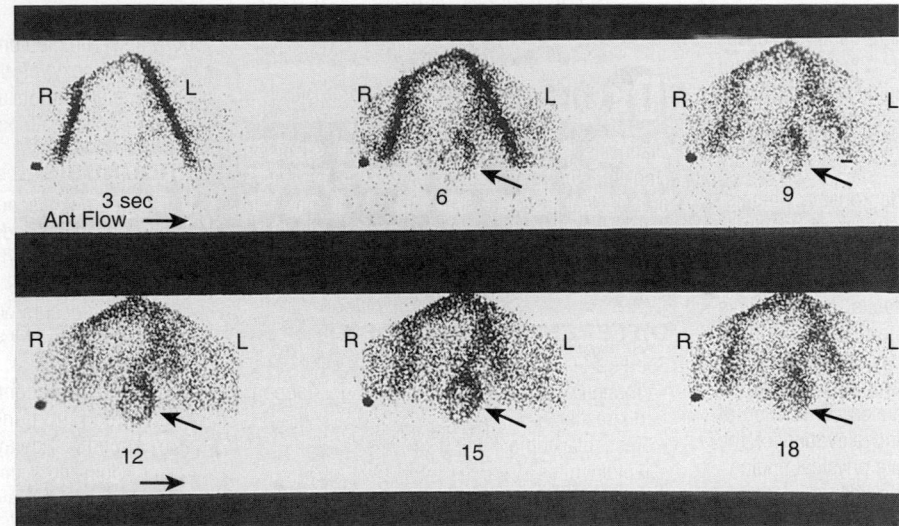

FIGURE 1T-13 Testicular torsion. Evaluation of blood flow to the testicle has been done by giving an intravenous bolus of radioactive material. The right and left iliac vessels are clearly identified, and sequential images are obtained every 3 sec. Here, increased flow is seen to the rim of the left testicle *(arrows)*, and there is no blood flow centrally. This is the appearance of a testicular torsion in which the torsion has been present for more than approximately 24 hr. (From Mettler FA [ed]: *Primary care radiology,* Philadelphia, 2000, Saunders.)

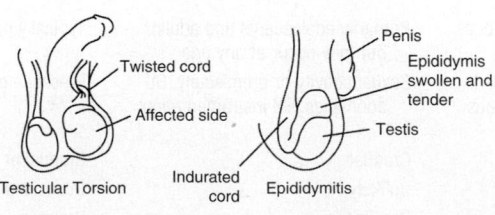

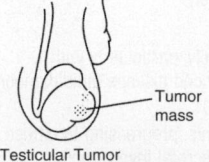

FIGURE 1T-14 Physical findings in acute scrotum. *Upper left,* Testicular torsion. *Upper right,* Epididymitis. *Lower,* Testicular tumor. Scrotal examination, which begins with palpation of the scrotal contents, should be performed in the following order: (1) testes, (2) epididymides, (3) spermatic cord structures, and (4) inguinal ring. (From Nseyo U, Weinman E, Lamm DL: *Urology for primary care physicians,* Philadelphia, 1999, WB Saunders.)

BASIC INFORMATION

DEFINITION

Tetralogy of Fallot (TOF) is a congenital heart deformity that consists of the following four features (Fig. 1T-19):
1. Malalignment ventricular septal defect (VSD).
2. Infundibular stenosis and/or pulmonary valve stenosis that leads to the obstruction of the right ventricular (RV) outflow tract.
3. An aorta that overrides the VSD by <50% of its diameter with rightward conal deviation.
4. Concentric RV hypertrophy.

SYNONYMS

TOF

ICD-10CM CODES
Q21.3 Tetralogy of Fallot

EPIDEMIOLOGY & DEMOGRAPHICS

INCIDENCE:
- TOF is the most common cyanotic congenital heart defect.

- TOF accounts for nearly 7% to 10% of all cases of congenital heart disease.
- Occurs in approximately 3.9/10,000 live births in the United States.
- It is the most common cyanotic malformation to reach adulthood without reparative surgery.

PREDOMINANT SEX: Slightly higher incidence in males than females.
GENETICS: Genetic influence is suspected.

PHYSICAL FINDINGS & CLINICAL PRESENTATION

- Of the four major features of TOF, infundibular and pulmonary stenosis that lead to RV outflow tract obstruction and the presence of a VSD are the defects that result in abnormal intracardiac circulation and lead to clinical manifestations:
  1. Right-to-left shunting and hypoxemia.
  2. Decreased pulmonary blood flow.
  3. Altered RV hemodynamics.
- The aforementioned pathophysiology results in common manifestations of TOF, including the following:
- Low birth weight and growth rate.
- Dyspnea on exertion.
- The child assuming a squatting position after exercise to increase systemic vascular

resistance, thereby decreasing right-to-left shunting.
1. Cyanosis of the nail beds and lips.
2. Digital clubbing.
3. Palpable RV impulse.
4. Systolic thrill along the left sternal border.
5. Single second heart sound comprised of aortic component only.
6. A grade 3 to 5 crescendo/decrescendo systolic murmur is heard along the left mid to upper sternal border with posterior radiation.
- In TOF with pulmonary atresia, murmur is softened/absent and the patient is deeply cyanotic.
- Paroxysmal episodes of worsening cyanosis and rapid and deep breathing ("tet" spells) may occur with when there is transient increase in right ventricular outflow tract obstruction.
- "Tet" spells, and sometimes syncope may be noticed after feeding and defecation.
- The degree of RV outflow obstruction determines the age and symptoms at presentation. In neonates with severe obstruction, profound cyanosis may result from insufficient pulmonary blood flow. Cases with mild to moderate obstruction and adequate pulmonary flow ("pink tet") may be diagnosed while patient is being evaluated for murmur or heart failure.
- After repair, patients may have a low-pitched diastolic murmur at the pulmonic area that is consistent with pulmonary regurgitation or occasionally a pansystolic murmur that is consistent with a VSD patch leak. If the patient only has a palliative shunt, a continuous murmur may be heard over the chest on the side of the shunt.
- Fig 1T-20 shows the pathophysiologic mechanisms of a hypoxic (tet) spell.

ETIOLOGY

TOF results from the abnormal septation of the embryologic conotruncus and is associated with some genetic disorders, but the exact molecular mechanism leading to the defect is unknown.

DIAGNOSIS

- The diagnosis of TOF is suspected in any neonate, infant, or child who presents with cyanosis and a heart murmur (see "Physical Findings & Clinical Presentation").
- TOF is associated with other cardiac defects:
  1. Persistent foramen ovale/atrial septal defect.
  2. Pulmonary artery anomalies.
  3. Right aortic arch.
  4. Left superior vena cava to coronary sinus.
  5. Additional VSDs.
  6. Coronary artery anomalies.
  7. Aortic valve regurgitation.
- Associated anomalies and syndromes include the following:
  1. DiGeorge.
  2. De Lange.
  3. Goldenhar.

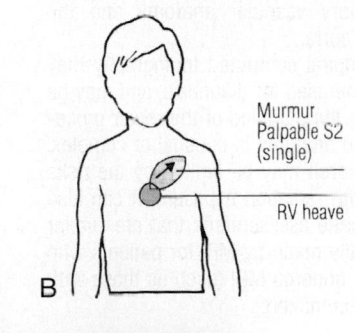

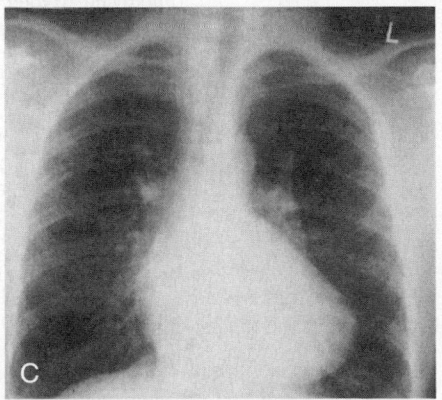

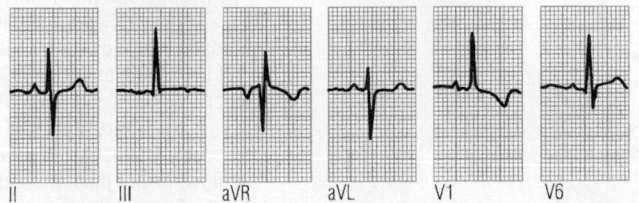

FIGURE 1T-19 Features of Fallot tetralogy. A, Diagram of abnormality. *Ao,* Aorta; *PA,* pulmonary artery; *VSD,* ventricular septal defect. **B,** Physical signs. **C,** Chest x-ray showing right ventricular hypertrophy, typical "coeur en sabot." **D,** ECG showing right atrial and ventricular hypertrophy and right axis deviation. (From Souhami RL, Moxham J: *Textbook of medicine,* ed 4, London, 2002, Churchill Livingstone.)

Diseases and Disorders

T

4. Klippel-Feil.
5. VACTERL.
6. CHARGE.
7. Pierre Robin.
8. Trisomies 21, 13, and 18.
9. Fetal alcohol.
10. Alagille.
11. MTHFR polymorphism.

DIFFERENTIAL DIAGNOSIS

- Asthma.
- Isolated VSD.
- Pulmonary atresia.
- Patent ductus arteriosus.
- Aortic stenosis.
- Pneumothorax.

WORKUP

- Detailed history and physical examination, including pulse oximetry.
- Echocardiogram, chest radiograph, 12-lead ECG, and routine laboratory tests.

LABORATORY TESTS

- Pulse oximetry to determine oxygenation.
- The CBC shows polycythemia from long-standing hypoxemia.
- Arterial blood gas levels show hypoxemia, normal pH, and pCO_2 (carbon dioxide levels).
- ECG commonly demonstrates right axis deviation, RV hypertrophy, and right atrial enlargement.
- Exercise testing may help to evaluate functional capacity and exertional arrhythmias.

IMAGING STUDIES

- Chest radiography reveals a boot-shaped heart that is commonly described as *coeur en sabot;* a prominent RV with decreased pulmonary vascularity; and a heart size that

is usually normal. However, in patients with increased aortopulmonary collateral blood flow or with associated large patent ductus arteriosus, the heart size is increased with increased pulmonary vascularity.

- Echocardiography demonstrates VSD(s), anatomy and severity of right ventricular outflow tract obstruction, aortic arch anatomy, coronary anatomy and other associated anomalies.
- Cardiac catheterization and angiography help to determine hemodynamics, the severity of right-to-left shunting, the localization of the VSD, coronary artery anatomy, right ventricular outflow obstruction, pulmonary artery stenosis, and assessment of aortopulmonary collaterals. However, it is infrequently required when the diagnosis is clear from noninvasive testing.
- Cardiac MRI can used for the localization of a residual VSD after prior surgery, the anatomic assessment of the RV outflow tract, the assessment of RV volumes and function, the quantification of degree of pulmonary regurgitation, and the detection of RV myocardial fibrosis. Magnetic resonance angiography (MRA) can be a noninvasive alternative to cardiac catheterization for the evaluation of pulmonary vascular anatomy and the ascending aorta.

Multislice spiral computed tomography may occasionally be used for diagnosis, and may be helpful during the planning of the repair procedure when the anatomy is unusual or complex. Its use in children may be limited by the risks associated with radiation exposure. It can also be used to make assessments that are similar to those usually made by MRI for patients who are unable to undergo MRI (such as those with permanent pacemakers).

Rx TREATMENT

NONPHARMACOLOGIC THERAPY

- Oxygen.
- Prostaglandins at time of birth to keep a patent ductus and to maintain ductal flow to the lungs.
- Knee-chest position during hypoxemic spells to help reduce venous return and to increase systemic vascular resistance, thereby decreasing right-to-left shunting.

ACUTE GENERAL Rx

- The acute treatment of any infant or child with TOF who is cyanotic with respiratory distress is aimed at increasing systemic vascular resistance and decreasing right-to-left shunting (e.g., phenylephrine 0.1-0.5 mcg/kg/min intravenously to increase systemic vascular resistance, and oxygen and morphine to decrease pulmonary vascular resistance).
- Intravenous sodium bicarbonate for metabolic acidosis and, if more is necessary, respiratory support with intubation and sedation are required to control respiratory distress in cyanotic spells.
- Intravenous b-blockers (e.g., propranolol 0.15 -0.25 mg/kg via slow intravenous push) are used to decrease RV outflow tract contractility.
- Emergent complete surgical repair or subclavian artery to pulmonary artery shunt (Blalock-Taussig shunt) is required if all of the above treatments fail.

CHRONIC Rx

- Palliative surgery includes procedures to increase pulmonary blood flow, thus improving oxygen saturation and allowing for pulmonary artery growth. Examples of palliative procedures include the modified Blalock-Taussig shunt, in which a Gore-Tex tube is used to create a connection between the subclavian artery and the pulmonary artery; the Waterston shunt, which attaches the ascending aorta to the right pulmonary artery; and the Potts shunt, which attaches the descending aorta to the left pulmonary artery (the latter two operations are no longer performed as they tended to lead to unpredictable pulmonary blood flow). These are generally performed in patients who are not candidates for complete surgical repair due to prematurity, hypoplastic pulmonary arteries, and/or coexistent cardiac anomalies.
- Complete surgical repair has good success and involves closing the VSD with a Dacron patch and relieving the RV outflow tract obstruction by resection of the infundibular stenosis, patch augmentation of the RV outflow, or the placement of a transannular patch. Frequently this is done before the age of 3 to 4 months but can be done in the neonatal period if the anatomy is suitable. Following surgical repair most patients have

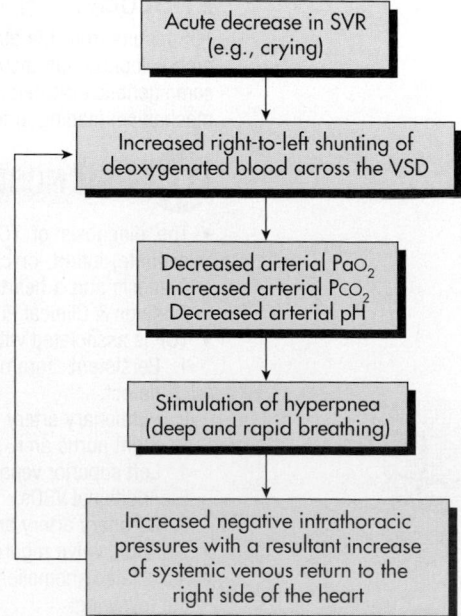

FIGURE 1T-20 Pathophysiologic mechanisms of a hypoxic (tet) spell. *SVR,* Systematic vascular resistance; *VSD,* ventricular septal defect. (From Marx et al: *Rosen's emergency medicine: concepts and clinical practice,* 7 ed, 2010, Elsevier.)

dramatic improvement in symptoms and are generally able to lead a relatively normal life.

- Postoperative issues include the following:
  1. Residual pulmonic regurgitation.
  2. Progressive RV dilation and dysfunction from pulmonary regurgitation leading to need for pulmonary valve replacement.
  3. Residual RV outflow tract obstruction.
  4. Branch pulmonary artery stenosis or hypoplasia.
  5. Sustained ventricular tachycardia.
  6. Sudden cardiac death.
  7. Atrioventricular block, atrial flutter, and atrial fibrillation.
  8. Progressive aortic regurgitation.
  9. Syndromal associations.

DISPOSITION

- In the current era, almost all patients with TOF have either palliative or complete surgical repair before they reach adulthood.
- <3% of patients with TOF survive to 40 yr without surgery.
- Survival after successful complete operative repair of TOF is excellent (35-yr survival rate for patients after TOF repair is 85%).

Adults who underwent palliative surgery during childhood can present with cyanosis and clubbing, polycythemia, and pulmonary hypertension where there is excessive pulmonary blood flow.

- Pulmonary regurgitation, residual pulmonary stenosis, and tricuspid regurgitation are the most common long-term sequelae in adults who underwent repair in childhood.
- Current guidelines and studies support pulmonary valve replacement with a bioprosthesis if the RV diastolic volume by cardiac MRI is >150 mL/m^2, RV systolic volume >80 mL/m^2, if there is evidence of RV dysfunction (RVEF <47%) or concomitant moderate or worse tricuspid regurgitation.
- Conduction disturbances; aortic root dilatation and aortic regurgitation are less common

long-term issues. Aortic dissection is extremely rare in patients with TOF.

- Ventricular arrhythmia can lead to sudden cardiac death in 8.3% of surgically repaired patients by the age of 35 yr. Monomorphic ventricular tachycardia is likely the result of a reentry circuit from RV scar caused by the surgery.
- A prolonged QRS duration on the preoperative ECG predicts an increased risk of postoperative supraventricular or ventricular arrhythmia. Prolongation of the QRS beyond 180 msec identifies patients who are at increased risk of ventricular tachycardia after surgery.
- Patients with signs or symptoms of arrhythmia may need to undergo invasive electrophysiologic testing and may require mapping and/or ablation of arrhythmias, antiarrhythmic medications, or the placement of an implantable cardiac defibrillator.
- Reduced exercise capacity is frequently the result of chronic pulmonary regurgitation or residual RV outflow tract obstruction.
- Patients with left ventricular dysfunction may benefit with angiotensin-converting enzyme inhibitors, diuretics, and digoxin.
- Women with repaired TOF should be assessed by a cardiologist before considering pregnancy to determine if pulmonic valve replacement is needed first, though many will tolerate pregnancy and delivery well.
- The offspring of patients with TOF are more likely than the general population to have congenital heart anomalies.
- Selected patients with normal RV pressures and function without evidence of residual shunt and without atrial or ventricular tachyarrhythmia are eligible to participate in competitive sports.

REFERRAL

- Infants and children with cyanotic heart disease should be referred to a pediatric cardiologist for further diagnostic evaluation. After

being diagnosed with TOF, patients should be referred to centers with experience in palliative and complete surgical repair.
- Adult patients with repaired TOF should be comanaged with a cardiologist who specializes in adults with congenital heart disease on at least an annual basis.

⚠ PEARLS & CONSIDERATIONS

- TOF was first described by the French physician Etienne Fallot in 1888.
- The first palliative surgical treatment for TOF was performed by Dr. Alfred Blalock at Johns Hopkins University in 1945 (i.e., the Blalock-Taussig shunt).
- The first surgical repair for TOF was performed by Dr. C. Walton Lillehei at the University of Minnesota in 1954.

COMMENTS

The severity of RV outflow tract obstruction is the primary determinant of clinical symptoms and outcomes.

- There is a 3% increased risk of congenital heart disease in the children of parents with TOF.
- Unrepaired TOF requires subacute bacterial endocarditis prophylaxis before any dental work or nonsterile surgical procedures (e.g., surgery of the bowel or bladder).
- Children with TOF are at risk for neurodevelopmental delay when they reach school age.

SUGGESTED READINGS

Available at www.expertconsult.com

RELATED CONTENT

Tetralogy of Fallot (Patient Information)

AUTHOR: **JONATHAN GINNS, M.D.**

BASIC INFORMATION

DEFINITION

Thalassemias are a heterogeneous group of disorders of hemoglobin synthesis that have in common a deficient synthesis of one or more of the polypeptide chains of the normal human hemoglobin, resulting in a quantitative abnormality of the hemoglobin thus produced. Table 1T-7 describes the various thalassemias. There are no qualitative changes such as those encountered in the hemoglobinopathies (e.g., sickle cell disease).

SYNONYMS

Mediterranean anemia
Cooley's anemia

ICD-10CM CODES

D56   Thalassemia
D56.0 Alpha thalassemia
D56.1 Beta thalassemia
D56.2 Delta-beta thalassemia
D56.3 Thalassemia trait
D56.4 Hereditary persistence of fetal hemoglobin (HPFH)
D56.8 Other thalassemias
D56.9 Thalassemia, unspecified

EPIDEMIOLOGY & DEMOGRAPHICS

- Thalassemia is among the most common genetic disorders worldwide. Approximately 4.83% of the world's population carry globin variants, including 1.67% of the population that are heterozygous for alpha-thalassemia and beta-thalassemia.
- The highest concentration of alpha-thalassemia is found in Southeast Asia and the African west coast. For example, the prevalence is 5% to 10% in Thailand. It is also common among blacks, with a prevalence of approximately 5%.
- The worldwide prevalence of beta-thalassemia is approximately 3%; in certain regions of Italy and Greece the prevalence reaches 15% to 30%. This high prevalence can be found in Americans of Italian or Greek descent.
- The distribution of thalassemia in Europe and Africa parallels that of malaria, suggesting that thalassemic persons are more resistant to the parasite, thus permitting evolutionary survival advantage.

CLASSIFICATION

Beta-thalassemia:
- Beta (+) thalassemia (suboptimal beta-globin synthesis)
- Beta (o) thalassemia (total absence of beta-globin synthesis)
- Delta-beta-thalassemia (total absence of both delta-globin and beta-globin synthesis)
- Lepore hemoglobin (synthesis of small amounts of fused delta-beta-globin and total absence of delta- and beta-globin)
- Hereditary persistence of fetal hemoglobin (HPHF) (increased hemoglobin F synthesis and reduced or absence of delta- and beta-globin)

Alpha-thalassemia:
- Silent carrier (three alpha-globin genes present)
- Alpha-thalassemia trait (two alpha-globin genes present)
- Hemoglobin H disease (one alpha-globin gene present)
- Hydrops fetalis (no alpha-globin gene)
- Hemoglobin constant sprint (elongated alpha-globin chain)

Thalassemic hemoglobinopathies:
- Hb Terre Haute, Hb Quong Sze, HbE, Hb Knossos

PHYSICAL FINDINGS & CLINICAL PRESENTATION

Beta-thalassemia:
- Heterozygous beta-thalassemia (thalassemia minor): no or mild anemia, microcytosis and hypochromia, mild hemolysis manifested by slight reticulocytosis and splenomegaly

TABLE 1T-7   The thalassemias

Thalassemia	Globin Genotype	Features	Expression	Hemoglobin Analysis
α-Thalassemia				
1 gene deletion	-,α/α,α	Normal	Normal	Newborn: Bart's 1%-2%
2 gene deletion trait	-,α/-,α -, -/α,α	Microcytosis, mild hypochromasia	Normal, mild anemia	Newborn: Bart's: 5%-10%
3 gene deletion hemoglobin H	-,-/-,α	Microcytosis, hypochromic	Mild anemia, transfusions not required	Newborn: Bart's: 20%-30%
2 gene deletion 1 Constant Spring	-,-/α,α$^{Constant Spring}$	Microcytosis, hypochromic	Moderate to severe anemia, transfusion, splenectomy	2%-3% Constant Spring, 10%-15% hemoglobin H
4 gene deletion	-,-/-,-	Anisocytosis, poikilocytosis	Hydrops fetalis	Newborn: 89%-90% Bart's with Gower 1 and 2 and Portland
Nondeletional	α,α/α,α^{variant}	Microcytosis, mild anemia	Normal	1%-2% variant hemoglobin
β-Thalassemia				
β^0 or β$^+$ heterozygote: trait	β^0/A, β$^+$/A	Variable microcytosis	Normal	Elevated A$_2$, variable elevation of F
β^0-Thalassemia	β^0/β^0, β$^+$/β^0, E/β^0	Microcytosis, nucleated RBC	Transfusion dependent	F 98% and A$_2$ 2% E 30%-40%
β$^+$-Thalassemia severe	β$^+$/β$^+$	Microcytosis, nucleated RBC	Transfusion dependent/thalassemia intermedia	F 70%-95%, A$_2$ 2%, trace A
Silent	β$^+$/A	Microcytosis	Normal with only microcytosis	A$_2$ 3.3%-3.5%
β$^+$/β$^+$	Hypochromic, microcytic	Mild to moderate anemia	A$_2$ 2%-5%, F 10%-30%	
Dominant (rare)	B^0/A	Microcytosis, abnormal RBCs	Moderately severe anemia, splenomegaly	Elevated F and A$_2$
d-Thalassemia	A/A	Normal	Normal	A$_2$ absent
(dβ)^0-Thalassemia	(dβ)^0/A	Hypochromic	Mild anemia	F 5%-20%
(dβ)$^+$-Thalassemia Lepore	β^{Lepore}/A	Microcytosis	Mild anemia	Lepore 8%-20%
Lepore	β^{Lepore}/β^{Lepore}	Microcytic, hypochromic	Thalassemia intermedia	F 80%, Lepore 20%
γdβ-Thalassemia	(γ^{A}dβ)^0/A	Microcytosis, microcytic, hypochromic	Moderate anemia, splenomegaly, homozygote: thalassemia intermedia	Decreased F and A$_2$ compared with db-thalassemia
γ-Thalassemia	(γ^{A}γ^G)^0/A	Microcytosis	Insignificant unless homozygote	Decreased F
Hereditary Persistence of Fetal Hemoglobin				
Deletional	A/A	Microcytic	Mild anemia	F 100% homozygotes
Nondeletional	A/A	Normal	Normal	F 20%-40%

From Kliegman RM et al: *Nelson textbook of pediatrics*, ed 19, Philadelphia, 2011, Saunders.

- Homozygous beta-thalassemia (thalassemia major): intense hemolytic anemia; transfusion dependency; bone deformities (skull and long bones); hepatomegaly; splenomegaly; iron overload leading to cardiomyopathy, diabetes mellitus, and hypogonadism; growth retardation; pigment gallstones; susceptibility to infection
- Thalassemia intermedia caused by combination of beta- and alpha-thalassemia or beta-thalassemia and Hb Lepore: resembles thalassemia major but is milder

Alpha-thalassemia:
- Silent carrier: no symptoms.
- Alpha-thalassemia trait: microcytosis only.
- Hemoglobin H disease: moderately severe hemolysis with microcytosis and splenomegaly.
- The loss of all four alpha-globin genes is incompatible with life (stillbirth of hydropic fetus). NOTE: Pregnancies with hydrops fetalis are associated with a high incidence of toxemia.

ETIOLOGY

- Beta-thalassemia: it is caused by more than 200 point mutations and, rarely, by deletions. The reduction of beta-globin synthesis results in redundant alpha-globin chains (Heinz bodies), which are cytotoxic and cause intramedullary hemolysis and ineffective erythropoiesis. The pathophysiology of beta-thalassemia is illustrated in Fig. E1T-21. Fetal hemoglobin may be increased.
- Alpha-thalassemia: duplication of the α-globin chain on chromosome 16 results in 4α-globin genes ($\alpha\alpha/\alpha\alpha$); α-thalassemia results from deletion of one or more of these. There are several mutations can result in insufficient amounts of alpha-globin available for combination with non–alpha-globins.

Dx DIAGNOSIS

LABORATORY TESTS

Beta-thalassemia:
- Microcytosis (mean cell volume: 55-80 fL)
- Normal red blood cell (RBC) distribution width index (RDW)

- Smear: nucleated RBCs, anisocytosis, poikilocytosis, polychromatophilia, Pappenheimer and Howell-Jolly bodies
- Hemoglobin electrophoresis: absent or reduced hemoglobin A, increased fetal hemoglobin, variable increase in the amount of hemoglobin A_2
- Markers of hemolysis: elevated indirect bilirubin and lactate dehydrogenase, decreased haptoglobin

Alpha-thalassemia:
- Microcytosis in the absence of iron deficiency
- Hemoglobin electrophoresis normal except for the presence of hemoglobin H in hemoglobin H disease (Table 1T-8)

Rx TREATMENT

- Thalassemia minor: no treatment, but avoid iron administration for incorrect diagnosis of iron deficiency.
- Beta-thalassemia major (and hemoglobin H disease):
  1. Transfusion therapy: monthly erythrocyte transfusions should be initiated for hemoglobin levels less than 7 g/dL (70 g/L). Guidelines for transfusion therapy recommend administration of 10 to 15 mL/kg of RBC every 2 to 4 weeks to maintain the pretransfusion hemoglobin level above 9 to 10.5 g/dl. Use of leukoreduced RBCs that have been stored for less than 7 to 10 days is preferred. Use of first degree relatives as blood donors should be avoided.
  2. Chelation therapy: Transfusion hemosiderosis is the major cause of late morbidity and mortality in patients with thalassemia major. Each unit of packed RBCs contains approximately 250 mg of iron. Chelation of iron can be accomplished with deoxferrioxamine (by IV or subcutaneous administration, 8-12 hr nightly, 5-6 days a week at a dose of 2-6 g/day with a portable infusion pump). Deferiprone, an oral chelating agent, can be used as a second-line treatment of iron overload caused by blood transfusions (transfusional hemosiderosis).
  3. Splenectomy for hypersplenism if present.
  4. Bone marrow transplantation. Allogenic hematopoietic stem cell transplantation (HSCT) should be considered in patients

with severe forms before the onset of end-organ damage. Although hematopoietic stem cell transplantation is the only curative approach for thalassemia, it has been limited by the high cost and scarcity of human leukocyte antigen–matched donors. Before transplantation, it is necessary to administer myeloablative regimens to eradicate the endogenous thalassemic bone marrow. Commonly used agents are hydroxyurea, azathioprine, fludarabine, busulfan, and cyclophosphamide.
  5. Hydroxyurea may increase the level of hemoglobin F.

! PEARLS & CONSIDERATIONS

- Polymerase chain reaction can be used to detect point mutations or deletions in chorionic villous samples, enabling first-trimester, DNA-based testing for thalassemia.
- Preimplantation genetic diagnosis can be extended to human leukocyte antigen typing on embryonic biopsies, allowing the selection of an embryo that is not affected by thalassemia and that may also serve as a stem cell donor for a previously affected child within the same family.

SUGGESTED READINGS

Available at www.expertconsult.com

AUTHOR: **FRED F. FERRI, M.D.**

TABLE 1T-8 Distinguishing Laboratory Features of α- and β-Thalassemias

Diagnosis*	BCB Prep[†]	HbA$_2$[‡]	HbF	HbH	Hb Barts in Newborn[§]
Normal	−	nl	nl	nl	−
α-Thalassemia	+	nl	nl	nl or ↑	+
β-Thalassemia	−	nl or ↑	nl or ↑	nl	−

Hb, Hemoglobin type; *nl*, normal; ↑, increased; −, negative; +, positive.
Can be negative for a one α-globin deletion (silent carrier), for compound heterozygotes with combined α- and β-thalassemia, and other hemoglobinopathies (e.g., HbE or HbS). Table shows typical results; exceptions occur.
*All forms of α -or β-thalassemia are pooled; specific results will vary.
[†]Brilliant cresyl blue (*BCB*) or inclusion body prep. Results vary by lab, but this can be done semiquantitatively. This can be negative when a one α-globin deletion (silent carrier) is present. This assay is unreliable in the presence of other hemoglobins (e.g., HbS or HbE). This can be negative when α- and β-thalassemia are simultaneously present.
[‡]HbA$_2$ results vary depending on laboratory method.
[§]Hb Barts increases with the degree of α-thalassemia.
From Fuhrman: *Pediatric critical care*, ed 4. Philadelphia, 2010, Elsevier.

BASIC INFORMATION

DEFINITION

Thoracic outlet syndrome (TOS) describes a condition producing upper extremity symptoms believed to result from neurovascular compression at the thoracic outlet (Fig. 1T-22). Three types are described on the basis of point of compression: (1) cervical rib and scalenus syndrome, in which abnormal scalene muscles or the presence of a cervical rib may cause compression; (2) costoclavicular syndrome, in which compression may occur under the clavicle; and (3) hyperabduction syndrome, in which compression may occur in the subcoracoid area. The compression occurs in three anatomical structures–arteries, veins, and nerves. TOS usually is caused by a combination of two factors: 1) having abnormal anatomy that creates compression in the thoracic outlet, 2) having some injury at the thoracic outlet.
- Neurogenic TOS: Caused by compression of brachial nerve plexus
- Arterial TOS: Caused by subclavian artery compression
- Venous TOS: Caused by compression of subclavian vein

SYNONYMS

TOS

ICD-10CM CODES
G54.0 Brachial plexus disorders

EPIDEMIOLOGY & DEMOGRAPHICS

PREVALENCE: TOS is an uncommon disorder. Varies from source to source; presence of cervical ribs in 0.5% to 1% of population (50% bilateral), but most are asymptomatic. Approximately 90% of all TOS disorders are neurogenic, and the remaining 10% are arterial or venous.
PREDOMINANT SEX: Females affected more often than males (ratio of 3.5:1)
PREDOMINANT AGE: Rare in those aged <20 yr

PHYSICAL FINDINGS & CLINICAL PRESENTATION

- Symptoms and signs are related to the degree of involvement of each of the various structures at the level of the first rib.
- True venous or arterial involvement is not common.
- Diagnosis is most often used in the consideration of neural pain affecting the arm, which suggests involvement of the brachial plexus.
  1. Arterial compression: pallor, paresthesias, diminished pulses, coolness, Raynaud's phenomenon, digital gangrene, supraclavicular bruit or mass, and stroke
  2. Venous compression: edema and pain; thrombosis causing superficial venous dilation in the shoulder area
  3. Neurologic compression: Pain and or paresthesia of neck, shoulder region, arm or hand, depending on the root involved with difficulty. Intrinsic weakness and diminished sensation on examination
  4. Possible supraclavicular tenderness

5. Provocative tests (Adson's, Wright's): may reproduce pain but are of disputed usefulness

ETIOLOGY

- Congenital cervical rib or fibrous extension of cervical rib (Fig. 1T-23)
- Abnormal scalene muscle insertion
- Drooping of shoulder girdle from generalized hypotonia or trauma
- Narrowed costoclavicular interval as a result of downward and backward pressure on shoulder (sometimes seen in individuals who carry heavy backpacks), poor posturing, pregnancy
- Acute venous thrombosis with exercise (effort thrombosis)
- Bony abnormalities of first rib
- Abnormal fibromuscular bands
- Malunion of clavicle fracture

DIAGNOSIS

DIFFERENTIAL DIAGNOSIS

- Carpal tunnel syndrome

- Cervical radiculopathy
- Brachial neuritis
- Ulnar nerve compression (cubital tunnel syndrome)
- Complex regional pain syndrome
- Superior sulcus tumor

WORKUP

Fig. 1T-24 describes a diagnostic algorithm for thoracic outlet syndrome. Except for venous or arterial pathology, no ancillary diagnostic tests are reliable for diagnostic confirmation.

IMAGING STUDIES

- Electromyography, nerve conduction velocity studies to rule out carpal tunnel syndrome, cervical radiculopathy
- Ultrasound for initial evaluation for arterial or venous thoracic outlet syndrome
- Cervical spine radiographs to rule out cervical disk disease
- Chest radiograph to rule out lung tumor
- Computed tomography (CT) for detailed anatomical relationship of vascular structure to surrounding muscles and bones

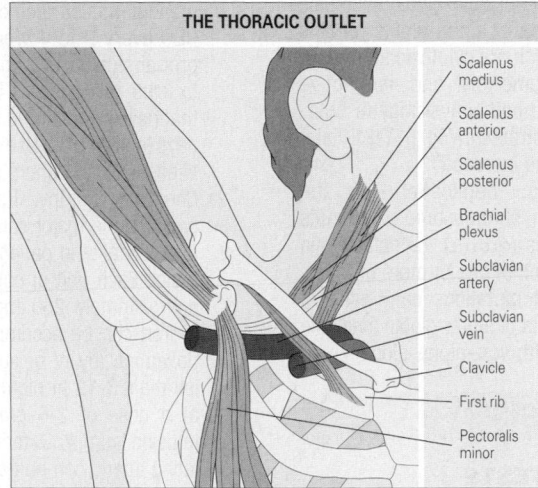

THE THORACIC OUTLET

Scalenus medius
Scalenus anterior
Scalenus posterior
Brachial plexus
Subclavian artery
Subclavian vein
Clavicle
First rib
Pectoralis minor

FIGURE 1T-22 The thoracic outlet. Three narrow channels of the outlet include the scalene triangle, the costoclavicular passage, and the pectoralis minor attachment at the coracoid process. (Hochberg MC et al: *Rheumatology,* ed 5, St Louis, 2011, Mosby.)

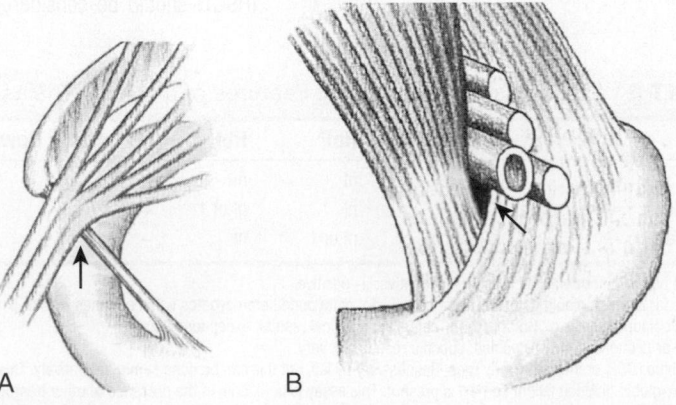

A   B

FIGURE 1T-23 A, Compression caused by a cervical rib *(arrow).* **B,** Abnormal scalene muscle insertions that may cause compression at the cervicobrachial region *(arrow).* (From Mercier LR: *Practical orthopedics,* ed 5, St Louis, 2000, Mosby.)

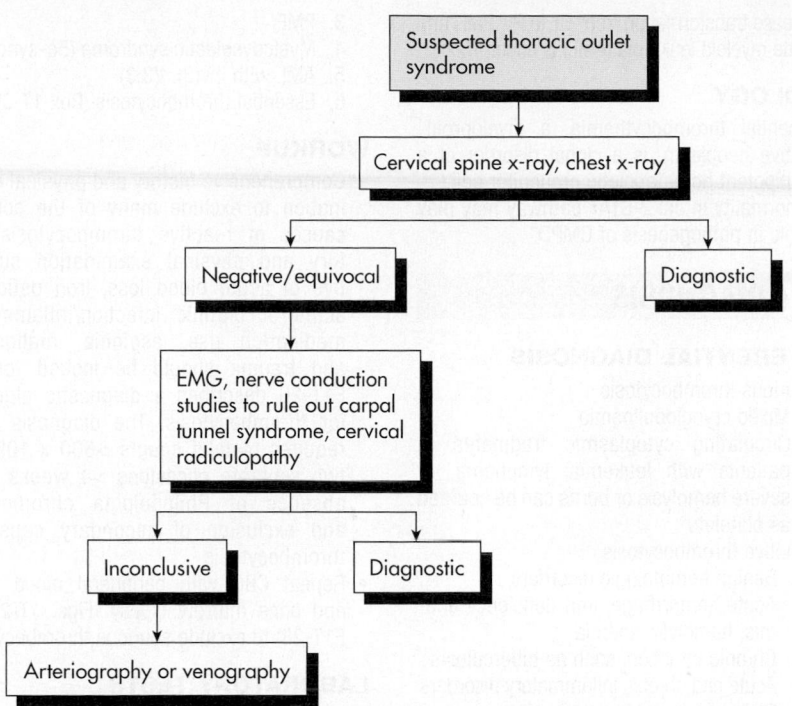

FIGURE 1T-24 Thoracic outlet syndrome. *EMG,* Electromyogram.

- Contrast-enhanced magnetic angiography can be very useful in assessing vessel imaging while using provocative arm positions.
- Arteriography or venography can be used for dynamic studies while performing upper extremity maneuvers and also performing thrombolysis if needed.

ACUTE GENERAL Rx

- Sling for pain relief
- Physical therapy modalities plus shoulder girdle–strengthening exercises

- Postural reeducation
- Nonsteroidal antiinflammatory drugs
- Muscle relaxants

CHRONIC Rx

Surgical treatment is indicated:
- After failure of physical therapy
- TOS with complications like thrombosis, aneurysms
- Neurologic compressions
- Sympathetic cervical rib

Surgical options include:
- Thoracic outlet decompression
- Cervical rib resection
- Thoracic sympathetectomy

- Vascular repair
- Catheter-directed thrombolysis

DISPOSITION

- Nonsurgical treatment: often successful for patients with pain as the primary symptom
- Complications of surgical treatment include transient dyesthesia, venous injury, arterial injuries, or brachial plexus injuries.

REFERRAL

For vascular surgery consultation when venous or arterial impairment is present

COMMENTS

- True thoracic outlet syndrome is probably an uncommon condition.
- Diagnosis is often used to describe a wide variety of clinical symptoms.
- Considerable disagreement exists regarding the frequency of this disorder.

SUGGESTED READINGS

Available at www.expertconsult.com

RELATED CONTENT

Thoracic Outlet Syndrome (Patient Information)

AUTHOR: **HISASHI TSUKADA, M.D., PH.D.**

T

Diseases and Disorders

BASIC INFORMATION

DEFINITION

Thrombocytosis is defined by an elevated platelet count (>450,000/mm³) in peripheral blood. It is caused by overproduction of platelets (reactive thrombocytosis), or it may be caused by clonal expansion of megakaryocytes (clonal thrombocytosis). Reactive thrombocytosis is driven by excessive cytokines induced by various stimuli, such as trauma or inflammation. The latter is defined as chronic myeloproliferative disorders (CMPD), of which four subgroups are well characterized: chronic myelogenous leukemia (CML), polycythemia vera (PV), primary myelofibrosis (PMF), and essential thrombocythemia (ET). In addition, platelet count can be spuriously elevated in some conditions (see differential diagnosis). Extreme thrombocytosis is defined as platelet count >1 million/mL.

SYNONYMS

Thrombocythemia
Essential thrombocythemia
ET

ICD-10CM CODES
D47.3 Essential (hemorrhagic) thrombocythemia
D75.89 Other specified diseases of blood and blood-forming organs
D75.9 Disease of blood and blood-forming organs, unspecified
D77 Other disorders of blood and blood-forming organs in diseases classified elsewhere

EPIDEMIOLOGY & DEMOGRAPHICS

Reactive thrombocytosis is much more frequent than clonal thrombocytosis (70% vs. 22% in one series).
Epidemiology for essential thrombocythemia:
INCIDENCE: 2.5 cases/100,000 population/yr
PREVALENCE: Estimated as 24 cases/100,000 population
PREDOMINANT SEX AND AGE: The median age at diagnosis is 60 yr. Female/male ratio is 2:1.

PHYSICAL FINDINGS & CLINICAL PRESENTATION

- Regardless of the cause, a high platelet count may be associated with vasomotor symptoms such as headache, visual disturbances, dizziness, atypical chest pain, acral dysesthesia, and erythromelalgia.
- Thrombotic and bleeding complications can occur.
- Symptoms and complications are much more likely to occur in association with autonomous thrombocytosis than reactive thrombocytosis.
- The degree of thrombocytosis does not predict the likelihood of autonomous thrombocytosis, and does not generally correlate to the risk of thrombosis.
- Splenomegaly is common with CMPD.
- Coexistent leukocytosis and erythrocytosis are common with CML and PV.

- Disease transformation from ET to PV, PMF, and acute myeloid leukemia (AML) is uncommon.

ETIOLOGY

- Essential thrombocythemia, a myeloproliferative neoplasm, is a clonal disorder of a multipotent hematopoietic progenitor cell.
- Abnormality in Jak2-STAT pathway may play a role in pathogenesis of CMPD.

DIAGNOSIS

DIFFERENTIAL DIAGNOSIS

- Spurious thrombocytosis
  1. Mixed cryoglobulinemia
  2. Circulating cytoplasmic fragments in patients with leukemia, lymphoma, or severe hemolysis or burns can be counted as platelets
- Reactive thrombocytosis
  1. Benign hematologic disorders
  2. Acute hemorrhage, iron deficiency anemia, hemolytic anemia
  3. Chronic infection, such as tuberculosis
  4. Acute and chronic inflammatory disorders
  5. Rheumatologic disorders
  6. Inflammatory bowel disease
  7. Celiac disease
  8. Functional and surgical asplenia
  9. Tissue damage
  10. Trauma, thermal burn
  11. Myocardial infarction
  12. Acute pancreatitis
  13. Recent surgery
  14. Renal failure, nephrotic syndrome
  15. Exercise
  16. Medications, such as vincristine, epinephrine
- Clonal thrombocytosis
  1. CML
  2. PV

3. PMF
4. Myelodysplastic syndrome (5q-syndrome)
5. AML with inv(3), t(3;3)
6. Essential thrombocytosis (Box 1T-3)

WORKUP

- Comprehensive history and physical examination to exclude many of the common causes of reactive thrombocytosis: history and physical examination suggestive of acute blood loss, iron deficiency, acute or chronic infection/inflammation, medication use, asplenia, malignancy, and trauma should be looked for. Fig. E1T-26 describes a diagnostic algorithm for thrombocytosis. The diagnosis of ET requires platelet counts >600 x 109/L on two separate occasions >4 weeks apart, absence of Philadelphia chromosome, and exclusion of secondary causes of thrombocytosis.
- Repeat CBC with peripheral blood smear and bone marrow biopsy (Figs. 1T-27 and E1T-28) to exclude spurious thrombocytosis.

LABORATORY TESTS

- CBC with peripheral blood smear: Howell-Jolly bodies and target cells are present in patients with asplenia; nucleated RBC, teardrop RBC and WBC precursors in patients with PMF
- Serum ferritin level: low ferritin level suggests iron deficiency
- Serum C-reactive protein (CRP), ESR, and plasma fibrinogen: nonspecific markers of infection or inflammation
- Philadelphia chromosome or BCR-ABL rearrangement: positive in CML
- Serum erythropoietin assay: low to normal in PV and ET
- JAK2 mutation analysis: PV and ET; JAK2 mutation is found in 95% to 99% of patient

---

BOX 1T-3 World Health Organization Diagnostic Criteria for Essential Thrombocythemia

Diagnosis requires that all of the following criteria be met:
- Sustained platelet count ≥450 × 10⁹/L[1]
- Bone marrow biopsy specimen showing proliferation mainly of the megakaryocytic lineage, with increased numbers of enlarged, mature megakaryocytes; no significant increase or left shift of neutrophil granulopoiesis or erythropoiesis
- Failure to meet the WHO criteria for polycythemia vera,[2] primary myelofibrosis,[3] BCR-ABL1–positive chronic myelogenous leukemia,[4] myelodysplastic syndrome,[5] or other myeloid neoplasms
- Demonstration of JAK2 V617F or other clonal marker; or, in the absence of JAK2 V617F, no evidence of reactive thrombocytosis[6]

[1] Sustained during the workup process.
[2] Requires the failure of iron replacement therapy to increase the hemoglobin level to the polycythemia vera range in the presence of decreased serum ferritin. Exclusion of polycythemia vera is based on hemoglobin and hematocrit levels; red cell mass measurement is not required.
[3] Requires the absence of relevant reticulin fibrosis, collagen fibrosis, peripheral blood leukoerythroblastosis, or markedly hypercellular marrow accompanied by megakaryocyte morphology typical for primary myelofibrosis—small to large megakaryocytes with an aberrant nuclear-to-cytoplasmic ratio and hyperchromatic, bulbous, or irregularly folded nuclei and dense clustering.
[4] Requires the absence of BCR-ABL1.
[5] Requires the absence of dyserythropoiesis and dysgranulopoiesis.
[6] Causes of reactive thrombocytosis include iron deficiency, splenectomy, surgery, infection, inflammation, connective tissue disease, metastatic cancer, and lymphoproliferative disorders. However, the presence of a condition associated with reactive thrombocytosis does not exclude the possibility of essential thrombocythemia if other criteria are met.
From Swerdlow SH et al (eds): WHO classification of tumours of haematopoietic and lymphoid tissues, Lyon, France, 2008, IARC Press.

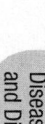

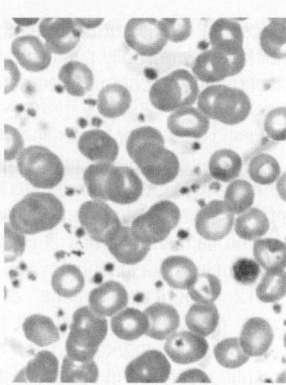

FIGURE 1T-27 Essential thrombocythemia: peripheral blood smear. The peripheral blood smear in ET shows a marked thrombocytosis with anisocytosis (varying sizes) of the platelets. (From Hoffman R et al: *Hematology: basic principles and practice,* ed 5, Philadelphia, 2009, Churchill Livingstone.)

with PV, in 40% to 60% of patients with PMF, and in about 50% of patients with ET
- MPL and CALR mutation analysis: Frequency is reported as 4% and 15% to 32%, respectively in ET
- Bone marrow chromosome analysis: 5q-syndrome and other myelodysplastic syndrome, CML
- Bone marrow exam in ET may show clusters of abnormal megakaryocytes and increased reticulin fibrosis (see Fig. E1T-28).

 **TREATMENT**

Treatment for ET will be addressed in this chapter. Reactive thrombocytosis has been rarely associated with thrombosis or bleeding and generally does not require specific therapy.

ACUTE GENERAL Rx
- Vasomotor symptoms easily manageable with low-dose aspirin (<100 mg/day)
- Bleeding
  1. Discontinue any platelet antiaggregating agent, such as aspirin or nonsteroidal anti-inflammatory agents.
  2. Evaluate for disseminated intravascular coagulopathy and coagulation factor deficiency. Acquired factor V deficiency is occasionally present in association with

autonomous thrombocytosis. In that case, treat with fresh frozen plasma infusion.
  3. In case of extreme thrombocytosis (platelet count generally >1,000,000/uL [1000×10⁹/L]), acquired von Willebrand disease may occur. Immediate platelet apheresis with definitive therapy with a platelet-lowering agent is essential in this instance.
- Thrombosis
  1. Arterial or venous thrombosis occurs in 20% to 30% of patients.
  2. If the platelet count is >800,000/mm³, platelet apheresis coupled with a platelet-lowering agent should be considered with the goal of platelet count <400,000/mm³.
  3. Initial workup should include additional thrombophilic diseases, such as proteins C and S abnormality, antithrombin, anticardiolipin antibody, mutations of factor V and II, and plasma homocysteine.
  4. Anticoagulant therapy for 3 to 9 mo based on the presence or absence of additional thrombophilic defects.

CHRONIC Rx
Treatment strategies for ET are based on the presence or absence of risk factors for thrombosis. Smoking cessation and obesity management should be discussed with all patients with ET. In low-risk patients (age <60 yr, no history of thrombosis or hemorrhage, platelet count <1 million/mL), observation may be adequate. Treatment with low-dose aspirin is indicated in low-risk patients with vasomotor symptoms or with other indications for aspirin use. The cytoreductive therapy along with low-dose aspirin therapy is indicated in high-risk patients (age >60 yr and/or with previous history of thrombosis).
- Low-dose aspirin (81 mg/day) may be safe and effective in preventing vascular events. It is also effective in preventing recurrent vascular events in high-risk patients and in treating the vasomotor symptoms.
- Cytoreductive therapy
  1. Hydroxyurea (HU) versus anagrelide: HU plus aspirin is suggested to be safer and more effective than anagrelide plus aspirin in regard to thrombosis, bleeding, and transformation to PMF at 5 yr in a randomized trial. Monitor liver function tests and the degree of neutropenia or anemia with HU therapy.

  2. The incidence of leukemic conversion in patients with ET treated with HU alone is reported as <1%. Interferon alpha may be effective for controlling platelet count in patients failing treatment with HU.

DISPOSITION
Although long survival is expected in patients with ET, it is inferior to the sex- and age-matched U.S. population.

An International Prognostic Score for Essential thrombocythemia (IPSET) was proposed by International Working Group on Myelofibrosis Research and Treatment based on age, WBC count, and history of thromboembolism at diagnosis.

REFERRAL
Refer to hematologist/oncologist when platelet count is consistently elevated >450,000/mm³ without causes for reactive thrombocytosis.

PEARLS & CONSIDERATIONS

COMMENTS
- Some patients with clinically apparent ET have Philadelphia chromosome or BCR-ABL rearrangement, even in the absence of other features of CML. It is suggested that it should be tested in all ET patients due to its potential therapeutic implications.
- The risk of bleeding with aspirin use in patients with ET is increased when the platelet count is >1 million/ml.
- A recent trial has shown rapid and durable hematologic response in patients with ET treated with the telomerase inhibitor imetelstat.[1]

PATIENT & FAMILY EDUCATION
Smoking cessation is encouraged in both patients with ET and reactive thrombocytosis.

SUGGESTED READINGS
Available at www.expertconsult.com

AUTHOR: **ETSUKO AOKI, M.D., PH.D.**

[1]Baerlocher G, et al: Telomerase inhibitor imetelstat in patients with essential thrombocythemia, *N Engl J Med* 373:920-928, 2015.

BASIC INFORMATION

DEFINITION

Superficial venous thrombophlebitis (SVT) is an inflammation of a vein with subsequent secondary thrombus formation. SVT most frequently involves superficial veins of the leg, but any superficial vein can be affected. SVT has been reported to occur in 125,000 people in the United States per year; however, the actual incidence is likely far greater. SVT is not always a benign condition. SVT should be regarded as the superficial venous manifestation of a systemic process known as venous thromboembolism (DVT, PE).

SYNONYMS

SVT
Superficial phlebitis
Superficial suppurative thrombophlebitis
Suppurative thrombophlebitis

ICD-10CM CODES

I80.00 Phlebitis and thrombophlebitis of superficial vessels of unspecified lower extremity
I80.8 Phlebitis and thrombophlebitis of other sites
I80.9 Phlebitis and thrombophlebitis of unspecified site

EPIDEMIOLOGY & DEMOGRAPHICS

- Approximately 30% to 45% of patients diagnosed with SVT are men with an average age of 54 yr.
- Approximately 55% to 70% of patients diagnosed with SVT are women with an average age of 58 yr.
- The overall recurrence of SVT is 18% over an average observation period of 15 mo, equally involving varicose and nonvaricose veins.
- The lifetime incidence of SVT in those with untreated varicose veins has been estimated at 25% to 50%.

PHYSICAL FINDINGS & CLINICAL PRESENTATION

- Subcutaneous vein is palpable as a tender cord or "wormlike" mass with increased warmth and erythema.
- Induration, redness, and tenderness are localized along the course of the vein. This linear appearance rather than circular appearance is useful to distinguish thrombophlebitis from other conditions (cellulitis, erythema nodosum).
- There is some swelling of the overlying skin and subcutaneous tissue but without generalized edema of the limb.
- Low-grade fever may be present.

ETIOLOGY

- In the lower extremity, 70% of SVT occurs in patients with varicose veins, with the great saphenous vein being most commonly involved (60%-80%).
- Intravenous catheters and infusion of caustic drugs are the most common cause of upper extremity SVT.
- Malignancy

- Pregnancy/puerperium
- Hypercoagulable states
- Previous
- DVT/SVT
- OCP (oral contraceptive pill)/HRT (hormone replacement therapy)

DIAGNOSIS

DIFFERENTIAL DIAGNOSIS

- Lymphangitis
- Cellulitis
- Erythema nodosum
- Panniculitis
- Acute lipodermatosclerosis

WORKUP

The clinical investigation includes not only the local findings but also the presence of varicose veins with or without the stigmata of chronic venous insufficiency. Today, duplex ultrasound is the most important additional diagnostic tool.

IMAGING STUDIES

- Duplex ultrasound offers the advantage of being inexpensive, noninvasive, and repeatable for follow-up examination.
- Ultrasonography confirms the diagnosis, shows the location of the thrombus and its location regarding the saphenofemoral and/or saphenopopliteal junctions.
- Ultrasound examination of patients with SVT has revealed that a concomitant DVT can exist in 15% to 20%.
- In up to 25% of these patients, the DVT may not be contiguous with the SVT and may be found in the contralateral leg.
- Therefore bilateral duplex exam is recommended in all cases of SVT that involve the main trunk of the great saphenous vein (GSV) or small saphenous vein (SSV).

TREATMENT

NONPHARMACOLOGIC THERAPY

- Warm, moist compresses
- Do not restrict activity. Immediate mobilization with walking exercises.

ACUTE GENERAL Rx

- Treatment guidelines for SVT are not well established because of the lack of controlled clinical trials. In general, the primary goal of management should be to prevent thrombus extension and the risk of venous thromboembolism. All other therapy is directed at patient comfort.
- In patients with migratory SVT, recurrent SVT, or SVT without varicose veins, the underlying condition should be investigated and treatment directed accordingly.
- The most common cause of upper extremity SVT is an intravenous catheter. Treatment starts with removal of the cannula and application of warm compresses. The resultant lump may persist for months. No anticoagulant therapy is required.
- In patients with lower extremity SVT in a varicose vein branch, control of pain with

analgesics and the use of gradient compression stockings are usually sufficient. Patients are encouraged to continue their usual daily activities.
- Many investigators favor systemic anticoagulation when there is superficial thrombosis of 5 cm or more in length, the thrombus is within 1 cm of the saphenous junctions, or more than 5 cm of the saphenous trunk is involved, as shown by duplex ultrasonography.
- The 2012 American College of Chest Physicians guidelines recommend the use of fondaparinux (1 mg/kg/day) for 45 days over no anticoagulation in patients with lower extremity SVT within 1 cm of the saphenofemoral or saphenopopliteal junction.
- In the case of patients with varicose veins secondary to saphenous vein reflux, a catheter vein ablation procedure should be performed only after the acute SVT episode is over in order to avoid the thromboembolic complications induced by such procedures.

DISPOSITION

Clinical improvement within 10 to 14 days

REFERRAL

Referral to vascular surgeon or phlebologist with vascular lab

PEARLS & CONSIDERATIONS

SUPERFICIAL SUPPURATIVE THROMBOPHLEBITIS

- Superficial suppurative thrombophlebitis is associated with an intravenous catheter or multiple puncture sites secondary to IV drug abuse and is located primarily in the upper extremity.
- Clinical presentation is similar to that of nonsuppurative SVT but with associated fever, leukocytosis, and/or septicemia.
- Most cases of intravenous catheter sepsis are not complicated by suppurative thrombophlebitis; local IV catheter site infections occur in about 7% of cases and septicemia is found in only 1 of every 400 IV catheterizations.
- The incidence of peripheral vein suppurative thrombophlebitis is highest in patients with specific risk factors such as burns, steroids, and IV drug abuse.
- Treatment consists of antibiotics with adequate coverage of gram-negative rods and *Staphylococcus aureus,* including MRSA. Initial empirical treatment is with IV vancomycin 1 g q12h *plus* ceftriaxone 1 g IV q24h. Alternative regimen consists of daptomycin 6 mg/kg IV q 12h *plus* ceftriaxone 1 g IV q24h.

SUGGESTED READINGS

Available at www.expertconsult.com

RELATED CONTENT

Thrombophlebitis (Patient Information)

AUTHOR: **FRANK G. FORT, M.D.**

BASIC INFORMATION

DEFINITION

Thrombotic thrombocytopenic purpura (TTP) is a rare disorder characterized by thrombocytopenia (often accompanied by purpura) and microangiopathic hemolytic anemia; neurologic impairment, renal dysfunction, and fever may also be present.

SYNONYMS

TTP

ICD-10CM CODES
M31.1 Thrombotic microangiopathy

EPIDEMIOLOGY & DEMOGRAPHICS

- TTP primarily affects females aged between 18 and 50 yr.
- The incidence of acquired TTP in adults is 2.9 cases per million per year. Incidence in children is 0.1 cases per million per year. There is increased incidence in HIV/AIDS and during pregnancy.

PHYSICAL FINDINGS & CLINICAL PRESENTATION

- The disease often begins as a flulike illness ultimately followed by clinical and laboratory abnormalities.
- Most patients present with nonspecific constitutional symptoms (weakness, nausea, abdominal pain, vomiting).
- Purpura (secondary to thrombocytopenia).
- Jaundice, pallor (from hemolysis).
- Mucosal bleeding.
- Fever.
- Fluctuating levels of consciousness (caused by thrombotic occlusion of the cerebral vessels). However, one third of patients have no neurologic abnormalities.
- Renal failure and neurologic events are usually end-stage features.

ETIOLOGY

- Acquired TTP is an autoimmune disorder caused by autoantibody inhibition of ADAMTS13 activity. Hereditary TTP (also called Upshaw-Schulman syndrome) is caused by homozygous or compound heterozygous ADAMTS13 mutations.
- Many drugs, including clopidogrel, penicillin, antineoplastic agents (gemcitabine, mitomycin C, cyclosporine) oral contraceptives, quinine, and ticlopidine, have been associated with TTP. Other precipitating causes include infectious agents, pregnancy, malignancies, allogeneic bone marrow transplantation, and neurologic disorders.

DIAGNOSIS

DIFFERENTIAL DIAGNOSIS

- Disseminated intravascular coagulation (DIC)
- Malignant hypertension
- Vasculitis
- Eclampsia or preeclampsia
- Hemolytic-uremic syndrome (typically encountered in children, often after a viral infection)
- Gastroenteritis as a result of a serotoxin-producing serotype of *Escherichia coli*
- Medications: clopidogrel, ticlopidine, penicillin, antineoplastic chemotherapeutic agents, oral contraceptives

WORKUP

- A comprehensive history, physical examination, and laboratory evaluation usually confirm the diagnosis. Fig. 1T-29 is an algorithm for diagnosis of TTP.

LABORATORY TESTS

- Severe anemia and thrombocytopenia (platelet count <50,000 or >50% reduction from previous counts). Peripheral blood smear (Fig. E1T-30) reveals numerous red cell fragments (schistocytes).
- Elevated blood urea nitrogen and creatinine.
- Evidence of hemolysis: elevated reticulocyte count, indirect bilirubin, lactate dehydrogenase, decreased haptoglobin.
- Urinalysis: hematuria (red blood cells [RBCs] and RBC casts in urine sediment) and proteinuria.
- Peripheral smear: severely fragmented RBCs (schistocytes). More than 4% RBC fragments in the peripheral blood.
- No laboratory evidence of DIC (normal fibrin degradation product, fibrinogen).
- The diagnosis of hereditary TTP requires documentation of ADAMTS13 deficiency and an absence of ADAMTS13 autoantibody inhibitor, and confirmation requires documentation of ADAMTS13 mutations. Diagnostic criteria for acquired TTP are the presence of microangiopathic hemolytic anemia and thrombocytopenia without another apparent cause. An ADAMTS13 level indicating less than 10% of normal activity supports the clinical diagnosis of acquired TTP.

Rx TREATMENT

ACUTE GENERAL Rx

- Discontinue potential offending agents. Initiate ADAMTS13 replacement by plasma infusion in patients with hereditary TTP.
- The American Association of Blood Banks, the American Society for Apheresis, and the British Committee for Standards in Haematology recommend daily plasma exchange with replacement of 1.0 to 1.5 times the predicted plasma volume of the patient as standard therapy for TTP. The British guidelines recommend that plasma exchange therapy be continued for a minimum of 2 days after the platelet count returns to normal (>150,000 cells/m³).
- High-dose plasma infusion (25 mL/kg/day) may be useful only if plasma exchange cannot be promptly started and for patients with very severe or refractory disease between plasma exchange sessions. High-dose plasma infusions can cause volume overload in patients with renal insufficiency.
- Patients with hereditary TTP who experience severe plasma allergic reactions have been effectively treated with plasma-derived factor VIII concentrate that contains ADAMTS13.
- Corticosteroids (prednisone 1 to 2 mg/kg/day) may be effective alone in patients with mild disease or may be administered concomitantly with plasmapheresis plus plasma exchange with fresh frozen plasma.
- The monoclonal antibody rituximab has also been used for treatment of TTP.
- Platelet transfusions are contraindicated except in severely thrombocytopenic patients with documented bleeding or those who are facing surgery or other invasive procedures in the setting of severe thrombocytopenia.
- Use of antiplatelet agents (acetylsalicylic acid, dipyridamole) is controversial.
- Splenectomy is performed in refractory cases.
- Dialysis is rarely required.

CHRONIC Rx

- Relapsing TTP may be treated with plasma exchange.
- Remission of chronic TTP that is unresponsive to conventional therapy has been reported after treatment with cyclophosphamide and the monoclonal antibody rituximab.
- Splenectomy done while the patients are in remission has been used in some centers to decrease the frequency of relapse in TTP.

DISPOSITION

- Survival of patients with TTP currently exceeds 80% with plasma exchange therapy.
- Relapse occurs in 20% to 40% of patients who have TTP in remission.

REFERRAL

Surgical referral for splenectomy in selected patients (see "Acute General Rx" and "Chronic Rx").

PEARLS & CONSIDERATIONS

COMMENTS

- The diagnosis of TTP/hemolytic-uremic syndrome should be considered in pregnant women with vague neurologic, gastrointestinal, or renal symptoms in either the obstetric triage or emergency department areas.
- TTP is fatal in 90% of patients without therapy.

SUGGESTED READINGS
Available at www.expertconsult.com

RELATED CONTENT
Hemolytic Uremic Syndrome (Related Key Topic)

AUTHOR: **FRED F. FERRI, M.D.**

Low platelet count
Hemolytic anemia
Fragmentation of RBC

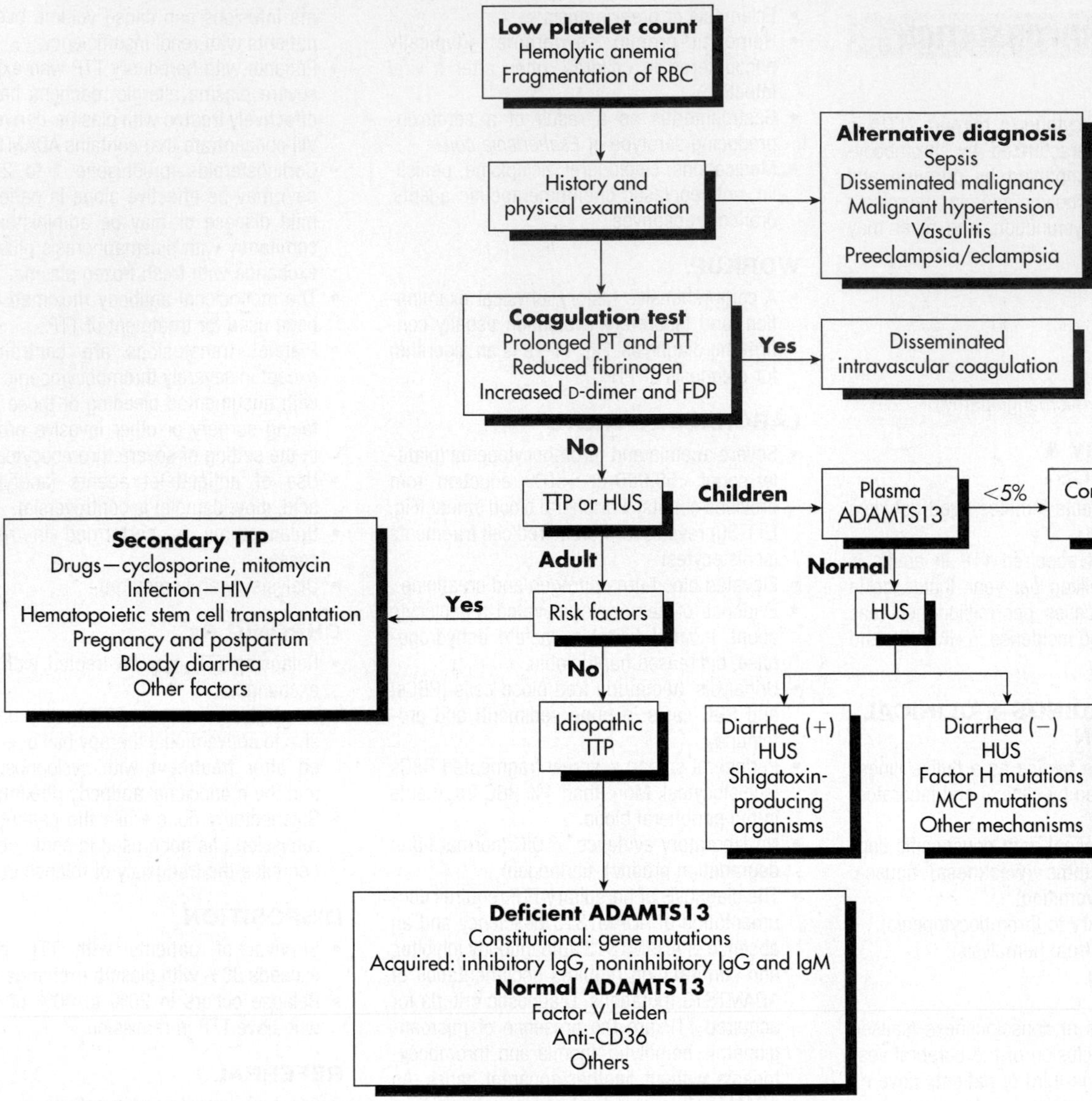

Alternative diagnosis
Sepsis
Disseminated malignancy
Malignant hypertension
Vasculitis
Preeclampsia/eclampsia

History and
physical examination

Coagulation test
Prolonged PT and PTT
Reduced fibrinogen
Increased D-dimer and FDP

Yes → Disseminated
intravascular coagulation

No

TTP or HUS → **Children** → Plasma ADAMTS13 → <5% → Congenital TTP

Adult

Normal

Secondary TTP
Drugs—cyclosporine, mitomycin
Infection—HIV
Hematopoietic stem cell transplantation
Pregnancy and postpartum
Bloody diarrhea
Other factors

Yes ← Risk factors

No

Idiopathic
TTP

HUS

Diarrhea (+)
HUS
Shigatoxin-
producing
organisms

Diarrhea (−)
HUS
Factor H mutations
MCP mutations
Other mechanisms

Deficient ADAMTS13
Constitutional: gene mutations
Acquired: inhibitory IgG, noninhibitory IgG and IgM
Normal ADAMTS13
Factor V Leiden
Anti-CD36
Others

FIGURE 1T-29 Algorithm for diagnosis of thrombotic thrombocytopenic purpura (TTP) and hemolytic-uremic syndrome (HUS). *MCP,* Membrane cofactor protein; *PT,* prothrombin time; *PTT,* partial thromboplastin time; *RBC,* red blood cell. (From Young NS et al [eds]: *Clinical hematology,* St Louis, 2006, Mosby.)

BASIC INFORMATION

DEFINITION

Thyroid carcinoma is a primary neoplasm of the thyroid. There are four major types of thyroid carcinoma: papillary, follicular, anaplastic, and medullary.

SYNONYMS

Papillary carcinoma of thyroid
Follicular carcinoma of thyroid
Anaplastic carcinoma of thyroid
Medullary carcinoma of thyroid

ICD-10CM CODES
C73   Malignant neoplasm of thyroid gland
D09.3 Carcinoma in situ of thyroid and other endocrine glands
D34   Benign neoplasm of thyroid gland
D44.0 Neoplasm of uncertain behavior of thyroid gland

EPIDEMIOLOGY & DEMOGRAPHICS

- Thyroid cancer is the most common endocrine cancer, with over 48,000 new cases in the United States and approximately 1100 deaths. The incidence of thyroid cancer is rising at a faster rate than any other type of malignancy.
- Female/male ratio is 3:1.
- Median age at diagnosis: 45 to 50 yr.
- Occult thyroid cancer is identified in 20% of autopsy specimens.

PHYSICAL FINDINGS & CLINICAL PRESENTATION

- Presence of thyroid nodule
- Hoarseness and cervical lymphadenopathy
- Painless swelling in the region of the thyroid

ETIOLOGY

- Risk factors: prior neck irradiation
- Multiple endocrine neoplasia II (medullary carcinoma)
- Inherited syndromes associated with thyroid cancer are described in Table 1T-9
- GLP-1 receptor agonists for the treatment of type 2 DM (e.g., exenatide, albiglutide) can increase the risk of medullary thyroid carcinoma (MTC)

TABLE 1T-9 Inherited Syndromes Associated With Thyroid Cancer

Multiple endocrine neoplasia (MEN) 2A and 2B
Isolated familial medullary thyroid cancer
Gardner syndrome
Familial adenomatous polyposis
Carney complex
Cowden syndrome
Familial nonmedullary thyroid cancer

From Cameron JL, Cameron AM: *Current surgical therapy*, ed 10, Philadelphia, 2011, Saunders.

DIAGNOSIS

DIFFERENTIAL DIAGNOSIS

- Multinodular goiter
- Lymphocytic thyroiditis
- Ectopic thyroid

WORKUP

The workup of thyroid carcinoma includes laboratory evaluation and diagnostic imaging. However, diagnosis is confirmed with fine-needle aspiration or surgical biopsy. At diagnosis the vast majority of thyroid cancers are well differentiated, with excellent prognosis. The characteristics of thyroid carcinoma vary with the type:

- Papillary carcinoma (85%):
  1. Most frequently occurs in women during second or third decades
  2. Histologically, psammoma bodies (calcific bodies present in papillary projections) are pathognomonic; found in 35% to 45% of papillary thyroid carcinomas
  3. Majority are not papillary lesions but mixed papillary follicular carcinomas
  4. Spread is by lymphatics and by local invasion
- Follicular carcinoma (10%):
  1. More aggressive than papillary carcinoma
  2. Incidence increases with age
  3. Tends to metastasize hematogenously to bone, producing pathologic fractures
  4. Tends to concentrate iodine (useful for radiation therapy)
- Anaplastic carcinoma (1%):
  1. Very aggressive neoplasm
  2. Two major histologic types: small cell (less aggressive, 5-yr survival approximately 20%) and giant cell (death usually within 6 mo of diagnosis)
- MTC (4%):
  1. Unifocal lesion: found sporadically in elderly patients
  2. Bilateral lesions: associated with pheochromocytoma and hyperparathyroidism; this combination is known as MEN-II and is inherited as an autosomal-dominant disorder

LABORATORY TESTS

- Thyroid function studies are generally normal. Thyroid-stimulating hormone (TSH), T4, and serum thyroglobulin levels should be obtained before thyroidectomy in patients with confirmed thyroid carcinoma. Serum thyroglobulin levels can be useful postoperatively to monitor recurrence of thyroid carcinoma (Fig. E1T-31).
- Increased plasma calcitonin assay in patients with medullary carcinoma (tumors produce thyrocalcitonin). RET proto-oncogene sequencing and measurement of plasma free metanephrine and normetanephrine levels to rule out coexistent pheochromocytoma are recommended in all patients with medullary thyroid cancer.
- Fine-needle aspiration biopsy is the best method to assess a thyroid nodule (see "Thyroid Nodule" in Section I).

IMAGING STUDIES (FIG. E1T-32)

- Thyroid ultrasound can detect solitary solid nodules that have a high risk of malignancy. However, a negative ultrasound does not exclude diagnosis of thyroid carcinoma.
- Thyroid scanning with iodine-123 or technetium-99m can identify hypofunctioning (cold) nodules, which are more likely to be malignant. However, warm nodules can also be malignant.

STAGING

- Stage I: thyroid cancer of any size without distal spread in patient under age 45. In patients 45 years or older, tumor size ≤2 cm without local invasion or positive cervical lymph nodes
- Stage II: distal spread in patient younger than 45 years. In patients 45 years or older, tumors >2 cm but <4 cm without local invasion or positive cervical lymph nodes
- Stage III: tumors >4 cm in patient over 45 years of age
- Stage IV: distal spread in patient over 45 years of age

TREATMENT

ACUTE GENERAL Rx

- Papillary carcinoma:
  1. Total thyroidectomy is indicated if the patient has:
     a. Extrapyramidal extension of carcinoma
     b. Papillary carcinoma limited to thyroid but a positive history of irradiation to the neck
     c. Lesion >2 cm
  2. Lobectomy with isthmectomy may be considered in patients with intrathyroid papillary carcinoma <2 cm and no history of neck or head irradiation; surgery should be followed with suppressive therapy with thyroid hormone because these tumors are TSH responsive. The accepted practice is to suppress serum TSH concentrations to <0.1 microunit/mL in patients with persistent disease, suppression to 0.1 to 0.5 microunit/ml in patients who are disease free but are at high risk of recurrence, and a goal TSH level of 0.3 to 2.0 microunits/mL in patients who are disease free and have a low risk of recurrence.
  3. Radioiodine ablation reduces rates of death and recurrence (Table 1T-10). Radioiodine is administered for stages III and IV disease.
- Follicular carcinoma:
  1. Total thyroidectomy followed by TSH suppression, as previously noted
  2. Radiotherapy with iodine-131 followed by thyroid suppression therapy with tri-iodothyronine is useful in patients with metastasis (Table 1T-10)
- Anaplastic carcinoma:
  1. At diagnosis, this neoplasm is rarely operable; palliative surgery is indicated for extremely large tumor compressing the trachea.

2. Management is usually restricted to radiation therapy or chemotherapy (combination of doxorubicin, cisplatin, and other antineoplastic agents) (Table 1T-10); these measures rarely provide significant palliation.

- Medullary carcinoma:
1. Thyroidectomy should be performed, followed by TSH suppression.
2. Vandetanib, an oral tyrosine kinase inhibitor, was recently FDA-approved for treatment of symptomatic or progressive, unresectable, locally advanced or metastatic medullary thyroid cancer. It is not recommended for treatment of asymptomatic or less aggressive disease due to its many serious side effects.
3. Patients and their families should be screened for pheochromocytoma and hyperparathyroidism.

DISPOSITION

Prognosis varies with the type of thyroid carcinoma: 5-yr survival approaches 80% for follicular carcinoma and is approximately 5% with anaplastic carcinoma (see Table 1T-11).

PEARLS & CONSIDERATIONS

COMMENTS

- Family members of patients with medullary carcinoma should be screened; DNA analysis for the detection of mutations in the *RET* gene structure permits the identification of *MEN IIA* gene carriers.
- Motesanib, an oral inhibitor of vascular endothelial growth factor (VEGF) receptors, has been reported effective in inducing partial responses in patients with advanced or metastatic differentiated thyroid cancer that is progressive.
- While there is little controversy regarding the benefit of radioactive iodine in iodine-avid advanced-stage well-differentiated thyroid cancer, the indications for radioactive iodine following total thyroidectomy in patients with very low risk disease is controversial. Proponents argue that its use may destroy microscopic metastases while opponents counter that the risk of secondary cancer due to radioactive iodine is not

warranted in patients whose prognosis is typically excellent.
- Metastatic thyroid cancers that are refractory to radioiodine (iodine-131) are associated with a poor prognosis. Recent trials have shown that the selective mitogen-activated protein kinase (MAPK) pathway antagonist selumetinib produces clinically meaningful increases in iodine uptake and retention in some patients with thyroid cancer that is refractory to radioiodine. In recent phase 2 trials, lenvatinib has also shown significant improvements in progression-free survival and response rate among patients with iodine-131 refractory thyroid cancer.

SUGGESTED READINGS
Available at www.expertconsult.com

RELATED CONTENT
Thyroid Cancer (Patient Information)

AUTHOR: **FRED F. FERRI, M.D.**

TABLE 1T-10 Indications for Iodine-131 Treatment in Patients With Papillary, Follicular, or Hürthle Cell Thyroid Carcinoma after Initial Definitive Near-Total Thyroidectomy

No Indication

Adult patients at very low risk for cause-specific mortality or relapse: complete surgical resection, favorable histology, and limited extent of disease (e.g., PTC patients with MACIS scores <6; patients with tumor size <1 cm, N0, and M0).

Definite Indications

Distant metastasis at diagnosis

Incomplete tumor resection

Complete tumor resection but high risk for mortality or recurrence (e.g., PTC patients with MACIS scores ≥6 and pTNM stage II/III FTC or HCC)

Probable Indications

Incomplete surgery (less than near-total thyroidectomy, no lymph node dissection)

PTC or FTC in a child younger than 16 yr

If PTC, tall cell or columnar cell variant and diffuse sclerosing variant

If FTC, widely invasive or poorly differentiated tumor

Bulky nodal metastases

FTC, Follicular thyroid carcinoma; *HCC,* Hürthle cell carcinoma; *MACIS,* scoring system based on metastasis, age, completeness of resection, invasion, and size; *PTC,* papillary thyroid carcinoma; *pTNM,* pathologic tumor-node-metastasis classification.
From Melmed S et al (eds): *Williams textbook of endocrinology,* ed 12, Philadelphia, 2011, Saunders.

TABLE 1T-11 Characteristics of Thyroid Cancers

Type of Cancer	Percentage of Thyroid Cancers	Age of Onset (Yr)	Treatment	Prognosis
Papillary	88	40-80	Thyroidectomy, followed by radioactive iodine ablation and TSH suppression	Good
Follicular	10	45-80	Thyroidectomy, followed by radioactive iodine ablation and TSH suppression	Fair to good
Medullary	3-4	20-50	Thyroidectomy and central compartment lymph node dissection and TSH suppression	Fair
Anaplastic	1	50-80	Isthmusectomy followed by palliative x-ray treatment	Poor
Lymphoma	<1	25-70	X-ray therapy and/or chemotherapy	Fair

From Andreoli TE et al: *Andreoli and Carpenter's Cecil essentials of medicine,* ed 8, Philadelphia, 2010, Saunders.

BASIC INFORMATION

DEFINITION

A thyroid nodule is an abnormality found on physical examination of the thyroid gland; nodules can be benign (70%) or malignant.

ICD-10CM CODES
E04.1   Nontoxic single thyroid nodule.
E05.2   Thyrotoxicosis with toxic single thyroid nodule.
E05.11 Thyrotoxicosis with toxic single thyroid nodule with thyrotoxic crisis or storm

EPIDEMIOLOGY & DEMOGRAPHICS

- Palpable thyroid nodules occur in 4% to 7% of the population.
- Thyroid nodules can be found in 50% of autopsies; however, only one in 10 is palpable.
- Malignancy is present in 5% to 15% of all thyroid nodules and in 7% to 9% of palpable nodules.
- Incidence of thyroid nodules increases after 45 yr. They are found more frequently in women (5% of women; 1% of men).
- History of prior head and neck irradiation increases the risk of thyroid cancer.
- Increased likelihood that nodule is malignant: nodule increasing in size or >3 cm, regional lymphadenopathy, fixation to adjacent tissues, age <40 yr, symptoms of local invasion (dysphagia, hoarseness, neck pain, male sex, family history of thyroid cancer or polyposis [Gardner syndrome]), rapid growth during levothyroxine therapy, microcalcification within the nodule, and high intranodular vascular flow.

PHYSICAL FINDINGS & CLINICAL PRESENTATION

- Palpable, firm, and nontender nodule in the thyroid area should prompt suspicion of carcinoma. Signs of metastasis are regional lymphadenopathy and inspiratory stridor.
- Signs and symptoms of thyrotoxicosis can be found in functioning nodules.

ETIOLOGY

- History of prior head and neck irradiation.
- Family history of pheochromocytoma, carcinoma of the thyroid, and hyperparathyroidism (medullary carcinoma of the thyroid is a component of MEN-II).

DIAGNOSIS

DIFFERENTIAL DIAGNOSIS

- Thyroid carcinoma.
- Multinodular goiter.
- Thyroglossal duct cyst.
- Epidermoid cyst.
- Laryngocele.
- Nonthyroid neck neoplasm.
- Branchial cleft cyst.

WORKUP

- Ultrasonography is inexpensive and effective modality to stratify malignancy risk.
- Fine-needle aspiration (FNA) biopsy is the best diagnostic study; the accuracy can be >90%, but it is directly related to the level of experience of the physician and the cytopathologist interpreting the aspirate. FNA is not routinely recommended for thyroid nodules <1 cm in diameter unless there are significant risk factors (see above).
- FNA biopsy is less reliable with thyroid cystic lesions; surgical excision should be considered for most thyroid cysts not abolished by aspiration.
- A diagnostic approach to thyroid nodule is described in Fig. 1T-33. Preoperative, ultrasonically guided FNA accurately classifies 62% to 85% of thyroid nodules as benign; however, 15% to 30% of aspirations yield indeterminate cytologic findings. Table 1T-12 describes the probability of malignancy at histology based on FNA biopsy cytology.

LABORATORY TESTS

- Serum TSH should be obtained in all patients with thyroid nodules. If suppressed, obtain free T4 and free T3 and thyroid scan to rule out "hot nodule," indicative of hyperthyroid adenoma. Less than 1% of hyperfunctioning nodules are malignant. Typically FNA biopsy is not necessary in hot nodules.
- Thyroid-stimulating hormone (TSH), T4, and serum thyroglobulin levels should be obtained before thyroidectomy in patients with confirmed thyroid carcinoma on FNA biopsy.
- Serum calcitonin at random or after pentagastrin stimulation is useful when suspecting medullary carcinoma of the thyroid and in anyone with a family history of medullary thyroid carcinoma.
- Serum thyroid autoantibodies (see "Thyroiditis" in Section I) are useful in patients with multinodular goiter and when suspecting thyroiditis.
- Molecular analysis of thyroid tissue for the presence of BRAF and RAS mutations and for RET/PTC and PAX8-PPAR gamma 1 gene rearrangements can be used as a diagnostic tool, since 60% to 70% of thyroid cancers harbor at least one genetic mutation. The gene expression classifier profile can be used to identify a subpopulation of patients with a low likelihood of cancer, thereby avoiding unnecessary surgery in patients with indeterminate FNA. The gene expression classifier test has a high negative predictive value for cytologically indeterminate nodules (95% for an atypical or follicular lesion of undetermined significance, 94% for a follicular neoplasm, and 85% for a lesion suggestive of cancer).

IMAGING STUDIES

- Thyroid ultrasound (Fig. E1T-34) is useful to evaluate the size of the thyroid and the number, composition (solid versus cystic), and dimensions of the thyroid nodule; solid thyroid nodules have a higher incidence of malignancy, but cystic nodules can also be malignant.

The three characteristics on thyroid ultrasound most predictive of cancer are nodules >2 cm, microcalcifications, and entirely solid nodules.
- Thyroid scan can be performed with technetium-99m pertechnetate, iodine-123, or iodine-131. Iodine isotopes are preferred because up to 35% of nodules that appear functioning on pertechnetate scanning may appear nonfunctioning on radioiodine scanning. A thyroid scan:
  1. Classifies nodules as hyperfunctioning (hot), normally functioning (warm), or nonfunctioning (cold); cold nodules have a higher incidence of malignancy.
  2. Scan has difficulty evaluating nodules near the thyroid isthmus or at the periphery of the gland.
  3. Normal tissue over a nonfunctioning nodule might mask the nodule as "warm" or normally functioning.
- Both thyroid scan and ultrasound provide information about the risk of malignant neoplasia based on the characteristics of the thyroid nodule, but their value in the initial evaluation of a thyroid nodule is limited because neither provides a definite tissue diagnosis.

TREATMENT

GENERAL Rx

- Evaluation of results of FNA:
  1. Normal cells: may repeat biopsy during present evaluation or reevaluate patient after 3 to 6 mo of suppressive therapy (L-thyroxine, prescribed in doses to suppress the TSH level to 0.1-0.5).
     a. Failure to regress indicates increased likelihood of malignancy.
     b. Reliance on repeat FNA biopsy is preferable to routine surgery for nodules not responding to thyroxine.
- Indeterminate: use of gene expression classifier profile. If suspicious, perform surgery; if benign, monitor with subsequent repeat FNA and gene expression classifier profile.
- Malignant cells: surgery.

DISPOSITION

Variable with results of FNA biopsy.

REFERRAL

Surgical referral for FNA biopsy.

PEARLS & CONSIDERATIONS

COMMENTS

- Most solid, benign nodules grow; therefore, an increase in nodule volume alone is not a reliable predictor of malignancy.
- Thyroid nodules incidentally identified on fluorodeoxyglucose-PET (FDG-PET) scan done for other disorders has a much higher malignancy rate (30% to 50%).
- Surgery is indicated in hard or fixed nodule, presence of dysphagia or hoarseness, and

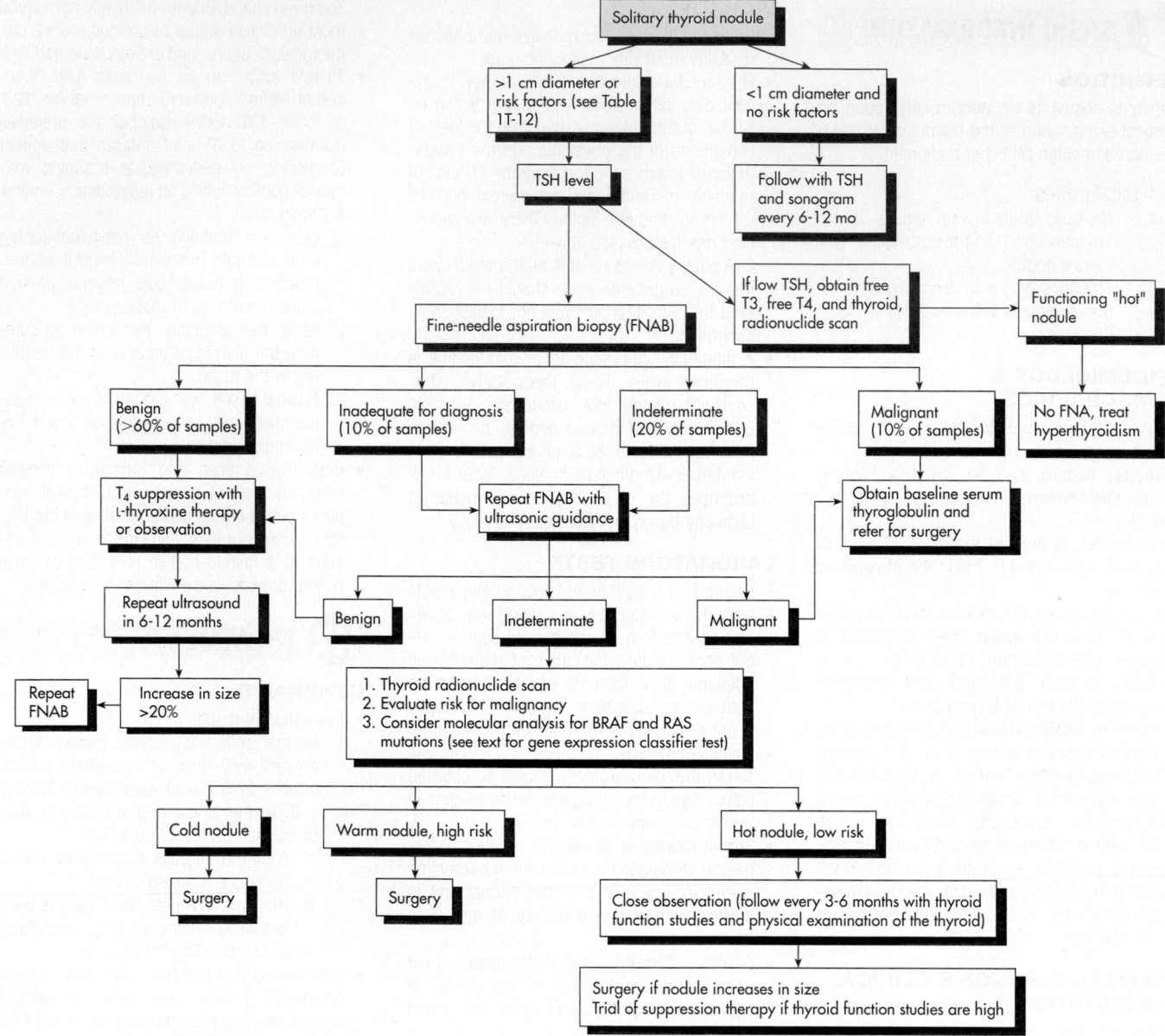

FIGURE 1T-33 Diagnostic algorithm for thyroid nodule. (From Ferri, F: *Ferri's best test*, 3rd ed, Philadelphia, Elsevier, 2014.)

TABLE 1T-12 Clinical and Ultrasound Findings in Favor of Malignant Thyroid Nodules

Clinical Features	Ultrasound Findings
History	Higher Suspicion
Young age (<20 yr) or older age (>60 yr)	Hypoechoic lesions
Male gender	Irregular margins
Neck irradiation during childhood or adolescence	Presence of microcalcifications
Rapid growth	Absence of halo
Recent changes in speaking, breathing, or swallowing	Internal or central blood flow
Family history of thyroid malignancy or MEN2	
Physical Examination	Low Suspicion
Firm and irregular consistency of nodule	Echo-free (cystic) lesion
Fixation to underlying or overlying tissues	Spongiform lesion
Vocal cord paralysis	
Regional lymphadenopathy	

From Melmed S, Polonsky KS, Larsen PR, et al: *Williams textbook of endocrinology*, ed 12, Philadelphia, 2011, Elsevier.

- rapidly growing solid masses regardless of "benign" results on FNA.
- Suppressive therapy of malignant thyroid nodules postoperatively with thyroxine is indicated. The use of suppressive therapy for benign solitary nodules is controversial.

SUGGESTED READINGS

Available at www.expertconsult.com

RELATED CONTENT

Thyroid Nodule (Patient Information)
Thyroiditis (Related Key Topic)

AUTHOR: **FRED F. FERRI, M.D.**

 BASIC INFORMATION

DEFINITION

Thyroiditis is an inflammatory, disease of the thyroid. It is a multifaceted disease with various etiologies, different clinical characteristics (depending on the stage), and distinct histopathology. Thyroiditis can be subdivided into three common types (Hashimoto's, painful, and painless) and two rare forms (suppurative and Riedel's). To add to the confusion, there are various synonyms for each form, and there is no internationally accepted classification of autoimmune thyroid disease.

SYNONYMS

Hashimoto's thyroiditis: chronic lymphocytic thyroiditis, chronic autoimmune thyroiditis, lymphadenoid goiter

Painful subacute thyroiditis: subacute thyroiditis, giant cell thyroiditis, de Quervain's thyroiditis, subacute granulomatous thyroiditis, pseudogranulomatous thyroiditis

Painless postpartum thyroiditis: subacute lymphocytic thyroiditis, postpartum thyroiditis

Painless sporadic thyroiditis: silent sporadic thyroiditis, subacute lymphocytic thyroiditis

Infectious thyroiditis: acute suppurative thyroiditis, bacterial thyroiditis, microbial inflammatory thyroiditis, pyogenic thyroiditis

Riedel's thyroiditis: fibrous thyroiditis

ICD-10CM CODES
E06.3 Autoimmune thyroiditis
E06.1 Subacute thyroiditis
E06.9 Thyroiditis, unspecified
E06.0 Acute thyroiditis
E06.5 Other chronic thyroiditis

PHYSICAL FINDINGS & CLINICAL PRESENTATION

- Hashimoto's: patients may have signs of hyperthyroidism (tachycardia, diaphoresis, palpitations, weight loss) or hypothyroidism (fatigue, weight gain, delayed reflexes) depending on the stage of the disease. Usually there is diffuse, firm enlargement of the thyroid gland; the gland may also be of normal size (atrophic form with clinically manifested hypothyroidism).
- Painful subacute: exquisitely tender, enlarged thyroid, fever; signs of hyperthyroidism are initially present; signs of hypothyroidism can subsequently develop.
- Painless thyroiditis: clinical features are similar to subacute thyroiditis except for the absence of tenderness of the thyroid gland.
- Suppurative: patient is febrile with severe neck pain, focal tenderness of the involved portion of the thyroid, erythema of the overlying skin.
- Riedel's: slowly enlarging hard mass in the anterior neck; often mistaken for thyroid cancer; signs of hypothyroidism occur in advanced stages.

ETIOLOGY

- Hashimoto's: autoimmune disorder that begins with the activation of CD4 (helper) T-lymphocytes specific for thyroid antigens. The etiologic factor for the activation of these cells is unknown.
- Painful subacute: possibly postviral; usually follows a respiratory illness not considered to be a form of autoimmune thyroiditis
- Painless thyroiditis: frequently occurs postpartum
- Infectious (suppurative): infectious etiology, generally bacterial, although fungi and parasites have also been implicated; often occurs in immunocompromised hosts or after a penetrating neck injury
- Riedel's: fibrous infiltration of the thyroid; etiology unknown
- Drug induced: typically painless due to lithium, interferon-alfa, amiodarone, interleukin-2
- Radiation thyroiditis: occurs 5 to 10 days after treatment with radioactive iodine; it is painful and may result in transient exacerbation of hyperthyroidism

 DIAGNOSIS

DIFFERENTIAL DIAGNOSIS

- The hyperthyroid phase of Hashimoto's, subacute, and silent thyroiditis can be mistaken for Graves' disease.
- Riedel's thyroiditis can be mistaken for carcinoma of the thyroid.
- Painful subacute thyroiditis can be mistaken for infections of the oropharynx and trachea or for suppurative thyroiditis.
- Factitious hyperthyroidism can mimic silent thyroiditis.

WORKUP

- The diagnostic workup includes laboratory and radiologic evaluation to rule out other conditions that may mimic thyroiditis (see previously) and differentiate the various forms of thyroiditis.
- The patient's medical history may be helpful in differentiating the various types of thyroiditis (e.g., presentation after childbirth is suggestive of silent [postpartum, painless] thyroiditis; occurrence after a viral respiratory infection suggests subacute thyroiditis; history of penetrating injury to the neck indicates suppurative thyroiditis) (Table E1T-13).

LABORATORY TESTS

- Thyroid-stimulating hormone, free T_4: may be normal or indicative of hypothyroidism or hyperthyroidism depending on the stage of the thyroiditis.
- White blood cell (WBC) with differential: increased WBC with left shift occurs with subacute and suppurative thyroiditis.
- Antimicrosomal antibodies: detected in >90% of patients with Hashimoto's thyroiditis and 50% to 80% of patients with silent thyroiditis.
- Serum thyroglobulin levels are elevated in patients with subacute and silent thyroiditis; this test is nonspecific but may be useful in monitoring the course of subacute thyroiditis and distinguishing silent thyroiditis from factitious hyperthyroidism (low or absent serum thyroglobulin level).

IMAGING STUDIES

Twenty-four–hour radioactive iodine uptake (RAIU) is useful to distinguish Graves' disease (increased RAIU) from thyroiditis (normal or low RAIU). Table E1T-14 summarizes factors that influence 24-hr thyroid iodide uptake.

Rx TREATMENT

ACUTE GENERAL Rx

- The duration of the thyrotoxic phase of thyroiditis is usually 3 to 6 wk. This phase is followed by a hypothyroid phase typically lasting up to 12 wk.
- Treat hypothyroid phase with levothyroxine 25 to 50 mcg/day initially and monitor serum thyroid-stimulating hormone initially every 6 to 8 wk.
- Control symptoms of hyperthyroidism with beta-blockers (e.g., propranolol 20-40 mg PO q6h).
- Control pain in patients with subacute thyroiditis with nonsteroidal anti-inflammatory drugs. Prednisone 20 to 40 mg qd may be used if nonsteroidals are insufficient, but it should be gradually tapered off over several weeks.
- Use IV antibiotics and drain abscess (if present) in patients with suppurative thyroiditis.

DISPOSITION

- Hashimoto's thyroiditis: long-term prognosis is favorable; most patients recover their thyroid function.
- Painful subacute thyroiditis: permanent hypothyroidism occurs in 10% of patients.
- Painless thyroiditis: 6% of patients have permanent hypothyroidism.
- Infectious thyroiditis: there is usually full recovery after treatment.
- Riedel's thyroiditis: hypothyroidism occurs when fibrous infiltration involves the entire thyroid.

REFERRAL

Surgical referral in patients with compression of adjacent neck structures and in some patients with infectious (suppurative) thyroiditis

EBM EVIDENCE

Available at www.expertconsult.com

SUGGESTED READINGS
Available at www.expertconsult.com

RELATED CONTENT
Thyroiditis (Patient Information)

AUTHOR: **FRED F. FERRI, M.D.**

BASIC INFORMATION

DEFINITION

Tinea capitis is a dermatophyte infection of hair shaft and follicles of the scalp, eyebrows, and eyelashes. It is a form of superficial mycosis. Etiologic agents are fungal species of the genera *Microsporum* and *Trichophyton*.

SYNONYMS

Ringworm of the scalp, ringworm of the head, gray patch tinea capitis, black dot tinea capitis, tinea tonsurans, herpes tonsurans, kerion, favus

ICD-10CM CODES
B35.0 Tinea barbae and tinea capitis

EPIDEMIOLOGY & DEMOGRAPHICS

Tinea capitis primarily affects prepubertal children with peak age between 3 and 7 yr old. Adult cases are rare, possibly because of the fungistatic effect of the sebum found in older persons. Urban living, large family size, low socioeconomic status, and crowded living conditions may contribute to an increased incidence of tinea capitis. The elderly and immunocompromised individuals have an increased risk of infection. The incidence of the disease varies worldwide; however, it has is relatively low in the United States. It is reportedly widespread in parts of central and South America, India, and Africa.

In the United States, peak incidence occurs in school-aged children of low socioeconomic status, with African-American male children accounting for the greatest proportion of cases. About 3% to 8% of American children are affected, and 34% of household contacts are asymptomatic carriers.

PHYSICAL FINDINGS & CLINICAL PRESENTATION

- Classic triad of scalp scaling, alopecia, and cervical adenopathy
- Most forms of tinea capitis begin with one or few round patches of scale or alopecia.
- Primary lesions include plaques, papules, pustules, or nodules on the scalp (usually occipital region).
- Secondary lesions include scales, alopecia (usually reversible), erythema, exudates, and edema.
- Scalp pruritus may be present.

- Fever, pain, and lymphadenopathy (commonly postcervical) may occur with inflammatory lesions.
- Different clinical patterns of tinea capitis have been described:
  1. Gray patch: Lesions are scaly and well demarcated. The hairs within the patch break off a few millimeters above the scalp. One or several lesions may be present; sometimes the lesions join to form larger ones.
  2. Black dot: Early lesions with erythema and scaling patch are easily overlooked until areas of alopecia develop. Hairs within the patches break at the surface of the scalp, leaving behind a pattern of swollen black dots.
  3. Kerion (Fig. 1T-35): inflamed, exudative, pustular, boggy, tender nodules exhibiting marked edema, and hair loss seen in severe tinea capitis. Caused by immune response to the fungus. May lead to some scarring.
  4. Favus: production of scutula (hair matted together with dermatophyte hyphae and keratin debris), characterized by yellow cup-shaped crusts around hair shafts. A fetid odor may be present.

ETIOLOGY

Although fungi of the *Microsporum* or *Trichophyton* genera cause most cases of tinea capitis, causative species vary between geographical areas and across time. *T. tonsurans* is the predominant cause of tinea capitis, present in more than 90% of cases in North and Central America. *Microsporum canis, M. audouinii,* and *Trichophyton mentagrophytes* are less common. The most common causative species for black dot tinea capitis is *T. tonsurans,* while gray patch tinea capitis tends to be caused by *M. andouinii* and *M. canis.* Infection of the hair shaft is preceded by invasion of the stratum corneum of the scalp. Transmission of *T. tonsurans* occurs from person-to-person via infected persons or asymptomatic carriers, fallen infected hairs, animal vectors, and fomites. *M. audouinii* is commonly spread by dogs and cats. Infectious fungal particles may remain viable for many months. Even though the organism remains viable on combs, hairbrushes, and other fomites for long periods of time, the role of fomites in spreading the infection may vary in different geographic areas.

DIAGNOSIS

DIFFERENTIAL DIAGNOSIS

Seborrheic dermatitis and psoriasis may be confused with tinea capitis. Other conditions that resemble tinea capitis include alopecia areata, impetigo, pediculosis, trichotillomania, traction alopecia, folliculitis, pseudopelade, seborrhea/atopic dermatitis, psoriasis, carbuncles, pyoderma, lichen ruber planus, lupus erythematosus should also be considered in the differential. Table 1T-15 highlights distinctive features of conditions that may be confused for tinea capitis.

WORKUP

- KOH testing of hair shaft extracted from the lesion, not the scale, because the *T. tonsurans* spores attach to or reside inside hair shafts and will rarely be found in the scales.
- Wood's ultraviolet light fluoresces blue-green on hair shafts for Microsporum infections but will fail to identify *T. tonsurans.*
- Fungal culture of hairs and scales on fungal medium such as Sabouraud's agar may be used to confirm the diagnosis, especially if uncertain.
- Histology of biopsies with fungal staining in cases where mycology tests are negative because of treatment initiation.

TREATMENT

- Griseofulvin is the gold standard FDA-approved treatment. Published studies show mean efficacy for griseofulvin treatment of about 68% for *Trichophyton* species and 88% for *Microsporum.* It is less costly than other drug options and has an excellent long-term safety profile. Micronized and ultramicronized preparations are absorbed better, and side effects are infrequent, especially when administered with fatty meals. Periodic monitoring of hematologic, liver, and renal function may be indicated, especially in prolonged treatment over 8 wk.

  Children: Griseofulvin is approved for children older than 2 yr of age: microsize griseofulvin 10 to 25 mg/kg PO per day in one single dose or two divided doses (maximum, 1 g/day; for tinea capitis, higher doses [20-25 mg/kg/day] have been recommended) or ultramicrosize griseofulvin, 5 to 15 mg/kg PO per day (maximum, 750 mg/day), in one single dose or two divided doses. Optimally, griseofulvin is given after a meal containing fat (e.g., peanut butter or ice cream). Recommended treatment length is 6 to 8 wk and should be continued 2 wk beyond clinical resolution (until hair regrowth occurs). Some children may require higher doses to achieve clinical cure.

  Adults and elderly persons: microsize griseofulvin 500 mg PO per day in one single dose or divided doses. The other option is ultramicrosize griseofulvin 375 mg PO per

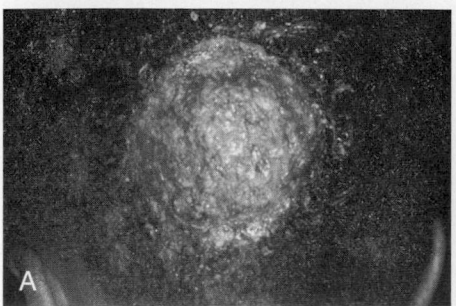
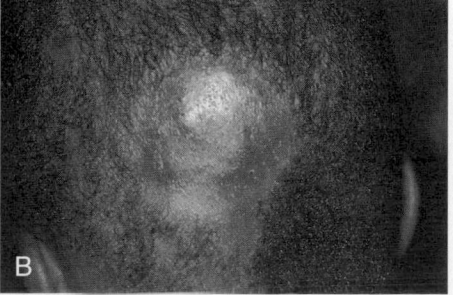

FIGURE 1T-35 A, Kerion. Boggy granulomatous mass of the scalp. **B,** Scarring after kerion. (From Kliegman RM et al: *Nelson textbook of pediatrics,* ed 19, Philadelphia, 2011, Saunders.)

TABLE 1T-15   Differential Diagnosis of Tinea Capitis

Disorder	Differentiating Features
Psoriasis	Red skin with thick, uniform, silvery scale, sharply demarcated; often psoriasis at other body sites also
Dermatitis	Main possibility is seborrheic dermatitis: usually more diffuse and has uniform fine scaling, rather than localized areas; doesn't typically cause alopecia or significant inflammation. May also be present on the face, especially the nasolabial fold, or as otitis externa. Atopic dermatitis is generally diffuse on scalp and almost inevitably present at other sites, but may coexist with tinea capitis, especially in children.
Pityriasis amiantacea	Thick sheets of asbestos-like scale, very adherent, generally a solitary patch. This may occur in various dermatoses.
Lichen simplex	Usually nape of neck; cobblestoned or lichenified skin thickening, with broken hairs that are not coated with scale
Alopecia areata	Usually not inflamed (may be mildly so), not scaly, usually sharply defined. "Exclamation mark" hairs occur but are not coated with fungus; "cadaverized" hairs especially cause difficulty, as they mimic black dot alopecia.
Scarring alopecias	Examples: discoid lupus erythematosus, lichen planus of scalp; cause perifollicular inflammation around intact hairs; usually associated with lesions at other sites also. Dissecting cellulitis of scalp is also in this differential.
Bacterial infections	Impetigo causes crusting but little inflammation, and hairs are intact; carbuncle is deeper and very tender but may be in the differential of kerion
Trichotillomania	Broken hairs of unequal length, but hair shafts themselves and the scalp are normal
Damage from hairdressing processes	Usually clear from the timescale
Neoplasm	May be in the differential of kerion; usually slower-growing and mainly on elderly, balding scalp, whereas kerion is in children or young adults with previously intact hair

From White GM, Cox NH (eds): *Diseases of the skin, a color atlas and text,* ed 2, St Louis, 2006, Mosby.

day in one single dose or divided doses. Recommended treatment length is 4 to 6 weeks.

- New alternative treatments: oral terbinafine, itraconazole, or fluconazole are comparable in efficacy and safety to griseofulvin, with possibly shorter treatment and better patient compliance. Preferred when resistant or when an allergy to griseofulvin is of concern. Monitoring of CBC, liver function tests, and renal function may be indicated.
  1. Terbinafine—4-wk course of therapy as effective as with griseofulvin. Dosages are 67.5 mg/day for patients weighing <20 kg; 125 mg/day for patients weighing 20 to 40 kg; and 250 mg for patients weighing >40 kg.
  2. Itraconazole—3.5 mg/kg daily for 4 to 6 wk or pulse therapy of 5 mg/kg daily for 1 wk each month for 2 to 3 mo (not approved for children)
  3. Fluconazole the only oral antifungal agent approved for children <2 yr, 6 mg/kg/day for 6 wk in children (3 to 6 wk in adults) or 8 mg/kg weekly for 8 to 12 wk (cap at 150 mg weekly for adults)
- The adjuvant use of antifungal shampoos may be recommended for all patients and household contacts. Shampoo like selenium sulfide 2.5% used for 5 min or ketoconazole shampoo used 2 to 3 times/wk can help prevent infection or eradicate asymptomatic carrier state by inhibiting fungal growth.
- Severe inflammatory kerion can be managed with additional prednisone 40 mg daily (1 mg/kg/day in children) and tapering over 2 wk.

- Prompt treatment is indicated, as is examination of siblings and other household contacts for evidence of tinea capitis.
- Recommend follow-up visit every 2 to 4 wk with Wood's light, microscopic study, and fungal culture. A mycologic documented cure is the goal of treatment.
- Pets that are infected or asymptomatic carriers should be treated.
- Children receiving treatment for tinea capitis may attend school once they start therapy with griseofulvin or other effective systemic agent.

⊘ PEARLS & CONSIDERATIONS

- Systemic antifungal therapy is required for tinea capitis because topical antifungal medications are not effective.
- Shaving of the head, haircuts, or wearing a cap or scarf during treatment is unnecessary.
- Sharing of combs, hair ribbons, and hairbrushes should be discouraged.

COMMENTS

- Confirming the diagnosis of tinea capitis with a laboratory specimen is important because misdiagnosis will result in delay or improper treatment.
- Patients and their families should look for sources of infections and disinfect contaminated objects such as combs, brushes, towels, and headgear. Avoid sharing personal hygiene utensils.
- Culture of hairs and scalp dander facilitates carrier identification and prevention.

SUGGESTED READINGS
Available at www.expertconsult.com

RELATED CONTENT
Tinea Capitis (Patient Information)

AUTHORS: **PRIYA SARIN GUPTA, M.D., M.P.H.,**
NADINE MBUYI, M.D., and
ALVARO M. RIVERA, M.D.

BASIC INFORMATION

DEFINITION

Tinea corporis is a dermatophyte fungal infection caused by the genera *Trichophyton* or *Microsporum*. Tinea corporis includes all superficial dermatophyte infections of the skin other than those invloving the scalp, beard, face, hands, feet, and groin.

SYNONYMS

Ringworm
Body ringworm
Tinea circinata

ICD-10CM CODES

B35.4 Tinea corporis

EPIDEMIOLOGY & DEMOGRAPHICS

- The disease is more common in warm climates.
- There is no predominant age or sex.

PHYSICAL FINDINGS & CLINICAL PRESENTATION

- Typically appears as single or multiple annular lesions with an advancing scaly border (Fig. 1T-36); the margin is slightly raised, reddened, and may be pustular.
- The central area becomes hypopigmented and less scaly as the active border progresses outward (Fig. 1T-37), thus the name "ringworm".
- The trunk and legs are primarily involved.
- Pruritus is variable.
- It is important to remember that recent topical corticosteroid use can significantly alter the appearance of the lesions.

- Tinea gladiatorum is a common problem for wrestlers.

ETIOLOGY

Trichophyton rubrum is the most common pathogen. Other common causes in the U.S. are *M. canis* and *T. mentagrophytes*.

DIAGNOSIS

DIFFERENTIAL DIAGNOSIS

- Pityriasis rosea
- Erythema multiforme
- Psoriasis
- Cutaneous systemic lupus erythematosus
- Secondary syphilis
- Nummular eczema
- Eczema
- Granuloma annulare
- Lyme disease
- Tinea versicolor
- Contact dermatitis

WORKUP

Diagnosis is usually made on clinical grounds. It can be confirmed by direct visualization under the microscope of a small fragment of the scale using wet mount preparation and potassium hydroxide solution; dermatophytes appear as translucent branching filaments (hyphae) with lines of separation appearing at irregular intervals.

LABORATORY TESTS

- Microscopic examination of hyphae
- Mycotic culture is usually not necessary.
- Biopsy is indicated only when the diagnosis is uncertain and the patient has not responded to treatment.
- HIV (widespread tinea corporis may be a presenting sign of AIDS)

TREATMENT

NONPHARMACOLOGIC THERAPY

Affected areas should be kept clean and dry.

ACUTE GENERAL Rx

- Various creams are effective; the application area should include normal skin approximately 2 cm beyond the affected area:
  1. Butenafine cream applied qd for 14 days
  2. Terbinafine cream applied bid for 7-14 days
  3. Other effective topical agents are sulconazole, miconazole, clotrimazole, ketoconazole, naftifine, cyclopirox olamine, and efinaconazole.
- Systemic therapy is reserved for severe cases and is usually given up to 4 wk; commonly used agents:
  1. Fluconazole, 150 mg once a week for 4 wk
  2. Terbinafine, 250 mg qd for 7-14 days
  3. Itraconazole 200 mg/day for 1 wk

DISPOSITION

Majority of cases resolve without sequelae within 3 to 4 wk of therapy.

REFERRAL

Dermatology referral in patients with persistent or recurrent infections

SUGGESTED READINGS

Available at www.expertconsult.com

RELATED CONTENT

Ringworm (Patient Information)

AUTHOR: **FRED F. FERRI, M.D.**

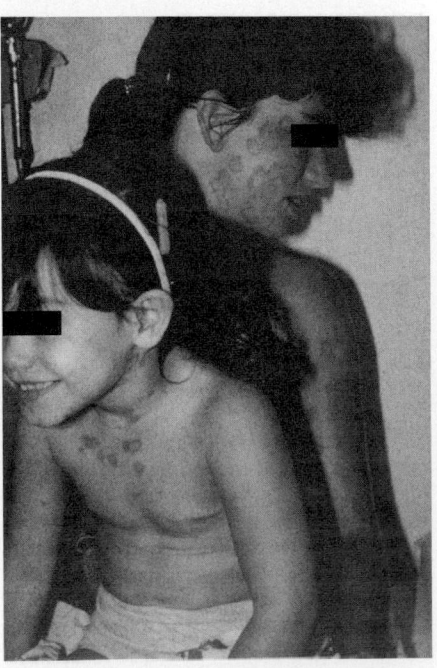

FIGURE 1T-36 Tinea corporis. (Courtesy of David Effron, MD.)

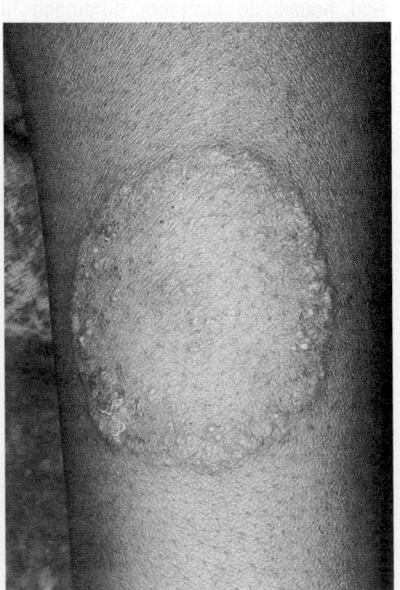

FIGURE 1T-37 Annular lesion (tinea corporis). Note raised erythematous, scaling border and central clearing. (From Noble J et al: *Textbook of primary care medicine,* ed 3, St Louis, 2001, Mosby.)

BASIC INFORMATION

DEFINITION
Tinea cruris is a dermatophyte infection of the groin.

SYNONYMS
Jock itch
Groin ringworm
Crotch itch

ICD-10CM CODES
B35.6 Tinea cruris

EPIDEMIOLOGY & DEMOGRAPHICS
- Most common during the summer in adolescent and young adult males.
- Males are affected more frequently than females; however, it has become more common in postpubertal females who are overweight or who often wear tight jeans or pantyhose.
- The infection often coexists with tinea pedis.

PHYSICAL FINDINGS & CLINICAL PRESENTATION
- It begins as a small erythematous, and scaling or crusted patch that spreads peripherally.
- Erythematous plaques have a half-moon shape and a scaling border.
- The acute inflammation tends to move down the inner thigh and usually spares the scrotum; in severe cases the fungus may spread onto the buttocks.
- Itching may be severe.
- Red papules, vesicles, and pustules may be present.
- An important diagnostic sign is the advancing well-defined border with a tendency toward central clearing (Fig. 1T-38).

ETIOLOGY
- Dermatophytes of the genera *Trichophyton, Epidermophyton,* and *Microsporum. T. rubrum* and *E. floccosum* are the most common infecting agents.
- Transmission from direct contact (e.g., infected persons, animals). The patient's feet should be evaluated as a source of infection because tinea cruris is often associated with tinea pedis.

DIAGNOSIS

DIFFERENTIAL DIAGNOSIS
- Candidal intertrigo
- Psoriasis
- Seborrheic dermatitis
- Erythrasma
- Contact dermatitis
- Tinea versicolor

WORKUP
Diagnosis is based on clinical presentation and demonstration of hyphae microscopically using potassium hydroxide.

LABORATORY TESTS
- Microscopic examination
- Cultures are generally not necessary.

TREATMENT

NONPHARMACOLOGIC THERAPY
- Keep infected area clean and dry.
- Boxer shorts are preferred to briefs. The reduction of perspiration and enhancement of evaporation from the crural area are necessary prophylactic measures.

ACUTE GENERAL Rx
- Various topical antifungal agents are available:
  1. Butenafine cream, applied qd × 14 days
  2. Terbinafine cream, applied bid × 14 days
- Drying powders (e.g., miconazole nitrate) may be useful in patients with excessive perspiration.
- Oral antifungal therapy is generally reserved for cases unresponsive to topical agents or can be used along with topical agents in severe cases. Effective medications are fluconazole 200 mg qd × 7 days or 150 mg once a week for 4 wks, terbinafine 250 mg qd × 14 days, or itraconazole 200 mg/day for 7 days.

DISPOSITION
Most cases respond promptly to therapy with complete resolution within 2 to 3 wk.

SUGGESTED READINGS
Available at www.expertconsult.com

RELATED CONTENT
Tinea Cruris (Patient Information)

AUTHOR: **FRED F. FERRI, M.D.**

Diseases and Disorders

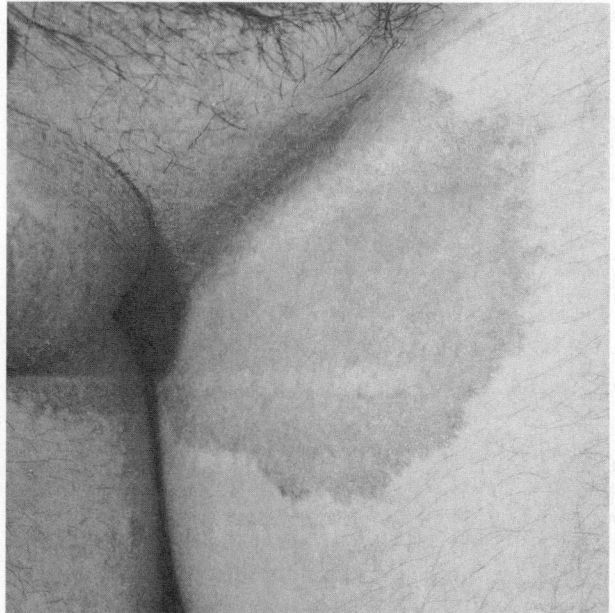

FIGURE 1T-38 Tinea cruris. A half-moon–shaped plaque has a well-defined, scaling border. (From Habif TB: *Clinical dermatology: a color guide to diagnosis and therapy,* ed 3, St Louis, 1996, Mosby.)

i BASIC INFORMATION

DEFINITION
Tinea pedis is a dermatophyte infection of the feet.

SYNONYMS
Athlete's foot

ICD-10CM CODES
B35.3 Tinea pedis

EPIDEMIOLOGY & DEMOGRAPHICS
- Most common dermatophyte infection
- Increased incidence in hot humid weather; occlusive footwear is a contributing factor
- Occurrence is rare before adolescence
- More common in adult males

PHYSICAL FINDINGS & CLINICAL PRESENTATION
- Typical presentation is variable and ranges from erythematous scaling plaques (Fig. 1T-39) and isolated blisters to interdigital maceration.
- The infection usually starts in the interdigital spaces of the foot. Most infections are found in the toe webs or on the soles.
- Fourth or fifth toes are most commonly involved.
- Pruritus is common and is most intense after removal of shoes and socks.
- Infection with *Trichophyton rubrum* often manifests with a "moccasin" distribution affecting the soles and lateral feet.

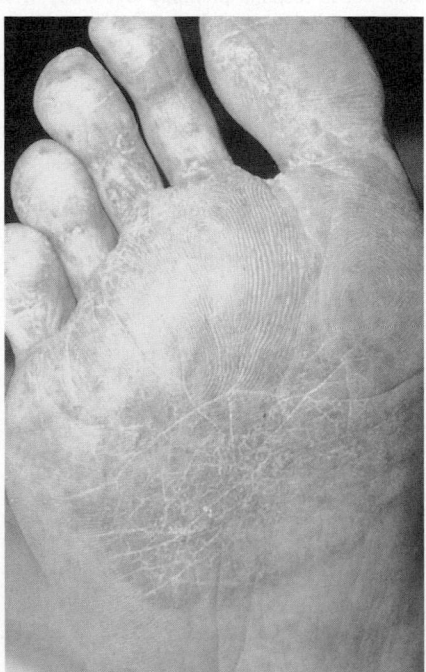

FIGURE 1T-39 Tinea pedis. (From Goldstein BG, Goldstein AO: *Practical dermatology*, ed 2, St Louis, 1997, Mosby.)

Tinea pedis caused by trichophyton mentagrophytes (interdigitale) can present with:
1. Erythema and desquamation between the toes.
2. Multilocular bullae involving the thin skin of the plantar arch and along the sides of the feet and heel.
3. White superficial onychomycosis.

ETIOLOGY
- Dermatophyte infection caused by *T. rubrum, Trichophyton mentagrophytes,* or less commonly *Epidermophyton floccosum*
- There may be an autosomal dominant predisposition to this form of infection.

Dx DIAGNOSIS

DIFFERENTIAL DIAGNOSIS
- Contact dermatitis
- Toe web infection (bacterial or candidal infection)
- Eczema
- Psoriasis
- Keratolysis exfoliativa
- Juvenile plantar dermatosis

WORKUP
- Diagnosis is usually made by clinical observation.
- Laboratory testing, when performed, generally consists of a simple potassium hydroxide preparation with mycologic examination under a light microscope to confirm the presence of dermatophytes.

LABORATORY TESTS
- Microscopic examination of a scale or the roof of a blister with 10% KOH under low or medium power will reveal hyphae.
- Mycologic culture is rarely indicated in the diagnosis of tinea pedis.
- Biopsy is reserved for when the diagnosis remains in question after testing or failure to respond to treatment.

Rx TREATMENT

NONPHARMACOLOGIC THERAPY
- Hyperhydrosis is a predisposing factor for tinea pedis. Keep infected area clean and dry. Aerate feet by using sandals when possible.
- Use 100% cotton socks rather than nylon socks to reduce moisture.
- Areas likely to become infected should be dried completely before being covered with clothes.

ACUTE GENERAL Rx
- Benzylamines: butenafine HCl 1% cream applied bid for 1 wk or qd for 4 wk is effective in interdigital tinea pedis.
- Allylamines: terbinafine cream applied bid × 14 days, or naftifine 1% cream applied qd or naftifine gel applied bid for 4 wk produces a significantly high cure rate.
- Imidazoles: econazole, ketoconazole, miconazole, luliconazole, and clotrimazole cream are also effective agents. Clotrimazole 1% cream is an over-the-counter treatment. It should be applied to affected and surrounding area bid for up to 4 wk.
- Ciclopirox and tolnaftate are other antifungal agents available in cream, suspension, or gel. Tolnaftate is also available as a lotion, spray, or powder.
- When using topical preparations, the application area should include normal skin approximately 2 cm beyond the affected area.
- Areas of maceration can be treated with Burow's solution soaks for 10 to 20 min bid followed by foot elevation.
- Oral agents (fluconazole 150 mg once per week for 4 wk, terbinafine 250 mg/day for 14 days, itraconazole 200 mg bid × 7 days, or griseofulvin 500-1000 mg/day for 14 days) can be used in combination with topical agents in resistant cases.

! PEARLS & CONSIDERATIONS

- Use of tolnaftate powder (Tinactin) or zeasorb medicated powder on the feet after bathing may be helpful in preventing recurrent tinea pedis in susceptible persons.
- Combination therapy of antifungal and corticosteroid (clotrimazole/betamethasone [Lotrisone]) should only be used when the diagnosis of fungal infection is confirmed and inflammation is a significant issue.
- Nystatin is not effective and should not be used.

SUGGESTED READING
Available at www.expertconsult.com

RELATED CONTENT
Athlete's Foot (Patient Information)

AUTHOR: **FRED F. FERRI, M.D.**

BASIC INFORMATION

DEFINITION

Tinea versicolor is a fungal infection of the skin caused by the yeast *Pityrosporum orbiculare* (*Malassezia furfur*).

SYNONYMS

Pityriasis versicolor

ICD-10CM CODES
B36.0 Pityriasis versicolor

EPIDEMIOLOGY & DEMOGRAPHICS

- Increased incidence in adolescence and young adulthood
- More common during the summer (hypopigmented lesions are more evident when the skin is tanned)

PHYSICAL FINDINGS & CLINICAL PRESENTATION

- Most lesions begin as multiple small, circular macules of various colors (Fig. 1T-40) on the trunk and upper arms.
- The macules may be darker or lighter than the surrounding normal skin and will scale with scraping.
- Most frequent site of distribution is trunk.
- Facial lesions are more common in children (forehead is most common facial site).
- Eruption is generally of insidious onset and asymptomatic.
- Lesions may be hyperpigmented in blacks.
- Lesions may be inconspicuous in fair-complexioned individuals, especially during the winter.
- Most patients become aware of the eruption when the involved areas do not tan (Fig. 1T-41).
- Mild itching and inflammation around the patches may be present.
- Facial lesions may occur in infants and immunocompromised patients.

ETIOLOGY

The infection is caused by *Malassezia* species (*M. globosa, M. restricta, M. sympodialis, M. furfur, M. obtusa,* and *M. slooffiae*) Factors that favor proliferation are pregnancy, malnutrition, immunosuppression, oral contraceptives, and excess heat and humidity.

DIAGNOSIS

DIFFERENTIAL DIAGNOSIS

- Vitiligo
- Pityriasis alba
- Secondary syphilis
- Pityriasis rosea
- Seborrheic dermatitis
- Postinflammatory hyperpigmentation or hypopigmentation
- Pityriasis rubra pilaris
- Syphilis
- Hansen's disease

WORKUP

Diagnosis is based on clinical appearance. The *Malassezia* fungus is easily demonstrated in

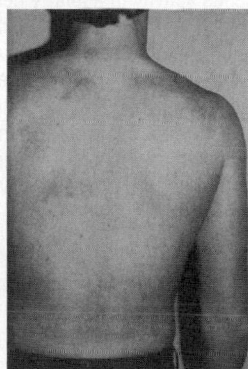

FIGURE 1T-40 Tinea versicolor. (Courtesy David Effron, M.D.)

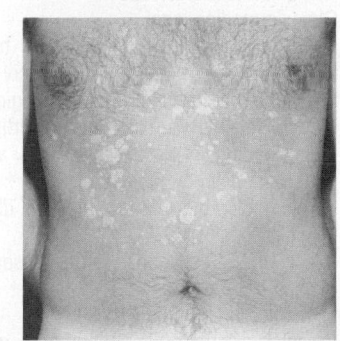

FIGURE 1T-41 The classic presentation of tinea versicolor with white, oval, or circular patches on tan skin. (From Habif TB: *Clinical dermatology: a color guide to diagnosis and therapy,* ed 3, St Louis, 1996, Mosby.)

scraping of the profuse scales that cover the lesions. Identification of hyphae and budding spores ("spaghetti and meatballs" appearance) with microscopy confirms diagnosis.

LABORATORY TESTS

Microscopic examination with potassium hydroxide confirms diagnosis.

TREATMENT

NONPHARMACOLOGIC THERAPY

Sunlight accelerates repigmentation of hypopigmented areas.

ACUTE GENERAL Rx

- Topical treatment: selenium sulfide 2.5% suspension (Selsun or Exsel) applied daily for 30 min for 7 consecutive days results in a cure rate of 80% to 90%. The scalp can be shampooed monthly with selenium sulfide to reduce scalp colonization.
- Antifungal topical agents (e.g., miconazole, ciclopirox, clotrimazole) are also effective.
- Oral treatment can be given along with topical agents but is generally reserved for resistant cases. Effective agents are ketoconazole 200 mg qd for 5 days, or single 400-mg dose (cure rate >80%), fluconazole 400 mg given as a single dose (cure rate >70% at 3 wk after treatment), or itraconazole 200 mg/day for 7 days.

DISPOSITION

The prognosis is good, with eradication of the fungus usually occurring within 3 to 4 wk of treatment; however, recurrence is common. After initial therapy, use of monthly application of selenium sulfide may lower risk of recurrence.

PEARLS & CONSIDERATIONS

COMMENTS

Patients should be informed that the hypopigmented areas will not disappear immediately after treatment and that several months may be necessary for the hypopigmented areas to regain their pigmentation.

RELATED CONTENT

Tinea Versicolor (Patient Information)

AUTHOR: **FRED F. FERRI, M.D.**

BASIC INFORMATION

DEFINITION

Tinnitus is a perceived sound in the absence of acoustic stimulus external to the head. It may be unilateral, bilateral, or lateral dominant. It is commonly described as a ringing, buzzing, roaring, hissing, whistling, humming, cricket-like, or pulsing sound. It is frequently a symptom associated with hearing loss, Meniere's disease, acoustic neuroma, drug toxicity, depression, or an autoimmune inner ear disease. The sound may be internal and perceived only by the patient, called subjective or tonal tinnitus, or it may be heard by both the patient and the examiner, called objective or nontonal tinnitus.

SYNONYMS

Ringing in the ear(s)

ICD-10CM CODES
H93.1   Tinnitus
H93.2   Other abnormal auditory perceptions
H93.11   Tinnitus, right ear
H93.12   Tinnitus, left ear
H93.13   Tinnitus, bilateral
H93.19   Tinnitus, unspecified ear

EPIDEMIOLOGY & DEMOGRAPHICS

PREVALENCE
- The American Tinnitus Association reports 50-60 million Americans have tinnitus for > 6 mo.
- Prevalence increases with age, peaking for persons aged 65 to 74 years.
- Prevalence in the United States based on National Health Interview Survey (NHIS) in 1996:
  1. 2.98% all ages
  2. 0.26% for persons <18 yr old
  3. 1.6% for persons aged 18-44 yr
  4. 5.96% for persons aged 45-64 yr: 7.7% males, 4.3% females
  5. 9.6% for persons aged 65-74 yr: 12% males, 7.7% females
  6. 7.6% for persons >75 yr old: 11.4% males, 5.3% females
  7. 2:1 South/Northeast regions
- Up to 18% of people in industrialized societies are mildly affected by chronic tinnitus, and 0.5% report tinnitus having a severe effect on their daily life.

PREDOMINANT SEX AND AGE: Persons most affected are male, Caucasian, elderly, persons with hearing impairment, persons living in southern United States. For military veterans, tinnitus is the third most common service-related disability.

RISK FACTORS: Any condition causing hearing loss or damage to the auditory system can produce tinnitus. Cochlear damage from exposure to noise is the most common cause. Exposure to ototoxic drugs is also important.

PHYSICAL FINDINGS & CLINICAL PRESENTATION

- History should focus on exposure to loud noises, evidence of hearing loss, and ototoxic drugs.
- Patient should be screened for depression.
- Patient who complains of sound in ear may also complain of ear pain or fullness.
- Objective tinnitus is pulsatile and coincides with patient's pulse.
- Physical examination should focus on HEENT, neck, and neurologic exam.
- There may be no significant physical findings.

ETIOLOGY

- The mechanism behind tinnitus is poorly understood. It may originate at any point along the auditory pathway. Causes of tinnitus include injured cochlear hair cells, spontaneous activity in auditory nerve fibers, hyperactivity in the auditory nuclei in the brain stem, or a reduction in the suppressive activity of the central auditory cortex.
- Medications implicated in causing tinnitus include: salicylates, NSAIDs, aminoglycosides, loop diuretics, valproate, quinine, chemotherapeutic agents, cisplatin, vincristine, heavy metals such as lead.

DIAGNOSIS

DIFFERENTIAL DIAGNOSIS

- Subjective/tonal tinnitus:
  1. Otologic: tympanic membrane disorder, inner ear disorder (hair cells, organ of Corti), Meniere's disease
  2. Ototoxic medications
  3. Neurologic: multiple sclerosis, head trauma, cochlear nerve lesion, acoustic schwannoma, neurofibroma, meningioma
  4. Metabolic: thyroid disorder, hyperlipidemia (leading to plaque formation), vitamin B_{12} deficiency
  5. Psychogenic: depression, anxiety, fibromyalgia
  6. Infectious: otitis media, Lyme disease, meningitis, syphilis
- Objective/nontonal tinnitus:
  1. Vascular: arterial bruit, venous hum, arteriovenous malformation, vascular tumors
  2. Neurologic: contraction of muscles of the eustachian tube, contraction of the stapedius muscle, contraction of the tensor tympani muscles, or a palatal myoclonus, glomus jugulare tumor
  3. Conductive: patulous (wide-open) eustachian tube

WORKUP

- Audiometry
- Tympanometry
- Electronystagmography is used to evaluate for Meniere's disease.
- Box E1T-4 describes useful diagnostic tests. An algorithm for tinnitus evaluation is described in Fig. E1T-42.

LABORATORY TESTS

Evaluate for metabolic abnormalities: TSH, CBC, B_{12}, and lipid panel.

IMAGING STUDIES

- CT/MRI: to evaluate for subjective tinnitus
- MRI/MRA: to evaluate objective tinnitus

TREATMENT

NONPHARMACOLOGIC THERAPY

- It is best to avoid exposure to excessive noise, ototoxic agents, and to wear protective equipment in noisy environments, or mask the tinnitus through amplification of normal sounds with a hearing aid. Habituation techniques such as tinnitus retraining therapy may help. Cognitive behavioral therapy helps patients cope with tinnitus distress through biofeedback.
- Recent trials involving brain stimulation in the form of repetitive transcranial magnetic stimulation (rTMS have shown reduction in the perception or severity of tinnitus).[1]

ACUTE GENERAL Rx

- If the tinnitus is severe enough to cause suicidal symptoms, immediate referral to a psychiatrist and an otolaryngologist is recommended to minimize the time to diagnosis and optimize treatment.
- Patients with persistent symptoms or tinnitus accompanied by visual changes or headache should be evaluated for tumors such as acoustic neuroma.

CHRONIC Rx

There is insufficient evidence to support the use of any medication, vitamin, or nutritional supplement to treat tinnitus.

COMPLEMENTARY & ALTERNATIVE MEDICINE

Possibly effective: acupuncture, relaxation therapy, hypnosis (based on systematic review)

DISPOSITION

Clinical course is variable. About 20% to 25% of patients with chronic tinnitus consider it a significant problem. Individualized tinnitus management programs can be beneficial in most patients.

PEARLS & CONSIDERATIONS

PREVENTION

- Avoid loud, chronic noise and ototoxic drugs.
- Higher caffeine intake is associated with a lower risk of incidence of tinnitus in women.

---

[1] Folmer RL, et al.: Repetitive Transcranial Magnetic Stimulation Treatment for Chronic Tinnitus: A Randomized Clinical Trial, *JAMA Otolaryngol Head Neck Surg* 141(8):716-722, 2015.

PATIENT & FAMILY EDUCATION

- American Tinnitus Association: 800-634-8978, http://www.ata.org

 EVIDENCE

Available at www.expertconsult.com

SUGGESTED READINGS

Available at www.expertconsult.com

RELATED CONTENT

Tinnitus (Patient Information)

AUTHORS: **VICKY H. BHAGAT, M.D., M.P.H.** and **DAWN HOGAN, M.D.**

Diseases and Disorders

BASIC INFORMATION

DEFINITION

The term *Torsade de Pointes* (TdP) refers to a polymorphic ventricular tachycardia (VT) associated with a prolonged QT interval and electrocardiographically characterized by QRS complexes of changing amplitude that appear to twist around the isoelectric line, hence the name *Torsade de Pointes*, or "twisting of the points" (Fig. 1T-43).

Torsade is typically initiated by a short-long-short sequence of ventricular beats but can also be initiated by a short-coupled variant. Typically, TdP occurs in the setting of a markedly prolonged QT interval (>500 msec); the QTc prolongs even further during the long diastolic interval of a compensatory pause, leading to a polymorphic VT with a ventricular rate of 160 to 250 beats per minute, irregular RR intervals, and a cycling of the QRS axis through 180 degrees every 5 to 20 beats. It may be repetitive, nonsustained, or sustained and may degenerate into ventricular fibrillation. In some cases, the result is sudden cardiac death.

SYNONYM(S)

Torsades
TdP

ICD-10-CM CODE(S)

I47.2 Ventricular tachycardia

EPIDEMIOLOGY & DEMOGRAPHICS

INCIDENCE: The precise incidence of TdP is unclear but accounts for fewer than 5% of all sudden cardiac arrests. In congenital long QT syndromes (LQTS), TdP may occur in up to 6%

cases at rest and 9% of cases during an exercise test. Among drug-induced causes of TdP, the incidence may vary between <1% in cases of antibiotics and antipsychotics to 2% to 4% when caused by class III anti-arrhythmics such as sotalol, ibutilide, and dofetilide.

PREDOMINANT SEX AND AGE: Because testosterone shortens the QT interval, women have a longer baseline QT interval, which is believed to be the reason for a two- to threefold increased incidence of TdP in women.

GENETICS: Of the congenital LQTS channelopathies, long QT syndromes 1, 2, and 3 account for >70% of all cases. In general, the risk of TdP increases as the QT lengthens; however, there are also genotype-phenotype relationships that help define risk; for example, LQTS3 carries a higher risk of TdP than LQTS1. Similarly, the Jervell and Lange-Nielsen syndrome and Romano-Ward syndrome may lead to TdP.

It is also likely that genetic factors are at play in acquired LQT and in the development of TdP. For example, in large populations, the QT interval prolongs very little with the administration of QT-prolonging drugs such as fluoroquinolones; however, certain individuals will have markedly exaggerated QT prolongation that leads to TdP; this is likely due to some underlying genetic factor.

RISK FACTORS: TdP in patients with congenital LQTS is often initiated by an external trigger (Table 1T-16). Triggers can include exercise, noise, emotion, sudden waking from sleep by an alarm clock, telephone ringing, thunder, swimming, or diving. TdP in LQT1 patients is classically triggered by vigorous exercise or swimming; in LQT2 by emotion, pregnancy, or noise; and in LQT3 when at rest or asleep. Risk factors for drug-induced TdP are outlined in Table 1T-17.

The risk factors for developing TdP in patients with acquired long QT are extensive and are outlined in Table 1T-18.

PATHOPHYSIOLOGY

- Changes in the balance of transmembrane ionic currents lead to lengthening of the QT interval and to abnormal action potentials called early afterdepolarizations (EADs). An EAD, in the setting of electrical instability induced by the prolonged QT, initiates the torsades. Perpetuation may be caused by transmural entry, triggered activity, or abnormal automaticity. A distinct group of cells called the M cells, located in the mid-myocardium, has a less rapid delayed rectifier potassium current (IKr), and the cells are central to the genesis of TdP.
- Drugs with the potential to cause TdP most frequently inhibit the rapid potassium channels and result in prolongation of the action potential duration, producing a prolonged QT on ECG.

PHYSICAL FINDINGS & CLINICAL PRESENTATION

- Clinical features depend on whether the TdP is caused by acquired or congenital long QT syndrome. Congenital LQTS patients may have certain specific triggers, such as noise, exercise, and emotions (see "Risk Factors").
- Symptoms of the tachycardia itself include palpitations, presyncope, syncope (sometimes with jerking movements from myoclonus, often misinterpreted as seizures), and sudden cardiac death (SCD).
- Patients resuscitated from SCD have an especially ominous prognosis, with a relative risk of 12.9% of experiencing another cardiac arrest.

ETIOLOGY

The etiology or triggers of TdP may be congenital or acquired causes of QT prolongation (see Table 1T-16). For a comprehensive list of drugs that can cause or have the potential to cause TdP, see "Patient/Family Education."

DIAGNOSIS

DIFFERENTIAL DIAGNOSIS

Other causes of syncope.
Other causes of broad complex tachycardia such as:

- Polymorphic VT.
- Wolff-Parkinson-White (WPW) syndrome with rapid atrial fibrillation.
- ECG artifact.

WORKUP

- ECG and telemetry are the mainstays of diagnosing TdP as they detect the arrhythmia, the preceding prolonged QT interval, and the long-short cycles that trigger it.
- Determination and treatment of the etiology of TdP (see Table 1T-16) is key.

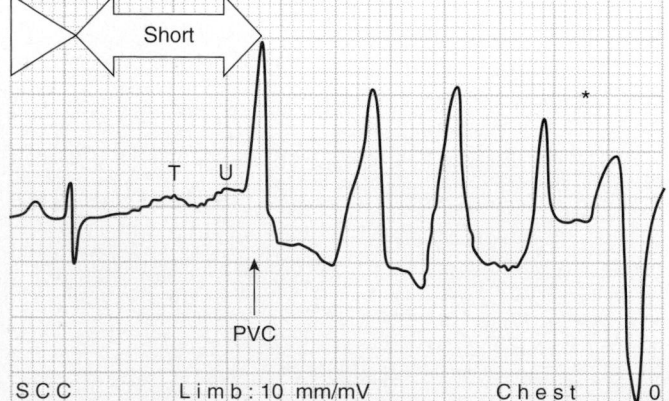

FIGURE 1T-43 Onset of Torsade de Pointes during the recording of a standard 12-lead ECG in a young male with a history of drug addiction treated with chronic methadone therapy who presented to a hospital emergency department after ingesting an overdose of prescription and over-the-counter drugs from his parent's drug cabinet. Classic ECG features evident in this rhythm strip include a prolonged QT interval with distorted T-U complex, initiation of the arrhythmia after a short-long-short cycle sequence by a PVC that falls near the peak of the distorted T-U complex, "warm-up" phenomenon with initial R-R cycles longer than subsequent cycles, and abrupt switching of QRS morphology from predominantly positive to predominantly negative complexes (asterisk). (From Drew BJ et al: Prevention of Torsade de Pointes in hospital settings: a scientific statement from the American Heart Association and the American College of Cardiology Foundation, *J Am Coll Cardiol* 55;934-947, 2010.)

TABLE 1T-16 Causes and Triggers of Torsade de Pointes

Congenital	• Romano-Ward syndrome [autosomal dominant] • Jervell and Lange-Nielsen syndrome [autosomal recessive] • LQTS channelopathies
Acquired	
Metabolic syndromes	• Hypokalemia • Hypocalcemia • Hypomagnesemia • Starvation • Anorexia nervosa • Liquid protein diets • Hypothyroidism
Bradyarrhythmias	• Sinus node dysfunction • Second- or third-degree AV block
Antiarrhythmic drugs	• Quinidine • Procainamide • Disopyramide • Amiodarone and dronedarone • Sotalol • Dofetilide, ibutilide, azimilide
Antimicrobial drugs	• Erythromycin, clarithromycin, azithromycin • Pentamidine • Azole antifungals like voriconazole • Fluoroquinolones such as levofloxacin & moxifloxacin • Chloroquine
Antihistaminics	• Terfenadine • Astemizole
Psychiatric drugs	• Phenothiazines • Thioridazine • Tricyclic antidepressants • Haloperidol • Risperidone • Selective serotonin reuptake inhibitors
Antineoplastic agents	• Tyrosine kinase inhibitors such as sunitinib, dasatinib • Vorinostat • Arsenic
Gastric motility agents	• Cisapride, domperidone
Opioid dependence drugs	• Methadone
Other factors	• Myocardial ischemia • Hypothermia • Intracranial disease • HIV infection • Connective tissue disease with anti-Ro/SSA antibodies • Periodic paralysis (Andersen syndrome) • Cocaine

LABORATORY TESTS

- Electrolytes: assess for hypokalemia, hypocalcemia, and hypomagnesemia.
- Thyroid function tests.
- Genetic studies if suspicion of congenital LQT syndrome.

IMAGING STUDIES

- Echocardiography to rule out structural heart disease as a cause of VT.
- Stress test to rule out myocardial ischemia. Stress ECG with dynamic assessment of the QT interval during varying heart rates may be diagnostic of long QT syndromes and related TdP.
- CT scan of the head if intracranial disease is suspected.
- Fig. 1T-44 shows TdP in a teenage patient with long QT syndrome.

(Rx) TREATMENT

The cornerstone of treatment comprises intravenous magnesium and acceleration of the heart rate, either by mechanical overdrive pacing or by infusion of isoproterenol. Withdrawal of causative drugs and correction of underlying causes such as electrolyte imbalances, hypothermia, and ischemia are also important.

NONPHARMACOLOGIC THERAPY

- Withdrawal of any offending drugs and correction of electrolyte abnormalities are recommended in patients presenting with TdP (Class I recommendation).
- Temporary atrial or ventricular overdrive pacing is a Class I recommendation for all causes of TdP if intravenous magnesium fails.

TABLE 1T-17 Risk Factors for Drug-Induced Torsade de Pointes

- Congenital long QT
- Female gender
- Electrolyte abnormalities (hypokalemia, hypomagnesemia, hypocalcemia)
- Diuretic use
- Bradycardia
- Cardiac hypertrophy
- Myocardial fibrosis
- Congestive heart failure
- Renal and liver insufficiency
- Coadministration of drugs blocking P450 isoenzyme CYP3A4
- High doses or rapid intravenous infusion of the drug
- Baseline electrocardiographic abnormalities (prolonged QT, T-wave lability)

From Gowda RM et al: Torsades de Pointes: the clinical considerations, *Int J Cardiol* 96(1):1-6, 2004.

TABLE 1T-18 Risk Factors for Torsade de Pointes in Hospitalized Patients

- Clinically recognizable risk factors
- QTc >500 msec
- LQT2-type repolarization: notched or "bifid" T-wave
- Use of QT-prolonging drugs
- Concurrent use of more than one QT-prolonging drug
- Rapid infusion by intravenous route
- Structural heart disease
- Congestive heart failure
- Myocardial infarction
- Advanced age
- Female sex
- Hypokalemia
- Hypomagnesemia
- Hypocalcemia
- Treatment with diuretics
- Impaired hepatic drug metabolism
- Bradycardia
- Sinus bradycardia, heart block, incomplete heart block with pauses
- Premature QRS complexes leading to short-long-short cycles
- Multiple clinically recognizable risk factors
- Occult (latent) congenital LQTS
- Genetic polymorphisms

From Drew BJ et al. Prevention of Torsade de Pointes in hospital settings: a scientific statement from the American Heart Association and the American College of Cardiology Foundation, *Circulation* 121(8):1047, 2010.

- Acute and long-term pacing is recommended for patients presenting with TdP due to heart block and symptomatic bradycardia (Class 1) or those with recurrent pause-dependent torsades (Class IIa).
- Active internal and external rewarming if hypothermia is the etiology.
- If TdP degenerates into ventricular fibrillation, defibrillation and advanced cardiac life support protocol should be followed.

Diseases and Disorders

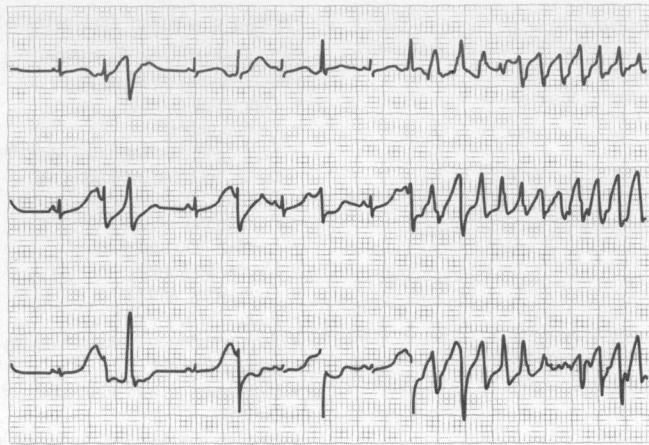

FIGURE 1T-44 Torsade de Pointes in a teenage patient with long QT syndrome. This arrhythmia is associated with no pulse and results in syncope. It often terminates spontaneously, but otherwise rapidly degenerates to ventricular fibrillation. (From Fuhrman: *Pediatric critical care*, ed 4, 2010, Elsevier.)

ACUTE Rx

- Intravenous magnesium sulfate 1 to 2 g given over 1 to 2 min is first-line therapy for patients who present with LQTS and few episodes of TdP (Class IIa). Magnesium is not likely to be effective in patients with a normal QT interval
- Isoproterenol is reasonable as temporary treatment in patients with acute disease who present with recurrent pause-dependent TdP and who do not have congenital LQTS (Class IIa).
- Beta-blockade combined with pacing is reasonable acute therapy for patients who present with TdP and sinus bradycardia (Class IIa).
- Potassium repletion to 4.5 to 5 mmol/L may be considered for patients who present with TdP and hypokalemia (Class IIb).
- Intravenous lidocaine, oral mexiletine, or phenytoin may be considered in patients who present with LQT3 and TdP (Class IIb).
- TdP is usually self-limited, and cardioversion should be performed only as a last resort in the setting of pulseless VF because of the high likelihood of immediate recurrence of the TdP after cardioversion.

CHRONIC Rx

- TdP resulting from congenital LQTS is treated with beta-blockade, pacing, and implantable cardioverter-defibrillator (ICD) in high-risk cases. For patients who continue to have syncope despite maximal drug therapy, cervical-thoracic sympathectomy may be considered.

- Long-term pacing is recommended for patients presenting with TdP due to heart block and symptomatic bradycardia.
- Avoid use of QT-prolonging drugs.
- Lifestyle modification in case of congenital LQTS.
- In patients with eating disorders, nutritional rehabilitation will correct the QT prolongation over the long term (3 to 18 mo).
- Psychiatric evaluation of patients with drug overdose and eating disorders.

DISPOSITION

Patients with TdP should be monitored in an intensive care setting.

REFERRAL

Patients should have an urgent cardiology consultation.

PEARLS & CONSIDERATIONS

COMMENTS

- Identification of the etiology for TdP is key in diagnosis, management, and prognosis of this condition.
- Drugs associated with TdP vary greatly in their risk for arrhythmia; an updated list can be found at https://crediblemeds.org. The risk-benefit ratio should be assessed for each individual to determine whether the potential therapeutic benefit of a drug outweighs the risk for TdP.

- Risk factors for drug-induced TdP include older age, female sex, heart disease, electrolyte disorders (especially hypokalemia and hypomagnesemia), renal or hepatic dysfunction, bradycardia or rhythms with long pauses, treatment with more than one QT-prolonging drug, and genetic predisposition.
- After initiation of a drug associated with TdP, ECG signs indicative of risk for arrhythmia include an increase in QTc from pre-drug baseline of >60 msec, marked QTc interval prolongation >500 msec, T-U wave distortion that becomes more exaggerated in the beat after a pause, visible T-wave alternans, new-onset ventricular ectopy, and couplets and nonsustained polymorphic ventricular tachycardia initiated in the beat after a pause.

PREVENTION

The 2011 AHA/ACC scientific statement on prevention of TdP suggests a strategy of documenting the QTc interval before and at least every 8 to 12 hr after the initiation, increased dose, or overdose of QT-prolonging drugs. If QTc prolongation is observed, documentation of more frequent measurements is recommended. The duration of QTc monitoring depends upon the duration of treatment with the QT-prolonging drug and the drug half-life.

PATIENT/FAMILY EDUCATION

- Patients should be educated about avoiding use of QT-prolonging drugs. A complete list of these drugs can be found at https://crediblemeds.org
- First-degree relatives of all patients with congenital LQTS should undergo genetic testing.
- Congenital LQTS patients should avoid certain specific triggers (e.g., swimming and exercise in LQTS 1 and LQTS 2 and acoustic stimuli in LQTS 2).
- It is recommended that all patients affected by LQTS avoid competitive sports activity.

RELATED TOPICS

Long QT Syndrome (Related Key Topic)

AUTHOR: **CHRISTOPHER PICKETT, M.D.**

Diseases and Disorders

 BASIC INFORMATION

DEFINITION

Tics are sudden, brief, intermittent involuntary or semi-voluntary movements (motor tics) or sounds (phonic or vocal tics) that mimic fragments of normal behavior.

Tourette's syndrome (TS) is an inherited neuropsychiatric disorder characterized by motor, vocal, and phonic tics that change during the course of illness. Onset is typically before age 18.

SYNONYMS

Gilles de la Tourette syndrome
TS
Tourette's disorder

ICD-10CM CODES
F95.2 Combined vocal and multiple motor tic disorder [de la Tourette]

EPIDEMIOLOGY & DEMOGRAPHICS

PREVALENCE (IN U.S.): Unknown; estimates range from 0.7% to 5%.
PREDOMINANT SEX: Approximate male/female ratio of 3:1.
PREDOMINANT AGE: Typical age of onset is between 2 and 15 yr (mean 5-7 yr).

PHYSICAL FINDINGS & CLINICAL PRESENTATION

- Neurologic examination is normal.
- Vocal and/or phonic tics could be simple (clearing of throat, sniffing, grunting or sucking sounds) or complex (repetitive short phrases, e.g., "you bet," swearing [coprolalia]).
- Motor tics can be simple (e.g., blinking, grimacing, head jerking) or complex (e.g., gesturing). Tics wax, wane, and change over time. Often they can be suppressed for short periods. Commonly they are preceded by an urge to perform the tic.
- TS is often associated with a variety of behavioral symptoms, most commonly attention deficit hyperactivity disorder (ADHD) and obsessive-compulsive disorder (OCD).

TS can be diagnosed using the DSM 5 criteria as follows:
1. Both multiple motor and one or more vocal tics must be present at some time during the illness, although not necessarily concurrent.
2. The tics may wax and wane in frequency but have persisted for >1 year since first tic onset.
3. Age at onset is <18 yr.
4. Disturbance is not attributable to the direct physiologic effects of a substance (e.g., stimulants) or a general medical condition (e.g., Huntington's disease or postviral encephalitis).

ETIOLOGY

Exact pathogenesis is unknown. Genetic predisposition is likely as there is a strong family history of OCD or TS in patients with tics, and twin studies provide evidence for the importance of genetic factors. Recent analysis of linkage in a two-generation pedigree has led to the identification of a mutation in the HDC gene encoding l-histidine decarboxylase, the rate-limiting enzyme in histamine biosynthesis, pointing to a role for histaminergic neurotransmission in the mechanism and modulation of Tourette's syndrome and tics (Fig. 1T-46). Immunologic dysfunction is being explored in the pathogenesis of this complex disorder.

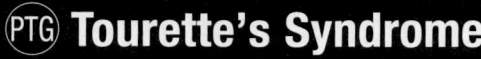 DIAGNOSIS

DIFFERENTIAL DIAGNOSIS

- Sydenham's chorea: occurs after infection with group A *Streptococcus.*
- PANDAS: pediatric autoimmune neuropsychiatric disorder associated with streptococcal infection.
- Sporadic tic disorders: tend to be motor or vocal but not both.
- Head trauma.
- Drug intoxication: many drugs are known to induce or exacerbate tic disorder, including

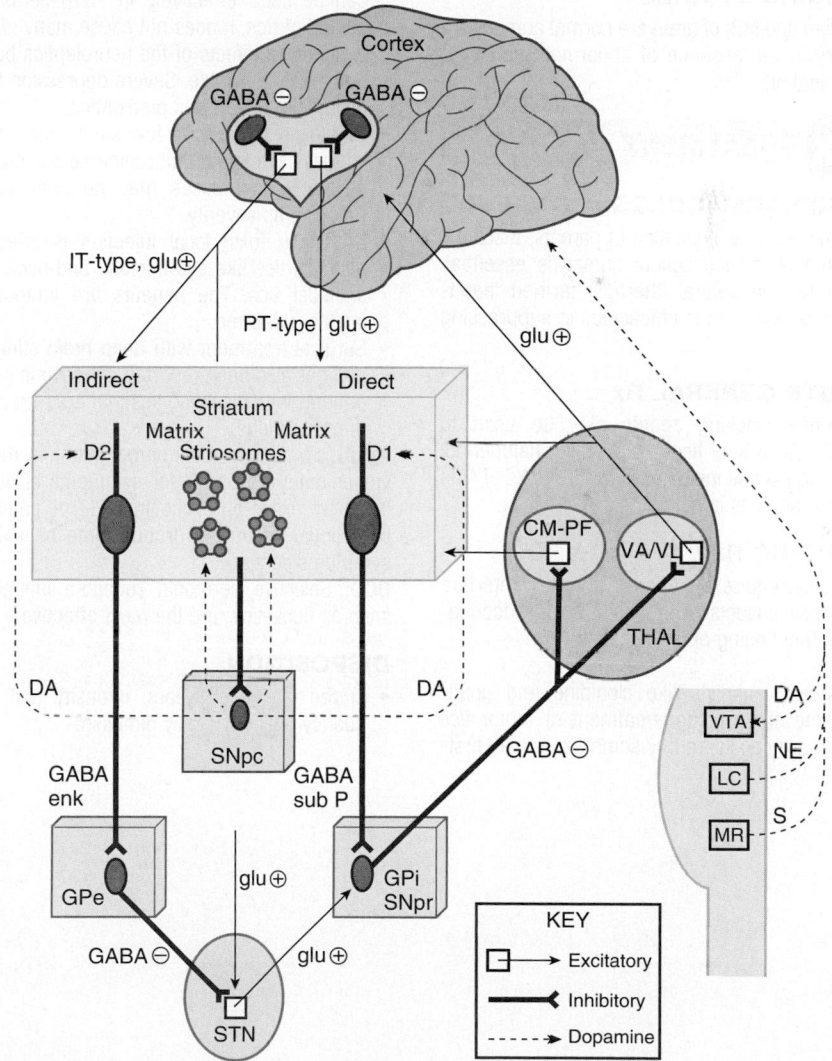

FIGURE 1T-46 The cortico-striatal-thalamo-cortical pathway and ascending cortical inputs. Hypothesized abnormalities have included disorders of excess excitation or diminished inhibition, disruptions in frontal cortex, striatum, or striosomes, and abnormalities of various synaptic neurotransmitters. *CM-PF,* Centromedian-parafascicular complex; *DA,* dopamine; *enk,* enkephalins; *GABA,* gamma-aminobutyric acid; *glu,* glutamate; *GPe,* globus pallidus externa; *GPi,* globus pallidus interna; *IT,* intra telencephalic; *LC,* locus coeruleus; *MR,* median raphe; *NE,* norepinephrine; *PT,* pyramidal tract; *S,* serotonin; *SNpc,* substantia nigra pars compacta; *SNpr,* substantia nigra pars reticulata; *STN,* subthalamic nucleus; *sub P,* substance P; *THAL,* thalamus; *VA/VL,* ventral anterior/ventral lateral nuclei; *VTA,* ventral tegmental area. (From Harris K and Singer HS. Tic disorders: Neural circuits, neurochemistry, and neuroimmunology. *J Child Neurology* 2006;21:678–689.)

methylphenidate, amphetamines, pemoline, anticholinergics, and antihistamines.
- Postinfectious encephalitis.
- Inherited disorders: Huntington's disease, Hallervorden-Spatz disease, and neuroacanthocytosis. All these conditions should have other observed abnormalities on neurologic examination.

WORKUP

Clinical observation and history to confirm diagnosis.

LABORATORY TESTS

No definitive laboratory tests.

IMAGING STUDIES

CT scan and MRI of brain are normal and unnecessary in the absence of abnormal neurologic examination.

℞ TREATMENT

NONPHARMACOLOGIC THERAPY

Multidisciplinary: education of parents, teachers, psychologists, and school nurses is essential. Cognitive behavioral therapy termed habit-reversal treatment is efficacious in suppressing tics.

ACUTE GENERAL Rx

Dopamine-blocking agents may be used to reduce severity of tics acutely (e.g., haloperidol 0.25 mg PO qhs initially). There are risks of side effects, such as acute dystonic reactions.

CHRONIC Rx

Tics only require treatment when they interfere with psychosocial, educational, and occupational functioning of a person.

TICS:
- Alpha-2 agonists like clonidine and guanfacine are used for treatment of motor tics and are considered by some experts as first-

line medications because of their favorable adverse effect profile. However, they are more beneficial for treatment of behavioral symptoms and should be preferred for patients with predominant psychiatric problems.
- Haloperidol and pimozide are the only neuroleptics that are approved by U.S. FDA for the treatment of tics in TS. Pimozide is started as 0.5 to 1.0 mg at night and increased every 5 to 7 days to therapeutic dose of 2 to 8 mg. Haloperidol is started as 0.25 to 0.5 mg and can be increased to 1 to 4 mg depending on response and side effects. Use of neuroleptics carries a small but significant risk of tardive dyskinesia.
- Tetrabenazine: dopamine-depleting agent can be used effectively in TS patients for control of tics. It does not cause many of the typical side effects of the neuroleptics but is not readily available. Severe depression may occur with use of this medication.
- Dopamine agonists: a few small, open-label studies have found that ropinirole and pramipexole in low doses may be effective in reducing tic severity.
- Botulinum toxin local injection is effective for focal tics like eye blinking and neck and shoulder tics. The benefits are temporary, lasting 3 to 6 mo.
- Surgical treatment with deep brain stimulation has also been reported effective in some patients with disabling tics that are refractory to medications.

ADHD: Stimulants (dextroamphetamine, methylphenidate) are useful for symptoms of ADHD but may exacerbate tics in 25% of patients, but should be used if troublesome behavioral symptoms persist.

OCD: Selective serotonin reuptake inhibitors, such as fluoxetine, are the most effective.

DISPOSITION

- In the later teen years, intensity and frequency of tics typically diminish.

- One third of patients will achieve significant remission, although complete, lifelong remission is rare.
- One third will have mild, persistent, but "nonimpairing" tics.

REFERRAL

To a neurologist to confirm initial diagnosis and for treatment in difficult cases.

⚠ PEARLS & CONSIDERATIONS

- Tics do not need treatment unless they interfere with an individual's ability to function.
- Greater improvement in symptom severity among children with Tourette's and chronic tic disorder has been reported with a comprehensive behavioral intervention compared with supportive therapy and education.
- An important part of treatment is appropriate evaluation and therapy of coexisting conditions (e.g., ADHD, OCD).
- Deep brain stimulation (DBS) has shown some promising results as an alternative therapy in patients with medically refractory disease.

COMMENTS

Patient education may be obtained from the Tourette's Syndrome Association, 4240 Bell Blvd., Bayside, NY 11361-2864; 800-237-0717 or 718-224-2999; http://www.tsa-usa.org.

SUGGESTED READINGS

Available at www.expertconsult.com

RELATED CONTENT

Tourette's Syndrome (Patient Information)

AUTHOR: **FARIHA ZAHEER, M.D.**

Diseases
and Disorders

BASIC INFORMATION

DEFINITION

Toxic epidermal necrolysis (TEN) is a rare, acute, life-threatening mucocutaneous disease that is characterized by whole epidermal keratinocyte death resulting in dermal-epidermal separation of more than 30% body surface area (BSA). TEN and Steven-Johnson Syndrome (SJS) were initially described as separate entities, but are now considered to be variants of the same spectrum of disease, with similar clinical, histopathologic, and pathogenic features. SJS involves less than 10% BSA, SJS-TEN overlap involves 10% to 30% BSA, and TEN involves more than 30% BSA. TEN and SJS are caused by a hypersensitivity reaction to medications.

SYNONYMS

Lyell's syndrome

ICD-10CM CODES
L51.2 Toxic epidermal necrolysis

EPIDEMIOLOGY & DEMOGRAPHICS

INCIDENCE: Annual incidence is two to seven cases per million per year
PREDOMINANT SEX AND AGE: Women/men ratio 1.5:1
GENETICS: Some ethnic groups are more susceptible to developing TEN to certain medications when having specific human leukocyte antigen (HLA) alleles: e.g., to carbamazepine in Asians and East Indians with HLA-B*1502 and Europeans with HLA-A*3101, or to allopurinol in Han Chinese with HLA-B*5801.
RISK FACTORS: Slow acetylator genotypes, immunosuppression, and concomitant administrations of radiotherapy and anticonvulsants increase the risk for TEN.

PHYSICAL FINDINGS & CLINICAL PRESENTATION

The lesions in TEN are dynamic and follow a sequence of changes characterized below.
- *Early*: Fever, stinging eyes, pain upon swallowing may precede cutaneous manifestations by 2 to 7 days.
- *Later*: Generalized, dusky red, purpuric macules of irregular size and shape, with tendency to coalesce (Fig. 1T-47). Nikolsky sign positive (top layers of the skin slip away from the lower layers when slightly rubbed), detachment of large sheets of necrotic epidermis, extreme skin pain, mucosal involvement, anxiety, and asthenia. As the necrotic epidermis detaches from the underlying dermis, flaccid blisters form. The blisters can be extended sideways by slight pressure with a finger as more necrotic epidermis is displaced laterally (Asboe–Hansen sign). TEN patients resemble burn victims clinically, as well as in morbidity and mortality.
- *Resolution*: Scarring may develop when healing (joint contractures, eye complications, strictures of esophagus, anus, vagina, urethra).

ETIOLOGY

Exfoliation of the epidermis is due to extensive keratinocyte apoptosis. Several mechanisms have been postulated to explain the keratinocyte apoptosis. These include drug- or cytotoxic T-cell–mediated expression of FasL, perforin, granulysin, and granzyme B by keratinocytes via a molecular bridge involving tumor necrosis factor alpha (TNF-α), interferon gamma (IFN-γ), and inducible nitric oxide synthase (iNOS).

Medications most commonly associated with the development of TEN are shown in Table 1T-19. Medications other than those listed in Table 1T-19 have been classified to carry a lower risk, a doubtful risk, or being without evidence for a risk to induce TEN (see "Suggested Readings").

DIAGNOSIS

DIFFERENTIAL DIAGNOSIS

- Steven-Johnson syndrome +SJS/TEN overlap
- Erythema multiforme-major (mostly postinfectious)
- Staphylococcal scalded skin syndrome
- Generalized fixed drug eruptions
- Paraneoplastic pemphigus
- Drug-induced linear IgA bullous dermatosis

WORKUP

Identification of TEN is based on the clinical findings of epidermal detachment of more than 30% BSA, mucous membrane involvement, and full-thickness epidermal necrolysis, as described by pathology. A complete medication history should be taken including a time line outlining when new medications were started before the onset of the clinical symptoms. TEN most commonly occurs between 1 and 4 weeks after starting a new

TABLE 1T-19 Medications Most Commonly Causing TEN

Allopurinol	Cotrimoxazole
Sulfa-drugs	Aminopenicillins
Carbamazepine	Cephalosporins
Phenobarbital	Quinolones
Phenytoin	Minocycline
Phenylbutazone	Trimethoprim-
Lamotrigine	Sulfamethoxazole
Nevirapine	Amithiozone (thioacetazone)
Oxicam NSAIDS	Antiretroviral drugs, especially
Thiacetazone	NNRTIs

drug, but can occur at any time. Risk assessment should be done by using the SCORTEN mortality prognostic indicator (see Table 1T-20). Workup for the patient is similar to burn patients.

LABORATORY TESTS

In addition to the skin biopsy, no specific laboratory test is available to diagnose TEN. Standard chemistry to monitor electrolyte and fluid balance and organ function (e.g., serum urea, bicarbonate, glucose; see Table 1T-20) should be monitored as in burn patients.

IMAGING STUDIES
N/A

 TREATMENT

Withdrawing the offending drug reduces the risk of death by 30% per day and is the single most important measure in the management of TEN.

NONPHARMACOLOGIC THERAPY
- *Symptomatic treatment:*
  1. SCORTEN >1: transfer to intensive care unit / burn unit
  2. Fluid replacement
  3. Peripheral venous access (preferably in non-involved areas)
  4. Increased environmental temperature (30°C)
  5. Air-fluidized bed
  6. Early nutritional support through nasogastric tube
  7. Aseptic procedures, frequent culturing of skin, blood, urine specimens
  8. No prophylactic antibiotics
  9. Prophylactic anticoagulation
  10. Nonadhesive wound dressings, porcine xenografts, human allografts, autologous skin grafts, skin substitutes
  11. Daily ophthalmologic exam/consultation; artificial tears, antibiotic eyedrops every 2 hours; early mechanical disruption of synechia
  12. Regular mouth washes with antiseptic/antifungal solutions

ACUTE GENERAL Rx

There is no consensus for the optimal pharmacologic treatment of TEN.
- High-dose steroids may be effective in the initial course of the disease, but probably increase mortality later on due to infectious complications (sepsis).

TABLE 1T-20 SCORTEN Mortality Prognostic Indicator

Prognostic Factor	Points	Scorten	Mortality (%)
Age >40 yrs	1	0-1	3.2
Heart rate >120 bpm	1	2	12.1
Cancer/hematologic malignancy	1	3	35.8
BSA involved more than 10% on day 1	1	4	58.3
Serum urea level >28 mg/dL	1	>5	90
Serum bicarbonate level <20 mEq/L	1		
Serum glucose level >252 mg/dL	1		

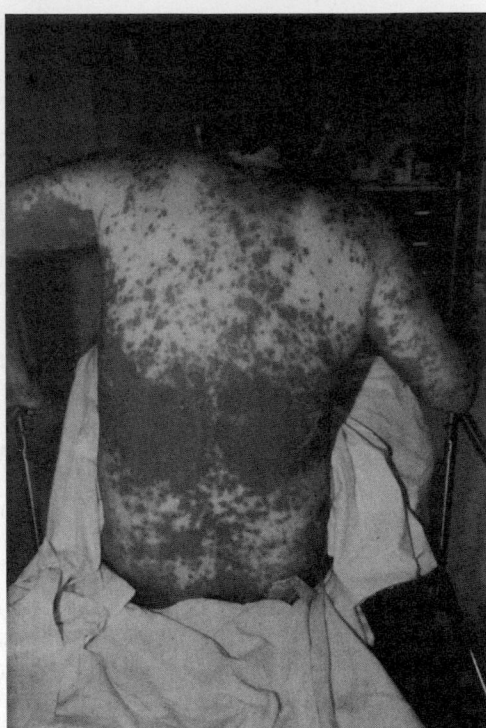

FIGURE 1T-47 Toxic epidermal necrolysis. (Courtesy David Effron, MD.) (Marx JA et al: *Rosen's emergency medicine,* ed 8, Philadelphia, 2014, WB Saunders.)

- Administration of high-dose IVIg over 3 to 4 days may reduce TEN-associated mortality (e.g., by blocking Fas-FasL interaction).
- Other agents that may also be effective in the treatment of TEN include cyclosporine, cyclophosphamide, plasmapheresis, and N-acetylcysteine.
- Several reports in the literature suggest efficacy of TNF-α inhibitors, notably infliximab and etanercept.

DISPOSITION

Late withdrawal of the causative drug is associated with a less favorable outcome/increased mortality. If he/she survives, the patient may suffer debilitating and disfiguring scars and contractures, requiring extensive physical therapy and/or surgical interventions.

PEARLS & CONSIDERATIONS

COMMENTS

Early recognition and prompt discontinuation of the culprit drug saves lives.

PREVENTION

In order to prevent recurrences, it is of pivotal importance that patients are never again exposed to the drug that caused TEN. This also includes chemically related medications. Avoiding any drugs that have caused less severe drug reactions in the past is important for primary prevention of TEN.

RELATED CONTENT

Erythema Multiforme-Major (Related Key Topic)
Steven-Johnson Syndrome (Related Key Topic)

DRUG REACTIONS

Third-Degree Burns

SUGGESTED READINGS

Available at www.expertconsult.com

AUTHORS: **GANARY DABIRI, M.D., Ph.D.,**
and **THOMAS M. RÜNGER, M.D., Ph.D.**

 BASIC INFORMATION

DEFINITION

Toxic megacolon is a rare but severe complication of colonic inflammation, usually inflammatory bowel disease (IBD). It is characterized by total or segmental nonobstructive colonic distention (>6 cm) associated with systemic toxicity of inflammatory or infectious etiology.

SYNONYMS

Toxic dilatation of the colon

ICD 10-CM CODES
K59.3 Megacolon, not elsewhere classified
A04.7 Megacolon due to *Clostridium difficile*

EPIDEMIOLOGY & DEMOGRAPHICS

INCIDENCE: Varies depending on etiology. Incidence in patients with ulcerative colitis (UC) is between 7% and 10% and approximately 1% and 5% in patients with Crohn's. *Clostridium difficile* infections may be complicated by toxic megacolon in up to 3% of cases.
PEAK INCIDENCE: N/A
PREVALENCE: N/A
PREDOMINANT SEX AND AGE: With increasing rates of *Clostridium difficile* (*C. diff*) infections due to overuse of antibiotics and hypervirulent strains, patients aged 65 and older are at higher risk for developing toxic megacolon as a result of *C. diff* infection.
GENETICS: There are no known genetic factors that predispose patients to developing toxic megacolon associated with an inflammatory or infectious etiology.
RISK FACTORS: Major risk factors include inflammatory, infectious, and ischemic conditions of the colon, especially in individuals who are immunocompromised. Other risk factors include hypokalemia, use of narcotics or antidiarrheal agents, pregnancy, and recent instrumentation (such as colonoscopy).

PHYSICAL FINDINGS & CLINICAL PRESENTATION

- Patients with toxic megacolon usually appear severely ill. Clinical symptoms are similar to those of IBD and acute colitis and may include abdominal pain, diarrhea (usually bloody), and vomiting.
- Physical exam findings may include a distended, tender, and tympanic abdomen with reduced or absent bowel sounds. The patient may also present with signs of shock such as fever, tachycardia, mental status changes, and hypovolemia.
- Laboratory findings may include leukocytosis, anemia, and electrolyte abnormalities such as hypokalemia and hypoalbuminemia.

ETIOLOGY

- Most common etiologies are inflammatory conditions such as UC, Crohn's, and Behcet's disease.

- Infections such as *C. diff, Salmonella, Shigella, E. coli,* cytomegalovirus, and *Entamoeba* can also be complicated by toxic megacolon.
- Other less common etiologies include ischemic colitis, malignancy such as lymphoma, and Kaposi's sarcoma. In general, toxic megacolon is more likely to be associated with pancolitis than segmental colitis (Box 1T-5).

DIAGNOSIS

DIFFERENTIAL DIAGNOSIS

- Ischemic colitis, Crohn's disease, ulcerative colitis

WORKUP

- General principles of workup include physical examination to evaluate for an acute abdomen, laboratory testing to detect electrolyte abnormalities, and plain radiography to evaluate for colonic dilatation.
- Clinical criteria for toxic megacolon, proposed by Jalan et al in 1969, are still used. A diagnosis can be made if radiographic evidence of colonic distention >6 cm is present with at least three of the following: fever >38°C, heart rate >120, leukocytosis >10.5, or anemia. In addition, at least one of the following must also be present: dehydration, altered level of consciousness, electrolyte abnormalities, or hypotension.

LABORATORY TESTS

- Initial testing should include a CBC, full chemistry panel, lactic acid, coagulation panel, liver function panel, and a type and screen

IMAGING STUDIES

- All patients should initially receive a plain abdominal radiograph to assess for colonic dilatation. Common findings include mucosal irregularity, loss of haustrations, "thumb printing" due to bowel wall edema, and thickening of the colonic wall with a continuous segment of air-filled colon >6 cm in diameter. The transverse or right colon is usually the most dilated segment seen.

BOX 1T-5 Disorders Associated With Toxic Megacolon

Inflammatory bowel disease
  ○ Ulcerative colitis
  ○ Crohn's disease
Infectious colitis
  ○ *Salmonella, Shigella,* amoebic colitis
  ○ *Clostridium difficile*
  ○ Cytomegalovirus colitis
  ○ HIV infection
Cancer chemotherapy
Ischemia

HIV, Human immunodeficiency virus.
From Vincent JL, Abraham E, Moore FA, Kochanek PM, Fink MP: *Textbook of critical care,* ed 6, Philadelphia, 2011, Saunders.

- Computed tomography (CT) has been increasingly used to assess disease extent and for surgical planning (Fig. 1T-48). It can also be helpful when differentiating between the various etiologies of toxic megacolon and to assess for complications such as intraabdominal hemorrhage or abscess.

TREATMENT

Treatment includes both medical and surgical options. Principles of initial management include treating the underlying cause and managing symptoms of shock with early surgical and gastroenterology consultation.

NONPHARMACOLOGIC THERAPY

- Surgery may be required in up to 50% of patients with toxic megacolon who do not show clinical improvement within 24 to 48 hours. The preferred first-line surgical treatment is subtotal colectomy with an end ileostomy. Other options include total proctocolectomy or colon decompression via the Turnbull method.
- Timing of surgical treatment is still controversial, with many advocating for aggressive medical treatment and observation before surgical intervention. Definitive indications for early surgical treatment include perforation, persistent colonic hemorrhage, or rapid clinical deterioration.

ACUTE GENERAL Rx

- Medications that impact colonic motility such as anticholinergics, opioids, and antidiarrheal agents should be discontinued and avoided.
- Electrolyte abnormalities, dehydration, and anemia are common clinical findings and should be addressed early. Fluid resuscitation with an isotonic solution (normal saline or lactated Ringer's) and correction of electrolyte disturbances (especially hypokalemia) can help prevent worsening atony of the colonic wall. Patients with anemia from colonic hemorrhage should receive blood transfusion.
- Patients with systemic signs of infection or a suspected infectious etiology should receive broad-spectrum antibiotics. Infections due to *C. diff* should be treated with vancomycin (oral or rectal) or metronidazole (oral or IV). Toxic megacolon due to cytomegalovirus should be treated with ganciclovir IV.
- Patients with inflammatory etiologies such as UC or Crohn's should receive high-dose IV steroids, either hydrocortisone 100 mg IV or methylprednisolone 60 mg IV. Steroids should not be used in patients with a confirmed infectious etiology.
- There are no data to currently support empiric treatment of toxic megacolon due to IBD with cyclosporine or infliximab. These treatment options should be reserved for patients who are not steroid responsive, and should be limited to one attempt at clinical improvement so as not to delay surgical intervention.

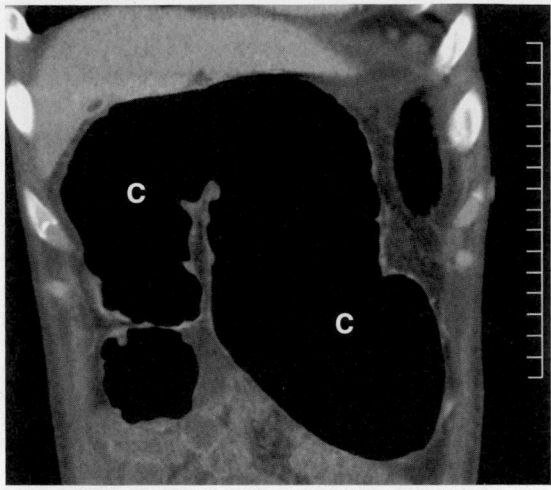

FIGURE 1T-48 Toxic megacolon. In a young patient with severe ulcerative colitis, coronal computed tomography demonstrates marked dilatation of the colon (*C*) with thinning of its walls. The diameter of the lumen of the colon exceeds 7 cm. This finding places the patient at high risk of colon perforation. (Webb WR et al: *Fundamentals of body CT*, ed 4, Philadelphia, 2015, WB Saunders.)

CHRONIC Rx

- Patients with IBD will need continued treatment for the underlying disease process once the acute processes associated with toxic megacolon have resolved.

COMPLEMENTARY AND ALTERNATIVE MEDICINE

- N/A

DISPOSITION

- All patients with toxic megacolon will require admission, possibly to the intensive care unit depending on their clinical presentation.

REFERRAL

- Surgical consultation in all cases.
- All patients with toxic megacolon due to newly diagnosed IBD who are discharged from the hospital should be referred to a gastroenterologist for continued treatment.

PEARLS & CONSIDERATIONS

COMMENTS

- Early recognition and treatment of toxic megacolon is critical given the associated high morbidity and mortality.
- Anticholinergic medications, antidiarrheal agents, and opioids can precipitate or worsen toxic megacolon.
- Management includes medical and surgical treatment with inpatient hospitalization and treatment of the underlying cause.

PREVENTION

- Prevention focuses on treatment of underlying causes of colitis to prevent complications such as toxic megacolon.

SUGGESTED READINGS

Available at www.expertconsult.com

RELATED CONTENT

Crohn's Disease (Related Key Topic)
Clostridium Difficile Infection (Related Key Topic)
Small Bowel Obstruction (Related Key Topic)
Ulcerative Colitis (Related Key Term)

AUTHOR: **STEVEN ROUGAS, M.D., M.S.**

 **BASIC INFORMATION**

DEFINITION

Toxic shock syndrome (TSS) is an acute febrile illness resulting in multiple organ system dysfunction caused most commonly by a bacterial exotoxin. Disease characteristics also include hypotension, vomiting, myalgia, watery diarrhea, vascular collapse, and an erythematous sunburnlike cutaneous rash that desquamates during recovery.

SYNONYMS

TSS

ICD-10CM CODES
A48.3 Toxic shock syndrome

EPIDEMIOLOGY & DEMOGRAPHICS

- Case reported incidence peak: 14 cases per 100,000 menstruating women annually in 1980; has since fallen to 1 case per 100,000 persons
- Occurs most commonly between ages 10 and 30 yr in healthy, young, menstruating white females
- Case fatality ratio of 3%

PHYSICAL FINDINGS & CLINICAL PRESENTATION

- Fever (>38.0° C)
- Diffuse macular erythrodermatous rash that involves both skin and mucous membranes, resembles sunburn, and also involves the palms and soles. The rash then desquamates 1 to 2 wk after disease onset in survivors
- Orthostatic hypotension
- Gastrointestinal symptoms: vomiting, diarrhea, abdominal tenderness
- Constitutional symptoms: myalgia, headache, photophobia, rigors, altered sensorium, conjunctivitis, arthralgia
- Respiratory symptoms: dysphagia, pharyngeal hyperemia, strawberry tongue
- Genitourinary symptoms: vaginal discharge, vaginal hyperemia, adnexal tenderness
- End-organ failure
- Severe hypotension and acute renal failure
- Hepatic failure
- Cardiovascular symptoms: disseminated intravascular coagulation, pulmonary edema, acute respiratory distress syndrome (ARDS), endomyocarditis, heart block

ETIOLOGY

- Menstruation-associated TSS: 45% of cases associated with tampons, diaphragm, or vaginal sponge use.
- Non–menstruation-associated TSS: 55% of cases associated with puerperal sepsis, post–cesarean section endometritis, mastitis, sinusitis, wound or skin infection, septorhinoplasty (nasal packings), pelvic inflammatory disease, respiratory infections following influenza, enterocolitis, and burns.

- Causative agent: *Staphylococcus aureus* infection of a susceptible individual (10% of population lacking sufficient levels of antitoxin antibodies), which liberates the disease mediator TSST-1 (exotoxin). While most cases are caused by methicillin-susceptible *S. aureus* (MSSA), cases of TSS from methicillin-resistant *S. aureus* (MRSA) have occurred, particularly those due to the more virulent community-associated MRSA strains.
- *S. aureus* exotoxins are superantigens that can activate large numbers of T cells (up to 20% at one time) resulting in a massive cytokine production: interleukin (Il-1), Il-2, TNF, and interferon gamma that then mediate the signs and symptoms of the disease.
- Other causative agents: coagulase-negative streptococci producing enterotoxins B or C, and exotoxin A–producing group A beta-hemolytic streptococci.

DIAGNOSIS

DIFFERENTIAL DIAGNOSIS

- Staphylococcal food poisoning
- Septic shock
- Mucocutaneous lymph node syndrome
- Scarlet fever
- Rocky Mountain spotted fever
- Meningococcemia
- Toxic epidermal necrolysis
- Kawasaki syndrome
- Leptospirosis
- Legionnaires' disease
- Hemolytic-uremic syndrome
- Stevens-Johnson syndrome
- Scalded skin syndrome
- Erythema multiforme
- Acute rheumatic fever

WORKUP

Broad-spectrum syndrome with multiorgan system involvement and variable but acute clinical presentation, including the following diagnostic criteria for staphylococcal toxic shock syndrome:
- Fever (>38° C)
- Classic desquamating rash (1-2 wk)

- Hypotension/orthostatic systolic blood pressure ≤90 mm Hg
- Syncope
- Negative throat and cerebrospinal fluid cultures
- Negative serologic test for Rocky Mountain spotted fever, rubeola, and leptospirosis
- Clinical involvement of three or more of the following:
  1. Cardiopulmonary: ARDS, pulmonary edema, endomyocarditis, second- or third-degree atrioventricular block
  2. Central nervous system: altered sensorium without focal neurologic findings
  3. Hematologic: thrombocytopenia (platelets <100,000)
  4. Liver: elevated liver function test results
  5. Renal: >5 cells/high-power field, negative urine cultures, azotemia, and increased creatinine (double normal)
  6. Mucous membrane involvement: vagina, oropharynx, conjunctiva
  7. Musculoskeletal: myalgia, creatine phosphokinase twice normal
  8. Gastrointestinal: vomiting, diarrhea

For streptococcal toxic shock syndrome the diagnostic criteria is as follows:
- Definite case: Isolation of group A β-hemolytic streptococci (GABHS) from a sterile site
- Probably case: Isolation of GABHS from a nonsterile site.
- Hypotension: Presence of two of the following findings:
  - Acute kidney injury or failure
  - Elevated aminotransferase
  - Erythematous macular rash, soft tissue necrosis
  - Coagulopathy, including thrombocytopenia and disseminated intravascular coagulation
  - Acute respiratory distress syndrome

LABORATORY TESTS

- Pan culture (cervix and vagina, throat, nasal passages, urine, blood, cerebrospinal fluid, wound) for *Staphylococcus, Streptococcus* (Table 1T-21), and other pathogenic organisms
- Electrolytes to detect hypokalemia, hyponatremia
- Complete blood count with differential and clotting profile for anemia (normocytic or

---

TABLE 1T-21 Staphylococcal versus Streptococcal Toxic Shock Syndrome

Feature	Staphylococcal	Streptococcal
Age	Primarily 15-35 yr	Primarily 20-50 yr
Gender	Higher frequency in women	Men and women equally affected
Severe pain	Rare	Common
Hypotension	100%	100%
Erythroderma rash	Very common	Less common
Renal failure	Common	Common
Bacteremia	Low frequency	60%
Tissue necrosis	Rare	Common
Predisposing factors	Tampons, surgery	Cuts, burns, varicella
Thrombocytopenia	Common	Common
Mortality rate	<3%	30%-70%

From Mandell GL et al: *Principles and practice in infectious diseases,* ed 7, Philadelphia, 2008, Churchill Livingstone.

normochromic), thrombocytopenia, leukocytosis, coagulopathy, and bacteremia
- Chemistry profile to detect decreased protein, increased aspartate aminotransferase, increased alanine aminotransferase, hypocalcemia, elevated blood urea nitrogen and creatinine, hypophosphatemia, increased lactate dehydrogenase, increased creatine phosphokinase
- Urinalysis to detect white blood cells (>5 cells/high-power field), proteinemia, microhematuria
- Arterial blood gases to assess respiratory function and acid-base status
- Serologic tests considered for Rocky Mountain spotted fever, rubeola, and leptospirosis

IMAGING STUDIES

- Chest x-ray to evaluate pulmonary edema
- ECG to evaluate arrhythmia
- Sonography, CT scan, or MRI considered if pelvic abscess or tubo-ovarian abscess suspected

Rx TREATMENT

NONPHARMACOLOGIC THERAPY

- For optimal outcome: high index of suspicion and early and aggressive supportive management in an ICU setting
- Aggressive fluid resuscitation (maintenance of circulating volume, cardiac output, systolic blood pressure)
- Thorough search for a localized infection or nidus: incision and drainage, debridement, removal of tampon or vaginal sponge
- Central hemodynamic monitoring, Swan-Ganz catheter, and arterial line for surveillance of hemodynamic status and response to therapy
- Foley catheter to monitor hourly urine output
- Possible military antishock trousers as temporary measure
- Acute ventilator management if severe respiratory compromise
- Renal dialysis for severe renal impairment
- Surgical intervention for indicated conditions (i.e., ruptured tubo-ovarian abscess, wound abscess, mastitis)
- Hyperbaric oxygen treatment can be used adjunctively.

ACUTE GENERAL Rx

- Isotonic crystalloid (normal saline solution) for volume replacement following "7-3" rule (refers to the response in millimeters of mercury [mm Hg] of the pulmonary artery wedge pressure to volume replacement).

- Electrolyte replacement (K+, C+)
- Packed red blood cells, coagulation factor replacement, fresh frozen plasma to treat anemia or dilation and curettage.
- Vasopressor therapy for hypotension refractory to fluid volume replacement (e.g., dopamine beginning at 2 to 5 μg/kg/min)
- Steroids have been used but are not generally recommended due to lack of evidence of benefit.
- It is not clear whether antibiotics alter the course of acute TSS. Most authors recommend that patients receive 10 to 14 days of combination antibiotic therapy. In staphylococcal TSS, effective agents are clindamycin (900 mg IV every 8 hr in adults or 25 to 40 mg/kg per day in children) plus vancomycin (adults: 30 mg/kg per day IV in two divided doses; children: 40 mg/kg per day IV in four divided doses). Oxacillin or nafcillin sodium (2 g IV every 4 hr in adults; children: 100 to 150 mg/kg per 24 hr divided in four doses) can be used instead of vancomycin if TSS due to MSSA. An alternative to vancomycin is linezolid.
- In streptococcal TSS, effective agents are penicillin G 24 million units/day in divided doses *plus* clindamycin 900 mg IV q8h. Alternative agents are ceftriaxone 2 g IV q24h *plus* clindamycin 900 mg IV q8h.
- Broad-spectrum antibiotic including gram-negative coverage added if concurrent sepsis suspected with TSS.
- Intravenous immune globulin (IVIG): while no controlled trials exist, most authors recommend IVIG (400 mg/kg in a single dose administered over several hours) in severe cases of TSS that are not responding to fluids or vasopressors. It may neutralize superantigen and decrease tissue damage.
- Tetracycline added if considering Rocky Mountain spotted fever.

CHRONIC Rx

- Severely ill patient: may require prolonged hospitalization and supportive management with gradual recovery and/or sequelae from severe end-organ involvement (ARDS or renal failure requiring dialysis)
- Majority of patients: complete recovery
- Early-onset complications (within 2 wk):
  1. Skin desquamation
  2. Impaired digit sensation
  3. Denuded tongue
  4. Vocal cord paralysis
  5. Acute tubular necrosis
  6. ARDS
- Late-onset complications (after 8 wk):
  1. Nail splitting and loss
  2. Alopecia

3. Central nervous system sequelae
4. Renal impairment
5. Cardiac dysfunction
- Recurrent TSS:
  1. More common in menstruation-related cases.
  2. Less common in patients treated with beta-lactamase–resistant antistaphylococcal antibiotics.
  3. Patients with history of TSS: if suspect signs and symptoms occur, have high index of suspicion and low threshold for evaluation and treatment.
  4. Screen for nasal carriage of *S. aureus* in patients with *S. aureus* TSS and treat with mupirocin in those with positive cultures.

PREVENTION

- Avoidance of tampons or use of low-absorbency tampons only (<4 hr in situ) and alternate with napkins
- Education for patients concerning signs and symptoms of TSS
- Avoidance of tampons for patients with history of TSS

DISPOSITION

- Complete recovery for most patients
- Long-term management of early- and late-onset complications for minority of patients

REFERRAL

- For multidisciplinary management, involving primary physician, gynecologist, internist, infectious disease specialist, and other supportive care specialists
- To tertiary-level hospital

 PEARLS & CONSIDERATIONS

COMMENTS

Antibiotic prophylaxis against invasive group A streptococcal infection with benzathine penicillin G plus rifampin, clindamycin, or azithromycin is recommended for immunocompromised household contacts of patients with streptococcal TSS-like syndrome.

SUGGESTED READINGS
Available at www.expertconsult.com

RELATED CONTENT
Toxic Shock Syndrome (Patient Information)

AUTHOR: **GLENN G. FORT, M.D., M.P.H.**

BASIC INFORMATION

DEFINITION

Toxoplasmosis is an infection caused by the protozoal parasite *Toxoplasma gondii*.

ICD-10CM CODES
B58.9	Toxoplasmosis, unspecified
B58.3	Pulmonary toxoplasmosis
B58.89	Toxoplasmosis with other organ involvement
P37.1	Congenital toxoplasmosis

EPIDEMIOLOGY & DEMOGRAPHICS

INCIDENCE (IN U.S.):
- 3% to >50% of healthy adults (seroprevalence)
- Increases with age
- Increases with certain activities
  1. Slaughterhouse workers
  2. Cat owners
- Increases with certain geographic locations: high prevalence of cats

PREDOMINANT SEX: Equal gender distribution
PREDOMINANT AGE:
- Infancy (congenital infection)
- Prevalence increases with age

PEAK INCIDENCE: Temperate climates
GENETICS: Congenital infection: 400 to 4000 cases/yr in the U.S.
- Incidence and severity vary with the trimester of gestation during which the mother acquired infection.
  1. 10% to 25% (first trimester)
  2. 30% to 54% (second trimester)
  3. 60% to 65% (third trimester)
- Congenital infection occurring in the first trimester is the most severe.
- 89% to 100% of infections in the third trimester are asymptomatic.
- Risk to the fetus is not correlated with symptoms in the mother.

PHYSICAL FINDINGS & CLINICAL PRESENTATION

- Acquired (immunocompetent host)
  1. 80% to 90% asymptomatic
  2. Adenopathy (usually cervical)
  3. Fever
  4. Myalgias
  5. Malaise
  6. Sore throat
  7. Maculopapular rash
  8. Hepatosplenomegaly
  9. Chorioretinitis rare
- Acquired (in patients with AIDS, CD4 count <100)
  1. 89% of symptomatic cases
     a. Encephalitis
     b. Intracerebral mass lesions
  2. Pneumonitis
  3. Chorioretinitis
  4. Other end organ
- Acquired (immunocompromised patients)
  1. Encephalitis
  2. Myocarditis (especially in heart transplant patients)
  3. Pneumonitis

- Ocular infection in the immunocompetent host
  1. Congenital infection
  2. Blurred vision
  3. Photophobia
  4. Pain
  5. Loss of central vision if macula involved
  6. Focal necrotizing retinitis
  7. Typically presents in second or third decade
- Congenital
  1. Results from acute infection acquired by the mother within 6 to 8 wk before conception or during gestation
  2. Usually, asymptomatic mother
  3. No sign of disease
  4. Chorioretinitis
  5. Blindness
  6. Epilepsy
  7. Psychomotor or mental retardation
  8. Intracranial calcifications
  9. Hydrocephalus
  10. Microcephaly
  11. Encephalitis
  12. Anemia
  13. Thrombocytopenia
  14. Hepatosplenomegaly
  15. Lymphadenopathy
  16. Jaundice
  17. Rash
  18. Pneumonitis
  19. Most infected infants are asymptomatic at birth

ETIOLOGY

- *Toxoplasma gondii*
  1. Ubiquitous intracellular protozoan
  2. Present worldwide
  3. Cat is definitive host (Fig. E1T-49)
- Human infection
  1. Ingestion of oocysts shed by cats in soil, litter boxes, vegetables
  2. Ingestion of inadequately cooked meat containing tissue cysts
  3. Vertical transmission

DIAGNOSIS

DIFFERENTIAL DIAGNOSIS

- Lymphadenopathy
  1. Infectious mononucleosis
  2. Cytomegalovirus (CMV) mononucleosis
  3. Cat-scratch disease
  4. Sarcoidosis
  5. Tuberculosis
  6. Lymphoma
  7. Metastatic cancer
- Cerebral mass lesions in immunocompromised host
  1. Lymphoma
  2. Tuberculosis
  3. Bacterial abscess
- Pneumonitis in immunocompromised host
  1. *Pneumocystis jiroveci (carinii)* pneumonia
  2. Tuberculosis
  3. Fungal infection
- Chorioretinitis
  1. Syphilis
  2. Tuberculosis

3. Histoplasmosis (competent host)
4. CMV
5. Syphilis
6. Herpes simplex
7. Fungal infection
8. Tuberculosis (AIDS patient)
- Myocarditis
  1. Organ rejection in heart transplant recipients
- Congenital infection
  1. Rubella
  2. CMV
  3. Herpes simplex
  4. Syphilis
  5. Listeriosis
  6. Erythroblastosis fetalis
  7. Sepsis

WORKUP

- Acute infection, immunocompetent host
  1. CBC
  2. *Toxoplasma* serology (IgG, IgM) in serial blood specimens 3 wk apart
  3. Lymph node biopsy if diagnosis uncertain
- Immunocompromised host
  1. CNS symptoms
     a. Cerebral CT scan or MRI if CNS symptoms present
     b. Spinal tap, if safe
     c. Brain biopsy if no response to empiric therapy
  2. Ocular symptoms
     a. Funduscopic examination
     b. Serologic studies
     c. Rarely, vitreous tap
  3. Pulmonary symptoms
     a. Chest x-ray examination
     b. Bronchoalveolar lavage
     c. Transbronchial or open-lung biopsy
  4. Myocarditis
     a. Cardiac enzymes
     b. Electrocardiogram
     c. Endomyocardial biopsy for definitive diagnosis
- Toxoplasmosis in pregnancy (Fig. 1T-50)
  1. Initial maternal screening with IgM and IgG
     a. If negative, mother at risk of acute infection and should be retested monthly
     b. If both IgG and IgM positive, obtain IgA and IgE ELISA, AC/HS test
     c. IgA and IgE ELISA, AC/HS test elevated in acute infection
     d. Ig high for 1 yr or more
     e. IgG repeated 3 to 4 wk later to determine if titer is stable
  2. Acute maternal infection not excluded or documented
     a. Fetal blood sampling (for culture, Ig, IgA, IgE)
     b. Amniotic fluid polymerase chain reaction (PCR)
  3. Fetal ultrasound every other wk if maternal infection documented
- Congenital toxoplasmosis (Fig. 1T-51)
  1. Placental histology
  2. Specific IgM or IgA in infant's blood

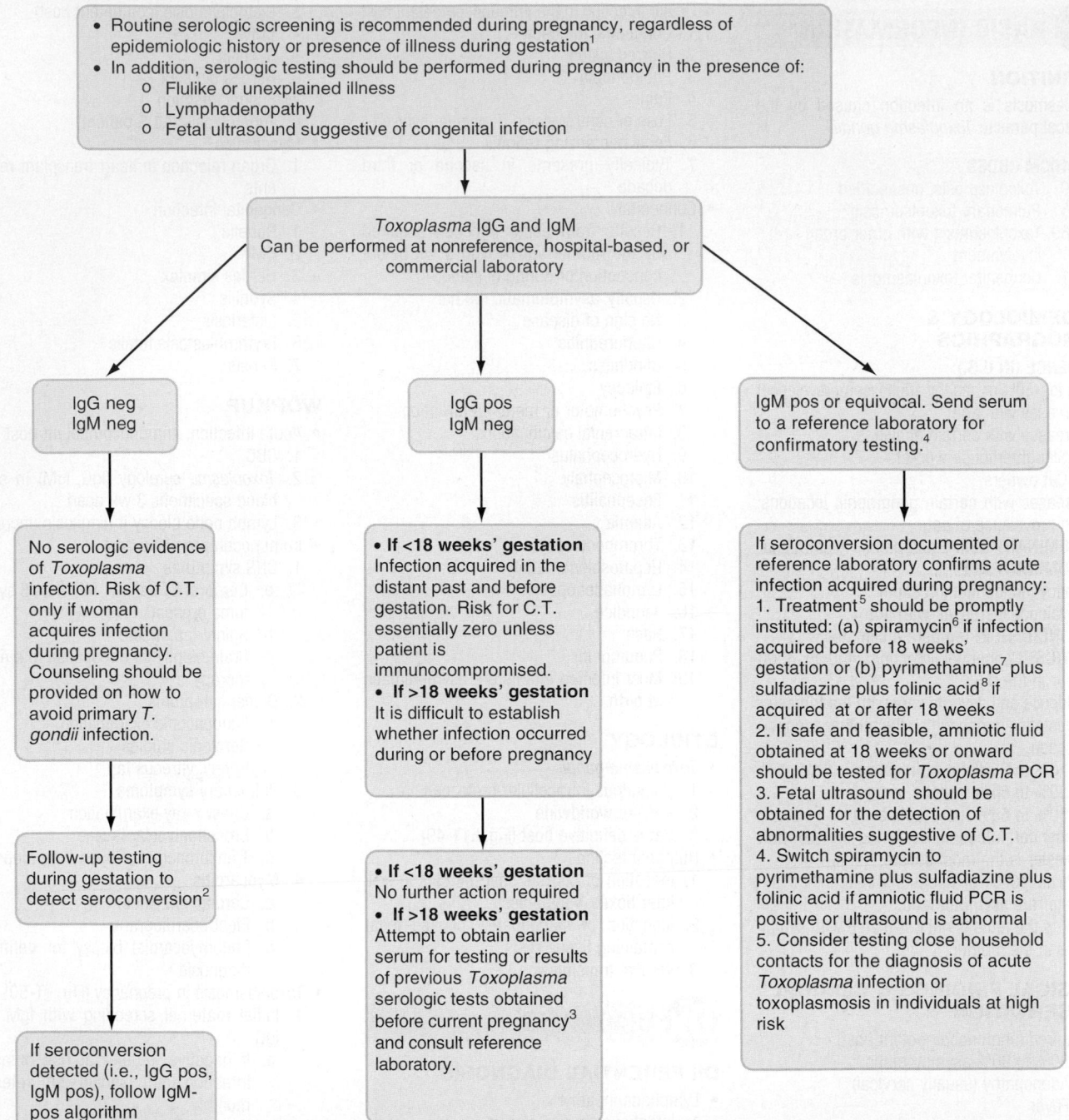

FIGURE 1T-50 Diagnostic approach and management algorithm of toxoplasmosis during pregnancy. Most of the initial serologic screening can be accomplished by nonreference or commercial laboratories. Only positive immunoglobulin M results should be considered for additional testing and consultation with medical experts at a reference laboratory. *CT*, Congenital toxoplasmosis; *IgG*, immunoglobulin G; *IgM*, immunoglobulin M; *neg*, negative test result; *pos*, positive test result.[1] Up to 50% of women who acquire *Toxoplasma* infection during gestation do not have a known risk factor for acute infection or an illness suggestive of toxoplasmosis. Thus, to identify all women at risk, serologic screening should be performed in all pregnant women, along with other routine screening tests.[2] In a recent study from Lyon, France, monthly screening of seronegative pregnant women was reported to significantly decrease the risk of vertical transmission and of clinical signs at 3 years of age. Consider consultation with a physician expert in management of toxoplasmosis during pregnancy (e.g., in the U.S., Palo Alto Medical Foundation–*Toxoplasma* Serology Laboratory [PAMF-TSL], www.pamf.org/serology/; 650-853-4828; e-mail, toxolab@pamf.org; or U.S. [Chicago] National Collaborative Treatment Trial Study [NCCTS]; 773-834-4152).[4] Consider sending serum sample to a reference laboratory (e.g., PAMF-TSL).[5] Treatment regimens vary by country. The pyrimethamine-sulfadiazine–folinic acid regimen should not be offered to any pregnant woman before 12 weeks of gestation because of potential teratogenicity. In some centers in Europe, this regimen is offered at 14 weeks of gestation or later; in the U.S., it is recommended at 18 weeks or later.[6] Spiramycin is not commercially available in the U.S. It can be obtained at no cost and after consultation (with PAMF-TSL or the NCCTS through the U.S. Food and Drug Administration).[7] When using pyrimethamine, folic acid should be discontinued from the prenatal multivitamins. Folic acid can potentially counteract the antiparasitic effect of the drug.[8] Folic acid should not be erroneously used instead of folinic acid. (Bennett JE et al: *Mandell, Douglas, and Bennett's principles and practice of infectious diseases*, ed 8, Philadelphia, 2015, WB Saunders.)

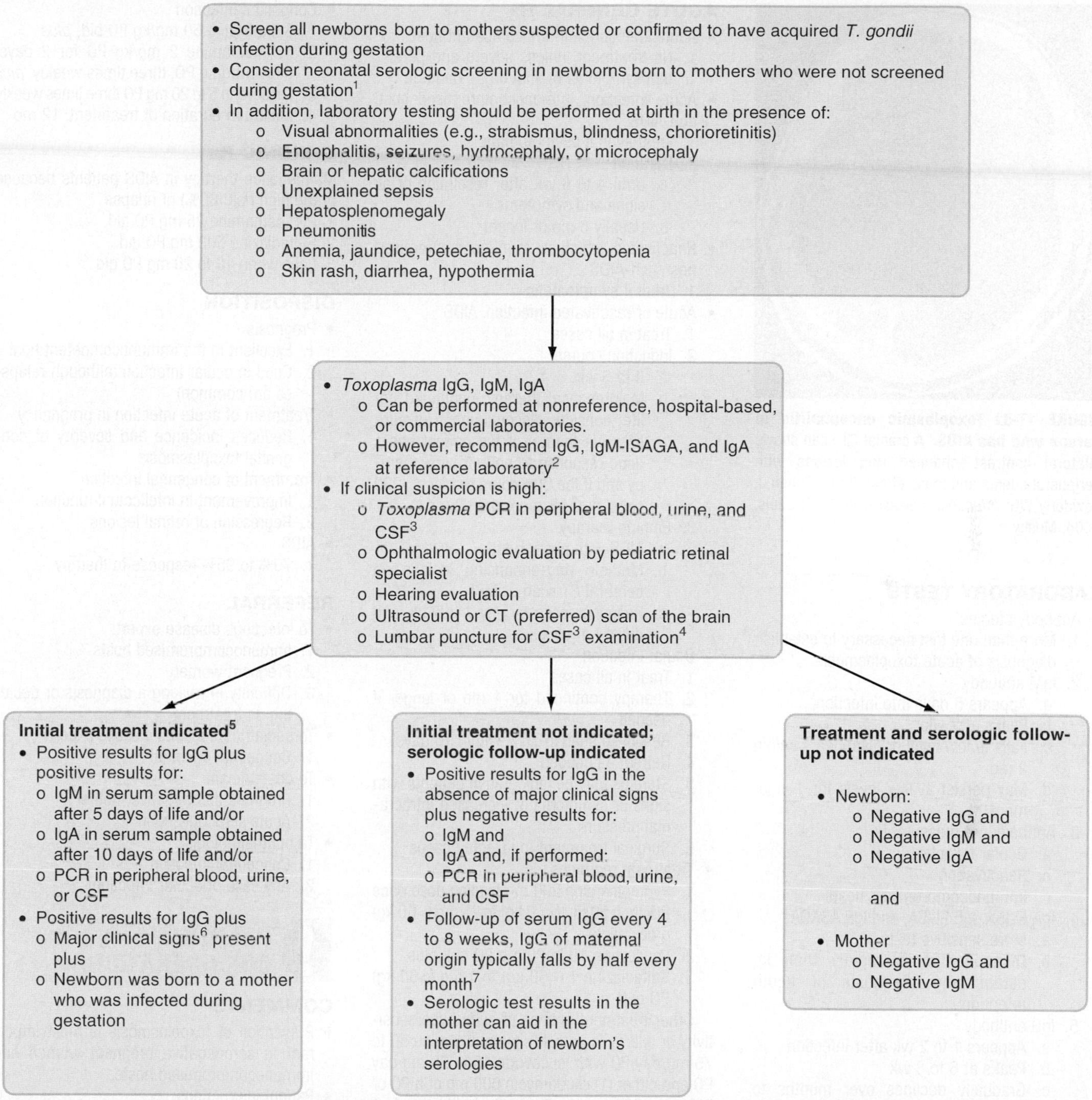

- Screen all newborns born to mothers suspected or confirmed to have acquired *T. gondii* infection during gestation
- Consider neonatal serologic screening in newborns born to mothers who were not screened during gestation[1]
- In addition, laboratory testing should be performed at birth in the presence of:
  - Visual abnormalities (e.g., strabismus, blindness, chorioretinitis)
  - Encephalitis, seizures, hydrocephaly, or microcephaly
  - Brain or hepatic calcifications
  - Unexplained sepsis
  - Hepatosplenomegaly
  - Pneumonitis
  - Anemia, jaundice, petechiae, thrombocytopenia
  - Skin rash, diarrhea, hypothermia

- *Toxoplasma* IgG, IgM, IgA
  - Can be performed at nonreference, hospital-based, or commercial laboratories.
  - However, recommend IgG, IgM-ISAGA, and IgA at reference laboratory[2]
- If clinical suspicion is high:
  - *Toxoplasma* PCR in peripheral blood, urine, and CSF[3]
  - Ophthalmologic evaluation by pediatric retinal specialist
  - Hearing evaluation
  - Ultrasound or CT (preferred) scan of the brain
  - Lumbar puncture for CSF[3] examination[4]

Initial treatment indicated[5]
- Positive results for IgG plus positive results for:
  - IgM in serum sample obtained after 5 days of life and/or
  - IgA in serum sample obtained after 10 days of life and/or
  - PCR in peripheral blood, urine, or CSF
- Positive results for IgG plus
  - Major clinical signs[6] present plus
  - Newborn was born to a mother who was infected during gestation

Initial treatment not indicated; serologic follow-up indicated
- Positive results for IgG in the absence of major clinical signs plus negative results for:
  - IgM and
  - IgA and, if performed:
  - PCR in peripheral blood, urine, and CSF
- Follow-up of serum IgG every 4 to 8 weeks, IgG of maternal origin typically falls by half every month[7]
- Serologic test results in the mother can aid in the interpretation of newborn's serologies

Treatment and serologic follow-up not indicated

- Newborn:
  - Negative IgG and
  - Negative IgM and
  - Negative IgA

  and

- Mother
  - Negative IgG and
  - Negative IgM

FIGURE 1T-51 Diagnostic approach and management algorithm of the newborn whose mother has been suspected or confirmed to have acquired toxoplasmosis during gestation. *CSF,* Cerebrospinal fluid; *CT,* computed tomography; *IgG, IgM,* and *IgA,* immunoglobulins G, M, and A, respectively; *ISAGA,* immunosorbent agglutination assay; *PCR,* polymerase chain reaction.[1] Consider consultation with a physician expert in management of toxoplasmosis during pregnancy (e.g., in the U.S., Palo Alto Medical Foundation–*Toxoplasma* Serology Laboratory [PAMF-TSL], www.pamf.org/serology/; 650-853-4828; e-mail, toxolab@pamf.org; or U.S. [Chicago] National Collaborative Treatment Trial Study, 773-834-4152).[2] Consider sending serum sample to a reference laboratory (e.g., PAMF-TSL).[3] If lumbar puncture is clinically indicated, deemed safe, and feasible.[4] In an attempt to confirm the diagnosis of congenital toxoplasmosis, CSF should be sent for cell count and differential (congenital toxoplasmosis is one of the few causes of eosinophilic meningitis), protein (congenital toxoplasmosis is one of the few causes of extreme elevation of CSF protein), glucose, and *T. gondii* PCR.[5] The recommended regimen is pyrimethamine plus sulfadiazine plus folinic acid (see text).[6] Major clinical signs are referred here: chorioretinitis, brain calcifications, and hydrocephalus.[7] Maternally transferred IgG antibodies usually decline and disappear within 6 to 12 months of life. (Bennett JE et al: *Mandell, Douglas, and Bennett's principles and practice of infectious diseases,* ed 8, Philadelphia, 2015, WB Saunders.)

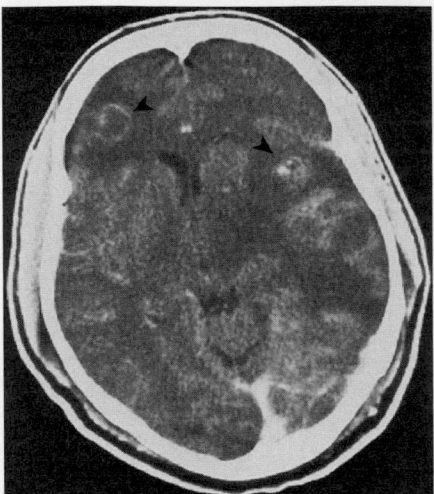

FIGURE 1T-52 Toxoplasmic encephalitis in person who has AIDS. A cranial CT scan shows bilateral contrast-enhanced ring lesions with peripheral edema and mass effect. (From Cohen J, Powderly WG: *Infectious diseases*, ed 2, St Louis, 2004, Mosby.)

LABORATORY TESTS

- Antibody studies
  1. More than one test necessary to establish diagnosis of acute toxoplasmosis
  2. IgM antibody
     a. Appears 5 days into infection
     b. Peaks at 2 wk
     c. Falls to low level or disappears within 2 mo
     d. May persist at low levels for 1 yr or more
  3. Antibody not measurable
     a. Ocular toxoplasmosis
     b. Reactivation
     c. Immunocompromised hosts
  4. IgA ELISA, IgE ELISA, and IgE ASAGA
     a. More sensitive tests
     b. Disappear more rapidly than Ig, establishing diagnosis of acute infection
  5. IgG antibody
     a. Appears 1 to 2 wk after infection
     b. Peaks at 6 to 8 wk
     c. Gradually declines over months to years

IMAGING STUDIES

- Chest x-ray if pulmonary involvement suspected
- Cerebral CT scan (Fig. 1T-52) or MRI if encephalitis suspected

Rx TREATMENT

NONPHARMACOLOGIC THERAPY

- Selected cases of ocular infection
  1. Photocoagulation
  2. Vitrectomy
  3. Lentectomy
- Selected cases of congenital cerebral infection
  1. Ventricular shunting

ACUTE GENERAL Rx

- Acute infection, immunocompetent host
  1. No treatment, unless severe and persistent symptoms or vital organ damage
- Acute infection, immunocompromised host, non-AIDS
  1. Treat even if asymptomatic
  2. Duration
     a. Until 4 to 6 wk after resolution of all signs and symptoms
     b. Usually 6 mo or longer
- Reactivated infection, immunocompromised host, non-AIDS
  1. Treat if symptomatic
- Acute or reactivated infection, AIDS
  1. Treat in all cases
  2. Induction course
     a. 3 to 6 wk.
     b. Maintenance therapy continued for life; consider discontinuation of suppressive therapy if the patient has a good response to antiretroviral therapy and if the CD4 count remains >200 cells/mm³ for more than 3 mo.
  3. Empiric therapy
     a. AIDS with positive IgG
     b. Multiple ring-enhancing lesions on cerebral CT scan or MRI
     c. Response seen by day 7 in 71% and day 14 in 91%
- Ocular infection
  1. Treat in all cases
  2. Therapy continued for 1 mo or longer if needed
  3. Response seen in 70% within 10 days
  4. Retreat as needed
  5. Steroids may be indicated in patients with signs or symptoms of increased intracranial pressure
  6. Surgical treatment in selected cases
- Treatment regimens
  1. Pyrimethamine 200 mg loading dose once PO, then 50 mg (<60 kg) to 75 mg (>60 kg) q day; plus
  2. Leucovorin 10 to 20 mg PO qid, plus
  3. Sulfadiazine 1 (<60 kg) to 1.5 g (>60 kg) PO q6h

  Other treatment options (if sulfa hypersensitivity or allergy is present): pyrimethamine 50 to 75 mg/day PO with leucovorin 10 to 20 mg/day PO and either (1) clindamycin 600 mg q6h PO or IV (up to 1200 mg IV) q6h, or (2) clarithromycin 1 g PO bid, or (3) dapsone 100 mg/day PO, or (4) atovaquone 750 mg PO q6h.
- Acute infection in pregnancy
  1. Treat immediately
  2. Risk of fetal infection reduced by 60% with treatment
     a. First trimester
        i. Spiramycin 3 g PO qid in two to four divided doses
        ii. Sulfadiazine 4 g PO qid in four divided doses
     b. Second and third trimester
        i. Sulfadiazine as previously described, *plus*
        ii. Pyrimethamine 25 mg PO qid, *plus*
        iii. Leucovorin 5 to 15 mg PO qid
        iv. Spiramycin as previously described

- Congenital infection
  1. Sulfadiazine 50 mg/kg PO bid, *plus*
  2. Pyrimethamine 2 mg/kg PO for 2 days, then 1 mg/kg PO, three times weekly, *plus*
  3. Leucovorin 5 to 20 mg PO three times weekly
  4. Minimum duration of treatment: 12 mo

CHRONIC Rx

Maintenance therapy in AIDS patients because of the high risk (80%) of relapse
1. Pyrimethamine 25 mg PO qid
2. Sulfadiazine 500 mg PO qid
3. Leucovorin 10 to 20 mg PO qid

DISPOSITION

- Prognosis
  1. Excellent in the immunocompetent host
  2. Good in ocular infection (although relapses are common)
- Treatment of acute infection in pregnancy
  1. Reduces incidence and severity of congenital toxoplasmosis
- Treatment of congenital infection
  1. Improvement in intellectual function
  2. Regression of retinal lesions
- AIDS
  1. 70% to 95% response to therapy

REFERRAL

- To infectious disease expert:
  1. Immunocompromised hosts
  2. Pregnant women
  3. Difficulty in making a diagnosis or deciding on treatment
- To pediatric infectious disease expert:
  1. Congenital infection
- To obstetrician:
  1. Pregnant seronegative mother
  2. Acute seroconversion
- To ophthalmologist:
  1. Congenital infection
  2. Any case of ocular infection

❗ PEARLS & CONSIDERATIONS

COMMENTS

- Prevention of toxoplasmosis is most important in seronegative pregnant women and immunocompromised hosts.
- Patient instructions:
  1. Cook meat to 66° C.
  2. Cook eggs.
  3. Do not drink unpasteurized milk.
  4. Wash hands thoroughly after handling raw meat.
  5. Wash kitchen surfaces that come in contact with raw meat.
  6. Wash fruits and vegetables.
  7. Avoid contact with materials potentially contaminated with cat feces.

SUGGESTED READINGS

Available at www.expertconsult.com

RELATED CONTENT

Toxoplasmosis (Patient Information)

AUTHOR: **PHILIP A. CHAN, M.D., M.S.**

BASIC INFORMATION

DEFINITION

Acute hemolytic transfusion reaction (AHTR) is acute intravascular hemolysis caused by mismatches in the ABO system. It is caused by complement-fixing immunoglobulin (Ig) and IgG antibodies to group A and B red blood cells. Hemolytic transfusion reactions can also be caused by minor antigen systems; however, they are usually less severe. In delayed serologic transfusion reactions, hemolysis with hemoglobinemia is unusual. Delayed hemolytic reactions are usually caused by an anamnestic alloantibody response upon re-exposure to an erythrocyte antigen. They usually occur 2 to 10 days after transfusion. In delayed reactions the only manifestations may be the development of a newly positive direct antiglobulin (Coombs test) and fever. The clinical severity of an ABO-incompatible blood transfusion is significantly influenced by the degree of complement activation and cytokine stimulation. In an extravascular hemolytic transfusion reaction, complement is either not fixed at all or is fixed only to C3b. This presentation is commonly associated with Rh antibodies, but can be seen with any number of non–ABO antigen–antibody complexes.

SYNONYMS

AHTR
Acute hemolytic transfusion reaction

ICD-10CM CODES
T80.9 Unspecified complication following infusion, transfusion and therapeutic injection
T80.3 ABO incompatibility reaction
T80.4 Rh incompatibility reaction
T80.8 Other complications following infusion, transfusion, and therapeutic injection

EPIDEMIOLOGY & DEMOGRAPHICS

- Acute intravascular hemolysis occurs in one to five per 50,000 transfusions.

PHYSICAL FINDINGS & CLINICAL PRESENTATION

- Hypotension
- Pain at the infusion site
- Fever, tachycardia, chest pain, dyspnea, dizziness, bronchospasm
- Lower back pain due to ischemic muscle pain or vasospasm rather than kidney pain from developing renal failure
- Severe reactions often occur in surgical patients under anesthesia who are unable to give any warning signs.
- Table 1T-22 summarizes signs and symptoms of acute adverse reactions to blood transfusion
- Patients with acute extravascular hemolytic transfusion reactions typically do not present as a clinical emergency. In most cases presentation is with a low-grade fever from the generation of IL-1 or other proinflammatory cytokines. Hemoglobinuria and hemoglobinemia are rarely present unless the amount of incompatible blood infused is excessive.

ETIOLOGY

Most fatal hemolytic reactions are caused by clerical errors and mislabeled specimens.

DIAGNOSIS

DIFFERENTIAL DIAGNOSIS

- Bacterial contamination of blood
- Hemoglobinopathies

WORKUP

The transfusion must be stopped immediately. The blood bank must be notified, and the donor transfusion bag must be returned to the blood bank along with a freshly drawn posttransfusion specimen.

LABORATORY TESTS

- The direct antiglobulin test (DAT) usually becomes positive in an immune hemolytic reaction (if tested before all the incompatible RBCs are destroyed). Preparation of an antibody eluate is necessary to identify the offending antibody.
- Analyze urine for hemoglobinuria (wine-colored urine), observe plasma for hemoglobinemia (pink plasma).
- Labs: Decreased hematocrit and serum haptoglobin (haptoglobin low to 0 mg/dL). Elevated BUN, creatinine, LDH, bilirubin.
- Monitor coagulation status (PT, aPTT, fibrinogen).

TREATMENT

NONPHARMACOLOGIC THERAPY

- Stop transfusion immediately. Test anticoagulated blood from the recipient for the presence of free hemoglobin in the plasma.
- Monitor vital signs closely, and maintain IV access with a suitable crystalloid or colloid solution.
- Maintain an adequate airway.

ACUTE GENERAL Rx

- Treatment is supportive and consists of fluid resuscitation, vasopressor support, and mannitol.
- Vigorous IV hydration (0.9% NaCl or some other suitable crystalloid solution) to maintain urine flow at >100 mL/hr until hypotension is corrected and hemoglobinuria clears. IV furosemide may be necessary to maintain adequate renal flow.
- The addition of mannitol may prevent renal damage (controversial). Mannitol, if chosen, must be used with caution; if acute tubular necrosis occurs before mannitol infusion, pulmonary edema may occur as a result of the acute increase in intravascular volume secondary to fluid expansion.
- Monitor for the presence of disseminated intravascular coagulation. PT, aPTT, and fibrinogen levels should be closely monitored.
- If sepsis is suspected, culture as appropriate.

Diseases and Disorders

TABLE 1T-22 Signs and Symptoms of Acute Adverse Reactions to Blood Transfusion

Reaction	Fever	Chills/ Rigors	Nausea/ Vomiting	Chest Discomfort/ Pain	Facial Flushing	Wheezing/ Dyspnea	Back/ Lumbar Pain	Discomfort at Infusion Site	Hypotension
Acute hemolytic	X	X	X	X	X	X	X	X	X
Febrile nonhemolytic	X	X		X	X				
Nonimmune hemolysis									
Acute lung injury	X			X		X			X
Allergic									
Massive transfusion complications									
Anaphylaxis	X	X	X	X	X	X	X	X	X
Passive cytokine infusion	X	X	X			X			
Hypervolemia						X			
Bacterial sepsis	X	X	X				X	X	X
Air embolus				X		X			

From Goldman L, Bennett JC [eds]: *Cecil's textbook of medicine*, ed 22, Philadelphia, 2004, Saunders.

DISPOSITION

Mortality rate exceeds 50% in severe transfusion reactions.

PEARLS & CONSIDERATIONS

COMMENTS

Hemolysis caused by minor antigen systems is generally less severe and may be delayed 2 to 10 days after transfusion.

SUGGESTED READINGS

Available at www.expertconsult.com

AUTHOR: **FRED F. FERRI, M.D.**

 **BASIC INFORMATION**

DEFINITION

Transient ischemic attack (TIA) is a transient episode of neurologic dysfunction caused by focal brain, spinal cord, or retinal ischemia without acute infarction on MRI. TIA symptoms typically resolve within 60 min and almost always within 24 hr.

SYNONYMS

TIA
Amaurosis fugax
"Mini-stroke"
Pre-stroke

ICD-10CM CODES
G45.9   Transient cerebral ischemic attack, unspecified
G45.8   Other transient cerebral ischemic attacks and related syndromes
Z86.73   Personal history of transient ischemic attack (TIA), and cerebral infarction without residual deficits

EPIDEMIOLOGY & DEMOGRAPHICS

INCIDENCE: 49 to 83 cases per 100,000 persons annually
PEAK INCIDENCE: After age 60 yr
PREVALENCE: 200,000 to 500,000 persons in the United States. The annual risk of stroke after a TIA or minor stroke is 3% to 4% approximately.
PREDOMINANT SEX AND RACE: Males > females; African American > Caucasian
RISK FACTORS: Same as for ischemic stroke

PHYSICAL FINDINGS & CLINICAL PRESENTATION

TIAs often present with ipsilateral transient monocular blindness (amaurosis fugax), contralateral numbness or weakness, contralateral homonymous hemianopsia, and/or aphasia.

ETIOLOGY

Embolic (cardioembolism in 10%-15%), large vessel atherothrombotic disease (20%-25%), lacunar disease, hypoperfusion, hypercoagulable state, arteritis

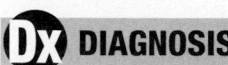 **DIAGNOSIS**

DIFFERENTIAL DIAGNOSIS

Seizures, hypoglycemia, complicated migraine, intracranial hemorrhage, mass lesion, vestibular disease, Bell's palsy, meningitis, multiple sclerosis, subdural hematoma, brain abscess, cervical or lumbar spine disease, conversion disorder

WORKUP

Given the high risk of stroke within the first 48 hr following TIA (up to 10%), hospital admission for workup is advised. Fig 1T-53 describes a TIA algorithm. The American Heart Association recommends that the ABCD2 score be used in the evaluation of TIA. It consists of 1 point for age ≥60 years, 1 point for BP ≥140 mm Hg systolic or ≥90 mm Hg diastolic, clinical features (2 points for unilateral weakness, 1 point for speech impairment), duration of TIA (2 points for duration ≥60 min, 1 point for duration 10-59 min), presence of diabetes mellitus (1 point). According to the guidelines, it is reasonable to hospitalize patients with TIA if they present within 72 hours and have an ABCD2 score ≥3. There is some debate about the usefulness of this scale since it fails to account for changes seen on echocardiogram, carotid Dopplers, or ECG that may place the patient at more imminent risk of stroke (carotid stenosis, Afib, cardiac thrombus, etc.). Alternatives to this scoring system are being investigated.

LABORATORY TESTS

Complete blood count, basic metabolic panel, prothrombin time, activated partial thromboplastin time, sedimentation rate, fasting lipid panel, serum glucose and hemoglobin A_{1c} (to detect latent diabetes mellitus)

IMAGING STUDIES

- CT scan should be obtained to exclude hemorrhage; MRI with diffusion weighting if immediately available.
- Imaging of the vessels should be obtained via magnetic resonance angiography (MRA), computed tomography angiography (CTA), or carotid Doppler/transcranial Doppler (CD/TCD).
  1. If symptoms are referable to the posterior circulation, MRA or CTA should be obtained in lieu of CD/TCD.
  2. Transthoracic echocardiogram should be obtained.
  3. An echocardiogram with bubble should be obtained in all patients younger than 50 yr with TIA symptoms.
- Electrocardiogram should be obtained to exclude the presence of arrhythmias, namely atrial fibrillation.
At least 24 hr of heart rhythm monitoring should be accomplished to screen for arrhythmia. Many stroke centers now utilize prolonged ambulatory cardiac rhythm monitoring over several weeks to months to identify paroxysmal atrial fibrillation in select patients when there is a high index of clinical suspicion.
- Paroxysmal atrial fibrillation is common in patients with TIA. A recent study found that noninvasive ambulatory ECG monitoring for 30 days significantly improved the detection of atrial fibrillation by a factor of more than five and nearly doubled the rate of anticoagulant treatment as compared with the standard practice of short-duration ECG monitoring.

 TREATMENT

NONPHARMACOLOGIC THERAPY

- Carotid endarterectomy or carotid stenting should be considered for patients found to have carotid stenosis as the cause for TIA.

Please refer to "Carotid Stenosis" chapter for more information.
- The practice of intracranial angioplasty and stenting has largely declined following the publication of negative results from clinical trials and is only used in select patients who fail maximal medical management with aggressive platelet inhibition, strict risk factor control such as hyperlipidemia, hypertension, diabetes mellitus, weight loss, treatment of sleep apnea and smoking cessation among others.

ACUTE GENERAL Rx

- In the absence of contraindications, patients who are identified to have atrial fibrillation should be considered for anticoagulation with intravenous heparin (or therapeutic lovenox) along with warfarin until target INR between 2.0 and 3.0 is achieved.
- Although no compelling evidence exists for the use of heparin in the acute treatment of TIAs without cardioembolic source, patients who develop recurrent symptoms within the same vascular territory that increase in duration, severity, and/or frequency (crescendo TIA/stuttering TIA) may benefit from its use pending cardiac and vascular imaging and identification of a possible source.

CHRONIC Rx

- Chronic therapy should be aimed at modifying the four major risk factors: hypertension, dyslipidemia, diabetes mellitus, and smoking cessation.
- Antiplatelet therapy should be used to reduce the risk of recurrent TIAs or subsequent stroke. Three antiplatelet agents are commonly used in stroke prevention: aspirin, aspirin/dipyridamole, and clopidogrel. All are reasonable choices but practitioners should consider their individual patient's comorbidities when selecting an antiplatelet agent.
- Dose-adjusted warfarin (INR 2.0-3.0) is indicated for prevention of future strokes in atrial fibrillation patients. The direct thrombin inhibitor dabigatran and the direct factor Xa inhibitors apixaban and rivaroxaban have been approved as alternative treatments to warfarin for stroke prevention in atrial fibrillation.

PEARLS & CONSIDERATIONS

- Despite complete symptom resolution, 20% to 50% of patients clinically suspected to have suffered a TIA have evidence of acute tissue infarction on MRI.
- Dual antiplatelet therapy in acute TIA and minor stroke is being evaluated. A recent trial revealed that among patients with TIA or minor stroke who can be treated within 24 hr after the onset of symptoms, the combination of clopidogrel and aspirin is superior to aspirin alone for reducing the risk of stroke in the first 90 days and does not increase the risk of hemorrhage.

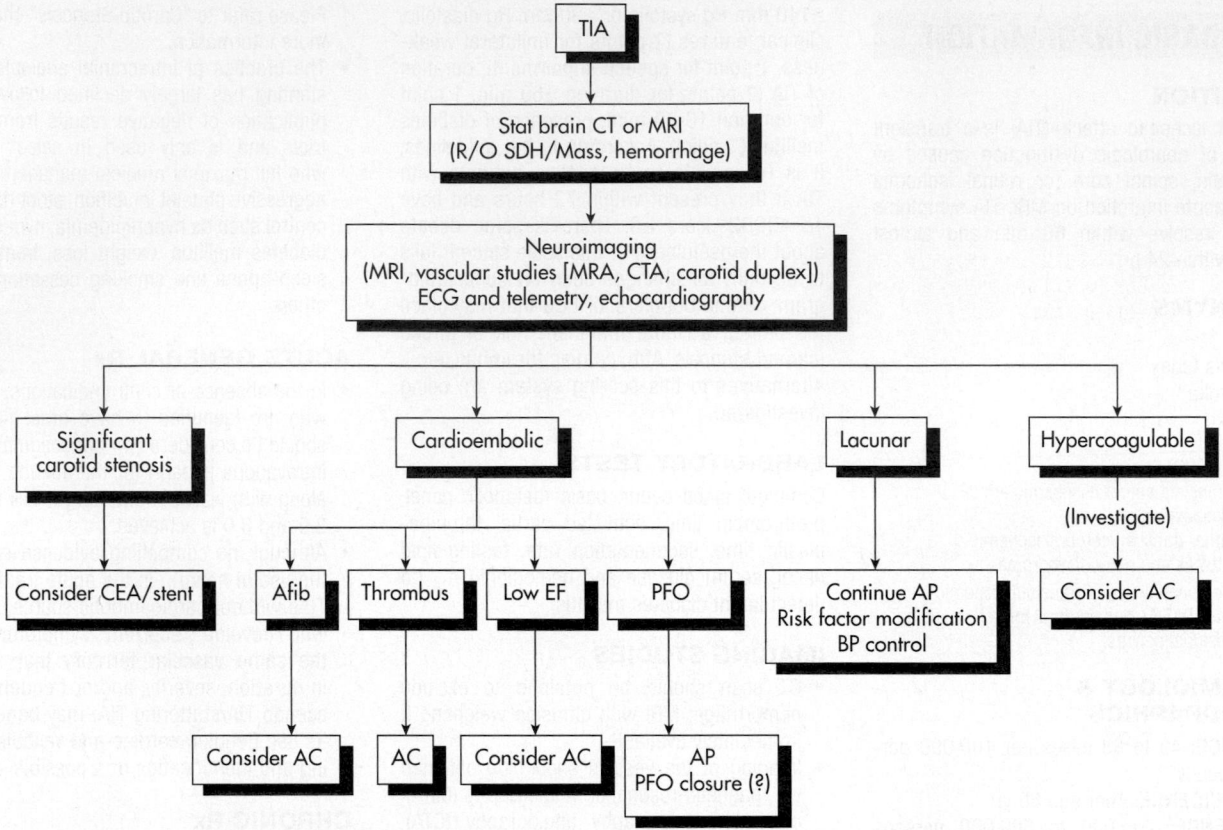

FIGURE 1T-53 Transient ischemic attack (TIA). *AC*, Anticoagulation; *AP*, antiplatelet; *ASA*, aspirin; *BP*, blood pressure; *CEA*, carotid endarterectomy; *CTA*, CT angiography; *EF*, ejection fraction; *MRA*, magnetic resonance angiography; *PFO*, patent foramen ovale; *SDH*, subdural hematoma.

PREVENTION

- A healthy lifestyle and management of cardiovascular risk factors should be encouraged.
- The identification of insulin resistance as a risk factor for stroke and myocardial infarction raises the possibility that pioglitazone which improves insulin sensitivity might benefit patients with cerebrovascular disease. In a recent trial involving patients without diabetes who had insulin resistance along with a recent history of ischemic stroke or TIA, the risk of stroke or MI was lower among patients who received pioglitazone than among those who received placebo. Pioglitazone was also associated with a lower risk of diabetes but with a higher risk of weight gain, edema, and fracture.[1]

PATIENT/FAMILY EDUCATION

Patients should be counseled on the early signs of stroke symptoms and instructed to promptly seek medical attention if they develop symptoms concerning for stroke. Patients should be encouraged to pursue a healthy lifestyle to include exercise and smoking cessation. In addition, patients should take an active role in controlling blood pressure and blood glucose. Further educational materials can be found online at http://www.strokecenter.org/.

[1] Kernan WN, et al.: Pioglitazone after Ischemic Stroke or Transient Ischemic Attack, *N Engl J Med* 374:1321-1331, 2016.

SUGGESTED READINGS

Available at www.expertconsult.com

RELATED CONTENT

Transient Ischemic Attack (TIA) (Patient Information)

AUTHOR: **PRASHANTH KRISHNAMOHAN, M.B.B.S., M.D.**

BASIC INFORMATION

DEFINITION

Demyelination in a transverse region of the spinal cord due to an inflammatory process that leads to sensory and motor changes below the lesion. The term "transverse myelitis" of late refers to any cause of inflammatory myelopathy, irrespective of severity or degree of structural or functional interruption of pathways through a transverse spinal cord section. The pathologic hallmark of transverse myelitis is the presence of focal collections of lymphocytes and monocytes with varying degrees of demyelination, axonal injury, and astroglial and microglial activation within the spinal cord.

SYNONYMS

Idiopathic transverse myelitis
TM

ICD-10CM CODES
G37.3 Acute transverse myelitis in demyelinating disease of central nervous system
G04.89 Other myelitis

EPIDEMIOLOGY & DEMOGRAPHICS

INCIDENCE: Annual incidence ranges from 1.3 to 8 cases per million. The incidence increases to 24.6 cases per million annually if causes of acquired demyelination such as multiple sclerosis (MS) are included.
PREVALENCE: Unknown
PREDOMINANT SEX: None
GENETICS: No genetic predisposition has been shown.
PEAK INCIDENCE: Bimodal peak in the incidence between 10 to 19 yr and 30 to 39 yr
RISK FACTORS: Infection, vaccination

PHYSICAL FINDINGS & CLINICAL PRESENTATION

- The clinical signs are caused by an interruption in ascending and descending neuroanatomic pathways in the transverse plane of the spinal cord, and a resulting sensory level is characteristic of transverse myelitis.
- Rapid onset of symmetric or asymmetric paraparesis or paraplegia of the lower extremities over a few days, ascending paresthesia, sensory level at the trunk, back pain, sphincter dysfunction, and positive Babinski, which can be bilateral. The arms may also be involved but less than the legs in most cases. In the acute phase the weakness is flaccid, with diminished deep tendon reflexes mimicking a peripheral neuropathy.
- One third to one half of patients present with localizing back pain.
- There is progression to nadir of clinical deficits between 4 hr and 21 days after symptom onset.
- Urinary incontinence or retention, GI disturbances (incontinence or constipation), and sexual dysfunction are common.

ETIOLOGY

- Can be idiopathic demyelination (15%-30%) or demyelination secondary to neurologic and systemic conditions.
- Secondary causes include postinfection, postvaccination, acute demyelinating encephalomyelitis (where transverse myelitis tends to be monophasic), and others such as multiple sclerosis, neuromyelitis optica (NMO), mixed connective tissue disorders, sarcoidosis, and paraneoplastic conditions, which can be progressive or relapsing.
- About 50% of patients have had a recent upper respiratory infection.
- Epstein-Barr virus and cytomegalovirus are most common viral infections.
- Hepatitis B, varicella, enterovirus, rhinovirus, mycoplasma, syphilis, measles, Lyme disease are less common.

DIAGNOSIS

DIFFERENTIAL DIAGNOSIS

- MS
- Neuromyelitis optica (NMO)
- Spinal cord tumors
- Herniated or slipped discs
- Spinal stenosis
- Abscess
- Vascular malformation

WORKUP

Transverse myelitis (TM) should be suspected in patients with a history of rapid (hours to days) onset of motor weakness and sensory abnormalities with bladder or bowel dysfunction that is referable to the spinal cord. The dysfunction is bilateral (not necessarily symmetric) and there is a clearly defined sensory (dermatomal) level. It is important to distinguish idiopathic TM from TM due to MS or neuromyelitis optica because idiopathic TM does not relapse and does not require long-term immunomodulatory therapy.

IMAGING STUDIES

- Gadolinium-enhanced magnetic resonance imaging (MRI) of brain and MRI of the entire spine (Fig. E1T-54). This will show demyelinating lesion on T_2 with contrast enhancement. In MS there is a short segment lesion (less than three vertebral segments) that is dorsally located.
- Computed tomography (CT) of the spine should be obtained if MRI is unavailable.
- CT myelogram may also be obtained.
- Chest CT scan if sarcoidosis is suspected.

LABORATORY TESTS

- Lumbar puncture looking for oligoclonal bands for MS or infection such as varicella zoster virus PCR and enterovirus PCR.
- ANA, hepatitis B serology, Lyme disease titer, VDRL, SSA, SSB, anticardiolipin antibody, copper, vitamin B_{12}, treponemal antibody.
- Serum NMO-IgG to evaluate for neuromyelitis optica.

TREATMENT

Corticosteroids (IV methylprednisone 1 g/day for 3 to 7 days) are the first-line treatment for transverse myelitis; IVIG, plasma exchange, and cyclophosphamide are other acute therapies, although there is no evidence-based medicine for use of corticosteroids, plasma exchange, or IVIG.

NONPHARMACOLOGIC THERAPY

- Physical therapy
- Respiratory and oropharyngeal support

ACUTE GENERAL Rx

- High-dose IV corticosteroid (e.g., methylprednisolone 1000 mg/day for 3-5 days).
- Rescue therapy with plasma exchange may be helpful in patients who do not respond to corticosteroids.
- Combination therapy with plasmapheresis and corticosteroids or other immunosuppressive agents (e.g., cyclophosphamide) may also be effective.
- Naproxen, ibuprofen for pain.

CHRONIC Rx

- Baclofen, tizanidine, or some other muscle relaxant for muscle spasms
- Gabapentin for pain
- Low-molecular-weight heparin for DVT prophylaxis in patients with immobility

DISPOSITION

- One third of patients with transverse myelitis will have complete recovery, one third will have fair recovery, and one third have permanent disability and do not recover. Recurrence or relapse is possible.
- Patients who need further care, including those with urinary retention, may need home nursing assistance. Some patients may benefit from rehabilitation, either inpatient or outpatient.

REFERRAL

- Consider physical therapy.
- Consider occupational therapy.
- Consider rehabilitation services.
- Consider psychiatric consultation (high incidence of long-term mood and anxiety disorders).

SUGGESTED READINGS

Available at www.expertconsult.com

AUTHOR: **PADMAJA SUDHAKAR, M.B.B.S.**

Hippocrates: 'No head injury is too severe to be despaired of, nor too trivial to be ignored'

ℹ️ BASIC INFORMATION

DEFINITION

Impact to the head resulting in varying levels of cellular and macroscopic changes, detected with clinical examination supplemented by imaging studies. Maas et al have proposed this definition: "brain damage resulting from external forces, as a consequence of direct impact, rapid acceleration or deceleration, a penetrating object (e.g., gunshot) or blast waves from an explosion. The nature, intensity, direction, and duration of these forces determine the pattern and extent of damage."

SYNONYMS

TBI
Head injury
Concussion
Intracranial contusion

ICD-10CM CODES
S06.9	X0AIntracranial injury
S06.1X7A	Traumatic cerebral edema with loss of consciousness of any duration with death due to brain injury prior to regaining consciousness, initial encounter
S06.2X9A	Diffuse traumatic brain injury with loss of consciousness of unspecified duration, initial encounter
S06.300A	Unspecified focal traumatic brain injury without loss of consciousness, initial encounter
S06.305A	Unspecified focal traumatic brain injury with loss of consciousness greater than 24 hours with return to pre-existing conscious level, initial encounter
S06.309A	Unspecified focal traumatic brain injury with loss of consciousness of unspecified duration, initial encounter

EPIDEMIOLOGY & DEMOGRAPHICS

Traumatic brain injury (TBI) is a worldwide leading cause of mortality in young individuals. Urbanization and increasing use of motor vehicles has led to an overall increase in TBI, especially in high income and developing countries.
INCIDENCE: Globally, more than 10 million people suffer TBI resulting in mortality or requiring hospitalization each year. By the year 2020, it is projected that TBI will surpass many diseases as the major cause of death and disability worldwide. It has been estimated that TBI accounts for 9% of global mortality and is a threat to health in every country in the world. The financial burden of TBI has been estimated to be greater than $60 billion per year in the United States alone. According to estimates from the CDC, about 2.5 million emergency department visits, including deaths and hospitalizations, were associated with TBI in 2010.

PREVALENCE: The prevalence of TBI in the United States has been estimated at approximately 5.3 million. In the European Union with 330 million inhabitants, approximately 7,775,000 new TBI cases occur each year.
PEAK INCIDENCE: Approximate incidence in the US per CDC data is 103/100,000 population. In the European Union, this is estimated to be at 235/100,000.
PREDOMINANT SEX AND AGE: TBI occurs more frequently in young adults, particularly males 15 to 25 years of age, and has a high cost to society because of life years lost as a result of death and disability.
GENETICS: Work on the genetic basis and the susceptibility it affords in traumatic brain injury is being currently studied. The most recognized association between a genetic polymorphism and outcome involves the apolipoprotein E (apo E) gene. The ε4 allele has been associated with poorer outcome after TBI. The same isoform is associated with Alzheimer's and increased deposition of amyloid beta lipoprotein after TBI. TBI and apo E ε4 synergistically are also associated with a 10-fold increased risk for Alzheimer's as well as larger intracerebral hematomas and greater ischemia after TBI.
RISK FACTORS: N/A.

PHYSICAL FINDINGS & CLINICAL PRESENTATION

TBI patients can present with a spectrum of clinical symptoms including nausea, vomiting, headache, seizures, altered mental status, and/or coma. Stigmata of trauma, including bruises, scalp lacerations, periorbital or mastoid ecchymosis suggesting skull base fractures are telltale signs of possible underlying traumatic brain injury. Box 1T-6 describes risk stratification in patients with minor head trauma. The spectrum of TBI is most commonly assessed using the Glasgow Coma Scale (GCS), which ranges from 3 to 15 and utilizes eye, motor, and verbal exams (Table 1T-23).

ETIOLOGY

Etiology, in most cases is impact related. Mechanical falls, motor vehicle accidents, and assaults resulting in direct or indirect trauma to the head from acceleration and rotational forces results in brain injury.

🅓🅧 DIAGNOSIS

DIFFERENTIAL DIAGNOSIS

Differential diagnosis of traumatic brain injury is quite limited; however, there are several considerations and diagnoses, which are considered as a possibility within the realm of TBI. These are enumerated in the imaging section.

WORKUP

TBI workup is always a part of the advanced trauma life support (ATLS) protocol. Primary and secondary survey followed by imaging studies constitutes the standardized approach to TBI. Focused TBI workup includes:

- History: including timing of injury, duration of loss of consciousness if applicable, seizures (if any), comorbidities, use of anticoagulants and antiplatelet agents (requires reversal in the event of intracranial blood on imaging).
- Neurological examination: Glasgow Coma Scale, cranial nerves, motor/sensory exam. Assess for scalp lacerations, specifically overlying a skull fracture. CSF otorrhea or rhinorrhea.
- CT imaging of the head if there is a significant history of impact to the head, polytrauma, positive loss of consciousness, or stigmata of trauma to the head.

LABORATORY TESTS

Basic labs including CBC, basic metabolic panel, prothrombin time, activated partial thromboplastin time, urinary drug screen. Upcoming tests for platelet function analysis for unknown antiplatelet use are also being performed for

---

BOX 1T-6   Risk Stratification in Patients With Minor Head Trauma

High Risk
Focal neurologic findings
Asymmetrical pupils
Skull fracture on clinical examination
Multiple trauma
Serious, painful, distracting injuries
External signs of trauma above the clavicles
Initial Glasgow Coma Scale score of 14 or 15
Loss of consciousness
Posttraumatic confusion or amnesia
Progressively worsening headache
Vomiting
Posttraumatic seizure
History of bleeding disorder or anticoagulation
Recent ingestion of intoxicants
Unreliable or unknown history of injury
Previous neurologic diagnosis
Previous epilepsy
Suspected child abuse
Age above 60 years or below 2 years

Medium Risk
Initial Glasgow Coma Scale score of 15
Brief loss of consciousness
Posttraumatic amnesia
Vomiting
Headache
Intoxication

Low Risk
Currently asymptomatic
No other injuries
No focality on examination
Normal pupils
No change in consciousness
Intact orientation and memory
Initial Glasgow Coma Scale score of 15
Accurate history
Trivial mechanism
Injury less than 24 hours ago
No or mild headache
No vomiting
No preexisting high-risk factors

From Marx JA et al: *Rosen's emergency medicine,* ed 8, Philadelphia, 2014, WB Saunders.

early reversal with platelet replacement. These tests focus on an individual's responsiveness to antiplatelet agents and are available at most academic institutions. There are no current laboratory biomarkers for TBI severity, but this is an area of intense research.

IMAGING STUDIES (TABLE 1T-24)

CT imaging of the forms the current cornerstone of imaging modalities for head trauma. Usually in addition to a plain CT of the head (Fig. 1T-55), CTA head/neck and CT of the spine is helpful if arterial or C-spine injury is suspected, respectively. Other imaging modalities such as MRI can be helpful in certain situations, but are typically adjuncts in the acute setting to CT-guided man-

agement. Canadian CT head rules are a useful guide in determining utility of obtaining a CT scan. These are based on risk factors[11]:

HIGH-RISK
1. Failure to reach GCS of 15 within 2 hours
2. Suspected open or any signs of basal skull fracture
3. More than two episodes of vomiting
4. Age older than 65

LOW RISK
1. Dangerous mechanism of injury or polytrauma
2. Loss of consciousness lasting >30 minutes
   Pathologies that can be identified with imaging are noted below:
   - Primary extra-axial: epidural, subdural, subarachnoid and intraventricular hemorrhage

- Primary intra-axial: axonal injury, cortical contusion, intracerebral hemorrhage, encephalomalacia (from prior TBI or vascular insult)
- Skull fracture: Linear, depressed, open, involving frontal sinus or skull base
- Penetrating brain injury: Gunshot wounds, sharp objects resulting in parenchymal and vascular injury
- Vascular injury: dissection, traumatic carotid-cavernous fistula (CCF), dural arteriovenous fistula (dAVF), pseudoaneurysm formation
- Secondary acute injury: diffuse cerebral swelling/dysautoregulation (seen more commonly in children from posttraumatic hyperemia), infarction, infection from penetrating trauma, brain herniation from mass lesion or cerebral edema
- Secondary chronic injury: hydrocephalus (posttraumatic due to disruption of normal CSF absorption pathways), encephalomalacia, CSF leak (from skull base fractures, manifests as otorrhea or rhinorrhea, leptomeningeal cyst (seen most commonly in infants, skull fracture resulting in underlying dural injury)

Rx TREATMENT

Prevention of secondary injury is the primary goal of prehospital and early in-hospital management. Most common mechanisms of secondary injury are either intracranial (ICP, hematoma) or systemic (hypoxia, hypovolemia, hypotension). Early categorization of head trauma patients according to the severity (based on GCS) and transport to facilities equipped with personnel and technology to deal with issues pertaining to head trauma has improved the overall management of head injury patients and prevention of secondary injury. Airway, breathing, and circulation, however, still remain the most important parameters to be stabilized which directly or indirectly can effect GCS and overall outcome. Trauma guidelines suggest intubation should be performed in any patient with a GCS of 8 or less to prevent hypoxemia and hypercapnia. Intravenous fluid resuscitation should

TABLE 1T-23 Glasgow Coma Scale (GCS)

Adult		Infant	
Eye Opening	**E**	**Eye Opening**	
Spontaneous	4	Spontaneous	
To speech	3	To speech	
To pain	2	To pain	
No response	1	No response	
Best Motor Response	**M**	**Best Motor Response**	
Obeys verbal command	6	Normal movements	
Localizes to pain	5	Localizes to pain	
Withdraws to pain	4	Withdraws to pain	
Flexion (decorticate)	3	Flexion (decorticate)	
Extension (decerebrate)	2	Extension (decerebrate)	
No response	1	No response	
Best Verbal Response	**E**	**Best Verbal Response**	
Oriented speech	5	Coos, babbles	
Disoriented speech	4	Cries but consolable	
Inappropriate words	3	Persistently irritable	
Incomprehensible sounds	2	Grunts to pain/restless	
No response	1	No response	

Mild TBI: GCS 13-15, Moderate TBI: GCS 9-12, Severe TBI GCS 8 or less.
GCS can range from 3 to 15. If intubated, then verbal component is replaced by 'T'. Best possible score if intubated is 10T, and worse is 3T.
In obtunded patients, pain stimulus can be central or peripheral. In patients with suspected spinal cord injury and paralysis, central stimulus to elicit facial grimace can be used to assess motor and eye component.

TABLE 1T-24 Comparison of Head Imaging Modalities

	Computed Tomography Scans	Magnetic Resonance Imaging	Angiography	Skull Radiography
Advantages	Fast Patient accessible for monitoring Defines acute hemorrhages, mass effects, bone injuries, hydrocephalus, intraventricular blood, edema	Defines contusions and pericontusion edema, posttraumatic ischemic infarction, brainstem injuries	Helps localize acute traumatic lesions Defines vascular injuries, injuries to venous sinuses Detects mass effects	Readily available May help screen some patients for further imaging studies
Disadvantages	Artifacts arise from patient's movement, foreign bodies Streak artifacts may obscure brainstem or posterior fossa	Slow Patients not easily accessible for monitoring Does not define most acute hemorrhagic lesions Not useful for bone injuries	Does not define nature of acute lesion Does not detect infratentorial masses	Does not indicate presence or absence of intracranial injury
Indications	Acute severe head trauma Acute moderate head trauma Suspected depressed skull fracture High-risk minor head trauma Suspected child abuse in minor head trauma Deteriorating neurologic status	Persistent symptoms with postconcussive syndrome Suspected post-traumatic ischemic infarction Suspected contusions not seen on CT scan	Suspected vascular injury CT scan not available	CT scan may not be done Penetrating head trauma

CT, Computed tomography.
From Marx: *Rosen's emergency medicine: concepts and clinical practice*, J.A. Marx, R.S. Hockberger, R.M. Walls, et al. (eds.) 7 ed, 2010, Elsevier.

also be started early to prevent hypovolemia resulting in hypotension which has been shown to double the mortality. Transfer and care in a Level I trauma center has shown to be associated with better outcomes.

Details of in-hospital management including critical care and surgical intervention is beyond the scope of this text. Some important points are summarized below.

1. ATLS protocol (airway, breathing, circulation, disability, exposure)
2. Ventilatory support
3. Optimization of oxygenation, ventilation and fluid status
4. CT head (Fig. E1T-56) to evaluate for mass lesion (hematoma) or cerebral edema which may necessitate surgical intervention or ICP monitor placement. ATLS guidelines recommend maximum 30 minutes between initial assessment and CT head.
5. In case of severe TBI (GCS 8 or less) or moderate TBI (GCS 8 to 13) with unreliable neurological exam, patients should be admitted to the intensive care unit for frequent neurological checks. TBI guidelines suggest ICP monitor placement for GCS 8 or less to closely monitor intracranial pressure. This is being researched further to determine flexibility with GCS score in placement of ICP monitors. ICP monitors are of various kinds; most commonly used: external ventricular drain, intraparenchymal pressure monitor, bolt device with brain tissue oxygen pressure monitoring with fiberoptic pressure monitor. Recent research has also supported the use of brain tissue oxygen monitoring for severe TBI patients. Devices such as the Licox monitor (Integra) are in clinical use for this. Surgical decompression may involve evacuation of hematoma (epidural, subdural [images attached] intraparenchymal contusion) through craniotomy alone (replace-

ment of bone after completion of operation) versus decompressive craniectomy (complete removal of bone without replacement) in certain cases where cerebral edema is out of proportion to the presence of mass lesion. Skull fractures are treated depending on the morphology of the fracture. Open, depressed fractures require surgical debridement and elevation in most cases in addition to broad-spectrum antibiotics.

6. Avoiding electrolyte imbalance, especially hyponatremia and hyperglycemia, which may contribute to cerebral edema and increase intracranial pressure.
7. Elevation of head of bed to allow better venous drainage, in an attempt to reduce intracranial pressure.
8. ICP management, which may include: surgical hematoma evacuation, administration of hyperosmotic fluids to reduce edema, pharmacologic sedation and paralysis, pentobarbital-induced coma, and surgical decompression of the brain. In patients with traumatic brain injury, hypothermia can reduce intracranial hypertension, but recent trials in patients with an intracranial pressure of more than 20 mm Hg after TBI, therapeutic hypothermia, plus standard care to reduce intracranial pressure did not result in outcomes better than those with standard care alone.[1]
9. Prevention of seizures in the acute setting. The most commonly used and studied drug is phenytoin. Indications for acute seizure prophylaxis in severe head trauma are described in Box 1T-7. Levetiracetam (Keppra) is also a beneficial antiepileptic now commonly used in the TBI setting.
10. DVT prophylaxis is recommended in almost all patients on hospital day 1, in addition to sequential compression devices (SCDs) on admission, for immobile or bed bound patients to prevent DVTs.
11. Early initiation of parentral nutrition.

CHRONIC Rx

- Patients suffering from TBI are shown to benefit from neurocognitive occupational

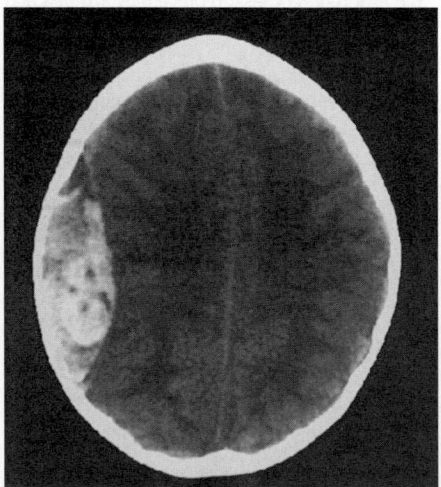

FIGURE 1T-55 Non–contrast-enhanced computed tomography scan of acute epidural hematoma at the level of right midconvexity. There is an associated mass effect and moderate midline shift. (From Marx: *Rosen's emergency medicine: concepts and clinical practice*, J.A. Marx, R.S. Hockberger, R.M. Walls, et al. (eds.) 7 ed, 2010, Elsevier.)

BOX 1T-7   Indications for Acute Seizure Prophylaxis in Severe Head Trauma

Depressed skull fracture
Paralyzed and intubated patient
Seizure at the time of injury
Seizure at emergency department presentation
Penetrating brain injury
Severe head injury (Glasgow Coma Scale score ≤8)
Acute subdural hematoma
Acute epidural hematoma
Acute intracranial hemorrhage
Prior history of seizures

---

[1]Andrews PJD, et al: Hypothermia for intracranial hypertension after traumatic brain injury, *N Engl J Med* 373:2103-2112, 2015.

and physical therapy. The Glasgow Outcome Scale is a comprehensive measure of severity and eventual outcome of brain injury. Posttraumatic amnesia, age, length of coma, GCS score within the first 24 hours, imaging study scales are some of the factors that affect outcome and dictate long-term prognosis.

- Chronic treatment addresses several sequelae of TBI, including (but not limited to): dysautonomia, agitation, sleep disturbance, posttraumatic epilepsy, spasticity, dysphagia, syndrome of the trephined, posttraumatic hydrocephalus, apathy, fecal/urinary incontinence, headache, and neuropathic pain syndromes.

COMPLEMENTARY AND ALTERNATIVE MEDICINE

Currently, there are no proven drugs that improve outcomes after TBI. Several pro-drugs are under study, with the hopes to have a single TBI cocktail that would enhance repair at the cellular and molecular pathway level. Neurostimulants such as amantadine, bromocriptine, amphetamine and methylphenidate are used in the rehabilitation phase with anecdotal data, but good RCTs are lacking in this area.

DISPOSITION

Depending on severity of head injury, patients may require admission to a rehabilitation facility or discharge to home with outpatient neurocognitive therapy.

REFERRAL

Early transfer to a Level 1 Trauma Center with neurosurgical personnel, if high risk findings are noted on clinical exam or CT head, is associated with better outcomes.

PEARLS & CONSIDERATIONS

TBI is major healthcare issue. Guidelines have been developed to address TBI in a timely and effective fashion. Clinical acumen and judgment, however, is irreplaceable and should be exercised for better patient care and outcomes. Early recognition of high-risk patients, early imaging and early evaluation at a Level 1 Trauma Center by a specialist is associated with good outcomes. The goal of healthcare providers in the field or in the community is to identify patients who need this attention.

PATIENT/FAMILY EDUCATION

Brain Injury Association of America http://www.biausa.org/
Brain Injury Resource Center http://www.headinjury.com/linktbisup.htm

SUGGESTED READINGS

Available at www.expertconsult.com

RELATED CONTENT

Concussion (Related Key Topic)

AUTHORS: **FARHAN A. MIRZA, M.B.B.S.,** and **JUSTIN F. FRASER, M.D.**

BASIC INFORMATION

DEFINITION

Traveler's diarrhea (TD) is defined as 3 or more loose-to-watery stools, with or without associated fever, abdominal cramps, and vomiting, within a 24-hr period. It develops during or within 10 days of traveling to developing areas of the world.

SYNONYMS

Enterotoxigenic *E. coli*
Enteroaggregative *E. coli*
Infectious diarrhea
Postinfectious irritable bowel syndrome

ICD-10CM CODES
A09 Infectious diarrhea

EPIDEMIOLOGY & DEMOGRAPHICS

Traveler's diarrhea is mostly caused by bacteria and other pathogens in food and water

At least 1 episode of diarrhea occurs in 40% to 50% of travelers during their stay abroad. Table 1T-25 describes pathogens and epidemiologic features associated with traveler's diarrhea

INCIDENCE: High risk (>20%): South and Southeast Asia, Africa (except South Africa), South and Central America, and Mexico

Moderate risk (10%-20 %): Caribbean Islands, South Africa, Central and East Asia (including Russia and China), Eastern Europe, and the Middle East, including Israel.

Low risk (<10%): Northern and Western Europe, Australia, New Zealand, United States, Canada, Singapore, Japan.

PEAK INCIDENCE:
- Peak incidence occurs during the first week of travel and progressively declines after that
- Seasonal variation does exist for TD, with lower rates in the winter months

PREVALENCE: Acute and chronic diarrhea account for a third of medical visits by returned travelers as per the GeoSentinel database.

PREDOMINANT SEX AND AGE:
- Travelers in their 30s are at highest risk, possibly secondary to more adventurous travel
- Gender does not seem to influence the risk for TD
- Infants and toddlers are more likely to have a more severe form of TD and are more likely to need hospitalization

GENETICS: Travelers with the O blood group are at higher risk for diarrhea caused by Norovirus and *Shigella*

RISK FACTORS:
- Gastric acid protects against enteropathogens, so medications that reduce gastric acid secretion (i.e., PPI or H2-receptor blockers) are known to increase risk for TD by a factor of 12
- Immunocompromised travelers such as those with HIV/AIDS are at higher risk for parasitic infections
- Backpackers are at higher risk than those staying at a resort
- Food bought from street vendors or prepared by persons not wearing gloves carries a higher risk

PHYSICAL FINDINGS & CLINICAL PRESENTATION

- The clinical presentation does not allow determination of infectious cause
- 90% of cases occur within 2 weeks of stay
- Acute watery diarrhea predominates in 90% of patients
- Signs of invasive infection, including fever and bloody/mucoid diarrhea, occur in 3% to 30%
- Most patients report 3 to 5 bowel movements a day, but in 20% a higher frequency of up to 20 daily bowel movements occurs
- Nausea (10%-70%), vomiting (4%-36%), abdominal cramps/tenesmus (80%) urgency (90%)
- Other: myalgia, arthralgia, headache
- Average episode resolves in 3 to 5 days

- Prolonged symptoms lasting more than a week: 8% to 15%; chronic diarrhea >30 days: 1% to 3%
- Severe episodes may result in electrolyte imbalance (K+ loss)
- 50% of all travelers are incapacitated for at least 24 hours, but up to 20% are ill in bed for 1 to 2 days.

ETIOLOGY

- *E. coli* (Table E1T-26): Accounts for up to 60% of all cases of TD and is most prevalent in Central and South America, South Asia, and Africa. Table E1T-27 summarizes etiology of traveler's diarrhea in Latin America, Africa, and Asia.
  - Enterotoxigenic *E. coli* (ETEC): produce heat labile and heat stable toxin and are the most common cause, accounting for 10% to 45% of cases. Frequently seen in Latin America, Africa and South Asia.
  - Enteroaggregative *E. coli* (EAEC): more commonly seen in Latin America.
  - Other *E. coli* (enteropathogenic [EPEC], enteroinvasive [EIEC], enterohemorrhagic [EHEC]: Shiga toxin-producing or diffuse adhering *E. coli* are much less common.
- *Campylobacter*: 2% to 32% of cases. More common in Southeast Asia, where it is more frequent than ETEC.
- Shigella: 2% to 9%. More common in Africa.
- Salmonella: <5% of cases except in Asia, where it is seen in up to 10% of cases.
- Other bacteria: *Aeromonas, Arcobacter, Plesiomonas*, enterotoxigenic *Bacteroides fragilis, Vibrio cholera*, noncholera vibrios.
- Viral pathogens:
  - Norovirus: up to 17% of cases from Caribbean and Africa.
  - Rotavirus: 4% to 7% of cases.
- Protozoans:
  - *Entamoeba histolytica*: more common in South and Southeast Asia.
  - *Giardia lamblia*: more common in South and Southeast Asia especially Nepal.
  - *Cryptosporidium, Cyclospora, Isospora*.

TABLE 1T-25 Pathogens and Epidemiologic Features Associated With Traveler's Diarrhea

Organism	Approximate Percentage of Cases (%)	Epidemiologic Features
Enterotoxigenic *Escherichia coli*	15-50	Most important causative agent of traveler's diarrhea overall; not diagnosed by routine microbiologic methods
Enteroaggregative *E. coli*	20-35	Not diagnosed by routine microbiologic methods
Shigella spp. and enteroinvasive *E. coli*	10-25	Most important causes of dysentery. Enteroinvasive *E. coli* not diagnosed by routine microbiologic methods
Nontyphoidal *Salmonella* spp.	5-10	
Campylobacter jejuni	3-15	More common in Asia; antimicrobial resistance a concern
Aeromonas	5	
Plesiomonas	5	
Giardia lamblia	<2	Affects hikers and campers who drink from contaminated freshwater streams
Cryptosporidium hominis/parvum	<2	Occasional large-scale waterborne outbreaks
Cyclospora cayetanensis	<2	
Vibrio cholerae		Ongoing outbreaks in Haiti and Zimbabwe, and endemic in many countries in Asia; rare cause of disease in travelers
Norovirus		Outbreaks on cruise ships
Entamoeba histolytica		May cause liver abscess

From Bennett JE et al: *Mandell, Douglas, and Bennett's principles and practice of infectious diseases*, ed 8, Philadelphia, 2015, WB Saunders.)

Diseases and Disorders

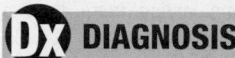 **DIAGNOSIS**

DIFFERENTIAL DIAGNOSIS

- Malaria
- Dengue fever
- Influenza
- Rocky Mountain spotted fever
- Irritable bowel syndrome
- Inflammatory bowel disease
- Shellfish poisoning
- Mushroom poisoning

WORK-UP

- Most cases of TD are self-limiting, do not require workup, and are treated symptomatically without regard to etiologic agent.
- In patients with diarrhea, fever, and colitic symptoms (bloody stools, cramping), a stool culture should be obtained to look for specific bacterial pathogens.

LABORATORY TESTS

- Stool culture ×3 for bacterial pathogens.
- Stool for ova and parasites to help identify protozoans. Special stains such as modified acid fast or trichrome stain may be necessary for *Cryptosporidium*, *Cyclospora*, and *Isospora*
- Blood cultures in patients with systemic illness to rule out *Salmonella* species

 **TREATMENT**

NONPHARMACOLOGIC THERAPY

- Fluid replacement to treat volume depletion of diarrhea is important.
- Mild cases: alternate fluids that contain salts and fluids that contain sugars, such as broths or fruit juices. Pedialyte is effective as an over the counter product.
- Severe cases: Oral rehydration solution (ORS) packets are available in most pharmacies. They should be mixed with clean water to replace lost electrolytes and are used until patient is urinating regularly. An alternative home-based solution can be made with: ½ teaspoon of salt, ½ teaspoon of baking soda, and 4 tablespoons of sugar in one liter of clean water.

ACUTE GENERAL Rx

- Antisecretory agents may reduce symptoms but do not treat underlying cause
  - Bismuth subsalicylate: 1 dose of 525 mg (2 tablets of Pepto-Bismol) po every 30 min up to 8 doses a day. Can reduce number of bowel movements by 50%

- Loperamide: 4 mg po, then 2 mg after each loose bowel movement, not to exceed 16 mg per day. Use for up to 48 hrs. Has antisecretory and antimotility effect. Antimotility drugs should not be used in cases of bloody diarrhea or dysentery (increased risk of colitis and colonic perforation). When used, they should be given only in conjunction with antimicrobial therapy.
- Antibiotics are warranted only for moderate to severe diarrhea (i.e., >4 bowel movements a day, fever, or blood, pus, or mucus in stool. Antibiotics can reduce duration of diarrhea by 1 to 2 days.
  - Fluoroquinolones are considered first line agents for bacterial causes of TD. Cannot be used in children under 15 and in pregnant women
    1. Ciprofloxacin: 500 mg twice a day for 1 to 3 days
    2. Levaquin: 500 mg a day for 1 to 3 days
  - Azithromycin: preferred agent for children and pregnant women. Dose of 1 gram po single dose. Particularly effective against quinolone resistant *Campylobacter* infections in Southeast Asia.
  - Rifaximin: 200 mg po TID for 3 days for children age>12 and adults is effective for afebrile, noncolitic diarrhea such as ETEC. Does not treat *Salmonella*, *Shigella*, or *Campylobacter*
- Concerns of use of antibiotics
  - Widespread use of antibiotics has led to resistance. Tetracycline and sulfa agents such as Bactrim are no longer used due to widespread resistance
  - Antibiotic treatment may lead to prolonged colonization in infections with *Salmonella* and nontyphoid *Salmonella*
  - In cases of EHEC (Shiga toxin production) treatment with quinolones, but not rifaximin, may increase risk of complications such as hemolytic uremic syndrome
  - *Clostridia difficile* infection can occur with use of antibiotics

PREVENTION BY ANTIBIOTICS AND NONANTIBIOTIC AGENTS

- Antibiotic prophylaxis can be considered for certain groups, such as persons with underlying illness, athletes, and politicians for up to 2 to 3 weeks. Ciprofloxacin 250 to 500 mg a day is effective in preventing 90% of TD. Rifaximin dosed daily has been shown to help prevent TD for U.S. travelers to Mexico, but not as effectively as Ciprofloxacin

- Bismuth subsalicylate can be used. It must be given 4× daily and can cause black tongue and stools. As it contains salicylates, it can interact with anticoagulants and lead to toxicity in patients on long term salicylate therapy
- Probiotics are being studied for their potential use but evidence of their effectiveness is limited

REFERRAL

- Infectious diseases physician for more difficult cases lasting more than 72 hours.

! PEARLS & CONSIDERATIONS

- Travelers on cruises have lower incidence of TD than land-based trips, but cruise ship passengers and staff are at higher risk of large outbreaks of Norovirus that are difficult to contain. Norovirus infection needs only a low inoculum of virus to cause illness, and the virus is relatively resistant to cleaning
- In up to 40% of cases of TD, no pathogen is identified
- *Giardia* is the most frequent cause of long-lasting TD

PREVENTION

- There are oral and injectable vaccines against *Salmonella typhi* available in the U.S.
- Dukoral oral vaccine is available in some countries such as Canada and Australia and in Europe to help prevent cholera and ETEC

PATIENT/FAMILY EDUCATION

- Food hygiene education: Wash hands often, especially after going to bathroom and before eating. Avoid raw fruits and vegetables (unless peeled and washed in clean water). Avoid undercooked meats, fish, and seafood. Avoid tap water and ice. Choose beverages in factory sealed containers (such as bottled water and carbonated soft drinks). Try to avoid buffet-style foods.

SUGGESTED READINGS

Available at www.expertconsult.com

RELATED CONTENT

Traveler's Diarrhea (Patient Information)

AUTHOR: **GLENN G. FORT, M.D., M.P.H.**

T

 BASIC INFORMATION

DEFINITION

Trigeminal neuralgia is an intense, usually unilateral, paroxysmal, stabbing pain in the sensory distribution of the fifth cranial nerve.

SYNONYMS

Tic douloureux ("painful tics/spasms")

ICD-10CM CODES
G50.0 Trigeminal neuralgia

EPIDEMIOLOGY & DEMOGRAPHICS

INCIDENCE: 4 per 100,000
PEAK INCIDENCE: Incidence increases with age and peaks at 67 yr; onset in 90% of patients is after age 40.
PREVALENCE: 155 in 1 million
PREDOMINANT SEX AND AGE: Male/female ratio is 1:1.5.
RISK FACTORS: Most cases are idiopathic; age and multiple sclerosis are risk factors.

PHYSICAL FINDINGS & CLINICAL PRESENTATION

- Patients present with paroxysmal, unilateral facial pain that is usually described as shock-like, stabbing, or electric (Fig. 1T-61).
- Pain can be spontaneous or triggered by touch, an air current, or activities such as shaving, eating, or brushing teeth.
- In severe cases, facial spasms can accompany the pain.
- Pain is usually described in distribution of the second (V2-maxillary) and third (V3-mandibular) divisions of the trigeminal nerve.
- The pain seldom lasts more than a few seconds to a minute.
- There is usually no sensory or motor loss.

ETIOLOGY

- Idiopathic or "classical": cause usually unknown, likely an aberrant artery or vein compressing cranial nerve V at or near

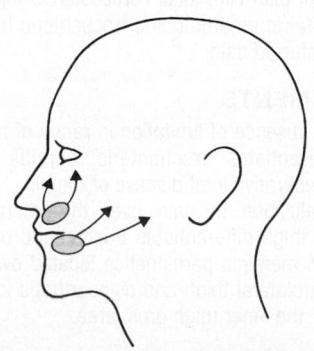

FIGURE 1T-61 Trigeminal neuralgia. The two most common sites of origin and radiation of pain are shown: mouth-ear and nose-orbit. Pain usually starts in the region of the encircled area and radiates in the directions shown. (From Souhami RL, Moxham J: *Textbook of medicine,* ed 4, London, 2002, Churchill Livingstone.)

the pons. Neurovascular contact is also commonly found incidentally on imaging in asymptomatic individuals.
- Secondary: accounts for up to 15% of cases; caused by nonvascular lesions such as a demyelinating plaque from multiple sclerosis, or compression from a tumor near the pons.
- Box 1T-8 summarizes causes of trigeminal neuralgia

 DIAGNOSIS

DIFFERENTIAL DIAGNOSIS

- Trigeminal neuropathy
- Primary stabbing headache
- Short-lasting unilateral neuralgiform headache with conjunctival injection and tearing (SUNCT)
- Postherpetic neuralgia
- Glossopharyngeal neuralgia
- Dental pain

WORKUP

Trigeminal neuralgia is a clinical diagnosis (see previously).

IMAGING STUDIES

Neuroimaging (MRI) should be considered in young patients (<40 years) with atypical symptoms (sensory loss, bilateral symptoms). MRI is useful to identify potential compressors or demyelinating causes.

Rx TREATMENT

PHARMACOLOGIC Rx

- Carbamazepine 400 to 800 mg, 2 to 3 times daily divided dosing is the recommended initial treatment. This can be titrated to pain relief by 100 to 200 mg every 3 days to a maximum of 1200 mg divided bid or tid.
- Oxcarbazepine can be used if carbamazepine is not tolerated due to side effects. Other medica-

---

BOX 1T-8   Causes of Trigeminal Neuralgia

Classical
Neurovascular compression by an artery or vein

Symptomatic
Saccular aneurysm
Arteriovenous malformation
Tumors/mass-lesions at cerebellopontine angle
- Vestibular schwannoma
- Meningioma
- Epidermoid
Primary demyelinating disorders
- Multiple sclerosis
- Charcot-Marie-Tooth disease (rare)
Infiltrative disorders
- Trigeminal amyloidoma
Nondemyelinating lesions
- Small infarct or angioma in the brainstem
Familial

Modified from Adams JG et al: *Emergency medicine, clinical essentials,* ed 2, Philadelphia, 2013, Elsevier.

---

tions include baclofen, phenytoin, gabapentin, clonazepam, lamotrigine, and levetiracetam.
- Drug combinations can be tried when one medication is partially effective before proceeding with secondary intervention.
- Spontaneous remissions may be seen in trigeminal neuralgia, and therefore periodic medication tapers should be considered if the patient is pain free.
- In the elderly population, caution should be used when initiating and titrating the above medications. Caution and extensive counseling should also be used in women of childbearing age when initiating treatment with antiseizure medications.

NONPHARMACOLOGIC THERAPY

Patients with refractory pain eventually need secondary intervention such as microvascular decompression, selective nerve fiber destruction (rhizotomy), glycerol injection, thermal lesioning, chemical ablation, or gamma knife radiosurgery. Microvascular decompression is the only available nondestructive procedure, and is effective in 75% of patients, with observed long-term benefits.

DISPOSITION

- Most patients are responsive to initial pharmacologic treatment. Spontaneous remission is possible.
- Medical management is eventually ineffective in 30% to 50% of patients.

REFERRAL

Referral to a neurologist is appropriate if there is uncertainty about diagnosis or if symptoms are refractory to conservative management.

! PEARLS & CONSIDERATIONS

In a young patient with trigeminal neuralgia, secondary causes such as multiple sclerosis should be considered, and an MRI of the head obtained. In secondary disease, initial therapy should address underlying secondary causes.

SUGGESTED READINGS
Available at www.expertconsult.com

RELATED CONTENT
Trigeminal Neuralgia (Patient Information)

AUTHOR: **JONATHAN H. SMITH, M.D.**

i BASIC INFORMATION

DEFINITION

Greater trochanteric pain syndrome (GTPS) is a term used to describe chronic pain overlying lateral aspect of the hip. Previously described as trochanteric bursitis, it often mimics pain generated from other sources, including myofascial pain, degenerative joint disease, and spinal pathology. Components of GTPS include tendinopathies, tendinous tears, bursal inflammation, and effusion.

SYNONYMS

GTPS
Trochanteric bursitis
Trochanteric syndrome

ICD-10CM CODES
M70.60 Trochanteric bursitis, unspecified hip
M70.61 Trochanteric bursitis, right hip
M70.62 Trochanteric bursitis, left hip

EPIDEMIOLOGY & DEMOGRAPHICS

- This commonly diagnosed regional pain syndrome is estimated to affect between 10% and 25% of the general population.
- In the primary care setting, the incidence of greater trochanteric pain is reported to be around 1.8 patients per 1000 per year.
- Incidence peaks between the fourth and sixth decades of life but can occur at any age.
- Occurs in females more often than males (ratio of 4:1).
- One study found the prevalence of GTPS to be 17.6%, being higher in women and in patients with coexisting LBP, OA, ITB tenderness and obesity.

PHYSICAL FINDINGS & CLINICAL PRESENTATION

- GTPS typically presents as chronic, persistent pain in the lateral hip and/or buttock that is exacerbated by lying on affected side, prolonged standing, climbing stairs, running, or other high-impact activities.
- Pain may radiate along lateral aspect to the knee.
- Tenderness along the lateral or posterior aspect of the greater trochanter (Fig. 1T-64).
- Pain is reproduced with resisted hip abduction.
- Pain at the extreme of rotation, abduction, or adduction, especially positive Patrick's/FABERE test in trochanteric bursitis.

FIGURE 1T-64 Typical location of pain in trochanteric bursitis syndrome. This is also a frequent pain radiation site for lumbar spine lesion, various nerve compression syndromes, and hip disease, particularly in osteonecrosis of the femoral head. (From Canoso JJ: *Rheumatology in primary care*, Philadelphia, 1997, Saunders.)

ETIOLOGY

- GTPS can be caused by repetitive high-intensity use of the tensor fasciae and gluteus medius over the outer femur; trauma, falls, infection (tuberculosis and bacterial), and crystal deposition can precipitate the disease.
- It can occur when other conditions such as osteoarthritis of the knee and hip, RA, sacroiliac joint disorders, leg length discrepancy, ankle sprain, and bunions of the feet cause changes in the patient's gait, placing varus stress on the hip joint.
- It can also occur as a complication resulting from arthroscopic surgery of the hip (estimated 1.4% of cases).

DIFFERENTIAL DIAGNOSIS

- GTPS: Gluteus medius dysfunction or tendinopathy, piriformis tendinopathy, iliotibial tract friction syndrome
- L2-L3 lumbar radiculopathy
- Lumbar facet syndrome
- Osteoarthritis of the hip
- Osteonecrosis of the hip
- Stress fracture of the
- Meralgia paresthetica
- Acetabular labral tear
- Fibromyalgia
- Iliopsoas bursitis
- Trochanteric tendonitis
- Trauma
- Osteomyelitis
- Metastatic bone disease
- Septic arthritis
- Gluteal medius tendon tears

WORKUP

Since there is a wide differential for lateral hip pain, GTPS can be a challenging diagnosis to reach. Complete neuromuscular exam should be performed, including gait observation. A history of lateral hip pain, tenderness on palpation of the lateral hip, and pain while lying on the affected side are the most common complaints.

LABORATORY TESTS

Generally not indicated in clear cases.

IMAGING STUDIES

- Plain radiography: Plain x-rays are usually normal, but other potential causes can be excluded, including OA, femoroacetabular impingement, fractures. Calcifications over the greater trochanter may be seen in 40% of patients presenting with GTPS.
- Ultrasound: Simple, dynamic, inexpensive test that can be very useful in establishing cause of lateral hip pain.
- CT and MRI will depict both osseous and soft tissue pathology but are usually not warranted unless suspect associated conditions that would affect treatment decisions. MRI shows increased signal in bursitis.

Rx TREATMENT

Most cases of GTPS are self-limiting and tend to resolve with conservative measures.

NONPHARMACOLOGIC THERAPY

- Physical therapy and iliotibial band stretching exercises can reduce irritation of the trochanteric bursa area.
- Ice application
- Ultrasound therapy
- Relative rest
- Treat gait disturbance by knee brace, shoe lift, ankle supports, foot orthotics for the specific underlying conditions

ACUTE GENERAL Rx

- NSAIDs for pain relief: ibuprofen 800 mg PO tid or naproxen 500 mg PO bid
- Topical corticosteroids delivered by percutaneous phonophoresis
- Corticosteroid injection
- Regional anesthetic block can be used as a treatment and may also help differentiate from referred pain.

CHRONIC Rx

Although rarely done, surgical removal of the bursa or with also lengthening of iliotibial band with bursectomy is possible for patients with refractory symptoms or infection.

DISPOSITION

- Most patients respond to NSAIDs and/or nonpharmacologic therapy.
- Steroid injection: ~70% of patients respond after first injection and >90% respond to two injections.
- 25% of patients receiving steroid injection may develop a relapse.

REFERRAL

- Physical therapy
- Rheumatology or orthopedics referral if steroid injection therapy is indicated.

! PEARLS & CONSIDERATIONS

Patients with GTPS will commonly report "hip" pain. The physical examination readily distinguishes GTPS from other hip pathologies. Relief of pain with local corticosteroid injection is helpful in differentiating trochanteric bursitis from referred pain.

COMMENTS

- The absence of limitation in range of motion differentiates trochanteric bursitis from degenerative joint disease of the hip.
- Localization of pain over the lateral hip and thigh differentiates trochanteric bursitis from meralgia paresthetica located over the anterolateral thigh and osteoarthritis located over the inner thigh groin area.

SUGGESTED READINGS

Available at www.expertconsult.com

RELATED CONTENT

Trochanteric Bursitis (Patient Information)

AUTHORS: **SAMAN ALI, M.D.**

 **BASIC INFORMATION**

DEFINITION

Miliary tuberculosis (TB) is an infection of disseminated hematogenous disease, caused by the bacterium *Mycobacterium tuberculosis* (Mtb), and is often characterized as resembling millet seeds on pathologic or radiologic examination. Extrapulmonary disease may occur in virtually every organ site.

SYNONYM

Disseminated TB

ICD-10CM CODES
A19.9 Miliary tuberculosis, unspecified

EPIDEMIOLOGY & DEMOGRAPHICS

INCIDENCE (IN U.S.): >38% of AIDS patients with TB have disseminated disease, often with concurrent pulmonary and extrapulmonary active sites. (See "Tuberculosis, Pulmonary" in Section I.)
PREVALENCE (IN U.S.)
- Undetermined
- Highest prevalence
  1. AIDS patients
  2. Minorities
  3. Children
  4. Foreign-born persons
  5. Elderly
PREDOMINANT SEX
- No specific predilection
- Male predominance in AIDS, shelters, and prisons reflected in disproportionate male TB incidence
PREDOMINANT AGE: Predominantly among 24 to 45 yr
PEAK INCIDENCE: HIV-positive patients, regardless of age

PHYSICAL FINDINGS & CLINICAL PRESENTATION
- See also "Etiology"
- Common symptoms
  1. High intermittent fever (93%)
  2. Night sweats (79%)
  3. Weight loss (85%)
  4. Dyspnea (64%)
  5. Cough (82%)
- Symptoms referable to individual organ systems may predominate
  1. Meninges
  2. Pericardium
  3. Liver
  4. Kidney
  5. Bone
  6. GI tract
  7. Lymph nodes
  8. Serous spaces
     a. Pleural
     b. Pericardial
     c. Peritoneal
     d. Joint
  9. Skin
  10. Lung: cough, shortness of breath
- Adrenal insufficiency possible, caused by infection of adrenal gland

- Pancytopenia
  1. With fever and weight loss *or*
  2. Without other localizing symptoms or signs *or*
  3. With only splenomegaly
- TB hepatitis
  1. Tender liver
  2. Obstructive enzymes (alkaline phosphatase) elevated out of proportion to minimal hepatocellular enzymes (SGOT, SGPT) and bilirubin
- TB meningitis
  1. Gradual-onset headache
  2. Minimal meningeal signs
  3. Malaise
  4. Low-grade fever (may be absent)
  5. Sudden stupor or coma
  6. Cranial nerve VI palsy
- TB pericarditis
  1. Effusions resembling TB pleurisy
  2. Cardiac tamponade
- Skeletal TB
  1. Large joint arthritis (with effusions resembling TB pericarditis)
  2. Bone lesions (especially ribs)
  3. Pott's disease
     a. TB spondylitis, especially of lower thoracic spine
     b. Paraspinous TB abscess
     c. Possible psoas abscess
     d. Frequent cord compression (often relieved by steroids)
- Genitourinary TB
  1. Renal TB
     a. Papillary necrosis
     b. Destruction of renal pelvis
     c. Strictures of upper third of ureters
     d. Hematuria
     e. Pyuria with misleading bacterial cultures
     f. Preserved renal function
  2. TB orchitis or epididymitis
     a. Scrotal mass
     b. Draining abscess
  3. Chronic prostatic TB
- GI TB
  1. Diarrhea
  2. Pain
  3. Obstruction
  4. Bleeding
  5. Especially common with AIDS
  6. Bowel lesions
     a. Circumferential ulcers
     b. Short strictures
     c. Calcified granulomas
     d. TB mesenteric caseous adenitis
     e. Abscess, but rare fistula formation
     f. Often difficult to distinguish from granulomatous bowel disease (Crohn's disease)
- TB peritonitis
  1. Fluid resembles TB pleurisy
  2. PPD often negative
  3. Tender abdomen
  4. Doughy peritoneal consistency, often with ascites
  5. Peritoneal biopsy indicated for diagnosis
- TB lymphadenitis (scrofula)
  1. May involve all node groups

  2. Common adenopathies
     a. Cervical
     b. Supraclavicular
     c. Axillary
     d. Retroperitoneal
  3. Biopsy generally needed for diagnosis
  4. Surgical resection of nodes may be necessary
  5. Especially common with AIDS
- Cutaneous TB
  1. Skin infection from autoinoculation or dissemination
  2. Nodules or abscesses
  3. Tuberculids (possibly allergic reactions)
  4. Erythema nodosum
- Miscellaneous presentations
  1. TB laryngitis
  2. TB otitis
  3. Ocular TB
     a. Choroidal tubercles
     b. Iritis
     c. Uveitis
     d. Episcleritis
  4. Adrenal TB
  5. Breast TB

ETIOLOGY
- See also "Pulmonary Tuberculosis" in Section I.
- Mtb, a slow-growing, aerobic, non–spore forming, nonmotile acid-fast bacillus
- Humans are the only reservoir for Mtb.
- Pathogenesis:
  1. Acid-fast bacilli (AFB) (Mtb) are ingested by macrophages in alveoli, then transported to regional lymph nodes where spread is contained.
  2. Some AFB reach the bloodstream and disseminate widely.
  3. Immediate active disseminated disease may ensue or a latent period may develop.
  4. During latent period, T-cell immune mechanisms contain infection in granulomas until later reactivation occurs as a result of immunosuppression or other undefined factors in conjunction with reactivated pulmonary TB or alone.
- Miliary TB may occur as a consequence of the following:
  1. Primary infection: inability to contain primary infection leads to a hematogenous spread and progressive disseminated disease.
  2. In late chronic TB and in those with advanced age or poor immunity, a continuous seeding of the blood may develop and lead to disseminated disease.

Dx DIAGNOSIS

DIFFERENTIAL DIAGNOSIS

Widespread sites of possible dissemination associated with myriad differential diagnostic possibilities:
- Lymphoma
- Typhoid fever
- Brucellosis
- Other tumors
- Collagen-vascular disease

WORKUP

- Prompt evaluation is essential
- Sputum for AFB stain and culture and chest x-ray
- High-resolution CT is more sensitive for miliary TB than CXR
- PPD, which may be negative in immunocompromised patients
- Fluid analysis and mycobacterial culture wherever available
  1. Sputum
  2. Blood: particularly helpful in patients with AIDS
  3. Urine
  4. CSF
  5. Pleural
  6. Pericardial
  7. Peritoneal
  8. Gastric aspirates
- Biopsy of any involved tissue is advisable to make immediate diagnosis
  1. Transbronchial biopsy preferred and easily accessible
  2. Bone marrow
  3. Lymph node
  4. Scrotal mass if present
  5. Any other involved site
  6. Positive granuloma or AFB on biopsy specimen is diagnostic
- Imaging studies as needed

LABORATORY TESTS

- Culture and fluid analysis as described previously
- Smear-negative sputum often is positive weeks later on culture
- CBC is usually normal
- ESR is usually elevated

IMAGING STUDIES

- Chest x-ray examination (may or may not be positive) (see "Tuberculosis, Pulmonary" in Section I)
- CT scan or MRI of brain and spinal cord (Fig. 1T-65)
  1. Tuberculoma
  2. Basilar arachnoiditis
- Barium studies of bowel

 **TREATMENT**

NONPHARMACOLOGIC THERAPY

- Bed rest during acute phase of treatment
- High-calorie, high-protein diet to reverse malnutrition and enhance immune response to TB
- Isolation in negative-pressure rooms with high-volume air replacement and circulation (with health care provider wearing proper protective 0.5- to 1-micron filter respirators)
  1. Until three consecutive sputum AFB smears are negative, if pulmonary disease coexists
  2. Isolation not required for closed-space TB infections

ACUTE GENERAL Rx

- See "Tuberculosis, Pulmonary" in Section I.
- Therapy should be initiated immediately. Do not wait for definitive diagnosis.
- More rapid response to chemotherapy by disseminated TB foci than cavitary pulmonary TB.
- Treatment for 6 mo with INH plus rifampin plus PZA.
  1. Treatment for 12 mo often required for bone and renal TB.
  2. Prolonged treatment often required for CNS and pericardial.
  3. Prolonged treatment often required for all disseminated TB in infants.
- Compliance (rigid adherence to treatment regimen) is the chief determinant of success.
  1. Supervised directly observed therapy (DOT) is recommended for all patients.
  2. Supervised DOT is mandatory for unreliable patients.
- Steroids are often helpful additions in fulminant miliary disease with the hypoxemia and DIC.

CHRONIC Rx

- Generally not indicated beyond treatment described previously
- Prolonged treatment supervised by infectious disease expert required in a few complicated infections caused by resistant organisms

DISPOSITION

- Monthly follow-up by physician experienced in TB treatment
- Confirm sensitivity testing, and alter treatment appropriately (see "Tuberculosis, Pulmonary" in Section I)

REFERRAL

- To infectious disease expert for:
  1. HIV-positive patient
  2. Patient with suspected drug-resistant TB
  3. Patient previously treated for TB
  4. Patient whose fever has not decreased and sputum (if positive) has not converted to negative in 2 to 4 wk
  5. Patients with overwhelming pulmonary or extrapulmonary TB
- To pulmonary, orthopedic, or GI physicians for examinations or biopsy

 **PEARLS & CONSIDERATIONS**

COMMENTS

- Consider acute TB in critically ill patients with enigmatic acute respiratory distress syndrome, shock, or DIC.
- All contacts (especially close household contacts and infants) should be properly tested for PPD conversions >3 mo following exposure.
- Those with positive PPD should be evaluated for active TB and properly treated or given prophylaxis.

EBM **EVIDENCE**

Available at www.expertconsult.com

SUGGESTED READINGS
Available at www.expertconsult.com

RELATED CONTENT
Pulmonary Tuberculosis (Related Key Topic)

AUTHOR: **GLENN G. FORT, M.D., M.P.H.**

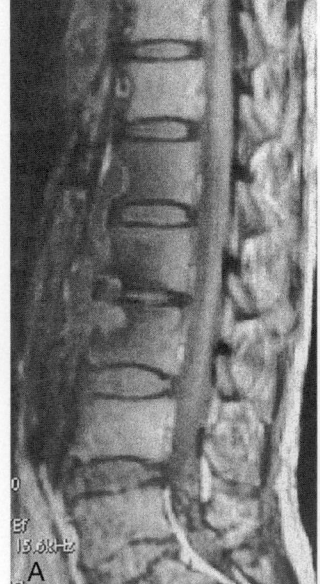
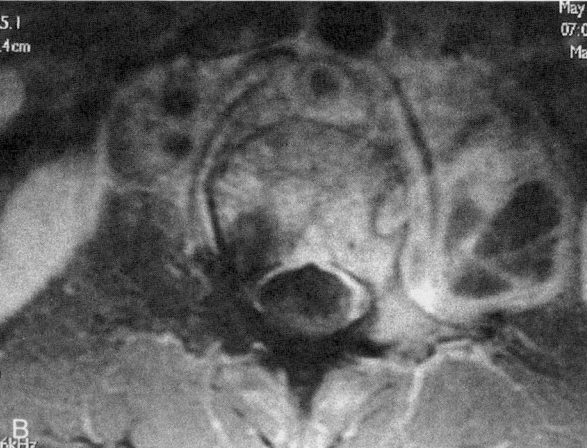

FIGURE 1T-65 A and **B,** Magnetic resonance images of tuberculous spinal osteomyelitis with scalloping of the vertebrae (tuberculous caries) and paraspinal "cold" abscesses. (From Grainger RG, Allison D: *Grainger & Allison's diagnostic radiology, a textbook of medical imaging,* ed 4, London, 2001, Churchill Livingstone.)

 BASIC INFORMATION

DEFINITION

Acute tubular necrosis (ATN) is a form of acute kidney injury (AKI) characterized by acute tubular cell injury and dysfunction. It is the most common form of AKI. ATN may be secondary to ischemic injury, nephrotoxic injury, or septic injury or may be multifactorial.

SYNONYMS

ATN
Acute tubular injury
Ischemic or nephrotoxic acute renal failure (ARF)
Tubular necrosis, acute

ICD-10CM CODES
N17.0 Acute kidney failure with tubular necrosis
N19 Unspecified kidney failure

EPIDEMIOLOGY & DEMOGRAPHICS

- Most common cause of AKI among hospitalized patients.
- Risk factors: advanced age, diabetes mellitus, chronic kidney disease, preexisting hypovolemia or poor renal perfusion.
- Early identification of ATN is paramount as many etiologies are reversible.

PHYSICAL FINDINGS & CLINICAL PRESENTATION

- Physical examination is nonspecific.
- Suspect ischemic ATN in the setting of hemorrhage, hypotension, recent surgery, and/or sepsis
- Suspect nephrotoxic ATN in the setting of contrast imaging, nephrotoxic medications, rhabdomyolysis, hemolysis, or myeloma
- The classic progression of ATN includes three phases, but can be highly variable:
  1. Initiation phase (hours to days): Renal hypoperfusion, evolving ischemia. Acute decrease in glomerular filtration rate (GFR), sudden rise in BUN and serum creatinine, and/or decrease in urine output.
  2. Maintenance phase (1-2 wk): Renal cell injury established, GFR stabilizes and at its nadir (5-10 mL/min/1.73 m²), urine output is at its lowest rate (usually 40-400 mL/day). ATN is complicated by hyperkalemia, metabolic acidosis, uremia, salt, and/or fluid overload. Patients are at an increased risk of infection, and approximately 25% of deaths from ATN occur during the maintenance phase.
  3. Recovery phase (>2 wk): Tubular cell repair and regeneration, with gradual partial or complete return of kidney function to baseline levels; associated with marked osmotic diuresis.

PATHOLOGIC FINDINGS

- Vacuolization and loss of brush border in proximal tubular cells, basement membrane disruption, sloughing of tubular cells, and occlusion of the tubular lumen by casts. Interstitial edema and mild leukocyte accumulation are variably present.

ETIOLOGY

- Diagnosis of exclusion. Prerenal, postrenal, and other intrinsic parenchymal causes of AKI must be ruled out.
- Ischemic processes that contribute to ATN include hypotension, shock, prolonged prerenal azotemia, and surgery
- Renal hypoperfusion may occur without systemic hypotension (normotensive AKI)
- Medications: NSAIDs, COX-2 inhibitors, antimicrobial drugs (acyclovir, foscarnet, tenofovir, cidofovir, adefovir, aminoglycosides, amphotericin B, pentamidine), calcineurin inhibitors, cisplatin, ifosfamide, angiotensin converting enzyme inhibitors, angiotensin II receptor blockers, intravenous immunoglobulin
- Radiocontrast (contrast nephropathy)
- Hemoglobin and myoglobin (rhabdomyolysis, transfusion reactions)
- Heavy metals
- Synthetic cannabinoids
- Cast nephropathy

 **DIAGNOSIS**

DIFFERENTIAL DIAGNOSIS

Prerenal disease, obstructive nephropathy, intrinsic renal vascular diseases (thrombotic thrombocytopenic purpura [TTP], hemolytic uremic syndrome [HUS], scleroderma, and malignant hypertension, renal infarction from aortic dissection or systemic thromboembolism), acute glomerulonephritis, acute interstitial nephritis, atheroembolic renal disease

LABORATORY TESTS & FINDINGS

- Urinalysis with specific gravity <1.015 and low-grade albuminuria with more severe ATN.
- Urine sediment examination with muddy brown casts and tubular epithelial cells.
- Fractional excretion of sodium (FE$_{Na}$) typically is >1%-2% (= [(U_{Na} × P_{Cr}) / (P_{Na} × U_{Cr})] × 100%).
- Multiple biomarkers for early diagnosis of ATN are currently under investigation, but none are yet replacements for serum creatinine.

IMAGING STUDIES

No specific studies are indicated, but appropriate studies may be ordered to diagnose the etiology of ATN (e.g., CT scan for abdominal abscess).

 **TREATMENT**

ACUTE GENERAL Rx

Treatment is etiology-specific. Hemodynamic abnormalities should be corrected and potentially nephrotoxic agents discontinued. Peritoneal or hemodialysis may be required until renal function is restored. Diuretic use is not recommended.

DISPOSITION

Kidney function typically recovers within 1 to 2 weeks of ATN, but outcomes are variable and depend on premorbid kidney function and mechanism of injury. Ischemic ATN with severe multiorgan failure has a mortality rate that exceeds 50%. However, in patients who survive the inciting incident, up to 95% will recover, with GFR approaching premorbid levels. The absence of oliguria (nonoliguric ATN) has a better prognosis.

REFERRAL

Nephrology consultation

PEARLS & CONSIDERATIONS

COMMENTS

Select patients with ATN may have FE$_{Na}$ <1%: patients taking ACEIs, ARBs, or NSAIDs; cirrhosis; heart failure; radiocontrast injury; heme pigment–induced injury (e.g., myoglobinuria or hemoglobinuria); and early sepsis

PREVENTION

- Aggressive restoration of intravascular volume in surgical/trauma patients may prevent ischemic ATN
- Appropriate medication of potentially nephrotoxic agents
- Low-volume of non-ionic radiocontrast agents with isotonic intravenous fluid administration before and after contrast delivery

SUGGESTED READINGS
Available at www.expertconsult.com

RELATED CONTENT
Acute Kidney Injury (Related Key Topic)

AUTHOR: **LENAR YESSAYAN, M.D., M.S.**

BASIC INFORMATION

DEFINITION

- Tumor lysis syndrome (TLS) is a potentially deadly constellation of metabolic derangements that can occur in tumors before or after starting cancer treatment. Rarely, TLS may occur spontaneously. TLS is one of the major oncologic emergencies.
- TLS usually occurs in patients with bulky, rapidly proliferating, and treatment-responsive tumors.
- TLS is associated with acute leukemias, high-grade non-Hodgkin's lymphoma, solid tumors, and hematologic cancers.
- TLS occurs when large numbers of cancer cells are destroyed either spontaneously or during cancer treatment. The result is the release of large amounts of intracellular ions and other metabolic products into the blood. This may lead to any or all of the following:
  1. Hyperkalemia
  2. Hypocalcemia
  3. Hyperphosphatemia
  4. Hyperuricemia
  5. Acute renal failure

Cairo and Bishop classification of TLS:
1. **Laboratory TLS** is defined by the presence of at least two of the following biochemical variables (hyperkalemia, hypocalcemia, hyperphosphatemia, hyperuricemia) within 3 days before or 7 days after initiation of chemotherapy despite adequate hydration and the use of uric acid lowering agents. Laboratory TLS is clinically silent.
2. **Clinical TLS** occurs when at least one of the clinical complications such as seizure, acute renal failure, or cardiac dysrhythmias occurs, and it is not believed to be caused by chemotherapy.

ICD-10CM CODES
E88.3 Tumor lysis syndrome

EPIDEMIOLOGY & DEMOGRAPHICS

INCIDENCE: Unknown, but it is the most common disease-related emergency encountered by physicians who treat children or adults with hematologic cancers. The incidence depends on cancer mass (the greater the mass, the greater the content released at cell death), patient characteristics (e.g., preexisting renal insufficiency, dehydration, hypotension), and supportive care.

PREVALENCE:
- Varies
- Increased frequency is associated with bulky, aggressive, and treatment-sensitive tumors

PREDOMINANT SEX AND AGE:
- No sex predilection exists.
- Occurs in all age groups. Older adults are more susceptible because of impaired renal function with age.

GENETICS: No known racial predilection

RISK FACTORS:
- Bulky tumor and large tumor burden, as in:
  1. Acute leukemias with elevated leukocyte count

2. Large, bulky, rapidly proliferating solid tumors
3. High-grade lymphomas
- Tumors that are treatment sensitive
- Dehydration
- Hypotension
- Exogenous potassium, phosphate
- CHF
- Exposure to nephrotoxic substances
- Impaired kidney function
- Older patients (i.e., reduced glomerular filtration rate)

PHYSICAL FINDINGS & CLINICAL PRESENTATION

CLINICAL PRESENTATION: Patients may present with a number of symptoms either before starting chemotherapy or commonly within 3 days after initiating cytotoxic treatment. Common symptoms include:
- Nausea
- Vomiting
- Edema
- Shortness of breath (from fluid overload or CHF)
- Lethargy or weakness
- Seizure
- Syncope
- Muscle cramps
- Tetany

PHYSICAL FINDINGS: Physical findings are associated with specific metabolic derangement. Patients with TLS variably present with hyperkalemia, hyperuremia, hypocalcemia, and hyperphosphatemia.
- Hyperkalemia:
  1. Weakness
  2. Paresthesia
  3. Paralysis
  4. ECG changes
  5. Cardiac arrhythmias
  6. Cardiac arrest
- Hyperuremia:
  1. Weakness
  2. Malaise
  3. Vomiting
  4. Pruritus
  5. Restless legs
  6. Ecchymoses
  7. Hiccups
  8. Paresthesia
  9. Pericarditis
  10. Dyspnea
  11. Hypertension
- Hypocalcemia:
  1. Paresthesia
  2. Tetany
  3. Bronchospasm
  4. Heart block
  5. Muscle twitching
- Hyperphosphatemia:
  1. Oliguria
  2. Anuria
  3. Acute kidney injury

ETIOLOGY
- Can occur spontaneously or after initiation of therapy in patients with:
  1. Acute leukemias
  2. Bulky solid tumors

3. High-grade lymphomas
- Administration of certain agents:
  1. Paclitaxel
  2. Hydroxyurea
  3. Etoposide
  4. Fludarabine
- It has been reported in some cancer patients who received:
  1. Intrathecal administration of chemotherapy
  2. Rare causes: pregnancy, fever, and rarely general anesthesia in predisposed individuals

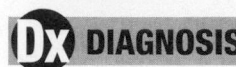
DIAGNOSIS

DIFFERENTIAL DIAGNOSIS
See "Acute Kidney Injury" topic in Section I.

LABORATORY TESTS
Early identification of abnormal laboratory values is required because this may prevent or reduce complications of TLS.
- Monitor BUN, creatinine phosphate, potassium, calcium, uric acid, LDH in high-risk patients before and up to 72 hr after initiating therapy. If evidence of TLS develops, check laboratory parameters at least twice a day.
- Closely monitor urine output for signs of oliguria. Increased urine flow rates inhibits crystal deposition in the renal tubules.
- Perform frequent ECGs or continuous cardiac monitoring for arrhythmia detection from potassium or calcium abnormalities.

IMAGING STUDIES
- Radiology: Examine for large thoracic tumors. Ultrasound and CT scanning for abdominal masses or if kidney failure is present.

TREATMENT

GENERAL PRINCIPLES
- "Prevention is always better than cure" is very relevant in the treating patients with TLS. Therefore, it is very important to identify high-risk patients (by assessing the extent of tumor burden, renal function, and pathologic findings) in order to initiate prophylactic measures before starting treatment. Delay in doing this may lead to life-threatening conditions.
- Optimal treatment involves preservation of renal function. It also includes the prevention of cardiac dysrhythmias and neuromuscular irritability.
- In patients with pretreatment TLS:
  1. Correct all metabolic derangement before starting cancer treatment, if possible.
- Careful and frequent laboratory and clinical monitoring. Check:
  1. Baseline ECG and continuous cardiac monitoring
  2. Renal and fluid status by checking vital signs, daily weights, fluid intake and output
  3. For high-risk patients and those with overt TLS, check the following at least twice daily:
     1. Basic metabolic panel
     2. Calcium

3. Uric acid
4. Phosphate
5. LDH

Treatment Options (Preventive Measures) for High-Risk Patients without Tumor Lysis Syndrome

Prompt and vigorous hydration and the use of uricosuric agents are the mainstays of treatment.

- **Hydration:** Prevent volume depletion and help correct electrolyte derangement.
  1. Start 24-48 hr before initiating cancer treatment and continue for up to 72 hr after treatment.
  2. May use D_5W plus 2 amps of $NaCO_3$.
- **Control of hyperuricemia:** Use allopurinol or rasburicase.
  1. Allopurinol (xanthine oxidase inhibitor prevents the conversion of xanthine and hypoxanthine to uric acid)
     1. Give 600 mg/day PO or IV for prophylaxis and 600 to 900 mg/day PO or IV to treat TLS.
  2. Rasburicase (recombinant urate oxidase) is used when uric acid levels cannot be lowered by standard procedures.
  3. Given IV or IM at dosages from 50 to 100 U/kg/day for 1 to 5 days.
     1. Do not give together with allopurinol.
     2. Alkalization is not necessary.
     3. Contraindicated in glucose-6-phosphate dehydrogenase deficiency (because rasburicase can cause severe hemolysis in patients with this condition) and pregnancy.
- Diuretics: indicated for well-hydrated patients with poor or inadequate diuresis.
  1. Furosemide may be used in well-hydrated patients with elevated potassium or in patients with fluid overload.

TREATMENT OF PATIENTS WITH TUMOR LYSIS SYNDROME

- Principles:
  1. General and preventive measures as mentioned in General Principles and Treatment Options.
  2. Aggressively treat electrolyte disturbances to prevent cardiac dysrhythmias and neuromuscular irritability.

3. Treat renal failure if the previous fail.
- Treating electrolyte disturbances:
  1. Hyperuricemia: as outlined previously
  2. Hyperkalemia:
     1. Restrict dietary potassium.
     2. Stop potassium in IV fluid.
     3. IV infusion of glucose and insulin (to move K to intracellular space).
     4. IV gluconate (cardioprotective effect).
     5. PO potassium-exchange resins.
     6. If above measures fail, then immediate dialysis is needed.
  3. Hyperphosphatemia
     1. Decrease dietary intake.
     2. IV glucose plus insulin.
     3. Oral phosphate binders.
  4. Hypocalcemia
     1. Treat only if symptomatic (e.g., neuromuscular irritability as in positive Chvostek or Trousseau sign).
     2. Calcium gluconate only when symptomatic.
     3. Calcitrol can be used only if serum phosphate level is normal.

TREAT RENAL FAILURE

- Consider early dialysis if above methods fail.
- Dialysis prevents life-threatening complications and irreversible renal failure.
- Hemodialysis is the preferred procedure.

REFERRAL

- Nephrology
- Critical care

ⓘ PEARLS & CONSIDERATIONS

COMMENTS

- High-risk patients should have prophylactic measures 24 to 48 hr before starting cytotoxic drugs. Low-intensity initial therapy is also recommended in patients at high risk for tumor lysis syndrome.
- Prophylactic measures include:
  1. IV hydration
  2. Administration of allopurinol
  3. Urinary alkalization

- Monitor blood chemistry and fluid status.
- Complications of tumor lysis syndrome include:
  1. Uremia
  2. Renal failure
  3. Electrolyte disturbances
  4. Cardiac arrhythmia
  5. Pulmonary edema secondary to aggressive hydration
  6. Metabolic alkalosis from IV bicarbonate administration

SUGGESTED READINGS

Available at www.expertconsult.com

AUTHOR: **DANIEL K. ASIEDU, M.D., Ph.D.**

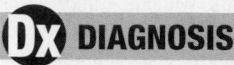 **BASIC INFORMATION**

DEFINITION

Ulcerative colitis (UC) is an idiopathic, remitting and relapsing, chronic inflammatory bowel disease that starts in the rectum and extends proximally.

SYNONYMS

UC
Inflammatory bowel disease (IBD)
Idiopathic proctocolitis
Pancolitis

ICD-10CM CODES
K51.0	Ulcerative pancolitis
K51.2	Ulcerative proctitis
K51.3	Ulcerative rectosigmoiditis
K51.5	Left-sided colitis
K51.90	Ulcerative colitis, unspecified, without complications
K51.80	Other ulcerative colitis without complications
K51.811	Other ulcerative colitis with rectal bleeding
K51.812	Other ulcerative colitis with intestinal obstruction
K51.813	Other ulcerative colitis with fistula
K51.814	Other ulcerative colitis with abscess
K51.818	Other ulcerative colitis with other complication
K51.819	Other ulcerative colitis with unspecified complications
K51.911	Ulcerative colitis, unspecified with rectal bleeding
K51.912	Ulcerative colitis, unspecified with intestinal obstruction
K51.913	Ulcerative colitis, unspecified with fistula
K51.914	Ulcerative colitis, unspecified with abscess
K51.918	Ulcerative colitis, unspecified with other complication
K51.919	Ulcerative colitis, unspecified with unspecified complications

EPIDEMIOLOGY & DEMOGRAPHICS

INCIDENCE: The incidence of UC is 9 to 12 cases per 100,000 persons per year in the U.S.; worldwide, the estimated incidence ranges from 1.2 to 20.3 cases per 100,000 person-years and its prevalence ranges from 7.6 to 246.0 per 100,000 persons. It is most common between ages 15 and 40 yr, with a second peak between 50 and 80 yr. The disease affects men and women at similar rates. Infection with nontyphoid salmonella or campylobacter is associated with an 8-10 time higher risk of developing ulcerative colitis in the following year. Worldwide UC is more common than Crohn's disease.

PREVALENCE: The prevalence of UC is 7.6 to 246.0 cases per 100,000 per year. Higher prevalence in Ashkenazi Jewish descendants.

GEOGRAPHIC DISTRIBUTION: The highest incidence and prevalence of IBD are seen in northern Europe and North America, and the lowest in continental Asia.

GENETICS

- Both specific and nonspecific gene variants are associated with UC.
- There are 47 loci associated with UC, of which 19 are specific for UC and 28 are shared with Crohn's disease.
- Abnormalities in humoral and cellular adaptive immunity are also found in UC.

ETIOLOGY AND PATHOGENESIS

Accumulating evidence suggests that it may result from an inappropriate inflammatory response to environmental triggers and immune dysregulation involving CD4+ T-cell Th2 response in a genetically susceptible host.

PHYSICAL FINDINGS & CLINICAL PRESENTATION

- Patients with UC often present with acute onset of bloody diarrhea accompanied by tenesmus, fever, and dehydration. At presentation 40% of adults have proctitis, 40% have left-sided colitis, and 20% have pancolitis.
- Abdominal distention and tenderness may indicate the presence of complications such as toxic megacolon.
- The onset of symptoms is typically acute and is generally followed by periods of spontaneous remission and frequent relapses.
- Fever, evidence of dehydration may be present during the acute flare-up.
- Evidence of extraintestinal manifestations may be present in nearly 25% of patients: liver disease, sclerosing cholangitis, iritis, uveitis, episcleritis, arthritis, erythema nodosum, pyoderma gangrenosum, aphthous stomatitis.

Dx DIAGNOSIS

DIFFERENTIAL DIAGNOSIS

- Crohn's disease (Table 1U-1)
- Bacterial infections (Table 1U-2)
  1. Acute: *Campylobacter, Yersinia, Salmonella, Shigella, Chlamydia, Escherichia coli, Clostridium difficile,* gonococcal proctitis
  2. Chronic: Whipple's disease, tuberculosis, enterocolitis
- Irritable bowel syndrome
- Protozoal and parasitic infections (amebiasis, giardiasis, cryptosporidiosis)
- Neoplasm (intestinal lymphoma, carcinoma of colon)
- Ischemic bowel disease
- Diverticulitis
- Celiac sprue, lymphocytic or collagenous colitis, radiation enteritis, endometriosis
- Solitary rectal ulcer
- Acute self-limited colitis
- Medication (NSAIDs, chemotherapy)

WORKUP

An accurate diagnosis of UC should define the extent and severity of inflammation. Diagnostic workup includes:

- Comprehensive history, physical examination

TABLE 1U-1 Comparison of Crohn's Disease and Ulcerative Colitis

Feature	Crohn's Disease	Ulcerative Colitis
Rectal bleeding	Sometimes	Common
Diarrhea, mucus, pus	Variable	Common
Abdominal pain	Common	Variable
Abdominal mass	Common	Not present
Growth failure	Common	Variable
Perianal disease	Common	Rare
Rectal involvement	Occasional	Universal
Pyoderma gangrenosum	Rare	Present
Erythema nodosum	Common	Less common
Mouth ulceration	Common	Rare
Thrombosis	Less common	Present
Colonic disease	50%-75%	100%
Ileal disease	Common	None except backwash ileitis
Stomach-esophageal disease	More common	Chronic gastritis can be seen
Strictures	Common	Rare
Fissures	Common	Rare
Fistulas	Common	Rare
Toxic megacolon	None	Present
Sclerosing cholangitis	Less common	Present
Risk for cancer	Increased	Greatly increased
Discontinuous (skip) lesions	Common	Not present
Transmural involvement	Common	Unusual
Crypt abscesses	Less common	Common
Granulomas	Common	None
Linear ulcerations	Uncommon	Common

From Kliegman RM et al: *Nelson textbook of pediatrics,* ed 19, Philadelphia, 2011, Saunders.

TABLE 1U-2 Infectious Agents Mimicking Inflammatory Bowel Disease

Agent	Manifestations	Diagnosis	Comments
Bacterial			
Campylobacter jejuni	Acute diarrhea, fever, fecal blood, and leukocytes	Culture	Common in adolescents, may relapse
Yersinia enterocolitica	Acute → chronic diarrhea, right lower quadrant pain, mesenteric adenitis-pseudoappendicitis, fecal blood, and leukocytes Extraintestinal manifestations, mimics Crohn's disease	Culture	Common in adolescents as fever of unknown origin, weight loss, abdominal pain
Clostridium difficile	Postantibiotic onset, watery → bloody diarrhea, pseudomembrane on sigmoidoscopy	Cytotoxin assay	May be nosocomial Toxic megacolon possible
Escherichia coli 0157:H7	Colitis, fecal blood, abdominal pain	Culture and typing	Hemolytic-uremic syndrome
Salmonella	Watery → bloody diarrhea, food borne, fecal leukocytes, fever, pain, cramps	Culture	Usually acute
Shigella	Watery → bloody diarrhea, fecal leukocytes, fever, pain, cramps	Culture	Dysentery symptoms
Edwardsiclla tarda	Bloody diarrhea, cramps	Culture	Ulceration on endoscopy
Aeromonas hydrophila	Cramps, diarrhea, fecal blood	Culture	May be chronic Contaminated drinking water
Plesiomonas	Diarrhea, cramps	Culture	Shellfish source
Tuberculosis	Rarely bovine, now Mycobacterium tuberculosis Ileocecal area, fistula formation	Culture, purified protein derivative, biopsy	Can mimic Crohn's disease
Parasites			
Entamoeba histolytica	Acute bloody diarrhea and liver abscess, colic	Trophozoite in stool, colonic mucosal flask ulceration, serologic tests	Travel to endemic area
Giardia lamblia	Foul-smelling, watery diarrhea, cramps, flatulence, weight loss; no colonic involvement	"Owl"-like trophozoite and cysts in stool; rarely duodenal intubation	May be chronic
AIDS-Associated Enteropathy			
Cryptosporidium	Chronic diarrhea, weight loss	Stool microscopy	Mucosal findings not like inflammatory bowel disease
Isospora belli	As in Cryptosporidium		Tropical location
Cytomegalovirus	Colonic ulceration, pain, bloody diarrhea	Culture, biopsy	More common when on immunosuppressive medications

From Kliegman RM et al: *Nelson textbook of pediatrics*, ed 19, Philadelphia, 2011, Saunders.

- Laboratory tests (see "Laboratory Tests")
- Colonoscopy to establish the presence of mucosal inflammation; typical endoscopic findings in UC are areas of continuous friable mucosa; diffuse, uniform erythema replacing the usual mucosal vascular pattern; and pseudopolyps. The transition from abnormal to normal tissue tends to be abrupt. Rectal involvement is invariably present if the disease is active. Pathologic findings suggestive of UC include crypt abscesses and atrophy, mucin depletion, basal plasmacytosis, basal lymphoid aggregates, increased lamina propria cellularity, and Paneth cell metaplasia.

LABORATORY TESTS

- Anemia and high erythrocyte sedimentation rate (in severe colitis) are common but normal levels do not rule out the disorder.
- Potassium, magnesium, calcium, and albumin may be decreased.
- Antineutrophil cytoplasmic antibodies (ANCA) with a perinuclear staining pattern (pANCA) can be found in >45% of patients; there is an increased frequency in treatment-resistant left-

sided colitis, suggesting a possible association between these antibodies and a relative resistance to medical therapy in patients with UC.
- Calprotectin is a protein that is measured in feces as a marker of intestinal mucosa leukocyte activity that may be useful for screening of patients with suspected IBD. Trials have shown that based on a pretest probability of IBD of 32% in adults, an abnormal fecal calprotectin test would increase the posttest probability to 91% and a normal result would reduce the probability to 3%.
- Fecal lactoferrin is also a sensitive marker of intestinal inflammation.
- Stool examinations for ova and parasites, stool culture, and testing for *Clostridium difficile* toxin and *E. coli* 0157:H7 may be useful to eliminate other causes of diarrhea in selected patients with risk factors.

IMAGING STUDIES

Image studies (plain radiography, CT scan [Fig. 1U-1]) are generally reserved for suspected complications such as perforation of bowel or toxic megacolon.

 **TREATMENT**

NONPHARMACOLOGIC THERAPY

- Correct nutritional deficiencies; total parenteral nutrition with bowel rest may be necessary in severe cases. Folate supplementation may reduce the incidence of dysplasia and cancer in chronic UC.
- Avoid oral feedings during acute exacerbation to decrease colonic activity; a low-roughage diet may be helpful in early relapse.
- Psychotherapy is useful in most patients. Referral to self-help groups is also important because of the chronicity of the disease and the young age of the patients.

ACUTE GENERAL Rx

The therapeutic options vary with the degree of disease (mild, severe, fulminant) and areas of involvement (distal, extensive).

- Mild disease can be treated with 5-aminosalicylate agents (mesalamine, olsalazine, balsalazide, sulfasalazine). It can be administered as an enema (40 mg once

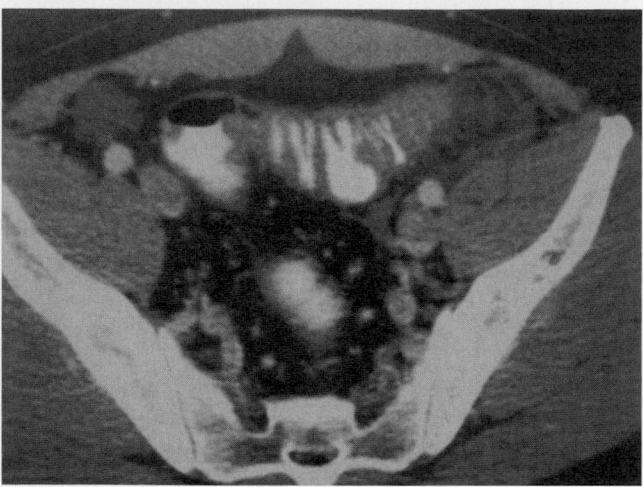

FIGURE 1U-1 Computed tomography scan showing colonic wall thickening in a patient with ulcerative colitis. (From Adams JG, et al: *Emergency medicine, clinical essentials*, ed 2, Philadelphia, 2013, Elsevier.)

daily at bedtime for 3-6 wk) or suppository (500 mg bid) for patients with distal colonic disease. Oral forms in which the 5-acetyl salicylic acid is in a slow-release or pH-dependent matrix (Pentasa 1 g qid, Asacol 800 mg PO tid) can deliver therapeutic concentrations to the more proximal small bowel or distal ileum. Olsalazine can be useful for maintenance of remission of UC in patients intolerant to sulfasalazine. Usual dose is 500 mg bid taken with food. Balsalazide is indicated for mild to moderately active UC. Usual dose is three 750-mg capsules tid. Probiotics may also be helpful in inducing remission in mild-to-moderate UC.

- Mild-to-moderate UC is often treated with a combination of rectal and oral 5-aminosalicylate. Refractory patients are candidates for oral glucocorticoids or immunosuppressive agents (e.g., cyclosporine).
- Severe disease usually responds to oral corticosteroids (e.g., prednisone 40-60 mg/day); the FDA has recently approved an extended-release formulation of the corticosteroid budesonide for induction of remission in mild to moderate ulcerative colitis. Corticosteroid suppositories or enemas are also useful for distal colitis. The immunosuppressant azathioprine also provides effective long-term treatment for Crohn's disease.

- Biological agents are emerging treatment options for the management of ulcerative colitis. Infliximab, a chimeric monoclonal antibody, has been shown to be effective in patients who have not responded to corticosteroid therapy. Newer TNF inhibitors include adalimumab (ADA), golimumab, and vedolizumab for treatment of moderate-to-severe ulcerative colitis. Head-to-head trials of these biologic agents are necessary to establish the best therapeutic option.
- Fulminant disease generally requires hospital admission and parenteral corticosteroids (e.g., IV hydrocortisone 100 mg q6h). When bowel movements have returned to normal and the patient is able to eat normally, oral prednisone is resumed. IV cyclosporine can also be used in severe refractory cases; renal toxicity is a potential complication.
- Surgery is indicated in patients who do not respond to intensive medical therapy. Proctocolectomy is usually curative in these patients and also eliminates the high risk of developing adenocarcinoma of the colon (10%-20% of patients develop it after 10 yr with the disease). Total proctocolectomy with ileal pouch-anal anastomosis (IPAA) is the procedure of choice for most patients who require elective surgery, since it preserves anal sphincter function. Continent ileostomy is an alternative procedure.

CHRONIC Rx

- Colonoscopic surveillance and multiple biopsies should be instituted approximately 10 yr after diagnosis because of the increased risk of colon carcinoma.
- Erythropoietin is useful in patients with anemia refractory to treatment with iron and vitamins.
- In patients on long-term steroid therapy, periodic bone density scans are recommended to screen for glucocorticoid-induced osteoporosis.

DISPOSITION

- The natural history of the disease is one of remission and episodic flares.
- The clinical course is variable. ~66% of patients will achieve clinical remission with medical therapy, and nearly 80% of treatment-compliant patients maintain remission. 15% to 20% of patients eventually require colectomy. Pouchitis is the most common long-term complication of IPAA (up to 40% of patients). >75% of patients treated medically will experience relapse.

REFERRAL

- Gastrointestinal consultation for initial diagnostic sigmoidoscopy/colonoscopy in suspected cases
- Surgical referral for patients with severe disease unresponsive to medical therapy

 **EVIDENCE**

Available at www.expertconsult.com

SUGGESTED READINGS

Available at www.expertconsult.com

RELATED CONTENT

Ulcerative Colitis (Patient Information)

AUTHOR: **FRED F. FERRI, M.D.**

Diseases and Disorders

I

BASIC INFORMATION

DEFINITION

Urethritis is a well-defined clinical syndrome manifested by dysuria, a urethral discharge, or both.

SYNONYMS

Gonnococcal urethritis

ICD-10CM CODES
A54.00 Gonococcal infection of lower genitourinary tract, unspecified

EPIDEMIOLOGY & DEMOGRAPHICS

- The major single specific etiology of acute urethritis is *Neisseria gonorrhoeae,* producing gonococcal urethritis (GCU). Urethritis of all other etiologies is called *nongonococcal urethritis* (NGU).
- NGU is twice as common as GCU in the U.S. NGU is the most common sexually transmitted disease (STD) syndrome occurring in men, accounting for 6 million office visits annually. NGU is more frequently encountered in higher socioeconomic groups. GCU is more common in homosexual males than heterosexual males with acute urethritis.
- *N. gonorrhoeae* is a gram-negative, kidney-shaped diplococcus with flattened opposed margins. The urethra is the most common site of infection in all men. In the United States, the rates of gonorrhea are 40 times higher in black adolescent males than in white adolescent males. In heterosexual men, the pharynx is infected in 7%, and in homosexual men the pharynx is infected in 40% and the rectum in 25%. A single episode of intercourse with an infected partner carries a transmission risk of 20% for males; female partners of an infected male will contract the disease 80% of the time.

PHYSICAL FINDINGS & CLINICAL PRESENTATION

- Symptoms of GCU: urethral discharge and dysuria are the most common symptoms. There is complaint of urethral itching. Prostatic involvement can cause frequency, urgency, and nocturia. It can involve the epididymis through spreading down the vas deferens, causing acute epididymitis.
- Incubation period: 3 to 10 days. Without treatment, urethritis persists for 3 to 7 wk, with 95% of men becoming asymptomatic after 3 mo. GCU is asymptomatic in up to 60% of contacts.
- Signs of GCU: yellow-brown discharge, meatal edema, urethral tenderness to palpation. Rectal bleeding with pus is seen with gonococcal proctitis. Periurethritis leading to urethral stenosis can occur. Disseminated infection can occur. Tenosynovitis and arthritis can occur. Rarely, hepatitis, myocarditis, endocarditis, and meningitis can occur.

DIAGNOSIS

DIFFERENTIAL DIAGNOSIS
- NGU
- Herpes simplex virus

LABORATORY TESTS
- Nucleic acid amplification tests (NAATs): these tests have largely replaced culture in many settings where persons are screened for asymptomatic genital infection. They are not more sensitive than culture for detecting *N. gonorrhoeae* in cervical or urethral specimen; however, they have specificities of >99% and retain sensitivity when used to test voided urine or self-collected vaginal swabs. The performance of NAATs with respect to overall sensitivity, specificity, and ease of specimen transport is better than that of any of the other tests available for the diagnosis of chlamydial and gonococcal infections. NAATs should be used to detect chlamydia and gonorrhea except in cases of child sexual assault involving boys and rectal and oropharyngeal infections in prepubescent girls and when evaluating a potential gonorrhea treatment failure, in which case culture and susceptibility testing might be required.
- Calcium alginate or rayon swab on a metal shaft (not cotton-tipped swabs, which are bactericidal) of the urethra should be performed anywhere from 2 to 4 hr after voiding to prevent bacterial washout with voiding. Gram staining with modified Thayer-Martin media is indicated. Cultures of the pharynx and rectum when indicated.
- Concomitant serologic testing for syphilis on all patients.
- Concomitant *Chlamydia* testing on all patients.
- Offer of HIV counseling and testing to all patients.

 TREATMENT

NONPHARMACOLOGIC THERAPY

Behavioral management: avoid intercourse until cure has been attained and sexual partners have been evaluated and treated.

ACUTE GENERAL Rx
- Ceftriaxone 250 mg IM × 1 dose *plus* azithromycin 1 g orally single dose. Doxycycline 100 mg orally twice/day for 7 days can be substituted for azithromycin in cases of allergy to azithromycin.

Alternative regimens:
- Cefixime 400 mg PO × 1 dose *plus* azithromycin 1 g orally single dose. Cure rate with this regimen is lower than ceftriaxone plus azithromycin because cefixime does not provide as high, nor as sustained, bactericidal blood levels as a 250 mg dose or ceftriaxone. Doxycycline 100 mg orally twice/day for 7 days can be substituted for azithromycin in cases of allergy to azithromycin.

- Resistance to penicillins, fluoroquinolones, sulfonamides, cephalosporins, and tetracyclines is now widespread.
- The use of azithromycin as the second antimicrobial is preferred over doxycycline due to the high prevalence of tetracycline resistance.
- The proportion of gonorrhea cases in heterosexual men that are fluoroquinolone resistant (QRNG) has reached 6.7%, an elevenfold increase from 0.6% in 2001. Fluoroquinolone antibiotics are no longer recommended to treat gonorrhea in the U.S.
- Dual treatment for gonococcal and chlamydial infections is based on theory and expert opinion rather than evidence from clinical trials.

CHRONIC Rx

Postgonococcal urethritis (PGU): reinfection is the most common cause of recurrence. Repeat swab and culture of the urethra, pharynx, and rectum (where applicable) are mandatory. Persistence of polymorphonuclear cells (PMNs) with the absence of gram-negative intracellular diplococci suggests a diagnosis of PGU. This occurs when GCU is treated with a regimen that is ineffective against coincident chlamydial infection; it represents NGU after GCU. The syndrome should be treated as NGU. Persistence of *N. gonorrhoeae* by smear or culture requires treatment for *N. gonorrhoeae*.

PEARLS & CONSIDERATIONS

COMMENTS

- Partner notification: the names and contact information of sexual partners should be gathered at the time of the visit and referred to the health department or the patient notifies the contact directly. Expedited partner treatment is recommended by the Centers for Disease Control and Prevention (CDC) and approved in several states. This consists of giving prescriptions to the infected patient for their partner(s) who has not been evaluated by a physician and is unlikely to seek medical care.
- On examination of the urethral smear, the presence of small numbers of PMNs provides objective evidence of urethritis. The complete absence of PMNs on a urethral smear argues against urethritis. If in addition to the PMNs there are gram-negative, intracellular diplococci, the diagnosis of gonorrhea is established.

SUGGESTED READINGS
Available at www.expertconsult.com

RELATED CONTENT
Evaluation of patients with dysuria and/or urethral/vaginal discharge (Algorithm, Section III)
Gonococcal Urethritis (Patient Information)

AUTHOR: **RUBEN ALVERO, M.D.**

BASIC INFORMATION

DEFINITION
Nongonococcal urethritis (NGU) is urethral inflammation caused by any of several organisms.

SYNONYMS
NGU
Nongonococcal urethritis

ICD-10CM CODES
A56.0 Chlamydial infection of lower genitourinary tract
N34.1 Nonspecific urethritis

EPIDEMIOLOGY & DEMOGRAPHICS
- Occurrence is 50% in sexually transmitted disease clinics. *Chlamydia trachomatis* is the most common notifiable disease in the U.S., with >1.3 million infections reported to the CDC in 2010.
- NGU most commonly affects men in a higher socioeconomic class, affecting heterosexual men more frequently than homosexual men.
- NGU carries a greater morbidity rate than gonococcal urethritis (GCU).

PHYSICAL FINDINGS & CLINICAL PRESENTATION
- Incubation period: 2 to 35 days
- Symptoms: dysuria, whitish-clear urethral discharge (Fig. 1U-2), and urethral itching. The onset of symptoms in NGU is less acute than GCU. The majority of persons with *C. trachomatis* infection are not aware of their infection because they do not have symptoms that would prompt them to seek medical care.
- Signs: whitish-clear urethral discharge, meatal edema, and erythema. Infected women manifest pyuria, and the disease can present as acute urethral syndrome.

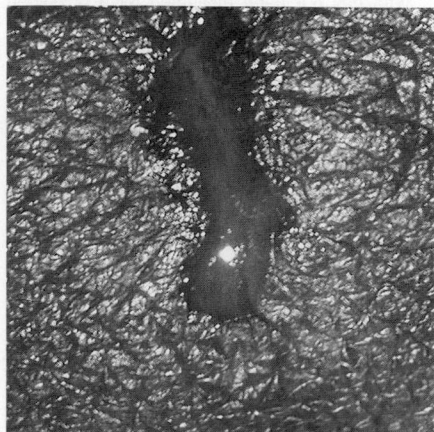

FIGURE 1U-2 Urethral discharge from a man with nongonococcal urethritis. (From Mandell GL et al: *Principles and practice of infectious diseases*, ed 7, Philadelphia, 2009, Churchill Livingstone.)

COMPLICATIONS
Epididymitis in heterosexual men may be linked to nonbacterial prostatitis, proctitis in homosexual men, or Reiter's syndrome.

ETIOLOGY
- Most common agent is *Chlamydia* spp., an obligate intracellular parasite possessing both DNA and RNA, which replicates by binary fission. It causes 20% to 50% of NGU cases. Two species exist:
  1. *Chlamydia psittaci*
  2. *Chlamydia trachomatis* with its 15 serotypes
     Serotypes A through C cause hyperendemic-blinding trachoma.
     Serotypes D through K cause genital tract infection.
     Serotypes L1 through L3 cause lymphogranuloma venereum.
- Other causes of NGU: *Mycoplasma genitalium*(found in 44% of treatment failures); *Ureaplasma urealyticum*, causing 15% to 30% of the cases of NGU; *Trichomonas vaginalis*; and herpes simplex virus. The cause of 20% of the cases of NGU has not been identified.
- Asymptomatic infection occurs in 28% of the contacts of women with chlamydial cervical infection.

 DIAGNOSIS

DIFFERENTIAL DIAGNOSIS
- GCU
- Herpes simplex virus
- Trichomoniasis

LABORATORY TESTS
- Requires demonstration of urethritis and exclusion of infection with *N. gonorrhoeae*.
- Nucleic acid amplification tests (NAATs): these tests have replaced culture in many settings where persons are screened for asymptomatic genital infection. The performance of NAATs with respect to overall sensitivity, specificity, and ease of specimen transport is better than that of any of the other tests available for the diagnosis of chlamydial and gonococcal infections. NAATs should be used to detect chlamydia and gonorrhea except in cases of child sexual assault involving boys, rectal and oropharyngeal infections in prepubescent girls, and when evaluating a potential gonorrhea treatment failure, in which case culture and susceptibility testing might be required.
- Chlamydia culture: The appearance of PMNs on urethral smear confirms the diagnosis of urethritis. Because *Chlamydia* is an intracellular parasite of the columnar epithelium, the best specimen for culture is an endourethral swab taken from an area 2 to 4 cm inside the urethra. For culture, a Dacron-tipped swab is used; avoid calcium alginate or cotton swabs. The organism can only be grown in tissue culture, which is expensive.

Rx TREATMENT

Because it is impossible to differentiate among the common etiologies of NGU, the condition is treated syndromically, including in the initial treatment regimen those drugs effective against the common causative agents. In patients with isolated uncomplicated NGU, recommended regimens are azithromycin 1 g orally single dose or doxycycline 100 mg bid × 7 days. In patients with confirmed urethritis and unclear etiology, concurrent treatment for gonorrhea and *Chlamydia* is recommended. In these patients, uncomplicated infections of the urethra can be treated with combination of a single 1-g dose of oral azithromycin or 100 mg doxycycline bid ×7 days *plus*
- Cefixime 400 mg PO ×1 dose (ceftriaxone is preferred over cefixime) or
- Ceftriaxone 250 mg IM ×1 dose or
  Recommended regimen in pregnancy is azithromycin, 1 g orally as a single dose. Repeat test 3 weeks after completion of treatment to confirm cure.
- In areas where *T. vaginitis* is prevalent, men who have sex with women and have persistent or recurrent urethritis should be presumably treated with metronidazole 2 g orally in a single dose of tinidazole 2 g orally in a single dose.

! PEARLS & CONSIDERATIONS

COMMENTS
Partner notification: The names and contact information of all sexual partners within preceding 60 days should be gathered at the time of the visit and referred to the health department or the patient notifies the contact directly. Expedited partner treatment is recommended by the CDC and approved in several states. This consists of giving prescriptions to the infected patient for their partner(s) who has not been evaluated by a physician and is unlikely to seek medical care.

SUGGESTED READINGS
Available at www.expertconsult.com

RELATED CONTENT
Evaluation of Patients with Dysuria and/or Urethral or Vaginal Discharge (Algorithm in Section III)
Nongonococcal Urethritis (Patient Information)
Cervicitis (Related Key Topic)
Chlamydia Genital Infections (Related Key Topic)

AUTHORS: **RUBEN ALVERO, M.D.,** and **PHILIP J. ALIOTTA, M.D.**

BASIC INFORMATION

DEFINITION

Urinary tract infection (UTI) is a term that encompasses a broad range of clinical entities that have in common a positive urine culture. A conventional threshold is growth of >100,000 colony-forming units per milliliter from a midstream-catch urine sample. In symptomatic patients, a smaller number of bacteria (between 100 and 10,000 colony-forming units per milliliter of midstream urine) is recognized as an infection.

SYNONYM

UTI

ICD-10CM CODES

N39.0	Urinary tract infection, site not specified
N99.521	Infection of other external stoma of urinary tract
N99.531	Infection of other stoma of urinary tract
N30.00	Acute cystitis without hematuria
N30.30	Trigonitis without hematuria
N30.20	Other chronic cystitis without hematuria

CLASSIFICATION

- Uncomplicated UTI: occurs in a normal urinary tract and resolves rapidly with conventional antimicrobials.
- Complicated UTI: occurs in patients with coexisting pathology (strictures, stones, comorbidities [diabetes mellitus, multiple sclerosis, spinal cord injuries]).
- First infection: the first documented UTI; tends to be uncomplicated and is easily treated.
- Unresolved bacteriuria: UTI in which the urinary tract is not sterilized during therapy. Main causes are bacterial resistance, patient noncompliance with medication, mixed bacterial infection, rapid reinfection, azotemia, infected stones, Münchausen syndrome, and papillary necrosis.
- Bacterial persistence: UTI in which the urine cultures become sterile during therapy, but a persistent source of infection from a site within the urinary tract that was excluded from the high urinary concentrations gives rise to reinfection by the same organism. Causes include infected stone, chronic bacterial prostatitis, atrophic infected kidney, vesicovaginal or enterovesical fistulas, obstructive uropathy, infected pyelocaliceal diverticula, infected ureteral stump after nephrectomy, infected necrotic papillae from papillary necrosis, infected urachal cysts, infected medullary sponge kidney, urethral diverticula, and foreign bodies.
- Reinfection: UTI in which a new infection occurs with new pathogens at variable intervals after a previous infection has been eradicated.

- Relapse: the less common form of recurrent infection; occurs within 2 wk of treatment when the same organism reappears in the same site as the previous infection. Relapsing infections of the urinary tract most commonly occur in pyelonephritis, kidney obstruction from a stone, and prostatitis.

EPIDEMIOLOGY & DEMOGRAPHICS

INCIDENCE

- UTI is the most common bacterial infection encountered in the ambulatory care setting in the U.S. The self-reported annual incidence of UTI in women is 12%, and by age 32 half of all women report having had at least one UTI.
- In neonates: more common in boys as a result of anatomic abnormalities such as the posterior urethral valves.
- In preschool children: more common in girls (4.5% vs. 0.5% for boys).
- In adulthood: more common in women, with a 1% to 3% prevalence in nonpregnant women. Table 1U-3 describes factors modulating risk for acute uncomplicated UTIs in women. In pregnancy at 12 wk, the incidence of asymptomatic bacteriuria is similar to nonpregnant women, at 2% to 10%. However, 25% to 30% of pregnant women with untreated asymptomatic bacteriuria develop acute pyelonephritis, especially in the second and third trimesters, and have a pyelonephritic recurrence rate of 10%. In adults aged ≥65 yr, at least 10% of men and 20% of women have bacteriuria.

PHYSICAL FINDINGS & CLINICAL PRESENTATION

- UTI presentation is inconsistent and cannot be relied on to diagnose UTI accurately or to localize the site of infection. Patients report:
  1. Urinary frequency, urgency
  2. Dysuria
  3. Urge incontinence
  4. Suprapubic pain
  5. Gross or microscopic hematuria
- When negative cultures are associated with significant pyuria, vaginal discharge, or hematuria, infections with *Chlamydia trachomatis, Neisseria gonorrhoeae,* and *Trichomonas vaginalis* should be considered.

- Acute pyelonephritis presents with fever, flank or abdominal pain, chills, malaise, vomiting, and diarrhea. It is these systemic symptoms that distinguish pyelonephritis from cystitis. Complications of acute pyelonephritis are renal abscess, perinephric abscess, emphysematous pyelonephritis, and pyonephrosis.

ETIOLOGY & PATHOGENESIS

- Four major pathways:
  1. Ascending from the urethra
  2. Lymphatic
  3. Hematogenous
  4. Direct extension from another organ system
- Other risk factors: neurologic diseases, renal failure, diabetes, anatomic abnormalities, bladder outlet obstruction, urethral stricture, vesicoureteral reflux, fistula, urinary diversion, megacystis, infected stones, age, pregnancy, instrumentation, poor patient compliance, poor hygiene, infrequent voiding, diaphragm contraceptives, tampon use, douches, and catheters.
- Catheters: all patients who require a long-term Foley catheter eventually develop significant levels of bacteriuria. Treatment is reserved for individuals who become symptomatic (leukocytosis, fever, chills, malaise, loss of appetite, etc.) Using prophylactic antibiotics to treat patients who have chronic catheters is to be discouraged because of the risk of acquiring bacteria resistant to antibiotic therapy.
- Once bacteria reach the urinary tract, three factors determine whether the infection occurs (Box E1U-1). These factors also determine the anatomic level of the UTI:
  1. Virulence of the microorganism
  2. Inoculum size
  3. Adequacy of the host defense mechanisms
- Urinary pathogens: in 95% of UTIs the infecting organism is a member of the Enterobacteriaceae, enterococci, or, in young women, *Staphylococcus saprophyticus. Escherichia coli* is the most common pathogen (85% of UTI cases). In contrast, the organisms that commonly colonize the distal urethra and skin of both men and women and the vagina

---

TABLE 1U-3 Factors Modulating Risk for Acute Uncomplicated Urinary Tract Infections in Women

Host Determinants	Uropathogen Determinants
Behavioral: sexual intercourse, use of spermicidal products, recent antimicrobial use, suboptimal voiding habits	*Escherichia coli* virulence determinants: P, S, Dr, and type I fimbriae; hemolysin; aerobactin; serum resistance
Genetic: innate and adaptive immune response, enhanced epithelial cell adherence, antibacterial factors in urine and bladder mucosa, nonsecretor of ABO blood group antigens, P$_1$ blood group phenotype, reduced CXCR1 expression, previous history of recurrent cystitis	
Biologic: estrogen deficiency in postmenopausal women, micturition	

From Floege J et al: *Comprehensive clinical nephrology,* ed 4, Philadelphia, 2010, Saunders.

of women are *Staphylococcus epidermidis*, diphtheroids, lactobacilli, *Gardnerella vaginalis*, and a variety of anaerobes that rarely cause UTIs. In general, the isolation of two or more bacterial species from a urine culture signifies a contaminated specimen unless the patient is being managed with an indwelling catheter or urinary diversion or has a chronic complicated infection.

- Defense mechanisms against cystitis: low pH and high osmolarity, mucopolysaccharide glycosaminoglycan protective layer, normal bladder that empties completely and has no incontinence, and the presence of estrogen.

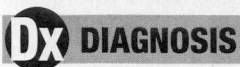 **DIAGNOSIS**

DIFFERENTIAL DIAGNOSIS

- Interstitial cystitis
- Vaginitis
- Urethritis (gonococcal, nongonococcal, *Trichomonas*)
- Frequency-urgency syndrome, prostatitis (acute and chronic)
- Obstructive uropathy
- Infected stones
- Fistulas
- Papillary necrosis
- Vesicoureteral reflux
- Irritation

LABORATORY TESTS

- Urinalysis with microscopic evaluation of clean-catch urine for bacteria and pyuria. The presence of ≥10 leukocytes/μl of unspun urine from a midstream catch indicates UTI. If urine dipsticks are used, the presence of positive nitrite and positive leukocyte esterase is indicative of UTI in a symptomatic patient.
- Urine culture and sensitivity are useful in complicated UTIs but generally not needed in uncomplicated UTIs.
- Complete blood count with differential (shows leukocytosis)
- Antibody-coated bacteria are seen with pyelonephritis

IMAGING STUDIES

- Warranted only if renal infection or genitourinary abnormality is suspected
- KUB (kidneys, ureter, and bladder); voiding cystourethrogram; renal sonogram; intravenous pyelogram; CT scan; nuclear scan
- Specialty examination: cystoscopy with occasional retrograde pyelography to rule out obstructive uropathy; stenting the obstruction possibly required

 **TREATMENT**

NONPHARMACOLOGIC THERAPY

- Hot sitz baths, anticholinergics, urinary analgesics
- For pyelonephritis: bed rest, analgesics, antipyretics, and IV hydration

ACUTE GENERAL Rx

- Conventional therapy of 7 days; short-term therapy of 3 or 5 days (Fig. E1U-3).
- Agents of choice: nitrofurantoin, fluoroquinolones, trimethoprim plus sulfonamide (TMP-SMX), amoxicillin/clavulanate, and cephalosporins. Drug resistance needs to be considered when choosing antibiotic therapy. Currently, in the U.S., fluoroquinolone resistance exceeds 20% and TMP-SMX resistance 40% in some regions, but resistance is much lower for nitrofurantoin.
- For pyelonephritis: hospitalization until afebrile and stable, then at home by home care agency with IV antibiotic composed of aminoglycoside plus cephalosporin for 1 wk followed by oral agents (based on sensitivity) for 2 wk. Moderate forms of pyelonephritis may be successfully treated with fluoroquinolone therapy for 21 days without requiring hospitalization. Most important, complicating factors such as obstructive uropathy or infected stones must be identified and treated.
- A urinary analgesic (e.g., phenazopyridine) can also be used along with antibiotics in patients with significant dysuria.

 **PEARLS & CONSIDERATIONS**

COMMENTS

- Asymptomatic bacteriuria: occurs in both anatomically normal and abnormal urinary tracts. It is uncommon among younger men but is present in nearly 10% of community-dwelling men over age 80 and in up to 40% of male residents of long-term care facilities. This can clear spontaneously, persist, or lead to symptomatic kidney infection. Treatment is recommended in patients with vesicoureteral reflux, stones, obstructive uropathy, parenchymal renal disease, or diabetes mellitus and in pregnant or immunocompromised patients.
- Pregnancy: 25% to 30% of pregnant women with asymptomatic untreated bacteriuria develop pyelonephritis. This is associated with prematurity and low-birth-weight infants. Confirmed significant bacteriuria should be treated with an aminopenicillin and cephalosporin.
- Recurrent UTI: caused by an unresolved infection, vaginal colonization of the originally infecting organism, or reinfection with a new strain. Management of recurrent UTI includes continuous antibiotic prophylaxis, intermittent self-treatment, and postcoital prophylaxis. Prophylaxis is recommended for women who have two or more symptomatic UTIs over a 6-mo period or three or more episodes over a 12-mo period.
  1. Changes after menopause: lower levels of lactobacilli, decreased estrogen, senile atrophy of the genitalia, and loss of bladder elasticity (compliance).
  2. Biologic factors altering defense systems: the presence of sialosyl galactosyl globo-

side on the surface of the kidney acts as a powerful receptor for *Escherichia coli* and increases the risk for UTI; the presence of the blood group P_1 causes increased binding of *E. coli* that is resistant to normal infection-fighting mechanisms in the body. It is believed that some individuals are deficient in a compound called human beta-defensin-1, a naturally occurring antibiotic that fights *E. coli* within the urinary tract.
  3. Cranberry juice is often used as a remedy for the prevention of UTIs; however, randomized placebo-controlled trials have shown that it is no better than placebo for preventing UTIs.

RESISTANCE

- Because of the overuse of antibiotics, organisms once sensitive to a number of antimicrobial agents are now increasingly resistant, making effective management of UTI and pyelonephritis more difficult and potentially more dangerous. Most important has been the increasing resistance to trimethoprim plus sulfamethoxazole (TMP-SMX), the current primary care provider drug of choice for acute uncomplicated UTI in women.
- When choosing a treatment regimen, physicians should consider such factors as:
  1. In vitro susceptibility
  2. Adverse effects
  3. Cost effectiveness
  4. Resistance rates in their respective communities

 EVIDENCE

Available at www.expertconsult.com

SUGGESTED READINGS

Available at www.expertconsult.com

RELATED CONTENT

Urinary Tract Infection (Patient Information)
Urinary Tract Infection (Child) (Patient Information)
Pyelonephritis (Related Key Topic)

AUTHORS: **RUBEN ALVERO, M.D.,** and **PHILIP J. ALIOTTA, M.D.**

BASIC INFORMATION

DEFINITION

Urolithiasis is the presence of calculi within the urinary tract from the kidney to the urethra. The five major types of urinary stones are calcium oxalate (70%-80%), calcium phosphate (10%-20%), uric acid (10%), struvite (7%), and cystine (1%) (Table 1U-4).

SYNONYMS

Kidney stones
Renal colic
Nephrolithiasis

ICD-10CM CODES

N20.9 Urinary calculus, unspecified
N20.0 Calculus of kidney
N20.1 Calculus of ureter
N20.2 Calculus of kidney with calculus of ureter
N21.0 Calculus in bladder
N21.1 Calculus in urethra
N21.8 Other lower urinary tract calculus
N21.9 Calculus of lower urinary tract, unspecified

EPIDEMIOLOGY & DEMOGRAPHICS

- In the U.S., the lifetime prevalence of nephrolithiasis is approximately 13% in men and 7% in women.
- Stone prevalence is likely increasing.
- Between 1% and 1.7% of emergency department visits (1 to 2 million visits annually) are accounted for by a primary diagnosis of renal colic or calculus.
- The incidence of symptomatic nephrolithiasis is greatest during the summer as a result of increased humidity and temperatures, with an increased risk of dehydration and urinary concentration.
- Calcium oxalate or mixed calcium oxalate/calcium phosphate stones account for nearly 70% of stones.

PHYSICAL FINDINGS & CLINICAL PRESENTATION

Stones may be asymptomatic, or they may cause the following signs and symptoms as a result of obstruction:
- Acute flank tenderness
- Nausea and vomiting
- Patient moves constantly in an attempt to alleviate pain, whereas patients with an acute abdomen are usually still because movement exacerbates pain.
- Pain radiating downward and anteriorly with referred pain in the genitalia with stone progression down the ureter
- Fever and chills accompany acute colic only if there is a superimposed infection
- Pain that may radiate anteriorly over to the abdomen and result in intestinal ileus

ETIOLOGY

CALCIUM STONES

- Supersaturation, often expressed as the ratio of urinary calcium oxalate or calcium phosphate concentration to its solubility, is the driving force in calcium kidney stone formation. At ratios exceeding 1, crystals can nucleate, grow, and become stones. All urine is supersaturated for calcium salts, accounting for the relatively high prevalence of stones.
- Idiopathic hypercalciuria. This is the most common diagnosis for patients with calcium stones; the diagnosis is made only if there is no hypercalcemia and no known cause of the hypercalciuria. These patients generally have increased intestinal calcium absorption and decrease in renal calcium reabsorption.
- Heterozygous mutations in the proximal tubule phosphate transporter NPT2a gene leads to hypophosphatemia by enhanced urinary phosphate loss.
- Hyperparathyroidism with resulting hypercalcemia.
- Malabsorption (e.g., inflammatory bowel disease) with increased oxalate absorption.

- Primary hyperoxaluria.
- Low urine pH due to metabolic syndrome (e.g., overweight, diabetes).
- Medullary sponge kidney.
- Hyperuricosuria (e.g., metabolic defects, dietary excess) (Box E1U-2).
- Type I (distal tubule) renal tubular acidosis (>1% of calcium stones).
- Chronic infections with urease-producing organisms (e.g., *Proteus, Providencia, Pseudomonas, Klebsiella*). Struvite, or magnesium ammonium phosphate crystals, is produced when the urinary tract is colonized by bacteria, thus producing elevated concentrations of ammonia (Box E1U-3).
- Cystinuria.
- Abnormal cystine excretion.

 DIAGNOSIS

DIFFERENTIAL DIAGNOSIS

- Urinary tract infection
- Pyelonephritis
- Diverticulitis
- Pelvic inflammatory disease
- Ovarian pathology
- Dysmenorrhea
- Factitious (illicit substance-seeking behavior)
- Appendicitis
- Small-bowel obstruction
- Ectopic pregnancy
  The differential diagnosis of obstructive uropathy is described in Section II.

WORKUP

- Fig. E1U-4 describes an algorithm for evaluation of suspected renal colic.
- Stone composition of recovered stones should be determined by infrared spectroscopy or X-ray crystallography.
- A clinical algorithm for the evaluation of nephrolithiasis is described in Fig. E1U-5.
- Box 1U-4 describes events in the medical history that may be significant with regard to urolithiasis.

TABLE 1U-4 Stone Composition and Relative Occurrence

Stone Composition	Occurrence (%)
Calcium-containing stones	
Ca oxalate	60
Mixed Ca oxalate/ hydroxyapatite	20
Brushite	2
Non–calcium containing stones	
Uric acid	7
Magnesium ammonium phosphate (struvite)	7
Cystine	1-3 (10% of stones in children)
Xanthine	<1
Medication-related stones	<1

From Lipshultz LI et al: *Urology and the primary care practitioner,* ed 3, Philadelphia, 2008, Elsevier.

BOX 1U-4 Components of the Medical History That Are Significant for Urolithiasis

- Diseases associated with disturbances of calcium metabolism: primary hyperparathyroidism, Wilson's disease, medullary sponge kidney, osteoporosis, immobilization, sarcoidosis, osteolytic metastases, plasmacytoma, neuroendocrine tumors, Paget's disease
- Dietary history: purine gluttony, calcium excess, milk alkali, oxalate excess, sodium excess, low citrus fruit intake
- Medications: uricosurics, diuretics, analgesics, vitamins C and D, antacids (especially phosphorus-binding agents), acetazolamide, calcium channel blockers, triamterene, estrogens, theophylline, protease inhibitors (indinavir), sulfonamides
- Diseases associated with disturbances of oxalate metabolism: primary hyperoxaluria types I and II, Crohn's disease, ulcerative colitis, intestinal bypass surgery (especially jejunoileal bypass), ileal resection
- Diseases associated with disturbances of purine metabolism
- Intrinsic metabolic disorders: anemia, neoplastic disorders (especially leukemias), intoxication, myocardial infarction, irradiation, cytotoxic chemotherapy
- Enzyme deficiency: primary gout, Lesch-Nyhan syndrome
- Altered excretion: renal insufficiency, metabolic acidosis
- Infectious history: organisms (particularly *Proteus* and *Klebsiella*), febrile, upper tract involvement, and dates (if hospitalized)

Modified from Nseyo UO (ed): *Urology for primary care physicians,* Philadelphia, 1999, Saunders.

LABORATORY TESTS

- Urinalysis: Hematuria may be present, but its absence does not exclude stones. Urine pH facilitates identification of stone type: pH >7.5 is associated with struvite stones, pH <5 is generally associated with uric acid stones, and low serum bicarbonate concentration with urine pH ≥6 is consistent with a renal tubular acidosis.
- Urine culture and sensitivity results should be obtained for all patients
- Serum chemistries include calcium, electrolytes, creatinine, phosphate, and uric acid.
- Additional tests: 24-hr urine collection for calcium, uric acid, phosphate, oxalate, and citrate excretion is generally reserved for patients with recurrent stones. A 24-hr urine collection may be appropriate for motivated, first-time stone patients interested in preventing recurrent stones.

IMAGING STUDIES

- Common diagnostic modalities for renal colic are summarized in Table 1U-5. Noncontrast CT scan has the greatest sensitivity and specificity. However, ultrasonography may be adequate in many instances, especially in patients known to have a history of stones.
- Kidney ultrasound (Fig. 1U-6): Initial ultrasonography is associated with lower cumulative radiation exposure than initial CT, without significant differences in high-risk diagnoses with complications, serious adverse events, pain scores, return emergency department visits, or hospitalizations. It is reasonable to use ultrasonography as the initial imaging modality in suspected nephrolithiasis. Accuracy of sonography in detecting distal ureteral stones can be high but is variable due to stone size and expertise of the technician and radiologist.
- Unenhanced (noncontrast) helical CT scanning can visualize calculi (Fig. E1U-7), identified by a "rim sign" or "halo," representing the edematous ureteral wall around the stone. The test is rapid and accurate (sensitivity, nearly 100%; specificity, 94%-96%) and can identify all stone types in all locations except for indinavir stones. These stones are not radiopaque, and signs of obstruction are usually minimal or absent. Contrast-enhanced CT may be required to diagnose them.
- Abdominal radiography can identify radiopaque stones (e.g., calcium-containing but not radiolucent uric acid stones) ≥5 mm in diameter.
- CT urograms may be ordered by urologists in considering whether an intervention is required for complex stones.

TABLE 1U-5 Common Diagnostic Imaging Modalities for Renal Colic

Modality	Information Provided	Radiation Dose	Contrast	Approximate Cost	Time
CT	Renal stones, including size and position of stones and evidence of obstruction Alternative diagnoses, such as AAA, appendicitis, and free air	4-10 mSv	No	$750-$1000	Less than 5 min to perform, 30 min for interpretation
CT with IV contrast	Same as noncontrast CT Delineation of renal mass lesions Additional information about vascular dissections and mesenteric ischemia	4-10 mSv	Yes	$750-$1000	Less than 5 min, after delay to measure creatinine
CT with IV and oral contrast	Same as CT with IV contrast Potentially improved diagnosis of bowel abnormalities	4-10 mSv	Yes	$750-$1000	Less than 5 min, after delay of approximately 2 hr to ingest oral contrast
Intravenous urogram	Structural and functional information about obstruction Rarely, identification of other pathology, such as AAA	1.5 mSv	Yes	$350	Approximately 75 min
X-ray	Possible identification of stone, but not useful for hydronephrosis or most other pathology	0.5-1 mSv	No	$250	Less than 5 min
Ultrasound	Identification of hydronephrosis or hydroureter Possible identification of stone Used to assess for AAA or biliary disease	No	No	$150	Approximately 15-30 min—bedside ultrasound is quicker

CT, Computed tomography; *IV,* intravenous.
From Lipshultz LI et al: *Urology and the primary care practitioner,* ed 3, Philadelphia, 2008, Elsevier.

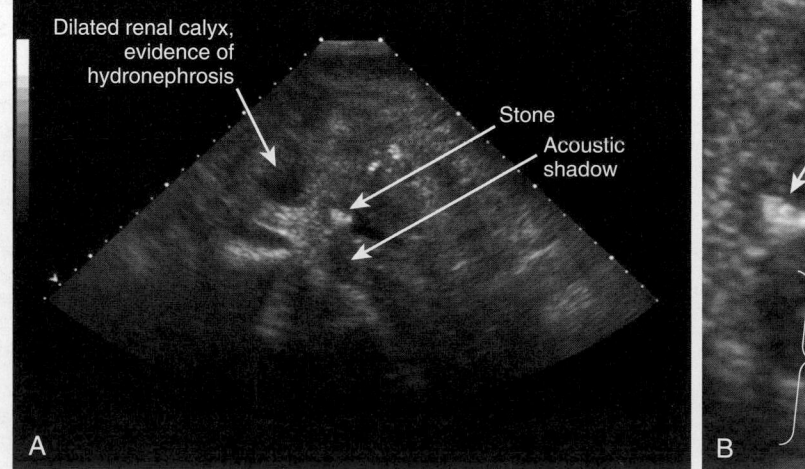

FIGURE 1U-6 Ultrasound of renal stone. Ultrasound can be used to assess for renal stones and complications such as hydronephrosis. Stones can be difficult to detect, whereas hydronephrosis is usually readily observed. Because stones are dense, they reflect sound and prevent its through transmission. As a result, stones are echogenic (bright) on ultrasound, and cast an acoustic shadow (black). **A,** Short-axis view of kidney. **B,** Close-up. (From Broder JS: *Diagnostic imaging for the emergency physician,* Philadelphia, 2011, Saunders.)

Diseases and Disorders

Rx TREATMENT

NONPHARMACOLOGIC THERAPY: CALCIUM STONES

- Increase water or other fluid intake. Doubling of previous fluid intake should occur unless the patient has a history of congestive heart failure or fluid overload. Generally, patients at increased risk for the development of stones should increase fluid intake to >2.5 L/day (68-96 oz/day) to maintain a urine volume of ≥ 2.5 L/day.
- Higher dietary calcium intake of 1000 to 2000 mg/day is recommended. Lower calcium consumption results in less gut oxalate binding and more colonic oxalate absorption. The increased oxalate load and urinary excretion increases the risk of calcium stones. Calcium supplements are not effective for prevention of recurrent kidney stones and may increase the risk.
- Less animal protein intake and restriction of dietary oxalate are recommended, particularly to address abnormal 24-hr urine chemistry results.
- Greater fruit and vegetable intake increases urinary excretion of citrate (stone inhibitor).
- Dietary sodium restriction is recommended. Decreases calcium excretion.
- Decrease protein intake to 1 g/kg/day to lower uric acid, calcium, and oxalate excretion..
- Limit sucrose and fructose intake. .

ACUTE GENERAL Rx

- Pain control: ketorolac (60 mg IM) for moderate pain. Narcotics are generally reserved for severe pain.
- Medical expulsive therapy with smooth muscle relaxants (tamsulosin, nifedipine) is commonly prescribed to patients with renal colic; however, trials have shown that it is no more effective or better than placebo.[1]

PREVENTION

- Therapy is specifically tailored to stone type:
  1. Uric acid calculi: Principal concept is to increase urinary pH with potassium citrate (10-mEq tablets). Taking the drug once nightly is sufficient to prevent: dosing two or three times daily alkalinizes the urine throughout the day and can dissolve stones.
  2. Serum urate-lowering therapy with allopurinol or febuxostat is reserved for patients who have difficulty alkalinizing their urine and those with gout.
  3. Calcium stones:
     1. Chlorthalidone 25 to 50 mg/day in patients with hypercalciuria. Hydrochlorothiazide 25 to 50 mg twice daily or indapamide 2.5 to 5.0 mg once daily may also be effective and better tolerated in patients with lower blood pressures.
     2. Potassium citrate supplementation for patients with calcium stones and

low 24-hr urine citrate excretion. Potassium citrate may also be effective with calcium stones even if urine citrate excretion is not low.
     3. Urate-lowering treatment for patients with hyperuricosuria but not hypercalciuria.
  4. Struvite stones:
     1. Characteristically large, branched, staghorn calculi that often causes obstruction. .
     2. Urologic interventions are always required. Extracorporeal shock wave lithotripsy (ESWL) is not preferred. Percutaneous nephrolithotomy and ureteroscopy, depending on stone size and urologist's preference.
     3. Prolonged antibiotic treatment (6 months or more) directed against the predominant urinary tract organism may prevent recurrent infections and reduce struvite stone recurrence. Suppressive doses of antibiotics for 6 mo or more may be required.
     4. Urease inhibitor treatment by aceto hydroxamic acid in patients who are not rendered stone free.
  5. Cystine stones
- High fluid intake of 3 to 4 L daily is the principal therapy. Urine alkalinization to pH >6.5 with potassium citrate; sodium citrate may increase cystine excretion. Thiol drugs penicillamine and tiopronin reduce the poorly soluble cystine to a soluble cysteine–drug complex. Captopril is not recommended for cystine stone prophylaxis but can still be used for its blood pressure–lowering effects in cystinuric patients.
- Passage of stones <10 mm diameter in the distal ureter may be facilitated by tamsulosin and nifedipine Tamsulosin (α-adrenergic antagonist) represents propulsive therapy, and nifedipine enhances ureteral dilation and relaxation. Tamsulosin may cause dizziness, and nifedipine may cause hypotension.
- Administer antibiotics if fever, sepsis, or pyuria (>5-20 leukocytes/hpf) is present.
- Surgical treatment for patients with severe pain unresponsive to medication, persistent fever or nausea, or significant impediment of urine flow:
  1. Ureteroscopic stone extraction as first-line therapy for most nephrolithiasis cases that require surgical intervention. Indications for percutaneous nephrolithotomy are described in Table E1U-6.
  2. ESWL for most kidney stones: first-line therapy for non–lower pole renal calculi <2 cm diameter and lower pole renal calculi <1 cm diameter. Contraindications include pregnancy, active UTI, coagulopathies, and distal obstruction. Spinal or orthopedic deformities and morbid obesity may preclude ESWL because of the inability to properly position patient or inadequate stone visualization.
- Fig. E1U-8 describes the management of ureteral stones.

- Guidelines for ureteral stone treatment:
  1. Proximal ureteral stones <1 cm diameter: ESWL, percutaneous nephroureterolithotomy, or ureteroscopy.
  2. Proximal ureteral stones >1 cm diameter: ESWL, percutaneous nephroureterolithotomy, and ureteroscopy. Ureteral stent placement is considered if the stone is causing high-grade obstruction.
  3. Distal ureteral stones <1 cm diameter: most stones pass spontaneously. ESWL and ureteroscopy are two accepted modes of therapy.
  4. Distal ureteral stones >1 cm diameter: nonsurgical monitoring, ESWL, and ureteroscopy after stone fragmentation.

  Fig. E1U-8 describes an approach to the management of ureteral calculi.

CHRONIC Rx

Maintenance of proper hydration and dietary restrictions (see "Acute General Rx")

DISPOSITION

- >50% of patients will pass the stone within 48 hours
- Stones recur in approximately 50% of patients within 5 years when no medical treatment is provided.

REFERRAL

Urology referral is made for complicated or recurrent stones. Most small, uncomplicated ureteral or renal calculi are followed on an outpatient basis. Inpatient monitoring is recommended for persistent vomiting, suspected urinary tract infection, pain unresponsive to oral analgesics, or an obstructing calculus associated with a solitary kidney.

! PEARLS & CONSIDERATIONS

COMMENTS

- Early identification and aggressive treatment of urinary tract infections is indicated for patients with struvite stones.
- Alkalinization of urine (i.e., achieving pH >7.5 with concurrent D-penicillamine or tiopronin therapy) is recommended for recurrent cystine stones.
- Stones <5 mm in diameter often pass spontaneously. Stones >10 mm diameter usually do not.
- In patients with asymptomatic renal stones, during average follow-up of 3.5 years, 20% grew by >50% and 28% became symptomatic.

SUGGESTED READINGS

Available at www.expertconsult.com

RELATED CONTENT

Kidney Stones (Patient Information)
Urinary Tract Infection (Patient Information)

AUTHOR: **LAMA NAZZAL, M.D., M.SC.**

[1]Picard R, et al: Medical expulsive therapy in adults with ureteric colic: a mutlicentre, randomised, placebo-controlled trial, *Lancet May* 18, 2015.

BASIC INFORMATION

DEFINITION

Uterine fibroids are benign tumors of muscle cell origin. They are discrete nodular tumors that vary in size and number and that may be found as subserosal, intramural, or submucosal masses. They can also be located in the cervix, broad ligament, or on a stalk (pedunculated) (Fig. 1U-13). They can also be parasitic, acquiring a blood supply from a nonuterine source.

SYNONYMS

Uterine leiomyomas
Uterine myomas

ICD-10CM CODES
D25.9 Leiomyoma of uterus, unspecified
D25.0 Submucous leiomyoma of uterus
D25.1 Intramural leiomyoma of uterus
D25.2 Subserosal leiomyoma of uterus

EPIDEMIOLOGY & DEMOGRAPHICS

- Estimated prevalence of 20% to 40% of reproductive age women
- The most common benign uterine tumor
- More common in black women than white women
- Asymptomatic fibroids may be present in 40% to 50% of women aged >40 yr
- May occur singly but are often multiple
- Less than half of all fibroids are estimated to produce symptoms
- Frequently diagnosed incidentally on pelvic examination
- There is increased familial incidence
- Potential to enlarge during pregnancy as well as regress after menopause
- <Symptomatic fibroids are the primary indication for approximately 30% of all hysterectomies
- Approximately 200,000 hysterectomies, 30,000 myomectomies, and thousands of selective uterine-artery embolizations and high-intensity focused ultrasound procedures are performed annually in the U.S. to remove or destroy uterine fibroids.[1]

PHYSICAL FINDINGS & CLINICAL PRESENTATION

- Enlarged, irregular uterus on pelvic examination
- Presenting symptoms:
  1. Menorrhagia (most common)
  2. Chronic pelvic pain (dysmenorrhea, dyspareunia, pelvic pressure)
  3. Acute pain (torsion of pedunculated fibroid, infarction, and degeneration)
  4. Urinary symptoms (frequency from bladder pressure, partial ureteral obstruction, complete ureteral obstruction)
  5. Rectosigmoid compression with constipation or intestinal obstruction
  6. Prolapse through cervix of pedunculated submucosal tumor
  7. Venous stasis of lower extremities
  8. Polycythemia
  9. Ascites

ETIOLOGY

Incompletely understood. It is suggested that fibroids arise from an original single smooth muscle cell in the myometrium. Each individual fibroid is monoclonal (all the cells are derived from one progenitor myocyte). Malignant degeneration of preexisting leiomyoma is extremely uncommon (<0.5%).

DIAGNOSIS

DIFFERENTIAL DIAGNOSIS

- Leiomyosarcoma
- Ovarian mass (neoplastic, nonneoplastic, endometrioma)
- Inflammatory mass
- Pregnancy

---

[1]Bulun SE: Uterine fibroids, *N Engl J Med* 369:1344-1355, 2013.

WORKUP

- Complete pelvic examination, rectovaginal examination
- Estimation of size of mass in centimeters and location of fibroids
- Endometrial sampling may be indicated (biopsy or dilation and curettage) when abnormal bleeding and pelvic mass are present
- If significant urinary symptoms are prominent, cystometry, cystoscopy to rule out bladder lesions, intravenous pyelogram to rule out impingement on urinary system

LABORATORY TESTS

- Pregnancy test
- Complete blood count, erythrocyte sedimentation rate

IMAGING STUDIES

- Pelvic ultrasound (Fig. 1U-14) is useful as a primary diagnostic modality. Transvaginal ultrasound commonly has higher diagnostic accuracy.
- MRI scan is helpful in planning treatment if malignancy is strongly suspected. Also important to localize fibroids, especially if myomectomy is contemplated. Size, number, and location of fibroids are also important if a minimally invasive myomectomy is considered.
- Saline infusion sonography is helpful in determining location and degree of intrusion into uterine cavity. Important if hysteroscopic resection is contemplated. Typically at least 50% of the fibroid must be intracavitary for a hysteroscopic approach to be successful.
- Hysteroscopy may provide direct evidence of intrauterine pathology or submucosal leiomyoma that distorts uterine cavity, and surgical resection may be performed during the same procedure.

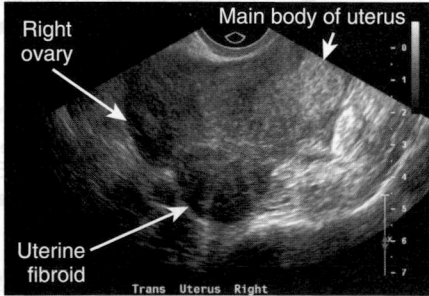

FIGURE 1U-14 Fibroid uterus: endovaginal ultrasound. Ultrasound is the primary modality used for evaluation of uterine fibroids (leiomyomas). Typical features include a well-circumscribed appearance. Fibroids may be hypoechoic or hyperechoic relative to the uterus. They may be exophytic or intramural, or they may project into the uterine cavity. Whereas malignant uterine tumors may invade adjacent structures, a fibroid is contained within the uterine serosa. Uterine tumors, both benign and malignant, can show central necrosis, which usually appears hypoechoic with ultrasound. In this 38-year-old woman, the fibroid is exophytic. The right ovary lies adjacent and is difficult to distinguish in this case. (From Broder JS: *Diagnostic imaging for the emergency physician*, Philadelphia, 2011, Saunders.)

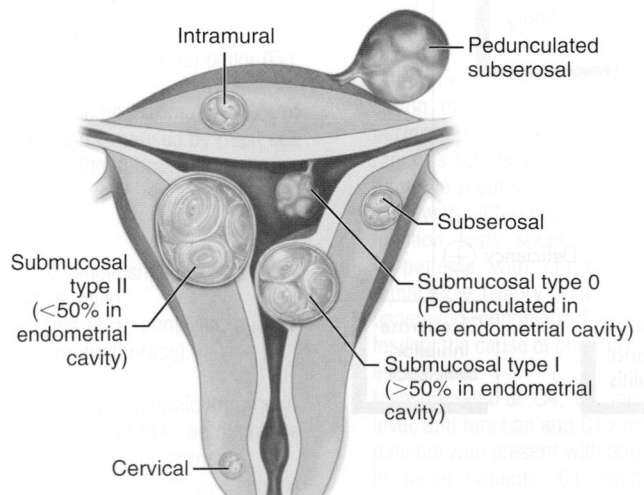

FIGURE 1U-13 Drawing of uterus in the coronal plane, illustrating possible location of uterine leiomyomas. (From Fielding JR et al: *Gynecologic imaging*, Philadelphia, 2011, Saunders.)

 **TREATMENT**

Management should be based on primary symptoms and may include observation with close follow-up, temporizing surgical therapies, embolization, medical management, or definitive surgical procedures. Treatment is generally indicated only when symptoms are present and are severe enough to be unacceptable to the patient.

NONSURGICAL Rx

- Patient observation and follow-up with periodic repeat pelvic examinations to ensure that tumors are not growing rapidly.
- Gonadotropin-releasing hormone (GnRH) agonist use results in 40% to 60% reduction in uterine volume. Hyperestrogenism, reversible bone loss, and hot flushes are associated with use. Limit to short-term use and consider low-dose hormonal replacement to minimize hypoestrogenic effects.
- Regrowth occurs in approximately 50% of women treated within a few months after cessation.
- Indications for GnRH:
  1. Fertility preservation in women with large myomas before attempting conception or preoperative myectomy treatment
  2. Anemia treatment to normalize hemoglobin before surgery
  3. Women approaching menopause to avoid surgery
  4. Preoperative for large myomas to make vaginal hysterectomy, hysteroscopic resection/ablation, or laparoscopic destruction more feasible
  5. Women with medical contraindications for surgery
  6. Personal or medical indications for delaying surgery
- Use of GnRH agonists may alter the consistency of the fibroid, making myomectomy more challenging.
- Progestational agents may also result in decrease in uterine size and amenorrhea, allowing iron therapy to treat anemia with limited success. Ulipristal acetate is a selective progesterone-receptor modulator that acts on progesterone receptors in myometrial and endometrial tissue and inhibits ovulation without causing large effects on estradiol levels or antiglucocorticoid activity. Recent trials have shown that treatment with ulipristal acetate for 13 wk effectively controlled excessive bleeding due to uterine fibroids and reduced the size of the fibroids.
- Other drugs used and under investigation:
  1. Danazol: androgen and multienzyme inhibitor of steroidogenesis
  2. Mifepristone: antiprogestogen shown to reduce the fibroid volume by 40% to 50% with amenorrhea
  3. Raloxifene: selective estrogen receptor modulator, either alone or with a GnRHa, shown to reduce the fibroid volume 70% up to 1 yr but only in postmenopausal women
  4. Fadrozole: aromatase inhibitor reported to have produced a 71% reduction in volume

SURGICAL Rx

- Indications
  1. Abnormal uterine bleeding with anemia refractory to hormonal therapy
  2. Chronic pain with severe dysmenorrhea, dyspareunia, or lower abdominal pressure/pain
  3. Acute pain, torsion, or prolapsing submucosal fibroid
  4. Urinary symptoms or signs such as hydronephrosis
  5. Rapid uterine enlargement premenopausal or any growth after menopause
  6. Infertility or recurrent pregnancy loss with submucous leiomyoma as only finding
  7. Enlarged uterus with compression symptoms or discomfort
- Procedures
  1. Hysterectomy (definitive procedure): Nearly 15% of women with uterine fibroids and a mean age of 45 yr require hysterectomy
  2. Abdominal myomectomy (to preserve fertility or due to patient preference)
  3. Vaginal myomectomy for prolapsed pedunculated submucous fibroid
  4. Hysteroscopic resection
  5. Laparoscopic/robotic myomectomy
  6. Uterine artery embolization (UAE): safe and effective short-term alternative to surgery, but its less invasive nature should be balanced against a higher rate for treatment failure or complications at 5 yr (32%) versus the surgery group (4%). Age 40 yr and under at embolization and history of previous myomectomy are significant predictors of embolization failure. If the patient wishes to preserve future fertility, UAE should not be performed.

COMPLICATIONS

- Red degeneration.
- Leiomyosarcoma (<0.1%). Recent concern has been voiced by the FDA regarding the use of morcellation in minimally invasive surgery because of the possibility of spreading malignancy in the peritoneal cavity.

REFERRAL

Consultation with gynecologic oncologist if suspicion of malignancy

SUGGESTED READINGS

Available at www.expertconsult.com

RELATED CONTENT

Uterine Fibroids (Patient Information)
Dysfunctional Uterine Bleeding (Related Key Topic)

AUTHOR: **RUBEN ALVERO, M.D.**

BASIC INFORMATION

DEFINITION
Uterine malignancy includes tumors from the endometrium and sarcomas. Uterine sarcoma is an abnormal proliferation of cells originating from the mesenchymal, or connective tissue, elements of the uterine wall (myometrium).

SYNONYMS
Leiomyosarcomas
Endometrial stromal sarcoma
Malignant mixed Müllerian tumors
Adenosarcomas

ICD-10CM CODES
C54.1 Malignant neoplasm of endometrium
C54.0 Malignant neoplasm of isthmus uteri
C54.8 Malignant neoplasm of overlapping sites of corpus uteri

EPIDEMIOLOGY & DEMOGRAPHICS
INCIDENCE: 17.1 cases per 1 million females. Endometrial cancer remains the most common gynecologic malignancy in the U.S.
PREVALENCE: Uterine sarcoma accounts for 4.3% of all cancers of the uterine corpus and is the most lethal gynecologic malignancy.
MEAN AGE AT DIAGNOSIS: 52 yr
RISK FACTORS: Box 1U-5 describes risk factors for uterine sarcoma

PHYSICAL FINDINGS & CLINICAL PRESENTATION
- Abnormal vaginal bleeding is the most common symptom.
- May also present as pelvic pain or pressure and pelvic mass on examination.

BOX 1U-5   Risk Factors for Uterine Sarcoma

Nulliparity
Obesity
History of pelvic radiation
Exposure to tamoxifen

From Fielding JR et al: *Gynecologic imaging*, Philadelphia, 2011, Saunders.

- May appear as tumor protruding through the cervix.
- Vaginal discharge may also be a presenting symptom.
- Rapidly enlarging uterus or pelvic mass.

ETIOLOGY
- The exact etiology is unknown.
- Prior pelvic radiation is a risk factor for sarcoma.
- Black women may be at higher risk.

DIAGNOSIS

DIFFERENTIAL DIAGNOSIS
Leiomyoma

WORKUP
Diagnosis is made histologically by biopsy for abnormal bleeding.

BOX 1U-6   Uterine Sarcoma Prognostic Factors

Tumor stage
Tumor grade
Tumor size
Patient age
Vascular space involvement
Mitotic count
Residual disease at surgery
Adjuvant chemotherapy

From Fielding JR et al: *Gynecologic imaging*, Philadelphia, 2011, Saunders.

BOX 1U-7   Uterine Sarcoma: Key Points

The disease mainly affects postmenopausal women.
Most patients present early with postmenopausal bleeding.
The primary treatment is hysterectomy.
Adjuvant radiotherapy to the pelvis is used if poor prognosis features in stage 1 or if spread has occurred beyond the corpus.

From Greer IA et al: *Mosby's color atlas and text of obstetrics and gynecology*, London, 2001, Harcourt.

LABORATORY TESTS
Chest radiography, CT scans, and MRI are used to evaluate metastatic lesions.

IMAGING STUDIES
- Chest x-ray is usually done as routine preoperative testing.
- CT scans (Fig. E1U-15) and MRI are useful for assessing tumor spread once diagnosis is made.

TREATMENT

NONPHARMACOLOGIC THERAPY
- Surgical excision is the mainstay of treatment.
- Grade and stage of tumor affect prognosis.
- The benefit of adjuvant radiotherapy in stage I endometrial adenocarcinoma to improve pelvic disease control and improve survival remains controversial despite several phase 3 trials.
- Chemotherapeutic agents have produced only partial and short-term responses.

DISPOSITION
- Survival varies with each type of sarcoma but is generally very poor. Box 1U-6 describes uterine prognostic factors.
- Five-year survival for leiomyosarcoma ranges from 48% for stage I to 0% for stage IV.
- Five-year survival for malignant mixed mesodermal tumor ranges from 36% for stage I to 6% for stage IV.

REFERRAL
Uterine sarcoma should be managed by a gynecologic oncologist and radiation oncologist. Key points in the management of uterine sarcoma are described in Box 1U-7.

SUGGESTED READINGS
Available at www.expertconsult.com

RELATED CONTENT
Uterine Cancer (Patient Information)
Endometrial Cancer (Related Key Topic)

AUTHOR: **RUBEN ALVERO, M.D.**

 **BASIC INFORMATION**

DEFINITION

Uveitis is inflammation of the uveal tract, including the iris, ciliary body, and choroid. It may also involve other contiguous structures such as the sclera, cornea, retina, and vitreous humor (Fig. 1U-16).

SYNONYMS

Anterior uveitis (iritis, iridocyclitis)
Intermediate uveitis (pars planitis)
Posterior uveitis (choroiditis)
Acute or chronic uveitis
Granulomatous or nongranulomatous uveitis

ICD-10CM CODES

H20.0	Acute and subacute iridocyclitis
H20.1	Chronic iridocyclitis
20.8	Other iridocyclitis
H20.9	Unspecified iridocyclitis
H44.131	Sympathetic uveitis, right eye
H44.132	Sympathetic uveitis, left eye
H44.133	Sympathetic uveitis, bilateral
H44.139	Sympathetic uveitis, unspecified eye

EPIDEMIOLOGY & DEMOGRAPHICS

INCIDENCE (IN U.S.): Common; busy ophthalmologist will see two or more cases per week.
PEAK INCIDENCE: Middle age or older.
PREVALENCE (IN U.S.): 17 cases per 100,000 persons
PREDOMINANT SEX: None
PREDOMINANT AGE: 38 yr. Although uveitis is less common in children than adults, it is believed to be more severe with an increased risk for vision-threatening complications.

PHYSICAL FINDINGS & CLINICAL PRESENTATION

- Symptoms of uveitis depend on the site of involvement and whether process is acute or insidious:
  1. Acute anterior uveitis: pain and photophobia. Vision may not be affected initially.

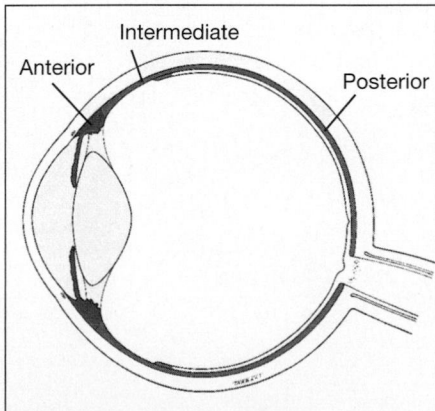

FIGURE 1U-16 Anatomic classification of uveitis. (From Kanski JJ, Bowling B: *Clinical ophthalmology, a systematic approach,* ed 7, Philadelphia, 2010, Saunders.)

2. Posterior uveitis: floaters, hazy vision. Involvement of the retina may produce blind spots or flashing lights.
3. Insidious anterior uveitis: symptoms may not be present until scarring cataracts and loss of vision occur.
- Photophobia
- Blurred visual acuity
- Irregular pupil
- Hazy cornea
- Abnormal cells and flare in anterior chamber or vitreous humor ("flare cells") noted with slit lamp examination
- Retinal hemorrhage, vascular sheathing
- Conjunctival injection
- Ciliary flush
- Keratitic precipitates (white precipitates on the posterior surface of the cornea)
- Hazy vitreous
- Retinal inflammation
- Iris nodules

ETIOLOGY

- Infections: herpes simplex virus, cytomegalovirus, toxoplasmosis, tuberculosis, syphilis, HIV
- Systemic disorders (autoimmunity): sarcoidosis, Behçet's syndrome, HLA-B27–associated diseases (e.g., ankylosing spondylitis, psoriatic arthritis), inflammatory bowel disease, juvenile idiopathic arthritis (Fig. E1U-17)
- Idiopathic (>50% of patients)

 **DIAGNOSIS**

DIFFERENTIAL DIAGNOSIS

- Glaucoma
- Conjunctivitis
- Retinal detachment
- Retinopathy
- Keratitis
- Scleritis
- Episcleritis
- Masquerading syndromes: lymphoma, uveal melanoma, metastases (breast, lung, renal), leukemia, retinitis pigmentosa, retinoblastoma

WORKUP

- Comprehensive eye examination including slit lamp exam, dilated ophthalmoscopy

LABORATORY TESTS

- Complete blood count
- Laboratory tests for specific inflammatory causes cited previously in "Workup" (e.g., antinuclear antibody, erythrocyte sedimentation rate, syphilis (VDRL), HLA-B27, purified protein derivative, Lyme titer, angiotensin converting enzyme [ACE])

IMAGING STUDIES

- Chest radiograph in suspected sarcoidosis, tuberculosis, histoplasmosis
- Sacroiliac radiograph in suspected ankylosing spondylitis

 **TREATMENT**

ACUTE GENERAL Rx

- Corticosteroids are the mainstay of therapy for noninfectious causes. The route and dosage of medication depends on the location of inflammation, the severity, and the presence of systemic disease. Cycloplegic drops (cyclopentolate, homatropine BID to QID) and topical steroids (prednisone acetate 1% 1 gtt qh during day, prn at night until favorable response, then q4 to 6h); avoid topical corticosteroids in infectious uveitis. Periocular corticosteroid injections can be used for posterior disease; they have the advantage of achieving high intraocular levels of steroids without the systemic side effects of oral corticosteroids.
- Antibiotics for bacterial infections and antiviral agents, when infection is suspected, should be started to prevent retinal damage.
- Systemic steroids if appropriate for the underlying disease. Systemic corticosteroid therapy is generally reserved for patients with systemic disorders and those with bilateral disease that is refractory to local medication or those with major ocular disability or retinitis.
- Antimetabolites when indicated. Immunosuppressive medications used in steroid-dependent or refractory uveitis include methotrexate, sulfasalazine, azathioprine, cyclosporine, and tacrolimus. These medications can have significant toxicity and should be prescribed only by physicians experienced with their use.
- High-dose IV daclizumab has been reported as effective in reducing active inflammation in active juvenile idiopathic arthritis (JIA)-associated anterior uveitis. Additional trials are needed to better assess efficacy and safety.

REFERRAL

Urgent referral to ophthalmologist for diagnosis and treatment

PEARLS & CONSIDERATIONS

COMMENTS

Chronic anterior uveitis is the most common form of intraocular inflammation in children. JIA is the most common cause.

SUGGESTED READINGS

Available at www.expertconsult.com

AUTHOR: **R. SCOTT HOFFMAN, M.D.**

BASIC INFORMATION

DEFINITION

Bleeding per vagina at any time during pregnancy must be regarded as abnormal and is associated with an increased likelihood of pregnancy complications.

SYNONYM

Hemorrhage

ICD-10CM CODES

O20.8	Other hemorrhage in early pregnancy
O20.9	Hemorrhage in early pregnancy, unspecified
O03.9	Complete or unspecified spontaneous abortion
O44.10	Placenta previa with hemorrhage, unspecified trimester
O45.8X9	Other premature separation of placenta, unspecified trimester

EPIDEMIOLOGY & DEMOGRAPHICS

- Common in U.S.; 20% to 25% of patients have vaginal spotting/bleeding in first trimester; of those, miscarriage occurs in 50%.
- Occurs in women of childbearing age.
- Between 1% and 2% of all pregnancies in the U.S. are ectopic.
- After one ectopic pregnancy, the chance of another is 7% to 15%.
- Ectopic pregnancy is the leading cause of maternal mortality in the first trimester.
- Average reported frequency for placental abruption is about 1 in 150 deliveries.
- Incidence of placenta previa is 1 in 200 deliveries (0.5%).

PHYSICAL FINDINGS & CLINICAL PRESENTATION

- Bleeding: ranges from scant to life-threatening with hemodynamic instability
- Color: brown to bright red
- Can be painless or painful (cramps, back pain, severe abdominal pain)
- Fetal compromise: ranges from none to fetal demise

ETIOLOGY

- Influenced by gestational age
- Vaginal
- Cervical
- Uterine

DIAGNOSIS

DIFFERENTIAL DIAGNOSIS

- Any gestational age:
  1. Cervical lesions: polyps, decidual reaction, neoplasia
  2. Vaginal trauma
  3. Cervicitis/vulvovaginitis
  4. Postcoital trauma
  5. Bleeding dyscrasias

- Gestation <20 wk:
  1. Spontaneous abortion
  2. Presence of intrauterine device
  3. Ectopic pregnancy
  4. Molar pregnancy
  5. Implantation bleeding
  6. Low-lying placenta
- Gestation >20 wk:
  1. Molar pregnancy
  2. Placenta previa
  3. Placental abruption
  4. Vasa previa
  5. Marginal separation of the placenta
  6. Bloody show at term
  7. Preterm labor
- Section II describes the differential diagnosis of vaginal bleeding in pregnancy.

WORKUP

- Gestation<20 wk (Section III, "Bleeding, Early Pregnancy"):
  1. Pelvic examination
  2. Laparoscopy
  3. Laparotomy (rarely required)
  4. Ultrasound to verify viable intrauterine pregnancy when beta hCG levels achieve threshold values (≥1500 mIU/mL for transvaginal sonography)
- Gestation >20 wk:
  1. Ultrasound to locate placenta before pelvic examination
  2. If placenta previa, no speculum or bimanual examination
  3. If preterm labor, appropriate evaluation done

LABORATORY TESTS

- Urine pregnancy test: If positive, get quantitative beta human chorionic gonadotropin (βhCG). The following are typical although not entirely exclusive patterns:
  1. Early pregnancy: follow serially every 48 hr
  2. Normal pregnancy: βhCG doubles approximately every 48 hr
  3. Spontaneous abortion: βhCG level will fall
  4. Ectopic pregnancy: βhCG level will rise inappropriately (less than expected; threshold increase over 48 hr should be ≥66%)
  5. Molar pregnancy: βhCG level is higher than expected for gestational age
- CBC
- Blood type and screen (Rh-negative patients need RhoGAM)
- Coagulation profile (useful in missed abortion and abruption)
- Cervical cultures/wet mount
- Pap smear for cervical malignancy; caution with biopsy, because cervix can bleed extensively

IMAGING STUDIES

Ultrasound:
- 5 to 6 wk: gestational sac (transvaginally); βhCG >>1500 mIU/mL is discriminatory level for seeing a singleton gestation
- 6 to 7 wk: fetal cardiac activity
- Molar pregnancy: characteristic cluster of cysts

- Location of placenta
- Degree of placental separation: difficult to assess
- Evidence of subchorionic hemorrhage

 TREATMENT

NONPHARMACOLOGIC THERAPY

- Pelvic rest: no coitus, douching, or tampons
- Bed rest, if >20 wk
- Counseling: genetic, bereavement

ACUTE GENERAL Rx

- Hemodynamic stabilization
- Emergency D&C, laparotomy, or cesarean section as necessary

CHRONIC Rx

Depends on diagnosis

DISPOSITION

Depends on diagnosis

REFERRAL

- If patient is unstable and needs emergency OB/GYN management and/or surgery
- If patient has diagnosis of ectopic or molar pregnancy, because immediate surgical treatment or medical intervention is indicated
- Perinatal consultation for high-risk pregnancy

SUGGESTED READINGS

Available at www.expertconsult.com

RELATED CONTENT

Abruptio Placentae (Related Key Topic)
Cervical Insufficiency (Related Key Topic)
Ectopic Pregnancy (Related Key Topic)
Molar Pregnancy (Related Key Topic)
Placenta Previa (Related Key Topic)
Sheehan's Syndrome (Related Key Topic)
Spontaneous Miscarriage (Related Key Topic)

AUTHOR: **RUBEN ALVERO, M.D.**

BASIC INFORMATION

DEFINITION

An abnormal passageway between the vagina and another epithelialized surface (Fig. 1V-1)

SYNONYM

Vaginal sinus

ICD-10CM CODES
N82 Fistulae involving the female genital tract
N82.2 Fistula of vagina to small intestine
N82.3 Fistula of vagina to large intestine

EPIDEMIOLOGY & DEMOGRAPHICS

INCIDENCE: After benign hysterectomy: <1% (0.08%-0.26%); after radical hysterectomy: 1% to 4%. Incidence is difficult to estimate in developing countries because of lack of medical care and medical follow-up after obstetric care.

PREVALENCE: Rare in the developed world from obstetric complications, but in developing countries, the best estimate of prevalence is as high as 124 in 100,000.

RISK FACTORS: *In developing countries*
- Obstetric trauma
- Prolonged labor
- Cephalopelvic disproportion causing ischemia and necrosis of the tissue between the fetal head and maternal pubic bone

In developed countries
- Fistula resulting from obstetric trauma are primarily related to vaginal lacerations, for which the risk factors include:
  1. Primiparity
  2. Midline episiotomies
  3. Increasing birth weights
  4. Use of vaginal forceps
- Abdominal hysterectomy, especially with the following:
  1. Extensive bladder dissection
  2. Iatrogenic injury of the bowel or bladder

3. Prolonged operating times
4. Large blood loss
5. Large volume uterus
6. Coexisting pelvic adhesions distorting the normal pelvic anatomy
- Invasive cancer
- Pelvic radiation, reported to be dependent on dosimetry
- Chronic inflammatory disease
  1. Crohn disease
  2. Diverticulitis
- Pelvic infection
- `Tuberculosis
  1. Syphilis
  2. Lymphogranuloma venereum
- Trauma
- Previous pelvic surgery
- Diabetes mellitus
- Age >50, likely as a result of poor tissue quality from menopausal estrogen deficiency, although some studies have refuted this.
- Tobacco usage
- Foreign bodies

PHYSICAL FINDINGS & CLINICAL PRESENTATION

- Flatus, stool, or urine per vagina
- Frequent urinary tract infections
- Mucopurulent malodorous discharge per vagina
- Dyspareunia
- Perineal pain
- Recurrent vaginal infections

ETIOLOGY

- Obstetric
  1. Incompletely repaired or unidentified vaginal lacerations
  2. Prolonged pressure between the fetal head and the maternal pubic bone, causing tissue necrosis
- Gynecologic
  1. Poor-quality tissue with prolonged healing as a result of estrogen deficiency, infection, malignancy, or prior radiation therapy

DIAGNOSIS

DIFFERENTIAL DIAGNOSIS

- Rectal or urinary incontinence
- Pelvic inflammatory disease
- Vaginal infection
- Vaginal fistula
  1. Vesicovaginal
  2. Urethrovaginal
  3. Ureterovaginal
  4. Rectovaginal
- Urinary tract infection

WORKUP

- Thorough history and physical exam, specifically, questioning about Crohn disease symptomology; constitutional symptoms such as weight loss and fatigue, with malignancy in mind
- Obtaining of past medical records specific to obstetric and surgical procedures
- Evaluation of patient's rectal and urinary continence
- Physical exam, looking for extraintestinal signs consistent with Crohn disease; lymphadenopathy; inspection of perineum and perianal area for evidence of abscess, obvious fistula, or scarring; pelvic exam including lighted speculum exam for any vulvar, vaginal, or cervical anomaly, excluding PID
- Biopsy of fistula tract

LABORATORY TEST(S)

- Urinalysis
- Urine culture
- Complete blood count
- Administration of IV indigo carmine (if seen vaginally, diagnostic of vesicovaginal fistula)

IMAGING STUDIES

- Proctoscopy for suspected rectovaginal fistula
- Vaginogram (Fig. 1V-2)
- Cystoscopy
- CT of the abdomen and pelvis to exclude malignancy (especially in women with no history of obstetric trauma, previous fistula, IBD, or known pelvic malignancy) (Fig. 1V-2)
- Endoanal ultrasound, with or without hydrogen peroxide contrast injected into the suspected fistula tract
- Magnetic resonance imaging
- Intravenous urogram
- Retrograde ureteropyelography

TREATMENT

NONPHARMACOLOGIC THERAPY

- Surgical repair, with multiple documented approaches
  1. Transvaginal
  2. Perineal
  3. Abdominal
  4. Laparoscopic
  5. Robot assisted
  6. Transrectal
- If vesicovaginal identified early
  1. Prolonged urinary catheter placement, greater than 3 weeks

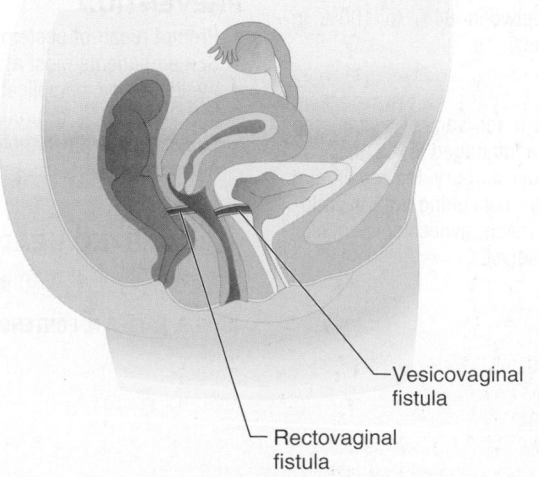

Vesicovaginal fistula

Rectovaginal fistula

FIGURE 1V-1 The two most common types of vaginal fistulas are vesicovaginal and rectovaginal. (From Fielding JR et al: *Gynecologic imaging,* Philadelphia, 2011, Saunders.)

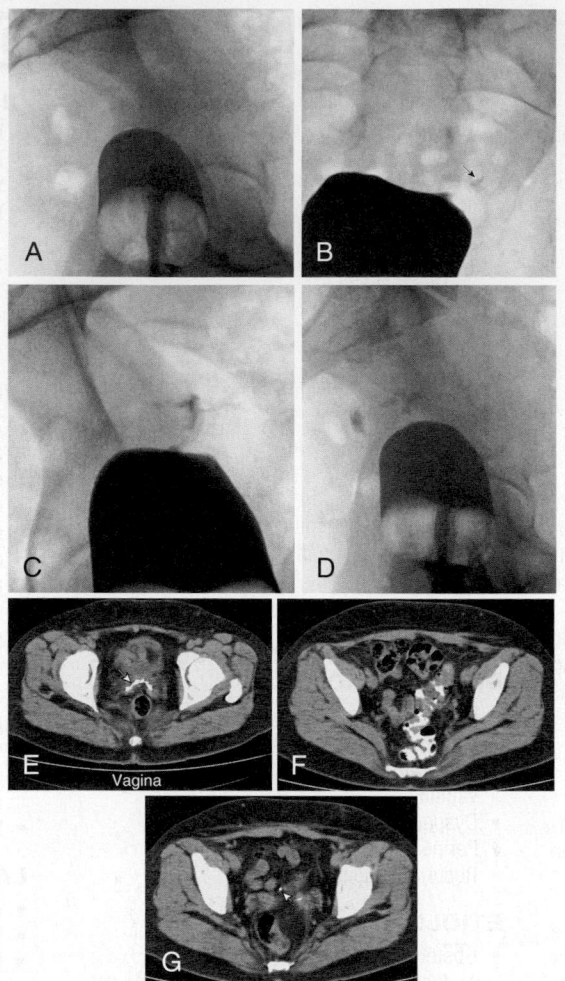

FIGURE 1V-2 A 44-year-old woman with gas and stool per vaginum 1 year after hysterectomy. Vaginal fistula was treated medically. **A,** Vaginogram, patient in left lateral position. **B,** Vaginogram, patient supine. The left apical vaginal fistula has just started to fill with contrast agent (*arrow*). **C,** Contrast agent is extending horizontally, likely in a loop of bowel. **D,** Vaginogram, patient in left lateral position, demonstrates small fistula to a loop of bowel, likely the rectosigmoid colon based on its relationship to the sacrum. **E,** Unenhanced computed tomographic (CT) scan of the pelvis immediately after the vaginogram demonstrates residual contrast agent in the vagina (*arrow*). **F,** CT scan confirms contrast agent from the vagina in the rectosigmoid colon. **G,** CT scan demonstrates 3 mm diameter short fistula to the rectosigmoid (*arrow*). (From Fielding JR et al: *Gynecologic imaging,* Philadelphia, 2011, Saunders.)

ACUTE GENERAL Rx

- Treatment of urinary or vaginal infection
- Estrogen replacement therapy, local vs. systemic if no contraindications
- Surgical repair of fistula with subsequent pelvic rest for 4 to 6 wk
- Minimizing Valsalva maneuvers

CHRONIC Rx

- If initial surgical management fails, repeat operations tailored to the cause of the fistula would be indicated, such as advancement flaps, sphincteroplasty, coloanal anastomosis (for rectovaginal fistula), gracilis flap.

DISPOSITION

- Cure rates after surgical repair vary in the literature, especially with the type of fistula repaired. With early intervention, estimated cure rates are between 84% to 100% in developed countries.

REFERRAL

- If there is concern for vaginal fistula, the patient should be managed by a surgeon familiar with fistula surgery for repair and follow-up. Consider consulting with a urologist, colorectal surgeon, gynecologic oncologist, or urogynecologist.

PEARLS & CONSIDERATIONS

PREVENTION

- Prompt repair of obstetric lacerations
- Screen patients most at risk before surgery
- Avoid urologic complications in surgery (e.g., injury to bladder or ureters)
- Cystoscopy with complicated hysterectomy dissections

SUGGESTED READINGS

Available online at www.expertconsult.com

AUTHOR: **AMBER N. FONTENOT FERRISS, M.D.**

BASIC INFORMATION

DEFINITION

Vaginal malignancy is an abnormal proliferation of vaginal epithelium demonstrating malignant cells below the basement membrane.

SYNONYMS

Squamous cell carcinoma of the vagina
Adenocarcinoma of the vagina
Melanoma of the vagina
Sarcoma of the vagina
Endodermal sinus tumor

ICD-10CM CODE

C52 Malignant neoplasm of vagina

EPIDEMIOLOGY & DEMOGRAPHICS

INCIDENCE: 0.42 cases per 100,000 persons
PREVALENCE: Vaginal cancer is the second rarest gynecologic cancer. It comprises 2% of malignancies of the female genital tract.
MEAN AGE AT DIAGNOSIS: Predominantly a disease of menopause. Mean age at diagnosis is 60 yr.

PHYSICAL FINDINGS & CLINICAL PRESENTATION

- Majority of cases are asymptomatic
- Postmenopausal vaginal bleeding and/or vaginal discharge are the most common symptoms
- May also present as pelvic pain or pressure, dyspareunia, dysuria, malodor, or postcoital bleeding
- May present as a vaginal lesion or abnormal Pap smear

ETIOLOGY

- The exact etiology is unknown.
- Most vaginal cancers are related to infection with HPV. HPV is implicated in 9 of 10 vaginal cancers and vaginal intraepithelial neoplasias. Cervical cancers have a similar risk factor. Vaginal intraepithelial neoplasia is believed to be a precursor for squamous cell carcinoma of the vagina.
- Long-term pessary use has been associated with vaginal malignancy.
- Prior pelvic radiation may be a risk factor.
- Clear-cell adenocarcinoma may be related to in utero diethylstilbestrol exposure (DES). Treatment of pregnant women with DES ended in the early 1970s, and it is anticipated that this spike in clear cell tumors will abate in the future.

DIAGNOSIS

DIFFERENTIAL DIAGNOSIS

- Extension from other primary carcinoma more common than primary vaginal cancer
- Vaginitis

WORKUP

- Diagnosis is made histologically by biopsy.
- Colposcopy and biopsy should follow suspicious Pap smear.
- Cystoscopy, proctosigmoidoscopy, chest radiography, IV urography, and barium enema may be used for clinical staging.
- CT scan (Fig. 1V-3), FDG, PET scan, and MRI are used to evaluate spread.
- Staging I to IV (Fig. 1V-4).

IMAGING STUDIES

- Chest radiography, IV urography, and barium enema are used for staging.
- CT scan and MRI are good for assessing tumor spread.

TREATMENT

NONPHARMACOLOGIC THERAPY

- Radiation therapy is the mainstay of treatment.
- Stage I tumors that are small and confined to the posterior, upper third of the vagina may be treated with radical surgery.
- Other stages require a whole-pelvis, interstitial, and/or intracavitary radiation therapy.

- Chemotherapy is used in conjunction with radiotherapy in rare select cases.

DISPOSITION

Five-year survival ranges from 80% for stage I to 17% for stage IV.

REFERRAL

Vaginal cancer should be managed by a gynecologic oncologist and radiation oncologist.

SUGGESTED READINGS

Available at www.expertconsult.com

RELATED CONTENT

Vaginal Cancer (Patient Information)

AUTHOR: **RUBEN ALVERO, M.D.**

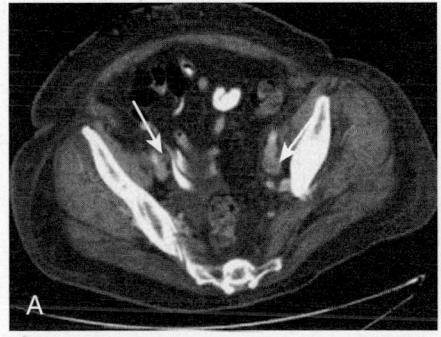
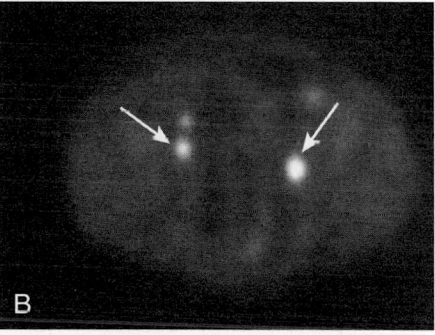

FIGURE 1V-3 Vaginal cancer with lymphadenopathy. A, CT of pelvis showing mildly enlarged external iliac nodes suggestive of metastases *(arrows).* **B,** Axial FDG PET scan showing hypermetabolic nodes as hyperintense spots confirming metastases. (From Abeloff MD: *Clinical oncology,* ed 3, Philadelphia, 2004, Churchill Livingstone.)

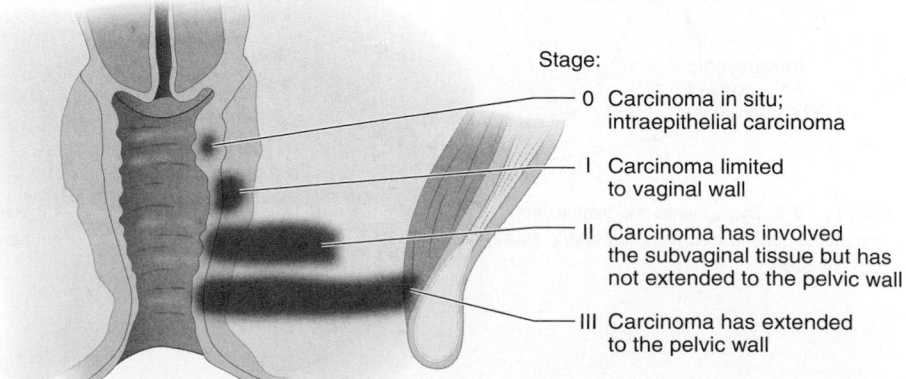

Stage:

0 Carcinoma in situ; intraepithelial carcinoma

I Carcinoma limited to vaginal wall

II Carcinoma has involved the subvaginal tissue but has not extended to the pelvic wall

III Carcinoma has extended to the pelvic wall

FIGURE 1V-4 Staging system for vaginal cancer. Metastatic disease that involves the bladder or rectum is stage IV-a. Metastatic disease beyond the pelvis is stage IV-b. (From Copeland LJ: *Textbook of gynecology,* ed 2, Philadelphia, 2000, Saunders.)

 BASIC INFORMATION

DEFINITION

Vaginismus refers to the involuntary spasm of the vaginal, introital, and/or levator ani muscles, preventing penetration or causing painful intercourse.

ICD-10CM CODES
N94.1 Vaginismus
F52.5 Non-organic vaginismus
F52.5 Vaginismus not due to a substance or known physiological condition

EPIDEMIOLOGY & DEMOGRAPHICS

INCIDENCE: Estimated at 11.7% to 42% of women presenting to sexual dysfunction clinics.
PREVALENCE: Affects approximately 1 in 200 women.
PREDOMINANT SEX: Affects only females.
RISK FACTORS: Any previous sexual trauma, including incest or rape.

PHYSICAL FINDINGS & CLINICAL PRESENTATION

- Fear of pain with coitus.
- Dyspareunia.
- Orgasmic dysfunction.

ETIOLOGY

- Learned conditioned response (Fig. 1V-5) to real or imagined painful vaginal experience (e.g., traumatic speculum examination, incest, rape)
- Vaginitis
- Pelvic inflammatory disease
- Endometriosis
- Anatomic anomalies
- Atrophic vaginitis
- Mucosal tears
- Inadequate lubrication
- Focal vulvitis
- Painful hymenal tags
- Scarring secondary to episiotomy
- Skin disorders
- Topical allergies
- Postherpetic neuralgia

DIAGNOSIS

WORKUP

- Thorough history (including sexual history)
- Careful pelvic examination
- Behavioral therapy

TREATMENT

NONPHARMACOLOGIC THERAPY

- Deconditioning the response by systematic self-administered progressive dilation techniques using fingers or dilators
- Behavioral and/or psychosexual therapy

ACUTE GENERAL Rx

- Botulinum toxin therapy given locally has been shown to relieve the perineal muscle spasms associated with vaginismus, allowing resumption of intercourse.
  1. Acts by preventing neuromuscular transmission, causing muscle weakness.
  2. Considered experimental treatment for vaginismus at this time.
- Cause should be determined by history and explained to the patient so that she understands the mechanics of the muscle spasms.
- Patient must be motivated to desire painless vaginal insertion for such reasons as pleasurable coitus, tampon insertion, or gynecologic examination.
- Patient (and her partner) must be willing to patiently undergo the process of systematic desensitization and counseling.

DISPOSITION

A high percentage of successfully treated patients

REFERRAL

To a gynecologist or sex therapist

PEARLS & CONSIDERATIONS

COMMENTS

- May uncover early sexual abuse or an aversion to sexuality in general
- American Association of Sex Educators, Counselors and Therapists, 11 Dupont Circle, NW, Washington, DC, 20036
- Sex Information and Education Council of the United States (SIECUS), 90 John St., New York, NY 10038

SUGGESTED READINGS

Available at www.expertconsult.com

RELATED CONTENT

Dyspareunia (Related Key Topic)

AUTHOR: **RUBEN ALVERO, M.D.**

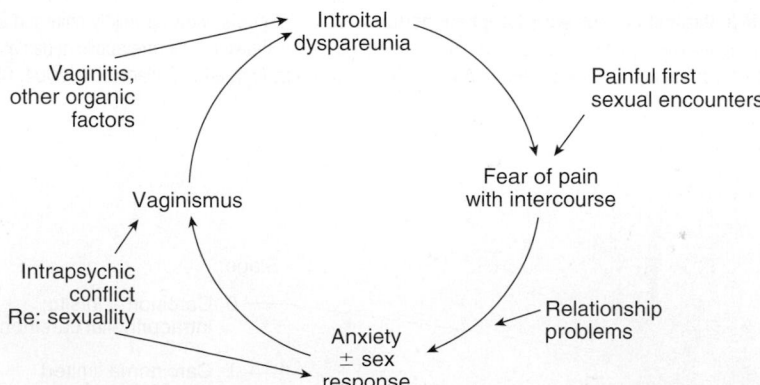

FIGURE 1V-5 Dyspareunia and vaginismus cycle. (From Lentz GM: *Emotional aspects of gynecology sexual dysfunction, eating disorders, substance abuse, depression, grief, loss; comprehensive gynecology*, St Louis, 2007, Mosby.)

BASIC INFORMATION

DEFINITION

Estrogen-deficient vulvovaginitis is the irritation and/or inflammation of the vulva and vagina because of progressive thinning and atrophic changes secondary to estrogen deficiency (Fig. 1V-6).

SYNONYMS

Atrophic vaginitis
Vulvovaginal atrophy

ICD-10CM CODE
N95.2 Post-menopausal atrophic vaginitis

EPIDEMIOLOGY & DEMOGRAPHICS

- Seen most often in postmenopausal women
- Average age of menopause is 52 yr
- Up to half of postmenopausal women are symptomatic, but a quarter of these will not seek treatment

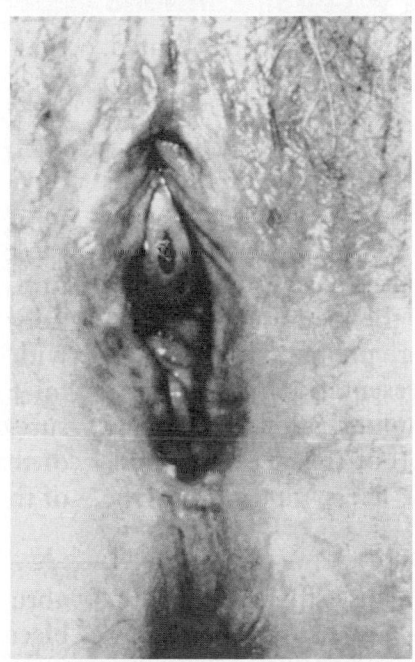

FIGURE 1V-6 Advanced postmenopausal atrophy of the vulva in a 72-year-old woman. (From Symonds EM, Macpherson MBA: *Color atlas of obstetrics and gynecology,* St Louis, 1994, Mosby.)

PHYSICAL FINDINGS & CLINICAL PRESENTATION

- Thinning of pubic hair, labia minora and majora
- Decreased secretions from the vestibular glands, with vaginal dryness
- Regression of subcutaneous fat
- Vulvar and vaginal itching
- Dyspareunia
- Dysuria and urinary frequency
- Vaginal spotting

ETIOLOGY

- Estrogen deficiency. Estrogen is essential to maintaining the urogenital environment. Postmenopausal thinning of the vaginal epithelium and increase in subepithelial connective tissue result in loss of rugal folds and elasticity. Reduced blood flow also contributes to a decline in vaginal secretions.
- Smoking and use of antiestrogen medications (e.g., aromatase inhibitors) increase the risk of vulvovaginal atrophy.

DIAGNOSIS

DIFFERENTIAL DIAGNOSIS

- Infectious vulvovaginitis
- Squamous cell hyperplasia
- Lichen sclerosus
- Vulvar malignancy
- Vaginal malignancy
- Cervical and endometrial malignancy
- Irritant contact dermatitis

WORKUP

- Pelvic examination
- Speculum examination
- Pap smear
- Possible endometrial biopsy if bleeding

LABORATORY TESTS

FSH and estradiol: generally after menopause, estradiol <15 pg/mL and FSH >40 mIU/mL (diagnosis of menopause usually made on a clinical basis and does not usually require FSH and/or estradiol testing)

TREATMENT

NONPHARMACOLOGIC THERAPY

- Avoidance of contact irritants such as scented soaps and feminine hygiene products
- Avoidance of synthetic undergarments, tight-fitting clothing

GENERAL Rx

- Regular use of vaginal moisturizers (e.g., Replens) can decrease vaginal itching and irritation.
- Use of water or silicone-based personal lubricants (e.g., Astroglide) during intercourse is useful to reduce dyspareunia.
- Conjugated estrogen vaginal cream intravaginally. Estradiol vaginal cream (Estrace).
  2 to 4 g/day × 2 wk then
  1 to 2 g/day × 2 wk then
  1 to 2 g × 2-3 days/wk
- Vagifem (estradiol vaginal tablets) 25 mg inserted intravaginally daily for 2 wk then twice weekly. May take up to 12 wk to feel the full benefits of the medication.
- Conjugated estrogen vaginal cream: 2 to 4 g qd (3 wk on, 1 wk off) for 3 to 5 mo.
- Hormone replacement therapy (HRT): use ultra-low doses. Estrogen use should be reviewed every 3 to 6 mo, with an attempt to taper or discontinue its use.
- Estraderm patch 0.05 mg ×2 per week.
- If uterus present:
  1. Estrogen +2.5 mg PO Provera qd *or*
  2. Estrogen +5 to 10 mg PO Provera 14 days each mo

DISPOSITION

The symptoms should be improved with the therapy. Caution for vaginal bleeding if uterus present.

REFERRAL

To obstetrician/gynecologist if vaginal bleeding

SUGGESTED READINGS
Available at www.expertconsult.com

Pruritus Vulvae (Related Key Topic)
AUTHOR: **RUBEN ALVERO, M.D.**

 **BASIC INFORMATION**

DEFINITION

Fungal vulvovaginitis is the inflammation of vulva and vagina caused by *Candida* spp.

SYNONYMS

Candidiasis, vulvovaginal
Monilial vulvovaginitis
Vulvovaginal candidiasis
VVC

ICD-10CM CODE
B37.3 Candidiasis of vulva and vagina

EPIDEMIOLOGY & DEMOGRAPHICS

- Second most common cause of vaginal infection
- 75% of women will have at least one episode during their childbearing years, and ~40% to 50% of these will have a second attack.
- No symptoms in 20% to 40% of women who have positive cultures

PHYSICAL FINDINGS & CLINICAL PRESENTATION

- Intense vulvar and vaginal pruritus
- Edema and erythema of vulva
- Thick, curd-like vaginal discharge ("cottage cheese" discharge)
- Adherent, dry, white, curdy patches attached to vaginal mucosa

ETIOLOGY

- *Candida albicans* is responsible for 80% to 95% of vaginal fungal infections.
- *Candida tropicalis* and *Torulopsis glabrata* (*Candida glabrata*) are the most common nonalbicans *Candida* species that can induce vaginitis.

PREDISPOSING HOST FACTORS

- Pregnancy
- Oral contraceptives (high-estrogen)
- Diabetes mellitus
- Antibiotics
- Immunosuppression (e.g., HIV)
- Tight, poorly ventilated, nylon underclothing, with increased local perineal moisture and temperature

 **DIAGNOSIS**

DIFFERENTIAL DIAGNOSIS

- Bacterial vaginosis
- *Trichomonas* vaginitis
- Atrophic vaginitis

Section II describes the differential diagnosis of vaginal discharges and infections.

WORKUP

- Pelvic examination
- Speculum examination
- Hyphae or budding spores on 10% KOH preparation (positive in 50%-70% of individuals with yeast infection)
- Normal vaginal pH
  Section III, "Vaginal Discharge," describes the evaluation of discharge.

LABORATORY TESTS

Culture, especially recurrence for identification

 **TREATMENT**

ACUTE GENERAL Rx

- Cure rate of the various azole derivatives 85% to 90%; little evidence of superiority of one azole agent over another.
- No significant differences in persistent symptoms with oral or vaginal treatment.
- Fluconazole 150 mg PO × 1 is preferred treatment.
- Cure rate of polyene cream, and suppositories: 75% to 80%.
- Miconazole 200-mg suppository, one suppository ×3 days or 2% vaginal cream, one applicatorful intravaginally qhs ×7.
- Clotrimazole 200-mg vaginal tablet, one tablet intravaginally qhs ×3 or 100-mg vaginal tablet one tablet intravaginally qhs ×7, or 1% vaginal cream intravaginally qhs ×7.
- Butoconazole 2% cream one applicator intravaginally qhs ×3.
- Terconazole 80-mg suppository or 0.8% vaginal cream, one suppository or one applicator intravaginally qhs ×3 or 0.4% vaginal cream, one applicator intravaginally qhs ×7.
- Gynecazole-1 vaginal cream, one applicator intravaginally ×1.
- Tioconazole 6.5% ointment (Vagi-stat), one applicator intravaginally ×1.
- In pregnant patient, treat with 7-day course of topical imidazole.

CHRONIC Rx (FOUR OR MORE SYMPTOMATIC EPISODES ANNUALLY)

- Resistance or recurrence
  1. 14- to 21-day course of 7-day regimens mentioned in "Acute General Rx"
  2. Fluconazole 150 mg PO ×2, 3 days apart
  3. Ketoconazole 200 mg PO bid ×5 to 14 days
  4. Itraconazole 200 mg PO qd ×3 days
  5. Boric acid 600-mg capsule intravaginally bid ×14 days

- Prophylactic regimens
  1. Clotrimazole one 500-mg vaginal tablet each month
  2. Ketoconazole 200 mg PO bid ×5 days each month
  3. Fluconazole 150 mg PO ×1 each month
  4. Miconazole 100-mg vaginal tablet ×2 weekly

DISPOSITION

- If symptoms do not resolve completely with treatment, or if they recur within a 2- to 3-mo period, further evaluation is indicated.
- Reexamination and possibly culture are necessary.
- Positive culture in absence of symptoms should not lead to treatment. Approximately 30% of women harbor *Candida* spp. and other species in the vagina.

REFERRAL

To obstetrician/gynecologist for recurrence

! **PEARLS & CONSIDERATIONS**

COMMENTS

- No evidence that treating a woman's male sexual partner significantly improves woman's infection or reduces her rate of relapse.
- Many *Candida albicans* strains produce hyaluronidase, which is an enzyme that degrades hyaluronan. Elevated hyaluronan levels in vaginal secretions are associated with increased itching, burning, and discharge in women with recurrent vulvovaginal candidiasis.
- Twenty percent of cases of recurrent vulvovaginal candidiasis are due to *Candida* species other than *C. albicans*.

SUGGESTED READINGS
Available at www.expertconsult.com

RELATED CONTENT
Candidiasis (Patient Information)
Vaginal Yeast Infection (Patient Information)
Pruritus Vulvae (Related Key Topic)
Vaginitis, Prepubescent (Related Key Topic)

AUTHOR: **RUBEN ALVERO, M.D.**

BASIC INFORMATION

DEFINITION

Prepubescent vulvovaginitis is an inflammatory condition of the vulva and vagina.

ICD-10CM CODES
N76.0 Acute vaginitis
N76.1 Subacute and chronic vaginitis

EPIDEMIOLOGY & DEMOGRAPHICS

- Most common gynecologic problem of pre-menarchal girls.
- Prepubertal girls are susceptible to irritation and trauma because of the absence of protective hair and labial fat pads and the lack of estrogenization with atrophic vaginal mucosa.
- Symptoms of vulvovaginitis and introital irritation and discharge account for 80% to 90% of gynecologic visits.
- Nonspecific etiology in approximately 75% of children with vulvovaginitis.
- Majority of vulvovaginitis in girls involves a primary irritation of the vulva with secondary involvement of the lower third of the vagina.

PHYSICAL FINDINGS & CLINICAL PRESENTATION

Vulvar pain, dysuria, pruritus
1. Discharge is not a primary symptom.
2. If present, vaginal discharge may be foul smelling or bloody.

ETIOLOGY

- Infections
  1. Bacterial
  2. Protozoal
  3. Mycotic
  4. Viral
- Endocrine disorders
- Labial adhesions
- Poor hygiene
- Sexual abuse
- Allergic substance
- Trauma
- Foreign body
- Masturbation
- Constipation

Section II describes the differential diagnosis of vaginal discharge in prepubertal girls.

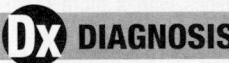

DIAGNOSIS

DIFFERENTIAL DIAGNOSIS

- Physiologic leukorrhea
- Foreign body
- Bacterial vaginosis
- Gonorrhea
- Fungal vulvovaginitis
- *Trichomonas* vulvovaginitis
- Sexual abuse
- Pinworms

WORKUP

- Pelvic, genital examination
- Speculum examination
- Rectal examination
- Vaginoscopy if considering a foreign body
- KOH and normal saline preparation of discharge
- Knee-chest position for examination may be easier for the child to tolerate during an examination

  Section III, "Vaginal Discharge," describes the evaluation of discharge.

LABORATORY TESTS

- Urinalysis to rule out urinary tract infection and diabetes
- Cultures including sexually transmitted diseases

TREATMENT

NONPHARMACOLOGIC THERAPY

- Avoid tight clothing
- Perineal hygiene
- Avoid irritant chemicals
- Reassurance

ACUTE GENERAL Rx

- Group A beta *Streptococcus* and *Streptococcus pneumoniae:* penicillin V potassium 125 to 250 mg PO qid ×10 days.
- *Chlamydia trachomatis:* azithromycin 1 g PO single dose.

- *Neisseria gonorrhoeae:* ceftriaxone 250 mg IM ×1 day.
  1. Children >8 yr should also be given doxycycline 100 mg bid PO ×7 days.
- *Staphylococcus aureus:* amoxicillin-clavulanate 20 to 40 mg/kg/day PO ×7 to 10 days.
- *Haemophilus influenzae:* amoxicillin 20 to 40 mg/kg/day PO ×7 days.
- *Trichomonas:* metronidazole 125 mg (15 mg/kg/day) tid PO ×7 to 10 days.
- Pinworms: mebendazole 100-mg tablet chewable, repeat in 2 wk.
- Labial agglutination: spontaneous resolution or topical estrogen cream for 7 to 10 days. High degree of efficacy with topical estrogen hormone.

CHRONIC Rx

See "Referral."

DISPOSITION

Further education:
- Young child: hygiene
- Adolescent: pregnancy prevention and safe sexual practices

REFERRAL

- To obstetrician/gynecologist
- To pediatrician

SUGGESTED READINGS
Available at www.expertconsult.com

RELATED CONTENT
Pruritus Vulvae (Related Key Topic)
Vaginitis, Fungal (Related Key Topic)
Vaginitis, *Trichomonas* (Related Key Topic)
Vaginosis, Bacterial (Related Key Topic)

AUTHOR: **RUBEN ALVERO, M.D.**

Diseases and Disorders

BASIC INFORMATION

DEFINITION
Trichomonas vulvovaginitis is the inflammation of vulva and vagina caused by *Trichomonas* spp.

SYNONYMS
Trichomonas vaginalis
Trichomoniasis
TV

ICD-10CM CODE
A59.01 Trichomonal vulvovaginitis

EPIDEMIOLOGY & DEMOGRAPHICS
- Acquired through sexual contact
- Diagnosed in
  1. 50% to 75% of prostitutes
  2. 5% to 15% of women visiting gynecology clinics
  3. 7% to 32% of women in sexually transmitted disease (STD) clinics
  4. 5% of women in family planning clinics
  5. 13% of black women, 1.8% of non-Hispanic white women
- Most prevalent nonviral sexually transmitted infection in the U.S.

PHYSICAL FINDINGS & CLINICAL PRESENTATION
- Profuse, yellow, malodorous vaginal discharge and severe vaginal itching
- Vulvar itching
- Dysuria
- Dyspareunia
- Intense erythema of the vaginal mucosa
- Cervical petechiae ("strawberry cervix")
- Some infected men may have symptoms of urethritis, epididymitis or prostatitis
- Asymptomatic in ~50% of women and 90% of men

ETIOLOGY
Single-cell protozoan *Trichomonas vaginalis*

RISK FACTORS
- Multiple sexual partners
- History of previous STDs

DIAGNOSIS

DIFFERENTIAL DIAGNOSIS (TABLE 1V-1)
- Bacterial vaginosis
- Fungal vulvovaginitis
- Cervicitis
- Atrophic vulvovaginitis

WORKUP
- Pelvic examination
- Speculum examination
- Mobile trichomonads seen on normal saline preparation (Fig. 1V-7): 70% sensitivity
- Elevated pH (>5) of vaginal discharge
- Culture is considered the traditional gold standard laboratory test for diagnosis of TV.

- Nucleic acid amplification tests (NAATs) have been developed that combine excellent performance characteristics with a more rapid turnaround time compared with culture.
- APTIMA assays utilize target capture and transcription-mediated amplification (TMA) to selectively purify, amplify, and detect species-specific 16 S ribosomal RNA. APTIMA *Trichomonas vaginalis* transcription-mediated amplification may be a better laboratory test than culture based on sensitivity and time frame for results.

LABORATORY TESTS
- NAAT is highly sensitive. The APTIMA *T. vaginalis* assay is FDA cleared for detection of *T. vaginalis* from vaginal, endocervical, and urine specimens from women (95%-100% clinical sensitivity and specificity). The OSOM Trichomonas Rapid Test on vaginal secretions provides results in 10 min with sensitivity of 82% to 95% and specificity of 97% to 100%.
- Microscopic evaluation of wet preparations of genital secretions: convenient and low cost but low sensitivity (51%-65%) in vaginal specimen with even lower sensitivity if there is a delay in evaluating slides.

TREATMENT

NONPHARMACOLOGIC THERAPY
Condom use: best way to prevent trichomoniasis is through consistent and correct use of condoms during all penile-vaginal sexual encounters

ACUTE GENERAL Rx
- Metronidazole 2 g PO × 1 *or* Tinidazole single 2-g oral dose in both sexes. Treatment of the sexual partner is essential to prevent reinfection.
- Alternative regimen: Metronidazole 500 mg PO BID ×7 days
- Alcohol consumption should be avoided during treatment with metronidazole (at least 24 hr after completion of therapy) and tinidazole (at least 72 hr after completion of therapy) to reduce possibility of disulfiram-like reaction

CHRONIC Rx
- Metronidazole gel: less likely to achieve therapeutic levels; therefore not recommended.
- Metronidazole (retreat): 500 mg PO bid ×7 days.
- Treatment of recurrences: metronidazole 2 g PO qd ×3 to 5 days.
- Allergy, intolerance, or adverse reactions: alternatives to metronidazole are not available. Patients who are allergic to metronidazole can be managed by desensitization.
- Pregnancy:
  1. Associated with adverse outcomes (i.e., premature rupture of membranes)
  2. Metronidazole 2 g PO ×1 day

DISPOSITION
- *Trichomonas* infection is considered an STD; therefore treatment of the sexual partner is necessary.
- *T. vaginalis* infection is associated with two- to threefold increased risk for HIV acquisition,

TABLE 1V-1 Differential Diagnosis of Vaginitis

Characteristics of Vaginal Discharge	*C. albicans* Vaginitis	*T. vaginalis* Vaginitis	Bacterial Vaginosis
pH	4.5	>5.0	>5.0
White curd	Usually	No	No
Odor with KOH	No	Yes	Yes
Clue cells	No	No	Usually
Motile trichomonads	No	Usually	No
Yeast cells	Yes	No	No

From Goldman L, Ausiello D (eds): *Cecil textbook of medicine*, ed 22, Philadelphia, 2004, Saunders.

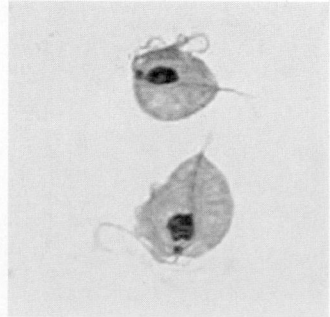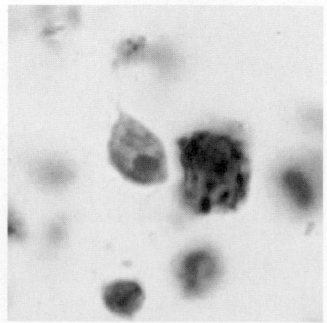

FIGURE 1V-7 *Trichomonas vaginalis* **trophozoites stained with Giemsa *(left)* and iron hematoxylin *(right)*.** (From the Centers for Disease Control and Prevention: *Laboratory identification of parasites of public health concern, Trichomoniasis.* www.dpd.cdc.gov/dpdx/HTML/ImageLibrary/Trichomoniasis_il.htm Accessed August 30, 2010.)

preterm birth, and other adverse pregnancy outcomes among pregnant women.

REFERRAL

To obstetrician/gynecologist for recurrence and pregnancy

SUGGESTED READINGS

Available at www.expertconsult.com

RELATED CONTENT

Trichomoniasis (Patient Information)
Pruritus Vulvae (Related Key Topic)

AUTHOR: **RUBEN ALVERO, M.D.**

BASIC INFORMATION

DEFINITION

Bacterial vaginosis (BV) is a polymicrobial clinical syndrome resulting from replacement of the normal hydrogen peroxide producing *Lactobacillus* spp. in the vagina, with high concentrations of anaerobic bacteria manifesting in thin, gray, homogeneous, malodorous vaginal discharge.

SYNONYM

Bacterial vaginosis
BV
Nonspecific Vaginitis
Haemophilus vaginalis vaginitis
Corynebacterium vaginalis vaginitis
Gardnerella vaginalis vaginitis

ICD-10 CODES
N76.0 Acute vaginitis
N77.1 Vaginitis, vulvitis and vulvovaginitis in diseases classified elsewhere

EPIDEMIOLOGY & DEMOGRAPHICS

- Most common vaginal infection
- *Gardnerella, Mycoplasma,* and *Mobiluncus* are harbored in the urethra of male partners; however:
  1. Male partners are asymptomatic.
  2. There is no improved cure rate or lower reinfection rate if the infected patient's male partner is treated.
  3. Abstinence from intercourse or condom use while the patient completes her treatment regimen may improve cure rates and lessen recurrences.
- Risk factors: BV is associated with having multiple male or female partners, a new sex partner, douching, lack of condom use, and lack of vaginal lactobacilli.

PHYSICAL FINDINGS & CLINICAL PRESENTATION

- 50% of patients are asymptomatic
- A thin, dark, or dull gray homogeneous discharge (Fig. E1V-8) that adheres to the vaginal walls
- An offensive, "fishy" odor that is accentuated after intercourse or menses
- Pruritus (only in 13%)

ETIOLOGY

- *Gardnerella vaginalis* is detected in 40% to 50% of vaginal secretions.
  1. Increase in vaginal pH caused by decrease in hydrogen peroxide–producing lactobacilli
  2. Anaerobes predominate and produce amines
- Amines, when alkalinized by semen, menstrual blood, the use of alkaline douches, or the addition of 10% potassium hydroxide, volatilize and cause the unpleasant "fishy" odor. This amine-whiff test is one of the diagnostic approaches used for BV.
- In BV:
  1. *Bacteroides* (anaerobes) species are increased 1000× the usual concentration.
  2. *G. vaginalis* are 100× normal.
  3. *Peptostreptococcus* are 10× normal.
  4. *Mycoplasma hominis* and Enterobacteriaceae members are present in increased concentrations.

DIAGNOSIS

WORKUP

Clinical criteria:
- The presence of three of the four following signs will diagnose 90% correctly, with <10% false-positive results:
  1. Thin, gray, homogeneous, malodorous discharge that adheres to the vaginal walls
  2. Elevated pH >4.5
  3. Positive potassium hydroxide whiff test (fishy odor of vaginal discharge before or after addition of 10% KOH)
  4. Clue cells (vaginal epithelial cells studded with adherent coccobacilli) present on wet mount
- Cultures are unnecessary.
- Pap smear will not identify *G. vaginalis.*
- Gram stain of vaginal secretions will reveal clue cells and abnormal mixed bacteria (Fig. 1V-9).
- Other tests include Affirm VP III, a DNA hybridization probe, and the OSOM BV Blue test.

TREATMENT

ACUTE GENERAL Rx
- Recommended regimens (equal efficacy):
  1. Metronidazole 500 mg PO bid for 7 days *or*

2. 0.75% metronidazole gel one full applicator (5 gm) intravaginally once a day for 5 days *or*
3. 2% clindamycin cream one full applicator (5 gm) intravaginally at bedtime for 7 days
- Alternate regimens (lower efficacy for BV):
  1. Tinidazole 2 g PO qd ×2 days or tinidazole 1 g PO qd ×5 day
  2. Clindamycin 300 mg PO bid for 7 days (increased incidence of diarrhea) or clindamycin ovules intravaginally once at bedtime for 3 days
- Patients should be advised to avoid alcohol while taking metronidazole and for 24 hr thereafter due to disulfiram-type (Antabuse) reaction when taken concurrently with alcohol.
- Treatment in pregnancy:
  1. All pregnant patients proved to have BV should be treated because of its association with preterm labor, chorioamnionitis, and premature rupture of membranes (PROM).
- Recommended regimens:
  1. Metronidazole 250 mg PO tid for 7 days
  2. Clindamycin 300 mg PO bid for 7 days
- Existing data do not support the use of topical agents during pregnancy.
- Multiple studies and meta-analyses have not demonstrated associations between metronidazole use during pregnancy and teratogenic effects in newborns.
  1. Tinidazole, an oral antiprotozoal drug, is now FDA approved for treatment of BV. Dosage is 2 g once/day for 2 days or 1 g qd ×5 days
- Recurrent BV:
  1. Condom use may help reduce the risk of recurrence.
  2. Concurrent treatment of male partner is controversial. Consider treating the male partner if there is recurrent vaginitis or any suspicion of associated upper genital tract infection.

PEARLS & CONSIDERATIONS

- BV has been associated with pelvic inflammatory disease, cystitis, posthysterectomy vaginal cuff cellulitis, postabortal infection, preterm delivery, PROM, amnionitis, chorioamnionitis, and postpartum endometritis. New evidence also shows BV increases women's risk of acquiring HIV.
- Higher cumulative cure rates have been found at 3 to 4 wk for a 7-day regimen of metronidazole (500 mg twice daily) than with a single dose (2 g).
- Persistent BV is associated with several bacteria in the Clostridiales order, *Megasphaera* phylotype 2, and *P. lacrimalis.*

SUGGESTED READINGS
Available at www.expertconsult.com

RELATED CONTENT
Bacterial Vaginal Infections (Patient Information)

AUTHOR: **RUBEN ALVERO, M.D.**

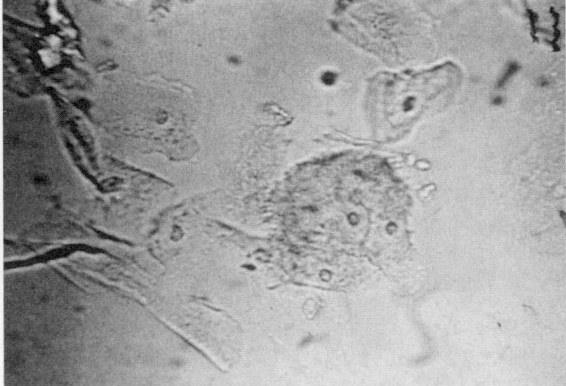

FIGURE 1V-9 Clue cells characteristic of bacterial vaginosis, squamous epithelial cells whose borders are obscured by bacteria. (From Carlson K [ed]: *Primary care of women,* St Louis, 1995, Mosby.)

 **BASIC INFORMATION**

DEFINITION

Enterococci are gram-positive, facultative anaerobic organisms usually oval in shape and can be seen as single cells, pairs, or chains. Vancomycin resistant *Enterococcus* (VRE) are enterococci that have become resistant to vancomycin and several antibiotics normally used to treat enterococcal infections.

SYNONYM

VRE

ICD-10CM CODES
Z16.39   Resistance to other specified antimicrobial drug

EPIDEMIOLOGY & DEMOGRAPHICS

INCIDENCE: VRE may be associated with the use of specific classes of antibiotics.
PEAK INCIDENCE: VRE was first reported in Europe in 1986, and there has been a steady rise in the incidence of enterococcal strains resistant to vancomycin. In 2007, 80% of *E. faecium* isolates and 7% of *E. faecalis* isolates were resistant to vancomycin.
PREVALENCE: 80% of *E. faecium* are VRE; 69% of *E. faecalis* are VRE.
RISK FACTORS
- Prior antimicrobial therapy, especially vancomycin
- Prolonged hospitalization
- Chronic medical conditions, renal failure
- Invasive devices
- ICU stay
- Colonization: VRE colonize the gastrointestinal tract; can be found on skin or perirectal swab culture or stool culture

PHYSICAL FINDINGS & CLINICAL PRESENTATION

Patients may be asymptomatic and have gastrointestinal colonization; it can be associated with diarrhea. In hospitalized patients, infection is associated with colonization and can cause wound infections, bacteremia, abscesses (intraabdominal), and, rarely, pneumonia and urinary tract infections.

ETIOLOGY

- The Clinical and Laboratory Standards Institute uses the following MIC definitions for vancomycin susceptibility and resistance in enterococci:
  1. Vancomycin susceptible: ≤4 mcg/mL
  2. Vancomycin resistant: ≥32 mcg/mL
  3. Vancomycin intermediate: 8 to 16 mcg/mL (vancomycin not recommended)

- Enterococci are primarily found in the human digestive tract and female genital tract, where they make up a significant portion of the normal bacterial population in healthy people. Enterococci can cause urinary tract, wound, bloodstream, heart valve, and brain infections. In the great majority of cases, VRE infections occur in hospitalized patients who have compromised immune systems. Most cases of VRE are caused by the *E. faecium* strains that have acquired resistance when they came in contact with other bacteria and shared genetic information.
- VRE is most commonly transmitted from one patient to another by health care workers whose hands have become contaminated inadvertently with feces or fluids of a person carrying the organism. VRE are not airborne but can survive on surfaces for several weeks.

 DIAGNOSIS

DIFFERENTIAL DIAGNOSIS

- Other bacterial pathogens in blood, wounds, or urine
- Once colonized, increased incidence to become infected

LABORATORY TESTS

- VRE rectal culture
- VRE stool culture
- Blood, urine, and wound cultures

Rx TREATMENT

- For rectal or stool colonization, therapy is not recommended
- Therapy is complicated by the fact that strains exhibit inherent resistance to many commonly used antibiotics.
- More than 80% of vancomycin-resistant *E. faecium* strains are also resistant to ampicillin.
- In symptomatic patients, if VRE strains are known to be susceptible, potential therapeutic agents include
  - Linezolid: 600 mg IV or PO q12h
  - Daptomycin: 4 mg/kg/day IV
  - Quinupristin-dalfopristin (Synercid) only effective for *E. faecium* strains with no activity for *E. faecalis* strains: 7.5 mg/kg q8 to 12h. Can cause severe myalgias and arthralgias and venous irritation that often requires use of a central line, which has limited the use of this antibiotic.
- The Healthcare Infection Control Practices Advisory Committee recommends that three negative stool/rectal cultures be obtained at weekly intervals to remove a patient from contact precautions.

REFERRAL

To infectious disease specialist

 **PEARLS & CONSIDERATIONS**

COMMENTS

- Patients who are colonized with VRE have about an 8% rate of developing a true VRE infection in hospital or after discharge. The rate is higher in immunocompromised and severely ill patients.
- Incidence increases with comorbidity and hospitalization.
- The number of patients already colonized with VRE in a defined geographic area (colonization pressure) is the most significant factor for predicting new acquisition of VRE.
- An association between VRE colonization and *Clostridium difficile* infection has been reported in patients with hematologic malignancies.

PREVENTION

- Hand hygiene: most important and practical method of preventing spread in hospital environment. Soap and water (used as a 30-sec wash) and alcohol-based hand rubs are effective, as is chlorhexidine.
- Cohorting and isolation techniques: use of private rooms and use of gowns and gloves has been shown to decrease the risk of spread of multidrug resistant bacteria.
- Cleaning contaminated objects or surfaces with standard hospital disinfectants, , antibiotic management (prudent vancomycin use), and surveillance also help prevent spread.

SUGGESTED READINGS
Available at www.expertconsult.com

RELATED CONTENT
Health Care-Related Infections (Related Key Topic)

AUTHOR: **GLENN G. FORT, M.D., M.P.H.**

V

Diseases and Disorders

BASIC INFORMATION

DEFINITION

Varicella is a viral illness that is characterized by the acute onset of a generalized vesicular rash and fever.

SYNONYM

Chickenpox

ICD-10CM CODES
B01.9	Varicella without complication
B01.8	Varicella with other complications
B01.0	Varicella meningitis
B01.11	Varicella encephalitis and encephalomyelitis
B01.12	Varicella myelitis
B01.2	Varicella pneumonia
B01.81	Varicella keratitis
B01.89	Other varicella complications
Z20.820	Contact with and (suspected) exposure to varicella

EPIDEMIOLOGY & DEMOGRAPHICS

- Varicella is extremely contagious. More than 90% of unvaccinated contacts become infected.
- The incubation period of chickenpox ranges from 9 to 21 days.
- The peak incidence is during the springtime.
- The predominant age is 5 to 10 yr.
- The infectious period begins 2 days before the onset of clinical symptoms and lasts until all of the lesions have crusted.
- Most patients will have lifelong immunity after an attack of chickenpox; protection from the virus after a varicella vaccine is approximately 6 yr.

PHYSICAL FINDINGS & CLINICAL PRESENTATION

- Findings vary with the clinical course. Initial symptoms consist of fever, chills, backache, generalized malaise, and headache.
- Symptoms are generally more severe in adults.
- Initial lesions generally occur on the trunk (centripetal distribution) and occasionally on the face; these lesions consist primarily of 3 to 4 mm red papules with an irregular outline and a clear vesicle (Fig. 1V-10) on the surface (i.e., the appearance of dewdrops on a rose petal).

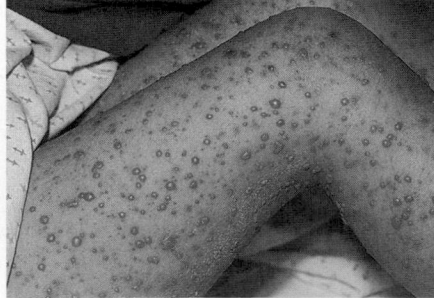

FIGURE 1V-10 Chickenpox. (From Swartz, MH: *Textbook of physical diagnosis*, 7 ed, Philadelphia, 2014, Saunders.)

- Intense pruritus generally accompanies the initial stage.
- New lesion development generally ceases by the fourth day, with subsequent crusting by the sixth day.
- Lesions generally spread to the face and the extremities (i.e., centrifugal spread).
- Patients generally present with lesions that are in different stages at the same time.
- Crusts generally fall off within 5 to 14 days.
- The fever is usually highest during the eruption of the vesicles; the patient's temperature generally returns to normal after the disappearance of vesicles.
- Signs of potential complications (e.g., bacterial skin infections, neurologic complications, pneumonia, hepatitis) may be present on physical examination.
- Mild constitutional symptoms (e.g., anorexia, myalgias, headaches, restlessness) may be present; these are most common among adults.
- Excoriations may be present if scratching is prominent.

ETIOLOGY

Varicella-zoster virus is a human herpes virus III that can manifest with either varicella or herpes zoster (i.e., shingles, which is a reactivation of varicella).

DIAGNOSIS

DIFFERENTIAL DIAGNOSIS

- Other viral infection.
- Impetigo.
- Scabies.
- Drug rash.
- Urticaria.
- Dermatitis herpetiformis.
- Smallpox.

WORKUP

The diagnosis is usually made on the basis of the patient's history and clinical presentation.

LABORATORY TESTS

- Laboratory evaluation is generally not necessary.
- The CBC may reveal leukopenia and thrombocytopenia.
- Serum varicella titers (i.e., a significant rise in the serum varicella immunoglobulin G antibody level), skin biopsies, or Tzanck smears are used only when diagnosis is in question.

TREATMENT

NONPHARMACOLOGIC THERAPY

- Use antipruritic lotions for symptomatic relief.
- Avoid scratching to prevent excoriations and superficial skin infections.
- Use a mild soap for bathing.
- Hands should be washed often.

ACUTE GENERAL Rx

- Use acetaminophen for fever and myalgias; aspirin should be avoided because of the associated increased risk of Reye's syndrome.
- Oral acyclovir (20 mg/kg qid for 5 days) initiated at the earliest sign (i.e., within 24 hr of illness) is useful for healthy, nonpregnant individuals 13 yr old or older to decrease the duration and severity of signs and symptoms. Immunocompromised hosts should be treated with intravenous acyclovir 500 mg/m^2 or 10 mg/kg q8h for 7 to 10 days.
- Varicella is most contagious from 2 days before to a few days after the onset of the rash. Varicella vaccine is available for children and adults; protection lasts at least 6 yr. Healthy, nonimmune adults and children exposed to varicella-zoster virus should receive prophylaxis with live attenuated varicella vaccine (Varivax). Patients with HIV or other immunocompromised patients should not receive the live attenuated vaccine.
- Exposed patients with contraindications to varicella vaccine can be treated with varicella-zoster immunoglobulin (VariZIG), which effectively prevents varicella in susceptible individuals. The dose is 12.5 U/kg IM up to a maximum of 625 U. VariZIG must be administered as early as possible after presumed exposure (i.e., within 10 days) for postexposure prophylaxis of varicella.
- Pruritus from chickenpox can be controlled with antihistamines (e.g., hydroxyzine 25 mg q6h) and oral antipruritic lotions (e.g., calamine).
- Oral antibiotics are not routinely indicated and should be used only in patients with secondary infection and infected lesions; the most common infective organisms are *Streptococcus* sp. and *Staphylococcus* sp.

DISPOSITION

- The course is generally benign in immunocompetent adults and children.
- Infants who develop chickenpox are incapable of controlling the infection and should be given varicella-zoster immunoglobulin or gamma globulin if VariZIG is not available.

PEARLS & CONSIDERATIONS

COMMENTS

- VariZIG can be obtained from the nearest regional Red Cross Blood Center or the Centers for Disease Control and Prevention in Atlanta.
- Varicella immunization is recommended for all who have not had chickenpox; the dosage for adults and adolescents (>13 yr old) is two 0.5 ml doses 4 to 8 wk apart.

EVIDENCE

Available at www.expertconsult.com

RELATED CONTENT

Chickenpox (Patient Information)

AUTHOR: **FRED F. FERRI, M.D.**

 **BASIC INFORMATION**

DEFINITION

Veins in the leg are soft, thin-walled tubes that return blood back to the heart. This is accomplished by the presence of one-way valves and the action of the calf pump. Superficial venous insufficiency develops when venous return is impaired by valvular incompetence, obstruction, or calf muscle pump failure.

Varicose veins, the most common clinical manifestation of chronic venous disease, are bulging (>3 mm in diameter), tortuous conduits (Fig. 1V-12). Reticular veins, often called "feeder veins," are bluish subdermal veins about 1 to 3 mm in diameter that give rise to telangiectasia. Spider veins or telangiectasias are very small (≤1 mm in diameter) thread veins found commonly in clusters on the surface of the skin.

SYNONYMS

Chronic venous disorder

ICD-10CM CODES
I83.90	Asymptomatic varicose veins of unspecified lower extremity
I83.899	Varicose veins of unspecified lower extremities with other complications

EPIDEMIOLOGY

PREVALENCE: One large U.S. cohort study found the biannual incidence of varicose veins was 3% in women and 2% in men.

The prevalence of varicose veins in Western populations was estimated in one study to be about 25% to 30% in women and 10% to 20% in men.

RISK FACTORS
Gender: female
Genetics: family history of varicose veins
Increasing age
Multiple pregnancies

SYMPTOMS AND PHYSICAL FINDINGS

Leg complaints consistent with chronic venous disease include aching, heaviness, subjective swelling, cramps, itching, tingling, and pain. These symptoms can be exacerbated by menses, heat, and prolonged standing.

CLINICAL PRESENTATION

- Chronic vein disease is the result of the introduction of high pressures into a normal low-pressure superficial venous system.
- This increased pressure or venous hypertension causes superficial veins to distend to such a degree that vein valves fail to close, causing reflux and pooling of blood in surface veins.
- Manifested clinically by two syndromes:
  1. Junctional: failure of the terminal valve at the intersection between the saphenous vein trunks and the deep system. If the great saphenous vein is involved, large varicose veins are found mainly above medial knee or calf. When the small saphenous vein is involved, large varicose veins are found in posterior knee or calf area. If the anterior accessory of great saphenous vein is involved, large varicose veins are found mainly in anterior or lateral thigh.
  2. Perforator: failure of valves located in perforating vein. Large varicose veins are found most commonly in medial calf and proximal thigh region.

CLASSIFICATION

Chronic venous disease can now be classified using the Clinical-Etiology-Anatomy-Pathophysiology (CEAP) criteria to allow a precise description of the type of venous disease being discussed and provide an orderly framework for decision making (Table 1V-3).

ETIOLOGY

- The underlying etiology of varicose veins remains uncertain.
- Important structural changes that occur: failure of vein valve function and vein wall dilation from fragmentation of the muscle layer.

COMPLICATIONS

- Superficial venous thrombophlebitis (SVT): a very common disorder with an incidence of 125,000 new cases per year in the U.S. The most frequent predisposing risk factors are varicose veins. The clinical findings include the presence of erythema, tenderness, and a palpable cord. Pain, increased warmth, and swelling are also present. Diagnosis is made by ultrasonography, which is useful to identify associated deep vein thrombosis that can occur in approximately 15% of patients. The location of the SVT determines the course of treatment; if the proximal great saphenous vein (GSV) is involved, a 1-mo course of low-molecular-weight heparin plus compression stockings has been found to be more effective than vein ligation. If SVT involves branch varicosities, treatment is usually symptomatic (control of pain).
- Bleeding is a more common complication than traditionally suspected. It is associated with thin-walled ectatic veins known as "blue blebs" that are found predominantly in the medial lower calf and ankle region. The best emergency treatment consists of pressure wrapping and not suture ligation, which results in delayed healing of the bleeding site. Sclerotherapy of these veins is the definitive treatment to prevent further bleeding.
- Dermal pathology of prolonged chronic venous disease (CEAP classes 4, 5, and 6).
  1. Varicose eczema: see "Venous Ulcers" section.
  2. Atrophie blanche: see "Venous Ulcers" section.
  3. Lipodermosclerosis: see "Venous Ulcers" section.
  4. Venous stasis ulcer: see "Venous Ulcers" section.

Dx **DIAGNOSIS**

DIFFERENTIAL DIAGNOSIS

Other conditions that cause leg pain:
- Stress fracture
- Arthritis hip/knee joint
- Gout
- Degenerative disk disease of lower back
- Intermittent claudication secondary to peripheral arterial disease (PAD)
- Medications such as allopurinol and statins

Other conditions that cause leg swelling:
- Cellulitis
- Soft tissue injury to leg/ankle/foot

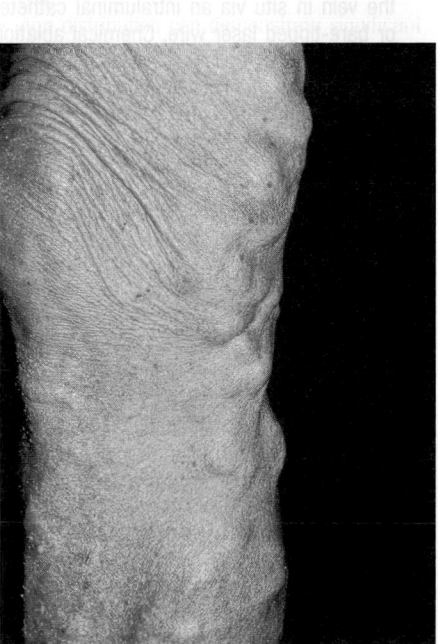

FIGURE 1V-12 Varicose veins. (From White GM, Cox NH [eds]: *Diseases of the skin, a color atlas and text,* ed 2, St Louis, 2006, Mosby.)

TABLE 1V-3 CEAP Classification of Chronic Venous Disease

C: Clinical

C_0: no visible or palpable signs of venous disease
C_1: telangiectasias or reticular veins
C_2: varicose veins
C_3: edema
C_4: pigmentation or eczema
C_5: healed venous ulcer
C_6: active venous ulcer

E: Etiology

c: congenital
p: primary
s: secondary or post thrombotic
n: no venous cause identified

A: Anatomy

s: superficial veins
p: perforator veins
d: deep veins
n: no venous location identified

P: Pathophysiology

r: reflux
o: obstruction
r,o: reflux and obstruction
n: no venous pathophysiology identified

TABLE 1V-6 Differential Diagnostic Features of Selected Forms of Small Vessel Vasculitis

Features	Microscopic Polyangiitis (MPA)	Granulomatosis with Polyangiitis (GPA)	Eosinophilic Granulomatosis with Polyangiitis	Henoch-Schönlein Purpura (HSP)	Cryoglobulinemic Vasculitis
Vasculitic signs and symptoms	+			+	+
IgA-dominant immune deposits	–			+	–
Cryoglobulins in blood and vessels	–		–	–	+
Antineutrophil cytoplasmic antibodies in blood	+	+	+	–	–
Necrotizing granulomas	–	+	+	–	–
Asthma and eosinophils	–	–	+	–	–

From Floege J et al: *Comprehensive clinical nephrology*, ed 4, Philadelphia, 2010, Saunders.

WORKUP

- The diagnosis of most forms of systemic vasculitis relies on the history and physical examination as well as supportive laboratory testing. Table 1V-6 describes differential diagnostic features of selected forms of small vessel vasculitis.
- Tissue biopsy is important in establishing an accurate diagnosis; biopsy sites should target affected tissues.
- Imaging such as mesenteric angiography can be supportive and may obviate the need for tissue biopsy.

LABORATORY TESTS

- Laboratory markers of systemic inflammation include an elevated erythrocyte sedimentation rate (ESR), C-reactive protein (CRP), and an anemia of chronic disease.
- ANCA targeting myeloperoxidase (MPO) and proteinase 3 (PR3) are frequently found in several small vessel vasculitides, including GPA (Wegener's), microscopic polyangiitis (MPA), and Churg-Strauss syndrome (CSS).
- Hepatitis C antibodies and rheumatoid factor are often present in cryoglobulinemic vasculitis.
- Urinalysis in patients with glomerulonephritis due to small vessel ANCA-associated vasculitis will generally demonstrate hematuria with active urinary sediment with red blood cell casts and proteinuria

IMAGING STUDIES

- Angiography can demonstrate vascular narrowing and aneurysm formation in suspected medium-size and large vessel vasculitis.
- Pulmonary and sinus CT scans can demonstrate active pulmonary and upper airway disease in ANCA-associated vasculitis.

 **TREATMENT**

Treatment of vasculitis depends on the specific type of vasculitis and is tailored to the severity of disease activity.

ACUTE GENERAL Rx

- Systemic corticosteroids are generally required to gain initial control of active disease although mild cases of drug-induced cutaneous leukocytoclastic vasculitis can often be treated with NSAIDs and cessation of the offending medication.
- GCA, HSP, and vasculitis limited to the skin including cutaneous PAN can often be managed without further immunosuppression.
- Major organ-threatening disease in systemic vasculitis has traditionally been treated with oral or intravenous cyclophosphamide.
- Studies have demonstrated noninferiority of rituximab compared to cyclophosphamide in ANCA-associated vasculitis with major organ involvement and it is approved for this use.
- Rituximab with prednisone has also recently been shown to be effective in the treatment of relapsing flares of disease activity in ANCA-associated vasculitis.
- Less severe disease such as granulomatosis with polyangiitis limited to the upper airways can be managed with methotrexate rather than cyclophosphamide.
- Trimethoprim/sulfamethoxazole should be used to prevent *Pneumocystis carinii* infection with concurrent immunosuppressive therapy.
- The goal of acute therapy is to induce remission of disease activity and is generally continued for 1 to 2 months once this is achieved, at which point chronic therapy is used to prevent disease relapse.

CHRONIC Rx

- The goal of chronic therapy is to prevent disease relapse and minimize medication side effects.
- Steroids are gradually tapered as allowed by disease activity.
- Immunomodulatory agents such as methotrexate or azathioprine are commonly used for maintenance therapy in place of cyclophosphamide to reduce side effects.

- Cryoglobulinemic vasculitis due to chronic hepatitis C will often improve with treatment of the underlying viral infection.
- Rituximab may also be an appropriate remission maintenance agent in ANCA-associated vasculitis, although frequency of dosing and duration of therapy are not yet well characterized.

DISPOSITION

Varies widely among the various vasculitides

REFERRAL

Systemic vasculitis care is generally coordinated by a rheumatologist. Renal, pulmonary, neurologic, and gastrointestinal consultation is often needed when vasculitis involves these organ systems. Isolated cutaneous leukocytoclastic vasculitis is often managed by dermatology.

SUGGESTED READINGS
Available at www.expertconsult.com

RELATED CONTENT
Churg-Strauss Syndrome (Related Key Topic)
Cogan's Syndrome (Related Key Topic)
Cryoglobulinemia (Related Key Topic)
Giant Cell Arteritis (Related Key Topic)
Granulomatosis with Polyangiitis (Related Key Topic)
Henoch-Schönlein Purpura (Related Key Topic)
Kawasaki Disease (Related Key Topic)
Microscopic Polyangiitis (Related Key Topic)
Polyarteritis Nodosa (Related Key Topic)
Takayasu's Arteritis (Related Key Topic)

AUTHORS: **NICOLE B. YANG, M.D.**, and **ANTHONY M. REGINATO, Ph.D., M.D.**

ⓘ BASIC INFORMATION

DEFINITION

The spectrum of chronic venous disease (CVD) ranges from varicose veins to leg edema and skin manifestations consisting of hyperpigmentation, eczema, lipodermatosclerosis, and venous ulcer. These latter venous specific skin changes constitute an advanced form of CVD known as chronic venous insufficiency (CVI).

SYNONYMS

Stasis dermatitis
Post-thrombotic syndrome (PTS)

ICD-10CM CODES

I87.2	Venous insufficiency (chronic) (peripheral)
I87.8	Other specified disorders of veins
I87.9	Disorder of vein, unspecified
I83.10	Varicose veins of unspecified lower extremity with inflammation

EPIDEMIOLOGY & DEMOGRAPHICS

- From 10% to 35% of adults in the United States have some form of CVI.
- Venous ulcers are the complication of CVI that results in the greatest morbidity and affects 4% of people over the age of 65.
- The population-based costs to the U.S. government for CVI treatment and venous ulcer care have been estimated at >$1 billion a year.
- In addition, 4.6 million workdays per year are lost to chronic venous-related diseases.

PHYSICAL FINDINGS & CLINICAL PRESENTATION

The spectrum of cutaneous changes of CVI in the affected leg include:

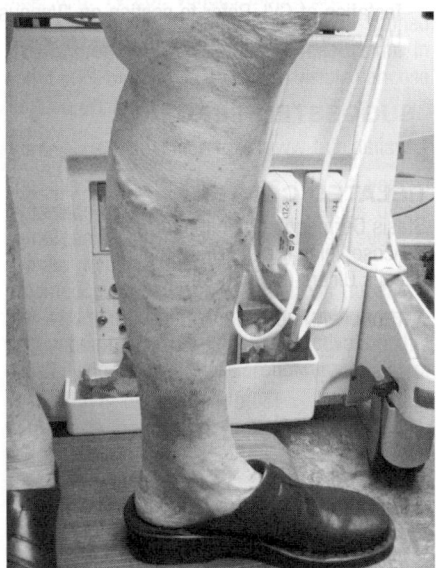

FIGURE 1V-15 Varicose eczema.

- Varicose eczema: the most common and earliest sign, this involves the skin above the medial ankle and consists of pruritic, red, and scaly eczematous patches and plaques (Fig. 1V-15).
- Hyperpigmentation: caused by the breakdown of red blood cells and leads to hemosiderin deposition and dark staining of the skin (Fig. 1V-16).
- Atrophie blanche: usually presents as hypopigmented white patches with focal red punctate dots or telangiectasia surrounded by hyperpigmentation. Skin in this condition is avascular and prone to ulceration (Fig. 1V-17).
- Lipodermatosclerosis: a chronic, brawny induration of the skin and underlying fat that usually involves the skin from medial malleolus up to the lower border of the calf. Progression of the disease leads to an "inverted champagne bottle" appearance. The induration and lack of perfusion of the skin in this area make it susceptible to ulcer formation (Fig. 1V-18).

ETIOLOGY

- CVI occurs as a result of sustained venous hypertension in the leg, which can be caused by the following:

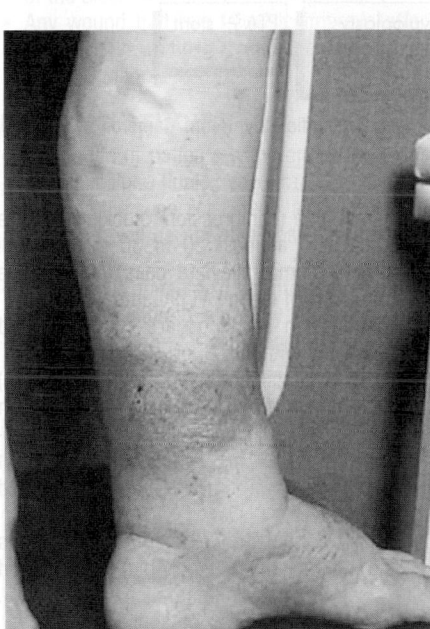

FIGURE 1V-16 Hyperpigmentation.

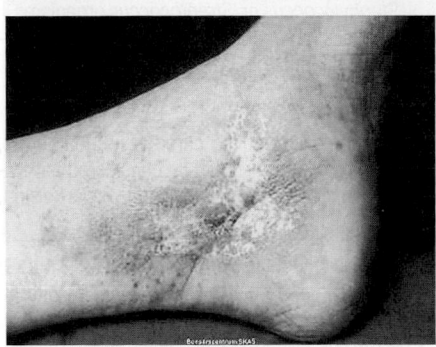

FIGURE 1V-17 Atrophie blanche.

1. Primary: vein valve failure with reflux in the superficial venous system or perforating veins (most common cause of CVI).
2. Secondary: post-thrombotic syndrome in which a deep vein thrombosis causes outflow obstruction or
3. Combination of the two previous processes.
- This sustained elevation in venous pressure or venous hypertension results in pathologic effects in the skin and subcutaneous tissues such as edema, eczema, hyperpigmentation, fibrosis, and ultimately venous ulceration.

ⒹⓍ DIAGNOSIS

The diagnosis and evaluation of CVI are directed primarily by a detailed history and physical examination.

DIFFERENTIAL DIAGNOSIS

- Contact dermatitis.
- Atopic dermatitis.
- Cellulitis.
- Dermatophyte infection.
- Pretibial myxedema.
- Nummular eczema.
- Xerosis.
- Asteatotic eczema.

WORKUP

The primary goal is to identify the cause of sustained venous hypertension. Fig. 1V-19 describes the evaluation and management of chronic venous insufficiency.

LABORATORY TESTS

Generally not indicated

IMAGING STUDIES

- Evaluation of the patient is performed in the standing position with duplex ultrasonography to identify reflux in the superficial, deep, and perforating veins as well as obstruction of the deep veins.

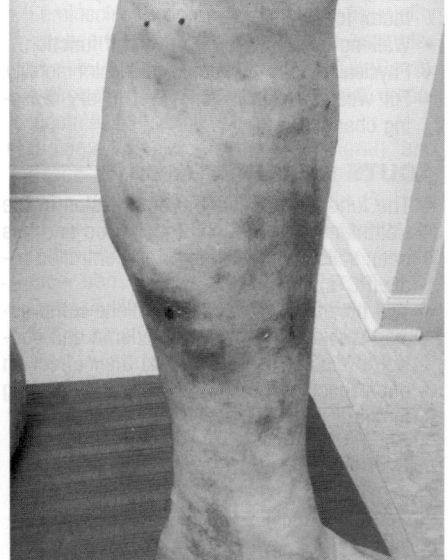

FIGURE 1V-18 Lipodermosclerosis.

shown effects on ulcer healing. Despite the lack of evidence to support their use, modern dressings remain a part of the standard of care. Decisions regarding their use should be based on local cost of the dressings and the physician's clinical experience.

- Trials involving the use of weekly, low-dose, high-frequency ultrasound for hard-to-heal venous leg ulcers do not support adding therapeutic ultrasound to standard care for venous leg ulcers.

DISPOSITION

The overall prognosis for this condition is poor; the healing rate depends on the initial size of the ulcer. Although 65% to 70% of venous ulcers are healed within 6 mo, the 5-yr recurrence rate of healed venous ulcers can be as high as 40%. Maintenance of lifelong compression therapy is recommended.

REFERRAL

All patients should be evaluated weekly during the first month of therapy. Nonhealing ulcers

with little to no improvement should also be referred to a wound care clinic.

 **EVIDENCE**

Available at www.expertconsult.com

SUGGESTED READINGS

Available at www.expertconsult.com

AUTHOR: **FRANK G. FORT, M.D.**

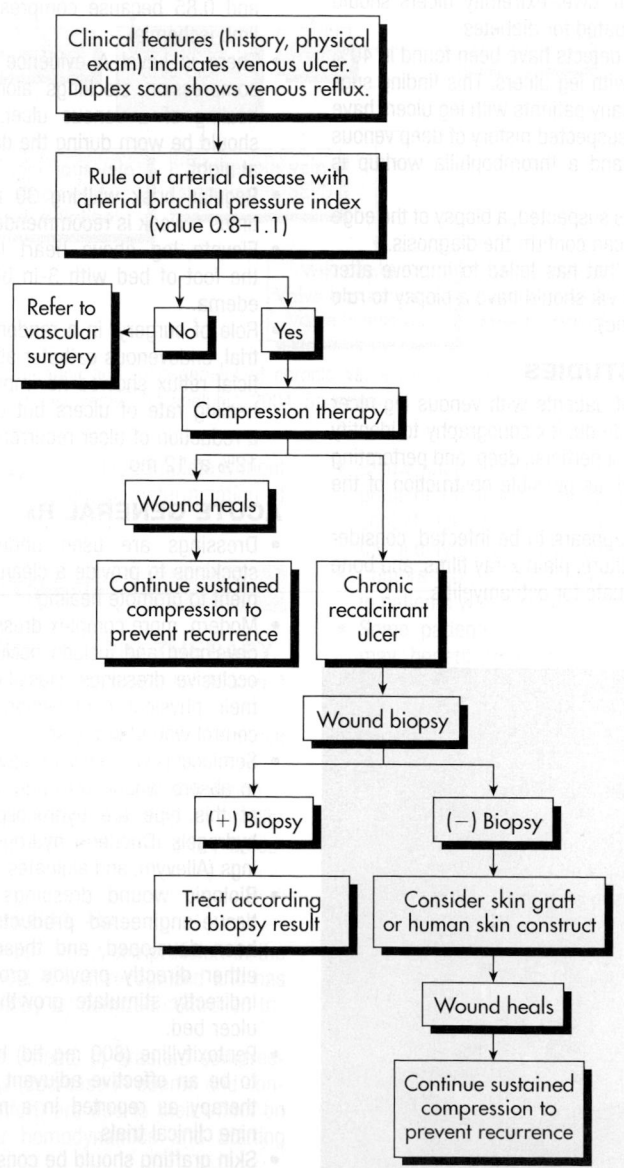

FIGURE 1V-21 Scheme for treatment of venous ulcer. (From *Venous Stasis Ulcers; Conn's Current Therapy*, St Louis 2008; Elsevier.)

BASIC INFORMATION

DEFINITION

Ventricular fibrillation (VF) is a rapid, disorganized ventricular arrhythmia that results in no meaningful cardiac output or blood pressure and, if not rapidly interrupted, death. The ECG appearance of VF can evolve rapidly over the course of minutes as the heart becomes more ischemic. Upon initiation, QRST complexes in VF often appear coarse with grossly irregular oscillating complexes of variable rate, axis and morphology. As VF continues, the QRST complexes become finer, lower amplitude, and slower, eventually resulting in asystole. VF is the leading mechanism of sudden cardiac death.

ICD-10CM CODES
I49.01 Ventricular fibrillation

EPIDEMIOLOGY & DEMOGRAPHICS

INCIDENCE: The true incidence of VF is impossible to know because the majority of these episodes result in sudden cardiac death in unmonitored patients. Sudden cardiac death, as determined by death certificate analysis, is estimated to account for 400,000 to 450,000 death per year in the U.S. In small studies in which patients were wearing monitoring at the time of death, the majority of sudden cardiac deaths were caused by VF (60%-70%). The true proportion of sudden cardiac deaths caused by VF is highly dependent on the population studied.

RISK FACTORS:
- The majority (~85%) of sudden cardiac death and VF occurs in patients with coronary artery disease or systolic dysfunction, with 15% of VF occurring in a "normal" heart at autopsy.
- After the age of 35 yr, coronary artery disease predominates as cause of VF; before the age of 35, inherited channelopathies and mild trauma-induced (comottio cordis) etiologies are more common.
- 60% to 70% of patients with VF have CAD.
- 50% of patients with sudden cardiac arrest presenting for cardiac catheterization have an acute artery occlusion.

RISK FACTORS FOR VF IN PATIENTS PRESENTING WITH ACUTE MI

- STEMI
- Baseline repolarization abnormalities
- Larger infarcts
- Hypokalemia
- Male sex
- Inferior infarcts
- Absence of pre-infarct angina

ETIOLOGIES OF VF IN ABSENCE OF STRUCTURAL OR CORONARY HEART DISEASE

- **Long QT syndrome:** estimated prevalence of 1:2000 to 1:5000; the diagnosis is made based on combination of ECG findings and clinical and family history collectively compiled as Schwartz criteria. Typically inherited as autosomal dominant mutation with variable penetrance, making genetic testing helpful for confirming diagnosis or screening family members.
- **Short QT syndrome:** inherited syndrome characterized by both a short Qtc (<350 ms in males and 360 ms in females) and symptomatic atrial fibrillation and VF.
- **Brugada syndrome:** prevalence is 5 to 50:10,000 of autosomal dominant inherited mutation characterized by a classic Brugada pattern on ECG in leads V1-2 combined with syncope or clinical sudden death. The ECG pattern is mutable and not always present within in the patient and genetic testing is limited.
- Wolff-Parkinson-White syndrome: 2% to 3% of sudden cardiac arrest due to WPW caused by AF conducting down bypass tract degenerating into VF.
- Idiopathic VF: diagnosis of exclusion typified by VF induced by early coupled PVCs typically emanating from conduction system. Notably suppressed by isopreteronol and quinidine.
- Early repolarization syndrome: typified by 1-mm ST elevation in two sequential inferior or lateral leads. This ECG pattern is quite nonspecific, occurring in 5% to 10% of general population and increasing risk of sudden death by threefold, or roughly 0.3%.
- Commotio cordis: VF as a result of low-velocity projectile impact on the chest wall inducing VF in the absence of sudden death. This is uncommon and occurs in young, typically male individuals.

PHYSICAL FINDINGS & CLINICAL PRESENTATION

- Patients are unconscious, without BP or pulse.
- Witnesses may describe a sudden loss of consciousness, without breathing along with a cyanotic appearance.
- Seizure activity may be witnessed after loss of consciousness caused by a lack of cerebral perfusion.
- History of structural heart disease, especially coronary artery disease and a prior myocardial infarction (MI), is a strong predictor of VF. Patents may also have a history of pacemaker or defibrillator implantation. A family history of sudden death must also be sought.

ETIOLOGY

The mechanism of VF is thought to involve multiple rotating spiral waves of microre-entry without any overall organized electrical activity. This is distinctly different from the predominant mechanism of monomorphic ventricular tachycardia, which is re-entry around a fixed zone of slow conduction typically ventricular scar. VF results from a substrate of heterogeneous repolarization and a triggering event such as critically timed PVC. Repolarization of the heart is an active process requiring ATP to obtain and maintain a negative resting membrane potential via NA/K ATPase ion channels. By depriving a significant amount of myocardium to oxygen and thus the ability to generate ATP, ischemia can provide both the substrate of VF by impairing the ischemic areas to fully repolarize and allow for a triggering event by allowing spontaneous depolarization. Genetic conditions such as Long QT syndrome can also predispose to VF in absence of ischemia by providing more heterogeneous repolarization within the myocardium.

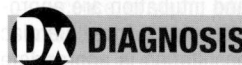

DIAGNOSIS

DIFFERENTIAL DIAGNOSIS

Differential diagnosis of an ECG suspicious of VF includes:
- ECG artifact
- Atrial fibrillation with aberration
- Polymorphic ventricular tachycardia

WORKUP

- Lab testing should especially focus on checking K and Mg levels as well as ischemia workup of cardiac biomarkers and ECG when sinus rhythm has been restored.
- A full 12-lead ECG of the tachycardia should always be obtained, whenever possible, and compared to the ECG in sinus rhythm if there is any uncertainty about the diagnosis.
- Ischemia evaluation is paramount, and cardiac catheterization should be performed in most cases.

LABORATORY TESTS

- Potassium, magnesium, and cardiac biomarkers.
- Genetic testing should be reserved for specific situations such as when there is a concern for genetically mediated conditions such as hypertrophic cardiomyopathy, catecholaminergic polymorphic ventricular tachycardia, or Brugada syndrome.

IMAGING STUDIES

An echocardiogram and ischemia evaluation with diagnostic coronary angiography and/or nuclear stress testing is recommended to rule out structural heart disease and ischemia. An MRI of the heart is indicated if these tests are unable to establish the cause of the arrhythmia and to rule out cardiomyopathies such as cardiac sarcoidosis, amyloid, LV noncompaction, arrhythmogenic right ventricular dysplasia, and so on.

TREATMENT

ACUTE GENERAL Rx

Patients with VF are hemodynamically unstable and require emergent unsynchronized defibrillation along with appropriate high quality CPR as per ACLS protocols.

Antiarrhythmic therapy with IV amiodarone and/or IV lidocaine is appropriate, particularly if patients have more than one event. IV lidocaine is particularly effective if VF is mediated by cardiac ischemia. Cardiac catheterization is recommended provided no mitral regurgitation, tricuspid regurgitation, aortic stenosis, pulmonary stenosis, and hypertrophic cardiomyopathy.

WORKUP

Any person who is suspected of having a VSD should undergo an ECG, a chest radiograph, and an echocardiogram.

LABORATORY TESTS

- Laboratory tests are not specific but may offer insight into the severity of the disease.
- The CBC may show polycythemia, especially in patients with Eisenmenger's complex.
- Arterial blood gas results may demonstrate hypoxemia.

IMAGING STUDIES

- ECG findings vary in accordance with the size of the VSD and depending on whether pulmonary hypertension is present. With large VSDs with pulmonary hypertension, right-axis deviation is seen, along with evidence of right ventricular hypertrophy.
- Chest x-ray findings in patients with VSD include the following:
  1. Cardiomegaly that results from left ventricular volume overload that directly relates to the magnitude of the shunt
  2. The enlargement of the proximal pulmonary arteries along with the redistribution and pruning of the distal pulmonary vessels as a result of sustained pulmonary hypertension (Fig. 1V-23, *A*)
- Echocardiography is the imaging modality of choice for the diagnosis of VSD:
  1. Two-dimensional echocardiography and color Doppler display the size and location of the VSD (Fig. 1V-23, *B*), the chamber sizes, ventricular function, the presence of aortic valve prolapse or regurgitation, outflow tract obstruction, and the presence of tricuspid regurgitation.
  2. Continuous-wave Doppler approximates the gradient between the left and right ventricles and estimates the pulmonary artery pressure.

3. The magnitude of the shunt can be determined by the calculation of the pulmonary-to-systemic flow ratio with the use of echocardiography.
- Heart catheterization is primarily indicated to assess operability of VSD patients with PAH based on their pulmonary vascular resistance (PVR) and in patients in whom the noninvasive testing was inconclusive, and further information, such as quantification of shunting and assessment of pulmonary pressures, is required.
- Ventriculography may help to locate the VSD:
  1. MRI and computed tomography scanning can be useful to assess the pulmonary artery, the pulmonary vein, and the aortic anatomy and to confirm the anatomy of unusual VSDs (e.g., inlet or apical defects) that are not seen well with echocardiography.

🆁🆇 TREATMENT

The decision to close a VSD depends on the type, size, and shunt severity as well as the patient's pulmonary vascular resistance, functional capacity, and associated valvular abnormalities.

NONPHARMACOLOGIC THERAPY

- Young children and adults with a small, asymptomatic VSD with a large left-to-right ventricular pressure gradient, a pulmonary-to-systemic blood flow ratio of less than 1.5:1, and no evidence of pulmonary hypertension can be observed (i.e., restrictive defect).
- Oxygen for hypoxemia and a low-salt diet are recommended for patients with congestive heart failure.

ACUTE GENERAL & CHRONIC Rx

Closure of the VSD is indicated for the following patients:
- Infants with congestive heart failure. Unrestrictive VSDs require surgical intervention within the first 2 yr of life to prevent pulmonary hypertension.

- Children between the ages of 1 and 6 yr with persistent VSD and a pulmonary-to-systemic blood flow ratio (Qp/Qs) of >2:1
- Adults with a Qp/Qs of ≥2 and clinical evidence of left ventricular volume overload (class I):
  1. Positive history of infective endocarditis (IE) (class I)
  2. Adults with a Qp/Qs of >1.5 with pulmonary artery pressure that is less than two thirds of the systemic pressure and pulmonary vascular resistance that is less than two thirds of the systemic vascular resistance (class IIa)
  3. Adults with a Qp/Qs of >1.5 in the presence of left ventricular systolic or diastolic failure (class IIa)
  4. Surgical closure is not indicated for VSD with severe irreversible PAH with high PVR.
  5. Although the exact PVR at which a child with VSD and pulmonary arterial hypertension is considered inoperable has not been determined, the consensus is that a PVR of <4 Wood units/m² is considered optimal. PVR of between 4 and 8 wood units/m² is considered on a case-by-case basis. There are no definitive guidelines on the use of vasoreactivity as a preoperative predictor, but a >20% decrease in PVR during vasodilator testing is considered a positive response.

Surgical closure with Dacron or Gore-Tex patches or primary surgical closure has long been the gold standard of therapy. It has low operative mortality (<2%) at experienced centers. However, surgery still carries a small risk of complete heart block (CHB), postpericardiotomy syndrome, wound infection, and neurologic sequelae related to cardiopulmonary bypass. Over the last two decades, the transcatheter approach to VSD closure has improved considerably and is becoming an increasingly accepted modality of treatment for appropriately selected patients. Some studies have shown similar success rates for both surgical and percutaneous closures, and there are significantly fewer complications, days in the hospital, and blood transfusions after percutaneous closures.

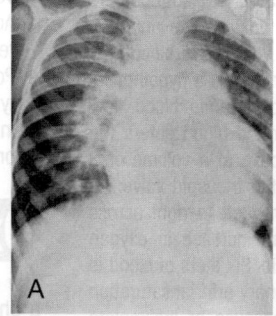
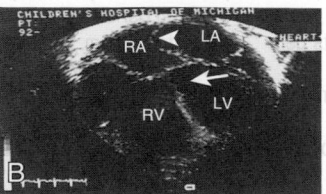

FIGURE 1V-23 A, Chest roentgenogram of a child with a large ventricular septal defect, large pulmonary blood flow, and pulmonary hypertension but only mild elevation of peripheral vascular resistance. This is reflected in the evidence of left and right ventricular enlargement, the enlargement of the main pulmonary artery, and a marked increase in pulmonary blood flow. **B,** Apical four-chamber echocardiographic view of ventricular septal defect *(large arrow)*. The small arrow points to the interatrial septum. *LA,* Left atrium; *LV,* left ventricle; *RA,* right atrium; *RV,* right ventricle. (**A** from Pacifico AD et al: Surgical treatment of ventricular septal defect. In Sabiston DC Jr, Spencer FC [eds]: *Surgery of the chest,* ed 5, Philadelphia, 1990, Saunders. **B** courtesy of Richard Humes, M.D., Children's Hospital of Michigan, Detroit.)

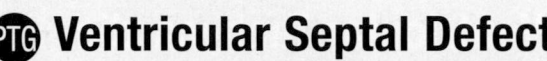

Catheter-based closure in muscular VSD may be considered, especially if the VSD is remote from the tricuspid valve and the aorta, if the VSD is associated with severe left-sided heart chamber enlargement, or if there is PAH (class IIb). Device closure is indicated in residual defects after prior attempts at surgical closure, restrictive VSDs with either a significant left-to-right shunt (Qp/Qs >1.5:1) or hx of IE, trauma, or iatrogenic artifacts after surgical replacement of the aortic valve.

Surgery still remains the treatment of choice in patients with large defects, coexistent congenital anomalies requiring surgical correction, and defects with close proximity to the aortic valve. Subpulmonic VSDs may require surgery due to the increased risk of aortic valve prolapse. Perimembranous VSD with more than trivial aortic regurgitation should be referred to surgery. PIVSDs (peri-infarct) usually carry a high mortality rate, and surgical closure remains the gold standard in the acute setting or for large (>15 mm) septal ruptures. In the subacute or chronic setting, small or medium PIVSD (<15 mm) can be treated with percutaneous closure with comparable mortality to surgery. VSDs post myocardial infarction generally arise within 1 wk of the acute event. Surgical management within 10 d has better outcomes than waiting for cardiac stabilization.

DISPOSITION

- The natural history of an isolated VSD depends on the type of defect, its size, and any associated abnormalities.
- ~75% to 80% of small VSDs close spontaneously by the time the patient reaches the age of 10 yr.
- Only 10% to 15% of large VSDs will close spontaneously.
- Large VSDs that are left untreated may lead to arrhythmias, congestive heart failure, pulmonary hypertension, and Eisenmenger's complex.
- Eisenmenger's complex carries a poor prognosis, with most patients dying before the age of 40 yr.
- Issues to monitor in adults with unrepaired or repaired and catheter-closed VSDs include the following:
  1. Development of aortic regurgitation
  2. Assessment of associated coronary artery disease
  3. Development of tricuspid regurgitation
  4. Assessment of the degree of left-to-right shunting (in unrepaired or residual VSD after repair)
  5. Ventricular dysfunction
  6. Assessment of pulmonary pressure
  7. Development of subpulmonary stenosis (usually as a result of a double-chambered right ventricle)

8. Development of discrete subaortic stenosis
9. Development of arrhythmia or heart block
10. Thromboembolic complications
11. Infective endocarditis
- After closure, late survival is excellent when ventricular function is normal. Pulmonary artery hypertension may improve, progress, or remain the same. Late operations may be required for tricuspid or aortic regurgitation.

REFERRAL

All infants and children diagnosed with VSD should be referred to a pediatric cardiologist. Adults with VSD should be referred to an adult cardiologist. Cardiothoracic surgeons who have experience with congenital heart disease surgery should be consulted if surgery is indicated.

FOLLOW-UP

- Adults with no residual VSD, no associated lesions, and normal pulmonary artery pressure do not require continued follow-up at a regional adult congenital heart disease (ACHD) center except on referral from the patient's cardiologist or physician.
- Adults with VSD with residual heart failure, shunts, PAH, AR, or RV outflow tract (RVOT) or LV outflow tract (LVOT) obstruction should be seen at least annually at an ACHD regional center (level of evidence: C).
- Adults with a small residual VSD and no other lesions should be seen every 3 to 5 yr at an ACHD regional center (level of evidence: C).
- Adults with device closure of a VSD should be followed up every 1 to 2 yr at an ACHD center depending on the location of the VSD and other factors.
- Patients who develop bifascicular block or transient trifascicular block after VSD closure are at risk in later years for the development of complete heart block and should be followed up yearly by history and ECG and have periodic ambulatory monitoring and/or exercise testing.

PEARLS & CONSIDERATIONS

COMMENTS

- A loud murmur does not imply a large VSD. Small, hemodynamically insignificant VSDs can cause loud murmurs.
- In patients with Eisenmenger's complex, the right-to-left shunting across the VSD is usually not associated with an audible murmur.
- The risk of patients with unrepaired VSD developing infective endocarditis is 4%. The risk is higher if aortic insufficiency is present.

- For patients with endocarditis, routine antibiotic prophylaxis for dental or surgical procedures is no longer indicated for isolated VSDs, except in the following circumstances:
  1. In the presence of complex congenital heart disease with cyanosis
  2. In the presence of a residual VSD after surgical closure
  3. During the first 6 mo after surgical patch or percutaneous transcatheter closure
- Any patient with a newly diagnosed murmur or hemodynamic compromise after a myocardial infarction should undergo evaluation for possible VSD.
- Pregnancy with a VSD is generally well tolerated in women with small VSDs, no pulmonary artery hypertension, and no associated lesions. Women with large shunts may experience arrhythmias, ventricular dysfunction, and the progression of pulmonary hypertension.
  1. Maternal use of valproic acid and phenytoin has also been suggested to cause structural defects.
- Women with VSDs and severe pulmonary artery hypertension or Eisenmenger's physiology should be counseled against pregnancy because of associated excessive maternal and fetal mortality.
  1. Small perimembranous VSDs (without left heart dilatation) and corrected VSDs have a good prognosis during pregnancy, when LV function is preserved. Prepregnancy evaluation of the presence of a (residual) defect, cardiac dimensions, and an estimation of pulmonary pressures is recommended. Pre-eclampsia may occur more often than in the normal population. Usually follow-up twice during pregnancy is sufficient, and spontaneous vaginal delivery is appropriate.
- Minimally invasive periventricular device closure of VSD without cardiopulmonary bypass under guidance of transesophageal echocardiography is a promising technique, but it needs long-term follow-up.

SUGGESTED READINGS

Available at www.expertconsult.com

RELATED CONTENT

Ventricular Septal Defect (VSD) (Patient Information)

AUTHOR: **RABIA ARSHAD, M.D.**

V

Diseases and Disorders

I

BASIC INFORMATION

DEFINITION

Ventricular tachycardia (VT) can be classified based on time (duration) or morphology.

Nonsustained ventricular tachycardia (NSVT) is defined as beats originating from the ventricle, lasting from 3 to 30 seconds or for <30 seconds, at a rate >100/min.

Sustained ventricular tachycardia is defined as above but lasts >30 seconds or produces symptoms in the patient and/or requires early intervention due to hemodynamic embarrassment.

Ventricular tachycardia can be monomorphic or polymorphic (see Fig. 1V-24), and the etiology, significance and treatment of these two types of VT are different.

SYNONYMS

- Nonsustained paroxysmal ventricular tachycardia (NSVT)
- Sustained ventricular tachycardia
- Ventricular tachycardia (VT)
- Ventricular tachycardia, monomorphic
- Ventricular tachycardia, nonsustained
- Ventricular tachycardia, paroxysmal
- Ventricular tachycardia, polymorphic
- Ventricular tachycardia, sustained

ICD-10CM CODES
I47.2 Ventricular tachycardia

EPIDEMIOLOGY & DEMOGRAPHICS

INCIDENCE: The actual incidence and prevalence of VT in the general population is unknown. VT, especially NSVT, can be seen in both structurally normal and abnormal hearts, although it is far more common in the latter. In apparently healthy, asymptomatic individuals, the incidence is estimated at 0% to 3% (1).

For details on incidence of NSVT in various cardiac conditions, please refer to Table 1V-7.

RISK FACTORS: The presence of structural heart disease is a strong risk factor for VT, but there are multiple, specific types of VT seen in patients without any structural heart disease.

PHYSICAL FINDINGS & CLINICAL PRESENTATION

- Patients may be asymptomatic, or they may present with any combination of palpitations, dizziness, syncope, chest pain, shortness of breath, seizures. or even cardiac arrest.

TABLE 1V-7 Reported Prevalence of Nonsustained Ventricular Tachycardia in Different Cardiac Conditions

CONDITION	PREVALENCE
Apparently healthy individuals	0-3%
Non-ST ACS (2 to 9 days after admission)	18-25%
Acute MI (early phase)	45-75%
Reperfused acute MI (later than 1 week)	7-13%
Heart failure (LVEF <30-40%)	30-80%
DCM	40-50%
HCM	25-80%
Significant valve disease	≤25%
Hypertension	8%
Hypertension and left ventricular hypertrophy	12%-28%

DCM, Dilated cardiomyopathy; *HCM*, hypertrophic cardiomyopathy; *LVEF*, left ventricular ejection fraction; *MI*, myocardial infarction; *Non-ST ACS*, non–ST-segment elevation acute coronary syndrome.
From Saksena S et al.: *Electrophysiological disorders of the heart,* ed 2, Philadelphia, Elsevier (Table 43-1).

- History of structural heart disease, especially coronary artery disease and a prior myocardial infarction, is a strong predictor of VT. Patents may also have a history of pacemaker or defibrillator implantation. A family history of sudden death must also be sought.
- Physical findings of AV dissociation may be seen by the astute observer. These include cannon A waves in the neck and variability in intensity of heart sounds. The patient may also present physical findings of congestive heart failure including an S3 gallop, pedal edema, or crackles at the lung bases.

Fig. E1V-25 shows initiation and termination of VT by means of programmed ventricular stimulation.

ETIOLOGY

Sustained monomorphic VT is mostly caused by re-entry around a scar in the ventricular wall. The scar is most commonly the result of an old myocardial infarction, but arrhythmogenic RV cardiomyopathy (ARVC), nonischemic dilated cardiomyopathy, sarcoidosis, Chagas disease, tuberculosis, surgical incisions for repair of congenital heart disease and ventricular volume reduction surgery can all cause scars in the myocardium. Fibrosis in the scar creates areas of anatomical conduction block, and fibrosis between surviving myocytes reduces cell-to-cell coupling, thereby distorting the path of propagation and causing areas of slow conduction, which promotes re-entry.

Monomorphic VT can also be seen in patients without any evidence of structural heart disease (idiopathic VT). This subgroup represents 10% of all patients with VT and includes RVOT VT and fascicular VT. Common sites of origin of idiopathic VT include the right ventricular outflow tract (most common), the left ventricular outflow tract, the regions near the anterior and posterior left fascicles, and the papillary muscles.

Polymorphic VT is usually the result of active myocardial ischemia, electrolyte abnormalities (hypokalemia, hypomagnesemia) or genetic conditions such as LQTS, BRS, and CPVT. It may also be seen in HCM, various types of nonischemic cardiomyopathy, and idiopathic VF. The mechanisms are poorly understood but likely involve an initiating trigger that interacts with multiple rotors in the substrate to maintain the arrhythmia.

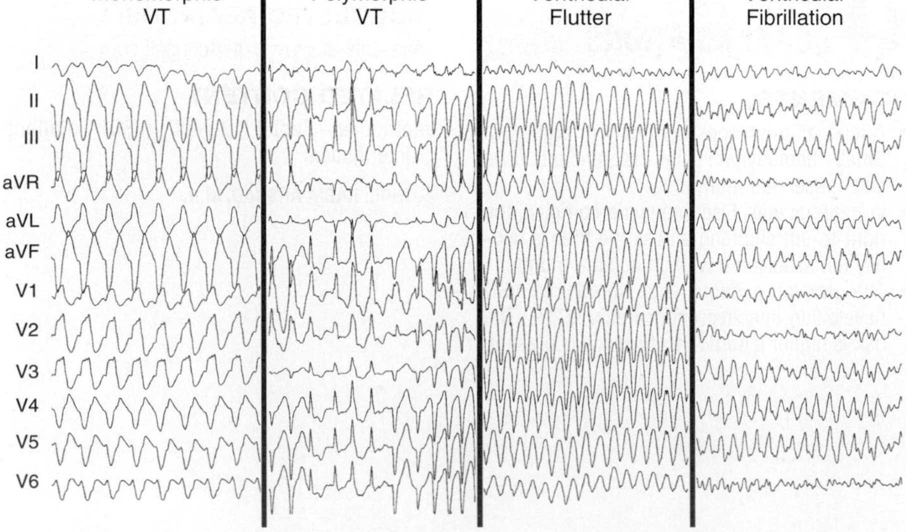

DIAGNOSIS

DIFFERENTIAL DIAGNOSIS

Differential diagnosis of an ECG suspicious of VT includes:
- SVT with aberrancy, either with a preexisting bundle branch block or a rate-related bundle branch block
- SVT in a patient taking anti-arrhythmic drugs, e.g., IA or IC agents
- Antidromic tachycardia from ventricular pre-excitation
- Ventricular paced rhythms
- ECG artifact

The following ECG characteristics strongly favor VT as opposed to SVT: Northwest axis, QRS

	Monomorphic VT	Polymorphic VT	Ventricular Flutter	Ventricular Fibrillation
I				
II				
III				
aVR				
aVL				
aVF				
V1				
V2				
V3				
V4				
V5				
V6				

FIGURE 1V-24 Surface ECG of different types of VT. (From Issa, Miller, Zipes [eds]; *Clinical Arrhythmology and Electrophysiology,* ed 1, p. 405, Figure 18-1, Philadelphia, Saunders, Elsevier.)

width >160 ms, AV dissociation, fusion beats, and capture beats. The last three are highly specific for VT.

WORKUP

- Lab testing should especially focus on checking K and Mg levels.
- A full 12-lead ECG of the tachycardia should always be obtained, whenever possible, and compared to the ECG in sinus rhythm if there is any uncertainty about the diagnosis.
- This should be followed by an echocardiogram and ischemia evaluation with diagnostic coronary angiography and/or nuclear stress testing. An MRI of the heart is indicated if these tests are unable to establish the cause of the arrhythmia.

LABORATORY TESTS

- Potassium, magnesium
- Genetic testing should be reserved for specific situations, i.e., when there is a concern for genetically mediated conditions such as HCM, CPVT, or BRS

IMAGING STUDIES

An echocardiogram and ischemia evaluation with diagnostic coronary angiography and/or nuclear stress testing is recommended to rule out structural heart disease and ischemia. An MRI of the heart is indicated if these tests are unable to establish the cause of the arrhythmia, to rule out cardiomyopathies such as cardiac sarcoidosis, amyloid, LV noncompaction, arrhythmogenic right ventricular dysplasia, etc.

 **TREATMENT**

ACUTE GENERAL Rx

Patients with VT may become hemodynamically unstable very quickly. In such situations emergency synchronized cardioversion (or defibrillation for polymorphic rhythms) is needed. Those who subsequently become pulseless or unresponsive should be managed as per standard ACLS resuscitation protocols.

If the patient is hemodynamically stable, either IV amiodarone, lidocaine (especially if there is a suspicion of ongoing ischemia) or procainamide may be used. In the case of a patient with sustained monomorphic VT and a known structurally normal heart, IV beta blockers or calcium blockers may be used. It must be remembered that use of all these agents may be associated with hemodynamic deterioration and an external defibrillator must be made available at all times.

Electrolyte supplementation is essential if hypokalemia or hypomagnesemia is detected.

CHRONIC Rx

An implantable cardioverter-defibrillator (ICD) is indicated for all cases of hemodynamically untolerated monomorphic VT in patients with structural heart disease or prior MI (in the absence of a successful catheter ablation that eliminates all VT, which is usually possible only in patients with normal LVEF and stable VT), since it indicates the presence of a scar and risk of subsequent arrhythmias. Patients with idiopathic VT and structurally normal hearts generally do not require an ICD, but in cases of syncope associated with VT that cannot be successfully treated with ablation, it may be considered. For polymorphic VT, a reversible cause such as ischemia or electrolyte disturbances can sometimes be found, and an ICD may not be appropriate under these circumstances.

Chronic therapy with antiarrhythmic medications such as amiodarone, mexiletine, or sotalol may be needed even after ICD implantation if the patient presents with multiple appropriate shocks. Cather ablation of VT, particularly if performed early after first appropriate ICD discharge, is also very effective in preventing further ICD discharges and is associated with improved acute and long-term outcomes.

DISPOSITION

Patients with sustained VT, either monomorphic or polymorphic, should always be managed in an intensive care unit due to the risk of degeneration to a hemodynamically unstable rhythm. An electrophysiologist should be consulted.

REFERRAL

All patients with VT or NSVT should be referred to a cardiologist or a cardiac electrophysiologist.

 **PEARLS & CONSIDERATIONS**

COMMENTS

- Use of antiarrhythmic drugs, especially IC agents, to treat NSVT is associated with increased mortality (CAST trial), while beta blockers have been shown to be helpful.
- In patients with coronary disease, NSVT has not been shown to have an adverse significance if LVEF is >40%. If the EF is below 40%, the MUSTT trial showed a benefit of EP-guided ICD therapy over antiarrhythmic agents such as mexiletine, propafenone, sotalol, or amiodarone. Patients with LVEF <35% are candidates for prophylactic ICD implantation based on the MADIT II and SCDHeFt trials.
- In hypertrophic cardiomyopathy, NSVT does seem to confer an increased risk of sudden death, especially if symptomatic, prolonged, or repetitive.
- There are certain conditions in which NSVT does not seem to have an adverse significance and does not predict sudden cardiac death. These include nonischemic dilated cardiomyopathy, mitral valve prolapse, mitral regurgitation, and absence of structural heart disease.

PATIENT/FAMILY EDUCATION

Patients with familial or genetic causes of ventricular tachycardia, should have family screening of first degree relatives.

RELATED TOPICS

Arrhythmogenic Right Ventricular Dysplasia (Related Key Topic)
Brugada Syndrome (Related Key Topic)
Long QT Syndrome (Related Key Topic)
Torsade de Pointes (Related Key Topic)

SUGGESTED READINGS

Available at www.expertconsult.com

AUTHOR: **JOYDEEP GHOSH, M.D.**

BASIC INFORMATION

DEFINITION

Vertebral compression fractures (VCFs) are defined as fractures of spinal vertebrae in which a bony surface is driven toward another bony surface. These fractures are classified as radiographic reductions in vertebral body height of more than 15%.

SYNONYMS

Thoracolumbar vertebral compression fractures
Osteoporotic fractures

ICD-10 CODES

M80.0	Post-menopausal osteoporosis with pathologic fracture
M80.4	Drug-induced osteoporosis with pathological fracture
M80.5	Idiopathic osteoporosis with pathological fracture
M80.8	Other osteoporosis with pathological fracture
M80.9	Unspecified osteoporosis with pathological fracture
S32.009A	Unspecified fracture of unspecified lumbar vertebra, initial encounter for closed fracture
S22.009A	Unspecified fracture of unspecified thoracic vertebra, initial encounter for closed fracture

EPIDEMIOLOGY & DEMOGRAPHICS

~700,000 VCFs occur in the United States each year, and they affect up to 25% of postmenopausal women. The prevalence increases with age, reaching a peak of 40% to 50% among women aged >80 yr. Compression fractures are also a major concern among men, although their rates of VCF are lower.

RISK FACTORS:

- Modifiable: tobacco or alcohol use, osteoporosis, estrogen deficiency (i.e., early menopause, bilateral oophorectomy, premenopausal amenorrhea for >1 yr), frailty, impaired vision, abusive situations, inadequate physical activity, low body mass index, and deficiency of vitamin D or calcium
- Nonmodifiable: advanced age, female gender, dementia, Caucasian descent, history of fractures in adulthood and among first-degree relatives, and falls

PHYSICAL FINDINGS & CLINICAL PRESENTATION

- Asymptomatic: Most VCFs are asymptomatic, except for height loss or kyphosis (i.e., dowager's hump [Fig. 1V-26]), which is often a sign of multiple VCFs and height loss of >6 cm has a sensitivity/specificity of 94% and 30%, respectively, for VCF.
- Symptomatic: When symptomatic, VCFs usually present as acute back pain after activity (e.g., bending, lifting) or coughing; neck strain and radicular rib pain may also be present.

ETIOLOGY

- VCFs take place when the combination of bending and the axial load on the spine exceed the strength of the vertebral body.
- The primary etiology of VCF is osteoporosis, though a pathologic fracture from an underlying malignancy, typically metastatic disease, must be ruled out.

Dx DIAGNOSIS

DIFFERENTIAL DIAGNOSIS

- Osteoporosis
- Malignancy, most often metastases
- Hyperparathyroidism
- Osteomalacia
- Granulomatous diseases (e.g., tuberculosis)
- Hematologic/oncologic diseases (e.g., multiple myeloma, primary bone malignancy)

WORKUP

- Only one third of VCFs are diagnosed. Guidelines for patient selection for vertebral fractural assessment are described in Box 1V-1.
- VCFs can be clinically suspected from the history and physical alone, though they are often diagnosed incidentally by imaging performed for another indication.
- There may or may not be a specific injury or a remembered event that led to the VCF.

LABORATORY TESTS

Tests to rule out infection or cancer may be helpful, such as a CBC, an erythrocyte sedimentation rate, an alkaline phosphatase level, and a C-reactive protein level; these tests can be reserved for individuals for whom there is clinical suspicion.

IMAGING STUDIES

- Plain frontal and lateral radiographs (x-rays) are the initial imaging method (Fig. 1V-26) and may be sufficient, particularly when no neurologic abnormalities are present. MRI and computed tomography (CT) scans may be uncomfortable or painful for the patient, especially during the acute phase.
- Although CT scans are not routinely necessary for the diagnosis, they can be helpful for visualizing fractures that are not seen on plain films, for evaluating the integrity of the posterior vertebral wall, for ruling out other causes of back pain, for detecting spinal canal narrowing, and for assessing instability.
- MRI may be useful when spinal cord compression is suspected, if neurologic symptoms are present, or to distinguish malignancy from osteoporosis (e.g., in patients <55 yr with VCF after minimal or no trauma).
- Bone density studies may be helpful to determine the severity of osteoporosis, which is a key risk factor for future fractures.

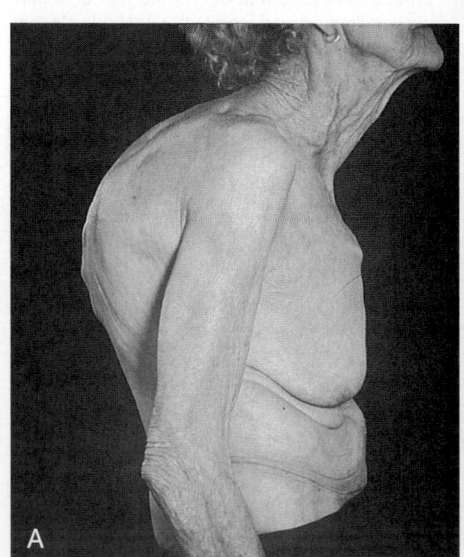
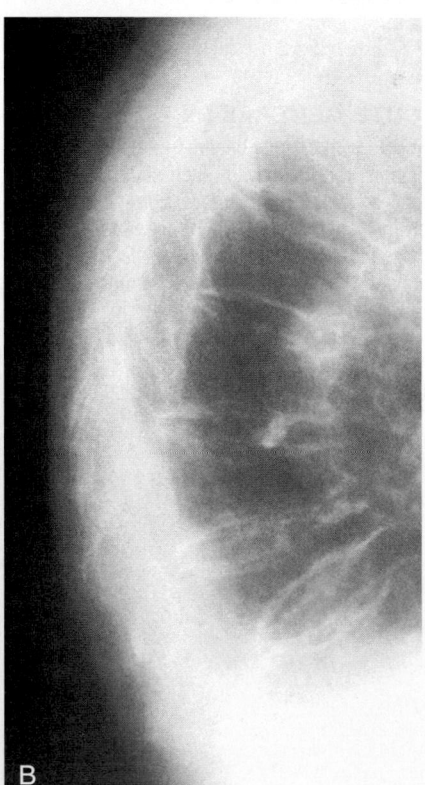

FIGURE 1V-26 Dowager's hump. A, Marked thoracic kyphosis due to multiple osteoporotic fractures in an elderly woman with corresponding radiograph (**B**). (From Hochberg MC et al [eds]: *Rheumatology*, ed 3, St Louis, 2003, Mosby.)

Rx TREATMENT

NONPHARMACOLOGIC THERAPY

- Physical therapy
- External back braces: Frequently recommended to relieve pain and improve mobility, however, controlled trials have not shown any effect in patients with vertebral compression fractures.
- Exercise programs: Getting active as soon as possible is extremely important for both short- and long-term recovery.

ACUTE GENERAL Rx

- Analgesics are first line for pain control, including acetaminophen and opioids (oral or parenteral), and pain can be expected to diminish over 4 to 6 wk.
- Nonsteroidal antiinflammatory drugs are helpful but must be used with caution among elderly patients or when contraindicated.
- Muscle relaxants should be used judiciously because they have significant side effects, particularly in the elderly.
- Intranasal calcitonin (200 units once daily, alternating nostrils) has been shown in some small trials to hasten relief from pain when used as an adjunct to oral analgesics, and a 2- to 4-wk course may be useful for patients who do not achieve adequate control with oral analgesics alone.
- Early mobilization with physical therapy is important for recovery and prevention of subsequent fractures.
- The efficacy of vertebroplasty versus kyphoplasty versus conservative treatment remains controversial.

- Percutaneous vertebroplasty involves the injection of acrylic bone cement into the affected vertebral body in an effort to stabilize the fracture and reduce pain, whereas in kyphoplasty, a high-pressure inflatable bone tamp or balloon is expanded within the body of the affected vertebra to restore prefracture vertebral height before the injection of bone cement. These two procedures were thought to be helpful in patients who did not respond to conservative therapy; however, further studies showed them to be no more effective than sham procedures (Buchbinder et al., 2009; Kallmes et al., 2009). Nonetheless, Klazen et al. (2010) demonstrated in an open-label prospective randomized trial that for the subgroup of patients with acute osteoporotic VCFs fractures and persistent pain, percutaneous vertebroplasty may provide immediate pain relief, sustained for at least a year, which may be significantly greater than that achieved with conservative treatment. Zampiri (2011) showed in a nonrandomized cohort study that elderly patients who underwent kyphoplasty were more likely to be discharged home. McCullough et al. (2013) analyzed Medicare claims of patients with VCF treated with kyphoplasty or vertebroplasty compared with medical management and found no difference in mortality or major medical outcomes but decreased health care utilization in the conservatively managed group. These procedures are still in their infancy, and more answers should be forthcoming as to their efficacy, as well as questions regarding the amount of time that conservative therapy alone should be pursued and which procedure, if any, should be advised. Most current guidelines recommend 4 to 6 wk of medical therapy before pursuing surgical intervention in neurologically intact VCF.

CHRONIC Rx

Osteoporosis should be treated with the reduction of risk factors (e.g., smoking, alcohol), diet, exercise, calcium and vitamin D supplements, and with medications used to treat osteoporosis (e.g., bisphosphonates).

REFERRAL

Referral is indicated for neurologic abnormalities, unremitting pain, instability, continued disability, or when the investigation of the cause of the fracture reveals serious underlying pathology.

! PEARLS & CONSIDERATIONS

Prevention of osteoporosis and conservative therapy remain the mainstays of treatment.

COMMENTS

- VCFs should be suspected in anyone aged >50 yr with the acute onset of low back pain. There are many opportunities for diagnosis and treatment that are easy to miss, especially for males.
- Solitary vertebral fractures higher than T7 are unusual and should raise suspicion for other pathologic causes.
- Diagnosing and treating osteoporosis reduce the incidence of VCFs.
- Getting people with VCF physically active as soon as possible will be efficacious both acutely and in the long term.
- In general, VCF will be best managed through a partnership of the patient, the primary care physician, an orthopedist, a physical therapist, a dietitian, and a social worker.

PREVENTION

Reducing the effects of modifiable risk factors is key.

EBM EVIDENCE

Available at www.expertconsult.com

SUGGESTED READINGS

Available at www.expertconsult.com

AUTHOR: **THOMAS J.T. ANDERSON, M.D.**

BOX 1V-1 **2007 ISCD Guidelines for Patient Selection for Vertebral Fractural Assessment**

- Postmenopausal women with low bone mass (osteopenia) by BMD criteria, *plus* any one of the following: age >70 yr, historical height loss >4 cm (1.6 in), or prospective height loss >2 cm (0.8 in), self-reported vertebral fracture (not previously documented)
- Two or more of the following: age 60 to 69 yr, self-reported prior non-vertebral fracture, historical height loss of 2 to 4 cm, or chronic systemic diseases associated with increased risk of vertebral fractures (e.g., moderate to severe COPD or COAD, seropositive rheumatoid arthritis, Crohn's disease)
- Men with low bone mass (osteopenia) by BMD criteria, *plus* any one of the following: age >80 yr, historical height loss >6 cm (2.4 in), prospective height loss >3 cm (1.2 in), self-reported vertebral fracture (not previously documented)
- Two or more of the following: age 70 to 79 yr, self-reported prior non-vertebral fracture, historical height loss of 3 to 6 cm, on pharmacologic androgen deprivation therapy or following orchiectomy, chronic systemic diseases associated with increased risk of vertebral fractures (e.g., moderate to severe COPD or COAD, seropositive rheumatoid arthritis, Crohn's disease)
- Women or men on chronic glucocorticoid therapy (equivalent to 5 mg or more of prednisone daily for 3 mo or longer)
- Postmenopausal women or men with osteoporosis by BMD criteria, if documentation of one or more vertebral fractures will alter clinical management

BMD, Bone mineral density; *COAD,* chronic obstructive airways disease; *COPD,* chronic obstructive pulmonary disease; *ISCD,* International Society for Clinical Densitometry.
Reproduced with permission from the International Society for Clinical Densitometry.
From Hochberg MC et al: *Rheumatology,* ed 5, St Louis, 2011, Mosby.

BASIC INFORMATION

DEFINITION

Vestibular neuronitis is a syndrome of sudden-onset dysfunction of the peripheral vestibular system, often severe, with prolonged vertigo, nausea, and vomiting.

SYNONYMS

Vestibular neuritis
Acute neuritis
Neurolabyrinthitis
Vestibular neuropathy

ICD-10CM CODES
H81.2   Vestibular neuronitis
H81.23 Vestibular neuronitis, bilateral
H81.20 Vestibular neuronitis, unspecified ear
H81.21 Vestibular neuronitis, right ear
H81.22 Vestibular neuronitis, left ear

EPIDEMIOLOGY & DEMOGRAPHICS

Vestibular neuritis is the second most common cause of peripheral vestibular vertigo with an incidence of about 3.5:100,000 population. Although etiology remains uncertain, thought to result from selective inflammation of the vestibular nerve, the etiology is presumed to be viral. Viral origin is supported by the fact that it occurs in epidemics, may affect several family members, and occurs more commonly in spring and early summer. The male-to-female ratio is nearly 1:1. There is selective damage to the superior part of the vestibular labyrinth, supplied by the superior vestibular portion of the eighth cranial nerve.

PHYSICAL FINDINGS & CLINICAL PRESENTATION

Course: develops, acutely, over period of hours and resolves over periods of days or weeks, although long-term sequelae may occur, such as residual imbalance and nonspecific dizziness persisting for months. Symptoms include vertigo, spontaneous peripheral nystagmus, positive head-thrust test, and imbalance. Patient reports intense sensation of rotation and difficulty standing and walking and tends to veer toward affected side; autonomic symptoms occur with pallor, sweating, nausea, and vomiting.

ETIOLOGY

Etiology remains uncertain. It is thought to be viral, or secondary to a post-viral inflammatory disorder, in origin, possibly due to herpes zoster, reactivation of herpes simplex, or other viruses, but evidence is circumstantial.

DIAGNOSIS

DIFFERENTIAL DIAGNOSIS

- Labyrinthitis: similar symptoms of vertigo, with the addition of unilateral hearing loss
- Labyrinthine infarction
- Acoustic neuroma
- Perilymph fistula
- Brain stem and cerebellar infarction
- Migraine-associated vertigo
- Meniere disease
- Multiple sclerosis

WORKUP

- Patient may fall toward affected side when attempting ambulation or during Romberg tests.
- Hallpike maneuver: checking for nystagmus and asking about recreation of vertigo symptoms
- Head-thrust test: grasp patient's head, apply brief small-amplitude rapid head turn, first to one side and then the other; patient fixates on examiner's nose: positive test is lack of corrective eye movements ("saccades") on affected side. A positive test supports the diagnosis of vestibular neuronitis.
- Laboratory testing and imaging are generally not indicated but may help rule out other etiologies

LABORATORY TESTS

- Electronystagmography (ENG): a battery of eye movement tests that may provide an objective assessment of the vestibular and oculomotor systems and may help localize the lesion's site
- Audiogram: normal

IMAGING STUDIES

Brain imaging: CT or MRI—normal

TREATMENT

NONPHARMACOLOGIC THERAPY

Vestibular exercises, when tolerated, will accelerate recovery.

ACUTE GENERAL Rx

Most treatments are empirical and related to symptoms. Further studies are needed.

- Corticosteroids: corticosteroids are often prescribed, although a recent Cochrane Review finds that there is insufficient evidence for administration. Some studies have shown that glucocorticoids administered within 3 days after onset of vestibular neuronitis may improve long-time recovery of vestibular function and reduce the length of hospital stay and may improve the caloric extent and recovery of canal paresis.

- Antihistamines: e.g., meclizine, dimenhydrinate, promethazine
- Anticholinergics: scopolamine
- Antiemetics: droperidol, prochlorperazine
- Benzodiazepines: e.g., diazepam, valium, lorazepam
- Valacyclovir, either alone or in combination, is likely ineffective in treating vestibular neuronitis.

CHRONIC Rx

- Vestibular rehabilitation exercises
- Anti-GABA agents
- Antihistamines

DISPOSITION

Most patients can be treated as outpatients, but inpatient care may be required in cases where vomiting is uncontrollable. If dehydrated because of severe vomiting, sufferers may require brief parenteral therapy.

REFERRAL

- ENT: if diagnosis uncertain, and if these patients are at risk for benign paroxysmal positional vertigo (BPPV) subsequently; also if symptoms linger
- Neurology: if question of central origin or migraine

PEARLS & CONSIDERATIONS

COMMENTS

- Diagnosis unlikely to be vestibular neuronitis if hearing is impaired or other neurologic signs and symptoms are present.
- Although patients may recover from dramatic acute symptoms, subtle vestibular deficits may linger for prolonged period, if not indefinitely (i.e., residual imbalance and nonspecific dizziness).
- Program of vestibular habituation head movement exercises can reduce imbalance symptoms.

PATIENT & FAMILY EDUCATION

Vestibular Disorders Association: http://www.vestibular.org

SUGGESTED READINGS
Available at www.expertconsult.com

RELATED CONTENT

Benign Paroxysmal Positional Vertigo (Related Key Topic)
Meniere's Disease (Related Key Topic)
Labyrinthitis (Related Key Topic)

AUTHOR: **ROCCO J. RICHARDS, M.D.**

BASIC INFORMATION

- Vitamin D is a hormone and a steroid and, by definition, not a vitamin. There are two forms of vitamin D: vitamin D_2 and vitamin D_3.
- Vitamin D_2 (ergocalciferol)is mainly found in some plant foods.
- Vitamin D_3 (cholecalciferol)is produced in skin exposed to ultraviolet (UV) B radiation from sunlight (Fig. 1V-27). Gloson, Whistler, and DeBoot independently described rickets in the mid-seventeenth century. Sniadecki first reported the association of rickets with inadequate exposure to sunlight in 1822.
- The major functions of vitamin D include:
  1. Increasing calcium and phosphorus absorption from the small intestines.
  2. Promoting the maturation of osteoclast to resorb calcium from bones.

DEFINITION

Vitamin D deficiency is characterized by impaired bone mineralization. It is classified as a serum 25-hydroxyvitamin D (25[OH]D) level of <20 ng/mL (50 nmol/L).

The consequences of vitamin D deficiency include:

- Bone disease (rickets, osteoporosis, low bone mass)
- May impair reproductive success
- Decrease the ability to combat infection (especially TB, influenza, viral infection)
- May induce or worsen autoimmune disorders
- May increase the incidence of death due to heart disease, IBD, fracture, and cancer of the breast, colon, and prostate

SYNONYMS

The sunshine vitamin
The antirachitic factor
Cholecalciferol

ICD-10CM CODES
E55.9 Vitamin D deficiency, unspecified

EPIDEMIOLOGY & DEMOGRAPHICS

INCIDENCE:
- Vitamin D insufficiency is very high among older adults and hospitalized and institutionalized people.
- Worldwide deficiency and insufficiency affect about 1 billion people.
- Children and young adults: 40% to 50% of preadolescent Caucasian girls, and Hispanic and African American adolescents, are vitamin D deficient.

PEAK INCIDENCE: In the United States, 40% to 100% of the elderly are vitamin D deficient.
60% of nursing home residents may be vitamin D deficient.

PREVALENCE: 42% of African American girls and women 15 to 49 yr old have 25(OH)D levels <20 ng/dl.

PREDOMINANT SEX AND AGE:
- Decreased skin production of vitamin D with age
- Increased prevalence among darker-skinned individuals

RISK FACTORS:
1. Age (due to decreased ability to produce D_3)
2. Sunshine-deficient areas (geographic location, living in higher latitudes)
3. Dark-skinned individuals (melanin competes with vitamin D_3 precursors for UV photons and thus decreases pre-D_3 formation)
4. Obese individuals
5. Institutionalized individuals
6. Pregnant and lactating women
7. Use of sunscreen (sun radiation that causes skin cancer also produces pre-vitamin D_3 in skin)
8. Patients on certain medications that antagonize vitamin D action (phenobarbital, phenytoin)
9. Intestinal resection
10. Severe chronic liver diseases (such as cirrhosis)
11. Kidney disease (e.g., nephritic syndrome)
12. Sarcoidosis and lymphomas (increased catabolism of 25[OH]D to 1,25[OH]2D)
13. Intestinal malabsorption disease (caused by celiac sprue, cystic fibrosis, Whipple's disease)

PHYSICAL FINDINGS & CLINICAL PRESENTATION

- Rickets—seen in children; caused by defective mineralization in the skeleton (Fig. 1V-28).
  1. Bowing of the legs
  2. Leg bone pain
  3. Delayed growth

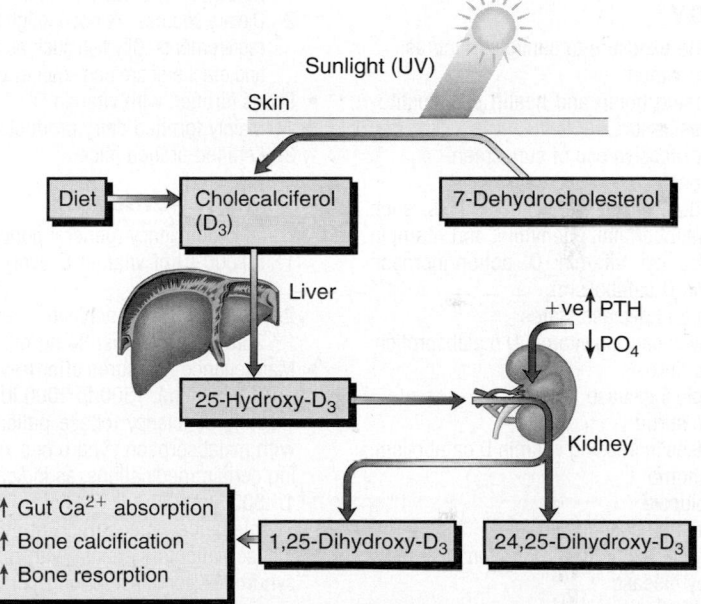

FIGURE 1V-27 The metabolism and actions of vitamin D. The primary source of vitamin D in humans is photoactivation in the skin of 7-dehydrocholesterol to cholecalciferol, which is then converted first in the liver to 25-hydroxyvitamin D and subsequently in the kidney to the much more active form, 1,25-dihydroxycholecalciferol $(1,25[OH]_2,D_3)$. Regulation of the latter step is by PTH, phosphate, and feedback inhibition by $1,25(OH)_2,D_3$. This step can also occur in lymphomatous and sarcoid tissue, resulting in the hypercalcemia that may complicate these diseases. (From Ballinger A: *Kumar & Clark's essentials of clinical medicine,* ed 6, Edinburgh, 2012, Saunders.)

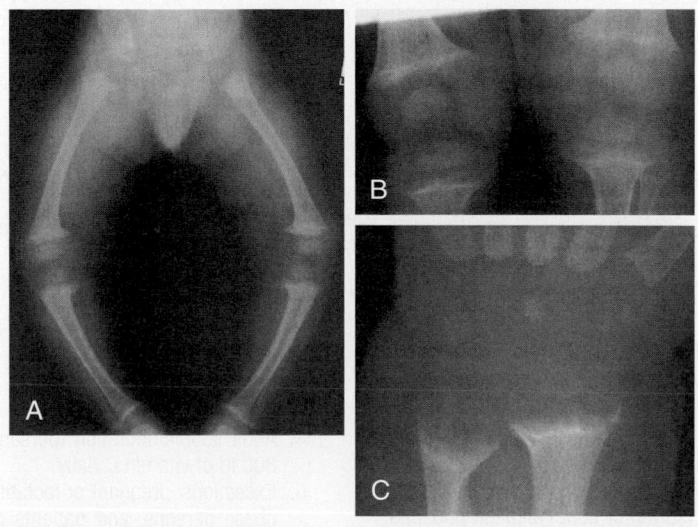

FIGURE 1V-28 Radiographs of a child with vitamin D–deficiency rickets demonstrating bowing of the femurs and tibias (**A**) and widened, frayed, demineralized epiphyseal plates (**B** and **C**). (From Hochberg MC et al: *Rheumatology,* ed 5, St Louis, 2011, Mosby.)

4. Seizure due to hypocalcemia
- Osteomalacia—seen in adults
  1. Periosteal bone pain (best detected by putting a firm pressure on tibia or sternal bones)
  2. Proximal muscle weakness
  3. Chronic muscle aches/pain
- Fracture with very minimal trauma (brittle and easily broken bones)
- Severe hypocalcemia—especially in late vitamin D deficiency leading to seizure tetany
- Hypophosphatemia
- Neuromuscular
- Paresthesia
- Tetany
- Muscle cramps

ETIOLOGY
- Inadequate exposure to sunlight, such as:
  1. During winter
  2. In nursing home and health care institution residents
  3. With excessive use of sunscreen
- Medications:
  1. Individuals on certain medications, such as phenobarbital, phenytoin, and rifampin (antagonize vitamin D action/increase vitamin D catabolism)
- Diseases and disease states:
  1. Diseases causing vitamin D malabsorption:
     Cystic fibrosis
     Whipple's disease
     Celiac sprue
  2. Diseases increasing vitamin D catabolism:
     Lymphoma
     Sarcoidosis
  3. Intestinal resection
  4. Decreased 25(OH)D production:
     Kidney disease
     Liver cirrhosis

DIAGNOSIS

DIFFERENTIAL DIAGNOSIS
- Arthritis
- Fibromyalgia

WORKUP
- Population-wide screening for vitamin D deficiency is not recommended because evidence to support this practice is lacking.
- Screening is needed for individuals at risk (osteoporosis, history of falls, obese persons, pregnant and lactating women, diseases causing vitamin D malabsorption, African Americans). Workup involves blood and urine tests as well as radiography, as outlined in the next section.

LABORATORY TESTS
- Serum 25(OH)D: this is the best test to determine vitamin D status.
- Parathyroid hormone (PTH): increased levels in vitamin D insufficiency. It is a marker of vitamin D insufficiency.
- Increased (serum or bone) alkaline phosphatase.
- Decreased 24-hour urine calcium (patient should not be on a thiazide).

IMAGING STUDIES
- Radiographs may show:
  1. Pseudofractures of the pelvis, femur, metatarsals
  2. Nontraumatic fractures
- Bone density:
  1. Decreased bone mineral density (osteopenia or osteoporosis).

TREATMENT

NONPHARMACOLOGIC THERAPY
- Natural sources of vitamin D. These include:
  1. Exposure to sunlight. A mild sunburn is equivalent to consuming 10,000 to 25,000 IU of dietary vitamin D.
  2. Dietary sources are not enough to meet daily requirements. Oily fish such as salmon, cod, and mackerel are rich sources of vitamin D₃.
- Foods fortified with vitamin D.
  1. Mainly fortified dairy products.
  2. Fortified orange juice.

ACUTE GENERAL Rx
- Treating deficiency (general population):
  1. 50,000 IU of vitamin D every week for 8 weeks, or
  2. 6000 IU daily to achieve a serum level of 25(OH)D of at least 30 ng/mL.
- Maintenance measures after treatment (general population): 1500 to 2000 IU daily.
- Treating deficiency (obese patients, patients with malabsorption syndromes, or those taking certain medications, as indicated earlier).
  1. 6000 to 10,000 IU daily.
- Maintenance measures after treatment (obese patients, patients with malabsorption syndromes, or those taking certain medications, as indicated earlier):
  1. 3000 to 6000 IU daily.
- After treating deficiency, recheck 25(OH)D in 12 to 14 weeks.

If deficiency persists after several attempts at treatment, try UV B light therapy

REFERRAL
Referral to an endocrinologist is recommended if there is no response to treatment.

PREVENTION
- Food fortification with vitamin D₂ or vitamin D₃.
- Adequate sun exposure, for example, exposure in the middle of the day (between 10:00 AM and 3:00 PM).
- Vitamin D supplementation (per the Endocrine Society):
  1. Infants (age range 1-12 mo) require at least 400 IU/day of vitamin D
  2. Children (age range 1-18 yr) require 600 IU/day of vitamin D
  3. Adult supplementation (adults 19-70 yr): 600 IU of vitamin D daily
  4. Adult supplementation (persons ≥70 yr): 800 IU of vitamin D daily
  5. Exceptions: pregnant or lactating women, obese persons, and patients on antiseizure medications, steroids, antifungals, and AIDS medications should be given 2× to 3× more vitamin D

- Screening: recommended only for individuals at high risk for vitamin D deficiency such as blacks and Hispanics, obese individuals (BMI >30 kg/m²), patients with osteoporosis, the elderly, and patients with certain chronic diseases (see "Risk Factors"). According to the U.S. Preventive Services Task Force (USPSTF), current evidence is insufficient to assess the balance of benefits and harms of screening for vitamin D deficiency in asymptomatic adults.

PEARLS & CONSIDERATIONS
- In the U.S., vitamin D supplements are available by prescription as vitamin D₂ (ergocalciferol) or over the counter as vitamin D₃ (cholecalciferol, usually in 400-1000-IU doses). Both vitamin D₂ and vitamin D₃ are acceptable as supplements. On average, oral vitamin D₃ raises blood levels more than does vitamin D₂.
- Upper limit of maintenance tolerability in healthy adults is 4000 IU a day. More than 4000 IU of vitamin D daily in nondeficient individuals increases the risk of harm. High-level supplements (>10,000 IU daily) are associated with kidney and tissue damage.
- Vitamin D supplementation is recommended for fall prevention. High-dose vitamin D supplementation (≥800 IU daily) has been shown to be favorable in the prevention of hip fracture and any nonvertebral fracture in persons 65 years of age or older.
- Prescribing more than the recommended daily amount to improve quality of life or prevent cardiovascular disease or death is not advised.
- Trials have shown that low vitamin D levels are associated with depressive symptoms, especially in persons with a history of depression. These findings suggest that vitamin D levels may be useful in patients with a history of depression.
- Vitamin D supplementation, administered with calcium, has been shown to lower the risk for falling and improve muscle strength in the elderly, especially in older vitamin D–deficient women who are at high baseline risk for falling.
- The treatment of vitamin D insufficiency in asymptomatic persons might reduce mortality risk in institutionalized elderly persons and risks for falls but not fractures.
- Recent data suggest that vitamin D deficiency is associated with the risk of developing certain cancers (including breast, colon, and prostate).
- Vitamin D deficiency is associated with some autoimmune diseases (types 1 and 2 diabetes, metabolic syndrome, multiple sclerosis).

EVIDENCE
Available at www.expertconsult.com

SUGGESTED READINGS
Available at www.expertconsult.com

RELATED CONTENT
Vitamin D Deficiency (Patient Information)

AUTHOR: **DANIEL K. ASIEDU, M.D., PH.D.**

BASIC INFORMATION

DEFINITION

Vitamins are organic compounds that cannot be synthesized by humans but are required as nutrients in minute amounts. Vitamins have several different functions: They may regulate cell growth and differentiation, as catalysts, as antioxidants, and as co-enzymes. Vitamins are classified as either fat soluble (vitamins A, D, E, K) or water soluble (B group of vitamins and C). Deficiency of most vitamins is rare in Western countries. Certain groups may be prone to vitamin deficiency, and these are discussed here. Vitamin D deficiency is discussed in a separate topic.

SYNONYMS

Vitamin A: retinol
Vitamin E: alpha tocopherol
Vitamin K: phytonadione or menadiol
Vitamin B_1: thiamine
Vitamin B_2: riboflavin
Niacin: vitamin B_3; nicotinic acid
Vitamin B_5: pantothenic acid
Vitamin B_6: pyridoxine; pyridoxal phosphate
Folic acid: vitamin B_9; folate
Vitamin B_{12}: cyanocobalamin
Vitamin C: ascorbic acid

ICD-10CM CODES
E50	Vitamin A deficiency
E51	Thiamine deficiency
E53	Deficiency of other B group vitamins
E55	Vitamin D deficiency
E56	Other vitamin deficiencies
E56.0	Deficiency of vitamin E
E56.1	Deficiency of vitamin K
E53.0	Riboflavin deficiency
E52	Niacin deficiency [pellagra]
E53.1	Pyridoxine deficiency
E53.8	Deficiency of other specified B group vitamins
E54	Ascorbic acid deficiency

EPIDEMIOLOGY & DEMOGRAPHICS

Deficiency can occur in all age groups but is most common in the elderly.
Vitamin A deficiency: Affects 250 million preschool children worldwide.
Vitamin K deficiency: Varies by geographic regions; no race predilection; affects both sexes equally. Encountered often in infants.
Vitamin B_1 (thiamine) deficiency: Incidence is unknown; no sex, race, or age predilection.
Vitamin B_5 (pantothenic acid) deficiency: Rare, as it is present in all foods.
Vitamin B_{12} (cobalamin) deficiency: Relatively common. Occurs in all age groups but more common in the elderly.
Vitamin B_9 (folic acid) deficiency: Mandatory fortification started in 1998. Prevalence before fortification 16% and after 0.5%. Neural tube defect associated with low maternal folate status during pregnancy. Pregnant women and the elderly are at greatest risk of folic acid deficiency.
Vitamin C (ascorbic acid) deficiency: Smokers and low-income persons are at increased risk. Fig. 1V-29 shows environmental and nutritional factors in disease.

PHYSICAL FINDINGS & CLINICAL PRESENTATION

- Vitamin A: xerophthalmia, xerosis of the cornea, keratomalacia, Bitot's spots (abnormal squamous cell proliferation and keratinization of the conjunctiva), nyctalopia (poor adaptation to darkness)/night blindness, poor bone growth, dry skin and hair, follicular hyperkeratosis (caused by blockage of hair follicles by keratin), pruritus, broken fingernails
- Vitamin K: clinical manifestation usually occurs if hypoprothrombinemia is present. Major symptom is bleeding to minor trauma. Also can show easy bruisability, epistaxis, hematoma, or gum bleeding.
- Vitamin E: nerve dysfunction (ataxia; hyporeflexia, peripheral neuropathy); bone weakness.
- Vitamin B_1 (thiamine):
  1. Nervous system (dry beriberi): peripheral neuropathy, Wernicke encephalopathy, Korsakoff syndrome.
  2. Cardiovascular (wet beriberi): edema, chest pain, increased heart rate (HR), lowered blood pressure (BP).
  3. Gastrointestinal (GI): anorexia; constipation.
- Vitamin B_2 (riboflavin):
  1. Cheilosis (chapping and fissure of the lip)
  2. Glossitis (sore red tongue)
  3. Oily, scaly rashes on nasolabial folds, eyelids, scrotum, labia majoris
  4. Red itchy eyes
  5. Anemia
  6. Peripheral neuropathy
- Vitamin B_3 (niacin):
  1. Pellagra (4 Ds—diarrhea, dermatitis, dementia, and ultimately death).
  2. Hyperpigmentation of sun-exposed skin.
  3. "Raw beef" swollen and painful tongue.
- Vitamin B_6: seborrheic dermatitis; glossitis, cheilosis, impaired proprioception; sensory ataxia, seizure.
- Vitamin B_{12}: Neurologic symptoms including peripheral neuropathy, ataxia, paresthesia; subacute degeneration of the spinal cord (demyelination of the dorsal column). Patients may also have dementia, depression, and weakness. Glossitis and GI symptoms such as nausea, vomiting, and anorexia are also common.
- Vitamin B_9 (folic acid):
  1. Patchy hyperpigmentation of skin (especially between fingers and toes) and mucous membranes
  2. Moderate fever (temp <102° F) despite the absence of infection
  3. Neural tube defect
  4. Angular stomatitis
  5. Red, beefy, smooth, and shiny tongue.
- Vitamin C: scurvy (poor wound healing, petechiae, follicular hyperkeratosis, fatigue, bleeding gums, weight loss, bone abnormalities [Fig. E1V-30]).

ETIOLOGY

- Fat-soluble vitamins (vitamins A, D, E, K):
  1. Decreased ingestion, malnutrition, eating disorders.
  2. Diseases that affect fat absorption decrease the absorption of fat-soluble vitamins—for example, cystic fibrosis, celiac sprue, inflammatory bowel disease, cholestasis, hepatobiliary disease, small bowel surgery.
  3. Change in vitamin metabolism:
     1. Alcoholism
     2. Drugs such as cholestyramine, warfarin, anticonvulsants, antibiotics (e.g., cephalosporins)
     3. Chronic kidney disease
  4. Increased risk in:
     1. Vegans
     2. Recent immigrants
     3. Refugees
     4. Toddlers/preschoolers living below the poverty line
- Water-soluble vitamins (the B group of vitamins and vitamin C)—there are several etiologic factors, including:
  1. Inadequate intake
  2. Decreased absorption
  3. Alcoholism
  4. Pregnancy/lactation
  5. Peritoneal dialysis
  6. Medications (e.g., isoniazid, phenothiazines, tricyclic antidepressants)
  7. Malabsorption
  8. Low income
  9. Advanced age
- Vitamin B_{12} deficiency—caused by:
  1. Insufficient dietary intake, as in strict vegans
  2. Decreased absorption secondary to intrinsic factor deficiency, decreased intrinsic factor secretion, gastric atrophy, gastrectomy
  3. Terminal ileum disease such as celiac disease, enteritis, tropical sprue
- Folic acid deficiency—increased needs can lead to deficiency (e.g., pregnancy, lactation, malignancy).
- Derangement of folate metabolism by:
  1. Medication (e.g., methotrexate)
  2. Disease (e.g., hypothyroidism)
  3. Increased excretion: as seen in alcoholics

DIAGNOSIS

WORKUP/LABORATORY TESTS

- General initial laboratory tests include:
  1. Complete blood cell count (CBC). Liver function tests (LFTs). Basic metabolic panel (BMP). Albumin.
  2. Measurement of serum levels of the specific vitamin in question.

Vitamin	Function	Consequences of deficiency
A	Retinal function, epithelial growth control	Night blindness, keratomalacia, xerophthalmia
B_1 (thiamine)	Co-enzyme	Beri beri, Wernicke's encephalopathy
B_2 (riboflavin)	Co-enzyme	Dermatitis, glossitis, keratitis, neuropathy, confusion
B_6 (pyridoxine)	Co-enzyme	Neuropathy
B_{12} (cobalamin)	Nucleic acid synthesis	Megaloblastic anemia Subacute combined degeneration of spinal cord
Niacin	Co-enzyme NAD, NADP	Pellagra (diarrhea, dermatitis, and dementia)
Folate	Co-enzyme in nucleic acid synthesis	Megaloblastic anemia, villous atrophy of gut
Vitamin C	Co-factor in hydroxylation	Scurvy
Vitamin D	Calcium and phosphate absorption	Rickets (childhood) Osteomalacia (adults)
Vitamin E	Antioxidant	Spinocerebellar degeneration
Vitamin K	Co-factor for coagulation factor synthesis	Bleeding due to coagulation defects

FIGURE 1V-29 Environmental and nutritional factors in disease. (From Stevens A: *Core pathology*, pp. 139-150, St. Louis, 2009, Elsevier Limited. All rights reserved.)

- Specific tests may be considered in the following cases:
1. Vitamin A:
2. Serum retinal level (best test, a direct measure, expensive)
   Retinol binding protein (easier to perform, less expensive)
   Dark-adaptation threshold test.
   Vitamin K:
      Prothrombin time/partial thromboplastin time (PT/PTT).
      Prothrombin.
      Des-gamma-carboxy prothrombin (most sensitive test).
   Niacin: urine-*N*-methylnicotinamide (level <0.8 mg/day indicates niacin deficiency).
   Vitamin B_{12}:
      Serum vitamin B_{12} <100 pg/mL is diagnostic of vitamin B_{12} deficiency.
      Serum methylmalonic acid, which is elevated in B_{12} deficiency.
      Antiparietal antibody.
      Intrinsic factor antibody is decreased.
      Blood smear shows macrocytosis and hypersegmentation of megaloblasts.
      CBC shows increased mean corpuscle volume (MCV).

Megaloblastic anemia.
Folic acid:
Check serum folate level
   Additional testing includes checking for serum homocysteine level, which will be elevated.
   Red cell folate level shows chronic folate status.

Rx TREATMENT

Most of the vitamins are available over the counter individually or in different multivitamin formulations.
Specific vitamins:
Vitamin A deficiency: treat with oral supplementation 10,000 IU daily.
1. Consume vitamin A–rich foods such as liver, beef, carrots, oranges, mangoes.
2. 5 servings of fruit and vegetables give enough carotenoids for a day.
Vitamin K deficiency: treatment depends on the severity of bleeding, administered subcutaneously (SQ) or intramuscularly (IM).
Vitamin B_1 (thiamine) deficiency: give intramuscular thiamine 50 mg for several days.

1. If B_1 deficiency is suspected and patient needs intravenous glucose, give thiamine first before intravenous glucose. This prevents the development of Korsakoff psychosis.
Vitamin B_{12} deficiency: give 1000 mcg IM daily for 7 days, then once a week for 1 month, then once a month indefinitely.
1. A potential option is oral supplementation.
Folic acid deficiency: daily requirement is 400 to 1000 mcg (1 mg) daily.
1. Centers for Disease Control and Prevention (CDC) recommend that women of child-bearing age take 400 mcg of folic acid daily.

SUGGESTED READINGS
Available at www.expertconsult.com

RELATED CONTENT
Anemia, Pernicious (Related Key Topic)
Rickets (Related Key Topic)
Vitamin D Deficiency (Related Key Topic)
Wernicke Syndrome (Related Key Topic)

AUTHOR: **DANIEL K. ASIEDU, M.D., Ph.D.**

V

BASIC INFORMATION

DEFINITION

Vitiligo is the acquired loss of epidermal pigmentation that is characterized histologically by the absence of epidermal melanocytes. There are 6 types based on the extent and distribution of the involved areas: localized (single or few macules in one anatomic area), segmental, generalized, universal (entire body surface is depigmented), acrofacial (fingers, lips), and mucosal.

ICD-10CM CODES
L80 Vitiligo

EPIDEMIOLOGY & DEMOGRAPHICS

PREVALENCE: Vitiligo affects 0.5% to 1% of the population; it is the most common depigmenting disorder.

PREDOMINANT AGE: Vitiligo can begin at any age, but the age at onset is <20 yr for half of patients. Peak onset is between ages 10 and 30. Onset is usually earlier in females.

GENETICS: A positive family history is present in 25% to 30% of patients, and both sexes are equally affected. There are no differences in the rates of occurrence with regard to skin type or race; however, it occurs in more than 8% in some regions of India.

PHYSICAL FINDINGS & CLINICAL PRESENTATION

- Hypopigmented and depigmented lesions (Fig. 1V-31) favor sun-exposed regions, intertriginous areas, genitalia, and sites over bony prominences.
- Areas around the body orifices are also frequently involved.
- The lesions tend to be symmetric.
- Segmental vitiligo (20% of childhood cases and 5% of adult cases) often has a dermatomal or quasidermatomal distribution.
- Vitiligo lesions may occur at trauma sites (i.e., Koebner's phenomenon).
- The hair in affected areas may be white.
- The margins of the lesions are usually well demarcated; when a ring of hyperpigmentation is seen, the term *trichrome vitiligo* is used.
- The term *marginal inflammatory vitiligo* is used to describe lesions with raised borders.

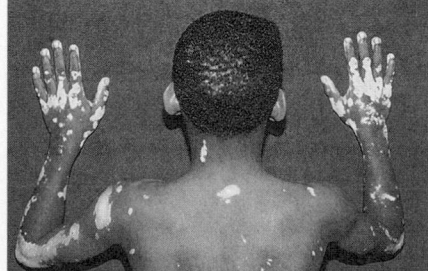

FIGURE 1V-31 Multiple, sharply demarcated, symmetric, depigmented areas of vitiligo. (From Behrman RE: *Nelson textbook of pediatrics,* Philadelphia, 2006, Saunders.)

- Initially the disease is limited, but the lesions tend to become more extensive over time.
- Focal vitiligo may affect nondermatomal areas (e.g., glans penis).
- Vitiligo may begin around pigmented nevi and produce a halo (i.e., Sutton's nevus); in such cases, the central nevus often regresses and disappears over time.

ETIOLOGY & PATHOGENESIS

- Three pathophysiologic theories:
  1. Autoimmune theory (i.e., autoantibodies against melanocytes)
  2. Neural theory (i.e., neurochemical mediators selectively destroy melanocytes)
  3. Self-destructive process in which melanocytes fail to protect themselves against cytotoxic melanin precursors
- Although vitiligo is considered to be an acquired disease, 25% to 30% of cases are familial. The mode of transmission is unknown; the condition seems to be polygenic or autosomal dominant with incomplete penetrance and variable expression.
- Associated disorders:
  1. Alopecia areata
  2. Type 1 diabetes mellitus
  3. Adrenal insufficiency
  4. Hyperthyroidism and hypothyroidism
  5. Mucocutaneous candidiasis
  6. Pernicious anemia
  7. Polyglandular autoimmune syndromes
  8. Melanoma
  9. Iritis and retinal pigmentary abnormalities

 DIAGNOSIS

DIFFERENTIAL DIAGNOSIS

- Acquired hypopigmentation disorders:
  1. Chemical-induced (e.g., chloroquine, imatinib, phenolic-catecholic derivatives [e.g., adhesives, deodorants, latex gloves, lacquer resins, varnish, soap antioxidants, insecticides, printing ink, paints, motor oil additives, disinfectants])
  2. Halo nevus
  3. Idiopathic guttate hypomelanosis
  4. Leprosy
  5. Leukoderma associated with melanoma
  6. Pityriasis alba
  7. Postinflammatory hypopigmentation
  8. Tinea versicolor
  9. Vogt-Koyanagi syndrome (i.e., vitiligo, uveitis, and deafness)
  10. Melasma
  11. Mycosis fungoides
- Congenital hypopigmentation disorders:
  1. Albinism, partial (piebaldism)
  2. Albinism, total
  3. Nevus anemicus
  4. Nevus depigmentosus
  5. Tuberous sclerosis
  6. Ito's hypomelanosis

WORKUP

- Inquire about a personal and family history of autoimmune disease.

- A Wood's light examination may enhance the lesions of light-skinned individuals.

TREATMENT

Treatment is indicated primarily for cosmetic purposes when depigmentation causes emotional or social distress. Depigmentation is more noticeable among patients with darker complexions.

- Cosmetic masking agents (e.g., Dermablend, Covermark) or stains (e.g., DY-O-Derm, Vitadye)
- Sunless tanning lotions (e.g., dihydroxyacetone)
- Repigmentation (This is achieved by the activation and migration of melanocytes from hair follicles; therefore, skin with little or no hair responds poorly to treatment.)
- Narrow-band ultraviolet B radiation (This is the preferred treatment for nonsegmental vitiligo. It is given twice weekly [not on successive days] during sessions that last from 5 to 10 min. The best results are achieved on the face, trunk, and limbs.)
- Psoralens and sunlight (e.g., PUVAsol)
- Topical mid-potency steroids (e.g., triamcinolone 0.1% or desonide 0.05% cream qd for 3 to 4 mo)
- Topical calcineurin inhibitors for face and neck lesions
- Intralesional steroid injection
- Systemic steroids (e.g., betamethasone 5 mg qd on two consecutive days per wk for 2 to 4 mo)
- Total depigmentation in cases of extensive vitiligo with 20% monobenzyl ether or hydroquinone (This is a permanent procedure, and patients will require lifelong protection from sun exposure.)
- Topical immunomodulators (e.g., tacrolimus, pimecrolimus) (These substances can also induce the repigmentation of vitiliginous skin lesions. However, their potential for systemic immunosuppression or for increasing the risk of skin cancer or other malignancies remains to be defined.)
- Calcipotriol, which is a synthetic analog of vitamin D_3 (This has also been used in combination with ultraviolet light or clobetasol, with limited results.)
- Surgical techniques can be applied to limited lesions

EVIDENCE

Available at www.expertconsult.com

SUGGESTED READING
Available at www.expertconsult.com

RELATED CONTENT
Vitiligo (Patient Information)

AUTHOR: **FRED F. FERRI, M.D.**

 BASIC INFORMATION

DEFINITION

Von Willebrand's disease is a congenital disorder of hemostasis characterized by defective or deficient Von Willebrand factor (vWF). There are several subtypes of Von Willebrand's disease. The most common type (80% of cases) is type I, which is caused by a quantitative decrease in vWF; type IIA and type IIB are results of qualitative protein abnormalities; and type III is a rare, autosomal recessive disorder characterized by a near-complete quantitative deficiency of vWF. Acquired Von Willebrand's disease is a rare disorder that usually occurs in elderly patients and usually presents with mucocutaneous bleeding abnormalities and no clinically meaningful family history. It is often accompanied by a hematoproliferative or autoimmune disorder. Successful treatment of the associated illness can reverse the clinical and laboratory manifestations.

SYNONYMS

Pseudohemophilia
vWD

ICD-10CM CODES
D68.0 Von Willebrand's disease

EPIDEMIOLOGY & DEMOGRAPHICS

- Autosomal-dominant disorder.
- Most common inherited bleeding disorder.
- Prevalence is 1% to 2% in general population, according to screening studies; estimates based on referral for symptoms of bleeding suggest a prevalence of 30 to 100 cases per million.

PHYSICAL FINDINGS & CLINICAL PRESENTATION

- Generally normal physical examination.
- Mucosal bleeding (gingival bleeding, epistaxis) and gastrointestinal bleeding may occur.
- Easy bruising.
- Postpartum bleeding, bleeding after surgery or dental extraction, menorrhagia.
- Increased incidence of endometriosis (likely related to backflow of menses), miscarriages.

ETIOLOGY

Quantitative or qualitative deficiency of vWF (see "Definition").

 **DIAGNOSIS**

The diagnosis of Von Willebrand's disease generally requires two criteria: (1) a personal history, family history, or physical evidence of mucocutaneous bleeding and (2) a qualitative or quantitative decrease in functional activity of Von Willebrand's disease. The American Society of Hematology states that a definitive diagnosis of vWD may be made if vWF antigen levels are <30 IU/dl. It also describes a gray zone of 30 to 50 IU/dl, designated as "low vWF."

DIFFERENTIAL DIAGNOSIS

Platelet function disorders, clotting factor deficiencies.

WORKUP

- Laboratory evaluation (see "Laboratory Tests").
- Initial testing includes prothrombin time (normal), partial thromboplastin time (normal or slightly increased), platelet count (normal), and bleeding time (prolonged).
- Subsequent tests include vWF level (decreased), factor VIII:C (decreased), and ristocetin agglutination (increased in type IIB) (Table 1V-10).

LABORATORY TESTS

- Decreased factor VIII coagulant activity.
- Decreased vWF antigen or ristocetin cofactor.
- Normal platelet number and morphology.
- Prolonged bleeding time.
- Prolonged platelet analyzer-100 (PFA-100®)
- Type IIA Von Willebrand's disease can be distinguished from type I by absence of ristocetin cofactor activity and abnormal multimer.
- Type IIB Von Willebrand's disease is distinguished from type I by abnormal multimer.

Rx TREATMENT

NONPHARMACOLOGIC THERAPY

- Avoidance of aspirin and other nonsteroidal antiinflammatory drugs.
- Evaluation for likelihood of bleeding (with measurement of bleeding time) before surgical procedures. When a patient undergoes surgery or receives repeated therapeutic doses of concentrates, factor VIII activity should be assayed every 12 hr on the day a dose is administered and every 24 hr thereafter.

GENERAL Rx

- The mainstay of treatment in Von Willebrand's disease is the replacement of the deficient protein at the time of spontaneous bleeding or before invasive procedures are performed.
- Desmopressin acetate (DDAVP) is useful to release stored vWF from endothelial cells. It is used to cover minor procedures and traumatic bleeding in mild type I Von

Willebrand's disease. Dose is 0.3 mcg/kg in 100 mL of normal saline solution IV infused >20 min. DDAVP is also available as a nasal spray (dose of 150 mcg spray administered to each nostril) as a preparation for minor surgery and management of minor bleeding episodes. DDAVP is not effective in type IIA Von Willebrand's disease and is potentially dangerous in type IIB (increased risk of bleeding and thrombocytopenia).
- In patients with severe disease, replacement therapy in the form of cryoprecipitate is the method of choice. The standard dose is 1 bag of cryoprecipitate per 10 kg of body weight.
- Factor VIII concentrate rich in vWF (Humate-P) is useful to correct bleeding abnormalities in type IIA, IIB, and type III Von Willebrand's disease without alloantibodies. Alloantibodies that inactivate vWF and form circulating immune complexes develop in 15% of patients with type III Von Willebrand's disease who have received multiple transfusions. In these patients, recombinant factor VIII is preferred because autoantibodies can elicit life-threatening anaphylactic reactions because of complement activation by immune complexes.
- Life-threatening hemorrhage unresponsive to therapy with cryoprecipitate or factor VIII concentrate may require transfusion of normal platelets.
- Women with menorrhagia may benefit from estrogen-containing oral contraceptives (increased vWF levels, improved regular menses). Antifibrinolytic agents (tranexamic acid, e-aminocaproic acid) can also be used for severe menorrhagia.
- Fig. 1V-33 summarizes the approach to the management of VWD.

SUGGESTED READINGS
Available at www.expertconsult.com

RELATED CONTENT
Von Willebrand's Disease (Patient Information)

AUTHOR: **FRED F. FERRI, M.D.**

TABLE 1V-10 Genetic and Laboratory Findings in Von Willebrand's Disease

Parameter Type	BT	VIII-C	vW-Ag	R-Cof	RIPA	Multimer Structure	Mode of Inheritance
I (classic)	P	R	R	R	R	Normal	AD
II							
A	P	N/R	N/R	R	R	Abnormal	AD
B	P	N/R	N/R	N/R	I	Abnormal	AD
III	P	R	R	R	R	Variable	AR

AD, Autosomal dominant; *AR,* autosomal recessive; *BT,* bleeding time; *I,* increased; *N/R,* normal or reduced; *P,* prolonged; *R,* reduced; *R-Cof,* ristocetin cofactor; *RIPA,* ristocetin-induced platelet aggregation (agglutination); *vW-Ag,* Von Willebrand antigen (protein); *VIII-C,* factor VIII coagulant activity.

From Behrman RE: *Nelson textbook of pediatrics,* ed 17, Philadelphia, 2004, Saunders.

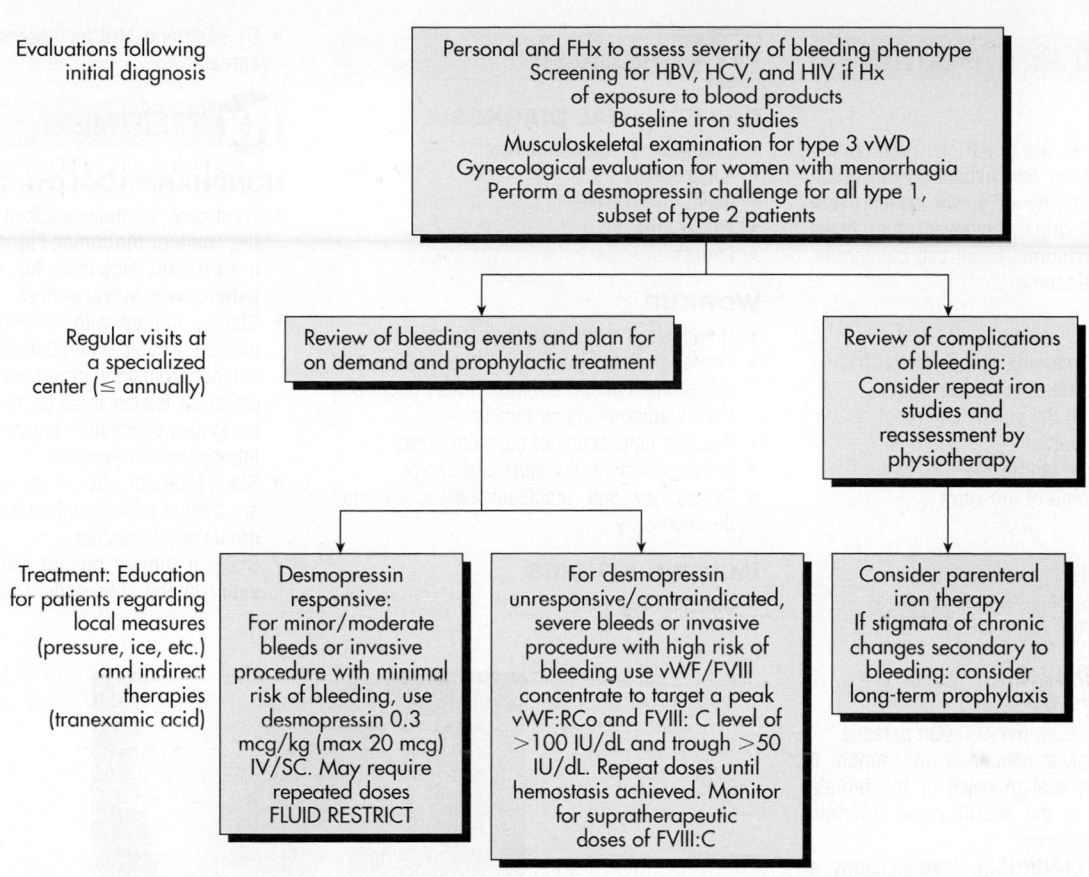

Evaluations following
initial diagnosis

Personal and FHx to assess severity of bleeding phenotype
Screening for HBV, HCV, and HIV if Hx
of exposure to blood products
Baseline iron studies
Musculoskeletal examination for type 3 vWD
Gynecological evaluation for women with menorrhagia
Perform a desmopressin challenge for all type 1,
subset of type 2 patients

Regular visits at
a specialized
center (≤ annually)

Review of bleeding events and plan for
on demand and prophylactic treatment

Review of complications
of bleeding:
Consider repeat iron
studies and
reassessment by
physiotherapy

Treatment: Education
for patients regarding
local measures
(pressure, ice, etc.)
and indirect
therapies
(tranexamic acid)

Desmopressin
responsive:
For minor/moderate
bleeds or invasive
procedure with minimal
risk of bleeding, use
desmopressin 0.3
mcg/kg (max 20 mcg)
IV/SC. May require
repeated doses
FLUID RESTRICT

For desmopressin
unresponsive/contraindicated,
severe bleeds or invasive
procedure with high risk of
bleeding use vWF/FVIII
concentrate to target a peak
vWF:RCo and FVIII: C level of
>100 IU/dL and trough >50
IU/dL. Repeat doses until
hemostasis achieved. Monitor
for supratherapeutic
doses of FVIII:C

Consider parenteral
iron therapy
If stigmata of chronic
changes secondary to
bleeding: consider
long-term prophylaxis

FIGURE 1V-33 Approach to the management of Von Willebrand's disease. (From Hoffman R: *Hematology, basic principles and practice,* ed 6, Philadelphia, 2013, Saunders.)

BASIC INFORMATION

DEFINITION

Vulvar cancer is an abnormal cell proliferation arising on the vulva and exhibiting malignant potential. The majority of vulvar cancers are of squamous cell origin; however, other types include adenocarcinoma, basal cell carcinoma, sarcoma, and melanoma.

SYNONYMS

Squamous cell carcinoma of the vulva (90%)
Basal cell carcinoma of the vulva
Adenocarcinoma of the vulva
Melanoma of the vulva
Bartholin gland carcinoma
Verrucous carcinoma of the vulva
Vulvar sarcoma

ICD-10CM CODE
C51.9 Malignant neoplasm of vulva, unspecified

EPIDEMIOLOGY & DEMOGRAPHICS

INCIDENCE: 2.2 cases per 100,000 persons
PREVALENCE: Vulvar cancer is uncommon. It comprises 4% of malignancies of the female genital tract. It is the fourth most common gynecologic malignancy.
MEAN AGE AT DIAGNOSIS: Predominantly a disease of menopause. Mean age at diagnosis is 65 yr.

PHYSICAL FINDINGS & CLINICAL PRESENTATION

- Vulvar pruritus or pain is present.
- May produce a malodorous discharge or present as bleeding.
- Raised lesion that may have fleshy (Fig. 1V-34), ulcerated, leukoplakic, or warty appearance; may have multifocal lesions.
- Lesions are usually located on labia majora but may be seen on labia minora, clitoris, and perineum.
- The lymph nodes of groin may be palpable.

ETIOLOGY

- The exact etiology is unknown.
- Vulvar intraepithelial neoplasia has been reported in 20% to 30% of invasive squamous cell carcinoma of the vulva, but the malignant potential is unknown.
- Human papillomavirus (HPV) is found in more than 50% of vulvar carcinoma, but its exact role is unclear. HPV is more likely to be found in younger women with vulvar cancer; older women are less likely to have HPV-associated cancer.
- Chronic pruritus, wetness, industrial wastes, arsenicals, hygienic agents, and vulvar dystrophies have been implicated as causative agents.
- Vulvar cancer in younger women is more directly dependent on HPV infection, vulvar dysplasia, and tobacco use.

DIAGNOSIS

DIFFERENTIAL DIAGNOSIS

- Lymphogranuloma inguinale
- Tuberculosis
- Vulvar dystrophies
- Vulvar atrophy
- Paget's disease

WORKUP

- Diagnosis is made histologically by biopsy
- Thorough examination of the lesion and assessment of spread. Table 1V-11 describes FIGO staging of vulvar cancer
- Possible colposcopy of adjacent areas
- Cytologic smear of vagina and cervix
- Cystoscopy and proctosigmoidoscopy may be necessary

IMAGING STUDIES

- Chest radiography
- CT scan and MRI for assessing local tumor spread

TREATMENT

NONPHARMACOLOGIC THERAPY

- Treatment is individualized depending on the stage of the tumor. Fig. 1V-35 describes a treatment algorithm for management of patients with vulvar cancer.
- Stage I tumors with <1 mm stromal invasion are treated with complete local excision without groin node dissection. Imiquimod 5% cream, a topical immune response modulator, is also effective in the treatment of vulvar intraepithelial neoplasia.
- Stage I tumors with >1 mm stromal invasion are treated with complete local excision with groin node dissection.
- Stage II tumors require radical vulvectomy with bilateral groin node dissection.

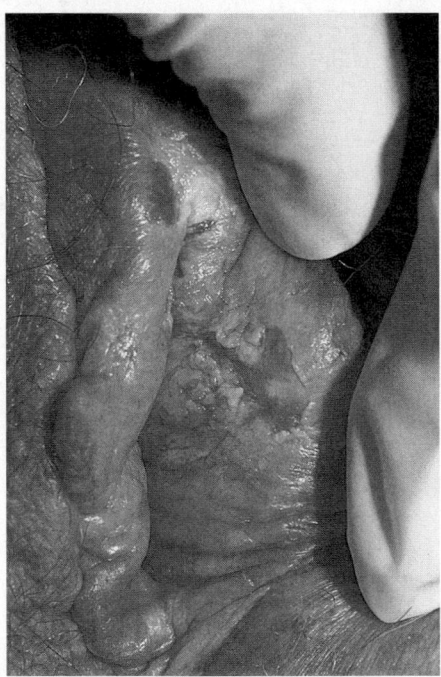

FIGURE 1V-34 Squamous cell carcinoma of the vulva. (From White GM, Cox NH [eds]: *Diseases of the skin, a color atlas and text,* ed 2, St Louis, 2006, Mosby.)

TABLE 1V-11 FIGO Staging of Vulval Cancer

Stage I	Tumor confined to the vulva—≤2 cm in diameter. Nodes are not involved.
	A. Lesions <1 mm depth invasion
	B. Other lesions <2 cm in diameter
Stage II	Tumor confined to the vulva—>2 cm in diameter. Nodes are not involved.
Stage III	Tumor of any size with:
	Adjacent spread to the lower urethra and/or the vagina, the perineum and the anus, and/or unilateral lymph node involvement.
Stage IV	Tumor of any size with bilateral groin lymph node involvement:
	A. Infiltrating the bladder mucosa or the rectal mucosa, or both, including the upper part of the urethral mucosa
	B. Fixed to the bone or other distant metastases. Fixed or ulcerated nodes in either one or both groins.

From Symonds EM, Symonds IM: *Essential obstetrics and gynecology,* ed 4, London, 2004, Churchill Livingstone.

- Advanced-stage disease may require the addition of radiation and chemotherapy to the surgical regimen.
- Fig. 1V-35 describes a treatment algorithm for management of vulvar cancer.

DISPOSITION
Five-year survival ranges from 90% for stage I to 15% for stage IV.

REFERRAL
Vulvar cancer should be managed by a gynecologic oncologist and radiation oncologist.

SUGGESTED READINGS
Available at www.expertconsult.com

RELATED CONTENT
Vulvar Cancer (Patient Information)

AUTHOR: **RUBEN ALVERO, M.D.**

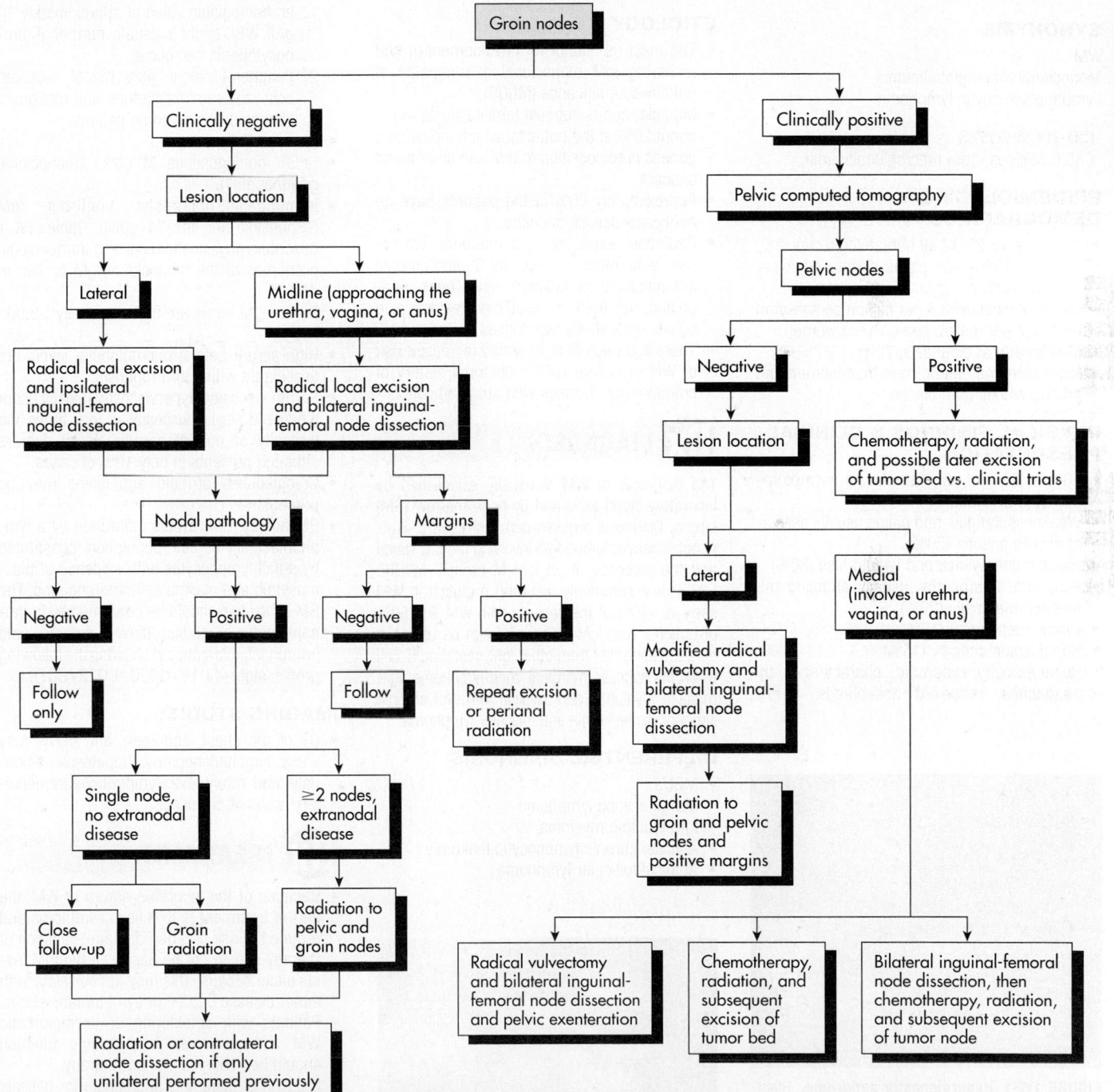

FIGURE 1V-35 Treatment algorithm for management of patients with vulvar cancer. (From Copeland LJ: *Textbook of gynecology,* ed 2, Philadelphia, 2000, Saunders.)

BASIC INFORMATION

DEFINITION
Waldenström macroglobulinemia (WM) is an indolent B-cell lymphoplasmacytic lymphoma (LPL)characterized by lymphoplasmacytic infiltration in the bone marrow (BM) or lymphatic tissue, and a monoclonal immunoglobulin M protein (IgM) in the serum. Less than 5% of LPL secrete IgG, IgA, or light chains.

SYNONYMS
WM
Monoclonal macroglobulinemia
Lymphoplasmacytic lymphoma

ICD-10CM CODES
C88.0 Waldenström macroglobulinemia

EPIDEMIOLOGY & DEMOGRAPHICS
- Accounts for 2% of all hematologic cancers
- 1000 to 1500 new cases diagnosed every year in the U.S.
- Overall incidence: 3.4 per million person-yr in men, 1.7 per million person-yr in women
- Median age at diagnosis: 70 yr
- More common among men than women and among whites than blacks

PHYSICAL FINDINGS & CLINICAL PRESENTATION
- 30% to 50% of patients can be asymptomatic at presentation.
- Weakness, fatigue, and pallor, usually associated with anemia (50%)
- Fever, night sweats, and weight loss (30%)
- Peripheral neuropathy, usually affecting the feet symmetrically (20%)
- Lymphadenopathy (15%)
- Hepatosplenomegaly (15%)
- Hyperviscosity syndrome, characterized by headaches, recurrent nosebleeds, blurry vision due to retinal hemorrhages (10%); retinal vein link: sausage shaped (Fig. 1W-1)
- Acrocyanosis, livedo reticularis, and purpura (Fig. 1W-2), usually associated with symptomatic cryoglobulinemia (5%-10%)
- Hemolytic anemia caused by cold agglutinin disease (5%)
- Amyloidosis causing renal dysfunction, neuropathy, and/or cardiac dysfunction (<5%)
- Meningeal signs caused by CNS involvement by WM (Bing Neel syndrome; 1%)

ETIOLOGY
- The main risk factor for development of WM is having IgM monoclonal gammopathy of unknown significance (MGUS).
- Multiple reports suggest familial clustering in about 20% of the patients, which indicates a genetic predisposition to WM and other blood cancers.
- Approximately 20% of the patients have an Ashkenazi Jewish ancestry.
- Radiation exposure, occupational chemicals, viral infection (hepatitis C), and chronic inflammatory stimulation have been suggested, but there is insufficient evidence to substantiate these hypotheses.
- There is a twofold to threefold increased risk of WM in people with a personal history of autoimmune diseases with autoantibodies.

DIAGNOSIS

The diagnosis of WM is usually established by laboratory blood tests and by bone marrow (BM) biopsy. Diagnosis requires demonstration of lymphoplasmacytic lymphoma involving the BM space and the presence of an IgM M protein. MYD88 L265P is a commonly recurring mutation in WM seen in >90% of the patients with WM and 50% of patients with IgM MGUS and can be useful in differentiating WM from other IgM-secreting B-cell disorders such as marginal zone lymphoma, IgM multiple myeloma, and atypical forms of chronic lymphocytic leukemia and follicular lymphoma.

DIFFERENTIAL DIAGNOSIS
- MGUS
- Marginal zone lymphoma
- IgM multiple myeloma
- Atypical chronic lymphocytic leukemia
- Atypical follicular lymphoma

WORKUP
In any patient suspected of having WM, specific blood tests (CBC, erythrocyte sedimentation rate [ESR], serum or urine protein electrophoresis [SPEP or UPEP, respectively], IgM level, beta 2-microglobulin, serum viscosity) should be ordered. BM biopsy confirms the diagnosis.

LABORATORY TESTS
- CBC with differential:
  1. Anemia is a common finding, with a median hemoglobin value of approximately 10 g/dl. WBC count is usually normal; thrombocytopenia can occur.
  2. Peripheral smear may reveal "stacked coin" rouleaux formations and malignant lymphoid cells in some patients.
- Elevated ESR.
- SPEP: homogeneous M spike (monoclonal gammopathy).
- Immunoelectrophoresis: confirms IgM responsible for the M spike. Table 1W-1 describes physicochemical and immunologic properties of the monoclonal IgM protein in WM.
- Serum IgM levels are high, generally >3,000 mg/dl.
- High serum beta 2-microglobulin levels are associated with poor prognosis.
- Serum viscosity. Hyperviscosity usually occur when the serum viscosity is four times the viscosity of normal serum; classic feature although presents in only 10% of cases.
- Cryoglobulins or cold agglutinins may be present.
- BM biopsy: BM reveals infiltration by a lymphoplasmacytic cell population constituted by small lymphocytes with evidence of plasmacytoid and plasma cell differentiation. The BM infiltration should be confirmed by immunophenotypic studies (flow cytometry and immunohistochemistry) showing the following profile: sIgM+CD19+CD20+CD22+CD79+.

IMAGING STUDIES
- CT of the chest, abdomen, and pelvis may show lymphadenopathy, hepatosplenomegaly, and rarely, extralymphatic/extramedullary areas of disease.

TREATMENT

- Because of the incurable nature of WM, the aim of treatment is to relieve symptoms and reduce the risk of organ damage. Initiation of therapy should not be based on the IgM levels alone because this may not correlate with either disease burden or symptomatic status. Patients with smoldering or asymptomatic WM and preserved hematologic function should be observed without therapy.
- Initiation of therapy is appropriate for patients with constitutional symptoms. Considerations for the initiation of treatment include the following: significant adenopathy or organomegaly, symptomatic hyperviscosity, severe neuropathy, amyloidosis, cryoglobulinemia, cold-agglutinin disease, hemoglobin concentration <10 g/dL, or evidence of disease transformation.

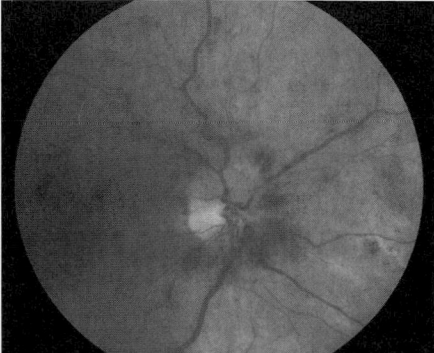

FIGURE 1W-1 Hyperviscosity syndrome. Right eye retinal image in a patient with Waldenström's macroglobulinemia and hyperviscosity syndrome showing sausaging (focal venular dilations), intraretinal hemorrhages, microaneurysms, and peripapillary cotton wool spots and disc swelling (papilledema). (From Goldman L, Schafer AI: *Goldman's Cecil medicine*, ed 24, Philadelphia, 2011, Saunders.)

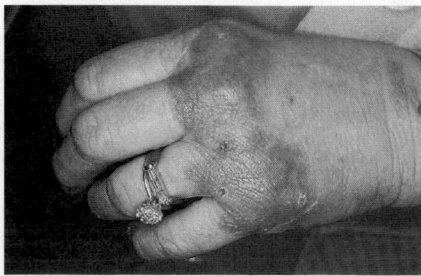

FIGURE 1W-2 Nonpalpable purpura of hyperglobulinemic purpura of Waldenström's hypergammaglobulinemia. (From Hochberg MC et al: *Rheumatology*, ed 5, St Louis, 2011, Mosby.)

TABLE 1W-1 Physicochemical and Immunologic Properties of Monoclonal Immunoglobulin Protein in Waldenström's Macroglobulinemia

Properties of Monoclonal Immunoglobulin Protein	Diagnostic Condition	Clinical Manifestations
Pentameric structure	Hyperviscosity	Headaches, blurred vision, epistaxis, retinal hemorrhages, impaired mentation, and intracranial hemorrhage
Prescription on cooling	Cryoglobulinemia (type I)	Raynaud's phenomenon, acrocyanosis, ulcers, purpura, and cold urticaria
Autoantibody activity to myelin-associated glyco-protein, ganglioside M1, and sulfatide moieties on peripheral nerve sheaths	Peripheral neuropa-thies	Sensorimotor neuropathies, painful neuropathies, ataxic gait, and bilateral foot drop
Autoantibody activity to immunoglobulin G	Cryoglobulinemia (type II)	Purpura, arthralgias, renal failure, and sensorimotor neuropathies
Autoantibody activity to red blood cell antigens	Cold agglutinins	Hemolytic anemia, Raynaud's phenomenon, acrocyanosis, and livedo reticularis
Tissue deposition as amorphous aggregates	Organ dysfunction	Skin: bullous skin disease, papules, and Schnitzler syndrome Gastrointestinal: diarrhea, malabsorption, and bleeding Kidney: proteinuria and renal failure (light-chain component)
Tissue deposition as amyloid fibrils (light-chain fibrils commonly the largest component)	Organ dysfunction	Fatigue, weight loss, edema, periorbital purpura, hepatomegaly, macroglossia, and organ dysfunc-tion of the involved organs: heart, kidney, liver, and peripheral sensory and autonomic nerves

From Hoffman R et al: *Hematology, basic principles and practice,* ed 5, Philadelphia, 2009, Churchill Livingstone.

- Treatment is directed at both hyperviscosity and the lymphoproliferative disorder itself.

NONPHARMACOLOGIC THERAPY

Asymptomatic patients do not require treatment, and these patients should be monitored periodically for the onset of symptoms or changes in blood tests (e.g., worsening anemia, thrombocytopenia, rising IgM levels, and serum viscosity). Plasmapheresis should be the initial treatment in patients with symptoms of hyperviscosity or cryoglobulinemia followed immediately by more definitive therapy.

INITIAL Rx

- Treatment of the lymphoproliferative disorder includes single or combination therapy. There is no universally agreed upon standard of care:
  1. Combination regimens include BDR (bortezomib, dexamethasone, rituximab), CaRD (carfilzomib, dexamethasone, rituximab), CDR (cyclophosphamide, dexamethasone, rituximab, cyclophosphamide), and bendamustine/rituximab. These should be used in patients with severe constitutional symptoms, symptomatic bulky disease,

hyperviscosity, or profound hematologic compromise. Response rates are >80%.
  2. Rituximab, a monoclonal anti-CD20 antibody, can be used in symptomatic patients with modest hematologic compromise, IgM-related neuropathy, or hemolytic anemia unresponsive to corticosteroids. Response rates are 40% to 50%.
  3. In April 2015, the FDA granted approval for the oral Bruton tyrosine kinase inhibitor ibrutinib to be used in patients with symptomatic WM. Response rates to ibrutinib are higher in patients with *MYD88* mutation.

RX ON RELAPSED/REFRACTORY DISEASE

- Rituximab is often used as maintenance therapy.
- Refractory patients can be retried on original therapy if length of response from initial therapy is >2 yr. If the response from the initial therapy was <2 yr, alternative first-line agents can be used. Trials with ibrutinib, a small molecule inhibitor of BTK that triggers apoptosis of Waldenström macroglobulinemia cells with MYD88 have shown that ibru-

tinib is highly active, associated with durable responses, and safe in pretreated patients with Waldenström macroglobulinemia.[1]
- Other treatment options: fludarabine, ofatumumab, thalidomide, everolimus, and clinical trials. Autologous stem cell transplantation should be considered in patients with highly refractory disease.

DISPOSITION

- The progression of WM is slow and insidious, with median survival from time of diagnosis of about 8 to 10 yr. About 10% to 20% of patients die from progression of the disease.
- Some patients develop acute myelogenous leukemia, usually secondary to exposure to chemotherapy, and some patients can develop more aggressive lymphomas.
- The risk of thyroid cancer, kidney cancer, and melanoma is increased in patients with WM.
- ~10% of patients will achieve complete remission, with prognosis being more favorable (median survival >10 yr).
- A staging system using serum beta 2-microglobulin concentration, hemoglobin concentration, and serum IgM concentration before treatment provides insight into prognosis and survival.
- Other factors can negatively affect the survival: age >65, male gender, the presence of organomegaly, and the presence of cytopenias.

REFERRAL

A Hematology consultation is helpful in guiding future workup, treatment, and monitoring. Participation in clinical trials is highly encouraged in patients with WM.

 **PEARLS & CONSIDERATIONS**

COMMENTS

- WM was first described in 1944 by the Swedish physician Jan Gösta Waldenström, who also described the X-linked Bruton agammaglobulinemia.

SUGGESTED READINGS

Available at www.expertconsult.com

AUTHOR: **JORGE J. CASTILLO, M.D.,** and **STEVEN P. TREON, M.D., PH.D.**

[1]Ibrutinib in previously treated Waldenström's macroglobulinemia, *N Engl J Med* 372:1430-1440, 2015.

BASIC INFORMATION

DEFINITION

Whiplash refers to a hyperextension injury to the neck, often the result of being struck from behind by a fast-moving vehicle.

SYNONYM

Acceleration flexion-extension neck injury

ICD-10CM CODES
S13.4 Sprain and strain of cervical spine

EPIDEMIOLOGY & DEMOGRAPHICS

- Whiplash occurs in more than 1 million people each year.
- Most injuries (40%) are the result of rear-end motor vehicle accidents.
- Whiplash occurs at all ages, in both sexes, and at all socioeconomic levels.
- Incidence is 4 per 1000 persons and is higher in women than men.
- Nearly 50% of patients with whiplash seek legal advice.
- Whiplash is also seen in shaken baby syndrome.

PHYSICAL FINDINGS & CLINICAL PRESENTATION

- Most present with a history of being involved in a motor vehicle accident and being rear-ended by another vehicle
- Pain not present initially but usually develops hr to a few days later
- Neck tightness and stiffness
- Occipital headache
- Shoulder, arm, and back pain
- Numbness in the arms
- Tinnitus
- Temporomandibular joint (TMJ) pain
- Dysphagia (retropharyngeal hematoma)
- Decreased range of motion of the neck
- Depressive symptoms

ETIOLOGY

- The mechanism of injury is the result of the sudden acceleration of the body forward, forcing the neck to hyperextend backward, causing injury to ligaments, muscles, bone, and/or intervertebral disk. At the end of the accident the head is thrust forward in a flexion position, sometimes causing injury to the cervical spine: C5-C6-C7.
- Motor vehicle accidents, trauma from falls, contact sports, physical abuse, and altercations are all possible causes of whiplash.

- The incidence of whiplash injury following polytrauma is low.
- Low-velocity crashes constitute a major cause of whiplash injury.

DIAGNOSIS

DIFFERENTIAL DIAGNOSIS

- Osteoarthritis
- Cervical disk disease
- Fibromyalgia
- Neuritis
- Torticollis
- Spinal cord tumor
- TMJ syndrome
- Tension headache
- Migraine headache

WORKUP

Any patient who presents with symptoms of whiplash and musculoskeletal or neurologic signs merits a workup to exclude cervical spine fracture or herniated disk disease.

LABORATORY TESTS

Laboratory studies are not helpful.

IMAGING STUDIES

- Plain cervical spine films (anteroposterior, lateral, and odontoid views)
- Flexion/extension x-rays
- CT scan to exclude fracture
- MRI as alternative or in addition to CT in selected cases

TREATMENT

NONPHARMACOLOGIC THERAPY

- Soft cervical collar for no longer than 72 hr
- Moist heat 15 to 20 min 4 to 6 times per day.
- Continue with usual activities.

ACUTE GENERAL Rx

- Analgesics
  1. NSAIDs
  2. Acetaminophen up to a maximum of 1 g tid
- Muscle relaxants (short-term use)

CHRONIC Rx

NSAIDs and Tylenol can be used on a long-term basis, as needed.

DISPOSITION

- Most patients recover from the acute whiplash injury within weeks.
- Factors associated with persistent and severe whiplash injuries are described in Table 1W-3.

TABLE 1W-3 Factors Associated with Persistent and Severe Whiplash Injuries

Severe Whiplash Injury
High-speed injury
Intense and rapid onset of pain
Severe restriction of movement at presentation
Abnormal neurology
Bony injuries

Persistent Whiplash Injury
High-speed injury
Intense and rapid onset of pain
Severe restriction of movement at presentation
Abnormal neurology
Bony injuries
Increasing age
Upper limb paresthesias
Cervical spondylosis

From Carr A, Hamilton W: *Orthopedics in primary care*, ed 2, Philadelphia, 2005, Saunders.

- 20% to 40% may develop chronic whiplash syndrome (symptoms of headache, neck pain, and psychiatric complaints that persist for 6 months).
- Older age, female gender, legal issues, and work status were found to be prognostic factors associated with a negative outcome.

REFERRAL

Orthopedic, physical therapy

PEARLS & CONSIDERATIONS

- Nearly one third of all personal injury cases involve cervical injuries.
- There is no relationship between trauma severity and incidence of whiplash injury.

COMMENTS

The entity of chronic whiplash syndrome remains elusive. Some authorities argue that financial motivation is a factor leading to persistent neck symptoms. Other studies do not substantiate this, showing a true chronic injury to the soft tissues of the neck.

SUGGESTED READINGS

Available at www.expertconsult.com

RELATED CONTENT

Whiplash (Patient Information)

AUTHOR: **JORGE A. VILLAFUERTE, M.D.**

W

I

 **BASIC INFORMATION**

DEFINITION

Wilson's disease is an autosomal recessive disorder of copper transport with inadequate biliary copper excretion, leading to an accumulation of the metal in liver, brain, kidneys, and corneas.

SYNONYM

Progressive hepatolenticular degeneration

ICD-10CM CODES
E83.00 Disorder of copper metabolism

EPIDEMIOLOGY & DEMOGRAPHICS

PREVALENCE: One case in 30,000
PREDOMINANT SEX: Affects men and women equally (autosomal recessive gene)
ONSET OF SYMPTOMS: Ages 3 to 40 yr

PHYSICAL FINDINGS & CLINICAL PRESENTATION

Most older patients present with chronic liver disease and/or neurologic manifestations, whereas younger patients may present with acute liver failure. Hepatic presentation:
- Acute hepatitis with malaise, anorexia, nausea, jaundice, elevated transaminase, prolonged prothrombin time; rarely fulminant hepatic failure
- Chronic active (or autoimmune) hepatitis with fatigue, malaise, rashes, arthralgia, elevated transaminase, elevated serum immunoglobulin G, positive antinuclear antibody and antismooth muscle antibody
- Chronic liver disease/cirrhosis with hepatosplenomegaly, ascites, low serum albumin, prolonged prothrombin time, portal hypertension

Neurologic presentation:
- Movement disorder: tremors, ataxia
- Spastic dystonia: masklike facies, rigidity, gait disturbance, dysarthria, drooling, dysphagia
- The most common neurologic presentation in a young adult is parkinsonism.

Ophthalmic:
- Kayser-Fleischer ring; indicates copper deposition in the Descemet's membrane of the iris. They are most common in patients with neurologic manifestations. Typically, they are only visualized with slit-lamp examination.
- Sunflower cataracts

Psychiatric presentation:
- Depression, obsessive-compulsive disorder, psychopathic behaviors, neuroses

Other organs:
- Hemolytic anemia due to the sudden release of copper from liver cells
- Renal disease (i.e., Fanconi's syndrome with hematuria, phosphaturia, renal tubular acidosis, vitamin D–resistant rickets)
- Cardiomyopathy
- Arthritis
- Hypoparathyroidism
- Hypogonadism

PHYSICAL FINDINGS:
- Ocular: the Kayser-Fleischer ring is a gold-yellow ring seen at the periphery of the iris (Fig. E1W-7); It is present in virtually all persons with neurologic involvement. These should be sought with slit-lamp examination by a skilled examiner.
- Stigmata of acute or chronic liver disease.
- Neurologic abnormalities: see previous.

ETIOLOGY & PATHOGENESIS
- Dietary copper is transported from the intestine to the liver, where normally it is metabolized into ceruloplasmin. In Wilson's disease, defective incorporation of copper into ceruloplasmin and a decrease of biliary copper excretion lead to accumulation of this mineral.
- The disease results from an autosomal recessive inborn error of metabolism caused by a mutation of the copper P-type adenosine triphosphatase encoded on chromosome *13q14.3* (*ATP7B* gene).

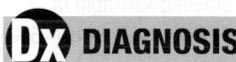 **DIAGNOSIS**

DIFFERENTIAL DIAGNOSIS
- Hereditary hypoceruloplasminemia
- Menkes' disease
- Consider the diagnosis of Wilson's disease in all cases of acute or chronic liver disease for which another cause has not been established.
- Consider Wilson's disease in patients with movement disorders or dystonia even without symptomatic liver disease.

LABORATORY TESTS
- Low serum ceruloplasmin level (<200 mg/L) present in 95% of affected patients
- 24-hr urinary copper excretion greater than 250 mcg (normal <60 mcg); increases to greater than 1200 mcg/24 hr after 500 mg of d-penicillamine (normal <500 mcg/24 hr)
- Low serum copper (<65 mcg/L)
- Abnormal liver function tests (note that aspartate aminotransferase may be higher than alanine aminotransferase)
- Low serum uric acid and phosphorus
- Abnormal urinalysis (hematuria)
- Molecular genetic testing for mutations of the *ATP7B* gene can also be used for diagnosis

BIOPSY
- Early:
  1. Steatosis, focal necrosis, glycogenated hepatocyte nuclei
  2. May reveal inflammation and piecemeal necrosis
- Late: cirrhosis
- Hepatic copper content (>250 mcg/g of dry weight) (normal is 20-50 mcg) gold standard for diagnosis

- Histochemical confirmation of excess copper can be helpful in diagnosis, but if absent, does not exclude Wilson's disease. The lack of immunoreactivity to copper-binding protein can occur because of the diffuse presence of copper in the cytoplasm and because of the assay's low sensitivity. Rhodamine and rubeanic acid stains can show dense granular lysosomal copper deposition in hepatocytes at the stage of cirrhotic nodular regeneration.

 **TREATMENT**

- Trientine (triethylenetetramine): (chelator therapy) preferred agent due to fewer side effects than penicillamine
  1. 1 to 2 g/day divided tid
  2. Monitor CBC
- Penicillamine: (chelator therapy)
  1. 0.75 to 1.5 g/day divided bid (with pyridoxine 25 mg/day)
  2. Monitor complete blood count (CBC) and urinalysis weekly
- Zinc: (inhibits intestinal copper absorption)
  1. 50 mg tid
  2. Monitor zinc level
- Ammonium tetrathiomolybdate for neurologic symptoms
- Antioxidants
- Liver transplantation (for severe hepatic failure unresponsive to chelation); liver transplantation corrects the underlying pathophysiology and can be lifesaving

PROGNOSIS

Good with early chelation treatment

REFERRAL

To gastroenterologist, neurologist

 **PEARLS & CONSIDERATIONS**

COMMENTS

Family screening of first-degree relatives must be undertaken. Genetic diagnosis is also useful in patients with indeterminate clinical and biochemical features.

EBM **EVIDENCE**

Available at www.expertconsult.com

SUGGESTED READINGS
Available at www.expertconsult.com

RELATED CONTENT
Wilson's Disease (Patient Information)

AUTHOR: **FRED F. FERRI, M.D.**

Differential Diagnosis

Acute gastroenteritis.
Appendicitis.
Intussusception.
Volvulus.
Meckel diverticulum.
Other: colic, trauma.

ABDOMINAL PAIN, LEFT LOWER QUADRANT

ICD-10CM # R10.814   Left Lower Quadrant Abdominal Tenderness
       R10.824   Left Lower Quadrant Rebound Abdominal Tenderness

Intestinal: diverticulitis, diverticulosis, intestinal obstruction, perforated ulcer, inflammatory bowel disease, perforated descending colon, inguinal hernia, neoplasm, appendicitis.
Reproductive: ectopic pregnancy, ovarian cyst, torsion of ovarian cyst, tuboovarian abscess, mittelschmerz, endometriosis, seminal vesiculitis.
Renal: renal or ureteral calculi, pyelonephritis, neoplasm.
Vascular: leaking aortic aneurysm.
Psoas abscess.
Trauma.

ABDOMINAL PAIN, LEFT UPPER QUADRANT

ICD-10CM # R19.02   Left Upper Quadrant Abdominal Swelling, Mass, and Lump

Gastric: PUD, gastritis, pyloric stenosis, hiatal hernia.
Pancreatic: pancreatitis, neoplasm, stone in pancreatic duct or ampulla.
Cardiac: MI, angina pectoris.
Splenic: splenomegaly, ruptured spleen, splenic abscess, splenic infarction.
Renal: calculi, pyelonephritis, neoplasm.
Pulmonary: pneumonia, empyema, pulmonary infarction.
Vascular: ruptured aortic aneurysm.
Cutaneous: herpes zoster.
Trauma.
Intestinal: high fecal impaction, perforated colon, diverticulitis.

ABDOMINAL PAIN, NONSURGICAL CAUSES

ICD-10CM # R19.8   Other Specified Symptoms and Signs Involving the Digestive System and Abdomen
       R10.817   Generalized abdominal tenderness

Irritable bowel syndrome.
Urinary tract infection, pyelonephritis, salpingitis, PID.
Gastroenteritis, gastritis, peptic ulcer.
Diverticular spasm.
Hepatitis, mononucleosis.
Pancreatitis.
Inferior wall myocardial infarction.

Basilar pneumonia, pulmonary embolism.
Diabetic ketoacidosis.
Strain or hematoma of rectus muscle.
Ruptured Graafian follicle.
Herpes zoster.
Nerve root compression.
Sickle cell crisis.
Acute adrenal insufficiency.
Other: acute porphyria, familial Mediterranean fever, tabes dorsalis, anxiety, sexual abuse.

ABDOMINAL PAIN, PERIUMBILICAL

ICD-10CM # R10.815   Periumbilic Abdominal Tenderness
       R10.825   Periumbilic Rebound Abdominal Tenderness

Intestinal: small bowel obstruction or gangrene, early appendicitis.
Vascular: mesenteric thrombosis, dissecting aortic aneurysm.
Pancreatic: pancreatitis.
Metabolic: uremia, DKA.
Trauma.

ABDOMINAL PAIN, POORLY LOCALIZED[49]

ICD-10CM # R10.819   Abdominal Tenderness, Unspecified Site

EXTRAABDOMINAL

Metabolic
DKA, acute intermittent porphyria, hyperthyroidism, hypothyroidism, hypercalcemia, hypokalemia, uremia, hyperlipidemia, hyperparathyroidism.

Hematologic
Sickle cell crisis, leukemia or lymphoma, Henoch-Schönlein purpura.

Infectious
Infectious mononucleosis, Rocky Mountain spotted fever, acquired immunodeficiency syndrome (AIDS), streptococcal pharyngitis (in children), herpes zoster.

Drugs and Toxins
Heavy metal poisoning, black widow spider bites, withdrawal syndromes, mushroom ingestion.

Referred Pain
Pulmonary: pneumonia, pulmonary embolism, pneumothorax.
Cardiac: angina, MI, pericarditis, myocarditis.
Genitourinary: prostatitis, epididymitis, orchitis, testicular torsion.
Musculoskeletal: rectus sheath hematoma.

Functional
Somatization disorder, malingering, hypochondriasis, Münchausen syndrome.

INTRAABDOMINAL

Early appendicitis, gastroenteritis, peritonitis, pancreatitis, abdominal aortic aneurysm, mesenteric insufficiency or infarction, intestinal obstruction, volvulus, ulcerative colitis.

ABDOMINAL PAIN, PREGNANCY

ICD-10CM # R10.817   Generalized Abdominal Tenderness
       R10.827   Generalized Rebound Abdominal Tenderness

GYNECOLOGIC (GESTATIONAL AGE IN PARENTHESES)

Miscarriage   (<20 wk; 80% <12 wk)
Septic abortion   (<20 wk)
Ectopic pregnancy   (<14 wk)
Corpus luteum cyst   (<12 wk)
   rupture
Ovarian torsion   (especially <24 wk)
Pelvic inflammatory   (<12 wk)
   disease
Chorioamnionitis   (>16 wk)
Abruptio placentae   (>16 wk)

NONGYNECOLOGIC

Appendicitis   (Throughout)
Cholecystitis   (Throughout)
Hepatitis   (Throughout)
Pyelonephritis   (Throughout)
Preeclampsia   (>20 wk)

ABDOMINAL PAIN, RIGHT LOWER QUADRANT

ICD-10CM # R10.813   Right Lower Quadrant Abdominal Tenderness
       R10.823   Right Lower Quadrant Rebound Abdominal Tenderness

Intestinal: acute appendicitis, regional enteritis, incarcerated hernia, cecal diverticulitis, intestinal obstruction, perforated ulcer, perforated cecum, Meckel diverticulitis.
Reproductive: ectopic pregnancy, ovarian cyst, torsion of ovarian cyst, salpingitis, tuboovarian abscess, mittelschmerz, endometriosis, seminal vesiculitis.
Renal: renal and ureteral calculi, neoplasms, pyelonephritis.
Vascular: leaking aortic aneurysm.
Cutaneous: herpes zoster.
Psoas abscess.
Trauma.
Cholecystitis.

ABDOMINAL PAIN, RIGHT UPPER QUADRANT

ICD-10CM # R10.811   Right Upper Quadrant Abdominal Tenderness
       R10.821   Right Upper Quadrant Rebound Abdominal Tenderness

Biliary: calculi, infection, inflammation, neoplasm.
Hepatic: hepatitis, abscess, hepatic congestion, neoplasm, trauma.
Gastric: PUD, pyloric stenosis, neoplasm, alcoholic gastritis, hiatal hernia.

Pancreatic: pancreatitis, neoplasm, stone in pancreatic duct or ampulla.

Renal: calculi, infection, inflammation, neoplasm, rupture of kidney.

Pulmonary: pneumonia, pulmonary infarction, right-sided pleurisy.

Intestinal: retrocecal appendicitis, intestinal obstruction, high fecal impaction, diverticulitis.

Cardiac: myocardial ischemia (particularly involving the inferior wall), pericarditis.

Cutaneous: herpes zoster.

Trauma.

Fitz-Hugh-Curtis syndrome (perihepatitis).

ABDOMINAL PAIN, RIGHT UPPER QUADRANT, DIFFERENTIAL DIAGNOSIS IN PREGNANCY[26]

| ICD-10CM # | R10.811 | Right Upper Quadrant Abdominal Tenderness |
| | R10.821 | Right Upper Quadrant Rebound Abdominal Tenderness |

DIFFERENTIAL DIAGNOSIS OF RIGHT UPPER QUADRANT ABDOMINAL PAIN DURING PREGNANCY

Hepatic Disorders:
Hepatitis.
Hepatic vascular engorgement.
Hepatic hematoma.
Hepatic malignancy.

Biliary Tract Disease:
Biliary colic.
Choledocholithiasis.
Cholangitis.
Cholecystitis.

Diseases Related to Pregnancy:
Preeclampsia or eclampsia.
Hemolysis, elevated liver enzymes, and low platelet count (HELLP) syndrome.
Acute fatty liver of pregnancy.
Hepatic hemorrhage or rupture.

Renal Disorders:
Pyelonephritis.
Nephrolithiasis.

Gastrointestinal Disorders:
Peptic ulcer disease.
Perforated duodenal ulcer.

Other Conditions in RUQ:
Rib fracture.
Shingles.

Referred Pain from Other Organ Disease:
Pneumonia.
Pulmonary embolus or infarct.
Pleural effusion.
Radiculopathy.
Inferior wall myocardial infarction.
Colon cancer.

ABDOMINAL PAIN, SUPRAPUBIC

| ICD-10CM # | R10.30 | Lower Abdominal Pain, Unspecified |

Intestinal: colon obstruction or gangrene, diverticulitis, appendicitis.

Reproductive system: ectopic pregnancy, mittelschmerz, torsion of ovarian cyst, PID, salpingitis, endometriosis, rupture of endometrioma.

Cystitis, rupture of urinary bladder.

ABDOMINAL WALL MASSES[67]

| ICD-10CM # | R19.00 | Intra-abdominal and Pelvic Swelling, Mass and Lump, Unspecified Site |

LUMPS ARISING IN THE SKIN AND SUBCUTANEOUS FAT (THAT COULD OCCUR ANYWHERE ON THE BODY)

Lipoma.
Sebaceous cyst.

LUMPS ARISING IN THE SKIN AND SUBCUTANEOUS FAT (SPECIFIC TO THE ANTERIOR ABDOMINAL WALL)

Tumor nodule of the umbilicus (secondary to the intraperitoneal malignancy, also called *Sister Mary Joseph nodule*).

LUMPS ARISING IN THE FASCIA AND MUSCLE

Rectus sheath hematoma (usually painful).
Desmoid tumor (associated with Gardner's syndrome).

HERNIA

Incisional:	It has an overlying scar. The sac may be very much larger than the neck of the hernia.
Umbilical:	The hernia is through the umbilical scar. Those presenting at birth commonly resolve in the first years of life.
Paraumbilical:	The neck is just lateral to the umbilical scar. Patients usually present later in life.
Epigastric:	It occurs in the midline between the xiphoid process and the umbilicus. They are usually small (<2 cm). They result when a knuckle of extraperitoneal fat extrudes through a small defect in the linea alba. Commonly irreducible and without an expansile cough impulse.
Spigelian:	A rare hernia found along the linea semilunaris at the lateral edge of the rectus sheath, most commonly a third of the way between the umbilicus and the pubis.

DIVARICATION OF THE RECTI

Supraumbilical elliptical swelling of the attenuated linea alba (no cough impulse).

ABORTION, RECURRENT

| ICD-10CM # | P01.8 | Newborn (Suspected to Be) Affected by Other Maternal Complications of Pregnancy |

Congenital anatomic abnormalities.
Adhesions (uterine synechiae).
Uterine fibroids.
Endometriosis.
Endocrine abnormalities (luteal phase insufficiency, hypothyroidism, uncontrolled diabetes mellitus [DM]).
Parenteral chromosome abnormalities.
Maternal infections (cervical mycoplasma, ureaplasma, chlamydia).
DES exposure, heavy metal exposure.
Thrombocytosis.
Allogenic immunity, autoimmunity, lupus anticoagulant.

ACHES AND PAINS, DIFFUSE[43]

| ICD-10CM # | M25.50 | Pain in Unspecified Joint |

Postviral arthralgias/myalgias.
Bilateral soft tissue rheumatism.
Overuse syndromes.
Fibrositis.
Hypothyroidism.
Metabolic bone disease.
Paraneoplastic syndrome.
Myopathy (polymyositis, dermatomyositis).
Rheumatoid arthritis (RA).
Sjögren's syndrome.
Polymyalgia rheumatica.
Hypermobility.
Benign arthralgias/myalgias.
Chronic fatigue syndrome.
Hypophosphatemia.

ACIDOSIS, HYPERCHLORIC METABOLIC[69]

| ICD-10CM # | E87.2 | Acidosis |

GASTROINTESTINAL BICARBONATE LOSS

Diarrhea.
External pancreatic or small bowel drainage.
Ureterosigmoidostomy, jejunal loop.
Drugs:
Calcium chloride (acidifying agent).
Magnesium sulfate (diarrhea).
Cholestyramine (bile acid diarrhea).

RENAL ACIDOSIS

Hypokalemic:
Proximal RTA (type 2).
Distal (classic) RTA (type 1).
Drug-induced hypokalemia:
- Acetazolamide (proximal RTA).
- Amphotericin B (distal RTA).

Differential Diagnosis

II

ADRENOCORTICAL HYPERFUNCTION[3]

ICD-10CM # E26.9 Hyperaldosteronism, Unspecified

SYNDROMES OF ADRENOCORTICAL HYPERFUNCTION

States of Glucocorticoid Excess
Physiologic states
Stress.
Strenuous exercise.
Last trimester of pregnancy.
Pathologic States
Psychiatric conditions (pseudo-Cushing's disorders):
  Depression.
  Alcoholism.
  Anorexia nervosa.
  Panic disorders.
  Alcohol and drug withdrawal.
ACTH-dependent states:
  Pituitary adenoma (Cushing's disease).
  Ectopic ACTH syndrome.
  Bronchial carcinoid.
  Thymic carcinoid.
  Islet cell tumor.
  Small cell lung carcinoma.
  Ectopic CRH secretion.
ACTH-independent states:
  Adrenal adenoma.
  Adrenal carcinoma.
  Micronodular adrenal disease.
Exogenous Sources
Glucocorticoid intake.
ACTH intake.
States of Mineralocorticoid Excess
Primary Aldosteronism
Aldosterone-secreting adenoma.
Bilateral adrenal hyperplasia.
Aldosterone-secreting carcinoma.
Glucocorticoid-suppressible hyperaldosteronism.
Adrenal Enzyme Deficiencies
11b-Hydroxylase deficiency.
17a-Hydroxylase deficiency.
11b-Hydroxysteroid dehydrogenase, type II.
Exogenous Mineralocorticoids
Licorice.
Carbenoxolone.
Fludrocortisone.
Secondary Hyperaldosteronism
Associated with hypertension:
  Accelerated hypertension.
  Renovascular hypertension.
  Estrogen administration.
  Renin-secreting tumors.
Without hypertension:
  Bartter syndrome.
  Sodium-wasting nephropathy.
  Renal tubular acidosis.
  Diuretic and laxative abuse.
  Edematous states (cirrhosis, nephrosis, congestive heart failure).

ACTH, Adrenocorticotropin hormone; *CRH,* corticotropin-releasing hormone.

ADRENOCORTICAL HYPOFUNCTION

ICD-10CM # E27.49 Other Adrenocortical Insufficiency

SYNDROMES OF ADRENOCORTICAL HYPOFUNCTION

Primary Adrenal Disorders
Combined Glucocorticoid and Mineralocorticoid Deficiency
Autoimmune:
  Isolated autoimmune disease (Addison disease).
  Polyglandular autoimmune syndrome, type I.
  Polyglandular autoimmune syndrome, type II.
Infectious:
  Tuberculosis.
  Fungal.
  Cytomegalovirus.
  Human immunodeficiency virus.
Vascular:
  Bilateral adrenal hemorrhage.
  Sepsis.
  Coagulopathy.
  Thrombosis; embolism.
  Adrenal infarction.
Infiltration:
  Metastatic carcinoma and lymphoma.
  Sarcoidosis.
  Amyloidosis.
  Hemochromatosis.
Congenital:
  Congenital adrenal hyperplasia.
    ■ 21-Hydroxylase deficiency.
    ■ 3b-ol Dehydrogenase deficiency.
    ■ 20,22-Desmolase deficiency.
  Adrenal unresponsiveness to ACTH.
  Congenital adrenal hypoplasia.
  Adrenoleukodystrophy.
  Adrenomyeloneuropathy.
Iatrogenic
Bilateral adrenalectomy.
Drugs:
  Metyrapone, aminoglutethimide, trilostane, ketoconazole, o,p¢-DDD, mifepristone.
Mineralocorticoid deficiency without glucocorticoid deficiency
Cortiscosterone methyl oxidase deficiency.
Isolated zona glomerulosa defect.
Heparin therapy.
Critical illness.
Converting-enzyme inhibitors.
Secondary Adrenal Disorders
Secondary Adrenal Insufficiency
Hypothalamic-pituitary dysfunction.
Exogenous glucocorticoids.
After removal of an ACTH-secreting tumor.
Hyporeninemic Hypoaldosteronism
Diabetic nephropathy.
Tubulointerstitial diseases.
Obstructive uropathy.
Autonomic neuropathy.
Nonsteroidal anti-inflammatory drugs.
β-Adrenergic drugs.

ACTH, Adrenocorticotropic hormone.

ADVERSE FOOD REACTIONS, DIFFERENTIAL DIAGNOSIS[45]

ICD-10CM # T78.1XXA Other Adverse Food Reactions, Not Elsewhere Classified, Initial Encounter

GASTROINTESTINAL DISORDERS (WITH VOMITING AND/OR DIARRHEA)

Structural abnormalities (pyloric stenosis, Hirschsprung's disease).
Enzyme deficiencies (primary or secondary):
  Disaccharidase deficiency—lactase, fructase, sucrase-isomaltase.
  Galactosemia.
Other: pancreatic insufficiency (cystic fibrosis), peptic disease.

CONTAMINANTS AND ADDITIVES

Flavorings and preservatives—rarely cause symptoms: Sodium metabisulfite, monosodium glutamate, nitrites.
Dyes and colorings—very rarely cause symptoms (urticaria, eczema): Tartrazine.
Toxins: Bacterial, fungal (aflatoxin), fish-related (scombroid, ciguatera).
Infectious organisms:
  Bacteria (*Salmonella, Escherichia coli, Shigella*).
  Virus (rotavirus, enterovirus).
  Parasites (*Giardia, Akis simplex* [in fish]).
Accidental contaminants: Heavy metals, pesticides.
Pharmacologic agents: Caffeine, glycosidal alkaloid solanine (potato spuds), histamine (fish), serotonin (banana, tomato), tryptamine (tomato), tyramine (cheese).

PSYCHOLOGIC REACTIONS

Food phobias.

ADYNAMIC ILEUS[49]

ICD-10CM # K56.0 Paralytic Ileus
                K56.7 Ileus, Unspecified

Abdominal trauma.
Infection (retroperitoneal, pelvic, intrathoracic).
Laparotomy.
Metabolic disease (hypokalemia).
Renal colic.
Skeletal injury (rib fracture, vertebral fracture).
Medications (e.g., narcotics).

AEROPHAGIA (BELCHING, ERUCTATION)

ICD-10CM # R14.0 Abdominal Distension (Gaseous)
                R14.1 Gas Pain
                R14.2 Eructation
                R14.3 Flatulence

Anxiety disorders.
Rapid food ingestion.
Carbonated beverages.
Nursing infants (especially when nursing in horizontal position).
Eating or drinking in supine position.

Gum chewing.
Poorly fitting dentures, orthodontic appliances.
Hiatal hernia, gastritis, nonulcer dyspepsia.
Cholelithiasis, cholecystitis.
Ingestion of legumes, onions, peppers.

AIR-SPACE OPACIFICATION ON X-RAY[32]

ICD-10CM # R91.8   Other nonspecific abnormal finding of lung field

CAUSES OF AIR-SPACE OPACIFICATION

Edema
Cardiogenic.
Non-cardiogenic.
Inflammation/Infection
Wegener's granulomatosis.
Cryptogenic organizing pneumonia.
Blood
Idiopathic pulmonary hemosiderosis.
Antibasement membrane antibody disease.
Systemic lupus erythematosus.
Miscellaneous Causes
Eosinophilic pneumonia.
Alveolar proteinosis.
Alveolar cell carcinoma.
Alveolar microlithiasis.
Lymphoma (MALToma).
Sarcoidosis.

AIRWAY OBSTRUCTION, PEDIATRIC AGE[37]

ICD-10CM #		
J44.9	Chronic Obstructive Pulmonary Disease, Unspecified
T17.900A	Unspecified Foreign Body in Respiratory Tract, Part Unspecified Causing Asphyxiation, Initial Encounter
T17.908A	Unspecified Foreign Body in Respiratory Tract, Part Unspecified Causing Other Injury, Initial Encounter
T17.910A	Gastric Contents in Respiratory Tract, Part Unspecified Causing Asphyxiation, Initial Encounter
T17.918A	Gastric Contents in Respiratory Tract, Part Unspecified Causing Other Injury, Initial Encounter
T17.920A	Food in Respiratory Tract, Part Unspecified Causing Asphyxiation, Initial Encounter
T17.928A	Food in Respiratory Tract, Part Unspecified Causing Other Injury, Initial Encounter
T17.990A	Other Foreign Object in Respiratory Tract, Part Unspecified in Causing Asphyxiation, Initial Encounter
T17.998A	Other Foreign Object in Respiratory Tract, Part Unspecified Causing Other Injury, Initial Encounter
J38.5	Laryngeal Spasm
J68.9	Unspecified Respiratory Condition Due To Chemicals, Gases, Fumes, and Vapors

CONGENITAL CAUSES

Craniofacial dysmorphism.
Hemangioma.
Laryngeal cleft/web.
Laryngoceles, cysts.
Laryngomalacia.
Macroglossia.
Tracheal stenosis.
Vascular ring.
Vocal cord paralysis.

ACQUIRED INFECTIOUS CAUSES

Acute laryngotracheobronchitis.
Epiglottitis.
Laryngeal papillomatosis.
Membranous croup (bacterial tracheitis).
Mononucleosis.
Retropharyngeal abscess.
Spasmodic croup.
Diphtheria.

ACQUIRED NONINFECTIOUS CAUSES

Anaphylaxis.
Foreign body aspiration.
Supraglottic hypotonia.
Thermal/chemical burn.
Trauma.
Vocal cord paralysis.
Angioneurotic edema.

AKINETIC/RIGID SYNDROME[3]

ICD-10CM # R29.8 Akinesis

Parkinsonism (idiopathic, drug-induced).
Catatonia (psychosis).

Progressive supranuclear palsy.
Multisystem atrophy (Shy-Drager syndrome, olivopontocerebellar atrophy).
Diffuse Lewy-body disease.
Toxins (MPTP, manganese, carbon monoxide).
Huntington's disease and other hereditary neurodegenerative disorders.

ALCOHOL-RELATED SEIZURES[50]

ICD-10CM # F10.232

DIFFERENTIAL DIAGNOSIS OF ALCOHOL-RELATED SEIZURES

Withdrawal (alcohol or drugs).
Exacerbation of idiopathic or posttraumatic seizures.
Acute intoxication (amphetamines, anticholinergics, cocaine, isoniazid, organophosphates, phenothiazines, tricyclic antidepressants, salicylates, lithium).
Metabolic (hypoglycemia, hyponatremia, hypernatremia, hypocalcemia, hepatic failure).
Infectious (meningitis, encephalitis, brain abscess).
Trauma (intracranial hemorrhage).
Cerebrovascular accident.
Sleep deprivation.
Noncompliance with anticonvulsants.

ALKALOSIS, METABOLIC

ICD-10CM # E87.3   Alkalosis

CAUSES OF METABOLIC ALKALOSIS

Exogenous HCO_3^- Loads
Acute alkali administration.
Milk-alkali syndrome.
Effective Extracellular Volume Contraction, Normotension, Hypokalemia, and Secondary Hyperreninemic Hyperaldosteronism
Gastrointestinal origin:
  Vomiting.
  Gastric aspiration.
  Congenital chloridorrhea.
  Villous adenoma.
  Combined administration of sodium polystyrene sulfonate (Kayexalate and aluminum hydroxide).
Renal origin:
  Diuretics (especially thiazides and loop diuretics).
  Acute.
  Chronic.
  Edematous states.
  Posthypercapnic state.
  Hypercalcemia-hypoparathyroidism.
  Recovery from lactic acidosis or ketoacidosis.
  Nonreabsorbable anions such as penicillin, carbenicillin.
  Mg^{++} deficiency.
  K^+ depletion.
  Bartter syndrome (loss-of-function mutation of Cl− transport in thick ascending limb of Henle loop).
  Gitelman syndrome (loss-of-function mutation in Na+/Cl− cotransporter).
  Carbohydrate refeeding after starvation.

II

ANAL INCONTINENCE[49]

ICD-10CM # R15.9 Full Incontinence of Feces

TRAUMATIC

Nerve injured in surgery.
Spinal cord injury.
Obstetric trauma.
Sphincter injury.

NEUROLOGIC

Spinal cord lesions.
Dementia.
Autonomic neuropathy (e.g., DM).
Obstetrics: pudendal nerve stretched during surgery.
Hirschsprung's disease.

MASS EFFECT

Carcinoma of anal canal.
Carcinoma of rectum.
Foreign body.
Fecal impaction.
Hemorrhoids.

MEDICAL

Procidentia.
Inflammatory disease.
Diarrhea.
Laxative abuse.

PEDIATRIC

Congenital.
Meningocele.
Myelomeningocele.
Spina bifida.
After corrective surgery for imperforate anus.
Sexual abuse.
Encopresis.

ANAPHYLAXIS[42]

ICD-10CM # T78.2 Anaphylactic Shock, Unspecified, Initial Encounter

PULMONARY

Laryngeal edema.
Epiglottitis.
Foreign body aspiration.
Pulmonary embolus.
Asphyxiation.
Hyperventilation.

CARDIOVASCULAR

Myocardial infarction.
Arrhythmia.
Hypovolemic shock.
Cardiac arrest.

CNS

Vasovagal reaction.
CVA.
Seizure disorder.
Drug overdose.

ENDOCRINE

Hypoglycemia.
Pheochromocytoma.

Carcinoid syndrome.
Catamenial (progesterone-induced anaphylaxis).

PSYCHIATRIC

Vocal cord dysfunction syndrome.
Münchausen syndrome.
Panic attack/globus hystericus.

OTHER

Hereditary angioedema.
Cord urticaria.
Idiopathic urticaria.
Mastocytosis.
Serum sickness.
Idiopathic capillary leak syndrome.
Sulfite exposure.
Scombroid poisoning (tuna, blue fish, mackerel).

ANAPHYLAXIS, PATHOPHYSIOLOGIC CLASSIFICATION[2]

ICD-10CM # T78.2 Anaphylactic shock, unspecified, initial encounter

PATHOPHYSIOLOGIC CLASSIFICATION OF ANAPHYLAXIS

IgE Dependent, Immunologic
Foods.
Drugs.
Insect stings and bites.
Exercise (food dependent).
Other causes
IgE Independent, Immunologic
Immune aggregates.
IgG anti-IgA.
Cytotoxic.
Disturbance of arachidonic acid metabolism:
- Aspirin.
- Other nonsteroidal antiinflammatory drugs.
Activation of kallikrein-kinin contact system:
- Dialysis membranes.
- Radiocontrast media.
Multimediator recruitment:
- Complement.
- Clotting.
- Clot lysis.
- Kallikrein-kinin contact system.
Other causes
Nonimmunologic
Direct mediator release from mast cells and basophils:
- Drugs, e.g., opiates.
- Physical factors, e.g., cold and sunlight.
Exercise
c-kit Mutation (D816V)
Other causes
Idiopathic

ANAPHYLACTOID SYNDROME OF PREGNANCY[1]

ICD-10CM # O88.113

CARDIOVASCULAR COLLAPSE, HYPOTENSION

Acute coronary syndromes, myocardial infarction.
Cardiomyopathy.

Pulmonary embolism.
Anesthesia complications, transfusion reaction.
Sepsis, systemic inflammatory response syndrome.

RESPIRATORY ARREST

Pulmonary embolism, air embolism.
Anesthesia complications, transfusion reaction.
Aspiration.

ALTERED MENTAL STATUS, SEIZURE

Eclampsia.
Cerebrovascular accident.
Hypoglycemia.

COAGULOPATHY

Disseminated intravascular coagulation.
Consumptive coagulopathy from hemorrhage.

ANDROGEN EXCESS, REPRODUCTIVE-AGE WOMAN

ICD-10CM # E28.1 Androgen Excess

Polycystic ovary syndrome.
Idiopathic.
Medications (e.g., anabolizing agents, testosterone, danazol).
Pregnancy (luteoma, hyperreaction luteinalis).
Sertoli-Leydig ovarian neoplasm.
Adrenal adenoma or hyperplasia.
Cushing's syndrome.
Glucocorticoid resistance.
Hypothyroidism.
Hyperprolactinemia.

ANDROGEN RESISTANCE[52]

ICD-10CM # E34.5 Androgen resistance syndrome

CONGENITAL OR DEVELOPMENTAL DISORDERS

Uncommon causes:
Kennedy disease (spinal and bulbar muscular atrophy).
Partial androgen insensitivity syndrome (AR mutations).
5α-reductase type 2 deficiency.
Complete androgen insensitivity syndrome (female phenotype).

ACQUIRED DISORDERS

Common causes:
AR antagonists (bicalutamide, nilutamide).
Drugs (spironolactone, cyproterone acetate, marijuana, histamine 2 receptor antagonists).
Uncommon causes:
Celiac disease.

ANEMIA, APLASTIC[39]

ICD-10CM # D61.09 Other Constitutional Aplastic Anemia

ACQUIRED APLASTIC ANEMIA

Secondary aplastic anemia.
Irradiation.
Drugs and chemicals.
Regular effects.
Cytotoxic agents.

Benzene.
Idiosyncratic reactions.
Chloramphenicol.
Nonsteroidal anti-inflammatory drugs.
Antiepileptics.
Gold.
Other drugs and chemicals.
Viruses.
Epstein-Barr virus (infectious mononucleosis).
Hepatitis virus (non-A, non-B, non-C, non-G hepatitis).
Parvovirus (transient aplastic crisis, some pure red cell aplasia).
Human immunodeficiency virus (acquired immunodeficiency syndrome).
Immune diseases.
Eosinophilic fasciitis.
Hyperimmunoglobulinemia.
Thymoma and thymic carcinoma.
Graft-versus-host disease in immunodeficiency.
Paroxysmal nocturnal hemoglobinuria.
Pregnancy.
Idiopathic aplastic anemia.

INHERITED APLASTIC ANEMIA

Fanconi anemia.
Dyskeratosis congenita.
Shwachman-Diamond syndrome.
Reticular dysgenesis.
Amegakaryocytic thrombocytopenia.
Familial aplastic anemias.
Preleukemia (e.g., monosomy 7).
Nonhematologic syndromes (e.g., Down, Dubowitz, Seckel).

ANEMIA, APLASTIC, DUE TO DRUGS AND CHEMICALS[1]

ICD-10CM #		
	D61.1	Drug-Induced Aplastic Anemia
	D61.2	Aplastic Anemia Due to Other External Agents
	D61.89	Other Specified Aplastic Anemias and Other Bone Marrow Failure Syndromes

Agents that regularly produce marrow depression as a major toxic effect when used in commonly employed doses or normal exposures:
Cytotoxic drugs used in cancer chemotherapy.
Alkylating agents (busulfan, melphalan, cyclophosphamide).
Antimetabolites (antifolic compounds, nucleotide analogs), antimitotics (vincristine, vinblastine, colchicine).
Some antibiotics (daunorubicin, doxorubicin [Adriamycin]).
Benzene (and less often benzene-containing chemicals; kerosene, carbon tetrachloride, Stoddard's solvent, chlorophenols).
Agents probably associated with aplastic anemia but with a relatively low probability relative to their use:
Chloramphenicol.
Insecticides.

Antiprotozoals (quinacrine and chloroquine).
Nonsteroidal anti-inflammatory drugs (including phenylbutazone, indomethacin, ibuprofen, sulindac, diclofenac, naproxen, piroxicam, fenoprofen, fenbufen, aspirin).
Anticonvulsants (hydantoins, carbamazepine, phenacemide, ethosuximide).
Gold, arsenic, and other heavy metals such as bismuth and mercury.
Sulfonamides as a class.
Antithyroid medications (methimazole, methylthiouracil, propylthiouracil).
Antidiabetes drugs (tolbutamide, carbutamide, chlorpropamide).
Carbonic anhydrase inhibitors (acetazolamide, methazolamide, mesalazine).
D-Penicillamine.
2-Chlorodeoxyadenosine.
Agents more rarely associated with aplastic anemia:
Antibiotics (streptomycin, tetracycline, methicillin, ampicillin, mebendazole and albendazole, sulfonamides, flucytosine, mefloquine, dapsone).
Antihistamines (cimetidine, ranitidine, chlorpheniramine).
Sedatives and tranquilizers (chlorpromazine, prochlorperazine, piperacetazine, chlordiazepoxide, meprobamate, methyprylon, remoxipride).
Antiarrhythmics (tocainide, amiodarone).
Allopurinol (can potentiate marrow suppression by cytotoxic drugs).
Ticlopidine.
Methyldopa.
Quinidine.
Lithium.
Guanidine.
Canthaxanthin.
Thiocyanate.
Carbimazole.
Cyanamide.
Deferoxamine.
Amphetamines.

ANEMIA, CAUSES IN PREGNANCY[26]

ICD-10CM #		
	D50.8	Other Iron Deficiency Anemias
	D50.9	Iron Deficiency Anemia, Unspecified
	D51.0	Vitamin B_{12} Deficiency Anemia Due to Intrinsic Factor Deficiency
	D51.1	Vitamin B_{12} Deficiency Anemia Due to Selective Vitamin B_{12} Malabsorption with Proteinuria
	D51.3	Other Dietary Vitamin B_{12} Deficiency Anemia
	D51.8	Other Vitamin B_{12} Deficiency Anemias
	D52.0	Dietary Folate Deficiency Anemia
	D52.1	Drug-Induced Folate Deficiency Anemia
	D52.8	Other Folate Deficiency Anemias
	D52.9	Folate Deficiency Anemia, Unspecified
	D53.1	Other Megaloblastic Anemias, Not Elsewhere Classified
	D53.0	Protein Deficiency Anemia
	D53.2	Scorbutic Anemia
	D53.8	Other Specified Nutritional Anemias
	D53.9	Nutritional Anemia, Unspecified
	D64.0	Hereditary Sideroblastic Anemia
	D64.1	Secondary Sideroblastic Anemia Due to Disease
	D64.2	Secondary Sideroblastic Anemia Due to Drugs and Toxins
	D64.3	Other Sideroblastic Anemias

CAUSES OF ANEMIA DURING PREGNANCY

Common Causes—85% of Anemia:
Physiologic anemia.
Iron deficiency.
Uncommon Causes:
Folic acid deficiency.
Vitamin B_{12} deficiency (due to the rapid increase in bariatric surgery).
Hemoglobinopathies:
- Sickle cell disease.
- Hemoglobin SC.
- β-Thalassemia minor.
Bariatric surgery.
Gastrointestinal bleeding.
Rare Causes:
Hemoglobinopathies.
- β-Thalassemia major.
- α-Thalassemia.
Syndromes of chronic hemolysis:
- Hereditary spherocytosis.
- Paroxysmal nocturnal hemoglobinuria.
Hematologic malignancy.

ANEMIA, DRUG-INDUCED[34]

ICD-10CM #		
	D61.1	Drug-Induced Aplastic Anemia

DRUGS THAT MAY INTERFERE WITH RED CELL PRODUCTION BY INDUCING MARROW SUPPRESSION OR APLASIA

Alcohol.
Antineoplastic drugs.
Antithyroid drugs.
Antibiotics.
Oral hypoglycemic agents.
Phenylbutazone.
Azidothymidine (AZT).

Differential Diagnosis

II

DRUGS THAT INTERFERE WITH VITAMIN B$_{12}$, FOLATE, OR IRON ABSORPTION OR UTILIZATION

Nitrous oxide.
Anticonvulsant drugs.
Antineoplastic drugs.
Isoniazid
Cycloserine A.

DRUGS CAPABLE OF PROMOTING HEMOLYSIS

Immune Mediated
Penicillins.
Quinine.
α-methyldopa.
Procainamide.
Mitomycin C.
Oxidative Stress
Antimalarials.
Sulfonamide drugs.
Nalidixic acid.

DRUGS THAT MAY PRODUCE OR PROMOTE BLOOD LOSS

Aspirin.
Alcohol.
Nonsteroidal anti-inflammatory agents.
Corticosteroids.
Anticoagulants.

ANEMIA, HYPOCHROMIC[39]

ICD-10CM #		
D50.8	Other Iron Deficiency Anemias
D50.9	Iron Deficiency Anemia, Unspecified
D64.0	Hereditary Sideroblastic Anemia
D64.1	Secondary Sideroblastic Anemia Due to Disease
D64.2	Secondary Sideroblastic Anemia Due to Drugs and Toxins
D64.3	Other Sideroblastic Anemias

DECREASED BODY IRON STORES

Iron-deficiency anemia.

NORMAL OR INCREASED BODY IRON STORES

Impaired iron metabolism.
Anemia of chronic disease.
Defective absorption, transport, or use of iron.
Disorders of globin synthesis:
  ○ Thalassemia.
  ○ Other microcytic hemoglobinopathies.
Disorders of heme synthesis: sideroblastic anemias:
  ○ Hereditary.
  ○ Acquired.

ANEMIA, LOW RETICULOCYTE COUNT[3]

ICD-10CM #	D64.9	Anemia, Unspecified

MICROCYTIC ANEMIA (MCV <80)

Iron deficiency.
Thalassemia minor.
Sideroblastic anemia.
Lead poisoning.

MACROCYTIC ANEMIA (MCV >100)

Megaloblastic anemias.
Folate deficiency.
Vitamin B$_{12}$ deficiency.
Drug-induced megaloblastic anemia.
Nonmegaloblastic macrocytosis.
Liver disease.
Hypothyroidism.

NORMOCYTIC ANEMIA (MCV 80-100)

Early iron deficiency.
Aplastic anemia.
Myelophthisic disorders.
Endocrinopathies.
Anemia of chronic disease.
Uremia.
Mixed nutritional deficiency.

ANEMIA, MEGALOBLASTIC[65]

ICD-10CM #		
D51.0	Vitamin B12 Deficiency Anemia Due to Intrinsic Factor Deficiency
D51.1	Vitamin B12 Deficiency Anemia Due to Selective Vitamin B12 Malabsorption with Proteinuria
D51.3	Other Dietary Vitamin B12 Deficiency Anemia
D51.8	Other Vitamin B12 Deficiency Anemias
D52.0	Dietary Folate Deficiency Anemia
D52.1	Drug-Induced Folate Deficiency Anemia
D52.8	Other Folate Deficiency Anemias
D52.9	Folate Deficiency Anemia, Unspecified
D53.1	Other Megaloblastic Anemias, Not Elsewhere Classified
D53.0	Protein Deficiency Anemia
D53.2	Scorbutic Anemia
D53.8	Other Specified Nutritional Anemias
D53.9	Nutritional Anemia, Unspecified

COBALAMIN (CBL) DEFICIENCY

Nutritional CBL Deficiency (Insufficient CBL Intake)
Vegetarians, vegans, breastfed infants of mothers with pernicious anemia.
Abnormal Intragastric Events (Inadequate Proteolysis of Food CBL)
Atrophic gastritis, partial gastrectomy with hypochlorhydria.

Loss/Atrophy of Gastric Oxyntic Mucosa (Deficient Intrinsic Factor [If] Molecules)
Total or partial gastrectomy, pernicious anemia (PA), caustic destruction (lye).
Abnormal Events in Small Bowel Lumen
Inadequate pancreatic protease (R-CBL not degraded, CBL not transferred to IF).
  ○ Insufficiency of pancreatic protease—pancreatic insufficiency.
  ○ Inactivation of pancreatic protease—Zollinger-Ellison syndrome.
Usurping of luminal CBL (inadequate CBL binding to IF).
  ○ By bacteria—stasis syndromes (blind loops, pouches of diverticulosis, strictures, fistulas, anastomoses); impaired bowel motility (scleroderma, pseudoobstruction), hypogammaglobulinemia.
  ○ By *Diphyllobothrium latum.*
Disorders of Ileal Mucosa/If Receptors (IF-CBL not Bound to IF Receptors)
Diminished or absent IF receptors—ileal bypass/resection/fistula.
Abnormal mucosal architecture/function—tropical/nontropical sprue, Crohn's disease, TB ileitis, infiltration by lymphomas, amyloidosis.
IF-/post IF-receptor defects—Imerslund-Graesbeck syndrome, TC II deficiency.
Drug-induced effects (slow K, biguanides, cholestyramine, colchicine, neomycin, PAS).

DISORDERS OF PLASMA CBL TRANSPORT (TC II-CBL NOT DELIVERED TO TC II RECEPTORS)

Congenital TC II deficiency, defective binding of TC II-CBL to TC II receptors (rare).

METABOLIC DISORDERS (CBL NOT UTILIZED BY CELL)

Inborn enzyme errors (rare).
Acquired disorders: (CBL oxidized to cob[III] alamin)—N$_2$O inhalation.

FOLATE DEFICIENCY

Nutritional Causes
Decreased dietary intake—poverty and famine (associated with kwashiorkor, marasmus), institutionalized individuals (psychiatric/nursing homes), chronic debilitating disease/goats' milk (low in folate), special diets (slimming), cultural/ethnic cooking techniques (food folate destroyed) or habits (folate-rich foods not consumed).
Decreased diet and increased requirements:
  ○ Physiologic: pregnancy and lactation, prematurity, infancy.
  ○ Pathologic: intrinsic hematologic disease (autoimmune hemolytic disease), drugs, malaria; hemoglobinopathies (SS, thalassemia), RBC membrane defects (hereditary spherocytosis, paroxysmal nocturnal hemoglobinopathy); abnormal hematopoiesis (leukemia/lymphoma, myelodysplastic syndrome, agnogenic myeloid metaplasia with myelofibrosis); infiltration with malignant disease; dermatologic (psoriasis).

Folate Malabsorption

With normal intestinal mucosa:
- Some drugs (controversial).
- Congenital folate malabsorption (rare).

With mucosal abnormalities—tropical and nontropical sprue, regional enteritis.

Defective Cellular Folate Uptake—Familial Aplastic Anemia (Rare), Inadequate Cellular Utilization

Folate antagonists (methotrexate).

Hereditary enzyme deficiencies involving folate.

Drugs (Multiple Effects on Folate Metabolism)

Alcohol, sulfasalazine, triamterene, pyrimethamine, trimethoprim-sulfamethoxazole, diphenylhydantoin, barbiturates.

MISCELLANEOUS MEGALOBLASTIC ANEMIAS (NOT CAUSED BY CBL OR FOLATE DEFICIENCY)

Congenital Disorders of DNA Synthesis (Rare)

Orotic aciduria, Lesch-Nyhan syndrome, congenital dyserythropoietic anemia.

Acquired Disorders of DNA Synthesis

Thiamine-responsive megaloblastosis (rare).

Malignancy—erythroleukemia—refractory sideroblastic anemias—all antineoplastic drugs that inhibit DNA synthesis.

Toxins—alcohol.

ANEMIA, MICROCYTIC, HYPOCHROMIC, DIFFERENTIAL DIAGNOSIS[38]

ICD-10CM #		
	D50.8	Other Iron Deficiency Anemias
	D50.9	Iron Deficiency Anemia, Unspecified
	D64.0	Hereditary Sideroblastic Anemia
	D64.1	Secondary Sideroblastic Anemia Due to Disease
	D64.2	Secondary Sideroblastic Anemia Due to Drugs and Toxins
	D64.3	Other Sideroblastic Anemias

DIFFERENTIAL DIAGNOSIS OF MICROCYTIC HYPOCHROMIC ANEMIA

Decreased Body Iron Stores

Iron-deficiency anemia.

Normal or Increased Body Iron Stores

Anemia of chronic disease.

Defective absorption, transport, or use of iron.

Iron-refractory, iron-deficiency anemia after parenteral iron.

Atransferrinemia.

Aceruloplasminemia.

Divalent metal transporter 1 (DMT1 or SLC11A2) deficiency.

Ferroportin-associated hemochromatosis with impaired iron export (type 4A).

Heme oxygenase 1 deficiency.

Disorders of globin synthesis.

Decreased Body Iron Stores

Thalassemia.
- Other microcytic hemoglobinopathies.
- Disorders of heme synthesis:

Sideroblastic anemias.
- Hereditary.
- Acquired.

ANERGY, CUTANEOUS[65]

ICD-10CM #	D89.9	Disorder Involving the Immune Mechanism, Unspecified

IMMUNOLOGIC

Acquired (AIDS, acute leukemia, carcinoma, CLL, Hodgkin's lymphoma, NHL).

Congenital (ataxia-telangiectasia, Di George's syndrome, severe combined immunodeficiency, Wiskott-Aldrich syndrome).

INFECTIONS

Bacterial (bacterial pneumonia, brucellosis).

Disseminated mycotic infections.

Mycobacterial (lepromatous leprosy, TB).

Viral (varicella, hepatitis, influenza, mononucleosis, measles, mumps).

IMMUNOSUPPRESSIVE MEDICATIONS

Systemic corticosteroids.

Methotrexate, cyclophosphamide.

Rifampin.

OTHER

Alcoholic cirrhosis, biliary cirrhosis, sarcoidosis, rheumatic disease.

Diabetes, Crohn's disease, uremia.

Anemia, pyridoxine deficiency, sickle cell anemia.

Burns, malnutrition, pregnancy, old age, surgery.

ANEURYSMS, THORACIC AORTA

ICD-10CM #	I71.2	Thoracic Aortic Aneurysm, Without Rupture

Trauma.

Infection.

Inflammatory (syphilis, Takayasu's disease).

Collagen vascular disease (RA, ankylosing spondylitis).

Annuloaortic ectasia (Marfan's syndrome, Ehlers-Danlos syndrome).

Congenital.

Coarctation.

Cystic medial necrosis.

ANHIDROSIS

ICD-10CM #	L74.0	Miliaria Rubra
	L74.1	Miliaria Crystallina
	L74.2	Miliaria Profunda

Drugs (anticholinergics).

Dehydration.

Hysteria.

Obstruction of sweat ducts (e.g., inflammation, miliaria).

Local radiant heat or pressure.

CNS lesions (medulla, hypothalamus, pons).

Spinal cord lesions.

Lesions of sympathetic nerves.

Congenital sweat gland disturbances.

ANION GAP ACIDOSIS[69]

ICD-10CM #	E87.2	Acidosis

CLINICAL CAUSES OF HIGH ANION GAP AND NORMAL ANION GAP ACIDOSIS

High Anion Gap

Ketoacidosis:

Diabetic ketoacidosis (acetoacetate).

Alcoholic (β-hydroxybutyrate).

Starvation.

Lactic acid acidosis:

L-Lactic acid acidosis (types A and B).

D-Lactic acid acidosis.

Renal failure: sulfate, phosphate, urate, hippurate.

Ingestions (toxins and their metabolites):

Ethylene glycol → glycolate, oxalate.

Methyl alcohol → formate.

Salicylate → ketones, lactate, salicylate.

Paraldehyde → organic anions.

Toluene → hippurate (commonly presents with normal anion gap).

Propylene glycol → lactate.

Pyroglutamic acidosis (acetaminophen use) → 5-oxoproline.

Normal Anion Gap

Gastrointestinal loss of HCO_3^- (negative urine anion gap):

Diarrhea.

Fistula, external.

Renal loss of HCO_3^- or failure to excrete NH_4^+ (positive urine anion gap):

Proximal renal tubular acidosis (RTA type 2).

Acetazolamide.

Classic distal renal tubular acidosis (low serum K^+) RTA type 1.

Generalized distal renal tubular defect (high serum K^+) RTA type 4.

Miscellaneous:

NH_4Cl ingestion.

Sulfur ingestion.

Dilutional acidosis.

Late stages in treatment of diabetic ketoacidosis.

ANION GAP INCREASE

ICD-10CM #	E87.8	Other Disorders of Electrolyte and Fluid Balance, Not Elsewhere Classified

Uremia.

Ketoacidosis (diabetic, starvation, alcoholic).

Lactic acidosis.

Ethylene glycol poisoning.

Salicylate overdose.

Methanol poisoning.

ANISOCORIA

ICD-10CM #	H57.02	Anisocoria

Mydriatic or miotic drugs.

Prosthetic eye.

Inflammation (keratitis, iridocyclitis).
Infections (herpes zoster, syphilis, meningitis, encephalitis, TB, diphtheria, botulism).
Subdural hemorrhage.
Cavernous sinus thrombosis.
Intracranial neoplasm.
Cerebral aneurysm.
Glaucoma.
CNS degenerative diseases.
Internal carotid ischemia.
Toxic polyneuritis (alcohol, lead).
Adie's syndrome.
Horner's syndrome.
DM.
Trauma.
Congenital.

ANOREXIA[67]

ICD-10CM # R63.0 Anorexia

SELECTED CAUSES OF ANOREXIA

Gastrointestinal Tract/Liver
Gastric outlet obstruction or small bowel obstruction.
Gastric cancer.
Hepatic metastases.
Acute viral hepatitis.
Metabolic
Addison's disease.
Hypopituitarism.
Hyperparathyroidism.
Functional
Extremely unpleasant sight/smell.
Systemic
Chronic pain.
Renal failure.
Severe congestive heart failure.
Respiratory failure.
Psychiatric
Depression.
Anorexia nervosa.
Medications
Digoxin.
Narcotic analgesics.
Diuretics.
Antihypertensives.
Chemotherapeutic agents.
Amphetamines.
Miscellaneous
Excessive smoking.
Excessive alcohol intake.
Oral cavity disease.
Thiamine deficiency.
Early pregnancy.
Hypogeusia or dysgeusia.

ANOVULATION

ICD-10CM # N97.0 Female Infertility Associated with Anovulation

Anorexia and bulimia.
Strenuous exercise.
Weight loss/malnutrition.
Empty sella syndrome.
Pituitary disorders (infarction, infection, trauma, irradiation, surgery, microadenomas, macroadenomas).
Idiopathic hypopituitarism.
Drug induced.
Thyroid dysfunction (hypothyroidism, hyperthyroidism).
Systemic diseases (e.g., liver disease).
Adrenal hyperfunction (Cushing's syndrome, congenital adrenal hyperplasia).
Polycystic ovarian syndrome.
Isolated gonadotropin deficiency.

APPENDICITIS, DIFFERENTIAL DIAGNOSIS IN PREGNANCY[26]

ICD-10CM # codes vary with specific

DIFFERENTIAL DIAGNOSIS OF APPENDICITIS DURING PREGNANCY

Gynecologic Conditions
Ruptured ovarian cyst.
Adnexal torsion.
Pelvic inflammatory disease or salpingitis.
Endometriosis.
Ovarian cancer.
Obstetrical Causes
Abruptio placentae.
Chorioamnionitis.
Endometritis.
Uterine fibroid degeneration.
Labor (preterm or term).
Viscus perforation after abortion.
Ruptured ectopic pregnancy.
Gastrointestinal Causes
Crohn's disease.
Colonic diverticulitis (right side).
Cholecystitis.
Pancreatitis.
Mesenteric lymphadenitis.
Gastroenteritis.
Colon cancer.
Intestinal obstruction.
Hernia (incarcerated inguinal or internal).
Colonic intussusception.
Ruptured Meckel's diverticulum.
Colonic perforation.
Acute mesenteric ischemia.
Other Causes
Pyelonephritis.
Urolithiasis.

APPETITE LOSS IN INFANTS AND CHILDREN[37]

ICD-10CM # R63.0 Anorexia
F50.8 Other Eating Disorders
F98.29 Other Feeding Disorders of Infancy and Early Childhood

ORGANIC DISEASE

Infection (Acute or Chronic) Neurologic
Congenital degenerative disease.
Hypothalamic lesion.
Increased intracranial pressure (including a brain tumor).
Swallowing disorders (neuromuscular).

Gastrointestinal
Oral lesions (e.g., thrush or herpes simplex).
Gastroesophageal reflux.
Obstruction (especially with gastric or intestinal distention).
Inflammatory bowel disease.
Celiac disease.
Constipation.
Cardiac
Congestive heart failure (especially associated with cyanotic lesions).
Metabolic
Renal failure and/or renal tubule acidosis.
Liver failure.
Congenital metabolic disease.
Lead poisoning.
Nutritional
Marasmus.
Iron deficiency.
Zinc deficiency.
Fever
RA.
Rheumatic fever.
Drugs
Morphine.
Digitalis.
Antimetabolites.
Methylphenidate.
Amphetamines.
Miscellaneous
Prolonged restriction of oral feedings, beginning in the neonatal period.
Systemic lupus erythematosus (SLE).
Tumor.

PSYCHOLOGIC FACTORS

Anxiety, fear, depression, mania (limbic influence on the hypothalamus).
Avoidance of symptoms associated with meals (abdominal pain, diarrhea, bloating, urgency, dumping syndrome).
Anorexia nervosa.
Excessive weight loss and food aversion in athletes, simulating anorexia nervosa.

ARTERIAL OCCLUSION[29]

ICD-10CM # I74.3 Embolism and Thrombosis of Arteries of the Lower Extremities
I74.2 Embolism and Thrombosis of Arteries of the Upper Extremities

Thromboembolism (post-MI, mitral stenosis, rheumatic valve disease, atrial fibrillation, atrial myxoma, marantic endocarditis, bacterial endocarditis, Libman-Sacks endocarditis).
Atheroembolism (microemboli composed of cholesterol, calcium, and platelets from proximal atherosclerotic plaques).
Arterial thrombosis (endothelial injury, altered arterial blood flow, trauma, severe atherosclerosis, acute vasculitis).
Vasospasm.
Trauma.
Hypercoagulable states.
Miscellaneous (irradiation, drugs, infections, necrotizing).

ARTHRITIS AND ABDOMINAL PAIN

ICD-10CM #	M00.9	Pyogenic Arthritis, Unspecified
	R10.817	Generalized Abdominal Tenderness
	M02.9	Reactive arthropathy

Viral syndrome.
Inflammatory bowel disease.
Celiac disease.
Vasculitis.
SLE.
RA.
Scleroderma.
Amyloidosis.
Chronic hepatitis C.
Whipple's disease.
Polyarteritis nodosa.
Behçet's disease.
Familial Mediterranean fever.
Blind loop syndrome.
Babesiosis.
Lyme disease.
Ehrlichiosis.

ARTHRITIS AND DIARRHEA

ICD-10CM #	M00.9	Pyogenic Arthritis, Unspecified
	R19.7	Diarrhea, Unspecified

Viral syndrome.
Inflammatory bowel disease.
Celiac disease.
Whipple's disease.
Enterogenic (bacterial) reactive arthritis.
Collagenous colitis.
Behçet's disease.
Hyperthyroidism.
Spondyloarthropathy.
Blind loop syndrome.

ARTHRITIS AND EYE LESIONS[15]

ICD-10CM #	M00.9	Pyogenic Arthritis, Unspecified
	M02.3	Reiter disease
	M02.9	Reactive arthropathy

SLE.
Sjögren's syndrome.
Behçet's syndrome.
Sarcoidosis.
Subacute bacterial endocarditis (SBE).
Lyme disease.
Granulomatosis with polyangiitis (Wegener's granulomatosis).
Giant cell arteritis.
Takayasu's arteritis.
RA, JRA.
Scleroderma.
Inflammatory bowel disease.
Whipple's disease.
Ankylosing spondylitis.
Reactive arthritis.
Psoriatic arthritis.

ARTHRITIS AND HEART MURMUR[15]

ICD-10CM #	M00.9	Pyogenic Arthritis, Unspecified
	I01.8	Other Acute Rheumatic Heart Disease
	M02.9	Reactive arthropathy

SBE.
Cardiac myxoma.
Ankylosing spondylitis.
Reactive arthritis.
Acute rheumatic fever.
RA.
SLE with Libman-Sacks endocarditis.
Relapsing polychondritis.

ARTHRITIS AND MUSCLE WEAKNESS[17]

ICD-10CM #	M00.9	Pyogenic Arthritis, Unspecified
	M62.9	Disorder of Muscle, Unspecified
	M02.9	Reactive arthropathy

RA.
Ankylosing spondylitis.
Polymyositis.
Dermatomyositis.
SLE, scleroderma, mixed connective tissue disease.
Sarcoidosis.
HIV-associated arthritis.
Whipple's disease.

ARTHRITIS AND RASH[15]

ICD-10CM #	M00.9	Pyogenic Arthritis, Unspecified
	R21	Rash and Other Nonspecific Skin Eruption
	M02.9	Reactive arthropathy

Chronic urticaria.
Vasculitic urticaria.
SLE.
Dermatomyositis.
Polymyositis.
Psoriatic arthritis.
Reactive arthritis.
Chronic sarcoidosis.
Serum sickness.
Sweet's syndrome.
Leprosy.

ARTHRITIS AND SUBCUTANEOUS NODULES[15]

ICD-10CM #	M00.9	Pyogenic Arthritis, Unspecified
	A18.4	Tuberculosis of Skin and Subcutaneous Tissue
	M02.9	Reactive arthropathy

RA.
Gout.

Pseudogout (rare).
Sarcoidosis.
Light chain (LA) amyloidosis (primary, multiple myeloma).
Acute rheumatic fever (ARF).
Hemochromatosis.
Whipple's disease.
Multicentric reticulohistiocytosis.

ARTHRITIS AND WEIGHT LOSS[15]

ICD-10CM #	M00.9	Pyogenic Arthritis, Unspecified
	R63.4	Abnormal Weight Loss
	M02.9	Reactive arthropathy

Severe RA.
RA with vasculitis.
Reactive arthritis.
RA or psoriatic arthritis or ankylosing spondylitis with amyloidosis.
Cancer.
Enteropathic arthritis (Crohn's, ulcerative colitis).
HIV infection.
Whipple's disease.
Blind loop syndrome.
Scleroderma with intestinal bacterial overgrowth.

ARTHRITIS OR EXTREMITY PAIN, IN CHILDREN AND ADOLESCENTS[45]

ICD-10CM #	M02.9	Reactive arthropathy

CAUSES OF ARTHRITIS OR EXTREMITY PAIN IN CHILDREN AND ADOLESCENTS

Rheumatic and Inflammatory Diseases
Juvenile idiopathic arthritis.
Systemic lupus erythematosus.
Juvenile dermatomyositis.
Polyarteritis.
Vasculitis.
Scleroderma.
Sjögren syndrome.
Behçet disease.
Overlap syndromes.
Granulomatosis with polyangiitis (Wegener granulomatosis).
Sarcoidosis.
Kawasaki syndrome.
Henoch-Schönlein purpura.
Chronic recurrent multifocal osteomyelitis.
Seronegative Spondyloarthropathies
Juvenile ankylosing spondylitis.
Inflammatory bowel disease.
Psoriatic arthritis.
Reactive arthritis associated with urethritis, iridocyclitis, and mucocutaneous lesions.
Infectious Illnesses
Bacterial arthritis (septic arthritis, *Staphylococcus aureus*, pneumococcus, gonococcus, *Haemophilus influenzae*).
Lyme disease.
Viral illness (parvovirus, rubella, mumps, Epstein-Barr virus, hepatitis B).
Fungal arthritis.

Differential Diagnosis

II

Mycobacterial infection.
Spirochetal infection.
Endocarditis.
Reactive Arthritis
Acute rheumatic fever.
Reactive arthritis (postinfectious due to *Shigella*, *Salmonella*, *Yersinia*, *Chlamydia*, or meningococcus).
Serum sickness.
Toxic synovitis of the hip.
Postimmunization.
Immunodeficiencies
Hypogammaglobulinemia.
Immunoglobulin A deficiency.
Human immunodeficiency virus.
Congenital and Metabolic Disorders
Gout.
Pseudogout.
Mucopolysaccharidoses.
Thyroid disease (hypothyroidism, hyperthyroidism).
Hyperparathyroidism.
Vitamin C deficiency (scurvy).
Hereditary connective tissue disease (Marfan syndrome, Ehlers-Danlos syndrome).
Fabry disease.
Farber disease.
Amyloidosis (familial Mediterranean fever).
Bone and Cartilage Disorders
Trauma.
Patellofemoral syndrome.
Hypermobility syndrome.
Osteochondritis dissecans.
Avascular necrosis (including Legg-Calvé-Perthes disease).
Hypertrophic osteoarthropathy.
Slipped capital femoral epiphysis.
Osteolysis.
Benign bone tumors (including osteoid osteoma).
Histiocytosis.
Rickets.
Neuropathic Disorders
Peripheral neuropathies.
Carpal tunnel syndrome.
Charcot joints.
Neoplastic Disorders
Leukemia.
Neuroblastoma.
Lymphoma.
Bone tumors (osteosarcoma, Ewing sarcoma).
Histiocytic syndromes.
Synovial tumors.
Hematologic Disorders
Hemophilia.
Hemoglobinopathies (including sickle cell disease).
Miscellaneous Disorders
Pigmented villonodular synovitis.
Plant-thorn synovitis (foreign body arthritis).
Myositis ossificans.
Eosinophilic fasciitis.
Tendinitis (overuse injury).
Raynaud phenomenon.
Pain Syndromes
Fibromyalgia.
Growing pains.
Depression (with somatization).
Reflex sympathetic dystrophy.
Regional myofascial pain syndromes.

ARTHRITIS, AXIAL SKELETON

ICD-10CM #	M45.9	Ankylosing Spondylitis of Unspecified Sites in Spine
	L40.54	Psoriatic Juvenile Arthropathy
	L40.59	Other Psoriatic Arthropathy
	M15.9	Polyosteoarthritis, Unspecified
	M45.9	Ankylosing Spondylitis of Unspecified Sites in Spine

RA.
Psoriatic arthritis.
Reiter's syndrome (reactive arthritis).
Ankylosing spondylitis.
Juvenile RA.
Degenerative disease of the nucleus pulposus.
Spondylosis deformans.
Diffuse idiopathic skeletal hyperostosis (DISH).
Alkaptonuria.
Infection.

ARTHRITIS, CHRONIC, MONOARTICULAR OR OLIGOARTICULAR, INFECTIOUS CAUSES[9]

| ICD-10CM # | varies with specific diagnosis |

INFECTIOUS CAUSES OF CHRONIC MONARTICULAR OR OLIGOARTICULAR ARTHRITIS

Bacterial
Borrelia burgdorferi.
Tropheryma whipplei.
Treponema pallidum.
Nocardia spp.
Fungi
Candida spp.
Cryptococcus neoformans.
Blastomyces dermatitidis.
Coccidioides spp.
Paracoccidioides brasiliensis.
Sporothrix schenckii.
Aspergillus spp. and other molds, including *Rhizopus*, *Scedosporium*, and *Fusarium*.
Mycobacteria
Mycobacterium tuberculosis.
M. kansasii.
M. marinum.
M. avium-intracellulare complex.
M. terrae.
M. fortuitum, M. chelonae, M. abscessus.
M. haemophilum.
M. leprae.
Parasites
Helminths.
Filariae.

ARTHRITIS, FEVER, AND RASH[15]

| ICD-10CM # | M00.9 | Pyogenic Arthritis, Unspecified |

	M02.9	Reactive arthropathy
	R21	Rash and Other Nonspecific Skin Eruption
	R50.9	Fever, Unspecified

Rubella, parvovirus B19.
Gonococcemia, meningococcemia.
Secondary syphilis, Lyme borreliosis.
Adult acute rheumatic fever, adult Still's disease, adult Kawasaki disease.
Vasculitic urticaria.
Acute sarcoidosis.
Familial Mediterranean fever.
Hyperimmunoglobulinemia D and periodic fever syndrome.

ARTHRITIS, MONOARTICULAR AND OLIGOARTICULAR[6]

ICD-10CM #	M19.90	Unspecified Osteoarthritis, Unspecified Site
	M01.X0	Direct Infection of Unspecified Joint in Infectious and Parasitic Diseases Classified Elsewhere
	M13.10	Monoarthritis, Not Elsewhere Classified, Unspecified Site

Septic arthritis (*S. aureus, Neisseria gonorrhoeae*, meningococci, streptococci, *Streptococcus pneumoniae*, enteric gram-negative bacilli).
Crystalline-induced arthritis (gout, pseudogout, calcium oxalate, hydroxyapatite and other basic calcium/phosphate crystals).
Traumatic joint injury.
Hemarthrosis.
Monoarticular or oligoarticular flare of an inflammatory polyarticular rheumatic disease (RA, psoriatic arthritis, Reiter's syndrome [reactive arthritis], SLE).

ARTHRITIS, PEDIATRIC AGE[37]

ICD-10CM #	M01.X0	Direct Infection of Unspecified Joint in Infectious and Parasitic Diseases Classified Elsewhere
	M08.00	Unspecified Juvenile Rheumatoid Arthritis of Unspecified Site
	M08.3	Juvenile Rheumatoid Polyarthritis (Seronegative)
	M08.40	Pauciarticular Juvenile Rheumatoid Arthritis, Unspecified Site

RHEUMATIC DISEASES OF CHILDHOOD

Acute rheumatic fever.
SLE.
Juvenile ankylosing spondylitis.

Polymyositis and dermatomyositis.
Vasculitis.
Scleroderma.
Psoriatic arthritis.
Mixed connective tissue disease and overlap syndromes.
Kawasaki disease.
Behçet's syndrome.
Familial Mediterranean fever.
Reiter's syndrome (reactive arthritis).
Reflex sympathetic dystrophy.
Fibromyalgia (fibrositis).

INFECTIOUS DISEASES

Bacterial arthritis.
Viral or postviral arthritis.
Fungal arthritis.
Osteomyelitis.
Reactive arthritis.

NEOPLASTIC DISEASES

Leukemia.
Lymphoma.
Neuroblastoma.
Primary bone tumors.

NONINFLAMMATORY DISORDERS

Trauma.
Avascular necrosis syndromes.
Osteochondroses.
Slipped capital femoral epiphysis.
Diskitis.
Patellofemoral dysfunction (chondromalacia patellae).
Toxic synovitis of the hip.
Overuse syndromes.

GENETIC OR CONGENITAL SYNDROMES

Hematologic Disorders
Sickle cell disease.
Hemophilia.

INFLAMMATORY BOWEL DISEASE

Miscellaneous
Growing pains.
Psychogenic arthralgias (conversion reactions).
Hypermobility syndrome.
Villonodular synovitis.
Foreign body arthritis.

ARTHRITIS, POLYARTICULAR

ICD-10CM #	M15.0	Primary Generalized (Osteo)Arthritis
	M12.89	Other Specific Arthropathies, Not Elsewhere Classified, Multiple Sites
	M08.3	Juvenile Rheumatoid Polyarthritis (Seronegative)

RA, juvenile (rheumatoid) polyarthritis.
SLE, other connective tissue diseases, erythema nodosum, palindromic rheumatism, relapsing polychondritis.
Psoriatic arthritis, ankylosing spondylitis.
Sarcoidosis.

Lyme arthritis, bacterial endocarditis, *Neisseria gonorrhoeae* infection, rheumatic fever, Reiter's disease (reactive arthritis).
Crystal deposition disease.
Hypersensitivity to serum or drugs.
Hepatitis B, HIV, rubella, mumps.
Other: serum sickness, leukemias, lymphomas, enteropathic arthropathy, Whipple's disease, Behçet's syndrome, Henoch-Schönlein purpura, familial Mediterranean fever, hypertrophic pulmonary osteoarthropathy.

ASCITES

ICD-10CM #	R18.0	Malignant Ascites
	C78.6	Secondary Malignant Neoplasm of Retroperitoneum and Peritoneum
	I89.8	Other Specified Noninfective Disorders of Lymphatic Vessels and Lymph Nodes

Hypoalbuminemia: nephrotic syndrome, protein-losing gastroenteropathy, starvation.
Cirrhosis.
Hepatic congestion: CHF, constrictive pericarditis, tricuspid insufficiency, hepatic vein obstruction (Budd-Chiari syndrome), inferior vena cava or portal vein obstruction.
Peritoneal infections: TB and other bacterial infections, fungal diseases, parasites.
Neoplasms: primary hepatic neoplasms, metastases to liver or peritoneum, lymphomas, leukemias, myeloid metaplasia.
Lymphatic obstruction: mediastinal tumors, trauma to the thoracic duct, filariasis.
Ovarian disease: Meigs' syndrome, struma ovarii.
Chronic pancreatitis or pseudocyst: pancreatic ascites.
Leakage of bile: bile ascites.
Urinary obstruction or trauma: urine ascites.
Myxedema.
Chylous ascites.

ASPIRATION LUNG INJURY, CHILDREN[45]

ICD-10CM #	P24.8	Neonatal aspiration syndromes

CONDITIONS PREDISPOSING TO ASPIRATION LUNG INJURY IN CHILDREN

Anatomic and Mechanical
Tracheoesophageal fistula.
Laryngeal cleft.
Vascular ring.
Cleft palate.
Micrognathia.
Macroglossia.
Achalasia.
Esophageal foreign body.
Tracheostomy.
Endotracheal tube.
Nasoenteric tube.
Collagen vascular disease (scleroderma, dermatomyositises).

Gastroesophageal reflux disease.
Obesity.

Neuromuscular
Altered consciousness.
Immaturity of swallowing/prematurity.
Dysautonomia.
Increased intracranial pressure.
Hydrocephalus.
Vocal cord paralysis.
Cerebral palsy.
Muscular dystrophy.
Myasthenia gravis.
Guillain-Barré syndrome.
Werdnig-Hoffmann disease.
Ataxia-telangiectasia.
Cerebral vascular accident.

Miscellaneous
Poor oral hygiene.
Gingivitis.
Prolonged hospitalization.
Gastric outlet or intestinal obstruction.
Poor feeding techniques (bottle propping, overfeeding, inappropriate foods for toddlers).
Bronchopulmonary dysplasia.
Viral infection.

ASTHENIA

ICD-10CM #	G93.3	Postviral Fatigue Syndrome
	R53.1	Weakness
	R53.81	Other Malaise
	R53.83	Other Fatigue

Depression.
Chronic fatigue syndrome.
Sleep disorders.
Anemia.
Hypothyroidism.
Sedentary lifestyle.
Medications (e.g., narcotics, sedatives).
Infections.
Dehydration/electrolyte disorders.
COPD and other pulmonary disorders.
Renal failure.
CHF.
Diabetes.
Addison's disease.
Paraneoplastic syndrome.

ASTHMA, CHILDHOOD[8]

ICD-10CM #	J45.20	Mild Intermittent Asthma, Uncomplicated
	J45.22	Mild Intermittent Asthma with Status Asthmaticus

INFECTIONS

Bronchiolitis (RSV).
Pneumonia.
Croup.
Tuberculosis, histoplasmosis.
Bronchiectasis.
Bronchiolitis obliterans.
Bronchitis.
Sinusitis.

Differential Diagnosis

ANATOMIC, CONGENITAL

Cystic fibrosis.
Vascular rings.
Ciliary dyskinesia.
B-lymphocyte immune defect.
Congestive heart failure.
Laryngotracheomalacia.
Tumor, lymphoma.
H-type tracheoesophageal fistula.
Repaired tracheoesophageal fistula.
Gastroesophageal reflux.

VASCULITIS, HYPERSENSITIVITY

Allergic bronchopulmonary aspergillosis.
Allergic alveolitis, hypersensitivity pneumonitis.
Churg-Strauss syndrome.
Periarteritis nodosa.

OTHER

Foreign body aspiration.
Pulmonary thromboembolism.
Psychogenic cough.
Sarcoidosis.
Bronchopulmonary dysplasia.
Vocal cord dysfunction.

ATAXIA

ICD-10CM #		
	R27.0	Ataxia, Unspecified
	R27.8	Other Lack of Coordination
	R27.9	Unspecified Lack of Coordination
	F10.229	Alcohol Dependence with Intoxication, Unspecified
	F10.20	Alcohol Dependence, Uncomplicated
	G11.1	Early-Onset Cerebellar Ataxia
	G31.89	Other Specified Degenerative Diseases of Nervous System
	F44.4	Conversion Disorder with Motor Symptom or Deficit
	F44.6	Conversion Disorder with Sensory Symptom or Deficit

Vertebral-basilar artery ischemia.
Diabetic neuropathy.
Tabes dorsalis.
Vitamin B_{12} deficiency.
Multiple sclerosis and other demyelinating diseases.
Meningomyelopathy.
Cerebellar neoplasms, hemorrhage, abscess, infarct.
Nutritional (Wernicke's encephalopathy).
Paraneoplastic syndromes.
Parainfectious: Guillain-Barré syndrome, acute ataxia of childhood and young adults.
Toxins: phenytoin, alcohol, sedatives, organophosphates.
Wilson's disease (hepatolenticular degeneration).
Hypothyroidism.
Myopathy.
Cerebellar and spinocerebellar degeneration: ataxia/telangiectasia, Friedreich's ataxia.

Frontal lobe lesions: tumors, thrombosis of anterior cerebral artery, hydrocephalus.
Labyrinthine destruction: neoplasm, injury, inflammation, compression.
Hysteria.
AIDS.

ATAXIA, ACUTE OR RECURRENT[20]

ICD-10CM #		
	R27.0	Ataxia, Unspecified
	R27.8	Other Lack of Coordination
	R27.9	Unspecified Lack of Coordination
	F10.229	Alcohol Dependence with Intoxication, Unspecified
	F10.20	Alcohol Dependence, Uncomplicated
	G11.1	Early-Onset Cerebellar Ataxia
	G31.89	Other Specified Degenerative Diseases of Nervous System
	F44.4	Conversion Disorder with Motor Symptom or Deficit
	F44.6	Conversion Disorder with Sensory Symptom or Deficit

Drug ingestion (e.g., phenytoin, carbamazepine, sedatives, hypnotics, and phencyclidine) or intoxication (e.g., alcohol, ethylene glycol, hydrocarbon fumes, lead, mercury, or thallium).
Postinfectious (cerebellitis [e.g., varicella], acute disseminated encephalomyelitis).
Head trauma.
Basilar migraine.
Benign paroxysmal vertigo (migraine equivalent).
Brain tumor or neuroblastoma (if accompanied by opsoclonus or myoclonus [i.e., "dancing eyes, dancing feet"]).
Hydrocephalus.
Infection (e.g., labyrinthitis, abscess).
Seizure (ictal or postictal).
Vascular events (e.g., cerebellar hemorrhage or stroke).
Miller-Fisher variant of Guillain-Barré syndrome (ataxia, ophthalmoplegia, and areflexia). Warning: If bulbar signs present, disease is likely progressive; patient may lose ability to protect airway and/or ability to breathe.
Inherited ataxias.
Inborn errors of metabolism (e.g., mitochondrial disorders, amino-acidopathies, urea cycle defects).
Conversion reaction.
Multiple sclerosis.

ATAXIA, CEREBELLAR, ADULT ONSET[63]

ICD-10CM #		
	G11.0	Congenital Nonprogressive Ataxia
	G11.2	Late-Onset Cerebellar Ataxia

CAUSES OF ADULT ONSET CEREBELLAR ATAXIA

Inherited
Later onset SCA syndromes.
Rarely Friedreich's ataxia.
Congenital
Arnold–Chiari malformation (cerebellar ectopia).
Inflammatory
Multiple sclerosis.
Sarcoidosis.
Infections (TB, viral).
Neoplastic
Often metastatic in adults.
Meningioma, neurofibroma.
Hemangioblastoma.
Paraneoplastic
Usually with small cell bronchial carcinoma.
Vascular
Infarction, hemorrhage.
Arteriovenous malformations.
Trauma
Head injury.
Postsurgical.
Toxic
Alcohol, phenytoin, solvent abuse.
Endocrine
Hypothyroidism (very rare).
Degenerative
Multiple system atrophy (MSA).

ATAXIA, CEREBELLAR, CHILDREN[63]

ICD-10CM #		
	G11.0	Congenital Nonprogressive Ataxia
	G11.2	Late-Onset Cerebellar Ataxia

CAUSES OF CEREBELLAR ATAXIA IN CHILDREN

Congenital Malformations
Cerebellar agenesis/hypoplasia.
Dandy–Walker syndrome.
Arnold–Chiari malformation.
Hereditary Ataxias
Friedreich's ataxia.
Trauma
Birth trauma.
Head injury in childhood.
Infectious
Secondary to bacterial meningitis.
Secondary to encephalitis.
Hydrocephalus
Tumors
Medulloblastoma.
Astrocytoma.
Hemangioblastoma.

ATAXIA, CHRONIC OR PROGRESSIVE[20]

ICD-10CM #		
	R27.0	Ataxia, Unspecified
	R27.8	Other Lack of Coordination
	R27.9	Unspecified Lack of Coordination

G11.1	Early-Onset Cerebellar Ataxia
G11.0	Congenital Nonprogressive Ataxia
G11.2	Late-Onset Cerebellar Ataxia
G11.3	Cerebellar Ataxia with Defective DNA Repair
G11.8	Other Hereditary Ataxia

Hydrocephalus.
Hypothyroidism.
Tumor or paraneoplastic syndrome.
Low vitamin E levels (e.g., cystic fibrosis).
Wilson disease.
Inborn errors of metabolism.
Inherited ataxias (e.g., ataxia-telangiectasia, Friedreich's ataxia).

ATELECTASIS

ICD-10CM # J98.11 Atelectasis

Lung neoplasm (primary or metastatic).
Infection (pneumonia, TB, fungal, histoplasmosis).
Postoperative (lower lobes).
Sarcoidosis.
Mucoid impaction.
Foreign body.
Postinflammatory (middle lobe syndrome).
Pneumothorax.
Pleural effusion.
Pneumoconiosis.
Interstitial fibrosis.
Bulla.
Mediastinal or adjacent mass.

ATRIAL ENLARGEMENT, LEFT ATRIUM[32]

ICD-10CM # I51.7 Cardiomegaly

CAUSES OF LARGE LEFT ATRIUM

Causes Due to Volume Overload
Mitral regurgitation (often with left ventricular failure).
Ventricular septal defect.
Patent ductus arteriosus.
Atrial septal defect with shunt reversal (i.e., pulmonary hypertension).
ASD with tricuspid atresia (obligatory shunt reversal).
Aortopulmonary window.
Causes Due to Pressure Overload
Mitral stenosis.
Noncompliant left ventricle: hypertension, hypertrophic cardiomyopathy, aortic stenosis.
Left ventricular failure (often with secondary mitral regurgitation).
Left atrial myxoma.
Other Causes (Both Rare)
Atrial fibrillation.
Isolated/idiopathic.

ATRIAL ENLARGEMENT, RIGHT ATRIUM

ICD-10CM # I51.7 Cardiomegaly

Right ventricular failure.
Atrial septal defect.
Tricuspid regurgitation.
Tricuspid stenosis.
Pulmonary hypertension.
Restrictive cardiomyopathy.
Right atrial myxoma.
Ebstein's anomaly.
Anomalous pulmonary venous drainage to the right atrium.
Endomyocardial fibrosis.
Sinus of Valsalva fistula.
Arrhythmogenic right ventricular dysplasia.

ATYPICAL LYMPHOCYTOSIS, HETEROPHIL NEGATIVE, INFECTIOUS CAUSES[3]

ICD-10CM # D72.820 Lymphocytosis (Symptomatic)

MOST COMMON INFECTIOUS CAUSES OF HETEROPHIL-NEGATIVE ATYPICAL LYMPHOCYTOSIS

Babesiosis.
Cytomegalovirus.
Epstein-Barr virus (particularly in children).
Human herpesvirus 6.
Human immunodeficiency virus (especially during acute seroconversion).
Infectious mononucleosis.
Malaria.
Measles.
Toxoplasmosis.
Varicella.
Infectious hepatitis.

AV NODAL BLOCK[29]

ICD-10CM # I44.30 Unspecified Atrioventricular Block
I44.2 Atrioventricular Block, Complete

Idiopathic fibrosis (Lenègre's disease).
Sclerodegenerative processes (e.g., Lev's disease with calcification of the mitral and aortic annuli).
AV node radiofrequency ablation procedure.
Medications (e.g., digoxin, beta-blockers, calcium channel blockers, class III antiarrhythmics).
Acute inferior wall MI.
Myocarditis.
Infections (endocarditis, Lyme disease).
Infiltrative diseases (e.g., hemochromatosis, sarcoidosis, amyloidosis).
Trauma (including cardiac surgical procedures).
Collagen vascular diseases.
Aortic root diseases (e.g., spondylitis).
Electrolyte abnormalities (e.g., hyperkalemia).

BACK PAIN

ICD-10CM #	M54.89	Other Dorsalgia
	M54.9	Dorsalgia, Unspecified
	M54.5	Low Back Pain
	F45.42	Pain Disorder with Related Psychological Factors
	M54.08	Panniculitis Affecting Regions of Neck and Back, Sacral and Sacrococcygeal Region
	S23.9XXA	Sprain of Unspecified Parts of Thorax, Initial Encounter
	M43.27	Fusion of Spine, Lumbosacral Region
	M43.28	Fusion of Spine, Sacral and Sacrococcygeal Region
	M53.2X7	Spinal Instabilities, Lumbosacral Region
	M53.3	Sacrococcygeal Disorders, Not Elsewhere Classified

Trauma: injury to bone, joint, or ligament.
Mechanical: pregnancy, obesity, fatigue, scoliosis.
Degenerative: osteoarthritis.
Infections: osteomyelitis, subarachnoid or spinal abscess, TB, meningitis, basilar pneumonia.
Metabolic: osteoporosis, osteomalacia.
Vascular: leaking aortic aneurysm, subarachnoid or spinal hemorrhage/infarction.
Neoplastic: myeloma, Hodgkin's disease, carcinoma of pancreas, metastatic neoplasm from breast, prostate, lung.
GI: penetrating ulcer, pancreatitis, cholelithiasis, inflammatory bowel disease.
Renal: hydronephrosis, calculus, neoplasm, renal infarction, pyelonephritis.
Hematologic: sickle cell crisis, acute hemolysis.
Gynecologic: neoplasm of uterus or ovary, dysmenorrhea, salpingitis, uterine prolapse.
Inflammatory: ankylosing spondylitis, psoriatic arthritis, Reiter's syndrome (reactive arthritis).
Lumbosacral strain.
Psychogenic: malingering, hysteria, anxiety.
Endocrine: adrenal hemorrhage or infarction.

BACK PAIN, CHILDREN AND ADOLESCENTS[45]

ICD-10CM # M54.5 Low Back Pain
M54.9 Dorsalgia

INFLAMMATORY OR INFECTIOUS

Diskitis.
Vertebral osteomyelitis (pyogenic, tuberculous).

Spinal epidural abscess.
Pyelonephritis.
Pancreatitis.

RHEUMATOLOGIC

Pauciarticular juvenile rheumatoid arthritis.
Reiter syndrome (reactive arthritis).
Ankylosing spondylitis.
Psoriatic arthritis.

DEVELOPMENTAL

Spondylolysis.
Spondylolisthesis.
Scheuermann disease.
Scoliosis.

TRAUMATIC (ACUTE VERSUS REPETITIVE)

Hip-pelvis anomalies.
Herniated disk.
Overuse syndromes.
Vertebral stress fractures.
Upper cervical spine instability.

NEOPLASTIC

Vertebral Tumors
Benign
Eosinophilic granuloma.
Aneurysmal bone cyst.
Osteoid osteoma.
Osteoblastoma.
Malignant
Osteogenic sarcoma.
Leukemia.
Lymphoma.
Metastatic tumors.
Spinal Cord, Ganglia, and Nerve Roots
Intramedullary spinal cord tumor.
Sympathetic chain.
Ganglioneuroma.
Ganglioneuroblastoma.
Neuroblastoma.

OTHER

Intraabdominal or pelvic pathology.
Following lumbar puncture.
Conversion reaction.
Juvenile osteoporosis.

BACK PAIN, LOW, ACUTE[6]

ICD-10CM #   M54.5   Low Back Pain

DIFFERENTIAL CONSIDERATIONS IN ACUTE LOW BACK PAIN

Emergent
Aortic dissection.
Cauda equina syndrome.
Epidural abscess or hematoma.
Meningitis.
Ruptured/expanding aortic aneurysm.
Spinal fracture or subluxation with cord or root impingement.
Urgent
Back pain with neurologic deficits.
Disk herniation causing neurologic compromise.
Malignancy.
Sciatica with motor nerve root compression.
Spinal fractures without cord impingement.

Spinal stenosis.
Transverse myelitis.
Vertebral osteomyelitis.
Common or Stable
Acute ligamentous injury.
Acute muscle strain.
Ankylosing spondylitis.
Degenerative joint disease.
Intervertebral disk disease without impingement.
Pathologic fracture without impingement.
Seropositive arthritis.
Spondylolisthesis.
Referred or Visceral
Cholecystitis.
Esophageal disease.
Nephrolithiasis.
Ovarian torsion, mass, or tumor.
Pancreatitis.
Peptic ulcer disease.
Pleural effusion.
Pneumonia.
Pulmonary embolism.
Pyelonephritis.
Retroperitoneal hemorrhage or mass.

BACK PAIN, VISCEROGENIC ORIGIN

ICD-10CM #	F45.41	Pain Disorder Exclusively Related to Psychological Factors
	M54	Dorsalgia
	M54.5	Low back pain

Urolithiasis.
Aortic aneurysm.
Colorectal carcinoma.
Endometriosis.
Tubal pregnancy.
Prostatitis.
Peptic ulcer.
Pancreatitis.
Diverticular spasm.
Metastatic neoplasm (e.g., bladder, uterus, ovary, kidney).

BACTERIAL OVERGROWTH, SMALL INTESTINE[67]

ICD-10CM #   A04.9   Bacterial intestinal infection, unspecified

Gastric surgery—Billroth II.
Small bowel diverticula.
Small bowel stricture:
   Crohn's disease.
   Radiation enteritis.
Impaired small intestinal motility:
   Scleroderma.
   Diabetes mellitus.
   Chronic intestinal pseudoobstruction.
Miscellaneous/multifactorial
   Elderly.
   Immune deficiency syndromes.
   Chronic pancreatitis.
   Cirrhosis.

BALLISM[9]

| ICD-10CM # | G25.4 | Drug-Induced Chorea |
| | G25.5 | Other Chorea |

Cerebral infarction or hemorrhage.
Medications (e.g., dopamine agonists, phenytoin).
CNS neoplasm (primary or metastatic).
Nonketotic hyperosmolar state.

BILE DUCT, DILATED[67]

ICD-10CM #   K83.1   Obstruction of bile duct

Normal variant.
Post-cholecystectomy.
Unsuspected bile duct stone.
Sphincter of Oddi stenosis.
Occult bile duct stricture.
Previous bile duct injury.
Early carcinoma of the pancreas, carcinoma of the bile duct, or carcinoma of the ampulla.
Extrinsic compression of the bile duct by a primary or secondary neoplasm.

BILIARY TREE, REFLUX OF GAS OR BOWEL[70]

ICD-10CM #   varies with specific diagnosis

CAUSES OF REFLUX OF GAS OR BOWEL CONTRAST INTO THE BILIARY TREE

Iatrogenic.
Sphincterotomy.
Choledochojejunostomy.
Gallstone fistula.
Cholecystoduodenal fistula.
Perforated ulcer.
Choledochoduodenal fistula.
Carcinoma.
Choledochoenteric fistula.

BLEEDING, LOWER GI

ICD-10CM #   K92.2   Gastrointestinal Hemorrhage, Unspecified

(ORIGINATING BELOW THE LIGAMENT OF TREITZ)

Small Intestine
Ischemic bowel disease (mesenteric thrombosis, embolism, vasculitis, trauma).
Small bowel neoplasm: leiomyomas, carcinoids.
Hereditary hemorrhagic telangiectasia (Rendu-Osler-Weber syndrome).
Meckel diverticulum and other small intestine diverticula.
Aortoenteric fistula.
Intestinal hemangiomas: blue rubber-bleb nevi, intestinal hemangiomas, cutaneous vascular nevi.
Hamartomatous polyps: Peutz-Jeghers syndrome (intestinal polyps, mucocutaneous pigmentation).
Infections of small bowel: tuberculous enteritis, enteritis necroticans.
Volvulus.

---

[9]Violent, flinging, nonpatterned rapid movements

Intussusception.
Lymphoma of small bowel, sarcoma, Kaposi's sarcoma.
Irradiation ileitis.
AV malformation of small intestine.
Inflammatory bowel disease.
Polyarteritis nodosa.
Other: pancreatoenteric fistulas, Henoch-Schönlein purpura, Ehlers-Danlos syndrome, SLE, amyloidosis, metastatic melanoma.

Colon
Carcinoma (particularly left colon).
Diverticular disease.
Inflammatory bowel disease.
Ischemic colitis.
Colonic polyps.
Vascular abnormalities: angiodysplasia, vascular ectasia.
Radiation colitis.
Infectious colitis.
Uremic colitis.
Aortoenteric fistula.
Lymphoma of large bowel.
Hemorrhoids.
Anal fissure.
Trauma, foreign body.
Solitary rectal/cecal ulcers.
Long-distance running.

BLEEDING, LOWER GI, PEDIATRIC[6]

ICD-10CM # K92.2 Gastrointestinal Hemorrhage, Unspecified

<3 MO
Swallowed maternal blood.
Infectious colitis.
Milk allergy.
Bleeding diathesis.
Intussusception.
Midgut volvulus.
Meckel diverticulum.
Necrotizing enterocolitis.

<2 YR
Anal fissure.
Infectious colitis.
Milk allergy.
Colitis.
Intussusception.
Meckel diverticulum.
Polyp.
Duplication.
Hemolytic-uremic syndrome.
Inflammatory bowel disease.
Pseudomembranous enterocolitis.

<5 YR
Infectious colitis.
Anal fissure.
Polyp.
Intussusception.
Meckel diverticulum.
Henoch-Schönlein purpura.
Hemolytic-uremic syndrome.
Inflammatory bowel disease.
Pseudomembranous enterocolitis.

5 TO 18 YR
Infectious colitis.
Inflammatory bowel disease.
Pseudomembranous enterocolitis.
Polyp.
Hemolytic-uremic syndrome.
Hemorrhoids.

BLEEDING, RECTAL[67]

ICD-10CM # K92.2 Gastrointestinal Hemorrhage, Unspecified

IN PATIENTS <40 YR
Very Common
Hemorrhoids.
Anal fissure.
Inflammatory bowel disease (mainly proctitis).
Less Common
Polyps (hamartomatous or adenomatous).
Infective colitis.
Meckel's diverticulum.
Intussusception.
Rare
Colorectal cancer.

IN PATIENTS >40 YR
Hemorrhoids.
Anal fissure.
Colorectal cancer.
Colorectal polyps (mostly adenomas).
Angiodysplasia.
Diverticular disease.
Inflammatory bowel disease.
Ischemic colitis.
Infective colitis.

BLEEDING, THIRD TRIMESTER[1]

ICD-10CM # N93.9 Abnormal uterine and vaginal bleeding, unspecified

Placental abruption.
Placenta previa.
Bloody show (extrusion of cervical mucus).
Vasa previa.
Disseminated intravascular coagulopathy.
Uterine rupture.
Cervicitis, cervical cancer, or other cervical abnormality.
Vaginal laceration.

BLEEDING, UPPER GI

ICD-10CM # K92.2 Gastrointestinal Hemorrhage, Unspecified

(ORIGINATING ABOVE THE LIGAMENT OF TREITZ)
Swallowed Hemoptysis
Oral or pharyngeal lesions: swallowed blood from nose or oropharynx.
Esophageal: varices, ulceration, esophagitis, Mallory-Weiss tear, carcinoma, trauma.
Gastric: peptic ulcer (including Cushing and Curling's ulcers), gastritis, angiodysplasia, gastric neoplasms, hiatal hernia, gastric diverticulum, pseudoxanthoma elasticum, Rendu-Osler-Weber syndrome.
Duodenal: peptic ulcer, duodenitis, angiodysplasia, aortoduodenal fistula, duodenal diverticulum, duodenal tumors, carcinoma of ampulla of Vater, parasites (e.g., hookworm), Crohn's disease.
Biliary: hematobilia (e.g., penetrating injury to liver, hepatobiliary malignancy, endoscopic papillotomy).

BLEEDING, UPPER GI, PEDIATRIC[6]

ICD-10CM # K92.2 Gastrointestinal Hemorrhage, Unspecified

<3 MO
Swallowed maternal blood.
Gastritis.
Ulcer, stress.
Bleeding diathesis.
Foreign body (NG tube).
Vascular malformation.
Duplication.

<2 YR
Esophagitis.
Gastritis.
Ulcer.
Pyloric stenosis.
Mallory-Weiss syndrome.
Vascular malformation.
Duplication.

<5 YR
Esophagitis.
Gastritis.
Ulcer.
Esophageal varices.
Foreign body.
Mallory-Weiss syndrome.
Hemophilia.
Vascular malformations.

5 TO 18 YR
Esophagitis.
Gastritis.
Ulcer.
Esophageal varices.
Mallory-Weiss syndrome.
Inflammatory bowel disease.
Hemophilia.
Vascular malformation.

BLEEDING, VAGINAL, NON-PREGNANT FEMALE[1]

ICD-10CM # N93.9 Abnormal uterine and vaginal bleeding, unspecified

TRAUMA
Blunt force.
Penetrating force.
Foreign bodies.

INFECTIOUS

Vaginitis.
Cervicitis.
Endometritis.

DYSFUNCTIONAL UTERINE BLEEDING

Ovulatory.
Anovulatory.
Adenomyosis.

BENIGN GROWTHS

Uterine leiomyomas.
Cervical polyps.

MALIGNANCY

Vulvar.
Cervical.
Uterine.
Ovarian.

SYSTEMIC DISEASE

Medications

Anticoagulation (warfarin [Coumadin], low-molecular-weight heparin, clopidogrel [Plavix]).
Antipsychotics.
Corticosteroids.
Tamoxifen.
Selective serotonin reuptake inhibitors.
Contraceptives (oral, intrauterine devices, intramuscular).

BLINDNESS, GERIATRIC AGE

ICD-10CM # H54.8 Legal Blindness, as Defined in USA

Cataracts.
Glaucoma.
Diabetic retinopathy.
Macular degeneration.
Trauma.
CVA.
Corneal scarring.
Giant cell arteritis.
Ocular herpes zoster.

BLINDNESS, MONOCULAR, TRANSIENT

ICD-10CM # H54.41 Blindness, Right Eye, Normal Vision Left Eye
H54.42 Blindness, Left Eye, Normal Vision Right Eye

Migraine (vasospasm).
Embolic cerebrovascular disease.
Intermittent angle-closure glaucoma.
Partial retinal vein occlusion.
Hyphema.
Optic disc edema.
Giant cell arteritis.
Psychogenic.
Hypotension.
Hypercoagulopathy disorders.
Multiple sclerosis.

BLINDNESS, PEDIATRIC AGE[46]

ICD-10CM # H54.41 Blindness, Right Eye, Normal Vision Left Eye
H54.42 Blindness, Left Eye, Normal Vision Right Eye

CONGENITAL

Optic nerve hypoplasia or aplasia.
Optic coloboma.
Congenital hydrocephalus.
Hydranencephaly.
Porencephaly.
Microencephaly.
Encephalocele, particularly occipital type.
Morning glory disc.
Aniridia.
Anterior microphthalmia.
Peter's anomaly.
Persistent pupillary membrane.
Glaucoma.
Cataracts.
Persistent hyperplastic primary vitreous.

PHAKOMATOSES

- Tuberous sclerosis.
- Neurofibromatosis (special association with optic glioma).
- Sturge-Weber syndrome.
- von Hippel–Lindau disease.

TUMORS

Retinoblastoma.
Optic glioma.
Perioptic meningioma.
Craniopharyngioma.
Cerebral glioma.
Posterior and intraventricular tumors when complicated by hydrocephalus.
Pseudotumor cerebri.

NEURODEGENERATIVE DISEASES

- Cerebral storage disease.
- Gangliosidoses, particularly Tay-Sachs disease (infantile amaurotic familial idiocy), Sandhoff's variant, generalized gangliosidosis.
- Other lipidoses and ceroid lipofuscinoses, particularly the late-onset amaurotic familial idiocies such as those of Jansky-Bielschowsky and of Batten-Mayou-Spielmeyer-Vogt.
- Mucopolysaccharidoses, particularly Hurler's syndrome and Hunter's syndrome.
- Leukodystrophies (dysmyelination disorders), particularly metachromatic leukodystrophy and Canavan's disease.
- Demyelinating sclerosis (myelinoclastic diseases), especially Schilder's disease and Devic's neuromyelitis optica.
- Special types: Dawson's disease, Leigh's disease, Bassen-Kornzweig syndrome, Refsum's disease.
- Retinal degenerations: retinitis pigmentosa and its variants, Leber's congenital type.
- Optic atrophies: congenital autosomal recessive type, infantile and congenital autosomal dominant types, Leber's disease, and atrophies associated with hereditary ataxias—the types of Behr, of Marie, and of Sanger-Brown.

INFECTIOUS PROCESSES

Encephalitis, especially in the prenatal infection syndromes caused by *Toxoplasma gondii*, cytomegalovirus, rubella virus, *Treponema pallidum*, herpes simplex.
Meningitis, arachnoiditis.
Chorioretinitis.
Endophthalmitis.
Keratitis.

HEMATOLOGIC DISORDERS

Leukemia with central nervous system involvement.

VASCULAR AND CIRCULATORY DISORDERS

Collagen vascular diseases.
Arteriovenous malformations—intracerebral hemorrhage, subarachnoid hemorrhage.
Central retinal occlusion.

TRAUMA

- Contusion or avulsion of optic nerves, chiasm, globe, cornea.
- Cerebral contusion or laceration.
- Intracerebral, subarachnoid, or subdural hemorrhage.

DRUGS AND TOXINS OTHER

- Retinopathy of prematurity.
- Sclerocornea.
- Conversion reaction.
- Optic neuritis.
- Osteopetrosis.

BLISTERS, SUBEPIDERMAL

ICD-10CM # T07 Unspecified Multiple Injuries

Burns.
Porphyria cutanea tarda.
Bullous pemphigoid.
Bullous drug reaction.
Arthropod bite reaction.
Toxic epidermal necrosis.
Dermatitis herpetiformis.
Polymorphous light eruption.
Variegate porphyria.
SLE.
Epidermolysis bullosa.
Pseudoporphyria.
Acute graft-versus-host reaction.
Linear IgA disease.
Leukocytoclastic vasculitis.
Pressure necrosis.
Urticaria pigmentosa.
Amyloidosis.

BONE AND/OR SOFT TISSUE HYPERTROPHY[58]

ICD-10CM # M85.80 Other specified disorders of bone density and structure, unspecified site

DISORDERS ASSOCIATED WITH BONE AND/OR SOFT TISSUE HYPERTROPHY

Conditions Associated with Generalized Overgrowth

Pituitary gigantism and acromegaly.
Other endocrine disorders.
Cerebral gigantism (Sotos).

Conditions Associated with Limb Hemihypertrophy

Lipomatosis.
Idiopathic congenital hemihypertrophy (associated with tumors, e.g., Wilms tumor, adrenocortical tumors, hepatoblastoma).
Proteus syndrome (capillary port-wine hemangiomas, lymphangiomas, lipomas, epidermal nevi, hypertrophy hands and feet, macroccphaly).
Maffucci syndrome (enchondromas, exostosis, lymphangiomas, venous angiomas).
Klippel-Trenaunay syndrome (capillary port-wine hemangiomas, varicosities, lymphangiomas).
Parkes Weber syndrome (capillary port-wine hemangiomas, varicosities, arteriovenous fistula).
Blue rubber bleb nevus syndrome (cavernous hemangiomas of skin, gastrointestinal tract).
Other angiodysplasias (e.g., Servelle-Martorell syndrome; venous arterial malformations with limb hypertrophy and bony hypoplasia).
Beckwith-Wiedemann syndrome (macroglossia, visceromegaly, omphaloceles, hemihypertrophy, etc.).

Conditions Associated with Macrodactyly

Neurofibromatosis.
Macrodystrophia lipomatosa.
Proteus syndrome.
Bannayan-Zonana syndrome (lipomatosis, angiomatosis, macrocephaly).
Hemangiomatosis and other vascular malformations (Klippel-Trenaunay and Parkes Weber).
Lymphangiomatosis.
Arteriovenous malformation.
Maffucci syndrome, Ollier disease.
Epidermal nevus syndrome.

BONE DENSITY, DECREASED, GENERALIZED[32]

ICD-10CM #	M85.80	Other Specified Disorders of Bone Density and Structure, Unspecified Site

DISORDERS ASSOCIATED WITH GENERALIZED LOSS OF BONE DENSITY

Disorders of Multiple or Uncertain Cause

Senile osteoporosis.[10]
Juvenile osteoporosis.
Osteogenesis imperfecta.[11]

Secondary Bone Disorders

Endocrine
Adrenal cortex.
  Cushing's disease.

---

[10]Patients who cannot synthesize Lewis blood group antigens (~5% of the population) do not produce CA-19-9 antigen.
*Common cause of decrease in bone density in adults.
[11]Common cause of decrease in bone density in children.

Addison's disease.
Gonadal disorders.
  Postmenopausal osteoporosis.
  Hypogonadism.
Pituitary.
  Acromegaly.
  Hypopituitarism.
Pancreas.
  Diabetes mellitus.
Thyroid.
  Hyperthyroidism.
  Hypothyroidism.
Parathyroid.
  Hyperparathyroidism.

Marrow Replacement and Expansion

Myeloma.
Leukemia.
Lymphoma.
Metastatic disease.
Gaucher's disease.
Anemias (sickle cell, thalassaemia, hemophilia).

Drugs And Other Substances

Steroids.
Heparin (osteoporosis).
Anticonvulsants (ostcomalacia).
Immunosuppressants.
Alcohol.

Chronic Disease

Chronic renal disease.
Hepatic insufficiency.
GI malabsorption syndromes.
Chronic inflammatory polyarthropathies.
Chronic debility or immobilization.

BONE DENSITY, DECREASED, LOCALIZED[32]

ICD-10CM #	Z82.62	Family History of Osteoporosis
	M85.80	Other specified disorders of bone density and structure, unspecified site

DISORDERS ASSOCIATED WITH LOCALIZED LOSS OF BONE DENSITY

Disuse osteoporosis.[12]
Reflex sympathetic dystrophy (Sudeck's).
Osteolytic syndromes.
  Acro-osteolysis, primary and secondary.
  Massive osteolysis of Gorham.
  Carpotarsal osteolysis.
Transient regional osteoporosis.
Neuromuscular disorders.
Infection.
Arthropathies.
Tumors, primary and secondary, myelomatosis.

BONE LESIONS, PREFERENTIAL SITE OF ORIGIN[64]

ICD-10CM #	C41.0	Malignant Neoplasm of Bones of Skull and Face
	C41.1	Malignant Neoplasm of Mandible

---

[12]Common causes.

	C41.2	Malignant Neoplasm of Vertebral Column
	C41.3	Malignant Neoplasm of Ribs, Sternum and Clavicle
	C40.00	Malignant Neoplasm of Scapula and Long Bones of Unspecified Upper Limb
	C40.10	Malignant neoplasm of Short Bones of Unspecified Upper Limb
	C41.4	Malignant Neoplasm of Pelvic Bones, Sacrum and Coccyx
	C40.20	Malignant Neoplasm of Long Bones of Unspecified Lower Limb
	C40.30	Malignant Neoplasm of Short Bones of Unspecified Lower Limb
	C41.9	Malignant Neoplasm of Bone and Articular Cartilage, Unspecified
	C79.51	Secondary Malignant Neoplasm of Bone
	C79.52	Secondary Malignant Neoplasm of Bone Marrow

EPIPHYSIS

Chondroblastoma.
Giant cell tumor—after fusion of growth plate.
Langerhans' cell histiocytosis.
Clear cell chondrosarcoma.
Osteosarcoma.

METAPHYSIS

Parosteal sarcoma.
Chondrosarcoma.
Fibrosarcoma.
Nonossifying fibroma.
Giant cell tumor—before fusion of growth plate.
Unicameral bone cyst.
Aneurysmal bone cyst.

DIAPHYSIS

Myeloma.
Ewing's tumor.
Reticulum cell sarcoma.

METADIAPHYSEAL

Fibrosarcoma.
Fibrous dysplasia.
Enchondroma.
Osteoid osteoma.
Chondromyofibroma.

BONE MARROW FAILURE SYNDROMES, INHERITED[39]

ICD-10CM #	D61.89	Other Specified Aplastic Anemias and Other Bone Marrow Failure Syndromes

Differential Diagnosis

II

BI-LINEAGE AND TRI-LINEAGE CYTOPENIAS

Fanconi anemia.
Shwachman-Diamond syndrome.
Dyskeratosis congenita.
Amegakaryocytic thrombocytopenia:
  Other inherited thrombocytopenia disorders.
Other genetic syndromes:
  Down syndrome.
  Dubowitz syndrome.
  Seckel syndrome.
  Reticular dysgenesis.
  Schimke immunoosseous dysplasia.
  Noonan syndrome.
  Cartilage-hair hypoplasia.
  Familial marrow failure (non-Fanconi).

UNI-LINEAGE CYTOPENIA

Diamond-Blackfan anemia.
Kostmann syndrome/Congenital neutropenia:
  ELA2 mutations.
  HAX1 mutations.
  GFI1 mutations.
  WASP mutations.
  Constitutive cell surface G-CSF-R mutations.
Other inherited neutropenia syndromes:
  Barth syndrome.
  Glycogen storage disease 1b.
  Miscellaneous.
Thrombocytopenia with absent radii.
Congenital dyserythropoietic anemias (CDAs):
  Types I, II, III, IV.
  Variants.
  Nonclassifiable CDAs.
  Groups IV, V, VI, VII.

BONE MARROW FIBROSIS[28]

ICD-10CM # D75.9 Disease of Blood and
                   Blood-Forming Organs,
                   Unspecified

MYELOID DISORDERS

Myelofibrosis with myeloid metaplasia.
Metastatic cancer.
Chronic myeloid leukemia.
Myelodysplastic syndrome.
Atypical myeloid disorder.
Acute megakaryocytic leukemia.
Other acute myeloid leukemias.
Gray platelet syndrome.

LYMPHOID DISORDERS

Hairy cell leukemia.
Multiple myeloma.
Lymphoma.

NONHEMATOLOGIC DISORDERS

Connective tissue disorder.
Infections (tuberculosis, kala-azar).
Vitamin D deficiency (rickets).
Renal osteodystrophy.

BONE MASS, LOW[3]

ICD-10CM # M85.80 Other specified
                    disorders of bone
                    density and structure,
                    unspecified site

SECONDARY CAUSES OF LOW BONE MASS

Endocrine Diseases

Female hypogonadism.
Hyperprolactinemia.
Hypothalamic amenorrhea.
Anorexia nervosa.
Premature and primary ovarian failure.
Female athlete triad.
Male hypogonadism.
Primary gonadal failure (e.g., Klinefelter's syndrome).
Secondary gonadal failure (e.g., idiopathic hypogonadotropic hypogonadism, androgen deprivation therapy for prostate cancer).
Hyperthyroidism.
Hyperparathyroidism.
Hypercortisolism.
Vitamin D insufficiency or deficiency.

Gastrointestinal Diseases

* Subtotal gastrectomy.
* Gastric bypass surgery.
* Malabsorption syndromes.
* Chronic obstructive jaundice.
* Primary biliary cirrhosis and other cirrhoses.

Bone Marrow Disorders

Multiple myeloma.
Monoclonal gammopathy of unknown significance (MGUS).
Lymphoma.
Leukemia.
Hemolytic anemias.
Systemic mastocytosis.
Disseminated carcinoma.

Connective Tissue Diseases

Osteogenesis imperfecta.
Ehlers-Danlos syndrome.
Marfan's syndrome.
Homocystinuria.

Drugs

Alcohol.
Antiseizure medications.
Aromatase inhibitors.
Chemotherapy.
Cyclosporine.
Depo-medroxyprogesterone.
Excess thyroid hormone.
Glucocorticoids.
Gonadotropin-releasing hormone agonists.
Heparin.

Miscellaneous Causes

Immobilization.
Rheumatoid arthritis.
Chronic obstructive pulmonary disease.
Weight loss.

BONE MINERAL DENSITY, INCREASED

ICD-10CM # M89.30   Hypertrophy of Bone,
                     Unspecified Site
            M89.8X9 Other Specified
                     Disorders of Bone,
                     Unspecified Site
            M94.8X9 Other Specified
                     Disorders
                     of Cartilage,
                     Unspecified Sites

Paget's disease of bone.
Skeletal metastases.
DISH.
Osteonecrosis.
Sarcoidosis.
Hypoparathyroidism, pseudohypoparathyroidism.
Milk-alkali syndrome.
Osteopetrosis.
Hypervitaminosis A or D.
Dysplasias (craniodiaphyseal, craniometaphyseal, frontometaphyseal).
Endosteal hyperostosis.
Fluorosis.
Heavy metal poisoning.
Ionizing radiation.
Other: lymphoma, leukemia, mastocytosis, multiple myeloma, polycythemia vera.

BONE PAIN

ICD-10CM # M89.8 Pain, bone

Trauma.
Neoplasm (primary or metastatic).
Osteoporosis with compression fracture.
Paget's disease of bone.
Infection (osteomyelitis, septic arthritis).
Osteomalacia.
Viral syndrome.
Sickle cell disease.
Anxiety.

BONE RESORPTION[64]

ICD-10CM # M89.9 Disorder of Bone,
                   Unspecified
            M94.9 Disorder of Cartilage,
                   Unspecified

DISTAL CLAVICLE

Hyperparathyroidism.
RA.
Scleroderma.
Posttraumatic osteolysis.
Progeria.
Pycnodysostosis.
Cleidocranial dysplasia.

INFERIOR ASPECT OF RIBS

Vascular impression, associated with but not limited to coarctation of the aorta.
Hyperparathyroidism.
Neurofibromatosis.

TERMINAL PHALANGEAL TUFTS

Scleroderma.
Raynaud's phenomenon.
Vascular disease.
Frostbite, electrical burns.
Psoriasis.
Tabes dorsalis.
Hyperparathyroidism.

GENERALIZED RESORPTION

Paraplegia.
Myositis ossificans.
Osteoporosis.

BOWEL WALL THICKENING[70]

ICD-10CM # varies with specific diagnosis

BENIGN VERSUS MALIGNANT BOWEL WALL THICKENING

Benign
Homogeneous attenuation.
Symmetrical.
Circumferential.
Thickening <1 cm.
Segmental or diffuse involvement.
Double halo sign.
Dark inner ring.
Bright outer ring.
Target sign.
Bright inner ring.
Dark middle ring.
Bright outer ring.

Malignant
Heterogeneous attenuation.
Asymmetrical.
Eccentric.
Thickening >1 to 2 cm.
Focal mass.
Abrupt transition.
Lobulated contour.
Spiculated contour.
Narrowed bowel lumen.
Enlarged lymph nodes.
Liver metastases.

BOW LEGS (GENU VARUM), CLASSIFICATION[45]

ICD-10CM # E64.3 Genu varum, acquired
Q74.1 Congenital malformation of knee

PHYSIOLOGIC

Asymmetric Growth
Tibia vara (Blount disease).
  Infantile.
  Juvenile.
  Adolescent.
Focal fibrocartilaginous dysplasia.
Physeal injury.
Trauma.
Infection.
Tumor.

METABOLIC DISORDERS
Vitamin D deficiency (nutritional rickets).
Vitamin D–resistant rickets.
Hypophosphatasia.

SKELETAL DYSPLASIA
Metaphyseal dysplasia.
Achondroplasia.
Enchondromatosis.

BRADYCARDIA, SINUS[29]

ICD-10CM # I49.8 Other Specified Cardiac Arrhythmias
R00.1 Bradycardia, Unspecified

Idiopathic.
Degenerative processes (e.g., Lev's disease, Lenègre's disease).

Medications
β-Blockers.
Some calcium channel blockers (diltiazem, verapamil).
Digoxin (when vagal tone is high).
Class I antiarrhythmic agents (e.g., procainamide).
Class III antiarrhythmic agents (amiodarone, sotalol).
Clonidine.
Lithium carbonate.

ACUTE MYOCARDIAL ISCHEMIA AND INFARCTION
Right or left circumflex coronary artery occlusion or spasm.
High vagal tone (e.g., athletes).

BRAIN MASS[1]

ICD-10CM # C71 Malignant neoplasm of brain
D33 Benign neoplasm of brain
I61.9 Intracranial hemorrhage, unspecified

METASTATIC BRAIN TUMOR

Primary brain tumor
Meningioma.
Glioma.
Pituitary adenoma.
Vestibular schwannoma.
Primary or secondary central nervous system lymphoma.
Infections
Abscess.
Toxoplasmosis.
Neurocysticercosis.
Tuberculoma.
Progressive multifocal leukoencephalopathy.

VASCULAR DISEASE

Hemorrhage
Anomalies (arteriovenous malformation).
Intratumoral.
Hypertensive.
Infarct
Embolism.
Thrombosis (sinus venous).
Inflammatory
Multiple sclerosis.
Encephalomyelitis.

BREAST INFLAMMATORY LESION[21]

ICD-10CM # N61 Inflammatory Disorders of Breast
N60.19 Diffuse Cystic Mastopathy of Unspecified Breast
P39.0 Neonatal Infective Mastitis
P83.4 Breast Engorgement of Newborn

Mastitis (*S. aureus*, β-hemolytic *Streptococcus*).
Trauma.
Foreign body (sutures, breast implants).

Granuloma (TB, fungal).
Fat necrosis post biopsy.
Necrosis or infarction (anticoagulant therapy, pregnancy).
Breast malignancy.

BREAST MASS

ICD-10CM # N63 Unspecified Lump in Breast

Fibrocystic breasts.
Benign tumors (fibroadenoma, papilloma).
Mastitis (acute bacterial mastitis, chronic mastitis).
Malignant neoplasm.
Fat necrosis.
Hematoma.
Duct ectasia.
Mammary adenosis.

BREATH ODOR[62]

ICD-10CM # R19.6 Halitosis

Sweet, fruity: DKA, starvation ketosis.
Fishy, stale: uremia (trimethylamines).
Ammonia-like: uremia (ammonia).
Musty fish, clover: fetor hepaticus (hepatic failure).
Foul, feculent: intestinal obstruction/diverticulum.
Foul, putrid: nasal/sinus pathology (infection, foreign body, cancer), respiratory infections (empyema, lung abscess, bronchiectasis).
Halitosis: tonsillitis, gingivitis, respiratory infections, Vincent's angina, gastroesophageal reflux, achalasia, certain foods (garlic, onions, protein drinks, etc.)
Cinnamon: pulmonary TB.

BREATHING, NOISY[62]

ICD-10CM # R06.00 Dyspnea, Unspecified
R06.09 Other Forms of Dyspnea
R06.3 Periodic Breathing
R06.83 Snoring
R06.89 Other Abnormalities of Breathing
R06.1 Stridor

Infection: upper respiratory infection, peritonsillar abscess, retropharyngeal abscess, epiglottitis, laryngitis, tracheitis, bronchitis, bronchiolitis.
Irritants and allergens: hyperactive airway, asthma (reactive airway disease), rhinitis, angioneurotic edema.
Compression from outside of the airway: esophageal cysts or foreign body, neoplasms, lymphadenopathy.
Congenital malformation and abnormality: vascular rings, laryngeal webs, laryngomalacia, tracheomalacia, hemangiomas within the upper airway, stenoses within the upper airway, cystic fibrosis.
Acquired abnormality (at every level of the airway): nasal polyps, hypertrophied adenoids and/or tonsils, foreign body, intraluminal tumors, bronchiectasis.
Neurogenic disorder: vocal cord paralysis.

Differential Diagnosis

BRONCHIAL OBSTRUCTION[32]

ICD-10CM #   J98.0   Tracheobronchial collapse

CAUSES OF BRONCHIAL OBSTRUCTION

Outside the Bronchus
Lymph nodes and other masses.
In the Wall of the Bronchus
Tumors
Lung carcinoma (commonly squamous cell).
Bronchial carcinoid.
Metastasis.
Hamartoma.
Inflammation
Tuberculosis.
Sarcoidosis.
Granulomatosis with polyangiitis (Wegener's granulomatosis).
Inflammatory bowel disease.
Bronchomalacia
Broncholith.
Inside the Bronchus
Mucus plug.
Inhaled foreign body.

BRONCHOPLEURAL FISTULA[32]

ICD-10CM #   J86.0   Bronchopleural fistula

CAUSES OF BRONCHOPLEURAL FISTULA

Trauma
Penetrating.
Iatrogenic (especially post-pneumonectomy, post-lobectomy, post-biopsy).
Infection
Necrotizing pneumonia.
Empyema.
Tuberculosis.
Septic embolus.
Infected pulmonary infarct.

BROWN URINE

ICD-10CM #   R82   Other abnormal findings in urine

Bile pigments.
Myoglobin.
Concentrated urine.
Use of multivitamin supplements.
Medications (antimalarials, metronidazole, nitrofurantoin, levodopa, methyldopa, phenazopyridine).
Diet rich in fava beans.
Urinary tract infection.

BRUISING

ICD-10CM #   I99.8   Other Disorder of Circulatory System

Medication-induced (warfarin, aspirin, NSAIDs, prednisone).
Alcohol abuse.
Senile purpura.
Purpura simplex.
Physical abuse.

Vasculitis.
Platelet disorders.
Coagulation factor deficiencies.
Cushing's disease.
Vitamin C deficiency.
Marfan's syndrome.
Ehlers-Danlos syndrome.
Disseminated intravascular coagulation.
Leukemia.
Hereditary hemorrhagic telangiectasia.

BULLOUS DISEASES

ICD-10CM #		
	L13.9	Bullous Disorder, Unspecified
	L12.0	Bullous Pemphigoid
	L12.8	Other Pemphigoid
	L10.0	Pemphigus Vulgaris
	L10.1	Pemphigus Vegetans
	L10.2	Pemphigus Foliaceous
	L10.4	Pemphigus Erythematosus
	L10.9	Pemphigus, Unspecified
	L10.0	Pemphigus Vulgaris
	L10.1	Pemphigus Vegetans
	L10.2	Pemphigus Foliaceous
	L10.4	Pemphigus Erythematosus
	L10.9	Pemphigus, Unspecified

Bullous pemphigoid.
Pemphigus vulgaris.
Pemphigus foliaceus.
Paraneoplastic pemphigus.
Cicatricial pemphigoid.
Erythema multiforme.
Dermatitis herpetiformis.
Herpes gestationis.
Impetigo.
Erosive lichen planus.
Linear IgA bullous dermatosis.
Epidermolysis bullosa acquisita.

CAFÉ-AU-LAIT SPOTS[45]

ICD-10CM #   L81.3   Cafe au lait spots

Neurofibromatosis types 1 and 2.
McCune-Albright syndrome.
Russell-Silver syndrome.
Ataxia-telangiectasia.
Fanconi anemia.
Tuberous sclerosis.
Bloom syndrome.
Basal cell nevus syndrome.
Gaucher disease.
Chédiak-Higashi syndrome.
Hunter syndrome.
Maffucci syndrome.
Multiple mucosal neuroma syndrome.
Watson syndrome.
Proteus syndrome.
Turner syndrome.
Ring chromosome syndrome.
Jaffe-Campanacci syndrome.

CALCIFICATION ON CHEST X-RAY

ICD-10CM #		
	J98.4	Calcification of lung
	M51.84	Other Intervertebral Disc Disorders, Thoracic Region
	M51.85	Other Intervertebral Disc Disorders, Thoracolumbar Region

Lung neoplasm (primary or metastatic).
Silicosis.
Idiopathic pulmonary fibrosis.
Tuberculosis.
Histoplasmosis.
Disseminated varicella infection.
Mitral stenosis (end-stage).
Secondary hyperparathyroidism.

CALCIFICATIONS, ABDOMINAL, NONVISCERAL ON X-RAY[32]

ICD-10CM #   M61.9   Calcification and Ossification of Muscle, Unspecified

NONVISCERAL ABDOMINAL CALCIFICATION

Common
Atherosclerosis.
Mesenteric lymph nodes.
Phleboliths.
Aneurysm.
Dermoid cyst.
Differentiate
Rib cartilage.
Injections in the buttocks.
Uncommon
Infestations.
   Armillifer armillatus.
   Cysticercosis.
   Guinea worm.
   Hydatid.
Tumors.
   Lipoma.
   Hemangioma.
   Neuroblastoma.
   Osteo/chondrosarcoma of soft tissues.
   Retroperitoneal sarcoma of soft tissues.
   Peritoneal metastases.
   Pheochromocytoma.
Tuberculosis.
   Peritonitis.
   Psoas abscess.
Meconium peritonitis.
Pseudomyxoma Peritonei
Mesenteric cyst.
Pancreatitis with saponification.
Lithopedion.
Appendices Epiploicae
Ligaments.
Foreign bodies.
Posttraumatic buttock cysts.

CALCIFICATIONS, ADRENAL GLAND ON X-RAY[32]

ICD-10CM #   E27.4   Calcification, adrenal gland

ADRENAL GLAND CALCIFICATION

Common
Idiopathic.
Hemorrhage.
Tuberculosis.
Neuroblastoma/ganglioneuroma.
Pheochromocytoma.
Uncommon
Other tumors:
  Adenoma.
  Carcinoma.
  Dermoid.
Addison's disease.
Cyst.
Histoplasmosis.

CALCIFICATIONS, CARDIAC ON X-RAY[32]

ICD-10CM #   I51.5   Calcification, myocardium
                 I25.1   Calcification, arteriosclerotic

CAUSES OF VISIBLE CALCIFICATION WITHIN THE HEART

Coronary Artery
Atherosclerosis.
Aortic Root
Atherosclerotic aorta.
Thrombus.
Syphilis.
Ankylosing spondylitis.
Homograft calcification.
Pericardium
Chronic pericarditis, tuberculosis, hemopericardium, pyogenic or viral pericarditis.
Posttraumatic.
Postoperative.
Uremic pericarditis.
Asbestosis (may be pleural calcification applied to pericardium).
Myocardium
Ventricular aneurysm (may mimic pericardial calcification).
Calcified myocardial infarction.
Postmyocarditis.
Endocardium
Endomyocardial fibrosis.
Thrombus.
Valve Cusps
Calcified valves (particularly mitral and aortic valves).
Mitral annulus calcification.
Homograft calcification.
Old vegetation.
Valve Annulus
Submitral.
Mitral.
Aortic.

Left Atrium
Wall.
Thrombus.
Atrial myxoma.
Pulmonary Artery
Pulmonary hypertension.
Postoperative.
    Postoperative Serumoma Calcified Hydatid Cyst

CALCIFICATIONS, CUTANEOUS

ICD-10CM #   L94.2   Calcinosis Cutis
                 L98.8   Other Specified Disorders of the Skin and Subcutaneous Tissue

Calcification, Raynaud's phenomenon, esophageal dysmotility, sclerodactyly, and telangiectasia (CREST) syndrome.
Trauma.
Pancreatitis or pancreatic cancer.
Chronic renal failure.
Sarcoidosis.
Hyperparathyroidism.
Milk-alkali syndrome.
Hypervitaminosis D.
Panniculitis.
Idiopathic.
Iatrogenic (e.g., application of calcium alginate dressing to skin).
Multiple myeloma.
Dermatomyositis.
Parasitic infections.
Leukemia.
Lymphoma.

CALCIFICATIONS, GENITAL TRACT, FEMALE ON X-RAY[32]

ICD-10CM #   E83.59   Other Disorders of Calcium Metabolism

FEMALE GENITAL TRACT CALCIFICATION

Uterus
Leiomyomas.
Squamous cell carcinoma.
Adenocarcinoma of endometrium.
Leiomyosarcoma.
Lithopedion.
Fallopian Tubes
Ovary.
Dermoid cyst.
Serous cystadenoma/carcinoma.
Tuberculosis.
Cysts.
Autoamputation.

CALCIFICATIONS, LIVER ON X-RAY[32]

ICD-10CM #   K76.89   Other Specified Diseases of Liver
                 NEC   Granuloma, hepatic
                 K75.3

LIVER CALCIFICATION

Common
Granuloma (tuberculosis, histoplasmosis, brucellosis).
  Multiple scattered round densities.
Hydatid cyst.
  Fine curvilinear in wall, or dense and irregular if contracted.
Primary liver tumor (hemangioma, hepatoblastoma, hepatoma, cholangiocarcinoma).
  Irregular patterns or multiple nodules.
Metastases (mucinous primary of colon or breast, cystadenocarcinoma of ovary).
  Finely stippled, may be extensive.
Uncommon
Hepatic artery aneurysm.
Armillifer armillatus infestation.
Chronic granulomatous disease of childhood.
Cyst (congenital or acquired).
Hematoma.
Intrahepatic gallstones.
Old liver abscess.
Portal vein thrombosis.
Differentiate
Hemochromatosis.
Thorotrast, thallium, iron.

CALCIFICATIONS, PANCREAS ON X-RAY[32]

ICD-10CM #   K86.8   Calcification, pancreas

PANCREATIC CALCIFICATION

Common
Chronic pancreatitis.
Uncommon
Acute pancreatitis (saponification).
Tumors.
  Cystadenoma.
  Cystadenocarcinoma.
  Islet cell tumor.
  Metastases.
Hereditary pancreatitis (large clumps).
Hemorrhage.
Hyperparathyroidism.
Pseudocyst.
Cavernous lymphangioma.
Mucoviscidosis.
Kwashiorkor.

CALCIFICATIONS, SPLEEN ON X-RAY[32]

ICD-10CM #   D73.8   Calcification, spleen

SPLENIC CALCIFICATION

Larger than 10 mm
Splenic artery aneurysm.
Splenic artery atheroma.
Cyst.
  Posttraumatic.
  Dermoid.
  Epidermoid.
  Hydatid.
Hematoma.
Infarct.
Abscess.
Tuberculosis.

Differential Diagnosis

II

NECROTIZING INFECTIONS

Bacteria: anaerobes, *Staphylococcus aureus*, enteric gram-negative bacteria, *Pseudomonas aeruginosa*, *Legionella* species, *Haemophilus influenzae*, *Streptococcus pyogenes*, *Streptococcus pneumoniae*, *Rhodococcus*, *Actinomyces*.

Mycobacteria: *Mycobacterium tuberculosis*, *Mycobacterium kansasii*, MAI.

Bacteria-like: *Nocardia* species.

Fungi: *Coccidioides immitis*, *Histoplasma capsulatum*, *Blastomyces hominis*, *Aspergillus* species, *Mucor* species.

Parasitic: *Entamoeba histolytica*, *Echinococcus*, *Paragonimus westermani*.

CAVITARY INFARCTION

Bland infarction (with or without superimposed infection).

Lung contusion.

SEPTIC EMBOLISM

S. aureus, anaerobes, others.

VASCULITIS

Wegener's granulomatosis, periarteritis.

NEOPLASMS

Bronchogenic carcinoma, metastatic carcinoma, lymphoma.

MISCELLANEOUS LESIONS

- Cysts, blebs, bullae, or pneumatocele with or without fluid collections.
- Sequestration.
- Empyema with air-fluid level.
- Bronchiectasis.

CEREBRAL INFARCTION SECONDARY TO INHERITED DISORDERS

ICD-10CM # I63.50 Cerebral Infarction Due to Unspecified Occlusion or Stenosis of Unspecified Cerebral Artery

Homocystinuria.
Marfan's syndrome.
Ehlers-Danlos syndrome.
Rendu-Osler-Weber syndrome.
Pseudoxanthoma elasticum.
Fabry's disease.

CEREBRAL VASCULITIS, CAUSES[25]

ICD-10CM # varies with specific diagnosis

PRIMARY CEREBRAL VASCULITIDES

Takayasu arteritis.
Primary cerebral vasculitis.
Polyarteritis nodosa.

SECONDARY VASCULITIDES

Immune Disorders

Systemic lupus erythematosus.
Wegner granulomatosis.
Kawasaki syndrome.
Sarcoidosis.
Henoch-Schönlein purpura.

Primary Intracranial Infections

Bacterial meningitis (especially *Diplococcus pneumoniae*).
Tuberculous meningitis.
Mycotic infections.
Cat-scratch disease.
Human immunodeficiency virus/acquired immunodeficiency syndrome.
Malaria.
Lyme disease.
Rickettsial infections.
Brucellosis.

CEREBROVASCULAR DISEASE, ISCHEMIC[72]

ICD-10CM # I67.9 Cerebrovascular Disease, Unspecified

VASCULAR DISORDERS

Large-vessel atherothrombotic disease.
Lacunar disease.
Arterial-to-arterial embolization.
Carotid or vertebral artery dissection.
Fibromuscular dysplasia.
Migraine.
Venous thrombosis.
Radiation.
Complications of arteriography.
Multiple, progressive intracranial arterial occlusions.

INFLAMMATORY DISORDERS

Giant cell arteritis.
Polyarteritis nodosa.
SLE.
Granulomatous angiitis.
Takayasu's disease.
Arteritis associated with amphetamine, cocaine, or phenylpropanolamine.
Syphilis, mucormycosis.
Sjögren's syndrome.
Behçet's syndrome.

CARDIAC DISORDERS

Rheumatic heart disease.
Mural thrombus.
Arrhythmias.
Mitral valve prolapse.
Prosthetic heart valve.
Endocarditis.
Myxoma.
Paradoxical embolus.

HEMATOLOGIC DISORDERS

Thrombotic thrombocytopenic purpura.
Sickle cell disease.
Hypercoagulable states.
Polycythemia.
Thrombocytosis.
Leukocytosis.
Lupus anticoagulant.

CERVICAL INSTABILITY, PEDIATRIC

ICD-10CM # M50 Cervical disc disorders

CONGENITAL

Vertebral (Bony Anomalies)

Cranio-occipital defects (occipital vertebrae, basilar impression, occipital dysplasias, condylar hypoplasia, occipitalized atlas).
Atlantoaxial defects (aplasia of atlas arch, aplasia of odontoid process).
Subaxial anomalies (failure of segmentation and/or fusion, spina bifida, spondylolisthesis).

Ligamentous or Combined Anomalies

Found at birth as an element of somatogenic aberration.

Syndromic Disorders

Down syndrome.
Klippel-Feil syndrome.
22q11.2 deletion syndrome.
Larsen syndrome.
Marfan syndrome.
Ehlers-Danlos syndrome.

ACQUIRED

Trauma.
Infection (pyogenic, granulomatous).
Tumor (including neurofibromatosis).
Inflammatory conditions (e.g., juvenile rheumatoid arthritis).
Osteochondrodysplasias (e.g., achondroplasia, diastrophic dysplasia, metatropic dysplasia, spondyloepiphyseal dysplasia).
Storage disorders (e.g., mucopolysaccharidoses).
Metabolic disorders (rickets).
Miscellaneous (including osteogenesis imperfecta, sequela of surgery).

CHEST PAIN, CHILDREN[8]

ICD-10CM #	R07.9	Chest Pain, Unspecified
	R07.82	Intercostal Pain
	R07.89	Other Chest Pain
	R07.1	Chest Pain on Breathing
	R07.81	Pleurodynia

MUSCULOSKELETAL (COMMON)

Trauma (accidental, abuse).
Exercise, overuse injury (strain, bursitis).
Costochondritis (Tietze's syndrome).
Herpes zoster (cutaneous).
Pleurodynia.
Fibrositis.
Slipping rib.
Sickle cell anemia vasoocclusive crisis.
Osteomyelitis (rare).
Primary or metastatic tumor (rare).

PULMONARY (COMMON)

Pneumonia.
Pleurisy.
Asthma.
Chronic cough.
Pneumothorax.
Infarction (sickle cell anemia).

Foreign body.
Embolism (rare).
Pulmonary hypertension (rare).
Tumor (rare).

GASTROINTESTINAL (LESS COMMON)

Esophagitis (gastroesophageal reflux).
Esophageal foreign body.
Esophageal spasm.
Cholecystitis.
Subdiaphragmatic abscess.
Perihepatitis (Fitz-Hugh-Curtis syndrome).
Peptic ulcer disease.

CARDIAC (LESS COMMON)

Pericarditis.
Postpericardiotomy syndrome.
Endocarditis.
Mitral valve prolapse.
Aortic or subaortic stenosis.
Arrhythmias.
Marfan's syndrome (dissecting aortic aneurysm).
Anomalous coronary artery.
Kawasaki disease.
Cocaine, sympathomimetic ingestion.
Angina (familial hypercholesterolemia).

IDIOPATHIC (COMMON)

Anxiety, hyperventilation.
Panic disorder.

OTHER (LESS COMMON)

Spinal cord or nerve root compression.
Breast-related pathologic condition.
Castleman's disease (lymph node neoplasm).

CHEST PAIN, NONPLEURITIC[18]

ICD-10CM #	R07.9	Chest Pain, Unspecified
	R07.82	Intercostal Pain
	R07.89	Other Chest Pain

Cardiac: myocardial ischemia/infarction, myocarditis.
Esophageal: spasm, esophagitis, ulceration, neoplasm, achalasia, diverticula, foreign body.
Referred pain from subdiaphragmatic GI structures.
Gastric and duodenal: hiatal hernia, neoplasm, PUD.
Gallbladder and biliary: cholecystitis, cholelithiasis, impacted stone, neoplasm.
Pancreatic: pancreatitis, neoplasm.
Dissecting aortic aneurysm.
Pain originating from skin, breasts, and musculoskeletal structures: herpes zoster, mastitis, cervical spondylosis.
Mediastinal tumors: lymphoma, thymoma.
Pulmonary: neoplasm, pneumonia, pulmonary embolism/infarction.
Psychoneurosis.
Chest pain associated with mitral valve prolapse.

CHEST PAIN, PLEURITIC

| ICD-10CM # | R07.1 | Chest Pain on Breathing |
| | R07.81 | Pleurodynia |

Cardiac: pericarditis, postpericardiotomy/Dressler's syndrome.
Pulmonary: pneumothorax, hemothorax, embolism/infarction, pneumonia, empyema, neoplasm, bronchiectasis, pneumomediastinum, TB, carcinomatous effusion.
GI: liver abscess, pancreatitis, esophageal rupture, Whipple's disease with associated pericarditis or pleuritis.
Subdiaphragmatic abscess.
Pain originating from skin and musculoskeletal tissues: costochondritis, chest wall trauma, fractured rib, interstitial fibrositis, myositis, strain of pectoralis muscle, herpes zoster, soft tissue and bone tumors.
Collagen vascular diseases with pleuritis.
Psychoneurosis.
Familial Mediterranean fever.

CHEST WALL TUMORS, PRIMARY[14]

ICD-10CM # varies with specific diagnosis

SOFT TISSUE

Benign
Lipoma.
Hemangioma.
Lymphangioma.
Fibroma.
Rhabdomyoma.
Neurofibroma.
Desmoid tumor.
Malignant
Malignant fibrous histiocytoma.
Rhabdosarcoma.
Liposarcoma.
Neurofibrosarcoma.
Leiomyosarcoma.

BONY AND CARTILAGINOUS

Benign
Fibrous dysplasia.
Osteochondroma.
Chondroma.
Askin tumor.
Plasmacytoma.
Malignant
Chondrosarcoma.
Osteogenic sarcoma.
Ewing sarcoma.

CHIASMAL DISEASE[11]

ICD-10CM # varies with specific diagnosis

CAUSES OF CHIASMAL DISEASE

Tumors
Pituitary adenomas.
Craniopharyngioma.
Meningioma.
Glioma.
Chordoma.
Dysgerminoma.
Nasopharyngeal tumors.
Metastases.
Non-neoplastic masses
Aneurysm.
Rathke pouch cysts.
Fibrous dysplasia.

Sphenoidal sinus mucocele.
Arachnoid cysts.
Miscellaneous
Demyelination.
Inflammation (e.g., sarcoidosis).
Trauma.
Radiation-induced necrosis.
Toxicity (e.g., ethambutol).
Vasculitis.

CHILDHOOD EOSINOPHILIA

ICD-10CM # D72.1 Eosinophilia

PHYSIOLOGIC

Prematurity.
Infants receiving hyperalimentation.
Familial.

INFECTIOUS

Parasitic (with tissue-invasive helminths, e.g., trichinosis, strongyloidiasis, pneumocystosis, filariasis, cysticercosis, cutaneous and visceral larva migrans, echinococcosis).
Bacterial (brucellosis, tularemia, cat-scratch disease, *Chlamydia*).
Fungal (histoplasmosis, blastomycosis, coccidioidomycosis, allergic bronchopulmonary aspergillosis).
Mycobacterial (tuberculosis, leprosy).
Viral (hepatitis A, hepatitis B, hepatitis C, Epstein-Barr virus).

PULMONARY

Allergic (rhinitis, asthma).
Loeffler syndrome.
Hypersensitivity pneumonitis.
Eosinophilic pneumonia.
Pulmonary interstitial eosinophilia.

DERMATOLOGIC

Atopic dermatitis.
Pemphigus.
Dermatitis herpetiformis.
Infantile eosinophilic pustular folliculitis.
Episodic angioedema and urticaria.
Eosinophilic fasciitis (Schulman syndrome).
Eosinophilic cellulitis (Wells syndrome).
Kimura disease.

ONCOLOGIC

Neoplasm (lung, gastrointestinal, uterine).
Hodgkin disease.
Leukemia.
Myelofibrosis.

IMMUNOLOGIC

T-cell immunodeficiencies.
Hyperimmunoglobulin E (Job) syndrome.
Wiskott-Aldrich syndrome.
Graft-versus-host disease.
Drug hypersensitivity.
Post-irradiation.
Post-splenectomy.

ENDOCRINE

Post-adrenalectomy.
Addison disease.
Panhypopituitarism.

Uterine:
  Missed abortion.
  Parturition.
  Period pain.

COLOR CHANGES, CUTANEOUS[62]

ICD-10CM # L81.9 Disorder of Pigmentation, Unspecified

BROWN

Generalized: pituitary, adrenal, liver disease, ACTH-producing tumor (e.g., oat cell lung carcinoma).
Localized: nevi, neurofibromatosis.

WHITE

Generalized: albinism.
Localized: vitiligo, Raynaud's syndrome.

RED (ERYTHEMA)

- Generalized: fever, polycythemia, urticaria, viral exanthems.
- Localized: inflammation, infection, Raynaud's syndrome.

YELLOW

- Generalized: liver disease, chronic renal disease, anemia.
- Generalized (except sclera): hypothyroidism, increased intake of vegetables containing carotene.
- Localized: resolving hematoma, infection, peripheral vascular insufficiency.

BLUE

Lips, mouth, nail beds: cardiovascular and pulmonary diseases, Raynaud's.

COMA

ICD-10CM # R40.20 Unspecified Coma

Vascular: hemorrhage, thrombosis, embolism.
CNS infections: meningitis, encephalitis, cerebral abscess.
Cerebral neoplasms with herniation.
Head injury: subdural hematoma, cerebral concussion, cerebral contusion.
Drugs: narcotics, sedatives, hypnotics.
Ingestion or inhalation of toxins: CO, alcohol, lead.
Metabolic disturbances.
Hypoxia.
Acid-base disorders.
Hypoglycemia, hyperglycemia.
Hepatic failure.
Electrolyte disorders.
Uremia.
Hypothyroidism.
Hypothermia, hyperthermia.
Hypotension, malignant hypertension.
Postictal.

COMA, NORMAL COMPUTED TOMOGRAPHY[3]

ICD-10CM # R40.20 Unspecified coma

MENINGEAL DISORDERS

Subarachnoid hemorrhage (uncommon).
Bacterial meningitis.
Encephalitis.
Subdural empyema.

EXOGENOUS TOXINS

Sedative drugs and barbiturates.
Anesthetics and γ-hydroxybutyrate.[13]
Alcohols.
Stimulants:
  o Phencyclidines.[14]
  o Cocaine and amphetamines.[15]
- Psychotropic drugs:
  o Cyclic antidepressants.
  o Phenothiazines.
  o Lithium.
- Anticonvulsants.
- Opioids.
- Clonidine.[16]
- Penicillins.
- Salicylates.
- Anticholinergics.
- Carbon monoxide, cyanide, and methemoglobinemia.

ENDOGENOUS TOXINS/ DEFICIENCIES/DERANGEMENTS

Hypoxia and ischemia.
Hypoglycemia.
Hypercalcemia.
Osmolar:
  Hyperglycemia.
  Hyponatremia.
  Hypernatremia.
Organ system failure:
  Hepatic encephalopathy.
  Uremic encephalopathy.
  Pulmonary insufficiency (carbon dioxide narcosis).

SEIZURES

Prolonged postictal state.
Spike-wave stupor.

HYPOTHERMIA OR HYPERTHERMIA

- Brain stem ischemia.
- Basilar artery stroke.
- Brain stem or cerebellar hemorrhage.
- Conversion or malingering.

COMA, PEDIATRIC POPULATION[59]

ICD-10CM # R40.20 Unspecified coma

[13]General anesthetic, similar to g-aminobutyric acid; recreational drug and body building aid. Rapid onset, rapid recovery often with myoclonic jerking and confusion. Deep coma (2-3 hr; Glasgow Coma Scale = 3) with maintenance of vital signs.
[14]Coma associated with cholinergic signs: lacrimation, salivation, bronchorrhea, and hyperthermia.
[15]Coma after seizures or status (i.e., a prolonged postictal state).
[16]An antihypertensive agent active through the opiate receptor system; frequent overdose when used to treat narcotic withdrawal.

ANOXIA

Birth asphyxia.
Carbon monoxide poisoning.
Croup/epiglottitis.
Meconium aspiration.

INFECTION

- Hemolysis.
- Blood loss.
- Hydrops fetalis.
- Infection.
- Meningoencephalitis.
- Sepsis.
- Postimmunization encephalitis.

INCREASED INTRACRANIAL PRESSURE

Anoxia.
Inborn metabolic errors.
Toxic encephalopathy.
Reye's syndrome.
Head trauma/intracranial bleed.
Hydrocephalus.
Posterior fossa tumors.

HYPERTENSIVE ENCEPHALOPATHY

Coarctation of aorta.
Nephritis.
Vasculitis.
Pheochromocytoma.

ISCHEMIA

Hypoplastic left heart.
Shunting lesions.
Aortic stenosis.
Cardiovascular collapse (any cause).

PURPURIC CAUSES

Disseminated intravascular coagulation.
Hemolytic-uremic syndrome.
Leukemia.
Thrombotic purpura.

HYPERCAPNIA

Cystic fibrosis.
Bronchopulmonary dysplasia.
Congenital lung anomalies.

NEOPLASM

Medulloblastoma.
Glioma of brain stem.
Posterior fossa tumors.

DRUGS/TOXINS

Maternal sedation.
Alcohol.
Any drug.
Lead.
Salicylism.
Arsenic.
Pesticides.

ELECTROLYTE ABNORMALITIES

Hypernatremia (diarrhea, dehydration, salt poisoning).
Hyponatremia (SIADH, androgenital syndrome, gastroenteritis).

Hyperkalemia (renal failure, salicylism, andro-genitalism).
Hypokalemia (diarrhea, hyperaldosteronism, salicylism, DKA).
Hypocalcemia (vitamin D deficiency, hyperparathyroidism).
Severe acidosis (sepsis, cold injury, salicylism, DKA).

HYPOGLYCEMIA

Birth injury or stress.
Diabetes.
Alcohol.
Salicylism.
Hyperinsulinemia.
Iatrogenic.

POSTSEIZURE

Renal Causes
Nephritis.
Hypoplastic kidneys.

Hepatic Causes
Acute hepatitis.
Fulminant hepatic failure.
Inborn metabolic errors.
Bile duct atresia.

CONGESTIVE HEART FAILURE AND CARDIOMYOPATHY[3]

ICD-10CM # I50.9 Heart failure, unspecified
                I42.7 Cardiomyopathy due to drug and external agent

CAUSES OF CONGESTIVE HEART FAILURE AND CARDIOMYOPATHY

Coronary Artery Disease
Acute ischemia.
Myocardial infarction.
Ischemic cardiomyopathy with hibernating myocardium.

Idiopathic
Idiopathic dilated cardiomyopathy.
Idiopathic restrictive cardiomyopathy.
Peripartum.

Pressure Overload
Hypertension.
Aortic stenosis.

Volume Overload
Mitral regurgitation.
Aortic insufficiency.
Anemia.
Atrioventricular fistula.

Toxins
Ethanol.
Cocaine.
Doxorubicin (Adriamycin).
Methamphetamine.

Metabolic-Endocrine
Thiamine deficiency.
Diabetes.
Hemochromatosis.
Thyrotoxicosis.
Obesity.

Infiltrative
Amyloidosis.

Inflammatory
Viral myocarditis.

Hereditary
Hypertrophic.
Dilated.

*Genetic bases for these cardiomyopathies have been identified in a large number of individual patients and families. Most of the mutations have been found in cardiac contractile or structural proteins.

CONGESTIVE HEART FAILURE, INFANT[1]

ICD-10CM # I05.9 Heart failure, unspecified

Critical coarctation of the aorta.
Interrupted aortic arch.
Congenital aortic stenosis.
Hypoplastic left heart syndrome.
Large ventricular septal defect.
Truncus arteriosus.
Unrecognized supraventricular tachycardia.
Cardiac tamponade.
Myocarditis.

CONJUNCTIVAL NEOPLASM

ICD-10CM # varies with specific diagnosis

MALIGNANT
Squamous cell carcinoma.
Melanoma.
Sebaceous carcinoma.
Kaposi's sarcoma.
Metastatic neoplasms.

BENIGN
Melanocytic nevus.
Squamous papilloma.
Hemangioma.
Lymphangioma.
Myxoma.

CONSCIOUSNESS IMPAIRMENT, ACUTE, IN CRITICALLY ILL PATIENT

ICD-10CM # F05.9 Delirium, unspecified

GENERAL CAUSES OF ACUTELY IMPAIRED CONSCIOUSNESS IN THE CRITICALLY ILL

Infection
Sepsis encephalopathy.
Central nervous system infection.

Drugs
Narcotics.
Benzodiazepines.
Anticholinergics.
Anticonvulsants.
Tricyclic antidepressants.
Selective serotonin uptake inhibitors.
Phenothiazines.
Steroids.
Immunosuppressants (cyclosporine, FK-506, OKT3).
Anesthetics.

Electrolyte and Acid-Base Disturbances
Hyponatremia.
Hypernatremia.
Hypercalcemia.

Hypermagnesemia.
Severe acidemia and alkalemia.

Organ System Failure
Shock.
Renal failure.
Hepatic failure.
Pancreatitis.
Respiratory failure (hypoxia, hypercapnia).

Endocrine Disorders
Hypoglycemia.
Hyperglycemia.
Hypothyroidism.
Hyperthyroidism.
Pituitary apoplexy.

Drug Withdrawal
Alcohol.
Opiates.
Barbiturates.
Benzodiazepines.

Vascular Causes
Shock.
Hypotension.
Hypertensive encephalopathy.
Central nervous system vasculitis.
Cerebral venous sinus thrombosis.

Central Nervous System Disorders
Hemorrhage.
Stroke.
Brain edema.
Hydrocephalus.
Increased intracranial pressure.
Meningitis.
Ventriculitis.
Brain abscess.
Subdural empyema.
Seizures.
Vasculitis.

Seizures
Convulsive and nonconvulsive status epilepticus.

Miscellaneous
Fat embolism syndrome.
Neuroleptic malignant syndrome.
Thiamine deficiency (Wernicke encephalopathy).
Psychogenic unresponsiveness.

CONSTIPATION

ICD-10CM # K59.00 Constipation, unspecified

Intestinal obstruction.
Fecal impaction.
Diverticular disease.
GI neoplasm.
Strangulated femoral hernia.
Gallstone ileus.
Tuberculous stricture.
Adhesions.
Ameboma.
Volvulus.
Intussusception.
Inflammatory bowel disease.
Hematoma of bowel wall, secondary to trauma or anticoagulants.
Poor dietary habits: insufficient bulk in diet, inadequate fluid intake.
Change from daily routine: travel, hospital admission, physical inactivity.

Acute abdominal conditions: renal colic, salpingitis, biliary colic, appendicitis, ischemia.

Hypercalcemia or hypokalemia, uremia.

Irritable bowel syndrome, pregnancy, anorexia nervosa, depression.

Painful anal conditions: hemorrhoids, fissure, stricture.

Decreased intestinal peristalsis: old age, spinal cord injuries, myxedema, diabetes, multiple sclerosis, Parkinsonism and other neurologic diseases.

Drugs: codeine, morphine, antacids with aluminum, verapamil, anticonvulsants, anticholinergics, disopyramide, cholestyramine, alosetron, iron supplements.

Hirschsprung's disease, meconium ileus, congenital atresia in infants.

CONSTIPATION, ADULT PATIENT[67]

ICD-10CM # K59.00 Constipation, unspecified

NO GROSS STRUCTURAL ABNORMALITY

Inadequate fiber intake.

Irritable bowel syndrome (associated with abdominal pain) or functional constipation.

Idiopathic slow-transit constipation.

"Obstructed defecation" pelvic floor dysfunction (or dyssynergia).

STRUCTURAL DISORDERS

Anal fissure, infection, or stenosis.

Colon cancer or stricture.

Aganglionosis and/or abnormal myenteric plexus:
  Hirschsprung's disease.
  Chagas' disease.
  Neuropathic pseudoobstruction.

Abnormal colonic muscle:
  Myopathy.
  Dystrophia myotonica.
  Systemic sclerosis.

Idiopathic megarectum and/or megacolon.

Proximal megacolon.

NEUROLOGIC CAUSES

Diabetic autonomic neuropathy.

Damage to the sacral parasympathetic outflow.

Spinal cord damage or disease (e.g., multiple sclerosis).

Parkinson's disease.

Blunting of consciousness, mental retardation, psychosis.

Pain induced by straining (e.g., sciatic nerve compression).

ENDOCRINE OR METABOLIC CAUSES

Hypothyroidism.

Hypercalcemia.

Porphyria.

Pregnancy.

PSYCHOLOGIC DISORDERS

Depression.

Anorexia nervosa.

Denied bowel habit.

DRUG SIDE EFFECTS

COPD DECOMPENSATION[50]

ICD-10CM # J44.1s

CAUSES OF ACUTE DECOMPENSATION IN THE PATIENT WITH CHRONIC OBSTRUCTIVE PULMONARY DISEASE

Acute Exacerbations
Infectious

Viral.

Rhinovirus, respiratory syncytial virus, coronavirus, influenza virus.

Bacterial.

Haemophilus influenzae, Streptococcus pneumoniae, Moraxella (Branhamella) catarrhalis, Pseudomonas aeruginosa.

Atypical bacteria.

Chlamydia pneumoniae, Legionella.

Air Pollution

Nitrogen dioxide.

Ozone.

Particulates, dust.

Other Critical Events

Pneumothorax.

Pulmonary embolism.

Lobar atelectasis.

Congestive heart failure.

Pneumonia.

Pulmonary compression (e.g., obesity, ascites, gastric distention, pleural effusion).

Trauma (e.g., rib fractures, pulmonary contusion).

Neuromuscular and metabolic disorders.

Unrelated treatable chronic pulmonary disease (bronchiectasis, tuberculosis, sarcoidosis).

Noncompliance with prescribed treatment regimens.

Iatrogenic.
  Inadequate therapy.
  Inappropriate therapy (e.g., deleterious drugs).

CORNEAL SENSATION, DECREASED

ICD-10CM # H18.899 Other specified disorders of cornea, unspecified eye

Herpes (simplex, zoster).

Contact lens wear.

Topical agents (NSAIDs, anesthetics, beta-blockers).

Diabetes.

Eye trauma.

Postsurgery.

COUGH

ICD-10CM # R05 Cough

Infectious process (viral, bacterial).

Postinfectious.

"Smoker's cough."

Rhinitis (allergic, vasomotor, postinfectious).

Asthma.

Exposure to irritants (noxious fumes, smoke, cold air).

Drug-induced (especially ACE inhibitors, beta-blockers).

GERD.

Interstitial lung disease.

Lung neoplasms.

Lymphomas, mediastinal neoplasms.

Bronchiectasis.

Cardiac (CHF, pulmonary edema, mitral stenosis, pericardial inflammation).

Recurrent aspiration.

Inflammation of larynx, pleura, diaphragm, mediastinum.

Cystic fibrosis.

Anxiety.

Other: pulmonary embolism, foreign body inhalation, aortic aneurysm, Zenker's diverticulum, osteophytes, substernal thyroid, thyroiditis, PMR.

COUGH, CHRONIC, ADULT PATIENT[2]

ICD-10CM # R05

CAUSES OF CHRONIC COUGH IN ADULTS

Intrathoracic Causes
Lungs and Airways

Asthma.

Nonasthmatic eosinophilic bronchitis.

Chronic bronchitis.

Bronchiectasis.

ACEIs.

Inhaled medications.

Chronic exposure to environmental and occupational irritants.

Bronchogenic and metastatic carcinoma.

Bronchial carcinoid.

Foreign body or endobronchial suture.

Broncholith.

Infectious and noninfectious bronchiolitis.

Chronic infectious pneumonias (e.g., bacterial, tuberculous, fungal, parasitic).

Chronic infectious tracheobronchitis (as in tuberculosis or aspergillosis).

Chronic interstitial lung disease (e.g., sarcoidosis, HSP, IPF, asbestosis).

Pulmonary vasculitis (as in granulomatosis with polyangiitis).

Sjögren syndrome with xerotrachea.

Relapsing polychondritis.

Pleura

Chronic effusion.

Diaphragm

Transvenous pacemaker stimulation.

Mediastinum

Neural tumors.

Thymoma.

Teratoma.

Lymphoma.

Metastatic lymphadenopathy.

Intrathoracic goiter.

Bronchogenic cyst.

Cardiovascular

Mitral stenosis.

Left ventricular failure.

Pulmonary thromboembolism.

Enlarged left atrium.

Vascular ring.

Aberrant innominate artery.

Aortic aneurysm.

Pericardial stimulation by transvenous pacemaker.

Extrathoracic Causes
Head and Neck
Rhinitis and sinusitis.
Nasal polyps.
Rhinolith.
Oropharyngeal dysphagia.
Laryngeal disorders (e.g., vocal fold dysfunction, laryngomalacia).
Postviral vagal neuropathy.
Recurrent aspiration.
Elongated uvula.
Chronically infected tonsils.
Neurilemmoma of vagus nerve.
Neuroma of internal laryngeal nerve.
Ascending palatine artery aneurysm.
Osteophytes of cervical spine.
Mammomanogamus (Syngamus) laryngeus infection.
Thyroiditis.
Upper Gastrointestinal
Gastroesophageal reflux disease.
Esophageal cyst or diverticulum.
Tracheoesophageal fistula.
Central Nervous System
Psychogenic or habit cough.
Tic disorders.
Gilles de la Tourette syndrome.

ACEI, Angiotensin-converting enzyme inhibitor; *HSP*, hypersensitivity pneumonitis; *IPF*, idiopathic pulmonary fibrosis.

CUTANEOUS INFECTIONS, ATHLETES

ICD-10CM # L08.9 Local infection of the skin and subcutaneous tissue, unspecified

Tinea pedis.
Tinea cruris.
Molluscum contagiosum.
Herpes simplex.
Verruca vulgaris.
Folliculitis.
Impetigo.
Furuncles.
Otitis externa.
Erythrasma.

CYANOSIS[6]

ICD-10CM # R23.0 Cyanosis

DIFFERENTIAL DIAGNOSIS OF CYANOSIS
Peripheral Cyanosis
Low cardiac output states
Shock.
Left ventricular failure.
Hypovolemia.
Environmental exposure (cold)
Air or water.
Arterial occlusion
Thrombosis.
Embolism.
Vasospasm (Raynaud's phenomenon).
Peripheral vascular disease.

Venous obstruction
Redistribution of blood flow from extremities
Central Cyanosis
Decreased arterial oxygen saturation
High altitude (>8000 ft).
Impaired pulmonary function.
　Hypoventilation.
　Impaired oxygen diffusion.
　Ventilation-perfusion mismatching.
　　Pulmonary embolism.
　　Acture respiratory distress syndrome.
　　Pulmonary hypertension.
　Respiratory compromise.
　　Upper airway obstruction.
　　Pneumonia.
　　Diaphragmatic hernia.
　　Tension pneumothorax.
　　Polycythemia.
Anatomic Shunts
Pulmonary arteriovenous fistulae and intrapulmonary shunts.
Cerebral, hepatic, peripheral arteriovenous fistulae.
Cyanotic congenital heart disease.
　Endocardial cushion defects.
　Ventricular septal defects.
　Coarctation of aorta.
　Tetralogy of Fallot.
　Total anomalous pulmonary venous drainage.
　Hypoplastic left ventricle.
　Pulmonary vein stenosis.
　Tricuspid atresia and anomalies.
　Premature closure of foramen ovale.
　Dextrocardia.
　Pulmonary stenosis of atrial septal defect.
　Patent ductus arteriosus with reversed shunt.
Abnormal Hemoglobin
Methemoglobinemia.
　Hereditary.
　Acquired.
Sulfhemoglobinemia.
Mutant hemoglobin with low oxygen affinity (e.g., hemoglobin Kansas).

CYANOSIS, NEONATAL[1]

ICD-10CM # R23.0 Cyanosis

RESPIRATORY
Upper Airway
Choanal atresia.
Macroglossia.
Glossoptosis (secondary to micrognathia).
Laryngomalacia.
Laryngeal web or cyst.
Vascular anomalies (e.g., cystic hygromas, rings).
Subglottic stenosis (commonly secondary to intubation).
Foreign body.
Lower Airway
Pneumonia.
Bronchiolitis.
Pulmonary edema.
Atelectasis.
Bronchopulmonary dysplasia.

SYSTEMIC
Sepsis.
Trauma.
Poisons.

CARDIAC
Cyanotic congenital heart diseases.
Transposition of the great vessels (most common neonatal).
Tetralogy of Fallot.
Truncus arteriosus.
Tricuspid atresia.
Total anomalous pulmonary venous return.
Ebstein anomaly.
Gastrointestinal.
Gastroesophageal reflux.

NEUROLOGIC
Seizures.
Central hypoventilation syndrome (Ondine curse).
Spinal muscular atrophy type I (Werdnig-Hoffmann).
Botulism.
Congenital myopathies.

HEMATOLOGIC
Methemoglobinemia.

DAYTIME SLEEPINESS

ICD-10CM # R53.82 Chronic fatigue, unspecified

Sleep deprivation.
Medication Induced (e.g., benzodiazepines, beta-blockers, narcotics, sedative antidepressants, gabapentin).
Depression.
Obstructive sleep apnea.
Medical illness (e.g., severe anemia, hypothyroidism, COPD, hepatic failure, renal insufficiency, CHF, electrolyte disturbances).
Circadian rhythm abnormalities (e.g., jet lag, shift work sleep disorder).
Restless legs syndrome.
Posttrauma.
Narcolepsy.
Neurologic disorders (e.g., neurodegenerative disorders; parkinsonism; multiple sclerosis; lesions affecting thalamus, hypothalamus, or brain stem).

DELAYED PASSAGE OF MECONIUM[32]

ICD-10CM # P76.0 Meconium plug syndrome

Ileal atresia.
Meconium ileus.
Functional immaturity of the colon.
Colon atresia.
Anorectal malformations.
Hirschsprung's disease.
Megacystis-microcolon-intestinal hypoperistalsis syndrome.
Extrinsic compression of the distal bowel by a mass lesion.
　Mesenteric cyst.
　Enteric duplication cyst.
Paralytic ileus, sepsis, drugs, and metabolic upset.

Differential Diagnosis

DELIRIUM[49]

ICD-10CM #	R40.0	Somnolence
	R40.1	Stupor
	F05	Delirium due to known physiological condition

PHARMACOLOGIC AGENTS

Anxiolytics (benzodiazepines).
Antidepressants (e.g., amitriptyline, doxepin, imipramine).
Cardiovascular agents (e.g., methyldopa, digitalis, reserpine, propranolol, procainamide, captopril, disopyramide).
Antihistamine.
Cimetidine.
Corticosteroids.
Antineoplastics.
Drugs of abuse (alcohol, cannabis, amphetamines, cocaine, hallucinogens, opioids, sedative-hypnotics, phencyclidine).

METABOLIC DISORDERS

Hypercalcemia.
Hypercarbia.
Hypoglycemia.
Hyponatremia.
Hypoxia.

INFLAMMATORY DISORDERS

Sarcoidosis.
SLE.
Giant cell arteritis.

ORGAN FAILURE

Hepatic encephalopathy.
Uremia.

NEUROLOGIC DISORDERS

Alzheimer's disease.
CVA.
Encephalitis (including HIV).
Encephalopathies.
Epilepsy.
Huntington's disease.
Multiple sclerosis.
Neoplasms.
Normal-pressure hydrocephalus.
Parkinson's disease.
Pick's disease.
Wilson's disease.

ENDOCRINE DISORDERS

Addison's disease.
Cushing's disease.
Panhypopituitarism.
Parathyroid disease.
Postpartum psychosis.
Recurrent menstrual psychosis.
Sydenham's chorea.
Thyroid disease.

DEFICIENCY STATES

Niacin.
Thiamine, vitamin B_{12}, and folate.

DELIRIUM AND AGITATION, DRUG-INDUCED

| ICD-10CM # | F05.9 | Delirium, unspecified |

COMMONLY USED DRUGS ASSOCIATED WITH DELIRIUM AND AGITATION

Benzodiazepines.
Opiates (especially meperidine).
Anticholinergics.
Antihistamines.
H_2 blockers.
Antibiotics.
Corticosteroids.
Metoclopramide.

DELIRIUM, AGITATED[6]

| ICD-10CM # | F05 | Delirium due to known physiological condition |

Metabolic causes:
  Electrolyte abnormalities.
  Hypoglycemia.
  Hypoxia.
  Uremia/hyperammonemia.
Structural lesions of the CNS:
  Trauma.
  Stroke.
  Hemorrhage.
  Mass.
Endocrine disease:
  Thyrotoxicosis.
Infections:
  Bacterial/viral meningitis/encephalitis.
Toxicologic causes:
  Sympathomimetic/stimulants.
  Cocaine.
  Amphetamines and derivatives.
  Caffeine.
  Phencyclidine/ketamine.
  Anticholinergics.
  Serotonin syndrome.
  Sedative-hypnotic withdrawal.
Heatstroke.
Postictal state.

CNS, Central nervous system.

DELIRIUM, DIALYSIS PATIENT[49]

| ICD-10CM # | F05 | Delirium due to known physiological condition |
| | F06.8 | Other specified mental disorders due to known physiological condition |

STRUCTURAL

Cerebrovascular accident (particularly hemorrhage).
Subdural hematoma.
Intracerebral abscess.
Brain tumor.

METABOLIC

Disequilibrium syndrome.
Uremia.

Drug effects.
Meningitis.
Hypertensive encephalopathy.
Hypotension.
Postictal state.
Hypernatremia or hyponatremia.
Hypercalcemia.
Hypermagnesemia.
Hypoglycemia.
Severe hyperglycemia.
Hypoxemia.
Dialysis dementia.

DEMYELINATING DISEASES[72]

| ICD-10CM # | G37.9 | Demyelinating disease of central nervous system, unspecified |

MULTIPLE SCLEROSIS

Relapsing and chronic progressive forms.
Acute multiple sclerosis.
Neuromyelitis optica (Devic's disease).

DIFFUSE CEREBRAL SCLEROSIS

Schilder's encephalitis periaxialis diffusa.
Baló's concentric sclerosis.

ACUTE DISSEMINATED ENCEPHALOMYELITIS

After measles, chickenpox, rubella, influenza, mumps.
After rabies or smallpox vaccination.

NECROTIZING HEMORRHAGIC ENCEPHALITIS

Hemorrhagic leukoencephalitis.

LEUKODYSTROPHIES

Krabbe's globoid leukodystrophy.
Metachromatic leukodystrophy.
Adrenoleukodystrophy.
Adrenomyeloneuropathy.
Pelizaeus-Merzbacher leukodystrophy.
Canavan's disease.
Alexander's disease.

DIAPHRAGM ELEVATION, BILATERAL, SYMMETRICAL[32]

| ICD-10CM # | J98.6 | Disorders of diaphragm |

CAUSES OF BILATERAL SYMMETRICAL ELEVATION OF THE DIAPHRAGM

Supine position.
Poor inspiration.
Obesity.
Pregnancy.
Abdominal distention (ascites, intestinal obstruction, abdominal mass).
Diffuse pulmonary fibrosis.
Lymphangitis carcinomatosa.
Disseminated lupus erythematosus.
Bilateral basal pulmonary emboli.
Painful conditions (after abdominal surgery).
Bilateral diaphragmatic paralysis.

DIAPHRAGM ELEVATION, UNILATERAL[32]

ICD-10CM # J98.6 Disorders of diaphragm

CAUSES OF UNILATERAL ELEVATION OF THE DIAPHRAGM

Posture—lateral decubitus position (dependent side).
Gaseous distention of stomach or colon.
Dorsal scoliosis.
Pulmonary hypoplasia.
Pulmonary collapse.
Phrenic nerve palsy.
Eventration.
Pneumonia or pleurisy.
Pulmonary thromboembolism.
Rib fracture and other painful conditions.
Subphrenic infection.
Subphrenic mass.

DIARRHEA, ACUTE WATERY AND BLOODY[67]

ICD-10CM #	K52.2	Allergic and dietetic gastroenteritis and colitis
	K52.89	Other specified noninfective gastroenteritis and colitis
	R19.7	Diarrhea, unspecified

ACUTE WATERY DIARRHEA

Gastrointestinal infections:
    Protozoal (e.g., *Giardia*).
    Bacterial (e.g., enterotoxigenic *Escherichia coli*, cholera).
    Viral (e.g., rotavirus, Norwalk virus).
Drugs.
Toxins.
Dietary constituents (e.g., lactose intolerance).
Onset of chronic diarrheal illness.

ACUTE BLOODY DIARRHEA

Infectious colitis:
    Confluent proctocolitis (e.g., *Shigella, Campylobacter, Salmonella, Entamoeba histolytica*).
    Segmental colitis (e.g., *Campylobacter, Salmonella,* enteroinvasive *E. coli, Aeromonas, E. histolytica*).
    Drug-induced colitis (e.g., nonsteroidal anti-inflammatory drugs [NSAIDs]).
    Inflammatory bowel disease.
    Ischemic colitis (usually elderly patient with underlying heart disease or arrhythmias).
    Antibiotic-associated colitis.

DIARRHEA, INFECTIOUS[6]

ICD-10CM # A09 Infectious gastroenteritis and colitis, unspecified

ETIOLOGIC AGENTS OF INFECTIOUS DIARRHEA

Viral (60% of Cases)
Astrovirus.
Calicivirus.
Coronavirus.
Cytomegalovirus.[17]
Enteric adenovirus.
Hepatitis A through G.
Herpes simplex virus.
HIV enteropathy.
Norwalk-like agents.
Pararotavirus.
Norwalk virus.
Picornavirus.
Rotavirus.
Small round viruses.
Bacterial (20% of Cases)

Invasive

Aeromonas spp.
Campylobacter spp.
Clostridium difficile.
Enteroinvasive *E. coli.*
Mycobacterium spp.
Plesiomonas shigelloides.
Salmonella spp.
Shigella spp.
Vibrio fluvialis.
Vibrio parahaemolyticus.
Vibrio vulnificus.
Yersinia enterocolitica.
Yersinia pseudotuberculosis.

Toxigenic

Food poisoning with preformed toxins.
    Bacillus cereus.
    Clostridium botulinum.
    Staphylococcus aureus.
Toxin formation after colonization.
    Aeromonas hydrophila.
    Clostridium perfringens.
    Enterohemorrhagic *E. coli* O157:H7.
    Enterotoxigenic *E. coli.*
    Klebsiella pneumoniae.
    Shigella spp.
    Vibrio cholerae.
Other bacteria
Parasitic (5% of Cases)
Protozoa
Balantidium coli.
Blastocystis hominis.
Cryptosporidium.
Cyclospora.
Dientamoeba fragilis.
Entamoeba histolytica.
Entamoeba polecki.
Enteromonas hominis.
Giardia lamblia.
Isospora belli.
Microsporidia.
Sarcocystis hominis.
Helminths
Angiostrongylus costaricense.
Anisakiasis.
Ascaris lumbricoides.
Diphyllobothrium latum.
Enterobius vermicularis.
Hookworms.
Schistosoma spp.
Strongyloides stercoralis.

Taenia spp.
Trichinella spiralis.
Trichuris trichiura.

DIARRHEA, NONINFECTIOUS[6]

ICD-10CM # K59.1 Functional diarrhea

CAUSES OF NONINFECTIOUS DIARRHEA

Toxins
Drugs
ACE inhibitors.
Alprazolam.
Antacids (Mg).
Antibiotics.
Antidepressants.
Antiepileptic drugs.
Antihypertensives.
Antiparkinson drugs.
Beta-blockers.
Caffeine.
Cardiac antiarrhythmics.
Chemotherapy agents.
Cholesterol-lowering drugs.
Cholinergic agents.
Cholinesterase inhibitors.
Colchicine.
Digitalis.
Diuretics.
Flurouracil.
Fluoxetine.
Histamine H_2-receptor antagonists.
Hydralazine.
Lactulose.
Laxatives/cathartics.
Levodopa.
Lithium.
NSAIDs.
Neomycin.
Podophyllin.
Procainamide.
Prostaglandins.
Quinidine.
Ricinoleic acid.
Theophylline.
Thyroid hormone.
Valproic acid.
Dietetic foods
Mannitol.
Sorbitol.
Xylitol.
Fish-associated toxins
Amnestic shellfish poisoning.
Ciguatera.
Echinoderms.
Neurotoxic shellfish poisoning.
Paralytic shellfish poisoning.
Scombroid.
Tetroton.
Plant-associated toxins
Herbal preparations.
Horse chestnut.
Mushrooms—*Amanita* spp.
Nicotine.
Other plant toxins:
    Pesticides—organophosphates.
    Pokeweed.
    Rhubarb.

---

[17]Associated with fever, abdominal pain, and fecal red blood cells or white blood cells. % indicates the estimated contribution to total cases.

Miscellaneous:
    Allergic reactions.
    Carbon monoxide poisoning.
    Ethanol.
    Heavy metals.
    Monosodium glutamate (MSG).
    Opiate withdrawal.

Gastrointestinal Pathology
Appendicitis.
Autonomic dysfunction.
Bile acid malabsorption.
Blind loop.
Bowel obstruction.
Celiac disease.
Cirrhosis.
Defects in amino acid transport.
Diverticular disease.
Familial dysautonomia.
Fecal impaction.
Fecal incontinence.
GI bleed.
GI cancer.
Hirschsprung's disease.
Inflammatory bowel disease (ulcerative colitis, Crohn's disease).
Intussusception.
Irritable bowel syndrome.
Ischemic bowel.
Lactose/fructose intolerance.
Malabsorption syndromes.
Malrotation.
Postsurgical.
Postvagotomy.
Radiation therapy.
Short gut syndrome.
Small bowel resection.
Strictures.
Toxic megacolon.
Tropical sprue.
Volvulus.
Whipple's disease.

Endocrine Related
Carcinoid syndrome (serotonin).
Hormonal hypersecretion.
Hyperthyroidism (thyroid hormone).
Medullary carcinoma of the thyroid (calcitonin).
Pancreatic cholera (VIP).
Somatostatinoma (somatostatin).
Systemic mastocytosis (histamine).
Zollinger-Ellison syndrome (gastrin).

Endocrine pathology
Adrenal insufficiency.
Diabetes enteropathy.
Hypoparathyroidism.
Pancreatic insufficiency.

Systemic Illness/Other
Alcoholism.
Amyloidosis.
Connective tissue disease.
Cystic fibrosis.
Ectopic pregnancy.
Hemolytic-uremic syndrome.
Henoch-Schönlein purpura.
Lymphoma.
Otitis media—infants.
Pelvic inflammatory disease.
Pneumonia/sepsis.
Pyelonephritis.
Scleroderma/SLE.

Severe malnutrition.
Stevens-Johnson syndrome.
Toxic shock syndrome.
Wilson's disease.
Miscellaneous:
    ○ Factitious diarrhea.
    ○ Runner's diarrhea.

ACE, Angiotensin-converting enzyme; *GI,* gastrointestinal; *NSAIDs,* nonsteroidal anti-inflammatory drugs; *SLE,* systemic lupus erythematosus; *VIP,* vasoactive intestinal polypeptide.

DIARRHEA, TUBE-FED PATIENT[28]
ICD-10CM # K91.89   Other postprocedural complications and disorders of digestive system

COMMON CAUSES UNRELATED TO TUBE FEEDING
Elixir medications containing sorbitol.
Magnesium-containing antacids.
Antibiotic-induced sterile gut.
Pseudomembranous colitis.

POSSIBLE CAUSES RELATED TO TUBE FEEDING
- Inadequate fiber to form stool bulk.
- High fat content of formula (in the presence of fat malabsorption syndrome).
- Bacterial contamination of enteral products and delivery systems (causal association with diarrhea not documented).
- Rapid advancement in rate (after the GI tract is unused for prolonged periods).

UNLIKELY CAUSES RELATED TO TUBE FEEDING
Formula hyperosmolality (proven not to be the cause of diarrhea).
Lactose (absent from nearly all enteral feeding formulas).

DIPLOPIA, BINOCULAR
ICD-10CM # H53.2   Diplopia

Cranial nerve palsy (3rd, 4th, 6th).
Thyroid eye disease.
Myasthenia gravis.
Decompensated strabismus.
Orbital trauma with blowout fracture.
Orbital pseudotumor.
Cavernous sinus thrombosis.

DIPLOPIA, MONOCULAR
ICD-10CM # H53.2   Diplopia

Postoperative corrected longstanding tropia.
Defective contact lenses.
Poorly fitting bifocals.
Trauma to iris.
Corneal disorder (e.g., dry eye, astigmatism).
Cataracts.
Lens subluxation.
Nystagmus.
Eyelid twitching.

Foreign body in aqueous or vitreous media.
Migraine.
Lesions of occipital cortex.
Psychogenic.

DIPLOPIA, VERTICAL
ICD-10CM # H53.2   Diplopia

- Myasthenia.
- Superior oblique palsy.
- Myositis or pseudotumor with orbital involvement.
- Lymphoma or metastases affecting the orbits.
- Brain stem or cerebellar lesions.
- Hydrocephalus.
- Third nerve palsy.
- Botulism.
- Wernicke's encephalopathy.
- Dysthyroid orbitopathy (muscle infiltration).

DYSENTERY AND INFLAMMATORY ENTEROCOLITIS[9]
ICD-10CM # varies with specific diagnosis

DIFFERENTIAL DIAGNOSIS OF ACUTE BACTERIAL DYSENTERY AND INFLAMMATORY ENTEROCOLITIS

Specific Infectious Processes
Bacillary dysentery (*Shigella dysenteriae, Shigella flexneri, Shigella sonnei, Shigella boydii; invasive Escherichia coli*).
Campylobacteriosis (*Campylobacter jejuni*).
Amebic dysentery (*Entamoeba histolytica*).
Ciliary dysentery (*Balantidium coli*).
Vibriosis (*Vibrio parahaemolyticus*).
Salmonellosis (*Salmonella typhimurium*).
Typhoid fever (*Salmonella typhi*).
Enteric fever (*Salmonella choleraesuis, Salmonella paratyphi*).
Yersiniosis (*Yersinia enterocolitica*).

Proctitis
Gonococcal (*Neisseria gonorrhoeae*).
Herpetic (herpes simplex virus).
Chlamydial (*Chlamydia trachomatis*).
Syphilitic (*Treponema pallidum*).

Other Syndromes
Necrotizing enterocolitis of the newborn.
Enteritis necroticans.
Pseudomembranous enterocolitis or *Clostridium difficile* colitis without overt pseudomembranes (*C. difficile*).
Diverticulitis.
Typhlitis.

Chronic Inflammatory Processes
Enteropathogenic and enteroaggregative *E. coli*.
Syphilis.
Gastrointestinal tuberculosis.
Gastrointestinal mycosis (including *Basidiobolus ranarum*).
Parasitic enteritis.

Syndromes without Known Infectious Cause
Idiopathic ulcerative colitis.
Crohn's disease.
Radiation enteritis.

Ischemic colitis.
Allergic enteritis.
Brainerd diarrhea.

DIZZINESS

ICD-10CM # R42 Dizziness and giddiness

- Viral syndrome.
- Anxiety, hyperventilation.
- Benign positional paroxysmal vertigo.
- Medications (e.g., sedatives, antihypertensives, analgesics).
- Withdrawal from medications (e.g., benzodiazepines, SSRIs).
- Alcohol or drug abuse.
- Postural hypotension.
- Hypoglycemia, hyperglycemia.
- Hematologic disorders (e.g., anemia, polycythemia, leukemia).
- Head trauma.
- Menière's disease.
- Vertebrobasilar ischemia.
- Cervical osteoarthritis.
- Cardiac abnormalities (arrhythmias, cardiomyopathy, CHF, pericarditis).
- Multiple sclerosis.
- Peripheral vestibulopathy.
- Air or sea travel.
- Electrolyte abnormalities.
- Eye problems (cornea, lens, retina).
- Migraine.
- Brain stem infarct.
- Autonomic neuropathy.
- Chronic otomastoiditis.
- Complex partial seizures.
- Ramsey Hunt syndrome.
- Arteritis.
- Syncope and presyncope.
- Perilymph fistula.
- Cerebellopontine tumor.
- Hepatic or renal disease.

DRY EYE

ICD-10CM # H04.129 Dry eye syndrome of unspecified lacrimal gland

Contacts.
Medications (antihistamines, clonidine, beta-blockers, ibuprofen, scopolamine).
Keratoconjunctivitis sicca.
Trauma.
Environmental causes (air conditioning in patient with contacts).

DYSLIPOPROTEINEMIAS, SECONDARY CAUSES[10]

ICD-10CM # E78.4 Other hyperlipidemia

Cause	Disorder
Metabolic	Diabetes
	Lipodystrophy
	Glycogen storage disorders
Renal	Chronic renal failure
	Glomerulonephritis with nephritic syndrome

Cause	Disorder
Hepatic	Cirrhosis
	Biliary obstruction
	Porphyria
Hormonal	Estrogens
	Progesterones
	Growth hormone
	Thyroid disorders (hypothyroidism)
	Corticosteroids
Lifestyle	Physical inactivity
	Obesity
	Diet rich in fats, saturated fats
	Alcohol intake
	Smoking
Medications	Retinoic acid derivatives
	Glucocorticoids
	Exogenous estrogens
	Thiazide diuretics
	Beta-adrenergic blockers (non-selective)
	Testosterone and other anabolic steroids
	Immunosuppressive medications (cyclosporine)
	Antiviral medications (human immunodeficiency virus protease inhibitors)
	Antischizophrenic agents

DYSPAREUNIA[21]

ICD-10CM #		
	N94.1	Dyspareunia
	N44.8	Other noninflammatory disorders of the testis
	N50.8	Other specified disorders of male genital organs
	N53.12	Painful ejaculation
	F52.6	Dyspareunia not due to a substance or known physiological condition

INTROITAL

Vaginismus.
Intact or rigid hymen.
Clitoral problems.
Vulvovaginitis.
Vaginal atrophy: hypoestrogen.
Vulvar dystrophy.
Bartholin or Skene gland infection.
Inadequate lubrication.
Operative scarring.

MIDVAGINAL

Urethritis.
Trigonitis.
Cystitis.
Short vagina.
Operative scarring.
Inadequate lubrication.

DEEP

Endometriosis.
Pelvic infection.

Uterine retroversion.
Ovarian pathology.
GI.
Orthopedic.
Abnormal penile size or shape.

DYSPEPSIA AND PYROSIS, DIFFERENTIAL DIAGNOSIS DURING PREGNANCY[26]

ICD-10CM #		
	K30	Dyspepsia, atonic
	F45.3	Dyspepsia, psychogenic

DIFFERENTIAL DIAGNOSIS OF DYSPEPSIA OR PYROSIS DURING PREGNANCY

Gastroesophageal reflux disease.
Peptic ulcer disease.
Nausea and vomiting of pregnancy.
Hyperemesis gravidarum.
Pancreatitis.
Biliary colic.
Acute cholecystitis.
Viral hepatitis.
Appendicitis.
Acute fatty liver of pregnancy (in late pregnancy).
Irritable bowel syndrome/nonulcer dyspepsia.

DYSPHAGIA

ICD-10CM # R13.10 Dysphagia, unspecified

Esophageal obstruction: neoplasm, foreign body, achalasia, stricture, spasm, esophageal web, diverticulum, Schatzki's ring.
Peptic esophagitis with stricture, Barrett's stricture.
External esophageal compression: neoplasms (thyroid neoplasm, lymphoma, mediastinal tumors), thyroid enlargement, aortic aneurysm, vertebral spurs, aberrant right subclavian artery (dysphagia lusoria).
Hiatal hernia, GERD.
Oropharyngeal lesions: pharyngitis, glossitis, stomatitis, neoplasms.
Hysteria: globus hystericus.
Neurologic and/or neuromuscular disturbances: bulbar paralysis, myasthenia gravis, ALS, multiple sclerosis, Parkinsonism, CVA, diabetic neuropathy.
Toxins: poisoning, botulism, tetanus, postdiphtheritic dysphagia.
Systemic diseases: scleroderma, amyloidosis, dermatomyositis.
Candida and herpes esophagitis.
Presbyesophagus.

DYSPHAGIA, OROPHARYNGEAL[67]

ICD-10CM # R13.12 Dysphagia, oropharyngeal phase

FUNCTIONAL DISORDERS

Central Nervous System

Stroke.
Head injury.
Parkinson's disease.
Motor neuron disease.
Multiple sclerosis.
Tumor.
Drugs (e.g., phenothiazines).
Malformations (e.g., syrinx, Arnold–Chiari).

Neural

Motor neuron disease.
Myasthenia gravis.
Radiotherapy.
Poliomyelitis.
Familial dysautonomia.

Muscle

Autoimmune myopathy (polymyositis, derma-
   tomyositis, systemic lupus erythematosus).
Thyrotoxic myopathy.
Guillain-Barré motor neuropathy.
Muscular dystrophies.

STRUCTURAL DISORDERS

Head/neck surgery.
Stricture.
Radiotherapy.
Tumor.
Pharyngeal pouch.
Web.
Extrinsic (e.g., osteophytes).

MISCELLANEOUS

Xerostomia.

DYSPNEA

ICD-10CM #   R06.9   Unspecified
                            abnormalities of
                            breathing

Upper airway obstruction: trauma, neoplasm,
   epiglottitis, laryngeal edema, tongue retrac-
   tion, laryngospasm, abductor paralysis of
   vocal cords, aspiration of foreign body.
Lower airway obstruction: neoplasm, COPD,
   asthma, aspiration of foreign body.
Pulmonary infection: pneumonia, abscess,
   empyema, TB, bronchiectasis.
Pulmonary hypertension.
Pulmonary embolism/infarction.
Parenchymal lung disease.
Pulmonary vascular congestion.
Cardiac disease: ASHD, valvular lesions, cardiac
   dysrhythmias, cardiomyopathy, pericardial
   effusion, cardiac shunts.
Space-occupying lesions: neoplasm, large hiatal
   hernia, pleural effusions.
Disease of chest wall: severe kyphoscoliosis,
   fractured ribs, sternal compression, morbid
   obesity.
Neurologic dysfunction: Guillain-Barré syn-
   drome, botulism, polio, spinal cord injury.
Interstitial pulmonary disease: sarcoidosis, col-
   lagen vascular diseases, DIP, Hamman-Rich
   pneumonitis, etc.
Pneumoconioses: silicosis, berylliosis, etc.
Mesothelioma.
Pneumothorax, hemothorax, pleural effusion.

Inhalation of toxins.
Cholinergic drug intoxication.
Carcinoid syndrome.
Hematologic: anemia, polycythemia, hemoglo-
   binopathies.
Thyrotoxicosis, myxedema.
Diaphragmatic compression caused by abdomi-
   nal distention, subphrenic abscess, ascites.
Lung resection.
Metabolic abnormalities: uremia, hepatic coma,
   DKA.
Sepsis.
Atelectasis.
Psychoneurosis.
Diaphragmatic paralysis.
Pregnancy.

DYSURIA

ICD-10CM #   R30.0   Dysuria
                            R30.9   Painful micturition,
                                         unspecified

Urinary tract infection.
Estrogen deficiency (in postmenopausal female).
Vaginitis.
Genital infection (e.g., herpes, condyloma).
Interstitial cystitis.
Chemical irritation (e.g., deodorant aerosols,
   douches).
Meatal stenosis or stricture.
Reiter's syndrome.
Bladder neoplasm.
GI etiology (diverticulitis, Crohn's disease).
Impaired bladder or sphincter action.
Urethral caruncle.
Chronic fibrosis posttrauma.
Radiation therapy.
Prostatitis.
Urethritis (gonococcal, *Chlamydia*).
Behçet's syndrome.
Stevens-Johnson syndrome.

EARACHE[61]

ICD-10CM #   H92.09   Otalgia, unspecified
                               ear

Otitis media.
Serous otitis media.
Eustachitis.
Otitis externa.
Otitic barotrauma.
Mastoiditis.
Foreign body.
Impacted cerumen.
Referred otalgia, as with TMJ dysfunction, den-
   tal problems, and tumors.

ECTOPIC ACTH SECRETION[28]

ICD-10CM #   E34.2   Ectopic hormone
                            secretion, not
                            elsewhere classified

Small cell carcinoma of lung.
Endocrine tumors of foregut origin.
   Thymic carcinoid.
   Islet cell tumor.
   Medullary carcinoid, thyroid.
   Bronchial carcinoid.

Pheochromocytoma.
Ovarian tumors.

EDEMA, CHILDREN[37]

ICD-10CM #   R60.0   Localized edema
                            R60.1   Generalized edema
                            R60.9   Edema, unspecified

CARDIOVASCULAR

Congestive heart failure.
Acute thrombi or emboli.
Vasculitis of many types.

RENAL

Nephrotic syndrome.
Glomerulonephritis of many types.
End-stage renal failure.

ENDOCRINE OR METABOLIC

Thyroid disease.
Starvation.
Hereditary angioedema.

IATROGENIC

Drugs (diuretics and steroids).
Water or salt overload.

HEMATOLOGIC

Hemolytic disease of the newborn.

GASTROINTESTINAL

Hepatic cirrhosis.
Protein-losing enteritis.
Lymphangiectasis.
Cystic fibrosis.
Celiac disease.
Enteritis of many types.

LYMPHATIC ABNORMALITIES

Congenital (gonadal dysgenesis).
Acquired.

EDEMA, GENERALIZED

ICD-10CM #   R60.0   Localized edema
                            R60.1   Generalized edema
                            R60.9   Edema, unspecified

Congestive heart failure (CHF).
Cirrhosis.
Nephrotic syndrome.
Pregnancy.
Idiopathic.
Acute nephritic syndrome.
Myxedema.
Medications (NSAIDs, estrogens, vasodilators).

EDEMA, LEG, UNILATERAL[49]

ICD-10CM #   R60.0   Localized edema
                            R60.9   Edema, unspecified

WITH PAIN

DVT.
Postphlebitic syndrome.
Popliteal cyst rupture.
Gastrocnemius rupture.
Cellulitis.
Psoas or other abscess.

WITHOUT PAIN

DVT.
Postphlebitic syndrome.
Other venous insufficiency (after saphenous vein harvest, varicosities).
Lymphatic obstruction/lymphedema (carcinoma, lymphoma, sarcoidosis, filariasis, retroperitoneal fibrosis).

EDEMA OF LOWER EXTREMITIES

| ICD-10CM # | R60.0 | Localized edema |
| | R60.9 | Edema, unspecified |

CHF (right-sided).
Hepatic cirrhosis.
Nephrosis.
Myxedema.
Lymphedema.
Pregnancy.
Abdominal mass: neoplasm, cyst.
Venous compression from abdominal aneurysm.
Varicose veins.
Bilateral cellulitis.
Bilateral thrombophlebitis.
Vena cava thrombosis, venous thrombosis.
Retroperitoneal fibrosis.

EJECTION SOUND OR CLICK

| ICD-10CM # | R01.2 | Other cardiac sounds |

Aortic regurgitation.
Aortic root dilatation.
Systemic hypertension.
Chronic pulmonary hypertension.
Tetralogy of Fallot.
Atrial septal defect.
Pulmonary valve stenosis.
Aortic aneurysm.

ELBOW PAIN

| ICD-10CM # | M25.529 | Pain in unspecified elbow |

Trauma.
Infection.
Inflammatory arthritis.
Lateral or medial epicondylitis.
Entrapment neuropathy.
Olecranon bursitis.
Osteoarthritis.
Gout.
Cervical disease (referred pain).
Shoulder disease (referred pain).
Partial subluxation.
Synovial osteochondromatosis.
Loose body.

ELEVATED HEMIDIAPHRAGM

ICD-10CM #	J98.6	Disorders of diaphragm
	Q79.0	Congenital diaphragmatic hernia
	Q79.1	Other congenital malformations of diaphragm

Neoplasm (bronchogenic carcinoma, mediastinal neoplasm, intrahepatic lesion).
Substernal thyroid.
Infectious process (pneumonia, empyema, TB, subphrenic abscess, hepatic abscess).
Atelectasis.
Idiopathic.
Eventration.
Phrenic nerve dysfunction (myelitis, myotonia, herpes zoster).
Trauma to phrenic nerve or diaphragm (e.g., surgery).
Aortic aneurysm.
Intraabdominal mass.
Pulmonary infarction.
Pleurisy.
Radiation therapy.
Rib fracture.

EMBOLI, ARTERIAL[49]

| ICD-10CM # | I74.3 | Embolism and thrombosis of arteries of the lower extremities |
| | I74.2 | Embolism and thrombosis of arteries of the upper extremities |

Myocardial infarction with mural thrombi.
Atrial fibrillation.
Cardiomyopathies.
Prosthetic heart valves.
CHF.
Endocarditis.
Left ventricular aneurysm.
Left atrial myxoma.
Sick sinus syndrome.
Paradoxical embolus from venous thrombosis.
Aneurysms of large blood vessels.
Atheromatous ulcers of large blood vessels.

EMESIS, PEDIATRIC AGE[37]

ICD-10CM #	R11.10	Vomiting, unspecified
	R11.11	Vomiting without nausea
	R11.12	Projectile vomiting

INFANCY

Gastrointestinal Tract Congenital:
Regurgitation—chalasia, gastroesophageal reflux.
Atresia—stenosis (tracheoesophageal fistula, prepyloric diaphragm, intestinal atresia).
Duplication.
Volvulus (errors in rotation and fixation, Meckel diverticulum).
Congenital bands.
Hirschsprung's disease.
Meconium ileus (cystic fibrosis), meconium plug.
Acquired:
Acute infectious gastroenteritis, food poisoning (staphylococcal, clostridial).
Pyloric stenosis.
Gastritis, duodenitis.
Intussusception.
Incarcerated hernia—inguinal, internal secondary to old adhesions.

Cow's milk protein intolerance, food allergy, eosinophilic gastroenteritis.
Disaccharidase deficiency.
Celiac disease—presents after introduction of gluten in diet; inherited risk.
Adynamic ileus—the mediator for many nongastrointestinal causes.
Neonatal necrotizing enterocolitis.
Chronic granulomatous disease with gastric outlet obstruction.
Nongastrointestinal Tract
Infectious—otitis, urinary tract infection, pneumonia, upper respiratory tract infection, sepsis, meningitis.
Metabolic—aminoaciduria and organic aciduria, galactosemia, fructosemia, adrenogenital syndrome, renal tubular acidosis, diabetic ketoacidosis, Reye's syndrome.
Central nervous system—trauma, tumor, infection, diencephalic syndrome, rumination, autonomic responses (pain, shock).
Medications—anticholinergics, aspirin, alcohol, idiosyncratic reaction (e.g., codeine).

CHILDHOOD

Gastrointestinal Tract
Peptic ulcer—vomiting is a common presentation in children younger than 6 yr old.
Trauma—duodenal hematoma, traumatic pancreatitis, perforated bowel.
Pancreatitis—mumps, trauma, cystic fibrosis, hyperparathyroidism, hyperlipidemia, organic acidemias.
Crohn's disease.
Idiopathic intestinal pseudoobstruction.
Superior mesenteric artery syndrome.
Nongastrointestinal Tract
Central nervous system—cyclic vomiting, migraine, anorexia nervosa, bulimia.

ENCEPHALOMYELITIS, NONVIRAL CAUSES[49]

| ICD-10CM # | G04.81 | Other encephalitis and encephalomyelitis |

Subacute bacterial endocarditis.
Rocky Mountain spotted fever.
Typhus.
Ehrlichia.
Q fever.
Chlamydia.
Mycoplasma.
Legionella.
Brucellosis.
Listeria.
Whipple's disease.
Cat-scratch disease.
Syphilis (meningovascular).
Relapsing fever.
Lyme disease.
Leptospirosis.
Nocardia.
Actinomycosis.
Tuberculosis.
Cryptococcus.
Histoplasma.
Toxoplasma.

Plasmodium falciparum.
Trypanosomiasis.
Behçet's disease.
Vasculitis.
Carcinoma.
Drug reactions.

ENCEPHALOPATHY, HYPERTENSIVE[69]

ICD-10CM #	varies with specific diagnosis

Cerebral infarction.
Subarachnoid hemorrhage.
Intracerebral hemorrhage.
Subdural or epidural hematoma.
Brain tumor or other mass lesion.
Seizure disorder.
Central nervous system vasculitis.
Encephalitis/meningitis.
Drug ingestion.
Drug withdrawal.

ENCEPHALOPATHY, METABOLIC[65]

ICD-10CM #	F10.27	Alcohol dependence with alcohol-induced persisting dementia
	K72.90	Hepatic failure, unspecified without coma
	K72.91	Hepatic failure, unspecified with coma
	G92	Toxic encephalopathy
	T56.0X1A	Toxic effect of lead and its compounds, accidental (unintentional), initial encounter
	T56.0X2A	Toxic effect of lead and its compounds, intentional self-harm, initial encounter

Substrate deficiency: hypoxia/ischemia, carbon monoxide poisoning, hypoglycemia.
Cofactor deficiency: thiamine, vitamin B_{12}, pyridoxine (INH administration).
Electrolyte disorders: hyponatremia, hypercalcemia, carbon dioxide narcosis, dialysis, hypermagnesemia, disequilibrium syndrome.
Endocrinopathies: DKA, hyperosmolar coma, hypothyroidism, hyperadrenocorticism, hyperparathyroidism.
Endogenous toxins: liver disease, uremia, porphyria.
Exogenous toxins: drug overdose (sedative/hypnotics, ethanol, narcotics, salicylates, tricyclic antidepressants), drug withdrawal, toxicity of therapeutic medications, industrial toxins (e.g., organophosphates, heavy metals), sepsis.
Heat stroke.
Epilepsy (postictal).

ENTHESOPATHY

ICD-10CM #	M46.00	Spinal enthesopathy, site unspecified

Viremia or bacteremia.
Ankylosing spondylitis.
Psoriatic arthritis.
Drug-induced (quinolones, etretinate).
Reactive arthritis.
DISH.
Reiter's syndrome.

EOSINOPHILIA, DISEASE ASSOCIATIONS[48]

ICD-10CM #	D72.1	Eosinophilia NEC
	J82	Eosinophilia, pulmonary

DISEASES, SYNDROMES, AND CONDITIONS COMMONLY ASSOCIATED WITH PERIPHERAL BLOOD EOSINOPHILIA AND/OR TISSUE EOSINOPHILIA

***Infectious Agents* Parasitic Infections**
Tropical eosinophilia.
Visceral larval migrans (VLM, toxocariasis).
Helminth infections.
Filariasis (*Wuchereria bancrofti, Brugia malay*).
Onchocerciasis.
Schistosomiasis.
Fascioliasis.
Paragonimiasis.
Strongyloidiasis.
Trichinosis.
Hookworm.
Ascariasis.
Echinococcosis/hydatid disease.
  Fungal Infections
Coccidioidomycosis.
Cryptococcosis (CSF eosinophilia) in HIV.
Allergic Diseases
Asthma (atopic and intrinsic, nasal polyps, aspirin intolerance syndromes).
Bronchopulmonary aspergillosis.
Allergic rhinitis.
Urticarias (acute allergic and chronic idiopathic).
Atopic dermatitis.
Acute drug (hypersensitivity) reactions (interstitial nephritis, cholestatic hepatitis, exfoliative dermatitis).
Respiratory Tract Disorders
Hypersensitivity pneumonitis (rare).
Allergic bronchopulmonary aspergillosis.
Eosinophilic pneumonia.
Transient pulmonary infiltrates (Löeffler syndrome).
Prolonged pulmonary infiltrates with eosinophilia (PIE syndrome).
Tropical pulmonary eosinophilia (TPE).
Bronchiectasis.
Cystic fibrosis.
Endocrinologic Disorders
Addison disease.
Gastrointestinal Diseases
Inflammatory bowel disease (IBD).
Eosinophilic gastroenteritis, eosinophilic esophagitis (EE).

Allergic gastroenteritis (young children).
Celiac disease (when associated with EE).
Toxic Reactions to Ingested Agents
Eosinophil myalgia syndrome (L-tryptophan).
Toxic oil syndrome.
Reactions to Cytokine Therapies
IL-2 and IL-2 plus lymphokine activated killer (LAK) cells.
GM-CSF therapy.
Cutaneous Disorders
Atopic dermatitis.
Immunologic skin diseases.
Scabies.
Myiasis.
Chlamydial pneumonia of infancy.
Scarlet fever and pneumococcal pneumonia (convalescent phase).
Cat scratch disease.
Eosinophilic cellulitis (Wells syndrome).
Episodic angioedema with eosinophilia.
Chronic idiopathic urticaria.
Bullous pemphigoid.
Herpes gestationis.
Angioblastic lymphoid hyperplasia (Kimura disease).
Immunodeficiency Syndromes
Wiskott-Aldrich syndrome.
Selective IgA deficiency with atopy.
Hyper-IgE recurrent infection syndrome (Job syndrome).
Swiss-type and sex-linked combined immunodeficiency.
Nezelof syndrome.
Graft-versus-host-disease (GVHD).
Connective Tissue Diseases
• **Vasculitis/Collagen Vascular Disorders**
  Hypersensitivity vasculitis.
  Allergic granulomatosis with angiitis (Churg-Strauss syndrome).
  Serum sickness.
  Eosinophilic fasciitis.
  Sjögren syndrome.
  Rheumatoid arthritis (severe).
Neoplastic, Myeloproliferative, and Ly Neoplasms and Syndromes
• *Neoplastic*
  Ovarian carcinoma.
  Solid tumors (mucin-secreting, epithelial cell origin).
Chronic eosinophil leukemia.
Idiopathic hypereosinophilic syndromes (HES).
Systemic mastocytosis.
Myeloproliferative
  Chronic myelogenous leukemia (CML) acute myelogenous leukemia (AML) and myelodysplastic syndrome (MDS).
  Myelomonocytic leukemia with bone marrow eosinophilia (M4Eo, inversion 16).
Lymphoproliferative
  T-cell lymphocytic leukemia.
  Lymphomas (T cell, Hodgkin disease).
  Angioimmunoblastic lymphadenopathy.
Rare Causes
○ Chronic active hepatitis.
○ Chronic dialysis.
○ Acute pancreatitis.
○ Postirradiation.
○ Hypopituitarism.

EOSINOPHILIC LUNG DISEASE[32]

ICD-10CM # NEC J82 Eosinophilia, pulmonary

IDIOPATHIC

Simple pulmonary eosinophilia (Löffler's syndrome).
Acute eosinophilic pneumonia.
Chronic eosinophilic pneumonia.
Hypereosinophilic syndrome.

DRUG-INDUCED

Aminosalicylic acid.
Para-aminosalicylic acid.
NSAIDs.
Captopril.
Cocaine.
Minocycline.
Nitrofurantoin.
Phenytoin.

INFECTION

Parasitic (ascariasis, paragonimiasis, tropical eosinophilia).
Fungal (aspergillus).
Bacterial (TB, atypical mycobacterial infection, brucella).
Viral (respiratory syncytial virus).

IMMUNOLOGIC DISEASES

Wegener's granulomatosis.
Churg–Strauss syndrome.
Rheumatoid disease.
Sarcoidosis.

NEOPLASMS

Bronchogenic carcinoma.
Bronchial carcinoid.
Lymphoma (Hodgkin's, non-Hodgkin's).

EOSINOPHILIA, PARASITIC CAUSES[9]

ICD-10CM # varies with specific diagnosis

PARASITIC CAUSES OF EOSINOPHILIA

Widespread Geographic Distribution
Ascariasis (migratory phase).
Hookworm.[†]
Strongyloidiasis.[*‡]
Tropical pulmonary eosinophilia.[*]
Lymphatic filariasis.
Schistosomiasis.
Toxocariasis.[*]
Cysticercosis (Taenia solium).
Echinococcosis (cyst rupture).
Trichinosis.[*]
Trichuriasis.
Aberrant helminthiasis from animals.

[†]Moderate to marked during larval migration in early infection; most often absent or very mild during chronic infection.

[*]Most frequent parasitic causes of massive eosinophilia (>5000/mm³).

[‡]Absent in disseminated infection in compromised hosts.

Limited Geographic Distribution
Clonorchiasis.[†]
Paragonimiasis.[†]
Fascioliasis.[†]
Angiostrongyliasis.
Opisthorchiasis.[†]
Onchocerciasis, loiasis, and other nonlymphatic filariases.
Gnathostomiasis.
Capillariasis.
Trichostrongyliasis.

EPIGASTRIC PAIN[67]

ICD-10CM # R10.816 Epigastric abdominal tenderness
R10.826 Epigastric rebound abdominal tenderness

Peptic ulceration (uncomplicated).[18]
Peptic ulceration (perforated).
Biliary colic.
Acute pancreatitis.
Abdominal aortic aneurysm.
Anxiety.
Inferior wall MI.

EPILEPSY

ICD-10CM # G40.909 Epilepsy, unspecified, not intractable, without status epilepticus

Psychogenic spells.
Transient ischemic attack.
Hypoglycemia.
Syncope.
Narcolepsy.
Migraine.
Paroxysmal vertigo.
Arrhythmias.
Drug reaction.

EPISTAXIS

ICD-10CM # R04.0 Epistaxis

Trauma.
Medications (nasal sprays, NSAIDs, anticoagulants, antiplatelets).
Nasal polyps.
Cocaine use.
Coagulopathy (hemophilia, liver disease, DIC, thrombocytopenia).
Systemic disorders (hypertension, uremia).
Infections.
Anatomic malformations.
Rhinitis.
Nasal polyps.
Local neoplasms (benign and malignant).
Desiccation.
Foreign body.

ERECTILE DYSFUNCTION, ORGANIC[59]

ICD-10CM # N52.9 Male erectile dysfunction, unspecified

---

[18]Conditions that also cause right upper quadrant pain

Neurogenic abnormalities: Somatic nerve neuropathy, central nervous system abnormalities.
Psychogenic causes: Depression, performance anxiety, marital conflict.
Endocrine causes: Hyperprolactinemia, hypogonadotropic hypogonadism, testicular failure, estrogen excess.
Trauma: Pelvic fracture, prostate surgery, penile fracture.
Systemic disease: DM, renal failure, hepatic cirrhosis.
Medications: Diuretics, antidepressants, H_2 blockers, exogenous hormones, alcohol, antihypertensives, nicotine abuse, finasteride, etc.
Structural abnormalities: Peyronie's disease.

EROSIONS, GENITALIA

ICD-10CM # N36.8 Other specified disorders of urethra

Candidiasis.
Intraepithelial neoplasia.
Squamous cell carcinoma.
Lichen planus.
Pemphigus vulgaris.
Erythema multiforme.
Lichen sclerosus.
Bullous pemphigoid.
Extramammary Paget's disease.
Impetigo.

ERYTHEMATOUS ANNULAR SKIN LESIONS

ICD-10CM # L53.8 Other specified erythematous conditions

Tinea corporis.
Warfarin plaques.
Erythema multiforme.
Erythema annulare.
Cutaneous lupus.
Cutaneous sarcoidosis.
Trauma.
Acute febrile neutrophilic dermatosis (Sweet's syndrome).

ERYTHROCYTOSIS[39]

ICD-10CM # D75.0 Familial erythrocytosis

CAUSES OF ERYTHROCYTOSIS

Relative or Spurious Erythrocytosis (Normal Red Cell Mass)
Hemoconcentration secondary to dehydration (diarrhea, diaphoresis, diuretics, water deprivation, emesis, ethanol, hypertension, preeclampsia, pheochromocytoma, carbon monoxide intoxication).

True or Absolute Erythrocytosis
Polycythemia vera.
Primary congenital polycythemia.
Secondary erythrocytosis caused by:
Congenital causes (e.g., activating mutation of erythropoietin receptor).
Hypoxia caused by carbon monoxide poisoning, high oxygen affinity hemoglobin,

high-altitude residence, chronic pulmonary disease, hypoventilation syndromes such as sleep apnea, right to left cardiac shunt, neurologic defects involving the respiratory center.

Nonhypoxic causes with pathologic erythropoietin production.

Renal disease (cysts, hydronephrosis, renal artery stenosis, focal glomerulonephritis, renal transplantation).

Tumors (renal cell cancer, hepatocellular carcinoma, cerebellar hemangioblastoma, uterine fibromyoma, adrenal tumors, meningioma, pheochromocytoma).

Drug-associated causes:

Androgen therapy.

Exogenous erythropoietin growth factor therapy.

ERYTHRODERMA

ICD-10CM # L53.9 Erythematous condition, unspecified

Drug reaction (e.g., allopurinol, ampicillin, phenytoin, vancomycin, dapsone, omeprazole, carbamazepine).
Atopic dermatitis.
Psoriasis.
Contact dermatitis.
Idiopathic.
Pityriasis rubra.
Chronic actinic dermatitis.
Bullous pemphigoid.
Paraneoplastic.
Cutaneous T-cell lymphoma.
Connective tissue disease.
Hypereosinophilia syndrome.

ESOPHAGEAL PERFORATION[49]

ICD-10CM # K22.3 Perforation of esophagus
S27.819A Unspecified injury of esophagus (thoracic part), initial encounter

Trauma.
Caustic burns.
Iatrogenic.
Foreign bodies.
Spontaneous rupture (Boerhaave's syndrome).
Postoperative breakdown of anastomosis.

ESOPHAGITIS[49]

ICD-10CM # K20.9 Esophagitis, unspecified

INFECTIOUS
Candidiasis.
Cytomegalovirus.
Herpes simplex virus.
HIV infection, acute.

NONINFECTIOUS
Gastroesophageal reflux.
Mucositis from cancer chemotherapy.

Mucositis from radiation therapy.
Aphthous ulcers.

ESOTROPIA

ICD-10CM # H50.00 Unspecified esotropia
H50.43 Accommodative component in esotropia
H50.05 Alternating esotropia

Congenital.
Accommodative esotropia.
Myasthenia gravis.
Abducens palsy.
Pseudo-sixth nerve palsy.
Medial rectus entrapment (e.g., blowout fracture).
Posterior internuclear ophthalmoplegia.
Wernicke's encephalopathy.
Thyroid myopathy.
Chiari malformation.

EXANTHEMS[54]

ICD-10CM # R21 Rash and other nonspecific skin eruption

Measles.
Rubella.
Erythema infectiosum (fifth disease).
Roseola exanthema.
Varicella.
Enterovirus.
Adenovirus.
Epstein-Barr virus.
Kawasaki disease.
Staphylococcal scalded skin.
Scarlet fever.
Meningococcemia.
Rocky Mountain spotted fever.

EYELID NEOPLASM

ICD-10CM # C44.101 Unspecified malignant neoplasm of skin of unspecified eyelid, including canthus

MALIGNANT
Melanoma.
Basal cell carcinoma.
Squamous cell carcinoma.
Bowen's disease.
Sebaceous cell carcinoma.
Metastatic lymphoma/leukemia.

BENIGN
Melanocytic nevus.
Pilar, eccrine, or apocrine tumor.
Neurofibroma.
Keratosis.
Squamous papilloma.
Keratoacanthoma.

EYELID RETRACTION

ICD-10CM # H02.89 Other specified disorders of eyelid

Congenital.
Graves' ophthalmopathy.
Myasthenia gravis.
Postsurgical.
Guillain-Barré syndrome.
Cerebellar disease.
Horizontal gaze palsy.
Partial palsy of superior rectus muscle.
Encephalitis.
Closed head injury.
Disseminated sclerosis.
Eye trauma.
Contact lens wear.
Proptosis.
Eyelid neoplasm.
Atopic dermatitis.
Herpes zoster ophthalmicus.
Botulinum toxin injection.
Cyclic oculomotor paralysis.
Spheroid wing meningioma.
Hepatic cirrhosis.
Down syndrome.
Essential hypertension.
Meningitis.
Paget's disease of bone.

EYE PAIN

ICD-10CM # H57.13 Ocular pain, bilateral

Foreign body.
Herpes zoster.
Trauma.
Conjunctivitis.
Iritis.
Iridocyclitis.
Uveitis.
Blepharitis.
Ingrown lashes.
Orbital or periorbital cellulitis/abscess.
Sinusitis.
Headache.
Glaucoma.
Inflammation of lacrimal gland.
Tic douloureux.
Cerebral aneurysm.
Cerebral neoplasm.
Entropion.
Retrobulbar neuritis.
UV light.
Dry eyes.
Irritation or inflammation from eye drops, dust, cosmetics, etc.

FACIAL PAIN

ICD-10CM # G50.1 Atypical facial pain

Infection, abscess.
Postherpetic neuralgia.
Trauma, posttraumatic neuralgia.
Tic douloureux.
Cluster headache, "lower-half headache."
Geniculate neuralgia.
Anxiety, somatization syndrome.
Glossopharyngeal neuralgia.
Carotidynia.

FACIAL PARALYSIS[54]

ICD-10CM # G51.0 Bell's palsy

INFECTION

Bacterial: otitis media, mastoiditis, meningitis, Lyme disease.
Viral: herpes zoster, mononucleosis, varicella, rubella, mumps, Bell's palsy.
Mycobacterial: TB, meningitis, leprosy.
Miscellaneous: syphilis, malaria.

TRAUMA

Temporal bone fracture, facial laceration.
Surgery.

NEOPLASM

Malignant: squamous cell carcinoma, basal cell and adenocystic tumors, leukemia, parotid neoplasms, metastatic tumors.
Benign: facial nerve neuroma, vestibular schwannoma, congenital cholesteatoma.

IMMUNOLOGIC

Guillain-Barré syndrome, periarteritis nodosa.
Reaction to tetanus antiserum.

METABOLIC

Pregnancy.
Hypothyroidism.
DM.

FAILURE TO THRIVE

ICD-10CM # R62.50 Unspecified lack of expected normal physiological development in childhood

PSYCHOSOCIAL/BEHAVIORAL

Inadequate diet because of poverty/food insufficiency, errors in food preparation.
Poor parenting skills (lack of knowledge of sufficient diet).
Child/parent interaction problems (autonomy struggles, coercive feeding, maternal depression).
Food refusal.
Rumination.
Parental cognitive or mental health problems.
Child abuse or neglect; emotional deprivation.

NEUROLOGIC

Cerebral palsy.
Hypothalamic and other CNS tumors (diencephalic syndrome).
Neuromuscular disorders.
Neurodegenerative disorders.

RENAL

Recurrent urinary tract infection.
Renal tubular acidosis.
Renal failure.

ENDOCRINE

Diabetes mellitus.
Diabetes insipidus.
Hypothyroidism/hyperthyroidism.
Growth hormone deficiency.
Adrenal insufficiency.

GENETIC/METABOLIC/CONGENITAL

Sickle cell disease.
Inborn errors of metabolism (organic acidosis, hyperammonemia, storage disease).
Fetal alcohol syndrome.
Skeletal dysplasias.
Chromosomal disorders.
Multiple congenital anomaly syndromes (VATER [vertebral defects, imperforate anus, tracheoesophageal fistula, radial and renal dysplasia], CHARGE [coloboma, heart disease, atresia choanae, retarded growth and retarded development and/or central nervous system anomalies, genital hypoplasia, ear anomalies and/or deafness]).

GASTROINTESTINAL

Pyloric stenosis.
Gastroesophageal reflux.
Repair of tracheoesophageal fistula.
Malrotation.
Malabsorption syndromes.
Celiac disease.
Milk intolerance: lactose, protein.
Pancreatic insufficiency syndromes (cystic fibrosis).
Chronic cholestasis.
Inflammatory bowel disease.
Chronic congenital diarrhea states.
Short bowel syndrome.
Pseudoobstruction.
Hirschsprung disease.
Food allergy.

CARDIAC

Cyanotic heart lesions.
Congestive heart failure.
Vascular rings.

PULMONARY/RESPIRATORY

Severe asthma.
Cystic fibrosis; bronchiectasis.
Chronic respiratory failure.
Bronchopulmonary dysplasia.
Adenoid/tonsillar hypertrophy.
Obstructive sleep apnea.

MISCELLANEOUS

Collagen vascular disease.
Malignancy.
Primary immunodeficiency.
Transplantation.

INFECTIONS

Perinatal infection (TORCHES [toxoplasma, other, rubella, cytomegalovirus, herpes simplex]).
Occult/chronic infections.
Parasitic infestation.
Tuberculosis.
HIV.

FATIGUE

ICD-10CM # R53.83 Other fatigue
F48.0 Neurasthenia

Depression.
Anxiety, emotional stress.
Inadequate sleep.

Chronic fatigue syndrome.
Prolonged physical activity.
Pregnancy and postpartum period.
Anemia.
Hypothyroidism.
Medications (β-blockers, anxiolytics, antidepressants, sedating antihistamines, clonidine, methyldopa).
Viral or bacterial infections.
Sleep apnea syndrome.
Dieting.
Renal failure, CHF, COPD, liver disease.

FATIGUE, CHRONIC

ICD-10CM # R53.83 Other fatigue
F48.0 Neurasthenia

CHRONIC INFECTIONS

Hepatitis C.
Lyme disease.
Parasitic and fungal infections.
Tuberculosis.
Human immunodeficiency virus.
Xenotropic murine leukemia retrovirus.

SLEEP DISORDERS

Obstructive sleep apnea.
Restless leg syndrome.
Circadian rhythm disorder.
Upper airway resistance syndrome.
Narcolepsy/parasomnias.
Alpha-delta sleep disorder.

ENDOCRINE/METABOLIC DISORDERS

Addison's disease.
Cushing's syndrome.
Poorly controlled diabetes.
Thyroid disorders.
Hemochromatosis.
Hypopituitarism.
Diabetes insipidus.

GENERAL MEDICAL DISORDERS

Anemia (any cause).
Chronic renal/hepatic failure.
Malnutrition.
Medication side effects.
Chronic pain disorders.

PSYCHOLOGICAL

Mood disorders (depression, anxiety, bipolar).
Schizophrenia.
Posttraumatic stress disorder.
Anorexia nervosa/bulimia.
Childhood abuse and/or neglect.

CHRONIC INFLAMMATION

Rheumatoid arthritis.
Systemic lupus erythematosus.
Sjögren's syndrome.
Polymyositis/dermatomyositis.
Vasculitis.
Sarcoidosis.

CARDIOPULMONARY

Congestive heart failure.
Neurally mediated hypotension.

Differential Diagnosis

II

Postural orthostatic tachycardia syndrome.
Pulmonary hypertension.
Chronic obstructive pulmonary disease.
Mitral valve prolapse.

GASTROINTESTINAL

Celiac disease.
Inflammatory bowel disease.
Autoimmune hepatitis.
Hepatic cirrhosis.

MALIGNANCY

Lymphoma and occult malignancies.
Postchemotherapy syndrome.

NEUROLOGIC DISORDERS

Multiple sclerosis.
Myasthenia gravis.
Muscular dystrophies.
Parkinson's disease.
Early dementia.

LIFESTYLE FACTORS

Chronic overwork.
Persistent unresolved stress.
Inadequate exercise.
Morbid obesity (body mass index >40).
Alcoholism/drug abuse.

FATTY LIVER

| ICD-10CM # | K76.0 | Fatty (change of) liver, not elsewhere classified |
| | K76.89 | Other specified diseases of liver |

Obesity.
Alcohol abuse.
DM.
Acute fatty liver of pregnancy.
Medications (tetracycline, valproic acid, glucocorticoids, amiodarone, estrogen, methotrexate).
Reye's syndrome.
Wilson's disease.
Nonalcoholic steatosis.

FEVER AND CARDIOPULMONARY FAILURE[22]

| ICD-10CM # | R50.9 | Fever, unspecified |

DIFFERENTIAL DIAGNOSIS OF FEVER AND RAPIDLY PROGRESSIVE CARDIOPULMONARY FAILURE

Bacterial Infection

Severe community-acquired pneumonia.
Meningitis, endocarditis.
Rickettsial disease (babesiois, ehrlichiosis, Rocky Mountain spotted fever, scrub typhus, Mediterranean spotted fever).
Q-Fever (*Coxiella burnetii*).
Brucellosis.
Plague (*Yersinia pestis*).
Tularemia (*Francisella tularensis*).
Typhoid fever/salmonellosis.
Leptospirosis (*Leptospira interrogans*).
Anthrax.

Mycobacterial infections.
Viral Infections
Viral pneumonia (influenza, CMV, EBV, VZV, SARS).
Hantavirus.
Dengue fever and yellow fever.
Hemorrhagic fever (Lassa, Marburg, or Ebola viruses).
Fungal infections
Coccidiomycosis.
Cryptococcus.
Histoplasmosis.
Blastomycosis.
Parasitic infections
Malaria.
Leishmaniasis.
Schistosomiasis.
Strongyloides.
Noninfectious causes
Inflammatory:
- Rapid-onset interstitial pneumonia (acute interstitial pneumonia, acute hypersensitivity pneumonitis).
- Acute eosinophilic pneumonia.
- ARDS due to other causes (inhalation injury, drug overdose, trauma).
Rheumatologic disorders:
- Wegener granulomatosis, Churg-Strauss disease, Goodpasture's syndrome.
- Systemic lupus erythematosus, antiphospholipid syndrome.
Other:
- Malignancy, lymphoma, lymphoproliferative disease, leukemia.
- Pulmonary embolism, aortic dissection, acute myocardial infarction.
- Adrenal insufficiency, thyroid storm.

ARDS, acute respiratory distress syndrome; *CMV,* Cytomegalovirus; *EBV,* Epstein-Barr virus; *SARS,* severe acute respiratory syndrome; *VZV,* varicella zoster virus.

FEVER AND JAUNDICE

| ICD-10CM # | R50.9 | Fever, unspecified |
| | R17 | Unspecified jaundice |

Bacterial sepsis.
Cholangitis.
Hepatic abscess.
Leptospirosis.
Malaria.
Viral hepatitis.
Yellow fever.

FEVER AND LYMPHADENOPATHY

| ICD-10CM # | R59.9 | Enlarged lymph nodes, unspecified |
| | R50.9 | Fever, unspecified |

Regional
Cervical
Streptococci.
Tuberculosis.
Viral upper respiratory infection.
Peripheral
Bartonella henselae.
Herpesviruses.
Lymphoma.
Metastatic cancer.

Sporotrichosis.
Streptococci.
Inguinal
Chancroid.
Herpes.
Lymphogranuloma venereum.
Syphilis (primary).
GENERALIZED
Cytomegalovirus.
Epstein-Barr virus.
HIV.
Lymphoma.
Sarcoidosis.
Syphilis (secondary).
Toxoplasmosis.
Viral hepatitis.

FEVER AND RASH

ICD-10CM #	R21	Rash and other nonspecific skin eruption
	R21	Rash and other nonspecific skin eruption
	R50.9	Fever, unspecified

Drug hypersensitivity: penicillin, sulfonamides, thiazides, anticonvulsants, allopurinol.
Viral infection: measles, rubella, varicella, erythema infectiosum, roseola, enterovirus infection, viral hepatitis, infectious mononucleosis, acute HIV.
Other infections: meningococcemia, staphylococcemia, scarlet fever, typhoid fever, *Pseudomonas* bacteremia, Rocky Mountain spotted fever, Lyme disease, secondary syphilis, bacterial endocarditis, babesiosis, brucellosis, listeriosis.
Serum sickness.
Erythema multiforme.
Erythema marginatum.
Erythema nodosum.
SLE.
Dermatomyositis.
Allergic vasculitis.
Pityriasis rosea.
Herpes zoster.

FEVER AND RASH IN ICU[67]

| ICD-10CM # | R21 | Rash and other nonspecific skin eruption |
| | R50.9 | Fever, unspecified |

DIFFERENTIAL DIAGNOSTIC CLINICAL FEATURES OF FEVER AND RASH IN THE ICU

Rash with Shock

Infectious causes: toxic shock syndrome, meningococcemia, postsplenectomy sepsis, overwhelming *Staphylococcus aureus* bacteremia/acute bacterial endocarditis, arboviral hemorrhagic fevers, hemorrhagic smallpox, *Vibrio vulnificus,* gas gangrene, dengue fever.
Noninfectious cause: systemic lupus erythematosus (on steroids).

RASH WITH MENTAL CHANGES

Infectious causes: Rocky Mountain spotted fever, meningococcemia (with meningitis), *S. aureus* acute bacterial endocarditis, Chikungunya fever, typhus.
Noninfectious cause: systemic lupus erythematosus.

RASH WITH CONJUNCTIVAL SUFFUSION

Infectious causes: Rocky Mountain spotted fever, dengue fever, arboviral hemorrhagic fevers, toxic shock syndrome.
Noninfectious cause: adult Kawasaki's disease.

RASH WITH RELATIVE BRADYCARDIA

Infectious causes: Rocky Mountain spotted fever, typhus, dengue fever, typhoid, arboviral hemorrhagic fevers.
Noninfectious cause: drug rash.

RASH WITH ABDOMINAL PAIN

Infectious causes: V. vulnificus, gas gangrene, Clostridium sordelli, scarlet fever.
Noninfectious causes: cholesterol emboli syndrome, systemic lupus erythematosus.

RASH ON PALMS AND SOLES

Infectious causes: Rocky Mountain spotted fever, toxic shock syndrome, chickenpox, smallpox, monkeypox, scarlet fever.
Noninfectious cause: drug rash.

RASH WITH DIARRHEA

Infectious causes: V. vulnificus, gas gangrene, toxic shock syndrome, dengue fever, arboviral hemorrhagic fevers.
Noninfectious cause: none.

RASH WITH EDEMA OF DORSUM OF HANDS/FEET

Infectious causes: Rocky Mountain spotted fever, toxic shock syndrome.
Noninfectious cause: adult Kawasaki's disease.

RASH WITH BULLAE

Infectious causes: V. vulnificus, S. aureus complicated skin/skin structure infection, gas gangrene.
Noninfectious cause: none.

RASH WITH HEART MURMUR

Infectious cause: acute bacterial endocarditis.
Noninfectious cause: systemic lupus erythematosus.
Rash with gangrene of nose tip
Infectious cause: S. aureus acute bacterial endocarditis.
Noninfectious causes: systemic lupus erythematosus, vasculitis.

RASH WITH CEREBROVASCULAR ACCIDENT

• Infectious causes: cholesterol emboli syndrome, S. aureus acute bacterial endocarditis.
• Noninfectious cause: none.

RASH WITH SPLENOMEGALY

Infectious causes: Rocky Mountain spotted fever, typhus.
Noninfectious causes: systemic lupus erythematosus, adult Kawasaki's disease.

RASH WITH DEAFNESS

• Infectious causes: Rocky Mountain spotted fever, typhus, meningococcal meningitis.
• Noninfectious cause: none.

RASH WITH HEPATOSPLENOMEGALY

Infectious causes: Rocky Mountain spotted fever, typhus.
Noninfectious cause: atypical measles.

RASH WITH HEPATOMEGALY

Infectious cause: typhus.
Noninfectious cause: none.

FEVER, AFTER TRAVEL TO THE TROPICS[3]

ICD-10CM # R50.81 Fever presenting with conditions classified elsewhere

CAUSES OF FEVER AFTER TRAVEL TO THE TROPICS

80% of Specific Infections Causing Fever (Includes Respiratory and Urinary Tract Infection)
Malaria.
Viral hepatitis.
Febrile illness unrelated to foreign travel.
Dengue fever.
Enteric fever (typhoid and paratyphoid fevers).

Other Causes
• Gastroenteritis.
• Rickettsia.
• Leptospirosis.
• Schistosomiasis.
• Amebic liver abscess.
• Tuberculosis.
• Acute HIV infection.
• Others.

FEVER, DRUG-INDUCED[30]

ICD-10CM # R50.2 Drug induced fever

SELECTED AGENTS ASSOCIATED WITH DRUG-INDUCED FEVER

Common
• Antimicrobial:
  • Amphotericin B.
  • β-Lactams.
  • Sulfonamides.
• Cardiovascular:
  • Procainamide.
  • Quinidine.
• Central nervous system:
  • Carbamazepine.
  • Phenytoin.
• Miscellaneous:
  • Bleomycin.
  • Interferon-α.
  • Interleukin-2.

Less Common
Antimicrobial:
  Clindamycin.
  Fluoroquinolones.
  Rifampin.
Cardiovascular:
  Diltiazem.
  Hydralazine.
Central nervous system:
  Haloperidol.
  Serotonin reuptake inhibitors.

Miscellaneous:
  Allopurinol.
  Cimetidine.
  Tacrolimus.

FEVER, HOSPITAL ASSOCIATED[30]

ICD-10CM # R50.2 Drug induced fever
            R50.9 Fever, unspecified

SELECTED CAUSES OF HOSPITAL-ASSOCIATED FEVER

Common
Infectious:
  Clostridium difficile enterocolitis.
  Pneumonia.
  Surgical wound.
  Urinary tract.
  Vascular catheter.
Noninfectious:
  Drug-induced fever.
  Hematoma.
  Immediate postoperative state.
  Transfusion reaction.
  Venous thromboembolism.
Less Common
Infectious:
  Biliary tract disease.
  Endometritis.
  Intraabdominal abscess.
  Mediastinitis.
  Sinusitis.
Noninfectious:
  Adrenal insufficiency.
  Gout.
  Myocardial infarction.
  Organ infarction.
  Pancreatitis.

FEVER IN RETURNING TRAVELERS AND IMMIGRANTS[54]

ICD-10CM # R50.81 Fever presenting with conditions classified elsewhere

Differential diagnosis of some selected systemic febrile illnesses to consider in returned travelers and immigrants.[19]

COMMON

Acute respiratory tract infection (worldwide).
Gastroenteritis (worldwide) [foodborne, waterborne, fecal-oral].
Enteric fever, including typhoid (worldwide) [food, water].
Urinary tract infection (worldwide) [sexual contact].

[19]Diagnoses for which particular symptoms are indicative are in *italics*. Exposure to regions of the world that are most likely to be significant to the diagnosis are presented in (parentheses). Vectors, risk behaviors, and sources associated with acquisition are presented in [brackets]. Special clinical characteristics are listed within {braces}.

Differential Diagnosis

II

Drug reactions [antibiotics, prophylactic agents, other] {rash frequent}.

Malaria (tropics, limited areas of temperate zones) [mosquitoes].

Arboviruses (Africa; tropics) [mosquitoes, ticks, mites].

Dengue (Asia, Caribbean, Africa) [mosquitoes].

Viral hepatitis (worldwide).

Hepatitis A (worldwide) [food, fecal-oral].

Hepatitis B (worldwide, especially Asia, sub-Saharan Africa) [sexual contact] {long incubation period}.

Hepatitis C (worldwide) [blood or sexual contact].

Hepatitis E (Asia, North Africa, Mexico, others) [food, water].

Tuberculosis (worldwide) [airborne, milk] {long period to symptomatic infection}.

Sexually transmitted diseases (worldwide) [sexual contact].

LESS COMMON

Filariasis (Asia, Africa, South America) [biting insects] {long incubation period, eosinophilia}.

Measles (developing world) [airborne] {in susceptible individual}.

Amebic abscess (worldwide) [food].

Brucellosis (worldwide) [milk, cheese, food, animal contact].

Listeriosis (worldwide) [foodborne] {meningitis}.

Leptospirosis (worldwide) [animal contact, open fresh water] {jaundice, meningitis}.

Strongyloidiasis (warm and tropical areas) [soil contact] {eosinophilia}.

Toxoplasmosis (worldwide) [undercooked meat].

RARE

Relapsing fever (western Americas, Asia, northern Africa) [ticks, lice].

Hemorrhagic fevers (worldwide) [arthropod and nonarthropod transmitted].

Yellow fever (tropics) [mosquitoes] {hepatitis}.

Hemorrhagic fever with renal syndrome (Europe, Asia, North America) [rodent urine] {renal impairment}.

Hantavirus pulmonary syndrome (western North America, other) [rodent urine] {respiratory distress syndrome}.

Lassa fever (Africa) [rodent excreta, person to person] {high mortality rate}.

Other—chikungunya, Rift Valley, Ebola-Marburg, etc. (various) [insect bites, rodent excreta, aerosols, person to person] {often severe}.

Rickettsial infections {rashes and eschars}.

Leishmaniasis, visceral (Middle East, Mediterranean, Africa, Asia, South America) [biting flies] {long incubation period}.

Acute schistosomiasis (Africa, Asia, South America, Caribbean) [fresh water].

Chagas' disease (South and Central America) [reduviid bug bites] {often asymptomatic}.

African trypanosomiasis (Africa) [tsetse fly bite] {neurologic syndromes, sleeping sickness}.

Bartonellosis (South America) [sandfly bite] {skin nodules}.

HIV infection/AIDS (worldwide) [sexual and blood contact].

Trichinosis (worldwide) [undercooked meat] {eosinophilia}.

Plague (temperate and tropical plains) [animal exposures and fleas].

Tularemia (worldwide) [animal contact, fleas, aerosols] {ulcers, lymph nodes}.

Anthrax (worldwide) [animal, animal product contact] {ulcers}.

Lyme disease (North America, Europe) [tick bites] {arthritis, meningitis, cardiac abnormalities}.

FEVER, NONINFECTIOUS CAUSES[6]

ICD-10CM # R50.9 Fever, unspecified

DIFFERENTIAL DIAGNOSIS—NONINFECTIOUS CAUSES OF FEVER

Critical Diagnoses

Acute myocardial infarction.

Pulmonary embolism/infarction.

Intracranial hemorrhage.

Cerebrovascular accident.

Neuroleptic-malignant syndrome.

Thyroid storm.

Acute adrenal insufficiency.

Transfusion reaction.

Pulmonary edema.

Emergent Diagnoses

Congestive heart failure.

Dehydration.

Recent seizure.

Sickle cell disease.

Transplant rejection.

Pancreatitis.

Deep vein thrombosis.

Nonemergent Diagnoses

Drug fever.

Malignancy.

Gout.

Sarcoidosis.

Crohn's disease.

Postmyocardiotomy syndrome.

FEVER, POSTPARTUM[1]

ICD-10CM # R50.9 Fever, unspecified

MOST COMMON

Metritis.

Urinary tract infection.

Pneumonia.

Wound infection.

Mastitis.

Superficial or deep vein thrombosis.

MOST THREATENING

Toxic shock syndrome.

Necrotizing fasciitis.

Pelvic phlegmon.

Pelvic abscess.

Peritonitis.

Septic pelvic thrombosis.

Breast abscess.

FEVER, PERIODIC[25]

ICD-10CM # R50.9 Fever, unspecified

HEREDITARY

Nonhereditary

Infectious

Hidden infectious focus (e.g., aortoenteric fistula, Caroli's disease).

Recurrent reinfection (e.g., chronic meningococcemia, host defense defect).

Specific infection (e.g., Whipple's disease, malaria).

Noninfectious inflammatory disorder, e.g.:
  Adult-onset Still's disease.
  Juvenile chronic rheumatoid arthritis.
  Periodic fever, aphthous stomatitis, pharyngitis, and adenitis.
  Schnitzler syndrome.
  Behçet's syndrome.
  Crohn's disease.
  Sarcoidosis.
  Extrinsic alveolitis.
  Humidifier lung, polymer fume fever.
  Neoplastic.

Lymphoma (e.g., Hodgkin's disease, angioimmunoblastic lymphoma).

Solid tumor (e.g., pheochromocytoma, myxoma, colon carcinoma).

Vascular (e.g., recurrent pulmonary embolism)

Hypothalamic.

Psychogenic periodic fever.

Factitious or fraudulent.

FEVER, PEDIATRIC, ACUTE[1]

ICD-10CM # R50.9 Fever, unspecified

COMMON VIRAL INFECTIONS

Central Nervous System

Meningitis.

Encephalitis.

Tumor.

Brain abscess.

Head, Ears, Eyes, Nose, and Throat

Otitis media.

Pharyngitis.

Retropharyngeal abscess.

Peritonsillar abscess.

Lateral pharyngeal wall abscess.

Stomatitis.

Influenza.

Sinusitis.

Parotitis.

Cervical adenitis.

Periorbital cellulitis.

Orbital cellulitis or abscess.

Respiratory System

Bronchiolitis.

Croup.

Epiglottitis.

Pneumonia.

Upper respiratory infection.

Cardiovascular System

Myocarditis.

Pericarditis.

Endocarditis.

Genitourinary System
Urinary tract infection.
Tuboovarian abscess.

Gastrointestinal Tract
Acute viral gastroenteritis.
Bacterial enteritis.
Appendicitis.

Focal Soft Tissue Infections
Cellulitis.

Musculoskeletal System
Osteomyelitis.
Septic arthritis.

Rheumatologic Disorders
Acute rheumatic fever.
Juvenile rheumatoid arthritis.
Henoch-Schönlein purpura.

Vasculitis
Behçet syndrome.

Malignancy
Leukemia.
Lymphoma.
Sarcoma.

Systemic Illness
Bacteremia.
Viremia.
Sepsis.
Kawasaki disease.
Toxic shock syndrome.
Rocky Mountain spotted fever.
Meningococcemia.

MISCELLANEOUS DISORDERS

Toxicologic
Anticholinergic toxidromes.
Salicylate overdose.
Amphetamine.
Cocaine.

Endocrine
Thyrotoxicosis.

FEVER, RECURRENT OR PERIODIC, IN CHILDREN[45]

ICD-10CM #		
	R50.2	Drug induced fever
	R50.9	Fever, unspecified

INFECTIOUS DISEASES
Brucellosis.
Rat-bite fever.
Relapsing fever.

RHEUMATIC DISEASES
Juvenile idiopathic arthritis (systemic onset).
Behçet disease.
Systemic lupus erythematosus.
Relapsing polychondritis.
Crohn's disease.

HEREDITARY AUTOINFLAMMATORY SYNDROMES
Familial Mediterranean fever (FMF).
Cryopyrinopathies:
    Familial cold autoinflammatory syndrome (FCAS).
    Muckle-Wells syndrome (MWS).
    Chronic infantile neurologic cutaneous and articular (CINCA) syndrome, also called neonatal-onset multisystem inflammatory disease (NOMID).

Tumor necrosis factor receptor–associated periodic syndrome (TRAPS).
Hyperimmunoglobulinemia D with periodic fever syndrome (HIDS).

CYCLIC HEMATOPOIESIS
Hereditary form.
Acquired form.

IDIOPATHIC CONDITIONS
Periodic fever with aphthous stomatitis, pharyngitis, and adenitis (PFAPA).

FINGER LESIONS, INFLAMMATORY

ICD-10CM #		
	B08.8	Other specified viral infections characterized by skin and mucous membrane lesions
	L03.0	Cellulitis of finger and toe

Paronychia.
Herpes simplex type 1 (herpetic whitlow).
Dyshidrotic eczema (pompholyx).
Herpes zoster.
Bacterial endocarditis (Osler's nodes).
Psoriatic arthritis.

FLACCID PARALYSIS, ACUTE, DIFFERENTIAL DIAGNOSIS[45]

ICD-10CM #		
	G83.9	Paralytic syndrome, unspecified

Brain stem stroke.
Brain stem encephalitis.
Acute anterior poliomyelitis.
    Caused by poliovirus.
    Caused by other neurotropic viruses.
Acute myelopathy.
    Space-occupying lesions.
    Acute transverse myelitis.
Peripheral neuropathy.
    Guillain-Barré syndrome.
    Post-rabies vaccine neuropathy.
    Diphtheritic neuropathy.
    Heavy metals, biologic toxins, or drug intoxication.
    Acute intermittent porphyria.
    Vasculitic neuropathy.
    Critical illness neuropathy.
    Lymphomatous neuropathy.
Disorders of neuromuscular transmission.
    Myasthenia gravis.
    Biologic or industrial toxins.
    Tic paralysis.
Disorders of muscle.
    Hypokalemia.
    Hypophosphatemia.
    Inflammatory myopathy.
    Acute rhabdomyolysis.
    Trichinosis.
    Periodic paralyses.

FLATULENCE AND BLOATING[61]

ICD-10CM #		
	R14.0	Abdominal distension (gaseous)
	R14.1	Gas pain
	R14.2	Eructation
	R14.3	Flatulence

Ingestion of nonabsorbable carbohydrates.
Ingestion of carbonated beverages.
Malabsorption: pancreatic insufficiency, biliary disease, celiac disease, bacterial overgrowth in small intestine.
Lactase deficiency.
Irritable bowel syndrome.
Anxiety disorders.
Food poisoning, giardiasis.

FLUSHING[53]

ICD-10CM #		
	R23.2	Flushing

Physiologic flushing: menopause, ingestion of monosodium glutamate (Chinese restaurant syndrome), ingestion of hot drinks.
Drugs: alcohol (with or without disulfiram, metronidazole, or chlorpropamide), nicotinic acid, diltiazem, nifedipine, levodopa, bromocriptine, vancomycin, amyl nitrate.
Neoplastic disorders: carcinoid syndrome, VIPoma syndrome, medullary carcinoma of thyroid, systemic mastocytosis, basophilic chronic myelocytic leukemia, renal cell carcinoma.
Anxiety.
Agnogenic flushing.

FOLATE DEFICIENCY[39]

ICD-10CM #		
	D52.0	Dietary folate deficiency anemia
	D52.1	Drug-induced folate deficiency anemia
	D52.8	Other folate deficiency anemias
	D52.9	Folate deficiency anemia, unspecified

ETIOPATHOPHYSIOLOGIC CLASSIFICATION OF FOLATE DEFICIENCY
Nutritional causes:
    Decreased dietary intake:
        Poverty and famine.
        Institutionalized individuals (e.g., psychiatric, nursing homes), chronic debilitating disease.
        Prolonged feeding of infants with goat's milk, special slimming diets or food fads (i.e., folate-rich foods not consumed), cultural or ethnic cooking techniques (i.e., food folate destroyed).
    Decreased diet and increased requirements:
        Physiologic (e.g., pregnancy and lactation, prematurity, hyperemesis gravidarum, infancy).
        Pathologic (e.g., intrinsic hematologic diseases involving hemolysis with compensatory erythropoiesis, abnormal hematopoiesis, or bone marrow infiltration with malignant disease and dermatologic disease such as psoriasis).

Folate malabsorption:
  With normal intestinal mucosa:
    Some drugs (controversial).
    Congenital folate malabsorption (rare).
    With mucosal abnormalities (e.g., tropical and nontropical sprue, regional enteritis).
Defective cellular folate uptake:
  Familial aplastic anemia (rare).
  Acute cerebral folate deficiency.
Inadequate cellular use:
  Folate antagonists (e.g., methotrexate).
  Hereditary enzyme deficiencies involving folate.
Drugs:
  Multiple effects on folate metabolism (e.g., alcohol, sulfasalazine, triamterene, pyrimethamine, trimethoprim-sulfamethoxazole, diphenylhydantoin, barbiturates).
Acute folate deficiency:
  Intensive care unit setting.
  Uncertain origin.

FOOT AND ANKLE PAIN[23]

| ICD-10CM # | M25.5 | Pain in joint |
| | M25.9 | Joint disorder, unspecified |

TENDON, LIGAMENT, AND MUSCLE

Gastrocnemius-soleus strain.
Plantaris rupture.
Anterior talofibular ligament tear.
Calcaneofibular ligament tear.
Deltoid ligament tear.
Anterolateral impingement due to complete tear of anterior talofibular ligament and anterior inferior tibiofibular ligament.
Syndesmotic impingement due to tear of syndesmosis.
Sinus tarsi syndrome (lateral hindfoot pain and instability due to injury of contents of the sinus and tarsal tunnel).
Achilles tendinitis.
Achilles rupture.
Plantar fasciitis.
Posterior tibial tendon dysfunction.
Flexor hallucis longus dysfunction.
Tibialis anterior tendon tear.
Peroneus brevis tendon tear.

BONE

Fracture of talus.
Calcaneal fracture.
Navicular fractures.
Lisfranc fracture-dislocation (fracture of the first metatarsal base with dislocation of medial cuneiform).
Metatarsal stress fracture.
Freiberg's infraction (sclerosis and flattening of the second metatarsal head due to trauma or microtrauma).
Avascular necrosis of the talus.
Fracture of the phalanges.
Fracture of the sesamoids.
Sesamoiditis.
Metatarsalgia.

JOINT

Osteoarthritis.
Gout.
Rheumatoid arthritis.
Other inflammatory arthritides.
Charcot's joint.
Osteochondral lesion of the talus.

PERIARTICULAR STRUCTURES

Shin splint (periosteal avulsion and periostitis at the insertion of the medial soleus due to repetitive overuse, such as in running and hiking).
Hallux rigidus.
Hallux valgus.
Ingrown toenail.
Toe deformities.
Turf toe (sprain of the first metatarsophalangeal joint due to hyperextension forces).
Plantar fasciitis.
Plantar fibromatosis.

NERVES

Anterior tarsal tunnel syndrome (involvement of deep peroneal nerve under the superficial fascia of the ankle).
Morton's neuroma.

VESSELS

Atherosclerosis.
Compartment syndrome.

REFERRED PAIN

Complex regional pain syndrome.

FOOT AND ANKLE PAIN, IN DIFFERENT AGE GROUPS[17]

| ICD-10CM # | M25.579 | Pain in unspecified ankle and joints of unspecified foot |

COMMON CAUSES OF FOOT AND ANKLE PAIN IN DIFFERENT AGE GROUPS

Childhood (2-10 yr)
Intraarticular
Club foot.
Congenital midfoot and forefoot deformities.
Septic arthritis.
Periarticular
Osteomyelitis.
Adolescence (10-18 yr)
Intraarticular
Arch disorders (pes cavus, pes planus).
Periarticular
Osteomyelitis.
Tumors.
Early Adulthood (18-30 yr)
Intraarticular
Metatarsalgia.
Hallux valgus.
Hallux rigidus.
Osteochondritis.
Accessory ossicles.
Periarticular
Achilles tendonitis.
Achilles tendon rupture.
Fasciitis.

Referred
Lumbar spine.
Knee.
Adulthood (30-50 yr)
Intraarticular
• Osteoarthritis.
• Inflammatory arthritis.
• Gout.
• Metatarsalgia.
• Hallux valgus.
• Hallux rigidus.
• Osteochondritis.
• Accessory ossicles.
Periarticular
• Ischemic foot pain.
• Diabetes.
• Bursitis.
• Tendonitis.
• Plantar fasciitis.
• Corns.
Referred
Lumbar spine.
Knee.
Old Age (>50 yr)
Intraarticular
Osteoarthritis.
Inflammatory arthritis.
Gout.
Metatarsalgia.
Hallux valgus.
Hallux rigidus.
Periarticular
Ischemic foot pain.
Diabetes.
Bursitis.
Tendonitis.
Plantar fasciitis.
Corns.
Referred
Lumbar spine.
Knee.

FOOT DERMATITIS

| ICD-10CM # | B35.3 | Tinea pedis |
| | K25 | Unspecified contact dermatitis |

Tinea pedis.
Dyshidrotic eczema.
Tylosis (mechanically induced hyperkeratosis, fissuring, and dryness).
Allergic contact dermatitis.
Psoriasis.
Peripheral vascular insufficiency.
Neuropathic foot ulcers (DM, poorly fitting shoes).
Acquired plantar keratoderma.
Sézary's syndrome.

FOOTDROP

| ICD-10CM # | M21.379 | Foot drop, unspecified foot |

Peripheral neuropathy.
L5 radiculopathy.
Peroneal nerve compression.
Sciatic nerve palsy.
Scapuloperoneal syndromes.
Spasticity.

Peroneal nerve compression.
Myopathy.
Dystonia.

FOOT LESION, ULCERATING

ICD-10CM #		
	S90.929A	Unspecified superficial injury of unspecified foot, initial encounter
	S90.933A	Unspecified superficial injury of unspecified great toe, initial encounter
	S90.936A	Unspecified superficial injury of unspecified lesser toe(s), initial encounter
	L08.89	Other specified local infections of the skin and subcutaneous tissue

Cellulitis.
Plantar wart.
Squamous cell carcinoma.
Actinomycosis (Madura foot).
Plantar fibromatosis.
Pseudoepitheliomatous hyperplasia.

FOOT PAIN

ICD-10CM #		
	M25.579	Pain in unspecified ankle and joints of unspecified foot

Trauma (fractures, musculoskeletal and ligamentous strain).
Inflammation (plantar fasciitis, Achilles tendonitis or bursitis, calcaneal apophysitis).
Arterial insufficiency, Raynaud's phenomenon, thromboangiitis obliterans.
Gout, pseudogout.
Calcaneal spur.
Infection (cellulitis, abscess, lymphangitis, gangrene).
Decubitus ulcer.
Paronychia, ingrown toenail.
Thrombophlebitis, postphlebitic syndrome.

FOOT PAIN BY AGE[45]

ICD-10CM #		
	M25.579	Pain in unspecified ankle and joints of unspecified foot

0-6 YEARS
Poorly fitting shoes.
Foreign body.
Fracture.
Osteomyelitis.
Leukemia.
Puncture wound.
Drawing of blood.
Dactylitis.
Juvenile rheumatoid arthritis (JRA).

6-12 YEARS
Poorly fitting shoes.
Sever disease.
Enthesopathy (JRA).
Foreign body.
Accessory navicular.
Tarsal coalition.
Ewing sarcoma.
Hypermobile flatfoot.
Trauma (sprains, fractures).
Puncture wound.

12-20 YEARS
Poorly fitting shoes.
Stress fracture.
Foreign body.
Ingrown toenail.
Metatarsalgia.
Plantar fasciitis.
Osteochondroses (avascular necrosis).
Freiberg infarction.
Köhler disease.
Achilles tendinitis.
Trauma (sprains).
Plantar warts.
Tarsal coalition.

FOREARM AND HAND PAIN

ICD-10CM #		
	S59.809A	Other specified injuries of unspecified elbow, initial encounter
	S59.919A	Unspecified injury of unspecified forearm, initial encounter
	S69.80XA	Other specified injuries of unspecified wrist, hand and finger(s), initial encounter
	S69.90XA	Unspecified injury of unspecified wrist, hand and finger(s), initial encounter

Epicondylitis.
Tenosynovitis.
Osteoarthritis.
Cubital tunnel syndrome.
Carpal tunnel syndrome.
Trauma.
Herpes zoster.
Peripheral vascular insufficiency.
Infection (cellulitis, abscess).

FOREARM FRACTURES[3A]

ICD-10CM #		
	S52	Fracture of forearm

TRAUMATIC
Wrist sprain, elbow sprain.
Ligamentous injuries, forearm contusions, hematomas.
Dislocations of the elbow or wrist (including nursemaid's elbow).

INFECTIOUS
Cellulitis of the forearm, abscesses.
Necrotizing fasciitis.

VASCULAR
Acute arterial occlusion.
Venous thrombosis.

NEUROLOGIC
Neurapraxias, carpal tunnel syndrome.
Systemic neurologic syndromes involving the nerves of the upper extremities.

ARTHRITIS
Septic joint, gonococcal arthritis, rheumatoid arthritis, osteoarthritis.
Pseudogout, gout.
Systemic lupus erythematosus, rheumatic fever, viral syndrome.
Reiter syndrome, Lyme disease, serum sickness.

OTHER
Olecranon bursitis, soft tissue masses.
Normal growth plates, nutrient vessels.

GAIT ABNORMALITY

ICD-10CM #		
	R26.0	Ataxic gait
	R26.1	Paralytic gait
	R26.89	Other abnormalities of gait and mobility
	R26.9	Unspecified abnormalities of gait and mobility

Parkinsonism.
Degenerative joint disease (hips, back, knees).
Multiple sclerosis.
Trauma, foot pain.
CVA.
Cerebellar lesions.
Infections (tabes, encephalitis, meningitis).
Sensory ataxia.
Dystonia, cerebral palsy, neuromuscular disorders.
Metabolic abnormalities.

GALACTORRHEA[54]

ICD-10CM #		
	N64.3	Galactorrhea not associated with childbirth

Prolonged suckling.
Drugs (INH, phenothiazines, reserpine derivatives, amphetamines, spironolactone and tricyclic antidepressants).
Major stressors (surgery, trauma).
Hypothyroidism.
Pituitary tumors.

GASTRIC DILATATION[32]

ICD-10CM #		
	K31.0	Acute dilatation of stomach

CAUSES OF A MASSIVELY DILATED STOMACH

Mechanical Gastric Outlet Obstruction
Duodenal or pyloric canal ulceration.

Carcinoma of pyloric antrum.
Extrinsic compression.
Paralytic Ileus
Surgery.
Trauma.
Peritonitis.
Pancreatitis.
Cholecystitis.
Diabetes mellitus.
Hepatic coma.
Drugs.
Gastric Volvulus
Intubation.
Air swallowing.

GASTRIC EMPTYING, DELAYED[3]

ICD-10CM # K30 Functional dyspepsia

CAUSES OF DELAYED GASTRIC EMPTYING

Mechanical Causes
Peptic ulcer disease, scarred pylorus.
Malignancy: gastric cancer, gastric lymphoma, pancreatic cancer.
Gastric surgery: vagotomy, gastric resection, Roux-en-Y anastomosis.
Crohn's disease.
Endocrine and Metabolic Causes
Diabetes mellitus.
Hypothyroidism.
Hypoadrenal states.
Electrolyte abnormalities.
Chronic renal failure.
Medications.
Anticholinergics.
Opiates.
Dopamine agonists.
Tricyclic antidepressants.
Abnormalities of Gastric Smooth Muscle
Scleroderma.
Polymyositis, dermatomyositis.
Amyloidosis.
Pseudoobstruction.
Myotonic dystrophy.
Neuropathy.
Scleroderma.
Amyloidosis.
Autonomic neuropathy.
Central Nervous System or Psychiatric Disorders
Brain stem tumors.
Spinal cord injury.
Anorexia nervosa.
Stress.
Miscellaneous
Idiopathic gastroparesis.
Gastroesophageal reflux disease.
Nonulcer (functional) dyspepsia.
Cancer cachexia or anorexia.

GASTRIC EMPTYING, RAPID

ICD-10CM # K30 Functional dyspepsia

Pancreatic insufficiency.
Dumping syndrome.
Peptic ulcer.
Celiac disease.

Promotility agents.
Zollinger-Ellison disease.

GENITAL DISCHARGE, FEMALE[21]

ICD-10CM # N94.9 Unspecified condition associated with female genital organs and menstrual cycle

Physiologic discharge: cervical mucus, vaginal transudation, bacteria, squamous epithelial cells.
Individual variation.
Pregnancy.
Sexual response.
Menstrual cycle variation.
Infection.
Foreign body: tampon, cervical cap, other.
Neoplasm.
Fistula.
IUD.
Cervical ectropion.
Spermicide.
Nongenital causes: urinary incontinence, urinary tract fistula, Crohn's disease, rectovaginal fistula.

GENITAL LESIONS, INFECTIOUS CAUSES[9]

ICD-10CM # varies with specific diagnosis

INFECTIOUS CAUSES OF GENITAL LESIONS

Sexually Transmitted Infections
Syphilis:
  • Primary (chancre).
  • Secondary (condyloma latum).
Herpes simplex virus types 1 and 2.
Chancroid (*Haemophilus ducreyi*).
Lymphogranuloma venereum.
Granuloma inguinale (donovanosis).
Human papillomavirus.
Sarcoptes scabiei.
Molluscum contagiosum.
Nonsexually Transmitted Infections
Folliculitis.
Tuberculosis.
Tularemia.
Histoplasmosis.
Candida (balanitis or vaginitis).
Amebiasis.

GENITAL LESIONS, NONINFECTIOUS CAUSES[9]

ICD-10CM # varies with specific diagnosis

NONVENEREAL CAUSES OF GENITAL LESIONS

Trauma.
Malignancies (e.g., squamous cell carcinoma).
Behçet's syndrome.
Lipschütz's vulvar ulcers.
Peyronie's disease.
Fixed-drug eruption.
Eczema.
Psoriasis.
Inflammatory bowel disease.

Contact dermatitis.
Lichen planus.
Hidradenitis suppurativa.
Postinflammatory hypopigmentation.
Aphthous ulcers (associated with human immunodeficiency virus).

GENITAL SORES[3]

ICD-10CM #	A60.9	Anogenital herpesviral infection, unspecified
	A51.0	Primary genital syphilis
	A63.0	Anogenital (venereal) warts
	A57	Chancroid
	A58	Granuloma inguinale
	A55	Chlamydial lymphogranuloma (venereum)
	N94.89	Other specified conditions associated with female genital organs and menstrual cycle
	N50.8	Other specified disorders of male genital organs

Herpes genitalis.
Syphilis.
Chancroid.
Lymphogranuloma venereum.
Granuloma inguinale.
Condyloma acuminatum.
Neoplastic lesion.
Trauma.

GLOMERULONEPHRITIS, RAPIDLY PROGRESSIVE[3]

ICD-10CM # N05.9 Unspecified nephritic syndrome with unspecified morphologic changes

DIFFERENTIAL DIAGNOSIS OF RAPIDLY PROGRESSIVE GLOMERULONEPHRITIS

Linear Immune Staining
Anti-GBM disease.
Goodpasture's syndrome.
Rarely membranous glomerulonephritis.
Granular Immune Staining
Subacute bacterial endocarditis (past infectious).
Lupus nephritis.
Cryoglobulinemia.
Membranoproliferative glomerulonephritis (type II more than type I).
Immunoglobulin A nephropathy, Henoch-Schönlein purpura.
Idiopathic.
No Immune Staining (Pauci-immune)
Antineutrophil cytoplasmic antibody-associated vasculitis (Wegener granulomatosis, microscopic polyangiitis, Churg-Strauss syndrome).
Idiopathic.

GLOMERULOPATHIES, THROMBOTIC, MICROANGIOPATHIC[3]

ICD-10CM # M31.1 Thrombotic microangiopathy

THROMBOTIC MICROANGIOPATHIC GLOMERULOPATHIES

Thrombotic thrombocytopenic purpura.
Hemolytic-uremic syndrome.
Malignant hypertension.
Scleroderma renal crisis.
Preeclampsia, eclampsia.
HELLP syndrome (hemolysis, elevated liver enzymes, low platelets).
Antiphospholipid antibody syndrome.
Drugs: oral contraceptives, quinine, cyclosporine, tacrolimus, ticlopidine, clopidogrel.

GLOMERULOSCLEROSIS, FOCAL SEGMENTAL[3]

ICD-10CM # N03.3 Chronic nephritic syndrome with diffuse mesangial proliferative glomerulonephritis

ETIOLOGY OF FOCAL SEGMENTAL GLOMERULOSCLEROSIS (FSGS)

Primary idiopathic FSGS.
Secondary FSGS.
HIV (usually collapsing variant).
Reflux nephropathy.
Heroin abuse.
Sickle cell disease.
Oligomeganephronia.
Renal dysgenesis or agenesis (low nephron mass).
Radiation nephritis.
Familial podocytopathies.
NPHS1 (nephrin) mutation.
NPHS2 (podocin) mutation.
TRPC6 (cation channel) mutation.
ACTN4 (a-actinin 4 mutation).

GLOSSODYNIA[67]

ICD-10CM # K14.6 Glossodynia

DENTURE-RELATED

Dentures (ill-fitting, monomer from denture base).
Dental plaque.
Oral parafunction.

INFECTIVE/DERMATOLOGIC

Candidiasis.
Lichen planus.

DEFICIENCY STATES

Iron, B12, folate, B2 (riboflavin), B6 (pyridoxine), zinc.

ENDOCRINE

Diabetes.
Myxedema.

Hormonal changes occurring during menopause.

NEUROLOGICALLY MEDIATED

Referred from tonsils, teeth.
Lingual nerve neuropathy.
Glossopharyngeal neuralgia.
Esophageal reflux.

IATROGENIC

Mouthwash.

XEROSTOMIA
PSYCHOGENIC
IDIOPATHIC

GLUCOCORTICOID DEFICIENCY[28]

ICD-10CM # E27.1 Primary adrenocortical insufficiency
E27.3 Drug-induced adrenocortical insufficiency

ACTH-independent causes.
TB.
Autoimmune (idiopathic).
Other rare causes:
  Fungal infection.
  Adrenal hemorrhage.
  Metastases.
  Sarcoidosis.
  Amyloidosis.
  Adrenoleukodystrophy.
  Adrenomyeloneuropathy.
  HIV infection.
  Congenital adrenal hyperplasia.
  Medications (e.g., ketoconazole).
ACTH-dependent causes:
  Hypothalamic-pituitary-adrenal suppression.
  Exogenous.
  Glucocorticoid.
  ACTH.
  Endogenous—cure of Cushing's syndrome.
Hypothalamic-pituitary lesions.
  Neoplasm:
    Primary pituitary tumor.
    Metastatic tumor.
    Craniopharyngioma.
  Infection:
    Tuberculosis.
    Actinomycosis.
    Nocardiosis.
Sarcoid.
Head trauma.
Isolated ACTH deficiency.

GOITER

ICD-10CM # E01.2 Iodine-deficiency related (endemic) goiter, unspecified
E04.9 Nontoxic goiter, unspecified
E04.9 Nontoxic goiter, unspecified
E07.1 Dyshormogenetic goiter

E01.2 Iodine-deficiency related (endemic) goiter, unspecified
E04.9 Nontoxic goiter, unspecified
E04.2 Nontoxic multinodular goiter
E04.0 Nontoxic diffuse goiter
E05.10 Thyrotoxicosis with toxic single thyroid nodule without thyrotoxic crisis or storm

Thyroiditis.
Toxic multinodular goiter.
Graves' disease.
Medications (PTU, methimazole, sulfonamides, sulfonylureas, ethionamide, amiodarone, lithium, etc.).
Iodine deficiency.
Sarcoidosis, amyloidosis.
Defective thyroid hormone synthesis.
Resistance to thyroid hormone.

GRANULOMATOUS DERMATITIDES

ICD-10CM # L92.9 Granulomatous disorder of the skin and subcutaneous tissue, unspecified

Granuloma annulare.
Sarcoidosis.
Necrobiosis lipoidica diabeticorum.
Cutaneous Crohn's disease.
Rheumatoid nodules.
Annular elastolytic giant cell granuloma (actinic granuloma).
Foreign body granuloma.

GRANULOMATOUS DISORDERS[60]

ICD-10CM # M31.30 Wegener's granulomatosis without renal involvement
K75.3 Granulomatous hepatitis
L92.9 Granulomatous disorder of skin and subcutaneous tissue, unspecified

INFECTIONS

Fungi
Histoplasma.
Coccidioides.
Blastomyces.
Sporothrix.
Aspergillus.
Cryptococcus.
Protozoa
Toxoplasma.
Leishmania.
Metazoa
Toxocara.
Schistosoma.

Spirochetes
Treponema pallidum.
T. pertenue.
T. carateum.
Mycobacteria
M. tuberculosis.
M. leprae.
M. kansasii.
M. marinum.
M. avian.
Bacille Calmette-Guérin (BCG) vaccine.
Bacteria
Brucella.
Yersinia.
Other Infections
Cat-scratch disease.
Lymphogranuloma.

NEOPLASIA

Carcinoma.
Reticulosis.
Pinealoma.
Dysgerminoma.
Seminoma.
Reticulum cell sarcoma.
Malignant nasal granuloma.

CHEMICALS

Beryllium.
Zirconium.
Silica.
Starch.

IMMUNOLOGIC ABERRATIONS

Sarcoidosis.
Crohn's disease.
Primary biliary cirrhosis.
Wegener's granulomatosis.
Giant cell arteritis.
Peyronie's disease.
Hypogammaglobulinemia.
SLE.
Lymphomatoid granulomatosis.
Histiocytosis X.
Hepatic granulomatous disease.
Immune complex disease.
Rosenthal-Melkersson syndrome.
Churg-Strauss allergic granulomatosis.

LEUKOCYTE OXIDASE DEFECT

Chronic granulomatous disease of childhood.

EXTRINSIC ALLERGIC ALVEOLITIS

Farmer's lung.
Bird fancier's.
Mushroom worker's.
Suberosis (cork dust).
Bagassosis.
Maple bark stripper's.
Paprika splitter's.
Coffee bean.
Spatlese lung.

OTHER DISORDERS

Whipple's disease.
Pyrexia of unknown origin.
Radiotherapy.
Cancer chemotherapy.
Panniculitis.

Chalazion.
Sebaceous cyst.
Dermoid.
Sea urchin spine injury.

GRANULOMATOUS LIVER DISEASE

ICD-10CM # K75.3 Granulomatous hepatitis

Sarcoidosis.
Wegener's granulomatosis.
Vasculitis.
Inflammatory bowel disease.
Allergic granulomatosis.
Erythema nodosum.
Infections (fungal, viral, parasitic).
Primary biliary cirrhosis.
Lymphoma.
Hodgkin's disease.
Drugs (e.g., allopurinol, hydralazine, sulfonamides, penicillins).
Toxins (copper sulfate, beryllium).

GREEN OR BLUE URINE

ICD-10CM # R82 Other abnormal findings in urine

Pseudomonal urinary tract infection
Medications: triamterene, amitriptyline, IV cimetidine, IV promethazine.
Biliverdin.
Dyes (methylene blue, indigo carmine).

GROIN LUMP[67]

ICD-10CM # R19.09 Other intraabdominal and pelvic swelling, mass and lump
R22.9 Localized swelling, mass and lump, unspecified

COMMON CAUSES

Inguinal hernia.
Femoral hernia.
Lymph node.

OTHER CAUSES

Saphena varix.
Femoral artery aneurysm/pseudoaneurysm.
Psoas abscess.
Lipoma of the cord.
Encysted hydrocele of the cord (male).
Testicular maldescent (male).
Hydrocele of canal of Nuck (female).

GROIN MASSES

ICD-10CM # R22.9 Localized swelling, mass and lump, unspecified
S39.848A Other specified injuries of external genitals, initial encounter

Hernia (inguinal, femoral).
Hydrocele.
Varicocele.
Sebaceous cyst.
Hidradenitis of inguinal apocrine glands.
Neoplasm: lymphoma, metastases.
Lipoma.
Hematoma.
Reactive inguinal adenopathy, femoral adenitis.
Folliculitis, psoas abscess.
Epididymitis, testicular torsion, ectopic testes.
Aneurysm or pseudoaneurysm of femoral artery.

GROIN PAIN[14]

ICD-10CM # R52 Pain, unspecified

DIFFERENTIAL DIAGNOSIS OF GROIN PAIN

Surgery
Workers' Compensation.
Hernia.
Recurrent hernia.
Posthernia.
Orthopedic
Hip disorders.
  Acetabular labral tears.
  Avascular necrosis.
  Chondritis dissecans.
  Legg-Calvé-Perthes disease.
  Osteoarthritis.
  Pelvic stress fractures.
  Slipped femoral capital epiphysis.
  Synovitis.
Urology
Cystitis.
Epididymitis.
Nephrolithiasis.
Prostate cancer.
Prostatitis.
Torsion of testes.
Urethral extravasation.
Urinary tract infection.
Vas granuloma/fibrosis.
Dermatology
Lymphadenitis.
Psoriasis/burn.
Sebaceous cyst/hidradenitis.
Thrombophlebitis/cellulitis.
Neurosurgery
Disk disease.
Spinal injuries, inflammation, tumors.
Spondylolisthesis.
Spondylolysis.
Rheumatology
Connective tissue disorders.
Iliopsoas bursitis.
Osteitis pubis.
Systemic lupus erythematosus.
Neurology
Lumbosacral disorders.
Neurofibromatosis.
Infectious Disease
Herpes zoster.
HIV/tuberculosis.
Lyme disease.
Psoas abscess.
Sports Medicine
"Sports hernia" (adductor strains).
Gilmore's groin.

Vascular

Abscess hematoma.
Post-vein stripping.
Pseudoaneurysm.
Vascular graft.

Gastroenterology

Appendicitis/adhesions.
Diverticulitis.
Inflammatory retroperitoneal phlegmon (pancreatitis).
Meckel diverticulum.
Granulomatous colitis.

Gynecology

Cesarean section.
Cervical cancer.
Endometriosis.
Tubal/ovarian disorders.

GROIN PAIN, ACTIVE PATIENT[66]

| ICD-10CM # | S39.848A | Other specified injuries of external genitals, initial encounter |
| | R52 | Pain, unspecified |

MUSCULOSKELETAL

Avascular necrosis of the femoral head.
Avulsion fracture (lesser trochanter, anterior superior iliac spine, anterior inferior iliac spine).
Bursitis (iliopectineal, trochanteric).
Entrapment of the ilioinguinal or iliofemoral nerve.
Gracilis syndrome.
Muscle tear (adductors, iliopsoas, rectus abdominis, gracilis, sartorius, rectus femoris).
Myositis ossificans of the hip muscles.
Osteitis pubis.
Osteoarthritis of the femoral head.
Slipped capital femoral epiphysis.
Stress fracture of the femoral head or neck and pubis.
Synovitis.

HERNIA-RELATED

Avulsion of the internal oblique muscle in the conjoined tendon.
Defect at the insertion of the rectus abdominis muscle.
Direct inguinal hernia.
Femoral ring hernia.
Indirect inguinal hernia.
Inguinal canal weakness.

UROLOGIC

Epididymitis.
Fracture of the testis.
Hydrocele.
Kidney stone.
Posterior urethritis.
Prostatitis.
Testicular cancer.
Torsion of the testis.
Urinary tract infection.
Varicocele.

GYNECOLOGIC

Ectopic pregnancy.
Ovarian cyst.
Pelvic inflammatory disease.
Torsion of the ovary.
Vaginitis.

LYMPHATIC ENLARGEMENT IN GROIN

GYNECOMASTIA

| ICD-10CM # | N62 | Hypertrophy of breast |

Physiologic (puberty, newborns, aging).
Drugs (estrogen and estrogen precursors, 5-a reductase inhibitors, digitalis, testosterone and exogenous androgens, clomiphene, cimetidine, spironolactone, ketoconazole, amiodarone, ACE inhibitors, isoniazid, phenytoin, methyldopa, metoclopramide, phenothiazine).
Increased prolactin level (prolactinoma).
Liver disease.
Adrenal disease.
Thyrotoxicosis.
Increased estrogen production (hCG-producing tumor, testicular tumor, bronchogenic carcinoma).
Secondary hypogonadism.
Primary gonadal failure (trauma, castration, viral orchitis, granulomatous disease).
Defects in androgen synthesis.
Testosterone deficiency.
Klinefelter's syndrome.

HAIR LOSS[33]

ICD-10CM #	L63.8	Other alopecia areata
	L63.9	Alopecia areata, unspecified
	L64.0	Drug-induced androgenic alopecia
	L64.8	Other androgenic alopecia

GENERALIZED*

Acute blood loss.
Childbirth.
Crash diets (inadequate protein).
Drugs:
- Coumarin.
- Heparin.
- Propranolol.
- Vitamin A.
- High fever.

Hypothyroidism and hyperthyroidisms.
Physical stress (e.g., surgery).
Physiologic stress (e.g., neonate).
Psychologic stress.
Severe illness (e.g., systemic lupus erythematosis).
Cancer chemotherapeutic agents.
Poisoning:
- Thallium (rat poison).
- Arsenic.

Radiation therapy.
Secondary syphilis: "moth eaten" alopecia.

LOCALIZED†

Androgenetic alopecia:
- Male pattern.
- Female pattern.

*Diffuse, uniform loss, but many hairs left randomly distributed in area of loss.
†Most or all hair missing from involved area.

Hirsutism.
Alopecia areata.
Trichotillomania.
Traction alopecia.
Scarring alopecia:
- Developmental defects: aplasia cutis.

Physical injury: burns, pressure.
Infection:
- Fungal: kerion.
- Bacterial: folliculitis, furuncle.
- Viral: herpes zoster.

Neoplasms:
- Metastatic carcinoma.
- Sclerosing basal cell carcinoma.

Lupus erythematosus.
Lichen planus.
Cicatricial pemphigoid.
Scleroderma.

HALITOSIS

| ICD-10CM # | R19.6 | Halitosis |

Tobacco use.
Alcohol use.
Dry mouth (mouth breathing, inadequate fluid intake).
Foods (onion, garlic, meats, nuts, protein drinks).
Disease of mouth or nose (infections, cancer, inflammation).
Medications (antihistamines, antidepressants).
Systemic disorders (diabetes, uremia).
GI disorders (esophageal diverticula, hiatal hernia, GERD, achalasia).
Sinusitis.
Pulmonary disorders (bronchiectasis, pneumonia, neoplasms, TB).

HAND PAIN AND SWELLING[15]

| ICD-10CM # | 729.5 | Pain in limb |

Trauma.
Gout.
Pseudogout.
Cellulitis.
Lymphangitis.
DVT of upper extremity.
Thrombophlebitis.
RA.
Remitting seronegative symmetrical synovitis with pitting edema (RS3PE).
Polymyalgia rheumatica.
Mixed connective tissue disease.
Scleroderma.
Rupture of the olecranon bursa.
Metzger's syndrome (neoplasia).
The puffy hand of drug addiction.
Reflex sympathetic dystrophy.
Eosinophilic fasciitis.
Sickle cell (hand-foot syndrome).
Leprosy.
Factitial (the rubber band syndrome).

HEADACHE[27]

ICD-10CM #	G44.1	Vascular headache, not elsewhere classified
	R51	Headache
	G44.209	Tension-type headache, unspecified, not intractable

Differential Diagnosis

	G44.009	Cluster headache syndrome, unspecified, not intractable
	G43.909	Migraine, unspecified, not intractable, without status migrainosus
	G44.1	Vascular headache, not elsewhere classified

Vascular: migraine, cluster headaches, temporal arteritis, hypertension, cavernous sinus thrombosis.

Musculoskeletal: neck and shoulder muscle contraction, strain of extraocular and/or intraocular muscles, cervical spondylosis, temporomandibular arthritis.

Infections: meningitis, encephalitis, brain abscess, sepsis, sinusitis, osteomyelitis, parotitis, mastoiditis.

Cerebral neoplasm.

Subdural hematoma.

Cerebral hemorrhage/infarct.

Pseudotumor cerebri.

Normal-pressure hydrocephalus (NPH).

Postlumbar puncture.

Cerebral aneurysm, arteriovenous malformations.

Posttrauma.

Dental problems: abscess, periodontitis, poorly fitting dentures.

Trigeminal neuralgia, glossopharyngeal neuralgia.

Otitis and other ear diseases.

Glaucoma and other eye diseases.

Metabolic: uremia, carbon monoxide inhalation, hypoxia.

Pheochromocytoma, hypoglycemia, hypothyroidism.

Effort induced: benign exertional headache, cough, headache, coital cephalalgia.

Drugs: alcohol, nitrates, histamine antagonists.

Paget's disease of the skull.

Emotional, psychiatric.

HEADACHE, ACUTE[20]

ICD-10CM # R51 Headache

DIFFERENTIAL DIAGNOSIS OF ACUTE HEADACHE

Evaluation of the first acute headache should exclude pathologic causes listed here before consideration of more common etiologies.

Increased intracranial pressure (ICP): Trauma, hemorrhage, tumor, hydrocephalus, pseudotumor cerebri, abscess, arachnoid cyst, cerebral edema.

Decreased ICP: After ventriculoperitoneal shunt, lumbar puncture, cerebrospinal fluid leak from basilar skull fracture.

Meningeal inflammation: Meningitis, leukemia, subarachnoid or subdural hemorrhage.

Vascular: Vasculitis, arteriovenous malformation, hypertension, cerebrovascular accident.

Bone, soft tissue: Referred pain from scalp, eyes, ears, sinuses, nose, teeth, pharynx, cervical spine, temporomandibular joint.

Infection: Systemic infection, encephalitis, sinusitis, etc.

First migraine.

HEADACHE AND FACIAL PAIN[65]

ICD-10CM # R51 Headache
G44.1 Vascular headache, not elsewhere classified

VASCULAR HEADACHES

Migraine

Migraine with headaches and inconspicuous neurologic features:

Migraine without aura ("common migraine").

Migraine with headaches and conspicuous neurologic features:

With transient neurologic symptoms:

Migraine with typical aura ("classic migraine").

Sensory, basilar, and hemiplegic migraine.

With prolonged or permanent neurologic features ("complicated migraine"):

Ophthalmoplegic migraine.

Migrainous infarction.

Migraine without headaches but with conspicuous neurologic features ("migraine equivalents"):

Abdominal migraine.

Benign paroxysmal vertigo of childhood.

Migraine aura without headache ("isolated auras," transient migrainous accompaniments).

Cluster Headaches

Episodic cluster headache ("cyclic cluster headaches").

Chronic cluster headaches.

Chronic paroxysmal hemicrania.

Other Vascular Headaches

Headaches of reactive vasodilation (fever, drug-induced, postictal, hypoglycemia, hypoxia, hypercarbia, hyperthyroidism).

Headaches associated with arterial hypertension:

Chronic severe hypertension (diastolic 120 mm Hg).

Paroxysmal severe hypertension (pheochromocytoma, some coital headaches).

Headaches caused by cranial arteritis:

Giant cell arteritis ("temporal arteritis").

Other vasculitides.

HEADACHES ASSOCIATED WITH DEMONSTRABLE MUSCLE SPASM

Headache caused by posturally induced or perilesional muscle spasm:

Headaches of sustained or impaired posture (e.g., prolonged close work, driving).

Headaches associated with cervical spondylosis and other diseases of cervical spine.

Myofascial pain dysfunction syndrome (headache or facial pain associated with disorders of teeth, jaws, and related structures, or "TMJ syndrome").

Headaches caused by psychophysiologic muscular contraction ("muscle contraction headaches," or tension-type headache associated with disorder of pericranial muscles).

HEADACHES AND FACIAL PAIN WITHOUT DEMONSTRABLE PHYSICAL SUBSTRATE

Headaches of uncertain etiology:

"Tension headaches" (tension-type headache unassociated with disorder of pericranial muscles).

Some forms of posttraumatic headache.

Psychogenic headaches (e.g., hypochondriacal, conversional, delusional, malingered).

Facial pain of uncertain etiology ("atypical facial pain").

COMBINED TENSION-MIGRAINE HEADACHES

Episodic migraine superimposed on chronic tension headaches.

Chronic daily headaches:

Associated with analgesic and/or ergotamine overuse ("rebound headaches").

Not associated with drug overuse.

Headaches And Head Pains Caused By Diseases of Eyes, Ears, Nose, Sinuses, Teeth, or Skull

HEADACHES CAUSED BY MENINGEAL INFLAMMATION

Subarachnoid hemorrhage.

Meningitis and meningoencephalitis.

Others (e.g., meningeal carcinomatosis).

HEADACHES ASSOCIATED WITH ALTERED INTRACRANIAL PRESSURE ("TRACTION HEADACHES")

Increased Intracranial Pressure

Intracranial mass lesions (neoplasm, hematoma, abscess, etc.).

Hydrocephalus.

Benign intracranial hypertension.

Venous sinus thrombosis.

Decreased Intracranial Pressure

Post–lumbar puncture headaches.

Spontaneous hypoliquorrheic headaches.

HEADACHES AND HEAD PAINS CAUSED BY CRANIAL NEURALGIAS

Presumed Irritation of Superficial Nerves

Occipital neuralgia.

Supraorbital neuralgia.

Presumed Irritation of Intracranial Nerves

Trigeminal neuralgia ("tic douloureux").

Glossopharyngeal neuralgia.

HEADACHE, CHRONIC[20]

ICD-10CM # R51 Headache

DIFFERENTIAL DIAGNOSIS OF RECURRENT OR CHRONIC HEADACHES

Migraine (with or without aura).

Tension.

Analgesic rebound.

Caffeine withdrawal.

Sleep deprivation (e.g., in children with sleep apnea) or chronic hypoxia.

Tumor.

Psychogenic: Conversion disorder, malingering. Cluster headache.

HEAD AND NECK, SOFT TISSUE MASSES

ICD-10CM # R22.0 Localized swelling, mass and lump, head
R22.1 Localized swelling, mass and lump, neck

Lipoma.
Pilar cyst.
Epidermal inclusion cyst.
Dermoid cyst.
Bone cyst.
Hemangioma.
Eosinophilic granuloma.
Other: facial nerve neuroma, teratoma, rhabdomyoma, rhabdomyosarcoma, branchial cleft cyst.

HEARING LOSS, ACUTE[49]

ICD-10CM # H91.23 Sudden idiopathic hearing loss, bilateral

Infectious: mumps, measles, influenza, herpes simplex, herpes zoster, CMV, mononucleosis, syphilis.
Vascular: macroglobulinemia, sickle cell disease, Berger's disease, leukemia, polycythemia, fat emboli, hypercoagulable states.
Metabolic: diabetes, pregnancy, hyperlipoproteinemia.
Conductive: cerumen impaction, foreign bodies, otitis media, otitis externa, barotrauma, trauma.
Medications: aminoglycosides, loop diuretics, antineoplastics, salicylates, vancomycin.
Neoplasm: acoustic neuroma, metastatic neoplasm.

HEARTBURN AND INDIGESTION[61]

ICD-10CM # R12 Heartburn
K30 Functional dyspepsia

Reflux esophagitis.
Gastritis.
Nonulcer dyspepsia.
Functional GI disorder (anxiety disorder, social/environmental stresses).
Excessive intestinal gas (ingestion of flatulogenic foods, GI stasis, constipation).
Gas entrapment (hepatitis or splenic flexure syndrome).
Neoplasm (adenocarcinoma of stomach or esophagus, lymphoma).
Gallbladder disease.

HEART FAILURE WITH PRESERVED LEFT VENTRICULAR EJECTION FRACTION[30]

ICD-10CM # I50.9 Heart failure, unspecified

CAUSES OF (AND ALTERNATIVE EXPLANATIONS FOR) HEART FAILURE WITH PRESERVED LEFT VENTRICULAR EJECTION FRACTION (>45%-50%)

Inaccurate diagnosis of heart failure (e.g., pulmonary disease, obesity).
Inaccurate measurements of ejection fraction.
Systolic function overestimated by ejection fraction (e.g., mitral regurgitation).
Episodic, unrecognized systolic dysfunction.
Intermittent ischemia.
Arrhythmia.
Severe hypertension.
Alcohol abuse.
Diastolic dysfunction.
Abnormalities of myocardial relaxation:
  Ischemia.
  Hypertrophy.
Abnormalities of myocardial compliance:
  Hypertrophy.
  Aging.
  Fibrosis.
  Diabetes mellitus.
  Infiltrative disease (amyloidosis, sarcoidosis).
  Storage disease (hemochromatosis).
  Endomyocardial disease (endomyocardial fibrosis, radiation, anthracyclines).
Pericardial disease (constriction, tamponade).

HEART FAILURE, ACUTE[6]

ICD-10CM # I50.9 Heart failure, unspecified

COMMON PRECIPITATING CAUSES OF ACUTE HF

Systemic hypertension.
Myocardial infarction or ischemia.
Dysrhythmia.
Systemic infection.
Anemia.
Dietary, physical, environmental, and emotional excesses.
Pregnancy.
Thyrotoxicosis or hypothyroidism.
Acute myocarditis.
Acute valvular dysfunction.
Pulmonary embolus.
Pharmacologic complications.

HEART FAILURE, CHRONIC[10]

ICD-10CM # I50.9 Heart failure, unspecified

Myocardial disease.
Coronary artery disease.
  Myocardial infarction.[20]
  Myocardial ischemia.
Chronic pressure overload.
  Hypertension.
  Obstructive valvular disease.
Chronic volume overload.
  Regurgitant valvular disease.
  Intracardiac (left-to-right) shunting.
  Extracardiac shunting.

[20]Indicates conditions that can also lead to HF with a preserved EF.

Nonischemic dilated cardiomyopathy.
  Familial or genetic disorders.
  Infiltrative disorders.
  Toxic or drug-induced damage.
  Metabolic disorder.
  Viral or other infectious agents.
Disorders of rate and rhythm.
  Chronic bradyarrhythmias.
  Chronic tachyarrhythmias.
Pulmonary heart disease
  Cor pulmonale.
  Pulmonary vascular disorders.
High-output states.
Metabolic disorders.
  Thyrotoxicosis.
  Nutritional disorders (beriberi).
Excessive blood flow requirements.
  Systemic arteriovenous shunting.
  Chronic anemia.

HEART FAILURE, CONGENITAL HEART DISEASE CAUSES[57]

ICD-10CM # I50.9 Heart failure, unspecified

CAUSES OF CONGESTIVE HEART FAILURE RESULTING FROM CONGENITAL HEART DISEASE

Age of Onset	Cause
At birth:	HLHS.
	Volume overload lesions:
	• Severe tricuspid or pulmonary insufficiency.
	• Large systemic arteriovenous fistula.
First week	TGA.
	PDA in small premature infants.
	HLHS (with more favorable anatomy).
	TAPVR, particularly those with pulmonary venous obstruction.
	Others.
	Systemic arteriovenous fistula.
	Critical AS or PS.
1-4 wk	COA with associated anomalies.
	Critical AS.
	Large left-to-right shunt lesions (VSD, PDA) in premature infants.
	All other lesions previously listed.
4-6 wk	Some left-to-right shunt lesions such as ECD.
6 wk-4 mo	Large VSD.
	Large PDA.
	Others, such as anomalous left coronary artery from the PA.

AS, Aortic stenosis; *COA*, coarctation of the aorta; *ECD*, endocardial cushion defect; *HLHS*, hypoplastic left heart syndrome; *PA*, pulmonary artery; *PDA*, patent ductus arteriosus; *PS*, pulmonary stenosis; *TAPVR*, total anomalous pulmonary venous return; *TGA*, transposition of the great arteries; *VSD*, ventricular septal defect.

Differential Diagnosis

II

HEART FAILURE, PATHOGENIC CAUSES[30]

ICD-10CM # I50.9   Heart failure, unspecified

IMPAIRED SYSTOLIC (CONTRACTILE) FUNCTION

Ischemic damage or dysfunction:
    Myocardial infarction.
    Persistent or intermittent myocardial ischemia.
    Hypoperfusion (shock).
Chronic pressure overloading:
    Hypertension.
    Obstructive valvular disease.
Chronic volume overload:
    Regurgitant valvular disease.
    Intracardiac left-to-right shunting.
    Extracardiac shunting.
Nonischemic dilated cardiomyopathy:
    Familial/genetic disorders.
    Toxic/drug-induced damage
    Immunologically mediated necrosis.
    Infectious agents.
    Metabolic disorders.
    Infiltrative processes.
    Idiopathic conditions.

IMPAIRED DIASTOLIC FUNCTION (RESTRICTED FILLING, INCREASED STIFFNESS)

- Pathologic myocardial hypertrophy:
    Primary (hypertrophic cardiomyopathies).
    Secondary (hypertension).
Aging.
Ischemic fibrosis.
Restrictive cardiomyopathy:
    ○ Infiltrative disorders (amyloidosis, sarcoidosis).
    ○ Storage diseases (hemochromatosis, genetic abnormalities).
- Endomyocardial disorders.

MECHANICAL ABNORMALITIES

Intracardiac:
    Obstructive valvular disease.
    Regurgitant valvular disease.
    Intracardiac shunts.
    Other congenital abnormalities.
Extracardiac:
    Obstructive (coarctation, supravalvular aortic stenosis).
    Left-to-right shunting (patent ductus arteriosus).

DISORDERS OF RATE AND RHYTHM

- Bradyarrhythmias (sinus node dysfunction, conduction abnormalities).
- Tachyarrhythmias (ineffective rhythms, chronic tachycardia).

PULMONARY HEART DISEASE

- Cor pulmonale.
- Pulmonary vascular disorders.

HIGH-OUTPUT STATES

Metabolic disorders:
    Thyrotoxicosis.
    Nutritional disorders (beriberi).
    Excessive blood flow requirements:
        Chronic anemia.
        Systemic arteriovenous shunting.

HEART FAILURE, PREGNANCY

ICD-10CM # I50.9   Heart failure, unspecified

Congenital valvular heart disease exacerbated by pregnancy.
Peripartum cardiomyopathy.
Untreated thyrotoxicosis.
Hypothyroidism.
Pulmonary hypertension.
Myocardial infarction.

HEAT STROKE[1]

ICD-10CM # T67.0   Heatstroke and sunstroke

Sepsis.
Encephalitis.
Meningitis.
Brain abscess.
Malaria (cerebral falciparum).
Typhoid fever.
Tetanus.
Alcohol withdrawal syndrome.
Neuroleptic malignant syndrome (see Tips and Tricks box).
Anticholinergic toxicity.
Salicylate toxicity.
Phencyclidine hydrochloride (PCP), cocaine, or amphetamine toxicity.
Status epilepticus.
Cerebral hemorrhage.
Diabetic ketoacidosis.
Thyroid storm.

HEEL PAIN

ICD-10CM # M25.50   Pain in unspecified joint

Achilles tendonitis/tendinopathy (insertional, noninsertional).
Retrocalcaneal bursitis (superficial, deep).
Plantar fasciopathy.
Neuropathy (tarsal tunnel, posterior tibial nerve [medial calcaneal branch], abductor digiti quinti).
Calcaneal stress fracture.
Puncture wound, foreign body.
Cellulitis.
Spondyloarthropathy.
Fat pad atrophy.
Soft tissue tumor.
S1 radiculopathy.
Paget's disease of bone.
Haglund deformity.
Primary or metastatic bone tumor.

HEEL PAIN, PLANTAR[43]

ICD-10CM # M79.609   Pain in unspecified limb

SKIN

Keratoses.
Verruca.
Ulcer.
Fissure.

CONNECTIVE TISSUE

Fat
Atrophy.
Panniculitis.
Dense Connective Tissue
Inflammatory fasciitis.
Fibromatosis.
Enthesopathy.
Bursitis.
Bone (Calcaneus)
Stress fracture.
Paget's disease.
Benign bone cyst/tumor.
Malignant bone tumor.
Metabolic bone disease (osteopenia).
Nerve
Tarsal tunnel.
Plantar nerve entrapment.
S1 nerve root radiculopathy.
Painful peripheral neuropathy.

INFECTION

Dermatomycoses.
Acute osteomyelitis.
Plantar abscess.

MISCELLANEOUS

Foreign body.
Nonunion calcaneus fracture.
Psychogenic.
Idiopathic.

HEMARTHROSIS

ICD-10CM # T14.90   Injury, unspecified

Trauma.
Anticoagulant therapy.
Thrombocytopenia, thrombocytosis.
Bleeding disorders (e.g., von Willebrand's disease).
Charcot's joint.
Idiopathic.
Other: pigmented villonodular synovitis, hemangioma, synovioma, AV fistula, ruptured aneurysm.

HEMATEMESIS[67]

ICD-10CM # K92.0   Hematemesis

CAUSES OF HEMATEMESIS

Very Common
Gastric or duodenal ulcer or erosions.
Common
Mallory-Weiss tear (a laceration at the gastroesophageal junction).
Ulcerative esophagitis.
Esophageal varices.

Uncommon
Vascular malformations.
Ulcerated gastrointestinal stromal tumor.
Carcinoma of esophagus or stomach.
Aortoenteric fistula.

HEMATURIA

ICD-10CM # R31.9 Hematuria, unspecified

Use the mnemonic TICS:

T (trauma): blow to kidney, insertion of Foley catheter or foreign body in urethra, prolonged and severe exercise, very rapid emptying of overdistended bladder.

(tumor): hypernephroma, Wilms' tumor, papillary carcinoma of the bladder, prostatic and urethral neoplasms.

(toxins): turpentine, phenols, sulfonamides and other antibiotics, cyclophosphamide, NSAIDs.

I (infections): glomerulonephritis, TB, cystitis, prostatitis, urethritis, *Schistosoma haematobium,* yellow fever, blackwater fever.

(inflammatory processes): Goodpasture's syndrome, periarteritis, postirradiation.

C (calculi): renal, ureteral, bladder, urethra.

(cysts): simple cysts, polycystic disease.

(congenital anomalies): hemangiomas, aneurysms, AVM.

S (surgery): invasive procedures, prostatic resection, cystoscopy.

(sickle cell disease and other hematologic disturbances): hemophilia, thrombocytopenia, anticoagulants.

(somewhere else): bleeding genitals, factitious (drug addicts).

HEMATURIA, DIFFERENTIAL BASED ON AGE AND SEX

ICD-10CM # R31.9 Hematuria, unspecified

0 TO 20 YR
Acute urinary tract infections.
Acute glomerulonephritis.
Congenital urinary tract anomalies with obstruction.
Trauma to genitals.

20 TO 40 YR
Acute urinary tract infection.
Trauma to genitals.
Urolithiasis.
Bladder cancer.

40 TO 60 YR (WOMEN)
Acute urinary tract infection.
Bladder cancer.
Urolithiasis.

40 TO 60 YR (MEN)
Acute urinary tract infection.
Bladder cancer.
Urolithiasis.

60 YR AND OLDER (WOMEN)
Acute urinary tract infection.
Bladder cancer.
Vaginal trauma or irritation.
Urolithiasis.

60 YR AND OLDER (MEN)
Acute urinary tract infection.
Benign prostatic hyperplasia.
Bladder cancer.
Urolithiasis.
Trauma.

HEMATURIA, IN CHILDREN[6]

ICD-10CM # R31.9 Hematuria, unspecified

EXTRARENAL
Trauma.
Meatal stenosis or posterior urethral valves.
Exercise.
Menstruation or rectal bleeding.
Foreign bodies.
Cystitis, urethritis, or epididymitis.

INTRARENAL
Pyelonephritis.
Renal or bladder stones or tumors.
Poststrepotococcal or idiopathic glomerulonephritis.
Acute interstitial nephritis.
Acute tubular necrosis.
Basement membrane glomerular disease.
Renal vein or arterial thrombosis.
Recurrent familial hematuria.
Polycystic kidney disease.

SYSTEMIC
Henoch-Schönlein purpura.
Systemic lupus erythematosus.
Hemolytic-uremic syndrome.
Infectious mononucleosis.
Sickle cell disease or other hemoglobinopathies.
Bacterial endocarditis or artificial cardiac valves.
Bleeding disorders, warfarin, or aspirin.
Medications such as amitriptyline or chlorpromazine, radiocontrast dyes.
Munchausen syndrome or factitious.

HEMIPARESIS/HEMIPLEGIA

ICD-10CM # G81.00 Flaccid hemiplegia affecting unspecified side
G81.10 Spastic hemiplegia affecting unspecified side

CVA.
Transient ischemic attack.
Cerebral neoplasm.
Multiple sclerosis or other demyelinating disorder.
CNS infection.
Migraine.
Hypoglycemia
Subdural hematoma.
Vasculitis.
Todd's paralysis.
Epidural hematoma.
Metabolic (hyperosmolar state, electrolyte imbalance).
Psychiatric disorders.
Congenital disorders.
Leukodystrophies.

HEMOLYSIS AND HEMOGLOBINURIA

ICD-10CM # P55.8 Other hemolytic diseases of newborn
P55.9 Hemolytic disease of newborn, unspecified
R82.3 Hemoglobinuria

Erythrocyte trauma (prosthetic cardiac valves, marching and severe trauma, extensive burns).
Infections (malaria, *Bartonella, Clostridium welchii*).
Brown recluse spider bite.
Incompatible blood transfusions.
Hemolytic-uremic syndrome.
Thrombotic thrombocytopenic purpura (TTP).
Paroxysmal nocturnal hemoglobinuria (PNH).
Drugs (penicillins, quinidine, methyldopa, sulfonamides, nitrofurantoin).
Erythrocyte enzyme deficiencies (e.g., exposure to fava beans in patients with glucose-6-phosphate dehydrogenase deficiency).

HEMOLYSIS, INTRAVASCULAR

ICD-10CM # D59.6 Hemoglobinuria due to hemolysis from other external causes
D59.8 Other acquired hemolytic anemias

- Infections.
- Exertional hemolysis (e.g., prolonged march).
- Valve hemolysis.
- Microangiopathic hemolytic anemia.
- Osmotic and chemical agents.
- Thermal injury.
- Cold agglutinins.
- Venoms (snakes, spiders).
- Paroxysmal nocturnal hemoglobinuria (PNH).

HEMOLYSIS, MECHANICAL

ICD-10CM # D59.4 Other nonautoimmune hemolytic anemias

Prosthetic heart valves.
Aortic stenosis.
Malignant hypertension.
Metastatic adenocarcinoma.
Traumatic exercise.
Renal transplants.
Renal cortical necrosis.
Glomerulonephritis.
Thrombotic thrombocytopenic purpura (TTP), hemolytic-uremic syndrome (HUS).
Renal vasculitis.
Scleroderma.
Diabetes mellitus.

HEMOPERITONEUM

ICD-10CM # K66.1 Hemoperitoneum

Ruptured Graafian follicle.
Ruptured spleen.
Ectopic pregnancy.
Traumatic laceration of liver.
Ruptured aneurysm.
Ruptured bladder.
Traumatic laceration of bowel, pancreas, uterus.

Differential Diagnosis

HEMOPTYSIS

ICD-10CM #   R04.2   Hemoptysis

CARDIOVASCULAR

Pulmonary embolism/infarction.
Left ventricular failure.
Mitral stenosis.
AV fistula.
Severe hypertension.
Erosion of aortic aneurysm.

PULMONARY

Neoplasm (primary or metastatic).
Infection.
Pneumonia: *Streptococcus pneumoniae, Klebsiella pneumoniae, Staphylococcus aureus, Legionella pneumophila.*
Bronchiectasis.
Abscess.
TB.
Bronchitis.
Fungal infections (aspergillosis, coccidioidomycosis).
Parasitic infections (amebiasis, ascariasis, paragonimiasis).
Vasculitis: Wegener's granulomatosis, Churg-Strauss syndrome, Henoch-Schönlein purpura.
Goodpasture's syndrome.
Trauma (needle biopsy, foreign body, right-sided heart catheterization, prolonged and severe cough).
Cystic fibrosis, bullous emphysema.
Pulmonary sequestration.
Pulmonary AV fistula.
SLE.
Idiopathic pulmonary hemosiderosis.
Drugs: aspirin, anticoagulants, penicillamine.
Pulmonary hypertension.
Mediastinal fibrosis.

OTHER

Epistaxis, trauma.
Laryngeal bleeding (laryngitis, laryngeal neoplasm).
Hematologic disorders (clotting abnormalities, DIC, thrombocytopenia).

HEPATIC CYSTS[65]

ICD-10CM #   Q44.6   Cystic disease of liver
             B67.8   Echinococcosis, unspecified, of liver

CONGENITAL HEPATIC CYSTS

Parenchymal: solitary cyst, polycystic disease.
Ductal: localized dilatation, multiple cystic dilatations of intrahepatic ducts (Caroli's disease).

ACQUIRED HEPATIC CYSTS

Inflammatory cysts: retention cysts, echinococcal cyst, amebic cyst.
Neoplastic cyst.
Peliosis hepatis.

HEPATIC GRANULOMAS[3]

ICD-10CM #   K75.3   Granulomatous hepatitis

INFECTIONS

Bacterial, spirochetal: TB and atypical mycobacterial infections, tularemia, brucellosis, leprosy, syphilis, Whipple's disease, listeriosis.
Viral: mononucleosis, CMV.
Rickettsial: Q fever.
Fungal: coccidioidomycosis, histoplasmosis, cryptococcal infections, actinomycosis, aspergillosis, nocardiosis.
Parasitic: schistosomiasis, clonorchiasis, toxocariasis, ascariasis, toxoplasmosis, amebiasis.

HEPATOBILIARY DISORDERS

Primary biliary cirrhosis, granulomatous hepatitis, jejunoileal bypass.

SYSTEMIC DISORDERS

Sarcoidosis, Wegener's granulomatosis, inflammatory bowel disease, Hodgkin's disease, lymphoma.

DRUGS/TOXINS

Beryllium, parenteral foreign material (starch, talc, silicone, etc.), phenylbutazone, α-methyldopa, procainamide, allopurinol, phenytoin, nitrofurantoin, hydralazine.

HEPATITIS, ACUTE[49]

ICD-10CM #   B17.8   Acute viral hepatitis, unspecified
             B15   Acute hepatitis A
             B16   Acute hepatitis B
             B17.1   Acute hepatitis C
             B17.2   Acute hepatitis E

Infectious:
   Hepatitis A, B, C, D, G.
   Epstein-Barr virus.
   Cytomegalovirus.
   Herpes simplex virus.
   Yellow fever.
   Leptospirosis.
   Q fever.
   HIV.
   Brucellosis.
   Lyme disease.
   Syphilis.
Noninfectious:
   Drug induced.
   Autoimmune.
   Ischemic.
   Acute fatty liver of pregnancy.
   Acute Budd-Chiari syndrome.
   Wilson's disease.

HEPATITIS, CHRONIC[49]

ICD-10CM #   K73.9   Chronic hepatitis, unspecified
             B18.0   Chronic viral hepatitis B with δ-agent
             B18.2   Chronic viral hepatitis C

Chronic viral hepatitis:
   Hepatitis B.
   Hepatitis C.
   Hepatitis D.
Autoimmune hepatitis and variant syndromes.
Hereditary hemochromatosis.
Wilson's disease.
α_1-Antitrypsin deficiency.
Fatty liver and nonalcoholic steatohepatitis.
Alcoholic liver disease.
Drug-induced liver disease.
Hepatic granulomas:
   Infectious.
   Drug induced.
   Neoplastic.
   Idiopathic.

HEPATITIS, IN CHILDREN[45]

ICD-10CM #   B17.9   Acute viral hepatitis, unspecified
             K73.9   Chronic hepatitis, unspecified

CAUSES AND DIFFERENTIAL DIAGNOSIS OF HEPATITIS IN CHILDREN

Infectious
Hepatotropic viruses:
   HAV.
   HBV.
   HCV.
   HDV.
   HEV.
   Hepatitis non–A-E viruses.
Systemic infection that can include hepatitis:
   Adenovirus.
   Arbovirus.
   Coxsackievirus.
   Cytomegalovirus.
   Enterovirus.
   Epstein-Barr virus.
   "Exotic" viruses (e.g., yellow fever).
   Herpes simplex virus.
   Human immunodeficiency virus.
   Paramyxovirus.
   Rubella.
   Varicella zoster.
Other.
Nonviral liver infections
Abscess.
Amebiasis.
Bacterial sepsis.
Brucellosis.
Fitz-Hugh-Curtis syndrome.
Histoplasmosis.
Leptospirosis.
Tuberculosis.
Other.
Autoimmune
Autoimmune hepatitis.
Sclerosing cholangitis.
Other (e.g., systemic lupus erythematosus, juvenile rheumatoid arthritis).
Metabolic
α1-Antitrypsin deficiency.
Tyrosinemia.
Wilson disease.
Other.

Toxic

Iatrogenic or drug induced (e.g., acetaminophen).

Environmental (e.g., pesticides).

Anatomic

Choledochal cyst.

Biliary atresia.

Other.

Hemodynamic

Shock.

Congestive heart failure.

Budd-Chiari syndrome.

Other.

Nonalcoholic Fatty Liver Disease

Idiopathic.

Reye syndrome.

Other.

HEPATOMEGALY

ICD-10CM # R16.0 Hepatomegaly, not elsewhere classified

FREQUENT JAUNDICE

Infectious hepatitis.

Toxic hepatitis.

Carcinoma: liver, pancreas, bile ducts, metastatic neoplasm to liver.

Cirrhosis.

Obstruction of common bile duct.

Alcoholic hepatitis.

Biliary cirrhosis.

Cholangitis.

Hemochromatosis with cirrhosis.

INFREQUENT JAUNDICE

CHF.

Amyloidosis.

Liver abscess.

Sarcoidosis.

Infectious mononucleosis.

Alcoholic fatty infiltration.

Nonalcoholic steatohepatitis.

Lymphoma.

Leukemia.

Budd-Chiari syndrome.

Myelofibrosis with myeloid metaplasia.

Familial hyperlipoproteinemia type 1.

Other: amebiasis, hydatid disease of liver, schistosomiasis, kala-azar (Leishmania donovani), Hurler's syndrome, Gaucher's disease, kwashiorkor.

HEPATOMEGALY, BY SHAPE OF LIVER[67]

ICD-10CM # R16.0 Hepatomegaly, not elsewhere classified

DIFFUSELY ENLARGED AND SMOOTH

Massive

Metastatic disease.

Alcoholic liver disease with fatty infiltration.

Myeloproliferative diseases (e.g., polycythemia rubra vera, myelofibrosis).

Moderate

The above causes.

Hemochromatosis.

Hematologic disease (e.g., chronic myeloid leukemia, lymphoma).

Fatty liver (e.g., diabetes mellitus, obesity).

Infiltrative disorders (e.g., amyloid).

Mild

The above causes.

Hepatitis (viral, drugs).

Cirrhosis.

Biliary obstruction.

Granulomatous disorders (e.g., sarcoid).

HIV infection.

DIFFUSELY ENLARGED AND IRREGULAR

Metastatic disease.

Cirrhosis.

Hydatid disease.

Polycystic liver disease.

LOCALIZED SWELLINGS

Riedel's lobe (a normal variant—the lobe may be palpable in the right lumbar region).

Metastasis.

Large simple hepatic cyst.

Hydatid cyst.

Hepatoma.

Liver abscess (e.g., amebic abscess).

HERMAPHRODITISM[8]

ICD-10CM # Q56.3 Pseudohermaphroditism, unspecified
Q56.4 Indeterminate sex, unspecified

FEMALE PSEUDOHERMAPHRODITISM

Androgen exposure:

Fetal source:

21-Hydroxylase (P450 c21) deficiency.

11β-Hydroxylase (P450 c11) deficiency.

3β-Hydroxysteroid dehydrogenase II (3β-HSD II) deficiency.

Aromatase (P450arom) deficiency.

Maternal source:

Virilizing ovarian tumor.

Virilizing adrenal tumor.

Androgenic drugs.

Undetermined origin:

Associated with genitourinary and GI tract defects.

MALE PSEUDOHERMAPHRODITISM

- Defects in testicular differentiation:
  ○ Denys-Drash syndrome (mutation in WT1 gene).
  ○ WAGR syndrome (Wilms tumor, aniridia, genitourinary malformation, retardation).
  ○ Deletion of 11p13.
  ○ Camptomelic syndrome (autosomal gene at 17q24.3-q25.1) and SOX 9 mutation.
  ○ XY pure gonadal dysgenesis (Swyer syndrome).
  ○ Mutation in SRY gene.
  ○ Unknown cause.
  ○ XY gonadal agenesis.
- Deficiency of testicular hormones:
  ○ Leydig cell aplasia.
  ○ Mutation in LH receptor.

○ Lipoid adrenal hyperplasia (P450 scc) deficiency; mutation in StAR (steroidogenic acute regulatory protein).

○ 3α-HSD II deficiency.

○ 17-Hydroxylase/17, 20-lyase (P450 c17) deficiency.

○ Persistent Müllerian duct syndrome.

○ Gene mutations, Müllerian-inhibiting substance (MIS).

○ Receptor defects for MIS.

Defect in androgen action:

5α-Reductase II mutations.

Androgen receptor defects:

Complete androgen insensitivity syndrome.

Partial androgen insensitivity syndrome.

Reifenstein and other syndromes.

Smith-Lemli-Opitz syndrome.

Defect in conversion of 7-dehydrocholesterol to cholesterol.

TRUE HERMAPHRODITISM

XX.

XY.

XX/XY chimeras.

HICCUPS[42]

ICD-10CM # R06.6 Hiccough

TRANSIENT HICCUPS

Sudden excitement, emotion.

Gastric distention.

Esophageal obstruction.

Alcohol ingestion.

Sudden change in temperature.

PERSISTENT OR CHRONIC HICCUPS

Toxic/metabolic: uremia, DM, hyperventilation, hypocalcemia, hypokalemia, hyponatremia, gout, fever.

Drugs: benzodiazepines, steroids, α-methyldopa, barbiturates.

Surgery/general anesthesia.

Thoracic/diaphragmatic disorders: pneumonia, lung cancer, asthma, pleuritis, pericarditis, myocardial infarction, aortic aneurysm, esophagitis, esophageal obstruction, diaphragmatic hernia or irritation.

Abdominal disorders: gastric ulcer or cancer, hepatobiliary or pancreatic disease, IBD, bowel obstruction, intraabdominal or subphrenic abscess, prostatic infection or cancer.

Central nervous system disorders: traumatic, infectious, vascular, structural.

Ear, nose, and throat disorders: pharyngitis, laryngitis, tumor, irritation of auditory canal.

Psychogenic disorders.

Idiopathic disorders.

HILAR AND MEDIASTINAL LYMPH NODE ENLARGEMENT[30]

ICD-10CM # R59.0 Mediastinal adenopathy

Differential Diagnosis

II

DISORDERS ASSOCIATED WITH HILAR AND MEDIASTINAL LYMPH NODE ENLARGEMENT

Sarcoidosis.
Lymphoma.
Fungal disease.
Tuberculosis.
Metastatic cancer.
Silicosis, coal worker's pneumoconiosis, beryllium lung.

HIP PAIN, CHILDREN[49]

ICD-10CM #	S79.819A	Other specified injuries of unspecified hip, initial encounter
	S79.829A	Other specified injuries of unspecified thigh, initial encounter
	S79.919A	Unspecified injury of unspecified hip, initial encounter

TRAUMA

Hip or pelvis fractures.
Overuse injuries.

INFECTION

Septic arthritis.
Osteomyelitis.

INFLAMMATION

Transient synovitis.
Juvenile RA.
Rheumatic fever.

NEOPLASM

Leukemia.
Osteogenic or Ewing's sarcoma.
Metastatic disease.

HEMATOLOGIC DISORDERS

Hemophilia.
Sickle cell anemia.

MISCELLANEOUS

Legg-Calvé-Perthes disease.
Slipped capital femoral epiphysis.

HIP PAIN, DIFFERENTIAL DIAGNOSIS[36]

| ICD-10CM # | M25.559 | Pain in unspecified hip |

ARTICULAR

Inflammatory joint diseases.
Rheumatoid arthritis.
Spondyloarthropathies.
Polymyalgia rheumatica.
Degenerative joint disease.
  Primary osteoarthritis.
  Secondary osteoarthritis.
Metabolic joint diseases.
  Gout.
  Pseudogout.
  Ochronosis.

Hemochromatosis.
Wilson's disease.
Acromegaly.
Femoroacetabular impingement.
Acetabular labral tear.
Infections.
Tumors.
  Benign.
  Pigmented villonodular sclerosis.
  Osteochondromatosis.
  Malignant.
  Synovial sarcoma.
  Synovial metastasis.
Hemarthrosis.
In children:
  Toxic synovitis.
  Juvenile chronic arthritis.

REFERRED PAIN

Thoracolumbar spine.
  Intraabdominal structures.
  Retroperitoneal structures.

PERIARTICULAR

Bursitis.
  Trochanteric.
  Iliopsoas.
  Ischiogluteal.
Tendinitis.
  Trochanteric.
  Adductor.
Acute calcific periarthritis.
Heterotropic ossification.

OSSEOUS

Bone lesions.
Fractures.
Neoplasms.
Infection.
Osteonecrosis of the femoral head.
Paget's disease.
Metabolic bone disease.
Stress fracture.
Transient osteoporosis.
In children:
  Congenital dislocation of the hip.
  Acetabular dysplasia.
  Coxa vara.
  Slipped capital femoral epiphysis.
  Legg-Calvé-Perthes disease.
  Rickets.

NEUROLOGIC

Entrapment neuropathies.
Lateral femoral cutaneous nerve (meralgia paresthetica).
Lumbar nerve root compression.
L2, L3, and L4.

VASCULAR

Atherosclerosis of aorta, iliac vessels.

HIP PAIN, IN DIFFERENT AGE GROUPS[17]

| ICD-10CM # | M25.559 | Pain in unspecified hip |

COMMON CAUSES OF HIP PAIN IN DIFFERENT AGE GROUPS

Childhood (2-10 yr)
Intraarticular
Developmental dislocation of the hip.
Perthes' disease.
Irritable hip.
Rickets.
Periarticular
Osteomyelitis.
Referred
Abdominal.
Adolescence (10-18 yr)
Intraarticular
Slipped upper femoral epiphysis.
Torn labrum.
Periarticular
• Trochanteric bursitis.
• Snapping hip.
• Osteomyelitis.
• Tumors.
Referred
Abdominal.
Lumbar spine.
Early Adulthood (18-30 yr)
Intraarticular
• Inflammatory arthritis.
• Torn labrum.
Periarticular
• Bursitis.
Referred
Abdominal.
Lumbar spine.
Adulthood (30-50 yr)
Intraarticular
Osteoarthritis.
Inflammatory arthritis.
Osteonecrosis.
Transient osteoporosis.
Periarticular
Bursitis.
Referred
Abdominal.
Lumbar spine.
Old Age (>50 yr)
Intraarticular
Osteoarthritis.
Inflammatory arthritis.
Referred
Abdominal.
Lumbar spine.

HIP PAIN WITHOUT OBVIOUS FRACTURE[6]

| ICD-10CM # | R52 | Pain, unspecified |
| | M25.559 | Pain in unspecified hip |

DIFFERENTIAL DIAGNOSIS OF A PAINFUL HIP WITHOUT OBVIOUS FRACTURE

Referred pain (lumbar spine, hip, or knee).
Avascular necrosis of the femoral head.
Degenerative joint disease or osteoarthritis.
Herniation of a lumbar disk.
Diskitis.
Toxic synovitis of the hip.

Septic arthritis.
Bursitis.
Tendonitis.
Ligamentous injuries of the knee or hip.
Occult fracture.
Slipped capital femoral epiphysis.
Perthes' disease.
Tumor (lymphoma).
Deep venous thrombosis.
Arterial insufficiency.
Osteomyelitis.
Iliopsoas abscess.
Retroperitoneal hematoma.
Inguinal hernia.
Inguinal lymphadenopathy.
Genitourinary complaints.
Sports-related hernia.

HIRSUTISM

ICD-10CM #   L68.0   Hirsutism

- Idiopathic: familial, possibly increased sensitivity to androgens.
- Menopause.
- Polycystic ovarian syndrome.
- Drugs: androgens, anabolic steroids, methyltestosterone, minoxidil, diazoxide, phenytoin, glucocorticoids, cyclosporine.
- Congenital adrenal hyperplasia.
- Adrenal virilizing tumor.
- Ovarian virilizing tumor: arrhenoblastoma, hilus cell tumor.
- Pituitary adenoma.
- Cushing's syndrome.
- Hypothyroidism (congenital and juvenile).
- Acromegaly.
- Testicular feminization.

HIV INFECTION, ANORECTAL LESIONS[49]

ICD-10CM #   B20   Human immunodeficiency virus [HIV] disease
          Z21   Asymptomatic human immunodeficiency virus [HIV] infection status

COMMON CONDITIONS

- Anal fissure.
- Abscess and fistula.
- Hemorrhoids.
- Pruritus ani.
- Pilonidal disease.

COMMON STDS

Gonorrhea.
Chlamydia.
Herpes.
Chancroid.
Syphilis.
Condylomata acuminata.

ATYPICAL CONDITIONS

Infectious: TB, CMV, actinomycosis, cryptococcus.
Neoplastic: lymphoma, Kaposi's sarcoma, squamous cell carcinoma.
Other: idiopathic and ulcer.

HIV INFECTION, CHEST RADIOGRAPHIC ABNORMALITIES[49]

ICD-10CM #   B20   Human immunodeficiency virus [HIV] disease
          Z21   Asymptomatic human immunodeficiency virus [HIV] infection status

DIFFUSE INTERSTITIAL INFILTRATION

Pneumocystis jiroveci.
Cytomegalovirus.
Mycobacterium tuberculosis.
Mycobacterium avium complex.
Histoplasmosis.
Coccidioidomycosis.
Lymphoid interstitial pneumonitis.

FOCAL CONSOLIDATION

Bacterial pneumonia.
Mycoplasma pneumoniae.
Pneumocystis jiroveci.
Mycobacterium tuberculosis.
Mycobacterium avium complex.

NODULAR LESIONS

- Kaposi's sarcoma.
- *Mycobacterium tuberculosis.*
- *Mycobacterium avium* complex.
- Fungal lesions.
- Toxoplasmosis.

CAVITARY LESIONS

- *Pneumocystis jiroveci.*
- *Mycobacterium tuberculosis.*
- Bacterial infection.

PLEURAL EFFUSION

Kaposi's sarcoma.
(Small effusion may be associated with any infection).

ADENOPATHY

Kaposi's sarcoma.
Lymphoma.
Mycobacterium tuberculosis.
Cryptococcus.

PNEUMOTHORAX

Kaposi's sarcoma.

HIV INFECTION, COGNITIVE IMPAIRMENT[49]

ICD-10CM #   B20   Human immunodeficiency virus [HIV] disease

EARLY TO MID-STAGE HIV DISEASE

Depression.
Alcohol and substance abuse.
Medication-induced cognitive impairment.
Metabolic encephalopathies.
HIV-related cognitive impairment.

ADVANCED HIV DISEASE (CD4+ <100/MM³)

- Opportunistic infection of CNS.
- Neurosyphilis.
- CNS lymphoma.
- Progressive multifocal leukoencephalopathy.
- Depression.
- Metabolic encephalopathies.
- Medication-induced cognitive impairment.
- Stroke.
- HIV dementia.

HIV INFECTION, CUTANEOUS MANIFESTATIONS[42]

ICD-10CM #   B20   Human immunodeficiency virus [HIV] disease
          Z21   Asymptomatic human immunodeficiency virus [HIV] infection status

BACTERIAL INFECTION

Bacillary angiomatosis: Numerous angiomatous nodules associated with fever, chills, weight loss.
Staphylococcus aureus: Folliculitis, ecthyma, impetigo, bullous impetigo, furuncles, carbuncles.
Syphilis: May occur in different forms (primary, secondary, tertiary); chancre may become painful because of secondary infection.

FUNGAL INFECTION

- Candidiasis: Mucous membranes (oral, vulvovaginal), less commonly candida intertrigo or paronychia.
- Cryptococcoses: Papules or nodules that strongly resemble molluscum contagiosum; other forms include pustules, purpuric papules, and vegetating plaques.
- Seborrheic dermatitis: Scaling and erythema in the hair-bearing areas (eyebrows, scalp, chest, and pubic area).

ARTHROPOD INFESTATIONS

Scabies: Pruritus with or without rash, usually generalized but can be limited to a single digit.

VIRAL INFECTION

Herpes simplex: Vesicular lesion in clusters; perianal, genital, orofacial, or digital; can be disseminated.
Herpes zoster: Painful dermatomal vesicles that may ulcerate or disseminate.
HIV: Discrete erythematous macules and papules on the upper trunk, palms, and soles are the most characteristic cutaneous finding of acute HIV infection.
Human papillomavirus: Genital warts (may become unusually extensive).
Kaposi's sarcoma (herpesvirus): Erythematous macules or papules; enlarge at varying rates; violaceous nodules or plaques; occasionally painful.
Molluscum contagiosum: Discrete umbilicated papules commonly on the face, neck, and intertriginous sites (axilla, groin, or buttocks).

Differential Diagnosis

II

NONINFECTIOUS

Drug reactions: More frequent and severe in HIV patients.

Nutritional deficiencies: Mainly seen in children and patients with chronic diarrhea; diffuse skin manifestations, depending upon the deficiency.

Psoriasis: Scaly lesions; diffuse or localized; can be associated with arthritis.

Vasculitis: Palpable purpuric eruption (can resemble septic emboli).

HIV INFECTION, ESOPHAGEAL DISEASE

ICD-10CM # B20 Human immunodeficiency virus [HIV] disease
K21.9 Gastro-esophageal reflux disease without esophagitis

Candida infection.
Cytomegalovirus infection.
Aphthous ulcer.
Herpes simplex.

HIV INFECTION, HEPATIC DISEASE[49]

ICD-10CM # B20 Human immunodeficiency virus [HIV] disease

VIRUSES

Hepatitis A.
Hepatitis B.
Hepatitis C.
Hepatitis D (with HBV).
Epstein-Barr virus.
Cytomegalovirus.
Herpes simplex virus.
Adenovirus.
Varicella-zoster virus.

MYCOBACTERIA

Mycobacterium avium complex.
Mycobacterium tuberculosis.

FUNGI

Histoplasma capsulatum.
Cryptococcus neoformans.
Coccidioides immitis.
Candida albicans.
Pneumocystis jiroveci.
Penicillium marneffei.

PROTOZOA

Toxoplasma gondii.
Cryptosporidium parvum.
Microsporida.
Schistosoma.

BACTERIA

Bartonella henselae (peliosis hepatis).

MALIGNANCY

Kaposi's sarcoma (HHV-8).
Non-Hodgkin's lymphoma.
Hepatocellular carcinoma.

MEDICATIONS

Zidovudine.
Didanosine.
Ritonavir.
Other HIV-1 protease inhibitors.
Fluconazole.
Macrolide antibiotics.
Isoniazid.
Rifampin.
Trimethoprim-sulfamethoxazole.

HIV INFECTION, LOWER GI TRACT DISEASE[49]

ICD-10CM # B20 Human immunodeficiency virus [HIV] disease

CAUSES OF ENTEROCOLITIS

Bacteria
Campylobacter jejuni and other spp.
Salmonella spp.
Shigella flexneri.
Aeromonas hydrophila.
Plesiomonas shigelloides.
Yersinia enterocolitica.
Vibrio spp.
Mycobacterium avium complex.
Mycobacterium tuberculosis.
Escherichia coli (enterotoxigenic, enteroadherent).
Bacterial overgrowth.
Clostridium difficile (toxin).

Parasites
Cryptosporidium parvum.
Microsporida (Enterocytozoon bieneusi, Septata intestinalis).
Isospora belli.
Entamoeba histolytica.
Giardia lamblia.
Cyclospora cayetanensis.

Viruses
Cytomegalovirus.
Adenovirus.
Calicivirus.
Astrovirus.
Picobirnavirus.
Human immunodeficiency virus.

Fungi
Histoplasma capsulatum.

CAUSES OF PROCTITIS

Bacteria
Chlamydia trachomatis.
Neisseria gonorrhoeae.
Treponema pallidum.

Viruses
Herpes simplex.
Cytomegalovirus.

HIV INFECTION, MUSCULOSKELETAL DISORDERS[58]

ICD-10CM # B20 Human immunodeficiency virus [HIV] disease

MUSCULOSKELETAL DISORDERS ASSOCIATED WITH HIV INFECTION

Joints, Ligaments, and Soft Tissues
Painful articular syndrome.

HIV-associated arthritis.
Reactive arthritis.
Septic arthritis.
Psoriatic arthritis.
Diffuse infiltrative lymphocytosis syndrome.
Systemic lupus erythematosus.
Rheumatoid arthritis.
Vasculitis (polyarteritis nodosa, drug induced).
Immune reconstitution inflammatory syndrome.
Cellulitis and soft tissue abscesses.
Fasciitis (including necrotizing fasciitis).
Bursitis and tenosynovitis.

Muscles
HIV myopathy.
Nucleoside reverse transcriptase inhibitor (NRTI) myopathy.
Muscle infections (pyomyositis, toxoplasmosis).
Other (rhabdomyolysis, non-Hodgkin's lymphoma, myasthenia gravis, nemaline [rod] myopathy, and inclusion body myositis).

Bones
Osteomyelitis.
Osteopenia and osteoporosis.
Osteonecrosis.
Hypertrophic osteoarthropathy.

Opportunistic Infections, HIV/AIDS-Defining Neoplastic Disorders, and Other Disorders Affecting Any Part of the Musculoskeletal System in HIV Infection

Neoplasia:
- Kaposi sarcoma.
- Non-Hodgkin's lymphoma.
- Hodgkin's lymphoma.
- Leiomyosarcoma.
- Ewing sarcoma.

Infection:
- Tuberculosis.
- Disseminated Mycobacterium avium complex infection.
- Coccidioidomycosis.
- Toxoplasmosis.
- Bacillary angiomatosis.

Other:
HIV-related lipodystrophy.
- HIV wasting syndrome.

HIV INFECTION, OCULAR MANIFESTATIONS[65]

ICD-10CM # B20 Human immunodeficiency virus [HIV] disease
Z21 Asymptomatic human immunodeficiency virus [HIV] infection status

EYELIDS

Molluscum contagiosum.
Kaposi's sarcoma.

CORNEA/CONJUNCTIVA

Keratoconjunctivitis sicca.
Bacterial/fungal ulcerative keratitis.
Herpes simplex.
Herpes zoster ophthalmicus.
Conjunctival microvasculopathy.
Kaposi's sarcoma.

RETINA, CHOROID, AND VITREOUS

Microvasculopathy.
Endophthalmitis.
Cytomegalovirus retinitis.
Acute retinal necrosis.
Syphilis.
Toxoplasmosis.
Pneumocystis choroidopathy.
Cryptococcosis.
Mycobacterial infection.
Intraocular lymphoma.
Candidiasis.
Histoplasmosis.

DRUGS ASSOCIATED WITH OCULAR TOXICITY

Rifabutin.
Didanosine.

NEUROOPHTHALMIC

Disc edema.
Primary or secondary optic neuropathy.
Cranial nerve palsies.

ORBITAL

Lymphoma.
Infection.
Pseudotumor.

HIV INFECTION, PULMONARY DISEASE[9,49]

ICD-10CM #   B20   Human immunodeficiency virus [HIV] disease
       I28.8   Other diseases of pulmonary vessels

RADIOGRAPHIC APPEARANCE

Diffuse Interstitial Infiltrates

Pneumocystis jiroveci.
Mycobacterium tuberculosis, especially with advanced human immunodeficiency virus disease.
Histoplasma capsulatum.
Coccidioides spp.
Cryptococcus neoformans.
Toxoplasma gondii.
Cytomegalovirus.
Influenza.
Lymphocytic interstitial pneumonitis.
Abacavir hypersensitivity.

Focal Consolidation

Pyogenic bacterial pneumonia from *Streptococcus pneumoniae, Haemophilus influenzae.*
M. tuberculosis.
Legionella spp.
Rhodococcus equi.

Hilar Adenopathy

M. tuberculosis.
H. capsulatum.
Coccidioides spp.
Non-Hodgkin's or Hodgkin's lymphoma.
Mycobacterium avium complex.

Cavitary Disease

Pyogenic bacterial pneumonia from *Pseudomonas aeruginosa, Staphylococcus aureus,* Enterobacteriaceae.

M. tuberculosis.
C. neoformans.
R. equi.
Aspergillus spp.
Nocardia spp.
Mycobacterium avium complex.
P. jiroveci.

Nodules or Masses

M. tuberculosis.
C. neoformans.
Aspergillus spp.
H. capsulatum.
Nocardia spp.
Non-Hodgkin's lymphoma.
Kaposi sarcoma.
Lung cancer.

Normal Radiograph

P. jiroveci.
M. tuberculosis.

CAUSES

Mycobacterial

M. tuberculosis.
M. kansasii.
M. avium complex.
Other nontuberculous mycobacteria.

Other Bacterial

Streptococcus pneumoniae.
Staphylococcus aureus.
Haemophilus influenzae.
Enterobacteriaceae.
Pseudomonas aeruginosa.
Moraxella catarrhalis.
Group A *Streptococcus.*
Nocardia spp.
Rhodococcus equi.
Chlamydia pneumoniae.

Fungal

Pneumocystis carinii.
Cryptococcus neoformans.
Histoplasma capsulatum.
Coccidioides immitis.
Aspergillus spp.
Blastomyces dermatitidis.
Penicillium marneffei.

Viral

Cytomegalovirus.
Herpes simplex virus.
Adenovirus.
Respiratory syncytial virus.
Influenza viruses.
Parainfluenza virus.

Other

Toxoplasma gondii.
Strongyloides stercoralis.
Kaposi's sarcoma.
Lymphoma.
Lung cancer.
Lymphocytic interstitial pneumonitis.
Nonspecific interstitial pneumonitis.
Bronchiolitis obliterans with organizing pneumonia.
Pulmonary hypertension.
Emphysema-like or bullous disease.
Pneumothorax.
Congestive heart failure.
Diffuse alveolar damage.
Pulmonary embolus.

HOARSENESS

ICD-10CM #   R49.8   Other voice and resonance disorders

Allergic rhinitis.
Infections (laryngitis, epiglottitis, tracheitis, croup).
Vocal cord polyps.
Voice strain.
Irritants (tobacco smoke).
Vocal cord trauma (intubation, surgery).
Neoplastic involvement of vocal cord (primary or metastatic).
Neurologic abnormalities (multiple sclerosis, ALS, parkinsonism).
Endocrine abnormalities (puberty, menopause, hypothyroidism).
Other (laryngeal webs or cysts, psychogenic, muscle tension abnormalities).

HYDROCEPHALUS

ICD-10CM #   G91.1   Obstructive hydrocephalus

Head trauma.
Brain neoplasm (primary or metastatic).
Spinal cord tumor.
Cerebellar infarction.
Exudative or granulomatous meningitis.
Cerebellar hemorrhage.
Subarachnoid hemorrhage.
Aqueductal stenosis.
Third ventricle colloid cyst.
Hindbrain malformation.
Viral encephalitis.
Metastases to leptomeninges.

HYPERCALCEMIA

ICD-10CM #   E83.52   Hypercalcemia

Malignancy: increased bone resorption via osteoclast-activating factors, secretion of PTH-like substances, prostaglandin E_2, direct erosion by tumor cells, transforming growth factors, colony-stimulating activity. Hypercalcemia is common in the following neoplasms:
   Solid tumors: breast, lung, pancreas, kidneys, ovary.
   Hematologic cancers: myeloma, lymphosarcoma, adult T-cell lymphoma, Burkitt's lymphoma.
Hyperparathyroidism: increased bone resorption, GI absorption, and renal absorption; etiology:
   Parathyroid hyperplasia, adenoma.
   Hyperparathyroidism or renal failure with secondary hyperparathyroidism.
Granulomatous disorders: increased GI absorption (e.g., sarcoidosis).
Paget's disease: increased bone resorption, seen only during periods of immobilization.
Vitamin D intoxication, milk-alkali syndrome; increased GI absorption.
Thiazides: increased renal absorption.
Other causes: familial hypocalciuric hypercalcemia, thyrotoxicosis, adrenal insufficiency, prolonged immobilization, vitamin A intoxi-

cation, recovery from acute renal failure, lithium administration, pheochromocytoma, disseminated SLE.

HYPERCALCEMIA, MALIGNANCY-INDUCED

ICD-10CM # E83.52   Hypercalcemia

Lung carcinoma	(6% frequency, 35% of hypercalcemic cases)
Breast carcinoma	(10% frequency, 25% of hypercalcemic cases)
Multiple myeloma	(33% frequency, 10% of hypercalcemic cases)
Lymphoma	(4% of hypercalcemic cases)
Genitourinary cancer	(6% of hypercalcemic cases)

HYPERCAPNIA, PERSISTENT[65]

ICD-10CM # R06.00   Dyspnea, unspecified
R06.09   Other forms of dyspnea
R06.89   Other abnormalities of breathing

Hypercapnia with normal lungs: CNS disturbances (CVA, parkinsonism, encephalitis), metabolic alkalosis, myxedema, primary alveolar hypoventilation, spinal cord lesions.
Diseases of the chest wall (e.g., kyphoscoliosis, ankylosing spondylitis).
Neuromuscular disorders (e.g., myasthenia gravis, Guillain-Barré syndrome, amyotrophic lateral sclerosis, muscular dystrophy, poliomyelitis).
COPD.

HYPERCOAGULABLE STATE, ASSOCIATED DISORDERS[39]

ICD-10CM # D68.69   Other thrombophilia

Systemic lupus erythematosus in association with the presence of a lupus anticoagulant or antiphospholipid antibodies.

MALIGNANCY

Disease-related: includes migratory superficial thrombophlebitis (Trousseau syndrome), nonbacterial thrombotic endocarditis, thrombosis associated with chronic DIC, thrombotic microangiopathy.
Treatment-related: associated with the administration of various chemotherapeutic agents (L-asparaginase, mitomycin, some adjuvant chemotherapeutic agents for treatment of breast cancer, thalidomide or lenalidomide in conjunction with high doses of dexamethasone).
Infusion of prothrombin complex concentrates.
Nephrotic syndrome.

Heparin-induced thrombocytopenia.
Myeloproliferative disorders.
Paroxysmal nocturnal hemoglobinuria.
DIC, Disseminated intravascular coagulopathy.

HYPERGASTRINEMIA

ICD-10CM # E16.4   Abnormal secretion of gastrin

Decreased gastrin release inhibition from medications (proton pump inhibitors [PPIs], H_2 receptor antagonists), vagotomy.
Chronic renal failure.
Hypochlorhydria due to atrophic gastritis, gastric carcinoma, pernicious anemia.
Gastrinoma (Zollinger-Ellison syndrome).
Pyloric obstruction.
Hyperplasia of antral G cells.
RA.

HYPERHIDROSIS[8]

ICD-10CM # R61   Generalized hyperhidrosis

CORTICAL

Emotional.
Familial dysautonomia.
Congenital ichthyosiform erythroderma.
Epidermolysis bullosa.
Nail-patella syndrome.
Jadassohn-Lewandowsky syndrome.
Pachyonychia congenita.
Palmoplantar keratoderma.

HYPOTHALAMIC

Drugs
Antipyretics.
Emetics.
Insulin.
Meperidine.
Exercise Infection
Defervescence.
Chronic illness.
Metabolic
Debility.
DM.
Hyperpituitarism.
Hyperthyroidism.
Hypoglycemia.
Obesity.
Porphyria.
Pregnancy.
Rickets.
Infantile scurvy.
Cardiovascular
Heart failure.
Shock.
Vasomotor
Cold injury.
Raynaud phenomenon.
RA.
Neurologic
Abscess.
Familial dysautonomia.
Postencephalitic.
Tumor.

Miscellaneous
Chédiak-Higashi syndrome.
Compensatory.
Phenylketonuria.
Pheochromocytoma.
Vitiligo.
Medullary
Physiologic gustatory sweating.
Encephalitis.
Granulosis rubra nasi.
Syringomyelia.
Thoracic sympathetic trunk injury.
Spinal
Cord transection.
Syringomyelia.
Changes in Blood Flow
Mallucci syndrome.
Arteriovenous fistula.
Klippel-Trenaunay syndrome.
Glomus tumor.
Blue rubber bleb nevus syndrome.

HYPERKALEMIA

ICD-10CM # E87.5   Hyperkalemia

Pseudohyperkalemia.
    Hemolyzed specimen.
    Severe thrombocytosis (platelet count 0.106 ml).
    Severe leukocytosis (white blood cell count 0.105 ml).
    Fist clenching during phlebotomy.
Excessive potassium intake (often in setting of impaired excretion).
    Potassium replacement therapy.
    High potassium diet.
    Salt substitutes with potassium.
    Potassium salts of antibiotics.
Decreased renal excretion.
    Potassium-sparing diuretics (e.g., spironolactone, triamterene, amiloride).
    Renal insufficiency.
    Mineralocorticoid deficiency.
    Hyporeninemic hypoaldosteronism.
    Tubular unresponsiveness to aldosterone (e.g., SLE, multiple myeloma, sickle cell disease).
    Type 4 RTA.
    ACE inhibitors.
    Heparin administration.
    NSAIDs.
    Trimethoprim-sulfamethoxazole.
    Beta-blockers.
    Pentamidine.
Redistribution (excessive cellular release).
    Acidemia (each 0.1 decrease in pH increases the serum potassium by 0.4 to 0.6 mEq/L). Lactic acidosis and ketoacidosis cause minimal redistribution.
    Insulin deficiency.
    Drugs (e.g., succinylcholine, markedly increased digitalis level, arginine, beta-adrenergic blockers).
    Hypertonicity.
    Hemolysis.
    Tissue necrosis, rhabdomyolysis, burns.
    Hyperkalemic periodic paralysis.

HYPERKALEMIA, DRUG-INDUCED[69]

ICD-10CM #   E87.5   Hyperkalemia

IMPAIRED RENIN-ALDOSTERONE ELABORATION/FUNCTION

Cyclooxygenase inhibitors (NSAIDs).
β-Adrenergic antagonists.
Spironolactone.
Angiotensin-converting enzyme inhibitors and angiotensin II receptor blockers.
Heparin.

INHIBITORS OF RENAL POTASSIUM SECRETION

Potassium-sparing diuretics (amiloride, triamterene).
Trimethoprim.
Pentamidine.
Cyclosporine.
Digitalis overdose.
Lithium.

ALTERED POTASSIUM DISTRIBUTION

Insulin antagonists (somatostatin, diazoxide).
β-Adrenergic antagonists.
α-Adrenergic agonists.
Hypertonic solutions.
Digitalis.
Succinylcholine.
Arginine hydrochloride, lysine hydrochloride.

HYPERKINETIC MOVEMENT DISORDERS[56]

ICD-10CM #		
	F90.8	Attention-deficit hyperactivity disorder, other type
	E83.00	Disorder of copper metabolism, unspecified
	E83.01	Wilson's disease
	E83.09	Other disorders of copper metabolism
	G24.02	Drug induced acute dystonia
	G24.1	Genetic torsion dystonia

Chorea, choreoathetosis: drug-induced, Huntington's chorea, Sydenham's chorea.
Tardive dyskinesia (e.g., phenothiazines).
Hemiballismus (lacunar CVA near subthalamic nuclei in basal ganglia, metastatic lesions, toxoplasmosis [in AIDS]).
Dystonia (idiopathic, familial, drug-induced [prochlorperazine, metoclopramide]), Wilson's disease.
Liver failure.
Thyrotoxicosis.
SLE, polycythemia.

HYPERMAGNESEMIA

ICD-10CM #		
	E83.40	Disorders of magnesium metabolism, unspecified
	E83.41	Hypermagnesemia

Renal failure (decreased GFR).
Decreased renal excretion secondary to salt depletion.
Abuse of antacids and laxatives containing magnesium in patients with renal insufficiency.
Endocrinopathies (deficiency of mineralocorticoid or thyroid hormone).
Increased tissue breakdown (rhabdomyolysis).
Redistribution: acute DKA, pheochromocytoma.
Other: lithium, volume depletion, familial hypocalciuric hypercalcemia.

HYPEROSTOSIS, CORTICAL BONE[32]

ICD-10CM #		
	M48.19	Ankylosing hyperostosis [Forestier], multiple sites in spine

DISORDERS ASSOCIATED WITH HYPEROSTOSIS OF CORTICAL BONE

Progressive diaphyseal dysplasia.
Endosteal hyperostosis.
Pachydermoperiostosis.
Hypertrophic oseoarthropathy.
Thyroid acropachy.
Hypervitaminosis A.
Paget's disease.
Infantile cortical hyperostosis.

HYPERPHOSPHATEMIA

ICD-10CM #		
	E83.30	Disorder of phosphorus metabolism, unspecified

Excessive phosphate administration.
Excessive oral intake or IV administration.
Laxatives containing phosphate (phosphate tablets, phosphate enemas).
Decreased renal phosphate excretion.
Acute or chronic renal failure.
Hypoparathyroidism or pseudohypoparathyroidism.
Acromegaly, thyrotoxicosis.
Bisphosphonate therapy.
Tumor calcinosis.
Sickle cell anemia.
Transcellular shift out of cells.
Chemotherapy of lymphoma or leukemia, tumor lysis syndrome, hemolysis.
Acidosis.
Rhabdomyolysis, malignant hyperthermia.
Artifact: in vitro hemolysis.
Pseudohyperphosphatemia: hyperlipidemia, paraproteinemia, hyperbilirubinemia.

HYPERPIGMENTATION[13]

ICD-10CM #		
	L81.4	Other melanin hyperpigmentation

Addison's disease.[21]
Arsenic ingestion.
ACTH- or MSH-producing tumors (e.g., oat cell carcinoma of the lung).

Drug induced (e.g., antimalarials, some cytotoxic agents).
Hemochromatosis ("bronze" diabetes).
Malabsorption syndrome (Whipple's disease and celiac sprue).
Melanoma.
Melanotropic hormone injection.
Pheochromocytoma.
Porphyrias (porphyria cutanea tarda and variegate porphyria).
Pregnancy.
Progressive systemic sclerosis and related conditions.
PUVA therapy (psoralen administration) for psoriasis and vitiligo.

ACTH, Adrenocorticotropic hormone; *MSH*, melanocyte-stimulating hormone; *PUVA*, psoralen plus ultraviolet A.

HYPERPROLACTINEMIA[52]

ICD-10CM #   E22.1   Hyperprolactinemia

PHYSIOLOGIC

Pregnancy.
Lactation.
Stress.
Sleep.
Coitus.
Exercise.

PATHOLOGIC

Hypothalamic-Pituitary Stalk Damage

Tumors: craniopharyngioma, suprasellar pituitary mass extension, meningioma, dysgerminoma, hypothalamic metastases.
Granulomas.
Infiltrations.
Rathke's cyst.
Irradiation.
Trauma: pituitary stalk section, sellar surgery, head trauma.

Pituitary

1. Prolactinoma.
2. Acromegaly.
3. Macroadenoma (compressive).
4. Idiopathic.
5. Plurihormonal adenoma.
6. Lymphocytic hypophysitis or parasellar mass.
7. Macroprolactinemia.

Systemic Disorders

Chronic renal failure.
Polycystic ovary syndrome.
Cirrhosis.
Pseudocyesis.
Epileptic seizures.
Cranial irradiation.
Chest: neurogenic chest wall trauma, surgery, herpes zoster.

PHARMACOLOGIC

Neuropeptide

Thyrotropin-releasing hormone.

Drug-Induced Hypersecretion

Dopamine receptor blockers:
  Phenothiazines: chlorpromazine, perphenazine.
  Butyrophenones: haloperidol.
  Thioxanthenes.
  Metoclopramide.

---

[21]Accentuation on sun-exposed surfaces.

Dopamine synthesis inhibitors:
α-Methyldopa.
Catecholamine depleters:
Reserpine.
Cholinergic Agonist
Physostigmine.
Antihypertensives
Labetalol.
Reserpine.
Verapamil.
H_2 Antihistamines
Cimetidine.
Ranitidine.
Estrogens
Oral contraceptives.
Oral contraceptive withdrawal.
Anticonvulsant
Phenytoin.
Anesthetics
Neuroleptics
Chlorpromazine.
Risperidone.
Promazine.
Promethazine.
Trifluoperazine.
Fluphenazine.
Butaperazine.
Perphenazine.
Thiethylperazine.
Thioridazine.
Haloperidol.
Pimozide.
Thiothixene.
Molindone.
Opiates and Opiate Antagonists
Heroin.
Methadone.
Apomorphine.
Morphine.
Antidepressants
Tricyclic antidepressants: chlorimipramine, amitriptyline.
Selective serotonin reuptake inhibitors: fluoxetine.

HYPERSPLENISM, ASSOCIATED CONDITIONS

ICD-10CM # D73.1 Hypersplenism

Cirrhosis.
Portal vein thrombosis.
Myeloproliferative diseases.
Lymphomas.
Leukemias.
Splenic vein thrombosis.
Autoimmune disease.
Sickle cell disease.
Thalassemias.
Gaucher's disease.
Niemann-Pick disease.

HYPERTENSION, ADRENOCORTICAL CAUSES[52]

ICD-10CM # I15.8 Other secondary hypertension

LOW RENIN AND HIGH ALDOSTERONE

Primary Aldosteronism

Aldosterone-producing adenoma (APA)	35% of cases
Bilateral idiopathic hyperplasia (IHA)	60% of cases
Primary (unilateral) adrenal hyperplasia	2% of cases
Aldosterone-producing adrenocortical carcinoma	<1% of cases
Familial hyperaldosteronism (FH)	
Glucocorticoid-remediable aldosteronism (FH type I)	<1% of cases
FH type II (APA or IHA)—<2% of cases	
Ectopic aldosterone-producing adenoma or carcinoma	<0.1% of cases

LOW RENIN AND LOW ALDOSTERONE

Hyperdeoxycorticosteronism
Congenital adrenal hyperplasia.
11β-Hydroxylase deficiency.
17α-Hydroxylase deficiency.
Deoxycorticosterone-producing tumor.
Primary cortisol resistance.
Apparent mineralocorticoid excess (AME)/11β-HSD[22] deficiency.
Genetic: Type 1 AME.
Acquired: Licorice or carbenoxolone ingestion (type 1 AME), Cushing's syndrome (type 2 AME).
Cushing's Syndrome
Exogenous glucocorticoid administration—most common cause.
Endogenous.
ACTH[23]-dependent—85% of cases: Pituitary, ectopic.
ACTH-independent—15% of cases: Unilateral adrenal disease (adenoma or carcinoma), bilateral adrenal disease (massive macronodular hyperplasia [rare], primary pigmented nodular adrenal disease [rare]).

HYPERTENSION, ENDOCRINE CAUSES[52]

ICD-10CM # I15.8 Other secondary hypertension

ADRENAL-DEPENDENT CAUSES

Pheochromocytoma.
Primary aldosteronism.
Hyperdeoxycorticosteronism.
Congenital adrenal hyperplasia: 11β-Hydroxylase deficiency, 17α-hydroxylase deficiency.
Deoxycorticosterone-producing tumor.
Primary cortisol resistance.
Cushing's syndrome.

---

[22]HSD, hydroxysteroid dehydrogenase
[23]ACTH, corticotropin

AME/11β-HSD (HYDROXYSTEROID DEHYDROGENASE) DEFICIENCY

Genetic.
Type 1 apparent mineralocorticoid excess (AME).
Acquired.
Licorice or carbenoxolone ingestion (type 1 AME).
Cushing's syndrome (type 2 AME).

THYROID-DEPENDENT CAUSES

Hypothyroidism.
Hyperthyroidism.

PARATHYROID-DEPENDENT CAUSES

Hyperparathyroidism.

PITUITARY-DEPENDENT CAUSES

Acromegaly.
Cushing's syndrome.

HYPERTENSION, IN CHILDREN[6]

ICD-10CM # I10 Essential (primary) hypertension

PRIMARY

Essential hypertension.

SECONDARY

Renal
Glomerulonephritis.
Henoch-Schönlein purpura.
Pyelonephritis.
Obstruction of reflux.
Polycystic kidney disease.
Diabetic nephropathy.
Trauma.
Renal transplant or hemodialysis.
Tuberous sclerosis.
Systemic lupus nephritis.
Endocrine
Pheochromocytoma.
Cushing's syndrome.
Congenital adrenal hyperplasia.
Corticosteroid treatment.
Hyperthyroidism.
Neuroblastoma.
Ovarian tumor.
Cardiac
Congestive heart failure.
Coarctation of the aorta.
Vascular
Hemolytic-uremic syndrome.
Kawasaki syndrome.
Renal artery thrombosis or stenosis.
Neurologic
Central nervous system tumor or infection.
Central nervous system trauma or abuse.
Increased intracranial pressure.
Guillain-Barré syndrome.
Neoplastic
Neuroblastoma.
Wilms' tumor.
Pheochromocytoma.
Adrenal carcinoma.

Drugs

Corticosteroids.
Cocaine.
Sympathomimetics.
Oral contraceptives.
Phencyclidine.
Beta-blocker or clonidine withdrawal.
Lead, mercury.

Others

Iatrogenic fluid overload.
Volume overload from end-stage renal disease.

HYPERTENSIVE CRISIS SYNDROMES[69]

ICD-10CM # I13 Hypertensive heart and renal disease
I15 Secondary hypertension

Malignant hypertension.
Nonmalignant hypertension with target organ disorders:
Patient requiring emergency surgery with poorly controlled hypertension.
Hyperviscosity syndrome.
Postoperative patient.
Renal transplant patient: acute rejection, transplant renal artery stenosis.
Quadriplegic patient with autonomic hyper-reflexia.
Severe burns.
Acute aortic dissection.
Intracranial hemorrhage, ischemic stroke, or subarachnoid hemorrhage.
Hypertensive encephalopathy.
Myocardial ischemia/acute left ventricular failure.
Preeclampsia/eclampsia.
Antiphospholipid antibody syndrome.
Acute renal failure:
Scleroderma renal crisis.
Chronic glomerulonephritis.
Reflux nephropathy.
Analgesic nephropathy.
Acute glomerulonephritis.
Radiation nephritis.
Ask-Upmark kidney.
Chronic lead intoxication.
Renovascular hypertension:
Fibromuscular dysplasia.
Atherosclerosis.
Endocrine hypertension:
Congenital adrenal hyperplasia.
Pheochromocytoma.
Oral contraceptives.
Aldosteronism.
Cushing disease.
Systemic vasculitis.
Atheroembolic renal crisis.
Drugs:
Oral contraceptives.
Nonsteroidal antiinflammatory agents.
Atropine.
Corticosteroids.
Sympathomimetics.
Cyclosporine.
Erythropoietin.
Lead intoxication.
Catecholamine excess states:

Pheochromocytoma.
MAO/tyramine interaction.
Antihypertensive withdrawal.
Cocaine intoxication, sympathomimetic overdose.

HYPERTRICHOSIS[16]

ICD-10CM # L68.0 Hirsutism
L68.1 Acquired hypertrichosis lanuginosa
L68.3 Polytrichia
L68.9 Hypertrichosis, unspecified
Q84.1 Congenital morphological disturbances of hair, not elsewhere classified

DRUGS

Dilantin.
Streptomycin.
Hexachlorobenzene.
Penicillamine.
Diazoxide.
Minoxidil.
Cyclosporine.

SYSTEMIC ILLNESS

Hypothyroidism.
Anorexia nervosa.
Malnutrition.
Porphyria.
Dermatomyositis.

IDIOPATHIC

HYPERTROPHIC OSTEOARTHROPATHY

ICD-10CM # M89.40 Other hypertrophic osteoarthropathy, unspecified site

Idiopathic.
Pulmonary disease (e.g., pulmonary fibrosis, cystic fibrosis, sarcoidosis).
Bronchogenic carcinoma.
AIDS.
GI neoplasm (e.g., esophagus, colon).
Hepatic neoplasm, cirrhosis.
Cardiovascular diseases, aortic aneurysm, aortic prosthesis.
Congenital cyanotic heart disease, patent ductus arteriosus.
Pulmonary infections, bacterial endocarditis, amebic dysentery.
Inflammatory bowel disease.
Connective tissue diseases.
Lymphomas.
Thyroid acropachy.

HYPERVENTILATION, PERSISTENT[65]

ICD-10CM # R06.4 Hyperventilation

Fibrotic lung disease.
Metabolic acidosis (e.g., diabetes, uremia).

CNS disorders (midbrain and pontine lesions).
Hepatic coma.
Salicylate intoxication.
Fever.
Sepsis.
Psychogenic (e.g., anxiety).

HYPOCALCEMIA

ICD-10CM # E83.51 Hypocalcemia

Renal insufficiency: hypocalcemia caused by:
Increased calcium deposits in bone and soft tissue secondary to increased serum phosphate level.
Decreased production of 1,25-dihydroxyvitamin D.
Excessive loss of 25-OHD (nephrotic syndrome).
Hypoalbuminemia: each decrease in serum albumin (g/L) will decrease serum calcium by 0.8 mg/dl but will not change free (ionized) calcium.
Vitamin D deficiency:
Malabsorption (most common cause).
Inadequate intake.
Decreased production of 1,25-dihydroxyvitamin D (vitamin D–dependent rickets, renal failure).
Decreased production of 25-OHD (parenchymal liver disease).
Accelerated 25-OHD catabolism (phenytoin, phenobarbital).
End-organ resistance to 1,25-dihydroxyvitamin D.
Hypomagnesemia: hypocalcemia caused by:
Decreased PTH secretion.
Inhibition of PTH effect on bone.
Pancreatitis, hyperphosphatemia, osteoblastic metastases: hypocalcemia is secondary to increased calcium deposits (bone, abdomen).
Pseudohypoparathyroidism (PHP): autosomal recessive disorder characterized by short stature, shortening of metacarpal bones, obesity, and mental retardation; the hypocalcemia is secondary to congenital end-organ resistance to PTH.
Idiopathic hypoparathyroidism, surgical removal of parathyroids (e.g., neck surgery).
"Hungry bones syndrome": rapid transfer of calcium from plasma into bones after removal of a parathyroid tumor.
Sepsis.
Massive blood transfusion (as a result of EDTA in blood).

HYPOCAPNIA

ICD-10CM # R06.8 Hypoventilation

Hyperventilation.
Pneumonia, pneumonitis.
Fever, sepsis.
Medications (salicylates, beta-adrenergic agonists, progesterone, methylxanthines).
Pulmonary disease (asthma, interstitial fibrosis).
Pulmonary embolism.
Hepatic failure.
Metabolic acidosis.
High altitude.
CHF.

Defects in H_2O_2 generation: mutations in DUOXA2 maturation factor or *DUOX2* gene.
Thyroglobulin synthesis defect: mutation in thyroglobulin gene.
Deiodination defect: mutation in *DEHAL1* gene.
TSH unresponsiveness:
　$G_s\alpha$ mutation (e.g., type 1A pseudohypothyroidism).
　Mutation in TSH receptor.
Defect in thyroid hormone transport: mutation in monocarboxylate transporter 8 *(MCT8)* gene.
Iodine deficiency (endemic goiter).
Maternal antibodies: thyrotropin receptor–blocking antibody (TRBAb, also termed *thyrotropin-binding inhibitor immunoglobulin*).
Maternal medications:
　Iodides, amiodarone.
　Propylthiouracil, methimazole.
　Radioiodine.

CENTRAL (HYPOPITUITARY) HYPOTHYROIDISM

PIT-1 mutations:
　Deficiency of thyroid-stimulating hormone (TSH).
　Deficiency of growth hormone.
　Deficiency of prolactin.
PROP-1 mutations:
　Deficiency of TSH.
　Deficiency of growth hormone.
　Deficiency of prolactin.
　Deficiency of luteinizing hormone.
　Deficiency of follicle-stimulating hormone.
　±Deficiency of adrenocorticotropic hormone.
TSH deficiency: mutation in TSH β subunit gene (manifests as primary hypothyroidism with elevated TSH level).
Multiple pituitary deficiencies (e.g., craniopharyngioma).
Thyroid-releasing hormone (TRH) deficiency:
　Isolated.
　Multiple hypothalamic deficiencies (e.g., septooptic dysplasia).
TRH unresponsiveness.
Mutations in TRH receptor.

HYPOTONIA, INFANTILE, DIFFERENTIAL DIAGNOSIS[45]

ICD-10CM #　H44.40　Unspecified hypotony of eye

Cerebral hypotonia.
　Benign congenital hypotonia.
　Chromosome disorders.
　Prader-Willi syndrome.
　Trisomy.
　Chronic nonprogressive encephalopathy.
　Cerebral malformation.
　Perinatal distress.
　Postnatal disorders.
　Peroxisomal disorders.
　Cerebrohepatorenal syndrome (Zellweger syndrome).
　Neonatal adrenoleukodystrophy.
　Other genetic defects.
　Familial dysautonomia.
　Oculocerebrorenal syndrome (Lowe syndrome).

Other metabolic defects.
Acid maltase deficiency (see "Metabolic Myopathies").
Infantile G_M, gangliosidosis.
Spinal cord disorders.
Spinal muscular atrophies.
　Acute infantile.
　Autosomal dominant.
　Autosomal recessive.
　Cytochrome-*c* oxidase deficiency.
　X-linked.
Chronic infantile.
　• Autosomal dominant.
　• Autosomal recessive.
　• Congenital cervical spinal muscular atrophy.
　• Infantile neuronal degeneration.
　• Neurogenic arthrogryposis.
Polyneuropathies.
　Congenital hypomyelinating neuropathy.
　Giant axonal neuropathy.
　Hereditary motor-sensory neuropathies.
Disorders of neuromuscular transmission.
　Familial infantile myasthenia.
　Infantile botulism.
　Transitory myasthenia gravis.
　Fiber-type disproportion myopathies.
　Central core disease.
　Congenital fiber-type disproportion myopathy.
　Myotubular (centronuclear) myopathy.
　Acute.
　Chronic.
　Nemaline (rod) myopathy.
　Autosomal dominant.
　Autosomal recessive.
Metabolic myopathies.
　Acid maltase deficiency.
　Cytochrome-*c* oxidase deficiency.
Muscular dystrophies.
　• Bethlem myopathy.
　• Congenital dystrophinopathy.
　• Congenital muscular dystrophy.
　• Merosin deficiency, primary.
　• Merosin deficiency, secondary.
　• Merosin positive.
　• Congenital myotonic dystrophy.

HYPOVOLEMIC SHOCK, PEDIATRIC POPULATION[25]

ICD-10CM #　R57.1　Hypovolemic shock
　　　　　　　　R57.8　Other shock

ETIOLOGIES OF HYPOVOLEMIC SHOCK

Whole blood loss.
Absolute loss: hemorrhage.
External bleeding.
Internal bleeding.
　○ Gastrointestinal.
　○ Intraabdominal (spleen, liver).
　○ Major vessel injury.
　○ Intracranial (in infants).
　○ Fractures.
Relative loss.
　Pharmacologic (barbiturates, vasodilators).
　Positive pressure ventilation.
　Spinal cord injury.

Sepsis.
Anaphylaxis.
Plasma loss.
Burns.
Capillary leak syndromes.
　Inflammation, sepsis.
　Anaphylaxis.
Protein-losing syndromes.
Fluid and electrolyte loss.
Vomiting and diarrhea.
Excessive diuretic use.
Endocrine:
　Adrenal insufficiency.
　Diabetes insipidus.
　Diabetes mellitus.

ILIAC FOSSA PAIN, LEFT SIDED[67]

ICD-10CM #　M25.5　Pain in joint

GASTROINTESTINAL CAUSES OF ACUTE LEFT ILIAC FOSSA PAIN

Nonspecific left iliac fossa pain including constipation.
Acute gastroenteritis.
Acute diverticulitis.
Colonic carcinoma.
Colonic ischemia.
Localized small bowel perforation.

ILIAC FOSSA PAIN, RIGHT SIDED[67]

ICD-10CM #　M25.5　Pain in joint

DIFFERENTIAL DIAGNOSIS OF RIGHT ILIAC FOSSA PAIN

Gastrointestinal Causes
Nonspecific right iliac fossa pain.
Acute appendicitis.
Mesenteric adenitis.
Terminal ileitis.
Acute inflammation of Meckel's diverticulum.
Crohn's disease of the terminal ileum.
Cecal carcinoma.
Inflammatory cecal lesion (e.g., diverticulitis in a solitary cecal diverticulum).
Inflammatory lesion of the terminal ileum (e.g., foreign body perforation).
Non-Gastrointestinal Causes
Ruptured ovarian follicle (mittelschmerz).
Acute salpingitis (pelvic inflammatory disease).
Rupture/torsion or hemorrhage of an ovarian cyst.
Endometriosis.
Ectopic pregnancy.
Urinary tract infection.

IMMUNODEFICIENCY, CONGENITAL (PRIMARY)

ICD-10CM #　D80.0　Hereditary hyopgammaglobulinemia
　　　　　　　　D80.1　Nonfamilial hypogammaglobulinemia
　　　　　　　　D80.2　Selective deficiency of IgA

D80.3 Selective deficiency of IgG
D80.4 Selective deficiency of IgM

CONGENITAL (PRIMARY) CAUSES OF IMMUNODEFICIENCY

T-lymphocyte Deficiencies

DiGeorge syndrome (thymic aplasia with reduced CD4 and CD3 cells).
Purine nucleoside phosphorylase deficiency (marked T-cell depletion).

B-lymphocyte Deficiencies

Bruton X-linked agammaglobulinemia (absence of B cells, plasma cells, and antibody).
Selective immunoglobulin G (IgG) subclass deficiencies.
Selective IgA deficiency.
Hyper-IgM immunodeficiency (elevated IgM but reduced IgG and IgA).

Mixed T- and B-lymphocyte Deficiencies

Common variable immunodeficiency (leads to various B-cell activation or differentiation defects and gradual deterioration of T-cell number and function).
Severe combined immunodeficiency (severe reduction in IgG and absence of T cells).
Wiskott-Aldrich syndrome (decreased T-cell number and function, low IgM, occasionally low IgG).
Ataxia-telangiectasia (decreased T-cell number and function; IgA, IgE, IgG$_2$, and IgG$_4$ deficiency).

Disorders of Complement

C3 deficiency (congenital absence of C3 or consumption of C3 due to deficiency of C3b inactivator).

Phagocyte Defects

Chronic granulomatous disease (defect in nicotinamide adenine dinucleotide phosphate oxidase in phagocytic cells).
Chédiak-Higashi syndrome (impaired microbicidal activity of phagocytes).
Kostmann syndrome, Shwachman-Diamond syndrome, cyclic neutropenia (low neutrophil count).

IMPOTENCE[53]

ICD-10CM # F52.21 Male erectile disorder
F52.8 Other sexual dysfunction not due to a substance or known physiological condition
N52.9 Male erectile dysfunction, unspecified

Psychogenic.
Endocrine: hyperprolactinemia, DM, Cushing's syndrome, hypothyroidism or hyperthyroidism, abnormality of hypothalamic-pituitary-testicular axis.
Vascular: arterial insufficiency, venous leakage, AV malformation, local trauma.
Medications.
Neurogenic: autonomic or sensory neuropathy, spinal cord trauma or tumor, CVA, multiple sclerosis, temporal lobe epilepsy.

Systemic illness: renal failure, COPD, cirrhosis of liver, myotonic dystrophy.
Peyronie's disease.
Prostatectomy.

INCONTINENCE, FECAL[67]

ICD-10CM # R15.9 Full incontinence of feces

NORMAL SPHINCTER

Diarrhea.
Anorectal conditions:
    Rectal carcinoma.
    Inflammatory bowel disease.
    Hemorrhoids.
    Mucosal prolapse.
    Fissure-in-ano.
    Abnormal rectal sensation.

ABNORMAL SPHINCTER

Congenital abnormalities.
Anal sepsis.
Neurologic conditions.
Rectal prolapse.
Sphincter trauma.
Neurogenic (idiopathic) incontinence.

INFERTILITY, FEMALE[28]

ICD-10CM # N97.9 Female infertility, unspecified

FALLOPIAN TUBE PATHOLOGY

PID or puerperal infection.
Congenital anomalies.
Endometriosis.
Secondary to past peritonitis of nongenital origin.
Amenorrhea and anovulation.
Minor anovulatory disturbances.

CERVICAL AND UTERINE FACTORS

Leiomyomas and polyps.
Uterine anomalies.
Intrauterine synechiae (Asherman's syndrome).
Destroyed endocervical glands (postsurgery or postinfection).

VAGINAL FACTORS

Congenital absence of vagina.
Imperforate hymen.
Vaginismus.
Vaginitis.

IMMUNOLOGIC FACTORS

Sperm-immobilizing antibodies.
Sperm-agglutinating antibodies.

NUTRITIONAL AND METABOLIC FACTORS

Thyroid disorders.
DM.
Severe nutritional disturbances.

INFERTILITY, MALE[28]

ICD-10CM # N46.9 Male infertility, unspecified

DECREASED PRODUCTION OF SPERMATOZOA

Varicocele.
Testicular failure.
Endocrine disorders.
Cryptorchidism.
Stress, smoking, caffeine, nicotine, recreational drugs.

DUCTAL OBSTRUCTION

Epididymal (postinfection).
Congenital absence of vas deferens.
Ejaculatory duct (postinfection).
Postvasectomy.

INABILITY TO DELIVER SPERM INTO VAGINA

Ejaculatory disturbances.
Hypospadias.
Sexual problems (i.e., impotence), medical or psychological.

ABNORMAL SEMEN

Infection.
Abnormal volume.
Abnormal viscosity.
Abnormal sperm motion.

IMMUNOLOGIC FACTORS

Sperm-immobilizing antibodies.
Sperm-agglutinating antibodies.

INSOMNIA[61]

780.51 Insomnia with Sleep Apnea
ICD-10CM # G47.00 Insomnia, unspecified
F51.01 Primary insomnia
F51.03 Paradoxical insomnia
F51.09 Other insomnia not due to a substance or known physiological condition

Anxiety disorder, psychophysiologic insomnia.
Depression.
Drugs (e.g., caffeine, amphetamines, cocaine), hypnotic-dependent sleep disorder.
Pain, fibromyalgia.
Inadequate sleep hygiene.
Restless leg syndrome.
Obstructive sleep apnea.
Sleep bruxism.
Medical illness (e.g., GERD, sleep-related asthma, parkinsonism and movement disorders).
Narcolepsy.
Other: periodic leg movement of sleep, central sleep apnea, REM behavioral disorder.

INTESTINAL PSEUDOOBSTRUCTION[65]

ICD-10CM # K56.0 Paralytic ileus
K56.7 Ileus, unspecified
K59.9 Functional intestinal disorder, unspecified

"PRIMARY" (IDIOPATHIC INTESTINAL PSEUDOOBSTRUCTION)

Hollow visceral myopathy:
  Familial.
  Sporadic.
Neuropathic:
  Abnormal myenteric plexus.
  Normal myenteric plexus.

SECONDARY

Scleroderma.
Myxedema.
Amyloidosis.
Muscular dystrophy.
Hypokalemia.
Chronic renal failure.
DM.
Drug toxicity caused by:
  Anticholinergics.
  Opiate narcotics.
Ogilvie's syndrome.

INTRAABDOMINAL MASS LESION, NEONATAL[32]

ICD-10CM # R19.00 Intraabdominal and pelvic swelling, mass and lump, unspecified site

CAUSES OF A NEONATAL INTRAABDOMINAL MASS LESION

Complicated meconium ileus.
Dilated bowel proximal to an obstruction.
Mesenteric or duplication cyst.
Abscess.
GU causes:
  Hydronephrosis.
  Renal cystic disease.
  Mesoblastic nephroma.
  Wilms' tumor.
  Adrenal hemorrhage.
  Neuroblastoma.
  Retroperitoneal teratoma.
  Ovarian cyst.
  Hydrometrocolpos.
Hemangioendothelioma.
Hepatoblastoma.
Choledochal, hepatic, or splenic cysts.

INTRACEREBRAL HEMORRHAGE, NONHYPERTENSIVE CAUSES

ICD-10CM # I61.9 Nontraumatic intracerebral hemorrhage, unspecified

Trauma.
Anticoagulation.
Intracranial tumors.
Vascular malformations.
Bleeding disorders.
Vasculitides (e.g., polyarteritis nodosa, granulomatous angiitis).
Cocaine and other sympathomimetic agents.
Cerebral amyloid angiopathy.

INTRACRANIAL LESION

ICD-10CM # G93.89 Other specified disorders of brain

Tumor (primary or metastatic).
Abscess.
Stroke.
Intracranial hemorrhage.
Angioma.
Multiple sclerosis (initial single lesion).
Granuloma.
Herpes encephalitis.
Artifact.

INTRAOCULAR NEOPLASM

ICD-10CM # C69.9 Malignant disorder of eye, unspecified

MALIGNANT

Retinoblastoma.
Melanoma.
Reticulum cell sarcoma.
Metastatic tumor.

BENIGN

Melanocytic nevus.
Hemangioma.
Reactive lymphoid hyperplasia.

IRON OVERLOAD[39]

ICD-10CM # E83.10 Disorder of iron metabolism, unspecified

HEREDITARY IRON OVERLOAD

Hereditary hemochromatosis:
  HFE-associated (type 1).
  Non–HFE-associated:
    Transferrin receptor 2–associated (type 3).
Juvenile hemochromatosis (type 2):
  Hemojuvelin-associated (type 2A).
  Hepcidin-associated (type 2B).
Autosomal dominant hemochromatosis:
  Ferroportin-associated (type 4).
  DMT1-associated hemochromatosis.
  Atransferrinemia.
  Aceruloplasminemia.

ACQUIRED IRON OVERLOAD

Iron-loading anemias (refractory anemias with hypercellular erythroid marrow).
Chronic liver disease.
Porphyria cutanea tarda.
Insulin resistance–associated hepatic iron overload.
African dietary iron overload.[24]
Medical iron ingestion.
Parenteral iron overload:
  Transfusional iron overload.
  Inadvertent iron overload from therapeutic injections.

PERINATAL IRON OVERLOAD

Neonatal hemochromatosis.
Trichohepatoenteric syndrome.

Cerebrohepatorenal syndrome.
GRACILE[25] (Fellman) syndrome.

FOCAL SEQUESTRATION OF IRON

Idiopathic pulmonary hemosiderosis.
Renal hemosiderosis.
Associated with neurologic abnormalities:
  Pantothenate kinase–associated neurodegeneration (formerly called Hallervorden-Spatz syndrome).
  Neuroferritinopathy.
  Friedreich's ataxia.

ISCHEMIA, UPPER EXTREMITY, CAUSES[14]

ICD-10CM # S45.809A Unspecified injury of other specified blood vessels at shoulder and upper arm level, unspecified arm, initial encounter

VASOSPASM

Raynaud disease.
Medication induced: vasopressors, b-blockers.
Ergot poisoning.

INTRINSIC ARTERIAL DISEASE

- Atherosclerosis.
- Radiation arteritis.
- Azotemic arteriopathy.
- Spontaneous dissection.
- Fibromuscular dysplasia.

INFLAMMATORY DISEASES

Connective tissue disorders.
Buerger disease.
Takayasu arteritis.
Temporal (giant cell) arteritis.
Hypersensitivity angiitis.

NONINFLAMMATORY MEDICAL DISEASE

- Thrombophilic states.
- Myeloproliferative disorders.
- Cold injury.
- Hepatitis-associated vasculitis.
- Cryoglobulinemia.
- Vinyl chloride exposure.

EMBOLISM

Cardiac (most common).
Proximal aneurysm.
Arterial thoracic outlet syndrome.
Atheroembolism.
Paradoxic embolus (with accompanying septal defect).

TRAUMA

Iatrogenic.
Blunt arterial injury.
Penetrating arterial injury.
Hypothenar hammer syndrome.
Vibration.

---

[24]May have a genetic component.

[25]GRACILE, Growth retardation, aminoaciduria, cholestasis, iron overload, lactic acidosis, and early death.

ISCHEMIC BOWEL DISEASE[1]

ICD 10CM #	K55.1	Vascular disorder of intestine
	I99	Other and unspecified disorders of circulatory system

Abdominal aortic aneurysm: rupture or expansion.
Perforated ulcer or viscus.
Ruptured ectopic pregnancy (woman of child-bearing age).
Incarcerated or strangulated hernia.
Septic shock.
Intussusception.
Volvulus.
Salpingitis or tuboovarian abscess.
Torsion of the ovary or testicle.
Appendicitis.
Pelvic mass or torsion.
Pancreatitis.
Diverticulitis.
Ruptured ovarian cyst.
Renal colic.
Biliary colic.
Also consider atypical manifestations of:
- ○ Inferior wall myocardial infarction.
- ○ Pulmonary embolism.
- ○ Pneumonia.
- ○ Diabetic ketoacidosis.
- ○ Acute glaucoma.
- • Differential diagnoses are listed in order of urgency.

ISCHEMIC COLITIS, NONOCCLUSIVE[42]

ICD-10CM #	K55.1	Chronic vascular disorders of intestine

ACUTE DIMINUTION OF COLONIC INTRAMURAL BLOOD FLOW

Small Vessel Obstruction
Collagen-vascular disease.
Vasculitis, diabetes.
Oral contraceptives.
Nonocclusive Hypoperfusion
Hemorrhage.
CHF, MI, arrhythmias.
Sepsis.
Vasoconstricting agents: vasopressin, ergot.
Increased viscosity: polycythemia, sickle cell disease, thrombocytosis.

INCREASED DEMAND ON MARGINAL BLOOD FLOW

Increased Motility
Mass lesion, stricture.
Constipation.
Increased Intraluminal Pressure
Bowel obstruction.
Colonoscopy.
Barium enema.

ISCHEMIC NECROSIS OF CARTILAGE AND BONE[28]

ICD-10CM #	M89.9	Disorder of bone, unspecified
	M94.9	Disorder of cartilage, unspecified

ENDOCRINE/METABOLIC

Ethanol abuse.
Glucocorticoid therapy.
Cushing's disease.
DM.
Hyperuricemia.
Osteomalacia.
Hyperlipidemia.

STORAGE DISEASES (E.G., GAUCHER'S DISEASE)

Hemoglobinopathies (e.g., sickle cell disease).
Trauma (e.g., dislocation, fracture).
HIV infection.
Dysbaric conditions (e.g., caisson disease).
Collagen-vascular disorders.
Irradiation.
Pancreatitis.
Organ transplantation.
Hemodialysis.
Burns.
Intravascular coagulation.
Idiopathic, familial.

JAUNDICE

ICD-10CM #	R17	Unspecified jaundice
	K83.8	Other specified diseases of biliary tract
	E80.7	Disorder of bilirubin metabolism, unspecified

PREDOMINANCE OF DIRECT (CONJUGATED) BILIRUBIN

Extrahepatic obstruction.
Common duct abnormalities: calculi, neoplasm, stricture, cyst, sclerosing cholangitis.
Metastatic carcinoma.
Pancreatic carcinoma, pseudocyst.
Ampullary carcinoma.
Hepatocellular disease: hepatitis, cirrhosis.
Drugs: estrogens, phenothiazines, captopril, methyltestosterone, labetalol.
Cholestatic jaundice of pregnancy.
Hereditary disorders: Dubin-Johnson syndrome, Rotor's syndrome.
Recurrent benign intrahepatic cholestasis.

PREDOMINANCE OF INDIRECT (UNCONJUGATED) BILIRUBIN

Hemolysis: hereditary and acquired hemolytic anemias.
Inefficient marrow production.
Impaired hepatic conjugation: chloramphenicol.
Neonatal jaundice.
Hereditary disorders: Gilbert's syndrome, Crigler-Najjar syndrome.

JAUNDICE, CLASSIFICATION[3]

ICD-10CM #	R17	Unspecified jaundice

PREHEPATIC (PREDOMINANTLY UNCONJUGATED HYPERBILIRUBINEMIA)

Overproduction
Hemolysis (e.g., spherocytosis, sickle cell disease, hemolysis of the newborn, autoimmune disorders).
Ineffective erythropoiesis (e.g., megaloblastic anemias).
Hematomas.
Pulmonary emboli.

HEPATIC (UNCONJUGATED HYPERBILIRUBINEMIA)

Decreased Hepatic Uptake
Gilbert syndrome.
Drugs (e.g., rifampin, radiographic contrast agents).
Neonatal jaundice.
Posthepatitis.
Decreased cystolic binding proteins (e.g., newborn or premature infants).
Portacaval shunt.
Prolonged fasting.
Decreased Conjugation Due to Limited Glucuronyl Transferase Activity
Gilbert's disease.
Crigler-Najjar syndrome, types I and II.
Neonatal jaundice.
Breast-milk jaundice.
Chronic persistent hepatitis.
Wilson's disease.
Noncirrhotic portal fibrosis.
Drug inhibition (e.g., chloramphenicol).

PREDOMINANTLY CONJUGATED HYPERBILIRUBINEMIA

Impaired Hepatic Excretion
Familial disorders (Dubin-Johnson syndrome, Rotor syndrome, benign recurrent cholestasis, cholestasis of pregnancy).
Hepatocellular infiltrative disorders.
Liver metastasis.
Liver cirrhosis.
Hepatitis (viral, bacterial, parasitic, autoimmune, ethanol, and drug-induced).
Drug-induced cholestasis (especially chlorpromazine, erythromycin estolate, isoniazid, halothane).
Primary biliary cirrhosis.
Primary sclerosing cholangitis.
Pericholangitis.
Congestive heart failure.
Shock.
Toxemia of pregnancy.
Sarcoidosis.
Hepatic trauma.
Amyloidosis.
Autoimmune cholangiopathy.
Vanishing bile duct syndrome.
Sepsis.
Postoperative complications.

EXTRAHEPATIC

Extrahepatic Biliary Obstruction
Gallstones, choledocholithiasis.
Cholecystitis.
Tumors of the head of the pancreas (adenocarcinoma, mucinous duct ectasia, neuroendocrine tumors, metastasis).

Differential Diagnosis

II

Tumors of bile ducts (cholangiocarcinoma, Klatskin tumor: cholangiocarcinoma at the bifurcation).

Gallbladder cancer.

Tumors of the ampulla of Vater (adenoma, adenocarcinoma).

Tumors of the duodenum (adenocarcinoma, lymphoma).

Hemobilia (blood in the biliary tree).

Biliary strictures (postcholecystectomy, post-liver transplantation, primary sclerosing cholangitis).

Congenital disorders (biliary atresia, idiopathic dilation of common bile duct, cystic fibrosis).

Metastasis to the hepatic hilum.

Primary bile duct lymphoma.

Cholangiopathy of acquired immunodeficiency syndrome.

Choledochal cysts.

Infectious cholangiopathy (*Clonorchis sinensis, Ascaris lumbricoides, Fasciola hepatica*).

Chronic pancreatitis (fibrosis of the head of the pancreas).

JAUNDICE, NEONATAL[3]

ICD-10CM # P59.9 Neonatal jaundice, unspecified

PREHEPATIC

Hereditary spherocytosis.

Nonspherocytic hemolytic anemia (glucose-6-phosphate dehydrogenase deficiency, α-thalassemia, vitamin K_3–induced hemolysis, pyruvate kinase deficiency).

HEPATIC

Crigler-Najjar syndrome, types I and II.

α_1-Antitrypsin deficiency.

Sepsis.

Drug-induced.

Hypothyroidism.

Breast-milk jaundice.

Fetomaternal blood group incompatibility (Rhesus, Landsteiner groups ABO).

POSTHEPATIC

Extrahepatic biliary obstruction.

Biliary atresia.

Bile duct paucity.

Alagille syndrome.

JOINT AND PERIARTICULAR PAIN, ACUTE[23]

ICD-10CM # M25.50 Joint pain

COMMON ACUTE MONOARTHRITIS

Septic arthritis (nongonococcal, gonococcal).

Crystal arthritis (gout, pseudogout).

Reactive arthritides.

Lyme disease.

Plant thorn synovitis.

Other infections (mycobacterial, viral, soft tissue).

TRAUMA OR INTERNAL DERANGEMENT

Loose bodies.

Stress fractures.

Ischemic necrosis.

Hemarthrosis.

ACUTE MONOARTHRITIS OF POLYARTHRITIS

Psoriatic arthritis.

Enteropathic arthritis.

Rheumatoid arthritis/palindromic rheumatism.

Juvenile inflammatory arthritides.

MONOARTHROPATHIES FROM NONINFLAMMATORY DISEASE

Osteoarthritis.

Charcot's joints.

Storage diseases (hemochromatosis, ochronosis).

SYNOVIAL DISEASES

Pigmented villonodular synovitis.

Lipoma arborescens.

Synovial osteochondromatosis.

Reflex sympathetic dystrophy.

Sarcoidosis.

Amyloid.

ACUTE MONOARTHRITIS OF SYSTEMIC DISEASE

Systemic lupus erythematosus.

Vasculitides (antineutrophil cytoplasmic antibody positive and negative).

Henoch-Schönlein purpura.

Behçet's disease.

Bacterial endocarditis.

Familial Mediterranean fever.

Relapsing polychondritis.

SOFT TISSUE LESIONS

Bone Diseases

Paget's disease.

Osteomyelitis (Brodie's abscess).

Osteogenic/osteoid tumors.

Metastatic disease.

Pulmonary hypertrophic osteoarthropathy.

This table shows the causes of inflammation in any one joint (monoarthritis) and pain around the joint that presents without inflammation (monoarthropathy).

JOINT PAIN, ANTERIOR HIP, MEDIAL THIGH, KNEE[54]

ICD-10CM #	M25.50	Pain in unspecified joint
	M25.559	Pain in unspecified hip
	M25.569	Pain in unspecified knee

ACUTE

Acute rheumatic fever.

Adductor muscle strain.

Avascular necrosis.

Crystal arthritis.

Femoral artery (pseudo) aneurysm.

Fracture (femoral neck or intertrochanteric).

Hemarthrosis.

Hernia.

Herpes zoster.

Iliopectineal bursitis.

Iliopsoas tendinitis.

Inguinal lymphadenitis.

Osteomalacia.

Painful transient osteoporosis of hip.

Septic arthritis.

SUBACUTE AND CHRONIC

Adductory muscle strain.

Amyloidosis.

Acute rheumatic fever.

Femoral artery aneurysm.

Hernia (inguinal or femoral).

Iliopectineal bursitis.

Iliopsoas tendinitis.

Inguinal lymphadenopathy.

Osteochondromatosis.

Osteomyelitis.

Osteitis deformans (Paget's disease).

Osteomalacia (pseudofracture).

Postherpetic neuralgia.

Sterile synovitis (e.g., RA, psoriatic, SLE).

JOINT PAIN, HIP, LATERAL THIGH[54]

ICD-10CM #	S79.919A	Unspecified injury of unspecified hip, initial encounter
	S79.929A	Unspecified injury of unspecified thigh, initial encounter
	M25.9	Joint disorder, unspecified

ACUTE

Herpes zoster.

Iliotibial tendinitis.

Impacted fracture of femoral neck.

Lateral femoral cutaneous neuropathy (meralgia paresthetica).

Radiculopathy: L4-5.

Trochanteric avulsion fracture (greater trochanter).

Trochanteric bursitis.

Trochanteric fracture.

SUBACUTE AND CHRONIC

Lateral femoral cutaneous neuropathy (meralgia paresthetica).

Osteomyelitis.

Postherpetic neuralgia.

Radiculopathy: L4-5.

Tumors.

JOINT PAIN, POLYARTICULAR

| **ICD-10CM #** | M25.50 | Pain in unspecified joint |

Osteoarthritis.

RA.

Fibromyalgia.

Viral syndrome (e.g., human parvovirus B19 infection).
SLE.
Psoriatic arthritis.
Ankylosing spondylitis.

JOINT PAIN, POSTERIOR HIPS, THIGH, BUTTOCKS[54]

ICD-10CM #	M25.50	Pain in unspecified joint
	M25.559	Pain in unspecified hip
	M25.569	Pain in unspecified knee

ACUTE

Gluteal muscle strain.
Herpes zoster.
Ischial bursitis.
Ischial or sacral fracture.
Osteomalacia (pseudofracture).
Sciatic neuropathy.
Radiculopathy: L5-S1.

SUBACUTE AND CHRONIC

Gluteal muscle strain.
Ischial bursitis.
Lumbar spinal stenosis.
Osteoarthritis of hip.
Osteitis deformans (Paget's disease).
Osteomyelitis.
Osteochondromatosis.
Osteomalacia (pseudofracture).
Postherpetic neuralgia.
Radiculopathy: L5-S1.
Tumors.

JOINT SWELLING

| ICD-10CM # | M25.40 | Effusion, unspecified joint |

Trauma.
Osteoarthritis.
Gout.
Pyogenic arthritis.
Pseudogout.
RA.
Viral syndrome.

JUGULAR VENOUS DISTENTION

| ICD-10CM # | I99.8 | Other disorder of circulatory system |

Right-sided heart failure.
Cardiac tamponade.
Constrictive pericarditis.
Goiter.
Tension pneumothorax.
Pulmonary hypertension.
Cardiomyopathy (restrictive).
Superior vena cava syndrome.
Valsalva maneuver.
Right atrial myxoma.
COPD.

KERATITIS, NONINFECTIOUS

| ICD-10CM # | H16.9 | Unspecified keratitis |

Collagen vascular disease.
Atopic keratoconjunctivitis.
Chemical injury.
Thermal injury.
Ectropion/entropion.
Lid defects.
Exophthalmos.
Keratoconjunctivitis sicca.
Erythema multiforme.
Mucous membrane pemphigoid.
DM (delayed epithelial healing).
Neuroparalytic (cranial nerve VII).
Neurotrophic (diabetes, cranial nerve V).

KIDNEY ENLARGEMENT, UNILATERAL[67]

| ICD-10CM # | N13.30 | Unspecified hydronephrosis |

Hydronephrosis (may be bilateral).
Polycystic kidney (may be bilateral).
Simple cyst of kidney.
Renal cell carcinoma.
Pyonephrosis (may be bilateral).
Acute renal vein thrombosis.

KNEE PAIN[54]

ICD-10CM #	S83.419A	Sprain of medial collateral ligament of unspecified knee, initial encounter
	S83.509A	Sprain of unspecified cruciate ligament of unspecified knee, initial encounter
	M23.50	Chronic instability of knee, unspecified knee
	M23.8X9	Other internal derangements of unspecified knee
	S83.289A	Other tear of lateral meniscus, current injury, unspecified knee, initial encounter
	S83.249A	Other tear of medial meniscus, current injury, unspecified knee, initial encounter
	M25.669	Stiffness of unspecified knee, not elsewhere classified

DIFFUSE

Articular.
Anterior.
Prepatellar bursitis.
Patellar tendon enthesopathy.
Chondromalacia patellae.

Patellofemoral osteoarthritis.
Cruciate ligament injury.
Medial plica syndrome.

MEDIAL

Anserine bursitis.
Spontaneous osteonecrosis.
Osteoarthritis.
Medial meniscal tear.
Medial collateral ligament bursitis.
Referred pain from hip and L3.
Fibromyalgia.

LATERAL

Iliotibial band syndrome.
Meniscal cyst.
Lateral meniscal tear.
Collateral ligament.
Peroneal tenosynovitis.

POSTERIOR

Popliteal cyst (Baker's cyst).
Tendinitis.
Aneurysms, ganglions, sarcoma.

KNEE PAIN, IN DIFFERENT AGE GROUPS[17]

| ICD-10CM # | M25.569 | Pain in unspecified knee |

COMMON CAUSES OF KNEE PAIN IN DIFFERENT AGE GROUPS

Childhood (2-10 yr)
Intraarticular
Juvenile arthritis.
Osteochondritis dissecans.
Infection.
Torn discoid meniscus.
Periarticular
Osteomyelitis.
Referred
Perthes' disease.
Irritable hip.
Adolescence (10-18 yr)
Intraarticular
Osteochondritis dissecans.
Torn meniscus.
Anterior knee pain syndrome.
Patellar instability.
Periarticular
Osgood–Schlatter disease.
Sinding–Larsen–Johansson syndrome.
Osteomyelitis.
Bone tumors.
Referred
Slipped upper femoral epiphysis.
Early Adulthood (18-30 yr)
Intraarticular
Torn meniscus.
Patellar instability.
Anterior knee pain syndrome.
Inflammatory arthritis.
Periarticular
Ligament injuries.
Bursitis.
Adulthood (30-50 yr)
Intraarticular
Degenerate meniscal tears.

Osteoarthritis.
Inflammatory arthritis.
Periarticular
Bursitis.
Referred
Osteoarthritis of hip.
Spinal disorders.
Old Age (>50 yr)
Intraarticular
Osteoarthritis.
Inflammatory arthritis.
Periarticular
Bursitis.
Referred
Osteoarthritis of hip.
Spinal disorders.

LARGE BOWEL STRICTURE[32]

ICD-10CM # S36.5 Injury of colon

CAUSES OF LARGE BOWEL STRICTURES

Physiologic:
    Spasm.
    Distended bladder.
Maligant:
    Annular carcinoma.
    Scirrhous carcinoma.
    Lymphoma.
Diverticular disease:
    Muscle thickening.
    Pericolic abscess.
    Superimposed malignancy.
Ischemia.
Radiation colitis.
Inflammatory bowel disease:
    Ulcerative colitis.
    Crohn's disease.
    Tuberculosis.
    Lymphogranuloma venereum.
    Amebiasis.
Extrinsic disease:
    Intraabdominal masses.
    Metastatic carcinoma.
    Endometriosis.
    Pelvic lipomatosis.
    Cholecystitis.
    Pancreatitis.
Miscellaneous:
    Postoperative anastomosis.
    Trauma.
    Hirschsprung's disease.

LEFT AXIS DEVIATION[44]

ICD-10CM #	I44.7	Left bundle-branch block, unspecified
	I44.4	Left anterior fascicular block
	I44.5	Left posterior fascicular block
	I44.60	Unspecified fascicular block
	I44.69	Other fascicular block

Normal variation.
Left anterior fascicular block (hemiblock).
Left bundle branch block.
Left ventricular hypertrophy.

Mechanical shifts causing a horizontal heart, high diaphragm, pregnancy, ascites.
Some forms of ventricular tachycardia.
Endocardial cushion defects and other congenital heart disease.

LEFT BUNDLE BRANCH BLOCK

ICD-10CM # I44.7 Left bundle-branch block, unspecified

Ischemic heart disease.
Electrolyte abnormalities (e.g., hyperkalemia).
Cardiomyopathy.
Idiopathic.
LVH.
Pulmonary embolism.
Cardiac trauma.
Bacterial endocarditis.

LEG CRAMPS, NOCTURNAL

ICD-10CM # R25.2 Cramp and spasm

Diabetic neuropathy.
Medications.
Electrolyte abnormalities (hypokalemia, hyponatremia, hypocalcemia, hyperkalemia, hypophosphatemia).
Respiratory alkalosis.
Uremia.
Hemodialysis.
Peripheral nerve injury.
ALS.
Alcohol use.
Heat cramps.
Vitamin B_{12} deficiency.
Hyperthyroidism.
Contractures.
DVT.
Hypoglycemia.
Peripheral vascular insufficiency.
Baker's cyst.

LEG LENGTH DISCREPANCIES[46]

ICD-10CM #	M21.759	Unequal limb length (acquired), unspecified femur
	M21.769	Unequal limb length (acquired), unspecified tibia and fibula
	Q72.899	Other reduction defects of unspecified lower limb

CONGENITAL

Proximal femoral local deficiency.
Coxa vara.
Hemiatrophy-hemihypertrophy (anisomelia).
Developmental dysplasia of the hip.

DEVELOPMENTAL

Legg-Calvé-Perthes disease.

NEUROMUSCULAR

Polio.
Cerebral palsy (hemiplegia).

INFECTIOUS

Pyogenic osteomyelitis with physeal damage.

TRAUMA

Physeal injury with premature closure.
Overgrowth.
Malunion (shortening).

TUMOR

Physeal destruction.
Radiation-induced physeal injury.
Overgrowth.

LEG MOVEMENT WHEN STANDING, INVOLUNTARY

ICD-10CM # R25.8 Other abnormal involuntary movements

Benign essential tremor.
Orthostatic tremor.
Spastic ataxia.
Cerebellar truncal tremor.
Postanoxic myoclonus.

LEG PAIN WITH EXERCISE

ICD-10CM # R25.2 Cramp and spasm

Shin splints.
Arteriosclerosis obliterans.
Neurogenic (spinal cord compression or ischemia).
Venous claudication.
Popliteal cyst.
DVT.
Thromboangiitis obliterans.
Adventitial cysts.
Popliteal artery entrapment syndrome.
McArdle syndrome.

LEG SWELLING[1]

ICD-10CM # R60.0

Deep vein thrombosis.
Cellulitis.
Baker cyst rupture or inflammation.
Congestive heart failure.
Renal failure.
Liver failure.
Inferior vena cava compression.
Musculoskeletal trauma.
Polyarteritis nodosa.
Erythema nodosum.
Myositis.
Tendinitis.
Lymphedema.
Superficial thrombophlebitis.
Compartment syndrome.

LEG ULCERS[54]

ICD-10CM # I70.25 Atherosclerosis of native arteries of other extremities with ulceration

L97.909	Non-pressure chronic ulcer of unspecified part of unspecified lower leg with unspecified severity

VASCULAR

Arterial: arteriosclerosis, thromboangiitis obliterans, AV malformation, cholesterol emboli.
Venous: superficial varicosities, incompetent perforators, DVT, lymphatic abnormalities.

VASCULITIS HEMATOLOGIC

Sickle cell anemia, thalassemia, polycythemia vera, leukemia, cold agglutinin disease.
Macroglobulinemia, protein C and protein S deficiency, cryoglobulinemia, lupus anticoagulant, antiphospholipid syndrome.

INFECTIOUS

Fungal: Blastomycosis, coccidioidomycosis, histoplasmosis, sporotrichosis.
Bacterial: Furuncle, ecthyma, septic emboli.
Protozoal: leishmaniasis.

METABOLIC

Necrobiosis lipoidica diabeticorum.
Localized bullous pemphigoid.
Gout, calcinosis cutis, Gaucher's disease.

TUMORS

Basal cell carcinoma, squamous cell carcinoma, melanoma.
Mycosis fungoides, Kaposi's sarcoma, metastatic neoplasms.

TRAUMA

Burns, cold injury, radiation dermatitis.
Insect bites.
Factitial, excessive pressure.

NEUROPATHIC

Diabetic trophic ulcers.
Tabes dorsalis, syringomyelia.

DRUGS

Warfarin, IV colchicine extravasation, methotrexate, halogens, ergotism, hydroxyurea.

PANNICULITIS

Weber-Christian disease.
Pancreatic fat necrosis, alpha-antitrypsinase deficiency.

LEPTOMENINGEAL LESIONS

ICD-10CM # G03.9 Leptomeningitis

Metastases.
Multiple sclerosis.
Bacterial or viral meningitis.
Vasculitis.
Lyme disease.
Tuberculosis.
Fungal infections (e.g., *Cryptococcus*).
Sarcoidosis.
Wegener's granulomatosis.
Neurocysticercosis.

Rheumatoid nodules.
Histiocytosis.

LEUKOCORIA

ICD-10CM # H57.9 Unspecified disorder of eye and adnexa

Cataract.
Retinal detachment.
Retinoblastoma.
Retinal telangiectasia.
Retrolenticular vascularized membrane.
Familial exudative vitreoretinopathy.

LID RETRACTION, CAUSES[41]

ICD-10CM # H02.539 Eyelid retraction unspecified eye, unspecified lid

Thyroid eye disease.
Neurogenic:
    Contralateral unilateral ptosis.
    Unopposed levator action due to facial palsy.
    3rd nerve misdirection.
    Marcus Gunn jaw-winking syndrome.
    Collier sign of the dorsal midbrain (Parinaud syndrome).
    Infantile hydrocephalus (setting sun sign).
    Parkinsonism.
    Sympathomimetic drops.
Mechanical:
    Surgical over-correction of ptosis.
    Scarring of upper lid skin.
Congenital:
    Isolated.
    Duane retraction syndrome.
    Down syndrome.
    Transient "eye popping" reflex in normal infants.
Miscellaneous:
    Prominent globe (pseudo-lid retraction).
    Uremia (Summerskill sign).
    Idiopathic.

LIGHT-NEAR DISSOCIATION[11]

ICD-10CM # varies with specific diagnosis

CAUSES OF LIGHT-NEAR DISSOCIATION

Unilateral
Afferent conduction defect.
Adie pupil.
Herpes zoster ophthalmicus.
Aberrant regeneration of the third cranial nerve.
Bilateral
Neurosyphilis.
Type 1 diabetes mellitus.
Myotonic dystrophy.
Parinaud (dorsal midbrain) syndrome.
Familial amyloidosis.
Encephalitis.
Chronic alcoholism.

LIMB ISCHEMIA, ACUTE, NONTRAUMATIC[14]

ICD-10CM # Atherosclerosis of arteries of extremities

CAUSES OF NONTRAUMATIC ACUTE LIMB ISCHEMIA

Atherosclerotic
In situ thrombosis.
Atheroembolism from thoracic aortic aneurysm/abdominal aortic aneurysm.
Femoral/popliteal aneurysm with or without compression.
Dissection.
Nonatherosclerotic
Embolism from cardiac thrombosis (atrial fibrillation, post–myocardial infarction akinesis).
Graft thrombosis, graft aneurysm.
Mycotic emboli.
Raynaud syndrome.
Arteritis with thrombosis.
Inherited and acquired hypercoagulable states.
Drug-induced vasospasm.
External compression (Baker cyst, popliteal entrapment).
Mimics
Phlegmasia cerulea dolens.
Acute neuropathy.
Hypovolemia.
Systemic shock.

LIMP

ICD-10CM #		
	R26.0	Ataxic gait
	R26.1	Paralytic gait
	R26.89	Other abnormalities of gait and mobility
	R26.9	Unspecified abnormalities of gait and mobility
	M25.80	Other specified joint disorders, unspecified joint
	F44.4	Conversion disorder with motor symptom or deficit
	F44.6	Conversion disorder with sensory symptom or deficit

Degenerative joint disease, osteochondritis dissecans, chondromalacia patellae.
Trauma to extremities, vertebral disk, hips.
Poorly fitting shoes, foreign body in shoe, unequal leg length.
Splinter in foot.
Joint infection (septic arthritis, osteomyelitis), viral arthritis.
Abdominal pain (e.g., appendicitis, incarcerated hernia), testicular torsion.
Polio, neuromuscular disorders, Guillain-Barré syndrome, multiple sclerosis.
Osgood-Schlatter disease.
Legg-Calvé-Perthes disease.
Factitious, somatization syndrome.
Neoplasm (local or metastatic).
Other: diskitis, periostitis, sickle cell disease, hemophilia.

LIMPING, PEDIATRIC AGE[46]

ICD-10CM #		
	R26.0	Ataxic gait
	R26.1	Paralytic gait
	R26.89	Other abnormalities of gait and mobility

R26.9	Unspecified abnormalities of gait and mobility

TODDLER (1-3 YR)

Infection:
  Septic arthritis:
    Hip.
    Knee.
  Osteomyelitis.
  Diskitis.
Occult trauma:
  Toddler's fracture.
Neoplasia.

CHILDHOOD (4-10 YR)

Infection:
  Septic arthritis:
    ■ Hip.
    ■ Knee.
  Osteomyelitis.
  Diskitis.
  Transient synovitis, hip.
LCPD.
Tarsal coalition.
Rheumatologic disorder:
  JRA.
Trauma.
Neoplasia.

ADOLESCENCE (11 + YR)

● SCFE.
● Rheumatologic disorder:
  JRA.
Trauma.
Tarsal coalition.
Hip dislocation (DDH).
Neoplasia.

DDH, Developmental dysplasia of the hip; *JRA*, juvenile RA; *LCPD*, Legg-Calvé-Perthes disease; *SCFE*, slipped capital femoral epiphysis.

LIVEDO RETICULARIS

ICD-10CM # L95.0 Livedoid vasculitis

Emboli (SBE, left atrial myxoma, cholesterol emboli).
Thrombocythemia or polycythemia.
Antiphospholipid antibody syndrome.
Cryoglobulinemia, cryofibrinogenemia.
Leukocytoclastic vasculitis.
SLE, RA, dermatomyositis.
Pancreatitis.
Drugs (quinine, quinidine, amantadine, catecholamines).
Physiologic (cutis marmorata).
Congenital.

LIVER DISEASE, PREGNANCY[67]

ICD-10CM # K75.89 Other specified inflammatory liver diseases

INCIDENTAL TO PREGNANCY

Viral hepatitis.
Alcohol related.
Autoimmune chronic active hepatitis.

RELATED TO PREGNANCY (POSSIBLY INFLUENCED BY HORMONES PRESENT IN PREGNANCY)

● Complicated gallstone disease.
● Hepatic adenoma.
● Focal nodular hyperplasia.
● Budd-Chiari syndrome.

SPECIFIC TO PREGNANCY

● Severe hyperemesis gravidarum.
● Benign intrahepatic cholestasis.
● Acute fatty liver of pregnancy.
● Preeclampsia (HELLP).

LIVER LESIONS, BENIGN, OFTEN CONFUSED WITH MALIGNANCY

| **ICD-10CM #** | K76.1 | Chronic passive congestion of liver |
| | K76.89 | Other specified diseases of liver |

Fatty infiltration.
Adenoma.
Hemangioma.
Cysts.
Flow artifacts.
Focal nodular hyperplasia.
Nonenhanced vessels.

LOW-VOLTAGE ECG

ICD-10CM # R94.31 Abnormal electrocardiogram [ECG] [EKG]

Hypothyroidism.
Obesity.
Pericardial effusion.
Anasarca.
Pleural effusion.
Pneumothorax.
Amyloidosis.
Aortic stenosis.

LUNG CANCER, OCCUPATIONAL CAUSES[32]

ICD-10CM # C34.90 Malignant neoplasm of unspecified part of unspecified bronchus or lung

CAUSES OF OCCUPATIONAL LUNG CANCER

Asbestos	Lagging, insulation
Arsenic	Metal smelting, pesticide manufacture
Beryllium	Electronics, dental prosthetic manufacture
Chromium	Coloring pigment production, electroplating
Nickel	Electroplating
Silica	Grinding, quarrying, sandblasting
Radon	Mining
Uranium	Mining

LUNG DISEASE AND GASTROINTESTINAL AND LIVER INVOLVEMENT[51]

ICD-10CM # codes vary with specific diagnosis

ESOPHAGEAL REFLUX

Aspiration pneumonia.
Asthma.
Scleroderma.
Bronchitis.
Bronchiectasis.
Cough.
Pulmonary fibrosis.
Mycobacterial disease.

INFLAMMATORY BOWEL DISEASE

Bronchitis.
Bronchiectasis.
Bronchiolitis.
Colobronchial fistula.
Desquamative interstitial lung disease.
Drug reactions for agents that treat inflammatory bowel disease.
Eosinophilic lung disease.
Interstitial lung disease.
Necrobiotic nodules.
Obstructive lung disease.
Organizing pneumonia.
Reduced diffusing capacity.
Sarcoidosis.
Serositis affecting pleura or pericarditis.
Tracheal stenosis.

LIVER

Alpha1-antitrypsin deficiency.
Chronic active hepatitis.
Hepatopulmonary syndrome.
Portapulmonary hypertension.
Primary biliary cirrhosis.
Hepatosplenomegaly.
  Amyloidosis.
  Collagen vascular disease.
  Eosinophilic granulomatosis.
  Lymphatic interstitial pneumonia.
  Sarcoidosis.

LUNG DISEASE AND RENAL INVOLVEMENT[51]

ICD-10CM # codes vary with specific diagnosis

LUNG DISEASE WITH RENAL INVOLVEMENT

Glomerulonephritis
Systemic vasculitis.
Collagen vascular disease.
Antibasement membrane.
Sarcoidosis.

Nephrotic Syndrome
Amyloidosis.
Disseminated Langerhans cell histiocytosis.
Drug-induced lung disease.
Paraneoplastic syndrome.
Post transplantation.
Pulmonary hydatid disease.
Systemic lupus erythematosus.
Vasculitis.
Venous thrombosis.

Renal Mass
Lymphangioleiomyomatosis.
Metastasis neoplasm.
Renal carcinoid.
Tuberous sclerosis.
Wegener's granulomatosis.

Nephrolithiasis
Alveolar proteinosis.
Cystic fibrosis.
Hypercalcemic syndromes.
Osteolysis from mycobacteria or fungi.
Sarcoidosis.

Systemic Hypertension
Collagen vascular disease.
Diffuse alveolar hemorrhage.
Pulmonary renal syndromes.
Neurofibromatosis.
Sleep apnea.

LUNG DISEASE AND SKIN AND SUBCUTANEOUS LESIONS[51]

ICD-10CM #	codes vary with specific diagnosis

SKIN AND SUBCUTANEOUS LESIONS ASSOCIATED WITH LUNG DISEASE

Skin Lesions
Diffuse pigment change.
  Acanthosis nigricans—lung neoplasm.
  Albinism—Hermansky-Pudlak syndrome.
  Bronze pigmentation—hemosiderosis.
  Gray-brown—Whipple's disease.
Cutaneous draining sinus.
  Fungal infections (especially histoplasmosis).
  Mycobacterial infections (especially tuberculosis).
  Neoplasms (especially mesothelial tumors).
  Necrotizing vasculitis.
  Other bacterial infections (especially actinomycosis).
Cutaneous ulcers.
  Beryllium disease.
  Chronic venous insufficiency.
  Fungal infections (especially histoplasmosis).
  Mycobacterial disease.
  Necrotizing vasculitis.
  Parasitic disease.
  Polycythemia.
  Sickle cell disease.
  Tularemia.
Cutaneous vasculitis.
  Behçet's syndrome.
  Churg-Strauss syndrome.
  Collagen vascular disease.
  Sarcoidosis.
  Wegener's granulomatosis.

Erythema multiforme.
  Drug reactions.
  Fungi (especially coccidiomycosis).
  Mycoplasma and other infectious agents.
  Neoplasms.
  Exfoliative dermatitis.
  Adverse drug reactions.
  Chemotherapy.
  Disseminated malignancy.
  Graft-versus-host disease.
  Radiation therapy.
Flushing.
  Bronchial carcinoid, pheochromocytoma, other neoplasms.
  Carbon dioxide, cyanide, and other toxins.
  Drugs.
  Foods and vasodilatory substances.
  Hormones.
  Mastocytosis.
  Metabolic states (e.g., hyperthyroidism, fever).
Macular rash.
  Anti-basement membrane disease.
  Café-au-lait spots (neurofibromatosis).
  Coal miner's scars.
  Collagen vascular disease.
  Idiopathic pulmonary fibrosis.
  Rose spots (psittacosis).
  Sarcoidosis.
  Syphilis.
  Viral pneumonia.
Maculopapular rash.
  Amyloidosis.
  Drug-induced lung disease.
  Collagen vascular disease.
  Gaucher's disease.
  Kaposi's sarcoma.
  Lung neoplasm.
  Lymphomatoid granulomatosis.
  Lymphoma.
  Parasites.
  Sarcoidosis.
  Syphilis.
  Vasculitis.
  Viral pneumonia
Telangiectasia
  Arteriovenous malformation.
  Ataxia-telangiectasia.
  Carcinoid syndrome.
  Cushing's disease.
  Hepatopulmonary syndrome and other chronic liver diseases.
  Hereditary hemorrhagic telangiectasia (Osler-Weber-Rendu).
  Mastocytosis.
  Systemic sclerosis and other collagen vascular diseases.
Urticaria
  Asthma.
  Drug reactions.
  Cystic fibrosis.
  Exercise-induced urticaria.
  Food allergy.
  Hereditary angioneurotic edema.
  Inhaled antigens.
  Insect bites and stings.
  Infectious agents, such as mycoplasma and helicobacter.
  Mastocytosis.

  Occupational sensitization.
  Parasites.
  Vasculitis.

Nail Changes with Lung Disease
Color changes:
  Cigarette smoking discoloration.
  Splinter hemorrhages.
  Yellow nail syndrome.
Beau's lines (any severe illness):
  Dermatomyositis.
  Sarcoidosis.
  Seronegative arthropathies.
  Systemic sclerosis.

Lung Disease with Subcutaneous Involvement
Adenopathy:
  Environmental mycobacteria.
  Fungal infections.
  Human immunodeficiency visurs infections.
  Metastatic neoplasm.
  Leukemia.
  Lymphoma.
  Sarcoidosis.
  Tuberculosis.
Calcinosis:
  ■ Dermatomyositis.
  ■ Metastatic osteosarcoma.
  ■ Mixed connective tissue disease.
  ■ Scleroderma.
  ■ Tuberculosis.
  ■ Uremic metastatic calcification.
  ○ Erythema induratum (Bazin's disease):
  Aortic stenosis.
  Cryoglobulinemia.
  Nodular vasculitis.
  Panniculitis.
  Peripheral neuropathy.
  Takayasu's disease.
  Streptococcus infection.
  Tuberculosis and other mycobacterial disease.
  Weber-Christian disease.
Erythema nodosa:
  Neoplasm.
  Other infectious and inflammatory diseases.
  Primary coccidiomycosis, histoplasmosis.
  Primary tuberculosis.
  Psittacosis.
  Sarcoidosis.
Subcutaneous nodules:
  Amyloidosis.
  Neoplasm.
  Neurofibromatosis.
  Rheumatoid arthritis.
  Tuberous sclerosis (angiofibromas).
  von Recklinghausen.
  Weber-Christian disease.

Lung Disease with Salivary Gland Enlargement
Bulimia and aspiration.
Gaucher's disease.
Lymphoid interstitial pneumonitis.
Lymphatic carcinoma.
Lymphoma.
Other causes of lymphadenopathy.
Sarcoidosis.
Sjögren disease.

LUNG DISEASE WITH BONE, JOINT, NERVE, AND MUSCLE INVOLVEMENT[51]

ICD-10CM # codes vary with specific diagnosis

ARTHRITIS

Ankylosing spondylitis.
Collagen vascular diseases.
Reactive arthritis.
Sarcoidosis.
Systemic vasculitis.
Tuberculosis.

BONE LESIONS

Ankylosing spondylitis.
Blastomycosis and other fungal disease.
Collagen vascular diseases.
Eosinophilic granulomatosis.
Fibrous histiocytoma.
Gaucher's disease.
Neoplasm.
Sarcoidosis.
Tuberculosis.

MUSCLE DISEASE

Collagen vascular disease.
L-Tryptophan.
Diabetes insipidus.
Eosinophilic granulomatosis.
Polymyositis.
Sarcoidosis.

NEUROLOGIC DISEASE

Acute inflammatory polyneuropathy.
Amyotrophic lateral sclerosis.
Aspiration.
Botulism.
Lambert-Eaton syndrome.
Myasthenia gravis.
Organophosphate poisoning.
Polio and postpolio syndrome.
Sarcoidosis.
Churg-Strauss syndrome.
Wegener's granulomatosis.

LUNG VOLUMES IN DIFFUSE LUNG DISEASE[30]

ICD-10CM # varies with specific disorder

LARGE LUNG VOLUMES

Emphysema.
Chonic asthma.
Diffuse bronchiolitis obliterans.
Highly trained athletes.
Lymphangioleiomyomatosis.

SMALL LUNG VOLUMES

End-stage lung fibrosis.
Bilateral diaphragmatic paralysis.
Massive ascites.

NORMAL LUNG VOLUMES

Sarcoidosis.
Langerhans cell histiocytosis.
Neurofibromatosis.
Emphysema with pulmonary fibrosis.

LYMPHADENOPATHY[28]

ICD-10CM # R59.9 Enlarged lymph nodes, unspecified

GENERALIZED

AIDS.
Lymphoma: Hodgkin's disease, non-Hodgkin's lymphoma.
Leukemias, reticuloendotheliosis.
Infectious mononucleosis, CMV, and other viral infections.
Diffuse skin infection: generalized furunculosis, multiple tick bites.
Parasitic infections: toxoplasmosis, filariasis, leishmaniasis, Chagas' disease.
Serum sickness.
Collagen vascular diseases (RA, SLE).
Dengue (arbovirus infection).
Sarcoidosis and other granulomatous diseases.
Drugs: INH, hydantoin derivatives, antithyroid and antileprosy drugs.
Secondary syphilis.
Hyperthyroidism, lipid-storage diseases.

LOCALIZED

Cervical Nodes
Infections of the head, neck, ears, sinuses, scalp, pharynx.
Mononucleosis.
Lymphoma.
TB.
Malignancy of head and neck.
Rubella.
Scalene/Supraclavicular Nodes
Lymphoma.
Lung neoplasm.
Bacterial or fungal infection of thorax or retroperitoneum.
GI malignancy.
Axillary Nodes
Infections of hands and arms.
Cat-scratch disease.
Neoplasm (lymphoma, melanoma, breast carcinoma).
Brucellosis.
Epitrochlear Nodes
Infections of the hand.
Lymphoma.
Tularemia.
Sarcoidosis, secondary syphilis (usually bilateral).
Inguinal Nodes
Infections of leg or foot, folliculitis (pubic hair).
LGV, syphilis.
Lymphoma.
Pelvic malignancy.
Pasteurella pestis.
Hilar Nodes
Sarcoidosis.
TB.
Lung carcinoma.
Fungal infections, systemic.
Mediastinal Nodes
Sarcoidosis.
Lymphoma.
Lung neoplasm.
TB.
Mononucleosis.
Histoplasmosis.

Abdominal/Retroperitoneal Nodes
Lymphoma.
TB.
Neoplasm (ovary, testes, prostate, and other malignancies).

LYMPHANGITIS[49]

ICD-10CM # I89.1 Lymphangitis

Acute:
  Group A streptococci.
  Staphylococcus aureus.
  Pasteurella multocida.
Chronic:
  Sporothrix schenckii (sporotrichosis).
  Mycobacterium marinum (swimming pool granuloma).
  Mycobacterium kansasii.
  Nocardia brasiliensis.
  W. bancrofti.

LYMPHEDEMA[40]

ICD-10CM # i89.0 Lymphedema, not elsewhere classified
          I97.2 Postmastectomy lymphedema syndrome
          Q82.0 Hereditary lymphedema

CLASSIFICATION OF LYMPHEDEMA

Primary lymphedema
Congenital lymphedema (Milroy's disease).
Lymphedema praecox.
Lymphedema tarda.
Syndromes associated with primary lymphedema
Yellow nail syndrome.
Turner syndrome.
Noonan syndrome.
Pes cavus.
Phakomatosis pigmentovascularis.
Distichiasis-lymphedema.
Emberger syndrome.
WILD syndrome.
Hypotrichosis-telangiectasia-lymphedema syndrome.
Cutaneous disorders sometimes associated with primary lymphedema
Yellow nails.
Hemangiomas.
Xanthomatosis and chylous lymphedema.
Congenital absence of nails.
Secondary lymphedema
Postmastectomy lymphedema.
Melphalan isolated limb perfusion.
Malignant occlusion with obstruction.
Extrinsic pressure.
Factitial lymphedema.
Postradiation therapy.
Following recurrent lymphangitis/cellulitis.
Lymphedema of upper limb in recurrent eczema.
Granulomatous disease.
Rosaceous lymphedema.
Primary amyloidosis.
Complications of lymphedema
Cellulitis of lymphedema.
Elephantiasis nostra verrucosa.

Ulceration.
Lymphangiosarcoma.

LYMPHOCYTOSIS, ATYPICAL[49]

ICD-10CM # D72.89 Other specified disorders of white blood cells

Epstein-Barr virus primary infection (infectious mononucleosis).
Cytomegalovirus primary infection (heterophile-negative mono).
Human herpesvirus 6 primary infection (roseola).
Primary HIV infection.
Toxoplasmosis.
Acute viral hepatitis.
Rubella, mumps.
Drug reactions (e.g., phenytoin, sulfa).

MACROTHROMBOCYTOPENIA, INHERITED[39]

ICD-10CM #   varies with specific disorder

Bernard-Soulier syndrome.
MHY9-related disorders:
    May-Hegglin anomaly.
    Sebastian syndrome.
    Fechtner syndrome.
    Epstein syndrome.
Gray platelet syndrome.
Montreal platelet syndrome.
Mediterranean macrothrombocytopenia.
Mediterranean stomatocytosis/macrothrombo-cytemia.
GATA1 mutations.
Sialyl-Lewis-S antigen deficiency.
Paris-Trousseau syndrome.
Platelet-type von Willebrand's disease.

MACULAR CRYSTALS[11]

ICD-10CM # varies with specific diagnosis

OTHER CAUSES OF MACULAR CRYSTALS

Primary hyperoxaluria.
Bietti corneoretinal crystalline dystrophy.
Cystinosis.
Sjögren–Larsson syndrome.
Gyrate atrophy.
Acquired parafoveal telangiectasis.
Talc-corn starch emboli.
West African crystalline maculopathy.

MADAROSIS[11]

ICD-10CM # H02.729 Madarosis of unspecified eye, unspecified eyelid and periocular area

CAUSES OF MADAROSIS

Local
Chronic anterior lid margin disease.
Infiltrating lid tumours.
Burns.
Radiotherapy or cryotherapy of lid tumours.
Skin disorders
Generalized alopecia.

Psoriasis.
Systemic diseases.
Myxoedema.
Systemic lupus erythematosus.
Acquired syphilis.
Lepromatous leprosy.
Following removal
Procedures for trichiasis.
Trichotillomania (psychiatric disorder of hair removal).

MALABSORPTION[67]

ICD-10CM # K90.89 Other intestinal malabsorption

CAUSES OF MALABSORPTION

More Common
Celiac disease.
Chronic pancreatitis.
Post gastrectomy.
Crohn's disease.
Small bowel resection.
Small intestinal bacterial overgrowth.
Lactase deficiency.
Less Common
AIDS (*Myobacterium avium* intracellulare, AIDS enteropathy).
Whipple's disease.
Intestinal lymphoma.
Immunoproliferative small intestinal disease (alpha heavy chain disease).
Radiation enteritis.
Collagenous sprue.
Tropical sprue.
Non-granulomatous ulcerative jejunoileitis.
Eosinophilic gastroenteritis.
Amyloidosis.
Zollinger-Ellison syndrome.
Intestinal lymphangiectasia.
Systemic mastocytosis.
Chronic mesenteric ischemia.
Abetalipoproteinemia (autosomal recessive).

MALNUTRITION, CAUSES IN EARLY LIFE[45]

ICD-10CM # E46 Unspecified protein-energy malnutrition

0-6 MO

Breastfeeding difficulties.
Improper formula preparation.
Impaired parent/child interaction.
Congenital syndromes.
Prenatal infections or teratogenic exposures.
Poor feeding (sucking, swallowing) or feeding refusal (aversion).
Maternal psychological disorder (depression or attachment disorder).
Congenital heart disease.
Cystic fibrosis.
Neurologic abnormalities.
Child neglect.
Recurrent infections.

6-12 MO

Celiac disease.
Food intolerance.
Child neglect.

Delayed introduction of age-appropriate foods or poor transition to food.
Recurrent infections.
Food allergy.

AFTER INFANCY

Acquired chronic diseases.
Highly distractible child.
Inappropriate mealtime environment.
Inappropriate diet (e.g., excessive juice consumption, avoidance of high-calorie foods).
Recurrent infections.

MEDIASTINAL COMPARTMENTS, ANATOMY AND PATHOLOGY[71]

ICD-10CM #   varies with specific disorder

ANTERIOR

Normal Structures
Lymph nodes.
Connective tissue.
Thymus (remnant in adults).
Masses
Thymoma.
Germ cell neoplasm.
Lymphoma.
Thyroid enlargement (intrathoracic goiter).
Other tumors.

MIDDLE

Normal Structures
Pericardium.
Heart.
Vessels: Ascending aorta, venae cavae, main pulmonary arteries.
Trachea.
Lymph nodes.
Nerves: Phrenic, upper vagus.
Masses
Carcinoma.
Lymphoma.
Pericardial cyst.
Bronchogenic cyst.
Benign lymph node enlargement (granulomatous disease).

POSTERIOR

Normal Structures
Vessels: Descending aorta.
Esophagus.
Vertebral column.
Nerves: Sympathetic chain, lower vagus.
Lymph nodes.
Connective tissue.
Masses
Neurogenic tumor.
Diaphragmatic hernia.

MEDIASTINAL MASSES OR WIDENING ON CHEST X-RAY

ICD-10CM # R59.9 Enlarged lymph nodes, unspecified
                 J98.5 Diseases of mediastinum, not elsewhere classified

Differential Diagnosis

II

Lymphoma: Hodgkin's disease and non-Hodgkin's lymphoma.
Sarcoidosis.
Vascular: aortic aneurysm, ectasia, or tortuosity of aorta or bronchocephalic vessels.
Carcinoma: lungs, esophagus.
Esophageal diverticula.
Hiatal hernia.
Achalasia.
Prominent pulmonary outflow tract: pulmonary hypertension, pulmonary embolism, right-to-left shunts.
Trauma: mediastinal hemorrhage.
Pneumomediastinum.
Lymphadenopathy caused by silicosis and other pneumoconioses.
Leukemias.
Infections: TB, viral (rare), *Mycoplasma* (rare), fungal, tularemia.
Substernal thyroid.
Thymoma.
Teratoma.
Bronchogenic cyst.
Pericardial cyst.
Neurofibroma, neurosarcoma, ganglioneuroma.

MEDIASTINAL MASSES, SITES OF ORIGIN[70]

ICD-10CM #   varies with specific diagnosis

DIFFERENTIAL DIAGNOSIS OF MEDIASTINAL MASSES BASED ON COMMON SITES OF ORIGIN

Prevascular space (anterior mediastinum)
Thymic masses.
Thymoma.
Thymic carcinoma.
Thymic neuroendocrine tumor.
Thymolipoma.
Thymic cyst.
Thymic hyperplasia.
Thymic lymphoma.
Germ cell tumors.
Teratoma and dermoid cyst.
Seminoma.
Nonseminomatous germ cell tumors.
Thyroid abnormalities (goiter and neoplasm).
Parathyroid tumor or hyperplasia.
Lymph node masses (particularly Hodgkin's lymphoma).
Vascular abnormalities (aorta and great vessels).
Mesenchymal abnormalities (e.g., lipomatosis, lipoma).
Foregut cyst.
Lymphangioma.
Hemangioma.
Retrosternal space (anterior mediastinum)
Lymph node masses.
Pretracheal space (middle mediastinum)
Lymph node masses.
Lung carcinoma.
Sarcoidosis.
Lymphoma (particularly Hodgkin's disease).
Metastases.
Infections (e.g., tuberculosis).
Foregut cyst.
Tracheal tumor.

Mesenchymal masses (e.g., lipomatosis, lipoma).
Thyroid abnormalities.
Vascular abnormalities (aorta and great vessels).
Lymphangioma and hemangioma.
Aortopulmonary window (middle mediastinum)
Lymph node masses.
Lung carcinoma.
Sarcoidosis.
Lymphoma.
Metastases.
Infections (e.g., tuberculosis).
Mesenchymal masses (e.g., lipomatosis, lipoma).
Vascular abnormalities (aorta or pulmonary artery).
Chemodectoma.
Foregut cyst.
Subcarinal space and azygoesophageal recess (middle mediastinum)
Lymph node masses.
Lung carcinoma.
Sarcoidosis.
Lymphoma.
Metastases.
Infections (e.g., tuberculosis).
Foregut cyst.
Dilated azygos vein.
Esophageal masses.
Varices.
Hernia.
Paravertebral masses (posterior mediastinum)
Neurogenic tumor.
Nerve sheath tumors.
Sympathetic ganglia tumors.
Paraganglioma.
Meningocele.
Foregut cyst.
Neurenteric cyst.
Thoracic spine abnormalities.
Extramedullary hematopoiesis.
Fluid collections and pseudocyst.
Vascular abnormalities.
Hernias.
Esophageal masses.
Varices.
Mesenchymal masses (e.g., lipomatosis, lipoma).
Lymph node masses.
Lymphoma (particularly non-Hodgkin's).
Metastases.
Dilated azygos or hemiazygos vein.
Hernia.
Lymphangioma and hemangioma.
Thymic mass or germ cell tumor.
Anterior cardiophrenic angle masses.
Lymph node masses (particularly lymphoma and metastases).
Pericardial cyst.
Fat pad.
Morgagni hernia.
Thymic masses.
Germ cell tumors.

MEDIASTINITIS, ACUTE[49]

ICD-10CM #   J98.5   Diseases of mediastinum, not elsewhere classified

Esophageal perforation.
Iatrogenic.
EGD, esophageal dilation, esophageal variceal sclerotherapy, nasogastric tube, Sengstaken-Blackmore tube, endotracheal intubation, esophageal surgery, paraesophageal surgery, transesophageal echocardiography, anterior stabilization of cervical vertebral bodies.
Swallowed foreign bodies.
Trauma.
Spontaneous perforation (e.g., emesis, carcinoma).
Head and neck infections (e.g., tonsillitis, pharyngitis, parotitis, epiglottitis, odontogenic).
Infections originating at another site (e.g., TB, pneumonia, pancreatitis, osteomyelitis of sternum, clavicle, ribs).
Cardiothoracic surgery (median sternotomy) (e.g., CABG, valve replacement, other types of cardiothoracic surgery).

MELANONYCHIA

ICD-10CM #   NEC L81.4   Melanin hyperpigmentation

Pregnancy.
Trauma.
Medications (e.g., AZT, 5-fluorouracil, doxorubicin, psoralens).
Nail matrix nevus.
HIV infection.
Onychomycosis.
Melanocyte hyperplasia.
Verrucae.
Pustular psoriasis.
Lichen planus.
Basal cell carcinoma.
Nail matrix melanoma.
Subungual keratosis.
Addison's disease.
Bowen's disease.

MEMORY LOSS SYMPTOMS, ELDERLY PATIENTS

ICD-10CM #   R41.2   Retrograde amnesia

Age-related mild cognitive impairment.
Depression (pseudodementia).
Medications (e.g., anticholinergics, sedatives).
Hypothyroidism.
Chronic hypoxia.
Cerebrovascular infarcts.
Alzheimer's disease.
Hepatic disease.
Chronic renal failure.
Hyperthyroidism.
Frontotemporal dementia.
Lewy body dementia.

MENINGITIS, CHRONIC[49]

ICD-10CM #   G03.1   Chronic meningitis

TB.
Fungal CNS infection.
Tertiary syphilis.
CNS neoplasm.
Metabolic encephalopathies.
Multiple sclerosis.

Chronic subdural hematoma.
SLE cerebritis.
Encephalitides.
Sarcoidosis.
NSAIDs.
Behçet's syndrome.
Anatomic defects (traumatic, congenital, post-operative).
Granulomatous angiitis.

MENINGITIS, RECURRENT[49]

ICD-10CM # G03.2 Benign recurrent meningitis [Mollaret]

Drug induced (with rechallenge).
Parameningeal focus.
  Infection (sinusitis, mastoiditis, osteomyelitis, brain abscess).
  Tumor (epidermoid cyst, craniopharyngioma).
Posttraumatic (bacterial).
Mollaret's meningitis.
SLE.
Herpes simplex virus.

MENTAL STATUS CHANGES AND COMA[6]

ICD-10CM # R41.82 Altered mental status, unspecified

METABOLIC/SYSTEMIC ETIOLOGY OF ALTERED MENTAL STATUS AND COMA

Hypoxia
Severe pulmonary disease (hypoventilation).
Severe anemia.
Environmental/toxin:
  Methemoglobinemia.
  Cyanide.
  Carbon monoxide.
  Decreased atmospheric oxygen (high altitude).
  Near-drowning.

Disorders of Glucose
Hypoglycemia:
  Chronic alcohol abuse and liver disease.
  Excessive use of insulin or other hypoglycemic agents.
  Insulinoma.
Hyperglycemia:
  Diabetic ketoacidosis.
  Nonketotic hyperosmolar coma.

Decreased Cerebral Blood Flow
Hypovolemic shock.
Cardiac:
  Vasovagal syncope.
  Arrhythmias.
  Myocardial infarction.
  Valvular disorders.
  Congestive heart failure.
  Pericardial effusion/tamponade.
  Myocarditis.
Infectious:
  Septic shock.
  Bacterial meningitis.
Vascular/hematologic:
  Hypertensive encephalopathy.
  Pseudotumor cerebri.

Hyperviscosity (sickle cell, polycythemia).
Hyperventilation.
Cerebral lupus vasculitis.
Thrombotic thrombocytopenic purpura.
Disseminated intravascular coagulation.

Metabolic Cofactor Deficiency
Thiamine (Wernicke-Korsakoff syndrome).
Pyridoxine (isoniazid overdose).
Folic acid (chronic alcohol abuse).
Cyanocobalamin.
Niacin.

Electrolye/pH Disturbances
Acidosis/alkalosis.
Hypernatremia/hyponatremia.[26]
Hypercalcemia/hypocalcemia.
Hypophosphatemia.
Hypermagnesemia/hypomagnesemia.

Endocrine Disorders
Myxedema coma, thyrotoxicosis.
Hypopituitarism.
Addison's disease (primary or secondary).
Cushing's disease.
Pheochromocytoma.
Hyperparathyroidism/hypoparathyroidism.

Endogenous Toxins
Hyperammonemia (liver failure).
Uremia (renal disease).
Carbon dioxide narcosis (pulmonary disease).
Porphyria.

Exogenous Toxins
Alcohols:
  Ethanol, isopropyl alcohol, methanol, ethylene glycol.
Acid poisons:
  Salicylates.
  Paraldehyde.
  Ammonium chloride.
Antidepressant medications:
  Lithium.
  Tricyclic antidepressants (TCAs).
  Selective serotonin reuptake inhibitors (SSRIs).
  Monamine oxidase inhibitors (MAOIs).
Stimulants:
  Amphetamines/methamphetamines.
  Cocaine.
  Over-the-counter sympathomimetics.
Narcotics/opiates:
  Morphine.
  Heroin.
  Codeine, oxycodone, meperidine, hydrocodone.
  Methadone.
  Fentanyl.
  Propoxyphene.
Sedative-hypnotics:
  Benzodiazepines.
  Barbiturates.
  Rohypnol.
  Bromide.
Hallucinogens:
  Lysergic acid diethylamide (LSD).
  Marijuana.
  Mescaline, peyote.
  Mushrooms.
  Phencyclidine (PCP).

Herbs/plants
  Aconite.
  Jimson weed.
  Morning glory.
Volatile substances:
  Hydrocarbons (gasoline, butane, toluene, benzene, chloroform).
  Nitrites.
  Anesthetic agents (nitrous oxide, ether).
Other:
  γ-Hydroxybutyrate (GHB).
  Ketamine.
  Penicillin.
  Cardiac glycosides.
  Anticonvulsants.
  Steroids.
  Heavy metals.
  Cimetidine.
  Organophosphates.

Disorders of Temperature Regulation/ Environmental
- Hypothermia.
- Heat stroke.
- Malignant hyperthermia.
- Neuroleptic malignant syndrome.
- High-altitude cerebral edema (HACE).
- Dysbarism.

Primary Glial or Neuronal Disorders
Adrenoleukodystrophy.
Creutzfeldt-Jakob disease.
Progressive multifocal leukoencephalopathy.
Marchiafava-Bignami disease.
Gliomatosis cerebri.
Central pontine myelinolysis.

Other Disorders of Unknown Etiology
- Seizures.
- Postictal states.
- Reye's syndrome.[27]
- Intussusception.

MENTAL STATUS CHANGES AND COMA, STRUCTURAL CAUSES[1]

ICD-10CM # R40.1

COMMON AGE-RELATED CAUSES OF ALTERED MENTAL STATUS AND COMA

Infant
Infection.
Trauma, abuse.
Metabolic.

Child
Toxic ingestion.

Adolescent, Young Adult
Toxic ingestion.
Recreational drug use.
Trauma.

Elderly
- Medication changes.
- Over-the-counter medications.
- Infection.
- Alterations in living environment.
- Stroke.
- Trauma.

[26]Can be associated with dilution of formula in infant feeding.

[27]Prominent in the pediatric population

MENTAL STATUS CHANGES AND COMA, METABOLIC AND SYSTEMIC CAUSES[1]

ICD-10CM # CM40.1

METABOLIC AND SYSTEMIC CAUSES OF ALTERED MENTAL STATUS AND COMA

Hypoxia, Hypercapnia
- Severe pulmonary disease (hypoventilation).
- Severe anemia.
- Environmental, toxic.
- Methemoglobinemia.
- Cyanide.
- Carbon monoxide.
- Decreased atmospheric oxygen (high altitude).
- Near-drowning.

Glucose Disorders
Hypoglycemia:
    Chronic alcohol abuse and liver disease.
    Excessive dosage of insulin or other hypoglycemic agents.
    Insulinoma.
Hyperglycemia:
    Diabetic ketoacidosis.
    Nonketotic hyperosmolar coma.

Decreased Cerebral Blood Flow
Hypovolemic shock.
Cardiac:
    Vasovagal syncope.
    Arrhythmias.
    Myocardial infarction.
    Valvular disorders.
    Congestive heart failure.
    Pericardial effusion, tamponade.
    Myocarditis.
Infectious
    Septic shock.
    Bacterial meningitis.
Vascular, hematologic
    Hypertensive encephalopathy.
    Pseudotumor cerebri.
    Hyperviscosity (sickle cell, polycythemia).
    Hyperventilation.
    Cerebral vasculitis as a manifestation of systemic lupus erythematosus.
    Thrombotic thrombocytopenic purpura.
    Disseminated intravascular coagulation.

Metabolic Cofactor Deficiency
Thiamine (Wernicke-Korsakoff syndrome).
Pyridoxine (isoniazid overdose).
Folic acid (chronic alcohol abuse).
Cyanocobalamin.
Niacin.

Electrolyte, pH Disturbances
Acidosis, alkalosis.
Hypernatremia, hyponatremia.[28]
Hypercalcemia, hypocalcemia.
Hypophosphatemia.
Hypermagnesemia, hypomagnesemia.

Endocrine Disorders
Myxedema coma, thyrotoxicosis.
Hypopituitarism.
Addison disease (primary or secondary).
Cushing disease.

Pheochromocytoma.
Hyperparathyroidism, hypoparathyroidism.

Endogenous Toxins
Hyperammonemia (liver failure).
Uremia (renal disease).
Carbon dioxide narcosis (pulmonary disease).
Porphyria.

Exogenous Toxins
Alcohols:
    Ethanol, isopropyl alcohol, methanol, ethylene glycol.
Acid poisons:
    Salicylates.
    Paraldehyde.
    Ammonium chloride.
Antidepressant medications:
    Lithium.
    Tricyclic antidepressants.
    Selective serotonin reuptake inhibitors.
    Monoamine oxidase inhibitors.
Stimulants:
    Amphetamines, methamphetamines.
    Cocaine.
    Over-the-counter sympathomimetics.
Narcotics, opiates:
    Morphine.
    Heroin.
    Codeine, oxycodone, meperidine, hydrocodone.
    Methadone.
    Fentanyl.
    Propoxyphene.
Sedative-hypnotics:
    Benzodiazepines.
    Barbiturates.
    Rohypnol.
    Bromide.
Hallucinogens:
    Lysergic acid diethylamide.
    Marijuana.
    Mescaline, peyote.
    Mushrooms.
    Phencyclidine.
Herbs, plants:
    Aconite.
    Jimsonweed.
    Morning glory.
Volatile substances:
    Hydrocarbons (gasoline, butane, toluene, benzene, chloroform).
    Nitrites.
    Anesthetic agents (nitrous oxide, ether).
Other:
    γ-Hydroxybutyrate.
    Ketamine.
    Penicillin.
    Cardiac glycosides.
    Anticonvulsants.
    Steroids.
    Heavy metals.
    Cimetidine.
    Organophosphates.

Disorders of Temperature Regulation, Environmental
Hypothermia.
Heat stroke.
Malignant hyperthermia.
Neuroleptic malignant syndrome.
High-altitude cerebral edema.
Dysbarism.

Primary Glial or Neuronal Disorders
Adrenoleukodystrophy.
Creutzfeldt-Jakob disease.
Progressive multifocal leukoencephalopathy.
Marchiafava-Bignami disease.
Gliomatosis cerebri.
Central pontine myelinolysis.

Other Disorders with Unknown Etiology
Seizures.
Postictal states.
Reye syndrome.[29]
Intussusception.

MESENTERIC ARTERIAL EMBOLISM, ASSOCIATED FACTORS[6]

ICD-10CM # I74.09   Other arterial embolism and thrombosis of abdominal aorta

FACTORS ASSOCIATED WITH MESENTERIC ARTERIAL EMBOLISM

Coronary artery disease.
    Post-myocardial infarction mural thrombi.
    Congestive heart failure.
Valvular heart disease.
    Rheumatic mitral valve disease.
    Nonbacterial endocarditis.
Arrhythmias.
    Chronic atrial fibrillation.
Aortic aneurysms or dissections.
Coronary angiography.

MESENTERIC ISCHEMIA, NONOCCLUSIVE[49]

ICD-10CM #	K55.0	Acute vascular disorders of intestine
	K55.1	Chronic vascular disorders of intestine
	S35.8X9A	Unspecified injury of other blood vessels at abdomen, lower back and pelvis level, initial encounter

- Cardiovascular disease resulting in low-flow states (CHF, cardiogenic shock, post cardiopulmonary bypass, dysrhythmias).
- Septic shock.
- Drug induced (cocaine, vasopressors, ergot alkaloid poisoning).

MESENTERIC VENOUS THROMBOSIS[49]

ICD-10CM # I82.91   Chronic embolism and thrombosis of unspecified vein

Hypercoagulable states (protein C or S deficiency, antithrombin III deficiency, Factor

---

[28]Can be associated with dilution of formula in infant feeding.

[29]Prominent in the pediatric population.

V Leyden, malignancy, polycythemia vera, sickle cell disease, homocystinemia, lupus anticoagulant, cardiolipin antibody).

Trauma (operative venous injury, abdominal trauma, postsplenectomy).

Inflammatory conditions (pancreatitis, diverticulitis, appendicitis, cholangitis).

Other: CHF, renal failure, portal hypertension, decompression sickness.

METASTATIC NEOPLASMS

ICD-10CM #		
	C79.51	Secondary malignant neoplasm of bone
	C79.52	Secondary malignant neoplasm of bone marrow
	C79.31	Secondary malignant neoplasm of brain
	C78.7	Secondary malignant neoplasm of liver and intrahepatic bile duct
	C78.00	Secondary malignant neoplasm of unspecified lung

To: Bone	To: Brain
Breast	Lung
Lung	Breast
Prostate	Melanoma
Thyroid	GU tract
Kidney	Colon
Bladder	Sinuses
Endometrium	Sarcoma
Cervix	Skin
Melanoma	Thyroid
To: Liver	**To: Lung**
Colon	Breast
Stomach	Colon
Pancreas	Kidney
Breast	Testis
Lymphomas	Stomach
Bronchus	Thyroid
Lung	Melanoma
Sarcoma	
Choriocarcinoma	
Kidney	

METHAEMOGLOBINAEMIA, DRUG INDUCED[38]

ICD-10CM #	D74	Methaemoglobinaemia

SUBSTANCES ASSOCIATED WITH METHAEMOGLOBINAEMIA

Acetaminophen (nitrobenzene derivative).
Acetanilide.
Local anesthetics.
  Benzocaine.
  Lidocaine.
  Prilocaine.
Aniline dyes.
Celecoxib.
Dapsone.
Flutamide.
Ifosfamide.
Metoclopramide.
Nitric oxide.

Nitrites.
  Amyl nitrite.
  Isobutyl nitrite.
  Sodium nitrite.
  Nitrates (bacterial conversion to nitrites).
Nitrobenzenes/nitrobenzoates.
Nitroethane (nail polish remover).
Nitrofurans.
Nitroglycerin.
Paraquat/monolinuron.
Phenacetin.
Phenazopyridine (pyridium).
Primaquine.
Rasburicase.
Sulfamethoxazole.

MICROCEPHALY[8]

ICD-10CM #	Q02	Microcephaly

PRIMARY (GENETIC)

Familial (autosomal recessive).
Autosomal dominant.
Syndromes:
  Down (21-trisomy).
  Edward (18-trisomy).
  Cri-du-chat (5 p-).
  Cornelia de Lange.
  Rubinstein-Taybi.
  Smith-Lemli-Opitz.

SECONDARY (NONGENETIC)

Radiation.
Congenital infections:
  Cytomegalovirus.
  Rubella.
  Toxoplasmosis.
Drugs:
  Fetal alcohol.
  Fetal hydantoin.
Meningitis/encephalitis.
Malnutrition.
Metabolic.
Hyperthermia.
Hypoxic-ischemic encephalopathy.

MICROPENIS[53]

ICD-10CM #	N48.89	Other specified disorders of penis
	Q55.62	Hypoplasia of penis

HYPOGONADOTROPIC HYPOGONADISM (HYPOTHALAMIC OR PITUITARY DEFICIENCIES)

Kallmann's syndrome: autosomal dominant; associated with hyposmia.
Prader-Willi syndrome: hypotonia, mental retardation, obesity, small hands and feet.
Rud syndrome: hyposomia, ichthyosis, mental retardation.
De Morsier's syndrome (septooptic dysplasia): hypopituitarism, hypoplastic optic discs, absent septum pellucidum.

HYPERGONADOTROPIC HYPOGONADISM

Primary testicular defect: disorders of testicular differentiation or inborn errors of testosterone synthesis.
Klinefelter's syndrome.
Other X polysomies (i.e., XXXXY, XXXY).
Robinow's syndrome: brachymesomelic dwarfism, dysmorphic facies.

PARTIAL ANDROGEN INSENSITIVITY

IDIOPATHIC

Defective morphogenesis of the penis.

MIOSIS

ICD-10CM #	H57.03	Miosis

Medications (e.g., morphine, pilocarpine).
Neurosyphilis.
Congenital.
Iritis.
CNS pontine lesion.
CNS infections.
Cavernous sinus thrombosis.
Inflammation/irritation of cornea or conjunctiva.

MONOARTHRITIS, ACUTE

ICD-10CM #	M13.10	Monoarthritis, not elsewhere classified, unspecified site

Overuse.
Trauma.
Gout.
Pseudogout.
Osteoarthritis.
Infectious arthritis (e.g., gonococcal, Lyme disease, viral, mycobacteria, fungi).
Osteomyelitis.
Avascular necrosis of bone.
Hemarthrosis.
Bowel disease-associated arthritis.
Bone malignancy.
Psoriatic arthritis.
Juvenile RA.
Sarcoidosis.
Hemoglobinopathies.
Vasculitic syndromes.
Behçet's syndrome.
Foreign body synovitis.
Hypertrophic pulmonary osteoarthropathy.
Amyloidosis, familial Mediterranean fever.

MONOCYTOSIS[39]

ICD-10CM #	D72.821	Monocytosis (symptomatic)

Inflammatory diseases:
  Infectious diseases:
    Tuberculosis.
    Syphilis.
    Subacute bacterial endocarditis.
    Fever of unknown origin.
      Autoimmune/granulomatous.
      Systemic lupus erythematosus.
      Rheumatoid arthritis.
      Temporal arteritis.

Myositis.
Polyarteritis.
Ulcerative colitis.
Regional enteritis.
Sarcoidosis.
Malignant disorders:
  Preleukemia.
  Nonlymphocytic leukemia.
  Histiocytoses.
  Hodgkin's disease.
  Non-Hodgkin's lymphoma.
  Carcinomas.
Miscellaneous:
  Chronic neutropenia.
  Post splenectomy.

MONONEUROPATHY

ICD-10CM #   G58.9   Mononeuropathy, unspecified

Herpes zoster.
Herpes simplex.
Vasculitis.
Trauma, compression.
Diabetes.
Postinfectious or inflammatory.

MONONEUROPATHY, ISOLATED[6]

ICD-10CM #   G56.90   Unspecified mononeuropathy of unspecified upper limb

UPPER EXTREMITY

Radial nerve.
  Axilla.
  Humerus.
  Elbow (posterior interosseous neuropathy).
  Wrist (superficial cutaneous radial neuropathy).
Ulnar nerve.
  Axilla.
  Humerus.
  Elbow.
  Condylar groove.
  Cubital tunnel.
Wrist (Guyon's canal).
Hand.
  Superficial terminal ulnar neuropathy.
  Deep terminal ulnar neuropathy.
    Proximal hypothenar.
    Distal hypothenar.
Median nerve.
Axilla.
Humerus (musculocutaneous mononeuropathy).
Forearm.
  Anterior interosseus.
  Pronator syndrome.
Wrist (carpal tunnel).
Hand (recurrent motor branch).
Suprascapular mononeuropathy.
  Axillary mononeuropathy.

LOWER EXTREMITY

Sciatic nerve.
Femoral nerve.
  Iliacus compartment (proximal).
  Saphenous mononeuropathy (distal).

Lateral femoral cutaneous (meralgia paresthetica).
Peroneal nerve.
  Common peroneal mononeuropathy (fibular head, popliteal fossa).
  Deep peroneal mononeuropathy (anterior compartment).
Tibial nerve.
  Popliteal fossa (proximal).
  Tarsal tunnel (distal).
Sural nerve.
  Popliteal fossa, calf (proximal).
  Fifth metatarsal base (distal).
Plantar nerve.
  Distal to tarsal tunnel.
  Interdigital neuropathies (Morton's neuroma).
Obturator mononeuropathy.

MONONEUROPATHY MULTIPLEX[50]

ICD-10CM #   G58.9   Mononeuropathy, unspecified

MONONEUROPATHY MULTIPLEX

Vasculitis
Systemic vasculitis:
  Polyarteritis nodosa.
  Rheumatoid arthritis.
  Systemic lupus erythematosus.
  Sjögren's syndrome (keratoconjunctivitis sicca).
Nonsystemic vasculitis
Diabetes mellitus
Neoplastic
Paraneoplastic.
Direct infiltration.
Infectious
Lyme disease.
HIV infection.
Sarcoid
Toxic (lead)
Transient (polycythemia vera)
Cryoglobulinemia (hepatitis C)

MONONUCLEOSIS, MONOSPOT NEGATIVE[3]

ICD-10CM #   B27.90   Infectious mononucleosis, unspecified without complication

DIFFERENTIAL DIAGNOSIS OF MONOSPOT-NEGATIVE MONONUCLEOSIS

Acute HIV infection.
EBV mononucleosis (particularly in children).
Cytomegalovirus.
Acute toxoplasmosis.
Streptococcal pharyngitis.
Acute hepatitis B infection.

EBV, Epstein-Barr virus; *HIV,* human immunodeficiency virus.

MUSCLE DISEASE[63]

ICD-10CM #   M60.009   Infective myositis, unspecified site

CLASSIFICATION OF MUSCLE DISEASE

Muscular Dystrophies
Duchenne.
Becker.
Limb girdle.
Childhood.
Facioscapulohumeral.
Myotonic Disorders
Dystrophia myotonica.
Myotonica congenita.
Inflammatory
Infective: bacterial, viral, parasitic.
Unknown cause: polymyositis, dermatomyositis, sarcoidosis.
Endocrine
Thyroid disease—hyper- and hypothyroidism.
Cushing's disease.
Addison's disease.
Hyperparathyroidism.
Metabolic
- Glycogen storage diseases.
- Periodic paralyses.
- Mitochondrial diseases.
Drug-induced
- Corticosteroids.
- Chloroquine.
- Amiodarone.
- Penicillamine.
- Alcohol.
- Zidovudine.
- Clofibrate.
Other
- Inclusion body myositis.

MUSCLE WEAKNESS

ICD-10CM #   M62.9   Disorder of muscle, unspecified

Physical deconditioning.
Impaired cardiac output (e.g., mitral stenosis, mitral regurgitation).
Uremia, liver failure.
Electrolyte abnormalities (hypokalemia, hyperkalemia, hypophosphatemia, hypercalcemia), hypoglycemia.
Drug induced (e.g., statin myopathy).
Muscular dystrophies.
Steroid myopathy.
Alcoholic myopathy.
Myasthenia gravis, Lambert-Eaton syndrome.
Infections (polio, botulism, HIV, hepatitis, diphtheria, tick paralysis, neurosyphilis, brucellosis, TB, trichinosis).
Pernicious anemia, other anemias, beriberi.
Psychiatric illness (depression, somatization syndrome).
Organophosphate or arsenic poisoning.
Inflammatory myopathies (e.g., collagen vascular disease, RA, sarcoidosis).
Endocrinopathies (e.g., adrenal insufficiency, hypothyroidism), diabetic neuropathy.
Other: motor neuron disease, mitochondrial myopathy, l-tryptophan (eosinophilia-myalgia), rhabdomyolysis, glycogen storage disease, lipid storage disease.

MUSCLE WEAKNESS, LOWER MOTOR NEURON VERSUS UPPER MOTOR NEURON[72]

ICD-10CM #   M62.9   Disorder of muscle, unspecified

LOWER MOTOR NEURON

Weakness, usually severe.
Marked muscle atrophy.
Fasciculations.
Decreased muscle stretch reflexes.
Clonus not present.
Flaccidity.
No Babinski sign.
Asymmetric and may involve one limb only in the beginning to become generalized as the disease progresses.

UPPER MOTOR NEURON

Weakness, usually less severe.
Minimal disuse muscle atrophy.
No fasciculations.
Increased muscle stretch reflexes.
Clonus may be present.
Spasticity.
Babinski sign.
Often initial impairment of only skilled movements.
In the limbs the following muscles may be the only ones weak or weaker than the others: triceps; wrist and finger extensors; interossei; iliopsoas; hamstrings; and foot dorsiflexors, inverters, and extroverters.

MUSCULOSKELETAL BENIGN TUMORS AND TUMOR-LIKE LESIONS[58]

ICD-10CM #   varies with specific diagnosis

BENIGN TUMORS AND TUMOR-LIKE CONDITIONS THAT MAY BE MULTIFOCAL

Fibrous dysplasia.
Enchondromatosis.
Osteochondromatosis.
Synovial cysts.
Brown tumors in hyperparathyroidism.
Langerhans cell histiocytosis (eosinophilic granuloma).
Hemangiomatosis.
Bone islands, osteoma (Gardner syndrome).
Fibrous cortical defect, nonossifying fibroma.
Giant cell tumor.
Neurofibromatosis.
Amyloidosis.
Mastocytosis.
SAPHO, chronic multifocal osteomyelitis.

SAPHO, Synovitis, acne, pustulosis, hyperostosis, osteitis.

MUSCULOSKELETAL MALIGNANT TUMORS AND TUMOR-LIKE LESIONS[58]

ICD-10CM #   varies with specific diagnosis

MALIGNANT OSSEOUS TUMORS THAT MAY BE MULTIFOCAL

Metastases.
Myeloma.
Angiosarcoma.
Leukemia.
Neuroblastoma.
Ewing sarcoma.
Osteosarcomatosis.
Lymphoma.

MYDRIASIS

ICD-10CM #   H57.04   Mydriasis

Coma.
Medications (cocaine, atropine, epinephrine, etc.).
Glaucoma.
Cerebral aneurysm.
Ocular trauma.
Head trauma.
Optic atrophy.
Cerebral neoplasm.
Iridocyclitis.

MYELIN DISORDERS

ICD-10CM #   varies with specific diagnosis

Multiple sclerosis.
Vitamin B_{12} deficiency.
Radiation.
Hypoxia.
Toxicity from carbon monoxide, alcohol, mercury.
Progressive multifocal encephalopathy.
Acute disseminated encephalomyelitis.
Acute hemorrhagic leukoencephalopathy.
Phenylketonuria.
Adrenoleukodystrophy.
Krabbe's disease.

MYELOPATHY AND MYELITIS[65]

ICD-10CM #   M51.9   Unspecified thoracic, thoracolumbar and lumbosacral intervertebral disc disorder
           G95.9   Disease of spinal cord, unspecified

INFLAMMATORY

Infectious: spirochetal TB, zoster, rabies, HIV, polio, rickettsial, fungal, parasitic.
Noninfectious: idiopathic transverse myelitis, multiple sclerosis.

TOXIC/METABOLIC

DM, pernicious anemia, chronic liver disease, pellagra, arsenic.

TRAUMA COMPRESSION

Spinal neoplasm, cervical spondylosis, epidural abscess, epidural hematoma.

VASCULAR

AV malformation, SLE, periarteritis nodosa, dissecting aortic aneurysm.

PHYSICAL AGENTS

Electrical injury, irradiation.

NEOPLASTIC

Spinal cord tumors, paraneoplastic myelopathy.

MYOCARDIAL ISCHEMIA[65]

ICD-10CM #   I25.5   Ischemic cardiomyopathy
           I25.89   Other forms of chronic ischemic heart disease
           I25.9   Chronic ischemic heart disease, unspecified
           I24.8   Other forms of acute ischemic heart disease

Atherosclerotic obstructive coronary artery disease.
Nonatherosclerotic coronary artery disease:
   Coronary artery spasm.
   Congenital coronary artery anomalies:
     Anomalous origin of coronary artery from pulmonary artery.
     Aberrant origin of coronary artery from aorta or another coronary artery.
     Coronary arteriovenous fistula.
     Coronary artery aneurysm.
Acquired disorders of coronary arteries:
   Coronary artery embolism.
   Dissection:
     Surgical.
     During percutaneous coronary angioplasty.
     Aortic dissection.
     Spontaneous (e.g., during pregnancy).
   Extrinsic compression:
     Tumors.
     Granulomas.
     Amyloidosis.
   Collagen-vascular disease:
     Polyarteritis nodosa.
     Temporal arteritis.
     RA.
     SLE.
     Scleroderma.
   Miscellaneous disorders:
     Irradiation.
     Trauma.
     Kawasaki disease.
Syphilis.
Hereditary disorders:
   Pseudoxanthoma elasticum.
   Gargoylism.
   Progeria.
   Homocystinuria.
   Primary oxaluria.
"Functional" causes of myocardial ischemia in absence of anatomic coronary artery disease:
   Syndrome X.
   Hypertrophic cardiomyopathy.
   Dilated cardiomyopathy.

Muscle bridge.
Hypertensive heart disease.
Pulmonary hypertension.
Valvular heart disease; aortic stenosis, aortic regurgitation.

MYOCLONUS

ICD-10CM # G25.3 Myoclonus

Physiologic (e.g., exercise or anxiety induced).
Renal failure.
Hepatic failure.
Hyponatremia.
Hypoglycemia or severe hyperglycemia.
Postdialysis.
Epileptic myoclonus.
Postencephalitis.
CNS lesion (stroke, neoplasm).
CNS trauma.
Parkinson's disease.
Medications (e.g., tricyclics, L-dopa).
Friedreich's ataxia.
Ataxia-telangiectasia.
Wilson's disease.
Huntington's disease.
Progressive supranuclear palsy.
Heavy metal poisoning.
Benign familial.

MYOPATHIC SYNDROMES, DRUG-INDUCED[36]

ICD-10CM # G72.9 Myopathy, unspecified

TYPE OF MYOPATHY

Necrotizing myopathy.
Inflammatory myopathy.
Mitochondrial myopathy.
Hypokalemic myopathy.
Antimicrotubular myopathy.
Lysosomal storage myopathy.
Corticosteroid myopathy.
Others.

DRUGS

HMG-CoA reductase inhibitors (statins), fibrates, alcohol.
Penicillamine, interferon-a, procainamide.
Zidovudine.
Diuretics, laxatives, licorice, amphotericin B, alcohol.
Colchicine, vincristine.
Chloroquine, hydroxychloroquine, quinacrine, amiodarone, perhexiline.
Corticosteroids, especially fluorinated.
Ipecac syrup, emetine.

MYOPATHIES ASSOCIATED WITH REST PAIN[36]

ICD-10CM # G72.9 Myopathy, unspecified

Childhood dermatomyositis.
Hypothyroid myopathy.
Acute alcoholic myopathy.
Drug-induced myopathies.
Infectious myopathies.
Myopathies associated with metabolic bone disease.

Carnitine palmitoyl transferase deficiency.
Rhabdomyolysis from any cause.

MYOPATHIES, HIV ASSOCIATED[23]

ICD-10CM # R25.2

HIV-Associated Myopathies	Myopathies Secondary to Antiretrovirals	Others
HIV poly-myositis.	Zidovudine myopathy.	Opportunistic infections involving muscle (toxo-plasmosis).
Inclusion body myositis.	Toxic mito-chondrial myopathies related to other NRTIs.[a]	
Nemaline myopathy.		Tumor infiltra-tions of skel-etal muscle.
Diffuse infiltrative lympho-cytosis syndrome.	HIV-associated lipodystrophy syndrome.	Rhabdomyo-lysis.
HIV wasting syndrome.	Immune recon-stitution syndrome related to HAART.[b]	
Vasculitic pro-cesses.		
Myasthenia gravis and other myas-thenic syn-dromes.		
Chronic fatigue and fibro-myalgia.		

[a]NRTIs, nucleoside reverse transcriptase inhibitors.
[b]HAART, highly active antiretroviral therapy.

MYOPATHIES, INFECTIOUS

ICD-10CM # G72.9 Myopathy, unspecified

HIV.
Viral myositis.
Trichinosis.
Toxoplasmosis.
Cysticercosis.

MYOPATHIES, INFLAMMATORY

ICD-10CM # G72.9 Myopathy, unspecified

SLE, RA.
Sarcoidosis.
Paraneoplastic syndrome.
Polymyositis, dermatomyositis.
Polyarteritis nodosa.
Mixed connective tissue disease.
Scleroderma.
Inclusion body myositis.
Sjögren's syndrome.
Cimetidine, D-penicillamine.

MYOPATHIES, METABOLIC[36]

ICD-10CM # G72.9 Myopathy, unspecified

DISORDERED GLYCOGEN METABOLISM

Myophosphorylase deficiency (McArdle disease).
Phosphorylase b kinase deficiency.
Phosphofructokinase deficiency.
Debrancher enzyme deficiency.
Brancher enzyme deficiency.
Phosphoglycerate kinase deficiency.
Phosphoglycerate mutase deficiency.
Lactate dehydrogenase deficiency.
Acid maltase deficiency.
Aldolase deficiency.
b-Enolase deficiency.

DISORDERED LIPID METABOLISM

Carnitine deficiencies.
Carnitine palmitoyltransferase deficiency.
Fatty acid acyl-CoA dehydrogenase deficiencies.

MITOCHONDRIAL MYOPATHIES

Coenzyme Q10 deficiency.
Respiratory chain complex deficiencies.

ENDOCRINE

- Acromegaly.
- Hypothyroidism.
- Hyperthyroidism.
- Hyperparathyroidism.
- Cushing disease.
- Addison disease.
- Hyperaldosteronism.

METABOLIC-NUTRITIONAL

Uremia.
Hepatic failure.
Malabsorption.
Periodic paralysis.
Vitamin D deficiency.
Vitamin E deficiency.

ELECTROLYTE DISORDERS

- Sodium: hypernatremia and hyponatremia.
- Potassium: hyperkalemia and hypokalemia.
- Calcium: hypercalcemia and hypocalcemia.
- Phosphate: hypophosphatemia.
- Magnesium: hypomagnesemia.

MYOPATHIES, TOXIC[3]

ICD-10CM # G72.2 Myopathy due to other toxic agents

- Inflammatory: cimetidine, D-penicillamine.
- Noninflammatory necrotizing or vacuolar: cholesterol-lowering agents, chloroquine, colchicine.
- Acute muscle necrosis and myoglobinuria: cholesterol-lowering drugs, alcohol, cocaine.
- Malignant hyperthermia: halothane, ethylene, others; succinylcholine.
- Mitochondrial: zidovudine.
- Myosin loss: nondepolarizing neuromuscular blocking agents; glucocorticoids.

MYOSITIS, INFECTIOUS CAUSES[36]

ICD-10CM # M60.009 Infective myositis, unspecified site

VIRAL

Influenza A and B viruses.
Enteroviruses (coxsackieviruses, echoviruses).
Human immunodeficiency virus.
Human T-cell lymphotrophic virus type 1.
Hepatitis B and C viruses.
Cytomegalovirus.
Epstein-Barr virus.
Adenovirus.
Varicella-zoster virus.
Parainfluenza.

PARASITIC

Trichinella species.
Echinococcus species.
Schistosoma species.
Toxoplasma gondii.
Trypanosoma cruzi.
Sarcocystis species.

BACTERIAL

Staphylococcus aureus.
Streptococcus, groups A and B.
Aeromonas hydrophila.
Borrelia burgdorferi.
Clostridium perfringens.
Anaerobic streptococci.
Mycobacterium species.
Rickettsia species.

FUNGAL

Candida species.
Cryptococcus neoformans.
Microsporida.

MYOSITIS, INFLAMMATORY[3]

ICD-10CM #	M60.009	Infective myositis, unspecified site
	M60.9	Myositis, unspecified
	M60.10	Interstitial myositis of unspecified site

INFECTIOUS

Viral myositis:
   Retroviruses (HIV, HTLV-I).
   Enteroviruses (echovirus, Coxsackievirus).
   Other viruses (influenza, hepatitis A and B, Epstein-Barr virus).
Bacterial: pyomyositis.
Parasites: trichinosis, cysticercosis.
Fungi: candidiasis.

IDIOPATHIC

Granulomatous myositis (sarcoid, giant cell).
Eosinophilic myositis.
Eosinophilia-myalgia syndrome.

ENDOCRINE/METABOLIC DISORDERS

- Hypothyroidism.
- Hyperthyroidism.
- Hypercortisolism.
- Hyperparathyroidism.
- Hypoparathyroidism.
- Hypocalcemia.
- Hypokalemia.

METABOLIC MYOPATHIES

- Myophosphorylase deficiency (McArdle's disease).
- Phosphofructokinase deficiency.
- Myoadenylate deaminase deficiency.
- Acid maltase deficiency.
- Lipid storage diseases.
- Acute rhabdomyolysis.

DRUG-INDUCED MYOPATHIES

Alcohol.
D-Penicillamine.
Zidovudine.
Colchicine.
Chloroquine, hydroxychloroquine.
Lipid-lowering agents.
Cyclosporine.
Cocaine, heroin, barbiturates.
Corticosteroids.

NEUROLOGIC DISORDERS

Muscular dystrophies.
Congenital myopathies.
Motor neuron disease.
Guillain-Barré syndrome.
Myasthenia gravis.

NAIL CLUBBING

ICD-10CM # R68.3 Clubbing of nails

COPD.
Pulmonary malignancy.
Cirrhosis.
Inflammatory bowel disease.
Chronic bronchitis.
Congenital heart disease.
Endocarditis.
AV malformations.
Asbestosis.
Trauma.
Idiopathic.

NAIL, HORIZONTAL WHITE LINES (BEAU'S LINES)

ICD-10CM # L60.4 Beau's lines

Malnutrition.
Idiopathic.
Trauma.
Prolonged systemic illnesses.
Pemphigus.
Raynaud's disease.

NAIL KOILONYCHIA

ICD-10CM # L60.8 Other nail disorders

Trauma.
Iron deficiency.
SLE.
Hemochromatosis.
Raynaud's disease.
Nail-patella syndrome.
Idiopathic.

NAIL ONYCHOLYSIS

ICD-10CM # L60.1 Onycholysis

Infection.
Trauma.
Psoriasis.
Connective tissue disorders.
Sarcoidosis.
Hyperthyroidism.
Amyloidosis.
Nutritional deficiencies.

NAIL PITTING

ICD-10CM # L60.8 Other nail disorders

Psoriasis.
Alopecia areata.
Reiter's syndrome.
Trauma.
Idiopathic.

NAIL SPLINTER HEMORRHAGE

ICD-10CM # L60.8 Other nail disorders

SBE.
Trauma.
Malignancies.
Oral contraceptives.
Pregnancy.
SLE.
Antiphospholipid syndrome.
Psoriasis.
RA.
Peptic ulcer disease.

NAIL STRIATIONS

ICD-10CM # L60.8 Other nail disorders

Psoriasis.
Alopecia areata.
Trauma.
Atopic dermatitis.
Vitiligo.

NAIL TELANGIECTASIA

ICD-10CM # L60.8 Other nail disorders

RA.
Scleroderma.
Trauma.
SLE.
Dermatomyositis.

NAIL WHITENING (TERRY'S NAILS)

ICD-10CM # L60.8 Other nail disorders

Malnutrition.
Trauma.
Liver disease (cirrhosis, hepatic failure).
DM.
Hyperthyroidism.
Idiopathic.

NAIL YELLOWING

ICD-10CM # L60.8 Other nail disorders

Differential Diagnosis

II

Tobacco abuse.
Nephrotic syndrome.
Chronic infections (TB, sinusitis).
Bronchiectasis.
Lymphedema.
Raynaud's disease.
RA.
Pleural effusions.
Thyroiditis.
Immunodeficiency.

NASAL AND PARANASAL SINUS TUMORS[32]

ICD-10CM # C30.0 Malignant neoplasm of nasal cavity

BENIGN AND MALIGNANT NASAL AND PARANASAL SINUS TUMORS

Epithelial Tumors

BENIGN

Papilloma.
Adenoma.
Inverting papilloma.

MALIGNANT

Squamous carcinoma.
Adenocarcinoma.
Melanoma.
Adenoid cystic carcinoma.
Malignant salivary tumors.

MESENCHYMAL TUMORS

Benign
Osteoma.
Ossifying fibroma complex.
Angiofibroma.
Chondroma.
Malignant
Osteogenic sarcoma.
Fibrosarcoma.
Angiosarcoma.
Chondrosarcoma.
Lymphoma.
Rhabdomyosarcoma.

NASAL MASSES, CONGENITAL[32]

ICD-10CM # J34.1 Cyst and mucocele of nose and nasal sinus
J34.89 Other specified disorders of nose and nasal sinuses

Dermoid.
Nasal cerebral heterotopia (glioma).
Frontal meningoencephalocele.
Nasolacrimal duct mucocele.
Nasal hamartoma.
Nasal hemangioma.

NAUSEA AND VOMITING

ICD-10CM # R11.2 Nausea with vomiting, unspecified

Infections (viral, bacterial).
Intestinal obstruction.

Metabolic (uremia, electrolyte abnormalities, DKA, acidosis, etc.).
Severe pain.
Anxiety, fear.
Psychiatric disorders (bulimia, anorexia nervosa).
Pregnancy.
Medications (NSAIDs, erythromycin, morphine, codeine, aminophylline, chemotherapeutic agents, etc.).
Withdrawal from substance abuse (drugs, alcohol).
Head trauma.
Vestibular or middle ear disease.
Migraine headache.
CNS neoplasms.
Radiation sickness.
PUD.
Carcinoma of GI tract.
Reye's syndrome.
Eye disorders.
Abdominal trauma.

NAUSEA AND VOMITING, CAUSES DURING PREGNANCY[26]

ICD-10CM # R11.2 Nausea with vomiting, unspecified

DIFFERENTIAL DIAGNOSIS OF NAUSEA AND VOMITING DURING PREGNANCY

Nausea and vomiting of pregnancy.
Hyperemesis gravidarum.
Pancreatitis.
Symptomatic cholelithiasis.
Viral hepatitis.
Peptic ulcer disease.
Gastric cancer.
Intestinal obstruction.
Intestinal pseudo-obstruction.
Gastroparesis diabeticorum.
Gastritis.
Gastroesophageal reflux disease.
Acute pyelonephritis.
Drug toxicity.
Vagotomy.
Preeclampsia/eclampsia.
Acute fatty liver of pregnancy.
Hemolysis, elevated liver enzymes, and low platelets (HELLP) syndrome.
Anorexia nervosa/bulimia.
Other neuropsychiatric disorders.

NECK AND ARM PAIN

ICD-10CM # M54.2 Cervicalgia
S46.919A Strain of unspecified muscle, fascia and tendon at shoulder and upper arm level, unspecified arm, initial encounter

Cervical disk syndrome.
Trauma, musculoskeletal strain.
Rotator cuff syndrome.

Bicipital tendonitis.
Glenohumeral arthritis.
Acromioclavicular arthritis.
Thoracic outlet syndrome.
Pancoast tumor.
Infection (cellulitis, abscess).
Angina pectoris.

NECK MASS[54]

ICD-10CM # R22.1 Localized swelling, mass and lump, neck

CONGENITAL ANOMALIES

Thyroglossal duct cyst.
Bronchial apparatus anomalies.
Teratomas.
Ranula.
Dermoid cysts.
Hemangioma.
Laryngoceles.
Cystic hygroma.

NONNEOPLASTIC INFLAMMATORY ETIOLOGIES

Folliculitis.
Adenopathy secondary to peritonsillar abscess.
Retropharyngeal or parapharyngeal abscess.
Salivary gland infections.
Viral infections (mononucleosis, HIV, CMV).
TB.
Cat-scratch disease.
Toxoplasmosis.
Actinomyces.
Atypical mycobacterium.
Jugular vein thrombus.

NEOPLASM (PRIMARY OR METASTATIC)

Lipoma.

NECK PAIN[54]

ICD-10CM # M54.2 Cervicalgia

INFLAMMATORY DISEASES

RA.
Spondyloarthropathies.
Juvenile RA.

NONINFLAMMATORY DISEASE

Cervical osteoarthritis.
Diskogenic neck pain.
Diffuse idiopathic skeletal hyperostosis.
Fibromyalgia or myofascial pain.

INFECTIOUS CAUSES

Meningitis.
Osteomyelitis.
Infectious diskitis.

NEOPLASMS

Primary.
Metastatic.

REFERRED PAIN

Temporomandibular joint pain.
Cardiac pain.
Diaphragmatic irritation.
GI sources (gastric ulcer, gallbladder, pancreas).

NECK PAIN FROM RHEUMATOLOGIC DISORDERS[23]

ICD-10CM # M54.2 Cervicalgia

Rheumatoid arthritis
   Without disease of the C1-C2 joint.
   With structural cervical abnormalities: C1-C2 subluxation, C1-C2 facet involvement.
Spondyloarthropathies.
Reactive arthritis.
Psoriatic arthritis.
Enteropathic arthritis.
Polymyalgia rheumatica.
Osteoarthritis.
Fibromyalgia.
Nonspecific musculoskeletal pain.
Miscellaneous spondyloarthropathies.
   Whipple's disease.
   Behçet's disease.
   Paget's disease.
   Acromegaly.
   Ossification of the posterior longitudinal ligament.
   Diffuse idiopathic skeletal hyperostosis.

NECROTIZING PNEUMONIAS[3]

ICD-10CM # J15.8 Pneumonia due to other specified bacteria

COMMON

Tuberculosis.
Staphylococcus.
Gram-negative bacilli.
Anaerobes.
Fungi.
Pneumocystis jirovecii.

RARE

Streptococcus pneumoniae.
Legionella.
Viruses.
Mycoplasma pneumoniae.

NEPHRITIC SYNDROME, ACUTE[3]

ICD-10CM # N00.8 Acute nephritic syndrome with other morphologic changes

LOW SERUM COMPLEMENT LEVEL

Acute postinfectious glomerulonephritis.
Membranoproliferative glomerulonephritis.
SLE.
Subacute bacterial endocarditis.
Visceral abscess "shunt" nephritis.
Cryoglobulinemia.

NORMAL SERUM COMPLEMENT LEVEL

IgA nephropathy.
Antiglomerular basement membrane disease.
Polyarteritis nodosa.
Wegener's glomerulonephritis.
Henoch-Schönlein purpura.
Goodpasture's syndrome.

NEPHROCALCINOSIS

ICD-10CM # E83.59 Other disorders of calcium metabolism

Sarcoidosis.
Hyperparathyroidism.
Chronic glomerulonephritis.
Milk-alkali syndrome.
Distal renal tubular acidosis.
Medullary sponge kidney.
Bartter's syndrome.
Hypervitaminosis D.
Idiopathic hypercalciuria.
Hyperoxaluria.
Cortical necrosis.
Tuberculosis.
Idiopathic hypercalciuria.
Rapidly progressive osteoporosis.

NEUROGENIC BLADDER[55]

ICD-10CM # N31.9 Neuromuscular dysfunction of bladder, unspecified

SUPRATENTORIAL

CVA.
Parkinson's disease.
Alzheimer's disease.
Cerebral palsy.

SPINAL CORD

Spinal cord injury.
Spinal stenosis.
Central cord syndrome.
ALS.
Multiple sclerosis.
Myelodysplasia.

PERIPHERAL NEUROPATHY

Diabetes.
Alcohol.
Shingles.
Syphilis.

NEUROLOGIC DEFICIT, FOCAL[49]

ICD-10CM # G45.9 Transient cerebral ischemic attack, unspecified
            I67.848 Other cerebrovascular vasospasm and vasoconstriction

TRAUMATIC: INTRACRANIAL, INTRASPINAL

Subdural hematoma.
Intraparenchymal hemorrhage.
Epidural hematoma.
Traumatic hemorrhagic necrosis.

INFECTIOUS

Brain abscess.
Epidural and subdural abscesses.
Meningitis.

NEOPLASTIC

Primary central nervous system tumors.
Metastatic tumors.
Syringomyelia.
Vascular.
Thrombosis.
Embolism.
Spontaneous hemorrhage: arteriovenous malformation, aneurysm, hypertensive.

METABOLIC

Hypoglycemia.
B_{12} deficiency.
Postseizure.
Hyperosmolar nonketotic.

OTHER

Migraine.
Bell's palsy.
Psychogenic.

NEUROLOGIC DEFICIT, MULTIFOCAL[49]

ICD-10CM # I67.89 Other cerebrovascular disease
            G45.9 Transient cerebral ischemic attack, unspecified
            I67.848 Other cerebrovascular vasospasm and vasoconstriction

Acute disseminated encephalomyelitis: postviral or postimmunization.
Infectious encephalomyelitis: poliovirus, enteroviruses, arbovirus, herpes zoster, Epstein-Barr virus.
Granulomatous encephalomyelitis: sarcoid.
Autoimmune: SLE.
Other: familial spinocerebellar degenerations.

NEUROMUSCULAR JUNCTION DYSFUNCTION[3]

ICD-10CM # N31.9 Neuromuscular dysfunction of bladder, unspecified

DISORDERS OF THE NEUROMUSCULAR JUNCTION

Autoimmune
Myasthenia gravis.
Lambert-Eaton myasthenic syndrome.
Congenital
Presynaptic defects in ACh resynthesis, packaging, or release.
Synaptic defect: congenital end plate AChE deficiency.
Postsynaptic defects: slow-channel syndromes.
Postsynaptic defects: decreased response to ACh.
   ○ Fast-channel syndromes.
   ○ AChR deficiency without kinetic abnormality.
• Familial limb-girdle myasthenia.

Toxic
Botulism.
Drug-induced disorders.
Organophosphate intoxication.

Ach, Acetylcholine; *AChE,* acetylcholinesterase; *AChR,* acetylcholine receptor.

NEURONOPATHIES, SENSORY (GANGLIONOPATHIES)[6]

ICD-10CM # G60.0 Hereditary motor and sensory neuropathy

- Herpes:
  Herpes simplex I and II.
  Varicella zoster (shingles).
Inflammatory sensory polyganglionopathy (ISP).
Paraneoplastic.
Primary biliary cirrhosis.
Sjögren's syndrome (keratoconjunctivitis sicca).
Toxin-induced:
  Pyridoxine (vitamin B_6) overdose.
  Metals:
    Platinum (cisplatin).
    Methyl mercury.
Vitamin E deficiency.

NEUROPATHIC BLADDER

ICD-10CM # N31.9 Neuromuscular dysfunction of bladder, unspecified

- Diabetes.
- Stroke.
- Multiple sclerosis.
- Parkinson's disease.
- Dementia.
- Encephalopathy.
- Brain trauma.
- Spinal cord trauma.
- Pelvic surgery.
- Spina bifida.

NEUROPATHIES WITH FACIAL NERVE INVOLVEMENT

ICD-10CM # G51.8 Other disorders of facial nerve

- Sarcoidosis.
- HIV.
- Lyme disease.
- Guillain-Barré.
- Others: chronic inflammatory polyneuropathy, Tangier disease, amyloidosis.

NEUROPATHIES, AUTONOMIC[45]

ICD-10CM # G63 Polyneuropathy in diseases classified elsewhere

GUILLAIN-BARRÉ SYNDROME
Non–Gulllain-Barré syndrome autoimmunity.
Paraneoplastic (type I antineuronal nuclear antibody).
Lambert-Eaton syndrome.

Antibodies to neuronal nicotinc acetylcholine receptors.
Antibodies to P/Q type calcium channels.
Other autoantibodies.
Systemic lupus erythematosus.

HEREDITARY
Type I autosomal dominant.
Type II autosomal recessive (Morvan disease).
Type III autosomal recessive (Riley-Day).
Type IV autosomal recessive (congenital insensitivity to pain with anhidrosis).
Type V absence of pain.

METABOLIC
Fabry disease.
Diabetes mellitus.
Tangier disease.
Porphyria.

INFECTIOUS
HIV.
Chagas' disease.
Botulism.
Leprosy.
Diphtheria.

OTHER
Triple A (Allgrove) syndrome.
Navajo Indian neuropathy.
Multiple endocrine neoplasia type 2b.

TOXINS

NEUROPATHIES, AUTONOMIC, PERIPHERAL, CAUSES[30]

ICD-10CM # G90.09 Other idiopathic peripheral autonomic neuropathy

METABOLIC
Diabetes mellitus.
Alcohol.
Acute intermittent porphyria.
Uremia.

AUTOIMMUNE
Autoimmune autonomic ganglionopathy.
Guillain-Barré syndrome.
Morvan's syndrome.
Lambert-Eaton myasthenic syndrome.
Chronic inflammatory demyelinating polyradiculoneuropathy.
Sjögren syndrome.
Systemic lupus erythematosus.
Mixed connective tissue diseases.

PARAPROTEINEMIC
Amyloidosis.

NUTRITIONAL
Cyanocobalamin deficiency.
Thiamine deficiency.
Gluten-sensitive neuropathy.

TOXIC
Heavy metals.
Organic solvents.

Organophosphates.
Vacor.
Acrylamide.

DRUG INDUCED
Cisplatin.
Vincristine.
Amiodarone.
Metronidazole.
Perhexiline.
Paclitaxel.

INFECTIOUS
Human immunodeficiency virus.
Leprosy.
Chagas' disease.
Botulism.
Diphtheria.
Lyme disease.

GENETIC
Hereditary sensory and autonomic neuropathies.
  Types I and II.
  Type III (familial dysautonomia).
  Type IV (congenital insensitivity to pain).
  Type V.
Fabry disease.

IDIOPATHIC
Adie's syndrome.
Ross' syndrome.
Acute cholinergic neuropathy.
Chronic idiopathic anhidrosis.
Amyotrophic lateral sclerosis.

NEUROPATHIES, PAINFUL[72]

ICD-10CM # G58.9 Mononeuropathy, unspecified
G62.1 Alcoholic polyneuropathy
G61.89 Other inflammatory polyneuropathies
G60.0 Hereditary motor and sensory neuropathy
G60.0 Hereditary motor and sensory neuropathy
E11.42 Type 2 diabetes mellitus with diabetic polyneuropathy
E10.42 Type 1 diabetes mellitus with diabetic polyneuropathy

MONONEUROPATHIES
Compressive neuropathy (carpal tunnel, meralgia paresthetica).
Trigeminal neuralgia.
Ischemic neuropathy.
Polyarteritis nodosa.
Diabetic mononeuropathy.
Herpes zoster.
Idiopathic and familial brachial plexopathy.

POLYNEUROPATHIES
DM.
Paraneoplastic sensory neuropathy.
Nutritional neuropathy.
Multiple myeloma.

Amyloid.
Dominantly inherited sensory neuropathy.
Toxic (arsenic, thallium, metronidazole).
AIDS-associated neuropathy.
Tangier disease.
Fabry's disease.

NEUROPATHIES, PERIPHERAL, ASYMMETRICAL PROXIMAL/DISTAL[6]

ICD-10CM # G99.0 Autonomic neuropathy in diseases classified elsewhere

BRACHIAL PLEXOPATHY

Open
Direct plexus injury (knife or gunshot wound).
Neurovascular (plexus ischemia).
Iatrogenic (central line insertion).
Closed
Traction injuries:
  "Stingers."
  Traction neurapraxia.
  Partial or complete nerve root avulsion.
Radiation.
Neoplastic.
Idiopathic brachial plexitis.
Thoracic outlet.

LUMBOSACRAL PLEXOPATHIES

Open
Closed
Traction injuries:
  Pelvic double vertical shearing fracture.
  Posterior hip dislocation.
  Retroperitoneal hemorrhage.
Vasospastic (deep buttock injection).
Neoplastic.
Radiation.
Idiopathic lumbosacral plexitis.
Infectious:
  Herpesvirus (sacrococcygeal).
  Herpes simplex II.
  Herpes zoster.
Cytomegalovirus (CMV) polyradiculopathy (HIV).

NEUROPATHIES, TOXIC AND METABOLIC[45]

ICD-10CM # NEC G62.2 Toxic neuropathy

METALS

Arsenic (insecticide, herbicide).
Lead (paint, batteries, pottery).
Mercury (metallic, vapor).
Thallium (rodenticides).
Gold.

OCCUPATIONAL OR INDUSTRIAL CHEMICALS

Acrylamide (grouting, flocculation).
Carbon disulfide (solvent).
Cyanide.
Dichlorophenoxyacetate.
Dimethylaminopropionitrile.
Ethylene oxide (gas sterilization).

Hexacarbons (glue, solvents).
Organophosphates (insecticides, petroleum additive).
Polychlorinated biphenyls.
Tetrachlorbiphenyl.
Trichloroethylene.

DRUGS

Amiodarone.
Chloramphenicol.
Chloroquine.
Cisplatin.
Colchicine.
Dapsone.
Ethambutol.
Ethanol.
Gold.
Hydralazine.
Isoniazid.
Metronidazole.
Nitrofurantoin.
Nitrous oxide.
Nucleosides (antiretroviral agents ddC, ddI, d4T, others).
Penicillamine.
Pentamidine.
Phenytoin.
Pyridoxine (excessive).
Statins.
Stilbamidine.
Suramin.
Taxanes (paclitaxel, docetaxel).
Thalidomide.
Tryptophan (eosinophilia-myalgia syndrome).
Vincristine.

METABOLIC DISORDER

Fabry disease.
Krabbe disease.
Leukodystrophies.
Porphyria.
Tangier disease.
Tyrosinemia.
Uremia.

NEUROPENIA, DRUG-INDUCED[38]

ICD-10CM # D70

DRUGS COMMONLY ASSOCIATED WITH NEUTROPENIA

Antibiotics:
  Vancomycin.
  Semisynthetic penicillins.
  Chloramphenicol.
  Sulfa.
  Linezolid.
Antithyroid drugs:
  ○ Methimazole.
  ○ Propylthiouracil.
• Cardiovascular:
  Ticlopidine.
  Procainamide.
Antipsychotics:
  Clozapine.
  Olanzapine.
  Chlorpromazine.

Anticonvulsants:
  Phenytoin.
  Carbamazepine
  Valproic acid.
Anti-inflammatory agents:
  Indomethacin.
  Sulfasalazine.
  Phenylbutazone.
H2 blockers:
  Cimetidine.
  Ranitidine.
Analgesics:
  Dipyrone.
Antineoplastic:
  Rituximab.
Anthelminthic:
  Levamisole.

NEUTROPENIA WITH DECREASED MARROW RESERVE[39]

ICD-10CM # D70.8 Other neutropenia

PRIMARY

Severe congenital neutropenia.
Shwachman–Diamond syndrome.
Cyclic neutropenia.

SECONDARY

Lymphoproliferative disorder of granular lymphocytes.
Chemotherapy.
Drug induced (nonimmune).
Nutritional.
Viral infection (varicella, EBV, measles, CMV, hepatitis, HIV).

NEUTROPENIA WITH NORMAL MARROW RESERVE[39]

ICD-10CM # D70.9 Neutropenia, unspecified

Chronic benign neutropenia of infancy and childhood.
Ethnic or benign familial neutropenia.
Autoimmune neutropenia.
Alloimmune neutropenia.
Drug-induced neutropenia.
Infection-related neutropenia.
Hypersplenism.

NEUTROPENIA, IN CHILDHOOD[68]

ICD-10CM # D70.8 Other neutropenia
               D70.9 Neutropenia unspecified

ACQUIRED

Infection.
Immune mediated.
Hypersplenism.
Vitamin B_{12}, folate, copper deficiency.
Drugs or toxic substances.
Aplastic anemia.
Malignancies or preleukemic disorders.
Ionizing radiation.

CONGENITAL
Cyclic neutropenia.
Severe congenital neutropenia (Kostmann syndrome).
Chronic benign neutropenia of childhood.
Shwachman-Diamond syndrome.
Fanconi anemia.
Metabolic disorders (amino acidopathies, Barth syndrome, glycogen storage disorders).
Osteopetrosis.
Neutropenia with pigmentation abnormalities, e.g., Chédiak-Higashi.

NEUTROPHILIA[39]

ICD-10CM #	D72.0	Neutrophilia, hereditary giant
	D71	Functional disorders of polymorphonuclear neutrophils

CLASSIFICATION OF NEUTROPHILIA
Primary (No Other Evident Associated Disease)
Hereditary neutrophilia.
Chronic idiopathic neutrophilia.
Chronic myelogenous leukemia (CML) and other myeloproliferative diseases.
Familial myeloproliferative disease.
Congenital anomalies and leukemoid reaction.
Leukocyte adhesion factor deficiency (LAD).
Familial cold urticaria and leukocytosis.
Secondary
Infection.
Stress neutrophilia.
Chronic inflammation.
Drug induced.
Nonhematologic malignancy.
Generalized marrow stimulation as in hemolysis.
Asplenia and hyposplenism.

NIPPLE LESIONS

ICD-10CM #	varies with specific diagnosis

Contact dermatitis.
Trauma.
Paget's disease.
Sebaceous hyperplasia.
Neurofibroma.
Accessory nipple.
Papillary adenoma.
Nevoid hyperkeratosis.
Cellulitis.

NODULAR LESIONS, SKIN

ICD-10CM #	R22.9	Localized swelling, mass and lump, unspecified

Lipoma.
Cherry angioma.
Angiokeratoma.
Hemangioma.
Classic Kaposi's sarcoma.
Nodular melanoma.
Pyogenic granuloma.
Angiosarcoma.
Eccrine poroma.

NODULES, PAINFUL

ICD-10CM #	R22.9	Localized swelling, mass and lump, unspecified

Arthropod bite or sting.
Erythema nodosum.
Glomus tumor.
Neuroma.
Leiomyoma.
Angiolipoma.
Dermatofibroma.
Osler's node.
Blue rubber bleb nevus.
Vasculitis.
Sweet's syndrome.

NYSTAGMUS

ICD-10CM #	H55.00	Unspecified nystagmus
	H55.89	Other irregular eye movements

Medications (meperidine, barbiturates, phenytoin, phenothiazines, etc.).
Multiple sclerosis.
Congenital.
Neoplasm (cerebellar, brain stem, cerebral).
Labyrinthine or vestibular lesions.
CNS infections.
Optic atrophy.
Other: Arnold–Chiari malformation, syringobulbia, chorioretinitis, meningeal cysts.

NYSTAGMUS, MONOCULAR

ICD-10CM #	H55.09	Other forms of nystagmus
	H55.00	Unspecified nystagmus

Amblyopia.
Strabismus.
Multiple sclerosis.
Monocular blindness.
Internuclear ophthalmoplegia.
Lid fasciculations.
Brain stem infarct.

ODYNOPHAGIA[67]

ICD-10CM #	varies with specific diagnosis

CAUSES OF ODYNOPHAGIA
Infections
Herpes simplex virus.
Cytomegalovirus.
Candidiasis.
Chemical, Inflammatory
Gastroesophageal reflux.
Drug induced (Slow-K, tetracyclines, quinidine).
Radiation.
Graft-versus-host disease.
Crohn's disease.
Dermatologic diseases (pemphigus and pemphigoid).

OPACIFICATION OF HEMIDIAPHRAGM ON X-RAY[32]

ICD-10CM #	varies with specific diagnosis

CAUSES OF OPACIFICATION OF A HEMITHORAX
Pleural effusion.
Consolidation.
Collapse.
Massive tumor.
Fibrothorax.
Combination of above lesions.
Pneumonectomy.
Lung agenesis.

OPHTHALMOPLEGIA[3]

ICD-10CM #	H51.9	Unspecified disorder of binocular movement
	H49.00	Third [oculomotor] nerve palsy, unspecified eye

BILATERAL
Botulism.
Myasthenia gravis.
Wernicke's encephalopathy.
Acute cranial polyneuropathy.
Brain stem stroke.

UNILATERAL
Carotid-posterior (3rd cranial nerve, pupil involved communicating aneurysm).
Diabetic-idiopathic (3rd or 6th cranial nerve, pupil spared).
Myasthenia gravis.
Brain stem stroke.

OPSOCLONUS[30]

ICD-10CM #	H55.89	Other irregular eye movements

Multiple sclerosis.
Encephalitis.
CNS lymphoma.
Hydrocephalus.
Pontine hemorrhage.
Thalamic disorder (glioma, hemorrhage).
Hyperosmolar coma.
Carcinoma, paraneoplastic.
Cocaine.
Medications (e.g., phenytoin, haloperidol, amitriptyline, diazepam, vidarabine).

OPTIC ATROPHY[63]

ICD-10CM #	H47.20	Unspecified optic atrophy

CAUSES OF OPTIC ATROPHY
Optic Nerve Compression
Pituitary tumor.
Carotid aneurysm.
Glaucoma.

---

[30]Spontaneous, multivector, chaotic eye movement

Optic nerve tumor.
Sphenoid meningioma.
Olfactory groove meningioma.
Optic Neuritis Following Longstanding Papilledema Central Retinal Artery Occlusion Toxic/Metabolic
Diabetes.
Methyl alcohol.
Tobacco.
Quinine.
Ethambutol.
Lead and arsenic.
Anemia.
Secondary to Retinal Disease
Senile macular degeneration.
Retinitis pigmentosa.
Severe chorioretinitis.
Secondary to Trauma
Orbital fracture.
Hereditary
Leber's optic atrophy.
Hereditary ataxias.
Spinocerebellar degeneration.

OPTIC DISC ELEVATION[11]

ICD-10CM #   varies with specific diagnosis

CAUSES OF OPTIC DISC ELEVATION
Papilloedema.
Accelerated hypertension.
Anterior optic neuropathy.
Ischemic.
Inflammatory.
Infiltrative.
Compressive, including orbital disease.
Pseudopapilloedema.
Disc drusen.
Tilted optic disc.
Peripapillary myelinated nerve fibers.
Crowded disc in hypermetropia.
Mitochondrial optic neuropathies.
Leber hereditary optic neuropathy.
Methanol poisoning.
Intraocular disease.
Central retinal vein occlusion.
Uveitis.
Posterior scleritis.
Hypotony.

ORAL MUCOSA, ERYTHEMATOUS LESIONS[18]

ICD-10CM #		
	K12.2	Cellulitis and abscess of mouth
	K13.70	Unspecified lesions of oral mucosa
	K13.79	Other lesions of oral mucosa

Allergy.
Erythroplakia.
Candidiasis.
Geographic tongue.
Stomatitis areata migrans.
Plasma cell gingivitis.
Pemphigus vulgaris.

ORAL MUCOSA, PIGMENTED LESIONS[18]

ICD-10CM #		
	K12.2	Cellulitis and abscess of mouth
	K13.70	Unspecified lesions of oral mucosa
	K13.79	Other lesions of oral mucosa
	K13.5	Oral submucous fibrosis

Racial pigmentation.
Oral melanotic macule.
Peutz-Jeghers syndrome.
Neurofibromatosis.
Albright's syndrome.
Addison's disease.
Chloasma.
Drug reaction: quinacrine, Minocin, chlorpromazine, Myleran.
Amalgam tattoo.
Lead line.
Smoker's melanosis.
Nevi.
Melanoma.

ORAL MUCOSA, PUNCTATE EROSIVE LESIONS[18]

ICD-10CM #		
	K12.2	Cellulitis and abscess of mouth
	K13.70	Unspecified lesions of oral mucosa
	K13.79	Other lesions of oral mucosa

Viral lesion: Herpes simplex, coxsackievirus (A, B, A16), herpes zoster.
Aphthous stomatitis.
Sutton's disease (giant aphthae).
Behçet's syndrome.
Reiter's syndrome.
Neutropenia.
Acute necrotizing ulcerative gingivostomatitis (ANUG).
Drug reaction.
Inflammatory bowel disease.
Contact allergy.

ORAL MUCOSA, WHITE LESIONS[18]

ICD-10CM #		
	K12.2	Cellulitis and abscess of mouth
	K13.70	Unspecified lesions of oral mucosa
	K13.79	Other lesions of oral mucosa
	K13.5	Oral submucous fibrosis

Leukoplakia.
White, hairy leukoplakia.
Squamous cell carcinoma.
Lichen planus.
Stomatitis nicotinica.
Benign intraepithelial dyskeratosis.
White spongy nevus.
Leukoedema.
Darier-White disease.

Pachyonychia congenital.
Candidiasis.
Allergy.
SLE.

ORAL ULCERS, ACUTE

ICD-10CM #		
	K13.70	Unspecified lesions of oral mucosa
	K13.79	Other lesions of oral mucosa

Trauma (including thermal trauma).
Aphthous stomatitis.
Syphilis.
Herpes simplex infection.
Herpes zoster.

ORAL VESICLES AND ULCERS[3]

ICD-10CM #		
	K13.70	Unspecified lesions of oral mucosa
	K13.79	Other lesions of oral mucosa

Aphthous stomatitis.
Primary herpes simplex infection.
Vincent's stomatitis.
Syphilis.
Coxsackievirus A (herpangina).
Fungi (histoplasmosis).
Behçet's syndrome.
SLE.
Reiter's syndrome.
Crohn's disease.
Erythema multiforme.
Pemphigus.
Pemphigoid.

ORBITAL INFLAMMATION[11]

ICD-10CM #		
	H05.019	Cellulitis of unspecified orbit
	C69.10	Malignant neoplasm of unspecified orbit
	D31.60	Benign neoplasm of unspecified orbit
	H05.029	Osteomyelitis of unspecified orbit
	H05.049	Tenonitis of unspecified orbit
	H05.229	Edema of unspecified orbit
	H05.239	Hemorrhage of unspecified orbit

DIFFERENTIAL DIAGNOSIS OF AN ACUTELY INFLAMED ORBIT
Infection
Bacterial orbital cellulitis.
Fungal orbital infection.
Dacryocystitis.
Infective dacryoadenitis.
Vascular lesions
Acute orbital hemorrhage,
Cavernous sinus thrombosis.
Carotid–cavernous fistula.
Neoplasia
Rapidly progressive retinoblastoma.

Differential
Diagnosis

II

Hereditary pancreatitis.
Cystoadenoma.
Cystoadenocarcinoma.
Cavernous lymphangioma.
Hemorrhage.
Acute pancreatitis (saponification).

PANCREATIC CYSTIC LESIONS[70]

| ICD-10CM # | K86.2 | Cyst of pancreas |
| | K86.3 | Pseudocyst of pancreas |

Pseudocyst.
Serous cystadenoma.
Mucinous cystic neoplasm.
Intraductal papillary mucinous neoplasm.
Solid and papillary epithelial neoplasm.
True epithelial cyst.
Duodenal diverticulum.
Cystic neuroendocrine tumors.
Ductal adenocarcinoma with cystic degeneration.
Cystic metastases.
Cystic degeneration in sarcoma, hemangioma, and paraganglioma.

PANCREATIC SOLID LESIONS[70]

| ICD-10CM # | C25.9 | Malignant neoplasm of pancreas, unspecified |
| | D13.6 | Benign neoplasm of pancreas |

Neoplastic solid tumors.
Ductal adenocarcinoma.
Pancreatic neuroendocrine tumor.
Pancreatic lymphoma.
Metastases to the pancreas.
Solid pseudopapillary tumor.
Pancreaticoblastoma.
Acinar cell carcinoma.
Mesenchymal tumors (sarcoma, fibrous histiocytoma, etc.).
Nonneoplastic solid lesions.
Focal chronic pancreatitis.
Autoimmune pancreatitis.
Groove pancreatitis.
Focal sparing of diffuse pancreatic fatty infiltration.
Intrapancreatic accessory spleen.
Developmental pancreas lobulation.
Sarcoidosis of the pancreas.

PANCREATITIS, ACUTE, IN CHILDREN[45]

| ICD-10CM # | K85 | Acute pancreatitis |

CAUSES OF ACUTE PANCREATITIS IN CHILDREN

Drugs and Toxins
Acetaminophen overdose.
Alcohol.
L-Asparaginase.
Azathioprine.
Carbamazepine.
Cimetidine.
Corticosteroids.
Enalapril.
Erythromycin.

Estrogen.
Furosemide.
Isoniazid.
Lisinopril.
6-Mercaptopurine.
Methyldopa.
Metronidazole.
Organophosphate poisoning.
Pentamidine.
Retrovirals: DDC, DDI, tenofovir.
Sulfonamides: mesalamine, 5-aminosalicylates, sulfasalazine, trimethoprim/sulfamethoxazole.
Sulindac.
Tetracycline.
Thiazides.
Valproic acid.
Venom (spider, scorpion, Gila monster lizard).
Vincristine.

Genetic
Cationic trypsinogen gene (PRSS1).
Chymotrypsin C gene (CTRC).
Cystic fibrosis gene (CFTR).
Trypsin inhibitor gene (SPINK1).

Infectious
Ascariasis.
Coxsackie B virus.
Epstein-Barr virus.
Hepatitis A, B.
Influenza A, B.
Leptospirosis.
Malaria.
Measles.
Mumps.
Mycoplasma.
Reye syndrome: varicella, influenza B.
Rubella.
Rubeola.
Septic shock.

Obstructive
Ampullary disease.
Ascariasis.
Biliary tract malformations.
Choledochal cyst.
Choledochocele.
Cholelithiasis, microlithiasis, and choledocholithiasis (stones or sludge).
Duplication cyst.
Endoscopic retrograde cholangiopancreatography (ERCP) complication.
Pancreas divisum.
Pancreatic ductal abnormalities.
Postoperative.
Sphincter of Oddi dysfunction.
Tumor.

Systemic Disease
Autoimmune pancreatitis.
Brain tumor.
Collagen vascular diseases.
Crohn disease.
Diabetes mellitus.
Head trauma.
Hemochromatosis.
Hemolytic-uremic syndrome.
Hyperlipidemia: type I, IV, V.
Hyperparathyroidism/Hypercalcemia.
Kawasaki disease.
Malnutrition.
Organic acidemia.
Peptic ulcer.

Periarteritis nodosa.
Renal failure.
Systemic lupus erythematosus.
Transplantation: bone marrow, heart, liver, kidney, pancreas.
Vasculitis.

Traumatic
Blunt injury.
Burns.
Child abuse.
Hypothermia.
Surgical trauma.
Total body cast.

PANCREATITIS, DRUG-INDUCED[6]

| ICD-10CM # | K85.3 | Drug induced acute pancreatitis |

DEFINITE
Acetaminophen.
Azathioprine.
Cimetidine.
Cisplatin.
Corticosteroids.
Didanosine.
Erythromycin.
Estrogens.
Ethyl alcohol.
Furosemide.
L-Asparaginase.
Mercaptopurine.
Metronidazole.
Methyldopa.
Nitrofurantoin.
Octreotide.
Organophosphates.
Pentamidine.
Ranitidine.
Tetracycline.
Salicylates.
Sulfonamides, trimethoprim-sulfamethoxazole, sulfasalazine.
Sulindac.
Valproic acid.

POSSIBLE
Bumetanide.
Carbamazepine.
Chlorthalidone.
Clonidine.
Colchicine.
Cyclosporine.
Cytarabine.
Diazoxide.
Enalapril.
Ergotamine.
Ethacrynic acid.
Indomethacin.
Isoniazid.
Isotretinoin.
Mefenamic acid.
Opiates.
Phenformin.
Piroxicam.
Procainamide.
Rifampin.
Thiazides.

PANCYTOPENIA[39]

ICD-10CM #   D61.818   Other pancytopenia

PANCYTOPENIA WITH HYPOCELLULAR BONE MARROW

Acquired aplastic anemia.
Inherited aplastic anemia (Fanconi anemia and others).
Some myelodysplasia syndromes.
Rare aleukemic leukemia (acute myelogenous leukemia).
Some acute lymphoblastic leukemias.
Some lymphomas of bone marrow.

PANCYTOPENIA WITH CELLULAR BONE MARROW

Primary bone marrow diseases.
Myelodysplasia syndromes.
Paroxysmal nocturnal hemoglobinuria.
Myelofibrosis.
Some aleukemic leukemias.
Myelophthisis.
Bone marrow lymphoma.
Hairy cell leukemia.
Secondary to systemic diseases.
Systemic lupus erythematosus, Sjögren syndrome.
Hypersplenism.
Vitamin B_{12}, folate deficiency (familial defect).
Overwhelming infection.
Alcohol.
Brucellosis.
Ehrlichiosis.
Sarcoidosis.
Tuberculosis and atypical mycobacteria.

HYPOCELLULAR BONE MARROW ± CYTOPENIA

Q fever.
Legionnaires disease.
Mycobacteria.
Tuberculosis.[33]
Anorexia nervosa, starvation.
Hypothyroidism.

PANCYTOPENIA SYNDROME, INHERITED[45]

ICD-10CM #   D61.818   Other pancytopenia

Fanconi anemia.
Shwachman-Diamond syndrome.
Dyskeratosis congenita.
Congenital amegakaryocytic thrombocytopenia.
Unclassified inherited bone marrow failure syndromes.
Other genetic syndromes:
    Down syndrome.
    Dubowitz syndrome.
    Seckel syndrome.
    Reticular dysgenesis.
    Schimke immunoosseous dysplasia.
    Familial aplastic anemia (non-Fanconi).
    Cartilage-hair hypoplasia.
    Noonan syndrome.

[33]Pancytopenia in tuberculosis only rarely is associated with a hypocellular bone marrow at biopsy or autopsy. Marrow failure in the setting of tuberculosis is almost always fatal; exceptional patients probably had underlying myelodysplasia or acute leukemia.

PAPILLEDEMA

ICD-10CM #   H47.10   Unspecified papilledema

CNS infections (viral, bacterial, fungal).
Medications (lithium, cisplatin, corticosteroids, tetracycline, etc.).
Head trauma.
CNS neoplasm (primary or metastatic).
Pseudotumor cerebri.
Cavernous sinus thrombosis.
SLE.
Sarcoidosis.
Subarachnoid hemorrhage.
Carbon dioxide retention.
Arnold–Chiari malformation and other developmental or congenital malformations.
Orbital lesions.
Central retinal vein occlusion.
Hypertensive encephalopathy.
Metabolic abnormalities.

PAPULOSQUAMOUS DISEASES[28]

ICD-10CM #   L98.8   Other specified disorders of the skin and subcutaneous tissue

Psoriasis.
Pityriasis rubra pilaris.
Pityriasis rosea.
Lichen planus.
Lichen nitidus.
Secondary syphilis.
Pityriasis lichenoides.
Parapsoriasis.
Mycosis fungoides.
Dermatophytosis.
Tinea versicolor.

PARANEOPLASTIC NEUROLOGIC SYNDROMES

ICD-10CM #   G13.0   Paraneoplastic neuromyopathy and neuropathy

Lambert-Eaton myasthenic syndrome.
Myasthenia gravis.
Guillain-Barré syndrome.
Amyotrophic lateral sclerosis.
Dermatomyositis.
Carcinoid myopathy.
Cerebellar degeneration.
Encephalomyelitis.
Optic neuritis, uveitis, retinopathy.
Stiff-man syndrome.
Autonomic neuropathy.
Brachial neuritis.
Sensory neuropathy.
Progressive multifocal leukoencephalopathy.

PARANEOPLASTIC SYNDROMES, ENDOCRINE[65]

ICD-10CM #   G13.0   Paraneoplastic neuromyopathy and neuropathy

Hypercalcemia.
Syndrome of inappropriate secretion of antidiuretic hormone.
Hypoglycemia.
Zollinger-Ellison syndrome.
Ectopic secretion of human chorionic gonadotropin.
Cushing's syndrome.

PARANEOPLASTIC SYNDROMES, NONENDOCRINE[65]

ICD-10CM #   G13.0   Paraneoplastic neuromyopathy and neuropathy

CUTANEOUS

Dermatomyositis.
Acanthosis nigricans.
Sweet's syndrome.
Erythema gyratum repens.
Systemic nodular panniculitis (Weber-Christian disease).

RENAL

Nephrotic syndrome.
Nephrogenic diabetes insipidus.

NEUROLOGIC

Subacute cerebellar degeneration.
Progressive multifocal leukoencephalopathy.
Subacute motor neuropathy.
Sensory neuropathy.
Ascending acute polyneuropathy (Guillain-Barré syndrome).
Myasthenic syndrome (Eaton-Lambert syndrome).

HEMATOLOGIC

Microangiopathic hemolytic anemia.
Migratory thrombophlebitis (Trousseau's syndrome).
Anemia of chronic disease.

RHEUMATOLOGIC

Polymyalgia rheumatica.
Hypertrophic pulmonary osteoarthropathy.

PARAPARESIS, ACUTE OR SUBACUTE[63]

ICD-10CM #   G82.2   Paraparesis

CAUSES OF ACUTE OR SUBACUTE PARAPARESIS

Trauma to a Previously Normal Spine
Vertebral Disease
Metastatic carcinoma.
Cervical spondylosis.
Dorsal disk prolapse.
Paget's disease.
Rheumatoid arthritis.
Pott's disease of spine.
Tumors
Extradural or intradural carcinoma, lymphoma, myeloma, leukemia.
Dorsal meningioma.
Neurofibroma.

Trichomonas cervicitis or vaginitis.
Tuboovarian abscess.

PREGNANCY-RELATED

First Trimester
Ectopic pregnancy.
Abortion.
Corpus luteum hematoma.
Late Pregnancy
Placental problems.
Preeclampsia.
Premature labor.

MISCELLANEOUS

Endometriosis.
Foreign objects.
Pelvic adhesions.
Pelvic neoplasm.
Primary dysmenorrhea.

PELVIC PAIN, NON-PREGNANT FEMALE[1]

ICD-10CM #	N94.89	Other specified conditions associated with female genital organs and menstrual cycle
	R10.2	Pelvic and perineal pain
	R10.10	Upper abdominal pain, unspecified
	R10.30	Lower abdominal pain, unspecified

DIFFERENTIAL DIAGNOSIS OF PELVIC PAIN IN NONPREGNANT FEMALES

Gynecologic Diagnoses
Infectious:
 Vaginitis.
 Cervicitis.
 Endometritis.
 Tuboovarian abscess.
 Pelvic inflammatory disease.
Ovarian:
 Ovarian torsion.
 Ruptured ovarian cyst.
 Ovarian tumor.
 Degenerating ovarian tumor.
 Mittelschmerz.
Cervical:
 Cervical polyps.
 Cervical stenosis.
 Cervical cancer.
Uterine:
 Uterine fibroids.
 Degenerating uterine fibroids.
 Adenomyosis.
 Endometrial carcinoma.
Extrauterine:
 Endometriosis.
 Adhesions.
 Residual accessory ovary.
Nongynecologic Diagnoses
• Gastrointestinal:
 Acute appendicitis.
 Mesenteric lymphadenitis.
 Diverticulitis.
 Inflammatory bowel disease.

 Irritable bowel syndrome.
 Bowel obstruction.
 Intraabdominal abscess.
 Colorectal carcinoma.
Urinary:
 Cystitis.
 Renal colic.
 Bladder cancer.
Musculoskeletal:
 Abdominal wall pain.
 Lumbar back pain.
 Fibromyalgia.
 Muscular strain.
 Piriformis syndrome.
Neurologic:
 Lumbar radiculopathy.
 Shingles.
 Spondylosis.
Psychologic:
 Personality disorders.
 Major depressive disorder.

PENILE RASH

ICD-10CM #	R21	Rash and other nonspecific skin eruption

Herpes simplex 2.
Balanitis (Candida).
Condyloma acuminatum.
Molluscum contagiosum.
Scabies.
Pediculosis pubis.
Pearly penile papules.
Lichen nitidus.
Fox-Fordyce disease (follicular papules).
Trauma.

PERIANAL PAIN[67]

ICD-10CM #	K62.89	Other specified diseases of anus and rectum

Fissure-in-ano
Anal sepsis
 Anal abscess
 Anal fistula
Hemorrhoids
 Internal hemorrhoids
 External hemorrhoids
Pruritus ani
Proctalgia fugax
Chronic perianal pain syndromes
 Coccygodynia
 Descending perineum syndrome
 Levator ani syndrome
 Idiopathic perineal pain

PERICARDIAL EFFUSION

ICD-10CM #	I30.9	Acute pericarditis, unspecified
	I31.3	Pericardial effusion

Pericarditis.
Uremia.
Myxedema.
Neoplasm (leukemia, lymphoma, metastatic).
Hemorrhage (trauma, leakage of thoracic aneurysm).
SLE, rheumatoid disease.
Myocardial infarction

PERIODIC PARALYSIS, HYPERKALEMIC

ICD-10CM #	G83.9	Paralytic syndrome, unspecified

Chronic renal failure.
Renal insufficiency with excessive potassium supplementation.
Potassium-sparing diuretics.
Endocrinopathies (hypoaldosteronism, adrenal insufficiency).

PERIODIC PARALYSIS, HYPOKALEMIC

ICD-10CM #	G83.9	Paralytic syndrome, unspecified

Chronic diarrhea (laxative abuse, sprue, villous adenoma).
Potassium-depleting diuretics.
Medications (amphotericin B, corticosteroids).
Chronic licorice ingestion.
Thyrotoxicosis.
Renal tubular acidosis.
Conn's syndrome.
Barter's syndrome.
Barium intoxication.

PERITONEAL CARCINOMATOSIS[28]

ICD-10CM #	C78.6	Secondary malignant neoplasm of retroperitoneum and peritoneum

PRIMARY DISORDERS OF THE PERITONEUM: MESOTHELIOMA

Metastatic spread from:
 Stomach.
 Colon.
 Pancreas.
 Carcinoid.
Other Intraabdominal Organs
Ovary.
Pseudomyxoma peritonei.
Extraabdominal Primary Tumors
Breast.
Lung.
Hematologic Malignancy
Lymphoma.

PERITONEAL EFFUSION[35]

ICD-10CM #	R18	Ascites
	R85.9	Unspecified abnormal finding in specimens from digestive organs and abdominal cavity
	R88.8	Abnormal findings in other body fluids and substances

TRANSUDATES

Increased hydrostatic pressure or decreased plasma oncotic pressure.
Congestive heart failure.
Hepatic cirrhosis.
Hypoproteinemia.

EXUDATES

Increased capillary permeability or decreased lymphatic resorption.

Infections (TB, spontaneous bacterial peritonitis, secondary bacterial peritonitis).

Neoplasms (hepatoma, metastatic carcinoma, lymphoma, mesothelioma).

Trauma.

Pancreatitis.

Bile peritonitis (e.g., ruptured gallbladder).

CHYLOUS EFFUSION

Damage or obstruction to thoracic duct.

Trauma.

Lymphoma.

Carcinoma.

Tuberculosis.

Parasitic infection.

PERIUMBILICAL SWELLING

ICD-10CM # R19.00 Intraabdominal and pelvic swelling, mass and lump, unspecified site

Umbilical hernia.

Lipoma.

Epigastric hernia.

Umbilical granuloma.

Omphalocele.

Gastroschisis.

Caput medusae.

PHARYNGEAL OBSTRUCTION, CAUSES[51]

ICD-10CM # varies with specific diagnosis

CAUSES OF PHARYNGEAL OBSTRUCTION

Malignant or benign tumors (e.g., papillomas, polyps).

Infection (e.g., croup, epiglottitis, tonsillar abscess).

Edema or hypertrophy (e.g., angioneurotic edema, anaphylactic reactions, postradiation therapy, obstructive sleep apnea).

Trauma (e.g., cricoid fracture, cervical subluxation, precervical hematoma).

Burn injury.

Extrinsic compression (e.g., goiter or pregnancy-related thyroid enlargement).

Foreign body.

Congenital web (infants).

Sarcoidosis and other granulomatous diseases.

Amyloid.

PHEOCHROMOCYTOMA-TYPE SPELLS[52]

ICD-10CM # I15.2 Hypertension due to pheochromocytoma

DIFFERENTIAL DIAGNOSIS OF PHEOCHROMOCYTOMA-TYPE SPELLS

Endocrine Causes

Carbohydrate intolerance.

Hyperadrenergic spells.

Hypoglycemia.

Pancreatic tumors (e.g., insulinoma).

Pheochromocytoma.

Primary hypogonadism (menopausal syndrome).

Thyrotoxicosis.

Cardiovascular Causes

Angina.

Cardiovascular deconditioning.

Labile essential hypertension.

Orthostatic hypotension.

Paroxysmal cardiac arrhythmia.

Pulmonary edema.

Renovascular disease.

Syncope (e.g., vasovagal reaction).

Psychologic Causes

Factitious (e.g., drugs, Valsalva).

Hyperventilation.

Severe anxiety and panic disorders.

Somatization disorder.

Pharmacologic Causes

Chlorpropamide-alcohol flush.

Combination of a monoamine oxidase inhibitor and a decongestant.

Illegal drug ingestion (cocaine, phencyclidine, lysergic acid diethylamide).

Sympathomimetic drug ingestion.

Vancomycin ("red man syndrome").

Withdrawal of adrenergic-inhibitor.

Neurologic Causes

Autonomic neuropathy.

Cerebrovascular insufficiency.

Diencephalic epilepsy (autonomic seizures).

Migraine headache.

Postural orthostatic tachycardia syndrome.

Stroke.

Other Causes

Carcinoid syndrome.

Mast cell disease.

Recurrent idiopathic anaphylaxis.

Unexplained flushing spells.

PHOTODERMATOSES[28]

ICD-10CM #	L56.0	Drug phototoxic response
	L56.1	Drug photoallergic response
	L56.2	Photocontact dermatitis [berloque dermatitis]

Polymorphous light eruption.

Chronic actinic dermatitis.

Solar urticaria.

Phototoxicity and photoallergy.

Porphyrias.

PHOTOSENSITIVITY

ICD-10CM #	L56.0	Drug phototoxic response
	L56.1	Drug photoallergic response
	L56.2	Photocontact dermatitis [berloque dermatitis]

Solar urticaria.

Photoallergic reaction.

Phototoxic reaction.

Polymorphous light eruption.

Porphyria cutanea tarda.

SLE.

Drug induced (e.g., tetracyclines).

PIGMENTURIA[6]

ICD-10CM # R82 Other abnormal findings in urine

HEMOGLOBINURIA

Hemolysis.

HEMATURIA

Renal causes.

Trauma.

ACUTE INTERMITTENT PORPHYRIA

Bilirubinuria

Food

Beets.

Drugs

Vitamin B$_{12}$.

Rifampin.

Phenytoin.

Laxatives.

PITUITARY REGION TUMORS[32]

ICD-10CM # varies with specific diagnosis

PRIMARY TUMORS IN THE SELLAR AND PARASELLAR REGION

Tumor

Pituitary macroadenoma.

Meningioma.

Schwannoma (e.g., of fifth nerve).

Chordoma.

Chondrosarcoma.

Crangiopharyngioma.

Rathke's cleft cyst.

Dermoid.

Epidermoid.

Tuber cinereum hamartoma.

Optic glioma.

Germ cell tumors.

PLEURAL EFFUSIONS

ICD-10CM # J91.8 Pleural effusion in other conditions classified elsewhere

EXUDATIVE

Neoplasm: bronchogenic carcinoma, breast carcinoma, mesothelioma, lymphoma, ovarian carcinoma, multiple myeloma, leukemia, Meigs' syndrome.

Infections: viral pneumonia, bacterial pneumonia, *Mycoplasma,* TB, fungal and parasitic diseases, extension from subphrenic abscess.

Trauma.

Collagen vascular diseases: SLE, RA, scleroderma, polyarteritis, granulomatosis with polyangiitis (Wegener's granulomatosis).

Pulmonary infarction.

Pancreatitis.

Postcardiotomy/Dressler's syndrome.

Drug-induced SLE (hydralazine, procainamide).

Postabdominal surgery.

Ruptured esophagus.

Chronic effusion secondary to congestive failure.

TRANSUDATIVE

CHF.
Hepatic cirrhosis.
Nephrotic syndrome.
Hypoproteinemia from any cause.
Meigs' syndrome.

PLEURAL EFFUSIONS, MALIGNANCY-ASSOCIATED

ICD-10CM #	C78.2	Secondary malignant neoplasm of pleura

Lung cancer	(30% to 40%)
Breast cancer	(20% to 25%)
Lymphoma	(10% to 15%)
Leukemia	(5% to 10%)
GI tract	(5%)
GU tract	(5%)
Reproductive	(3%)

PNEUMATOSIS INTESTINALIS IN NEONATE AND OLDER CHILD[32]

ICD-10CM #	varies with specific diagnosis

CAUSES OF PNEUMATOSIS INTESTINALIS IN THE NEONATE AND THE OLDER CHILD

- Necrotizing enterocolitis.
- Bowel ischemia, inflammation, and obstruction.
- Cyanotic congenital heart disease.
- Hirschsprung's disease.
- Gastroschisis.
- Anorectal atresia.
- Inflammatory bowel disease.
- Lymphoma.
- Leukemia.
- CMV and rotavirus gastroenteritis.
- Colonoscopy.
- Caustic ingestion.
- Short bowel syndrome.
- Congenital immune deficiency states.
- *Clostridium* infection.
- Chronic steroid use.
- Posthepatic, renal, or bone marrow transplant.
- Collagen vascular disease.
- Graft-versus-host disease.
- AIDS.

PNEUMONIA, CHRONIC[9]

ICD-10CM #	J15.9	Unspecified bacterial pneumonia
	J12.9	Viral pneumonia, unspecified
	B25.0	Cytomegaloviral pneumonitis
	J18.0	Bronchopneumonia, unspecified organism

INFECTIOUS AGENTS THAT TYPICALLY CAUSE CHRONIC PNEUMONIA

Bacteria
Mixed aerobic and anaerobic bacteria.
Actinomyces spp.
Nocardia spp.
Rhodococcus equi.

Burkholderia pseudomallei.
Mycobacteria
Mycobacterium tuberculosis.
Mycobacterium kansasii.
Mycobacterium avium complex.
Mycobacterium abscessus.
Mycobacterium terrae.
Fungi
Aspergillus spp.
Blastomyces dermatitidis.
Coccidioides spp.
Cryptococcus neoformans.
Cryptococcus gattii.
Dark-walled molds.
Emmonsia parvum var. crescens.
Histoplasma capsulatum.
Sporothrix schenckii complex.
Paracoccidioides brasiliensis.
Penicillium marneffei.
Scedosporium apiospermum.
Parasites
Dirofilaria.
    Echinococcus granulosus.
    Filaria (tropical pulmonary eosinophilia).
    Paragonimus westermani.

NONINFECTIOUS CAUSES OF CHRONIC PNEUMONIA

Neoplasia
Carcinoma (primary or metastatic).
Hodgkin's disease and non-Hodgkin's lymphoma.
Other lymphoproliferative disorders.
Cystic Fibrosis
Sarcoidosis
Amyloidosis
Vasculitis (Autoimmune Diseases).
Systemic lupus erythematosus.
Polyarteritis nodosa.
Granulomatosis with polyangiitis (Wegener's granulomatosis).
Allergic angiitis and granulomatosis (Churg-Strauss syndrome).
Goodpasture's syndrome.
Microscopic polyangiitis.
Lymphomatoid granulomatosis.
Progressive systemic sclerosis.
Rheumatoid arthritis.
Mixed connective tissue syndrome (overlap syndrome).
Chemicals, Drugs
Radiation
Recurrent Pulmonary Emboli
Bronchial Obstruction with Atelectasis (e.g., Tumor, Foreign Body)
Pulmonary Sequestration
Pulmonary Infiltration with Eosinophilia Syndrome
Löffler's syndrome—usually transient.
Pneumonia plus asthma (e.g., allergic bronchopulmonary aspergillosis).
Bronchocentric granulomatosis.
Chronic eosinophilic pneumonia.
Pneumoconiosis
Asbestosis.
Berylliosis.
Silicosis.
Anthracosilicosis.
    Chronic Form of Extrinsic Allergic Alveolitis (Hypersensitivity Pneumonitis)

OTHER LUNG DISEASES: CAUSE UNKNOWN

Chronic Organizing Pneumonia
Chronic Interstitial Pneumonia (Fibrosing Alveolitis, Idiopathic Pulmonary Fibrosis)
Usual interstitial pneumonia (UIP).
Desquamative interstitial pneumonia (DIP).
Lymphocytic interstitial pneumonia (LIP).
Giant cell interstitial pneumonia (GIP).
Eosinophilic granuloma (histiocytosis X).
Lymphangioleiomyomatosis.
Pulmonary alveolar proteinosis.
Pulmonary alveolar microlithiasis.
Idiopathic pulmonary hemosiderosis.
Angiocentric immunoproliferative lesions.

PNEUMONIA MIMICS[12]

ICD-10CM #	varies with specific diagnosis

NONINFECTIOUS CAUSES THAT MAY PRESENT AS PNEUMONIA

Radiologic Technique
Inadequate inspiration.
Breast shadow.
Thymus.
Uneven grid on film.
Underpenetrated film.
Primary Pulmonary
Asthma.
Bronchiectasis.
Atelectasis.
Bronchopulmonary dysplasia.
Cystic fibrosis.
Pulmonary sequestration.
Congenital cystic adenomatoid malformation.
α_1-Antitrypsin deficiency.
Aspiration
Foreign body.
Chemical.
Recurrent caused by anatomic or physiologic disorders.
Primary Cardiac
Congenital heart disease.
Congestive heart failure.
Pulmonary Infarction
Sickle cell vasoocclusive crisis.
Pulmonary embolism.
Collagen Vascular Disorders
Acute Respiratory Distress Syndrome
Pleural Effusion
Neoplasm
. From Boyer KM: Nonbacterial pneumonia. In Feigin RD, Cherry JD (eds): Textbook of Pediatric Infectious Diseases, 4th ed. Philadelphia, WB Saunders, 1998, pp 260-273.

PNEUMONIA, NONRESPONDING, CAUSES[51]

ICD-10CM #	J15.9	Unspecified bacterial pneumonia
	J12.9	Viral pneumonia, unspecified
	B25.0	Cytomegaloviral pneumonitis
	J18.0	Bronchopneumonia, unspecified organism

CAUSES OF NONRESPONDING PNEUMONIA

Infectious Pneumonia

- Resistant microorganisms:
  - Community-acquired pneumonia (e.g., *Streptococcus pneumoniae*, *Staphylococcus aureus*).
  - Nosocomial pneumonia (e.g., *Acinetobacter*, *methicillin-resistant Staphylococcus aureus* (MRSA), *Pseudomonas aeruginosa*).
- Uncommon microorganisms (e.g., *Mycobacterium tuberculosis*, *Nocardia* spp., fungi, *Pneumocystis jirovecii*).
- Complications of pneumonia:
  Empyema.
  Abscess or necrotizing pneumonia.
  Metastatic infection.

Noninfectious Pneumonia

Neoplasms.
Pulmonary hemorrhage.
Pulmonary embolism.
Sarcoidosis.
Eosinophilic pneumonia.
Pulmonary edema.
Acute respiratory distress syndrome.
Bronchiolitis obliterans with organizing pneumonia.
Drug-induced pulmonary disease.
Pulmonary vasculitis.

PNEUMONIA, RECURRENT

ICD-10CM #	J15.9	Unspecified bacterial pneumonia
	J12.9	Viral pneumonia, unspecified
	B25.0	Cytomegaloviral pneumonitis
	J18.0	Bronchopneumonia, unspecified organism

Mechanical obstruction from neoplasm.
Chronic aspiration (tube feeding, alcoholism, CVA, neuromuscular disorders, seizure disorder, inability to cough).
Bronchiectasis.
Kyphoscoliosis.
COPD, CHF, asthma, silicosis, pulmonary fibrosis, cystic fibrosis.
Pulmonary TB, chronic sinusitis.
Immunosuppression (HIV, corticosteroids, leukemia, chemotherapy, splenectomy).

PNEUMOPERITONEUM, NEONATAL[32]

ICD-10CM #   varies with specific diagnosis

CAUSES OF NEONATAL PNEUMOPERITONEUM

Necrotizing enterocolitis.
Spontaneous perforation of a hollow viscus.
   Stomach.
   Duodenum.
   Ileum.
   Colon.
Malrotation and volvulus.
Distal obstruction.

Perforation of Meckel's diverticulum.
Anterior abdominal wall defects.
   Pentalogy of Cantrell.
   Omphalocele.
   Gastroschisis.
   Cloacal exstrophy.
Stress and peptic ulcers.
Mechanical ventilation (air leak) or resuscitation ("bagging").
Post-laparotomy.
Iatrogenic gastric perforation with an orogastric tube.
Iatrogenic colon perforation.
   Thermometer.
   During an enema.
Indomethacin.
Dexamethasone treatment.

PNEUMOTHORAX, IN CHILDREN[45]

ICD-10CM #	J93.0	Spontaneous tension pneumothorax
	J93	Pneumothorax
	J93.9	Pneumothorax unspecified

SPONTANEOUS

Primary idiopathic—usually resulting from ruptured subpleural blebs.
Secondary blebs.
Congenital lung disease:
   Congenital cystic adenomatoid malformation.
   Bronchogenic cysts.
   Pulmonary hypoplasia.
Conditions associated with increased intrathoracic pressure:
   Asthma.
   Bronchiolitis.
   Air-block syndrome in neonates.
   Cystic fibrosis.
   Airway foreign body.
Infection:
   Pneumatocele.
   Lung abscess.
   Bronchopleural fistula.
Diffuse lung disease:
   Langerhans cell histiocytosis.
   Tuberous sclerosis.
   Marfan syndrome.
   Ehlers-Danlos syndrome.
Metastatic neoplasm—usually osteosarcoma (rare).

TRAUMATIC

Noniatrogenic.
   Penetrating trauma.
   Blunt trauma.
   Loud music (air pressure).
Iatrogenic.
   Thoracotomy.
   Thoracoscopy, thoracentesis.
   Tracheostomy.
   Tube or needle puncture.
Mechanical ventilation.

POLIOSIS[11]

ICD-10CM #   varies with specific diagnosis

CAUSES OF POLIOSIS

Ocular

Chronic anterior blepharitis.
Sympathetic ophthalmitis.
Idiopathic uveitis.

Systemic

Vogt–Koyanagi–Harada syndrome.
Waardenburg syndrome.
Vitiligo.
Marfan syndrome.
Tuberous sclerosis.

POLYCYTHEMIA

ICD-10CM #	D45	Polycythemia primary
	D75.1	Polycythemia secondary

Tobacco abuse.
Chronic lung disease.
High altitude.
Sleep apnea.
Right-to-left cardiac shunts.
Erythropoietin administration.
Androgens/anabolic steroids.
Polycystic kidney disease.
Renal cell carcinoma.
Hepatocellular carcinoma.
Polycythemia vera.
Carbon monoxide exposure.
Primary familial and congenital polycythemia.
High-oxygen–affinity hemoglobins.
Uterine leiomyoma, meningioma, pheochromocytoma, parathyroid carcinoma.
Cobalt exposure.

POLYCYTHEMIAS, DIFFERENTIAL DIAGNOSIS[38]

ICD-10CM #	D45	Polycythemia primary
	D75.1	Polycythemia secondary

DIFFERENTIAL DIAGNOSIS OF THE POLYCYTHEMIAS

Relative or Spurious Polycythemia

Decreased plasma volume—reduced fluid intake, marked loss of body fluids (diaphoresis, vomiting, diarrhea, "third spacing").
Gaisböck syndrome.
Overfilling of blood in collection vacuum tubes.
Absolute polycythemia
Secondary polycythemia.
Acquired.
Hypoxia.
   Pulmonary disease.
   Cyanotic congenital heart disease.
   Hypoventilation syndromes:
      Sleep apnea.
      Pickwickian syndrome.
      High altitude.
      Smokers' polycythemia, hookah polycythemia, carbon monoxide intoxication caused by industrial exposure.
Postrenal transplantation erythrocytosis.
Aberrant erythropoietin production.

Differential Diagnosis

II

Tumors:
    Renal cell carcinoma.
    Wilms tumor.
    Hepatic carcinoma.
    Uterine leiomyomata.
    Virilizing ovarian tumors.
    Vascular cerebellar tumors.
    Miscellaneous renal and hepatic disorders:
        Solitary renal cysts.
        Polycystic kidney disease.
        Renal artery stenosis hydronephrosis.
        Viral hepatitis.
Endocrine disorders:
    Cushing syndrome.
    Primary aldosteronism.
    Androgen use.
    Erythropoietin use.
    Congenital Polycythemias:
        Abnormal high-affinity hemoglobin variants.
        Bisphosphoglycerate deficiency.
        Congenital methemoglobinemia.
        Chuvash polycythemia (von Hippel Lindau mutations).
        Prolyl hydroxylase mutations.
        Hypoxia-inducible factor gene mutations.
Primary polycythemias:
    Primary congenital and familial polycythemia.
    Polycythemia vera.

POLYCYTHEMIA, RELATIVE VERSUS ABSOLUTE[39]

ICD-10CM # D75.1 Secondary polycythemia

RELATIVE OR SPURIOUS POLYCYTHEMIA

Decreased plasma volume—reduced fluid intake, marked loss of body fluids (diaphoresis, vomiting, diarrhea, "third-spacing").
Gaisböck syndrome.
Overfilling of blood in collection vacuum tubes.

ABSOLUTE POLYCYTHEMIA

Primary Congenital and Familial Polycythemia
Secondary Polycythemia Acquired:
Hypoxia:
    Pulmonary disease.
    Cyanotic congenital heart disease.
    Hypoventilation syndromes—sleep apnea, Pickwickian syndrome.
High altitude.
Smokers' polycythemia, carbon monoxide intoxication due to industrial exposure.
Postrenal transplantation erythrocytosis.
Aberrant erythropoietin production:
    Tumors—renal cell carcinoma, Wilms' tumor, hepatic carcinoma, uterine leiomyomata, virilizing ovarian tumors, vascular cerebellar tumors.
    Miscellaneous renal and hepatic disorders—solitary renal cysts, polycystic kidney disease, renal artery stenosis, hydronephrosis, viral hepatitis.
Endocrine disorders—Cushing's syndrome, primary aldosteronism.
Androgen use.
Erythropoietin use.

Congenital:
    Abnormal high-affinity hemoglobin variants.
    Bisphosphoglycerate deficiency.
    Congenital methemoglobinemia.
    Chuvash polycythemia (von Hippel–Lindau mutations).
    Prolyl hydroxylase mutations.

POLYCYTHEMIA VERA

POLYMYALGIAS[36]

ICD-10CM # M35.3 Polymyalgia rheumatica

DISEASE ENTITIES WITH POLYMYALGIAS

Rheumatoid arthritis.
Rotator cuff syndrome.
Osteoarthritis of shoulder and hip joints.
Fibromyalgia.
Polymyositis/dermatomyositis.
Spondyloarthritis.
Systemic lupus erythematosus.
Vasculitides.
Paraneoplastic myalgias.
Infection-associated myalgias.
Statin therapy.
RS3PE (remitting seronegative symmetric synovitis and pitting edema).
Parkinson's disease.
Hypothyroidism.

POLYNEUROPATHY[72]

ICD-10CM # G61.9 Inflammatory polyneuropathy, unspecified

PREDOMINANTLY MOTOR

- Guillain-Barré syndrome.
- Porphyria.
- Diphtheria.
- Lead.
- Hereditary sensorimotor neuropathy, types I and II.
- Paraneoplastic neuropathy.

PREDOMINANTLY SENSORY

Diabetes.
Amyloidosis.
Leprosy.
Lyme disease.
Paraneoplastic neuropathy.
Vitamin B_{12} deficiency.
Hereditary sensory neuropathy, types I-IV.

PREDOMINANTLY AUTONOMIC

- Diabetes.
- Amyloidosis.
- Alcoholic neuropathy.
- Familial dysautonomias.

MIXED SENSORIMOTOR

- Systemic diseases: renal failure, hypothyroidism, acromegaly, RA, periarteritis nodosa, SLE, multiple myeloma, macroglobulinemia, remote effect of malignancy.
- Medications: isoniazid, nitrofurantoin, ethambutol, chloramphenicol, chloroquine, vincristine, vinblastine, dapsone, disulfiram, diphenylhydantoin, cisplatin, 1-tryptophan.

- Environmental toxins: N-hexane, methyl N-butyl ketone, acrylamide, carbon disulfide, carbon monoxide, hexachlorophene, organophosphates.
- Deficiency disorders: malabsorption, alcoholism, vitamin B_1 deficiency, Refsum's disease, metachromatic leukodystrophy.

POLYNEUROPATHY, DEMYELINATING[6]

ICD-10CM # G37.9 Demyelinating disease of central nervous system, unspecified

Guillain-Barré syndrome.
    Acute inflammatory demyelinating polyradiculoneuropathy (AIDP).
    Acute motor axonal neuropathy (AMAN).
    Acute motor and sensory axonal neuropathy (AMSAN).
    Miller Fisher syndrome.
Chronic inflammatory demyelinating polyradiculoplexo-neuropathy.
Malignancy.
HIV.
Hepatitis B.
Buckthorn.
Diphtheria.

POLYNEUROPATHY, DISTAL SENSORIMOTOR[6]

ICD-10CM # G63 Polyneuropathy in diseases classified elsewhere

Diabetes mellitus.
Alcoholism.
Neoplastic or paraneoplastic.
Hereditary motor and sensory neuropathies (Charcot-Marie-Tooth).
Cryptogenic sensorimotor polyneuropathies (CSPN).
HIV.
Toxins:
    Organic or industrial agents:
        Acrylamide.
        Allyl chloride.
        Carbon disulfide.
        Ethylene oxide.
        Hexacarbons.
        Methyl bromide.
        Organophosphate-induced delayed polyneuropathy (OPIDP).
        Polychlorinated biphenyls (PCBs).
        Trichloroethylene.
        Vacor.
    Metals:
        Arsenic.
        Gold.
        Mercury (inorganic).
        Thallium.
    Therapeutic agents:
        Amiodarone.
        Antiretrovirals.
        Dapsone.
        Disulfiram.
        Isoniazid.
        Metronidazole.
        Nitrofurantoin.

Paclitaxel (Taxol).
Phenytoin.
Statins (HMG-CoA reductase inhibitors).
Thalidomide.
Vinca alkaloids (vincristine, vinblastine).
Nutritional:
   Beriberi (thiamine or vitamin B_1).
   Pellagra (niacin, B vitamins).
   Pernicious anemia (vitamin B_{12}).
   Pyridoxine deficiency (vitamin B_6).
End-organ dysfunction
   ○ Acromegaly.
   ○ Chronic pulmonary disease.
   ○ Hypothyroidism.
   ○ Renal failure (uremic neuropathy).
Paraproteinemias:
   ○ Amyloidosis.
   ○ Monoclonal gammopathy of unknown significance (MGUS).
   ○ Multiple myeloma.
   ○ Waldenström's macroglobulinemia.
Porphyria.

HMG-CoA, Hydroxymethylglutaryl coenzyme A.

POLYNEUROPATHY, DRUG-INDUCED[72]

ICD-10CM #   G62.0   Drug-induced polyneuropathy

DRUGS IN ONCOLOGY

Vincristine.
Procarbazine.
Cisplatin.
Misonidazole.
Metronidazole (Flagyl).
Taxol.

DRUGS IN INFECTIOUS DISEASES

Isoniazid.
Nitrofurantoin.
Dapsone.
ddC (dideoxycytidine).
ddI (dideoxyinosine).

DRUGS IN CARDIOLOGY

Hydralazine.
Perhexiline maleate.
Procainamide.
Disopyramide.

DRUGS IN RHEUMATOLOGY

Gold salts.
Chloroquine.

DRUGS IN NEUROLOGY AND PSYCHIATRY

• Diphenylhydantoin.
• Glutethimide.
• Methaqualone.

MISCELLANEOUS

• Disulfiram (Antabuse).
• Vitamin: (pyridoxine in megadoses).

POLYNEUROPATHY, SYMMETRIC[72]

ICD-10CM #   G61.9   Inflammatory polyneuropathy, unspecified

ACQUIRED NEUROPATHIES

Toxic:
   Drugs.
   Industrial toxins.
   Heavy metals.
   Abused substances.
Metabolic/endocrine:
   Diabetes.
   Chronic renal failure.
   Hypothyroidism.
   Polyneuropathy of critical illness.
Nutritional deficiency:
   Vitamin B_{12} deficiency.
   Alcoholism.
   Vitamin E deficiency.
Paraneoplastic:
   ○ Carcinoma.
   ○ Lymphoma.
• Plasma cell dyscrasia:
   Myeloma, typical, atypical, and solitary forms.
   Primary systemic amyloidosis.
Idiopathic chronic inflammatory demyelinating polyneuropathies.
Polyneuropathies associated with peripheral nerve autoantibodies.
Acquired immunodeficiency syndrome.

INHERITED NEUROPATHIES

Neuropathies with Biochemical Markers
• Refsum's disease.
• Bassen-Kornzweig disease.
• Tangier disease.
• Metachromatic leukodystrophy.
• Krabbe's disease.
• Adrenomyeloneuropathy.
• Fabry's disease.

Neuropathies without Biochemical Markers or Systemic Involvement
Hereditary motor neuropathy.
Hereditary sensory neuropathy.
Hereditary sensorimotor neuropathy.

POLYURIA

ICD-10CM #   R35.8   Other polyuria

DM.
Diabetes insipidus.
Primary polydipsia (compulsive water drinking).
Hypercalcemia.
Hypokalemia.
Postobstructive uropathy.
Diuretic phase of renal failure.
Drugs: diuretics, caffeine, alcohol, lithium.
Sickle cell trait or disease, chronic pyelonephritis (failure to concentrate urine).
Anxiety, cold weather.

POPLITEAL SWELLING

ICD-10CM #	I87.1	Compression of vein
	I72.4	Aneurysm of artery of lower extremity
	S85.009A	Unspecified injury of popliteal artery, unspecified leg, initial encounter
	I77.3	Arterial fibromuscular dysplasia
	M71.20	Synovial cyst of popliteal space [Baker], unspecified knee
	I80.3	Phlebitis and thrombophlebitis of lower extremities, unspecified
	M66.369	Spontaneous rupture of flexor tendons, unspecified lower leg

Phlebitis (superficial).
Lymphadenitis.
Trauma: fractured tibia or fibula, contusion, traumatic neuroma.
DVT.
Ruptured varicose vein.
Baker's cyst.
Popliteal abscess.
Osteomyelitis.
Ruptured tendon.
Aneurysm of popliteal artery.
Neoplasm: lipoma, osteogenic sarcoma, neurofibroma, fibrosarcoma.

PORTAL HYPERTENSION[3]

ICD-10CM #   K76.6   Portal hypertension

INCREASED RESISTANCE TO FLOW

Presinusoidal
Portal or splenic vein occlusion (thrombosis, tumor).
Schistosomiasis.
Congenital hepatic fibrosis.
Sarcoidosis.
Sinusoidal
Cirrhosis (all causes).
Alcoholic hepatitis.
Postsinusoidal
Venoocclusive disease.
Budd-Chiari syndrome.
Constrictive pericarditis.

INCREASED PORTAL BLOOD FLOW

Splenomegaly not caused by liver disease.
Arterioportal fistula.

POSTMENOPAUSAL BLEEDING

ICD-10CM # N95.0 Postmenopausal bleeding

Hormone replacement therapy.
Neoplasm (uterine, ovarian, cervical, vaginal, vulvar).
Atrophic vaginitis.
Vaginal infection.
Polyp.
Extragenital (GI, urinary).
Tamoxifen.
Trauma.

POSTURAL HYPOTENSION, NONNEUROLOGIC CAUSES

ICD-10CM # I95.1 Orthostatic hypotension

Diuretics and hypertensive agents.
GI hemorrhage.
Alcohol.
Excessive heat.
Rapid volume loss from diarrhea, vomiting.
Hemodialysis.
Extensive burns.
Pyrexia.
Aortic stenosis (impaired output).
Constrictive pericarditis, atrial myxoma (impaired cardiac filling).
Adrenal insufficiency.
Diabetes insipidus.
Vasodilator agents (e.g., nitrates).

PREMATURE GRAYING, SCALP HAIR

ICD-10CM # varies with specific diagnosis

Chemical exposure (e.g., phenol/catechol derivatives, sulfhydryls, arsenic).
Physical agents (e.g., ionizing radiation, lasers).
Hyperthyroidism.
Vitamin B_{12} deficiency.
Down syndrome.
Chronic and severe protein deficiency.
Vitiligo.
Idiopathic.
Myotonic dystrophy.
Ataxia-telangiectasia.
Progeria.
Werner's syndrome.

PREMATURE VENTRICULAR CONTRACTIONS AND VENTRICULAR TACHYCARDIA[6]

ICD-10CM # I49.40 Unspecified premature depolarization
I47.2 Ventricular tachycardia

CAUSES OF PREMATURE VENTRICULAR CONTRACTIONS AND VENTRICULAR TACHYCARDIA

Acute or previous myocardial infarction/ischemia.

Hypokalemia.
Hypoxemia.
Ischemic heart disease.
Valvular disease.
Catecholamine excess.[35]
Other drug intoxications (especially cyclic antidepressants).
Idiopathic causes.[36]
Digitalis toxicity.
Hypomagnesemia.
Hypercapnia.
Class I antidysrhythymic agents.
Ethanol.
Myocardial contusion.
Cardiomyopathy.
Acidosis.
Alkalosis.
Methylxanthine toxicity.

PROLONGED QT SYNDROMES[50]

ICD-10CM # I45.81 Long QT syndrome

CLASSIFICATION AND CAUSES OF PROLONGED QT SYNDROMES THAT PRODUCE TORSADES DE POINTES

Pause Dependent (Acquired)
Drug induced: Class IA and IC antidysrhythmics; many phenothiazines and butyrophenones (notably haloperidol and droperidol), cyclic antidepressants, antibiotics (especially macrolides), organophosphates, antihistamines, antifungals, antiseizure and antiemetic agents.
Electrolyte abnormalities: hypokalemia, hypomagnesemia, hypocalcemia (rarely).
Diet related: starvation, low protein.
Severe bradycardia or atrioventricular block.
Hypothyroidism.
Contrast injection.
Cerebrovascular accident (especially intraparenchymal).
Myocardial ischemia.

Adrenergic Dependent (Tachycardia Prompted)
Congenital:
   Jervell and Lange-Nielsen syndrome (deafness, autosomal recessive).
   Romano-Ward syndrome (normal hearing, autosomal dominant).
   Sporadic (normal hearing, no familial tendency).
   Mitral valve prolapse.
Acquired (Rare):
   Cerebrovascular disease (especially subarachnoid hemorrhage).
   Autonomic surgery: radical neck dissection, carotid endarterectomy, truncal vagotomy.

---

[35]Relative increase in sympathetic tone from drugs (direct or indirect) or conditions that augment catecholamine release or decrease parasympathetic tone.
[36]Isolated premature ventricular contractions (PVCs) can occur in up to 50% of young subjects without obvious cardiac or noncardiac disease; however, multiform and repetitive PVCs and ventricular tachycardia are rarely seen in this population.

PROPTOSIS[56]

ICD-10CM # H05.20 Unspecified exophthalmos
H05.2 Ocular proptosis

Thyrotoxicosis.
Orbital pseudotumor.
Optic nerve tumor.
Cavernous sinus AV fistula, cavernous sinus thrombosis.
Cellulitis.
Metastatic tumor to orbit.

PROPTOSIS AND PALATAL NECROTIC ULCERS

ICD-10CM # K13.70 Unspecified lesions of oral mucosa
K13.79 Other lesions of oral mucosa
H05.20 Unspecified exophthalmos

Cavernous sinus thrombosis.
Bacterial orbital cellulitis.
Metastatic neoplasm.
Rhinocerebral mucormycosis.
Ecthyma gangrenosum.
CNS aspergillosis.

PROTEIN-LOSING ENTEROPATHY, PEDIATRIC AGE[45]

ICD-10CM # E44.0 Moderate proteinenergy malnutrition

CAUSES OF PROTEIN-LOSING ENTEROPATHY

Mucosal inflammation:
Infection:
   Cytomegalovirus.
   Bacterial overgrowth.
   Invasive bacterial infection.
Gastric inflammation:
   Ménétrier disease.
   Eosinophilic gastroenteropathy.
Intestinal inflammation:
   Celiac disease.
   Crohn disease.
Eosinophilic gastroenteropathy:
   Tropical sprue.
   Radiation enteritis.
Primary intestinal lymphangiectasia.
Secondary intestinal lymphangiectasia:
   Constrictive pericarditis.
   Congestive heart failure.
   Post–Fontan procedure.
   Malrotation.
   Lymphoma.
   Sarcoidosis.
   Radiation therapy.
Colonic inflammation:
   Inflammatory bowel diseases.
   Necrotizing enterocolitis.
Congenital disorders of glycosylation.

PROTEINURIA

ICD-10CM # R80.9 Proteinuria, unspecified

'Nephrotic syndrome as a result of primary renal diseases.
Malignant hypertension.
Malignancies: multiple myeloma, leukemias, Hodgkin's disease.
CHF.
DM.
SLE, RA.
Sickle cell disease.
Goodpasture's syndrome.
Malaria.
Amyloidosis, sarcoidosis.
Tubular lesions: cystinosis.
Functional (after heavy exercise).
Pyelonephritis.
Pregnancy.
Constrictive pericarditis.
Renal vein thrombosis.
Toxic nephropathies: heavy metals, drugs.
Radiation nephritis.
Orthostatic (postural) proteinuria.
Benign proteinuria: fever, heat, or cold exposure.

PRURITUS

ICD-10CM # L29.9 Pruritus, unspecified
L29.3 Anogenital pruritus, unspecified

Dry skin.
Drug-induced eruption, fiberglass exposure.
Scabies.
Skin diseases.
Myeloproliferative disorders: mycosis fungoides, Hodgkin's lymphoma, multiple myeloma, polycythemia vera.
Cholestatic liver disease.
Endocrine disorders: DM, thyroid disease, carcinoid, pregnancy.
Carcinoma: breast, lung, gastric.
Chronic renal failure.
Iron deficiency.
AIDS.
Neurosis.
Sjögren's syndrome.

PRURITUS ANI[50]

ICD-10CM # L29.0 Pruritus ani

FECAL IRRITATION
Poor hygiene.
Anorectal conditions (fissure, fistula, hemorrhoids, skin tags, perianal clefts).
Spicy foods, citrus foods, caffeine, colchicine, quinidine.

CONTACT DERMATITIS
Anesthetic agents, topical corticosteroids, perfumed soap.

DERMATOLOGIC DISORDERS
Psoriasis, seborrhea, lichen simplex or sclerosus.

SYSTEMIC DISORDERS
Chronic renal failure, myxedema, DM, thyrotoxicosis, polycythemia vera, Hodgkin's disease.

SEXUALLY TRANSMITTED DISEASES
Syphilis, herpes simplex virus, human papillomavirus.

OTHER INFECTIOUS AGENTS
Pinworms.
Scabies.
Bacterial infection, viral infection.

PRURITUS VULVAE[63]

ICD-10CM # L29.3 Anogenital pruritus, unspecified

CAUSES OF PRURITUS VULVAE
Diseases Special to Vulval Skin
Lichen sclerosus et atrophicus.
Leukoplakia.
Carcinoma.
Skin Disease
Psoriasis.
Atopic dermatitis.
Irritant and allergic contact dermatitis (especially medicaments).
Infection
Candidiasis.
Trichomonas.
Infestation
Pediculosis.
Psychogenic
Anxiety.
Depression.
Unknown

PSEUDOCYANOSIS, ETIOLOGY

ICD-10CM # varies with etiology

Medications: amiodarone, minocycline, chlorpromazine.
Heavy metals:
Gold (systemic absorption).
Silver (systemic absorption).
Local contact with color dyes, gold, silver.

PSEUDOHERMAPHRODITISM, FEMALE

ICD-10CM # E25.0 Congenital adrenogenital disorders associated with enzyme deficiency
E25.8 Other adrenogenital disorders
E25.9 Adrenogenital disorder, unspecified
Q56.3 Pseudohermaphroditism, unspecified
Q56.4 Indeterminate sex, unspecified

Congenital adrenal hyperplasia.
Maternal use of testosterone or related steroids.
Virilizing ovarian or adrenal tumor.
Virilizing luteoma of pregnancy.
Disturbances in differentiation of urogenital structures, non-androgen related.
Maternal virilizing adrenal hyperplasia.
Fetal P450 aromatase deficiency.

PSEUDOHERMAPHRODITISM, MALE

ICD-10CM # E25.0 Congenital adrenogenital disorders associated with enzyme deficiency
E25.8 Other adrenogenital disorders
E25.9 Adrenogenital disorder, unspecified
Q56.3 Pseudohermaphroditism, unspecified
Q56.4 Indeterminate sex, unspecified

Maternal ingestion of progestogens.
End-organ resistance to androgenic hormones.
5-α-reductase-2 deficiency.
XY gonadal dysgenesis.
Testicular regression syndrome.
Defects in testosterone metabolism by peripheral tissues.
Testosterone biosynthesis defects.

PSEUDOINFARCTION[44]

ICD-10CM # varies with specific diagnosis

Cardiac tumors, primary and secondary.
Cardiomyopathy (particularly hypertrophic and dilated).
Chagas' disease.
Chest deformity.
COPD (particularly emphysema).
HIV infection.
Hyperkalemia.
Left anterior fascicular block.
Left bundle branch block.
Left ventricular hypertrophy.
Myocarditis and pericarditis.
Normal variant.
Pneumothorax.
Poor R wave progression, rotational changes, and lead placement.
Pulmonary embolism.
Trauma to chest (nonpenetrating).
Wolff-Parkinson-White syndrome.
Rare causes: pancreatitis, amyloidosis, sarcoidosis, scleroderma.

PSYCHOSIS[54]

ICD-10CM # # F29 Unspecified psychosis not due to a substance or known physiological condition
F29 Unspecified psychosis not due to a substance or known physiological condition
F10.231 Alcohol dependence with withdrawal delirium
F01.51 Vascular dementia with behavioral disturbance

PRIMARY

Schizophrenia related.[37]
Major depression.
Dementia.
Bipolar disorder.

SECONDARY

Drug use.[38]
Drug withdrawal.[39]
Drug toxicity.[40]
Charles Bonnet syndrome.
Infections (pneumonia).
Electrolyte imbalance.
Syphilis.
Congestive heart failure.
Parkinson's disease.
Trauma to temporal lobe.
Postpartum psychosis.
Hypothyroidism/hyperthyroidism.
Hypomagnesemia.
Epilepsy.
Meningitis.
Encephalitis.
Brain abscess.
Herpes encephalopathy.
Hypoxia.
Hypercarbia.
Hypoglycemia.
Thiamine deficiency.
Postoperative states.

PSYCHOSIS, MEDICAL DISORDERS-INDUCED[50]

| ICD-10CM # | F29 | Unspecified psychosis not due to a substance or known physiological condition |
| | F53 | Puerperal psychosis |

MEDICAL DISORDERS THAT MAY CAUSE ACUTE PSYCHOSIS

Metabolic Disorders

Hypercalcemia.
Hypercarbia.
Hypoglycemia.
Hyponatremia.
Hypoxia.

Inflammatory Disorders

Sarcoidosis.
Systemic lupus erythematosus.
Temporal (giant cell) arteritis.

Organ Failure

Hepatic encephalopathy.
Uremia.

Neurologic Disorders

Alzheimer's disease.
Cerebrovascular disease.
Encephalitis (including HIV infection).
Encephalopathies.
Epilepsy.

---

[37]Includes schizophrenia, schizophreniform disorder, brief reactive psychosis.
[38]Includes hypnotics, glucocorticoids, marijuana, phencyclidine, atropine, dopaminergic agents (e.g., amantadine, bromocriptine, l-dopa), immunosuppressants.
[39]Includes alcohol, barbiturates, benzodiazepines.
[40]Includes digitalis, theophylline, cimetidine, anticholinergics, glucocorticoids, catecholaminergic agents.

Huntington's disease.
Multiple sclerosis.
Neoplasms.
Normal-pressure hydrocephalus.
Parkinson's disease.
Pick's disease.
Wilson's disease.

Endocrine disorders

Addison's disease.
Cushing's disease.
Panhypopituitarism.
Parathyroid disease.
Postpartum psychosis.
Recurrent menstrual psychosis.
Sydenham's chorea.
Thyroid disease.

Deficiency States

Niacin.
Thiamine.
Vitamin B_{12} and folate.

PSYCHOSIS, MEDICATION-INDUCED[50]

| ICD-10CM # | F10.5 | Psychotic disorder due to psychoactive substance use |

PHARMACOLOGIC AGENTS THAT MAY CAUSE ACUTE PSYCHOSIS

Antianxiety Agents

Alprazolam.
Chlordiazepoxide.
Clonazepam.
Clorazepate.
Diazepam.
Ethchlorvynol.

Antibiotics

Isoniazid.
Rifampin.

Anticonvulsants

Ethosuximide.
Phenobarbital.
Phenytoin.
Primidone.

Antidepressants

Amitriptyline.
Doxepin.
Imipramine.
Protriptyline.
Trimipramine.

Cardiovascular Drugs

Captopril.
Digitalis.
Disopyramide.
Methyldopa.
Procainamide.
Propranolol.
Reserpine.

Drugs of Abuse

Alcohol.
Amphetamines.
Cannabis.
Cocaine.
Hallucinogens.
Opioids.
Phencyclidine.
Sedative-hypnotics.

Miscellaneous Drugs

Antihistamines.

Antineoplastics.
Bromides.
Cimetidine.
Corticosteroids.
Disulfiram.
Heavy metals.

PTOSIS

ICD-10CM #	H02.409	Unspecified ptosis of unspecified eyelid
	Q10.0	Congenital ptosis
	H02.419	Mechanical ptosis of unspecified eyelid
	H02.429	Myogenic ptosis of unspecified eyelid
	H02.439	Paralytic ptosis unspecified eyelid

Third nerve palsy.
Myasthenia gravis.
Horner's syndrome.
Senile ptosis.

PUBERTY, DELAYED[53]

| ICD-10CM # | E30.0 | Delayed puberty |

NORMAL OR LOW SERUM GONADOTROPIN LEVELS

Constitutional delay in growth and development.
Hypothalamic and/or pituitary disorders:
  Isolated deficiency of growth hormone.
  Isolated deficiency of Gn-RH.
  Isolated deficiency of LH and/or FSH.
  Multiple anterior pituitary hormone deficiencies.
  Associated with congenital anomalies: Kallmann's syndrome; Prader-Willi syndrome; Laurence-Moon-Biedl syndrome; Friedreich's ataxia.
  Trauma.
  Postinfection.
  Hyperprolactinemia.
  Postirradiation.
  Infiltrative disease (histiocytosis).
  Tumor.
  Autoimmune hypophysitis.
  Idiopathic.
Functional:
  Chronic endocrinologic or systemic disorders.
  Emotional disorders.
  Drugs: cannabis.

INCREASED SERUM GONADOTROPIN LEVELS

Gonadal abnormalities:
Congenital:
  Gonadal dysgenesis.
  Klinefelter's syndrome.
  Bilateral anorchism.
  Resistant ovary syndrome.
  Myotonic dystrophy in males.
  17-Hydroxylase deficiency in females.
  Galactosemia.
Acquired:
  Bilateral gonadal failure resulting from trauma or infection or after surgery, irradiation, or chemotherapy.
  Oophoritis: isolated or with other autoimmune disorders.

Uterine or vaginal disorders:
  Absence of uterus and/or vagina.
  Testicular feminization: complete or incomplete androgen insensitivity.

PUBERTY, PRECOCIOUS

ICD-10CM #	E25.0	Congenital adrenogenital disorders associated with enzyme deficiency
	E25.8	Other adrenogenital disorders
	E25.9	Adrenogenital disorder, unspecified

Idiopathic.
Congenital virilizing adrenal hyperplasia.
Hypothalamic tumors.
Head trauma.
Hydrocephalus.
Degenerative CNS disease.
Arachnoid cyst.
Sex chromosome abnormalities (e.g., 47, XXY, 48, XXXY).
Perinatal asphyxia.
CNS infection (e.g., meningitis, encephalitis).

PULMONARY CRACKLES

ICD-10CM #	R09.8	Friction sounds, chest

Pneumonia.
Left ventricular failure.
Asbestosis, silicosis, interstitial lung disease.
Chronic bronchitis.
Alveolitis (allergic, fibrosing).
Neoplasm.

PULMONARY CYSTS ON X-RAY[32]

ICD-10CM #	Q33.0	Polycystic lungs, congenital
	J98.4	Pulmonary manifestations

CAUSES OF CYSTS IN THE LUNG ON CHEST RADIOGRAPH

Cystic fibrosis.
Cystic bronchiectasis.
Bronchopulmonary dysplasia (neonate and older).
Tuberculosis (apical thick walled).
Pulmonary abscess (thick wall, fluid level).
Empyema.
Streptococcal pneumatocele (thin wall, postinfective).
Cavitating pneumonia.
Mycetoma (apical cyst with contents).
Cystic congenital adenomatoid malformation (basal cysts of varying size).
Diaphragmatic hernia (cysts of similar size).
Hiatal hernia (posterior).
Morgagni hernia (midline anterior).
Bronchopulmonary sequestration (basal).
Congenital lobar emphysema.
Hydatid disease (in endemic areas).
Kerosene inhalation (pneumatocele).
Histiocytosis and other causes of interstitial disease.

PULMONARY EDEMA, NONCARDIOGENIC[32]

ICD-10CM #	J81.0	Acute pulmonary edema

CAUSES OF NONCARDIOGENIC PULMONARY EDEMA

Adult respiratory distress syndrome.
Drowning.
Asphyxia.
Upper airway obstruction (usually with cardiomegaly).
High altitude.
Increased intracranial pressure.
Postictal.
Noxious gases:
  Smoke.
  Nitrous dioxide (silo filler's disease).
  Sulfur dioxide.
  Nitrogen mustard.
Drugs:
  Asprin.
  Diazepam, chlordiazepoxide, barbiturates.
  Narcotics (heroin, methadone, morphine).
  β-adrenergic drugs (terbutaline).
  Contrast media.
  Colchicine.
  Fluorescein.
  Hydrochlorothiazide.
  Nitrofurantoin.
  Propoxyphene.
Poisons:
  Parathion.
Transfusion reactions.
Renal failure: transplantation.
Bone marrow transplantation.
Fat embolism.
Pancreatitis.

PULMONARY EOSINOPHILIA[2]

ICD-10CM #	NEC J82	Eosinophilia, pulmonary

TYPES AND CAUSES OF PULMONARY EOSINOPHILIA

Drug- and toxin-induced eosinophilic lung diseases.
Helminth and fungal infection-related eosinophilic lung diseases:
  Transpulmonary passage of larvae (i.e., Löffler syndrome): *Ascaris*, hookworm, *Strongyloides*.
  Pulmonary parenchymal invasion: mostly helminths, paragonimiasis.
  Heavy hematogenous seeding with helminths: trichinellosis, disseminated strongyloidiasis, cutaneous and visceral larva migrans, schistosomiasis.
  Tropical pulmonary eosinophilia: filaria.
  Allergic bronchopulmonary aspergillosis.
Chronic eosinophilic pneumonia.
Acute eosinophilic pneumonia.
Churg-Strauss syndrome (vasculitis).
Other: neoplasia, idiopathic hypereosinophilic syndrome, bronchocentric granulomatosis.

PULMONARY HEMORRHAGE, PEDIATRIC AGE

ICD-10CM #	P26.9	Pulmonary hemorrhage newborn

CAUSES OF PULMONARY HEMORRHAGE (HEMOPTYSIS)

Focal Hemorrhage

Bronchitis and bronchiectasis (especially cystic fibrosis related).
Infection (acute or chronic), pneumonia, abscess.
Tuberculosis.
Trauma.
Pulmonary arteriovenous malformation.
Foreign body (chronic).
Neoplasm including hemangioma.
Pulmonary embolus with or without infarction.
Bronchogenic cysts.
Diffuse hemorrhage
Idiopathic of infancy.
Congenital heart disease (including pulmonary hypertension, venoocclusive disease, congestive heart failure).
Prematurity.
Cow's milk hyperreactivity (Heiner syndrome).
Goodpasture syndrome.
Collagen vascular diseases (systemic lupus erythematosus, rheumatoid arthritis).
Henoch-Schönlein purpura and vasculitic disorders.
Granulomatous disease (Wegener granulomatosis).
Celiac disease.
Coagulopathy (congenital or acquired).
Malignancy.
Immunodeficiency.
Exogenous toxins.
Hyperammonemia.
Pulmonary hypertension.
Pulmonary alveolar hemosiderosis.
Tuberous sclerosis.
Lymphangiomyomatosis or lymphangioleiomyomatosis.
Physical injury or abuse.

PULMONARY HEMORRHAGIC SYNDROMES, DIFFUSE[32]

ICD-10CM #	P26.1	Massive pulmonary hemorrhage originating in the perinatal period
	R04.8	Pulmonary hemorrhage

CLASSIFICATION OF DIFFUSE PULMONARY HEMORRHAGE SYNDROMES

Non-immunocompromised patients

Antibasement membrane antibody disease/Goodpasture's syndrome.
Diseases of presumed immune etiology, with or without nephropathy:
  Systemic lupus erythematosus.
  Rheumatoid arthritis.
  Systemic sclerosis.
  Systemic necrotizing vasculitis.
  Granulomatosis with polyangiitis (Wegener's granulomatosis).
  Microscopic polyarteritis.
Diseases with no known immune etiology:
  Idiopathic pulmonary hemosiderosis.
  Rapidly progressive glomerulonephritis without immune complexes.
  Fibrillary glomerulonephritis.

Drug-induced (anticoagulants, trimellitic anhydride, cocaine, lymphangiography).
Valvular heart disease.
Disseminated intravascular coagulation.
Acute lung injury.
Tumors.
Immunocompromised Patients
Blood dyscrasias.
Infection.
Tumors.

PULMONARY INFILTRATES, IMMUNOCOMPROMISED HOST[71]

ICD-10CM #	J82	Pulmonary eosinophilia, not elsewhere classified
	J98.4	Other disorders of lung

CAUSES OF PULMONARY INFILTRATES IN THE IMMUNOCOMPROMISED HOST

Infections:
Bacteria:
  Gram-positive cocci, especially *Staphylococcus.*
  Gram-negative bacilli.
  Mycobacterium tuberculosis.
  Nontuberculous mycobacteria.
  Nocardia.
Viruses:
  Cytomegalovirus.
  Herpesvirus.
Fungi:
  Aspergillus.
  Cryptococcus.
  Candida.
  Mucor.
  Pneumocystis jiroveci.
Protozoa:
  Toxoplasma gondii (rare).
Pulmonary effects of therapy:
1. Chemotherapeutic agents.
2. Radiation therapy.
3. Pulmonary hemorrhage.
4. Congestive heart failure.
5. Disseminated malignancy.
6. Nonspecified interstitial pneumonitis (no defined etiology).

PULMONARY LESIONS

ICD-10CM #	J82	Pulmonary eosinophilia, not elsewhere classified
	J98.4	Other disorders of lung
	J70.9	Respiratory conditions due to unspecified external agent
	S27.309A	Unspecified injury of lung, unspecified, initial encounter

TB.
Legionella pneumonia.
Mycoplasma pneumonia.

Viral pneumonia.
Pneumocystis carinii.
Hypersensitivity pneumonitis.
Aspiration pneumonia.
Fungal disease (aspergillosis, histoplasmosis).
ARDS associated with pneumonia.
Psittacosis.
Sarcoidosis.
Septic emboli.
Metastatic cancer.
Multiple pulmonary emboli.
Rheumatoid nodules.

PULMONARY MASS, SOLITARY, CAUSES[32]

ICD-10CM #	R91.1	Solitary pulmonary nodule

CAUSES OF A SOLITARY PULMONARY MASS

Bronchial carcinoma.
Bronchial carcinoid.
Granuloma.
Hamartoma.
Metastasis.
Chronic pneumonia or abscess.
Hydatid cyst.
Pulmonary hematoma.
Bronchocele.
Fungus ball.
Massive fibrosis in coal workers.
Bronchogenic cyst.
Sequestration.
Arteriovenous malformation.
Pulmonary infarct.
Round atelectasis.

PULMONARY MASS, SOLITARY, MIMICS[32]

ICD-10CM #	varies with specific diagnosis

SIMULANTS OF A SOLITARY PULMONARY MASS

Extrathoracic artifacts.
Cutaneous masses.
Bony lesions.
Pleural tumors or plaques.
Encysted pleural fluid.
Pulmonary vessels.

PULMONARY NODULE, SOLITARY

ICD-10CM #	J98.4	Other disorders of lung

Bronchogenic carcinoma.
Granuloma from histoplasmosis.
TB granuloma.
Granuloma from coccidioidomycosis.
Metastatic carcinoma.
Bronchial adenoma.
Bronchogenic cyst.
Hamartoma.
AV malformation.
Other: fibroma, intrapulmonary lymph node, sclerosing hemangioma, bronchopulmonary sequestration.

PULMONARY–RENAL SYNDROMES, CAUSES[24]

ICD-10CM #	varies with specific diagnosis	
Systemic vasculitis	Anti-GBM disease (Goodpasture's). ANCA associated: Granulomatosis with poly-angiitis (Wegener's granulomatosis). Microscopic polyarteritis. Churg-Strauss syndrome. Drugs (penicillamine, hydralazine, propyl-thiouracil). Immune complex disease. Lupus erythematosus. Henoch-Schönlein purpura. Mixed cryoglobulinemia. Rheumatoid vasculitis.	
Infection	Severe bacterial pneumonia; postinfectious glomerulonephritis; *Legionella;* hantavirus; opportunistic infection in immunocompromised patients; infective endocarditis.	
Pulmonary edema and AKI	Volume overload; severe left ventricular failure.	
Multiorgan failure	Acute respiratory distress syndrome and AKI.	
Other	Paraquat poisoning; renal vein or IVC thrombosis with pulmonary emboli.	

AKI, Acute kidney injury; *ANCA,* anti-neutrophil cytoplasmic antibody; *GBM,* glomerular basement membrane; *IVC,* inferior vena cava.

PULSELESS ELECTRICAL ACTIVITY

ICD-10CM #	I46.9	Cardiac arrest, cause unspecified

Hypovolemia.
Hypoxia.
Hyperkalemia.
Acidosis.
Cardiac tamponade.
Tension pneumothorax.
Pulmonary embolus.
Drug overdose.
Hypothermia.

PUPILLARY DILATATION, POOR RESPONSE TO DARKNESS

ICD-10CM #	H21.569	Pupillary abnormality, unspecified eye

Drugs (narcotics, general anesthetics, cholinergics).

Acute trauma (spasm from prostaglandin release).

Inflammation, infection (interruption of inhibitory fibers to the Edinger-Westphal nucleus).

Old age (loss of inhibition at midbrain from reticular activating formation).

Horner's syndrome (sympathetic neuron interruption).

Adie's syndrome tonic pupil.

Lymphoma.

Congenital miosis.

PURPURA

ICD-10CM #	D69.2	Other nonthrombocytopenic purpura
	D69.0	Allergic purpura
	D69.49	Other primary thrombocytopenia
	M31.1	Thrombotic microangiopathy

THROMBOTIC

Trauma.

Septic emboli, atheromatous emboli.

DIC.

Thrombocytopenia.

Meningococcemia.

Rocky Mountain spotted fever.

Hemolytic-uremic syndrome.

Viral infection: echo, coxsackie.

Scurvy.

Other: left atrial myxoma, cryoglobulinemia, vasculitis, hyperglobulinemic purpura.

PURPURA, NONPALPABLE[39]

| ICD-10CM # | D69.2 | Other nonthrombocytopenic purpura |

INCREASED TRANSMURAL PRESSURE GRADIENT

Acute (Valsalva, coughing, vomiting, high altitude, weight lifting).

Chronic—Venous stasis.

DECREASED MECHANICAL INTEGRITY OF MICROCIRCULATION AND SUPPORTING TISSUES

Age related (infancy and actinic purpura).

Glucocorticoid excess—Cushing syndrome and glucocorticoid therapy.

Vitamin C deficiency (scurvy).

Abnormal connective tissue—Ehlers-Danlos syndrome.

Amyloid infiltration of blood vessels.

Colloid milium.

Hormonal—Female easy bruising syndrome (purpura simplex).

Lorenzo's oil.

MELAS syndrome.

TRAUMA TO BLOOD VESSELS

Physical:
  Injuries.
  Child abuse.
  Factitial purpura.
Ultraviolet purpura:
  Purpuric sunburn.
  Solar purpura.
Infectious:
  Bacterial.
  Rickettsial.
  Fungal.
  Viral.
  Parasitic.
Embolic:
  Infectious organisms.
  Atheroemboli (cholesterol crystal emboli).
  Fat emboli.
Allergic and/or inflammatory:
  Serum sickness.
  Pigmented purpuric eruptions.
  Pyoderma gangrenosum.
  Contact dermatitis.
  Familial Mediterranean fever.
Neoplastic.
Metabolic:
  Erythropoietic porphyria.
  Calciphylaxis.
Immunoglobulin related (hyperglobulinemic purpura of Waldenström and light-chain vasculitis).
Drug related.
Thrombotic:
  Disseminated intravascular coagulation.
  Warfarin (Coumadin)-induced skin necrosis.
  Protein C or protein S deficiency, factor V Leiden, prothrombin G20201A.
  Purpura fulminans.
  Paroxysmal nocturnal hemoglobinuria.
  Antiphospholipid antibody syndrome.
  Hemangioma with thrombocytopenia and consumptive coagulopathy (Kasabach-Merritt syndrome).

UNKNOWN CAUSE—PSYCHOGENIC PURPURA

PURPURA, NONPURPURIC DISORDERS SIMULATING PURPURA[3]

| ICD-10CM # | varies with specific diagnosis |

Disorders with telangiectasias:
  Cherry angiomas.
  Hereditary hemorrhagic telangiectasia.
  Chronic actinic telangiectasia.
  Scleroderma.
  CREST syndrome.
  Ataxia-telangiectasia.
  Chronic liver disease.
  Pregnancy-related telangiectasia.
Kaposi sarcoma and other vascular sarcomas.
Fabry disease.
Neonatal extramedullary hematopoiesis.
Angioma serpiginosum.

PURPURA, PALPABLE[39]

| ICD-10CM # | D69.2 | Other nonthrombocytopenic purpura |

Cutaneous vasculitis:
  Systemic vasculitides.
  Paraneoplastic vasculitis.
  Henoch-Schönlein purpura.
  Acute hemorrhagic edema of infancy.
  Livedoid vasculitis.
  Idiopathic.
  Urticarial.
Cryoglobulinemia.
Cryofibrinogenemia.
Primary cutaneous diseases.

QT INTERVAL PROLONGATION[44]

| ICD-10CM # | R94.31 | Abnormal electrocardiogram [ECG] [EKG] |
| | I45.81 | Long QT syndrome |

Drugs:
  Class I antiarrhythmics (e.g., disopyramide, procainamide, quinidine).
  Class III antiarrhythmics.
  Tricyclic antidepressants.
  Phenothiazines.
  Astemizole.
  Terfenadine.
  Adenosine.
  Antibiotics (e.g., erythromycin and other macrolides).
  Antifungal agents.
  Pentamidine, chloroquine.
Ischemic heart disease.
Cerebrovascular disease.
Rheumatic fever.
Myocarditis.
Mitral valve prolapse.
Electrolyte abnormalities.
Hypocalcemia.
Hypothyroidism.
Liquid protein diets.
Organophosphate insecticides.
Congenital prolonged QT syndrome.

RADIATION-INDUCED NEOPLASMS[58]

| ICD-10CM # | varies with specific diagnosis |

RADIATION-INDUCED NEOPLASMS

Osteochondroma

Benign.

Exclusively with childhood irradiation.

Histologically identical to spontaneous osteochondroma.

Sarcoma

Malignant.

Latent period of 4 years or more.

Histologically identical to spontaneous sarcoma.

Commonly malignant fibrous histiocytoma or osteosarcoma.

Occurs in either bone or soft tissue.

Tumors in Other Organ Systems

Squamous cell cancer of the skin.

Breast cancer.

Leukemia, with shorter latent period than sarcoma.

RECTAL MASS, PALPABLE[67]

ICD-10CM # R22.9 Localized swelling, mass and lump, unspecified

Rectal carcinoma.
Rectal polyp.
Hypertrophied anal papilla.
Diverticular phlegmon (prolapsing into the pouch of Douglas).
Sigmoid colon carcinoma (prolapsing into the pouch of Douglas).
Metastatic deposits at the pelvic reflection (Blumer's shelf).
Primary pelvic malignancy (uterine, ovarian, prostatic, or cervical).
Mesorectal lymph nodes.
Endometriosis.
Solitary rectal ulcer syndrome.
Foreign body.
Feces.
Presacral cyst.
Amebic granuloma.
Vaginal tampon and even the pubic bone may be mistaken for a rectal mass.

RECTAL PAIN

ICD-10CM # K62.89 Other specified diseases of anus and rectum

Anal fissure.
Thrombosed hemorrhoid.
Anorectal abscess.
Foreign bodies.
Fecal impaction.
Endometriosis.
Neoplasms (primary or metastatic).
Pelvic inflammatory disease.
Inflammation of sacral nerves.
Compression of sacral nerves.
Prostatitis.
Other: proctalgia fugax, uterine abnormalities, myopathies, coccygodynia.

RED BLOOD CELL APLASIA, ACQUIRED, ETIOLOGY

ICD-10CM # D61.01 Constitutional (pure) red blood cell aplasia

Idiopathic (>50% of cases).
Medications (most frequent with phenytoin).
Non-Hodgkin's lymphoma.
Viral infections (parvovirus B19, EB virus, mumps, hepatitis).
Myelodysplastic syndromes.
Thymoma.
Autoimmune diseases.
Allogenic bone marrow transplant from ABO incompatible donor.
Pregnancy.

RED BLOOD CELL FRAGMENTATION HEMOLYSIS, CAUSES[38]

ICD-10CM # varies with specific disorder

CAUSES OF RED BLOOD CELL FRAGMENTATION HEMOLYSIS

Damaged microvasculature.
Thrombotic thrombocytopenic purpura–hemolytic uremic syndrome (TTP–HUS).
Associated with pregnancy: preeclampsia or eclampsia; hemolysis plus elevated liver enzymes plus low platelets (HELLP syndrome).
Associated with malignancy, with or without mitomycin C treatment.
Vasculitis: polyarteritis, Wegener granulomatosis, acute glomerulonephritis, or *Rickettsia*-like infections.
Systemic lupus erythematosus.
Abnormalities of renal vasculature: malignant hypertension, acute glomerulonephritis, scleroderma, or allograft rejection with or without cyclosporine treatment.
Disseminated intravascular coagulation.
Malignant hypertension.
Catastrophic antiphospholipid antibody syndrome.
Atrioventricular malformations.
Kasabach-Merritt syndrome.
Hemangioendotheliomas.
Atrioventricular shunts for congenital and acquired conditions (e.g., stents, coils, transjugular intrahepatic portosystemic shunt, Levine shunts).
Cardiac abnormalities:
   Replaced valve, prosthesis, graft, or patch.
   Aortic stenosis or regurgitant jets (e.g., in ruptured sinus of Valsalva).
Drugs:
Cyclosporine.
Mitomycin.
Ticlopidine.
Clopidogrel.
Tacrolimus.
Cocaine.
Systemic infection:
Bacterial endocarditis.
Brucellosis.
Cytomegalovirus.
Human immunodeficiency virus.
Ehrlichiosis.
Rocky Mountain spotted fever

RED EYE

ICD-10CM # H57.8 Other specified disorders of eye and adnexa

Infectious conjunctivitis (bacterial, viral).
Allergic conjunctivitis.
Acute glaucoma.
Keratitis (bacterial, viral).
Iritis.
Trauma.

RED EYE, ACUTE[4]

ICD-10CM # H57.8

Obvious open globe.
Corneal abrasion.
Corneal ulcer.
Subconjunctival hemorrhage.

Hyphema.
Occult open globe.
Herpes simplex virus glaucoma.
Iritis, traumatic iritis.
Scleritis.
Conjunctivitis.
Blepharitis.
Ultraviolet keratitis.
Episcleritis.
Conjunctival foreign body.
Dry eye.
Contact lens overwear syndrome.

RED HOT JOINT

ICD-10CM # varies with specific diagnosis

Trauma.
Gout.
Infection (septic joint).
Pseudogout (calcium pyrophosphate dehydrate crystal deposition).
Psoriatic arthropathy.
Reactive arthritis.
Palindromic rheumatism.

RED URINE

ICD-10CM # R39.19 Other difficulties with micturition

Hematuria.
Porphyrins.
Hemoglobinuria.
Myoglobinuria.
Medications (phenazopyridine, aminosalicylic acid, deferoxamine, phenazopyridine, phenolphthalein, NSAIDs, rifampin, phenytoin, methyldopa, doxorubicin, phenacetin).
Foods (beets, berries, maize).
Urate crystalluria.

RENAL ALLOGRAFT DYSFUNCTION[30]

ICD-10CM # T86.1 Complications of renal allograft

IMMEDIATE/DELAYED GRAFT FUNCTION (1-3 DAYS)

Acute tubular necrosis.
Hyperacute humoral rejection.
Urinary leak or obstruction.
Renal artery or vein thrombosis.
Recurrence of disease (e.g., focal segmental glomerulosclerosis).

EARLY POSTTRANSPLANTATION PERIOD (FIRST MONTH)

Acute cellular rejection.
Acute humoral rejection.
Calcineurin inhibitor toxicity.
Urinary tract obstruction.
Volume depletion.
Recurrence of disease.
Late Acute Dysfunction
Acute rejection.
Cyclosporine or tacrolimus toxicity.
Recurrence of primary disease.
Tubulointerstitial nephritis, drug-induced.
Renal artery stenosis.

Infection (bacterial urinary tract infection [UTI], cytomegalovirus, BK virus).

Hemodynamic (volume; use of angiotensin-converting enzyme inhibitor, angiotensin II receptor blocker).

Chronic Dysfunction

Chronic rejection.
Cyclosporine or tacrolimus toxicity.
Recurrent renal disease.
De novo renal disease.
Urinary tract obstruction.
Bacterial UTI.
Hypertensive nephrosclerosis.

RENAL ARTERY OCCLUSION, CAUSES

ICD-10CM #   N28.0   Ischemia and infarction of kidney

Atrial fibrillation.
Angiography or stent placement.
Abdominal aortic surgery.
Trauma.
Renal artery aneurysm/dissection.
Vasculitis.
Thrombosis in patient with fibromuscular dysplasia.
Atherosclerosis.
Septic embolism.
Mural thrombus thromboembolism.
Atrial myxoma thromboembolism.
Mitral stenosis thromboembolism.
Prosthetic valve thromboembolism.
Renal cell carcinoma.

RENAL COLIC[4]

ICD-10CM #   N23

Vascular:
   Abdominal aortic aneurysm.
   Aortic dissection.
   Renal artery dissection.
   Renal artery stenosis.
   Renal vein thrombosis.
   Renal infarct.
   Mesenteric ischemia.
   Retroperitoneal hemorrhage.
Gastrointestinal:
   Incarcerated hernia.
   Appendicitis.
   Cholecystitis.
   Biliary colic.
   Pancreatitis.
   Bowel obstruction.
   Diverticulitis.
Gynecologic:
   Ectopic pregnancy.
   Ovarian torsion.
   Tuboovarian abscess.
   Pelvic inflammatory disease.
   Endometriosis.
Genitourinary:
   Testicular torsion.
   Pyelonephritis.
   Perinephric abscess.
   Urinary tract tumor.
   Renal papillary necrosis.
   Upper urinary tract hemorrhage.

Musculoskeletal:
   Lumbar strain.
   Radiculopathy.
   Disk herniation.
   Vertebral compression fracture.
Dermatologic:
   Herpes zoster.
Miscellaneous:
   Factitious.

RENAL CYSTIC DISORDERS

ICD-10CM #   Q61.01   Congenital single renal cyst

Simple cysts.
Acquired cystic kidney disease.
Autosomal dominant polycystic kidney disease.
Autosomal recessive polycystic kidney disease.
Medullary cystic disease.
Medullary sponge kidney.

RENAL FAILURE, ACUTE, PIGMENT-INDUCED[6]

ICD-10CM #   N19   Unspecified kidney failure

CAUSES OF PIGMENT-INDUCED ACUTE RENAL FAILURE

Rhabdomyolysis and myoglobinuria.
Vigorous exercise.
Arterial embolization.
Status epilepticus.
Status asthmaticus.
Coma-induced and pressure-induced myonecrosis.
Heat stress.
Diabetic ketoacidosis.
Myopathy.
Alcoholism.
Hypokalemia.
Hypophosphatemia.
Hemoglobinuria.
Transfusion reactions.
Snake envenomation.
Malaria.
Mechanical destruction of RBCs by prosthetic valves.
G6PD deficiency.

G6PD, Glucose-6-phosphate dehydrogenase; *RBCs,* red blood cells.

RENAL FAILURE, CHRONIC[30]

ICD-10CM #   N18.9   Chronic kidney disease, unspecified

CAUSES OF CHRONIC RENAL FAILURE

Diabetic glomerulosclerosis (systemic disease involving the kidney).
Hypertensive nephrosclerosis.
Glomerular disease:
   Glomerulonephritis.
   Amyloidosis, light chain disease (systemic disease involving the kidney).
   Systemic lupus erythematosus, Wegener granulomatosis (systemic disease involving the kidney).

Tubulointerstitial disease:
   Reflux nephropathy (chronic pyelonephritis).
   Analgesic nephropathy.
   Obstructive nephropathy (stones, benign prostatic hypertrophy).
   Myeloma kidney (systemic disease involving the kidney).
Vascular disease:
   Scleroderma (systemic disease involving the kidney).
   Vasculitis (systemic disease involving the kidney).
   Renovascular renal failure (ischemic nephropathy).
   Atheroembolic renal disease (systemic disease involving the kidney).
Cystic disease:
   Autosomal dominant polycystic kidney disease.
   Medullary cystic kidney disease.

RENAL FAILURE, INTRINSIC OR PARENCHYMAL CAUSES[65]

ICD-10CM #   N17.0   Acute kidney failure with tubular necrosis
      N17.1   Acute kidney failure with acute cortical necrosis
      N17.2   Acute kidney failure with medullary necrosis
      N17.8   Other acute kidney failure
      N17.9   Acute kidney failure, unspecified
      N18.9   Chronic kidney disease, unspecified

ABNORMALITIES OF THE VASCULATURE

Renal arteries: atherosclerosis, thromboembolism, arteritis.
Renal veins: thrombosis.
Microvasculature: vasculitis, thrombotic microangiopathy.

ABNORMALITIES OF GLOMERULI (ACUTE GLOMERULONEPHRITIS)

Antiglomerular membrane disease (Goodpasture's syndrome).
Immune complex glomerulonephritis: SLE, postinfectious, idiopathic, membranoproliferative.

ABNORMALITIES OF INTERSTITIUM (ACUTE INTERSTITIAL NEPHRITIS)

Drugs (e.g., antibiotics, NSAIDs, diuretics, anticonvulsants, allopurinol).
Infectious pyelonephritis.
Infiltrative: lymphoma, leukemia, sarcoidosis.

ABNORMALITIES OF TUBULES

Physical obstruction (uric acid, oxalate, light chains).
Acute tubular necrosis:
   Ischemic.
   Toxic (antibiotics, chemotherapy, immunosuppressives, radiocontrast dyes, heavy metals, myoglobin, hemolyzed RBCs).

RENAL FAILURE, POSTRENAL CAUSES[65]

ICD-10CM # N17.0 Acute kidney failure with tubular necrosis
N17.1 Acute kidney failure with acute cortical necrosis
N17.2 Acute kidney failure with medullary necrosis
N17.8 Other acute kidney failure
N17.9 Acute kidney failure, unspecified
N18.9 Chronic kidney disease, unspecified

URETER AND RENAL PELVIS

Intrinsic obstruction:
Blood clots.
Stones.
Sloughed papillae: diabetes, sickle cell disease, analgesic nephropathy.
Inflammatory: fungus ball.
Extrinsic obstruction:
Malignancy.
Retroperitoneal fibrosis.
Iatrogenic: inadvertent ligation of ureters.

BLADDER

Prostatic hypertrophy or malignancy.
Neuropathic bladder.
Blood clots.
Bladder cancer.
Stones.

URETHRAL

Strictures.
Congenital valves.

RENAL FAILURE, PRERENAL CAUSES[65]

ICD-10CM # N17.0 Acute kidney failure with tubular necrosis
N17.1 Acute kidney failure with acute cortical necrosis
N17.2 Acute kidney failure with medullary necrosis
N17.8 Other acute kidney failure
N17.9 Acute kidney failure, unspecified
N18.9 Chronic kidney disease, unspecified

DECREASED CARDIAC OUTPUT

CHF.
Arrhythmias.
Pericardial constriction or tamponade.
Pulmonary embolism.

HYPOVOLEMIA

GI tract loss (vomiting, diarrhea, nasogastric suction).
Blood losses (trauma, GI tract surgery).
Renal losses (diuretics, mineralocorticoid deficiency, postobstructive diuresis).
Skin losses (burns).

VOLUME REDISTRIBUTION (DECREASE IN EFFECTIVE BLOOD VOLUME)

Hypoalbuminemic states (cirrhosis, nephrosis).
Sequestration of fluid in "third" space (ischemic bowel, peritonitis, pancreatitis).
Peripheral vasodilation (sepsis, vasodilators, anaphylaxis).

ALTERED RENAL VASCULAR RESISTANCE

Increase in afferent vascular resistance (NSAIDs, liver disease, sepsis, hypercalcemia, cyclosporine).
Decrease in efferent arteriolar tone (ACE inhibitors).

RENAL INFARCTION[24]

ICD-10CM # N28.0 Ischemia and infarction of kidney

CAUSES OF RENAL INFARCTION

Thrombosis: Spontaneous
Atherosclerotic disease of aorta and renal artery.
Fibromuscular dysplasia of renal artery.
Aneurysms of aorta or renal artery.
Dissection of aorta or renal artery.
Marfan's syndrome.
Ehlers-Danlos syndrome.
Vasculitis involving renal artery.
○ Polyarteritis nodosa.
○ Takayasu's arteritis.
○ Kawasaki disease.
○ Thromboangiitis obliterans.
○ Other necrotizing vasculitides.
• Inflammatory disease of the aorta or renal artery.
Syphilis.
Tuberculosis.
Mycoses.
Hypercoagulable states.
○ Nephrotic syndrome.
○ Antiphospholipid syndrome.
○ Antithrombin III deficiency.
○ Homocystinuria.
• Thrombotic microangiopathies.
Hemolytic-uremic syndrome.
Thrombotic thrombocytopenic purpura.
Antiphospholipid syndrome.
Malignant hypertension.
Scleroderma.
Sickle cell nephropathy.
Polycythemia vera.
Postpartum hemolytic-uremic syndrome.
Hyperacute vascular allograft rejection.
Thrombosis: Induced
Traumatic.
Following endovascular intervention.
Post renal transplantation.
Embolism
Cardiac source.
○ Atrial fibrillation or other arrhythmias.
○ Native and prosthetic valvular heart disease.
○ Infective endocarditis.
○ Marantic endocarditis.

• Myocardial infarction with mural thrombi.
○ Left atrial myxoma or other tumor.
• Noncardiac sources.
Atheromatous embolic disease.
Paradoxical emboli.
Fat emboli.
Tumor emboli.
Therapeutic renal embolization.
Segmental renal infarction of childhood.
Cisplatinum and gemcitabine.
Sickle cell disease or sickle cell trait.

RENAL PARENCHYMAL DISEASE, CHRONIC[32]

ICD-10CM # N28.9 Disorder of kidney and ureter, unspecified

DIFFERENTIAL DIAGNOSIS OF CHRONIC RENAL PARENCHYMAL DISEASE

No Papillary/Caliceal Abnormality
Diffuse Parenchymal Loss
Bilateral:
Chronic glomerulonephritis.
Diffuse small-vessel disease.
Hereditary nephropathies.
Unilateral:
Renal artery stenosis.
Postirradiation.
Rare:
Hypoplastic kidney.
Postobstructive atrophy.

FOCAL PARENCHYMAL LOSS
Infarct.
Previous trauma.
Papillary/Caliceal Abnormality
Diffuse Parenchymal Loss
Obstructive nephropathy.
Generalized reflux nephropathy.
No Parenchymal Loss
Papillary necrosis.
TB.
Medullary sponge kidney.
Megacalices.
Pelvicaliceal cyst.
Focal Parenchymal Loss
Focal reflux nephropathy (chronic atrophic pyelonephritis).
TB.
Calculus disease.

RENAL VEIN THROMBOSIS, CAUSES

ICD-10CM # I82.3 Embolism and thrombosis of renal vein

Nephrotic syndrome.
Renal cell carcinoma.
Aortic aneurysm causing compression.
Lymphadenopathy.
Retroperitoneal fibrosis.
Estrogen therapy.
Pregnancy.
Renal cell carcinoma with vein invasion.
Severe dehydration.

RESPIRATORY DISTRESS IN THE NEWBORN, CAUSES[26]

ICD-10CM #   J96.00   Acute respiratory failure

RESPIRATORY DISTRESS IN THE NEWBORN

Noncardiopulmonary
Hypothermia or hyperthermia.
Hypoglycemia.
Metabolic acidosis.
Drug intoxications; withdrawal.
Polycythemia.
Central nervous system insult.
Asphyxia.
Hemorrhage.
Neuromuscular disease.
Werdnig-Hoffman disease.
Myopathies.
Phrenic nerve injury.
Skeletal abnormalities.
Asphyxiating thoracic dystrophy.
Cardiovascular
Left-sided outflow obstruction.
Hypoplastic left heart.
Aortic stenosis.
Coarctation of the aorta.
Cyanotic lesions.
Transposition of the great vessels.
Total anomalous pulmonary venous return
Tricuspid atresia.
Right-sided outflow obstruction.
Pulmonary
Upper airway obstruction.
Choanal atresia.
Vocal cord paralysis.
Meconium aspiration.
Clear fluid aspiration.
Transient tachypnea.
Pneumonia.
Pulmonary hypoplasia.
Primary.
Secondary.
Hyaline membrane disease.
Pneumothorax.
Pleural effusions.
Mass lesions.
Lobar emphysema.
Cystic adenomatoid malformation.

RESPIRATORY FAILURE, HYPOVENTILATORY[54]

ICD-10CM #   J96.00   Acute respiratory failure, unspecified whether with hypoxia or hypercapnia
       J96.90   Respiratory failure, unspecified, unspecified whether with hypoxia or hypercapnia

ABNORMAL RESPIRATORY CAPACITY (NORMAL RESPIRATORY WORKLOADS)

Acute depression of central nervous system:
    Various causes.

Chronic central hypoventilation syndromes:
    Obesity-hypoventilation syndrome.
    Sleep apnea syndrome.
    Hypothyroidism.
    Shy-Drager syndrome (multisystem atrophy syndrome).
Acute toxic paralysis syndromes:
    Botulism.
    Tetanus.
    Toxic ingestion or bites.
    Organophosphate poisoning.
Neuromuscular disorders (acute and chronic):
    Myasthenia gravis.
    Guillain-Barré syndrome.
    Drugs.
    Amyotrophic lateral sclerosis.
    Muscular dystrophies.
    Polymyositis.
    Spinal cord injury.
    Traumatic phrenic nerve paralysis.

ABNORMAL PULMONARY WORKLOADS

Chronic obstructive pulmonary disease:
    Chronic bronchitis.
    Asthmatic bronchitis.
    Emphysema.
Asthma and acute bronchial hyperreactivity syndromes.
Upper airway obstruction.
Interstitial lung diseases.

ABNORMAL EXTRAPULMONARY WORKLOADS

Chronic thoracic cage disorders:
    Severe kyphoscoliosis.
    After thoracoplasty.
    After thoracic cage injury.
Acute thoracic cage trauma and burns.
Pneumothorax.
Pleural fibrosis and effusions.
Abdominal processes.

RETINOPATHY, HYPERTENSIVE

ICD-10CM #   H35.039   Hypertensive retinopathy, unspecified eye

Retinal venous obstruction.
Diabetic retinopathy.
Ocular ischemic syndrome.
Hyperviscosity.
Tortuosity of retinal artery.

RHINITIS

ICD-10CM #	J31.0	Chronic rhinitis
	J30.0	Vasomotor rhinitis
	J30.1	Allergic rhinitis due to pollen
	J30.2	Other seasonal allergic rhinitis
	J30.5	Allergic rhinitis due to rood
	J30.89	Other allergic rhinitis
	J30.9	Allergic rhinitis, unspecified

Allergic rhinitis.
Infectious rhinitis.
Vasomotor rhinitis.
Exercise-induced rhinitis.
Emotional rhinitis.
Rhinitis medicamentosa.
Hormone-mediated rhinitis (menses, pregnancy, oral contraceptives, hypothyroidism).
GERD.
Chemical- or irritant-induced rhinitis.
Rhinitis mimics:
    Deviated septum.
    Enlarged adenoids.
    Nasal polyps/tumors.
    Foreign bodies.
    CSF rhinorrhea.
    Sarcoidosis.
    Midline granuloma.
    Granulomatosis with polyangiitis (Wegener's granulomatosis).
    SLE.
    Sjögren's syndrome.

RHINITIS, CHRONIC[2]

ICD-10CM #   J31.0   Chronic rhinitis

CLASSIFICATION OF CHRONIC RHINITIS

Allergic
Systemic.
Local (entopy).
Work-Related
Irritant.
Corrosive.
Immunologic.
Infectious (Rhinosinusitis)
Allergic.
Nonallergic.
Nonallergic
Idiopathic.
Nonallergic with eosinophilia.
Atrophic.
Primary.
Secondary.
Medication-related.
Topical vasoconstrictors (rhinitis medicamentosa).
Oral medications.
Exercise-induced.
Cold air–induced.
Gustatory.
Hormonal.
Aging.
Systemic diseases.

RHINOSINUSITIS, DIFFERENTIAL DIAGNOSIS[51]

ICD-10CM #   varies with specific diagnosis

DIFFERENTIAL DIAGNOSIS OF RHINOSINUSITIS

Allergic Rhinitis
Seasonal.
Perennial.
Combined seasonal and perennial.
Allergic fungal rhinosinusitis.
Nonallergic Rhinitis
Nonallergic, noninflammatory idiopathic rhinopathy (vasomotor rhinitis).

Nonallergic rhinitis with eosinophilia syndrome (NARES).
Cold dry air–induced rhinitis.
Gustatory rhinitis.
Infectious Rhinosinusitis
Bacterial.
Viral.
Fungal.
Granulomatous.
Drug-Induced Rhinitis
Oral contraceptives.
Various antihypertensives and ocular β-blockers.
Topical decongestants (rhinitis medicamentosa).
Phosphodiesterase-5 antagonists.
Mechanical Causes of Rhinosinusitis
• Septal deviation.
• Nasal foreign body.
• Choanal atresia or stenosis.
• Adenoid hypertrophy.
• Encephalocele.
• Glioma.
• Dermoid.
Innate and Acquired Immunity Disorders
Congenital or acquired immunodeficiencies.
Cystic fibrosis.
Immotile cilia syndrome.
Systemic Inflammatory Disorders
Sarcoidosis.
Wegener's granulomatosis.
Vasculitis.
Neoplastic Causes
Benign:
Polyps.
Nasopharyngeal angiofibroma.
Inverting papilloma.
Malignant:
Adenocarcinoma.
Squamous cell carcinoma.
Aesthesioneuroblastoma.
Lymphoma.
Rhabdomyosarcoma.

RIB DEFECTS ON X-RAY[32]

ICD-10CM # varies with specific diagnosis

CAUSES OF SUPERIOR MARGINAL RIB DEFECTS

Normal
Isolated defects.
Projectional artifacts (due to lordosis).
Neurologic
Paralytic poliomyelitis.
Quadriparesis.
Collagen Vascular Disease
Rheumatoid arthritis.
SLE.
Systemic sclerosis.
Local Pressure
Chest drainage tube.
Osteochondroma.
Neural tumor.
Coarctation of aorta.
Hyperparathyroidism Miscellaneous
Osteogenesis imperfecta.
Marfan's syndrome.

RIB NOTCHING ON X-RAY[32]

ICD-10CM # varies with specific diagnosis

CAUSES OF INFERIOR RIB NOTCHING

ARTERIAL

AORTIC OBSTRUCTION

Aortic coarctation.
Aortic thrombosis.
Aortitis.

SUBCLAVIAN ARTERY OBSTRUCTION

Blalock-Taussig operation.
Arteritis.
Atherosclerotic occlusion.

PULMONARY OLIGEMIA

Pulmonary atresia.
Tetralogy of Fallot.
Multiple pulmonary arterial stenoses.
Venous

CHRONIC SUPERIOR VENA CAVAL OBSTRUCTION

Arteriovenous
Arteriovenous Malformation
Pulmonary.
Chest wall.
Neural
Neurofibromas

RIGHT AXIS DEVIATION[44]

ICD-10CM # varies with specific diagnosis

Normal variation.
Right ventricular hypertrophy.
Left posterior fascicular block.
Lateral myocardial infarction.
Pulmonary embolism.
Dextrocardia.
Mechanical shifts or emphysema causing a vertical heart.

SALIVARY GLAND ENLARGEMENT

ICD-10CM # K11.1 Hypertrophy of salivary gland

Neoplasm.
Sialolithiasis.
Infection (mumps, bacterial infection, HIV, TB).
Sarcoidosis.
Idiopathic.
Acromegaly.
Anorexia/bulimia.
Chronic pancreatitis.
Medications (e.g., phenylbutazone).
Cirrhosis.
DM.

SALIVARY GLAND SECRETION, DECREASED

ICD-10CM # K11.7 Disturbances of salivary secretion
R68.2 Dry mouth, unspecified

Medications (antihistamines, antidepressants, neuroleptics, antihypertensives).
Dehydration.

Anxiety.
Sjögren's syndrome.
Sarcoidosis.
Mumps.
Amyloidosis.
CNS disorders.
Head and neck radiation.

SCLERODERMA-LIKE SYNDROMES[3]

ICD-10CM # varies with specific diagnosis

OTHER DISEASES

Morphea.
Eosinophilic fasciitis.
Scleredema (of Buschke).
Scleromyxedema.
Graft-versus-host disease.
Nephrogenic-fibrosing dermopathy.

ENVIRONMENTAL AGENTS AND DRUGS

Bleomycin.
L-Tryptophan.
Organic solvents.
Pentazocine.
Toxic oil syndrome.
Vinyl chloride disease.
Gadolinium.

SCROTAL MASSES, BOYS AND ADOLESCENTS[45]

ICD-10CM # R22.9 Localized swelling, mass and lump, unspecified

PAINFUL

Testicular torsion.
Torsion of appendix testis.
Epididymitis.
Trauma: ruptured testis, hematocele.
Inguinal hernia (incarcerated).
Mumps orchitis.

PAINLESS

Hydrocele.
Inguinal hernia.[41]
Varicocele.
Spermatocele.
Testicular tumor.
Henoch-Schönlein purpura.
Idiopathic scrotal edema.

SCROTAL PAIN[54]

ICD-10CM # S31.30XA Unspecified open wound of scrotum and testes, initial encounter
N50.9 Disorder of male genital organs, unspecified
R10.2 Pelvic and perineal pain

---

[41]May be associated with discomfort.

N49.9		Inflammatory disorder of unspecified male genital organ
N50.1		Vascular disorders of male genital organs
N49.9		Inflammatory disorder of unspecified male genital organ

Torsion:
  Appendages.
  Spermatic cord.
Infection:
  Orchitis.
  Abscess.
  Epididymitis.
Neoplasia:
  Benign.
  Malignant.
Incarcerated hernia.
Trauma.
Hydrocele.
Spermatocele.
Varicocele.

SCROTAL SWELLING

ICD-10CM # N50.8 Other specified disorders of male genital organs

Hydrocele.
Varicocele.
Neoplasm.
Acute epididymitis.
Orchitis.
Trauma.
Hernia.
Torsion of spermatic cord.
Torsion of epididymis.
Torsion of testis.
Insect bite.
Folliculitis.
Sebaceous cyst.
Thrombosis of spermatic vein.
Other: lymphedema, dermatitis, fat necrosis, Henoch-Schönlein purpura, idiopathic scrotal edema.

SEIZURE

ICD-10CM # R56.9 Unspecified convulsions

Syncope.
Alcohol abuse/withdrawal.
TIA.
Hemiparetic migraine.
Psychiatric disorders.
Carotid sinus hypersensitivity.
Hyperventilation, prolonged breath holding.
Hypoglycemia.
Narcolepsy.
Movement disorders (tics, hemiballismus).
Hyponatremia.
Brain tumor (primary or metastatic).
Tetanus.
Strychnine, phencyclidine poisoning.

SEIZURE, PEDIATRIC[6]

ICD-10CM # R56.9 Unspecified convulsions
P90 Convulsions of newborn

FIRST MONTH OF LIFE
First Day
Hypoxia.
Drugs.
Trauma.
Infection.
Hyperglycemia.
Hypoglycemia.
Pyridoxine deficiency.
Day 2-3
Infection.
Drug withdrawal.
Hypoglycemia.
Hypocalcemia.
Developmental malformation.
Intracranial hemorrhage.
Inborn error of metabolism.
Hyponatremia or hypernatremia.
Day >4
Infection.
Hypocalcemia.
Hyperphosphatemia.
Hyponatremia.
Developmental malformation.
Drug withdrawal.
Inborn error of metabolism.

1 TO 6 MO
As above.

6 MO TO 3 YR
Febrile seizures.
Birth injury.
Infection.
Toxin.
Trauma.
Metabolic disorder.
Cerebral degenerative disease.

>3 YR
Idiopathic.
Infection.
Trauma.
Cerebral degenerative disease.

SEIZURE MIMICS[3]

ICD-10CM # varies with specific diagnosis

NON-EPILEPTIC EPISODIC DISORDERS THAT MAY RESEMBLE SEIZURES

Movement disorders: myoclonus, paroxysmal choreoathetosis, episodic ataxias, hyperexplexia (startle disease).
Migraine: confusional, vertebrobasilar, visual auras.
Syncope.
Behavioral and psychiatric: psychogenic non-epileptic attacks (pseudoseizures), hyperventilation syndrome, panic or anxiety disorder, dissociative states.
Cataplexy (usually associated with narcolepsy).

Transient ischemic attack.
Alcoholic blackouts.
Hypoglycemia.

SEXUAL DYSFUNCTION, FEMALE[3]

ICD-10CM # R37 Sexual dysfunction, unspecified

FACTORS THAT MAY INFLUENCE SEXUAL FUNCTIONING IN WOMEN
Biological
Medications (e.g., antidepressants, antihypertensives).
Vaginal atrophy, pain with intercourse.
Low testosterone levels (e.g., bilateral oophorectomy).
Illness (e.g., diabetes, hypothyroidism, cerebrovascular accident).
Sleep disturbances, fatigue.
Disability or pain from illness (e.g., arthritis).
Incontinence.
Psychological
Depression.
Body image.
Interpersonal
Marital issues.
Poor communication.
Partner's sexual problems (e.g., erectile dysfunction).
Partner's health problems (e.g., myocardial infarction).
Sociocultural
Ageism ("too old" to want sex).
Multiple other obligations and commitments.
Lack of partner.

SEXUALLY TRANSMITTED DISEASES, ANORECTAL REGION[50]

ICD-10CM # K62.89 Other specified diseases of anus and rectum

ULCERATIVE
Lymphogranuloma venereum.
Herpes simplex virus.
Early (primary) syphilis.
Chancroid (*Haemophilus ducreyi*).
Cytomegalovirus.
Idiopathic (usually HIV positive).

NONULCERATIVE
Condyloma acuminatum.
Gonorrhea.
Chlamydia (*Chlamydia trachomatis*).
Syphilis.

SEXUAL PRECOCITY[73]

ICD-10CM # E30.1 Precocious puberty
E30.8 Other disorders of puberty

TRUE PRECOCIOUS PUBERTY
Premature reactivation of LHRH pulse generator.

INCOMPLETE SEXUAL PRECOCITY

(Pituitary gonadotropin independent).

Males

Chorionic gonadotropin-secreting tumor.
Leydig cell tumor.
Familial testotoxicosis.
Virilizing congenital adrenal hyperplasia.
Virilizing adrenal tumor.
Premature adrenarche.

Females

Granulosa cell tumor (follicular cysts may be manifested similarly).
Follicular cyst.
Feminizing adrenal tumor.
Premature thelarche.
Premature adrenarche.
Late-onset virilizing congenital adrenal hyperplasia.

In Both Sexes

McCune-Albright syndrome.
Primary hypothyroidism.

SHOULDER PAIN

ICD-10CM #	M24.819	Other specific joint derangements of unspecified shoulder, not elsewhere classified
	M75.80	Other shoulder lesions, unspecified shoulder
	S43.409A	Unspecified sprain of unspecified shoulder joint, initial encounter
	S46.919A	Strain of unspecified muscle, fascia and tendon at shoulder and upper arm level, unspecified arm, initial encounter

WITH LOCAL FINDINGS IN SHOULDER

Trauma: contusion, fracture, muscle strain, trauma to spinal cord.
Arthrosis, arthritis, RA, ankylosing spondylitis.
Bursitis, synovitis, tendinitis, tenosynovitis.
Aseptic (avascular) necrosis.
Local infection: septic arthritis, osteomyelitis, abscess, herpes zoster, TB.

WITHOUT LOCAL FINDINGS IN SHOULDER

Cardiovascular disorders: ischemic heart disease, pericarditis, aortic aneurysm.
Subdiaphragmatic abscess, liver abscess.
Cholelithiasis, cholecystitis.
Pulmonary lesions: apical bronchial carcinoma, pleurisy, pneumothorax, pneumonia.
GI lesions: PUD, gastric neoplasm, peptic esophagitis.
Pancreatic lesions: carcinoma, calculi, pancreatitis.
CNS abnormalities: neoplasm, vascular abnormalities.
Multiple sclerosis.
Syringomyelia.

Polymyositis/dermatomyositis.
Psychogenic.
Polymyalgia rheumatica.
Ectopic pregnancy.

SHOULDER PAIN BY LOCATION

ICD-10CM #	M75.80	Other shoulder lesions, unspecified shoulder
	S43.499A	Other sprain of unspecified shoulder joint, initial encounter
	S46.019A	Strain of muscle(s) and tendon(s) of the rotator cuff of unspecified shoulder, initial encounter
	S46.819A	Strain of other muscles, fascia and tendons at shoulder and upper arm level, unspecified arm, initial encounter

TOP OF SHOULDER (C4)

Cervical source.
Acromioclavicular.
Sternoclavicular.
Diaphragmatic.

SUPEROLATERAL (C5)

Rotator cuff tendinitis.
Impingement.
Adhesive capsulitis.
Glenohumeral arthritis.

ANTERIOR

Bicipital tendinitis and rupture.
Glenoid labral tear.
Adhesive capsulitis.
Glenohumeral arthritis.
Osteonecrosis.

AXILLARY

Neoplasm (Pancoast's, mediastinal).
Herpes zoster.

SHOULDER PAIN, IN DIFFERENT AGE GROUPS[17]

| ICD-10CM # | M25.519 | Pain in unspecified shoulder |

COMMON CAUSES OF SHOULDER PAIN IN DIFFERENT AGE GROUPS

Childhood (2-10 yr)
Intraarticular
Instability.
Periarticular
Osteochondromas.
Adolescence (10-18 yr)
Intraarticular
Instability.

Early Adulthood (18-30 yr)
Intraarticular
Instability.
Acromioclavicular joint sprain.
Periarticular
Calcific tendonitis.
Impingement.
Referred
Cervical.
Adulthood (30-60 yr)
Intraarticular
Osteochondritis.
Osteoarthritis.
Frozen shoulder.
Inflammatory arthritis.
Periarticular
Calcific tendonitis.
Impingement.
Rotator cuff tear.
Bicipital tendonitis.
Referred
Cervical.
Old Age (>60 yr)
Intraarticular
Osteochondritis.
Osteoarthritis.
Frozen shoulder.
Inflammatory arthritis.
Periarticular
• Impingement.
• Rotator cuff tear.
Referred
Cervical.

SINUS NODE DYSFUNCTION[30]

| ICD-10CM # | varies with specific diagnosis |

CAUSES OF SINUS NODE DYSFUNCTION

Intrinsic
• Hypothyroidism.
• Fibrocalcific degeneration.
• Increased vagal tone, especially in sleep apnea.
• Congenital mutations.
• Scleroderma.
• Amyloidosis.
• Chagas disease.

Extrinsic
Trauma, including cardiac surgery.
Drugs:
  Calcium-channel blockers.
  β-Blockers.
  Digoxin.
  Antiarrhythmic medications (amiodarone, dronedarone, sotalol, flecainide, propafenone).
  Lithium.

SINUS OSTIAL OBSTRUCTION[9]

| ICD-10CM # | Codes vary with specific diagnosis |

FACTORS THAT PREDISPOSE TO SINUS OSTIAL OBSTRUCTION

Mucosal Swelling
Systemic factors:
  Viral upper respiratory infection.
  Allergic inflammation.

Cystic fibrosis.
Immune disorders.
Ciliary dyskinesia.
Tobacco smoke.
Local insult:
Facial trauma.
Swimming, diving.
Rhinitis medicamentosa.
Nasal intubation.
Mechanical Obstruction
Choanal atresia.
Deviated septum.
Nasal polyps.
Foreign body.
Tumor.
Ethmoid bullae.

SKIN INDURATION, CHRONIC[36]

ICD-10CM #   varies with specific diagnosis

CONDITIONS ASSOCIATED WITH CHRONIC SKIN INDURATION

Systemic sclerosis.
Localized scleroderma.
Scleroderma variants.
Scleredema.
   o Scleredema adultorum of Buschke.
   o Scleredema diabeticorum.
   o Scleredema neonatorum.
• Scleromyxedema.
• Nephrogenic fibrosing dermopathy.
• Eosinophilic syndromes.
   o Eosinophilic fasciitis (diffuse fasciitis with
     oosinophilia, Schulman dicoaco).
   o Eosinophilia-myalgia syndrome.
   o Toxic oil syndrome.
• Chronic graft-versus-host disease.
• Pseudoscleroderma (local injection of vitamin
   K, bleomycin, pentazocine).
• Metabolic diseases.
   Porphyria cutanea tarda.
   Phenylketonuria.
   Werner syndrome.
   Acromegaly.
Pachydermoperiostitis.
Polyneuropathy, organomegaly, endocrinopathy,
   monoclonal gammopathy (POEMS).
Stiff skin syndrome.
Reflex sympathetic dystrophy.
Hemiplegia.

SMALL BOWEL MASSES[67]

ICD-10CM #   varies with specific diagnosis

Cyst:
   Mesenteric cyst.
Tumor:
   Benign.
   Malignant.
Intussusception.
Inflammation:
   Crohn's disease.

SMALL BOWEL OBSTRUCTION[50]

ICD-10CM #   K56.5   Intestinal adhesions [bands] with obstruction (postprocedural) (postinfection)
           Q41.9   Congenital absence, atresia and stenosis of small intestine, part unspecified

INTRINSIC

Congenital (atresia, stenosis).
Inflammatory (Crohn's, radiation enteritis).
Neoplasms (metastatic or primary).
Intussusception.
Traumatic (hematoma).

EXTRINSIC

Hernias (internal and external).
Adhesions.
Volvulus.
Compressing masses (tumors, abscesses, hematomas).

INTRALUMINAL

Foreign body.
Gallstones.
Bezoars.
Barium.
Ascaris infestation.

SMALL INTESTINE ULCERATION

ICD-10CM #   K63.3   Ulcer of intestine

Inflammatory bowel disease.
Celiac disease.
Vasculitis, SLE, Behçet's syndrome.
Uremia.
Infections (*Campylobacter*, TB, *Yersinia*, parasites, typhoid, cytomegalovirus [CMV], *Clostridium*).
Mesenteric insufficiency.
Neoplasms.
Radiation.
Drugs (salicylates, potassium, indomethacin, antimetabolites).
Meckel diverticulum.
Zollinger-Ellison syndrome.
Lymphocytic enterocolitis.
Stomal ulceration.

SMELL DISTURBANCE

ICD-10CM #   R43.8   Other disturbances of smell and taste

Upper respiratory tract infection.
Nasal or paranasal sinus disease.
Exposure to noxious vapors.
Head trauma.
Idiopathic.
Dental caries, periodontal disease.
Medications.

SOFT TISSUE MASS MIMICKING MALIGNANCY[58]

ICD-10CM #   varies with specific diagnosis

OVERVIEW OF DISEASES THAT CAN PRESENT AS A SOFT TISSUE MASS MIMICKING MALIGNANCY

Etiology	Disease Entity
Trauma:	Muscle contusion.
	Hematoma.
	Muscle herniation.
	Calcific myonecrosis.
	Hypothenar hammer syndrome.
	Myositis ossificans.
Metabolic:	Diabetic myopathy.
	Gout.
	Pseudogout.
	Calcific tendinosis.
Congenital:	Accessory muscle.
Infectious:	Necrotizing fasciitis.
	Abscess.
	Pyomyositis.
	Hydatid cystic disease.
	Cat-scratch disease.
	Actinomycosis.
Inflammation:	Bursitis.
	Sarcoidosis.
	Foreign body reaction.
	Injection granuloma.
	Granuloma annulare.
	Epidermal inclusion cyst.
Vascular:	Adventitial cystic disease.
	Pseudoaneurysm.
	Thrombosed vein.
	Arteriovenous vascular malformation.
Miscellaneous:	Focal myositis.
	Amyloid tumor of soft tissue.

SOFT TISSUE TUMORS, PEDIATRIC PATIENTS[58]

ICD-10CM #   varies with specific diagnosis

PEDIATRIC SOFT TISSUE TUMORS

Vascular lesions:
   Hemangioma of infancy.*
   Congenital hemangioma.*
   Hemangioendothelioma (Kasabach-Merritt syndrome).*
   Arteriovenous malformation.*
   Venous malformations.*
   Lymphatic malformation (lymphangioma, cystic hygroma).*
   Capillary malformation.*
Adipocytic tumors:
   Lipoma.*
   Lipoblastoma.*
   Liposarcoma.*
Fibrohistiocytic tumors:
   Pigmented villonodular synovitis.*
   Giant cell tumor of tendon sheath.*

*Lesions with MR-specific features.

Fibroblastic and myofibroblastic tumors:
Nodular fasciitis.
Fibrous hamartoma of infancy.
Myofibroma, myofibromatosis.
Infantile fibrosarcoma.
Fibromatosis colli.*
Neurogenic tumors:
Schwannoma.*
Neurofibroma.*
Malignant nerve sheath tumor.
Leiomyoma
Rhabdomyosarcoma
Tumors of uncertain differentiation
Synovial cell sarcoma.
Primitive neuroectodermal tumor (Ewing sarcoma).
Pilomatricoma*

SORE THROAT[6]

ICD-10CM #   J02   Acute pharyngitis

DIFFERENTIAL DIAGNOSIS FOR SORE THROAT

Infectious Causes
Aerobes
Common:
Streptococcus pyogenes (GABHS).
GABHS.
Peptostreptococcus spp.
Non–group A streptococcus.
Neisseria gonorrhoeae.
Neisseria meningitides.
Mycoplasma pneumoniae.
Arcanobacterium hemolyticum.
Chlamydia trachomatis.
Staphylococcus aureus.
Uncommon:
Haemophilus influenzae.
Haemophilus parainfluenzae.
Coccidioides spp.
Corynebacterium diphtheriae.
Streptococcus pneumoniae.
Yersinia enterocolitica.
Treponema pallidum.
Francisella tularensis.
Legionella pneumophila.
Mycobacterium spp.

ANAEROBES

Bacteroides spp.
Peptococcus spp.
Clostridium spp.
Fusobacterium spp.
Prevotella spp.

OTHER

Candida spp.

VIRAL

Rhinovirus.
Adenovirus.
Coronavirus.
Herpes simplex 1, 2.
Influenza A, B.
Parainfluenza.
Cytomegalovirus.
Epstein-Barr.
Varicella-zoster.
Hepatitis virus.

Noninfectious Causes

SYSTEMIC

Kawasaki disease.
Stevens-Johnson syndrome.
Cyclic neutropenia.
Thyroiditis.
Connective tissue disease.

TRAUMA, MISCELLANEOUS

Penetrating injury.
Angioneurotic edema.
Retained foreign body.
Anomalous aortic arch.
Laryngeal fracture.
Calcific retropharyngeal tendinitis.
Retropharyngeal hematoma.
Caustic exposure.

TUMOR

Tongue.
Larynx.
Thyroid.
Leukemia.

SPASTIC PARAPLEGIAS

ICD-10CM #   G82.20   Paraplegia, unspecified

Cervical spondylosis.
Friedreich's ataxia.
Multiple sclerosis.
Spinal cord tumor.
HIV.
Tertiary syphilis.
Vitamin B_{12} deficiency.
Spinocerebellar ataxias.
Syringomyelia.
Spinal cord AV malformations.
Adrenoleukodystrophy.

SPINAL CORD COMPRESSION, EPIDURAL

ICD-10CM #   varies with specific diagnosis

Osteoarthritis.
Meningioma.
Spinal epidural abscess.
Spinal epidural hematoma.
Spinal epidural vascular malformations.
RA.
Metastatic cancer (vertebral, intramedullary, leptomeninges).
Radiation myelopathy.
Neurofibroma.
Sarcoidosis.
Paraneoplastic myelopathy.
Histiocytosis.

SPINAL CORD DYSFUNCTION

ICD-10CM #		
	G95.9	Disease of spinal cord, unspecified
	G95.9	Disease of spinal cord, unspecified
	Q07.9	Congenital malformation of nervous system, unspecified
	D51.1	Vitamin B_{12} deficiency anemia due to selective vitamin B_{12} malabsorption with proteinuria
	D51.3	Other dietary vitamin B_{12} deficiency anemia
	D51.8	Other vitamin B_{12} deficiency anemias
	G95.89	Other specified diseases of spinal cord
	G95.19	Other vascular myelopathies

Trauma.
Multiple sclerosis.
Transverse myelitis.
Neoplasm (primary, metastatic).
Syringomyelia.
Spinal epidural abscess.
HIV myelopathy.
Diskitis.
Spinal epidural hematoma.
Spinal cord infarction.
Spinal AV malformation.
Subarachnoid hemorrhage.

SPINAL CORD DYSFUNCTION, NONTRAUMATIC[6]

ICD-10CM #   Q07.9   Congenital malformation of nervous system, unspecified

NONTRAUMATIC ETIOLOGIES OF SPINAL CORD DYSFUNCTION

Processes Affecting the Spinal Cord or Blood Supply Directly
Multiple sclerosis.
Transverse myelitis.
Spinal arteriovenous malformation/subarachnoid hemorrhage.
Syringomyelia.
HIV myelopathy.
Other myelopathies.
Spinal cord infarction.
Compressive Lesions Affecting the Spinal Cord
Spinal epidural abscess.
Spinal epidural hematoma.
Diskitis.
Neoplasm.
Metastatic.
Primary CNS.

HIV, Human immunodeficiency virus; CNS, central nervous system.

SPINAL CORD ISCHEMIC SYNDROMES

ICD-10CM #   varies with specific diagnosis

Systemic hypotension.
Venous or arterial occlusion.
Arterial dissection.
Thromboembolism.
Endovascular procedures.

Vasculitis.
Fibrocartilaginous embolism.
Regional hemodynamic compromise.

SPINAL TUMORS[28]

ICD-10CM # varies with specific diagnosis

EXTRADURAL

Metastases.
Primary bone tumors arising in spine.

INTRADURAL EXTRAMEDULLARY

Meningiomas.
Neurofibromas.
Schwannomas.
Lipomas.
Arachnoid cysts.
Epidermoid cysts.
Metastasis.

INTRAMEDULLARY

Ependymoma.
Glioma.
Hemangioblastoma.
Lipoma.
Metastases.

SPLENIC CYSTS, CLASSIFICATION[14]

ICD-10CM # D73.4 Cyst of spleen

Primary (true).
Parasitic.
Nonparasitic.
Congenital.
Epidermoid.
Dermoid.
Mesothelial (serous).
Transitional.
Neoplastic.
Secondary (false): pseudocysts.
Traumatic.
Degenerative.
Inflammatory.
Hemorrhagic.

SPLENIC TUMORS, CLASSIFICATION[14]

ICD-10CM # C26.1 Malignant neoplasm of spleen

- Malignant.
- Lymphoproliferative disease.
- Non-Hodgkin lymphoma.
- Hodgkin disease.
- Hairy cell leukemia.
- Chronic lymphocytic leukemia.
- Myeloproliferative disease.
- Chronic myelogenous leukemia.
- Myelofibrosis.
- Primary tumors.
- Angiosarcoma.
- Metastatic tumors.
- Benign.
- Hemangiomas.
- Hamartomas.
- Lymphangiomas.

- Sclerosing angiomatoid nodular transformation (SANT).

SPLENOMEGALY

ICD-10CM #	R16.1	Splenomegaly, not elsewhere classified
	D73.2	Chronic congestive splenomegaly
	R16.1	Splenomegaly, not elsewhere classified

Hepatic cirrhosis.
Neoplastic involvement: CML, CLL, lymphoma, multiple myeloma.
Bacterial infections: TB, infectious endocarditis, typhoid fever, splenic abscess.
Viral infections: infectious mononucleosis, viral hepatitis, HIV.
Gaucher's disease and other lipid storage diseases.
Sarcoidosis.
Parasitic infections (malaria, kala-azar, histoplasmosis).
Hereditary and acquired hemolytic anemias.
Idiopathic thrombocytopenic purpura (ITP).
Collagen vascular disorders: SLE, RA (Felty's syndrome), polyarteritis nodosa.
Serum sickness, drug hypersensitivity reaction.
Splenic cysts and benign tumors: hemangioma, lymphangioma.
Thrombosis of splenic or portal vein.
Polycythemia vera, myeloid metaplasia.

SPLENOMEGALY AND HEPATOMEGALY[67]

| ICD-10CM # | R16.1 | Splenomegaly, not elsewhere classified |
| | R16.0 | Hepatomegaly, not elsewhere classified |

CAUSES OF SPLENOMEGALY AND HEPATOSPLENOMEGALY

Massive Splenomegaly
Hematologic disease (e.g., chronic myeloid leukemia, myelofibrosis).
Moderate Splenomegaly
The above causes.
Portal hypertension.
Hematologic disease (e.g., lymphoma, leukemia, thalassemia).
Storage disease (e.g., Gaucher's disease).
Small Splenomegaly
The above causes.
Infective (hepatitis, leptospirosis, malaria, bacterial endocarditis).
Hematologic disease (e.g., hemolytic anemias, essential thrombocythemia, polycythemia rubra vera).
Connective tissue diseases or vasculitis (e.g., rheumatoid arthritis, systemic lupus erythematosus, polyarteritis nodosa).
Solitary cyst, polycystic syndrome, hydatid cyst.
Infiltration (amyloid, sarcoid).
Hepatosplenomegaly
Chronic liver disease with portal hypertension.
Hematologic disease (e.g., myeloproliferative disease, lymphoma).

Infection (e.g., amyloid, sarcoid).
Connective tissue disease (e.g., systemic lupus erythematosus).

SPLENOMEGALY, CHILDREN[39]

ICD-10CM # R16.1 Splenomegaly, not elsewhere classified

DISORDERS OF THE BLOOD

Hemolytic anemia: congenital/acquired.
Thalassemia.
Sickle cell disease.
Leukemia.
Osteopetrosis.
Myelofibrosis/myeloid metaplasia/thrombocythemia.

INFECTIONS: ACUTE AND CHRONIC

Viral:
  Congenital (e.g., TORCH association).
  Mononucleosis (e.g., EBV, CMV infection).
  Virus-associated hemophagocytic syndrome.
  Human immunodeficiency virus.
Bacterial:
  Sepsis/abscess.
  Brucellosis.
  Salmonellosis.
  Tularemia.
  Tuberculosis.
  Subacute bacterial endocarditis.
  Syphilis.
  Lyme disease.
Fungal:
  Histoplasmosis (disseminated).
Rickettsial:
  Rocky Mountain spotted fever.
  Cat scratch disease.
Parasitic:
  Toxoplasmosis.
  Malaria.
  Leishmaniasis (kala-azar).
  Schistosomiasis.
  Echinococcosis.

HEPATIC/PORTAL SYSTEM DISORDERS

Acute/chronic active hepatitis.
Cirrhosis/hepatic fibrosis/biliary atresia.
Portal or splenic venous obstruction (Banti syndrome).

AUTOIMMUNE DISEASE

Juvenile rheumatoid arthritis.
Systemic lupus erythematosus.
Autoimmune lymphoproliferative syndrome (Canale–Smith syndrome).

NEOPLASMS/CYSTS

Lymphomas (Hodgkin and non-Hodgkin).
Hemangiomas/lymphangiomas.
Hamartomas.
Congenital or acquired (posttraumatic) cysts.

STORAGE DISEASES/INBORN ERRORS OF METABOLISM

Lipidoses: Gaucher disease, Niemann–Pick disease, others.

Mucopolysaccharidoses.
Defects in carbohydrate metabolism: galactosemia, fructose intolerance.
Sea-blue histiocyte syndrome.

MISCELLANEOUS DISORDERS

Histiocytoses:
  Reactive.
  Langerhans cell.
  Malignant.
Sarcoidosis.
Congestive heart failure.
Familial Mediterranean fever.

CMV, Cytomegalovirus; *EBV,* Epstein-Barr virus; *TORCH,* toxoplasmosis, other infections, rubella, cytomegalovirus infection, herpes simplex.

SPONTANEOUS PNEUMOTHORAX[50]

ICD-10CM #	J93.0	Spontaneous tension pneumothorax
	J93.11	Primary spontaneous pneumothorax
	J93.12	Secondary spontaneous pneumothorax

CAUSES OF SECONDARY SPONTANEOUS PNEUMOTHORAX

Airway Disease
Chronic obstructive pulmonary disease.
Asthma.
Cystic fibrosis.
Infections
Necrotizing bacterial pneumonia, lung abscess.
Pneumocystis jiroveci pneumonia.
Tuberculosis.
Interstitial Lung Disease
Sarcoidosis.
Idiopathic pulmonary fibrosis.
Lymphangiomyomatosis.
Tuberous sclerosis.
Pneumoconioses.
Neoplasms
Primary lung cancers.
Pulmonary or pleural metastases.
Miscellaneous
Connective tissue diseases.
Pulmonary infarction.
Endometriosis, catamenial pneumothorax.

STATURAL OVERGROWTH[52]

| ICD-10CM # | E34.4 |
| | |

FETAL OVERGROWTH

Maternal diabetes mellitus.
Cerebral gigantism (Sotos syndrome).
Weaver's syndrome.
Beckwith-Wiedemann syndrome.
Other insulin-like growth factor 2 (IGF2) excess syndromes.

POSTNATAL OVERGROWTH LEADING TO CHILDHOOD TALL STATURE

Familial (constitutional) tall stature.
Cerebral gigantism.

Beckwith-Wiedemann syndrome.
Exogenous obesity.
Excess growth hormone (GH) secretion (pituitary gigantism).
McCune-Albright syndrome or multiple endocrine neoplasia (MEN) associated with excess GH secretion.
Precocious puberty.
Marfan's syndrome.
Klinefelter's syndrome (XXY).
Weaver's syndrome.
Fragile X syndrome.
Homocystinuria.
XYY.
Hyperthyroidism.

POSTNATAL OVERGROWTH LEADING TO ADULT TALL STATURE

Familial (constitutional) tall stature.
Androgen or estrogen deficiency/estrogen resistance (in males).
Testicular feminization.
Excess GH secretion.
Marfan's syndrome.
Klinefelter's syndrome (XXY).
XYY.

STEATOHEPATITIS

| ICD-10CM # | K76.0 | Fatty (change of) liver, not elsewhere classified |
| | K76.89 | Other specified diseases of liver |

Alcohol abuse.
Obesity.
DM.
Parenteral nutrition.
Medications (high-dose estrogen, amiodarone, corticosteroids, methotrexate, nifedipine).
Jejunoileal bypass.
Abetalipoproteinemia.
Wilson's disease, Weber-Christian disease.

STOMATITIS, BULLOUS

| ICD-10CM # | K12.30 | Oral mucositis (ulcerative), unspecified |

Erythema multiforme.
Erosive lichen planus.
Bullous pemphigoid.
SLE.
Pemphigus vulgaris.
Mucous membrane pemphigoid.

STRIDOR IN NEONATES[1]

| ICD-10CM # | R06.1 | Stridor |

INTRINSIC LESIONS

Larynx
Laryngomalacia.
Infection (laryngitis).
Vocal cord paralysis.
Laryngeal web.
Laryngocele or laryngeal cyst.
Laryngotracheal esophageal cleft.
Foreign body.

Trachea
Tracheomalacia.
Tracheal stenosis.
Tracheoesophageal fistula.
Subglottic hemangioma.
Tracheal web.
Extrinsic Compression
Vascular ring.
Anomalous innominate artery.
Mediastinal mass.
Esophageal foreign body.
Other
Macroglossia.
Gastroesophageal reflux.

STRIDOR, PEDIATRIC AGE[8]

| ICD-10CM # | R06.1 | Stridor |

RECURRENT

Allergic (spasmodic) croup.
Respiratory infections in a child with otherwise asymptomatic anatomic narrowing of the large airways.
Laryngomalacia.

PERSISTENT

Laryngeal obstruction:
  Laryngomalacia.
  Papillomas, other tumors.
  Cysts and laryngoceles.
  Laryngeal webs.
  Bilateral abductor paralysis of the cords.
  Foreign body.
Tracheobronchial disease:
  Tracheomalacia.
  Subglottic tracheal webs.
Endotracheal, endobronchial tumors.
Subglottic tracheal stenosis.
Congenital.
Acquired.
Extrinsic masses.
Mediastinal masses.
Vascular ring.
Lobar emphysema.
Bronchogenic cysts.
Thyroid enlargement.
Esophageal foreign body.
Tracheoesophageal fistulas.
Other.
Gastroesophageal reflux.
Macroglossia, Pierre Robin syndrome.
Cri-du-chat syndrome.
Hysterical stridor.
Hypocalcemia.

STROKE[65]

| ICD-10CM # | I64 | Stroke |
| | I67.89 | Other cerebrovascular disease |

Hypoglycemia.
Drug overdose or intoxication.
Hysterical conversion reaction.
Hyperventilation.
Metabolic encephalopathy.
Migraine.
Syncope.
Transient global amnesia.

Seizures.
Vestibular vertigo.

STROKE, PEDIATRIC AGE[46]

ICD-10CM # I67.89 Other cerebrovascular disease

CARDIAC DISEASE

Congenital:
    Aortic stenosis.
    Mitral stenosis; mitral prolapse.
    Ventricular septal defects.
    Patent ductus arteriosus.
    Cyanotic congenital heart disease involving right-to-left shunt.
Acquired:
    Endocarditis (bacterial, SLE).
    Kawasaki disease.
    Cardiomyopathy.
    Atrial myxoma.
    Arrhythmia.
    Paradoxical emboli through patent foramen ovale.
    Rheumatic fever.
    Prosthetic heart valve.

HEMATOLOGIC ABNORMALITIES

Hemoglobinopathies:
    Sickle cell (SS) disease.
    Sickle (SC) disease.
Polycythemia.
Leukemia/lymphoma.
Thrombocytopenia.
Thrombocytosis.
Disorders of coagulation:
    Protein C deficiency.
    Protein S deficiency.
    Factor V Leiden.
    Antithrombin III deficiency.
    Lupus anticoagulant.
Oral contraceptive pill use.
Pregnancy and the postpartum state.
Disseminated intravascular coagulation.
Paroxysmal nocturnal hemoglobinuria.
Inflammatory bowel disease (thrombosis).

INFLAMMATORY DISORDERS

- Meningitis:
    - Viral.
    - Bacterial.
    - Tuberculosis.
- Systemic infection:
    - Viremia.
    - Bacteremia.
    - Local head and neck infections.
- Drug-induced inflammation:
    Amphetamine.
    Cocaine.
Autoimmune disease:
    SLE.
    Juvenile RA.
    Takayasu's arteritis.
    Mixed connective tissue disease.
    Polyarteritis nodosum.
    Primary CNS vasculitis.
    Sarcoidosis.
    Behçet's syndrome.
    Granulomatosis with polyangiitis (Wegener's granulomatosis).

METABOLIC DISEASE ASSOCIATED WITH STROKE

Homocystinuria.
Pseudoxanthoma elasticum.
Fabry's disease.
Sulfite oxidase deficiency.
Mitochondrial disorders:
    MELAS.
    Leigh syndrome.
Ornithine transcarbamylase deficiency.

INTRACEREBRAL VASCULAR PROCESSES

Ruptured aneurysm.
Arteriovenous malformation.
Fibromuscular dysplasia.
Moyamoya disease.
Migraine headache.
Postsubarachnoid hemorrhage vasospasm.
Hereditary hemorrhagic telangiectasia.
Sturge-Weber syndrome.
Carotid artery dissection.
Postvaricella.

TRAUMA AND OTHER EXTERNAL CAUSES

Child abuse.
Head trauma/neck trauma.
Oral trauma.
Placental embolism.
ECMO therapy.

CNS, Central nervous system; *ECMO,* extracorporeal membrane oxygenation; *MELAS,* mitochondrial encephalomyopathy, lactic acidosis, and stroke.

STROKE, YOUNG ADULT, CAUSES[3]

ICD-10CM # I64 Stroke
                 I67.89 Other cerebrovascular disease

Cardiac factors (ASD, MVP, patent foramen ovale).
Inflammatory factors (SLE, polyarteritis nodosa).
Infections (endocarditis, neurosyphilis).
Drugs (cocaine, heroin, oral contraceptives, decongestants).
Arterial dissection.
Hematolic factors (DIC, TTP, deficiency of protein S, protein C, antithrombin III).
Migraine.
Postpartum angiopathy.
Other: premature atherosclerosis, fibromuscular dysplasia.

ST-SEGMENT DEPRESSION, NONCORONARY CAUSES[10]

ICD-10CM # R94.31

NONCORONARY CAUSES OF ST-SEGMENT DEPRESSION

Anemia.
Cardiomyopathy.
Digitalis use.
Glucose load.
Hyperventilation.
Hypokalemia.
Intraventricular conduction disturbance.

Left ventricular hypertrophy.
Mitral valve prolapse.
Preexcitation syndrome.
Severe aortic stenosis.
Severe hypertension.
Severe hypoxia.
Severe volume overload (aortic, mitral regurgitation).
Sudden excessive exercise.
Supraventricular tachyarrhythmias.

ST-SEGMENT ELEVATION[1]

ICD-10CM # R94.31 Abnormal ECG

DIFFERENTIAL DIAGNOSIS OF ST-SEGMENT ELEVATION ON ELECTROCARDIOGRAPHY

ST-segment elevation myocardial infarction.
Pericarditis.
Benign early repolarization.
Left bundle branch block.
Left ventricular hypertrophy.
Left ventricular aneurysm.
Paced ventricular rhythms.
Prinzmetal angina.
Hyperkalemia.
Hypothermia with Osborne waves.
Intracranial hemorrhage.
Brugada syndrome.
Normal variant.

ST SEGMENT ELEVATIONS, NONISCHEMIC

ICD-10CM # R94.31 Abnormal electrocardiogram [ECG] [EKG]

Early repolarization.
Acute pericarditis.
LVH.
Normal pattern variant.
LBBB.
Pulmonary embolism.
Hyperkalemia.
Postcardioversion.

SUDDEN DEATH, PEDIATRIC AGE[8]

ICD-10CM # R99 Ill-defined and unknown cause of mortality

SIDS AND SIDS "MIMICS"

SIDS.
Long QT syndromes.
Inborn errors of metabolism.
Child abuse.
Myocarditis.
Duct-dependent congenital heart disease.

CORRECTED OR UNOPERATED CONGENITAL HEART DISEASE

Aortic stenosis.
Tetralogy of Fallot.
Transposition of great vessels (postoperative atrial switch).
Mitral valve prolapse.
Hematologic left heart syndrome.
Eisenmenger's syndrome.

CORONARY ARTERIAL DISEASE

Anomalous origin.
Anomalous tract.
Kawasaki disease.
Periarteritis.
Arterial dissection.
Marfan's syndrome.
Myocardial infarction.

MYOCARDIAL DISEASE

Myocarditis.
Hypertrophic cardiomyopathy.
Dilated cardiomyopathy.
Arrhythmogenic right ventricular dysplasia.

CONDUCTION SYSTEM ABNORMALITY/ARRHYTHMIA

Long Q-T syndromes.
Proarrhythmic drugs.
Preexcitation syndromes.
Heart block.
Commotio cordis.
Idiopathic ventricular fibrillation.
Heart tumor.

MISCELLANEOUS

Pulmonary hypertension.
Pulmonary embolism.
Heat stroke.
Cocaine.
Anorexia nervosa.
Electrolyte disturbances.

SIDS, Sudden infant death syndrome.

SUDDEN DEATH, YOUNG ATHLETE

ICD-10CM # R99 Ill-defined and unknown cause of mortality

Hypertrophic cardiomyopathy.
Coronary artery anomalies.
Myocarditis.
Ruptured aortic aneurysm (Marfan's syndrome).
Arrhythmias.
Aortic valve stenosis.
Asthma.
Trauma (cerebral, cardiac).
Drug and alcohol abuse.
Heat stroke.
Cardiac sarcoidosis.
Atherosclerotic coronary artery disease.
Dilated cardiomyopathy.

SWOLLEN LIMB

ICD-10CM # M79.89 Other specified soft tissue disorders

Trauma.
Insect bite.
Abscess.
Lymphedema.
Thrombophlebitis.
Lipoma.
Neurofibroma.
Postphlebitic syndrome.
Myositis ossificans.
Nephrosis, cirrhosis, CHF.
Hypoalbuminemia.
Varicose veins.

TALL STATURE[53]

ICD-10CM # E22.0 Acromegaly and pituitary gigantism

Constitutional (familial or genetic)—most common cause

ENDOCRINE CAUSES

Growth hormone excess—gigantism.
Sexual precocity (tall as children, short as adults):
True sexual precocity.
Pseudosexual precocity.
Androgen deficiency:
Klinefelter's syndrome.
Bilateral anorchism.

GENETIC CAUSES

Klinefelter's syndrome.
Syndromes of XYY, XXYY.

MISCELLANEOUS SYNDROMES AND DISORDERS

Cerebral gigantism or Sotos' syndrome: prominent forehead, hypertelorism, high arched palate, dolichocephaly, mental retardation, large hands and feet, and premature eruption of teeth. Large at birth, with most rapid growth in first 4 yr of life.
Marfan's syndrome: disorder of mesodermal tissues, subluxation of the lenses, arachnodactyly, and aortic aneurysm.
Homocystinuria: same phenotype as Marfan's syndrome.
Obesity: tall as infants, children, and adolescents.
Total lipodystrophy: large hands and feet, generalized loss of subcutaneous fat, insulin-resistant DM, and hepatomegaly.
Beckwith-Wiedemann syndrome: neonatal tallness, omphalocele, macroglossia, and neonatal hypoglycemia.
Weaver-Smith syndrome: excessive intrauterine growth, mental retardation, megalocephaly, widened bifrontal diameter, hypertelorism, large ears, micrognathia, camptodactyly, broad thumbs, and limited extension of elbows and knees.
Marshall-Smith syndrome: excessive intrauterine growth, mental retardation, blue sclerae, failure to thrive, and early death.

TARDIVE DYSKINESIA[27]

ICD-10CM # R27.9 Unspecified lack of coordination
F44.4 Conversion disorder with motor symptom or deficit
F44.6 Conversion disorder with sensory symptom or deficit
G24.4 Idiopathic orofacial dystonia

DIFFERENTIAL DIAGNOSIS

Medications (antidepressants, anticholinergics, amphetamines, lithium, I-dopa, phenytoin).
Brain neoplasms.

Ill-fitting dentures.
Huntington's disease.
Idiopathic dystonias (tics, blepharospasm, aging).
Wilson's disease.
Extrapyramidal syndrome (postanoxic or postencephalitic).
Torsion dystonia.

TASTE AND SMELL LOSS[3]

ICD-10CM # R43.0 Anosmia
R43.1 Parosmia
R43.2 Parageusia

TASTE

Local: radiation therapy.
Systemic: cancer, renal failure, hepatic failure, nutritional deficiency (vitamin B_{12}, zinc), Cushing's syndrome, hypothyroidism, DM, infection (influenza), drugs (antirheumatic and antiproliferative).
Neurologic: Bell's palsy, familial dysautonomia, multiple sclerosis.

SMELL

Local: allergic rhinitis, sinusitis, nasal polyposis, bronchial asthma.
Systemic: renal failure, hepatic failure, nutritional deficiency (vitamin B_{12}), Cushing's syndrome, hypothyroidism, DM, infection (viral hepatitis, influenza), drugs (nasal sprays, antibiotics).
Neurologic: head trauma, multiple sclerosis, Parkinson's disease, frontal brain tumor.

TELANGIECTASIA

ICD-10CM # I78.8 Other diseases of capillaries
I78.9 Disease of capillaries, unspecified

Oral contraceptive agents.
Pregnancy.
Rosacea.
Varicose veins.
Trauma.
Drug induced (corticosteroids, systemic or topical).
Spider telangiectases.
Hepatic cirrhosis.
Mastocytosis.
SLE, dermatomyositis, systemic sclerosis.

TENDINOPATHY[50]

ICD-10CM # M67.90 Unspecified disorder of synovium and tendon, unspecified site
M71.9 Bursopathy, unspecified

INTRINSIC FACTORS

Anatomic Factors
Malalignment.
Muscle weakness or imbalance.
Muscle inflexibility.
Decreased vascularity.

Systemic Factors
Inflammatory conditions (e.g., SLE).
Pregnancy.
Quinolone-induced tendinopathy.
Age-Related Factors
Tendon degeneration.
Increased tendon stiffness.
Tendon calcification.
Decreased vascularity.

EXTRINSIC FACTORS
Repetitive Mechanical Load
Excessive duration.
Excessive frequency.
Excessive intensity.
Poor technique.
Workplace factors.
Equipment Problems
Footwear.
Athletic field surface.
Equipment factors (e.g., racquet size).
Protective gear.

TESTICULAR FAILURE[19]

ICD-10CM # E29 Testicular dysfunction

PRIMARY
Klinefelter's syndrome (XXY).
XYY.
Vanishing testes syndrome (in utero or early postnatal torsion).
Noonan's syndrome.
Varicocele.
Myotonic dystrophy.
Orchitis (mumps, gonorrhea).
Cryptorchidism.
Chemical exposure.
Irradiation to testes.
Spinal cord injury.
Polyglandular failure.
Idiopathic oligospermia or azoospermia.
Germinal cell aplasia (Sertoli cell–only syndrome).
Idiopathic testicular failure.
Testicular torsion.
Testicular trauma.
Diethylstilbestrol (maternal use during pregnancy leading to in utero estrogen exposure).
Testicular tumor with subsequent irradiation therapy, chemotherapy, or surgery (retroperitoneal lymph node dissection or orchiectomy).

SECONDARY
Delayed puberty.
Kallmann's syndrome.
Isolated gonadotropin deficiency.
Prader-Labhart-Willi syndrome.
Lawrence-Moon-Biedl syndrome.
Central nervous system irradiation.
Prepubertal panhypopituitarism.
Postpubertal panhypopituitarism.
Hypogonadism secondary to hyperprolactinemia.
Adrenogenital syndrome.
Chronic liver disease.
Chronic renal failure/uremia.
Hemochromatosis.
Cushing's syndrome.

Malnutrition.
Massive obesity.
Sickle cell anemia.
Hyper/hypothyroidism.
Anabolic steroid use.

TESTICULAR PAIN

| ICD-10CM # | N50.9 | Disorder of male genital organs, unspecified |
| | R10.2 | Pelvic and perineal pain |

Testicular torsion.
Trauma.
Epididymitis.
Orchitis.
Neoplasm.
Urolithiasis.
Inguinal hernia.
Infection (cellulitis, abscess, folliculitis).
Anxiety.

TESTICULAR SIZE VARIATIONS[19]

ICD-10CM #	N50.0	Atrophy of testis
	N44.2	Benign cyst of testis
	N44.8	Other noninflammatory disorders of the testis
	N50.3	Cyst of epididymis
	N50.8	Other specified disorders of male genital organs
	N53.12	Painful ejaculation
	E29.1	Testicular hypofunction

SMALL TESTES
Hypothalamic-pituitary dysfunction.
Gonadotropin deficiency.
Growth hormone deficiency.
Normal variant.
Primary hypogonadism.
Autoimmune destruction.
Chemotherapy.
Cryptorchidism.
Irradiation.
Klinefelter's syndrome.
Orchiditis.
Testicular regression syndrome.
Torsion.
Trauma.

LARGE TESTES
Adrenal rest tissue.
Compensatory.
Fragile X syndrome.
Idiopathic.
Tumor.

TETANUS[50]

ICD-10CM # A35 Other tetanus

Acute abdomen.
Black widow spider bite.
Dental abscess.
Dislocated mandible.

Dystonic reaction.
Encephalitis.
Head trauma.
Hyperventilation syndrome.
Hypocalcemia.
Meningitis.
Peritonsillar abscess.
Progressive fluctuating muscular rigidity (stiffman syndrome).
Psychogenic.
Rabies.
Sepsis.
Subarachnoid hemorrhage.
Status epilepticus.
Strychnine poisoning.
Temporomandibular joint syndrome.

THROMBOCYTOPENIA

ICD-10CM #	D47.3	Essential (hemorrhagic) thrombocythemia
	D69.59	Other secondary thrombocytopenia
	D69.6	Thrombocytopenia, unspecified

INCREASED DESTRUCTION
Immunologic
Drugs: quinine, quinidine, digitalis, procainamide, thiazide diuretics, sulfonamides, phenytoin, aspirin, penicillin, heparin, gold, meprobamate, sulfa drugs, phenylbutazone, nonsteroidal anti-inflammatory drugs (NSAIDs), methyldopa, cimetidine, furosemide, INH, cephalosporins, chlorpropamide, organic arsenicals, chloroquine, platelet glycoprotein IIb/IIIa receptor inhibitors, ranitidine, indomethacin, carboplatin, ticlopidine, clopidogrel.
Idiopathic thrombocytopenic purpura (ITP).
Transfusion reaction: transfusion of platelets with plasminogen activator (PLA) in recipients without PLA-1.
Fetal/maternal incompatibility.
Collagen vascular diseases (e.g., SLE).
Autoimmune hemolytic anemia.
Lymphoreticular disorders (e.g., CLL).
Nonimmunologic
Prosthetic heart valves.
Thrombotic thrombocytopenic purpura (TTP).
Sepsis.
DIC.
Hemolytic-uremic syndrome (HUS).
Giant cavernous hemangioma.

DECREASED PRODUCTION
Abnormal marrow.
Marrow infiltration (e.g., leukemia, lymphoma, fibrosis).
Marrow suppression (e.g., chemotherapy, alcohol, radiation).
Hereditary disorders.
Wiskott-Aldrich syndrome: X-linked disorder characterized by thrombocytopenia, eczema, and repeated infections.
May-Hegglin anomaly: increased megakaryocytes but ineffective thrombopoiesis.
Vitamin deficiencies (e.g., vitamin B_{12}, folic acid).

TREMOR, IN CHILDREN, CAUSES[45]

ICD-10CM #	R25.0	Abnormal head movements
	R25.1	Tremor, unspecified
	R25.2	Cramp and spasm
	R25.3	Fasciculation
	R25.9	Unspecified abnormal involuntary movements

BENIGN

Enhanced physiologic tremor.
Shuddering attacks.
Jitteriness.
Spasmus nutans.

STATIC INJURY/STRUCTURAL

Cerebellar malformation.
Stroke (particularly in the midbrain or cerebellum).
Multiple sclerosis.

HEREDITARY/DEGENERATIVE

Familial essential tremor.
Fragile X premutation.
Wilson disease.
Huntington disease.
Juvenile parkinsonism (tremor is rare).
Pallidonigral degeneration.

METABOLIC

Hyperthyroidism.
Hyperadrenergic state (including pheochromocytoma and neuroblastoma).
Hypomagnesemia.
Hypocalcemia.
Hypoglycemia.
Hepatic encephalopathy.
Vitamin B_{12} deficiency.
Inborn errors of metabolism.
Mitochondrial disorders.

DRUGS/TOXINS

Valproate, phenytoin, carbamazepine, lamotrigine, gabapentin, lithium, tricyclic antidepressants, stimulants (cocaine, amphetamine, caffeine, thyroxine, bronchodilators), neuroleptics, cyclosporin, toluene, mercury, thallium, amiodarone, nicotine, lead, manganese, arsenic, cyanide, naphthalene, ethanol, lindane, serotonin reuptake inhibitors.

PERIPHERAL NEUROPATHIES
PSYCHOGENIC

TRICHOMEGALY[11]

ICD-10CM #	Not available

CAUSES OF TRICHOMEGALY

Drug-induced: topical prostaglandin analogues, phenytoin and cyclosporine.
Malnutrition.
AIDS.
Porphyria.
Hypothyroidism.
Familial.
Congenital: Oliver–McFarlane, Cornelia de Lange, Goldstein–Hutt, Hermansky–Pudlak syndromes.

TUBULOINTERSTITIAL DISEASE, ACUTE[28]

ICD-10CM #	N17.0	Acute kidney failure with tubular necrosis

DRUGS

Antibiotics, penicillins, cephalosporins, rifampin.
Sulfonamides: cotrimoxazole, sulfamethoxazole.
NSAIDs: propionic acid derivatives.
Miscellaneous: phenytoin, thiazides, allopurinol, cimetidine, ifosfamide.

INFECTIONS

Invasion of renal parenchyma.
Reaction to systemic infections: streptococcal, diphtheria, hantavirus.

SYSTEMIC DISEASES

Immune mediated: SLE, transplanted kidney, cryoglobulinemias.
Metabolic: Urate, oxalate.
Neoplastic: Lymphoproliferative diseases.

IDIOPATHIC

TUBULOINTERSTITIAL KIDNEY DISEASE[28]

ICD-10CM #	N17.0	Acute kidney failure with tubular necrosis

Ischemic and toxic acute tubular necrosis.
Allergic interstitial nephritis.
Interstitial nephritis secondary to immune complex-related collagen vascular disease (e.g., SLE, Sjögren's).
Granulomatous diseases (sarcoidosis, uveitis).
Pigment-related tubular injury (myoglobinuria, hemoglobinuria).
Hypercalcemia with nephrocalcinosis.
Tubular obstruction (drugs such as indinavir, uric acid in tumor lysis syndrome).
Myeloma kidney or cast nephropathy.
Infection-related interstitial nephritis: *Legionella, Leptospira.*
Infiltrative diseases (e.g., lymphoma).

TUMOR MARKERS ELEVATION[67]

ICD-10CM #	R97.8	Other abnormal tumor markers

CAUSES OF ELEVATED LEVELS OF TUMOR MARKERS

Carcinoembryonic Antigen (CEA)
Colonic cancer (higher levels if the tumor is more differentiated or is extensive or has spread to the liver).
Lung or breast cancer; seminoma.
Cigarette smokers.
Cirrhosis, inflammatory bowel disease, rectal polyps, pancreatitis.
Advanced age.
Alpha-Fetoprotein
Hepatocellular cancer: very high titers or a rising titer is strongly suggestive, but >10% of patients do not have an elevated level.
Hepatic regeneration (e.g., cirrhosis, alcoholic or viral hepatitis).

Cancer of the stomach, colon, pancreas, or lung.
Teratocarcinoma or embryonal cell carcinoma (testis, ovary, extragonadal).
Pregnancy.
Ataxia-telangiectasia.
Normal variant.
Prostate-Specific Antigen
Prostate carcinoma (localized disease).
Prostatic hyperplasia.
Prostatitis.
Prostatic infarction.
Cancer-Associated Antigen (CA-19-9)[43]
Pancreatic carcinoma (80% with advanced, well-differentiated cancer have an elevated level).
Other gastrointestinal cancers: colon, stomach, bile duct.
Acute or chronic pancreatitis.
Chronic liver disease.
Biliary tract disease.

[43]Patients who cannot synthesize Lewis blood group antigens (~5% of the population) do not produce CA-19–9 antigen.

UREMIC ENCEPHALOPATHY, DIFFERENTIAL DIAGNOSIS[24]

ICD-10CM #	G93.40	Encephalopathy, unspecified

Differential Diagnosis	Comment
Hypertensive encephalopathy	
Systemic inflammatory response syndrome (SIRS):	Observed in septic patients
Systemic vasculitis:	Vasculitis or lupus with cerebral involvement
Drug-induced neurotoxicity	
Analgesics:	Meperidine, codeine, morphine, gabapentin
Antibiotics:	High-dose penicillins (may cause seizures), acyclovir, ethambutol (optic nerve damage), erythromycin and aminoglycosides (may cause ototoxicity), nitrofurantoin and isoniazid (peripheral neuropathy)
Psychotropics:	Lithium, haloperidol, clonazepam, diazepam, chlorpromazine
Immunosuppressants:	Cyclosporine, tacrolimus
Chemotherapeutics:	Cisplatinum, ifosfamide
Others:	High doses of loop diuretics (ototoxic), ephedrine, methyldopa, aluminum

Differential Diagnosis	Comment
Cerebral atheroembolic disease:	Follows recent aortic or cardiac angiography; associated with peripheral manifestations, including lower extremity cyanosis, livedo reticularis, and eosinophilia
Subdural hematoma	
Posterior leukoencephalopathy:	Observed particularly following renal transplantation due to reversible, abnormal permeability of the blood-brain barrier
	Often manifests as headache followed by mental depression, visual loss, and seizures in the context of volume expansion, acute hypertension, and often treatment with corticosteroids or calcineurin inhibitors
	Lesions in the parietal, temporal, and occipital lobes may be seen on imaging studies

URETERAL COLIC[47]

ICD-10CM # R33.8 Other retention of urine
N13.8 Other obstructive and reflux uropathy

DIAGNOSTIC DIFFERENTIALS OF RENAL OR URETERAL COLIC

Acute cholecystitis, acute cholelithiasis.
Acute appendicitis.
Pelvic inflammatory disease.
Diverticulosis and/or diverticulitis.
Intestinal obstruction.
Leaking abdominal aortic aneurysm.
Musculoskeletal sprains.
Herniated disk.
Hepes zoster (shingles).
Gastrointestinal dysfunction with ileus and/or toxic colonic dilatation.

URETERIC OBSTRUCTION, CONGENITAL[32]

ICD-10CM # N13.8 Other obstructive and reflux uropathy
N20.9 Urolithiasis

CONGENITAL CAUSES OF URETERIC OBSTRUCTION

Primary megaureter.
Ureterocele (ectopic and orthotopic).
Ureteric valve.
Distal ureteric stenosis.
Ureteric atresia.
Circumcaval ureter and variants.
Bladder diverticulum.

URETHRAL DISCHARGE AND DYSURIA

ICD-10CM # R36.0 Urethral discharge without blood
R36.9 Urethral discharge, unspecified
N36.9 Urethral disorder, unspecified
N39.9 Disorder of urinary system, unspecified
R30.0 Dysuria
R30.9 Painful micturition, unspecified

Urethritis (gonococcal, chlamydial, trichomonal).
Cystitis.
Prostatitis.
Vaginitis (candidiasis, chemical).
Meatal stenosis.
Interstitial cystitis.
Trauma (foreign body, masturbation, horseback or bike riding).

URETHRAL OBSTRUCTION, CHILDREN[32]

ICD-10CM # N13.8 Other obstructive and reflux uropathy

CAUSES OF URETHRAL OBSTRUCTION IN CHILDREN

Intrinsic Lesions
Valve (posterior, anterior, saccular diverticulum).
Stenosis, atresia.
Inflammatory stricture.
Traumatic stricture:
    External trauma (saddle injury, and so on).
    Iatrogenic trauma (catheter, cystoscopy, surgery).
Urethral "tumors":
    Girls: leiomyoma.
    Boys: polyp, rhabdomyosarcoma.
Miscellaneous (epidermolysis bullosa).

Extrinsic Lesions
Presacral mass dissecting inferiorly (tumor, cyst).
Fecal impaction (Hirschsprung's, postrepair anal atresia, habitual constipation, neuropathy).
Mass originating in genital organs:
    Boys: utricle cyst, prostate rhabdomyosarcoma, seminal vesicle cyst, Cowper's duct cyst.
    Girls: hydrometrocolpos, hydrocolpos, fused labia.

URIC ACID STONES

ICD-10CM # N20.9 Urolithiasis

Hyperuricemia.
Excessive dietary purine.
Medications (salicylates, allopurinol, probenecid).
Urine pH <5.5 (e.g., diarrhea, high animal protein diet).
Decreased urine output (dehydration, malabsorption, diarrhea, inadequate fluid intake).
Tumor lysis.
Hemolytic anemia.
Myeloproliferative disorders.

URINARY INCONTINENCE, CHILDREN[45]

ICD-10CM # R32 Unspecified urinary incontinence

CAUSES OF URINARY INCONTINENCE IN CHILDHOOD

Overactive bladder.
Infrequent voiding.
Detrusor-sphincter dyssynergia.
Non-neurogenic neurogenic bladder (Hinman syndrome).
Vaginal voiding.
Giggle incontinence.
Cystitis.
Bladder outlet obstruction (posterior urethral valves).
Ectopic ureter and fistula.
Sphincter abnormality (epispadias, exstrophy; urogenital sinus abnormality).
Neuropathic.
Overflow incontinence.
Traumatic.
Iatrogenic.
Behavioral.
Combination.

URINARY RETENTION[47]

ICD-10CM # R33.9 Retention of urine, unspecified

COMMON CAUSES OF URINARY RETENTION

Obstructive Cause
Urethral stricture.
Enlarged prostate.
Lower genitourinary tract malignancy.
Pelvic malignancy.
Bladder stones.
Foreign body.
Blood clot.
Posterior urethral valves.
Ureterocele.

Primary Detrusor Insufficiency
Detrusor areflexia.
Multiple sclerosis.
Iatrogenic injury during abdominal or back surgery.
Spinal cord injury.
Myelomeningocele.

URINARY RETENTION, ACUTE

ICD-10CM # R33.9 Retention of urine, unspecified

Mechanical obstruction: urethral stone, foreign body, urethral stricture, BPH, prostate carcinoma, prostatitis, trauma with hematoma formation.
Neurogenic bladder.
Neurologic disease (MS, parkinsonism, tabes dorsalis, CVA).
Spinal cord injury.
CNS neoplasm (primary or metastatic).
Spinal anesthesia.
Lower urinary tract instrumentation.

THIRD TRIMESTER

Placenta previa.
Placental abruption.
Premature labor.
Choriocarcinoma.

VAGINAL DISCHARGE, PREPUBERTAL GIRLS[37]

ICD-10CM # N89.8 Other specified noninflammatory disorders of vagina

Irritative (bubble baths, sand).
Poor perineal hygiene.
Foreign body.
Associated systemic illness (group A streptococci, chickenpox).
Infections.
Escherichia coli with foreign body.
Shigella organisms.
Yersinia organisms.
Infections (consider sexual abuse).
 Chlamydia trachomatis.
 Neisseria gonorrhoeae.
 Trichomonas vaginalis.
Tumor (rare).

VALVULAR HEART DISEASE[3]

ICD-10CM # varies with specific diagnosis

MAJOR CAUSES OF VALVULAR HEART DISEASE IN ADULTS

Aortic Stenosis
Bicuspid aortic valve.
Rheumatic fever.
Degenerative stenosis.
Aortic Regurgitation
Bicuspid aortic valve.
Aortic dissection.
Endocarditis.
Rheumatic fever.
Aortic root dilation.
Mitral Stenosis
Rheumatic fever.
Mitral Regurgitation

CHRONIC

Mitral valve prolapse.
Left ventricular dilation.
Posterior wall myocardial infarction.
Rheumatic fever.
Endocarditis.

ACUTE

Posterior wall or papillary muscle ischemia.
Papillary muscle or chordal rupture.
Endocarditis.
Prosthetic valve dysfunction.
Systolic anterior motion of mitral valve.

TRICUSPID REGURGITATION

Functional (annular) dilation.
Tricuspid valve prolapse.
Endocarditis.
Carcinoid heart disease.

VASCULITIS, CLASSIFICATION[50]

ICD-10CM # I77.6 Arteritis, unspecified

LARGE VESSEL DISEASE

Arteritis
Giant cell arteritis.
Takayasu's arteritis.
Arteritis associated with Reiter's syndrome (reactive arthritis), ankylosing spondylitis.

MEDIUM AND SMALL VESSEL DISEASE

Polyarteritis Nodosa
Primary (idiopathic).
Associated with viruses (hepatitis B or C, CMV, HIV, herpes zoster).
Associated with malignancy (hairy cell leukemia).
Familial Mediterranean fever.
Granulomatous Vasculitis
Granulomatosis with polyangiitis (Wegener's granulomatosis).
Lymphomatoid granulomatosis.
Behçet's Disease
Kawasaki Disease (Mucocutaneous Lymph Node Syndrome)

PREDOMINANTLY SMALL VESSEL DISEASE

Hypersensitivity Vasculitis (Leukocytoclastic Vasculitis)
Henoch-Schönlein purpura.
Mixed cryoglobulinemia.
Serum sickness.
Vasculitis associated with connective tissue diseases (SLE, Sjögren's syndrome).
Vasculitis associated with specific syndromes:
 Primary biliary cirrhosis.
 Lyme disease.
 Chronic active hepatitis.
 Drug-induced vasculitis.
Churg-Strauss Syndrome
Goodpasture's Syndrome
Erythema Nodosum
Panniculitis
Buerger's Disease (Thrombophlebitis Obliterans)

VASCULITIS (DISEASES THAT MIMIC VASCULITIS)[54]

ICD-10CM # varies with specific diagnosis

EMBOLIC DISEASE

Infectious or marantic endocarditis.
Cardiac mural thrombus.
Atrial myxoma.
Cholesterol embolization syndrome.

NONINFLAMMATORY VESSEL WALL DISRUPTION

Atherosclerosis.
Arterial fibromuscular dysplasia.
Drug effects (vasoconstrictors, anticoagulants).
Radiation.

Genetic disease (neurofibromatosis, Ehlers-Danlos syndrome).
Amyloidosis.
Intravascular malignant lymphoma.

DIFFUSE COAGULATION

Disseminated intravascular coagulation.
Thrombotic thrombocytopenic purpura.
Hemolytic-uremic syndrome.
Protein C and S deficiencies, factor V/Leiden mutation.
Antiphospholipid syndrome.

VEGETATIVE STATE, PERSISTENT[3]

ICD-10CM # R40.3 Persistent vegetative state

PERSISTENT VEGETATIVE STATE: COMMON CAUSES[44]

Trauma (diffuse axonal injury).
Cardiac arrest and hypoperfusion (laminar necrosis of cortical mantle and/or thalamic necrosis).
Bihemispheric infarctions.
Purulent meningitis or encephalitis (cortical injury).
Carbon monoxide.
Prolonged hypoglycemic coma.

VENTILATION–PERFUSION MISMATCH ON LUNG SCAN

ICD-10CM # varies with specific diagnosis

Pulmonary embolism.
Emphysema.
Irradiation.
Pulmonary hypertension.
AV malformations.
Pulmonary thrombosis.
External compression of pulmonary artery (neoplasm, cysts, fibrosing mediastinitis).
Vasculitis.
Tuberculosis.
Pulmonary thrombosis.
Congenital (pulmonary artery hypoplasia, congenital heart disease with upper lobe diversion).
Sequestered segment.
Parasitic lung disease.
Intraluminal obstruction from catheter fragments.

VENTRICULAR FAILURE

ICD-10CM # I51.9 Heart disease, unspecified

LEFT VENTRICULAR FAILURE

Systemic hypertension.
Valvular heart disease (AS, AR, MR).

---

[44]A vegetative state may not necessarily begin with coma but can also develop as the end stage of neurodegenerative diseases (e.g., Alzheimer's disease) of adults or children and can accompany severe congenital developmental abnormalities of the brain such as anencephaly.

Cardiomyopathy, myocarditis.
Bacterial endocarditis.
Myocardial infarction.
Idiopathic hypertrophic subaortic stenosis.

RIGHT VENTRICULAR FAILURE

Valvular heart disease (mitral stenosis).
Pulmonary hypertension.
Bacterial endocarditis (right-sided).
Right ventricular infarction.

BIVENTRICULAR FAILURE

Left ventricular failure.
Cardiomyopathy.
Myocarditis
Arrhythmias.
Anemia.
Thyrotoxicosis.
Arteriovenous fistula.
Paget's disease.
Beriberi.

VERRUCOUS LESIONS

ICD-10CM #	varies with specific diagnosis

Warts.
Seborrheic keratosis.
Lichen simplex.
Acanthosis nigricans.
Scabies (Norwegian, crusted).
Verrucous carcinoma.
Nevus sebaceous.
Deep fungal infection.

VERTIGO

ICD-10CM #	R42	Dizziness and giddiness
	H81.13	Benign paroxysmal vertigo, bilateral
	H81.49	Vertigo of central origin, unspecified ear
	II01.399	Other peripheral vertigo, unspecified ear
	H81.23	Vestibular neuronitis, bilateral

PERIPHERAL

Otitis media.
Acute labyrinthitis.
Vestibular neuronitis.
Benign positional vertigo.
Meniere's disease.
Ototoxic drugs: streptomycin, gentamicin.
Lesions of the eighth nerve: acoustic neuroma, meningioma, mononeuropathy, metastatic carcinoma.
Mastoiditis.

CNS OR SYSTEMIC

Vertebrobasilar artery insufficiency.
Posterior fossa tumor or other brain tumors.
Infarction/hemorrhage of cerebral cortex, cerebellum, or brain stem.
Basilar migraine.
Metabolic: drugs, hypoxia, anemia, fever.

Hypotension/severe hypertension.
Multiple sclerosis.
CNS infections: viral, bacterial.
Temporal lobe epilepsy.
Arnold–Chiari malformation, syringobulbia.
Psychogenic: ventilation, hysteria.

VERTIGO, CENTRAL[1]

ICD-10CM #	R42

MAJOR CAUSES OF CENTRAL VERTIGO

Demyelination.
　Acquired.
　Leukodystrophies.
　Multiple sclerosis.
Familial disorders.
　Friedreich ataxia.
　Spinocerebellar ataxia.
　Familial episodic ataxia (type 1 and type 2).
　Olivopontocerebellar atrophy.
Central nervous system infections.
　Lyme neuroborreliosis.
　Meningitis.
　Tuberculosis.
Intrinsic brainstem lesion.
　Tumor.
　Arteriovenous malformation.
　Trauma.
Migraine.
　Basilar.
　Benign paroxysmal positional vertigo of childhood.
Toxins.
　Drugs, alcohol.
　Analgesics.
　Anticonvulsants.
　Antihypertensives.
　Hypnotics.
　Tranquilizers.
Metabolic and endocrine disorders.
　Hyperinsulinism.
　Impaired glucose tolerance.
　Diabetes mellitus.
　Hypertriglyceridemia.
　Hypothyroidism.
Systemic conditions.
　Paget disease.
Stroke/ischemia.
　Vertebrobasilar.
　Cerebellar.
　Posterior inferior cerebellar artery syndrome.
　Lateral medullary syndrome.
　Medial medullary infarct.
　Basilar artery syndrome.
　Anterior inferior cerebellar artery.
Other causes of posterior ischemia.
　Subclavian steal syndrome.
　Rotational vertebral artery occlusion syndrome.
　Vertebral artery dissection.
　Vertebral or basilar artery dolichoectasia.
　Neoplasm of the fourth ventricle.
　Chiari malformation.
　Superficial siderosis of the central nervous system.
　Vestibular epilepsy.

VESICULOBULLOUS DISEASES[28]

ICD-10CM #	L94.2	Calcinosis cutis
	L98.8	Other specified disorders of the skin and subcutaneous tissue

IMMUNOLOGICALLY MEDIATED DISEASES

Bullous pemphigoid.
Herpes gestationis.
Mucous membrane pemphigoid.
Epidermolysis bullosa acquisita.
Dermatitis herpetiformis.
Pemphigus (vulgaris, foliaceus, paraneoplastic).

HYPERSENSITIVITY DISEASES

Erythema multiforme minor.
Erythema multiforme major (Stevens-Johnson syndrome).
Toxic epidermal necrolysis.

METABOLIC DISEASES

Porphyria cutanea tarda.
Pseudoporphyria.
Diabetic blisters.

INHERITED GENETIC DISORDERS

Epidermolysis bullosa.
　Simplex.
　Junctional.
　Dystrophic.

INFECTIOUS DISEASES

Impetigo.
Staphylococcal scalded skin syndrome.
Herpes simplex.
Varicella.
Herpes zoster.

VISION LOSS, ACUTE, PAINFUL

ICD-10CM #	H53.139	Sudden visual loss, unspecified eye

Acute angle-closure glaucoma.
Corneal ulcer.
Uveitis.
Endophthalmitis.
Factitious.
Somatization syndrome.
Trauma.

VISION LOSS, ACUTE, PAINLESS

ICD-10CM #	H53.139	Sudden visual loss, unspecified eye

Retinal artery occlusion.
Optic neuritis.
Retinal vein occlusion.
Vitreous hemorrhage.
Retinal detachment.
Exudative macular degeneration.
CVA.

Differential Diagnosis

II

Ischemic optic neuropathy.
Factitious.
Somatization syndrome, anxiety reaction.

VISION LOSS AFTER DIVING[4]

ICD-10CM # H53.139

DIFFERENTIAL DIAGNOSIS OF DECREASED VISION AFTER DIVING

- Decompression sickness.
- Arterial gas embolism.
- Bubbles under contact lenses.
- Displaced contact lens.
- Antifog agent keratopathy.
- Contact lens adherence syndrome.
- Transdermal scopolamine
- Hyperoxic myopia.
- Oxymetazoline optic neuropathy.
- Diving-induced migraine phenomena.
- Eye disorders not related to diving.

VISION LOSS, CHILDREN

ICD-10CM # H53.9 Unspecified visual disturbance

Craniopharyngioma.
Hereditary optic atrophy.
Optic nerve glioma.
Glioma of chiasm.
Albinism.
Optic nerve hypoplasia.

VISION LOSS, CHRONIC, PROGRESSIVE

ICD-10CM # H54.7 Unspecified visual loss

- Cataract.
- Macular degeneration.
- Cerebral neoplasm.
- Refractive error.
- Open-angle glaucoma.

VISION LOSS, MONOCULAR, TRANSIENT

ICD-10CM # H54.7 Unspecified visual loss

Thromboembolism.
Vasculitis.
Migraine (vasospasm).
Anxiety reaction.
CNS tumor.
Temporal arteritis.
Multiple sclerosis.

VITREOUS HEMORRHAGE[41]

ICD-10CM # H43.13 Vitreous hemorrhage, bilateral

CAUSES OF VITREOUS HEMORRHAGE

Acute posterior vitreous detachment associated either with a retinal tear or avulsion of a peripheral vessel.
Proliferative retinopathies.
  Diabetic.
  Following retinal vein occlusion.

Sickle cell disease.
Eales disease.
Vasculitis.
Miscellaneous retinal disorders.
  ○ Macroaneurysm.
  ○ Telangiectasis.
  ○ Capillary hemangioma.
Trauma.
  ○ Blunt.
  ○ Penetrating.
  ○ Iatrogenic.
Systemic.
  Bleeding disorders.
  Terson syndrome.

VOCAL CORD PARALYSIS

ICD-10CM # J38.00 Paralysis of vocal cords and larynx, unspecified
             J38.01 Paralysis of vocal cords and larynx, unilateral
             J38.02 Paralysis of vocal cords and larynx, bilateral

Neoplasm: primary or metastatic (e.g., lung, thyroid, parathyroid, mediastinum).
Neck surgery (parathyroid, thyroid, carotid endarterectomy, cervical spine).
Idiopathic.
Viral, bacterial, or fungal infection.
Trauma (intubation, penetrating neck injury).
Cardiac surgery.
RA.
Multiple sclerosis.
Parkinsonism.
Toxic neuropathy.
CVA.
CNS abnormalities: hydrocephalus, Arnold–Chiari malformation, meningomyelocele.

VOLUME DEPLETION[3]

ICD-10CM # E86.9 Volume depletion, unspecified

GI losses:
  Upper: bleeding, nasogastric suction, vomiting.
  Lower: bleeding, diarrhea, enteric or pancreatic fistula, tube drainage.
Renal losses:
  Salt and water: diuretics, osmotic diuresis, postobstructive diuresis, acute tubular necrosis (recovery phase), salt-losing nephropathy, adrenal insufficiency, renal tubular acidosis.
Water loss: diabetes insipidus.
Skin and respiratory losses:
  Sweat, burns, insensible losses.
Sequestration without external fluid loss:
  Intestinal obstruction, peritonitis, pancreatitis, rhabdomyolysis, internal bleeding.

VOLUME EXCESS[3]

ICD-10CM #   varies with specific diagnosis

PRIMARY RENAL SODIUM RETENTION (INCREASED EFFECTIVE CIRCULATING VOLUME)

Renal failure, nephritic syndrome, acute glomerulonephritis.
Primary hyperaldosteronism.
Cushing's syndrome.
Liver disease.

SECONDARY RENAL SODIUM RETENTION (DECREASED EFFECTIVE CIRCULATING VOLUME)

Heart failure.
Liver disease.
Nephrotic syndrome (minimal change disease).
Pregnancy.

VOMITING

ICD-10CM # R11.10 Vomiting, unspecified
             R11.11 Vomiting without nausea
             R11.12 Projectile vomiting

GI disturbances:
  Obstruction: esophageal, pyloric, intestinal.
  Infections: viral or bacterial enteritis, viral hepatitis, food poisoning, gastroenteritis.
  Pancreatitis.
  Appendicitis.
  Biliary colic.
  Peritonitis.
  Perforated bowel.
  Diabetic gastroparesis.
Other: gastritis, PUD, IBD, GI tract neoplasms.
Drugs: morphine, digitalis, cytotoxic agents, bromocriptine.
Severe pain: MI, renal colic.
Metabolic disorders: uremia, acidosis/alkalosis, hyperglycemia, DKA, thyrotoxicosis.
Trauma: blows to the testicles, epigastrium.
Vertigo.
Reye's syndrome.
Increased intracranial pressure.
CNS disturbances: trauma, hemorrhage, infarction, neoplasm, infection, hypertensive encephalopathy, migraine.
Radiation sickness.
Nausea and vomiting of pregnancy, hyperemesis gravidarum.
Motion sickness.
Bulimia, anorexia nervosa.
Psychogenic: emotional disturbances, offensive sights or smells.
Severe coughing.
Pyelonephritis.
Boerhaave's syndrome.
Carbon monoxide poisoning.

VOMITING, NEONATAL[1]

ICD-10CM # R11.10

CAUSES OF NEONATAL VOMITING

Anatomic Causes
Esophagus, trachea, great vessels:
  Stricture.
  Web.

Tracheoesophageal fistula.
Laryngeal cleft.
Double aortic arch.
Stomach and duodenum:
Pyloric stenosis.
Duodenal atresia (usually noted on the first day of life)
Small and large intestine:
Volvulus secondary to malrotation.
Incarcerated hernia.
Hirschsprung disease (secondary to obstipation).
Necrotizing enterocolitis.
Genitourinary:
Testicular torsion.

Nonanatomic Causes

Infection:
Septicemia.
Meningitis.
Urinary tract infection.
Gastroenteritis.
Otitis media
Increased intracranial pressure:
Cerebral edema.
Subdural hematoma.
Hydrocephalus.
Brain tumor.
Congenital adrenal hyperplasia (salt-losing variety).
Inborn errors of metabolism.
Renal disease.

VULVAR LESIONS[21]

ICD 10CM #	N77.0	Ulceration of vulva in diseases classified elsewhere
	N90.7	Vulvar cyst
	N90.89	Other specified noninflammatory disorders of vulva and porinoum
	D07.1	Carcinoma in situ of vulva
	N90.89	Other specified noninflammatory disorders of vulva and perineum
	N90.5	Atrophy of vulva

RED LESION

Infection/Infestation

Fungal infection:
Candida.
Tinea cruris.
Intertrigo.
Pityriasis versicolor.
Sarcoptes scabiei.
Erythrasma: Corynebacterium minutissimum.
Granuloma inguinale: Calymmatobacterium granulomatis.
Folliculitis: Staphylococcus aureus.
Hidradenitis suppurativa.
Behçet's syndrome.

Inflammation

Reactive vulvitis.
Chemical irritation:
Detergent.
Dyes.

Perfume.
Spermicide.
Lubricants.
Hygiene sprays.
Podophyllum.
Topical 5-FU.
Saliva.
Gentian violet.
Semen.
Mechanical trauma: scratching.
Vestibular adenitis.
Essential vulvodynia.
Psoriasis.
Seborrheic dermatitis.

Neoplasm

Vulvar intraepithelial neoplasia (VIN):
Mild dysplasia.
Moderate dysplasia.
Severe dysplasia.
Carcinoma-in-situ.
Vulvar dystrophy.
Bowen's disease.
Invasive cancer:
Squamous cell carcinoma.
Malignant melanoma.
Sarcoma.
Basal cell carcinoma.
Adenocarcinoma.
Paget's disease.
Undifferentiated.

WHITE LESION

Vulvar dystrophy:
Lichen sclerosus.
Vulvar dystrophy.
Vulvar hyperplasia.
Mixed dystrophy.
VIN.
Vitiligo.
Partial albinism.
Intertrigo.
Radiation treatment.

DARK LESION

Lentigo.
Nevi (mole).
Neoplasm (see "Neoplasm, Vulvar," below).
Reactive hyperpigmentation.
Seborrheic keratosis.
Pubic lice.

ULCERATIVE LESION

Infection

Herpes simplex.
Vaccinia.
Treponema pallidum.
Granuloma inguinale.
Pyoderma.
Tuberculosis.

Noninfectious

Behçet's disease.
Crohn's disease.
Pemphigus.
Pemphigoid.
Hidradenitis suppurativa (see "Neoplasm, Vulvar," below).

Neoplasm

• Basal cell carcinoma.
• Squamous cell carcinoma.

• Vulvar tumor <1 cm:
Condyloma acuminatum.
Molluscum contagiosum.
Epidermal inclusion.
Vestibular cyst.
Mesonephric duct.
VIN.
Hemangioma.
Hidradenoma.
Neurofibroma.
Syringoma.
Accessory breast tissue.
Acrochordon.
Endometriosis.
Fox-Fordyce disease.
Pilonidal sinus.
Vulvar tumor >1 cm:
Bartholin cyst or abscess.
Lymphogranuloma venereum.
Fibroma.
Lipoma.
Verrucous carcinoma.
Squamous cell carcinoma.
Hernia.
Edema.
Hematoma.
Acrochordon.
Epidermal cysts.
Neurofibromatosis.
Accessory breast tissue.

WEAKNESS, ACUTE, EMERGENT[50]

| ICD-10CM # | M62.81 | Muscle weakness (generalized) |

Demyelinating disorders (Guillain-Barré, chronic inflammatory demyelinating polyneuropathy [CIDP]).
Myasthenia gravis.
Infectious (poliomyelitis, diphtheria).
Toxic (botulism, tick paralysis, paralytic shellfish toxin, puffer fish, newts).
Metabolic (acquired or familial hypokalemia, hypophosphatemia, hypermagnesemia).
Metal poisoning (arsenic, thallium).
Porphyria.

WEAKNESS, GRADUAL ONSET

| ICD-10CM # | M62.81 | Muscle weakness (generalized) |

Depression.
Malingering.
Anemia.
Hypothyroidism.
Medications (e.g., sedatives, antidepressants, narcotics).
CHF.
Renal failure.
Liver failure.
Respiratory insufficiency.
Alcoholism.
Nutritional deficiencies.
Disorders of motor unit.
Basal ganglia disorders.
Upper motor neuron lesions.

WEAKNESS, NONNEUROMUSCULAR CAUSES

ICD-10CM #	G93.3	Postviral fatigue syndrome
	R53.1	Weakness
	R53.81	Other malaise
	R53.83	Other fatigue

Anxiety disorder.
Infectious process.
Anemia.
Renal insufficiency.
Hyperventilation.
Malignancy.
Hypothyroidism.
Hypotension.
Hypercapnia.
Hypoglycemia.
Cardiac arrhythmias.
Hepatic insufficiency.
Electrolyte imbalance.
Malnutrition.
Cerebrovascular insufficiency.

WEIGHT GAIN

ICD-10CM #	R63.5	Abnormal weight gain
	E66.9	Obesity, unspecified

Sedentary lifestyle.
Fluid overload.
Discontinuation of tobacco abuse.
Endocrine disorders (hypothyroidism, hyperinsulinism associated with maturity-onset DM, Cushing's syndrome, hypogonadism, insulinoma, hyperprolactinemia, acromegaly).
Medications (nutritional supplements, oral contraceptives, glucocorticoids, etc.).
Anxiety disorders with compulsive eating.
Laurence-Moon-Biedl syndrome, Prader-Willi syndrome, other congenital diseases.
Hypothalamic injury (rare; <100 cases reported in medical literature).

WEIGHT LOSS

ICD-10CM #	R63.4	Abnormal weight loss

Malignancy.
Psychiatric disorders (depression, anorexia nervosa).
New-onset DM.
Malabsorption.
COPD.
AIDS.
Uremia, liver disease.
Thyrotoxicosis, pheochromocytoma, carcinoid syndrome.
Addison's disease.
Intestinal parasites.
Peptic ulcer disease.
Inflammatory bowel disease.
Food faddism.
Postgastrectomy syndrome.

WHEEZING

ICD-10CM #	R06.2	Wheezing

Asthma.
COPD.
Interstitial lung disease.
Infections (pneumonia, bronchitis, bronchiolitis, epiglottitis).
Cardiac asthma.
GERD with aspiration.
Foreign body aspiration.
Pulmonary embolism.
Anaphylaxis.
Obstruction of airway (neoplasm, goiter, edema or hemorrhage from trauma, aneurysm, congenital abnormalities, strictures, spasm).
Carcinoid syndrome.

WHEEZING, PEDIATRIC AGE[8]

ICD-10CM #	R06.2	Wheezing

Reactive airways disease.
Atopic asthma.
Infection-associated airway reactivity.
Exercise-induced asthma.
Salicylate-induced asthma and nasal polyposis.
Asthmatic bronchitis.
Other hypersensitivity reactions:
    Hypersensitivity pneumonitis.
    Tropical eosinophilia.
    Visceral larva migrans.
    Allergic bronchopulmonary aspergillosis.
Aspiration:
    Foreign body.
    Food, saliva, gastric contents.
    Laryngotracheoesophageal cleft.
    Tracheoesophageal fistula, H-type.
    Pharyngeal incoordination or neuromuscular weakness.
Cystic fibrosis.
Primary ciliary dyskinesia.
Cardiac failure.
Bronchiolitis obliterans.
Extrinsic compression of airways:
    Vascular ring.
    Enlarged lymph node.
    Mediastinal tumor.
    Lung cysts.
Tracheobronchomalacia.
Endobronchial masses.
Gastroesophageal reflux.
Pulmonary hemosiderosis.
Sequelae of bronchopulmonary dysplasia.
"Hysterical" glottic closure.
Cigarette smoke, other environmental insults.

WRIST AND HAND PAIN, IN DIFFERENT AGE GROUPS[17]

ICD-10CM #	S69.80XA	Other specified injuries of unspecified wrist, hand and finger(s), initial encounter
	S69.90XA	Unspecified injury of unspecified wrist, hand and finger(s), initial encounter

COMMON CAUSES OF WRIST AND HAND PAIN IN DIFFERENT AGE GROUPS

Childhood (2-10 yr)
Intraarticular
Infection.
Periarticular
Fracture.
Osteomyelitis.
Adolescence (10-18 yr)
Intraarticular
Infection.
Periarticular
Trauma.
Osteomyelitis.
Tumors.
Ganglion.
Idiopathic wrist pain.
Early Adulthood (18-30 yr)
Intraarticular
Inflammatory arthritis.
Infection.
Osteoarthritis.
Periarticular
Peripheral nerve entrapment.
Tendonitis.
Referred
Cervical.
Adulthood (30-50 yr)
Intraarticular
Inflammatory arthritis.
Infection.
Osteoarthritis.
Periarticular
Peripheral nerve entrapment.
Tendonitis.
Referred
Cervical.
Chest.
Cardiac.
Old age (>50 yr)
Intraarticular
Inflammatory arthritis.
Osteoarthritis.
Periarticular
Peripheral nerve entrapment.
Tendonitis.
Referred
Cervical.
Chest.
Cardiac.

WRIST PAIN

ICD-10CM #	S69.80XA	Other specified injuries of unspecified wrist, hand and finger(s), initial encounter
	S69.90XA	Unspecified injury of unspecified wrist, hand and finger(s), initial encounter

MECHANICAL

Osteoarthritis.
Ligament tear.
Fracture.

Ganglion.
De Quervain's tenosynovitis.
Avascular necrosis (scaphoid, lunate).
Nonunion of scaphoid or lunate.
Neoplasm.

METABOLIC

Pregnancy.
Diabetes.
Gout.
Pseudogout.
Paget's disease.
Acromegaly.
Hypothyroidism.
Hyperparathyroidism.

INFECTIOUS

Osteomyelitis.
Septic arthritis.
Cat-scratch disease.
Tick bite (Lyme disease, babesiosis).
Tuberculosis.

NEUROLOGIC

Peripheral neuropathy.
Nerve injury (median, ulnar, radial nerve).
Thoracic outlet compression syndrome.
Distal posterior interosseous nerve syndrome.

RHEUMATOLOGIC

Psoriasis.
RA.
SLE, mixed connective tissue disorder (MCTD).
Scleroderma.

MISCELLANEOUS

Granulomatous (sarcoidosis).
Amyloidosis.
Multiple myeloma.
Leukemia.

XEROPHTHALMIA[54]

ICD-10CM # H11.149 Conjunctival
xerosis, unspecified,
unspecified eye

MEDICATIONS

Tricyclic antidepressants: amitriptyline (Elavil),
doxepin (Sinequan).
Antihistamines: diphenhydramine (Benadryl),
chlorpheniramine (Chlor-Trimeton), promethazine (Phenergan), and many cold and
decongestant preparations.
Anticholinergic agents: antiemetics such as
scopolamine, antispasmodic agents such as
oxybutynin chloride (Ditropan).

ABNORMALITIES OF EYELID FUNCTION

Neuromuscular disorders.
Aging.
Thyrotoxicosis.

ABNORMALITIES OF TEAR PRODUCTION

Hypovitaminosis A.
Stevens-Johnson syndrome.
Familial diseases affecting sebaceous secre-
tions.

ABNORMALITIES OF CORNEAL SURFACES

Scarring from past injuries and herpes simplex
infection.

XEROSTOMIA[54]

ICD-10CM # K11.7 Disturbances of
salivary secretion
R68.2 Dry mouth, unspecified

MEDICATIONS

Tricyclic antidepressants: amitriptyline (Elavil),
doxepin (Sinequan).
Antihistamines: diphenhydramine (Benadryl),
chlorpheniramine (Chlor-Trimeton), promethazine (Phenergan), and many cold and
decongestant preparations.
Anticholinergic agents: antiemetics such as
scopolamine, antispasmodic agents such as
oxybutynin chloride (Ditropan).

DEHYDRATION

Debility.
Fever.

POLYURIA

Alcohol intake.
Arrhythmia.
Diabetes.

PREVIOUS HEAD AND NECK IRRADIATION SYSTEMIC DISEASES

Sjögren's syndrome.
Sarcoidosis.
Amyloidosis.
Human immunodeficiency virus (HIV) infection.
Graft-versus-host disease.

YELLOW URINE

ICD-10CM # R82 Other abnormal findings
in urine

Normal coloration.
Concentrated urine.
Use of multivitamin supplements.
Diet rich in carrots.
Use of Cascara.
Urinary tract infection

REFERENCES

1. Adams JG, et al.: *Emergency medicine, clinical essentials*, ed 2, Philadelphia, Elsevier.
2. Adkinson NF, et al.: *Middleton's Allergy Principles and Practice*, ed 8, Philadelphia, 2014, Saunders.
3. Andreoli TE: *Cecil essentials of medicine*, ed 5, Philadelphia, Saunders.
4. Auerbach P: *Wilderness medicine*, Philadelphia, Saunders.
5. Ballinger A: *Kumar & Clark's essentials of clinical medicine*, ed 6, Edinburgh, Saunders.
6. Barkin RM, Rosen P: *Emergency pediatrics: a guide to ambulatory care*, ed 5, St Louis, Mosby.
7. Baude AI: Infectious diseases and medical micro-biology, ed 2, Philadelphia, Saunders.
8. Behrman RE: *Nelson textbook of pediatrics*, ed 16, Philadelphia, Saunders.
9. Bennett JE, Dolin R, Blaser MJ: *Mandell, Douglas, and Bennett's Principles and Practice of Infectious Diseases*, ed 8, Philadelphia, 2015, Saunders.
10. Bonow RO, et al.: *Braunwauld's heart disease*, ed 9, Philadelphia, Elsevier.
11. Bowling B: *Kanski's Clinical Ophthalmology*, ed 8, Philadelphia, 2016, Elsevier.
12. Boyer KM: Nonbacterial pneumonia. In Feigin RD, Cherry JD, editors: *Textbook of Pediatric Infectious Diseases*, ed 4, Philadelphia, 1998, WB Saunders, pp 260–273.
13. Callen JP: *Color atlas of dermatology*, ed 2, Philadelphia, WB Saunders.
14. Cameron JL, Cameron AM: *Current surgical therapy*, ed 10, Philadelphia, Saunders.
15. Canoso J: *Rheumatology in primary care*, Philadelphia, Saunders.
16. Carlson KJ: *Primary care of women*, ed 2, St Louis, Mosby.
17. Carr A, Hamilton W: *Orthopedics in primary care*, ed 2, Philadelphia, Saunders.
18. Conn R: *Current diagnosis*, ed 9, Philadelphia, Saunders.
19. Copeland LJ: *Textbook of gynecology*, ed 2, Philadelphia, Saunders.
20. Custer JW, Rau RE: *The Harriet Lane handbook*, ed 18, St Louis, Mosby.
21. Danakas G: *Practical guide to the care of the gynecologic/obstetric patient*. St Louis, Mosby.
22. Eberlein M, et al.: A fall in Ghana, *Am J Med* 122:1091, 2009.
23. Firestein GS, Budd RC, Gabriel SE, et al.: *Kelly's textbook of rheumatology*, ed 9, Philadelphia, Saunders.
24. Floege J, et al.: *Comprehensive clinical nephrology*, ed 4, Philadelphia, Saunders.
25. Fuhrman BP, et al.: *Pediatric critical care*, ed 4, Philadelphia, Saunders.
26. Gabbe SG: *Obstetrics*, ed 6, Philadelphia, Saunders.
27. Goldberg RJ: *The care of the psychiatric patient*, ed 3, St Louis, Mosby.
28. Goldman L, Ausiello D: *Cecil textbook of medicine*, ed 21, Philadelphia, Saunders.
29. Goldman L, Braunwald E: *Braunwauld Primary cardiology*, Philadelphia, Saunders.
30. Goldman L, Schafer AI: *Goldman's Cecil medicine*, ed 24, Philadelphia, Saunders.
31. Gorbach SL: *Infectious diseases*, ed 2, Philadelphia, Saunders.
32. Grainger RG, Allison D: *Grainger & Allison's diagnostic radiology, a textbook of medical imaging*, ed 4, London, Churchill Livingstone.
33. Habif TP: *Clinical Dermatology*, ed 6, Philadelphia, 2016, Elsevier.
34. Harrington J: *Consultation in internal medicine*, ed 2, St Louis, Mosby.
35. Henry JB: *Clinical diagnosis and management by laboratory methods*, ed 20, Philadelphia, Saunders.
36. Hochberg MC, et al.: *Rheumatology*, ed 5, Mosby: St. Louis.
37. Hoekelman R: *Primary pediatric care*, ed 3, St Louis, Mosby.
38. Hoffman R: *Hematology, basic principles and practice*, ed 6, Philadelphia, Saunders.
39. Hoffmann R, et al.: *Hematology: basic principles and practice*, ed 5, Philadelphia, Churchill Livingstone.

II

Differential
Diagnosis

40. James WD, et al.: *Andrews' Diseases of the skin*, ed 12, Philadelphia, 2016, Saunders.

41. Kanski JJ, Bowling B: *Clinical ophthalmology, a systematic approach*, ed 7, Philadelphia, Saunders.

42. Kassirer J: *Current therapy in adult medicine*, ed 4, St Louis, Mosby.

43. Kassirer J: *Practical rheumatology*, London, Mosby.

44. Khan MG: *Rapid ECG interpretation*, Philadelphia, Saunders.

45. Kliegman RM, et al.: *Nelson textbook of pediatrics*, ed 19, Philadelphia, Saunders.

46. Kliegman R: *Practical strategies in pediatric diagnosis and therapy*, Philadelphia, Saunders.

47. Lipshultz LI, Khera M, Atwal DT: *Urology and the primary care practitioner*, ed 3, Philadelphia, Saunders.

48. Mahanty S, Nutman TB: Eosinophilia and eosinophil-related disorders. In Middleton EJ, Reed CE, Ellis EF, et al. *Allergy: Principles and practice. ed 4, editors:* Mosby-Year Book: St Louis, p. 1077.

49. Mandell GL: *Mandell, Douglas, and Bennett's principles and practice of infectious diseases*, ed 6, New York, Churchill Livingstone.

50. Marx JA, et al.: *Rosen's Emergency Medicine*, ed 8, Philadelphia, 2014, Saunders.

51. Mason RJ: *Murray & Nadel's Textbook of Respiratory Medicine*, ed 5, Philadelphia, Saunders.

52. Melmed S, Polonsky KS, Larsen PR, Kronenberg HM: *Williams textbook of endocrinology*, ed 12, Philadelphia, Saunders.

53. Moore WT, Eastman RC: *Diagnostic endocrinology*, ed 2, St Louis, Mosby.

54. Noble J: *Primary care medicine*, ed 3, St Louis, Mosby.

55. Nseyo UO: *Urology for primary care physicians*, Philadelphia, Saunders.

56. Palay D: *Ophthalmology for the primary care physician*, St Louis, Mosby.

57. Park MK: *Park's Pediatric cardiology for practitioners*, ed 6, Philadelphia, 2014, Saunders.

58. Pope TL, Bloem HL, Beltran J, Morrison WB, Wilson DJ: *Musculoskeletal imaging*, ed 2, Philadelphia, 2014, Saunders.

59. Rakel RE: *Principles of family practice*, ed 6, Philadelphia, Saunders.

60. Schwarz MI: *Interstitial lung disease*, ed 2, St Louis, Mosby.

61. Seller RH: *Differential diagnosis of common complaints*, ed 4, Philadelphia, Saunders.

62. Siedel HM: *Mosby's guide to physical examination*, ed 4, St Louis, Mosby.

63. Souhami RL, Moxham J: *Textbook of medicine*, ed 4, London, Churchill Livingstone.

64. Specht N: *Practical guide to diagnostic imaging*, St Louis, Mosby.

65. Stein JH: *Internal medicine*, ed 5, St Louis, Mosby.

66. Swain R, Snodgrass JG: Managing groin pain, *Phys Sportmed* 23(56), 1995.

67. Talley NJ, Martin CJ: *Clinical gastroenterology*, ed 2, Sydney, Churchill Livingstone.

68. Tschudy MM, Arcara KM: *The Harriet Lane handbook*, ed 19, Philadelphia, Mosby.

69. Vincent JL, et al.: *Textbook of critical care*, ed 6, Philadelphia, Saunders.

70. Webb WR, Brant WE, Major NM: *Fundamentals of body CT*, ed 4, Philadelphia, 2015, Saunders.

71. Weinberg SE, et al.: *Principles of pulmonary medicine*, ed 5, Philadelphia, Saunders.

72. Wiederholt WC: *Neurology for non-neurologists*, ed 4, Philadelphia, Saunders.

73. Wilson JD: *Williams textbook of endocrinology*, ed 9, Philadelphia, Saunders.

SECTION III

Clinical Algorithms

PLEASE NOTE: These algorithms are designed to assist clinicians in the evaluation and treatment of patients. They may not apply to all patients with a particular disorder and are not intended to replace the clinician's individual judgment.

Additional algorithms available at www.expertconsult.com

Clinical Algorithms

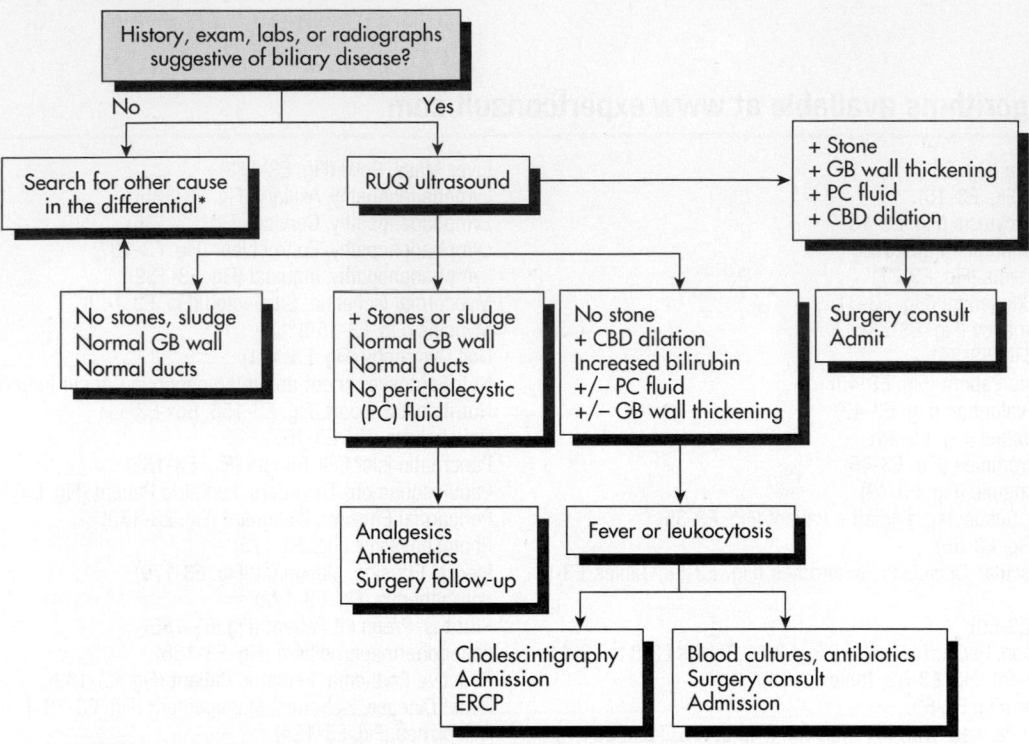

FIGURE 3-1 Treatment algorithm for right upper quadrant (RUQ) pain. *Refer to Section II, Differential Diagnosis, Abdominal Pain Right Upper Quadrant. *CBD*, Common bile duct; *ERCP*, endoscopic retrograde cholangiopancreatography; *GB*, gallbladder; *RUQ*, right upper quadrant; +, with; −, without; ±, with or without. (From Adams JG et al: *Emergency medicine, clinical essentials,* ed 2, Philadelphia, 2013, Elsevier.)

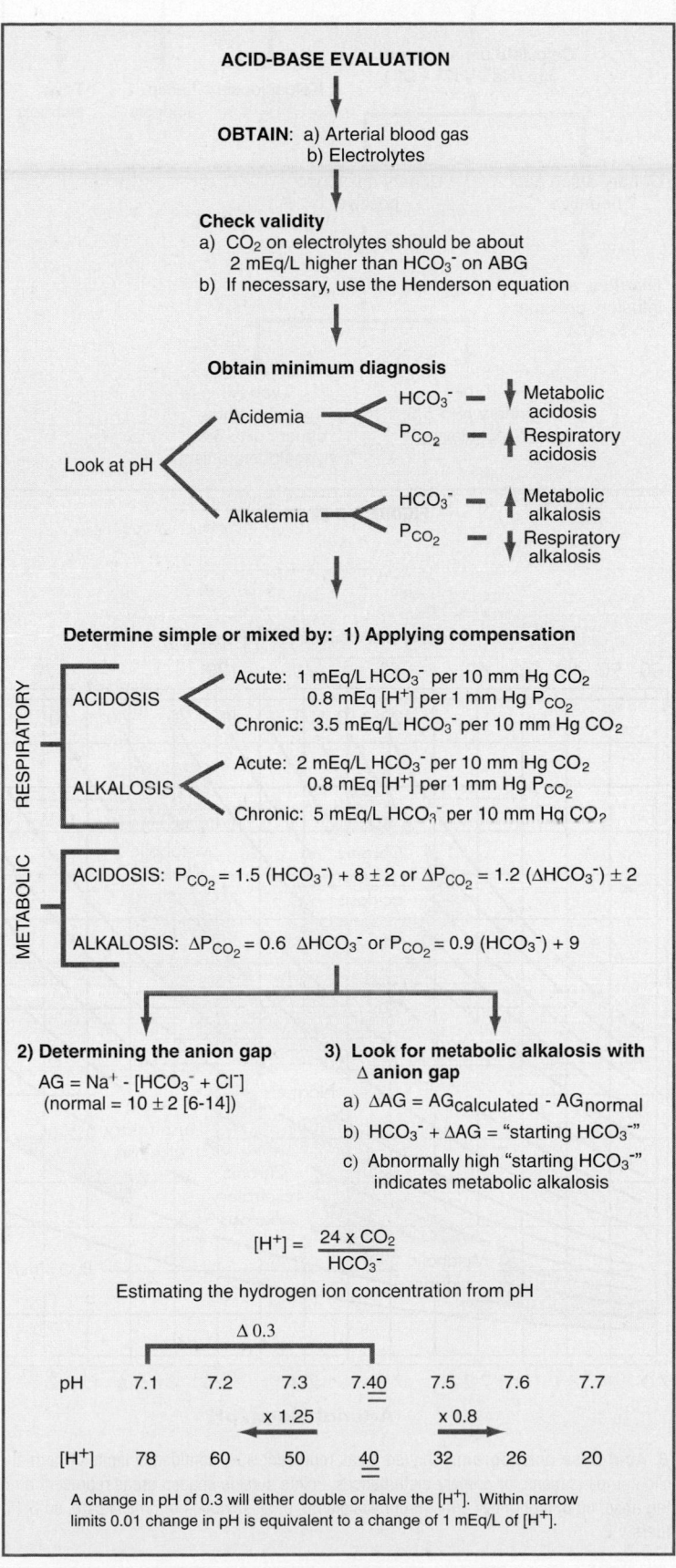

FIGURE 3-2 Scheme for assessing acid-base homeostasis. (Modified from Andreoli TE [ed]: *Cecil essentials of medicine,* ed 7, Philadelphia, 2008, Saunders.)

Continued on next page

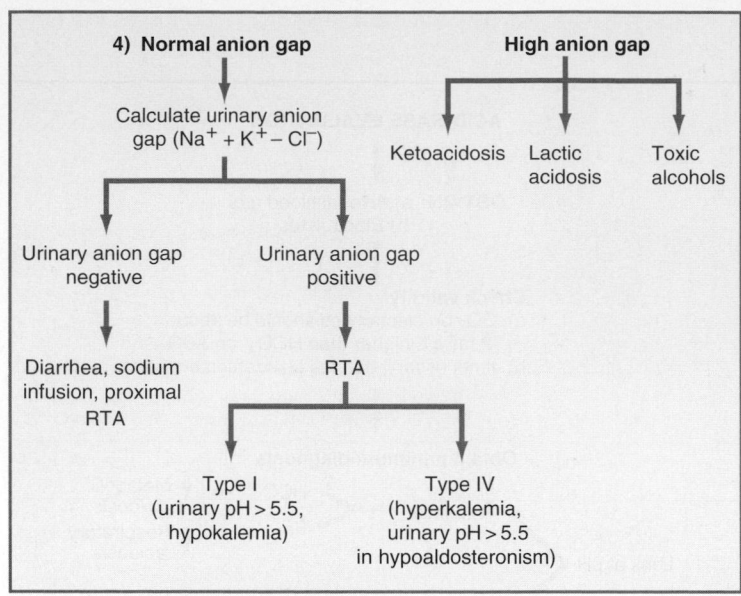

FIGURE 3-2 (Continued)

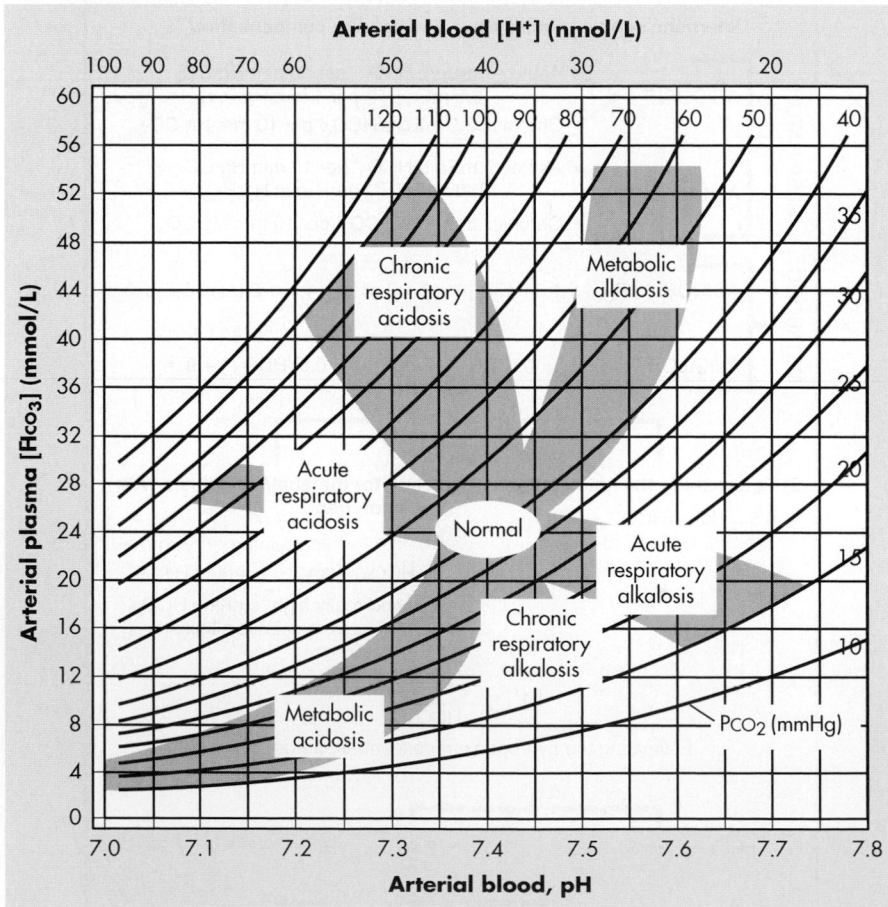

FIGURE 3-3 Acid base normogram. Shaded areas represent 95% confidence limits of normal respiratory and metabolic compensations for primary disturbances. Points outside shaded areas represent a mixed disorder, assuming absence of laboratory error. (From Vincent JL, et al: *Textbook of critical care*, ed 6, Philadelphia, 2011, Saunders.)

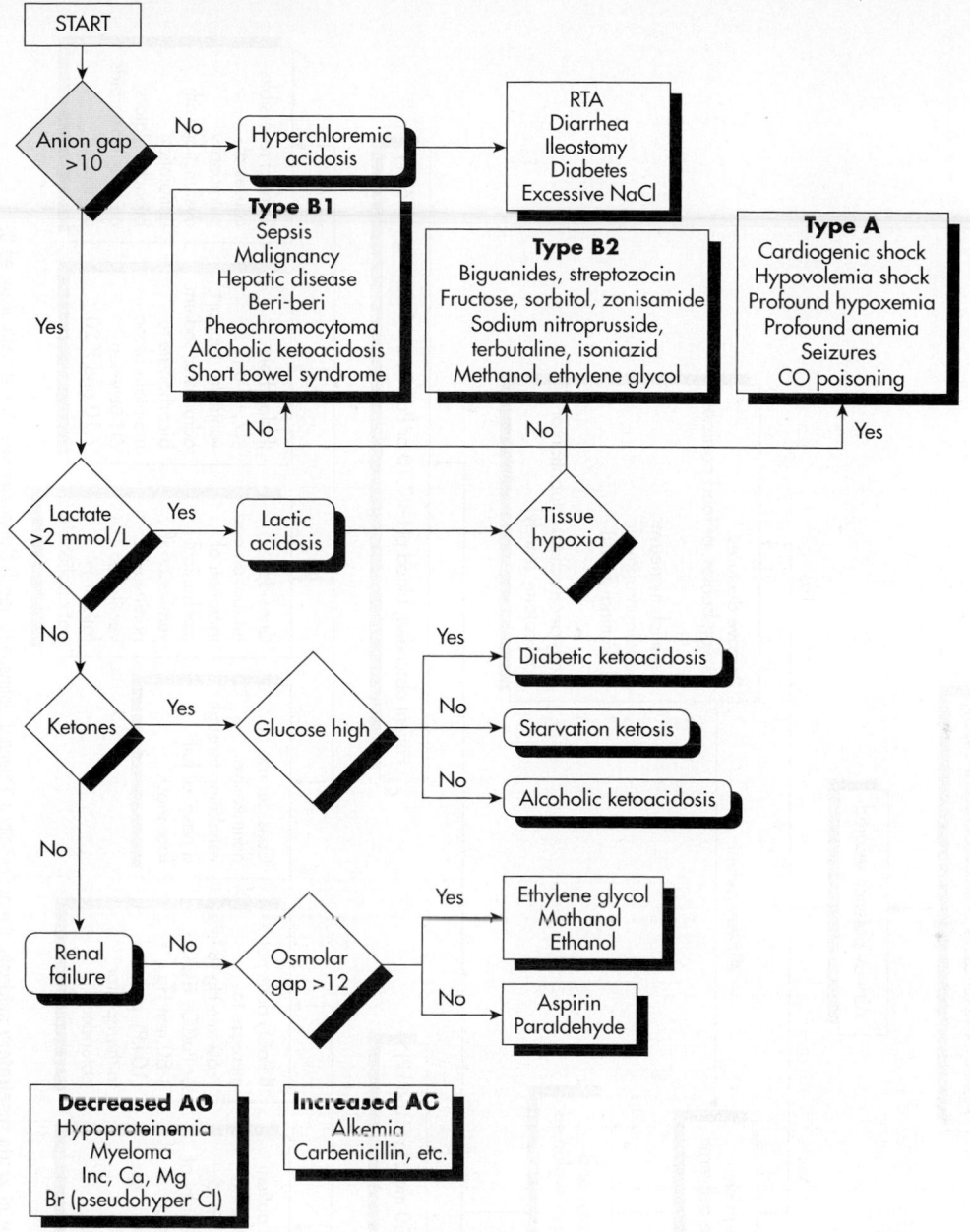

FIGURE 3-4 Diagnostic approach to metabolic acidosis. (Modified from Vincent JL, Ahraham E, Moore FA, et al: *Textbook of critical care*, ed 6, Philadelphia, 2011, Saunders.)

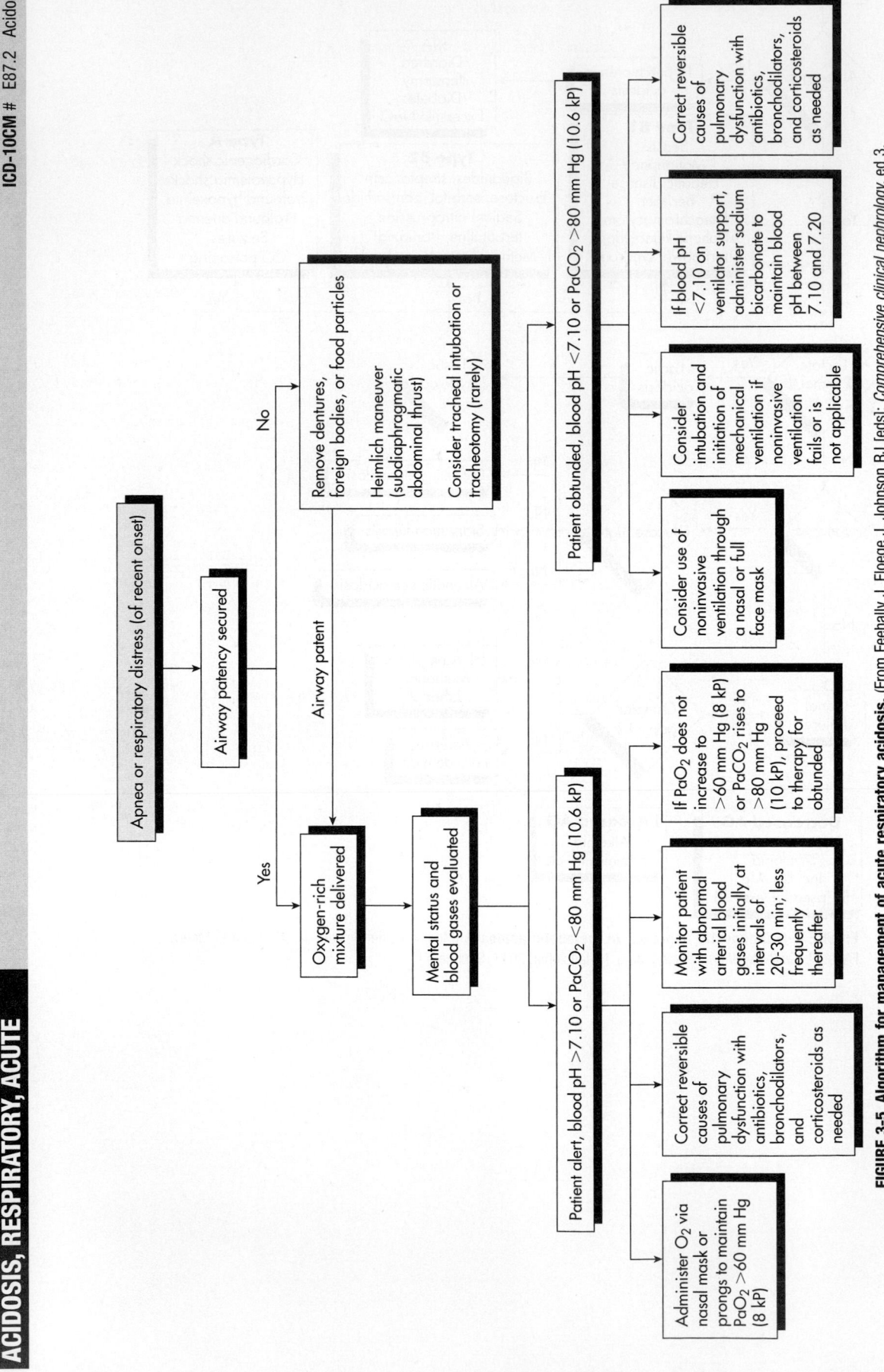

FIGURE 3-5 Algorithm for management of acute respiratory acidosis. (From Feehally J, Floege J, Johnson RJ [eds]: *Comprehensive clinical nephrology,* ed 3, St Louis, 2007, Mosby.)

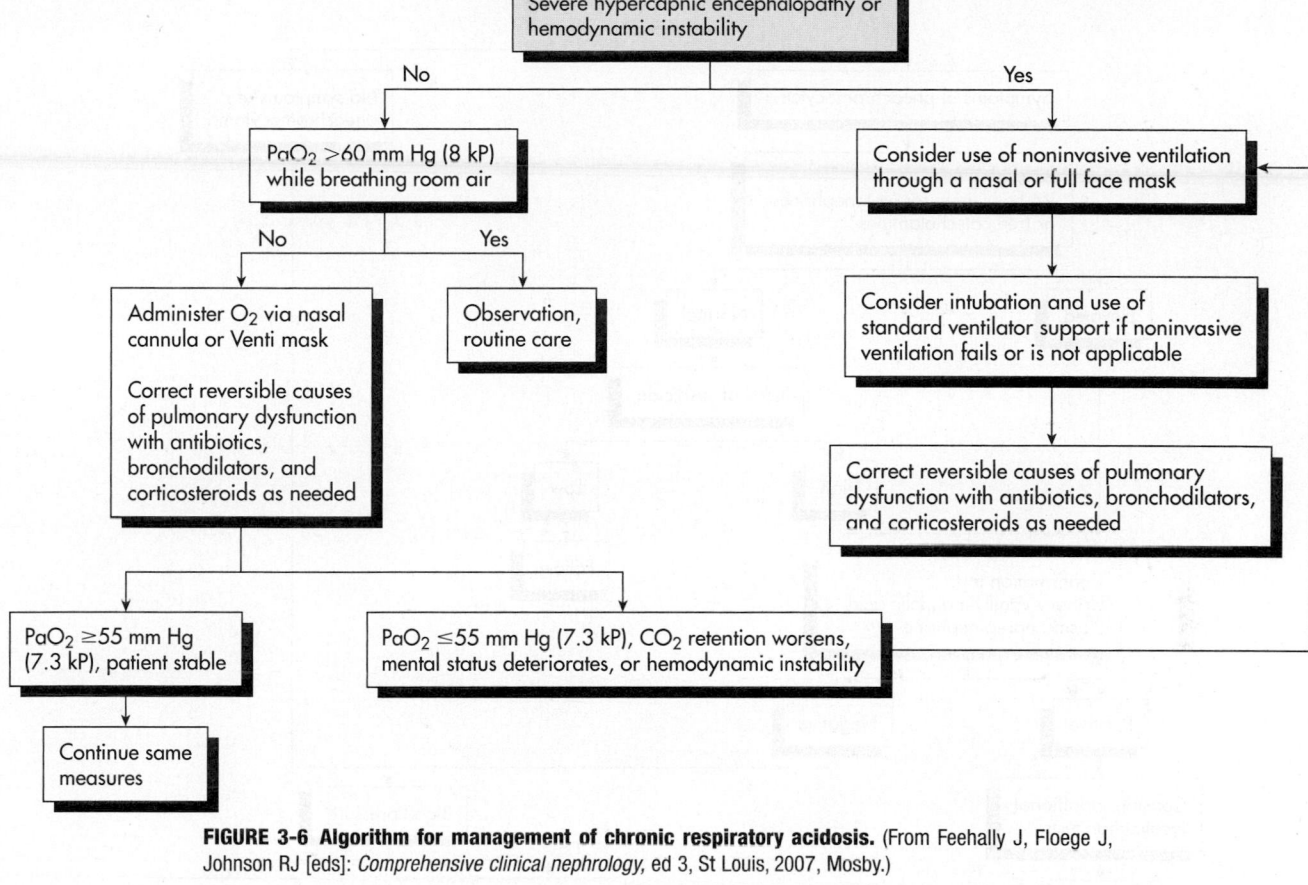

FIGURE 3-6 Algorithm for management of chronic respiratory acidosis. (From Feehally J, Floege J, Johnson RJ [eds]: *Comprehensive clinical nephrology,* ed 3, St Louis, 2007, Mosby.)

ICD-10CM # C74.90 Malignant neoplasm of unspecified part of unspecified adrenal gland
E27.8 Other specified disorders of adrenal gland

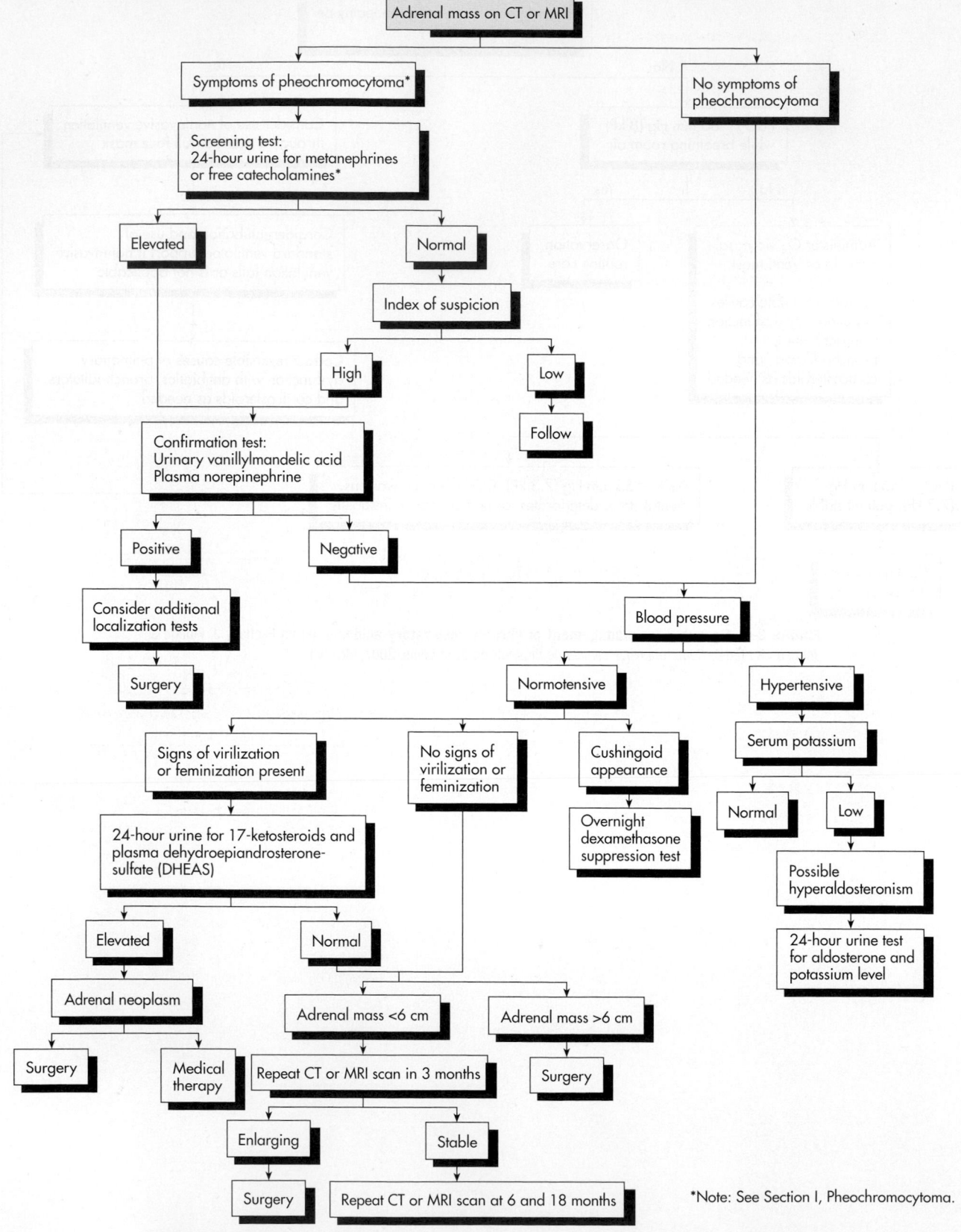

FIGURE 3-8 Evaluation of adrenal mass. *CT,* Computed tomography; *MRI,* magnetic resonance imaging.
(Modified from Greene HL, Johnson WP, Lemcke D [eds]: *Decision making in medicine,* ed 2, St Louis, 1998, Mosby.)

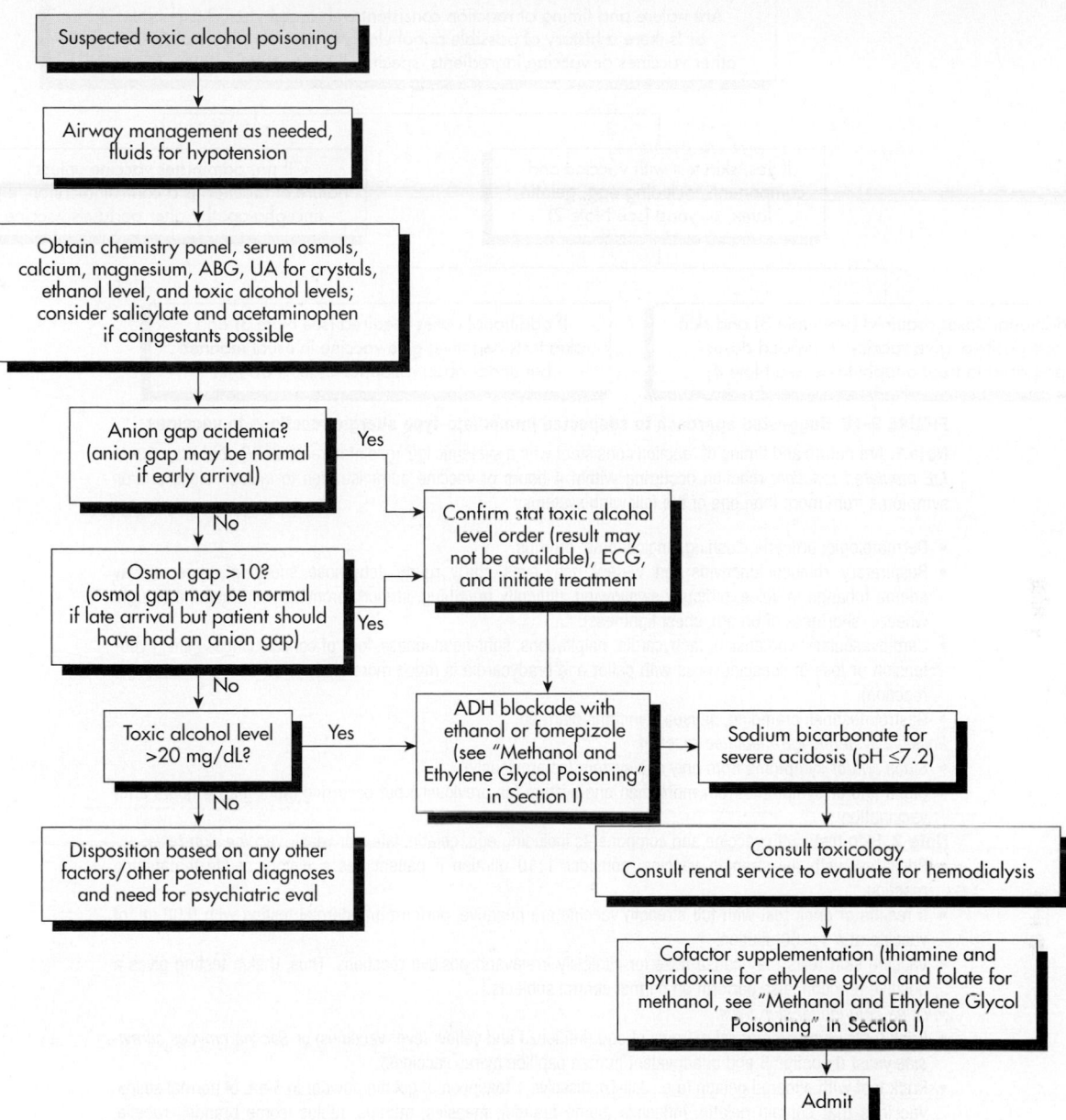

FIGURE 3-9 Treatment algorithm for toxic alcohol poisoning. *ABG,* arterial blood gas measurements; *ADH,* alcohol dehydrogenase; *ECG,* electrocardiography; *UA,* urinalysis. (From Adams JG et al: *Emergency medicine, clinical essentials,* ed 2, Philadelphia, 2013, Elsevier.)

Clinical
Algorithms

III

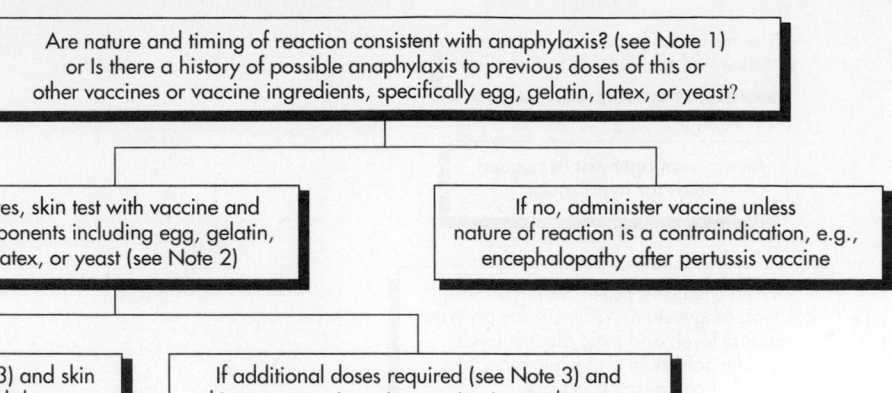

FIGURE 3-10 Suggested approach to suspected immediate-type allergic reactions to vaccines.

Note 1. Are nature and timing of reaction consistent with a systemic IgE-mediated reaction? *Probable systemic IgE-mediated reaction:* reaction occurring within 4 hours of vaccine administration to include signs and/or symptoms from more than one of the following systems:

- Dermatologic: urticaria, flushing, angioedema, pruritus.
- Respiratory: rhinoconjunctivitis (red, watery, itchy eyes, stuffy, runny, itchy nose, sneezing), upper airway edema (change in voice, difficulty swallowing, difficulty breathing, stridor), bronchospasm/asthma (cough, wheeze, shortness of breath, chest tightness).
- Cardiovascular: hypotension, tachycardia, palpitations, light-headedness, loss of consciousness (NOTE: hypotension or loss of consciousness with pallor and bradycardia is much more likely to be due to a vasovagal reaction).
- Gastrointestinal: cramping, nausea, vomiting, diarrhea.

Possible systemic IgE-mediated reaction:
- Signs and/or symptoms from only one system (as previously)
- Signs and/or symptoms from more than one system (as previously) but occurring more than 4 hours after vaccination

Note 2. Skin tests with vaccine and components including egg, gelatin, latex, or yeast. *Vaccine skin tests:*
- Prick test with full-strength vaccine; consider 1:10 dilution if patient has a history of life-threatening reaction.
- If results of prick test with full-strength vaccine are negative, perform intradermal testing with 0.02 mL of vaccine at a 1:100 dilution.
- Vaccine skin tests may cause false (or clinically irrelevant) positive reactions. Thus, if skin testing gives a positive reaction, also perform on normal control subjects.

Vaccine component skin tests:
- Prick tests with commercial extracts of egg (influenza and yellow fever vaccines) or *Saccharomyces cerevisiae* yeast (hepatitis B and quadrivalent human papillomavirus vaccines).
- Prick test with sugared gelatin (e.g., Jell-O): dissolve 1 teaspoon of gelatin powder in 5 mL of normal saline. Vaccines that contain gelatin: influenza (some brands), measles, mumps, rabies (some brands), rubella, typhoid (capsule), varicella, yellow fever, zoster.
- Prick test with latex: soak 2 fingers of latex glove or a toy balloon in 5 ml of normal saline. Vaccines that contain latex in packaging: available at http://www.cdc.gov/vaccines/pubs/pinkbook/downloads/appendices/B/latex-table.pdf.
- In vitro assays for specific IgE antibody to egg, gelatin, latex, and yeast also are commercially available as an alternative or complement to skin testing.

Note 3. If fewer than the recommended number of doses are received, consider measuring level of IgG antibodies to immunizing agent. If the measured level is associated with protection from disease, consider withholding additional doses, although magnitude and duration of immunity may be less than if all doses received. **Note 4.** Vaccine administration in graded doses:
- With a vaccine for which the usual dose is 0.5 mL, administer graded doses of vaccine at 15-minute intervals: 0.05 mL of 1:10 dilution, 0.05 mL of full strength, 0.10 mL of full strength, 0.15 mL of full strength, 0.20 mL of full strength. (From Adkinson NF, et al: *Middleton's allergy principles and practice*, ed 8, Philadelphia, 2014, Saunders.)

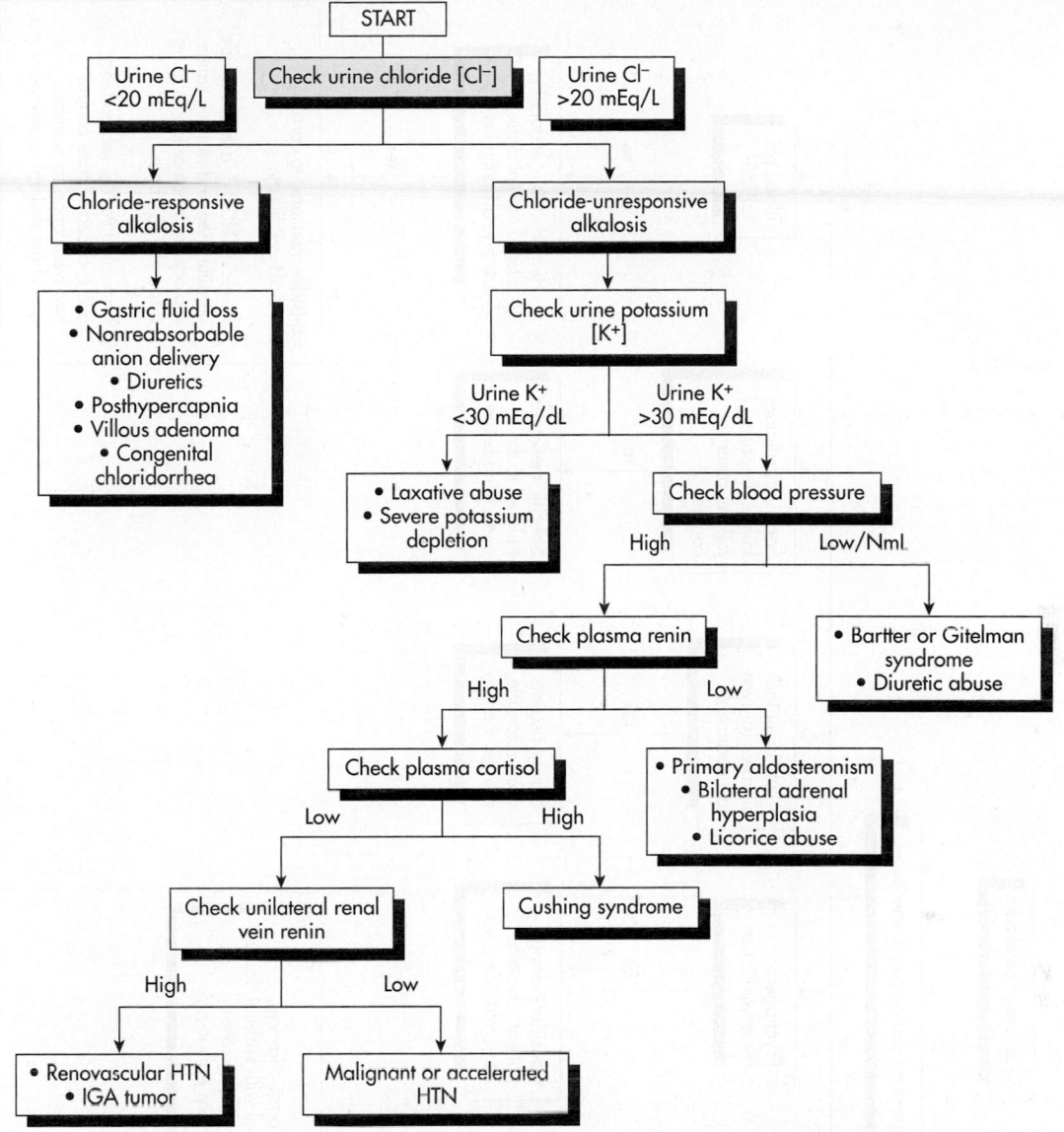

FIGURE 3-11 Workup of metabolic alkalosis. (Data from DuBose TD Jr. Acid-base disorders. In: Brenner BM (ed). *Brenner and Rector's the kidney*, ed 8, Philadelphia, 2008, Saunders, p. 513.)

Clinical
Algorithms

ALKALOSIS, RESPIRATORY TREATMENT

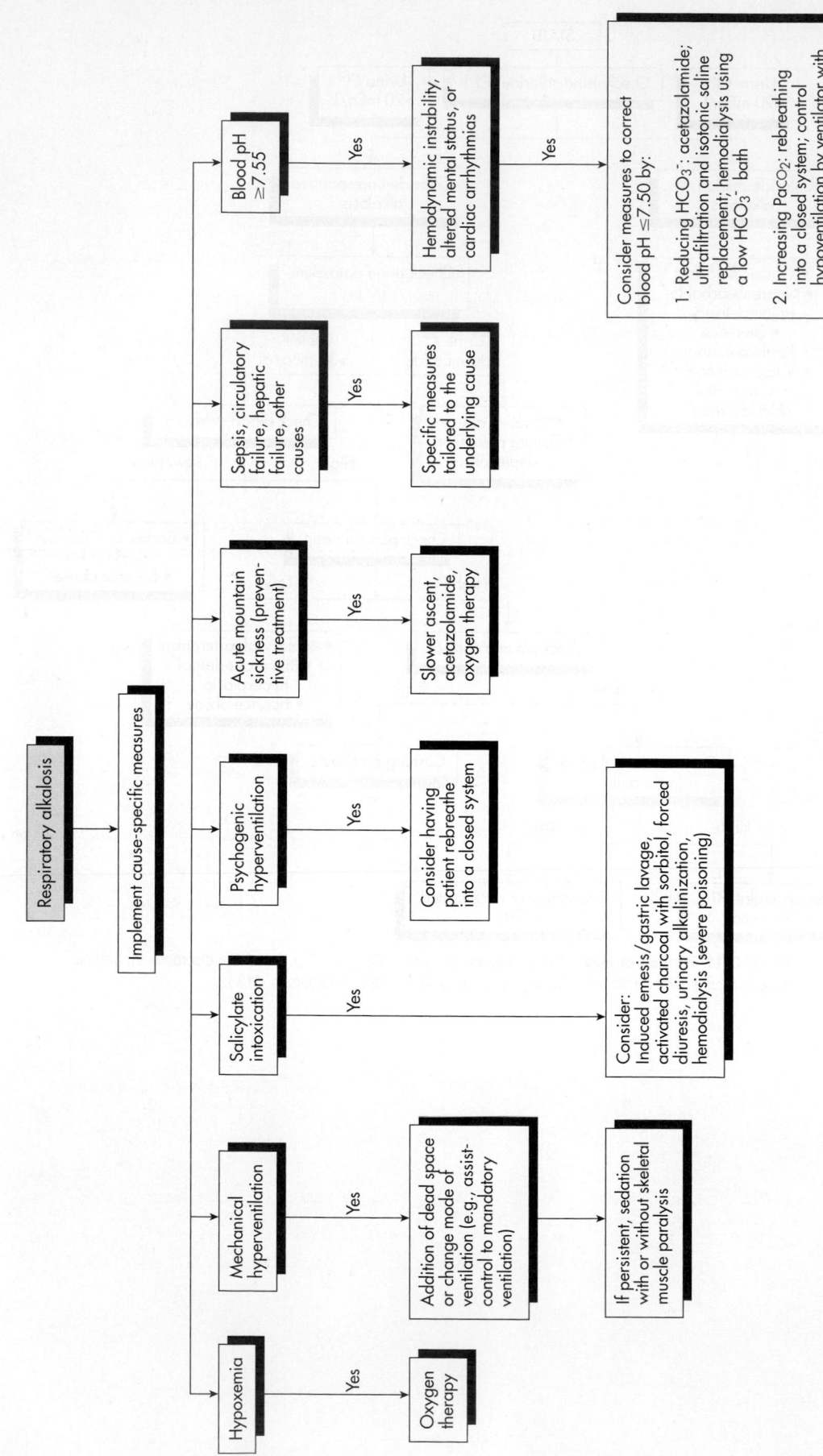

FIGURE 3-12 Recommended treatment of respiratory alkalosis. (From Feehally J, Floege J, Johnson RJ [eds]: *Comprehensive clinical nephrology*, ed 3, St Louis, 2007, Mosby.)

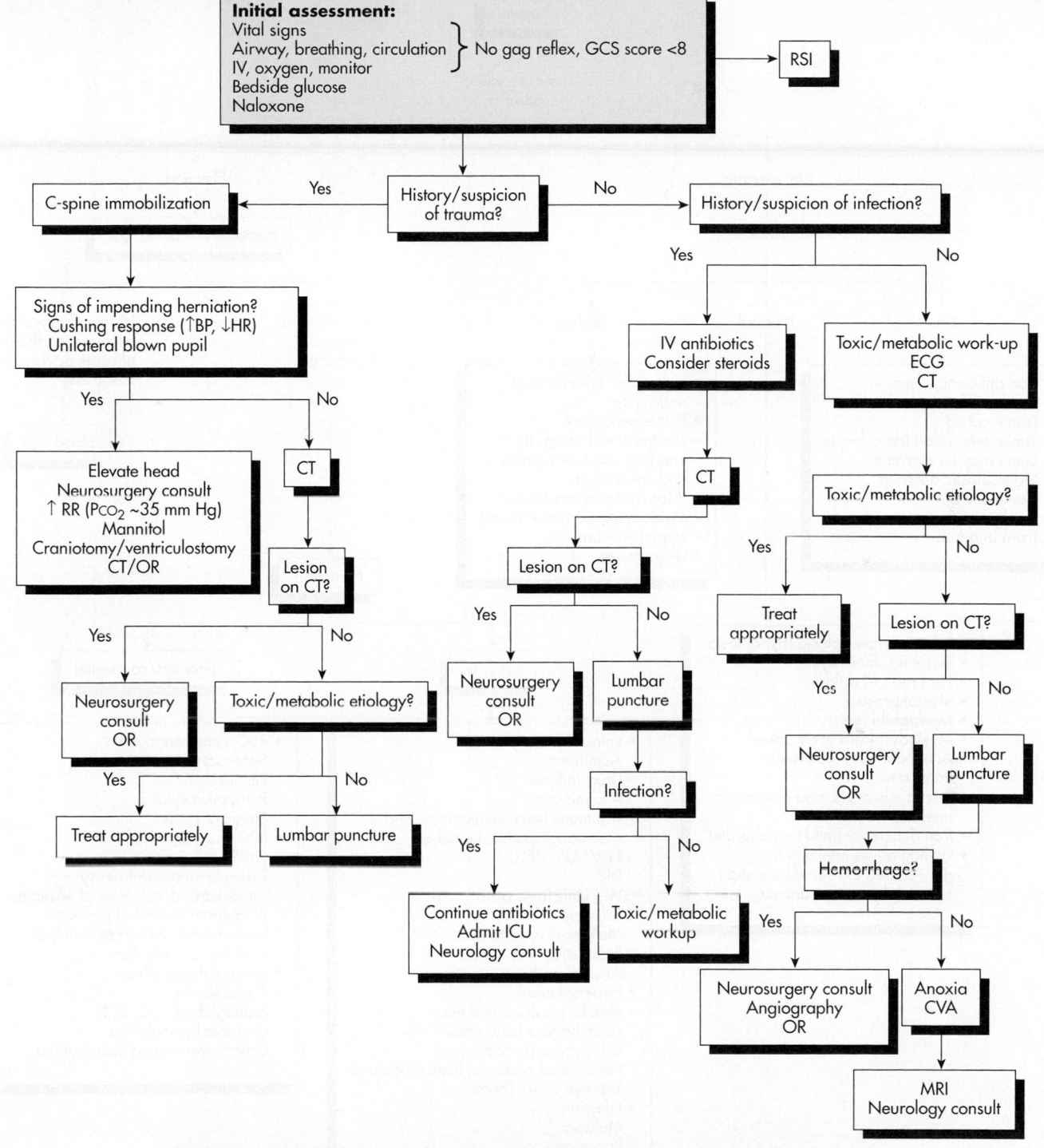

FIGURE 3-13 Diagnostic approach to altered mental status and coma. *BP*, Blood pressure; *CT*, computed tomography; *CVA*, cerebrovascular accident; *ECG*, electrocardiography; *GCS*, Glasgow Coma Scale; *HR*, heart rate; *ICU*, intensive care unit; *MRI*, magnetic resonance imaging; *OR*, operating room; *RR*, respiratory rate; *RSI*, rapid-sequence intubation. (From Adams JG et al: *Emergency medicine, clinical essentials,* ed 2, Philadelphia, 2013, Elsevier.)

Clinical
Algorithms

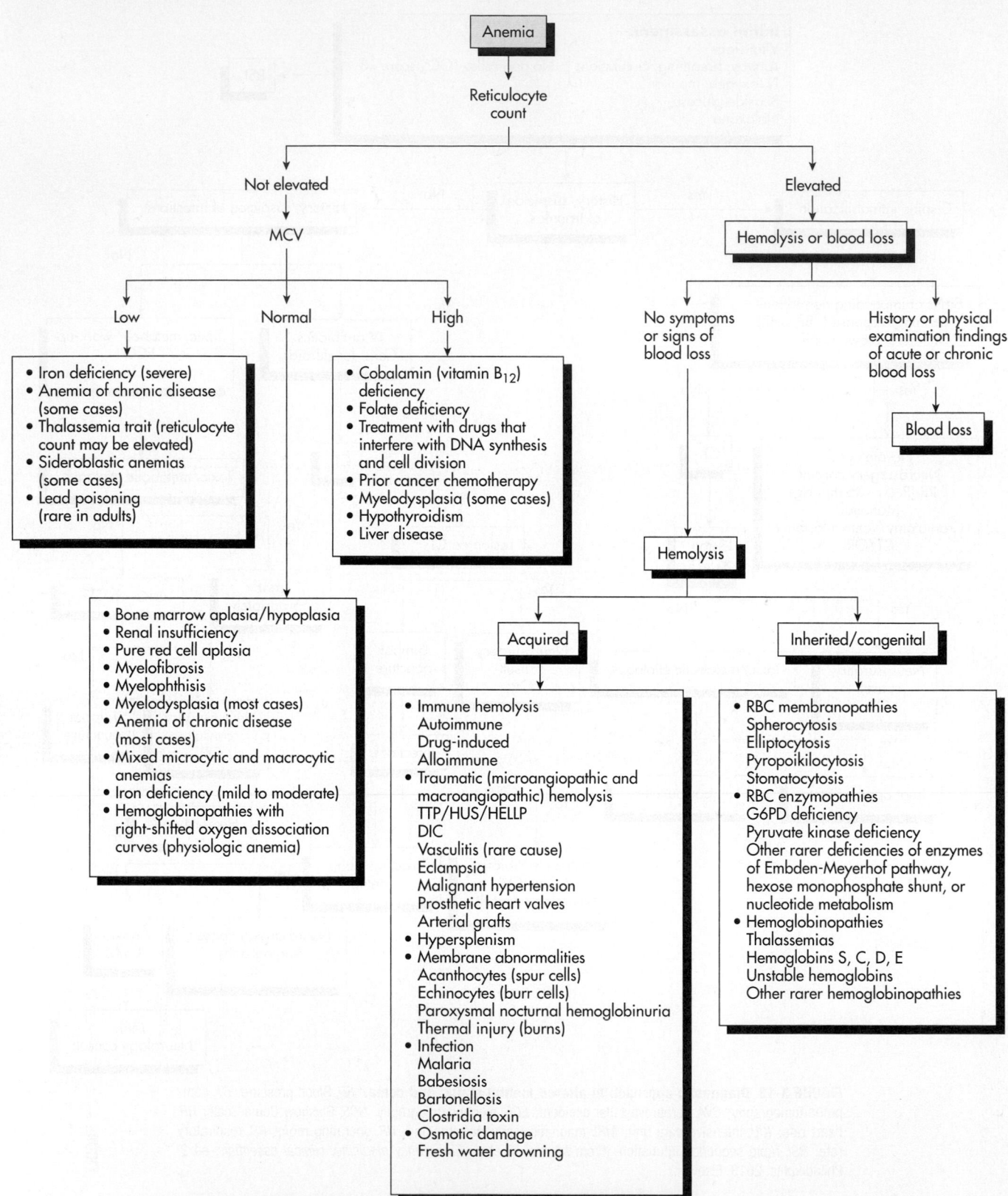

FIGURE 3-14 Algorithm for diagnosis of anemias. *DIC,* Disseminated intravascular coagulation; *G6PD,* glucose-6-phosphate-dehydrogenase; *HELLP, h*epatomegaly-*e*levated *l*iver (function tests)-*l*ow *p*latelets; *HUS,* hemolytic-uremic syndrome; *MCV,* mean corpuscular volume; *RBC,* red blood cell; *TTP,* thrombotic thrombo-cytopenic purpura. (From Goldman L, Ausiello D [eds]: *Cecil textbook of medicine,* ed 23, Philadelphia, 2008, Saunders.)

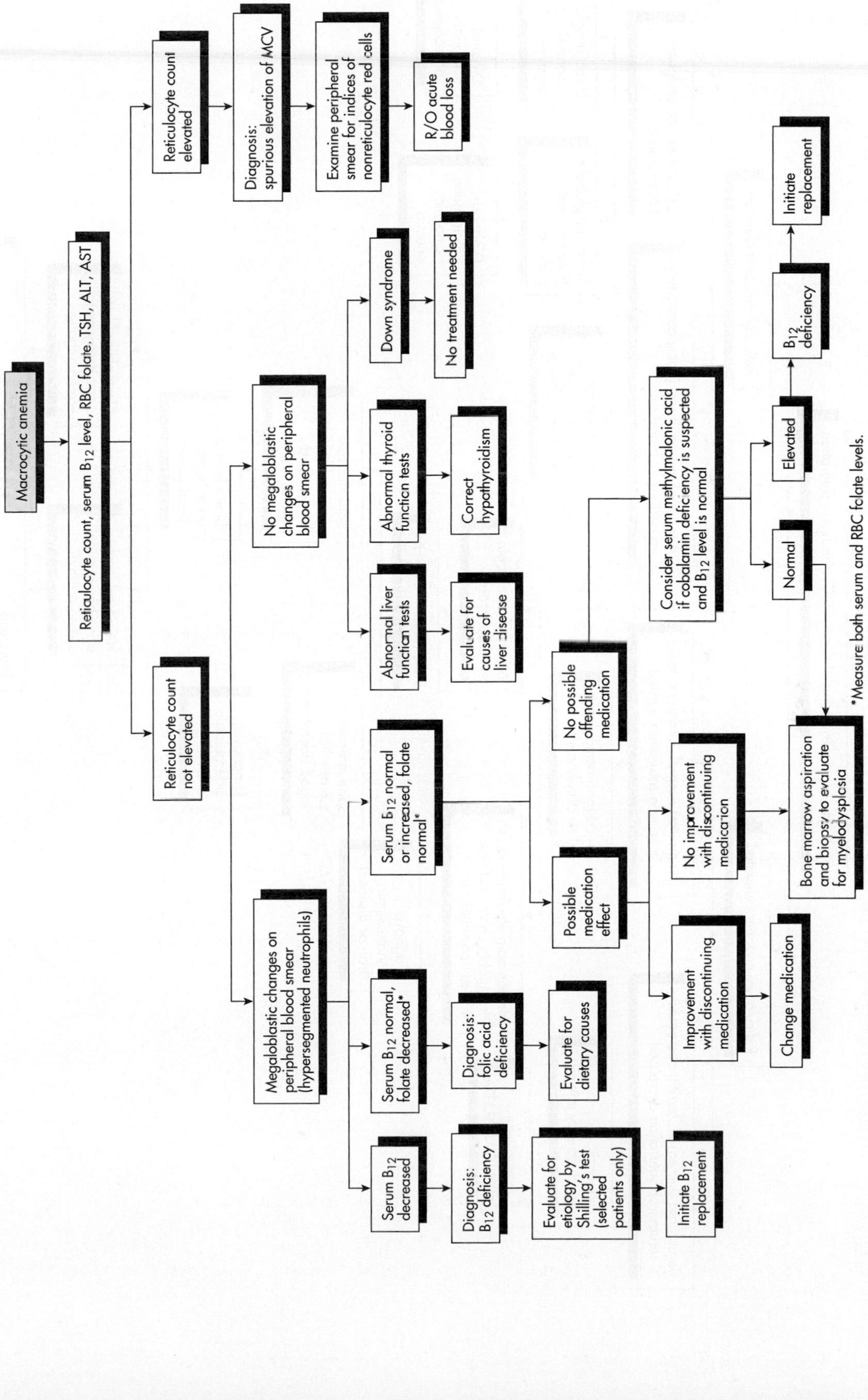

Macrocytic anemia

Reticulocyte count, serum B$_{12}$ level, RBC folate, TSH, ALT, AST

Reticulocyte count elevated

Diagnosis: spurious elevation of MCV

Examine peripheral smear for indices of nonreticulocyte red cells

R/O acute blood loss

Reticulocyte count not elevated

No megaloblastic changes on peripheral blood smear

Down syndrome

No treatment needed

Abnormal thyroid function tests

Correct hypothyroidism

Abnormal liver function tests

Evaluate for causes of liver disease

Megaloblastic changes on peripheral blood smear (hypersegmented neutrophils)

Serum B$_{12}$ normal or increased, folate normal*

No possible offending medication

Consider serum methylmalonic acid if cobalamin deficiency is suspected and B$_{12}$ level is normal

Normal

Elevated

B$_{12}$ deficiency

Initiate replacement

Serum B$_{12}$ normal, folate decreased*

Diagnosis: folic acid deficiency

Evaluate for dietary causes

Possible medication effect

No improvement with discontinuing medication

Improvement with discontinuing medication

Change medication

Bone marrow aspiration and biopsy to evaluate for myelodysplasia

Serum B$_{12}$ decreased

Diagnosis: B$_{12}$ deficiency

Evaluate for etiology by Shilling's test (selected patients only)

Initiate B$_{12}$ replacement

*Measure both serum and RBC folate levels.

FIGURE 3-16 Differential diagnosis of macrocytic anemia. *MCV,* Mean corpuscular volume. (Modified from Rakel RE [ed]: *Principles of family practice,* ed 7, Philadelphia, 2007, Saunders.)

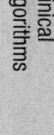

Clinical Algorithms

III

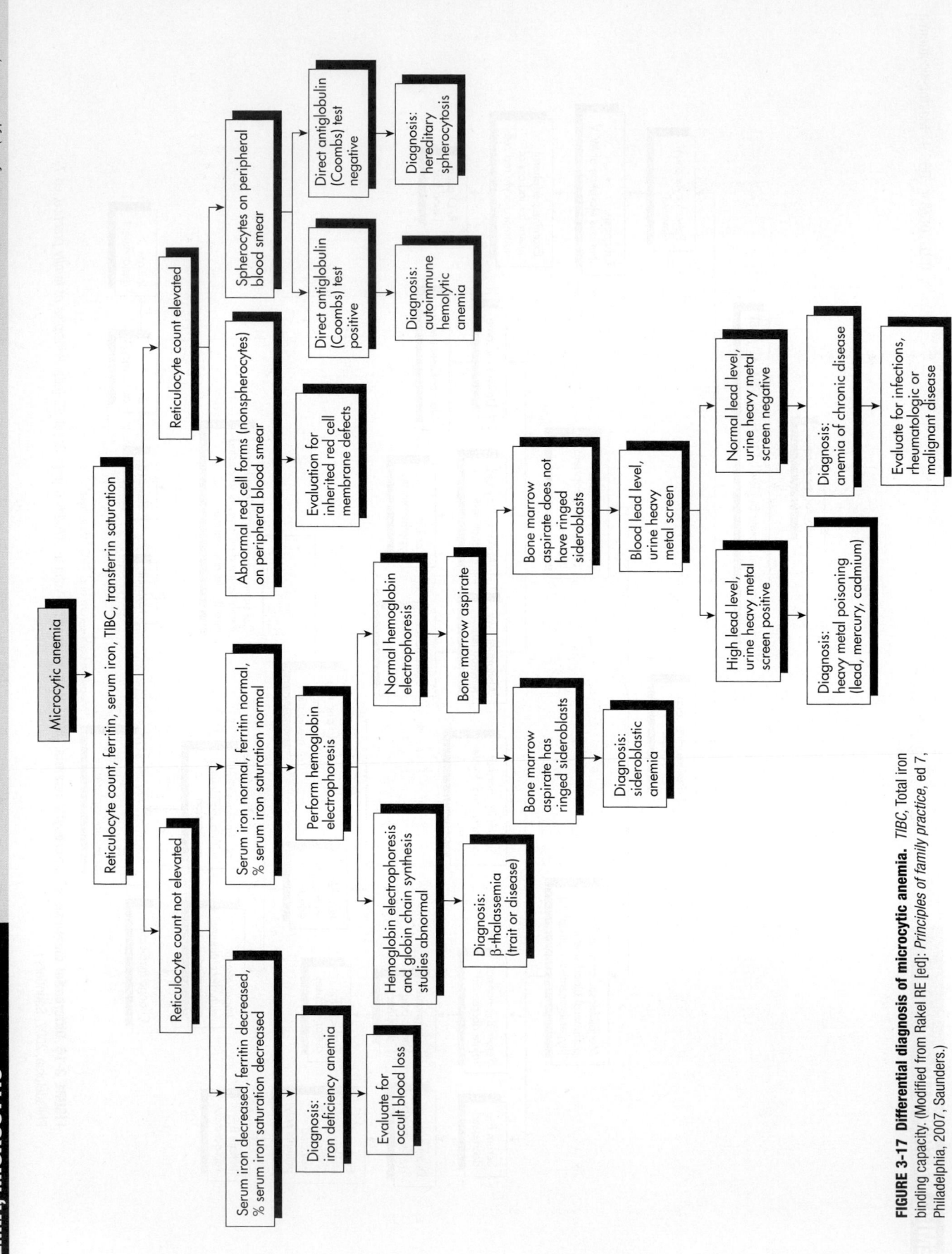

FIGURE 3-17 Differential diagnosis of microcytic anemia. *TIBC,* Total iron binding capacity. (Modified from Rakel RE [ed]: *Principles of family practice,* ed 7, Philadelphia, 2007, Saunders.)

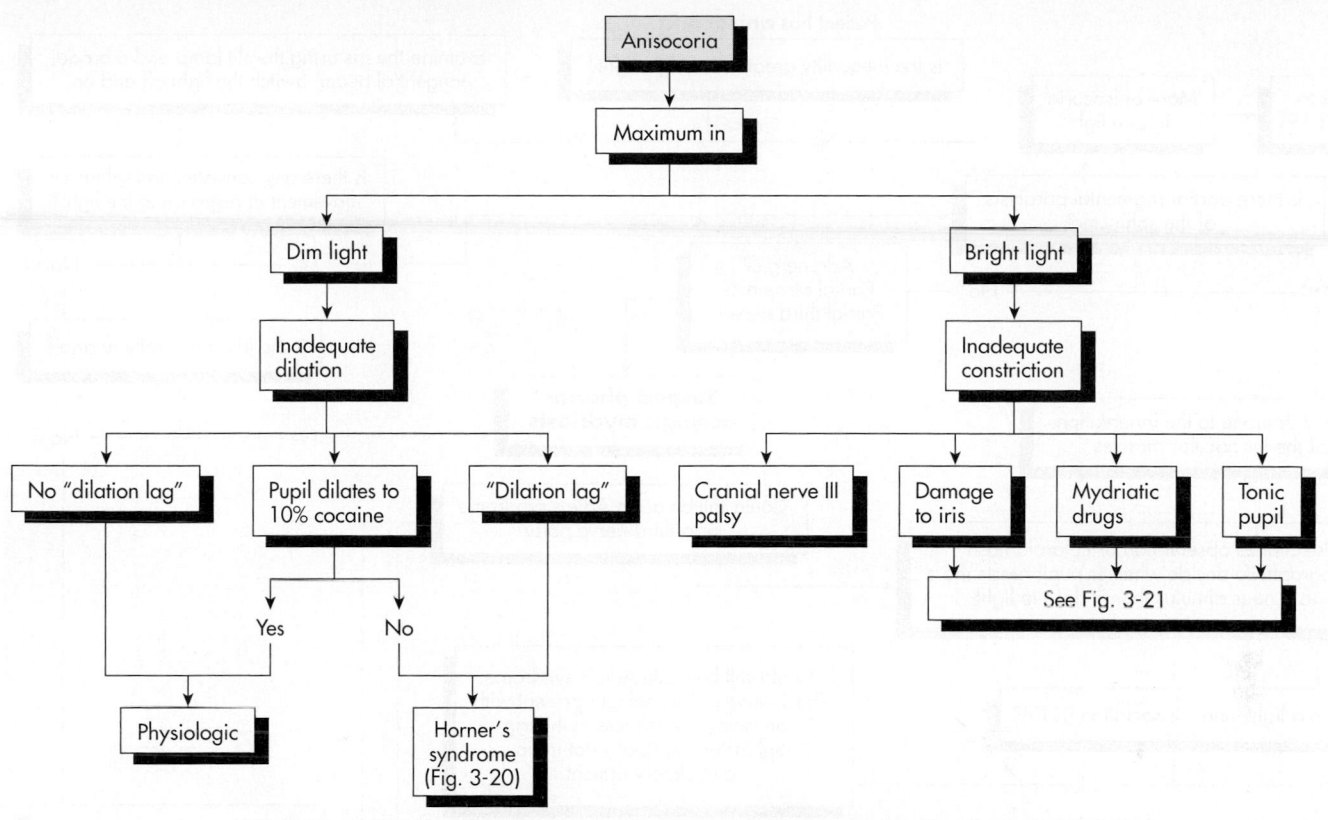

FIGURE 3-19 Algorithm for the approach to unequal pupils (anisocoria). (From Andreoli TE [ed]: *Cecil essentials of medicine,* ed 7, Philadelphia, 2008, Saunders.)

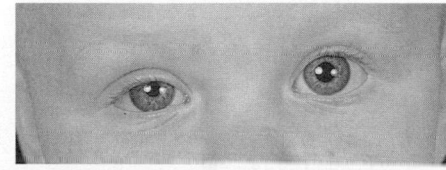

FIGURE 3-20 Horner's syndrome clearly acquired in infancy must be evaluated for neuroblastoma, a treatable tumor. This baby, with a right ptosis and miosis, developed a flush during cycloplegia that made the vasomotor abnormality very clear—the Horner's side remained pale. The baby had no sign of Horner's syndrome during her first 8 months, but at 16 months Horner's syndrome is obvious (ptosis, miosis, and upside-down ptosis). Because the syndrome was acquired, a chest radiograph was ordered; it showed a mass in the pulmonary apex. Magnetic resonance imaging confirmed the lesion. Surgery showed it to be a neuroblastoma. (From Yanoff M, Duker JS: *Ophthalmology,* ed 2, St Louis, 2004, Mosby.)

Clinical
Algorithms

III

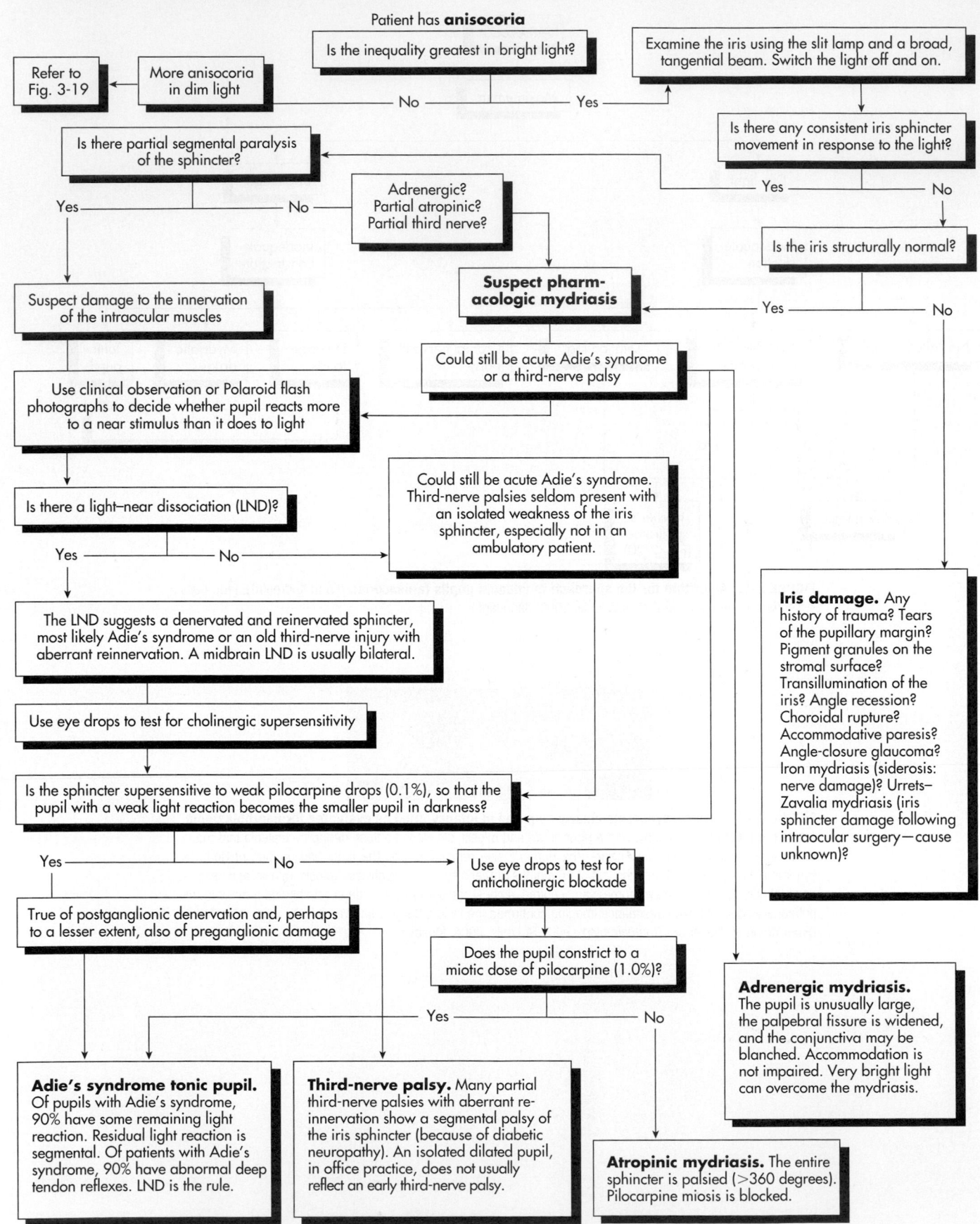

FIGURE 3-21 Diagnosis of pupillary abnormalities in which anisocoria increases in bright light. Initial pupillary inequality is greater in bright light than in darkness, which indicates that the sphincter of the large pupil is weak or that a parasympathetic lesion is present on that side. (From Yanoff M, Duker JS: *Ophthalmology*, ed 2, St Louis, 2004, Mosby.)

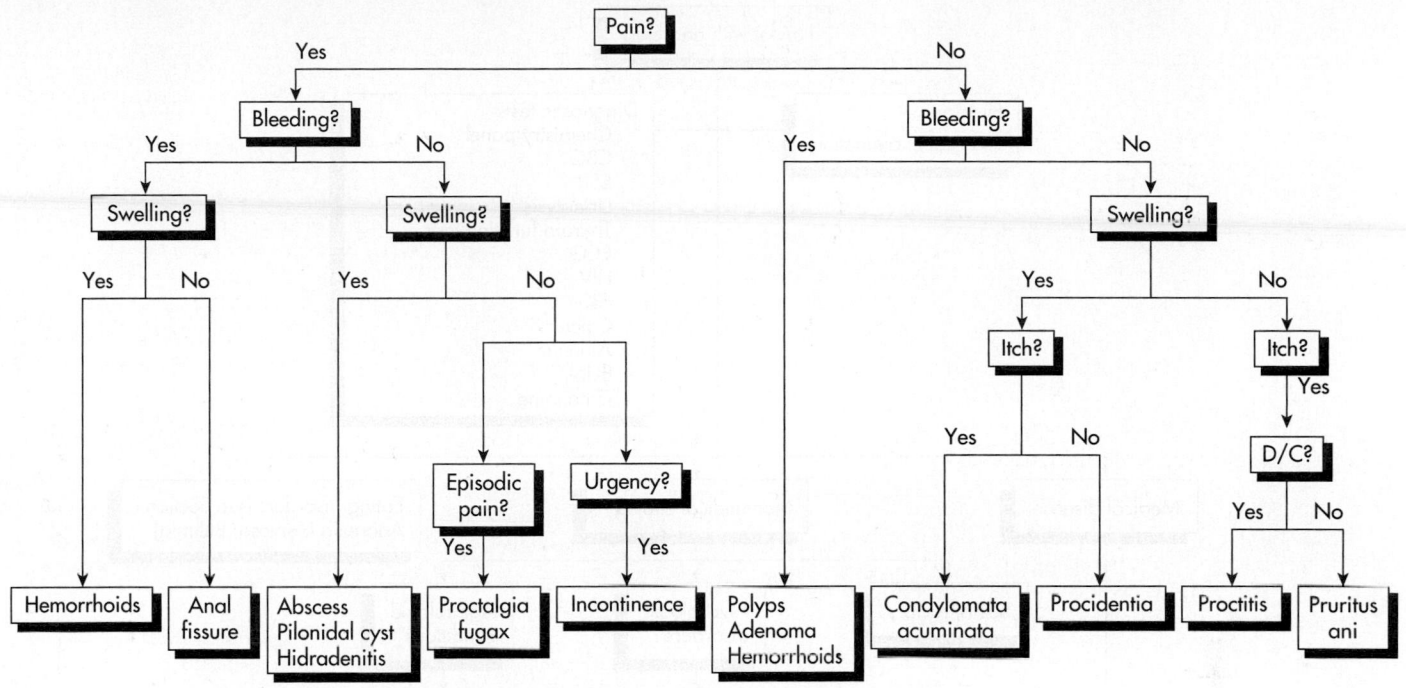

FIGURE 3-22 Algorithm for anorectal complaints. *D/C,* discharge. (From Marx JA, et al: *Rosen's emergency medicine*, ed 8, Philadelphia, 2014, Saunders.)

BOX 3-1, A   The WASH Regimen for Management of Hemorrhoids

- *W*arm water
- *A*nalgesic agents
- *S*tool softeners
- *H*igh-fiber diet

From Marx JA, et al: *Rosen's emergency medicine*, ed 8, Philadelphia, 2014, Saunders.

BOX 3-1, B   Medical History in Diagnosis of Anorectal Disorders

Anorectal History
Pain
Bleeding
Swelling
Itching
Discharge
Urgency

Gastrointestinal History
Change in bowel habits (straining, flatus, color, consistency, frequency)
Nausea or vomiting
Incontinence of stool
Underlying GI disease (Crohn's disease, cancer, polyps)

Systemic Disease History
Diabetes mellitus
Coagulopathy
Cancer
HIV infection

Sexual History of the Anus
Penetration
Known STDs
Assault

GI, Gastrointestinal; *HIV,* human immunodeficiency virus; *STD,* sexually transmitted disease.
From Marx JA, et al: *Rosen's emergency medicine,* ed 8, Philadelphia, 2014, Saunders.

Clinical Algorithms

III

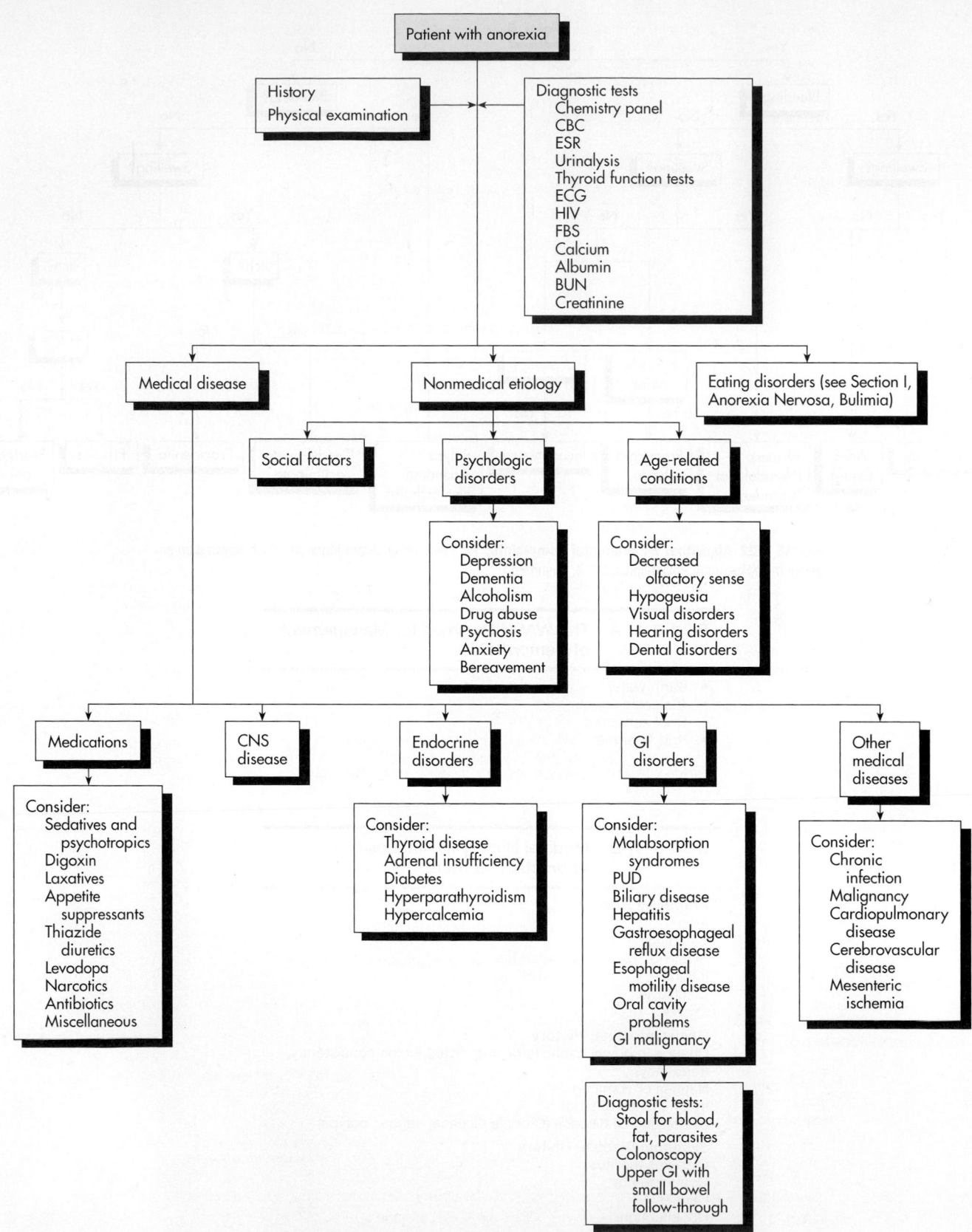

FIGURE 3-23 Evaluation of anorexia. *BUN,* Blood urea nitrogen; *CBC,* complete blood count; *CNS,* central nervous system; *ECG,* electrocardiogram; *ESR,* erythrocyte sedimentation rate; *FBS,* fasting blood sugar; *GI,* gastrointestinal; *PUD,* peptic ulcer disease. (Modified from Greene HL, Johnson WP, Lemcke D [eds]: *Decision making in medicine,* ed 2, St Louis, 1998, Mosby.)

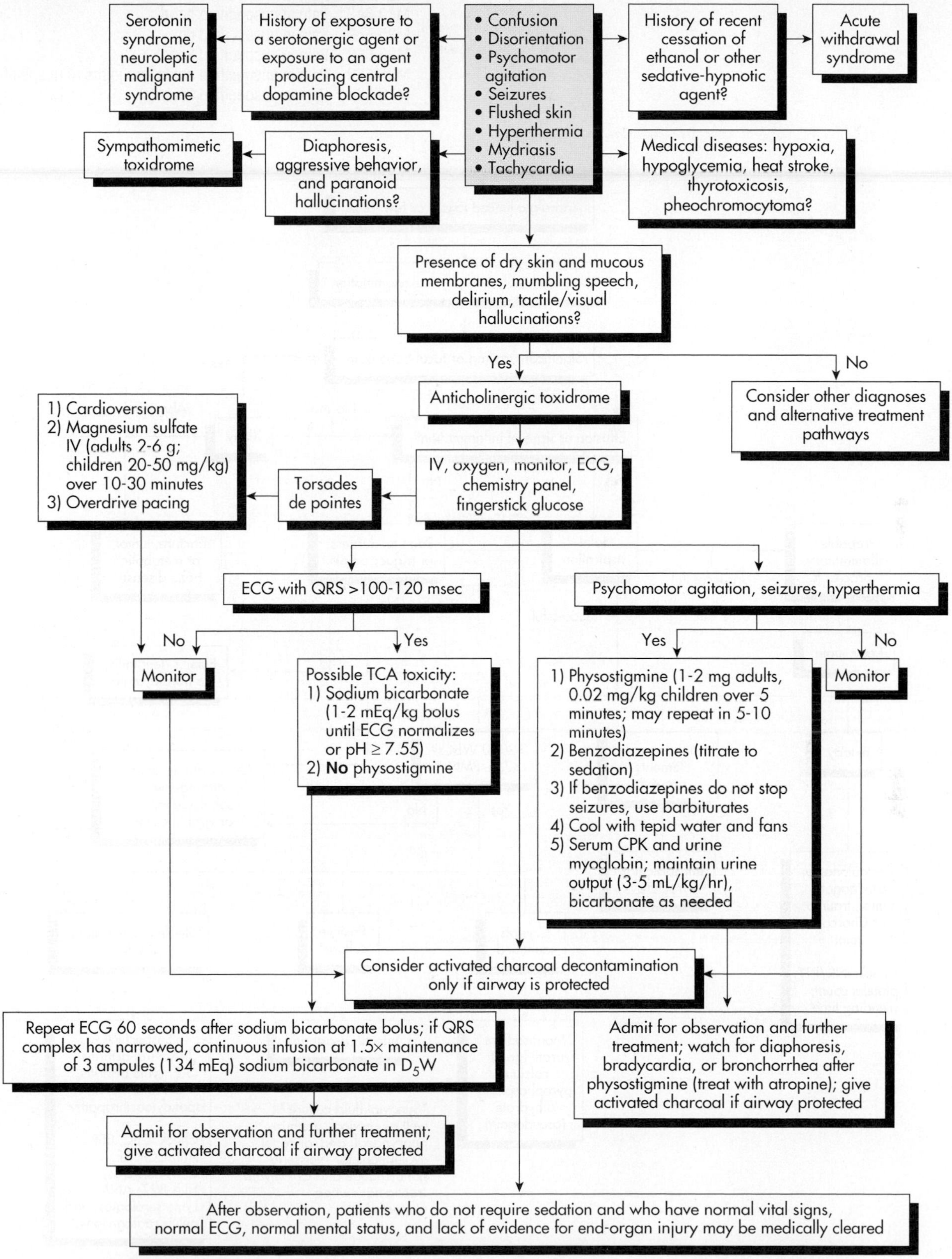

Serotonin syndrome, neuroleptic malignant syndrome ← History of exposure to a serotonergic agent or exposure to an agent producing central dopamine blockade? ←

- Confusion
- Disorientation
- Psychomotor agitation
- Seizures
- Flushed skin
- Hyperthermia
- Mydriasis
- Tachycardia

→ History of recent cessation of ethanol or other sedative-hypnotic agent? → Acute withdrawal syndrome

Sympathomimetic toxidrome ← Diaphoresis, aggressive behavior, and paranoid hallucinations? ← [Confusion box] → Medical diseases: hypoxia, hypoglycemia, heat stroke, thyrotoxicosis, pheochromocytoma?

Presence of dry skin and mucous membranes, mumbling speech, delirium, tactile/visual hallucinations?

Yes ↓   No →

Anticholinergic toxidrome   Consider other diagnoses and alternative treatment pathways

1) Cardioversion
2) Magnesium sulfate IV (adults 2-6 g; children 20-50 mg/kg) over 10-30 minutes
3) Overdrive pacing

← Torsades de pointes ← IV, oxygen, monitor, ECG, chemistry panel, fingerstick glucose

ECG with QRS >100-120 msec   Psychomotor agitation, seizures, hyperthermia

No ←   ↓ Yes   Yes ↓   No →

Monitor   Possible TCA toxicity:
1) Sodium bicarbonate (1-2 mEq/kg bolus until ECG normalizes or pH ≥ 7.55)
2) **No** physostigmine

1) Physostigmine (1-2 mg adults, 0.02 mg/kg children over 5 minutes; may repeat in 5-10 minutes)
2) Benzodiazepines (titrate to sedation)
3) If benzodiazepines do not stop seizures, use barbiturates
4) Cool with tepid water and fans
5) Serum CPK and urine myoglobin; maintain urine output (3-5 mL/kg/hr), bicarbonate as needed

Monitor

Consider activated charcoal decontamination only if airway is protected

Repeat ECG 60 seconds after sodium bicarbonate bolus; if QRS complex has narrowed, continuous infusion at 1.5× maintenance of 3 ampules (134 mEq) sodium bicarbonate in D_5W

Admit for observation and further treatment; watch for diaphoresis, bradycardia, or bronchorrhea after physostigmine (treat with atropine); give activated charcoal if airway protected

Admit for observation and further treatment; give activated charcoal if airway protected

After observation, patients who do not require sedation and who have normal vital signs, normal ECG, normal mental status, and lack of evidence for end-organ injury may be medically cleared

FIGURE 3-24 Algorithm for the recognition and treatment of anticholinergic toxicity. *CPK,* Creatine phosphokinase; *D_5W,* 5% dextrose in water; *ECG,* electrocardiogram; *IV,* intravenous line; *TCA,* tricyclic antidepressant. (From Adams JG et al: *Emergency medicine, clinical essentials,* ed 2, Philadelphia, 2013, Elsevier.)

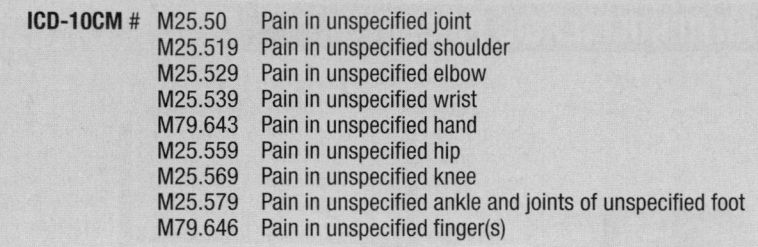

ICD-10CM #	M25.50	Pain in unspecified joint
	M25.519	Pain in unspecified shoulder
	M25.529	Pain in unspecified elbow
	M25.539	Pain in unspecified wrist
	M79.643	Pain in unspecified hand
	M25.559	Pain in unspecified hip
	M25.569	Pain in unspecified knee
	M25.579	Pain in unspecified ankle and joints of unspecified foot
	M79.646	Pain in unspecified finger(s)

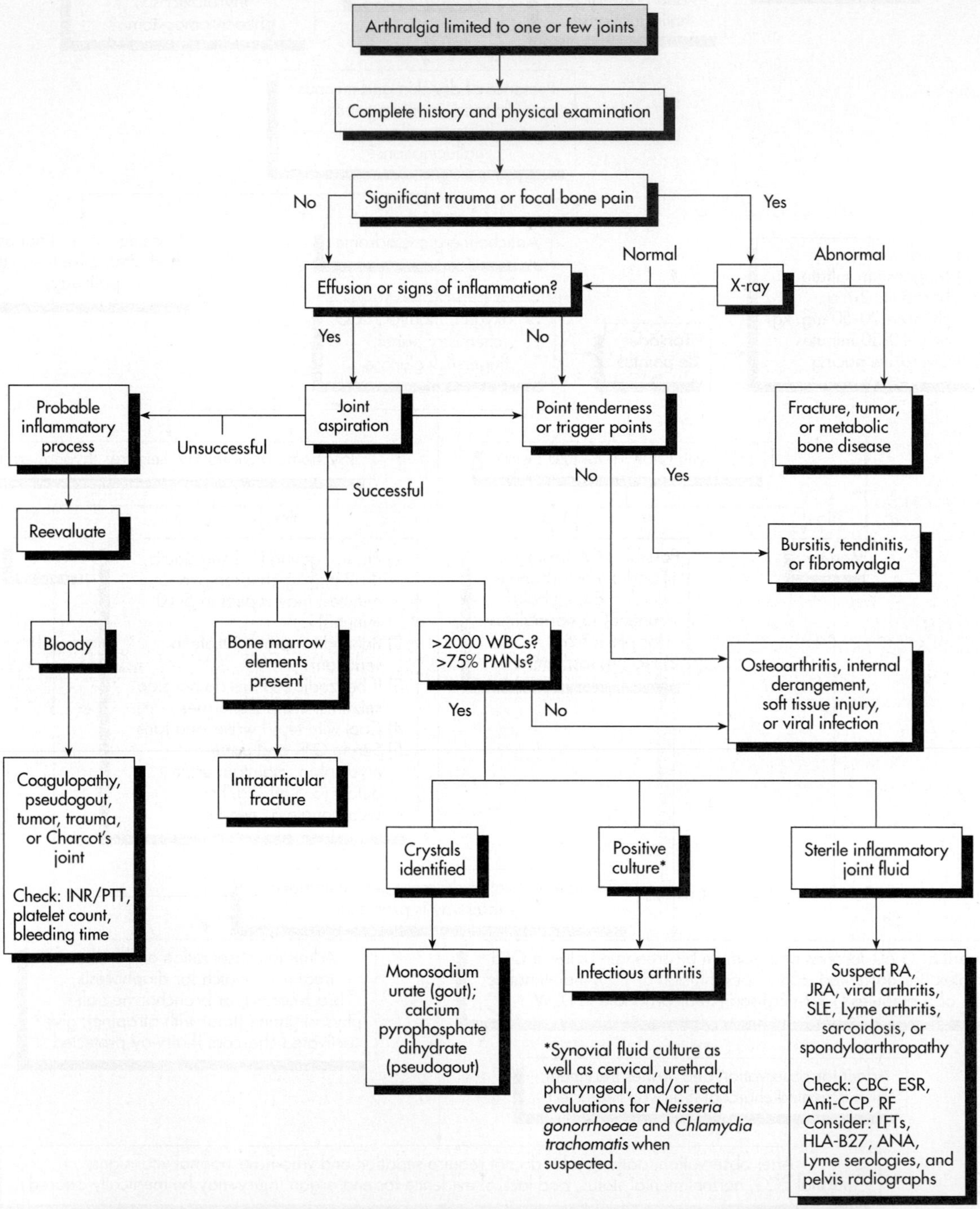

Arthralgia limited to one or few joints
↓
Complete history and physical examination
↓
Significant trauma or focal bone pain
— No → Effusion or signs of inflammation?
— Yes → X-ray
- X-ray Normal → Effusion or signs of inflammation?
- X-ray Abnormal → Fracture, tumor, or metabolic bone disease

Effusion or signs of inflammation?
- Yes → Joint aspiration
- No → Point tenderness or trigger points

Joint aspiration
- Unsuccessful → Probable inflammatory process → Reevaluate
- Successful ↓

Point tenderness or trigger points
- No → Osteoarthritis, internal derangement, soft tissue injury, or viral infection
- Yes → Bursitis, tendinitis, or fibromyalgia

Joint aspiration (Successful):
- Bloody → Coagulopathy, pseudogout, tumor, trauma, or Charcot's joint. Check: INR/PTT, platelet count, bleeding time
- Bone marrow elements present → Intraarticular fracture
- >2000 WBCs? >75% PMNs?
  - Yes ↓
  - No → Osteoarthritis, internal derangement, soft tissue injury, or viral infection

>2000 WBCs? >75% PMNs? (Yes):
- Crystals identified → Monosodium urate (gout); calcium pyrophosphate dihydrate (pseudogout)
- Positive culture* → Infectious arthritis
- Sterile inflammatory joint fluid → Suspect RA, JRA, viral arthritis, SLE, Lyme arthritis, sarcoidosis, or spondyloarthropathy. Check: CBC, ESR, Anti-CCP, RF. Consider: LFTs, HLA-B27, ANA, Lyme serologies, and pelvis radiographs

*Synovial fluid culture as well as cervical, urethral, pharyngeal, and/or rectal evaluations for *Neisseria gonorrhoeae* and *Chlamydia trachomatis* when suspected.

FIGURE 3-25 A diagnostic approach to arthralgia in a few joints. *ANA,* Antinuclear antibodies; *Anti-CCP,* anti-cyclic cintrullinated peptide; *CBC,* complete blood count; *ESR,* erythrocyte sedimentation rate; *JRA,* juvenile rheumatoid arthritis; *LFTs,* liver function tests; *PMNs,* polymorphonuclear neutrophils; *PT,* prothrombin time; *PTT,* partial thromboplastin time; *RA,* rheumatoid arthritis; *RF,* rheumatoid factor; *SLE,* systemic lupus erythematosus; *WBCs,* white blood cells. (Modified from American College of Rheumatology Ad Hoc Committee on Clinical Guidelines: *Arthritis Rheum* 39:1, 1996.)

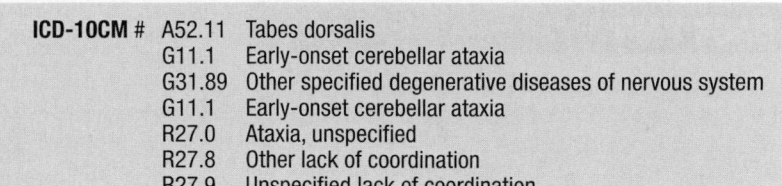

ICD-10CM #
A52.11	Tabes dorsalis
G11.1	Early-onset cerebellar ataxia
G31.89	Other specified degenerative diseases of nervous system
G11.1	Early-onset cerebellar ataxia
R27.0	Ataxia, unspecified
R27.8	Other lack of coordination
R27.9	Unspecified lack of coordination

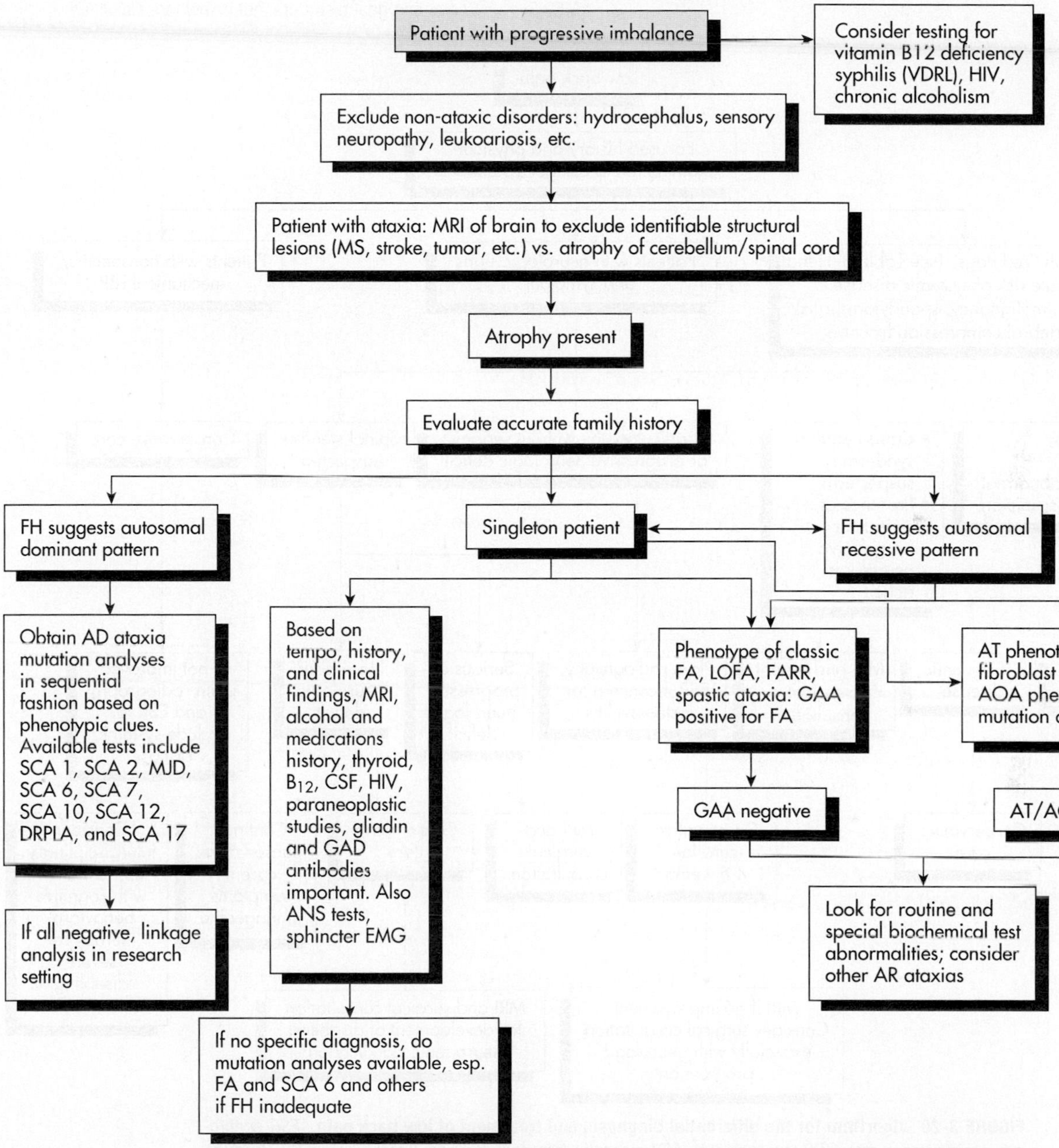

Patient with progressive imbalance → Consider testing for vitamin B12 deficiency syphilis (VDRL), HIV, chronic alcoholism

Exclude non-ataxic disorders: hydrocephalus, sensory neuropathy, leukoariosis, etc.

Patient with ataxia: MRI of brain to exclude identifiable structural lesions (MS, stroke, tumor, etc.) vs. atrophy of cerebellum/spinal cord

Atrophy present

Evaluate accurate family history

FH suggests autosomal dominant pattern

Singleton patient

FH suggests autosomal recessive pattern

Obtain AD ataxia mutation analyses in sequential fashion based on phenotypic clues. Available tests include SCA 1, SCA 2, MJD, SCA 6, SCA 7, SCA 10, SCA 12, DRPLA, and SCA 17

Based on tempo, history, and clinical findings, MRI, alcohol and medications history, thyroid, B12, CSF, HIV, paraneoplastic studies, gliadin and GAD antibodies important. Also ANS tests, sphincter EMG

Phenotype of classic FA, LOFA, FARR, spastic ataxia: GAA positive for FA

AT phenotype: α-fetoprotein, fibroblast survival; AOA phenotype: consider mutation analysis

If all negative, linkage analysis in research setting

GAA negative

AT/AOA not present

Look for routine and special biochemical test abnormalities; consider other AR ataxias

If no specific diagnosis, do mutation analyses available, esp. FA and SCA 6 and others if FH inadequate

FIGURE 3-28 An algorithm for a diagnostic approach to patients with progressive ataxia. *AD,* Autosomal dominant; *AOA,* ataxia with oculomotor apraxia; *AR,* autosomal recessive; *AT,* ataxia-telangiectasia; *CSF,* cerebrospinal fluid; *DRPLA,* dentatorubral-pallidoluysian atrophy; *EMG,* electromyelography; *FA,* Friedreich's ataxia; *FH,* family history; *GAD,* glutamate decarboxylase; *HIV,* human immunodeficiency virus; *MRI,* magnetic resonance imaging; *MS,* multiple sclerosis; *SCA,* spinocerebellar ataxia. (Modified from Bradley WG et al [eds]: *Neurology in clinical practice,* ed 4, Philadelphia, 2004, Butterworth Heinemann.)

Clinical Algorithms

ICD-10CM #	M54.89	Other dorsalgia
	M54.9	Dorsalgia, unspecified
	M54.5	Low back pain
	F45.42	Pain disorder with related psychological factors
	M54.08	Panniculitis affecting regions of neck and back, sacral and sacrococcygeal region
	S23.9XXA	Sprain of unspecified parts of thorax, initial encounter
	M43.27	Fusion of spine, lumbosacral region
	M43.28	Fusion of spine, sacral and sacrococcygeal region
	M53.2X7	Spinal instabilities, lumbosacral region
	M53.3	Sacrococcygeal disorders, not elsewhere classified

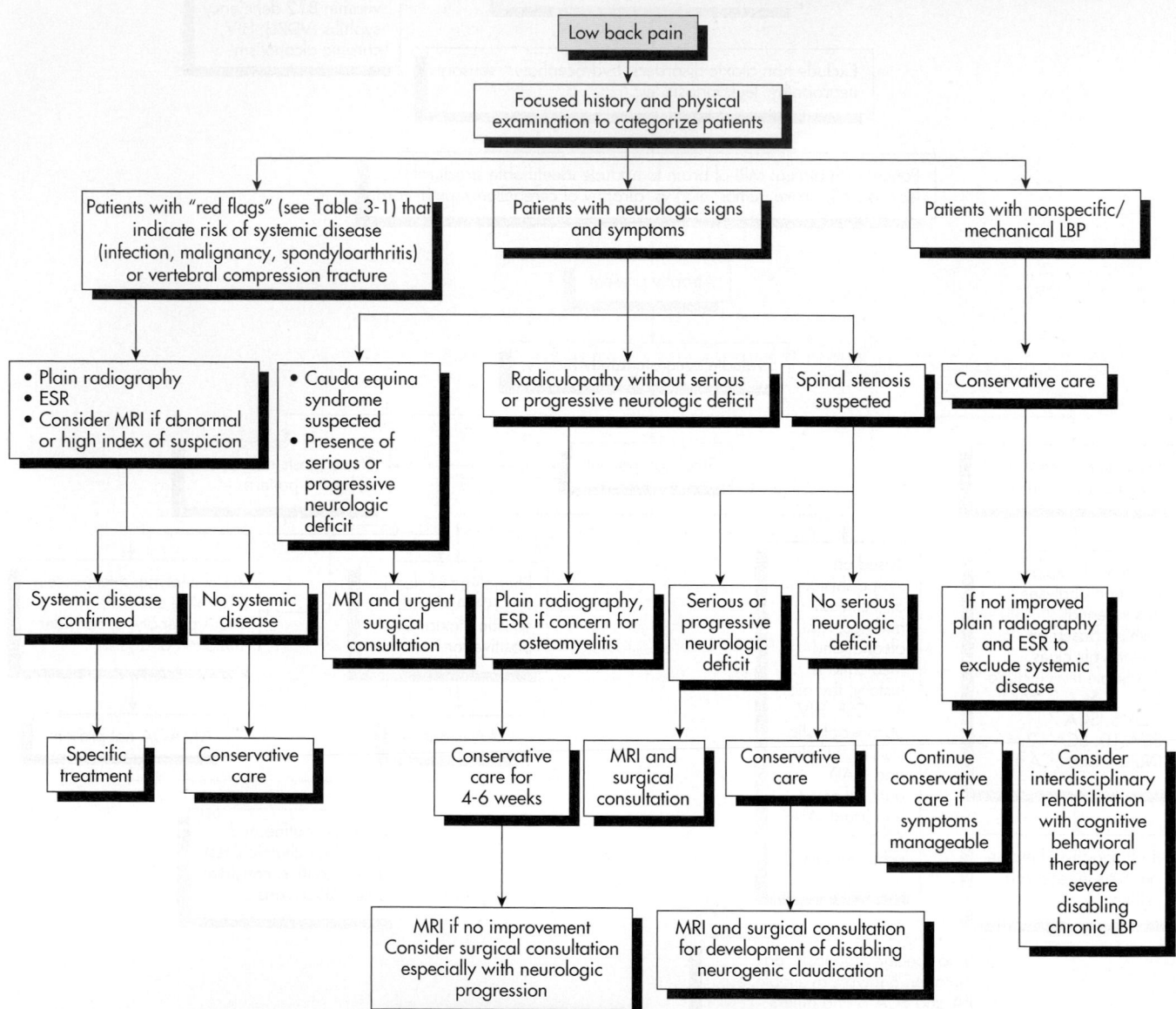

FIGURE 3-29 Algorithm for the differential diagnosis and treatment of low back pain. *ESR*, erythrocyte sedimentation rate; *LBP*, low back pain; *MRI*, magnetic resonance imaging. (From Firestein GS, Budd RC, Gabriel SE, et al: *Kelley's textbook of rheumatology,* ed 9, Philadelphia, 2013, Saunders.)

TABLE 3-1 Red Flags for Potentially Serious Conditions

Possible Fracture	Possible Tumor or Infection	Possible Cauda Equina Syndrome
From Medical History		
Major trauma, such as vehicle accident or fall from height	Age over 50 or under 20 yr	Saddle anesthesia
	History of cancer	Recent onset of bladder dysfunction, such as urinary retention, increased frequency, or overflow incontinence
Minor trauma or even strenuous lifting (in older or potentially osteoporotic patient)	Constitutional symptoms, such as recent fever or chills or unexplained weight loss	
	Risk factors for spinal infection: recent bacterial infection (e.g., urinary tract infection), intravenous drug abuse, or immune suppression (from steroids, transplant, or human immunodeficiency virus)	Severe or progressive neurologic deficit in the lower extremity
	Pain that worsens when supine; severe nighttime pain	

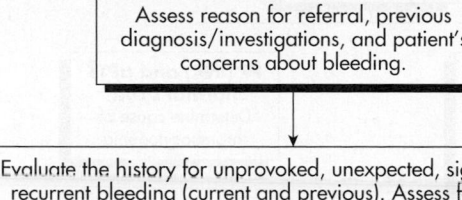

Assess reason for referral, previous diagnosis/investigations, and patient's concerns about bleeding.

Evaluate the history for unprovoked, unexpected, significant, and recurrent bleeding (current and previous). Assess for symptoms of bruising, prolonged bleeding with cuts, nosebleeds, gum and oral bleeding, gastrointestinal bleeding, joint or muscle bleeds, urinary tract bleeding, and other bleeding (e.g., intracranial, umbilical stump). Evaluate the drug history and family history of bleeding problems. Evaluate other medical problems. Determine the nature and timing of any abnormal bleeding with challenges (right away, within hours or days after) and the severity (e.g., required transfusion, longer hospital stay, developed large hematomas).

If symptoms suggest an underlying bleeding problem, evaluate whether the cause could be an acquired or congenital problem (e.g., symptoms from childhood, positive family history).

If bleeding problems are new, consider potential reasons and triggers (e.g., a first major hemostatic challenge could be the first presentation of a mild bleeding disorder; trigger could be drugs, development of an immune disorder, or blood, endocrine, liver, or renal disease).

Formulate a differential diagnosis for the potential inherited and acquired causes that should be investigated.

FIGURE 3-30 Steps to evaluate bleeding and bruising problems. (From Hoffman R: *Hematology, basic principles and practice,* 6th ed, Philadelphia, Saunders, 2013, Figure 130-1.)

Clinical
Algorithms

III

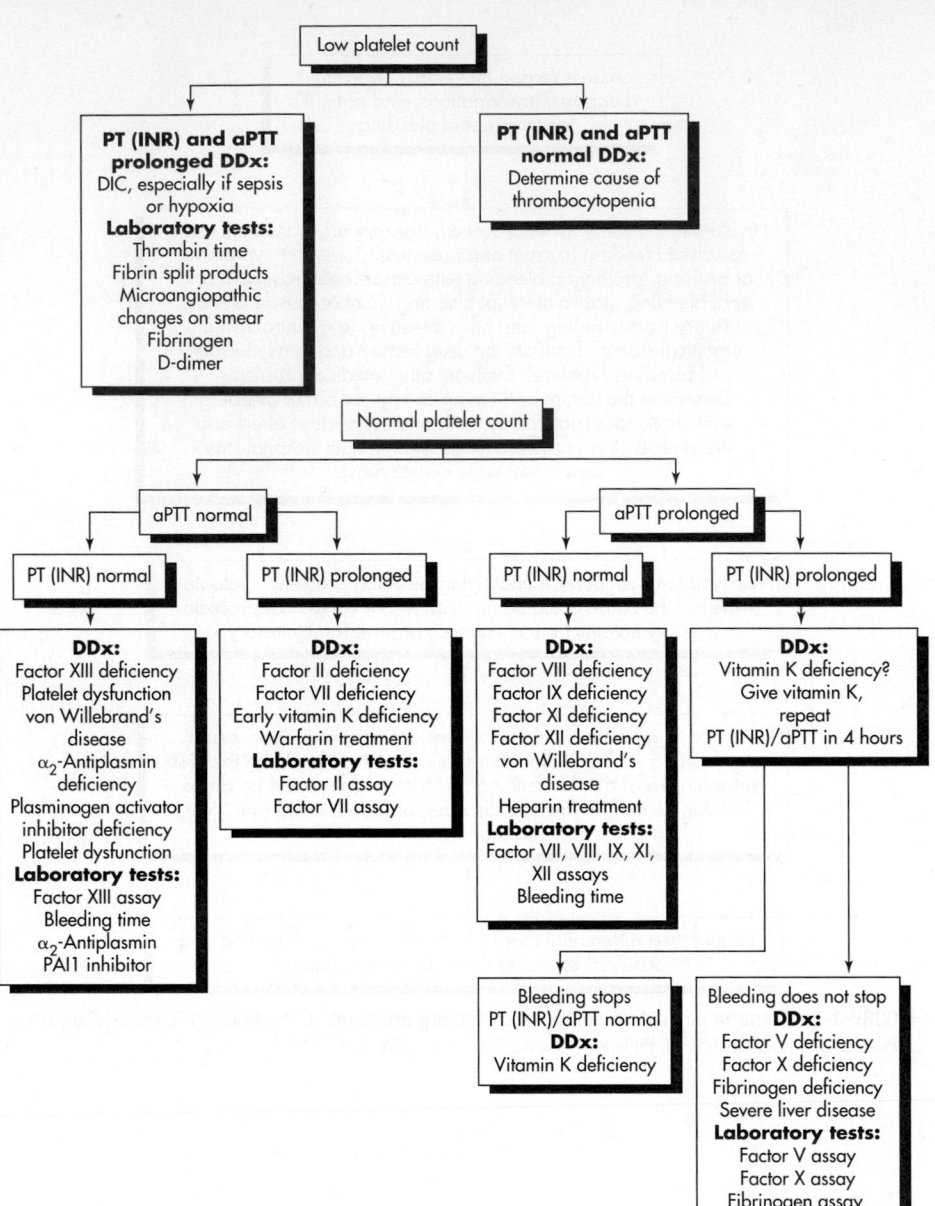

FIGURE 3-32 Differential diagnosis (DDx) of bleeding disorders. (From Cluster JW, Rau RE: *The Harriet Lane handbook,* ed 18, St Louis, 2009, Mosby.)

BOX 3-2   Bleeding Disorders

Congenital

Disorder of platelet number or function

Thrombocytopenia: Secondary to bone marrow disease or defective megakaryocyte maturation

Disorders of platelet function: Bernard-Soulier syndrome, Glanzmann thrombasthenia, storage pool diseases

Factor VIII deficiency: See text (Section I)

Factor IX deficiency: See text (Section I)

von Willebrand's disease: See text (Section I)

Acquired

Disseminated intravascular coagulation: Characterized by prolonged PT and aPTT, decreased fibrinogen and platelets, increased fibrin degradation products, and elevated D-dimers. Treatment includes identifying and treating underlying disorder. Replacement of depleted coagulation factors with FFP may be necessary in severe cases, especially when bleeding is present; 10-15 ml/kg will raise clotting factors 20%. Fibrinogen, if depleted, can be given as cryoprecipitate. Platelet transfusions may also be necessary.

Liver disease: The liver is the major site of synthesis of factors V, VII, IX, X, XI, XII, XIII, prothrombin, plasminogen, fibrinogen, protein C and S, and ATIII. Treatment with FFP and platelets may be needed, but this will increase hepatic protein load. Vitamin K should be given to patients with liver disease and clotting abnormalities.

Vitamin K deficiency: Factors II, VII, IX, X, protein C, and protein S are vitamin K dependent. Early vitamin K deficiency may present with isolated prolonged PT because factor VII has the shortest half-life. Fibrinogen should be normal.

Hemolytic-uremic syndrome/thrombotic thrombocytopenic purpura (HUS/TTP): Characterized by the triad of microangiopathic hemolytic anemia, uremia, and thrombocytopenia. HUS/TTP is often triggered by bacterial enteritis, especially caused by *Escherichia coli* O157:H7, although there are a variety of causes. HUS does not typically include coagulation abnormalities, such as those seen in DIC. Avoid blood products in patients with HUS thought to be secondary to pneumococcal infection. TTP includes the triad of HUS in addition to fever and CNS changes and is more common in older adolescents and adults.

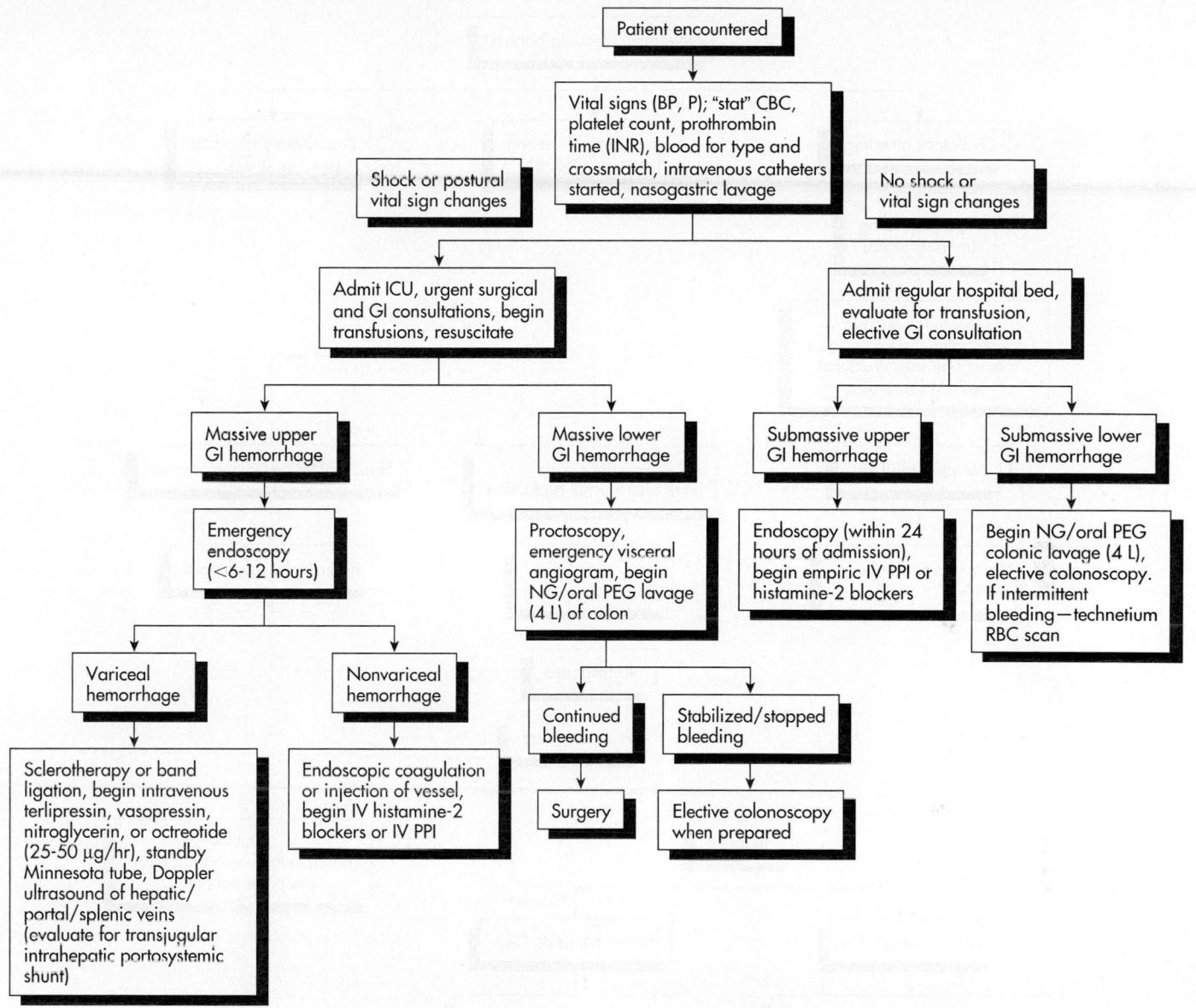

FIGURE 3-34 Approach to the patient with gastrointestinal hemorrhage. *BP,* Blood pressure; *CBC,* complete blood count; *GI,* gastrointestinal; *ICU,* intensive care unit; *IV,* intravenous; *INR,* International Normalized Ratio; *NG,* nasogastric; *P,* weight; *PEG,* percutaneous endoscopic gastrostomy; *PPI,* proton pump inhibitor; *RBC,* red blood cell. (Modified from Goldman L, Ausiello D [eds]: *Cecil textbook of medicine,* ed 23, Philadelphia, 2008, Saunders.)

Clinical
Algorithms

III

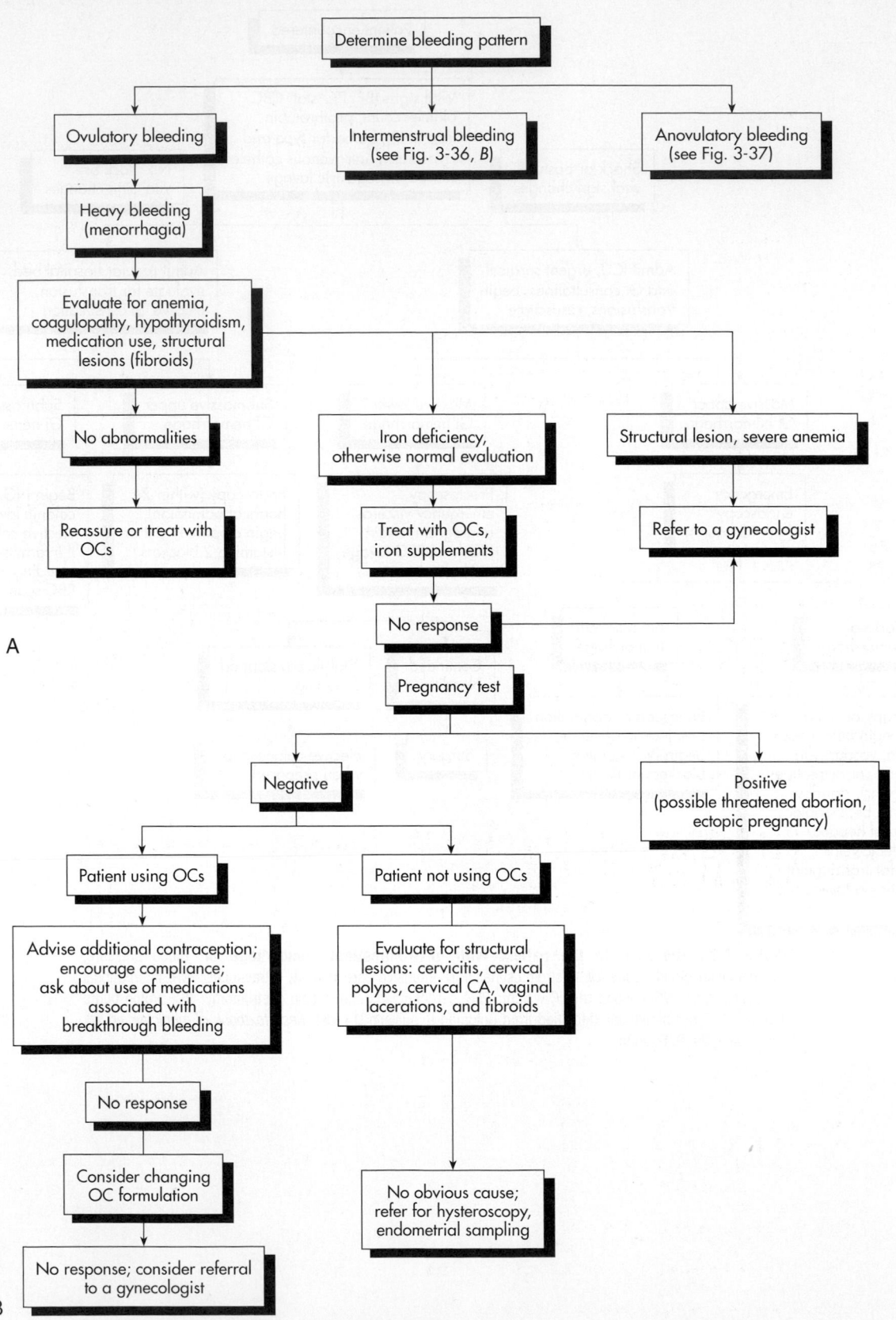

FIGURE 3-36 A, Evaluation of ovulatory bleeding. B, Evaluation of intermenstrual bleeding.
OCs, Oral contraceptives. (Modified from Appleby J, Henderson M, Wathen PI: *Intern Med* Sept:17, 1996.)

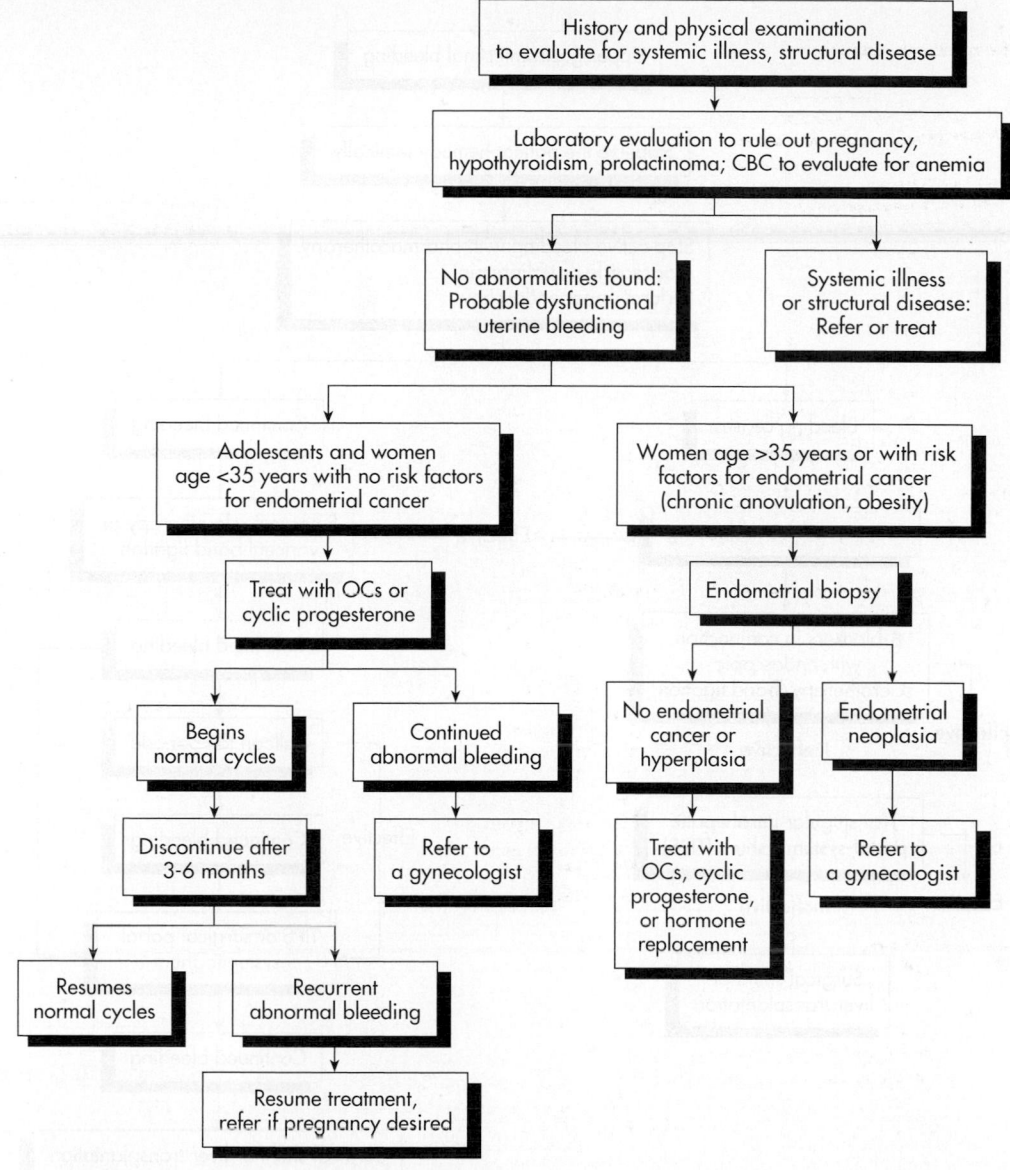

FIGURE 3-37 Evaluation of anovulatory bleeding. *CBC*, Complete blood count; *OCs*, oral contraceptives. (From Appleby J, Henderson M, Wathen PI: *Intern Med*, Sept:17, 1996.)

ICD-10CM # D68.8 Other specified coagulation defects
K92.2 Gastrointestinal bleeding

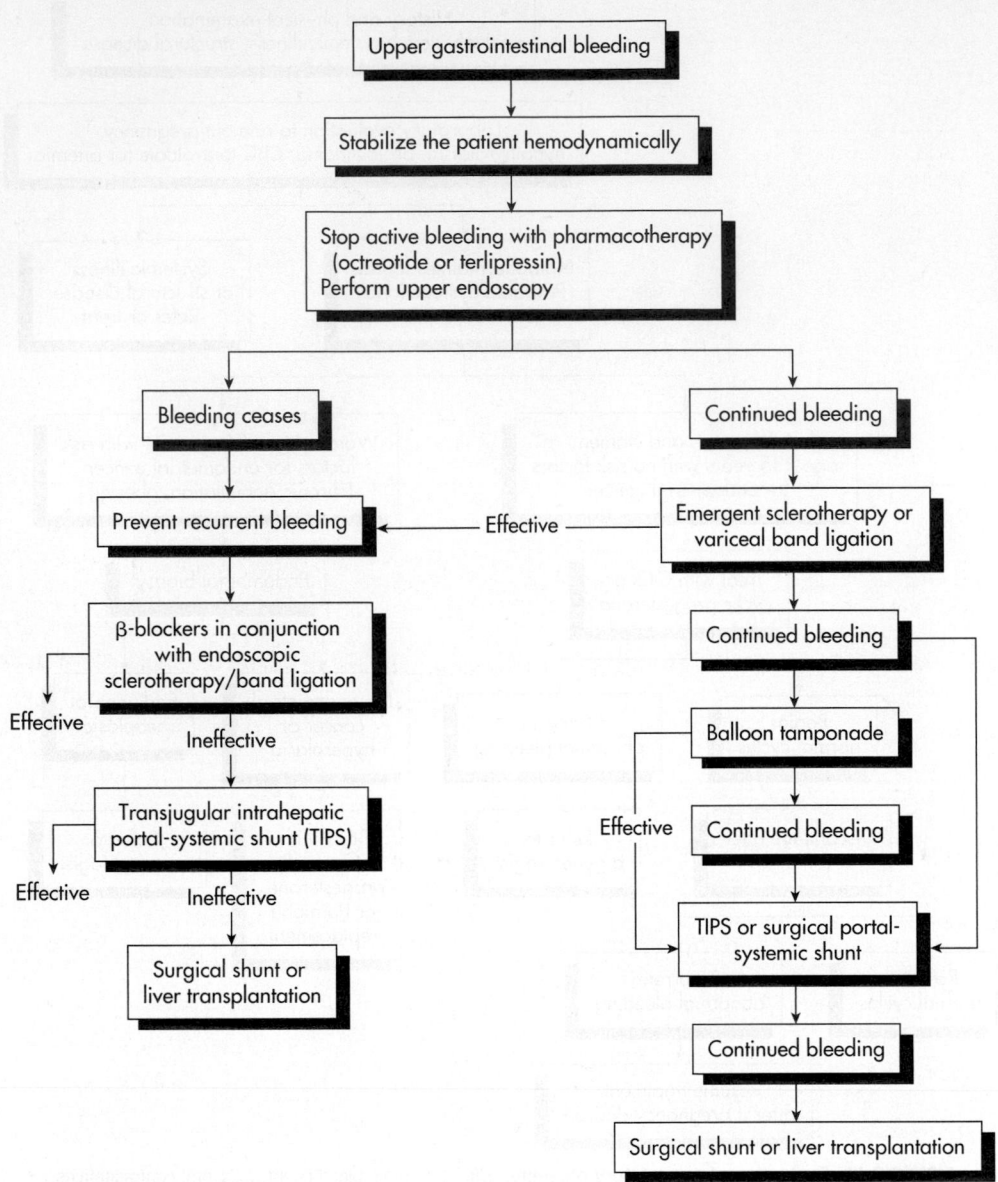

FIGURE 3-38 Management algorithm for variceal bleeding. (From Goldman L, Schafer AL [eds]: *Cecil textbook of medicine,* ed 24, Philadelphia, 2012, Saunders.)

BRADYCARDIA

ICD-10CM # R00.1 Bradycardia
         I49.8   Other specified cardiac arrhythmias
         I49.5   Sick sinus syndrome

1553

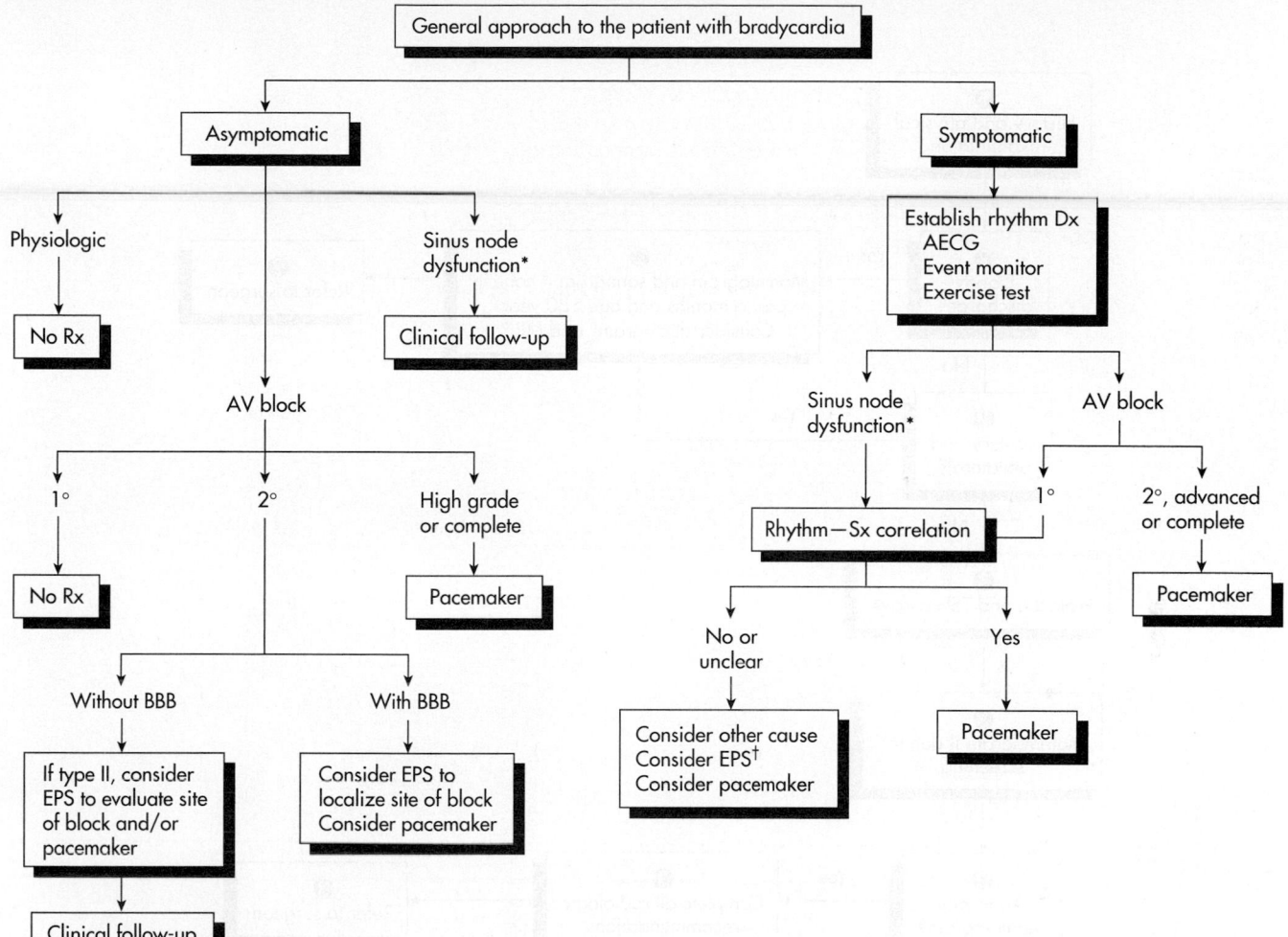

*Includes bradycardia-tachycardia syndrome.
†EPS includes sinus node function and ventricular arrhythmia induction studies.

FIGURE 3-39 General approach to the patient with bradycardia. *AECG,* Ambulatory electrocardiography; *AV,* atrioventricular; *BBB,* bundle branch block; *Dx,* diagnostic; *EPS,* electrophysiologic study, *Rx,* treatment; *Sx,* symptoms; *1°,* first-degree; *2°,* second-degree. (From Goldman L, Braunwald E [eds]: *Primary cardiology,* ed 2, Philadelphia, 2003, Saunders.)

Clinical
Algorithms

III

BREAST, NIPPLE DISCHARGE EVALUATION

ICD-10CM #   N64.52   Nipple discharge
N64.51   Induration of breast
N64.53   Retraction of nipple
N64.59   Other signs and symptoms in breast

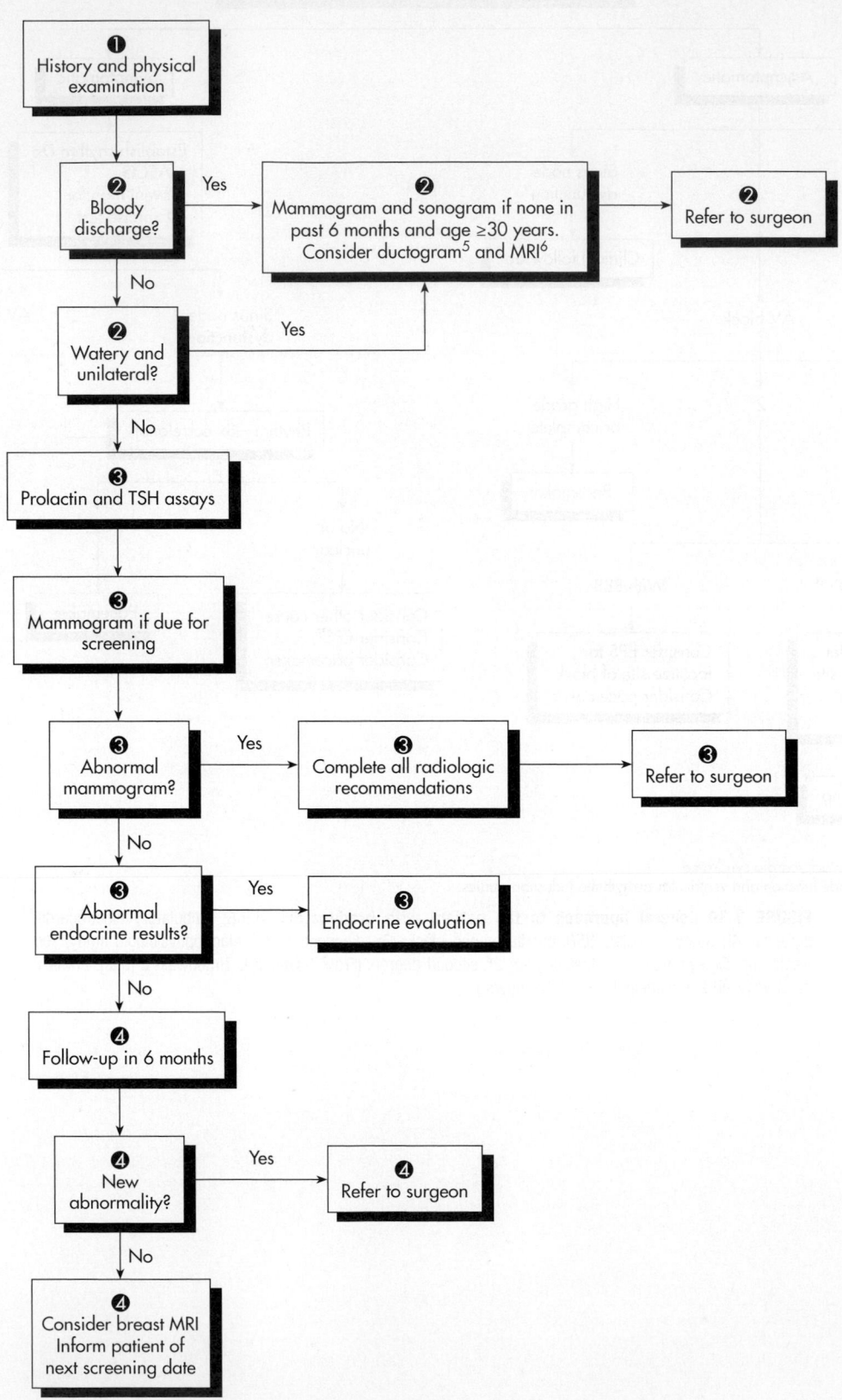

❶ History and physical examination

❷ Bloody discharge? — Yes → ❷ Mammogram and sonogram if none in past 6 months and age ≥30 years. Consider ductogram[5] and MRI[6] → ❷ Refer to surgeon

No ↓

❷ Watery and unilateral? — Yes →

No ↓

❸ Prolactin and TSH assays

❸ Mammogram if due for screening

❸ Abnormal mammogram? — Yes → ❸ Complete all radiologic recommendations → ❸ Refer to surgeon

No ↓

❸ Abnormal endocrine results? — Yes → ❸ Endocrine evaluation

No ↓

❹ Follow-up in 6 months

❹ New abnormality? — Yes → ❹ Refer to surgeon

No ↓

❹ Consider breast MRI Inform patient of next screening date

*Without palpable mass.

FIGURE 3-41 Breast cancer screening and evaluation. The primary goal of evaluation and management of nipple discharge is separation of patients with pathological causes of discharge from those with benign

BREAST, NIPPLE DISCHARGE
EVALUATION—cont'd

ICD-10CM #	N64.52	Nipple discharge
	N64.51	Induration of breast
	N64.53	Retraction of nipple
	N64.59	Other signs and symptoms in breast

1555

FIGURE 3-41 (Continued)

physiologic findings. Physiologic discharge is usually bilateral, involves multiple ducts, tests negative for blood regardless of color, and can be associated with nipple stimulation or breast compression. Approximately 50%-80% of women in their reproductive years can express some type of fluid from the breast. During the normal hormonal stimulation caused by pregnancy and breast feeding, the mammary glands often produce physiologic discharge of milk and colostrum. This discharge can be seen for up to 1 year postpartum after the cessation of breastfeeding. Nipple discharge is classified as pathologic if it is spontaneous, unilateral, bloody, serous, clear, or associated with a mass. Common causes of pathologic discharge are intraductal papilloma, duct ectasia, carcinoma, and infection. Of these, the most commonly seen is a benign papilloma, identified in up to 57% of cases of pathologic nipple discharge. A papilloma is a benign epithelial neoplasm that can be a cause of clear or bloody discharge. Papilloma can be classified as a spectrum of lesions that may be associated with atypical cells and low-grade carcinomas. The management of benign papilloma remains controversial. Duct ectasia is another common cause of pathologic discharge, seen in approximately 33% of cases. Malignancy is found in only 5%-15% of cases of pathologic nipple discharge, and is most commonly ductal carcinoma in situ.[2] (Modified from Institute for Clinical Systems Integration, Minneapolis: *Postgrad Med* 100:182, 1996.)

1. **History and physical examination**[1]. Patients who present with a complaint of nipple discharge should be evaluated with breast-related history taking and a physical examination. History taking is aimed at uncovering and characterizing any other breast-related symptom. A risk assessment should also be undertaken for identified risk factors, including patient age over 50 years, any past personal history of breast cancer, history of hyperplasia on previous breast biopsies, and family history of breast cancer in first-degree relatives (mother, sister, daughter). Physical examination should include inspection of the breast for any evidence of ulceration or contour changes and inspection of the nipple for Paget's disease. Palpation should be performed with the patient in both the upright and the supine positions to determine the presence of any palpable mass.

2. **Bloody discharge?** If the discharge appears frankly bloody, the patient should be referred to a surgeon for evaluation. At the time of referral, a mammogram of the involved breast should be obtained if the patient is over 40 years of age and has not had a mammogram within the preceding 6 months. Similarly, patients with a watery, unilateral discharge should be referred to a surgeon for evaluation and possible biopsy.

3. **Endocrine tests. Mammogram.** If the discharge appears frankly milky or is bilateral, serum prolactin and serum thyroid-stimulating hormone *(TSH)* assays should be performed to rule out the presence of an endocrinologic basis for the symptoms. At the time of that visit, a mammogram should also be performed if the patient is due for routine mammographic screening according to the recommended intervals. Mammography has a low positive predictive value of only 16.7%, and low sensitivity of 59% in the diagnosis of malignant duct pathology associated with nipple discharge.[2] A patient with an abnormal mammogram should be further evaluated radiologically to better characterize the lesion and then be referred to a surgeon if appropriate. Make certain that all recommended additional views, ultrasound examinations, and follow-up studies have been obtained before referral to a surgeon. Should the mammogram appear normal, results of the assays for TSH and prolactin should be reviewed. If the results are abnormal, the patient should undergo appropriate evaluation for etiology, either by a primary care physician or by an endocrinologist.

4. **Six-month follow-up results.** If results of the mammogram and the endocrinologic screening studies are normal, the patient should return for a follow-up visit in 6 months to ensure that there has been no specific change in the character of the discharge, such as development of frank bleeding or Paget's disease, that would warrant surgical evaluation. If the evaluation at that follow-up visit fails to reveal any palpable or visible abnormalities, the patient should be returned to the routine screening process with studies performed at the recommended intervals.

5. **Ultrasound.** Breast ultrasound is complementary to mammography and is noninvasive, free of ionizing radiation, and is extremely useful in the evaluation of patients with nipple discharge. Ultrasound is used primarily to detect masses and determine whether a palpable or mammographically identified mass is cystic, solid, or within a duct. It can also be used to delineate the relationship of the mass within the involved ductal system and the number of ducts involved. It has been reported that a benign physical examination and a negative subareolar ultrasound virtually exclude the possibility of malignancy in patients with pathologic nipple discharge. In patients with pathologic discharge, ultrasound has a reported sensitivity of 97%, specificity of 60%, and positive predictive values of 95%.[2]

6. **Contrast-enhanced MRI.** The role of MRI in the evaluation of nipple discharge is emerging as a preferred, less invasive alternative to ductography. MRI has a high sensitivity (94%-100%) for the detection of breast cancer. MRI requires the intravenous injection of a gadolinium-based contrast agent. As opposed to ductography, MRI is able to characterize lesions and provide a means for histologic diagnosis via percutaneous MRI-guided core biopsy.[2]

[1]ICSI health care guidelines are designed to assist clinicians by providing an analytic framework for the evaluation and treatment of patients. They are not intended either to replace a clinician's judgment or to establish a protocol for all patients with a particular condition. A guideline will rarely establish the only approach to a problem. In addition, guidelines are "living documents" that are expected to be imperfect and are subject to annual review and revision.

[2]From Patel BK, Falcon S, Drukteinis J: Management of nipple discharge and the associated imaging findings. *Am J Med* 128(4), 2015.

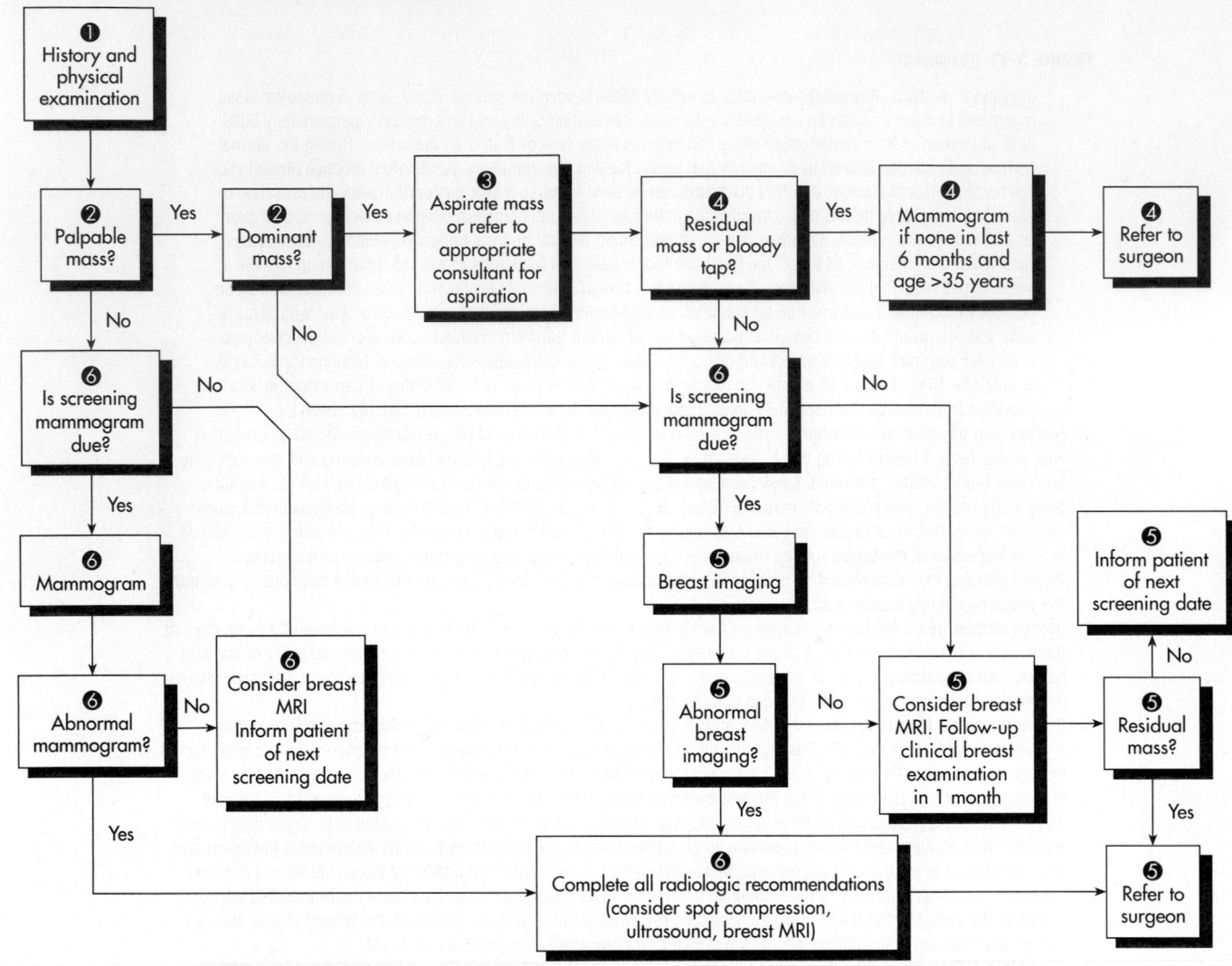

FIGURE 3-43 Breast cancer screening and evaluation. (Modified from Institute for Clinical Systems Integration, Minneapolis: *Postgrad Med* 100:182, 1996.)

1. **History and physical examination.**[3] Primary care evaluation is initiated with history taking aimed at uncovering and characterizing any breast-related symptom. A risk assessment should also be undertaken for identified risk factors, including patient age over 50 years, any past personal history of breast cancer, history of hyperplasia on previous breast biopsies, and family history of breast cancer in first-degree relatives (mother, sister, daughter). Physical examination should include inspection of the breast for any evidence of ulceration or contour changes and inspection of the nipple for Paget's disease. Palpation should be performed with the patient in both the upright and supine positions to determine the presence of any palpable mass.

2. **Palpable mass? Dominant mass?** A dominant mass is a palpable finding that is discrete and clearly different from the surrounding parenchyma. If a palpable mass is identified, it should be determined whether it represents a dominant (i.e., discrete) mass, which requires immediate evaluation. The primary care physician or appropriate consultant should attempt to aspirate any dominant mass because a simple cyst may be uncovered, in which case aspiration completes the evaluation process.

3. **Aspirate mass or refer for aspiration.** Aspiration of a dominant palpable mass should be performed by the primary care physician or by the appropriate consultant. The breast skin is prepped with alcohol. Then, with the lesion immobilized by the nonoperating hand, an 18- to 25-gauge needle mounted on a 10-ml syringe is directed to the central portion of the mass for a single attempt at aspiration. Successful aspiration of a simple cyst would yield a nonbloody fluid with complete resolution of the dominant mass. Typical watery fluid may be discarded. However, cyst fluid that is bloody or unusually tenacious should be examined cytologically.

[3]CSI health care guidelines are designed to assist clinicians by providing an analytic framework for the evaluation and treatment of patients. They are not intended either to replace a clinician's judgment or to establish a protocol for all patients with a particular condition. A guideline will rarely establish the only approach to a problem. In addition, guidelines are living documents that are expected to be imperfect and are subject to annual review and revision.

FIGURE 3-43 (Continued)

4. **Residual mass or bloody tap?** Mammogram if none in past 6 months. Refer to surgeon. Should the mass remain after the attempt at aspiration or should frank blood be aspirated during the process, the presence of a malignant process cannot be ruled out. Patients with a residual mass or bloody tap should be referred to a surgeon for possible biopsy. Before the referral, a mammogram should be obtained for any patient over age 35 years who has not had a mammogram within the preceding 6 months. In patients 35 years and under, obtaining any other breast-imaging studies should be left to the discretion of the surgeon or radiologist.

5. **Is screening mammogram due?** Breast imaging. Follow-up clinical breast examination. Refer to surgeon. Should physical examination demonstrate a palpable mass that is not clearly a discrete and dominant mass, its size, location, and character should be documented in anticipation of a follow-up examination. A screening mammogram should be obtained if one has not been done within the recommended interval. If no mammogram is required or if a required mammogram demonstrates no abnormality, a follow-up examination in 1 month is indicated. Breast MRI should be considered. Should any residual mass be identified, the patient should be referred to a surgeon for possible biopsy. Patients with a persisting nondominant palpable mass that does not resolve within 1 month and those with any recurring cystic mass should be referred for surgical evaluation. If no mass is apparent at the time of the follow-up examination, the patient should then be informed of the appropriate date for her next screening examination, according to the recommended intervals.

6. **Screening mammogram and results.** After completion of the physical examination, the appropriateness of a routine screening mammogram should be determined. If a mammogram is done, the radiologist should provide the results to the primary care physician for reporting to the patient. Should any abnormalities be uncovered, it will be the responsibility of the radiologist to complete any additional imaging studies required for the complete radiographic characterization of the lesion. The radiologist should make certain that all recommended additional views, follow-up studies, and ultrasound examinations have been completed before referral to a surgeon. However, it is important that the primary care physician who ordered the mammogram review the results of these studies to understand fully the opinion of the radiologist and to ensure that all recommendations of the radiologist have been completed. Should the radiologist recommend that surgical consultation is warranted, it will be the responsibility of the primary care physician to establish this referral.

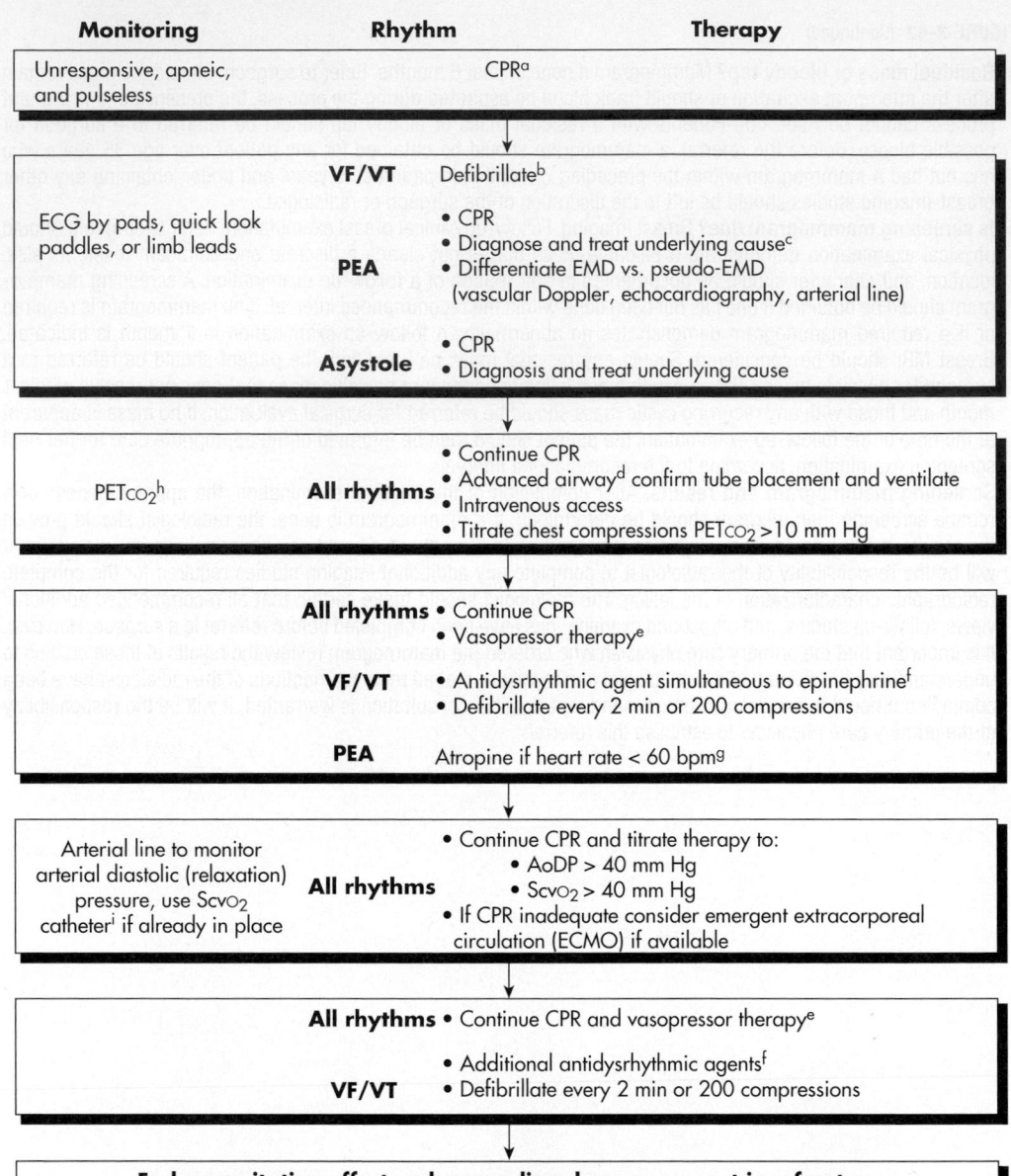

Monitoring	Rhythm	Therapy
Unresponsive, apneic, and pulseless		CPR[a]

	VF/VT	Defibrillate[b]
ECG by pads, quick look paddles, or limb leads	PEA	• CPR • Diagnose and treat underlying cause[c] • Differentiate EMD vs. pseudo-EMD (vascular Doppler, echocardiography, arterial line)
	Asystole	• CPR • Diagnosis and treat underlying cause

PETco2[h]	All rhythms	• Continue CPR • Advanced airway[d] confirm tube placement and ventilate • Intravenous access • Titrate chest compressions PETco2 >10 mm Hg

	All rhythms	• Continue CPR • Vasopressor therapy[e]
	VF/VT	• Antidysrhythmic agent simultaneous to epinephrine[f] • Defibrillate every 2 min or 200 compressions
	PEA	Atropine if heart rate < 60 bpm[g]

Arterial line to monitor arterial diastolic (relaxation) pressure, use Scvo2 catheter[i] if already in place	All rhythms	• Continue CPR and titrate therapy to:
		  • AoDP > 40 mm Hg
		  • Scvo2 > 40 mm Hg
		• If CPR inadequate consider emergent extracorporeal circulation (ECMO) if available

	All rhythms	• Continue CPR and vasopressor therapy[e]
	VF/VT	• Additional antidysrhythmic agents[f] • Defibrillate every 2 min or 200 compressions

End resuscitative efforts when cardiopulmonary arrest is refractory to optimized therapy and reversible causes have been corrected.

FIGURE 3-46 Emergency treatment algorithm for treatment of cardiac arrest. [a]If arrest is witnessed and known to be of short duration, immediate rhythm assessment and defibrillation or ventricular fibrillation/ventricular tachycardia (VF/VT) precede cardiopulmonary resuscitation (CPR). In cases of prolonged untreated VF/VT, 1 to 2 minutes of CPR before defibrillation may enhance the ability to achieve return of spontaneous circulation. *EMD,* Electromechanical dissociation; *PEA,* pulseless electrical activity. [b]Biphasic defibrillation should use manufacturer-recommended energy versus monophasic defibrillation (360 J). [c]See Section I, Pulseless Electrical Activity. [d]Endotracheal intubation or supraglottic airway when feasible with minimal interruption in chest compressions. [e]Epinephrine, initial dose of 1 mg intravenously (IV) or intraosseously (IO), or 2.5 mg by endotracheal tube (ETT). Repeat every 3 to 5 minutes. Subsequent doses may be increased up to 0.1 mg/kg. An alternative to epinephrine is vasopressin, 40 U via IV push. Vasopressin is potentially more effective if the presenting rhythm is asystolic. The dose (40 U) can be repeated once in 3 minutes, followed by administration of epinephrine every 3 to 5 minutes. [f]Amiodarone, 300 mg via IV push, followed by 150 mg every 30 minutes. Lidocaine is an alternative antidysrhythmic if amiodarone is not available. Magnesium sulfate, 1 to 2 g via IV push in torsades de pointes or known hypomagnesemia. [g]Atropine, 1 mg via IV push or 2.5 mg by ETT. Repeat dose every 3 to 5 minutes to a total dose of 0.04 mg/kg. *AoDP,* Aortic diastolic pressure; *ECG,* electrocardiogram; *Scvo2,* central venous oxygen saturation. [h]Changes in the partial pressure of end-tidal carbon dioxide (PETco2) may not be predictive of myocardial blood flow in the setting of high-dose vasopressor therapy. [i]Invasive monitoring should be performed only if adequate personnel are available and if it would not delay therapeutic interventions. (From Marx JA, et al: *Rosen's emergency medicine,* ed 8, Philadelphia, 2014, Saunders.)

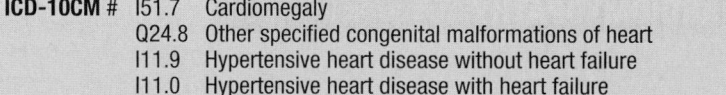

Evaluation of cardiomegaly on chest x-ray

↓

Review history
Examination
ECG

↓

Echocardiogram

| Left ventricular dilation | Biventricular dilation | Right ventricular dilation | Pericardial effusion/thickening/mass | No abnormalities |

Left ventricular dilation

Evaluate for:
  Valvular heart disease
  Coronary artery disease
  Cardiomyopathy

Biventricular dilation

Consider right heart failure secondary to left heart failure from various causes of left ventricular dilation

Right ventricular dilation

Pulmonary hypertension?

Pericardial effusion/thickening/mass

R/O tamponade → ? Pericardiocentesis

? Cause → Consider:
  CT
  MRI
  Surgery/biopsy

No abnormalities

No further workup

Yes:
Evaluate for:
  Pulmonary emboli
  Mitral stenosis
  Primary pulmonary hypertension
  Eisenmenger's syndrome

No:
Evaluate for:
  Atrial septal defect
  Tricuspid regurgitation

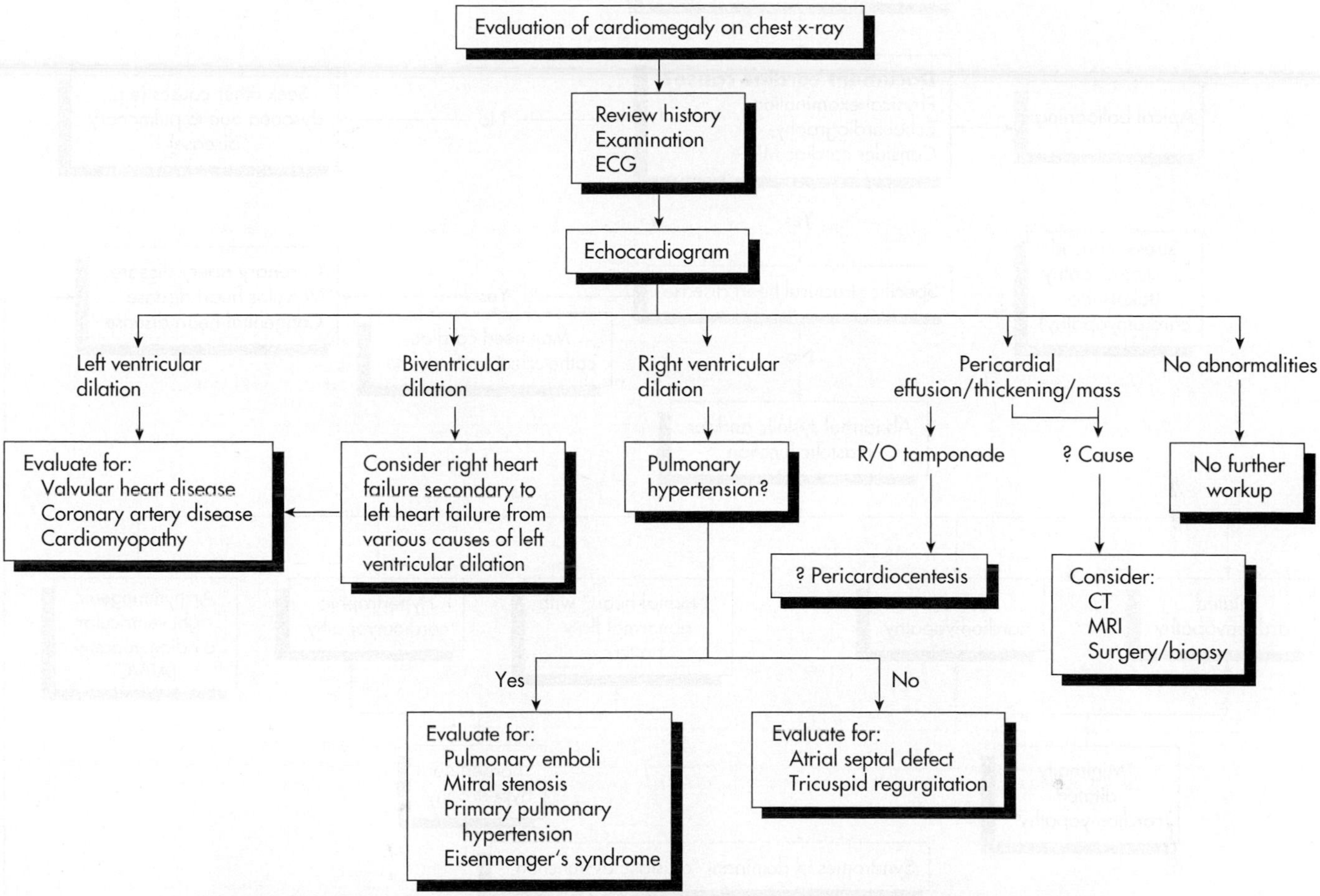

FIGURE 3-47 Approach to the patient with cardiomegaly. When cardiomegaly is found on the chest radiograph, the history and physical examination should be reviewed and an electrocardiogram *(ECG)* performed before obtaining a two-dimensional Doppler echocardiographic study. Cardiomegaly may be explained by left ventricular dilation, biventricular dilation, right ventricular dilation, or pericardial abnormalities, or it may be found to be spurious on the echocardiogram. Rarely, isolated abnormalities of the atrium, particularly the left atrium, may cause abnormalities on the chest radiograph but will not cause true cardiomegaly. Depending on the echocardiographic findings, further tests can help elucidate the cause of echocardiographically confirmed cardiomegaly. *CT,* Computed tomography; *MRI,* magnetic resonance imaging; *R/O,* rule out. (From Goldman L, Braunwald E [eds]: *Primary cardiology,* ed 2, Philadelphia, 2003, Saunders.)

Clinical Algorithms

III

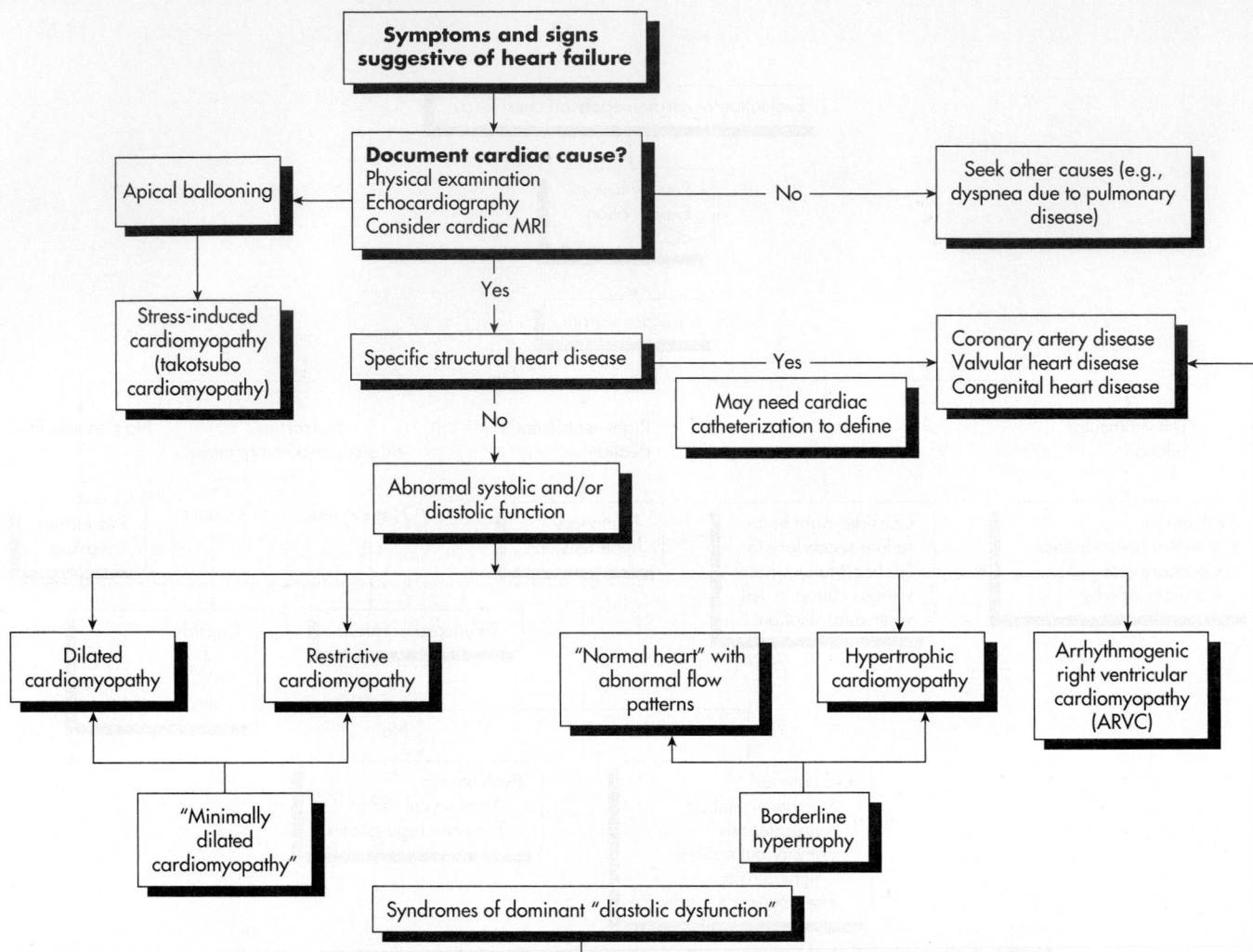

FIGURE 3-48 Initial approach to classification of cardiomyopathy. The evaluation of symptoms or signs consistent with heart failure first includes confirmation that they can be attributed to a cardiac cause. Although this conclusion is often apparent from routine physical examination, echocardiography serves to confirm cardiac disease and provides clues to the presence of other cardiac disease, such as focal abnormalities, suggesting primary valve disease or congenital heart disease. Having excluded these conditions, cardiomyopathy is generally considered to be dilated, restrictive, or hypertrophic. Patients with apparently normal cardiac structure and contraction are occasionally found to demonstrate abnormal intracardiac flow patterns consistent with diastolic dysfunction but should also be evaluated carefully for other causes of their symptoms. Most patients with so-called diastolic dysfunction also demonstrate at least borderline criteria for left ventricular hypertrophy, frequently in the setting of chronic hypertension and diabetes. A moderately decreased ejection fraction without marked dilation or a pattern of restrictive cardiomyopathy is sometimes referred to as "minimally dilated cardiomyopathy," which may represent either a distinct entity or a transition between acute and chronic disease. (From Goldman L, Ausiello D [eds]: *Cecil textbook of medicine*, ed 23, Philadelphia, 2008, Saunders.)

Table 3-2 Profiles of Myocardial Disease

	Hypertrophic	Dilated	Restrictive	ARVC
Causes	Genetic	Myocarditis Metabolic/endocrine Genetic	Infiltrative or storage diseases Endomyocardial (e.g., Löffler's, carcinoid)	Genetic
Ejection fraction	Increased	Reduced	25%-50%	Normal until end stage 30% regional LV disease
Left ventricular End-diastolic dimension	Usually decreased	Increased	Normal	Normal until end stage Right ventricle dilated
Left ventricular wall thickness	Increased	Normal	Normal or mildly increased	Normal
Atrial size	Increased	Increased	Increased; may be massive	Left atrium normal; right dilated in severe disease
Valvular disease	Mitral regurgitation (SAM)	Mitral (functional); tricuspid regurgitation in late stages	Mitral and tricuspid regurgitation, rarely severe	Tricuspid regurgitation in severe disease
Common symptoms	Dyspnea; chest pain, syncope Late: orthopnea, PND	Dyspnea, fatigue Late: orthopnea, PND	Dyspnea Late: orthopnea, PND, right heart failure	Palpitations, syncope Late: right heart failure
Arrhythmia	Atrial fibrillation, ventricular tachycardia; conduction block in PRKAG2, mitochondrial; Fabry's disease	Ventricular tachyarrhythmias; heart block in Chagas' disease, giant cell myocarditis, laminopathies	Atrial fibrillation; conduction block in sarcoid, amyloidosis, desminopathy	Ventricular ectopy and tachycardia

ARVC, Arrhythmogenic right ventricular cardiomyopathy; *LV,* left ventricular; *SAM,* systolic anterior motion of mitral valve; *PND,* paroxysmal nocturnal dyspnea.
From Goldman L, Schafer AI [eds]: *Goldman's Cecil medicine,* ed 24, Philadelphia, 2012, Saunders.

Clinical
Algorithms

III

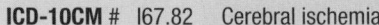

ICD-10CM #	I67.82	Cerebral ischemia
	I67.81	Acute cerebrovascular insufficiency
	I67.89	Other cerebrovascular disease
	I67.848	Other cerebrovascular vasospasm and vasoconstriction
	G45.9	Transient cerebral ischemic attack, unspecified

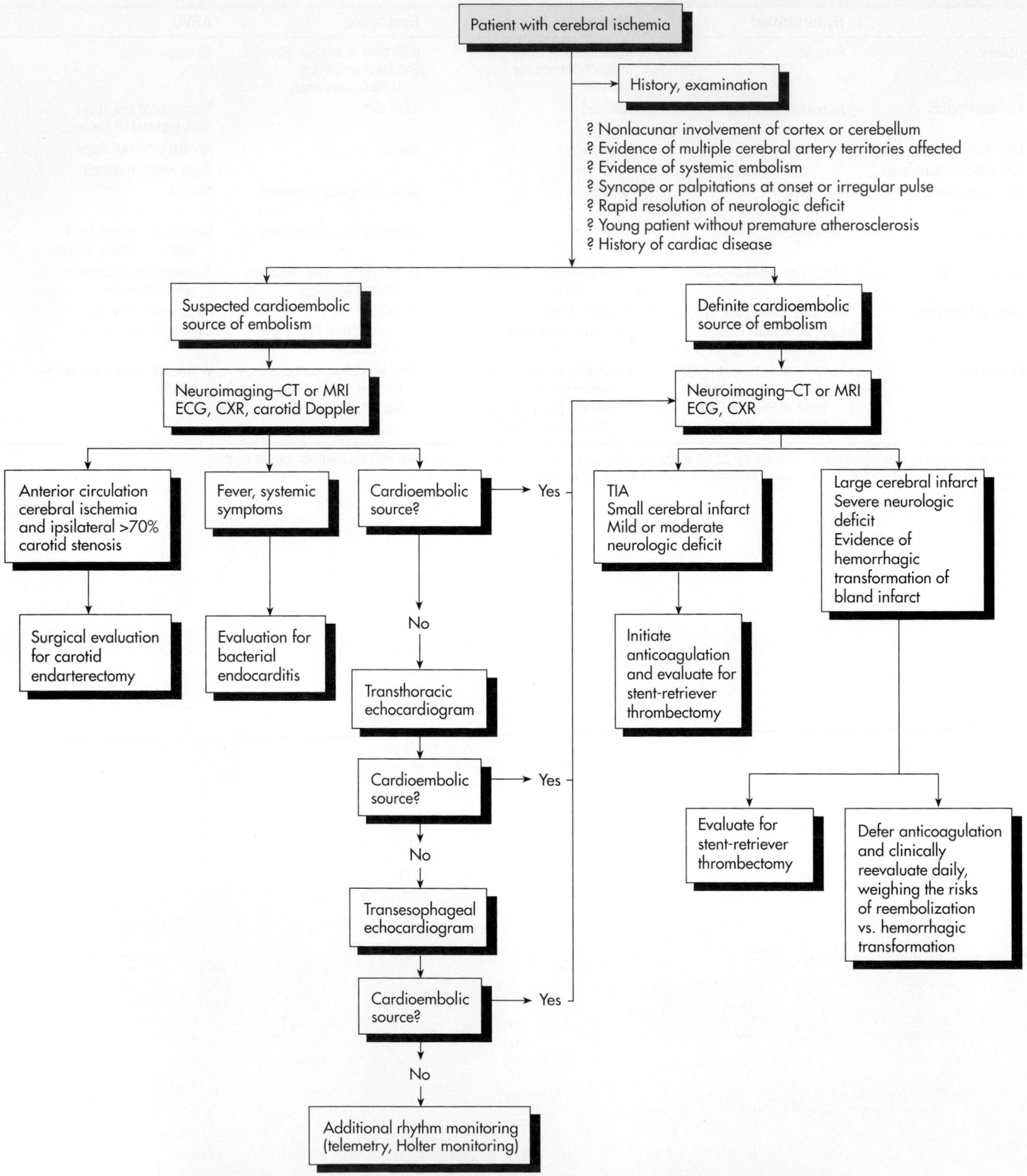

Patient with cerebral ischemia

History, examination

? Nonlacunar involvement of cortex or cerebellum
? Evidence of multiple cerebral artery territories affected
? Evidence of systemic embolism
? Syncope or palpitations at onset or irregular pulse
? Rapid resolution of neurologic deficit
? Young patient without premature atherosclerosis
? History of cardiac disease

Suspected cardioembolic source of embolism

Definite cardioembolic source of embolism

Neuroimaging—CT or MRI
ECG, CXR, carotid Doppler

Neuroimaging—CT or MRI
ECG, CXR

Anterior circulation cerebral ischemia and ipsilateral >70% carotid stenosis

Fever, systemic symptoms

Cardioembolic source? → Yes

TIA
Small cerebral infarct
Mild or moderate neurologic deficit

Large cerebral infarct
Severe neurologic deficit
Evidence of hemorrhagic transformation of bland infarct

Surgical evaluation for carotid endarterectomy

Evaluation for bacterial endocarditis

No

Initiate anticoagulation and evaluate for stent-retriever thrombectomy

Transthoracic echocardiogram

Cardioembolic source? → Yes

No

Evaluate for stent-retriever thrombectomy

Defer anticoagulation and clinically reevaluate daily, weighing the risks of reembolization vs. hemorrhagic transformation

Transesophageal echocardiogram

Cardioembolic source? → Yes

No

Additional rhythm monitoring (telemetry, Holter monitoring)

FIGURE 3-50 Evaluation of patients with cerebral ischemia for a cardioembolic source. *CT,* Computed tomography; *CXR,* chest radiograph; *ECG,* electrocardiogram; *MRI,* magnetic resonance imaging; *TIA,* transient ischemic attack. (Modified from Johnson R [ed]: *Current therapy in neurologic disease,* ed 5, St Louis, 1997, Mosby.)

CHEST PAIN

ICD-10CM # R07.2 Pain(s) heart
R07.3 Pain(s) chest anterior wall
R07.4 Pain(s) chest

1563

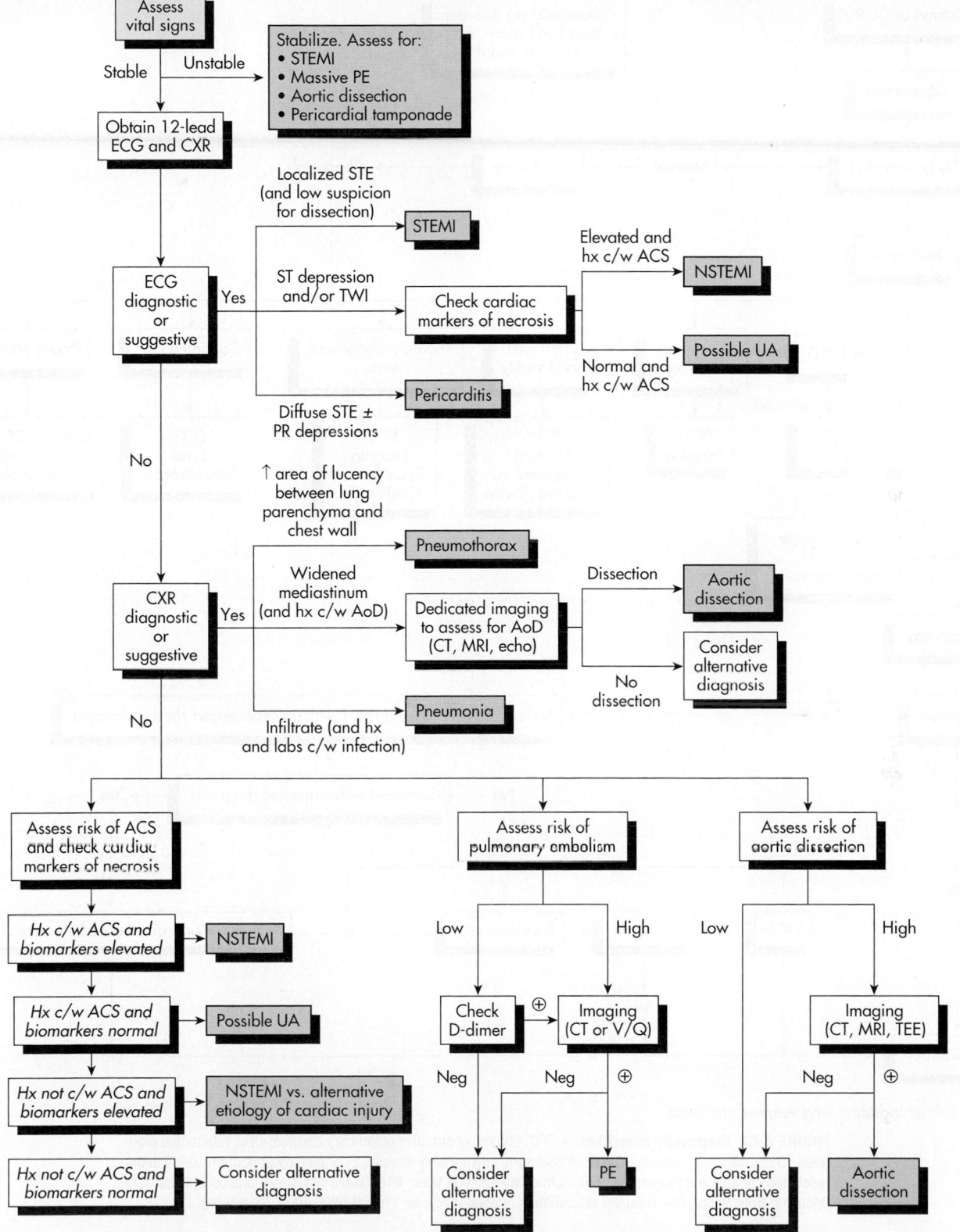

FIGURE 3-51 Algorithm for the initial diagnostic approach to a patient with chest pain. *AoD,* Aortic dissection; *c/w,* consistent with; *CXR,* chest x-ray; *hx,* history; *NSTEMI,* non–ST-segment myocardial infarction; *PE,* pulmonary embolism; *STE,* ST elevation; *STEMI,* ST-segment myocardial infarction; *TEE,* transesophageal echocardiography; *UA,* unstable angina; *V/Q,* ventilation-perfusion scan. (From Bonow RO et al: *Braunwauld's heart disease,* ed 9, Philadelphia, 2012, Elsevier.)

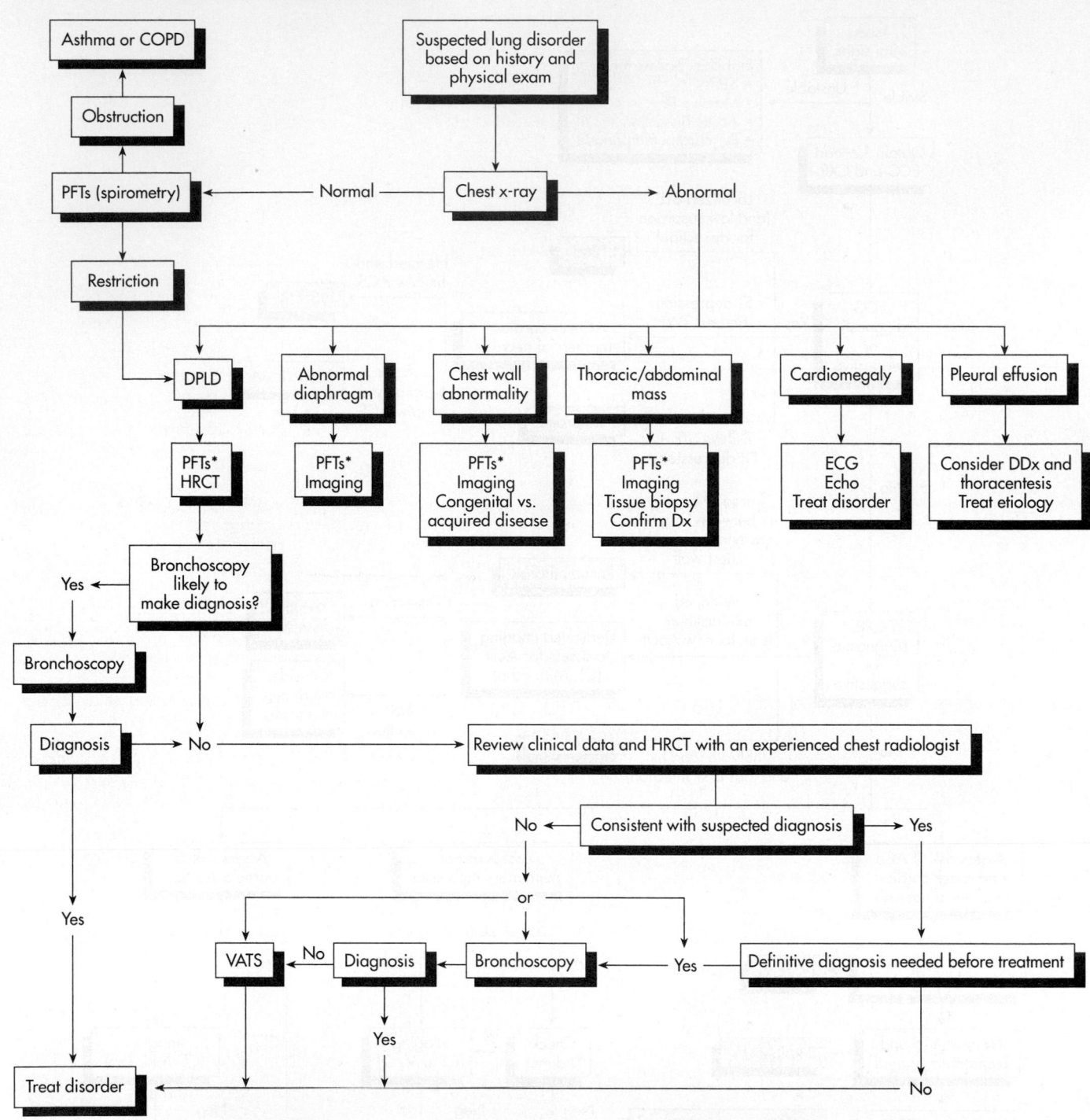

FIGURE 3-52 Diagnostic algorithm. *COPD,* Chronic obstructive pulmonary disease; *DDx,* differential diagnosis; *D LCO,* diffusion capacity; *DPLD,* diffuse parenchymal lung disease; *ECG,* electrocardiogram; *HRCT,* high-resolution computed tomography; *PFTs,* pulmonary function tests; *VATS,* video-assisted thoracoscopic surgery. (Modified from Runge MS, Greganti MA: *Netter's internal medicine,* Philadelphia, 2008, Saunders.)

*PFTs = Full set including lung volumes and DLCO

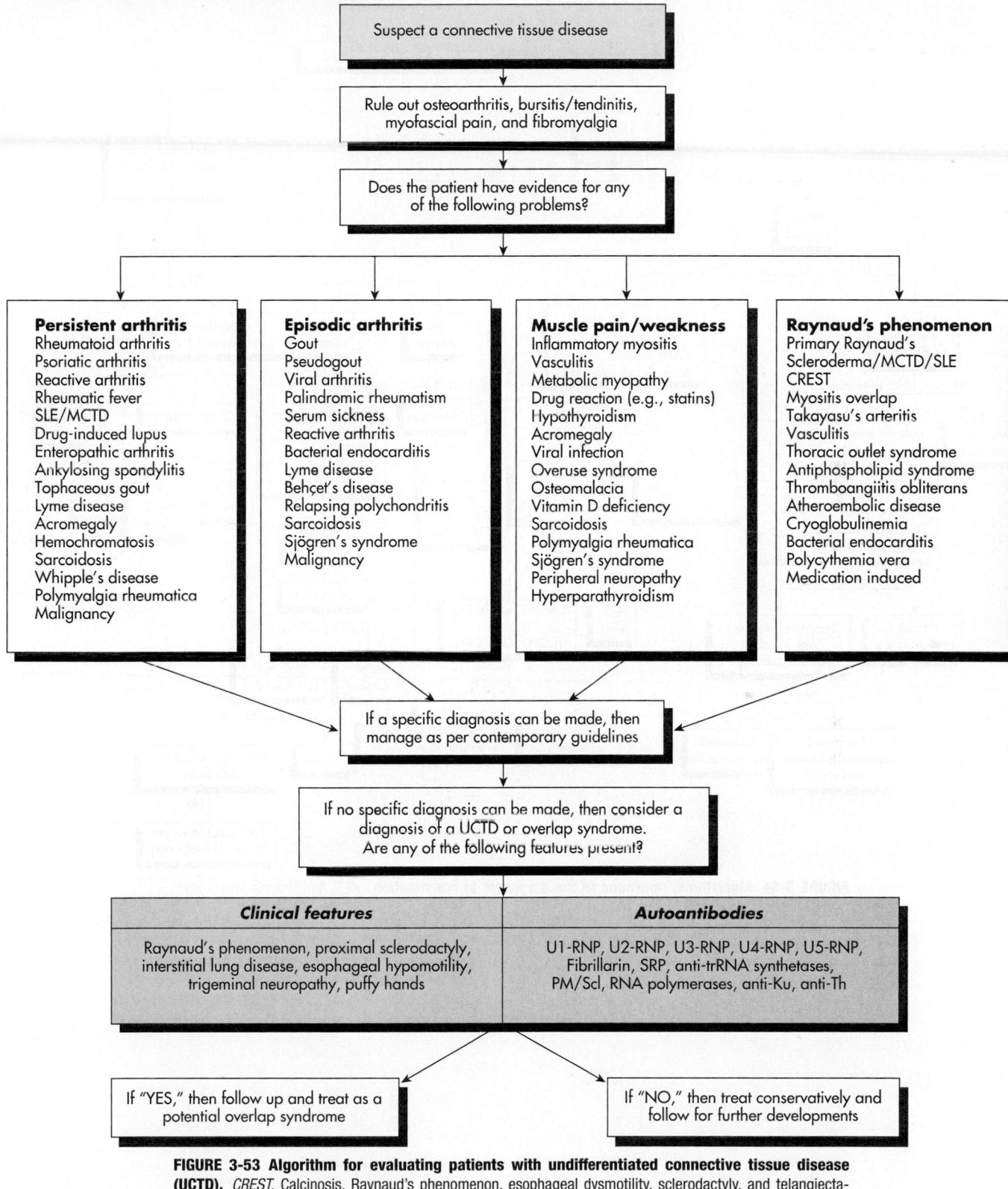

FIGURE 3-53 Algorithm for evaluating patients with undifferentiated connective tissue disease (UCTD). *CREST,* Calcinosis, Raynaud's phenomenon, esophageal dysmotility, sclerodactyly, and telangiectasia; *MCTD,* mixed connective tissue disease; *SLE,* systemic lupus erythematosus. (From Firestein GS, Budd RC, Gabriel SE, et al: *Kelley's textbook of rheumatology,* ed 9, Philadelphia, 2013, Saunders. [Original credit: Courtesy Dr. George Raj, Non Surgical Spine and Joint Clinic PS, Bellingham, Wash.])

Clinical Algorithms

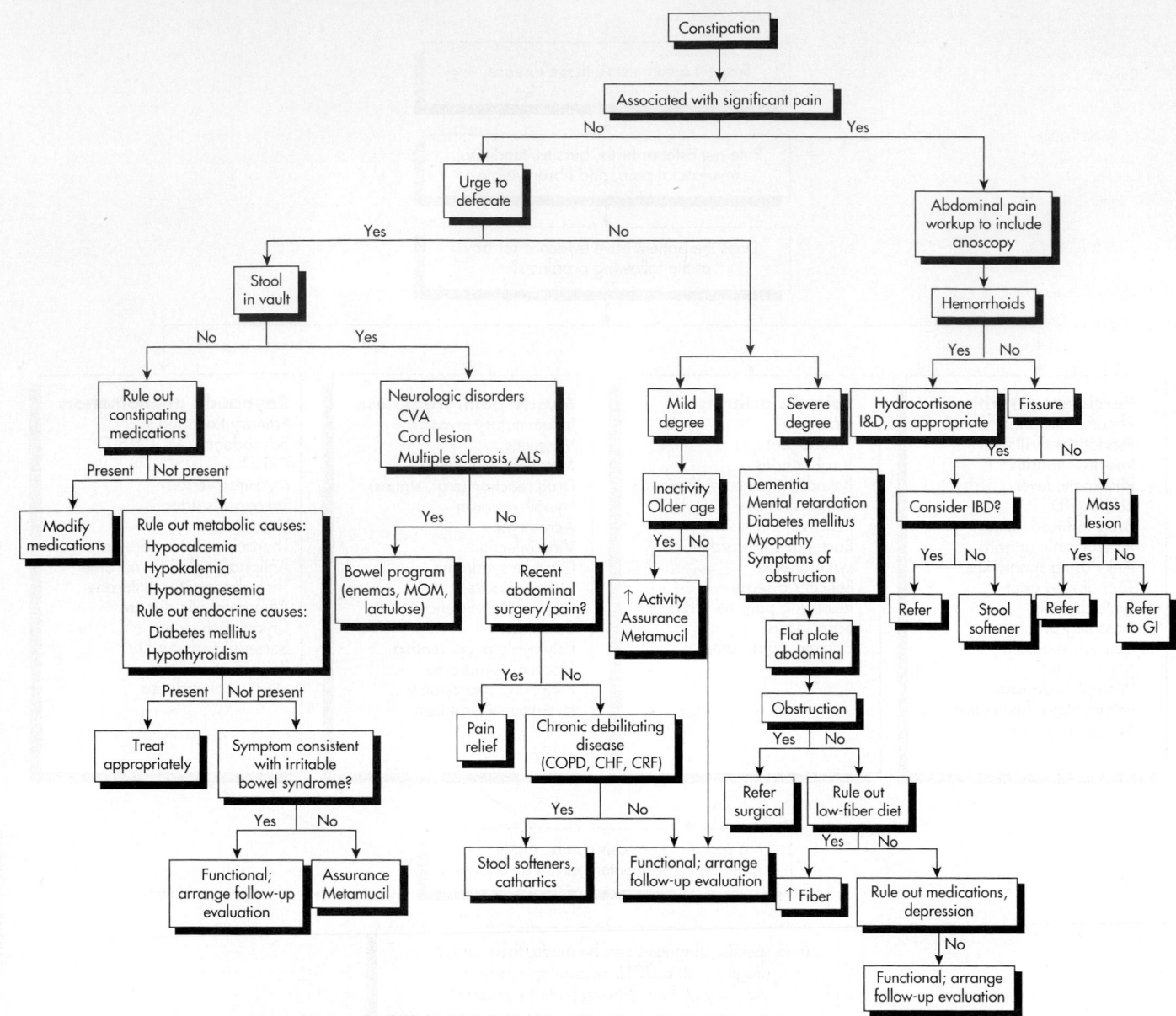

FIGURE 3-54 Algorithmic approach to the diagnosis of constipation. *ALS,* Amyotrophic lateral sclerosis; *CHF,* congestive heart failure; *COPD,* chronic obstructive pulmonary disease; *CRF,* chronic renal failure; *CVA,* cerebrovascular accident; *GI,* gastroenterology; *IBD,* inflammatory bowel disease; *I&D,* incision and drainage; *MOM,* milk of magnesia. (From Marx JA et al: *Rosen's emergency medicine,* ed 8, Philadelphia, 2014, Saunders.)

Table 3-3 Preparations Used in the Symptomatic Treatment of Constipation

Medication	Maximal Recommended Dose	Onset of Action	Comments
Bulk Laxatives			Indigestible fiber attracts water, which leads to larger, softer fecal mass.
Psyllium (Metamucil)	Titrate up to 20 g	12-72 hr	Natural fiber that undergoes bacterial degradation, which may contribute to bloating and flatus. Should be taken with plenty of water to avoid intestinal obstruction.
Methylcellulose (Citrucel)	Titrate up to 20 g		Semisynthetic cellulose fiber that is relatively resistant to colonic bacterial degradation.
Polycarbophil (Fibercon)	Titrate up to 20 g		Synthetic fiber of polymer of acrylic acid, resistant to bacterial degradation.
Osmotic Laxatives			Draw water into the intestines along osmotic gradient.
Magnesium or Sodium Salts			
Magnesium hydroxide (milk of magnesia)	30-45 ml once daily	1-6 hr	A small percentage of magnesium is absorbed—use caution in patients with renal insufficiency and in children.
Magnesium citrate	150-300 ml as needed	3-6 hr	
Sodium phosphate (Fleet Phospho-soda)	20-45 ml with 12 oz of water as needed		Hyperphosphatemia may result if patient has renal insufficiency. Commonly used before colonoscopy.
Poorly Absorbed Sugars			
Lactulose	15-30 ml once or twice a day	24-48 hr	Synthetic disaccharide not absorbed by the small intestine. Gas and bloating common.
Sorbitol	15-30 ml once or twice a day		Poorly absorbed by small intestine.
Polyethylene glycol and electrolytes (GoLYTELY, MiraLax)	17 g two or three times a day	12-24 hr	Organic polymers that are poorly absorbed and not metabolized by bacteria, thus may cause less bloating and cramping. Can be mixed with noncarbonated beverages.
Stimulant Laxatives			Stimulate intestinal motility or secretion.
Senna (Senokot, Ex-Lax)	8-34 mg daily	6-12 hr	Stimulates secretion and motility of small intestine and colon.
Bisacodyl (Dulcolax, Correctol)	5-10 mg daily		
Stool Softeners			Increase water penetration and soften stool.
Docusate sodium (Colace)	100 mg twice a day; some use higher doses	24-48 hr	In many studies, no better than placebo. Not recommended as first-line or solo therapy.
Mineral oil (Fleet mineral oil)	5-15 ml orally at night		Provides lubrication for the passage of stool. Long-term use is not recommended. Lipid pneumonia can occur in patients predisposed to aspiration.
Newer Agents			
Lubiprostone (Amitiza)	24 µg once or twice per day	1 hr	A chloride channel activator. FDA approved for treatment of chronic idiopathic constipation in adults. Adverse effects: headache, nausea, diarrhea.
Methylnaltrexone (Relistor)	8-12 mg SQ		Used in refractory opioid-induced constipation.
Linaclotide (Linzess)	145 mcg daily 30 min prior to meals	2-6 hr	Peptide agonist of the guanylate cyclase 2C. It increases smooth muscle contractions. Useful in IBS with constipation.

FDA, U.S. Food and Drug Administration; *SQ,* subcutaneously.
From Marx JA et al: *Rosen's emergency medicine,* ed 8, Philadelphia, 2014, Saunders.

BOX 3-3 General Approach to Treatment of Constipation

For specific agents, dosages, and precautions, see Table 3-3.

I. Core Program for All Patients
- Adequate intake of fluid and fiber is one key to preventing constipation. Fiber is available primarily from grains and bran cereals. Flatulence, bloating, and cramps are common side effects encountered when bran fiber is introduced.
- Another source of bulk is from synthetic bulk agents (e.g., psyllium). Bulk agents require an adequate amount of fluid intake; otherwise, they may worsen constipation.
- Avoid irritant laxatives as part of a core program because long-term use may decrease bowel motility. Encourage the patient to exercise and respond promptly to the urge to defecate.

II. Individualized Program-Specific Indications and General Comments
- *Stimulant laxatives (e.g., senna, bisacodyl):* Many believe that long-term use of these agents leads to dependency and habituation, but this is not substantiated. When used appropriately, these medications are not harmful and are very effective. Senna is probably the first-line choice among this class of laxatives.

- *Osmotic laxatives (e.g., polyethylene glycol [PEG], lactulose, milk of magnesia, magnesium citrate):* These agents are most commonly used for colonic preparation before bowel procedures. These agents are safe and well tolerated. PEG has been shown to be slightly more effective than lactulose and causes less bloating and flatus.
- *Lubricants and stool softeners:* Oral mineral oil lubricants and stool softeners are particularly helpful in patients who have acute painful perianal lesions. The softening and coating of the stool can make passage much easier and less painful, preventing constipation. Mineral oil is contraindicated in patients with swallowing problems or in those who are particularly debilitated, to prevent aspiration leading to lipid pneumonia.
- *Suppositories and enemas:* These agents may be helpful in patients who tend to have trouble expelling soft stool from the rectum. Glycerin suppositories may have a soothing effect and be helpful in patients with constipation caused by local, painful perianal lesions. Tap-water enemas are helpful when disimpaction is necessary.

From Marx JA et al: *Rosen's emergency medicine,* ed 8, Philadelphia, 2014, Saunders.

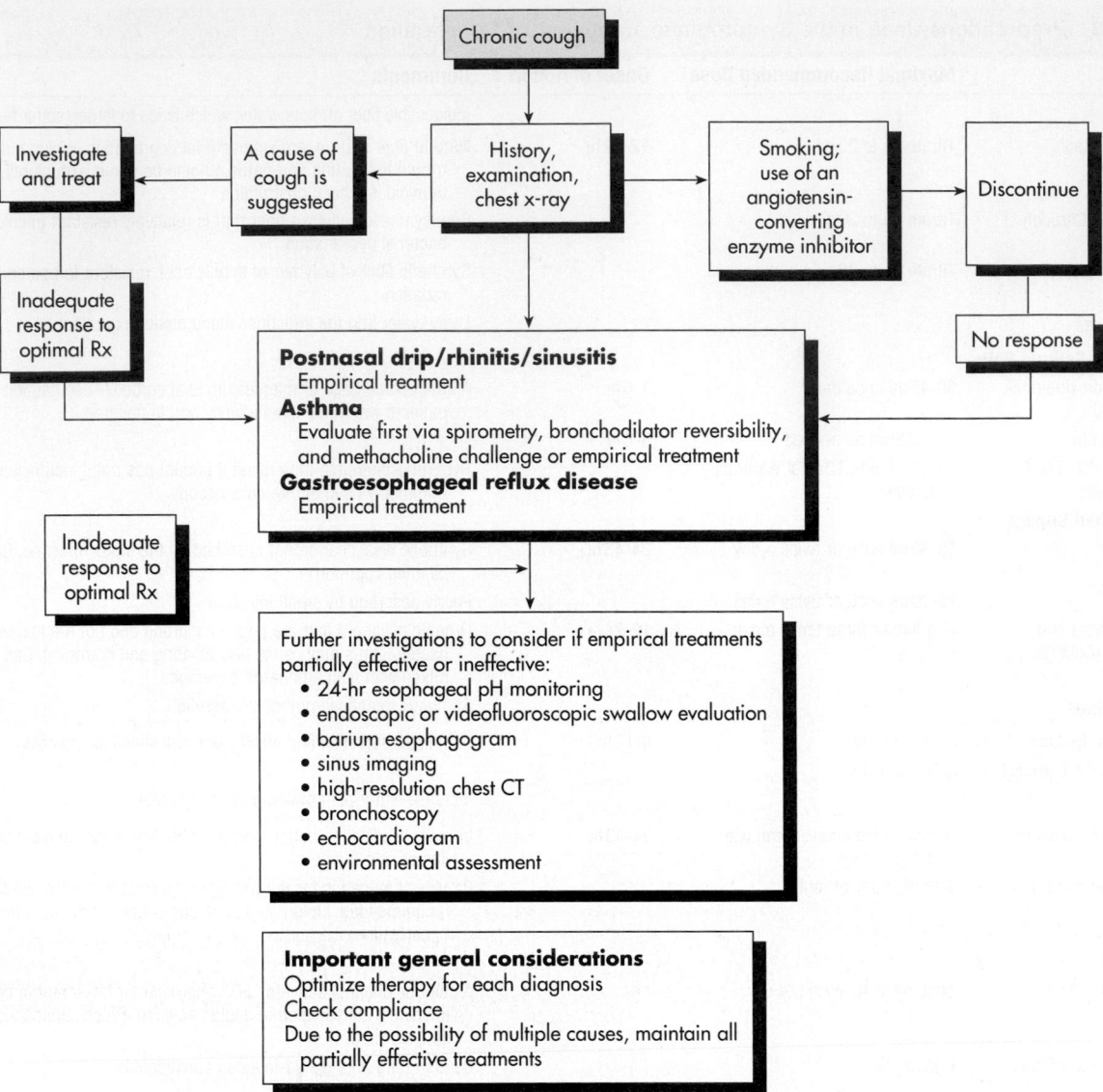

FIGURE 3-57 Algorithm for the management of chronic cough lasting >8 weeks. *CT,* Computed tomography; *Rx,* prescription. (From Goldman L, Schafer AI: *Goldman's Cecil medicine,* ed 24, Philadelphia, 2012, Saunders.)

Table 3-4   Testing Characteristics of Diagnostic Protocol for Evaluation of Chronic Cough

Tests	Diagnosis	Positive Predictive Value (%)	Negative Predictive Value (%)
Sinus radiograph	Sinusitis	57-81	95-100
Methacholine inhalation challenge	Asthma	60-82	100
Modified barium esophagography	GERD, esophageal stricture	38-63	63-93
Esophageal pH*	GERD	89-100	>100
Bronchoscopy	Endobronchial mass/lesion	50-89	100

*24-Hour esophageal pH monitoring. *GERD,* Gastroesophageal reflux disease.
From Goldman L, Schafer AI [eds]: *Goldman's Cecil medicine,* ed 24, Philadelphia, 2012, Saunders.

Table 3-5   Definitions and Common Causes of Cough in Adults and Children

Age Group	Type of Cough	Duration	Common Causes
Adults	Acute	<3 weeks	• Common cold • Exacerbation of lung disease (e.g., asthma) • Acute environmental exposure • Acute cardiopulmonary disease
	Subacute	3-8 weeks	• Postinfectious cough • Pertussis infection • Exacerbation of underlying lung disease (e.g., asthma, COPD, bronchiectasis)
	Chronic	>8 weeks	• ACEI therapy • Smoking/chronic bronchitis • Underlying lung disease • UACS • Asthma • NAEB • GERD
Children	Acute	<4 weeks	• Common cold • Exacerbation of underlying lung disease • Acute cardiopulmonary disease
	Chronic	>4 weeks	• Asthma • Protracted bacterial bronchitis • Tracheobronchomalacia • Chronic rhinosinusitis • Recurrent aspiration • GERD • Underlying lung disease (e.g., bronchiectasis) • Pulmonary infections (e.g., pertussis)

ACEI, Angiotensin-converting enzyme inhibitor; *COPD,* chronic obstructive pulmonary disease; *GERD,* gastroesophageal reflux disease; *NAEB,* nonasthmatic eosinophilic bronchitis; *UACS,* upper airway cough syndrome.
From Adkinson NF et al: *Middleton's allergy principles and practice,* ed 8, Philadelphia, 2014, Saunders.

BOX 3-4   Pitfalls and Errors in the Diagnosis and Management of Chronic Cough in Adults

General Considerations
• Failing to consider that UACS, asthma/NAEB, and/or GERD are likely when the chest radiograph is normal or near-normal in appearance and the patient is a nonsmoker and is not taking an ACEI
• Failing to include UACS, asthma/NAEB, and/or GERD in the differential diagnosis because clinical or radiographic evidence confirms the presence of an "obvious" cause of the patient's cough (e.g., solitary pulmonary nodule, idiopathic pulmonary fibrosis)
• Not recognizing multiple simultaneous causes of cough
• Failing to continue treatment trials long enough to accurately assess their effectiveness
• Prematurely diagnosing "unexplained" cough before a bronchoscopy has been performed to assess for unsuspected airway disease
• Mistakenly diagnosing "unexplained" cough or diagnosing psychogenic cough before a complete evaluation for cough has been performed

Upper Airway Cough Syndrome
• Failing to realize that UACS can manifest as cough productive of phlegm
• Not recognizing that chronic cough can be the sole manifestation of UACS in at least 20% of the cases
• Failing to consider sinusitis as a cause of UACS
• Mistakenly assuming that selective histamine H_1 receptor antagonists are effective in treating nonallergic causes of UACS
• Missing allergic rhinitis because symptoms are perennial
• Missing aspirin-exacerbated disease in a patient with nasal polyps

Asthma/NAEB
• Failing to realize that these conditions can sometimes manifest as cough productive of phlegm

• Not recognizing that chronic cough can sometimes be the sole manifestation of asthma (so-called cough variant asthma)
• Mistakenly assuming that a positive result on bronchial challenge (e.g., methacholine challenge) is diagnostic of asthma when it is merely *consistent* with the diagnosis
• Failing to consider NAEB when the bronchial challenge test yields a negative result
• Not recognizing that inhaled medications can sometimes provoke cough
• Failing to consider occupational and environmental causes of asthma/NAEB

Gastroesophageal Reflux Disease
• Failing to realize that GERD can sometimes manifest as cough productive of phlegm
• Not recognizing that chronic cough can sometimes be the sole manifestation of GERD (so-called silent GERD)
• Mistakenly concluding that cough cannot be due to GERD simply because cough does not resolve with relief of gastrointestinal symptoms
• Not considering nonacid reflux and mistakenly assuming that cough will always respond to acid suppression
• Failing to assess the adequacy of GERD treatment by using 24-hour monitoring of esophageal pH and impedance
• Not recognizing coexisting diseases (e.g., sleep apnea) and medications (e.g., nitrates, progesterone) that may impair the effectiveness of GERD treatment
• Failing to recognize that surgery may help when intensive medical therapy has failed

Angiotensin-Converting Enzyme Inhibitor
• Failing to consider ACEI therapy as a cause of chronic cough simply because the cough predated initiation of the ACEI
• Mistakenly concluding that ACEI therapy is not the cause of chronic cough because the cough did not resolve within 1 to 3 weeks of stopping the ACEI

ACEI, Angiotensin-converting enzyme inhibitor; *GERD,* gastroesophageal reflux disease; *NAEB,* nonasthmatic eosinophilic bronchitis; *UACS,* upper airway cough syndrome.
From Adkinson NF et al: *Middleton's allergy principles and practice,* ed 8, Philadelphia, 2014, Saunders.

Clinical Algorithms

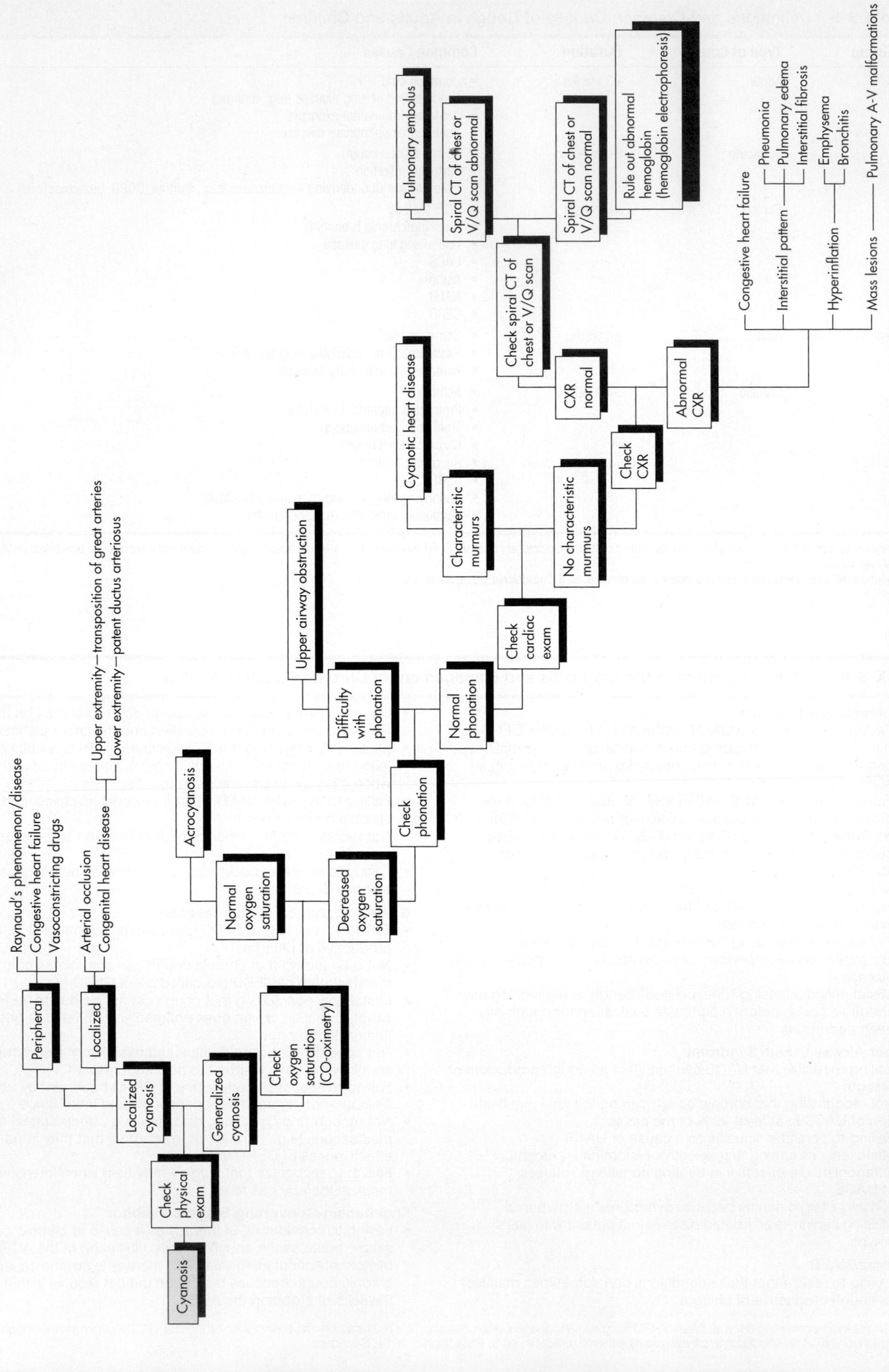

FIGURE 3-59 Cyanosis. *A-V,* Arteriovenous; *CXR,* chest x-ray; *V/Q,* ventilation-perfusion. (From Healey PM: *Common medical diagnosis: an algorithmic approach,* ed 3, Philadelphia, 2000, Saunders.)

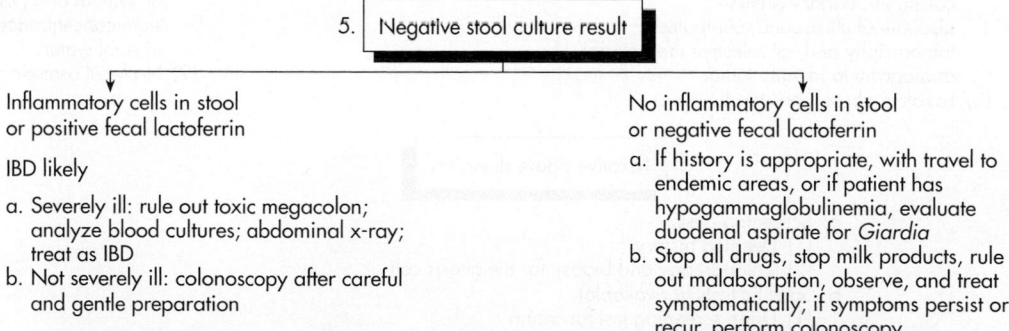

1. Physical examination

Hydrate as necessary

2. Stool examination*

Inflammatory cells (Fecal lactoferrin testing has largely replaced testing for fecal leukocytes as a screen for inflammatory diarrhea)

Present: suggests mucosal disease
a. IBD
b. Invasive bacterial infections (such as *Shigella* spp., *Salmonella* spp., amebiasis, *Campylobacter*), or
Absent: suggests viral gastroenteritis, toxin (*Staphylococcus, Escherichia coli, Aeromonas Plesiomonas* spp.), or drug-related diarrhea or IBS

Ova and parasites

Blood: if present, consider:
a. IBD
b. Bacterial infections:
Salmonella spp.
Shigella spp.
Amebiasis
Campylobacter
Clostridium difficile toxin
E. coli O157:H7

3. Culture stool*

Positive culture result

Treat appropriately, except for *Salmonella* infections in which treatment may prolong the carrier state

Negative culture result

See step 5

4. Flexible sigmoidoscopy†

Abnormal mucosa

a. Pseudomembranes: check for *C. difficile* toxin: treat with metronidazole or vancomycin
b. Ulcerations/granularity
(1) Proctitis only: culture for *Chlamydia trachomatis, Neisseria gonorrhoeae*; Gram stain and culture urethra and pharynx; biopsy as in (2)
(2) More extensive: culture; biopsy to look for amebae, granulomas, or nonspecific finding of IBD

Normal mucosa

Wait for culture results

5. Negative stool culture result

Inflammatory cells in stool or positive fecal lactoferrin

IBD likely

a. Severely ill: rule out toxic megacolon; analyze blood cultures; abdominal x-ray; treat as IBD
b. Not severely ill: colonoscopy after careful and gentle preparation

No inflammatory cells in stool or negative fecal lactoferrin

a. If history is appropriate, with travel to endemic areas, or if patient has hypogammaglobulinemia, evaluate duodenal aspirate for *Giardia*
b. Stop all drugs, stop milk products, rule out malabsorption, observe, and treat symptomatically; if symptoms persist or recur, perform colonoscopy

FIGURE 3-64 Diagnostic steps in the assessment of acute diarrhea. *For most cases of acute diarrhea, testing is not indicated. Stool examination and culture should be reserved for patients with severe illness, bloody stool, severe dehydration, immunosuppression, and for suspected nosocomial infection. †The role of lower endoscopy in acute diarrhea is limited. It should be considered only if the diagnosis is unclear after blood and stool tests in severely symptomatic patients. ‡Acute diarrhea is defined as stool with increased water content, volume, or frequency that lasts less than 14 days. *IBD,* Inflammatory bowel disease; *IBS,* irritable bowel syndrome. (Modified from Stein JH [ed]: *Internal medicine,* ed 5, St Louis, 1998, Mosby.)

Clinical Algorithms

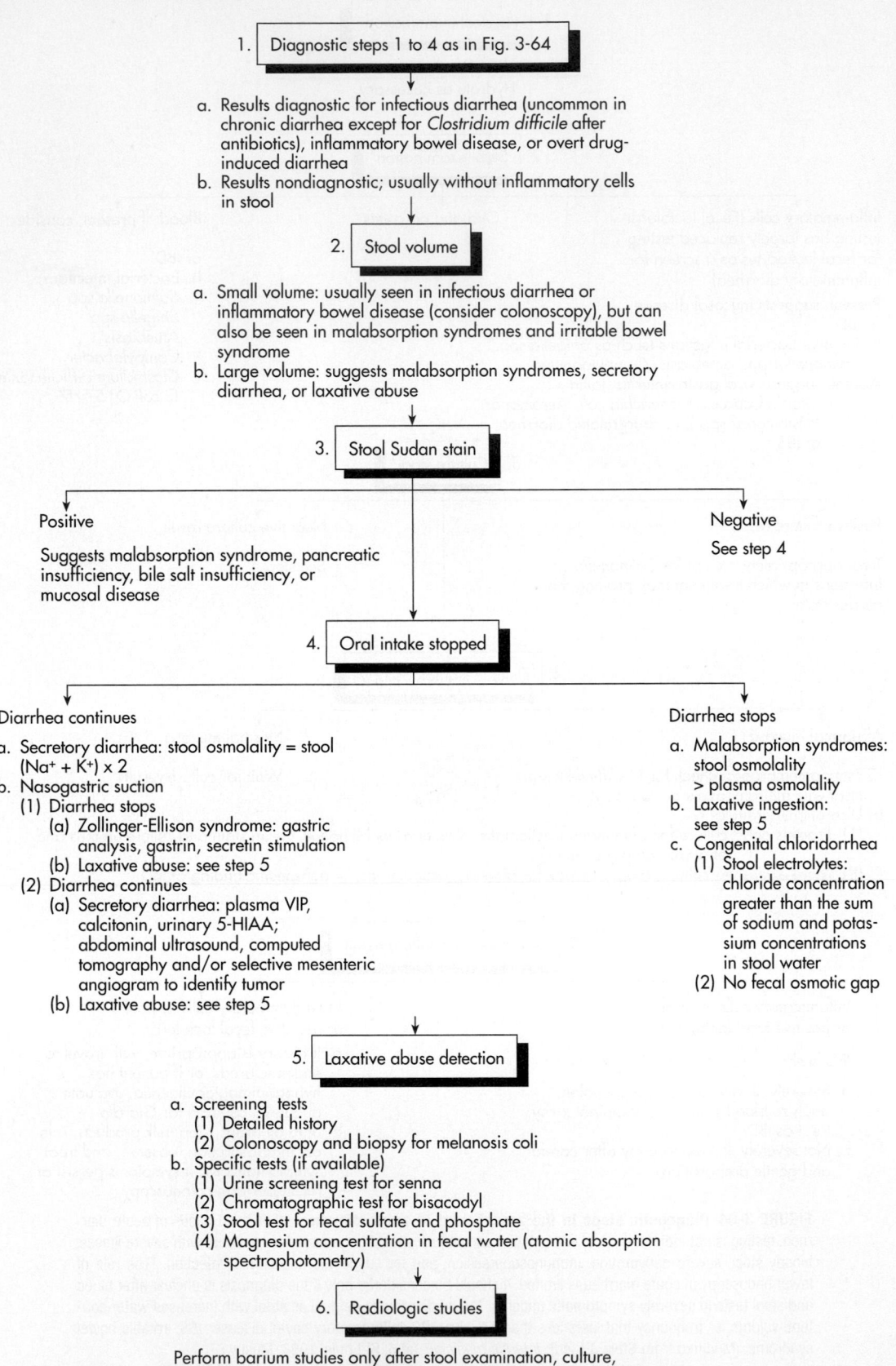

FIGURE 3-65 Diagnostic approach to the patient with chronic diarrhea (patients who are HIV negative). *5-HIAA*, 5-Hydroxyindoleacetic acid; *VIP*, vasoactive intestinal polypeptide. (Modified from Stein JH [ed]: *Internal medicine*, ed 5, St Louis, 1998, Mosby.)

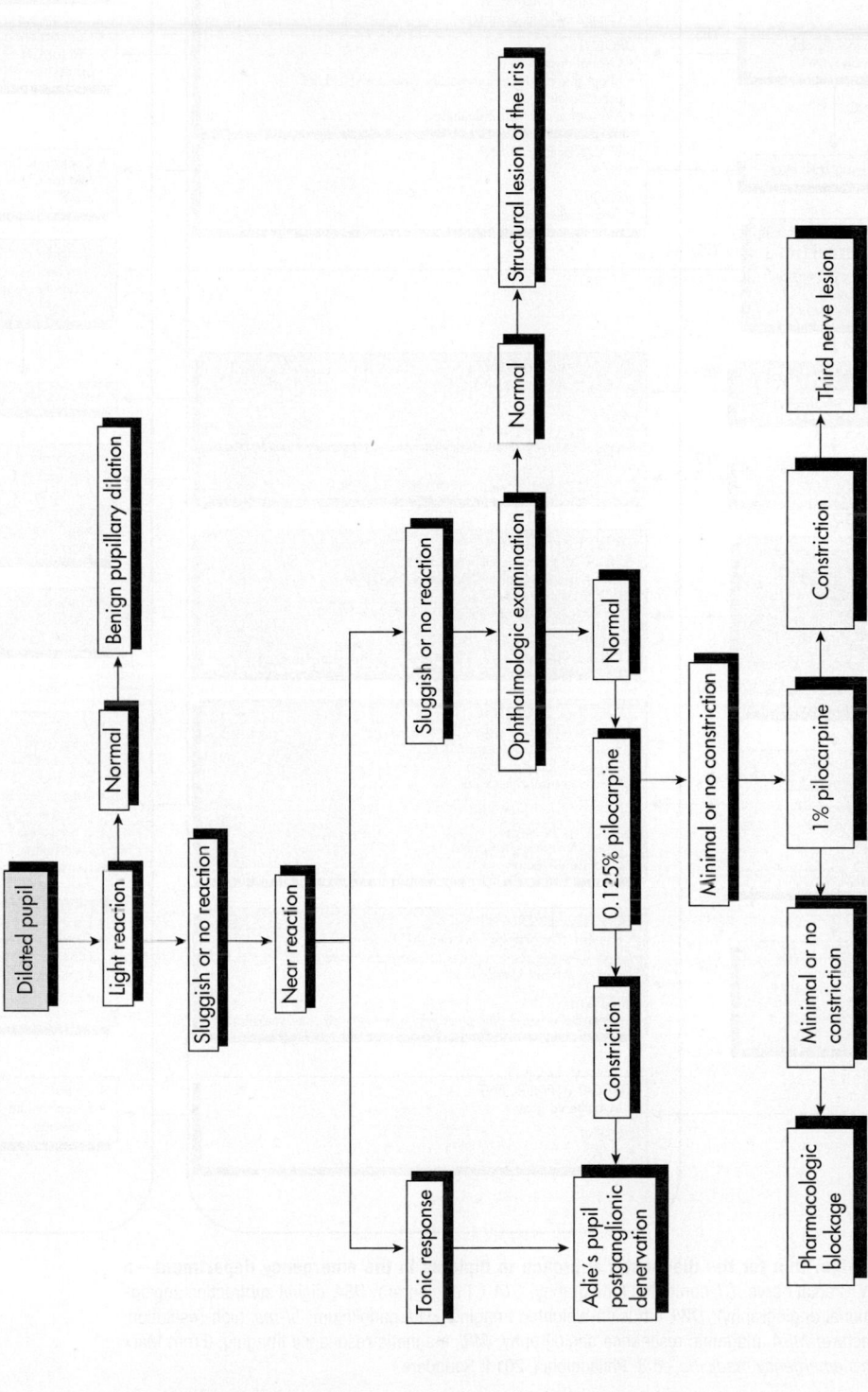

FIGURE 3-68 Use of pilocarpine to help differentiate between different causes of a dilated pupil. (From Goldman L, Ausiello D [eds]: *Cecil textbook of medicine*, ed 23, Philadephia, 2008, Saunders.)

Clinical
Algorithms

III

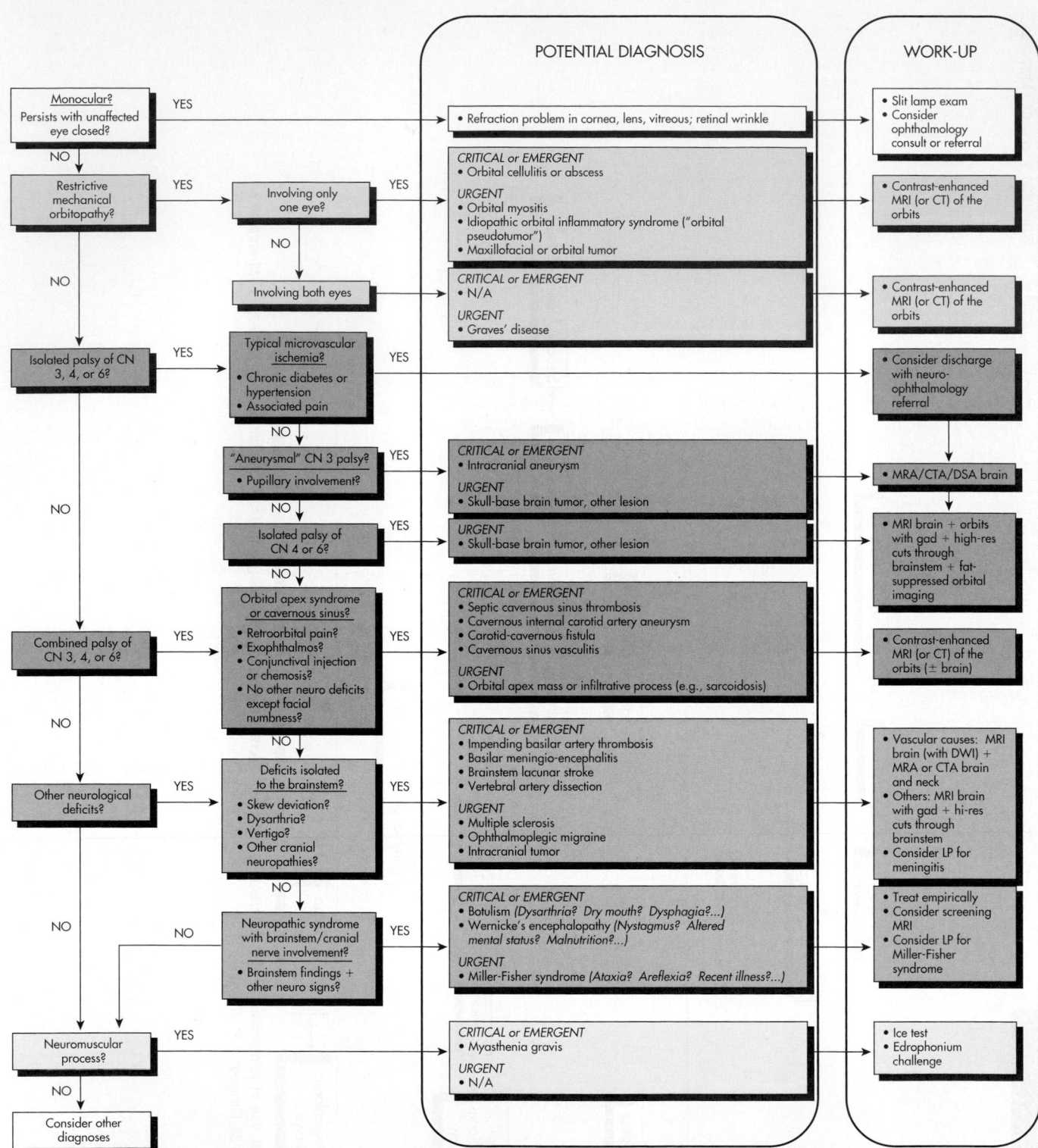

FIGURE 3-69 Algorithm for the diagnostic approach to diplopia in the emergency department—a guideline. *CN,* Cranial nerve; *CT,* computed tomography; *CTA,* CT angiogram; *DSA,* digital subtraction angiography (conventional angiography); *DWI,* diffusion-weighted imaging; *gad,* gadolinium; *hi-res,* high-resolution; *LP,* lumbar puncture; *MRA,* magnetic resonance angiography; *MRI,* magnetic resonance imaging. (From Marx JA et al: *Rosen's emergency medicine,* ed 8, Philadelphia, 2014, Saunders.)

Table 3-14   Important Causes of Diplopia

Diplopia-Causing Entity	Mechanism and Mortality	Distinguishing Features
Tier 1—Critical		
Basilar artery thrombosis	Acute thrombosis of the basilar artery with brainstem ischemia; untreated, mortality 70-90%	Vertigo, dysarthria, other cranial nerve involvement; risk factors for stroke
Botulism	Toxin inhibits of release of acetylcholine (ACh) at cholinergic synapses and presynaptic myoneural junctions; untreated, mortality 60%	Dysarthria, dysphagia, autonomic dysreflexia, pupillary dysfunction
Basilar meningitis	Infection; untreated, mortality close to 100% if bacterial (25-40% if treated)	Headache, meningismus, fever
Aneurysm	Enlarging aneurysm directly compresses cranial nerve; untreated, rupture risk is 1% per year; mortality 26-50% per rupture	CN III palsy with pupillary involvement
Tier 2—Emergent		
Vertebral dissection	Dissection causes vertebrobasilar ischemia; acute untreated, mortality 28% (2-5% if neurologically asymptomatic)	Neck pain, vertigo; risk factors for vertebral dissection
Myasthenia gravis	Autoantibodies develop against ACh nicotinic postsynaptic receptors; untreated, crisis mortality 42% (5% if treated)	Fluctuating muscle weakness, ptosis, and diplopia worsen with activity and improve with rest
Wernicke's encephalopathy	Thiamine-dependent metabolic failure and tissue injury; untreated, mortality 20%	Nystagmus, ataxia, altered mental status, and ophthalmoplegia; risk factors and nutritional deficiency
Orbital apex syndrome, cavernous sinus process	Inflammation or infection in the orbital apex or cavernous sinus directly affects oculomotor cranial nerves; acute mortality low unless infectious and complicated by meningitis	A combination of palsies of CN III, IV, or VI, with retroorbital pain, conjunctival injection, and possible periorbital or facial numbness
Tier 3—Urgent		
Brainstem tumor	Tumor involvement at the supranuclear level; acute mortality low (long-term mortality variable)	Skew deviation vertical diplopia, internuclear ophthalmoplegia
Miller-Fisher syndrome	Autoantibodies develop to a cranial nerve ganglioside, GQ1b; acute mortality low if fully differentiated from GBS; mortality 2-12% if GBS	Ophthalmoplegia, ataxia, areflexia
Multiple sclerosis	Demyelinating lesions; acute mortality low	Internuclear ophthalmoplegia
Thyroid myopathy (Graves' disease)	Autoimmune myopathy; acute mortality low with regard to ocular complaints	Proptosis, restriction of elevation and abduction of the eye, signs of Graves' disease
Ophthalmoplegic migraine	Inflammatory cranial neuropathy; low mortality—self-limited disease	Ipsilateral headache, CN (usually III) palsy
Ischemic neuropathy	Microvascular ischemia; mortality low—self-limited disease	Isolated CN palsy (pupil-sparing if CN III)
Orbital myositis, pseudotumor	Autoimmune or idiopathic myositis; acute mortality low with regard to ocular complaints	Eye pain, restriction of movement, periorbital edema; exophthalmos and chemosis when more severe
Orbital apex mass	A tumor, infiltration, or mass effect in the orbital apex or cavernous sinus directly compresses oculomotor cranial nerves; acute mortality low	A combination of palsies of CN III, IV, or VI, and possible periorbital or facial numbness, with retroorbital pain, proptosis, signs of venous congestion

CN, Cranial nerve; *GBS,* Guillain-Barre syndrome.
From Marx JA et al: *Rosen's emergency medicine*, ed 8, Philadelphia, 2014, Saunders.

Clinical
Algorithms

III

Table 3-15   Differential Diagnoses for Acute Dyspnea

Organ System	Critical Diagnoses	Emergent Diagnoses	Nonemergent Diagnoses
Pulmonary	Airway obstruction	Spontaneous pneumothorax	Pleural effusion
	Pulmonary embolus	Asthma	Neoplasm
	Noncardiogenic edema	Cor pulmonale	Pneumonia (CAP score ≤ 70)
	Anaphylaxis	Aspiration	COPD
	Ventilatory failure	Pneumonia (CAP score >70)	
Cardiac	Pulmonary edema	Pericarditis	Congenital heart disease
	Myocardial infarction		Valvular heart disease
	Cardiac tamponade		Cardiomyopathy
Primarily Associated with Normal or Increased Respiratory Effort			
Abdominal		Mechanical interference	Pregnancy
		Hypotension, sepsis from ruptured viscus, bowel obstruction, inflammatory or infectious process	Ascites
			Obesity
Psychogenic			Hyperventilation syndrome
			Somatization disorder
			Panic attack
Metabolic or endocrine	Toxic ingestion	Renal failure	Fever
	DKA	Electrolyte abnormalities	Thyroid disease
		Metabolic acidosis	
Infectious	Epiglottitis	Pneumonia (CAP score >70)	Pneumonia (CAP score ≤70)
Traumatic	Tension pneumothorax	Simple pneumothorax, hemothorax	Rib fractures
	Cardiac tamponade	Diaphragmatic rupture	
	Flail chest		
Hematologic	Carbon monoxide poisoning	Anemia	
	Acute chest syndrome		
Primarily Associated with Decreased Respiratory Effort			
Neuromuscular	CVA, intracranial insult	Multiple sclerosis	ALS
	Organophosphate poisoning	Guillain-Barré syndrome	Polymyositis
		Tick paralysis	Porphyria

ALS, Amyotrophic lateral sclerosis; *CAP,* community-acquired pneumonia; *COPD,* chronic obstructive pulmonary disease; *CVA,* cerebrovascular accident; *DKA,* diabetic ketoacidosis.
From Marx JA et al: *Rosen's Emergency Medicine,* ed 8, Philadelphia, 2014, Saunders.

Table 3-16 Pivotal Findings in Physical Examination

Sign	Physical Finding	Diagnoses to Consider
Vital signs	Tachypnea	Pneumonia, pneumothorax
	Hypopnea	Intracranial insult, drug or toxin ingestion
	Tachycardia	PE, traumatic chest injury
	Hypotension	Tension pneumothorax
	Fever	Pneumonia, PE
General appearance	Cachexia, weight loss	Malignancy, acquired immune disorder, mycobacterial infection
	Obesity	Hypoventilation, sleep apnea, PE
	Pregnancy	PE
	Barrel chest	COPD
	"Sniffing" position	Epiglottitis
	"Tripoding" position	COPD or asthma with severe distress
	Traumatic injury	Pneumothorax (simple, tension), rib fractures, flail chest, hemothorax, pulmonary contusion
Skin and nails	Tobacco stains or odor	COPD, malignancy, infection
	Clubbing	Chronic hypoxia, intracardiac shunts, or pulmonary vascular anomalies
	Pallid skin or conjunctivae	Anemia
	Muscle wasting	Neuromuscular disease
	Bruising	Chest wall: rib fractures, pneumothorax
		Diffuse: thrombocytopenia, chronic steroid use, anticoagulation
	Subcutaneous emphysema	Rib fractures, pneumothorax, tracheobronchial disruption
	Hives, rash	Allergic reaction, infection, tick-borne illness
Neck	Stridor	Upper airway edema or infection, foreign body, traumatic injury, anaphylaxis
	JVD	Tension pneumothorax, COPD or asthma exacerbation, fluid overload or CHF, PE
Lung examination	Wheezes	CHF, anaphylaxis
		Bronchospasm
	Rales	CHF, pneumonia, PE
	Unilateral decrease	Pneumothorax, pleural effusion, consolidation, rib fractures or contusion, pulmonary contusion
	Hemoptysis	Malignancy, infection, bleeding disorder, CHF
	Sputum production	Infection (viral, bacterial)
	Friction rub	Pleurisy
	Abnormal respiratory pattern (e.g., Cheyne-Stokes)	Intracranial insult
Chest examination	Crepitance or pain on palpation	Rib or sternal fractures
	Subcutaneous emphysema	Pneumothorax, tracheobronchial rupture
	Thoracoabdominal desynchrony	Diaphragmatic injury with herniation; cervical spinal cord trauma
	Flail segment	Flail chest, pulmonary contusion
Cardiac examination	Murmur	PE
	S_3 or S_4 gallop	PE
	S_2 accentuation	PE
	Muffled heart sounds	Cardiac tamponade
Extremities	Calf tenderness, Homans' sign	PE
	Edema	CHF
Neurologic examination	Focal deficits (motor, sensory, cognitive)	Stroke, intracranial hemorrhage causing central abnormal respiratory drive; if long-standing, risk of aspiration pneumonia
	Symmetrical deficits	Neuromuscular disease
	Diffuse weakness	Metabolic or electrolyte abnormality (hypocalcemia, hypomagnesemia, hypophosphatemia), anemia
	Hyporeflexia	Hypermagnesemia
	Ascending weakness	Guillain-Barré syndrome

CHF, Congestive heart failure; *COPD*, chronic obstructive pulmonary disease; *JVD*, jugular venous distention; *PE*, pulmonary embolism.
From Marx JA et al: *Rosen's Emergency Medicine*, ed 8, Philadelphia, 2014, Saunders.

Clinical Algorithms

Table 3-17 Diagnostic Table: Patterns of Diseases Often Resulting in Dyspnea

Disease	History (Dyspnea)	Associated Symptoms	Signs and Physical Findings	Tests
Pulmonary embolism	• HPI: abrupt onset, pleuritic pain, immobility (travel, recent surgery) • PMH: malignancy, DVT, PE, hypercoagulability, oral contraception, obesity	Diaphoresis, exertional dyspnea	Tachycardia, tachypnea, low-grade fever	• Pulse oximetry, ABG (A-a gradient), D-dimer • ECG (dysrhythmia, right-sided heart strain) • CXR (Westermark sign, Hampton's hump), spiral CT, MRV • Pulmonary angiogram • Ultrasound positive for DVT
Pneumonia	Fever, productive cough, chest pain	Anorexia, chills, nausea, vomiting, exertional dyspnea, cough	Fever, tachycardia, tachypnea, rales or decreased breath sounds	CXR, CBC, sputum and blood cultures
Bacterial	SH: tobacco use			Pulse oximetry Waveform capnography if altered mental status, ABG if capnography unavailable and acid-base derangement or hypercarbia suspected
Viral	Exposure (e.g., influenza, varicella)			
Opportunistic	Immune disorder, chemotherapy			
Fungal or parasitic	Exposure (e.g., birds), indolent onset	Episodic fever, nonproductive cough		
Pneumothorax	Abrupt onset: trauma, chest pain, thin males more likely to have spontaneous pneumothorax	Localized chest pain	Decreased breath sounds, subcutaneous emphysema, chest wall wounds or instability	• CXR: pneumothorax, rib fractures, hemothorax • Ultrasound: pneumothorax, pleural effusion
Simple				Ultrasound positive for pneumothorax
Tension	Decompensation of simple pneumothorax	Diaphoresis	JVD, tracheal deviation, muffled heart sounds, cardiovascular collapse	Clinical diagnosis: requires immediate decompression. May verify via bedside ultrasound
COPD or asthma	Tobacco use, medication noncompliance, URI symptoms, sudden weather change	Air hunger, diaphoresis	• Retractions, accessory muscle use, tripoding, cyanosis • "Shark fin" capnograph	• CXR: rule out infiltrate, pneumothorax, atelectasis (mucus plug) • Ultrasound: distinguish from heart failure
	PMH: environmental allergies FH: asthma			Waveform capnography
Malignancy	Weight loss, tobacco, or other occupational exposure	Dysphagia	Hemoptysis	CXR, chest CT: mass, hilar adenopathy, focal atelectasis
Fluid overload	• Gradual onset, dietary indiscretion or medication noncompliance, chest pain • PMH: recent MI, diabetes, CHF	Worsening orthopnea, PND	JVD, peripheral edema, S_3 or S_4 gallop, new cardiac dysrhythmia, hepatojugular reflux	• CXR and/or ultrasound: pleural effusion, interstitial edema, Kerley B lines, cardiomegaly • ECG: ischemia, dysrhythmia • NT-proBNP
Anaphylaxis	Abrupt onset, exposure to allergen	Dysphagia	Oral swelling, stridor, wheezing, hives	

A-a, Alveolar-arterial; *ABG,* arterial blood gas; *CBC,* complete blood count; *CHF,* congestive heart failure; *CT,* computed tomography; *CXR,* chest x-ray examination; *DVT,* deep vein thrombosis; *ECG,* electrocardiogram; *FH,* family history; *HPI,* history of present illness; *JVD,* jugular venous distention; *MI,* myocardial infarction; *MRV,* magnetic resonance venography; *NT-proBNP,* amino-terminal pro-B–type natriuretic peptide; *PE,* pulmonary embolism; *PMH,* past medical history; *PND,* paroxysmal nocturnal dyspnea; *SH,* social history; *URI,* upper respiratory infection.
From Marx JA et al: Rosen's Emergency Medicine, ed 8, Philadelphia, 2014, Saunders.

DYSURIA AND/OR URETHRAL/ VAGINAL DISCHARGE

ICD-10CM # R30.0 Dysuria
R30.9 Painful micturition, unspecified
R36.0 Urethral discharge without blood
R36.9 Urethral discharge, unspecified
N89.8 Other specified noninflammatory disorders of vagina

1581

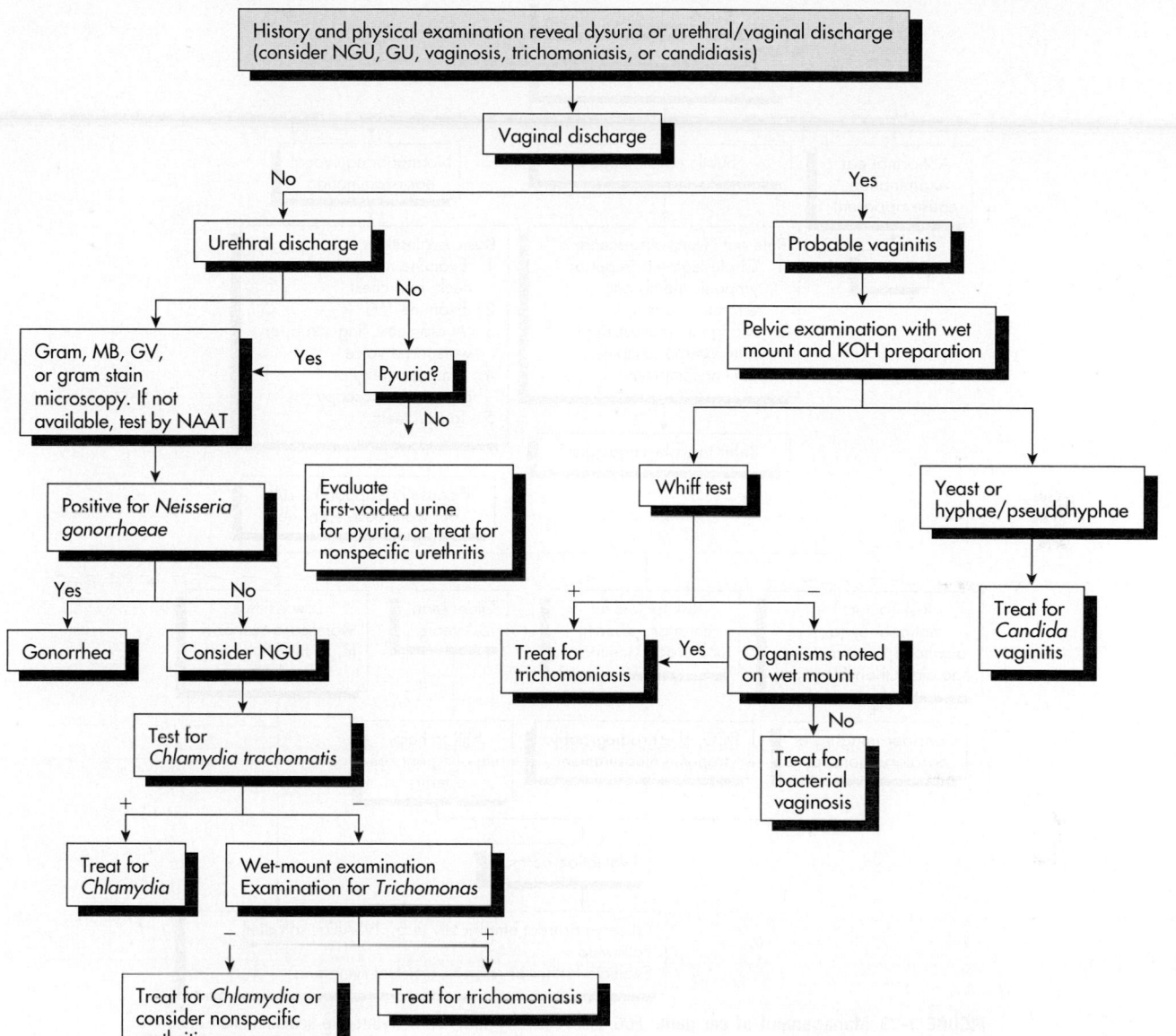

FIGURE 3-72 Evaluation of patients with dysuria and/or urethral/vaginal discharge. *GU,* Gonococcal urethritis; *GV,* gentian violet; *KOH,* potassium hydroxide; *MB,* methylene blue; *NAAT,* nucleic amplification test; *NGU,* nongonococcal urethritis. (Modified from Nseyo UO [ed]: Urology for primary care physicians, Philadelphia, 1999, Saunders.)

Clinical
Algorithms

III

Management of Ear Pain

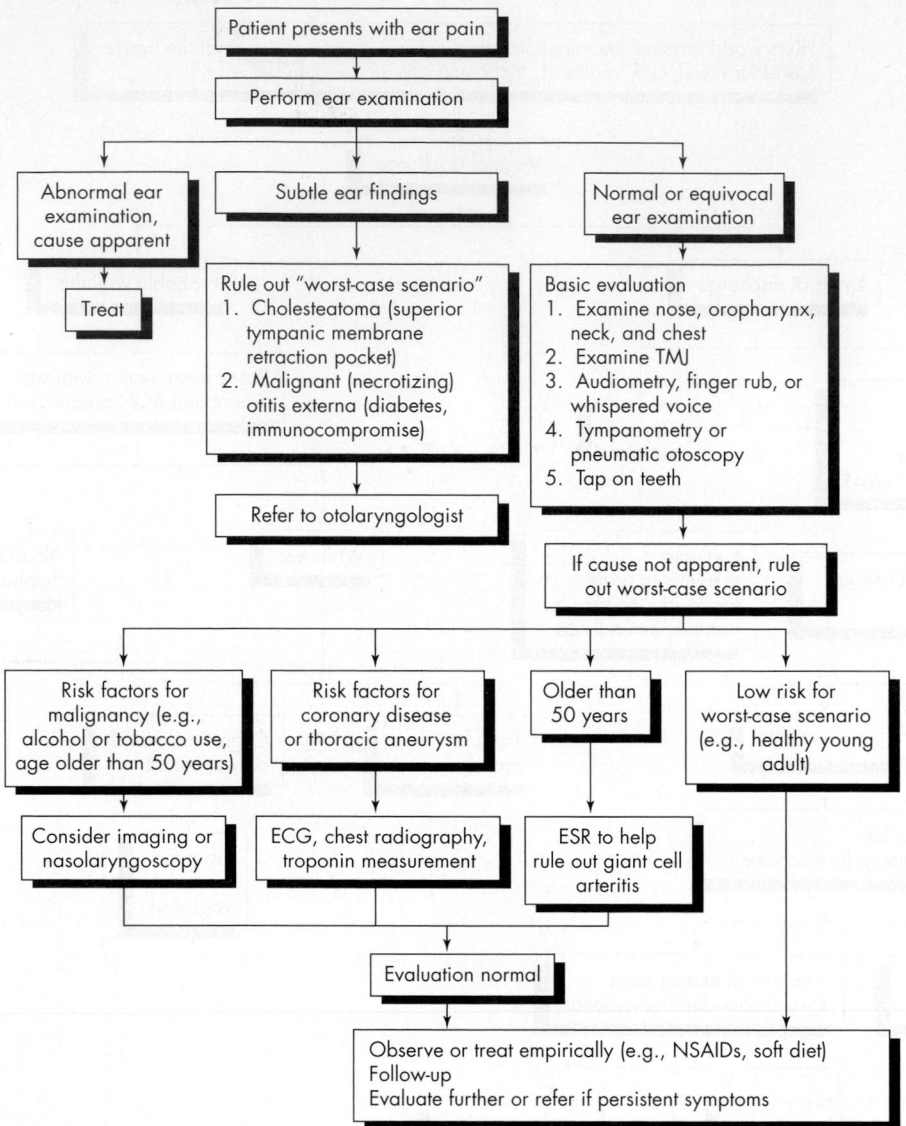

FIGURE 3-73 Management of ear pain. *ECG,* Electrocardiography; *ESR,* erythrocyte sedimentation rate; *NSAIDs,* nonsteroidal anti-inflammatory drugs; *TMJ,* temporomandibular joint. (Modified from Ely JW et al: Diagnosis of ear pain, *Am Fam Physician* 77[5]:622, 2008.)

FIGURE 3-74 Evaluation of generalized edema. *BNP,* B-type natriuretic peptide; *BUN,* blood urea nitrogen; *CHF,* congestive heart failure; *JVP,* jugular venous pressure; *LFT,* liver function tests; *TFTs,* thyroid function tests. (Modified from Greene HL, Johnson WP, Lemcke D [eds]: *Decision making in medicine,* ed 2, St Louis, 1998, Mosby.)

Clinical
Algorithms

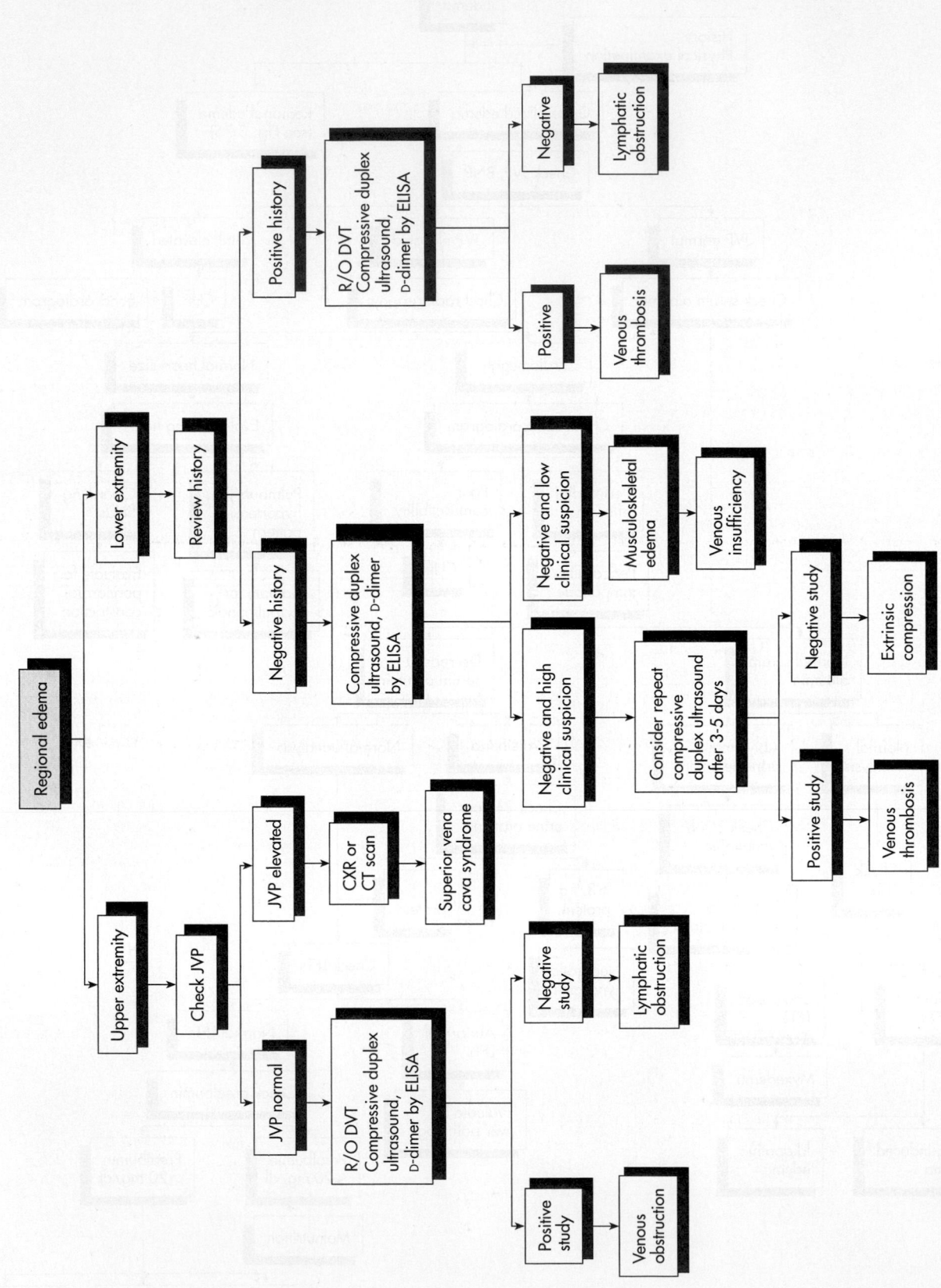

FIGURE 3-75 Evaluation of regional edema. *CT,* Computed tomography; *CXR,* chest x-ray examination; *DVT,* deep venous thrombosis; *ELISA,* enzyme-linked immunosorbent assay; *JVP,* jugular venous pressure. (Modified from Greene HL, Johnson WP, Lemcke D [eds]: *Decision making in medicine,* ed 2, St Louis, 1998, Mosby.)

ERYTHROCYTOSIS, ACQUIRED

ICD-10CM # D75.1 Secondary polycythemia
D75.0 Familial erythrocytosis
D45 Polycythemia vera
P61.1 Polycythemia neonatorum

1585

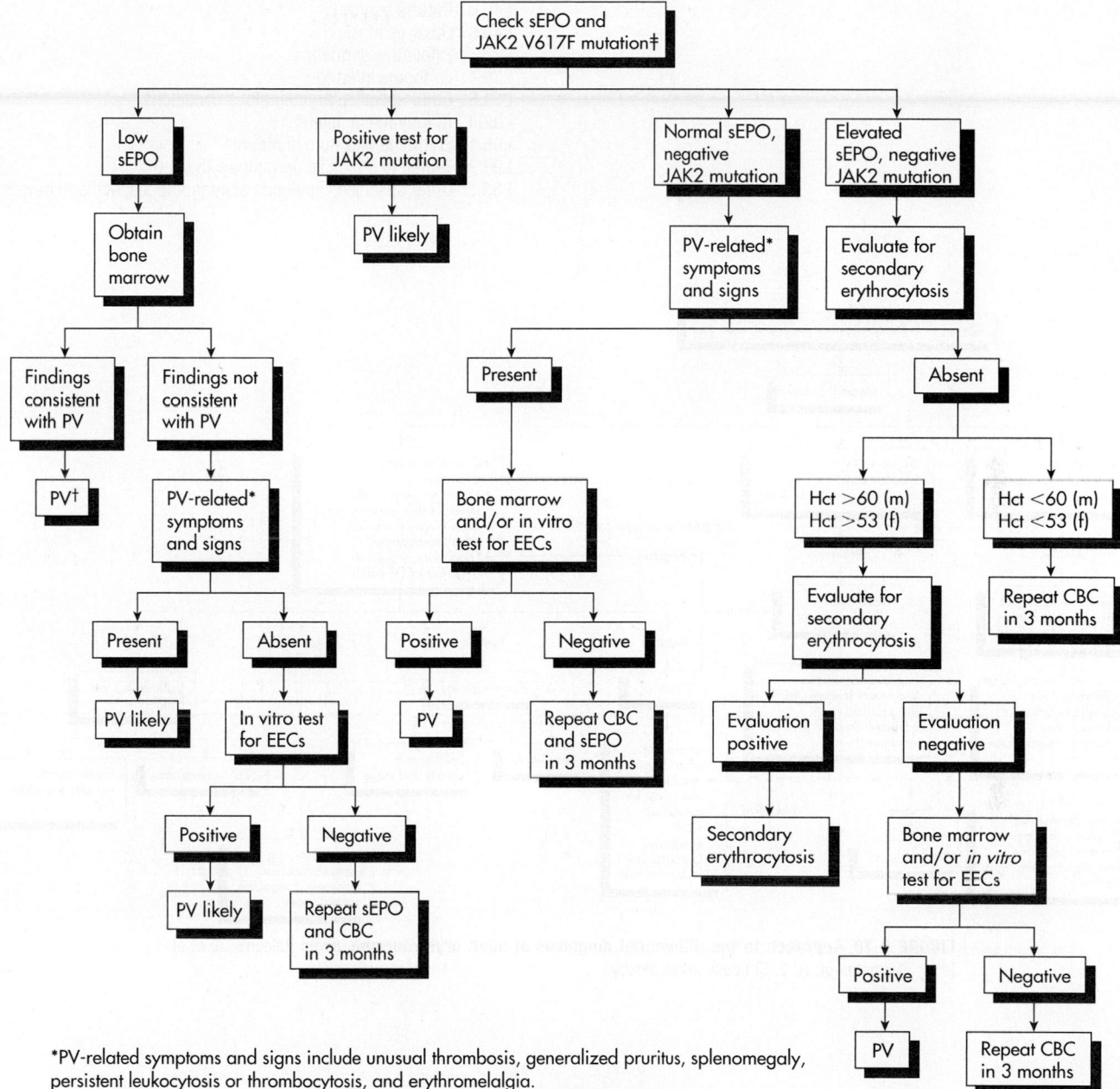

*PV-related symptoms and signs include unusual thrombosis, generalized pruritus, splenomegaly, persistent leukocytosis or thrombocytosis, and erythromelalgia.
†Note: Refer to Section I, Polycythemia Vera, for additional information on this topic.
‡The JAK2 mutation is found in >95% of patients with PV and can be used for diagnostic purposes.

FIGURE 3-77 A diagnostic approach to acquired erythrocytosis. *CBC,* Complete blood cell count; *EEC,* endogenous (spontaneous) erythroid colonies; *f,* female; *Hct,* hematocrit; *m,* male; *PV,* polycythemia vera; *sEPO,* serum erythropoietin level. (Modified from Goldman L, Schafer AL [eds]: *Cecil textbook of medicine,* ed 24, Philadelphia, 2012, Saunders.)

Clinical Algorithms

III

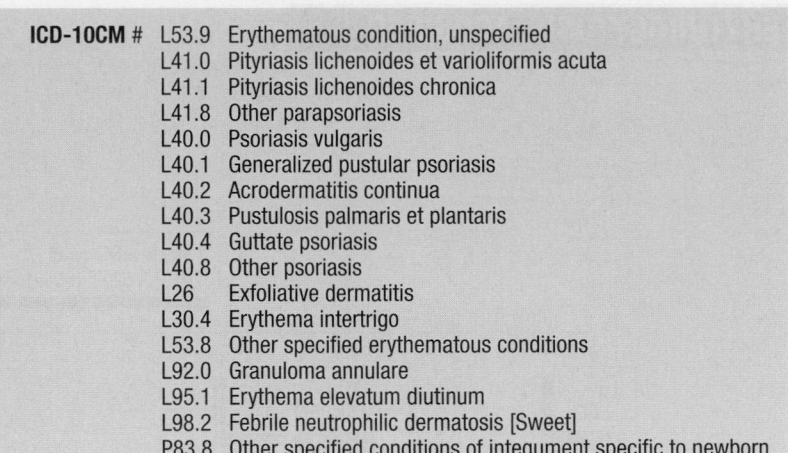

ICD-10CM #		
	L53.9	Erythematous condition, unspecified
	L41.0	Pityriasis lichenoides et varioliformis acuta
	L41.1	Pityriasis lichenoides chronica
	L41.8	Other parapsoriasis
	L40.0	Psoriasis vulgaris
	L40.1	Generalized pustular psoriasis
	L40.2	Acrodermatitis continua
	L40.3	Pustulosis palmaris et plantaris
	L40.4	Guttate psoriasis
	L40.8	Other psoriasis
	L26	Exfoliative dermatitis
	L30.4	Erythema intertrigo
	L53.8	Other specified erythematous conditions
	L92.0	Granuloma annulare
	L95.1	Erythema elevatum diutinum
	L98.2	Febrile neutrophilic dermatosis [Sweet]
	P83.8	Other specified conditions of integument specific to newborn

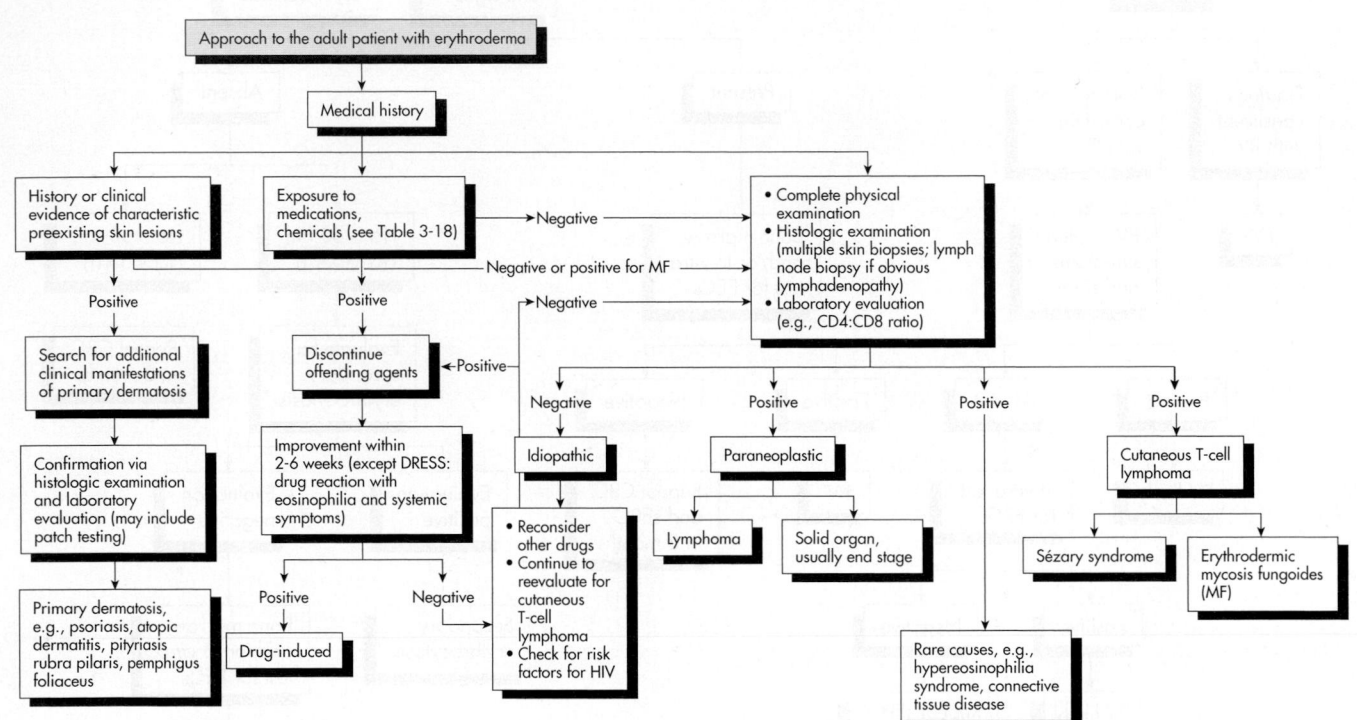

FIGURE 3-78 Approach to the differential diagnosis of adult erythroderma. (From Bolognia JL et al [eds]: *Dermatology*, ed 2, St Louis, 2008, Mosby.)

ICD-10CM #

L53.9	Erythematous condition, unspecified
L41.0	Pityriasis lichenoides et varioliformis acuta
L41.1	Pityriasis lichenoides chronica
L41.8	Other parapsoriasis
L40.0	Psoriasis vulgaris
L40.1	Generalized pustular psoriasis
L40.2	Acrodermatitis continua
L40.3	Pustulosis palmaris et plantaris
L40.4	Guttate psoriasis
L40.8	Other psoriasis
L26	Exfoliative dermatitis
L30.4	Erythema intertrigo
L53.8	Other specified erythematous conditions
L92.0	Granuloma annulare
L95.1	Erythema elevatum diutinum
L98.2	Febrile neutrophilic dermatosis [Sweet]
P83.8	Other specified conditions of integument specific to newborn

Table 3-18 Drugs Associated with Erythroderma

Common	Rare
• Allopurinol	Amiodarone
• Ampicillin/amoxicillin/penicillin G	Aztreonam
• Carbamazeplne/oxcarbazepine	Cimetidine
• Dapsone	Chlorpromazine
• Omeprazole/lansoprazole	Clofazimine
• Phenobarbital	Codeine
• Phenothiazines	Diltiazem
• Phenytoin	Erythropoietin
• Sulfasalazine	Fluorouracil
• Sulfonamides	Indinavir sulfate
• Vancomycin	Lithium
Less Common	Mitomycin C
Captopril	Pentostatin
Carboplatin/cisplatin	Piroxicam
Cytokines (IL-2/GM-CSF)	Practolol
Diflunisal	Ranltldlne
Gold	Rifampin (rifampicin)
Hydroxychloroquine/mefloquine	Tear gas (CS gas)
Isoniazid	Teicoplanin
Mercury	Terbinafine
Minocycline	Tobramycin
Nifedipine	Tramadol
Thalidomide	Vinca alkaloids
	Zidovudine

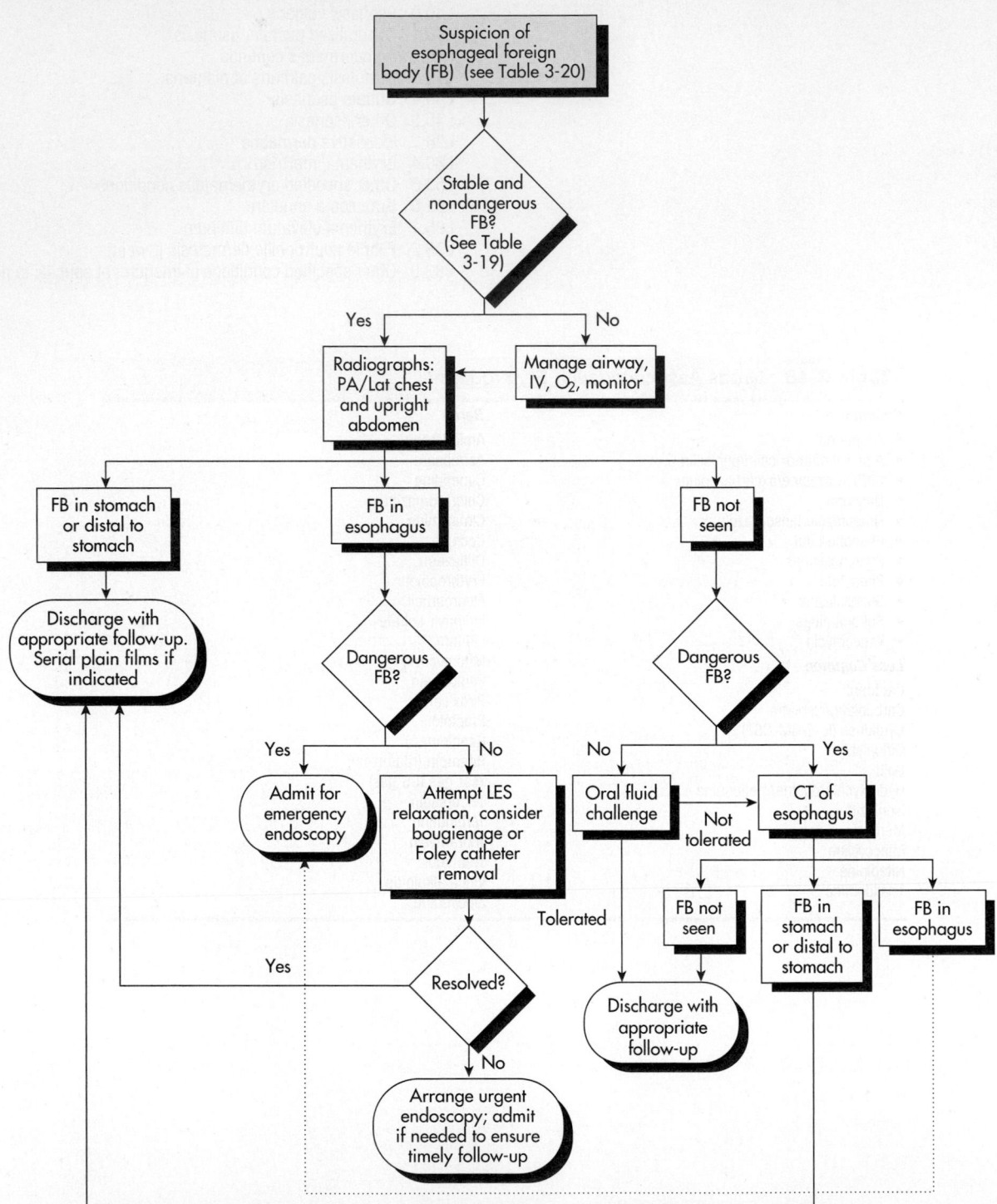

FIGURE 3-79 Diagnostic algorithm for the evaluation of a suspected esophageal foreign body. *CT*, Computed tomography; *IV*, intravenous line; *Lat*, lateral; *LES*, lower esophageal sphincter; *PA*, posteroanterior. (From Adams JG et al: *Emergency medicine, clinical essentials*, ed 2, Philadelphia, 2013, Elsevier.)

Table 3-19 Most Threatening and Most Common Esophageal Foreign Bodies

Most Threatening

In Children

Disc batteries
Bones
Needles
Other sharp objects

In Adults

Disc batteries
Bones
Packets of illicit drugs
Toothpicks

Most Common

In Children

Coins
Marbles
Buttons
Toys

In Adults

Food boluses
Bones
Dentures
Oral piercings

From Adams JG, et al: *Emergency medicine, clinical essentials*, ed 2, Philadelphia, 2013, Elsevier.

Table 3-20 Differential Diagnosis for Esophageal Foreign Bodies

In Children

Perforation
Abrasion or laceration
Airway foreign body
Esophagitis
Epiglottitis
Globus hystericus
Reactive airways disease

In Adults

Perforation
Abracion or laceration
Spasm
Esophagitis
Diverticulum
Malignancy
Myocardial infarction
Globus hystericus

From Adams JG, et al: *Emergency medicine, clinical essentials*, ed 2, Philadelphia, 2013, Elsevier.

Clinical Algorithms

III

ICD-10CM #   R53.83   Other fatigue
F48.8   Other specified nonpsychotic mental disorders
R53.83   Other fatigue

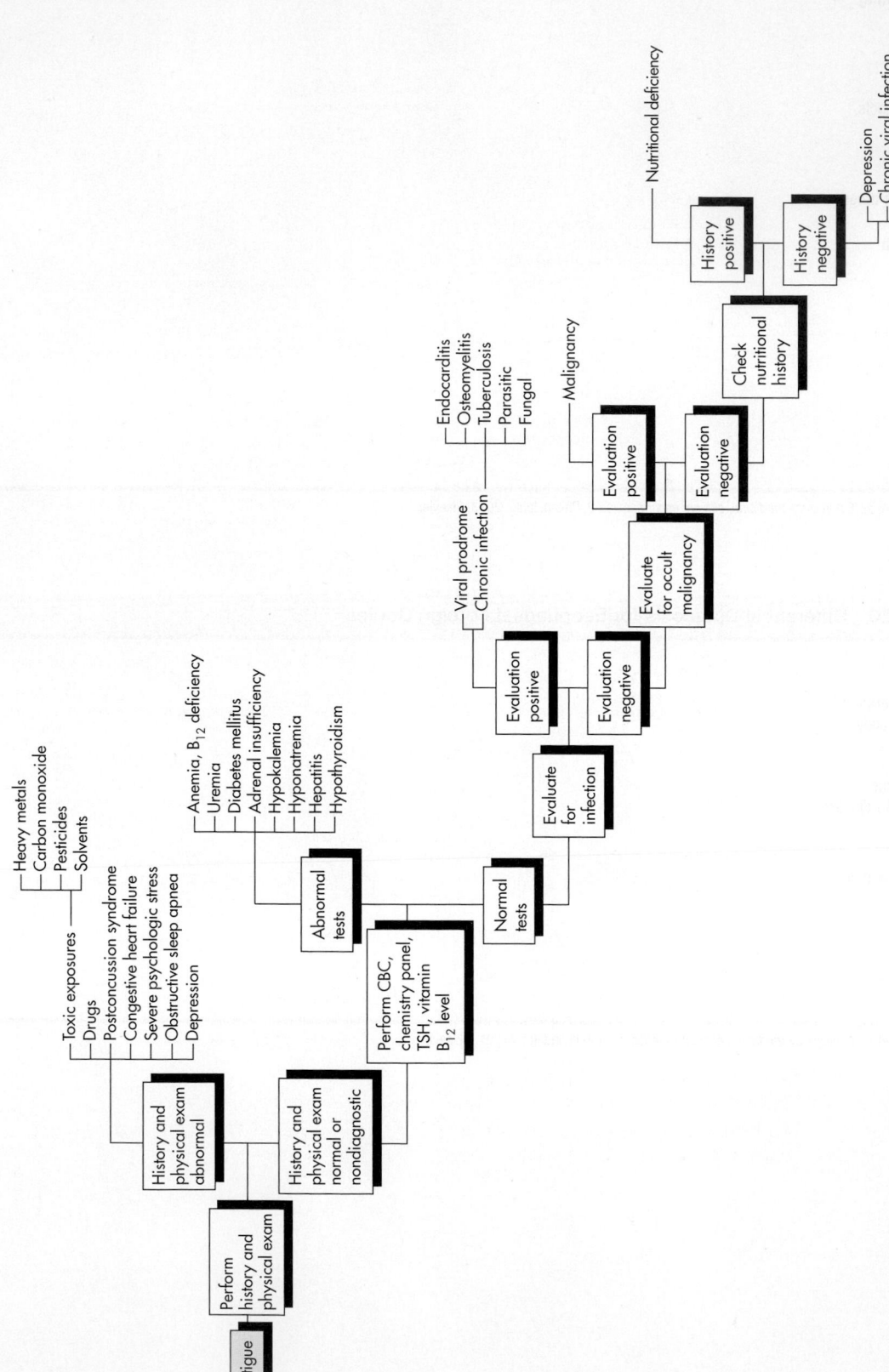

FIGURE 3-80 **Evaluation of fatigue.** *CBC,* Complete blood count. (Modified from Healey PM: *Common medical diagnosis: an algorithmic approach,* ed 3, Philadelphia, 2000, Saunders.)

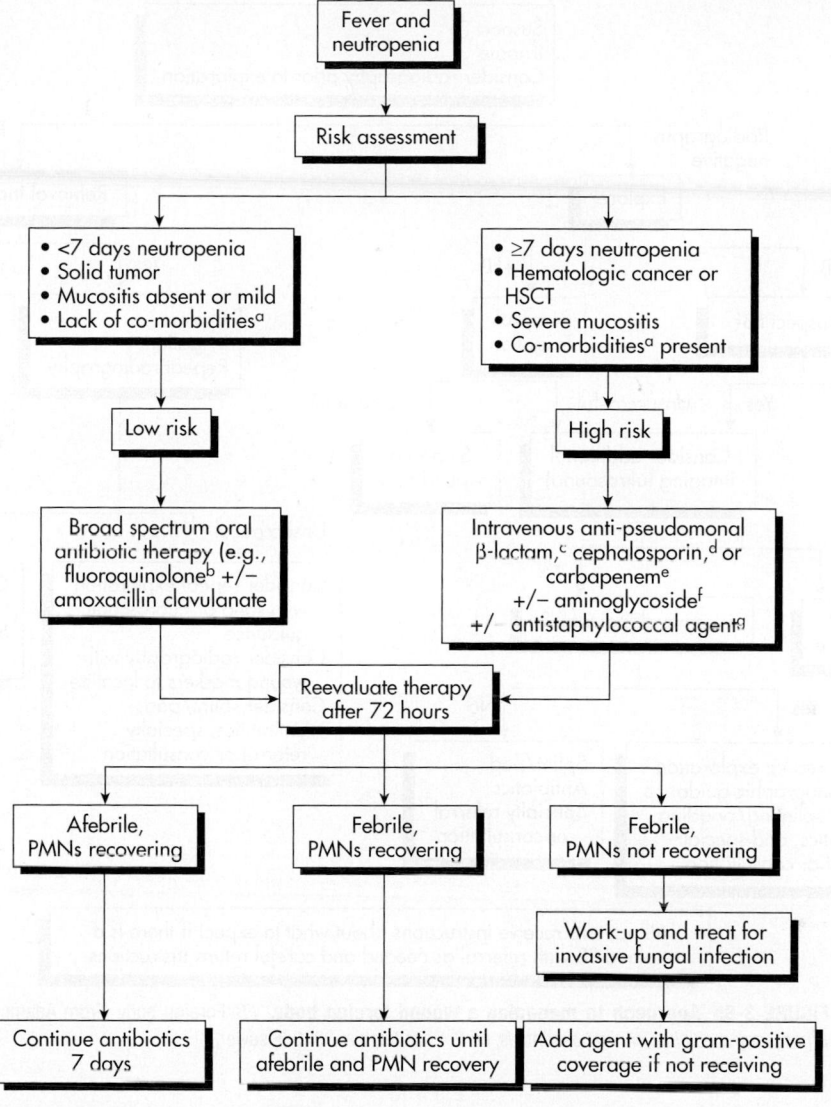

^a Hypotension, altered mental status, neurologic changes, respiratory failure, abdominal pain, hemorrhage,
   cardiac compromise or new arrythmia, catheter tunnel infection, extensive cellulitis,
   acute renal or liver failure
^b Institution-sensitivity dependent, ciprofloxacin, levofloxacin, moxifloxacin
^c Drug selection and dosing institution-specific: piperacillin tazobactam, ticarcillin/clavulanate
^d Drug selection and dosing institution-specific: ceftazidime, cefepime, ^eimipenem/cilastatin,
   meropenem, doripenem
^f Gentamin, tobramycin, or amakacin
^g Drug selection and institution-specific: vancomycin, linezolid, daptomycin, ceftaroline

FIGURE 3-82 Approach to patient with fever and neutropenia. (From Hoffman R: Hematology, basic
principles and practice, 6th ed, Philadelphia, Saunders, 2013, Figure 88-3.)

Clinical
Algorithms

III

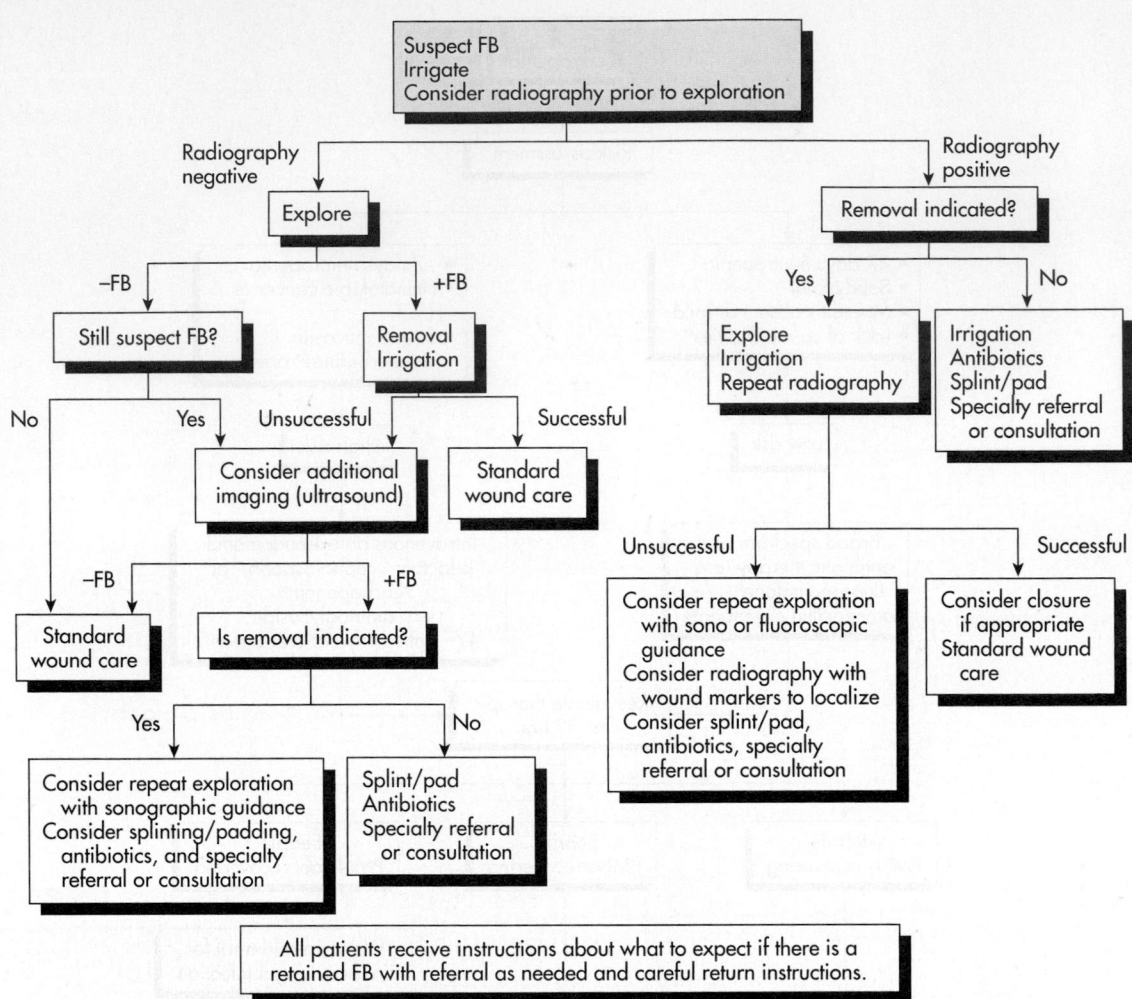

FIGURE 3-85 Approach to managing a wound foreign body. *FB*, Foreign body (From Adams JG et al: *Emergency medicine, clinical essentials*, ed 2, Philadelphia, 2013, Elsevier.)

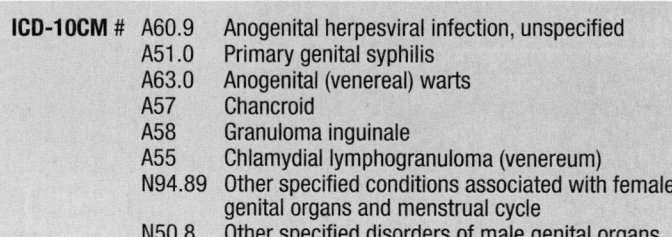

ICD-10CM #
A60.9 Anogenital herpesviral infection, unspecified
A51.0 Primary genital syphilis
A63.0 Anogenital (venereal) warts
A57   Chancroid
A58   Granuloma inguinale
A55   Chlamydial lymphogranuloma (venereum)
N94.89 Other specified conditions associated with female
       genital organs and menstrual cycle
N50.8 Other specified disorders of male genital organs

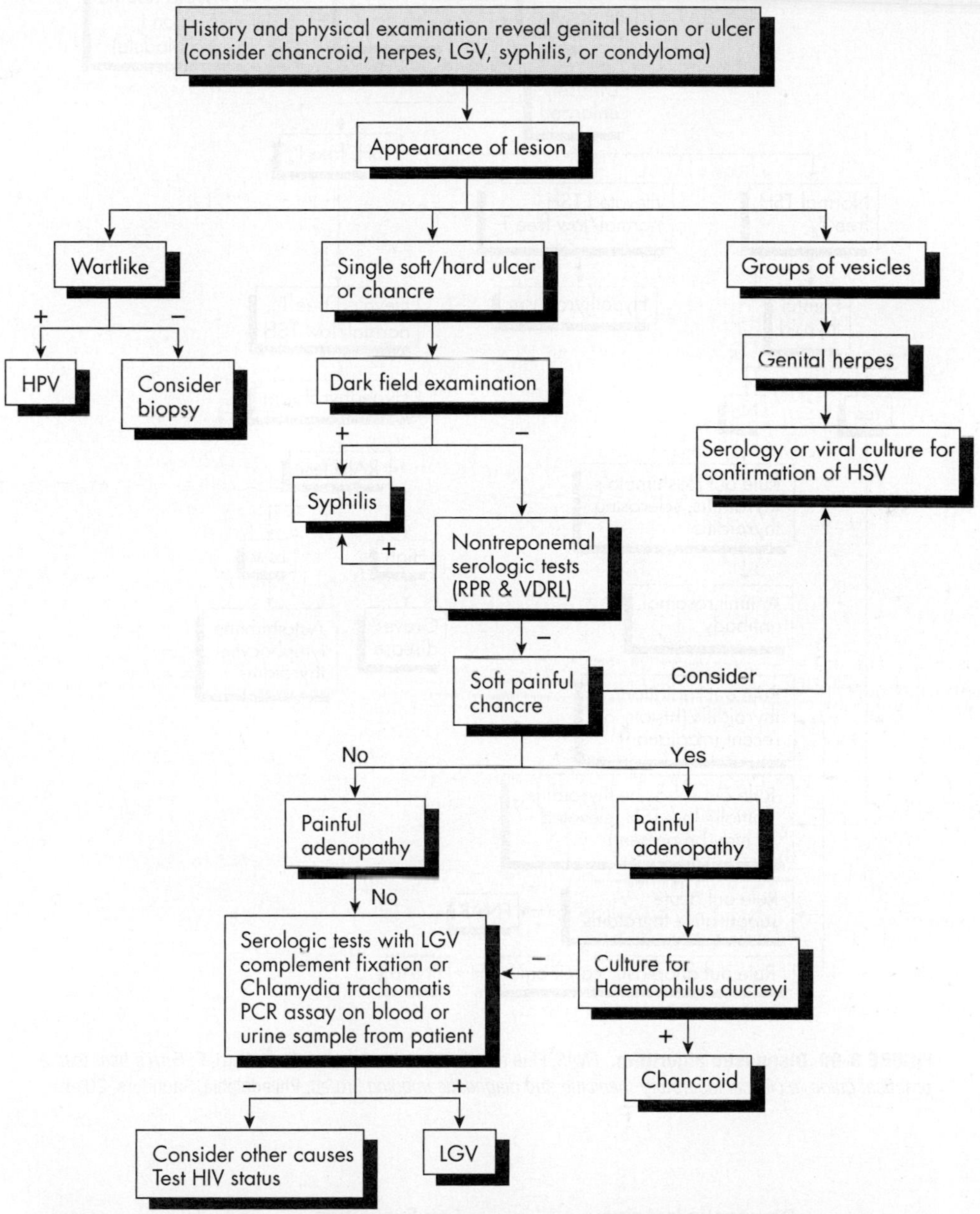

History and physical examination reveal genital lesion or ulcer
(consider chancroid, herpes, LGV, syphilis, or condyloma)

Appearance of lesion

Wartlike → + → HPV

Wartlike → − → Consider biopsy

Single soft/hard ulcer or chancre → Dark field examination

Dark field examination → + → Syphilis

Dark field examination → − → Nontreponemal serologic tests (RPR & VDRL)

Nontreponemal serologic tests (RPR & VDRL) → + → Syphilis

Nontreponemal serologic tests (RPR & VDRL) → − → Soft painful chancre

Groups of vesicles → Genital herpes → Serology or viral culture for confirmation of HSV

Soft painful chancre → Consider → Serology or viral culture for confirmation of HSV

Soft painful chancre → No → Painful adenopathy

Soft painful chancre → Yes → Painful adenopathy

Painful adenopathy (No side) → No → Serologic tests with LGV complement fixation or Chlamydia trachomatis PCR assay on blood or urine sample from patient

Painful adenopathy (Yes side) → Culture for Haemophilus ducreyi

Culture for Haemophilus ducreyi → − → Serologic tests with LGV complement fixation or Chlamydia trachomatis PCR assay on blood or urine sample from patient

Culture for Haemophilus ducreyi → + → Chancroid

Serologic tests... → − → Consider other causes Test HIV status

Serologic tests... → + → LGV

FIGURE 3-87 Evaluation of patients with genital lesions or ulcers. *HIV,* Human immunodeficiency virus; *HPV,* human papillomavirus; *HSV,* herpes simplex virus; *LGV,* lymphogranuloma venereum; *RPR,* rapid plasma reagin; *VDRL,* Venereal Disease Research Laboratory. (Modified from Nseyo UO [ed]: *Urology for primary care physicians,* Philadelphia, 1999, Saunders.)

Clinical
Algorithms

ICD-10CM # E04.0 Nontoxic diffuse goiter
E04.1 Nontoxic uninodular goiter
E04.2 Nontoxic multinodular goiter
E05.0 Toxic goiter

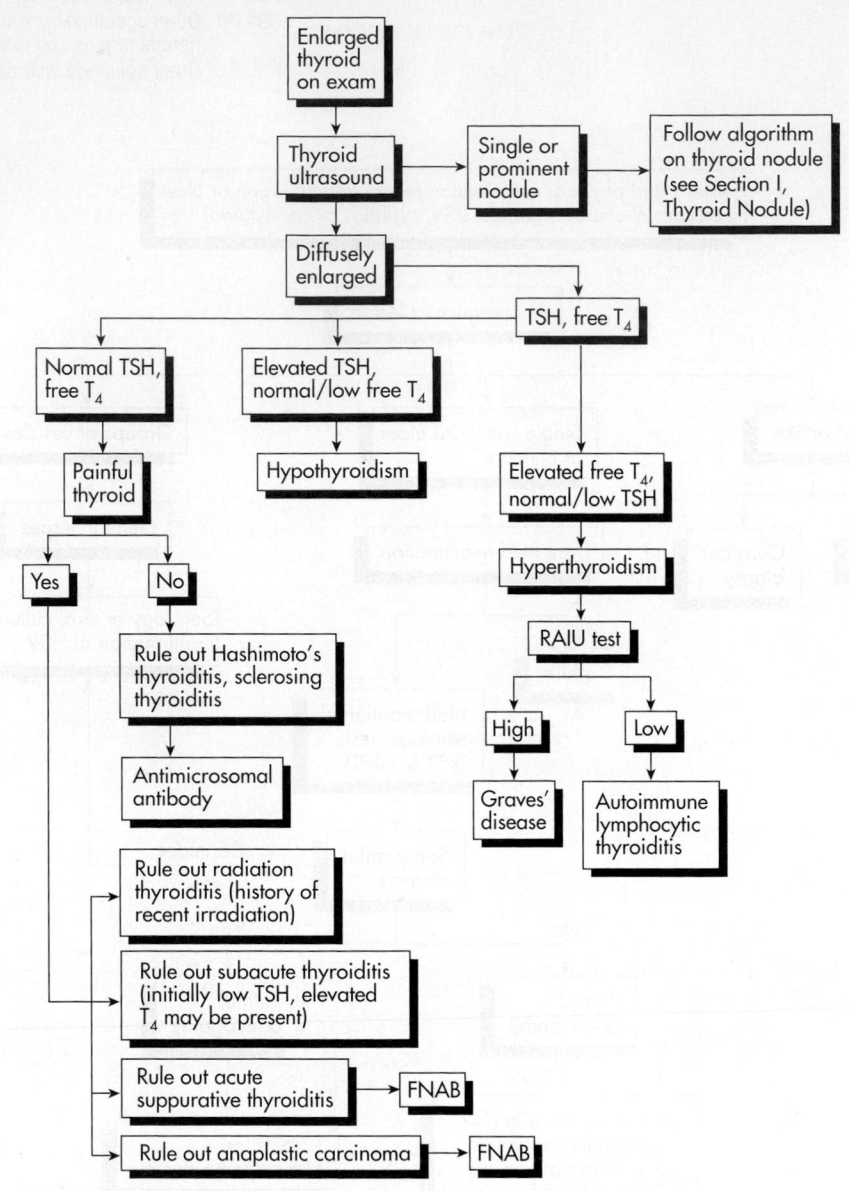

FIGURE 3-90 Diagnostic algorithm. *FNAB,* Fine needle aspiration biopsy. (From Ferri, F: *Ferri's best test: a practical guide to clinical laboratory medicine and diagnostic imaging* 3rd ed, Philadelphia, Saunders, 2014.)

Diagnostic Imaging
Best Test(s)
Ultrasound of thyroid

Ancillary Tests
• RAIU scan of thyroid

Lab Evaluation
Best Test(s)
TSH, free T$_4$

Ancillary Tests
CBC with differential
Antimicrosomal Ab
Thyroglobulin level

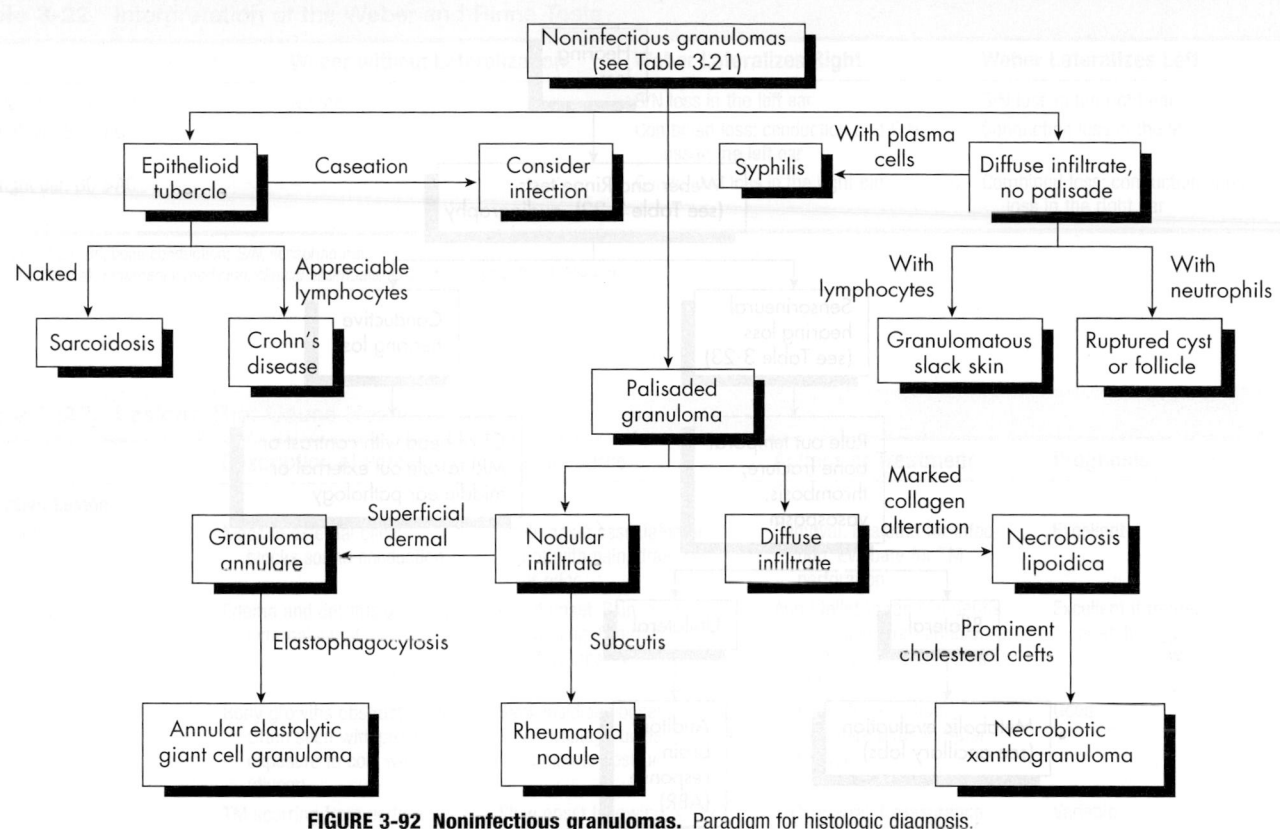

FIGURE 3-92 Noninfectious granulomas. Paradigm for histologic diagnosis.

Table 3-21   Clinical Features of the Major Granulomatous Dermatitides

	Sarcoidosis	Classic GA*	NLD	AEGCG	Crohn's Disease	Rheumatoid Nodule
Average age (years)	25-35, 45-65	<30		40	35	30-40
Sex	Female	Female	Female	Female	Female	Female
Racial predilection in United States	African American	None	None	Caucasian	None	None
Site	Symmetric on face, neck, upper trunk, extremities	Hands, feet, extremities	Anterior and lateral distal lower extremities	Face, neck, forearms	Genital areas, lower >upper extremities	Juxtaarticular areas, elbows, hands, ankles, feet
Appearance	Red to red-brown papules and plaques	Papules coalescing into annular plaques	Plaques with elevated borders, telangiectasias centrally	Annular plaques	Dusky erythema and swelling, ulceration	Skin-colored, firm, mobile subcutaneous nodules
Size of lesions	1-5 cm	1-2 mm papules, <5 cm annular plaques	>10 cm	1-6 cm	Variable	1-3 cm
Number of lesions	Variable	1-10	1-10	1-10	1-5	1-10
Associations	Systemic manifestations of sarcoidosis	Rare diabetes mellitus, malignancy	Diabetes mellitus	Actinic damage	Intestinal Crohn's disease	Rheumatoid arthritis
Special clinical characteristics	Occasional central atrophy and hypopigmentation	Central hyperpigmentation	Yellow-brown atrophic centers, ulceration	Central atrophy and hypopigmentation	Draining sinuses and fistulae	Occasional ulceration, especially at site of trauma

AEGCG, Annular elastolytic giant cell granuloma; *GA,* granuloma annulare; *NLD,* necrobiosis lipoidica diabeticorum.
*Clinical variants include generalized, micropapular, nodular, perforating, subcutaneous, and patch GA.
From Bolognia JL et al: *Dermatology,* ed 2, St Louis, 2008, Mosby.

Table 3-23 Lesions That Cause Hearing Loss—cont'd

	Description of Pathology	Onset/Course	Actions or Treatment	Prognosis
Viral cochleitis	Cochlear inflammation. Often following URI	Rapid onset. Often following URI	Steroids often used (no good data)	Variable
Presbycusis	Age-related hearing loss. May be related to previous chronic noise exposure	Slow onset. Usually symmetric. High frequencies most affected. Tinnitus may occur	Hearing aid may help with both hearing loss and tinnitus	Variable
Acoustic neuroma	Benign schwannoma of 8th cranial nerve	Slow onset. Usually unilateral. May exhibit tinnitus, vertigo. May exhibit facial hyperesthesias or twitching	May require surgical excision if symptoms debilitating	Variable
Ototoxic agents	Direct toxicity to inner ear structures	Variable onset. High frequency most affected. Exposure to ototoxic drugs. May have associated tinnitus	Stop use of offending agent	Variable. Hearing loss at time of stopping offending agent is usually permanent
Multiple sclerosis	Multiple demyelinating lesions interfere with nerve conduction	Often other associated neurologic findings. May wax and wane	Standard multiple sclerosis treatment (steroids, cytotoxic agents)	Variable
Stroke/CVA	Focal ischemic lesion of auditory nerve or auditory cortex	Sudden onset. Often associated with other neurologic deficits	Treat CVA risk factors (ASA, anticoagulants, glycemic control, BP control)	Variable
Meningitis	Infection enters inner ear through CNS-perilymph connection. Damages organ of Corti	Follows clinical picture of meningitis	Treat infection. Steroids may limit inflammation and damage	Variable
Meniere's disease (endolymphatic hydrops)	Abnormal homeostasis of inner ear fluids (clinical diagnosis; definitive diagnosis made histologically)	Episodic spells of vertigo. Associated sensation of fullness, tinnitus, and SNHL or auditory distortion. Low-frequency ranges most affected	Reduce salt, caffeine, nicotine (vasoconstrictors) intake. Consider diuretics, antihistamines, anticholinergics. ENT referral	Variable
Chronic noise exposure	Direct mechanical damage to cochlear structures and hair cells	Slow onset. Usually high frequency most affected	Prevention measures (earplugs). Stop exposure	Usually permanent
Skull trauma	Interruption of cranial nerve VIII, ossicle disruption, or shearing effects on organ of Corti	Sudden onset after trauma	ENT consultation for possible surgical repair	Variable: ossicle disruption has better prognosis than nerve or organ of Corti damage
Autoimmune causes	Vascular or neuronal inflammatory changes	Bilateral asymmetric SNHL. May be fluctuating or progressive. Often other systemic autoimmune findings	Outpatient autoimmune evaluation. Steroids and cytotoxic agents may slow progression	Variable

ASA, Acetylsalicylic acid; *BP*, blood pressure; *CNS*, central nervous system; *CSF*, cerebrospinal fluid; *CVA*, cerebrovascular accident; *ENT*, ear, nose, and throat; *SNHL*, sensorineural hearing loss; *TM*, tympanic membrane; *URI*, upper respiratory infection.

From Adams JG et al: *Emergency medicine, clinical essentials*, ed 2, Philadelphia, 2013, Elsevier.

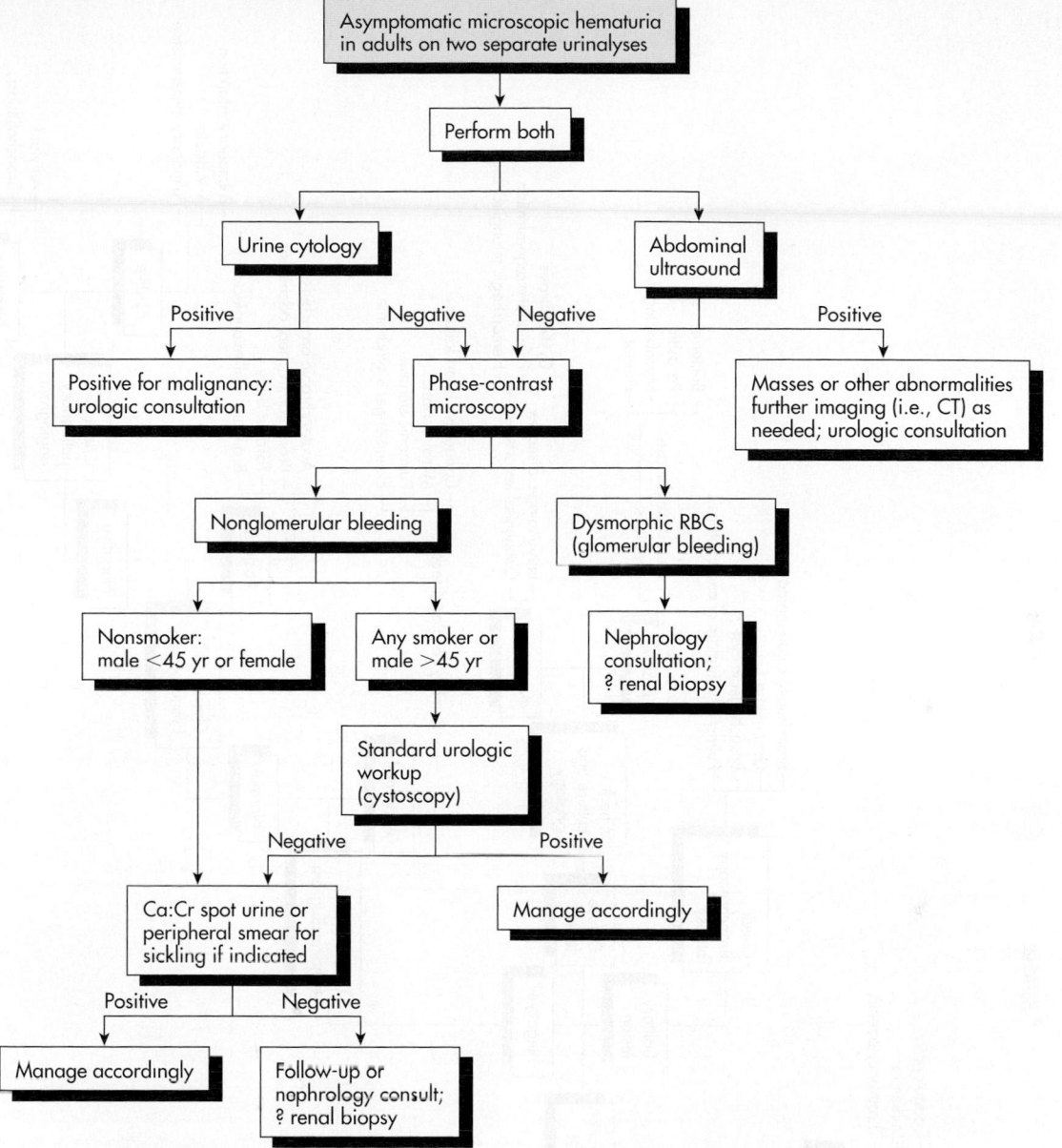

FIGURE 3-95 Suggested algorithm for the evaluation of adult asymptomatic microscopic hematuria. These patients must have no symptoms referable to the hematuria and a negative urinalysis except for red blood cells *(RBCs)*. Adults with gross hematuria require a full urologic evaluation. *Ca:Cr,* Calcium:creatinine ratio. (Modified from Nseyo UO [ed]: *Urology for primary care physicians,* Philadelphia, 1999, Saunders.)

Clinical
Algorithms

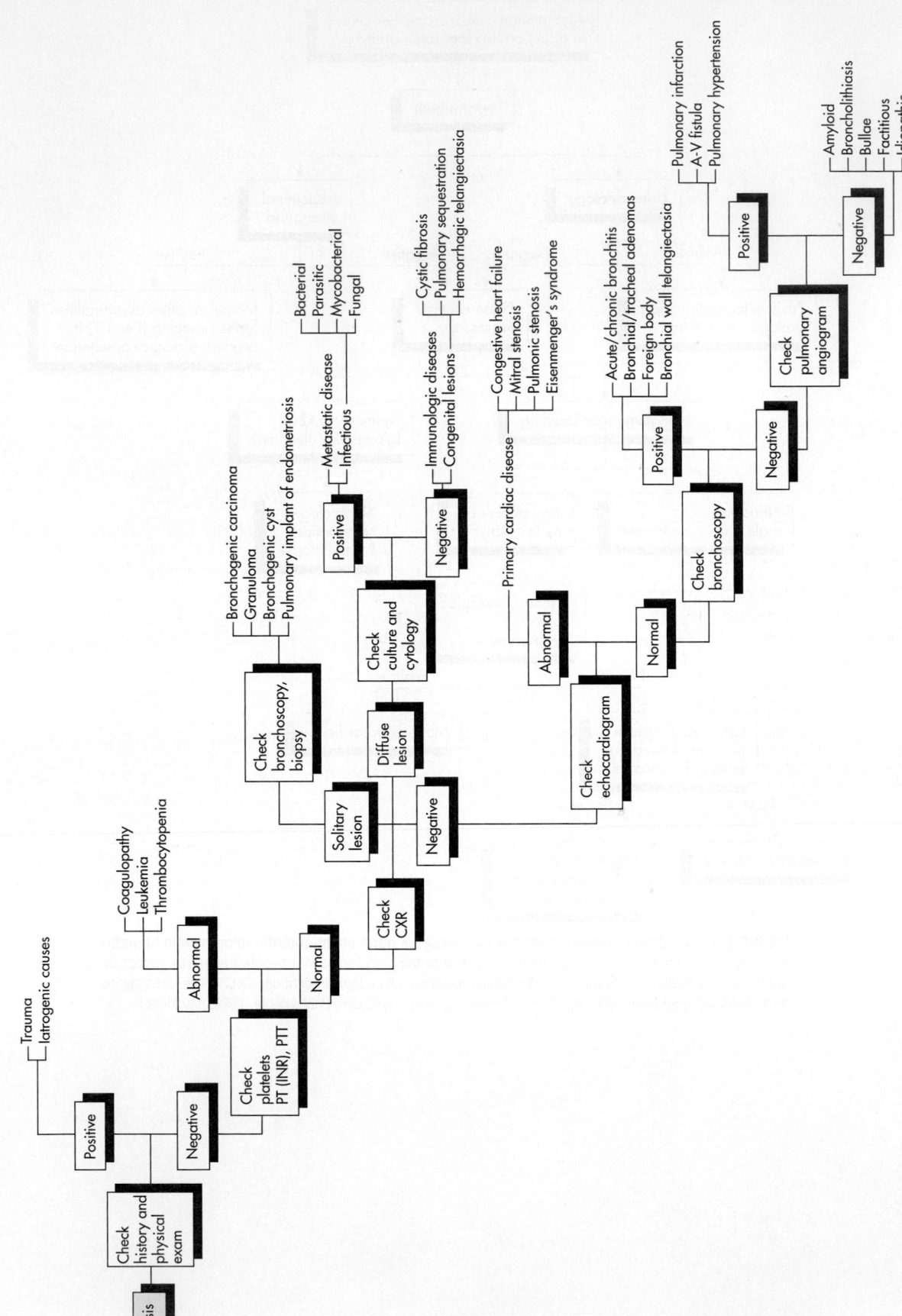

FIGURE 3-97 Evaluation of hemoptysis. *A-V,* Arteriovenous; *CXR,* chest x-ray; *INR,* International Normalized Ratio; *PT,* prothrombin time; *PTT,* partial thromboplastin time. (From Healey PM: *Common medical diagnosis: an algorithmic approach,* ed 3, Philadelphia, 2000, Saunders.)

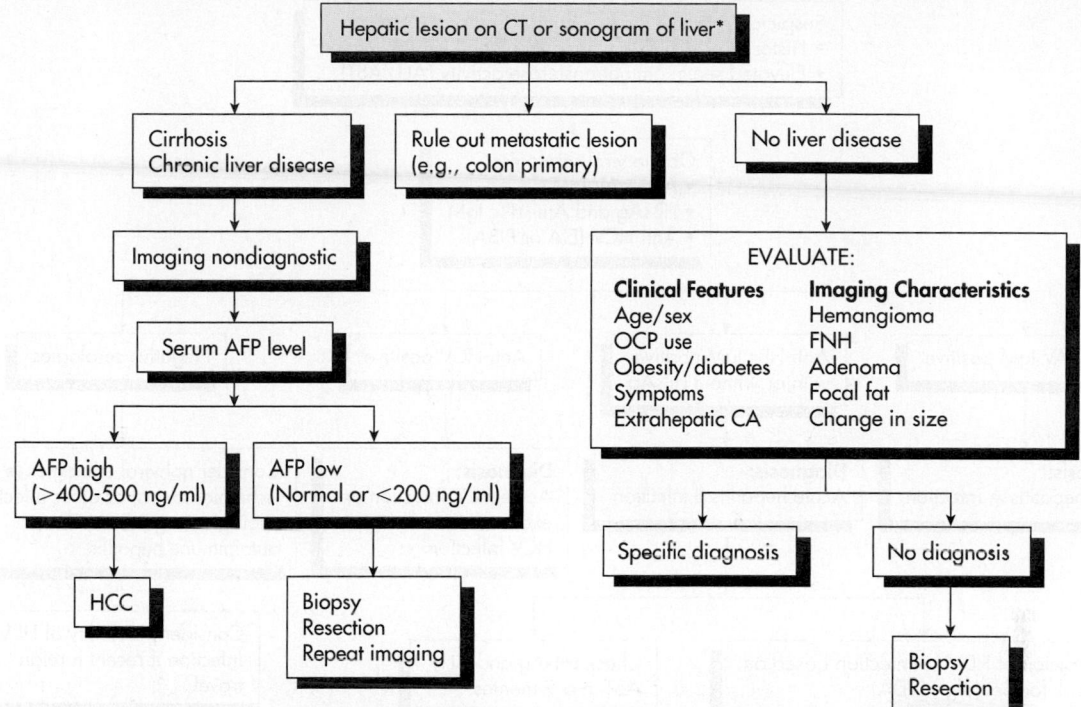

FIGURE 3-98 Diagnostic approach to space-occupying lesions of the liver. *AFP,* α-Fetoprotein; *CA,* cancer antigen; *FNH,* focal nodular hyperplasia; *HCC,* hepatocellular carcinoma; *OCP,* oral contraceptives. *Please refer also to algorithm for Liver Mass, Solid. (Modified from Goldman L, Schafer AL [eds]: *Cecil textbook of medicine,* ed 24, Philadelphia, 2012, Saunders.)

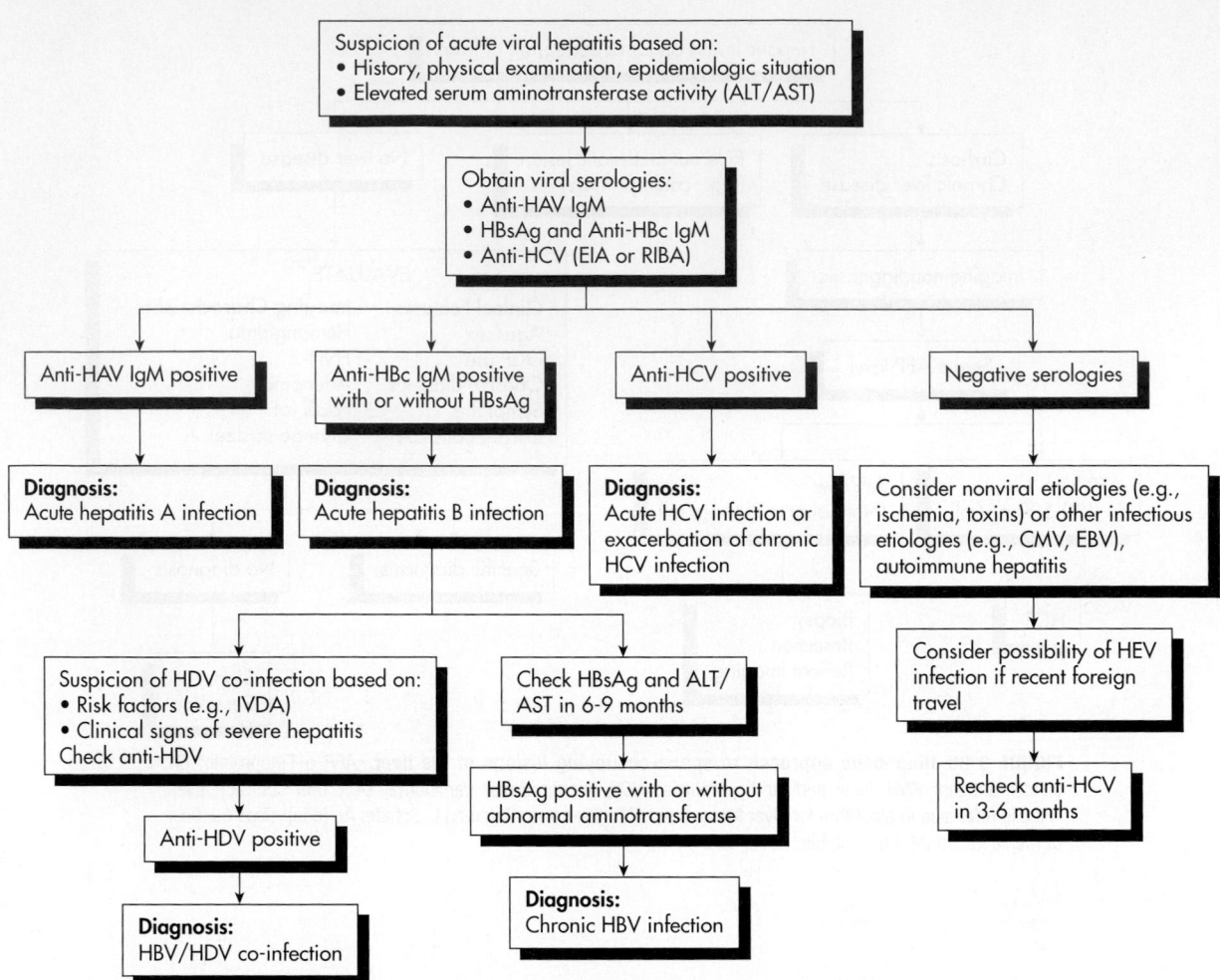

FIGURE 3-99 A flow diagram showing the use of specific serologic tests for the diagnosis of acute viral hepatitis in relation to the clinical and epidemiologic setting. Co-infections and superinfections of chronic hepatitis B or C patients should always be considered in cases that do not fit well with the clinical or serologic picture. *CMV,* Cytomegalovirus; *EBV,* Epstein-Barr virus; *EIA,* enzyme immunoassay; *HBV,* hepatitis B virus; *HCV,* hepatitis C virus; *HDV,* hepatitis D virus; *HEV,* hepatoencephalomyelitis virus; *IVDA,* intravenous drug abuse; *RIBA,* recombinant immunoblot assay. (Modified from Mandell GL et al: *Mandell, Douglas, and Bennett's principles and practice of infectious diseases,* ed 7, New York, 2008, Churchill Livingstone.)

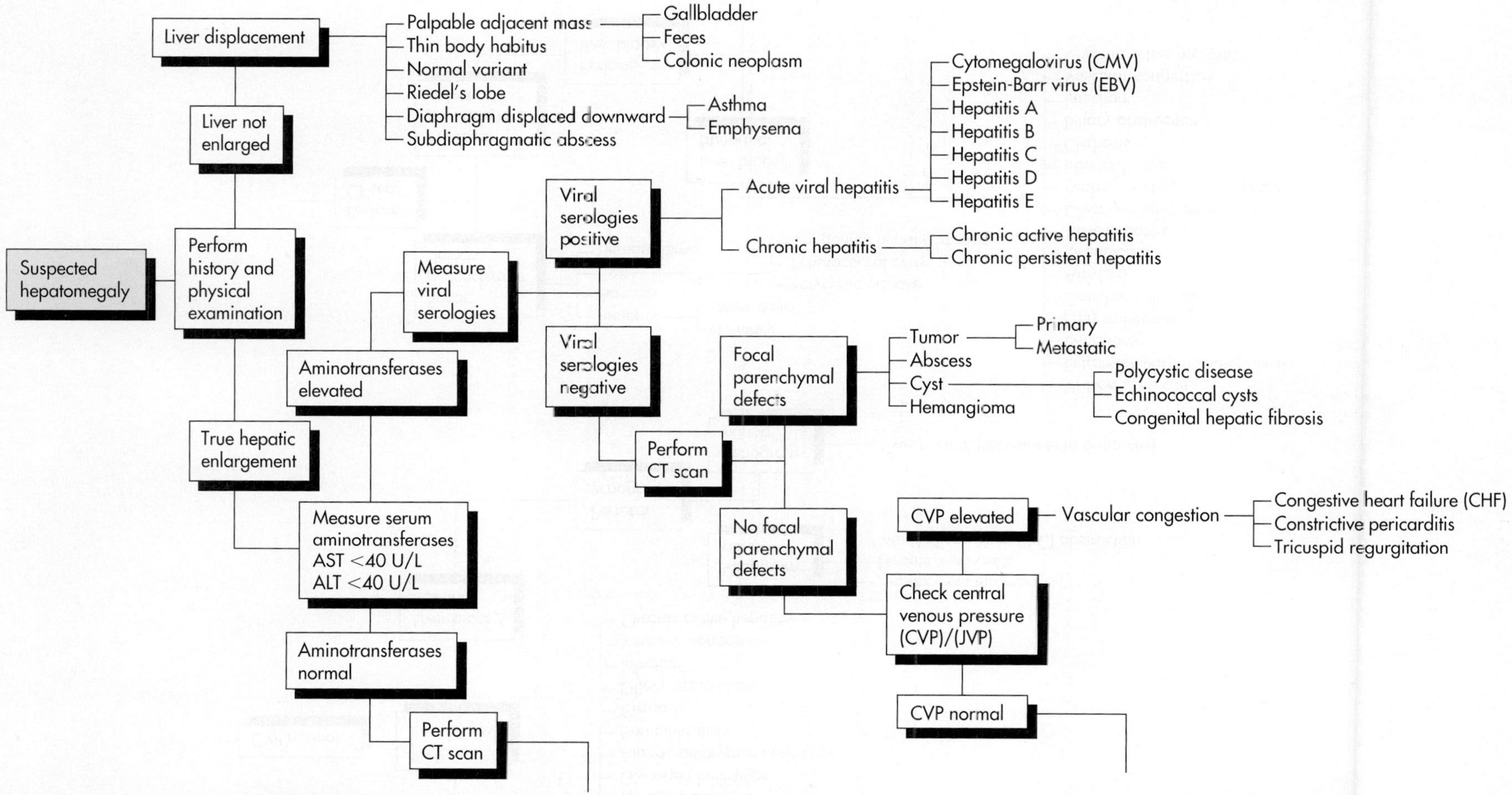

HEPATOMEGALY

Suspected hepatomegaly

Perform history and physical examination

Liver displacement
- Palpable adjacent mass
  - Gallbladder
  - Feces
  - Colonic neoplasm
- Thin body habitus
- Normal variant
- Riedel's lobe
- Diaphragm displaced downward
  - Asthma
  - Emphysema
- Subdiaphragmatic abscess

Liver not enlarged

True hepatic enlargement

Aminotransferases elevated

Measure serum aminotransferases
AST <40 U/L
ALT <40 U/L

Aminotransferases normal

Perform CT scan

Measure viral serologies

Viral serologies positive

Acute viral hepatitis
- Cytomegalovirus (CMV)
- Epstein-Barr virus (EBV)
- Hepatitis A
- Hepatitis B
- Hepatitis C
- Hepatitis D
- Hepatitis E

Chronic hepatitis
- Chronic active hepatitis
- Chronic persistent hepatitis

Viral serologies negative

Perform CT scan

Focal parenchymal defects

Tumor
- Primary
- Metastatic
Abscess
Cyst
- Polycystic disease
- Echinococcal cysts
- Congenital hepatic fibrosis
Hemangioma

No focal parenchymal defects

Check central venous pressure (CVP)/(JVP)

CVP elevated

Vascular congestion
- Congestive heart failure (CHF)
- Constrictive pericarditis
- Tricuspid regurgitation

CVP normal

FIGURE 3-100 Hepatomegaly. *ALT,* Alanine aminotransferase; *AST,* aspartate aminotransferase; *CT,* computed tomography; *JVP,* jugular venous pressure. (Modified from Healey PM: *Common medical diagnosis: an algorithmic approach,* ed 3, Philadelphia, 2000, Saunders.)

Continued

Clinical Algorithms

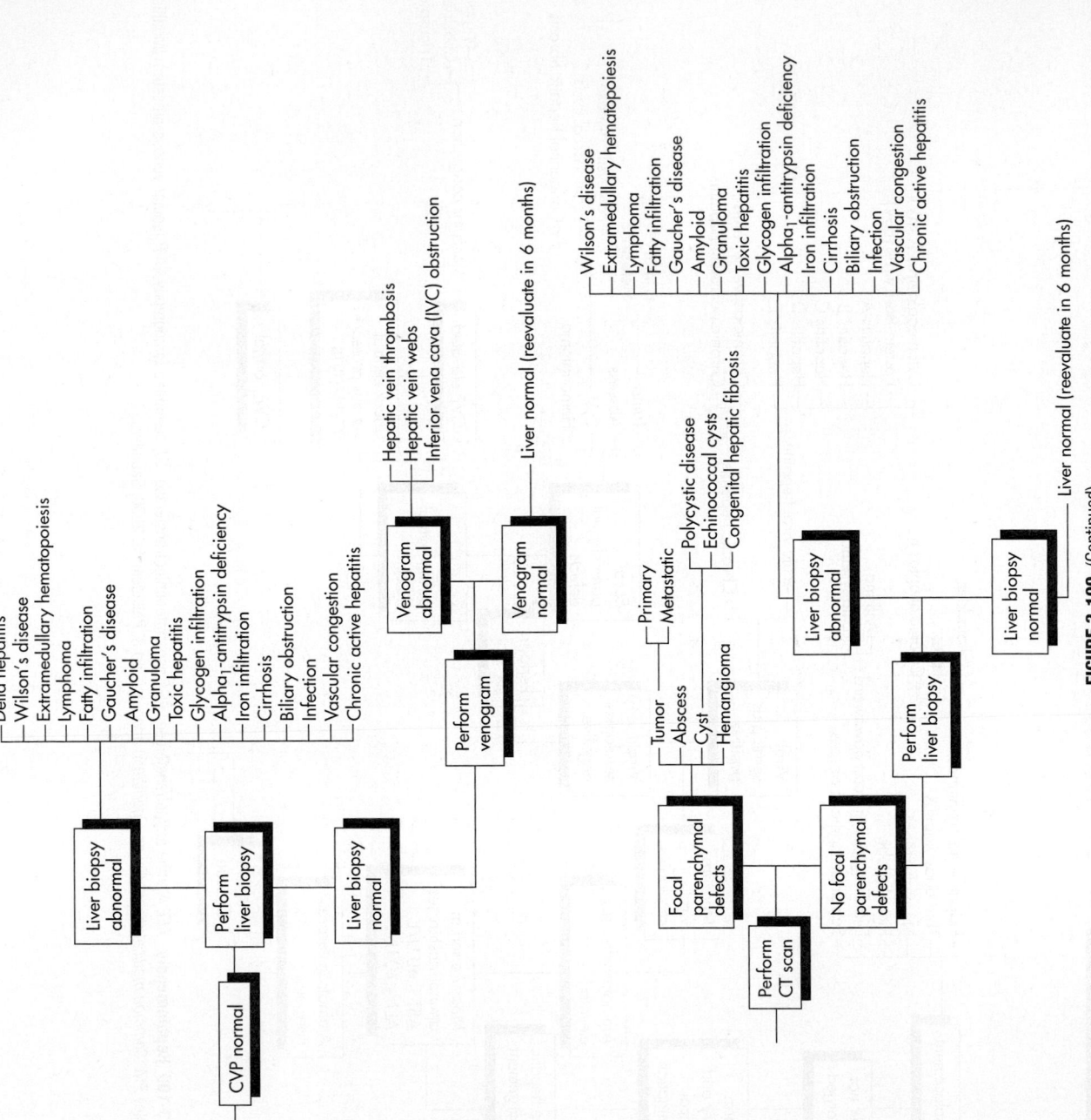

FIGURE 3-100   (Continued)

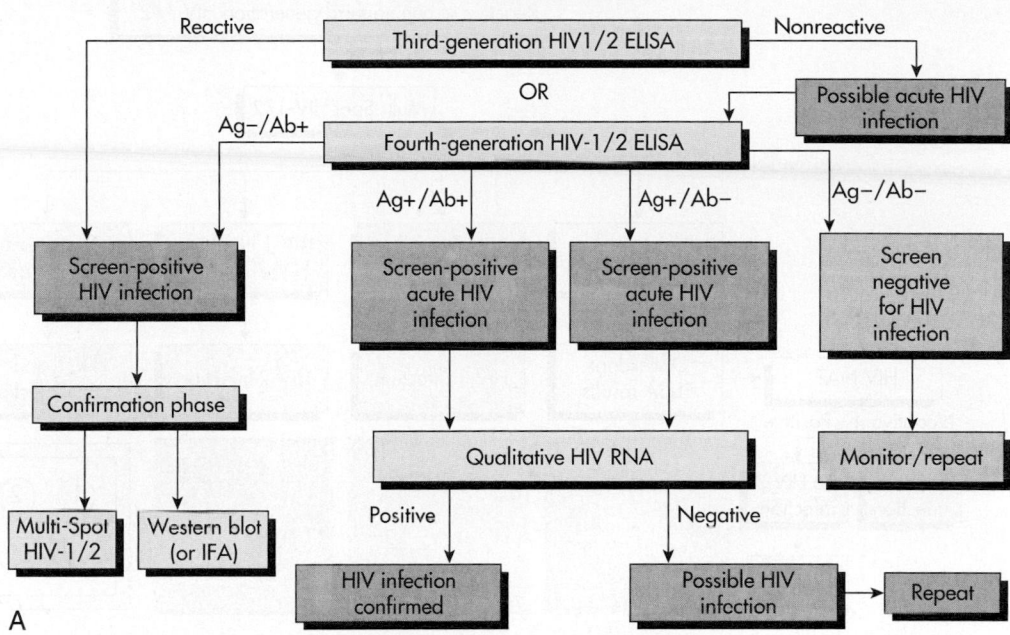

HIV Screening Phase

A

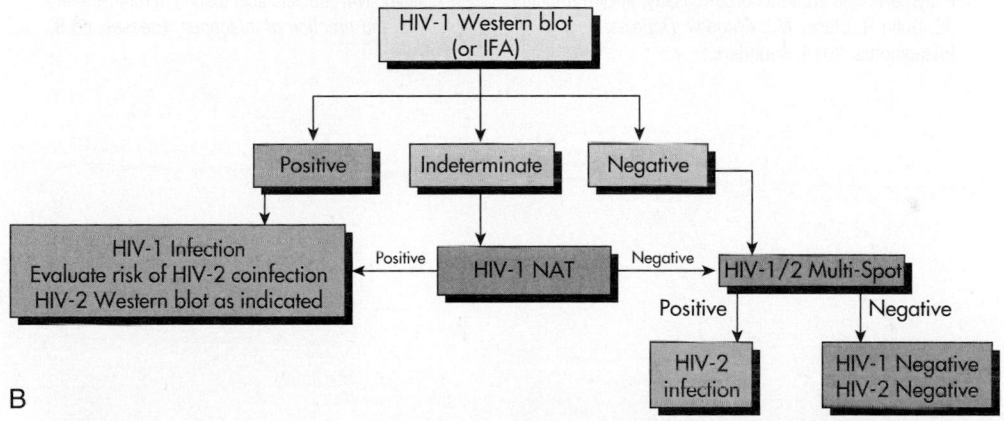

Confirmation Phase: Western Blot

B

FIGURE 3-101 Algorithms for human immunodeficiency virus (HIV) detection in patients at risk for HIV infection. In the absence of documented infection (noted in *yellow*), all individuals with HIV risk factors should be monitored and followed as indicated with routine testing. **A,** Screening algorithm. HIV screening should be considered for all patients at elevated risk for infection. The choice of screening test may be guided by clinical circumstances. **B,** Confirmation algorithm: Western blot. Negative and indeterminate results require discussion and consideration for alternative possibilities, especially the presence of acute HIV infection.

PROPOSED CONFIRMATION PHASE: MULTI-SPOT ALGORITHM

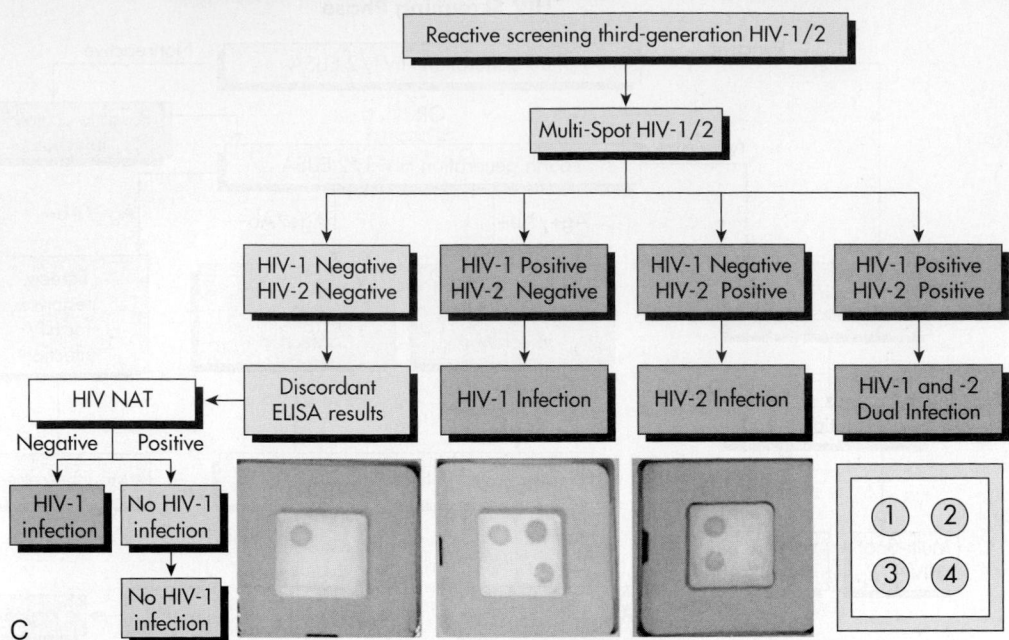

FIGURE 3-101 (Continued) **C,** Confirmation algorithm: proposed Multi-Spot algorithm, enabling screening and confirmation to be performed using rapid testing. It distinguishes HIV-1 from HIV-2 or dual infection. *ELISA,* Enzyme-linked immunosorbent assay; *IFA,* immunofluorescence assay; *NAT,* nucleic acid testing. (From Bennett JE, Dolin R, Blaser MJ: *Mandell, Douglas, and Bennett's principles and practice of infectious diseases,* ed 8, Philadelphia, 2015, Saunders.)

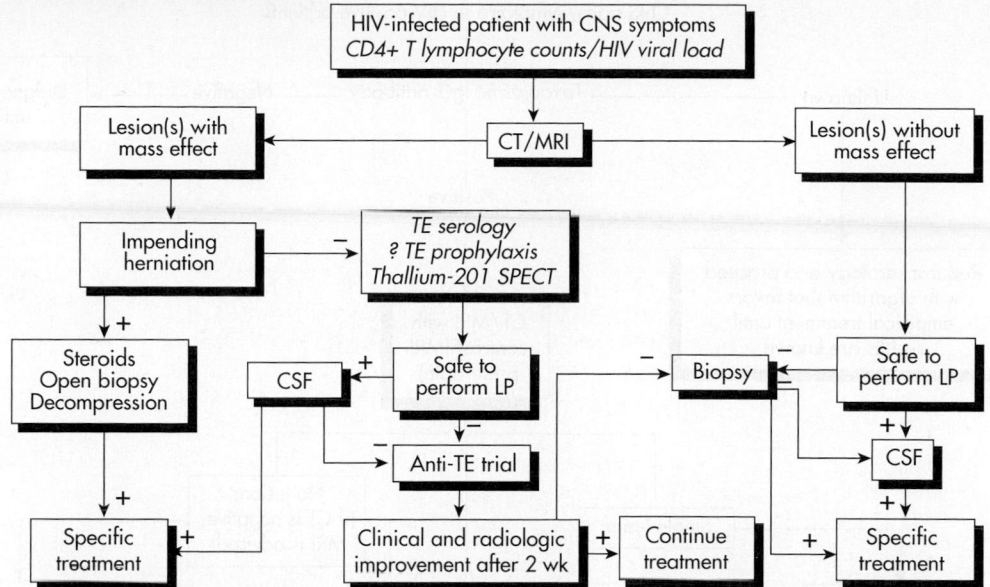

FIGURE 3-102 Management of the human immunodeficiency virus (HIV) type 1–infected patient with central nervous system (CNS) mass lesions. The elements in italics represent data that contribute to the decision-making process (see text for details). *CSF,* Cerebrospinal fluid; *CT,* computed tomography; *LP,* lumbar puncture; *MRI,* magnetic resonance imaging; *SPECT,* single-photon emission computed tomography; *TE, Toxoplasma* encephalitis. (From Bennett JE, Dolin R, Blaser MJ: *Mandell, Douglas, and Bennett's principles and practice of infectious diseases,* ed 8, Philadelphia, 2015, Saunders.)

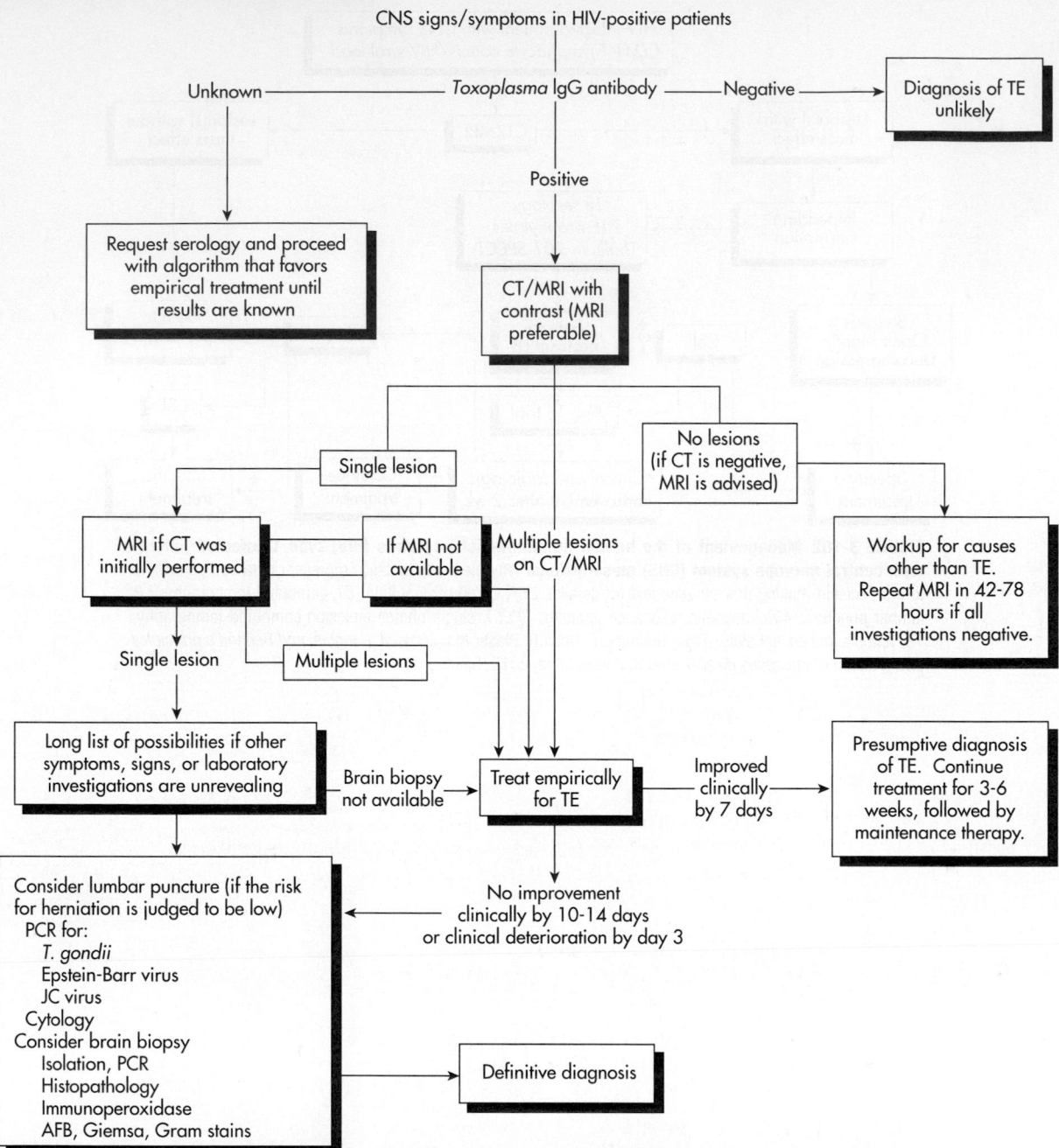

FIGURE 3-103 Diagnostic approach and management algorithm for human immunodeficiency virus (HIV)-infected patients with central nervous system (CNS) symptoms or signs that might potentially be toxoplasmic encephalitis (TE). *AFB,* Acid-fast bacilli; *CT,* computed tomography; *IgG,* immunoglobulin G; *MRI,* magnetic resonance imaging; *PCR,* polymerase chain reaction. (From Bennett JE, Dolin R, Blaser MJ: *Mandell, Douglas, and Bennett's principles and practice of infectious diseases,* ed 8, Philadelphia, 2015, Saunders.)

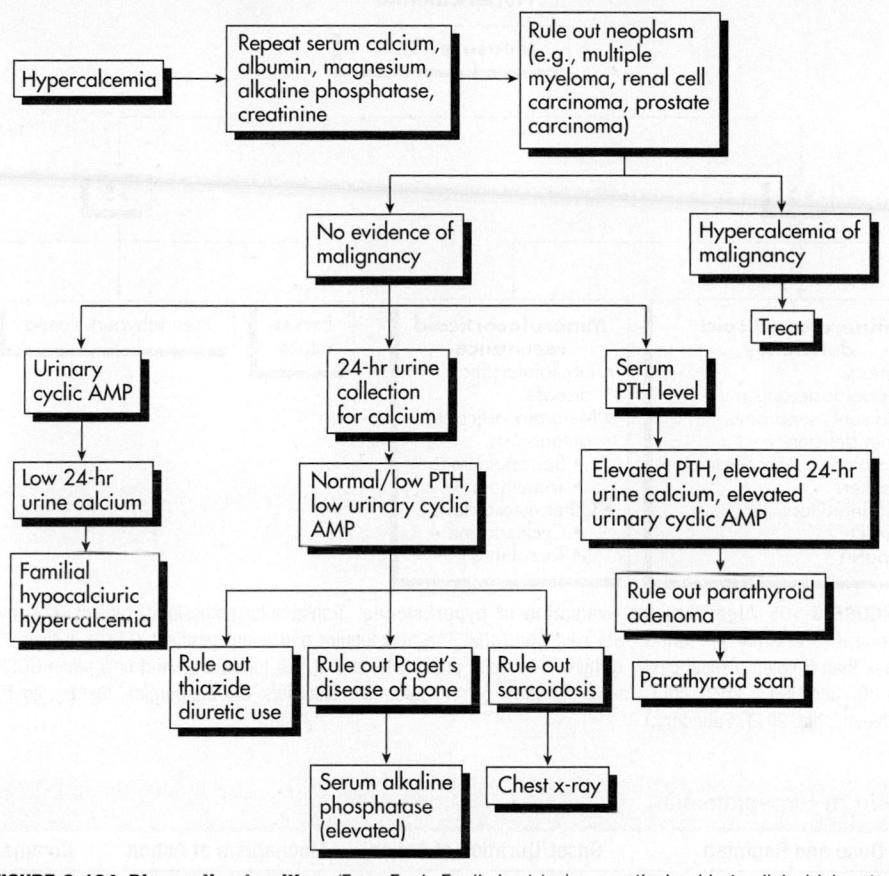

FIGURE 3-104 Diagnostic algorithm. (From Ferri, *Ferri's best test: a practical guide to clinical laboratory medicine and diagnostic imaging,* ed 3, Philadelphia, Saunders, 2014.)

Diagnostic Imaging
Best Test(s)
None

Ancillary Tests
Radiograph of painful bones (r/o bone neoplasm, multiple myeloma)
Tc-99m parathyroid scan (r/o parathyroid adenoma)
Ultrasound of parathyroid glands
Ultrasound of kidneys (r/o renal cell carcinoma)

Lab Evaluation
Best Test(s)
Serum calcium level
PTH level

Ancillary Tests
Serum phosphate, magnesium, alkaline phosphatase, albumin
Electrolytes, BUN, creatinine
24-hour urine collection for calcium
Urinary cyclic AMP
PSA (if prostate carcinoma is suspected)
Serum and urine protein immunoelectrophoresis (if multiple myeloma suspected)

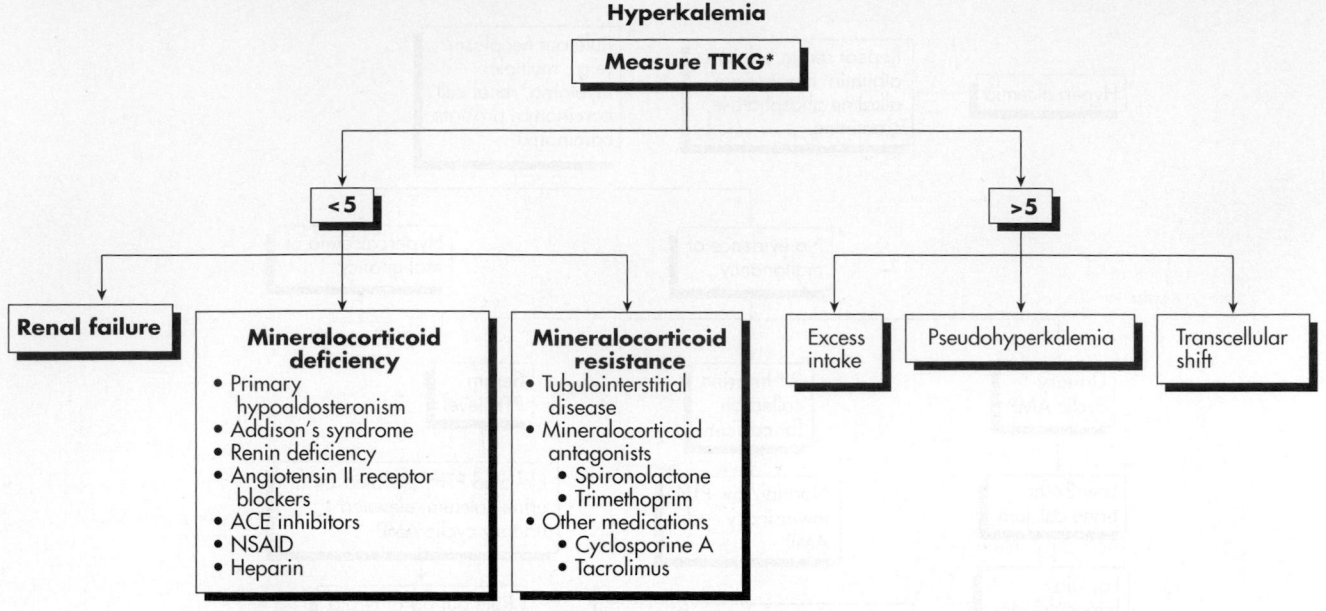

FIGURE 3-105 Algorithm for evaluation of hyperkalemia. Transtubular potassium gradient (TTKG) = Urine K$^+$ / Plasma K$^+$ / Urine OSM / Plasma OSM. The transtubular potassium gradient (TTKG) is typically less than 5 when a renal cause of hyperkalemia is present. Note that this formula is valid only when UOSM > 300 and UNa > 25. (From Cameron JL, Cameron AM: *Electrolyte disorders, Current surgical therapy,* ed 10, Philadelphia, 2011, Saunders.)

Table 3-24 Treatment of Hyperkalemia

Agent or Modality	Dose and Regimen	Onset/Duration of Action	Mechanism of Action	Comments
Calcium gluconate (10%) or calcium chloride (10%)	10 mL IV (may repeat × 2 prn every 5-10 min)	1-5 min/~1 hr	Antagonizes membrane effects of K	ECG monitoring required Do not mix with HCO$_3^-$ *Beware:* Hypercalcemia
Albuterol	10-20 mg (nebulized) by inhalation	30 min/2+ hr	Intracellular movement of K	Relatively free of significant side effects; tachycardia
Glucose and insulin	10-20 units regular insulin per 100 g glucose	30 min/while infusion continued	Intracellular movement of K	*Beware:* Hyperglycemia Hypoglycemia Infused volume may be decreased by giving D$_{10}$W, D$_{20}$W, or D$_{50}$W
Sodium bicarbonate	150 mEq/L IV infusion (rate variable)	Approximately 10-15 min/1-2 hr	Possible intracellular movement of K	Sodium bicarbonate
Kayexalate	25 g in 25 mL 70% sorbitol PO q6h ± 50 g in 50 mL 70% sorbitol by retention enema q6h	Hours/while continued	Exchange of K for Na	Slow and modest effect *Beware:* Na overload Enema must be retained × 30-45 min
Dialysis	HD PD	Minutes/while continued	Removal of K from blood	HD may remove 50 mEq/hr (*beware:* K rebound) PD may remove 15 mEq/hr
Intravenous diuretics (intravenous fluid if patient is hypovolemic)		Minutes/while diuresis continued (depending on renal function)	Urinary K excretion	Only in patients with some residual renal function

$D_{10}W$, 10% dextrose in water; $D_{20}W$, 20% dextrose in water; $D_{50}W$, 50% dextrose in water; *ECG*, electrocardiogram; *HD*, hemodialysis; *IV*, intravenously; *PD*, peritoneal dialysis; *PO*, orally.
From Marx JA et al: *Rosen's emergency medicine*, ed 8, Philadelphia, 2014, Saunders.

Diagnostic Imaging
Best Test(s)
None

Ancillary Tests
None
Lab Evaluation
Best Test(s)
Heparinized potassium level

Ancillary Tests
- Serum electrolytes, BUN, plasma osmolality, urine osmolality creatinine, urine potassium, calculation of TTKG (see Fig. E3-105)
- Glucose, CBC
- CPK (when rhabdomyolysis is suspected)

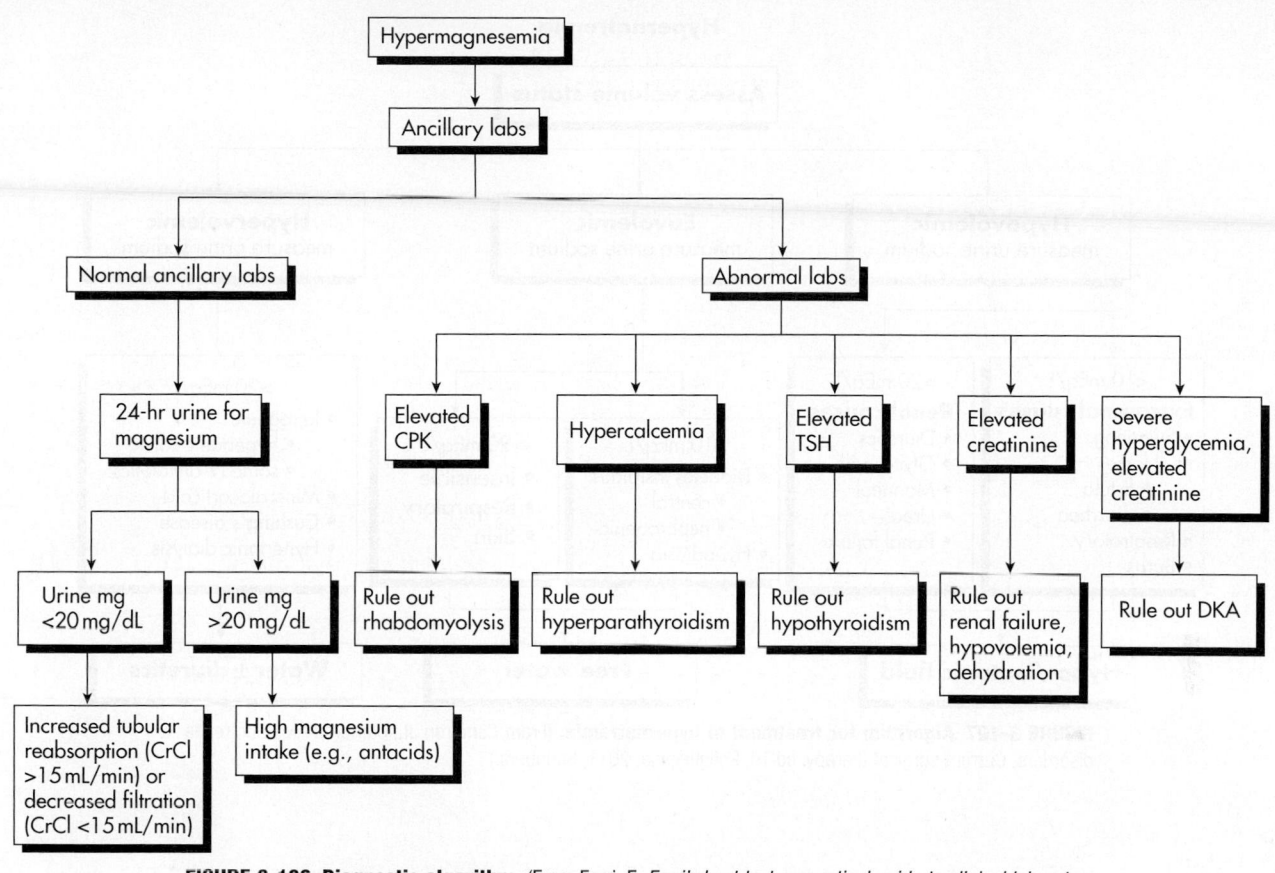

FIGURE 3-106 Diagnostic algorithm. (From Ferri, F: *Ferri's best test: a practical guide to clinical laboratory medicine and diagnostic imaging,* ed 3, Philadelphia, 2014, Saunders.)

Diagnostic Imaging
Best Test(s)
None

Ancillary Tests
• None
Lab Evaluation
Best Test(s)
• 24-hour urine magnesium level

Ancillary Tests
• Serum electrolytes, calcium
• BUN, creatinine, glucose
• TSH
• CPK

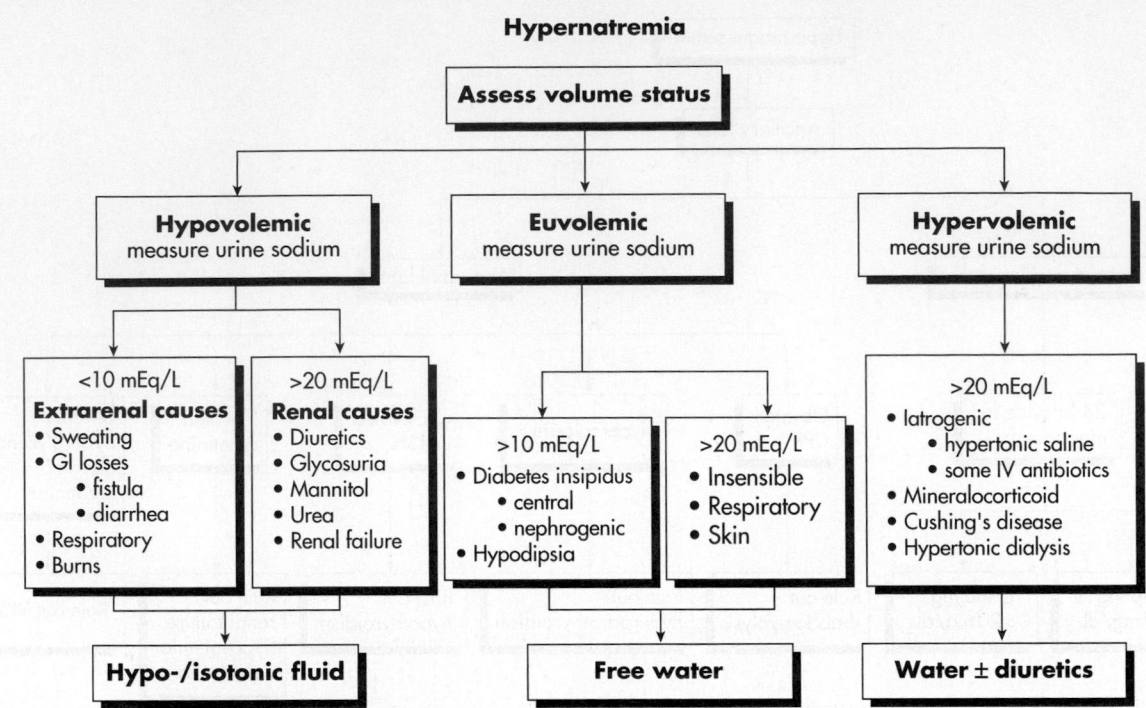

FIGURE 3-107 Algorithm for treatment of hypernatremia. (From Cameron JL, Cameron AM: Electrolyte disorders, Current surgical therapy, ed 10, Philadelphia, 2011, Saunders.)

Diagnostic Imaging	**Ancillary Tests**
Best Test(s)	Urine osmolality
None	BUN, creatinine
Ancillary Tests	
None	
Lab Evaluation	
Best Test(s)	
Serum electrolytes, urine sodium	

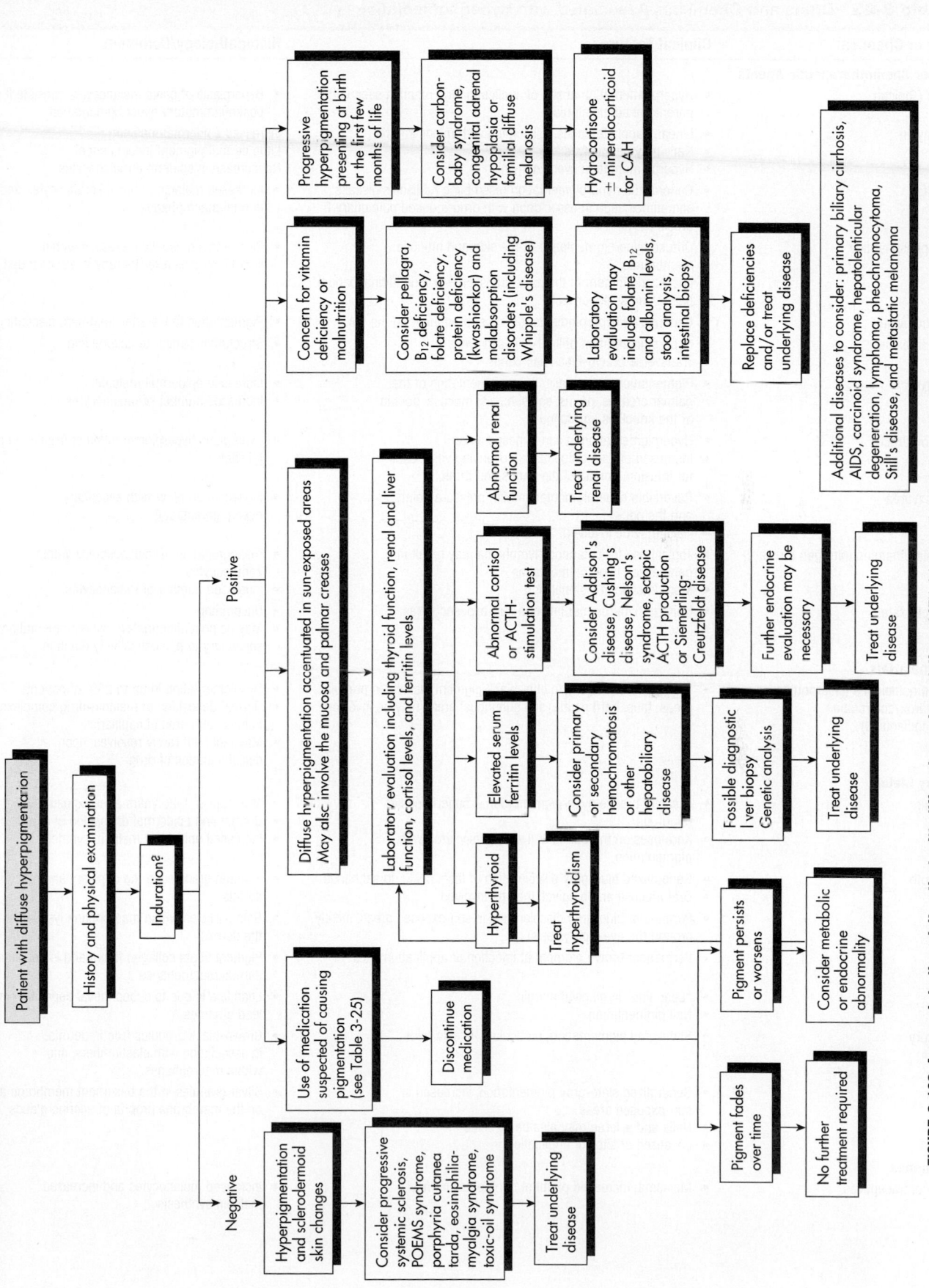

FIGURE 3-108 Approach to the adult patient with diffuse hyperpigmentation. *ACTH,* Adrenocorticotropic hormone; *AIDS,* acquired immunodeficiency syndrome; *CAH,* congenital adrenal hyperplasia; *POEMS,* polyneuropathy, organomegaly, endocrinopathies, monoclonal gammopathy, skin changes. (From Bolognia JL et al [eds]: *Dermatology,* ed 2, St Louis, 2008, Mosby.)

Clinical Algorithms

III

Table 3-25   Drugs and Chemicals Associated with Hyperpigmentation

Drug or Chemical	Clinical Features	Histopathology/Comment
Cancer Chemotherapeutic Agents		
BCNU (Topical)	• Hyperpigmentation at site of application (no reaction seen with parenteral administration)	• Hyperplasia of basal melanocytes consistent with postinflammatory hyperpigmentation
Bleomycin	• Linear, flagellate bands, associated with minor trauma • Nails may be involved • Hyperpigmentation overlying joints	Increased epidermal melanin Little dermal pigment incontinence No increase in epidermal melanocytes
Busulfan	• Generalized hyperpigmentation resembling Addison's disease; sometimes seen in association with drug-induced pulmonary fibrosis	• Increased melanin in basal keratinocytes and in dermal macrophages
Cyclophosphamide	• Diffuse hyperpigmentation of the skin and mucous membranes • Localized pigment of the nails (transverse or longitudinal bands), palms and soles, or teeth	• Pigmentation usually regresses within 6 to 12 months after therapy is discontinued
Dactinomycin	• Generalized hyperpigmentation, most prominent on the face	• Pigmentation fades after treatment discontinued
Daunorubicin	• Hyperpigmentation of light-exposed areas • Transverse brown-black nail bands	• Structurally similar to doxorubicin
Doxorubicin	• Pigmentation of the nails; hyperpigmentation of the palmar creases, palms, soles, buccal mucosa, dorsae of the knuckles and tongue	• Increased epidermal melanin • Increased number of melanocytes
5-Fluorouracil	• Hyperpigmentation in sun-exposed areas • Increased pigmentation of skin overlying veins used for infusion, dorsae of the hands and trunk	• Synergistic hyperpigmentation of irradiation portal sites
Hydroxyurea	• Reversible hyperpigmentation over pressure points and the back • Nails may be involved	• Lichenoid eruption with secondary hyperpigmentation
Mechlorethamine (nitrogen mustard)	• Topical use for cutaneous lymphoma may result in generalized hyperpigmentation • More intense in lesional skin	• Disaggregation of melanosomes within keratinocytes • Increased number of melanocytes
Methotrexate	• Uniform hyperpigmentation in sun-exposed areas	• Uncommon • May be postinflammatory hyperpigmentation secondary to photosensitivity reaction
Antimalarials		
Amino quinolones (chloroquine, hydroxychloroquine, amodiaquine)	• Yellow-brown or gray to blue-black pigment, usually in pretibial areas; face, hard palate, and subungual areas may be involved	• Dyspigmentation in up to 25% of patients • Dermal deposition of melanin-drug complexes; hemosiderin around capillaries • May fade, but rarely resolves, upon discontinuation of drug
Heavy Metals		
Arsenic	• Areas of bronze hyperpigmentation ± superimposed raindrops • Keratoses on the palms and soles associated with pigmentation	• May appear 1-20 years after exposure • Dermal and epidermal deposition of arsenic • Increased epidermal melanin synthesis
Bismuth	• Generalized blue-gray discoloration of face, neck, dorsal hands • Oral mucosa and gingivae may be involved	• Bismuth granules in the papillary and reticular dermis
Gold	• Permanent blue-gray discoloration in sun-exposed areas, mostly around the eyes (chrysiasis)	• Gold particles within macrophage lysosomes in the dermis
Iron	• Permanent brown pigment at injection or application sites	• Pigment coats collagen fibers and is deposited in dermal macrophages
Lead	• "Lead line" in gingival margin • Nail pigmentation	• Lead line is due to subepithelial deposition of lead granules
Mercury	• Slate-gray pigmentation, particularly in skin folds	• Brown-black granules free in dermis, in association with elastic fibers, and within macrophages
Silver	• Generalized slate-gray pigmentation, increased in sun-exposed areas • Nails and sclerae may also be involved • Localized at sites of application	• Silver granules in the basement membrane and on the membrana propria of eccrine glands
Hormones		
Oral contraceptives	• Melasma; increased pigment of nipples and nevi	• Increased melanocytes and increased melanin synthesis

Table 3-25 Drugs and Chemicals Associated with Hyperpigmentation—cont'd

Drug or Chemical	Clinical Features	Histopathology/Comment
ACTH/MSH	• Diffuse brown or bronze pigmentation; seen in Addison's disease and Cushing's syndrome	• Increased melanin synthesis
Miscellaneous Compounds		
Amiodarone	• Slate-gray to violaceous discoloration of sun-exposed skin	• Yellow-brown granules in dermis, mostly perivascular • Lysosomal inclusions with a lipid-like substance
Azidothymidine (zidovudine, AZT)	• Nail and mucocutaneous hyperpigmentation	• Skin biopsy shows increased epidermal and dermal melanin
Clofazimine	• Diffuse red to red-brown discoloration of skin • Violet-brown to bluish discoloration, especially lesional skin	• Redness secondary to drug in fat • Phagolysosomes with lipofuscin material
Dioxins	• Chloracne most common skin finding • Hyperpigmentation may occur in sun-exposed areas	• Rare, except in accidental exposure
Hydroquinone	• Hyperpigmentation in areas of application due to exogenous ochronosis	• Yellow-brown banana-shaped fibers in papillary dermis
Minocycline	• Blue-black discoloration in old acne scars or sites of inflammation as well as lower extremities • May also involve nails, sclerae, oral mucosa, bones, and teeth • Generalized "muddy brown" pigmentation pattern in some patients	• Iron-containing granules and/or increased melanin, depending on clinical type
Psoralens	• Increased pigmentation after exposure to UVA light (PUVA)	• Proliferation of follicular melanocytes • Increased synthesis and transfer of melanin
Psychotropic drugs (phenothiazine, chlorpromazine, imipramine, desipramine)	• Slate-gray discoloration in sun-exposed areas	• Golden-brown granules in the upper dermis • Electron-dense inclusion bodies

From Bolognia JL et al [eds]: *Dermatology,* ed 2, St Louis, 2008, Mosby.

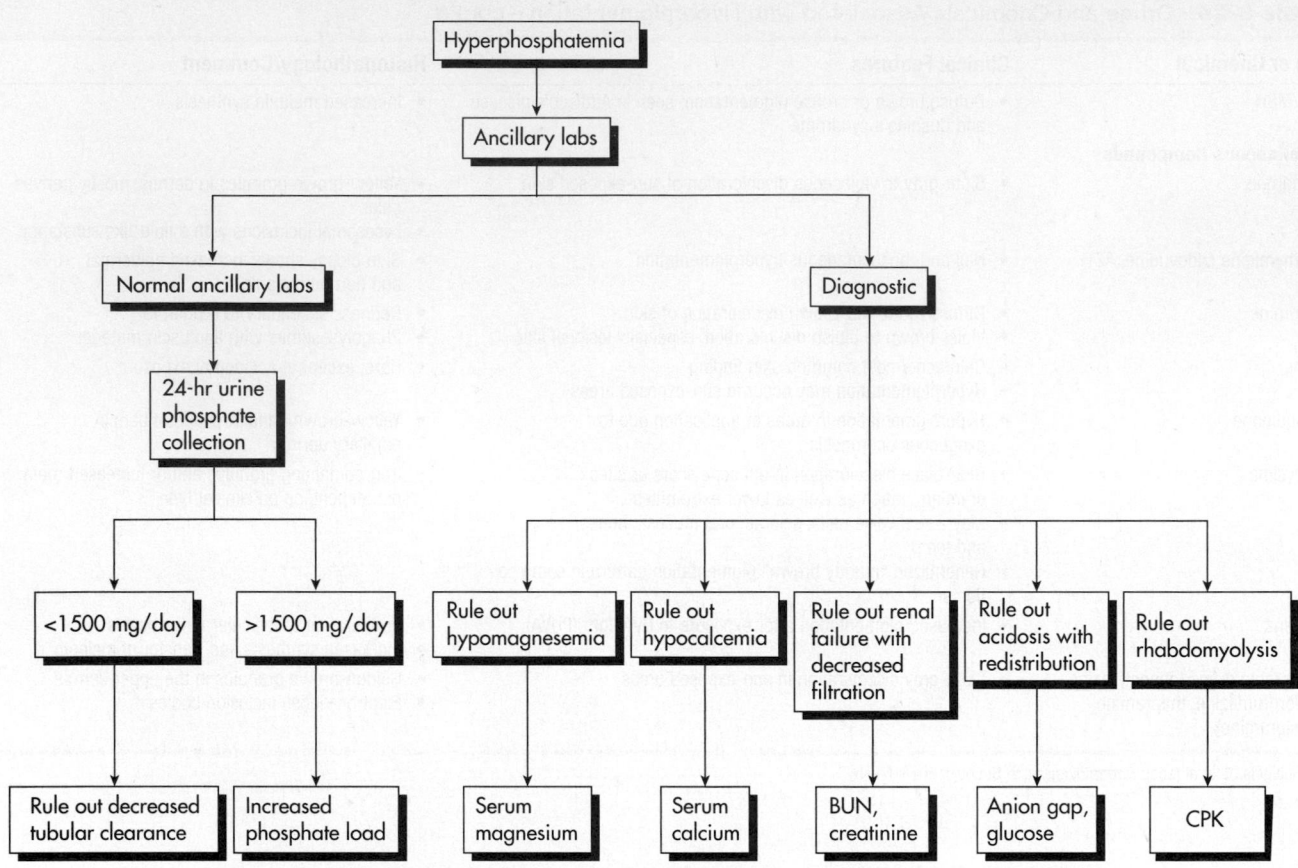

FIGURE 3-109 Diagnostic algorithm. (From Ferri, F: *Ferri's best test: a practical guide to clinical laboratory medicine and diagnostic imaging,* ed 3, Philadelphia, 2014, Saunders.)

Diagnostic Imaging
Best Test(s)
- None

Ancillary Tests
- None

Lab Evaluation
Best Test(s)
- 24-hour urine phosphate collection

Ancillary Tests
- Serum electrolytes, BUN, creatinine, magnesium, calcium, glucose
- Urinalysis, CPK

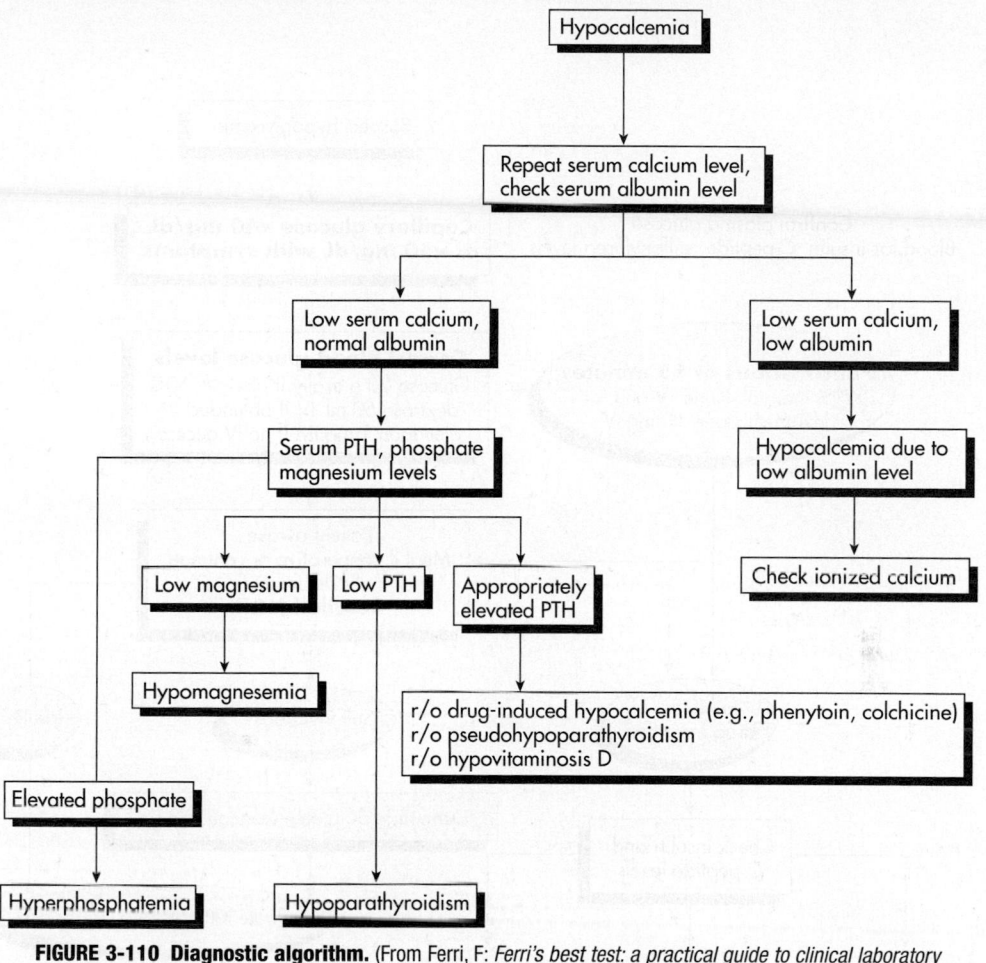

FIGURE 3-110 Diagnostic algorithm. (From Ferri, F: *Ferri's best test: a practical guide to clinical laboratory medicine and diagnostic imaging,* ed 3, Philadelphia, 2014, Saunders.)

Diagnostic Imaging
Best Test(s)
- None

Ancillary Tests
- None

Lab Evaluation
Best Test(s)
- PTH

Ancillary Tests
- Serum albumin level
- Serum phosphate, magnesium level

Clinical
Algorithms

III

ICD-10CM # E16.2 Hypoglycemia, spontaneous
E16.0 Hypoglycemia, drug-induced
E16.1 Hypoglycemia, reactive
E16.3 Hypersecretion, glucagon

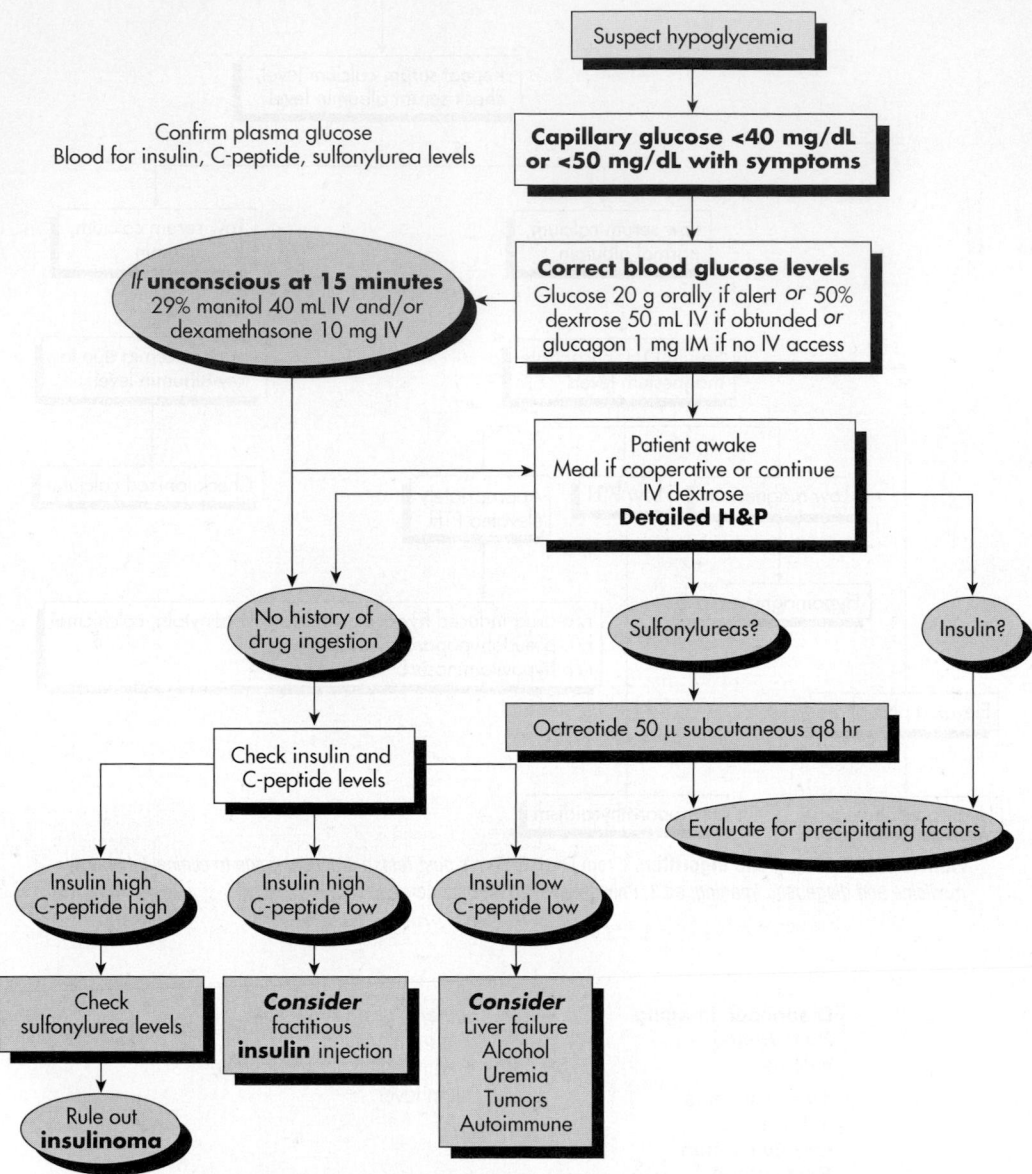

FIGURE 3-111 Decision tree for suspected hypoglycemia in adults. (From Vincent JL, Abraham E, Moore FA, et al: *Textbook of critical care*, ed 6, Philadelphia, 2011, Saunders.)

HYPOGONADISM

ICD-10CM #
E28.310	Symptomatic premature menopause
E29.1	Testicular hypofunction
E28.39	Other primary ovarian failure
E23.6	Other disorders of pituitary gland

1619

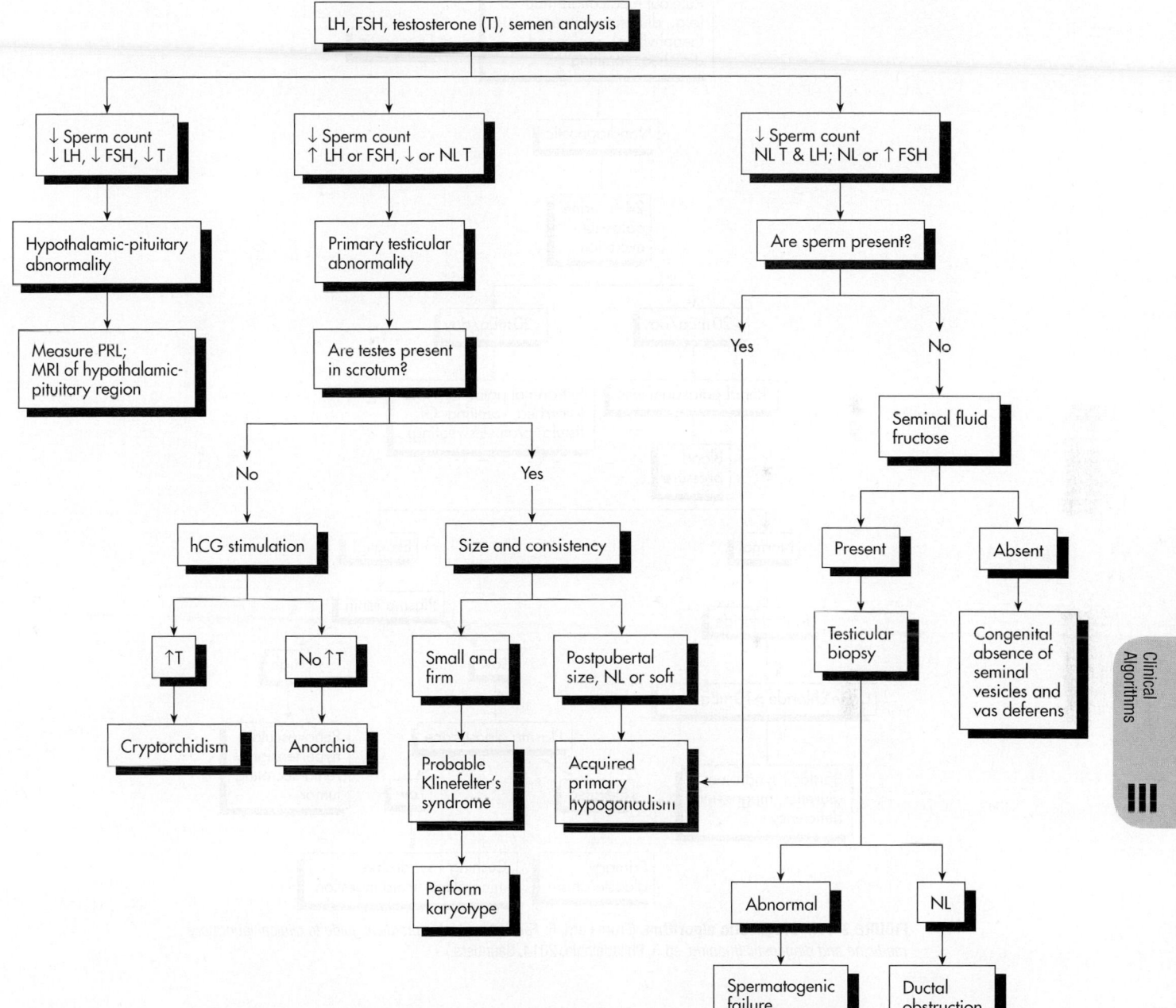

FIGURE 3-112 Laboratory evaluation of hypogonadism in men. *FSH*, Follicle-stimulating hormone; *hCG*, human chorionic gonadotropin; *LH*, luteinizing hormone; *MRI*, magnetic resonance imaging; *NL*, normal; *PRL*, prolactin; ↑, elevated; ↓, decreased or low. (From Andreoli TE [ed]: *Cecil essentials of medicine*, ed 7, Philadelphia, 2008, Saunders.)

Clinical Algorithms

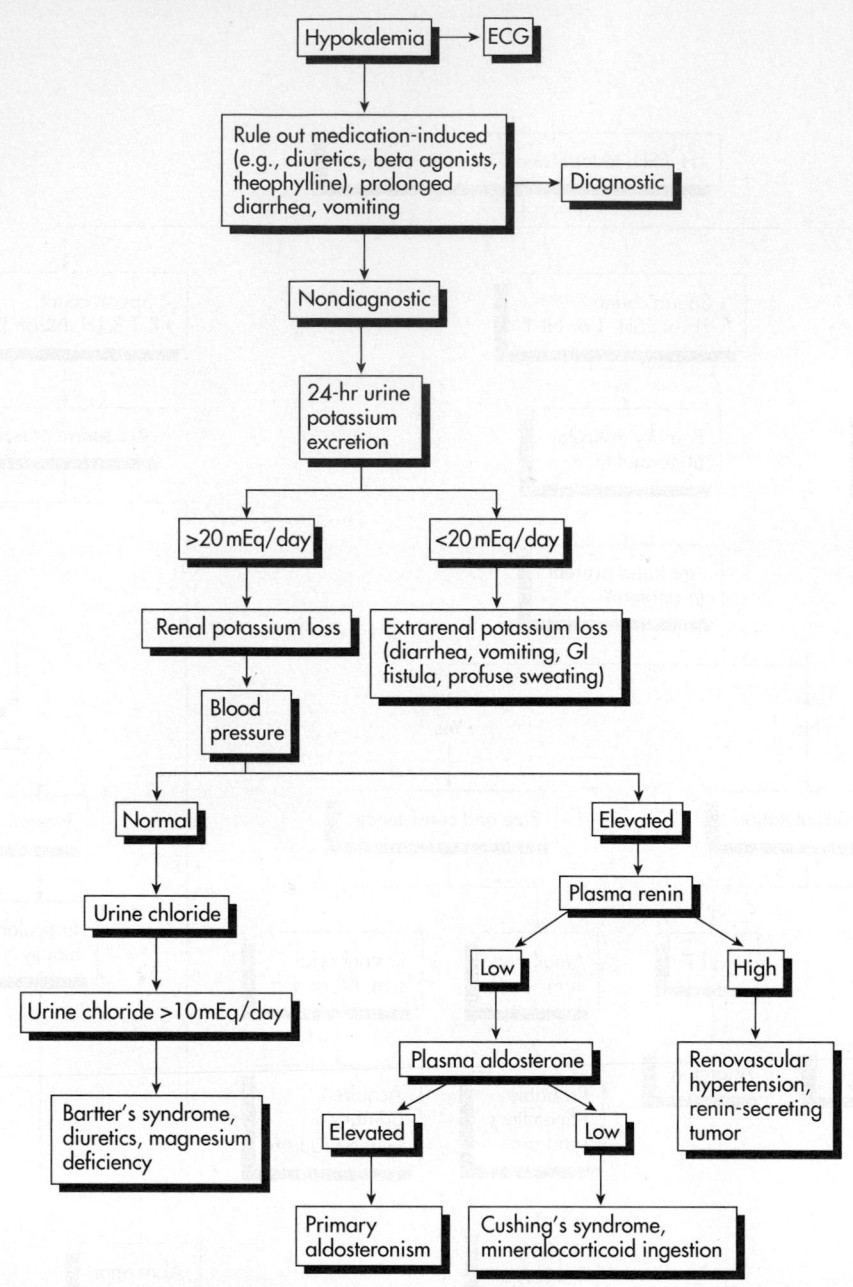

FIGURE 3-113 Diagnostic algorithm. (From Ferri, F: *Ferri's best test: a practical guide to clinical laboratory medicine and diagnostic imaging*, ed 3, Philadelphia, 2014, Saunders.)

Diagnostic Imaging
Best Test(s)
• None
Ancillary Tests
• ECG
Lab Evaluation
Best Test(s)
• 24-hour urine potassium excretion

Ancillary Tests
• Serum electrolyte, BUN, creatinine
• Urine chloride
• Plasma renin, aldosterone

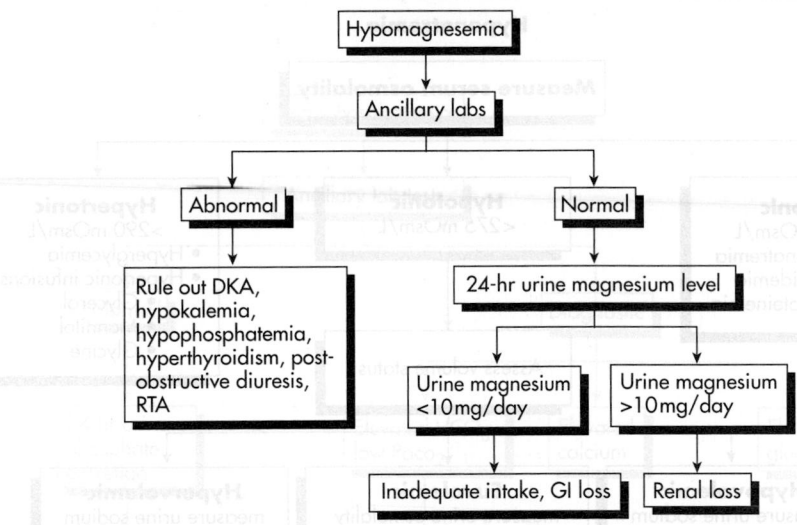

FIGURE 3-114 Diagnostic algorithm. (From Ferri, F: *Ferri's best test: a practical guide to clinical laboratory medicine and diagnostic imaging*, ed 3, Philadelphia, 2014, Saunders.)

Diagnostic Imaging
Best Test(s)
- None

Ancillary Tests
- None

Lab Evaluation
Best Test(s)
- 24-hour urine magnesium level

Ancillary Tests
- Serum electrolytes, calcium, phosphate, glucose, albumin
- BUN, creatinine
- TSH
- Urine sodium

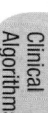

BOX 3-7   Screening Tests for T Cell Immunity

Screening Tests
- Newborn screening for TREC analysis (not available in all states)
- Absolute lymphocyte count
- Chest radiograph for thymus shadow in newborns
- Delayed skin hypersensitivity to recall antigens
- Quantification of T cell subsets

Advanced Testing
- Lymphocyte proliferative responses to mitogens, antigens, and allogeneic cells in MLC
- Lymphocyte-mediated cytotoxicity: NK and ADCC activity
- Production of cytokines
- Functional response to cytokines
- Signal transduction studies
- Molecular analysis for specific defects

ADCC, Antibody-dependent cellular cytotoxicity; *MLC,* mixed lymphocyte culture; *NK,* natural killer; *TREC,* T cell receptor excision circles.
From Adkinson NF et al: *Middleton's allergy principles and practice,* ed 8, Philadelphia, 2014, Saunders.

BOX 3-8   Screening Tests for B Cell Immune Function

Screening Tests
- Quantitative serum immunoglobulins
- Specific antibodies to vaccine responses
  - Tetanus, diphtheria (IgG1)
  - Pneumococcal and meningococcal polysaccharides (IgG2)
  - Viral respiratory pathogens (IgG1 and IgG3)
  - Other vaccines: hepatitis B, influenza, MMR, polio (killed vaccine)
- Isohemagglutinins (IgM antibodies to A and B blood group antigens)
- B cell quantitation by flow cytometry

Advanced Testing
- In vitro B cell immunoglobulin production
- Regulation of immunoglobulin synthesis
- CD40 ligand-CD40 interactions
- B-cell subsets: non-switched and switched memory B cells
- Molecular analysis for gene deletions or mutations

IgG, Immunoglobulin G; *MMR,* measles, mumps, rubella vaccine.
From Adkinson NF et al: *Middleton's allergy principles and practice,* ed 8, Philadelphia, 2014, Saunders.

Table 3-26 Physical Examination of Patients with Recurrent Infection

Diagnosis and Physical Findings	Associated Pathology
Growth Failure	
SCID	T/B cell combined deficiency
Dysmorphisms	
Micrognathia, short philtrum, ear anomalies	T cell deficiency (DiGeorge anomaly)
Short-limbed dwarfism	T cell deficiency (cartilage-hair hypoplasia)
Hypertelorism, epicanthal folds, flat nasal bridge	ICF syndrome
Ectodermal dysplasia	NEMO defect
Coarse facies	HIES
Skin and Oral Mucosa	
Rashes	
Lupus-like malar rash	Early complement pathway defect
Dermatomyositis rash	Bruton disease (XLA)
Erythroderma	Omenn syndrome
Eczema	Wiskott-Aldrich, hyper-IgE syndrome
Petechiae	Wiskott-Aldrich syndrome
Pyoderma, abscesses	Neutrophil or B cell defects
Poor wound healing	LAD
Candidiasis	T cell or T/B cell combined deficiency, APECED, IPEX, CMC
Telangiectasia	Ataxia-telangiectasia
Delayed umbilical cord separation	Neutrophil adhesion defect
Abnormal hair	Cartilage-hair hypoplasia, NEMO defect, Chediak-Higashi syndrome, Griscelli syndrome
Ears, Nose, Throat, and Mouth	
Chronic otitis media	B cell deficiency; mannose-binding lectin deficiency
Dull tympanic membranes	
Poor light reflex	
Scarring	
Perforations of the tympanic membrane	
Sinusitis	B cell deficiency
Purulent nasal discharge	
Purulent post-pharyngeal exudate	
Pharyngeal cobblestoning	
Dentition, gums	NEMO defect
Conical teeth	NEMO defect
Periodontitis	LAD, neutropenia
Respiratory Tract	
Digital clubbing	Defect in any immune component
Rales	Defect in any immune component
Wheezing	B cell (IgA) deficiency
Cardiac System	
Heart murmur (conotruncal abnormalities)	DiGeorge anomaly
Lymphatic System	
Absent tonsils, lymph nodes	Bruton disease (XLA), T/B cell combined deficiencies
Diffuse lymphoid hyperplasia	CVID, CGD, HIV infection, ALPS, XLP
Lymphadenitis	CGD
Musculoskeletal System	
Arthralgia, arthritis	B cell deficiency
Dermatomyositis	B cell or complement deficiency
Lupus-like syndrome	Complement (early classic pathway), CVID or IgA deficiency
Short-limb dwarfism	Cartilage-hair syndrome
Craniosynostosis	Hyper-IgE syndrome
Neurologic System	
Ataxia	Ataxia-telangiectasia
Enteroviral meningoencephalitis	B cell deficiency (Bruton disease [XLA])
Neuropathies	Chediak-Higashi and Griscelli syndromes
Pernicious anemia	CVID

ALPS, Autoimmune lymphoproliferative disease; *APECED*, autoimmune polyendocrinopathy candidiasis, ectodermal dystrophy syndrome; *CGD*, chronic granulomatous disease; *CMC*, chronic mucocutaneous candidiasis; *CVID*, common variable immunodeficiency; *HIES*, hyperimmunoglobulin E (hyper-IgE) syndrome; *HIV*, human immunodeficiency virus; *ICF*, immunodeficiency, centromere instability, and facial anomalies; *Ig*, immunoglobulin; *LAD*, leukocyte adhesion deficiency; *NEMO*, nuclear factor-κB (NF-κB) essential modulator; *SCID*, severe combined immunodeficiency disease; *XLA*, X-linked agammaglobulinemia; *XLP*, X-linked lymphoproliferative disease.

From Adkinson NF et al: *Middleton's allergy principles and practice*, ed 8, Philadelphia, 2014, Saunders.

Clinical Algorithms

III

ICD-10CM #	
M00.9	Pyogenic arthritis, unspecified
M86.9	Osteomyelitis unspecified
T84.3	Infection and inflammatory reaction
M79.9	Soft tissue disorder, unspecified

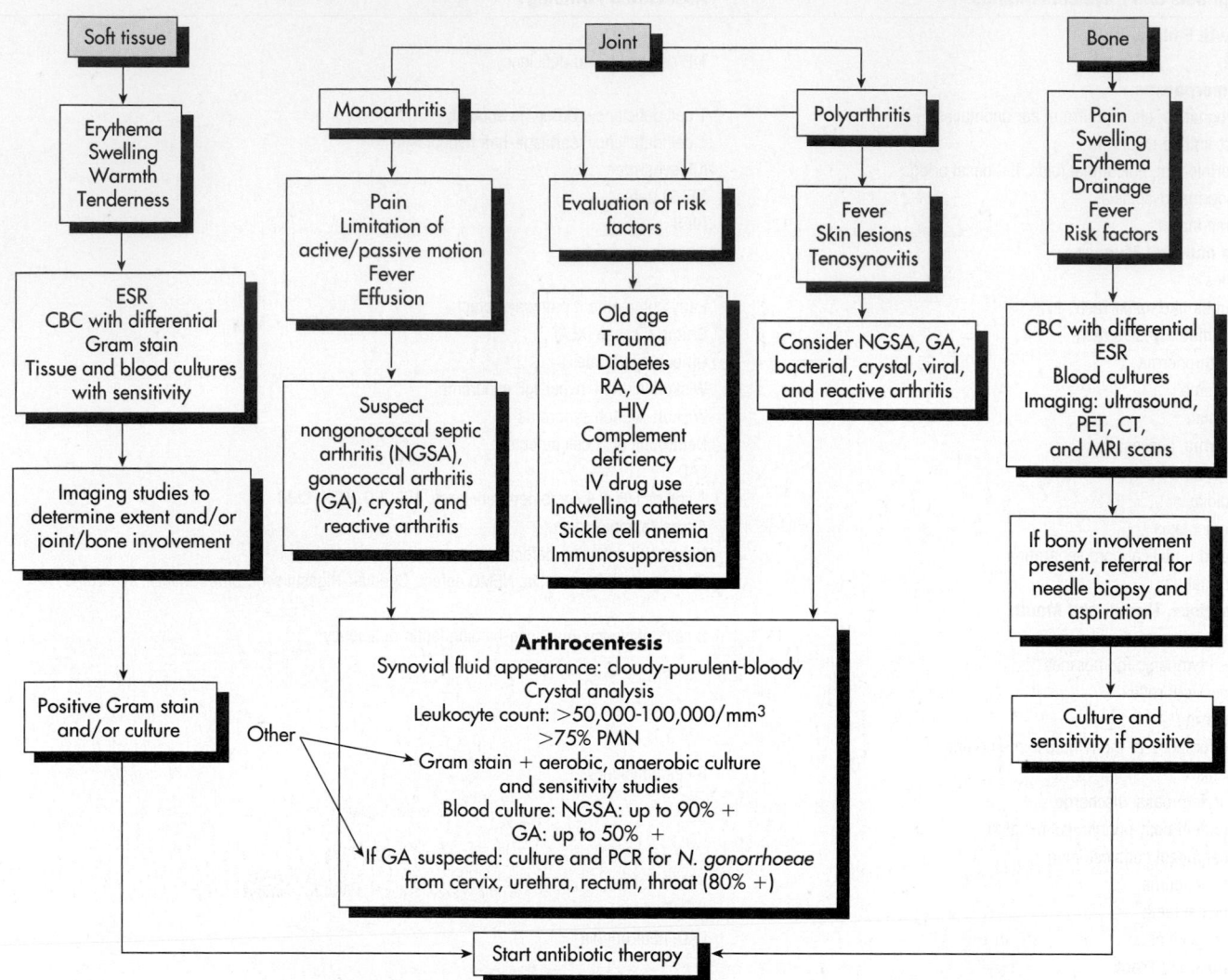

FIGURE 3-119 Clinical evaluation of infections of soft tissues, joints, and bone. *CBC,* Complete blood count; *CT,* computed tomography; *ESR,* erythrocyte sedimentation rate; *GA,* gonococcal arthritis; *HIV,* human immunodeficiency virus; *IV,* intravenous; *MRI,* magnetic resonance imaging; *NGSA,* nongonococcal septic arthritis; *OA,* osteoarthritis; *PCR,* polymerase chain reaction; *PET,* positron emission tomography; *PMN,* polymorphonuclear leukocyte; *RA,* rheumatoid arthritis. (From Goldman L, Schafer AI: *Goldman's Cecil medicine,* ed 24, Philadelphia, 2012, Saunders.)

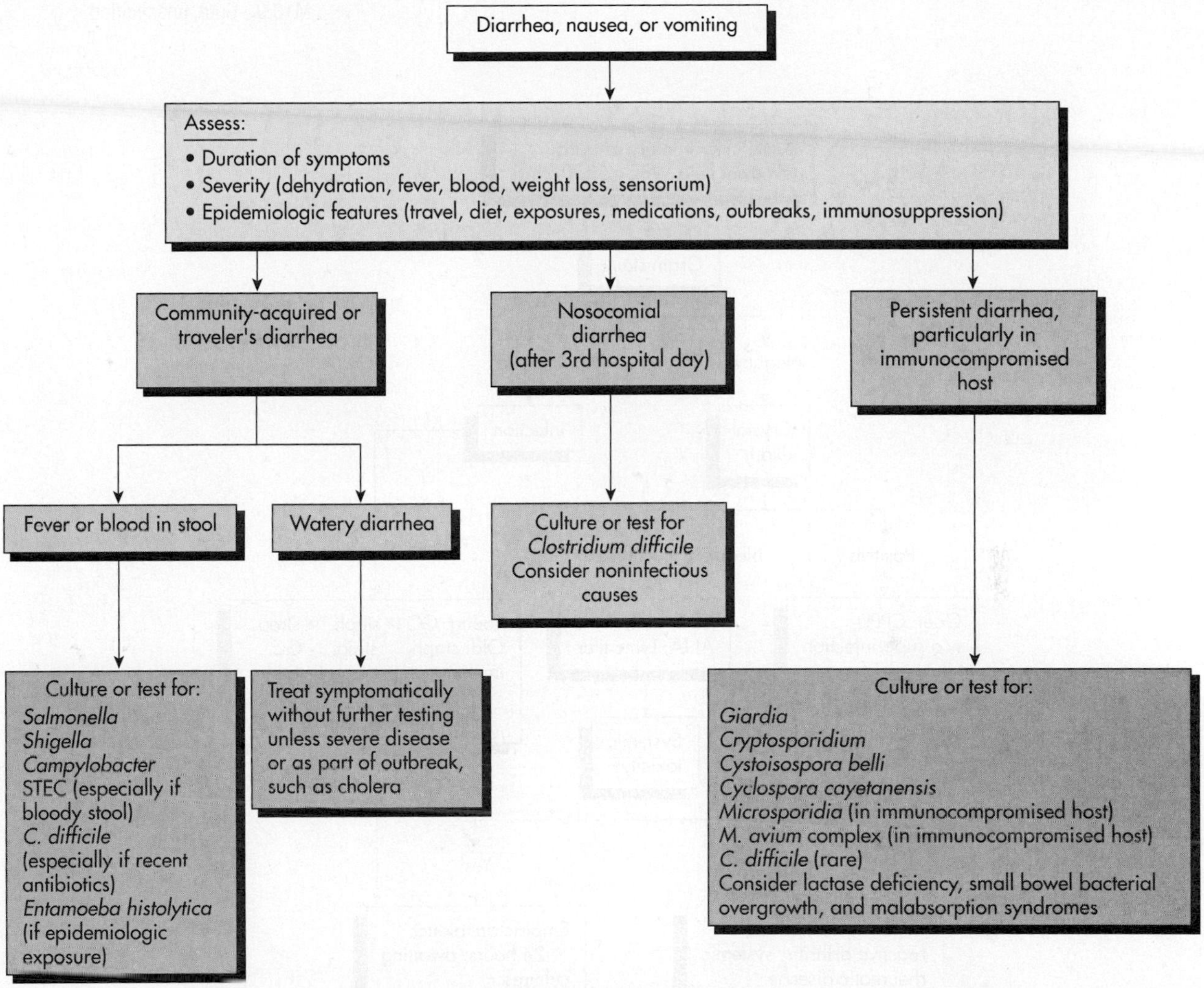

Diarrhea, nausea, or vomiting

Assess:
- Duration of symptoms
- Severity (dehydration, fever, blood, weight loss, sensorium)
- Epidemiologic features (travel, diet, exposures, medications, outbreaks, immunosuppression)

Community-acquired or traveler's diarrhea

Nosocomial diarrhea (after 3rd hospital day)

Persistent diarrhea, particularly in immunocompromised host

Fever or blood in stool

Watery diarrhea

Culture or test for
Clostridium difficile
Consider noninfectious causes

Culture or test for:
Salmonella
Shigella
Campylobacter
STEC (especially if bloody stool)
C. difficile
(especially if recent antibiotics)
Entamoeba histolytica
(if epidemiologic exposure)

Treat symptomatically without further testing unless severe disease or as part of outbreak, such as cholera

Culture or test for:
Giardia
Cryptosporidium
Cystoisospora belli
Cyclospora cayetanensis
Microsporidia (in immunocompromised host)
M. avium complex (in immunocompromised host)
C. difficile (rare)
Consider lactase deficiency, small bowel bacterial overgrowth, and malabsorption syndromes

FIGURE 3-120 Approach to diagnosis of infectious diarrhea. *STEC*, Shiga toxin producing *Escherichia coli.* (From Bennett JE, Dolin R, Blaser MJ: *Mandell, Douglas, and Bennett's principles and practice of infectious diseases,* ed 8, Philadelphia, 2015, Saunders.)

Clinical
Algorithms

ICD-10CM # M00.9 Pyogenic arthritis, unspecified
M01.1 Tuberculous arthritis
M01.2 Arthritis in Lyme disease
M01.5 Arthritis in viral disease
M02.9 Reactive arthropathy, unspecified
M08.9 Juvenile arthritis, unspecified
M10.9 Gout, unspecified

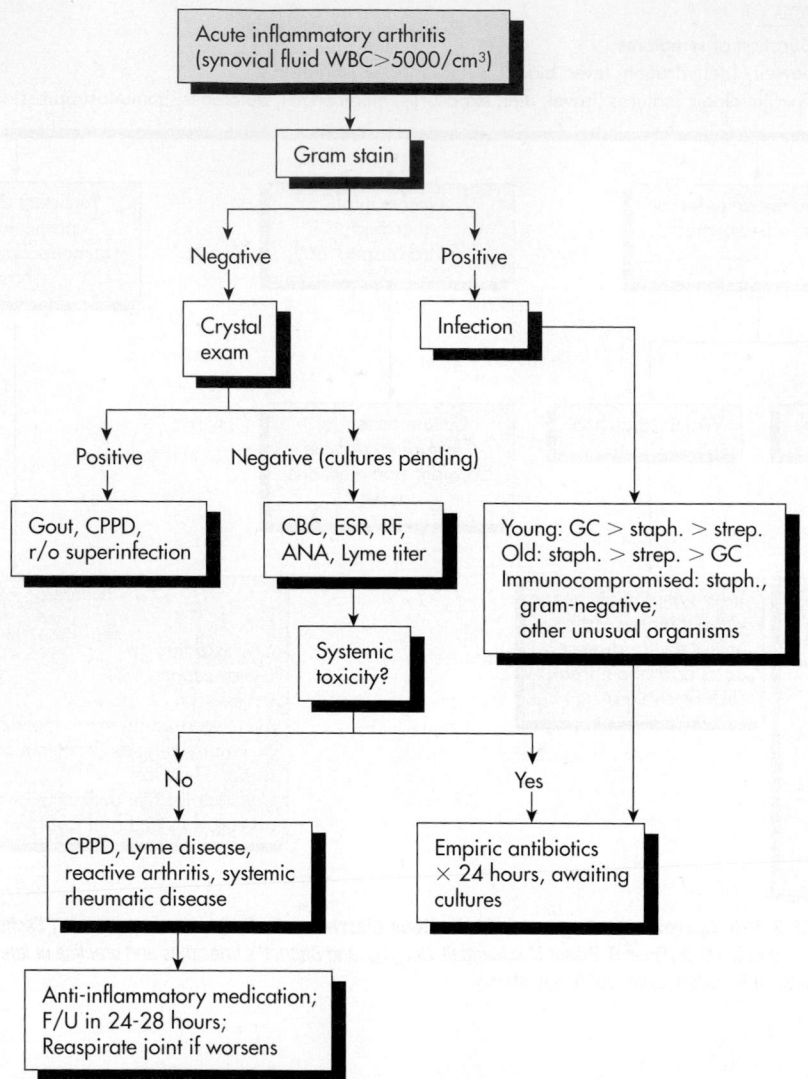

FIGURE 3-121 Approach to acute inflammatory arthritis. *ANA,* Antinuclear antibody test; *CBC,* complete blood count; *CPPD;* calcium pyrophosphate deposition disease; *ESR,* erythrocyte sedimentation rate; *F/U,* follow-up; *GC,* gonococcal infection; *RF,* rheumatoid factor; *r/o,* rule out; *staph.,* staphylococcal infection; *strep.,* streptococcal infection; *WBC,* white blood cell count. (From Harris ED et al [eds]: *Kelley's textbook of rheumatology,* ed 7, Philadelphia, 2005, Saunders.)

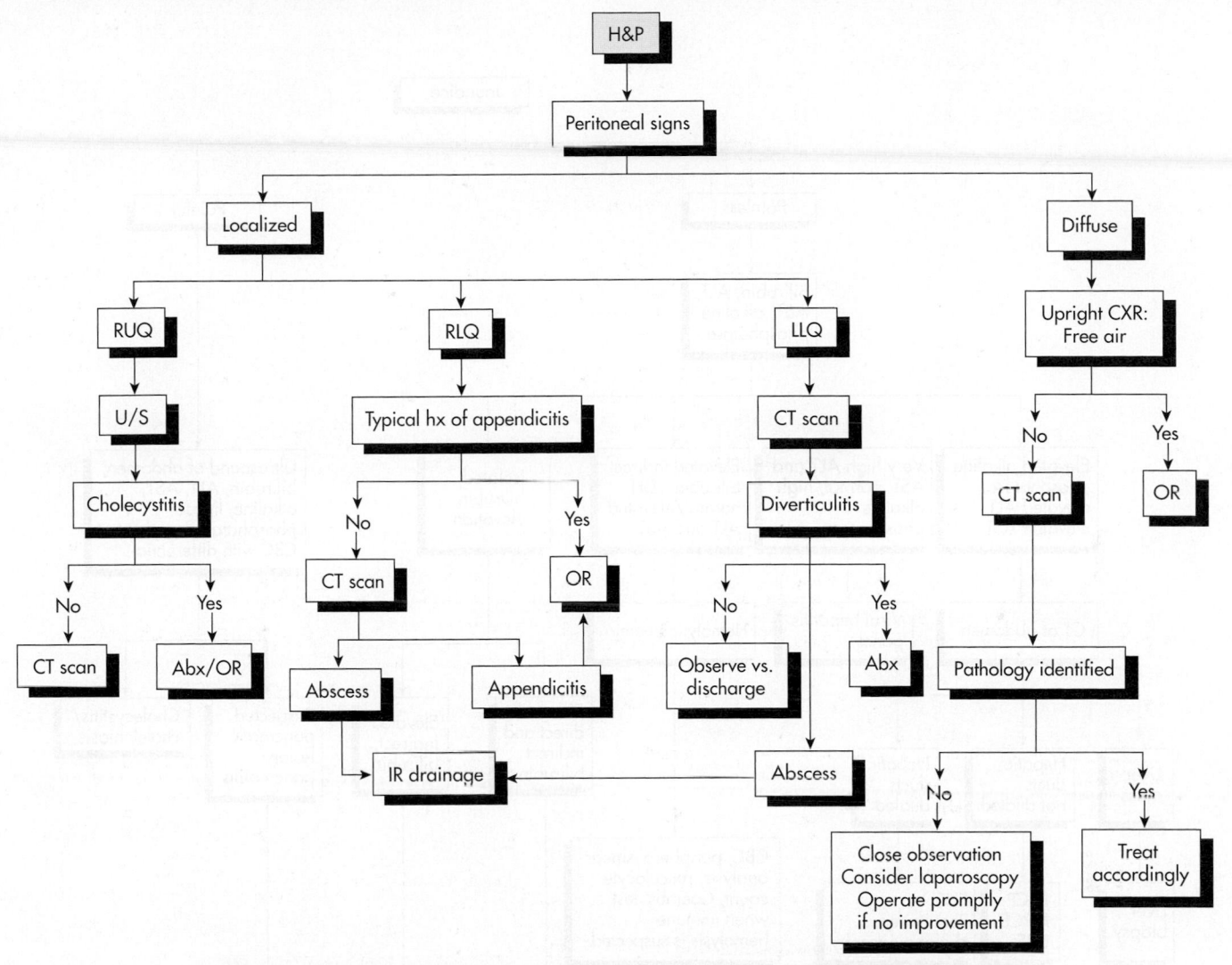

FIGURE 3-122 Algorithm for the diagnosis and management of patients with suspected intraabdominal infection. *H&P,* History and physical exam; *Abx,* antibiotics; *CXR,* chest radiograph; *hx,* history; *IR,* interventional radiology; *LLQ,* left lower quadrant; *RLQ,* right lower quadrant; *RUQ,* right upper quadrant; *U/S,* ultrasound. (From Cameron JL, Cameron AM: *Current surgical therapy,* ed 10, Philadelphia, 2011, Saunders.)

ICD-10CM# R17 Unspecified jaundice
K83.2 Other specified diseases of biliary tract
E80.7 Disorder of bilirubin metabolism, unspecified

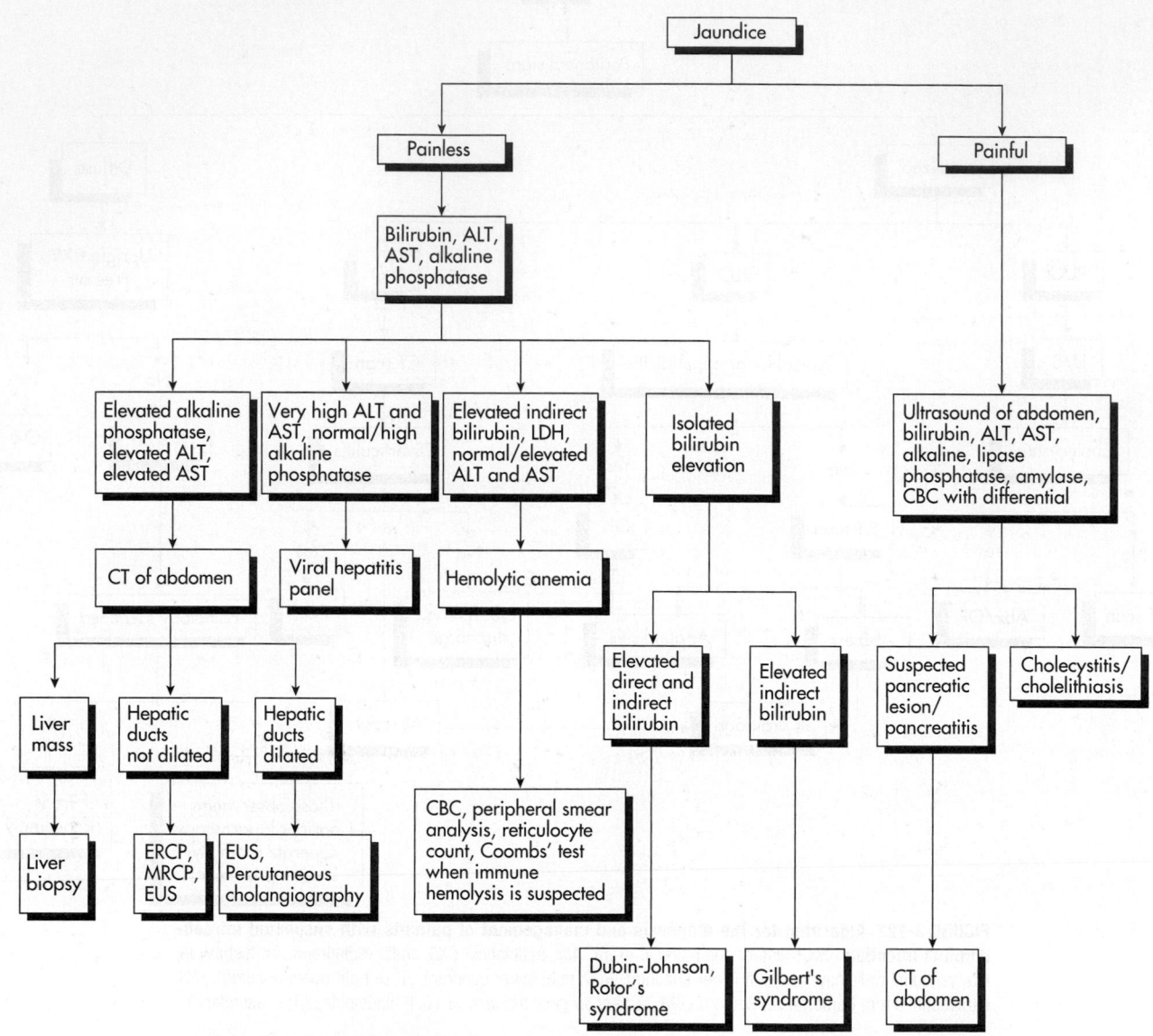

FIGURE 3-125 Diagnostic algorithm. (From Ferri, F: *Ferri's best test: a practical guide to clinical laboratory medicine and diagnostic imaging*, ed 3, Philadelphia, 2014, Saunders.)

Diagnostic Imaging	Lab Evaluation
Best Test(s)	**Best Test(s)**
• CT of abdomen with contrast if painless jaundice	• Bilirubin with fractionation
• Ultrasound of abdomen if painful jaundice	• Alkaline phosphatase, ALT, AST
	• Viral hepatitis panel
Ancillary Tests	**Ancillary Tests**
• MRCP	• Serum amylase, lipase, LDH
• ERCP	• CBC, reticulocyte count, Coombs' test
• EUS	• BUN, creatinine, electrolytes
	• Liver biopsy

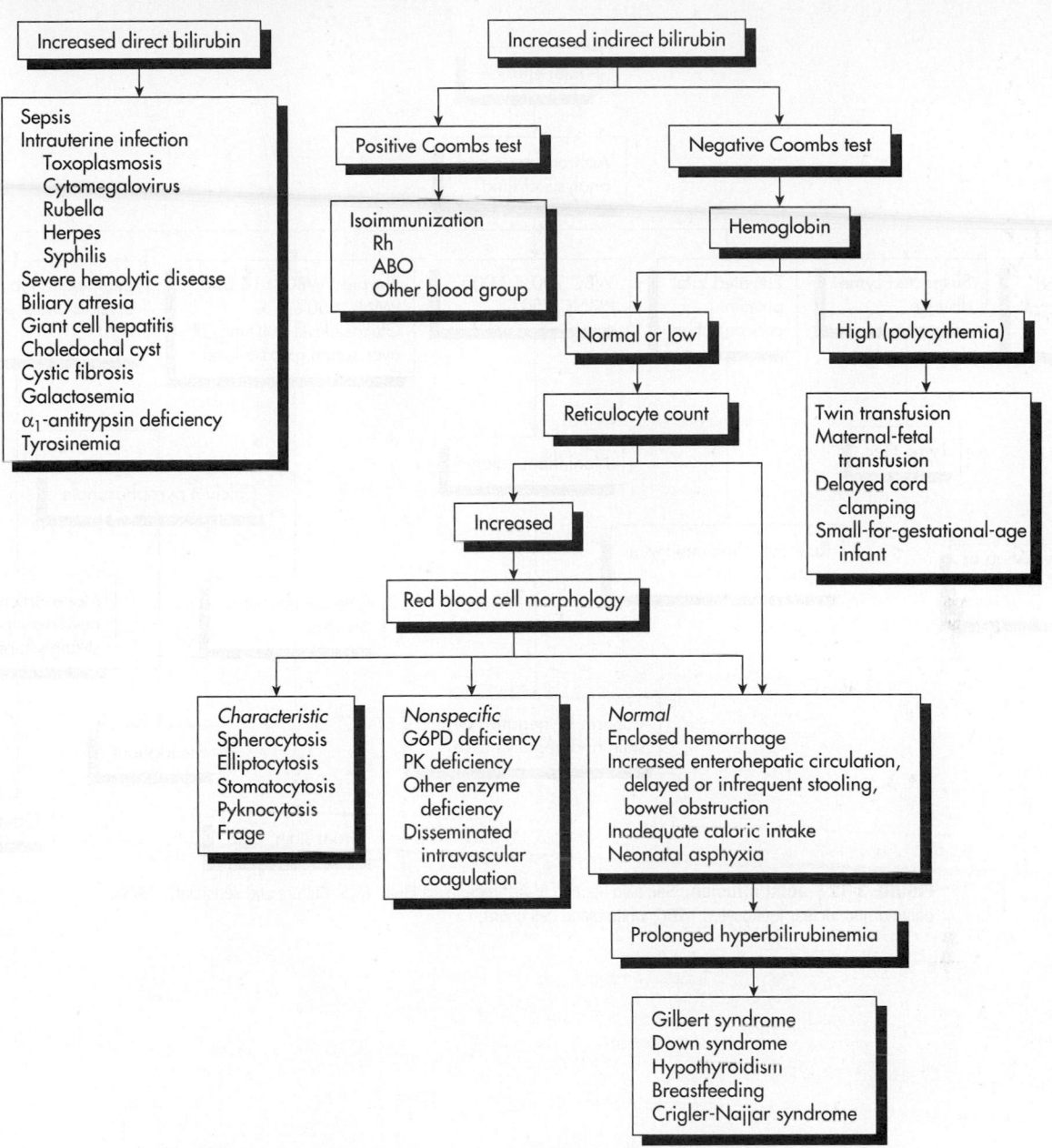

FIGURE 3-126 Schematic approach to the diagnosis of neonatal jaundice. *G6PD,* Glucose-6-phosphate dehydrogenase; *PK,* pyruvate kinase. (From Oski FA: Differential diagnosis of jaundice. In Taeusch HW, Ballard RA, Avery MA [eds]: *Schaffer and Avery's diseases of the newborn,* ed 6, Philadelphia, 1991, Saunders.)

Clinical
Algorithms

III

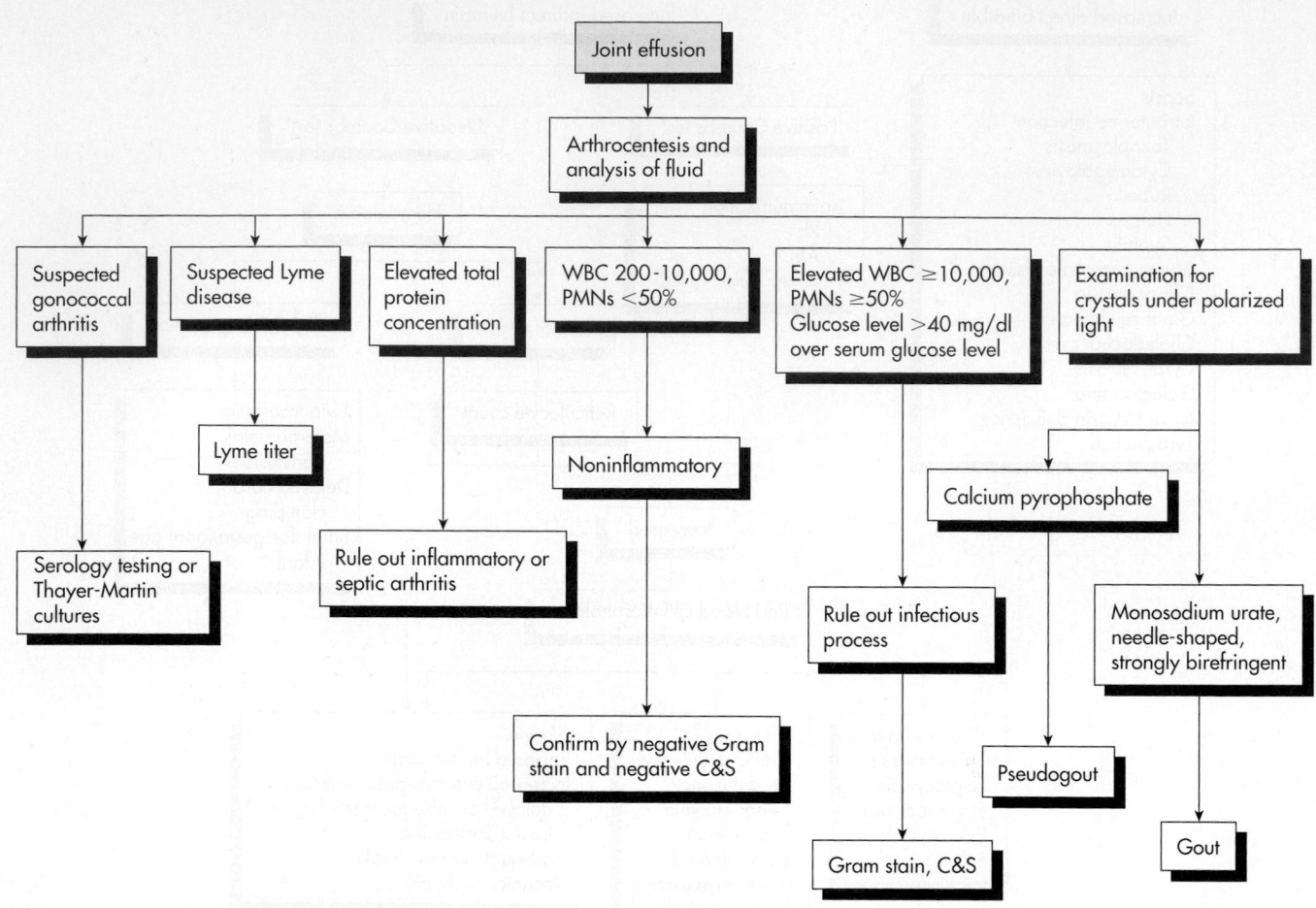

FIGURE 3-127 Joint effusion. See also Section IV, Arthrocentesis Fluid. *C&S,* Culture and sensitivity; *PMNs,* polymorphonuclear leukocytes; *WBC,* white blood cell count.

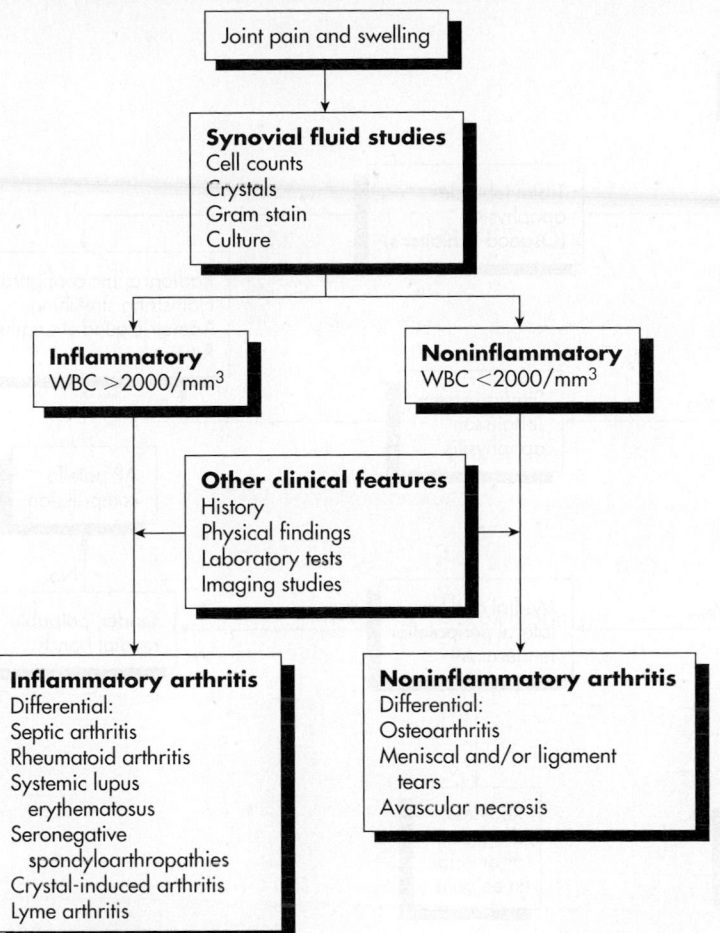

FIGURE 3-128 Diagnostic approach for swollen joints. *WBC,* White blood cell count. (From Goldman L, Schafer AL [eds]: *Cecil textbook of medicine,* ed 24, Philadelphia, 2012, Saunders.)

ICD-10CM #	M12.9	Arthropathy, unspecified
	S99.919A	Unspecified injury of unspecified ankle, initial encounter
	M25.669	Stiffness of unspecified knee, not elsewhere classified
	M25.469	Effusion, unspecified

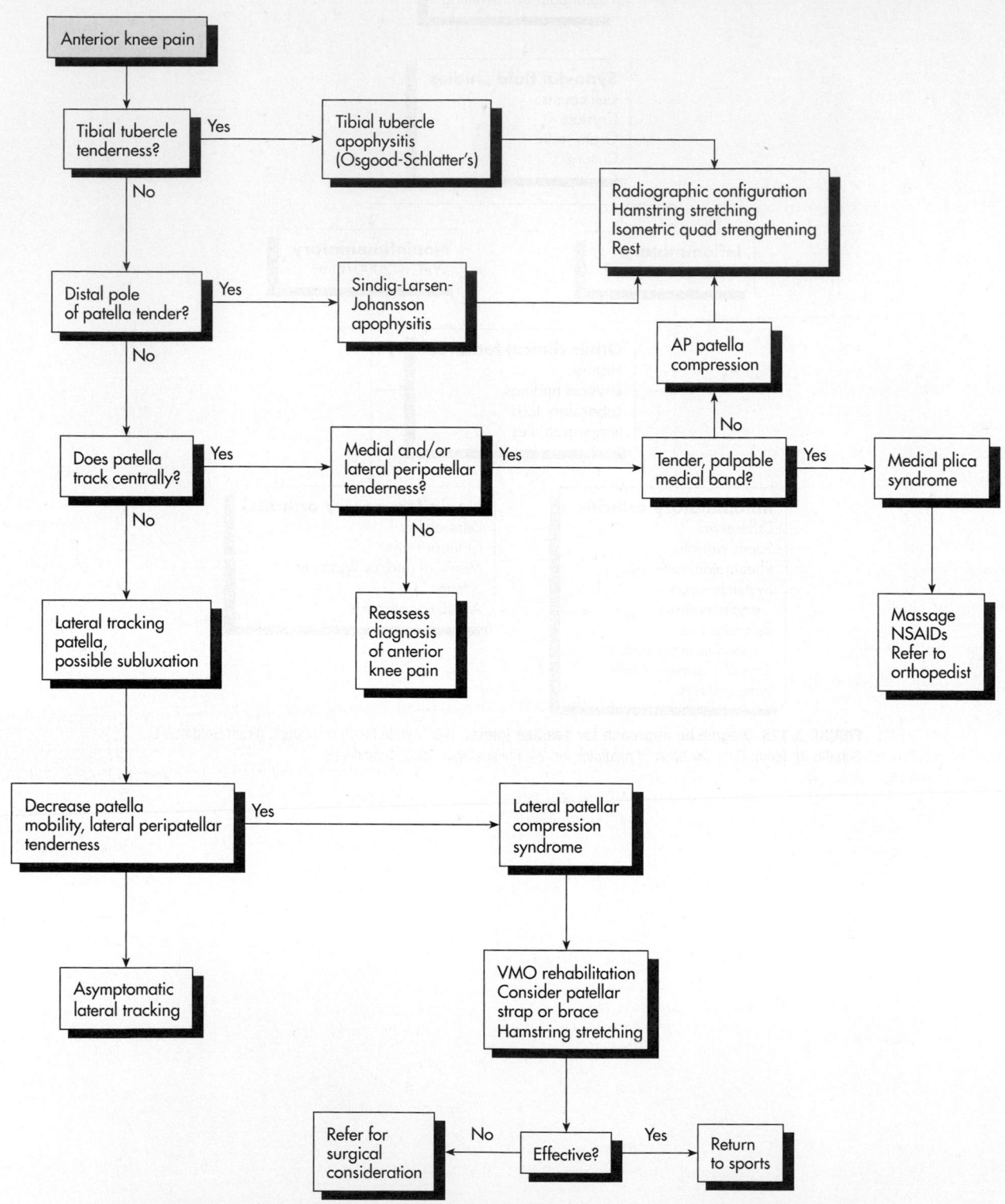

FIGURE 3-130 Evaluation and management of knee extensor mechanism pain. Focused treatment based on specific etiology will prevent recurrence. *AP,* Anteroposterior; *NSAIDs,* nonsteroidal anti-inflammatory drugs; *VMO,* vastus medialis obliquus muscle. (From Scudieri G [ed]: *Sports medicine, principles of primary care,* St Louis, 1997, Mosby.)

LEG ULCER

ICD-10CM # I70.25   Atherosclerosis of native arteries of other extremities with
                     ulceration
            L97.909 Non-pressure chronic ulcer of unspecified part of unspecified
                     lower leg with unspecified severity
            L98.499 Non-pressure chronic ulcer of skin of other sites with unspecified
                     severity
            L89.90   Pressure ulcer of unspecified site, unspecified stage

1637

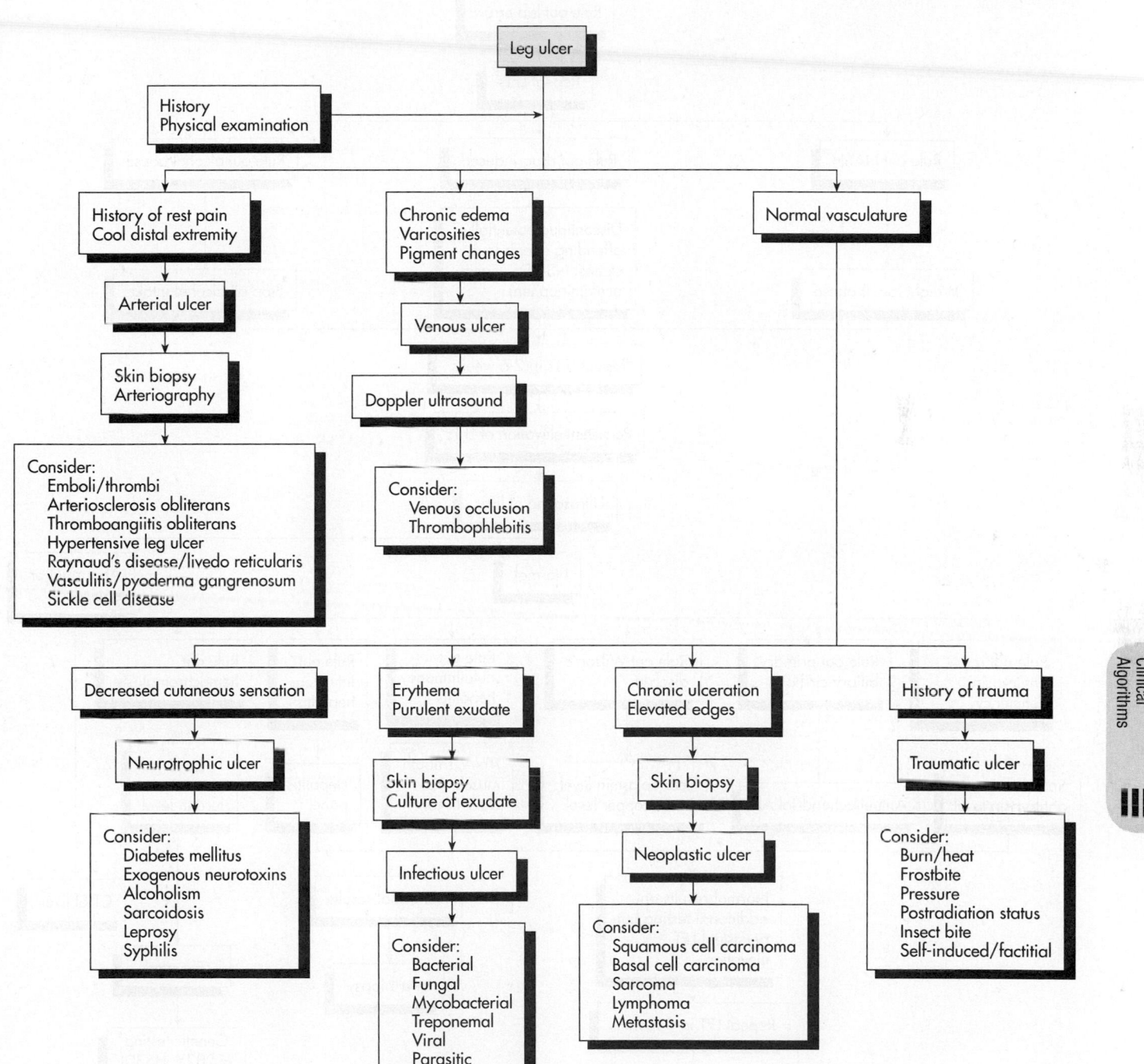

FIGURE 3-131 Leg ulcer. (From Greene HL, Johnson WP, Lemcke D [eds]: *Decision making in medicine,* ed 2, St Louis, 1998, Mosby.)

Clinical
Algorithms

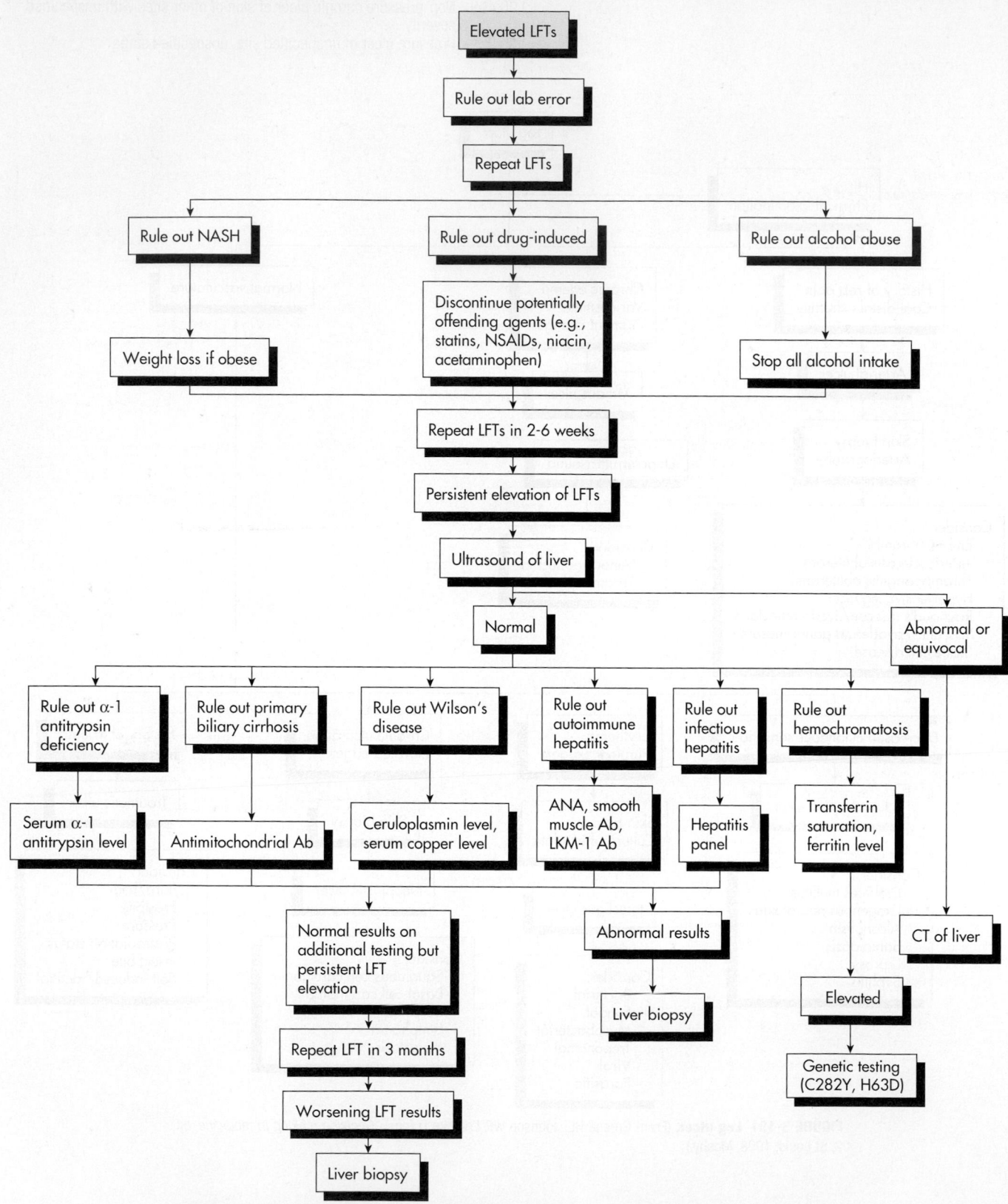

FIGURE 3-132 Liver function test elevations. *Ab,* Antibody; *ANA,* antibody to nuclear antigens; *CT,* computed tomography; *IEP,* immuno-electrophoresis; *LFTs,* liver function tests; *LKM,* liver-kidney microsome; *NASH,* nonalcoholic steatohepatitis; *NSAIDs,* nonsteroidal anti-inflammatory drugs.

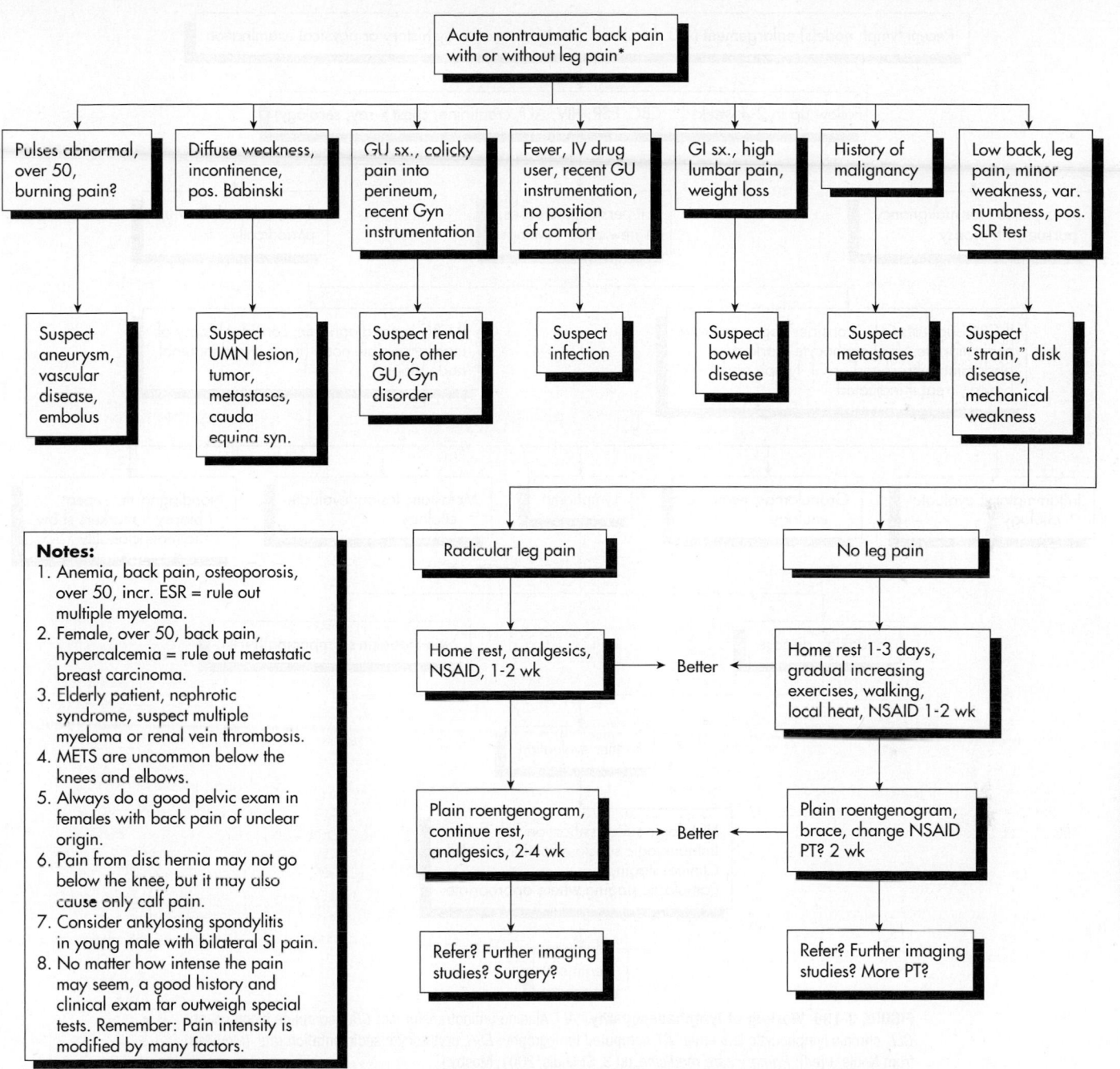

Notes:
1. Anemia, back pain, osteoporosis, over 50, incr. ESR = rule out multiple myeloma.
2. Female, over 50, back pain, hypercalcemia = rule out metastatic breast carcinoma.
3. Elderly patient, nephrotic syndrome, suspect multiple myeloma or renal vein thrombosis.
4. METS are uncommon below the knees and elbows.
5. Always do a good pelvic exam in females with back pain of unclear origin.
6. Pain from disc hernia may not go below the knee, but it may also cause only calf pain.
7. Consider ankylosing spondylitis in young male with bilateral SI pain.
8. No matter how intense the pain may seem, a good history and clinical exam far outweigh special tests. Remember: Pain intensity is modified by many factors.

FIGURE 3-134 Algorithm for low back and/or leg pain. *Also refer to Section I, Lumbar Disk Syndrome. *GI*, Gastrointestinal; *GU*, genitourinary; *IV*, intravenous; *METS*, metabolic equivalents; *NSAID*, nonsteroidal anti-inflammatory drug; *PT*, physical therapy; *SI*, sacroiliac; *SLR*, straight-leg raising; *UMN*, upper motor neuron. (From Mercier LR: *Practical orthopedics*, ed 2, St Louis, 2000, Mosby.)

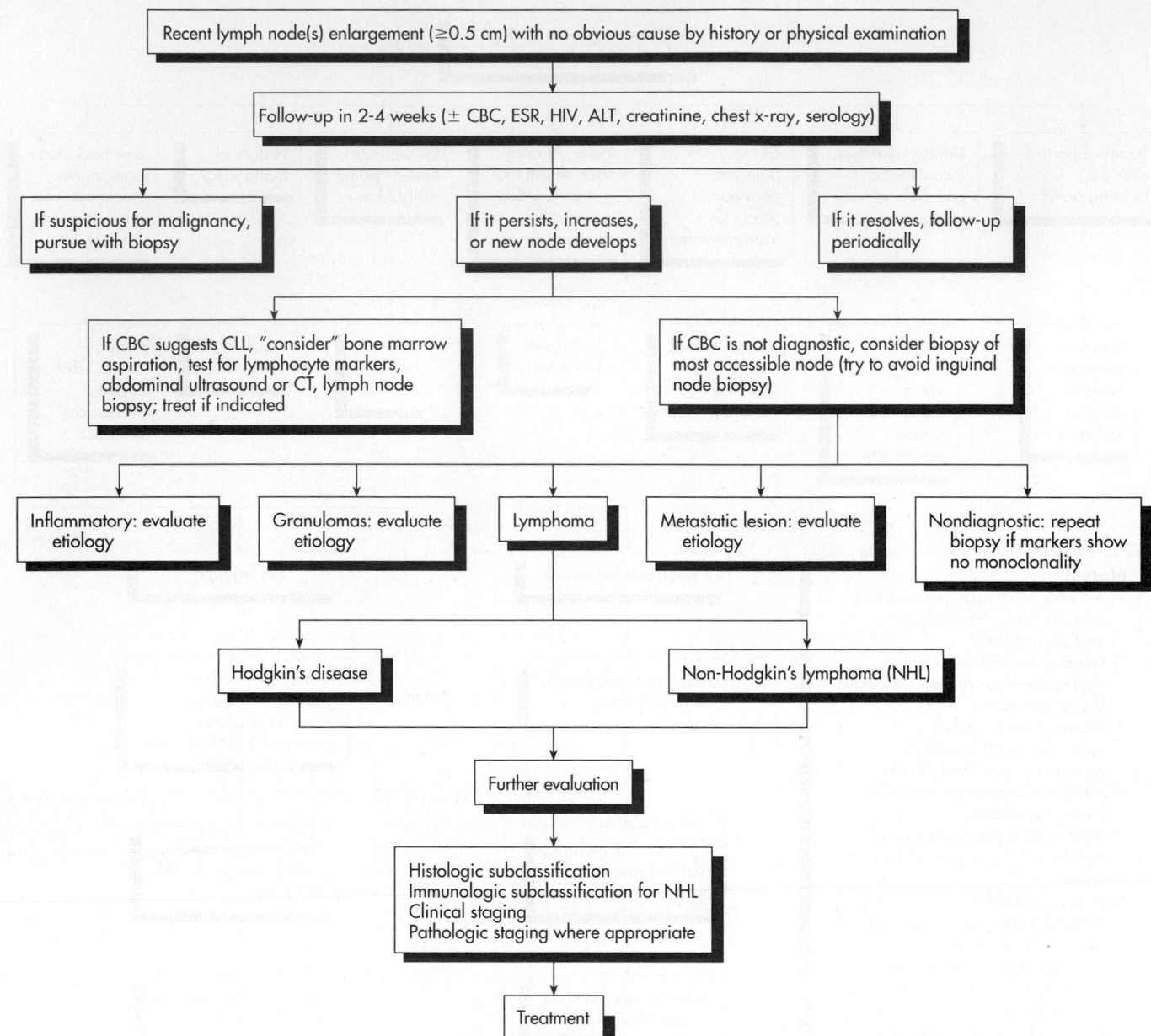

FIGURE 3-138 Workup of lymphadenopathy. *ALT*, Alanine aminotransferase; *CBC*, complete blood count; *CLL*, chronic lymphocytic leukemia; *CT*, computed tomography; *ESR*, erythrocyte sedimentation rate. (Modified from Noble J [ed]: *Primary care medicine*, ed 3, St Louis, 2001, Mosby.)

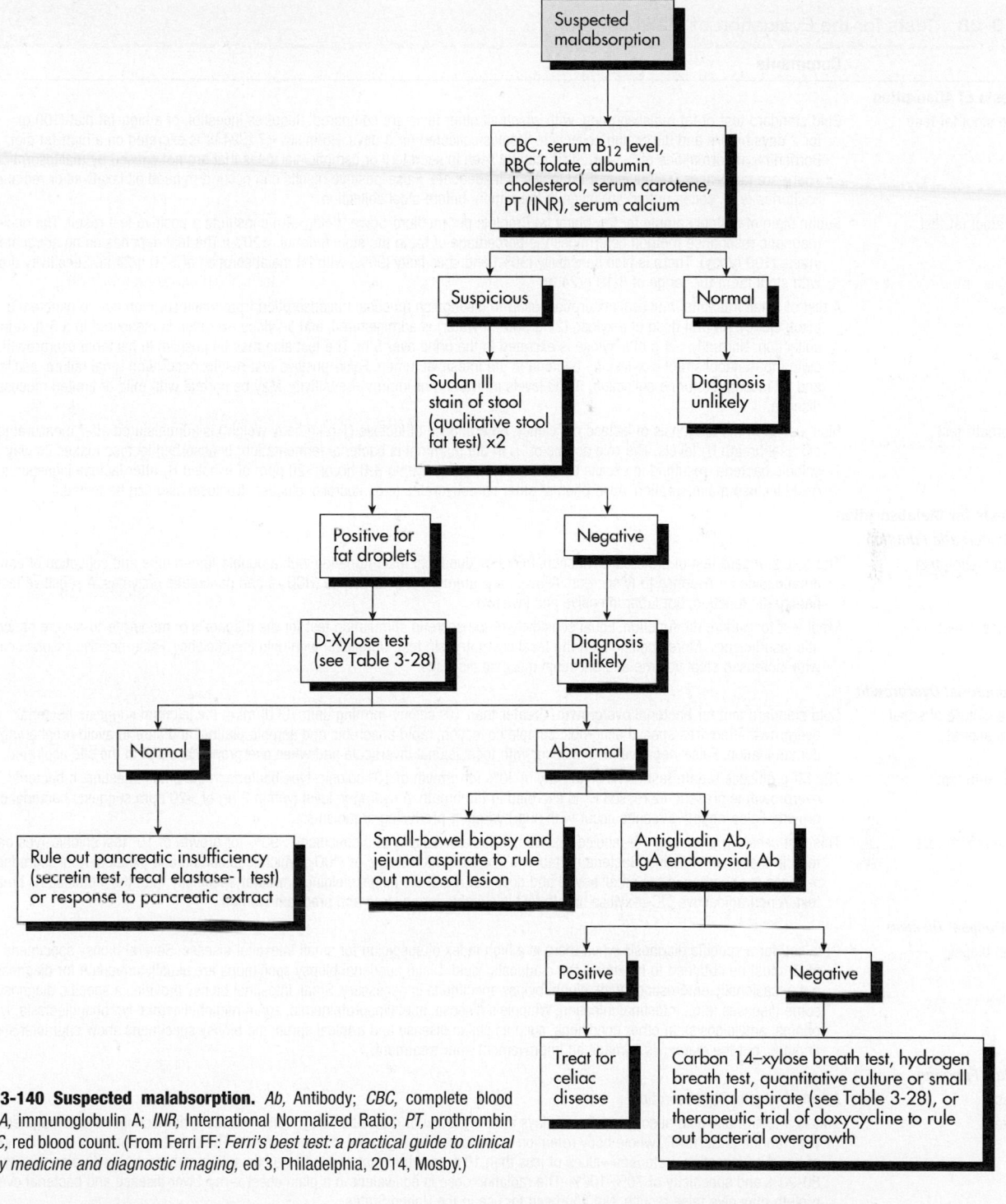

FIGURE 3-140 Suspected malabsorption. *Ab,* Antibody; *CBC,* complete blood count; *IgA,* immunoglobulin A; *INR,* International Normalized Ratio; *PT,* prothrombin time; *RBC,* red blood count. (From Ferri FF: *Ferri's best test: a practical guide to clinical laboratory medicine and diagnostic imaging,* ed 3, Philadelphia, 2014, Mosby.)

Clinical Algorithms

III

BOX 3-9   Malabsorption, Suspected

Diagnostic Imaging **Best Test** Small-bowel series **Ancillary Test** CT of pancreas with IV contrast **Lab Evaluation** **Best Test** Biopsy of small bowel	**Ancillary Tests** Albumin, total protein ALT, AST, PT Serum lytes, BUN, creatinine Sudan III stain of stool for fecal leukocytes CBC, RBC folate, serum iron, serum carotene, cholesterol, serum calcium Hydrogen 14-C xylose breath test D-Xylose test, secretin test Quantitative fecal test Antigliadin antibody, IgA endomysial antibody

---

ALT, Alanine aminotransferase; AST, aspartate aminotransferase; BUN, blood urea nitrogen; CBC, complete blood count; CT, computed tomography; IgA, immunoglobulin A; IV, intravenous; PT, prothrombin time; RBC, red blood count.

From Ferri FF: *Ferri's best test: a practical guide to clinical laboratory medicine and diagnostic imaging,* ed 3, Philadelphia, 2014, Elsevier Mosby.

Table 3-28   Tests for the Evaluation of Malabsorption*

Test	Comments
General Tests of Absorption	
Quantitative stool fat test	Gold standard test of fat malabsorption, with which all other tests are compared. Requires ingestion of a high-fat diet (100 g) for 2 days before and during the collection. Stool is collected for 3 days. Normally, <7 g/24 hr is excreted on a high-fat diet. Borderline abnormalities of 8-14 g/24 hr may be seen in secretory or osmotic diarrheas that are not caused by malabsorption. There are false-negative findings if fat intake is inadequate. False-positive results can occur if mineral oil laxatives or rectal suppositories (e.g., cocoa butter) are given to the patient before stool collection.
Qualitative stool fat test	Sudan stain of a stool sample for fat. Many fat droplets per medium-power field (×40) constitute a positive test result. The nuclear magnetic resonance method determines the percentage of fat in the stool (normal, <20%). The test depends on an adequate fat intake (100 g/day). There is high sensitivity (90%) and specificity (90%) with fat malabsorption of >10 g/24 hr. Sensitivity drops with stool fat in the range of 6-10 g/24 hr.
D-Xylose test	A test of small intestinal mucosal absorption, used to distinguish mucosal malabsorption from malabsorption due to pancreatic insufficiency. An oral dose of D-xylose (24 g/500 ml water) is administered, and D-xylose excretion is measured in a 5-hr urine collection. Normally, >4 g of D-xylose is excreted in the urine over 5 hr. The test also may be positive in bacterial overgrowth owing to metabolism of D-xylose by bacteria in the intestinal lumen. False-positive test results occur with renal failure, ascites, and an incomplete urine collection. Blood levels at 1 and 3 hr improve sensitivity. May be normal with mild or limited mucosal disease.
Hydrogen breath test	Most useful in the diagnosis of lactase deficiency. An oral dose of lactose (1 g/kg body weight) is administered after measurement of basal breath H_2 levels. The sole source of H_2 in the mammal is bacterial fermentation; unabsorbed lactose makes its way to colonic bacteria, resulting in excess breath H_2. A *late peak* (within 3-6 hr) of >20 ppm of exhaled H_2 after lactose ingestion suggests lactose malabsorption. Absorption of other carbohydrates (e.g., sucrose, glucose, fructose) also can be tested.
Specific Tests for Malabsorption	
Tests for Pancreatic Function	
Secretin stimulation test	The gold standard test of pancreatic function. Requires duodenal test intubation with a double-lumen tube and collection of pancreatic juice in response to IV secretin. Allows measurement of bicarbonate (HCO_3-) and pancreatic enzymes. A sensitive test of pancreatic function, but labor intensive and invasive.
Fecal elastase-1 test	Stool test for pancreatic function. Equal sensitivity to the secretin stimulation test for the diagnosis of moderate-to-severe pancreatic insufficiency. More specific than the fecal chymotrypsin test. Unreliable with mild insufficiency. False-positive results occur with increased stool volume and intestinal mucosal diseases.
Tests for Bacterial Overgrowth	
Quantitative culture of small intestinal aspirate	Gold standard test for bacterial overgrowth. Greater than 10^5 colony-forming units (CFU)/ml in the jejunum suggests bacterial overgrowth. Requires special anaerobic sample collection, rapid anaerobic and aerobic plating, and care to avoid oropharyngeal contamination. False-negative results occur with focal jejunal diverticula and when overgrowth is distal to the site aspirated.
Hydrogen breath test	The 50-g glucose breath test has a sensitivity of 90% for growth of 10^5 colonic-type bacteria in the small intestine. If bacterial overgrowth is present, increased H_2 is excreted in the breath. A hydrogen level (within 2 hr) of >20 ppm suggests bacterial overgrowth. False-negative results occur with non-hydrogen-producing organisms.
^{14}C-D-xylose breath test	This test uses 1 g of carbon 14–labeled D-xylose. It has a sensitivity and specificity >90% for growth of 10^5 test colonic-type bacteria in the small intestine. Bacteria metabolize D-xylose with release of $^{14}CO_2$, which is absorbed and exhaled. Non-degraded D-xylose is absorbed in the small bowel and does not reach the colon, yielding a greater specificity than the lactulose H_2 breath test. A nonradioactive ^{13}C-D-xylose breath test is suitable for children and pregnant women.
Tests for Mucosal Disease	
Small bowel biopsy	Obtained for a specific diagnosis when there is a high index of suspicion for small intestinal disease. Several biopsy specimens (4-5) must be obtained to maximize the diagnostic yield. Distal duodenal biopsy specimens are usually adequate for diagnosis, but occasionally enteroscopy with jejunal biopsy specimens is necessary. Small intestinal biopsy provides a specific diagnosis in some diseases (e.g., intestinal infection, Whipple's disease, abetalipoproteinemia, agammaglobulinemia, lymphangiectasia, lymphoma, amyloidosis). In other conditions, such as celiac disease and tropical sprue, the biopsy specimens show characteristic findings, but the diagnosis is made on improvement after treatment.
Tests of Ileal Function	
Schilling test	A test of vitamin B_{12} absorption
^{75}SeHCAT test	This is a test of bile acid absorption. Seven days after ingestion of radiolabeled synthetic selenium-homocholic acid conjugated with taurine (^{75}SeHCAT), whole body retention is measured by a gamma-counting device. The result is expressed as a fraction of baseline ingestion. Retention values of less than 10% are abnormal and indicate bile acid malabsorption with a sensitivity of 80-90% and specificity of 70%-100%. The radiation dose is equivalent to a plain chest x-ray. Liver disease and bacterial overgrowth may give false results. Not approved for use in the United States.

*Not all these tests are readily available. A strong suspicion for any disease may warrant foregoing an extensive work-up and obtaining the test with highest diagnostic yield. In some cases, empirical treatment, such as removing lactose from the diet of an otherwise healthy individual with lactose intolerance, is warranted without any testing.

From Goldman L, Schafer AI: *Goldman's Cecil Medicine,* ed 24, Philadelphia, 2012, Saunders.

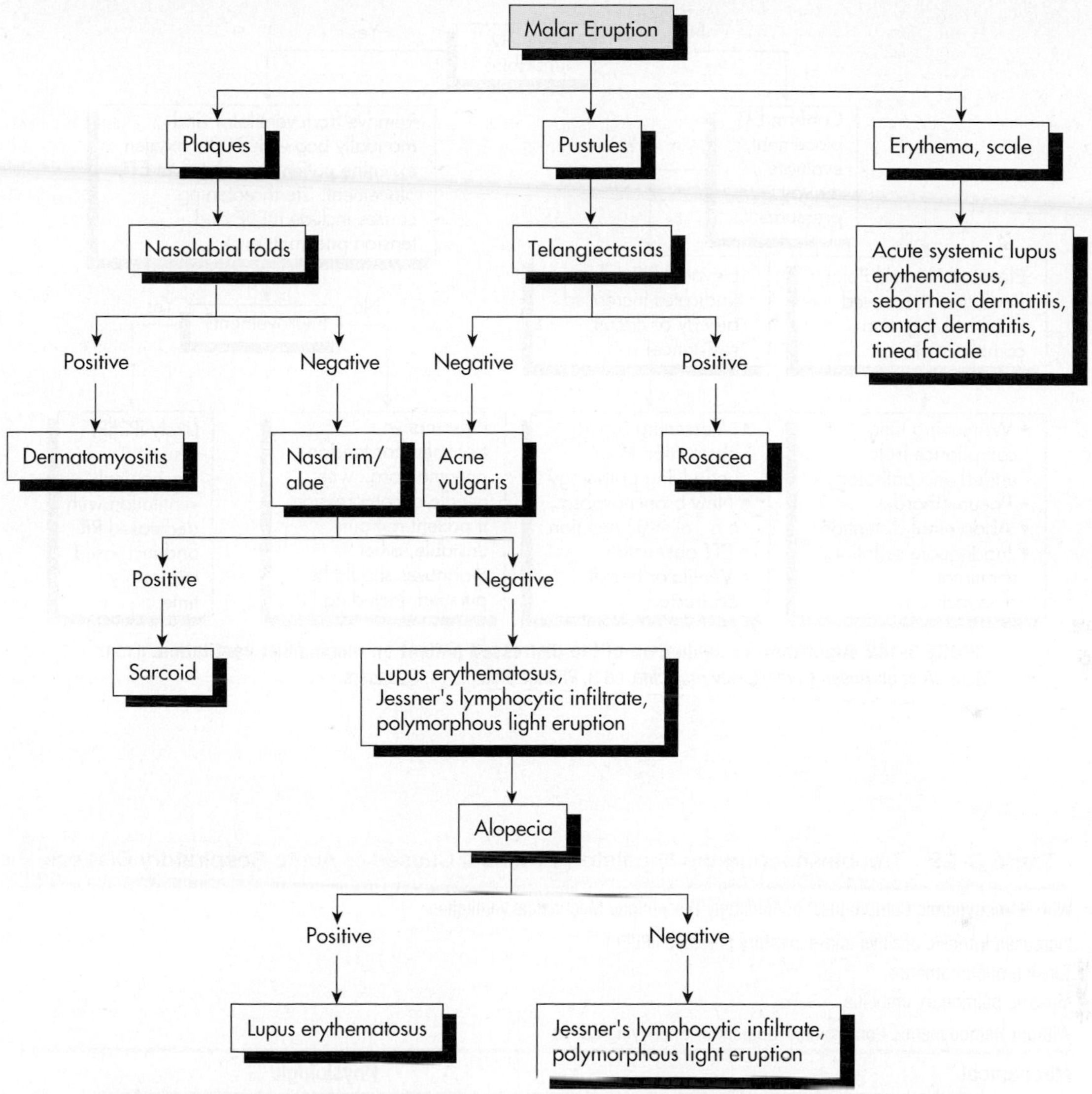

Malar Eruption

Plaques

Pustules

Erythema, scale

Nasolabial folds

Telangiectasias

Acute systemic lupus erythematosus, seborrheic dermatitis, contact dermatitis, tinea faciale

Positive

Negative

Negative

Positive

Dermatomyositis

Nasal rim/ alae

Acne vulgaris

Rosacea

Positive

Negative

Sarcoid

Lupus erythematosus, Jessner's lymphocytic infiltrate, polymorphous light eruption

Alopecia

Positive

Negative

Lupus erythematosus

Jessner's lymphocytic infiltrate, polymorphous light eruption

FIGURE 3-141 Clinical algorithm for diagnosis of a malar eruption, which must be confirmed by appropriate cultures, serology, and biopsy. (From Harris ED et al [eds]: *Kelley's textbook of rheumatology,* ed 7, Philadelphia, 2005, Saunders.)

Clinical Algorithms

EVALUATION OF THE DISTRESSED PATIENT ON MECHANICAL VENTILATION

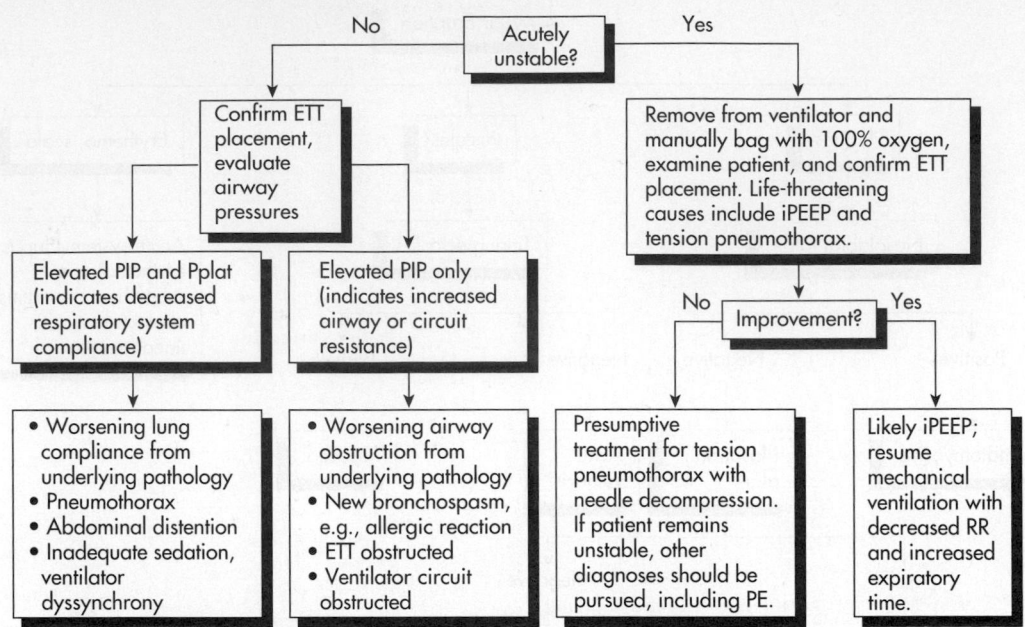

FIGURE 3-142 Algorithm for evaluation of the distressed patient on mechanical ventilation. (From Marx JA et al: *Rosen's emergency medicine*, ed 8, Philadelphia, 2014, Saunders.)

Table 3-29 Troubleshooting the Ventilator: Potential Causes of Acute Respiratory Distress

With Hemodynamic Compromise: Immediately Discontinue Mechanical Ventilation

Increased intrinsic positive end-expiratory pressure (iPEEP)

Tension pneumothorax

Massive pulmonary embolus

Without Hemodynamic Compromise: Search for Underlying Cause

Mechanical	Physiologic
Endotracheal tube migration into bronchus	Worsening lung compliance
Endotracheal tube obstruction	Worsening airway obstruction
Endotracheal tube cuff leak	Abdominal distention
Inadvertent extubation	Pulmonary embolus
Discontinuity in ventilator circuit	Pain or inadequate sedation

From Marx JA et al: *Rosen's emergency medicine*, ed 8, Philadelphia, 2014, Saunders.

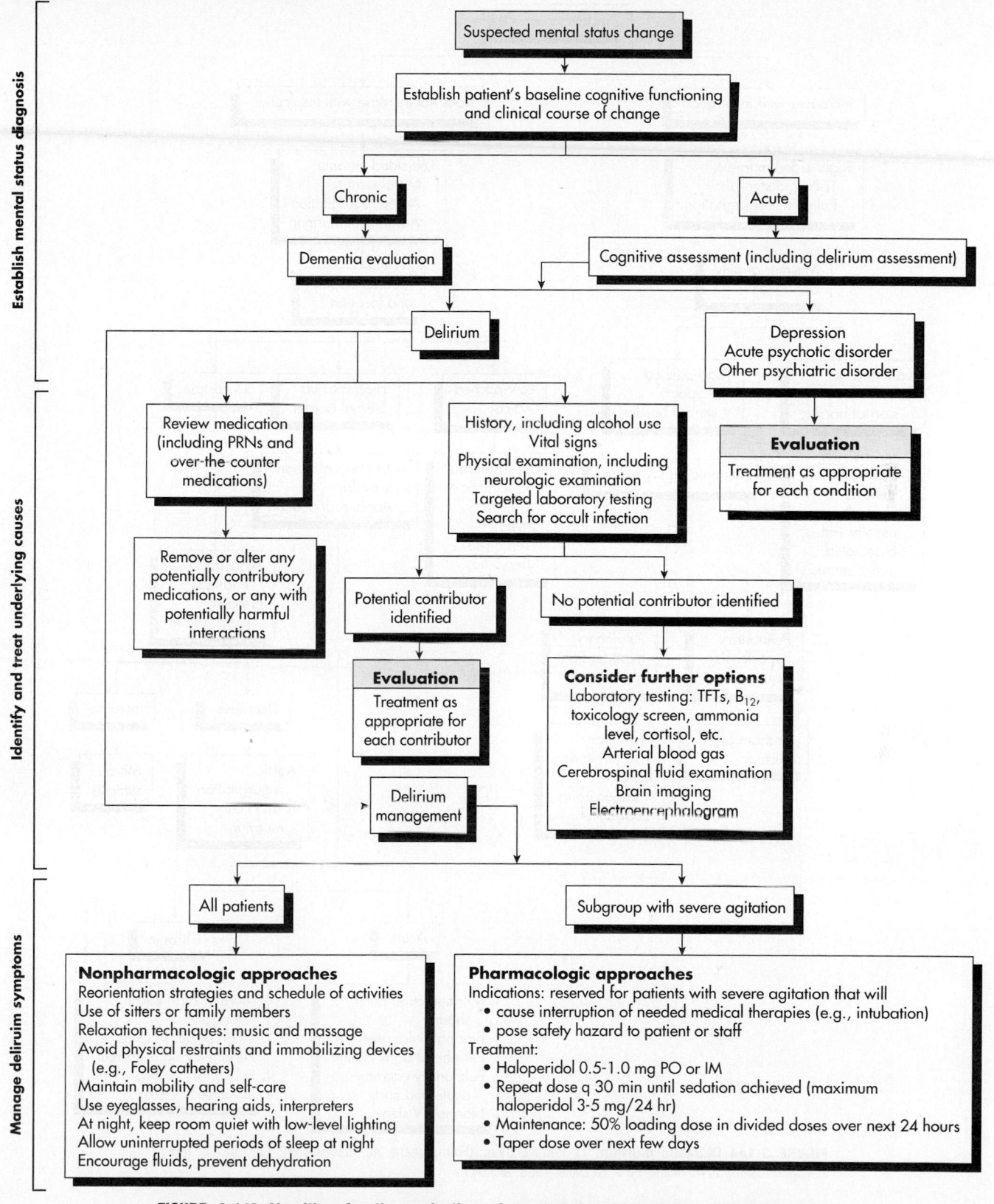

FIGURE 3-143 Algorithm for the evaluation of suspected mental status change in older patients. *PRN,* As needed; *TFTs,* thyroid function tests. (From Goldman L, Schafer AI: *Goldman's Cecil medicine,* ed 24, Philadelphia, 2012, Saunders.)

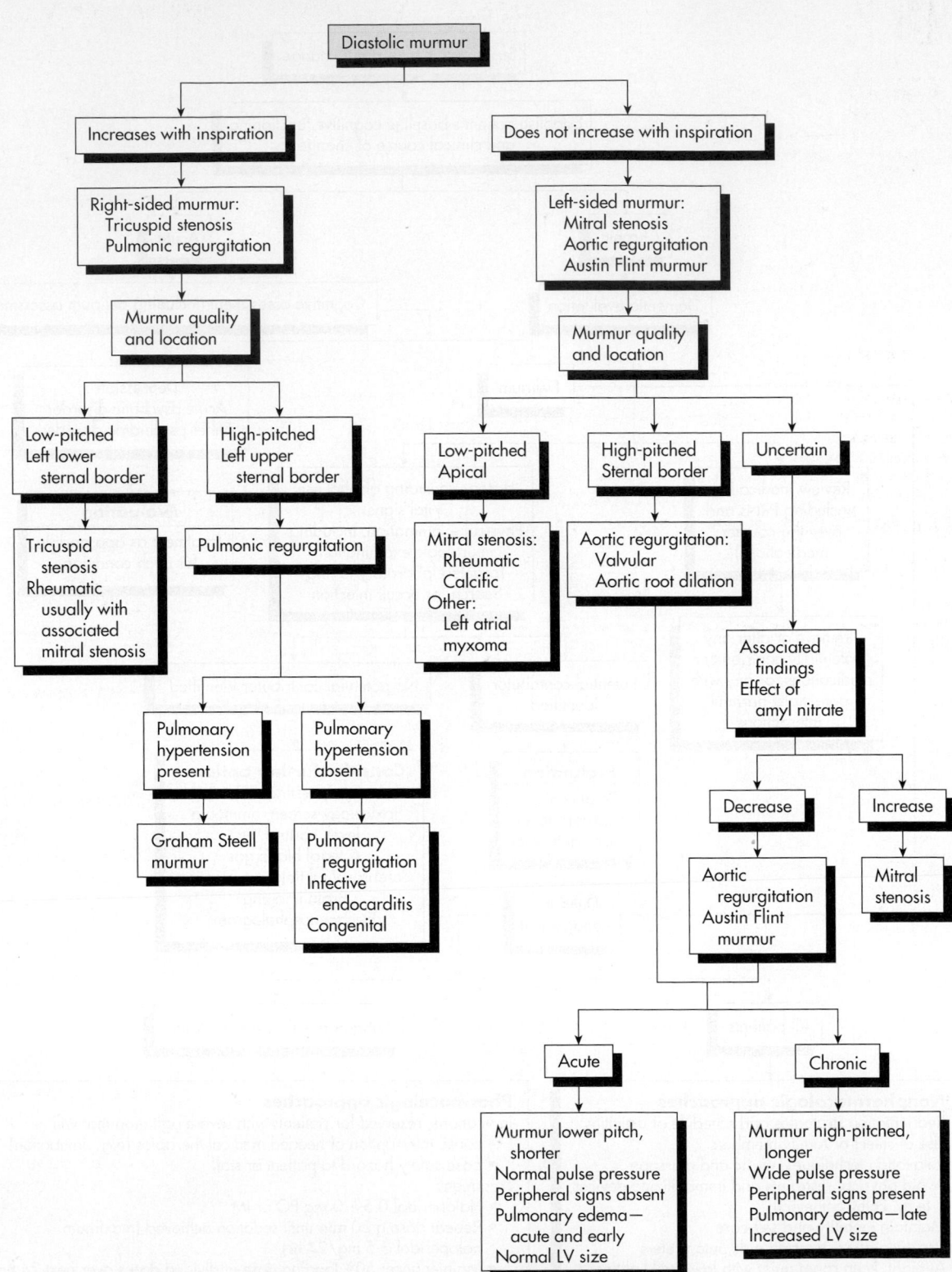

FIGURE 3-144 Diastolic murmur. *LV,* Left ventricle. (From Greene HL, Johnson WP, Lemcke DL [eds]: *Decision making in medicine,* ed 2, St Louis, 1998, Mosby.)

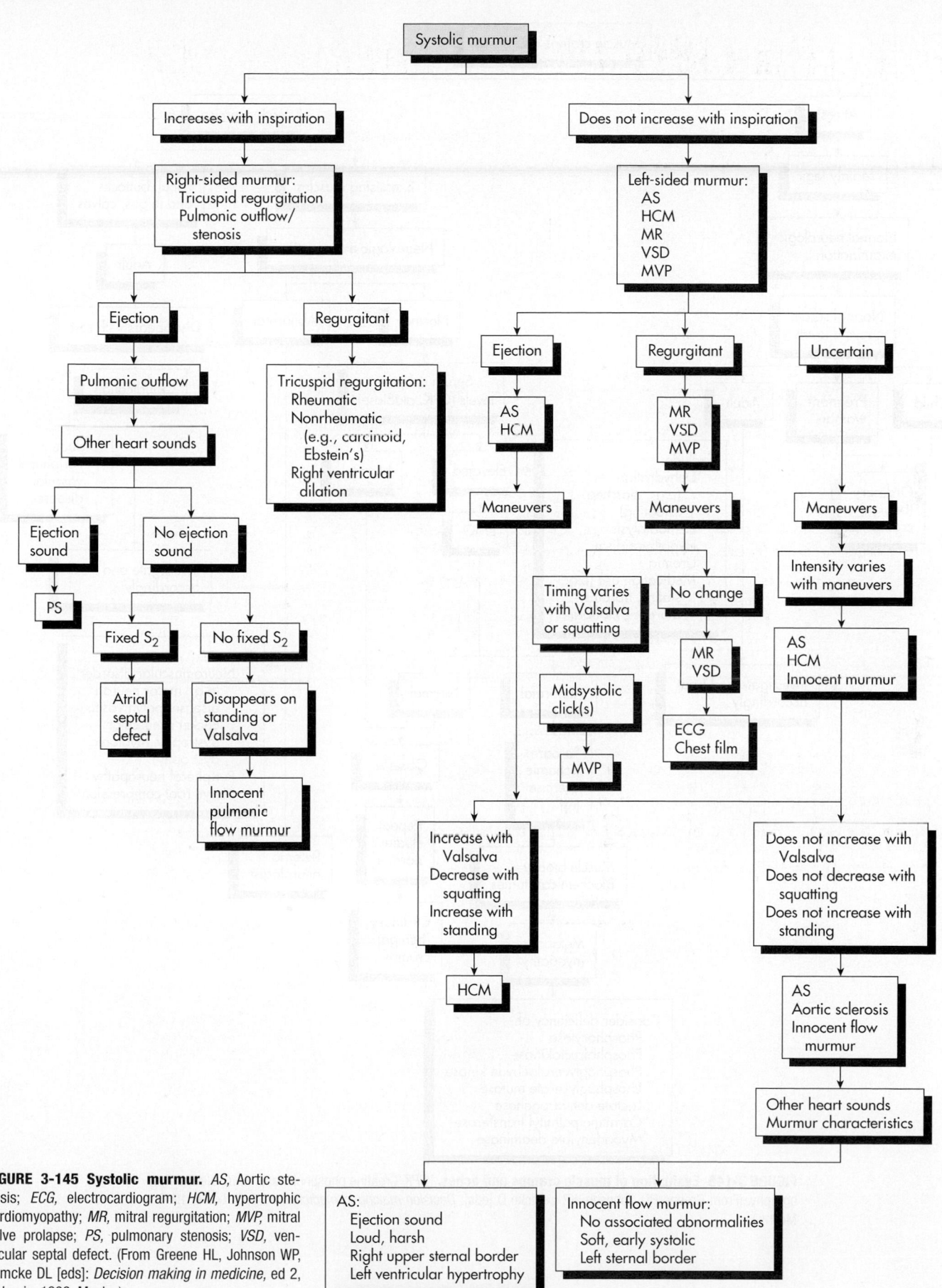

FIGURE 3-145 Systolic murmur. *AS,* Aortic stenosis; *ECG,* electrocardiogram; *HCM,* hypertrophic cardiomyopathy; *MR,* mitral regurgitation; *MVP,* mitral valve prolapse; *PS,* pulmonary stenosis; *VSD,* ventricular septal defect. (From Greene HL, Johnson WP, Lemcke DL [eds]: *Decision making in medicine,* ed 2, St Louis, 1998, Mosby.)

Clinical Algorithms

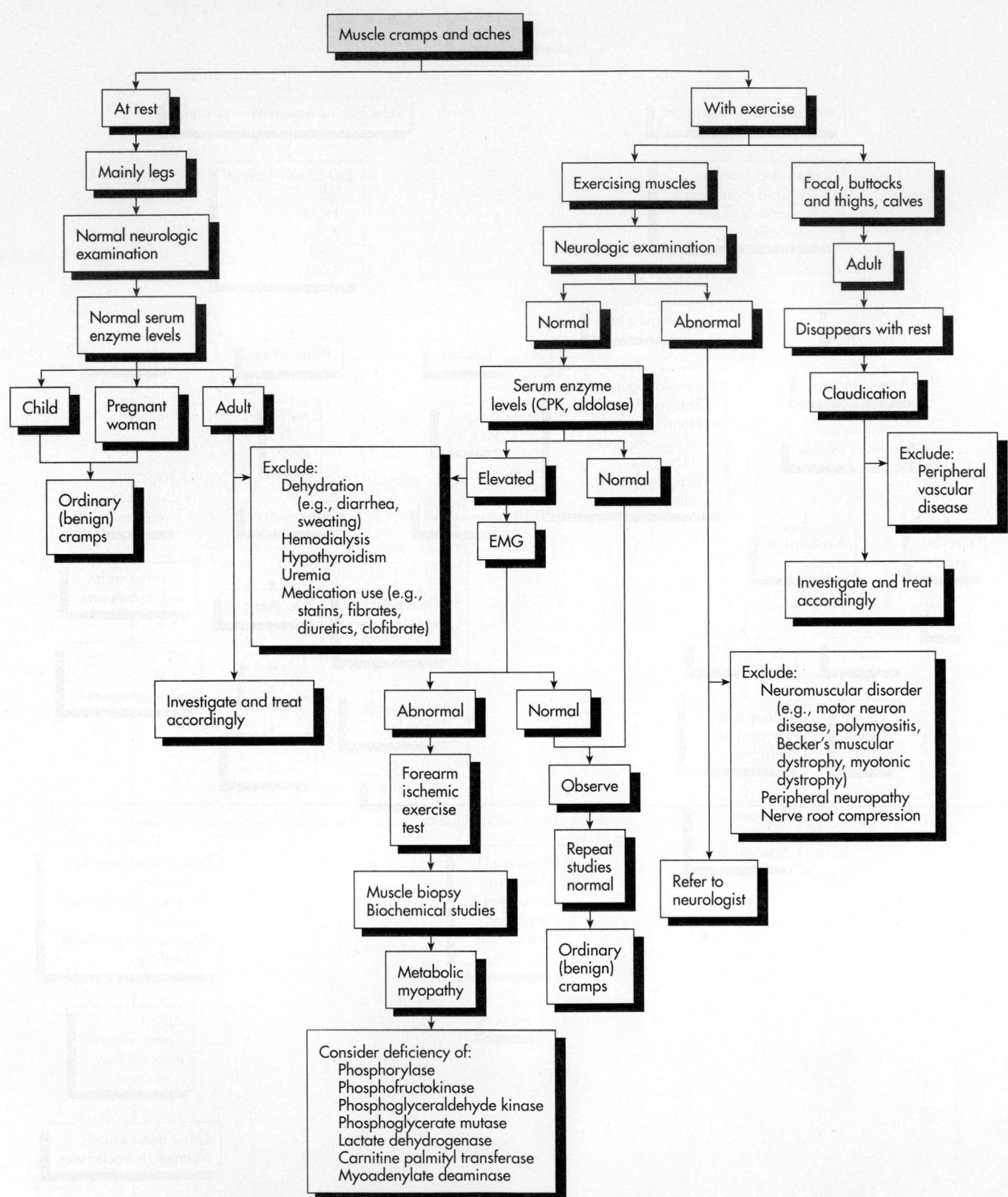

FIGURE 3-146 Evaluation of muscle cramps and aches. *CPK,* Creatine phosphokinase; *EMG,* electromyography. (From Greene HL, Johnson WP, Lemcke D [eds]: *Decision making in medicine,* ed 2, St Louis, 1998, Mosby.)

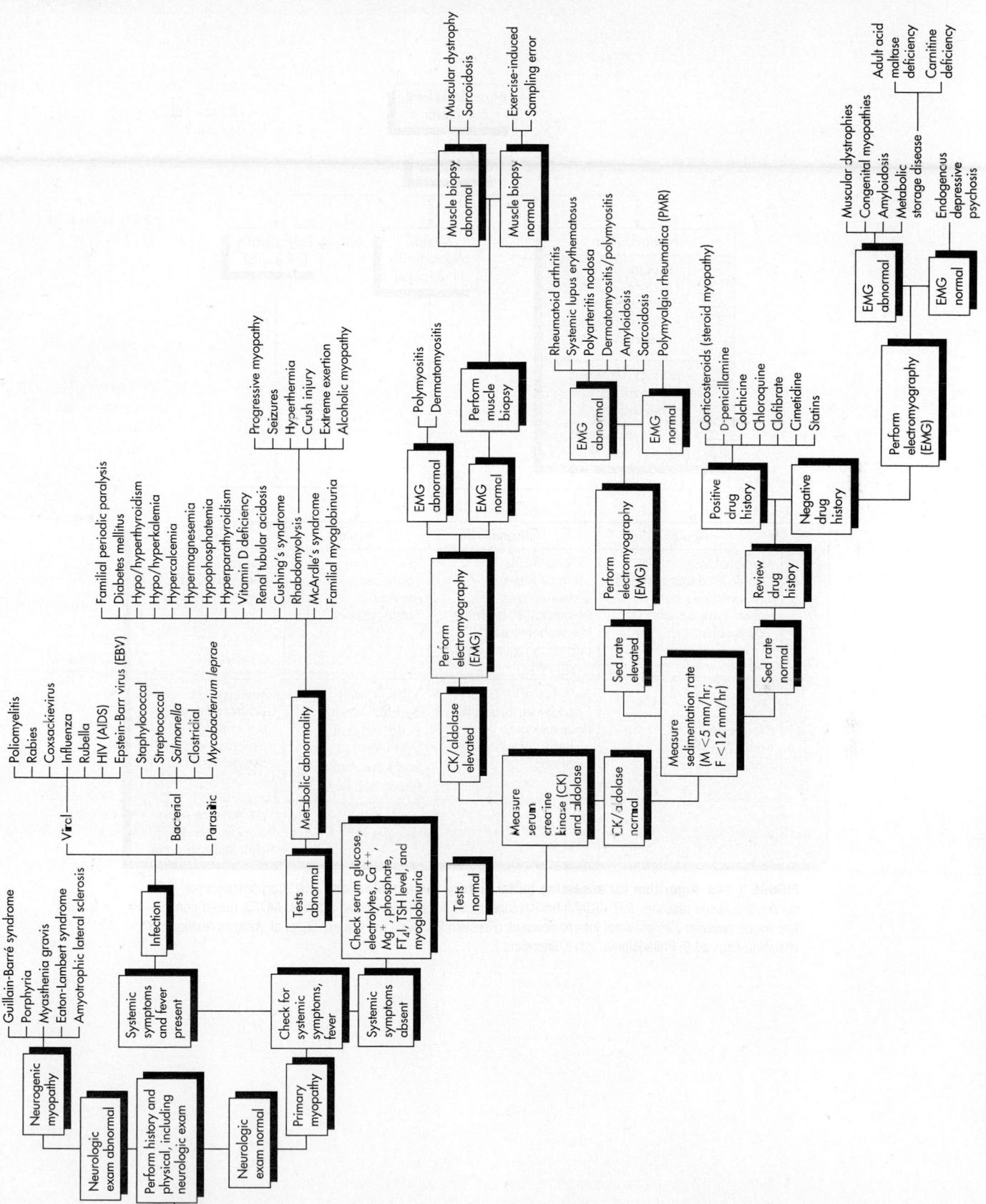

FIGURE 3-147 Muscle weakness. *AIDS,* Acquired immunodeficiency syndrome; *F,* female; *HIV,* human immunodeficiency virus; *M,* male. (From Healey PM: *Common medical diagnosis: an algorithmic approach,* ed 3, Philadelphia, 2000, Saunders.)

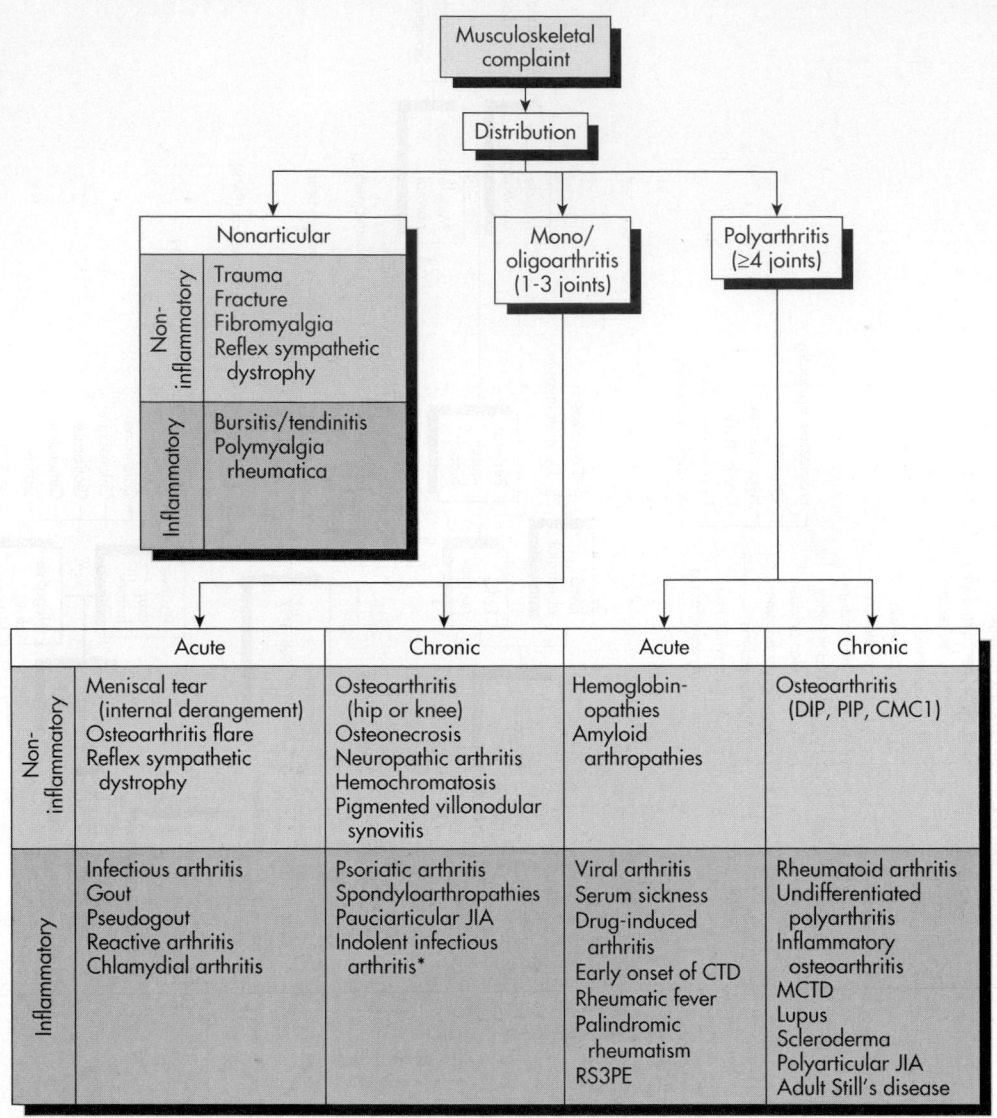

FIGURE 3-148 Algorithm for assessing initial history and examination. *CMC*, Carpometacarpal; *CTD*, connective tissue disease; *DIP*, distal interphalangeal; *JIA*, juvenile idiopathic arthritis; *MCTD*, mixed connective tissue disease; *PIP*, proximal interphalangeal. (Firestein GS, Budd RC, Gabriel SE, et al: *Kelley's textbook of rheumatology*, ed 9, Philadelphia, 2013, Saunders.)

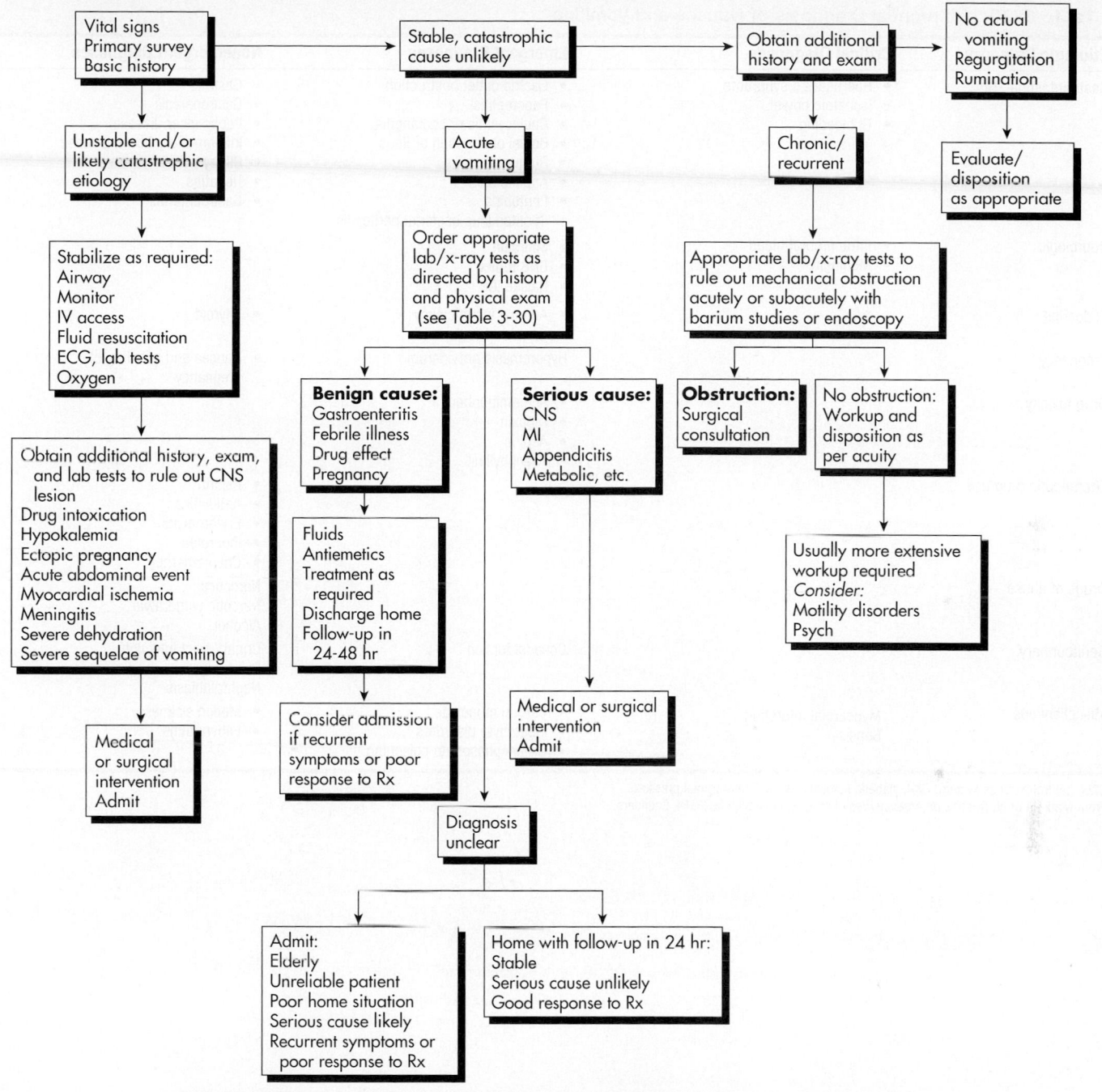

FIGURE 3-152 Approach to the patient with nausea and vomiting. *CNS,* Central nervous system; *ECG,* electrocardiogram; *IV,* intravenous; *MI,* myocardial infarction; *Psych,* psychogenic; *Rx,* treatment. (From Marx JA et al: *Rosen's emergency medicine,* ed 8, Philadelphia, 2014, Saunders.)

Table 3-30 Differential Diagnosis of Nausea and Vomiting

Etiologic Category	Critical Diagnoses	Emergent Diagnoses	Nonemergent Diagnoses
Gastrointestinal (GI)	• Boerhaave's syndrome • Ischemic bowel • GI bleeding	• Gastric outlet obstruction • Pancreatitis • Cholecystitis or cholangitis • Bowel obstruction or ileus • Ruptured viscus • Appendicitis • Peritonitis • Spontaneous bacterial peritonitis	• Gastritis • Gastroparesis • Peptic ulcer disease • Inflammatory bowel disease • Biliary colic • Hepatitis • Gastroenteritis
Neurologic	• Intracerebral bleed • Meningitis	• Migraine • CNS tumor • Raised ICP	
Endocrine	• DKA	• Adrenal insufficiency • Uremia	• Thyroid
Pregnancy		Hyperemesis gravidarum	• Nausea and vomiting of pregnancy
Drug toxicity		• Acetaminophen • Digoxin • Aspirin • Theophylline	
Therapeutic drug use			• Aspirin • Antibiotics • Erythromycin • Ibuprofen • Chemotherapy
Drugs of abuse			Narcotics Narcotic withdrawal Alcohol
Genitourinary		Gonadal torsion	Urinary tract infection Poisoning Nephrolithiasis
Miscellaneous	Myocardial infarction Sepsis	• Carbon monoxide • Electrolyte disorders • Organophosphate poisoning	• Motion sickness • Labyrinthitis

CNS, Central nervous system; *DKA,* diabetic ketoacidosis; *ICP,* intracranial pressure.
From Marx JA et al: *Rosen's emergency medicine,* ed 8, Philadelphia, 2014, Saunders.

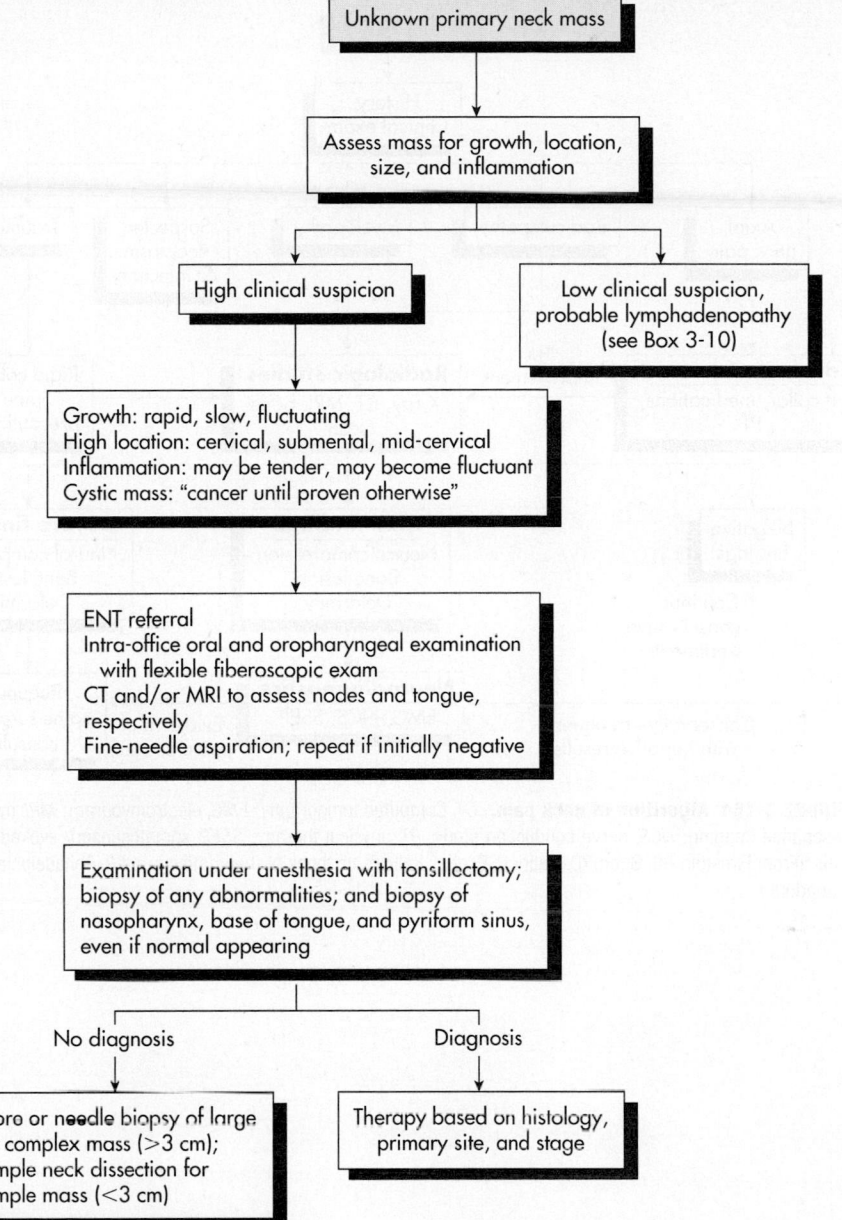

Unknown primary neck mass

Assess mass for growth, location, size, and inflammation

High clinical suspicion

Low clinical suspicion, probable lymphadenopathy (see Box 3-10)

Growth: rapid, slow, fluctuating
High location: cervical, submental, mid-cervical
Inflammation: may be tender, may become fluctuant
Cystic mass: "cancer until proven otherwise"

ENT referral
Intra-office oral and oropharyngeal examination with flexible fiberoscopic exam
CT and/or MRI to assess nodes and tongue, respectively
Fine-needle aspiration; repeat if initially negative

Examination under anesthesia with tonsillectomy; biopsy of any abnormalities; and biopsy of nasopharynx, base of tongue, and pyriform sinus, even if normal appearing

No diagnosis

Diagnosis

Core or needle biopsy of large or complex mass (>3 cm); simple neck dissection for simple mass (<3 cm)

Therapy based on histology, primary site, and stage

FIGURE 3-153 Evaluation of an unknown primary neck mass. *CT,* Computed tomography; *ENT,* ear, nose, and throat; *MRI,* magnetic resonance imaging. (From Goldman L, Schafer AL [eds]: *Cecil textbook of medicine,* ed 24, Philadelphia, 2012, Saunders.)

Clinical
Algorithms

BOX 3-10   An Approach to the Patient with Lymphadenopathy

- Does the patient have a known illness that causes lymphadenopathy? Treat and monitor for resolution.
- Is there an obvious infection to explain the lymphadenopathy (e.g., infectious mononucleosis)? Treat and monitor for resolution.
- Are the nodes very large and/or very firm and thus suggestive of malignancy? Perform a biopsy.
- Is the patient very concerned about malignancy and unable to be reassured that malignancy is unlikely? Perform a biopsy.
- If none of the preceding are true, perform a complete blood cell count and if it is unrevealing, monitor for a predetermined period (usually 2 to 6 weeks). If the nodes do not regress or if they increase in size, perform a biopsy.

From Goldman L, Ausiello D (eds): *Cecil textbook of medicine,* ed 23, Philadelphia, 2008, Saunders.

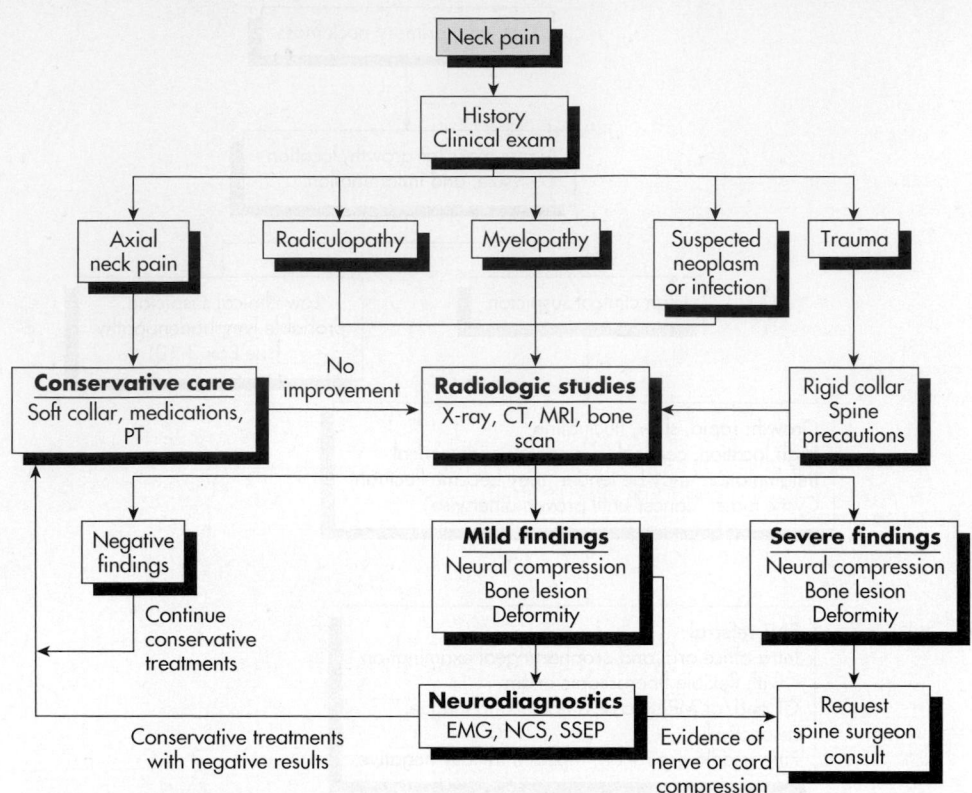

FIGURE 3-154 Algorithm of neck pain. *CT*, Computed tomography; *EMG*, electromyogram; *MRI*, magnetic resonance imaging; *NCS*, nerve conduction study; *PT,* physical therapy; *SSEP*, somatosensory evoked potentials. (From Firestein GS, Budd RC, Gabriel SE, et al: Kelley's textbook of rheumatology, ed 9, Philadelphia, 2013, Saunders.)

NYSTAGMUS

ICD-10CM # H55.00 Unspecified nystagmus
H81.13 Benign paroxysmal vertigo, bilateral
H81.49 Vertigo of central origin, unspecified ear
H55.89 Other irregular eye movements

1655

Identification of Types of Nystagmus

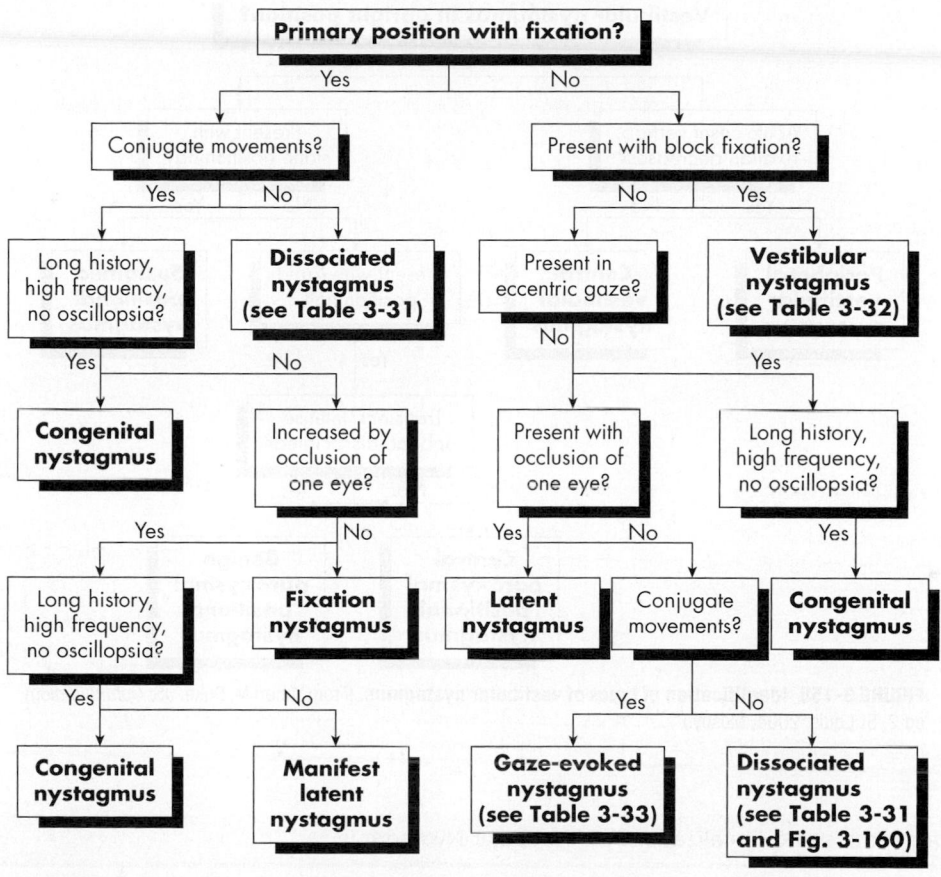

FIGURE 3-157 Identification of types of nystagmus. (From Yanoff M, Duker JS: *Ophthalmology,* ed 2, St Louis, 2004, Mosby.)

Table 3-31 Characteristics and Localizations of Dissociated Nystagmus

Nystagmus	Characteristics	Localization
Acquired pendular in adults	Pendular, horizontal, vertical, torsional, disconjugate (coexisting palatal myoclonus)	Brain stem, cerebellum
Superior oblique myokymia	Pendular, jerk, torsional, vertical, high frequency, small amplitude, monocular	Trochlear nucleus
See-saw	Pendular, vertical, torsional, rising eye intorts, falling eye extorts; rarely jerk	Midbrain (interstitial nucleus of Cajal)
Abducting "nystagmus" of internuclear ophthalmoplegia	Jerk, horizontal, decreasing velocity slow components, larger in abducting eye	Medial longitudinal fasciculus in pons, midbrain horizontal gaze
Abducting nystagmus of myasthenia gravis	Gaze-paretic nystagmus in horizontal gaze, greater paresis of medial rectus muscle	Myoneural junction—myasthenia gravis

From Yanoff M, Duker JS: *Ophthalmology,* ed 2, St Louis, 2004, Mosby.

Clinical Algorithms

III

ICD-10CM # H55.00 Unspecified nystagmus
            H81.13 Benign paroxysmal vertigo, bilateral
            H81.49 Vertigo of central origin, unspecified ear
            H55.89 Other irregular eye movements

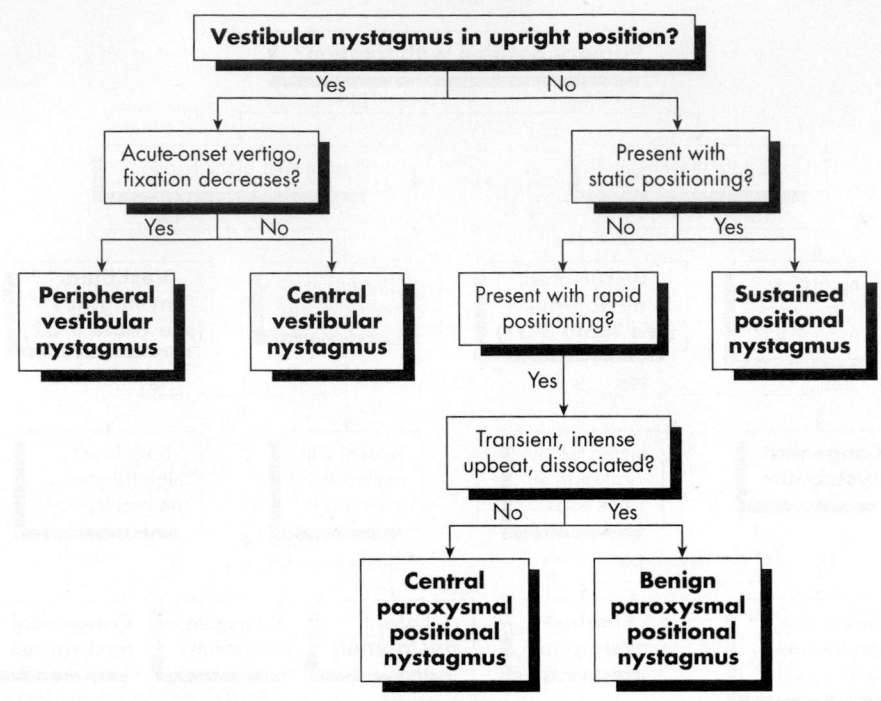

FIGURE 3-158 Identification of types of vestibular nystagmus. (From Yanoff M, Duker JS: *Ophthalmology,* ed 2, St Louis, 2004, Mosby.)

Table 3-32 Characteristics and Localizations of Vestibular Nystagmus

Nystagmus	Characteristics	Localization
Spontaneous peripheral vestibular	Jerk, horizontal, small torsional, inhibited by fixation	Labyrinth, eighth nerve (acute)
Central vestibular (fixation) nystagmus	Jerk, pendular, horizontal, vertical, torsional, not inhibited by fixation	Brain stem, cerebellum
Sustained positional vestibular	Jerk, horizontal, small torsional, direction fixed, direction changing (static positioning)	Labyrinth, eighth nerve or brain stem, cerebellum
Benign paroxysmal positional	Jerk, dissociated upbeat, latency, not inhibited by fixation, fatigue (Nylen–Barany maneuver)	Posterior vertical canal
Central paroxysmal positional	Jerk, symmetric, upbeat, downbeat	Brain stem, cerebellum

From Yanoff M, Duker JS: *Ophthalmology,* ed 2, St Louis, 2004, Mosby.

Table 3-33 Characteristics and Localizations of Gaze-Evoked Nystagmus

Nystagmus	Characteristics	Localization
Physiologic, endpoint	Jerk, small amplitude, intermittent, extremes of horizontal and up gaze	Physiologic
Gaze-paretic (symmetric)	Jerk (decreasing velocity slow components) at 30° eccentric gaze	Nonlocalizing (drugs, mental fatigue)
Gaze-paretic (asymmetric)	Jerk (decreasing velocity slow components), horizontal, at 30° eccentric gaze, larger amplitude toward side of lesion	Lesions of brain stem, cerebellum, cerebral hemisphere
Rebound	Jerk, horizontal, decreases and direction can reverse in eccentric gaze, transient jerk nystagmus on return to primary gaze, fast components beating toward eccentric gaze	Cerebellum
Myasthenia gravis	Jerk, horizontal or vertical, gradual onset in prolonged eccentric gaze	Myoneural junction (fatigue—increasing transmission block)

From Yanoff M, Duker JS: *Ophthalmology,* ed 2, St Louis, 2004, Mosby.

NYSTAGMUS—cont'd

ICD-10CM # H55.00 Unspecified nystagmus
H81.13 Benign paroxysmal vertigo, bilateral
H81.49 Vertigo of central origin, unspecified ear
H55.89 Other irregular eye movements

1657

Identification
of Types of Gaze-Evoked Nystagmus

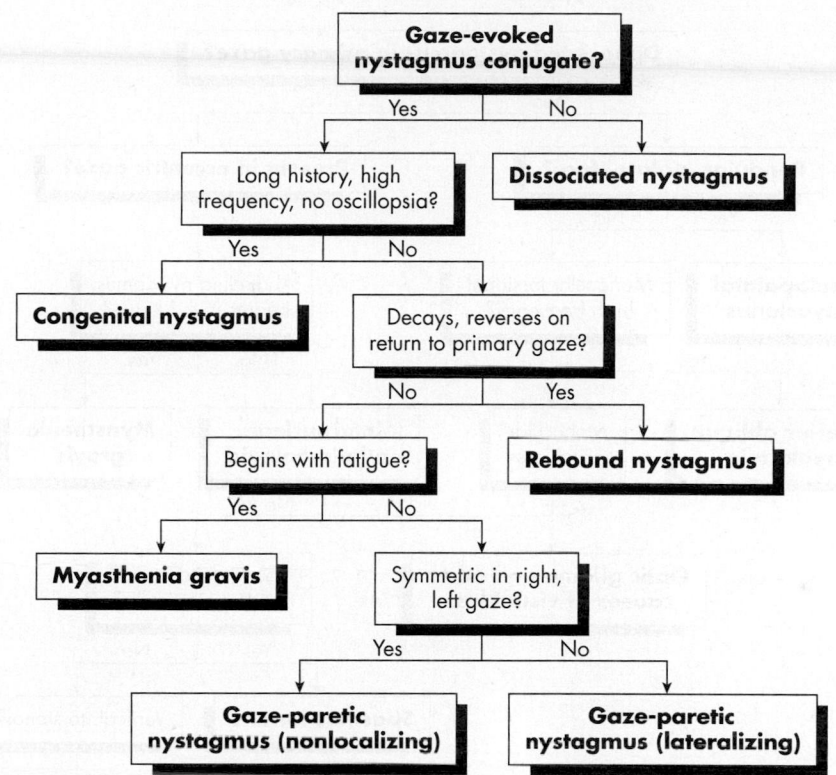

FIGURE 3-159 Identification of types of gaze-evoked nystagmus. (From Yanoff M, Duker JS: *Ophthalmology,* ed 2, St Louis, 2004, Mosby.)

ICD-10CM #   H55.00   Unspecified nystagmus
H81.13   Benign paroxysmal vertigo, bilateral
H81.49   Vertigo of central origin, unspecified ear
H55.89   Other irregular eye movements

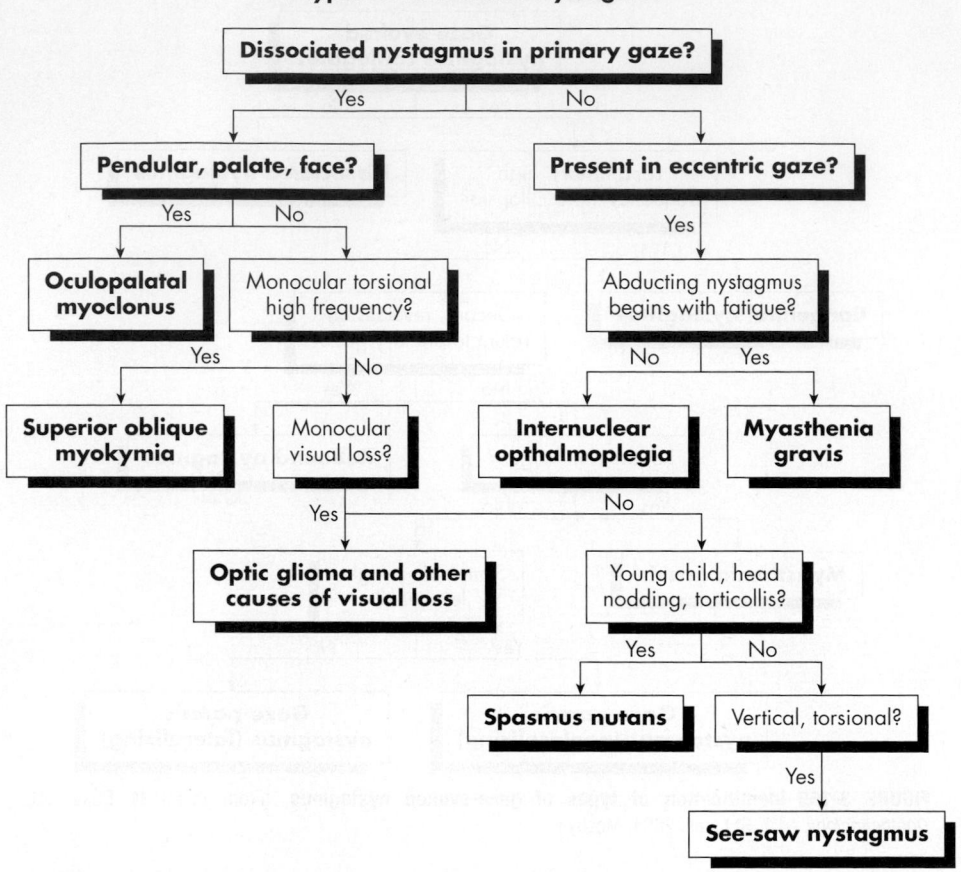

FIGURE 3-160 Identification of types of dissociated nystagmus. (From Yanoff M, Duker JS: *Ophthalmology*, ed 2, St Louis, 2004, Mosby.)

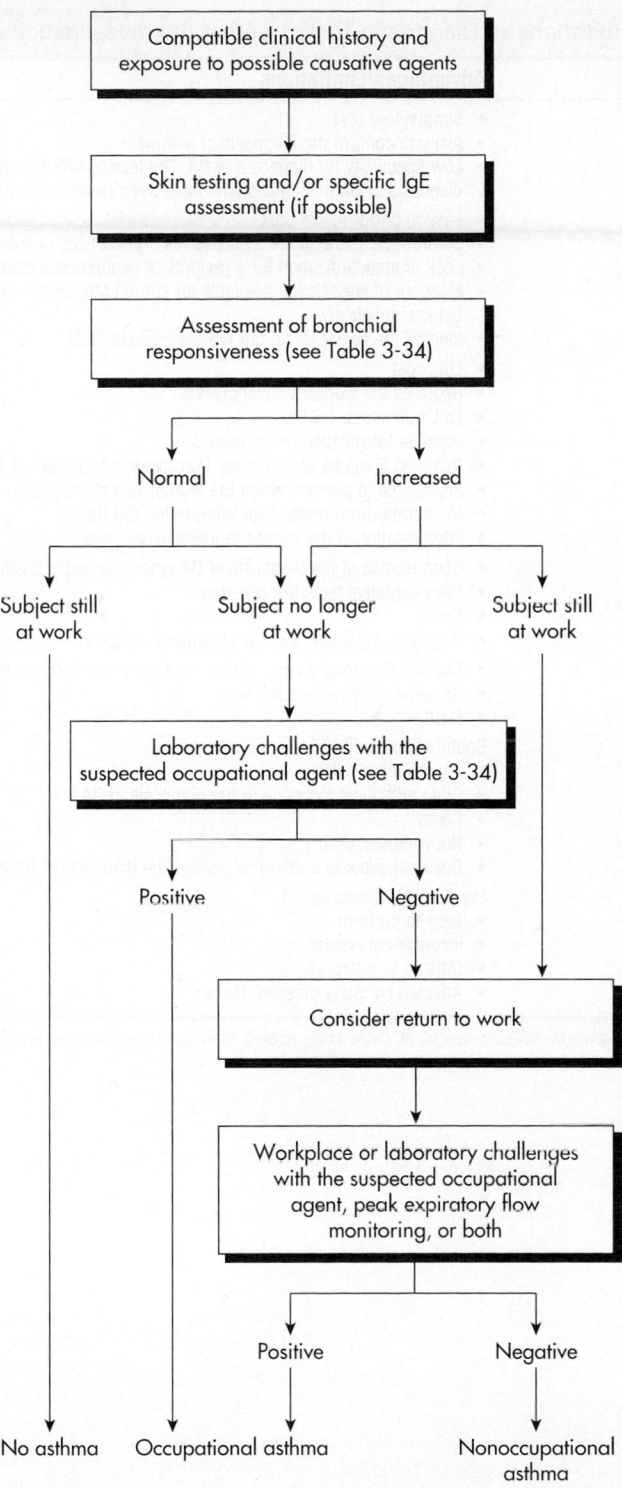

FIGURE 3-161 Algorithm for the investigation of occupational asthma. *IgE,* Immunoglobulin E. (From Adkinson NF et al: *Middleton's allergy principles and practice*, ed 8, Philadelphia, 2014, Saunders.)

Table 3-34 Advantages and Limitations of Diagnostic Tests Used in the Investigation of Occupational Asthma (OA)

Diagnostic Test(s)	Advantages/Limitations
Assessment of bronchial responsiveness	• Simple, low cost • Allow to confirm the diagnosis of asthma • Low specificity for diagnosis of OA. The lack of NSBHR does not allow discarding the diagnosis of OA in subjects who have been removed from the workplace.
Immunologic tests	• Easy to perform, low cost • Commercial extracts are available (skin-prick tests or specific IgE for HMW agents). • Lack of standardization for a majority of occupational allergens except latex • Measure of specific IgE available for some LMW agents (anhydrides, acids, isocyanates, aldehydes), but low sensitivity • Identify the sensitization but not the disease itself
PEF monitoring	• Low cost • Requires the worker's collaboration • Low adherence (<60%) • Possible falsification of the results • Requires 2 weeks at and away from work, which are not always possible for the workers • Impossible to perform when the worker has already been removed from exposure • No standardized method for interpreting the results • Interpretation of the results requires experience.
Specific inhalation challenges in the laboratory	• Confirmation of the diagnosis of OA when the test is positive • False-negative tests are possible. • Costly • Available in a small number of centers worldwide
Specific inhalation challenges at the workplace	• Exclude diagnosis if response is negative when performed in the usual work conditions • Requires usual work condition • Costly
Noninvasive measures of airway inflammation	Sputum cell counts • Impossible to falsify • Bring additional evidence to the diagnosis of OA • Costly • Not widely available • Does not allow to confirm or discard the diagnosis of OA by itself Exhaled NO measurement • Easy to perform • Inconsistent results • Difficult to interpret • Affected by many different factors

HMW, High-molecular-weight; *IgE,* immunoglobulin E; *LMW,* low-molecular-weight; *NO,* nitric oxide; *NSBHR,* nonspecific bronchial hyperresponsiveness; *PEF,* peak expiratory flow.
From Adkinson NF et al: *Middleton's allergy principles and practice,* ed 8, Philadelphia, 2014, Saunders.

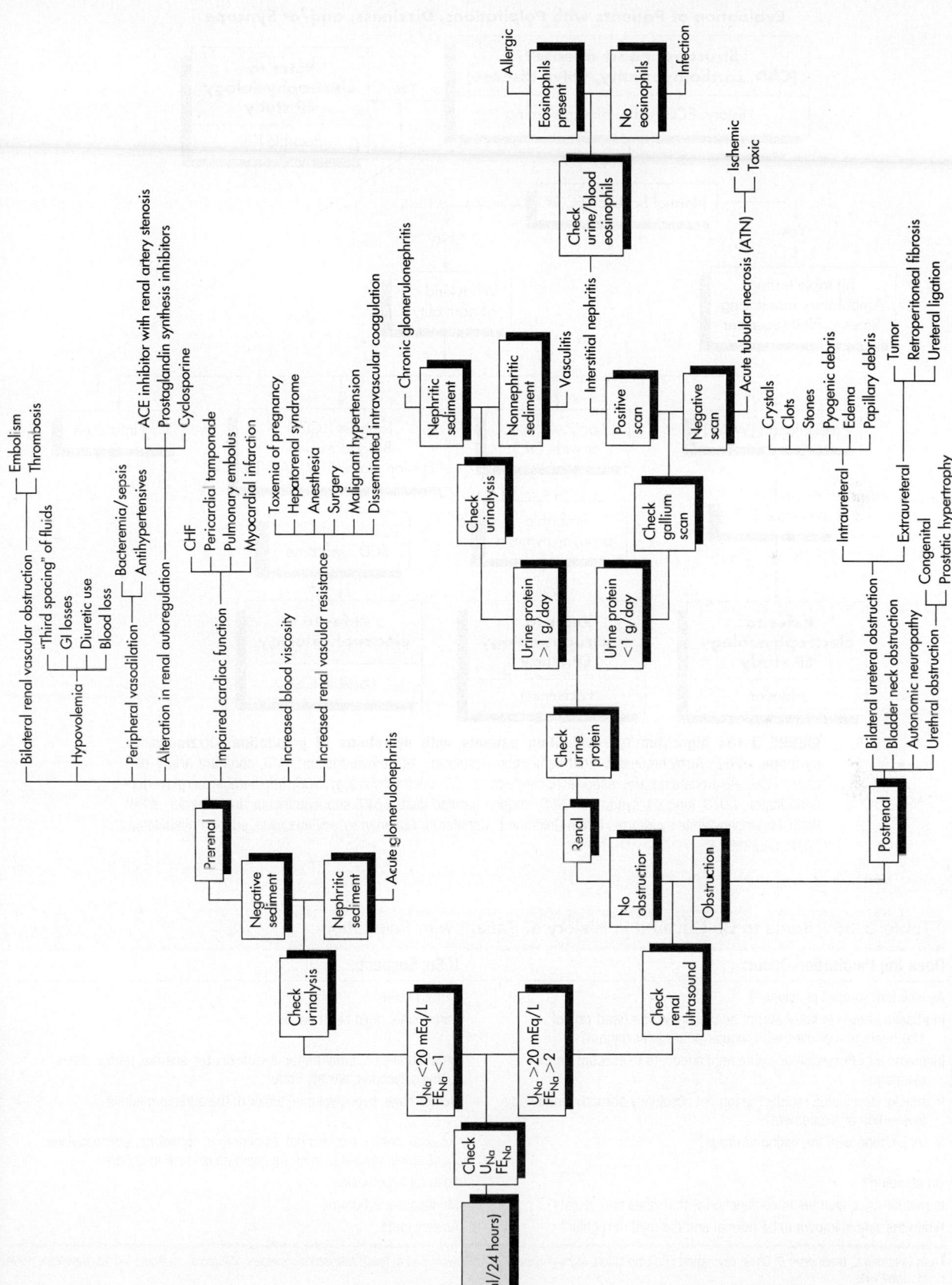

FIGURE 3-162 Evaluation of oliguria. *ACE,* Angiotensin-converting enzyme; *CHF,* congestive heart failure; *GI,* gastrointestinal. (From Healey PM: *Common medical diagnosis: an algorithmic approach,* ed 3, Philadelphia, 2000, Saunders.)

Evaluation of Patients with Palpitations, Dizziness, and/or Syncope

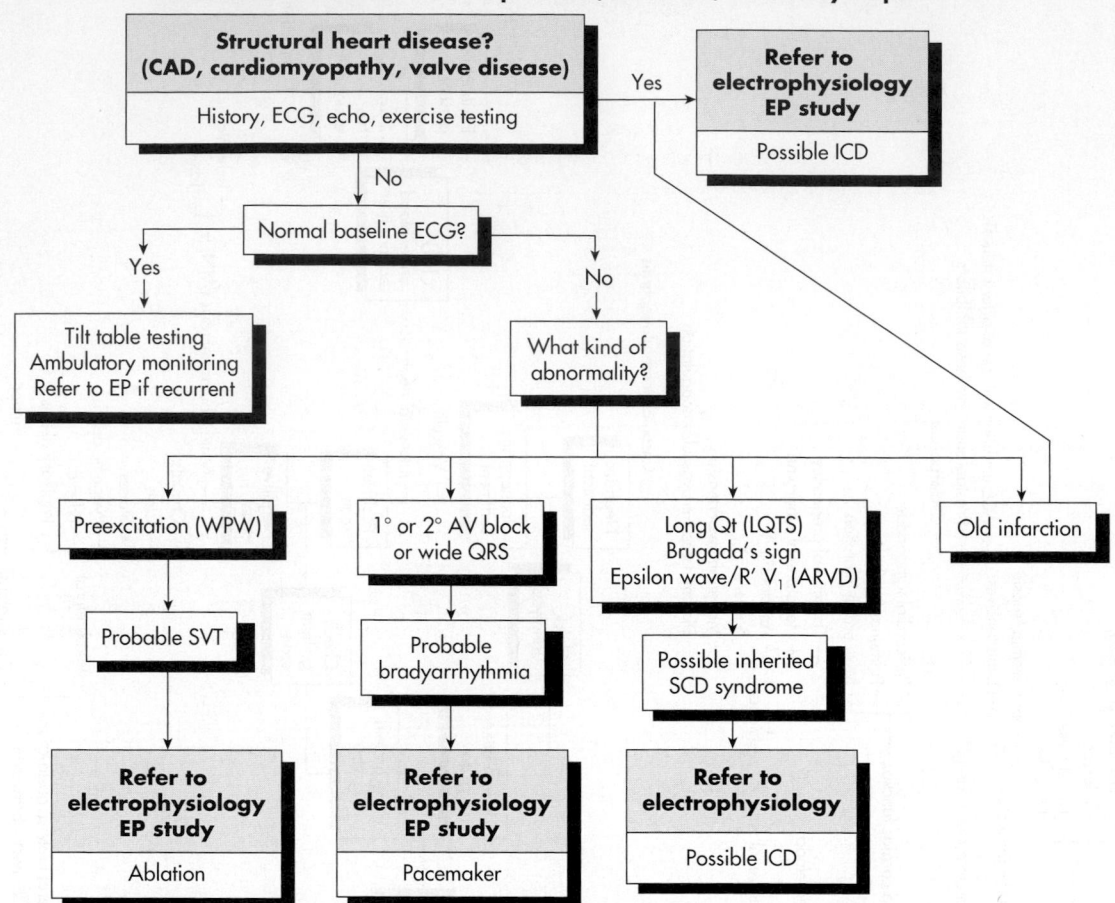

FIGURE 3-164 Algorithm for evaluating patients with symptoms of palpitation, dizziness, or syncope. *ARVD,* Arrhythmogenic right ventricular dysplasia; *AV,* atrioventricular; *CAD,* coronary artery disease; *ECG,* electrocardiogram; *echo,* echocardiogram; *EP,* electrophysiology; *ICD,* implantable cardioverter-defibrillator; *LQTS,* long QT syndrome; *SCD,* sudden cardiac death; *SVT,* supraventricular tachycardia; *WPW,* Wolff-Parkinson-White syndrome. (From Goldman L, Schafer AI: *Goldman's Cecil medicine,* ed 24, Philadelphia, 2012, Saunders.)

Table 3-35 Items to Be Covered in History of Patient with Palpitation

Does the Palpitation Occur:	If So, Suspect:
As isolated "jumps" or "skips"?	Extrasystoles
In attacks known to be of abrupt beginning, with a heart rate of 120 beats/min or over, with regular or irregular rhythm?	Paroxysmal rapid heart action
Independent of exercise or excitement adequate to account for the symptom?	Atrial fibrillation, atrial flutter, thyrotoxicosis, anemia, febrile states, hypoglycemia, anxiety state
In attacks developing rapidly though not absolutely abruptly, unrelated to exertion or excitement?	Hemorrhage, hypoglycemia, tumor of the adrenal medulla
In conjunction with the taking of drugs?	Tobacco, coffee, tea, alcohol, epinephrine, ephedrine, aminophylline, atropine, thyroid extract, monoamine oxidase inhibitors
On standing?	Postural hypotension
In middle-aged women, in conjunction with flushes and sweats?	Menopausal syndrome
When the rate is known to be normal and the rhythm regular?	Anxiety state

From Goldman L, Braunwald E: Chest discomfort and palpitation. In Isselbacher KJ, Braunwald E et al [eds]: *Harrison's principles of internal medicine,* ed 13, New York, 1994, McGraw-Hill.

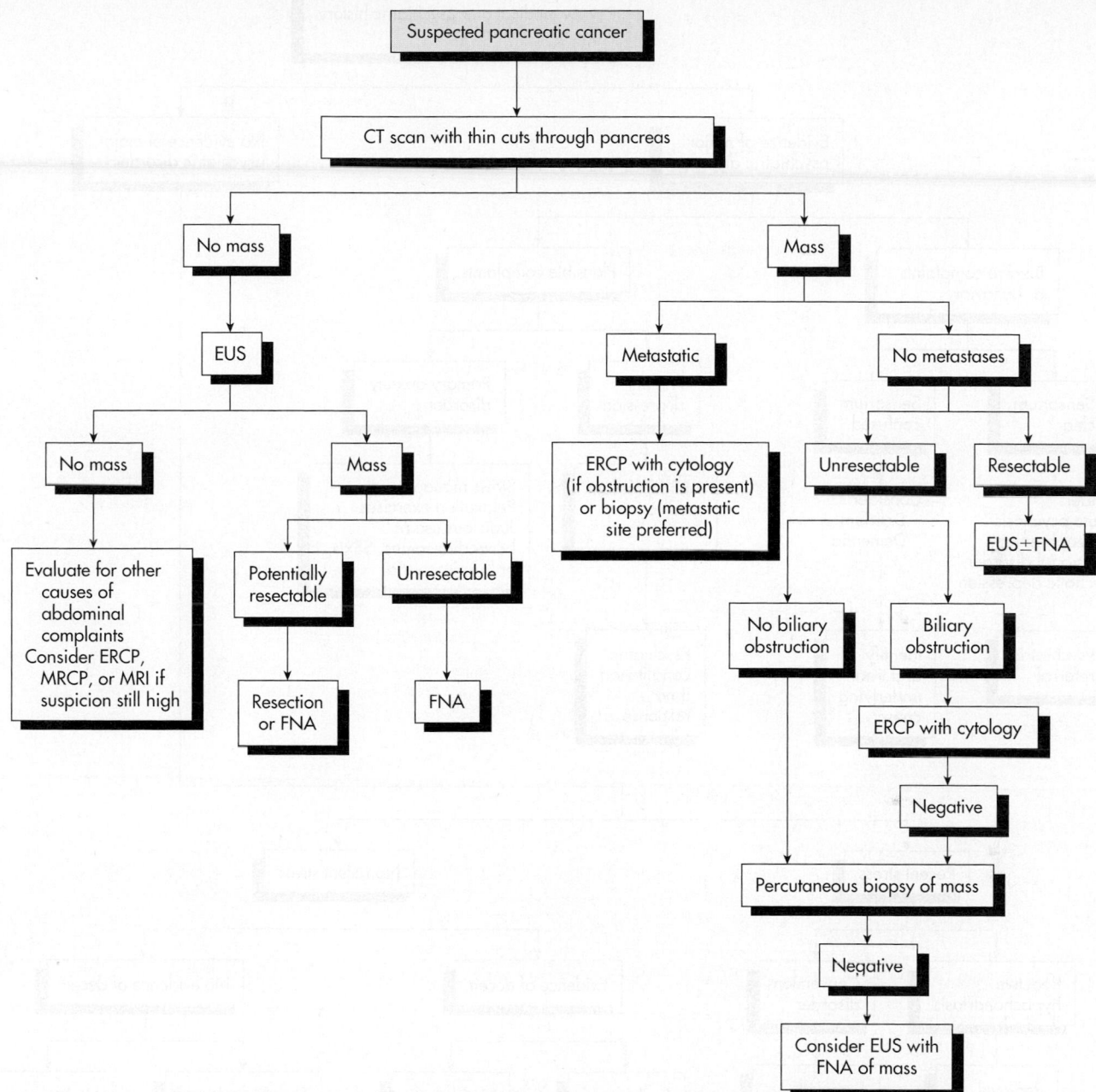

FIGURE 3-166 Diagnostic algorithm for pancreatic cancer. Intraoperative fine-needle aspiration (FNA) if found inoperable during surgery. *CT,* Computed tomography; *ERCP,* endoscopic retrograde cholangiopancreatography; *EUS,* endoscopic ultrasonography; *MRI,* magnetic resonance imaging. (From Goldman L, Schafer AL [eds]: *Cecil textbook of medicine,* ed 24, Philadelphia, 2012, Saunders.)

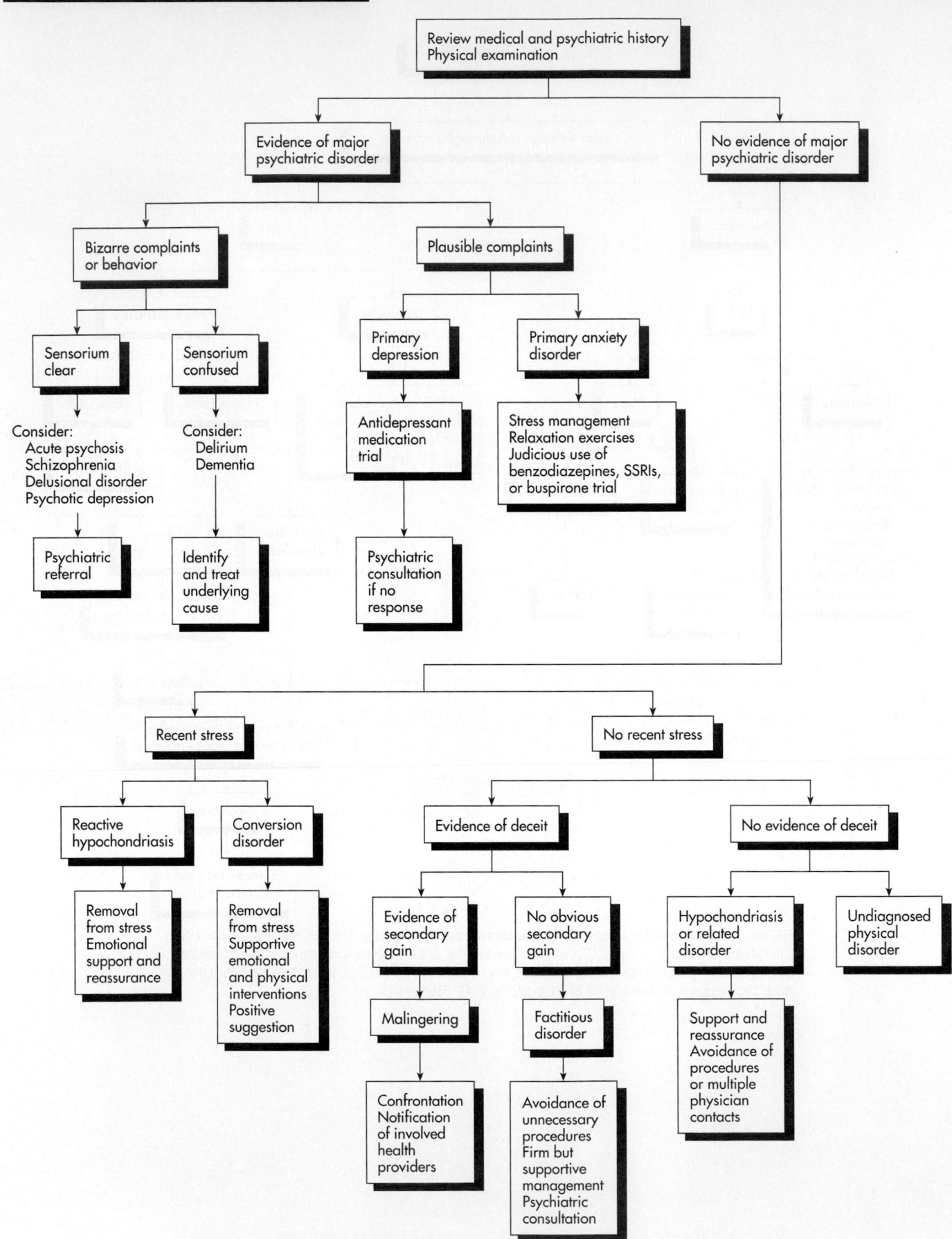

FIGURE 3-168 Patient with ill-defined physical complaints. Previous or recent evaluations are noncontributory. *SSRIs,* Selective serotonin reuptake inhibitors. (From Greene H, Johnson WP, Lemcke D [eds]: *Decision making in medicine,* ed 2, St Louis, 1998, Mosby.)

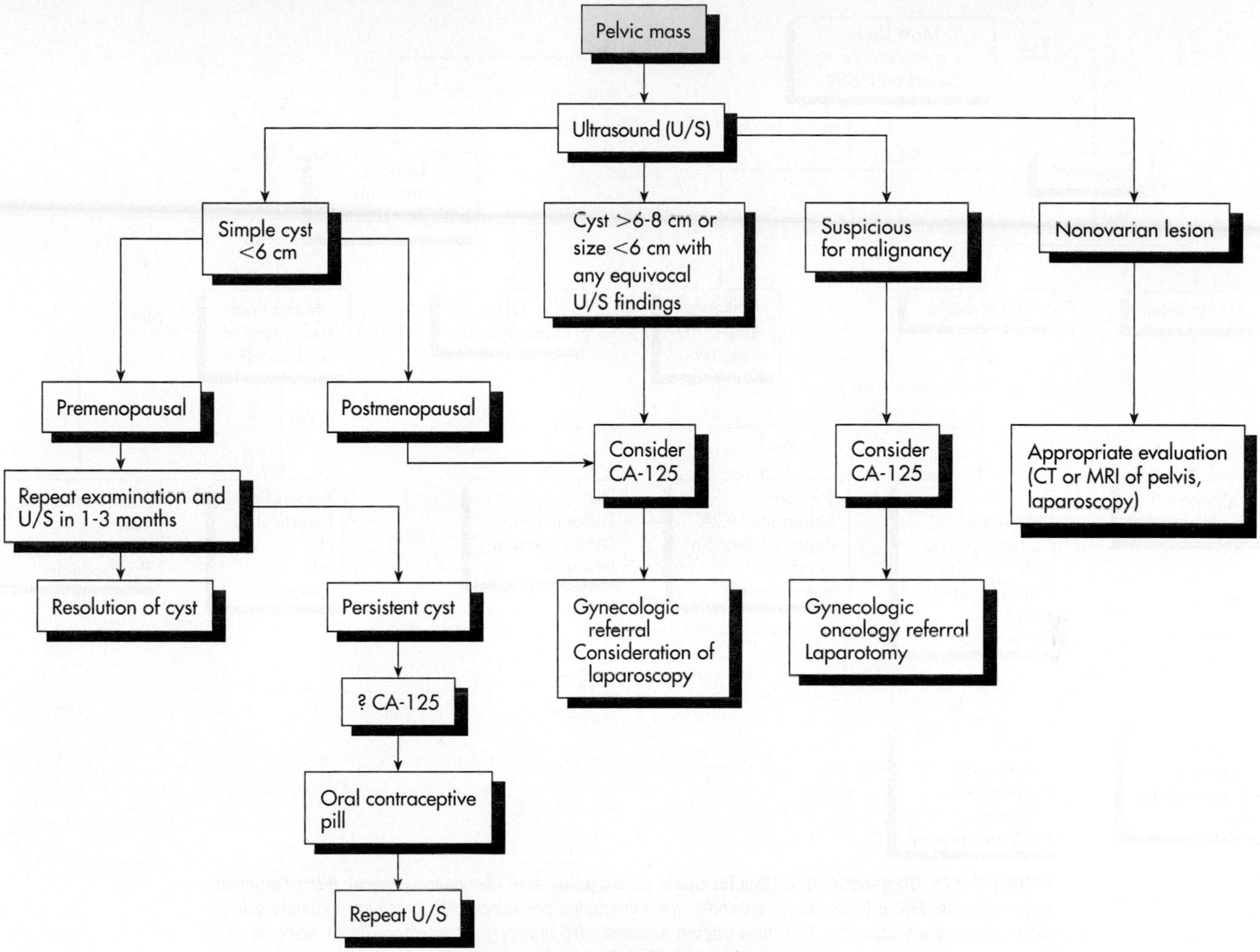

```
                              ┌──────────────┐
                              │  Pelvic mass │
                              └──────┬───────┘
                                     │
                              ┌──────┴───────┐
          ┌───────────┬───────┤ Ultrasound (U/S) ├────────┬────────────┐
          │           │       └──────────────┘            │            │
   ┌──────┴─────┐  ┌──────────────────┐  ┌──────────────┐  ┌──────────────┐
   │ Simple cyst│  │ Cyst >6-8 cm or  │  │  Suspicious  │  │ Nonovarian   │
   │   <6 cm    │  │ size <6 cm with  │  │ for malignancy│  │   lesion     │
   └──┬──────┬──┘  │ any equivocal    │  └──────┬───────┘  └──────┬───────┘
      │      │     │  U/S findings    │         │                 │
      │      │     └────────┬─────────┘         │                 │
┌─────┴───┐ ┌───────────┐   │          ┌────────┴──┐     ┌─────────┴────────┐
│Pre-     │ │Post-      │   │          │ Consider  │     │ Appropriate      │
│menopausal││menopausal │   │          │ CA-125    │     │ evaluation       │
└────┬────┘ └─────┬─────┘   │          └────┬──────┘     │ (CT or MRI of    │
     │            │   ┌──────┴────┐         │            │ pelvis,          │
┌────┴──────────┐ │   │ Consider  │         │            │ laparoscopy)     │
│Repeat examina-│ │   │ CA-125    │    ┌────┴───────┐    └──────────────────┘
│tion and U/S   │ │   └────┬──────┘    │ Gynecologic│
│in 1-3 months  │ │        │           │ oncology   │
└────┬──────────┘ │   ┌────┴───────┐   │ referral   │
     │            │   │ Gynecologic│   │ Laparotomy │
┌────┴──────┐     │   │ referral   │   └────────────┘
│Resolution │     │   │Consideration│
│ of cyst   │     │   │ of          │
└───────────┘     │   │laparoscopy │
          ┌───────┴──┐└────────────┘
          │Persistent│
          │  cyst    │
          └────┬─────┘
          ┌────┴─────┐
          │? CA-125  │
          └────┬─────┘
          ┌────┴──────────┐
          │Oral contracep-│
          │ tive pill     │
          └────┬──────────┘
          ┌────┴─────┐
          │Repeat U/S│
          └──────────┘
```

FIGURE 3-169 Approach to the patient with a pelvic mass. *CT,* Computed tomography; *MRI,* magnetic resonance imaging. (Modified from Carlson KJ et al: *Primary care of women,* ed 2, St Louis, 2002, Mosby.)

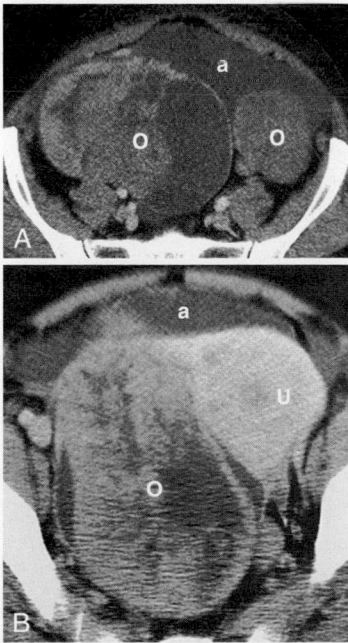

FIGURE 3-170 Ovarian carcinoma. A, Both ovaries (O) are replaced and enlarged by tumors with predominant solid components. Ascites (a) is present providing strong evidence of tumor spread to the peritoneal cavity. **B,** A large mass (O) with predominant solid components arises from the right ovary and displaces the uterus (U) anteriorly and leftward. Ascites (a) is present. (From Webb WR, Brant WE, Major NM: *Fundamentals of body CT,* ed 4, Philadelphia, 2015, Saunders.)

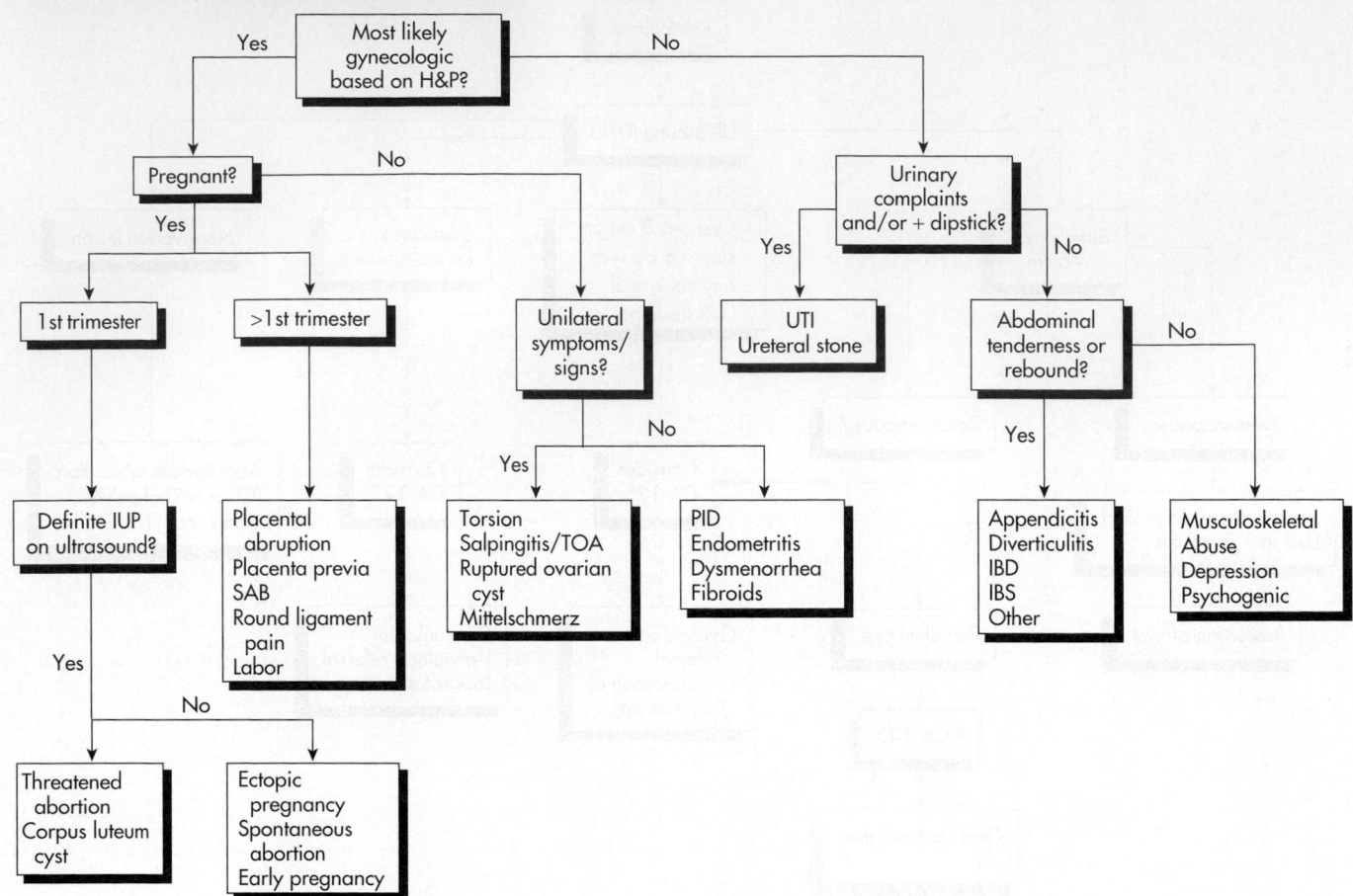

FIGURE 3-171 Diagnostic algorithm for acute pelvic pain. *H&P,* History and physical; *IBD,* inflammatory bowel disease; *IBS,* irritable bowel syndrome; *IUP,* intrauterine pregnancy; *PID,* pelvic inflammatory disease; *SAB,* spontaneous abortion; *TOA,* tubo-ovarian abscess; *UTI,* urinary tract infection. (From Marx JA et al: *Rosen's emergency medicine,* ed 8, Philadelphia, 2014, Saunders.)

PELVIC PAIN, WOMEN, DIAGNOSTIC EVALUATION—cont'd

Table 3-36 Differentiation of Common or Potentially Catastrophic Causes of Pelvic Pain

Causative Disorder or Condition	Pain History	Associated Symptoms	Supporting History	Prevalence in ED	Physical Examination	Useful Tests	Atypical or Additional Aspects
Ectopic pregnancy (critical if ruptured)	Classically severe, sharp, lateral pelvic pain, but severity, location, and quality highly variable.	Vaginal bleeding (often mild, can be absent).	Missed period; history of previous ectopic pregnancy, infertility, pelvic surgery, PID, or IUD use.	Common	Classically unilateral adnexal tenderness, adnexal mass, and CMT.	Pelvic US, quantitative β-hCG, T&C, laparoscopy.	Cannot reliably exclude diagnosis based on history and physical examination. Severe pain, hypotension, or peritonitis suggests rupture.
Ruptured ovarian cyst (emergent—critical with significant hemorrhage; otherwise, urgent)	Abrupt moderate to severe lateral pain.	Light-headedness if bleeding is severe; rectal pain arises from fluid in cul-de-sac.		Uncommon	Hypotension and tachycardia if blood loss is significant; possible peritonitis.	Pelvic US, CBC, T&C.	Physical examination findings often do not correlate with volume of blood in pelvis at US.
Ovarian torsion (emergent)	Acute onset of moderate to severe lateral pain.	Nausea and vomiting.	History of ovarian mass or cyst.	Uncommon	Adnexal mass and tenderness, possible peritonitis.	US with Doppler flow studies, laparoscopy.	Torsion can be intermittent.
Appendicitis (emergent)	Duration often <48 hr, generalized followed by localized RLQ pain.	Low-grade fever, nausea, anorexia.	Migration of pain to RLQ from center, abdominal pain before vomiting.	Common	RLQ tenderness, possible peritonitis.	US or CT in unclear cases.	Early in course, tenderness may be minimal or poorly localized.
PID, TOA (TOA: emergent; PID: urgent-emergent)	Without TOA, pain usually bilateral. May manifest acutely within 48 hr or subacutely with up to 3 wk of pain.	Fever, vaginal discharge.	Vaginal discharge, history of PID, history of unprotected intercourse or multiple partners.	PID: common TOA: uncommon	Pus from cervical os, CMT, adnexal tenderness. Peritonitis suggests severe PID or TOA.	CBC, ESR, CRP, pelvic US, laparoscopy, cervical cultures, cervical smear for WBCs.	History and physical examination may be inaccurate for diagnosis, particularly in patients with subacute presentation.
UTI (urgent)	Pain with urination. Patient may have flank pain from associated pyelonephritis.	Urinary urgency and frequency; fever and vomiting if patient has associated pyelonephritis.	Recent urologic procedure, prior history of UTI.	Common	Suprapubic tenderness, flank tenderness and fever with pyelonephritis.	Urinalysis, urine culture (if recurrent or complicated).	WBCs can be present in urine with PID and appendicitis. RBCs present in urine with hemorrhagic cystitis.
Ureteral colic (urgent)	Acute onset, manifests within hours. Pain is lateral, usually moderate to severe. Often radiates into the groin or costovertebral angle or flank.	Nausea and vomiting.	Prior history of stones.	Common	Patient often appears uncomfortable, but physical examination can be otherwise unremarkable.	Urinalysis: hematuria present in approximately 80% of cases. Renal ultrasound for hydronephrosis. Abdominal CT.	If stone is at ureterovesicular junction, patient can have localized pain that can mimic appendicitis or other acute pelvic pathology.
Unruptured ovarian cyst or tumor	Lateral ache, gradual onset.	Often minimal.	Prior history of similar pain.	Common	Lateral pelvic tenderness, with or without a mass.	Pelvic US.	
Endometriosis	Unilateral or bilateral pelvic pain, often recurrent.	Dysmenorrhea, dyspareunia.	Prior history of same type of pain in association with menstrual cycle.	Common	Unilateral or bilateral adnexal tenderness, occasionally pelvic mass present, peritoneal findings uncommon.	Pelvic US, laparoscopy.	Symptoms can mimic other types of pelvic pathology; laparoscopy often is needed for confirmation.

β-hCG, β-Human chorionic gonadotropin; CBC, complete blood count; CMT, cervical motion tenderness; CRP, C-reactive protein; CT, computed tomography; ED, emergency department; ESR, erythrocyte sedimentation rate; IUD, intrauterine device; PID, pelvic inflammatory disease; RBC, red blood cell; RLQ, right lower quadrant; T&C, type and crossmatch; TOA, tubo-ovarian abscess; US, ultrasonography; UTI, urinary tract infection; WBC, white blood cell.
From Marx JA et al: Rosen's emergency medicine, ed 8, Philadelphia, 2014, Saunders.

Clinical Algorithms

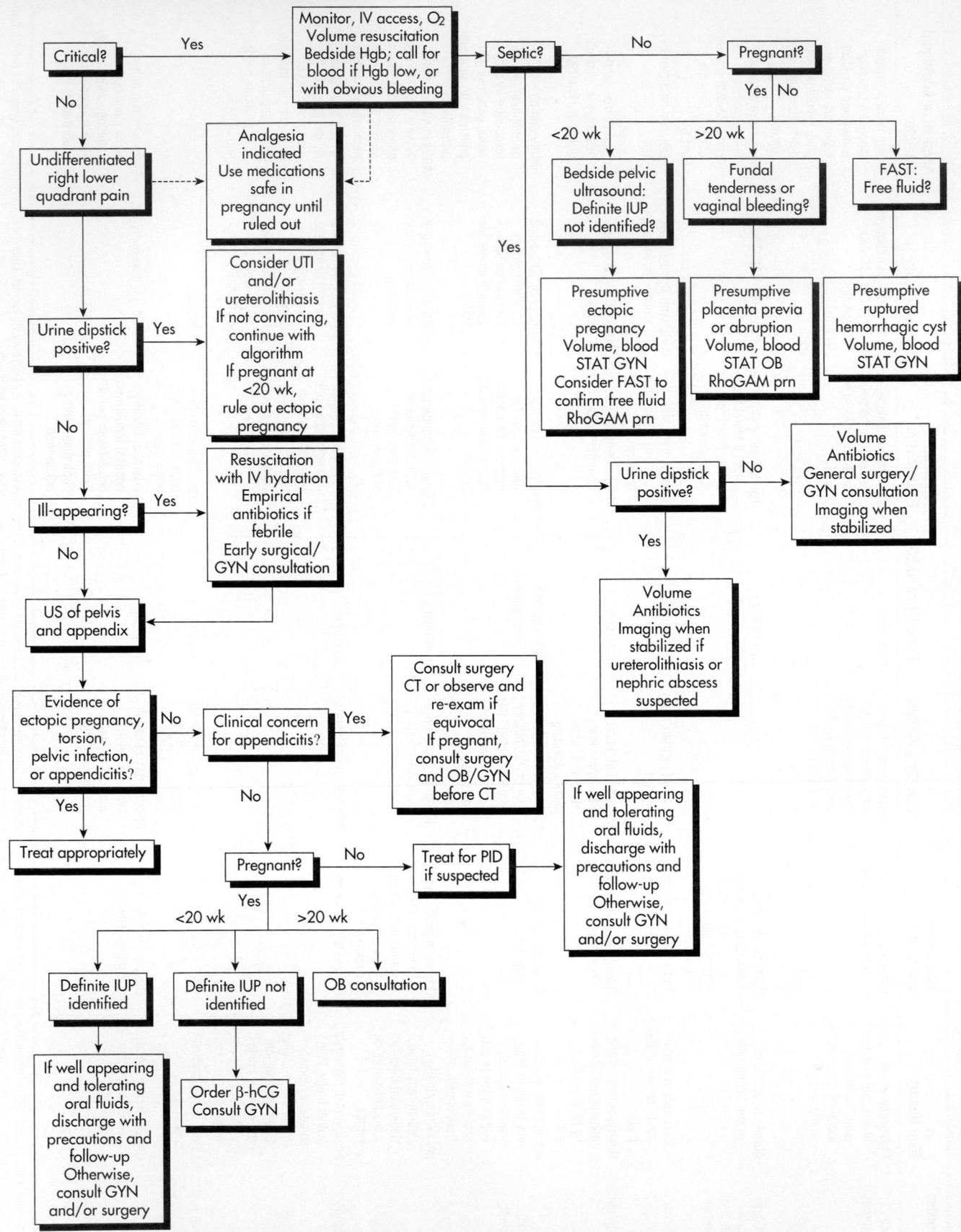

FIGURE 3-172 Management algorithm for acute pelvic pain: critical patients and right lower quadrant pain presentations. β-*hCG*, β-Human chorionic gonadotropin; *CT*, computed tomography; *FAST*, focused assessment with sonography for trauma; *GYN*, gynecology; *Hgb*, hemoglobin; *IUP*, intrauterine pregnancy; *IV*, intravenous; *OB*, obstetrics; *PID*, pelvic inflammatory disease; *STAT*, immediately; *US*, ultrasound; *UTI*, urinary tract infection. (From Marx JA et al: *Rosen's emergency medicine*, ed 8, Philadelphia, 2014, Saunders.)

ICD-10CM # G60.9 Hereditary and idiopathic neuropathy, unspecified
                    G57.10 Meralgia paresthetica, unspecified lower limb
                    G90.09 Other idiopathic peripheral autonomic neuropathy

1669

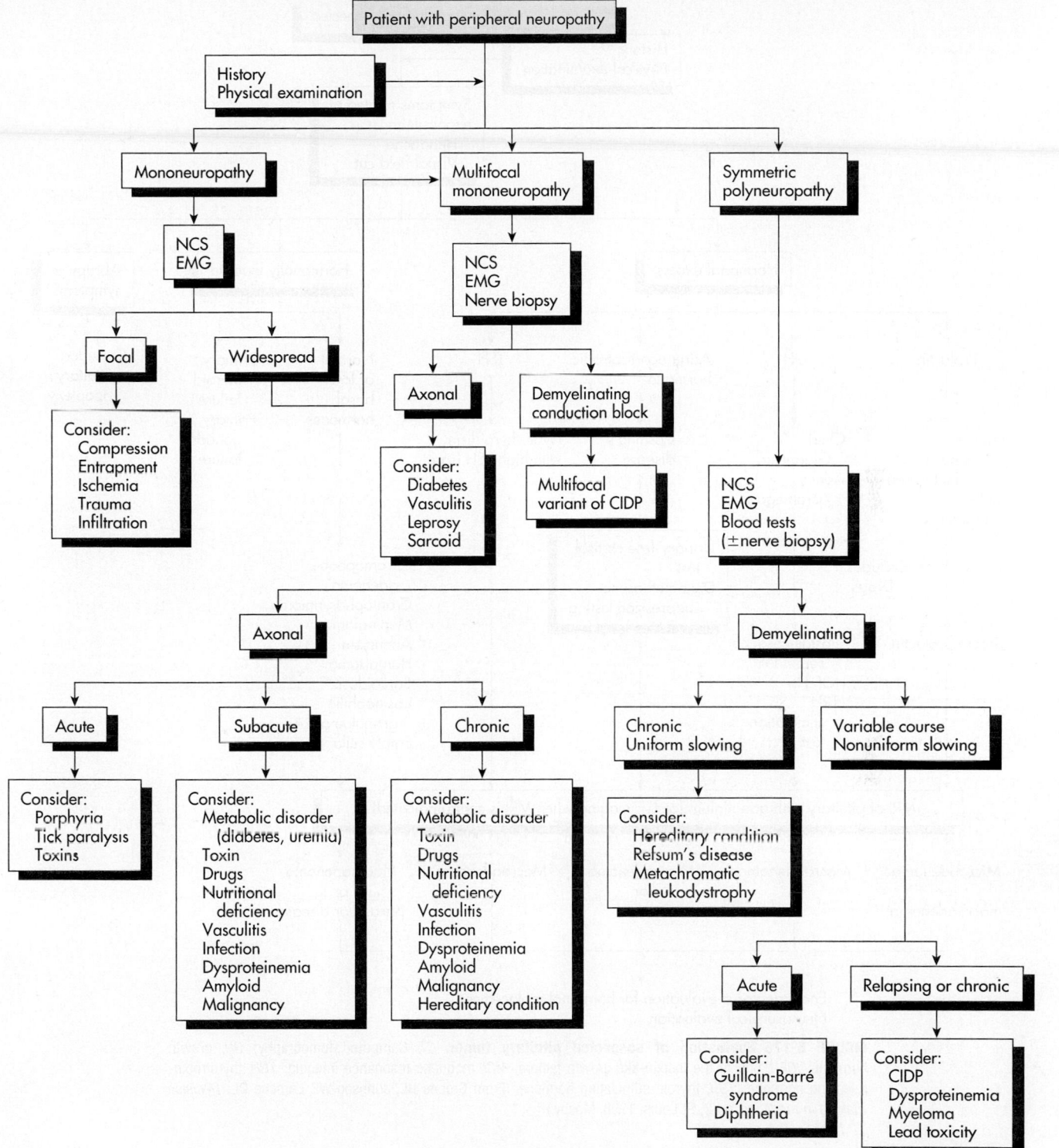

FIGURE 3-174 Approach to the patient with peripheral neuropathy. *CIDP,* Chronic inflammatory demyelinating polyradiculopathy; *EMG,* electromyogram; *NCS,* nerve conduction studies. (From Greene HL, Johnson WP, Lemcke DL: *Decision making in medicine,* ed 2, St Louis, 1988, Mosby.)

Clinical
Algorithms

III

ICD-10CM #   D44.3   Neoplasm of uncertain behavior of pituitary gland
E22.8   Other hyperfunction of pituitary gland
E22.0   Acromegaly and pituitary gigantism

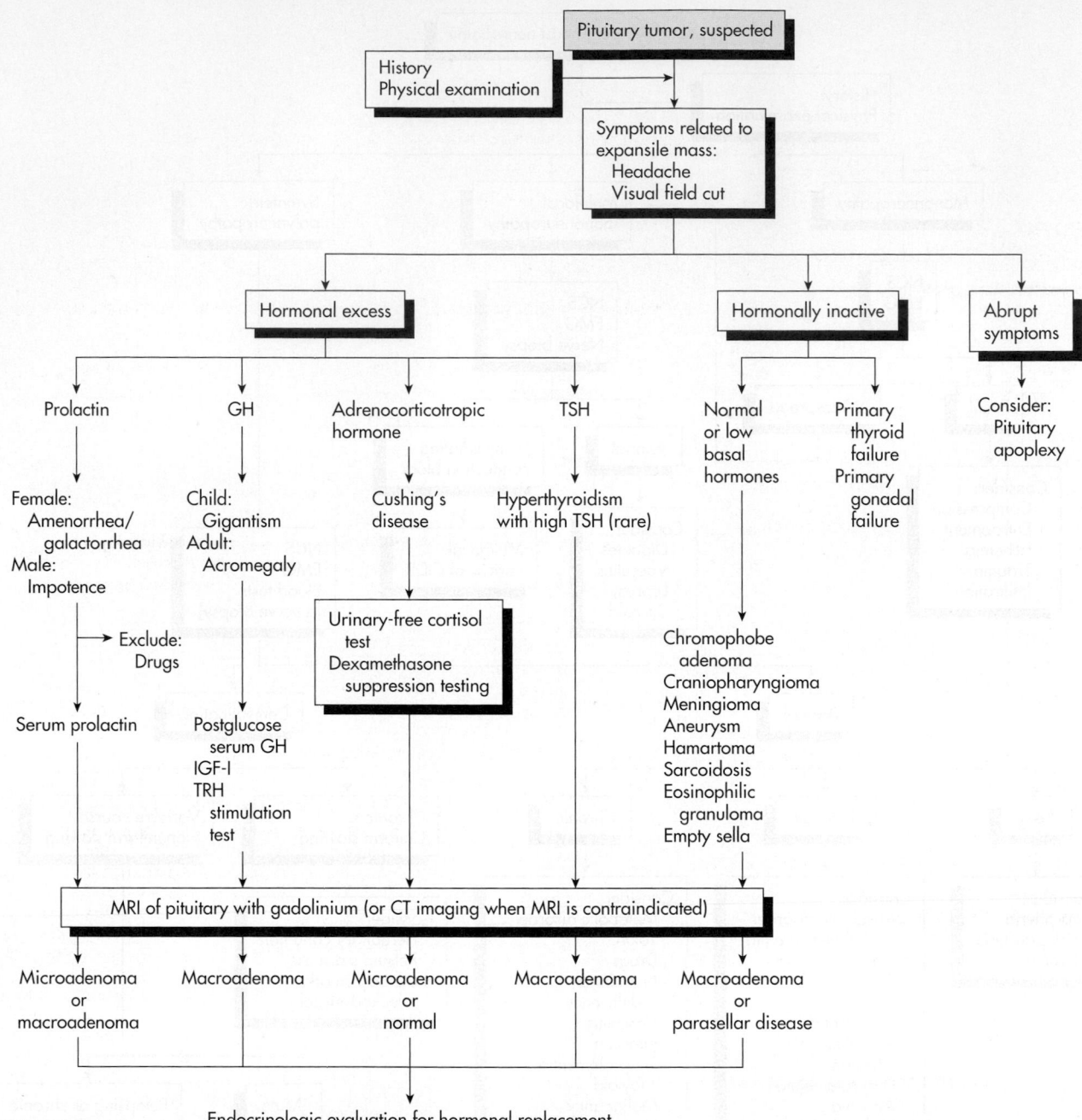

FIGURE 3-176 Evaluation of suspected pituitary tumor. *CT,* Computed tomography; *GH,* growth hormone; *IGF-I,* one of the insulin-like growth factors; *MRI,* magnetic resonance imaging; *TRH,* thyrotropin-releasing hormone; *TSH,* thyroid-stimulating hormone. (From Greene HL, Johnson WP, Lemcke DL: *Decision making in medicine,* ed 2, St Louis, 1998, Mosby.)

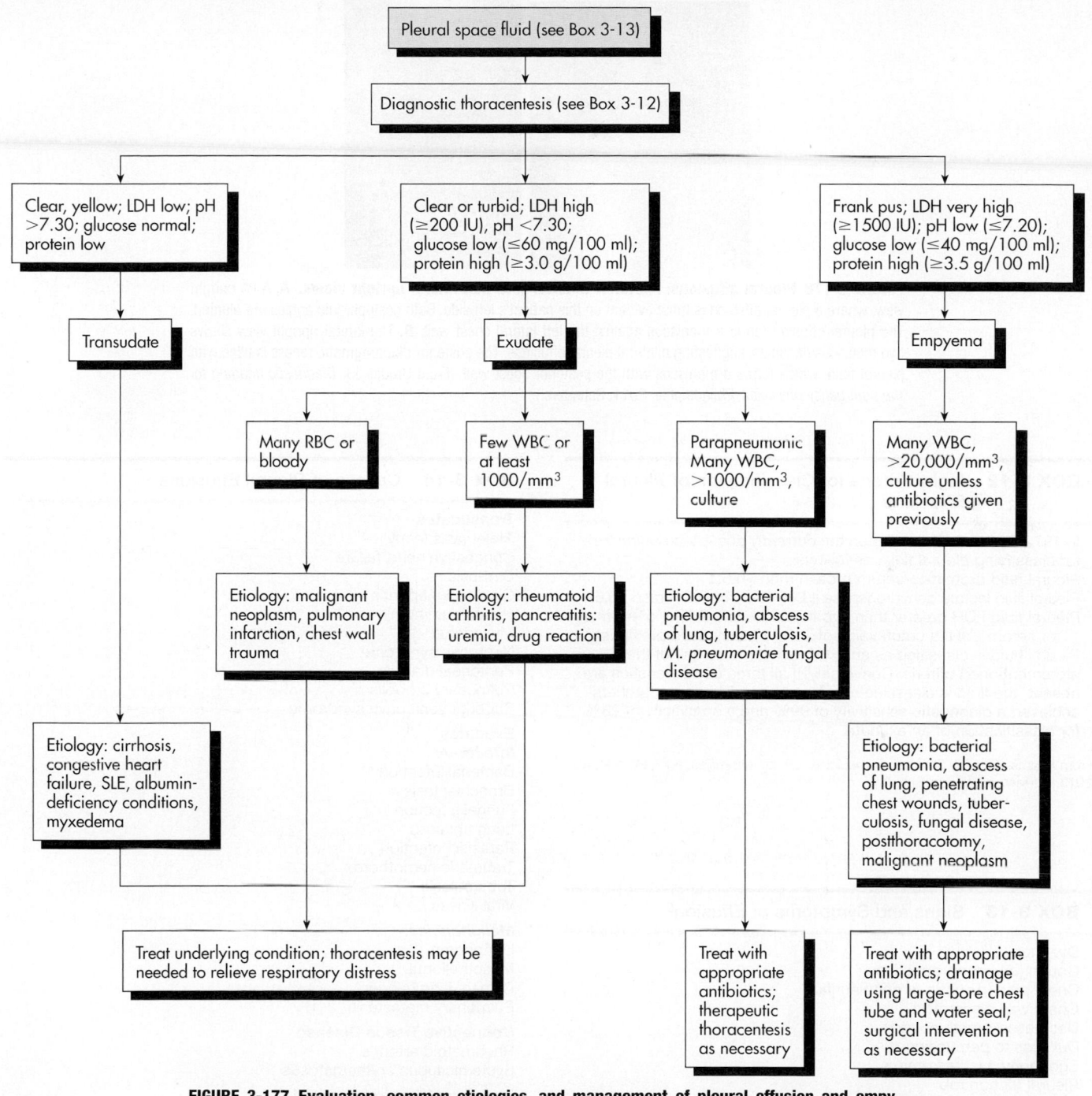

FIGURE 3-177 Evaluation, common etiologies, and management of pleural effusion and empyema. Additional information on empyema is available in Section I, Empyema. *LDH,* Lactate dehydrogenase; *RBC,* red blood cells; *SLE,* systemic lupus erythematosus; *WBC,* white blood cells. (From Kassirer J [ed]: *Current therapy in adult medicine,* ed 4, St Louis, 1998, Mosby.)

Clinical Algorithms

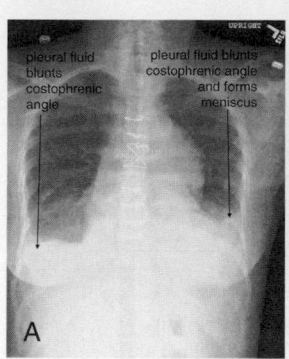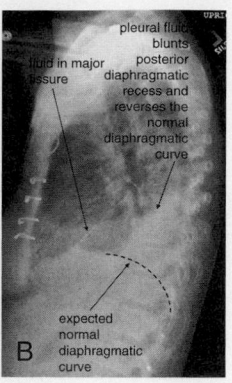

FIGURE 3-178 Pleural effusions: Posterior-anterior (PA) and lateral upright views. A, A PA upright view, where a pleural effusion is most evident on this patient's left side. Both costophrenic angles are blunted. The pleural effusion forms a meniscus against the left lateral chest wall. **B,** The lateral upright view shows two meniscus densities, suggesting bilateral pleural effusions. The posterior diaphragmatic recess is filled with pleural fluid, which forms a meniscus with the posterior chest wall. (From Broder JS: *Diagnostic imaging for the emergency physician*, Philadelphia, 2011, Saunders.)

BOX 3-12   Light Criteria for Classification of Pleural Effusions

In 1972, Light et al. developed the currently accepted benchmark for classifying pleural fluid, as follows:
Pleural fluid protein-to-serum protein ratio >0.5:1
Pleural fluid lactate dehydrogenase (LDH)-to-serum LDH ratio >0.6:1
Pleural fluid LDH greater than two thirds the upper limit of normal for serum LDH (a cutoff value of 200 IU/L was used previously)
Pleural fluid is classified as an exudate if it meets any of the aforementioned criteria. Conversely, if all three characteristics are absent, the fluid is classified as a transudate. These researchers achieved a diagnostic sensitivity of 99% and a specificity of 98% for classification of an exudate.

From Adams JG, et al: *Emergency medicine, clinical essentials*, ed 2, Philadelphia, 2013, Elsevier.

BOX 3-13   Signs and Symptoms of Effusion[5]

Dyspnea
Cough (dry, nonproductive)
Chest pain (pleuritic or nonpleuritic)
Chest wall discomfort
Decreased breath sounds
Dullness to percussion
Egophony, tactile fremitus
Pleural friction rub
Disease-specific signs and symptoms may include:
Orthopnea
Paroxysmal nocturnal dyspnea
Fever
Night sweats

[5]A detailed past medical history may uncover the cause of the effusion.
From Adams JG, et al: *Emergency medicine, clinical essentials*, ed 2, Philadelphia, 2013, Elsevier.

BOX 3-14   Causes of Pleural Effusions

Transudates
Atelectasis (early)
Congestive heart failure
Cirrhosis
Glomerulonephritis
Hypoalbuminemia
Myxedema
Nephrotic syndrome
Peritoneal dialysis
Pulmonary embolism
Superior vena cava syndrome

Exudates
Infectious
Bacterial infection
Bronchiectasis
Fungal infection
Lung abscess
Parasitic infection
Traumatic hemothorax
Tuberculosis
Viral illness

Malignancies
Lymphoma
Mesothelioma
Primary lung cancer
Pulmonary metastasis

Connective Tissue Disease
Rheumatoid arthritis
Systemic lupus erythematosus

Abdominal/Gastrointestinal
Esophageal rupture
Pancreatic disorders
Subphrenic abscess

Other
Atelectasis (chronic)
Chylothorax
Drug reactions (amiodarone)
Postpartum state
Pulmonary infarction or embolism
Uremia

From Adams JG, et al: *Emergency medicine, clinical essentials*, ed 2, Philadelphia, 2013, Elsevier.

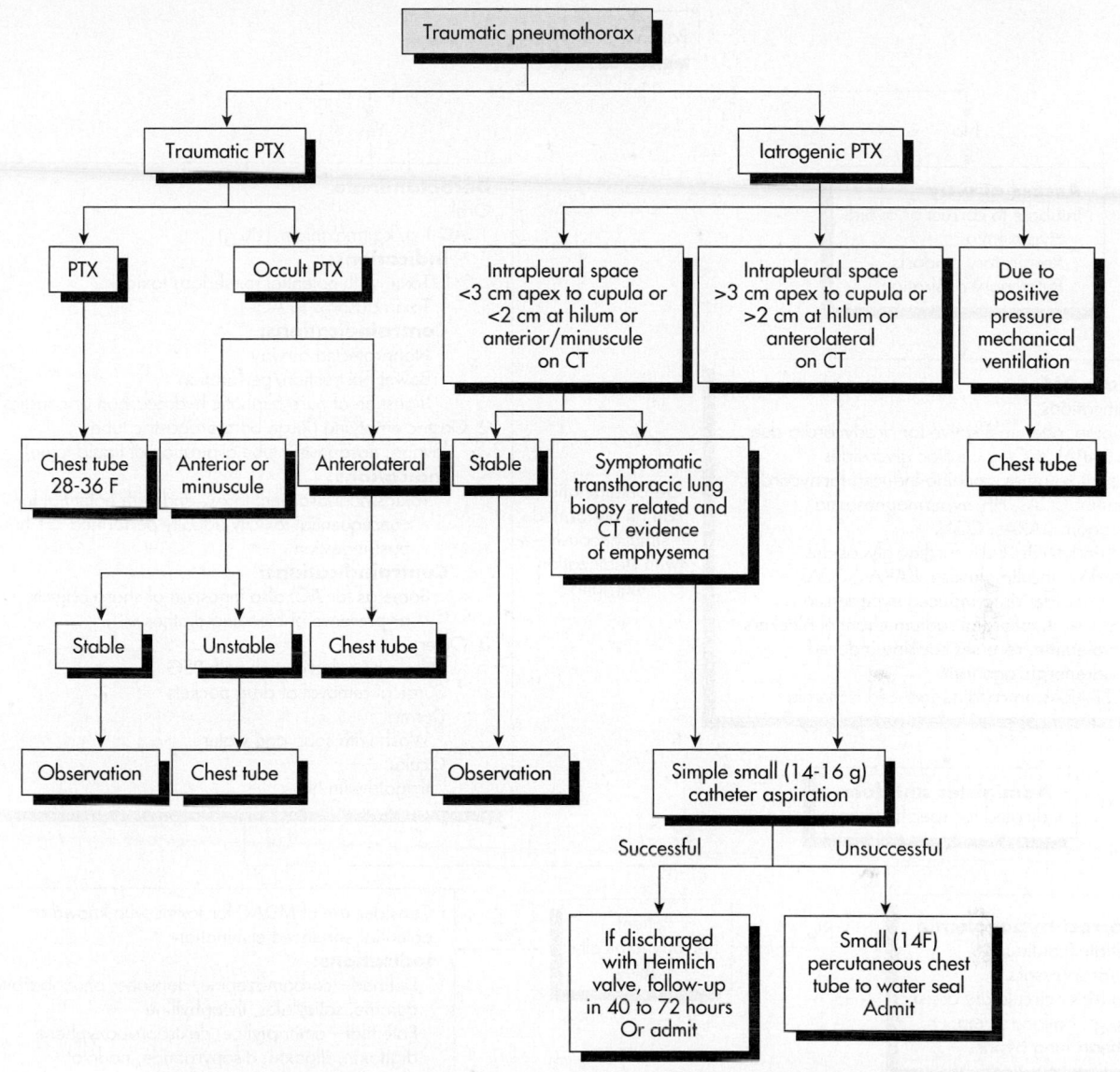

FIGURE 3-180 Algorithmic approach to the treatment of traumatic pneumothorax. *CT*, Computed tomography; *PTX*, pneumothorax. (From Adams JG, et al: *Emergency medicine, clinical essentials*, ed 2, Philadelphia, 2013, Elsevier.)

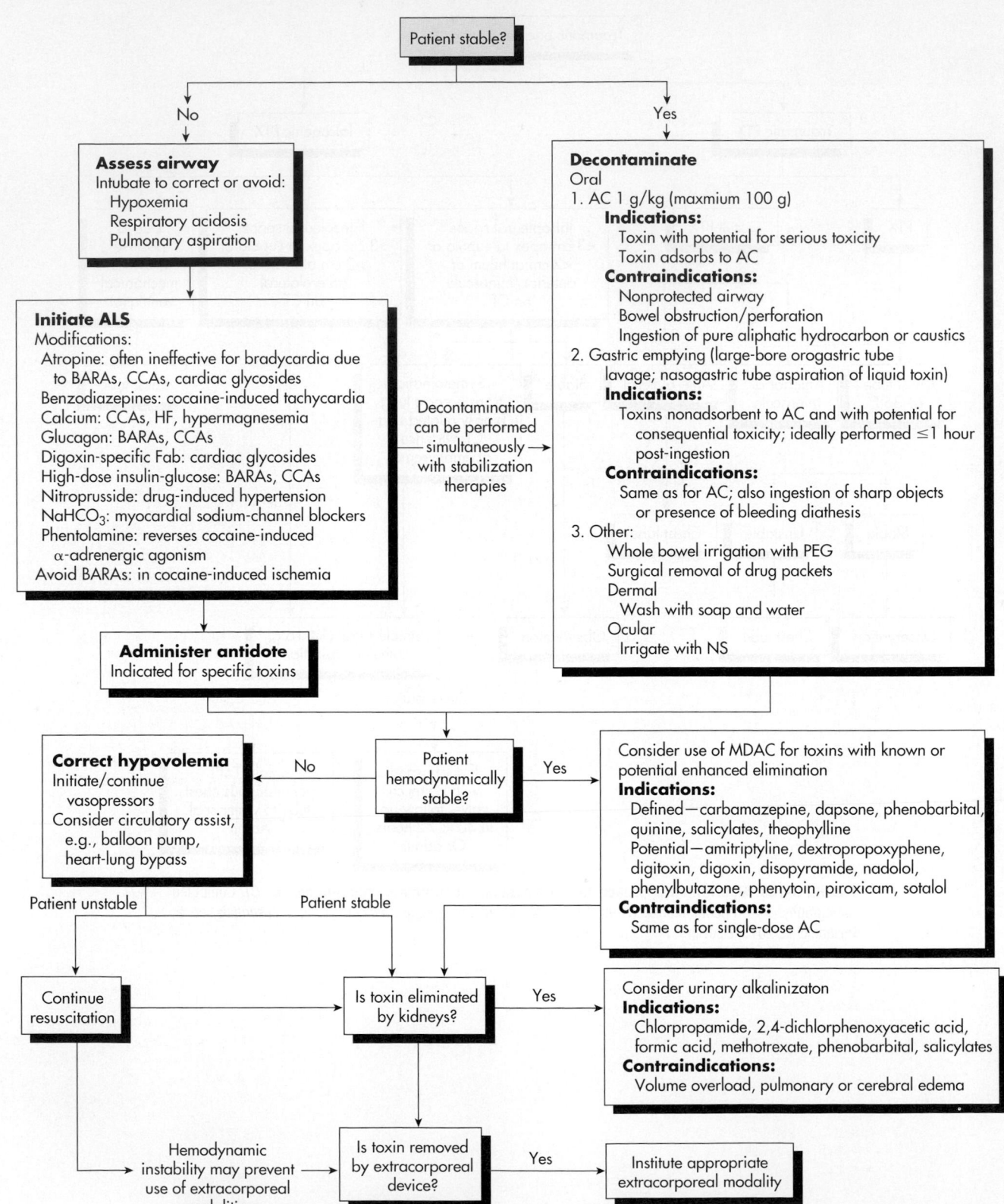

FIGURE 3-181 Algorithm for the management of acute poisoning. See also Table 3-37. *AC,* Activated charcoal; *ALS,* advanced life support; *BARAs,* β-adrenergic receptor antagonists; *CCAs,* L-type calcium-channel antagonists; *HF,* hydrofluoric acid; *MDAC,* multidose activated charcoal; *NS,* 0.9% saline solution; *PEG,* nonabsorbable polyethylene glycol solution. (From Goldman L, Schafer AI: *Goldman's Cecil medicine,* ed 24, Philadelphia, 2012, Saunders.)

Table 3-37   Pathophysiology, Clinical Effects, and Management of Specific Drugs and Toxicants

Drug or Toxicant	Pathophysiology	Clinical Effects	Laboratory	Specific Therapy
Acetaminophen	NAPQI (toxic metabolite) binds hepatic and renal tubular cells; acetaminophen itself induces transient decrease in functional factor VII	• Initial: nausea, vomiting, coma, lactic acidosis in severe cases • Days 1-3: elevated INR, aminotransferase, and bilirubin levels; RUQ tenderness; increased creatinine level in severe cases • Days 4-14: gradual recovery or continued increase in INR and creatinine, lactic acidosis, coma, cerebral edema, death	• Potentially toxic level ≥150 μg/ml 4 hr after ingestion* • INR may be transiently elevated in first 24 hr because of decrease in functional factor VII; further increases indicate hepatic necrosis; elevated aminotransferase and bilirubin levels not predictive of hepatic failure • Creatinine elevated in severe cases	NAC can increase INR but not aPTT[†]
Amphetamines	• Increased release of presynaptic norepinephrine and dopamine • Increased serotonin release (especially MDMA, PMA, DOB, other synthetic amphetamines)	• Mild: euphoria, decreased appetite, repetitive behavior • Moderate: vomiting, agitation, hypertension, tachycardia, mydriasis, bruxism, diaphoresis • Severe: hypertension or hypotension, arrhythmias, hyperthermia, seizures, coma, hepatotoxicity, rhabdomyolysis, DIC, hyponatremia (SIADH), renal failure, cerebral infarction or hemorrhage	Not helpful; many false-positives and false-negatives on screening tests	• IV crystalloids • External cooling • Benzodiazepines or barbiturates to control agitation or seizures • Benzodiazepines or nitroprusside for hypertension • See SSRIs/SRIs for features and treatment of serotonin syndrome
β-Adrenergic receptor antagonists	Blocks catecholamines from β-adrenergic receptors • α- and β-adrenergic receptor antagonism: carvedilol, labetalol • Delayed rectifier potassium-channel blockade: sotalol	Bradyarrhythmias, decreased myocardial contractility, hypotension, respiratory depression, decreased consciousness with seizures or coma (lipophilic agents, e.g., propranolol), prolonged QT interval (sotalol)	• ECG • No specific tests	• IV glucagon, 3.5-5 mg over 2-min period; if no increase in BP or HR, can repeat up to 10 mg; if effective, immediately start continuous infusion at 2-10 mg/hr; if still unstable, options include (1) regular insulin, 1 U/kg by IV bolus, followed by 1 U/kg/hr, plus dextrose to maintain euglycemia; (2) norepinephrine or dobutamine infusion titrated to desirable BP and HR; (3) IV milrinone, 50 μg/kg over 10-min period, then 0.375-0.75 μg/kg/min based on hemodynamic status[†] • Electrical pacing and IABP in refractory cases
L-type calcium-channel antagonists	• Blocks L-type voltage-sensitive calcium channels, thereby decreasing calcium entry into myocardial and vascular smooth muscle cells • Decreases pancreatic insulin release and increases insulin resistance	Bradyarrhythmias (verapamil, diltiazem), hypotension, hyperglycemia	• ECG • No specific tests	• IV 10% calcium chloride, 10-20 mg/kg (0.1-0.2 ml/kg); can repeat once; if BP improves, continuous infusion at 0.2-0.5 ml/kg/hr (20-50 mg/kg/hr) • Ionized Ca²⁺ levels should not exceed 2× normal (severe cases will be refractory to calcium therapy) • Glucagon, high-dose insulin and dextrose, catecholamines, and milrinone (as for β-adrenergic antagonists)

Table 3-37 Pathophysiology, Clinical Effects, and Management of Specific Drugs and Toxicants—cont'd

Drug or Toxicant	Pathophysiology	Clinical Effects	Laboratory	Specific Therapy
Cardiac glycosides, including digoxin, bufadienolides (toxic toad venom), or cardenolides (e.g., oleander, lily of the valley, dogbane)	• Inhibits Na^+, K^+-ATPase • Decreased CNS sympathetic output • Decreased baroreceptor sensitivity • Increased vagal acetylcholine discharge	• Bradyarrhythmias, including second- and third-degree AV block and asystole • Ventricular ectopy, tachycardia, fibrillation • Junctional tachycardia, paroxysmal atrial tachycardia with block • Weakness, visual disturbances, nausea, vomiting	• Serum digoxin level • Serum potassium (hyperkalemia occurs in acute poisoning; hypokalemia may be present in chronic poisoning), magnesium, and creatinine levels	• Correct hypokalemia and hypomagnesemia; do not give calcium • Digoxin-specific antibody fragments (Fab) indicated if patient has hemodynamically significant arrhythmias, serum potassium ≥5 mg/L, Mobitz II or third-degree AV block, ingestion of bufadienolide- or cardenolide-containing agents, or renal insufficiency • Empirical dose • Chronic: 2-5 vials • Acute: 10-20 vials • Calculated dose • Chronic: number of vials = 2 × serum digoxin level (ng/ml) × 5.6 × weight (kg)/1000 • Acute: number of vials = 2 × oral digoxin dose (mg) × 0.8
Cyclic antidepressants	• Myocardial sodium- and potassium-channel blockade • Blockade of α-adrenergic and cholinergic muscarinic receptors • Inhibition of norepinephrine re-uptake	• Decreased level of consciousness (can develop rapidly), myoclonus, seizures, coma • Anticholinergic toxidrome • Sinus tachycardia, ventricular conduction delays, ventricular arrhythmias, asystole • Hypotension	Serum levels not helpful in management	• Intermittent IV boluses of $NaHCO_3$ (1 mEq/kg) to maintain arterial pH at 7.5 because acidemia can worsen cardiovascular complications • Intubation and neuroparalytic drugs may be useful to ameliorate acidemia from muscular hyperactivity while seizures are being treated • Contraindicated drugs: types IA and IC antiarrhythmic agents; physostigmine, flumazenil
Ethylene glycol, methanol (e.g., antifreeze, window cleaners, camping stove fuels)	• Ethylene glycol: toxic metabolites produce cytotoxicity in CNS, kidneys, lungs, heart, liver, muscles; metabolic acidosis is due to glycolate accumulation; oxalate complexes with calcium, so hypocalcemia can develop • Methanol: metabolized to formic acid, which is responsible for metabolic acidosis and inhibition of cytochrome aa_3; target organs include retina, optic nerve, CNS	• Ethylene glycol: CNS depression, cerebral edema, seizures, anion gap metabolic acidosis, renal failure with acute tubular necrosis, pulmonary edema, myositis • Methanol: nausea, vomiting; cerebral edema, hemorrhage, infarcts; necrosis of thalamus and putamen; anion gap metabolic acidosis; visual disturbances, papilledema, hyperemic optic disc, nonreactive pupils	• Serum ethylene glycol and methanol levels; levels may be low or undetectable if significant metabolism has occurred • Ethylene glycol: serum calcium, creatinine, BUN levels; examine urine for calcium oxalate crystals; false hyperlactatemia occurs with certain analyzers using L-lactate oxidase, which cross-reacts with glycolic and glyoxylic acids	• For both: fomepizole (which inhibits alcohol dehydrogenase and blocks formation of toxic metabolites), 15 mg/kg IV loading dose, then 10 mg/kg IV for 4 doses during the next 48 hr, then 15 mg/kg for subsequent doses; interval dosing is q12h (q4h during hemodialysis, with dosing interval adjustments at start and finish); continue until ethylene glycol or methanol is no longer detectable • Use of ethanol is no longer recommended • Hemodialysis: initiate if level is ≥50 mg/dl or metabolic acidosis with end-organ toxicity; continue until acidosis resolves and serum level of ethylene glycol or methanol is undetectable • Monitor for cerebral edema with possible herniation • Ethylene glycol: IV calcium for symptomatic hypocalcemia • Methanol: folinic acid, 50 mg IV q4h until methanol not detectable and acidosis cleared
γ-Hydroxybutyrate (GHB) and its precursors (γ-butyrolactone and 1,4-butanediol [1,4-BD])	Agonist effect on CNS GHB receptors; indirect action with opioid receptors (may increase proenkephalins); metabolized to GABA, interacts with $GABA_B$ receptors; decreases dopamine release	• CNS: rapid loss of consciousness, with recovery typical within 2-4 hr; myoclonus (possible seizures) • Respiratory depression; bradycardia; nausea, vomiting	No specific tests	• Supportive care, including respiratory support as needed • Withdrawal resembles sedative-hypnotic withdrawal and can be treated with benzodiazepines or pentobarbital

Continued

Table 3-37   Pathophysiology, Clinical Effects, and Management of Specific Drugs and Toxicants—cont'd

Drug or Toxicant	Pathophysiology	Clinical Effects	Laboratory	Specific Therapy
Lithium	Decreases brain inositol; alters CNS serotonin, dopamine, and norepinephrine; inhibits adenylate cyclases, including those that mediate vasopressin-induced renal concentration and thyroid function	• Chronic toxicity usually more severe than acute toxicity: tremor, hyperreflexia, drowsiness, incoordination, clonus, confusion, ataxia; in severe cases, seizures, coma, death; recovery may take weeks, and CNS deficits may persist • Sinus node dysfunction, QT prolongation, T wave abnormalities, U waves • Nephrogenic diabetes insipidus, hypothyroidism, hyperthyroidism, hypercalcemia, pseudotumor cerebri • Acute toxicity: nausea, vomiting, diarrhea, and milder neurologic findings	• Peak serum levels: • Normal dose 2-3 hr; up to 5 hr for sustained-release lithium • Acute overdose: peak may be delayed ≥4-12 hr	• Replenish intravascular volume, maintain urinary output at 1-2 ml/kg/hr • Consider GI decontamination with oral polyethylene glycol electrolyte solution within 1-2 hr after acute overdose of sustained-release drug • Hemodialysis§ in patients with altered mental status, ataxia, seizures, or coma or in patients with mild symptoms in the setting of acute overdose or renal insufficiency • Ineffective or contraindicated therapies include oral activated charcoal, diuretics, and aminophylline
Opioids (e.g., heroin, morphine, oxycodone, fentanyl)	Agonist effect at CNS μ, κ, and δ opioid receptors; result is cell hyperpolarization and decreased neurotransmitter release	• CNS depression, respiratory depression, miosis • Dextromethorphan increases CNS serotonin and inhibits NMDA receptors, which causes hallucinations • Propoxyphene and its metabolite norpropoxyphene block sodium channels and can cause seizures and wide-complex arrhythmias similar to cyclic antidepressants; NaHCO₃ treats arrhythmias • Seizure risk with tramadol, meperidine, propoxyphene • Rapid, powerful heroin-like effect when sustained-release oxycodone is crushed before ingestion, snorting, or smoking • QTc prolongation and torsades de pointes with methadone	Rapid urine drug screens detect morphine and codeine but may not detect semisynthetic and synthetic opioids; some interferents/irrelevants	• IV naloxone, 0.4-2 mg; can repeat up to 10 mg if no response • Continuous infusion for recurrent symptoms or sustained-release opioid ingestion; give 50% of dose that produces desired effect 15 min after initial effect is obtained, then infuse two thirds of this dose every hr; infusion rate can be increased or decreased to maintain normal respiration and avoid withdrawal symptoms • Contraindicated therapies: nalmefene and naltrexone should not be used for acute opioid reversal
Organophosphorus compounds and carbamates (e.g., diazinon, mevinphos, fenthion, aldicarb)	Inhibits acetylcholinesterase, resulting in excessive acetylcholine stimulation of nicotinic and muscarinic receptors in autonomic and somatic motor nervous systems and CNS	• Nicotinic-mediated effects: tachycardia, mydriasis, hypertension, delirium, coma, seizures, muscle weakness, fasciculations • Muscarinic-mediated effects: salivation, lacrimation, urination, vomiting, defecation, miosis, bronchorrhea, bronchospasm, bradycardia	• Serum (butyrylcholinesterase) or RBC (acetylcholinesterase) activity <50% of normal • Clinical recovery occurs before serum cholinesterase levels normalize	• Atropine, 1-2 mg by initial IV bolus; double the dose every 5 min (2 mg, 4 mg, 8 mg, 16 mg, etc.) until drying of bronchial secretions, adequate oxygenation, pulse >80 bpm, systolic blood pressure >80 mm Hg achieved; continuous infusion at 10%-20% of total stabilizing dose per hr; stop infusion if patient develops any signs or symptoms of anticholinergic toxidrome; restart infusion at lower rate when signs or symptoms abate • Pralidoxime chloride 30 mg/kg (maximum 2 g) IV bolus over 30 min, then 8-10 mg/kg/hr (maximum 650 mg/hr) continuous infusion; administer as soon as possible after poisoning; continue 12-24 hr after atropine no longer required and symptoms resolve

Clinical Algorithms

III

Table 3-37 Pathophysiology, Clinical Effects, and Management of Specific Drugs and Toxicants—cont'd

Drug or Toxicant	Pathophysiology	Clinical Effects	Laboratory	Specific Therapy
Salicylates	Inhibits cyclooxygenase; decreases formation of prostaglandins and thromboxane A_2; stimulates CNS medullary respiratory receptor and chemoreceptor trigger zone; impairs platelet function; disrupts carbohydrate metabolism; uncouples oxidative phosphorylation; increases vascular permeability	• Acute toxicity • Mild: nausea, vomiting, diaphoresis, tinnitus, decreased hearing, hyperpnea, tachypnea • Moderate–severe: confusion, delirium, coma, seizures, hyperthermia, ALI; death can occur within hours of overdose • Chronic toxicity: same as acute, but may not have diaphoresis or vomiting • Consider diagnosis in patients with new-onset confusion, anion gap metabolic acidosis, or ALI	• Serum salicylate level: toxic ≥30 mg/dl; level ≥100 mg/dL indicates life-threatening toxicity with possible sudden, rapid clinical deterioration; in chronic toxicity, levels may be minimally elevated (>30 mg/dl), and clinical evaluation is more reliable for gauging degree of toxicity • Arterial blood gases: respiratory alkalosis with metabolic acidosis • Anion gap metabolic acidosis • Prolonged PT and PTT, ketonuria, ketonemia	Multidose activated charcoal q2-3h in acute overdose with progressive symptoms or rising salicylate level
SSRIs/SRIs	• Inhibits re-uptake of serotonin • SRIs have additional effects (e.g., duloxetine inhibits norepinephrine re-uptake, nefazodone inhibits serotonergic 5-HT2 receptors, trazodone inhibits peripheral α-adrenergic receptors, venlafaxine inhibits norepinephrine and dopamine re-uptake)	• Vomiting, blurred vision, CNS depression, tachycardia • Seizures and coma rare • Torsades de pointes reported with citalopram • Serotonin syndrome: clonus, agitation, tremor, diaphoresis, hyperreflexia; hyperthermia and hypertonicity in severe cases	• No specific tests • If serotonin syndrome suspected: electrolytes, BUN, glucose, liver enzymes, coagulation panel, blood gases, chest radiograph	• Respiratory support as needed • Benzodiazepines for agitation or seizures • Serotonin syndrome: consider cyproheptadine, 12 mg PO initial dose then 2 mg PO q2h (to a maximum of 32 mg/day) until symptoms resolve • Critical care therapies for hyperthermia, rhabdomyolysis, DIC, ARDS, renal and hepatic dysfunction, torsades de pointes

ALI, Acute lung injury; *aPTT,* activated partial thromboplastin time; *ARDS,* acute respiratory distress syndrome; *AV,* atrioventricular; *BP,* blood pressure; *bpm,* beats per minute; *BUN,* blood urea nitrogen; *CNS,* central nervous system; *DIC,* disseminated intravascular coagulation; *DOB,* 4-bromo-2,5-dimethoxyamphetamine; *ECG,* electrocardiogram; *GABA,* α-aminobutyric acid; *GI,* gastrointestinal; *HR,* heart rate; *IABP,* intra-aortic balloon counterpulsation; *INR,* international normalized ratio; *IV,* intravenous; *MDMA,* 3,4-methylenedioxymethamphetamine; *Na^1,K^1-ATPase,* sodium, potassium adenosine triphosphatase; *NAC,* N-acetylcysteine; *NAPQI,* N-acetyl-p-benzoquinone imine; *NMDA,* N-methyl-D-aspartate; *PMA,* paramethoxyamphetamine; *PT,* prothrombin time; *PTT,* partial thromboplastin time; *RBC,* red blood cell; *RUQ,* upper right quadrant (abdomen); *SIADH,* syndrome of inappropriate antidiuretic secretion; *SRI,* serotonin re-uptake inhibitor; *SSRI,* selective serotonin re-uptake inhibitor.

* A nomogram to evaluate the potential toxicity of levels drawn more than 4 hours after ingestion is provided in Fig. 3-3, from Rumack BH, Matthew H: Acetaminophen poisoning and toxicity, *Pediatrics* 1975(55):871-876. The nomogram is valid only for levels drawn after a single acute ingestion.

†NAC can be discontinued in patients with uncomplicated disease after a loading dose plus six maintenance doses if hepatic aminotransferase levels are normal and acetaminophen is not detected; otherwise, the full regimen should be administered.

‡Adjust infusion for reduced renal function.

§Continue hemodialysis until the serum lithium level is less than 1 mEq/L. Recheck the level 8 hr after dialysis, and restart hemodialysis if the level is higher than 1 mEq/L. Repeat this cycle until the serum lithium level remains lower than 1 mEq/L.

IIA double-blind, randomized, placebo-controlled trial of pralidoxime in acute organophosphorus poisoning found no significant difference in mortality rates or need for intubation.

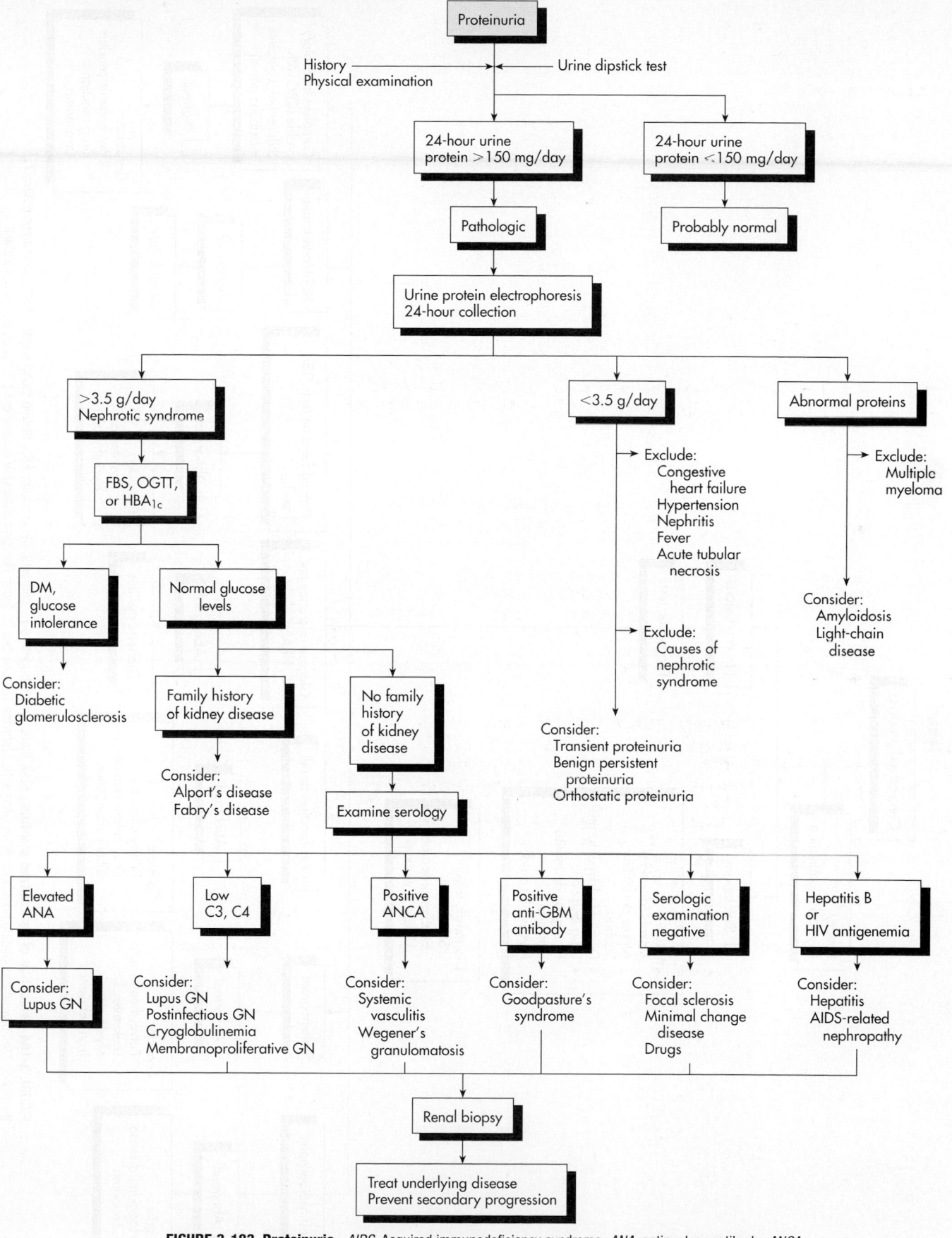

FIGURE 3-183 Proteinuria. *AIDS,* Acquired immunodeficiency syndrome; *ANA,* antinuclear antibody; *ANCA,* antineutrophil cytoplasmic autoantibody; *anti-GBM,* anti-glomerular basement membrane; *FBS,* fasting blood sugar; *GN,* glomerulonephritis; *OGTT,* oral glucose tolerance test. (Modified from Greene HL, Johnson WP, Lemcke DL [eds]: *Decision making in medicine,* ed 2, St Louis, 1998, Mosby.)

Clinical Algorithms

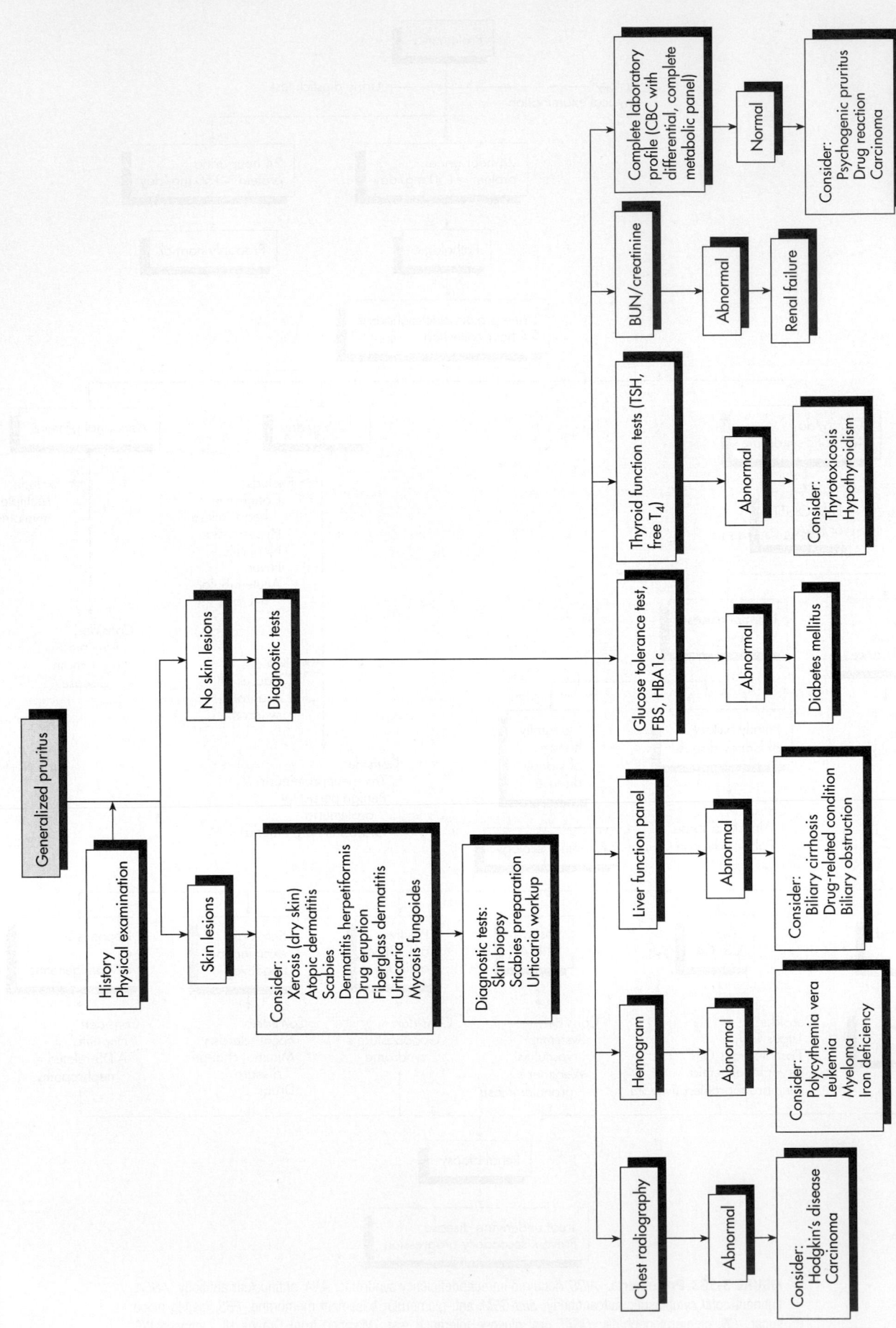

FIGURE 3-184 Evaluation of generalized pruritus. *BUN,* Blood urea nitrogen; *CBC,* complete blood count; *FBS,* fasting blood sugar; *HBA1c,* hemoglobin A1c; *T₄,* thyroxine; *TSH,* thyroid-stimulating hormone. (From Greene HL, Johnson WP, Lemcke DL [eds]: *Decision making in medicine,* ed 2, St Louis, 1998, Mosby.)

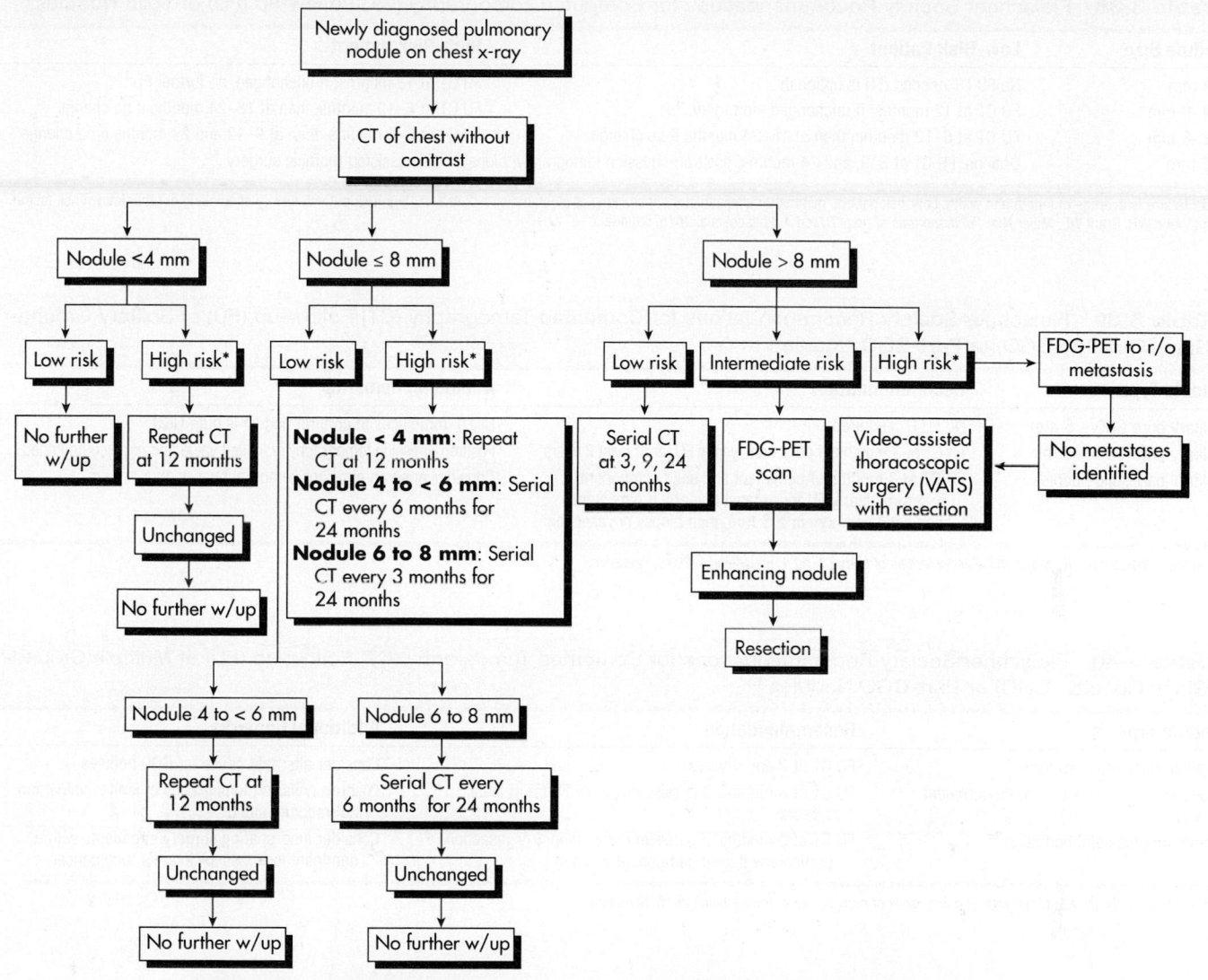

FIGURE 3-187 Diagnostic algorithm. *High risk: history of smoking, history of malignancy, age > 40. (From Ferri, F: *Ferri's best test: a practical guide to clinical laboratory medicine and diagnostic imaging,* ed 3, Philadelphia, 2014, Saunders.)

Diagnostic Imaging	Lab Evaluation
Best Test(s)	**Best Test(s)**
• CT of chest without contrast	• Needle biopsy of nodule
Ancillary Tests	**Ancillary Tests**
• PET scan	• None

Table 3-38 Fleischner Society Recommendations for Computed Tomography (CT) Follow-up (FU) of Solid Nodules *

Nodule Size	Low-Risk Patient	High-Risk patient
≤ 4 mm	No FU CT needed (FU is optional)	FU CT at 12 months; if unchanged, no further FU
> 4–6 mm	FU CT at 12 months; if unchanged, no further FU	FU CT at 6–12 months, then at 18–24 months if no change
> 6–8 mm	FU CT at 6–12 months, then at 18–24 months if no change	FU CT at 3–6 months, then at 9–12 and 24 months if no change
> 8 mm	Options: FU CT at 3, 9, and 24 months; positron emission tomography; biopsy; video-assisted thoracic surgery	

*Nodule size is average of length and width. Low-risk patient, minimal or absent history of smoking or other known risk factors; high-risk patient, history of smoking or other known risk factors.
From Webb WR, Brant WE, Major NM: *Fundamentals of body CT*, ed 4, Philadelphia, 2015, Saunders.

Table 3-39 Fleischner Society Recommendations for Computed Tomography (CT) Follow-up (FU) of Solitary Ground-Glass Opacity (GGO) or Part-GGO Nodules

Nodule Type	Recommendation	Additional Remarks
Solitary pure GGO ≤ 5 mm	No FU CT required	Use 1-mm slices to confirm nodule is pure GGO
Solitary pure GGO > 5 mm	FU CT at 3 months; if persistent, yearly FU for at least 3 years	Positron emission tomography of limited value and not recommended
Solitary part-solid nodules	FU CT at 3 months; if persistent and solid component < 5 mm, yearly FU for at least 3 years; if persistent and solid component ≥ 5 mm, then biopsy or resection	Consider positron emission tomography if nodule > 1 cm

From Webb WR, Brant WE, Major NM: *Fundamentals of body CT*, ed 4, Philadelphia, 2015, Saunders.

Table 3-40 Fleischner Society Recommendations for Computed Tomography (CT) Follow-up (FU) of Multiple Ground-Glass Opacity (GGO) or Part-GGO Nodules

Nodule Type	Recommendation	Additional Remarks
Multiple pure GGO ≤ 5 mm	FU CT at 2 and 4 years	Consider alternate cause for GGO nodules
Multiple pure GGO > 5 mm; no dominant lesion	FU CT at 3 months; if persistent, yearly FU for at least 3 years	Positron emission tomography of limited value and not recommended
Dominant part-solid nodule(s)	FU CT at 3 months; if persistent, then biopsy or resection, particularly if solid component ≥ 5 mm	Consider lung-sparing surgery in patients with a dominant lesion suspicious for lung cancer

From Webb WR, Brant WE, Major NM: *Fundamentals of body CT*, ed 4, Philadelphia, 2015, Saunders.

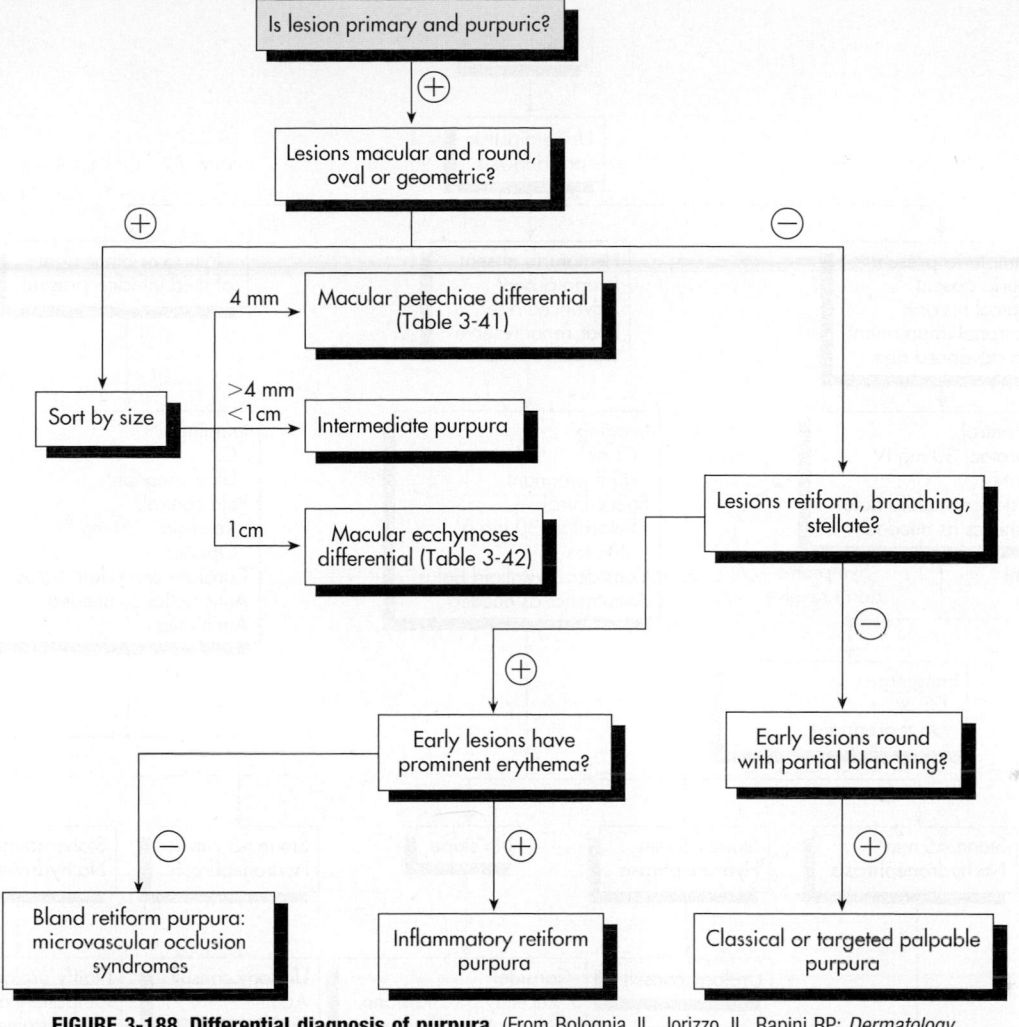

FIGURE 3-188 Differential diagnosis of purpura. (From Bolognia JL, Jorizzo JL, Rapini RP: *Dermatology*, St Louis, 2003, Mosby.)

Table 3-41 Differential Diagnosis of Petechial Hemorrhage—Non-Palpable, Non-Retiform and ≤4 mm in Diameter

Pathophysiology: Hemostatically Relevant Thrombocytopenia (<550,000/mm³) **

Major etiologies*
Idiopathic thrombocytopenic purpura
Thrombotic thrombocytopenic purpura
Disseminated intravascular coagulation
Other acquired thrombocytopenias, including drug-related
   Peripheral destruction (e.g., quinine, quinidine)
   Decreased production, idiosyncratic or dose-related (e.g., chemotherapy)
   Bone marrow infiltration, fibrosis or failure

Pathophysiology: Abnormal Platelet Function

Major etiologies*
Congenital or hereditary platelet function defects
Acquired platelet function defects
   Aspirin, nonsteroidal antiinflammatory drugs
   Renal insufficiency
   Monoclonal gammopathy
Thrombocytosis in myeloproliferative disease (often >1,000,000/mm³)

Pathophysiology: Non-Platelet Etiologies

- Major etiologies*
- Spiking elevations of intravascular venous pressure (Valsalva maneuver-like, e.g., repetitive vomiting, childbirth, paroxysmal coughing, seizure)
- Fixed increased pressure (e.g., stasis, ligatures)
- Trauma (often linear)
- Perifollicular (vitamin C deficiency)
- Mildly inflammatory conditions
  - ○ Chronic pigmented purpura
  - ○ Hypergammaglobulinemic purpura of Waldenström

Table 3-42 Differential Diagnosis for Macular Purpura and Ecchymoses—Non-Palpable and Non-Retiform

Intermediate Macular Purpura (>4 mm, <1 cm in diameter)

- Major etiologies*
- Hypergammaglobulinemic purpura of Waldenström
- Infection/inflammation in patients with thrombocytopenia
- Rarely, minimally inflamed immune complex vasculitis (usually dependent distribution)

Ecchymoses (≥1 cm in diameter)

Pathophysiology: procoagulant defect plus minor trauma*
- ○ Anticoagulant use
- ○ Hepatic insufficiency with poor procoagulant synthesis
- ○ Vitamin K deficiency
- ○ Disseminated intravascular coagulation (some)

Pathophysiology: poor dermal support of vessels plus minor trauma*
- ○ Actinic (solar, senile) purpura
- ○ Corticosteroid therapy, topical or systemic
- ○ Vitamin C deficiency (scurvy)
- ○ Systemic amyloidosis (light chain-related, some familial types)
- ○ Ehlers-Danlos syndrome (primarily type IV)

Pathophysiology: other causes plus minor trauma*
- ○ Hypergammaglobulinemic purpura of Waldenström
- ○ Platelet function defects, including von Willebrand disease, medications, metabolic diseases
- ○ Acquired or congenital thrombocytopenia

*Partial list.
** Most patients do not have petechiae until platelets ≤20,000/mm³.

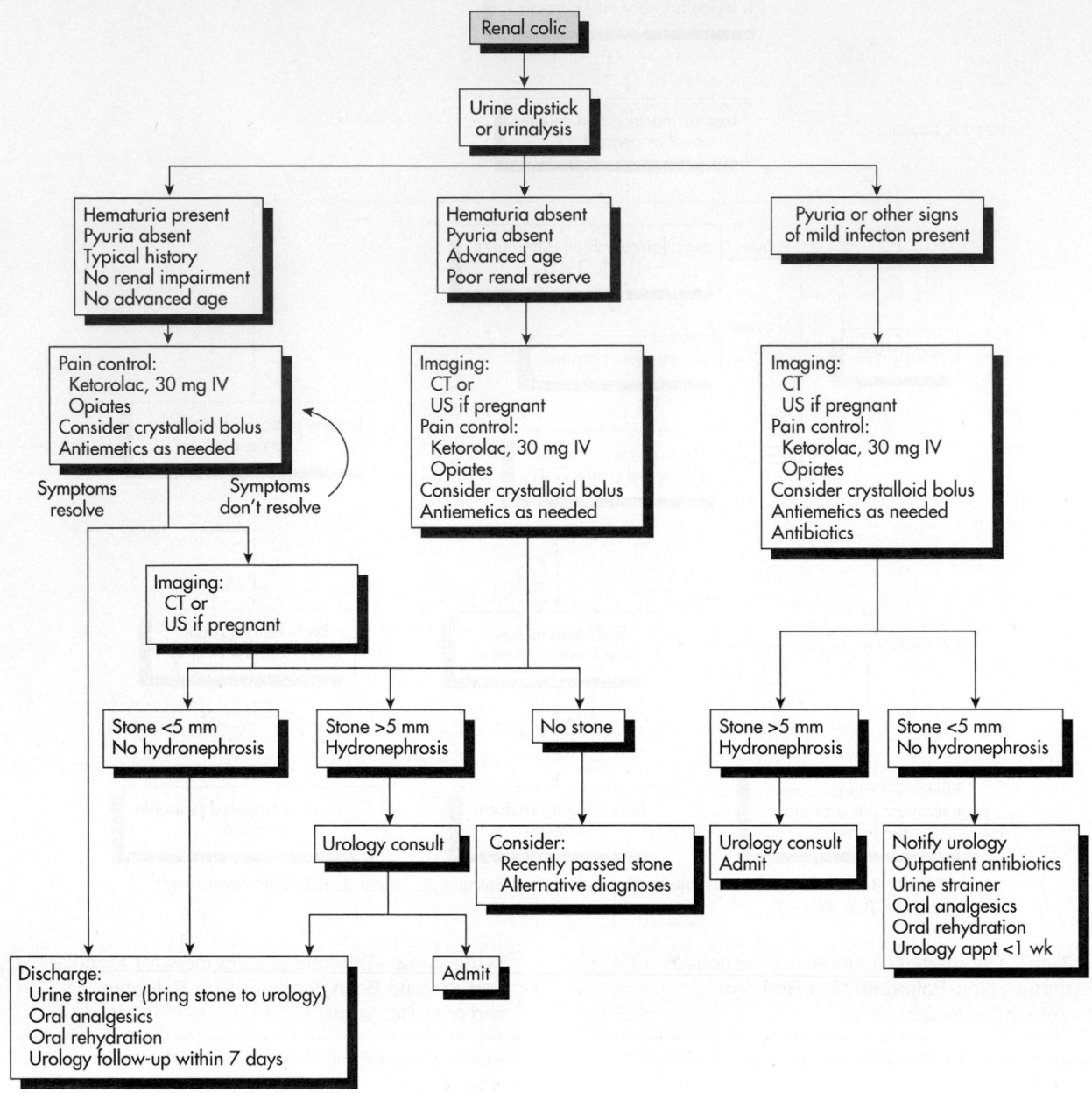

FIGURE 3-190 Guideline algorithm for the evaluation, treatment, and disposition of patients with presumed renal colic. *CT*, Computed tomography; *IV*, intravenously; *US*, ultrasonography. (From Adams JG, et al: *Emergency medicine, clinical essentials*, ed 2, Philadelphia, 2013, Elsevier.)

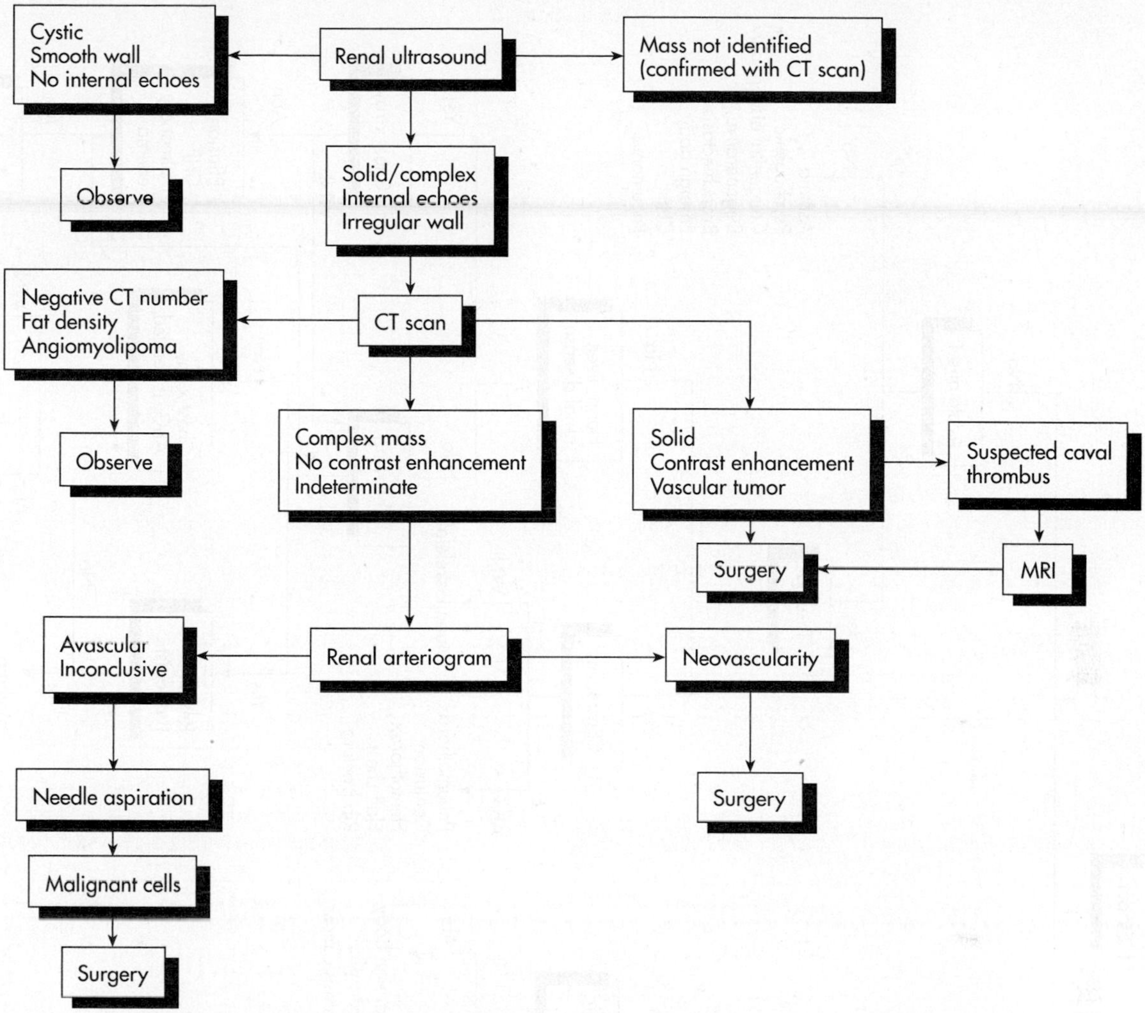

```
                    Cystic              ┌─────────────────┐              Mass not identified
                    Smooth wall    ◄────│ Renal ultrasound│────►        (confirmed with CT scan)
                    No internal echoes  └─────────────────┘
                         │                        │
                         ▼                        ▼
                    ┌─────────┐           Solid/complex
                    │ Observe │           Internal echoes
                    └─────────┘           Irregular wall
                                                  │
                                                  ▼
  Negative CT number    ◄───────────────   ┌─────────┐
  Fat density                              │ CT scan │──────────────────┐
  Angiomyolipoma                           └─────────┘                  │
        │                                       │                       │
        ▼                                       ▼                       ▼
  ┌─────────┐                        Complex mass              Solid                    Suspected caval
  │ Observe │                        No contrast enhancement   Contrast enhancement ──► thrombus
  └─────────┘                        Indeterminate             Vascular tumor               │
                                            │                       │                       ▼
                                            │                       ▼                     ┌─────┐
                                            │                  ┌─────────┐  ◄──────────────│ MRI │
                                            │                  │ Surgery │                └─────┘
                                            ▼                  └─────────┘
  Avascular          ◄──────   ┌──────────────────┐   ──────►  Neovascularity
  Inconclusive                 │ Renal arteriogram│                  │
        │                      └──────────────────┘                  ▼
        ▼                                                       ┌─────────┐
  ┌──────────────────┐                                          │ Surgery │
  │ Needle aspiration│                                          └─────────┘
  └──────────────────┘
        │
        ▼
  ┌────────────────┐
  │ Malignant cells│
  └────────────────┘
        │
        ▼
  ┌─────────┐
  │ Surgery │
  └─────────┘
```

FIGURE 3-192 Evaluation of a patient with a renal mass on renal ultrasound. *CT,* Computed tomography; *MRI,* magnetic resonance imaging. (Modified from Williams RD: Tumors of the kidney, ureter, and bladder. In Goldman L, Schafer AL [eds]: *Cecil textbook of medicine,* ed 23, Philadelphia, 2008, Saunders.)

Clinical
Algorithms

III

RESPIRATORY DISTRESS

ICD-10CM #	
R06.00	Dyspnea, unspecified
R06.09	Other forms of dyspnea
R06.3	Periodic breathing
R06.89	Other abnormalities of breathing
J80	Acute respiratory distress syndrome

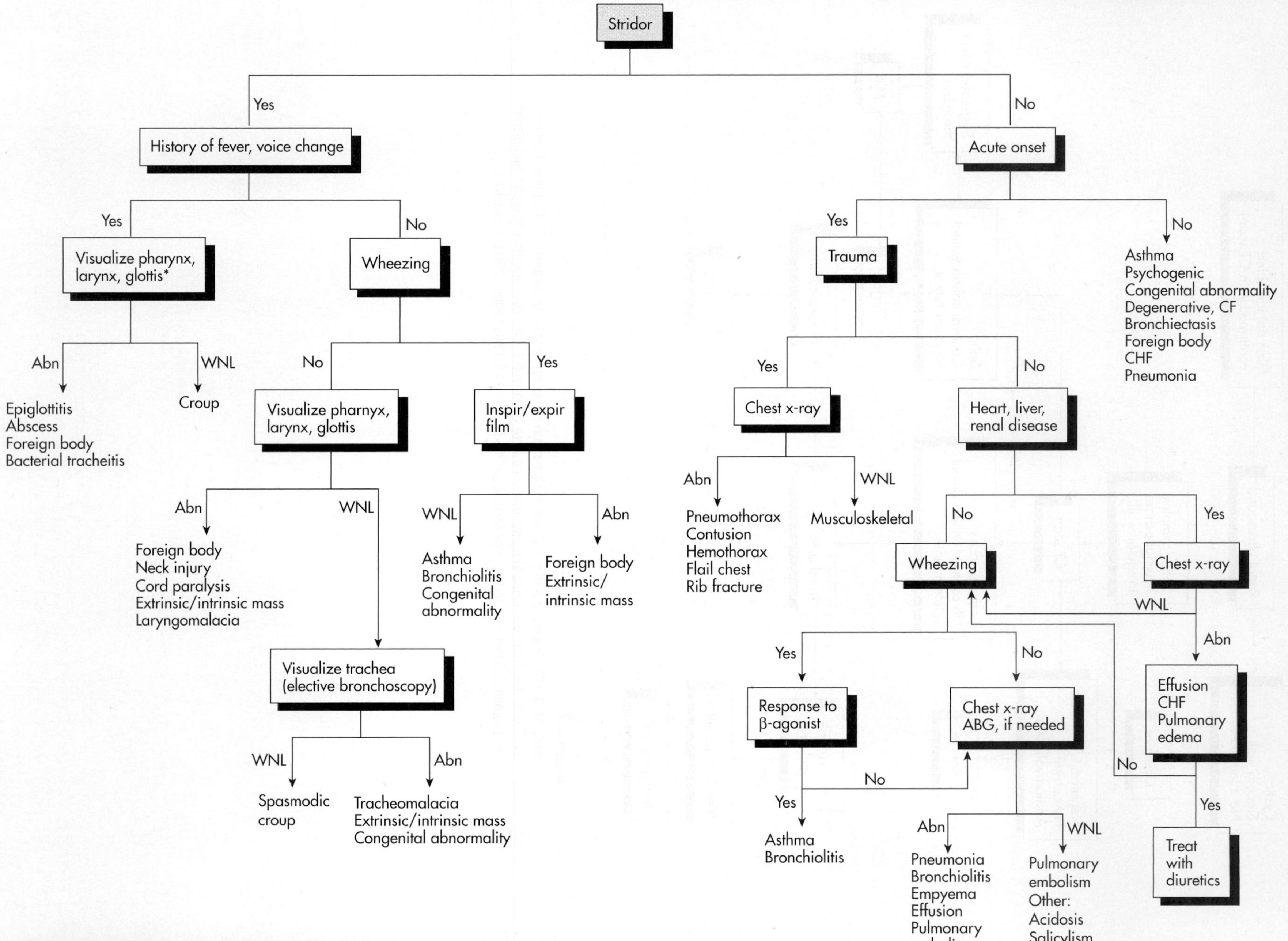

FIGURE 3-193 Respiratory distress in a pediatric patient. *ABG*, Arterial blood gas; *Abn*, abnormal; *CF*, cystic fibrosis; *CHF*, congestive heart failure; *WNL*, within normal limits. (From

ICD-10CM #	N44.2	Benign cyst of testis
	N44.8	Other noninflammatory disorders of the testis
	N50.3	Cyst of epididymis
	N50.8	Other specified disorders of male genital organs

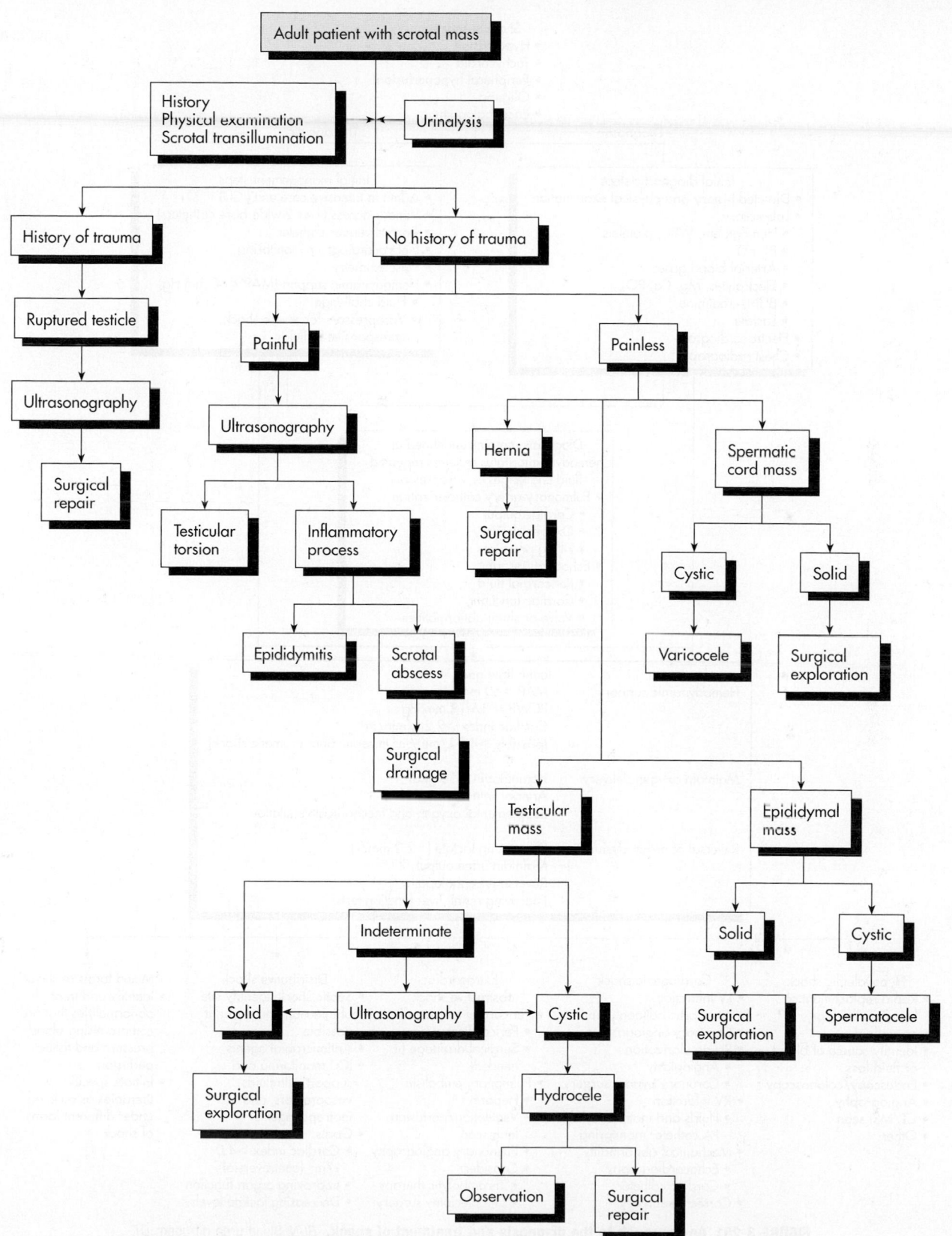

FIGURE 3-195 Evaluation of scrotal mass. (From Greene HL, Johnson WP, Lemcke DL [eds]: *Decision making in medicine,* ed 2, St Louis, 1998, Mosby.)

Clinical Algorithms

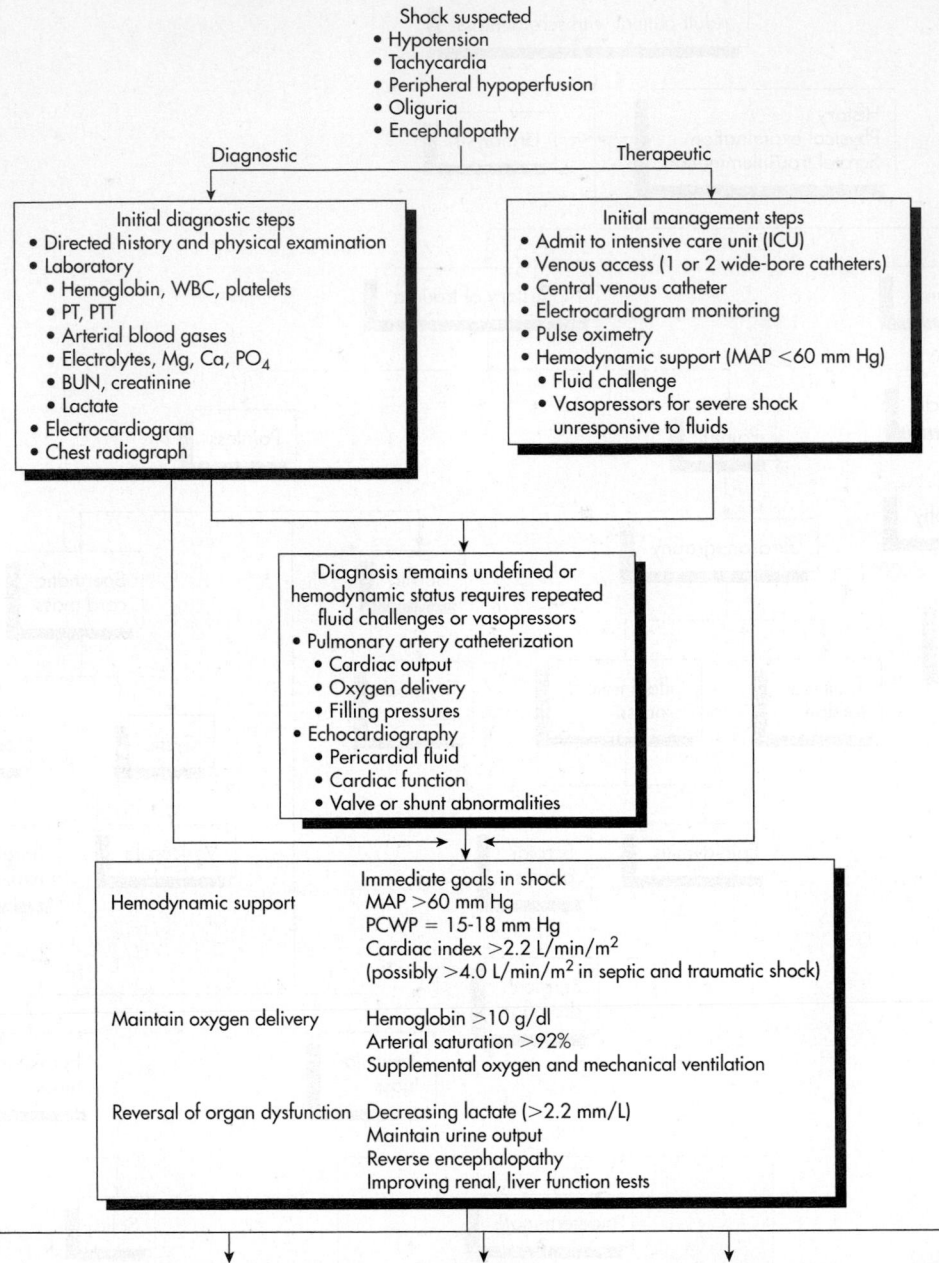

FIGURE 3-201 An approach to the diagnosis and treatment of shock. *BUN,* Blood urea nitrogen; *CT,* computed tomography; *LV,* left ventricular; *MAP,* mean arterial pressure; *MRI,* magnetic resonance imaging; *PA,* pulmonary arterial; *PCWP,* pulmonary capillary wedge pressure; *PT,* prothrombin time; *PTT,* partial thromboplastin time; *RV,* right ventricular; *WBC,* white blood cell count. (From Goldman L, Ausiello D [eds]: *Cecil textbook of medicine,* ed 24, Philadelphia, 2012, Saunders.)

SHOULDER PAIN

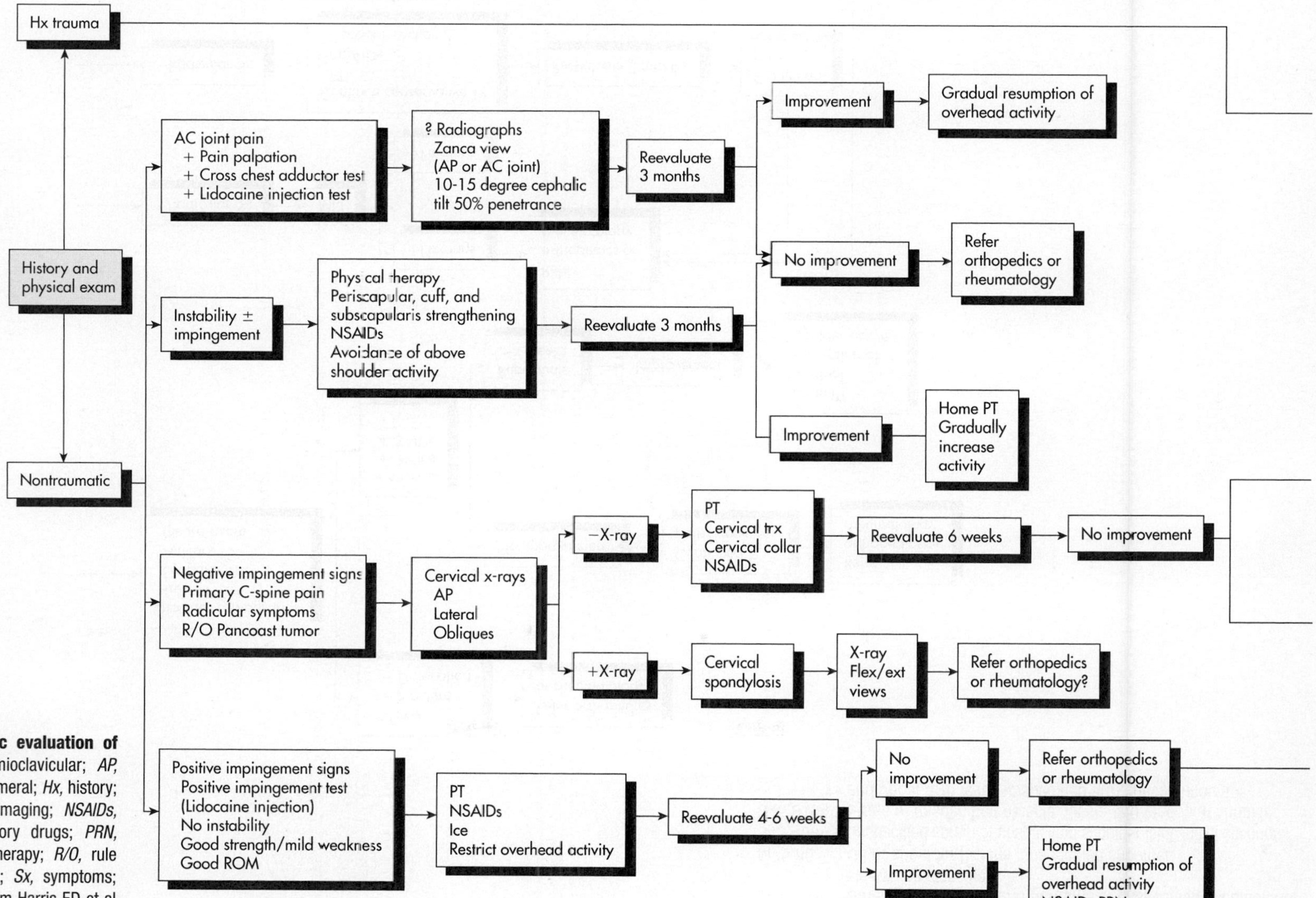

FIGURE 3-203 Algorithmic evaluation of shoulder pain. *AC,* Acromioclavicular; *AP,* anteroposterior; *GH,* glenohumeral; *Hx,* history; *MRI,* magnetic resonance imaging; *NSAIDs,* nonsteroidal anti-inflammatory drugs; *PRN,* as required; *PT,* physical therapy; *R/O,* rule out; *ROM,* range of motion; *Sx,* symptoms; *trx,* traction; *Tx,* therapy. (From Harris ED et al [eds]: *Kelley's textbook of rheumatology,* ed 7, Philadelphia, 2005, Saunders.)

Clinical Algorithms

SHOULDER PAIN—cont'd

ICD-10CM #	S34.109A	Unspecified injury to unspecified level of lumbar spinal cord, initial encounter
	M24.819	Other specific joint derangements of unspecified shoulder, not elsewhere classified
	M75.80	Other shoulder lesions, unspecified shoulder
	S43.409A	Unspecified sprain of unspecified shoulder joint, initial encounter
	S46.919A	Strain of unspecified muscle, fascia and tendon at shoulder and upper arm level, unspecified arm, initial encounter

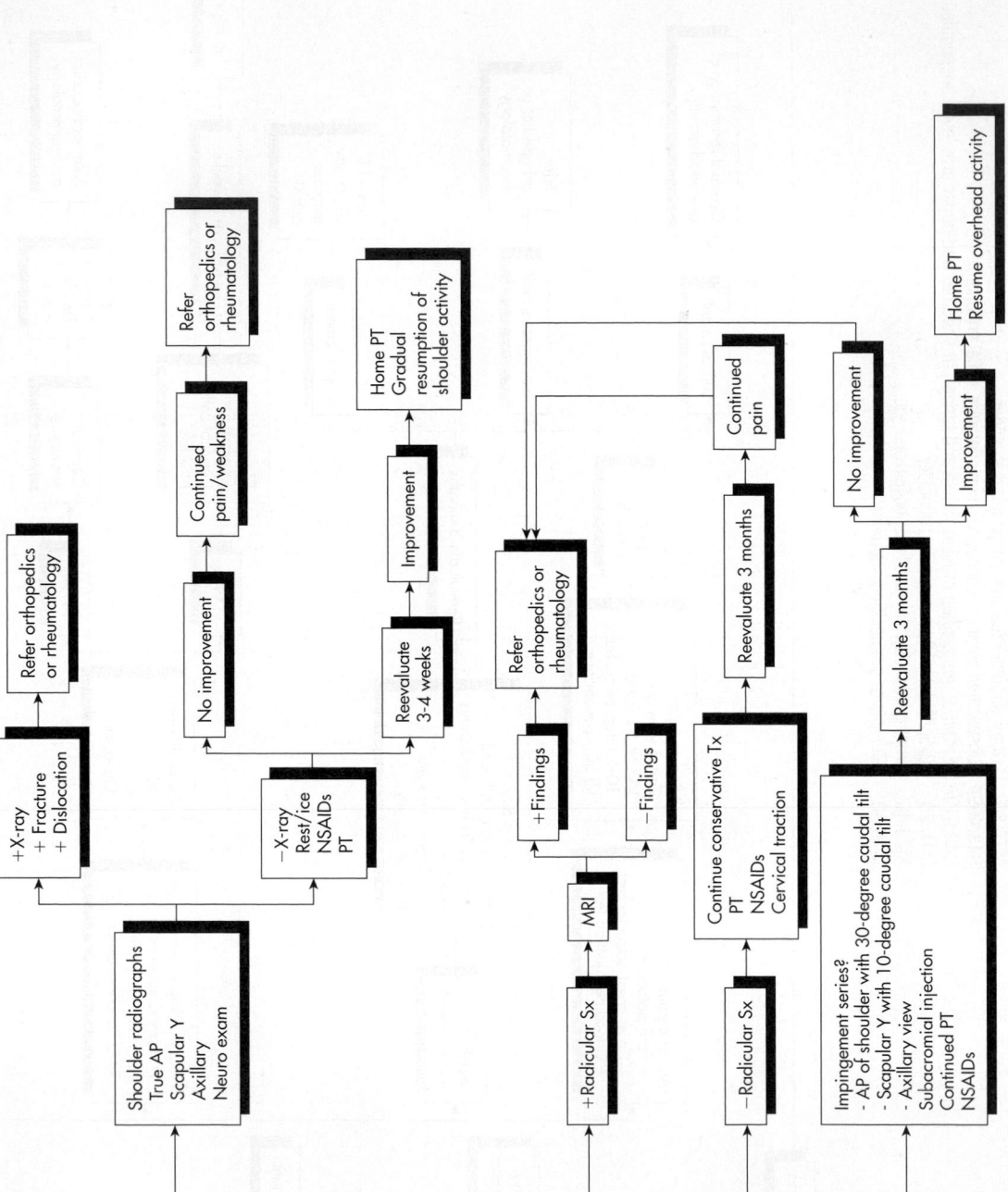

FIGURE 3-203 (Continued)

Continued on next page

ICD-10CM # S34.109A Unspecified injury to unspecified level of lumbar spinal cord, initial encounter
M24.819 Other specific joint derangements of unspecified shoulder, not elsewhere classified
M75.80 Other shoulder lesions, unspecified shoulder
S43.409A Unspecified sprain of unspecified shoulder joint, initial encounter
S46.919A Strain of unspecified muscle, fascia and tendon at shoulder and upper arm level, unspecified arm, initial encounter

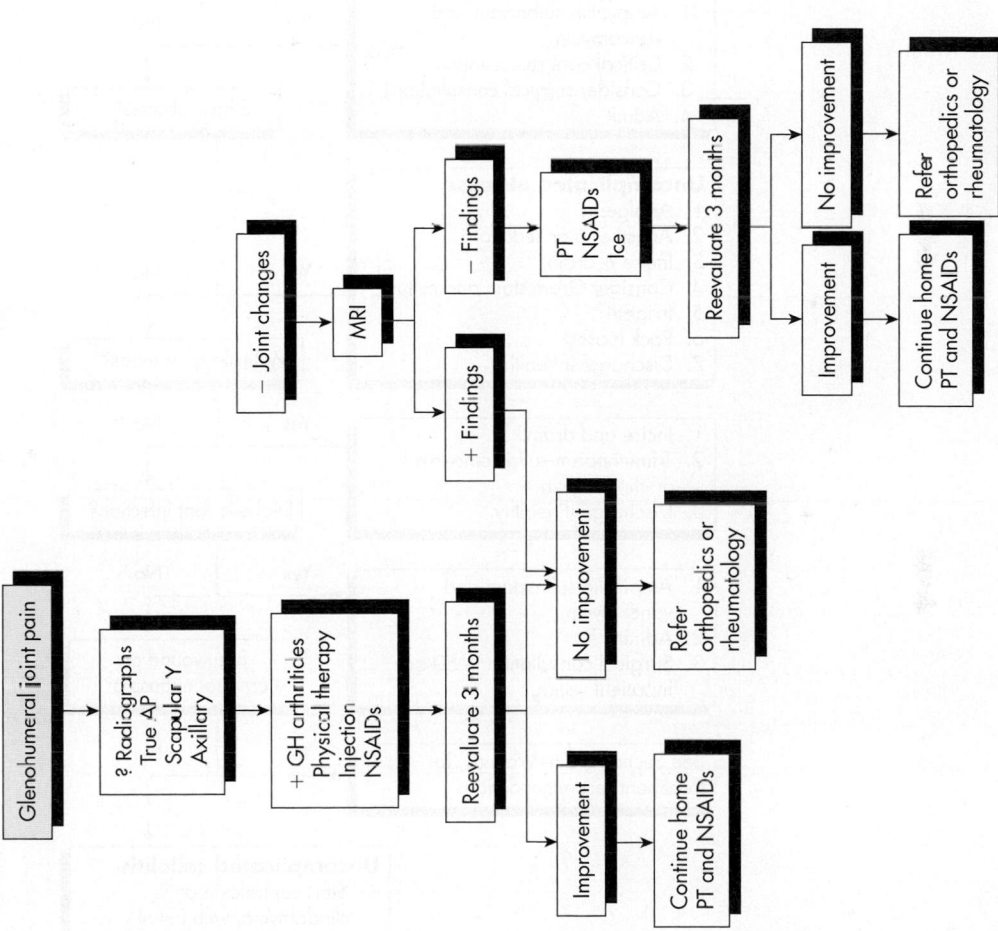

FIGURE 3-203 (Continued)

Clinical Algorithms

III

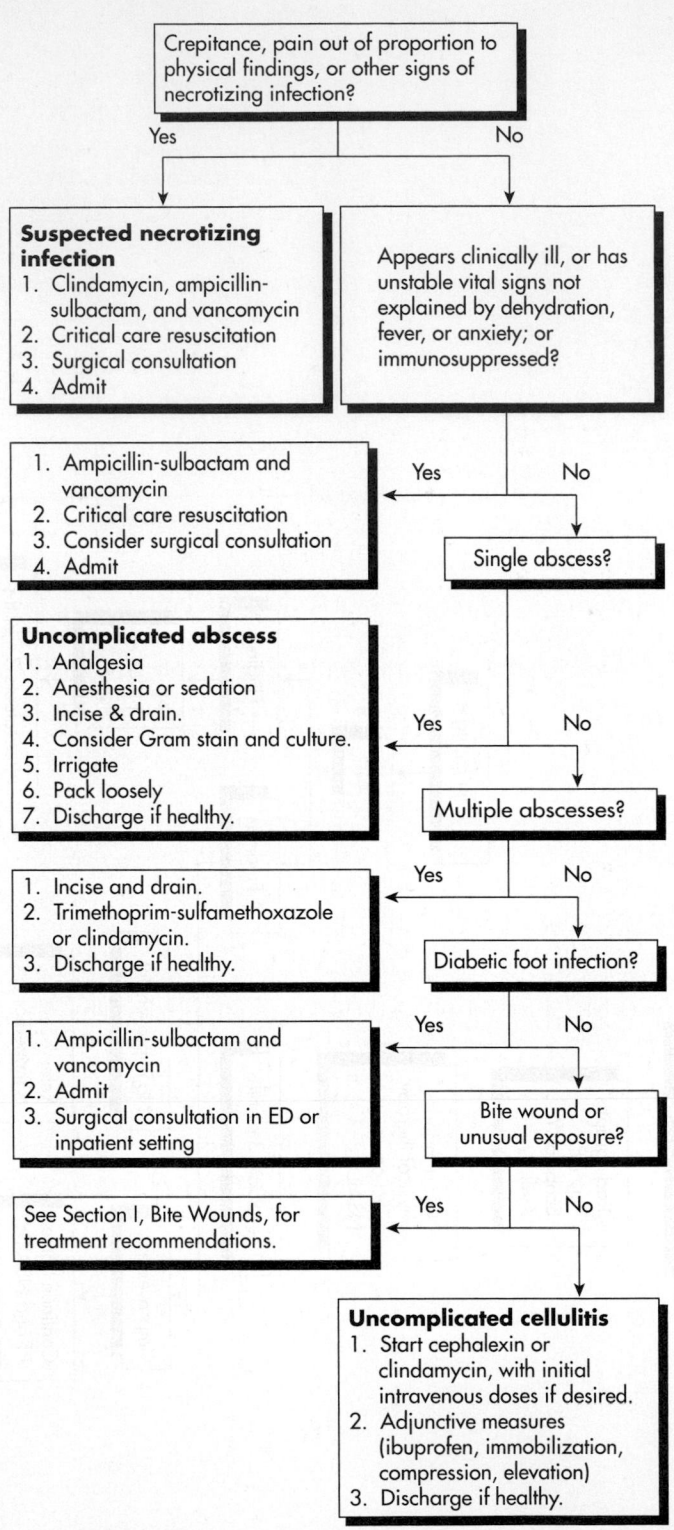

FIGURE 3-204 Universal algorithm for skin and soft tissue infections (assuming no prior treatment). (From Marx JA et al: *Rosen's emergency medicine*, ed 8, Philadelphia, 2014, Saunders.)

Sleep disturbance

History →

Insomnia | Hypersomnia | Sleep-associated affective and behavioral disturbance

See Algorithm **B**

See Algorithm **C**

Duration >3 weeks | Duration >3 weeks

Normal sleep hygiene | Poor sleep hygiene

Consider:
    Situational disorder
    Work shift change
    Jet lag syndrome

Advise on rules of better sleep hygiene

Spontaneous resolution
Reassurance
Possible short course of zolpidem

Stress related | Not stress related

Psychiatric | Psychophysiologic condition | Alcohol or drug use

Consider:
    Restless legs syndrome
    Periodic movements of sleep
    Central sleep apnea
    Chronic respiratory failure
    Alpha delta sleep pattern

Chronic pain syndrome

Psychiatric consultation and therapy

Abstention Counseling

Identify source

PSG to confirm diagnosis

Treat

Stress reduction
Relaxation techniques
Stimulus control
Daily exercise
Deconditioning

PSG may reassure and exclude other possibilities

A

FIGURE 3-206 A, Patient with sleep disturbance. *PSG,* Polysomnography. (Modified from Greene HL, Johnson WP, Lemcke DL [eds]: *Decision making in medicine,* ed 2, St Louis, 1998, Mosby.)

Continued on following page

Clinical Algorithms

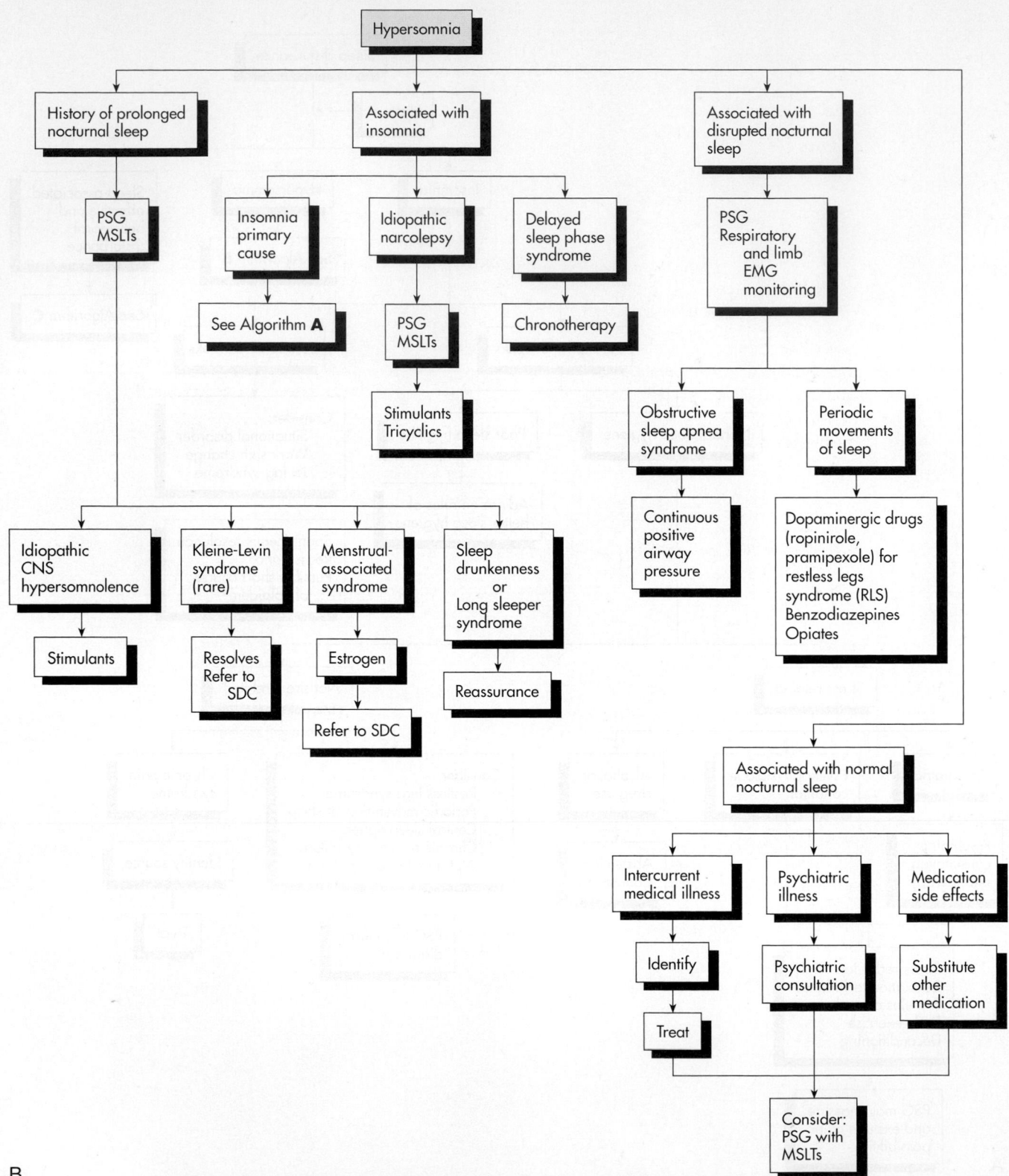

FIGURE 3-206 (Continued) **B, Hypersomnia.** *CNS,* Central nervous system; *EMG,* electromyelogram; *MSLTs,* multiple sleep latency tests; *PSG,* polysomnography; *SDC,* sleep disorders clinic. (Modified from Greene HL, Johnson WP, Lemcke DL [eds]: *Decision making in medicine,* ed 2, St Louis, 1998, Mosby.)

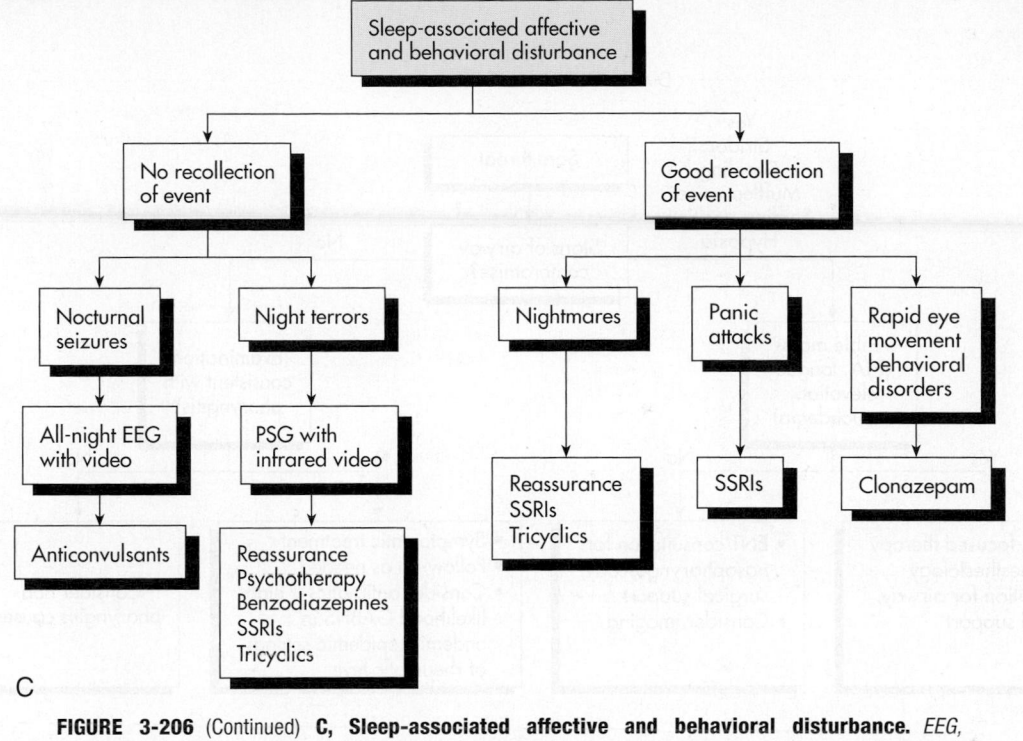

FIGURE 3-206 (Continued) **C, Sleep-associated affective and behavioral disturbance.** *EEG,* Electroencephalogram; *PSG,* polysomnography; *SSRIs,* selective serotonin reuptake inhibitors. (Modified from Greene HL, Johnson WP, Lemcke DL [eds]: *Decision making in medicine,* ed 2, St Louis, 1998, Mosby.)

ICD-10CM #   J02.9   Acute pharyngitis, unspecified
             J31.2   Chronic pharyngitis
             J02.0   Streptococcal pharyngitis

DIAGNOSTIC ALGORITHM

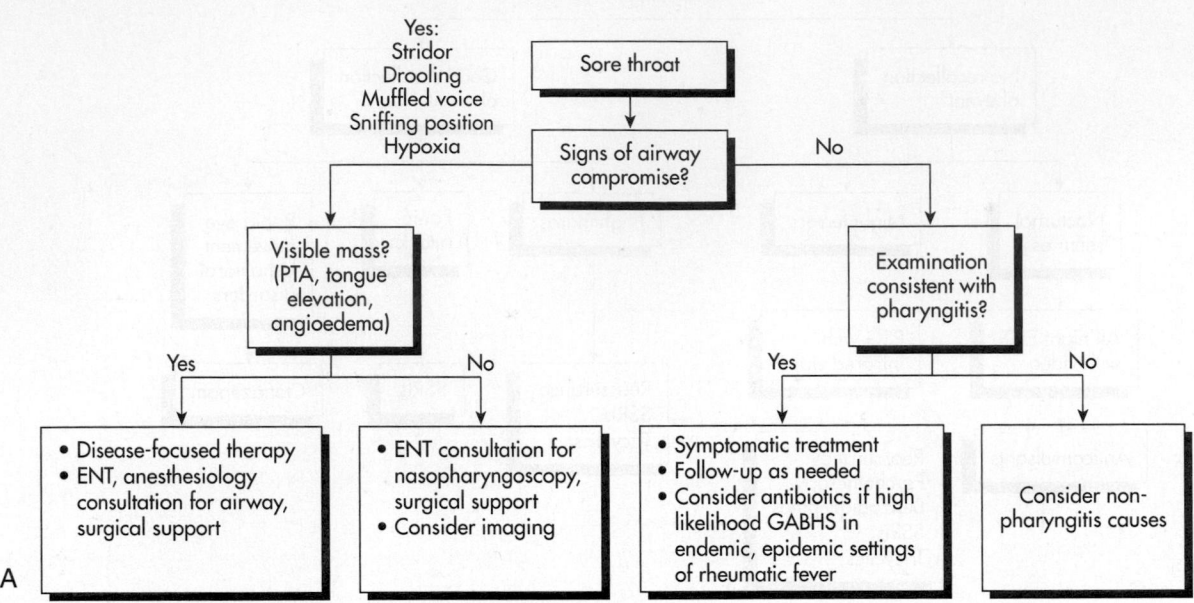

MANAGEMENT ALGORITHM

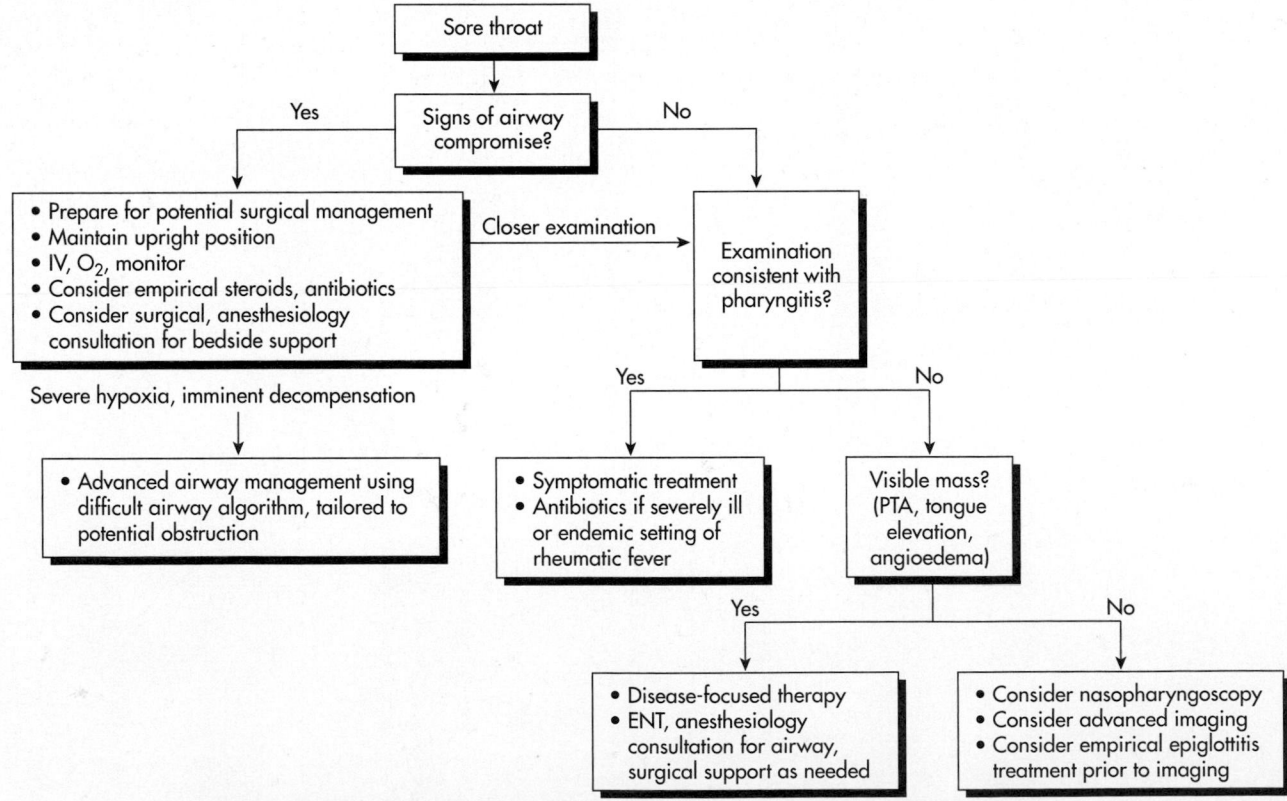

FIGURE 3-207 Clinical approach to the patient with sore throat—diagnosis and management. Refer to Section I, Pharyngitis/Tonsillitis and Epiglottitis, for additional information on this matter. *ENT*, Ear-nose-throat; *GABHS*, group A beta-hemolytic streptococcus; *IV*, intravenous; *PTA*, peritonsillar abscess. (From Marx JA et al: *Rosen's emergency medicine*, ed 8, Philadelphia, 2014, Saunders.)

SPLENOMEGALY

ICD-10CM #	
R16.1	Splenomegaly, not elsewhere classified
D73.2	Chronic congestive splenomegaly
Q89.01	Asplenia (congenital)
Q89.09	Congenital malformations of spleen
R16.1	Splenomegaly, not elsewhere classified

Splenomegaly

With lymphadenopathy
See Section III algorithm, Lymphadenopathy, Generalized

Without lymphadenopathy

Confirm
Spleen ultrasound or CT

Exclude
Portal hypertension
Congestive heart failure
Subacute bacterial endocarditis

Splenic cyst or displacement of normal-sized spleen excluded

Evaluate for immunologic disorders
Systemic lupus erythematosus
Rheumatoid arthritis
Felty's syndrome

Immunologic causes excluded

Examine peripheral blood smear
Hematologic malignancies
Nonmalignant hematologic disease
Parasitemia

Results negative or equivocal

Bone marrow aspiration, biopsy, and cultures
Hematologic conditions
Chronic fungal and mycobacterial infections
Gaucher's disease
Amyloidosis

Bone marrow nondiagnostic, cultures negative

Asymptomatic:
Follow

Symptomatic:
Splenectomy for diagnosis

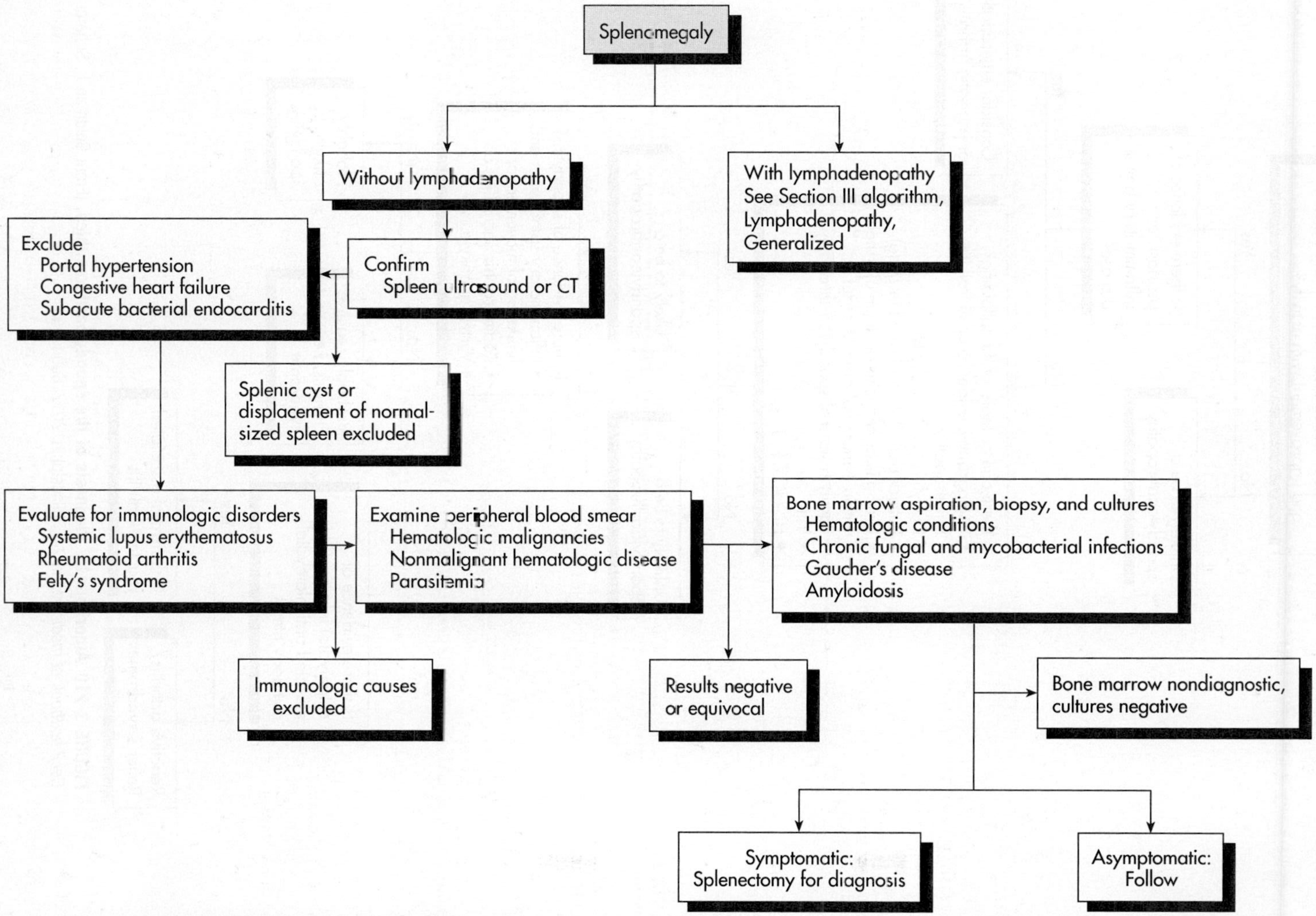

FIGURE 3-209 Clinical approach to patient with splenomegaly. *CT,* Computed tomography. (Modified from Stein JH [ed]: *Internal medicine,* ed 5, St Louis, 1998, Mosby.)

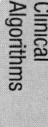

Clinical
Algorithms

III

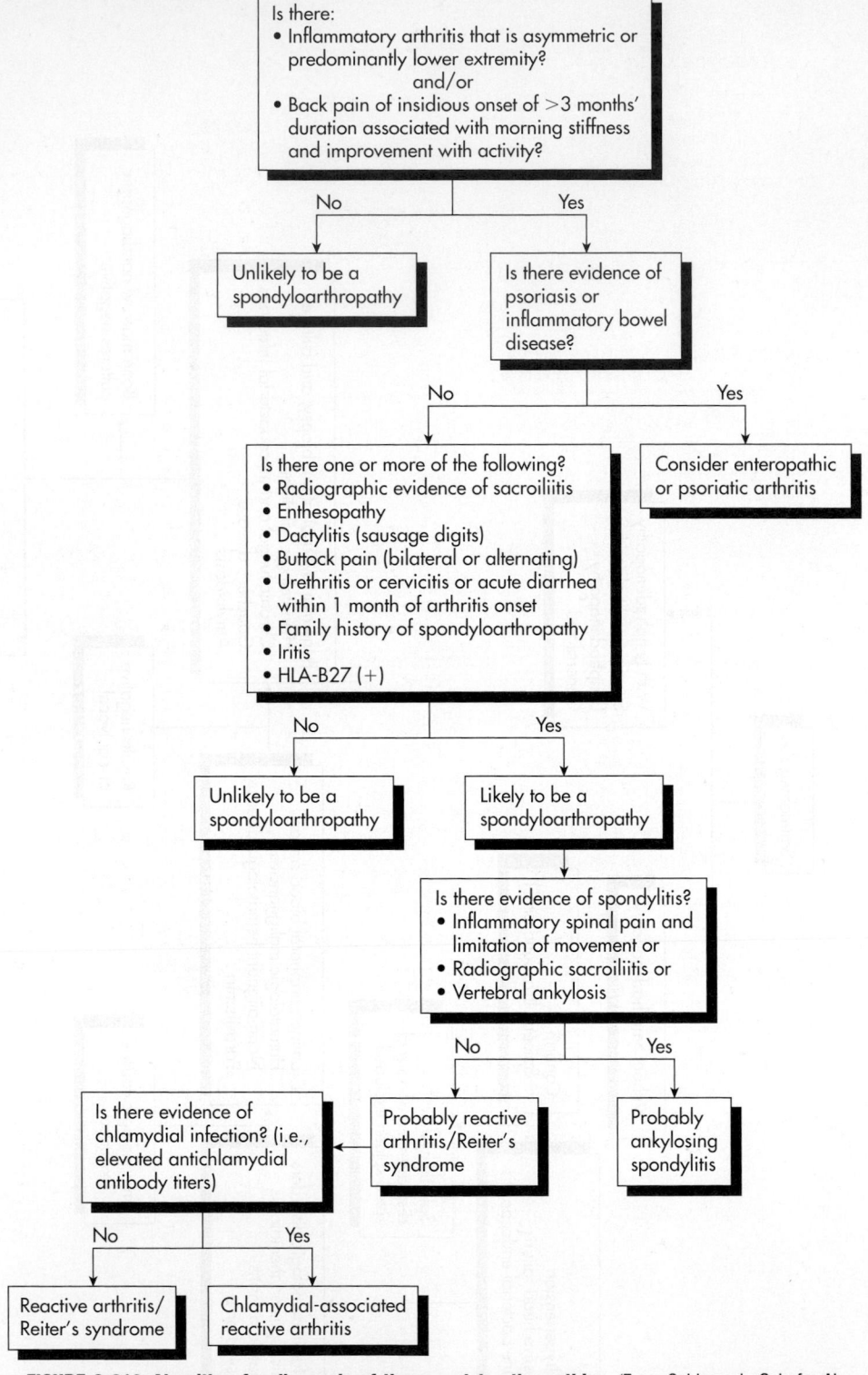

FIGURE 3-210 Algorithm for diagnosis of the spondyloarthropathies. (From Goldman L, Schafer AL: *Cecil textbook of medicine,* ed 24, Philadelphia, 2012, Saunders.)

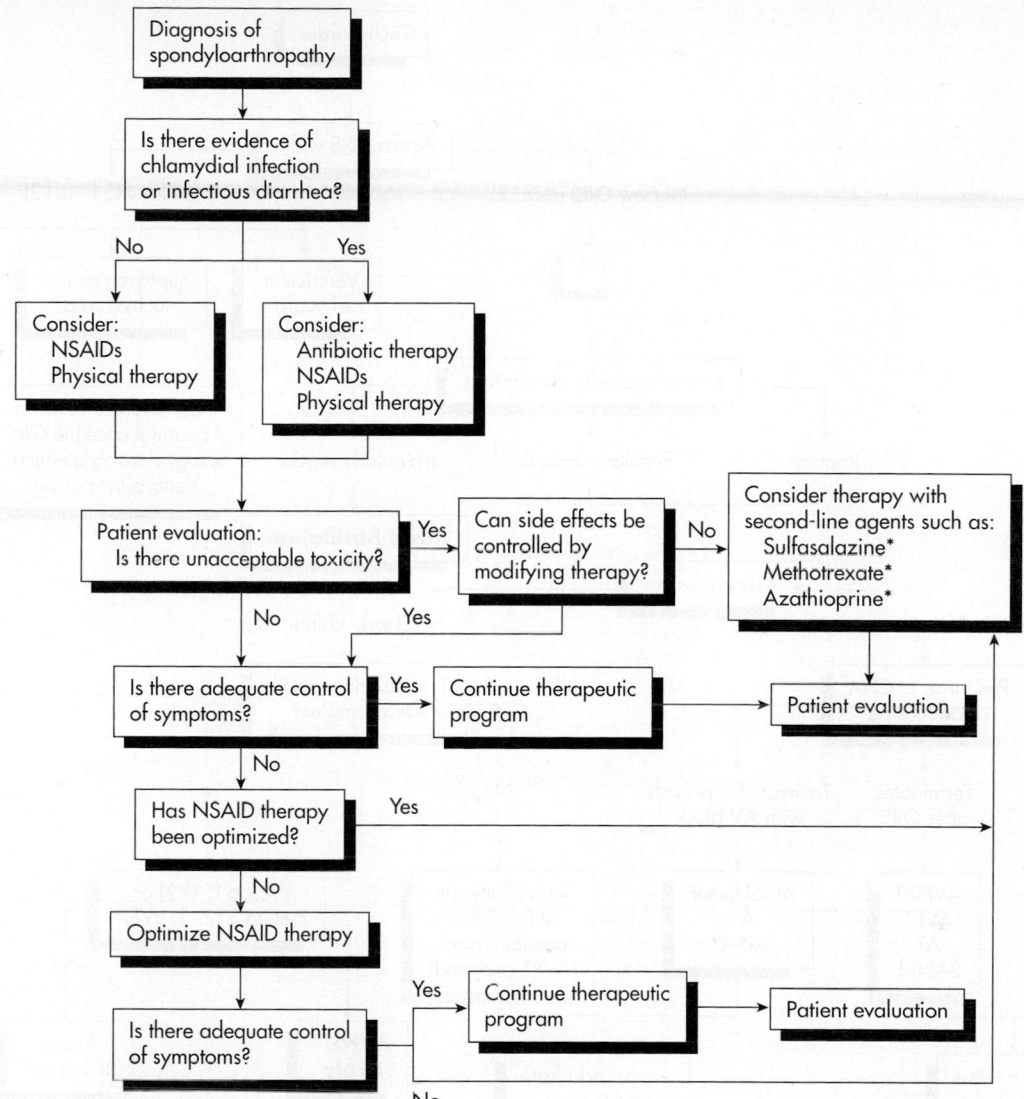

FIGURE 3-211 Treatment algorithm for patients with a spondyloarthropathy. *FDA,* Food and Drug Administration; *NSAID,* nonsteroidal anti-inflammatory drug. (From Goldman L, Schafer AL: *Cecil textbook of medicine,* ed 24, Philadelphia, 2012, Saunders.)

Clinical
Algorithms

III

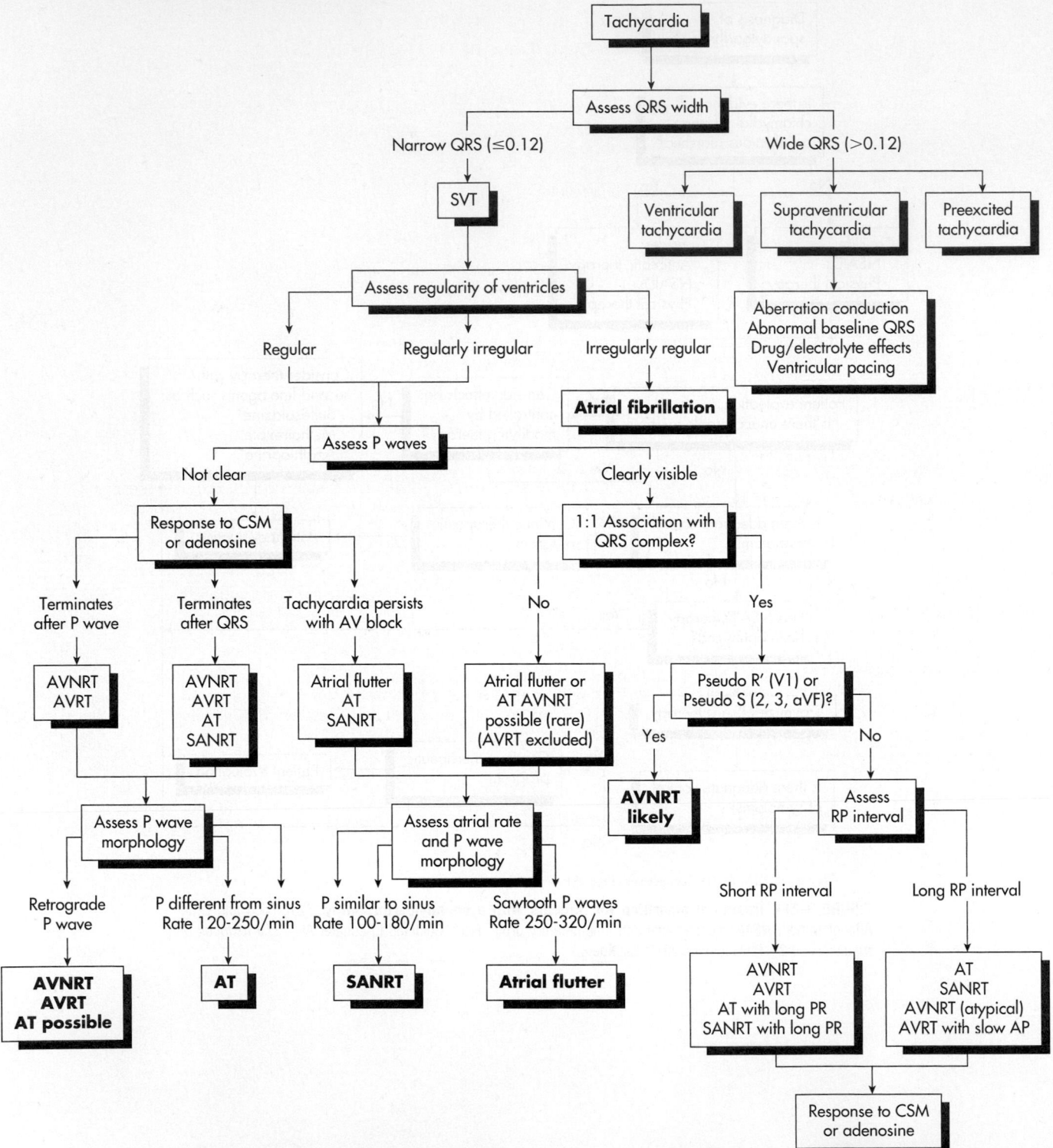

FIGURE 3-215 Stepwise approach to the diagnosis of type of tachycardia based on 12-lead electrocardiogram during the episode. The initial step is to determine whether the tachycardia has a wide or narrow QRS complex (see Fig. 3-216). For wide complex tachycardia, see Figure 3-218; the remainder of the algorithm is helpful in diagnosing the type of narrow-complex tachycardia. *AP,* Accessory pathway; *AT,* atrial tachycardia; *AV,* atrioventricular; *AVNRT,* AV nodal reentrant tachycardia; *AVRT,* AV reciprocating tachycardia; *CSM,* carotid sinus massage; *SANRT,* sinoatrial nodal reentry tachycardia; *SVT,* supraventricular tachycardia. (From Zipes DP, Libby P, Bonow RO, Braunwald E [eds]: *Braunwald's heart disease,* ed 7, Philadelphia, 2005, Saunders.)

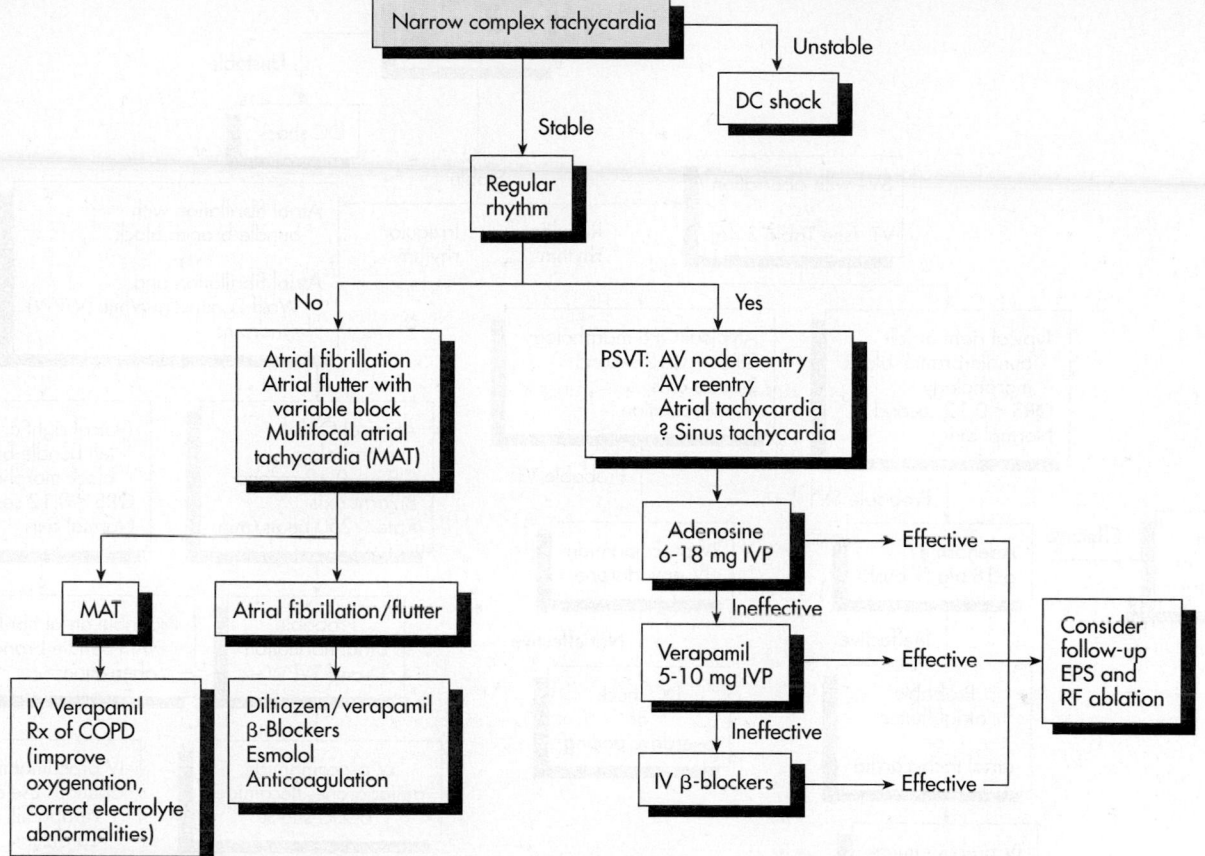

FIGURE 3-216 Evaluation and management of narrow complex tachycardia. *AV*, Atrioventricular; *COPD*, chronic obstructive pulmonary disease; *EPS*, electrophysiologic studies; *IV*, intravenous; *IVP*, intravenous push; *PSVT*, paroxysmal supraventricular tachycardia; *RF*, radiofrequency.

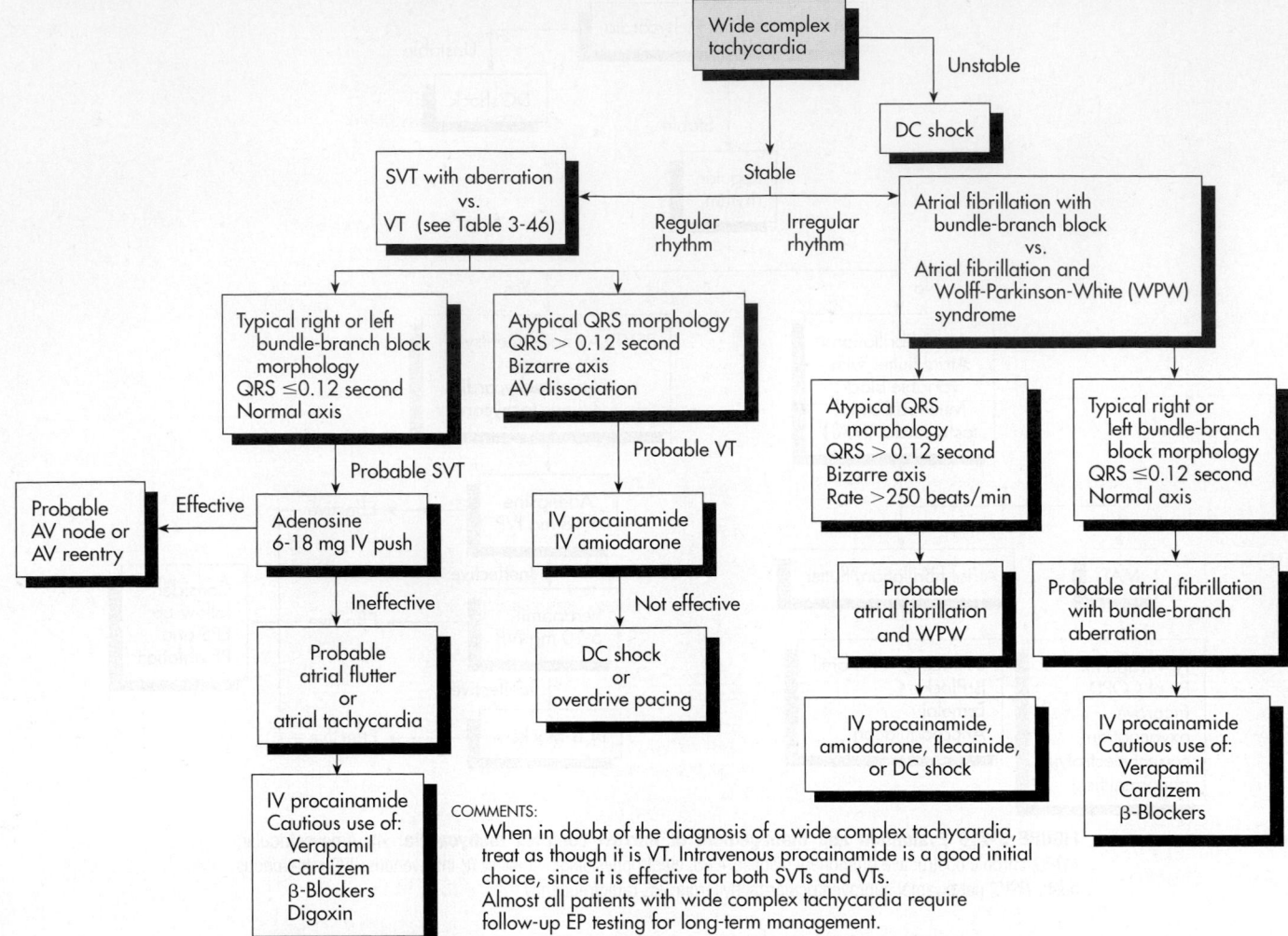

FIGURE 3-218 Evaluation and management of wide complex tachycardia. *AV,* Atrioventricular; *EP,* electrophysiologic; IV, intravenous; SVT, supraventricular tachycardia; VT, ventricular tachycardia. (From Driscoll CE et al: *The family practice desk reference,* ed 3, St Louis, 1996, Mosby.)

COMMENTS:
When in doubt of the diagnosis of a wide complex tachycardia, treat as though it is VT. Intravenous procainamide is a good initial choice, since it is effective for both SVTs and VTs.
Almost all patients with wide complex tachycardia require follow-up EP testing for long-term management.

Table 3-46 Major Features in the Differential Diagnosis of Wide QRS Beats

Supports SVT	Supports VT
Slowing or termination by vagal tone	Fusion beats
Onset with premature P wave	Capture beats
RP interval <100 msec	AV dissociation
P and QRS rate and rhythm linked to suggest that ventricular activation depends on atrial discharge, e.g., 2:1 AV block rSR′ V1	P and QRS rate and rhythm linked to suggest that atrial activation depends on ventricular discharge, e.g., 2:1 VA block
Long-short cycle sequence	• "Compensatory" pause
	• Left axis deviation; QRS duration >140 msec
	• Specific QRS contours (see text)

SVT, Supraventricular tachycardia; *VT,* ventricular tachycardia.
From Zipes DP et al [eds]: *Braunwald's heart disease,* ed 7, Philadelphia, 2005, Saunders.

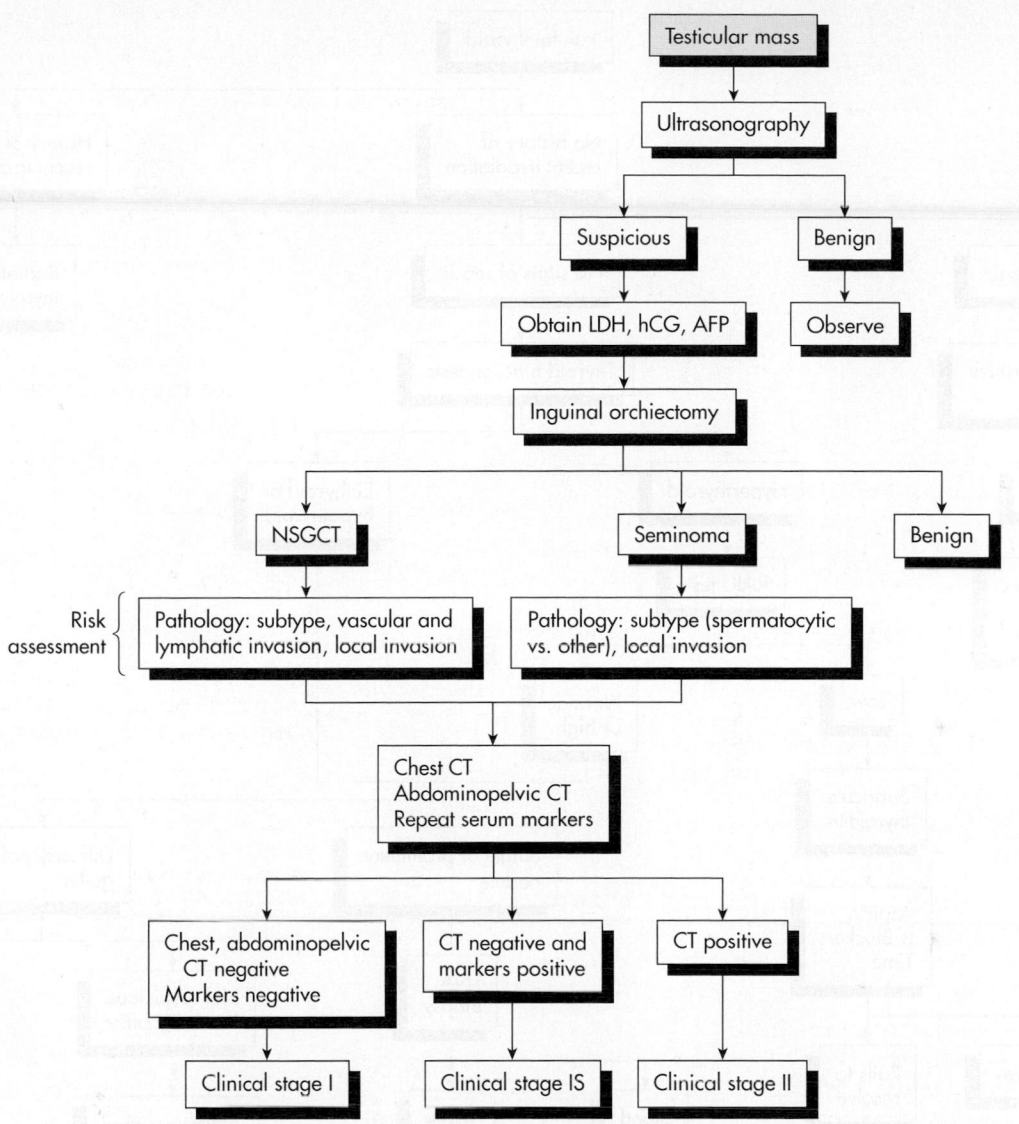

FIGURE 3-219 Diagnosis, staging, and risk assessment of patients with testicular germ cell tumor. See Section I, Testicular Cancer, for additional information. *AFP,* α-Fetoprotein; *CT,* computed tomography; *hCG,* human chorionic gonadotropin; *LDH,* lactic dehydrogenase; *NSGCT,* nonseminoma germ cell tumor. (From Abeloff MD: *Clinical oncology,* ed 4, New York, 2007, Churchill Livingstone.)

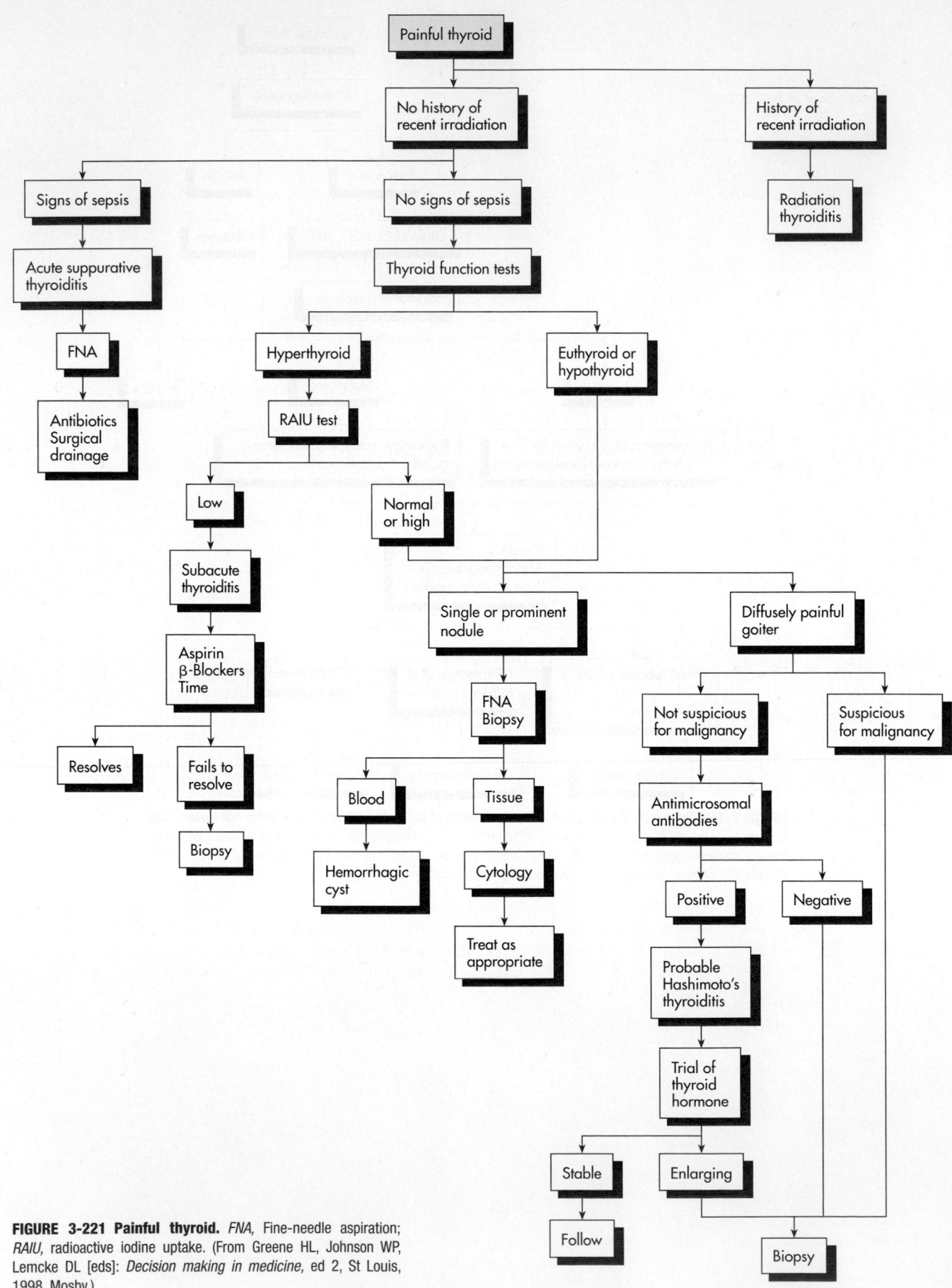

FIGURE 3-221 Painful thyroid. *FNA,* Fine-needle aspiration; *RAIU,* radioactive iodine uptake. (From Greene HL, Johnson WP, Lemcke DL [eds]: *Decision making in medicine,* ed 2, St Louis, 1998, Mosby.)

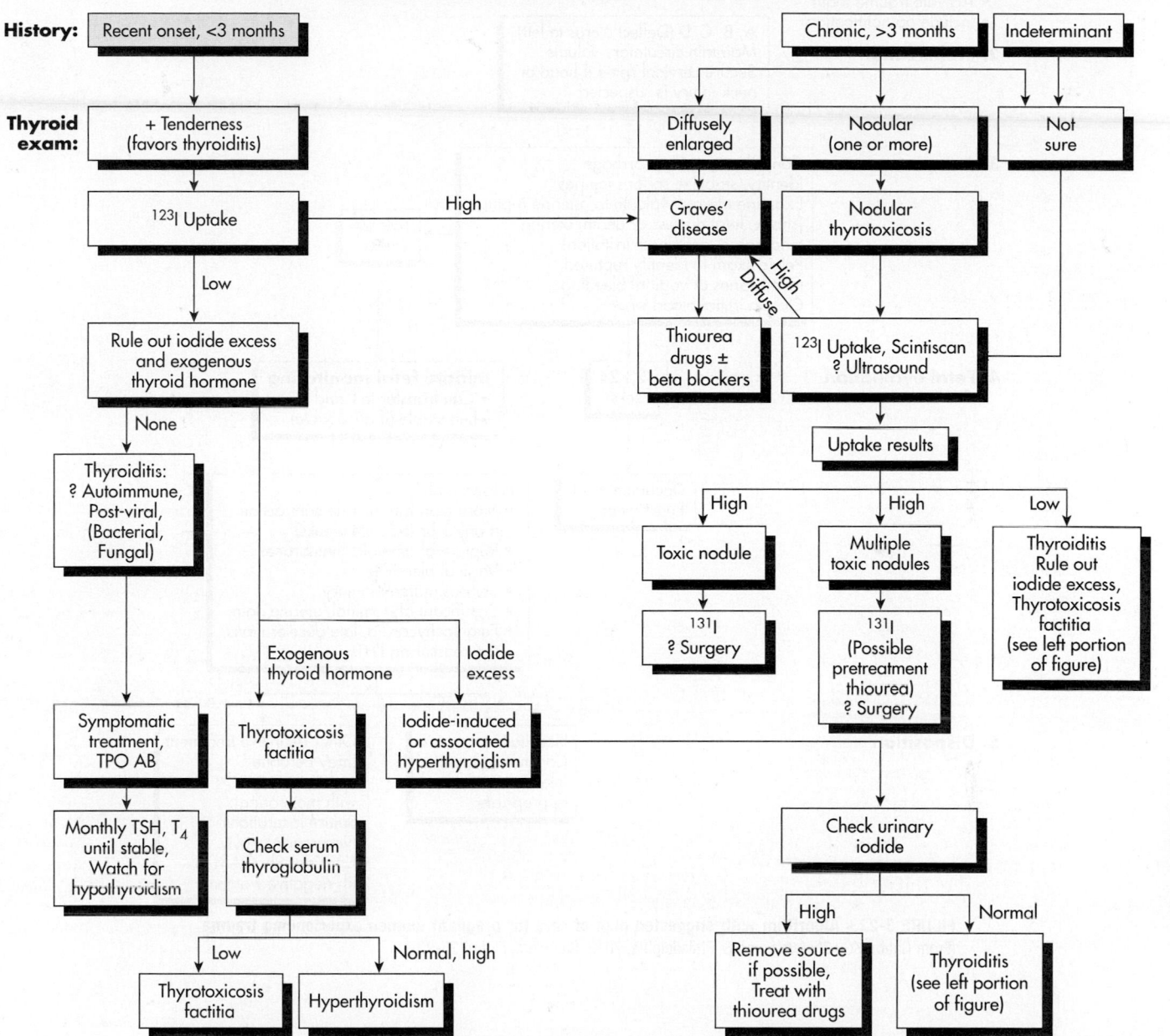

FIGURE 3-222 Algorithm for determining the cause of thyrotropin-independent thyrotoxicosis.
Additional information on thyrotoxicosis is available in Section I, topics Hyperthyroidism, Thyroid Nodule,
Thyroiditis, Thyroid Storm, and Graves Disease. T_3, Triiodothyronine; T_4, thyroxine; *TPO AB*, thyroid peroxidase
antibody; *TSH*, thyroid-stimulating hormone (thyrotropin). (From Melmed S, Polonsky KS, Larsen PR, Kronenberg
HM, *Williams textbook of endocrinology*, ed 12, Philadelphia, 2011, Saunders.)

Clinical
Algorithms

III

EMERGENCY DEPARTMENT MANAGEMENT: TRAUMA IN PREGNANCY

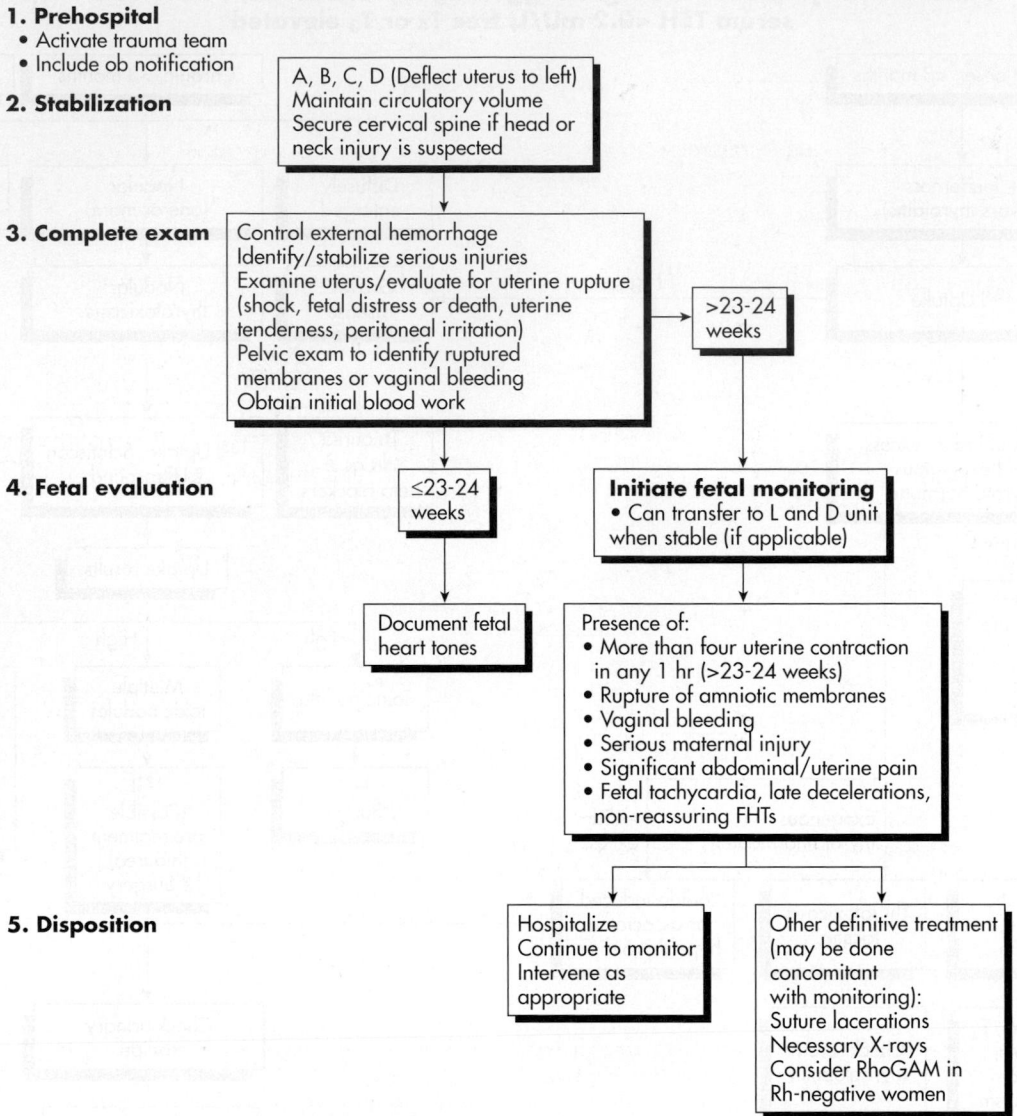

1. Prehospital
- Activate trauma team
- Include ob notification

2. Stabilization

A, B, C, D (Deflect uterus to left)
Maintain circulatory volume
Secure cervical spine if head or
neck injury is suspected

3. Complete exam

Control external hemorrhage
Identify/stabilize serious injuries
Examine uterus/evaluate for uterine rupture
(shock, fetal distress or death, uterine
tenderness, peritoneal irritation)
Pelvic exam to identify ruptured
membranes or vaginal bleeding
Obtain initial blood work

>23-24
weeks

4. Fetal evaluation

≤23-24
weeks

Initiate fetal monitoring
- Can transfer to L and D unit
  when stable (if applicable)

Document fetal
heart tones

Presence of:
- More than four uterine contraction
  in any 1 hr (>23-24 weeks)
- Rupture of amniotic membranes
- Vaginal bleeding
- Serious maternal injury
- Significant abdominal/uterine pain
- Fetal tachycardia, late decelerations,
  non-reassuring FHTs

5. Disposition

Hospitalize
Continue to monitor
Intervene as
appropriate

Other definitive treatment
(may be done
concomitant
with monitoring):
Suture lacerations
Necessary X-rays
Consider RhoGAM in
Rh-negative women

FIGURE 3-223 Algorithm with suggested plan of care for pregnant women experiencing trauma.
(From Gabbe SG: *Obstetrics,* ed 6, Philadelphia, 2012, Saunders, Figure 25-2.)

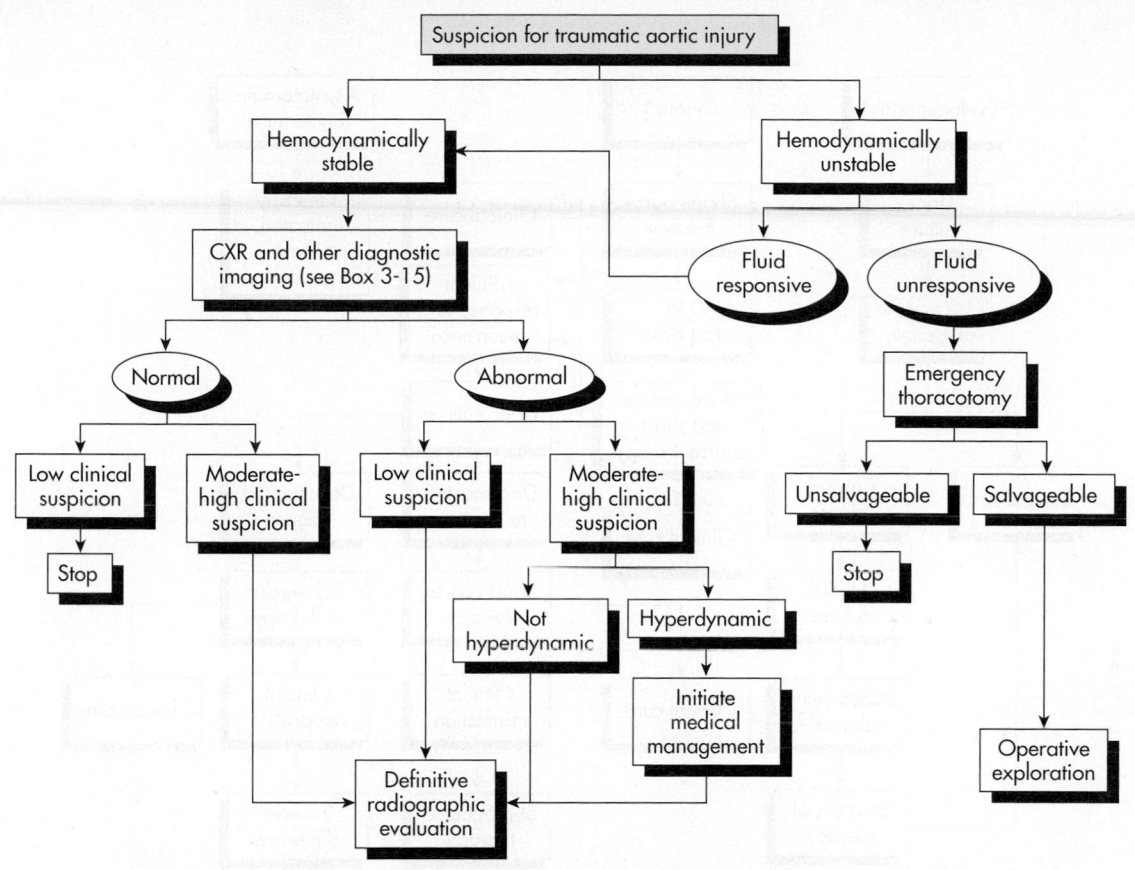

FIGURE 3-224 Diagnostic management algorithm for suspected traumatic aortic injury. *CXR,* Chest radiograph. (Modified from Adams JG, et al: *Emergency medicine, clinical essentials,* ed 2, Philadelphia, 2013, Elsevier.)

BOX 3-15   Pros and Cons of Imaging Modalities for Great Vessel Injury

Chest Radiography
Pros
Inexpensive
Performed at the bedside
Easy to interpret

Cons
Nonspecific
False-negative rate of 7% to 10% for traumatic aortic injury

Computed Tomographic Angiography
Pros
Identifies mediastinal hematoma and differentiates its causes
Identifies aortic injury, including intimal tears
Sensitivity and specificity approaching 100% for traumatic aortic injury

Cons
Poor delineation of nonaortic vascular injuries
Requires relative hemodynamic stability to obtain

Aortography
Pros
Traditional "gold standard"
Beneficial in the diagnosis of branch vessel injuries
Delineates equivocal computed tomographic angiographic findings

Cons
Difficult to obtain on an emergency basis
Requires relative hemodynamic stability

Transesophageal Echocardiography
Pros
May be performed at the bedside
Not limited by body habitus

Cons
Poor availability on an emergency basis
Contraindicated in patients with an unstable cervical spine or suspected esophageal trauma

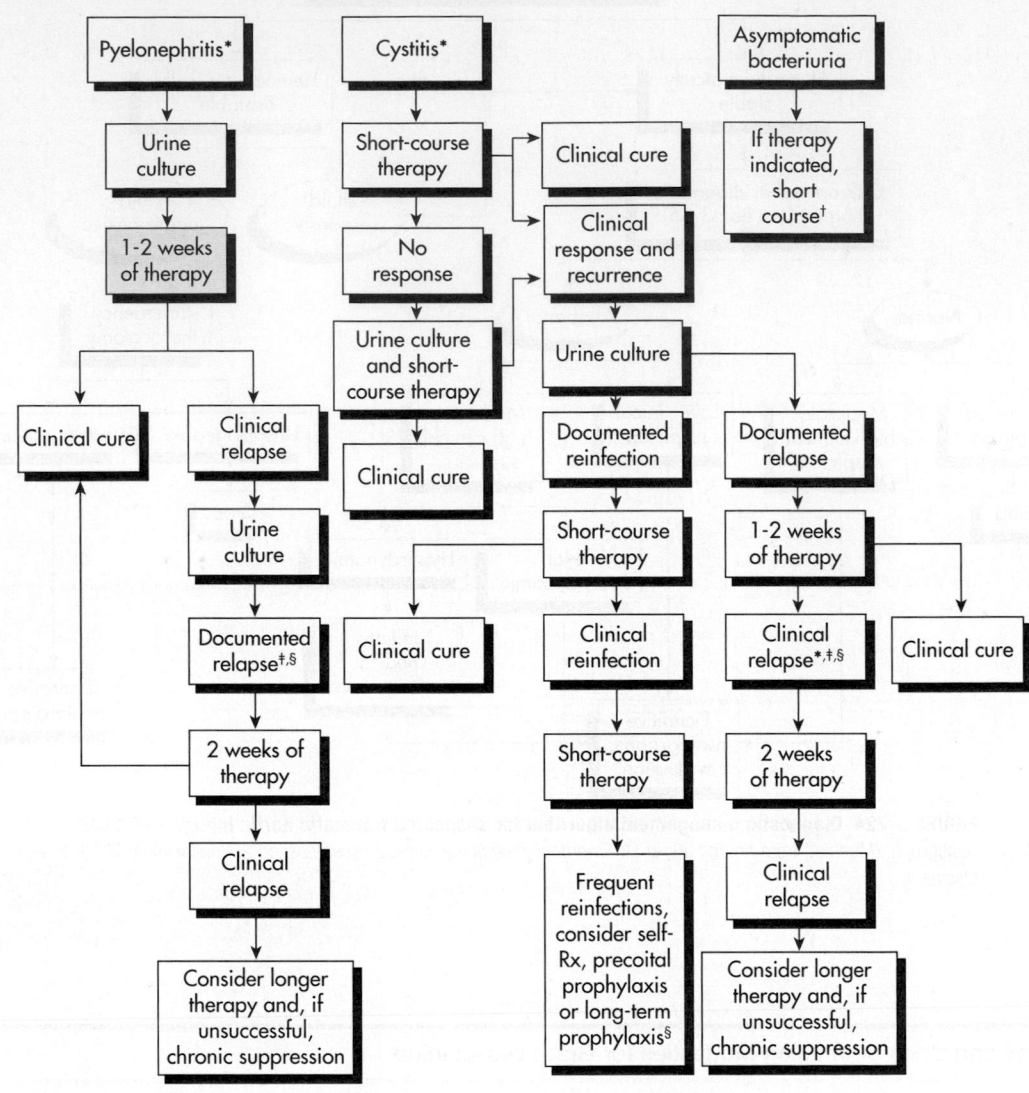

*Consider imaging studies in all men and in women with complicated urinary tract infection.
†No therapy except for renal transplant patients or prior to urologic procedures. Follow-up culture only in transplant patients.
‡Evaluate men for chronic bacterial prostatitis.
§Consider imaging studies in women.

FIGURE 3-226 Approach to the management of urinary tract infection in nonpregnant adults. (From Bennett JE , Dolin R, Blaser MJ: *Mandell, Douglas, and Bennett's principles and practice of infectious diseases*, ed 8, Philadelphia, 2015, Saunders.)

Table 3-47 Recommendations for Initial Therapy of Urinary Tract Infection in Adults

Parameter	Oral*	Parenteral (Switch to Oral when Response)
Uncomplicated Pyelonephritis		
GNB or no urine Gram stain available	CP 7 days, LV 5 days; if cannot use FQ, TMP-SMX 14 days ± 1 dose CT or AM	FQ 7 days or extended spectrum β-lactam (e.g., CT), 14 days ± AM
GPC in chains	Amoxicillin, 14 days	Ampicillin, 14 days
GPC in clusters	Linezolid or TMP-SMX, 14 days	Vancomycin, 14 days
Complicated Pyelonephritis		
Nonpregnant women or men	As for uncomplicated pyelonephritis	FQ, 7 days plus extended spectrum β-lactam initially ± AM
Pregnant women	Extended spectrum β-lactam; TMP-SMX† only if known sensitive both for 14 days	Extended spectrum β-lactam ± AM for 14 days
Uncomplicated Cystitis		
Nonpregnant women	Nitrofurantoin, 5 days or fosfomycin, 1 dose, or TMP-SMX, 3 days, or pivmecillinam, 3-7 days; FQ in reserve, 3 days	
Complicated Cystitis		
Women or men	FQ or nitrofurantoin, 7 days or fosfomycin, 1 dose	
Pregnant women	Cephalexin, 3-5 days or fosfomycin, 1 dose or nitrofurantoin, 7 days or TMP-SMX†, 3 days if sensitive	

GNB, Gram-negative bacilli; *GPC*, gram-positive cocci.
Drugs and Doses:
CP, ciprofloxacin orally 500 mg twice/day or 1000 mg once/day.
LV, levofloxacin orally 750 mg once/day.
TMP-SMX, trimethoprim-sulfamethoxazole orally 160/800 mg twice/day.
CT, ceftriaxone parenterally 1 g/day.
FQ, fluoroquinolone parenterally—ciprofloxacin 500 mg twice/day or levofloxacin 750 mg once/day.
FQ, fluoroquinolone orally—ciprofloxacin 500 mg twice/day or 1000 once/day or levofloxacin 750 mg once/day.
AM, aminoglycoside parenterally (e.g., gentamicin 5 mg/kg/day).
Amoxicillin orally 875 mg twice/day.
Ampicillin parenterally 2 g every 4 hr.
Linezolid orally 600 mg twice/day.
Vancomycin parenterally 15 mg/kg twice/day.
Nitrofurantoin orally 100 mg twice/day.
Fosfomycin orally 3 g once.
Pivmecillinam orally 400 mg twice/day.
Cephalexin orally 500 mg four times/day.
*Preferred if the patient is reliable, compliant, hemodynamically stable, and able to take oral therapy.
†TMP-SMX should be avoided in the third trimester.
From Bennett JF , Dolin R, Blaser MJ: *Mandell, Douglas, and Bennett's principles and practice of infectious diseases*, ed 8, Philadelphia, 2015, Saunders.

Investigation and Management of Suspected Urinary Tract Obstruction

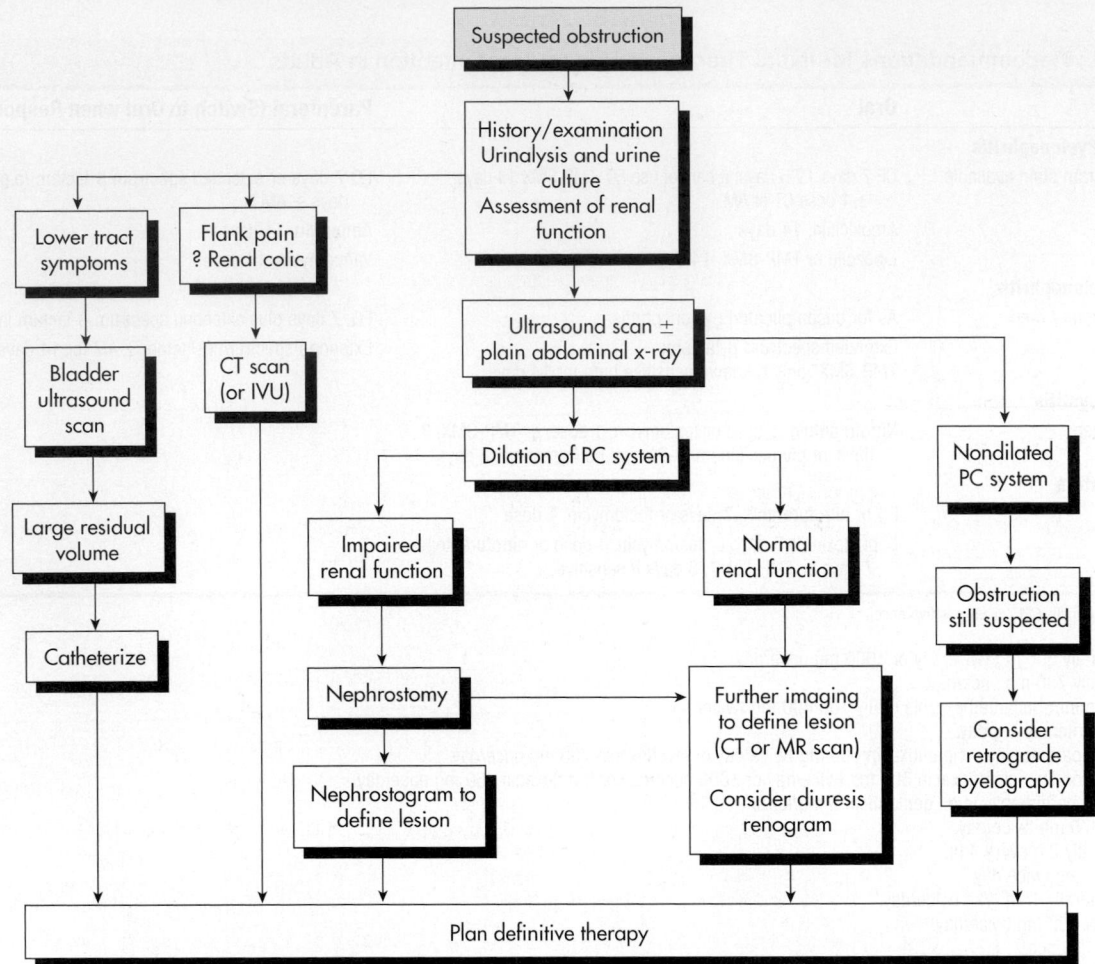

FIGURE 3-227 Investigation and management of suspected urinary tract obstruction. A full history and examination should be performed together with urinalysis, urine microscopy and culture, and measurement of renal function and serum electrolytes. Ultrasound is a useful first-line investigation for any patient with suspected urinary tract obstruction. Helical (spiral) computed tomography (CT) is now the preferred imaging technique when renal calculi are suspected. Either CT or magnetic resonance (MRI) urography can accurately diagnose both the site and the cause of obstruction in most cases. If there is renal impairment, insertion of a nephrostomy allows the effective relief of the obstruction and time for renal function to recover while definitive therapy is planned. *IVU,* Intravenous urography; *PC,* pelvicalyceal. (From Floege J et al: *Comprehensive clinical nephrology,* ed 4, Philadelphia, 2010, Saunders.)

BOX 3-16   Diagnostic Tests Used in Obstructive Uropathy

Upper Urinary Tract Obstruction
Sonography (ultrasound)
Plain films of the abdomen (KUB)
Excretory or intravenous pyelography (very rarely needed)
Retrograde pyelography
Isotopic renography
Computed tomography (helical CT)
Magnetic resonance imaging
Pressure flow studies (the Whitaker test)

Lower Urinary Tract Obstruction
• Some of the tests listed at left
• Cystoscopy
• Voiding cystourethrogram
• Retrograde urethrography
• Urodynamic tests
• Debimetry
• Cystometrography
• Electromyography
• Urethral pressure profile

KUB, Kidneys, ureter, bladder.

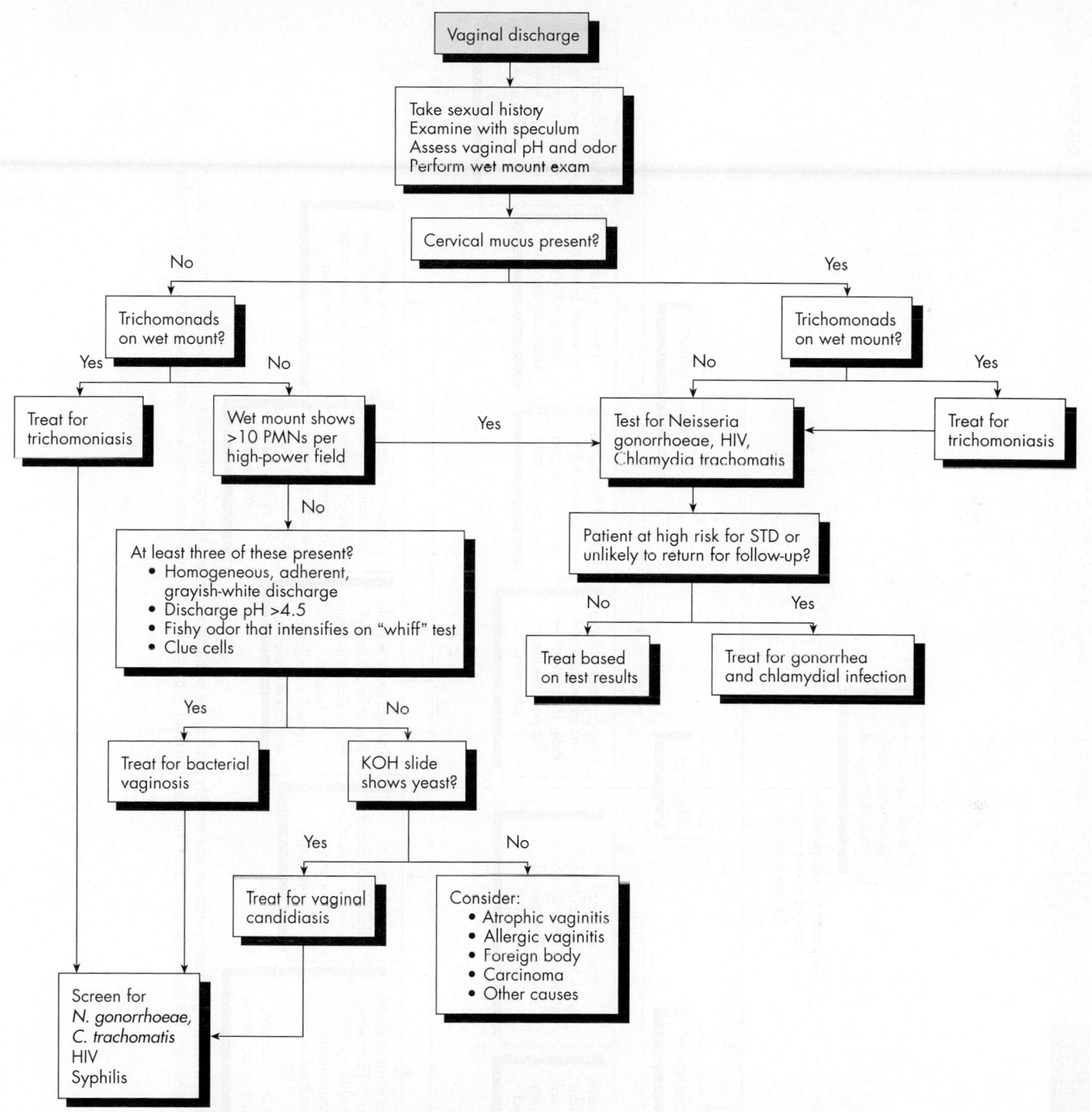

FIGURE 3-228 Evaluation of vaginal discharge. See Section I, Vaginitis, Fungal, and Vaginitis Trichomonas for additional information on vaginal discharge evaluation. *HIV,* Human immunodeficiency virus; *KOH,* potassium hydroxide; *PMN,* polymorphonuclear leukocyte; *STD,* sexually transmitted disease.

Clinical
Algorithms

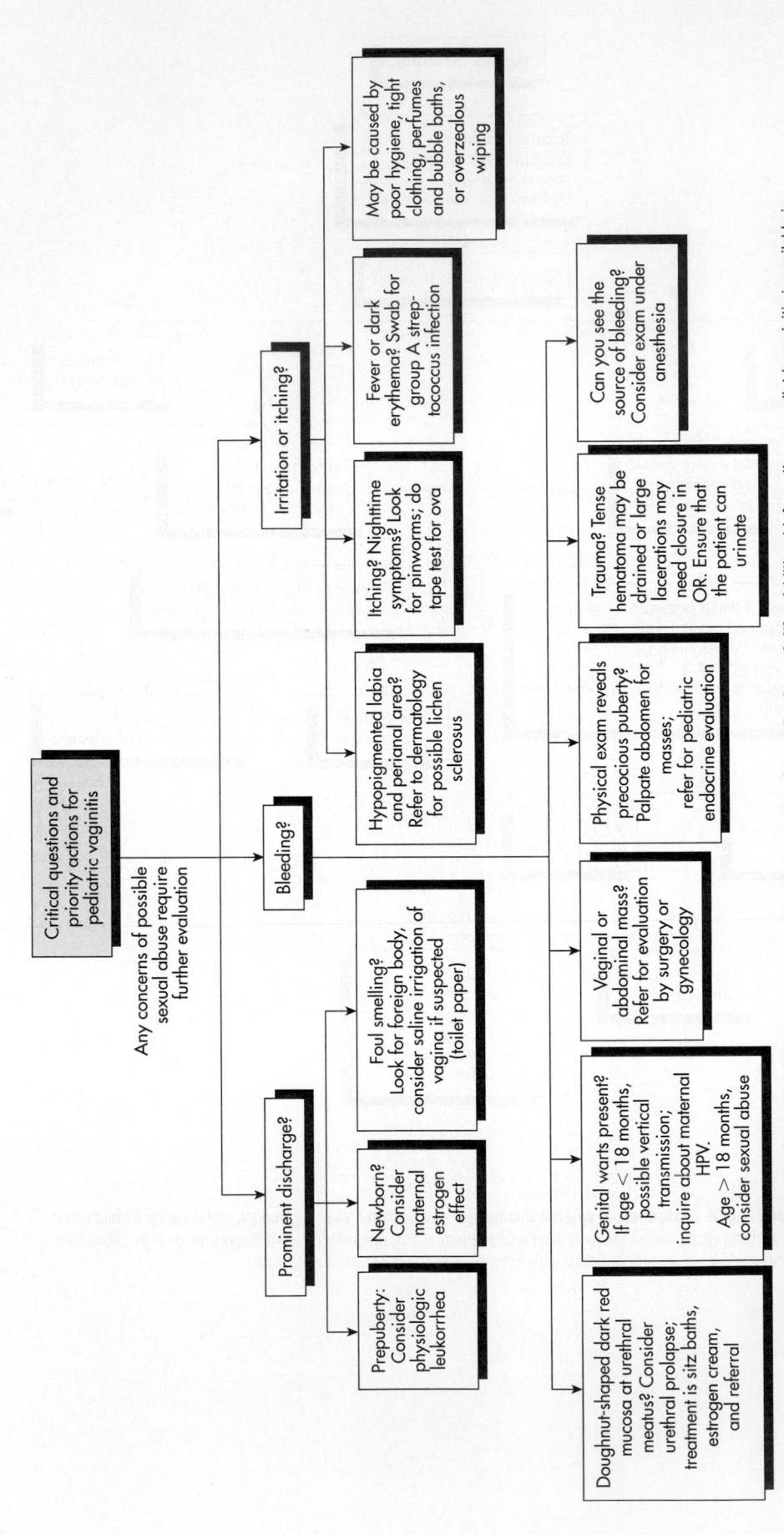

FIGURE 3-230 Algorithm showing critical questions and priority actions for pediatric vaginitis. Additional information on pediatric vaginitis is available in Section I, Vaginitis, Prepubescent. *HPV,* Human papillomavirus; *OR,* operating room. (From Adams JG, et al: *Emergency medicine, clinical essentials,* ed 2, Philadelphia, 2013, Elsevier.)

Critical questions and priority actions for pediatric vaginitis

Any concerns of possible sexual abuse require further evaluation

Prominent discharge?

Bleeding?

Irritation or itching?

Prepuberty: Consider physiologic leukorrhea

Newborn? Consider maternal estrogen effect

Foul smelling? Look for foreign body, consider saline irrigation of vagina if suspected (toilet paper)

Hypopigmented labia and perianal area? Refer to dermatology for possible lichen sclerosus

Itching? Nighttime symptoms? Look for pinworms; do tape test for ova

Fever or dark erythema? Swab for group A streptococcus infection

May be caused by poor hygiene, tight clothing, perfumes and bubble baths, or overzealous wiping

Doughnut-shaped dark red mucosa at urethral meatus? Consider urethral prolapse; treatment is sitz baths, estrogen cream, and referral

Genital warts present? If age < 18 months, possible vertical transmission; inquire about maternal HPV. Age > 18 months, consider sexual abuse

Vaginal or abdominal mass? Refer for evaluation by surgery or gynecology

Physical exam reveals precocious puberty? Palpate abdomen for masses; refer for pediatric endocrine evaluation

Trauma? Tense hematoma may be drained or large lacerations may need closure in OR. Ensure that the patient can urinate

Can you see the source of bleeding? Consider exam under anesthesia

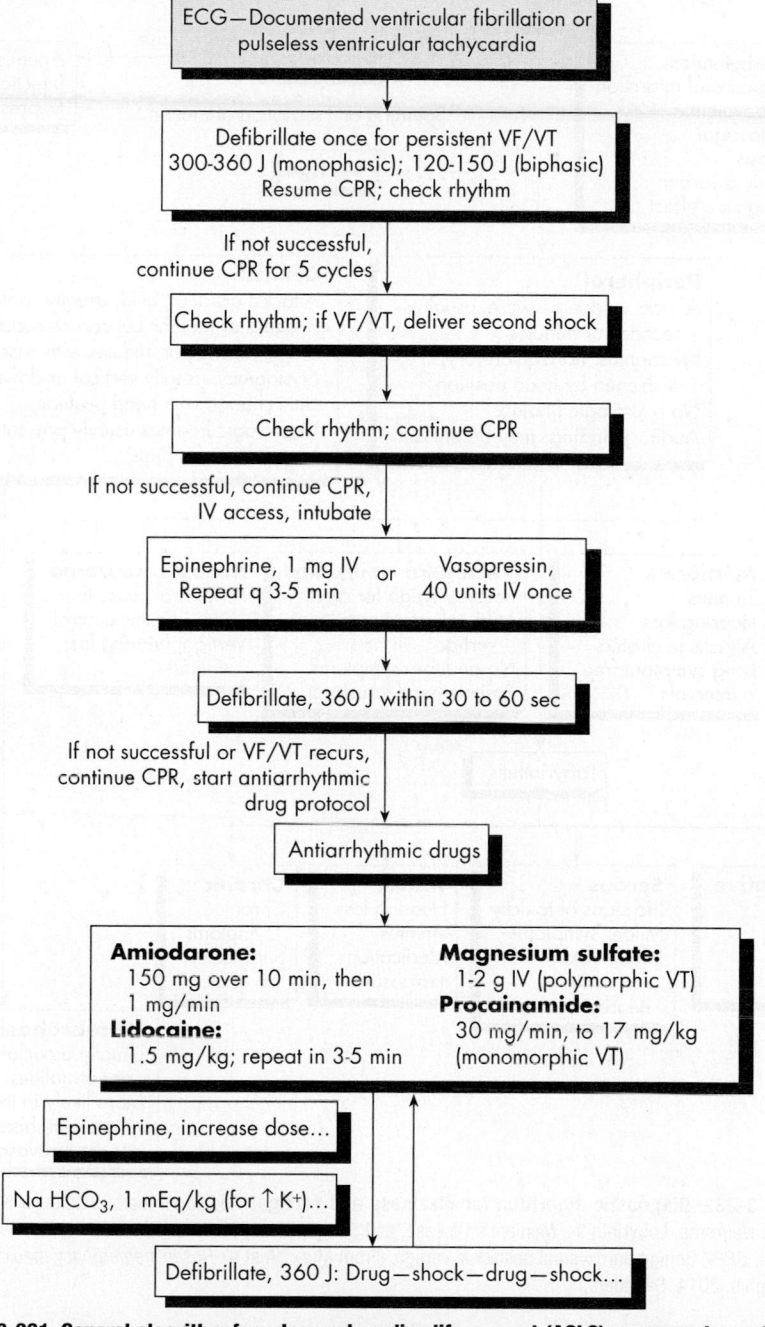

FIGURE 3-231 General algorithm for advanced cardiac life support (ACLS) response to ventricular fibrillation (VF) or pulseless ventricular tachycardia (VT). *Note:* In a 2008 advisory, 200 compression-only sequences were suggested as an alternative to standard CPR cycles between shocks, and this approach is under consideration for future guidelines. *CPR,* Cardiopulmonary resuscitation; *ECG,* electrocardiogram. (From Goldman L, Schafer AI: *Goldman's Cecil medicine,* ed 24, Philadelphia, 2012, Saunders.)

Clinical Algorithms

III

	ICD-10CM #	R42	Dizziness and giddiness
		H81.13	Benign paroxysmal vertigo, bilateral
		H81.49	Vertigo of central origin, unspecified ear
		H81.399	Other peripheral vertigo, unspecified ear
		H81.23	Vestibular neuronitis, bilateral

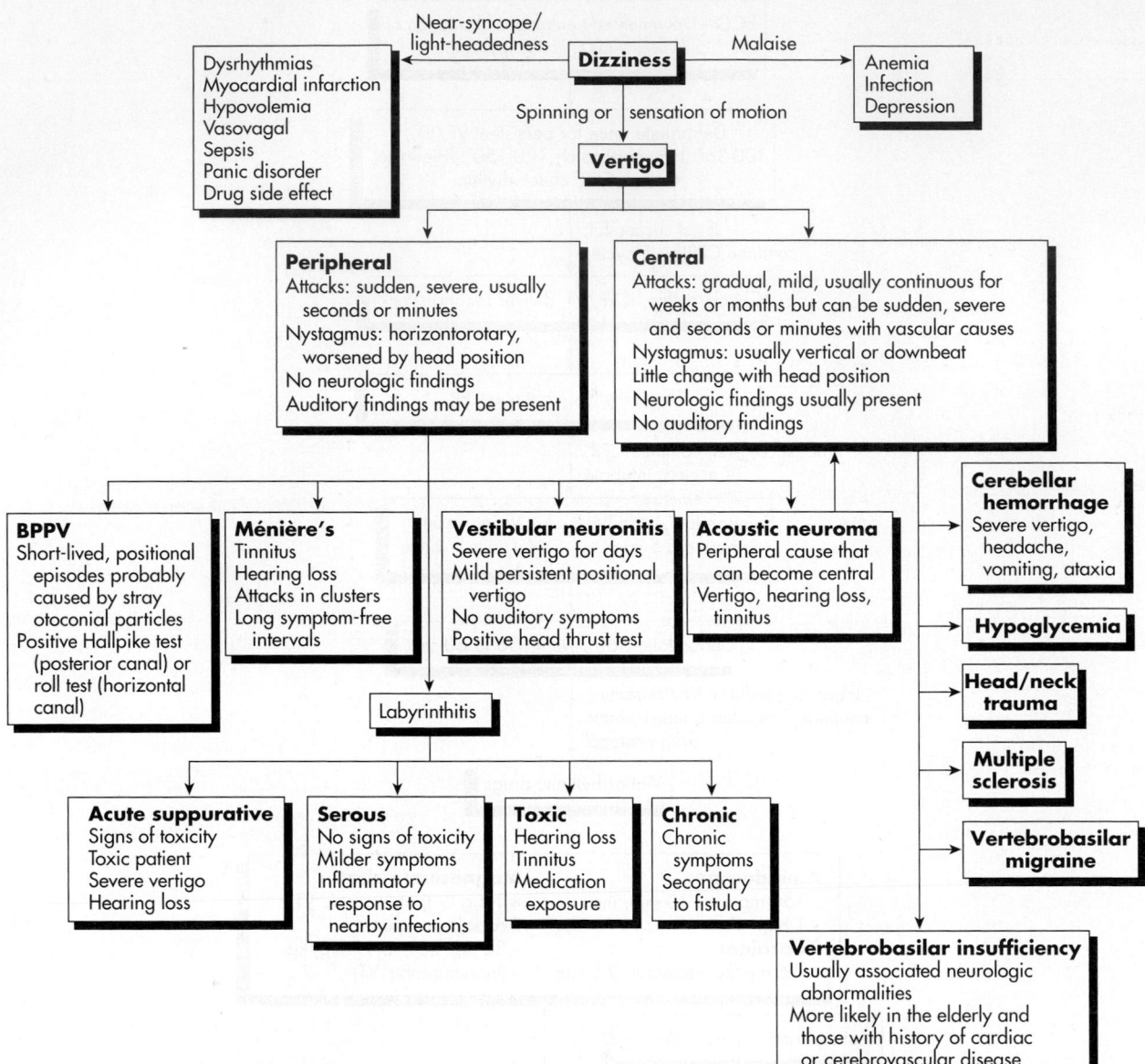

FIGURE 3-232 Diagnostic algorithm for dizziness and vertigo. Additional topics Vestibular Neuronitis, Acoustic Neuroma, Labyrinthitis, Meniere's Disease, and Benign Paroxysmal Positional Vertigo are available in Section I. *BPPV,* Benign paroxysmal positional vertigo. (From Marx JA et al: *Rosen's emergency medicine,* ed 8, Philadelphia, 2014, Saunders.)

VERTIGO—cont'd

ICD-10CM #		
R42	Dizziness and giddiness	
H81.13	Benign paroxysmal vertigo, bilateral	
H81.49	Vertigo of central origin, unspecified ear	
H81.399	Other peripheral vertigo, unspecified ear	
H81.23	Vestibular neuronitis, bilateral	

1715

Table 3-48 Differential Diagnosis of Patients with True Vertigo

Cause	History	Associated Symptoms	Physical
Peripheral			
1. Benign paroxysmal positional vertigo	Short-lived, positional, fatigable episodes	Nausea, vomiting	Single position can precipitate vertigo. Positive result on Hallpike test (posterior semicircular canal) or Roll test (horizontal canal).
2. Labyrinthitis			
A. Serous	Mild to severe positional symptoms. Usually coexisting or antecedent infection of ear, nose, throat, or meninges.	Mild to severe hearing loss can occur	Usually nontoxic patient with minimal fever elevation
B. Acute suppurative	Coexisting acute exudative infection of the inner ear. Severe symptoms.	Usually severe hearing loss, nausea, vomiting	Febrile patient showing signs of toxicity. Acute otitis media.
C. Toxic	Gradually progressive symptoms: Patients on medication causing toxicity.	Hearing loss that may become rapid and severe, nausea and vomiting	Hearing loss. Ataxia common feature in chronic phase.
3. Ménière's disease	Recurrent episodes of severe rotational vertigo usually lasting hours. Onset usually abrupt. Attacks may occur in clusters. Long symptom-free remissions.	Nausea, vomiting, tinnitus, hearing loss	Positional nystagmus not present
4. Vestibular neuritis	Sudden onset of severe vertigo, increasing in intensity for hours, then gradually subsiding over several days but can last weeks to months. Can be worsened with positional change. Sometimes history of infection or toxic exposure that precedes initial attack. Highest incidence is found in third and fifth decades.	Nausea, vomiting. Auditory symptoms do not occur.	Spontaneous nystagmus toward the involved ear may be present.
5. Acoustic neuroma	Gradual onset and increase in symptoms. Neurologic signs in later stages. Most occur in women aged 30 to 60.	Hearing loss, tinnitus. True ataxia and neurologic signs as tumor enlarges.	Unilateral decreased hearing. True truncal ataxia and other neurologic signs when tumor enlarges. May have diminution or absence of corneal reflex. Eighth cranial nerve deficit may be present.
Central			
1. Vascular disorders			
A. Vertebrobasilar insufficiency	Should be considered in any patient of advanced age with isolated new-onset vertigo without an obvious cause. More likely with history of atherosclerosis. Can occur with neck trauma. Initial episode usually lasts seconds to minutes.	Often headache. Usually neurologic symptoms including dysarthria, ataxia, weakness, numbness, double vision. Tinnitus and deafness uncommon.	Neurologic deficits usually present, but initially neurologic examination can be normal
B. Cerebellar hemorrhage	Sudden onset of severe symptoms	Headache, vomiting, ataxia	Signs of toxicity. Dysmetria, true ataxia. Ipsilateral sixth cranial nerve palsy may be present.
C. Occlusion of posterior inferior cerebellar artery (Wallenberg's syndrome)	Vertigo associated with significant neurologic complaints	Nausea, vomiting, loss of pain and temperature sensation, ataxia, hoarseness	Loss of pain and temperature sensation on the side of the face ipsilateral to the lesion and on the opposite side of the body, paralysis of the palate, pharynx, and larynx. Horner's syndrome (ipsilateral ptosis, miosis, and decreased facial sweating).
2. Head trauma	Symptoms begin with or shortly after head trauma. Positional symptoms most common type after trauma. Self-limited symptoms that can persist weeks to months.	Usually mild nausea	Occasionally, basilar skull fracture
3. Vertebrobasilar migraine	Vertigo almost always followed by headache. Patient has usually had similar episodes in past. Most patients have a family history of migraine. Syndrome usually begins in adolescence.	Dysarthria, ataxia, visual disturbances, or paresthesias usually precede headache	No residual neurologic or otologic signs are present after attack
4. Multiple sclerosis	Vertigo presenting symptom in 7-10% and appears in the course of the disease in a third. Onset may be severe and suggest labyrinth disease. Disease onset usually between ages 20 and 40. Often history of other attacks with varying neurologic signs or symptoms.	Nausea and vomiting, which may be severe	May have horizontal, rotary, or vertical nystagmus. Nystagmus may persist after the vertiginous symptoms have subsided. Bilateral internuclear ophthalmoplegia and ataxic eye movements suggest multiple sclerosis.
5. Temporal lobe epilepsy	Can be initial or prominent symptom in some patients with the disorder	Memory impairment, hallucinations, trancelike states, seizures	May have aphasia or convulsions
6. Hypoglycemia	Should be considered in diabetics and any other patient with unexplained symptoms	Sweating, anxiety	Tachycardia, mental status change may be present

From Marx JA et al: *Rosen's emergency medicine*, ed 8, Philadelphia, 2014, Saunders.

Clinical Algorithms

III

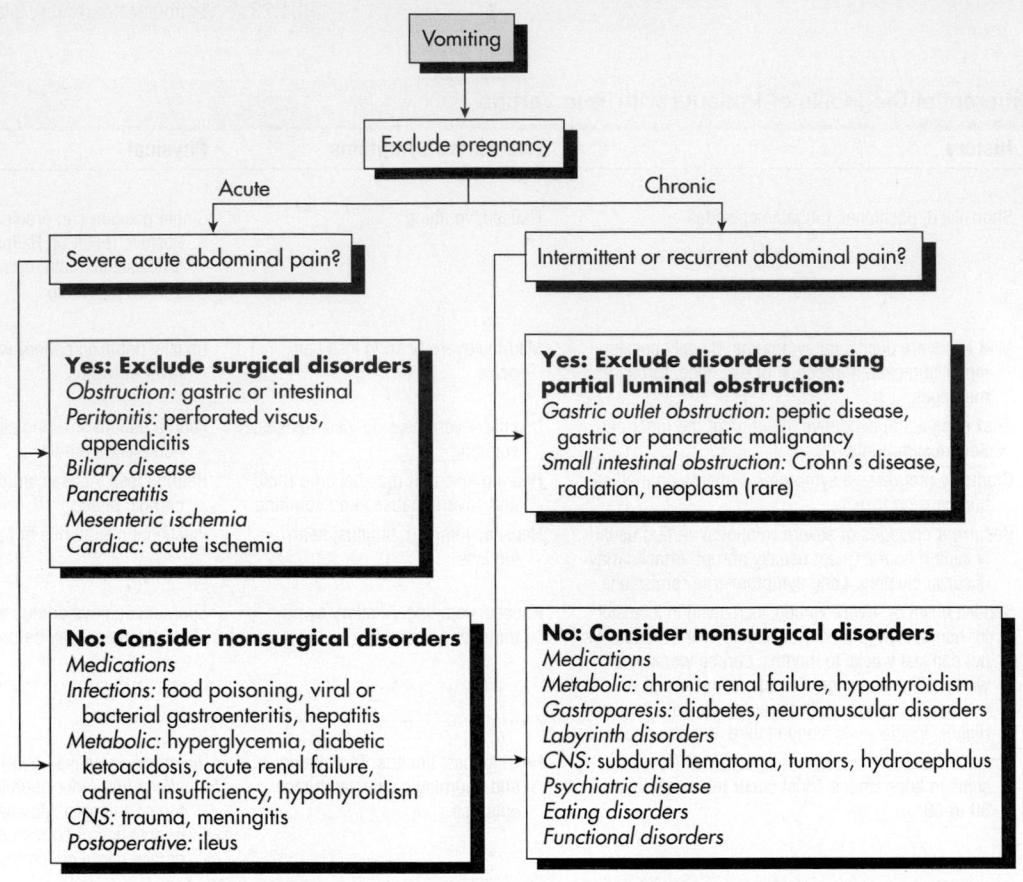

FIGURE 3-233 Approach to the patient with vomiting. *CNS*, Central nervous system. (From Goldman L, Schafer AI: *Goldman's Cecil medicine,* ed 24, Philadelphia, 2012, Saunders.)

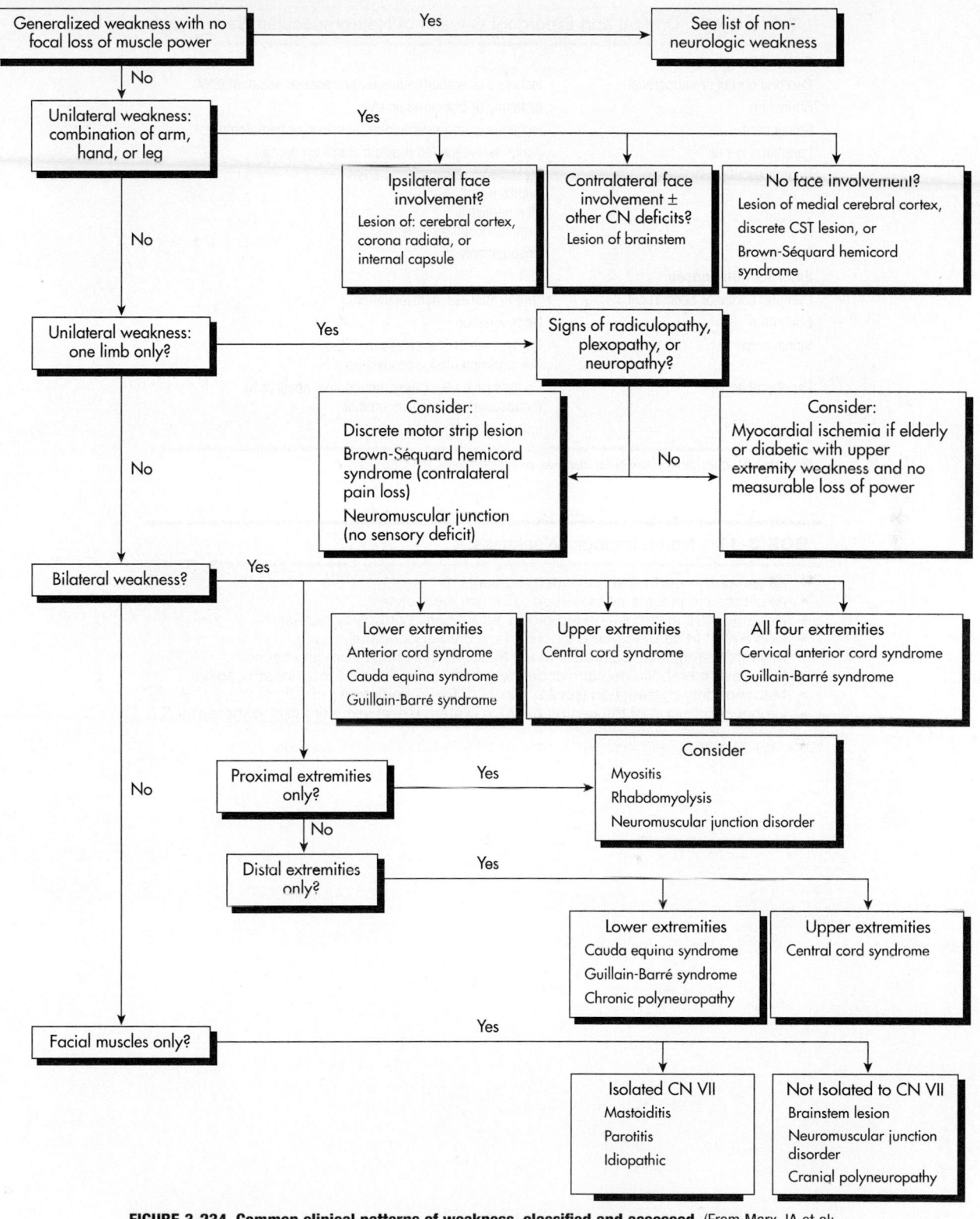

FIGURE 3-234 Common clinical patterns of weakness, classified and assessed. (From Marx JA et al: *Rosen's emergency medicine*, ed 8, Philadelphia, 2014, Saunders.)

Table 3-49 Critical and Emergent Causes of Neuromuscular Weakness

Critical Diagnoses

Cerebral cortex or subcortical	Ischemic or hemorrhagic cerebrovascular accident (CVA)
Brainstem	Ischemic or hemorrhagic CVA
Spinal cord	Ischemia, compression (disk, abscess, or hematoma)
Peripheral nerve	Acute demyelination (Guillain-Barré syndrome)
Neuromuscular junction	Myasthenic or cholinergic crisis
	Botulism
	Tick paralysis
	Organophosphate poisoning
Muscle	Rhabdomyolysis

Emergent Diagnoses

Cerebral cortex or subcortical	Tumor, abscess, demyelination
Brainstem	Demyelination
Spinal cord	Demyelination (transverse myelitis)
	Compression (disk, spondylosis)
Peripheral nerve	Compressive plexopathy (hematoma, aneurysm)
	Paraneoplastic vasculitis uremia
Muscle	Inflammatory myositis

From Marx JA et al: *Rosen's emergency medicine*, ed 8, Philadelphia, 2014, Saunders.

BOX 3-17 Nonneurologic Weakness

- Alterations in plasma volume (dehydration)
- Alterations in plasma composition (glucose, electrolytes).
- Derangement in circulating red blood cells (anemia or polycythemia)
- Decrement in cardiac pump function (myocardial ischemia)
- Drop in systemic vascular resistance (vasodilatory shock from any cause)
- Increased metabolic demand (local or systemic infection, endocrinopathy, toxin)
- Mitochondrial dysfunction (severe sepsis or toxin-mediated)
- Global depression of the central nervous system (sedatives, stimulant withdrawal)

From Marx JA et al: *Rosen's emergency medicine*, ed 8, Philadelphia, 2014, Saunders.

ICD-10CM # G93.3 Postviral fatigue syndrome
R53.1 Weakness
R53.81 Other malaise
R53.83 Other fatigue

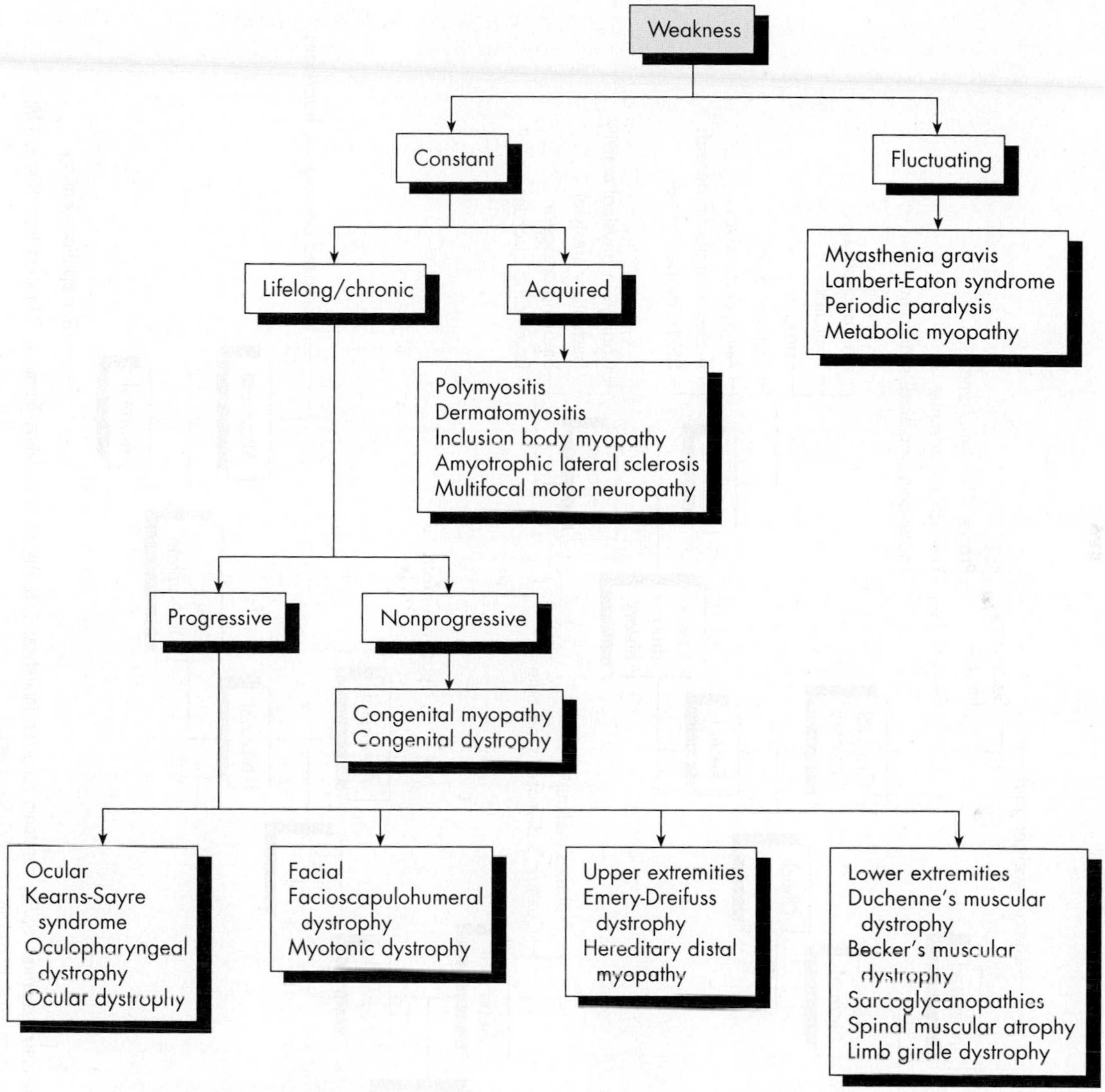

Weakness
Constant
Fluctuating
Myasthenia gravis
Lambert-Eaton syndrome
Periodic paralysis
Metabolic myopathy
Lifelong/chronic
Acquired
Polymyositis
Dermatomyositis
Inclusion body myopathy
Amyotrophic lateral sclerosis
Multifocal motor neuropathy
Progressive
Nonprogressive
Congenital myopathy
Congenital dystrophy
Ocular
Kearns-Sayre syndrome
Oculopharyngeal dystrophy
Ocular dystrophy
Facial
Facioscapulohumeral dystrophy
Myotonic dystrophy
Upper extremities
Emery-Dreifuss dystrophy
Hereditary distal myopathy
Lower extremities
Duchenne's muscular dystrophy
Becker's muscular dystrophy
Sarcoglycanopathics
Spinal muscular atrophy
Limb girdle dystrophy

FIGURE 3-235 An algorithm for the approach to the patient with weakness. (From Bradley WG, Daroff RB, Fenichel GM, Jankovic J [eds]: *Neurology in clinical practice,* ed 4, Philadelphia, 2004, Butterworth Heinemann.)

ICD-10CM # R63.5 Abnormal weight gain
E66.9 Obesity, unspecified

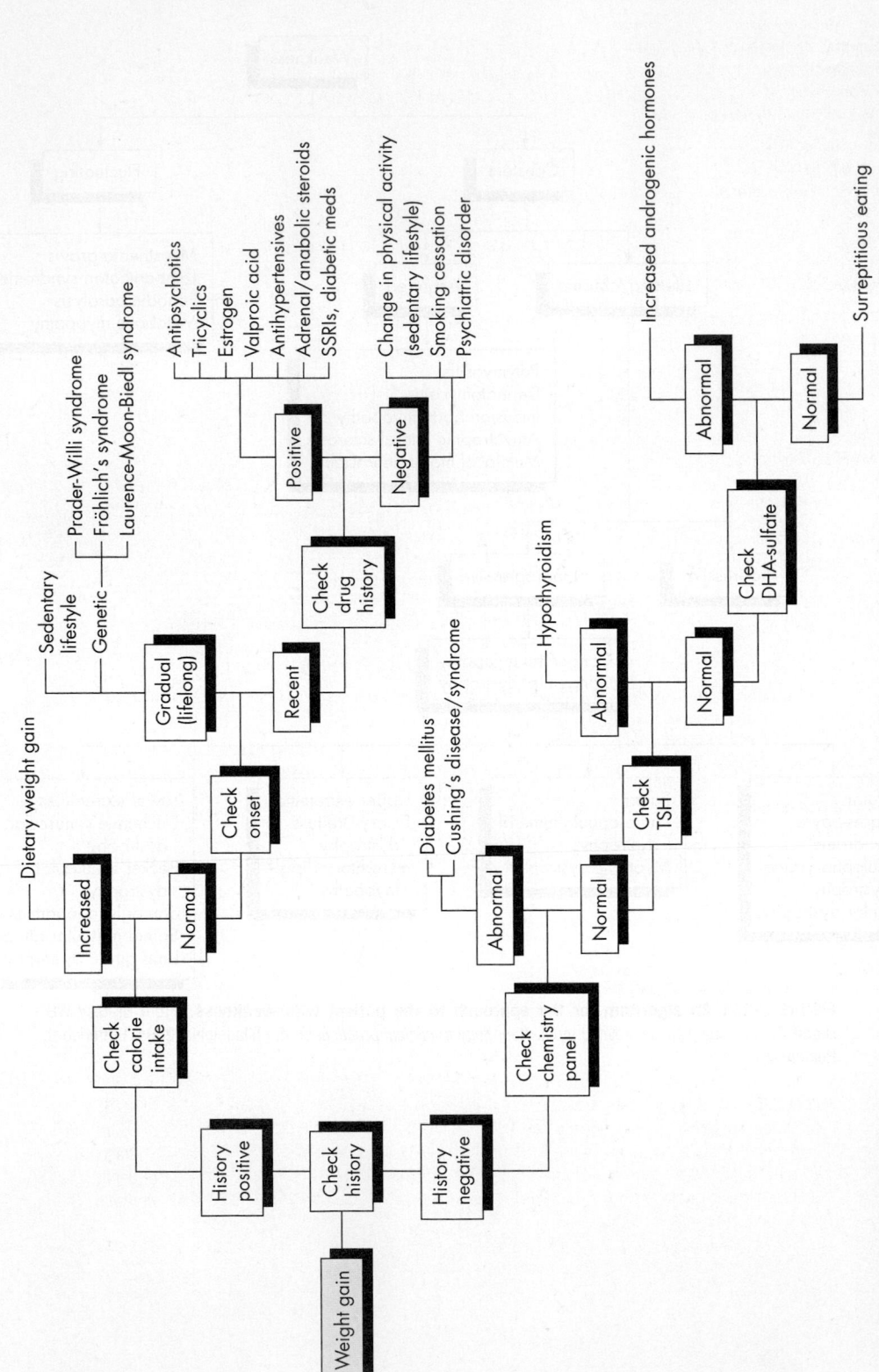

FIGURE 3-236 Weight gain. *DHA,* Dehydroepiandrosterone; *SSRIs,* serotonin reuptake inhibitors; *TSH,* thyroid-stimulating hormone. (Modified from Healey PM: *Common medical diagnosis: an algorithmic approach,* ed 3, Philadelphia, 2000, Saunders.)

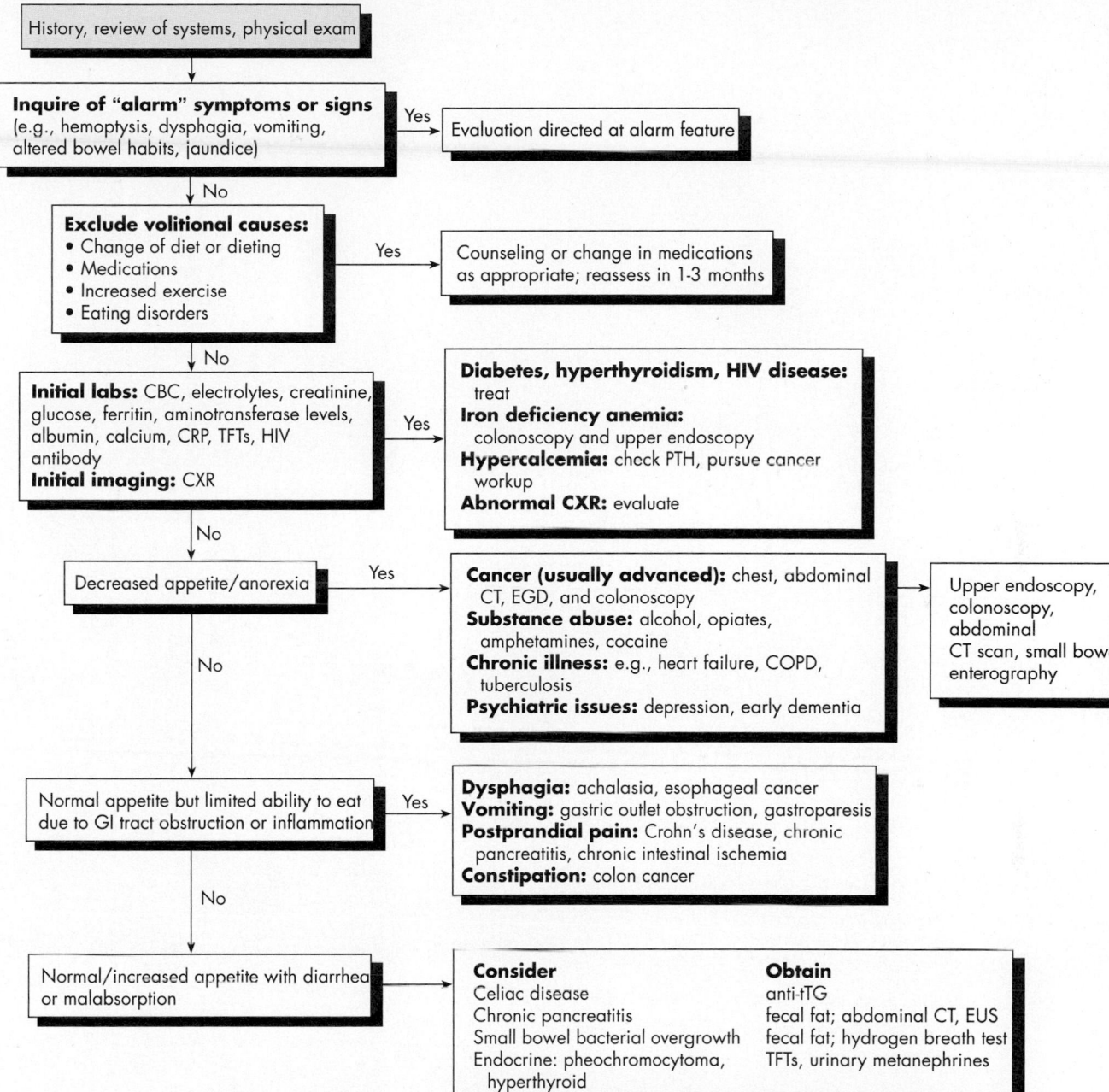

FIGURE 3-237 Approach to the patient with unintentional weight loss greater than 5%. *CBC,* Complete blood count; *COPD,* chronic obstructive pulmonary disease; *CRP,* C-reactive protein; *CT,* computed tomography; *CXR,* chest radiograph; *EGD,* esophagogastroduodenoscopy; *EUS,* endoscopic ultrasound; *GI,* gastrointestinal; *HIV,* human immunodeficiency virus; *PTH,* parathyroid hormone; *TFTs,* thyroid function tests; *tTG,* tissue transglutaminase; *U/A,* urinalysis. (From Goldman L, Schafer AI: *Goldman's Cecil medicine,* ed 24, Philadelphia, 2012, Saunders.)

SECTION IV

Laboratory Tests and Interpretation of Results

This section contains more than 300 commonly performed laboratory tests. In general, the tests are discussed in the following format:

1. Laboratory test.
2. Normal range in adult patients. Normal values are given using the present (traditional) reference interval, followed by the Système Internationale (SI) reference interval, the conversion factor (CF), and the suggested minimum increment (SMI).
3. Common abnormalities, such as positive test, increased, or decreased value.
4. Causes of abnormal result.

The normal ranges may differ slightly, depending on the laboratory. The reader should be aware of the "normal range" of the particular laboratory performing the test. Every attempt has been made to present current laboratory test data, with emphasis on practical considerations.

ACE LEVEL
See ANGIOTENSIN-CONVERTING ENZYME

ACETONE (serum or plasma)
Normal: Negative
Elevated in: DKA, starvation, isopropanol ingestion

ACETYLCHOLINE RECEPTOR (AChR) ANTIBODY
Normal: <0.03 nmol/L
Elevated in: Myasthenia gravis. Changes in AChR concentration correlate with the clinical severity of myasthenia gravis following therapy and during therapy with prednisone and immunosuppressants. False-positive AChR antibody results may be found in patients with Eaton-Lambert syndrome.

ACID-BASE REFERENCE VALUES
See Tables 4-1 and 4-2.

ACID PHOSPHATASE (serum)
Normal range: 0-5.5 U/L (0-90 nkat/L [CF: 16.67; SMI:2 nkat/L])
Elevated in: Carcinoma of prostate, other neoplasms (breast, bone), Paget's disease, osteogenesis imperfecta, malignant invasion of bone, Gaucher's disease, multiple myeloma, myeloproliferative disorders, benign prostatic hypertrophy, prostatic palpation or surgery, hyperparathyroidism, liver disease, chronic renal failure, idiopathic thrombocytopenic purpura, bronchitis

ACID SERUM TEST
See HAM TEST

ACTIVATED CLOTTING TIME (ACT)
Normal: This test is used to determine the dose of protamine sulfate to reverse the effect of heparin as an anticoagulant during angioplasty, cardiac surgery, and hemodialysis. The accepted goal during cardiopulmonary bypass surgery is usually 400-500 sec.

ACTIVATED PARTIAL THROMBOPLASTIN TIME (APTT, aPTT)
See PARTIAL THROMBOPLASTIN TIME

ADRENOCORTICOTROPIC HORMONE
Normal: 9-52 pg/ml
Elevated in: Addison's disease, ectopic ACTH-producing tumors, congenital adrenal hyperplasia, Nelson's syndrome, pituitary-dependent Cushing's disease
Decreased in: Secondary adrenocortical insufficiency, hypopituitarism, adrenal adenoma or adrenal carcinoma

ALANINE AMINOPEPTIDASE
Normal:
Male: 1.11-1.71 mcg/ml
Female: 0.96-1.52 mcg/ml
Elevated in: Liver or pancreatic disease, ethanol use, oral contraceptives use, malignancy, tobacco use, pregnancy
Decreased in: Abortion

ALANINE AMINOTRANSFERASE (ALT, SGPT)
See Fig. 4-1, an algorithm for evaluation of elevated ALT.
Normal range: 0-35 U/L (0.058 μkat/L [CF: 0.02 μkat/L])
Elevated in: Liver disease (hepatitis, cirrhosis, Reye's syndrome), hepatic congestion, infectious mononucleosis, myocardial infarction, myocarditis, severe muscle trauma, dermatomyositis/polymyositis, muscular dystrophy, drugs (antibiotics, narcotics, antihypertensive agents, heparin, labetalol, statins, NSAIDs, amiodarone, chlorpromazine, phenytoin), malignancy, renal and pulmonary infarction, seizures, eclampsia, shock liver

TABLE 4-1 Commonly Used Acid-Base Reference Values for Arterial and Venous Plasma or Serum (Averaged from Various Sources)

	ARTERIAL		VENOUS	
	Conventional Units	SI Units*	Conventional Units	SI Units*
pH	7.40 (7.35-7.45)	7.40 (7.35-7.45)	7.37 (7.32-7.42)	7.37 (7.32-7.42)
Pco₂	40 mm Hg (35-45)	5.33 kPa (4.67-6.10)	45 mm Hg (45-50)	6.10 kPa (5.33-6.67)
Po₂	80-100 mm Hg	10.66-13.33 kPa	40 mm Hg (37-43)	5.33 kPa (4.93-5.73)
HCO₃ (CO₂ combining power)	24 mEq/L (20-28)	24 mmol/L (20-28)	26 mEq/L (22-30)	26 mmol/L (22-30)
CO₂ content	25 mEq/L (22-28)	25 mmol/L (22-28)	27 mEq/L (24-30)	27 mmol/L(24-30)

From Ravel R: *Clinical laboratory medicine*, ed 6, St Louis, 1995, Mosby.
*International system.

TABLE 4-2 Summary of Laboratory Findings in Primary Uncomplicated Respiratory and Metabolic Acid-Base Disorders*

Disorder	Pco₂	pH	Base Excess
Acute primary respiratory hypoactivity (respiratory acidosis)	Increase	Decrease	Normal/positive
Acute primary respiratory hyperactivity (respiratory alkalosis)	Decrease	Increase	Normal/negative
Uncompensated metabolic acidosis	Normal	Decrease	Negative
Uncompensated metabolic alkalosis	Normal	Increase	Positive
Partially compensated metabolic acidosis	Decrease	Decrease	Negative
Partially compensated metabolic alkalosis	Increase	Increase	Positive
Chronic primary respiratory hypoactivity (compensated respiratory acidosis)	Increase	Normal	Positive
Fully compensated metabolic alkalosis	Increase	Normal	Positive
Chronic primary respiratory hyperactivity (compensated respiratory alkalosis)	Decrease	Normal	Negative
Fully compensated metabolic acidosis	Decrease	Normal	Negative

From Ravel R: *Clinical laboratory medicine*, ed 6, St Louis, 1995, Mosby.
*Base excess results refer to negative (–) values more than 22 and positive (+) values more than 12.

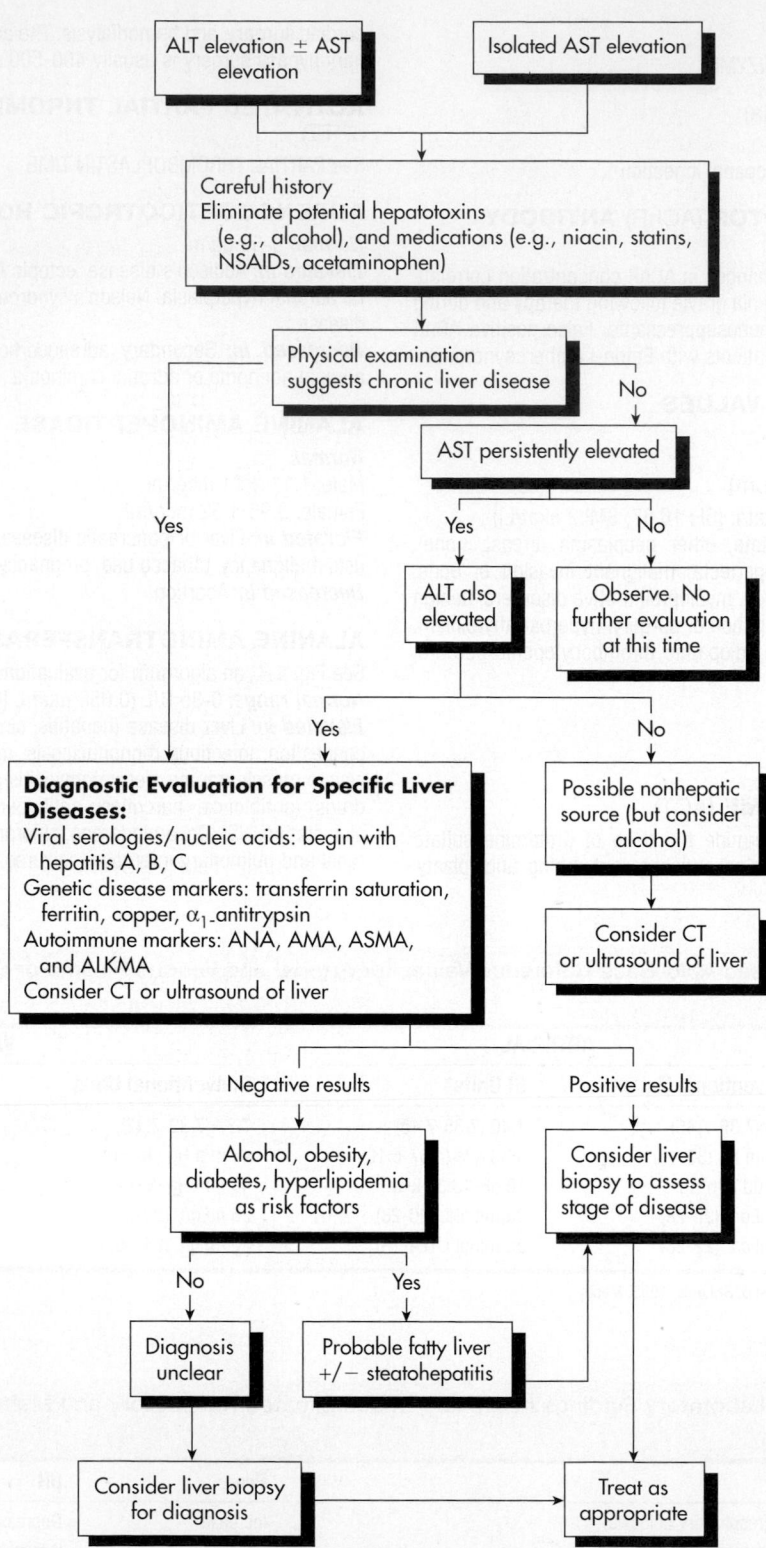

FIGURE 4-1 Approach to the evaluation of isolated elevated levels of serum alanine aminotrans-ferase *(ALT)* and/or aspartate aminotransferase *(AST)* in the asymptomatic patient. *ALKMA,* Anti–liver/kidney microsomal antibody; *AMA,* antimitochondrial antibody; *ANA,* antinuclear antibody; *ASMA,* anti–smooth muscle antibody; *NSAIDs,* nonsteroidal anti-inflammatory drugs. (Modified from Goldman L, Ausiello D [eds]: *Cecil textbook of medicine,* ed 24, Philadelphia, 2012, Saunders.)

ALBUMIN (serum)
Normal range: 4-6 g/dl (40-60 g/L [CF:10; SMI: 1 g/L])
Elevated in: Dehydration (relative increase)
Decreased in: Liver disease, nephrotic syndrome, poor nutritional status, rapid IV hydration, protein-losing enteropathies (e.g., inflammatory bowel disease), severe burns, neoplasia, chronic inflammatory diseases, pregnancy, oral contraceptives, prolonged immobilization, lymphomas, hypervitaminosis A, chronic glomerulonephritis

ALCOHOL DEHYDROGENASE
Normal: 0-7 U/L
Elevated in: Drug-induced hepatocellular damage, obstructive jaundice, malignancy, inflammation, infection

ALDOLASE (serum)
Normal range: 0-6 U/L (0-100 nkat/L [CF: 16.67; SMI: 20 nkat/L])
Elevated in: Muscular dystrophy, rhabdomyolysis, dermatomyositis/polymyositis, trichinosis, acute hepatitis and other liver diseases, myocardial infarction, prostatic carcinoma, hemorrhagic pancreatitis, gangrene, delirium tremens, burns
Decreased in: Loss of muscle mass, late stages of muscular dystrophy

ALDOSTERONE
Normal range:
Recumbent: 50-150 ng/L
Upright: 150-300 ng/L
(Highest levels in neonates, decreasing over time to adult levels)
Elevated in: Primary aldosteronism, secondary aldosteronism, pseudoprimary aldosteronism
Decreased in:
Patient with hypertension: diabetes mellitus, Turner's syndrome, acute alcohol intoxication, excess secretion of deoxycorticosterone, corticosterone, and 18-hydroxycorticosterone
Patient without hypertension: Addison's disease, hypoaldosteronism resulting from renin deficiency, isolated aldosterone deficiency

ALKALINE PHOSPHATASE (ALP) (serum)
See Fig. E4-2 for approach to elevated ALP.
Normal range: 30-120 U/L (0.5-2 µkat/L [CF:0.01667; SMI: 0.1 µkat/L])
Elevated in:
LIVER AND BILIARY TRACT ORIGIN
Extrahepatic bile duct obstruction
Intrahepatic biliary obstruction
Liver cell acute injury
Liver passive congestion
Drug-induced liver cell dysfunction
Space-occupying lesions
Primary biliary cirrhosis
Sepsis
BONE ORIGIN (OSTEOBLAST HYPERACTIVITY)
Physiologic (rapid) bone growth (childhood and adolescence)
Metastatic tumor with osteoblastic reaction
Fracture healing
Paget's disease of bone
CAPILLARY ENDOTHELIAL ORIGIN
Granulation tissue formation (active)
PLACENTAL ORIGIN
Pregnancy
Some parenteral albumin preparations
OTHER
Thyrotoxicosis
Benign transient hyperphosphatasemia
Primary hyperparathyroidism
Decreased in: Hypothyroidism, pernicious anemia, hypophosphatemia, hypervitaminosis D, malnutrition

ALPHA-1-ANTITRYPSIN (serum)
Normal range: 110-140 mg/dl
Decreased in: Homozygous or heterozygous deficiency

ALPHA-1-FETOPROTEIN (serum)
See α-1 FETOPROTEIN

ALT
See ALANINE AMINOTRANSFERASE

ALUMINUM (serum)
Normal range: 0-6 ng/ml
Elevated in: Chronic renal failure on dialysis, parenteral nutrition, industrial exposure

AMA
See ANTIMITOCHONDRIAL ANTIBODY

AMEBIASIS SEROLOGIC TEST
Test description: Test is used to support diagnosis of amebiasis caused by *Entamoeba histolytica*. Serum acute and convalescent titers are drawn 1-3 weeks apart. A fourfold increase in titer is the most indicative result.

AMINOLEVULINIC ACID (δ-ALA) (24-hr urine collection)
Normal: 1.5-7.5 mg/day
Elevated in: Acute porphyrias, lead poisoning, DKA, pregnancy, anticonvulsant drugs, hereditary tyrosinemia
Decreased in: Alcoholic liver disease

AMMONIA (serum)
See Fig. E4-3 for approach to hyperammonemia in pediatric patients.
Normal range: 10-80 µg/dl (5-50 µmol/L [CF: 0.5872; SMI:5 µmol/L])
Elevated in: Hepatic failure, hepatic encephalopathy, Reye's syndrome, portacaval shunt, drugs (diuretics, polymyxin B, methicillin)
Decreased in: Drugs (neomycin, lactulose, tetracycline), renal failure

AMYLASE (serum)
Normal range: 0-130 U/L (0-2.17 µkat/L [CF: 0.01667; SMI: 0.01 µkat/L])
Elevated in: Acute pancreatitis, pancreatic neoplasm, abscess, pseudocyst, ascites, macroamylasemia, perforated peptic ulcer, intestinal obstruction, intestinal infarction, acute cholecystitis, appendicitis, ruptured ectopic pregnancy, salivary gland inflammation, peritonitis, burns, diabetic ketoacidosis, renal insufficiency, drugs (morphine), carcinomatosis (of lung, esophagus, ovary), acute ethanol ingestion, mumps, prostate tumors, post-endoscopic retrograde cholangiopancreatography, bulimia, anorexia nervosa
Decreased in: Advanced chronic pancreatitis, hepatic necrosis, cystic fibrosis

AMYLASE, URINE
See URINE AMYLASE

AMYLOID A PROTEIN (serum)
Normal: <10 mcg/ml
Elevated in: Inflammatory disorders (acute phase–reacting protein), infections, acute coronary syndrome, malignancies

ANA
See ANTINUCLEAR ANTIBODY

ANCA
See ANTINEUTROPHIL CYTOPLASMIC ANTIBODY

ANDROSTENEDIONE (serum)
Normal:
Male: 75-205 ng/dl
Female: 85-275 ng/dl
Elevated in: Congenital adrenal hyperplasia, polycystic ovary syndrome, ectopic ACTH-producing tumor, Cushing's syndrome, hirsutism, hyperplasia of ovarian stroma, ovarian neoplasm
Decreased in: Ovarian failure, adrenal failure, sickle cell anemia

ANGIOTENSIN II
Normal: 10-60 pg/ml
Elevated in: Hypertension, CHF, cirrhosis, renin-secreting renal tumor, volume depletion
Decreased in: ACE inhibitor drugs, ARB drugs, primary aldosteronism, Cushing's syndrome

ANGIOTENSIN-CONVERTING ENZYME (ACE level)
Normal range: <40 nmol/ml/min (<670 nkat/L [CF: 16.67; SMI: 10 nkat/L])
Elevated in: Sarcoidosis, primary biliary cirrhosis, alcoholic liver disease, hyperthyroidism, hyperparathyroidism, diabetes mellitus, amyloidosis, multiple myeloma, lung disease (asbestosis, silicosis, berylliosis, allergic alveolitis, coccidioidomycosis), Gaucher's disease, leprosy

ANH
See ATRIAL NATRIURETIC HORMONE

ANION GAP
Normal range: 9-14 mEq/L
Elevated in: Lactic acidosis, ketoacidosis (diabetes, alcoholic starvation), uremia (chronic renal failure), ingestion of toxins (paraldehyde, methanol, salicylates, ethylene glycol), hyperosmolar nonketotic coma, antibiotics (carbenicillin)
Decreased in: Hypoalbuminemia, severe hypermagnesemia, IgG myeloma, lithium toxicity, laboratory error (falsely decreased sodium or overestimation of bicarbonate or chloride), hypercalcemia of parathyroid origin, antibiotics (e.g., polymyxin)

ANTICARDIOLIPIN ANTIBODY (ACA)
Normal range: Negative. Test includes detection of IgG, IgM, and IgA antibodies to phospholipid, cardiolipin
Present in: Antiphospholipid antibody syndrome, chronic hepatitis C

ANTICOAGULANT
See CIRCULATING ANTICOAGULANT

ANTIDIURETIC HORMONE
Normal range: mOsm/kg 295-300 (4-12 pg/ml)
Elevated in: SIADH, antipsychotic medications, ectopic ADH from systemic neoplasm, Guillain-Barré syndrome, CNS infections, brain tumors, nephrogenic diabetes insipidus
Decreased in: Central diabetes insipidus, nephritic syndrome, psychogenic polydipsias, demeclocycline, lithium, phenytoin, alcohol

ANTI-DNA
Normal range: Absent
Present in: Systemic lupus erythematosus, chronic active hepatitis, infectious mononucleosis, biliary cirrhosis

ANTI-DS DNA
Normal: <25 U
Elevated in: Systemic lupus erythematosus

ANTIGLOBULIN TEST
See COOMBS TEST

ANTIGLOMERULAR BASEMENT ANTIBODY
See GLOMERULAR BASEMENT MEMBRANE ANTIBODY

ANTIHISTONE
Normal: <1 U
Elevated in: Drug-induced lupus erythematosus

ANTIMITOCHONDRIAL ANTIBODY (AMA, Mitochondrial antibody)
Normal range: <1:20 titer
Elevated in: Primary biliary cirrhosis (85%-95%), chronic active hepatitis (25%-30%), cryptogenic cirrhosis (25%-30%)

ANTINEUTROPHIL CYTOPLASMIC ANTIBODY (ANCA)
Positive test: Cytoplasmic pattern (cANCA): positive in Wegener's granulomatosis (see Fig. E4-4 and Table E4-3 for approach to patient with positive c-ANCA)

Perinuclear pattern (pANCA): positive in inflammatory bowel disease, primary biliary cirrhosis, primary sclerosing cholangitis, autoimmune chronic active hepatitis, crescentic glomerulonephritis (see Fig. E4-5 and Table E4-3 for approach to patient with positive P-ANCA)

ANTINUCLEAR ANTIBODY (ANA)
See Fig. E4-6 for approach to positive ANA pattern
Normal range: <1:20 titer
Positive test: Systemic lupus erythematosus (more significant if titer >1:160), drugs (phenytoin, ethosuximide, primidone, methyldopa, hydralazine, carbamazepine, penicillin, procainamide, chlorpromazine, griseofulvin, thiazides), chronic active hepatitis, autoimmune thyroid disease (positive ANA is found in up to 45% of patients), idiopathic thrombocytopenic purpura, multiple sclerosis, rheumatoid arthritis, scleroderma, mixed connective tissue disease, necrotizing vasculitis, Sjögren's syndrome, tuberculosis, pulmonary interstitial fibrosis. Positive ANA results are nonspecific and can be found in healthy individuals (13.8% of the adult general population). Table 4-4 describes diseases associated with ANA subtypes. Fig. 4-7 illustrates various fluorescent ANA test patterns.

TABLE 4-4	Disease-Associated ANA Subtypes
Nuclear Location	**Disease(s)**
"Native" DNA (dsDNA, or dsDNA/ssDNA complex)	SLE (60%-70%; range, 35%-75%) Also PSS (5%-55%), MCTD (11%-25%), RA (5%-40%), DM (5%-25%), SS (5%)
sNP	SLE (50%) Also other collagen diseases
DNP (DNA-histone complex)	SLE (52%) Also MCTD (8%), RA (3%)
Histones	Drug-induced SLE (95%) Also SLE (30%), RA (15%-24%)
ENA Sm	SLE (30%-40%; range, 28%-40%) Also MCTD (0%-8%); RNP (U1-RNP) MCTD (in high titer without any other ANA subtype present: 95%-100%) Also SLE (26%-50%), PSS (11%-22%), RA (10%), SS (3%)
SS-A (Ro)*	SS without RA (60%-70%) Also SLE (26%-50%), neonatal SLE (over 95%), PSS (30%), MCTD (50%), SS with RA (9%), PBC (15%-19%)
SS-B (La)	SS without RA (40%-60%) Also SLE (5%-15%), SS with RA (5%)
Scl-70*	PSS (15%-43%)
Centromere*	CREST syndrome (70%-90%; range, 57%-96%) Also PSS (4%-20%), PBC (12%)
Nucleolar	PSS (scleroderma) (54%-90%) Also SLE (25%-26%), RA (9%)
RAP (RANA)	SS with RA (60%-76%) Also SS without RA (5%)
Jo-1	Polymyositis (30%)
PM-1	Polymyositis or PMS/PSS overlap syndrome (60%-90%) Also DM (17%)
ssDNA	SLE (60%-70%) Also CAH, infectious mononucleosis, RA, chronic GN, chronic infections, PBC

Cytoplasmic Location	**Disease(s)**
Mitochondrial	PBC (90%-100%) Also CAH (7%-30%), cryptogenic cirrhosis (30%), acute hepatitis, viral hepatitis (3%), other liver diseases (0%-20%), SLE (5%), SS and PSS (8%)
Microsomal†	Chronic active hepatitis (60%-80%), Hashimoto's thyroiditis (97%)
Ribosomal	SLE (5%-12%)
Smooth muscle‡	Chronic active hepatitis (60%-91%)

From Ravel R: *Clinical laboratory medicine*, ed 6, St Louis, 1995, Mosby.
*CAH,*Chronic active hepatitis; *DM,* dermatomyositis; *GN,* glomerulonephritis; *MS,* multiple sclerosis; *PBC,* primary biliary cirrhosis; *SS,* Sjögren's syndrome.
*Not detected using rat or mouse liver or kidney tissue method.
†Not detected by cultured cell method.
‡Detected by cultured cells but better with rat or mouse tissue.

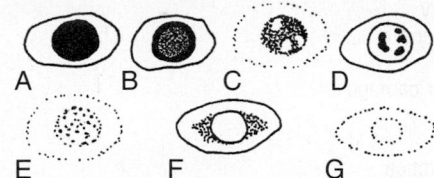

FIGURE 4-7 Fluorescent antinuclear antibody test patterns (HEP-2 cells). A, Solid (homogeneous). **B,** Peripheral (rim). **C,** Speckled. **D,** Nucleolar. **E,** Anticentromere. **F,** Antimitochondrial. **G,** Normal (nonreactive). (From Ravel R [ed]: *Clinical laboratory medicine*, ed 6, St Louis, 1995, Mosby.)

ANTI-RNP ANTIBODY

See EXTRACTABLE NUCLEAR ANTIGEN

ANTI-SCL-70

Normal: Absent
Elevated in: Scleroderma

ANTI-SM (anti-Smith) ANTIBODY

See EXTRACTABLE NUCLEAR ANTIGEN

ANTI-SMOOTH MUSCLE ANTIBODY

See SMOOTH MUSCLE ANTIBODY

ANTISTREPTOLYSIN O TITER (Streptozyme, ASLO titer)

Normal range for adults: <160 Todd units
Elevated in: Streptococcal upper airway infection, acute rheumatic fever, acute glomerulonephritis, increased levels of β-lipoprotein

NOTE: A fourfold increase in titer between acute and convalescent specimens is diagnostic of streptococcal upper airway infection regardless of the initial titer.

ANTITHROMBIN III

See Table 4-5.

TABLE 4-5 Assay Measurements in Heterozygous Antithrombin (ATIII) Deficiency for Diagnosis

Type	ACTIVITY		
	Antigen	Heparin Cofactor	Progressive ATIII
I	Low	Low	Low
II			
Active site defect	Normal	Low	Low
Heparin-binding site defect	Normal	Low	Normal

From Hoffman R et al: *Hematology: basic principles and practice*, ed 5, Philadelphia, 2009, Churchill Livingstone.

Normal range: 81%-120% of normal activity; 17-30 mg/dl
Decreased in: Hereditary deficiency of antithrombin III, disseminated intravascular coagulation, pulmonary embolism, cirrhosis, thrombolytic therapy, chronic liver failure, postsurgery, third trimester of pregnancy, oral contraceptives, nephrotic syndrome, IV heparin >3 days, sepsis, acute leukemia, carcinoma, thrombophlebitis
Elevated in: Warfarin drugs, post-myocardial infarction

APOLIPOPROTEIN A-1 (Apo A-1)

Normal: Desirable >120 mg/dl
Elevated in: Familial hyperalphalipoproteinemia, statins, niacin, estrogens, weight loss, familial cholesteryl ester transfer protein (CETP) deficiency
Decreased in: Familial hypoalphalipoproteinemia, Tangier disease, diuretics, androgens, cigarette smoking, hepatocellular disorders, chronic renal failure, nephritic syndrome, coronary heart disease, cholestasis

APOLIPOPROTEIN B (Apo B)

Normal: Desirable <100 mg/dl; high risk >120 mg/dl
Elevated in: High saturated fat diet, high-cholesterol diet, hyperapobetalipoproteinemia, familial combined hyperlipidemia, anabolic steroids, diuretics, beta-blockers, corticosteroids, progestins, diabetes, hypothyroidism, chronic renal failure, liver disease, Cushing's syndrome, coronary heart disease
Decreased in: Statins, niacin, low-cholesterol diet, malnutrition, abetalipoproteinemia, hypobetalipoproteinemia, hyperthyroidism

ARTERIAL BLOOD GASES

Normal range:
Po_2: 75-100 mm Hg
Pco_2: 35-45 mm Hg
HCO_3: 24-28 mEq/L
pH: 7.35-7.45
Abnormal values: Acid-base disturbances (see the following)
METABOLIC ACIDOSIS
Metabolic acidosis with increased AG (AG acidosis)
Lactic acidosis
Ketoacidosis (diabetes mellitus, alcoholic ketoacidosis)
Uremia (chronic renal failure)
Ingestion of toxins (paraldehyde, methanol, salicylate, ethylene glycol)
High-fat diet (mild acidosis)
Metabolic acidosis with normal AG (hyperchloremic acidosis)
Renal tubular acidosis (including acidosis of aldosterone deficiency)
Intestinal loss of HCO_3^- (diarrhea, pancreatic fistula)
Carbonic anhydrase inhibitors (e.g., acetazolamide)
Dilutional acidosis (as a result of rapid infusion of bicarbonate-free isotonic saline)
Ingestion of exogenous acids (ammonium chloride, methionine, cystine, calcium chloride)
Ileostomy
Ureterosigmoidostomy
Drugs: amiloride, triamterene, spironolactone, β-blockers
RESPIRATORY ACIDOSIS
Pulmonary disease (COPD, severe pneumonia, pulmonary edema, interstitial fibrosis)
Airway obstruction (foreign body, severe bronchospasm, laryngospasm)
Thoracic cage disorders (pneumothorax, flail chest, kyphoscoliosis)
Defects in muscles of respiration (myasthenia gravis, hypokalemia, muscular dystrophy)
Defects in peripheral nervous system (amyotrophic lateral sclerosis, poliomyelitis, Guillain-Barré syndrome, botulism, tetanus, organophosphate poisoning, spinal cord injury)
Depression of respiratory center (anesthesia, narcotics, sedatives, vertebral artery embolism or thrombosis, increased intracranial pressure)
Failure of mechanical ventilator
METABOLIC ALKALOSIS
Divided into chloride-responsive (urinary chloride <15 mEq/L) and chloride-resistant forms (urinary chloride level >15 mEq/L)
Chloride-responsive:
Vomiting
Nasogastric (NG) suction
Diuretics
Posthypercapnic alkalosis
Stool losses (laxative abuse, cystic fibrosis, villous adenoma)
Massive blood transfusion
Exogenous alkali administration
Chloride-resistant:
Hyperadrenocorticoid states (Cushing's syndrome, primary hyperaldosteronism, secondary mineralocorticoidism [licorice, chewing tobacco])
Hypomagnesemia
Hypokalemia
Bartter's syndrome
RESPIRATORY ALKALOSIS
Hypoxemia (pneumonia, pulmonary embolism, atelectasis, high-altitude living)
Drugs (salicylates, xanthines, progesterone, epinephrine, thyroxine, nicotine)
Central nervous system (CNS) disorders (tumor, cerebrovascular accident [CVA], trauma, infections)

Psychogenic hyperventilation (anxiety, hysteria)
Hepatic encephalopathy
Gram-negative sepsis
Hyponatremia
Sudden recovery from metabolic acidosis
Assisted ventilation

ARTHROCENTESIS FLUID
Interpretation of results:
1. **Color:** Normally it is clear or pale yellow; cloudiness indicates inflammatory process or presence of crystals, cell debris, fibrin, or triglycerides.
2. **Viscosity:** Normally it has a high viscosity because of hyaluronate; when fluid is placed on a slide, it can be stretched to a string >2 cm in length before separating (low viscosity indicates breakdown of hyaluronate [lysosomal enzymes from leukocytes] or the presence of edema fluid).
3. **Mucin clot:** Add 1 ml of fluid to 5 ml of a 5% acetic acid solution and allow 1 minute for the clot to form; a firm clot (does not fragment on shaking) is normal and indicates the presence of large molecules of hyaluronic acid (this test is nonspecific and infrequently done).
4. **Glucose:** Normally it approximately equals serum glucose level; a difference of more than 40 mg/dl is suggestive of infection.
5. **Protein:** Total protein concentration is <2.5 g/dl in the normal synovial fluid; it is elevated in inflammatory and septic arthritis.
6. **Microscopic examination for crystals**
   a. **Gout:** Monosodium urate crystals
   b. **Pseudogout:** Calcium pyrophosphate dihydrate crystals

ASLO TITER
See ANTISTREPTOLYSIN O TITER

ASPARTATE AMINOTRANSFERASE (AST, SGOT)
Normal range: 0-35 U/L (0-0.58 μkat/L [CF: 0.01667, SMI: 0.01μkat/L])
Elevated in:
HEART
Acute myocardial infarction
Pericarditis (active: some cases)
LIVER
Hepatitis virus, Epstein-Barr, or cytomegalovirus infection
Active cirrhosis
Liver passive congestion or hypoxia
Alcohol- or drug-induced liver dysfunction
Space-occupying lesions (active)
Fatty liver (severe)
Extrahepatic biliary obstruction (early)
Drug-induced
SKELETAL MUSCLE
Acute skeletal muscle injury
Muscle inflammation (infectious or noninfectious)
Muscular dystrophy (active)

Recent surgery
Delirium tremens
KIDNEY
Acute injury or damage
Renal infarct
OTHER
Intestinal infarction
Shock
Cholecystitis
Acute pancreatitis
Hypothyroidism
Heparin therapy (60%-80% of cases)
Fig. 4-1 describes an approach to the evaluation of AST elevation.

ATRIAL NATRIURETIC HORMONE (ANH)
Normal: 20-77 pg/ml
Elevated in: CHF, volume overload, cardiovascular disease with high filling pressure
Decreased with: Prazosin and other alpha blockers

B-TYPE NATRIURETIC PEPTIDE (BNP)
Normal range: up to 100 mcg/L. Natriuretic peptides are secreted to regulate fluid volume, blood pressure, and electrolyte balance. They have activity in both the central and peripheral nervous systems. In humans the main source of circulatory BNP is the heart ventricles.
Elevated in: Heart failure. This test is useful to differentiate heart failure patients from those with chronic obstructive pulmonary disease presenting with dyspnea. Levels are also increased in asymptomatic left ventricular dysfunction, arterial and pulmonary hypertension, cardiac hypertrophy, valvular heart disease, arrhythmia, and acute coronary syndrome. See Figure 4-8.

BASOPHIL COUNT
Normal range:
0.4%-1% of total WBC; 40-100/mm^3
Elevated in: Leukemia, inflammatory processes, polycythemia vera, Hodgkin's lymphoma, hemolytic anemia, after splenectomy, myeloid metaplasia, myxedema
Decreased in: Stress, hypersensitivity reaction, steroids, pregnancy, hyperthyroidism, postirradiation

BICARBONATE
Normal: Arterial: 21-28 mEq/L
Venous: 22-29 mEq/L
Elevated in: Metabolic alkalosis, compensated respiratory acidosis, diuretics, corticosteroids, laxative abuse
Decreased in: Metabolic acidosis, compensated respiratory alkalosis, acetazolamide, cyclosporine, cholestyramine, methanol or ethylene glycol poisoning

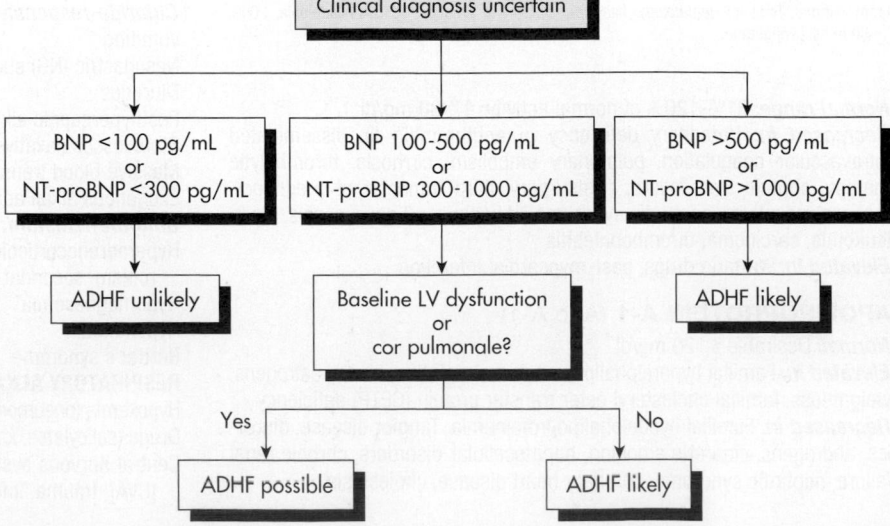

FIGURE 4-8 Interpretation of natriuretic peptide levels. *ADHF,* Acute decompensated heart failure; *BNP,* B-type natriuretic peptide; *NT-proBNP,* inactive N-terminal fragment of BNP. (From Adams JG, et al: *Emergency medicine, clinical essentials,* ed 2, Philadelphia, 2013, Elsevier.)

BILE, URINE
See URINE BILE

BILIRUBIN, DIRECT (conjugated bilirubin)
Normal range:
0-0.2 mg/dl (0-4 µmol/L [CF: 17.10; SMI: 2 µmol/L])
Elevated in: Hepatocellular disease, biliary obstruction, drug-induced cholestasis, hereditary disorders (Dubin-Johnson syndrome, Rotor's syndrome)

BILIRUBIN, INDIRECT (unconjugated bilirubin)
Normal range:
0-1.0 mg/dl (2-18 µmol/L [CF: 17.10; SMI: 2 µmol/L])
Elevated in:
Increased bilirubin production (if normal liver, serum unconjugated bilirubin is usually less than 4 mg/100 ml)
  Hemolytic anemia
    Acquired
    Congenital
  Resorption from extravascular sources
    Hematomas
    Pulmonary infarcts
  Excessive ineffective erythropoiesis
    Congenital (congenital dyserythropoietic anemias)
    Acquired (pernicious anemia, severe lead poisoning; if present, bilirubinemia is usually mild)
Defective hepatic unconjugated bilirubin clearance (defective uptake or conjugation)
  Severe liver disease
  Gilbert's syndrome
  Crigler-Najjar type I or II
  Drug-induced inhibition
  Portacaval shunt
  Congestive heart failure
  Hyperthyroidism (uncommon)

BILIRUBIN, TOTAL
See Fig. E4-9 and Table E4-6, for evaluation of hyperbilirubinemia and liver disease.
Normal range:
0-1.0 mg/dl (2-18 µmol/L [CF: 17.10, SMI: 2 µmol/L])
Elevated in: Liver disease (hepatitis, cirrhosis, cholangitis, neoplasm, biliary obstruction, infectious mononucleosis), hereditary disorders (Gilbert's disease, Dubin-Johnson syndrome), drugs (steroids, statins, niacin, acetaminophen, diphenylhydantoin, phenothiazines, penicillin, erythromycin, clindamycin, captopril, amphotericin B, sulfonamides, azathioprine, isoniazid, 5-aminosalicylic acid, allopurinol, methyldopa, indomethacin, halothane, oral contraceptives, procainamide, tolbutamide, labetalol), hemolysis, pulmonary embolism or infarct, hepatic congestion secondary to congestive heart failure

BILIRUBIN, URINE
See URINE BILE

BLADDER TUMOR ASSOCIATED ANTIGEN
Normal: ≤14 U/ml. Test is used to detect bladder cancer recurrence. Sensitivity 57%-83% and specificity 68%-72%.
Elevated in: Bladder cancer, renal stones, nephritis, UTI, hematuria, renal cancer, cystitis, recent bladder or urinary tract trauma

BLEEDING TIME (modified Ivy method)
See Fig. E4-10 for evaluation of patients with prolonged bleeding time.
Normal range: 2 to 9.5 min
Elevated in: Thrombocytopenia, capillary wall abnormalities, platelet abnormalities (Bernard-Soulier disease, Glanzmann's disease), drugs (aspirin, warfarin, anti-inflammatory medications, streptokinase, urokinase, dextran, β-lactam antibiotics, moxalactam), disseminated intravascular coagulation, cirrhosis, uremia, myeloproliferative disorders, von Willebrand's disease.

Bleeding time tests are no longer performed at many hospitals and have been replaced by the platelet function analyzer (PFA-100) assay.

BLOOD VOLUME, TOTAL
Normal:
60-80 ml/kg
Elevated in: Polycythemia vera, pulmonary disease, CHF, renal insufficiency, pregnancy, acidosis, thyrotoxicosis
Decreased In: Anemia, hemorrhage, vomiting, diarrhea, dehydration, burns, starvation

BNP
See B-TYPE NATRIURETIC PEPTIDE

BORDETELLA PERTUSSIS SEROLOGY
Test description: PCR of nasopharyngeal aspirates or secretions is used to identify *Bordetella pertussis,* the organism responsible for whooping cough.

BRCA ANALYSIS
DESCRIPTION OF ANALYSIS
Comprehensive BRCA analysis:
  BRCA1: Full sequence determination in both forward and reverse directions of approximately 5500 base pairs comprising 22 coding exons and one noncoding exon (exon 4) and approximately 800 adjacent base pairs in the noncoding intervening sequence (intron). Exon 1, which is noncoding, is not analyzed. The wild-type *BRCA1* gene encodes a protein comprising 1863 amino acids.
  BRCA2: Full sequence determination in both forward and reverse directions of approximately 10,200 base pairs comprising 26 coding exons and approximately 900 adjacent base pairs in the noncoding intervening sequence (intron). Exon 1, which is noncoding, is not analyzed. The wild-type *BRCA2* gene encodes a protein comprising 3418 amino acids.
  The noncoding intronic regions of *BRCA1* and *BRCA2* that are analyzed do not extend more than 20 base pairs proximal to the 5' end and 10 base pairs distal to the 3' end of each exon.
  Single-site BRCA analysis: DNA sequence analysis for a specified mutation in *BRCA1* and/or *BRCA2.*
  Multisite 3 BRCA analysis: DNA sequence analysis of specific portions of *BRCA1* exon 2, *BRCA1* exon 20, and *BRCA2* exon 11 designed to detect only mutations 187delAG and 5385insC in *BRCA1* and 6174delT in *BRCA2.*
Interpretive Criteria:
  "Positive for a deleterious mutation": Includes all mutations (nonsense, insertions, deletions) that prematurely terminate ("truncate") the protein product of *BRCA1* at least 10 amino acids from the C-terminus, or the protein product of *BRCA2* at least 110 amino acids from the C-terminus (based on documentation of deleterious mutations in *BRCA1* and *BRCA2*).
  In addition, specific missense mutations and noncoding intervening sequence (IVS) mutations are recognized as deleterious on the basis of data derived from linkage analysis of high-risk families, functional assays, biochemical evidence, and/or demonstration of abnormal mRNA transcript processing.
  "Genetic variant, suspected deleterious": Includes genetic variants for which the available evidence indicates a likelihood, but not proof, that the mutation is deleterious. The specific evidence supporting such an interpretation will be summarized for individual variants on each such report.
  "Genetic variant, favor polymorphism": Includes genetic variants for which available evidence indicates that the variant is highly unlikely to contribute substantially to cancer risk. The specific evidence supporting such an interpretation will be summarized for individual variants on each such report.
  "Genetic variant of uncertain significance": Includes missense mutations and mutations that occur in analyzed intronic regions whose clinical significance has not yet been determined, as well as chain-terminating mutations that truncate *BRCA1* and *BRCA2* distal to amino acid positions 1853 and 3308, respectively.

"No deleterious mutation detected": Includes nontruncating genetic variants observed at an allele frequency of approximately 1% of a suitable control population (providing that no data suggest clinical significance), as well as all genetic variants for which published data demonstrate absence of substantial clinical significance. Also includes mutations in the protein-coding region that neither alter the amino acid sequence nor are predicted to significantly affect exon splicing, and base pair alterations in noncoding portions of the gene that have been demonstrated to have no deleterious effect on the length or stability of the mRNA transcript.

There may be uncommon genetic abnormalities in *BRCA1* and *BRCA2* that will not be detected by *BRCA* analysis. This analysis, however, is believed to rule out the majority of abnormalities in these genes, which are believed responsible for most hereditary susceptibility to breast and ovarian cancer.

"Specific variant/mutation not identified": Specific and designated deleterious mutations or variants of uncertain clinical significance are not present in the individual being tested. If one (or rarely two) specific deleterious mutations have been identified in a family member, a negative analysis for the specific mutation(s) indicates that the tested individual is at the general population risk of developing breast or ovarian cancer.

BREATH HYDROGEN TEST (hydrogen breath test)

Normal: This test is for bacterial overgrowth. H_2 excretion fasting: 4.6 ± 5.1, after lactulose, early increase <12. Lactulose usually results in a colonic response >30 min after ingestion.

Elevated in: A high fasting breath H_2 level and an increase of at least 12 ppm within 30 min after lactulose challenge are indicative of bacterial overgrowth in the small intestine. The increase must precede the colonic response.

False positives in: Accelerated gastric emptying, laxative use

False negatives in: Use of antibiotics and patients who are nonhydrogen producers

BUN

See UREA NITROGEN, BLOOD

C282Y AND H63D MUTATION ANALYSIS

Procedure: Detection of the C282Y and H63D mutations is accomplished by amplification of exons 2 and 4 of the *HFE* gene on chromosome 6 by polymerase chain reaction (PCR) followed by allele-specific hybridization and chemiluminescent detection of hybridized probes. H63D is viewed by some as a polymorphism rather than a mutation because of its prevalence in the population, because 15% of the individuals affected with hereditary hemochromatosis (HH) are compound heterozygotes for C282Y and H63D and about 1% of patients are H63D homozygotes, which suggests that H63D may be causative in the development of the disorder at reduced penetrance.

Interpretation: Homozygosity for the C282Y mutation has been associated with an increased risk of being affected with HH compared with the general population. The genotype is observed in 60%-90% of individuals affected with HH and occurs in less than 1% of the general population. However, approximately 25% of asymptomatic individuals with this genotype do not develop the disorder.

C3

See COMPLEMENT

C4

See COMPLEMENT

CALCITONIN (serum)

Normal range: <100 pg/ml (<100 ng/L [CF: 1; SMI: 10 ng/L])

Elevated in: Medullary carcinoma of the thyroid (particularly if level >1500 pg/ml), carcinoma of the breast, apudomas, carcinoids, renal failure, thyroiditis

CALCIUM (serum)

Normal range: 8.8-10.3 mg/dl (2.2-2.58 µmol/L [CF: 0.2495; SMI: 0.02 µmol/L])

ELEVATED

Relatively common:

Neoplasia
Bone primary
Myeloma
Acute leukemia
Nonbone solid tumors
Breast
Lung
Squamous nonpulmonary
Kidney
Neoplasm secretion of parathyroid hormone-related protein (PTHrP, "ectopic PTH")
Primary hyperparathyroidism
Thiazide diuretics
Tertiary (renal) hyperparathyroidism
Idiopathic
Spurious (artifactual) hypercalcemia
Dehydration
Serum protein elevation
Laboratory technical problem (lab error)

Relatively uncommon:

Sarcoidosis
Hyperthyroidism
Immobilization (mostly seen in children and adolescents)
Diuretic phase of acute renal tubular necrosis
Vitamin D intoxication
Milk-alkali syndrome
Addison's disease
Lithium therapy
Idiopathic hypercalcemia of infancy
Acromegaly
Theophylline toxicity

Table 4-7 describes the laboratory differential diagnosis of hypercalcemia.

DECREASED

Artifactual
Hypoalbuminemia
Hemodilution
Primary hypoparathyroidism
Pseudohypoparathyroidism
Vitamin D related
Vitamin D deficiency
Malabsorption
Renal failure
Magnesium deficiency
Sepsis
Chronic alcoholism
Tumor lysis syndrome
Rhabdomyolysis
Alkalosis (respiratory or metabolic)
Acute pancreatitis
Drug-induced hypocalcemia
Large doses of magnesium sulfate
Anticonvulsants
Mithramycin
Gentamicin
Cimetidine

Table 4-8 describes the laboratory differential diagnosis of hypocalcemia.

CALCIUM, URINE

See URINE CALCIUM

CANCER ANTIGEN 15-3 (CA 15-3)

Normal: <30 U/ml

Elevated in: Approximately 80% of women with metastatic breast cancer. Clinical sensitivity is 0.60, specificity 0.87, positive predictive value 0.91. This test is generally used to predict recurrence of breast cancer and

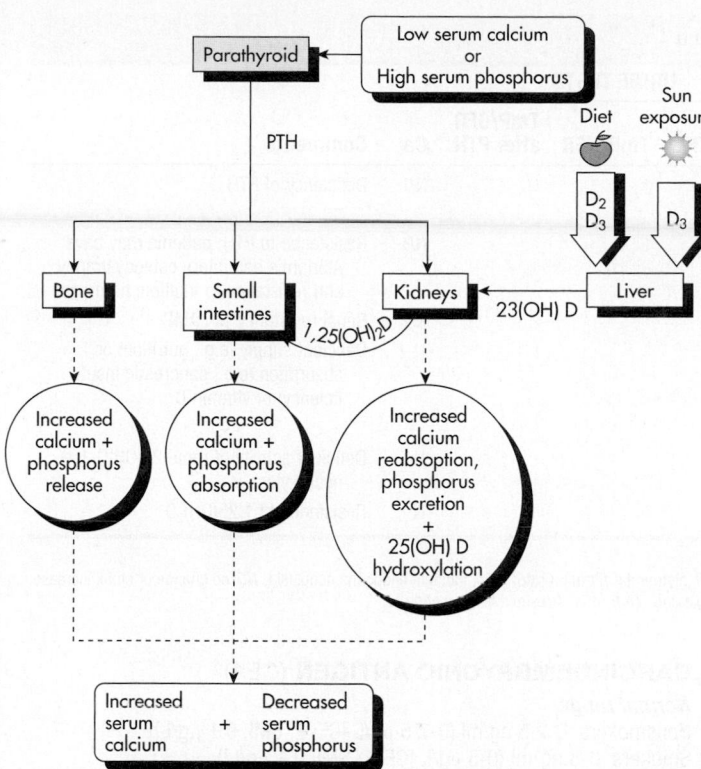

FIGURE 4-11 Calcium homeostasis. Parathyroid hormone (PTH) is released from the parathyroid glands in response to hypocalcemia and hyperphosphatemia. PTH acts on bone, the small intestines, and the kidneys to effect a rise in serum calcium and a net decrease in serum phosphorus. Hydroxylation of inactive forms of vitamin D occurs in the liver and kidneys. 1,25(OH)2D facilitates intestinal absorption of calcium and phosphorus. *1,25(OH)2D*, 1,25-Dihydroxyvitamin D; *25(OH) D*, 25-hydroxyvitamin D; *D2*, vitamin D2; *D3*, vitamin D3. (From Adams JG, et al: *Emergency medicine, clinical essentials*, ed 2, Philadelphia, 2013, Elsevier.)

evaluate response to therapy. May also be elevated in liver cancer, pancreatic cancer, ovarian cancer, colorectal cancer. Elevations can also occur with benign breast and liver disease.

CANCER ANTIGEN 27-29 (CA 27-29)

Normal: <38 U/ml

Elevated in: Approximately 75% of women with metastatic breast cancer. Clinical sensitivity is 0.57, specificity 0.97, positive predictive value 0.83, negative predictive value 0.92. This test is generally used to predict recurrence of breast cancer and evaluate response to therapy. May also be elevated in liver cancer, pancreatic cancer, ovarian cancer, colorectal cancer. Elevations can also occur with benign breast and liver disease.

CANCER ANTIGEN 72-4 (CA 72-4)

Normal: <4.0 ng/ml

Elevated in: Gastric cancer (elevated in >50% of patients). Often used in combination with CA 72-4, CA 19-9, and CEA to monitor gastric cancer after treatment.

CANCER ANTIGEN 125 (CA 125)

Normal range: <1.4%

This test uses an antibody against antigen from tissue culture of an ovarian tumor cell line. Various published evaluations report sensitivity of about 75%-80% in patients with ovarian carcinoma. There is also an appreciable incidence of elevated values in nonovarian malignancies and in certain benign conditions (see below). Test values may transiently increase during chemotherapy.

MALIGNANT

Epithelial ovarian carcinoma, 75%-80% (range, 25%-92%; better in serous than mucinous cystadenocarcinoma)

Endometrial carcinoma, 25%-48% (2%-90%)

Pancreatic carcinoma, 59%

Colorectal carcinoma, 20% (15%-56%)

Endocervical adenocarcinoma, 83%

Squamous cervical or vaginal carcinoma, 7%-14%

TABLE 4-7 Laboratory Differential Diagnosis of Hypercalcemia

Diagnosis	PLASMA TESTS					URINE TESTS			Comments
	Ca	PO₄	PTH	25(OH)D	1,25(OH)₂D	cAMP	TmP/GFR	Ca	
Primary hyperparathyroidism	↑	N/↓	↑	N	N/↑	↑	↓	↑	Parathyroid adenoma most common
MEN I									Parathyroid hyperplasia; also includes pituitary and pancreatic neoplasms
MEN IIa									Parathyroid hyperplasia; also includes medullary thyroid carcinoma and pheochromocytoma
MEN IIb									Parathyroid disease uncommon, primarily medullary thyroid carcinoma and pheochromocytoma
FHH	↑	N	N/↑	N	N	N/↑	N/↓	↓↓	Autosomal dominant inheritance; hypercalcemia present within first decade; benign
Malignancy									
Solid tumor, humoral	↑	N/↓	↓	N	N	↑	↓	↑↑	Primarily epidermoid tumors; PTH-related protein(s) is mediator
Solid tumor, osteolytic	↑	N/↑	↓	N	N	↓	↑	↑↑	
Lymphoma	↑	N/↑	↓	N/↓	↑	↓	↑	↑↑	
Granulomatous disease	↑	N/↑	↓	N/↓	↑↑	↓	↑	↑↑	Sarcoid most common etiology
Vitamin D intoxication	↑	N/↑	↓	↑↑	N	↓	↑	↑↑	
Hyperthyroidism	↑	N	↓	N	N	N	N	↑↑	Plasma concentrations of T₄ and/or T₃ are elevated

From Moore WT, Eastman RC: *Diagnostic endocrinology*, ed 2, St Louis, 1996, Mosby.

Ca, Calcium; *cAMP*, cyclic adenosine monophosphate; *FHH*, familial hypocalciuric hypercalcemia; *GFR*, glomerular filtration rate; *MEN*, multiple endocrine neoplasia; *25(OH)D*, 25 hydroxyvitamin D; *PO₄*, phosphate; *PTH*, parathyroid hormone; *T₃*, triiodothyronine; *T₄*, thyroxine; *TmP*, renal threshold for phosphorus.

TABLE 4-8 Laboratory Differential Diagnosis of Hypocalcemia

Diagnosis	PLASMA TESTS					URINE TESTS					Comments
	Ca	PO₄	PTH	25(OH)D	1,25(OH)₂D	cAMP	cAMP after PTH	TmP/GFR	TmP/GFR after PTH	Ca	

Diagnosis	Ca	PO$_4$	PTH	25(OH)D	1,25(OH)$_2$D	cAMP	cAMP after PTH	TmP/GFR	TmP/GFR after PTH	Ca	Comments
Hypoparathyroidism	↓	↑	N/↓	N	↓	↓	↑↑	↑	↓↓	N/↓	Deficiency of PTH
Pseudohypoparathyroidism											
Type I	↓	↑	↑↑	N	↓	↓	NC	↑	↑	N/↓	Resistance to PTH; patients may have Albright's hereditary osteodystrophy and resistance to multiple hormones
Type II	↓	N	↑↑	N	↓	↓	↑	↑	↑	N/↓	Renal resistance to cAMP
Vitamin D deficiency	↓	N/↓	↑↑	↓↓	N/↓	↑	↑	↓	↓	↓↓	Deficient supply (e.g., nutrition) or absorption (e.g., pancreatic insufficiency) of vitamin D
Vitamin D–dependent Rickets											
Type I	↓	N/↓	↑↑	N	↓	↑↑		↓		↓↓	Deficient activity of renal 25(OH)D-1α-hydroxylase
Type II	↓	N/↓	↑↑	N	↑↑	↑		↓		↓↓	Resistance to 1,25(OH)₂D

From Moore WT, Eastman RC: *Diagnostic endocrinology,* ed 2, St Louis, 1996, Mosby.
Ca, Calcium; *cAMP,* cyclic adenosine monophosphate; *FHH,* familial hypocalciuric hypercalcemia; *GFR,* glomerular filtration rate; *MEN,* multiple endocrine neoplasia; *NC,* no change or small increase; *(OH)D,* hydroxycalciferol D; *PO₄,* phosphate; *PTH,* parathyroid hormone; *T₃,* triiodothyronine; *T₄,* thyroxine; *TmP,* renal threshold for phosphorus.

Lung carcinoma, 32%
Breast carcinoma, 12%-40%
Lymphoma, 35%
BENIGN
Cirrhosis, 40%-80%
Acute pancreatitis, 38%
Acute peritonitis, 75%
Endometriosis, 88%
Acute pelvic inflammatory disease, 33%
Pregnancy first trimester, 2%-24%
During menstruation (occasionally)
Renal failure (?frequency)
Normal persons, 0.6%-1.4%

CAPTOPRIL STIMULATION TEST

Normal: Test performed by giving 25 mg captopril orally after overnight fast. Patient should be seated during test. After captopril, aldosterone <15 ng/dl, renin >2 ng angiotensin L/ml/hr.
Interpretation: In patients with primary aldosteronism, plasma aldosterone remains high and plasma renin activity remains low after captopril.

CARBAMAZEPINE (Tegretol)

Normal therapeutic range: 4-12 mcg/ml

CARBOHYDRATE ANTIGEN 19-9

Normal: <37.0 U/ml
Elevated in: GI cancer, most frequently pancreatic cancer. Amount of elevation has no relation to tumor mass. Elevations can also occur with cirrhosis, cholangitis, and chronic or acute pancreatitis.

CARBON DIOXIDE, PARTIAL PRESSURE

Normal:
Male: 35-48 mm Hg
Female: 32-45 mm Hg
Elevated in: Respiratory acidosis
Decreased in: Respiratory alkalosis

CARBON MONOXIDE

See CARBOXYHEMOGLOBIN

CARBOXYHEMOGLOBIN

Normal range: Saturation of hemoglobin <2%; smokers <9%
Elevated in: Smoking, exposure to smoking, exposure to automobile exhaust fumes, malfunctioning gas-burning appliances

CARCINOEMBRYONIC ANTIGEN (CEA)

Normal range:
Nonsmokers: 0-2.5 ng/ml (0-2.5 µg/L [CF: 1; SMI: 0.1 µg/L])
Smokers: 0-5 ng/ml (0-5 µg/L [CF: 1; SMI: 0.1 µg/L])
Elevated in:
Colorectal carcinomas, pancreatic carcinomas, and metastatic disease (usually produce higher elevations: >20 ng/ml)
Carcinomas of the esophagus, stomach, small intestine, liver, breast, ovary, lung, and thyroid (usually produce lesser elevations)
Benign conditions (smoking, inflammatory bowel disease, hypothyroidism, cirrhosis, pancreatitis, infections) (usually produce levels <10 ng/ml)

CAROTENE (serum)

Normal range: 50-250 µg/dl (0.9-4.6 µmol/L [CF: 0.01863; SMI: 0.1 µmol/L])
Elevated in: Carotenemia, chronic nephritis, diabetes mellitus, hypothyroidism, nephrotic syndrome, hyperlipidemia
Decreased in: Fat malabsorption, steatorrhea, pancreatic insufficiency, lack of carotenoids in diet, high fever, liver disease

CATECHOLAMINES, URINE

See URINE CATECHOLAMINES

CBC

See COMPLETE BLOOD COUNT

CD40 LIGAND

Normal: <5 mcg/L. CD40 ligand is a soluble protein that is shed from activated leukocytes and platelets and used in risk stratification for acute coronary syndrome.
Elevated in: Acute coronary syndrome. Increased CD40 ligand is associated with higher incidence of death or nonfatal MI.

CD4+ T-LYMPHOCYTE COUNT (CD4+ T-cells)

Calculated as total WBC × % lymphocytes × % lymphocytes stained with CD4.

This test is used primarily to evaluate immune dysfunction in HIV infection. It is useful as a prognostic indicator and as a criterion for initiating prophylaxis for several opportunistic infections that are sequelae of HIV infection. Progressive depletion of CD4+ T-lymphocytes is associated with an increased likelihood of clinical complications (Table 4-9).

CEA

See CARCINOEMBRYONIC ANTIGEN

TABLE 4-9 Relation of CD4 Lymphocyte Counts to the Onset of Certain HIV-Associated Infections and Neoplasms in North America

CD4 Count (Cells/mm³)*	Opportunistic Infection or Neoplasm	Frequency (%)†
>500	Herpes zoster, polydermatomal	5-10
200-500	*Mycobacterium tuberculosis* infection, pulmonary and extrapulmonary	2-20
	Oral hairy leukoplakia	40-70
	Candida pharyngitis (thrush)	40-70
	Recurrent *Candida* vaginitis	15-30 (F)
	Kaposi's sarcoma, mucocutaneous	15-30 (M)
	Bacterial pneumonia, recurrent	15-20
	Cervical neoplasia	1-2 (F)
100-200	*Pneumocystis carinii* pneumonia	15-60
	Herpes simplex, chronic, ulcerative	5-10
	Histoplasma capsulatum infection, disseminated	0-20
	Kaposi's sarcoma, visceral	3-8 (M)
	Progressive multifocal leukoencephalopathy	2-3
	Lymphoma, non-Hodgkin's	2-5
<100	*Candida* esophagitis	15-20
	Mycobacterium avium-intracellulare, disseminated	25-40
	Toxoplasma gondii encephalitis	5-25
	Cryptosporidium enteritis	2-10
	CMV retinitis	20-35
	Cryptococcus neoformans encephalitis	2-5
	CMV esophagitis or colitis	6-12
	Lymphoma, central nervous system	4-8

From Andreoli TE (ed): *Cecil essentials of medicine,* ed 5, Philadelphia, 2000, Saunders.

CMV, Cytomegalovirus; *F,* exclusively in women; *HIV,* human immunodeficiency virus; *M,* almost exclusively in men.

*Table indicates CD4 count at which specific infections or neoplasms generally begin to appear. Each infection may recur or progress during the subsequent course of HIV disease.

†Even within the United States, great regional differences in the incidence of specific opportunistic infections are apparent. For example, disseminated histoplasmosis is common in the Mississippi River drainage area but very rare in individuals who have lived exclusively on the East or West Coast.

CEREBROSPINAL FLUID (CSF)

Interpretation of results:

Appearance of the fluid

Clear: normal.

Yellow color (xanthochromia) in the supernatant of centrifuged CSF within 1 hour or less after collection is usually the result of previous bleeding (subarachnoid hemorrhage); it may also be caused by increased CSF protein, melanin from meningeal melanosarcomas, or carotenoids.

Pinkish color is usually the result of a bloody tap; the color generally clears progressively from tubes 1 to 4 (the supernatant is usually crystal clear in traumatic taps).

Turbidity usually indicates the presence of leukocytes (bleeding introduces approximately 1 WBC/500 RBCs into the CSF).

CSF pressure: elevated pressure can be seen with meningitis, meningoencephalitis, pseudotumor cerebri, mass lesions, and intracerebral bleeding.

Cell count: in the adult the CSF is normally free of cells (although up to 5 mononuclear cells/mm³ is considered normal); the presence of granulocytes is never normal.

Neutrophils: seen in bacterial meningitis, early viral meningoencephalitis, and early tuberculosis (TB) meningitis.

Increased lymphocytes: TB meningitis, viral meningoencephalitis, syphilitic meningoencephalitis, fungal meningitis.

Protein: serum proteins are generally too large to cross the normal blood–CSF barrier; however, increased CSF protein is seen with meningeal inflammation, traumatic tap, increased CNS synthesis, tissue degeneration, obstruction to CSF circulation, and Guillain-Barré syndrome.

Glucose

Decreased glucose is seen with bacterial meningitis, TB meningitis, fungal meningitis, subarachnoid hemorrhage, and some cases of viral meningitis.

A mild increase in CSF glucose can be seen in patients with very elevated serum glucose levels.

Table 4-10 describes CSF findings in central nervous system disorders.

CERULOPLASMIN (serum)

Normal range: 20-35 mg/dl (200-350 mg/L [CF: 10; SMI: 10 mg/L])

Elevated in: Pregnancy, estrogens, oral contraceptives, neoplastic diseases (leukemias, Hodgkin's lymphoma, carcinomas), inflammatory states, systemic lupus erythematosus, primary biliary cirrhosis, rheumatoid arthritis

Decreased in: Wilson's disease (values often <10 mg/dl), nephrotic syndrome, advanced liver disease, malabsorption, total parenteral nutrition, Menkes' syndrome

CHLAMYDIA GROUP ANTIBODY SEROLOGIC TEST

Test description: Acute and convalescent sera is drawn 2-4 weeks apart. A fourfold increase in titer between acute and convalescent sera is necessary for confirmation. A single titer ≥1:64 is considered indicative of psittacosis or LGV.

CHLAMYDIA TRACHOMATIS PCR

Test description: Test is performed on endocervical swab, urine, and intraurethral swab

Normal: Negative

CHLORIDE (serum)

Normal range: 95-105 mEq/L (95-105 mmol/L [CF: 1; SMI: 1 mmol/L])

Elevated in: Dehydration, excessive infusion of normal saline solution, cystic fibrosis (sweat test), hyperparathyroidism, renal tubular disease, metabolic acidosis, prolonged diarrhea, drugs (ammonium chloride administration, acetazolamide, boric acid, triamterene)

Decreased in: Congestive heart failure, syndrome of inappropriate antidiuretic hormone secretion, Addison's disease, vomiting, gastric suction, salt-losing nephritis, continuous infusion of D₅W, thiazide diuretic administration, diaphoresis, diarrhea, burns, diabetic ketoacidosis

CHLORIDE (sweat)

Normal: 0-40 mmol/L

Borderline/indeterminate: 41-60 mmol/L

Consistent with cystic fibrosis: >60 mmol/L

False low results can occur with edema, excessive sweating, and hypoproteinemia.

CHLORIDE, URINE

See URINE CHLORIDE

CHOLECYSTOKININ-PANCREOZYMIN (CCK, CCK-PZ)

Normal: <80 pg/ml

Elevated in: Pancreatic disease, celiac disease, gastric ulcer, postgastrectomy, IBS, fatty food intolerance

CHOLESTEROL, HIGH-DENSITY LIPOPROTEIN

See HIGH-DENSITY LIPOPROTEIN CHOLESTEROL

CHOLESTEROL, LOW-DENSITY LIPOPROTEIN

See LOW-DENSITY LIPOPROTEIN CHOLESTEROL

CHOLESTEROL, TOTAL

Normal range: Varies with age

Generally <200 mg/dl (<5.20 mmol/L [CF: 0.02586; SMI: 0.05 mmol/L])

Laboratory Tests

IV

TABLE 4-10 Cerebrospinal Fluid Findings in Central Nervous System Disorders

Condition	Pressure (mm H₂O)	Leukocytes (mm³)	Protein (mg/dl)	Glucose (mg/dl)	Comments
Normal	50-80	<5, ≥75% lymphocytes	20-45	>50 (or 75% serum glucose)	
Common Forms of Meningitis					
Acute bacterial meningitis	Usually elevated (100-300)	100-10,000 or more; usually 300-2000; PMNs predominate	Usually 100-500	Decreased, usually <40 (or <66% serum glucose)	Organisms usually seen on Gram stain and recovered by culture; latex agglutination of CSF usually positive
Partially treated bacterial meningitis	Normal or elevated	5-10,000; PMNs usual but mononuclear cells may predominate if pretreated for extended period	Usually 100-500	Normal or decreased	Organisms may be seen on Gram stain; latex agglutination CSF may be positive; pretreatment may render CSF sterile
Viral meningitis or meningoencephalitis	Normal or slightly elevated (80-150)	Rarely >1000 cells; eastern equine encephalitis and lymphocytic choriomeningitis may have cell counts of several thousand; PMNs early but mononuclear cells predominate through most of the course	Usually 50-200	Generally normal; may be decreased to <40 in some viral diseases, particularly mumps (15%-20% of cases)	HSV encephalitis is suggested by focal seizures or by focal findings on CT or MRI scans or EEG. Enteroviruses and HSV infrequently recovered from CSF. HSV and enteroviruses may be detected by PCR of CSF.
Uncommon Forms of Meningitis					
Tuberculous meningitis	Usually elevated	10-500; PMNs early but lymphocytes predominate through most of the course	100-3000; may be higher in presence of block	<50 in most cases; decreases with time if treatment is not provided	Acid-fast organisms almost never seen on smear; organisms may be recovered in culture of large volumes of CSF; *Mycobacterium tuberculosis* may be detected by PCR of CSF
Fungal meningitis	Usually elevated	5-500; PMNs early but mononuclear cells predominate through most of the course; cryptococcal meningitis may have no cellular inflammatory response	25-500	<50; decreases with time if treatment is not provided	Budding yeast may be seen; organisms may be recovered in culture; cryptococcal antigen (CSF and serum) may be positive in cryptococcal infection
Syphilis (acute) and leptospirosis	Usually elevated	50-500; lymphocytes predominate	50-200	Usually normal	Positive CSF serology; spirochetes not demonstrable by usual techniques of smear or culture; darkfield examination may be positive
Amebic (*Naegleria*) meningoencephalitis	Elevated	1000-10,000 or more; PMNs predominate	50-500	Normal or slightly decreased	Mobile amebae may be seen by hanging-drop examination of CSF at room temperature
Brain and Parameningeal Abscesses					
Brain abscess	Usually elevated (100-300)	5-200; CSF rarely acellular; lymphocytes predominate; if abscess ruptures into ventricle, PMNs predominate and cell count may reach >100,000	75-500	Normal unless abscess ruptures into ventricular system	No organisms on smear or culture unless abscess ruptures into ventricular system
Subdural empyema	Usually elevated (100-300)	100-5000; PMNs predominate	100-500	Normal	No organisms on smear or culture of CSF unless meningitis also present; organisms found on tap of subdural fluid
Cerebral epidural abscess	Normal to slightly elevated	10-500; lymphocytes predominate	50-200	Normal	No organisms on smear or culture of CSF
Spinal epidural abscess	Usually low, with spinal block	10-100; lymphocytes predominate	50-400	Normal	No organisms on smear or culture of CSF
Chemical (drugs, dermoid cysts, myelography dye)	Usually elevated	100-1000 or more; PMNs predominate	50-100	Normal or slightly decreased	Epithelial cells may be seen within CSF by use of polarized light in some children with dermoids
Noninfectious Causes					
Sarcoidosis	Normal or elevated slightly	0-100; mononuclear	40-100	Normal	No specific findings
Systemic lupus erythematosus with CNS involvement	Slightly elevated	0-500; PMNs usually predominate; lymphocytes may be present	100	Normal or slightly decreased	No organisms on smear or culture; LE preparation may be positive; positive neuronal and ribosomal P protein antibodies in CSF
Tumor, leukemia	Slightly elevated to very high	0-100 or more; mononuclear or blast cells	50-1000	Normal to decreased (20-40)	Cytology may be positive

From Behrman RE: *Nelson textbook of pediatrics*, ed 17, Philadelphia, 2004, Saunders.

CNS, Central nervous system; *CSF*, cerebrospinal fluid; *CT*, computed tomography; *EEG*, electroencephalogram; *HSV*, herpes simplex virus; *MRI*, magnetic resonance imaging; *PCR*, polymerase chain reaction; *PMN*, polymorphonuclear neutrophils.

Elevated in: Primary hypercholesterolemia, biliary obstruction, diabetes mellitus, nephrotic syndrome, hypothyroidism, primary biliary cirrhosis, high-cholesterol diet, pregnancy third trimester, myocardial infarction, drugs (steroids, phenothiazines, oral contraceptives)

Decreased in: Medications (statins, niacin), starvation, malabsorption, sideroblastic anemia, thalassemia, abetalipoproteinemia, hyperthyroidism, Cushing's syndrome, hepatic failure, multiple myeloma, polycythemia vera, chronic myelocytic leukemia, myeloid metaplasia, Waldenström's macroglobulinemia, myelofibrosis

CHORIONIC GONADOTROPINS, HUMAN (serum) (HCG)

Normal range, serum: Female, premenopausal: <0.8 IU/L; postmenopausal <3.3 IU/L
Male: <0.7 IU/L

Elevated in:

- Pregnancy, choriocarcinoma, gestational trophoblastic neoplasia (including molar gestations), placental site trophoblastic tumors; human anti-mouse antibodies (HAMA) can produce false serum assay for hCG.
- The principal use of this test is to diagnose pregnancy. The concentration of hCG increases significantly during the initial 6 weeks of pregnancy.

Normal range: Varies with gestational stage:
1 wk: 5-50 mU/ml
1-2 wk: 50-550 mU/ml
2-3 wk: up to 5000 mU/ml
3-4 wk: up to 10,000 mU/ml
4-5 wk: up to 50,000 mU/ml
2-3 mo: 10,000-100,000 mU/ml
Peak values approaching 100,000 IU/L occur 60-70 days following implantation.
hCG levels generally double every 1-3 days. In patients with concentration <2000 IU/L, an increase of serum hCG <66% after 2 days is suggestive of spontaneous abortion or ruptured ectopic gestation.

CHYMOTRYPSIN

Normal: <10 mcg/L
Elevated in: Acute pancreatitis, chronic renal failure, oral enzyme preparations, gastric cancer, pancreatic cancer
Decreased in: Chronic pancreatitis, late cystic fibrosis

CIRCULATING ANTICOAGULANT (lupus anticoagulant)

Normal: Negative
Detected in: Systemic lupus erythematosus, drug-induced lupus, long-term phenothiazine therapy, multiple myeloma, ulcerative colitis, rheumatoid arthritis, postpartum, hemophilia, neoplasms, chronic inflammatory states, AIDS, nephrotic syndrome

NOTE: The name is a misnomer because these patients are prone to hypercoagulability and thrombosis.

CK

See CREATINE KINASE

CLONIDINE SUPPRESSION TEST

Interpretation: Clonidine inhibits neurogenic catecholamine release and will cause a decrease in plasma norepinephrine into the reference interval in hypertensive subjects without pheochromocytoma. Test is performed by giving 4.3 mcg clonidine/kg orally after overnight fast. Norepinephrine is measured at 3 hr. Result should be within established reference range and decrease to <50% of baseline concentration. Lack of decrease in norepinephrine is suggestive of pheochromocytoma.

CLOSTRIDIUM DIFFICILE TOXIN ASSAY (stool)

Normal: Negative
Detected in: Antibiotic-associated diarrhea and pseudomembranous colitis

CO

See CARBOXYHEMOGLOBIN

COAGULATION FACTORS

See Table 4-11 for characteristics of coagulation factors.
See Table 4-12 for differential diagnosis of low factor VIII.
Factor reference ranges:
V: >10%
VII: >10%
VIII: 50%-170%
IX: 60%-136%
X: >10%
XI: 50%-150%
XII: >30%
Table 4-13 describes screening laboratory results in coagulation factor deficiencies.

COBALAMIN, SERUM

See VITAMIN B$_{12}$

COLD AGGLUTININS TITER

Normal range: <1:32
Elevated in:
Primary atypical pneumonia (*Mycoplasma* pneumonia), infectious mononucleosis, CMV infection

TABLE 4-11 Characteristics of Coagulation Factors

Factor	Descriptive Name	Source	Approximate Half-Life (hr)	Function
I	Fibrinogen	Liver	120	Substrate for fibrin clot (CP)
II	Prothrombin	Liver (VKD)	60	Serine protease (CP)
V	Proaccelerin, labile factor	Liver	12-36	Cofactor (CP)
VII	Serum prothrombin conversion accelerator, proconvertin	Liver (VKD)	6	(?) Serine protease (EP)
VIII	Antihemophilic factor or globulin	Endothelial cells and (?) elsewhere	12	Cofactor (IP)
IX	Plasma thromboplastin component, Christmas factor	Liver (VKD)	24	Serine protease (IP)
X	Stuart-Prower factor	Liver (VKD)	36	Serine protease (CP)
XI	Plasma thromboplastin antecedent	(?) Liver	40-84	Serine protease (IP)
XII	Hageman factor	(?) Liver	50	Serine protease contact activation (IP)
XIII	Fibrin-stabilizing factor	(?) Liver	96-180	Transglutaminase (CP)
Prekallikrein	Fletcher factor	(?) Liver	?	Serine protease contact activation (IP)
High-molecular-weight kininogen	Fitzgerald factor, Flaujeac or Williams factor	(?) Liver	?	Cofactor, contact activation (IP)

From Noble J (ed): *Primary care medicine*, ed 3, St Louis, 2001, Mosby.
CP, Common pathway; *EP*, extrinsic pathway; *IP*, intrinsic pathway; *VKD*, vitamin K dependent.

Laboratory Tests

IV

TABLE 4-12 Differential Diagnosis of a Low Factor VIII Level

1. FVIII <10%
   - Severe or moderately severe hemophilia A
   - Severe type 1 vWD
   - Type 3 vWD
   - Type 2N vWD
   - Acquired hemophilia A
   - Acquired vWD
2. FVIII: 10% to 50%
   - Mild hemophilia A
   - Type 1 vWD
   - Type 2N vWD
   - Combined FVIII and FV deficiency

From Hoffman R: *Hematology: basic principles and practice*, ed 6, Philadelphia, Saunders, 2013. *FV*, Factor V; *FVIII*, factor VIII; *VWD*, von Willebrand disease.

TABLE 4-13 Screening Laboratory Results in Coagulation Factor Deficiencies

Deficient Factor	Frequency	PT	PTT	TT
I (fibrinogen)	Rare	↑	↑	↑
II (prothrombin)	Very rare	↑	↑	↑
V 1:1,000,000	↑		↑	NL
VII	1:500,000	↑	NL	NL
VIII	1:5000 (male)	NL	↑	NL
IX	1:30,000 (male)	NL	↑	NL
X 1:500,000	↑		↑	NL
XI	Rare*	NL	↑	NL
XII or HMWK or PK†	Rare	NL	↑	NL
XIII	Rare	NL	NL	↑

From Andreoli TE (ed): *Cecil essentials of medicine*, ed 5, Philadelphia, 2001, Saunders.
↑Increased over normal range; *HMWK*, high-molecular-weight kininogen; *NL*, normal; *PK*, prekallikrein; *PT*, prothrombin time; *PTT*, partial thromboplastin time; *TT*, thrombin time.
*Except in those of Ashkenazi Jewish descent (approximately 4% are heterozygous for factor XI deficiency).
†Not associated with clinical bleeding.

Others: hepatic cirrhosis, acquired hemolytic anemia, frostbite, multiple myeloma, lymphoma, malaria

COMPLEMENT
Normal range:
C3: 70-160 mg/dl (0.7-1.6 g/L [CF: 0.01; SMI: 0.1 g/L])
C4: 20-40 mg/dl (0.2-0.4 g/L [CF: 0.01; SMI: 0.1 g/L])
Abnormal values:
Decreased C3: Active SLE, immune complex disease, acute glomerulonephritis, inborn C3 deficiency, membranoproliferative glomerulonephritis, infective endocarditis, serum sickness, autoimmune/chronic active hepatitis
Decreased C4: Immune complex disease, active SLE, infective endocarditis, inborn C4 deficiency, hereditary angioedema, hypergammaglobulinemic states, cryoglobulinemic vasculitis
Note: The complement system has daunting nomenclature; accordingly, some basic definitions are given in Box 4-1.

COMPLEMENT DEFICIENCY
Table 4-14 describes complement deficiency states.

COMPLETE BLOOD COUNT (CBC)
See Fig. 4-12, which describes an algorithm for the evaluation of patients with neutropenia.
White blood cells 3200-9800/mm³ (3.2-9.8 × 10⁹/L [CF: 0.001; SMI: 0.1 × 10⁹/L])
Red blood cells
   Male: 4.3-5.9 × 10⁶/mm³ (4.3-5.9 × 10¹²/L [CF: 0.001; SMI: 0.1 × 10¹²/L])

BOX 4-1 Definitions

Classical pathway: C1, C4, C2, C3, and the terminal components.
Alternative pathway: Factor B, factor D, properdin, and the terminal components.
Lectin activation pathway: MBL, MASP1, MASP2, C3, and the terminal components.
Anaphylatoxins: C3a, C4a, C5a. These are mediators of smooth muscle contraction, degranulation of mast cells, enhanced neutrophil aggregation, increased vascular permeability.
Opsonization: Renders a particle more easily phagocytosed.
C3 tickover: This term occasionally is used to describe spontaneous C3 hydrolysis.
Membrane attack complex (terminal components): C5, C6, C7, C8, C9.
CH50: Used to define the dilution of serum capable of lysing 50% of sensitized sheep red cells. This assay measures the intactness of the classical pathway through the terminal components.
AH50: Used to define the dilution of serum capable of lysing 50% of nonsensitized rabbit red cells. This assay measures the intactness of the alternative pathway through the terminal components.

From Adkinson NF et al: *Middleton's allergy principles and practice*, ed 8, Philadelphia, 2014, Saunders.

Female: 3.5-5 × 10⁶/mm³ (3.5-5 × 10¹²/L [CF: 0.001; SMI: 0.1 × 10¹²/L])
Hemoglobin
   Male: 13.6-17.7 g/dl (136-172 g/L [CF: 10; SMI: 1 g/L])
   Female: 12-15 g/dl (120-150 g/L [CF: 10; SMI: 1 g/L])
Hematocrit
   Male: 39%-49% (0.39-0.49 [CF: 0.01; SMI: 0.01])
   Female: 33%-43% (0.33-0.43 [CF: 0.01; SMI: 0.01])
Mean corpuscular volume (MCV): 76-100 μm³ (76-100 fL [CF: 1; SMI: 1 fL])
Mean corpuscular hemoglobin (MCH): 27-33 pg (27-33 pg [CF: 1; SMI: 1 pg])
Mean corpuscular hemoglobin concentration (MCHC): 33-37 g/dl (330-370 g/L [CF: 10; SMI: 10 g/L])
Red blood cell distribution width index (RDW): 11.5%-14.5%
Platelet count: 130-400 × 10³/mm³ (130-400 × 10⁹/L [CF: 1; SMI: 5 × 10⁹/L])
Differential:
   2-6 stabs (bands, early mature neutrophils)
   60-70 segs (mature neutrophils)
   1-4 eosinophils
   0-1 basophils
   2-8 monocytes
   25-40 lymphocytes

CONJUGATED BILIRUBIN
See BILIRUBIN, DIRECT

COOMBS (antiglobulin test), DIRECT
Normal: Negative
Positive: Autoimmune hemolytic anemia, erythroblastosis fetalis, transfusion reactions, drugs (α-methyldopa, penicillins, tetracycline, sulfonamides, levodopa, cephalosporins, quinidine, insulin)
False-positive: May be seen with cold agglutinins

COOMBS (antiglobulin test), INDIRECT
Normal: Negative
Positive: Acquired hemolytic anemia, incompatible cross-matched blood, anti-Rh antibodies, drugs (methyldopa, mefenamic acid, levodopa)

COPPER (serum)
Normal range: 70-140 μg/dl (11-22 μmol/L [CF: 0.1574, SMI: 0.2 μmol/L])
Decreased in: Wilson's disease, Menkes' syndrome, malabsorption, malnutrition, nephrosis, total parenteral nutrition, acute leukemia in remission
Elevated in: Aplastic anemia, biliary cirrhosis, systemic lupus erythematosus, hemochromatosis, hyperthyroidism, hypothyroidism, infection, iron

START

Complete blood count with differential and platelet count

Neutrophil count <1×10^9/L

Fever (>38° C) or signs of infection?

Yes → Hospitalize, obtain cultures, and consider empiric antibiotic Rx

No

Neutrophil count <2×10^9/L >1×10^9/L

Selective neutropenia?

No → Bi- or pancytopenia

Yes

Taking drugs?

Yes → Discontinue suspect drug. Response?

No → History of recurrent infections?

Examine peripheral blood smear and check MCV

Oval macrocytes or high MCV?

No → Toxins? Drugs?

No No / Yes

Yes → Obtain serum B_{12} and folate levels. Low?

Discontinue. Response?

No → Hypersegmented neutrophils?

No / Yes

No → B_{12}/folate deficiency

Yes → B_{12}/folate deficiency

History of recurrent infections?

No / Yes

Toxin exposure?

No → Family history of chronic neutropenia?

Stop exposure.

Family history of chronic neutropenia?
Yes → Familial neutropenia
No → Chronic inflammatory or autoimmune disease?
No → Idiopathic, congenital, pseudoneutropenia
Yes

Reconsider B_{12}/folate deficiency. Order RBC folate, methylmalonate, homocysteine. Abnormal?
No / Yes

Bone marrow examination

Hypocellular

Normal or increased cellularity

Aplastic anemia
AIDS
Drug-related
 Toxic
 Immunologically mediated
Immune injury
 Cytotoxic T cells (T)
 Antibody-mediated (Ab)
 Both T and Ab
Toxin-mediated injury
Certain viral infections
Mycobacterial infections
Myelodysplasia
Paroxysmal nocturnal hemoglobinuria
Hereditary neutropenia syndromes

Normal morphology?

No → Acute leukemia
Myelodysplasia
Lymphoma
Hairy cell leukemia
AIDS
Carcinoma
Fibrosis
Immune injury
Megaloblastic
(B_{12}/folate deficiency)

Yes → Neutrophil destruction
Neutrophil utilization
 Infection
 Trauma
Sequestration
Tissue necrosis
Hypersplenism

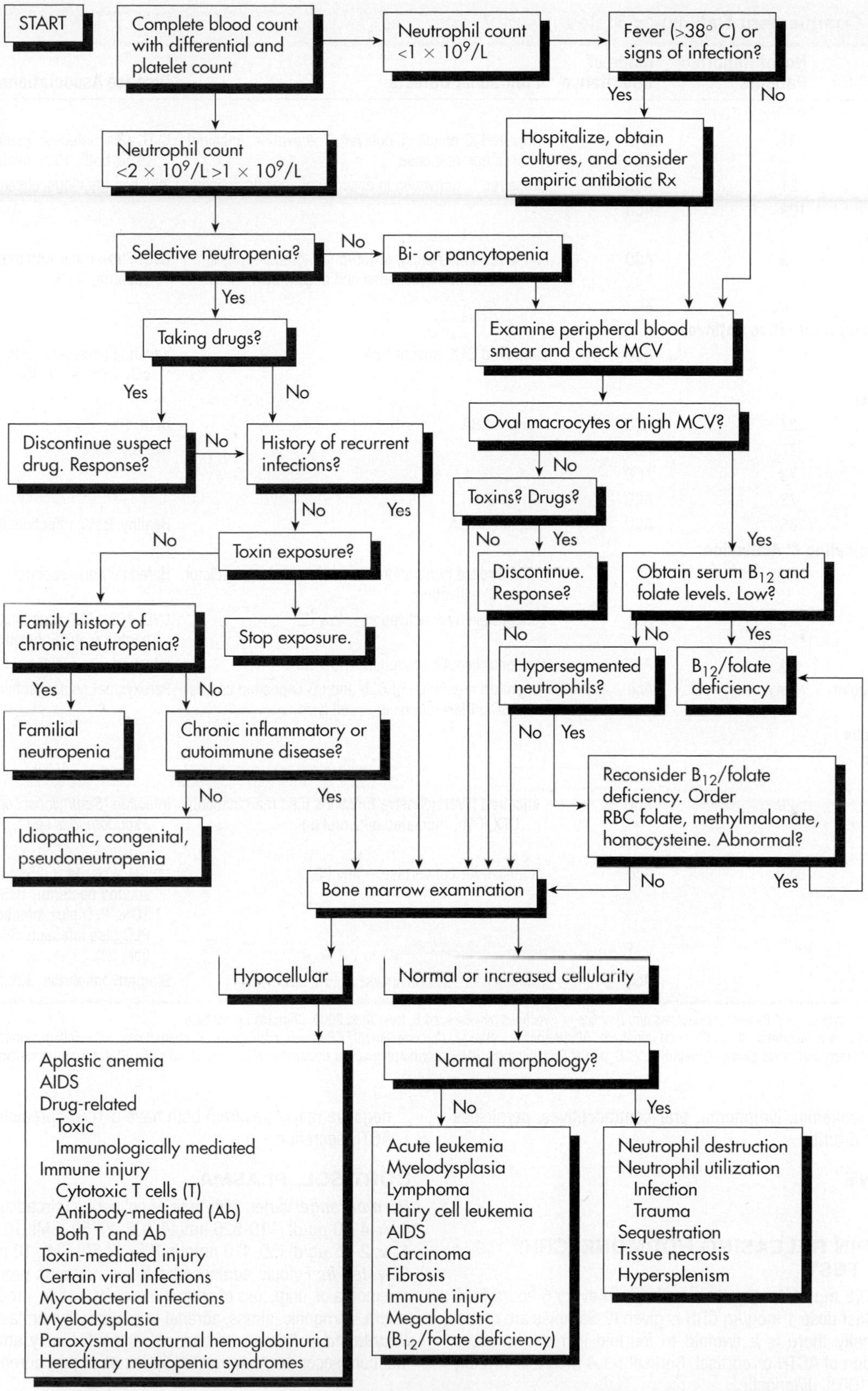

FIGURE 4-12 A practical algorithm for the evaluation of patients with neutropenia. The fundamental diagnostic principle is that for patients with severe neutropenia or for those with bicytopenia or pancytopenia, bone marrow examination will likely be necessary unless the following diagnoses are made: (1) a nutritional (folate or vitamin B_{12}) deficiency or (2) drug- or toxin-induced neutropenia in a patient whose neutropenia resolves after discontinuation of the offending agent. *AIDS,* Acquired immunodeficiency syndrome; *MCV,* mean corpuscular volume; *RBC,* red blood cell. (From Goldman L, Ausiello D [eds]: *Cecil textbook of medicine,* ed 24, Philadelphia, 2012, Saunders.)

Laboratory Tests

IV

TABLE 4-14 Complement Deficiency States

Component	No. of Reported Patients	Mode of Inheritance	Functional Defects	Disease Associations
Classic Pathway				
C1qrs	31	ACD	Impaired IC handling, delayed C' activation, impaired immune response	CVD, 48%; infection (encapsulated bacteria), 22%; both, 18%; healthy, 12%
C4	21	ACD	Impaired C' activation in absence of specific antibody	Infection (meningococcal), 74%; healthy, 26%
C2	109	ACD		
Alternative Pathway				
D	3	ACD	Impaired IC handling, opson/phag; granulocytosis, CTX, immune response and absent SBA	CVD, 79%; recurrent infection (encapsulated bacteria), 71%
P	70	XL		
Junction of Classic and Alternative Pathways				
C3	19	ACD	Impaired CTX; absent SBA	Infection (*Neisseria*, primarily meningococcal), 58%; CVD, 4%
Terminal Components				
C5	27	ACD	Absent SBA	Both, 1%
C6	77	ACD		Healthy, 25%
C7	73	ACD		
C8	73	ACD		
C9	165	ACD	Impaired SBA	Healthy, 91%; infection, 9%
Plasma Proteins Regulating C' Activation				
C1-INH	Many	AD	Uncontrolled generation of an inflammatory mediator on C' activation	Hereditary angioedema
H	13	Acq	Uncontrolled AP activation → low C3	CVD, 40%; CVD plus infection (encapsulated bacteria), 40%; healthy, 20%
I	14	ACD	Uncontrolled AP activation → low C3	Infection (encapsulated bacteria), 100%
Membrane proteins regulating C' activation	Many	Acq	Impaired regulation of C3b and C8 deposited on host RBCs; PMN, platelets → cell lysis	Paroxysmal nocturnal hemoglobinuria
Decay-accelerating factor				
Homologous restriction factor				
CD59	>20	ACD	Impaired PMN adhesive functions (i.e., margination), CTX, C3bi-mediated opson/phag	Infection (*Staphylococcus aureus, Pseudomonas* spp.), 100%
CR3 autoantibodies				
C3 nephritic factors	>59	Acq	Stabilize AP, convertase → low C3	MPGN, 41%; PLD, 25%; infection (encapsulated bacteria), 16%; MPGN plus PLD, 10%; PLD plus infection, 5%; MPGN plus PLD plus infection, 3%; MPGN plus infection, 2%
C4 nephritic factor		Acq	Stabilize CP, C3 convertase → low C3	Glomerulonephritis, 50%; CVD, 50%

From Mandell GL: *Mandell, Douglas, and Bennett's principles and practice of infectious diseases,* ed 6, New York, 2005, Churchill Livingstone.
ACD, Autosomal codominant; *Acq,* acquired; *AD,* autosomal dominant; *AP,* alternative pathway; *C,* complement; *CP,* classic pathway; *CTX,* chemotaxis; *CVD,* collagen-vascular disease; *IC,* immune complex, *MPGN,* membranoproliferative glomerulonephritis; *PLD,* partial lipodystrophy; *PMN,* polymorphonuclear neutrophil; *RBCs,* red blood cells; *SBA,* serum bactericidal activity; *XL,* X-linked.

deficiency anemia, leukemia, lymphoma, oral contraceptives, pernicious anemia, rheumatoid arthritis

COPPER, URINE

See URINE COPPER

CORTICOTROPIN RELEASING HORMONE (CRH) STIMULATION TEST

Normal: A dose of 0.5 mg of dexamethasone is given every 6 hours for 2 days; 2 hours after last dose 1 mcg/kg CRH is given IV. Samples are drawn after 15 min. Normally there is a twofold to fourfold increase in mean baseline concentration of ACTH or cortisol. Cortisol >1.4 mcg/L is virtually 100% specific and 100% diagnostic.
Interpretation:
Normal or exaggerated response: Pituitary Cushing's disease
No response: Ectopic ACTH-secreting tumor
A positive response to CRH or a suppressed response to high-dose dexamethasone has a 97% positive predictive value for Cushing's disease. However, a lack of response to either test excludes Cushing's disease in only 64%-78% of patients. When the tests are considered together,

negative responses from both have a 100% predictive value for ectopic ACTH secretion.

CORTISOL, PLASMA

Normal range: Varies with time of collection (circadian variation):
8 AM: 4-19 μg/dl (110-520 nmol/L [CF: 27.59; SMI: 10 nmol/L])
4 PM: 2-15 μg/dl (50-410 nmol/L [CF: 27.59; SMI: 10 nmol/L])
Elevated in: Ectopic adrenocorticotropic hormone production (i.e., oat cell carcinoma of lung), loss of normal diurnal variation, pregnancy, chronic renal failure, iatrogenic, stress, adrenal or pituitary hyperplasia, or adenomas
Decreased in: Primary adrenocortical insufficiency, anterior pituitary hypofunction, secondary adrenocortical insufficiency, adrenogenital syndromes

C-PEPTIDE

Elevated in: Insulinoma, sulfonylurea administration
Decreased in: Insulin-dependent diabetes mellitus, factitious insulin administration

CPK

See CREATINE KINASE

TABLE 4-15 Comparison of Erythrocyte Sedimentation Rate and C-Reactive Protein

	Erythrocyte Sedimentation Rate	C-Reactive Protein
Advantages	• Much clinical information in the literature • May reflect overall health status	• Rapid response to inflammatory stimuli • Wide range of clinically relevant values are detectable • Unaffected by age and gender • Reflects value of a single acute phase protein • Can be measured on stored sera • Quantitation is precise and reproducible
Disadvantages	• Affected by age and gender • Affected by red blood cell morphology • Affected by anemia and polycythemia • Reflects levels of many plasma proteins, not all of which are acute phase proteins • Responds slowly to inflammatory stimuli • Requires fresh sample • May be affected by drugs	• None

From Firestein GS, Budd RC, Gabriel SE, et al: *Kelley's textbook of rheumatology*, ed 9, Philadelphia, 2013, Saunders.

TABLE 4-16 Conditions Associated with Elevated C-Reactive Protein Levels

Normal or Minor Elevation (<1 mg/dL)	Moderate Elevation (1-10 mg/dL)	Marked Elevation (>10 mg/dL)
• Vigorous exercise • Common cold • Pregnancy • Gingivitis • Seizures • Depression • Insulin resistance and diabetes • Several genetic polymorphisms • Obesity	• Myocardial infarction • Malignancies • Pancreatitis • Mucosal infection (bronchitis, cystitis) • Most connective tissue diseases • Rheumatoid arthritis	• Acute bacterial infection (80%-85%) • Major trauma • Systemic vasculitis

From Firestein GS, Budd RC, Gabriel SE, et al: *Kelley's textbook of rheumatology*, ed 9, Philadelphia, 2013, Saunders.

C-REACTIVE PROTEIN

Normal range: 6.8-820 µg/dl (68-8200 µg/L [CF: 10; SMI: 10 µg/L])

Elevated in: Rheumatoid arthritis, rheumatic fever, inflammatory bowel disease, bacterial infections, myocardial infarction, oral contraceptives, third trimester of pregnancy (acute phase reactant), inflammatory and neoplastic diseases. Table 4-15 shows a comparison of erythrocyte sedimentation rate and C-reactive protein, and Table 4-16 shows conditions associated with elevated C-reactive protein levels.

C-REACTIVE PROTEIN, HIGH SENSITIVITY (hs-CRP, cardio-CRP)

This is a cardiac risk marker. It is increased in patients with silent atherosclerosis years before a cardiovascular event and is independent of cholesterol level and other lipoproteins. It can be used to help stratify cardiac risk.

INTERPRETATION OF RESULTS

Cardio-CRP result (mg/L)	Risk
0.6	Lowest risk
0.7-1.1	Low risk
1.2-1.9	Moderate risk
2.0-3.8	High risk
3.9-4.9	Highest risk
≥5.0	Results may be confounded by acute inflammatory disease. If clinically indicated, a repeat test should be performed in 2 or more weeks.

CREATINE KINASE (CK, CPK)

Fig. E4-13 describes a diagnostic approach to creatine kinase elevation.

Normal range: 0-130 U/L (0-2.16 µkat/L [CF: 0.01667; SMI: 0.01 µkat/L])

Elevated in: Myocardial infarction, myocarditis, rhabdomyolysis, myositis, crush injury/trauma, polymyositis, dermatomyositis, vigorous exercise, muscular dystrophy, myxedema, seizures, malignant hyperthermia syndrome, IM injections, cerebrovascular accident, pulmonary embolism and infarction, acute dissection of aorta

Decreased in: Corticosteroid use, decreased muscle mass, connective tissue disorders, alcoholic liver disease, metastatic neoplasms

CREATINE KINASE ISOENZYMES

CK-BB

Elevated In: Cerebrovascular accident, subarachnoid hemorrhage, neoplasms (prostate, gastrointestinal tract, brain, ovary, breast, lung), severe shock, bowel infarction, hypothermia, meningitis

CK-MB

Elevated In: Myocardial infarction (MI), myocarditis, pericarditis, muscular dystrophy, cardiac defibrillation, cardiac surgery, extensive rhabdomyolysis, strenuous exercise (marathon runners), mixed connective tissue disease, cardiomyopathy, hypothermia

NOTE: CK-MB exists in the blood in two subforms. MB_2 is released from cardiac cells and converted in the blood to MB_1. Rapid assay of CK-MB subforms can detect MI (CK-MB_2 ≥1.0 U/L, with a ratio of CK-MB_2/CK-MB_1 ≥1.5) within 6 hours of onset of symptoms.

Fig. 4-14 illustrates the time course of CK, AST, troponins, and LDH activity after acute MI.

CK-MM

Elevated In: Crush injury, seizures, malignant hyperthermia syndrome, rhabdomyolysis, myositis, polymyositis, dermatomyositis, vigorous exercise, muscular dystrophy, IM injections, acute dissection of aorta

CREATININE (serum)

See Fig. 4-15.

Normal range: 0.6-1.2 mg/dl (50-110 µmol/L [CF: 88.4; SMI: 10 µmol/L])

Elevated in: Renal insufficiency (acute and chronic), decreased renal perfusion (hypotension, dehydration, congestive heart failure), urinary tract infection, rhabdomyolysis, ketonemia

Drugs (antibiotics [aminoglycosides, cephalosporins], hydantoin, diuretics, methyldopa)

Laboratory Tests

IV

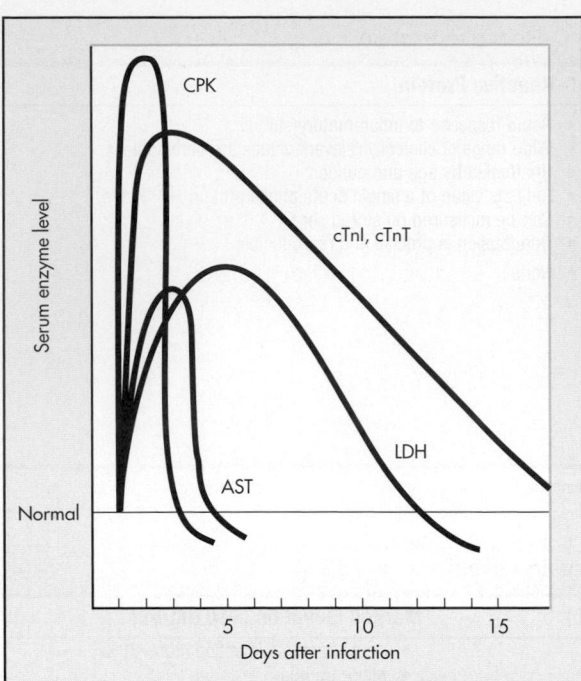

FIGURE 4-14 Evaluation of creatine kinase elevation. *AST,* Aspartate aminotransferase; *CPK,* creatine kinase; *cTnI,* cardiac troponin I; *cTnT,* cardiac troponin T; *LDH,* lactate dehydrogenase. (From Greene HL, Johnson WP, Lemcke D [eds]: *Decision making in medicine,* ed 2, St Louis, 1998, Mosby.)

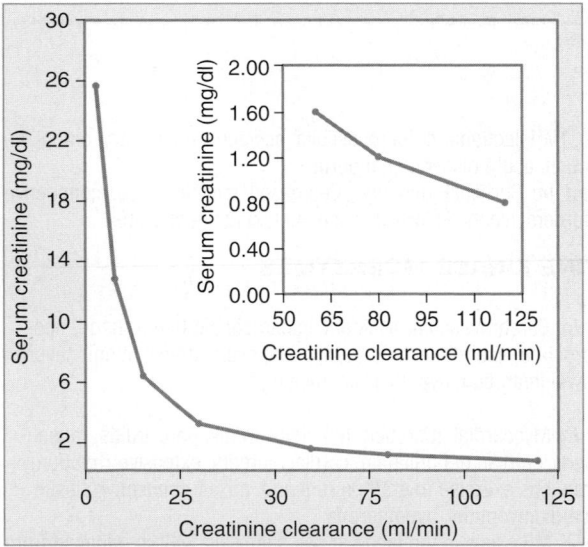

FIGURE 4-15 Relationship between creatinine clearance and serum creatinine. In steady state, serum creatinine should increase twofold for each 50% reduction in creatinine clearance. *Inset* represents enlarged view of changes in serum creatinine as creatinine clearance decreases from 120 to 60 ml/min. If serum creatinine is 0.8 mg/dl when creatinine clearance is 120 ml/min, creatinine clearance can decrease by 33% such that increased serum creatinine is still within normal range. (From Vincent JL et al: *Textbook of critical care,* ed 6, Philadelphia, 2011, Saunders.)

Falsely elevated in: Diabetic ketoacidosis, administration of some cephalosporins (e.g., cefoxitin, cephalothin)
Decreased in: Decreased muscle mass (including amputees and older persons), pregnancy, prolonged debilitation

CREATININE CLEARANCE

Normal range: 75-124 ml/min (1.24-2.08 ml/sec [CF: 0.01667; SMI: 0.02 ml/sec])

Box 4-2 describes a formula for calculation of creatinine clearance.

The Cockcroft-Gault formula to calculate creatinine clearance is described in Box 4-3.
Elevated in: Pregnancy, exercise
Decreased in: Renal insufficiency, drugs (cimetidine, procainamide, antibiotics, quinidine)

CREATININE, URINE
See URINE CREATININE

CRYOGLOBULINS (serum)
Normal range: Not detectable
Present in: Collagen vascular diseases, chronic lymphocytic leukemia, hemolytic anemias, multiple myeloma, Waldenström's macroglobulinemia, chronic active hepatitis, Hodgkin's disease

CRYPTOSPORIDIUM ANTIGEN BY EIA (stool)
Normal range: Not detected
Present in: Cryptosporidiosis

CSF
See CEREBROSPINAL FLUID

CYSTATIN C
Normal: Cystatin C is a cysteine protease inhibitor that is produced at a constant rate by all nucleated cells. It is freely filtered by the glomerulus and reabsorbed (but not secreted) by the renal tubules with no extrarenal excretion. Its concentration is not affected by diet, muscle mass, or acute inflammation. Normal range when measured by particle-enhanced nephelometric immunoassay (PENIA) is <0.28 mg/L.
Elevated in: Renal disorders. Good predictor of the severity of acute tubular necrosis. Cystatin C increases more rapidly than creatinine in the early stages of GFR impairment. The cystatin C concentration is an independent risk factor for heart failure in older adults and appears to provide a better measure of risk assessment than the serum creatinine concentration.

CYSTIC FIBROSIS PCR
Test description: Test can be performed on whole blood or tissue. Common mutations in the cystic fibrosis transmembrane regulator (CFTR) gene can be used to detect 75%-80% of mutant alleles.

CYTOMEGALOVIRUS BY PCR
Test description: Test can be performed on whole blood, plasma, or tissue. Qualitative PCR is highly sensitive but may not be able to differentiate between latent and active infection.

D-DIMER
Normal range:
<0.5 mcg/ml
Elevated in:
DVT, pulmonary embolism, high levels of rheumatoid factor, activation of coagulation and fibrolytic system from any cause

D-dimer assay by ELISA assists in the diagnosis of DVT and pulmonary embolism. This test has significant limitations because it can be elevated whenever the coagulation and fibrinolytic systems are activated and can also be falsely elevated with high rheumatoid factor levels.

A positive D-dimer is not diagnostic for PE. Patients with positive D-dimer and clinical suspicion for PE need additional tests such as chest CT to confirm diagnosis.

PE might be ruled out in patients with negative D-dimer and low pretest probability for PE.

DEHYDROEPIANDROSTERONE SULFATE
Normal:
Males:

Ages 19-30:	125-619 mcg/dl
31-50:	59-452 mcg/dl
51-60:	20-413 mcg/dl
61-83:	10-285 mcg/dl

Females:

Ages 19-30:	29-781 mcg/dl
31-50:	12-379 mcg/dl
Postmenopausal:	30-260 mcg/dl

Elevated in: Hirsutism, congenital adrenal hyperplasia, adrenal carcinomas, adrenal adenomas, polycystic ovary syndrome, ectopic ACTH-producing tumors, Cushing's disease, spironolactone

DEHYDROTESTOSTERONE (serum, urine)
Normal:
Serum: Males: 30-85 ng/dl; females: 4-22 ng/dl
Urine, 24 h: Males: 20-50 mcg/day; females: <8 mcg/day
Elevated in:
Hirsutism
Decreased in:
5-α-reductase deficiency, hypogonadism

DEOXYCORTICOSTERONE (11-deoxycorticosterone, DOC) (serum)
Normal:
2-19 ng/dl. Normal secretion depends on ACTH and is suppressible by dexamethasone.
Elevated in:
Adrenogenital syndromes due to 17- and 11-hydroxylase deficiencies, pregnancy
Decreased in:
Preeclampsia

DEXAMETHASONE SUPPRESSION TEST, OVERNIGHT
Normal: Test is performed by giving 1 mg dexamethasone orally at 11 PM and measuring serum cortisol at 8 AM the following morning. Normal response is cortisol suppression to <3 mcg/dl; If dose of 4 mg dexamethasone is given, cortisol suppression will be to <50% of baseline.
Interpretation: Cushing's syndrome (<10 mcg/dl), endogenous depression (half of patients suppress test values <5 mcg/dl). Most patients with pituitary Cushing's disease demonstrate suppression, whereas patients with adrenal adenoma, carcinoma, and ectopic ACTH-producing tumors do not.

DIGOXIN
Normal therapeutic range:
0.5-2 ng/ml
Elevated in: Impaired renal function, excessive dosing, concomitant use of quinidine, amiodarone, verapamil, fluoxetine, nifedipine. Toxicity may occur at a lower blood concentration in the presence of hypokalemia, hypomagnesemia, and hypercalcemia.

DILANTIN
See PHENYTOIN

DIRECT ANTIGLOBULIN TEST
See COOMBS, DIRECT

DISACCHARIDE ABSORPTION TESTS
Normal: Test is used to diagnose malabsorption due to disaccharide deficiency. It is performed by giving disaccharide orally 1 g/kg body weight to a total of 25 g. Blood is drawn at 0, 30, 60, 90, and 120 min. Normal response is a change in glucose from fasting value >30 mg/dl, inconclusive when increase is 20-30 mg/dl, abnormal when increase is >20 mg/dl. Test can also be performed by measuring air at 0, 30, 60, 90, and 120 min. Normal is H_2 >20 ppm above baseline level before a colonic response.
Decreased in: Disaccharide deficiency (lactose, fructose, sorbitol), celiac disease, sprue, acute gastroenteritis

DOC
See DEOXYCORTICOSTERONE

DONATH-LANDSTEINER (D-L) TEST FOR PAROXYSMAL COLD HEMOGLOBINURIA
Normal: No hemolysis
Interpretation: Hemolysis indicates presence of bithermic cold hemolysins or Donath-Landsteiner antibodies (D-L Ab)

DOPAMINE
Normal range:
175 pg/ml
Elevated in: Pheochromocytomas, neuroblastomas, stress, vigorous exercise, certain foods (bananas, chocolate, coffee, tea, vanilla)

D-XYLOSE ABSORPTION
Normal range:
21%-31% excreted in 5 hours
Decreased in:
Malabsorption syndrome

D-XYLOSE ABSORPTION TEST
Normal range:
a. **URINE:** ≥4 g/5 hours (5-hour urine collection in adults >12 years [25-g dose])
b. **SERUM:** ≥25 mg/dl (adult, 1 hour, 25-g dose, normal renal function)
Normal results: In patients with malabsorption, normal results suggest pancreatic disease as an etiology of the malabsorption.
Abnormal results: Celiac disease, Crohn's disease, tropical sprue, surgical bowel resection, AIDS. False-positives can occur with decreased renal function, dehydration/hypovolemia, surgical blind loops, decreased gastric emptying, vomiting.

ELECTROPHORESIS, HEMOGLOBIN
See HEMOGLOBIN ELECTROPHORESIS

ELECTROPHORESIS, PROTEIN
See PROTEIN ELECTROPHORESIS

ENA COMPLEX
See EXTRACTABLE NUCLEAR ANTIGEN

ENDOMYSIAL ANTIBODIES
Normal: Not detected
Present in:
Celiac disease, dermatitis herpetiformis

EOSINOPHIL COUNT
Normal range:
1%-4% eosinophils (0-440/mm^3)
Elevated in:
HELMINTHIC PARASITES
7. *Ascaris lumbricoides* (invasive larval stage)
8. Hookworms (invasive larval stage)
9. *Strongyloides stercoralis* (initial infection and autoinfection)
10. Trichinosis
11. Filariasis

TABLE 4-17 Eosinophilia Investigation in Returning Travelers

History	Allergies
	Drugs and vitamins (L-tryptophan)
	Regions, localities, and duration of exposure
Physical examination	Skin, subcutaneous tissues
	Liver/spleen
	Signs of other systemic disease
Initial investigations	Full blood count and differential white blood cell count
	Stool examination for ova and parasites (×3) Urine analysis
	Examination of midday urine for ova and parasites (×3) (in those who have traveled to Africa or the Middle East)
Further investigations as suggested by travel and exposure from history	*Strongyloides* culture and serologic testing
	Duodenal aspirate (strongyloidiasis, hookworm)
	Serologic testing (schistosomiasis, filariasis) Day/night blood films (filariasis)
Further studies if suggested by history and physical examination	Skin snips (onchocerciasis)
	Chest x-ray examination (hydatid cyst, tropical pulmonary eosinophilia, paragonimiasis)
	Soft tissue x-ray examination (cysticercosis) Sputum examination for ova and parasites (paragonimiasis)
	Abdominal ultrasound examination (hydatid cyst)
	Cystoscopy with or without biopsy (schistosomiasis)
	Rectal snips (schistosomiasis)

From Hoffman R: *Hematology: basic principles and practice*, ed 6, Philadelphia, Saunders, 2013.

12. *Echinococcus granulosus* and *E. multilocularis*
13. *Toxocara* species
14. Animal hookworms
15. *Angiostrongylus cantonensis* and *A. costaricensis*
16. Schistosomiasis
17. Liver flukes
18. *Fasciolopsis buski*
19. Anisakiasis
20. *Capillaria philippinensis*
21. *Paragonimus westermani*
22. "Tropical eosinophilia" (unidentified microfilariae)

OTHER INFECTIONS/INFESTATIONS
c. Pulmonary aspergillosis
d. Severe scabies

ALLERGIES
Asthma
Hay fever
Drug reactions
Atopic dermatitis

AUTOIMMUNE AND RELATED DISORDERS
Polyarteritis nodosa
Necrotizing vasculitis
Eosinophilic fasciitis
Pemphigus

NEOPLASTIC DISEASES
Hodgkin's disease
Mycosis fungoides
Note: Table 4-17 describes an approach to investigation of eosinophilia in a returning traveler
Chronic myelocytic leukemia
Eosinophilic leukemia
Polycythemia vera
Mucin-secreting adenocarcinomas

IMMUNODEFICIENCY STATES
Hyperimmunoglobulin E with recurrent infection
Wiskott-Aldrich syndrome

OTHER
Addison's disease
Inflammatory bowel disease
Dermatitis herpetiformis
Toxic/chemical syndrome
Eosinophilic myalgia syndrome, tryptophan, toxic oil syndrome
Hypereosinophilic syndrome (unknown etiology)

EPINEPHRINE, PLASMA
Normal range:
0-90 pg/ml
Elevated in: Pheochromocytomas, neuroblastomas, stress, vigorous exercise, certain foods (bananas, chocolate, coffee, tea, vanilla), hypoglycemia

EPSTEIN-BARR VIRUS SEROLOGY (Box 4-4)
Normal range: IgG anti-VCA <1:10 or negative>

BOX 4-4 Epstein-Barr Virus–Associated Malignancies

Malignancy	Epstein-Barr Virus Frequency
Hodgkin disease	≈40%
Non-Hodgkin lymphomas	
Burkitt lymphoma	20%-95%
Diffuse large B-cell lymphoma and CD30+ Ki-1+ anaplastic large cell lymphoma	10%-35%
Lymphomatoid granulomatosis	80%-95%
T cell–rich B-cell lymphoma	20%
Angioimmunoblastic lymphoma	>80%
T-cell, NK cell, and T/NK-cell lymphomas	30%-90%
Nasopharyngeal carcinoma	>95%
Gastric adenocarcinoma	5%-10%
Pyothorax-associated lymphoma	>95%
Leiomyosarcoma in immunocompromised patients	>95%

From Hoffman R: *Hematology: basic principles and practice*, ed 6, Philadelphia, Saunders, 2013.

Abnormal:
IgG anti-VCA >1:10 or positive indicates either current or previous infection
IgM anti-VCA >1:10 or positive indicates current or recent infection
Anti-EBNA ≥ 1.5 or positive indicates previous infection
Table 4-18 and Fig. 4-16 describe test interpretation.

ERYTHROCYTE SEDIMENTATION RATE (ESR, sed rate, sedimentation rate)
Normal range:
Male: 0-15 mm/hr
Female: 0-20 mm/hr
Elevated in: Collagen vascular diseases, infections, myocardial infarction, neoplasms, inflammatory states (acute phase reactant), hyperthyroidism, hypothyroidism, rouleaux formation
Decreased in: Sickle cell disease, polycythemia, corticosteroids, spherocytosis, anisocytosis, hypofibrinogenemia, increased serum viscosity

ERYTHROPOIETIN (EP)
Normal: 3.7-16.0 IU/L by radioimmunoassay
Erythropoietin is a glycoprotein secreted by the kidneys that stimulates RBC production by acting on erythroid-committed stem cells.
Increased in:
Extremely high: Generally seen in patients with severe anemia (Hct, <25; Hb<7) such as in cases of aplastic anemia, severe hemolytic anemia, hematologic cancers
Very high: Patients with mild to moderate anemia (Hct, 25-35; Hb, 7-10)
High: Patients with mild anemia (e.g., AIDS, myelodysplasia)

TABLE 4-18 Antibody Tests in Epstein-Barr Viral Infection

	Appearance	Peak	Disappears
Heterophil Ab	3-5 days after onset of Sx (range, 0-21 days)	During second wk after onset of Sx (1-4 wk)	2-3 mo after onset of Sx (still found at 1 yr in 20% of cases)
VCA-IgM	Beginning of Sx (1 wk before to 1 wk after Sx begin)	During first wk after onset of Sx (0-21 days)	2-3 mo after onset of Sx (1-6 mo)
VCA-IgG	3 days after onset of Sx (0-2 wk)	During second wk after onset of Sx (1-3 wk)	Decline to lower level, then persists for life
EBNA-IgG	3 wk after onset of Sx (1-4 wk)	8 mo after appearance (3-12 mo)	Lifelong
EA-D	5 days after onset of Sx (during first 1-2 wk after onset of Sx)	14-21 days after onset of Sx (1-4 wk)	9 wk after appearance (2-6 mo)
EBNA-IgM	Same as VCA-IgM	Same as VCA-IgM	Same as VCA-IgM

From Ravel R: *Clinical laboratory medicine,* ed 6, St Louis, 1995, Mosby.
Ab, Antibody; *EA,* early antigen; *EBNA,* Epstein-Barr virus nuclear antigen; *Sx,* symptoms; *VCA,* viral capsid antigen.

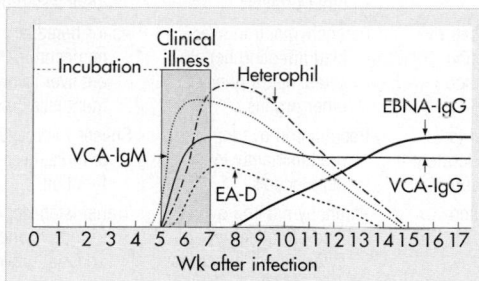

FIGURE 4-16 Tests in Epstein-Barr viral infection. See Table 4-18 for abbreviations. (From Ravel R [ed]: *Clinical laboratory medicine,* ed 6, St Louis, 1995, Mosby.)

Erythropoietin can be inappropriately elevated in patients with malignant neoplasms, renal cysts, postrenal transplant, meningioma, hemangioblastoma, and leiomyoma.
Decreased in: Renal failure, polycythemia vera, autonomic neuropathy

ESTRADIOL (serum)
Normal range:
Female, premenopausal: 30-400 pg/ml, depending on phase of menstrual cycle
Female, postmenopausal: 0-30 pg/ml
Male, adult: 10-50 pg/ml
Decreased in: Ovarian failure
Elevated in: Tumors of ovary, testis, adrenal, or nonendocrine sites (rare)

ESTROGEN
Normal range (serum):
Males:	20-80 pg/ml
Females:	
Follicular:	60-200 pg/ml
Luteal:	160-400 pg/ml
Postmenopausal:	<130 pg/ml

Normal Range (urine):
Males:	4-23 µg/g creatinine
Females:	
Follicular:	7-65 µg/g creatinine
Midcycle:	32-104 µg/g creatinine
Luteal:	8-135 µg/g creatinine

Elevated in: Hyperplasia of adrenal cortex, ovarian tumors producing estrogen, granulosa and thecal cell tumors, testicular tumors
Decreased in: Menopause, hypopituitarism, primary ovarian malfunction, anorexia nervosa, hypofunction of adrenal cortex, ovarian agenesis, psychogenic stress, gonadotropin-releasing hormone deficiency

ETHANOL (blood)
Normal range:
Negative (values <10 mg/dl are considered negative)
Ethanol is metabolized at 10-25 mg/dl/hr. Levels >80 mg/dl are considered evidence of impairment for driving. Fatal blood concentration is considered to be >400 mg/dl.

EXTRACTABLE NUCLEAR ANTIGEN (ENA complex, anti-RNP antibody, anti-SM, anti-Smith)
Normal: Negative
Present in:
Systemic lupus erythematosus, rheumatoid arthritis, Sjögren's syndrome, mixed connective tissue disease

FACTOR V LEIDEN
Test description: PCR test performed on whole blood or tissue. This single mutation, found in 2%-8% of the general Caucasian population, is the single most common cause of hereditary thrombophilia.

FASTING BLOOD SUGAR
See GLUCOSE, FASTING

FBS
See GLUCOSE, FASTING

FDP
See FIBRIN DEGRADATION PRODUCT

FECAL FAT, QUANTITATIVE (72-hr collection)
Normal range:
2-6 g/24 hr (7-21 mmol/dl [CF: 3.515; SMI: 1 mmol/dl])
Elevated in:
Malabsorption syndrome

FECAL GLOBIN IMMUNOCHEMICAL TEST
Normal: Negative. This test is performed by immunochromatography on a cellulose strip that has been impregnated with various antibodies. The test uses a small amount of toilet water as the specimen and is placed onto absorbent pads of card similar to traditional OB card. There is no direct handling of stool. This test is specific for the globin portion of the hemoglobin molecule, which confers lower GI bleeding specificity. It specifically detects blood from the lower GI tract; guaic tests are not lower GI specific. It is more sensitive than typical Hemoccult test (detection limit 50 mcg Hb/g feces versus >500 mcg Hb/g feces for Hemoccult). It has no dietary restrictions and gives no false-positives due to plant peroxidases and red meats. It has no medication restrictions. Iron supplements and NSAIDs do not cause false-positives. Vitamin C does not cause false-negatives.
Positive in: Lower GI bleeding

FERRITIN (serum)
Normal range: 18-300 ng/ml (18-300 µg/L [CF: 1; SMI: 10 µg/L])

TABLE 4-19 Hereditary Iron Overload Disorders

Disorder	Gene, Chromosome Location	Inheritance	Plasma Transferrin Saturation	Plasma Ferritin	Iron Deposition Sites	Clinical Manifestations
Hereditary hemochromatosis, *HFE*-associated (type 1; OMIM 235200)	*HFE*, 6p21	Autosomal recessive	Early increase; >45%	Later increase after third decade	Parenchymal iron overload affecting hepatocytes, heart, pancreas, other organs	Liver and heart disease, diabetes, gonadal failure, arthritis, skin pigmentation
Hereditary hemochromatosis, TfR2-associated (type 3; OMIM 604250)	*TFR2*, 7q22	Autosomal recessive	Early increase; >45%	Later increase after third decade	Parenchymal iron overload affecting hepatocytes, heart, pancreas, other organs	Liver and heart disease, diabetes, gonadal failure, arthritis, skin pigmentation
Juvenile hemochromatosis, hemojuvelin-associated (type 2A; OMIM 602390)	*HJV*, 1q21	Autosomal recessive	Early increase; >45%	Increased by second decade	Parenchymal iron overload affecting hepatocytes, heart, pancreas, other organs	As for hereditary hemochromatosis, but liver involvement less prominent
Juvenile hemochromatosis, hepcidin-associated (type 2B; OMIM 613313)	*HAMP*, 19q13	Autosomal recessive	Early increase; >45%	Increased by second decade	Parenchymal iron overload affecting hepatocytes, heart, pancreas, other organs	As for hereditary hemochromatosis, but liver involvement less prominent
Hemochromatosis, DMT1-associated (OMIM 206100)	*SCL11A2*, 12q13	Autosomal recessive	Early increase; >45%	Normal to moderately elevated	Hepatic iron overload, predominantly in hepatocytes	Severe microcytic anemia, liver dysfunction
Atransferrinemia (OMIM 209300)	*TF*, 3q22	Autosomal recessive	No plasma transferrin	Increased	Parenchymal iron overload affecting hepatocytes, heart, pancreas; no iron in bone marrow or spleen	Transfusion-dependent iron deficiency anemia, growth retardation, poor survival
Aceruloplasminemia (OMIM 604290)	*CP*, 3q24-q25	Autosomal recessive	Decreased	Increased	Marked iron accumulation in basal ganglia, liver, pancreas	Diabetes, progressive neurologic disease, retinal degeneration
Hemochromatosis, ferroportin-associated, with impaired iron export (type 4A; OMIM 606069)	*SLC40A1*, 2q32	Autosomal dominant	Remains normal or low	Early increase	Predominantly macrophage iron deposition	None
Hemochromatosis, ferroportin-associated, with hepcidin resistance (type 4B; OMIM 606069)	*SLC40A1*, 2q32	Autosomal dominant	Early increase; >45%	Early increase	Parenchymal iron overload affecting hepatocytes, heart, pancreas, other organs	Similar to HFE-associated hemochromatosis

From Hoffman R, et al: *Hematology, basic principles and practice*, ed 6, Philadelphia, 2013, Saunders.

Elevated in: Hyperthyroidism, inflammatory states, liver disease (ferritin elevated from necrotic hepatocytes), neoplasms (neuroblastomas, lymphomas, leukemia, breast carcinoma), iron replacement therapy, hemochromatosis, hemosiderosis. Table 4-19 summarizes hereditary iron overload disorders.
Decreased in: Iron deficiency anemia
Ferritin

α-1 FETOPROTEIN
Normal range:
0-20 ng/ml (0-20 μg/L [CF: 1; SMI: 1 μg/L])
Elevated in: Hepatocellular carcinoma (usually values >1000 ng/ml), germinal neoplasms (testis, ovary, mediastinum, retroperitoneum), liver disease (alcoholic cirrhosis, acute hepatitis, chronic active hepatitis), fetal anencephaly, spina bifida, basal cell carcinoma, breast carcinoma, pancreatic carcinoma, gastric carcinoma, retinoblastoma, esophageal atresia

FIBRIN DEGRADATION PRODUCT (FDP)
Normal range:
<10 μg/ml
Elevated in: Disseminated intravascular coagulation, primary fibrinolysis, pulmonary embolism, severe liver disease
NOTE: The presence of rheumatoid factor may cause falsely elevated FDP.

FIBRINOGEN
Normal range:
200-400 mg/dl (2-4 g/L [CF: 0.01; SMI: 0.1 g/L])
Elevated in: Tissue inflammation or damage (acute phase protein reactant), oral contraceptives, pregnancy, acute infection, myocardial infarction
Decreased in: Disseminated intravascular coagulation, hereditary afibrinogenemia, liver disease, primary or secondary fibrinolysis, cachexia

FOLATE (folic acid)
Normal range:
Plasma: 2-10 ng/ml (4-22 nmol/L [CF: 2.266; SMI: 2 nmol/L])
Red blood cells: 140-960 ng/ml (550-2200 nmol/L [CF: 2.266; SMI: 10 nmol/L])
Decreased in: Folic acid deficiency (inadequate intake, malabsorption), alcoholism, drugs (methotrexate, trimethoprim, phenytoin, oral contraceptives, Azulfidine), vitamin B$_{12}$ deficiency (defective red cell folate absorption), hemolytic anemia. Box 4-5 summarizes an etiophysiologic classification of folate deficiency.
Elevated in: Folic acid therapy

FOLLICLE-STIMULATING HORMONE (FSH)
Normal range: 5-20 mIU/ml

BOX 4-5 Etiopathophysiologic Classification of Folate Deficiency

Nutritional causes
    Decreased dietary intake—poverty and famine, institutionalized individuals (psychiatric/nursing homes)/chronic debilitating disease, prolonged feeding of infants with goat's milk, special slimming diets or food fads (folate-rich foods not consumed), cultural/ethnic cooking techniques (food folate destroyed)
    Decreased diet and increased requirements
        Physiologic—pregnancy and lactation, prematurity, hyperemesis gravidarum, infancy
        Pathologic
            Intrinsic hematologic diseases involving hemolysis with compensatory erythropoiesis, abnormal hematopoiesis, or bone marrow infiltration with malignant disease
            Dermatologic disease—psoriasis
Folate malabsorption
    With normal intestinal mucosa
    Drugs—sulfasalazine, pyrimethamine, proton pump inhibitors (via inhibition of proton-coupled folate transporter [PCFT])
    Hereditary folate malabsorption (mutations in PCFTs) (rare)
    With mucosal abnormalities—tropical and nontropical sprue, regional enteritis
Defective cerebral spinal fluid folate transport—cerebral folate deficiency (mutation or autoantibodies to folate receptors) (rare)
Inadequate cellular utilization
    Folate antagonists (methotrexate)
    Hereditary enzyme deficiencies involving folate
Drugs (multiple effects on folate metabolism)—alcohol, sulfasalazine, triamterene, pyrimethamine, trimethoprim-sulfamethoxazole, diphenylhydantoin, barbiturates

From Hoffman R: *Hematology: basic principles and practice*, ed 6, Philadelphia, Saunders, 2013.

Elevated in: Menopause, primary gonadal failure, alcoholism, castration, Klinefelter's syndrome, gonadotropin-secreting pituitary hormones
Decreased in: Pregnancy, polycystic ovary disease, anorexia nervosa, anterior pituitary hypofunction

FREE T4

See T_4, FREE

FREE THYROXINE INDEX

Normal range:
1.1-4.3
INCREASED THYROXINE OR FREE THYROXINE VALUES
Laboratory error
Primary hyperthyroidism (T4/T3 type)
Severe thyroxine-binding globulin elevation
Excess therapy of hypothyroidism
Excessive dose of levothyroxine
Active thyroiditis (subacute, painless, early active Hashimoto's disease)
Familial dysalbuminemic hyperthyroxinemia (some FT4 kits, especially analog types)
Peripheral resistance to T4 syndrome
Amiodarone or propranolol
Postpartum transient toxicosis
Factitious hyperthyroidism
Jod-Basedow (iodine-induced) hyperthyroidism
Severe nonthyroid illness
Acute psychosis (especially paranoid schizophrenia)
T4 sample drawn 2-4 hr after levothyroxine dose
Struma ovarii
Pituitary thyroid-stimulating hormone–secreting tumor
Certain x-ray contrast media (Telepaque and Oragrafin)
Acute porphyria
Heparin effect (some T4 and FT4 kits)
Amphetamine, heroin, methadone, and phencyclidine abuse

Perphenazine or 5-fluorouracil
Antithyroid or anti-IgG heterophil (HAMA) autoantibodies
"T4" hyperthyroidism
Hyperemesis gravidarum; about 50% of patients
High altitudes
DECREASED THYROXINE OR FREE THYROXINE VALUES
Laboratory error
Primary hypothyroidism
Severe nonthyroid illness
Lithium therapy
Severe thyroxine-binding globulin decrease (congenital, disease, or drug-induced) or severe albumin decrease
Dilantin, Depakene, or high-dose salicylate drugs
Pituitary insufficiency
Large doses of inorganic iodide (e.g., saturated solution of potassium iodide)
Moderate or severe iodine deficiency
Cushing's syndrome
High-dose glucocorticoid drugs
Pregnancy, third trimester (low normal or small decrease)
Addison's disease; some patients (30%)
Heparin effect (a few FT4 kits)
Desipramine or amiodarone drugs
Acute psychiatric illness

FTA-ABS (serum)

Normal:
Nonreactive
Reactive in:
Syphilis, other treponemal diseases (yaws, pinta, bejel), SLE, pregnancy

FUROSEMIDE STIMULATION TEST

Normal: Test is performed by giving 60 mg furosemide orally after overnight fast. Patient should be on a normal diet without medications the week before the test. Normal results: renin 1-6 ng angiotensin L/ml/hr.
Elevated in: Renovascular hypertension, Barrter's syndrome, high-renin essential hypertension, pheochromocytoma
No response in: Primary aldosteronism, low-renin essential hypertension, hyporeninemic hypoaldosteronism

GAMMA-GLUTAMYL TRANSFERASE (GGT)

See γ-GLUTAMYL TRANSFERASE

GASTRIN (serum)

Normal range: 0-180 pg/ml (0-180 ng/L [CF: 1; SMI: 10 ng/L])
Elevated in: Zollinger-Ellison syndrome (gastrinoma), pernicious anemia, hyperparathyroidism, retained gastric antrum, chronic renal failure, gastric ulcer, chronic atrophic gastritis, pyloric obstruction, malignant neoplasms of the stomach, H_2-blockers, omeprazole, calcium therapy, ulcerative colitis, rheumatoid arthritis

GASTRIN STIMULATION TEST

Normal: Gastrin stimulation test after calcium infusion is performed by giving a calcium infusion (15 mg/kg in 500 ml normal saline over 4 hours). Serum is drawn in fasting state before infusion and at 1, 2, 3, and 4 hr. Normal response is little or no increase over baseline gastrin level.
Elevated in: Gastrinoma (gastrin >400 pg/ml), duodenal ulcer (gastrin level increase <400 ng/L)
Decreased in: Pernicious anemia, atrophic gastritis

GLIADIN ANTIBODIES, IGA AND IGG

Normal: <25 U, equivocal 20-25 U, positive >25 U. Test is useful to monitor compliance with gluten-free diet in patients with celiac disease.
Elevated in: Celiac disease with dietary noncompliance

GLOMERULAR BASEMENT MEMBRANE (gBm) ANTIBODY

Normal: Negative
Present in: Goodpasture's syndrome

GLOMERULAR FILTRATION RATE

See Box 4-6 for a summary of common equations for calculating GFR or creatinine clearance.

Normal:

Ages 20-29	116 ml/min/1.73 m^2
Ages 30-39	107 ml/min/1.73 m^2
Ages 40-49	99 ml/min/1.73 m^2
Ages 50-59	93 ml/min/1.73 m^2
Ages 60-69	85 ml/min/1.73 m^2
Ages >75	75 ml/min/1.73 m^2

Decreased in: Renal insufficiency, decreased renal blood flow

---

BOX 4-6   Common Equations for Estimating Glomerular Filtration Rate or Creatinine Clearance

Cockcoft-Gault (C_{Cr} · BSA/1.73 m^2)
For men: $C_{Cr} = [(140 - age) \cdot weight\ (kg)]/S_{Cr} \cdot 72$
For women: $C_{Cr} = ([(140 - age) \cdot weight\ (kg)]/S_{Cr} \cdot 72) \cdot 0.85$

MDRD (1)
GFR = 170 · $[S_{Cr}]^{-0.999}$ · $[age]^{-0.176}$ · [0.762 if patient is female] · [1.18 if patient is black] · $[BUN]^{-0170}$ · $[Alb]^{0.318}$

MDRD (2)
GFR = 186 · $[S_{Cr.}]^{-1.154}$ · $[age]^{-0.203}$ · [0.742 if patient is female] · [1.212 if patient is black]

Jellife (1) (C_{Cr} · BSA/1.73 m^2)
For men: $(98 - [0.8 \cdot (age - 20)])/S_{Cr}$
For women: $(98 - [0.8 \cdot (age - 20)])S_{Cr} \cdot 0.90$

Jellife (2)
For men: $(100/S_{Cr}) - 12$
For women: $(80/S_{Cr}) - 7$

Mawer
For men: weight · $[29.3 - (0.203 \cdot age)] \cdot [1 - (0.03 \cdot S_{Cr})]$
For women: weight · $[25.3 - (0.175 \cdot age)] \cdot [1 - (0.03 \cdot S_{Cr})]$

Bjornsson
For men: $[27 - (0.173 \cdot age)] \cdot weight \cdot 0/S_{Cr}$
For women: $[25 - (0.175 \cdot age)] \cdot weight \cdot 0.07/S_{Cr}$

Gates
For men: $(89.4 \cdot S_{Cr}^{-1.2}) + (55 - age) \cdot (0.447 \cdot S_{Cr}^{-1.1})$
For women: $(89.4 \cdot S_{Cr}^{-1.2}) + (55 - age) \cdot (0.447 \cdot S_{Cr}^{-1.1})$

Salazar-Corcoran
For men: $[137 - age] \cdot [(0.285 \cdot weight) + (12.1 \cdot height^2)]/(51 \cdot S_{Cr})$
For women: $[146 - age] \cdot [(0.287 \cdot weight) + (9.74 \cdot height^2)]/(60 \cdot S_{Cr})$

From Vincent JL et al: *Textbook of critical care*, ed 6, Philadelphia, 2011, Saunders.

GLUCAGON

Normal: 20-100 pg/ml
Elevated in: Glucagonoma (900-7800 pg/ml), chronic renal failure, diabetes mellitus, glucocorticoids, insulin, nifedipine, danazol, sympathomimetic amines
Decreased in: Hyperlipoproteinemia (types III, IV), beta-blockers, secretin

GLUCOSE, FASTING (FBS, fasting blood sugar)

Fig. E4-17 describes the approach to hypoglycemia. An algorithm for evaluation of hypoglycemia in children is described in Fig. E4-18.
Normal range: 60-99 mg/dl (3.8-6.0 mmol/L [CF: 0.05551; SMI: 0.1 mmol/L])
Elevated in: Diabetes mellitus, stress, infections, myocardial infarction, cerebrovascular accident, Cushing's syndrome, acromegaly, acute pancreatitis, glucagonoma, hemochromatosis, drugs (glucocorticoids, diuretics [thiazides, loop diuretics]), glucose intolerance, impaired fasting glucose
Decreased in: Sulfonylurea therapy, insulin therapy, reactive hypoglycemia (e.g., subtotal gastrectomy), starvation, insulinoma, glycogen storage disorders, severe liver disease or renal disease, ethanol-induced hypoglycemia, mesenchymal tumors that secrete insulin-like hormones

GLUCOSE, POSTPRANDIAL

Normal range: <140 mg/dl (<7.8 mmol/L [CF: 0.05551; SMI: 0.1 mmol/L])
Elevated in: Diabetes mellitus, glucose intolerance

Decreased in: Post-gastrointestinal resection, reactive hypoglycemia, hereditary fructose intolerance, galactosemia, leucine sensitivity

GLUCOSE TOLERANCE TEST

Normal values above fasting:
23. 30 min: 30-60 mg/dl (1.65-3.3 mmol/L [CF: 0.05551; SMI: 0.1 mmol/L])
24. 60 min: 20-50 mg/dl (1.1-2.75 mmol/L [CF: 0.05551; SMI: 0.1 mmol/L])
25. 120 min: 5-15 mg/dl (0.28-0.83 mmol/L [CF: 0.05551; SMI: 0.1 mmol/L])
26. 180 min: fasting level or below
Abnormal in: Glucose intolerance, diabetes mellitus, Cushing's syndrome, acromegaly, pheochromocytoma, gestational diabetes

GLUCOSE-6-PHOSPHATE DEHYDROGENASE (G6PD)
Screen (blood)

Normal: G6PD enzyme activity detected
Abnormal: If a deficiency is detected, quantitation of G6PD is necessary; a G6PD screen may be falsely interpreted as "normal" after an episode of hemolysis because most G6PD-deficient cells have been destroyed.

γ-GLUTAMYL TRANSFERASE (GGT)

Normal range: 0-30 U/L (0.050 μkat/L [CF: 0.01667; SMI: 0.01 μkat/L])
Elevated in: Chronic alcoholic liver disease, neoplasms (hepatoma, metastatic disease to the liver, carcinoma of the pancreas), systemic lupus erythematosus, congestive heart failure, trauma, nephrotic syndrome, sepsis, cholestasis, drugs (phenytoin, barbiturates)

GLYCOHEMOGLOBIN (glycated glycosylated]
hemoglobin), (HbA$_{1c}$)

Normal range: 4.0%-5.9%
Elevated in: Uncontrolled diabetes mellitus (glycated hemoglobin levels reflect the level of glucose control over the preceding 120 days), lead toxicity, alcoholism, iron deficiency anemia, hypertriglyceridemia
Decreased in: Hemolytic anemias, decreased red blood cell survival, pregnancy, acute or chronic blood loss, chronic renal failure, insulinoma, congenital spherocytosis, hemoglobin S, C, and D diseases

GROWTH HORMONE

Normal: Male: 1-9 ng/ml; female: 1-16 ng/ml
Elevated in: Pituitary gigantism, acromegaly, ectopic GH secretion, cirrhosis, renal failure, anorexia nervosa, stress, exercise, prolonged fasting, amphetamines, beta-blockers, insulin, levodopa, metoclopramide, clonidine, vasopressin, human growth hormone (HGH) supplementation
Decreased in: Hypopituitarism, pituitary dwarfism, adrenocortical hyperfunction, bromocriptine, corticosteroids, glucose

GROWTH HORMONE RELEASING HORMONE (GHRH)

Normal: <50 pg/ml
Elevated in: Acromegaly caused by GHRH secretion by neoplasms

GROWTH HORMONE SUPPRESSION TEST (after glucose)

Normal: Test is done by giving 1.75 g glucose/kg orally after overnight fast. Blood is drawn at baseline, after 60 min, and after 120 min of glucose load. Normal response is growth hormone suppression to <2 ng/ml or undetectable levels.
Abnormal: There is no or incomplete suppression from the high basal level in gigantism or acromegaly.

HAM TEST (acid serum test)

Normal: Negative
Positive in: Paroxysmal nocturnal hemoglobinuria
False-positive in: Hereditary or acquired spherocytosis, recent transfusion with aged red blood cells, aplastic anemia, myeloproliferative syndromes, leukemia, hereditary dyserythropoietic anemia type II

HAPTOGLOBIN (serum)

Normal range: 50-220 mg/dl (0.50-2.2 g/L [CF: 0.01; SMI: 0.01 g/L])

Elevated in: Inflammation (acute phase reactant), collagen vascular diseases, infections (acute phase reactant), drugs (androgens), obstructive liver disease
Decreased in: Hemolysis (intravascular more than extravascular), megaloblastic anemia, severe liver disease, large tissue hematomas, infectious mononucleosis, drugs (oral contraceptives)

HBA$_{1C}$
See GLYCOHEMOGLOBIN

HDL
See HIGH-DENSITY LIPOPROTEIN CHOLESTEROL

HELICOBACTER PYLORI (serology, stool antigen)
Normal range: Not detected
Detected in: H. pylori infection. Positive serology can indicate current or past infection. Positive stool antigen test indicates acute infection (sensitivity and specificity >90%). Stool testing should be delayed at least 4 weeks after eradication therapy.

HEMATOCRIT
Normal range:
Male: 39%-49% (0.39-0.49 [CF: 0.01; SMI: 0.01])
Female: 33%-43% (0.33-0.43 [CF: 0.01; SMI: 0.01])
Elevated in: Polycythemia vera, smoking, chronic obstructive pulmonary disease, high altitudes, dehydration, hypovolemia
Decreased in: Blood loss (gastrointestinal, genitourinary) anemia

HEMOGLOBIN
Normal range:
Male: 13.6-17.7 g/dl (136-172 g/L [CF: 10; SMI: 1 g/L])
Female: 12.0-15.0 g/dl (120-150 g/L [CF: 10; SMI: 1 g/L])
Elevated in: Hemoconcentration, dehydration, polycythemia vera, chronic obstructive pulmonary disease, high altitudes, false elevations (hyperlipemic plasma, white blood cells >50,000/mm^3), stress
Decreased in: Hemorrhagic (gastrointestinal, genitourinary) anemia

HEMOGLOBIN A$_{1C}$
See GLYCOHEMOGLOBIN

HEMOGLOBIN ELECTROPHORESIS
Table 4-20 describes neonatal hemoglobin electrophoresis patterns, Table 4-21 summarizes types of hemoglobin, and Table 4-22 describes classifications of hemoglobinopathies.
Normal range:
HbA$_1$: 95%-98%
HbA$_2$: 1.5%-3.5%
HbF: <2%
HbC: absent
HbS: absent

HEMOGLOBIN, GLYCATED
See GLYCOHEMOGLOBIN

HEMOGLOBIN, GLYCOSYLATED
See GLYCOHEMOGLOBIN

HEMOGLOBIN H
See Table 4-21.
Normal: Negative
Present in:
Hemoglobin H disease, alpha-thalassemia trait, unstable hemoglobin disorders

HEMOGLOBIN, URINE
See URINE HEMOGLOBIN, FREE

HEMOSIDERIN, URINE
See URINE HEMOGLOBIN, FREE

TABLE 4-20   Neonatal Hemoglobin (Hb) Electrophoresis Patterns*

FA	Fetal Hb and adult normal Hb; the normal newborn pattern.
FAV	Indicates the presence of both HbF and HbA. However, an anomalous band (V) is present, which does not appear to be any of the common Hb variants.
FAS	Indicates fetal Hb, adult normal HbA, and HbS, consistent with benign sickle cell trait.
FS	Fetal and sickle HbS without detectable adult normal HbA. Consistent with clinically significant homozygous sickle Hb genotype (S/S) or sickle β-thalassemia, with manifestations of sickle cell anemia during childhood.
FC†	Designates the presence of HbC without adult normal HbA. Consistent with clinically significant homozygous HbC genotype (C/C), resulting in a mild hematologic disorder presenting during childhood.
FSC	HbS and HbC present. This heterozygous condition could lead to the manifestations of sickle cell disease during childhood.
FAC	HbC and adult normal HbA present, consistent with benign HbC trait.
FSA	Heterozygous HbS/β-thalassemia, a clinically significant sickling disorder.
F†	Fetal HbF is present without adult normal HbA. Although this may indicate a delayed appearance of HbA, it is also consistent with homozygous β-thalassemia major, or homozygous hereditary persistence of fetal HbF.
FV†	Fetal HbF and an anomalous Hb variant (V) are present.
AF	May indicate prior blood transfusion. Submit another filter paper blood specimen when the infant is 4 mo of age, at which time the transfused blood cells should have been cleared.

From Tschudy MM, Arcara KM: *The Harriet Lane handbook,* ed 19, Philadelphia, 2012, Mosby.
NOTE: HbA: α2β2; HbF: α2γ2; HbA2: α2δ2.
*Hemoglobin variants are reported in order of decreasing abundance; for example, FA indicates more fetal than adult hemoglobin.
†Repeat blood specimen should be submitted to confirm the original interpretation.

TABLE 4-21   Types of Hemoglobin

	Hemoglobin	Structure	Comment
Normal	A	$\alpha_2\beta_2$	97% of adult hemoglobin
	A$_2$	$\alpha_2\delta_2$	2% of adult Hb; elevated in β-thalassemia
	F	$\alpha_2\gamma_2$	Normal Hb in fetus from 3rd to 9th month; increased in β-thalassemia
Abnormal chain production	H	β_4	Found in α-thalassemia, biologically useless
	Barts	γ_4	Found in α-thalassemia, biologically useless
Abnormal chain structure	S	$\alpha_2\beta_2$	Substitution of valine for glutamic acid in position 6 of β chain
	C	$\alpha_2\beta_2$	Substitution of lysine for glutamic acid in position 6 of β chain

From Ballinger A: *Kumar & Clark's essentials of clinical medicine,* ed 6, Edinburgh, 2012, Saunders.

HEPARIN-INDUCED THROMBOCYTOPENIA ANTIBODIES
Normal: Antigen assay: Negative, <0.45; weak, 0.45-1.0; strong, >1.0
Elevated in: Heparin-induced thrombocytopenia

HEPATITIS A ANTIBODY
Normal: Negative
Present in: Viral hepatitis A; can be IgM or IgG (if IgM, acute hepatitis A; if IgG, previous infection with hepatitis A)
See Fig. 4-19 for serologic tests in HAV infection.

Laboratory Tests

IV

TABLE 4-22 Classification of Hemoglobinopathies

Structural hemoglobinopathies—hemoglobins with altered amino acid sequenc-
es that result in deranged function or altered physical or chemical properties
Abnormal Hemoglobin Polymerization—HBS
Altered Oxygen Affinity
High affinity—polycythemia
Low affinity—cyanosis, pseudoanemia
Hemoglobins That Oxidize Readily
Unstable hemoglobins, hemolytic anemia, jaundice
M hemoglobins—methemoglobinemia, cyanosis
Thalassemias—Defective Production of Globin Chains
α-Thalassemias
β-Thalassemias
$\delta\beta$-, $\gamma\delta\beta$-, $\alpha\beta$-Thalassemias
Structural hemoglobinopathies—structurally abnormal Hb associated with
coinherited thalassemia phenotype
HbE
Hb Constant Spring
Hb Lepore
Hereditary Persistence of Fetal Hemoglobin—Persistence of High Levels of Hbf
Into Adult Life
Pancellular—all red blood cells contain elevated HbF levels
Nondeletion forms
Deletion forms
Hb Kenya
Heterocellular—only specific subpopulation of red blood cells contain elevated
levels of HbF
Acquired Hemoglobinopathies
Methemoglobin due to toxic exposures
Sulfhemoglobin due to toxic exposures
Carboxyhemoglobin
HbH in erythroleukemia
Elevated HbF in states of erythroid stress and bone marrow dysplasia, usually
heterocellular

From Hoffman R: *Hematology: basic principles and practice*, ed 6, Philadelphia, 2013, Saunders.
Hb, Hemoglobin.

HAV-IGM ANTIBODY

Appearance: About the same time as clinical symptoms (3-4 weeks after
exposure; range, 14-60 days), or just before beginning of AST/ALT elevation
(range, 10 days before to 7 days after)
Peak: About 3-4 weeks after onset of symptoms (1-6 weeks)
Becomes nondetectable: 3-4 months after onset of symptoms (1-6 months).
In a few cases HAV-IgM antibody can persist as long as 12-14 months.

HAV TOTAL ANTIBODY

Appearance: About 3 weeks after IgM becomes detectable (therefore
about the middle of clinical symptom period to early convalescence)

Peak: About 1-2 months after onset
Becomes nondetectable: Remains elevated for life but can somewhat
slowly fall

HEPATITIS A VIRAL INFECTION

Best all-purpose test(s) to diagnose acute HAV infection = HAV-Ab (IgM)
Best all-purpose test(s) to demonstrate past HAV infection/immunity =
HAV-Ab (total)

HEPATITIS B SURFACE ANTIGEN (HBsAg)

Normal: Not detected
Detected in: Acute viral hepatitis type B, chronic hepatitis B
Appearance: 2-6 weeks after exposure (range, 6 days to 6 months);
5%-15% of patients are negative at onset of jaundice
Peak: 1-2 weeks before to 1-2 weeks after onset of symptoms
Becomes nondetectable: 1-3 months after peak (range, 1 week to 5
months)

HEPATITIS B VIRAL INFECTION

See Table 4-23
    Figs. 4-20, 4-21, and 4-22 illustrate antigens and antibodies in hepatitis
B infection.
HB$_S$
-Ag:
HB$_S$Ag: shows current active HBV infection.
Persistence over 6 months indicates carrier/chronic HBV infection.
HBV nucleic acid probe: present before and longer than HB$_S$Ag.
More reliable marker for increased infectivity than HB$_S$Ag and/or HB$_e$Ag.
-Ab:
HB$_S$Ab-total: shows previous healed HBV infection and evidence of
immunity.
HB$_C$
-Ab:
HB$_C$Ab-IgM: shows either acute or very recent infection by HBV.
In convalescent phase of acute HBV, may be elevated when HB$_S$Ag has
disappeared (core window).
Negative HB$_C$Ab-IgM with positive HB$_S$Ag suggests either very early acute
HBV or carrier/chronic HBV.
HB$_C$Ab-total: only useful to show past HBV infection if HB$_S$Ag and HB$_C$Ab-
IgM are both negative.
HB$_E$
-Ag:
HB$_e$-AbAg: when present, especially without HB$_e$Ab, suggests increased
patient infectivity.
HB$_e$Ab-total: when present, suggests less patient infectivity.
    HB$_S$Ag positive, HB$_C$Ab negative
        About 5% (range, 0%-17%) of patients with early-stage HBV acute
        infection (HB$_C$Ab rises later)

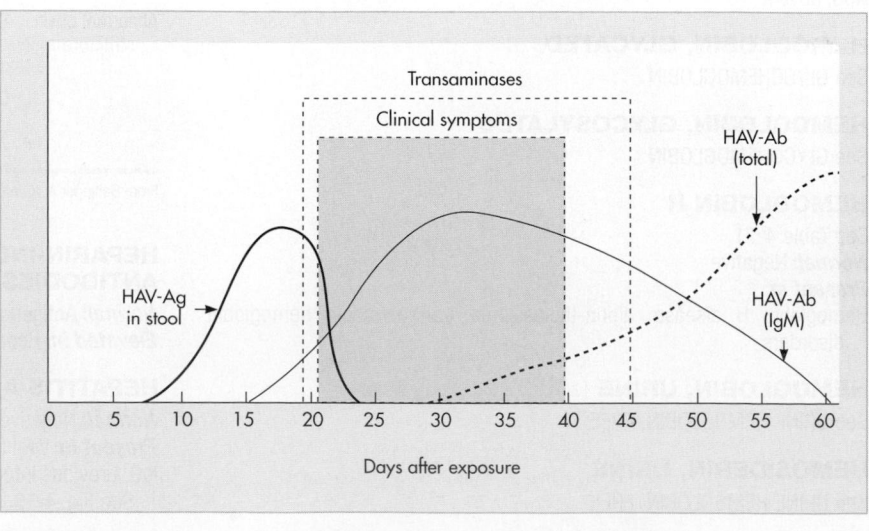

FIGURE 4-19 Serologic tests in HAV infection. (From
Ravel R [ed]: *Clinical laboratory medicine*, ed 6, St Louis,
1995, Mosby.)

TABLE 4-23 Serologic Markers of Hepatitis B Infection

	HBsAg	anti-HBc	anti-HBs	IgM anti-HBc
Susceptible to infection	Negative	Negative	Negative	Negative
Immune due to natural infection	Negative	Positive	Positive	Negative
Immune due to hepatitis B vaccination	Negative	Negative	Positive	Negative
Acutely infected	Positive	Positive	Negative	Positive
Chronically infected	Positive	Positive	Negative	Negative

From Ballinger A: *Kumar & Clark's essentials of clinical medicine*, ed 6, Edinburgh, 2012, Saunders.

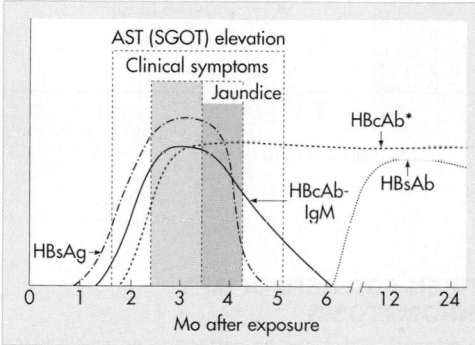

FIGURE 4-20 HBV surface antigen-antibody and core antibodies. Note "core window." *HB$_C$Ab = HB$_C$Ab-IgM + HBCAb-IgG (combined). (From Ravel R [ed]: *Clinical laboratory medicine*, ed 6, St Louis, 1995, Mosby.)

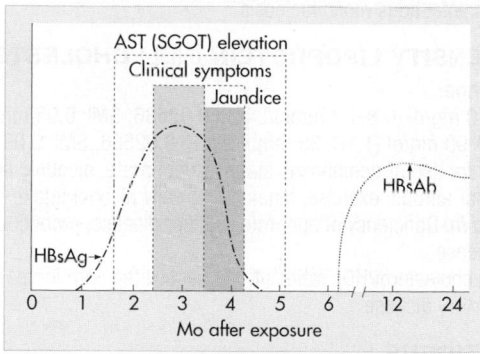

FIGURE 4-21 HBV surface antigen and antibody (HB$_S$Ag and HB$_S$Ab-total). (From Ravel R [ed]: *Clinical laboratory medicine,* ed 6, St Louis, 1995, Mosby.)

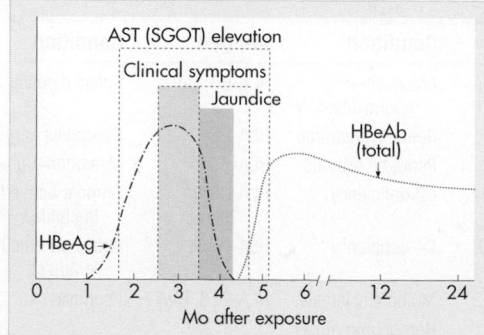

FIGURE 4-22 HBVe antigen and antibody. (From Ravel R [ed]: *Clinical laboratory medicine,* ed 6, St Louis, 1995, Mosby.)

HB$_S$Ag positive, HB$_C$Ab positive, HB$_S$Ab negative
  Most of the clinical symptom stage
  Chronic HBV carriers without evidence of liver disease ("asymptomatic carriers")
  Chronic HBV hepatitis (chronic persistent type or chronic active type)
HB$_S$Ag negative, HB$_C$Ab positive,* HB$_S$Ab negative
  Late clinical symptom stage or early convalescence stage (core window)
  Chronic HBV infection with HB$_S$Ag below detection levels with current tests
  Old previous HBV infection
HB$_S$Ag negative, HB$_C$Ab positive, HB$_S$Ab positive
  Late convalescence to complete recovery
  Old infection

HEPATITIS C VIRAL INFECTION

Fig. 4-23 illustrates antigens and antibodies in hepatitis C infection.

HEPATITIS C RNA

Normal: Negative
Elevated in: Hepatitis C. Detection of hepatitis C-RNA is used to confirm current infection and to monitor treatment. Quantitative assays (viral load) are needed before treatment to assess response (<2 log decrease after 12-week treatment indicates lack of response).

HCV
-Ag:
HCV nucleic acid probe: shows current infection by HCV (especially with PCR amplification).
-Ab:
HCV-Ab (IgG): current, convalescent, or old HCV infection.
HAV
-Ag:
HAV-Ag by EM: shows presence of virus in stool early in infection.
-Ab:
HAV-Ab (IgM): current or recent HAV infection.
HAV-Ab (total): convalescent or old HAV infection.

HEPATITIS D VIRAL INFECTION

Fig. 4-24 illustrates antigens and antibodies in hepatitis D infection.
Best current all-purpose screening test = HDV-Ab (total)
Best test to differentiate acute from chronic infection = HDV-Ab (IgM)

DELTA HEPATITIS COINFECTION (acute HDV1 acute HBV) or Superinfection (acute HDV1 chronic HBV)

HDV
-Ag:
9. HDV-Ag: shows current infection (acute or chronic) by HDV.
10. HDV nucleic acid probe: detects antigen before and longer than HDV-Ag by EIA.

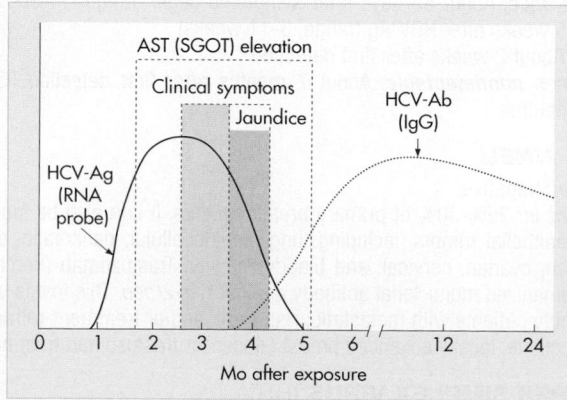

FIGURE 4-23 HCV antigen and antibody. (From Ravel R [ed]: *Clinical laboratory medicine,* ed 6, St Louis, 1995, Mosby.)

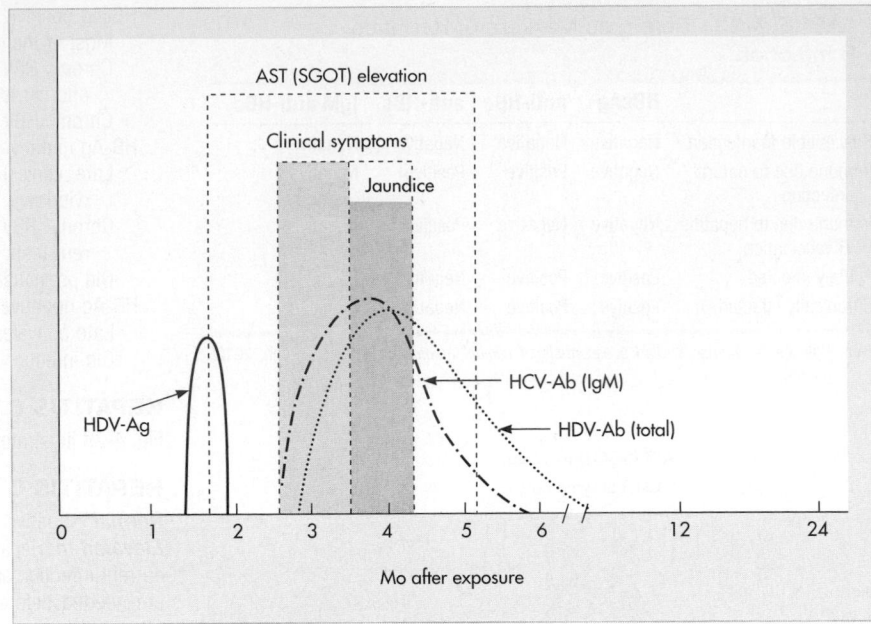

FIGURE 4-24 HDV antigen and antibodies. (From Ravel R [ed]: *Clinical laboratory medicine,* ed 6, St Louis, 1995, Mosby.)

-Ab:

j. HDV-Ab (IgM): high elevation in acute HDV; does not persist.

k. Low or moderate elevation in convalescent HDV; does not persist.

l. Low to high persistent elevation in chronic HDV (depends on degree of cell injury and sensitivity of the assay).

m. HDV-Ab (total): high elevation in acute HDV; does not persist.

n. High persistent elevation in chronic HDV.

HDV-AG

Detected by DNA probe, less often by immunoassay

Appearance: Prodromal stage (before symptoms); just at or after initial rise in ALT (about a week after appearance of HB$_S$Ag and about the time HB$_C$Ab-IgM level begins to rise)

Peak: 2-3 days after onset

Becomes nondetectable: 1-4 days (may persist until shortly after symptoms appear)

HDV-AB (IgM)

Appearance: About 10 days after symptoms begin (range, 1-28 days)

Peak: About 2 weeks after first detection

Becomes nondetectable: About 35 days (range, 10-80 days) after first detection (most other IgM antibodies take 3-6 months to become nondetectable)

HDV-AB (total)

Appearance: About 50 days after symptoms begin (range, 14-80 days); about 5 weeks after HDV-Ag (range, 3-11 weeks)

Peak: About 2 weeks after first detection

Becomes nondetectable: About 7 months after first detection (range, 4-14 months)

HER-2/NEU

Normal: Negative

Present in: 25%-30% of primary breast cancers. It can also be found in other epithelial tumors, including lung, hepatocellular, pancreatic, colon, stomach, ovarian, cervical, and bladder cancer. Trastuzumab (Herceptin) is a humanized monoclonal antibody against Her-2/*neu*. This test is useful to identify patients with metastatic; recurrent; and/or treatment-refractory, unresectable, locally advanced breast cancer for trastuzumab treatment.

HERPES SIMPLEX VIRUS (HSV)

Test description: The PCR test can be performed on serum biopsy samples, CSF, vitreous humor.

HFE SCREEN FOR HEREDITARY HEMOCHROMATOSIS

Test description: PCR test can be performed on whole blood or tissue. One mutation (C282Y) and two polymorphisms (H63D, S65C) account for the majority of alleles associated with this disease.

HETEROPHIL ANTIBODY

Normal: Negative

Positive in: Infectious mononucleosis

HIGH-DENSITY LIPOPROTEIN (HDL) CHOLESTEROL

Normal range:

Male: 40-70 mg/dl (0.8-1.8 mmol/L [CF: 0.02586; SMI: 0.05 mmol/L])

Female: 50-90 mg/dl (1.1-2.35 mmol/L [CF: 0.02586; SMI: 0.05 mmol/L])

Increased in: Use of gemfibrozil, statins, fenofibrate, nicotinic acid, estrogens, regular aerobic exercise, small (1 oz) daily alcohol intake

Decreased in: Deficiency of apoproteins, liver disease, probucol ingestion, Tangier disease

NOTE: A cholesterol/HDL ratio >4.0 is associated with increased risk of coronary artery disease.

HLA ANTIGENS

Associated disorders: see Table 4-24.

TABLE 4-24 **HLA Antigens Associated with Specific Diseases**

Antigen	Condition	Antigen	Condition
HLA-B27	Ankylosing spondylitis	HLA-B8, Dw3	Celiac disease
	Reiter's syndrome	HLA-B8, Dw3	Dermatitis herpetiformis
	Psoriatic arthritis	HLA-B8	Myasthenia gravis
HLA-A10, B18, Dw2	C2 deficiency	HLA-B8	Chronic active hepatitis in children
HLA-A2, B40, Cw3	C4 deficiency	HLA-Drw4	Active chronic hepatitis in adults
HLA-B7, Dw2	Multiple sclerosis	HLA-B13, Bw17	Psoriasis
HLA-A3	Hemochromatosis		

From Cerra FB: *Manual of critical care,* St Louis, 1987, Mosby.
HLA, Human leukocyte antigen.

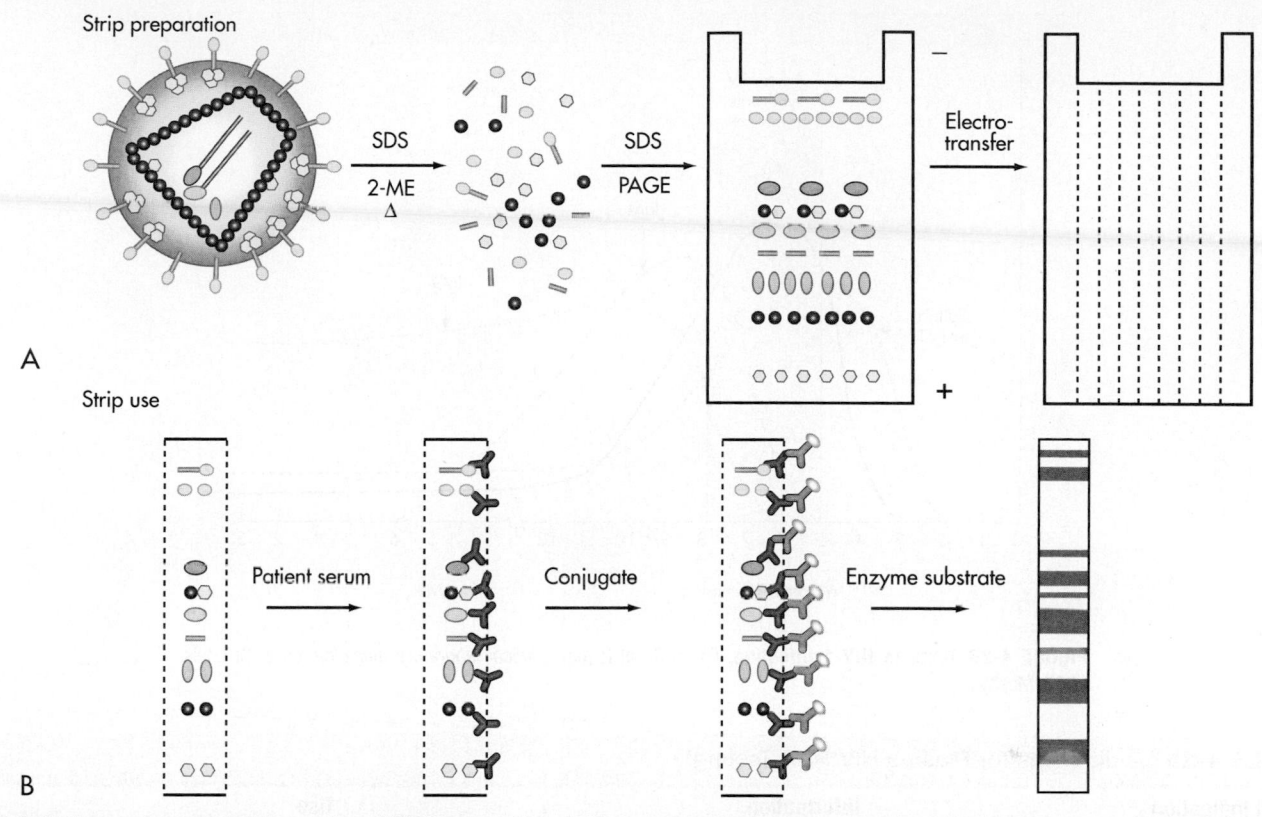

FIGURE 4-25 Human immunodeficiency virus (HIV) Western blot. A, Western blot strips are prepared with purified HIV virions that are disrupted with ionic detergent and reducing agent, subjected to sodium dodecyl sulfate–polyacrylamide gel electrophoresis (SDS-PAGE), and electrotransferred to solid strips, typically of nitrocellulose. **B,** Strips are sequentially incubated with patient sample (serum, plasma, saliva, or urine); enzyme-conjugated antihuman IgG; and enzyme substrate. The positions of enzymes bound identify the presence of antibody to individual HIV proteins. (From Bennett JE , Dolin R, Blaser MJ: *Mandell, Douglas, and Bennett's principles and practice of infectious diseases,* ed 8, Philadelphia, 2015, Saunders.)

HOMOCYSTEINE (plasma)

Normal range:

0-30 years:	4.6-8.1 mcmol/L
30-59 years:	6.3-11.2 mcmol/L (males), 4.5-7.9 mcmol/L (females)
>59 years:	5.8-11.9 mcmol/L

Increased: Thrombophilic states, B_6, B_{12}, folic acid, riboflavin deficiency, pregnancy, homocystinuria

NOTE: An increased homocysteine level is an independent risk factor for atherosclerosis.

HUMAN CHORIONIC GONADOTROPIN (hCG)

Normal range: Varies with gestational stage:

1 wk:	5-50 mU/ml
1-2 wk:	50-550 mU/ml
2-3 wk:	up to 5000 mU/ml
3-4 wk:	up to 10,000 mU/ml
4-5 wk:	up to 50,000 mU/ml
2-3 mo:	10,000-100,000 mU/ml

Elevated in: Normal pregnancy, hydatidiform mole, choriocarcinoma, germ cell tumors of testicle, some nontrophoblastic neoplasms (e.g., neoplasms of cervix, gastrointestinal tract, ovary, lung, breast)

HUMAN HERPES VIRUS 8 (HHV8)

Test description: PCR test can be performed on whole blood, tissue, bone marrow, and urine. HHV8 is found in all forms of Kaposi's sarcoma.

HUMAN IMMUNODEFICIENCY VIRUS ANTIBODY, TYPE 1 (HIV-1)

Normal range: Not detected
Abnormal result: HIV antibodies usually appear in the blood 1-4 months after infection.

Testing sequence:
ELISA is the recommended initial screening test. Sensitivity and specificity are >99%. False-positive ELISA may occur with autoimmune disorders, administration of immune globulin manufactured before 1985, within 6 weeks of testing, in the presence of rheumatoid factor, in the presence of DLA-DR antibodies in multigravida female, with administration of influenza vaccine within 3 months of testing, with hemodialysis, with positive plasma reagin test, and with certain medical disorders (hemophilia, hypergammaglobulinemia, alcoholic hepatitis).

A positive ELISA is confirmed with Western blot (Fig. 4-25). False-positive Western blot may result from connective tissue disorders, human leukocyte antigen antibodies, polyclonal gammopathies, hyperbilirubinemia, presence of antibody to another human retrovirus, or cross-reaction with other non-virus-derived proteins in healthy persons. Undetermined Western blot may occur in AIDS patients with advanced immunodeficiency (caused by loss of antibodies) and in recent HIV infections.

PCR is used to confirm indeterminate Western blot results or negative results in persons with suspected HIV infection.

Fig. 4-26 describes tests in HIV infection; indications for plasma HIV RNA testing are described in Table 4-25.

HUMAN IMMUNODEFICIENCY VIRUS TYPE 1 (HIV-1)
Antigen (p24), Qualitative (p24 antigen)

Normal range: Negative. This test detects uncomplexed HIV-1 p24 antigen. The core protein p24 is the first detectable protein encoded by the group-specific antigen *(gag)* gene. This protein is a marker for viremia. This test should not be used in place of HIV-1 antibody testing as a screen for HIV-1 infection. HIV-1 p24 may be detectable in the first month of acute HIV-1 infection and generally falls to undetectable levels during the asymptomatic stage of HIV-1 infection. A negative result does not exclude the possibility of infection or exposure to HIV-1. It is recommended that a negative result be followed with repeat testing at least 8 weeks after the original test. This test is used primarily for screening of donated blood and plasma and as an aid for the prognosis of HIV-1 infection.

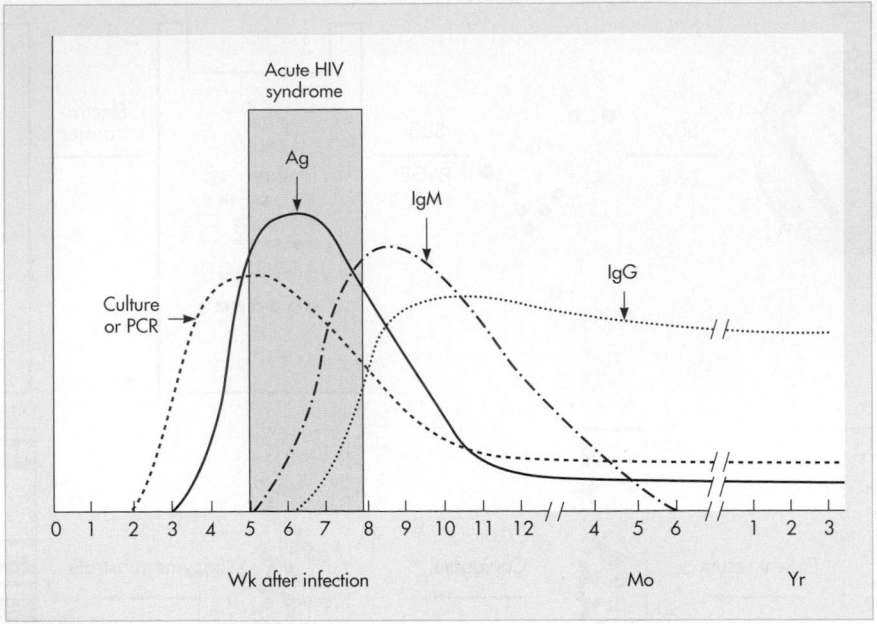

FIGURE 4-26 Tests in HIV-1 infection. (From Ravel R [ed]: *Clinical laboratory medicine,* ed 6, St Louis, 1995, Mosby.)

TABLE 4-25   Indications for Plasma HIV RNA Testing*

Clinical Indication	Information	Use
Syndrome consistent with acute HIV infection	Establishes diagnosis when HIV antibody test is negative or indeterminate	Diagnosis[†]
Initial evaluation of newly diagnosed HIV infection	Baseline viral load set point	Decision to start or defer therapy
Every 3-4 mo in patients not on therapy	Changes in viral load	Decision to start therapy
4-8 wk after initiation of antiretroviral therapy	Initial assessment of drug efficacy	Decision to continue or change therapy
3-4 mo after start of therapy	Maximal effect of therapy	Decision to continue or change therapy
Every 3-4 mo in patients on therapy	Durability of antiretroviral effect	Decision to continue or change therapy
Clinical event or significant decline in CD4+ T cells	Association with changing or stable	Decision to continue, initiate, or change

From Report of the NIH Panel to Define Principles of Therapy of HIV Infection, *MMWR Recomm Rep* 47(RR-5):1-41, 1998.

*Acute illness (e.g., bacterial pneumonia, tuberculosis, HSV, PCP) and immunizations can cause increase in plasma HIV RNA for 2-4 wk; viral load testing should not be performed during this time. Plasma HIV RNA results should usually be verified with a repeat determination before starting or making changes in therapy. HIV RNA should be measured using the same laboratory and the same assay.

[†]Diagnosis of HIV infection determined by HIV RNA testing should be confirmed by standard methods (e.g., Western blot serology) performed 2-4 mo after the initial indeterminate or negative test.

HUMAN IMMUNODEFICIENCY VIRUS TYPE 1 (HIV-1) VIRAL LOAD

Normal range: HIV-1 RNA, quant. bDNA 3: less than 50 copies/ml or less than 1.7 log copies/ml

This test should be used only in individuals with documented HIV-1 infection for monitoring the progression of infection, response to antiretroviral therapy, and disease prognosis. It is not indicated for diagnosis of HIV infection.

HUMAN PAPILLOMA VIRUS (HPV)

Test description: PCR test can be performed on cervical smears, biopsies, scrapings, liquid cytology specimen, and anogenital tissues.

HUNTINGTON'S DISEASE PCR

Test description: PCR can be performed on whole blood. Huntington's disease is caused by the expansion of the trinucleotide repeat CAG within IT 15 (huntingtin). Pre- and post-test counseling should be performed when ordering this test.

HYDROGEN BREATH TEST

See BREATH HYDROGEN TEST

5-HYDROXYINDOLE-ACETIC ACID, URINE

See URINE 5-HYDROXYINDOLE-ACETIC ACID

IMMUNE COMPLEX ASSAY

Normal: Negative

Detected in: Collagen vascular disorders, glomerulonephritis, neoplastic diseases, malaria, primary biliary cirrhosis, chronic acute hepatitis, bacterial endocarditis, vasculitis

IMMUNOGLOBULINS

Normal range:

IgA: 50-350 mg/dl (0.5-3.5 g/L [CF: 0.01; SMI: 0.01 g/L])
IgD: <6 mg/dl (<60 mg/L [CF: 0.01; SMI: 0.01 g/L])
IgE: <25 μg/dl (<0.00025 g/L [CF: 0.01; SMI: 0.01 g/L])
IgG: 800-1500 mg/dl (8-15 g/L [CF: 0.01; SMI: 0.01 g/L])
IgM: 45-150 mg/dl (0.45-1.5 g/L [CF: 0.01; SMI: 0.01 g/L])

Table 4-26 summarizes biologic properties of human immunoglobulin isotopes.

Elevated in:

27. **IgA:** Lymphoproliferative disorders, Berger's nephropathy, chronic infections, autoimmune disorders, liver disease
28. **IgE:** Allergic disorders, parasitic infections, immunologic disorders, IgE myeloma (see Box 4-7 for summary of nonallergic diseases associated with high levels of IgE. Box 4-8 summarizes conditions with very high IgE levels)

TABLE 4-26 Selected Biologic Properties of Human Immunoglobulin Isotypes

Characteristics	IgG1	IgG2	IgG3	IgG4	IgM	IgA1	IgA2	IgD	IgE
Physical Properties									
Molecular weight (kD)	146	146	165	146	970*	160	160	170	190
Serum half-life (days)	29	27	7	16	5	6	6	–	2
Anatomic Distribution									
Mean serum level (mg/mL)	5-12	2-6	0.5-1.0	0.2-1.0	0.5-1.5	0.5-2.0	0-0.2	0-0.4	0-0.002
Transport across placenta	+++	+	++	±	–	–	–	–	–
Transport across epithelium	–	–	–	–	+	+++†	+++†	–	–
Extravascular diffusion	+++	+++	+++	+++	±	++‡	++‡	+	+
Functional Activity									
Antigen neutralization	++	++	++	++	++	++	++	–	–
Complement fixation	++	+	++	–	+++	+	+	–	–
ADCC	+	+	+	±	–	–	–	–	+
Immediate hypersensitivity	–	–	–	–	–	–	–	–	+++

From Adkinson NF et al: *Middleton's allergy principles and practice*, ed 8, Philadelphia, 2014, Saunders.
ADCC, Antibody-dependent cellular cytotoxicity; –, no effect; ±, no effect or negligible degree; +, small degree; ++, moderate degree; +++, large degree.
*Pentameric IgM plus J chain.
†Dimer.
‡Monomer.

BOX 4-7 Nonallergic Diseases Associated with Altered Total Serum Immunoglobulin E Levels

Increased Levels (≥500 IU/ml)
Parasitic Diseases
Ascariasis
Visceral larva migrans
Capillariasis
Paragonimiasis
Fascioliasis
Schistosomiasis
Hookworm
Trichinosis
Filariasis
Strongyloidiasis
Echinococcosis
Onchocerciasis
Malaria
Infections
Allergic bronchopulmonary mycosis
Systemic candidiasis
Coccidioidomycosis
Leprosy
Epstein-Barr virus mononucleosis
Cytomegalovirus mononucleosis
Viral respiratory infections
Human immunodeficiency virus (HIV) type 1 infections
Pertussis
Cutaneous Diseases
Alopecia areata
Bullous pemphigoid
Chronic acral dermatitis
Streptococcal erythema nodosum
Other Diseases and Disorders
Nephrotic syndrome
Drug-induced interstitial nephritis

Liver disease
Cystic fibrosis
Kawasaki disease
Infantile polyarteritis nodosa
Primary pulmonary hemosiderosis
Guillain-Barré syndrome
Burns
Rheumatoid arthritis
Bone marrow transplantation
Cigarette smoking
Alcoholism
Neoplastic Diseases
Hodgkin disease
Immunoglobulin E (IgE) myeloma
Bronchial carcinoma
Immunodeficiency Diseases
Wiskott-Aldrich syndrome
Hyper-IgE syndrome
Thymic hypoplasia (DiGeorge syndrome)
Cellular immunodeficiency with immunoglobulins (Nezelof syndrome)
Selective IgA deficiency
Medications
Enfuvirtide
Pholcodine
Decreased Levels (<5 IU/ml)
Familial IgE deficiency and recurrent sinopulmonary infections
Human T cell lymphotropic virus type 1 infections
Primary biliary cirrhosis

From Adkinson NF et al: *Middleton's allergy principles and practice*, ed 8, Philadelphia, 2014, Saunders.

29. **IgG:** Chronic granulomatous infections, infectious diseases, inflammation, myeloma, liver disease
30. **IgM:** Primary biliary cirrhosis, infectious diseases (brucellosis, malaria), Waldenström's macroglobulinemia, liver disease
Decreased in:
e. **IgA:** Nephrotic syndrome, protein-losing enteropathy, congenital deficiency, lymphocytic leukemia, ataxia-telangiectasia, chronic sinopulmonary disease
f. **IgE:** Hypogammaglobulinemia, neoplasms (breast, bronchial, cervical), ataxia-telangiectasia, primary biliary cirrhosis (see Box 4-7)

g. **IgG:** Congenital or acquired deficiency, lymphocytic leukemia, phenytoin, methylprednisolone, nephrotic syndrome, protein-losing enteropathy
h. **IgM:** Congenital deficiency, lymphocytic leukemia, nephrotic syndrome

INFLUENZA A AND B TESTS

Test description: PCR can be performed on nasopharyngeal swab, wash, or aspirate
Normal: Negative

Laboratory Tests

IV

BOX 4-8 Conditions Associated with Unusually High Serum Immunoglobulin E Concentrations (≥500 IU/ml)

Allergic bronchopulmonary mycosis
Allergic fungal sinusitis
Atopic dermatitis
Human immunodeficiency virus (HIV) infection
Hyperimmunoglobulin E (hyper-IgE) syndrome
Immunoglobulin E myeloma
Kimura disease
Lymphoma
Netherton syndrome
Systemic helminthic parasitosis
Tuberculosis

From Adkinson NF et al: *Middleton's allergy principles and practice*, ed 8, Philadelphia, 2014, Saunders.

INSULIN AUTOANTIBODIES

Normal: Negative
Present in: Exogenous insulin from insulin therapy. The presence of islet cell antibodies indicates ongoing beta cell destruction. This test is useful in the early diagnosis of type 1a diabetes mellitus and in the identification of patients at high risk for type 1a diabetes.

INSULIN, FREE

Normal: <17 mcU/ml
Elevated in: Insulin overdose, insulin resistance syndromes, endogenous hyperinsulinemia
Decreased in: Inadequately treated type 1 diabetes mellitus

INSULIN-LIKE GROWTH FACTOR-1 (IGF-1) (Serum)

Normal range:

Ages 16-24:	182-780 ng/ml
Ages 25-39:	114-492 ng/ml
Ages 40-54:	90-360 ng/ml
Ages >55:	71-290 ng/ml

Elevated in: Adolescence, acromegaly, pregnancy, precocious puberty, obesity
Decreased in: Malnutrition, delayed puberty, diabetes mellitus, hypopituitarism, cirrhosis, old age

INSULIN-LIKE GROWTH FACTOR-II

Normal range: 288-736 ng/ml
Elevated in: Hypoglycemia associated with non–islet cell tumors, hepatoma, and Wilms' tumor
Decreased in: Growth hormone deficiency

INTERNATIONAL NORMALIZED RATIO (INR)

The INR is a comparative rating of prothrombin time (PT) ratios. The INR represents the observed PT ratio adjusted by the International Reference Thromboplastin. It provides a universal result indicative of what the patient's PT result would have been if measured using the primary World Health Organization International Reference reagent. For proper interpretation of INR values, the patient should be on stable anticoagulant therapy.

RECOMMENDED INR RANGES:

Proximal deep vein thrombosis:	2-3
Pulmonary embolism:	2-3
Transient ischemic attacks:	2-3
Atrial fibrillation:	2-3
Mechanical prosthetic valves:	2.5-3.5
Recurrent venous thromboembolic disease:	2.5-3.5

INTRINSIC FACTOR ANTIBODIES

Normal: Negative

Present in: Pernicious anemia (>50% of patients). Cyanocobalamin may give false-positive results.

IRON (Serum)

Normal: Male: 65-175 mcg/dl; female: 50-1170 mcg/dl
Elevated in: Hemochromatosis, excessive iron therapy, repeated transfusions, lead poisoning, hemolytic anemia, aplastic anemia, pernicious anemia
Decreased in: Iron deficiency anemia, hypothyroidism, chronic infection

IRON-BINDING CAPACITY, TOTAL (TIBC)

Normal range: 250-460 μg/dl (45-82 μmol/L [CF: 0.1791; SMI: 1 μmol/L])
Elevated in: Iron deficiency anemia, pregnancy, polycythemia, hepatitis, weight loss
Decreased in: Anemia of chronic disease, hemochromatosis, chronic liver disease, hemolytic anemias, malnutrition (protein depletion)

Table 4-27 describes TIBC and serum iron abnormalities.

TABLE 4-27 Serum Iron and Total Iron-Binding Capacity Patterns

SI↓	TIBC↓	Chronic diseases Uremia
SI↓	TIBC↑	Chronic iron deficiency anemia Pregnancy in third trimester
SI↑	TIBC↓	Hemachromatosis iron therapy overload (TIBC may be normal) Hemolytic anemia; thalassemia; lead poisoning; megaloblastic anemia; aplastic, pyridoxine deficiency, or other sideroblastic anemias
SI↑	TIBC↑	Oral contraceptives Acute hepatitis (some report TIBC is low normal) Chronic hepatitis (some patients)
SI↑	TIBCNL	B₁₂ or folate deficiency
SI↓	TIBCNL	Chronic iron deficiency (some patients) Acute infection, surgery, tissue damage
SI NL	TIBC↑	B₁₂/folate deficiency plus iron deficiency

From Ravel R: *Clinical laboratory medicine*, ed 6, St Louis, 1995, Mosby.
NL, Normal; *SI,* serum iron; *TIBC,* total iron-binding capacity.

IRON SATURATION (% Transferrin Saturation)

Normal:
Male: 20%-50%
Female: 15%-50%
Elevated in: Hemochromatosis, excessive iron intake, aplastic anemia, thalassemia, vitamin B_6 deficiency
Decreased in: hypochromic anemias, GI malignancy

LACTATE (blood)

Normal range: 0.5-2.0 mEq/L
Elevated in: Tissue hypoxia (shock, respiratory failure, severe CHF, severe anemia, carbon monoxide or cyanide poisoning), systemic disorders (liver or renal failure, seizures), abnormal intestinal flora (d-lactic acidosis), drugs or toxins (salicylates, ethanol, methanol, ethylene glycol), G6PD deficiency

LACTATE DEHYDROGENASE (LDH)

Normal range: 50-150 U/L (0.82-2.66 μkat/L [CF: 0.01667; SMI: 0.02 μkat/L])
Elevated in:
31. Infarction of myocardium, lung, kidney
32. Diseases of cardiopulmonary system, liver, collagen, central nervous system
33. Hemolytic anemias, megaloblastic anemias, transfusions, seizures, muscle trauma, muscular dystrophy, acute pancreatitis, hypotension, shock, infectious mononucleosis, inflammation, neoplasia, intestinal obstruction, hypothyroidism

LACTATE DEHYDROGENASE ISOENZYMES

Normal range:
LDH₁: 22%-36% (cardiac, red blood cell) (0.22-0.36 [CF: 0.01, SMI: 0.01])
LDH₂: 35%-46% (cardiac, red blood cell) (0.35-0.46)
LDH₃: 13%-26% (pulmonary) (0.15-0.26)
LDH₄: 3%-10% (striated muscle, liver) (0.03-0.1)
LDH₅: 2%-9% (striated muscle, liver) (0.02-0.09)

Normal ratios:
$LDH_1 < LDH_2$
$LDH_5 < LDH_4$

Abnormal values:
$LDH_1 > LDH_2$: Myocardial infarction (can also be seen with hemolytic anemias, pernicious anemia, folate deficiency, renal infarct)
$LDH_5 > LDH_4$: Liver disease (cirrhosis, hepatitis, hepatic congestion)

LACTOSE TOLERANCE TEST (serum)

Normal: Test is performed by giving 2 g/kg body weight lactose orally and drawing glucose level at 0, 30, 45, 60, and 90 min. Normal response is change in glucose from fasting value to >30 mg/dl. Inconclusive response is increase of 20-30 mg/dl, abnormal response is increase <20 mg/dl.
Abnormal in: Lactase deficiency

LAP SCORE

See LEUKOCYTE ALKALINE PHOSPHATASE

LEAD

Normal: Child, <10 mcg/dl; adult, <25 mcg/dl; acceptable for industrial exposure, <50 mcg/dl
Elevated in: Lead exposure, lead poisoning

LDH

See LACTATE DEHYDROGENASE

LDL

See LOW-DENSITY LIPOPROTEIN CHOLESTEROL

LEGIONELLA PNEUMOPHILA PCR

Test description: PCR can be performed on lung tissue, water sputum, bronchoalveolar lavage, and other respiratory fluids.

LEGIONELLA TITER

Normal: Negative
Positive in: Legionnaire's disease (presumptive: ≥1:256 titer; definitive: fourfold titer increase to ≥1:128)

LEUKOCYTE ALKALINE PHOSPHATASE (LAP)

Normal range: 13-100 (33-188 U)
Elevated in: Leukemoid reactions, neutrophilia secondary to infections (except in sickle cell crisis—no significant increase in LAP score), Hodgkin's disease, polycythemia vera, hairy cell leukemia, aplastic anemia, Down syndrome, myelofibrosis
Decreased in: Acute and chronic granulocytic leukemia, thrombocytopenic purpura, paroxysmal nocturnal hemoglobinuria, hypophosphatemia, collagen disorders

LEUKOCYTE COUNT

See COMPLETE BLOOD COUNT

LIPASE

Normal range: 0-160 U/L (0-2.66 μkat/L [CF: 0.01667; SMI: 0.02 μkat/L])
Elevated in: Acute pancreatitis, perforated peptic ulcer, carcinoma of pancreas (early stage), pancreatic duct obstruction, bowel infarction, intestinal obstruction

LIPOPROTEIN(a)

Normal: Male: 1.35-19.6 mg/dl; female: 1.24-20.1 mg/dl

Elevated in: Coronary artery disease, uncontrolled diabetes, hypothyroidism, chronic renal failure, pregnancy, tobacco use, infections, nephritic syndrome
Decreased in: Niacin, omega-3 fatty acids, estrogens, tamoxifen, statins

LIPOPROTEIN CHOLESTEROL, HIGH-DENSITY

See HIGH-DENSITY LIPOPROTEIN CHOLESTEROL

LIPOPROTEIN CHOLESTEROL, LOW-DENSITY

See LOW-DENSITY LIPOPROTEIN CHOLESTEROL

LIVER KIDNEY MICROSOME TYPE 1 ANTIBODIES (LKM1)

Normal: <20 U
Elevated in: Autoimmune hepatitis type 2

LKM1

See LIVER KIDNEY MICROSOME TYPE 1 ANTIBODIES

LOW-DENSITY LIPOPROTEIN (LDL) CHOLESTEROL

Normal range: 50-130 mg/dl (1.30-1.68 mmol/L [CF: 0.02586; SMI: 0.05 mmol/L])

<70	Optimal in diabetics, prior MI, and patients with cardiac risk factors
100-129	Near or above optimal
130-159	Borderline high
160-189	High
≥190	Very high

LUPUS ANTICOAGULANT

See CIRCULATING ANTICOAGULANT

LUTEINIZING HORMONE

Normal range: 5-25 mIU/ml
Elevated in: Postmenopause, pituitary adenoma, primary gonadal dysfunction, polycystic ovary syndrome
Decreased in: Severe illness, anorexia nervosa, malnutrition, pituitary or hypothalamic impairment, severe stress

LYME DISEASE ANTIBODY TITER

Normal range: Negative
Positive result: Figure 4-27 illustrates the usual serologic response in Lyme disease.
A serologic test is not necessary or helpful for several days after a tick bite because it is only 40%-50% sensitive in this stage, and a negative test does not rule out the diagnosis.

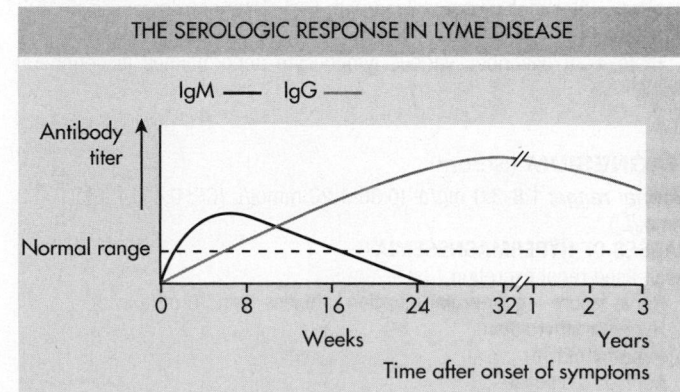

FIGURE 4-27 IgM and IgG responses in Lyme disease.

LYMPHOCYTES

Normal range: 15%-40%
  Total lymphocyte count = 800-2600/mm³
  Total T lymphocyte = 800-2200/mm³
  CD4 lymphocytes = ≥ 400/mm³

Laboratory Tests   IV

TABLE 4-28　Differential Diagnosis of Abnormal Lymphocytes in Peripheral Blood

Lymphocyte Type	Usual Disease Association	Cytologic Features	Laboratory Features	Clinical Features
Small lymphocyte	Chronic lymphocytic leukemia	B-cell surface markers with low concentration of surface immunoglobulin, CD5 antigen	Hypogammaglobulinemia in 50%; positive direct Coombs test in 15%; on node biopsy, diffuse, well-differentiated lymphocytic infiltrate	Elderly adults; presentation runs gamut from asymptomatic with lymphocytosis only to bulky disease with adenopathy, splenomegaly, and "packed" bone marrow
Atypical lymphocyte	Infectious mononucleosis, other viral illnesses	Suppressor T-cell markers	Heterophil agglutinin; positive serology for Epstein-Barr virus, cytomegalovirus, toxoplasma, HBsAg	Pharyngitis, fever, adenopathy, rash, splenomegaly, palatal petechiae, jaundice
Plasmacytoid lymphocyte	Waldenström's macroglobulin anemia	Cytoplasmic IgM, periodic acid-Schiff positivity	IgM paraprotein, rouleaux, cryoglobulins	Adenopathy, splenomegaly, absence of bone lesions, hyperviscosity syndrome, cryopathic phenomena
Lymphoblast	ALL	Terminal transferase positivity, common ALL antigen, B- or T-precursor markers	Anemia, granulocytopenia, thrombocytopenia, hyperuricemia, diffuse bone marrow infiltration	Peak incidence in childhood, acute onset, bone pain frequent
Lymphosarcoma cell	Lymphocytic lymphoma	B-cell surface markers with high concentration of monoclonal surface immunoglobulin	Nodular or diffuse, poorly differentiated lymphocytic lymphoma on node biopsy, patchy, peritrabecular bone marrow involvement	Middle-aged to older adults, generalized adenopathy, constitutional symptoms
Sézary cell	Cutaneous lymphomas	T-lymphocyte surface markers	Skin biopsy is diagnostic	Exfoliative erythroderma, cutaneous plaques or tumors
Hairy cell	Hairy cell leukemia	B-lymphocyte markers, cytoplasmic projections, tartrate-resistant acid phosphatase, interleukin-2 receptors, CD11 antigen	Pancytopenia	Middle-aged males, moderate to marked splenomegaly without adenopathy
Prolymphocyte	Prolymphocytic leukemia	B-cell surface markers with high concentration of surface immunoglobulin, CD5 negative	Marked lymphocytosis (frequently $>100 \times 10^9$/L)	Elderly adults, massive splenomegaly, minimum adenopathy, poor response to therapy

From Stein JH (ed): *Internal medicine*, ed 5, St Louis, 1998, Mosby.
ALL, Acute lymphoblastic leukemia.

CD8 lymphocytes = 200-800/mm³
Normal CD4/CD8 ratio is 2.0.
Elevated in: Chronic infections, infectious mononucleosis and other viral infections, chronic lymphocytic leukemia, Hodgkin's disease, ulcerative colitis, hypoadrenalism, idiopathic thrombocytopenia
Decreased in:
AIDS, bone marrow suppression from chemotherapeutic agents or chemotherapy, aplastic anemia, neoplasms, steroids, adrenocortical hyperfunction, neurologic disorders (multiple sclerosis, myasthenia gravis, Guillain-Barré syndrome)
CD4 lymphocytes are calculated as total white blood cells × % lymphocytes × % lymphocytes stained with CD4. They are decreased in AIDS and other immune dysfunction.
Table 4-28 describes various lymphocyte abnormalities in peripheral blood.

MAGNESIUM (Serum)

Normal range: 1.8-3.0 mg/dl (0.80-1.20 mmol/L [CF: 0.4114; SMI: 0.02 mmol/L])
CAUSES OF HYPERMAGNESEMIA
Decreased renal excretion
　Renal failure—glomerular filtration rate less than 30 ml/min
　Hyperparathyroidism
　Hypothyroidism
　Addison's disease
　Lithium intoxication
　Familial hypocalciuric hypercalcemia
Other causes: usually in association with decrease in glomerular filtration rate
　Endogenous loads
　　Diabetic ketoacidosis
　　Severe tissue injury—burns
　Exogenous loads
　　Gastrointestinal
　　　Magnesium-containing laxatives and antacids
　　　High-dose vitamin D analogs
　　Parenteral: management of toxemia of pregnancy
CAUSES OF HYPOMAGNESEMIA
Alcoholic abuse
Diuretic use
Renal losses
Acute and chronic renal failure
Postobstructive diuresis
Acute tubular necrosis
Chronic glomerulonephritis
Chronic pyelonephritis
Interstitial nephropathy
Renal transplantation
Gastrointestinal losses
Chronic diarrhea
Nasogastric suctioning
Short bowel syndrome
Protein-calorie malnutrition
Bowel fistula
Total parenteral nutrition
Acute pancreatitis
Endocrine
Diabetes mellitus
Hyperaldosteronism
Hyperthyroidism
Hyperparathyroidism
Acute intermittent porphyria
Pregnancy
Drugs
Aminoglycosides

Amphotericin
β-agonists
Cisplatin
Cyclosporine
Diuretics
Foscarnet
Pentamidine
Theophylline
Congenital disorders
Familial hypomagnesemia
Maternal diabetes
Maternal hypothyroidism
Maternal hyperparathyroidism

MEAN CORPUSCULAR VOLUME (MCV) (Table 4-29)

Normal range: 76-100 μm^3 (76-100 fL) (76-100 fL [CF: 1; SMI: 1 fL])
See Tables 4-30, 4-31, and 4-32 for descriptions of MCV abnormalities.

TABLE 4-29   Clinical Conditions Not to Be Confused With Megaloblastosis

Macrocytosis* Without Megaloblastosis[†]

Reticulocytosis
Liver disease
Aplastic anemia
Myelodysplastic syndromes (especially 5q-)
Multiple myeloma
Hypoxemia
Smokers

Spurious Increases In MCV Without Macro-Ovalocytosis[‡]

Cold agglutinin disease
Marked hyperglycemia
Leukocytosis
Older individuals

From Hoffman R: *Hematology: basic principles and practice,* ed 6, Philadelphia, 2013, Saunders.
MCV, Mean corpuscular volume.
*The central pallor that normally occupies about one-third of the normal red blood cell is decreased in macro-ovalocytes. This contrasts with the finding of thin macrocytes, in which the central pallor is increased.
[†]Although megaloblastosis implies that a bone marrow test has been performed, with the addition of highly sensitive tests for the specific diagnosis of cobalamin and folate deficiency, the need for a bone marrow test is often dictated by the urgency to make the diagnosis.
[‡]When the Coulter counter readings of a high MCV are not confirmed by looking at the peripheral smear.

METANEPHRINES, URINE

See URINE METANEPHRINES

METHYLMALONIC ACID (Serum)

Normal: <0.2 mcmol/L
Elevated in: Vitamin B_{12} deficiency, pregnancy, methylmalonic acidemia

MITOCHONDRIAL ANTIBODY (AMA)

Normal: Negative
Present in: Primary biliary cirrhosis (>90% of patients)

MONOCYTE COUNT

Normal range: 2%-8%
Elevated in: Viral diseases, parasites, infections, neoplasms, inflammatory bowel disease, monocytic leukemia, lymphomas, myeloma, sarcoidosis
Decreased in: Aplastic anemia, lymphocytic leukemia, glucocorticoid administration
See Table 4-33 for changes in monocyte number.

TABLE 4-30   Some Causes of Increased Mean Corpuscular Volume (Macrocytosis)

Causes	% of all Macrocytosis Patients*	% of Macrocytosis in Each Disease[†]
Common		
Folate or B_{12} deficiency	20-30 (5-50)[‡]	80-90 (4-100)
Chronic liver disease	15-20 (6-28)	25-30 (8-65)
Chronic alcoholism	10-12 (3-15)	60 (26-90)
Cytotoxic chemotherapy	10-15 (2-20)	30-40 (13-82)
Cardiorespiratory abnormality	8 (7-9.5)	?
Reticulocytosis	6-7 (0-15)	Depends on severity
Myelodysplastic syndromes	Frequent over age 40 yr	>60 in RAEB and RARS
Unexplained	25 (22.5-27)	—
Normal newborn		
Less Common	**<4%**	
Noncytotoxic drugs		
> Zidovudine		
Phenytoin		30 (14-50)
Azathioprine		
Hypothyroidism		20-30 (8-55)
Chronic leukemia/myelofibrosis		
Radiotherapy for malignancy		
Chronic renal disease (occasional patients)		
Distance-runner macrocytosis (some persons)		
Down syndrome		
Artifactual (e.g., cold agglutinins)		

From Ravel R: *Clinical laboratory medicine,* ed 6, St Louis, 1995, Mosby.
RAEB, Refractory anemia with excessive blasts; *RARS,* refractory anemia with ring sideroblasts (formerly called "IASA," or idiopathic acquired sideroblastic anemia).
*Percentage of all patients with macrocytosis.
[†]Percentage of patients with each condition listed who have macrocytosis.
[‡]Numbers in parentheses are literature range.

TABLE 4-31   Some Causes of Decreased Mean Corpuscular Volume (Microcytosis)

Common	Less Common
Chronic iron deficiency	Some cases of polycythemia
α- or β-thalassemia (minor)	Some cases of lead poisoning
Anemia of chronic disease	Some cases of congenital spherocytosis Some cases of sideroblastic anemia Certain abnormal hemoglobins (HbE, Hb Lepore)

From Ravel R: *Clinical laboratory medicine,* ed 6, St Louis, 1995, Mosby.

MYCOPLASMA PNEUMONIAE PCR

Test description: PCR can be performed on sputum, bronchoalveolar lavage, nasopharyngeal and throat swabs, other respiratory fluids, and lung tissue

MYELIN BASIC PROTEIN, CEREBROSPINAL FLUID

Normal: <2.5 ng/ml
Elevated in: Multiple sclerosis, CNS trauma, stroke, encephalitis

MYOGLOBIN, URINE

See URINE MYOGLOBIN

Laboratory Tests

IV

TABLE 4-32 Differential Diagnosis of Microcytic Hypochromic Anemia

Decreased Body Iron Stores

- Iron-deficiency anemia

Normal or Increased Body Iron Stores

- Anemia of chronic disease
- Defective absorption, transport, or use of iron
- Iron-refractory, iron-deficiency anemia after parenteral iron
- Atransferrinemia
- Aceruloplasminemia
- Divalent metal transporter 1 (DMT1 or SLC11A2) deficiency
- Ferroportin-associated hemochromatosis with impaired iron export (type 4A)
- Heme oxygenase 1 deficiency
- Disorders of globin synthesis
  - Thalassemia
  - Other microcytic hemoglobinopathies
- Disorders of heme synthesis: sideroblastic anemias
  - Hereditary
  - Acquired

From Hoffman R, et al: *Hematology, basic principles and practice*, ed 6, Philadelphia, 2013, Saunders.

TABLE 4-33 Changes in Monocyte Number

Monocytosis
Infections: tuberculosis, granulomatous infection, brucellosis, subacute bacterial endocarditis
Connective tissue disorder
Recovery from myelosuppression
Hematologic malignancies
   MDS, MPD, MDS–MPD overlap, CMML
   Acute and chronic monocytic leukemia, myelomonocytic leukemia
   Hodgkin and non-Hodgkin lymphomas
Monocytopenia
Hairy cell leukemia
MonoMAC syndrome
Aplastic anemia
Drugs: chemotherapy, IFN-α, glucocorticoids (transient)
Radiation therapy

From Hoffman R: *Hematology, basic principles and practice*, ed 6, Philadelphia, 2013, Saunders. *CMML*, Chronic myelomonocytic leukemia; *IFN*, interferon; *MDS*, myelodysplastic syndrome; *monoMAC*, monocytopenia and mycobacterium avium complex syndrome; *MPD*, myeloproliferative disorder.

NEISSERIA GONORRHOEAE PCR

Test description: Test can be performed on endocervical swab, urine, and intraurethral swab
Normal: Negative

NEUTROPHIL COUNT

Normal range: 50%-70%
Subsets:
1. Stabs (bands, early mature neutrophils): 2%-6%
2. Segs (mature neutrophils): 60%-70%
Elevated in: Acute bacterial infections, acute myocardial infarction, stress, neoplasms, myelocytic leukemia
Decreased in: Viral infections, aplastic anemias, immunosuppressive drugs, radiation therapy to bone marrow, agranulocytosis, drugs (antibiotics, antithyroidals, clopidogrel), lymphocytic and monocytic leukemias
   Box 4-9 describes various drugs that can cause neutropenia. Table 4-34 describes miscellaneous inherited neutropenia disorders.

NOREPINEPHRINE

Normal range: 0-600 pg/ml
Elevated in: Pheochromocytomas, neuroblastomas, stress, vigorous exercise, certain foods (bananas, chocolate, coffee, tea, vanilla)

BOX 4-9 Drugs That Cause Neutropenia

k. Antiarrhythmics: tocainide, procainamide, propranolol, quinidine
l. Antibiotics: chloramphenicol, penicillins, sulfonamides, *p*-aminosalicylic acid (PAS), rifampin, vancomycin, isoniazid, nitrofurantoin
m. Antimalarials: dapsone, quinine, pyrimethamine
n. Anticonvulsants: phenytoin, mephenytoin, trimethadione, ethosuximide, carbamazepine
o. Hypoglycemic agents: tolbutamide, chlorpropamide
p. Antihistamines: cimetidine, brompheniramine, tripelennamine
q. Antihypertensives: methyldopa, captopril
r. Anti-inflammatory agents: aminopyrine, phenylbutazone, gold salts, ibuprofen, indomethacin
s. Antithyroid agents: propylthiouracil, methimazole, thiouracil
t. Diuretics: acetazolamide, hydrochlorothiazide, chlorthalidone
u. Phenothiazines: chlorpromazine, promazine, prochlorperazine
v. Immunosuppressive agents: antimetabolites
w. Cytotoxic agents: alkylating agents, antimetabolites, anthracyclines, *Vinca* alkaloids, cisplatin, hydroxyurea, dactinomycin
x. Other agents: recombinant interferons, allopurinol, ethanol, levamisole, penicillamine, zidovudine, streptokinase, carbamazepine, clopidogrel, ticlopidine

Modified from Goldman L, Ausiello D (eds): *Cecil textbook of medicine*, ed 22, Philadelphia, 2004, Saunders.

5′-NUCLEOTIDASE

Normal range: 2-16 IU/L (3-27 × 10^8 kat/L [CF: 1.67 × 10^8; SMI: 1 × 10^8 kat/L])
Elevated in: Biliary obstruction, metastatic neoplasms to liver, primary biliary cirrhosis, renal failure, pancreatic carcinoma, chronic active hepatitis

OSMOLALITY (serum)

Normal range: 280-300 mOsm/kg (280-300 mmol/kg [CF: 1; SMI: 1 mmol/kg])
   It can also be estimated by the following formula:

$$2([Na + [K] + glucose/18 + BUN/2.8)$$

Elevated in: Dehydration, hypernatremia, diabetes insipidus, uremia, hyperglycemia, mannitol therapy, ingestion of toxins (ethylene glycol, methanol, ethanol), hypercalcemia, diuretics
Decreased in: Syndrome of inappropriate diuretic hormone secretion, hyponatremia, overhydration, Addison's disease, hypothyroidism

OSMOLALITY, URINE

See URINE OSMOLALITY

OSMOTIC FRAGILITY TEST

Normal: Hemolysis begins at 0.50, w/v [5.0 g/L] and is complete at 0.30, w/v [3.0 g/L] NaCl.
Elevated in: Hereditary spherocytosis, hereditary stomatocytosis, spherocytosis associated with acquired immune hemolytic anemia
Decreased in: Iron deficiency anemia, thalassemias, liver disease, leptocytosis associated with asplenia

PARACENTESIS FLUID

Testing and evaluation of results:
Process the fluid as follows:
   Tube 1: LDH, glucose, albumin
   Tube 2: protein, specific gravity
   Tube 3: cell count and differential
   Tube 4: save until further notice
Draw serum LDH, protein, albumin.
Gram stain, AFB stain, bacterial and fungal cultures, amylase, and triglycerides should be ordered only when clearly indicated; bedside inoculation

TABLE 4-34   Miscellaneous Inherited Neutropenia Disorders

Diagnosis	Genetics	Mapping	Mutant Gene	Additional Features
Hyper IgM syndrome, type 1	X-L	Xq26	*CD40L*	↓IgG, IgA, IgE, autoimmune cytopenias
Hermansky-Pudlak syndrome, type 2	AR	5q14.1	*AP3B1*	↓IgG, partial albinism, platelet dysfunction
Griscelli syndrome, type 1	AR	15q21	*MYO5A*	Neurologic dysfunction, partial albinism
Griscelli syndrome, type 2	AR	15q21	*RAB27A*	Same as type 1 plus hemophagocytosis
Chediak-Higashi syndrome	AR	1q42.1-q42.2	*LYST (CHSI)*	Immunodeficiency, partial albinism
Poikiloderma with neutropenia	AR	16q13	*C16ORF57*	Rash, short stature, dystrophic nails
P14 deficiency	AR	1q22	*MAPBPIP*	Immunodeficiency, hypopigmentation
Cohen syndrome	AR	8q22-q23	*VPS13B/COH1*	Retinopathy, retardation, skeletal anomalies
Charcot-Marie-Tooth syndrome, type 2	AD	19p13.2	*DMN2*	Axonal demyelinating neuropathy

Data compiled from Online Mendelian Inheritance in Man (http://ncbi.nlm.nih.gov/omim); From Hoffman R: *Hematology: basic principles and practice*, ed 6, Philadelphia, 2013, Saunders. *AD*, Autosomal dominant; *AR*, autosomal recessive; *Ig*, immunoglobulin; *X-L*, X-linked recessive.

of blood-culture bottles with ascitic fluid improves sensitivity in detecting bacterial growth.

If malignant ascites is suspected, consider a carcinoembryonic antigen level on the paracentesis fluid and cytologic evaluation.

In suspected spontaneous bacterial peritonitis (SBP) the incidence of positive cultures can be increased by injecting 10 to 20 ml of ascitic fluid into blood culture bottles.

Peritoneal effusion can be subdivided as exudative or transudative based on its characteristics (see Section II).

The serum-ascites albumin gradient (serum albumin level–ascitic fluid albumin level [SAAG]) correlates directly with portal pressure and can also be used to classify ascites. Patients with gradients ≥1.1 g/dl have portal hypertension, and those with gradients ≤1.1 g/dl do not; the accuracy of this method is >95%.

For the differential diagnosis of ascites, refer to Section II.

An ascitic fluid polymorphonuclear leukocyte count >500/μl is suggestive of SBP.

A blood-ascitic fluid albumin gradient.

PARATHYROID HORMONE (PTH)

Normal:
Serum, intact molecule 10-65 pg/ml
Plasma 1.0-5.0 pmol/L
Elevated in: Hyperparathyroidism (primary or secondary), pseudohypoparathyroidism, anticonvulsants, corticosteroids, lithium, INH, rifampin, phosphates, Zollinger-Ellison syndrome, hereditary vitamin D deficiency
Decreased in: Hypoparathyroidism, sarcoidosis, cimetidine, beta-blockers, hyperthyroidism, hypomagnesemia

PARIETAL CELL ANTIBODIES

Normal: Negative
Present in: Pernicious anemia (>90%), atrophic gastritis (up to 50%), thyroiditis (30%), Addison's disease, myasthenia gravis, Sjögren's syndrome, type 1 DM

PARTIAL THROMBOPLASTIN TIME (PTT), Activated Partial Thromboplastin Time (APTT)

See Table 4-35.
Normal range: 25-41 sec
Elevated in: Heparin therapy, coagulation factor deficiency (I, II, V, VIII, IX, X, XI, XII), liver disease, vitamin K deficiency, disseminated intravascular coagulation, circulating anticoagulant, warfarin therapy, specific factor inhibition (PCN reaction, rheumatoid arthritis), thrombolytic therapy, nephrotic syndrome
NOTE: Useful to evaluate the intrinsic coagulation system.

PEPSINOGEN I

Normal: 124-142 ng/ml
Elevated in: ZE syndrome, duodenal ulcer, acute gastritis
Decreased in: Atrophic gastritis, gastric carcinoma, myxedema, pernicious anemia, Addison's disease

TABLE 4-35   Clinical Peculiarities of Coagulation Protein Screening Tests

Long aPTT, normal or long PT, no bleeding	Normal aPTT, PT, *with bleeding*
Long aPTT Only	
Factor XII deficiency	Factor XIII deficiency or inhibitor
Prekallikrein deficiency	α₂-Antiplasmin deficiency or defect
High-molecular-weight kininogen	Plasminogen activator inhibitor defiency or defect
Lupus anticoagulant	α₁-Antitrypsin Pittsburgh defect
Long aPTT and PT	
Dysfibrinogenemia with fibrinopeptide B release	
Lupus anticoagulant	

From Hoffman R et al: *Hematology: basic principles and practice*, ed 5, Philadelphia, 2009, Churchill Livingstone.

pH, BLOOD

Normal values:
Arterial: 7.35-7.45
Venous: 7.32-7.42
For abnormal values, refer to ARTERIAL BLOOD GASES.

pH, URINE

See URINE pH

PHENOBARBITAL

Normal therapeutic range: 15-30 mcg/ml for epilepsy control

PHENYTOIN (Dilantin)

Normal therapeutic range: 10-20 mcg/ml

PHOSPHATASE, ACID

See ACID PHOSPHATASE

PHOSPHATASE, ALKALINE

See ALKALINE PHOSPHATASE

PHOSPHATE (serum)

Normal range: 2.5-5 mg/dl (0.8-1.6 mmol/L [CF: 0.3229; SMI: 0.05 mmol/L])
DECREASED
Parenteral hyperalimentation
Diabetic acidosis
Alcohol withdrawal
Severe metabolic or respiratory alkalosis

Antacids that bind phosphorus
Malnutrition with refeeding using low-phosphorus nutrients
Renal tubule failure to reabsorb phosphate (Fanconi's syndrome; congenital disorder; vitamin D deficiency)
Glucose administration
Nasogastric suction
Malabsorption
Gram-negative sepsis
Primary hyperthyroidism
Chlorothiazide diuretics
Therapy of acute severe asthma
Acute respiratory failure with mechanical ventilation

INCREASED

Renal failure
Severe muscle injury
Phosphate-containing antacids
Hypoparathyroidism
Tumor lysis syndrome

PLASMINOGEN

Normal: Immunoassay (antigen): <20 mg/dl
Elevated in: Infection, trauma, neoplasm, myocardial infarction (acute phase reactant), pregnancy, bilirubinemia
Decreased in: DIC, severe liver disease, thrombolytic therapy with streptokinase or urokinase, alteplase

PLATELET AGGREGATION

Normal: Full aggregation (generally >60%) in response to epinephrine, thrombin, ristocetin, ADP, collagen
Elevated in: Heparin, hemolysis, lipemia, nicotine, hereditary and acquired disorders of platelet adhesion, activation, and aggregation
Decreased in: Aspirin, some penicillins, chloroquine, chlorpromazine, clofibrate, captopril, Glanzmann's thrombasthenia, Bernard-Soulier syndrome, Wiskott-Aldrich syndrome, cyclooxygenase deficiency. In von Willebrand's disease there is normal aggregation with ADP, collagen, and epinephrine but abnormal agglutination with ristocetin.

PLATELET ANTIBODIES

Normal: Absent
Present in: ITP (>90% of patients with chronic ITP). Patients with nonimmune thrombocytopenias may have false-positive results.

PLATELET COUNT

See Fig. E4-28 for evaluation of thrombocytosis. Box E4-10 describes testing for thrombocytopenia. See Table 4-36 for differential diagnosis.
Normal range: $130-400 \times 10^3/mm^3$ ($130-400 \times 10^9/L$ [CF: 1; SMI: $5 \times 10^9/L$])
Elevated in

Reactive Thrombocytosis

Infections or inflammatory states: vasculitis, allergic reactions, etc.
Surgery and tissue damage: myocardial infarction, pancreatitis, etc.
Postsplenectomy state
Malignancy: solid tumors, lymphoma
Iron deficiency anemia, hemolytic anemia, acute blood loss
Uncertain etiology
Rebound effect after chemotherapy or immune thrombocytopenia
Renal disorders: renal failure, nephrotic syndrome

Myeloproliferative Disorders

Chronic myeloid leukemia
Primary thrombocythemia
Polycythemia vera
Idiopathic myelofibrosis

Decreased:

Increased destruction
 Immunologic
  Drugs: quinine, quinidine, digitalis, procainamide, thiazide diuretics, sulfonamides, phenytoin, aspirin, penicillin, heparin, gold, meprobamate, sulfa drugs, phenylbutazone, NSAIDs, methyldopa, cimetidine, furosemide, INH, cephalosporins, chlorpropamide, organic arsenicals, chloroquine

TABLE 4-36 Differential Diagnosis of Thrombocytopenia in Suspected Disseminated Intravascular Coagulation

Differential Diagnosis	Additional Diagnostic Clues
DIC	Prolonged aPTT and PT, increased FDP, low levels of AT or protein C
Sepsis without DIC	Positive (blood) cultures, positive sepsis criteria, hematophagocytosis in BM aspirate
Massive blood loss	Major bleeding, low hemoglobin, prolonged aPTT and PT
Thrombotic microangiopathy	Schistocytes in blood smear, Coombs-negative hemolysis, fever, neurologic symptoms, renal insufficiency, coagulation test results usually normal, ADAMTS13 levels decreased
Heparin-induced thrombocytopenia	Use of heparin, venous or arterial thrombosis, positive HIT test (usually immunoassay for heparin-platelet factor 4 antibodies), increase in platelet count after cessation of heparin; coagulation tests usually normal
Immune thrombocytopenia	Antiplatelet antibodies, normal or increased number of megakaryocytes in BM aspirate, TPO decreased; coagulation tests usually normal
Drug-induced thrombocytopenia	Decreased number of megakaryocytes in BM aspirate or detection of drug-induced antiplatelet antibodies, increase in platelet count after cessation of drug; coagulation test results usually normal

From Hoffman R: *Hematology, basic principles and practice,* ed 6, Philadelphia, Saunders, 2013. *ADAMTS13,* A disintegrin and metalloproteinase with a thrombospondin type 1 motif, member 13; *aPTT,* activated partial thromboplastin time; *AT,* antithrombin; *BM,* bone marrow; *DIC,* disseminated intravascular coagulation; *FDP,* fibrin degradation product; *HIT,* heparin-induced thrombocytopenia; *PT,* prothrombin time; *TPO,* thrombopoietin.

Idiopathic thrombocytopenic purpura
Transfusion reaction: transfusion of platelets with platelet antigen HPA-1a (PL^{A1}) in recipients without PL^{A1}
Fetal/maternal incompatibility
Vasculitis (e.g., systemic lupus erythematosus)
Autoimmune hemolytic anemia
Lymphoreticular disorders (e.g., chronic lymphocytic leukemia)
Nonimmunologic
 Prosthetic heart valves
 Thrombotic thrombocytopenic purpura
 Sepsis
 Disseminated intravascular coagulation
 Hemolytic-uremic syndrome
 Giant cavernous hemangioma
Decreased production
 Abnormal marrow
  Marrow infiltration (e.g., leukemia, lymphoma, fibrosis)
  Marrow suppression (e.g., chemotherapy, alcohol, radiation)
 Hereditary disorders
  Wiskott-Aldrich syndrome: X-linked disorder characterized by thrombocytopenia, eczema, and repeated infections
  May-Hegglin anomaly: increased megakaryocytes but ineffective thrombopoiesis
  Vitamin deficiencies (e.g., vitamin B_{12}, folic acid)
Splenic sequestration, hypersplenism
Dilutional, secondary to massive transfusion

PLATELET FUNCTION ANALYSIS 100 ASSAY (PFA)

Normal: This test is a two-component assay where blood is aspirated through two capillary tubes, one of which is coated with collagen and ADP (COL/ADP) and the other with collagen and epinephrine (COL/EPI). The test measures the ability of platelets to occlude an aperture in a biologically active membrane treated with COL/ADP and COL/EPI. During the test, the platelets adhere to the surface of the tube and cause blood flow to cease.

The closing time refers to the cessation of blood flow and is reported in conjunction with the hematocrit and platelet count. Hematocrit count must be >25% and platelet count >50 K/microliter for the test to be performed
COL/ADP: 70-120 sec
COL/EPI: 75-120 sec
Elevated in: Acquired platelet dysfunction, von Willebrand's disease, anemia, thrombocytopenia, use of aspirin and NSAIDs

PLEURAL FLUID
Testing and evaluation of results:
Pleural effusion fluid should be differentiated in exudate or transudate. The initial laboratory studies should be aimed only at distinguishing an exudate from a transudate.
Tube 1: protein, LDH, albumin.
Tubes 2, 3, 4: save the fluid until further notice. In selected patients with suspected empyema, a pH level may be useful (generally ≤7.0). See following for proper procedure to obtain a pH level from pleural fluid.
A serum/effusion albumin gradient of ≤1.2 g/dl is indicative of exudative effusions, especially in patients with congestive heart failure (CHF) treated with diuretics.
Note the appearance of the fluid:
A grossly hemorrhagic effusion can be a result of a traumatic tap, neoplasm, or an embolus with infarction.
A milky appearance indicates either of the following:
Chylous effusion: caused by trauma or tumor invasion of the thoracic duct; lipoprotein electrophoresis of the effusion reveals chylomicrons and triglyceride levels >115 mg/dl.
Pseudochylous effusion: often seen with chronic inflammation of the pleural space (e.g., TB, connective tissue diseases).
If transudate, consider CHF, cirrhosis, chronic renal failure, and other hypoproteinemic states and perform subsequent workup accordingly.
If exudate, consider ordering these tests on the pleural fluid:
Cytologic examination for malignant cells (for suspected neoplasm).
Gram stain, cultures (aerobic and anaerobic), and sensitivities (for suspected infectious process).
AFB stain and cultures (for suspected TB).
pH: a value <7.0 suggests parapneumonic effusion or empyema; a pleural fluid pH must be drawn anaerobically and iced immediately; the syringe should be prerinsed with 0.2 ml of 1:1000 heparin.
Glucose: a low glucose level suggests parapneumonic effusions and rheumatoid arthritis.
Amylase: a high amylase level suggests pancreatitis or ruptured esophagus.
Perplexing pleural effusions are often a result of malignancy (e.g., lymphoma, malignant mesothelioma, ovarian carcinoma), TB, subdiaphragmatic processes, prior asbestos exposure, and postcardiac injury syndrome.

TABLE 4-37 Features Differentiating Exudative from Transudative Pleural Effusion

FEATURE	TRANSUDATE	EXUDATE
Appearance	Serous	Cloudy
Leukocyte count	<10,000/mm^3	>50,000/mm^3
pH	>7.2	<7.2
Protein	<3.0 g/dL	>3.0 g/dL
Ratio of pleural fluid protein to serum	<0.5	>0.5
Lactate dehydrogenase (LDH)	<200 IU/L	>200 IU/L
Ratio of pleural fluid LDH to serum	<0.6	>0.6
Glucose	≥60 mg/dL	<60 mg/dL

From Bennett JE, Dolin R, Blaser MJ: *Mandell, Douglas, and Bennett's principles and practice of infectious diseases*, ed 8, Philadelphia, 2015, Saunders.

POTASSIUM (serum)
Normal range: 3.5-5 mEq/L (3.5-5 mmol/L [CF: 1; SMI: 0.1 mmol/L])
CAUSES OF HYPERKALEMIA
See Fig. E4-29 for evaluation and treatment of hyperkalemia, and Fig. E4-30 for electrocardiographic changes in hyperkalemia.)

Pseudohyperkalemia
  Hemolysis of sample
  Thrombocytosis
  Leukocytosis
  Laboratory error
Increased potassium intake and absorption
  Potassium supplements (oral and parenteral)
  Dietary: salt substitutes
  Stored blood
  Potassium-containing medications
Impaired renal excretion
  Acute renal failure
  Chronic renal failure
  Tubular defect in potassium secretion
    1. Renal allograft
    2. Analgesic nephropathy
    3. Sickle cell disease
    4. Obstructive uropathy
  Hypoaldosteronism
    ■ Primary (Addison's disease)
    ■ Secondary
      • Hyporeninemic hypoaldosteronism (type IV RTA)
      • Congenital adrenal hyperplasia
      • Drug-induced
        ○ NSAIDs
        ○ ACE inhibitors
        ○ Heparin
        ○ Cyclosporine
Transcellular shifts
  ○ Acidosis
  ○ Hypertonicity
  ○ Insulin deficiency
  ○ Drugs
    ■ β-blockers
    ■ Digitalis toxicity
    ■ Succinylcholine
  ○ Exercise
  ○ Hyperkalemic periodic paralysis
Cellular injury
  ○ Rhabdomyolysis
  ○ Severe intravascular hemolysis
  ○ Acute tumor lysis syndrome
  ○ Burns and crush injuries
CAUSES OF HYPOKALEMIA
• Decreased intake
  ○ Decreased dietary potassium
  ○ Impaired absorption of potassium
  ○ Clay ingestion
  ○ Kayexalate
• Increased loss
  ○ Renal
  Hyperaldosteronism
  Primary
    (1) Conn's syndrome
    (2) Adrenal hyperplasia
  Secondary
    (1) Congestive heart failure
    (2) Cirrhosis
    (3) Nephrotic syndrome
    (4) Dehydration
  Bartter's syndrome
  Glycyrrhizic acid (licorice, chewing tobacco)
  Excessive adrenal corticosteroids
    a. Cushing's syndrome
    b. Steroid therapy
    c. Adrenogenital syndrome
  Renal tubular defects
    a. Renal tubular acidosis
    b. Obstructive uropathy
    c. Salt-wasting nephropathy

Drugs
- a. Diuretics
- b. Aminoglycosides
- c. Mannitol
- d. Amphotericin
- e. Cisplatin
- f. Carbenicillin
○ Gastrointestinal
  1. Vomiting
  2. Nasogastric suction
  3. Diarrhea
  4. Malabsorption
  5. Ileostomy
  6. Villous adenoma
  7. Laxative abuse
○ Increased losses from the skin
  1. Excessive sweating
  2. Burns
- Transcellular shifts
  A. Alkalosis
     1. Vomiting
     2. Diuretics
     3. Hyperventilation
     4. Bicarbonate therapy
  B. Insulin
     1. Exogenous
     2. Endogenous response to glucose
  C. β₂-Agonists (albuterol, terbutaline, epinephrine)
  D. Hypokalemia periodic paralysis
     1. Familial
     2. Thyrotoxic
- Miscellaneous
  A. Anabolic state
  B. Intravenous hyperalimentation
  C. Treatment of megaloblastic anemia
  D. Acute mountain sickness

POTASSIUM, URINE

See URINE POTASSIUM

PROCAINAMIDE

Normal therapeutic range: 4-10 mcg/ml

PROGESTERONE (serum)

Normal:
Female: Follicular phase: 15-70 ng/dl
Luteal phase: 200-2500 ng/dl
Male: 15-70 ng/dl
Elevated in: Congenital adrenal hyperplasia, clomiphene, corticosterone, 11-deoxycortisol, dihydroprogesterone, molar pregnancy, lipoid ovarian tumor
Decreased in: Primary or secondary hypogonadism, oral contraceptives, ampicillin, threatened abortion

PROLACTIN

See Fig. E4-31 for the evaluation of hyperprolactinemia.
Normal range: <20 ng/ml (<20 μg/L [CF: 1; SMI: 1 μg/L])
Elevated in: Prolactinomas (level >200 micrograms/L highly suggestive), drugs (phenothiazines, cimetidine, tricyclic antidepressants, metoclopramide, estrogens, antihypertensives [methyldopa], verapamil, haloperidol), postpartum, stress, hypoglycemia, hypothyroidism, chronic liver disease, end-stage renal disease, brain radiation therapy, polycystic ovary syndrome, seizures, exercise, coitus, lactation. Mild hyperprolactinemia (<100 micrograms/L) can also be caused by large sellar masses, including nonfunctioning pituitary adenoma.

PROSTATE-SPECIFIC ANTIGEN (PSA)

Normal range: 0-4 ng/ml
Table 4-38 describes age-specific reference ranges for PSA.

TABLE 4-38	Age-Specific Reference Ranges for PSA		
	SERUM PSA (NG/ML)		
Age (yr)	**Whites**	**Japanese**	**African Americans**
40-49	0-2.5	0-2.0	0-2.0
50-59	0-3.5	0-3.0	0-4.0
60-69	0-4.5	0-4.0	0-4.5
70-79	0-6.5	0-5.0	0-5.5

From Nseyo UO (ed): *Urology for primary care physicians*, Philadelphia, 1999, Saunders.
PSA, Prostate-specific antigen.

TABLE 4-39	Factors Affecting Serum PSA
Factors Affecting Serum PSA	**Duration of Effect**
Prostate cell number	NA
Prostate size	NA
Recent ejaculation	6-48 hours
Prostate manipulation	
Vigorous massage	1 week
Cystoscopy	1 week
Prostate biopsy	4-6 weeks
Prostatitis	
Acute	3-6 months
Chronic	Unknown
Prostate cancer	NA
Drugs: finasteride*	3-6 months

From Nseyo UO (ed): *Urology for primary care physicians*, Philadelphia, 1999, Saunders.
NA, Not applicable; *PSA*, prostate-specific antigen.
*Lowers PSA for as long as patient is on the medication.

Elevated in: Benign prostatic hypertrophy, carcinoma of prostate, prostatitis, postrectal examination, prostate trauma.
Factors affecting serum PSA are described in Table 4-39.
NOTE: Measurement of free PSA is useful to assess the probability of prostate cancer in patients with normal digital rectal examination and total PSA between 4 and 10 ng/ml. In these patients, the global risk of prostate cancer is 25%; however, if the free PSA is >25%, the risk of prostate cancer decreases to 8%, whereas if the free PSA is <10%, the risk of cancer increases to 56%. Free PSA is also useful to evaluate the aggressiveness of prostate cancer. A low free PSA percentage generally indicates a high-grade cancer, whereas a high free PSA percentage is generally associated with a slower-growing tumor.
Decreased in: 5-α reductase inhibitors (finasteride, dutasteride), saw palmetto use, antiandrogens

PROSTATIC ACID PHOSPHATASE

Normal: 0-0.8 U/L
Elevated in: Prostate cancer (especially in metastatic prostate cancer), BPH, prostatitis, post-prostate surgery or manipulation, hemolysis, androgens, clofibrate
Decreased in: Ketoconazole

PROTEIN (serum)

Normal range: 6-8 g/dl (60-80 g/L [CF: 10; SMI: 1 g/L])
Elevated in: Dehydration, multiple myeloma, Waldenström's macroglobulinemia, sarcoidosis, collagen vascular diseases
Decreased in: Malnutrition, low-protein diet, overhydration, malabsorption, pregnancy, severe burns, neoplasms, chronic diseases, cirrhosis, nephrosis

PROTEIN C ASSAY

See Table 4-40.
Normal: 70%-140%
Elevated in: Oral contraceptives, stanozol

TABLE 4-40 Assay Measurement in Heterozygote Protein C Deficiency

Type	ACTIVITY		
	Antigen	Amidolytic	Coagulant
I	Low	Low	Low
II	Normal	Low	Low
	Normal	Normal	Low

From Hoffman R et al: *Hematology: basic principles and practice,* ed 5, Philadelphia, 2009, Churchill Livingstone.

Decreased in: Congenital protein C deficiency, warfarin therapy, Vitamin K deficiency, renal insufficiency, consumptive coagulopathies

PROTEIN ELECTROPHORESIS (serum)

Normal range:
Albumin: 60%-75% (0.6-0.75 [CF: 0.01; SMI: 0.01])
α-1: 1.7%-5% (0.02-0.05)
α-2: 6.7%-12.5% (0.07-0.13)
β: 8.3%-16.3% (0.08-0.16)
γ: 10.7%-20% (0.11-0.2)

Albumin: 3.6-5.2 g/dl (36-52 g/L [CF: 0.01; SMI: 1 g/L])
α-1: 0.1-0.4 g/dl (1-4 g/L)
α-2: 0.4-1 g/dl (4-10 g/L)
β: 0.5-1.2 g/dl (5-12 g/L)
γ: 0.6-1.6 g/dl (6-16 g/L)

Elevated in:
Albumin: dehydration
α-1: neoplastic diseases, inflammation
α-2: neoplasms, inflammation, infection, nephrotic syndrome
β: hypothyroidism, biliary cirrhosis, diabetes mellitus
γ: See IMMUNOGLOBULINS

Decreased in:
Albumin: malnutrition, chronic liver disease, malabsorption, nephrotic syndrome, burns, systemic lupus erythematosus
α-1: emphysema (α-1 antitrypsin deficiency), nephrosis
α-2: hemolytic anemias (decreased haptoglobin), severe hepatocellular damage
β: hypocholesterolemia, nephrosis
γ: See IMMUNOGLOBULINS
Fig. 4-32 describes serum protein electrophoretic patterns.

PROTEIN S ASSAY

See Table 4-41.

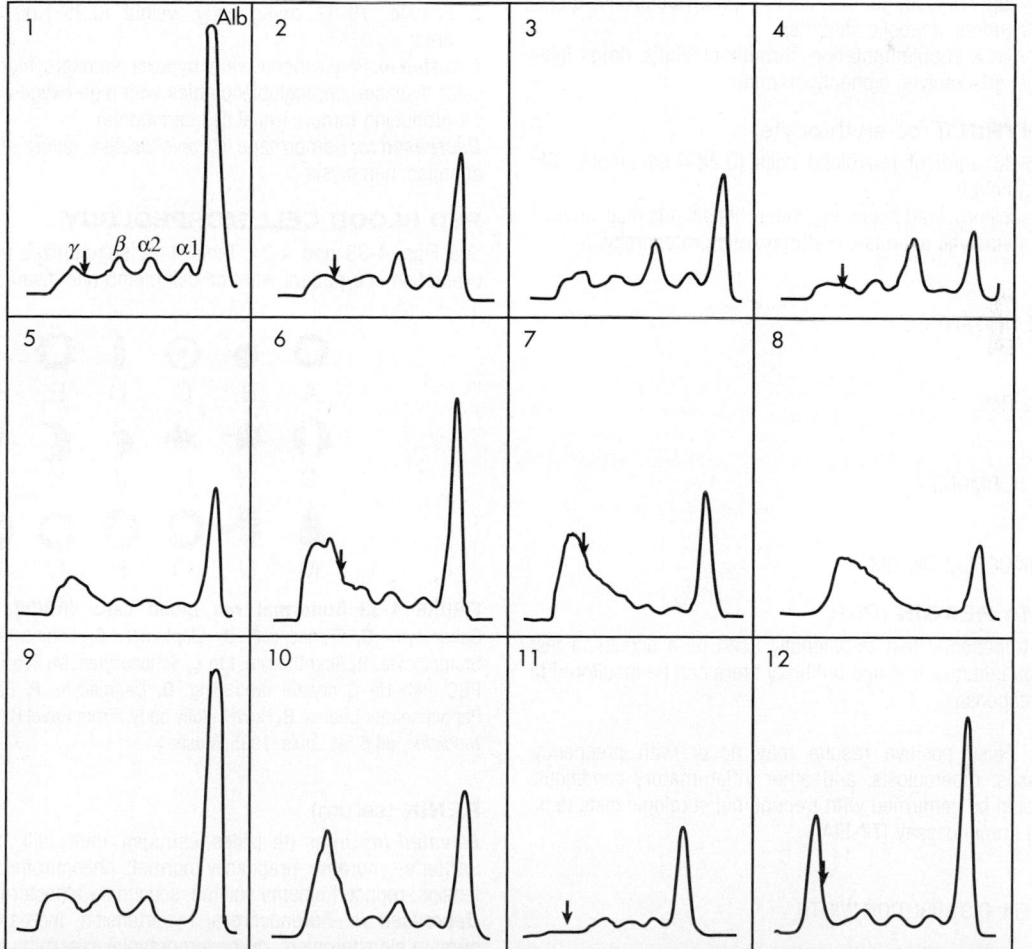

FIGURE 4-32 Typical serum protein electrophoretic patterns. *1,* Normal (*arrow* near γ region indicates serum application point). *2,* Acute reaction pattern. *3,* Acute reaction or nephrotic syndrome. *4,* Nephrotic syndrome. *5,* Chronic inflammation, cirrhosis, granulomatous diseases, rheumatoid-collagen group. *6,* Same as 5, but γ elevation is more pronounced. There is also partial (but not complete) β-γ fusion. *7,* Suggestive of cirrhosis but could be found in the granulomatous diseases or the rheumatoid-collagen group. *8,* Characteristic pattern of cirrhosis. *9,* α-1 Antitrypsin deficiency with mild γ elevation suggesting concurrent chronic disease. *10,* Same as 5, but the γ elevation is marked. The configuration of the γ peak superficially mimics that of myeloma, but is more broad-based. There are superimposed acute reaction changes. *11,* Hypogammaglobulinemia or light-chain myeloma. *12,* Myeloma, Waldenström's macroglobulinemia, idiopathic or secondary monoclonal gammopathy. (From Ravel R [ed]: *Clinical laboratory medicine,* ed 6, St Louis, 1995, Mosby.)

TABLE 4-41 Assay Measurements in Heterozygote Protein S Deficiency

| | ACTIVITY | | |
Type	Protein S Total Antigen	Protein S Free Antigen	Protein S Activity
I (classic)	Low	Low	Low
II	Normal	Normal	Low
III	Normal	Low	Low

From Hoffman R et al: *Hematology: basic principles and practice,* ed 5, Philadelphia, 2009, Churchill Livingstone.

Normal: 65%-140%
Elevated in: Presence of lupus anticoagulant
Decreased in: Hereditary deficiency, acute thrombotic events, DIC, surgery, oral contraceptives, pregnancy, hormone replacement therapy, l-asparaginase treatment

PROTHROMBIN TIME (PT)
Normal range: 10-12 sec
Elevated in: Liver disease, oral anticoagulants (warfarin), heparin, factor deficiency (I, II, V, VII, X), disseminated intravascular coagulation, vitamin K deficiency, afibrinogenemia, dysfibrinogenemia, drugs (salicylate, chloral hydrate, diphenylhydantoin, estrogens, antacids, phenylbutazone, quinidine, antibiotics, allopurinol, anabolic steroids)
Decreased in: Vitamin K supplementation, thrombophlebitis, drugs (glutethimide, estrogens, griseofulvin, diphenhydramine)

PROTOPORPHYRIN (Free erythrocyte)
Normal range: 16-36 μg/dl of red blood cells (0.28-0.64 μmol/L [CF: 0.0177; SMI: 0.02 μmol/L])
Elevated in: Iron deficiency, lead poisoning, sideroblastic anemias, anemia of chronic disease, hemolytic anemias, erythropoietic protoporphyria

PSA
See PROSTATE-SPECIFIC ANTIGEN

PT
See PROTHROMBIN TIME

PTH
See PARATHYROID HORMONE

PTT
See PARTIAL THROMBOPLASTIN TIME

RAPID PLASMA REAGIN (RPR)
Description: Non-treponemal test traditionally used as a screening test for syphilis. It is a quantitative test and antibody titers can be monitored to assess treatment response.
Normal: Negative
Positive: Syphilis. False positive results may occur with pregnancy, autoimmune diseases, tuberculosis, and other inflammatory conditions. Positive results should be confirmed with treponemal serologic tests (e.g., T-pallidum enzyme immunoassay [TP-EIA])

RDW
See RED BLOOD CELL DISTRIBUTION WIDTH

RED BLOOD CELL (RBC) COUNT
Normal range:
36. Male: $4.3-5.9 \times 10^6/mm^3$ ($4.3-5.9 \times 10^{12}/L$ [CF: 1; SMI: $0.1 \times 10^{12}/L$])
37. Female: $3.5-5 \times 10^6/mm^3$ ($3.5-5 \times 10^{12}/L$ [CF: 1; SMI: $0.1 \times 10^{12}/L$])
Elevated in: Polycythemia vera, smokers, high altitude, cardiovascular disease, renal cell carcinoma and other erythropoietin-producing neoplasms, stress, hemoconcentration/dehydration

Decreased in: Anemias, hemolysis, chronic renal failure, hemorrhage, failure of marrow production

RED BLOOD CELL DISTRIBUTION WIDTH (RDW)
Measures variability of red cell size (anisocytosis)
Normal range: 11.5-14.5
Normal RDW and elevated mean corpuscular volume (MCV): Aplastic anemia, preleukemia
Normal MCV: Normal, anemia of chronic disease, acute blood loss or hemolysis, chronic lymphocytic leukemia (CLL), chronic myelocytic leukemia, nonanemic enzymopathy or hemoglobinopathy
Decreased MCV: Anemia of chronic disease, heterozygous thalassemia
Elevated RDW and elevated MCV: Vitamin B_{12} deficiency, folate deficiency, immune hemolytic anemia, cold agglutinins, CLL with high count, liver disease
Normal MCV: Early iron deficiency, early vitamin B_{12} deficiency, early folate deficiency, anemic globinopathy
Decreased MCV: Iron deficiency, red blood cell fragmentation, HbH disease, thalassemia intermedia

RED BLOOD CELL FOLATE
See FOLATE

RED BLOOD CELL MASS (volume)
Normal range:
y. Male: 20-36 ml/kg body weight ($1.15-1.21$ L/m^2 body surface area)
z. Female: 19-31 ml/kg body weight ($0.95-1.00$ L/m^2 body surface area)
Elevated in: Polycythemia vera, hypoxia (smokers, high altitude, cardiovascular disease), hemoglobinopathies with high oxygen affinity, erythropoietin-producing tumors (renal cell carcinoma)
Decreased in: Hemorrhage, chronic disease, failure of marrow production, anemias, hemolysis

RED BLOOD CELL MORPHOLOGY
See Figs. 4-33 and 4-34. Table 4-42 summarizes peripheral blood film evaluation in a patient with red cell membrane disorder.

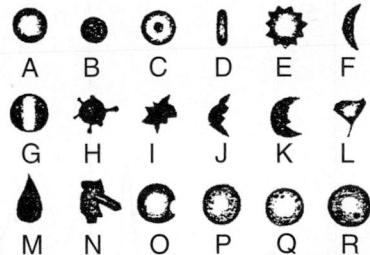

FIGURE 4-33 Abnormal red blood cells (RBCs). A, Normal RBC. **B,** Spherocyte. **C,** Target cell. **D,** Elliptocyte. **E,** Echinocyte. **F,** Sickle cell. **G,** Stomatocyte. **H,** Acanthocyte. **I** to **L,** Schistocytes. **M,** Teardrop RBC. **N,** Distorted RBC with Hb C crystal protruding. **O,** Degmacyte. **P,** Basophilic stippling. **Q,** Pappenheimer bodies. **R,** Howell-Jolly body. (From Ravel R [ed]: *Clinical laboratory medicine,* ed 6, St Louis, 1995, Mosby.)

RENIN (serum)
Elevated in: Drugs (thiazides, estrogen, minoxidil), chronic renal failure, Bartter's syndrome, pregnancy (normal), pheochromocytoma, renal hypertension, reduced plasma volume, secondary aldosteronism
Decreased in: Adrenocortical hypertension, increased plasma volume, primary aldosteronism, drugs (propranolol, reserpine, clonidine)
   Table 4-43 describes typical renin-aldosterone patterns in various conditions.

RESPIRATORY SYNCYTIAL VIRUS (RSV) SCREEN
Test description: PCR test can be performed on nasopharyngeal swab, wash, or aspirate

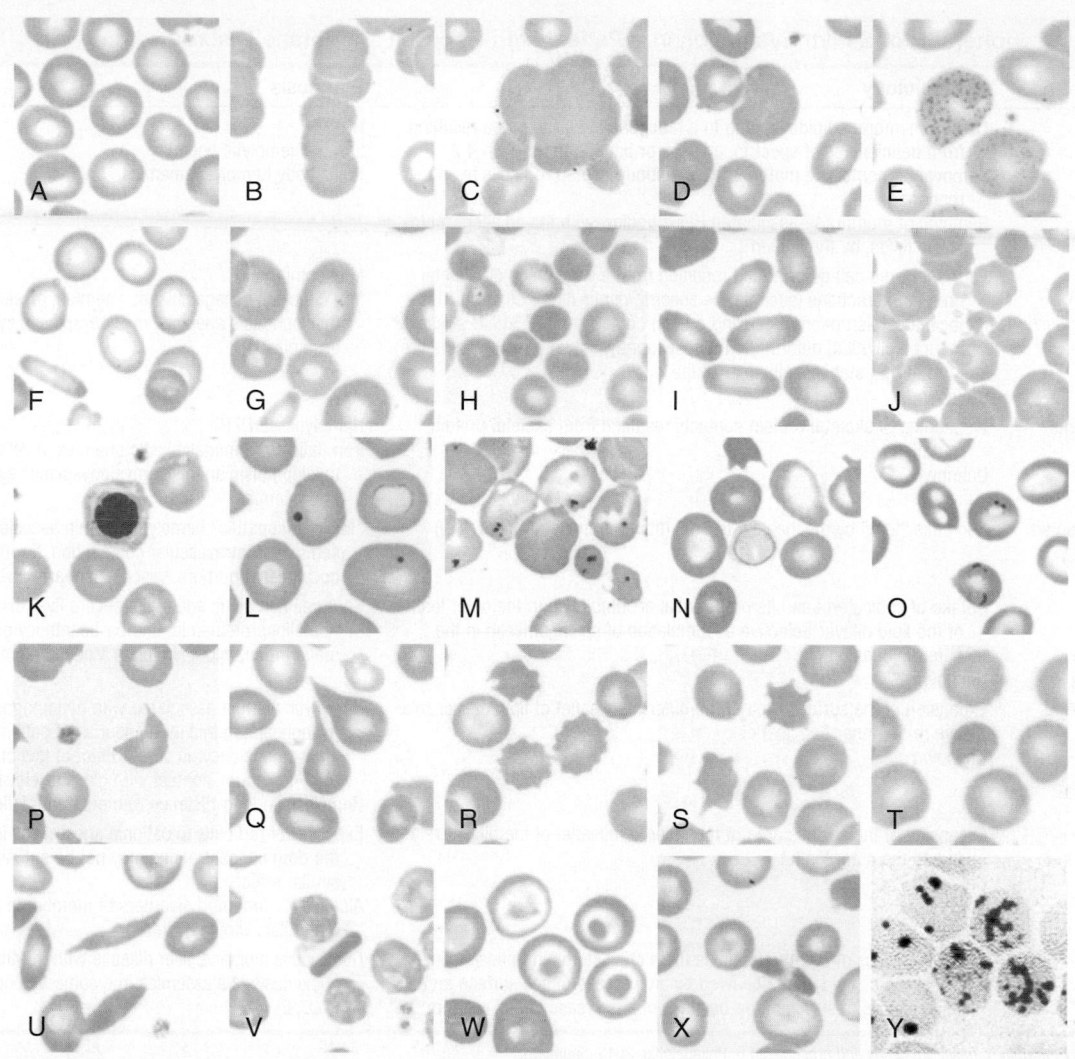

FIGURE 4-34 Useful peripheral blood and red blood cell features in the evaluation of anemia. A, Normal red blood cells (RBCs). Note the central pallor is one-third the diameter of the entire cell. **B,** Rouleaux formation is indicative of increased plasma protein. **C,** Agglutination indicates an antibody-mediated process such as cold agglutinin disease. **D,** Polychromatophilic cell. The gray-blue color is attributable to RNA and the cell is equivalent to a reticulocyte, which must be identified with a reticulocyte stain. **E,** Basophilic stippling. This also is attributable to increased RNA caused either by a left shift in erythroid cells or lead toxicity. **F,** Hypochromic microcytic cells typical of iron-deficiency anemia. Note the widened central pallor and the "pencil" cell in the lower left. **G,** Macroovalocyte as can be seen in either megaloblastic anemia or myelodysplastic syndrome. **H,** Microspherocytes typical of hereditary spherocytosis. **I,** Elliptocytes (ovalocytes) from a patient with hereditary elliptocytosis. **J,** RBC fragments from thermal injury (burn patient). **K,** Nucleated RBC. **L,** Howell-Jolly bodies indicative of splenic dysfunction or absence. **M,** Pappenheimer bodies from a patient with sideroblastic anemia. **N,** Cabot ring, as can be seen in megaloblastic anemia or myelodysplastic syndromes. **O,** Malarial parasites *(Plasmodium falciparum).* **P,** Schistocyte typical of a microangiopathic hemolytic anemia. **Q,** Tear-drop form indicates marrow fibrosis and extramedullary hematopoiesis. **R,** Echinocyte (Burr cell) with rounded edges. **S,** Acanthocyte (spur cell) with more irregular pointed ends. This was from a patient with neuroacanthocytosis. They can also be seen in patients with liver disease and lipid abnormalities. **T,** "Bite" cell from a patient with glucose-6-phosphate dehydrogenase (G6PD) deficiency. **U,** Sickle cell, from a patient with homozygous sickle cell disease. **V,** Hemoglobin C crystal. **W,** Target cells. **X,** Hemoglobin C disease. Note that the RBC in center has condensed hemoglobin at each pole. **Y,** Heinz body preparation (supravital stain) from a patient with G6PD deficiency. Note that the cells to the right have increased precipitated hemoglobin. From Hoffman R, et al: *Hematology, basic principles and practice,* ed 6, Philadelphia, 2013, Saunders.

RETICULOCYTE COUNT

See Fig. E4-35 and Table 4-44.

Normal range: 0.5%-1.5%

Elevated in: Hemolytic anemia (sickle cell crisis, thalassemia major, autoimmune hemolysis), hemorrhage, postanemia therapy (folic acid, ferrous sulfate, vitamin B_{12}), chronic renal failure

Decreased in: Aplastic anemia, marrow suppression (sepsis, chemotherapeutic agents, radiation), hepatic cirrhosis, blood transfusion, anemias of disordered maturation (iron deficiency anemia, megaloblastic anemia, sideroblastic anemia, anemia of chronic disease)

RHEUMATOID FACTOR

Normal: Negative. Present in titer >1:20

RHEUMATIC DISEASES

Rheumatoid arthritis
Sjögren's syndrome
Systemic lupus erythematosus
Polymyositis/dermatomyositis
Mixed connective tissue disease
Scleroderma

INFECTIOUS DISEASES

Subacute bacterial endocarditis
Tuberculosis
Infectious mononucleosis
Hepatitis
Syphilis

TABLE 4-42 Peripheral Blood Film Evaluation in a Patient with Red Cell Membrane Disorder

Shape	Pathobiology	Diagnosis
Microspherocytes	Loss of membrane lipids leading to a reduction of surface area resulting from deficiencies of spectrin, ankyrin, or band 3 and protein 4.2 Removal of membrane material from antibody-coated red cells by macrophages Removal of membrane-associated Heinz bodies, with the adjacent membrane lipids, by the spleen	HS Immunohemolytic anemias Heinz body hemolytic anemias
Elliptocytes	Permanent red cell deformation resulting from a weakening of skeletal protein interactions (such as the spectrin dimer-dimer contact). This facilitates disruption of existing protein contacts during shear stress–induced elliptical deformation. Subsequently, new protein contacts are formed that stabilize elliptical shape Unknown	Mild common HE Iron deficiency, megaloblastic anemias, myelofibrosis, myelophthisic anemias, myelodysplastic syndrome, thalassemias
Poikilocytes/Fragments	Weakening of skeletal protein contacts resulting from skeletal protein mutations Unknown	Hemolytic HE/HPP Iron deficiency, megaloblastic anemias, myelofibrosis, myelophthisic anemias, myelodysplastic syndrome, thalassemias
Schistocytes, fragmented red cells	Red cells "torn" by mechanical trauma (fibrin strands, turbulent flow)	"Microangiopathic" hemolytic anemia associated with disseminated intravascular coagulation, thrombotic thrombocytopenic purpura, vasculitis, heart valve prostheses
Acanthocytes	Uptake of cholesterol and its preferential accumulation in the outer leaflet of the lipid bilayer Selective accumulation of sphingomyelin in the outer lipid leaflet Unknown	Spur cell hemolytic anemia in severe liver disease Abetalipoproteinemia, Chorea-acanthocytosis syndrome, malnutrition, hypothyroidism McLeod phenotype
Echinocytes	Expansion of the surface area of the outer hemileaflet of lipid bilayer relative to the inner hemileaflet Unknown	Hemolytic anemia associated with hypomagnesemia and hypophosphatemia in malnourished patients, pyruvate kinase deficiency; in vitro artifact of low blood storage (ATP depletion), contact with glass or elevated pH Hemolysis in long-distance runners, renal failure
Stomatocytes	Expansion of the surface area of the inner hemileaflet of the bilayer relative to the outer leaflet Unknown	Exposure of red cells to cationic anesthetics in vitro; in vivo the drug concentrations may not be sufficient to produce similar effect Alcoholism, inherited disorders of membrane permeability (hereditary stomatocytosis)
Target cells	Absolute excess of membrane lipids (both cholesterol and phospholipids: "symmetric" lipid gain), followed by an increase of cell surface area Relative excess of surface area because of a decrease in cell volume	Obstructive jaundice, liver disease with intrahepatic cholestasis Thalassemias and some hemoglobinopathies (C, D, E)

From Hoffman R, et al: *Hematology, basic principles and practice*, ed 6, Philadelphia, 2013, Saunders.
ATP, Adenosine triphosphate; *HE*, hereditary elliptocytosis; *HPP*, hereditary pyropoikilocytosis; *HS*, hereditary spherocytosis.

TABLE 4-43 Typical Renin-Aldosterone Patterns in Various Conditions

	Plasma Renin	Aldosterone
Primary aldosteronism	Low	High
"Low-renin" essential hypertension	Low	Normal
Cushing's syndrome	Low	Low-normal
Licorice ingestion syndrome	Low	Low
High-salt diet	Low	Low
Oral contraceptives	High	Normal
Cirrhosis	High	High
Malignant hypertension	High	High
Unilateral renal disease	High	High
"High-renin" essential hypertension	High	High
Pregnancy	High	High
Diuretic overuse	High	High
Juxtaglomerular tumor (Bartter's syndrome)	High	High
Low-salt diet	High	High
Addison's disease	High	Low
Hypokalemia	High	Low

From Ravel R: *Clinical laboratory medicine*, ed 6, St Louis, 1995, Mosby.

TABLE 4-44 Combining the Reticulocyte Count and Red Blood Cell Parameters for Diagnosis

MCV, RDW	Reticulocyte Count <75,000/µL	Reticulocyte Count >100,000/µL
Low, Normal	Anemia of chronic disease	
Normal, Normal	Anemia of chronic disease	
High, Normal	Chemotherapy/antivirals/alcohol Aplastic anemia	Chronic liver disease
Low, High	Iron deficiency anemia	Sickle cell-β-thalassemia
Normal, High	Early iron, folate, vitamin B$_{12}$ deficiency Myelodysplasia	Sickle cell anemia, sickle cell disease
High, High	Folate or vitamin B$_{12}$ deficiency Myelodysplasia	Immune hemolytic anemia Chronic liver disease

From Hoffman R et al: *Hematology: basic principles and practice*, ed 5, Philadelphia, 2009, Churchill Livingstone.
MCV, Mean corpuscular volume; *RDW*, red blood cell distribution width.

Leprosy
Influenza
MALIGNANCIES
Lymphoma
Multiple myeloma
Waldenström's macroglobulinemia
Postradiation or postchemotherapy
MISCELLANEOUS
Normal adults, especially the elderly
Sarcoidosis
Chronic pulmonary disease (interstitial fibrosis)
Chronic liver disease (chronic active hepatitis, cirrhosis)
Mixed essential cryoglobulinemia
Hypergammaglobulinemic purpura

RNP

See EXTRACTABLE NUCLEAR ANTIGEN

RPR

See RAPID PLASMA REAGIN

ROTAVIRUS SEROLOGY

Test description: PCR test is performed on stool specimen
Normal: Negative

SED RATE

See ERYTHROCYTE SEDIMENTATION RATE

SEDIMENTATION RATE

See ERYTHROCYTE SEDIMENTATION RATE

SEMEN ANALYSIS

Table 4-45 describes semen analysis reference ranges.

TABLE 4-45   Semen Analysis Reference Ranges

Color	Grayish white
pH	7.3-7.8 (literature range, 7.0-7.8)
Volume	2.0-5.0 ml (literature range, 1.5-6.0 ml)
Sperm count	20-250 million/ml (literature range for upper limit varies from 100-250 million/ml)
Motility	>60% motile <3 hours after specimen is obtained (literature range, >40% to >70%)
% Normal sperm	>60% (literature range, >60% to >70%)
Viscosity	Can be poured from a pipet in droplets rather than a thick strand

From Ravel R (ed): *Clinical laboratory medicine*, ed 6, St Louis, 1995, Mosby.

SGOT

See ASPARTATE AMINOTRANSFERASE

SGPT

See ALANINE AMINOTRANSFERASE

SICKLE CELL TEST

Normal: Negative
Positive in: Sickle cell anemia, sickle cell trait, combination of *Hb S* gene with other disorders such as alpha-thalassemia, beta-thalassemia.

SMOOTH MUSCLE ANTIBODY

Normal: Negative
Present in: Chronic acute hepatitis, primary sclerosing cholangitis, primary biliary cirrhosis, autoimmune hepatitis, infectious mononucleosis

SODIUM (serum)

Normal range: 135-147 mEq/L (135-147 mmol/L [CF: 1; SMI: 1 mmol/L])

HYPONATREMIA
Table E4-46 describes drugs associated with hyponatremia.
Sodium and water depletion (deficit hyponatremia)
 Loss of gastrointestinal secretions with replacement of fluid but not electrolytes
  Vomiting
  Diarrhea
  Tube drainage
 Loss from skin with replacement of fluids but not electrolytes
  Excessive sweating
  Extensive burns
 Loss from kidney
  Diuretics
  Chronic renal insufficiency (uremia) with acidosis
 Metabolic loss
  Starvation with acidosis
  Diabetic acidosis
 Endocrine loss
  Addison's disease
  Sudden withdrawal of long-term steroid therapy
 Iatrogenic loss from serous cavities
  Paracentesis or thoracentesis
Excessive water (dilution hyponatremia)
 Excessive water administration
 Congestive heart failure
 Cirrhosis
 Nephrotic syndrome
 Hypoalbuminemia (severe)
 Acute renal failure with oliguria
Inappropriate antidiuretic hormone (IADH) syndrome
Intracellular loss (reset osmostat syndrome)
False hyponatremia (actually a dilutional effect)
 Marked hypertriglyceridemia
 Marked hyperproteinemia
 Severe hyperglycemia
HYPERNATREMIA
Dehydration is the most frequent overall clinical finding in hypernatremia.
Deficient water intake (either orally or intravenously)
Excess kidney water output (diabetes insipidus, osmotic diuresis)
Excess skin water output (excess sweating, loss from burns)
Excess gastrointestinal tract output (severe protracted vomiting or diarrhea without fluid therapy)
Accidental sodium overdose
High-protein tube feedings

STREPTOZYME

See ANTISTREPTOLYSIN O TITER

SUCROSE HEMOLYSIS TEST (sugar water test)

Normal: Absence of hemolysis
Positive in:
Paroxysmal nocturnal hemoglobinuria
False-positive: autoimmune hemolytic anemia, megaloblastic anemias
False-negative: may occur with use of heparin or EDTA

SUDAN III STAIN (qualitative screening for fecal fat)

Normal: Negative. Test should be preceded by diet containing 100-150 g of dietary fat/day for 1 week, avoidance of high-fiber diet, and avoidance of suppositories or oily material before specimen collection.
Positive in: Steatorrhea, use of castor oil or mineral oil droplets

SYNOVIAL FLUID ANALYSIS

Table 4-47 describes the classification and interpretation of synovial fluid analysis.

Laboratory Tests

IV

TABLE 4-47 Classification and Interpretation of Synovial Fluid Analysis

Group	Diseases	Appearance	Viscosity	Mucin Clot	WBC/mm³	% PMN	Glucose (mg/dl) (Blood-Synovial Fluid)	Protein (g/dl)
Normal	—	Clear	↑	Firm	<200	<25	<10	<2.5
I (noninflammatory)	Osteoarthritis, aseptic necrosis, traumatic arthritis, erythema nodosum, osteochondritis dissecans	Clear, yellow (may be xanthochromic if traumatic arthritis)	↑	Firm	↑ Up to 10,000	<25	<10	<2.5
II (inflammatory)	Crystal-induced arthritis, rheumatoid arthritis, Reiter's syndrome, collagen vascular disease, psoriatic arthritis, serum sickness, rheumatic fever	Clear, yellow, turbid	↓	Friable	↑↑ Up to 100,000	40-90	<40	<2.5
III (septic)	Bacterial (staphylococcal, gonococcal, tuberculosis)	Turbid	↓/↑	Friable	↑↑↑ Up to 5 million	40-100	20-100	>2.5

↑, Elevated; ↑↑ >markedly high; ↓, decreased; *PMN*, polymorphonuclear leukocytes. Note that there is considerable overlap in the numbers listed above.

T₃ (triiodothyronine)

See Table 4-48 for T₃ abnormalities.
Normal range: 75-220 ng/dl (1.2-3.4 nmol/L [CF: 0.01536; SMI: 0.1 nmol/L])
Abnormal values:
Elevated in hyperthyroidism (usually earlier and to a greater extent than serum T₄).
Useful in diagnosing:
T₃ hyperthyroidism (thyrotoxicosis): increased T₃, normal FTI.
Toxic nodular goiter: increased T₃, normal or increased T₄.
Iodine deficiency: normal T₃, possibly decreased T₄.
Thyroid replacement therapy with liothyronine (Cytomel): normal T₄, increased T₃ if patient is symptomatically hyperthyroid.
Not ordered routinely but indicated when hyperthyroidism is suspected and serum-free T₄ or FTI inconclusive.

T₃ RESIN UPTAKE (T₃RU)

Normal range: 25%-35%
Abnormal values: Increased in hyperthyroidism. T₃ resin uptake (T₃RU or RT₃U) measures the percentage of free T₄ (not bound to protein); it does not measure serum T₃ concentration; T₃RU and other tests that reflect thyroid hormone binding to plasma protein are also known as *thyroid hormone-binding ratios* (THBR).

T₄, FREE (Free thyroxine)

Normal range: 0.8-2.8 ng/dl
Elevated in:
Graves' disease, toxic multinodular goiter, toxic adenoma, iatrogenic and factitious causes, transient hyperthyroidism

Serum-free T₄ directly measures unbound thyroxine. Free T₄ can be measured by equilibrium dialysis (gold standard of free T₄ assays) or by immunometric techniques (influenced by serum levels of lipids, proteins, and certain drugs). The free thyroxine index (FTI) can also be easily calculated by multiplying T₄ times T₃RU and dividing the result by 100; the FTI corrects for any abnormal T₄ values secondary to protein binding: FTI = T₄ × T₃RU/100.
Normal values equal 1.1 to 4.3.

T₄, SERUM T₄

Normal range: 0.8-2.8 ng/dl (10-36 pmol/L [CF: 12.87; SMI: 1 pmol/L])
Abnormal values: Serum thyroxine (T₄)
Elevated in:
Graves' disease
Toxic multinodular goiter
Toxic adenoma
Iatrogenic and factitious
Transient hyperthyroidism
    Subacute thyroiditis
    Hashimoto's thyroiditis
    Silent thyroiditis
Rare causes: hypersecretion of TSH (e.g., pituitary neoplasms), struma ovarii, ingestion of large amounts of iodine in a patient with preexisting thyroid hyperplasia or adenoma (Jod-Basedow phenomenon), hydatidiform mole, carcinoma of thyroid, amiodarone therapy of arrhythmias.
Serum thyroxine test measures both circulating thyroxine bound to protein (represents >99% of circulating T₄) and unbound (free) thyroxine. Values vary with protein binding; changes in the concentration of T₄ secondary

TABLE 4-48 Findings in Thyroid Function Tests in Various Clinical Conditions

Condition	T₄	FT₄I	T₃	FT₃I	TSH	TSI	TRH Stimulation
Hyperthyroidism							
Graves' disease	↑	↑	↑	↑	↓	+	↓
Toxic nodular goiter	↑	↑	↑	↑	↓	–	↓
Pituitary TSH-secreting tumors	↑	↑	↑	↑	↑	–	↓
T₃ thyrotoxicosis	N	N	↑	↑	↓	+, –	↓
T₄ thyrotoxicosis	↑	↑	N	N	↓	+, –	↓
Hypothyroidism							
Primary	↓	↓	↓	↓	↑	+, –	↑
Secondary	↓	↓	↓	↓	↓ N	–	↓
Tertiary	↓	↓	↓	↓	↓, N	–	N
Peripheral unresponsiveness	↑, N	↑, N	↑, N	↑	↑, N	–	N,↑

From Tilton RC, Barrows A: *Clinical laboratory medicine,* St Louis, 1992, Mosby.
↑, Increased; ↓, decreased; +, – variable; N, normal.

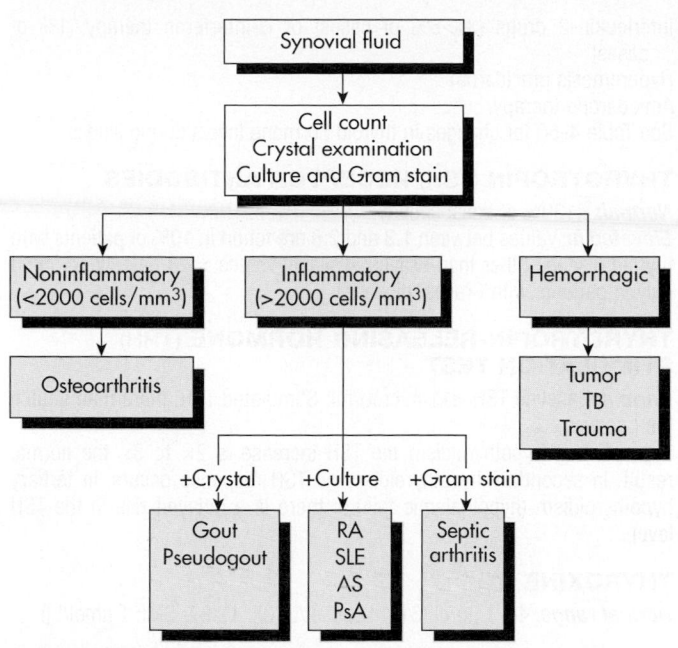

FIGURE 4-36 Algorithm for analysis of joint fluid. Examples of inflammatory arthritis are indicated, although many conditions can produce these findings. *AS,* ankylosing spondylitis; *PsA,* psoriatic arthritis; *RA,* rheumatoid arthritis; *SLE,* systemic lupus erythematosus; *TB,* tuberculosis. (From Goldman L, Schafer AI: *Goldman's Cecil medicine,* ed 24, Philadelphia, 2012, Saunders.)

to changes in thyroxine-binding globulin (TBG) can be caused by the following:

Increased TBG (↑T4)	Decreased TBG (↓T4)
Pregnancy	Androgens, glucocorticoids
Estrogens	Nephrotic syndrome, cirrhosis
Acute infectious hepatitis	Acromegaly
Oral contraceptives	Hypoproteinemia
Familial	Familial
Fluorouracil, clofibrate	Phenytoin, ASA and other NSAIDs, heroin, methadone, high-dose penicillin, asparaginase, chronic debilitating illness

To eliminate the suspected influence of protein binding on thyroxine values, two additional tests are available: T₃ resin uptake and serum free thyroxine. Table 4-49 summarizes the effects of pregnancy on thyroid physiology, and Table 4-50 describes changes in thyroid hormone levels during illness.

TEGRETOL

See CARBAMAZEPINE.

TESTOSTERONE (total testosterone)

Normal range: Variable with age and sex. Testosterone circulates in plasma mostly bound to plasma proteins and sex hormone-binding globulin (SHBG). Approximately 2% of testosterone circulates in free form (biologically active form). Low testosterone levels in obese patients may be due to reduced levels of SHBG; therefore, it is essential to measure free testosterone when evaluating androgen deficiency in obese patients.

Serum/plasma

Males: 280-1100 ng/dl   Females: 15-70 ng/dl

Urine

Males: 50-135 µg/day   Females: 2-12 µg/day

Elevated in: Testicular tumors, ovarian masculinizing tumors, testosterone replacement therapy

Decreased in: Hypogonadism, obesity, insulin resistance, sleep apnea. Figure 4-37 illustrates testosterone level changes with age. The diagnosis of androgen deficiency should be based on at least 2 morning testosterone measurements (collected on separate days) in a symptomatic patient.

TABLE 4-49   Effects of Pregnancy on Thyroid Physiology

Physiologic Change	Thyroid-Related Consequences
↑ Serum thyroxine-binding globulin	↑ Total T₄ and T₃; ↑ T₄ production
↑ Plasma volume	↑ T₄ and T₃ pool size; ↑ T₄ production; ↑ cardiac output
D3 expression in placenta and (?) uterus	↑ T₄ production
First-trimester ↑ in hCG	↑ Free T₄; ↓ basal thyrotropin; ↑ T₄ production
↑ Renal I– clearance	↑ Iodine requirements
↑ T₄ production; fetal T₄ synthesis during second and third trimesters	
↑ Oxygen consumption by fetoplacental unit, gravid uterus, and mother	↑ Basal metabolic rate; ↑ cardiac output

From Melmed S, Polonsky KS, Larsen PR, Kronenberg HM: *Williams textbook of endocrinology,* ed 12, Philadelphia, 2011, Saunders.
D3, type 3 iodothyronine deiodinase; *I–,* plasma iodide; *hCG,* human chorionic gonadotropin; *T₃,* triiodothyronine; *T₄,* thyroxine.

TABLE 4-50   Changes in Thyroid Hormone Levels during Illness

Severity of Illness	Free T₃	Free T₄	Reverse T₃	TSH	Probable Cause
Mild	↓	N	↑	N	↓ D2, D1
Moderate	↓↓	N, ↑↓	↑↑	N, ↓	↓↓ D2, D1,?↑ D3
Severe	↓↓↓	↓	↑	↓↓	↓↓ D2, D1, ↑D3
Recovery	↓	↓	↑	↑	?

From Melmed S, Polonsky KS, Larsen PR, Kronenberg HM: *Williams textbook of endocrinology,* ed 12, Philadelphia, 2011, Saunders.
D1 through *D3,* iodothyronine deiodinases; *N,* no change; *T₃,* triiodothyronine; *T₄,* thyroxine; *TSH,* thyroid-stimulating hormone.

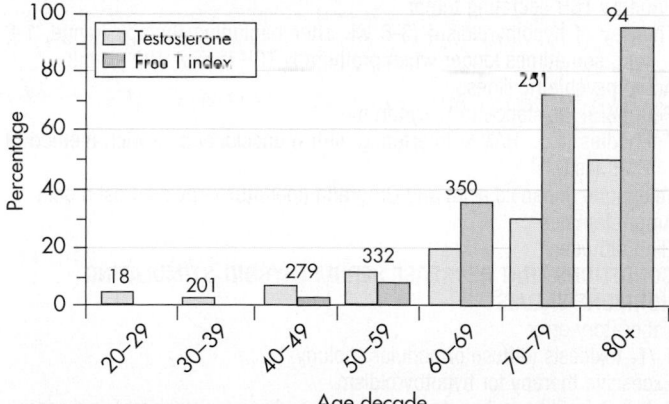

FIGURE 4-37 Hypogonadism in aging men. Bar height indicates the percentage of men in each 10-year interval, from the third to the ninth decades, with at least one testosterone value in the hypogonadal range. The criteria used for these determinations are total testosterone less than 11.3 nmol/L (325 ng/dL) and testosterone and sex hormone–binding globulin (free T index) less than 0.153 nmol/nmol. The numbers above each pair of bars indicate the number of men studied in the corresponding decade. The fraction of men who are hypogonadal increases progressively after age 50 years by either criterion. More men are hypogonadal by free T index than by total testosterone after 50 years, and there seems to be a progressively greater difference with increasing age between the two criteria. (From Goldman L, Schafer AI: *Goldman's Cecil medicine,* ed 24, Philadelphia, 2012, Saunders.)

Laboratory Tests

IV

THEOPHYLLINE
Normal therapeutic range: 10-20 mcg/ml

THORACENTESIS FLUID
See PLEURAL FLUID

THROMBIN TIME (TT)
Normal range: 11.3-18.5 sec
Elevated in: Thrombolytic and heparin therapy, disseminated intravascular coagulation, hypofibrinogenemia, dysfibrinogenemia

THYROGLOBULIN
Normal: 3-40 ng/ml. Thyroglobulin is a tumor marker for monitoring the status of patients with papillary or follicular thyroid cancer following resection.
Elevated in: Papillary or follicular thyroid cancer, Hashimoto's thyroiditis, Graves' disease, subacute thyroiditis

THYROID MICROSOMAL ANTIBODIES
Normal: Undetectable. Low titers may be present in 5%-10% of normal individuals
Elevated in: Hashimoto's disease, thyroid carcinoma, early hypothyroidism, pernicious anemia

THYROID-STIMULATING HORMONE (TSH)
See Fig. 4-38 for an algorithmic approach to thyroid testing.
Normal range: 2-11 μU/ml (2-11 mU/L [CF: 1; SMI: 1 mU/L])
CONDITIONS THAT INCREASE SERUM THYROID-STIMULATING HORMONE VALUES
Laboratory error
Primary hypothyroidism
Synthroid therapy with insufficient dose
Lithium or amiodarone; some patients
Hashimoto's thyroiditis in later stage
Large doses of inorganic iodide (e.g., SSKI)
Severe nonthyroid illness in recovery phase
Iodine deficiency (moderate or severe)
Addison's disease
TSH specimen drawn in evening (peak of diurnal variation)
Pituitary TSH-secreting tumor
Therapy of hypothyroidism (3-6 wk after beginning therapy [range, 1-8 wk]; sometimes longer when pretherapy TSH is over 100 μU/ml)
Acute psychiatric illness
Peripheral resistance to T_4 syndrome
Antibodies (e.g., HAMA) interfering with monoclonal sandwich method of TSH assay
Telepaque (iopanoic acid) and Oragrafin (ipodate) x-ray contrast media
Amphetamines
High altitudes
CONDITIONS THAT DECREASE SERUM THYROID-STIMULATING HORMONE VALUES
Laboratory error
T_4/T_3 toxicosis (diffuse or nodular etiology)
Excessive therapy for hypothyroidism
Active thyroiditis (subacute, painless, or early active Hashimoto's disease)
Multinodular goiter containing areas of autonomy
Severe nonthyroid illness (especially acute trauma, dopamine, or glucocorticoid)
T_3 toxicosis
Pituitary insufficiency
Cushing's syndrome (and some patients on high-dose glucocorticoid)
Jod-Basedow (iodine-induced) hyperthyroidism
Thyroid-stimulating hormone drawn 2-4 hr after levothyroxine dose
Postpartum transient toxicosis
Factitious hyperthyroidism
Struma ovarii
Radioimmunoassay, surgery, or antithyroid drug therapy for hyperthyroidism 4-6 weeks (range, 2 wk to 2 yr) after the treatment

Interleukin-2 drugs (3%-6% of cases) or α-interferon therapy (1% of cases)
Hyperemesis gravidarum
Amiodarone therapy.
See Table 4-50 for changes in thyroid hormone levels during illness.

THYROTROPIN (TSH) RECEPTOR ANTIBODIES
Normal: <130% of basal activity
Elevated in: Values between 1.3 and 2.0 are found in 10% of patients with thyroid disease other than Graves' disease. Values >2.8 have been found only in patients with Graves' disease.

THYROTROPIN-RELEASING HORMONE (TRH) STIMULATION TEST
Normal: Baseline TSH <11 microU/ml; Stimulated TSH: more than double the baseline.
  In primary hypothyroidism the TSH increase is 2× to 3× the normal result. In secondary hypothyroidism no TSH response occurs. In tertiary hypothyroidism (hypothalamic failure) there is a delayed rise in the TSH level.

THYROXINE (T_4)
Normal range: 4-11 μg/dl (51-142 nmol/L [CF: 12.87; SMI: 1 nmol/L])

TIBC
See IRON-BINDING CAPACITY, TOTAL

TISSUE TRANSGLUTAMINASE ANTIBODY
Normal: Negative
Present in: Celiac disease (specificity; 94%-97%, sensitivity, 90%-98%), dermatitis herpetiformis

TRANSFERRIN
Normal range: 170-370 mg/dl (1.7-3.7 g/L [CF: 0.01; SMI: 0.01 g/L])
Elevated in: Iron deficiency anemia, oral contraceptive administration, viral hepatitis, late pregnancy
Decreased in: Nephrotic syndrome, liver disease, hereditary deficiency, protein malnutrition, neoplasms, chronic inflammatory states, chronic illness, thalassemia, hemochromatosis, hemolytic anemia

TRIGLYCERIDES
Normal range: <150 mg/dl (<1.80 mmol/L [CF: 0.01129; SMI: 0.02 mmol/L])
Elevated in: Hyperlipoproteinemias (types I, IIb, III, IV, V), hypothyroidism, pregnancy, estrogens, acute myocardial infarction, pancreatitis, alcohol intake, nephrotic syndrome, diabetes mellitus, glycogen storage disease
Decreased in: Malnutrition, congenital abetalipoproteinemias, drugs (e.g., gemfibrozil, fenofibrate, nicotinic acid, clofibrate)

TRIIODOTHYRONINE
See T_3

TROPONINS (serum)
See Box 4-11 for causes of troponin elevations.
Normal range: 0-0.4 ng/ml (negative). If there is clinical suspicion of evolving acute MI or ischemic episode, repeat testing in 5-6 hours is recommended.
Indeterminate: 0.05-0.49 ng/ml. Suggest further tests. In a patient with unstable angina and this troponin I level, there is an increased risk of a cardiac event in the near future.
Strong probability of acute MI:
$\geq$ 0.05 ng/ml
Cardiac troponin T (cTnT) is a highly sensitive marker for myocardial injury for the first 48 hours after MI and for up to 5-7 days (see Fig. 4-15, under "Creatine Kinase Isoenzymes"). It may also be elevated in renal failure, chronic muscle disease, and trauma.
Cardiac troponin I (cTnI) is highly sensitive and specific for myocardial injury ($\geq$ CK-MB) in the initial 8 hours, peaks within 24 hours and lasts

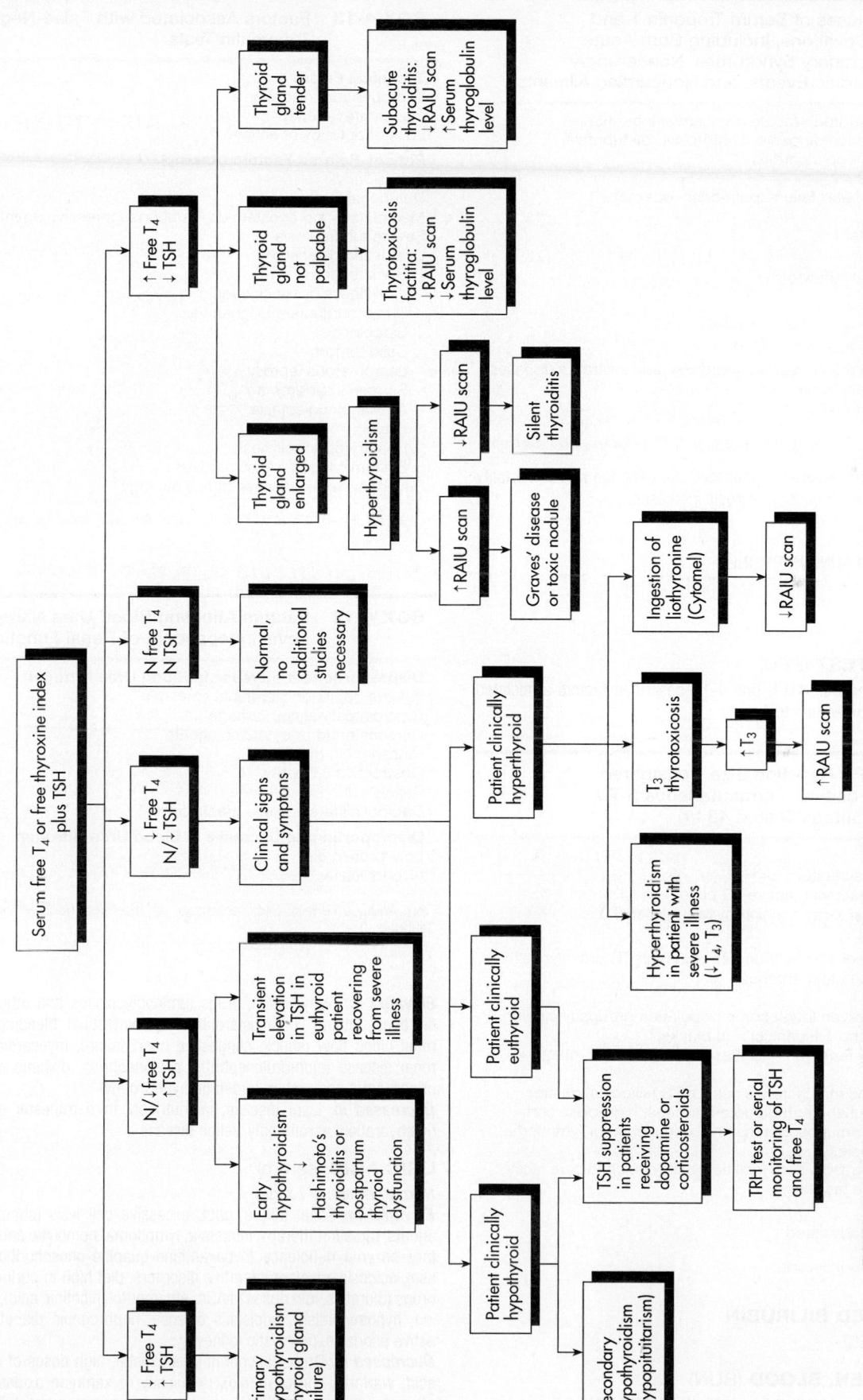

FIGURE 4-38 Diagnostic approach to thyroid testing. *N*, Normal; *RAIU*, radioactive iodine uptake; *TRH*, thyrotropin-releasing hormone; *TSH*, thyroid-stimulating hormone. (From Ferri FF: *Practical guide to the care of the medical patient*, ed 8, St Louis, 2011, Mosby.)

BOX 4-11	Causes of Serum Troponin T and I Elevations, Including Both Acute Coronary Syndromes, Noncoronary Cardiac Events, and Noncardiac Ailments

Acute coronary syndrome/acute myocardial infarction
Shock of any form (cardiogenic, obstructive, distributive)
Myocarditis and myopericarditis
Cardiomyopathies
Acute congestive heart failure (pulmonary edema)
Sepsis
Pulmonary embolism
Renal failure
Sympathomimetic ingestions
Polytrauma
Burns
Acute CNS event
Rhabdomyolysis
Cardiac neoplasm, inflammatory syndromes, and infiltrative diseases
Congenital coronary anomalies
Extreme physical exertion

From Vincent JL et al: *Textbook of critical care,* ed 6, Philadelphia, 2011, Saunders.

up to 7 days. With progressively higher levels of cTnI, the risk of mortality increases because the amount of necrosis increases.

TSH
See THYROID-STIMULATING HORMONE

TT
See THROMBIN TIME

TUBERCULIN TEST (PPD)
Abnormal results: see Box 4-12. Box 4-13 describes factors associated with false-negative tuberculin tests.

BOX 4-12	PPD Reaction Size Considered "Positive" (Intracutaneous 5 TU Mantoux Test at 48 hr)

5 mm or More
HIV infection or risk factors for HIV
Close recent contact with active TB case
Persons with chest x-ray consistent with healed TB

10 mm or More
Foreign-born persons from countries with high TB prevalence in Asia, Africa, and Latin America
IV drug users
Medically underserved low-income population groups (including Native Americans, Hispanics, and blacks)
Residents of long-term care facilities (nursing homes, mental institutions)
Medical conditions that increase risk for TB (silicosis, gastrectomy, undernourishment, diabetes mellitus, high-dose corticosteroids or immunosuppression Rx, leukemia or lymphoma, other malignancies)
Employees of long-term care facilities, schools, child care facilities, health care facilities

15 mm or More
All others not already listed

TB, Tuberculosis; *TU,* tuberculin units.

UNCONJUGATED BILIRUBIN
See BILIRUBIN, DIRECT

UREA NITROGEN, BLOOD (BUN)
Normal range: 8-18 mg/dl (3-6.5 mmol/L [CF: 0.357; SMI: 0.5 mmol/L])
Box 4-14 describes factors affecting BUN level independent of renal function.

BOX 4-13	Factors Associated with False-Negative Tuberculin Tests

Technical Errors
Improper administration
Inaccurate reading
Loss of potency of antigen
Patient-Related Factors (Anergy)
Age (elderly)
Nutritional status
Medications: corticosteroids, immunosuppressive agents
Severe tuberculosis
Coexisting diseases
  HIV infection
  Viral illness or vaccination
  Lymphoreticular malignancies
  Sarcoidosis
  Solid tumors
  Lepromatous leprosy
  Sjögren's syndrome
  Ataxia telangiectasia
  Uremia
  Primary biliary cirrhosis
  Systemic lupus erythematosus
Severe systemic disease of any etiology

From Stein JH (ed): *Internal medicine,* ed 4, St Louis, 1994, Mosby.

BOX 4-14	Factors Affecting Blood Urea Nitrogen Level Independent of Renal Function

Disproportionate Increase in Blood Urea Nitrogen
Volume depletion ("prerenal azotemia")
Gastrointestinal hemorrhage
Corticosteroid or cytotoxic agents
High-protein diet
Obstructive uropathy
Sepsis
Catabolic states, tissue breakdown
Disproportionate Decrease in Blood Urea Nitrogen
Low-protein diet
Liver disease

From Andreoli TE (ed): *Cecil essentials of medicine,* ed 5, Philadelphia, 2001, Saunders.

Elevated in: Dehydration, drugs (aminoglycosides and other antibiotics, diuretics, lithium, corticosteroids), gastrointestinal bleeding, decreased renal blood flow (shock, congestive heart failure, myocardial infarction), renal disease (glomerulonephritis, pyelonephritis, diabetic nephropathy), urinary tract obstruction (prostatic hypertrophy)
Decreased in: Liver disease, malnutrition, third trimester of pregnancy, overhydration, acromegaly, celiac disease

URIC ACID (serum)
Normal range: 2-7 mg/dl
Elevated in: Renal failure, gout, excessive cell lysis (chemotherapeutic agents, radiation therapy, leukemia, lymphoma, hemolytic anemia), hereditary enzyme deficiency (hypoxanthine-guanine-phosphoribosyl transferase), acidosis, myeloproliferative disorders, diet high in purines or protein, drugs (diuretics, low doses of ASA, ethambutol, nicotinic acid), lead poisoning, hypothyroidism, Addison's disease, nephrogenic diabetes insipidus, active psoriasis, polycystic kidneys
Decreased in: Drugs (allopurinol, febuxostat, high doses of ASA, probenecid, warfarin, corticosteroid), deficiency of xanthine oxidase, syndrome of inappropriate antidiuretic hormone secretion, renal tubular deficits (Fanconi's syndrome), alcoholism, liver disease, diet deficient in protein or purines, Wilson's disease, hemochromatosis

URINALYSIS

Normal range:
aa. Color: light straw
bb. Appearance: clear
cc. Ketones: absent
dd. pH: 4.5-8 (average, 6)
ee. Protein: absent
ff. Glucose: absent
gg. Specific gravity: 1.005-1.030
hh. Occult blood absent
ii. Microscopic examination:
Red blood cells: 0-5 (high-power field)

TABLE 4-51 Microscopic Examination of the Urine

Finding	Associations
Casts	
Red blood cell	Glomerulonephritis, vasculitis
White blood cell	Interstitial nephritis, pyelonephritis
Epithelial cell	Acute tubular necrosis, interstitial nephritis, glomerulonephritis
Granular	Renal parenchymal disease (nonspecific)
Waxy, broad	Advanced renal failure
Hyaline	Normal finding in concentrated urine
Fatty	Heavy proteinuria
Cells	
Red blood cell	Urinary tract infection, urinary tract inflammation
White blood cell	Urinary tract infection, urinary tract inflammation
Eosinophil	Acute interstitial nephritis
(Squamous) epithelial cell	Contaminants
Crystals	
Uric acid	Acid urine, acute uric acid nephropathy, hyperuricosuria
Calcium phosphate	Alkaline urine
Calcium oxalate	Acid urine, hyperoxaluria, ethylene glycol poisoning
Cystine	Cystinuria
Sulfur	Sulfa-containing antibiotics

From Andreoli TE (ed): *Cecil essentials of medicine*, ed 5, Philadelphia, 2001, Saunders.

White blood cells: 0-5 (high-power field)
Bacteria (spun specimen): absent
Casts: 0-4 hyaline (low-power field)
Abnormalities in the microscopic examination of urine are described in Table 4-51.

URINE AMYLASE

Normal range: 35-260 U Somogyi/hr (6.5-48.1 U/hr [CF: 0.185; SMI: 1 U/hr])
Elevated in: Pancreatitis, carcinoma of the pancreas

URINE BILE

Normal: Absent
Abnormal:
Urine bilirubin: hepatitis (viral, toxic, drug-induced), biliary obstruction
Urine urobilinogen: hepatitis (viral, toxic, drug-induced), hemolytic jaundice, liver cell dysfunction (cirrhosis, infection, metastases)

URINE CALCIUM

Normal range: <250 mg/24 hr (<6.2 mmol/dl [CF: 0.02495; SMI: 0.1 mmol/dl])
Elevated in: Primary hyperparathyroidism, hypervitaminosis D, bone metastases, multiple myeloma, increased calcium intake, steroids, prolonged immobilization, sarcoidosis, Paget's disease, idiopathic hypercalciuria, renal tubular acidosis
Decreased in: Hypoparathyroidism, pseudohypoparathyroidism, vitamin D deficiency, vitamin D–resistant rickets, diet low in calcium, drugs (thiazide diuretics, oral contraceptives), familial hypocalciuric hypercalcemia, renal osteodystrophy, potassium citrate therapy

URINE cAMP

Elevated in: Hypercalciuria, familial hypocalciuric hypercalcemia, primary hyperparathyroidism, pseudohypoparathyroidism, rickets
Decreased in: Vitamin D intoxication, sarcoidosis

URINE CATECHOLAMINES

Normal range:
Norepinephrine: <100 μg/24 hr (<590 nmol/day [CF: 5.911; SMI: 10 nmol/day])
Epinephrine: <10 μg/24 hr (55 nmol/day [CF: 5.458; SMI: 5 nmol/day])
Elevated in: Pheochromocytoma, neuroblastoma, severe stress

URINE CHLORIDE

Normal range: 110-250 mEq/day (110-250 mmol/day [CF: 1; SMI: 1 mmol/day])
Elevated in: Corticosteroids, Bartter's syndrome, diuretics, metabolic acidosis, severe hypokalemia
Decreased in: Chloride depletion (vomiting), colonic villous adenoma, chronic renal failure, renal tubular acidosis

URINE COPPER

Normal range: <40 μg/24 hr (<0.6 μmol/day [CF: 0.01574; SMI: 0.2 μmol/day])

URINE CORTISOL, FREE

Normal range: 10-110 μg/24 hr (30-300 nmol/day [CF: 2.759; SMI: 10 nmol/day])
Elevated: See CORTISOL, PLASMA

URINE CREATININE (24 hr)

Normal range:
Male: 0.8-1.8 g/day (7-16 mmol/day [CF: 8.840; SMI: 0.1 mmol/day])
Female: 0.6-1.6 g/day (5.3-14 mmol/day)
NOTE: Useful test as an indicator of completeness of 24-hr urine collection.

URINE CRYSTALS

Uric acid: acid urine, hyperuricosuria, uric acid nephropathy
Sulfur: antibiotics containing sulfa
Calcium oxalate: ethylene glycol poisoning, acid urine, hyperoxaluria
Calcium phosphate: alkaline urine
Cystine: cystinuria

URINE EOSINOPHILS

Normal: Absent
Present in: Interstitial nephritis, acute tubular necrosis, urinary tract infection, kidney transplant rejection, hepatorenal syndrome

URINE GLUCOSE (qualitative)

Normal: Absent
Present in: Diabetes mellitus, renal glycosuria (decreased renal threshold for glucose), glucose intolerance

URINE HEMOGLOBIN, FREE

Normal: Absent
Present in: Hemolysis (with saturation of serum haptoglobin binding capacity and renal threshold for tubular absorption of hemoglobin)

URINE HEMOSIDERIN

Normal: Absent
Present in: Paroxysmal nocturnal hemoglobinuria, chronic hemolytic anemia, hemochromatosis, blood transfusion, thalassemias

URINE 5-HYDROXYINDOLE-ACETIC ACID (Urine 5-HIAA)

Normal range: 2-8 mg/24 hr (10-40 μmol/day [CF: 5.23; SMI: 5 μmol/day])
Elevated in: Carcinoid tumors, after ingestion of certain foods (bananas, plums, tomatoes, avocados, pineapples, eggplant, walnuts), drugs (monoamine

Laboratory Tests

IV

TABLE 4-52 Factors That Interfere with Determination of Urinary 5-HIAA

Foods	Drugs
Factors That Produce False-Positive Results	
Avocado	Acetaminophen
Banana	Acetanilid
Chocolate	Caffeine
Coffee	Fluorouracil
Eggplant	Guaifenesin
Pecan	l-Dopa
Pineapple	Melphalan
Plum	Mephenesin
Tea	Methamphetamine
Walnuts	Methocarbamol
	Methysergide maleate
	Phenmetrazine
	Reserpine
	Salicylates
Factors That Cause False-Negative Results	
None	Corticotropin
	p-Chlorophenylalanine
	Chlorpromazine
	Heparin
	Imipramine
	Isoniazid
	Methenamine mandelate
	Methyldopa
	Monoamine oxidase inhibitors
	Phenothiazine
	Promethazine

From Melmed S, Polonsky KS, Larsen PR, Kronenberg HM: *Williams textbook of endocrinology,* ed 12, Philadelphia, 2011, Saunders.
5-HIAA, 5-hydroxyindoleacetic acid.

oxidase inhibitors, phenacetin, methyldopa, glycerol guaiacolate, acetaminophen, salicylates, phenothiazines, imipramine, methocarbamol, reserpine, methamphetamine). See Table 4-52.

URINE INDICAN
Normal: Absent
Present in: Malabsorption secondary to intestinal bacterial overgrowth

URINE KETONES (semiquantitative)
Normal: Absent
Present in: Diabetic ketoacidosis, alcoholic ketoacidosis, starvation, isopropanol ingestion

URINE METANEPHRINES
Normal range: 0-2.0 mg/24 hr (0-11.0 μmol/day [CF: 5.458; SMI: 0.5 μmol/day])
Elevated in: Pheochromocytoma, neuroblastoma, drugs (caffeine, phenothiazines, monoamine oxidase inhibitors), stress. Table 4-53 summarizes medications that may increase metanephrine levels.

URINE MYOGLOBIN
Normal: Absent
Present in: Severe trauma, hyperthermia, polymyositis/dermatomyositis, carbon monoxide poisoning, drugs (narcotic and amphetamine toxicity), hypothyroidism, muscle ischemia

URINE NITRITE
Normal: Absent
Present in: Urinary tract infections

TABLE 4-53 Medications That May Increase Measured Levels of Fractionated Catecholamines and Metanephrines

Tricyclic antidepressants (including cyclobenzaprine)
Levodopa
Drugs containing adrenergic receptor agonists (e.g., decongestants)
Amphetamines
Buspirone and antipsychotic agents
Prochlorperazine
Reserpine
Withdrawal from clonidine and other drugs (e.g., illicit drugs)
Illicit drugs (e.g., cocaine, heroin)
Ethanol

From Melmed S, Polonsky KS, Larsen PR, Kronenberg HM: *Williams textbook of endocrinology,* ed 12, Philadelphia, 2011, Saunders.

URINE OCCULT BLOOD
Normal: Negative
Positive in: Trauma to urinary tract, renal disease (glomerulonephritis, pyelonephritis), renal or ureteral calculi, bladder lesions (carcinoma, cystitis), prostatitis, prostatic carcinoma, menstrual contamination, hematopoietic disorders (hemophilia, thrombocytopenia), anticoagulants, ASA

URINE OSMOLALITY
Normal range: 50-1200 mOsm/kg (50-1200 mmol/kg [CF: 1; SMI: 1 mmol/kg])
Elevated in: Syndrome of inappropriate antidiuretic hormone secretion, dehydration, glycosuria, adrenal insufficiency, high-protein diet
Decreased in: Diabetes insipidus, excessive water intake, IV hydration with D$_5$W, acute renal insufficiency, glomerulonephritis

URINE pH
Normal range: 4.6-8 (average, 6)
Elevated in: Bacteriuria, vegetarian diet, renal failure with inability to form ammonia, drugs (antibiotics, sodium bicarbonate, acetazolamide)
Decreased in: Acidosis (metabolic, respiratory), drugs (ammonium chloride, methenamine mandelate), diabetes mellitus, starvation, diarrhea

URINE PHOSPHATE
Normal range: 0.8-2.0 g/24 hr
Elevated in: Acute tubular necrosis (diuretic phase), chronic renal disease, uncontrolled diabetes mellitus, hyperparathyroidism, hypomagnesemia, metabolic acidosis, metabolic alkalosis, neurofibromatosis, adult-onset vitamin D–resistant hypophosphatemic osteomalacia
Decreased in: Acromegaly, acute renal failure, decreased dietary intake, hypoparathyroidism, respiratory acidosis

URINE POTASSIUM
Normal range: 25-100 mEq/24 hr (25-100 mmol/day [CF: 1; SMI: 1 mmol/day])
Elevated in: Aldosteronism (primary, secondary), glucocorticoids, alkalosis, renal tubular acidosis, excessive dietary potassium intake
Decreased in: Acute renal failure, potassium-sparing diuretics, diarrhea, hypokalemia

URINE PROTEIN (quantitative)
Normal range: <150 mg/24 hr (<0.15 g/day [CF: 0.001; SMI: 0.01 g/day])
Elevated in:
Nephrotic syndrome as a result of primary renal diseases
Malignant hypertension
Malignancies: multiple myeloma, leukemias, Hodgkin's disease
Congestive heart failure
Diabetes mellitus
Systemic lupus erythematosus, rheumatoid arthritis
Sickle cell disease
Goodpasture's syndrome
Malaria

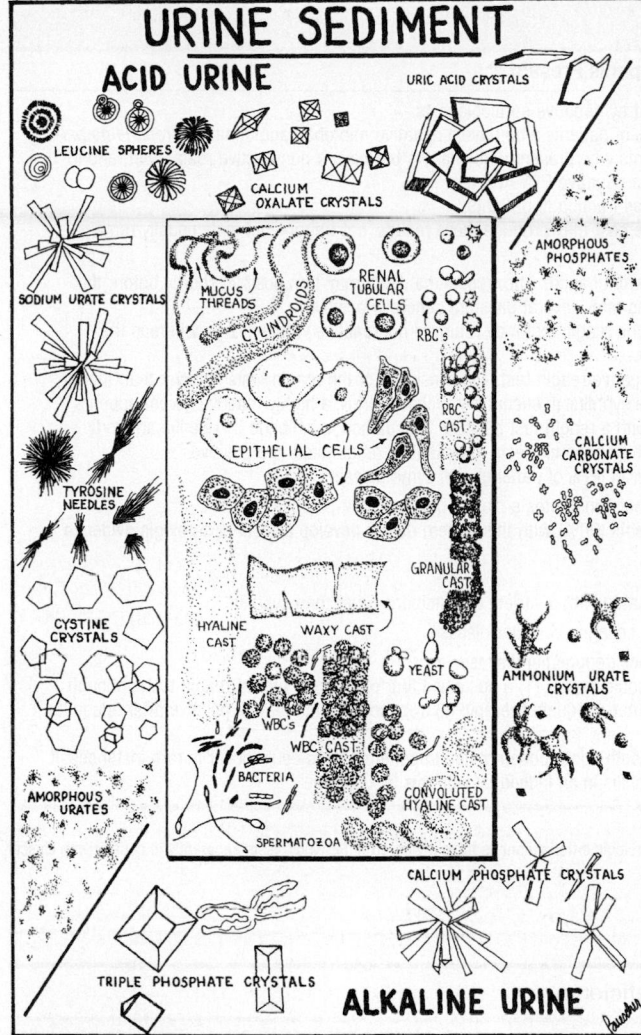

FIGURE 4-39 Microscopic examination of urinary sediment. (From Grigorian Greene M: *The Harriet Lane handbook: a manual for pediatric house officers*, ed 17, St Louis, 2007, Mosby.)

Amyloidosis, sarcoidosis
Tubular lesions: cystinosis
Functional (after heavy exercise)
Pyelonephritis
Pregnancy
Constrictive pericarditis
Renal vein thrombosis
Toxic nephropathies: heavy metals, drugs
Radiation nephritis
Orthostatic (postural) proteinuria
Benign proteinuria: fever, heat or cold exposure

URINE SEDIMENT

See Fig. 4-39 for evaluation of common abnormalities.

URINE SODIUM (quantitative)

See Table 4-54 for use of urine electrolytes in the differential diagnosis of hypokalemia.
Normal range: 40-220 mEq/day (40-220 mmol/day [CF: 1; SMI: 1 mmol/day])
Elevated in: Diuretic administration, high sodium intake, salt-losing nephritis, acute tubular necrosis, vomiting, Addison's disease, syndrome of inappropriate antidiuretic hormone secretion, hypothyroidism, congestive heart failure, hepatic failure, chronic renal failure, Bartter's syndrome, glucocorticoid deficiency, interstitial nephritis caused by analgesic abuse,

---

TABLE 4-54	Urine Electrolytes* in the Differential Diagnosis of Hypokalemia	
Condition	**URINE ELECTROLYTE**	
	Na⁺	Cl⁻
Vomiting		
Recent	High†	Low‡
Remote	Low	Low
Diuretics		
Recent	High	High
Remote	Low	Low
Diarrhea or Laxative Abuse	Low	High
Bartter's or Gitelman's Syndrome	High	High

From Vincent JL et al: *Textbook of critical care*, ed 6, Philadelphia, 2011, Saunders.
*Do not use the urine electrolytes in this fashion during polyuric states.
†High = urine concentration >15 mmol/L.
‡Low = urine concentration <15 mmol/L.

mannitol, dextran, or glycerol therapy, milk-alkali syndrome, decreased renin secretion, postobstructive diuresis
Decreased In: Increased aldosterone, glucocorticoid excess, hyponatremia, prerenal azotemia, decreased salt intake

URINE SPECIFIC GRAVITY

Normal range: 1.005-1.030
Elevated in: Dehydration, excessive fluid losses (vomiting, diarrhea, fever), x-ray contrast media, diabetes mellitus, congestive heart failure, syndrome of inappropriate antidiuretic hormone secretion, adrenal insufficiency, decreased fluid intake
Decreased in: Diabetes insipidus, renal disease (glomerulonephritis, pyelonephritis), excessive fluid intake or IV hydration

URINE VANILLYLMANDELIC ACID (VMA)

Normal range: <6.8 mg/24 hr (<35 μmol/day [CF: 5.046; SMI: 1 μmol/day])
Elevated in: Pheochromocytoma, neuroblastoma, ganglioblastoma, drugs (isoproterenol, methocarbamol, levodopa, sulfonamides, chlorpromazine), severe stress, after ingestion of bananas, chocolate, vanilla, tea, coffee
Decreased In: Drugs (monoamine oxidase inhibitors, reserpine, guanethidine, methyldopa)

VARICELLA-ZOSTER VIRUS (VZV) SEROLOGY

Test description: Test can be performed on whole blood, tissue, skin lesions, and CSF

VASOACTIVE INTESTINAL PEPTIDE (VIP)

Normal: <50 pg/ml
Elevated in: Pancreatic VIP-omas, neuroblastoma, pancreatic islet cell hyperplasia, liver disease, MEN I, ganglioneuroma, ganglioneuroblastoma

VDRL

Normal range: Negative
Positive test: Syphilis, other treponemal diseases (yaws, pinta, bejel)
    NOTE: A false-positive test may be seen in patients with systemic lupus erythematosus and other autoimmune diseases, infectious mononucleosis, HIV, atypical pneumonia, malaria, leprosy, typhus fever, rat-bite fever, relapsing fever.
    NOTE: See Table 4-55 for interpretation of serologic tests for syphilis.

VISCOSITY (serum)

Normal range: 1.4-1.8 relative to water (1.10-1.22 centipoise)
Elevated in: Monoclonal gammopathies (Waldenström's macroglobulinemia, multiple myeloma), hyperfibrinogenemia, systemic lupus erythematosus, rheumatoid arthritis, polycythemia, leukemia

VITAMIN B₁₂ (cobalamin)

See Fig. E4-40 for the Schilling test. See Box 4-15 for etiopathophysiologic classification of cobalamin deficiency. Causes of false-positive and false-negative serum cobalamine levels are summarized in Table 4-56.

TABLE 4-55 Interpretation of Serologic Tests for Syphilis*

Nontreponemal Tests	Treponemal Tests	Interpretation of Finding: Is Syphilis Present?*
Nonreactive	Nonreactive	Early primary syphilis is not ruled out by negative serologic tests.
		Early syphilis is present in 13%-30% of patients who have a negative microhemagglutination *Treponema pallidum* test; in about 30% of patients who present with chancre but have a nonreactive reagin test; and in about 10% of patients who have a negative FTA-ABS test.
		Late syphilis is present in a very small fraction of patients.
		Adequately treated syphilis in remote past may produce these results, but treponemal tests usually remain reactive.
	Reactive	Observed in about 10% of patients with chancre. The treponemal tests may turn positive shortly before the reagin tests. Reagin tests repeated after several days are generally positive.
		In adequately treated early syphilis, the reagin test may return to nonreactive within 1-2 yr, whereas the treponemal tests generally do not.
		Late syphilis is not ruled out by a negative reagin test. The sensitivity of the reagin tests is lower than that of treponemal tests in untreated late syphilis. In secondary syphilis, rarely, a highly reactive serum appears negative when tested undiluted with a reagin test because flocculation is inhibited by relative antibody excess. Not reported to occur with treponemal tests. Quantitative reagin tests are positive.
		False-positive treponemal tests occur in 40% of patients with Lyme disease.
Reactive	Nonreactive borderline (FTA-ABS)	Finding is not diagnostic of syphilis but constitutes a classic biologic false-positive reaction.
		Not diagnostic of syphilis; most patients (90%) with this pattern do not develop clinical or serologic evidence of syphilis.
		Repeat test is indicated.
		Chronic borderline results are associated with a variety of conditions other than syphilis.
	Beaded (FTA-ABS)	Not diagnostic of syphilis. Seen with collagen vascular disease.
	Reactive	Findings diagnostic of syphilis or other treponemal disease.
		In adequately treated syphilis, one would expect (1) a sustained fourfold drop in titer of reagin test, although reagin test may remain positive after adequate therapy; (2) treponemal tests remain positive after adequate therapy.
		Concurrent false-positive results on both nontreponemal and treponemal tests could occur in rare instances. It may be impossible to rule out syphilis in an individual with this test profile.

From Stein JH (ed): *Internal medicine*, ed 4, St Louis, 1994, Mosby.

*Serologic data must always be interpreted in the light of a total clinical evaluation. Diagnosis based on serologic criteria alone is fraught with error. Serologic tests apparently in conflict with clinical diagnosis should be confirmed by repetition or possibly referral to a reference laboratory.

FTA-ABS, Fluorescent treponemal antibody, absorbed.

BOX 4-15 Etiopathophysiologic Classification of Cobalamin Deficiency

Nutritional cobalamin deficiency (insufficient cobalamin intake)—vegetarians, poverty-imposed near-vegetarians, breastfed infants of mothers with pernicious anemia

Abnormal intragastric events (inadequate proteolysis of food cobalamin)—atrophic gastritis, hypochlorhydria, proton pump inhibitors, H$_2$ blockers

Loss/atrophy of gastric oxyntic mucosa (deficient intrinsic factor [IF] molecules)—total or partial gastrectomy, adult and juvenile pernicious anemia, caustic destruction (lye)

Abnormal events in the small bowel lumen

  Inadequate pancreatic protease (R factor–cobalamin not degraded, cobalamin not transferred to IF)

  Insufficient pancreatic protease—pancreatic insufficiency

  Inactivation of pancreatic protease—Zollinger-Ellison syndrome

  Usurping of luminal cobalamin (inadequate binding of cobalamin to IF)

  By bacteria-stasis syndromes (blind loops, pouches of diverticulosis, strictures, fistulas, anastomosis), impaired bowel motility (scleroderma), hypogammaglobulinemia

  By *Diphyllobothrium latum* (fish tapeworm)

Disorders of ileal mucosa/IF-cobalamin receptors (IF-cobalamin not bound to IF-cobalamin receptors [cubam receptors])

  Diminished or absent cubam receptors—ileal bypass/resection/fistula

  Abnormal mucosal architecture/function—tropical/nontropical sprue, Crohn disease, tuberculous ileitis, amyloidosis

  Cubam receptor defects—Imerslund-Gräsbeck syndrome

  Drug-effects—metformin, cholestyramine, colchicine, neomycin

Disorders of plasma cobalamin transport (transcobalamin [TCII]-cobalamin not delivered to TCII receptors)—congenital TCII deficiency, defective binding of TCII-cobalamin to TCII receptors (rare)

Metabolic disorders (cobalamin not used by cell)

Inborn enzyme errors—cblA to cblG disorders

Acquired disorders (cobalamin inactivated by irreversible oxidation)—nitrous oxide

From Hoffman R: *Hematology: basic principles and practice*, ed 6, Philadelphia, Saunders, 2013.

TABLE 4-56 Serum Cobalamin: False-Positive and False-Negative Test Results

Falsely Low Serum Cobalamin in the Absence of True Cobalamin Deficiency

Folate deficiency (one-third of patients)
Multiple myeloma
TCI deficiency
Megadose vitamin C therapy

Falsely Raised Cobalamin Levels in the Presence of True Deficiency*

Cobalamin binders (TCI and II) increased (e.g., myeloproliferative states, hepatomas, and fibrolamellar hepatic tumors)
TCII-producing macrophages are activated (e.g., autoimmune diseases, monoblastic leukemias and lymphomas)
Release of cobalamin from hepatocytes (e.g., active liver disease)
High serum anti-IF antibody titer

From Hoffman R, et al: *Hematology, basic principles and practice*, ed 6, Philadelphia, 2013, Saunders.

*Although a low serum cobalamin level is not synonymous with cobalamin deficiency, 5% of patients with true cobalamin deficiency have low-normal cobalamin levels, a potentially serious problem because the patient's underlying cobalamin deficiency will progress if uncorrected.

IF, Intrinsic factor; *TC,* transcobalamin.

Normal:
190-900 ng/ml
Causes of vitamin B$_{12}$ deficiency:
    Pernicious anemia (antibodies against intrinsic factor and gastric parietal cells)
    Dietary (strict lacto-ovovegetarians, food faddists)

Malabsorption (achlorhydria, gastrectomy, ileal resection, pancreatic insufficiency, drugs [omeprazole, cholestyramine])
Falsely low levels occur in patients with severe folate deficiency, in patients using high doses of ascorbic acid, and when cobalamin levels are measured after nuclear medicine studies (radioactivity interferes with cobalamin radioimmunoassay).
Falsely high or normal levels in patients with cobalamin deficiency can occur in severe liver disease and chronic granulocytic leukemia.
The absence of anemia or macrocytosis does not exclude the diagnosis of cobalamin deficiency.

VITAMIN D, 1,25 DIHYDROXY CALCIFEROL

Normal: 16-65 pg/ml
Elevated in: Tumor calcinosis, primary hyperparathyroidism, sarcoidosis, tuberculosis, idiopathic hypercalciuria
Decreased in: Nutritional deficiency, postmenopausal osteoporosis, chronic renal failure, hypoparathyroidism, tumor-induced osteomalacia, rickets, elevated blood lead levels

VITAMIN K

Normal: 0.10-2.20 ng/ml
Decreased in: Primary biliary cirrhosis, anticoagulants, antibiotics, cholestyramine, GI disease, pancreatic disease, cystic fibrosis, obstructive jaundice, hypoprothrombinemia, hemorrhagic disease of the newborn

VON WILLEBRAND FACTOR

Normal: Levels vary according to blood type; blood type O: 50-150 U/dl; blood type non-O: 90-200 U/dl
Decreased in: von Willebrand's disease (however, in type II von Willebrand's disease the antigen may be normal but the function is impaired)

SECTION V

Clinical Practice Guidelines

PART A • THE PERIODIC HEALTH EXAMINATION

Age-Specific Charts

TABLE 5-1   Birth to 10 Years

Interventions considered and recommended for the Periodic Health Examination	Leading causes of death
	Conditions originating in perinatal period
	Congenital anomalies
	Sudden infant death syndrome
	Unintentional injuries (non–motor vehicle)
	Motor vehicle injuries

INTERVENTIONS FOR THE GENERAL POPULATION

Screening

Height and weight

Blood pressure

Vision screen (ages 3-4 yr)

Hemoglobinopathy screen (birth)[1]

Phenylalanine level (birth)[2]

Thyroxine and/or thyroid-stimulating hormone (birth)[3]

Lead level

Counseling

Injury prevention

Child safety car seats (age <5 yr)

Lap/shoulder belts (age ≥5 yr)

Bicycle helmet; avoid bicycling near traffic

Smoke detector, flame-retardant sleepwear

Hot water heater temperature <120°-130° F

Window/stair guards, pool fence

Safe storage of drugs, toxic substances, firearms, and matches

Syrup of ipecac, poison control phone number

CPR training for parents/caretakers

Diet and exercise

Breastfeeding, iron-enriched formula and foods (infants and toddlers)

Limit fat and cholesterol; maintain caloric balance; emphasize grains, fruits, vegetables (age ≥2 yr)

Regular physical activity*

Substance use

Effects of passive smoking*

Antitobacco message*

Dental health

Regular visits to dental care provider*

Floss, brush with fluoride toothpaste daily*

Advice about baby bottle tooth decay*

Immunizations

Diphtheria-tetanus-pertussis (DTaP)[4]

Inactivated poliovirus vaccine (IPV)[5]

Measles-mumps-rubella (MMR)[6]

Haemophilus influenzae type b (Hib) conjugate[7]

Hepatitis A vaccine (HR4)

Hepatitis B[8]

Varicella[9]

Pneumococcal vaccine[10]

Influenza[11]

Meningococcal conjugate vaccine (MCV)[12]

Rotavirus (RV)[13]

Human papillomavirus vaccine (HPV)[14]

Chemoprophylaxis

Ocular prophylaxis (birth)

INTERVENTIONS FOR HIGH-RISK POPULATIONS

Population	Potential Interventions (see detailed high-risk definitions)
Preterm or low birth weight	Hemoglobin/hematocrit (HR1)
Infants of mothers at risk for HIV	HIV testing (HR2)
Low income; immigrants	Hemoglobin/hematocrit (HR1); PPD (HR3)
TB contacts	PPD (HR3)
Native American/Alaska Native	Hemoglobin/hematocrit (HR1); PPD (HR3); pneumococcal vaccine (HR5)
Residents of long-term care facilities	PPD (HR3); hepatitis A vaccine (HR4); influenza vaccine (HR6)
Certain chronic medical conditions	PPD (HR3); pneumococcal vaccine (HR5); influenza vaccine (HR6)
Increased individual or community lead exposure	Blood lead level (HR7)
Inadequate water fluoridation	Daily fluoride supplement (HR8)
Family history of skin cancer; nevi; fair skin, eyes, hair	Avoid excess/midday sun, use protective clothing* (HR9)

CPR, Cardiopulmonary resuscitation; *HR*, high risk; *PPD*, purified protein derivative; *STDs*, sexually transmitted diseases; *TB*, tuberculosis.

[1]Whether screening should be universal or targeted to high-risk groups depends on the proportion of high-risk individuals in the screening area and other considerations. [2]If done during first 24 hr of life, repeat by age 2 wk. [3]Optimally between day 2 and 6, but in all cases before newborn nursery discharge. [4]2, 4, 6, and 12-18 mo; once between age 4-6 yr. [5]2, 4, 6-18 mo; once between age 4-6 yr. [6]12-15 mo and 4-6 yr. [7]2, 4, 6 and 12-15 mo; no dose needed at 6 mo if PRP-OMP vaccine is used for first 2 doses. [8]Birth, 1 mo, 6 mo; or, 0-2 mo, 1-2 mo later, and 6-18 mo. If not done in infancy: current visit, and 1 and 6 mo later. [9]12-18 mo; or any child without history of chickenpox or previous immunization. Include information on risk in adulthood, duration of immunity, and potential need for booster doses. Administer a second dose of varicella vaccine at age 4-6 yr. [10]Pneumococcal polysaccharide vaccine (PPSV) can be administered at the same time as the other childhood vaccines at a separate site. [11]Influenza vaccine is recommended in children 6 mo-18 yr of age. [12]Administer meningococcal conjugate vaccine (MCV) to children aged 2 through 10 yr with terminal complement component deficiency, anatomic or functional asplenia, and certain other high-risk groups (see *MMWR* 54[RR-7], 2005). Persons who received MPSV 3 or more years previously and who remain at increased risk for meningococcal disease should be revaccinated with MCV. [13]Administer first dose at 2 mo. If Rotarix® is administered at ages 2 and 4 mo, a dose at 6 mo is not indicated. [14]HPV4 may be administered in a 3-dose series to males aged 9 through 26 yr and females aged 11 to 26 yr to reduce the likelihood of acquiring genital warts.

*The ability of clinician counseling to influence this behavior is unproven.

HR1: Infants aged 6-12 mo who are living in poverty, black, Native American or Alaska Native, immigrants from developing countries, preterm and low-birth-weight infants, infants whose principal dietary intake is unfortified cow's milk.

HR2: Infants born to high-risk mothers whose HIV status is unknown. Women at high risk include past or present injection drug users; persons who exchange sex for money or drugs and their sex partners; injection drug–using, bisexual, or HIV-positive sex partners currently or in past; persons seeking treatment for STDs; persons who received a blood transfusion between 1978 and 1985.

HR3: Persons infected with HIV, close contacts of persons with known or suspected TB, persons with medical risk factors associated with TB, immigrants from countries with high TB prevalence, medically underserved low-income populations (including homeless), residents of long-term care facilities.

HR4: Hepatitis A vaccine (Hep A) is recommended for all children at 1 yr of age (i.e., 12-23 mo). The two doses in the series should be administered at least 6 mo apart. Children who are not vaccinated by 2 yr of age can be vaccinated at subsequent visits.

HR5: Immunocompetent persons ≥2 yr with certain medical conditions, including chronic cardiac or pulmonary disease, diabetes mellitus, and anatomic asplenia, as well as cochlear implant candidates and recipients. Immunocompetent persons ≥2 yr living in high-risk environments or social settings (e.g., certain Native American and Alaska Native populations).

HR6: Annual vaccinations of children ≥6 mo who are residents of chronic care facilities or who have chronic cardiopulmonary disorders, metabolic diseases (including diabetes mellitus), hemoglobinopathies, immunosuppression, or renal dysfunction.

HR7: Children approximately age 12 mo who (1) live in communities in which the prevalence of lead levels requiring individual intervention, including residential lead hazard control or chelation, is high or undefined; (2) live in or frequently visit a home built before 1950 with dilapidated paint or with recent or ongoing renovation or remodeling; (3) have close contact with a person who has an elevated lead level; (4) live near lead industry or heavy traffic; (5) live with someone whose job or hobby involves lead exposure; (6) use lead-based pottery; or (7) take traditional ethnic remedies that contain lead.

HR8: Children living in areas with inadequate water fluoridation (<0.6 ppm).

HR9: Persons with a family history of skin cancer; a large number of moles; atypical moles; poor tanning ability; or light skin, hair, and eye color.

TABLE 5-2 Ages 11 to 24 Years

Interventions considered and recommended for the Periodic Health Examination	Leading causes of death
	Motor vehicle accidents/other unintentional injuries
	Homicide
	Suicide
	Malignant neoplasms
	Heart diseases

INTERVENTIONS FOR THE GENERAL POPULATION

Screening

Height and weight
Blood pressure[1]
Papanicolaou (Pap) test[2] (females)
Chlamydia screen[3] (females <25 yr)
HIV screening
Lipid panel (in high-risk young adults only)
Rubella serology or vaccination history[4] (females >12 yr)
Assess for problem drinking
Lead level

Counseling

Injury prevention

Lap/shoulder belts
Bicycle/motorcycle/ATV helmets*
Smoke detector*
Safe storage/removal of firearms*

Substance use

Avoid tobacco use
Avoid underage drinking and illicit drug use*
Avoid alcohol/drug use while driving, swimming, boating, etc.*

Sexual behavior

STD prevention: abstinence*; avoid high-risk behavior*; condoms/female barrier with spermicide*
Unintended pregnancy: contraception

Diet and exercise

Limit fat and cholesterol; maintain caloric balance; emphasize grains, fruits, vegetables
Adequate calcium intake (females)
Regular physical activity*

Dental health

Regular visits to dental care provider*
Floss, brush with fluoride toothpaste daily

Immunizations

Tetanus, diphtheria, pertussis†
Hepatitis B[5]
Measles-mumps-rubella (MMR) (11-12 yr)[6]
Varicella (11-12 yr)[7]
Rubella (females >12 yr)[4]
Meningococcal[8]
Human papilloma virus (females 11-26 yr, males 9-26 yr)[9]
Influenza[10]
Pneumococcal polysaccharide vaccine (PPSV)[11]

Chemoprophylaxis

Multivitamin with folic acid (females)

INTERVENTIONS FOR HIGH-RISK POPULATIONS

Population	Potential Interventions (see detailed high-risk definitions)
High-risk sexual behavior	RPR/VDRL (HR1); screen for gonorrhea (female) (HR2), HIV (HR3), chlamydia (female) (HR4); hepatitis A vaccine (HR5)
Injection or street drug use	RPR/VDRL (HR1); HIV screen (HR3); hepatitis A vaccine (HR5); PPD (HR6); advice to reduce infection risk (HR7)
TB contacts; immigrants; low income	PPD (HR6)
Native Americans/Alaska Natives	Hepatitis A vaccine (HR5); PPD (HR6); pneumococcal vaccine (HR8)
Travelers to developing countries	Hepatitis A vaccine (HR5)
Certain chronic medical conditions	PPD (HR6); pneumococcal vaccine (HR8); influenza vaccine (HR9)
Settings where adolescents and young adults congregate	Second MMR (HR10)
Susceptible to varicella, measles, mumps	Varicella vaccine (HR11); MMR (HR12)
Institutionalized persons; health care/lab workers	Hepatitis A vaccine (HR5); PPD (HR6); influenza vaccine (HR9)
Family history of skin cancer; nevi; fair skin, eyes, hair	Avoid excess/midday sun, use protective clothing* (HR13)
Prior pregnancy with neural tube defect	Folic acid 4.0 mg (HR14)
Inadequate water fluoridation	Daily fluoride supplement (HR15)
Pregnancy	HIV screen, Tdap vaccine (given in second or early third trimester of pregnancy)
Infants 6-11 mo of age travelling internationally	MMR

ATV, All-terrain vehicle; *HR*, high risk; *PPD*, purified protein derivative; *RPR*, rapid plasmin reagin; *STD*, sexually transmitted disease; *TB*, tuberculosis; *VDRL*, Venereal Disease Research Laboratory.
[1]Periodic blood pressure for persons aged ≥21 yr. [2]Screening for cervical cancer should begin at 21 years of age, regardless of sexual behaviors and risk factors. Cytology without HPV testing should be performed every 3 years. [3]If sexually active, Table 5-6 summarizes cervical cancer screening guidelines. [4]Serologic testing, documented vaccination history, and routine vaccination against rubella (preferably with MMR) are equally acceptable alternatives. [5]If not previously immunized: current visit and 1 and 6 mo later. [6]If no previous second dose of MMR. [7]If susceptible to chicken-pox. [8]Meningococcal conjugate vaccine (MCV) can be administered at 11-12 yr visit, at high school entry, or at beginning of college (especially indicated in students living in college dormitories). Meningococcal group B vaccine (Trumenba) is approved for use in individuals 10 through 25 years of age for active immunization to prevent invasive disease caused by *Neisseria meningitidis* serogroup B. [9]Quadrivalent human papillomavirus (types 6, 11, 16, 18) recombinant vaccine (Gardasil) should be given to all females aged 11-26 yr who have not been previously vaccinated. The vaccine is indicated for the prevention of cervical cancer and genital warts caused by the human papilloma virus (HPV) 6, 11, 16, or 18. Gardasil is an intramuscular injection for administration to the thigh or upper arm. The schedule consists of three 0.5-ml doses, with the second dose given 2 mo after the first, and the final dose administered 6 mo after the initial dose. HPV4 may also be administered in a 3-dose series to males aged 9 through 26 years to reduce their likelihood of acquiring genital warts. A bivalent HPV vaccine is available for prevention of cervical dysplasia in females. [10]Influenza vaccine is recommended for children 6 mo to 18 yr of age and all adults. [11]Administer to children with certain underlying medical conditions (see *MMWR* 46[RR-8], 1997), including a cochlear implant. A single revaccination should be administered to children with functional or anatomic asplenia or other immunocompromising condition after 5 yr.
*The ability of clinician counseling to influence this behavior is unproven.
†Tdap vaccine is recommended for adolescents aged 11-12 yr who have completed the recommended childhood DTP/DTaP vaccination series and have not received a Td booster dose. Adolescents aged 13-18 yr who missed the 11-12-yr Td/Tdap booster dose should also receive a single dose of Tdap if they have completed the recommended childhood DTP/DTaP vaccination series. A 5-yr interval from the last Td dose is encouraged when Tdap is used as a booster drug; however, a shorter interval may be used if pertussis immunity is needed. For pregnant patients, the Tdap vaccine is recommended with each pregnancy between 27 and 36 weeks of gestation.

HR1: Persons who exchange sex for money or drugs and their sex partners, persons with other STDs (including HIV), and sexual contacts of persons with active syphilis. Clinicians should also consider local epidemiology.

HR2: Females who have had two or more sex partners in the last year or a sex partner with multiple sexual contacts; exchanged sex for money or drugs; or have a history of repeated episodes of gonorrhea. Clinicians should also consider local epidemiology.

HR3: Males who had sex with males after 1975; past or present injection drug users; persons who exchange sex for money or drugs and their sex partners; injection drug–using, bisexual, or HIV-positive sex partner currently or in the past; recipients of a blood transfusion between 1978 and 1985; persons seeking treatment for STDs. Clinicians should also consider screening for HIV in general population.

HR4: Sexually active females with multiple risk factors, including history of prior STD, new or multiple sex partners, age <25 yr, nonuse or inconsistent use of barrier contraceptives, or cervical ectopy. Clinicians should consider local epidemiology of the disease in identifying other high-risk groups.

HR5: Persons living in, traveling to, or working in areas where the disease is endemic and where periodic outbreaks occur (e.g., countries with high or intermediate endemicity; certain Alaska Native, Pacific Island, Native American, and religious communities); men who have sex with men; injection or street drug users; persons with clotting factor disorders or chronic liver disease, diabetics. Vaccine may be considered for institutionalized persons and workers in these institutions; military personnel; and day-care, hospital, and laboratory workers. Clinicians should also consider local epidemiology.

HR6: HIV-positive, close contacts of persons with known or suspected TB, health care workers, persons with medical risk factors associated with TB, immigrants from countries with high TB prevalence, medically underserved low-income populations (including homeless), alcoholics, injection drug users, and residents of long-term care facilities.

HR7: Persons who continue to inject drugs.

HR8: Immunocompetent persons with certain medical conditions, including chronic cardiac, renal, or pulmonary disease; diabetes mellitus; cochlear implant candidates and recipients; and anatomic asplenia. Immunocompetent persons who live in high-risk environments or social settings (e.g., certain Native American and Alaska Native populations). Adults who smoke cigarettes, persons with asymptomatic or symptomatic HIV infection.

HR9: Annual vaccination of residents of chronic care facilities; persons with chronic cardiopulmonary disorders, metabolic diseases (including diabetes mellitus), hemoglobinopathies, immunosuppression, or renal dysfunction; and health care providers for high-risk patients.

HR10: Adolescents and young adults in settings where such individuals congregate (e.g., high schools and colleges) if they have not previously received a second dose.

HR11: Healthy persons aged ≥13 yr without a history of chickenpox or previous immunization. Consider serologic testing for presumed susceptible persons aged ≥13 yr.

HR12: Persons born after 1956 who lack evidence of immunity to measles or mumps (e.g., documented receipt of live vaccine on or after the first birthday, laboratory evidence of immunity, or a history of physician-diagnosed measles or mumps).

HR13: Persons with a family or personal history of skin cancer; a large number of moles; atypical moles; poor tanning ability; or light skin, hair, and eye color.

HR14: Women with prior pregnancy affected by neural tube defect who are planning pregnancy.

HR15: Persons aged <17 yr living in areas with inadequate water fluoridation (<0.6 ppm).

TABLE 5-3 Ages 25 to 64 Years

Interventions considered and recommended for the Periodic Health Examination	Leading causes of death
	Malignant neoplasms
	Heart diseases
	Motor vehicle and other unintentional injuries
	HIV infection
	Suicide and homicide

INTERVENTIONS FOR THE GENERAL POPULATION

Screening

Blood pressure

Height and weight

Lipid panel (men aged 35-64 yr, women aged 45-64 yr)

HIV screening

Papanicolaou (Pap) test (women)[1]

Cytology without HPV testing starting at age 21

Cytology with HPV testing starting at 30 years of age

Fecal occult blood test[2] and/or colonoscopy (≥50 yr)

Mammogram ± clinical breast examination[3] (women 40-69 yr)[8]

Bone density scan in postmenopausal women

Assess for problem drinking

Rubella serology or vaccination history[4] (women of childbearing age)

Counseling

Substance use

Tobacco cessation

Avoid alcohol/drug use while driving, swimming, boating, etc.*

Diet and exercise

Limit fat and cholesterol; maintain caloric balance; emphasize grains, fruits, vegetables

Adequate calcium intake (women)

Regular physical activity*

Injury prevention

Lap/shoulder belts

Motorcycle/bicycle/ATV helmets*

Smoke detector*

Safe storage/removal of firearms*

Sexual behavior

STD prevention: avoid high-risk behavior*; condoms/female barrier with spermicide*

Unintended pregnancy: contraception

Dental health

Regular visits to dental care provider*

Floss, brush with fluoride toothpaste daily*

Immunizations

Tetanus-diphtheria-pertussis (Tdap) booster[7]

Rubella[4] (women of childbearing age)

Influenza vaccine†

Human papillomavirus[5]

Herpes zoster (≥60 yr)[6]

Chemoprophylaxis

Multivitamin with folic acid (women planning or capable of pregnancy)

INTERVENTIONS FOR HIGH-RISK POPULATIONS

Population	Potential Interventions (see detailed high-risk definitions)
High-risk sexual behavior	RPR/VDRL (HR1); screen for gonorrhea (female) (HR2), HIV (HR3), chlamydia (female) (HR4); hepatitis B vaccine (HR5); hepatitis A vaccine (HR6)
Injection or street drug use	RPR/VDRL (HR1); HIV screen (HR3); hepatitis B vaccine (HR5); hepatitis A vaccine (HR6); PPD (HR7); advice to reduce infection risk (HR8)
Low income; TB contacts; immigrants; alcoholics	PPD (HR7)
Native Americans/Alaska Natives	Hepatitis A vaccine (HR6); PPD (HR7); pneumococcal vaccine (HR9)
Travelers to developing countries	Hepatitis B vaccine (HR5); hepatitis A vaccine (HR6)
Certain chronic medical conditions	PPD (HR7); pneumococcal vaccine (HR9); influenza vaccine (HR10)
Blood product recipients	HIV screen (HR3); hepatitis B vaccine (HR5); hepatitis C screen
Susceptible to measles, mumps, or varicella	MMR (HR11); varicella vaccine (HR12)
Institutionalized persons	Hepatitis A vaccine (HR6); PPD (HR7); pneumococcal vaccine (HR9); influenza vaccine (HR10)
Health care/lab workers	Hepatitis B vaccine (HR5); hepatitis A vaccine (HR6); PPD (HR7); influenza vaccine (HR10)
Family history of skin cancer; fair skin, eyes, hair	Avoid excess/midday sun, use protective clothing* (HR13)
Previous pregnancy with neural tube defect	Folic acid 4.0 mg (HR14)
Cardiovascular risk factors	Lipid panel (HR 15)
Pregnancy	HIV screen, Tdap vaccine (in second or early third trimester of pregnancy)
Diabetes mellitus	Hepatitis B vaccine (HR5)

ATV, All-terrain vehicle; *HPV,* human papillomavirus; *HR,* high risk; *MMR,* measles-mumps-rubella; *PPD,* purified protein derivative; *RPR,* rapid plasma reagin; *STD,* sexually transmitted disease; *TB,* tuberculosis; *Tdap,* tetanus and diphtheria toxoids and acellular pertussis; *VDRL,* Venereal Disease Research Laboratory.

[1]Women who are or have been sexually active and who have a cervix: q ≤3 yr. Routine Pap smear screening is unnecessary for women who have undergone a complete hysterectomy for benign disease. The American College of Obstetricians and Gynecologists (ACOG) recommends that routine Pap smears should start at age 21. Women 30 and older should wait 3 yrs between paps once they have had three consecutive clear tests. For women 21-29 years old, cervical cytology alone should be performed every 3 years. For women 30-65 years old, co-testing with cervical cytology and human papilloma virus (HPV) testing should be performed every 5 years. Screening should occur more frequently in women who have established risk factors for cervical cancer (including immunocompromised status, HIV infection, history of cervical intraepithelial neoplasia, exposure to diethylstilbestrol in utero). [2]Annually. [3]Mammogram q1-2 yr, or mammogram q1-2 yr with annual clinical breast examination. [4]Serologic testing, documented vaccination history, and routine vaccination (preferably with MMR) are equally acceptable. [5]Quadrivalent human papillomavirus (types 6, 11, 16, 18) recombinant vaccine (Gardasil) should be given to all females aged 9-26 yr who have not been previously vaccinated. The vaccine is indicated for the prevention of cervical cancer and genital warts caused by the human papillomavirus (HPV) 6, 11, 16, or 18. Gardasil is an intramuscular injection for administration to the thigh or upper arm. The schedule consists of three 0.5-ml doses, with the second dose given 2 mo after the first, and the final dose administered 6 mo after the initial dose. Gardasil is also indicated in males aged 9 to 26 yr for prevention of genital warts. A bivalent HPV vaccine is available for prevention of cervical dysplasia in females. [6]Herpes zoster vaccine (Zostavax) is indicated for prevention of herpes zoster (shingles) in individuals 60 yr or older. Zostavax is administered as a single dose subcutaneously. It is a lyophilic preparation of the Oka/Merck strain of live, attenuated varicella-zoster virus (VZV). It should not be administered to individuals with a history of primary or acquired immunodeficiency states, persons on immunosuppressive therapy (including high-dose corticosteroids), those with active untreated tuberculosis, and those who may be pregnant. [7]For pregnant patients, the Tdap is recommended with each pregnancy between 27 and 36 weeks of gestation. [8]American Cancer Society guidelines for average risk women recommend optional annual screening mammography at age 40-44, screening (strong recommendation) beginning at age 45, annual screening 45-54, biannual screening with option to continue annual screening, continue screening as long as overall health is good and life expectancy is ≥10 years. Clinical breast examination for screening is not recommended.

*The ability of clinician counseling to influence this behavior is unproven.

†A live attenuated influenza vaccine (LAIV, FluMist) administered intranasally is available for healthy persons aged 2 to 49 yr.

HR1: Persons who exchange sex for money or drugs and their sex partners, persons with other STDs (including HIV), and sexual contacts of persons with active syphilis. Clinicians should also consider local epidemiology.

HR2: Women who exchange sex for money or drugs or who have had repeated episodes of gonorrhea. Clinicians should also consider local epidemiology.

HR3: Men who had sex with men after 1975; past or present injection drug users; persons who exchange sex for money or drugs and their sex partners; persons with current or past injection drug–using, bisexual, or HIV-positive sex partners; recipients of a blood transfusion between 1978 and 1985; persons seeking treatment for STDs. Clinicians should also consider local epidemiology and HIV screening in the general population.

HR4: Sexually active women with multiple risk factors, including history of STD, new or multiple sex partners, nonuse or inconsistent use of barrier contraceptives, or cervical ectopy. Clinicians should also consider local epidemiology.

HR5: Blood product recipients (including hemodialysis patients), persons with frequent occupational exposure to blood or blood products, men who have sex with men, injection drug users and their sex partners, persons with multiple recent sex partners, persons with other STDs (including HIV), travelers to countries with endemic hepatitis B, all diabetics age 19 to 59.

HR6: Persons living in, traveling to, or working in areas where the disease is endemic and where periodic outbreaks occur (e.g., countries with high or intermediate endemicity; certain Alaska Native, Pacific Island, Native American, and religious communities); men who have sex with men; injection or street drug users; patients with clotting factor disorders or chronic liver disease. Consider for institutionalized persons and workers in these institutions; military personnel; and day-care, hospital, and laboratory workers. Clinicians should also consider local epidemiology.

HR7: HIV-positive, close contacts of persons with known or suspected TB, health care workers, persons with medical risk factors associated with TB, immigrants from countries with high TB prevalence, medically underserved low-income populations (including homeless), alcoholics, injection drug users, and residents of long-term care facilities.

HR8: Persons who continue to inject drugs.

HR9: Immunocompetent institutionalized persons and immunocompetent persons with certain medical conditions, including chronic cardiac, renal, or pulmonary disease; anatomic asplenia; diabetes mellitus; or cochlear implant candidates and recipients. Immunocompetent persons who live in high-risk environments or social settings (e.g., certain Native American and Alaska Native populations), adults who smoke cigarettes, persons with asymptomatic or symptomatic HIV infection.

HR10: Annual vaccination of residents of long-term care facilities; persons with chronic cardiopulmonary disorders, metabolic diseases (including diabetes mellitus), hemoglobinopathies, immunosuppression, or renal dysfunction; and health care providers of high-risk patients.

HR11: Persons born after 1956 who lack evidence of immunity to measles or mumps (e.g., documented receipt of live vaccine on or after the first birthday, laboratory evidence of immunity, or a history of physician-diagnosed measles or mumps).

HR12: Healthy adults without a history of chickenpox or previous immunization. Consider serologic testing for presumed susceptible adults.

HR13: Persons with a family or personal history of skin cancer; a large number of moles; atypical moles; poor tanning ability; or light skin, hair, and eye color.

HR14: Women with previous pregnancy affected by neural tube disorder who are planning pregnancy.

HR15: Clinicians should consider a fasting serum lipid panel on a case-by-case basis.

TABLE 5-4 Ages 65 and Older

Interventions considered and recommended for the Periodic Health Examination	Leading causes of death
	Heart diseases
	Malignant neoplasms (lung, colorectal, breast)
	Cerebrovascular disease
	Chronic obstructive pulmonary disease
	Pneumonia and influenza

INTERVENTIONS FOR THE GENERAL POPULATION

Screening
Blood pressure
Height and weight
Fecal occult blood test[1] and/or colonoscopy
Mammogram ± clinical breast examination[2] (women ≤69 yr)
Papanicolaou (Pap) test (women)[3]
Bone density scan in postmenopausal patients
Vision screening
Assess for hearing impairment
Assess for problem drinking
Offer HIV screen

Counseling
Substance use
Tobacco cessation
Avoid alcohol/drug use while driving, swimming, boating, etc.*
Diet and exercise
Limit fat and cholesterol; maintain caloric balance; emphasize grains, fruits, vegetables
Adequate calcium intake (women)
Regular physical activity*

Injury prevention
Lap/shoulder belts
Motorcycle and bicycle helmets*
Fall prevention*
Safe storage/removal of firearms*
Smoke detector*
Set hot water heater to <120°-130° F
CPR training for household members
Dental health
Regular visits to dental care provider*
Floss, brush with fluoride toothpaste daily*
Sexual behavior
STD prevention: avoid high-risk sexual behavior*; use condoms
Immunizations
Pneumococcal vaccine[5]
Influenza[1]
Tetanus-diphtheria (Td) boosters every 10 years, with 1 substitute Tdap dose
Herpes zoster[4]

INTERVENTIONS FOR HIGH-RISK POPULATIONS

Population	*Potential Interventions (see detailed high-risk definitions)*
Institutionalized persons	PPD (HR1); hepatitis A vaccine (HR2); amantadine/rimantadine (HR4)
Chronic medical conditions; TB contacts; low income; immigrants; alcoholics	PPD (HR1)
Persons ≥75 yr or ≥70 yr with risk factors for falls	Fall prevention intervention (HR5)
Cardiovascular disease risk factors	Consider lipid screening (HR6)
Family history of skin cancer; nevi; fair skin, eyes, hair	Avoid excess/midday sun, use protective clothing* (HR7)
Native Americans/Alaska Natives	PPD (HR1); hepatitis A vaccine (HR2)
Travelers to developing countries	Hepatitis A vaccine (HR2); hepatitis B vaccine (HR8)
Blood product recipients	HIV screen (HR3); hepatitis B vaccine (HR8)
High-risk sexual behavior	Hepatitis A vaccine (HR2); HIV screen (HR3); hepatitis B vaccine (HR8); RPR/VDRL (HR9)
Injection or street drug use	PPD (HR1); hepatitis A vaccine (HR2); HIV screen (HR3); hepatitis B vaccine (HR8); RPR/VDRL (HR9); advice to reduce infection risk (HR10)
Health care/lab workers	PPD (HR1); hepatitis A vaccine (HR2); amantadine/rimantadine (HR4); hepatitis B vaccine (HR8)
Persons susceptible to varicella	Varicella vaccine (HR11)
Men aged 65 to 75 who have ever smoked	Ultrasound of abdominal aorta (HR12)

HR, High risk; *PPD*, purified protein derivative; *RPR*, rapid plasma reagin; *STD*, sexually transmitted disease; *TB*, tuberculosis; *VDRL*, Venereal Disease Research Laboratory.

[1]Annually. [2]Mammogram q1-2 yr, or mammogram q1-2 yr with annual clinical breast exam. [3]The American Cancer Society (ACS) recommends that Pap testing can be discontinued at age 65 after three negative Pap tests or two negative HPV tests in past three years. ACOG (American College of Obstetricians and Gynecologists) recommends discontinuing Pap testing at age 65 to 70 after three negative tests in preceding 10 years. [4]Herpes zoster vaccine (Zostavax) is indicated for prevention of herpes zoster (shingles) in individuals age ≥60 yr. Zostavax is administered as a single dose subcutaneously. It is a lyophilic preparation of the Oka/Merck strain of live, attenuated varicella zoster virus (VZV). It should not be administered to individuals with a history of primary or acquired immunodeficiency states, persons on immunosuppressive therapy (including high-dose corticosteroids), those with active untreated tuberculosis, and those who may be pregnant. [5]Healthy adults 65 years and older receiving a pneumococcal vaccine for the first time should receive PCV13 and then PPSV23 6 to 12 months later. If a patient has already received the PPSV23 vaccine after 65 years of age, the PCV13 dose should be administered at least one year after the PPSV23 dose.
*The ability of clinician counseling to influence this behavior is unproven.

HR1: HIV-positive persons, close contacts of persons with known or suspected TB, health care workers, persons with medical risk factors associated with TB, immigrants from countries with high TB prevalence, medically underserved low-income populations (including homeless), alcoholics, injection drug users, and residents of long-term care facilities.

HR2: Persons living in, traveling to, or working in areas where the disease is endemic and where periodic outbreaks occur (e.g., countries with high or intermediate endemicity; certain Alaska Native, Pacific Island, Native American, and religious communities); men who have sex with men; injection or street drug users; persons with clotting factor disorders or chronic liver disease. Consider for institutionalized persons and workers in these institutions and day care, hospital, and laboratory workers. Clinicians should also consider local epidemiology and HIV screening in the general population.

HR3: Men who had sex with men after 1975; past or present injection drug users; persons who exchange sex for money or drugs and their sex partners; persons with current or past injection drug–using, bisexual, or HIV-positive sex partners; recipients of a blood transfusion between 1978 and 1985; persons seeking treatment for STDs. Clinicians should also consider local epidemiology.

HR4: Consider for persons who have not received influenza vaccine or are vaccinated late, when the vaccine may be ineffective because of major antigenic changes in the virus; for unvaccinated persons who provide home care for high-risk persons; as supplemental protection in persons who are expected to have a poor antibody response; and for high-risk persons in whom the vaccine is contraindicated.

HR5: Persons aged ≥75 yr or 70-74 yr with one or more additional risk factors, including use of certain psychoactive and cardiac medications (e.g., benzodiazepines, antihypertensives); use of four or more prescription medications; impaired cognition, strength, balance, or gait. Intensive individualized, home-based multifactorial fall prevention intervention is recommended in settings where adequate resources are available to deliver such services.

HR6: Clinicians should consider fasting lipid panel screening on a case-by-case basis for persons aged 65 to 75 yr, especially in those with additional risk factors (e.g., smoking, diabetes, or hypertension).

HR7: Persons with a family or personal history of skin cancer; a large number of moles; atypical moles; poor tanning ability; or light skin, hair, and eye color.

HR8: Blood product recipients (including hemodialysis patients), persons with frequent occupational exposure to blood or blood products, men who have sex with men, injection drug users and their sex partners, persons with multiple recent sex partners, persons with other STDs (including HIV), travelers to countries with endemic hepatitis B.

HR9: Persons who exchange sex for money or drugs and their sex partners, persons with other STDs (including HIV), and sexual contacts of persons with active syphilis. Clinicians should also consider local epidemiology.

HR10: Persons who continue to inject drugs.

HR11: Healthy adults without a history of chickenpox or previous immunization. Consider serologic testing for presumed susceptible adults.

HR12: Consider ultrasound of abdominal aorta to screen for abdominal aortic aneurysm in all men aged 65 to 75 yr who have ever smoked.

TABLE 5-5 Pregnant Women*

Interventions considered and recommended for the Periodic Health Examination

INTERVENTIONS FOR THE GENERAL POPULATION

Screening

First visit

Blood pressure

Hemoglobin/hematocrit

Hepatitis B surface antigen (HBsAg)

RPR/VDRL

Chlamydia screen (<25 yr)

Rubella serology or vaccination history

D(Rh) typing, antibody screen

Offer CVS (<13 wk)[1] or amniocentesis (15-18 wk)[1] (age ≥35 yr)

Offer hemoglobinopathy screening

Assess for problem or risk drinking

Offer HIV screening[2]

Follow-up visits

Blood pressure

Urine culture (12-16 wk)

Offer amniocentesis (15-18 wk)[1] (age ≥35 yr)

Offer multiple marker testing[1] (15-18 wk)

Offer serum α-fetoprotein[1] (16-18 wk)

Counseling

Tobacco cessation; effects of passive smoking

Alcohol/other drug use

Nutrition, including adequate calcium intake

Encourage breastfeeding

Lap/shoulder belts

Infant safety car seats

STD prevention: avoid high-risk sexual behavior†; use condoms†

Chemoprophylaxis

Multivitamin with folic acid[3]

Immunizations

Influenza

Tdap[4]

INTERVENTIONS FOR HIGH-RISK POPULATIONS

Population	*Potential Interventions (see detailed high-risk definitions)*
High-risk sexual behavior	Screen for chlamydia (first visit) (HR1), gonorrhea (first visit) (HR2), HIV (first visit) (HR3); HBsAg (third trimester) (HR4); RPR/VDRL (third trimester) (HR5)
Blood transfusion between 1978 and 1985	HIV screen (first visit) (HR3)
Injection drug use	HIV screen (HR3); HBsAg (third trimester) (HR4); advice to reduce infection risk (HR6)
Unsensitized D-negative women	D(Rh) antibody testing (24-28 wk) (HR7)
Risk factors for Down syndrome	Offer CVS (first trimester), amniocentesis (15-18 wk)[1] (HR8)
Prior pregnancy with neural tube defect	Offer amniocentesis (15-18 wk),[1] folic acid 4.0 mg[3] (HR9)

CVS, Chorionic villus sampling; *HR*, high risk; *RPR*, rapid plasma reagin; *VDRL*, Venereal Disease Research Laboratory.

[1]Women with access to counseling and follow-up services, reliable standardized laboratories, skilled high-resolution ultrasound and, for those receiving serum marker testing, amniocentesis capabilities. [2]Universal screening is recommended. [3]Beginning at least 1 mo before conception and continuing through the first trimester. [4]For pregnant patients, the Tdap vaccine is recommended with each pregnancy between 27 and 36 weeks of gestation.

*See Tables 5-2 and 5-3 for other preventive services recommended for women of this age group.

†The ability of clinician counseling to influence this behavior is unproven.

HR1: Women with history of STD or new or multiple sex partners. Clinicians should also consider local epidemiology. Chlamydia screen should be repeated in third trimester if at continued risk.

HR2: Women younger than 25 yr with two or more sex partners in the last year or whose sex partner has multiple sexual contacts, women who exchange sex for money or drugs, and women with a history of repeated episodes of gonorrhea. Clinicians should also consider local epidemiology. Gonorrhea screen should be repeated in the third trimester if at continued risk.

HR3: Universal screening for HIV infection is recommended for all pregnant women. It is especially important in women with the following individual risk factors: past or present injection drug use; history of exchanging sex for money or drugs; injection drug–using, bisexual, or HIV-positive sex partner currently or in the past; recipients of a blood transfusion between 1978 and 1985; persons seeking treatment for STDs.

HR4: Women who are initially HBsAg negative who are at high risk because of injection drug use, who have suspected exposure to hepatitis B during pregnancy, and who have had multiple sex partners.

HR5: Women who exchange sex for money or drugs, women with other STDs (including HIV), and sexual contacts of persons with active syphilis. Clinicians should also consider local epidemiology.

HR6: Women who continue to inject drugs.

HR7: Unsensitized D-negative women.

HR8: Prior pregnancy affected by Down syndrome, advanced maternal age (≥35 yr), known carriage of chromosome rearrangement.

HR9: Women with previous pregnancy affected by neural tube defect.

TABLE 5-6 Cervical Cancer Screening Guidelines*

Group	ACOG 2009	USPSTF 2012	ACS 2012
Women age <21	No screening	No screening	No screening
Women age 21-29	Cytology every 2 years; HPV testing not recommended	Cytology every 3 years; HPV testing not recommended	Cytology every 3 years; HPV testing not recommended
Women age 30-65	Cytology every 3 years if three consecutive normal results; addition of HPV testing also appropriate	Cytology every 3 years or cytology plus HPV testing every 5 years	Cytology plus HPV every 5 years (preferred) or cytology alone every 3 years; both are regardless of screening history
Women age <65	Following three normal screening results and no abnormal results in the last 10 years, screening may be discontinued	If adequately screened in the past, screening should be discontinued	If adequately screened in the past, screening should be discontinued
Women with total hysterectomy and no prior history of high-grade CIN	No need to continue screening if hysterectomy was for benign indication	Screening should be discontinued	Screening should be discontinued

ACOG, American College of Obstetricians and Gynecologists; *ACS,* American Cancer Society; *CIN,* Cervical intraepithelial neoplasia; *HPV,* human papillomavirus; *USPSTF,* U.S. Preventive Services Task Force.
*The American College of Physicians (ACP) recommends the following: (1) Cytology without HPV testing every three years starting at age 21; (2) cytology with HPV testing may be performed starting at 30 years of age once every 5 years in average-risk women 30 years or older who prefer longer screening intervals; and (3) screening should stop after 65 years of age in the setting of three consecutive negative cytology results or two consecutive negative cytology plus HPV cotesting results, with the most recent test performed within the previous five years.

PART B • IMMUNIZATIONS AND CHEMOPROPHYLAXIS

Childhood and Adolescent Immunizations

> **TABLE 5-7** Recommended Immunization Schedule for Persons Aged 0 Through 18 Years: United States, 2016 (For those who fall behind or start late, see the schedule below and the catch-up schedule [Table 5-8])

These recommendations must be read with the footnotes that follow. For those who fall behind or start late, provide catch-up vaccination at the earliest opportunity as indicated by the divided bars. To determine minimum intervals between doses, see the catch-up schedule (Table 5-8). School entry and adolescent vaccine age groups are in bold.

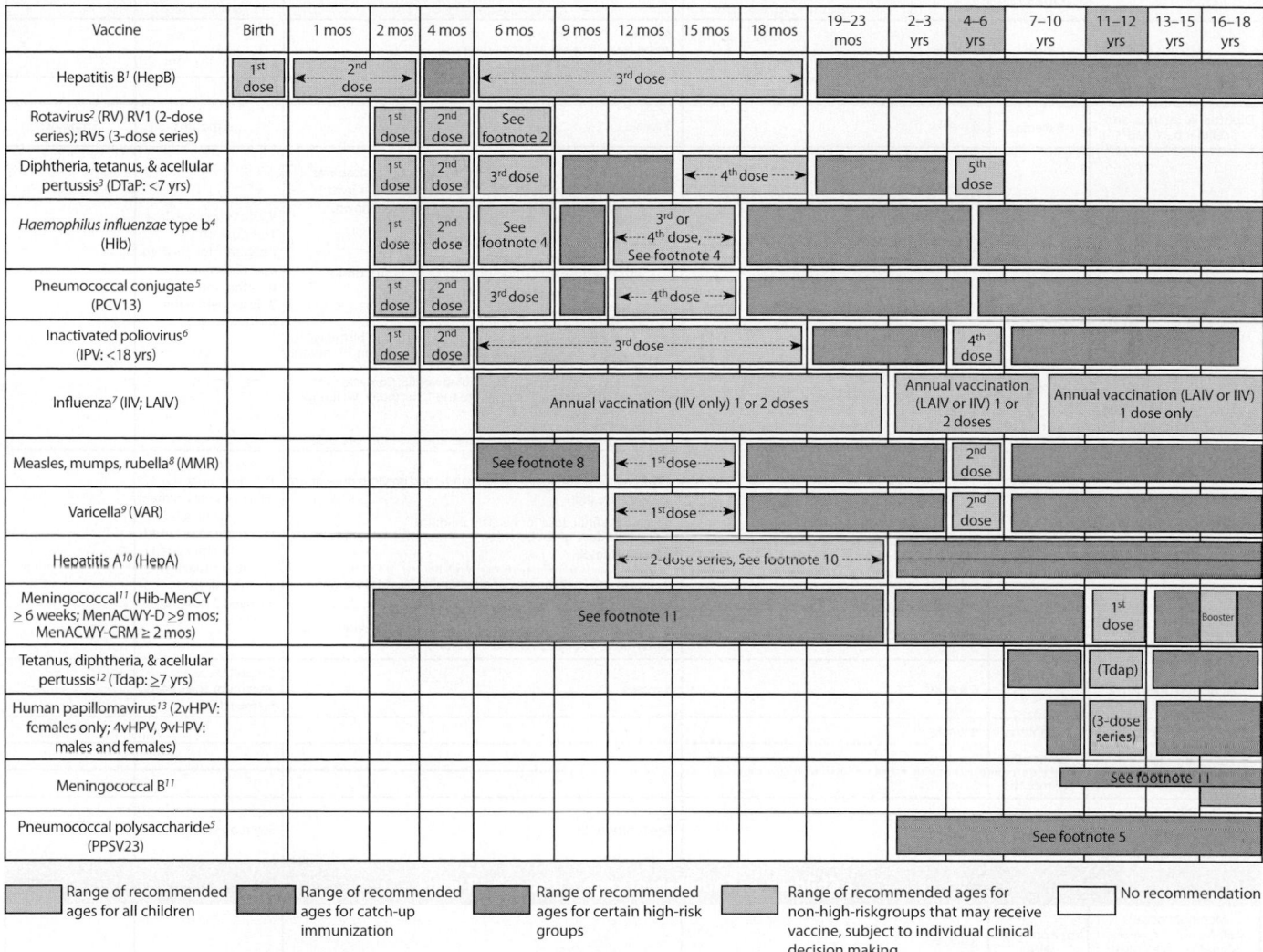

| Range of recommended ages for all children | Range of recommended ages for catch-up immunization | Range of recommended ages for certain high-risk groups | Range of recommended ages for non-high-riskgroups that may receive vaccine, subject to individual clinical decision making | No recommendation |

This schedule includes recommendations in effect as of January 1, 2016. Any dose not administered at the recommended age should be administered at a subsequent visit, when indicated and feasible. The use of a combination vaccine generally is preferred over separate injections of its equivalent component vaccines. Vaccination providers should consult the relevant Advisory Committee on Immunization Practices (ACIP) statement for detailed recommendations, available online at http://www.cdc.gov/vaccines/hcp/acip-recs/index.html. Clinically significant adverse events that follow vaccination should be reported to the Vaccine Adverse Event Reporting System (VAERS) online (http://www.vaers.hhs.gov) or by telephone (800-822-7967). Suspected cases of vaccine-preventable diseases should be reported to the state or local health department. Additional information, including precautions and contraindications for vaccination, is available from CDC online (http://www.cdc.gov/vaccines/recs/vac-admin/contraindications.htm) or by telephone (800-CDC-INFO [800-232-4636]).

This schedule is approved by the Advisory Committee on Immunization Practices (http://www.cdc.gov/vaccines/acip), the American Academy of Pediatrics (http://www.aap.org), the American Academy of Family Physicians (http://www.aafp.org), and the American College of Obstetricians and Gynecologists (http://www.acog.org).

NOTE: The above recommendations must be read along with the footnotes of this schedule.

TABLE 5-8 Catch-up Immunization Schedule for Persons Aged 4 Months Through 18 Years Who Start Late or Who Are More Than 1 Month Behind: United States, 2016

The table below provides catch-up schedules and minimum intervals between doses for children whose vaccinations have been delayed. A vaccine series does not need to be restarted, regardless of the time that has elapsed between doses. Use the section appropriate for the child's age. Always use this table in conjunction with Table 5-7 and the footnotes that follow.

		Children age 4 months through 6 years			
Vaccine	Minimum Age for Dose 1	Minimum Interval Between Doses			
		Dose 1 to Dose 2	Dose 2 to Dose 3	Dose 3 to Dose 4	Dose 4 to Dose 5
Hepatitis B[1]	Birth	4 weeks	8 weeks *and* at least 16 weeks after first dose. Minimum age for the final dose is 24 weeks.		
Rotavirus[2]	6 weeks	4 weeks	4 weeks[2]		
Diphtheria, tetanus, and acellular pertussis[3]	6 weeks	4 weeks	4 weeks	6 months	6 months[3]
Haemophilus influenzae type b[4]	6 weeks	4 weeks if first dose was administered before the 1st birthday. 8 weeks (as final dose) if first dose was administered at age 12 through 14 months. No further doses needed if first dose was administered at age 15 months or older.	4 weeks[4] if current age is younger than 12 months **and** first dose was administered at younger than age 7 months, **and** at least 1 previous dose was PRP-T (ActHib, Pentacel) or unknown. 8 weeks *and* age 12 through 59 months (as final dose)[4] • if current age is younger than 12 months **and** first dose was administered at age 7 through 11 months (wait until at least 12 months old); OR • if current age is 12 through 59 months **and** first dose was administered before the 1st birthday, **and** second dose administered at younger than 15 months; OR • if both doses were PRP-OMP (PedvaxHIB; Comvax) **and** were administered before the 1st birthday (wait until at least 12 months old) No further doses needed if previous dose was administered at age 15 months or older.	8 weeks (as final dose) This dose only necessary for children age 12 through 59 months who received 3 doses before the 1st birthday.	
Pneumococcal[5]	6 weeks	4 weeks if first dose administered before the 1st birthday. 8 weeks (as final dose for healthy children) if first dose was administered at the 1st birthday or after. No further doses needed for healthy children if first dose administered at age 24 months or older.	4 weeks if current age is younger than 12 months and previous dose given at <7months old. 8 weeks (as final dose for healthy children) if previous dose given between 7-11 months (wait until at least 12 months old); OR if current age is 12 months or older and at least 1 dose was given before age 12 months. No further doses needed for healthy children if previous dose administered at age 24 months or older.	8 weeks (as final dose) This dose only necessary for children aged 12 through 59 months who received 3 doses before age 12 months or for children at high risk who received 3 doses at any age.	
Inactivated poliovirus[6]	6 weeks	4 weeks[6]	4 weeks[6]	6 months[6] (minimum age 4 years for final dose).	
Measles, mumps, rubella[8]	12 months	4 weeks			
Varicella[9]	12 months	3 months			
Hepatitis A[10]	12 months	6 months			
Meningococcal[11] (Hib-MenCY ≥ 6 weeks; MenACWY-D ≥9 mos; MenACWY-CRM ≥ 2 mos)	6 weeks	8 weeks[11]	See footnote 11	See footnote 11	
		Children and adolescents age 7 through 18 years			
Meningococcal[11] (Hib-MenCY ≥ 6 weeks; MenACWY-D ≥9 mos; MenACWY-CRM ≥ 2 mos)	Not Applicable (N/A)	8 weeks[11]			
Tetanus, diphtheria; tetanus, diphtheria, and acellular pertussis[12]	7 years[12]	4 weeks	4 weeks if first dose of DTaP/DT was administered before the 1st birthday. 6 months (as final dose) if first dose of DTaP/DT or Tdap/Td was administered at or after the 1st birthday.	6 months if first dose of DTaP/DT was administered before the 1st birthday.	
Human papillomavirus[13]	9 years	Routine dosing intervals are recommended.[13]			
Hepatitis A[10]	N/A	6 months			
Hepatitis B[1]	N/A	4 weeks	8 weeks **and** at least 16 weeks after first dose.		
Inactivated poliovirus[6]	N/A	4 weeks	4 weeks[6]	6 months[6]	
Measles, mumps, rubella[8]	N/A	4 weeks			
Varicella[9]	N/A	3 months if younger than age 13 years. 4 weeks if age 13 years or older.			

NOTE: The above recommendations must be read along with the footnotes of this schedule.

Footnotes — Recommended immunization schedule for persons aged 0 through 18 years—United States, 2016

For further guidance on the use of the vaccines mentioned below, see: http://www.cdc.gov/vaccines/hcp/acip-recs/index.html.
For vaccine recommendations for persons 19 years of age and older, see the adult immunization schedule.

Additional information

- For contraindications and precautions to use of a vaccine and for additional information regarding that vaccine, vaccination providers should consult the relevant ACIP statement available online at http://www.cdc.gov/vaccines/hcp/acip-recs/index.html.
- For purposes of calculating intervals between doses, 4 weeks = 28 days. Intervals of 4 months or greater are determined by calendar months. Vaccine doses administered 4 days or less before the minimum interval are considered valid. Doses of any vaccine administered ≥5 days earlier than the minimum interval or minimum age should not be counted as valid doses and should be repeated as age-appropriate. The repeat dose should be spaced after the invalid dose by the recommended minimum interval. For further details, see *MMWR, General Recommendations on Immunization and Reports* / Vol. 60 / No. 2; Table 1. *Recommended and minimum ages and intervals between vaccine doses* available online at http://www.cdc.gov/mmwr/pdf/rr/rr6002.pdf.
- Information on travel vaccine requirements and recommendations is available at http://wwwnc.cdc.gov/travel/destinations/list.
- For vaccination of persons with primary and secondary immunodeficiencies, see Table 13, "Vaccination of persons with primary and secondary immunodeficiencies," in General Recommendations on Immunization (ACIP), available at http://www.cdc.gov/mmwr/pdf/rr/rr6002.pdf.; and American Academy of Pediatrics. "Immunization in Special Clinical Circumstances," in Kimberlin DW, Brady MT, Jackson MA, Long SS eds. *Red Book: 2015 report of the Committee on Infectious Diseases*. 30th ed. Elk Grove Village, IL: American Academy of Pediatrics.

1. **Hepatitis B (HepB) vaccine. (Minimum age: birth)**
   Routine vaccination:
   At birth:
   - Administer monovalent HepB vaccine to all newborns before hospital discharge.
   - For infants born to hepatitis B surface antigen (HBsAg)-positive mothers, administer HepB vaccine and 0.5 mL of hepatitis B immune globulin (HBIG) within 12 hours of birth. These infants should be tested for HBsAg and antibody to HBsAg (anti-HBs) at age 9 through 18 months (preferably at the next well-child visit) or 1 to 2 months after completion of the HepB series if the series was delayed; CDC recently recommended testing occur at age 9 through 12 months; see http://www.cdc.gov/mmwr/preview/mmwrhtml/mm6439a6.htm.
   - If mother's HBsAg status is unknown, within 12 hours of birth administer HepB vaccine regardless of birth weight. For infants weighing less than 2,000 grams, administer HBIG in addition to HepB vaccine within 12 hours of birth. Determine mother's HBsAg status as soon as possible and, if mother is HBsAg-positive, also administer HBIG for infants weighing 2,000 grams or more as soon as possible, but no later than age 7 days.

   Doses following the birth dose:
   - The second dose should be administered at age 1 or 2 months. Monovalent HepB vaccine should be used for doses administered before age 6 weeks.
   - Infants who did not receive a birth dose should receive 3 doses of a HepB-containing vaccine on a schedule of 0, 1 to 2 months, and 6 months starting as soon as feasible. See Table 5-8.
   - Administer the second dose 1 to 2 months after the first dose (minimum interval of 4 weeks), administer the third dose at least 8 weeks after the second dose AND at least 16 weeks after the **first** dose. The final (third or fourth) dose in the HepB vaccine series should be administered no **earlier than age 24 weeks.**
   - Administration of a total of 4 doses of HepB vaccine is permitted when a combination vaccine containing HepB is administered after the birth dose.

   Catch-up vaccination:
   - Unvaccinated persons should complete a 3-dose series.
   - A 2-dose series (doses separated by at least 4 months) of adult formulation Recombivax HB is licensed for use in children aged 11 through 15 years.
   - For other catch-up guidance, see Table 5-8.

2. **Rotavirus (RV) vaccines. (Minimum age: 6 weeks for both RV1 [Rotarix] and RV5 [RotaTeq])**
   Routine vaccination:
   Administer a series of RV vaccine to all infants as follows:
   - If Rotarix is used, administer a 2-dose series at 2 and 4 months of age.
   - If RotaTeq is used, administer a 3-dose series at ages 2, 4, and 6 months.
   - If any dose in the series was RotaTeq or vaccine product is unknown for any dose in the series, a total of 3 doses of RV vaccine should be administered.

   Catch-up vaccination:
   - The maximum age for the first dose in the series is 14 weeks, 6 days; vaccination should not be initiated for infants aged 15 weeks, 0 days or older.
   - The maximum age for the final dose in the series is 8 months, 0 days.
   - For other catch-up guidance, see Table 5-8.

3. **Diphtheria and tetanus toxoids and acellular pertussis (DTaP) vaccine. (Minimum age: 6 weeks. Exception: DTaP-IPV [Kinrix, Quadracel]: 4 years)**
   Routine vaccination:
   - Administer a 5-dose series of DTaP vaccine at ages 2, 4, 6, 15 through 18 months, and 4 through 6 years. The fourth dose may be administered as early as age 12 months, provided at least 6 months have elapsed since the third dose.
   - Inadvertent administration of 4th DTaP dose early: If the fourth dose of DTaP was administered at least 4 months, but less than 6 months, after the third dose of DTaP, it need not be repeated.

   Catch-up vaccination:
   - The fifth dose of DTaP vaccine is not necessary if the fourth dose was administered at age 4 years or older.
   - For other catch-up guidance, see Table 5-8.

4. ***Haemophilus influenzae* type b (Hib) conjugate vaccine. (Minimum age: 6 weeks for PRP-T [ACTHIB, DTaP-IPV/Hib (Pentacel) and Hib-MenCY (MenHibrix)], PRP-OMP [PedvaxHIB or COMVAX], 12 months for PRP-T [Hiberix])**
   Routine vaccination:
   - Administer a 2- or 3-dose Hib vaccine primary series and a booster dose (dose 3 or 4 depending on vaccine used in primary series) at age 12 through 15 months to complete a full Hib vaccine series.
   - The primary series with ActHIB, MenHibrix, or Pentacel consists of 3 doses and should be administered at 2, 4, and 6 months of age. The primary series with PedvaxHib or COMVAX consists of 2 doses and should be administered at 2 and 4 months of age; a dose at age 6 months is not indicated.
   - One booster dose (dose 3 or 4 depending on vaccine used in primary series) of any Hib vaccine should be administered at age 12 through 15 months. An exception is Hiberix vaccine. Hiberix should only be used for the booster (final) dose in children aged 12 months through 4 years who have received at least 1 prior dose of Hib-containing vaccine.
   - For recommendations on the use of MenHibrix in patients at increased risk for meningococcal disease, please refer to the meningococcal vaccine footnotes and also to *MMWR* February 28, 2014 / 63(RR01);1-13, available at http://www.cdc.gov/mmwr/PDF/rr/rr6301.pdf.

   Catch-up vaccination:
   - If dose 1 was administered at ages 12 through 14 months, administer a second (final) dose at least 8 weeks after dose 1, regardless of Hib vaccine used in the primary series.

- If both doses were PRP-OMP (PedvaxHIB or COMVAX), and were administered before the first birthday, the third (and final) dose should be administered at age 12 through 59 months and at least 8 weeks after the second dose.
- If the first dose was administered at age 7 through 11 months, administer the second dose at least 4 weeks later and a third (and final) dose at age 12 through 15 months or 8 weeks after second dose, whichever is later.
- If first dose is administered before the first birthday and second dose administered at younger than 15 months, a third (and final) dose should be administered 8 weeks later.

For unvaccinated children aged 15 months or older, administer only 1 dose.

For other catch-up guidance, see Table 5-8. For catch-up guidance related to MenHibrix, please see the meningococcal vaccine footnotes and also *MMWR* February 28, 2014 / 63(RR01);1-13, available at http://www.cdc.gov/mmwr/PDF/rr/rr6301.pdf.

Vaccination of persons with high-risk conditions:

- Children aged 12 through 59 months who are at increased risk for Hib disease, including chemotherapy recipients and those with anatomic or functional asplenia (including sickle cell disease), human immunodeficiency virus (HIV) infection, immunoglobulin deficiency, or early component complement deficiency, who have received either no doses or only 1 dose of Hib vaccine before 12 months of age, should receive 2 additional doses of Hib vaccine 8 weeks apart; children who received 2 or more doses of Hib vaccine before 12 months of age should receive 1 additional dose.
- For patients younger than 5 years of age undergoing chemotherapy or radiation treatment who received a Hib vaccine dose(s) within 14 days of starting therapy or during therapy, repeat the dose(s) at least 3 months following therapy completion.
- Recipients of hematopoietic stem cell transplant (HSCT) should be revaccinated with a 3-dose regimen of Hib vaccine starting 6 to 12 months after successful transplant, regardless of vaccination history; doses should be administered at least 4 weeks apart.
- A single dose of any Hib-containing vaccine should be administered to unimmunized* children and adolescents 15 months of age and older undergoing an elective splenectomy; if possible, vaccine should be administered at least 14 days before procedure.
- Hib vaccine is not routinely recommended for patients 5 years or older. However, 1 dose of Hib vaccine should be administered to unimmunized* persons aged 5 years or older who have anatomic or functional asplenia (including sickle cell disease) and unvaccinated persons 5 through 18 years of age with HIV infection.

  Patients who have not received a primary series and booster dose or at least 1 dose of Hib vaccine after 14 months of age are considered unimmunized.

5. **Pneumococcal vaccines. (Minimum age: 6 weeks for PCV13, 2 years for PPSV23)**

Routine vaccination with PCV13:

- Administer a 4-dose series of PCV13 vaccine at ages 2, 4, and 6 months and at age 12 through 15 months.
- For children aged 14 through 59 months who have received an age-appropriate series of 7-valent PCV (PCV7), administer a single supplemental dose of 13-valent PCV (PCV13).

Catch-up vaccination with PCV13:

- Administer 1 dose of PCV13 to all healthy children aged 24 through 59 months who are not completely vaccinated for their age.
- For other catch-up guidance, see Table 5-8.

Vaccination of persons with high-risk conditions with PCV13 and PPSV23:

- All recommended PCV13 doses should be administered prior to PPSV23 vaccination if possible.
- For children 2 through 5 years of age with any of the following conditions: chronic heart disease (particularly cyanotic congenital heart disease and cardiac failure); chronic lung disease (including asthma if treated with high-dose oral corticosteroid therapy); diabetes mellitus; cerebrospinal fluid leak; cochlear implant; sickle cell disease and other

hemoglobinopathies; anatomic or functional asplenia; HIV infection; chronic renal failure; nephrotic syndrome; diseases associated with treatment with immunosuppressive drugs or radiation therapy, including malignant neoplasms, leukemias, lymphomas, and Hodgkin disease; solid organ transplantation; or congenital immunodeficiency:

1. Administer 1 dose of PCV13 if any incomplete schedule of 3 doses of PCV (PCV7 and/or PCV13) were received previously.
2. Administer 2 doses of PCV13 at least 8 weeks apart if unvaccinated or any incomplete schedule of fewer than 3 doses of PCV (PCV7 and/or PCV13) were received previously.
3. Administer 1 supplemental dose of PCV13 if 4 doses of PCV7 or other age-appropriate complete PCV7 series was received previously.
4. The minimum interval between doses of PCV (PCV7 or PCV13) is 8 weeks.
5. For children with no history of PPSV23 vaccination, administer PPSV23 at least 8 weeks after the most recent dose of PCV13.

- For children aged 6 through 18 years who have cerebrospinal fluid leak; cochlear implant; sickle cell disease and other hemoglobinopathies; anatomic or functional asplenia; congenital or acquired immunodeficiencies; HIV infection; chronic renal failure; nephrotic syndrome; diseases associated with treatment with immunosuppressive drugs or radiation therapy, including malignant neoplasms, leukemias, lymphomas, and Hodgkin disease; generalized malignancy; solid organ transplantation; or multiple myeloma:

1. If neither PCV13 nor PPSV23 has been received previously, administer 1 dose of PCV13 now and 1 dose of PPSV23 at least 8 weeks later.
2. If PCV13 has been received previously but PPSV23 has not, administer 1 dose of PPSV23 at least 8 weeks after the most recent dose of PCV13.
3. If PPSV23 has been received but PCV13 has not, administer 1 dose of PCV13 at least 8 weeks after the most recent dose of PPSV23.

- For children aged 6 through 18 years with chronic heart disease (particularly cyanotic congenital heart disease and cardiac failure), chronic lung disease (including asthma if treated with high-dose oral corticosteroid therapy), diabetes mellitus, alcoholism, or chronic liver disease, who have not received PPSV23, administer 1 dose of PPSV23. If PCV13 has been received previously, then PPSV23 should be administered at least 8 weeks after any prior PCV13 dose.
- A single revaccination with PPSV23 should be administered 5 years after the first dose to children with sickle cell disease or other hemoglobinopathies; anatomic or functional asplenia; congenital or acquired immunodeficiencies; HIV infection; chronic renal failure; nephrotic syndrome; diseases associated with treatment with immunosuppressive drugs or radiation therapy, including malignant neoplasms, leukemias, lymphomas, and Hodgkin disease; generalized malignancy; solid organ transplantation; or multiple myeloma.

6. **Inactivated poliovirus vaccine (IPV). (Minimum age: 6 weeks)**

Routine vaccination:

- Administer a 4-dose series of IPV at ages 2, 4, 6 through 18 months, and 4 through 6 years. The final dose in the series should be administered on or after the fourth birthday and at least 6 months after the previous dose.

Catch-up vaccination:

- In the first 6 months of life, minimum age and minimum intervals are only recommended if the person is at risk of imminent exposure to circulating poliovirus (i.e., travel to a polio-endemic region or during an outbreak).
- If 4 or more doses are administered before age 4 years, an additional dose should be administered at age 4 through 6 years and at least 6 months after the previous dose.
- A fourth dose is not necessary if the third dose was administered at age 4 years or older and at least 6 months after the previous dose.
- If both OPV and IPV were administered as part of a series, a total of 4 doses should be administered, regardless of the child's current age. If only OPV were administered, and all doses were given prior to 4 years of age, one dose of IPV should be given at 4 years or older, at least 4 weeks after the last OPV dose.
- IPV is not routinely recommended for U.S. residents aged 18 years or older.
- For other catch-up guidance, see Table 5-8.

7. **Influenza vaccines. (Minimum age: 6 months for inactivated influenza vaccine [IIV], 2 years for live, attenuated influenza vaccine [LAIV])**
   Routine vaccination:

   - Administer influenza vaccine annually to all children beginning at age 6 months. For most healthy, nonpregnant persons aged 2 through 49 years, either LAIV or IIV may be used. However, LAIV should NOT be administered to some persons, including 1) persons who have experienced severe allergic reactions to LAIV, any of its components, or to a previous dose of any other influenza vaccine; 2) children 2 through 17 years receiving aspirin or aspirin-containing products; 3) persons who are allergic to eggs; 4) pregnant women; 5) immunosuppressed persons; 6) children 2 through 4 years of age with asthma or who had wheezing in the past 12 months; or 7) persons who have taken influenza antiviral medications in the previous 48 hours. For all other contraindications and precautions to use of LAIV, see *MMWR* August 7, 2015 / 64(30):818-25 available at http://www.cdc.gov/mmwr/pdf/wk/mm6430.pdf.

   For children aged 6 months through 8 years:

   - For the 2015-16 season, administer 2 doses (separated by at least 4 weeks) to children who are receiving influenza vaccine for the first time. Some children in this age group who have been vaccinated previously will also need 2 doses. For additional guidance, follow dosing guidelines in the 2015-16 ACIP influenza vaccine recommendations, *MMWR* August 7, 2015 / 64(30):818-25, available at http://www.cdc.gov/mmwr/pdf/wk/mm6430.pdf.
   - For the 2016-17 season, follow dosing guidelines in the 2016 ACIP influenza vaccine recommendations.

   For persons aged 9 years and older:
   - Administer 1 dose.

8. **Measles, mumps, and rubella (MMR) vaccine. (Minimum age: 12 months for routine vaccination)**
   Routine vaccination:

   - Administer a 2-dose series of MMR vaccine at ages 12 through 15 months and 4 through 6 years. The second dose may be administered before age 4 years, provided at least 4 weeks have elapsed since the first dose.
   - Administer 1 dose of MMR vaccine to infants aged 6 through 11 months before departure from the United States for international travel. These children should be revaccinated with 2 doses of MMR vaccine, the first at age 12 through 15 months (12 months if the child remains in an area where disease risk is high), and the second dose at least 4 weeks later.
   - Administer 2 doses of MMR vaccine to children aged 12 months and older before departure from the United States for international travel. The first dose should be administered on or after age 12 months and the second dose at least 4 weeks later.

   Catch-up vaccination:

   - Ensure that all school-aged children and adolescents have had 2 doses of MMR vaccine; the minimum interval between the 2 doses is 4 weeks.

9. **Varicella (VAR) vaccine. (Minimum age: 12 months)**
   Routine vaccination:

   - Administer a 2-dose series of VAR vaccine at ages 12 through 15 months and 4 through 6 years. The second dose may be administered before age 4 years, provided at least 3 months have elapsed since the first dose. If the second dose was administered at least 4 weeks after the first dose, it can be accepted as valid.

   Catch-up vaccination:

   - Ensure that all persons aged 7 through 18 years without evidence of immunity (see *MMWR* 2007 / 56 [No. RR-4], available at http://www.cdc.gov/mmwr/pdf/rr/rr5604.pdf) have 2 doses of varicella vaccine. For children aged 7 through 12 years, the recommended minimum interval between doses is 3 months (if the second dose was administered at least 4 weeks after the first dose, it can be accepted as valid); for persons aged 13 years and older, the minimum interval between doses is 4 weeks.

10. **Hepatitis A (HepA) vaccine. (Minimum age: 12 months)**
    Routine vaccination:

    - Initiate the 2-dose HepA vaccine series at 12 through 23 months; separate the 2 doses by 6 to 18 months.
    - Children who have received 1 dose of HepA vaccine before age 24 months should receive a second dose 6 to 18 months after the first dose.
    - For any person aged 2 years and older who has not already received the HepA vaccine series, 2 doses of HepA vaccine separated by 6 to 18 months may be administered if immunity against hepatitis A virus infection is desired.

    Catch-up vaccination:

    - The minimum interval between the 2 doses is 6 months.

    Special populations:

    - Administer 2 doses of HepA vaccine at least 6 months apart to previously unvaccinated persons who live in areas where vaccination programs target older children, or who are at increased risk for infection. This includes persons traveling to or working in countries that have high or intermediate endemicity of infection; men having sex with men; users of injection and non-injection illicit drugs; persons who work with HAV-infected primates or with HAV in a research laboratory; persons with clotting-factor disorders; persons with chronic liver disease; and persons who anticipate close personal contact (e.g., household or regular babysitting) with an international adoptee during the first 60 days after arrival in the United States from a country with high or intermediate endemicity. The first dose should be administered as soon as the adoption is planned, ideally 2 or more weeks before the arrival of the adoptee.

11. **Meningococcal vaccines. (Minimum age: 6 weeks for Hib-MenCY [MenHibrix], 9 months for MenACWY-D [Menactra], 2 months for MenACWY-CRM [Menveo], 10 years for serogroup B meningococcal [MenB] vaccines: MenB-4C [Bexsero] and MenB-FHbp [Trumenba])**
    Routine vaccination:

    - Administer a single dose of Menactra or Menveo vaccine at age 11 through 12 years, with a booster dose at age 16 years.
    - Adolescents aged 11 through 18 years with human immunodeficiency virus (HIV) infection should receive a 2-dose primary series of Menactra or Menveo with at least 8 weeks between doses.
    - For children aged 2 months through 18 years with high-risk conditions, see the following.

    Catch-up vaccination:

    - Administer Menactra or Menveo vaccine at age 13 through 18 years if not previously vaccinated.
    - If the first dose is administered at age 13 through 15 years, a booster dose should be administered at age 16 through 18 years with a minimum interval of at least 8 weeks between doses.
    - If the first dose is administered at age 16 years or older, a booster dose is not needed.
    - For other catch-up guidance, see Table 5-8.

    Clinical discretion:

    - Young adults aged 16 through 23 years (preferred age range is 16 through 18 years) may be vaccinated with either a 2-dose series of Bexsero or a 3-dose series of Trumenba vaccine to provide short-term protection against most strains of serogroup B meningococcal disease. The two MenB vaccines are not interchangeable; the same vaccine product must be used for all doses.

    Vaccination of persons with high-risk conditions and other persons at increased risk of disease:
    Children with anatomic or functional asplenia (including sickle cell disease):
    Meningococcal conjugate ACWY vaccines:

    1. Menveo
       o *Children who initiate vaccination at 8 weeks:* Administer doses at 2, 4, 6, and 12 months of age.

o *Unvaccinated children who initiate vaccination at 7 through 23 months:* Administer 2 doses, with the second dose at least 12 weeks after the first dose AND after the first birthday.

o *Children 24 months and older who have not received a complete series:* Administer 2 primary doses at least 8 weeks apart.

2. MenHibrix

o *Children who initiate vaccination at 6 weeks:* Administer doses at 2, 4, 6, and 12 through 15 months of age.

o If the first dose of MenHibrix is given at or after 12 months of age, a total of 2 doses should be given at least 8 weeks apart to ensure protection against serogroups C and Y meningococcal disease.

3. Menactra

o *Children 24 months and older who have not received a complete series:* Administer 2 primary doses at least 8 weeks apart. If Menactra is administered to a child with asplenia (including sickle cell disease), do not administer Menactra until 2 years of age and at least 4 weeks after the completion of all PCV13 doses.

Meningococcal B vaccines:

1. Bexsero or Trumenba

o *Persons 10 years or older who have not received a complete series.* Administer a 2-dose series of Bexsero, at least 1 month apart. Or a 3-dose series of Trumenba, with the second dose at least 2 months after the first and the third dose at least 6 months after the first. The two MenB vaccines are not interchangeable; the same vaccine product must be used for all doses.

Children with persistent complement component deficiency (includes persons with inherited or chronic deficiencies in C3, C5-9, properidin, factor D, factor H, or taking eculizumab (Soliriis®):
Meningococcal conjugate ACWY vaccines:

1. Menveo

o *Children who initiate vaccination at 8 weeks:* Administer doses at 2, 4, 6, and 12 months of age.

o *Unvaccinated children who initiate vaccination at 7 through 23 months:* Administer 2 doses, with the second dose at least 12 weeks after the first dose AND after the first birthday.

o *Children 24 months and older who have not received a complete series:* Administer 2 primary doses at least 8 weeks apart.

2. MenHibrix

o *Children who initiate vaccination at 6 weeks:* Administer doses at 2, 4, 6, and 12 through 15 months of age.

o If the first dose of MenHibrix is given at or after 12 months of age, a total of 2 doses should be given at least 8 weeks apart to ensure protection against serogroups C and Y meningococcal disease.

3. Menactra

o *Children 9 through 23 months:* Administer 2 primary doses at least 12 weeks apart.

o *Children 24 months and older who have not received a complete series:* Administer 2 primary doses at least 8 weeks apart.

Meningococcal B vaccines:

1. Bexsero or Trumenba

o *Persons 10 years or older who have not received a complete series.* Administer a 2-dose series of Bexsero, at least 1 month apart. Or a 3-dose series of Trumenba, with the second dose at least 2 months after the first and the third dose at least 6 months after the first. The two MenB vaccines are not interchangeable; the same vaccine product must be used for all doses.

For children who travel to or reside in countries in which meningo-coccal disease is hyperendemic or epidemic, including countries in the African meningitis belt or the Hajj

• Administer an age-appropriate formulation and series of Menactra or Menveo for protection against serogroups A and W meningo-coccal disease. Prior receipt of MenHibrix is not sufficient for children traveling to the meningitis belt or the Hajj because it does not contain serogroups A or W.

For children at risk during a community outbreak attributable to a vaccine serogroup

• Administer or complete an age- and formulation-appropriate series of MenHibrix, Menactra, or Menveo, Bexsero or Trumenba.

For booster doses among persons with high-risk conditions, refer to *MMWR* 2013 / 62(RR02);1-22, available at http://www.cdc.gov/mmwr/preview/mmwrhtml/rr6202a1.htm.

For other catch-up recommendations for these persons, and complete information on use of meningococcal vaccines, including guidance related to vaccination of persons at increased risk of infection, see *MMWR* March 22, 2013 / 62(RR02);1-22, and *MMWR* October 23, 2015 / 64(41); 1171-1176 available at http://www.cdc.gov/mmwr/pdf/rr/rr6202.pdf, and http://www.cdc.gov/mmwr/pdf/wk/mm6441.pdf.

12. **Tetanus and diphtheria toxoids and acellular pertussis (Tdap) vaccine. (Minimum age: 10 years for both Boostrix and Adacel)**
Routine vaccination:

• Administer 1 dose of Tdap vaccine to all adolescents aged 11 through 12 years.

• Tdap may be administered regardless of the interval since the last tetanus and diphtheria toxoid-containing vaccine.

• Administer 1 dose of Tdap vaccine to pregnant adolescents during each pregnancy (preferred during 27 through 36 weeks gestation) regardless of time since prior Td or Tdap vaccination.

Catch-up vaccination:

• Persons aged 7 years and older who are not fully immunized with DTaP vaccine should receive Tdap vaccine as 1 (preferably the first) dose in the catch-up series; if additional doses are needed, use Td vaccine. For children 7 through 10 years who receive a dose of Tdap as part of the catch-up series, an adolescent Tdap vaccine dose at age 11 through 12 years should NOT be administered. Td should be administered instead 10 years after the Tdap dose.

• Persons aged 11 through 18 years who have not received Tdap vaccine should receive a dose followed by tetanus and diphtheria toxoids (Td) booster doses every 10 years thereafter.

• Inadvertent doses of DTaP vaccine: If administered inadvertently to a child aged 7 through 10 years may count as part of the catch-up series. This dose may count as the adolescent Tdap dose, or the child can later receive a Tdap booster dose at age 11 through 12 years.

• If administered inadvertently to an adolescent aged 11 through 18 years, the dose should be counted as the adolescent Tdap booster. For other catch-up guidance, see Table 5-8.

13. **Human papillomavirus (HPV) vaccines. (Minimum age: 9 years for 2vHPV [Cervarix], 4vHPV [Gardasil] and 9vHPV [Gardasil 9])**
Routine vaccination:

• Administer a 3-dose series of HPV vaccine on a schedule of 0, 1-2, and 6 months to all adolescents aged 11 through 12 years. 9vHPV, 4vHPV or 2vHPV may be used for females, and only 9vHPV or 4vHPV may be used for males.

• The vaccine series may be started at age 9 years.

• Administer the second dose 1 to 2 months after the first dose (minimum interval of 4 weeks); administer the third dose 16 weeks after the second dose (minimum interval of 12 weeks) and 24 weeks after the first dose.

• Administer HPV vaccine beginning at age 9 years to children and youth with any history of sexual abuse or assault who have not initiated or completed the 3-dose series.

Catch-up vaccination:

• Administer the vaccine series to females (2vHPV or 4vHPV or 9vHPV) and males (4vHPV or 9vHPV) at age 13 through 18 years if not previously vaccinated.

• Use recommended routine dosing intervals (see Routine vaccination previously) for vaccine series catch-up.

General Recommendations on Immunization

TABLE 5-9 Recommended and Minimum Ages and Intervals between Vaccine Doses*†

Vaccine and Dose Number	Recommended Age for this Dose	Minimum Age for this Dose	Recommended Interval to Next Dose	Minimum Interval to Next Dose
HcpB 1§	Birth	Birth	1-4 months	4 weeks
HepB-2	1-2 months	4 weeks	2-17 months	8 weeks
HepB-3¶	6-18 months	24 weeks	—	—
DTaP-1§	2 months	6 weeks	2 months	4 weeks
DTaP-2	4 months	10 weeks***	2 months	4 weeks
DTaP-3	6 months	14 weeks	6-12 months	6 months**††
DTaP-4	15-18 months	12 months	3 years	6 months**
DTaP-5	4-6 years	4 years	—	—
Hib-1§§§	2 months	6 weeks	2 months	4 weeks
Hib-2	4 months	10 weeks	2 months	4 weeks
Hib-3¶¶	6 months	14 weeks	6-9 months	8 weeks
Hib-4	12-15 months	12 months	—	—
IPV-1§	2 months	6 weeks	2 months	4 weeks
IPV-2	4 months	10 weeks	2-14 months	4 weeks
IPV-3	6-18 months	14 weeks	3-5 years	6 months
IPV-4***	4-6 years	4 years	—	—
PCV-1§§	2 months	6 weeks	8 weeks	4 weeks
PCV-2	4 months	10 weeks	8 weeks	4 weeks
PCV-3	6 months	14 weeks	6 months	8 weeks
PCV-4	12-15 months	12 months	—	—
MMR-1†††	12-15 months	12 months	3-5 years	4 weeks
MMR-2†††	4-6 years	13 years	—	—
Varicella-1†††	12-15 months	12 months	3-5 years	12 weeks§§§
Varicella-2†††	4-6 years	15 months	—	—
HepA-1	12-23 months	12 months	6-18 months**	6 months**
HepA-2	≥18 months	18 months	—	—
Influenza inactivated¶¶¶	≥6 months	6 months****	1 month	4 weeks
LAIV (intranasal)¶¶¶	2-49 years	2 years	1 month	4 weeks
MCV4-1††††	11-12 years	2 years	5 years	8 weeks
MCV4-2	16 years	11 years (+8 weeks)	—	—
MPSV4-1††††	—	2 years	5 years	5 years
MPSV4-2	—	7 years	—	—
Td	11-12 years	7 years	10 years	5 years
Tdap§§§§	≥11 years	7 years	—	—
PPSV-1	—	2 years	5 years	5 years
PPSV-2¶¶¶¶	—	7 years	—	—
HPV-1*****	11-12 years	9 years	2 months	4 weeks
HPV-2	11-12 years (+2 months)	9 years (+4 weeks)	4 months	12 weeks†††††
HPV-3†††††	11-12 years (+6 months)	9 years (+24 weeks)	—	—
Rotavirus-1§§§§§	2 months	6 weeks	2 months	4 weeks
Rotavirus-2	4 months	10 weeks	2 months	4 weeks
Rotavirus-3¶¶¶¶¶	6 months	14 weeks	—	—
Herpes zoster******	≥60 years	60 years	—	—
Pneumococcal vaccine††††††	—	—	—	—

DTaP, Diphtheria and tetanus toxoids and acellular pertussis; *HepA,* hepatitis A; *HepB,* hepatitis B; *Hib, Haemophilus influenzae* type b; *HPV,* human papillomavirus; *IPV,* inactivated poliovirus; *LAIV,* live, attenuated influenza vaccine; *MCV4,* quadrivalent meningococcal conjugate vaccine; *MMR,* measles, mumps, and rubella; *MMRV,* measles, mumps, rubella, and varicella; *MPSV4,* quadrivalent meningococcal polysaccharide vaccine; *PCV,* pneumococcal conjugate vaccine; *PPSV,* pneumococcal polysaccharide vaccine; *PRP-OMB,* polyribosylribitol phosphate-meningococcal outer membrane protein conjugate; *Td,* tetanus and diphtheria toxoids; *Tdap,* tetanus toxoid, reduced diphtheria toxoid, and acellular pertussis.

*Combination vaccines are available. Use of licensed combination vaccines is generally preferred to separate injections of their equivalent component vaccines. When administering combination vaccines, the minimum age for administration is the oldest age for any of the individual components; the minimum interval between doses is equal to the greatest interval of any of the individual components.

†Information on travel vaccines, including typhoid, Japanese encephalitis, and yellow fever, is available at http://www.cdc.gov/travel. Information on other vaccines that are licensed in the United States but not distributed, including anthrax and smallpox, is available at http://www.bt.cdc.gov.

§Combination vaccines containing the hepatitis B component are available. These vaccines should not be administered to infants aged <6 weeks because of the other components (i.e., Hib, DTaP, HepA, and IPV).

¶HepB-3 should be administered at least 8 weeks after HepB-2 and at least 16 weeks after HepB-1 and should not be administered before age 24 weeks.

**Calendar months.

††The minimum recommended interval between DTaP-3 and DTaP-4 is 6 months. However, DTaP-4 need not be repeated if administered at least 4 months after DTaP-3.

§§For Hib and PCV, children receiving the first dose of vaccine at age ≥7 months require fewer doses to complete the series.

¶¶If PRP-QMP (Pedvax-Hib, Merck Vaccine Division) was administered at ages 2 and 4 months, a dose at age 6 months is not necessary.

***A fourth dose is not needed if the third dose was administered at ≥4 years and at least 6 months after the previous dose.

†††Combination MMRV vaccine can be used for children aged 12 months to 12 years.

§§§The minimum interval from Varicella-1 to Varicella-2 for persons beginning the series at age ≥13 years is 4 weeks.

¶¶¶One dose of influenza vaccine per season is recommended for most persons. Children aged <9 years who are receiving influenza vaccine for the first time or who received only 1 dose the previous season (if it was their first vaccination season) should receive 2 doses this season.

****The minimum age for inactivated influenza vaccine varies by vaccine manufacturer. See package insert for vaccine-specific minimum ages.

††††Revaccination with meningococcal vaccine is recommended for previously vaccinated persons who remain at high risk for meningococcal disease. (Source: CDC. Updated recommendations from the Advisory Committee on Immunization Practices (ACIP) for revaccination of persons at prolonged increased risk for meningococcal disease. *MMWR* 2009;58:[1042-3]).

§§§§Only 1 dose of Tdap is recommended. Subsequent doses should be given as Td. For one brand of Tdap, the minimum age is 11 years. For management of a tetanus-prone wound in persons who have received a primary series of tetanus-toxoid–containing vaccine, the minimum interval after a previous dose of any tetanus-containing vaccine is 5 years.

¶¶¶¶A second dose of PPSV 5 years after the first dose is recommended for persons aged ≤65 years at highest risk for serious pneumococcal infection and those who are likely to have a rapid decline in pneumococcal antibody concentration. (Source: CDC. Prevention of pneumococcal disease: recommendations of the Advisory Committee on Immunization Practices [ACIP]. *MMWR* 1997;46[No. RR-8]).

*****Bivalent HPV vaccine is approved for females aged 10-25 years. Quadrivalent HPV vaccine is approved for males and females aged 9-26 years.

†††††The minimum age for HPV-3 is based on the baseline minimum age for the first dose (i.e., 108 months) and the minimum interval of 24 weeks between the first and third dose. Dose 3 need not be repeated if it is administered at least 16 weeks after the first dose.

§§§§§The first dose of rotavirus must be administered at age 6 weeks through 14 weeks and 6 days. The vaccine series should not be started for infants aged ≥15 weeks, 0 days. Rotavirus should not be administered to children older than 8 months, 0 days of age regardless of the number of doses received between 6 weeks and 8 months, 0 days of age.

¶¶¶¶¶If 2 doses of Rotarix (GlaxoSmithKline) are administered as age appropriate, a third dose is not necessary.

******Herpes zoster vaccine is recommended as a single dose for persons aged ≥60 years.

TABLE 5-10 Guidelines for Spacing of Live and Inactivated Antigens

Antigen Combination	Recommended Minimum Interval between Doses
Two or more inactivated*	May be administered simultaneously or at any interval between doses
Inactivated and live	May be administered simultaneously or at any interval between doses
Two or more live intranasal or injectable†	28 days minimum interval, if not administered simultaneously

From Centers for Disease Control and Prevention: General recommendations on immunization: recommendations of the Advisory Committee on Immunization Practices (ACIP), *MMWR* 60(2):38, 2011.
*Certain experts suggest a 28-day interval between tetanus toxoid, reduced diphtheria toxoid, and acellular pertussis (Tdap) vaccine and tetravalent meningococcal conjugate vaccine if they are not administered simultaneously.
†Live oral vaccines (e.g., Ty21a typhoid vaccine and rotavirus vaccine) may be administered simultaneously or at any interval before or after inactivated or live injectable vaccines.

TABLE 5-11 Guidelines for Administering Antibody-Containing Products* and Vaccines

Type of Administration	PRODUCTS ADMINISTERED		Recommended Minimum Interval Between Doses
Simultaneous (during the same office visit)	Antibody-containing products and inactivated antigen		Can be administered simultaneously at different anatomic sites or at any time interval between doses
	Antibody-containing products and live antigen		Should not be administered simultaneously.† If simultaneous administration of measles-containing vaccine or varicella vaccine is unavoidable, administer at different sites and revaccinate or test for seroconversion after the recommended interval
Nonsimultaneous	**Administered First**	**Administered Second**	
	Antibody-containing products	Inactivated antigen	No interval necessary
	Inactivated antigen	Antibody-containing products	No interval necessary
	Antibody-containing products	Live antigen	Dose related†‡
	Live antigen	Antibody-containing products	2 weeks†

From Centers for Disease Control and Prevention: General recommendations on immunization: recommendations of the Advisory Committee on Immunization Practices (ACIP), *MMWR* 60: (RR-2), 2011.
*Blood products containing substantial amounts of immune globulin include intramuscular and intravenous immune globulin, specific hyperimmune globulin (e.g., hepatitis B immune globulin, tetanus immune globulin, varicella zoster immune globulin, and rabies immune globulin), whole blood, packed red blood cells, plasma, and platelet products.
†Yellow fever vaccine; rotavirus vaccine; oral Ty21a typhoid vaccine; live, attenuated influenza vaccine; and zoster vaccine are exceptions to these recommendations. These live, attenuated vaccines can be administered at any time before or after or simultaneously with an antibody-containing product.
‡The duration of interference of antibody-containing products with the immune response to the measles component of measles-containing vaccine, and possibly varicella vaccine, is dose related.

TABLE 5-12 Recommended Intervals between Administration of Antibody-Containing Products and Measles- or Varicella-Containing Vaccine, by Product and Indication for Vaccination

Product/Indication	Dose (mg IgG/kg) and Route*	Recommended Interval before Measles- or Varicella-Containing Vaccine† Administration (months)
Tetanus IG	250 units (10 mg IgG/kg) IM	3
Hepatitis A IG		
Contact prophylaxis	0.02 ml/kg (33 mg IgG/kg) IM	3
International travel	0.06 ml/kg (10 mg IgG/kg) IM	3
Hepatitis B IG	0.06 ml/kg (10 mg IgG/kg) IM	3
Rabies IG	20 IU/kg (22 mg IgG/kg) IM	4
Varicella IG	125 units/10 kg (60–200 mg IgG/kg) IM, maximum 625 units	5
Measles prophylaxis IG		
Standard (i.e., nonimmunocompromised) contact	0.25 ml/kg (40 mg IgG/kg) IM	5
Immunocompromised contact	0.50 ml/kg (80 mg IgG/kg) IM	6
Blood transfusion		
RBCs, washed	10 ml/kg negligible IgG/kg IV	None
RBCs, adenine-saline added	10 ml/kg (10 mg IgG/kg) IV	3
Packed RBCs (hematocrit 65%)§	10 ml/kg (60 mg IgG/kg) IV	6
Whole blood (hematocrit 35%-50%)§	10 ml/kg (80-100 mg IgG/kg) IV	6
Plasma/platelet products	10 ml/kg (160 mg IgG/kg) IV	7
Cytomegalovirus IGIV	150 mg/kg maximum	6
IGIV		
Replacement therapy for immune deficiencies¶	300-400 mg/kg IV¶	8
Immune thrombocytopenic purpura treatment	400 mg/kg IV	8
Postexposure varicella prophylaxis**	400 mg/kg IV	8
Immune thrombocytopenic purpura treatment	1000 mg/kg IV	10
Kawasaki disease	2 g/kg IV	11
Monoclonal antibody to respiratory syncytial virus	15 mg/kg IM	None
F protein (Synagis [MedImmune])††		

From Centers for Disease Control and Prevention: General recommendations on immunization: recommendations of the Advisory Committee on Immunization Practices (ACIP), *MMWR* 60: (RR-2), 2011.

HIV, human immunodeficiency virus; *IG*, immune globulin; *IgG*, immune globulin G; *IGIV*, intravenous immune globulin; *mg IgG/kg*, milligrams of immune globulin G per kilogram of body weight; *IM*, intramuscular; *IV*, intravenous; *RBCs*, red blood cells.

*This table is not intended for determining the correct indications and dosages for using antibody-containing products. Unvaccinated persons might not be protected fully against measles during the entire recommended interval, and additional doses of IG or measles vaccine might be indicated after measles exposure. Concentrations of measles antibody in an IG preparation can vary by manufacturer's lot. Rates of antibody clearance after receipt of an IG preparation also might vary. Recommended intervals are extrapolated from an estimated half-life of 30 days for passively acquired antibody and an observed interference with the immune response to measles vaccine for 5 months after a dose of 80 mg IgG/kg.

†Does not include zoster vaccine. Zoster vaccine may be given with antibody-containing blood products.

§Assumes a serum IgG concentration of 10 mg/ml

¶Measles and varicella vaccinations are recommended for children with asymptomatic or mildly symptomatic HIV infection but are contraindicated for persons with severe immunosuppression from HIV or any other immunosuppressive disorder.

**The investigational VariZIG, similar to licensed varicella-zoster IG (VZIG), is a purified human IG preparation made from plasma containing high levels of antivaricella antibodies (IgG). The interval between VariZIG and varicella vaccine (Var or MMRV) is 5 months.

††Contains antibody only to respiratory syncytial virus.

TABLE 5-13 Contraindications and Precautions* to Commonly Used Vaccines

Vaccine	Contraindications	Precautions
DTaP	Severe allergic reaction (e.g., anaphylaxis) after a previous dose or to a vaccine component Encephalopathy (e.g., coma, decreased level of consciousness, or prolonged seizures), not attributable to another identifiable cause, within 7 days of administration of previous dose of DTP or DTaP	Progressive neurologic disorder, including infantile spasms, uncontrolled epilepsy, progressive encephalopathy; defer DTaP until neurologic status clarified and stabilized Temperature of ≥105° F (≥40° C) within 48 hours after vaccination with a previous dose of DTP or DTaP Collapse or shock-like state (i.e., hypotonic hyporesponsive episode) within 48 hours after receiving a previous dose of DTP/DTaP Seizure ≤3 days after receiving a previous dose of DTP/DTaP Persistent, inconsolable crying lasting ≥3 hours within 48 hours after receiving a previous dose of DTP/DTaP GBS <6 weeks after previous dose of tetanus toxoid-containing vaccine History of Arthus-type hypersensitivity reactions after a previous dose of tetanus toxoid-containing vaccine; defer vaccination until at least 10 years have elapsed since the last tetanus-toxoid–containing vaccine Moderate or severe acute illness with or without fever
DT, Td	Severe allergic reaction (e.g., anaphylaxis) after a previous dose or to a vaccine component	GBS <6 weeks after previous dose of tetanus toxoid-containing vaccine History of Arthus-type hypersensitivity reactions after a previous dose of tetanus toxoid-containing vaccine; defer vaccination until at least 10 years have elapsed since the last tetanus-toxoid–containing vaccine Moderate or severe acute illness with or without fever
Tdap	Severe allergic reaction (e.g., anaphylaxis) after a previous dose or to a vaccine component Encephalopathy (e.g., coma, decreased level of consciousness, or prolonged seizures), not attributable to another identifiable cause, within 7 days of administration of previous dose of DTP, DTaP, or Tdap	GBS <6 weeks after a previous dose of tetanus toxoid-containing vaccine Progressive or unstable neurologic disorder, uncontrolled seizures, or progressive encephalopathy until a treatment regimen has been established and the condition has stabilized History of Arthus-type hypersensitivity reactions after a previous dose of tetanus toxoid-containing vaccine; defer vaccination until at least 10 years have elapsed since the last tetanus toxoid-containing vaccine Moderate or severe acute illness with or without fever
IPV	Severe allergic reaction (e.g., anaphylaxis) after a previous dose or to a vaccine component	Pregnancy Moderate or severe acute illness with or without fever
MMR[†§]	Severe allergic reaction (e.g., anaphylaxis) after a previous dose or to a vaccine component Pregnancy: Known severe immunodeficiency (e.g., from hematologic and solid tumors, receipt of chemotherapy, congenital immunodeficiency, or long-term immunosuppressive therapy[¶] or patients with HIV infection who are severely immunocompromised)[§]	Recent (≤11 months) receipt of antibody-containing blood product (specific interval depends on product) History of thrombocytopenia or thrombocytopenic purpura Need for tuberculin skin testing[††] Moderate or severe acute illness with or without fever
Hib	Severe allergic reaction (e.g., anaphylaxis) after a previous dose or to a vaccine component Age <6 weeks	Moderate or severe acute illness with or without fever
Hepatitis B	Severe allergic reaction (e.g., anaphylaxis) after a previous dose or to a vaccine component	Infant weight <2000 g[§§] Moderate or severe acute illness with or without fever
Hepatitis A	Severe allergic reaction (e.g., anaphylaxis) after a previous dose or to a vaccine component	Pregnancy: Moderate or severe acute illness with or without fever
Varicella	Severe allergic reaction (e.g., anaphylaxis) after a previous dose or to a vaccine component Known severe immunodeficiency (e.g., from hematologic and solid tumors, receipt of chemotherapy, congenital immunodeficiency, or long-term immunosuppressive therapy[¶] or patients with HIV infection who are severely immunocompromised)[§] Pregnancy	Recent (≤11 months) receipt of antibody-containing blood product (specific interval depends on product)[¶¶] Moderate or severe acute illness with or without fever
PCV	Severe allergic reaction (e.g., anaphylaxis) after a previous dose (of PCV7, PCV13, or any diphtheria toxoid-containing vaccine) or to a component of a vaccine (PCV7, PCV13, or any diphtheria toxoid-containing vaccine)	Moderate or severe acute illness with or without fever
TIV	Severe allergic reaction (e.g., anaphylaxis) after a previous dose or to vaccine component, including egg protein	GBS <6 weeks after a previous dose of influenza vaccine Moderate or severe acute illness with or without fever
LAIV	Severe allergic reaction (e.g., anaphylaxis) after a previous dose or to vaccine component, including egg protein Pregnancy Immunosuppression Certain chronic medical conditions***	GBS <6 weeks after a previous dose of influenza vaccine Moderate or severe acute illness with or without fever
PPSV	Severe allergic reaction (e.g., anaphylaxis) after a previous dose or to a vaccine component	Moderate or severe acute illness with or without fever

TABLE 5-13 Contraindications and Precautions* to Commonly Used Vaccines—cont'd

Vaccine	Contraindications	Precautions
MCV4	Severe allergic reaction (e.g., anaphylaxis) after a previous dose or to a vaccine component	Moderate or severe acute illness with or without fever
MPSV4	Severe allergic reaction (e.g., anaphylaxis) after a previous dose or to a vaccine component	Moderate or severe acute illness with or without fever
HPV	Severe allergic reaction (e.g., anaphylaxis) after a previous dose or to a vaccine component	Pregnancy: Moderate or severe acute illness with or without fever
Rotavirus	Severe allergic reaction (e.g., anaphylaxis) after a previous dose or to a vaccine component SCID	Altered immunocompetence other than SCID: History of intussusception Chronic gastrointestinal disease[†††] Spina bifida or bladder exstrophy[†††] Moderate or severe acute illness with or without fever
Zoster	Severe allergic reaction (e.g., anaphylaxis) after a previous dose or to a vaccine component Substantial suppression of cellular immunity Pregnancy	Moderate or severe acute illness with or without fever

From Centers for Disease Control and Prevention: General recommendations on immunization: recommendations of the Advisory Committee on Immunization Practices (ACIP), *MMWR* 60: (RR-2), 2011.

DT, diphtheria and tetanus toxoids; *DTaP*, diphtheria and tetanus toxoids and acellular pertussis; *GBS*, Guillain-Barré syndrome; *HBsAg*, hepatitis B surface antigen; *Hib*, *Haemophilus influenzae* type b; *HIV*, human immunodeficiency virus; *HPV*, human papillomavirus; *IPV*, inactivated poliovirus; *LAIV*, live, attenuated influenza vaccine; *MCV4*, quadrivalent meningococcal conjugate vaccine; *MMRV*, measles, mumps, rubella; *MPSV4*, quadrivalent meningococcal polysaccharide vaccine; *PCV*, pneumococcal conjugate vaccine; *PPSV*, pneumococcal polysaccharide vaccine; *SCID*, severe combined immunodeficiency; *Td*, tetanus and diphtheria toxoids; *Tdap*, tetanus toxoid, reduced diphtheria toxoid, and acellular pertussis; *TIV*, trivalent inactivated influenza vaccine.

*Events or conditions listed as precautions should be reviewed carefully. Benefits of and risks for administering a specific vaccine to a person under these circumstances should be considered. If the risk from the vaccine is believed to outweigh the benefit, the vaccine should not be administered. If the benefit of vaccination is believed to outweigh the risk, the vaccine should be administered. Whether and when to administer DTaP to children with proven or suspected underlying neurologic disorders should be decided on a case-by-case basis.

[†]HIV-infected children may receive varicella and measles vaccine if CD4+ T-lymphocyte count is <15%. (Source: Adapted from American Academy of Pediatrics. Passive immunization. In: Pickering LK, ed. *Red book: 2009 report of the committee on infectious diseases*. 28th ed. Elk Grove Village. IL: American Academy of Pediatrics: 2009.)

[§]MMR and varicella vaccines can be administered on the same day. If not administered on the same day, these vaccines should be separated by at least 28 days.

[¶]Substantially immunosuppressive steroid dose is considered to be ≥2 weeks of daily receipt of 20 mg or 2 mg/kg body weight of prednisone or equivalent.

[††]Measles vaccination might suppress tuberculin reactivity temporarily. Measles-containing vaccine can be administered on the same day as tuberculin skin testing. If testing cannot be performed until after the day of MMR vaccination, the test should be postponed for ≥4 weeks after the vaccination. If an urgent need exists to skin test, do so with the understanding that reactivity might be reduced by the vaccine.

[§§]Hepatitis B vaccination should be deferred for infants weighing <2000 g if the mother is documented to be HBsAg-negative at the time of the infant's birth. Vaccination can commence at chronological age 1 month or at hospital discharge. For infants born to HBsAg-positive women, hepatitis B immune globulin and hepatitis B vaccine should be administered within 12 hours after birth, regardless of weight.

[¶¶]Vaccine should be deferred for the appropriate interval if replacement immune globulin products are being administered.

[***]Source: CDC. Prevention and control of seasonal influenza with vaccines: recommendations of the Advisory Committee on Immunization Practices (ACIP), 2010. *MMWR* 2010;59(No. RR-8).

[†††]For details see CDC. Prevention of rotavirus gastroenteritis among infants and children: recommendations of the Advisory Committee on Immunization Practices. *MMWR* 2009;58(No. RR-2).

TABLE 5-14 Conditions Commonly Misperceived as Contraindications to Vaccination

Vaccine	Conditions Commonly Misperceived as Contraindications (i.e., Vaccination May be Administered under These Conditions)
General for all vaccines, including DTaP, pediatric DT, adult Td, adolescent-adult Tdap, IPV, MMR, Hib, hepatitis A, hepatitis B, varicella, rotavirus, PCV, TIV, LAIV, PPSV, MCV4, MPSV4, HPV, and herpes zoster	Mild acute illness with or without fever
	Mild-to-moderate local reaction (i.e., swelling, redness, soreness); low-grade or moderate fever after previous dose
	Lack of previous physical examination in well-appearing person
	Current antimicrobial therapy*
	Convalescent phase of illness
	Preterm birth (hepatitis B vaccine is an exception in certain circumstances)†
	Recent exposure to an infectious disease
	History of penicillin allergy, other nonvaccine allergies, relatives with allergies, or receiving allergen extract immunotherapy
DTaP	Fever of <105° F (<40° C), fussiness or mild drowsiness after a previous dose of DTP/DTaP
	Family history of seizures
	Family history of sudden infant death syndrome
	Family history of an adverse event after DTP or DTaP administration
	Stable neurologic conditions (e.g., cerebral palsy, well-controlled seizures, or developmental delay)
Tdap	Fever of ≥105° F (≥40° C) for <48 hours after vaccination with a previous dose of DTP or DTaP
	Collapse or shock-like state (i.e., hypotonic hyporesponsive episode) within 48 hours after receiving a previous dose of DTaP
	Seizure <3 days after receiving a previous dose of DTP/DTaP
	Persistent, inconsolable crying lasting <3 hours within 48 hours after receiving a previous dose of DTP/DTaP
	History of extensive limb swelling after DTP/DTaP/Td that is not an Arthus-type reaction
	Stable neurologic disorder
	History of brachial neuritis
	Latex allergy that is not anaphylactic
	Breastfeeding
	Immunosuppression
IPV	Previous receipt of ≥1 dose of oral polio vaccine
MMR§,¶	Positive tuberculin skin test
	Simultaneous tuberculin skin testing**
	Breastfeeding
	Pregnancy of recipient's mother or other close or household contact
	Recipient is female of childbearing age
	Immunodeficient family member or household contact
	Asymptomatic or mildly symptomatic HIV infection
	Allergy to eggs
Hepatitis B	Pregnancy
	Autoimmune disease (e.g., systemic lupus erythematosus or rheumatoid arthritis)
Varicella	Pregnancy of recipient's mother or other close or household contact
	Immunodeficient family member or household contact††
	Asymptomatic or mildly symptomatic HIV infection
	Humoral immunodeficiency (e.g., agammaglobulinemia)
TIV	Nonsevere (e.g., contact) allergy to latex, thimerosal, or egg
	Concurrent administration of Coumadin or aminophylline
LAIV	Health care providers that see patients with chronic diseases or altered immunocompetence (an exception is providers for severely immunocompromised patients requiring care in a protected environment)
	Breastfeeding
	Contacts of persons with chronic disease or altered immunocompetence (an exception is contacts of severely immunocompromised patients requiring care in a protected environment)
PPSV	History of invasive pneumococcal disease or pneumonia
HPV	Immunosuppression
	Previous equivocal or abnormal
	Papanicolaou test
	Known HPV infection
	Breastfeeding
	History of genital warts
Rotavirus	Prematurity
	Immunosuppressed household contacts
	Pregnant household contacts

TABLE 5-14 Conditions Commonly Misperceived as Contraindications to Vaccination—cont'd

Vaccine	Conditions Commonly Misperceived as Contraindications (i.e., Vaccination May be Administered under These Conditions)
Zoster	Therapy with low-dose methotrexate (≤0.4 mg/kg/week), azathioprine (≤3.0 mg/kg/day), or 6-mercaptopurine (≤1.5 mg/kg/day) for treatment of rheumatoid arthritis, psoriasis, polymyositis, sarcoidosis, inflammatory bowel disease, or other conditions
	Health care providers of patients with chronic diseases or altered immunocompetence
	Contacts of patients with chronic diseases or altered immunocompetence
	Unknown or uncertain history of varicella in a U.S.-born person

From Centers for Disease Control and Prevention: General recommendations on immunization: recommendations of the Advisory Committee on Immunization Practices (ACIP), *MMWR* 60: (RR-2), 2011.
DT, Diphtheria and tetanus toxoids; *DTP,* diphtheria toxoid, tetanus toxoid, and pertussis; *DTaP,* diphtheria and tetanus toxoids and acellular pertussis; *HBsAg,* hepatitis B surface antigen; *Hib, Haemophilus influenzae* type b; *HPV,* human papillomavirus; *IPV,* inactivated poliovirus; *LAIV,* live, attenuated influenza vaccine; *MCV4,* quadrivalent meningococcal conjugate vaccine; *MMR,* measles, mumps, and rubella; *MPSV4,* quadrivalent meningococcal polysaccharide vaccine; *PCV,* pneumococcal conjugate vaccine; *PPSV,* pneumococcal polysaccharide vaccine; *Td,* tetanus and diphtheria toxoids; *Tdap,* tetanus toxoid, reduced diphtheria toxoid, and acellular pertussis; *TIV,* trivalent inactivated influenza vaccine.
*Antibacterial drugs might interfere with Ty21a oral typhoid vaccine, and certain antiviral drugs might interfere with varicella-containing vaccines and LAIV.
†Hepatitis B vaccination should be deferred for infants weighing <2000 g if the mother is documented to be HBsAg-negative at the time of the infant's birth. Vaccination can commence at chronologic age 1 month or at hospital discharge. For infants born to HBsAg-positive women, hepatitis B immune globulin and hepatitis B vaccine should be administered within 12 hours after birth, regardless of weight.
§MMR and varicella vaccines can be administered on the same day. If not administered on the same day, these vaccines should be separated by at least 28 days.
¶HIV-infected children should receive immune globulin after exposure to measles. HIV-infected children can receive varicella and measles vaccine if CD4+ T-lymphocyte count is >15%. (Source: Adapted from American Academy of Pediatrics. Passive immunization. In: Pickering LK, ed. *Red book: 2009 report of the Committee on Infectious Diseases,* 28th ed. Elk Grove Village, IL: American Academy of Pediatrics; 2009.)
**Measles vaccination might suppress tuberculin reactivity temporarily. Measles-containing vaccine can be administered on the same day as tuberculin skin testing. If testing cannot be performed until after the day of MMR vaccination, the test should be postponed for at least 4 weeks after the vaccination. If an urgent need exists to skin test, do so with the understanding that reactivity might be reduced by the vaccine.
††If a vaccinee experiences a presumed vaccine-related rash 7-25 days after vaccination, the person should avoid direct contact with immunocompromised persons for the duration of the rash.

VACCINE ADMINISTRATION*

INFECTION CONTROL AND STERILE TECHNIQUE

Persons administering vaccines should follow appropriate precautions to minimize risk for spread of disease. Hands should be cleansed with an alcohol-based, waterless antiseptic hand rub or washed with soap and water between each patient contact. Occupational Safety and Health Administration (OSHA) regulations do not require that gloves be worn when administering vaccinations unless persons administering vaccinations are likely to come into contact with potentially infectious body fluids or have open lesions on their hands. Needles used for injections must be sterile and disposable to minimize the risk for contamination. A separate needle and syringe should be used for each injection. Changing needles between drawing vaccine from a vial and injecting it into a recipient is not necessary. Different vaccines should never be mixed in the same syringe unless specifically licensed for such use, and no attempt should be made to transfer between syringes.

For all intramuscular injections, the needle should be long enough to reach the muscle mass and prevent vaccine from seeping into subcutaneous tissue, but not so long as to involve underlying nerves, blood vessels, or bone. Vaccinators should be familiar with the anatomy of the area where they are injecting vaccine. Intramuscular injections are administered at a 90-degree angle to the skin, preferably into the anterolateral aspect of the thigh or the deltoid muscle of the upper arm depending on the age of the patient.

Decision on needle size and site of injection must be made for each person on the basis of the size of the muscle, the thickness of adipose tissue at the injection site, the volume of the material to be administered, injection technique, and the depth below the muscle surface into which the material is to be injected (Fig. E5-1). Aspiration before injection of vaccines or toxoids (i.e., pulling back on the syringe plunger after needle insertion before injection) is not required because no large blood vessel exists at the recommended injection sites.

INFANTS (AGED <12 MONTHS)

For the majority of infants, the anterolateral aspect of the thigh is the recommended site for injection because it provides a large muscle mass (Fig. E5-2). The muscles of the buttock have not been used for administration of vaccines in infants and children because of concern about potential injury to the sciatic nerve, which is well documented after injection of antimicrobial agents into the buttock. If the gluteal muscle must be used, care should be taken to define the anatomic landmarks.† Injection technique is the most important parameter to ensure efficient intramuscular vaccine delivery. If the subcutaneous and muscle tissue are bunched to minimize the chance of striking bone, a 1-inch needle is required to ensure intramuscular administration in infants. For the majority of infants, a 1-inch, 22- to 25-gauge needle is sufficient to penetrate muscle in an infant's thigh. For newborn (first 28 days of life) and premature infants, a 5/8-inch-long needle usually is adequate if the skin is stretched flat between thumb and forefinger and the needle inserted at a 90-degree angle to the skin.

TODDLERS AND OLDER CHILDREN (AGED 12 MONTHS TO 10 YEARS)

The deltoid muscle should be used if the muscle mass is adequate. The needle size for deltoid site injections can range from 22 to 25 gauge and from 5/8 to 1 inch on the basis of the size of the muscle and the thickness of adipose tissue at the injection site (Fig. E5-3). A 5/8-inch needle is adequate only for the deltoid muscle and only if the skin is stretched flat between the thumb and forefinger and the needle inserted at a 90-degree angle to the skin. For toddlers, the anterolateral thigh can be used, but the needle should be at least 1 inch in length.

ADOLESCENTS AND ADULTS (AGED >11 YEARS)

For adults and adolescents, the deltoid muscle is recommended for routine intramuscular vaccinations. The anterolateral thigh also can be used. For men and women weighing <130 lb (<60 kg) a 5/8- to 1-inch needle is sufficient to ensure intramuscular injection. For women weighing 130 to 200 lb (60 to 90 kg) and men 130 to 260 lb (60 to 118 kg), a 1- to 1½-inch needle is needed. For women weighing >200 lb (>90 kg) or men weighing >260 lb (>118 kg), a 1½-inch needle is required.

SUBCUTANEOUS INJECTIONS

Subcutaneous injections are administered at a 45-degree angle, usually into the thigh for infants younger than 12 months and in the upper-outer triceps area of persons aged 12 months and older. Subcutaneous injections can be administered into the upper-outer triceps area of an infant if necessary. A 5/8-inch, 23- to 25-gauge needle should be inserted into the subcutaneous tissue (Figs. E5-4 and E5-5).

TABLE 5-15 Treatment of Anaphylaxis in Children and Adults with Drugs Administered Intramuscularly or Orally

Drug	Dosage
Children	
Primary Regimen	
Epinephrine 1:1000 (aqueous) (1 mg/ml)*	0.01 mg/kg up to 0.5 mg (administer 0.01 ml/kg/dose up to 0.5 mL) IM repeated every 10-20 minutes up to 3 doses
Secondary Regimen	
Diphenhydramine	1-2 mg/kg oral, IM, or IV, every 4-6 hours (100 mg, maximum single dose)
Hydroxyzine	0.5-1 mg/kg oral, IM, every 4-6 hours (100 mg, maximum single dose)
Prednisone	1.5-2 mg/kg oral (60 mg, maximum single dose); use corticosteroids as long as needed
Adults	
Primary Regimen	
Epinephrine 1:1000 (aqueous)*	0.01 mg/kg up to 0.5 mg (administer 0.01 ml/kg/dose up to 0.5 ml) IM repeated every 10-20 minutes up to 3 doses
Secondary Regimen	
Diphenhydramine	1-2 mg/kg up to l00 mg IM or oral, every 4-6 hours

From Centers for Disease Control and Prevention: General recommendations on immunization: recommendations of the Advisory Committee on Immunization Practices (ACIP), *MMWR* 60:(RR-2), 2011. Adapted from American Academy of Pediatrics. Passive immunization. In: Pickering LK, Baker CJ, Kimberlin DW, Long SS, eds: *Red book: 2009 report of the Committee on Infectious Diseases*, 28th ed. Elk Grove Village, IL: American Academy of Pediatrics, 2009:66-7; Immunization Action Coalition. Medical management of vaccine reactions in adult patients (available at www.immunize.org/catg.d/p3082.pdf); and *Mosby's drug consult*, St Louis, 2005, Mosby.

IM, Intramuscular; *IV,* intravenous.

*If the agent causing the anaphylactic reaction was administered by injection, epinephrine may be injected into the same site to slow absorption.

TABLE 5-16 Vaccination of Persons with Primary and Secondary Immunodeficiencies

Primary	Specific Immunodeficiency	Contraindicated Vaccines*	Risk-Specific Recommended Vaccines*	Effectiveness and Comments
B-lymphocyte (humoral)	Severe antibody deficiencies (e.g., X-linked agammaglobulinemia and common variable immunodeficiency)	OPV[†] Smallpox LAIV BCG Ty21a (live typhoid) Yellow fever	Pneumococcal Consider measles and varicella vaccination	The effectiveness of any vaccine is uncertain if it depends only on the humoral response (e.g., PPSV or MPSV4). IVIG interferes with the immune response to measles vaccine and possibly varicella vaccine.
	Less severe antibody deficiencies (e.g., selective IgA deficiency and IgG subclass deficiency)	OPV[†] BCG Yellow fever Other live vaccines appear to be safe.	Pneumococcal	All vaccines likely effective; immune response might be attenuated.
T-lymphocyte (cell-mediated and humoral)	Complete deficits (e.g., severe combined immunodeficiency [SCID] disease, complete DiGeorge syndrome)	All live vaccines[§,¶,**]	Pneumococcal	Vaccines might be ineffective.
	Partial defects (e.g., most patients with DiGeorge syndrome, Wiskott-Aldrich syndrome, ataxia-telangiectasia)	All live vaccines[§,¶,**]	Pneumococcal Meningococcal Hib (if not administered in infancy)	Effectiveness of any vaccine depends on degree of immune suppression.
Complement	Persistent complement, properdin, or factor B deficiency	None	Pneumococcal Meningococcal	All routine vaccines likely effective.
Phagocytic function	Chronic granulomatous disease, leukocyte adhesion defect, and myeloperoxidase deficiency	Live bacterial vaccines[§]	Pneumococcal[††]	All inactivated vaccines safe and likely effective. Live viral vaccines likely safe and effective.
Secondary	HIV/AIDS	OPV[†] Smallpox BCG LAIV Withhold MMR and varicella in severely immunocompromised persons. Yellow fever vaccine might have a contraindication or a precaution depending on clinical parameters of immune function***	Pneumococcal Consider Hib (if not administered in infancy) and meningococcal vaccination.	MMR, varicella, rotavirus, and all inactivated vaccines, including inactivated influenza, might be effective.[§§]
	Malignant neoplasm, transplantation, immunosuppressive or radiation therapy	Live viral and bacterial, depending on immune status[§,¶]	Pneumococcal	Effectiveness of any vaccine depends on degree of immune suppression.
	Asplenia	None	Pneumococcal Meningococcal Hib (if not administered in infancy)	All routine vaccines likely effective.
	Chronic renal disease	LAIV	Pneumococcal Hepatitis B[¶¶]	All routine vaccines likely effective.

From Centers for Disease Control and Prevention: General recommendations on immunization: recommendations of the Advisory Committee on Immunization Practices (ACIP), *MMWR* 60:(RR-2), 2011. Adapted from American Academy of Pediatrics. Passive immunization. In: Pickering LK, Baker CJ, Kimberlin DW, Long SS, eds: *Red book: 2009 report of the Committee on Infectious Diseases*, 28th ed. Elk Grove Village, IL: American Academy of Pediatrics; 2009:74–5.

AIDS, acquired immunodeficiency syndrome; *BCG*, bacille Calmette-Guérin; *Hib, Haemophilus influenzae* type b; *HIV*, human immunodeficiency virus; *Ig*, immunoglobulin; *IGIV*, immune globulin intravenous; *LAIV*, live, attenuated influenza vaccine; *MMR*, measles, mumps, and rubella; *MPSV4*, quadrivalent meningococcal polysaccharide vaccine; *OPV*, oral poliovirus polysaccharide vaccine; *PPSV*, pneumococcal polysaccharide vaccine.

*Other vaccines that are universally or routinely recommended should be given if not contraindicated.

[†]OPV is no longer available in the United States.

[§]Live bacterial vaccines: BCG and oral Ty21a *Salmonella typhi* vaccine.

[¶]Live viral vaccines: MMR, MMRV, OPV, LAIV, yellow fever, zoster, rotavirus, varicella, and vaccinia (smallpox). Smallpox vaccine is not recommended for children or the general public.

**Regarding T-lymphocyte immunodeficiency as a contraindication for rotavirus vaccine, data exist only for severe combined immunodeficiency.

[††]Pneumococcal vaccine is not indicated for children with chronic granulomatous disease beyond age-based universal recommendations for PCV. Children with chronic granulomatous disease are not at increased risk for pneumococcal disease.

[§§]HIV-infected children should receive IG after exposure to measles and may receive varicella and measles vaccine if CD4+ T-lymphocyte count is ≥15%.

[¶¶]Indicated based on the risk from dialysis-based bloodborne transmission.

***Symptomatic HIV infection or CD4+ T-lymphocyte count of <200/mm³ or <15% of total lymphocytes for children aged <6 years is a contraindication to yellow fever vaccine administration. Asymptomatic HIV infection with CD4+ T-lymphocyte count of 200–499/mm³ for persons aged ≥6 years or 15%–24% of total lymphocytes for children aged <6 years is a precaution for yellow fever vaccine administration. Details of yellow fever vaccine recommendations are available from CDC. (CDC. Yellow fever vaccine recommendations of the Advisory Committee on Immunization Practices [ACIP]. *MMWR* 2010;59[No. RR-7].)

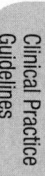

Clinical Practice Guidelines

V

TABLE 5-17 Immunizations for Pediatric Oncology Patients

Vaccine	Indications and Comments
DTaP	Indicated for incompletely immunized children <7 yr, even during active chemotherapy
Td	Indicated 1 yr after completion of therapy in children 7 yr
Hib	Indicated for incompletely immunized children if <7 yr
HBV	Indicated for incompletely immunized children
23PS	Indicated for asplenic patients
PCV13	Indicated for incompletely immunized children <5 yr
Meningococcus	Consider in asplenic patients
IPV	Indicated for incompletely immunized children; also recommended for all household contacts requiring immunization to reduce the risk of vaccine-associated polio
MMR	Contraindicated until child is in remission and finished with all chemotherapy for 3-6 mo; may need to reimmunize after chemotherapy if titers have fallen below protective levels
Influenza	Defer in active chemotherapy; may give as early as 3-4 wk after remission and off chemotherapy if during influenza season; peripheral granulocyte and lymphocyte counts should be >1000/μL; should also be given to household contact of children with cancer
Varicella	Consider immunizing children who have remained in remission and have finished chemotherapy for >1 yr; with absolute lymphocyte count of >700/μl and platelet count of >100,000/μL within 24 hr of immunization; check titers of previously immunized children to verify protective levels of antibodies

From *MMWR* 49(RR-10):1-147, 2000.

DTaP, Diphtheria, tetanus, and pertussis; *HBV,* hepatitis B virus; *Hib, Haemophilus influenzae* type b; *IPV,* inactivated polio vaccine; *MMR,* measles, mumps, rubella; *PCV13,* pneumococcal conjugate vaccine; *Td,* tetanus, diphtheria; *23PS,* 23-valent pneumococcal polysaccharide vaccine.

TABLE 5-18 Approaches to the Evaluation and Vaccination of Persons Vaccinated Outside the United States Who Have No (or Questionable) Vaccination Records

Vaccine	Recommended Approach	Alternative Approach*
MMR	Revaccination with MMR	Serologic testing for IgG antibodies to measles, mumps, and rubella
Hib	Age-appropriate revaccination	—
Hepatitis A	Age-appropriate revaccination	Serologic testing for IgG antibodies to hepatitis A
Hepatitis B	Age-appropriate revaccination and serologic testing for HBsAg†	—
Poliovirus	Revaccinate with inactivated poliovirus vaccine	Serologic testing for neutralizing antibody to poliovirus types 1, 2, and 3 (limited availability)
DTaP	Revaccination with DTaP, with serologic testing for specific IgG antibody to tetanus and diphtheria toxins in the event of a severe local reaction	Persons whose records indicate receipt of ≥3 doses: serologic testing for specific IgG antibody to diphtheria and tetanus toxins before administering additional doses, or administer a single booster dose of DTaP, followed by serologic testing after 1 month for specific IgG antibody to diphtheria and tetanus toxins with revaccination as appropriate
Tdap	Age-appropriate vaccination of persons who are candidates for Tdap vaccine on the basis of time since last diphtheria and tetanus-toxoid–containing vaccines.	—
Varicella	Age-appropriate vaccination of persons who lack evidence of varicella immunity	—
Pneumococcal conjugate	Age-appropriate vaccination	—
Rotavirus	Age-appropriate vaccination	—
HPV	Age-appropriate vaccination	—
Zoster	Age-appropriate vaccination	—

From Centers for Disease Control and Prevention: General recommendations on immunization: recommendations of the Advisory Committee on Immunization Practices (ACIP), *MMWR* 60:(RR-2), 2011. *DTaP*, Diphtheria and tetanus toxoids and acellular pertussis; *HBsAg*, hepatitis B surface antigen; *Hib, Haemophilus influenzae* type b; *HPV*, human papillomavirus; *IgG*, immune globulin G; *MMR*, measles, mumps, and rubella; *Tdap*, tetanus toxoid, reduced diphtheria toxoid, and acellular pertussis.

*There is a recommended approach for all vaccines and an alternative approach for some vaccines.

†In rare instances, hepatitis B vaccine can give a false-positive HBsAg result up to 18 days after vaccination; therefore, blood should be drawn to test for HBsAg before vaccinating. (Source: CDC. A comprehensive immunization strategy to eliminate transmission of hepatitis B virus infection in the United States: recommendations of the Advisory Committee on Immunization Practices [ACIP]; Part I. Immunization in infants, children, and adolescents, *MMWR* 2005;54(No. RR-16.])

Immunizations for Adults

TABLE 5-19 Recommended Adult Immunization Schedule, by Vaccine and Age Group[1]

These recommendations must be read with the footnotes that follow.

VACCINE ▼ AGE GROUP ▶	19-21 years	22-26 years	27-49 years	50-59 years	60-64 years	≥ 65 years
Influenza[*,2]	1 dose annually					
Tetanus, diphtheria, pertussis (Td/Tdap)[*,3]	Substitute Tdap for Td once, then Td booster every 10 yrs					
Varicella[*,4]	2 doses					
Human papillomavirus (HPV) Female[*,5]	3 doses					
Human papillomavirus (HPV) Male[*,5]	3 doses					
Zoster[6]					1 dose	
Measles, mumps, rubella (MMR)[*,7]	1 or 2 doses depending on indication					
Pneumococcal 13-valent conjugate (PCV13)[*,8]					1 dose	
Pneumococcal 23-valent polysaccharide (PPSV23)[8]	1 or 2 doses depending on indication					1 dose
Hepatitis A[*,9]	2 or 3 doses depending on vaccine					
Hepatitis B[*,10]	3 doses					
Meningococcal 4-valent conjugate (MenACWY) or polysaccharide (MPSV4)[*,11]	1 or more doses depending on indication					
Meningococcal B (MenB)[11]	2 or 3 doses depending on vaccine					
Haemophilus influenzae type b (Hib)[*,12]	1 or 3 doses depending on indication					

*Covered by the Vaccine Injury Compensation Program

	Recommended for all persons who meet the age requirement, lack documentation of vaccination, or lack evidence of past infection; zoster vaccine is recommended regardless of past episode of zoster
	Recommended for persons with a risk factor (medical, occupational, lifestyle, or other indication)
	No recommendation

Report all clinically significant postvaccination reactions to the Vaccine Adverse Event Reporting System (VAERS). Reporting forms and instructions on filing a VAERS report are available at www.vaers.hhs.gov or by telephone, 800-822-7967.

Information on how to file a Vaccine Injury Compensation Program claim is available at www.hrsa.gov/vaccinecompensation or by telephone, 800-338-2382. To file a claim for vaccine injury, contact the U.S. Court of Federal Claims, 717 Madison Place, N.W., Washington, D.C. 20005; telephone, 202-357-6400.

Additional information about the vaccines in this schedule, extent of available data, and contraindications for vaccination is also available at www.cdc.gov/vaccines or from the CDC-INFO Contact Center at 800-CDC-INFO (800-232-4636) in English and Spanish, 8:00 a.m. - 8:00 p.m. Eastern Time, Monday - Friday, excluding holidays.

Use of trade names and commercial sources is for identification only and does not imply endorsement by the U.S. Department of Health and Human Services.

The recommendations in this schedule were approved by the Centers for Disease Control and Prevention's (CDC) Advisory Committee on Immunization Practices (ACIP), the American Academy of Family Physicians (AAFP), the America College of Physicians (ACP), the American College of Obstetricians and Gynecologists (ACOG), and the American College of Nurse-Midwives (ACNM).

TABLE 5-20A Vaccines That Might Be Indicated for Adults Based on Medical and Other Indications: United States[1]

Note: These recommendations *must* be read with the footnotes that follow containing number of doses, intervals between doses, and other important information.

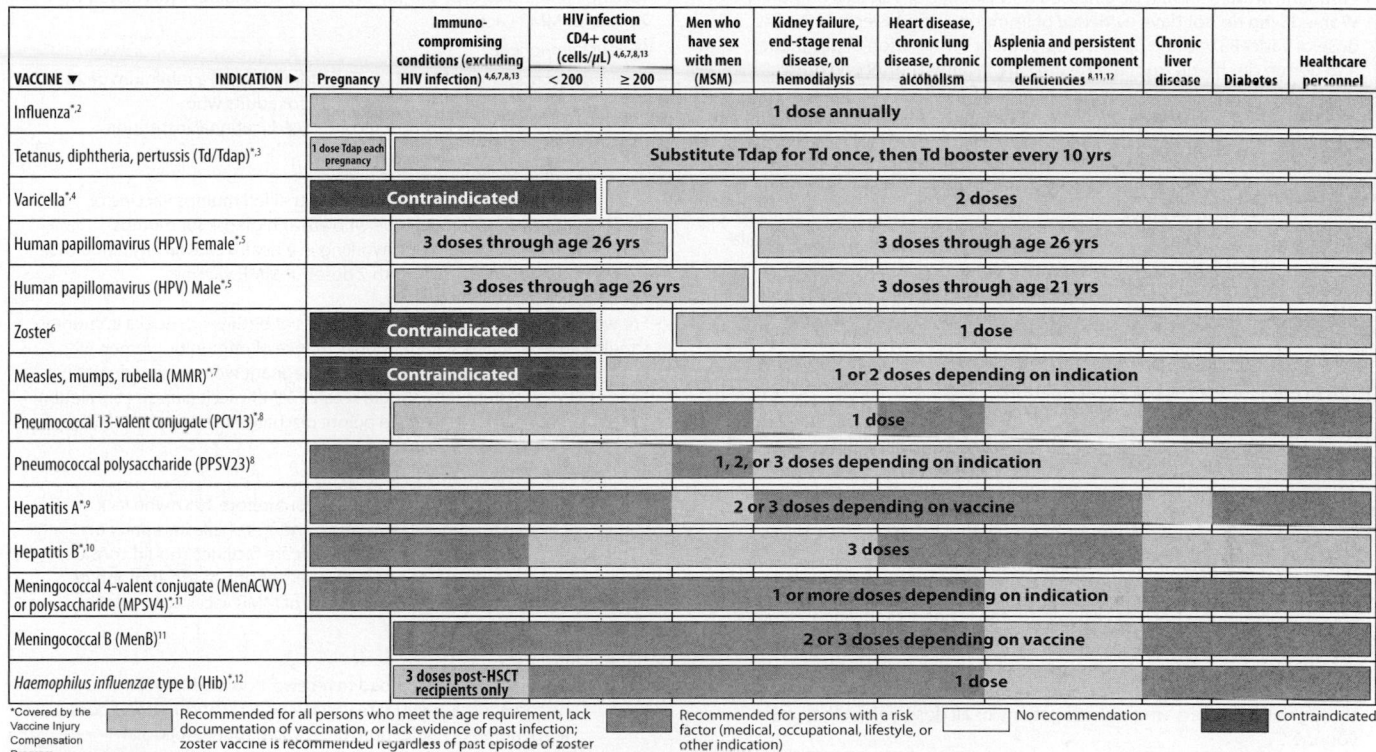

VACCINE ▼ INDICATION ▶	Pregnancy	Immuno-compromising conditions (excluding HIV infection) [4,6,7,8,13]	HIV infection CD4+ count (cells/µL) [4,6,7,8,13] < 200	HIV infection CD4+ count (cells/µL) [4,6,7,8,13] ≥ 200	Men who have sex with men (MSM)	Kidney failure, end-stage renal disease, on hemodialysis	Heart disease, chronic lung disease, chronic alcoholism	Asplenia and persistent complement component deficiencies [8,11,12]	Chronic liver disease	Diabetes	Healthcare personnel
Influenza[*,2]	1 dose annually										
Tetanus, diphtheria, pertussis (Td/Tdap)[*,3]	1 dose Tdap each pregnancy	Substitute Tdap for Td once, then Td booster every 10 yrs									
Varicella[*,4]	Contraindicated			2 doses							
Human papillomavirus (HPV) Female[*,5]		3 doses through age 26 yrs				3 doses through age 26 yrs					
Human papillomavirus (HPV) Male[*,5]		3 doses through age 26 yrs				3 doses through age 21 yrs					
Zoster[6]	Contraindicated			1 dose							
Measles, mumps, rubella (MMR)[*,7]	Contraindicated			1 or 2 doses depending on indication							
Pneumococcal 13-valent conjugate (PCV13)[*,8]						1 dose					
Pneumococcal polysaccharide (PPSV23)[8]						1, 2, or 3 doses depending on indication					
Hepatitis A[*,9]						2 or 3 doses depending on vaccine					
Hepatitis B[*,10]						3 doses					
Meningococcal 4-valent conjugate (MenACWY) or polysaccharide (MPSV4)[*,11]						1 or more doses depending on indication					
Meningococcal B (MenB)[11]						2 or 3 doses depending on vaccine					
Haemophilus influenzae type b (Hib)[*,12]	3 doses post-HSCT recipients only			1 dose							

*Covered by the Vaccine Injury Compensation Program

■ Recommended for all persons who meet the age requirement, lack documentation of vaccination, or lack evidence of past infection; zoster vaccine is recommended regardless of past episode of zoster

■ Recommended for persons with a risk factor (medical, occupational, lifestyle, or other indication)

☐ No recommendation

■ Contraindicated

U.S. Department of Health and Human Services
Centers for Disease Control and Prevention

These schedules indicate the recommended age groups and medical indications for which administration of currently licensed vaccines is commonly recommended for adults aged ≥19 years, as of February 2016. For all vaccines being recommended on the Adult Immunization Schedule: a vaccine series does not need to be restarted, regardless of the time that has elapsed between doses. Licensed combination vaccines may be used whenever any components of the combination are indicated and when the vaccine's other components are not contraindicated. For detailed recommendations on all vaccines, including those used primarily for travelers or that are issued during the year, consult the manufacturers' package inserts and the complete statements from the Advisory Committee on Immunization Practices (www.cdc.gov/vaccines/hcp/acip-recs/index.html). Use of trade names and commercial sources is for identification only and does not imply endorsement by the U.S. Department of Health and Human Services.

Footnotes—Recommended Immunization Schedule for Adults Aged 19 Years or Older: United States, 2016

1. Additional information
- Additional guidance for the use of the vaccines described in this supplement is available at www.cdc.gov/vaccines/hcp/acip-recs/index.html.
- Information on vaccination recommendations when vaccination status is unknown and other general immunization information can be found in the General Recommendations on Immunization at www.cdc.gov/mmwr/preview/mmwrhtml/rr6002a1.htm.
- Information on travel vaccine requirements and recommendations (e.g., for hepatitis A and B, meningococcal, and other vaccines) is available at wwwnc.cdc.gov/travel/destinations/list.
- Additional information and resources regarding vaccination of pregnant women can be found at www.cdc.gov/vaccines/adults/rec-vac/pregnant.html.

2. Influenza vaccination
- Annual vaccination against influenza is recommended for all persons aged ≥6 months. A list of currently available influenza vaccines can be found at http://www.cdc.gov/flu/protect/vaccine/vaccines.htm.
- Persons aged ≥6 months, including pregnant women, can receive the inactivated influenza vaccine (IIV). An age-appropriate IIV formulation should be used.
- Intradermal IIV is an option for persons aged 18 through 64 years.
- High-dose IIV is an option for persons aged ≥65 years.
- Live attenuated influenza vaccine (LAIV [FluMist]) is an option for healthy, non-pregnant persons aged 2 through 49 years.
- Recombinant influenza vaccine (RIV [Flublok]) is approved for persons aged ≥18 years.
- RIV, which does not contain any egg protein, may be administered to persons aged ≥18 years with egg allergy of any severity; IIV may be used with additional safety measures for persons with hives-only allergy to eggs.

- Health care personnel who care for severely immunocompromised persons who require care in a protected environment should receive IIV or RIV; health care personnel who receive LAIV should avoid providing care for severely immunosuppressed persons for 7 days after vaccination.

3. Tetanus, diphtheria, and acellular pertussis (Td/Tdap) vaccination
- Administer 1 dose of Tdap vaccine to pregnant women during each pregnancy (preferably during 27–36 weeks' gestation) regardless of interval since prior Td or Tdap vaccination.
- Persons aged ≥11 years who have not received Tdap vaccine or for whom vaccine status is unknown should receive a dose of Tdap followed by tetanus and diphtheria toxoids (Td) booster doses every 10 years thereafter. Tdap can be administered regardless of interval since the most recent tetanus or diphtheria-toxoid-containing vaccine.
- Adults with an unknown or incomplete history of completing a 3-dose primary vaccination series with Td-containing vaccines should begin or complete a primary vaccination series including a Tdap dose.
- For unvaccinated adults, administer the first 2 doses at least 4 weeks apart and the third dose 6–12 months after the second.
- For incompletely vaccinated (i.e., less than 3 doses) adults, administer remaining doses.
  Refer to the ACIP statement for recommendations for administering Td/Tdap as prophylaxis in wound management (see footnote 1).

4. Varicella vaccination
- All adults without evidence of immunity to varicella (as defined below) should receive 2 doses of single-antigen varicella vaccine or a second dose if they have received only 1 dose.
- Vaccination should be emphasized for those who have close contact with persons at high risk for severe disease (e.g., health care personnel and family contacts of persons with immunocompromising conditions) or are

at high risk for exposure or transmission (e.g., teachers; child care employees; residents and staff members of institutional settings, including correctional institutions; college students; military personnel; adolescents and adults living in households with children; nonpregnant women of childbearing age; and international travelers).

- Pregnant women should be assessed for evidence of varicella immunity. Women who do not have evidence of immunity should receive the first dose of varicella vaccine upon completion or termination of pregnancy and before discharge from the health care facility. The second dose should be administered 4–8 weeks after the first dose.
- Evidence of immunity to varicella in adults includes any of the following:
  - documentation of 2 doses of varicella vaccine at least 4 weeks apart;
  - U.S.-born before 1980, except health care personnel and pregnant women;
  - history of varicella based on diagnosis or verification of varicella disease by a health care provider;
  - history of herpes zoster based on diagnosis or verification of herpes zoster disease by a health care provider; or
  - laboratory evidence of immunity or laboratory confirmation of disease.

5. Human papillomavirus (HPV) vaccination

- Three HPV vaccines are licensed for use in females (bivalent HPV vaccine [2vHPV], quadrivalent HPV vaccine [4vHPV], and 9-valent HPV vaccine [9vHPV]) and two HPV vaccines are licensed for use in males (4vHPV and 9vHPV).
- For females, 2vHPV, 4vHPV, or 9vHPV is recommended in a 3-dose series for routine vaccination at age 11 or 12 years and for those aged 13 through 26 years, if not previously vaccinated.
- For males, 4vHPV or 9vHPV is recommended in a 3-dose series for routine vaccination at age 11 or 12 years and for those aged 13 through 21 years, if not previously vaccinated. Males aged 22 through 26 years may be vaccinated.
- HPV vaccination is recommended for men who have sex with men through age 26 years who did not get any or all doses when they were younger.
- Vaccination is recommended for immunocompromised persons (including those with HIV infection) through age 26 years who did not get any or all doses when they were younger.
- A complete HPV vaccination series consists of 3 doses. The second dose should be administered 4–8 weeks (minimum interval of 4 weeks) after the first dose; the third dose should be administered 24 weeks after the first dose and 16 weeks after the second dose (minimum interval of 12 weeks).
- HPV vaccines are not recommended for use in pregnant women. However, pregnancy testing is not needed before vaccination. If a woman is found to be pregnant after initiating the vaccination series, no intervention is needed; the remainder of the 3-dose series should be delayed until completion or termination of pregnancy.

6. Zoster vaccination

- A single dose of zoster vaccine is recommended for adults aged ≥60 years regardless of whether they report a prior episode of herpes zoster. Although the vaccine is licensed by the U.S. Food and Drug Administration for use among and can be administered to persons aged ≥50 years, ACIP recommends that vaccination begin at age 60 years.
- Persons aged ≥60 years with chronic medical conditions may be vaccinated unless their condition constitutes a contraindication, such as pregnancy or severe immunodeficiency.

7. Measles, mumps, rubella (MMR) vaccination

- Adults born before 1957 are generally considered immune to measles and mumps.
- All adults born in 1957 or later should have documentation of 1 or more doses of MMR vaccine unless they have a medical contraindication to the vaccine or laboratory evidence of immunity to each of the three diseases. Documentation of provider-diagnosed disease is not considered acceptable evidence of immunity for measles, mumps, or rubella.

Measles component:

- A routine second dose of MMR vaccine, administered a minimum of 28 days after the first dose, is recommended for adults who:
  - are students in postsecondary educational institutions,
  - work in a health care facility, or
  - plan to travel internationally.
- Persons who received inactivated (killed) measles vaccine or measles vaccine of unknown type during 1963–1967 should be revaccinated with 2 doses of MMR vaccine.

Mumps component:

- A routine second dose of MMR vaccine, administered a minimum of 28 days after the first dose, is recommended for adults who:
  - are students in a postsecondary educational institution,
  - work in a health care facility, or
  - plan to travel internationally.
- Persons vaccinated before 1979 with either killed mumps vaccine or mumps vaccine of unknown type who are at high risk for mumps infection (e.g., persons who are working in a health care facility) should be considered for revaccination with 2 doses of MMR vaccine.

Rubella component:

- For women of childbearing age, regardless of birth year, rubella immunity should be determined. If there is no evidence of immunity, women who are not pregnant should be vaccinated. Pregnant women who do not have evidence of immunity should receive MMR vaccine upon completion or termination of pregnancy and before discharge from the health care facility.

Health care personnel born before 1957:

- For unvaccinated health care personnel born before 1957 who lack laboratory evidence of measles, mumps, and/or rubella immunity or laboratory confirmation of disease, health care facilities should consider vaccinating personnel with 2 doses of MMR vaccine at the appropriate interval for measles and mumps or 1 dose of MMR vaccine for rubella.

8. Pneumococcal vaccination

- General information
  - Adults are recommended to receive 1 dose of 13-valent pneumococcal conjugate vaccine (PCV13) and 1, 2, or 3 doses (depending on indication) of 23-valent pneumococcal polysaccharide vaccine (PPSV23).
  - PCV13 should be administered at least 1 year after PPSV23.
  - PPSV23 should be administered at least 1 year after PCV13, except among adults with immunocompromising conditions, anatomical or functional asplenia, cerebrospinal fluid leak, or cochlear implant, for whom the interval should be at least 8 weeks; the interval between PPSV23 doses should be at least 5 years.
  - No additional dose of PPSV23 is indicated for adults vaccinated with PPSV23 at age ≥65 years.
  - When both PCV13 and PPSV23 are indicated, PCV13 should be administered first; PCV13 and PPSV23 should not be administered during the same visit.
  - When indicated, PCV13 and PPSV23 should be administered to adults whose pneumococcal vaccination history is incomplete or unknown.
- Adults aged ≥65 years (immunocompetent) who:
  - have not received PCV13 or PPSV23: administer PCV13 followed by PPSV23 at least 1 year after PCV13.
  - have not received PCV13 but have received a dose of PPSV23 at age ≥65 years: administer PCV13 at least 1 year after PPSV23.
  - have not received PCV13 but have received 1 or more doses of PPSV23 at age <65 years: administer PCV13 at least 1 year after the most recent dose of PPSV23. Administer a dose of PPSV23 at least 1 year after PCV13 and at least 5 years after the most recent dose of PPSV23.
  - have received PCV13 but not PPSV23 at age <65 years: administer PPSV23 at least 1 year after PCV13.
  - have received PCV13 and 1 or more doses of PPSV23 at age <65 years: administer PPSV23 at least 1 year after PCV13 and at least 5 years after the most recent dose of PPSV23.
- Adults aged ≥19 years with immunocompromising conditions or anatomical or functional asplenia (defined in the following) who:

- have not received PCV13 or PPSV23: administer PCV13 followed by PPSV23 at least 8 weeks after PCV13. Administer a second dose of PPSV23 at least 5 years after the first dose of PPSV23.
- have not received PCV13 but have received 1 dose of PPSV23: administer PCV13 at least 1 year after the PPSV23. Administer a second dose of PPSV23 at least 8 weeks after PCV13 and at least 5 years after the first dose of PPSV23.
- have not received PCV13 but have received 2 doses of PPSV23: administer PCV13 at least 1 year after the most recent dose of PPSV23.
- have received PCV13 but not PPSV23: administer PPSV23 at least 8 weeks after PCV13. Administer a second dose of PPSV23 at least 5 years after the first dose of PPSV23.
- have received PCV13 and 1 dose of PPSV23: administer a second dose of PPSV23 at least 8 weeks after PCV13 and at least 5 years after the first dose of PPSV23.
- If the most recent dose of PPSV23 was administered at age <65 years, at age ≥65 years, administer a dose of PPSV23 at least 8 weeks after PCV13 and at least 5 years after the last dose of PPSV23.
- Immunocompromising conditions that are indications for pneumococcal vaccination are: congenital or acquired immunodeficiency (including B- or T-lymphocyte deficiency, complement deficiencies, and phagocytic disorders excluding chronic granulomatous disease), HIV infection, chronic renal failure, nephrotic syndrome, leukemia, lymphoma, Hodgkin disease, generalized malignancy, multiple myeloma, solid organ transplant, and iatrogenic immunosuppression (including long-term systemic corticosteroids and radiation therapy).
- Anatomical or functional asplenia that are indications for pneumococcal vaccination are: sickle cell disease and other hemoglobinopathies, congenital or acquired asplenia, splenic dysfunction, and splenectomy. Administer pneumococcal vaccines at least 2 weeks before immunosuppressive therapy or an elective splenectomy, and as soon as possible to adults who are newly diagnosed with asymptomatic or symptomatic HIV infection.
- Adults aged ≥19 years with cerebrospinal fluid leaks or cochlear implants: administer PCV13 followed by PPSV23 at least 8 weeks after PCV13; no additional dose of PPSV23 is indicated if aged <65 years. If PPSV23 was administered at age <65 years, at age ≥65 years, administer another dose of PPSV23 at least 5 years after the last dose of PPSV23.
- Adults aged 19 through 64 years with chronic heart disease (including congestive heart failure and cardiomyopathies, excluding hypertension), chronic lung disease (including chronic obstructive lung disease, emphysema, and asthma), chronic liver disease (including cirrhosis), alcoholism, or diabetes mellitus, or who smoke cigarettes: administer PPSV23. At age ≥65 years, administer PCV13 at least 1 year after PPSV23, followed by another dose of PPSV23 at least 1 year after PCV13 and at least 5 years after the last dose of PPSV23.
- Routine pneumococcal vaccination is not recommended for American Indian/Alaska Native or other adults unless they have an indication as above; however, public health authorities may consider recommending the use of pneumococcal vaccines for American Indians/Alaska Natives or other adults who live in areas with increased risk for invasive pneumococcal disease.

9. Hepatitis A vaccination

- Vaccinate any person seeking protection from hepatitis A virus (HAV) infection and persons with any of the following indications:
  - men who have sex with men;
  - persons who use injection or noninjection illicit drugs;
  - persons working with HAV-infected primates or with HAV in a research laboratory setting;
  - persons with chronic liver disease and persons who receive clotting factor concentrates;
  - persons traveling to or working in countries that have high or intermediate endemicity of hepatitis A (see footnote 1); and

- unvaccinated persons who anticipate close personal contact (e.g., household or regular babysitting) with an international adoptee during the first 60 days after arrival in the United States from a country with high or intermediate endemicity of hepatitis A (see footnote 1). The first dose of the 2-dose hepatitis A vaccine series should be administered as soon as adoption is planned, ideally 2 or more weeks before the arrival of the adoptee.
- Single-antigen vaccine formulations should be administered in a 2-dose schedule at either 0 and 6–12 months (Havrix), or 0 and 6–18 months (Vaqta). If the combined hepatitis A and hepatitis B vaccine (Twinrix) is used, administer 3 doses at 0, 1, and 6 months; alternatively, a 4-dose schedule may be used, administered on days 0, 7, and 21–30 followed by a booster dose at 12 months.

10. Hepatitis B vaccination

- Vaccinate any person seeking protection from hepatitis B virus (HBV) infection and persons with any of the following indications:
  - sexually active persons who are not in a long-term, mutually monogamous relationship (e.g., persons with more than 1 sex partner during the previous 6 months); persons seeking evaluation or treatment for a sexually transmitted disease (STD); current or recent injection drug users; and men who have sex with men;
  - health care personnel and public safety workers who are potentially exposed to blood or other infectious body fluids;
  - persons who are aged <60 years with diabetes as soon as feasible after diagnosis; persons with diabetes who are aged ≥60 years at the discretion of the treating clinician based on the likelihood of acquiring HBV infection, including the risk posed by an increased need for assisted blood glucose monitoring in long-term care facilities, the likelihood of experiencing chronic sequelae if infected with HBV, and the likelihood of immune response to vaccination;
  - persons with end-stage renal disease (including patients receiving hemodialysis), persons with HIV infection, and persons with chronic liver disease;
  - household contacts and sex partners of hepatitis B surface antigen–positive persons, clients and staff members of institutions for persons with developmental disabilities, and international travelers to regions with high or intermediate levels of endemic HBV infection (see footnote 1); and
  - all adults in the following settings: STD treatment facilities, HIV testing and treatment facilities, facilities providing drug abuse treatment and prevention services, health care settings targeting services to injection drug users or men who have sex with men, correctional facilities, end-stage renal disease programs and facilities for chronic hemodialysis patients, and institutions and nonresidential day care facilities for persons with developmental disabilities.
- Administer missing doses to complete a 3-dose series of hepatitis B vaccine to those persons not vaccinated or not completely vaccinated. The second dose should be administered at least 1 month after the first dose; the third dose should be administered at least 2 months after the second dose (and at least 4 months after the first dose). If the combined hepatitis A and hepatitis B vaccine (Twinrix) is used, give 3 doses at 0, 1, and 6 months; alternatively, a 4-dose Twinrix schedule may be used, administered on days 0, 7, and 21–30, followed by a booster dose at 12 months.
- Adult patients receiving hemodialysis or with other immunocompromising conditions should receive 1 dose of 40 mcg/mL (Recombivax HB) administered on a 3-dose schedule at 0, 1, and 6 months or 2 doses of 20 mcg/mL (Engerix-B) administered simultaneously on a 4-dose schedule at 0, 1, 2, and 6 months.

11. Meningococcal vaccination

- General information
  - Serogroup A, C, W, and Y meningococcal vaccine is available as a conjugate (MenACWY [Menactra, Menveo]) or a polysaccharide (MPSV4 [Menomune]) vaccine.

- Serogroup B meningococcal (MenB) vaccine is available as a 2-dose series of MenB-4C vaccine (Bexsero) administered at least 1 month apart or a 3-dose series of MenB-FHbp (Trumenba) vaccine administered at 0, 2, and 6 months; the two MenB vaccines are not interchangeable, i.e., the same MenB vaccine product must be used for all doses.
- MenACWY vaccine is preferred for adults with serogroup A, C, W, and Y meningococcal vaccine indications who are aged ≤55 years, and for adults aged ≥56 years: 1) who were vaccinated previously with MenACWY vaccine and are recommended for revaccination or 2) for whom multiple doses of vaccine are anticipated; MPSV4 vaccine is preferred for adults aged ≥56 years who have not received MenACWY vaccine previously and who require a single dose only (e.g., persons at risk because of an outbreak).
- Revaccination with MenACWY vaccine every 5 years is recommended for adults previously vaccinated with MenACWY or MPSV4 vaccine who remain at increased risk for infection (e.g., adults with anatomical or functional asplenia or persistent complement component deficiencies, or microbiologists who are routinely exposed to isolates of *Neisseria meningitidis*).
- MenB vaccine is approved for use in persons aged 10 through 25 years; however, because there is no theoretical difference in safety for persons aged >25 years compared to those aged 10 through 25 years, MenB vaccine is recommended for routine use in persons aged ≥10 years who are at increased risk for serogroup B meningococcal disease.
- There is no recommendation for MenB revaccination at this time.
- MenB vaccine may be administered concomitantly with MenACWY vaccine but at a different anatomic site, if feasible.
- HIV infection is not an indication for routine vaccination with MenACWY or MenB vaccine; if an HIV-infected person of any age is to be vaccinated, administer 2 doses of MenACWY vaccine at least 2 months apart.
- Adults with anatomical or functional asplenia or persistent complement component deficiencies: administer 2 doses of MenACWY vaccine at least 2 months apart and revaccinate every 5 years. Also administer a series of MenB vaccine.

- Microbiologists who are routinely exposed to isolates of *Neisseria meningitidis:* administer a single dose of MenACWY vaccine; revaccinate with MenACWY vaccine every 5 years if remain at increased risk for infection. Also administer a series of MenB vaccine.
- Persons at risk because of a meningococcal disease outbreak: if the outbreak is attributable to serogroup A, C, W, or Y, administer a single dose of MenACWY vaccine; if the outbreak is attributable to serogroup B, administer a series of MenB vaccine.
- Persons who travel to or live in countries in which meningococcal disease is hyperendemic or epidemic: administer a single dose of MenACWY vaccine and revaccinate with MenACWY vaccine every 5 years if the increased risk for infection remains (see footnote 1); MenB vaccine is not recommended because meningococcal disease in these countries is generally not caused by serogroup B.
- Military recruits: administer a single dose of MenACWY vaccine.
- First-year college students aged ≤21 years who live in residence halls: administer a single dose of MenACWY vaccine if they have not received a dose on or after their 16th birthday.
- Young adults aged 16 through 23 years (preferred age range is 16 through 18 years): may be vaccinated with a series of MenB vaccine to provide short-term protection against most strains of serogroup B meningococcal disease.

12. *Haemophilus influenzae* **type b (Hib) vaccination**

- One dose of Hib vaccine should be administered to persons who have anatomical or functional asplenia or sickle cell disease or are undergoing elective splenectomy if they have not previously received Hib vaccine. Hib vaccination 14 or more days before splenectomy is suggested.
- Recipients of a hematopoietic stem cell transplant (HSCT) should be vaccinated with a 3-dose regimen 6–12 months after a successful transplant, regardless of vaccination history; at least 4 weeks should separate doses.
- Hib vaccine is not recommended for adults with HIV infection since their risk for Hib infection is low.

13. **Immunocompromising conditions**

- Inactivated vaccines (e.g., pneumococcal, meningococcal, and inactivated influenza vaccines) generally are acceptable and live vaccines generally should be avoided in persons with immune deficiencies or immunocompromising conditions. Information on specific conditions is available at www.cdc.gov/vaccines/hcp/acip-recs/index.html.

TABLE 5-20B   Contraindications and Precautions to Commonly Used Vaccines in Adults*†‡

Vaccine	Contraindications	Precautions
Influenza, inactivated vaccine (IIV)§	Severe allergic reaction (e.g., anaphylaxis) after previous dose of any influenza vaccine or to a vaccine component, including egg protein.	Moderate or severe acute illness with or without fever. History of Guillain-Barré Syndrome (GBS) within 6 weeks of previous influenza vaccination. Adults with egg allergy of any severity may receive RIV; adults with hives-only allergy to eggs may receive IIV with additional safety measures.§
Influenza, recombinant (RIV)	Severe allergic reactions (e.g., anaphylaxis) after previous dose of RIV or to a vaccine component. RIV does not contain any egg protein.§	Moderate or severe acute illness with or without fever. History of Guillain-Barre syndrome within 6 weeks of previous influenza vaccination.
Influenza, live attenuated (LAIV)§,‖	Severe allergic reaction (e.g., anaphylaxis) to any component of the vaccine, or to a previous dose of any influenza vaccine. In addition, ACIP recommends that LAIV not be used in the following populations: -pregnant women; -immunosuppressed adults; -adults with egg allergy of any severity; or -adults who have taken influenza antiviral medications (amatadine, rimantadine, zanamivir, or oseltamivir) within the previous 48 hours; avoid use of these antiviral drugs for 14 days after vaccination.	Moderate or severe acute illness with or without fever. History of GBS within 6 weeks of previous influenza vaccination. Asthma in persons aged 5 years or older. Other chronic medical conditions (e.g., other chronic lung diseases, chronic cardiovascular disease [excluding isolated hypertension], diabetes, chronic renal or hepatic disease, hematologic disease, neurologic disease, and metabolic disorders).
Tetanus, diphtheria, acellular pertussis (Tdap); tetanus, diphtheria (Td)	Severe allergic reaction (e.g., anaphylaxis) after a previous dose or to a vaccine component. For pertussis-containing vaccines: encephalopathy (e.g., coma, decreased level of consciousness, or prolonged seizures) not attributable to another identifiable cause within 7 days of administration of a previous dose of Tdap, diphtheria and tetanus toxoids and pertussis (DTP), diphtheria and tetanus toxoids and acellular pertussis (DTaP) vaccine.	Moderate or severe acute illness with or without fever. GBS within 6 weeks after a previous dose of tetanus toxoid–containing vaccine. History of Arthus-type hypersensitivity reactions after a previous dose of tetanus or diptheria toxoid–containing vaccine; defer vaccination until at least 10 years have elapsed since the last tetanus toxoid-containing vaccine. For pertussis-containing vaccines: progressive or unstable neurologic disorder, uncontrolled seizures, or progressive encephalopathy until a treatment regimen has been established and the condition has stabilized.
Varicella‖	Severe allergic reaction (e.g., anaphylaxis) after a previous dose or to a vaccine component. Known severe immunodeficiency (e.g., from hematologic and solid tumors, receipt of chemotherapy, congenital immunodeficiency, or long-term immunosuppressive therapy¶ or patients with human immunodeficiency virus (HIV) infection who are severely immunocompromised). Pregnancy.	Recent (within 11 months) receipt of antibody-containing blood product (specific interval depends on product).** Moderate or severe acute illness with or without fever. Receipt of specific antivirals (i.e., acyclovir, famciclovir, or valacyclovir) 24 hours before vaccination; avoid use of these antiviral drugs for 14 days after vaccination.
Human papillomavirus (HPV), 9-valent (9vHPV), quadrivalent (4vHPV), bivalent (2vHPV)	Severe allergic reaction (e.g., anaphylaxis) after a previous dose or to a vaccine component.	Moderate or severe acute illness with or without fever. Pregnancy.
Zoster‖	Severe allergic reaction (e.g., anaphylaxis) to a vaccine component. Known severe immunodeficiency (e.g., from hematologic and solid tumors, receipt of chemotherapy or long-term immunosuppressive therapy or patients with HIV infection who are severely immunocompromised). Pregnancy.	Moderate or severe acute illness with or without fever. Receipt of specific antivirals (i.e., acyclovir, famciclovir, or valacyclovir) 24 hours before vaccination; avoid use of these antiviral drugs for 14 days after vaccination.

TABLE 5-20B Contraindications and Precautions to Commonly Used Vaccines in Adults*†‡—cont'd

Vaccine	Contraindications	Precautions
Measles, mumps, rubella (MMR)‖	Severe allergic reaction (e.g., anaphylaxis) after a previous dose or to a vaccine component. Known severe immunodeficiency (e.g., from hematologic and solid tumors, receipt of chemotherapy, congenital immunodeficiency, or long-term immunosuppressive therapy ¶ or patients with HIV infection who are severely immunocompromised). Pregnancy.	Moderate or severe acute illness with or without fever. Recent (within 11 months) receipt of antibody-containing blood product (specific interval depends on product).** History of thrombocytopenia or thrombocytopenic purpura. Need for tuberculin skin testing.††
Pneumococcal, 13-valent conjugate (PCV13)	Severe allergic reaction (e.g., anaphylaxis) after a previous dose or to a vaccine component, including to any vaccine containing diphtheria toxoid.	Moderate or severe acute illness with or without fever.
Pneumococcal, 23-valent polysaccharide (PPSV23)	Severe allergic reaction (e.g., anaphylaxis) after a previous dose or to a vaccine component.	Moderate or severe acute illness with or without fever.
Meningococcal serogroup ACWY, conjugate (MenACWY); meningococcal serogroup ACWY, polysaccharide (MPSV4)	Severe allergic reaction (e.g., anaphylaxis) after a previous dose or to a vaccine component.	Moderate or severe acute illness with or without fever.
Meningococcal serogroup B (MenB)	Severe allergic reaction (e.g., anaphylaxis) after a previous dose or to a vaccine component.	Moderate or severe acute illness with or without fever.
Hepatitis A	Severe allergic reaction (e.g., anaphylaxis) after a previous dose or to a vaccine component.	Moderate or severe acute illness with or without fever.
Hepatitis B	Severe allergic reaction (e.g., anaphylaxis) after a previous dose or to a vaccine component.	Moderate or severe acute illness with or without fever.
Haemophilus influenzae type b (Hib)	Severe allergic reaction (e.g., anaphylaxis) after a previous dose or to a vaccine component.	Moderate or severe acute illness with or without fever.

* Adapted from "Table 6. Contraindications and precautions to commonly used vaccines," in CDC. General recommendations on immunization: recommendations of the Advisory Committee on Immunization Practices. MMWR Recomm Rep. 2011;60:40-1; and from Appendix A in Hamborsky J, Kroger A, Wolfe C, eds. *Epidemiology and Prevention of Vaccine Preventable Diseases.* 13th ed. Washington, DC: Public Health Foundation; 2015 (available at www.cdc.gov/vaccines/pubs/pinkbook/index.html).

†Regarding latex allergy. Consult the package insert for any vaccine administered.

‡Vaccine package inserts and the full ACIP recommendations for these vaccines should be consulted for additional information on vaccine-related contraindications and precautions and for more information on vaccine excipients. Events or conditions listed as precautions should be reviewed carefully. Benefits of and risks for administering a specific vaccine to a person under these circumstances should be considered. If the risk from the vaccine is believed to outweigh the benefit, the vaccine should not be administered. If the benefit of vaccination is believed to outweigh the risk, the vaccine should be administered. A contraindication is a condition in a recipient that increases the chance of a serious adverse reaction. Therefore, a vaccine should not be administered when a contraindication is present.

§For more information on use of influenza vaccines among persons with egg allergies and a complete list of conditions that CDC considers to be reasons to avoid receiving LAIV, see CDC. Prevention and control of seasonal influenza with vaccines: recommendations of the Advisory Committee on Immunization Practices (ACIP)-United States, 2015-16 influenza season. MMWR. 2015;64(30):818-25.

‖LAIV, MMR, varicella, and zoster vaccines can be administered on the same day. If not administered on the same day, these live vaccines should be separated by at least 28 days.

¶Immunosuppressive steroid dose is considered to be 2 or more weeks of daily receipt of 20 mg prednisone or the equivalent. Vaccination should be deferred for at least 1 month after discontinuation of such therapy. Providers should consult ACIP recommendations for complete information on the use of specific live vaccines among persons on immune-suppressing medications or with immune suppression because of other reasons.

**Vaccine should be deferred for the appropriate interval if replacement immune globulin products are being administered. See CDC. General recommendations on immunization: recommendations of the Advisory Committee on Immunization of Practices (ACIP). MMWR Recomm Rep. 2011;60;1-64 (available at www.cdc.gov/vaccines/pubs/pinkbook/index.html).

††Measles vaccination might suppress tuberculin reactivity temporarily. Measles-containing vaccine may be administered on the same day as tuberculin skin testing. If testing cannot be performed until after the day of MMR vaccination, the test should be postponed for at least 4 weeks after the vaccination. If an urgent need exists to skin test, do so with the understanding that reactivity might be reduced by the vaccine.

TABLE 5-21 Immunization and Pregnancy

Vaccine	Before Pregnancy	During Pregnancy	After Pregnancy	Type of Vaccine	Route
Hepatitis A	If at high risk for disease	If at high risk for disease	If at high risk for disease	Inactivated	IM
Hepatitis B	Yes, if at risk	Yes, if at risk	Yes, if at risk	Inactivated	IM
Human papillomavirus (HPV)	Yes, if 9 to 26 years of age	No, under study	Yes, if 9 to 26 years of age	Inactivated	IM
Influenza TIV	Yes	Yes	Yes	Inactivated	IM
Influenza LAIV	Yes, if <50 years and healthy; avoid conception for 4 weeks	No	Yes, if <50 years and healthy; avoid conception for 4 weeks	Live	Nasal spray
MMR	Yes, avoid conception for 4 weeks	No	Yes, give immediately postpartum if susceptible to rubella	Live	SC
Meningococcal:	If indicated	If indicated	If indicated		
Polysaccharide				Inactivated	SC
Conjugate				Inactivated	IM
Pneumococcal polysaccharide	If indicated	If indicated	If indicated	Inactivated	IM or SC
Tetanus/diphtheria Td	Yes, Tdap preferred	If indicated	Yes, Tdap preferred	Toxoid	IM
Tdap, one dose only	Yes, preferred	If high risk of pertussis; otherwise, Td preferred	Yes, preferred	Toxoid/inactivated	IM
Varicella	Yes, avoid conception for 4 weeks	No	Yes, give immediately postpartum if susceptible	Live	SC

IM, Intramuscular; *LAIV,* live, attenuated influenza vaccine; *SC,* subcutaneous; *Tdap,* tetanus and diphtheria toxoids and acellular pertussis; *TIV,* trivalent inactivated influenza vaccine.

TABLE 5-22 Immunizing Agents and Immunization Schedules for Health Care Workers (HCWs)*

Generic Name	Primary Schedule and Booster(s)	Indications	Major Precautions and Contraindications	Special Considerations
Immunizing Agents Strongly Recommended for Health Care Workers				
Hepatitis B (HB) recombinant vaccine	Two doses IM 4 wk apart; third dose 5 mo after second; booster doses not necessary	**Preexposure:** HCWs at risk for exposure to blood or body fluids	Based on limited data no risk of adverse effects to developing fetuses is apparent. Pregnancy should *not* be considered a contraindication to vaccination of women. Previous anaphylactic reaction to common baker's yeast is a contraindication to vaccination.	The vaccine produces neither therapeutic nor adverse effects on HB-infected persons. Prevaccination serologic screening is not indicated for persons being vaccinated because of occupational risk. HCWs who have contact with patients or blood should be tested 1-2 mo after vaccination to determine serologic response.
Hepatitis B immune globulin (HBIG)	0.06 ml/kg IM as soon as possible after exposure. A second dose of HBIG should be administered 1 mo later if the HB vaccine series has not been started.	**Postexposure prophylaxis:** For persons exposed to blood or body fluids containing HBsAg and who are not immune to HBV infection—0.06 ml/kg IM as soon as possible (but no later than 7 days after exposure)		
Influenza vaccine (inactivated whole-virus and split-virus vaccines)	Annual vaccination with current vaccine Administered IM	HCWs who have contact with patients at high risk for influenza or its complications; HCWs who work in long-term care facilities; HCWs with high-risk medical conditions or who are aged ≥65 yr	History of anaphylactic hypersensitivity to egg ingestion	No evidence exists of risk to mother or fetus when the vaccine is administered to a pregnant woman with an underlying high-risk condition. Influenza vaccination is recommended during second and third trimesters of pregnancy because of increased risk for hospitalization.
Measles live-virus vaccine	One dose SC; second dose at least 1 mo later	HCWs[†] born during or after 1957 who do not have documentation of having received two doses of live vaccine on or after the first birthday **or** a history of physician-diagnosed measles or serologic evidence of immunity. Vaccination should be considered for all HCWs who lack proof of immunity, including those born before 1957.	Pregnancy; immunocompromised persons,[‡] including HIV-infected persons who have evidence of severe immunosuppression; anaphylaxis after gelatin ingestion or administration of neomycin; recent administration of immune globulin	MMR is the vaccine of choice if recipients are likely to be susceptible to rubella and/or mumps as well as measles. Persons vaccinated between 1963 and 1967 with a killed measles vaccine alone, killed vaccine followed by live vaccine, or with a vaccine of unknown type should be revaccinated with two doses of live measles virus vaccine.
Mumps live-virus vaccine	One dose SC; second dose at least 1 mo later	HCWs[†] believed to be susceptible can be vaccinated. Adults born before 1957 can be considered immune.	Pregnancy; immunocompromised persons,[‡] history of anaphylactic reaction after gelatin ingestion or administration of neomycin	MMR is the vaccine of choice if recipients are likely to be susceptible to measles and rubella, as well as mumps.
Hepatitis A virus (HAV) vaccine	Two doses of vaccine either 6-12 mo apart (HAVRIX), or 6 mo apart (VAQTA)	Not routinely indicated for HCWs in the United States. Persons who work with HAV-infected primates or with HAV in a research laboratory setting should be vaccinated.	History of anaphylactic hypersensitivity to alum or, for HAVRIX, the preservative 2-phenoxyethanol. The safety of the vaccine in pregnant women has not been determined; the risk associated with vaccination should be weighed against the risk for hepatitis A in women who may be at high risk for exposure to HAV.	

TABLE 5-22 Immunizing Agents and Immunization Schedules for Health Care Workers (HCWs)*—cont'd

Generic Name	Primary Schedule and Booster(s)	Indications	Major Precautions and Contraindications	Special Considerations
Meningococcal vaccine	One dose in volume and by route specified by manufacturer; single booster for adults 19 to 21 years of age if the first dose was given before age 16	Laboratory personnel and others with exposure risk.	The safety of the vaccine in pregnant women has not been evaluated; it should not be administered during pregnancy unless the risk for infection is high.	
Typhoid vaccine, IM, SC, and oral	IM vaccine: One 0.5-ml/dose, booster 0.5 ml every 2 yr SC vaccine: Two 0.5-ml doses, ≥4 wk apart, booster 0.5 ml SC or 0.1 ID every 3 yr if exposure continues Oral vaccine: Four doses on alternate days. The manufacturer recommends revaccination with the entire 4-dose series every 5 yr	Workers in microbiology laboratories who frequently work with *Salmonella typhi*	Severe local or systemic reaction to a previous dose. Ty21a (oral) vaccine should not be administered to immunocompromised persons[†] or to persons receiving antimicrobial agents.	Vaccination should not be considered an alternative to the use of proper procedures when handling specimens and cultures in the laboratory.
Vaccinia vaccine (smallpox)	One dose administered with a bifurcated needle; boosters administered every 10 yr	Laboratory workers who directly handle cultures with vaccinia, recombinant vaccinia viruses, or orthopox viruses that infect human beings	The vaccine is contraindicated in pregnancy, in persons with eczema or a history of eczema, and in immunocompromised persons[†] and their household contacts.	Vaccination may be considered for HCWs who have direct contact with contaminated dressings or other infectious material from volunteers in clinical studies involving recombinant vaccinia virus.
Other Vaccine-Preventable Diseases				
Tetanus and diphtheria and pertussis (Tdap)	Two IM doses 4 wk apart or tetanus and diphtheria toxoid for adults with uncertain or incomplete primary vaccination; third dose 6-12 mo after second dose; booster every 10 yr. Substitute a one-time dose of Tdap for one of the doses of Td, either in the primary series or for the routine booster, whichever comes first.	All adults	Except in the first trimester, pregnancy is not a precaution. History of a neurologic reaction or immediate hypersensitivity reaction after a previous dose. History of severe local (Arthus-type) reaction after a previous dose. Such persons should not receive further routine or emergency doses of Td for 10 yr.	Tetanus prophylaxis in wound management[‡]
Pneumococcal polysaccharide vaccine (23 valent)	One dose, 0.5 ml, IM or SC; revaccination recommended for those at highest risk ≥5 yr after the first dose	Adults who are at increased risk of pneumococcal disease and its complications because of underlying health conditions; older adults, especially those age ≥65 who are healthy	The safety of vaccine in pregnant women has not been evaluated; it should not be administered during pregnancy unless the risk for infection is high. Previous recipients of any type of pneumococcal polysaccharide vaccine who are at highest risk for fatal infection or antibody loss may be revaccinated ≥5 yr after the first dose.	

Continued

TABLE 5-22   Immunizing Agents and Immunization Schedules for Health Care Workers (HCWs)*—cont'd

Generic Name	Primary Schedule and Booster(s)	Indications	Major Precautions and Contraindications	Special Considerations
Rubella live-virus vaccine	One dose SC; second dose at least 1 mo later	Indicated for HCWs,[†] both men and women, who do not have documentation of having received live vaccine on or after their first birthday **or** laboratory evidence of immunity. Adults born before 1957, **except women who can become pregnant,** can be considered immune.	Pregnancy; immunocompromised persons[†]; history of anaphylactic reaction after administration of neomycin	The risk for rubella vaccine–associated malformations in the offspring of women pregnant when vaccinated or who become pregnant within 3 mo after vaccination is negligible. Such women should be counseled regarding the theoretic basis of concern for the fetus. MMR is the vaccine of choice if recipients are likely to be susceptible to measles or mumps as well as rubella.
Varicella-zoster live-virus vaccine	Two 0.5-ml doses SC 4-8 wk apart if ≥13 yr	Indicated for HCWs[†] who do not have either a reliable history of varicella or serologic evidence of immunity	Pregnancy, immunocompromised persons,[‡] history of anaphylactic reaction after receipt of neomycin or gelatin. Avoid salicylate use for 6 wk after vaccination.	Vaccine is available from the manufacturer for certain patients with acute lymphocytic leukemia in remission. Because 71%-93% of persons without a history of varicella are immune, serologic testing before vaccination is likely to be cost effective.
Varicella-zoster immune globulin (VZIG)	Persons <50 kg: 125 µg/10 kg IM; persons ≥50 kg: 625 µg[§]	Persons known or likely to be susceptible (particularly those at high risk for complications, e.g., pregnant women) who have close and prolonged exposure to a contact case or to an infectious hospital staff worker or patient		Serologic testing may help in assessing whether to administer VZIG. If use of VZIG prevents varicella disease, patient should be vaccinated subsequently.

BCG Vaccination

Generic Name	Primary Schedule and Booster(s)	Indications	Major Precautions and Contraindications	Special Considerations
Bacille Calmette-Guérin (BCG) vaccine (TB)	One percutaneous dose of 0.3 ml; no booster dose recommended	Should be considered only for HCWs in areas where multidrug TB is prevalent, a strong likelihood of infection exists, and where comprehensive infection control precautions have failed to prevent TB transmission to HCWs	Should not be administered to immunocompromised persons,[‡] pregnant women	In the United States TB-control efforts are directed toward early identification, treatment of cases, and preventive therapy with isoniazid.

Other Immunobiologics That Are or May Be Indicated for HCWs

Generic Name	Primary Schedule and Booster(s)	Indications	Major Precautions and Contraindications	Special Considerations
Immune globulin (hepatitis A)	**Postexposure**—One IM dose of 0.02 ml/kg administered ≤2 wk after exposure	Indicated for HCWs exposed to feces of infectious patients	Contraindicated in persons with IgA deficiency; do not administer within 2 wk after MMR vaccine or 3 wk after varicella vaccine. Delay administration of MMR vaccine for ≥3 mo and varicella vaccine ≥5 mo after administration of immune globulin	Administer in large muscle mass (deltoid, gluteal).

Modified from *MMWR* 46(RR-18), 1998.

HBsAg, Hepatitis B surface antigen; *HBV,* hepatitis B virus; *HIV,* human immunodeficiency virus; *IM,* intramuscular; *MMR,* measles, mumps, rubella vaccine; *SC,* subcutaneous; *TB,* tuberculosis.

*Persons who provide health care to patients or work in institutions that provide patient care (e.g., physicians, nurses, emergency medical personnel, dental professionals and students, medical and nursing students, laboratory technicians, hospital volunteers, and administrative and support staff in health care institutions).

[†]All HCWs (i.e., medical or nonmedical, paid or volunteer, full time or part time, student or nonstudent, with or without patient-care responsibilities) who work in health care institutions (e.g., inpatient and outpatient, public and private) should be immune to measles, rubella, and varicella.

[‡]Persons immunocompromised because of immune deficiency diseases, HIV infection, leukemia, lymphoma or generalized malignancy, or immunosuppressed as a result of therapy with corticosteroids, alkylating drugs, antimetabolites, or radiation.

[§]Some experts recommend 125 µg/10 kg regardless of total body weight.

TABLE 5-23 Recommendations for Persons with Medical Conditions Requiring Special Vaccination Considerations

Condition	Tdap	MMR	Varicella	HBV	HAV	Pneumovax[a]	Influenza[b]	HbCV	Meningococcal	IPV	Other Live Vaccines[c]	Other Killed Vaccines[d]
HIV infection	Rou	Rou/Contr[e]	Contr[f]	Rou[g]	Rou	Rec	Rec	Cons	Rou	Rou	Contr	Rou
Severe immunocompromise[h]	Rou	Contr	Contr[f]	Rou[g]	Rou	Rec	Rec	Rou[i]	Rou	Rou	Contr	Rou
Renal failure	Rou	Rou	Rou	Rec[g]	Rou	Rec	Rec	Rou	Rou	Rou	Rou	Rou
Diabetes	Rou	Rou	Rou	Rou	Rou	Rec	Rec	Rou	Rou	Rou	Rou	Rou
Chronic liver disease	Rou	Rou	Rou	Rou	Rec	Rec	Rec	Rou	Rou	Rou	Rou	Rou
Cardiac disease	Rou	Rou	Rou	Rou	Rou	Rec	Rec	Rou	Rou	Rou	Rou	Rou
Pulmonary disease	Rou	Rou	Rou	Rou	Rou	Rec	Rec	Rou	Rou	Rou	Rou	Rou
Alcoholism	Rou	Rou	Rou	Rou	Rou	Rec	Rec	Rou	Rou	Rou	Rou	Rou
Functional/anatomic asplenia	Rou	Rou	Rou	Rou	Rou	Rec[j]	Rec	Rec[j]	Rec[j]	Rou	Rou	Rou
Terminal complement deficiency	Rou	Rou	Rou	Rou	Rou	Rou	Rou	Rou	Rec	Rou	Rou	Rou
Clotting factor disorders	Rou	Rou	Rou	Rec	Rec	Rou	Rou	Rou	Rou	Rou	Rou	Rou

Modified and updated from *MMWR* 42(RR-4):16, 1993.

Cons, Consider vaccination; *Contr,* contraindicated; *HAV,* hepatitis A virus; *HbCV, Haemophilus influenzae* conjugate vaccine; *HBV,* hepatitis B virus; *IPV,* inactivated poliomyelitis vaccine; *MMR,* measles-mumps-rubella; *Rec,* recommended; *Rou,* routine as outlined for all adults; *Tdap,* tetanus and diphtheria toxoids and acellular pertussis.

[a] Pneumovax should be repeated in 5 yr for patients in whom vaccine is recommended. Asthma without chronic obstructive pulmonary disease is not an indication for the vaccine.

[b] Influenza vaccine should also be given to caregivers and household members.

[c] Includes bacille Calmette-Guérin, vaccinia, oral typhoid, yellow fever (if exposure cannot be avoided; persons with HIV can be given yellow fever vaccine; see text).

[d] Includes rabies (check postvaccination titers in HIV or severely immunocompromised persons), Lyme disease, inactivated typhoid, cholera, plague, and anthrax.

[e] For asymptomatic, nonseverely immunocompromised persons with HIV, MMR can be used; it is contraindicated in severely immunocompromised persons. MMR can be considered in symptomatic HIV patients without severe immunocompromise.

[f] Varicella can be given to household members and caregivers, but if varicella-like rash develops after vaccination, contact should be avoided.

[g] Recommended for persons with severe chronic renal failure approaching or already receiving dialysis and higher doses should be given. Antibody titers should be measured after vaccination in these patients and in those with HIV or severe immunocompromise (who may require higher doses) to ensure adequate response. Yearly titers should be measured in dialysis patients.

[h] Severe immunocompromise can result from congenital immunodeficiency, leukemia, lymphoma, malignancy, organ transplant, chemotherapy, radiation therapy, or high-dose corticosteroids.

[i] Only for persons with Hodgkin's disease.

[j] Give at least 2 wk in advance of elective splenectomy.

TABLE 5-24 Vaccinations for International Travel

Disease*	Areas Affected†	Prophylaxis Recommended	Ideal Time between Last Vaccine Dose and Travel
Tetanus	All	All travelers; vaccine series/booster	Probably 30 days for series; anamnestic response to booster
Measles	All	If born after 1956; ensure immunity by antibody titer, diagnosed measles, or two doses of vaccine	As MMR, 7-14 days
Rubella	All	If born after 1956 and any female of childbearing age; rubella titer or one dose of vaccine	As MMR, 7-14 days
Mumps	All	If born after 1956; ensure immunity by antibody titer, diagnosed mumps, or one dose of vaccine	As MMR, 7-14 days
Varicella	All	All travelers; antibody titer, reported illness, or vaccine series	7-14 days
Hepatitis B	5%-20% of population are carriers in Africa, Middle East except Israel, all Southeast Asia, Amazon basin, Haiti, and Dominican Republic; 1%-5% of population are carriers in south-central and southwest Asia, Israel, Japan, Americas, Russia, and eastern and southern Europe	Travelers for more than 6 mo in close contact with population or for less time but with high-risk activities (close household contact, seeking dental or medical care, sex); vaccine series	Probably 30 days
Hepatitis A	Developing countries	Travelers to rural areas; eating and drinking in settings of poor sanitation; vaccine or pooled immune globulin	Vaccine, 30 days Pooled IG, 2 days
Influenza	Tropics throughout the year; southern hemisphere from April to September	Travelers for whom vaccine is otherwise indicated; give current vaccine and revaccinate in fall as usual	7-14 days
Meningococcus*	Sub-Saharan Africa "belt" (Senegal to Ethiopia) from December to June; required for pilgrims to Saudi Arabia during Hajj; epidemics reported in other African nations, India, Nepal, and Mongolia	All travelers; vaccine	7-10 days
Rabies	Endemic dog rabies exists in Mexico, El Salvador, Guatemala, Peru, Colombia, Ecuador, India, Nepal, Philippines, Sri Lanka, Thailand, and Vietnam	Travelers staying for more than 30 days or at high risk of exposure to domestic or wild animals; vaccine series/booster	7-14 days
Poliomyelitis	Developing countries not in western hemisphere; at risk all year in tropics; in temperate zones, incidence increases in summer and fall	All travelers; vaccine series/booster	Parenteral vaccine series, 28 day
Typhoid fever	Many countries in Asia, Africa, Central America, and South America	Travelers with prolonged stay in rural areas with poor sanitation; vaccine series/booster	Oral vaccine, 7 days Parenteral vaccine, probably 14 days
Yellow fever*	North and central South America, forest-savannah zones of Africa; some countries in Africa, Asia, and Middle East require travelers from endemic areas to be vaccinated	All travelers; vaccine/booster at approved yellow fever vaccination center.	10 days
Japanese encephalitis	Seasonally in most areas of Asia, Indian subcontinent, and western Pacific islands; in temperate zones, incidence increases in summer and early fall; in tropics, year-round incidence	Travelers staying for more than 30 days in high-risk rural areas; staying outdoors during transmission season; vaccine series	10 days
Cholera*	Certain undeveloped countries	If required by local authorities, one dose usually suffices; primary series only for those living in high-risk areas under poor sanitary conditions or those with compromised gastric defense mechanisms (achlorhydria, antacid therapy, previous ulcer surgery); booster every 6 mo	Probably 30 days
Plague	Africa, Asia, and Americas in rural mountainous or upland areas	Travelers whose research or field activities bring them in contact with rodents; vaccine series/booster; consider taking tetracycline (500 mg four times a day) for chemoprophylaxis (inferred from clinical experience in treating plague)	Probably 30 days

From Noble J: *Primary care medicine*, ed 3, St Louis, 2001, Mosby.
IG, Immune globulin; *MMR*, measles-mumps-rubella.
*Only yellow fever vaccine is required for entry by any country; cholera vaccine may be required by some local authorities. Meningococcus vaccine is required for pilgrims to Mecca, in Saudi Arabia, during Hajj. However, it is important to follow Centers for Disease Control and Prevention (CDC) recommendations for all vaccines to prevent disease. If a required vaccine is contraindicated or withheld for any reason, attempts should be made to obtain a waiver from the country's consulate or embassy.
†Because areas affected can change, and for more specific details, consult the CDC's traveler's hotline.

Recommendations and Implementation Strategies for Hepatitis B Vaccination of Adults

BOX 5-1 Adults Recommended to Receive Hepatitis B Vaccination

Persons at Risk for Infection by Sexual Exposure
Sex partners of persons who are HBsAg positive
Sexually active persons who are not in a long-term, mutually monogamous relationship (e.g., persons who have had more than one sex partner during the previous 6 months)
Persons seeking evaluation or treatment for a sexually transmitted disease
Men who have sex with men

Persons at Risk for Infection by Percutaneous or Mucosal Exposure to Blood
Current or recent users of injection drugs
Household contacts of persons who are HBsAg positive

Residents and staff of facilities for developmentally disabled persons
Health care and public safety workers with reasonably anticipated risk for exposure to blood or blood-contaminated body fluids
Persons with end-stage renal disease, including predialysis, hemodialysis, peritoneal dialysis, and home dialysis patients

Others
International travelers to regions with high or intermediate levels (HBsAg prevalence of ≥2%) of endemic HBV infection
Persons with chronic liver disease
Persons with HIV infection
All other persons seeking protection from HBV infection

From CDC: A comprehensive immunization strategy to eliminate transmission of hepatitis B virus infection in the United States: recommendations of the Advisory Committee on Immunization Practices (ACIP), *MMWR* 55(RR-16):15, 2006.
HBsAg, Hepatitis B surface antigen; *HBV,* hepatitis B virus.

BOX 5-2 Hepatitis B Vaccine Schedules for Adults (Aged ≥20 yr)[1]

0, 1, and 6 months
0, 1, and 4 months
0, 2, and 4 months
0, 1, 2, and 12 months[2]

From CDC: A comprehensive immunization strategy to eliminate transmission of hepatitis B virus infection in the United States: recommendations of the Advisory Committee on Immunization Practices (ACIP), *MMWR* 55(RR-16):15, 2006.
[1]All schedules are applicable to single-antigen hepatitis B vaccines; Twinrix (combined hepatitis A and hepatitis B vaccine) may be administered at 0, 1, and 6 months.
[2]A 4-dose schedule of Engerix-B is licensed for all age groups.

TABLE 5-25 Recommended Doses of Currently Licensed Formulations of Adult Hepatitis B Vaccine by Group and Vaccine Type

| | SINGLE-ANTIGEN VACCINE | | | | COMBINATION VACCINE | |
| | RECOMBIVAX HB[a] | | ENGERIX-B[b] | | TWINRIX[b,c] | |
Group	Dose (µg)[d]	Vol. (ml)	Dose (µg)[d]	Vol. (ml)	Dose (µg)[d]	Vol. (ml)
Adults (aged ≥20 yr)	10	1.0	20	1.0	20	1.0
Hemodialysis patients and other immunocompromised persons aged ≥20 yr	40[e]	1.0	40[f]	2.0	—[g]	—

From Centers for Disease Control and Prevention: A comprehensive immunization strategy to eliminate transmission of hepatitis B virus infection in the United States: recommendations of the Advisory Committee on Immunization Practices (ACIP), *MMWR* 55(RR-16):10, 2006.

HB, Hepatitis B.

[a]Merck & Co., Inc., Whitehouse Station, New Jersey.

[b]GlaxoSmithKline Biologicals, Rixensart, Belgium.

[c]Combined hepatitis A and hepatitis B vaccine, recommended for persons aged >18 yr who are at increased risk for both hepatitis B virus and hepatitis A virus infections.

[d]Recombinant hepatitis B surface antigen protein dose.

[e]Dialysis formulation administered on a 3-dose schedule at 0, 1, and 6 mo.

[f]Two 1.0-ml doses administered in 1 or 2 injections on a 4-dose schedule at 0, 1, 2, and 6 mo.

[g]Not applicable.

TABLE 5-26 Recommended HIV/AIDS, Sexually Transmitted Disease (STD), and Viral Hepatitis Prevention Services by Risk Population

Risk Population[a]	Recommended Services
High-Risk Heterosexuals	
Persons seeking sexually transmitted disease evaluation or treatment	Hepatitis B vaccination
	Testing for HIV infection[b]
	Testing for syphilis, gonorrhea, and chlamydia, as clinically indicated[c]
Sexually active men not in a long-term, mutually monogamous relationship	Hepatitis B vaccination
	Annual testing for HIV infection[b,d]
Sexually active women not in a long-term, mutually monogamous relationship	Hepatitis B vaccination[e]
	Annual testing for HIV infection[b,d]
	Annual testing for chlamydia (NOTE: Also recommended for all sexually active females aged <25 yr)[c]
Men Who Have Sex with Men (MSM)	
All MSM	Hepatitis A vaccination
	Hepatitis B vaccination[e]
Sexually active MSM not in a long-term, mutually monogamous relationship	Hepatitis A vaccination
	Hepatitis B vaccination[e]
	Annual testing for HIV infection[b]
	Annual testing for syphilis, gonorrhea, and chlamydia[c]
Injection-Drug Users	
	Hepatitis A vaccination[f]
	Hepatitis B vaccination
	Testing for hepatitis C virus infection[g]
	Annual testing for HIV infection[b]
	Substance-abuse treatment[h]

From Centers for Disease Control and Prevention (CDC): A comprehensive immunization strategy to eliminate transmission of hepatitis B virus infection in the United States: recommendations of the Advisory Committee on Immunization Practices (ACIP), *MMWR* 55(RR-16):17, 2006.

[a]Testing for HIV infection, chlamydia, gonorrhea, syphilis, and hepatitis B surface antigen also is recommended for pregnant women. (CDC: Revised recommendations for HIV testing of adults, adolescents, and pregnant women in health care settings, *MMWR* 55[RR-14], 2006; CDC: Sexually transmitted diseases treatment guidelines, *MMWR* 55[RR-11], 2006; CDC: A comprehensive immunization strategy to eliminate transmission of hepatitis B virus infection in the United States: recommendations of the Advisory Committee on Immunization Practices [ACIP]. Part 1: immunization of infants, children, and adolescents, *MMWR* 54[RR-16], 2005.)

[b]CDC: Revised recommendations for HIV testing of adults, adolescents, and pregnant women in health care settings, *MMWR* 55(RR-14), 2006.

[c]CDC: Sexually transmitted diseases treatment guidelines 2006, *MMWR* 55(RR-11), 2006.

[d]HIV screening is recommended for all persons aged 13-64 yr. Repeat screening is recommended at least annually for persons likely to be at high risk for HIV infection, including MSM or heterosexuals who themselves or whose sex partners have had more than one partner since their most recent HIV test.

[e]Hepatitis B vaccination is recommended for persons who have had more than one sex partner during the previous 6 mo.

[f]Prevention of hepatitis A through active or passive immunization: recommendations of the Advisory Committee on Immunization Practices (ACIP), *MMWR* 55(RR-7), 2006.

[g]CDC: Recommendations for prevention and control of hepatitis C virus (HCV) infection and HCV-related chronic disease, *MMWR* 47(RR-19), 1998. Recommended frequency of testing for hepatitis C virus infection has not been determined.

[h]CDC: *Substance abuse treatment for injection drug users: a strategy with many benefits,* Atlanta, 2002, U.S. Department of Health and Human Services, CDC. Available at http://www.cdc.gov/idu/facts/treatment.htm.

TABLE 5-27 Guidelines for Postexposure Prophylaxis* of Persons with Nonoccupational Exposures† to Blood or Body Fluids That Contain Blood by Exposure Type and Vaccination Status

	TREATMENT	
Exposure	Unvaccinated Person‡	Previously Vaccinated Person§
HBsAg-Positive Source		
Percutaneous (e.g., bite or needlestick) or mucosal exposure to HBsAg-positive blood or body fluids	Administer hepatitis B vaccine series and hepatitis B immune globulin (HBIG)	Administer hepatitis B vaccine booster dose
Sex or needle-sharing contact with a person who is HBsAg positive	Administer hepatitis B vaccine series and HBIG	Administer hepatitis B vaccine booster dose
Victim of sexual assault/abuse by a perpetrator who is HBsAg positive	Administer hepatitis B vaccine series and HBIG	Administer hepatitis B vaccine booster dose
Source with Unknown HBsAg Status		
Victim of sexual assault/abuse by a perpetrator with unknown HBsAg status	Administer hepatitis B vaccine series	No treatment
Percutaneous (e.g., bite or needlestick) or mucosal exposure to potentially infectious blood or body fluids from a source with unknown HBsAg status	Administer hepatitis B vaccine series	No treatment
Sexual or needle-sharing contact with person with unknown HBsAg status	Administer hepatitis B vaccine series	No treatment

From Centers for Disease Control and Prevention: A comprehensive immunization strategy to eliminate transmission of hepatitis B virus infection in the United States: recommendations of the Advisory Committee on Immunization Practices (ACIP), *MMWR* 55(RR-16):30, 2006.

HBsAg, Hepatitis B surface antigen.

*When indicated, immunoprophylaxis should be initiated as soon as possible, preferably within 24 hours. Studies are limited on the maximum interval after exposure during which postexposure prophylaxis is effective, but the interval is unlikely to exceed 7 days for percutaneous exposures or 14 days for sexual exposures. The hepatitis B vaccine series should be completed.

†These guidelines apply to nonoccupational exposures. Guidelines for management of occupational exposures have been published separately and also can be used for management of nonoccupational exposures if feasible.

‡A person who is in the process of being vaccinated but has not completed the vaccine series should complete the series and receive treatment as indicated.

§A person who has written documentation of a complete hepatitis B vaccine series and did not receive postvaccination testing.

TABLE 5-28 Typical Interpretation of Serologic Test Results for Hepatitis B Virus Infection

SEROLOGIC MARKER				
HBsAg	Total Anti-HBc	IgM Anti-HBc	Anti-HBs	Interpretation
−*	−	−	−	Never Infected
+†‡	−	−	−	Early acute infection; transient (up to 18 days) after vaccination
+	+	+	−	Acute infection
−	+	+	+ or −	Acute resolving infection
−	+	−	+	Recovered from past infection and immune
+	+	−	−	Chronic infection
−	+	−	−	False-positive (i.e., susceptible), past infection, "low-level" chronic infection,§ or passive transfer of anti-HBc to infant born to mother who is HBsAg positive
−	−	−	+	Immune if concentration is >10 mIU/ml after vaccine series completion‖; passive transfer after hepatitis B immune globulin administration

From Centers for Disease Control and Prevention: A comprehensive immunization strategy to eliminate transmission of hepatitis B virus infection in the United States: recommendations of the Advisory Committee on Immunization Practices (ACIP), *MMWR* 55(RR-16):4, 2006.

HBc, Antibody to hepatitis B core antigen; *HBs*, antibody to HBsAg; *HBsAg*, hepatitis B surface antigen; *Ig*, immunoglobulin.

*Negative test result.

†Positive test result.

‡To ensure that an HBsAg-positive test result is not a false-positive, samples with reactive HBsAg results should be tested with a licensed neutralizing confirmatory test if recommended in the manufacturer's package insert.

§Persons positive only for anti-HBc are unlikely to be infectious except under unusual circumstances in which they are the source for direct percutaneous exposure of susceptible recipients to large quantities of virus (e.g., blood transfusion or organ transplant).

‖Milli-international units per milliliter.

Hepatitis A Prophylaxis

TABLE 5-29   Recommended Dosages of Hepatitis A Immune Globulin

Setting	Duration of Coverage	Dose
Preexposure prophylaxis	Short term (<3 mo)	0.02 ml/kg
	Long term (3-5 mo)*	0.06 ml/kg
Postexposure prophylaxis	—	0.02 ml/kg

NOTE: Immune globulin should be administered intramuscularly into the deltoid or gluteal muscle in children younger than 24 mo; it may be administered in the anterolateral thigh muscle.
*Repeat every 5 mo if continued exposure to hepatitis A virus occurs.
Modified from Centers for Disease Control and Prevention: Prevention of hepatitis A through active or passive immunization: recommendations of the Advisory Committee on Immunization Practices (ACIP), *MMWR* 55(RR-07):9, 2006.

TABLE 5-30   Licensed Dosages of Hepatitis A Vaccines

Vaccine	Patient's Age	Dose	Volume (ml)	Number of Doses	Schedule (mo)*
Hepatitis A vaccine, inactivated (Havrix)	12 mo to 18 yr	720 EL.U.	0.5	2	0, 6-12
	≥19 yr	1440 EL.U.	1.0	2	0, 6-12
Hepatitis A vaccine, inactivated (Vaqta)	12 mo to 18 yr	25 U	0.5	2	0, 6-18
	≥19 yr	50 U	1.0	2	0, 6-18
Combined hepatitis A and hepatitis B vaccine (Twinrix)	≥18 yr	720 EL.U. of hepatitis A antigen and 20 mcg of hepatitis B surface antigen protein	1.0	3	0, 1, and 6

Modified from Centers for Disease Control and Prevention: Prevention of hepatitis A through active or passive immunization: recommendations of the Advisory Committee on Immunization Practices (ACIP), *MMWR* 55(RR-07):10, 2006.
*Zero represents the timing of the initial dose; subsequent numbers represent months after the initial dose.

Influenza Treatment and Prophylaxis

| BOX 5-3 | Summary of Seasonal Influenza Vaccination Recommendations |

Children	Adults

All children aged 6 months to 18 years should be vaccinated annually. Children and adolescents at higher risk for influenza complications should continue to be a focus for vaccination efforts as providers and programs transition to routinely vaccinating all children and adolescents, including those who:
 	
  are aged 6 months to 4 years (59 months)
  have chronic pulmonary (including asthma), cardiovascular (except hypertension), renal, hepatic, cognitive, neurologic/neuromuscular, hematologic, or metabolic disorders (including diabetes mellitus)
  are immunosuppressed (including immunosuppression caused by medications or by human immunodeficiency virus)
  are receiving long-term aspirin therapy and therefore might be at risk for experiencing Reye's syndrome after influenza virus infection
  are residents of long-term care facilities
  will be pregnant during the influenza season
Note: Children aged <6 months cannot receive influenza vaccination. Household and other close contacts (e.g., day-care providers) of children aged <6 months, including older children and adolescents, should be vaccinated.
	Annual vaccination against influenza is recommended for any adult who wants to reduce the risk of becoming ill with influenza or of transmitting it to others. Vaccination is recommended for all adults without contraindications in the following groups, because these persons either are at higher risk for influenza complications, or are close contacts of the persons at higher risk:
	
	• persons aged ≥50 years
	• women who will be pregnant during the influenza season
	• persons who have chronic pulmonary (including asthma), cardiovascular (except hypertension), renal, hepatic, cognitive, neurologic/neuromuscular, hematologic, or metabolic disorders (including diabetes mellitus)
	• persons who have immunosuppression (including immunosuppression caused by medications or by human immunodeficiency virus)
	• residents of nursing homes and other long-term care facilities
	• health care personnel
	• household contacts and caregivers of children aged <5 years and adults aged ≥50 years, with particular emphasis on vaccinating contacts of children aged <6 months
	• household contacts and caregivers of persons with medical conditions that put them at higher risk for severe complications from influenza

Modified from *MMWR* 58:(RR-8), 2009.

RECOMMENDED VACCINES FOR DIFFERENT AGE GROUPS

When vaccinating children aged 6 to 35 months with TIV, health care providers should use TIV that has been licensed by the FDA for this age group (i.e., TIV manufactured by Sanofi Pasteur [FluZone]). TIV from Novartis (Fluvirin) is FDA approved in the United States for use among persons aged 4 years and older. TIV from GlaxoSmithKline (Fluarix and FluLaval) or CSL Biotherapies (Afluria) is labeled for use in persons aged 18 years and older because data to demonstrate efficacy among younger persons have not been provided to the FDA. LAIV from MedImmune (FluMist) is licensed for use by healthy, nonpregnant persons aged 2 to 49 years. A vaccine dose does not need to be repeated if inadvertently administered to a person who does not have an age indication for the vaccine formulation given. Expanded age and risk group indications for licensed vaccines are likely over the next several years, and vaccination providers should be alert to these changes. In addition, several new vaccine formulations are being evaluated in immunogenicity and efficacy trials; when licensed, these new products will increase the influenza vaccine supply and provide additional vaccine choices for practitioners and their patients.

INFLUENZA VACCINES AND USE OF INFLUENZA ANTIVIRAL MEDICATIONS

Administration of TIV and influenza antivirals during the same medical visit is acceptable. The effect on safety and effectiveness of LAIV coadministration with influenza antiviral medications has not been studied. However, because influenza antivirals reduce replication of influenza viruses, LAIV should not be administered until 48 hours after cessation of influenza antiviral therapy, and influenza antiviral medications should not be administered for 2 weeks after receipt of LAIV. Persons receiving antivirals within the period 2 days before to 14 days after vaccination with LAIV should be revaccinated at a later date.

PERSONS WHO SHOULD NOT BE VACCINATED WITH TIV

TIV should not be administered to persons known to have anaphylactic hypersensitivity to eggs or other components of the influenza vaccine. Prophylactic use of antiviral agents is an option for preventing influenza among such persons. Information about vaccine components is located in package inserts from each manufacturer. Persons with moderate to severe acute febrile illness usually should not be vaccinated until their symptoms have abated. However, minor illnesses with or without fever do not contraindicate use of influenza vaccine. Guillain-Barré syndrome within 6 weeks after a previous dose of TIV is considered a precaution for use of TIV.

CONSIDERATIONS WHEN USING LAIV

LAIV is an option for vaccination of healthy, nonpregnant persons aged 2 to 49 years, including health care providers and other close contacts of high-risk persons (except severely immunocompromised persons who require care in a protected environment). No preference is indicated for LAIV or TIV when considering vaccination of healthy, nonpregnant persons aged 2 to 49 years. Use of the term *healthy* in this recommendation refers to persons who do not have any of the underlying medical conditions that confer high risk for severe complications (see "Persons Who Should Not Be Vaccinated with LAIV"). However, during periods when inactivated vaccine is in short supply, use of LAIV is encouraged when feasible for eligible persons (including health care providers) because use of LAIV by these persons might increase availability of TIV for persons in groups targeted for vaccination but who cannot receive LAIV. Possible advantages of LAIV include its potential to induce a broad mucosal and systemic immune response in children, its ease of administration, and possibly increased acceptability of an intranasal rather than intramuscular route of administration.

If the vaccine recipient sneezes after administration, the dose should not be repeated. However, if nasal congestion is present that might impede delivery of the vaccine to the nasopharyngeal mucosa, deferral of administration should be considered until resolution of the illness, or TIV should be administered instead. No data exist about concomitant use of nasal corticosteroids or other intranasal medications.

Although FDA licensure of LAIV excludes children aged 2 to 4 years with a history of asthma or recurrent wheezing, the precise risk, if any, of wheezing caused by LAIV among these children is unknown because experience with LAIV among these young children is limited. Young children might not have a history of recurrent wheezing if their exposure to respiratory viruses has been limited because of their age. Certain children might have a history of wheezing with respiratory illnesses but have not had asthma diagnosed. The following screening recommendations should be used to assist persons who administer influenza vaccines in providing the appropriate vaccine for children aged 2 to 4 years.

Clinicians and vaccination programs should screen for possible reactive airways diseases when considering use of LAIV for children aged 2 to 4 years and should avoid use of this vaccine in children with asthma or a recent wheezing episode. Health care providers should consult the medical record, when available, to identify children aged 2 to 4 years with asthma or recurrent wheezing that might indicate asthma. In addition, to identify children who might be at greater risk for asthma and possibly at increased risk for wheezing after receiving LAIV, parents or caregivers of children aged 2 to 4 years should be asked, "In the past 12 months, has a health care provider ever told you that your child had wheezing or asthma?" Children whose parents or caregivers answer "yes" to this question and children who have asthma or who had a wheezing episode noted in the medical record during the preceding 12 months should not receive LAIV. TIV is available for use in children with asthma or possible reactive airways diseases.

LAIV can be administered to persons with minor acute illnesses (e.g., diarrhea or mild upper respiratory tract infection with or without fever). However, if nasal congestion is present that might impede delivery of the vaccine to the nasopharyngeal mucosa, deferral of administration should be considered until resolution of the illness.

PERSONS WHO SHOULD NOT BE VACCINATED WITH LAIV

The effectiveness or safety of LAIV is not known for the following groups, who should not be vaccinated with LAIV:

- Persons with a history of hypersensitivity, including anaphylaxis, to any of the components of LAIV or eggs

- Persons younger than 2 years or aged 50 years or older
- Persons with any of the underlying medical conditions that serve as an indication for routine influenza vaccination, including asthma, reactive airways disease, or other chronic disorders of the pulmonary or cardiovascular systems; other underlying medical conditions, including metabolic diseases such as diabetes, renal dysfunction, and hemoglobinopathies; or known or suspected immunodeficiency diseases or immunosuppressed states
- Children aged 2 to 4 years whose parents or caregivers report that a health care provider has told them during the preceding 12 months that their child had wheezing or asthma, or whose medical record indicates a wheezing episode has occurred during the preceding 12 months
- Children or adolescents receiving aspirin or other salicylates (because of the association of Reye syndrome with wild-type influenza virus infection)
- Persons with a history of Guillain-Barré syndrome after influenza vaccination
- Pregnant women

CONCURRENT ADMINISTRATION OF INFLUENZA VACCINE WITH OTHER VACCINES

Use of LAIV concurrently with measles, mumps, rubella (MMR) alone, and MMR and varicella vaccine among children aged 12 to 15 months has been studied, and no interference with immunogenicity to antigens in any of the vaccines was observed. Among adults aged 50 years or older, the safety and immunogenicity of zoster vaccine and TIV were similar whether administered simultaneously or spaced 4 weeks apart. In the absence of specific data indicating interference, following ACIP's general recommendations for vaccination is prudent. Inactivated vaccines do not interfere with the immune response to other inactivated vaccines or to live vaccines. Inactivated or live vaccines can be administered simultaneously with LAIV. However, after administration of a live vaccine, at least 4 weeks should pass before another live vaccine is administered.

TABLE 5-31 Live, Attenuated Influenza Vaccine (LAIV) Compared with Inactivated Influenza Vaccine (TIV) for Seasonal Influenza, United States Formulations

Factor	LAIV	TIV
Route of administration	Intranasal spray	Intramuscular injection
Type of vaccine	Live virus	Noninfectious virus (i.e., inactivated)
Number of included virus strains	3 (2 influenza A, 1 influenza B)	3 (2 influenza A, 1 influenza B)
Vaccine virus strains updated	Annually	Annually
Frequency of administration	Annually*	Annually*
Approved age	Persons aged 2-49 yr	Persons aged ≥6 mo
Interval between 2 doses recommended for children aged ≥6 mo to 8 yr who are receiving influenza vaccine for the first time	4 wk	4 wk
Can be administered to persons with medical risk factors for influenza-related complications[†]	No	Yes
Can be administered to children with asthma or children aged 2-4 yr with wheezing during the preceding year[§]	No	Yes
Can be administered to family members or close contacts of immunosuppressed persons not requiring a protected environment	Yes	Yes
Can be administered to family members or close contacts of immunosuppressed persons requiring a protected environment (e.g., hematopoietic stem cell transplant recipient)	No	Yes
Can be administered to family members or close contacts of persons at high risk but not severely immunosuppressed	Yes	Yes
Can be simultaneously administered with other vaccines	Yes[¶]	Yes**
If not simultaneously administered, can be administered within 4 wk of another live vaccine	Prudent to space 4 wk apart	Yes
If not simultaneously administered, can be administered within 4 wk of an inactivated vaccine	Yes	Yes

Modified from *MMWR* 56(RR-6), 2007.

*Children aged 6 months to 8 years who have never received influenza vaccine before should receive 2 doses. Those who only receive 1 dose in their first year of vaccination should receive 2 doses in the following year, spaced 4 weeks apart.

[†]Persons at higher risk for complications of influenza infection because of underlying medical conditions should not receive LAIV. Persons at higher risk for complications of influenza infection because of underlying medical conditions include adults and children with chronic disorders of the pulmonary or cardiovascular systems; adults and children with chronic metabolic diseases (including diabetes mellitus), renal dysfunction, hemoglobinopathies, or immunosuppression; children and adolescents receiving long-term aspirin therapy (at risk for developing Reye's syndrome after wild-type influenza infection); persons who have any condition (e.g., cognitive dysfunction, spinal cord injuries, seizure disorders, or other neuromuscular disorders) that can compromise respiratory function or the handling of respiratory secretions or that can increase the risk for aspiration; pregnant women; and residents of nursing homes and other chronic-care facilities that house persons with chronic medical conditions.

[§]Clinicians and immunization programs should screen for possible reactive airways diseases when considering use of LAIV for children aged 2-4 years and should avoid use of this vaccine in children with asthma or a recent wheezing episode. Health care providers should consult the medical record, when available, to identify children aged 2-4 years with asthma or recurrent wheezing that might indicate asthma. In addition, to identify children who might be at greater risk for asthma and possibly at increased risk for wheezing after receiving LAIV, parents or caregivers of children aged 2-4 years should be asked: "In the past 12 months, has a health care provider ever told you that your child had wheezing or asthma?" Children whose parents or caregivers answer "yes" to this question and children who have asthma or who had a wheezing episode noted in the medical record during the preceding 12 months should not receive LAIV.

[¶]LAIV coadministration has been evaluated systematically only among children aged 12-15 months who received measles, mumps, and rubella vaccine or varicella vaccine.

**TIV coadministration has been evaluated systematically only among adults who received pneumococcal polysaccharide or zoster vaccine.

INDICATIONS FOR USE OF ANTIVIRALS

PERSONS FOR WHOM ANTIVIRAL TREATMENT SHOULD BE CONSIDERED

If possible, antiviral treatment should be started within 48 hours of influenza illness onset. The effectiveness of initiating antiviral treatment more than 48 hours after illness onset has not been established. Persons for whom antiviral treatment should be considered include:

- Persons hospitalized with laboratory-confirmed influenza (limited data suggest benefit even for persons whose antiviral treatment is initiated more than 48 hours after illness onset)
- Persons with laboratory-confirmed influenza pneumonia
- Persons with laboratory-confirmed influenza and bacterial coinfection
- Persons with laboratory-confirmed influenza infection who are at higher risk for influenza complications
- Persons presenting to medical care with laboratory-confirmed influenza within 48 hours of influenza illness onset who want to decrease the duration or severity of their symptoms and transmission of influenza to others at higher risk for complications

PERSONS FOR WHOM ANTIVIRAL CHEMOPROPHYLAXIS SHOULD BE CONSIDERED DURING PERIODS OF INCREASED INFLUENZA ACTIVITY IN THE COMMUNITY

- Persons at high risk during the 2 weeks after influenza vaccination (after the second dose for children younger than 9 years who have not previously been vaccinated) if influenza viruses are circulating in the community
- Persons at high risk for whom influenza vaccine is contraindicated
- Family members or health care providers who are unvaccinated and are likely to have ongoing, close exposure to persons at high risk or unvaccinated persons or infants younger than 6 months
- Persons and their family members and close contacts and health care workers when circulating strains of influenza virus in the community are not matched with vaccine strains
- Persons with immune deficiencies or those who might not respond to vaccination (e.g., persons infected with HIV or other immunosuppressed conditions or who are receiving immunosuppressive medications)
- Unvaccinated staff and persons during response to an outbreak in a closed institutional setting with residents at high risk (e.g., extended-care facilities)

Modified from *MMWR* 57(RR-7), 2008.

NOTE: Recommended antiviral medications (neuraminidase inhibitors) are not licensed for chemoprophylaxis of children younger than 1 year (oseltamivir) or younger than 5 years (zanamivir). Updates or supplements to these recommendations (e.g., expanded age or risk group indications for licensed vaccines) might be required. Health care providers should be alert to announcements of recommendation updates and should check the CDC influenza website periodically for additional information (http://www.cdc.gov/flu).

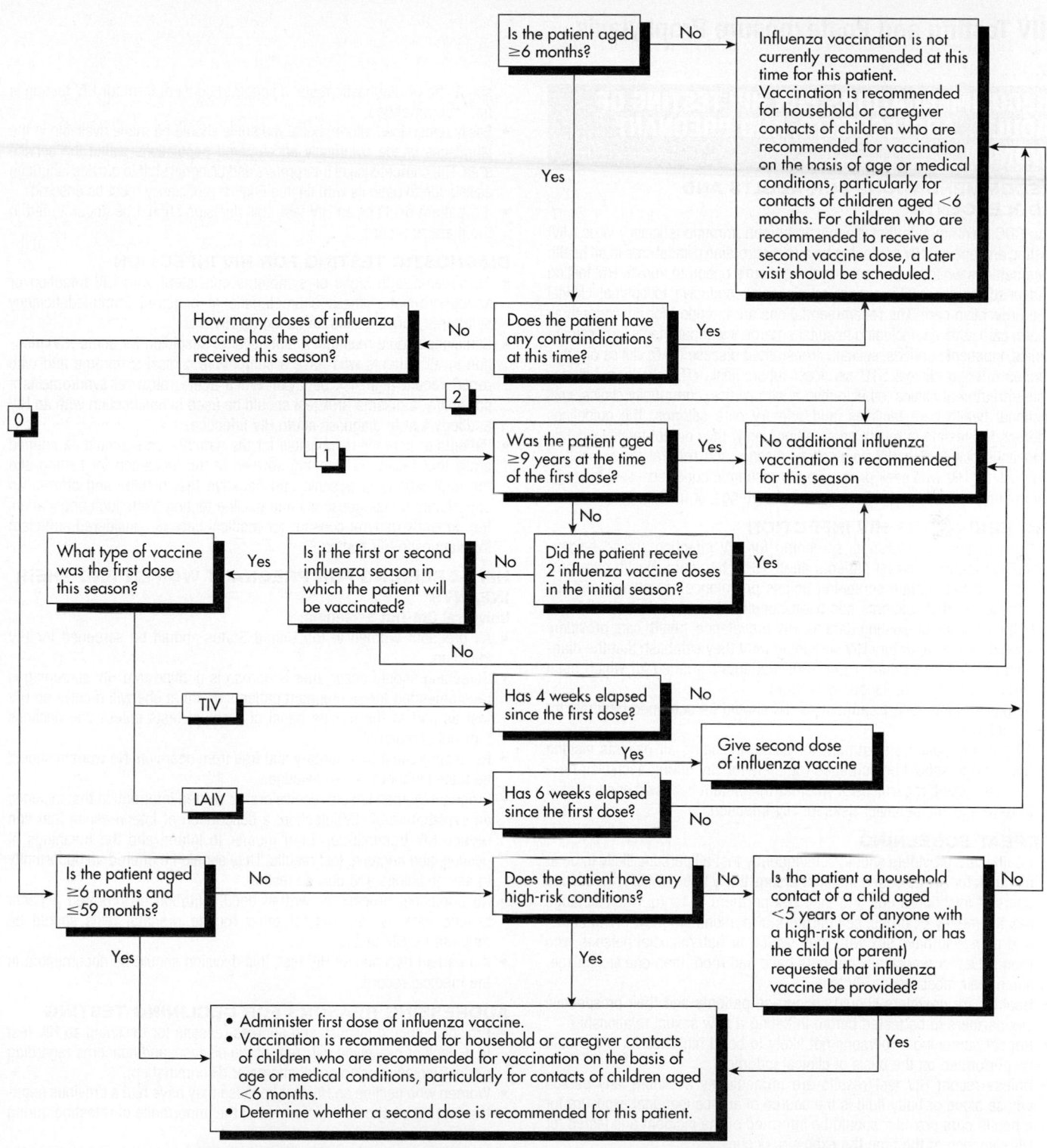

FIGURE 5-6 Algorithm for determining recommended influenza immunization actions for children. *TIV,* Trivalent inactivated influenza vaccine; *LAIV,* Live attenuated influenza vaccine. (Modified with permission from the American Academy of Pediatrics' Committee on Infectious Diseases: Prevention of influenza: recommendations for influenza immunization of children, 2006-2007, *Pediatrics* 119:846-51, 2007.)

Clinical Practice Guidelines

V

HIV Testing and Postexposure Prophylaxis

RECOMMENDATIONS FOR HIV TESTING OF ADULTS, ADOLESCENTS, AND PREGNANT WOMEN

RECOMMENDATIONS FOR ADULTS AND ADOLESCENTS[4]

The CDC recommends that diagnostic human immunodeficiency virus (HIV) testing and opt-out HIV screening be a part of routine clinical care in all health care settings while also preserving the patient's option to decline HIV testing and ensuring a provider-patient relationship conducive to optimal clinical and preventive care. The recommendations are intended for providers in all health care settings, including hospital emergency departments, urgent-care clinics, inpatient services, sexually transmitted disease (STD) clinics or other venues offering clinical STD services, tuberculosis (TB) clinics, substance abuse treatment clinics, other public health clinics, community clinics, correctional health care facilities, and primary care settings. The guidelines address HIV testing in health care settings only; they do not modify existing guidelines concerning HIV counseling, testing, and referral for persons at high risk for HIV who seek or receive HIV testing in nonclinical settings (e.g., community-based organizations, outreach settings, or mobile vans).

SCREENING FOR HIV INFECTION
- In all health care settings, screening for HIV infection should be performed routinely for all patients aged 13 to 64 years. Health care providers should initiate screening unless prevalence of undiagnosed HIV infection in their patients has been documented to be less than 0.1%. In the absence of existing data for HIV prevalence, health care providers should initiate voluntary HIV screening until they establish that the diagnostic yield is less than 1 per 1000 patients screened, at which point such screening is no longer warranted.
- All patients initiating treatment for TB should be screened routinely for HIV infection.
- All patients seeking treatment for STDs, including all patients visiting STD clinics, should be screened routinely for HIV during each visit for a new complaint, regardless of whether the patient is known or suspected to have specific behavior risks for HIV infection.

REPEAT SCREENING
- Health care providers should subsequently test all persons likely to be at high risk for HIV at least annually. Persons likely to be at high risk include users of injection drugs and their sex partners, persons who exchange sex for money or drugs, sex partners of persons who are HIV infected, and men who have sex with men (MSM) or heterosexual persons who themselves or whose sex partners have had more than one sex partner since their most recent HIV test.
- Health care providers should encourage patients and their prospective sex partners to be tested before initiating a new sexual relationship.
- Repeat screening of persons not likely to be at high risk for HIV should be performed on the basis of clinical judgment.
- Unless recent HIV test results are immediately available, any person whose blood or body fluid is the source of an occupational exposure for a health care provider should be informed of the incident and tested for HIV infection at the time the exposure occurs.

CONSENT AND PRETEST INFORMATION
- Screening should be voluntary and undertaken only with the patient's knowledge and understanding that HIV testing is planned.
- Patients should be informed orally or in writing that HIV testing will be performed unless they decline (opt-out screening). Oral or written information should include an explanation of HIV infection and the meanings of positive and negative test results, and the patient should be offered an opportunity to ask questions and decline testing. With such notification, consent for HIV screening should be incorporated into the patient's general informed consent for medical care on the same basis as are other

screening or diagnostic tests; a separate consent form for HIV testing is not recommended.
- Easily understood informational materials should be made available in the languages of the commonly encountered populations within the service area. The competence of interpreters and bilingual staff to provide language assistance to patients with limited English proficiency must be ensured.
- If a patient declines an HIV test, this decision should be documented in the medical record.

DIAGNOSTIC TESTING FOR HIV INFECTION
- All patients with signs or symptoms consistent with HIV infection or an opportunistic illness characteristic of acquired immunodeficiency syndrome (AIDS) should be tested for HIV.
- Clinicians should maintain a high level of suspicion for acute HIV infection in all patients who have a compatible clinical syndrome and who report recent high-risk behavior. When acute retroviral syndrome is a possibility, a plasma RNA test should be used in conjunction with an HIV antibody test to diagnose acute HIV infection.
- Patients or persons responsible for the patient's care should be notified orally that testing is planned, advised of the indication for testing and the implications of positive and negative test results, and offered an opportunity to ask questions and decline testing. With such notification, the patient's general consent for medical care is considered sufficient for diagnostic HIV testing.

HIV SCREENING FOR PREGNANT WOMEN AND THEIR INFANTS*
Universal Opt-Out Screening:
- All pregnant women in the United States should be screened for HIV infection.
- Screening should occur after a woman is notified that HIV screening is recommended for all pregnant patients and that she will receive an HIV test as part of the routine panel of prenatal tests unless she declines (opt-out screening).
- HIV testing must be voluntary and free from coercion. No woman should be tested without her knowledge.
- Pregnant women should receive oral or written information that includes an explanation of HIV infection, a description of interventions that can reduce HIV transmission from mother to infant, and the meanings of positive and negative test results. They should be offered an opportunity to ask questions and decline testing.
- No additional process or written documentation of informed consent beyond what is required for other routine prenatal tests should be required for HIV testing.
- If a patient declines an HIV test, this decision should be documented in the medical record.

ADDRESSING REASONS FOR DECLINING TESTING
- Providers should discuss and address reasons for declining an HIV test (e.g., lack of perceived risk, fear of the disease, and concerns regarding partner violence or potential stigma or discrimination).
- Women who decline an HIV test because they have had a previous negative test result should be informed of the importance of retesting during each pregnancy.
- Logistical reasons for not testing (e.g., scheduling) should be resolved.
- Certain women who initially decline an HIV test might accept at a later date, especially if their concerns are discussed. Certain women will continue to decline testing, and their decisions should be respected and documented in the medical record.

Timing of HIV Testing:
- To promote informed and timely therapeutic decisions, health care providers should test women for HIV as early as possible during each pregnancy. Women who decline the test early in prenatal care should be encouraged to be tested at a subsequent visit.
- A second HIV test during the third trimester, preferably less than 36 weeks of gestation, is cost effective even in areas of low HIV prevalence

---

[4]Data from *MMWR* 57(RR-10), 2008.

and may be considered for all pregnant women. A second HIV test during the third trimester is recommended for women who meet one or more of the following criteria:

1. Women who receive health care in jurisdictions with elevated incidence of HIV or AIDS among women aged 15 to 45 years. In 2004, these jurisdictions included Alabama, Connecticut, Delaware, the District of Columbia, Florida, Georgia, Illinois, Louisiana, Maryland, Massachusetts, Mississippi, Nevada, New Jersey, New York, North Carolina, Pennsylvania, Puerto Rico, Rhode Island, South Carolina, Tennessee, Texas, and Virginia.[5]

2. Women who receive health care in facilities in which prenatal screening identifies at least one pregnant woman who is infected with HIV per 1000 women screened.

3. Women who are known to be at high risk for acquiring HIV (e.g., users of injection drugs and their sex partners, women who exchange sex for money or drugs, women who are sex partners of persons who are infected with HIV, and women who have had a new or more than one sex partner during this pregnancy).

4. Women who have signs or symptoms consistent with acute HIV infection. When acute retroviral syndrome is a possibility, a plasma RNA test should be used in conjunction with an HIV antibody test to diagnose acute HIV infection.

Rapid Testing During Labor:

- Any woman with undocumented HIV status at the time of labor should be screened with a rapid HIV test unless she declines (opt-out screening).

---

[5]A second HIV test in the third trimester is as cost effective as other common health interventions when HIV incidence among women of childbearing age is =17 HIV cases per 100,000 person-years. In 2004, in jurisdictions with available data on HIV case rates, a rate of 17 new HIV diagnoses per year per 100,000 women aged 15 to 45 years was associated with an AIDS case rate of at least nine AIDS diagnoses per year per 100,000 women aged 15 to 45 years (CDC, unpublished data, 2005). As of 2004, the jurisdictions listed above exceeded these thresholds. The list of specific jurisdictions where a second test in the third trimester is recommended will be updated periodically based on surveillance data.

- Reasons for declining a rapid test should be explored (see "Addressing Reasons for Declining Testing").
- Immediate initiation of appropriate antiretroviral prophylaxis should be recommended to women on the basis of a reactive rapid test result without waiting for the result of a confirmatory test.

Postpartum/Newborn Testing:

- When a woman's HIV status is still unknown at the time of delivery, she should be screened immediately postpartum with a rapid HIV test unless she declines (opt-out screening).
- When the mother's HIV status is unknown postpartum, rapid testing of the newborn as soon as possible after birth is recommended so that antiretroviral prophylaxis can be offered to infants exposed to HIV. Women should be informed that identifying HIV antibodies in the newborn indicates that the mother is infected.
- For infants whose HIV exposure status is unknown and who are in foster care, the person legally authorized to provide consent should be informed that rapid HIV testing is recommended for infants whose biologic mothers have not been tested.
- The benefits of neonatal antiretroviral prophylaxis are best realized when it is initiated within 12 hours after birth.

Confirmatory Testing:

- Whenever possible, uncertainties regarding laboratory test results indicating HIV infection status should be resolved before final decisions are made regarding reproductive options, antiretroviral therapy, cesarean delivery, or other interventions.
- If the confirmatory test result is not available before delivery, immediate initiation of appropriate antiretroviral prophylaxis should be recommended to any pregnant patient whose HIV screening test result is reactive to reduce the risk for perinatal transmission.

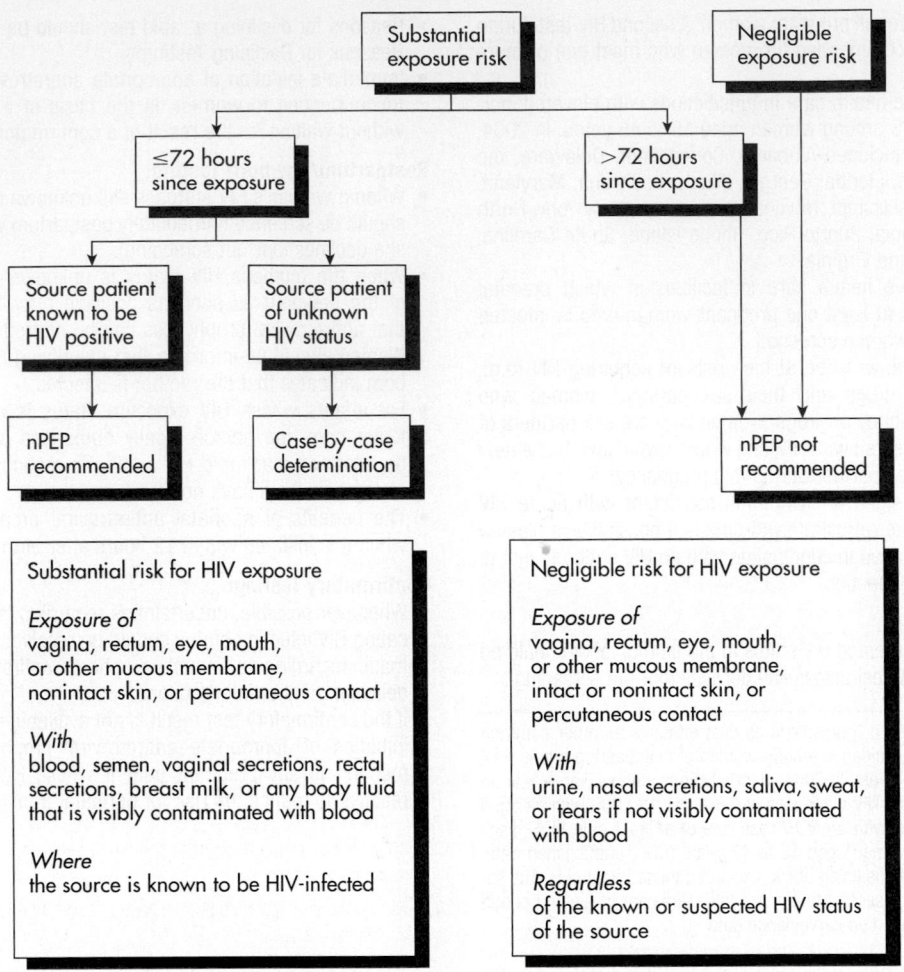

FIGURE 5-7 Algorithm for evaluation and treatment of possible nonoccupational HIV exposure. *nPEP,* Nonoccupational postexposure prophylaxis. (Modified from *MMWR* 54[RR-2], 2005.)

TABLE 5-32 HIV Exposure, Estimated Per-Act Risk

Exposure Route	Risk per 10,000 Exposures to an Infected Source
Blood transfusion	9000
Needle-sharing injection drug use	67
Receptive anal intercourse	50
Percutaneous needle stick	30
Receptive penile-vaginal intercourse	10
Insertive anal intercourse	6.5
Insertive penile-vaginal intercourse	5
Receptive oral intercourse	1
Insertive oral intercourse	0.5

Modified from *MMWR* 54(RR-2), 2005.
NOTE: Estimates of risk for transmission from sexual exposures assume no condom use. Source refers to oral intercourse performed on a man.

TABLE 5-33 Regimens for 28-Day Postexposure Prophylaxis for HIV Infection*

Regimen	Dose	Daily Pill Burden[†]no.	Advantages	Disadvantages
Two-Drug Regimens				
Tenofovir–emtricitabine (Truvada)[‡]	One tablet (300 mg of tenofovir with 200 mg of emtricitabine) once daily	1	Well-tolerated; once-daily dosing	Potential nephrotoxicity
Zidovudine–lamivudine (Combivir)[§]	One tablet (300 mg of zidovudine with 150 mg of lamivudine) twice daily	2	Preferred In pregnancy	Twice-daily dosing; less well-tolerated than tenofovir–emtricitabine (nausea, asthenia, neutropenia, anemia, abnormal liver-enzyme levels)
Three-Drug Regimens[¶]				
Ritonavir–lopinavir (Kaletra) (plus either tenofovir–emtricitabine or zidovudine–lamivudine)	Two tablets (50 mg of ritonavir with 200 mg of lopinavir per tablet) twice daily, or four tablets once daily	5 or 6	Either once-daily or twice-daily dosing; one copayment; no refrigeration required; most experience in pregnancy; high genetic barrier to resistance	Gastrointestinal side effects such as diarrhea; may cause elevated liver-enzyme levels or hepatitis
Ritonavir plus atazanavir (plus either tenofovir–emtricitabine or zidovudine–lamivudine)	100 mg of ritonavir plus 300 mg of atazanavir once daily	3 or 4	Once-daily dosing; well tolerated	Ritonavir must be refrigerated; potential for asymptomatic jaundice, renal stones; may cause elevated liver-enzyme levels or hepatitis
Ritonavir plus darunavir (plus either tenofovir–emtricitabine or zidovudine–lamivudine)	100 mg of ritonavir plus two tablets, each containing 400 mg of darunavir, once daily	4 or 5	Once-daily dosing; high genetic barrier to resistance	Ritonavir must be refrigerated; gastrointestinal side effects; may cause elevated liver-enzyme levels or hepatitis

From Landovitz RJ, Currier JS: Postexposure prophylaxis for HIV infection, *N Engl J Med* 361:1768-75, 2009.

*Tenofovir, emtricitabine, and lamivudine all have activity against hepatitis B. Patients with chronic active hepatitis B (i.e., patients who are positive for hepatitis B surface antigen) may have flares of hepatitis on withdrawal of these agents at the completion of postexposure prophylaxis treatment. Referral to a hepatitis specialist or serial monthly monitoring of liver-enzyme levels for up to 6 months after treatment should be considered.

[†]The daily pill burden in the three-drug regimens depends on which two-drug regimen is chosen.

[‡]The dose of tenofovir–emtricitabine should be reduced to one tablet every 48 hours in patients with a creatinine clearance of 30 to 49 ml per mlnute. Tenofovir–emtricitabine is not recommended in patients with a creatinine clearance of less than 30 ml per minute or in patients who are undergoing hemodialysis; see the guidelines from the Department of Health and Human Services for considerations regarding doses of individual agents in patients with advanced renal dysfunction.

[§]Zidovudine–lamivudine is not recommended in patients with a creatinine clearance of less than 50 ml per minute; see the guidelines from the Department of Health and Human Services for considerations regarding doses of individual agents in patients with renal dysfunction.

[¶]The boosting agent ritonavir is not considered to be an active drug in tabulating the number of agents in the three-drug regimen.

TABLE 5-34 Antiretroviral Therapy Medications, Adult Dosage, and Side Effects

Medication	Adult Dosage*	Side Effects and Toxicities
Combination Tablets		
Lopinavir/ritonavir (Kaletra)‡	3 tablets twice daily 400 mg lopinavir/100 mg ritonavir	Diarrhea, nausea, vomiting; asthenia; elevated transaminases; hyperglycemia; fat redistribution; lipid abnormalities; possible increased bleeding in persons with hemophilia; pancreatitis
Zidovudine/lamivudine (Combivir)	1 tablet twice daily 300 mg zidovudine/150 mg lamivudine	See following individual medications
Zidovudine/lamivudine/ abacavir (Trizivir)	1 tablet twice daily 300 mg zidovudine/150 mg lamivudine/300 mg abacavir	See following individual medications
Lamivudine/abacavir (Epzicom)	1 tablet once daily 300 mg lamivudine/600 mg abacavir	See following individual medications
Emtricitabine/tenofovir (Truvada)	1 tablet once daily 200 mg emtricitabine/300 mg tenofovir	See following individual medications
Single Agents		
Nucleoside and nucleotide reverse transcriptase inhibitors (side effects as a class: lactic acidosis, severe hepatomegaly with steatosis, including some fatal cases)		
Abacavir (Ziagen, ABC)‡	300 mg twice daily or 600 mg once daily	Severe hypersensitivity reaction (can be fatal); nausea; vomiting
Didanosine (Videx, ddI)‡	>60 kg (132 lb) body weight: 200 mg twice daily or 400 mg daily; if with tenofovir, 250 mg/daily	Pancreatitis; nausea, diarrhea; peripheral neuropathy
	<60 kg (132 lb): 125 mg twice daily or 250 mg daily; if with tenofovir, dose not established	
	Do not use with stavudine (d4T, Zerit) during pregnancy; avoid ddI/ d4T combination in general because of increased risk for adverse events (e.g., neuropathy, pancreatitis, and hyperlactatemia)	
Emtricitabine (Emtriva, FTC)	200 mg once daily	Minimal toxicity; lactic acidosis and hepatic steatosis a rare but possibly life-threatening event
Lamivudine (Epivir, 3TC)‡	150 mg twice daily or 300 mg once daily	Minimal toxicity; lactic acidosis and hepatic steatosis a rare but possibly life-threatening event
Stavudine (Zerit, d4T)‡	>60 kg (132 lb) body weight: 40 mg twice daily	Pancreatitis; peripheral neuropathy; rapidly progressive ascending neuromuscular weakness (rare)
	<60 kg (132 lb) body weight: 30 mg twice daily	
	Do not use with didanosine (ddI, Videx) during pregnancy; avoid ddI/ d4T combination in general because of increased risk of adverse events (e.g., neuropathy, pancreatitis, and hyperlactatemia)	
Tenofovir (Viread)	300 mg daily	Nausea, vomiting, diarrhea; headache; asthenia; flatulence; renal impairment
Zidovudine (Retrovir, AZT)‡	200 mg three times daily or 300 mg twice daily	Bone marrow suppression (anemia, neutropenia); gastrointestinal intolerance; headache; insomnia; asthenia; and myopathy
Nonnucleoside reverse transcriptase inhibitors (side effects as a class: Stevens-Johnson syndrome)		
Efavirenz (Sustiva)	600 mg daily at bedtime	Rash; central nervous system symptoms (e.g., dizziness, impaired concentration, insomnia, and abnormal dreams); transaminase elevation; false-positive cannabinoid test
Protease inhibitors (side effects as a class: gastrointestinal intolerance, hyperlipidemia, hyperglycemia, diabetes, fat redistribution, and possible increased bleeding in hemophiliacs; do not use during known or possible pregnancy)		
Atazanavir (Reyataz)	400 mg once daily; if administered with tenofovir plus ritonavir, 300 mg once daily	Indirect hyperbilirubinemia; prolonged PR interval (use caution in patients with underlying cardiac conduction defects or on concomitant medications that can cause PR prolongation)
Fosamprenavir (Lexiva)‡	1400 mg twice daily	Gastrointestinal intolerance, nausea, vomiting, diarrhea; rash; elevated transaminases; headache
Indinavir (Crixivan)	800 mg q8h	Gastrointestinal intolerance, nausea; nephrolithiasis; headache; asthenia; blurred vision; metallic taste; thrombocytopenia; hemolytic anemia; indirect hyperbilirubinemia (inconsequential)
	With ritonavir (might increase risk for renal adverse events): 800 mg indinavir and 100 mg ritonavir q12h or 800 mg indinavir and 200 mg ritonavir every q12h	
Nelfinavir (Viracept)‡	750 mg three times daily or one 250 mg twice daily	Diarrhea; elevated transaminases
Ritonavir (Norvir)‡	See doses used in combination with other specific protease inhibitors	Gastrointestinal intolerance; nausea, vomiting, diarrhea; paresthesias; hepatitis; pancreatitis; asthenia; taste perversion; many drug interactions
Saquinavir (hard-gel capsule) (Invirase)	With ritonavir: 400 mg saquinavir and 400 mg ritonavir twice daily or 1000 mg saquinavir and 100 mg ritonavir twice daily	Gastrointestinal intolerance; nausea, diarrhea; headache; elevated transaminases
Saquinavir (soft-gel capsule) (Fortovase)	With ritonavir: 400 mg saquinavir and 400 mg ritonavir twice daily or 1000 mg saquinavir and 100 mg ritonavir twice daily	Gastrointestinal intolerance; nausea, diarrhea; abdominal pain; dyspepsia; headache; elevated transaminases

Sources: Modified from U.S. Department of Health and Human Services and the Henry J. Kaiser Family Foundation: *Guidelines for the use of antiretroviral agents in HIV-infected adults and adolescents.* Available at http://www.aidsinfo.nih.gov/guidelines/default_db2.asp?id=50 (refer to website for updated versions); Bartlett JG, Finkbeiner AK: HIV drugs: the guide to living with HIV infection, 2001. Available at http://www.thebody.com/jh/bartlett/drugs.html.
*For pediatric dosing information, see *Guidelines for use of antiretroviral agents in pediatric HIV infection.* Available at http://www.aidsinfo.nih.gov/guidelines/default_db2.asp?id=51.
‡Pediatric formulation available.

TABLE 5-35 Laboratory Tests Generally Recommended for Persons after Exposure to HIV*

| Test | RECOMMENDED DURING TREATMENT | | RECOMMENDED AT FOLLOW-UP | | |
	Baseline	Symptom-Directed[†]	4-6 wk	12 wk	24 wk
ELISA for HIV antibodies	Yes	Yes	Yes	Yes	Yes
Creatinine, liver function, and complete blood count with differential count	Yes	Yes	No	No	No
HIV viral load	No	Yes	No	No	No
Anti-HBs antibodies	Yes[‡]	No	No	No	No
HBsAg	Yes[‡§]	No	No	No	No
HCV antibodies	Yes	No	Yes	Yes	Yes
HCV RNA[∥]	No	Yes	Yes	Yes	Yes
Screening, including rapid plasma reagin test, for other sexually transmitted infections[¶]	Yes	Yes	No	Yes	No

From Landovitz RJ, Currier JS: Postexposure prophylaxis for HIV infection, *N Engl J Med* 361:1768-1775, 2009.

Anti-HBs antibodies, Hepatitis B virus surface antibodies; *ELISA,* enzyme-linked immunosorbent assay; *HBsAg,* hepatitis B surface antigen; *HCV,* hepatitis C virus.

*Patients who receive zidovudine plus lamivudine–based regimens should have a complete blood count and measurement of liver-enzyme levels at 2 weeks of treatment, irrespective of the presence or absence of clinical symptoms. Tenofovir plus emtricitabine–based regimens generally involve few side effects, and symptom-directed assessment of serum creatinine or liver-enzyme levels should be considered. The addition of a ritonavir-boosted protease inhibitor should be followed by symptom-directed assessment of liver-enzyme levels, serum glucose levels, or both.

[†]Symptom-directed tests are for signs or symptoms of toxic effects (rash, nausea, vomiting, or abdominal pain) or HIV seroconversion (fever, fatigue, lymphadenopathy, rash, or oral or genital ulcers).

[‡]If tests for anti-HBs antibodies and HBsAg are both negative, a vaccination series against HBV infection should be initiated and completed.

[§]If the patient is HBsAg-positive, he or she should have monthly follow-up of liver function tests after discontinuation of postexposure prophylactic regimens containing tenofovir, lamivudine, or emtricitabine; referral to a specialist in viral hepatitis should be considered.

[∥]HCV RNA testing may identify early HCV seroconversion; early detection and treatment during acute HCV infection may avert or ameliorate chronic disease. Data are from Dienstag and McHutchison.

[¶]Rapid plasma reagin testing and testing of urethral-swab and rectal-swab specimens for gonorrhea and chlamydia and of pharyngeal-swab specimens for gonorrhea should be performed as appropriate, according to the patient's sexual risk-taking behaviors and the type of exposure to HIV.

BOX 5-4 Situations for Which Expert Consultation for HIV Postexposure Prophylaxis Is Advised[6]

- Delayed (i.e., later than 24-36 hours) exposure report
  1. The interval after which there is no benefit from postexposure prophylaxis (PEP) is undefined
- Unknown source (e.g., needle in sharps disposal container or laundry)
  1. Decide use of PEP on a case-by-case basis
  2. Consider the severity of the exposure and the epidemiologic likelihood of HIV exposure
  3. Do not test needles or other sharp instruments for HIV
- Known or suspected pregnancy in the exposed person
  1. Does not preclude the use of optimal PEP regimens
  2. Do not deny PEP solely on the basis of pregnancy
- Resistance of the source virus to antiretroviral agents
  1. Influence of drug resistance on transmission risk is unknown
  2. Selection of drugs to which the source person's virus is unlikely to be resistant is recommended if the source person's virus is known or suspected to be resistant to one or more of the drugs considered for the PEP regimen
  3. Resistance testing of the source person's virus at the time of the exposure is not recommended
- Toxicity of the initial PEP regimen
  1. Adverse symptoms such as nausea and diarrhea are common with PEP
  2. Symptoms often can be managed without changing the PEP regimen by prescribing antimotility and/or antiemetic agents
  3. Modification of dose intervals (i.e., administering a lower dose of drug more frequently throughout the day, as recommended by the manufacturer) in other situations might help alleviate symptoms

[6]Local experts and/or the National Clinicians' Postexposure Prophylaxis Hotline (PEPline [888-448-4911]).

BOX 5-5 Occupational Exposure Management Resources

National Clinicians' Postexposure Prophylaxis Hotline (PEPline)
Run by University of California–San Francisco/San Francisco General Hospital staff; supported by the Health Resources and Services Administration, Ryan White CARE Act, HIV/AIDS Bureau, AIDS Education and Training Centers, and CDC

Phone: 888-448-4911
Internet: http://www.ucsf.edu/hivcntr

Needlestick!
A website to help clinicians manage and document occupational blood and body fluid exposures. Developed and maintained by the University of California, Los Angeles (UCLA), Emergency Medicine Center, UCLA School of Medicine, and funded in part by CDC and the Agency for Healthcare Research and Quality

Internet: http://www.needlestick.mednet.ucla.edu

Hepatitis Hotline

Phone: 888-443-7232
Internet: http://www.cdc.gov/ncidod/diseases/hepatitis/index.htm

Reporting to CDC: Occupationally acquired HIV infections and failures of PEP

Phone: 800-893-0485

HIV Antiretroviral Pregnancy Registry

Phone: 800-258-4263
Fax: 800-800-1052
Address: 1410 Commonwealth Dr., Suite 215, Wilmington, NC 28405
Internet: http://www.glaxowellcome.com/preg_reg/antiretroviral

Food and Drug Administration Report unusual or severe toxicity to antiretroviral agents

Phone: 800-332-1088
Address: MedWatch, HF-2, FDA, 5600 Fishers Lane, Rockville, MD 20857
Internet: http://www.fda.gov/medwatch

HIV/AIDS Treatment Information Service

Internet: http://www.hivatis.org

BOX 5-6 Management of Occupational Blood Exposures

Provide Immediate Care to the Exposure Site
- Wash wounds and skin with soap and water
- Flush mucous membranes with water

Determine Risk Associated with Exposure
- Type of fluid (e.g., blood, visibly bloody fluid, other potentially infectious fluid or tissue, and concentrated virus)
- Type of exposure (e.g., percutaneous injury, mucous membrane or nonintact skin exposure, and bites resulting in blood exposure)

Evaluate Exposure Source
- Assess the risk of infection using available information
- Test known sources for HBsAg, anti-HCV, and HIV antibodies (consider using rapid testing)
- For unknown sources, assess risk of exposure to HBV, HCV, or HIV infection
- Do not test discarded needles or syringes for virus contamination

Evaluate the Exposed Person
- Assess immune status for HBV infection (i.e., by history of hepatitis B vaccination and vaccine response)

Give PEP for Exposures Posing Risk of Infection Transmission
- HBV: See Table 5-27
- HCV: PEP not recommended
- HIV: See Tables 5-33, 5-34, and 5-35 and Figure 5-7
  1. Initiate PEP as soon as possible, preferably within hours of exposure
  2. Offer pregnancy testing to all women of childbearing age not known to be pregnant
  3. Seek expert consultation if viral resistance is suspected
  4. Administer PEP for 4 weeks if tolerated

Perform Follow-up Testing and Provide Counseling
- Advise exposed persons to seek medical evaluation for any acute illness occurring during follow-up

HBV Exposures
- Perform follow-up anti-HBs testing in persons who receive hepatitis B vaccine
  1. Test for anti-HBs 1 to 2 months after last dose of vaccine
  2. Anti-HBs response to vaccine cannot be ascertained if HBIG was received in the previous 3 to 4 months

HCV Exposures
- Perform baseline and follow-up testing for anti-HCV and alanine aminotransferase 4 to 6 months after exposure
- Perform HCV RNA at 4 to 6 weeks if earlier diagnosis of HCV infection desired
- Confirm repeatedly reactive anti-HCV enzyme immunoassays with supplemental tests

HIV Exposures
- Perform HIV-antibody testing for at least 6 months after exposure (e.g., at baseline, 6 weeks, 3 months, and 6 months)
- Perform HIV-antibody testing if illness compatible with an acute retroviral syndrome occurs
- Advise exposed persons to use precautions to prevent secondary transmission during the follow-up period
- Evaluate exposed persons taking PEP within 72 hr after exposure and monitor for drug toxicity for at least 2 weeks

HBIG, Hepatitis B immune globulin; *HBsAg,* hepatitis B surface antigen; *HBV,* hepatitis B virus; *HCV,* hepatitis C virus; *HIV,* human immunodeficiency virus; *PEP,* postexposure prophylaxis; *RNA,* ribonucleic acid.

Endocarditis Prophylaxis[7]

TABLE 5-36 Cardiac Conditions Associated with the Highest Risk of Adverse Outcome from Endocarditis for Which Prophylaxis with Dental Procedures Is Recommended

---

Prosthetic cardiac valve

Previous infective endocarditis

CHD*

Unrepaired cyanotic CHD, including palliative shunts and conduits

Completely repaired congenital heart defect with prosthetic material or device, whether placed by surgery or by catheter intervention, during the first 6 mo after the procedure[†]

Repaired CHD with residual defects at the site or adjacent to the site of a prosthetic patch or prosthetic device (that inhibit endothelialization)

Cardiac transplant recipients who develop cardiac valvulopathy

---

CHD, Congenital heart disease.

*Except for the conditions listed above, antibiotic prophylaxis is no longer recommended for any other form of CHD.

[†]Prophylaxis is recommended because endothelialization of prosthetic material occurs within 6 mo after the procedure.

TABLE 5-37 Dental Procedures for Which Endocarditis Prophylaxis Is Recommended for Patients in Table 5-36

All dental procedures that involve manipulation of gingival tissue or the periapical region of teeth or perforation of the oral mucosa*

---

*The following procedures and events do not need prophylaxis: routine anesthetic injections through noninfected tissue, taking dental radiographs, placement of removable prosthodontic or orthodontic appliances, adjustment of orthodontic appliances, placement of orthodontic brackets, shedding of deciduous teeth, and bleeding from trauma to the lips or oral mucosa.

TABLE 5-38 Regimens for a Dental Procedure

Situation		REGIMEN: SINGLE DOSE 30-60 MIN BEFORE PROCEDURE		
	Agent	**Adults**	**Children**	
Oral	Amoxicillin	2 g	50 mg/kg	
Unable to take oral medication	Ampicillin	2 g IM or IV	50 mg/kg IM or IV	
	OR			
	Cefazolin or ceftriaxone*	1 g IM or IV	50 mg/kg IM or IV	
Allergic to penicillins or ampicillin, oral	Cephalexin*[†]	2 g	50 mg/kg	
	OR			
	Clindamycin	600 mg	20 mg/kg	
	OR			
	Azithromycin or clarithromycin	500 mg	15 mg/kg	
Allergic to penicillins or ampicillin and unable to take oral medicine	Cefazolin or ceftriaxone[†]	1 g IM or IV	50 mg/kg IM or IV	
	OR			
	Clindamycin	600 mg IM or IV	20 mg/kg IM or IV	

IM, Intramuscular; *IV*, intravenous.

*Or other first-generation or second-generation oral cephalosporin in equivalent adult or pediatric dosage.

[†]Cephalosporins should not be used in an individual with a history of anaphylaxis, angioedema, or urticaria with penicillins or ampicillin.

---

[7]From Prevention of infective endocarditis. A guideline from the American Heart Association Rheumatic Fever, Endocarditis, and Kawasaki Disease Committee, Council on Cardiovascular Disease in the Young, and the Council on Clinical Cardiology, Council on Cardiovascular Surgery and Anesthesia, and the Quality of Care and Outcomes Research Interdisciplinary Working Group. Circulation published online Apr 19, 2007, DOI: 10.1161/CIRCULATIONAHA.106.183095. Copyright © 2007 American Heart Association. All rights reserved. Print ISSN: 0009-7322. Online ISSN: 1524-4539.

TABLE 5-39 Summary of Major Changes in Updated Recommendations

We concluded that bacteremia resulting from daily activities is much more likely to cause IE than bacteremia associated with a dental procedure.

We concluded that only an extremely small number of cases of IE might be prevented by antibiotic prophylaxis even if prophylaxis is 100% effective.

Antibiotic prophylaxis is not recommended based solely on an increased lifetime risk of acquisition of IE.

Limit recommendations for IE prophylaxis only to those conditions listed in Table 5-36.

Antibiotic prophylaxis is no longer recommended for any other form of CHD, except for the conditions listed in Table 5-36.

Antibiotic prophylaxis is recommended for all dental procedures that involve manipulation of gingival tissues or periapical region of teeth or perforation of oral mucosa only for patients with underlying cardiac conditions associated with the highest risk of adverse outcome from IE (see Table 5-36).

Antibiotic prophylaxis is recommended for procedures on respiratory tract or infected skin, skin structures, or musculoskeletal tissue only for patients with underlying cardiac conditions associated with the highest risk of adverse outcome from IE (see Table 5-36).

Antibiotic prophylaxis solely to prevent IE is not recommended for GU or GI tract procedures.

The writing group reaffirms the procedures noted in the 1997 prophylaxis guidelines for which endocarditis prophylaxis is not recommended and extends this to other common procedures, including ear and body piercing, tattooing, and vaginal delivery and hysterectomy.

NOTE: A guide to the clinical preventive services described is available online at http://www.ahrq.gov/clinic/pocketgd07/.
CHD, Congenital heart disease; *GI*, gastrointestinal; *GU*, genitourinary; *IE*, infective endocarditis.

Hepatitis C Testing

BOX 5-7 Recommendations for Prevention and Control of Hepatitis C Virus (HCV) Infection and HCV-Related Chronic Diseases

Recommendations for the Identification of Chronic Hepatitis C Virus Infection Among Persons Born During 1945–1965[8]
- Adults born during 1945-1965 should receive one-time testing for HCV without prior ascertainment of HCV risk.
- All persons with identified HCV infection should receive a brief alcohol screening and intervention as clinically indicated, followed by referral to appropriate care and treatment services for HCV infection and related conditions.

Guidelines for Prevention and Treatment of Opportunistic Infections in HIV-Infected Adults and Adolescents[9,10]
- HIV-infected patients should be tested routinely for evidence of chronic HCV infection. Initial testing for HCV should be performed using the most sensitive immunoassays licensed for detection of antibody to HCV (anti-HCV) in blood.

Recommendations for Prevention and Control of Hepatitis C Virus (HCV) Infection and HCV-Related Chronic Disease
Routine HCV testing is recommended for
- Persons who ever injected illegal drugs, including those who injected once or a few times many years ago and do not consider themselves drug users.
- Persons with selected medical conditions, including:
  1. persons who received clotting factor concentrates produced before 1987;
  2. persons who were ever on chronic (long-term) hemodialysis;
  3. persons with persistently abnormal alanine aminotransferase levels.
- Prior recipients of transfusions or organ transplants, including:
  1. persons who were notified that they received blood from a donor who later tested positive for HCV infection;
  2. persons who received a transfusion of blood or blood components before July 1992; and
  3. persons who received an organ transplant before July 1992.

Routine HCV testing is recommended for persons with recognized exposures, including
- Health care, emergency medical, and public safety workers after needle sticks, sharps, or mucosal exposures to HCV-positive blood.
- Children born to HCV-positive women.

From Centers for Disease Control and Prevention: Recommendations for the identification of chronic hepatitis C virus infection among persons born during 1945-1965. *MMWR* 2012:61(4).
[8]Source: Centers for Disease Control and Prevention: Recommendations for the identification of chronic hepatitis C virus infection among persons born during 1945–1965. *MMWR* 2012;61(No. RR–4).
[9]Source: Centers for Disease Control and Prevention: Recommendations for prevention and control of hepatitis C virus (HCV) infection and HCV-related chronic disease. *MMWR* 1998;47(No. RR–19).
[10]Source: Centers for Disease Control and Prevention: Guidelines for prevention and treatment of opportunistic infections in HIV-infected adults and adolescents: Recommendations from CDC, the National Institutes of Health, and the HIV Medicine Association of the Infectious Diseases Society of America. *MMWR* 2009;58(No. RR–4).

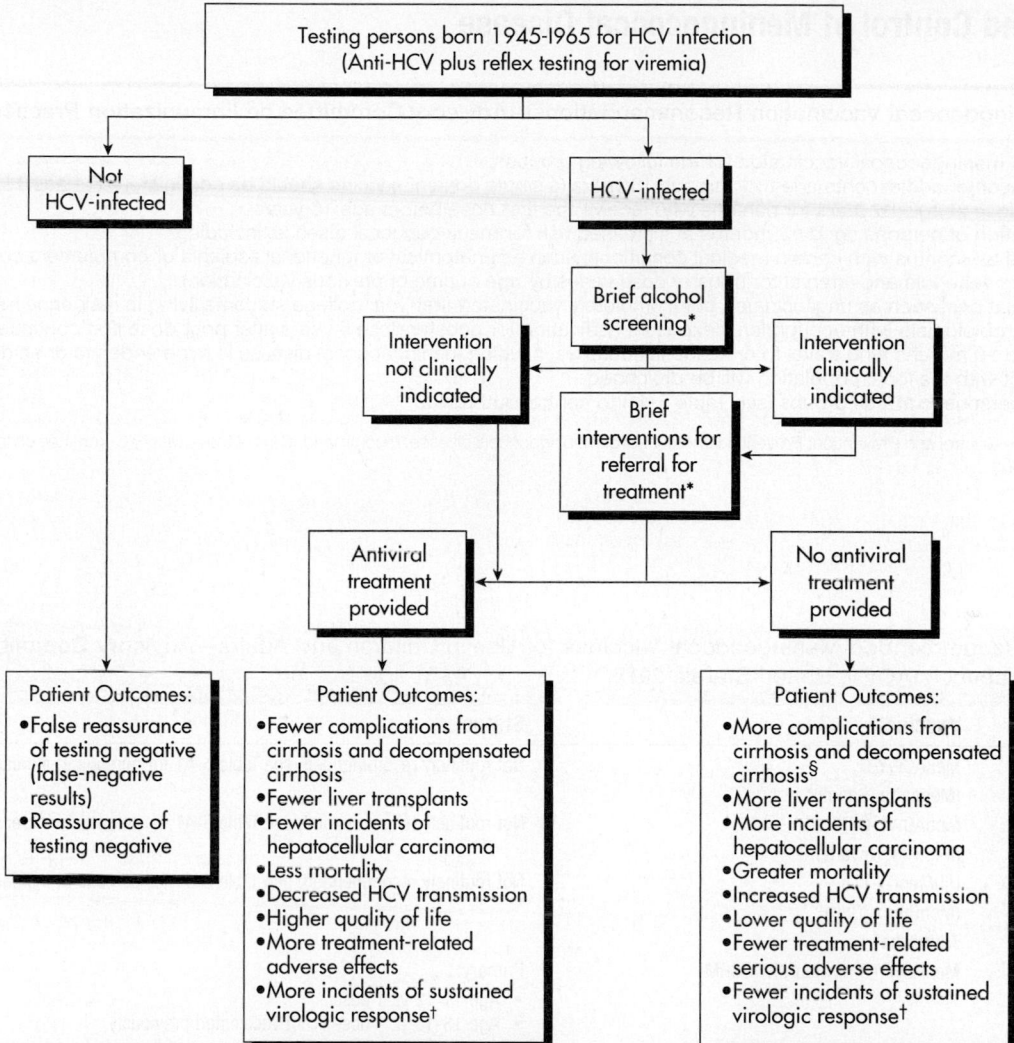

FIGURE 5-8 Analytic Framework for Guiding HCV Testing Among Persons Born During 1945-1965 *Together, these interventions are known as alcohol screening and brief interventions (SBI) for referral for treatment. †Viral eradication after treatment completion. §Cirrhosis with the diagnosis of at least one of the following: ascites, variceal bleeding, encephalopathy, or impaired hepatitis synthetic function. From Centers for Disease Control and Prevention: Recommendations for the identification of chronic hepatitis C virus infection among persons born during 1945-1965. *MMWR* 2012:61(4).

Prevention and Control of Meningococcal Disease

BOX 5-8 Meningococcal Vaccination Recommendations—Advisory Committee on Immunization Practices, 2013

ACIP recommends meningococcal vaccination for the following groups:
- Routine vaccination of adolescents aged 11 through 18 years (a single dose of vaccine should be administered at age 11 or 12 years, with a booster dose at age 16 years for persons who receive the first dose before age 16 years).
- Routine vaccination of persons aged ≥2 months at increased risk for meningococcal disease, including:
    1. Persons aged ≥2 months with certain medical conditions, such as anatomical or functional asplenia or complement component deficiency (dosing schedule and interval for booster dose varies by age at time of previous vaccination).
    2. Special populations, such as unvaccinated or incompletely vaccinated first-year college students living in residence halls, military recruits, or microbiologists with occupational exposure (indication for booster dose 5 years after prior dose if at continued risk).
    3. Persons aged ≥9 months who travel to or reside in countries in which meningococcal disease is hyperendemic or epidemic, particularly if contact with the local population will be prolonged.
- Vaccination of persons in at-risk groups (see Table 5-41) to control outbreaks.

From Centers for Disease Control and Prevention: Prevention and control of meningococcal disease, recommendations of the Advisory Committee on Immunization Practices (ACIP). *MMWR* 2013:63(2).

TABLE 5-40 Recommended Meningococcal Vaccines for Use in Children and Adults—Advisory Committee on Immunization Practices (ACIP), United States, 2012

Age Group	Vaccine	Status
2 mo-10 yr	MenACWY-D (Menactra, Sanofi)*	Not routinely recommended; see Table 5-41 for persons at increased risk
	MenACWY-CRM (Menveo, Novartis)[†]	Not routinely recommended; see Table 5-41 for persons at increased risk
	HibMenCY-TT (MenHibrix, GSK)[‡]	Not routinely recommended; see Table 5-41 for persons at increased risk
10-25 yr	Trumenba[§]	
11-21 yr	MenACWY-D or MenACWY-CRM	Primary: • Age 11-12 yr, 1 dose • Age 13-18 yr, 1 dose if not vaccinated previously • Age 19-21 yr, not routinely recommended but may be administered as catch-up vaccination for those who have not received a dose after their 16th birthday Booster: • 1 dose recommended if first dose administered before 16th birthday
22-55 yr	MenACWY-D or MenACWY-CRM	Not routinely recommended; see Table 5-41 for persons at increased risk
≥56 yr	MPSV4, MenACWY-D, or MenACWY-CRM	Not routinely recommended; see Table 5-41 for persons at increased risk

Adapted from American Academy of Pediatrics. Meningococcal infections. In: Pickering LK, Baker CJ, Kimberlin DW, eds. *Red book: 2012 report of the Committee on Infectious Diseases*. 29th ed. Elk Grove, IL: American Academy of Pediatrics; 2012:500-9; From Centers for Disease Control and Prevention: Prevention and control of meningococcal disease, Recommendations of the Advisory Committee on Immunization Practices (ACIP). *MMWR* 2013:63(2).
*Licensed only for persons aged 9 months-55 years.
[†]Licensed only for persons aged 2-55 years. Under investigation for use at ages 2, 4, 6, and 12-15 months.
[‡]Licensed only for children aged 6 weeks-18 months.
[§]Meningococcal group B vaccine (Trumenba) is indicated for active immunization to prevent invasive disease caused by *Neisseria meningitidis* serogroup B in individuals 10-25 years of age.

TABLE 5-41 Recommended Immunization Schedule and Intervals for Persons at Increased Risk for Meningococcal Disease—Advisory Committee on Immunization Practices (ACIP), United States, 2012*

Age Group	Subgroup	Primary Vaccination	Booster Dose[†]
2-18 mo with high-risk conditions[‡]	Children who: • have persistent complement deficiencies • have functional or anatomic asplenia • are at risk during a community outbreak attributable to a vaccine serogroup	Four doses of Hib-MenCY-TT (MenHibrix), at 2, 4, 6, and 12-15 mo	Person remains at increased risk and completed the primary dose or series at age: • 2 mo-6 yr:Should receive additional dose of MenACWY 3 yr after primary immunization; boosters should be repeated every 5 yr thereafter • ≥7 yrs:Should receive additional dose of MenACWY 5 yr after primary immunization; boosters should be repeated every 5 yr thereafter
9-23 mo with high-risk conditions[§]	Children who: • have persistent complement deficiencies • travel to or are residents of countries where meningococcal disease is hyperendemic or epidemic • are at risk during a community outbreak attributable to a vaccine serogroup	Two doses of MenACWY-D (Menactra), 12 weeks apart[‖]	
2-55 yr with high-risk conditions and not vaccinated previously	Persons who: • have persistent complement deficiencies • have functional or anatomic asplenia • have HIV, if another indication for vaccination exists	Two doses of MenACWY, 8-12 wk apart[¶]	
	Persons who: • are first-year college students aged ≤21 yr living in residential housing • travel to or are residents of countries where meningococcal disease is hyperendemic or epidemic • are at risk during a community outbreak attributable to a vaccine serogroup • are microbiologists routinely exposed to isolates of *Neisseria meningitidis*	One dose of MenACWY[‖]	

Adapted from American Academy of Pediatrics. Meningococcal infections. In: Pickering LK, Baker CJ, Kimberlin DW, Long SS, eds. *Red book: 2012 report of the Committee on Infectious Diseases.* 29th ed. Elk Grove, IL: American Academy of Pediatrics; 2012: 500-9; Centers for Disease Control and Prevention: Prevention and control of meningococcal disease, recommendations of the Advisory Committee on Immunization Practices (ACIP). *MMWR* 62(2).

*Includes persons who have persistent complement deficiencies (e.g., C5-C9, properdin, factor H, or factor D), and anatomic or functional asplenia; travelers to or residents of countries in which meningococcal disease is hyperendemic or epidemic; and persons who are part of a community outbreak of a vaccine-preventable serogroup.

[†]If the person remains at increased risk for meningococcal disease.

[‡]Infants and children who received Hib-MenCY-TT and are travelling to areas with high endemic rates of meningococcal disease such as the African "meningitis belt" are not protected against serogroups A and W-135 and should receive a quadrivalent meningococcal vaccination licensed for children aged ≥9 mo prior to travel.

[§]Because of high risk for invasive pneumococcal disease, children with functional or anatomic asplenia should not be immunized with MenACWY-D (Menactra) before age 2 yr to avoid interference with the immune response to the pneumococcal conjugate vaccine (PCV) series.

[‖]If an infant is receiving the vaccine prior to travel, 2 doses may be administered as early as 8 wk apart.

[¶]If MenACWY-D is used, it should be administered at least 4 wk after completion of all PCV doses.

TABLE 5-42 Recommended Chemoprophylaxis Regimens for Protection Against Meningococcal Disease—Advisory Committee on Immunization Practices (ACIP), United States, 2012

Drug	Age Group	Dosage	Duration and Route of Administration
Rifampin[†]	Children aged <1 mo	5 mg/kg every 12 hr	2 d
	Children aged ≥1 mo	10 mg/kg every 12 hr	2 d
	Adults	600 mg every 12 hr	2 d
Ciprofloxacin[‡]	Adults	500 mg	Single dose
Ceftriaxone	Children age <15 yr	125 mg	Single IM dose
Ceftriaxone	Adults	250 mg	Single IM dose

IM, Intramuscular.

* Oral administration unless indicated otherwise.

[†]Rifampin is not recommended for pregnant women because the drug is teratogenic in laboratory animals. Because the reliability of oral contraceptives might be affected by rifampin therapy, consideration should be given to using alternative contraceptive measures while rifampin is being administered.

[‡]Ciprofloxacin is not generally recommended for persons aged <18 yr or for pregnant and lactating women because the drug causes cartilage damage in immature laboratory animals. However, ciprofloxacin may be used for chemoprophylaxis of children when no acceptable alternative therapy is available. A recent review identified no reports of irreversible cartilage toxicity or age-associated adverse events in children and adolescents.

Burstein GR, Berman SM, Blumer JL, Moran JS. Ciprofloxacin for the treatment of uncomplicated gonorrhea infection in adolescents: does the benefit outweigh the risk? *Clin Infect Dis* 2002;35:S191-9; Centers for Disease Control and Prevention: Prevention and control of meningococcal disease, recommendations of the Advisory Committee on Immunization Practices (ACIP). *MMWR* 62(2).

Hepatitis B Virus Postexposure Protection for Health Care Personnel

TABLE 5-43 Postexposure Management of Health Care Personnel After Occupational Percutaneous and Mucosal Exposure to Blood and Body Fluids, by Health Care Personnel HepB Vaccination and Response Status

Health Care Personnel Status	POSTEXPOSURE TESTING		POSTEXPOSURE PROPHYLAXIS		Postvaccination Serologic Testing[†]
	Source Patient (HBsAg)	HCP Testing (anti-HBs)	HBIG*	Vaccination	
Documented responder[‡] after complete series (≥3 doses)	No action needed				
Documented nonresponder[§] after 6 doses	Positive/unknown	—ᶦ	HBIG ×2 separated by 1 mo	—	No
	Negative	No action needed			
Response unknown after 3 doses	Positive/unknown	<10 mIU/mLᶦ	HBIG ×1	Initiate revaccination	Yes
	Negative	<10 mIU/mL	None		
	Any result	≥10 mIU/mL	No action needed		
Unvaccinated/incompletely vaccinated or vaccine refusers	Positive/unknown	—ᶦ	HBIG ×1	Complete vaccination	Yes
	Negative	—	None	Complete vaccination	Yes

From Centers for Disease Control and Prevention: CDC guidance for evaluating health-care personnel for hepatitis B virus protection and for administering post-exposure management. *MMWR* 2013;62(10).

anti-HBs, Antibody to hepatitis B surface antigen; *HBIG*, hepatitis B immune globulin; *HBsAg*, hepatitis B surface antigen; *HCP*, health care personnel.

*HBIG should be administered transmuscularly as soon as possible after exposure when indicated. The effectiveness of HBIG when administered >7 d after percutaneous, mucosal, or nonintact skin exposures is unknown. HBIG dosage is 0.06 mL/kg.

†Should be performed 1-2 mo after the last dose of the HepB vaccine series (and 4-6 mo after administration of HBIG to avoid detection of passively administered anti-HBs) using a quantitative method that allows detection of the protective concentration of anti-HBs (≥10 mIU/mL).

‡A responder is defined as a person with anti-HBs ≥10 mIU/mL after ≥3 doses of HepB vaccine.

§A nonresponder is defined as a person with anti-HBs <10 mIU/mL after ≥6 doses of HepB vaccine.

ᶦHCP who have anti-HBs <10 mIU/mL, or who are unvaccinated or incompletely vaccinated, and sustain an exposure to a source patient who is HBsAg-positive or has unknown HBsAg status, should undergo baseline testing for HBV infection as soon as possible after exposure, and follow-up testing approximately 6 mo later. Initial baseline tests consist of total anti-HBc; testing at approximately 6 months consists of HBsAg and total anti-HBc.

APPENDIX

I. Complementary and Alternative Medicine

II. Nutrition

III. Acute Poisoning

IV. Impairment and Disability Issues

V. Primary Care Procedures (available online)

VI. Patient Teaching Guides (available online)

APPENDIX

Definitions of Complementary and Alternative Medicine Terms

Acupuncture Thin needles are inserted superficially on the skin at locations throughout the body. These points are located along "channels" of energy. Heat can be applied by burning (moxibustion), electric current (electroacupuncture), or pressure (acupressure). Healing is proposed by the restoration of a balance of energy flow called *Qi*. Another explanation suggests that, possibly, the stimulation activates endorphin receptors.

Alexander Technique A bodywork technique in which rebalancing of "postural sets" (i.e., physical alignment) is taught by mentally focusing on the way correct alignments should look and feel and through verbal and tactile guidance by the practitioner.

Applied Kinesiology A form of treatment that uses nutrition, physical manipulation, vitamins, diets, and exercise to restore and energize the body. Weak muscles are proposed as a source of dysfunctional health.

Aromatherapy A form of herbal medicine that uses various oils from plants. Route of administration can be through absorption in the skin or inhalation. The aromatic biochemical structures of certain herbs are thought to act in areas of the brain related to past experiences and emotions (e.g., limbic system).

Ayurveda A major health system that originated in India and incorporates the body, mind, and spirit to prevent and treat disease. Includes special types of diets, herbs, and minerals.

Biofeedback A mind body therapy procedure in which sensors are placed on the body to measure muscle tension, heart rate, and sweat responses or neural activity. Information is provided by visual, auditory, or body-muscle cell activation so as to teach either to increase or decrease physiologic activity, which, when reconstituted, is proposed to improve health problems (e.g., pain, anxiety, or high blood pressure). In some cases, relaxation exercises complement this procedure.

Chelation Therapy Involves the removal—through intravenous infusion of a chelating agent (synthetic amino acid ethylenediamine tetraacetic acid [EDTA])—of heavy metals, including lead, nickel, and cadmium, as a way to treat certain diseases. Ancillary treatments include the use of vitamins, changes in diet, and exercise.

Cognitive Therapy Psychological therapy in which the major focus is altering and changing irrational beliefs through a type of Socratic dialogue and self-evaluation of certain illogical thoughts. Conditioning and learning are important components of this therapy.

Craniosacral Therapy A form of gentle manual manipulation used for diagnosis and for making corrections in a system made up of cerebrospinal fluid, cranial and dural membranes, cranial bones, and sacrum. This system is proposed to be dynamic, with its own physiologic frequency. Through touch and pressure, tension is proposed to be reduced and cranial rhythms normalized, leading to improvement in health and disease.

Diathermy The use of high-frequency electrical currents as a form of physical therapy and in surgical procedures. The term *diathermy,* derived from the Greek words *dia* and *therma,* literally means "heating through." The three forms of diathermy used by physical therapists are short wave, ultrasound, and microwave.

Eye Movement Desensitization and Reprocessing (EMDR) A technique that proposes to remove painful memories by behavioral techniques. Rhythmic, multisaccadic eye movements are produced by allowing the patient to track and follow a moving object while imagining a stressful memory or event. By using deconditioning, including verbal interaction with the therapist, the painful memory is extinguished and health improved.

Feldenkrais Method A bodywork technique that integrates physics, judo, and yoga. The practitioner directs sequences of movement using verbal or hands-on techniques or teaches a system of self-directed exercise to treat physical impairments through the learning of new movement patterns.

Hatha Yoga The branch of yoga practice that involves physical exercise, breathing practices, and movement. These exercises are designed to have a salutary effect on posture, flexibility, and strength and are intended ultimately to prepare the body to remain still for long periods of meditation.

Hellerwork A bodywork technique that treats and improves proper body alignment through the development of a more complete awareness of the physical body. The goal is to realign fascia for improvement of standing, sitting, and breathing using "body energy," verbal feedback, and changing emotions and attitudes.

Homeopathy A form of treatment in which substances (minerals, plant extracts, chemicals, or disease-producing germs), which in sufficient doses would produce a set of illness symptoms in healthy individuals, are given in microdoses to produce a "cure" of those same symptoms. The *symptom* is not thought to be part of the illness but part of a curative process.

Hyperbaric Oxygen A therapy in which 100% oxygen is given at or above atmospheric pressure. An increase in oxygen in the tissue is proposed to increase blood circulation and improve healing and health and influence the course of disease.

Jin Shin Jyutsu An ancient bodywork technique to harmonize body, mind, and spirit by gentle touch that uses specific "healing points" at the body surface. The points are proposed to overlie flowing energy (Qi). The therapist's fingers are used to "redirect, balance, and provide a more efficient energy flow" to and throughout the body.

Light Therapy Natural light or light of specified wavelengths is used to treat disease. This may include ultraviolet light, colored light, or low-intensity laser light. Generally, the eye is the initial entry point for the light because of its direct connection to the brain.

Magnetic Therapy Magnets are placed directly on the skin, theoretically stimulating living cells and increasing blood flow by ionic currents that are created from polarities on the magnets.

Modified from Spencer JW: *Complementary/alternative medicine: an evidence-based approach,* St Louis, 1999, Mosby.

Mediterranean Diet A diet that is thought to provide optimal distribution of daily caloric intake of different nutrients and includes 50% to 60% carbohydrates, 30% fats, and 10% proteins. The diet is derived from the eating habits of people in the Mediterranean area, who were shown to have reduced rates of cardiovascular disease.

Mind-Body Therapies A group of therapies that emphasize using the mind or brain in conjunction with the body to assist healing. Mind-body therapies can involve varying degrees of levels of consciousness, including *hypnosis,* in which selective attention is used to induce a specific altered state (trance) for memory retrieval, relaxation, or suggestion; *visual imagery,* in which the focus is on a target visual stimulus; *yoga,* which involves integration of posture and controlled breathing, relaxation, and/or meditation; *relaxation,* which includes lighter levels of altered states of consciousness through indirect or direct focus; and *meditation,* in which there is an intentional use of posture, concentration, contemplation, and visualization.

Muscle Energy Technique A manual therapy in osteopathic medicine that includes both passive mobilization and muscle reeducation. Diagnosis of somatic dysfunction is performed by the practitioner, after which the patient is guided to provide corrective muscle contraction.

Music Therapy The use of music in an either active or passive mode. Used mainly to reduce stress, anxiety, and pain.

Naturopathy A major health system that includes practices that emphasize diet, nutrition, homeopathy, acupuncture, herbal medicine, manipulation, and various mind-body therapies. Focal points include self-healing and treatment through changes in lifestyle and emphasis on health prevention.

Ornish Diet A life-choice program based on eating a vegetarian diet containing less than 10% fat. The diet is high in complex carbohydrates and fiber. Meat and fish are generally avoided.

Oslo Diet An eating plan that emphasizes increased intake of fish and reduced total fat intake. Diet is combined with regular endurance exercise.

Pilates An educational and exercise approach using the proper body mechanics, movements, truncal and pelvic stabilization, coordinated breathing, and muscle contractions to promote strengthening. Attention is paid to the entire musculoskeletal system.

Prayer The use of prayer(s) that are offered to "some higher being" or authority to heal and/or arrest disease. May be practiced by the individual patient, by groups, or by other(s) with or without the patient's knowledge (e.g., intercessory).

Pritikin Diet A weight management plan that is based on a vegetarian framework. Meals are low in fat, high in fiber, and high in complex carbohydrates.

Qi Gong A form of Chinese exercise-stimulation therapy that proposes to improve health by redirecting mental focus, breathing, coordination, and relaxation. The goal is to "rebalance" the body's own healing capacities by activating proposed electrical or energetic currents that flow along meridians located throughout the body. These meridians, however, do not follow conventional nerve or muscle pathways. In Chinese medical training and practice this therapy includes "external Qi," which is energy transmitted from one person to another so as to heal.

Raja Yoga Yoga practice that includes all of the other forms of yoga. The practitioner is instructed to follow moral directives, physical exercises, breathing exercises, meditation, devotion, and service to others to facilitate religious awakening.

Reflexology A bodywork technique that uses reflex points on the hands and feet. Pressure is applied at points that correspond to various body parts, to eliminate blockages thought to produce pain or disease.

Reiki Comes from the Japanese word meaning "universal life force energy." The practitioner serves as a conduit for healing energy directed into the body or energy field of the recipient without physical contact with the body.

Rolfing A bodywork technique that involves the myofascia. The body is realigned by using the hands to apply deep pressure and friction that allow more sufficient posture, movement, and the "release" of emotions from the body.

Shiatsu A Japanese bodywork technique involving finger pressure at specific points on the body mainly to balance "energy" in the body. The major focus is on prevention by keeping the body healthy. The therapy uses more than 600 points on the skin that are proposed to be connected to pathways through which energy flows.

T'ai Chi A technique that uses slow, purposeful motor-physical movements of the body to control and achieve a more balanced physiologic and psychological state.

Therapeutic Touch A body energy field technique in which hands are passed over the body without actually touching to recreate and change proposed "energy imbalances" for restoring innate healing forces. Verbal interaction between patient and therapist helps maximize effects.

Traditional Chinese Medicine An ancient form of medicine that focuses on prevention and secondarily treats disease with an emphasis on maintaining balance through the body by stimulating a constant, smooth-flowing Qi energy. Herbs, acupuncture, massage, diet, and exercise are also used.

Trager Psychophysical Integration A bodywork technique in which the practitioner enters a meditative state and guides the client through gentle, light, rhythmic, nonintrusive movements. "Mentastics" exercises using self-healing movements are taught to the clients.

AUTHOR: **ANNE L. HUME, PHARM.D.**

Relaxation Techniques

Relaxation Techniques

Relaxation Technique	Summary	Further Resources
Breathing exercise	This is the foundation of most relaxation techniques. Have patients place one hand on the chest and the other on the abdomen. Instruct them to take a slow, deep breath, as if they were sucking in all the air in the room. While doing this, the hand on the abdomen should rise higher than the hand on the chest. This promotes diaphragmatic breathing that increases alveolar expansion in the bases of the lungs. Have them hold the breath for a count of 7 and then exhale. Exhalation should take twice as long as inhalation. Repeat this for a total of five breaths, and encourage patients to do this three times a day.	*Conscious Breathing* by Gay Hendricks is one of many good resources on using breathing for relaxation and health.
Meditation		
Transcendental/The relaxation response	To prevent distracting thoughts, the subject repeats a mantra (a word or sound) over and over again while sitting in a comfortable position. If a distracting thought comes to mind, it is accepted and let go, with the mind focusing again on the mantra.	www.mindbody.harvard.edu or *The Relaxation Response* by Herbert Benson; www.tm.org for information on transcendental meditation.
Mindful meditation	This represents the philosophy of living in the present or in the moment. The *body scan* is one technique where the subject uses breathing to obtain a relaxed state while lying or sitting. The mind progressively focuses on different parts of the body, where it feels any and all sensations intentionally but nonjudgmentally before moving on to another part of the body. A patient with back pain may focus on the quality and characteristics of the pain as if to better understand it and bring it under control.	*Full Catastrophe Living* by Jon Kabat-Zinn describes this technique in full and the program for stress reduction at the University of Massachusetts Medical Center.
Centering prayer	This is a form similar to transcendental meditation that has a more religious foundation. The subject repeats a "sacred word" similar to a mantra. As thoughts come to mind, they are accepted and let go, clearing the mind to become more centered on the spirit within, as if the mind's preoccupied thoughts are the layers of an onion that are peeled away, allowing better understanding of the spirit at the core.	www.centeringprayer.com; look under "method of centering prayer" for a nondenominational discussion.
Progressive muscle relaxation (PMR)	A form of relaxation in which the subject is attuned to the difference in feeling when the muscles are tensed and then relaxed. In a comfortable position, start by tensing the whole body from head to toe. While doing this, notice the feelings of tightness. Take a deep breath in and as you let it out, let the tension release and the muscles relax. This is then followed by progressive tension and relaxation throughout the body. One may start by clenching the fists and then tensing the arms, shoulders, chest, abdomen, hips, legs, and so on, with each step followed by relaxation.	www.uaex.edu/publications/pub/fshei28.htm is a good review of PMR as well as other relaxation exercises. It is sponsored by the University of Arkansas. *You Must Relax* is a book by the founder of this technique, Edmund Jacobson.
Visualization/Self-hypnosis	The subject uses visualization to recruit images that create a relaxed state. For example, if a person is anxious, visualizing images of a place and a time that were peaceful and comforting would help induce relaxation. This is best used in conjunction with a breathing exercise.	There are many CDs, MP3s, and DVDs that can guide people through a visualization "script" that can result in relaxation. Emmett Miller is one well-known author.
Autogenic training	This induces a physiologic response by using simple phrases. For example, "My legs are heavy and warm" is meant to increase the blood flow to this area, resulting in relaxation. This is done progressively from head to toe with the use of deep breathing and repetition of the phrase. After completing this, focus attention on any body part that may still be tense, and then focus the breath and phrase to that area until the whole body is relaxed.	The British Autogenic Society at www.autogenictherapy.org.uk is a good resource for more information.

Continued on following page

Relaxation Techniques—cont'd

Relaxation Technique	Summary	Further Resources
Exercise/Movement		
Aerobic	While performing an aerobic exercise, focus attention on a phrase, sound, word, or prayer and passively disregard other thoughts that may enter the mind. Some may focus on their breathing, saying to themselves, "In" with inhalation and "Out" with exhalation, or repeating "one-two, one-two" with each step they take with jogging. Doing this will help the mind focus, preventing other thoughts that may cause tension.	*Beyond the Relaxation Response* by Herbert Benson includes discussion of his research on inducing the relaxation response while exercising.
Yoga	This has been practiced for thousands of years in India. In America, it has been divided into three aspects: breathing (pranayama yoga), bodily postures or asanas (hatha yoga), and meditation to maintain balance and health. Regular practice induces relaxation.	For Yoga, t'ai chi, and qi gong therapies, it is best to encourage patients to take a class at a local community center or gym and to pick up an introductory book at a library or bookstore.
T'ai chi	An ancient Chinese martial art that uses slow, graceful movements combined with inner mindfulness and breathing techniques to help bring balance between the mind and body.	See above.
Qi gong	A traditional Chinese practice that uses movement, meditation, and controlled breathing to balance the body's vital energy force, Qi.	See above.

From Rakel RE (ed): *Principles of family practice,* ed 6, Philadelphia, 2002, Saunders.

Overview of Selected Natural Products

This table includes a few of the common uses and side effects of selected natural products. The evidence supporting the uses and side effects of these products varies considerably and may be based on anecdotal information or theoretical concerns with the natural products.

Natural Products	Common Use(s)	Adverse Effects/Potential Concerns
African plum (Pygeum)	Benign prostatic hyperplasia	Nausea and abdominal pain have been reported, but pygeum is generally well tolerated. Pygeum does not decrease prostate size or influence PSA concentrations.
Andrographis	Prevention and treatment of viral respiratory infections	Headache, fatigue, rash, diarrhea, and vomiting. Products are standardized to 4%-6% andrographolide; this botanical is commonly used in combination products.
Black cohosh	Menopausal symptoms (hot flashes), induction of labor in pregnant women, premenstrual syndrome	Dyspepsia, rash, weight gain, headache, and cramping have been reported. Concern exists that black cohosh causes liver toxicity. The potential development of mild estrogen-like adverse effects, especially endometrial hyperplasia, is of concern.
Butterbur	Prevention of migraine headaches; allergic rhinitis; urinary tract spasms; pain	Diarrhea, stomach upset, fatigue, belching, headache, and drowsiness may occur. Due to concern about hepatotoxicity, butterbur products should be free of pyrrolizidine alkaloids. Products should be standardized to 15% petasin and isopetasin.
Chamomile (German)	Motion sickness, anxiety, insomnia; gastrointestinal spasms; mucositis	Allergic reactions occur on rare occasion. Patients with a ragweed allergy should use chamomile with caution.
Chasteberry	Premenstrual dysphoric disorder, premenstrual syndrome, menopausal symptoms, female infertility, mastalgia	Gastrointestinal upset, headache, rash, acne, weight gain, and menstrual bleeding have been reported.
Chitosan	Weight loss, Crohn's disease, hypercholesterolemia, anemia	Gastrointestinal upset, nausea, flatulence, and constipation have been reported. Patients with a shellfish allergy should avoid the use of chitosan.
Chondroitin sulfate	Osteoarthritis, osteoporosis, hyperlipidemia	Gastrointestinal upset, nausea, diarrhea, constipation, and alopecia. Concern exists that chondroitin may have anticoagulant activity due to its structural similarity to part of heparin.
Cinnamon	Type 2 diabetes mellitus, flatulence, gastrointestinal spasms, anorexia, menopausal symptoms, impotence	Cassia cinnamon is one of three types of cinnamon in commercial food products; this is the only type that may have minor effects to improve blood glucose concentrations.
Coenzyme Q10	Congestive heart failure, angina, dilated cardiomyopathy, statin-induced myopathy, Parkinson's disease, chronic fatigue syndrome, HIV/AIDS	Nausea, vomiting, diarrhea, anorexia, heartburn, and rash have been reported. Coenzyme Q10 is structurally similar to vitamin K; concern exists about potential interaction with warfarin.
Cranberry	Prevention and treatment of urinary tract infections; type 2 diabetes mellitus; chronic fatigue syndrome; pleurisy	Gastrointestinal upset and diarrhea have been reported with large doses of cranberry. Uric acid kidney stone formation is also possible with large doses of cranberry over prolonged periods of time.
Dehydroepiandrosterone (DHEA)	Slow or reverse aging, weight loss, metabolic syndrome, erectile dysfunction, immune stimulant, osteoporosis, systemic lupus erythematosus, multiple sclerosis, depression, schizophrenia	Acne and other androgenic effects commonly occur in women. Alopecia, insulin resistance, hepatic dysfunction, and hypertension have been reported. Ingested wild yam and soy cannot be converted into DHEA by humans.
Devil's claw	Osteoarthritis, atherosclerosis, gout, myalgias, fever, migraines	Diarrhea, nausea, and vomiting, as well as allergic reactions, have been reported.
Echinacea	Prevention and treatment of viral respiratory infections; urinary tract infections; chronic fatigue syndrome; attention deficit hyperactivity disorder	Nausea, vomiting, diarrhea, heartburn, headaches, dizziness, arthralgias, and allergic reactions have been reported with echinacea. Patients with a ragweed allergy should use echinacea with caution because the risk of allergic reactions may be increased.

Natural Products	Common Use(s)	Adverse Effects/Potential Concerns
Eleuthero (Siberian ginseng)	Maintenance of a normal blood pressure; athero-sclerosis; Alzheimer's disease; chronic fatigue syndrome; diabetes; herpes simplex infections	Drowsiness, anxiety, and irritability have been reported.
Evening primrose oil (EPO)	Premenstrual syndrome, mastalgia, osteoporosis, asthma, menopausal symptoms, eczema, chronic fatigue syndrome	EPO is well tolerated.
Fenugreek	Type 2 diabetes mellitus, anorexia, atherosclerosis; also used as galactogogue	Gastrointestinal upset, flatulence, and hypoglycemia are possible side effects. Patients with a peanut allergy (and an allergy to related plants) should use fenu-greek with caution. Nursing mothers who use fenugreek may notice a "maple syrup" smell in their sweat and in the urine of their infants. This may be mistaken to be maple syrup urine disease in the infant.
Feverfew	Prevention of migraines; fever; menstrual-related problems; arthritis; infertility; asthma	Gastrointestinal side effects are the most common with feverfew. A "post-feverfew syndrome" has been reported in individuals who have taken feverfew for pro-longed periods of time and then have abruptly stopped the herbal.
Fish oil	Hypertriglyceridemia, coronary heart disease, hypertension, asthma, depression, rheumatoid arthritis, osteoporosis, psoriasis	Heartburn, nausea, rash, and a "fishy" aftertaste can occur. Contamination with pesticides (as well as with mercury and other heavy metals) is a potential concern, although this is unlikely.
Garlic	Hyperlipidemia, hypertension, peripheral arterial disease, type 2 diabetes mellitus	Nausea, vomiting, heartburn, and body odor are most common. "Deodorized" garlic products may lack the active ingredient, allicin.
Ginger	Nausea and vomiting secondary to pregnancy, che-motherapy, motion sickness, surgery	Heartburn, belching, and dermatitis have been reported. In overdoses, ginger has been associated with central nervous system depression and arrhythmias. Efficacy for hyperemesis gravidarum is unknown, and use is not recommended.
Ginkgo	Alzheimer's disease, vascular dementias, tinnitus, acute mountain sickness, intermittent claudication	Gastrointestinal side effects, headaches, dizziness, and allergic skin reactions. Seizures have been reported in several case reports. Products should contain 24% ginkgo flavone glycosides and 6% terpenoids.
Ginseng (Panax)	Increased resistance to stress and improved well-being; increased physical stamina; depression; diabetes; erectile dysfunction	Insomnia has been reported with ginseng. Vaginal bleeding, mastalgia, and amenorrhea have also been reported.
Glucosamine sulfate	Osteoarthritis	Nausea, heartburn, skin reactions, and headache have been reported. Increased glucose concentrations have been a concern but have not been well documented. Patients with a shellfish allergy should use glucosamine with caution.
Green tea	Improve cognitive performance; prevention of breast, prostate, and colon cancer; hyperlipid-emia; Parkinson's disease; obesity; diabetes; cardiovascular disease	Nausea, vomiting, dyspepsia, dizziness, insomnia, and nervousness have been reported. Side effects may be a result of the large amount of caffeine in green tea products. Hepatotoxicity has been a potential concern with green tea.
Hawthorn	Mild heart failure, angina, arrhythmias, hypertension	Mild gastrointestinal effects, dizziness, rash, palpitations, and nervousness have been reported.
Hoodia	Obesity	Side effects have not been reported. Many products lack the actual ingredient.
Horse chestnut	Chronic venous insufficiency, including varicose veins; benign prostate hyperplasia; diarrhea	Mild nausea, vomiting, dizziness, headache, and itching. Products are standardized to 16%-20% aescin.
Huperzine	Alzheimer's disease, increased alertness and energy, myasthenia gravis, memory enhancement	Nausea, vomiting, diarrhea, sweating, and blurred vision as a result of the cholin-ergic effects of huperzine have been reported.
Kava	Anxiety, insomnia, restlessness, seizure disorders, depression, chronic fatigue syndrome	Gastrointestinal upset, headache, dizziness, "kava" dermopathy, and allergic skin reactions. Hepatotoxicity is the primary concern with kava; some countries have banned the use of kava.
Melatonin	Jet lag, insomnia, migraine, chronic fatigue syn-drome, breast cancer, osteoporosis; also used for insomnia in children with ADHD	Daytime drowsiness, headache, and dizziness have been reported. Vaginal bleed-ing has occurred in perimenopausal women. Melatonin from animal sources should be avoided.
Melissa	Cold sores (topically), anxiety, insomnia, Alzheimer's disease, hypertension, dyspepsia	Nausea, vomiting, dizziness, and wheezing have occurred with oral melissa.
Methylsulfonylmethane (MSM)	Chronic pain, arthritis, diabetes, osteoporosis, aller-gies, obesity, premenstrual syndrome	Nausea, bloating, diarrhea, fatigue, and insomnia have been associated with MSM. This substance is used frequently in combination with glucosamine and chondroitin.
Milk thistle	Protective agent against liver damage due to alco-hol, acetaminophen, and carbon tetrachloride; hepatitis C	Nausea, abdominal fullness, diarrhea, and allergic reactions. Patients with a ragweed allergy should use milk thistle with caution.
Peppermint	Irritable bowel syndrome, sinusitis, morning sick-ness, dysmenorrhea	Heartburn has been reported, as well as laryngeal and bronchial spasm in infants and children.
Policosanol	Hyperlipidemia, intermittent claudication, athero-sclerosis	Migraines, insomnia, dizziness, skin rash, and bleeding have been reported with policosanol. The product has antiplatelet effects.
Probiotics	Treatment and prevention of diarrhea including antibiotic-associated diarrhea; irritable bowel syndrome; atopic dermatitis; Crohn's disease	Theoretically, probiotic products may increase risk of infections in immunocompro-mised individuals.
Red clover phytoestrogens	Menopausal symptoms, premenstrual syndrome, asthma	Rash, myalgias, headaches, and vaginal bleeding have been reported. Theoretically, endometrial hyperplasia is an adverse effect from the use of these compounds.
Red yeast rice	Hyperlipidemia, indigestion, diarrhea, circulatory conditions, HIV/AIDS	Gastrointestinal upset and dizziness may occur. Red yeast rice may contain lovastatin-like compounds and potentially cause rhabdomyolysis.

Natural Products	Common Use(s)	Adverse Effects/Potential Concerns
S-adenosylmethionine (SAM-e)	Depression, anxiety, dementia, osteoarthritis, heart disease	Nausea, vomiting, diarrhea, headache, and nervousness have been reported. Concern exists that SAM-e raises homocysteine levels.
St. John's wort	Depression, anxiety, chronic fatigue syndrome, HIV/AIDS	Anxiety, gastrointestinal upset, vaginal bleeding, neuropathy, and rash can occur. Hypomania has been induced by St. John's wort.
Tea tree oil	Topical use for acne, fungal infections, lice, scabies	Local inflammation and contact dermatitis may occur.
Valerian	Insomnia, depression, chronic fatigue syndrome, menstrual cramps	Headaches, gastrointestinal upset, and drowsiness can occur. Hepatotoxicity is a potential concern with valerian.

AIDS, Acquired immune deficiency syndrome; *HIV,* human immunodeficiency virus.

AUTHOR: **ANNE L. HUME, PHARM.D.**

Appendix Id

Natural Products and Drug Interactions

This table lists interactions between selected natural products and prescription and nonprescription drugs. Although many of the listed interactions are theoretical in nature and have not been documented to occur in humans, those involving St. John's wort are potentially life threatening in nature, depending on the individual drug. Other interactions are based on small studies of healthy volunteers and use pharmaceutical-quality natural products that may or may not be commercially available.

Natural Products	Drugs	Interactions
Andrographis	Immune suppressants	Andrographis may stimulate immune function, potentially decreasing the effectiveness of drugs such as cyclosporine, tacrolimus, and prednisone.
	Antihypertensive agents	Andrographis may lower blood pressure, potentiating the hypotensive effects of antihypertensive agents.
	Antiplatelet and anticoagulant agents	Andrographis may have antiplatelet activity, potentially increasing the risk of bleeding.
Black cohosh	Hepatotoxic drugs	Concern exists that the risk of hepatotoxicity with black cohosh is increased in the presence of hepatotoxic drugs such as acetaminophen.
	Cisplatin	Animal studies suggest that the efficacy of cisplatin against breast cancer cells may be decreased by black cohosh.
	CYP2D6 substrates	Black cohosh may modestly inhibit CYP2D6 enzyme activity to result in higher drug concentrations.
Butterbur	CYP3A4 inducers (rifampin, carbamazepine, etc.)	Drugs that induce the activity of CYP3A4 increase the risk of the formation of hepatotoxic metabolites from pyrrolizidine alkaloids from some butterbur products.
Chamomile	CNS depressants (benzodiazepines, opiates, barbiturates, etc.)	Chamomile may have additive CNS depressant effects.
	CYP1A2 substrates	Chamomile may inhibit CYP1A2 enzyme activity to result in higher drug concentrations.
	CYP3A4 substrates	Chamomile may inhibit CYP3A4 enzyme activity to result in higher drug concentrations.
	Estrogens	Chamomile may compete for estrogen receptors.
	Tamoxifen	Chamomile may interfere with the effects of tamoxifen because of its estrogenic effects.
Chaste tree berry	Antipsychotic agents	Chaste tree berry may antagonize the effects of antipsychotic agents through its dopaminergic activity.
	Metoclopramide	Chaste tree berry may antagonize the effects of metoclopramide through its dopaminergic activity.
	Dopamine agonists	Chaste tree berry may possess additive effects to drugs such as levodopa and ropinirole through its dopaminergic activity.
	Oral contraceptives/estrogens	Chaste tree berry may possess additive hormonal effects.
Chondroitin	Warfarin	High-dose chondroitin has structural similarity to a heparinoid and may possess weak anticoagulant effects.
Cinnamon	Hypoglycemic agents	Cinnamon may possess additive effects on blood glucose to those of hypoglycemic agents.
Coenzyme Q10	Antihypertensive agents	Coenzyme Q10 may possess additive effects on blood pressure to those of antihypertensive agents.
	Warfarin	Coenzyme Q10 may lessen the anticoagulant effects of warfarin because of its structural similarity to vitamin K.
	Chemotherapy	The antioxidant effects of coenzyme Q10 may blunt the efficacy of certain chemotherapeutic agents that depend on the formation of free radicals.
Cranberry	CYP2C9 substrates (warfarin)	Cranberry may inhibit CYP2C9 enzyme activity to result in higher drug concentrations; evidence with warfarin is contradictory.
Dehydroepiandrosterone (DHEA)	Tamoxifen and aromatase inhibitors such as anastrozole and exemestane	DHEA may interfere with the antiestrogenic effects of these drugs.
	CYP3A4 substrates	DHEA may slightly inhibit CYP3A4 enzyme activity to result in higher drug concentrations.

Natural Products	Drugs	Interactions
Devil's claw	Antihypertensive agents	Devil's claw may possess additive effects on blood pressure to those of antihypertensive agents.
	Hypoglycemic agents	Devil's claw may possess additive effects on blood glucose to those of hypoglycemic agents.
	H₂ antagonists and PPIs	Devil's claw may raise gastric pH and blunt the efficacy of H_2 antagonists and PPIs.
	CYP3A4 substrates	Devil's claw may inhibit CYP3A4 enzyme activity to result in higher drug concentrations.
	CYP2C9 substrates	Devil's claw may inhibit CYP2C9 enzyme activity to result in higher drug concentrations.
	CYP2C19 substrates	Devil's claw may inhibit CYP2C19 enzyme activity to result in higher drug concentrations.
	Warfarin	Devil's claw may inhibit CYP2C9 enzyme activity to result in higher concentrations of warfarin; purpura has been reported.
Echinacea	Immune suppressants	Echinacea may stimulate immune function, potentially decreasing the effectiveness of drugs such as cyclosporine, tacrolimus, and prednisone.
	CYP3A4 substrates	Echinacea may modestly induce hepatic CYP3A4 enzyme activity to result in lower drug concentrations.
	CYP1A2 substrates	Echinacea may inhibit CYP1A2 enzyme activity to result in higher drug concentrations.
Eleuthero (Siberian ginseng)	CNS depressants (benzodiazepines, opiates, barbiturates, etc.)	Eleuthero may have additive CNS depressant effects.
	Antiplatelet and anticoagulant agents	Eleuthero may have antiplatelet activity, potentially increasing the risk of bleeding.
	CYP3A4 substrates	Eleuthero may inhibit CYP3A4 enzyme activity to result in higher drug concentrations.
	CYP1A2 substrates	Eleuthero may modestly inhibit CYP1A2 enzyme activity to result in higher drug concentrations.
	CYP2C9 substrates	Eleuthero may modestly inhibit CYP2C9 enzyme activity to result in higher drug concentrations.
	CYP2D6 substrates	Eleuthero may inhibit CYP2D6 enzyme activity to result in higher drug concentrations.
	Digoxin	Concentration of digoxin has been reported to increase but without evidence of toxicity.
Evening primrose oil (EPO)	Antiplatelet and anticoagulant agents	EPO may have anticoagulant activity, potentially increasing the risk of bleeding.
Fenugreek	Antiplatelet and anticoagulant agents	Fenugreek may have antiplatelet activity, potentially increasing the risk of bleeding.
	Hypoglycemic agents	Fenugreek may potentially lower blood glucose concentrations and have additive effects with hypoglycemic agents.
Feverfew	Antiplatelet and anticoagulant agents	Feverfew may have antiplatelet activity, potentially increasing the risk of bleeding.
	CYP3A4 substrates	Feverfew may inhibit CYP3A4 enzyme activity to result in higher drug concentrations.
	CYP1A2 substrates	Feverfew may inhibit CYP1A2 enzyme activity to result in higher drug concentrations.
	CYP2C9 substrates	Feverfew may inhibit CYP2C9 enzyme activity to result in higher drug concentrations.
	CYP2C19 substrates	Feverfew may inhibit CYP2C19 enzyme activity to result in higher drug concentrations.
Fish oils (omega-3 fatty acids)	Antiplatelet and anticoagulant agents	Fish oils may have antiplatelet activity, potentially increasing the risk of bleeding, although this has not been documented in humans.
	Antihypertensive agents	Fish oils may possess additive effects on blood pressure to those of antihypertensive agents.
	Oral contraceptives	Oral contraceptives may potentially interfere with the triglyceride-lowering effects of fish oil.
Garlic	Antiplatelet and anticoagulant agents	Garlic may have antiplatelet activity, potentially increasing the risk of bleeding.
	CYP3A4 substrates	Garlic may potentially induce CYP3A4 enzyme activity to result in lower drug concentrations; evidence is contradictory.
	CYP2E1 substrates	Garlic may modestly inhibit CYP2E1 enzyme activity to result in higher drug concentrations.
Ginger	Antiplatelet and anticoagulant agents	Ginger may have antiplatelet activity, potentially increasing the risk of bleeding.
	Hypoglycemic agents	Ginger may potentially lower blood glucose concentrations and have additive effects with hypoglycemic agents.
Ginkgo	Antiplatelet and anticoagulant agents	Ginkgo may have antiplatelet activity, potentially increasing the risk of bleeding.
	CYP2C19 substrates	Ginkgo may induce CYP2C19 enzyme activity to result in lower drug concentrations.
	CYP1A2 substrates	Ginkgo may modestly inhibit CYP1A2 enzyme activity to result in higher drug levels.
	CYP2C9 substrates	Ginkgo may modestly inhibit CYP2C9 enzyme activity to result in higher drug concentrations.
	CYP2D6 substrates	Ginkgo may inhibit CYP2D6 enzyme activity to result in higher drug concentrations.
Ginseng (Panax)	Antiplatelet and anticoagulant agents	Panax ginseng may have antiplatelet properties; American ginseng may decrease the effectiveness (international normalized ration [INR]) of warfarin.
	CYP2D6 substrates	Panax ginseng may modestly inhibit CYP2D6 enzyme activity to result in higher drug concentrations.
	Immune suppressants	Panax ginseng may stimulate immune function, potentially decreasing the effectiveness of drugs such as cyclosporine, tacrolimus, and prednisone.
	Hypoglycemic agents	Panax ginseng may potentially lower blood glucose levels and have additive effects with hypoglycemic agents.
Glucosamine	Warfarin	High-dose glucosamine (along with high-dose chondroitin) may have additive effects to those of warfarin because of structural similarity to heparin.

Continued on following page

Natural Products	Drugs	Interactions
Green tea extract	Antiplatelet agents	Green tea possesses compounds that may have antiplatelet activity, potentially increasing the risk of bleeding.
	Amphetamines	Caffeine in green tea may increase the risk of CNS toxicity.
	Cocaine	Caffeine in green tea may increase the risk of CNS toxicity.
	Oral contraceptives	Oral contraceptives may decrease the clearance of caffeine in green tea.
	Warfarin	Small amounts of vitamin K have been reported to be present in green tea, potentially decreasing the effectiveness of warfarin.
	Theophylline	Caffeine potentially decreases theophylline clearance.
	Verapamil	Verapamil decreases caffeine clearance, resulting in increased concentrations.
	Quinolone antibiotics	Some quinolone antibiotics decrease the clearance of caffeine.
	Hepatotoxic drugs	Concern exists that the risk of hepatotoxicity with green tea is increased in the presence of hepatotoxic drugs such as acetaminophen.
Hawthorn	β-Blockers	Hawthorn and β-blockers may have additive effects on blood pressure and heart rate.
	CCBs, nitrates	Hawthorn and CCBs (or nitrates) may have additive effects due to coronary vasodilation.
	Digoxin	Hawthorn may have additive effects to those of digoxin.
	Phosphodiesterase inhibitors	Hawthorn may have additive vasodilatory and hypotensive effects with sildenafil, tadalafil, and vardenafil.
Horse chestnut seed extract (HCSE)	Antiplatelet and anticoagulant agents	HCSE may have antiplatelet activity, potentially increasing the risk of bleeding.
	Hypoglycemic agents	HCSE may potentially lower blood glucose concentrations and have additive effects with hypoglycemic agents.
Huperzine	AChE inhibitors (donepezil, etc.)	Huperzine may have additive effects when combined with AChE inhibitors.
	Anticholinergic drugs	The effectiveness of huperzine and/or the anticholinergic drug may be decreased by their concomitant administration.
	Cholinergic drugs (bethanechol, neostigmine, etc.)	Huperzine may have additive effects when combined with cholinergic drugs.
Kava	CYP3A4 substrates	Kava may inhibit CYP3A4 enzyme activity to result in higher drug concentrations.
	CYP1A2 substrates	Kava may inhibit CYP1A2 enzyme activity to result in higher drug concentrations.
	CYP2C9 substrates, CYP2C19 substrates	Kava may inhibit CYP2C9 and CYP2C19 enzyme activity to result in higher drug concentrations.
	CYP2D6 substrates	Kava may inhibit CYP2D6 enzyme activity to result in higher drug concentrations.
	P-glycoprotein substrates (digoxin; etoposide, paclitaxel, vinblastine, vincristine; itraconazole; diltiazem, verapamil; and many other drugs)	Kava may inhibit P-glycoprotein transporter systems.
	Hepatotoxic drugs	Concern exists that the risk of hepatotoxicity from kava is increased in the presence of hepatotoxic drugs such as acetaminophen.
Melatonin	Antiplatelet and anticoagulant agents	Melatonin may potentiate the effects of antiplatelets and anticoagulants, although the mechanism is unknown.
	CNS depressants	Melatonin may have additive CNS depressant effects.
	Fluvoxamine	Fluvoxamine may increase levels of melatonin.
	Immune suppressants	Melatonin may stimulate immune function, potentially decreasing the effectiveness of drugs such as cyclosporine, tacrolimus, and prednisone.
	Hypoglycemic agents	Melatonin may impair glucose utilization and may decrease the efficacy of hypoglycemic agents.
Milk thistle	Estrogens (and other drugs that undergo glucuronidation)	Silymarin may increase the clearance of estrogens.
	CYP2C9 substrates	Milk thistle may modestly inhibit CYP2C9 enzyme activity to result in higher drug concentrations.
Peppermint oil	H_2 antagonists and proton pump inhibitors	Peppermint oil may raise gastric pH and blunt efficacy of H_2 antagonists and PPIs.
	CYP3A4 substrates	Peppermint oil may modestly inhibit CYP3A4 enzyme activity to result in higher drug concentrations.
	CYP1A2 substrates	Peppermint oil may modestly inhibit CYP1A2 enzyme activity to result in higher drug concentrations.
	CYP2C9 substrates, CYP2C19 substrates	Peppermint oil may modestly inhibit CYP2C9 and CYP2C19 enzyme activity to result in higher drug concentrations.
Policosanol	Antiplatelet and anticoagulant agents	Policosanol may have antiplatelet activity, potentially increasing the risk of bleeding.
Probiotics	Antibiotics	Antibiotics may kill the live organisms in different probiotic preparations.
	Immune suppressants	Theoretically, probiotics may cause bacterial or fungal infections in patients who are taking immune suppressants chronically.

Natural Products	Drugs	Interactions
Red clover phytoestrogens	Antiplatelet and anticoagulant agents	Theoretically, red clover may possess coumarins, which increase the risk of bleeding with antiplatelet and anticoagulants.
	CYP3A4 substrates	Red clover may inhibit CYP3A4 enzyme activity to result in higher drug concentrations.
	CYP2C9 substrates, CYP2C19 substrates	Red clover may inhibit CYP2C9 and CYP2C19 enzyme activity to result in higher drug concentrations.
	CYP1A2 substrates	Red clover may inhibit CYP1A2 enzyme activity to result in higher drug concentrations.
Red yeast rice	CYP3A4 inhibitors	Drugs that inhibit CYP3A4 may decrease the metabolism of lovastatin in red yeast rice.
	Statins	Red yeast rice contains lovastatin and increases the risk of myopathy (and hepatotoxicity).
	Fibrates and niacin	Fibrates and niacin may increase concentrations of lovastatin in red yeast rice.
S-adenosylmethionine (SAM-e)	Antidepressants (including MAOIs)	Additive effects are possible, and there is potential for toxicity.
	Serotonergic drugs (triptans, SSRIs, tramadol, meperidine, dextromethorphan, etc.)	SAM-e may increase the risk of development of serotonin syndrome when used concomitantly.
Soy phytoestrogens	Antibiotics	Antibiotics may decrease the efficacy of soy because intestinal bacteria convert isoflavones into more active forms.
	Estrogens	Soy potentially may inhibit the effects of estrogen.
	Tamoxifen/aromatase inhibitors	Soy's estrogenic effects may antagonize the antitumor effects of tamoxifen/aromatase inhibitors.
	MAOIs	Fermented soy products may contain tyramine.
St. John's wort	CYP3A4 substrates	St. John's wort strongly induces CYP3A4 enzyme activity to result in lower drug concentrations.
	CYP1A2 substrates	St. John's wort modestly induces CYP1A2 enzyme activity to result in lower drug levels.
	CYP2C9 substrates	St. John's wort induces CYP2C9 enzyme activity to result in lower drug concentrations.
	P-glycoprotein substrates (digoxin; etoposide, paclitaxel, vinblastine, vincristine; itraconazole; diltiazem, verapamil; and other drugs)	St. John's wort induces P-glycoprotein transporter systems.
	Serotonergic drugs (triptans, SSRIs, tramadol, meperidine, dextromethorphan, etc.)	St. John's wort may increase the risk of development of serotonin syndrome when used concomitantly.
Valerian	CNS depressants (benzodiazepines, opiates, barbiturates, alcohol, etc.)	Valerian may increase the sedative effects of CNS depressants.
	CYP3A4 substrates	Valerian may modestly inhibit the CYP3A4 enzyme activity.

AChE, Acetylcholinesterase; *CCBs,* calcium channel blockers; *CNS,* central nervous system; *MAOIs,* monoamine oxidase inhibitor; *PPIs,* proton pump inhibitors; *SSRIs,* selective serotonin reuptake inhibitors.

EXAMPLES OF DRUGS METABOLIZED BY CYP ENZYMES

The following are examples of drugs that are metabolized through the different cytochrome P450 isoenzymes:

CYP1A2 substrates: theophylline, imipramine, clozapine, naproxen

CYP2C9 substrates: warfarin, tamoxifen, irbesartan, ibuprofen, glipizide

CYP2C19 substrates: omeprazole and other proton pump inhibitors, phenytoin, phenobarbital, cyclophosphamide

CYP2D6 substrates: S-metoprolol, propafenone, paroxetine, risperidone, tramadol

CYP2E1 substrates: acetaminophen, alcohol

CYP3A4 substrates: most statins, indinavir, amlodipine, verapamil, alprazolam, buspirone

(For a complete list of drugs and their respective metabolic pathways through the cytochrome P450 isoenzyme systems go to http://medicine.iupui.edu/flockhart.)

AUTHOR: **ANNE L. HUME, PHARM.D.**

Commonly Ingested Plants with Significant Toxic Potential

Plant	Symptoms	Management
Autumn crocus (Colchicum autumnale)	Vomiting Diarrhea Initial leukocytosis followed by bone marrow failure Multisystem organ failure	Activated charcoal decontamination Aggressive fluid resuscitation and supportive care
Belladonna alkaloids: jimson weed (Datura stramonium) Belladonna ("deadly nightshade"; Atropa belladonna)	Anticholinergic toxidrome Seizures	Supportive care, benzodiazepines Consider physostigmine if patient is a threat to self or others; only use if no conduction delays on ECG
Cardiac glycoside–containing plants (foxglove, lily of the valley, oleander, yellow oleander, etc.)	Nausea Vomiting Bradycardia Dysrhythmias (AV block, ventricular ectopy) Hyperkalemia	Digoxin-specific Fab fragments
Jequirity bean and other abrin-containing species (e.g., rosary pea, precatory bean)	Oral pain Vomiting Diarrhea Shock Hemolysis Renal failure	Supportive care, including aggressive volume resuscitation and correction of electrolyte abnormalities
Monkshood (Aconitum species)	Numbness and tingling of lips/tongue Vomiting Bradycardia	Atropine for bradycardia Supportive care
Oxalate-containing plants: Philodendron, Diffenbachia, Colocasia ("elephant ear")	Local tissue injury Oral pain Vomiting	Supportive care, pain control
Poison hemlock (Conium maculatum)	Vomiting Agitation followed by CNS depression Paralysis Respiratory failure	Supportive care
Pokeweed	Hemorrhagic gastroenteritis Burning of mouth and throat	Supportive care
Rhododendron	Vomiting Diarrhea Bradycardia	Atropine for symptomatic bradycardia Supportive care
Tobacco	Vomiting Agitation Diaphoresis Fasciculations Seizures	Supportive care
Water hemlock (Cicuta species)	Abdominal pain Vomiting Delirium Seizures	Supportive care, including benzodiazepines for seizures
Yew (Taxus species)	GI symptoms QRS widening Hypotension CV collapse	Supportive care Atropine for bradycardia Sodium bicarbonate does not appear to be effective

AV, Atrioventricular; CNS, central nervous system; CV, cardiovascular; ECG, electrocardiogram; Fab, fragment, antigen binding; GI, gastrointestinal.
From Kliegman RM et al: Nelson textbook of pediatrics, ed 19, Philadelphia, 2011, Saunders.

Herbs Associated with Toxicity

Herbal Product	Toxic Chemicals	Toxic Effects
Aconite (*Aconitum* spp.)	Aconitine alkaloids	Nausea, vomiting, paresthesias, weakness, hypotension, asystole, arrhythmias, bradycardia
Chamomile (*Matricaria chamomilla, Anthemis nobilis*)	Allergens	Anaphylaxis, contact dermatitis
Chapparal (*Larrea divaricate, Larrea tridentate*)	Nordihydroguaiaretic acid	Nausea, vomiting, lethargy, hepatitis
Cinnamon oil (*Cinnamomum* spp.)	Cinnamaldehyde	Dermatitis, abuse syndrome
Coltsfoot (*Tussilago farfara*)	Pyrrolizidines	HVOD
Comfrey (*Symphytum officinale*)	Pyrrolizidines	HVOD
Crotalaria spp.	Pyrrolizidines	HVOD
Echinacea (*Echinacea angustifolia*, Compositae spp.)	Polysaccharides	Asthma, atopy, angioedema, anaphylaxis, urticaria
Eucalyptus (*Eucalyptus globulus*)	1,8-cineole	Drowsiness, ataxia, nausea, vomiting, seizures, coma, respiratory failure
Garlic (*Allium sativum*)	Allicin	Dermatitis, chemical burns, oxidizing agent
Germander (*Teucrium chamaedrys*)		Hepatotoxicity
Ginseng (*Panax ginseng*)	Ginsenoside	Ginseng abuse, diarrhea, anxiety, insomnia, hypertension
Glycerated asafetida	Oxidants	Methemoglobinemia
Groundsel (*Senecio longilobus*)	Pyrrolizidines	HVOD
Heliotrope, turnsole (*Crotalaria tulva, Heliotropium, Cynoglossum officinale*)	Pyrrolizidines	HVOD
Jin bu huan (*Stephania* spp., *Corydalis* spp.)	L-Tetrahydropalmitine	Hepatitis, lethargy, coma
Kava-kava (*Piper methysticum*)	Kawain, methysticin	Hepatic failure, "kavaism," neurotoxicity
Kelp	Iodine	Thyroid dysfunction
Laetrile	Cyanide	Coma, seizures, death
Licorice (*Glycyrrhiza glabra*)	Glycyrrhetic acid	Hypertension, cardiac arrhythmias, hypokalemia
Ma huang (*Ephedra sinica*)	Ephedrine	Cardiac arrhythmias, seizures, stroke, hypertension
Monkshood (*Aconitum napellus, A. columbianum*)	Aconite	Cardiac arrhythmias, weakness, coma, shock, paresthesias, vomiting, seizures
Nutmeg (*Myristica fragrans*)	Myristicin, eugenol	Hallucinations, emesis, headache
Nux vomica	Strychnine	Seizures, abdominal pain, respiratory arrest
Pennyroyal (*Mentha pulegium* or *Hedeoma* spp.)	Pulegone	Centrilobular liver necrosis, fetotoxicity, seizures, shock
Ragwort (golden) (*Senecio aureus, Echium*)	Pyrrolizidines	HVOD
Wormwood (*Artemisia* spp.)	Thujone	Seizures, dementia, tremors, headache

HVOD, Hepatic venoocclusive disease.
From Fuhrman BP et al: *Pediatric critical care,* ed 4, Philadelphia, 2011, Saunders.

Appendix Ig

Websites Providing Data on Herbal Therapy Hazards

Web Address	Website
http://www.fda.gov or http://www.vmcfsan.fda.gov/-dms/aems/html	On the U.S. Food and Drug Administration website under the title "Medwatch," some herb warnings can be found ("special adverse event monitoring system" link)
http://www.faseb.org/aspet/H&MIG3.htm#top	ASPET Herbal and Medicinal Plant Interest Group: a site for an herb discussion group with pharmacologists
http://www.nnlm.nlm.nih.gov/pnr/uwmhg/	University of Washington Medicinal Herb Garden
http://www.nim.nih.gov/medlineplus/herbalmedicine.html	Provides an update on ongoing clinical studies involving herbal products, news, and many links
http://www.update-software.com/abstracts/mainindex.html	The Cochrane Collaboration maintains an updated international database of clinical trials involving complementary and alternative medicine
http://www.amfoundation.org/	Providing consumers and professionals with responsible evidence-based information on the integration of alternative and conventional medicine
http://www.herbmed.org/	An interactive electronic herbal database provides hyperlinked access to scientific data underlying the use of herbs for health; an evidence-based information resource for professionals, researchers, and the general public
http://nccam.nih.gov/	The National Center for Complementary and Alternative Medicine is 1 of 27 institutes and centers that make up the U.S. National Institutes of Health; their mission is to support rigorous research on complementary and alternative medicine, train researchers, and disseminate information to the general public and professionals
http://toxnet.nlm.nih.gov/	A cluster of databases on toxicology, hazardous chemicals, and related areas

From Floege J et al: *Comprehensive clinical nephrology*, ed 4, Philadelphia, 2010, Saunders.

Dietary Supplements: What Every Primary Care Provider Should Know

Primary care providers must be knowledgeable regarding the safety, efficacy, and drug interactions associated with common dietary supplements because of the following:

- An estimated 38% of adults ages 18 years and older reported the use of at least one form of complementary and alternative medicine (CAM) according to the National Health Interview Survey in 2007.
- Almost 17.8% of adults specifically reported the use of dietary supplements, with fish oil, glucosamine, echinacea, flaxseed, and ginseng most frequently used.
- Although the use of dietary supplements has plateaued as a result of consumer concerns about effectiveness and potential adverse effects, usage remains common and potentially dangerous.

COMMON TERMINOLOGY

- A *dietary supplement* is defined as an oral product containing vitamins, minerals, herbs, or other botanicals; amino acids; dietary substances used to supplement the diet by increasing the total dietary intake; or a concentrate, metabolite, constituent, extract, or combination.
- *CAM* refers to the broad domain of healing practices that include diverse health systems, modalities, and practices and their accompanying theories and beliefs (see glossary of terms in Appendix Ia).
- *Complementary therapies* are those that are used *in addition to* conventional therapies, whereas *alternative therapies* are those that are used *instead of* conventional therapies. Most consumers in the United States use dietary supplements as a complementary therapy.
- *Standardization* refers to the practice of producing dietary supplements with a specific amount of a given compound that may or may not include the actual active ingredient. For example, feverfew has been standardized to its parthenolide content.

LEGISLATION

The U.S. Food and Drug Administration (FDA) is frequently criticized for not closely regulating dietary supplements and monitoring their safety. However, although the agency regulates prescription drugs and over-the-counter (OTC) products, the FDA has limited regulatory authority over dietary supplements. This is because the Dietary Supplement and Health Education Act (DSHEA) of 1994 and its resulting regulations limit the FDA's authority. As a result of DSHEA, the FDA is able to act only when a dietary supplement has been documented to contain a prescription drug, as was the case with glyburide in a natural treatment for diabetes and diazepam in an osteoarthritis preparation. In addition, the FDA can act when safety issues related to a product have been clearly documented, although these cases are frequently challenged in the courts.

HEALTH CLAIMS

Dietary supplements generally are marketed under three types of health claims. The first category is the "nutrient content" claim, in which the product is identified as an excellent source of, typically, a mineral such as calcium, based on recommended daily values. The second type is the "significant scientific agreement" claim; these claims are used when some evidence of the product's efficacy exists (e.g., fish oil supplements). The third and most common type of health claim is called a "structure/function" claim; these claims state that the product has some effect on health—for example, "helps to maintain a healthy heart." However, dietary supplements are not permitted to carry claims stating that they are effective in preventing, treating, or curing diseases.

INFORMATION RESOURCES

Appendix Ic provides a brief overview of common dietary supplements. Until recently, few evidence-based resources on dietary supplements were available. Clinical studies and systematic reviews on dietary supplements are now widely available through PubMed, EMBASE, and the Cochrane Database of Systematic Reviews. Although more information is available, references on specific products vary in their interpretation of the available evidence and may exhibit an unintentional bias, either pro or con, regarding the safety and efficacy of dietary supplements.

"Gold standard" evidence-based databases on dietary supplements (subscription required) include the following:

- Natural Medicines Comprehensive Database (http://www.naturaldatabase.com): This database includes listings for many dietary supplements and is organized in a clinician-friendly manner. Monographs include the different common and scientific names; uses and likely effectiveness for different uses; chemical constituents; interactions with drugs, diseases, foods, and laboratory tests; adverse effects; and cautions. The information is extensively referenced and is updated on a daily basis. The primary limitation is that the evaluation of data on clinical effectiveness could be more rigorous.
- Natural Standard (http://www.naturalstandard.com): This database includes listings for dietary supplements and other forms of complementary and alternative medicine. The evidence supporting the assessments in this database is critically evaluated and rigorous in nature. The primary limitation is that many fewer dietary supplements are included in this database.

Evidence-based free websites on dietary supplements include the following:

- National Center for Complementary and Alternative Medicine (NCCAM) (http://nccam.nih.gov)
- Office of Dietary Supplements International Bibliographic Information on Dietary Supplements (http://dietary-supplements.info.nih.gov/Health_Information/IBIDS.aspx)
- Memorial Sloan-Kettering Cancer Center (http://www.mskcc.org/mskcc/html/11570.cfm)

DRUG INTERACTIONS

Clinically significant interactions have been documented between dietary supplements and prescription or OTC drugs. The challenge for primary care providers is to identify real, clinically relevant interactions versus potential or theoretical interactions. Data on interactions with dietary supplements are usually based on isolated case reports or on studies enrolling healthy volunteers. As with drug-drug interactions, the likelihood of an interaction and its severity are influenced especially by concomitant medical conditions, such as heart failure and presence or absence of impaired kidney and liver function.

Appendix Id lists interactions between selected natural products and prescription and nonprescription drugs. The following two broad interactions are particularly important in primary care practice:

- St. John's wort, commonly used for depression, is a potent inducer of cytochrome P450 3A4 isoenzymes and has been documented to increase the clearance of many drugs that are metabolized through this (and other) pathways. (For a list of common drugs cleared in this manner, readers should consult http://medicine.iupui.edu/flockhart/clinlist.htm.) In addition, St. John's wort may induce P-glycoprotein transporter systems that are important for digoxin and some chemotherapeutic agents. St. John's wort has also been associated with the development of serotonin syndrome when used with drugs that have significant serotonergic activity.

- Dietary supplements such as garlic, ginkgo, and feverfew, as well as many others, have been purported to either have antiplatelet activity or have effects on the clotting cascade. This may be important for adults also taking aspirin (and other platelet-active agents) or warfarin.

COUNSELING POINTS

The single most important counseling point related to dietary supplements is always to ask patients about their use of these products and to do so in an open, nonjudgmental manner. The approach should emphasize that many consumers have been interested in vitamins, minerals, herbs, teas, and so on, to maintain their health or to treat illness. If the clinician is unaware of the safety, efficacy, and interactions of a specific product, several websites are available to quickly scan for information. Also, access to drug information centers at colleges of pharmacy is almost always available, and some hospitals now offer programs in integrative medicine.

Patients should be asked about their goals in using the product, as well as how long they have taken it and in what dosage. Allergies to plants should be documented because cross-allergies are common. Clinicians should appreciate that individuals who use dietary supplements may be interested in making lifestyle changes and potentially decreasing their use of prescription drugs. In addition, if an individual is also consulting an alternative medicine practitioner, clinicians should recognize that some alternative health systems discourage the use of established therapies such as vaccines.

Although problems with safety and efficacy have been identified, many dietary supplements are benign except for their cost. Some patients are at higher risk for adverse outcomes from the use of dietary supplements (e.g., those with chronic kidney and liver disease). Patients should be counseled specifically to avoid purchasing dietary supplements over the Internet.

RESEARCH ISSUES

Many clinical and observational studies of dietary supplements have been published. In the past, clinicians frequently stated either that published studies of dietary supplements did not exist or that only a few were available. The reason for this finding was that until recently the National Library of Medicine did not abstract from the peer-reviewed alternative medicine literature. Fortunately, much more research is now readily available. As with all research, the more rigorous the study methodology, the less likely the dietary supplement is to demonstrate clinical benefit.

In evaluating published studies of dietary supplements, the following should be considered:

- Has the correct plant and part of the plant (root, stem, leaf) been used? This critical information may not be known to many clinicians. Consulting a resource such as the National Medicines Comprehensive Database can usually provide the needed information to judge this component of the study.

- Has the content of active ingredients been verified throughout the study? In a recent review of 81 major randomized controlled trials of herbal products, only 12 (15%) reported performing tests to quantify actual contents, and 3 (4%) provided adequate data to compare actual with expected content values of at least one chemical constituent.

- Is the severity of the disease appropriate for study? Negative studies with dietary supplements sometimes inappropriately enroll participants who have moderate-to-severe disease (e.g., those with depression or benign prostatic hyperplasia) when only mild disease would be appropriate.

- Is the duration of the study appropriate? Early studies comparing glucosamine and nonsteroidal anti-inflammatory agents (NSAIAs) demonstrated greater efficacy with the NSAIAs because of an inadequate study duration for glucosamine to show any benefit.

- Is a placebo group included? Recent studies with dietary supplements for menopausal symptoms and osteoarthritis have demonstrated placebo responses over 40% to 50%.

- Was the blinding maintained throughout the study? Some dietary supplements, such as saw palmetto, have distinctive odors and tastes that are not easily masked.

- Is the preparation commercially available? Most important, when a study with dietary supplements does show benefit, it frequently is difficult to use the product in practice because the specific formulation studied is not commercially available.

AUTHOR: **ANNE L. HUME, PHARM.D.**

Vitamins and Their Functions

	Biochemistry and Physiology	Deficiency [RDA*]	Toxicity [TUL†]	Assessment of Status
Fat-Soluble Vitamins				
Vitamin A	A family of the retinoid compounds, each member having biologic activity qualitatively similar to retinol. Carotenoids are structurally related to retinoids. Some carotenoids, most notably β-carotene, are metabolized into compounds with vitamin A activity and are therefore considered to be provitamin A compounds. Vitamin A is an integral component of rhodopsin and iodopsins, light-sensitive proteins in rod and cone cells in the retina. *Additional functions:* induction and maintenance of cellular differentiation in certain tissues; signal for appropriate morphogenesis in the developing embryo; maintenance of cell-mediated immunity. One microgram of retinol = 3.33 IU of vitamin A.	Follicular hyperkeratosis and night blindness are early indicators. Conjunctival xerosis, degeneration of the cornea (keratomalacia), and de-differentiation of rapidly proliferating epithelia are later indications of deficiency. *Bitot spots* (focal areas of the conjunctiva or cornea with foamy appearance) are an indication of xerosis. Blindness, due to corneal destruction and retinal dysfunction, ensues if left uncorrected. Increased susceptibility to infection is also a consequence. [F: 700 μg; M: 900 μg]	In adults, >150,000 μg may cause acute toxicity: fatal intracranial hypertension, skin exfoliation, and hepatocellular necrosis. *Chronic* toxicity may occur with habitual daily intake of >10,000 μg: alopecia, ataxia, bone and muscle pain, dermatitis, cheilitis, conjunctivitis, pseudotumor cerebri, hepatocellular necrosis, hyperlipidomia, and hyperostosis are common. Single, large doses of vitamin A (30,000 μg), or habitual intake of >4500 μg/day in early pregnancy can be teratogenic. Excessive intake of carotenoids causes a benign condition characterized by yellowish discoloration of the skin. Habitually large doses of canthaxanthin, a carotenoid, have the additional capability of inducing a retinopathy. [3000 μg]	Retinol concentration in the plasma and vitamin A concentrations in the milk and tears are reasonably accurate measures of adequate status. Toxicity is best assessed by elevated levels of retinyl esters in plasma. A quantitative measure of dark adaptation for night vision or an electroretinogram are useful functional tests.
Vitamin D	A group of sterol compounds whose parent structure is cholecalciferol (vitamin D_3). Cholecalciferol is formed in the skin from 7-dehydrocholesterol (provitamin D_3) by exposure to UVB radiation. A plant sterol, ergocalciferol (provitamin D_2) can be similarly converted into vitamin D_2 and has similar vitamin D activity. The vitamin undergoes sequential hydroxylations in the liver and kidney at the 25 and 1 positions, respectively, producing the most bioactive form of the vitamin, 1,25-dihydroxy vitamin D. Maintains intracellular and extracellular concentrations of calcium and phosphate by enhancing intestinal absorption of the two ions and, in conjunction with PTH, promoting their mobilization from bone mineral. Retards proliferation and promotes differentiation in certain epithelia. One microgram = 40 IU.	Deficiency results in disordered bone modeling called *rickets* in childhood and *osteomalacia* in adults. Expansion of the epiphyseal growth plates and replacement of normal bone with unmineralized bone matrix are the cardinal features of rickets; the latter feature also characterizes osteomalacia. Deformity of bone and pathologic fractures occur. Decreased serum concentrations of calcium and phosphate may occur. [15 μg, ages 19-70 yr; 20 μg, age >70 yr]	Excess amounts result in abnormally high concentrations of calcium and phosphate in the serum: metastatic calcifications, renal damage, and altered mentation may occur. [50 μg]	The serum concentration of the major circulating metabolite, 25-hydroxyvitamin D, is an excellent indicator of systemic status except in chronic renal failure, in which the impairment of renal L-hydroxylation results in disassociation of the mono- and dihydroxyvitamin concentrations. Measuring the serum concentration of 1,25-dihydroxyvitamin D is then necessary.

	Biochemistry and Physiology	Deficiency [RDA*]	Toxicity [TUL†]	Assessment of Status
Vitamin E	A group of at least 8 naturally occurring compounds, some of which are tocopherols and some of which are tocotrienols. At present, the only dietary form that is thought to be biologically active in humans is α-tocopherol. Acts as an antioxidant and free radical scavenger in lipophilic environments, most notably in cell membranes. Acts in conjunction with other antioxidants such as selenium.	Deficiency due to dietary inadequacy rare. Usually seen in (1) premature infants, (2) individuals with fat malabsorption, and (3) individuals with abetalipoproteinemia. Red blood cell fragility occurs and can produce a hemolytic anemia. Neuronal degeneration produces peripheral neuropathies, ophthalmoplegia, and destruction of posterior columns of spinal cord. Neurologic disease is frequently irreversible if deficiency is not corrected early enough. May contribute to the hemolytic anemia and retrolental fibroplasia seen in premature infants. Reported to suppress cell-mediated immunity. [15 mg]	Depressed levels of vitamin K-dependent procoagulants and potentiation of oral anticoagulants have been reported, as has impaired WBC function. Doses of 800 mg/day have been reported to increase slightly the incidence of hemorrhagic stroke. [1000 mg]	Plasma or serum concentration of α-tocopherol is most commonly used. Additional accuracy is obtained by expressing this value per mg of total plasma lipid. RBC peroxide hemolysis test is not entirely specific but is a useful functional measure of the antioxidant potential of cell membranes.
Vitamin K	A family of naphthoquinone compounds with similar biologic activity. Phylloquinone (vitamin K_1) is derived from plants; a variety of menaquinones (vitamin K_2) is derived from bacterial sources. Serves as an essential cofactor in the post-translational γ-carboxylation of glutamic acid residues in many proteins. These proteins include several circulating procoagulants and anticoagulants as well as proteins in a variety of tissues.	Deficiency syndrome, uncommon except in (1) breast-fed newborns, in whom it may cause "hemorrhagic disease of the newborn," (2) adults with fat malabsorption or who are taking drugs that interfere with vitamin K metabolism (e.g., coumarin, phenytoin, broad-spectrum antibiotics), and (3) individuals taking large doses of vitamin E and anticoagulant drugs. Excessive hemorrhage is the usual manifestation. [F: 90 μg; M: 120 μg]	Rapid intravenous infusion of K_1 has been associated with dyspnea, flushing, and cardiovascular collapse; this is likely related to the dispersing agents in the solution. Supplementation may interfere with coumarin-based anticoagulation. Pregnant women taking large amounts of the provitamin menadione may deliver infants with hemolytic anemia, hyperbilirubinemia, and kernicterus. [no TUL established]	Prothrombin time is typically used as a measure of functional K status; it is neither sensitive nor specific for vitamin K deficiency. Determination of undercarboxylated prothrombin in the plasma is more accurate but less widely available.

Water-Soluble Vitamins

	Biochemistry and Physiology	Deficiency [RDA*]	Toxicity [TUL†]	Assessment of Status
Thiamine (vitamin B_1)	A water-soluble compound containing substituted pyrimidine and thiazole rings and a hydroxyethyl side chain. The coenzyme form is thiamine pyrophosphate (TPP). Serves as a coenzyme in many α-ketoacid decarboxylation and transketolation reactions. Inadequate thiamine availability leads to impairments of above reactions, resulting in inadequate adenosine triphosphate synthesis and abnormal carbohydrate metabolism, respectively. May have an additional role in neuronal conduction independent of aforementioned actions.	Classic deficiency syndrome ("beriberi") described in Asian populations consuming polished rice diet. Alcoholism and chronic renal dialysis are also common precipitants. High carbohydrate intake increases need for B_1. *Mild deficiency:* irritability, fatigue, and headaches. *More severe deficiency:* combinations of peripheral neuropathy, cardiovascular dysfunction, and cerebral dysfunction. Cardiovascular involvement ("wet beriberi"): congestive heart failure and low peripheral vascular resistance. Cerebral disease: nystagmus, ophthalmoplegia, and ataxia (Wernicke's encephalopathy); hallucinations, impaired short-term memory, and confabulation ("Korsakoff's psychosis"). Deficiency syndrome responds within 24 hr to parenteral thiamine but is partially or wholly irreversible after a certain stage. [F: 1.1 mg; M: 1.2 mg]	Excess intake is largely excreted in the urine, although parenteral doses of > 400 mg/day are reported to cause lethargy, ataxia, and reduced tone of the gastrointestinal tract. [TUL not established]	The most effective measure of B_1 status is the erythrocyte transketolase activity coefficient, which measures enzyme activity before and after addition of exogenous TPP: RBCs from a deficient individual express a substantial increase in enzyme activity with addition of TPP. Thiamine concentrations in blood or urine are also used.
Riboflavin (vitamin B_2)	Consists of a substituted isoalloxazine ring with a ribitol side chain. Serves as a coenzyme for a diverse array of biochemical reactions. The primary coenzymatic forms are flavin mononucleotide (FMN) and flavin adenine dinucleotide (FAD). Riboflavin holoenzymes participate in oxidation-reduction reactions in a myriad of metabolic pathways.	Deficiency is usually seen in conjunction with deficiencies of other B vitamins. Isolated deficiency of riboflavin produces hyperemia and edema of nasopharyngeal mucosa, cheilosis, angular stomatitis, glossitis, seborrheic dermatitis, and a normochromic, normocytic anemia. [F: 1.1; M: 1.3]	Toxicity not reported in humans. [TUL not established]	The most common method of assessment is determining the activity coefficient of glutathione reductase in RBCs (the test is invalid for individuals with glucose-6-phosphate dehydrogenase [G6PD] deficiency). Measurements of blood and urine concentrations are less desirable methods.

	Biochemistry and Physiology	Deficiency [RDA*]	Toxicity [TUL†]	Assessment of Status
Niacin (vitamin B₃)	Refers to nicotinic acid and the corresponding amide, nicotinamide. The active coenzymatic forms are composed of nicotinamide affixed to adenine dinucleotide, forming NAD or NADP. More than 200 apoenzymes use these compounds as electron acceptors or hydrogen donors, either as a coenzyme or as a co-substrate. The essential amino acid tryptophan is a precursor of niacin; 60 mg of dietary tryptophan yields approximately 1 mg of niacin. Dietary requirements thus depend partly on tryptophan intake. Requirement is often determined on basis of caloric intake (i.e., niacin equivalents/1000 kcal). Large doses of nicotinic acid (1.5-3 g/day) effectively lower low-density lipoprotein cholesterol and elevate high-density lipoprotein cholesterol.	Pellagra is the classic deficiency syndrome and is often seen in populations in which corn is the major source of energy. Still endemic in parts of China, Africa, and India. Diarrhea, dementia (or associated symptoms of anxiety or insomnia), and a pigmented dermatitis that develops in sun-exposed areas are typical features. Glossitis, stomatitis, vaginitis, vertigo, and burning dysesthesias are early signs. Reported to occasionally occur in carcinoid syndrome because tryptophan is diverted to other synthetic pathways. [F: 14 mg; M: 16 mg]	Human toxicity known largely through studies examining hypolipidemic effects. Includes vasomotor phenomenon (flushing), hyperglycemia, parenchymal liver damage, and hyperuricemia. [35 mg]	Assessment of status is problematic: blood levels of vitamin not reliable. Measurement of urinary excretion of the niacin metabolites, N-methylnicotinamide and 2-pyridone, is thought to be the most effective means of assessment at present.
Vitamin B₆	Refers to several derivatives of pyridine, including pyridoxine (PN), pyridoxal (PL), and pyridoxamine (PM), which are interconvertible in the body. The coenzymatic forms are pyridoxal-5-phosphate (PLP) and pyridoxamine-5-phosphate (PMP). As a coenzyme, B₆ is involved in many transamination reactions (and thereby in gluconeogenesis), in the synthesis of niacin from tryptophan, in the synthesis of several neurotransmitters, and in the synthesis of δ-aminolevulinic acid (and therefore in heme synthesis). It also has functions unrelated to coenzymatic activity: PL and PLP bind to hemoglobin and alter O_2 affinity; PLP also binds to steroid receptors, inhibiting receptor affinity to DNA and thereby modulating steroid activity.	Deficiency usually seen in conjunction with other water-soluble vitamin deficiencies. Stomatitis, angular cheilosis, glossitis, irritability, depression, and confusion occur in moderate to severe depletion; normochromic, normocytic anemia has been reported in severe deficiency. Abnormal electroencephalograms and, in infants, convulsions have also been observed. Some sideroblastic anemias respond to B₆ administration. Isoniazid, cycloserine, penicillamine, ethanol, and theophylline can inhibit B₆ metabolism. [Ages 19-50 yr: 1.3 mg; >50 yr: 1.5 mg for women, 1.7 mg for men]	Long-term use with doses exceeding 200 mg/day (in adults) may cause peripheral neuropathies and photosensitivity. [100 mg]	Many useful laboratory methods of assessment exist. The plasma or erythrocyte PLP levels are most common. Urinary excretion of xanthurenic acid after an oral tryptophan load or activity indices of RBC alanine or aspartic acid transaminases (ALT and AST, respectively) are all functional measures of B₆-dependent enzyme activity.
Folate	A group of related pterin compounds. More than 35 forms of the vitamin are found naturally. The fully oxidized form, folic acid, is not found in nature but is the pharmacologic form of the vitamin. All folate functions relate to its ability to transfer one-carbon groups. It is essential in the *de novo* synthesis of nucleotides and in the metabolism of several amino acids, and is an integral component for the regeneration of the "universal" methyl donor, S-adenosylmethionine. Inhibition of bacterial and cancer cell folate metabolism is the basis for the sulfonamide antibiotics and chemotherapeutic agents such as methotrexate and 5-fluorouracil, respectively.	Women of childbearing age are most likely to be deficient. *Classic deficiency syndrome:* megaloblastic anemia, diarrhea. The hematopoietic cells in bone marrow become enlarged and have immature nuclei, reflecting ineffective DNA synthesis. The peripheral blood smear demonstrates macro-ovalocytes and polymorphonuclear leukocytes with an average of more than 3.5 nuclear lobes. Megaloblastic changes also occur in other epithelia that proliferate rapidly (e.g., oral mucosa, gastrointestinal tract), producing glossitis and diarrhea, respectively. Sulfasalazine and diphenytoin inhibit absorption and predispose to deficiency. [400 µg of dietary folate equivalents (DFE); 1 DFE = 1 µg food folate = 0.6 µg folic acid]	Doses >1000 µg/day may partially correct the anemia of D_{12} deficiency and may therefore mask (and perhaps exacerbate) the associated neuropathy. Large doses also reported to lower seizure threshold in individuals prone to seizures. Parenteral administration is rarely reported to cause allergic phenomena, which is probably due to dispersion agents. [1000 µg]	Serum folate measures short-term folate balance, whereas RBC folate is a better reflection of tissue status. Serum homocysteine rises early in deficiency but is nonspecific because B₁₂ or B₆ deficiency, renal insufficiency, and older age may also cause elevations.

Continued on following page

	Biochemistry and Physiology	Deficiency [RDA*]	Toxicity [TUL†]	Assessment of Status
Vitamin C (ascorbic and dehydroascorbic acid)	Ascorbic acid readily oxidizes to dehydroascorbic acid in aqueous solution. The latter can be reduced in vivo, so it possesses vitamin C activity. Total vitamin C is therefore the sum of ascorbic and dehydroascorbic acid content. It serves primarily as a biologic antioxidant in aqueous environments. Biosyntheses of collagen, carnitine, bile acids, and norepinephrine, as well as proper functioning of the hepatic mixed-function oxygenase system, depend on this property. Vitamin C in foodstuffs increases the intestinal absorption of nonheme iron.	Overt deficiency is uncommon in developed countries. The classic deficiency syndrome is scurvy: fatigue, depression, and widespread abnormalities in connective tissues, such as inflamed gingivae, petechiae, perifollicular hemorrhages, impaired wound healing, coiled hairs, hyperkeratosis, bleeding into body cavities. In infants, defects in ossification and bone growth may occur. Tobacco smoking lowers plasma and leukocyte vitamin C levels. [F: 75 mg; M: 90 mg; increase requirement for cigarette smokers by 35 mg/day]	≥500 mg/day (in adults) may cause nausea and diarrhea. >1 g/day modestly increases risk for oxalate kidney stones. Supplementation may interfere with laboratory tests based on redox potential (e.g., fecal occult blood testing, serum cholesterol, and glucose). Withdrawal from chronic ingestion of high doses of vitamin C supplements should be done gradually because accommodation appears to occur, raising a concern of "rebound scurvy." [2 g]	Plasma ascorbic acid concentration reflects recent dietary intake, whereas WBC levels more closely reflect tissue stores. Women's plasma levels are approximately 20% higher than men's for any given dietary intake.
Vitamin B$_{12}$	A group of closely related cobalamin compounds composed of a corrin ring (with a cobalt atom in its center) connected to a ribonucleotide through an aminopropanol bridge. Microorganisms are the ultimate source of all naturally occurring B$_{12}$. The two active coenzyme forms are deoxyadenosylcobalamin and methylcobalamin. These coenzymes are needed for the synthesis of succinyl coenzyme A (CoA), which is essential in lipid and carbohydrate metabolism, and for the synthesis of methionine. The latter reaction is essential for amino acid metabolism, for purine and pyrimidine synthesis, for many methylation reactions, and for the intracellular retention of folates.	Dietary inadequacy is a rare cause of deficiency except in strict vegetarians. Most deficiencies arise from loss of intestinal absorption, which may occur with pernicious anemia, pancreatic insufficiency, atrophic gastritis, small bowel bacterial overgrowth, or ileal disease. Megaloblastic anemia and megaloblastic changes in other epithelia (see "Folate") are the result of sustained depletion. Demyelination of peripheral nerves, posterior and lateral columns of spinal cord, and nerves within the brain may occur. Altered mentation, depression, and psychoses occur. Hematologic and neurologic complications may occur independently. Folate supplementation, in doses of 1000 µg/day, may partly correct the anemia, thereby masking (or perhaps exacerbating) the neuropathic complication. [2.4 µg]	A few allergic reactions have been reported to crystalline B$_{12}$ preparations and are probably due to impurities, not the vitamin. [TUL not established]	Serum, or plasma, concentrations are generally accurate. Subtle deficiency with neurologic complications, as described in the "Deficiency" column, can best be established by concurrently measuring the concentration of plasma B$_{12}$ and serum methylmalonic acid because the latter is a sensitive indicator of cellular deficiency.
Biotin	A bi-cyclic compound consisting of a ureido ring fused to a substituted tetrahydrothiophene ring. Endogenous synthesis by intestinal flora may contribute significantly to biotin nutriture. Most dietary biotin is linked to lysine, a compound called biotinyl lysine, or biocytin. The lysine must be hydrolyzed by an intestinal enzyme called biotinidase before intestinal absorption occurs. Acts primarily as a coenzyme for several carboxylases; each holoenzyme catalyzes an ATP-dependent CO$_2$ transfer. The carboxylases are critical enzymes in carbohydrate and lipid metabolism.	Isolated deficiency is rare. Deficiency in humans has been produced by prolonged total parenteral nutrition lacking the vitamin and by ingestion of large quantities of raw egg white, which contains avidin, a protein that binds biotin with such high affinity that it renders it bio-unavailable. Alterations in mental status, myalgias, hyperesthesias, and anorexia occur. Later, a seborrheic dermatitis and alopecia develop. Deficiency is usually accompanied by lactic acidosis and organic aciduria. [30 µg]	Toxicity has not been reported in humans with doses as high as 60 mg/day in children. [TUL not established]	Plasma and urine concentrations of biotin are diminished in the deficient state. Elevated urine concentrations of methyl citrate, 3-methylcrotonylglycine, and 3-hydroxyisovalerate are also observed in deficiency.

	Biochemistry and Physiology	Deficiency [RDA*]	Toxicity [TUL†]	Assessment of Status
Pantothenic acid	Consists of pantoic acid linked to β-alanine through an amide bond. An essential component of CoA and phosphopantetheine, which are essential for synthesis and β-oxidation of fatty acids, as well as synthesis of cholesterol, steroid hormones, vitamins A and D, and other isoprenoid derivatives. CoA is also involved in the synthesis of several amino acids and δ-aminolevulinic acid, a precursor for the corrin ring of vitamin B_{12}, the porphyrin ring of heme, and of cytochromes. CoA is also necessary for the acetylation and fatty acid acylation of a variety of proteins.	Deficiency rare: only reported as a result of feeding semisynthetic diets or an antagonist to the vitamin. Experimental, isolated deficiency in humans produces fatigue, abdominal pain, vomiting, insomnia, and paresthesias of the extremities. [5 mg]	In doses of 10 g/day, diarrhea is reported to occur. [TUL not established]	Whole blood and urine concentrations of pantothenate are indicators of status; serum levels are not thought to be accurate.

PTH, Parathyroid hormone; *UVB*, ultraviolet B.

*Recommended daily allowance (RDA) established for female (F) and male (M) adults by the U.S. Food and Nutrition Board, 1999-2001. In some instances, insufficient data exist to establish an RDA, in which case the adequate intake (AI) established by the board is listed.

†Tolerated upper intake (TUI) established for adults by the U.S. Food and Nutrition Board, 1999-2001.

From Goldman L, Schafer AI: *Goldman's Cecil medicine*, ed 24, Philadelphia, 2012, Saunders.

Nutritional Trace Elements and Their Clinical Implications

	Biochemistry and Physiology	Deficiency [RDA*]	Toxicity [TUL†]	Assessment of Status
Chromium	Dietary chromium consists of both inorganic and organic forms. Its primary function in humans is to potentiate insulin action. It accomplishes this function as a circulating complex called *glucose tolerance factor*, thereby affecting carbohydrate, fat, and protein metabolism.	Deficiency in humans only described in long-term total parenteral nutrition (TPN) patients receiving insufficient chromium. Hyperglycemia or impaired glucose tolerance occurs. Elevated plasma-free fatty acid concentrations, neuropathy, encephalopathy, and abnormalities in nitrogen metabolism are also reported. Whether supplemental chromium may improve glucose tolerance in glucose-intolerant individuals remains controversial. [F: 25 μg; M: 35 μg]	Toxicity after oral ingestion is uncommon and seems confined to gastric irritation. Airborne exposure may cause contact dermatitis, eczema, skin ulcers, and bronchogenic carcinoma. [no TUL established]	Plasma or serum concentration of chromium is a crude indicator of chromium status; it appears to be meaningful when the value is markedly above or below the normal range.
Copper	Copper is absorbed by a specific intestinal transport mechanism. It is carried to the liver where it is bound to ceruloplasmin, which circulates systemically and delivers copper to target tissues in the body. Excretion of copper is largely through bile, and then into the feces. Absorptive and excretory processes vary with the levels of dietary copper, providing a means of copper homeostasis. Copper serves as a component of many enzymes, including amine oxidases, ferroxidases, cytochrome c oxidase, dopamine β-hydroxylase, superoxide dismutase, and tyrosinase.	Dietary deficiency is rare; it has been observed in premature and low-birthweight infants fed exclusively a cow's milk diet and in individuals on long-term TPN without copper. Clinical manifestations include depigmentation of skin and hair, neurologic disturbances, leukopenia, hypochromic microcytic anemia, and skeletal abnormalities. Anemia arises from impaired utilization of iron and is therefore a conditioned form of iron deficiency anemia. The deficiency syndrome, except the anemia and leukopenia, is also observed in Menkes' disease, a rare inherited condition associated with impaired copper utilization. [900 μg]	Acute copper toxicity has been described after excessive oral intake and with absorption of copper salts applied to burned skin. Milder manifestations include nausea, vomiting, epigastric pain, and diarrhea; coma and hepatic necrosis may ensue in severe cases. Toxicity may be seen with doses as low as 70 μg/kg/day. Chronic toxicity is also described. Wilson's disease is a rare, inherited disease associated with abnormally low ceruloplasmin levels and accumulation of copper in the liver and brain, eventually leading to damage to these two organs. [10 mg]	Practical methods for detecting marginal deficiency are not available. Marked deficiency is reliably detected by diminished serum copper and ceruloplasmin concentrations as well as low red blood cell (RBC) superoxide dismutase activity.
Fluorine	Known more commonly by its ionic form, fluoride. It is incorporated into the crystalline structure of bone, thereby altering its physical characteristics.	Intake of <0.1 mg/day in infants and <0.5 mg/day in children is associated with an increased incidence of dental caries. Optimal intake in adults is between 1.5 and 4 mg/day. [F: 3 mg; M: 4 mg]	Acute ingestion of >30 mg/kg body weight is likely to cause death. Excessive chronic intake (0.1 mg/kg/day) leads to mottling of teeth (dental fluorosis), calcification of tendons and ligaments, and exostoses and may increase the brittleness of bones. [10 mg]	Estimates of intake or clinical assessment are used because no good laboratory test exists.

	Biochemistry and Physiology	Deficiency [RDA*]	Toxicity [TUL†]	Assessment of Status
Iodine	Readily absorbed from the diet, concentrated in the thyroid, and integrated into the thyroid hormones, thyroxine (T_4) and triiodothyronine (T_3). These hormones circulate largely bound to thyroxine-binding globulin. They modulate resting energy expenditure and, in the developing human, growth and development.	In the absence of supplementation, populations relying primarily on food from soils with low iodine content have endemic iodine deficiency. Maternal iodine deficiency leads to fetal deficiency, which produces spontaneous abortions, stillbirths, hypothyroidism, cretinism, and dwarfism. Permanent cognitive deficits may result from iodine deficiency during first 2 years of life. In the adult, compensatory hypertrophy of the thyroid goiter occurs along with varying degrees of hypothyroidism. [150 µg]	Large doses (>2 mg/day in adults) may induce hypothyroidism by blocking thyroid hormone synthesis. Supplementation with >100 mg/day to an individual who was formerly deficient occasionally induces hyperthyroidism. [1.1 mg]	Iodine status of a population can be estimated by the prevalence of goiter. Urinary excretion of iodine is an effective laboratory means of assessment. Thyroid-stimulating hormone (TSH) blood level is an indirect, and therefore not entirely specific, means of assessment.
Iron	Conveys the capacity to participate in redox reactions to a number of metalloproteins such as hemoglobin, myoglobin, cytochrome enzymes, and many oxidases and oxygenases. Primary storage form is ferritin and, to a lesser degree, hemosiderin. Intestinal absorption is 15%-20% for "heme" iron and 1%-8% for iron contained in vegetables. Absorption of the latter form is enhanced by the ascorbic acid in foodstuffs; by poultry, fish, or beef; and by an iron-deficient state. It is decreased by phytate and tannins.	The most common micronutrient deficiency in the world. Women of childbearing age are the highest-risk group because of menstrual blood losses, pregnancy, and lactation. The classic deficiency syndrome is hypochromic, microcytic anemia. Glossitis and koilonychia ("spoon" nails) are also observed. Easy fatigability often is an early symptom, before anemia appears. In children, mild deficiency of insufficient severity to cause anemia is associated with behavioral disturbances and poor school performance. [postmenopausal F and M: 8 mg; premenopausal F: 18 mg]	Iron overload typically occurs when habitual dietary intake is extremely high, intestinal absorption is excessive, repeated parenteral administration occurs, or a combination of these factors exists. Excessive iron stores usually accumulate in the reticuloendothelial tissues and cause little damage ("hemosiderosis"). If overload continues, iron eventually begins to accumulate in tissues such as the hepatic parenchyma, pancreas, heart, and synovium, causing hemochromatosis. Hereditary hemochromatosis results from homozygosity of a common recessive trait. Excessive intestinal absorption of iron is seen in homozygotes. [45 mg]	Negative iron balance initially leads to depletion of iron stores in the bone marrow: a bone marrow biopsy and the concentration of serum ferritin are accurate indicators of early depletion. As the severity of deficiency proceeds, serum iron (SI) decreases and total iron-binding capacity (TIBC) increases: an iron saturation (SI/TIBC) of <16% suggests iron deficiency. Microcytosis, hypochromia, and anemia ensue. Elevated levels of serum ferritin or an iron saturation of >60% suggest iron overload, although systemic inflammation elevates serum ferritin regardless of iron status.
Manganese	A component of several metalloenzymes. Most manganese is in mitochondria, where it is a component of manganese superoxide dismutase.	Manganese deficiency in the human has not been conclusively demonstrated. It is said to cause hypocholesterolemia, weight loss, hair and nail changes, dermatitis, and impaired synthesis of vitamin K dependent proteins. [F: 1.8 mg; M: 2.3 mg]	Toxicity by oral ingestion is unknown in humans. Toxic inhalation causes hallucinations, other alterations in mentation, and extrapyramidal movement disorders. [11 mg]	Until the deficiency syndrome is better defined, an appropriate measure of status will be difficult to develop.
Molybdenum	A cofactor in several enzymes, most prominently xanthine oxidase and sulfite oxidase.	A probable case of human deficiency is described as being secondary to parenteral administration of sulfite and resulted in hyperoxypurinemia, hypouricemia, and low sulfate excretion. [45 µg]	Toxicity not well described in humans, although it may interfere with copper metabolism at high doses. [2 mg]	Laboratory means of assessment not meaningful until deficiency syndrome is better described.
Selenium	Most dietary selenium is in the form of an amino acid complex. Nearly complete absorption of such forms occurs. Homeostasis is largely performed by the kidney, which regulates urinary excretion as a function of selenium status. Selenium is a component of several enzymes, most notably glutathione peroxidase and superoxide dismutase. These enzymes protect against oxidative and free radical damage of various cell structures. The antioxidant protection conveyed by selenium apparently operates in conjunction with vitamin E because deficiency of one seems to potentiate damage induced by a deficiency of the other. Selenium also participates in the enzymatic conversion of thyroxine to its more active metabolite, triiodothyronine.	Deficiency is rare in North America but has been observed in individuals on long-term TPN lacking selenium. Such individuals have myalgias and/or cardiomyopathies. Populations in some regions of the world, most notably some parts of China, have marginal intake of selenium. In these regions Keshan's disease, a condition characterized by cardiomyopathy, is endemic; it can be prevented (but not treated) by selenium supplementation. [55 µg]	Toxicity is associated with nausea, diarrhea, alterations in mental status, peripheral neuropathy, loss of hair and nails: such symptoms were observed in adults who inadvertently consumed 27-2400 mg. [400 µg]	Erythrocyte glutathione peroxidase activity and plasma, or whole blood, selenium concentrations are the most commonly used methods of assessment. They are moderately accurate indicators of status.

Continued on following page

	Biochemistry and Physiology	Deficiency [RDA*]	Toxicity [TUL†]	Assessment of Status
Zinc	Intestinal absorption occurs by a specific process that is enhanced by pregnancy and corticosteroids and diminished by coingestion of phytates, phosphates, iron, copper, lead, or calcium. Diminished intake of zinc leads to an increased efficiency of absorption and decreased fecal excretion, providing a means of zinc homeostasis. Zinc is a component of more than 100 enzymes, among which are DNA polymerase, RNA polymerase, and transfer RNA synthetase.	Zinc deficiency has its most profound effect on rapidly proliferating tissues. *Mild deficiency:* growth retardation in children. *More severe deficiency:* growth arrest, teratogenicity, hypogonadism and infertility, dysgeusia, poor wound healing, diarrhea, dermatitis on the extremities and around orifices, glossitis, alopecia, corneal clouding, loss of dark adaptation, and behavioral changes. Impaired cellular immunity is observed. Excessive loss of gastrointestinal secretions through chronic diarrhea and fistulas may precipitate deficiency. Acrodermatitis enteropathica is a rare, recessively inherited disease in which intestinal absorption of zinc is impaired. [F: 8 mg; M: 11 mg]	Acute zinc toxicity can usually be induced by ingestion of >200 mg of zinc in a single day (in adults). It is manifested as epigastric pain, nausea, vomiting, and diarrhea. Hyperpnea, diaphoresis, and weakness may follow inhalation of zinc fumes. Copper and zinc compete for intestinal absorption: long-term ingestion of >25 mg/day of zinc may lead to copper deficiency. Long-term ingestion of >150 mg/day has been reported to cause gastric erosions, low high-density lipoprotein cholesterol levels, and impaired cellular immunity. [40 mg]	No accurate indicators of zinc status exist for routine clinical use. Plasma, RBC, and hair zinc concentrations are often misleading. Acute illness, in particular, is known to diminish plasma zinc levels, in part by inducing a shift of zinc out of the plasma compartment and into the liver. Functional tests that determine dark adaptation, taste acuity, and rate of wound healing lack specificity.

*Recommended daily allowance (RDA) established for female (F) and male (M) adults by the U.S. Food and Nutrition Board, 1999-2001. In some instances, insufficient data exist to establish an RDA, in which case the adequate intake (AI) established by the board is listed.

†Tolerated upper limit (TUL) established for adults by the U.S. Food and Nutrition Board, 1999-2001.

From Goldman L, Schafer AI: *Goldman's Cecil medicine,* ed 24, Philadelphia, 2012, Saunders.

Summary of Vitamin and Mineral Deficiencies

Vitamin and Mineral Deficiencies	Neurologic Syndrome or Syndromes	Supporting Tests	Treatment	Causes (Other Than Malnutrition)
A (retinol)	Blindness from retinal or corneal damage	Visual fields, visual acuity Serum level <30-65 μg/dl	30,000 IU vitamin A daily × 1 wk	Hypothyroidism, diabetes, renal or liver failure
B₁ (thiamine)	Wernicke's encephalopathy: ataxia, nystagmus, ophthalmoparesis, confusion, delirium Korsakoff's syndrome: amnesia, confabulation Beriberi: axonal neuropathy	MRI: symmetric lesions of midbrain (periaqueductal area), pons, hypothalamus, thalamus, cerebellum MRI: necrosis of mammillary bodies, dorsomedial and anterior thalamus Nerve conduction tests: decreased amplitude Serum thiamine level <20 ng/dl Erythrocyte transketolase	Prevent by 100 mg PO daily before and 1 year after bariatric surgery, 100 mg IV before glucose administration or refeeding Treat Wernicke's encephalopathy with 5 days of thiamine, 100-500 mg IV or IM daily, then PO 100 mg daily Antioxidants (N-acetylcysteine)	Alcoholism, bariatric or other major GI surgery, prolonged vomiting, hemodialysis, diuretic treatment of heart failure, cachexia, 5-fluorouracil, other blockers of thiamine phosphate production
B₃ (niacin)	Pellagra: confusion, dementia, weakness, ataxia, spasticity, myoclonus, glossitis, dermatitis, photosensitivity	Erythrocyte NAD, plasma niacin, urinary N₁-methylnicotinamide	Nicotinic acid, 50 mg PO tid or 25 mg IV tid; nicotinamide, 50-100 mg IM or PO tid	Alcoholism, corn- or cereal-based diet, Hartnup's syndrome, carcinoid syndrome
B₅ (pantothenic acid)	Dysesthesias, foot paresthesias	Deficient coenzyme A	5 mg PO daily	Severe malnutrition
B₆ (pyridoxine)	Neuropathy, sensory ataxia, depression Infantile pyridoxine-deficient epilepsy	Plasma PLP <27 nmol/L; urinary 4-pyridoxic acid, <3 nmol ↑ Homocysteine after methionine loading challenge ↑ α-AASA in urine, plasma, CSF	50-100 mg PO daily for neuropathy (preventive use if taking B₆ antagonist) 100-200 mg daily for adult epilepsy	Diverticulosis, isoniazid, cycloserine, other antagonists Genetic defects in antiquitin (aldehyde dehydrogenase), pyridoxal synthesis
B₁₂ (cobalamin)	Myelopathy with spastic paraparesis and sensory ataxia, peripheral neuropathy, optic neuropathy, memory loss, dementia; indirect contributor to stroke	Blood level <200 pg/ml ↑ Methylmalonic acid >145 nmol/L Intrinsic factor antibodies Schilling test, megaloblastic anemia Delayed somatosensory evoked potentials ↑ Homocysteine, total >12.5 μmol/L	IM B₁₂, 1000 μg daily for 1 week, then weekly for 1 month, then monthly or oral B₁₂, 1000 μg daily, or nasal B₁₂, 500 μg weekly for lifetime if abnormal absorption, 50-100 μg daily if normal absorption	Achlorhydria, gastric or ileal resection, blind loop syndrome, sprue, HIV infection, nitrous oxide anesthesia (especially abuse), fish tapeworm, vegan diet
D (calciferol)	Proximal myopathy, often painful; cognitive impairment Secondary compression of spinal cord, plexus, or peripheral nerves from rickets or osteomalacia	25-(OH) vitamin D₃ level <10 ng/ml in urine Serum calcium ↑ PTH >54 pg/ml Osteopenia/porosis on bone densitometry	Daily supplementation with 400 IU, >50,000 IU 3 times per wk if malabsorption; use blood level or urine calcium excretion to guide (should be >100 mg/day)	Lack of exposure to sunlight, including sunblock protection; chronic antiepileptic drug use
E (tocopherol)	Spinal and cerebellar ataxia, Babinski's sign, ophthalmoplegia, peripheral neuropathy, retinitis pigmentosa	Vitamin E level <2.5 mg/L (normal, 6-15 with normal lipid level) ↑ A-β-lipoprotein levels, antigliadin antibodies Genetic analysis to rule out other spinocerebellar ataxias such as Friedreich's ataxia	Supplement with 6-800 IU, 5-10 mg/kg twice daily, for ataxia of genetic causes, water-soluble 200 mg/kg/day or IM α-tocopherol for malabsorption	Biliary atresia, celiac sprue, Genetic: ↓ α-tocopherol transport protein (8q13), microsomal triglyceride transfer protein

Continued on following page **1875**

Summary of Vitamin and Mineral Deficiencies

Vitamin and Mineral Deficiencies	Neurologic Syndrome or Syndromes	Supporting Tests	Treatment	Causes (Other Than Malnutrition)
Folate	Dementia, B_{12} deficiency, stroke	↑ Homocysteine, plasma level <2.5 µg/L	1 mg 3 times per day until normal level, then maintenance of 1 mg/day Pregnancy: additional 0.4 mg/day if taking a folate antagonist	Malabsorption or use of antagonist (methotrexate) or antiepileptic medication
K (phytonadione)	Intracranial hemorrhage	INR or PT elevation	IM phytonadione at birth, maternal vitamin K for last month of pregnancy	Medication use that increases metabolism, such as phenytoin
Copper	Myelopathy, neuropathy	Serum Cu <75 µg/dl, ↓ urinary Cu, ceruloplasmin <23 mg/dl MRI: ↑ T_2 signal in cervical cord, dorsal column Mutation in ATP7A gene (Menkes' disease)	Elemental Cu, 8 mg/day PO week 1, 6 mg/day week 2, 4 mg/day week 3, 2 mg/day ongoing malabsorption Menkes' disease: 250 mg SC bid	Wilson's disease, Menkes' disease, alcoholism, malabsorption, gastric bypass, zinc toxicity
Magnesium	Seizures, encephalopathy	Serum magnesium <1.5 mg/ dl, correct for low albumin	Magnesium sulfate IV or PO Avoid magnesium-wasting drugs	Alcoholism, especially beer
Potassium	Muscle weakness, chronic, acute	Serum potassium <3.5 mEq/L, ECG	IV or PO KCl until normalized	Diuretic use, bulimia

AASA, Aminoadipic semialdehyde; *CSF,* cerebrospinal fluid; *ECG,* electrocardiography; *GI,* gastrointestinal; *HIV,* human immunodeficiency virus; *IM,* intramuscularly; *INR,* international normalized ratio; *IU,* international units; *IV,* intravenously; *MRI,* magnetic resonance imaging; *NAD,* nicotinamide adenine dinucleotide; *PLP,* pyridoxal-5-phosphate (active coenzyme of pyridoxine); *PO,* by mouth; *PT,* prothrombin time; *PTH,* parathyroid hormone; *tid,* three times a day.

From Goldman *L,* Schafer AI: *Goldman's Cecil medicine,* ed 24, Philadelphia, 2012, Saunders.

Historical and Physical Findings in Poisoning

Sign	Toxin
Odor	
Bitter almonds	Cyanide
Acetone	Isopropyl alcohol, methanol, paraldehyde, salicylates
Alcohol	Ethanol
Wintergreen	Methyl salicylate
Garlic	Arsenic, thallium, organophosphates, selenium
Ocular Signs	
Miosis	Opioids (except propoxyphene, meperidine, and pentazocine), organophosphates and other cholinergics, clonidine, phenothiazines, sedative-hypnotics, olanzapine
Mydriasis	Atropine, cocaine, amphetamines, antihistamines, TCAs, carbamazepine, serotonin syndrome, PCP, LSD, postanoxic encephalopathy
Nystagmus	Phenytoin, barbiturates, sedative-hypnotics, alcohols, carbamazepine, PCP, ketamine, dextromethorphan
Lacrimation	Organophosphates, irritant gas or vapors
Retinal hyperemia	Methanol
Cutaneous Signs	
Diaphoresis	Organophosphates, salicylates, cocaine and other sympathomimetics, serotonin syndrome, withdrawal syndromes
Alopecia	Thallium, arsenic
Erythema	Boric acid, elemental mercury, cyanide, carbon monoxide, disulfuram, scombroid, anticholinergics
Cyanosis (unresponsive to oxygen)	Methemoglobinemia (e.g., benzocaine, dapsone, nitrites, phenazopyridine), amiodarone, silver
Oral Signs	
Salivation	Organophosphates, salicylates, corrosives, ketamine, PCP, strychnine
Oral burns	Corrosives, oxalate-containing plants
Gum lines	Lead, mercury, arsenic, bismuth
Gastrointestinal Signs	
Diarrhea	Antimicrobials, arsenic, iron, boric acid, cholinergics, colchicine, withdrawal
Hematemesis	Arsenic, iron, caustics, NSAIDs, salicylates
Cardiac Signs	
Tachycardia	Sympathomimetics (e.g., amphetamines, cocaine), anticholinergics, antidepressants, theophylline, caffeine, antipsychotics, atropine, salicylates, cellular asphyxiants (cyanide, carbon monoxide, hydrogen sulfide), withdrawal
Bradycardia	β-Blockers, calcium channel blockers, digoxin, clonidine and other central α_2 agonists, organophosphates, opioids, sedative-hypnotics
Hypertension	Sympathomimetics (amphetamines, cocaine, LSD), anticholinergics, clonidine (early), monoamine oxidase inhibitors
Hypotension	β-Blockers, calcium channel blockers, cyclic antidepressants, iron, phenothiazines, barbiturates, clonidine, theophylline, opioids, arsenic, amatoxin mushrooms, cellular asphyxiants (cyanide, carbon monoxide, hydrogen sulfide), snake envenomation
Respiratory Signs	
Depressed respirations	Opioids, sedative-hypnotics, alcohol, clonidine, barbiturates
Tachypnea	Salicylates, amphetamines, caffeine, metabolic acidosis (ethylene glycol, methanol, cyanide), carbon monoxide, hydrocarbons

1877

Continued on following page

Sign	Toxin
Central Nervous System Signs	
Ataxia	Alcohol, anticonvulsants, benzodiazepines, barbiturates, lithium, dextromethorphan, carbon monoxide, inhalants
Coma	Opioids, sedative-hypnotics, anticonvulsants, cyclic antidepressants, antipsychotics, ethanol, anticholinergics, clonidine, GHB, alcohols, salicylates, barbiturates
Seizures	Sympathomimetics, anticholinergics, antidepressants (especially TCAs, bupropion, venlafaxine), isoniazid, camphor, lindane, salicylates, lead, organophosphates, carbamazepine, tramadol, lithium, ginkgo seeds, water hemlock, withdrawal
Delirium/psychosis	Sympathomimetics, anticholinergics, LSD, PCP, hallucinogens, lithium, dextromethorphan, steroids, withdrawal
Peripheral neuropathy	Lead, arsenic, mercury, organophosphates

GHB, Gamma hydroxybutyrate; *LSD,* lysergic acid diethylamide; *NSAID,* nonsteroidal anti-inflammatory drug; *PCP,* phencyclidine; *TCA,* tricylic antidepressant.

From Goldman L, Schafer AI: *Goldman's Cecil medicine,* ed 24, Philadelphia, 2012, Saunders.

Recognizable Poison Syndromes

Poison Syndrome	Vital	Mental Status	Pupils	Skin	Bowel Sounds	Other	Possible Toxins
			SIGNS				
Sympathomimetic	Hypertension, tachycardia, hyperthermia	Agitated, psychosis, delirium	Dilated	Diaphoretic	Normal to increased		Amphetamines, cocaine, Ecstasy, pseudoephedrine, caffeine, theophylline
Anticholinergic	Hypertension, tachycardia, hyperthermia	Agitation, delirium, mumbling speech	Dilated	Dry	Decreased		Antihistamines, tricyclic antidepressants, atropine, jimson weed, phenothiazines
Cholinergic	Bradycardia (although may show tachycardia), BP and temp typically normal	Confusion, coma, fasciculations	Small	Diaphoretic	Hyperactive	Diarrhea, urination, bronchorrhea, bronchospasm, emesis, lacrimation, salivation	Organophosphates, nerve gases, Alzheimer medications
Opioids	Respiratory depression (hallmark of toxicity), bradycardia, hypotension, hypothermia	Depression, coma	Pinpoint	Normal	Normal to decreased		Methadone, suboxone, morphine, oxycodone, heroin, etc.
Sedative-hypnotics	Respiratory depression, HR normal to decreased, BP normal to decreased, temp normal to decreased	Somnolence, coma	Small	Normal	Normal		Barbiturates, benzodiazepines, ethanol
Serotonin syndrome	Hyperthermia, tachycardia, hypertension or hypotension (autonomic instability)	Agitation, confusion, coma	Dilated	Diaphoretic	Increased	Neuromuscular hyperexcitability: clonus, hyperreflexia (lower extremities > upper extremities)	SSRIs, lithium, MAOIs, linezolid, tramadol, meperidine, dextromethorphan
Salicylates	Tachypnea, hyperpnea, tachycardia, hyperthermia	Agitation, confusion, coma	Normal	Diaphoretic	Normal	Nausea, vomiting, tinnitus, ABG with primary respiratory alkalosis and primary metabolic acidosis	Aspirin, bismuth subsalicylate (Pepto-Bismol), methylsalicylates
Withdrawal	Tachycardia, tachypnea, hyperthermia	Lethargy, confusion, delirium	Dilated	Diaphoretic	Increased		Withdrawal from opioids, sedative-hypnotics, ethanol

ABG, Arterial blood gas; *BP*, blood pressure; *HR*, heart rate; *MAOI*, monoamine oxidase inhibitor; *SSRI*, selective serotonin reuptake inhibitor; *temp*, temperature.
From Kliegman RM et al: *Nelson textbook of pediatrics*, ed 19, Philadelphia, 2011, Saunders.

Antidotes and Indications for Use

Antidote	Indication for Use	Dose*	Treatment End Point	Comments
Antivenom (Fab)[†]	Crotalines	4-6 vials; repeat for persistent or worsening clinical condition; repeat doses of 2 vials at 6, 12, and 18 hr after initial antivenom dose(s) are recommended	Halt in progression of circumferential and proximal swelling Resolving systemic effects	Better safety profile than equine-derived antivenom Repetitive dosing indicated for recurrent soft tissue swelling
Antivenom, *Latrodectus* (equine)[†]	Black widow spider (*Latrodectus* sp.)	1 vial diluted in 100 ml NS, infused over 1 hr; can repeat	Resolution of symptoms, vital signs normal	Dilution and slow infusion rate are critical to avoid anaphylactoid reaction Indications include severe pain unresponsive to opioids and severe hypertension Serum sickness can occur IV calcium is ineffective
Atropine	Carbamates Nerve agents Organophosphorus compounds	2 mg IV; double the dose every 5 min to achieve atropinization and hemodynamic stability; then start continuous infusion of 10%-20% of total stabilizing dose per hr	Cessation of excessive oral and pulmonary secretions, >80 bpm, systolic blood pressure >80 mm Hg	Doubling of the dose every 5 min (e.g., 2 mg, 4 mg, 8 mg, 16 mg) estimated to achieve atropinization within 30 min Stop infusion if patient develops any signs or symptoms of anticholinergic toxidrome; restart infusion at lower rate when signs or symptoms abate
Calcium[‡]	Calcium-channel antagonists	Calcium chloride 10%, 20-50 mg (0.2-0.5 ml)/kg/hr	Reversal of hypotension; may not reverse bradycardia	All indications: Monitor ionized calcium levels IV extravasation causes tissue necrosis, especially with calcium chloride Can administer at faster than stated rates for immediate, life-threatening conditions Taper infusions and monitor for relapse of toxicity when discontinuing therapy Calcium chloride contains three times more elemental calcium than calcium gluconate does Calcium-channel antagonists may be ineffective in severe toxicity
	Hydrofluoric acid	Systemic toxicity: calcium gluconate 10%, 1-3 g (10-30 ml) per dose IV over 10-min period; repeat as needed every 5-10 min	Reversal of life-threatening manifestations of hypocalcemia and hyperkalemia	Can dilute and give intraarterially or IV with a Bier block for extremity exposures and burns
	Hyperkalemia (except cardiac glycosides)	Calcium gluconate 10%, 1 g (10 ml) per dose IV over 10-min period; repeat as needed every 5-10 min	Reversal of myocardial depression and conduction delays	May precipitate ventricular arrhythmias
	Hypermagnesemia	Calcium gluconate 10%, 1-2 g (10-20 ml) per dose IV over 10-min period; repeat as needed every 5-10 min	Reversal of respiratory depression, hypotension, and cardiac conduction blocks	Simultaneous therapies to increase magnesium elimination should be instituted
	Hypocalcemia (e.g., ethylene glycol)	Calcium gluconate 10%, 0.5-1.0 g (5-10 ml) per dose over 10-min period; repeat as needed every 10 min	Reversal of tetany	Correct symptomatic hypocalcemia; avoid excessive administration that may increase production of calcium oxalate crystals in ethylene glycol poisoning

Antidote	Indication for Use	Dose*	Treatment End Point	Comments
L-Carnitine	Valproate-induced hyperammonemia or hepatotoxicity	100 mg/kg (maximum 6 g) IV over 30 min, then 15 mg/kg IV over 30-min period q4h (max 6 g/day)	Treat until clinical improvement occurs	Levocarnitine is active form Adjust dose for end-stage renal disease
Cyanide antidote kit	Cyanide		Resolution of lactic acidosis and moderate to severe clinical signs and symptoms: seizures, coma, dyspnea, apnea, hypotension, bradycardia	
Amyl nitrate		Amyl nitrite: 0.3-ml pearls, crush and inhale over 30-sec period		Coordinate amyl nitrite with continued oxygenation and give only until sodium nitrite infusion is begun; nitrites may produce hypotension and excess methemoglobinemia
Sodium nitrite		Sodium nitrite 3%: 10 ml IV over 10-min period		Sodium nitrite dose must be adjusted if patient has hemoglobin <12 g/dl
Sodium thiosulfate		Sodium thiosulfate 25%: 50 ml (12.5 g) IV over 10-min period		Sodium thiosulfate dosing can be repeated
Deferoxamine	Iron	15 ml/kg/hr IV (max 8 g/day) Mild to moderate: administer for 6-12 hr Severe toxicity: administer 24 hr	Resolution of clinical signs and symptoms Do not use urine color, which is an unreliable marker for iron clearance	Indications: symptomatic patients with lethargy, severe abdominal pain, hypovolemia, acidosis, shock; any symptomatic patient with peak serum iron level >350 g/dl Prolonged therapy can cause pulmonary toxicity
Digoxin-specific antibody fragments (Fab)	Digoxin Digitalis Other cardiac glycosides (e.g., bufodienalides [Bufo toads], oleander)	Unknown digoxin dose or serum level or for plant or toad source: acute toxicity—10-20 vials; chronic toxicity—3-6 vials Digoxin dose known: number of vials = (mg ingested × 0.8) ÷ 0.5 Digoxin serum level known: number of vials = [serum level (ng/ml) × weight (kg)] ÷ 100	Resolution of hyperkalemia, symptomatic bradydysrhythmias, ventricular arrhythmias, Mobitz II or third-degree heart block	Each vial binds 0.5 mg of digoxin or digitoxin Monitor ECG and potassium levels Digoxin serum levels unreliable after antidote administered unless test is specific for free serum digoxin
Dimercaprol (BAL)	Arsenic Lead Mercury, elemental and inorganic salts	Arsenic: 3-5 mg/kg IM q4h Lead: 75 mg/m² (4 mg/kg) IM q4h for 5 days Inorganic mercury: 5 mg/kg IM, then 2.5 mg/kg IM q12h for 10 days or until patient clinically improved	Arsenic: 24-hr urinary arsenic <50 µg/L Lead: encephalopathy resolved, blood lead level <100 µg/dl, and succimer therapy can be started Mercury, elemental and inorganic: 24-hr urinary mercury <20 µg/L	Maximum adult dose is 3 g/day BAL started 4 hr before initiation of concomitant CaNa₂EDTA for lead encephalopathy Dosing not well established for arsenic and elemental or inorganic mercury toxicity; not used for organic mercury poisoning Adverse effects: painful injections, fever, diaphoresis, agitation, headache, salivation, nausea and vomiting, hemolysis in G6PD-deficient patients, chelation of essential metals Check essential metal levels if chelation is prolonged Succimer is replacing BAL for many indications except lead encephalopathy Treatment end points for arsenic and mercury include improving clinical condition
Edetate calcium disodium (CaNa₂EDTA)	Lead	1500 mg/m²/24 hr (max 3 g) by continuous infusion	Treat for 5 days, followed by 2-day hiatus; repeat until encephalopathy resolved, lead level <100 µg/dl, and succimer therapy can be started	Use in patients with lead encephalopathy or lead level >100 g/dl Administer BAL 4 hr before initiating CaNa₂EDTA Hydrate patient and establish good urinary output before starting therapy Avoid thrombophlebitis by diluting in NS or D₅W to a concentration ≤0.5% Substitution of Na₂EDTA can cause fatal hypocalcemia
Flumazenil	Benzodiazepines Venlafaxine	0.1 mg/min IV to a total dose of 1 mg	Reversal of respiratory depression	Limit use to reversal of inadequate respiration in benzodiazepine-toxic patients Increases intracranial pressure and risk for seizures in presence of underlying seizure disorder or ingestion of seizure-producing toxicants Monitor for resedation up to 2 hr after last dose

Continued on following page

Antidote	Indication for Use	Dose*	Treatment End Point	Comments
Folinate (tetrahydrofolic acid [leucovorin])	Methanol Methotrexate	Methanol: 50 mg IV q4h Methotrexate: 100 mg/m² IV q3-6h	Methanol: methanol undetectable, metabolic acidosis cleared Methotrexate: serum level $<1 \times 10^{-8}$ mol/L	Essential therapy for both toxicants Methotrexate: large ingestions may require increased dose Glucarpidase administered 2-4 hr before or after folinate
Fomepizole	Ethylene glycol Methanol	Dose 1: 15 mg/kg IV Doses over next 48 hr: 10 mg/kg IV All subsequent doses: 15 mg/kg IV Administer q12h, except when HD performed: HD initiation: ½ next dose if >6 hr since last dose HD ongoing: q4h End of HD (based on time of last dose): <1 hr, no dose; 1-3 hr, ½ next dose; >3 hr, next dose	For both: serum level <20 mg/dl and metabolic acidosis resolved	Start immediately if toxic alcohol suspected, without waiting for confirmatory levels Dose amount is not affected by interval timing of doses
Glucagon	β-Adrenergic receptor antagonists Calcium-channel antagonists	Bolus of 3.5-5 mg IV; can repeat to achieve clinical effect, then infusion of 2-10 mg/hr	Reversal of hypotension and bradycardia; taper infusion	Can precipitate vomiting; be prepared to protect airway Mild hyperglycemia occurs Maximum dosing amounts unknown; bolus doses up to 30 mg reported Duration of effect is 15 min; thus infusion must be started immediately
Hydroxocobalamin	Cyanide	Initial: 5 g IV over 15-min period Second dose: 5 g IV over 15 min–2 hr; maximum total dose is 10 g Follow each hydroxocobalamin dose with sodium thiosulfate 25%: 50 ml (12.5 g) IV over 10-min period	Resolution of lactic acidosis and moderate to severe clinical signs and symptoms: seizures, coma, dyspnea, apnea, hypotension, bradycardia	Can be administered IV push if patient is in cardiac arrest Do not give hydroxocobalamin and sodium thiosulfate through the same IV line Adverse effects: red discoloration of plasma, urine, mucous membranes, skin; transient hypertension Interference with laboratory colorometric assays: Levels increased: bilirubin; creatinine; glucose; hemoglobin; magnesium; co-oximetry total Hb, COHb%, MetHb% Levels decreased: AST, ALT, creatinine, co-oximetry O₂Hb%
Hyperbaric oxygen (HBO)	Carbon monoxide Experimental: carbon tetrachloride, cyanide, hydrogen sulfide	3.0 atm pressure for 60 min (25 min O₂, 5 min air, 25 min O₂, 5 min air), then 2.0 atm for 65 min (30 min O₂, 5 min air, 30 min O₂), then "surface" to 1.0 atm	One treatment Second treatment rarely administered (controversial)	Carbon monoxide: treatment protocols may vary HBO indicated for loss of consciousness; seizures; cerebellar dysfunction; impaired cognition; headache, nausea/vomiting persisting after 4 hr O₂ therapy regardless of carboxyhemoglobin level Experimental indications: treatment protocols not established
Insulin-glucose	Calcium-channel antagonists β-Adrenergic receptor antagonists	Regular insulin, 1 U/kg bolus, followed by 0.5-1 U/kg/hr Titrate 50% dextrose IV to avoid hypoglycemia	Reversal of myocardial depression	Beneficial in case series and reports Initiate if glucagon and vasopressor or inotropic drugs fail to reverse myocardial depression; more effective if used before onset of cardiogenic shock Monitor glucose and potassium; hypoglycemia can occur during and after therapy Hyperglycemia results from toxicant-induced insulin resistance, and initial dextrose requirements may be less than anticipated Recovery may be heralded by normalization of glucose levels, with increased dextrose required to avoid hypoglycemia
Intralipid	Cardiac toxicity from local anesthetics (e.g., bupivacaine, ropivacaine) Experimental: verapamil, diltiazem, tricyclic antidepressants, bupropion, propranolol	Use 20% formulation Initial bolus: 1.5 ml/kg IV over 1 min, followed immediately by infusion of 0.25 ml/kg/min for 30-60 min Can repeat bolus for asystole	Return of hemodynamic stability	Use based on animal experiments and human case reports; numerous dosing regimens have been used Use if advanced life support measures fail; continue CPR as needed during drug administration

Antidote	Indication for Use	Dose*	Treatment End Point	Comments
Methylene blue	Methemoglobin-producing agents	1-2 mg/kg body weight (0.1-0.2 ml/kg) of 1% methylene blue is administered over 5-min period; repeat dose for persistent or recurrent symptoms or signs	Resolution of dyspnea and altered mental status	Use if patient is symptomatic (i.e., dyspneic, altered mental status) Maximum dose should not exceed 7 mg/kg (0.7 ml/kg) Contraindicated in G6PD-deficient patients; may cause hemolysis Some toxicants (e.g., dapsone) may require prolonged therapy
N-Acetylcysteine (NAC)	Acetaminophen Experimental: carbon tetrachloride, chloroform, pennyroyal oil	Oral: Load—140 mg/kg Maintenance (starting 4 hr after load)—70 mg/kg q4h IV: Load—150 mg/kg over 1-hr period Maintenance infusion—12.5 mg/kg over 4-hr period, then 6.25 mg/kg per hour as continuous infusion	Administer 24 hr of NAC and repeat AST and APAP levels: if AST normal and APAP not detected, stop NAC; if AST normal and APAP detected, continue NAC for 12 hr, then reassess AST and APAP levels; if AST elevated, continue NAC for total of 72 hr of therapy After 72 hr of therapy, if INR <2.0, stop NAC After patient has received 72 hr of therapy, if INR ≥2.0 or severe hepatotoxicity present, continue NAC until INR <2.0	Most effective if initiated within 8 hr after ingestion; may be started any time after ingestion and is beneficial in severe hepatotoxic states Use IV in patients unable to tolerate PO or with severe hepatotoxicity; the dose and timing differ from the oral regimen Dosage and administration of FDA-approved IV formulation assume early treatment of acute overdose without hepatotoxicity; longer duration of treatment required in patients with hepatotoxicity Treatment end points simplified for ease of use INR result not valid indicator if FFP recently administered
Naloxone	Opioids	Bolus: 0.4-2 mg via IV, sublingual injection, or endotracheal instillation; 0.4-0.8 mg SC Continuous infusion: establish bolus dose required to reverse respiratory depression Begin infusing two thirds of reversal dose every hour, and titrate to maintain adequate respirations Rebolus with half of reversal dose 15 min after reversing respiratory depression	Initial: reversal of respiratory depression with resolution of hypoxia and hypercapnia Final: resolution of CNS and respiratory depression	Preventilate patients with respiratory depression by bag-valve mask or intubation before administration Use smaller doses in opioid-dependent patients; some opioids (e.g., propoxyphene, pentazocine, fentanyls) may require larger doses of naloxone; use continuous infusion for recurrent symptoms and prolonged action of some formulations (e.g., sustained-release morphine, methadone) Resedation can occur Do not use nalmefene or naltrexone to reverse acute toxicity
Octreotide	Sulfonylureas	50 mg SC q6h	Resolution of hypoglycemia and dextrose not required	Maintain dextrose infusion as needed
Physostigmine	Anticholinergic agents (e.g., diphenhydramine, jimsonweed [Datura sp.], scopolamine)	1-2 mg IV over 5-min period; can repeat once after 10-15 min if no effect	Reversal of anticholinergic effects	Duration of effect is 60-90 min Benzodiazepine used for subsequent treatment of agitation and seizures; additional physostigmine used rarely (e.g., refractory seizures or agitation) Adverse effects include seizures, excessive oral secretions, bradyarrhythmias; contraindicated in cyclic antidepressant toxicity
Pralidoxime chloride	Organophosphorus compounds Nerve agents—sarin, VX	30 mg/kg IV bolus (max 2 g) over 30 min, followed by continuous infusion of 8-10 mg/kg/hr (max 650 mg/hr)	Resolution of signs and symptoms, atropine no longer required	Can give initial dose over 2-min period for life-threatening clinical effects Administer early when diagnosis known or strongly suspected Efficacy variable, depending on the organophosphate Fat-soluble organophosphates may require prolonged treatment
Pyridoxine	Ethylene glycol (theoretical efficacy) Isoniazid Monomethylhydrazine mushrooms	100 mg IV 5 g IV, repeat for refractory seizures	One dose Resolution of seizures	Efficacy theoretical Pyridoxine may stop seizures, but patient can remain comatose (isoniazid, mushrooms); use benzodiazepines and phenobarbital concomitantly to manage seizures Excessive dosing can cause neuropathy

Continued on following page

Antidote	Indication for Use	Dose*	Treatment End Point	Comments
Sodium bicarbonate (NaHCO$_3$)	Reversal of myocardial sodium-channel blockers (e.g., cyclic antidepressants, cocaine, propoxyphene, sodium-channel-blocking antiarrhythmics with $\tau_{recovery}$ >1 sec, piperidine phenothiazines (thioridazine, mesoridazine)	1-2 mEq NaHCO$_3$/kg via intermittent bolus; repeat as needed	Narrowing of prolonged QRS, resolution of ventricular arrhythmias, reversal of hypotension	Monitor blood pH (optimal pH approximately 7.50); avoid pH >7.55
	Altered tissue distribution or enhanced elimination of salicylates; may be used in chlorophenoxy herbicides, chlorpropamide, formic acid, methotrexate, phenobarbital	1-2 mEq NaHCO$_3$/kg, followed by 3 ampules (150 ml) NaHCO$_3$ (44 mEq per 50 ml) in 850 ml of D$_5$W, infused at 2-3 times normal maintenance fluid rate	Serum salicylate <30 mg/dl and patient clinically stable	Monitor urinary pH hourly; adjust infusion to maintain urine pH of 7.5-8.0 (avoid blood pH >7.55) Monitor ABGs Maintain normokalemia
Succimer (DMSA)	All forms: Arsenic Lead Mercury	10 mg/kg/dose q8h for 5 days, followed by q12h for 14 days Drug holiday for 2 wk; repeat if treatment end point not reached	Arsenic: 24-hr urinary arsenic <50 µg/L Lead: resolution of encephalopathy, gastrointestinal symptoms, neuropathy, nephropathy, arthralgias, myalgias, and blood lead level <70 µg/dl Mercury, elemental and inorganic: 24-hr urinary mercury <20 µg/L Mercury, organic: end point not well established	Oral chelator; adverse effects include rash, transient AST and alkaline phosphatase elevations, and gastrointestinal distress; minimal chelation of essential metals occurs Dosing for arsenic and mercury not well established Therapeutic end point for organic mercury not established; neurotoxicity not responsive to chelation therapy; suggest chelation until blood mercury level within normal value range for reference laboratory
Vitamin K	Anticoagulants (e.g., warfarin, long-acting anticoagulant rodenticides [LAARs])	Subcutaneous: AquaMEPHYTON (K$_1$), 10-25 mg, repeat every 6-12 hr until oral vitamin K$_1$ started Oral: 25-50 mg q6h; larger doses may be required	INR is normal 48-72 hr after stopping vitamin K$_1$ therapy Can also monitor factor VII activity	Anaphylactoid reaction can occur with IV administration Severe bleeding may also require FFP or factor concentrates Base decision to treat on finding of elevated INR; do not administer prophylactic vitamin K$_1$ Oral therapy has been required for months with LAAR poisoning because of lipophilicity of toxicant, with slow body clearance

ABG, Arterial blood gas; *ALT*, alanine aminotransferase; *APAP*, acetyl-para-aminophenol (acetaminophen); *AST*, aspartate aminotransferase; *BAL*, British antilewisite; bpm, beats per minute; *CNS*, central nervous system; *COHb%*, percent carboxyhemoglobin; *CPR*, cardiopulmonary resuscitation; *D$_5$W*, 5% dextrose in water; *DMSA*, 2,3-dimercaptosuccinic acid; *ECG*, electrocardiogram; *FDA*, Food and Drug Administration; *FFP*, fresh-frozen plasma; *G6PD*, glucose-6-phosphate dehydrogenase; *Hb*, hemoglobin; *HD*, hemodialysis; *IM*, intramuscular; *INR*, international normalized ratio; *IV*, intravenous; *MetHb%*, percent methemoglobinemia; *NS*, normal saline; *O$_2$Hb%*, percent oxyhemoglobin; *PO*, per os (by mouth); *SC*, subcutaneous; $\tau_{recovery}$, drug blockade recovery rate.

*Dose concentrations and infusion times are not given. Drug dosages may require adjustment in patients with renal or hepatic failure.

†Administer antivenom in a monitored setting; antivenom must be reconstituted and then diluted; initially infuse at a rate of 2 to 5 ml/hr, and double the infusion rate every 5 minutes as tolerated to administer antivenom over a 1-hour period.

‡Ten percent calcium chloride solution = 100 mg/ml (27.2 mg/ml elemental calcium); 10% calcium gluconate solution = 100 mg/ml (9 mg/ml elemental calcium).

From Goldman L, Schafer AI: *Goldman's Cecil medicine*, ed 24, Philadelphia, 2012, Saunders.

Appendix IV

Impairment and Disability Issues

Impairment describes harm to anatomy and physiology, whereas *disability* denotes the difficulty a person has performing a function. Reporting disability for different sectors of society has its own nuances. Proper evaluation of impairment/disability starts with knowing who is asking for what. It is an area of practice in which an understanding of some basic concepts can make it rewarding rather than distressing.

- Ultimately, disability is a measure of function. Functional outcomes are becoming increasingly important in medicine, mirroring the shift towards patient-centeredness. All practitioners should have some facility with documenting the effects of an intervention on a patient's physical, psychological, and social functioning. For example, the continuation of an opioid analgesic should be predicated on meeting functional goals negotiated between the patient and physician before initiation of treatment. Even a brief comment on walking distance or work tolerance is better than nothing.
- Some concepts apply to all venues of disability. Primary care providers should rarely be in the position to determine whether a patient can be on or off a specific job. Rather, their task is to give general parameters about which physical exertions are medically dangerous. Try to be specific and use objective criteria where appropriate, but don't be intimidated by a form. Ballpark estimates can often suffice. For example, many chronic low back pain patients may conservatively and safely be described as able to lift/carry up 10 lbs, push/pull 25 lbs, and change positions as needed to keep comfortable. Have thorough medical records and be consistent; lawyers may focus on contradictions in your documentation to help their clients.
- Rehabilitation centers across the country are required to monitor function using a standardized set of criteria called the "Functional Independence Measure (FIM)," which categorizes activities of daily living into divisions such as mobility, transfers, feeding, grooming/hygiene, dressing, bathing, and toileting. In therapy notes, you may come across scores in these categories rating patients on a seven-point scale from totally dependent to moderate-assistance (mod A; patient can perform 50% of task) to modified-independent (patient requires an assistive device) to independent.
- Psychosocial contributing factors such medicolegal issues can profoundly influence patients' presentations through somatization from secondary gain. However, it is important to differentiate this from malingering, Munchausen's syndrome, or "gaming the system," which are remarkably less prevalent.
- The number of stakeholders expands in the disability system to include the employer, the government, the legal system, and the payer. Each sector has its own regulations. You may be required to fill out disability questionnaires as a condition of accepting payment for clinical services from a payer, such as in the workers' compensation system. Much more commonly, you will be seeing patients for clinical services paid for by an evaluation and management code. In these cases, you are not obligated to provide free medicolegal assessments. Settling payment issues in advance can avoid misunderstanding. Again, before assessing disability, understand who is asking and why.

GOVERNMENT-ADMINISTERED DISABILITY

State Temporary Disability Insurance (TDI) programs, the Family Medical Leave Act of 1993 (FMLA), the Social Security Administration (SSA), and the Department of Veterans Affairs offer disability benefits through the state and federal government.

- State TDI forms must be filled out for the patient to receive any income. They are generally very basic and just engage the social support network for a patient. This may not be the best venue to stipulate partial disability.
- The FMLA provides unpaid leave for qualified medical and family reasons. Because it is a federal program, the forms involved are standard across states and employers. They can be intimidating at first, but are reasonably easy to complete once the basic definitions used are understood. It is recommended that you familiarize yourself with this paperwork the first few times it is encountered. Completing the form for subsequent patients should not be overly burdensome.
- The SSA and the Department of Veterans Affairs have their own internal mechanisms for quantifying disability, but they may subpoena your records or request a summary narrative as part of their processes. If you've kept good clinical notes, your existing documentation should satisfy their requirements. Many patients choose to apply for Social Security Disability Insurance (SSDI) and/or Supplemental Security Income (SSI) through a legal representative. These lawyers may send you a lengthy questionnaire to prepare their case. There are physicians whose practices perform these services and who can be hired by attorneys to facilitate patients' applications. If this nonclinical work appeals to you, consider affiliating with the SSA or contracting your time to lawyers under separate indenture. If not, you may want to recommend the law office contact a suitable practice.

WORKERS' COMPENSATION

In workers' compensation, the payer and employer join the provider in trying to rehabilitate the injured worker. Confidentiality issues are handled differently because these stakeholders may have a right to protected health information.

- Each state has their own laws regarding reporting requirements, and the U.S. Department of Labor governs injured federal employees. If you plan on accepting workers' compensation patients, you must familiarize yourself with the necessary paperwork. Typically, this is a standard, short form that includes measures of function. It may make sense to copy your state's parameters and create a "work note" to be used uniformly in your practice for cases both inside and outside of the workers' compensation system. Functional limitations should pertain to any task, not just to the employee's vocation. In general, employees should not be labeled "on" or "off."
- A notification that an employee has reached "maximal medical improvement" should be made once an employee's condition is expected to change over months/years rather than days/weeks. At this juncture they will transition from temporary disability benefits to permanent disability benefits, possibly including vocational rehabilitation. If ongoing sequelae exist, a permanent impairment rating may be needed to resolve an employee's claim and allow them to progress to the next stage of their life. These are more sophisticated determinations, usually directed by the American Medical Association's (AMA) *Guides to the Evaluation of Permanent Impairment*, now in its sixth edition. Analysis of permanent impairment, causation, and apportionment generally fall out-

side of workers' compensation reporting requirements. Someone with appropriate training may be best suited to complete this task. Consider providing these more detailed services under a separate indenture, such as a consultation arrangement with the employee's attorney. Your state workers' compensation board may have specific guidelines governing these reports. In any case, the work should be done under a clear written agreement, not based on a verbal request by the employee. Very complex cases may also require a formal functional capacity evaluation through an appropriate rehabilitation resource.

PERSONAL INJURY

Patients hurt in car accidents or other personal injuries often are involved in legal cases covering medical care, personal damages, and pain and suffering. Most commonly, you will be helping these patients with their clinical issues under their regular medical insurance, although some providers agree to provide services under a legal lien on the claim. Regardless of your role in a personal injury case, it is helpful to document objective details about the injury and functional parameters. If you are asked to keep someone out of work, try to delineate functional limitations as you would in a workers' compensation employee.

- Similar to the workers' compensation system, it is helpful to state when a patient has reached maximal medical improvement. Personal injury claims can take longer to resolve than in the workers' compensation system, as the employer and insurance company are strongly incentivized to reach a resolution in those cases. In general, an ongoing legal case may hinder a patient from achieving a healthful balance of wellness. It is in the patient's best interest to move the claim toward completion.
- Quantifying permanent disability is a key component of resolving these cases. If a clinician is providing services under a legal lien, there may be a conflict of interest in having that provider quantify the permanent impairment. There may be financial implications to the degree of disability awarded, and this may influence whether or not the clinician will receive payment on their lien. These cases are almost always

contentious, and may be best handled by providers with special training, such as an independent medical examiner. Again, the determination typically follows the AMA's *Guides to the Evaluation of Permanent Impairment*. A clinician's role is to manage the patient's injuries, not to negotiate medicolegal issues. If you are not appropriately trained, consider deferring questions regarding disability to someone who is.

PRIVATE DISABILITY

Some patients purchase private insurance plans to provide income in addition to that offered through the government in the case of long-term disability. These forms vary by insurance carrier and change over time. They may need to be filled out periodically to maintain benefits. Many providers opt to charge a separate fee for the completion of this type of paperwork.

CONCLUSION

In summary, impairment and disability are measures of function and should be followed by all good doctors as part of patient-centered care. Providers can be most effective interacting with the various disability systems if they know when they are acting as clinicians and when they are acting as legal consultants. Understanding the principles involved with the different sectors will help you avoid confusion between obligations and opportunities when doing this work.

SUGGESTED READINGS

American Academy of Physical Medicine and Rehabilitation: Disability evaluation. Accessed March 7, 2014, at http://now.aapmr.org/rehab-essentials/special-assessment-mgmt-strategy/Pages/Disability-evaluation.aspx.

Holmes EB: Impairment rating and disability determination. Accessed March 7, 2014, at http://emedicine.medscape.com/article/314195-overview#a1.

Rondinelli R.D.. In: *Guides to the evaluation of permanent impairment*. American Medical Association: Arlington, VA.

AUTHOR: **MATTHEW J. SMITH, M.D.**

Page numbers followed by "b", "f" and "t" indicate
boxes, figures and tables respectively.

1887

Meningomyelocele I
Mental status changes and coma II
Meralgia paresthetica I
Migraine headache I
Mild cognitive impairment I
Mononeuropathies, isolated II
Motion sickness I
Multiple sclerosis I
Multiple system atrophy I
Muscle disease II
Muscle weakness, algorithm III
Muscular dystrophy I
Myasthenia gravis I
Myelin disorders II
Myoclonus I
Myotonia I
Narcolepsy I
Neuroblastoma I
Neuromuscular junction dysfunction II
Neuronopathies, sensory (ganglionopathies) II
Neuropathic bladder II
Neuropathic pain I
Neuropathies, peripheral, asymmetrical proximal/distal II
Neuropathies with facial nerve involvement II
Nystagmus, monocular II
Opsoclonus II
Optic atrophy II
Optic neuritis I
Osteosclerosis, diffuse II
Otosclerosis (otospongiosis) I
Paraneoplastic neurologic syndromes II
Paraparesis, acute or subacute II
Paraparesis, chronic progressive II
Paraphilic disorders I
Parkinsonism-plus syndromes II
Parkinson's disease I
Partial seizures I
Poliomyelitis I
Polyneuropathies, demyelinating II
Polyneuropathies, distal, sensorimotor II
Postconcussive syndrome I
Postherpetic neuralgia I
Postpoliomyelitis syndrome I
Progressive multifocal leukoencephalopathy I
Progressive supranuclear palsy I
Quadrilateral space syndrome I
Ramsay Hunt syndrome I
Restless legs syndrome I
Seizures, mimics II
Shaken baby syndrome I
Smell disturbance II
Spasticity I
Spina bifida I
Spinal cord compression I
Spinal cord compression, epidural II
Spinal cord dysfunction, non-traumatic II
Spinal cord ischemic syndromes II
Spinal stenosis I
Spinocerebellar ataxia I
Status epilepticus I
Stroke, acute ischemic I
Stroke, hemorrhagic I
Stroke, secondary prevention I
Subarachnoid hemorrhage I
Subclavian steal syndrome I
Subdural hematoma I
Syncope I
Syringomyelia I
Tabes dorsalis I
Tardive dyskinesia I
Tension-type headache I
Tics II
Tinnitus I
Transient ischemic attack I
Transverse myelitis I
Traumatic brain injury (TBI) I
Tremors II
Trigeminal neuralgia I
Tuberous sclerosis I
Unconscious patient III
Vegetative state, persistent II
Vertigo, algorithm III
Vestibular neuronitis I
Weakness, neuromuscular III
Wernicke's encephalopathy I
Whiplash I
Wilson's disease I

OPHTHALMOLOGY

Amaurosis fugax I
Amblyopia I
Anisocoria III
Blepharitis I
Blindness, monocular, transient II
Cataracts I
Conjunctival neoplasm II
Conjunctivitis I
Corneal abrasion I

Corneal disorders III
Corneal sensation, decreased II
Corneal ulceration I
Cytomegalovirus infection I
Diabetic retinopathy I
Dilated pupil III
Diplopia, monocular II
Diplopia, vertical II
Episcleritis I
Esotropia II
Eyelid neoplasm II
Eyelid retraction II
Glaucoma, open-angle I
Glaucoma, primary angle-closure I
Horner's syndrome I
Intraocular neoplasm II
Keratitis, noninfectious II
Macular degeneration I
Nystagmus, diagnosis III
Nystagmus, monocular II
Ocular foreign body I
Opsoclonus II
Optic atrophy I, II
Optic neuritis I
Orbital lesions, calcified II
Orbital lesions, cystic II
Pupillary dilatation, poor response to darkness II
Ramsay Hunt syndrome I
Red eye, acute III
Reiter's syndrome (reactive arthritis) I
Retinal detachment I
Retinal hemorrhage I
Retinitis pigmentosa I
Retinoblastoma I
Retinopathy, hypertensive II
Scleritis I
Sjögren's syndrome I
Strabismus I
Stye (hordeolum) I
Tuberous sclerosis I
Uveitis I
Von Hippel-Lindau disease I
Wilson's disease I

ORTHOPEDICS

Achilles tendon rupture I
Ankle fracture I
Ankle sprain I
Ankylosing spondylitis I
Arthralgia limited to one or few joints III
Aseptic necrosis I
Back pain, algorithm III
Back pain, low, acute II
Back pain, viscerogenic origin II
Baker's cyst I
Biceps tendonitis I
Bone tumor, primary malignant I
Bursitis I
Carpal tunnel syndrome I
Cervical disk syndromes I
Charcot's joint I
Compartment syndrome I
Complex regional pain syndrome I
Concussion I
Costochondritis I
Cubital tunnel syndrome I
De Quervain's tenosynovitis I
Diffuse idiopathic skeletal hyperostosis (DISH) I
Dupuytren's contracture I
Elbow pain II
Enteropathic arthritis I
Epicondylitis I
Fibromyalgia I
Foot and ankle pain, in different age groups II
Footdrop II
Foot lesion, ulcerating II
Fracture, bone III
Frozen shoulder I
Ganglia I
Glenohumeral dislocation I
Gout I
Granulomatous arthritis I
Heel pain II
Hip fracture I
Hip pain, in different age groups II
Hip pain without obvious fracture II
Hypertrophic osteoarthropathy I
Inflammatory arthritis III
Juvenile idiopathic arthritis I
Knee pain, anterior III
Knee pain, in different age groups II
Legg-Calvé-Perthes disease I
Lumbar disk syndrome I
Metatarsalgia I
Morton's neuroma I
Muscle cramps and aches III
Muscle weakness, algorithm III
Myofascial pain syndrome I
Osgood-Schlatter disease I

Osteoarthritis I
Osteochondritis dissecans I
Osteomyelitis I
Osteoporosis I
Osteoporosis, secondary causes II
Paget's disease of the bone I
Patellofemoral pain syndrome I
Piriformis syndrome I
Plantar fasciitis I
Pronator syndrome I
Psoriatic arthritis I
Pseudogout I
Rheumatoid arthritis I
Rib defects on x-ray II
Rib notching on x-ray II
Rotator cuff syndrome I
Scoliosis I
Septic arthritis I
Shin splints III
Shoulder pain III
Shoulder pain, in different age groups II
Slipped capital femoral epiphysis I
Spinal cord compression I
Spinal cord compression, epidural II
Spinal stenosis, lumbar I
Spine tumor III
Spondyloarthropathy, diagnosis III
Spondyloarthropathy, treatment III
Spondylosis, cervical III
Tarsal tunnel syndrome I
Temporomandibular joint syndrome I
Thoracic outlet syndrome I
Torticollis I
Trigger finger I
Trochanteric bursitis I
Vertebral compression fractures I
Whiplash I
Wrist and hand pain, in different age groups II
Wrist pain II

OTORHINOLARYNGOLOGY (ENT)

Acoustic neuroma I
Allergic rhinitis I
Behçet's disease I
Bruxism I
Burning mouth syndrome I
Cogan's syndrome I
Epiglottitis I
Epistaxis I
Gingivitis I
Glossitis I
Goiter evaluation and management III
Head and neck, soft tissue masses II
Hearing loss III
Hemoptysis, algorithm III
Herpangina I
Labyrinthitis I
Laryngeal carcinoma I
Laryngitis I
Mastoiditis I
Meneire's disease I
Mononucleosis I
Motion sickness I
Mucormycosis I
Mumps I
Oral cancer I
Otitis externa I
Otitis media I
Otosclerosis (otospongiosis) I
Peritonsillar abscess I
Pharyngitis/tonsillitis I
Rhinorrhea III
Salivary gland neoplasms I
Sialadenitis I
Sialolithiasis I
Sinusitis I
Sleep apnea I
Smell disturbance II
Stomatitis I
Temporomandibular joint syndrome I
Thyroid carcinoma I
Thyroid nodule I
Thyroid, painful III
Thyroiditis I
Tinnitus I
Torticollis I
Tracheitis I
Vertigo, algorithm III

PEDIATRICS

Absence seizures I
Anemia in newborn III
Asthma I
Ataxia, cerebellar, children II
Attention deficit hyperactivity disorder I
Autistic spectrum disorders I
Bleeding neonate III
Bone marrow failure syndromes, inherited II
Breastfeeding difficulties III